Dictionary of American Regional English

Dictionary of American Regional English

Volume III   I-O

Frederic G. Cassidy
Chief Editor

Joan Houston Hall
Associate Editor

The Belknap Press of Harvard University Press
Cambridge, Massachusetts, and London, England
1996

Design by Marianne Perlak

Library of Congress Cataloging in Publication Data

Dictionary of American regional English.

1. English language—Dialects—United States—Dictionaries.
2. English language—United States—Dictionaries.
3. Americanisms—Dictionaries.
I. Cassidy, Frederic Gomes, 1907–
II. Hall, Joan Houston.
PE2843.D52   1985   427′.973   84-29025
ISBN 0-674-20511-1 (v. 1 : alk. paper)
ISBN 0-674-20512-X (v. 2)
ISBN 0-674-20519-7 (v. 3)

Contents

DARE Staff, Volume III   VI

Preface   VII

Acknowledgments   VIII

The Anatomy of a *DARE* Entry   IX

List of Abbreviations   XI

Dictionary of American Regional English, I-O   1

DARE Staff, Volume III

IN REMEMBRANCE
John Calvin McGalliard
Scholar—Gentleman—Colleague
1906–1993

Preface

The discerning reader who has used the first two volumes of the *Dictionary of American Regional English* (*DARE*) will be on familiar ground in the third: the method of presentation of entries follows that used in Volumes I and II, as described in the introductory matter for those volumes. New users of the Dictionary are encouraged to read those prefatory essays in order to use *DARE* to the fullest. For all readers, however, the following reminders may be helpful:

The term "regional" in *DARE* refers to words and phrases whose forms or meanings are not used throughout the United States but only in a part or parts of the country; the term is also broadly used to include those words used more frequently by a particular social group (e.g., older speakers, Black speakers, women, rural people) than would be expected based on demographics; and it includes words that are "folk" in origin—that is, those that are learned from family and friends rather than teachers and books. For a full discussion of *DARE*'s criteria for inclusion and exclusion, see pp. xvi-xviii in Volume I.

The maps included in the text reflect the fieldwork done for *DARE* between 1965 and 1970. Each dot represents one of the 1,002 communities investigated in the survey, communities that were chosen to reflect settlement history, population density, and representative community types. The configuration of the map has been "adjusted" to reflect each state's population rather than its physical area, but as nearly as possible the spatial relations between the states have been retained, as have their approximate shapes. See "The *DARE* Map and Regional Labels" in Volume I (pp. xxiii-xxxv) for a full explanation.

In the Dictionary text, the questions asked by *DARE* fieldworkers are usually cited in abbreviated form. The full text of each question may be seen in Volume I (pp. lxii-lxxxv).

DARE informants are identified in the Dictionary text by state code and informant number. For each of these informants, specifics of age, sex, race, amount of education, and community type are listed in Volume I (pp. lxxxvi-cli).

Quotations from printed sources are identified by date, author, and an abbreviated title. This information is intended to be full enough to allow a reader to identify the exact source from which the quote was taken; full bibliographic details, however, will be provided in the final volume of *DARE*.

The illustrative quotes in the *DARE* entries come from a wide variety of sources covering a span of nearly four hundred years, from the time of the first English-speaking settlements up to the present. They represent the speech and writing of people of all social and educational groups, and include a broad range of observations and opinions. In choosing quotations, *DARE* editors try to illustrate as accurately as possible the use of each word over time and space, without regard to the sentiments expressed. Our task is to report usage, not to endorse it.

"The Anatomy of a *DARE* Entry," on p. ix, provides a graphic explanation of the features in a typical treatment of a word or phrase in the Dictionary. While not every entry will include each of these features, it will include all those justified by the evidence available to the editors.

A few abbreviations have been added to the original list; the expanded list is printed on pp. xi–xv.

Acknowledgments

Primary funding for the third volume of *DARE* has come from the National Endowment for the Humanities (an independent federal agency) and the Andrew W. Mellon Foundation. Without the support of these two organizations, the project could not have continued. All of us at *DARE* are grateful to them for their understanding of the meticulous work required in the production of a research tool of this kind; in particular, we give sincere thanks to Helen Agüera and Martha Chomiak at NEH and to Richard Ekman at the Mellon Foundation for their continued encouragement, patience, and assistance.

Additional funding has been provided by the National Science Foundation, the Horace W. Goldsmith Foundation, the Brittingham Fund, Inc., the Evjue Foundation, Inc., the Connemara Fund, the Quaker Oats Foundation, the New York Times Company Foundation, the Houghton Mifflin Company, and the Alexander Company. Many generous individuals have also contributed to the project, and their support as well as that of the organizations listed above is gratefully acknowledged.

Invaluable assistance of other kinds has come from many sources: Audrey R. Duckert, Professor of English at the University of Massachusetts at Amherst, has provided trenchant commentary on the editorial work in progress as well as unfailing concern for the project from its inception; Michael Agnes, Executive Editor of *Webster's New World Dictionaries,* has generously allowed us the use of an extensive file of notes and quotations compiled by Mitford M. Mathews following the 1954 publication of his *Dictionary of Americanisms;* E. Ward Gilman, Director of Defining for Merriam-Webster, Inc., and Jesse Sheidlower, Random House Reference Department, have provided valuable advice, citations, and corroboration of entries; Michael B. Montgomery, University of South Carolina, has graciously shared his extensive collection of Smoky Mountain speech; Lee A. Pederson, Emory University, has, in the materials of the *Linguistic Atlas of the Gulf States* and in personal communications, made available a wealth of data on speech of that region; Lester Seifert and C. Richard Beam have assisted with our treatments of Pennsylvania German words; stalwart volunteers from the Madison community have continued giving their gifts of time to do some invisible but invaluable tasks that make our lives easier.

At the University of Wisconsin–Madison, librarians across campus have been consistently helpful. Particular thanks go to Kenneth L. Frazier, Director of the General Library System; to Mary Tipton and Audrey Berns for allowing us access to and assisting us with the use of OCLC; to Judith L. Tuohy, J. L. Brandenburg, Madeline Quigley, and Alan K. Seeger in the Interlibrary Loan department, who have facilitated our access to arcane materials; to Elsa E. Althen, Jeanne M. Witte, and Edward L. Duesterhoeft, whose cooperation has been invaluable. Emeritus Professor of Botany Hugh Iltis has generously facilitated our use of rare books crucial to natural science entries.

DARE also expresses appreciation to David Ward, Chancellor of the University of Wisconsin–Madison, to W. Charles Read, Acting Dean of the Graduate School, to Phillip R. Certain, Dean of the College of Letters and Science, and to Associate Deans Fannie LeMoine and Joseph Wiesenfarth of the Graduate School, and Yvonne Ozzello of the College of Letters and Science, who have provided crucial advice, assistance, and support to the project.

The Anatomy of a *DARE* Entry

- **headword.**

- **part-of-speech abbreviation.**

- **variant form.** All variants are cross-referenced; a reader who looks up *drop egg* will find a reference to **dropped egg.**

- **etymology.** *DARE* doesn't try to trace every word back to its ultimate origin, but only to explain how it got into American English. This etymology suggests that *dropped egg* is from Scots dialect, and refers the reader to the relevant entry in the *Scottish National Dictionary,* where the earliest citation is from 1824.

- **regional label.** This generalization is based on all the available evidence, but especially, when possible, on evidence from the *DARE* survey.

- **social label.** Like the regional label, this is based on all available evidence, but especially on evidence from the *DARE* survey.

- **definition.**

- **map.** The computer-generated map is deliberately distorted so that the area of each state is roughly proportional to its population. If every informant who was asked question H35 had answered *dropped egg,* the map would show 1,002 evenly spaced dots, each representing one of the communities selected for the *DARE* survey. This uniform spacing makes it much easier to interpret the map, since any "bunching" of dots is potentially significant, though it does take a little practice to recognize the states in their distorted forms.

- **quotation block.** The quotations provide examples of the headword, beginning with the earliest known U.S. example. All quotations, unless explicitly attributed to a secondary source, have been verified in the original.

- **short-title.** The bibliography, to be published in the last volume, will give precise bibliographic details on every source cited in *DARE* (there are currently over 8,500), but the abbreviated titles allow the interested reader to identify the source.

- **regional label.** Whenever possible, regional information is given for individual quotations. In this example, the reader finds that the story quoted was set in Massachusetts.

- ***DARE* question.** This is the question to which *dropped egg* was a reply. The full questionnaire is printed in Volume I.

- **summary statement.** This summarizes the regional distribution of the informants who gave this response.

- **informant code.** Rarer responses are attributed to individual informants; a list in Volume I gives basic data on each one.

- **social statistics.** In this entry, this is the main evidence for the social label *"somewhat old-fash."* When there are more informants, more elaborate statistics may be justified.

dropped egg n Also *drop egg* [Prob from Scots dial; cf *SND drap* v. 5. (2) (b) 1824 →] **chiefly NEng** See Map *somewhat old-fash*
A poached egg.

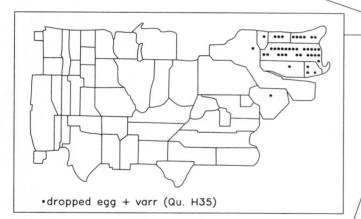

•dropped egg + varr (Qu. H35)

  1884 *Harper's New Mth. Mag.* 69.306/1 **MA, Martha was . . eating** her toast and a dropped egg. **1896** (c1973) Farmer *Orig. Cook Book* 93, *Dropped Eggs* (Poached). **1933** *Hanley Disks* **neMA,** Dropped egg—take and put a pan of milk on the stove and boil and drop the egg in and let it cook. **1941** *LANE* Map 295 (Poached Eggs), **throughout NEng,** *Dropped eggs.* . . 1 inf, **ceVT,** Drop eggs. **1948** Peattie *Berkshires* 323 **wMA,** In Berkshire . . you could not get a poached egg, but you could get a "dropped" egg, which was the same thing. **1965** *PADS* 43.24 **seMA,** 6 [infs] poached eggs, 4 [infs] dropped eggs, 1 [inf] dropped egg on toast. **1965–70** *DARE* (Qu. H35, *When eggs are taken out of the shell and cooked in boiling water, you call them _____ eggs*) 40 Infs, **chiefly NEng,** Dropped; **NH15,** Dropped egg on toast. [33 of 41 Infs old] **1975** Gould *ME Lingo* 82, *Dropped egg*—Maine for poached egg, usually on toast. **1977** *Yankee* Jan 73 **Isleboro ME,** The people on Isleboro eat dropped eggs instead of poached.

List of Abbreviations

Note: Periods are used for abbreviations in short-titles, but are generally omitted elsewhere.

a	ante (before); auxiliary informant	BBC	British Broadcasting Corporation
abbr(s)	abbreviated, abbreviation(s)	bd	board
absol	absolute(ly)	betw	between
abstr	abstract	bib	bibliographical, bibliography
acad	academy	biog	biographical, biography
acc	accusative	biol	biological, biology
accd	according to	bot	botanical
acct	account	Brit	Britain, Britannica, British
ADD	*American Dialect Dictionary*	bur	bureau
addit	addition(al)		
adj(s)	adjectival, adjective(s)	c	central; circa (about); copyright
adv(s)	adverb(s), adverbial	Can	Canadian
advent	adventure(s)	CanEngl	Canadian English (language)
advt	advertisement(s), advertiser	CanFr	Canadian French (language)
Afr	African	cap	capital
Afro-Amer	Afro-American	capt	captain
ag	agricultural, agriculture	CB	citizens band
agric	agriculturalist	cent(s)	central; century (-ies)
AHD	*American Heritage Dictionary*	*Cent D*	*Century Dictionary*
alt(s)	alternation(s), alternative	cf	confer (compare)
alter(s)	alteration(s)	ch	chapter; church
Amer	America(n), Americana	chem	chemical, chemistry
AmFr	American French	Chr	Christian
AmInd	American Indian (language)	chron	chronicle(s)
AmPort	American Portuguese (language)	co	company; county
AmSp	*American Speech*	cogn	cognate
AmSpan	American Spanish (language)	col	colonel
AND	*Australian National Dictionary*	coll	collected, collection(s), collective; college
anon	anonymous	colloq	colloquial
AN&Q	*American Notes & Queries*	comb(s)	combination(s), combine(s)
anthol	anthology	comm(s)	commission(ers); committee(s); community (-ies)
anthro	anthropological, anthropology	comp	compiler, compiled, composition
antiq	antiquarian, antiquity	compar	comparative
aphet	aphetic	concr	concrete(ly)
apoc	apocopated, apocopation	Cong	Congress
app	appendix	conj	conjunction
appar	apparent(ly)	conjug	conjugation
approx	approximate(ly)	cons	consonant
Apr	April	conserv	conservancy, conservation
arch	archaic	constr(s)	construct(ed), construction(s); construed
archeol	archeological, archeology	contemp	contemporary
art	article	contr	contracted, contraction
assim	assimilated, assimilation	contrib	contribution(s)
assoc	associate, association	conv	conversation(al)
asst	assistant	coop	cooperative
astron	astronomical, astronomy	Corn	Cornish, Cornwall
Atl	Atlantic	corr(s)	correct, corrected, correction(s)
attrib	attribution, attributive	correl	correlated, correlation, correlative
Aug	August	corresp	correspondence
Austr	Australia(n)	cpd	compound, compounded, compounding
autobiog	autobiographical, autobiography	crit	critical
aux	auxiliary	cv	cultivar
		cyclop	cyclopedia

d	died		ext	extended, extension
DA	*Dictionary of Americanisms*		eye-dial	eye-dialect
DAE	*Dictionary of American English*			
Dan	Danish		f, ff	and following
DARE	*Dictionary of American Regional English*		famil	familiar(izing)
DAS	*Dictionary of American Slang*		Feb	February
dat	dative		fem	feminine
DBE	*Dictionary of Bahamian English*		fig	figurative, figure
DCan	*Dictionary of Canadianisms*		Fin	Finnish
Dec	December		folk-etym	folk-etymological, folk-etymology
def art	definite article		folkl	folklore
defin	defining, definition, definitive		foll	follow(s), followed, following
Delmarva	DE, eMD, eVA		Fr	French
dem	demonstrative		Franco-Amer	Franco-American
dept	department		FrCan	French Canadian (people)
deriv	derivation, derived, derivative		freq	frequent(ly)
derog	derogatory		Fri	Friday
descr	description, descriptive		Fris	Frisian
dial(s)	dialect(s), dialectal		ft	foot (measures); fort
dicc	diccionario		funct	function(al)
dict	dictionary		fut	future
dimin(s)	diminutive(s)		*F&W*	*Funk and Wagnalls Standard Dictionary*
diss	dissertation(s)		FW	fieldworker
dissim	dissimilated, dissimilation			
distrib	distribute(d), distribution, distributive		Gael	Gaelic
div	division		gaz	gazette(er)
DJE	*Dictionary of Jamaican English*		gen	general(ly); genitive
DN	*Dialect Notes*		geneal	genealogical, genealogy
DNE	*Dictionary of Newfoundland English*		genl	general
doc	document(ary)		geog	geography
DOST	*Dictionary of the Older Scottish Tongue*		geogr(s)	geographer(s), geographic(al)
Dr	Doctor		geol	geological, geology
DS	Data Summary		Ger	German
DSL	*Dictionary of the Scottish Language*		Gk	Greek
DSNA	Dictionary Society of North America		gloss	glossary
Du	Dutch		Gmc	Germanic
			gov	governor
e	east(ern)		govt	government
ed	edition, editor, editorial		gram	grammar, grammatical
EDD	*English Dialect Dictionary*		gs	grade school
EDG	*English Dialect Grammar*		gt	great
educ	educated, education(al)			
ellip	ellipsis, elliptical(ly)		Haw	Hawaiian
EModE	Early Modern English		hdbk	handbook
encycl	encyclopedia		Heb	Hebrew
engin	engineering		herb	herbaceous
Engl	England, English		hist	historic, historical(ly), history
entomol	entomologica, entomological, entomology (-ist)		horticult	horticultural(ist), horticulture
epenth	epenthesis, epenthetic		hon	honorable
Episc	Episcopal		hs	high school
equiv	equivalence, equivalent		Hung	Hungarian
erron	erroneous(ly)		hydrog	hydrographical, hydrography
esp	especially			
est	established		ibid	ibidem (in the same place)
et al	et alii (and others)		ie	id est (that is)
etc	et cetera (and so forth)		illit	illiterate
etym(s)	etymological, etymology (-ies)		illustr	illustrate(d), illustration
euphem(s)	euphemism(s), euphemistic(ally)		imit	imitation, imitative
eve	evening		imper	imperative(ly)
evid	evident(ly)		imperf	imperfect(ly)
ex(x)	example(s)		impers	impersonal(ly)
exag	exaggerated		in	inch
exc	except		inc	incorporated
exclam	exclamation, exclamatory		incl	include(d), including, inclusive
excr	excrescent		Ind	Indian
exped	expedition(s)		indef	indefinite(ly)
exper	experiment(al)		indic	indicative(ly)
expl(s)	explain(ed), explanation(s)		inf(s)	informant(s)
explor	exploration(s)		infin	infinitive(ly)
expr(s)	expression(s)		infl	influence(d)

info	information
infreq	infrequent(ly)
init	initial(ly)
inst	institute, institution
interp	interpretation, interpreter
interrog	interrogative(ly)
intj	interjection
intr	intransitive(ly)
intro	introduced, introducing, introduction
Ir	Irish
irreg	irregular(ly)
is	island(s)
Ital	Italian
iter	iteration, iterative
Jan	January
jct	junction
joc	jocular(ly)
jrl(s)	journal(s)
l, ll	lake; line(s)
lab	laboratory
LaFr	Louisiana French
LAGS	*Linguistic Atlas of the Gulf States*
LAMSAS	*Linguistic Atlas of the Middle and South Atlantic States*
LANCS	*Linguistic Atlas of the North Central States*
LANE	*Linguistic Atlas of New England*
lang(s)	language(s)
Lat	Latin
LAUM	*Linguistic Atlas of the Upper Midwest*
LGer	Low German
lib	library
ling	linguistic(s)
lit	literature, literary
Luth(s)	Lutheran(s)
m	meter(s); monsieur
mag	magazine
malaprop	malapropism
Mar	March
masc	masculine
math	mathematical, mathematics
ME	Middle English (in etymologies; elsewhere = Maine)
med	medic(in)al, medicine
MED	*Middle English Dictionary*
mem(s)	memorial(s)
metall	metallurgical, metallurgy
metaph	metaphor, metaphorical(ly)
metath	metathesis, metathetic(ally)
Mex	Mexican, Mexico
MexSpan	Mexican Spanish
mfg(r)(s)	manufacture, manufacturer(s), manufacturing
mid	middle
mid-aged	middle-aged (of Infs: 40-59)
midl	midland
midwest	midwestern
misc	miscellaneous, miscellany
mispronc	mispronunciation
Missip	Mississippi
MJLF	*Midwestern Journal of Language and Folklore*
MLG	Middle Low German
MLJ	*Modern Language Journal*
MLN	*Modern Language Notes*
mod	modern
ModE	Modern English
Mon	Monday
monogr	monograph(s)
ms(s)	manuscript(s)
mt(s)	mountain(s)
mth(s)	monthly, month(s)

MW	midwest
n	noun; north(ern)
NADS	*Newsletter of the American Dialect Society*
N Amer	North America(n)
narr(s)	narrative(s)
nat	natural
natl	national
naut	nautical
NB	New Brunswick
nd	no date
ne	northeast
NEast	northeast
neg	negative
NEng	New England
neut	neuter
newsl	newsletter
newsp	newspaper(s)
Nfld	Newfoundland
no(s)	number(s)
nom	nominative
non-std	nonstandard
Norw	Norwegian
Nov	November
np	no page
N&Q	*Notes & Queries*
ns	new series
nth(n)	north(ern)
nw	northwest
NYC	New York City
NYT	*New York Times*
obj	objective
obs	obsolete
occas	occasional(ly)
Oct	October
OE	Old English
OED(S)	*Oxford English Dictionary (Supplement)*
OF	Old French
old-fash	old-fashioned
ON	Old Norse
orig	origin, original(ly)
ornith	ornithological, ornithologist, ornithology
Oxfd	Oxford
p, pp	post (after); page(s)
PADS	*Publication of the American Dialect Society*
PaGer	Pennsylvania German
pejor	pejorative
perf	perfect
perh	perhaps
pers	person
pert	pertaining
petrol	petroleum
philol	philological, philology
philos	philosopher, philosophical, philosophy
phon	phonetic
phr(r)	phrase(s)
phys	physical
pl	plate; plural
PMLA	*Publications of the Modern Language Association of America*
poet	poetical
Pol	Polish
pop	popular(ly)
Port	Portuguese
poss	possessive; possible
ppl	participial
pple(s)	participle(s)
prec	preceded, preceding

pred	predicate, predication, predicative(ly)	statist	statistical(ly)
pref	prefix(ation)	std	standard, standardized
prehist	prehistoric, prehistory	StdE	Standard English
prelim	preliminary	sth(n)	south(ern)
prep(s)	preposition(s)	subj	subject
pres	present	subjunc	subjunctive
pret	preterite	subseq	subsequent(ly)
prob	probable, probably	subsp(p)	subspecies
proc	proceedings	suff	suffix(ation)
progr	progressive	sugg	suggest(ed), suggestion
pron	pronoun	Sun	Sunday
pronc	pronounced, pronunciation	superl	superlative
pronc-sp	pronunciation-spelling	suppl	supplement(ary)
Prot	Protestant	surv	survey
prov	proverb(ial); provincial	sw	southwest
psych	psychological, psychology	Sw	Swedish
pt	part; port	syll	syllable
pub	public; publication(s), published, publisher, publishing	syn	synonym(ous)
punct	punctuation		
		tech	technical, technological, technology
QR	questionnaire	terr	territory (-ies)
qrly	quarterly	Thu	Thursday
qu, qq	question(s)	topog	topographic(al), topography
quot(s)	quotation(s)	tr	transitive
		trans	transaction(s)
r	recto; river	transcr	transcribe, transcription
rec	record(s)	transf	transfer(red)
recoll	recollections	transl	translate(d), translation, translator, translating
redund	redundant	treas	treasury
redup	reduplicated, reduplication, reduplicative	Tue	Tuesday
ref(s)	refer, reference(s)		
refl	reflexive	ult	ultimate(ly)
reg	register; regular(ly)	uncert	uncertain
rel	related, relation, relative	uncom	uncommon
relig	religion, religious	uncult	uncultivated
repet	repetition, repetitive	univ	university
repr	representative(s); represented, represent(s), representing; reprint(ed)	unpub	unpublished
		unstr	unstressed
rept	report(s)	US(A)	United States (of America)
resp(s)	response(s)	usu	usual(ly)
rev	review		
revol	revolution(ary)	v	verb; verso
rr	railroad(s)	var(r)	variant(s), various, varying; variety (-ies)
Russ	Russian	vbl	verbal
		vd	various dates
s	south(ern)	vet	veterinarian, veterinary
Sat	Saturday	viz	videlicet (namely)
Scan	Scandinavian	vocab(s)	vocabulary (-ies)
sci	science(s)	vol(s)	volume(s)
Scotl	Scotland	vs	versus
Scots	Scottish		
se	southeast	w	west(ern); weekly
sec(s)	section(s)	*W2*	*Webster's New International Dictionary,* 2nd ed
secy	secretary	*W3*	*Webster's Third New International Dictionary*
Sept	September	wd	word
ser	series	Wed	Wednesday
serv	service	*WELS*	*Wisconsin English Language Survey*
sess	session	wildfl	wildflower
sg	singular	wks	works
sig	signature	*WNID*	*Webster's New International Dictionary*
SND	*Scottish National Dictionary*	wrn	western
soc	society (-ies)	WWI, WWII	World War I (or II)
sociol	sociological, sociology		
sp(p)	spelling(s), spelled; species	yd	yard
Span	Spanish	yr(s)	year(s)
SpanAm	Spanish American (people)		
spec	specific(ally)	zool	zoological, zoology
sp-pronc	spelling-pronunciation		
st	saint; street		
sta	station		

State Abbreviations

AK	Alaska
AL	Alabama
AR	Arkansas
AZ	Arizona
CA	California
CO	Colorado
CT	Connecticut
DC	Washington DC
DE	Delaware
FL	Florida
GA	Georgia
HI	Hawaii
IA	Iowa
ID	Idaho
IL	Illinois
IN	Indiana
KS	Kansas
KY	Kentucky
LA	Louisiana
MA	Massachusetts
MD	Maryland
ME	Maine
MI	Michigan
MN	Minnesota
MO	Missouri
MS	Mississippi
MT	Montana
NC	North Carolina
ND	North Dakota
NE	Nebraska
NH	New Hampshire
NJ	New Jersey
NM	New Mexico
NV	Nevada
NY	New York
OH	Ohio
OK	Oklahoma
OR	Oregon
PA	Pennsylvania
RI	Rhode Island
SC	South Carolina
SD	South Dakota
TN	Tennessee
TX	Texas
UT	Utah
VA	Virginia
VT	Vermont
WA	Washington
WI	Wisconsin
WV	West Virginia
WY	Wyoming

Signs and Symbols

~ is used to avoid repetition of a previously spelled-out word or phrase

‡ is used to indicate a word or sense of questionable genuineness

* is used to indicate unattested or hypothetical forms

+ is used for "and"

→ is used with dates to indicate first or last attestation

< is used for "derived from"

> is used for "from which is derived"

= is used for "equals"

I

I pron Usu |aɪ, ɑɪ|; also **chiefly Sth, S Midl** |a·, aə, ɑ·|; for addit varr see quots Pronc-spp *ah, oy, u(h)* Cf Pronc Intro 3.II.13, 3.III.2

Std senses, var forms.

1904 *DN* 2.423 **Cape Cod MA** (as of a1857), The pronoun *I* when unemphatic is often pronounced ah, as *ah be*. **1914** *DN* 4.158 **cVA** (as of 1901–7), Ah can't bide cats. *Ibid* 159, Ah was jes' fixin' tuh go. **1916** *DN* 4.345, *I* [a]. . . So pronounced throughout the South. **1922** Gonzales *Black Border* 174 **sSC, GA coasts** [Gullah], Uh haffuh hab [=I have to have] wife fuh cook fuh me. *Ibid* 179, Uh binnuh sleep, ma'am. **1925** *DN* 5.356 **seGA, swSC** [Black], Ah's [əz] fo hunnahed yeahs ol. *Ibid*, Ah [ɑ] done wrap he feet. **1930** *DN* 6.80 **cSC** [Black], Uh sesso [=I said so]. **1930** *AmSp* 6.170 **eVA** [Black], [əɪ wʌks . . əɪ dʌz . . əɪ ləɪks . . əɪz bɔːn]. *Ibid* 171, [a mits əm . .], and [a dʌznt laɪjk]. **1934** in 1944 *ADD* **cVA**, *I*. . . [a] in 'Ah live . . Ah reckon' [Inf Black]. *Ibid* **cGA**, Ah'm ([am]) not certain . . Ah think Ah'll go . . Ah don't know. *Ibid* **OK**, [ɑ] in 'I didn't,' 'I wouldn't.' **1934** *AmSp* 9.213 **Sth**, *Simplification of Diphthongs* . . [ɑɪ] or [aɪ] > [ɑ]. . *by, fire, I, ice . . my.* . . [*AmSp* Ed: For [aɪ] we have heard [a], [aə], and [ae] as well as [ɑ].] **1936** *AmSp* 11.33 **eTX**, In . . words . . such as *I'll . . I'd . . bite . . my .* ., Webster [aɪ] is likely to be [a] in East Texas when the word is not especially emphatic. . . In . . 'I'm right well,' the first two words are [am rat] as often as they are [aɪm raɪt]. **1941** O'Donnell *Great Big Doorstep* 17 **sLA**, Ahm behine in my wuk [=work]. **1941** *AmSp* 16.12 **eTX** [Black], I decided . . I knew there wasn't nothing I could do, [. . ɑ ‚dsaːdəd . . ə nju ðə wʌdn nʌθn ə kəd du]. *Ibid* 116 **VA**, A Northerner somehow expects a Virginian to say 'ah' and 'mah' for *I* and *my*. It appears, however, that the change of [aɪ] to a simple vowel or to another diphthong is a fairly rare occurrence. . . among the [101] girls [=students in a state college for women] who took my test. . . [11] changed the diphthong to [a] before a voiced consonant in *I've*. **1942** Hall *Smoky Mt. Speech* 44 **eTN, wNC**, *I* . . [is] very often [a·], [ɑ]. . . Sometimes *I* shows complete reduction of the second element, whereas other words in the same sentence show retention: [ju ˈmaɪtɪ ˈdæ‚gɔn ˈraɪt a· ˈwʊd] . . But the reduction . . may reach even to the first element. Unstressed, *I* . . may be [ɪ], [ə]. **1968** Moody *Coming of Age MS* 18 [Black], I had to tote Adline and Junior all the way here. You must think um superman or something. **1990** Simpson *Gt. Dismal* 7 **nNC, sVA**, "Where in Dare County you from?" "Hatt'ras Oyland," he said, "but Oy been all over Virginia with the Corps of Engineers."

i prep Pronc-spp *aye, ey, hy, 'y* [By reduction of *by* in exclam phrr *by God, by Jesus* and varr (often with minced forms), but cf also *ay* or *ah* intj in similar phrr; cf *OED ay* int. 1, *SND ay* int. 6(3), and std *egad*] **chiefly Sth, S Midl** Cf **dad** n², **gonnies, gorry, jallus** n²

Used in var exclam phrr, usu with a euphem for *God* or *Jesus*, to express strong emotion; see quots.

1843 (1916) Hall *New Purchase* 146 **IN**, I says one day to Nancy . . "I dad 'spose we put out and live there." **1873** (1969) Smith *Bill Arp's Peace Papers* 203 **GA**, I golly, there aint many of us can say that. **a1883** (1911) Bagby *VA Gentleman* 80, Every time a train passes . . , Uncle Jim seldom fails to exclaim, "I George! she's a goin' uv it." **1894** Riley *Armazindy* 1 **IN**, Name ain't down in *History,—/* But, i jucks! it *ort* to be! *Ibid* 5, I gum! *Ibid* 45, I jacks! *Ibid* 68, And the strangest thing, i jing! **1905** *DN* 3.12 **nCT**, I dad! . . Exclamation of surprise. **1908** Johnson *Highways Pacific Coast* 319 **ID**, 'I golly!' I said, 'you're goin' to kill me, ain't you?' **1908** *S. Atl. Qrly.* 7.333 **eSC** [Gullah], Pul! senkah [=same as] one jack nag! I golly! **1913** Kephart *Highlanders* 287 **sAppalachians**, Ey God, a favorite expletive, is the original of egad,

and goes back to Chaucer. **1927** in 1928 Green *In the Valley* 165 **eNC**, 'Y God, I reckon so. *Ibid* 166, No, 'y God, I don't. **1929** Sale *Specialist* 7 **ceIL**, All mixed up with hollyhocks—/ Everything! . . I jocks. **1930** *AmSp* 5.268 **Ozarks**, One of the Ozarker's favorite exclamations is best spelled *i-God*. **1935** Sheppard *Cabins* 299 **cwNC**, Aye jallus. **1940** *Amer. Mercury* June 211 **Sth**, Aye gonnies, if that little 'un didn't grow up six feet two. **1940** in 1944 *ADD* **AR**, [Radio:] 'Y grannies, we'll try it! . . Hy grannies! . . 'y dogs, we kin try . . 'Y doggies! . . Hy doggie(s)! [haɪ ˈdɔgi(z)]. **1942** Hall *Smoky Mt. Speech* 28 **wNC, eTN**, A few old men have been heard to employ the 'by word' *Aye God*. **1943** *Sat. Eve. Post* 13 Feb 14 **MS**, I Godfrey, what a day! **1969** *DARE* (Qu. NN32, *Exclamations like 'I swear' or 'I vow'*: "I _____.") Inf **GA84**, Ganny. **1969** *DARE* FW Addit **GA13**, "I god, I played the devil!" *I-God* [is] used real often in this region. **1990** *Lutz Coll.* **nNJ**, Both her mother (a Bergen County woman) and Robert's step-father's mother (in . . Morris Co., N.J.) used an expression of surprise or amazement that meant something like, "Now what do you think of that?" or, "Well, of all things!" Their phrase sounded like "I guy!"

I-all pron [Facetious extension of *I* by analogy with **we-all, you-all**] *joc*

I.

1929 *AmSp* 4.348, One example of *I all* occurred a short time ago in the strip, "Freckles and His Friends." . . "Africa? Man! dat's where I all come from too. Yassh." A day or two later I saw the same thing in the *Literary Digest* in a joke. . . "Yessah, Ah-all did have a business, but Ah done lost my business." **1942** in 1944 *ADD*, [Radio:] [In resp to the question: "Did you-all break the door?"] No, I-all broke my shoulder.

I-am n [Cf Exodus 3:14 "I AM hath sent me unto you."]

1 in phrr *big* (or *great*) *I-am*: A boastful or self-important person.

1966–69 *DARE* (Qu. HH8, *A person who likes to brag*) Infs **CA166, MI4, 26**, Big I-am; (Qu. HH17, *A person who tries to appear important*) Infs **CT16, MA5, NY12, NC61**, Great I-am; **CA17**, Big I-am; [**NJ1**, I-am-it man;] (Qu. II35) Inf **MA5**, Big I-am.

2 in phr *great I-am*: Used as an exclam.

1965–68 *DARE* (Qu. NN29a, *Exclamations . . "Great _____!"*) Infs **MS64, VA11**, I-am. [Both Infs old]

I be phr **chiefly Sth, S Midl** Cf **be** B1a(3)

I'll be—used in var oaths and exclams.

a1883 (1911) Bagby *VA Gentleman* 90, I speak Virginian, not the lingo of Bosting, or even of Ingling (perhaps you'd like for me to say England. I be blamed if I do). **1914** *DN* 4.75 **ME, nNH**, Killed! I be. Exclamation of surprise. **1930** Faulkner *As I Lay Dying* 65 **MS**, I be durn if it didn't give me the creeps. **1966** *Wilson Coll.* **csKY**, I be dog! **1966–69** *DARE* (Qu. NN7, *Exclamations of surprise*) Infs **GA5, LA40**, I be darned; **AR55**, I be dog; (Qu. NN9a, *Exclamations showing great annoyance*) Inf **KY30**, I be darned; **LA3**, I be durned. **1986** Pederson *LAGS Concordance (Exclamations of surprise)* 1 inf, **ceLA**, I be dog.

I-bought-you teeth n pl Cf **bought 2, store-bought**

1965–70 *DARE* (Qu. X13b, . . *False teeth*) Infs **AL61, MS60**, I-bought-you teeth; [**NC86**, S.I.B.—some I bought; **FL2**, S.S.B.—some she bought]. [All Infs Black]

I brought back what I borrowed n Cf **hold fast what I give you**

1957 *Sat. Eve. Post Letters* **neWI**, I brought back what I borrowed—Parlor Game. The Lender sits in special chair. One monitor whispers names of common articles to each . . [player]; a second person gives to . . [each player] the name of some other person present. In turn each person takes the person named to him by the hand and leads him/her to the lender with the statement, "I've brought back what I borrowed." "What is it?" asks the lender. In reply, "An old broom," or, "hunk of cheese," "case of smallpox," etc. The lousiest object is made to sit as lender, and the game continues with another round of borrowed goods.

I catch you See **catch him**

iceberg n Cf **icebox pickle, ice-water pickle**
See quots.
    1969–70 *DARE* (Qu. H56, . . *Kinds of pickles*) Infs **CA**178, **PA**189, Iceberg(s). [**1972** *Foxfire Book* 179 **nGA**, Iceberg green tomato pickle. . . Soak the tomatoes in a mixture of 1½ cups lime to 1 gallon water. . . Drain and soak for four hours in fresh water. Make a syrup of the sugar, vinegar, and spices, and bring it to a boil. Pour it over the tomatoes . . , and let stand overnight.]

ice berm n [**berm 2b**]
See quot.
    1971 *WI Conserv. Bulletin* Jan–Feb 13, Wind driving across the un-obstructed surface can push on the ice as if it were a flat sail and, on a large open lake, generate a tremendous amount of pressure. This power can drive the ice many feet inland and push soil into a bank along shore that may reach heights of over 6 feet on some lakes. These "ice berms" are common on almost every large body of water in Wisconsin.

ice bird n [*OED* 1620 → applied to the dovekie] Cf *DNE*
Any of several sea birds: esp the **dovekie,** but also the **razor-billed auk,** the black guillemot *(Cepphus grylle),* or the common **murre 1** (here: *Uria aalge*).
    1898 (1900) Davie *Nests N. Amer. Birds* 24, Dovekie. *Alle alle.* . . The little Ice-bird of the fishermen and the Sea Dove of ornithologists. **1917** (1923) *Birds Amer.* 1.31, Dovekie—*Alle alle.* . . Other names.—Little Auk; Sea Dove; Alle; Rotch; Ice-bird. **1925** (1928) Forbush *Birds MA* 1.43, *Alca torda.* . . Razor-billed Auk. *Other names:* . . Ice-bird. **1946** Hausman *Eastern Birds* 334, Razor-billed Auk. . . Ice Bird. . . Arctic shores southward to Newfoundland and New Brunswick; formerly Maine. In winter southward as far as Long Island, and uncommonly along the coast of North Carolina. **1951** *AmSp* 26.276 **MA,** Names compounded with the prefix *ice,* as a rule, are applied to our hardiest species—those for which the frigid season seems to have no terrors. That is certainly true for all called simply *ice bird,* including the . . razor-billed auk . . common murre (Mass.), dovekie (Greenland, New-foundland, Labrador, New Brunswick, Nova Scotia, Maine, Mass.), and common guillemot (Mass.)

icebox n
1 also *ice chest:* A gas or electric refrigerator. [Transf from *icebox, ice chest* a refrigerator cooled by ice]
    1950 *WELS Suppl.* **csWI,** Icebox—used for both ice and mechanical models. *Ibid* **cwWI,** My girls object to my calling the G.E. [=General Electric refrigerator] an icebox. **1959** *VT Hist.* 27.143, Ice chest. . . Refrigerator. Occasional. **1961** McDavid *Coll.* **csOK,** Electric ice box—electric refrigerator. [Inf old] **1965–70** *DARE* (Qu. D10b, *The place to keep food cool if it is run by electricity or gas*) 116 Infs, **widespread,** Icebox; **CT**18, 26, **FL**15, Ice chest. **1982** *Greenfield Recorder* (MA) 22 May sec A 6, I always make up one large batch of pie paste, ready for the wetting and keep it in a large tin in the ice chest. **1989** *DARE* File **cIA** (as of 1950s–88), My grandmother always referred to every electric refrigerator she owned as "an icebox."
2 in phrr *icebox (is) open:* See quot. Cf **barn door 2b, endgate 1b**
    1970 *DARE* (Qu. W24c, *Sayings to warn a man that his trouser-fly is open*) Infs **GA**90, **IL**140, **VA**73, Icebox (is) open. [All Infs young, Black]
3 in phrr *tap (on) the icebox:* See **tap the icebox.**

icebox is open See **icebox 2**

icebox melon n Also *icebox watermelon* [Because it fits easily into a refrigerator] Cf **frigidaire watermelon, icebox tomato**
A round cultivar of the watermelon *(Citrullus lanatus).*
    1966–70 *DARE* (Qu. I26, . . *Kinds of melons*) Infs **AR**55, **OK**43, **SC**53, **TX**89, Icebox melon(s); **CO**20, Icebox melon—smallish one; **CT**2, Icebox melon—watermelon about the size of a head; **FL**6, Kinds

of watermelon—cannonballs, congos, icebox melon; **TX**102, Icebox melon—small watermelon; **FL**19, 37, **SC**7, Icebox watermelon(s). **1976** Olds Seed Co. *Seeds* 18 **csWI,** Sugar Baby. . . An icebox or midget melon of superior quality. . . Fruits are perfectly round, about 7 to 8 inches in diameter. [**1976** Bailey–Bailey *Hortus Third* 1169, Water-melon. . . Recently some small "icebox" cultivars of fairly good quality have become available.] **1986** Pederson *LAGS Concordance* **Gulf Region** (*Watermelons*) 21 infs, Icebox (melon or watermelon); 9 infs, Ice-box (melons or watermelons)—small; 5 infs, Icebox melons—small(er) and round; 1 inf, Icebox melons—small, round, dark; 1 inf, Icebox melons—you could put them in [the] refrigerator; 1 inf, Icebox melon—matures in sixty days; 1 inf, Icebox—small, yellow meat; 1 inf, Icebox melon—little, round, pinkish meat; 1 inf, Icebox melon—size of canta-loupe; 1 inf, Icebox melon—light green inside, make melon balls.

icebox open See **icebox 2**

icebox pickle n
A type of cucumber pickle intended to be kept in the refrig-erator rather than processed and stored at room temperature.
    1966–67 *DARE* (Qu. H56, . . *Kinds of pickles*) Infs **FL**19, **NC**38, Icebox pickles. [Both Infs old] **1989** *DARE* File **csWI,** Icebox pickles are chopped cucumbers mixed with condensed milk, vinegar and sugar. You put that overnight in the refrigerator. Those are icebox pickles. *Ibid* **csWI,** Icebox pickles are about the easiest pickles to make. You just cook up a brine with salt, vinegar, and spices on top of the stove and pour it over your sliced cucumbers. They keep for quite a while in the refrigerator. Some people call them refrigerator pickles.

icebox tomato n [Appar by analogy with **icebox melon**]
A small cultivar of the tomato *(Lycopersicon lycopersicum).*
    1986 Pederson *LAGS Concordance,* 2 infs, **TX,** Icebox tomatoes—small (ones).

icebox watermelon See **icebox melon**

icebreaker n [See quot 1923] Cf **ice duck 1**
=**mallard 1.**
    1923 U.S. Dept. Ag. *Misc. Circular* 13.8 **IL,** Mallard. . . *Vernacular Names.* . . *In local use.* . . Ice-breaker (. . . Applied to late migrants thought to be a race distinct from the fall flight). **1982** Elman *Hunter's Field Guide* 150, Mallard. . . *Common & regional names.* . . Ice-breaker.

ice bridge n **AK** Cf **ice road**
A roadway of artificially thickened ice across a river.
    1968 *DARE* File [*Anchorage Daily Times,* prob 31 Jan], Alaskan Ice Bridge: How Is It Put Up? . . Ice is built upon existing natural ice rather than on the ground. . . There may be numerous applications, letting one 3-inch layer of water become solid before another is spread upon it. **1973** *Fairbanks Daily News-Miner* (AK) 12 Dec (*Tabbert Coll.*), Alyeska Pipeline Service Company has awarded a contract . . to build an ice bridge across the Yukon River. . . The bridge will be five feet thick, 75 feet wide at the top and 150 feet wide at the base. A maximum of 10 men will be employed in the water spraying project to build layers of ice on the bridge. **1979** *Ibid* 30 Jan (*Tabbert Coll.*), Tons of military equipment have moved across an ice bridge spanning the Tanana River . . where the Army has built a four-foot-thick bridge. **1990** *Ibid* 4 Feb sec B 4 (*Tabbert Dict. Alaskan Engl.*), The timber is about 12 miles from Nenana in a roadless area. Harvesting will take place this winter and next over ice bridges and winter roads.

ice cactus n
Prob an **ice plant 1.**
    1969 *SC Market Bulletin* 25 Sept 4, Ginger lily, ice cactus, pink wax plant, . . 25¢ ea.

ice candle n [*EDD* (at *ice* sb. 1 (2)) 1736 →] Cf **ice candy,** *DNE*
An icicle.
    1950 *WELS* (*Long, pointed pieces of ice that hang down from the eaves*) 1 Inf, **WI,** Ice candles.

ice candy n Cf **ice candle**
See quots.
    1954 *Harder Coll.* **cwTN,** Ice candy—icicle. **1988** *DARE* File **cwTN,** [Letter:] We did not often have icicles; and when they were hanging from eaves, they were rather smallish, comparable to stick candy. . . I can recall, "It so cold this mornin', ice candy hangin' off roof."

ice chest See **icebox 1**

ice-cream n attrib

1 Of a suit or pair of trousers: white or light-colored.

   1890 *Road* (Denver) 19 April 1/3 *(DA),* Tenderness of heart perchance warns him against dragging a light colored ice cream suit into the ides of November with its chilling blasts. **1908** *Sat. Eve. Post* 5 Sept 15, Johnny ambled up, decorated with a blue coat, white vest an' ice-cream pants, an' his hair all slicked down. **1940** Faulkner *Hamlet* 151 **MS,** He had on the first white flannel trousers Frenchman's Bend ever saw. They were the last ones too. . . That night the night station agent told of a frightened and battered man in a pair of ruined ice cream pants. **1946** *AmSp* 21.34 **ceTX** [College slang], Ice cream pants. . . Pearl gray colored trousers and slacks worn by seniors. **1950** *WELS (Words . . for clothes)* 1 Inf, Ice-cream suit. **1965** *Liberator* (NY NY) Aug 23/1 **Detroit MI** [Black], Stacked broads rushed in on the arms of stiffies straight from the cornfields, you know—them cats with the cowboy hats and ice-cream suits. **1986** Pederson *LAGS Concordance,* 1 inf, **ceFL,** Ice-cream pants—white flannel, coat, 1920s style.

2 Of a browse plant: highly desirable; especially favored.

   1937 U.S. Forest Serv. *Range Plant Hdbk.* W107, Fernleaf loveroot . . seldom is abundant in any one place and, due to its high palatability but relative scarcity, is often referred to as an ice cream plant. **1949** *Pacific Discovery* Jan–Feb 7/2, In the parlance of U.S. deer managers this would put mahogany in the class of an "ice cream plant"—one so favored by deer that it is commonly overbrowsed regardless of the balance between deer and the total available forage. **1982** McGregor *Counting Sheep* 29 **NW,** As the native bunchgrasses and other perennial plants of these regions ("ice cream plants," as cattlemen called them) were replaced by exotic, early maturing annual forbs ("hard tack"), the lowland ranges produced . . smaller percentages of year-round feed. **1987** Henderson *Landscaping* 26 **Upper MW,** Many of these fruits are not immediately desirable as wildlife foods. Some summer and fall fruits like American elderberry and Nanking cherry are eaten as soon as they are ripe and are frequently referred to as "ice cream plants" for wildlife. **1990** *DARE* File **csWI,** In the last few years I've heard several Forest Service people use the term *ice-cream plant* when they were talking about deer browse.

3 See quots.

   1967 *DARE* (Qu. II24, . . *The part of a town where the well-off people live*) Inf **TX9,** Ice-cream section. **1986** Pederson *LAGS Concordance (Loam)* 1 inf, **cwMS,** Ice-cream land. [Inf is a farmer]

ice-cream bee n

Perh a **sweat bee.**

   1967 *DARE* (Qu. R21, . . *Other kinds of stinging insects*) Inf **IL26,** Ice-cream bees, or sand bees.

ice-cream cactus n Cf **ice-cream 2, pitahaya**

Any of var cacti having juicy edible fruits.

   1894 *Scribner's Mag.* 15.597 **Rio Grande Valley,** There is an almost unvarying succession of the . . "pitahaya," or ice-cream cactus.

ice-cream candy n Also *ice-cream drop,* ~ *nugget* [Prob from the appearance] *somewhat old-fash* Cf **ice-cream cone**

Any of var types of candy made from fondant; see quots.

   1873 Bailey *Life in Danbury* 273 **CT,** And a package of ice-cream candy. **1896** (1973) Farmer *Orig. Cook Book* 447, Ice Cream Candy. . . sugar. . . cream of tartar. . . boiling water. . . vinegar. Boil . . until, when tried in cold water, mixture will become brittle. . . As soon as it can be handled, pull until white and glossy. While pulling, flavor . . using vanilla, orange . . or melted chocolate. Cut in sticks or small pieces. **1967** *DARE* Tape **PA55** (as of c1900), My brother and I would sell ice-cream nuggets as they were called. He manufactured these little cubes that were about an inch and a half cube, wrap them in paper and pack them in a can. We'd take two tubs of these ice-cream nuggets on our express wagon, one chocolate and one vanilla, and peddle them around town for a penny apiece, ringing a bell. **1968** *DARE* (Qu. H82b, . . *Cheap candy . . sold years ago*) Inf **NY92,** Ice-cream drops—vanilla creams, chocolate covered.

ice-cream cloud See **ice-cream soda (cloud)**

ice-cream cone n Also *candy cone* Cf **ice-cream candy**

See quots.

   1967–68 *DARE* (Qu. H82b, . . *Cheap candy . . sold years ago*) Inf **MI61,** Ice-cream cones—little cones, "candy cones" we called them,

had sugar candy on the top, no ice cream; **CT**12, Penny ice-cream cones. [Both Infs old] **1992** *DARE* File **NYC** (as of early 1950s), An ice-cream cone was a smallish penny candy, shaped like an ice-cream cone, and which had the appearance and consistency of styrofoam. There were also bananas made of the same substance which were equally unpalatable.

ice-cream drop See **ice-cream candy**

ice-cream festival n *somewhat old-fash*
=**ice-cream social.**

   1893 *Harper's New Mth. Mag.* 86.593 **DC,** The groups gathered here and there enjoy themselves about as they do at church sociables and ice-cream and strawberry festivals in their home villages. **1968** *DARE* (Qu. FF1, . . *A 'social' or 'sociable'*) Inf **MD26,** Ice-cream festival—ice cream and cake sold by church out on lawn; **MD49,** Strawberry festival, ice-cream festival—given by church or school—[the] item named is sold, people socialize, sometimes there's a raffle or games; **NY45,** Ice-cream festival—ice cream and strawberries, in the summer; **NY61,** Ice-cream festival. [3 of 4 Infs old]

ice-cream melon n Also *ice-cream watermelon* [Perh from the color of the flesh]

A cultivar of the watermelon *(Citrullus lanatus).*

   1863 Burr *Field & Garden* 195, The Water-Melon. . . Ice-Cream. A large, very pale-green sort. . . Flesh white, very sweet and tender, and of remarkably fine flavor; seeds white. **1986** Pederson *LAGS Concordance,* 1 inf, **seGA,** Ice-cream melon—yellow meat—a watermelon; 1 inf, **cwAR,** Ice-cream melon—type of watermelon; 1 inf, **cwMS,** Ice-cream watermelon—yellow meat; 1 inf, **cLA,** Ice-cream watermelon—striped, inside yellow. **1990** *Seed Savers Yearbook* 258, [*Watermelons:*] *Ice Cream* . . a very old var., quite early.

ice-cream nugget See **ice-cream candy**

ice-cream party n
=**ice-cream social.**

   1904 M. Kelly *Little Citizens* 203 *(DA),* They expected some word of farewell—perhaps even an ice-cream party. **1968–70** *DARE* (Qu. FF1, . . *A 'social' or 'sociable'*) Inf **TX40,** Box socials, ice-cream parties; **TX80,** Box supper, ice-cream parties; (Qu. FF2, . . *Kinds of parties*) Inf **CA136,** Ice-cream parties—make homemade ice cream. [2 of 3 Infs old] **1986** Pederson *LAGS Concordance,* 1 inf, **cTX,** Ice-cream party; 1 inf, **ceGA,** Ice-cream parties. [Both Infs old]

ice-cream plant See **ice-cream 2**

ice-cream social n Also *ice-cream sociable;* for addit varr see quots **scattered, but chiefly Inland Nth, N Midl** See Map on p. 4 Cf **box social, cake social, ice-cream festival,** ~ **party,** ~ **supper**

A social gathering at which ice cream and sometimes other foods are sold to raise money for some benevolent purpose; occas a private party at which ice cream is served.

   1873 *Winfield Courier* (KS) 15 May np **seKS,** The Ladies of the Congregational church will hold an Ice Cream Sociable at the residence of Capt. John Lowrey. **1898** *Dly. Ardmoreite* (Ardmore, Okla.) 15 July 3/3 *(DA),* The ladies of the Methodist Church . . gave an ice cream social last night on the lawn at the parsonage. **1935** Sandoz *Jules* 179 **wNE** (as of c1895), Make the Niobrara feud look like one of them ice-cream socials gettin' so popular with the parson's hen yards. **1950** *WELS (A 'social' or 'sociable')* 23 Infs, **WI,** Ice-cream social(s); 2 Infs, Ice-cream sociable; 1 Inf, Pie-and-Ice-cream social. **1959** Lomax *Rainbow Sign* 160 **LA** [Black], I hadn't thought of even courtin till one night I went to a little ice-cream sociable. **1965–70** *DARE* (Qu. FF1) 190 Infs, **scattered, but chiefly Inland Nth, N Midl,** Ice-cream social; **NY12, PA104, SC11,** Ice-cream sociable; **PA148,** Ice-cream-and-cake social; (Qu. FF2, . . *Parties*) Inf **TX80,** Ice-cream socials; (Qu. FF16, . . *Celebrations*) Inf **MO35,** V.F.W. ice-cream social. **1967** *NE City News-Press* (NE) 11 Oct 2/6, The ice cream social Tuesday night . . was a huge success. . . The proceeds from the sales will be used for school and PTA projects at the school. **1967** *DARE* Tape **IL4,** Then when they come out [at a shivaree], they get 'em to give them something like a ice-cream social or something like a keg of beer; **IL23,** We still have socials . . ice-cream socials. **1991** *Waunakee Tribune* (WI) 1 Aug 4/1, The Waunakee Band Boosters will host an "Ice Cream Social" during the concert [of the Waunakee Community Band].

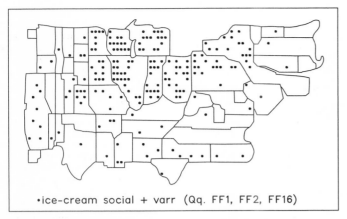

•ice-cream social + varr (Qq. FF1, FF2, FF16)

ice-cream soda (cloud) n Also *ice-cream cloud*
   1967–70 *DARE* (Qu. B9, . . *Big clouds that roll up high before a rainstorm*) Inf **NJ**45, Used to call them ice-cream sodas when [I] was a kid; **CA**4, Ice-cream soda clouds; (Qu. B11, . . *Other kinds of clouds*) Inf **NC**87, Ice-cream clouds—like puffs or scoops of ice cream on a cone.

ice-cream supper n Also *cream supper* **scattered, but esp Sth, S Midl, TX** See Map Cf **hot supper 1**
=**ice-cream social.**
   1892 *Canebrake Herald* 1 July 3/1 *(DA)* **cAL,** A delightful ice cream supper was given by the ladies. **1908** *DN* 3.322 **eAL, wGA,** Ice-cream supper. . . An evening entertainment at which ice-cream is sold. **1946** Wilson *Fidelity Folks* 98 **swKY,** Ice-cream suppers were long used as a means to raise money for churches and schools. **1965–70** *DARE* (Qu. FF1, . . *A 'social' or 'sociable'*) 38 Infs, **scattered, but esp Sth, S Midl, TX,** Ice-cream supper; **AL**20, Cream supper; (Qu. FF2, . . *Kinds of parties*) Infs **GA**8, **KY**7, **MS**22, Ice-cream suppers; **MS**1, Cream suppers. **1967** *DARE* Tape **TX**36, Once and a while . . they'd have a ice-cream supper, maybe every two or three years at somebody's house. **1986** Pederson *LAGS Concordance,* 1 inf, **nwGA,** Ice-cream suppers— social events [in] private homes; 1 inf, **ceMS,** Ice-cream suppers. **1989** *DARE* File **cAR** (as of 1945), There were ice-cream suppers when I was a kid, church suppers. These were like potlucks, only more desserts. People mostly brought desserts, not hot dish things.

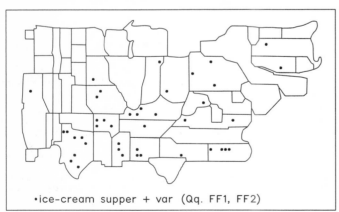

•ice-cream supper + var (Qq. FF1, FF2)

ice-cream watermelon See **ice-cream melon**

ice creeper See **creeper 7**

iced highway, iced road See **ice road**

ice duck n
   1 Any of var ducks; see quot 1951. Cf **icebreaker, ice mallard**
   1911 *Forest & Stream* 77.173, (European Widgeon) *Mareca penelope.* C.E. Brewster informs me that this species is known as Ice Duck at Crisfield, Md. **1923** U.S. Dept. Ag. *Misc. Circular* 13.8 **MO,** Mallard *(Anas platyrhyncha). . . Vernacular Names. . . In local use. . .* Ice duck. **1951** *AmSp* 26.276, Names compounded with the prefix *ice,* as a rule, are applied to our hardiest species—those for which the frigid season

seems to have no terrors. . . True ducks, to which the name *ice duck* has been given, embrace the mallard (Mo. . .), European widgeon (Md.), goldeneye (Ill., Tenn., Iowa), bufflehead (Ill.), old squaw (Tenn.), white-winged scoter (Va.), and goosander (Ill.) **1982** Elman *Hunter's Field Guide* 150, *Mallard. . . Common & Regional Names. . .* Ice duck. *Ibid* 250, *White-winged Scoter. . .* Ice duck.
   2 Brünnich's guillemot *(Uria lomvia lomvia).*
   1951 *AmSp* 26.276 **AK,** In the use of *ice duck. . .* as applied to Brünnich's guillemot . . , there is no variance as to implied hardiness, but the term is somewhat of a misnomer as to appearance of the bird.

ice gull n
=**glaucous gull.**
   1872 Coues *Key to N. Amer. Birds* 311, *Glaucous Gull. Ice Gull. Burgomaster. . .* Arctic America; S. coastwise in winter to the Middle States. **1917** (1923) *Birds Amer.* 1.41, *Larus hyperboreus. . . Other Names. . .* Ice Gull. **1951** *AmSp* 26.277 **ME, MA, NY,** Ice gull . . glaucous.

icehouse n
   1 A place where ice is made or sold. [By ext from *icehouse* a structure for the storage of ice]
   1830 Watson *Annals Philadelphia* 202, *Ice Houses.* These have all come into use among us since the war of Independence. After them came the use of ice creams. . . Public ice houses for the sale of ice, is a more modern enterprise than either. **1992** *DARE* File **TX,** Where I grew up in a tiny town in east Texas, every morning the men who were working in the piney woods would stop at the icehouse to get ice for their water barrels—otherwise the water would be hot by afternoon. The icehouse was a pretty big establishment where the ice was made as well as sold. They would chop it or break it to the size you wanted. *Ibid* **cwMS,** I assumed that it [=a tavern] continued to be called Jack's Icehouse because that had always been its name—since it had been an icehouse for many years. *Ibid* **MS,** Nick's Icehouse—a favorite watering hole. . . What better place to market beer than an icehouse?
   2 By ext: See below. **chiefly TX**
   a A convenience store.
   1967 *DARE* FW Addit **TX,** I heard a caller to a Houston radio station use *icehouse* in reference to the small, often open-fronted, grocery stores [which are] usually called stop-and-shop stores in this area. The caller was obviously not a native Texan. **1983** *DARE* File **cnTX,** Icehouse—A convenience grocery; said to be a Dallas-area word. Refrigerated foods are a staple, hence the name. **1984** *Cuisine* 13.10.15 **eTX,** I have just returned from the icehouse down the street with the fruit of a dime's wise investment. *Ibid,* I would sprint down to the icehouse, palm a Moon Pie off the pastry rack, and slide a bottle of Yoo-Hoo from the melting ice . . of the soda box. **1986** Pederson *LAGS Concordance* **San Antonio TX** *(Small neighborhood store)* 1 inf, Icehouse—open early and late; 1 inf, Icehouses—small, all-night grocery stores; 1 inf, An icehouse—convenience store with a glass front. **1991** *Contemp. S. Short Fiction* 118 **San Antonio TX,** "God damn," my father said, in the exact tone he'd say *Yes Ma'am* when my mother asked him to pick up a loaf of bread at the ice house, which is what convenience stores used to be called in San Antonio.
   b A tavern.
   1988 Black *Killin' Time* (Sound Recording) **eTX,** When the whistle blows at five o'clock / there's only one place I'll be found / Down at Ernie's Icehouse liftin' longnecks to that good old country sound. **1992** *DARE* File **seTX,** Icehouse is/was a frequent name for a beer joint— tavern was a literary acquisition for me in southeast Texas. *Ibid* **cTX,** They are a 'regional' occurrence in central TX and I'm primarily aware of the Icehouse/Izehouse label among the Chicano/Mexicano community in San Antonio where it prevails [over 'tavern'] on outside signs. *Ibid* **MS,** Jack's Icehouse in Jackson, Mississippi, became a tavern when the ice business got too slow. *Ibid* **MS,** In Hattiesgulch, Mississippi . . there is a fine drinking establishment: Nick's Icehouse. **1995** *Ibid* **csWI,** In the early 1980s, there was a tavern in Stoughton called the Ice House.

ice mallard n [See quot 1923] Cf **ice duck 1**
=**mallard 1.**
   1923 U.S. Dept. Ag. *Misc. Circular* 13.8 **MO,** Mallard. . . *Vernacular Names. . . In local use. . .* Ice mallard (. . applied to late migrants thought to be a race distinct from the fall flight). **1951** *AmSp* 26.276 **MO, AR,** Mallard . . *ice mallard.*

ice, mark it on the See **write it on (the) ice**

ice mitt See **icy mitt**

ice mouse n
=rat-tailed maggot.
 1970 *DARE* (Qu. P6, *Other kinds of worms also used for bait*) Inf **MI**112, Ice mice—for winter fishing.

icening n [Var of **icing** n 1; cf **-en** suff[5], *DBE, DJE*] Cf **frost-ening**
 1968 *DARE* (Qu. H64, *The sweet covering spread on top of a cake*) Inf **PA**29, [ˈɑɪsnɪn]; **PA**143, Icening [aɪsɪnɪŋ].

ice-out n chiefly **NEng** Cf *DCan* Also called **break-up** n 1
The breaking and melting of ice on rivers and lakes in the spring.
 1966 *Portsmouth Herald* (NH) 30 Apr 8/3, Windy weather of the past week hastened the clearing of Maine lakes and ponds of ice. . . The ice-out line now runs roughly from Danforth through Lincoln. **1966** *Monadnock Regionaire* Summer 17 **swNH**, Suckers go upstream to spawn, and soon after ice-out in the spring start back toward deep water. **1972** *Down East* Mar 57 **NEng**, The smelter who delays too long in getting his house ashore has the unsettling experience of taking part in the ice-out. **1982** Sternberg *Fishing* 50, Following ice-out, Great Lakes fishermen catch brown trout as large as 25 pounds. **1985** McPhee *Table of Contents* 252 **ME**, Just after breakup—or ice out, as they call it in Maine—a friend and I were on Allagash Lake. **1985** Clark *From Mailbox* 28 **ME**, Then the ice-out picnic and watching for the first sign of the loons—all part of the excitement of April.

ice pick n
1 **=horn snake 1.**
 1968 *DARE* (Qu. P25, . . *Kinds of snakes*) Inf **LA**34, Ice pick—a water snake with a real pointed tail and it's hard, hard, hard; book name is horn snake.
2 See quot.
 1970 *DARE* (Qu. W42a, . . *Men's sharp-pointed shoes*) Inf **VA**39, Ice picks—keen toes. [Inf Black]

ice pitcher n Cf **icy mitt**, *DS* II5b
Fig: a snub, "the cold shoulder."
 1900 *DN* 2.42 **eMA**, Ice-pitcher. . . Refusal to recognize an acquaintance. **1950** *WELS* (*If you meet someone who used to be a good friend, and he pretends not to know you . . "He _____."*) 1 Inf, **WI**, Gave me the ice pitcher.

ice plant n
1 also *ice vine, icicle plant*: A plant of the genus *Mesembryanthemum*, usu the naturalized *M. crystallinum*. [From the glistening papillae on the leaves which produce an effect like that of ice crystals; *OED* 1753 →] orig **CA**, now more widespread
 1817 Eaton *Botany* 56, Mesembryanthemum. . . crystallinum, ice plant. **1859** Emory *Rept. U.S. Mex. Boundary* 2.1.16 **coastal sCA**, Growing with the *Abronias* a species of ice-plant . . is frequently found. **c1887** Sturtevant *Notes Edible Plants* 363 (*DAE*), The ice plant . . is advertised in American seed lists of 1881 as a desirable vegetable for boiling like spinach, or for garnishing. **1914** Saunders *With Flowers in CA* 266, *M[esembryanthemum] crystallinum* . . found on Southern California sea beaches. . . is remarkable for its glittering, often reddish foliage which seems frosted with particles of ice and on this account it has long been one of the world's green-house curiosities under the name of ice-plant. **1949** Arnow *Hunter's Horn* 15 **KY**, The windows were covered with ancient vines—Virginia creeper, honeysuckle, hopvine and ice vine. **1961** Thomas *Flora Santa Cruz* 157 **cwCA**, Mesembryanthemum L. Ice Plant. . . *M. nodiflorum.* . . Slender-leaved Ice Plant. . . *M. crassifolium.* . . Common Ice Plant. **1966** *DARE* FW Addit **wCA**, Ice plant—a plant growing along the California coast; used often as a ground cover, has purple to blue flowers and the leaf contains water. **1970** *DARE* (Qu. I35, . . *Kitchen herbs . . grown and used . . around here*) Inf **TX**85, Ice plant; (Qu. S26e, *Other wildflowers*) Inf **CA**189, Ice plants. **1976** Bailey–Bailey *Hortus Third* 729, Mesembryanthemum. . . Icicle plant, ice plant.
2 **=Indian pipe 1.**
 1830 Rafinesque *Med. Flora* 2.243, Monotropa uniflora. . . Iceplant. . . Used by Indians and herbalists. **1873** in 1976 Miller *Shaker Herbs* 173, Ice Plant. . . The whole plant is ivory white, resembling frozen jelly,

and when handled, melts away like ice. **1892** (1974) Millspaugh *Amer. Med. Plants* 105-1, Ice Plant. . . This strange waxy or bluish-white, fleshy, inodorous, semi-parasitic herb, grows from 2 to 8 inches high. **1934** Haskin *Wild Flowers Pacific Coast* 247, The name, Indian pipe, is only one of its titles. . . Other names inspired by the color and texture of the stems are . . corpse plant, and ice plant. **1975** Hamel–Chiltoskey *Cherokee Plants* 40, Indian pipe, fit root, ice plant.
3 A **crownbeard** (here: *Verbesina virginica*).
 1940 Clute *Amer. Plant Names* 275, Verbesina virginica. . . Ice plant. [**1944** AL Geol. Surv. *Bulletin* 53.233, On frosty mornings in the fall ribbons of ice often exude from the lower part of the stem [of *Verbesina occidentalis* and *V. virginica*], an interesting phenomenon that city dwellers seldom see, because they are not likely to get out in the country on such mornings before the delicate ribbons melt.]
4 A **rockrose** (here: *Helianthemum canadense*).
 1958 Jacobs–Burlage *Index Plants NC* 39, Helianthemum canadense. . . Ice-plant. . . The American Indians used it as a[n] . . astringent. **1974** (1977) Coon *Useful Plants* 97, Helianthemum canadense . . Ice plant. . . The common name refers to the fact that in late fall crystals of ice may shoot from the base of the stem.

ice polo n
A game similar to ice hockey.
 1948 Coatsworth *South Shore* 52 **ceMA** (as of 1920s), One can hear the sharp smack of sticks on the puck as the boys play endless games of ice polo. **1967** *DARE* (Qu. EE27, *Games played on the ice*) Inf **OH**11, Ice polo—like ice hockey.

ice pop n esp **NYC** area
A confection made by freezing fruit juice or a similar liquid on a stick.
 1977–78 Foster *Lexical Variation* 97 **NJ**, Sticks of frozen water are known as *ices* (1), *icicles* (17), *(ice) pops* (20), . . *popsicle* (134 responses). **1980** *NADS Letters* **NYC**, In New York there were ice pops before there were popsicles. **1989** *DARE* File **Long Is. NY** (as of 1950s), My Mom made what she called ice pops. She put juice in an ice cube tray with tongue depressors in each division, and put the tray in the freezer. Making ice pops at home was a lot cheaper than buying commercially made popsicles and icicles. **1990** *Ibid* **Long Is. NY** (as of 1950s), An ice pop was an iced confection on a stick. You could either buy it from the ice cream vendor or make it at home with a special ice cube tray that had a place to put the stick.

ice potato n [Pronc-sp for **Irish potato** reflecting reduction of [ˈaɪrɪš > aɪš > aɪs], perh infl by folk-etym] esp freq among *Black speakers*
 1965 Brown *Manchild* 47 [Black], I learned some things down South too. . . Grandma told me what peckerwoods were and taught me not to call white potatoes white potaters, "because they ain't white potaters, they is ice potaters." **1970** *DARE* (Qu. I9, *Other names [including nicknames] for potatoes*) Inf **FL**49, Ice potato. [Inf Black] **1970** *DARE* FW Addit **VA**41, Ice taters [ˈaəs ˈtedəz] [FW: Inf has heard]. [Inf Black] **1991** Still *Wolfpen Notebooks* 128 **sAppalachians**, You ever heard of Luther Burbank, the man who messes with plants? I have, and he's going to Hell when he dies. He changed the ice potato from what it used to be. There's Scripture against changing nature.

ice, put it on (the) See **write it on (the) ice**

ice road n Also *iced road*, *~ highway* Cf **ice bridge**
A road maintained for winter hauling (esp of logs) by sprinkling water over frozen ground.
 1942 ME Univ. *Studies* 57.41 [Pulpwood operations], Ice roads . . must be frequently sprinkled and carefully maintained. *Ibid*, Large quantities of water are required to make a good iced road. . . A good iced road extends through a very few inches of snow down to the ground. *Ibid* 43, A truck is helpless unless it is on an iced road or highway. **1946** Newton *Paul Bunyan* 102 **cnMI**, Then he ordered the cookees to pump the gravy into a water tank which we used to sprinkle the ice roads in winter. **1966–70** *DARE* Tape **MI**27 (as of c1914), In the wintertime, I was on the sprinklers, makin' ice roads; **MI**125, [FW:] What does this refer to when they put water on it to make a place for the sleigh to go? [Inf:] That was an ice road where you had hard pulls, see, and that road was kept iced and clean. [FW:] This was going down hill? [Inf:] No, uphill. . . That had to be just so. And there was no—nothing on that road, no dirt nor nothin' because sleighs'll stick. [FW:] How about the horses? Don't they slip on that ice? [Inf:] Sure, but they

had sharp shoes. **1969** Sorden *Lumberjack Lingo* 60 **NEng, Gt Lakes,** A logger reported that an ice road at Rib Lake was used as late as May 15 one year with fifteen inches of ice still intact. **1976** *Fairbanks Daily News–Miner* (AK) 6 Dec sec A 7 (Tabbert *Dict. Alaskan Engl.*), Original plans were to move the rig in mid-November, but temperatures then were too warm to provide the frozen ground base needed to construct an ice road.

ice root n
=**goldenseal 1.**
   1940 Clute *Amer. Plant Names* 3, *H[ydrastis] canadensis*. . . Ice root.

ice tag n[1] [*tag* hanging piece of material] Cf **ice candle, tag**
An icicle.
   1954 *Harder Coll.* **cwTN,** *Ice tag*—icicle. **1966** *PADS* 46.26 **cnAR,** During the big freeze everything had ice tags on it. **1967** *DARE* FW Addit **cSC,** Ice tags—icicles.

ice tag n[2] **chiefly Nth, N Midl, esp PA** See Map
The game of tag played on ice.
   1965–70 *DARE* (Qu. EE27, *Games played on the ice*) 92 Infs, **chiefly Nth, N Midl, esp PA,** Ice tag.

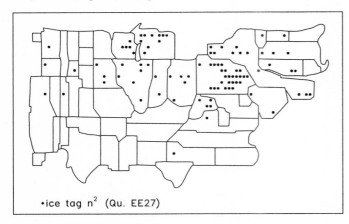

•ice tag n[2] (Qu. EE27)

ice vine See **ice plant 1**

ice-water pickle n Also *cold-water pickle*
A type of pickle made from cucumbers treated initially with ice water.
   1965 Levinson *Complete Book Pickles* 104, *Ice water pickles*. . . Soak cucumbers, sliced lengthwise, in ice water for 2 hours. Remove, drain and pack in hot sterilized jars with sliced onions, mustard seed and celery seed. **1967–69** *DARE* (Qu. H56, . . *Kinds of pickles*) Inf **CA**146, Ice-water pickles—also called cold-water pickles; **IA**13, Ice-water pickles—made from cucumbers; [**IN**41, Iced pickles].

ice worm n **AK** Cf *DCan*
See quots.
   1959 Hart *McKay's AK* 31, The "ice worm" began as a great fictional joke during the gold-rush days and was a source of many tall stories. Newcomers were treated to drinks with a bit of spaghetti in them and for many years the ice-worm legend was popular. . . Real ice worms do exist and specimens may be seen in the Territorial Museum in Juneau. **1968** *DARE* (Qu. CC17, *Imaginary animals*) Inf **AK**1, Ice worm; **AK**8, Ice worms—imaginary, but there's a real one in the sloughs. **1970** *DARE* FW Addit **AK,** I have heard two versions: spaghetti put in water in a pill jar . . to tease greenhorns; a strip of fur (rabbit, etc.) sold as "ice worm" to tourists. **1991** Tabbert *Dict. Alaskan Engl.* 264, Once again fact proves fiction true. Ice worms do exist, though the wags who created the mythical worm in Dawson at the turn of the century almost certainly did not know it. The real worm (*Mesenchytraeus solifugus* and several other species) are about three-quarters to an inch long and live near the surface of glaciers, feeding on airborne pollen and spores. The ice worm of the sourdoughs' imaginings was made widely known through the writings of Robert Service. . . Though strictly speaking of Canadian origin, the ice worm and ice worm cocktail have become part of Alaskan lore as well.

ice, write it on (the) See **write it on (the) ice**

ichiban adj [Japanese]
Number one; superlative.

1955 *AmSp* 30.46, If he [=American serviceman stationed in the Far East] can count, he knows *ichiban* 'number one' and finds it expressive ('This beer is *ichiban*'). **1960** *AmSp* 35.119 [Among American G.I.'s in Korea], *Ichi-ban,* or 'number one,' indicates what was superlatively good. . . Through extensive use, the phrase meaning 'number one' tended to lose its impact and to be used in the sense of merely 'good.' **1972** Carr *Da Kine Talk* 92 **HI,** Examples of Japanese words of wide currency in Hawaii . . *ichiban* 'number one.' **1989** *DARE* File **Honolulu HI,** I'm familiar with "ichiban"—"number one, best"—but I don't use it all the time. **1990** *DARE* File **cwCA,** There is a restaurant in San Francisco with *Ichiban* as part of its name, so some non-Japanese people know the meaning 'number one' through that source.

icicle n Pronc-sp *ishic(k)le;* for addit varr see quots
Std sense, var forms.
   1899 (1912) Green *VA Folk-Speech* 241, *Ishicle*. . . Icicle. **1925** Dargan *Highland Annals* 94 **cwNC,** We's well up Smoky, an' the coldest wind ablowin' that ever made an i-shickle out of a man's gizzard. **1949** *AmSp* 24.110 **neGA,** *Ishe-shicles* ['aɪʃˌʃɪklz]. . . Icicles. **1968** *DARE* FW Addit **VA**13, Icicle [ˌæɪs'šɪkl]—old-fashioned mountain pronunciation.

icicle mushroom n
An unidentified mushroom.
   1961 Douglas *My Wilderness* 277 **nME,** The icycle [sic] mushroom. . . we collected and broiled.

icicle pepper n [Perh from the shape; but cf quot 1972 at **icicle pickle**]
   1969 *DARE* (Qu. I22d, *Names for different kinds of peppers—large sweet*) Inf **MO**19, Icicle peppers.

icicle pickle n [From the shape]
A type of pickle made with cucumbers cut lengthwise.
   1951 Farmer *Cook Book* 784, *Icicle Pickles*. . . Peel *cucumbers,* remove seeds, and cut in strips ½ inch wide. Cover with ice water and let stand overnight. Drain. Pack upright in sterilized jars. Boil vinegar, water, and sugar 3 minutes. Add salt and pour over cucumbers. **1968–70** *DARE* (Qu. H56, . . *Kinds of pickles*) Infs **GA**70, **NY**104, 115, 153, **PA**143, 203, 221, Icicle pickle(s); **NY**230, Icicle pickles—small, made with alum; **VA**35, Icicle pickles—hot water, alum, pack with syrup—a very crisp pickle. **1972** *Foxfire Book* 177 **nGA,** *Icicle pickles (cucumbers, sweet bell peppers, and green tomatoes)*—This is a process that takes fourteen days, but is actually much easier than it sounds. Select and cut up a peck . . of the above. . . Cut cucumbers into six- to eight-inch strips. Put in a crock, and pour boiling water over the top . . and a half cup of salt per peck of vegetables. Let this mixture sit for nine days. **1989** *DARE* File **csWI** (as of early 1950s), My mother made icicle pickles—they were called that because of the shape. One recipe said to quarter the cucumbers lengthwise, another said to cut them into four-inch lengths. *Ibid* **ceWI,** To make icicle pickles you take two gallons of cucumbers and slice them the long way; that makes them look like icicles, I guess. . . Every day you make some syrup, pour it over the cucumber lengths, pour it off, and the next day do it again. All total it takes about a week.

icicle plant See **ice plant 1**

icing n
1 A sweet topping for cakes and baked goods; see quots. **widespread, but less freq Nth, Pacific** See Map and Map Section Cf **filling 1, frosting 1**
   1821 Willich *Domestic Encycl.* 3.127, *Iceing for Tarts.*—Beat the yolk of an egg and some melted butter well together, wash the tarts with a feather, and sift sugar over as you put them in the oven. **1896** (c1973) Farmer *Orig. Cook Book* 439 **eMA,** The mixture in which small cakes are dipped for icing is fondant. **1928** Peterkin *Scarlet Sister Mary* 30 **SC** [Gullah], You go on back to bed . . whilst I whips up de icin. Gawd'll help me fix dis cake. **1936** *AmSp* 11.314 **Ozarks,** I shore don't want th' icin' t' brickle off'n that 'ar cake. **c1960** *Wilson Coll.* **csKY.** **1965–70** *DARE* (Qu. H64, *The sweet covering . . on top of a cake*) 695 Infs, **widespread, but less freq Nth, Pacific,** Icing; **PA**167, Whipped-cream icing; (Qu. H28, . . *Doughnuts*) Inf **NC**88, Doughnut with icing; **MO**35, Icing doughnut; (Qu. GG22b, . . "*Well, that certainly _____.*") Inf **SC**54, Puts the icing on the cake.

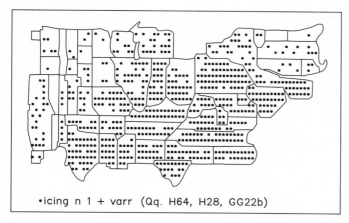

•icing n 1 + varr (Qq. H64, H28, GG22b)

2 A sweet sauce; see quots. **Sth, S Midl** Cf **filling 2, frosting 2**

1956 Ker *Vocab. W. TX* 261 *(Sweet liquid served with pudding)*, 1 inf, Icing. **1967–69** *DARE* (Qu. H21, . . *The sweet stuff that's poured over . . [pan]cakes)* Inf **IL**94, Icing [FW: Inf questions response]; (Qu. H66a, . . *Sweet liquid that you pour over a pudding)* Infs **KY**34, 52, **MO**17, **TX**36, Icing; (Qu. H66b, . . *Sweet liquid that you pour over ice cream)* Inf **MO**4, Chocolate icing. **1986** Pederson *LAGS Concordance* **Gulf Region** *(Sauce . . sweet liquid)* 17 infs, Icing; 1 inf, Icing—sauce over apple dumpling; 1 inf, Icing—sweet sauce, perhaps [same as] frosting [FW: Inf vague]; 1 inf, Icing—on top of pie; 1 inf, Icing—made from egg whites [FW suggests inf may mean meringue].

icing v Cf **icening**

1982 Barrick Coll. **csPA**, Icing . . ice (a cake). "To icing a cake."

ick See **icky**

ickity-ick adj Also *icky-icky* Cf **bookity-book, nippity-tuck** Nip and tuck.

1968 *DARE* (Qu. KK54, *Just about equal, very close: "They were both fast runners and it was _____ all the way.")* Inf **NJ**22, Icky-icky [ɪki-ɪki]; **NJ**39, Ickity-ick [ˈɪkɪti-ɪk].

icky adj Rarely *ick* [Hypocoristic; perh varr of *sticky*] **chiefly Nth, N Midl, Pacific** See Map *esp freq among young and mid-aged speakers and among women* Cf **ishy** Sticky, cloying; unpleasant, displeasing; uncomfortable—used as a generalized expression of distaste.

1929 in 1992 *DARE* File [From a song in the film "The Great Gabbo"], And when I eat my ice-cream cone / I get all over icky. **1935** *Vanity Fair* Nov 71 **NYC**, If the straight music is also oversweet, the term *icky* . . is frequently employed to denote this. **1941** in 1942 *AmSp* 17.13, [Song lyrics:] No ickeroo will do . . I'm . . in an icky plight. **1949** in 1986 *DARE* File **Sth**, Icky equals tacky or silly. "I certainly look icky." **1950** *WELS* **WI** ("I've got to wash my hands; they're all _____.") 1 Inf, Icky; *(A day when the air is very still, moist, and warm)* 1 Inf, Icky; *(They painted the house a(n) _____ color)* 2 Infs, Icky; *(On a day when you don't feel just right)* 2 Infs, Icky—about the weather. **1952** Kauffmann *Philanderer* (1953) 13 *(OEDS)*, 'It's just that—oh, I don't know—now everything's so icky.' . . Another of her dubious charms. The high-school words. **1959** Bellow *Henderson* 200 **CT**, Under the thickened rain clouds, a heated, darkened breeze sprang up. . . choky, sultry, icky. **1965–70** *DARE* (Qu. Y40a, . . *Sticky stuff: "I've got to wash my hands. They're all _____.")* 18 Infs, **scattered Nth, CA**, Icky; (Qu. B2, *If the weather is very unpleasant, you say it's a _____ day)* Infs **IL**45, **NJ**4, **PA**184, **VA**105, Icky; **IL**34, Ick; (Qu. B8, *When clouds come and go all day)* Inf **IL**45, Icky day; (Qu. X17, . . *A damp cellar)* Inf **WA**22, Icky; (Qu. Y39, . . *"The children have been eating candy and they've got their faces all _____.")* Infs **CA**32, 59, 112, **IN**35, **MA**2, **NJ**13, **WA**28, 33, Icky; (Qu. Y40b, . . *Sticky stuff)* Inf **NY**157, Icky stuff; (Qu. BB5, *A general feeling of discomfort or illness that isn't any one place in particular)* Infs **CA**82, 164 **IL**28, **MI**33, Feel(ing) icky; **CA**107, **MA**57, Icky (all over); (Qu. BB16b, *If something a person ate didn't agree with him, he might just feel a bit _____)* Infs **CA**53, **IL**102, **IN**15, 28, **KS**2, **MA**57, **WI**47, Icky; (Qu. BB39, . . *When you don't feel just right)* Infs **MA**57, **NY**199, **OH**45, Icky; (Qu. GG14, . . *Someone who fusses or worries a lot)* Inf **DC**11, Icky; (Qu. GG34b, *To feel depressed or in a gloomy mood)* Inf **RI**15, Icky; (Qu. HH16, *Uncomplimentary words with no definite meaning)* Inf **FL**16, He's icky;

(Qu. NN17, . . *"That _____ fly won't go away.")* Inf **IN**32, Icky. [36 of 47 total Infs female, 28 young or mid-aged] **1992** *DARE* File **OR**, It's a term showing disgust. . . In my variety one would use "ick" or "yuck" and "icky" or "yucky".

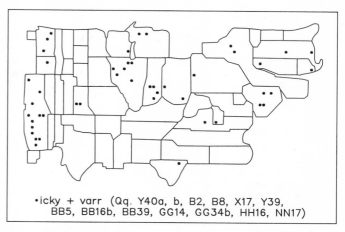

•icky + varr (Qq. Y40a, b, B2, B8, X17, Y39, BB5, BB16b, BB39, GG14, GG34b, HH16, NN17)

icky-acky-over n, exclam Cf **eevy-ivy-over, illy-ally-over, licka-licka-lacka** =**Antony-over.**

1967 *DARE* (Qu. EE22, . . *The game in which they throw a ball over a building)* Inf **DC**2, Icky-acky-over; (Qu. EE23a, . . *What do you call out when you throw the ball?)* Inf **DC**2, Icky-acky; other side would say "Over."

icky-icky See **ickity-ick**

icta n Also sp *icter, ikta, iktus* [Chinook Jargon; see quot 1863] **Pacific NW, AK** A thing, portable possession; goods, equipment; also fig.

1856 *Democratic State Jrl.* (Sacramento CA) 4 Oct 3/1 **OR**, They are getting short of blankets and other *ictas*. **1862** (1863) Winthrop *Canoe & Saddle* 53 **nwWA**, My motley retinue followed me humbly, bearing "ikta," my traps, and their own plunder. [**1863** Gibbs *Chinook Jargon* 6 **OR**, *Iktah*. . . A thing; goods; merchandise; clothing.] **1900** *Everybody's Mag.* Dec 539 **AK, nwCanada**, Either my life or my *ictas* (possessions) would have been required to make good the loss. . . A white man, I told them, . . always does as he chooses with his own *ictas*. **1918** *DN* 5.25 **Pacific NW**, *Icter*. . . A small or delicate thing or person. . . General. **1958** McCulloch *Woods Words* 93 **Pacific NW**, *Iktus*—(Various spellings) . . means stuff, gear, all the junk that a man carries around in his packsack.

icy mitt n Also *ice mitt, icy mit(ten)* somewhat old-fash Cf **ice pitcher, mitten** n Fig: a rejection or refusal; a snub—often in phr *give one the icy mit.*

1897 *KS Univ. Qrly.* (ser B) 6.88, Icy mitten: cool refusal. **1915** *DN* 4.244 **MT**, Give (one) the icy mit. . . To reject as a suitor. **1935** *AmSp* 10.17 (as of c1900) [Underworld argot], Ice or Icy mitt. A cold or hostile reception. **1968** *DARE* (Qu. II5b, *When you don't want to have anything to do with a certain person . . "I'd certainly like to give him the _____.")* Inf **IN**38, Icy mitt.

Idaho brainstorm See **Idaho rain**

Idaho rain n Also *Idaho brainstorm, ~ shower* joc Cf **Mormon rain(storm), Oklahoma rain, Oregon mist 2** A duststorm, sandstorm.

1934 (1940) Weseen *Dict. Amer. Slang* 100 **West**, Idaho brain storm—A twister; a cylindrical sandstorm. **c1971** Hall *Snake River Valley* **sID** *(A dry storm)* 1 inf, Idaho rain; 1 inf, Idaho shower.

iddicasion See **educate**

ide See **idea 2**

idea n Usu |ˌaɪˈdiə|; for varr see below Std senses, var forms.

1 |aɪˈdɪr, aɪˈdir|; pronc-sp *idear;* for addit pronc and sp varr see quots. **scattered, but esp NEng, NY** Cf Pronc Intro 3.II.26

1836 Smith *Col. Crockett's Exploits* 129, "Let us take an indeer." So we walked up to the bar, took a nip, and let the matter drop. [**1890** *DN* 1.37 **csME,** *Idea:* the added *r* [of colloquial English spoken in London] I look upon as vulgar and avoid.] **1904–22** in 1944 *ADD* **NEng,** *Idea.* . . "The idear of it!" Freq. **1905** *DN* 3.57 **eNE,** Pronunciations like *idear.* . are imported only. **1930** *AmSp* 6.96 **eVA,** *Idea* ['əɪdɪəɹ]. This is not uncommon in Peninsular speech, though the [ɹ] is lighter than that in New England coast speech. **1933** *AmSp* 8.2.45 **neNY,** The addition of [r] after vowels in unstressed syllables, as [aɪdɪər] for *idea* . . is occasionally heard, usually from older people of the more rural districts. **1942** *AmSp* 17.154 **seNY, NYC,** In . . *idea,* final [ə] frequently changes to [ɚ]. **1950** Stuart *Hie Hunters* 37 **eKY,** Slide back down. I've got a idear. **1959** *VT Hist.* 27.144 **eVT,** [aɪˈdɪr]. . . Common. **1965** *DARE* FW Addit **cwCA,** [aɪˈdiɚ]—reported as a common Bay Area pronunciation. **1966–67** *DARE* Tape **MA6,** [aɪˈdɪɚ]; **HI2,** That gave the idear [aɪˈdɪɚ] for later. **1979** *DARE* File **wCT,** [aɪˈdɪɚ].

2 |aɪˈdi, ˈaɪdi|; pronc-spp *idee, idy;* for addit pronc and sp varr see quots. **chiefly Sth, S Midl; also NEng**

1829 Kirkham *Engl. Grammar* 194, [Improper:] i de—[pronounced:] i de a. **1843** Thompson *Major Jones' Courtship* 58 **GA,** I hadn't no sort of a ide how she was gwine do it. **1861** Holmes *Venner* 1.124 **NEng,** He don't like the idee of dancin'. **1891** *DN* 1.160 **cNY,** ['aɪdi]. **1893** Shands *MS Speech* 39, Negroes and illiterate whites say *idy* and *idee* (['aɪdi] and ['aɪdi]). **1902** *DN* 2.237 **sIL** [Pioneer dialect], ['aɪdi]. **1903** *DN* 2.317 **seMO,** Idy [aɪdi]. **1906** *DN* 3.120 **sIN,** [aɪdi]. **1907** *DN* 3.223 **nwAR,** ['aɪdi]. **1908** *DN* 3.322 **eAL, wGA,** ['aɪdi] . . or ['aɪdi]. **1928** *AmSp* 3.402 **Ozarks,** The final unstressed *-a* is often turned into short *y.* . . *Idea* becomes either *idy* or *idee,* the latter form being the more emphatic. **1936** in 1952 Mathes *Tall Tales* 212 **sAppalachians,** "Cole," the officer said quietly, "I guess you know what I've come for." "No idy at all," drawled Grannison. **1951** *PADS* 15.66 **cwNH** (as of 1920s), *Idee.* **1967–68** *DARE* FW Addit **swAL,** ['a,dɪz]; **MD31,** [a'di]. **1970** *DARE* (Qu. JJ35a) Inf **IL126,** Idee [aɪˈdi]. **1970** *DARE* Tape **TX96,** That was the main ['aɪ,dɪ]. **1989** *New Yorker* 27 Feb 56 **nwTX,** We don't have no *i-dee.*

3 |ˈaɪdiə|; pronc-sp *aideah.* **chiefly Sth, S Midl** Cf Intro "Language Changes" IV.2

1890 *DN* 1.24 **SC,** ['aɪdiə] . . said to be general. **1892** *DN* 1.216 **Philadelphia PA,** *Idea.* . . The accent on the first syllable is very common. *Ibid* 239 **Kansas City MO,** *Idea.* Generally accented on the first syllable. **1893** Shands *MS Speech* 39, *Idea* ['aɪdiə]. This word has two or three different pronunciations among the various classes of people. The educated people generally pronounce it with the accent on the first syllable. **1908** *DN* 3.322 **eAL, wGA,** ['aɪdiə]. **1930** *DN* 6.80 **cSC** [Black], Uh done curryspon [=I have given up] de aideah o' goin'. **1944** *PADS* 2.15 **AL, GA, NC, SC, VA,** *Idea* ['aɪdiə]: Frequent pronunciation of many standard speakers, especially in black belt.

idear See **idea 1**

idee See **idea 2**

ideer See **idea 1**

identical adj Also aphet *'denticul, dentikul* Cf **dientical**
Std sense, var forms.

1843 (1916) Hall *New Purchase* 228 **IN,** That's the dentikul toone! **1922** Gonzales *Black Border* **sSC, GA coasts** [Gullah glossary], *'Denticul*—identical.

idiot n Usu |ɪdɪət|; also |ˈɪdjət, ˈɪjət, ˈɪjɪt| Pronc-spp *eediot, eejit, i(d)jit;* for addit varr see **A** below Cf Pronc Intro 3.I.5.a
A Forms.

1890 *Century Illustr. Mag.* Dec 249, You're two of the confoundest, dad-blastedest old eejits that ever was. **1893** Shands *MS Speech* 39 [Black], *Ijit.* **1905** *DN* 3.58 **NE,** The passing of [dj] into [j] is common: *ijjit.* **1908** *DN* 3.322 **eAL, wGA,** Idiot [ˈɪjət]. . . A common pronunciation. **1919** *DN* 5.39 **TN,** *Eegit.* **1923** *DN* 5.206 **swMO,** *Eediot.* **1928** *AmSp* 3.403 **Ozarks** (as of 1916–27), *Little, itch, inch, idiot,* and *oblige* have the sound of *ee.* **1934** *AmSp* 9.43 **Sth,** After *d* in such words as *idiom, idiot* . . one often hears [j] and sometimes, though rarely, [j] in the South, but some Southerners use [ɪ]. **1941** *LANE* Map 465, 1 inf, **nVT,** [ɪdjəˆt]; 1 inf, **ceVT,** [ɪdʒət]. **1944** *PADS* 2.29 **eKY,** *Eedient* ['ɪdɪənt]. . . Rural. Common. **1955** Stong *Blizzard* 16 **seIA,** I guess there's nothing we can do till the ijjut gets here. **c1960** *Wilson Coll.* **csKY,** *Idiot* [ɪjɪt]—rather common among elderly, and for fun. **1981** Pederson *LAGS Basic Materials* **Gulf Region,** 4 infs, ['ɪdʒɪt]; 3 infs, ['ɪdʒət]; 1 inf, ['ɪˈɪdjət]; 1 inf, ['ɪdɪˆənt]. **1984** Burns *Cold Sassy* 163

nGA (as of 1906), I told her she sounded like a idjit. **1991** *Macoupin Co. Enquirer* (Carlinville IL) 6, [From a 1961 issue quoting "oldsters":] A simpler minded person might be termed quar or be called a iggiot or ediot.
B Sense.
A channel rockfish (here: *Sebastolobus alascanus*).

1936 *AK Sportsman* Aug 17, Then there are such undesirable varieties as mud sharks, dog-fish, devil fish, turbot and a variety of red cod they call "idiots." **1953** Roedel *Common Fishes CA* 136, *Channel Rockfish.* . . *Unauthorized Names:* Idiot. **1973** Knight *Cook's Fish Guide* 383, Idiot—Rockfish, Channel. **1993** *Capital Times* (Madison WI) 25 Aug sec D 6/4 **Los Angeles CA,** Now he turns to something labelled "red ocean perch," a beautiful fish with mottled red skin. . . "It's short-spine thornyhead—fishermen call them 'idiots'—and they're hard to find because the big ones are all sold to Japan."

idiot stick n
1 Any of var hand tools, spec:
a also *idiot spoon,* ~ *tool;* Esp among loggers and miners: a shovel or other digging tool. **chiefly West** Cf **banjo B2, Irish banjo**

1930 Williams *Logger-Talk* 25 **Pacific NW,** *Idiot stick:* A shovel. **1937** *AmSp* 12.74 [Among Civilian Conservation Corps workers], *Idiot stick*—shovel, pick, axe. **1948** *PADS* 9.34 **OK,** *Idiot spoon.* . . *idiot stick.* . . Among men of greater skill, those who use such things as picks and shovels are idiots. The tools they use are therefore *idiot sticks.* **1954** *AmSp* 29.273 **NY,** An idiot-stick needs no brains to manipulate it—only muscle! **1958** McCulloch *Woods Words* 93 **Pacific NW,** *Idiot stick*—A large scoop shovel. **1966** *DARE* (Qu. HH42, . . *A common laborer;* total Infs questioned, 75) Inf **OK27,** Idiot-stick operator—idiot stick [is a] shovel. [Inf young] **1966** *DARE* FW Addit **SD,** *Idiot stick*—Black Hills miners' term for a shovel. They also call it a banjo. [FW: I have also used these terms myself when working in the mines of Idaho.] **1986** Pederson *LAGS Concordance,* 1 inf, **cwFL,** A set of idiot tools—post-hole diggers.
b See quot. [Cf *EDD idjit* sb., *nidget* sb.²]
1966–68 *DARE* (Qu. L35, *Hand tools used for cutting underbrush and digging out roots*) Inf **AR47,** Idiot stick—weed cutter with sharp edges on both sides; (Qu. L37, *A hand tool used for cutting weeds and grass*) Infs **AR40, 47, IN42, TX37,** Idiot stick; **KS12,** Idiot stick—straight stick, surrogated [sic] iron at the bottom—used around here, but no one knows another name.
c See quot.
1959 *AmSp* 34.78 **nCA** [Logger jargon], *Idiot stick.* . . A peeling bar.
2 =**gee-haw whimm(e)y-diddle.**
1970 *DARE* FW Addit **seKY,** *Idiot stick*—another name for a gee-haw whimmy-diddle—so called because only an idiot can make it work. [Inf worked at a craft shop.]

idiot tool See **idiot stick 1a**

idjit See **idiot A**

idjucation See **educate**

idle adj Also *idle-minded* [*OED idle* a.2.b *"Obs."*]
Slow-witted.
1899 (1912) Green *VA Folk-Speech* 237, *Idle.* . . Wandering in mind; light-headed. **1967** *DARE* (Qu. HH3, *A dull and stupid person*) Inf **TX26,** Idle-minded.

idle bread n [Cf Proverbs 31:27 "She . . eateth not the bread of idleness"]
Unearned sustenance.
1972 *DARE* File **seAR,** "Do you suppose I can get him to mend that fence?" "No, he prefers to live on idle bread."

idle-minded See **idle**

idlesome adj esp S Midl Cf **-some**
Lazy, shiftless.
1953 Randolph–Wilson *Down in Holler* 255 **Ozarks,** *Idlesome.* . . Given over to idleness and sloth. "Tom sure is idlesome nowadays." [One inf] says that "*idlesome* is an old word, and it means more than just idle." **1954** Harder Coll. **cwTN,** *Idlesome.* **1967** *DARE* (Qu. A9, . . *Wasting time by not working on the job*) Inf **LA9,** Being idlesome. **1986** Pederson *LAGS Concordance* (The poor whites—white man's terms) 1 inf, **cnAL,** An idlesome man = "a common man"—pejorative.

idol n

A duck or goose decoy.

1937 Pearson *Adventures* 120 **NC,** Daylight duck- and goose-hunting was carried on by use of decoys. A "stool" usually consisted of a few live geese, more rarely a few live ducks, and generally from a hundred to two hundred wooden decoys, or "idols," as some Carolina hunters called them. **1952** Brown *NC Folkl.* 1.553 **c,eNC,** *Idol. . .* A duck decoy.

idy See **idea 2**

-ie suff[1] See **-y**

-ie suff[2] [Prob back-formation from **-ies 1**]

See quot.

1929 *AmSp* 5.20 **Ozarks,** *Waistie. . .* Waist, shirt. This form is very common, and does not seem to be a diminutive, or a facetious term. *Ibid, Waspie. . .* Wasp.

-ie suff[3] Also sp *-y* [By ext from std use as dimin suff; cf **-ies 2, -sie**] Cf **aggie, alley** n[2], **commie, dropsie, glassie, immie**

Often preceded by *-s-:* Used to form names for types of marbles, actions in marble play, marble games, etc. Note: The form *-sie* appears in many cases to represent the plural *-s* + *-ie* (compare, for instance, *dropsie* with *drops* [at **drop** n C7a]); in others it may represent the dimin suff *-sie* (cf **-sie**).

1958 *PADS* 29.39 **WI,** *Potsy. . .* A marble game. **1958** *Sat. Eve. Post Letters* **GA** (as of c1905), "Onesies," also known as "chalkies," were the least expensive marbles, and were rarely played with. . . "Twosies" were by far the most popular, and cost more than "onesies." **1963** *KY Folkl. Rec.* 9.3.58, *Large marbles . .* aggie *.* tawey. . . *Stone marble . .* aggie *. .* stonie. *Ibid* 59, *Broken or chipped marble . .* chippie *. .* crackie *. . Colored glass marble, translucent . .* moonie *. .* purey. *. . White colored marble . .* creamy *. .* whitey. *Ibid* 62, Small pinch of dirt on which a marble is sometimes elevated: *hillie.* **1970** *Thompson Coll.* **cnAL** (as of 1920s), *Dropsy*—a marble game in which the marks try to drop marbles through a hole in the top of a cigar box. **c1970** Wiersma *Marbles Terms,* [Infs listed such terms for marbles as] darkies, glassie, milkies, moonie, peerie, purie, shinie, steelie. *Ibid* **seMI** (as of 1960), *Hopsy. . .* The name of a bouncing shot. *Ibid* **swMI,** *Keepsie*—when one player knocks out the majority of marbles from the circle he wins, gets to keep opponents' marbles. *Ibid* **swMI,** *Kneesy*—an illegal procedure which enables the player to get closer to the pit . . ; leads to the call: "No kneesies." *Ibid, Nudgie . .* a marble played with illegal wrist action. *Ibid* **swMI,** *Throwsy . .* a shot in which a marble is thrown overhand at another marble in an effort to hit it. . . "No throwsies this game." **1973** Ferretti *Marble Book* 29, *Marbles . . aggies . . alleys . . clayeys, commonies, commies, kimmies* or *immies . . Chinees, crockies* or *potteys . . steelies . . glassies.*

-ies suff

1 Pronc-sp for nonstd pl of nouns ending in |st, sp, sk|. Cf **-es** suff[1] **1a, -ie** suff[2]

1913 Kephart *Highlanders* 285 **sAppalachians,** The ancient syllabic plural is preserved in beasties (horses), nesties, posties . . (these are not diminutives). **1954** *Harder Coll.* **cwTN,** *Ghost.* Pl. *ghosties. Ibid,* The house wren builds *. .* nesties. **1968** *DARE* (Qu. CC17) Inf **VA**31, Ghosties. **c1970** Pederson *Dial. Surv. Rural GA* **seGA,** [In the words *nests, desks, fists,* and *ghosts,* plurals of the type ['nestɨz, 'deskɨz, 'fɨstɨz, 'goustɨz] occur frequently; those of the type ['nestɨz, 'deskɨz] occur only rarely.]

2 often with inserted *-s-;* In children's games: used to form names for actions, figures, and situations in games, or for games themselves; hence used to form exclams usu claiming the right to perform certain actions. Note: These words appear to be singular, but limited contexts make it difficult to be sure; some of them may belong rather at **-ie** suff[3]. Cf **burysies, clearsies, digsies, dubs** n pl, exclam, **easies, eyesies, fensies, footsies, guessies, halvsies** and also the entries for other terms listed in quots below

1942 Berrey–Van den Bark *Amer. Slang* 663.1, *Blindsies, hopscotch played with the eyes . . blindfolded . .* scotchies, *the figures traced on the ground. Ibid* 663.2, *Helpsies, helping to balance oneself; moochies, "mooching," or moving the hand . .* squirmies, *twisting the feet. Ibid* 665.6, *Interj. . .* changies!, *called for permission to change marbles . .* downsies! *. . said to a* [marble] *player who has lifted his hand off the ground to shoot.* **1963** *KY Folkl. Rec.* 9.3.60 **eKY,** *When marbles . . are not to be kept . .* fun *. .* funs *. .* funsies. *Ibid* 61, *When marbles . .*

change owners as they are won *. .* keeps *. .* keepsies. *Ibid* 63, *Demand for right to stay in ring once the marble has stuck . .* stick *. .* sticks *. .* sticksies *. .* stickies. *Ibid* 65, *To ask for permission to clean path of shooter . .* cleans *. .* cleansies. *Ibid, To ask for permission to move shooter . .* ennies *. .* movies. *Ibid* 66, *Command to keep shooting hand on the ground . .* no uppies. *Ibid, When shooter has landed in a good shooting position . .* shapes *. .* shapsies [sic]. **1965–70** *DARE* (Qu. EE7, *. . Marble games*) Inf **PA**163, Bombsies; **OR**10, Chasies; **AZ**8, Keepies; **WI**68, Keepsies; **MT**1, Potsies; **OR**10, Ringsies. **c1970** Wiersma *Marbles Terms,* Chipsies, dropsies, foursies, grannies, keepies, keepsies, kissies, potsies, tradies, [etc]. **1973** Ferretti *Marble Book* 43, *Eggies.* Short for "Can I borrow a few marbles?" as in "Eggies on aggies?" *Ibid* 51, *Rollsies!* A defensive call to force a player to roll his shooter . . rather than throw it. *Ibid* 66, *Chasies. Ibid* 67, In Iowa *. . bombsies. Ibid* 127, *Dicies.* **1975** Ferretti *Gt. Amer. Book Sidewalk Games* 44 **NYC,** For "onesies," throw the ball against the wall and, standing behind the line, catch it before it hits the ground. . . For "twosies," throw it against the wall, let it bounce once in the area between the wall and the line, then catch it [*DARE* Ed: similarly through "tensies"]. *Ibid* 101 **NYC,** In "strictsies," on the other hand, no "movsies" or "interference" or "kissies" or "haystacks" are permitted. . . If Jacks is being played near a curb and a jack or jacks falls into the street . . , any other player can call, "placies," and, with all the nastiness she can muster, can place it for example, right at the lip of the curb. **1979** *DARE* File **Queens NYC,** In South Ozone Park . . near JFK airport, eggies! for 'sharesies!'

if conj Usu |ɪf|; also **chiefly Sth, S Midl** |ɛf| Pronc-sp *ef* Cf **iffen, if so be**

Std sense, var form.

1839 in 1952 Green *Samuel Maverick* 94 **AL** [Black], [Letter:] I wish you would do me a favour and ef you will you will oblige your humble Servant Samuel very much. **1843** Thompson *Major Jones' Courtship* 54 **GA,** Ef the world does cum to a eend she couldn't bare the site. **1843** in 1956 Eliason *Tarheel Talk* 312 **wNC,** Ef. **1861** Holmes *Venner* 2.139 **NEng,** He *. .* acted as ef he was spyin' abaout. **1891** Garland *Main-Travelled Roads* 188 **WI,** I'm goin' to a hotel, ef I don't never lay up a cent. **1891** *PMLA* 6.165 **WV,** *Ef.* **1893** Shands *MS Speech* 72 [Black], Ef. **1895** *DN* 1.375 **seKY, eTN, wNC,** Ef. **1901** *DN* 2.182 **neKY** [Black], Ef. **1903** *DN* 2.291 **Cape Cod MA** (as of a1857), *Ef.* **1906** *DN* 3.120 **sIN,** Regularly *. . ef.* **1914** *DN* 4.72 **ME, nNH,** *Ef. . .* Common. **1919** *DN* 5.39 **KY, TN, VA,** *Ef.* **1922** Gonzales *Black Border* 143 **sSC, GA coasts** [Gullah], Ef de Lawd haffuh tek'um. **1967–68** *DARE* FW Addits **CT**15, **LA**8, Ef.

iffen conj Also *effen, ef'n, if-and, if'n, ifnd, ifnt* [Perh pronc-spp for *if* + **and** conj B1; cf *OED an* conj. 2 quot 1749] **chiefly Sth, S Midl** Cf **if, if so be**

If.

1909 *S. Atl. Qrly.* 8.41 **seSC** [Gullah], Ef'n yo' don' lak de tas'e er yo' bittle [=victuals], dash um 'way an' be done! **1931** *AmSp* 6.230 **neOR,** Such old forms of English as . . "effen" for "if" may be heard in the ordinary speech of the natives. **1938** Rawlings *Yearling* 24 **FL,** Iffen you'll learn yourself to work, you'll be your Pa all over. **1953** Brewer *Word Brazos* 14 **eTX** [Black], Ah tells you what to do, if'n you raily wants to be a true chile of Gawd. **1966** *Wilson Coll.* **csKY,** If'n I hear you say that. **1966** *DARE* Tape **DC5,** ['ɛfn] the market's open. **1967** Will *Dredgeman* 114 **FL,** If'n a man was out there naked he wouldn't last an hour. **1978** *Comments on Etym.* 8.2.2 **Ozarks,** I have heard the following types of sentences: *Ifnt he won't come. . . Ifnt it don't work. . . Ifnd I'd only known. . . Ifnd he'd have told us.* **1986** Pederson *LAGS Concordance,* 1 inf, **csGA,** Iffen you want to. **1993** Mason *Feather Crowns* 355 **KY,** Well, I thought it might be, and I thought I'd tell you if-and you didn't know.

iffen so be See **if so be**

-ification suff Cf **-ify**

Used as a noun-forming suff, often in place of std *-(ic)ation.* Note: Only non-std words ending in *-ification* are illustrated here.

1841 (1952) Cooper *Deerslayer* 212 **nNY,** "And what exaltification"—the reader will have remarked that the Deerslayer had not very critically studied his dictionary—"And what exaltification would it be to me . . to be bedizened and bescarleted like a Mingo chief?" **1843** (1916) Hall *New Purchase* 266 **IN,** "How is a child's spelling-book to be made any plainer?" "Why, sir, by clear explifications of the words in one column, by exemplifying illustrations in the other." **1904** (1913) Johnson *High-*

ways *South* 101 **GA**, The games of "Stealing Partners," "Twistification," and "Fancy Four" . . do not differ much from dancing, except in name. **1906** *DN* 3.129 **nwAR**, *Bustification.* . . Used facetiously of an explosion, disaster, or quarrel. **1954** *Harder Coll.* **cwTN**, Fornication. **1989** *AmSp* 64.141 [Black], That simplification / That newification / That purification. . . Has fixed him so that he's converted.

-ified suff *Also -fied* **chiefly Sth, S Midl** *Cf* **-ify**

Used as an adj-forming suff, often in place of std -*y* or -*ed*. Note: Only non-std words ending in -*(i)fied* are illustrated here.

1744 (1907) Hamilton *Itinerarium* 100 **NYC**, These gloves . . were fit for nothing but to be wore by itchified persons under a course of sulpher. **1851** Burke *Polly Peablossom* 72 **cwMS**, In about er minit I 'gin to get tired and disgustified. **1853** Bird *Nick of Woods* 274 **KY**, You exflunctified, perditioned rascal. **1919** *DN* 5.36 **NC**, Drappin' down on his bendified knees. **1933** *AmSp* 8.1.47 **Ozarks**, *Airyfied.* . . Inclined to put on airs, stuck-up, *fine-haired.* **1935** (1944) Rawlings *Golden Apples* 58 **FL**, Someway it jest don't look ricified [=suitable for rice-growing]. *Ibid* 136, Tain't nothin' but ol' trashified folks goes bare-footed on Sundays. **c1937** in 1972 *Amer. Slave* 2.131 **SC**, My missis . . learn me Christianified manners. **c1938** in 1970 Hyatt *Hoodoo* 1.158 **seVA**, He looked kind of *draggy-fied*, kind of ashamed, downcast. **1939** *Hench Coll.*, I heard a brakeman in the Washington, D.C., Union Station say, "I've been aguefied in my joints these cold nights." **1939** McGuire *FL Cracker Dial.* 179, *Pusslegutted.* . . Pot-bellied, "bustified." **1942** Rawlings *Cross Creek* 158 **FL**, Night overtakened me and I begun to feel a mite creepified. **1953** Randolph–Wilson *Down in Holler* 45 **Ozarks**, The hillman likes adjectives ending in *ified. Dressified* means particular about clothing, *fitified* means subject to *fits.* . . *Yankeefied.* . . *holyfied.* . . *rectified* . . meant corrected. . . *airified.* . . *eatified.* . . *rainified.* . . *witchified.* . . *hurtified.* . . *erectified.* . . *mister-fied.* **1962** Wilson *Folkways Mammoth Cave* 40 **csKY**, *Bigified.* Another term for being stuck up or smart-alec. **1966** *DARE* (Qu. GG18, . . '*Obstinate.*') Inf **MA6**, Jackassified; (Qu. HH2, . . *Nicknames for a citified person*) Inf **ME19**, A dud[e]ified chap. **1968** Haun *Hawk's Done Gone* 153 **TN**, Every time he got to feeling girlified and shamed because he had to cook supper, he would make himself think about the books in the library.

if'n, ifnd, ifnt See **iffen**

if so be conj *Also iffen so be, if so be as how, if so be that* Pronc-sp *efsobe* [*OED if* conj. 8.f "*arch.* and *dial.*"] **old-fash**

If.

1795 Dearborn *Columbian Grammar* 136, List of Improprieties. . . If so be for If. **1823** Cooper *Pioneers* 1.75 **nNY**, Yes, the squire is right, for if-so-be that he wasn't, how is it that the seventh son always is a doctor? *Ibid* 213, If-so-be he is thinking of putting any Johnny-raw over my head, why I shall resign. **1848** Bartlett *Americanisms* 187, *If so be or if so be as how.* A vulgar expression used by uneducated people in the interior parts of the country and in England. **1921** Haswell *Daughter Ozarks* 96 (as of 1880s), Efsobe he ever needs a man to stand with him agin man or devil, here I be. **1931** *PMLA* 46.1305 **sAppalachians**, He'll name it (mention) to Jones, if so be he's there. **1938** Matschat *Suwannee R.* 29 **neFL, seGA**, Shet yer ears quick, iffen so be ye hear one a-singin'!

-ify suff *Also -fy* **chiefly Sth, S Midl** *Cf* **argufy, -ification, -ified**

Used as a verb-forming suff, often added pleonastically to verbs or used to form verbs from nouns or adjectives. Note: Only non-std words ending in -*ify* are illustrated here.

1789 (1918) Low *Politician Outwitted* 366 **NYC**, What argufies your signifies, or your magnifies? **1844** Featherstonhaugh *Excursion Slave States* 71 **St. Louis MO**, Stranger, if that ar hoss don't go like a screamer, I'll give you leave to ex-flunctify me into no time of day at all. **1893** Shands *MS Speech* 35, *Happify.* . . Used by illiterate whites to mean *to make happy.* **1931** *AmSp* 6.269 **KY**, Redundant or curiously assorted suffixes occur in the . . suffixes argufy . . , temptify, exaltify, interprefy, aspersifyin'. **1953** Randolph–Wilson *Down in Holler* 45 **Ozarks**, There is a tendency to coin verbs ending in *fy* and *ify*: *argufy* instead of argue, *speechify* instead of orate. . . One of Rose O'Neill's neighbors near Walnut Shade, Missouri, boasted that he could *clockify*, . . *rightify* is sometimes used. **1966–69** *DARE* (Qu. X53a, . . *An oversize stomach*) Inf **SC10**, Bloatify; (Qu. Y3, *To say uncomplimentary things about somebody*) Inf **GA77**, Bitterfy someone.

igg v *Also sp ig* [Abbrs for *ignore*] **chiefly among Black speakers**

To ignore, snub; to reject; hence n *ig(g)* a rebuff, snub.

1946 (1972) Mezzrow–Wolfe *Really Blues* 334, [Glossary:] *Igg:* ignore. **1958** Hughes–Bontemps *Negro Folkl.* 485 **NYC** [Black], *Igg:* To ignore, to high hat. *Miss Dicty tried to igg me.* **1963** *Freedomways* 3.55 **Harlem NYC** [Black], And they kept leanin' over to one another, talkin' confidential—puttin' the *ig'* on the silks scattered amongs' 'em. *Ibid* 57 **Harlem NYC**, [Glossary:] *Silks: white folk.* . . *ig: to ignore.* **1965–70** *DARE* (Qu. II6, *If you meet somebody who used to be a friend, and he pretends not to know you: "When I met him on the street he _____."*) 16 Infs, **esp Sth, S Midl**, Igged me; (Qu. AA11, *If a man asks a girl to marry him and she refuses, you'd say she _____*) Inf **NY241**, Igged him, gave him the igg. [All Infs Black, 12 of 16 total Infs young or mid-aged] **1977** Smitherman *Talkin* 259 [Black], *Put the ig on*, also simply, *to ig*, to ignore somebody, act like you don't know them when you do.

ignorant adj Usu |'ɪgnərənt|; also **chiefly Sth, S Midl** |'ɪgnə(r)nt, 'ɪg-| Pronc-spp *eegnunt, ignoret, ignun, ignurnt;* for addit pronc and sp varr see quots Similarly n |'ɪgnə(r)ns|, pronc-spp *ignrunce, ignunce* Cf Intro "Language Changes" I.9 Note: The non-std proncs are often associated with sense **B** below. See, e.g., quot 1995 at **A** below

A Forms.

1851 Hooper *Widow Rugby's Husband* 68 **AL**, "It was all," he swore, "his *ignunce*"—(ignorance.) **1922** Gonzales *Black Border* 92 **sSC, GA coasts** [Gullah], Middletun dat eegnunt en' haa'dhead'. [=Middleton is so ignorant and hardheaded]. **1923** (1946) Greer–Petrie *Angeline Steppin'* 37 **csKY**, He's forever openin' his'n [=his mouth] and showin' his ignrunce. **1927** Kennedy *Gritny* 65 **sLA** [Black], Don' show people how ignun you is. **1936** *AmSp* 11.155 **eTX**, *Ignorant* is also ['ɪgnə(ə)nt], ['ɪgnənt]. *Ibid* 162, [*Unstressed vowels of final syllables:*] *Ignorant* has a variant pronunciation. While its normal form is ['ɪgnrənt] [sic], in less literate speech it is frequently heard also as ['ɪgnə̣nt]. *Ibid, Ignorance* is ['ɪgnə̣ns]. **1937** in 1972 *Amer. Slave* 2.1.88 **nwSC**, I is ig'nant. **1937** in 1976 *Weevils in the Wheat* 94 **VA** [Black], She kept mother ig'unt. Didn't tell her nothin'. **1941** *AmSp* 16.9 **eTX** [Black], Unstressed medial vowels are dropped or remain as [ə]. . . ignorant ['ɪgnənt]. *Ibid* 10, [Final syllables:] *Ignorance* . . ['ɪgnə̣ns] . . *ignorant* . . ['ɪgnə̣nt]. **1942** Hall *Smoky Mt. Speech* 71 **wNC, eTN**, The vowel of the final syllable is subject to loss after *r* especially before *n*. . . ignorance, ignorant. **1942** in 1944 *ADD* 315 **caIN**, [Radio:] *Ignorant.* . . ['ɪgnə̣nt] *ignernt.* **1981** Pederson *LAGS Basic Materials* Gulf Region, 5 infs, ['ɪgnə̣nt]; 5 infs, ['ɪ(ə)gnənt]; 2 infs, ['ɪgnɪ(n)t]; 1 inf, ['ɪgnəə̣nt]; 1 inf, ['ɪgnə̣nt]; 1 inf, ['ɪgrənt]. **1984** Erdrich *Love Medicine* 64 **ND**, It was . . them ignoret bush Crees who found her and couldn't figure out how she was raised. **1988** [see **B** below]. **1995** *DARE* File **seMO**, Ignorant /'ɪgnə̣t/—This pronunciation usually means eccentric or stupid behavior often intended by the perpetrator to raise dander in onlookers; or obstinacy about a point in contention. . . /'ɪgnə̣ənt/ is used when the textbook definition of ignorant is intended. *Ibid* **NM**, [Comment on preceding quot:] A college educated black woman in her mid-thirties . . often uses the pronunciation /'ɪgnənt/ in the same manner. She also uses the "correct" pronunciation for the textbook definition. *Ibid* **Ozarks**, I learned very quickly in my first public-school experience . . that I was no longer just 2-syllable ig-nert [no final nasalization anywhere, I'm still surprised to hear!] but now 3-syllable ig-nor-ant!

B Sense.

Coarse, crude, boorish.

1967 *DARE* File **eTN**, "Ignorant" is very common for a stupid or boorish person. "He's just ignorant." **1982** *Barrick Coll.* **csPA**, *Ignorant*—indelicate; obscene. "That's ignorant." Given to using dirty words. **1988** *DARE* File **cUT**, Ignorant ['ɪgnə̣nt] means "rude, uncouth." More common among kids than adults, though adults—especially females—will use it to describe typically "male" behavior that is objectionable. "Oh, those ignurnt boys!" "Oh, for ignurnt!" Often, young people learn the usual meaning only many years after they learn this one. **1994** *Ibid* **cwCA** (as of c1956), A childhood acquaintance who had moved to California (from Missouri, I think), used to like to say of other girls, "She's so ignorant ['ɪgnə̣nt]!" She didn't mean that the girl lacked knowledge, but that she seemed unsophisticated or uncouth. **1995** *Ibid*, The first time I ever heard the word [=*ignorant*] was from my grandmother's [Black] maid in Oklahoma in the 1940s, and it seemed clear from the context that it meant simply "rude." I learned the standard meaning only when I used the word in my grandmother's presence . . and was hastily corrected in tones that gently but clearly conveyed to me that there was something socially unacceptable about using it in that sense. The next time I heard the word in the meaning "rude" was in the 1980s in Ohio, again from an African American. **1995** [see **A** above].

I gonnies See **gonnies**

I-got-it n Cf **ice tag** n²

A game of tag played on the ice; see quots.

   1950 *WELS* (Games played on the ice) 1 Inf, **WI,** I-got-it—form of tag with one person holding mitten, cap or some such thing. **1950** *WELS Suppl.* neWI (as of 1890s), I-got-it. Skating game played on ice. This is the game of *tag,* but in reverse. The gang chases the person, who must keep shouting all the while, "I've got it." When tagged, the tagger acquires *it* and he in turn shouts, "I've got it," until he is tagged and this new tagger shouts, "I've got it." *Ibid* neIL, On the ice with skates we played . . *I-got-it.*

I'ish See **Irish** n¹, adj

iiwi n [Haw *'i'iwi*] **HI**

An orange-red Hawaiian honeycreeper *(Vestiaria coccinea)* with black wings and tail.

   [**1779** (1784) King *Voyage Pacific* 3.119 **HI,** The birds of these islands are as beautiful as any we have seen. . . Another is of an exceeding bright scarlet colour; . . its native name is *eeeeve.*] **1890** Wilson & Evans *Aves Hawaiienses* I.1 *(OEDS),* Vestiaria coccinea. Olokele or Iiwi. *Ibid* 3, The call-note of the 'Iiwi' is peculiar. **1930** Degener *Ferns of HI* 53, Idols. . . consisted of plaited heads covered usually with the red feathers of the *iiwi* to which the yellow and black of the *oo* were added to emphasize the features. **1944** Munro *Birds HI* 69, The great ohia trees . . were a mass of bloom and each of them was literally alive with hordes of crimson apapane and scarlet iiwi. **1967** *DARE* (QR near Qu. Q23) Inf **HI**14, Iiwi [iʔivi]—native Hawaiian birds—honey-eaters. **1970** Carlquist *Hawaii* 198, The iiwi, *Vestiaria coccinea,* is a bright red bird which represents a tendency toward nectar feeding. Iiwis do not eat nectar exclusively, though. **1980** Bushnell *Water of Kane* 370 **HI,** In a bower of ohia-lehuas, . . among the crimson blossoms and dark green leaves, the iiwi came home to nest.

i Jacks See **Jacks, by**

ij(j)it, ijjut See **idiot A**

Ike n [Dimin of *Isaac*]

1 An uncouth or rude fellow; a rustic. Cf **jake** n¹ **1, rube**

   1896 *DN* 1.419 cnNY, Ike [aɪk]: an uncouth fellow. "He's an awful Ike." **1915** *DN* 4.199 [Terms of disparagement], *Ike,* crazy Ike, an uncouth fellow. "The crazy Ike didn't know enough to tip his cap when I introduced him to mother." In general usage. **c1955** Reed–Person *Ling. Atlas Pacific NW,* 1 inf, Country Ike. **c1960** *Wilson Coll.* csKY, Ike. . . A crude, ignorant . . fellow. **1965–69** *DARE* (Qu. HH22a, *A mean or disagreeable person;* total Infs questioned, 75) Inf **MS**56, Smart Ike; (Qu. II36a, *Somebody who talks back or gives rude answers: "Did you ever see such a _____?")* Inf **KY**6, Crazy Ike. **1986** Pederson *LAGS Concordance* (Poor white) 1 inf, cTN, Country Ikes; (A rustic) 1 inf, neTX, Country Ike.

2 A self-important or pretentious person; see quots. See also **big Ike**

   1902 Harben *Abner Daniel* 72 **GA,** He's a big Ike in some church in Atlanta. **1942** Berrey–Van den Bark *Amer. Slang* 184.1, Big George, Big Ike . . *a conceited person.* **c1960** *Wilson Coll.* csKY, Ike—A self-important fellow. **1966–70** *DARE* (Qu. GG19b, . . *A person [who] acts . . important . . "He seems to think he's _____.")* Inf **MS**39, The big Ike; (Qu. HH17, *A person who tries to appear important, or who tries to lay down the law . . "He'd like to be the _____ around here.")* Infs **KY**42, 53, 91, Big Ike. **1986** Pederson *LAGS Concordance,* 1 inf, neMS, Big Ikes—pretentious people.

3 See **Ikey 1.**

4 See **Ikey 2.**

Ikey n Also sp *Ikie* [**Ike**]

1 also *Ike:* A Jew. *usu derog* Cf **Abie, Isaac, kike**

   1900 *DN* 2.42 New Orleans LA [College slang], Ikey. . . A Jew. **1941** *LANE* Map 455, Nicknames, derogatory or less commonly jocular applied to a Jew . . Ikey [48 infs, esp e,sNEng]; Ike [2 infs, wVT]. **1950** *WELS* (Jewish) 1 Inf cWI, Ikey. **1956** Ker *Vocab. W. TX* 368, Jew (nicknames) . . Ikey [2 of 67 infs]. **1960** Wentworth–Flexner *Slang* 279, Ikey, Ikie. . . A Jew. **1967–70** *DARE* (Qu. HH28, . . *People of foreign background . . Jewish*) Infs **CA**107, **NY**22, Ikey.

2 also *Ike;* Transf: a person of Italian background. [Prob by confusion with **Itie**] Cf **ack, hike** n

   1941 *LANE* Map 453 scattered NEng, The [seven] informants who offer . . [the term *Ikey* or *Ike*] as a nickname for Italians state positively

that they use it in this sense. **1966–69** *DARE* (Qu. HH28, . . *People of foreign background . . Italian*) Inf **PA**206, Ikey; [(Qu. HH28, . . *Irish*) Inf **WA**18, Ikey?]. **1986** Pederson *LAGS Concordance* (Italians) 1 inf, cTN, Ikes.

3 Transf from **1** above: A **puffin** (here: *Lunda cirrhata*). Cf **jewbird, jew duck 1**

   1956 *AmSp* 31.185 **AK,** Ikey—Puffin. . . That is, Jew, from prominent beak or 'nose.'

Ikie See **Ikey** n

ikta, iktus See **icta**

iky adj [Prob **Ike 2,** but cf *EDD ikey* adj. "Proud"]

   1906 *DN* 3.142 nwAR, Iky [aɪki]. . . Impertinent, impudent. "Don't get iky."

ilant See **island**

ile n¹ See **island B2**

ile n² See **oil**

ilet See **islet 2**

ili n [Haw *'ili*] **HI** Cf **ahupuaa**

A unit of land; see quot 1967.

   1955 Day *HI People* 291, In a letter written by William Richards in 1841 the annual tax on an *ili* or estate was said to be "a hog, a dog, a fish net, a fishline, a cluster of feathers, and twenty kapas." **1967** Reinecke-Tsuzaki *Hawaiian Loanwords* 98, Ili. . . A division of land (next) smaller than an *ahupuaa.* . . S[eldom].

ilima n [Haw *'ilima*] **HI**

A plant of the genus *Sida,* esp *S. fallax,* bearing flowers often used in leis.

   1888 Hillebrand *Flora Hawaiian Is.* 43, Sida. . . A large genus, distributed over the warmer regions of the entire globe.—Nat[ive] name of all species: 'Ilima.' **1929** Neal *Honolulu Gardens* 195, Ilima (Sida fallax . .). In many parts of Hawaii, from near sea level to an elevation of more than 2,000 feet, various forms of ilima plants, four feet or less high, open their bright flowers, which range in color from yellow to rich-orange to dull red. **1930** Degener *Ferns of HI* 209, The plants comprising *Sida* are generally called *ilima* by the Hawaiians. . . Their small, yellow flowers were formerly commonly strung into garlands, or *lei,* reserved for chiefs. **1955** Day *HI People* 301, The *lei* of early days was a garland of orange ilima, of feathery red ohia, of fragrant *maile* leaves, or of fern. **1970** Carlquist *Hawaii* 269, *Sida fallax,* the ilima, is a mat with yellow-orange flowers and finely hairy white leaves, common near the shores of all the islands. **1994** *WI State Jrl.* (Madison) 6 Nov sec H 3 **HI,** Ilima. . . Plants found in areas ranging from the beach coast to altitudes of more than 2,000 feet. . . Its colors are brilliant and they range from yellow to deep gold to rusty orange.

ilio n [Haw *'īlio*] **HI**

A dog.

   1954–60 Hance et al. *Hawaiian Sugar,* Ilio ['ilio] dog. **1955** Day *HI People* 310, Many Hawaiian words have been taken into English. . . ilio: dog.

ill adj

1 Vicious, bad-tempered, cross, fretful. [Cf *OED ill* a.2.b 1480 →; but appar Scots dial in ref to humans; cf *SND ill* adj. I.4.] chiefly Sth, S Midl See also **ill-minded, ~-turned**

   1857 (1859) Olmsted *Journey TX* 78, "Ill" for "vicious." "Is your dog ill?" **1865** Byrn *Advent. Fudge Fumble* 101 **TN,** This "old Grey" . . had a young colt, and all the country people know how ill a mare is then. **1887** *Scribner's Mag.* 2.476 **AR,** Bulah war mighty long-sufferin' with him. . . An't made me mad, seein' him so ill [Footnote: cross] with her. **1895** *DN* 1.372 seKY, eTN, wNC, Ill: cross. . . "The cow is ill when she is pestered." **1902** *DN* 2.237 sIL [Pioneer dialect], Ill. . . Cross; peevish; fretful; morose. **1903** *DN* 2.317 seMO, Ill. . . Cross; ill tempered. **1904** *DN* 2.398 AR, VA. **1905** *DN* 3.83 nwAR, 'The dog's ill.' Rare. **1917** *DN* 4.413 wNC, Ill. . . Ill-natured; vicious. **1939** *Hall Coll.* eTN, Ill as a hornet—is said of a person "who's been on a drunk or had a bad night of any kind." *Ibid,* Ill—having a bad disposition. "He was a awful ill teacher." Of a dog—"He's not ill of a day." **1942** *Hench Coll.* cVA, [Letter:] When I'd admire a rosy cheeked youngster in its mother's arms, she would always say, "Oh but he is so ill." After . . asking how long he had been sick I found that she meant "naughty." **1943** *Ibid* swVA, Ill—naughty, bad. **1946** *PADS* 6.18 ceNC (as of 1900–10), Ill. . . Cross, in a bad humor. Said of children. **1953** Randolph–Wilson *Down in Holler* 156 **Ozarks, Ill** . . vicious or bad-tempered. "My woman . . gits iller every day she lives!". . . "Them Tompkins boys is the illest critters on the creek." **c1960** *Wilson Coll.* **csKY, Ill**—angry, high-tempered. Not [used] for "sick" much until lately. **1967–68** *DARE* (Qu. K16, *A cow with a bad temper*) Inf **WV7**, Ill; (Qu. Z16, *A small child who is rough, misbehaves*) Inf **LA12**, Ill. **1969** *DARE* Tape **KY35**, A horse will get used to the [double-]bit [bridle], and it depends on how the rider handles—now some riders'll get a little ill sometimes, they *could* hurt their horse. **1986** Pederson *LAGS Concordance*, 1 inf, **nwFL**, He's ill—touchy; 1 inf, **seGA**, They're not ill at all—not mean, bad-tempered; 1 inf, **neGA**, They're not as ill as the wasp and yellow jacket; 1 inf, **cTX**, The illest snake of all them—meanest. **1990** *DARE* File **cAR**, Around here, if a man was mean to his children—beat them or abused them in some way—we'd say "he was ill to his children." That means the same as saying "he was bad to hurt them."

2 Of a woman: menstruating. *euphem* Cf *DS* AA27

1931 Randolph *Ozarks* 82, When the word *ill* is applied to a woman . . sometimes it refers to menstruation. . . The individual who is afflicted with a serious disease is neither *ill* nor *unwell*, but *sick*. [**1948** *Word* 4.185 [Terms for a menstruating woman], Unwell.] **c1960** *Wilson Coll.* **csKY, Ill** sometimes suggested a woman's sickness and was said in a whisper or behind the hand.

i'll n See **oil**

I'll be go-to-hell(ed) See **go-to-hell, I'll be**

ill convenient adj [*OED* (at *ill-* B) "now *vulgar*"; W3 "archaic"]
Inconvenient.

1837 Sherwood *Gaz.* GA 70, *Provincialisms.* . . *Illconvenient*, inconvenient. **1899** (1912) Green *VA Folk-Speech* 238, *Ill-convenient.* . . Inconvenient. **1901** *DN* 2.142 **cNY**, Illconvenient. **1917** *DN* 4.413 **wNC**, *Ill-convenient.* . . Inconvenient. **1952** Brown *NC Folkl.* 1.553, *Ill-convenient.*

illegal adj [*EDD* illegal sb. and adj. "A bastard. . Illegitimate"] **esp Sth, S Midl**
Of a child: illegitimate.

1961 Folk *Word Atlas N. LA* Map 1211 *(Illegitimate child)* Illegal child [is among ten responses given by 18 percent of the 275 informants]. **1966** Dakin *Dial. Vocab. Ohio R. Valley* 2.438, *Unlawful child, illegal* ∼, and *fatherless* ∼ appear occasionally. **1966–68** *DARE* (Qu. Z11a, . . *A child whose parents were not married—serious words*) 9 Infs, **scattered, but esp Sth, S Midl**, Illegal (child); (Qu. Z11b, *Nicknames and joking words*) Inf **KY21**, Illegal; **LA8**, Illegal? Unlegal? **1973** Allen *LAUM* 1.344 **IA** (as of c1950), Illegal child [1 inf]. **1983** *MJLF* 9.1.44 **ceKY**, Illegal child. . . an illegitimate child. **1986** Pederson *LAGS Concordance* **Gulf Region** *(Bastard)* 7 infs, Illegal (child). [6 of 7 infs old]

illegitimate adj Also *(le)gitimate, negitimate, inegitable;* for addit forms see quots Cf **illegal, illy**
Std sense, var forms.

1967–68 *DARE* (Qu. Z11a, . . *A child whose parents were not married—serious words*) Inf **MD24**, [ɪˈlɪ̌jəmɪt]; **NY96**, [əˈlɪ̌jəmət] [FW: Inf was conscious this was a mistake.]; **AK8, LA11**, Legitimate (child); **GA28**, Negitimate [nɪˈjɪtɪmɪt]; **NY61**, Inegitable; [(Qu. AA19, . . *A man and woman who are not married but live together as if they were*) Inf **AK8**, Legitimate]. **c1970** Pederson *Dial. Surv. Rural GA* **seGA** *(A child whose mother and father are not married)* 4 infs, [ɛlˈdʒɪtɪmət, ɛlə-, -mɪt]; 1 inf, [ɛlˈdʒɪtəmət]; 1 inf, [ɪləˈdʒɪtəmə̃]; 3 infs, [ɪˈdʒɪtəmət]; 3 infs, [ˈdʒɪtəmɪt, -mət]; 1 inf, [ˈdʒɪtəməˇ] child; 1 inf, [məˈdɪtɪmət]; 1 inf, [ˈdʒɪ·tɪ·ɪt]. **1989** Pederson *LAGS Tech. Index* 235 **Gulf Region**, [323 infs, Illegitimate (child or baby, etc); 29 infs, [Il]legitimate (child or baby); 3 infs, [Ille]gitimate (child). Examination of the *LAGS Basic Materials* shows that these generalized spp cover std proncs as well as many idiolectal varr, e.g., [əˈdʒɪˇtəmət, ɪ̂nəˈdʒɪˇtəmət, ˈiˈdʒɪˇlɪmət, ɪˇləməˈdʒɪˇtək, ɪ̂ˈdʒɪˇtəməs].]

Illinois n Usu |ɪləˈnɔɪ|; also |ɪləˈnɔɪz, ɛləˈnɔɪ(z)|; for addit varr see quots Pronc-spp *Elenoise, Illinoize* Cf Pronc Intro 3.I.3.a, 3.II.2
Std senses, var forms.

1829 in 1938 *AmSp* 13.264, [Letter of Edward Everett to J.E. Worcester:] Illenois is pronounced as you write it [=Il-li-noy] almost always; but Il-ye-nois & Il-le-nore are sometimes heard. **1864** (1868) Trowbridge *Cudjo's Cave* 25 **TN**, Ain't you from Ohio or Illinoize? **1903** *DN* 2.317 **seMO**, Illinois. . . Pronounced . . [ɪlɪnɔɪz]. **1921** Haswell *Daughter Ozarks* 18 (as of 1880s), [I] hev seed the perarys of Elenoise.

1942 Hall *Smoky Mt. Speech* 62 **eTN, wNC**, Medial . . *i.* . . Occasionally the vowel approaches or reaches [i]. Example . . *Illinois* [ˈɪlɪnɔɪz]. **1944** Kenyon-Knott *Pronc. Dict.* 214, *Illinois.* . . [ˌɪləˈnɔɪz], not infrequent generally, is esp. common in the S[outh]. **1965** Carmony *Speech Terre Haute* 50 **IN**, /ɛ/—[ɛ]. . . One pronunciation of *Illinois* [ɛˌɫəˈnɔɪˇ]. **1968** *DARE* File **wKY**, *Illinois*, among older people in western Kentucky, is [ɪləˈnɔɪz]. **1976** Allen *LAUM* 3.348 **Upper MW** (as of c1950), The conspicuous variable in the pronunciation of *Illinois* is the final consonant, sometimes occurring because of the spelling. The historical pronunciation without the consonant is most frequent among those UM infs. living closest to Illinois; that with the spelling pronunciation with final /z/ is most frequent in North Dakota. This variant also produces a social contrast. Where final /z/ occurs it is clearly more likely to be used by a Type I [=older, less educated] speaker. *Ibid,* For several speakers, mostly Midland, the medial vowel has become so weak as to quite vanish and hence leave a two-syllable variant /ɪlnɔɪ(z)/.

Illinois nut n Also *Illinois hickory*
=**pecan.**

a1782 (1788) Jefferson *Notes VA* 37, Paccan, or Illinois nut (Juglans alba). . . It grows on the Illinois, Wabash, Ohio, and Missisipi. **1785** Marshall *Arbustrum* 69, Juglans pecan. *The pecan, or Illinois Hickery.* This tree is said to grow plenty in the neighbourhood of the Illinois river, and other parts to the westward. **1786** (1925) Washington *Diaries* 3.54 **VA**, Also 21 of the Illinois Nuts. **1867** De Voe *Market Asst.* 400 **NEast**, Pecan nuts—These nuts are brought from the South and West, and are taken for a species of the *Hickory Nut*, known by some as the *Illinois Hickory.* **1884** Sargent *Forests of N. Amer.* 132, Carya olivæformis. . . Pecan. Illinois Nut. **1900** Lyons *Plant Names* 191, Illinois nut.

Illinois rose n
A wild rose (prob *Rosa carolina*).

1969 *DARE* (Qu. S26a, . . *Roadside flowers*) Inf **IL55**, Wild rose or Illinois rose—because native to Illinois; **IL78**, Illinois rose.

Illinoize See **Illinois**

ill-kept adj [Perh var of *ill-kempt* or by analogy with *well-kept*]
1966 *DARE* (QR, near Qu. W41) Inf **NM9**, Ill-kept; (Qu. HH36, . . *Careless, slovenly*) Inf **GA44**, Ill-kept.

ill-minded adj Cf **ill 1**
Bad-tempered; see quot.
1967 *DARE* (Qu. K16, *A cow with a bad temper*) Inf **MO38**, An ill-minded cow.

ill-scented trillium See **stinking trillium**

ill-turned adj Cf **ill 1**
See quot 1960.
1949 Arnow *Hunter's Horn* 279 **KY**, Used to be Nunn and Milly never quarreled, but lately, seemed like Nunn was so ill turned he quarreled at them all, even Milly. **1960** Criswell *Resp. to PADS 20* **Ozarks**, *Ill-turned*—unpleasant in disposition. Common from long ago.

illy n [Abbr for **illegitimate** or **illegal** child]
1970 *DARE* (Qu. Z11a, . . *A child whose parents were not married—serious words*) Inf **NY250**, Illies [ˈɪlɪz]—not used any more.

illy-ally-over n, exclam [Var of **alley(-alley)-over**] Cf **icky-acky-over**
=**Antony-over.**
1968 *DARE* (Qu. EE22, . . *The game in which they throw a ball over a building [a house or a barn] to a player on the other side*) Inf **NY92**, Illy-ally-over; (Qu. EE23a, . . *What do you call out when you throw the ball?*) Inf **NY92**, Illy-ally-over.

im pron See **him** pron

im adj See **him** adj

Ima See **go** v A4e

I'm a Dutchman See **Dutchman 3**

imagination n

1 pl; also *imaginaries:* See quot.
1966–69 *DARE* (Qu. BB28, *Joking names . . for imaginary diseases:* "He must have the _____.") Infs **ND2, TX36**, Imaginations; **IL86**, Imaginaries.

2 An intuitive feeling, hunch. [Perh for *intimation*]
1965–68 *DARE* (Qu. GG12, *To have an inner feeling that something is about to happen:* "There she comes now, I _____ she would.") Infs **MS63, NY83**, Had an imagination. [Both Infs old]

imaginitis See **-itis**

imbrawdry See **embroidery**

I mean exclam Cf **declare**

Used as an expression of surprise or strong assertion.

1933 Rawlings *South Moon* 14 **FL,** They guffawed, their mouths wide. "I mean!" **1968** *DARE* (Qu. LL35, *Words used to make a statement stronger:* "This cake tastes _____ good.") Inf **GA**19, I mean, this cake is good. **1986** Pederson *LAGS Concordance* **Gulf Region** *(Strong affirmation)* 4 infs, I mean; 1 inf, I mean—"they was pretty"—emphatic; 1 inf, I mean = and how!

imejuntly See **immediate**

I'm free See **free** exclam 2

imitate v

1 To come up to the standard of.

1937 *Hall Coll.* **ceTN,** *Imitate*—To compare with. "These apples we have don't imitate those we had."

2 To resemble in appearance.

1969 *DARE* (Qu. Z10, *If a child looks very much like his father, you might say, "He _____ his father.")* Inf **MO**39, Imitates; **NY**149, Resembles, imitates. **c1970** Pederson *Dial. Surv. Rural GA (If a boy is similar in appearance to his father, you would say that the boy _____ his father?)* 1 inf, **seGA,** Imitates. **1986** Pederson *LAGS Concordance,* 1 inf, **seAL,** He imitates his father—physical appearance.

imitation n [Abbr for *imitation agate*]

=immie 1.

1965–67 *DARE* (Qu. EE6d, *Special marbles*) Inf **OK**1, Imitation—a shooting marble; **TX**9, Imps—imitations, **TX**18, Imitations—glass.

imitation bird n

=mockingbird 1.

1970 *DARE* (Qu. Q14, *. . Other names . . for . . mockingbird)* Inf **PA**247, Imitation bird.

immatesticle adj Also sp *immatistical*

Immaterial, irrelevant.

1927 *Ruppenthal Coll.* **KS,** Immatistical . . indifferent; immaterial. **1967** *DARE* (Qu. KK26, *Something that makes no difference at all to you:* "He can think what he likes, it _____ me.") Inf **WA**30, It's immatesticle. **1986** Chapman *New Dict. Amer. Slang* 224, Immatesticle. . . Of no concern; not relevant; immaterial.

immediate adj Usu |ɪ'midiət, ə-|; also |ɪ'midjət, ɪ'mijət| Proncspp *immejate, immejit* Similarly adv *imejuntly, immegiately, immeje(n)tly;* for addit pronc and sp varr see quots Cf **idiot A**

Std senses, var forms.

1861 Holmes *Venner* 2.300 **NEng,** I have a minute of it I took down immed'ately after the intervoo. **1862** (1864) Browne *Artemus Ward Book* 181, Orfice seekers, all clameruss for a immejit interview with Old Abe. **1867** Harris *Sut Lovingood Yarns* 31 **TN,** She imejuntly sot in, an' biled a big pot ove paste. **1890** *DN* 1.39 **csME,** Immediately. . . [ɪ'midiətlɪ], not [ɪ'mijətlɪ], which I have also heard. **1890** Holley *Samantha among Brethren* 66 **NY,** Immegiately, or a very little after, I was calm again. **1905** *DN* 3.58 **eNE,** Intrusive *n . . immeje(n)tly.* Ibid, The passing of [dj] into [j] is common; *ijjit, immejiately.* **1906** *DN* 3.142 **nwAR,** Immejate. . . Immediate. **1908** *DN* 3.323 **eAL, wGA,** *Immediate(ly)* [ɪ'mijətlɪ]. . . Commonly so pronounced. **1934** *AmSp* 9.43 **Sth,** After *d* in such words as . . *idiot, immediately . .* one often hears [j] and sometimes, though rarely, [j] in the South, but some Southerners use [ɪ]. **1944** Kenyon–Knott *Pronc. Dict.* 215, Immediate [ɪ'midɪɪt], esp. *C[anad]* [ɪ'midjət]. **c1960** *Wilson Coll.* **csKY,** Immediate [ə'mijɪt], occasionally, now largely for fun.

immie n Also sp *im(m)y;* pronc-sp *emmy* [Abbr for **imitation** + **-ie** suff³]

1 Any of var types of playing marbles; see quots. Cf **agate, alley** n², **imp** n

1913 *Funk & Wagnalls Dict.,* Immy. . . A choice marble made in imitation, as of a carnelian or an agate. **1952** Steinbeck *East of Eden* 421 **cwCA,** Cal was able to develop his marble game and set about gathering in all the chalkies and immies, glassies and agates. **1957** *Sat. Eve. Post Letters* **AR,** We had "immies" which . . were not true china but a softer clay only partially baked. *Ibid* **IL** (as of 1930s), My cousins in Illinois had "pee-wees," "aggies," "immies," and "flinties" which we in Kentucky never heard of. **1967–68** *DARE* (Qu. EE6b, *Small marbles or marbles in general)* Inf **NY**67, Immies—brother used this term;

OR15, Immies ['ɪmiz]; (Qu. EE6c, *Cheap marbles*) Inf **NY**78, Immies—imitation allies; (Qu. EE6d, *Special marbles*) Inf **NJ**43, Immies. **c1970** Wiersma *Marbles Terms* **neIL** (as of 1928), *Emmy. . .* Name given to the small glass and wood marbles. **1971** Bright *Word Geog. CA & NV* 116 **sCA,** *(Marbles)* 5 infs, Imies. **1973** Ferretti *Marble Book* 47 **seNY,** *Immies.* Imitation agate. Initially of clay, later of ordinary glass. **1989** *DARE* File **NYC** (as of c1950), We played marbles with agates and clearies and immies. Your immie was your shooter. The other marbles were mostly clear, some with stuff inside, but an immie was usually solid, and larger. You rubbed it on the sidewalk so it had a good texture; you rubbed it to rough it up. If you were down to your immie, that meant you had lost all your marbles.

2 also pl: Any of var marble games; see quots.

1957 *Sat. Eve. Post Letters* **Chicago IL** (as of 1910–20), "Immies" was a marble game using imitation canicks instead of the real thing. **1973** Ferretti *Marble Book* 130 **NYC,** *Immie*—This game, a Brooklyn . . creation, was usually run by a fellow with an extensive collection of . . marbles which he would offer as bait. He would sit on the sidewalk with an *immie* in front of him and offer it to whoever could hit with a shooter from two sidewalk cement squares away. . . If it was hit, it was won. The *immie* owner, however, kept all the misses. *Ibid* 47, *Immies. . .* In eastern United States, a general term for all marble games.

immigrant shawl n Cf **babushka**

1950 *WELS (A square cloth that women fold and tie over their heads)* 1 Inf, **WI,** Scarf, babushka, immigrant shawl.

immunization n Usu |ˌɪmjənə'zešən|; also |ɪmənə'zešən| Pronc-sp *emonization*

Std sense, var form.

1936 *AmSp* 11.159 **eTX,** In another group [of words], the medial *u* is pronounced both [jə] and [ə], the latter sound being especially characteristic of less literate speech. . . One of the subjects of this study, an old country doctor, says . . [ɪmənə'zešən] for *immunization.* This word he spelled *emonization* in a personal letter to the author.

immy See **immie**

lmo See **go** v **A4e**

imp n

=immie 1.

1967 *DARE* (Qu. EE6c, *Cheap marbles)* Inf **TX**37, Imps—glass; (Qu. EE6d, *Special marbles)* Inf **TX**9, Imps—imitations.

imp v Cf **imp** n

1911 *DN* 3.538 **eKY,** Imp. . . To imitate.

impedent, impedin', imperent See **impudent**

imperial crab n Also *crab imperial, imperial deviled crab* **Chesapeake Bay area**

Baked, stuffed crab.

1932 Stieff *Eat in MD* 48, Imperial Deviled Crab—Simmer the flakes of two crabs and half a chopped onion in butter, season with salt and cayenne pepper, add . . thick cream sauce . . Worcestershire sauce . . English mustard . . chives, bring to a boil and bind with the yolks of two eggs. Add a little green and Spanish pepper. . . Fill crab shells, . . bake . . until brown. *Hotel Rennert, Baltimore.* **1952** Tracy *Coast Cookery* 263 **DC,** *Bishop's Imperial Crab.* . . Add capers and pepper to mayonnaise; mix gently with crabmeat. Pile the mixture into . . crab shells. . . Bake. **1964** *Favorite Recipes Virginias* 77 **VA,** Crab Imperial. . . Cook onion and green pepper in butter. . . Add milk. . . seasonings, eggs and crab meat. Place in 6 well-greased shells or 5-ounce custard cups. Bake. **1968** *DARE* (Qu. H45, *Dishes . . that everybody around here would know)* Infs **MD**14, 41, 50, Imperial crab; **MD**33, 37, 44, Crab imperial. **1968** *DARE* FW Addit **eMD,** Imperial crab.

impetigo n Usu |ˌɪmpə'taɪgo, 'ɪmpəˌtaɪgo, ɛm-|; also **chiefly NEng** |ˌɪmpə'tigo|; also, by folk-etym, |ˌɪnfən'taɪgo, 'ɪnfənˌtaɪgo, ɛn-| Pronc-spp *enfantigo, infantigo, infa(n)tigus;* abbr *'(pe)tigo;* for addit pronc and sp varr see quots

Std sense, var forms.

1950 *WELS* **WI** *(Common itching diseases)* 18 Infs, Impetigo; 1 Inf, Infantigo; 1 Inf, Infatigus. **1950** *WELS Suppl.* **csWI,** [ɪnfə'taɪgo, ɪnfən'taɪgo]—common for *impetigo.* Probably folk-etymology—because it is more common among children. **1954** *Harder Coll.* **cwTN,** *Infantigo*—A children's skin disease. **1965–70** *DARE* (Qu. BB25, *. . Common skin diseases)* 81 Infs, **scattered,** [ˌɪmpə'taɪgo, 'ɪmpəˌtaɪgo, ɛm-]; 33 Infs, **scattered,** [ˌɪnfən'taɪgo, 'ɪnfənˌtaɪgo]; 13 Infs, **scattered,** Impetigo [no pronc recorded]; **CT**5, 6, 8, 9, 12, 19, 29, **MA**3, 5, 12, **NY**34,

RI1, 6, 12, [,ɪmpə'tigo, 'ɛmpə,tigo]; **CA**59, **IA**8, 22, **NJ**16, **OH**17, **PA**36, 167, **RI**17, [,ɪmpə'tego, 'ɪmpə,tego, ɛm-]; **AL**6, **CA**1, **NY**141, **NC**82, **PA**209, 214, **VA**54, [,ɛnfə'taɪgo, 'ɛnfə,taɪgo, ɪn-]; **IN**60, 66, 69, **OH**8, **PA**133, 175, [,ɪmpə'tæ(ɪ)go]; **CA**166, **IA**34, **MI**75, **PA**216, **TX**29, [,ɪmpɛn'taɪgo, -ti-, -te-]; **CA**148, **FL**19, **IN**41, **PA**94, Enfantigo [,ɛnfən'taɪgo]; **AL**33, **CA**99, **NY**27, [,ɪnfə'tego, 'ɪnfən,tego, ,ɛnfən'tego]; **OR**6, **TX**26, [,ɪmpə'tego]; **CA**101, [,ɪmə'taɪgo] [FW: sic]; **IN**19, ['ɪnfən,tæɪgo]; **IN**3, Infantigus ['ɪnfən,taɪgɪs]; **IA**30, ['ɪnfrətego]; **MI**81, [ɪm'pɛtɪgo]; **NY**163, Enfantigo [no pronc recorded]; **NY**219, ['ɪfən,taɪgo]; **NC**50, ['ɛnfɪ'tægo]; **PA**14, 'Tigo ['taɪgə]; **TN**12, 'Petigo ['pɛtɪ,go]; **VT**16, [,ɪnfən'tigo]. [Of all Infs responding to the question, 29% were comm type 5; of those giving responses with [f] for [p], 47% were comm type 5.] **1988** *DARE* File **csWI**, They had a troublesome case of infantigo [,ɪnfən'taɪgo].

impident See **impudent**

‡impity adj [Perh blend of *impudent* + *uppity*] Cf **impudent**
  1967 *DARE* (Qu. II36a, *Somebody who talks back or gives rude answers: "Did you ever see such a _____?"*) Inf **TX**11, Impity ['ɪmpətɪ] person.

impodance See **impudent**

imp-of-the-devil n
=**stag beetle.**
  c1930 Brown *Amer. Folkl. Insect Lore* 5, Stag beetles, . . because of their formidable appearance, were sometimes called "Imps-of-the-Devil."

impositor n [By analogy with *depositor, repository,* etc]
An impostor.
  1916 *DN* 4.276 **NE**, Impositor . . [z]. . . Occasional for *impostor.* "I am sure the man is an impositor."

impotent See **impudent**

impressed ppl adj
Impelled, moved.
  1931 *PMLA* 46.1303 **sAppalachians**, Many formal words and terms are used glibly [by preachers], thus influencing everyday speech. . . My brethering, (or breethren), I feel *impressed* to tell ye the truth.

impty See **empty**

impudent adj Pronc-spp *impedin', impedent, imperent, impident, impotent* Similarly n *impodance* [Cf *EDD imperent* "A corruption of the word 'impudent' " and *EDD impident*]
Std sense, var forms.
  a1824 (1937) Guild *Jrl.* 264 **VT**, I think they got punished enough for their impodance. *Ibid* 312, Servant very impotent. **1844** Thompson *Major Jones's Courtship* 70 **GA**, Miss Mary went to meetin with that imperent cus. **1899** (1912) Green *VA Folk-Speech* 238, Impedent. . . Impudent. **1922** Gonzales *Black Border* 307 **sSC, GA coasts** [Gullah glossary], Impedin'—impudence, impudent. **1959** Faulkner *Mansion* 414 **MS**, That nigger . . got almost impident, durn nigh called a white man a liar to his face.

impudent lawyer n
=**butter-and-eggs 1.**
  1900 Lyons *Plant Names* 226, L[inaria] Linaria. . . Impudent-lawyer. **1940** Clute *Amer. Plant Names* 30, L[inaria] vulgaris. . . Impudent lawyer. **1949** Moldenke *Amer. Wild Flowers* 272, The common name of *butter-and-eggs* . . seems appropriate because of the colors of the corolla, but the names . . *impudent-lawyer* . . and *rabbitflower* are a bit more obscure in their application.

impure v Pronc-sp *impyo*
  1909 *S. Atl. Qrly.* 8.44 **seSC** [Gullah], Impure is used with the active sense of *to make pure: the frost* is said to impyo [=impure] *de groun'* by freezing the foulness out of it: *i.e., purifying it.*

imu n |'ɪmu, 'i-| [Haw] **HI** Cf **kalua**
A pit in which food is covered with earth and cooked over heated stones.
  1911 *Century Dict. Suppl.,* Imu. . . In the Hawaiian islands, a pit used for baking meat or vegetables by means of heated stones. **1938** Reinecke *Hawaiian Loanwords* 16, Imu ['ɪmu] ['imu]. . . An underground oven or pit for the baking or roasting of food in the Hawaiian manner. A layer of red-hot porous lava rocks is spread in the bottom of the pit; over this is placed the food, wrapped in *ti* or banana leaves; and earth is heaped over all until the food is cooked. V[ery] F[requent]. **1951** *AmSp* 26.21 **HI**, At a 'luau,' or Hawaiian feast. . . food is wrapped in 'ki' or 'ti'

leaves and baked in an 'imu' or underground oven in the steam rising from heated and drenched lava rocks. A whole pig is baked in this way, 'kalua' style. **1965** Krauss–Alexander *Grove Farm* 23 **HI**, Several days later George passed the Hawaiian's grass house to find "Smut's" hide on the ground near the imu where the family cooked its dinner in the underground oven. **1967** *DARE* (QR, near Qu. H38) Inf **HI**6, [kɑ'lua]—method [for cooking] pig in imu; (Qu. H45, *Dishes made with meat*) Inf **HI**1, Pig cooked in an imu ['ɪmu]—an underground oven. **1972** Carr *Da Kine Talk* 87 **HI**, *Hawaiian Words Commonly Heard In Hawaii's English. . . Imu.* Earth oven.

imy See **immie**

in prep, adv Usu |ɪn|; for varr see **A** below
A Forms.
1 |ɪn|; pronc-sp *een.* **chiefly Sth, S Midl**
  1888 Jones *Negro Myths* 9 **GA coast** [Gullah], Den Buh Rabbit butt de Tar Baby een eh face. **1922** Gonzales *Black Border* 51 **sSC, GA coasts** [Gullah], 'E jam 'e [=He jammed his] two spuhr een e' hawss' belly. **1933** *AmSp* 8.1.24 **s,cAppalachians**, Sometimes *in* is *een,* end is *eend,* and been is *bean.* **1942** Hall *Smoky Mt. Speech* 16 **wNC, eTN**, [ɪ^] or [i] may sometimes be heard in . . *in.* **1942** *Sat. Eve. Post* 3 Oct 68 **seSC**, It wouldn't be "in," it would be "een." . . All spirituals are sung in dialect. **1994** *DARE* File **swWI** (as of c1950), I have heard *in* pronounced [ɪn] by people in Richland County and the Kickapoo area (our Midland speech area in Wisconsin).
2 |ɪnd|; pronc-sp *ind.*
  1890 *DN* 1.11, [He] spoke of an insertion of *d* after the preposition *in* when the next word begins with a vowel; as, *ind another.* **1905** *DN* 3.57 **eNE**, The consonant *d* is occasionally added after *n* or *r*; as —*in(d) another place.*
B As prep.
1 Used where *into* is considered std. Note: Alternation of *in* with *into* has always been std with some verbs (see *OED in* prep. 30), but the details of idiom have been variable. Colloquial US usage accepts *in* with verbs of motion as long as either the semantics of the verb or the immediate context precludes a contrast between *into* and *within* (i.e., further context is necessary for a sentence such as "She ran in the house" to be unambiguous). Cf **into B1**
  1781 *PA Jrl. & Weekly Advt.* (Philadelphia) 16 May [np], The third class [of improprieties] consists of vulgarisms in America only. . . Walk *in* the house, for *into* the house. **1814** in 1816 Pickering *Vocab.* 112 **NY**, We get *in* the *stage,* and have the rheumatism *into* our knees. **1816** *Ibid* **PA**, In for *into.* . . An observing English friend at *Philadelphia* also speaks of its frequent use there . . : "The preposition *into* is almost unknown here. They say, *when did you come* in *town? I met him riding* in *town.*" **1847** Hurd *Grammatical Corrector* 43, [Common errors of speech:] *In,* for *into,* with verbs of action; as, "He got *in* the coach." "He went *in* the house." "He broke it *in* pieces." Action, movement, or transition, from one State or condition to another, requires *into;* repose, permanency, or a state of rest, requires *in.* **1887** in 1944 *ADD* **IN**, [They] can take & turn theirselves in anything they please! **1905** *DN* 3.12 **cCT**, *In.* . . Into. **1908** *DN* 3.323 **eAL, wGA**, *In.* . . Commonly used in locutions where *into* would be preferable. **1939** *Atlantic Mth.* 164.534 **eKY**, We walked in the barn. **1941** Stuart *Men of Mts.* 300 **neKY**, Cane was getting ripe to make in lassies [=molasses]. **c1965** *DARE* File **eTX**, "We welcome you in the community."—Rural communities in Nacogdoches Co.
2 in phr *in course:* Of course. [*OED course* 34.c 1722 →; "Now only in vulgar use."] **chiefly Sth, S Midl** *somewhat old-fash*
  1843 (1847) Field *Drama Pokerville* 101 **nIL**, Old Mrs. Cornfed . . asked me if I knew the cocks [=faucets], and I told her yes, *in* course, cause I'd bathed a few [times]. **1851** (1969) Burke *Polly Peablossom* 33 **GA**, And ef I do win it, why in course the old man can't claim more'n four hundred and fifty-one dollars. **1887** *Scribner's Mag.* 2.476 **AR**, An', in course, the baby mus' come in the thick er it! **1891** Page *Elsket* 136 **ceVA** [Black], I still reposed [=supposed], in co'se, 'twuz 'bout de ring. **1908** *DN* 3.301 **eAL, wGA**, Cose. . . Frequently *in cose.* **1911** Shute *Plupy* 22 **seNH** (as of 1860s), Why, in course, in course, sonny, come right over. **1955** Faulkner *Big Woods* 89, Ash said, "I got [shotgun] shells. . . Shoot? In course they'll shoot!"
3a Used in var contexts where *on* is std in US usage; see quots.
  1800 (1907) Thornton *Diary* 113 **PA**, A person in Phia will probably purchase a lot which he possesses in Pennsylvania avenue. **1844** Walker

in 1940 Drury *Pioneers Spokanes* 188 **ME**, It is a grief to me that Mrs. W. is disposed to read so much that is not devotional in the Sabbath. **1857** in 1923 *Jrl. Amer. Hist.* [New Haven] 17.228 **RI**, Land on this street is selling at $5.00 per square foot . . only rich people can live here. Indeed it is the only street fit to live in. **1966** *DARE* (Qu. CC11) Inf **AR**18, Setting in Easy Street. **1966** *DARE* FW Addit **SC**, "He lives in X street." Inf has heard it often—more frequently in days gone by. **1986** Pederson *LAGS Concordance* **Gulf Region,** 1 inf, City guy has no corns in his hands; 1 inf, There wasn't no meat in him; 2 infs, Corn in the cob; [1 inf, Corn in the ear;] *(Haunches)* 1 inf, Get down in my hunkers; 1 inf, Greasiest thing in God's earth. **1990** Brown *Big Bad Love* 57 **MS**, I knew it was about time for me to get in the road.

b spec, in phr *in the floor:* On the floor. [*OED in* prep. 2, quot 1480; *EDD in* prep. 8, quots 1835, 1877]
    1931 *Scribner's Mag.* Jan 50 **MS**, The screen-door crashed open. A man stood in the floor, his feet apart and his heavy-set body poised easily. *Ibid* 51, Plunkett stood in the floor and cursed the others. **1940** Stuart *Trees of Heaven* 243 **neKY**, Jest a chear broke down in the floor with me.

4 Within (a specified extent of distance or time).
    1807 (1919) Bedford *Tour to New Orleans* 5.52 **VA**, Claiborne arrived with the welcome intelligence that the boats were in 12 miles and approaching. **1859** (1931) Tuttle *CA Diary* 15.232 **WI**, We . . encamped in about a mile of the summit. **1871** Eggleston *Hoosier Schoolmaster* 19 **sIN**, I could whip you in an inch of your life with my left hand and never half try. **1928** *Ruppenthal Coll.* **KS**, No one can get in a mile of the fire. **1943** Writers' Program NC *Bundle of Troubles* 167 [Black], Her pa and ma both died in 'bout six months of t'other. **1967** *DARE* Tape **TX**35, They was four, five [schools] right around here in reach of Brookeland. **1984** Wilder *You All Spoken Here* 65 **Sth**, *In a little of:* Almost; damned near.

5 in phr *in one's:* For oneself, in one's own case; see quots.
    1867 in 1944 *ADD* **MT**, When a Western man declines any proposition, he [says] 'none of that in mine.' **1916** *DN* 4.324 **cKS**, *In mine (his, yours, etc.)* . . As my (his, etc.) part, share, portion, due, etc. . . "If I marry I don't want any divorce in mine." "Her folks wanted her to teach school, but she didn't want any teaching in hers." General slang.

6 in phr *in someone:* On the part of someone; see quots.
    1871 Eggleston *Hoosier Schoolmaster* 87 **sIN**, It was real good in Mr. Pearson to take me. **1890** Howells *Boy's Town* 88 **sOH**, It was considered mean in him.

7 also *into;* in phrr *in(to) the lip, in(to) the jaw, in the gum,* and varr; In ref to taking snuff: in or into the space between the lip and the gum. **scattered, but chiefly S Atl, Lower Missip Valley** See Map Note: In this context *under the lip, against the lip,* and varr are widespread.
    1950 Faulkner *Stories* 322 **MS**, A white man had shown him how to put the powder into his lip and scour it against his teeth with a twig. **1965–70** *DARE* (Qu. DD3b, *How do people take snuff around here?*) 104 Infs, **scattered, but esp S Atl, Lower Missip Valley**, (Put it, pour it, take it, etc) in (the, lower, etc) lip [and var phrr: see *DS*]; 12 Infs, **scattered Sth, S Midl**, Put (*or* pour) it in (the) jaw [and var phrr: see *DS*]; **NC**77, Take the pack and pour it into their jaw; **FL**5, 13, 30, 34, 35, 39, **MS**68, **NC**17, Pour (*or* put) it in gum(s) [and var phrr: see *DS*]. [Of all Infs responding to the question, 33% were comm type 5, 31% gs educ or less; of those giving these responses, 48% were comm type 5, 45% gs educ or less.]

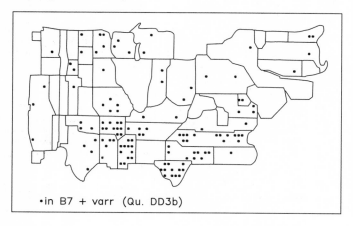
•in B7 + varr (Qu. DD3b)

C As adv.
Into a less settled area, esp Alaska or its interior. Cf **inside** adv **2, out** **B**1
    1898 Henderson *Rainbow's End AK* 242 (Tabbert *Dict. Alaskan Engl.*), It's astonishing what such things cost in Alaska. I met a man who went in last spring, taking an old black sleigh robe that cost $14 six years before, and showed it. When he came out, a miner eagerly asked him if he'd take three ounces ($41) for it. **1899** Hitchcock *2 Women in Klondike* 42, Entering Alaska is always spoken of as "going in;" leaving it, as "going out." **1925** *AmSp* 1.149 **NV**, "Out" and "in" are used with peculiar beauty. . . "In" is used as though it were a regional designation, and when a young Westerner speaks of going "in" for twenty miles it is as though he spoke of a place where the world has not yet penetrated. **1943** Brandt *AK Bird Trails* 10 (as of 1924), We were the only easterners 'going in,' which shows that Fairbanks is not exactly on the route of the winter tourists!

-in suff[1] See **-ing**

-in suff[2] See **-en** suff[3]

i'n See **iron**

in about adv phr Also *in and about* [Cf *SND in* adv. 9.(1) "before preps. as *in aboot,* . . *in at,* . . *in* has little more than intensive force"; *EDD in-almost* (at *in* adv. II.2.(2)) "almost"] **Sth, S Midl** Cf **nigh** adv, **nigh about**
Almost, nearly; approximately.
    1871 (1892) Johnston *Dukesborough Tales* 86 **cGA**, I've been nigh and in about a-dyin' to see you, especially sence night afore last. *Ibid* 83 **cGA**, I've heern him and mammy say so nigh and in and about a thousand times. **1883** (1971) Harris *Nights with Remus* 268 **GA** [Black], Ef he dast run, I'll inabout drapt out er my min'. **1887** (1967) Harris *Free Joe* 16 **GA**, It'd in-about drapt out er my min'. **1916** *DN* 4.343 **MD**, *In and about.* . . Approximately. . . "Half a bushel in and about." **1927** *AmSp* 2.358 **cwWV**, *In and about.* . . in the neighborhood of. "Here are certainly in and about ten bushels of potatoes."

in a hole See **hole** n 10c

in a horn See **horn** n 8a

in a manner See **manner** n 2

inamona n Also sp *inimona* [Haw *'inamona*] **HI** Cf **kukui**
A dish made from roasted candlenuts; see quot 1940.
    1930 Degener *Ferns of HI* 198, It is advisable for the visitor to partake sparingly of *inimona* until he has observed how this dish agrees with him. **1933** Bryan *Hawaiian Nature* 114, The poisonous properties, in the case of kukui kernels, are much modified by cooking. A much-prized relish, called *inimona*, is made by pounding the roasted kernels with salt, to which red peppers may also be added. **1938** Reinecke *Hawaiian Loanwords* 16, Inamona. . . The meat of the *kukui (Aleurites moluccana)* nut roasted and pounded up with salt as a relish for food. V[ery] S[eldom] (Also called simply *kukui*). **1940** Bazore *Hawaiian Foods* 40, *Characteristic Hawaiian Dishes.* . . Inamona—Roasted kukui nuts, shelled, and pounded with coarse salt until a smooth paste is obtained. This is served as a relish or mixed with fresh seaweed or raw liver. **1965** Neal *Gardens HI* 506, The white, oily kernels. . . are eaten as a relish ('inamona), after being baked, pounded, and mixed with salt and chili peppers.

in and about See **in about**

in and out adj phr, adv phr [Cf *EDD in and out* (at *in* adv. II.3.(7)(6)) "now and again, intermittently"; *OED in and out* adv. 1, 4]
Of weather or meteorological phenomena: variable, coming and going; intermittently, in fits and starts.
    1966–70 *DARE* (Qu. B8, *When clouds come and go all day, you say it's _____*) Infs **CA**210, **MA**10, In and out; **MA**34, Old farmers say it's "in and out"; **IL**34, They're in and out; **NY**61, Clouds are going in and out; (Qu. B14, *When the wind is blowing unevenly, sometimes strong and sometimes weak . . it's _____*) Inf **NJ**52, Coming in and out.

in-and-out n See **in-and-out-the-window 2**

in-and-out-the-window n
1 freq *go(ing)-in-and-out-the-window* and varr; also *in-and-out-the-door:* A ring game; see quots. Cf **marching around the levee**
    [**1903** (1963) Newell *Games & Songs* 128 **NY**, Go Round and Round

the Valley. A ring of dancers with clasped hands. A girl circles about the outside of the rest, who join in singing—Go round and round the val-ley [repeated three times] . . As we are all so gay. The players now let go hands, and she winds in and out of the circle, singing—Go in and out of the windows [repeated three times] As we are all so gay.] **1905** *DN* 3.81 **nwAR,** *Go in and out the window. . .* The name of a game. **1948** *WELS Suppl.* **IA,** We used to play a singing circle game—"Go In and Out the Window." . . Someone was "It" and would choose someone else and someone else would choose until there was a line of several girls. . . They went in and out the circle one behind the other. The song: Go in and out the window [three times] / For I am Jingle Bell / I made this dress to show you [three times] / That I am Jingle Bell / I made it cause I love you [three times] / For I am Jingle Bell. **1957** *Sat. Eve. Post Letters* **IL, KS, OH,** Go-in-and-out-the-window(s). **1965–70** *DARE* (Qu. EE1, . . *Games . . children play . . in which they form a ring, and either sing or recite a rhyme*) 20 Infs, **scattered, but esp Nth, N Midl,** Go-in-and-out-the-window(s); 15 Infs, **scattered, but esp Nth, N Midl,** In-and-out-the-window(s); **LA**17, **ME**11, **NH**17, Going-in-and-out-the-window; **GA**6, 33, (Go-)in-and-out-your-windows; **WI**18, In-and-out-the-door. **1966–68** *DARE* Tape **AL**6, Go-in-and-out-the-windows . . you know that one? . . Hold their hands up . . in a circle and . . I guess they had one that'd go in; **NY**88, As I recall, the tune went something like this: "Go in and out the window [three times] / As we have done before." The children were in a ring holding hands; then there was one who was "it" and he would go in and out between the children. **c1970** *DARE* FW Addit **swVA,** A five-verse rhyme was sung as Go-in-and-out-the-window was played. The first line of each verse was repeated three times. These were: "Go in and out the window / Go forth and face your lover / I stand because I love you / I measure my love to show you / Oh it breaks my heart to leave you." The fourth line of each verse was the refrain "For you have gained the day." This was nice to play when we had summer guests.

2 also *in-and-out:* Appar a game like **musical chairs.** Cf **Jerusalem, going to 1**
    1967–69 *DARE* (Qu. EE2, *Games that have one extra player—when a signal is given, the players change places, and the extra one tries to get a place*) Infs **KY**44, **NJ**13, **WA**25, Go-in-and-out-the-window(s); **TX**40, Going-in-and-out-the-window; **GA**23, In-and-out.

in'ards See **inwards**

Inca dove n Also *Inca*
A small, grayish dove *(Scardafella inca)* found in the Southwest, esp Arizona. Also called **Mexican dove 2**
    1887 Ridgway *N. Amer. Birds* 216, *S[cardafella] inca. . .* Inca dove. **1917** (1923) *Birds Amer.* 2.52, *Inca dove. . . Other Name.*—Scaled Dove. . . Southern Texas, southern Arizona, and Lower California and southward. . . We heard the Inca before we saw him. **1928** Bailey *Birds NM* 306, An adult male Inca Dove appeared in Silver City, May 26, 1924, and remained there until taken by Mr. Kellogg on July 17, 1924. **1964** Phillips *Birds AZ* 43, *Inca Dove. . .* Common resident of cities and towns of central and central-southern Arizona. . . This is one of the most friendly and delightful of Arizona birds. **1967** *DARE* (Qu. Q7, . . *Game birds*) Inf **TX**11, Doves—Inca.

incense bush n Cf **incienso**
=brittlebush.
    1967 *DARE* (Qu. S26a, . . *Roadside flowers*) Inf **CA**4, Encelia—incense bush (fragrant leaves).

incense cedar n [See quot 1917]
A tall conifer *(Libocedrus decurrens)* native to the Pacific coast. Also called **juniper 2e, pencil cedar, post cedar, red cedar, white cedar**
    1869 (1911) Muir *First Summer* 27 **cCA,** Another conifer was met to-day,—incense cedar *(Libocedrus decurrens),* a large tree with warm yellow-green foliage in flat plumes like those of arborvitae. **1884** Sargent *Forests of N. Amer.* 176, *Incense Cedar. . .* Largely used for fencing and in the construction of water-flumes. **1917** (1923) Rogers *Trees Worth Knowing* 270, The incense cedar . . has its name from its resinous, aromatic sap. **1923** Saunders *S. Sierras* 42 **sCA,** Silver firs, yellow pines, and incense cedars four and five feet in diameter made a contemplative twilight. **1968** *DARE* (Qu. T5, . . *Evergreens*) Inf **CA**97, Incense cedar.

incense shrub n [From its fragrance]
A **currant B1** (here: *Ribes sanguineum*).
    1897 Parsons *Wild Flowers CA* 214, *Ribes glutinosum. . .* We are made

aware of a strong, heavy fragrance emanating from this shrub . . which has gained for it the popular name of "incense-shrub" in some localities. **1934** Haskin *Wild Flowers Pacific Coast* 135, *Red-flowered Currant. Ribes sanguineum. . .* The whole plant . . is strongly permeated with a spicy, aromatic scent, giving it the occasionally used name of incense shrub.

inch n, v Usu |inč|; also **chiefly Sth, S Midl** |inč|; occas |ɛnč| Pronc-sp *eench* Cf Pronc Intro 3.I.5.a
Std senses, var forms.
    1923 *DN* 5.206 **swMO,** Eench over, John, so's I kin sot down. **1928** *AmSp* 3.403 **Ozarks,** *Little, itch, inch, idiot* and *oblige* have the sound of *ee.* **1934** *AmSp* 9.210 **Sth,** A great many words having standard [ɪ] before . . [g], [n], [ŋ], and possibly [č], change [ɪ] to [i]. . . *Finch, finger, flinch, inch.* Ibid 211 **NC,** Some persons . . pronounce [ɪ] of some words as [ɛ]. . . *Clinch, inch.* **c1960** *Wilson Coll.* **csKY,** *Inch* is nearly always [inč].

inch and a half n
See quot 1984.
    1950 *Western Folkl.* 9.118 **nwOR** [Logger speech], *Inch and a half.* Time and one half for overtime. **1958** McCulloch *Woods Words* 94 **Pacific NW. 1984** Weaver *TX Crude* 93, *Inch-and-a-half.* Time-and-a-half pay rate for overtime.

inch-a-night (grass) n Cf **foot-a-night**
A **bullgrass 1** (prob *Paspalum distichum*).
    1986 Pederson *LAGS Concordance* (*Undesirable grass in a cotton field*) 1 inf, **cwAL,** Inch-a-night grass; 1 inf, **cnAL,** Inch-a-night—formerly "water grass"—grows fast.

‡incher n
    1969 *DARE* (Qu. II18, *Someone who joins himself on to you and your group without being asked and won't leave*) Inf **NC**61, Incher.

inchie n [Abbr and var of **enchilada**] Cf Pronc Intro 3.I.4.a
    1987 *NADS Letters* **cOK,** At fast-food places around here . . enchiladas are *inchies.*

inching vbl n [Cf **inch up**]
In marble play:
a also pl: Moving the hand forward while shooting. [Cf *EDD inchin'* (at *inch* v. 4) "encroaching gradually. . . Boys cried out at play, 'No inchin, no inchin.' "] Cf **fudge** v, **hunch** v **2a**
    1881 *Amer. Grocer* 20 July (*OED*), Boys who did not play fair . . would keep reaching over the line in order to get nearer the marbles in the ring and have a better chance to knock them out. This was called 'inching', and 'fen inchings' was the warning against such unfair play. **1955** *PADS* 23.20 **cwTN,** *Inchings. . .* Fudging. **1968** *DARE* Tape **DE**3, You weren't allowed to put your hand beyond that line when you first shot, or, if you did, we'd call that inching. And, if you were plucking . . you didn't dare move your hand forward; if you did, we'd call that podging.
b pl: Denying an opponent the right to move a marble from an unfavorable position; see quot.
    1922 *DN* 5.187 **KY,** *Inchins. . .* A case of one's taw rolling up close to an opponent's taw (approximately within an inch). If one then cries out "Inchin's," the opponent must shoot from where his taw lies without moving back for better position. The opponent is not so bound if he cries out first, "Vence ye inchin's."

inchings See **inching a, b**

inchly n Also *inchling*
    1968 *DARE* (QR, near Qu. M12) Inf **MD**13, Inchlies—corn chopped into pieces about an inch long; **MD**18, Silo—stores inchlies ['ɪnčliz]— green corn, chopped up; **MD**20, Silo—contains inchlings ['ɪnčlɨŋz]— green corn cut in small pieces.

inch plum n [From its size]
A **wild plum** (here: *Prunus americana* var *lanata*).
    1960 Vines *Trees SW* 405, *Inch Plum. Prunus americana* var. *lanata. . . Fruit. . .* Deep red with a bloom, about 1 in. long, flesh juicy. **1962** Harrar–Harrar *Guide S. Trees* 352, *Inch Plum. Prunus lanata. . .* Inch plum, so called because of the length of its fruit, is a small tree of the lower Ohio River Valley, Missouri, Arkansas, eastern Oklahoma, eastern Texas, Louisiana, and south-central Alabama.

inch up v phr Cf **fudge** v, **inching**
In marble play: see quot 1942; hence n *inch-up;* see quot 1963.

1942 McAtee *Dial. Grant Co. IN* 36 (as of 1890s), *Inch up . .* move nearer surreptitiously, as to "fudge" in a game of marbles. **1963** *KY Folkl. Rec.* 9.3.65 **seKY** [Marbles terms], *Trying to get [a] closer shot by placing the hand in a position nearer to the marble being shot at:* close-up . . crow-hops . . inch-up.

inchworm n [See quot 1905] **widespread, but esp NEast, N Cent** See Map Cf **measuring worm**
=**looper.**

a1861 Winthrop *Open Air* 123 *(DA),* All the green inchworms vanish on the tenth of every June. **1881** *Harper's New Mth. Mag.* 63.656 **wMA, wCT,** A wriggling inch-worm . . awaiting . . an opportunity to measure the length of your nose. **1899** (1912) Green *VA Folk-Speech* 239, *Inch-worm.* . . A drop worm or measuring-worm. **1905** Kellogg *Amer. Insects* 395, Familiar to all observers . . are the inchworms, spanworms, or loopers. . . These three common names . . refer to the peculiar mode of locomotion affected by all the Geometrina. Each . . step is made by the bringing forward of the caudal extremity of the body quite to the thoracle feet, the portion of flexible body between bending up and out of the way each time during the process. **1949** *Sat. Eve. Post* 12 Mar 33 **Philadelphia PA,** One evening the Main Line local train hunched its cars together like an inchworm and skidded to a halt at Merion station. **1965–70** *DARE* (Qu. R27x, . . *Kinds of caterpillars or similar worms;* not asked in early QRs) 145 Infs, **widespread, but esp NEast, N Cent,** Inchworm; (Qu. R27y, . . *The soft worm that eats the leaves on plants and turns into a butterfly;* total Infs questioned, 75) Inf **DC2,** Inchworm. **1970** *NC Folkl.* 18.37, The measuring worm, known as inch worm in mountains of North Carolina, . . when measuring on you, was sign of your getting a new suit. **1980** Milne–Milne *Audubon Field Guide Insects* 765, The larvae are the familiar . . inchworms— slender caterpillars with . . a characteristic looping method of locomotion. **1986** Pederson *LAGS Concordance* **FL, LA,** 3 infs, Inch worm; 1 inf, Inch worms—green, not for fishing.

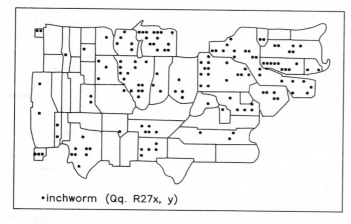

•inchworm (Qq. R27x, y)

incidence n [*W3 incidence* 1 *"now chiefly dial";* prob infl by use of *incidence* in other senses or by *coincidence*] Cf **instant, innocence 1**
An incident.

1906 *DN* 3.142 **nwAR,** Incidence. . . "A strange incidence happened while I was there." **1916** *DN* 4.276 **NE, MA.** **1933** *AmSp* 8.3.76, R.G. Greene asks whether there is no way to stop speakers from saying *"an incidence"* (plural *incidences*) instead of the proper *"an incident."* He thinks that the spurious singular form arises from confusion with *coincidence.* **1938** in 1976 *Weevils in the Wheat* 80 **VA,** His mind is fairly clear and he can readily recall incidences of his boyhood days. **1979** *DARE* File, [Radio:] Three people froze to death in my [Michigan] district last year. . . Three separate incidences.

incienso n [Span "incense"; see quot 1971] Cf **incense bush**
A **brittlebush** (here: *Encelia farinosa*).

1925 Jepson *Manual Plants CA* 1082, *E[ncelia] farinosa.* . . Incienso. . . Low hills or valleys or desert benches. **1931** U.S. Dept. Ag. *Misc. Pub.* 101.164, Other vernacular names include brittlebrush, . . incienso. . . It ranges from lower California to southern Utah and northern Sonora and is a typical desert plant of the plains and lower foothills. **1957** Jaeger *N. Amer. Deserts* 270, *Incienso.* . . Resinous-stemmed shrub with gray-green leaves. **1971** Dodge *100 Desert Wildflowers* 87, Stems of the low-growing, silvery-leaved shrub exude a gum which was

chewed by desert Indians and burned as incense by priests in mission churches, giving the plant the local name, *incienso.* . . *Encelia farinosa.*

in clear exclam Cf **all clear, in free**
In hide-and-seek A: =**all (in) free.**

1968 *DARE* (Qu. EE15, *When he has caught the first of those that were hiding what does the player who is 'it' call out to the others?*) Inf **NJ39,** In clear. **1977–78** Foster *Lexical Variation* 79 **NJ,** Free Calls— Hide and seek . . *in clear.*

inconnu n [Fr, literally "unknown"; *DCan* 1806 →]
A freshwater food fish *(Stenodus leucichthys)* native to Alaska and northwestern Canada. Also called **sheefish, shign, whitefish, Yukon char**

1882 U.S. Natl. Museum *Bulletin* 16.304, *S[tenodus] mackenzii.* . . *Inconnu.* . . Mackenzie's River and its tributaries. **1889** *Century Dict.* 3043, *Inconnu.* . . was an unknown fish to the Canadian voyageurs who first saw it, and the name perpetuates the impression first conveyed. **1896** U.S. Natl. Museum *Bulletin* 47.474, *Inconnu.* . . A fair food-fish, but the flesh is oily. **1946** Dufresne *AK's Animals* 257, The . . Inconnu . . is a sort of connecting link between the salmons and the great whitefishes of the polar cap. **1955** U.S. Arctic Info. Center *Gloss.* 43, *Inconnu.* . . A large fresh water food fish . . found in streams in Siberia, Alaska and northern Canada.

in course See **in** prep **B2**

increase of the moon n Also *increase* [*OED increase* sb. 1.b →1665; *EDD* has 1887 ex at *keep* v. 3(5)] Cf **dark of the moon**
The waxing of the moon.

1972 *Foxfire Book* 218 **nGA,** Plant all things which yield above the ground during the increase or growing of the moon. **1975** Dwyer *Thangs* 26 **Sth, S Midl,** Kraut should be made on the increase of the moon so the water will rise and it won't spoil. **1986** Pederson *LAGS Concordance,* 1 inf, **neTX,** Kill them [=hogs] on the increase—sign of the moon; 1 inf, **csLA,** We done passed the increase.

ind See **in** prep, adv **A2**

indeed and double adv phr Also *'deed and 'deed, 'deed and double* Cf **indeedy**
To be sure; really and truly—used to emphasize an assertion.

1890 *Harper's New Mth. Mag.* 81.142 **VA** [Black], "Where's the thimble?" said the colonel. "I drap it in de snow-bank out yer—'deed an' double I did—an' I 'most froze lookin' fur't." **1895** *DN* 1.386 **KY, OH,** *Deed and double:* an affirmation heard among children and illiterate women. **1916** Howells *Leatherwood God* 124 **sOH,** 'Deed and 'deed, I can tell you he ain't agoun' to do no such a thing. *Ibid* 144, 'Deed and 'deed, I'm not agoun' to speak at all. **1928** Ruppenthal *Coll.* **KS,** Indeed and double, it is so. **1928** in 1944 *ADD* **WV,** Indeed and double! **1930s** *Ibid* **eWV,** 'Deed and double. Common.

indeedy adv Also *indeedy-deedy* Cf **indeed and double**
Indeed, certainly—used to emphasize an affirmation or denial.

1856 *Knickerbocker* Dec 620 **NYC,** 'Is thy eyes not opened?' 'Yes, indeedy,' says I. **1872** Twain *Roughing It* 337, He never shook his mother. . . No indeedy. . . he looked after her and took care of her. **1890** *DN* 1.22 **DC,** *Indeedy,* for *indeed. Ibid* 78 **MA, ePA, sDE, KY,** *Indeedy* [reported in use by 5 infs]. **1892** *DN* 1.216 **DC,** *Indeedy.* . . used only in such phrases as *yes indeedy,* or *no indeedy.* We never said *indeedy* with no other word before it. **1914** Lewis *Our Mr. Wrenn* 253, "Ah-h, is it [=he] just fearful neglected when it [=he] comes home all tired out?" "No, indeedy. But you got to kiss me first, else I won't go at all." **1932** Cather *Obscure Destinies* 165, I'd like to, powerful well, Mrs. Harris. I would, indeedy. [**1943** *LANE* Map 590 *(Certainly!)* 1 inf, **cME,** Indeedly—heard as a hyperurbanism.] **1967–69** *DARE* (Qu. KK55c, . . *Expressions of strong denial*) Inf **TN12,** No indeedy-deedy; (Qu. NN4, . . *Ways of answering 'no'*) Inf **KY11,** No indeedy.

Independence tree n
A **catalpa B1.**

1902 Earle *Old Time Gardens* 31 **nNJ,** The fine line of Catalpa trees set out by Richard Stockton . . were in full flower when he rode up to his house on a memorable July day to tell his wife that he had signed the Declaration of American Independence. Since then Catalpa trees bear everywhere in that vicinity the name of Independence trees, and are believed to be ever in bloom on July 4th.

independent rich adj phr Cf Intro "Language Changes" II.8
Wealthy enough not to have to work for a living.

1906 *DN* 3.142 **nwAR,** *Independent rich.* . . Having income enough to live without work. "I wish I was him; he's independent rich." **1908** *DN* 3.323 **eAL, wGA,** *Independent(ly) rich.* . . Very rich, sufficiently rich to live without work. **1909** (1922) Norris *Third Circle* 23 **San Francisco CA,** [He] is independent rich by now, and the policeman's got a bank account. **1938** Stuart *Dark Hills* 51 **neKY,** You ought to be independent rich.

India n Pronc-spp *Inger, Ingia, Injy*

A Forms. Cf **Indian A**

   1799 in 1967 *PADS* 48.40 **NC,** *Ingia.* **1847** Hurd *Grammatical Corrector* 84, India ["incorrect" pronc = ['ɪnji]]. **1871** (1882) Stowe *Fireside Stories* 57 **MA,** She was a little thin woman, but tough as Inger rubber. **1904** *DN* 2.423 **Cape Cod MA** (as of a1857), *India* (Injy). **1908** Lincoln *Cy Whittaker* 11 **eMA,** Land! you're peppery as a West Injy omelet this mornin'.

B Senses.

1 In marble play: see quot.

   1958 *PADS* 29.35 **MI,** *India.* . . A marble of clear glass with an object in the center, usually a figure of an elephant, sometimes a Victorian lady, a turbaned Indian, etc.

2 also *game of India:* Pachisi. [From trademark *A Royal Game of India*]

   [**1918** U.S. Patent Office *Official Gaz.* 251.4.822, Essanar Company, Inc. . . Filed . . 1917. Under ten-year proviso. *A Royal Game of India* . . Board and Counter Games. Claims use since 1869. . . *Parcheesi.* . . Claims use since 1869.] **1966–69** *DARE* (Qu. DD37, . . *Table games*) Inf **NH**18, India—pachisi; (Qu. EE40, . . *Table games* . . *using dice*) Infs **FL**28, **IN**73, **IA**9, (Game of) India; **IA**13, Pachisi—also called India; **NY**94, Game of India—the dice tell you how far to move to see who gets home first.

Indian n Usu |'ɪndiən|; also |'ɪnjən, 'ɪndɪn| Pronc-spp *Indin(e), Indjon, Ingen, Ingin, Injin, Injun(n);* for addit pronc and sp varr see quots

A Forms.

   1617 in 1933 *VA Co. Records* 3.71, Indyan Corne. **1635** in 1853 **MA** (Colony) *Rec. of Gov.* 1.140, Indean corne. **1641** [see **B1a** below]. **1670** in 1887 East Hampton NY *Records* 1.330, Obadia the engiane was hiered. **1680** in 1866 NH Hist. Soc. *Coll.* 8.55, The ingens have showed themselves. **1758** in 1910 Essex Inst. *Coll.* 46.211 **eMA,** A hous wass Burnt down a lettell while afore by the Indjons. **1825** Neal *Brother Jonathan* 1.104 **CT,** Where's the injunn? **1835** (1927) Evans *Exped. Rocky Mts.* 14.201 **IN,** Passed today several Indin encampments. **1843** (1916) Hall *New Purchase* 79 **IN,** The Ingin grave. **1844** Uncle Sam *Peculiarities* 2.72 **sePA,** I . . grow all *my* own Indine corn. **1891** *DN* 1.127 **cNY,** [enjən] < *Indian.* **1904** *DN* 2.426 **Cape Cod MA** (as of a1857), *Injin.* **1907** [see **Indian bannock**]. **1909** *DN* 3.415 **nME,** Rye-and-Indian (Injun). **1916** *DN* 4.340 **seOH,** Big Injun. **1934** *AmSp* 9.43 **Sth,** After *d* in . . *Indian,* one often hears [j] and sometimes, though rarely, [dʒ] . . but some Southerners use [ɪ]. **1941** *LANE* Map 286 **NEng,** 8 infs, ['ɪndʒən, -dʒɪn, -dʒɪn]. *Ibid* Map 287, 10 infs, ['ɪndʒən, -dʒɪn, -dʒɪn, -dʒn]; 1 inf, **eCT,** ['ɪndɪn]; 1 inf, **sVT,** ['ɪndʒən]. *Ibid* Map 288, 21 infs, ['ɪndʒən, -dʒɪn, -dʒɪn]; 5 infs, **CT,** ['ɪndɪn]; 2 infs, **CT, cMA,** ['ɪndʒən]; 1 inf, **wMA,** ['ɛndʒɪn] meal. **1942** Hall *Smoky Mt. Speech* 66 **wNC, eTN,** In at least two words [ɪ] has palatalized the preceding dental stop and disappeared: *Indian* ['ɪndʒən], *tedious* ['tɪdʒəs]. This pronunciation of *Indian* may still be heard from a number of old people, but the current forms are ['ɪndɪn], as frequently in general American, and ['ɪndʒən]. **1960** Criswell *Resp. to PADS* 20 **Ozarks,** ['ɪnjən]—this old-time pron., now obsolete. **1967** *DARE* Tape **TX**13, ['ɪnjən] [corr to] ['ɪndɪn].

B Senses.

1a =**Indian corn 1,** cornmeal. **chiefly NEng** Note: Except in the attrib use treated at **1b** below, this sense appears to be virtually obs. Cf **rye and Indian**

   1641 in 1883 Dorchester MA *Town Rec.* 286, I Re[ceive]d in wheate and Indein 3l.8s. **1648** Shepard *Clear Sunshine* 15 **eMA,** A homely dinner, perhaps parcht Corne or *Indian* stalks. **1780** (1899) Parkman *Diary* 200 **MA,** Elias went today with a Bushel of Indian. **1817** Niles' *Natl. Reg.* 12.212 **sePA,** The cut worm, or grub, . . is if possible more destructive to the Indian crop this season than that of the last year. **1831** *Liberator* (Boston MA) 7 May 74/1, It is only to put a little more indian, or a few more potatoes, into the bread. **1849** Cooper *Sea Lions* 2.110, There were . . a few barrels of corn-meal, or 'injin,' as it is usually termed in American parlance. **1894** *Century Illustr. Mag.* 27.849 **eCT,**

The newcomer from another part of the country, when first he crosses the Connecticut River, is startled at being asked by an innocent-looking girl waiter in a village tavern if he will have some "fried Indian." **1941** *LANE* Map 287 *(Brown bread)* 1 inf, **ceMA,** Of rye and indian; 1 inf, **cMA,** Of rye, indian and graham meal.

b attrib; Of foods: made of corn or cornmeal. See also **Indian bannock, ~ bread 1, ~ cake, ~ meal, ~ pone 1, ~ pudding**

   1743 (1751) Bartram *Observations* 60, Last of all was served a great bowl, full of *Indian* dumplings, of new soft corn, cut or scraped off the ear. **1788** *Mass. Centinel* 18 Oct. 40/1 *(DA),* This milk may be used . . either with bread, or rice or Indian mush. **1851** *Knickerbocker* 38.392, He scattered far and wide corn-meal, with recipes for making pone and Indian dumplings. **1877** Bartlett *Americanisms* 312 **PA,** *Indian dab.* A kind of batter-cake. **1896** (c1973) Farmer *Orig. Cook Book* 500, *Indian Gruel*—2 tablespoons Indian meal. Cold water. **1938** Damon *Grandma* 11 **CT,** To make "injun porridge" perfectly—a very little "injun" meal boiled a very long while in a vast amount of water till all was of the consistency of whipped cream. **1941** *LANE* Map 288 **NEng** *(Corn meal mush)* 3 infs, Indian mush; 1 inf, Indian porridge; 1 inf, Indian squeal, cooked with pork and molasses. **1986** Pederson *LAGS Concordance (Breads and cakes made of cornmeal)* 1 inf, **cnGA,** Indian dumplings—in cheesecloth with greens.

2 Anger; a quick temper. Cf **African** n[1] **B1, Dutch** n **4, Irish** n[1] **B1**

   1893 Leland *Memoirs* 298, My "old Injun" was up, and I had "sailed in" for a fight by mere impulse. *Ibid* 302, When the "old Injun" and my High-Dutch ancestor are upon me, I reason not at all, and then I see visions and dream dreams, and it always comes true, without the *least* self-deception or delusion. **1897** Barrère–Leland *Slang* 1.460, *Irish, Indian, Dutch* (American), all of these words are used to signify anger or arousing temper. But to say that one has his *"Indian up,"* implies a great degree of vindictiveness, while *Dutch* wrath is stubborn but yielding to reason.

3 A child, esp an unruly one.

   1946 *Life* 29 July 102, [Advt:] He's [=a baby's] a regular Wild Indian, but *my* floor can take it! **1967–70** *DARE* (Qu. Z12, *Nicknames and joking words meaning 'a small child': "He's a healthy little _____."*) Inf **VA**102, Indian; (Qu. Z16, *A small child who is rough, misbehaves, and doesn't obey*) Inf **OR**1, Wild Indian; **PA**35, Young Indian.

4 A wild, unmanageable horse.

   1964 Jackman–Long *OR Desert* 394, [Glossary:] Indian—a horse completely dangerous to handle. **1967** *DARE* (Qu. K42, *A horse that is rough, wild, or dangerous*) Inf **PA**23, Outlaw or Indian.

5 The **hooded merganser** or the **red-breasted merganser.**

   1910 Eaton *Birds NY* 1.180, The Red-breasted merganser, Sawbill, Indian, or Pied sheldrake, as this species is called, is one of the most abundant ducks along the coast and on the inland waters. **1956** *AmSp* 31.180 **NY,** *Indian* or *Injun,* perhaps referring to the crest as a scalp lock, is a designation of the hooded merganser. *Ibid* **TX,** *Indian* or *Injun* . . red-breasted merganser.

6 in phrr *where the Indian(s) shot one:* The navel. **esp Gulf States, TX** See Map

   1965–70 *DARE* (Qu. X34, . . *The navel*) 22 Infs, **chiefly Gulf States, TX,** Where the Indian shot you; **OK**42, Where the Indians shot you; **MO**37, Where the Indian shot me; [**CO**36, Indian shot; **NY**34, Indian sign—family usage]. [16 of 24 Infs male]

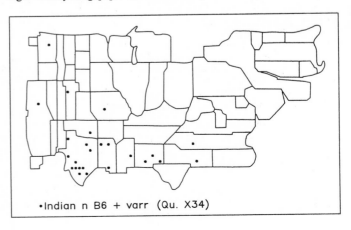

•Indian n B6 + varr (Qu. X34)

Indian v Also with *up*

To roam or move about, esp stealthily; to sneak up.

    1869 Stowe *Oldtown Folks* 189 **MA,** Jack Marshall and me has been Indianing round these 'ere woods more times 'n you could count. **1897** Lummis *King of Broncos* 41 **NM,** He intended to keep out of sight—to "Injun on 'em a little," as he would have said. **1944** Adams *Western Words* 83, *Indian up*—To approach without noise. Commonly used with reference to sneaking. [**1967** *DARE* (Qu. Y26a, *To walk very quietly*) Inf **DC1,** Tiptoe like an Indian.] **1975** Fink *Backpacking* 27 **TN,** I'd not yet learned how wary those fish were, how one had to "Injun up" on a pool.

Indiana n Usu |ˌɪndɪ'ænə|; for varr see below

Std sense, var forms.

    1 |ˌɪndi'æni|; pronc-spp *Indianny, Injianny;* for addit varr see quots. **NEng, S Midl** Cf Pronc Intro 3.I.12.b, Intro "Language Changes" IV.1.b, **-a, Africa A, Indian A**

    1862 (1864) Browne *Artemus Ward Book* 213 **NEng,** They air fully equal to the corn fed gals of Ohio and Injianny, and will make the bestest kind of wives. **1864** (1868) Trowbridge *3 Scouts* 26 **TN,** You can quit any time you choose: you can go to Indianny, and git a divorce there. **1871** Eggleston *Hoosier Schoolmaster* 133 **sIN,** Ole Pearson . . died a fightin' thieves on Rocky Branch in Hoopole Kyounty, State of Injeanny. **1942** Hall *Smoky Mt. Speech* 76 **wNC, eTN,** In the speech of most old people, of many middle-aged and young, both *-a* and *-ia* . . appear as [ɪ]. . . Indiana. **1949** Arnow *Hunter's Horn* 277 **KY,** You left your strength behind in Indianiee? **c1960** *Wilson Coll.* **csKY,** Indiana [ˌɪndɪ'æni]—older people.

    2 |ɪndɪ'ænɚ|; pronc-sp *Indianer.* Cf Pronc Intro 3.I.12.b, Intro "Language Changes" IV.1.b, **America A, -er 2**

    1986 Pederson *LAGS Concordance* **Gulf Region,** 1 inf, [ɪndɪˈ^'ænɚ]; 1 inf, [ɪndɪ'ænɚ]; 1 inf, ['ɪndɪænɚ].

Indiana dye n [Perh erron for **Indian dye**]

=**goldenseal 1.**

    1971 Krochmal *Appalachia Med. Plants* 144, *Hydrastis canadensis.* . . Indiana dye.

Indian agate n Cf **agate**

A type of playing marble.

    1957 *Sat. Eve. Post Letters* **wKY** (as of 1930s), "Indian agates" were brown and opaque. **1969** *DARE* FW Addit **ceKY,** Indian agates—an agate hand-carved from a type of stone, probably flint.

Indian alarm clock n

    1980 *DARE* File **csWI,** An Indian alarm clock is a glass of water taken before going to bed. That'll make sure you get up by morning!

Indian apple n

    1 A **mayapple 1** (here: *Podophyllum peltatum*).

    1847 *Knickerbocker* 29.310 **MO,** The rich flowers of the Indian-apple were there in profusion. **1876** Hobbs *Bot. Hdbk.* 56, Indian apple, May apple, Podophyllum peltatum. **1910** Graves *Flowering Plants* 194 **CT,** May, Indian, Hog or Devil's Apple. . . The fruit is edible and harmless but disagreeable to many persons. **1931** Clute *Common Plants* 35, The May-apple *(Podophyllum peltatum)* was known to the settlers as Indian apple, but it is really a berry. **1950** *WELS (Other names . . for the mayapple)* 5 Infs, **WI,** Indian apple. **1967** *DARE* (Qu. S26a, . . *Roadside flowers*) Inf **NE8,** Indian apple. **1971** Krochmal *Appalachia Med. Plants* 198.

    2 A wild apple (*Malus* spp).

    1930 Shoemaker *1300 Words* 32 **cPA Mts** (as of c1900), *Indian apple*—The native wild apple of the mountains. **1950** *WELS (Fruits that grow wild in your neighborhood)* 1 Inf, **ceWI,** Apples—called Indian apples.

    3 A **waxmallow** (here: *Malvaviscus drummondii*).

    1939 Tharp *Vegetation TX* 62, Indian Apple (*Malvaviscus*).

    4 A pomegranate *(Punica granatum).* Cf **Chinese apple**

    1967 *DARE* File **neMA,** Indian apple—a pomegranate.

    5 =**Osage orange.**

    1969 *DARE* (Qu. I46) Inf **IN63,** Indian apple—same as hedge apple.

    6 A **thorn apple** (here: either *Datura inoxia* or *D. meteloides*).

    1968 Schmutz et al. *Livestock-Poisoning Plants AZ* 80, Indianapple . . *(Datura meteloides).* . . The fruit is an oval or round . . prickly capsule. **1970** Correll *Plants TX* 1405, *Datura inoxia.* . . Indian apple. **1976**

Bailey–Bailey *Hortus Third* 365, *Indian apple.* . . Sw. U.S. and Mex.; introd. into the Old World.

Indian arrow See **Indian arrowwood 1**

Indian arrowhead See **Indian arrowwood 3**

Indian arrowwood n

    1 also *Indian arrow(root):* A **burning bush 1** (here: *Euonymus atropurpureus*).

    1815 Drake *Natural View Cincinnati* 77 **swOH,** [Plants growing in Miami country include] *Euonymus* carolinensis—*Indian arrow-wood.* **1843** Torrey *Flora NY* 1.141, Burning-bush, Indian Arrow, . . [grows in] moist woods and along rivers, in the western part of the state. **1892** *Jrl. Amer. Folkl.* 5.94 **csIN,** *Euonymus atropurpureus,* Indian arrow. **1940** Clute *Amer. Plant Names* 128, *E. atropurpureus.* . . Indian arrow. *Ibid* 258, *Euonymus atropurpureus.* . . Indian arrowroot. **1961** Sackett–Koch *KS Folkl.* 72, But we never forgot Famora, the prettiest queen this land ever knew, and the shrub she held in her hand, and which was changed into an arrow, is called to-day Indian arrow wood. **1971** Krochmal *Appalachia Med. Plants* 116, *Euonymus atropurpureus.* . . *Common Names:* Eastern wahoo, . . Indian arrow-wood.

    2 A **flowering dogwood** (here: *Cornus florida*).

    1900 Lyons *Plant Names* 118, *C[ornus] florida.* . . Indian Arrow-wood. **1930** Sievers *Amer. Med. Plants* 28, *Flowering Dogwood.* . . *Other common names.* . . Indian arrowwood. **1974** (1977) Coon *Useful Plants* 119, Indian arrow-wood. . . In looking at the names, we note the word "arrow-wood" and because the wood is very hard, it has a number of possible uses.

    3 also *Indian arrowhead:* A **mock orange 1b** (here: *Philadelphus lewisii*).

    1937 U.S. Forest Serv. *Range Plant Hdbk.* B109, Indian arrowwood is another name sometimes given to this plant [=*Philadelphus lewisii*] because the Indians used its slender shoots for arrow shafts. **1963** Craighead *Rocky Mt. Wildflowers* 77, *Philadelphus lewisii.* . . Other names . . Indian Arrowwood. . . The straight stems of the plant were used by Indians in making arrows. **1979** Spellenberg *Audubon Guide N. Amer. Wildflowers W. Region* 531, *Indian Arrowhead.* . . Indians used its straight stems in making arrows.

Indiana tobacco n Cf **Indian tobacco 4**

=**pussytoes.**

    1966 *DARE* FW Addit **cMA,** Indiana tobacco—pussytoes.

Indian ball n Also *Indian baseball*

A bat-and-ball game; see quots.

    1953 Brewster *Amer. Nonsinging Games* 80 **MO,** Indian Ball. . . A triangular playing field is used for this game. . . The players are divided into two teams of five men each. . . Any ball passing the infield on the ground is a hit, but if the ball is caught while in the air. . . Three outs constitute an inning, and five innings a game. No running is done by the batter. **1967–68** *DARE* (Qu. EE11, *Bat-and-ball games for just a few players*) Inf **MO26,** Indian ball—two players per team, boundaries 25 feet apart, the object is for the hitter to smash the ball past the infielder or hit it over the outfielder's head; if the infielder fields the ball cleanly or if either fielder catches a pop fly, it's an out, otherwise it's a hit; **PA94,** Indian baseball—roll the ball toward the bat—if hit, batter loses turn; **PA163,** Indian ball. **1968** *DARE* FW Addit **cwMD,** Indian baseball—bat-and-ball game with few players—hitter throws ball for himself, no pitcher. **1975** Ferretti *Gt. Amer. Book Sidewalk Games* 190 **PA,** In Philadelphia, *Indian Ball* is played. The batter hits by himself, then places the broomstick across whatever has been designated home plate. Whichever fielder of three or more retrieves the ball rolls it at the bat. If it hits and the batter catches it as it bounces up, he remains at bat. If he does not catch it, or if he drops it, whoever rolled the ball becomes the batter. **1983** *Wall St. Jrl.* (NY NY) 22 Aug 15/1 **St Louis MO,** Your article brought back childhood memories of a game we called "Indian Ball" . . any ground ball cleanly fielded within 20 feet in front of the line was . . an out, and the batter usually threw the baseball up himself rather than swinging at a pitch from a teammate. **1987** Dillard *Amer. Childhood* 123 **cwPA,** We are silent, waiting or running. . . Someone hits the ball, someone silent far up the street catches it on the bounce. . . Carefully the batter lays down the bat perpendicular to the street. Carefully the hushed player up the street rolls the ball down to the bat. The rolled ball hits the bat and flies up unpredictably; the batter misses his catch; he and the fielder switch positions. Indian Ball.

Indian balm n

A **trillium,** usu *Trillium erectum.*

1830 Rafinesque *Med. Flora* 2.98, *Trillium latifolium. Names. . . Vulgar.* Bethroot, . . Indian Balm. **1889** Lindley–Moore *Treas. Botany* 2.1171, *T[rillium] erectum* (sometimes called *T. pendulum*). . . is also called Indian Balm. **1907** Hodge *Hdbk. Amer. Indians* 1.605, *Indian balm.*—The erect trillium, or ill-scented wake-robin *(Trillium erectum).* **1970** *NC Folkl.* 18.6, Trillium (birthroot, sometimes called wood lily and recognized as "Indian balm,") was used to assuage the pangs of childbirth.

Indian balsam n
A **biscuit root 1** (here: *Lomatium dissectum*).
1936 McDougall–Baggley *Plants of Yellowstone* 95, Leaves finely dissected. Flowers purple or yellow. *Indian-balsam.* **1962** Balls *Early Uses CA Plants* 85, The root of Indian Balsam . . was thought to be particularly good for asthma and tuberculosis.

Indian banana n
1979 *Blair & Ketchum's Country Jrl.* 12 **cMA,** No one has referred to "Indian bananas." In the late summer, when what I assume to be bracken fiddle-head ferns matured, we would pull up a bundle of fern stems and at the bottom, encased in the base of the stems, was a small "banana" about two inches long, tapering from one-half inch in diameter at the bottom to a somewhat pulpy upper end. They had a bland but not disagreeable taste.

Indian bannock n chiefly **eNEng, esp ME, NH** *old-fash* Cf **bannock, Indian** n **B1b**
A thin bread or cake made of cornmeal.
1806 *Old Farmer's Almanac for 1807* Jan np **NEng,** Now for a good broiled sausage, a dish of pancakes, or an Indian bannock. **1809** in 1957 *Old Farmer's Almanac Sampler* 111 **NH,** An Indian bannock was said to be a favorite of Washington. **1907** *DN* 3.191 **seNH,** *Injun bannock. . .* Johnny cake. The latter the usual name. **1941** *LANE* Map 287 *([Indian] Bannock)* 19 infs, **ME, sNH,** Indian bannock; 1 inf, **RI,** Bannock, of wheat flour; *Indian bannock,* of corn meal; 1 inf, **neMA,** *Indian bannock,* father's term for *Johnnycake.*

Indian bark n Cf **Indian bitter 2**
A **sweet bay** (here: *Magnolia virginiana*).
1876 Hobbs *Bot. Hdbk.* 56, Indian bark, Sweet bay, Magnolia glauca. **1900** Lyons *Plant Names* 236, *M[agnolia] Virginiana. . .* Massachusetts, south to Florida and Texas, near Atlantic and Gulf sea-board. Laurel Magnolia, Small or Sweet Magnolia, . . Indian-bark. **1907** Hodge *Hdbk. Amer. Indians* 1.605, *Indian bark.*—The laurel magnolia, or sweet bay *(Magnolia virginiana).* **1960** Vines *Trees SW* 286, *Magnolia virginiana. . . Medicinal Uses.* Sweet-bay Magnolia bark was at one time the source of an official [sic] drug for the treatment of malaria and rheumatism, but its use has been abandoned. . . Vernacular names are Swamp-bay, . . and Indian-bark.

Indian baseball See **Indian ball**

Indian basket grass n [See quot 1974] **NW**
=**squaw grass.**
1922 *Country Life* June 45 **OR,** We camped two days . . in the ghost forest beyond the glorious and fragrant cream-white spikes of the Indian basket grass. **1936** Thompson *High Trails* 86 **nwMT,** The bear grass flower. . . is also listed as . . Indian basket grass. **1949** Peattie *Cascades* 248 **Pacific NW,** It is a member of the lily family, . . and has the tongue-twisting name of Xerophyllum tenax. In days gone by the Indians used its tough leaves in making their baskets, which accounts for its common names of squaw grass and Indian basket-grass. **1961** Thomas *Flora Santa Cruz* 116 **cwCA,** Indian Basket Grass. . . Known from only two localities in the Santa Cruz Mountains. **1974** (1977) Coon *Useful Plants* 177, Indian basket grass. . . The roots have been used for food but, as one common name indicates, it was used by the Indians for making clothing and weaving baskets.

Indian battercake See **Indian cake**

Indian bead n [From the shape]
A single part of the jointed stalk of a fossil crinoid. Also called **fish bone**
1966 *Wilson Coll.* **csKY,** Indian bead—a fossil stone ring. **1967** *Living Museum* 29.106 **IL,** Walking along the edge of a dusty road, wading along a cool creek, or exploring an old quarry, one may find what appear to be stone buttons. These small disks, often called "Indian beads," may be lying loose in the gravel or firmly attached to a large piece of rock. In fact, some limestone is composed almost entirely of these "beads," indicating that they are actually much older than the Indians.

Indian bean n
1 Any of var cultivated beans, sometimes supposed to have been in use among American Indians.
1637 in 1850 CT (Colony) *Pub. Rec.* 1.9, Weathersfeild [is to provide] 1 bushell of Indian Beanes; Windsor 50 peeces of Porke. **1793** MA Hist. Soc. *Coll.* 3d ser 5.129, His Indian beans [were] ready to be eaten as stringed beans. **a1936** in 1943 *Colorado Mag.* 20.144 **West** (as of 1852), We served mutton and goat meat, Indian beans or frijoles. **1950** *WELS* (*Flat beans that are striped or speckled with red*) 1 Inf, **seWI,** Indian beans. **1966** *DARE* (Qu. I20, *Other kinds of beans that are grown around here*) Inf **ND9,** Indian beans—red ones—grown in earlier days. **1978** *Wanigan Catalog* 11, *Indian Bean.* Known by this name in many New England areas. A bit shorter than Soldier, but growth is similar. Early.
2 =**catalpa B1;** also its seed pod.
1843 Torrey *Flora NY* 2.25, *Catalpa syringæfolia . .* Indian Bean. **1884** Sargent *Forests of N. Amer.* 115, *Indian Bean. . .* A decoction of the seeds and dried bark occasionally used in cases of asthma and bronchitis. **1897** Sudworth *Arborescent Flora* 335 **IL, MA, NJ, NY, NC, PA, RI,** *Catalpa. . .* Common Names. . . Indian Bean. **1931** Clute *Common Plants* 36, The slender cylindrical fruits of the catalpa tree *(C. speciosa)* are often known as Indian beans and Indian cigars. **1950** *WELS* (*The tree with large heart-shaped leaves, clusters of white blossoms, and long slender seed pods*) 1 Inf, **cWI,** Indian bean. **1968** *DARE* (Qu. T9) Inf **PA89,** Indian bean. **1968** Everett *Living Trees* 298, The Indian-bean has many more flowers in each cluster than the Western catalpa. **1976** Bruce *How to Grow Wildflowers* 158, *Catalpa bignonioides . .* [and] *C. speciosa. .* [have] long, slender, cylindrical seed capsules (the "Indian beans" of many a country boy's childhood) which are conspicuous in winter.
3 A **groundnut B1** (here: *Apios americana*).
1898 *Jrl. Amer. Folkl.* 11.225, *Apios tuberosa,* . . Indian bean, Morristown, N.J.
4 A **lupine** (here: *Lupinus perennis*).
1935 (1943) Muenscher *Weeds* 304, *Lupinus perennis. . .* Indian beans. . . Pistil forming a broad hairy 4–7-seeded legume. **1940** Clute *Amer. Plant Names* 263, *Lupinus perennis.* . . Indian bean.
5 A **coral tree** (here: *Erythrina flabelliformis*).
1960 Vines *Trees SW* 559, *Erythrina flabelliformis. . .* is also known under the vernacular names of Indian Bean, Coral-tree, and Chilicote. The . . red beans [are sometimes used] for necklaces. **1979** Little *Checklist U.S. Trees* 127, *Southwestern coralbean. . . Other common names . .* Indian-bean.

Indian beardgrass See **Indian grass 1b**

Indian bear grass n
=**squaw grass.**
1941 Writers' Program *Guide WA* 418, The slopes are often carpeted with Indian bear grass, its great white tufts like ice cream cones on two-foot stalks.

Indian bells n [From the shape of the flower]
A **mariposa lily** (here: *Calochortus albus*).
1923 in 1925 Jepson *Manual Plants CA* 238, *C[alochortus] albus. . . White Globe Lily. . .* Also called Snow-Drops, Indian Bells, and Satin Bells.

Indian berry n
A **yaupon** (here: *Ilex vomitoria*).
1951 *PADS* 15.36 **TX,** *Ilex vomitoria. . .* Indian berry . . used by the pioneers, to whom friendly Indians showed medicinal plants.

Indian bird See **Indian crow**

Indian biscuit n
A **biscuit root 1** (here: *Lomatium piperi*).
1925 Jepson *Manual Plants CA* 725, *L[omatium] piperi. . . Indian Biscuit. . .* Sierra Co. to Siskiyou Co., n. to Wash. **1939** Medsger *Edible Wild Plants* 190, Biscuitroot, or Indian Biscuit, or Cowas. . . Usually it is . . ground into a sort of flour and made into cakes. The cakes are said to have the taste of stale biscuits; hence by the white people the plant was generally called Biscuitroot.

Indian bitter n
1 A **burning bush 1** (here: *Euonymus atropurpureus*). *obs*
1859 Colton *Mt. Scenery* 97 **NC,** The wahoo, or Indian bitter, resembles both the cucumber and the linn. . . The bark, steeped in liquor, is said to have miraculous effect in curing the chills and fevers.

2 also pl: Either of two **magnolias:** *Magnolia acuminata* or *M. fraseri.* [See quot 1950]

1897 Sudworth *Arborescent Flora* 197 **NC**, *Magnolia fraseri. . . Common Names. . .* Indian Bitters. **1907** Hodge *Hdbk. Amer. Indians* 1.605, *Indian bitters.*—A North Carolina name of the Fraser umbrella or cucumber tree *(Magnolia fraseri).* **1950** Peattie *Nat. Hist. Trees* 275, *Magnolia acuminata. . .* Indian-bitter. [*Ibid* 276, François Michaux. . . [i]n July, 1802, . . makes a dry observation on the Cucumbertree: "The inhabitants of the remotest parts of Pennsylvania and Virginia and even the western countries, pick the cones when green, to infuse in whiskey, which gives it a pleasant bitter. This bitter is very much esteemed in this country as a preventative against intermittent fevers, but I have my doubts whether it would be so generally used if it had the same qualities when mixed with water."] **1958** Jacobs–Burlage *Index Plants NC* 143, *Magnolia Fraseri. . .* Indian bitters.

Indian blackbird n

Either the **phainopepla** or the **yellow-headed blackbird.**

1957 *AmSp* 32.182 **MO**, *Indian blackbird . .* yellow-headed blackbird. *Ibid* 32.183 **AZ**, *Indian blackbird . .* Phainopepla.

Indian black drink n

A **yaupon** (here: *Ilex vomitoria*); also the ceremonial and medicinal drink made from this plant by American Indians of the southeastern US.

1876 Hobbs *Bot. Hdbk.* 56, Indian black drink, South sea tea, Ilex vomitoria. **1907** Hodge *Hdbk. Amer. Indians* 1.605, *Indian black drink.*—The cassena, yaupon, black drink . . , or Carolina tea *(Ilex cassine).* **1960** Vines *Trees SW* 647, A medicinal tea was formerly prepared by the Indians from the leaves, which contain caffeine and also possess emetic and purgative qualities. The brew was known as the "Black Drink" and was ceremoniously taken once a year. . . Local names in use are . . Indian Black-drink, Christmas-berry.

Indian blanket n chiefly TX

1 also *Indian-blanket flower:* A **gaillardia B,** usu *Gaillardia pulchella.* [See quot c1979]

1936 Whitehouse *TX Flowers* 183, *Indian Blanket. . .* is the pride of Texas prairies. **1942** *Torreya* 42.166, *Gaillardia* sp.—Indian-blanket flower, Texas Panhandle. **1948** Stevens *KS Wild Flowers* 392, *Gaillardia pulchella.* . . 'Indian blanket' is an appropriate common name suggested by a colony of these plants in bloom, often widespread over the plains. **1961** Wills–Irwin *Flowers TX* 241, Indian-blanket is found throughout Texas. **1969–70** DARE (Qu. S21, . . *Weeds . . that are a trouble in gardens and fields*) Inf **TX**73, Indian blanket; (Qu. S26a, . . *Roadside flowers*) Infs **TX**12, 29, 43, 64, 78, 91, Indian blanket. **1970** Correll *Plants TX* 1671, *Gaillardia.* . . Indian Blanket. Blanket Flower. **c1979** TX Dept. Highways *Flowers* np, *Indian blanket . .* blooms over the state from April to June, with brilliant color combinations of red, orange and yellow which, when viewed in mass, resemble the bright tapestries of the Western Indians. **1993** Kingsolver *Pigs in Heaven* 175, Along the highways the cornfields . . reveal Oklahoma's . . orange velvet dirt. The uncultivated hills nearby show off . . wildflowers. The massed reds flecked with gold are Indian blanket.

2 An **Indian paintbrush 1,** esp *Castilleja coccinea.*

1940 Steyermark *Flora MO* 487, *Indian Blanket . . Castilleja coccinea.* . . corolla yellowish. . . Eastern, southern, and central Mo. **1940** Writers' Program *Guide TX* 24, Indian paintbrush and Indian blanket are known in other localities as Indian pink or paintcup. **1951** PADS 15.40 **TX**, *Castilleja* spp.—Indian blankets or Indian paint-brushes.

Indian-blanket flower See Indian blanket 1

Indian bluebells n Cf bluebell 1f

A **virgin's bower** (here: *Clematis hirsutissima*).

1967 DARE Wildfl QR (Craighead) Pl.7.1 Inf **CO**15, Indian bluebells.

Indian bokay See Indian bouquet

Indian bouquet n Eye-dial sp Indian bokay

1 =**butterfly weed 1.**

1951 PADS 15.38 **TX**, *Asclepias tuberosa.* . . Indian 'bokay.'

2 A **puccoon.**

1951 PADS 15.39 **TX**, *Batchia linearifolia.* . . Indian 'bokay.' . . *Lithospermum gmelinii.* . . Indian 'bokay.'

Indian boys and girls n

=**Dutchman's breeches 1.**

1896 *Jrl. Amer. Folkl.* 9.181, *Dicentra cucullaria.* . . Indian boys and girls, Madison, Wis. **1907** Hodge *Hdbk. Amer. Indians* 1.605, *Indian*

boys and girls.—A western name of the Dutchman's breeches *(Bikukulla cucullaria).* **1940** Clute *Amer. Plant Names* 121. **1959** Carleton *Index Herb. Plants* 64.

Indian bread n

1 also *Indian corn bread, ~ meal bread:* Corn bread. **esp NEng, NY** Cf **Indian n B1b**

1654 (1974) Johnson *Wonder-Working* 84 **ceMA**, The want of English graine . . proved a sore affliction to some stomachs, who could not live upon *Indian* Bread. **1765** Timberlake *Memoirs* 30 **ceTN**, Fried meats of several kinds, and very good Indian bread, baked in a very curious manner. **1796** (1799) Weld *Travels* 105 **eVA**, Indian corn bread . . is a coarse, strong kind of bread, which has something of the taste of that made from oats. **1856** Whitcher *Bedott Papers* 70 **cNY**, If I don't make a johnnycake every few days, he says to me, says he, "Mar, why don't you make some injin bread?" **1864** Nichols *40 Yrs.* 1.117 **nwNY**, The long narrow table . . is covered with Yankee luxuries—hot Indian-corn bread, milk-toast, hot rolls. **1895** (1900) Arnold *Century Cook Book* 236 **VT**, *Thin Indian Bread.* **1941** LANE Map 286 *(Corn bread)* 23 infs, **NEng exc RI**, Indian bread; 3 infs, **CT, ME, MA**, Indian meal bread. **1949** *AmSp* 24.110 **neFL**, *Indian bread. . .* Corn bread prepared in pones. **1968–70** DARE (Qu. H14, *Bread . . made with cornmeal*) Inf **MI**77, Indian bread—bought it in Florida; (Qu. H18, . . *Special kinds of bread*) Inf **MI**119, Indian bread—with cornmeal; **NY**105, Indian bread—made with white cornmeal and red beans, made into cakes and boiled.

2 Any of var other types of bread, which may or may not include cornmeal; see quots. [Perh from their resemblance in color to **1** above] Cf **brown bread, rye and Indian**

1887 Parloa *Miss Parloa's Kitchen Companion* 800, *Steamed Indian Bread.* . . Indian meal . . flour . . sweet milk . . sour [milk] . . molasses. . . Steam for three hours. **1896** (c1973) Farmer *Orig. Cook Book* 61, *Indian Bread.* . . Graham flour . . Indian meal . . molasses . . milk. Mix and steam as Boston Brown Bread. **1941** LANE Map 287 *(Brown bread)* 1 inf, **ceCT**, Indian bread, of corn meal, rye flour and molasses; 1 inf, **swVT**, Indian bread = brown bread. **1967** DARE (Qu. H18, . . *Special kinds of bread*) Inf **WA**27, Indian bread—molasses and graham, sourdough base. **1986** Pederson *LAGS Concordance*, 1 inf, **seGA**, Indian bread—flour, brown sugar; *(Bread made with flour)* 1 inf, **swAL**, Indian bread—wheat flour, mashed sweet potatoes.

3 also *Indian head, ~ loaf, ~ pone:* An edible fungus such as *Poria cocos.* [See quot 1920] Cf **tuckahoe**

1848 Bartlett *Americanisms* 366, *Tuckahoe. . .* The Virginia truffle. A curious vegetable, sometimes called by the name of Indian Bread, or Indian Loaf, found in the Southern States, bordering on the Atlantic. **1871** U.S. Dept. Ag. *Rept. of Secy. for 1870* 423, *Tuckahoe or Indian head, (Lycoperdon solidum.)* . . These singular fungous growths are subterranean and parasitic on roots of large trees. . . The form is irregularly globose, about the size of a man's head. **1883** U.S. Natl. Museum *Annual Rept. for 1881* 692, *P[achyma] cocos.* . . "Indian Bread," "Indian Head," and "Indian Loaf." **1891** *Century Dict.* 6522, *Tuckahoe. . .* A subterranean fungus, *Pachyma Cocos,* otherwise known as *Indian bread, Indian head,* and *Indian loaf,* found widely in the southern United States. **1894** DN 1.331 **sNJ**, *Indian bread.* **1903** DN 2.318 **seMO**, *Indian bread* or *Indian pone.* **1920** Saunders *Useful Wild Plants* 39, *Pachyma Cocos.* . . Inside the brown rind is a firm, white meat. . . Its most common name is Indian Bread, because of the Indian use of it as food. **1950** PADS 14.40 **SC**, *Indian bread.* . . The truffle. **1967** DARE (Qu. S26e, *Other wildflowers*) Inf **SC**46, Indian bread—solid, white, rounded.

4 An unidentified plant: see quot. Cf **Indian potato q**

1929 Bell *Some Contrib. KS Vocab.* 179, Indian bread. . . Reported from McPherson as a "plant growing close to the ground with rounded but much corrugated leaves and meaty roots." Reported from Hutchison, also.

5 An edible plant such as an **arrow arum** (here: *Peltandra virginica*).

1974 (1977) Coon *Useful Plants* 67, *Peltandra virginica . .* Indian bread. . . Much used by many Indians as a food plant after extracting the acrid principle.

Indian breadroot n [See quot 1967; DCan 1852 →] chiefly west of Missip R

A **scurf pea** such as *Psoralea castorea* or *P. hypogaea* (or the edible tubers of such a plant), but esp *Psoralea esculenta* which is also called **breadroot 1, Cree potato, Dakota turnip, ground apple 1, Indian turnip 2, Missouri breadroot,**

pomme blanche, pomme de prairie, pomme de terre, prairie apple, prairie potato, prairie turnip, tipsinna, white apple, wild potato, wild turnip

1900 Lyons *Plant Names* 309, P[*soralea*] *esculenta*. . . Manitoba to Texas. Indian . . Bread-root. . . *Tubers* esculent, as are the smaller ones of . . *P. hypogaea* . ., Nebraska to New Mexico, Smaller Indian Bread-root. **1907** Hodge *Hdbk. Amer. Indians* 1.605, *Indian bread-root.*—The prairie turnip, or pomme blanche *(Psoralea esculenta).* **1937** U.S. Forest Serv. *Range Plant Hdbk.* W157, *Psoralea castorea* . . Indian breadroot. **1938** FWP *Guide MN* 395 swMN. **1951** *PADS* 15.35 **TX**, *Psoralea hypogaea*. . . Indian breadroot. **1967** Harrington *Edible Plants Rocky Mts.* 203, *Indian Breadroot.* . . The starchy, tuber-like roots furnished a well-known food to the Indians, and the early white settlers soon discovered their value. **1973** Hitchcock–Cronquist *Flora Pacific NW* 273.

Indian brier n

A **greenbrier** (here: *Smilax rotundifolia*).

1892 Torrey *Foot-Path Way* 80 **seMA**, It [=*Smilax glauca*] . . had less of beauty than its familiar relatives, the common greenbrier (cat-brier, horse-brier, Indian-brier) of my boyhood.

Indian-broke ppl adj Also *Indian-broken* Cf cowboy-broke, Indian side

Of a horse: trained to be mounted from the right or from either side indifferently.

1929 *AmSp* 5.63 **NE** (as of 1860–1900), An "Indian pony," one "Indian broken," is approached and mounted on the right or "far side." *Ibid* 66, The Indians had them before there were any white settlers in the state and "broke" them to be approached and mounted on the right side, hence the term "Indian broke." **1940** Writers' Program *Guide NM* 114, Injun-broke horse. . . A horse broken for mounting from either side.

Indian broom n

A **groundsel tree** (here: *Baccharis sarothroides*).

1949 Curtin *By the Prophet* 65 **AZ**, *Baccharis sarothroides*. . . Common name: Broom baccharis, . . Indian broom. . . The Pima make brooms from the stalks.

Indian burn n Cf snakebite

The act of grasping a person's arm with both hands and twisting in opposite directions simultaneously; hence v *Indian burn* to twist someone's arm in this manner.

1960 Williams *Walk Egypt* 138 **GA**, He began twisting her arm one way with one hand, the other way with the other, Indian-burning. **1980** *Verbatim Letters* cwVT, Indian burn was used in Connecticut in the 1950's to describe that awful practice of wrist-twisting—and Vermont children still use it now. **1981** *NADS Letters* **neCT**, I . . grew up . . well acquainted with the term "Indian burn"—as well as with its practice. (Ouch.) **1985** *DARE* File (as of 1950–60), To grasp someone's arm with both hands and twist in opposite directions is called an "Indian burn" in central North Carolina. **1988** *Ibid*, One night we were horsing around and my friend, saying "Here's an Indian burn," grabbed my wrist with two hands and began rubbing it by turning his hands in opposite directions at the same time. "That hurts!" I said. Two others yelled "Indian burn! Indian burn!" Someone else said, "That's not an Indian burn, that's a snake bite." **1992** *Ibid* **NYC** (as of early 1950s), Growing up in the Bronx, what we called Indian burns and noogies were the chief torments which we kids inflicted on each other. **1995** *Ibid* **csWI** (as of 1930s), Indian burn.

Indian cabbage n

1 A **yucca** (here: *Yucca glauca*). Cf **banana yucca**

1939 Vestal–Schultes *Economic Botany* 18, *Yucca glauca*. . . Indian Cabbage. [*Ibid* 19, The central spike of the plant is also eaten as "cabbage."] **1943** Elmore *Ethnobotany Navajo* 33, *Yucca glauca*. . . Indian Cabbage. [*Ibid* 34, The fruits of this plant are either eaten as they are found, baked in ashes, or they are sliced and dried for winter use. . . They taste similar to a banana.]

2 A **prince's plume** (here: *Stanleya pinnata*). Cf **Paiute cabbage**

[**1878** *Amer. Naturalist* 12.604, *Caulanthus crassicaulis* and *Stanleya pinnatifida* are eaten raw in the spring by the Pah-Ute Indians, the young plants being tender, and when cooked taste like cabbage. For this reason these seeds are called cabbage by the settlers of Utah. The Indians gather the seeds and after reducing them to flour make them into mush.] **1987** Kindscher *Edible Wild Plants* 216, Prince's plume has been called Indian cabbage because it was reported as a cabbagelike food source of the Indians of the Southwest and the Great Basin.

Indian cake n Also *Indian battercake, ~ griddle cake, ~ hoecake, ~ johnnycake, ~ meal cake, ~ pancake* Cf Indian n B1b

A thin bread or pancake made of cornmeal.

1608 in 1860 Amer. Antiq. Soc. *Trans. & Coll.* 4.87 **VA**, And hee . . had bought some witnesses' handes against me to diuers artycles, wth Indian cakes . . perswations, and threats. **1719** in 1915 NJ Hist. Soc. *Proc.* 33.103, The Indians supplied them with Indian cakes. **1789** Morse *Amer. Geog.* 131 **VA**, He breakfasts . . on three small indian hoe-cakes. **1790** *Very Surprising Narr.* 4, She refreshed us with. . . some Indian cake, and excellent water. **1841** Steele *Summer Journey* 128 **nIL**, They soon placed upon the table cloth . . nice indian meal cakes. **1847** (1979) Rutledge *Carolina Housewife* 25, *Indian cakes*. . . eggs . . milk . . molasses, and meal enough to make a thick batter. . . Bake. **1847** (1853) Thompson *Locke Amsden* 22 **VT**, Then came the fine meal Indian Johnny-cake, mixed with cream, eggs, and sugar . . forming . . the most delectable esculent of the bread kind. **1867** *Common Sense Cook Book* 8 *(DA)*, [Recipe:] Indian Batter Cakes. **1879** (1965) Tyree *Housekeeping in Old VA* 56, Indian Griddle Cakes. **1939** Wolcott *Yankee Cook Book* 134 **neMA**, Fried Indian Cakes [Also called Cornmeal Slappers] 2 cups cornmeal, ½ teaspoon soda, ½ teaspoon salt, 2½ cups boiling water. . . Fry in skillet in hot fat. **1941** *LANE* Map 286 *(Corn bread)* 9 infs, **ME, eMA, NH**, *Indian cake*. . . [is the same as] *Johnny-cake*, sweetened corn bread. *Ibid* Map 289 *(Griddle cake*. . . *corn cake)* 2 infs, **swCT**, *Indian (pan)cake*.

Indian caraway n

A **yampah** (here: *Perideridia gairdneri*).

1951 Abrams *Flora Pacific States* 3.233, *Perideridia Gairdneri*. . . False or Indian Caraway. **1976** Bailey–Bailey *Hortus Third* 846, [*Perideridia] Gairdneri*. . . Indian c[araway].

Indian carrot n

A **wild carrot**.

1940 Smith *Puyallup–Nisqually* 251 **nwWA**, Additional food roots [included] the wild or Indian carrot.

Indian catch-blanket n Cf tear-blanket

A **prickly ash** (here: *Zanthoxylum americanum*).

1968 *Dallas Morning News* (TX) 10 Aug sec D 1/2, This small tree or bush has many common names, in addition to . . prickly ash. . . Clair A. Brown, professor of botany at Louisiana State, also mentions Indian catch blanket.

Indian cedar n

A **hop hornbeam 1** (here: *Ostrya virginiana*).

1900 Lyons *Plant Names* 270, O[*strya*] *virginiana*. . . Indian cedar. **1907** Hodge *Hdbk. Amer. Indians* 1.605, *Indian cedar.*—The hop-hornbeam, or ironwood *(Ostrya virginiana)*. **1940** Clute *Amer. Plant Names* 162. **1960** Vines *Trees SW* 145, *Ostrya virginiana*. . . Vernacular names are Ironwood, . . and Indian-cedar. The wood is used for posts, golf clubs, tool handles, mallets, and woodenware.

Indian celery n AK

A **cow parsnip 1** (here: *Heracleum lanatum*).

1939 FWP *Guide AK* 169, The waterfront street continues left to the Indian village, which smells of Indian celery and dandelion and drying salmon. **1955** U.S. Arctic Info. Center *Gloss.* 431 **AK**, *Indian celery*. The cow parsnip. **1968** *DARE* (Qu. S6) Inf **AK**1, Indian celery—Indian rhubarb—wild rhubarb.

Indian cherry n

1 A **buckthorn**: usu **Carolina buckthorn 1,** but also *Rhamnus cathartica*.

1884 Sargent *Forests of N. Amer.* 40, *Rhamnus Caroliniana*. . . *Indian Cherry.* . . The edible fruit sweet and agreeable. **1895** Gray–Bailey *Field Botany* 105, R[*hamnus*] *Caroliniana*. . . *Indian Cherry.* . . The 3-seeded fruit at first crimson, finally black. Wild in wet grounds, from N.J. and Ky. S. **1900** (1927) Keeler *Our Native Trees* 49, *Indian Cherry. Rhamnus caroliniana.* . . Its northern limit is Long Island, New York, where it is a shrub; it becomes a tree only in southern Arkansas and adjoining regions. **1901** Lounsberry *S. Wild Flowers* 328, Indian Cherry. Carolina Buckthorn. **1964** Batson *Wild Flowers SC* 74, *Indian cherry.* . . Small deciduous tree up to 25 ft. high. **1974** (1977) Coon *Useful Plants* 235, *Rhamnus cathartica* . . Indian cherry. . . As is true with other fruits of this genera [sic], they are laxative and purgative, and should be used with care.

2 A **serviceberry**, usu *Amelanchier canadensis*.

1897 Sudworth *Arborescent Flora* 212 **PA**, *Amelanchier canadensis*. . . Indian Cherry. **1911** *Century Dict. Suppl., Cherry*. . . *Indian cherry.* (a)

The Carolina buckthorn, *Rhamnus Caroliniana.* (b) The service-berry, *Amelanchier Canadensis.* **1940** Clute *Amer. Plant Names* 9, *A. Canadensis.* . . Indian cherry. **1960** Vines *Trees SW* 416, *Amelanchier arborea.* . . Vernacular names are . . June-plum, Indian-cherry.

3 A **jack-in-the-pulpit 1** (here: *Arisaema triphyllum*).
   1951 *PADS* 15.27 **TX,** *Arisaema triphyllum.* . . Indian cherries. . . The corm and fruits were boiled and drained before being eaten by the aborigines; birds also like the "cherries."

Indian chickweed n [See quots 1931, 1974]
   A **carpetweed 1,** usu *Mollugo verticillata.*
   1837 Darlington *Flora Cestrica* 96, *Verticillate Mollugo. Vulgo*—Carpet weed. Indian Chickweed. **1892** *Jrl. Amer. Folkl.* 5.89, *Mollugo verticillata* is thus called Indian chickweed, to distinguish it from the omnipresent common chickweed, *Stelleria media.* **1931** Clute *Common Plants* 34, The Indian chickweed *(Mollugo verticillata)* . . is a little mat-plant that came to us from the warmer parts of the world and has no association with America's primitive inhabitants. **1959** Gillespie *Compilation Edible Wild Plants WV* 45. **1974** (1977) Coon *Useful Plants* 52, *Mollugo verticillata*—Indian chickweed. . . Reputed to have been used by the Indians as a poultice, demulcent, and ointment and possibly also as a potherb, today it has relatively minor value.

Indian chief n
   1 A **shooting star** (here: *Dodecatheon meadia*).
   1894 *Jrl. Amer. Folkl.* 7.94, *Dodecatheon Meadia.* . . Indian chief, Rockford, Ill. **1900** Lyons *Plant Names* 138, *D[odecatheon] Meadia.* . . Pennsylvania to Georgia and west to Texas and Manitoba. Shooting-star, American Cowslip, . . Indian-chief. **1949** Moldenke *Amer. Wild Flowers* 234, Our best-loved species is the *indianchief* . . whose flowers are pink-purple. **1959** Carleton *Index Herb. Plants* 64, *Indian chief:* Dodecatheon meadia.
   2 A cultivated bean. Cf **Indian bean 1**
   1966 *DARE* (Qu. I20, . . *Beans . . grown around here*) Inf **ME**12, Indian chief.
   3 A children's game. [Perh from rhyme "Rich man, poor man, beggar man, thief / Doctor, lawyer, Indian chief"]
   1968 *DARE* (Qu. EE1, . . *Games . . children play . . , in which they form a ring, and either sing or recite a rhyme*) Inf **NY**81, Indian chief.

Indian chocolate n Also *Indian chocolate root* [See quot 1889]
   =**water avens;** also a decoction made from its root.
   1828 Rafinesque *Med. Flora* 1.222, All the Avens have nearly the same properties. . . They are the base of the Indian Chocolate of Empirics. The doses are a daily pint of the weak decoction. . . These roots are sometimes put in Ale, as stomachics. **1876** Hobbs *Bot. Hdbk.* 23, Chocolate, Indian, Avens Root, Geum rivale. **1889** *Century Dict.* 2504, The roots of . . the water-avens, *G. rivale,* . . from their reddish-brown color are sometimes known by the names of *chocolate-root* and *Indian chocolate.* **1910** Graves *Flowering Plants* 235 **CT,** *Geum rivale.* . . Indian Chocolate-root. Wet or boggy meadows. . . The root is used medicinally. **1959** Carleton *Index Herb. Plants* 64, *Indian-chocolate:* Geum rivale. **1976** Bailey–Bailey *Hortus Third* 509, *[Geum] rivale.* . . *Indian chocolate.* . . Calyx purple, petals . . dull orange-pink.

Indian chop n Cf **chop** n[1] **1, hominy B1**
   1840 *Daily Picayune* (New Orleans LA) 21 Aug 2/5, Ham and greens, ham and greens, and hominy and rice, rice and hominy all the time. The hominy is nothin' but Ingin-chop—but if I could larn to cook that are hominy!

Indian chub n
   =**hornyhead c.**
   1820 *Western Rev.* 2.238 **Ohio Valley,** *Kentuckian Shiner. Luxilus Kentuckiensis.* . . Vulgar names, Indian chub, Red-tail, Shiner, &c. **1896** U.S. Natl. Museum *Bulletin* 47.322, *Hybopsis kentuckiensis.* . . Horny Head; . . Indian Chub. **1983** Becker *Fishes WI* 485, Indian chub. . . A prominent reddish "ear spot," and orange on dorsal and anal fins.

Indian cigar n Also *Indian cigar tree* [See quot 1976] **chiefly Midl, Gt Lakes** See Map Cf **cigar tree, lady cigar, monkey cigar tree**
   A **catalpa B1,** usu *Catalpa bignonioides,* or its pod.
   1897 Sudworth *Arborescent Flora* 335 **PA,** *Catalpa bignonioides.* . . *Common Names.* . . Indian Cigar-tree. **1900** Lyons *Plant Names* 86, *C[atalpa] Catalpa.* . . Indian cigar. **1931** Clute *Common Plants* 36, The slender cylindrical fruits of the catalpa tree *(C. speciosa)* are often known as Indian beans and Indian cigars. **1950** *WELS* **WI** (*The tree with large heart-shaped leaves, clusters of white blossoms, and long slender seed pods*) 1 Inf, Indian cigar tree; 1 Inf, Indian cigar—[in] Kentucky. **c1960** Wilson *Coll.* **csKY,** *Indian cigar.* . . The seedpod of a catalpa. The tree itself is sometimes called Indian cigar tree. **1965–70** *DARE* (Qu. T9) 23 Infs, **chiefly Midl, Gt Lakes,** Indian cigar tree; **IN**73, Catalpa—the pods are "Indian cigars." **1976** Bruce *How to Grow Wildflowers* 159, My childhood memories include those of many expeditions to "Indian Cigar" trees, to collect the pods for later smoking in secret.

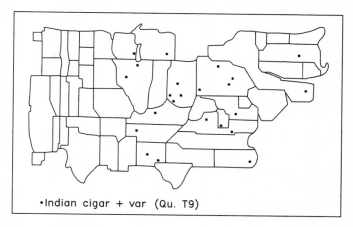

•Indian cigar + var (Qu. T9)

Indian clover n
   =**rancheria clover.**
   1925 Jepson *Manual Plants CA* 545, *T[rifolium] dichotomum.* . . Indian Clover. . . Corolla cream-tipped. . . Locally gregarious, covering patches a rod square or so, low hills. **1961** Thomas *Flora Santa Cruz* 216 **cwCA,** *T[rifolium] dichotomum.* . . Branched Indian Clover. Occasional in grasslands and on serpentine soils. . . *T. albopurpureum.* . . Common Indian . . Clover. Grassy slopes.

Indian club n [Perh from the shape]
   =**bottle gourd.**
   1967 *DARE* FW Addit **LA**2, Indian club—the gourd commonly used for dippers. Also known as water gourd.

Indian collard n Cf **wild collard**
   Prob a **skunk cabbage** (here: *Symplocarpus foetidus*).
   1937 (1963) Hyatt *Kiverlid* 79 **KY,** We picked wild mustard an' Shawnee an' Injun collards, polk [sic], blue-thistle, . . an' I don't know what all.

Indian corn n
   1 Std: a cereal grass *(Zea mays)* widely cultivated esp for food and fodder. Also called **Indian** n **B1a, Indian wheat 1.** For other names of the common table corn *(Zea mays var rugosa)* see **butter and sugar corn, sugar ~, sweet ~.** For other names of other varr see **bloody butcher, bread corn, Canada ~, chicken ~ 2, cow ~, dent ~, Dutton ~, flint ~, flour ~, fodder ~, gourdseed ~, guinea corn 3, hard ~, hog ~, horse ~, horsetooth ~, hull ~ 1, mule ~, mutton ~, ree ~, rice ~, sod ~, soft ~, squaw ~, stock ~, tucket**
   2 A dish made with corn; see quot. [Cf **1** above]
   1950 *WELS* **WI** (*Dishes made with corn*) 1 Inf, Indian corn; 1 Inf, Indian corn—sometimes called scalloped.
   3 A **bead lily** (here: *Clintonia borealis*).
   1968 *DARE* Tape **IN**14, [In discussion of wildflowers:] Indian corn, as it is called, or wild corn.
   4 =**green dragon.** Cf **Indian turnip 1**
   1967 *DARE* FW Addit **AR**44, Indian corn or dragon head—*Arisaena* [sic] *dracontium.*

Indian corn bread See **Indian bread 1**

Indian corn meal See **Indian meal**

Indian-corn pudding See **Indian pudding**

Indian cradle n
   A **jack-in-the-pulpit 1.**
   1892 *Garden and Forest* 5.614, We all know the significance of Jack-in-the-pulpit, but the same Arum is known as Indian Cradle, from a fancied resemblance to a pappoose with the hood drawn over its head.

Indian creeper n

=**trumpet creeper.**

1924 Deam *Shrubs IN* 289, Trumpet creeper. . . is also called Indian-creeper. **1940** Clute *Amer. Plant Names* 232, *Tecoma radicans.* . . Hellvine, Indian creeper, shoestrings.

Indian crow n Also *Indian bird* Cf **Indian hen 3**

=**pileated woodpecker.**

1957 *AmSp* 32.182 **SC**, Indian crow . . pileated woodpecker. **1966** *DARE* (Qu. Q17, . . *Kinds of woodpeckers*) Inf **FL34**, Indian bird—pileated.

Indian cucumber root n Also *Indian cucumber*

A liliaceous plant (*Medeola virginiana*), native to the eastern US, which produces an edible white root with a cucumberlike flavor. Also called **cucumber root 1, false hellebore 2**

1784 in 1785 Amer. Acad. Arts & Sci. *Memoirs* 1.437 **sePA**, *Medeola.* . . *Indian Cucumber.* . . The roots . . are esculent and of an agreeable taste. The Indians made them a part of their food. **1814** Pursh *Flora Americae* 1.244, *Medeola virginica.* . . This plant is known by the name *Indian Cucumber:* the roots have a strong resemblance in taste and flavour to cucumbers, and are eaten by the natives. **a1862** (1864) Thoreau *ME Woods* 309, The prevailing flowers and conspicuous small plants . . were . . *Medeola virginica* (Indian cucumber-root), [etc]. **1902** *Jrl. Amer. Folkl.* 15.108, *Indian cucumber.* **1947** *Amer. Midland Naturalist* 38.37 **MD**, *Medeola virginiana* (Indian cucumber-root). Common in terrace forest; occasional in seepage swamps and bluff forest. **1966** *DARE* (Qu. S26d, *Wildflowers that grow in meadows*) Inf **ME8**, Indian cucumber.

Indian cup n

1 also *Indian cup plant:* =**cup plant 1.** [See quot 1961]

1876 Hobbs *Bot. Hdbk.* 56, Indian cup plant, Silphium perfoliatum. **1907** [see **2** below]. **1936** Winter *Plants NE* 154, Indian-cup. Ranges throughout the prairie states. **1961** Smith *MI Wildflowers* 401, *Indian Cup.* . . Leaves . . (at least the upper leaves) joined by their bases or petioles, often forming a cuplike structure. **1976** Bruce *How to Grow Wildflowers* 236, One of these is the showy Cup-plant or Indian-cup, *Silphium perfoliatum.*

2 A **pitcher plant,** usu *Sarracenia purpurea.*

1837 P.H. Gosse in E.W. Gosse *Life* (1890) 108 (*OED*), That curious plant, the Indian cup or pitcher plant (*Sarracenia*). **1900** Lyons *Plant Names* 335, *S[arracenia] purpurea.* . . Indian-cup. **1907** Hodge *Hdbk. Amer. Indians* 1.605, *Indian cup.*—(1) The common pitcher plant (*Sarracenia purpurea*). (2) The cup-plant (*Silphium perfoliatum*). **1931** Clute *Common Plants* 37, Nor is it likely that the hollow leaves of the pitcher plant (*Sarracenia purpurea*) were used as cups by the Indians, though they are known as Indian cups. Possibly these are plants mentioned only to their disparagement. **1959** Carleton *Index Herb. Plants* 64, *Indian Cup:* Monotropa uniflora; Sarracenia (v); Silphium perfoliatum.

3 =**Indian pipe 1.**

1959 [see **2** above].

Indian cup plant See **Indian cup 1**

Indian currant n

1 A **coralberry 1** (here: *Symphoricarpos orbiculatus*).

1785 Marshall *Arbustrum* 82, *Lonicera Symphoricarpos. Indian Currants, or St. Peter's Wort.* This hath a shrubby stalk, which rises from four to five feet high. **1806** (1905) Clark *Orig. Jrls. Lewis & Clark Exped.* 5.327 **MT**, Deep purple berry of the large Cherry of the Current [sic] Species which is common. . . The engagees call it the Indian Current. **1859** (1968) Bartlett *Americanisms* 99, Coral Berry. (*Symphoricarpos vulgaris.*) The Indian Currant of Missouri. **1931** Clute *Common Plants* 37, We cannot imagine a real use by the aborigines of . . Indian currant (*Symphoricarpos orbiculatus*). **1976** Bailey–Bailey *Hortus Third* 1087.

2 A **currant B1** (here: *Ribes sanguineum* var *glutinosum*).

1948 *So. Sierran* Feb 2/2 (*DA*), 'Indian currant' was also in bloom.

Indian daisy n

=**black-eyed Susan 2.**

1966 *DARE* (Qu. S7, *A kind of daisy, bright yellow with a dark center, that grows along roadsides in late summer*) Inf **MO1**, An Indian daisy.

Indian devil n

1 =**mountain lion.** Cf **Indian panther**

1851 (1856) Springer *Forest Life* 66 **ME**, A dangerous specimen of the feline species, known by woodsmen as the 'Indian devil,' had prowled from time immemorial. **1901** Thompson *In ME Woods* 60, The cougar, or "Indian devil," is sometimes seen, but only rarely. **1909** *DN* 3.412 **nME**, *Indian devil.* . . The catamount.

2 =**wolverine.** [*DCan* 1853 →]

1916 Kephart *Camping & Woodcraft* 1.262, The wolverine, also called . . Indian devil, is the champion thief of the wilderness. **1946** Dufresne *AK's Animals* 95, The "Indian devil" . . as it is sometimes called gives way to no other animal in the north. **1949** Palmer *Nat. Hist.* 597, *Wolverine.* . . A great menace to trappers and campers, and a dangerous antagonist if cornered. . . Known as carcajou, . . Indian devil. **1949** *Sat. Eve. Post* 22 Jan 98, Once the Indian Devil has found the line he will give up his wider wanderings and settle down to working it as persistently as the trapper, and several days earlier.

Indian dream n Also *Indian's dream*

Either of two ferns: usu a **cliff brake** (here: *Pellaea atropurpurea*), but also *Cheilanthes siliquosa.*

1876 Hobbs *Bot. Hdbk.* 57, Indian dream, Rock brake, Pteris atropurpurea. **1900** Lyons *Plant Names* 279, *P[ellaea] atropurpurea.* . . Indian's-dream. **1907** Hodge *Hdbk. Amer. Indians* 1.607, *Indian's dream,* the purple-stemmed cliff-brake (*Pellaea atropurpurea*). **1923** Abrams *Flora Pacific States* 1.26, *Cheilanthes siliquosa.* . . Indian's Dream. . . Crevices of cliffs and rock outcrops. **1967** Gilkey–Dennis *Hdbk. NW Plants* 14, *Cheilanthes siliquosa.* . . Indian Dream. Oregon Cliff-brake.

Indian duck n

A **scoter.**

1956 *AmSp* 31.181, Indian duck. . . Scoters. . . General. **1982** Elman *Hunter's Field Guide* 237, *American Scoter.* . . *Common & Regional Names.* . . Indian duck. *Ibid* 240, *Surf Scoter.* . . Indian duck. *Ibid* 250, *White-winged Scoter.* . . Indian duck.

Indian dye n [See quot 1869]

=**goldenseal 1.**

1869 Porcher *Resources* 15 **Sth**, Indian Dye. . . Hydrastis Canadensis. . . The root was known to the Indians, from the brilliant yellow color which it yields. **1892** (1974) Millspaugh *Amer. Med. Plants* 9-1, *Hydrastis canadensis.* . . Indian Dye. [*Ibid* 9-2, The American aborigines valued the root highly as a tonic . . as well as a yellow dye for their clothing and implements of warfare.] **1907** Hodge *Hdbk. Amer. Indians* 1.605, *Indian dye.*—The yellow puccoon or orange-root (*Hydrastis canadensis*). **1933** Small *Manual SE Flora* 511. **1959** Carleton *Index Herb. Plants* 64, *Indian dye:* Hydrastis canadensis.

Indian elm n

=**slippery elm.**

c1873 in 1976 Miller *Shaker Herbs* 169, Red Elm. Indian Elm. . . The bark is chewed for sore throat. **1876** Hobbs *Bot. Hdbk.* 56, Indian elm, Slippery elm, Ulmus fulva. **1910** Graves *Flowering Plants* 152 **CT**, Indian . . elm. . . The inner bark is used extensively in medicine. **1930** Sievers *Amer. Med. Plants* 51. **1971** Krochmal *Appalachia Med. Plants* 260, Indian elm. . . In Appalachia, a tea made from the bark is used as a laxative.

Indianer See **Indiana 2**

Indian feather n Cf **Indian plume**

1 A **cardinal flower** (here: *Lobelia cardinalis*).

1844 Embury *Amer. Wild Flowers* 223 **NY**, *Lobelia cardinalis.* . . This . . Lobelia is one of the richest of American wild-flowers, glowing as it does in the brightest crimson hues. . . It is known by the name of Indian Feather, although more generally, perhaps, as the Cardinal Flower; the latter by no means an appropriate appellation.

2 =**Texas porlieria.**

1951 *PADS* 15.35 **TX**, *Porliera* [sic] *angustifolia.* . . Indian feather.

3 An **Indian paintbrush 1.**

1968 *DARE* (Qu. S26a, . . *Roadside flowers*) Inf **IN32**, Indian feather—paintbrush.

Indian field n Cf **old field 1**

A field cultivated by American Indians; an open area that is, or appears to be, a clearing made by American Indians and subsequently allowed to go wild; also fig.

1631 in 1940 *AmSp* 15.275 **VA**, Three hundred acres . . commonly called by the name of Indian ffield. **1696** (1977) Dickinson *God's Providence* 62, The place was an old *Indian-Field* on a high bleak hill, where had been a large *Indian house,* but it was tumbled down. **1791**

Bartram *Travels* 50 **S Atl,** An ancient Indian field, verdured o'er with succulent grass, and chequered with coppices of fragrant shrubs. **1837** (1962) Williams *Territory FL* 143, On the south side of Hillsborough, there is a large prairie, which may contain one thousand acres. It appears like an old Indian field, but the land is rather poor. **1877** Johnson *Hist. Anderson Co. KS* 19 (as of 1854), They . . planted a crop of corn, on an old Indian field, and raised a fair crop therefrom. **1899** (1912) Green *VA Folk-Speech* 239, *Indian-field.* . . A clearing used by the Indians for corn planting, and abandoned; then grown up in bushes and broomstraw. **1939** *LANE* Map 121 **Block Is. RI,** Indian field, grandfather's term for a garden overgrown with weeds (because the Indians let the weeds grow). **1942** Weygandt *Plenty* 48 **ePA,** On a ridge of poor soil above the Delaware in Bucks County there is an "Indian field" which in the memory of men still alive bore good crops because a shad, or a half shad, was planted to each hill under six grains of flint corn. **1954** Price *Johnny Appleseed* 58 **OH** (as of c1800), The Indian fields directly west of Andy Craig's shack on Center Run were a series of low, deep-soiled grassy flats that separated the river from the forest to the north. The Delawares had camped and planted there for generations and still came and went freely though their main villages had been moved above the treaty line fifteen miles north.

Indian fig n

1 Any of var **prickly pears;** also the fruit of such a plant.
  [**c1622** in 1918 *John Pory's Plymouth Colony* 25 **Bermuda,** The fruite it selfe is likened to a fig in respect of the thicknes and softnes of the rinde, and because of the graines within it, and hence it hath beene fitlie called the Indian-figge. *Ibid* 26, This description of the Indian figge . . exactlie agreeth with that fruite which in the Sommer-Islands we call the prickled-peare.] **1737** (1911) Brickell *Nat. Hist. NC* 23, The *Sun-Flower,* the *Indian-Figg,* or *Prickly-Pear,* the Fruit of this Vegetable is frequently eaten. **1802** Drayton *View of SC* 70, Common Indian fig, or prickly pear. (*Cactus* opuntia.) Grows plentifully on the sea islands. **1878** Campion *Frontier* 304 **SW,** Tunas are the fruit of the prickly pear or Indian fig. **1902** *Jrl. Amer. Folk.* 15.108, *Indian fig.* . . 1. The fruit of a large species of cactus (*Cereus giganteus*), found in New Mexico, Arizona, etc. 2. The *Opuntia Rafinesquii* of the Northeastern States. **1907** Hodge *Hdbk. Amer. Indians* 1.605, *Indian Fig.*—(1) The eastern prickly pear (*Opuntia opuntia*). (2) *Cereus giganteus,* or saguaro, the giant cereus of Arizona, California, Mexico, and New Mexico. **1920** Saunders *Useful Wild Plants* 107, The well-known Prickly Pears or Indian Figs, . . *Opuntia vulgaris,* . . and *O. Rafinesquii,* . . occur in sandy or sterile soil of the Atlantic seaboard. Their seedy, lean, insipid berries . . are edible in a way, but they are not at all in the same class with the fat, juicy "pears" of many of the species growing wild in the Southwestern desert country, where the genus is best represented. **1974** Angier *Field Guide Edible Plants* 178, The ripened colors of these Indian figs, as they are also known, range from yellowish-green and purplish-black to . . the large red fruits of the big *Opuntia megacantha* of the . . Southwest.

2 =**saguaro;** also its fruit.
  1859 (1968) Bartlett *Americanisms* 214, *Indian fig.* The fruit of a gigantic plant (*Cereus giganteus*) of the Cactus family, known among the Indians of New Mexico and Arizona as the Pitahaya, the fruit of which resembles the fig in taste. **1902** [see **1** above]. **1907** [see **1** above].

Indian fire n

1 A **sage** (here: *Salvia coccinea*).
  1936 Whitehouse *TX Flowers* 126, *Indian Fire (Salvia coccinea).* . . The red flowers are nearly an inch long. **1961** Wills-Irwin *Flowers TX* 197, Scarlet Sage or Indian-fire, with bright red flowers from April to October, grows mainly south of Travis and Harris counties, but is found in scattered localities northward to Grayson and Childress counties.

2 See quot. Cf **Indian smoke 2,** *DS* B19
  1954 *Harder Coll.* **cwTN,** *Indian fire*—Said of fog that is going up into the air. [Also] *Indians cooking in a pot.*

3 A skin disease; see quots. **Gulf States, esp LA**
  1961 Brown *NC Folkl.* 6.53 **New Orleans LA,** To cure "Indian fire," place the child in a cupboard or chiffonier and open and close the door several times. **1966–68** *DARE* (Qu. BB25, . . *Common skin diseases*) Infs **LA**15, 25, 35, 46, **MS**33, Indian fire; **LA**23, Indian fire—I never knew any other name for this until I took my children to a pediatrician and he called it "impetigo"; **LA**31, Indian fire—old-fashioned. **1968** Bradford *Red Sky* 26 **AL,** I began to get things like Indian fire and ringworm in the summer. *Ibid* 27, Indian fire is something all little boys

and girls get. . . He'll grow out of it. **1986** Pederson *LAGS Concordance,* 1 inf, **cLA,** Indian fire—a childhood disease.

‡**4** See quot. [Cf *firewater*]
  1970 *DARE* (Qu. DD21b, *General words . . for bad liquor*) Inf **MI**118, Indian fire.

Indian firebug n Cf *DS* P21

Appar a **spring peeper;** see quot.
  1986 Pederson *LAGS Concordance* (Spring frogs . . small, green) 1 inf, **seAR,** Indian firebug.

Indian firewheel See firewheel

Indianfish n

Either of two **sunfishes: pumpkinseed** (here: *Lepomis gibbosus*) or **warmouth** (here: *Lepomis gulosus*).
  1933 LA Dept. of Conserv. *Fishes* 342, The Warmouth Bass has come to bear many confusing names. These are: Warmouth, . . Indianfish. **1946** LaMonte *N. Amer. Game Fishes* 142, *Chaenobryttus coronarius.* . . Indianfish. . . Deep holes, muddy water, weed beds, around bridges. **1949** Caine *N. Amer. Sport Fish* 42, *Pumpkinseed.* . . *Colloquial Names.* . . Big-ear Bream, . . Indian Fish. **1973** Knight *Cook's Fish Guide* 383, Indianfish—Pumpkinseed.

Indian ginger n [See quot 1974]

A **wild ginger** (here: *Asarum canadense*).
  1828 Rafinesque *Med. Flora* 1.70, *Asarum Canadense.* . . *Vulgar Names*—Wild Ginger, Indian Ginger, . . Coltsfoot, &c. **1876** Hobbs *Bot. Hdbk.* 56, Indian ginger, Canada snake root, Asarum Canadensis. **1930** Sievers *Amer. Med. Plants* 19, *Canada Wildginger.* . . *Other common names.*—Asarum, Indian ginger, Canada snakeroot. . . It has a fragrant odor and spicy taste. **1931** Clute *Common Plants* 37, We cannot imagine a real use by the aborigines of Indian ginger (*Asarum Canadense*). **1966** *DARE* Wildfl QR Pl.46 Inf **WA**10, Ginger root . . wild or Indian ginger. **1974** (1977) Coon *Useful Plants* 70, Indian ginger. . . The dried root has often been used as a substitute for "tropical" ginger, a use in Colonial times that likely came from the Indians.

Indian grass n

1 Any of several grasses, as:
a A grass of the genus *Sorghastrum,* usu *S. nutans.* Also called **Indian reed 2.** For other names of *S. nutans* see **wild oat, wood grass**
  1764 Hutchinson *Hist. MA Bay* 1.480, The natural upland grass of the country commonly called Indian grass, is poor fodder. **1837** Darlington *Flora Cestrica* 88, *A[ndropogon] nutans.* . . Wood Grass. Indian Grass. **1894** Coulter *Botany W. TX* 494, *C[hrysopogon] nutans.* . . (*Indian Grass.*) . . Common in rather dry soil throughout the United States, but more abundant in the South. **1911** Walker *Lookout* 49 **seTN,** Indian grass is a tall wild grass, quite ornamental, and grows in various places on the side of the mountain near the base. **1966** *Badgerland* (Stoughton WI) 15 Oct 6/2, Prairie grasses (big bluestem, little bluestem, and Indian grass) change color in the fall just as do the shrubs and trees. **1967** *DARE* (Qu. L9a, . . *Grass . . grown for hay*) Inf **TX**42, Indian grass. **1976** Bailey-Bailey *Hortus Third* 1060, *Indian g[rass].* . . Important as a forage grass.

b also *Indian beardgrass:* A **beardgrass,** usu *Andropogon glomeratus.* Cf **finger Indian grass**
  1822 Eaton *Botany* 173, [*Andropogon*] *macrourus* . . Indian grass. **1837** Darlington *Flora Cestrica* 88, *A[ndropogon] macrourus.* . . Cluster-flowered Indian Grass. **1847** Wood *Class-Book* 622, *A. macrourus.* . . *Indian Grass.* . . Swamps, Mid[dle] States to Car[olina]. **1907** Hodge *Hdbk. Amer. Indians* 1.605, *Indian beard-grass.* . . The bushy beard-grass (*Andropogon glomeratus*). **1912** Baker *Book of Grasses* 53, This grass [=*Schizachyrium scoparium*], sometimes known as Indian Grass or Little Blue-stem, is late in starting and the leaves, often tinged with red and bronze, are seldom noticeable until June.

c A **holy grass** (here: *Hierochloe odorata*).
  1916 *Torreya* 16.236, *Hierochloë odorata.* . . Indian or sweet grass, matinicus [sic] Id., Me. **1941** Writers' Program *Guide MI* 555 **neMI,** On several points of land near by, marking the sites of Indian villages, is the Indian grass, long and tough-fibered, that was worked with split ash in basket weaving, giving a peculiarly sweet, characteristic odor to the baskets. **1950** Gray-Fernald *Manual of Botany* 186, *H[ierochloe] odorata.* . . Vanilla, Indian or Sweet Grass. . . The long leaves of vegetative shoots used for Indian baskets. **1969** *DARE* (Qu. S8) Inf **NJ**55, Indian grass.

2 A **pondweed** (here: *Potamogeton pectinatus*).

  1913 *Torreya* 13.226, *Potamogeton pectinatus*. . . Indian grass, Cayuga Lake, N.Y.

Indian grasshopper n

A **grasshopper 1** of the family Acrididae.

  1968 *DARE* (Qu. R6, . . *Names* . . *for grasshoppers*) Inf **GA54**, Indian grasshopper.

Indian gravelroot n

A **boneset 1** (here: *Eupatorium purpureum*).

  1894 *Jrl. Amer. Folkl.* 7.92 **WV**, *Eupatorium purpureum*, . . quill-wort, Indian gravel root. . . Apparently thought to be a remedy for calculi. **1971** Krochmal *Appalachia Med. Plants* 120, *Eupatorium purpureum*. . . *Common Names:* Bluestem Joe-pyeweed, . . Indian gravelroot. **1974** (**1977**) Coon *Useful Plants* 108, *Eupatorium purpureum* . . Indian gravel root. . . Among herbalists it is claimed to be of value as a diuretic and tonic.

Indian greens n pl

A **pokeweed** (here: *Phytolacca americana*).

  1951 *PADS* 15.30 **TX**, *Phytolacca americana*. . . Called also Indian greens, and still often used as "greens."

Indian griddle cake See **Indian cake**

Indian grip See **Indian hold**

Indian-hair fern n [From the black stipes]

The ebony spleenwort (*Asplenium platyneuron*).

  1951 *PADS* 15.26 **TX**, *Asplenium platyneuron*. . . Indian-hair fern.

Indian hair tonic n

A **sagebrush** (here: *Artemisia dracunculus*).

  1945 Wodehouse *Hayfever Plants* 159, Dragon sagewort . . , also called Indian hair tonic and green sagebrush. . . Its leaves and stems are nearly smooth and tinged with red, and not aromatic. It is found . . west of the Mississippi River . . on the plains and mountain slopes.

Indian head n

1 See **Indian bread 3.**

2 A **gaillardia B**; see quot.

  1929 Bell *Some Contrib. KS Vocab.* 179, Indian head. . . A kind of wild gaillardia growing in the region of the Saline River valley, having beautiful pink rays falling back from a brown comb-like center. The way in which the rays fall away from the brown comb suggests the name *Indian head.*

3 =**pileated woodpecker. Cf Indian hen 3**

  1986 Pederson *LAGS Concordance (Woodpecker)* 1 inf, **swLA**, Indian head—big as a chicken, brown, long legs; 1 inf, **nwTX**, Indian head—others' term for woodchuck [*DARE* Ed: =**pileated woodpecker**].

4 =**niggerhead 1.**

  1945 FWP *Lay My Burden Down* 260 **Sth** [Black], They throwed a lot of Indian-head rocks all over his grave, 'cause it was so shallow, and them rocks kept the wild animals from a-bothering Sam.

Indianhead root n

A **purple coneflower.**

  1940 Early *New Engl. Sampler* 317, Another remarkable weed is Echinacea (*Indian Head-root* or *Nigger-head*), a powerful drug, and an American cure-all for nearly three hundred years. Indians scraped the root, and used it as treatment for hydrophobia, insect, and snake bites.

Indian heart n [See quot 1889]

A **heartseed** such as **balloon vine.**

  1884 Miller *Dict. Engl. Names of Plants* 174, *Cardiospermum Corindum*, Heart-seed, Indian Heart. **1889** *Century Dict.* 3058, *Indian-heart*. . . A plant of the genus *Cardiospermum*, particularly *C. corindum*: so called from the prominent, white, heart-shaped scars on the seed, which mark the point of attachment. **1900** Lyons *Plant Names* 81, *C[ardiospermum] Halicacabum*. . . Balloon-vine, Heart-seed, Heart Pea, Indian-heart.

Indian hellebore n

An **Indian poke 1** (here: *Veratrum viride*).

  1917 Eaton *Green Trails* 88 **nwMT**, Associated with the woods, too, is . . the giant Indian hellebore (*[V]eratrum viride*), . . common in the East, as "false hellebore." **1922** *Country Life* June 45 **OR**, We passed into a second pasture, this time filled with tall Indian hellebore instead of

fern brake, but with the same vivid coloring. **1934** Haskin *Wild Flowers Pacific Coast* 47, Green, or Indian Hellebore. *Veratrum viride*. . . Among the Indians of the North Coast no plant was more highly valued for its magical potency than this.

Indian hemp n

1 =**dogbane a,** esp *Apocynum cannabinum* which is also called **amyroot, bowman's root 4, Choctaw root, dropsy weed, hemp dogbane, Indian physic 3, milkweed 3, rheumatism root, rheumatism weed, silkweed, squawroot, wild cotton.** [From its use by Amer Indians in making cordage]

  1619 in 1915 VA House of Burgesses *Jrls.* 10, For hempe also both *Englishe* & Indian . . , we doe require & enjoine all householders of this Colony, that have any of those seeds, to make tryal thereof the nexte season. **1637** (**1972**) Morton *New Engl. Canaan* 25, Matts . . made of their Indian hempe. **1739** (**1946**) Gronovius *Flora Virginica* 36, Indian Hemp. **1876** Hobbs *Bot. Hdbk.* 57, Indian hemp, black . . Apocynum cannabinum. . . Indian hemp, white, Asclepias incarnata. **1892** (**1974**) Millspaugh *Amer. Med. Plants* 132-1, *Apocynum androsæmifolium*. . . Com[mon] names. . . Indian hemp, . . spreading dog's bane. *Ibid* 133-1, *Apocynum cannabinum*. . . This plant is often termed Indian hemp, a name only applicable to *Cannabis Indica*, as it designates that plant alone. **1907** Hodge *Hdbk. Amer. Indians* 1.605, *Indian hemp*.—(1) The army-root (*Apocynum cannabinum*), called also black Indian hemp. (2) The swamp milkweed (*Asclepias incarnata*) and the hairy milkweed (*A. pulchra*), called also white Indian hemp. (3) A West Virginia name for the yellow toad-flax (*Linaria linaria*). (4) The velvet-leaf (*Abutilon abutilon*), called also Indian mallow. **1933** Harrington *Gypsum Cave NV* 41, Near the surface were two pieces of string, one of Indian hemp and one of sinew. **1974** Morton *Folk Remedies* 27 **SC**, *Indian Hemp*. . . *Apocynum cannabinum*. . . The stems yield strong, white fiber which the American Indians still use for thread, ropes, fish nets and clothing.

2 Std: a widely cultivated hemp (*Cannabis sativa*).

3 also *white Indian hemp*: A **milkweed 1,** usu *Asclepias incarnata*. [See quot 1783]

  1783 in 1785 Amer. Acad. Arts & Sci. *Memoirs* 1.424 **sePA**, *Indian Hemp*. Blossoms redish. . . The fibres of the bark are strong, and capable of being wrought into a fine soft thread; but it is very difficult to separate the bark from the stalk. It is said to have been used by the Indians for bow-strings. **1876** [see **1** above]. **1907** [see **1** above]. **1940** Clute *Amer. Plant Names* 90, *A[sclepias] incarnata*. . . White Indian hemp. . . *A. pulchra*. . . White Indian hemp. **1959** Carleton *Index Herb. Plants* 124, *White-Indian-hemp:* Asclepias (v).

4 A **flax** (here: *Linum virginianum*). *obs*

  1830 Watson *Annals Philadelphia* 444, The Indians made their ropes, bridles, and twine for nets, out of a wild weed, growing abundantly in old corn fields, commonly called Indian hemp—(i.e. Linum Virginianum.)

5 =**velvetleaf.**

  1900 Lyons *Plant Names* 8, *A[butilon] Abutilon*. . . Indian Hemp. **1907** [see **1** above]. **1933** Small *Manual SE Flora* 847, *A. Abutilon*. . . Indian-hemp. **1959** Carleton *Index Herb. Plants* 64, *Indian-hemp:* Apocynum cannabinum; Abutilon theoprasti [sic].

6 =**butter-and-eggs 1.**

  1907 [see **1** above]. **1940** Clute *Amer. Plant Names* 225, *Linaria vulgaris*. . . Indian hemp.

Indian hen n

1 =**bittern.**

  a1782 (**1788**) Jefferson *Notes VA* 74, *Ardea stellaris Americana* . . [is known as] Brown bittern. . . [and] Indian hen. **1824** Keating *Narrative* 1.169 **swMI**, Mr. Say observed, among others, the mallard, . . stellate heron or *Ardea minor*, (Ardea minor). **1844** Giraud *Birds Long Is.* 286 **seNY**, This species [=*Botaurus lentiginosus*] is said to have been the favorite bird of the Indians, and at this day is known to many persons by the name of "Indian Hen." **1897** *Oölogist* 14.81, For many years the peculiar habits and movements of the Indian Hen or Greater Bittern have offered special attractions for me. **1932** Howell *FL Bird Life* 110, *American bittern* . . Indian Hen. **1953** *AmSp* 28.280, *Indian hens* . . American bittern (rather generally). **1969** Longstreet *Birds FL* 27.

2 Any of var herons: see below. **chiefly Sth**

a =**night heron.**

  1835 Audubon *Ornith. Biog.* 3.275, The inhabitants of East Florida know it [=the night heron] under the name of "Indian Hen." **1953** *AmSp* 28.280, The *Indian hens* known at present comprise the little blue heron (Ala.), green heron (Va., N.C., Ga., Ala., Tenn., Ark.), black-crowned night heron (Pa., Ga., Fla.), yellow-crowned night heron (Ga., Fla.) **1955** *Oriole* 20.1.2 **GA,** *Green Heron. . . Indian Hen . .* (a wild bird, facetiously referred to as poultry of the Indians). . . *Black-crowned Night Heron. . . Indian Hen. . . Yellow-crowned Night Heron. . . Indian Hen.*

b =**green heron.**

1851 *De Bow's Rev.* 11.55 **LA,** *Blue Water Hen,* or *Indian Hen,* or *Heron,* of a bluish color on the back, brown belly; sits still over the water, on a log or stick, watching for fish. **1911** Howell *Birds AR* 26, *Green Heron. Butorides virescens.* This familiar bird, known to many by the curious name of "Indian hen," is a common and generally distributed summer resident. **1913** *Auk* 30.493 **Okefenokee GA,** *Green Heron . .* 'Indian Hen.' **1938** Matschat *Suwannee R.* 290 **neFL, seGA,** Indian hen: *Butorides virescens virescens.* **1953** [see **2a** above]. **1962** Imhof *AL Birds* 83, *Green Heron. . . Other names:* Indian Hen. . . A dark greenish-blue, crow-sized bird with chestnut neck and yellowish-green to orange legs.

c =**little blue heron.**

1908 *DN* 3.323 **eAL, wGA,** *Indian-hen. . .* The small blue heron. Also called *shide-poke* [sic]. **1953** [see **2a** above].

3 Either of two **woodpeckers:** the **pileated woodpecker** or the **ivory-billed woodpecker. chiefly Sth, S Midl**

1917 *Wilson Bulletin* 29.2.81 **LA,** *Phloetomus pileatus. . .* Indian hen, Marksville and Hamburg. **1924** Howell *Birds AL* 169, The pileated woodpecker. . . is known by a variety of names, including . . "Indian-hen." **1933** *AmSp* 8.1.50 **Ozarks,** *Indian hen. . .* The pileated woodpecker, also known as the woodhen. These birds are difficult to approach, and it is said that a boy *aint a rale hunterman till he's kilt him a Injun hen.* **1953** *AmSp* 28.280, *Indian hens . .* pileated woodpecker (from Pa. and Mo. southward), ivory-billed woodpecker (Ga., Ark., Texas). **1955** *Oriole* 20.1.10 **GA,** *Ivory-billed Woodpecker.—Indian Hen* (as a sizable bird; "Indian" in such names has the significance of "wild"). **1968** *DARE* FW Addit **AR,** I'd ask daddy what that was making that noise and he'd say, "It's a good-god." And I'd ask him what that was and he'd say, "Indian hen." **1986** Pederson *LAGS Concordance,* 14 infs, **Gulf Region,** Indian hen.

4 Any of several other birds; see quots.

1953 *AmSp* 28.279, *Indian hen.* For large enough birds, this term may have the meaning of 'wild hen,' or the hen that Indians might have favored if they had wanted hens, but for the smaller kinds, these suggestions do not seem satisfactory. Why the brown thrasher, for example, should be so called is a mystery. *The Indian hens . .* comprise . . purple and common gallinules (Texas), American coot (La., Texas), yellow-billed cuckoo (Pa.), . . and brown thrasher (Pa.) **1967–68** *DARE* (Qu. Q7, . . *Game birds*) Inf **DE4,** Indian hen or marsh hen—this is black; (Qu. Q9, *The bird that looks like a small, dull-colored duck and is commonly found on ponds and lakes*) Inf **LA7,** Indian hen—this one is brownish; (Qu. Q18) Inf **LA7,** Indian hen—on your [hunting] license . . they call him a woodcock.

Indian hippo n [**hippo** n[2]]

An **Indian physic 1** (here: *Gillenia trifoliata*).

1876 Hobbs *Bot. Hdbk.* 57, Indian hippo, Indian physic, Gillenia trifoliata. **1907** Hodge *Hdbk. Amer. Indians* 1.605, *Indian hippo.—*The bowman's root *(Porteranthus trifoliatum).* **1974** (1977) Coon *Useful Plants* 226, Indian hippo. . . The bark of the root is a mild and efficient emetic, with actions that are similar to ipecac.

Indian hoecake See **Indian cake**

Indian hold n Also *Indian grip*

See quots.

1947 Du Bois *Island in Square* 82 **NYC,** "Here comes a big one! Indian grip!" Hands locked at each other's wrists, they braced against the pull of the wave. **1968** *DARE* FW Addit **seID,** Indian hold—clasping hands wrist to wrist for double hold when playing red rover. **1991** *DARE* File **Chicago IL** (as of c1935), *Indian hold* is a term from my childhood. It was commonly used by both adults and children. The term referred to a handhold in which individuals grasped each other's lower arm and placed their thumbs on the wrists. It was intended to provide a more secure grip for certain games in which strong handgrips were a necessity in maintaining a defensive line. *Ibid* (as of c1941), In a different neighborhood [of Chicago] *Indian hold* [was a] new grip [that] required finger curling to grasp the competitor's hand for a game of *Indian wrestling.* **1991** *NADS Letters* **neOK** (as of c1920), One of our [=a rescue team's] drills was the "rescue chain." A number of us grasped each other with the Indian hold. This was to pull people out of a flooding river or those who had broken through ice. *Ibid* **swTX** (as of 1950s),

Indian hold . . is the approved [by Boy Scouts] grip for pulling up somebody who has fallen off a cliff or fallen into the river. *Ibid* **cnUT, ceWA** (as of c1955), I would like to report other instances of "Indian hold" and the variants "grab" or "hold Indian (or Injun) style." I can attest to its being used among gradeschool children . . that I played with in Spokane, Washington. . . [T]he expression was [also] common among gradeschool children in Salt Lake City. *Ibid* **wMA, NJ, Philadelphia PA,** Indian grip.

Indian horse See **Indian pony**

Indian horseradish n

A **jack-in-the-pulpit 1.**

1969 *DARE* (Qu. S1, . . *Other names . . for the jack-in-the-pulpit*) Inf **CT40,** Possibly Indian horseradish (the root).

Indian hug n *old-fash*

A type of wrestling in which opponents face one another and use their arms to grasp the other's body in a very tight hold; such a wrestling hold; also fig.

1825 Neal *Brother Jonathan* 1.257 **CT,** Carter went about . . giving out his challenge, on every side, in a loud voice, for "Indian hug; half hug; arm's length" or "close hug." **1830** Ames *Mariner's Sketches* 147 **MA,** He [=a seal] was so near that I felt his breath on my face and neck, at the same time it was not difficult to perceive that in the Indian hug or Kentucky bite, I should stand no chance at all. **1853** *S. Lit. Messenger* 19.471 **AL,** To start *in medias res . .* to give out and prove the law . . to wrestle with the subject Indian-hug fashion—to speak in plain English . . these qualities were possessed in an eminent degree. **1916** Du Puy *Uncle Sam* 46, Like a flash his head was in the tall man's chest, all his strength was in his arms, and he was administering that treatment known in his youth as the "Indian hug."

Indian hyacinth n

1 A **brodiaea** (here: *Triteleia grandiflora* [formerly *Brodiaea douglasii*]).

1915 (1926) Armstrong–Thornber *Western Wild Flowers* 24, *Indian Hyacinth . . (Brodiaea Douglasii). . .* Though the general appearance of the plant is very different, the individual flowers of this beautiful plant very much resemble the bells of a Hyacinth, for they have the same waxy, semi-translucent texture.

2 A **camas 1** (here: *Camassia scilloides*).

1951 *PADS* 15.28 **TX,** *Quamasia hyacintha. . .* Prairie hyacinth, Indian hyacinth (Indians ate the bulbs).

Indian jack-in-the-pulpit n Also *Indian jack*

A **jack-in-the-pulpit 1** (here: *Arisaema triphyllum*).

1968 Barkley *Plants KS* 85, Arisaema triphyllum. . . Indian Jack-in-the-Pulpit. **1969** *DARE* (Qu. S1, . . *Other names . . for the jack-in-the-pulpit*) Inf **NY207,** Indian jack. **1971** Krochmal *Appalachia Med. Plants* 62, Arisaema triphyllum. . . *Common Names. . .* Indian Jack-in-the-pulpit.

Indian johnnycake See **Indian cake**

Indian jug n

A **pitcher plant** (here: *Sarracenia purpurea*).

1940 Clute *Amer. Plant Names* 271, Sarracenia purpurea. . . Indian jug.

Indian ladder n

A ladderlike contrivance made from a small tree trunk, with footholds consisting either of the stubs of branches or of notches cut in the trunk.

1715 *NJ Hist. Soc. Proc.* 33.41 **nNJ,** S.G. and I went up . . to a rock which shoots from the hill . . about 20 foot high, against which we set an Indian ladder. **1791** Bartram *Travels* 247 **FL,** Having provided ourselves with a long snagged sapling, called an Indian ladder, and each of us a pole, by the assistance of these we both descended safely to the bottom. **1912** Green *VA Folk-Speech* 239, *Indian-ladder. . .* A ladder made by trimming off the limbs of a small, straight tree; cutting notches in the body; used by leaning against the straight tree to be climbed. **1929** Summers *Annals* 1517 **swVA,** It is very easy to ascend and descend, as the limbs usually begin at the ground, and being cut off about a foot from the trunk, a very convenient "Indian ladder" is formed.

Indian leek See **Indian onion 1**

Indian lemonade n

1 =**fragrant sumac.**

1898 *Jrl. Amer. Folkl.* 11.225 **CA,** *Rhus Canadensis . .* var. *trilobata, . .* squaw bush, Indian lemonade. **1907** Hodge *Hdbk. Amer. Indians* 1.605,

Indian lemonade.—A California name . . for the fragrant sumac *(Rhus trilobata).*

2 The lemonade-like drink made from **sumacs.**

1920 Saunders *Useful Wild Plants* 152, Equally refreshing and easy to decoct, is the woodland drink called "Indian lemonade," made from the crimson, berrylike fruits of certain species of Sumac. **1974** Angier *Field Guide Edible Plants* 218, Pick . . the red berries, drop them in a pan and mash them slightly, cover with . . water. . . Then strain. . . Sweeten to taste, then serve the so-called Indian lemonade hot or cold.

Indian lettuce n
1 =**columbo.**

1791 Bartram *Travels* 42 seGA, A very singular and elegant plant, of an unknown family, called Indian Lettuce, made its first appearance in these rich vales. **1876** Hobbs *Bot. Hdbk.* 57, Indian lettuce, American Columbo, Frasera Walteri. **1900** Lyons *Plant Names* 164, *F[rasera] Carolinensis.* . . Indian Lettuce. **1940** Clute *Amer. Plant Names* 223, *Frasera Carolinensis.* Ground centaury, Indian lettuce, meadow pride.

2 A **wintergreen** (here: *Pyrola rotundifolia*).

1876 Hobbs *Bot. Hdbk.* 57, Indian lettuce, Round leaved pyrola, Pyrola rotundifolia. **1897** Parsons *Wild Flowers CA* 100, We found . . *Pyrola rotundifolia.* . . This is called "Indian lettuce" and "canker lettuce," and a tincture of the fresh plant is used in medicine for the same purposes as chimaphila. **1907** Hodge *Hdbk. Amer. Indians* 1.606, *Indian lettuce.*—The round-leaved wintergreen *(Pyrola rotundifolia).* **1931** Clute *Common Plants* 37, We cannot imagine a real use by the aborigines of . . Indian lettuce *(Pyrola Americana).*

3 =**miner's lettuce,** esp *Montia perfoliata.* [See quot 1897] **chiefly Pacific**

1897 Parsons *Wild Flowers CA* 16, *Montia perfoliata.* . . The succulent leaves and stems are greedily eaten by the Indians, from which it is called "Indian lettuce." **1902** *Jrl. Amer. Folkl.* 15.109, *Indian lettuce.* A California name for the *Montia fontana.* **1915** (1926) Armstrong–Thornber *Western Wild Flowers* 120, *Miner's Lettuce. Montia parviflora.* . . It is also called Indian Lettuce and Squaw Cabbage. *M. perfoliata* is similar. **1939** Medsger *Edible Wild Plants* 145, The Indian Lettuce. . . is an odd and dainty plant which grows larger and coarser in cultivation. **1968–70** *DARE* (Qu. I28b, *Kinds of greens that are cooked*) Inf CA87, Miner's lettuce—a papery cup with a white flower in the center—also called Indian lettuce; (Qu. S20) Inf CA212, Indian lettuce.

4 =**vanilla plant.**

1980 *Verbatim Letters* ceFL (as of c1937), There were several plants called Indian Lettuce, only one of them Deer-Tongue. . . Flat leaves . . more or less lying on the ground. . . We boys would chew them. Rather spicy mild flavor. . . Deer-Tongue was also (I was told then) used . . as a source of an artificial vanilla-type flavoring.

Indian lice n
=**beggar ticks 1.**

1950 *WELS (Small flat weed seeds with two prongs that cling to clothing)* 1 Inf, cnWI, Indian lice.

Indian licorice n
=**crab's eye.**

1900 Lyons *Plant Names* 8, *A[brus] precatorius.* . . Indian Licorice (Liquorice). . . *Root,* a poor substitute for licorice root. **1933** Small *Manual SE Flora* 743 FL, *Indian-licorice.* . . Woods, thickets and road-sides. **1953** Greene-Blomquist *Flowers South* 61, *Indian-Licorice.* . . has become naturalized in peninsular Florida. **1976** Bailey-Bailey *Hortus Third* 3.

Indian lilac n
1 =**Chinaberry 1.**

1900 Lyons *Plant Names* 243, *M[elia] Azedarach.* . . Indian Lilac, Lilac tree. **1929** Neal *Honolulu Gardens* 175, *Indian lilac.* . . From March to June it is usually possible to find the small, pale-blue, fragrant flowers, which blossom profusely in graceful bunches. **1960** Vines *Trees SW* 602, *China-berry.* . . Vernacular names are . . Indian-lilac, and Pride-of-India.

2 =**crape myrtle.**

1900 Lyons *Plant Names* 213, *L[agerstroemia] Indica . . ,* China, is Crape Myrtle, Indian Lilac. [**1971** Carleton *Small Garden Book* 63, *Lagersroemia indica.* . . Welcomed by Northerners who move South and miss the lilacs, its huge trusses of bluish-violet, lavender, white, and red flowers create a lilac effect.]

Indian loaf See **Indian bread 3**

Indian mallow n Also *Indian mallows*
1 A plant of the genus *Abutilon.* [See quot 1931; *OED* 1754→] Also called **flowering maple 2, mountain lily.** For other names of var spp see **velvetleaf**

1822 Eaton *Botany* 458, *Sida. . . abutilon* (indian mallows). . . About gardens, roads, &c. **1847** Wood *Class-Book* 209, Sida Abutilon. . . *Indian Mallow.* . . Native in both Indies and naturalized in most of the states, inhabiting waste places &c. **1876** Hobbs *Bot. Hdbk.* 57, Indian mallow, . . Abutilon Avicennæ. Indian mallows, False mallows, Sida spinosa. **1891** Coulter *Botany W. TX* 41, *Abutilon. . . Indian mallow.* Herbs or shrubs. . . represented in Texas by several . . species which are, as yet, in considerable confusion. **1931** Clute *Common Plants* 34, It will not do, however, to assume that all plant names with the word Indian in them, relate to the American Aborigines. . . The *Indian mallow (Abutilon Theophrasti).* . . comes from the other side of the world. **1976** Bailey-Bailey *Hortus Third* 3, *Abutilon.* . . Flowering maple, parlor m[aple], Indian mallow.

2 A **teaweed** (here: *Sida rhombifolia* or *S. spinosa*).

1808 Ashe *Travels America* 57, *Popular name.* . . Indian Mallow.—*Linnean name.* . . Sida Rhombifolia. **1876** [see **1** above]. **1935** (1943) Muenscher *Weeds* 338, *Sida spinosa.* . . Indian mallow. . . Introduced from tropical America; possibly native in the southern states.

Indian manzanita n
A **manzanita** (here: *Arctostaphylos mewukka*).

1951 Abrams *Flora Pacific States* 3.316, Indian Manzanita. . . According to Dr. C.H. Merriam, "the Mu-wa Indians of Yosemite call this species *Muk-ko.*" **1959** Munz–Keck *CA Flora* 423, *A[rctostaphylos] mewukka.* . . Indian Manzanita. **1962** Sweet *Plants of West* 28, Indian Manzanita. . . will not fire-kill. . . Indians made many uses of the berries, eating them raw, cooked or ground into meal to be used as a porridge.

Indian marsh milkweed See **marsh milkweed**

Indian meal n Also *Indian corn meal* esp **NEng** Cf **Indian n B1b**
Cornmeal.

1609 in 1850 *Doc. Hist. State of NY* 3.5, They eat dried Indian meal which they steep in water like porridge. **1767** in 1953 Woodmason *Carolina Backcountry* 17 **SC,** [I] have lived all this Week on a little Milk and Indian Corn Meal. **1768** *Ibid* 44, How would they go without any Sustenance save Indian meal and Water? **1797** (1821) Asbury *Jrl.* 2.288 **VA,** My diet is chiefly tea, potatoes, Indian-meal gruel, and chicken broth. **1841** [see **Indian cake**]. **1896** (c1973) Farmer *Orig. Cook Book* 500, *Indian Gruel*—2 tablespoons Indian meal. Cold water. **1905** *DN* 3.12 cCT, *Indian meal.* . . Meal from maize. **1930** *AmSp* 5.419 sNH, *Injun meal.* **1941** [see **Indian bread 1**]. **1941** [see **Indian pudding**]. **1953** *NY Folkl. Qrly.* 7.192 **Long Is. NY** (as of c1905), Cornmeal was still called "Injun meal" here in my childhood. **1966–68** *DARE* (Qu. H50) Inf CT5, Indian meal pudding; (Qu. H64) Inf ME16, Indian meal pudding; (QR, near Qu. H64) Inf DC4, Indian meal is yellow, coarser, *not* white meal.

Indian meal bread See **Indian bread 1**

Indian meal cake See **Indian cake**

Indian meal pudding See **Indian pudding**

Indian melon n
A **barrel cactus.**

1898 *Jrl. Amer. Folkl.* 11.227 **CO,** *Echinocactus* (sp.), Indian melon. **1920** Rice–Rice *Pop. Studies CA Wild Flowers* 66, The next in number are the globe-shaped and vertically ribbed Indian Melons *(Echinocactus).*

Indian millet n
1 Std: common **sorghum** (here: *Sorghum bicolor*). [*OED* 1640 →]

2 A **mountain rice,** usu *Oryzopsis hymenoides.* [See quot 1920]

1888 U.S. Dept. Ag. Div. Botany *Bulletin* 6.53, *Oryzopsis cuspidata* (Indian millet) . . has a wide distribution . . through all the interior region of Utah, Nevada, New Mexico, Texas, Colorado and Nebraska to the Missouri River. It is a perennial, growing in dense tufts, whence its common name of bunch-grass. **1907** Hodge *Hdbk. Amer. Indians* 1.606, *Indian millet.*—The silky oryzopsis *(Oryzopsis cuspidata).* **1911** *Century Dict. Suppl.,* Millet. . . *Indian millet.* . . In the United States, one of the various mountain-rices, *Eriocoma cuspidata.* It is a valued bunchgrass of the Western arid country, thriving in soil too dry and sandy for most other grasses. *Oryzopsis micrantha*, of the Dakotas and Montana, has been called *small Indian millet.* **1920** Saunders *Useful Wild Plants* 55, A Southwestern grass of wide distribution . . is the so-called Indian Millet. . . It is a perennial . . with peculiar panicles whose . . branchlets are tipped with husks containing small, blackish seeds, which have long been valued by desert Indians for flour making. **1939** Medsger *Edible Wild Plants* 128, *Wild* or Indian Millet. . . is found on prairies, deserts, and dry hillsides. **1967** Harrington *Edible Plants Rocky Mts.* 320, *Indian Millet.* . . The seeds of these plants. . . were often ground to form a meal that was used in various ways, as a mush or gruel, to thicken soup or to make cakes. **1976** Bailey–Bailey *Hortus Third* 802, *Oryzopsis. . . hymenoides.* . . Indian millet.

Indian moccasin See **Indian shoe**

Indian mockingbird n

A **loggerhead shrike** (here: *Lanius ludovicianus ludovicianus*).

    1917 *Wilson Bulletin* 29.2.84, *Lanius ludovicianus.* . . Indian mockingbird, Marksville, La. **1957** *AmSp* 32.182 **LA, TX,** *Indian mockingbird* . . southern shrike.

Indian mountain rice n

A **mountain rice** (here: *Oryzopsis hymenoides*).

    1923 in 1925 Jepson *Manual Plants CA* 124, *O[ryzopsis] hymenoides.* . . Indian Mountain Rice. . . Deserts and plains. **1937** U.S. Forest Serv. *Range Plant Hdbk.* G88, *Oryzopsis hymenoides.* . . This hardy, densely tufted perennial is also commonly known as Indian mountain-rice. . . The nutritious seeds of this species were formerly one of the food staples of many western Indians. **1967** Harrington *Edible Plants Rocky Mts.* 320, *Indian Mountain-rice.* . . The seeds of these plants are rather large when compared with those of native grasses in general.

Indian mozemize n [*mozemize* var of **moosemise**]

A **mountain ash 1** (here: *Sorbus americana*).

    1893 *Jrl. Amer. Folkl.* 6.141, *Pyrus Americana*, Indian mozemize . . Ferrisburgh, Vt. **1907** Hodge *Hdbk. Amer. Indians* 1.606, *Indian mozemize.* . . The American mountain-ash . . (*Sorbus americana*). **1930** Sievers *Amer. Med. Plants* 7, *Sorbus americana.* . . *Other common names* . . Indian mozemize. **1971** Krochmal *Appalachia Med. Plants* 239, Indian mozemize. . . Bark preparations have been used for biliousness.

Indian mugwort n

A **guayule** (here: *Parthenium hysterophorus*).

    1900 Lyons *Plant Names* 276, *P[arthenium] Hysterophorus.* . . Indian Mugwort.

Indian-neck terrapin n

Perh the three-toed **box turtle** (*Terrapene carolina triunguis*), the male of which often has a red head and neck.

    1966 *DARE* (Qu. P24, . . *Kinds of turtles*) Inf **NC36,** Indian-neck terrapin.

Indian nosy See **Indian posy 2**

Indian nut n

=**pine nut.**

    1967 *DARE* (Qu. S26e, *Other wildflowers not yet mentioned*; not asked in early QRs) Inf **AZ2,** Indian nuts. **1976** Elmore *Shrubs & Trees SW* 14, They are some of the largest nuts produced by any of our pines and are sold throughout the country as pinyon or pine nuts, Indian nuts, or Christmas nuts.

Indianny See **Indiana 1**

Indian olive n

    1935 Davis *Honey* 175 **OR,** They ate Indian olives, which were a kind of pickled acorn, flavorsome enough if you didn't know what they were pickled in.

Indian onion n

1 also *Indian leek:* A **cattail 1** (here: *Typha latifolia*).

    [**1890** Healy & Bigelow *Kickapoo Indians* 54/1 *(DA)*, The Indian Onion . . contributes its leaves and root to the great Kickapoo Sagwa remedy.] **1951** *PADS* 15.27 **TX,** *Typha latifolia.* . . Indian onion or leek, the red men ate the tender white rootstocks.

2 =**brodiaea.**

    1962 Balls *Early Uses CA Plants* 31, Camas. . . is often found in great quantities, and the bulb is much larger than . . Indian Onion, *Brodiaea.*

3 A **wild onion** (here: *Allium* spp).

    1902 U.S. Natl. Museum *Contrib. Herbarium* 7.323 **CA,** *Allium unifolium.* . . The wild or Indian onion . . grows 1 to 2 feet high in rich, damp meadows throughout the region. **1968** *DARE* (Qu. I5, . . *Kind of onions that keep coming up without replanting year after year*) Inf **LA20,** Wild onions or Indian onions.

Indian oriole n

=**Baltimore oriole.**

    1957 *AmSp* 32.182 **IA,** *Indian oriole* . . Baltimore oriole.

Indian paint n

1 also *red Indian paint, red paintroot:* =**bloodroot 1.** [See quot 1971]

    1803 A.F.M. Willich *Domestic Encycl.* (Amer. ed.) IV.442/1 *(OEDS)*, Sanguinaria Canadensis, called commonly *Puccoon*, blood-wort, redroot, Indian paint, turmeric. **1837** Darlington *Flora Cestrica* 317 **ePA,** *Sanguinaria canadensis.* . . *Vulgo*—Red-root. Turmeric. Indian Paint. **1876** Hobbs *Bot. Hdbk.* 57, Indian paint, red, Blood root, Sanguinaria Canadensis. *Ibid* 97, Red paint root, Blood root, Sanguinaria Canadensis. **1900** Lyons *Plant Names* 332, *S[anguinaria] Canadensis.* . . Red Indian Paint. **1907** Hodge *Hdbk. Amer. Indians* 1.606, *Indian paint.*—(1) The strawberry-blite (*Blitum capitatum*). (2) The hoary puccoon (*Lithospermum canescens*). (3) A Wisconsin name, according to Bergen, for a species of *Tradescantia.* (4) Bloodroot (*Sanguinaria canadensis*), called red Indian paint. (5) The yellow puccoon (*Hydrastis canadensis*), called yellow Indian paint. **1931** Clute *Common Plants* 26, Possibly the original puccoon was the bloodroot (*Sanguinaria Canadensis*), because of its red juice. The plant is also called . . Indian paint. **1932** *Country Life* 62.67, One of the loveliest . . of the mountain wildings is . . Red Indian Paint. . . The Indians . . used its highly colored juice to stain the canes and white-oak laths for their baskets in times of peace, and in more troublous days it served as their war paint. **1971** Krochmal *Appalachia Med. Plants* 226, Red Indian paint. . . When combined with oak bark, the roots give a red dye.

2 also *yellow Indian paint, yellow paint(root):* =**goldenseal 1.** [See quot 1828]

    1828 Rafinesque *Med. Flora* 1.251, *Hydrastis canadensis.* . . Yellowpaint, . . Indian paint. [*Ibid* 253, This . . [yields] a juice of a brilliant yellow color, which they [=Amer Indians] use to stain skins and clothing; it may become a valuable dye.] **1876** Hobbs *Bot. Hdbk.* 57, Indian paint, yellow, Goldenseal root, Hydrastis Canadensis. *Ibid* 135, Yellow paint root, Goldenseal root, Hydrastis Canadensis. **1901** Lounsberry *S. Wild Flowers* 172 **TN,** *Yellow Indian Paint.* . . There the people in the autumn . . gather its rootlets and the rhizomes, which are known to them as having drastic properties. **1911** (1916) Porter *Harvester* 416 **IN,** "One of its [=goldenseal's] names is Indian paint," explained the harvester. "Probably it furnished the squaws of these woods with colouring matter." **1930** Sievers *Amer. Med. Plants* 31, *Hydrastis canadensis.* . . Yellow Indian paint. **1971** Krochmal *Appalachia Med. Plants* 144, *Hydrastis canadensis.* . . *Common Names:* Goldenseal, . . Indian paint, . . yellow paintroot.

3 A **puccoon:** usu *Lithospermum canescens*, but also *L. incisum.* [See quot 1967]

    1894 *Jrl. Amer. Folkl.* 7.95 **MN,** *Lithospermum canescens* . . Indian paint. **1897** *Ibid* 10.51 **swMO,** *Lithospermum canescens* . . Indian paint. . . From a tradition that the Indians thus utilized its root. **1899** Bergen *Animal Lore* 119 **swMO,** *Lithospermum canescens* is called "Indian paint," because the Indians are said to use it in painting themselves. **1907** [see **1** above]. **1940** Clute *Amer. Plant Names* 225, *Lithospermum canescens.* . . Indian paint. **1954** *Harder Coll.* **cwTN. 1959** Carleton *Index Herb. Plants* 65, *Indian paint:* Chenopodium capitatum; Lithospermum canescens; Sanguinaria canadensis. **1963** Craighead *Rocky Mt. Wildflowers* 158, *Lithospermum incisum.* . . Indianpaint. **1967** Dodge *Roadside Wildflowers* 59 **SW,** *Narrowleaf gromwell.* . . In some localities called Indian paint . . Indians used the roots to produce a purple dye. . . *Lithospermum incisum.*

4 =**strawberry blite.** [See quot 1894]

    1894 *Jrl. Amer. Folkl.* 7.97 **CO,** *Chenopodium Capitatum* . . Indian paint. . . Because of the bright color of the fruit. **1907** [see **1** above]. **1909** *DN* 3.412 **nME,** *Indian paint.* . . A plant whose fruit has a scarlet juice. **1950** Gray–Fernald *Manual of Botany* 595, *Chenopodium capitatum.* . . Indian paint. **1961** Smith *MI Wildflowers* 103, *Strawberry-blite, Indian-paint.* . . In fruit the clusters become large, juicy, and bright red, and are very conspicuous.

5 =**spiderwort.** [See quot 1897]

    1897 *Jrl. Amer. Folkl.* 10.146, *Tradescantia*, sp., Indian paint, Mineral

Point, Wis. . . The juice said to irritate the skin and make it red. **1907** [see **1** above].

6 =butterfly weed 1.
1920 *Torreya* 20.24, *Asclepias tuberosa*. . . Indian-paint, Traverse City, Mich.

7 A **prickly poppy** (here: prob *Argemone polyanthemos*).
1929 Bell *Some Contrib. KS Vocab.* 179, Indian paint. . . A name for a wild flower, a white poppy, several inches across, having prickly foliage and golden stamens which give it the effect of a pond lily. When the stems are broken, a rich yellow paint oozes out. The name arises from the story that the Indians painted themselves with the juice.

8 A **prairie coneflower** (here: *Ratibida columnifera*).
1967 *DARE* Tape **TX28**, Niggertoe . . I think is sometimes called Indian paint. **1967** *DARE* (Qu. S26a, . . *Wildflowers. . . Roadside flowers*) Inf **TX28**, Indian paints.

9 Prob **=Indian paintbrush 1.**
1969–70 *DARE* (Qu. S26e, *Other wildflowers*) Inf **CA204**, Indian paints; **IL55**, Indian paint—orangey-red.

Indian paintbox n
=butterfly weed 1.
1967 *DARE* (Qu. S26a, . . *Roadside flowers*) Inf **SC36**, Butterfly bush—same [as] Indian paintbox—bright orange.

Indian paintbrush n

1 also *Indian's paintbrush:* A plant of the genus *Castilleja*. [See quot 1915] Also called **devil's paintbrush 2, Indian blanket 2, ~ paintcup, ~ pink 3, ~ plume 1, paintbrush, painted cup, red feather.** For other names of *C. coccinea* see **election posy, fire pink 2, nosebleed 1, painted lady, prairie fire, red Indians, ~ robin, scarlet painted cup, squaw-flower, wickakee.** For other names of var spp see **desert paintbrush, honeysuckle 5d, Indian feather 3, scarlet cup, squawfeather**
1892 *Jrl. Amer. Folkl.* 5.101 **MA**, *Castilleja coccinea*. . . Indian paint-brush. **1898** *Atlantic Mth.* 82.497, The scarlet painted cup, otherwise known as the Indian's paint-brush and prairie fire, splendid for color. **1915** (1926) Armstrong–Thornber *Western Wild Flowers* 470, There are many kinds of Castilleja. . . These gaudy plants are well named Indian Paint Brush, for the flower-cluster and leaf-tips look as if they had been dipped in color. **1923** Sinclair *Parowan Bonanza* 21 **NV**, He plucked a bright red "Indian paintbrush" from beside a rock. **1950** *WELS Suppl.* **ceWI**, In Waupaca County the flower which we called Indian paintbrush is not at all like a red trillium. Its blossom looks like a rather ragged paintbrush—the tip of each 'bristle' a yellowish-red. **1951** *PADS* 15.40 **TX**, *Castilleja*. . . Indian blankets or Indian paintbrushes. **1965–70** *DARE* (Qq. S26a-e, . . *Wildflowers*) 62 Infs, **chiefly Nth, West,** Indian paintbrush; (Qu. S21, . . *Weeds . . that are a trouble in gardens and fields*) Infs **MI96, PA68, WI52, 72,** Indian paintbrush. **1974** (1977) Coon *Useful Plants* 245, *Castilleja (various species)*—Indian paint-brush. . . Mostly found in dry open ground in the West. . . The flowers are rated in most species as edible when picked raw and fresh.

2 A **tassel flower** (here: *Emilia javanica*).
1959 Carleton *Index Herb. Plants* 65, *Indian paintbrush:* Emilia sagittata (Cacalia coccinea); Castilleja coccinea. **1967** *DARE* (Qu. S21, . . *Weeds . . that are a trouble in gardens and fields*) Inf **HI2**, Emilia—Indian paintbrush.

3 =butterfly weed 1.
1967 *DARE* Wildfl QR Pl.171 Inf **AR46**, Indian paintbrush—I have that in three colors. **1969** *DARE* (Qu. S26d, *Wildflowers that grow in meadows*) Inf **KY24**, Indian paintbrush [same as] butterfly bush (book name is butterflyweed, *Asclepias tuberosa*). **1976** Bailey–Bailey *Hortus Third* 117, [*Asclepias*] *tuberosa*. . . Indian paintbrush. . . Corolla orange or occasionally red or yellow.

4 A **hawkweed,** usu *Hieracium aurantiacum*.
1968 *DARE* File **cnNY**, Indian paintbrush—a small flower the size of a penny. Plants have a grayish-green stem and little foliage. Flowers are red with some black or yellow with some black. They grow on poor ground. **1992** *Ibid* **nwMA** (as of late 1960s), As kids we used to pick the pretty orange and yellow, hairy-stemmed flowers we called Indian paintbrush and pretend to paint with them held as brushes. They always wilted soon after being picked. Now I know them to be identified in books as hawkweed.

5 Any of var other plants; see quots.
1967–68 *DARE* (Qu. S20, *A common weed that grows on open*

hillsides: It has velvety green leaves close to the ground, and a tall stalk with small yellow flowers on a spike at the top) Infs **CT11, OH2,** Indian paintbrush. **1967–68** *DARE* Wildfl QR Pl.54A [=*Lychnis flosculi*] Inf **OH37**, Indian paintbrush; Pl.167 [=*Gentiana crinita*] Inf **OR8**, Indian paintbrush; Pl.189 [=*Monarda didyma*] Inf **WA30**, Indian paintbrush.

Indian paintcup n Cf **painted cup**
=Indian paintbrush 1.
1940 Writers' Program *Guide TX* 24, Indian paintbrush and Indian blanket are known in other localities as Indian pink or paintcup.

Indian paint fungus n [From its use in dyeing]
A tooth fungus (*Echinodontium tinctorium*) native to the Rocky Mts and the Pacific NW.
1948 Boyce *Forest Pathology* 404, Brown stringy rot of the heartwood of living conifers in the western United States and Canada is caused by the Indian paint fungus. [*Ibid* 405, The Indians made a pigment from the substance of the conks, hence the common name.] **1972** Miller *Mushrooms* 186, *Echinodontium tinctorium*. . . The common name, Indian Paint Fungus, comes from the belief that it was used as a source of dye by the Indians of the Pacific Northwest. **1981** Lincoff *Audubon Field Guide Mushrooms* 429, *Indian Paint Fungus*. . . Its common name refers to the fact that Indians used this mushroom to make red war paint; it is still used by hobbyists as a yarn dye.

Indian paintroot n
A **redroot** (here: *Lachnanthes caroliniana*).
1900 Lyons *Plant Names* 181, *G[yrotheca] capitata*. . . Indian Paint-root.

Indian pancake See **Indian cake**

Indian panther n Cf **Indian devil 1**
=mountain lion.
1968 *DARE* (Qu. P31, . . *Names or nicknames . . for the . . panther*) Inf **NH14**, Mountain lion or Indian panther.

Indian parsnip n Cf **wild parsnip**
An umbelliferous plant (*Cymopterus longipes*).
1915 (1926) Armstrong–Thornber *Western Wild Flowers* 336, *Indian Parsnip*. . . This has a thick root and grows on dry sunny hills, in gravelly soil. **1959** Barnes *Nat. Hist. Wasatch Winter* 69 **UT**, February 22. . . Such early plants as the Indian parsnip (*Aulosperum* [sic] *longipes* [sic]) and the squirrel corn (*Dicentra uniflora*) are about to rise. *Ibid* 96, *March 20*. . . The only plant at all common is the Indian parsnip, a low perennial of the parsley family with yellow flowers. It appears somewhat like a mat, as we almost tread upon it.

Indian pea n
=ground plum 1.
1871 U.S. Dept. Ag. *Rept. of Secy. for 1870* 419, *Milk vetch (Astragalus)*. . . Several species . . are commonly called Indian pea [etc]. . . The pea is divested of the hull and boiled for food. **1943** Fernald–Kinsey *Edible Wild Plants E. N. Amer.* 248, Ground-Plum, Indian Pea, *Astragalus . . caryocarpus*.

Indian peach n

1 A peach (*Prunus persica*), usu a red **clingstone. Sth, S Midl**
1709 (1967) Lawson *New Voyage* 110 **NC**, Of this sort we make Vinegar; wherefore we call them Vinegar-Peaches, and sometimes *Indian-peaches.* **1737** (1911) Brickell *Nat. Hist. NC* 101, The *Indian-Peach* Tree, is a kind of Peach common amongst the *Indians,* which they claim as their own, and affirm that they had it growing amongst them before any *Europeans* came to *America*. . . Of this sort there is made *Vinegar;* therefore some call them *Vinegar Peaches.* **1801** *Hist. Review & Directory* I.261 *(DAE),* This is frequently called the *Indian Peach,* and is the first for flavor, size and beauty. **1881** *Harper's New Mth. Mag.* 62.745 **sLA**, A robe of gauze the color of an Indian peach, garlanded with pale clear blooms. **1906** *DN* 3.142 **nwAR**, *Indian peach*. . . A clingstone peach with red flesh. **1949** *AmSp* 24.110 **cSC**. **1950** *PADS* 14.40 **SC**, *Indian peach*. . . A cling-stone peach with reddish color and dusky-red streaks, the flesh of which is also streaked with red. **1954** Harder *Coll.* **cwTN**. **c1960** Wilson *Coll.* **csKY**, *Indian peach*. . . One that has red skin and red flesh. **1966–69** *DARE* (Qu. I51, *The kind of a peach where the hard center is loose*) Inf **VA9**, Indian peach; (Qu. I52, *The kind of a peach where the hard center is tight to the flesh*) Inf **OK43**, Indian peaches were pickling peaches; **TX9**, Indian peach; (Qu. I53, *Other fruits grown around here*) Inf **AR47**, Indian peach—dark red peaches; **GA85**, Indian peach—smaller than ordinary peaches; outside peeling is purple colored; it is a clingstone peach, is fast disappear-

ing; **NC**55, Indian peach—red and cling; **OK**51, Indian peaches. **1967** *DARE* Tape **AR**52, Now I remember the peach tree that grew out from under the old chair-factory house, Indian peach. **1993** Kingsolver *Pigs in Heaven* 220 **OK,** These here are Indian peaches, they call them. Blood red in the center.

2 =**osoberry. Pacific NW**

1934 Haskin *Wild Flowers Pacific Coast* 159, The oso-berry is a shrub. . . Other common names are . . Indian peach. . . The fruit which ripens in June is first orange and later bluish-black. **1967** Gilkey–Dennis *Hdbk. NW Plants* 212, *Indian peach.* . . Drupes becoming peach-colored, changing to deep blue-black.

Indian pear n [*OEDS* 1796→]

1 A **serviceberry,** usu *Amelanchier canadensis.*

1900 Lyons *Plant Names* 28, *A[melanchier] Canadensis.* . . Indian pear. **1907** Hodge *Hdbk. Amer. Indians* 1.606, *Indian pear.*—The service-berry *(Amelanchier Canadensis),* called also wild Indian pear. **1943** Fernald–Kinsey *Edible Wild Plants E. N. Amer.* 230, *Indian Pear, Amelanchier* (about 20 species). . . Few wild fruits of such excellent quality . . are less known to the modern American. **1955** U.S. Arctic Info. Center *Gloss.* 43 **AK,** *Indian pear.* The serviceberry. **1960** Vines *Trees SW* 416, *Amelanchier arborea.* . . Vernacular names are . . Indian-cherry, Indian-pear.

2 A **prickly pear.**

1929 Bell *Some Contrib. KS Vocab.* 179, Indian pear. . . A name for the cactus, usually known as *prickly pear.*

Indian physic n

1 A plant of the genus *Gillenia.* [See quots c1738, 1843] Also called **bowman's root 2.** For other names of *G. trifoliata* see **dropwort 1, Indian hippo**

c1738 (1929) Byrd *Histories* 156, In the Stony Grounds we rode over we found great Quantity of the true Ipocoacanna, which in this part of the World is call'd Indian-Physick. . It is not so strong as that from Brazil, but has the same happy Effects, If taken in Somewhat a larger Dose. **1788** in 1888 Cutler *Life* 2.285 **OH,** A plant called *Indian Physic,* or *Indian Root;* it blossoms, I believe, early in the year, for the seed was ripe in August. **1809** Kendall *Travels* 3.36 **NEng,** *Spiræa trifoliata,* otherwise called Indian Physic, with its pink blossoms and pale green leaves, is frequent, but is less conspicuous. **1843** Torrey *Flora NY* 1.200, *Gillenia trifoliata.* . . Indian Physic. Bowman's-root. . . [The root] acts as an emetic, or a cathartic, according to the dose. **1893** *Jrl. Amer. Folkl.* 6.141, *Gillenia stipulacea,* Injin physic. Banner Elk, N.C. **1907** Hodge *Hdbk. Amer. Indians* 1.606, *Indian physic.*—(1) The bowman's-root *(Porteranthus trifoliatus).* . . (2) American ipecac *(Porteranthus stipulatus).* (3) Fraser's magnolia, the long-leaved umbrella-tree *(Magnolia fraseri).* **1970** *DARE* Tape **VA**46, Indian physic is a herb. Picked with an upward motion [it] causes vomiting, and with a downward motion causes bowel movement. **1974** (1977) Coon *Useful Plants* 226, Indian physic. . . The bark of the root is a mild and efficient emetic, with actions that are similar to ipecac.

2 A **magnolia 1** (here: *Magnolia fraseri*). [See quot 1814]

1810 Michaux *Histoire des Arbres* 1.28 *The ear leaved magnolia.* . . *Indian phisic,* dénomination plus usitée par les habitans des montagnes de la Caroline du nord et de la Virginie, mais moins convenable. *Long leaved cucumber tree* . . secondairement en usage dans les mêmes contrées. [=*The ear leaved magnolia.* . . *Indian phisic,* the name more commonly used by the inhabitants of the mountains of North Carolina and Virginia, but less proper. *Long leaved cucumber tree* . . secondarily in use in the same regions.] **1814** Pursh *Flora Americae* 2.382, *Magnolia auriculata.* . . The bark of this and some of the foregoing species is esteemed a valuable medicine, particularly in intermitting fevers; from which circumstance it is known in some places by the name of *Indian Physic.* **1860** Curtis *Cat. Plants NC* 68, *Long-leaved Cucumber Tree.* . . Found only in ravines of the mountains where it is known by this name, and also as *Wahoo* and *Indian Physic.* **1897** Sudworth *Arborescent Flora* 197 **NC, TN,** *Magnolia fraseri.* . . *Common Names.* . . Indian Physic. **1907** [see **1** above]. **1933** Small *Manual SE Flora* 536.

3 An **Indian hemp 1** (here: *Apocynum cannabinum*). [See quots 1873, 1974]

1873 in 1976 Miller *Shaker Herbs* 187, *Indian Hemp, Black.* . . Indian Physic. . Use in dropsy, remittent and intermittent fevers, pneumonia, and obstructions of the kidneys, liver, and spleen. **1876** Hobbs *Bot. Hdbk.* 57, Indian physic, Black Indian hemp, Apocynum cannabinum. **1900** Lyons *Plant Names* 40. **1930** Sievers *Amer. Med. Plants* 34, Indian-physic. . . *Part used.*—The root, collected in autumn. In reasonably constant demand. **1974** Morton *Folk Remedies* 27 **SC,** *Indian*

Physic. . . *Apocynum cannabinum.* . . *South Carolina (Current use):* Root steeped with whisky which is taken to relieve colds and fever. Said to be very laxative. Root decoction taken to cause abortion; sometimes administered by midwives.

4 =**flowering spurge.**

1892 (1974) Millspaugh *Amer. Med. Plants* 148-1, *Euphorbia corollata.* . . *Indian physic.* . . The flowering spurge is a favorite medicine among the aborigines of America, being used as a purgative.

5 A **mayapple 1** (here: *Podophyllum peltatum*).

1912 Green *VA Folk-Speech* 239, Indian physic. . . The podophyllum.

6 as *Indian's physic:* =**culver's root 1.**

1956 in 1969 *DARE* File **Pipestone Co MN,** Culver's Root (Indians [sic] Physic) Veronicastrum virginicum.

7 also *Indian physic tea:* An emetic decoction made from any of the above plants.

1914 Applegate *Recollections* 6 **MO,** I have thought that if Socrates instead of the cup of hemlock, had had to take a dose of "Injin Fizic," he. . . would have skipped, not to save his life, but to avoid the dose. **1937** Hall Coll. **wNC,** Indian physic tea. "Good to clean your stomach off. . . Whenever we'ud get puny Mother would go to the woods to gather some herbs and make us some tea." **1949** Guthrie *Way West* 84, What cured me . . was Injun physic. . . It was brewed from a root and it would gag a hog. **1970** *DARE* (Qu. BB50d, *Favorite spring tonics*) Inf **VA**46, Indian physics [sic]—plant with scarlet leaf, white flower, grows in woods . . make tea with leaf.

Indian pine n

=**loblolly pine 1.**

1806 Shecut *Flora Carolinæensis* I.122 *(DA),* Almiggim wood, supposed to be the Indian pine. **1896** Mohr–Roth *Timber Pines* 106 **NC, VA,** *Pinus tæda.* . . *Common or Local Names.* . . Indian pine. **1907** Hodge *Hdbk. Amer. Indians* 1.606, *Indian pine.*—The loblolly, or old-field pine *(Pinus tæda).* **1950** Peattie *Nat. Hist. Trees* 24, Indian pine. . . Bark of the trunk of broad, flat, bright red-brown plates. **1960** Vines *Trees SW* 23, *Pinus taeda.* . . Other vernacular names are . . Indian Pine, . . and Old-field Pine.

Indian pink n

1 also *Indian pinkroot:* A **pinkroot** (here: *Spigelia marilandica*). Also called **Carolina pink 1, serpentine, snakeroot, spink-root, starbloom, worm grass, worm root, wormweed, wormwood**

1743 Catesby *Nat. Hist. Carolina* 2.78 **S Atl,** The *Indian Pink.* This Plant rises usually with four or five Stalks, of about twelve or fourteen Inches in Height, every one of which has three or four Pair of sharp-pointed Leaves, set opposite to each other. **1765** (1942) Bartram *Diary of a Journey* 5 Sept **seGA,** The Spegelia [sic], or *Indian pink-root.* **1831** Audubon *Ornith. Biog.* 1.361, *The Indian Pink-root or Worm-grass.* . . This plant is perennial, flowers in the summer months, and grows in rich soil by the margins of woods, in the Middle States. **1876** Hobbs *Bot. Hdbk.* 57, Indian pink, Spigelia Marilandica. **1907** Hodge *Hdbk. Amer. Indians* 1.606, *Indian pink.*—(1) The Carolina pink, or worm-grass *(Spigelia marylandica).* (2) The cypress-vine *(Quamoclit quamoclit).* (3) The fire pink *(Silene virginica).* (4) The cuckoo-flower, or ragged-robin *(Lychnis flos-cuculi).* (5) The fringed milkwort, or poly-gala *(Polygala paucifolia).* (6) The scarlet-painted cup *(Castilleja coccinea).* (7) The wild pink *(Silene pennsylvanica).* (8) *Silene californica.* **1942** Hylander *Plant Life* 437, Indian Pink . . is a small and rather rare . . plant with . . red flowers, marked with yellow on the inside of the corolla. **1967–70** *DARE* (Qu. S26a, . . *Roadside flowers*) Inf **DE**3, Indian pink—shaped like a gladiola only real small; **IN**38, **OH**47, **TN**22, Indian pink(s); (Qu. S26c, *Wildflowers that grow in woods*) Infs **MA**49, **OH**80, **TN**6, Indian pink(s); (Qu. S26d, *Wildflowers that grow in meadows*) Inf **KY**47, Indian pink. **1975** Hamel–Chiltoskey *Cherokee Plants* 40, Indian pink. . . Tea for worms.

2 A **cardinal flower** (here: *Lobelia cardinalis*).

1873 in 1976 Miller *Shaker Herbs* 147, *Lobelia cardinalis.* . . Indian Pink. [**1967** *DARE* FW Addit **AR**44, Indian pink—something like cardinal-flower.] **1976** Bailey–Bailey *Hortus Third* 675, [*Lobelia*] *cardinalis.* . . Indian pink.

3 An **Indian paintbrush 1,** usu *Castilleja coccinea.* **esp TX**

1888 Lindley–Widney *CA of South* 170, Indian pinks (castilleia) and others quite as pretty. **1894** *Jrl. Amer. Folkl.* 7.96, *Castillea coccinea.* . . Indian pink, Peoria, Ill. **1907** [see **1** above]. **1936** Whitehouse *TX Flowers* 133, Scarlet Paint-Brush *(Castilleja indivisa)* is also called . . Indian pink. **1940** [see **Indian paintcup**]. **1966** *Good Old Days* Apr 4 **sCA,**

There would be the old-fashioned Indian pink or paint brush, red bell, buttercup, Johnny-jump-up and many others. **1967–68** *DARE* (Qu. S26a, . . *Roadside flowers*) Infs **NV**8, **TX**11, 13, 19, Indian pink(s); (Qu. S26e, *Other wildflowers*) Inf **TX**17, Indian pink.

4 A **cypress vine 1** (here: *Quamoclit vulgaris*).
   1889 *Century Dict.* 3179, The cypress-vine, Indian-pink, American red bell-flower, or sweet-william of the Barbados . . is now widely naturalized. **1901** Lounsberry *S. Wild Flowers* 439, *Q. quamoclit*, cypress vine, Indian pink. . . about many old gardens from Florida to Virginia . . is seen growing spontaneously. **1907** [see **1** above].

5 =**fringed polygala.**
   1893 *Jrl. Amer. Folkl.* 6.140, *Polygala paucifolia*. . . Indian pink. Montague, Mass. **1907** [see **1** above]. **1940** Clute *Amer. Plant Names* 124, *P[olygala] paucifolia*. . . Indian pink. **1970** *DARE* (Qu. S26e, *Other wildflowers*) Inf **MI**116, May pinks or Indian pinks.

6 Any of var spp of **catchfly 1,** but esp *Silene californica*.
   1892 IN Dept. Geol. & Nat. Resources *Rept. for 1891* 268, *Silene virginica*. . . Fire Pink, Indian Pink. Next to the cardinal flower, this is the showiest of our wild flowers. **1896** *Jrl. Amer. Folkl.* 9.182 **CA,** *Silene California* . . Indian pink. **1897** Parsons *Wild Flowers CA* 354, The Indian pink is one of the most beautiful of our flowers. . . Its brilliant scarlet blossoms brighten the soft browns of our roadsides in early summer. **1898** *Jrl. Amer. Folkl.* 11.223, *Silene Pennsylvanica* . . Indian pink, Auburndale, Mass. **1953** Greene–Blomquist *Flowers South* 30, *Indian-* or *Fire-Pink (Silene virginica)*. . . is the showiest of our native pinks, having a relatively large flower with deep red or crimson petals. **1959** Carleton *Index Herb. Plants* 65, *Indian-pink:* Arethusa bulbosa; Castilleja coccinea; Dianthus sinensis; Lychnis flos-cuculi; Quamoclit pennata (Ipomaea quamoclit); Silene virginica. **1969** *DARE* FW Addit **KY**5, Indian pink—fire pink or *Silene virginica*. **1976** Bailey–Bailey *Hortus Third* 1043, *[Silene] californica*. . . Indian pink. *Ibid* 1044, *[Silene] laciniata*. . . Indian pink. **1990** *Plants SW* (Catalog) 94, *Silene laciniata*. Indian Pink. . . Red-orange, deeply cut flowers in summer.

7 A **ragged robin** (here: *Lychnis flos-cuculi*).
   1900 Lyons *Plant Names* 232, *L[ychnis] flos-cuculi*. . . Indian pink. **1940** Clute *Amer. Plant Names* 63, *L. flos-cuculi*. . . Indian pink. **1959** [see **6** above].

8 A **trillium** (here: *Trillium catesbaei*).
   1901 Lounsberry *S. Wild Flowers* 60, *Wake Robin. Indian Pink. Trillium stylosum*. . . *Colour.* Rose and white. . . This very pretty trillium . . is one that is peculiar to the south.

9 =**spiderflower.**
   1932 Rydberg *Flora Prairies* 385, *Peritoma*. . . Indian Pink. **1936** Winter *Plants NE* 69, *Cleome*. . . Bee Flower. Indian Pink.

10 A **garden pink** (*Dianthus* spp).
   1939 *Natl. Geogr. Mag.* Aug 232, The family name changed accordingly to Dianthaceae, which counts among its members the clove pinks or carnations, Indian pinks, and other attractive garden or florists' plants. **1959** [see **6** above].

11 A **swamp pink** (here: *Arethusa bulbosa*).
   1959 [see **6** above].

Indian pinkroot See **Indian pink 1**

Indian pipe n

1 also *Indian piper, ~ pipestem, ~ smoke-pipe:* A waxy white, leafless, saprophytic plant (*Monotropa uniflora*) with a single pipe-shaped flower. **chiefly Nth, esp NEast** See Map Also called **bird's nest 5, convulsion root, corpse plant, Dutchman's pipe 2, eyebright 8, fairy smoke, fitroot, ghost flower 1, ~ pipe 1, ~ plant 2, ice plant 2, Indian cup 3, ~ tobacco 12, nest plant, pinesap, pipe plant, tobacco ~, wax ~**
   1822 Eaton *Botany* 357, *Monotropa*. . . *uniflora* (birds-nest, indian-pipe . .). Whole plant ivory-white at first. **1869** *Amer. Naturalist* 3.6 **IL,** The Indian Pipestem (*Monotropa uniflora*) will be found rarely in low woods. **1897** IN Dept. Geol. & Nat. Resources *Rept. for 1896* 664, Indian Pipe. . . Dry wooded hillsides, in rich soil; scarce. **1915** (1926) Armstrong–Thornber *Western Wild Flowers* 358, Indian pipe. . . An odd plant, all translucent white, beautiful but unnatural, glimmering in the dark heart of the forest. **1937** Thornburgh *Gt. Smoky Mts.* 22, Less conspicuous are . . umbrella leaf . . ; Indian pipe or ghost flower, with its fragile, leafless, pipe-shaped blossoms. **1965–70** *DARE* (Qu. S26c, *Wildflowers . . in woods*) 11 Infs, **esp Nth,** Indian pipe(s); **PA**231, Indian pipers; (Qu. S26a) Infs **CT**21, **NY**134, **OH**37, Indian pipe(s); (Qu. S26b) Inf **VT**10, Indian pipes; (Qu. S26d) Inf **VT**16, Indian pipe; (Qu.

S26e) Infs **NY**232, **PA**60, **RI**15, **WI**78, Indian pipe(s); (Qu. S2) Inf **AL**20, Indian pipe—shape of a pipe on a stem; (Qu. S19) Inf **NY**165, Indian pipe—comes out of rotten wood in a dense woods, in beechwoods, especially. **1966–68** *DARE* Wildfl QR Pl.152B Infs **AR**44, **MI**57, **NH**4, **WA**10, Indian pipe; **OH**82, Indian smoke-pipe. **1972** Brown *Wildflowers LA* 129, *Indian Pipe*. . . Plants . . white when fresh, occasionally flesh to light purplish, turning black when picked.

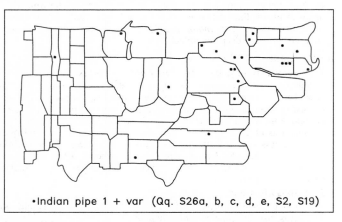

•Indian pipe 1 + var (Qq. S26a, b, c, d, e, S2, S19)

2 A **pinesap** (here: *Monotropa hypopitys*). [From the shape of the flowers]
   1949 Peattie *Cascades* 232 **Pacific NW,** The many-flowered Indian pipe, Monotropa Hypopitys, is similar to the Indian pipe but instead of being dead white it is yellowish to reddish and has a number of flowers near the top of the stem. **1966** *DARE* File, *Monotropa hypopitys*—Indian pipe.

3 A **virgin's bower** (here: *Clematis viorna*). [Prob from the shape of the flower and stem]
   1967 *DARE* Wildfl QR Pl.74 Inf **CO**29, Indian pipe—leather flower.

4 A **catalpa B1. Cf Indian cigar**
   1967 *DARE* (Qu. T9, *The common shade tree with large heart-shaped leaves, clusters of white blossoms, and long thin seed pods or 'beans'*) Inf **OH**16, Indian pipe.

5 A **mullein** (here: prob *Verbascum thapsus*). [Perh related to the use of its dried leaves as tobacco] Cf **Indian tobacco 3**
   1970 *DARE* (Qu. S20, *A common weed that grows on open hillsides: It has velvety green leaves close to the ground, and a tall stalk with small yellow flowers on a spike at the top*) Inf **MA**124, Indian pipe.

Indian piper, Indian pipestem See **Indian pipe 1**

Indian pipestone See **pipestone**

Indian pipe weed n [See quot 1937]
   =**desert trumpet.**
   1923 in 1925 Jepson *Manual Plants CA* 307, *E[riogonum] inflatum*. . . Also called Indian Pipe Weed. **1937** U.S. Forest Serv. *Range Plant Hdbk.* W70, Desert-trumpet . . , sometimes called Indianpipe weed, . . ranges from Colorado and New Mexico to California. . . The tubular stems . . , are inflated and trumpetlike near their ends, and somewhat resemble a cigarette holder. **1949** Moldenke *Amer. Wild Flowers* 73, An unusual species called . . *indianpipeweed*, . . has curiously inflated stems and small, yellowish flowers.

Indian pitcher n Also *Indian pitcher plant*
   A **pitcher plant 1,** usu *Sarracenia purpurea*.
   [**1892** *Jrl. Amer. Folkl.* 5.92 **NB,** *Sarracenia purpurea*, . . Indian pitcher.] **1900** Lyons *Plant Names* 335, *S. purpurea*. . . Canada and eastern U.S. . . Indian-pitcher. **1907** Hodge *Hdbk. Amer. Indians* 1.606, *Indian pitcher.*—The pitcher-plant or side-saddle flower (*Sarracenia purpurea*). **1933** Small *Manual SE Flora* 581, *S. purpurea*. . . Indian pitcher. **1959** Carleton *Index Herb. Plants* 65, *Indian-Pitcher-Plant:* Sarracenia (v.).

Indian plant n
1 =**goldenseal 1.**
   1876 Hobbs *Bot. Hdbk.* 57, Indian plant, Goldenseal, Hydrastis Canadensis. **1958** Jacobs–Burlage *Index Plants NC* 180, *Hydrastis canadensis*. . . Indian plant. . . The plant grows from Canada to Georgia west to Washington in rich shady woods and in the mountains of North Carolina and South Carolina. **1971** Krochmal *Appalachia Med. Plants*

144, *Hydrastis canadensis.* . . *Common Names:* Goldenseal, . . Indian plant.

2 =bloodroot 1. Cf Indian paint 1

1940 Clute *Amer. Plant Names* 271, *Sanguinaria Canadensis.* . . Indian plant.

Indian plantago n
=plantain.

1971 Krochmal *Appalachia Med. Plants* 196, *Plantago* L. *spp.* . . *Common Names* . . Indian plantago.

Indian plantain n [From the resemblance of the leaves to those of *Plantago*]

A plant of the genus *Cacalia.* Also called **wild caraway.** For other names of var spp see **wild cabbage, ~ collard**

1848 Gray *Manual of Botany* 239, *Cacalia.* . . Indian Plantain. **1876** Hobbs *Bot. Hdbk.* 57, Indian plantain, Cacalia tuberosa. **1894** *Jrl. Amer. Folkl.* 7.91 **WV,** *Cacalia,* sp., Indian plantain. **1897** IN Dept. Geol. & Nat. Resources *Rept. for 1896* 698, *C. atriplicifolius.* . . Pale Indian Plantain. Dry banks and wooded hillsides; frequent. **1907** Hodge *Hdbk. Amer. Indians* 1.606, *Indian plantain.*—(1) The great Indian plantain or wild collard (*Mesadenia* [=*Cacalia*] *reniformis*). (2) The pale Indian plantain (*M. atriplicifolia*). (3) The tuberous Indian plantain (*M. tuberosa*). (4) The sweet-scented Indian plantain (*Synosma suaveolens*). **1932** Rydberg *Flora Prairies* 873, *Mesadenia* [=*Cacalia*]. . . Indian Plantain. **1972** Brown *Wildflowers LA* 192, *Indian Plantain. Cacalia plantaginea.* . . A stout perennial up to 6 feet tall. . . Widely distributed, locally abundant, prairie and pineland. **1987** *Nature Conserv. News* 37.3.28 **MI,** Actually a peninsula on Bois Blanc Island, the area harbors . . prairie Indian-plantain (*Cacalia plantaginea*), and dwarf lake iris.

Indian plum n

1 A **wild plum** such as *Prunus americana.* [See quot 1788]

1788 Schöpf *Reise Staaten* 1.248, Sie lieben diese . . Früchte sehr, und pflanzen die Kerne überall. . . Man nennt dahero diese Pflaumen . . (Indian Plumbs [sic]), indianische Pflaumen. [=They [=Amer Indians] are very fond of these fruits, and plant the pits everywhere. . . Therefore these plums are called Indian plums.] **1930** Shoemaker *1300 Words* 32 **cPA Mts** (as of c1900), *Indian Plum*—The small, native wild plum.

2 =osoberry. Pacific NW

1920 *DN* 5.82 **NW,** *Indian plum.* Osmaronia cerasiformis. **1934** Haskin *Wild Flowers Pacific Coast* 159, The oso-berry is a shrub. . . Other common names are Indian plum [etc]. . . The fruit which ripens in June is first orange, and later bluish-black with a heavy bluish bloom. . . Each individual fruit is a flattish drupe, in which a single horny seed is encased in sweetish black pulp. **1961** Peck *Manual OR* 445, *Indian Plum.* . . Thickets west of the Cascades to B.C. and Calif. **1967** *DARE* FW Addit **WA**30, Indian plum. **1974** (1977) Coon *Useful Plants* 227, Indian plum. . . is found on the West Coast with rather poorly-flavored fruit, although the fruit is edible raw or cooked.

Indian plume n

1 =Indian paintbrush 1.

1888 Lindley *Calif. of South* 329 (DA) **sCA,** Here, too, is *Castilleia,* the painter's brush or Indian plume, identical with that of the East. **1897** Parsons *Wild Flowers CA* 344, *Indian Paint-Brush.* . . They are known in some localities as "Indian plume."

2 also *Indian's plume:* An **Oswego tea** (here: *Monarda didyma*).

1900 Lyons *Plant Names* 251, *M[onarda] didyma.* . . Canada to Georgia and Michigan. Oswego Tea, . . Indian's-plume. **1940** Clute *Amer. Plant Names* 26, Oswego Tea. . . Indian plume. **1971** Krochmal *Appalachia Med. Plants* 178, *Monarda didyma.* . . *Common Names:* Oswego beebalm, American bee balm, . . Indian's plume.

3 =butterfly weed 1.

1920 *Torreya* 20.24, *Asclepias tuberosa.* . . *Indian-plume,* . . Traverse City, Mich.

4 A **standing cypress** (here: *Ipomopsis rubra*).

1936 Whitehouse *TX Flowers* 105, *Standing Cypress.* . . (Gilia rubra). . . is sometimes known as Indian plume. **1946** Reeves–Bain *Flora TX* 131, Indian Plume. . . *I[pomopsis] rubra.* . . Flowers showy; . . usually scarlet-red.

Indian poke n

1 A **false hellebore 1:** usu *Veratrum viride,* but also *V. woodii.* For other names of *V. viride* see **bear corn 2, bugbane 2, corn lily 3a, crow poison 4, devil's bit c, duckretter, elleber,**

Indian hellebore, itchweed 1, pepperroot, poke, pokeroot, poor Annie, puppet root, rattlesnake weed, skunk cabbage, swamp hellebore, tickleweed, varebell, white hellebore, wolfbane

1784 in 1785 *Amer. Acad. Arts & Sci. Memoirs* 1.492 **sePA,** *Veratrum.* . . *White Helebore* [sic]. *Poke-root. Indian Poke.* . . The root is a most drastic cathartic and sternutatory. The fresh roots, beaten up with hog's lard, cures the itch. . . Crows may be destroyed by boiling Indian corn in a strong decoction of the fresh roots, and strewing it on the ground where they resort. **1830** Rafinesque *Med. Flora* 2.273, *Veratrum viride.* . . *Indianpoke.* . . Useful in epilepsy, gout, mania, cophosis, acute rheumatism. **1876** Hobbs *Bot. Hdbk.* 57, Indian poke, American hellebore, Veratrum Viride. **1907** Hodge *Hdbk. Amer. Indians* 1.606, *Indian poke.*—(1) American white hellebore (*Veratrum viride*). (2) False hellebore (*V. woodii*). **1961** Douglas *My Wilderness* 231 **NH,** The coarse orange hawkweed . . and a large-leafed plant called Indian poke are constant companions. **1967** *DARE* FW Addit ceNY, Indian poke, poke root, white (or) false hellebore—all are the root of *Veratrum viride.*

2 also *Indian pokeweed:* A **pokeweed** (here: *Phytolacca americana*).

1951 Voss–Eifert *IL Wild Flowers* 146, *Phytolacca americana.* . . Thrusting through the moist earth of the April woods comes the Indian pokeweed. . . Those who gather Indian poke, however, must carefully cut off the shoots above the ground . . because the . . root is poisonous and must never be included in the dish of greens. **1964** Batson *Wild Flowers SC* 42, *Indian Polk* [sic]. . . The very young leafy shoots . . are often eaten when properly cooked.

Indian pond lily n **Pacific**

A **spatterdock** (here: *Nuphar polysepalum*).

1901 Jepson *Flora CA* 193, *N[uphar] polysepalum.* . . *Indian Pond Lily.* . . The seeds were used as an article of food by the Klamath Indians. **1915** (1926) Armstrong–Thornber *Western Wild Flowers* 156, *Indian Pond Lily.* . . Like the eastern Spatter-dock, this is a coarse but rather handsome and decorative plant. **1949** Moldenke *Amer. Wild Flowers* 17, In the Northwest one finds the *Indian pondlily* . . with reddish-tinged flowers, which are . . 4 or 5 inches wide when the stamens mature. **1973** Hitchcock–Cronquist *Flora Pacific NW* 123, Indian pond lily. . . *N[uphar] polysepalum.*

Indian pone n

1 See quots. Cf **corn pone, Indian** n B1b

1881 Tourgée *Royal Gentleman & Zouri* 500 **Sth,** The fish with its red-clay case and Indian-pone cover lay exposed upon her lap. [*Ibid* 501, She ate Uncle Peter's red-horse [=a fish] and 'Zouri's corn-pone.] **1929** *AmSp* 5.19 **Ozarks,** Injun pone. **1953** Randolph–Wilson *Down in Holler* 256 **Ozarks,** Indian pone. . . A cake made of flour or meal, like biscuit, except that it contains eggs. Cut into squares, it is served with a *dip* of milk and molasses.

2 See **Indian bread 3.**

Indian pony n Also *Indian horse* [Cf *W3* Indian pony 1] Cf **appaloosa** n[1], **Chickasaw 1**

A spotted or calico horse or pony.

1944 Adams *Western Words* 83, *Indian pony*—What the old-timers of the Southwest called a paint or pinto horse. He was a favorite with the Indian. [**1949** *ND Hist.* 16.14 neND (as of 1884), Spotted Indian ponies grazed on the hill sides.] **1950** *WELS* (A horse of mixed colors) 3 Infs, **WI,** Indian pony. **1955** Harris *Look of Old West* 239, A pinto or paint horse was one variously spotted or splotched, bay, chestnut, red, or brown on gray or white. . . Appaloosas, Indian horses from the Nez Perce country, had leopard-like spots on the rump. . . The Indian pony, by the way, actually the old Spanish horse with a dash of wild in his blood . . was still called a chickasaw horse in the old Indian Territory where I was born. **1965–70** *DARE* (Qu. K37, . . *A horse of mixed colors*) Infs **AR**18, **KS**20, **MA**6, 15, **MI**19, **MO**2, 20, Indian pony (or ponies); **AK**8, Indian horses are spotted; **PA**141, Indian horse; **RI**3A, [My] black, tan, and white horse [is] a little Indian horse; **RI**7, Indian pony? [(Qu. K38, *A horse of a dirty white color*) Inf **AK**8, Indian pony;] (Qu. K39, . . *Names* . . *for horses according to their colors*) Inf **MO**5, Indian ponies; **MO**5A, Indian ponies—they're spotted.

Indian posy n Also *Indian posey*

1 A **cudweed** (here: usu *Gnaphalium obtusifolium*).

1846 *Knickerbocker* 27.287 **NY,** Sand and large pebbles, on which were scattered dwarf cedars interspersed with golden-rods, lobelias, Indian posies. **1876** Hobbs *Bot. Hdbk.* 57, Indian posey, White balsam, Gnaphalium polycephalum. **1894** *Jrl. Amer. Folkl.* 7.92, *Gnaphalium* *polycephalum, . .* Indian posy, Stonington, Ct. **1896** *Ibid* 9.192, *Gnaphalium polycephalum, . .* Indian posy, Southold, L[ong] I[sland]. **1907** Hodge *Hdbk. Amer. Indians* 1.606, *Indian posey.*—(1) Sweet life-everlasting *(Gnaphalium obtusifolium).* (2) Large-flowered everlasting *(Anaphalis margaritacea).* (3) The butterfly-weed *(Asclepias tuberosa).*

2 also, perh erron, *Indian nosy:* **=butterfly weed 1.**

1897 IN Dept. Geol. & Nat. Resources *Rept. for 1896* 666, *A[sclepias] tuberosa. . .* Indian Posey. . . frequent. **1900** Lyons *Plant Names* 50, *A[sclepias] tuberosa. . .* Indian Posy. **1907** [see **1** above]. **1930** Sievers *Amer. Med. Plants* 18. **1940** Clute *Amer. Plant Names* 90, *Butterfly-weed. . .* Indian posey. **1958** Jacobs–Burlage *Index Plants NC* 21, *Asclepias tuberosa. . .* Indian-nosy.

3 =pearly everlasting.

1900 Lyons *Plant Names* 32, *A[naphalis] margaritacea. . .* Indian-posy. **1907** [see **1** above]. **1931** Harned *Wild Flowers Alleghanies* 564, *Pearly Everlasting. . .* A number of household names cling to it, among them are Silverleaf, . . Indian posy.

Indian pot See **Indian stew**

Indian potato n

Any of numerous plants which produce edible tubers, bulbs, corms, or tuberous roots, as:

a A **groundnut B1** (here: *Apios americana*).

1788 in 1826 Biggs *Narrative* 21 **IL**, They had nothing to eat . . but indian potatoes—some people call them hoppines. **1830** Rafinesque *Med. Flora* 2.193, *Apios tuberosa. . . Indian Potato, Potato Pea.* Hopniss of the Delaware tribes. . . Valuable plant, formerly cultivated by the Indians (yet by the Creeks) for the roots, which are like potatoes, or rather like *Helianthus tuberosus,* and the seeds like peas and as good. **1876** Hobbs *Bot. Hdbk.* 57. **1907** Hodge *Hdbk. Amer. Indians* 1.606, *Indian potato.*—(1) The groundnut *(Apios apios).* (2) A western name for the squirrel-corn *(Bikukulla canadensis).* (3) A California name, according to Bergen, for *Brodiaea capitata;* but according to Barrett . . the term is indiscriminately given to many different species of bulbs and corms, which formed a considerable item in the food supply of the Californian Indians. **1931** Clute *Common Plants* 35, Among the more useful of the Indian's food plants are the Indian potatoes *(Apios tuberosa, Helianthus giganteus,* and *H. tuberosus).* These, even the white man has used on occasion. **1974** (1977) Coon *Useful Plants* 165, *Apios tuberosa*—Indian potato, ground nut. . . The nuts dug in the fall are edible uncooked, but the best way is to slice the unpeeled tubers and fry them like potatoes.

b A **sunflower:** either *Helianthus giganteus* or **Jerusalem artichoke;** also the tuber of the **Jerusalem artichoke.**

[**1824** West *Substance of a Jrl.* 109 **Canada,** There is a root which is found in large quantities, and generally called by the settlers, the Indian potatoe. It strongly resembles the Jerusalem artichoke, and is eaten by the natives in a raw state; but when boiled it is not badly flavoured.] **1912** Blackmar *Kansas* 1.41, The rich soil . . spontaneously afforded a variegated growth of grass, flowering plants, and native fruits, nuts, Indian potatoes, etc. **1920** Saunders *Useful Wild Plants* 7, *H[elianthus] giganteus* . . has thickened tuber-like roots which are . . edible. These are the "Indian potato" of the Assiniboine Indians. **1931** [see **a** above]. **1959** Carleton *Index Herb. Plants* 65, *Indian-potato:* Asclepias tuberosa; Apios tuberosa; Gnaphalium polycephalum; Helianthus tuberosa.

c =camas 1.

1837 Irving *Rocky Mts.* 1.40 **NE,** Game was scanty, and they had to eke out their scanty fare with wild roots and vegetables, such as the Indian potato, the wild onion, and the prairie tomato. **1902** U.S. Natl. Museum *Contrib. Herbarium* 7.326 **nwCA,** *Quamasia leichtlinii.* . . A specie of camas, 2 to 4 feet tall. . . The plant has an onion-like bulb about an inch in diameter. . . This is the largest and by all odds the best of all the Indian potatoes. . . They are dug up in June or July by squaws with a "potato stick." **1920** Saunders *Useful Wild Plants* 17, It is the Pacific Coast, however, that has a special fame for edible wild bulbs. . . There the Indians have, from before history began, been consuming such bulbs either raw or cooked. To some extent, also, they have been drawn upon for food by white travelers and settlers—the most palatable species being of the genera *Calochortus, Brodiaea* and *Camassia,* and commonly called "Indian potatoes."

d =mariposa lily. West

1890 *Century Dict.* 4648, *Potato. . . Indian potato. . .* The liliaceous genus *Calochortus:* so called from its bulb or corm. **1920** [see **c** above].

e =brodiaea. Pacific

1898 *Jrl. Amer. Folkl.* 11.281 **CA,** *Brodiœa capitata* . . Indian potato.

1902 (1974) Chestnut *Plants Indians* 327 **nwCA,** *Triteleia laxa.* . . The most abundant and widespread of all the Indian potatoes. **1907** [see **a** above]. **1920** [see **c** above].

f A **squirrel corn** (here: *Dicentra canadensis*).

1898 *Jrl. Amer. Folkl.* 11.222, *Dicentra Canadensis,* . . Indian potatoes, Bolivar, Ohio. **1902** *Ibid* 15.110 **OH,** *Indian potato. . . Dicentra canadensis,* or "squirrel corn." **1907** [see **a** above].

g A **yampah** (here: *Perideridia gairdneri*).

1937 U.S. Forest Serv. *Range Plant Hdbk.* W48, Yampa . . is also known as . . Indian-potato. . . The tubers have a sweet, nutty, creamlike flavor and were formerly eaten extensively by the Indians, but now are little used. Piper recognized yampa as the best food plant of the Northwestern Indians. . . Yampa roots are fleshy and tuberous, . . and resemble tiny sweetpotatoes.

h =arrowhead 1.

1940 Smith *Puyallup–Nisqually* 250 **nwWA,** Wappato or Indian potatoes grew only in land flooded by fresh water. **1951** *PADS* 15.27 **TX,** *Sagittaria.* . . Indian potatoes, duck potatoes; tubers eaten by both red men and birds.

i =turkey pea, usu *Orogenia linearifolia.* **esp Rocky Mts**

1951 Martin *Amer. Wildlife & Plants* 491, Indianpotato *(Orogenia).* **1963** Craighead *Rocky Mt. Wildflowers* 129, *Orogenia linearifolia. . . Other names:* . . Indian potato. . . Indians ate the tubers; raw they have a potato-like flavor. **1967** Harrington *Edible Plants Rocky Mts.* 312, *Orogenia linearifolia.* Indian Potato. [*Ibid* 313, The raw roots had a pleasant crisp taste. . . We then sliced and fried these raw roots in butter. We all pronounced them very good, somewhat nutty tasting, not really like fried potatoes, but possibly even better.] **1970** Kirk *Wild Edible Plants W. U.S.* 122, *Orogenia fusiformis* and *linearifolia.* . . Indian Potato. . . These are dwarf, non-hairy, perennial plants with fleshy roots. **1974** (1977) Coon *Useful Plants* 261, *Orogenia linearifolia* . . Indian potato. . . These roots are rubber-like and make a palatable food either fried, baked, or boiled.

j =butterfly weed 1.

1959 [see **b** above].

k A **cudweed 1** (here: *Gnaphalium obtusifolium*).

1959 [see **b** above].

l =man-of-the-earth 1. Sth

1961 Wills–Irwin *Flowers TX* 175, Indian-potato, *I[pomoea] pandurata* . . , is a milky-juiced perennial trailing and twining vine of sandy pine woods in East Texas, growing from an enormously thickened starchy root which in old plants may weigh as much as 25 lbs. This species too is a troublesome weed in fields. **1967–68** *DARE* (Qu. S5, . . *Wild morning glory*) Inf **AL**30, Indian potato; (Qu. S21, . . *Weeds . . that are a trouble in gardens and fields*) Inf **AL**30, Indian potato; (QR p126) Inf **NC**49, Indian tata—looks like sweet potato.

m A **sweet vetch** (here: *Hedysarum alpinum*).

1966 Heller *Wild Flowers AK* 101, *Indian Potato. . . Hedysarum alpinum* L. ssp. *americanum.* . . Tap root long, thick, with several tuberlike enlargements. . . Root edible.

n A **jack-in-the-pulpit 1. Cf Indian turnip 1**

1967 *DARE* (Qu. S1, . . *Jack-in-the-pulpit*) Inf **SC**43, Indian potato? not edible; (Qu. S26e, *Other wildflowers . . ;* not asked in early QRs) Inf **SC**43, Indian potato—grows like potatoes—not edible.

o A **wild potato** (here: *Solanum jamesii*).

1970 Kirk *Wild Edible Plants W. U.S.* 240, [*Solanum . . jamesii.* . . [has] tubers that are similar, though much smaller, to our cultivated potato, . . and may be prepared in the same way.] *Ibid* 241, *S. jamesii* (Indian Potato) is found in mountains in Colorado, Utah, New Mexico, and Arizona.

p =water chinquapin.

1974 (1977) Coon *Useful Plants* 193, *Nelumbium pentapetalum* . . water chinquipin [sic]. . . This . . is well-known for the edible quality of its seeds. . . Other values are found in the tubers, which were called the Indian potato of Iowa, for these tubers when dried and stored could be cooked with meat in winter.

q An unidentified plant; see quot. **Cf Indian bread 4**

1929 Bell *Some Contrib. KS Vocab.* 179, Indian potato. . . The name for a plant having geranium-like leaves, and a magenta, single-rose flower, growing close to the ground. It, also, has a meaty root. Sometimes called *prairie apple.* Perhaps the same as callirrhoe.

r A **chickweed wintergreen** (here: *Trientalis latifolia*).

1979 Spellenberg *Audubon Guide N. Amer. Wildflowers W. Region* 694,

Indian Potato (Trientalis latifolia). . . The name Indian Potato refers to the small underground swelling at the base of the stem; modern references do not mention edibility, so caution is advised.

Indian puccoon n

A **puccoon** (here: *Lithospermum canescens*).

1900 Lyons *Plant Names* 227, L[*ithospermum*] *canescens*. . . Indian puccoon. **1907** Hodge *Hdbk. Amer. Indians* 1.606, *Indian puccoon.*— The hoary puccoon (*Lithospermum canescens*). **1940** Clute *Amer. Plant Names* 226.

Indian pudding n Also *Indian-corn pudding, Indian meal pudding* **chiefly NEng** See Map *old-fash* Cf **Indian** n **B1b**

A dish consisting primarily of boiled or baked cornmeal, often sweetened with molasses and served for dessert.

1722 *New–Engl. Courant* (Boston MA) 26 Mar 2/2, A Plain Indian Pudding, being put into the Pot and boil'd the usual Time, it came out of a Blood-red colour, to the great Surprise of the whole Family. **1824** Irving *Hist. NY* 1.166 **NYC,** He was making his breakfast from a prodigious earthen dish, filled with milk and Indian pudding. **1905** *DN* 3.12 **cCT,** Indian pudding. . . A pudding of Indian meal and molasses. **1907** *DN* 3.191 **seNH,** *Injun pudd'n.* . . Pudding of corn meal, milk, and apples, commonly baked in a bean pot. **1932** (1946) Hibben *Amer. Regional Cookery* 234 **eMA,** The traditional accompaniment for Indian pudding is rich cream or hard sauce, but it is often served, even in Boston, with vanilla ice cream. **1941** *LANE* Map 288 **NEng,** Corn meal mush is made of corn meal stirred into salted boiling water and cooked till thick. It is eaten with milk, cream, butter, bacon grease or syrup. It is a 'whole meal' in itself. . . Corn meal pudding consists of corn meal, molasses and suet. . . It is baked for two or three hours and served as a dessert. . . Neither of these two dishes is popular at the present time . . , so that some of the informants, especially in urbanized areas, have only vague recollections of the difference between them and of their names. This uncertainty appears commonly in the term *Indian (meal) pudding,* which usually denotes the (baked) dessert, but is applied to the (boiled) breakfast dish by a fairly large number of our informants. **1950** *WELS* (*Kinds of pudding*) 1 Inf, **WI,** Indian pudding. **1965–70** *DARE* (Qu. H63, *Kinds of desserts*) 34 Infs, **chiefly NEng,** (Baked) Indian pudding; **ME**16, Indian meal pudding; (Qu. H23, . . *Hot cooked breakfast cereal*) Inf **MA**58, Injun pudding; (Qu. H24, . . *Boiled cornmeal*) Infs **CT**33, **MA**7, **NY**21, Indian pudding; **NH**15, Mush; Indian pudding [is] different—sweetened; **MA**58, Injun pudding; (Qu. H45) Inf **MA**50, Yorkshire pudding, plum pudding, Indian pudding; (Qu. H50, *Dishes made with . . corn*) Infs **OH**96, **RI**1, Indian pudding; **CT**5, Indian meal pudding; (Qu. HH30, *Things that are nicknamed for different nationalities*) Inf **OH**95, Indian pudding. [32 of 37 total Infs old] **1966** *DARE* Tape **NH**6, Indian pudding is still made a lot today. . . One that I make mostly has tapioca in it. . . It's cornmeal and molasses, and some sugar . . stirred into milk. . . It's baked, an hour or two. **1973** Allen *LAUM* 1.301 (as of c1950) 1 inf, **swMN,** Mush. . . Indian pudding. **1986** Pederson *LAGS Concordance* (Mush) 1 inf, **ceTX,** Indian-corn pudding—brown on top; 1 inf, **nwAL,** Indian pudding—boiled Indian meal; 1 inf, **csGA,** Indian pudding; 1 inf, **csGA,** Indian pudding [FW: apparently differs from mush, cush].

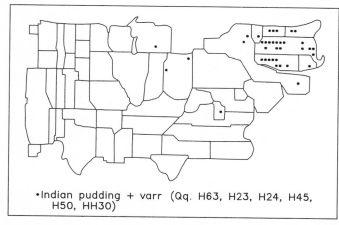

•Indian pudding + varr (Qq. H63, H23, H24, H45, H50, HH30)

Indian pullet n **chiefly FL, GA, SC**

1 =night heron.

1835 Audubon *Ornith. Biog.* 3.275, The Night Heron. . . in South

Carolina. . . is named "the Indian Pullet," in Lower Louisiana the Creoles call it *"Gros-bec,"* the inhabitants of East Florida know it under the name of "Indian Hen," and in our Eastern States its usual appellation is "Qua Bird." **1910** Wayne *Birds SC* 32, *Black-crowned Night Heron.* . . The local name of this species on the coast is "Indian Pullet." **1953** *AmSp* 28.277, With modifiers we have such titles as . . *Indian pullet* (green heron, Ga., Fla.; black-crowned and yellow-crowned night herons, S.C., Ga.; American bittern, N.Y., S.C., Ga., Fla.; limpkin, Fla.; king rail, S.C.; and purple gallinule, Ga.) **1954** Sprunt *FL Bird Life* 37, These herons [=black-crowned night herons] were once often shot as food, and known under the local name of Indian Pullet, particularly the brownish, streaked young. . . *Yellow-crowned Night Heron.* . . *Local Names:* Quock; Indian pullet. **1955** *Oriole* 20.1.2 **GA,** Black-crowned Night Heron. . . Indian Pullet. . . Yellow-crowned Night Heron. . . Indian Pullet.

2 =bittern.

1883 *Amer. Naturalist* 17.432, Other names [for *Botaurus lentiginosus*] are "Indian hen" and "Indian pullet." **1910** Wayne *Birds SC* 27, The Bittern, which is locally known as "Indian Pullet," . . is abundant during the winter months. **1911** *Forest & Stream* 77.174, *Botaurus lentiginosus.* . . Indian Pullet, Santee, S.C. **1932** Bennett *Check-list* 15 **MO,** *American bittern.* . . Indian pullet. . . C[ommon] S[ummer] R[esident] throughout the state. **1953** [see **1** above]. **1955** *Oriole* 20.1.2 **GA,** American Bittern. . . Indian Hen, Indian Pullet.

3 =green heron.

1913 *Auk* 30.493 **Okefenokee GA,** *Green Heron;* 'Indian Pullet'. . . A few were observed on the borders of the prairies and along the edge of Billy's Lake. **1926** *AmSp* 1.418 **Okefenokee GA,** Even the Injun Pullet [Footnote: Green Heron] wuz there. **1946** Hausman *Eastern Birds* 107, *Eastern Green Heron.* . . *Other Names* . . Indian Pullet, Minnow Fisher. **1955** *Oriole* 20.1.2 **GA,** *Green Heron.* . . *Indian Pullet* (a wild bird, facetiously referred to as poultry of the Indians). **1968** *DARE* (Qu. Q10, . . *Water birds and marsh birds*) Inf **GA**20, Indian pullet. **1969** Longstreet *Birds FL* 21, *Indian Pullet.* . . The green heron is the smallest of our true heron [sic], measuring from 15 to 22 inches in length.

4 =king rail 1.

1923 U.S. Dept. Ag. *Misc. Circular* 13.40 **SC,** *Rallus elegans.* . . *Vernacular Names.* . . *In local use* . . Indian pullet. **1950** *PADS* 14.40 **SC,** *Indian pullet.* . . The king rail. **1953** [see **1** above].

5 =limpkin.

1932 Howell *FL Bird Life* 199, *Limpkin.* . . *Other Names* . . Indian Pullet. **1946** Hausman *Eastern Birds* 233, *Limpkin.* . . *Other Names* . . Indian Pullet, Carau. . . From the Okefinokee Swamp, southern Georgia (rarely from South Carolina) southward to Florida. **1953** [see **1** above].

6 =purple gallinule.

1953 [see **1** above].

Indian purge n Cf **Indian black drink**

See quots.

1687 in 1744 Royal Soc. London *Philos. Trans. for 1739* 41.150 **VA,** There is another Herb, which they [=Virginians] call the *Indian Purge:* This Plant . . bears yellow Berries round about the Joints: they only make use of the Root of this Plant. [*DARE* Ed: This quot may refer to *Ilex opaca* var *xanthocarpa*, the root of which is still used in folk medicine.] **1911** *Century Dict. Suppl., Purge.* . . *Indian purge.* (a) The wild potato-vine, man-of-the-earth, or mecha-meck of the Indians, *Ipomoea pandurata.* (b) A plant of Virginia, probably *Triosteum perfoliatum,* the root of which was used as a purgative by the aborigines. **1951** *PADS* 15.36 **TX,** *Ilex vomitoria.* . . Indian purge; used by the pioneers, to whom the friendly Indians showed medicinal plants.

Indian quinine n

=**vervain**.

1951 *PADS* 15.39 **TX,** *Verbena* spp. . . Indian quinine.

Indian railroad See **Indian road**

Indian red bell n

Prob a **fritillary** (here: *Fritillaria recurva*).

1942 Whipple *Joshua* 116 **UT** (as of c1860), Clory spied even a wildflower with a tiny pink cup—Willie thought it was an Indian red bell.

Indian redroot n

A **redroot** (here: *Lachnanthes caroliniana*).

1876 Hobbs *Bot. Hdbk.* 57, Indian red root, Spirit weed, Lacnanthes [sic] tinctoria. **1907** Hodge *Hdbk. Amer. Indians* 1.606, *Indian red-*

root.—The red-root *(Gyrotheca capitata).* **1959** Carleton *Index Herb. Plants* 65, *Indian-red-root:* Lachnanthes tinctoria.

Indian reed n

1 =**Virginia willow.**

1927 Boston Soc. Nat. Hist. *Proc.* 38.240 **Okefenokee GA,** The following list of plants . . have been found in the prairie 'houses.' . . *Itea virginica* 'Indian reed.'

2 =**Indian grass 1a.**

1933 Small *Manual SE Flora* 47, *Sorghastrum.* . . Indian-reeds.

Indian relish n

1967 *DARE* (Qu. H50, *Dishes made with beans . . corn)* Inf **TN1,** Indian relish—beans, corn, tomatoes—canned.

Indian rhubarb n

1 A coarse-leaved plant *(Peltiphyllum peltatum)* which produces edible fleshy leafstalks and is native to California and Oregon. Also called **umbrella plant**

1897 Parsons *Wild Flowers CA* 244, This plant is commonly called "Indian rhubarb," because the Indians are extravagantly fond of the stalks of the leaves and flowers. **1898** *Jrl. Amer. Folkl.* 11.226 **CA,** *Saxifraga peltata,* . . Indian rhubarb, umbrella plant. **1907** Hodge *Hdbk. Amer. Indians* 1.606. **1939** Medsger *Edible Wild Plants* 154, Indian Rhubarb. . . The thick fleshy leafstalks. . . sometimes . . are cooked after the manner of asparagus. **1967** Gilkey–Dennis *Hdbk. NW Plants* 178, *Indian rhubarb.* . . On the margins of and in shallow streams from the Coast Ranges. **1970** Kirk *Wild Edible Plants W. U.S.* 201, Indian Rhubarb. . . The fleshy leafstalks may be peeled and eaten as is, or in salad. They may also be added to stews, or used alone as a potherb, but cooking destroys some of their flavor. **1992** *Wilderness* Winter 18 **sOR,** [Caption:] Indian rhubarb in the Illinois River Canyon.

2 A **cow parsnip 1** (here: *Heracleum lanatum).* **AK**

1938 (1958) Sharples *AK Wild Flowers* 68, *H[eracleum] lanatum.* . . "Indian Rhubarb." **1968** *DARE* (Qu. S6) Inf **AK1,** Indian celery—Indian rhubarb—wild rhubarb.

Indian rice n

1 A **wild rice** (here: *Zizania aquatica).*

1837 Darlington *Flora Cestrica* 93, *Z[izania] aquatica.* . . Indian Rice. . . Mr. *Elliott* thought it might be a valuable grass, in overflowed or marshy meadows,—as Stock of all descriptions are fond of it. **1889** Vasey *Ag. Grasses* 33, Indian Rice. . . abounds in the small lakes of Minnesota and the Northwest, and is there gathered by the Indians for food. **1901** Mohr *Plant Life AL* 362, Wild Rice. Indian Rice. . . Copious in water . . in the estuaries of the rivers emptying into Mobile Bay. **1902** *Jrl. Amer. Folkl.* 15.110, *Indian rice.* A name sometimes applied to the 'wild rice' *(Zizania aquatica)* of the region of the Great Lakes. **1956** St. John *Flora SE WA* 62, *Indian Rice.* . . Grain long cylindrical, black. . . A native of e. N. Am., introduced to attract waterfowl. **1976** Bailey–Bailey *Hortus Third* 1185, *Indian r[ice].* . . An aboriginal food plant still used for human food; also planted as a food and shelter for waterfowl. . . Que. to N. Dak., s. to N.Y. and Nebr.

2 also *Indian ricegrass:* A **mountain rice** (here: *Oryzopsis hymenoides).* **chiefly Desert SW**

1933 Jaeger *CA Deserts* 165 **sCA,** Indian rice *(Oryzopsis hymenoides)* is frequent in porous soils, particularly on blown sand. **1937** U.S. Forest Serv. *Range Plant Hdbk.* G88, This species [=*Oryzopsis hymenoides*] produces . . plump, oval seeds which supposedly resemble the seeds of common rice. . . The nutritious seeds . . were formerly one of the food staples of many western Indians; hence the common name, Indian ricegrass. Indians ground the seeds into meal or flour which was made into bread. **1948** *Ecological Monogr.* 18.171 **swUT,** Indian rice grass, *Oryzopsis hymenoides,* is common in certain small areas. **1957** Jaeger *N. Amer. Deserts* 161, Atop these hummocks may be seen . . scattered tufts of the beautiful big-seeded sandbinding grass sometimes called Indian rice *(Oryzopsis hymenoides).* **1957** *Plateau* 30.2.34 **cnAZ, csUT,** Indian rice-grass *(Oryzopsis hymenoides)* is relatively scarce in any one place but is to be found over most of the area visited. **1976** Bailey–Bailey *Hortus Third* 802, *Indian r[icegrass].* . . Man[itoba] to B[ritish] C[olumbia], s. to Tex., Calif., and n. Mex. **1990** *Plants SW* (Catalog) 8, *Indian Ricegrass. Oryzopsis hymenoides.* The leaves on this perennial bunch grass are long, slender, and green, curing to straw when dormant.

3 A **fritillary:** usu *Fritillaria camschatcensis,* but also *F. lanceolata.* **Pacific NW, AK**

1922 *Amer. Botanist* 28.81 **NW,** The native species of *Fritillaria* and especially *F. pudica* are known as . . "Indian rice," from the small

pearly-white bulblets, shaped almost exactly like grains of rice. **1934** Haskin *Wild Flowers Pacific Coast* 23, *Fritillaria lanceolata.* . . The name . . Indian rice comes from the fact that its large bulbs are covered with plump, white, rice-like scales. *Ibid* 25, Indian rice, *Fritillaria camtschatcensis* [sic]. . . is a more northern species having its flowers less mottled. . . Its range is from northern Washington northward. **1938** (1958) Sharples *AK Wild Flowers* 57, *F[ritillaria] camschatcensis.* . . Indian Rice. . . is a common article of food among the Indians. . . The bulbs are eaten boiled, and also from the dried bulbs is produced a flour which is made into cakes, cooked, and eaten as bread. The conical-shaped bulb is entirely covered with numerous bulblets, the whole resembling a cluster of boiled rice. **1959** Anderson *Flora AK* 154. **1963** Craighead *Rocky Mt. Wildflowers* 26, Other species, such as the Kamchatka Lily (or Indian Rice), are regularly gathered and eaten by Eskimos. **1973** Hitchcock–Cronquist *Flora Pacific NW* 691, Indian rice, black lily. . . *F. camschatcensis.*

Indian ricegrass n See **Indian rice 2**

Indian River chicken n Cf **Albany beef, Cape Cod turkey** =**striped mullet.**

1934 *AmSp* 9.236 **ceFL,** *Indian River chicken* is a purely local and facetious name for 'mullet.'

Indian road n Also *Indian railroad*

1973 Attwood *Length ME* 14, *Horseback*—A long ridge, narrow and with comparatively slight elevation above surrounding land. An esker. A whaleback, hogback, ridge, . . Indian road, Indian railroad.

Indian root n

1 A **spikenard** (here: *Aralia racemosa).*

1876 Hobbs *Bot. Hdbk.* 57, Indian root, Spikenard, American, Aralia racemosa. **1892** *Jrl. Amer. Folkl.* 5.97 **NH,** *Aralia racemosa,* Indian root. **1907** Hodge *Hdbk. Amer. Indians* 1.606, *Indian root.*—The American spikenard *(Aralia racemosa).* **1930** Sievers *Amer. Med. Plants* 63. **1968** *Foxfire* 2.2.49 **nGA,** *Aralia racemosa,* called . . indian-root, . . is a "cure-all." . . The roots were ground up with sowbugs and molasses for yellow jaundice, and also used in kidney ailments, female troubles, and for backaches. **1974** (1977) Coon *Useful Plants* 68, *Aralia racemosa*—Indian-root. . . Roots and rhizomes have been used to treat rheumatism, coughs and, in the Appalachian area, they have been used for backache.

2 A **redroot** (here: *Lachnanthes caroliniana).*

1951 Teale *North with Spring* 41 **FL,** The Kissimmee cranes are specialists at finding the underground tubers of . . the . . Indian root.

3 A **pickerelweed** (here: *Pontederia cordata).*

1969 *DARE* FW Addit **GA51,** Indian root—wampee [=*Pontederia cordata*].

Indian runner n [*Indian < India*]

1950 *PADS* 14.76, *Indian runner.* . . A Brahman cow in Florida.

Indian rye n

Perh a **wild rye.**

1969 *DARE* (Qu. S26b, *Wildflowers that grow in water or wet places)* Infs **TN33, 36,** Indian rye.

Indian sage n

1 A **boneset 1:** usu *Eupatorium perfoliatum,* but also *E. purpureum.*

1828 Rafinesque *Med. Flora* 1.174, *Eupatorium perfoliatum.* . . *Vulgar Names* . . Indian Sage, Agueweed. **1892** (1974) Millspaugh *Amer. Med. Plants* 79-1, Boneset, . . Indian Sage. . . The attic, or woodshed, of almost every country farm-house, has its bunches of the dried herb hanging tops downward from the rafters during the whole year, ready for immediate use should some member of the family . . be taken with a cold. **1907** Hodge *Hdbk. Amer. Indians* 1.606. **1930** Sievers *Amer. Med. Plants* 16, Indian sage. . . is a common weed in low, wet ground. **1959** Carleton *Index Herb. Plants* 65, *Indian-sage:* Eupatorium purpureum. **1975** Hamel–Chiltoskey *Cherokee Plants* 26, Indian sage. . . Tea for colds, sore throat, flu.

2 Scotch broom *(Cytisus scoparius).*

1904 (1913) Johnson *Highways South* 319 **VA** [Black], My driver called the broom "Indian sage," and said it was medicinal.

Indian salad n

A **waterleaf** (here: *Hydrophyllum virginianum).*

1939 Medsger *Edible Wild Plants* 166, Indian Salad, Hydrophyllum virginianum. . . is said to make good greens. **1976** Bailey–Bailey *Hor-*

tus Third 580, *Indian-salad*. . . The tender shoots were eaten by the Amer. Indians.

Indian salt n

1 A **sumac:** spec, the efflorescence produced by the hairs of the sumac berry; see quots.

[**1830** Rafinesque *Med. Flora* 2.256, *Rhus*. . . *Shumac*. . . Berries . . have an agreeable acid taste, make a cooling drink infused in water. Efflorescence on them used as salt and vinegar: it is malic acid.] **1876** Hobbs *Bot. Hdbk.* 56, Indian salt, Cane sugar, *Saccharum officinarium.* Indian salt, the powd'r on sumac berries, *Rhus glabrum.* **1881** *Harper's New Mth. Mag.* 62.526 **NY,** He saw moving with the wind a quantity of Indian salt, commonly known as sumac, which, when ripe, presents a red appearance. [**1892** (1974) Millspaugh *Amer. Med. Plants* 36-4, *Calcium bimalate.*—This salt is found clinging to the hair of the fruit [of *Rhus glabra*] as a concretion exuded from them; when soaked off the fruits are no longer sour.]

2 Sugar produced from sugarcane (*Saccharum officinarum*).

1876 [see **1** above].

Indian sanicle n

A **boneset 1:** usu *Eupatorium rugosum,* but also *E. pur-pureum.*

1876 Hobbs *Bot. Hdbk.* 57, Indian sanicle, White sanicle, Eupatorium ageratoides. **1900** Lyons *Plant Names* 155, E[upatorium] agera-toides. . . Indian Sanicle. . . *Root* aromatic, diuretic, vulnerary. **1935** (1943) Muenscher *Weeds* 487, *Eupatorium urticaefolium*. . . Indian sanicle. [*Ibid* 488, The plant . . causes the disease known as trembles in cattle or milk sickness in humans.] **1940** Clute *Amer. Plant Names* 82, *E. urticaefolium*. . . Indian sanicle. **1959** Carleton *Index Herb. Plants* 65, *Indian-sanicle:* Eupatorium purpureum.

Indian's dream   See **Indian dream**

Indian shamrock n

A **trillium,** usu *Trillium erectum.*

1876 Hobbs *Bot. Hdbk.* 57, Indian shamrock, Beth root, Trillium pendulum and species. **1907** Hodge *Hdbk. Amer. Indians* 1.606. **1930** Sievers *Amer. Med. Plants* 48, *Purple Trillium*. . . *Other common names*. . . Indian shamrock, nosebleed. . . Many of these names are applied also to other species of trillium. **1971** Krochmal *Appalachia Med. Plants* 256, Indian shamrock. . . has a single stout stem with a whorl of 3 broad leaves at the top. . . The Indians of Appalachia cooked pieces of the root in food as an aphrodisiac.

Indian sheldrake n Cf **Indian n B5**
=red-breasted merganser.

1923 U.S. Dept. Ag. *Misc. Circular* 13.5 **NY,** Red-breasted Merganser. . . *Vernacular Names*. . . *In local use*. . . Indian sheldrake. **1957** *AmSp* 32.182 **NY,** *Indian sheldrake* (red-breasted merganser . .) is possibly from the same idea [*DARE* Ed: that it is an inferior food species], or the name may refer to the bird's crest or 'scalp-lock.' **1982** Elman *Hunter's Field Guide* 230, Red-breasted Merganser. . . *Common & regional names* . . Indian sheldrake.

Indian shitepoke   See **shitepoke**

Indian shoe n Also *Indian moccasin,* ~ *slipper* [See quot 1915]
=lady's slipper 1.

[**1764** in 1925 Fries *Rec. Moravians* 2.569 **NC,** *Lady Shoes,* some call it *Indian Shoes.* It is a Snakeroot, and the Indians know how to use it for many things. Has a yellow or white blossom which is exactly the shape of a wooden shoe. Grows in rich Uplands.] **1876** Hobbs *Bot. Hdbk.* 57, Indian shoe, Yellow ladies' slipper, Cypripedium pubescens. **1897** *Jrl. Amer. Folkl.* 10.144, *Cypripedium acaule*. . . Indian slipper, Oxford County, M[ain]e. **1907** Hodge *Hdbk. Amer. Indians* 1.606, *Indian moccasin.*—The stemless lady's-slipper or moccasin-flower (*Cypripedium acaule*). . . *Indian shoe.*—The large yellow lady's-slipper or moccasin-flower (*Cypripedium hirsutum*). . . *Indian slipper.*—The pink lady's-slipper, or moccasin-flower (*Cypripedium acaule*). **1915** (1926) Armstrong–Thornber *Western Wild Flowers* 78, There are many kinds of Cypripedium. . . They are easily known by the curious lip, which is a large inflated sac, suggesting both the common names, Lady's Slipper and Indian Moccasin. **1938** FWP *Guide MN* 362 **nwMN,** In tamarack swamps of the area are pink and white moccasin flowers, also called . . Indian shoes. **1966–68** *DARE* (Qu. S26c, *Wildflowers that grow in woods*) Inf **AR**2, Indian slipper—little red flower; **WI**58, Pink

lady-slippers—another name is Indian moccasins. **1976** Bailey–Bailey *Hortus Third* 356, *Yellow Indian-shoe.*

Indian shoestrings n Cf **devil's shoestring, shoestring**

1968 McPhee *Pine Barrens* 132 **NJ,** Before the outing was over, the group had found Indian shoestrings, Turk's-cap lilies [etc].

Indian shutter n [From the idea that they served to repel Indian attacks] NEng

Any of var types of functional wooden window shutters.

1966 *Yankee* June 5 **csNH,** [Advt:] *Indian shutters, fireplaces, beamed ceilings.* An oldtime Cape with a mountain view. **1981** *NADS Letters* **MA** (as of c1920), Indian shutters are heavy wooden shutters which are on the outside of the house, but which can be fastened shut from the inside. . . The name came from their use during Indian attacks in Colonial days. **1983** *DARE* File, On the television program "This Old House" an architect talked about making Indian shutters to replicate those on an eighteenth-century house in Hollis, New Hampshire. They were low shutters, covering the bottom part of the window; they were made of slats, and closed accordion-wise. I recall this kind of shutters; some of the old houses in Deerfield, Massachusetts have them. **1985** *WI Alumnus Letters* **NEng,** *Indian Shutters*—This is a widely used term throughout New England. It is used to describe solid wooden shutters hung on the *inside* of the window, to be found usually in the large, elegant, 18th-century Colonial homes built by rich merchants, ship owners, and whaling captains. The shutters fold back against the wall when not in use, where they are concealed by the draperies or slide into especially built crevices on either side of the window. . . Contrary to usual belief they were not used to repel Indian attacks. That theory is a romantic myth. Their actual purpose is more mundane: to help deflect not Indian arrows but rather the humid heat of a New England summer or the icy blasts of a New England winter. **1986** *Ibid* **NEng,** *Indian Shutters* . . were protective wood shutters on 18th-century New England houses to protect the occupants during an Indian raid on the town. Presumably they were arrow-resistant.

Indian side n West Cf **far side, Indian-broke, siwash side**

The right-hand side, esp of a horse; hence, the wrong side or wrong way of doing something.

1942 Berrey–Van den Bark *Amer. Slang* 935 **West,** Injun side, *one's right side.* **1958** *AmSp* 33.272 **eWA,** Siwash side; Indian side. The right side of a horse, or the left side of a milch cow; said, therefore, of anything done backward or ineptly. **1984** Smith *SW Vocab.* 127, *Indian side:* The right side of a horse, so called because Indians habitually mounted on the right side instead of the left as the white man did (and does). Old timers attempting to emulate the Indian were usually thrown, bitten, or kicked by the horse.

Indian sign n

A hex or spell believed to render an opponent powerless or ineffective—often in phrr *have* (or *hang, hold, put*) *the Indian sign on (someone)*.

[**1850** Garrard *Wah-to-yah* 333 **cKS,** A California Indian, belonging to Colonel Russell, ran, with gun in hand, far out toward the foiled enemy, making the Indian sign of insult and derision; and, in Spanish, abusing them most scandalously.] **1908** *Baseball Mag.* June 28, Barney had lost that indefineable [sic] something called "nerve," and as one after another, the bases filled he kept chattering with unwitting appropriateness: "Got th' Indian sign on me—th' Indian sign!" **1916** *Boy Scouts' Year Bk.* (N.Y.) 93/2 *(OEDS),* He had proved that the Indian sign wasn't infalli-ble. . . After all, then, the Indian sign was a kind of superstition. **1929** Ellis *Ordinary Woman* 24 **CO** (as of 1880s), Judge Slaughter put the Indian sign on them by declaring, 'I've seen and settled more hell than you could ever raise.' **1939** *Tamony Coll.,* A.F. Williams says that, during his childhood in Minnesota (1895–1912), when one boy would put the Indian Sign on another he would make passes with his arms and pronounced meaningless words. The ritual was in the manner of the hocus-pocus and abracadabra of stage magicians, and was supposed to put the other person "on the spot." **1950** *WELS Suppl.* **cwWI,** Indian sign—"to have the Indian sign on someone" is (approximately) to hex. **1953** Goodwin *It's Good* 122 **sIL,** That was the beginning of the end. Spud couldn't miss for hitting. . . "Spud sure got the Indian sign on this game." **1955** Funk *Heavens to Betsy* 107, An expression familiarly used in my boyhood—"to put (or hang) the Injun sign on someone." By that we meant, to mark a person for injury or defeat in a contest; to put a jinx on one; to wish him ill luck. **1967** *San Francisco Examiner* (CA) 3 Apr *(Tamony Coll.),* [Headline:] Dragster Tommy Ivo Still Holds Indian Sign on Rival.

Indian slipper See **Indian shoe**

Indian smoke n

1 See quot.

1973 Allen *LAUM* 1.332 **cnIA** (as of c1950), *Spider web*. . . Iowa *mare's tail* and *Indian smoke* [1 inf], and probably *dangler* as well, refer to the single strands floating in the air during the fall months. *Ibid, Indian smoke:* Inf. says they . . signal six weeks of Indian summer.

2 See quots. [Because it resembles smoke rising from a signal fire] Cf **Indian fire 2**

1965 *DARE* File **nwMA,** *Indian smoke*—a wisp of mist that appears to rise from a hillside; a common upcountry term. 1986 *Ibid* **cwMA,** *Indian smokes*—they form over brooks, small ponds, even big puddles when the sun strikes the water and the atmospheric conditions are right.

Indian smoke-pipe See **Indian pipe 1**

Indian smoker n Cf **Indian cigar**

A **catalpa B1.**

1968 *DARE* (Qu. T9, *The common shade tree with large heart-shaped leaves, clusters of white blossoms, and long thin seed pods or 'beans'*) Inf **NJ21,** Indian smoker.

Indian's nerve n

=**funny bone 1.**

1969 *DARE* (Qu. X33, *The place in the elbow that gives you a strange feeling if you hit it against something*) Inf **GA77,** Indian's nerve—old-fashioned.

Indian snipe n

=**bluestocking 2.**

1957 *AmSp* 32.182 **TX,** *Injun snipe* . . avocet.

Indian snuffbox n Cf **devil's snuffbox 1, snuffbox**

A **puffball.**

1967 *DARE* (Qu. S18, *A kind of mushroom that grows like a globe . . sometimes gets as big as a man's head*) Inf **AR52,** Indian snuffbox.

Indian soap plant n Also *Indian soap(berry)* [See quot 1960]

A **soapberry** (here: *Sapindus saponaria* var *drummondii* or *S. marginatus*).

1876 Hobbs *Bot. Hdbk.* 57, Indian soap plant, Soap berry, Sapindus marginatus. 1907 Hodge *Hdbk. Amer. Indians* 1.606, *Indian soap-plant.*—The soap-berry, or wild China-tree (*Sapindus marginatus*). 1911 *Century Dict. Suppl., Indian-soap.* . . The American soapberry, *Sapindus marginatus.* 1940 Clute *Amer. Plant Names* 271, *Sapindus drummondi* [sic]. Indian soap-berry. 1960 Vines *Trees SW* 683, *Sapindus drummondii.* . . Used for soap. . . Vernacular names are . . Wild China-tree, and Indian Soap-plant.

Indian soap root n

A **soap plant** (here: *Chlorogalum pomeridianum*).

1962 Sweet *Plants of West* 33, *Indian soap root,* or *Amole.* . . The bulb. . . was also used as a soap for washing hair or clothes. Mashed and scattered in streams, it stupefied fish.

Indian's paintbrush See **Indian paintbrush 1**

Indian's physic See **Indian physic 6**

Indian spice n

=**chaste tree.**

1960 Vines *Trees SW* 898, *Vitex agnus-castus.* . . Vernacular names are . . Wild Pepper, Indian Spice, . . Chaste Lamb-tree. . . In Brazil . . the aromatic leaves are used to spice food. 1970 Correll *Plants TX* 1340, *Indian-spice.* . . Introd. from s. Eu[rope] and Orient; very widely cult.; naturalized in various parts of s. U.S. 1979 Little *Checklist U.S. Trees* 294, Indian-spice . . is a shrub or sometimes small tree to 16 ft. . . naturalized locally.

Indian spinach n

A **povertyweed** (here: *Monolepis nuttalliana*).

1949 Curtin *By the Prophet* 70 **AZ,** *Monolepis nuttalliana.* . . Common name: Indian spinach. . . Gathered while young, . . well washed and then boiled in a little water. . . the greens are salted, then fried in lard or any other fat.

Indian's plume See **Indian plume 2**

Indian spring n [By analogy with **Indian summer**]

A period of mild or warm weather in late winter or early spring.

1947 *VT Life* Spring 7, Comes Indian spring. . . March, early April. . . warm days and winter sun, and the enterprising Vermont farmer begins to stir toward the sugar bush. [1968 *DARE* (QR, near Qu. B32) Inf **CA90,** Indian February—we just had one. [*DARE* Ed: interview conducted in March]]

Indian squash n Also *old Indian squash*

A crookneck squash (*Cucurbita moschata*).

1967–68 *DARE* (Qu. I23, . . *Kinds of squash*) Inf **OH59,** Indian squash [*DARE* Ed: Drawing in text resembles a crookneck squash.]; **WA27,** Indian squash—large, yellow; like Hubbard, with red streaks; **CT4,** Old Indian squash = Canada crookneck = today's butternut.

Indian squaw grass See **squaw grass**

Indian squill n

A **camas 1** (here: *Camassia scilloides*).

1949 Moldenke *Amer. Wild Flowers* 325, A small group of plants related to the lilies is . . the genus *Camassia.* . . Our only eastern species . . is called . . *indiansquill.*

Indian stew n Also *Indian pot*

A type of stew; see quots.

1950 *WELS* (*Different kinds of stew*) 1 Inf, **WI,** Indian stew—much like Mulligan. 1968 *DARE* (Qu. H50, *Dishes made with beans, peas, or corn that everybody around here knows, but people in other places might not*) Inf **NC55,** Indian pot—varied vegetables.

Indian strawberry n

1 A naturalized plant (*Duchesnea indica*) which produces strawberrylike fruits. Also called **mock strawberry, snakeberry, strawberry geranium, yellow strawberry**

1868 (1870) Gray *Field Botany* 124, *F[ragaria] Indica, Indian S[trawberry]* . . running wild S[outh] E[ast], rather handsome both in flower and (red) fruit, which are produced all summer and autumn. 1903 Small *Flora SE U.S.* 520, *Indian Strawberry.* . . In waste places, New York to Florida to Alabama. . . Spring to fall. 1931 Clute *Common Plants* 34, The Indian strawberry (*Duchesnea Indica*) as its specific name indicates, is really entitled to be called Indian, but in this case the name refers to India and . . was not named for the "red" Indians. 1973 Hitchcock–Cronquist *Flora Pacific NW* 210, Indian strawberry. . . Fr[uit] up to 1 cm broad, strawberrylike, but of poor flavor.

2 =**strawberry blite.**

1844 Lapham *Geogr. Descr. WI* 82, *Blitum capitatum,* . . Indian strawberry. 1876 Hobbs *Bot. Hdbk.* 57, Indian strawberry, Blitum capitatum. 1907 Hodge *Hdbk. Amer. Indians* 1.606, *Indian strawberry.*—The strawberry-blite (*Blitum capitatum*). 1959 Carleton *Index Herb. Plants* 65, *Indian strawberry:* Chenopodium capitatum; Duchesnea indica.

3 A strawberry (here: *Fragaria virginiana*).

1971 Krochmal *Appalachia Med. Plants* 122, *Fragaria virginiana.* . . *Common Names:* Virginia strawberry, Indian strawberry.

Indian sugar n

Maple sugar.

1784 in 1842 Van Schaack *Life* 360 **NY,** Little Cornelius is her favorite; she convinces him of her affection by giving him a small present, as Indian sugar, cookies, &c. 1835 Hoffman *Winter in West* (NY) 1.225 **nwIN,** Indian sugar,—as that made from the maple-tree is called at the West,—was soon placed before us. 1947 *AmSp* 22.306 **IN** (as of c1900), The term Indian sugar was also in frequent use.

Indian summer n Cf **autumn summer, Indian spring, ~ weather, ~ winter**

A period of warm or mild weather, usu in late autumn, esp when preceded by harsher weather; also fig.

c1774 in 1925 Crèvecoeur *Sketches* 41 **NY,** A severe Frost succeeds [the autumn rains] which prepares it [=the earth] to receive the voluminous coat of snow which is soon to follow; though it is often preceded by a short interval of smoke and mildness, called the Indian Summer. 1832 Kennedy *Swallow Barn* 2.92 **VA,** That foggy tint which is said . . to spread such a charm over an Indian-summer landscape. 1857 *Natl. Intelligencer* (DC) 26 Nov 2/5, The short season of pleasant weather usually occurring about the middle of November is called the Indian summer, from the custom of the Indians to avail themselves of this delightful time for harvesting their corn. **1874** in 1983 *PADS* 70.38 **ce,sePA,** [Diary entry for 24 Oct:] It is splendid weather now for that kind of work as it appears to be Indian Summer. **1881** *Harper's New Mth. Mag.* 62.273, Perhaps in the Indian summer of his life he may put his heart into a poem. **1893** Frederic *Copperhead* 91 **nNY,** No one was ever quite sure when it *was* Indian summer. **1942** *AmSp* 17.210, Each autumn there is some public curiosity and speculation over the term 'Indian Summer.'. . The first of our American forefathers, then, whoever he or quite possibly she was, that may have said ' 'Tis but an Indian kind of summer . . ,' was only following the early habit among them of characterizing by the term Indian whatever in the new world looked something like the real thing but was not. **1965–70** *DARE* (Qu. B32, *A period of warm weather late in the fall*) 872 Infs, **widespread,** Indian summer; **MO**17, **NC**3, Indian-summer weather; (Qu. HH30, *Things that are nicknamed for different nationalities*) Inf **MO**10, Indian summer. **1977** *New Yorker* 2 May 52 **AK,** 7 a.m., and the water temperature is forty-four, the air fifty-six, the sky blue and clear—an Indian-summer morning, August 18th.

Indian sunburst n

A **gaillardia B** (here: *Gaillardia pulchella*).

1946 Reeves–Bain *Flora TX* 268, *G[aillardia] pulchella.* . . Indian Sunburst. . . Ray-flowers variously colored (dark-purple, red, orange, or yellow, or any combination, mostly red below and yellow above). **1967** *DARE* Wildfl QR (Wills-Irwin) Pl.61C Inf **TX**44, Indian sunburst.

Indian tea n

Any of several plants used for making a drink similar to tea, as:

a A **holly** n[1] **1** such as *Ilex vomitoria*. Cf **Indian black drink**

1709 (1967) Lawson *New Voyage* 98, This plant [=yaupon] is the *Indian* Tea, us'd and approv'd by all the Savages on the Coast of *Carolina.* **1737** (1911) Brickell *Nat. Hist. NC* 87, The *Indian-Tea* Tree, which in their Language is called *Yaupon,* and *Cassena,* grows in great plenty in this Province. **1925** Heming *Living Forest* 131 *(DA),* That evening, while we were talking about bears, the old woodsman infused some of the Indian tea he had gathered. **1951** *PADS* 15.36 **TX,** *Ilex vomitoria.* . . Indian tea . . used by the pioneers, to whom friendly Indians showed medicinal plants. **1974** (1977) Coon *Useful Plants* 64, *Ilex vomitoria.* . . Indian tea. . . The leaves of the plant are emetic, cathartic, and seemingly both stimulant and depressant.

b A **wintergreen** (here: *Gaultheria procumbens*).

1809 Kendall *Travels* 2.143 **MA,** Where the pine only is found, the ground beneath is nearly bare, sustaining but dwarfish plants, such as the *partridge-berry,* sometimes called the *tea plant* and *Indian tea.*

c A **ceanothus** (here: *Ceanothus greggii*).

1960 Vines *Trees SW* 691, *Ceanothus greggii.* . . Also known by the name of . . Indian-tea.

d A **bearberry 2** (here: *Arctostaphylos uva-ursi*). Cf **Indian tobacco 2**

1967 *DARE* FW Addit **WA**30, Indian tea—kinikinik . . , shiny green-leafed vine. Tea is purgative!

Indian teakettle n

A **pitcher plant 1** (here: *Sarracenia purpurea*).

1901 Lounsberry *S. Wild Flowers* 207, *S[arracenia] purpurea,* pitcher-plant, side saddle flower, or Indian tea-kettle, the latter a quaint and little known name, is a common species and the one on which the genus was founded. **1940** Clute *Amer. Plant Names* 145, *S. purpurea.* . . Indian teakettles. **1959** Carleton *Index Herb. Plants* 65.

Indian tea weed n Cf **Indian tea**

=**vervain.**

1951 *PADS* 15.39 **TX,** *Verbena* spp. . . Indian tea weed.

Indian thistle n

1 Teasel *(Dipsacus fullonum).*

1894 *Jrl. Amer. Folkl.* 7.90 **WV,** *Dipsacus sylvestris* . . Indian thistle. **1940** Clute *Amer. Plant Names* 105, *Common Teasel.* . . Indian thistle.

2 A **thistle** (here: *Cirsium edule*). **CA, Pacific NW**

1925 Jepson *Manual Plants CA* 1163, *C. edule.* . . Indian Thistle. . . Creeks and gulches. **1949** Peattie *Cascades* 258 **Pacific NW,** The composite family. . . includes even the prickly leaves and purple heads of the Indian thistle. **1954** Sharpe *101 Wildflowers* 37 **nwWA,** *Indian Thistle. Cirsium edule.* . . Lost or injured hikers, short of food, have

been known to survive on this plant for days. The young tender stalks are prepared by peeling and boiling. **1961** Thomas *Flora Santa Cruz* 379 **cwCA,** Indian Thistle. Wooded areas and brush-covered slopes. San Francisco southward. **1973** Hitchcock–Cronquist *Flora Pacific NW* 505, Indian t[histle], edible t[histle]. . . *C[irsium] edule.*

Indian time n *usu derog* Cf **colored people's time, Hawaiian time, Navajo time**

A flexible system of time; a lack of punctuality; see quots.

1963 *AmSp* 38.276 **KS** [Amer Ind student slang], An important distinction in the Indian's attitude toward time: there is *Indian time* and *white man's time.* The Indian considers that the white man is a slave to time. . . the Indian does not like to feel bound in this way; this is why he is not embarrassed when he is late for an appointment by white man's standards, for he kept that appointment by *Indian time.* **1966** *Navajo Times* (Window Rock AZ) 31 Mar 9/5, Immediately upon completion of the contests, an award ceremony will be held. . . "Indian time" will not be permitted! **1979** *DARE* File **nWI,** A regional planner hired as a consultant by a Wisconsin tribe was disturbed to find that mutually agreed upon deadlines were not being met by his Indian counterparts. Nobody had warned him, he said, that they would be going by Indian time. They turned in their data when they wanted to, and not a day before. **1989** Lesley *River Song* 289 **cnOR** [Amer Ind speaker], "He's probably running on Indian time." They all chuckled. **1990** *DARE* File **cnAZ,** They arrived pretty late. Two teachers in the carpool are Navajos, and there were a couple of cracks from the whites about "Indian time." You hear "Indian time" and "Navajo time" around this area [=Flagstaff], and it's always derogatory. You don't hear, say, "Hopi time" or "Indian time" in reference to the Hopis. **1991** *Ibid* **nwNE,** I mentioned to the campus recruiter that I didn't see many Indians on campus and he said, "Well, they're here, but they're running on Indian time." That means that, say, if school starts on Monday, they'll show up between Monday and Wednesday. Or they don't show up for the first two weeks. Or they show up on Monday, a month later go back to the Rosebud or wherever for two weeks, then come back. . . You don't hear "Sioux time" or "Cheyenne time." Always "Indian time," but people mean only Sioux and Cheyenne. **1993** *WI State Jrl.* (Madison) 28 Mar sec A 11/2 **ceWI,** Years ago you'd hear a lot of slurs in town, you know about 'Indian time' and all that. You don't hear that as much now.

Indian tobacco n

1 A **lobelia B1** (here: *Lobelia inflata*). [See quot 1942] Also called **asthma weed, bladderpod 2, eyebright 4, field lobelia, gagroot, lowbelia, obelia, pukeweed, vomitwort, wild tobacco**

[**1764** in 1925 Fries *Rec. Moravians* 2.568 **NC,** Indian Tobacco has leaves much like Brown Betonia, though rougher.] **1824** Bigelow *Florula Bostoniensis* 86, *Lobelia inflata.* . . *Indian Tobacco.* . . The whole plant operates as a violent emetic. **1859** (1968) Bartlett *Americanisms* 216, *Indian tobacco. (Lobelia inflata.)* A plant whose leaves contain a poisonous, white, viscid juice, of an acrid taste. **1891** Jesup *Plants Hanover NH* 25, *L.* inflata. . . (Indian Tobacco.) Fields; very common. **1912** Blatchley *IN Weed Book* 142, In gathering Indian tobacco for sale the leaves and tops should be collected in late summer, dried in the shade and then kept in covered vessels. **1942** Hylander *Plant Life* 634, Indian Tobacco is . . found from New England to Georgia, west to Kansas. . . The Indians are supposed to have smoked and chewed the leaves. **1968** *DARE* (Qu. S26a, . . *Roadside flowers*) Inf **VT**4, Indian tobacco. **1976** Bailey–Bailey *Hortus Third* 675, *Indian tobacco.* . . The dried st[em]s and l[ea]v[e]s are . . used medicinally.

2 A **bearberry 2,** usu *Arctostaphylos uva-ursi*. [See quot 1792]

1792 Belknap *Hist. NH* 3.126, One of these is a running vine, bearing a small red berry, and a round leaf, which Josselyn . . says, the fishermen called *poke;* it is known to the hunters by the name of *Indian tobacco,* and it was used by the natives . . for smoking. **1931** [see **13** below]. **1937** U.S. Forest Serv. *Range Plant Hdbk.* B17, *Arctostaphylos patula.* . . Greenleaf manzanita, sometimes called buckhorn (or small) manzanita and Indian-tobacco, is a widely branched shrub . . with crooked, very stout limbs, and smooth, dark red bark. **1990** *Plants SW* (Catalog) 65, *Arctostaphylos uva-ursi.* . . *Indian Tobacco.* . . Brilliant red berries.

3 A **mullein** (here: *Verbascum thapsus*).

1830 Watson *Annals Philadelphia* 470, The ancient Swedes . . called the mullein plant the Indian tobacco; they tied it round their arms and feet, as a cure when they had the ague. **1940** Clute *Amer. Plant Names*

274, *Verbascum thapsus*. . . Indian tobacco. **1950** *WELS* **WI** (*Weed with furry green leaves close to the ground and a tall stalk with small yellow flowers; grows on open hillsides*) 9 Infs, Indian tobacco; 1 Inf, Indian tobacco, sometimes, although regular Indian tobacco has blue flowers. **1965–70** *DARE* (Qu. S20) 70 Infs, **scattered, but somewhat less freq Sth,** Indian tobacco. **1971** Krochmal *Appalachia Med. Plants* 264, *Verbascum thapsus*. . . *Common Names:* Common mullein, Aaron's rod, . . Indian tobacco.

4 A pussytoes, esp *Antennaria plantaginifolia*. [See quot 1892] **chiefly Nth, esp NEast**

1892 *Jrl. Amer. Folkl.* 5.89, Not infrequently the "Indian" namesake of some well-known plant may be used as at least a nominal substitute for the latter, *e.g.* Indian tobacco, *Antennaria plantaginifolia*, is chewed by children. *Ibid* 5.98 **NEast, NE,** *Antennaria plantaginifolia,* Indian tobacco. **1899** Garland *Boy Life* 123 **nwIA** (as of 1870s), All things not positively poisonous were eaten, or at least tasted. The roots of ferns, black haws, chokeberries, sheep-sorrel, Indian tobacco, clams, dewberries, May-apples—anything at all that happened to be in season or handy. **1907** [see **5** below]. **1910** Graves *Flowering Plants* 389 **CT,** *Antennaria neglecta*. . . Indian Tobacco. Common. . . The earliest flowering and most plentiful of the genus. **1929** *Torreya* 29.151 **ME,** Antennaria was "*Indian Tobacco*" or "*Pussy Toes*." **1936** Winter *Plants NE* 152, *Antennaria*. . . Cat's-Paws. Pussy-toes. Everlasting. Indian Tobacco. **1966–70** *DARE* (Qu. S20) Inf **CT**12, Indian tobacco—grows about 3 inches tall and is white; **CT**30, Indian tobacco—2 inches high, looks like everlasting flower, white flower; **CT**40, Indian tobacco—tiny plant, little gray soft head; **ME**7, Indian tobacco—6 inches high, has 3 tiny white puffs; **NV**8, Indian tobacco—white flower and smaller than a mullein; **NJ**8, Indian tobacco—only about 6 inches high, white flowers; **WV**17, Indian tobacco—small, 1 foot high, gray leaves; **WI**20, Indian tobacco—a small (3 inches) white flower in patches in the spring; stalk and leaves also white; **WI**43, Indian tobacco—a small white flower, 3–4 inches high; (Qu. S26a, . . *Roadside flowers*) Inf **MI**64, Indian tobacco—white; (Qu. S26c, *Wildflowers that grow in woods*) Inf **NJ**66, Indian tobacco—little white flower, low to ground. [*DARE* Ed: Some of these Infs may refer instead to **6** below.] **1968** Barkley *Plants KS* 350, Antennaria plantaginifolia . . var. ambigens. . . Indian Tobacco. Rocky open woods and prairies.

5 Any of several **tobaccos:** see quots. [See quot 1925]

1804 (1905) Lewis *Orig. Jrls. Lewis & Clark Exped.* 6.157, The corolla of the Indian Tobacco as prepared for the purpose of smoking. **1894** *Jrl. Amer. Folkl.* 7.95 **NY,** *Nicotiana rustica*, . . Indian tobacco. **1907** Hodge *Hdbk. Amer. Indians* 1.606, *Indian tobacco*.—(1) The wild tobacco (*Lobelia inflata*). (2) Wild tobacco (*Nicotiana rustica*). (3) The plantain-leaf everlasting (*Antennaria plantaginifolia*). (4) A New Jersey name, according to Bartlett, of the common mullein (*Verbascum thapsus*). **1914** Saunders *With Flowers in CA* 65, It [=*Nicotiana glauca*] is popularly known in California as . . Indian tobacco, and is a real tobacco, cousin to Lady Nicotine. **1925** Jepson *Manual Plants CA* 889, *N[icotiana] bigelovii*. . . *Indian Tobacco*. . . This and N. attenuata were used by the Indians as a smoking tobacco; some of the tribes certainly cultivated these plants—their only strictly agricultural practice. **1928** [see **14** below]. **1951** *PADS* 15.39 **TX,** *Nicotiana repanda*. . . Indian tobacco. **1961** Thomas *Flora Santa Cruz* 309 **cwCA,** *N. bigelovii*. . . Indian Tobacco. Occasional on the eastern slopes of the Santa Cruz Mountains. **1962** Sweet *Plants of West* 54, Indian Tobacco, *Nicotiana* sp. . . Indians gathered the whole plant when seeds were ripe but leaves still green. They dried and crumbled the leaves for smoking.

6 =pearly everlasting.

1920 *Torreya* 20.25, *Anaphalis margaritacea*. . . Indian tobacco, Traverse City, Mich. **1937** U.S. Forest Serv. *Range Plant Hdbk.* W13, Pearl everlasting, . . also called pearly everlasting, . . Indian-tobacco, . . is often confused with the related pussytoes.

7 A crownbeard (here: *Verbesina virginica*).

1933 Small *Manual SE Flora* 1443, *Verbesina virginica*. . . Frostweed. Tickweed. Indian-tobacco.

8 A wild buckwheat (here: *Eriogonum heracleoides*).

1937 U.S. Forest Serv. *Range Plant Hdbk.* W70, Wyeth eriogonum (*E. heracleoides*), also called Indian-tobacco, . . has little or no forage value. **1963** Craighead *Rocky Mt. Wildflowers* 40, *Eriogonum heracleoides*. . . Wild Buckwheat, Indian-tobacco.

9 A cudweed 1 (here: *Gnaphalium obtusifolium*).

1949 *AmSp* 24.110 **cSC,** Indian tobacco. . . Rabbit tobacco (a species of weed often rolled into home-made cigarettes, especially by boys trying to learn to smoke).

10 A **dock** n[1]. [See quot 1967]

1959 Carleton *Index Herb. Plants* 65, *Indian-tobacco*: Lobelia inflata; Rumex (v). **1967** Harrington *Edible Plants Rocky Mts.* 92, Many people in this area have used the seed as a substitute for tobacco or in a mixture with it; in fact this dock [=*Rumex crispus*] is often called "Indian tobacco." **1967–68** *DARE* (Qu. S20) Inf **CO**4, Indian tobacco—same as sour dock; **OR**1, Indian tobacco or sour dock; (QR, near Qu. S21) Inf **IA**29, Sour dock—called "Indian tobacco" when it dried—could be smoked.

11 A **yarrow** (here: *Achillea millefolium*).

1966 *DARE* Wildfl QR Pl.260B Inf **WA**15, Yarrow, Indian tobacco.

12 =Indian pipe 1.

1968 *DARE* Wildfl QR Pl.152B Inf **IA**25, Indian tobacco.

13 Any of several other plants; see quot.

1931 Clute *Common Plants* 28, One of the kinnikinniks is still known as Indian tobacco (*Lobelis* [sic] *inflata*), but plants regarded as better entitled to the name are the bearberry (*Arctostaphylos uva-ursi*), the burning bush (*Euonymus atropurpureus*), the aromatic wintergreen (*Gaultheria procumbens*), the willow (*Salix*), and several species of cornel or dog-wood, especially *Cornus amomum, C. sueccia,* and *C. stolonifera.*

14 =kinnikinnick 1.

1928 Buffalo Child *Long Lance* 241 **nMT** [Amer Ind speaker], He dispatched a runner to the Crow Chief, who was coming with his band more than one hundred miles away, with a present of Indian tobacco—*kinikinik*. . . Six days later the runner returned with a present of "Eastern Indian tobacco"—tobacco like that used by the white man today.

15 Low-quality tobacco used in trade with American Indians.

1910 Johnson *Highways Rocky Mts.* 212, Often you couldn't get any but mouldy, strong old stuff that they called Indian tobacco, because it was chiefly used in trading with the Indians for furs.

16 Home-grown and home-cured tobacco.

1950 *WELS* (*Names and nicknames for home-grown and home-cured tobacco*) 3 Infs, **WI,** Indian tobacco.

Indian toby tree See **toby tree**

‡Indian-toed adj

1968 *DARE* (Qu. X37, . . *Words . . to describe people's legs if they're noticeably bent, or uneven, or not right*) Inf **MD**29, Indian-toed—toes straight ahead; nigger-toed—toes point out.

Indian toilet paper n Cf **woodman's Charmin**

A **false hellebore 1** (here: prob *Veratrum californicum*).

1969 *DARE* (Qu. S26e, *Other wildflowers; not asked in early QRs*) Inf **CA**140, Indian toilet paper—another name for skunk cabbage; it's very pliable, has small hairs on, and that's what the Indians used them for. There's smooth-leaved skunk cabbage and this kind with hairy leaves.

Indian trumpet n

A **gilia** (here: *Linanthus androsaceus*).

1968 *DARE* FW Addit **CO**7, Indian trumpet, Gilia androsacea; **CO**7A, Fairy trumpet—gilia. . . Gilia aggregata—phlox order and family—flower white—red-flowered one called Indian trumpet—not found on prairie.

Indian turmeric n

=goldenseal 1.

1892 (1974) Millspaugh *Amer. Med. Plants* 9-1, *Hydrastis canadensis*. . . *Indian turmeric*. . . The American aborigines valued the root highly as a tonic, stomachic, and application to sore eyes and general ulcerations. **1907** Hodge *Hdbk. Amer. Indians* 1.606, *Indian turmeric*.—The yellow puccoon, or orange-root (*Hydrastis canadensis*). **1930** Sievers *Amer. Med. Plants* 31. **1974** (1977) Coon *Useful Plants* 220, Indian turmeric. . . The roots are . . used . . in reputable medical practice as an alterative and bitter tonic.

Indian turnip n

1 =jack-in-the-pulpit 1, esp *Arisaema triphyllum*. [See quot 1936]

1802 in 1938 *Castanea* 3.110 **VA,** Mrs. M. Barton related to me the case of a negro-man, who was entirely cured of a consumption of his lungs, by giving him to drink . . milk in which was boiled the root of the recent Indian turnip (Arum triphyllum). **1806** in 1852 U.S. Congress *Debates & Proc.* 9th Cong 2d Sess 1142 **sAR, nLA,** Persicaria, Indian turnip, wild carrot, wild onion, . . and bastard indigo [grow near the

Ouachita River]. **1828** Rafinesque *Med. Flora* 1.66, *Arum triphyllum. . . Vulgar Names . .* Indian Turnip [etc]. . . Root perennial, round, flattened, tuberous. [*Ibid* 67, The vulgar names are common to all the North American species, which have similar roots.] **1897** Robinson *Uncle Lisha's Outing* 32 **wVT,** A crowded cluster of scarlet berries . . marked the place where the fiery bulb of the Indian turnip was hidden. **1907** *DN* 3.214 **nwAR, cCT,** *Indian turnip. . .* Jack-in-the-pulpit. **1936** IL Nat. Hist. Surv. *Wildflowers* 40, Jack in the Pulpit. . . The 2 leaves and the inflorescence come up in May from the corm, which because of its shape is called Indian Turnip. **1942** (1960) Robertson *Red Hills* 178 **SC,** She watched the white drift of the plum trees, the dogwood and the yellow jessamine and jewelweeds and the wild Indian turnips. **1965–70** *DARE* (Qu. S1, . . *Jack-in-the-pulpit*) 113 Infs, **chiefly Midl, Gt Lakes,** Indian turnip; (Qu. S2) Infs **OK**1, **TN**22, Indian turnip; (Qu. S16) Inf **IN**14, Indian turnip; (Qu. S26e, *Other wildflowers;* not asked in early QRs) Infs **IL**135, **VA**2, Indian turnip; **SC**31, Indian turnip—hot flavor, grows in bottoms, big leaves, makes a root that's much like a turnip; (Qu. I3) Inf **PA**163, Indian turnip—grows wild here; (Qu. I35, . . *Kitchen herbs*) Inf **KY**85, Indian turnip—hot as fire; (Qu. HH30) Inf **OH**95, Indian turnip. **1986** Pederson *LAGS Concordance,* 1 inf, **cwTN,** Indian turnip—a poisonous plant.

2 A **scurf pea,** usu *Psoralea esculenta.* [See quot 1872] Cf **Indian breadroot**

   1857 Gray *Manual of Botany* 94, *P[soralea] esculenta, . .* the *Indian Turnip, . .* used as food by the aborigines,—may possibly occur on the Wisconsin side of the Mississippi. **1872** Schele de Vere *Americanisms* 399, *Bread-root* (Psoralea esculenta) is . . a beet-like plant growing abundantly in the Rocky Mountains. . . The white pulpy substance within is . . farinaceous . . and nutritious. . . It has also the name of *Indian Turnip,* having been long used by the Sioux and other tribes . .; but it must be held carefully distinct from another *Indian Turnip* (Arum triphyllum), the root of which is acrid, and, when fresh, highly poisonous. **1907** Hodge *Hdbk. Amer. Indians* 1.606, *Indian turnip.*—(1) The jack-in-the-pulpit (*Arisaema triphyllum*), also called three-leaved Indian turnip. (2) The prairie potato, or pomme blanche (*Psoralea esculenta*). **1937** U.S. Forest Serv. *Range Plant Hdbk.* W157, Indian breadroot. . . This species [=*Psoralea esculenta*]. . . is known under a variety of names as . . Indian turnip. . . Slender scurfpea (*P. tenuiflora*), a native western species, erroneously called Indian turnip, is reputedly poisonous to horses and cattle. **1951** *PADS* 15.35 **TX,** *Psoralea hypogaea. . .* Indian turnip. **1974** (1977) Coon *Useful Plants* 169, Indian turnip. . . is a low-growing perennial plant with an edible root which. . . can be boiled or roasted or dried and stored for winter use.

3 A **blazing star 3** (here: *Liatris tenuifolia*).

   1927 Boston Soc. Nat. Hist. *Proc.* 38.221 **Okefenokee GA,** *Laciniaria tenuifolia* 'Indian turnip'.

Indian up See **Indian** v

Indian valley n, also attrib

Among railroad workers: a "happy hunting ground" where jobs are abundant; paradise.

   1932 *RR Mag.* Oct 368, *Indian Valley R.R.*—An imaginary line where one could always get a good job. **1945** Hubbard *Railroad Ave.* 348, *Indian Valley Line*—An imaginary railroad "at the end of the rainbow," on which you could always find a good job and ideal working conditions. . . *Boomers* resigning or being fired would say they were going to the *Indian Valley.* The term is sometimes used to mean death or the railroader's Heaven.

Indian walking cane n

   1978 Massey *Bittersweet Country* 382 **Ozarks,** The mountain dulcimer, also known as the Indian walking cane or Jacob's coffin. . . is a long, narrow, stringed instrument, sometimes rather resembling an elongated guitar without the neck.

Indian warrior n [See quot 1954]

Any of var western **louseworts,** but usu *Pedicularis densiflora.*

   1897 Parsons *Wild Flowers CA* 336, *Pedicularis densiflora. . .* Among the children of our mountain districts this flower is known as "Indian warrior." **1915** (1926) Armstrong–Thornber *Western Wild Flowers* 502, Indian Warrior. *Pedicularis densiflora. . .* A robust and very decorative plant with rich coloring. **1937** U.S. Forest Serv. *Range Plant Hdbk.* W142, Although several species of *Pedicularis,* such as . . Indian-warrior (*P. densiflora*), have fairly well-standardized common names, . . lousewort is frequently used. *Ibid* W143, Elephant-head [=*Pedicularis groenlandica*], also called . . Indian-warrior, . . is a conspicuous plant in wet meadows and grasslands. **1954** Sharpe *101 Wildflowers* 36

nwWA, Bracted Pedicularis. . . The flowering head resembles a type of Indian headdress, giving rise to another, more common name, that of Indian warrior. **1956** St. John *Flora SE WA* 376, *Pedicularis bracteosa . .* Indian Warrior. **1968** *DARE* (Qu. S26e, *Other wildflowers;* not asked in early QRs) Inf **CA**97, Indian warrior. **1976** Bailey–Bailey *Hortus Third* 832, *Indian-warrior. . .* Winter to late spring. S. Ore. to s. Calif.

Indian weather n Cf **Indian summer**

   1966 *DARE* (Qu. B32) Inf **AL**11, Indian weather—cold, then a hot day.

Indian weed n Cf **Indian tobacco 5** =tobacco.

   1730 in 1900 MD Hist. Soc. *Fund Pub.* 39 **MD,** Reduc'd to Penury indeed,/ By feeding on this *Indian* Weed,/ And tend a stinking *Indian* Weed,/ Scotch, English, and *Hybernians* wild. **1795** (1976) Freneau *Poems* 125, [Title:] Tobbaco. [Verse:] This *Indian weed,* that once did grow / On fair *Virginia's* fertile plain. **1844** *Knickerbocker* 24.394 **NY,** The 'Experiences of a Tobacco Smoker' will suggest to the lover of the Indian weed . . some important truths. **1867** Dixon *New Amer.* 56, The red men have taught the whole world how to smoke the Indian weed. **1896** Robinson *In New Engl. Fields* 105, The Indian weed has never such perfect flavor as when . . one lights his pipe with a coal. **1907** Hodge *Hdbk. Amer. Indians* 1.606, Indian weed.—An early term for tobacco.

Indian wheat n

1 =**Indian corn 1.** *arch*

   1601 in 1841 NY Hist. Soc. *Coll.* 2d ser 1.325, The people of the country came aboard of us, making show of love, and gave us tobacco and *Indian* wheat, and departed for that night. **1746** *London Mag. & Mth. Chronologer* 15.327 **GA,** I have known them [=horses] to go six Days Journey without a Feed of Corn; having nothing but the Stalks of *Indian* Wheat, and such other Litter as they could pick up. **1825** Neal *Brother Jonathan* 1.53 **CT,** After the maize, or Indian wheat, is gathered into the barn, the farmer . . puts a good face on the matter. **1899** (1912) Green *VA Folk-Speech* 239, *Indian wheat. . .* Corn; maize. **1907** Hodge *Hdbk. Amer. Indians* 1.605.

2 A **mule-ear 2** (here: *Wyethia mollis*).

   1897 Parsons *Wild Flowers CA* 157, *W[yethia] mollis, . .* "Indian wheat," is very abundant in the Sierras. . . The common name, "Indian wheat," has been bestowed upon it not because it in the least resembles wheat, but because the Indians gather the seed in great quantities and grind it into a flour.

3 A **plantain** such as *Plantago purshii.*

   1910 AZ Ag. Exp. Sta. *Bulletin* 264, The native plantains known widely as Indian wheat, rank next in importance. **1936** McDougall–Baggley *Plants of Yellowstone* 114, Indianwheat (*Plantago purshii*). **1948** Stevens *KS Wild Flowers* 148, *Plantago purshii. Woolly Indianwheat. . .* On account of its palatable nutritious spikes it has forage value for sheep, especially in the Southwest, when other forage is scant. **1949** Curtin *By the Prophet* 96 **AZ,** *Plantago fastigata. . .* Common name: Indianwheat. . . These annual herbs. . . bear a great quantity of mucilaginous, shiny brown seeds resembling the imported psyllium. **1974** Angier *Field Guide Edible Plants* 168, *Plantain. . . Other names . .* Indian Wheat. **1985** Dodge *Flowers SW Deserts* 34, The smaller winter annuals known as Indianwheat carpet . . [the] desert floor . . producing a straw-colored "pile" of tiny blossom spikes.

4 See quot. Cf **ant rice**

   1924 Austin *Land of Journeys' Ending* 132 **AZ,** After the first rains, around these clearings, spring up downy carpets of inch-high "Indian wheat," like hoar-frost, whose full-seeded heads are harvested by the ants the moment they are matured.

5 also *India wheat:* Tartarian buckwheat (*Fagopyrum tataricum*). [*Indian* < India]

   1839 Holmes *Rept. Aroostook R.* 60 **ME,** The variety called Indian wheat in Kennebec, but more commonly in this region, 'Rough Buckwheat,' is very extensively cultivated . . on the Aroostook. **1891** Jesup *Plants Hanover NH* 35, *F[agopyrum] Tataricum. . .* India Wheat. Asiatic. **1895** Gray–Bailey *Field Botany* 372, *F[agopyrum] tataricum, . .* Tartary or Indian wheat. Cult[ivated] for flour. **1943** Fernald–Kinsey *Edible Wild Plants E. N. Amer.* 167, The Buckwheat itself, *Fagopyrum esculentum,* and the India-Wheat, *F. tataricum,* are extensively cultivated in northern states and Canada, and occasionally persist about old fields and rubbish-heaps. **1959** *VT Hist.* 27.144, *Injy wheat. . .* Indian wheat, similar to buckwheat, except that its blossom is yellow instead of white. . . The flour is darker than that of buckwheat. Before western grains were bought, Vermont farmers raised the wheat for chicken feed.

Indian wicopy n Also *Indian wickape, ~ wickup* [**wicopy**]

1 A **leatherwood 1** (here: *Dirca palustris*).

   1832 Williamson *Hist. ME* 1.112, *Leatherwood* or *Indian Wickape* is a small tree which grows on the best hardwood land and none other. . . Even when dry, it is sufficiently limber and flexible to be used in lieu of twine or cords. Millers often lay by them a stock of its bark, for bag-strings, in supply of their customers; and the Indians used it for their cordage. **1898** *Bot. Gaz.* 26.253 **West**, *Dirca palustris,* . . Indian wickape.

2 A **willow herb,** usu *Epilobium angustifolium*.

   1876 Hobbs *Bot. Hdbk.* 129, Wicopy Indian, Epilobium spicatum and other spec. **1907** Hodge *Hdbk. Amer. Indians* 1.607, *Indian wickup.*— The great willow-herb or fireweed (Epilobium augifolium [sic]), although Algonquian Indians called the basswood *(Tilia americana)* wickup. **1974** (1977) Coon *Useful Plants* 196, *Epilobium angustifolium* . . Indian wicopy. . . The pith of stems is good in soups. . . Further, cotton from the seed pods makes an excellent tinder for campfires.

Indian winter n [By analogy with **Indian summer**] Cf **squaw winter**

A period of unseasonably cold weather.

   1931 *AmSp* 6.466 **wNE**, *Indian Summer* has long been an American name for the period of warm, pleasant weather which sometimes comes in the fall after a cold, disagreeable period. An analogous term, *Indian Winter,* is used in Nebraska to name a belated spell of winter coming in the late spring. **1966** *DARE* (Qu. B31, *A period of cold weather that comes early in the fall, after the first frost;* total Infs questioned, 75) Inf **GA**1, Indian winter.

India-rubber ice See **rubber ice**

India wheat See **Indian wheat 5**

indicator n [See quot 1952]

A grape fern *(Botrychium virginianum)*.

   1900 Lyons *Plant Names* 67 **VA**, *B[otrychium] Virginianum.* . . Indicator. **1952** Strausbaugh–Core *Flora WV* 10, *B. virginianum.* . . In Jackson County it has been called "Indicator," its growth thought to indicate the presence of Ginseng.

indigesting n [Var of *indigestion*] Cf Intro "Language Changes" II.12, **-ing B1**

See quots.

   1942 in 1944 *ADD* **sePA** [PaGer], *Indigestion.* . . [ɪndɑɪdʃɛsdɪŋ] [sic]. **1953** Randolph–Wilson *Down in Holler* 26, A physician at Pineville, Missouri, told me that he had often heard indigestion pronounced *indigesting* by his up-the-creek patients.

indigo n

1 Std: a dye-yielding plant of the genus *Indigofera*. Also called **indigo weed 1**

2 often with qualifying adj: Any of var plants which resemble **indigo 1** or produce a similar dye, as:

a =**wild indigo.**

   1828 Rafinesque *Med. Flora* 1.79, *Baptisia tinctoria.* . . *Vulgar Names* . . Yellow Indigo. **1900** Lyons *Plant Names* 57, *B[aptisia] australis.* . . Blue . . Indigo. . . *B. tinctoria.* . . Yellow or American Indigo. **1938** Matschat *Suwannee R.* 291 **neFL, seGA**, Indigo: *Indigo tinctoria.* **1949** Moldenke *Amer. Wild Flowers* 135, The *prairie-indigo* . . inhabits riverbanks, woods, pinelands, and prairies. . . The *pineland-indigo* . . makes a conspicuous display in the spring of the year. **1972** Brown *Wildflowers LA* 74, White Indigo. *Baptisia leucantha.* . . Entire plant turns black with maturity or drying. . . Nodding Indigo. *Baptisia leucophaea. Ibid* 75, Nuttall Indigo. *Baptisia nuttaliana.* . . Fruit a thick-walled, spherical pod, opening tardily.

b Any of var **false indigos 1;** see quots.

   1931 U.S. Dept. Ag. *Misc. Pub.* 101.83, *A[morpha] nana* . . *,* or dwarf-indigo, seldom over 1 foot high, is a smooth and nearly hairless species, with mostly solitary spikes of fragrant flowers. **1933** Small *Manual SE Flora* 689, *A[morpha] glabra.* . . Mountain-indigo. *Ibid* 690, *A. virgata.* . . Mountain-indigo. **1938** Van Dersal *Native Woody Plants* 51, *Amorpha glabra.* . . Mountain-indigo. . . *Amorpha schwerinii.* Schwerin-indigo. . . *Amorpha tennesseensis.* Tennessee-indigo. **1960** Vines *Trees SW* 519, Mountain-indigo Amorpha. *Amorpha glabra.*

c A **rattlebox** (here: *Sesbania drummondii* or *S. exaltata*).

   1920 *Torreya* 20.22 **LA**, *Daubentonia longifolia.* . . Seenie bean, Indigo, [in] Cameron Parish. **1942** *Ibid* 42.161 **LA**, *Sesban macrocarpa.* . . Indigo, acacie. **1966–68** *DARE* (Qu. S20) Inf **GA**7, Coffee weed—indigo; (Qu. S21, . . *Weeds* . . *that are a trouble in gardens and fields*) Inf **AL**38, Indigos.

d A **joint vetch** (here: *Aeschynomene virginica*).

   1920 *Torreya* 20.22 **GA**, *Aeschynomene virginica.* . . Indigo, [in] Savannah. **1935** (1943) Muenscher *Weeds* 52, *Some common weeds of rice fields.* . . Æschynomene virginica—Curly indigo.

3 See **indigo snake.**

indigo (blue)bird See **indigo bunting**

indigo broom n [See quot 1828]

A **wild indigo** (here: *Baptisia tinctoria*).

   1828 Rafinesque *Med. Flora* 1.79, *Baptisia tinctoria.* . . Indigo-broom. [*Ibid* 80, This plant has the appearance of a small shrub and broom.] **1876** Hobbs *Bot. Hdbk.* 57, Indigo broom, Wild indigo plant, Baptisia tinctoria. **1901** Lounsberry *S. Wild Flowers* 266, *B. tinctoria,* . . indigo broom, . . is again known by its very small three-foliate glabrous leaves, and its bright yellow flowers. **1940** Clute *Amer. Plant Names* 253, *Baptisia tinctoria.* . . Indigo broom. **1974** (1977) Coon *Useful Plants* 165, Indigo broom. . . has been used in the cure of ulcers.

indigo brush n

A **ceanothus** (here: *Ceanothus foliosus*).

   1961 Thomas *Flora Santa Cruz* 235 **cwCA**, *C[eanothus] foliosus.* . . Indigo Brush. . . Known from Loma Prieta and Mount Madonna. April-May.

indigo bunting n Also *indigo (blue)bird, ~ finch, ~ painted bunting*

A small finch *(Passerina cyanea),* the male of which is colored indigo blue in spring and summer. Also called **blue pop 1, green bird, little indigo, painted bunting, ~ finch 1, summer bluebird**

   1783 Latham *Gen. Synopsis Birds* II.205 *(DA),* Indigo B[unting]. . . It is common at New York. **1785** Pennant *Arctic Zool.* 2.365, Inhabits (according to *Catesby)* the interior parts of *Carolina.* . . It is found as low as *Mexico* where the *Spaniards* call it *Azul Lexos,* or the far-fetched bird: and the *Americans* call it the *Indigo* bird. **1828** Bonaparte *Amer. Ornith.* 2.91, Female Indigo Finch. *Fringilla Cyanea.* **1871** Lowell *Study Windows* 18 **MA**, Till within a fortnight, a pair of indigo-birds would keep up their lively *duo* for an hour together. **1917** (1923) *Birds Amer.* 3.71, *Indigo bunting. Passerina cyanea.* . . *Other Names.*—Indigo Bluebird; Indigo Painted Bunting; Indigo Bird; Indigo Finch. **1966–69** *DARE* (Qu. Q11) Inf **PA**104, Indigo bird—size of a robin, beautiful blue; (Qu. Q14) Infs **MI**2, 53, Indigo bunting; **IL**32, Indigo finch; (QR, near Qu. Q23) Inf **GA**18, Other South Georgia birds. . . Indigo bunting.

indigo bush n

1 also *indigo shrub:* =**false indigo 1,** esp *Amorpha fruticosa.* [See quots 1860, 1931]

   1860 Curtis *Cat. Plants NC* 104, Indigo Bush. (Amorpha fruticosa . .) . . . It is said to have been used for the manufacture of Indigo, but, I imagine, with not much profit. **1924** Deam *Shrubs IN* 155, *Amorpha fruticosa.* . . Indigobush. **1931** U.S. Dept. Ag. *Misc. Pub.* 101.82, *Indigobushes (Amorpha* spp.) About 15 species of this genus . . have been described . . , of which at least half occur in the Western States. *Ibid* 83, The generic type is the indigobush (*A. fruticosa*). . . It is said that the early settlers used this shrub as a substitute for true indigo. **1935** Rollins *Disc. Ore. Trail* 225 *(DA),* [A] title for this same stream . . given because the birdwood or indigo shrub, *Amorpha fruticosa,* was common along its banks. **1981** Benson–Darrow *Trees SW Deserts* 266, *Indigo Bush.* . . Shrubs; stems *not* prickly, spiny, or thorny; plant aromatic.

2 A plant of either the genus *Dalea* or the genus *Psorothamnus.* [See quots 1914, 1971] **Desert SW** For other names of var spp see **desert beauty, peabush, smokethorn;** for other names of var spp of *Dalea* see **feather peabush, goatweed, prairie clover, sheepweed, Texas heather, woods clover;** for other names of var spp of *Psorothamnus* see **ghost tree, mangle n[1] 2b, smoke tree** Note: *Psorothamnus* was formerly included in *Dalea*.

   1897 Sudworth *Arborescent Flora* 257 **CA**, *Dalea spinosa.* . . Indigo Bush. **1914** Saunders *With Flowers in CA* 75, *Dalea spinosa.* . . Indigo bush is another name I have heard for it, but you have to be here in mid-June to understand why. Then . . the whole tree bursts into glorious bloom—an almost solid mass of small pea-blossoms of the richest indigo blue. **1941** Jaeger *Wildflowers* 107 **Desert SW,** *Indigo-bush. Parosela Schottii. . . Fl[owers]:* deep indigo blue. . . A most handsome plant in flower. **1947** *So. Sierran* May 4/2 *(DA)* **sCA,** We were thrilled by the fine display of Indigo Bush. **1971** Dodge *100 Desert Wildflowers* 36, In common with other daleas . . it [=*Dalea fremontii*] is usually called "indigobush." . . There are many species of dalea in the desert, all characterized by deep blue to indigo and rose-violet flowers. **1981** Benson–Darrow *Trees SW Deserts* 262, *Dalea fremontii . . var. Saundersii. . . Indigo Bush. . .* Slopes and plains . . in the Mojave Desert.

indigo finch, indigo painted bunting See **indigo bunting**

indigo shrub See **indigo bush 1**

indigo snake n Also *indigo* [From its color] Cf **blue darter 3**
A large, usu blue-black snake *(Drymarchon corais)* native to the southern US. Also called **blue bullsnake, ~ gopher snake, ~ snake 2, chicken snake 4, gopher ~ 2, rat ~**
1853 Baird–Girard *N. Amer. Reptiles* 1.165, Indigo Snake *(Georg[ia] Coup[eri])*. **1885** Kingsley *Std. Nat. Hist.* 3.367, *S[piloles] Couperi* inhabiting the Gulf States and Georgia. . . is of a deep black, shading into yellow on the throat. It is known by the negroes as the indigo or gopher-snake. **1937** Pope *Snakes Alive* 132, It is hard to imagine a more gorgeous sight than an indigo snake with its five or six feet of glossy black scales. **1948** *Atlantic Mth.* Feb 87 **cKY,** The others—the hognosed viper, the indigo or gopher snake, the ringneck, the assorted grass and water snakes—we never got around to naming. **1966–70** DARE (Qu. P25, . . *Kinds of snakes*) Infs **FL**4, 34, **TX**11, Indigo (snakes); **FL**27, Indigo or black snake; **TN**65, Indigo snake—makes a nice pet. **1970** GA Dept. Ag. *Farmers Market Bulletin* 16 Dec 8/2 **cnFL,** Eradication of rattle snakes is simple. Get a pair of indigo snakes, good big ones about 5 feet long. Put them out in the spring and within two years—no more rattle snakes. **1979** Behler–King *Audubon Field Guide Reptiles* 603, Not a constrictor, the Indigo immobilizes food with its jaws. . . Habitat destruction, commercial collecting, and the practice of gassing tortoise burrows—the Indigo's favorite retreat—have drastically reduced its numbers.

indigo squill n
A **camas 1** (here: *Camassia scilloides*).
1933 Small *Manual SE Flora* 292, *Q[uamasia] hyacinthina. . . Indigo-squill. . .* Plants often become very abundant in abandoned fields and in fence-rows where the mass-effect of the delicate sky-blue flowers is exceedingly attractive. **1976** Bailey–Bailey *Hortus Third* 208, *Indigo squill. . . Fl[ower]s* regular, white, blue, or blue-violet.

indigo weed n
1 =**indigo 1.** *obs*
1784 in 1785 *Amer. Acad. Arts & Sci. Memoirs* 1.473 **sePA,** *Indigofera. . . Indigoweed. . .* A durable pale blue may be obtained from the leaves and small branches. Fomentations of the plant, it is said, will abate the swelling, and counteract the poison in the bite of rattle-snakes. **1789** Morse *Amer. Geog.* 429 **SC,** The soil. . . produces moderately good indigo weed.
2 A **wild indigo,** usu *Baptisia tinctoria.*
1828 Rafinesque *Med. Flora* 1.79, *Baptisia tinctoria. . .* Indigo Weed. [*Ibid* 80, It dyes a kind of blue like Indigo; but greatly inferior. . . It is often used to keep off the flies from horses, as these insects appear to avoid it.] **1852** MI State Ag. Soc. *Trans. for 1851* 3.197, My timber is generally oak, with some hickory, indigo weed[,] tea weed. **1892** (1974) Millspaugh *Amer. Med. Plants* 52-1, *Indigo Weed. . .* is indigenous to the Canadas and the United States. **1959** Carleton *Index Herb. Plants* 65, *Indigo-weed; Baptisia australis.* **1971** Krochmal *Appalachia Med. Plants* 72, Indigo weed. . . has value as a febrifuge, tonic, purgative, and antiseptic.
3 =**Colorado River hemp.**
1935 (1943) Muenscher *Weeds* 51, Some common weeds of rice fields. . . Sesbania macrocarpa [=*S. exaltata*]—Indigo weed.

indi-i-over n, exclam Also *inti-inti-i-over* [Varr of **anti-i-over**]
1966 DARE (Qu. EE22, . . *The game in which they throw a ball over a building . . to a player on the other side*) Inf **MI**34, I don't know what it's called, but we always said "inti-inti-i-over"; **SD**2, Indi-i-over; (Qu. EE23a, . . *What . . you call out when you throw the ball?*) Inf **SD**2, Indi-i-over; [**MI**14, I-over—I guess; I'm not sure].

Indin(e) See **Indian** n

inding See **inning**

Indjon See **Indian** n

indurance See **enduring** prep

industrious adj Pronc-spp *industris, industrous* Cf Intro "Language Changes" I.9
Std sense, var forms.
1861 Holmes *Venner* 1.163 **NEng,** She's an industris young woman,— yis, she *is* industris,—but perhaps she a'n't quite so spry a worker as some. **1899** (1912) Green *VA Folk-Speech* 239, *Industrous. . .* Marked by industry; done with or characterized by diligence. **1981** Pederson *LAGS Basic Materials,* 1 inf, **cnGA,** [ɪn'dʌˌstrɪˤs]; 1 inf, **cnAL,** [ɪn'dʌˤstrəs].

in earnest adj phr, adv phr Cf **earnest B, for keeps**
Of marble games: played with the understanding that marbles taken will be kept; on condition that marbles taken will be kept.
1877 Bartlett *Americanisms* 197, Boys call it playing marbles *in earnest,* when it is understood that the winners shall keep the marbles. **1883** Newell *Games & Songs* 186, The game, when played to win the marbles of the opponent, is said to be "in earnest." **1899** Champlin–Bostwick *Young Folks' Games* 484, The marbles he strikes out of the ring become his property if the game is "for keeps," or "in earnest," but are given back to their former owners at the close, if the game is "for fun." **1955** PADS 23.20 **cwTN,** *In earnest. . .* A game is said to be *in earnest* when the players keep the marbles they knock from the ring.

inegitable See **illegitimate**

infair See **infare**

in family way See **family way, in a**

infant baby n Also *infant child* **Sth** Cf **apron child**
A very young baby.
c1938 in 1970 Hyatt *Hoodoo* 1.416 **MD** [Black], You take a little *infant baby* wit you, cuz if you don't, you gon'a have trouble. *Ibid* **VA** [Black], I've also heard that spirits do not appear in a house where there is an infant baby. **1966** DARE Tape **NC**25, She had a baby, a infant baby, and then a baby that was just walkin' around. **1986** Pederson *LAGS Concordance,* 1 inf, **csGA,** Infant childrens [inf Black].

infantigo, infantigus See **impetigo**

infant's breath n
1 =**moneywort 1.**
1897 *Jrl. Amer. Folkl.* 10.49, *Lysimachia mummularia* [sic], . . infant's breath, Oxford Co., Me.
2 See **baby's breath 2b.**

infare n Also sp *infair;* for addit varr see quots [Scots, Ir, nEngl dial; cf *EDD, SND*]
1 A reception or celebration for a newly married couple, esp one given at the home of the groom's parents on the day following the wedding; hence n *infare wedding* a wedding that includes such a party. **chiefly Sth, S Midl** *old-fash* Cf **home-bringen**
[**1744** (1899) MacSparran *Letter Book* 18 **RI** [Scots writer], Dr. Hazard and Betty Gardiner went to . . Billy Hazard's weding. . . They are both gone again . . to the Infair.] **1794** in 1843 *Amer. Pioneer* 2.223, An infair was given to-day by Mason, to a fellow named Kuykendall, who had . . run off with Mason's daughter . . a few weeks ago. **1818** in 1824 Knight *Letters* 92 **KY,** On the day after the wedding, at the bridegroom's father's hall, is usually a sumptuous festival, called an *inn-fare.* **1848** in 1956 Eliason *Tarheel Talk* 278 **NC,** One of her daughters was married some days ago. . . and this was reception day—or what in old times [was called] the infair. **1870** *Nation* 28 July 56 **sePA,** There still exist in that region . . many words and idioms taken from Scotland to Ireland, and brought from Ireland here. . . "Infare," accented on the first syllable, was the term for the home-bringing of a bride and the wedding-reception. **1890** DN 1.70 **nLA, KY,** Infare. **1895** DN 1.383 **NJ,** Infare. **1903** DN 2.318 **seMO,** Infare. **1906** DN 3.142 **nwAR,** Infare dinner. . . A dinner given by the bridegroom's father in honor of a couple the day after their wedding. . . Now rare. **1908** DN 3.323 **eAL, wGA,** Infare. **1915** DN 4.184 **swVA,** Infare. **1921** DN 5.120 **sOH,** Infare. **1926** DN 5.400 **Ozarks,** Infare. . . Sometimes pronounced *enfare* or *onfare.* **1927** DN 5.469 **Appalachians,** Infare. **1927** AmSp 2.358 **cwWV,** Infare . . a celebration on the night of a wedding. **1932** Randolph *Ozark Mt. Folks*

65, Such dances are usually given in connection with weddings, en-fares, house-raisings, hog-killings, wood-choppings and similar gather-ings. **1941** *LANE* Map 409 **csME,** ['ɪn,fæᶜə], a party at the couple's house immediately after the wedding. **1942** Thomas *Blue Ridge Country* 151 **sAppalachians,** The infare wedding lasted all of three days and nights. **1944** *PADS* 2.27 **cwNC, cwOH,** *Infare.* **1946** *AmSp* 21.97 **sIL,** *Infare* . . is rarely used now. **1950** *PADS* 14.40 **SC,** *Infare.* . . Obsoles-cent. **1953** *AmSp* 28.249 **csPA,** *Infare.* . . The word has almost com-pletely disappeared although it is recognized by the elderly. **1955** Ritchie *Singing Family* 62 **seKY,** The old custom is to stay the first night at *her* father's house, have a party and the wedding breakfast and so on, then to go the next day to *his* father's house, for the infare. **1958** *PADS* 29.12 **TN,** *Infare.* . . used by elderly people. **1967–70** *DARE* (Qu. AA18, . . *A noisy neighborhood celebration after a wedding*) Inf **LA8,** Infare ['ɪn,fæə]—it's connected with the wedding; they eat at the infare, eat and drink; poor people have infares, rich people don't; **NC55,** Infare ['ɪn,fɛɚ]; **OH78,** Infare is a reception given by the groom's family to welcome the bride; **SC40,** End-fair [sic]—Negro word; feed, dance, etc; **SC46,** Infare ['ɪnfɚ]—go to the groom's home day after wedding, a feast; not done now; bride and groom present; **TN2,** Infare—old-fash-ioned; an open house for friends after wedding; forerunner of modern reception; **TN43,** Infare ['ɪnfæɚ]—a Scottish word; **TX95,** Infare ['ɛnfæɚ]. **1986** Pederson *LAGS Concordance,* 9 infs, **esp cAL, wMS,** Infare; 1 inf, **neTX,** Infare dinner; 1 inf, **cMS,** Infare dress—worn the day after the wedding.
2 By ext: Any kind of party or celebration.
1893 Shands *MS Speech* 39, *Infair.* . . Used by the illiterate whites of South Mississippi to mean a party or dance somewhat more elaborate than a *shindig.* **1945** Saxon *Gumbo Ya-Ya* 572 **LA,** '*Infares.*' Soirée, or small party. **1947** Ballowe *The Lawd* 133 **LA,** You are a heroine. You saved the crop. As soon as we get the brasses back in place there'll be an infare in the sugarhouse to celebrate what you did.

infare days n pl [**infare 1**] **S Midl**
A honeymoon.
1926 *DN* 5.400 **Ozarks,** *Infare days.* . . The period immediately sub-sequent to marriage, the honeymoon. "Hit aint right ner fittin' fer a woman t' grub sprouts endurin' of her infare days." **1954** *Harder Coll.* **cwTN,** *Infare day* [sic]. . . Honeymoon. **1983** *MJLF* 9.1.45 **ceKY** (as of 1956), *Infare days* . . the honeymoon. [Inf old]

infare wedding See **infare 1**

infatigus See **impetigo**

infested ppl adj [Cf *OED infest* v.² 1.b "sometimes confused with *infect.* . . *Obs.*"]
Infected.
1967–68 *DARE* (Qu. BB29, . . *The red flesh that sometimes grows in a wound and keeps it from healing right*) Inf **NY40,** Infested [flesh]—same as an infection; (Qu. BB36, *When there's an open sore and this yellowish stuff is coming out of it*) Infs **NV2, NY40,** Infested; (Qu. BB37, *When yellowish stuff comes out of a person's ear*) Inf **OR13,** Infested ear.

infirmary n
A poorhouse or **poor farm.**
1931–33 *LANE Worksheets* **cMA,** Infirmary—what used to be called a town farm or home farm. **1935** Horwill *Mod. Amer. Usage* 7 **OH,** Although *almshouse* is the legal name in New Eng. and is fairly con-sistently found in the East and South, in Ohio it is *infirmary,* in Indiana *asylum,* and in the Middle West *poor house, poor farm, county farm,* or *county house.*

in fix See **fix** n 2

in flew endways n Also *hen flew endways* [Joc varr of *influenza*] old-fash
1942 McAtee *Dial. Grant Co. IN* 36 (as of 1890s), *In-flew-endways* . . jocular rendering of influenza. **c1960** Wilson *Coll.* **csKY,** *In* (or *hen*) *flew endways.* . . Humorous name for influenza, esp. in its outbreaks before 1917–18; since then it has been flu.

in flower See **flower** n B2

influenza n Usu |ɪnflu'ɛnzə|; for addit varr see quots Pronc-sp *influansy*
Std sense, var forms.
1851 in 1956 Eliason *Tarheel Talk* 313 **cnNC,** Influansy. **1967–70** *DARE* (Qu. BB49) Inf **LA8,** [,ɪnflu'rɛnzə]; **NY250** [ɪn,flu'ɪnzə]. [Both

Infs Black] **1981** Pederson *LAGS Basic Materials,* 1 inf, **cwMS,** [hĩ^ᵊn,flʉʉ'rɪˀnzɨ] [inf Black]; 1 inf, **cTX,** [,ĩˀnflɜ̆ˀɪˀ·nzə̆].

‡influenza sparrow n
=A **goldfinch 1** (here: *Carduelis tristis*).
1966 *DARE* (Qu. Q14, . . *Names* . . *for* . . *goldfinch*) Inf **MS66,** Influenza sparrow.

infoxicated adj [Joc var of *intoxicated,* infl by **fox** v 1] Cf **foxy 1**
1962 *Mt. Life* 38.4.11 **sAppalachians,** The man who has drunk enough to glow, sing, and laugh freely but whose tongue might become twisted on a word now and then is "foxy." . . If he continues to drink but responds to his condition with humor and gaiety, he might finally become "infoxicated," however.

in free exclam Cf **home free**
In **hide-and-seek A:** =**all (in) free.**
1895 *DN* 1.397 **NY,** *In free:* same as *home free.* **1951** *PADS* 15.54 **neIN** (as of 1890s), *Free* . . or *in free.* . . A cry in games, the result of which was already decided, by an individual who desired to surrender without penalty, so as to shorten that particular phase of the play. **1967–70** *DARE* (Qu. EE15, *When he has caught the first of those that were hiding what does the player who is 'it' call out to the others?*) 11 Infs, **Nth, Midl,** In free. **1977–78** Foster *Lexical Variation* 79 **NJ,** Home free all (32 responses), *home free* (18), *in free* (4).

in front of prep phr
With ref to time: before.
1943 in 1944 *ADD* 235, [Radio announcer:] It is now . . 27 minutes in front of 7. **1950** *Milwaukee Talk,* And what is so bad, it should happen right in front of my vacation. **1979** *DARE* File **Madison WI,** [Radio announcer:] It's now ten minutes in front of the hour.

in full See **full** adj B1

-ing suff Pronc-spp *-en, -in, -(u)n*
A Forms.
c1820 in 1941 *AmSp* 16.157 **NYC,** Walk'n—walking. Fight'n—fighting. **1867** Lowell *Biglow* 25 '**Upcountry' MA,** Cairin' cotton-bales. . . financierin'. . . cornfiscatin' all debts [etc]. **1890** *DN* 1.33 **ME,** I was early trained to avoid various vulgarisms, such as pronouncing *-in* for *-ing.* **1891** *DN* 1.75 **cNY,** [ŋ]. . . in the formative ending *-ing* . . has regularly become [n]. **1894** Riley *Armazindy* 19 **IN,** Without no . . / . . giggle-un and winkin',/ Ner sizin' how each-other's dressed. **1895** *DN* 1.375 **seKY, eTN, wNC,** Present participles are in [n], instead of [ŋ], as in other dialects. *Ibid* 383 **NJ,** Hull. . . "He went a-hullen all over the country." **1941** Skidmore *Hawk's Nest* 50 **WV,** Kind of warm to be traipsen, ain't it. **1942** Hall *Smoky Mt. Speech* 83 **wNC, eTN,** *-ing.* . . varies [ən], [ɪn], [ɪn], [n̩], depending in most cases on the preceding sound; [ɪŋ] may be heard . . from educated speakers, but, on the whole, it is very rare, even among them. . . After vowels, the sound is usually [ən], as in *doing* ['duən]. . . After all consonants, except the dentals and *l,* [ə] is generally used. . . After *l,* [ɪ] or [ɨ] is more frequent than [ə], as in *cracklings* ['kræklɪnz]. . . After [t], [d], [s], [z], syllabic *n* is almost universal. **1942** McAtee *Dial. Grant Co. IN* 7 (as of 1890s), All "ing's" were rendered "in." **1953** Randolph–Wilson *Down in Holler* 25 **Ozarks,** The Ozarker says *sleepin'*—never *sleep'n', sleepen,* or *sleepun.* **1973** Gawthrop *Dial. Calumet* 105 **nwIN,** One judge felt it [=the narrator's pronunciation] was unusual for the Region, citing the informant's . . consistent use of [ŋ] for the *-ing* ending rather than the frequent Calumet [n]. **1975** Allen *LAUM* 2.44 **Upper MW** (as of c1950), *-ing.* . . The influence of the written form has contributed to its preference in the schools, a choice reflected in its greater frequency among cultured speakers in the eastern and North Central states and in its fifty-fifty status among . . speakers [with a high school education or its equivalent] in eastern New York, southeastern Pennsylvania, and southern New Eng-land. Elsewhere [ɪn] is the majority form for all except the cultured speakers. . . In the U[pper] M[idwest] as a whole slightly more than one-half of the infs. have [ɪŋ] but more than three-fourths have [ɪn], with a consequent overlap of the 31% of the total recorded number who use one form or the other at different times.
B Applications.
1 Used as a hypercorrect form of |-ən, -ɪn|; see quots. **chiefly Sth, S Midl** Cf Intro "Language Changes" II.12, **indigesting**
1636 in 1881 Boston Registry Dept. *Records* 2.12, The upper poast of his garding gap. **1800** in 1956 Eliason *Tarheel Talk* 314 **NC,** Mittings [=mittens]. **1837** *Ibid* 308 **NC,** Chickings. **1861** Holmes *Venner* 1.60

NEng, The foot of a mountain,—called by the working-folks of the place "*the* Maounting." **1871** Eggleston *Hoosier Schoolmaster* 103 **sIN,** "The mud isn't so deep at the East. When I was to Bosting—" but Ralph never heard what happened when she was to Bosting. **1895** *DN* 1.375 **seKY, eTN, wNC,** *Mounting* (mountain). **1903** *DN* 2.321 **seMO,** *Mountain.* . . Pronounced mounting. This pronunciation applies to quite a number of words ending in 'ain.' . . As 'founting,' 'certingly,' etc. **1917** Torrence *Granny Maumee* 69 **swOH** [Black], I'm goin' tek de burding . . off'n you. **1953** Randolph–Wilson *Down in Holler* 26 **Ozarks,** I once knew a jimson-weed preacher in Benton County, Arkansas, who always shouted *brethering* when he meant brethren and pronounced heaven as if it were spelled *heving.* . . *capting* for captain. . . Chicken is sometimes pronounced *chicking.* An old friend . . always said *muzzling* when he meant muslin. The word certain is generally *sartin* in the backwoods, but I have heard an Arkansas legislator . . pronounce it *sarting.* A stately lady near Cotter, Arkansas, spoke at length about the *herrings* [=herons] she had seen on White River.

2 Added redundantly to vbl nouns or progressive forms of verbs. Cf Intro "Language Changes" II.5, **-ed** suff **1**

  1928 Peterkin *Scarlet Sister Mary* 180 **SC** [Gullah], I didn' know you'd feel so bad about my gwinen [=*gwine* going + *-ing*]. **1929** *WV Review* Oct 30, An extra *in* has been given to some words: *loading,* or the contraction *loadin',* has been *loadinin,* and likewise *fiddling* has been *fiddlinin,* and *fishing, fishinin.* **1935** *AmSp* 8.1.25 **WV, KY,** A number of words ending in "ing" are given a double "in." *Riding* is *ridinin, hunting, huntinin, working, workinin,* and so on.

ingan See **onion** n

ingen n[1] See **Indian** n

ingen n[2] See **onion** n

in generally adv phr For pronc-spp see quots [*OED* (at *generally* 5) "*Obs.*"] **chiefly Sth, S Midl**
In general; usually.
  1851 (1969) Burke *Polly Peablossom* 68 **MS,** The wimmin folks an' my gal Sally is always, in generally, the skeerdest in the world uv 'em. **1886** *Century Illustr. Mag.* 31.430 **GA,** "In giner'lly," said Grandsir Hightower, "I hate for to make remarks 'bout folks." **1908** *DN* 3.323 **eAL, wGA,** *Ingenerly.* . . Generally: originally *in general.* "I most ingenerly plant my cotton when I see the first dog-wood blooms." Also *inginerly.* **1960** Bailey *Resp. to PADS 20* **KS,** Generally, in generally, most times. **1968–70** *DARE* (Qu. KK40, . . *'Usually':* "They come twice a month, _____.") Infs **MS88, TN34,** In generally; **IN45,** Most in generally. [All Infs old]

Inger See **India**

ingern See **onion** n

Ingia See **India**

Ingin n[1] See **Indian** n

ingin n[2] See **onion** n

ingine See **engine**

ingineer See **engineer**

Inglish hay See **English hay**

ingon See **onion** n

in good fashion See **good fashion**

in good fix See **fix** n **2**

in good order See **order** n **2**

ingrateful adj [*OED* "*Obs.*"]
Ungrateful.
  1694 in 1860 CT Hist. Soc. *Coll.* 1.115, It was an old Saying: *Say I am Ingrateful and say any thing.* **1828** Webster *Amer. Dict., Ingrateful.* . . Ungrateful; unthankful. **1916** *DN* 4.295 **sAppalachians,** *In, im,* and *un* are often used interchangeably. . . *in*grateful.

ingun See **onion** n

ingyne See **engine**

ingyon See **onion** n

in head of See **in the head of**

inia n **HI** [Appar var of *India*]
=Chinaberry 1.

  1929 Neal *Honolulu Gardens* 175, *Inia* . . *Melia azedarach.* . . has become naturalized. . . in many wild parts of Hawaii, because mynah birds use in building nests stems bearing seeds. **1940** Von Tempski *Paradise* 20 **HI** (as of 1900–25), I could see them seating themselves on the grass, under the spreading beauty of an *Inia* tree. . . The tree known elsewhere in the world as "Pride of India" is simply called "Inia" in Hawaii.

inimona See **inamona**

inion See **onion** n

initials on it, get one's v phr
In marble play: see quot 1955.
  1934 *AmSp* 9.75 **ND,** *Get your initials on it.* Expression used when one nearly gets a marble out; used as a good luck omen and supposed to help the one *with his initials on it* to secure the marble eventually. **1955** *PADS* 23.19 **cwTN,** *Get one's initials on it.* . . To strike the target [marble] without knocking it out of the boundary line of the ring.

initiation n Also *initiating (party)* **esp Sth**
A celebration for newlyweds; see quots; hence v *initiate* to provide such a celebration for.
  1965 *PADS* 43.22 **seMA,** A noisy celebration on a newly married couple: [1 inf] shivaree, initiation. **1966–69** *DARE* (Qu. AA18, . . *A noisy neighborhood celebration after a wedding, where the married couple is expected to give a treat*) Inf **GA28,** Initiate 'em, reception; **GA77,** Initiating party—a couple of months after the wedding, for the friends—old-fashioned; **MS16,** Initiating. **1986** Pederson *LAGS Concordance (Noisy, burlesque serenade after a wedding)* 1 inf, **seAL,** Initiate them—serenade, play pranks; 1 inf, **cGA,** (I)nitiate them at a wedding; 1 inf, **swAL,** (I)nitiate them—carry on a pole or in a barrel. [All infs old]

Injeanny, Injianny See **Indiana 1**

in jig('s) time See **jig** n[1] **2**

Injin See **Indian** n

injin(e) See **engine**

in jolly foot See **foot** n C5k

Injun(n) See **Indian** n

Injy See **India**

ink n Usu |ɪŋk|; also *esp Sth, S Midl* |iŋk, ɛŋk|; for addit varr see quots Pronc-sp *ank* Cf Pronc Intro 3.I.6.d
A Forms.
  1934 *AmSp* 9.210 **Sth,** A great many words having standard [ɪ] before [g], [n], [ŋ] . . change [ɪ] to [i]. . . *Big, blink,* . . *ink.* **1941** *AmSp* 16.4 **eTX** [Black], *Blink, drink, ink,* . . [blēŋk], [blēĩŋk], etc. **1942** Hall *Smoky Mt. Speech* 16 **eTN, wNC,** [ɛ^] or [ɛ] often occurs in *drink, finger,* . . *ink.* **1949** *PADS* 11.7 **wTX,** *Ink* [iŋk]. . . Common pronunciation. **c1960** *Wilson Coll.* **csKY,** Ink is usually |iŋk|. **1967–70** *DARE* (Qu. JJ10a) Inf **LA8,** Ink [ɛŋk] pencils; **VA72,** Ink [iŋk] pencil. **1976** Garber *Mountain-ese* 3 **sAppalachians,** *Ank-pen* . . ink pen.
B Sense.
Also *ink spot, inky dink(y):* A Black person, esp one with very dark skin. *sometimes derog*
  1915 *DN* 4.227 **wTX,** *Ink.* . . A negro. "We've got a new ink for a cook." **1942** *Amer. Mercury* 55.223.95 **Harlem NYC** [Black], *Inky dink*—very black person. **1955** *The Ink Spots: America's Greatest Vocal Quartet* (Phonodisc). [*DARE* Ed: Black vocal group] **1966** Dakin *Dial. Vocab. Ohio R. Valley* 2.449, Other miscellaneous terms, all clearly derogatory in intent . . *burr head, wooly ~, kinky ~* (Ky.); and *ink spot* (O[hio]). **1970** Major *Dict. Afro-Amer. Slang* 69, *Inky-dinky:* (loosely used) a negative connotation, sometimes refers to a very dark Afro-American who happens also to be untidy.

ink-ball oak n [From the use of the galls in making ink]
=scarlet oak.
  1822 Eaton *Botany* 419, [*Quercus*] *coccinea.* . . Ink-ball oak. . . Produces brownish-purple nut-galls. [**1888** *Century Illustr. Mag.* 36.765 **Sth,** The distillation of a vegetable product known as "ink balls," usurped the place of ink.]

inkberry n
1 Any of var **hollies** n[1] **1** or their berries, but usu *Ilex glabra* which is also called **Appalachian tea 1, bear bush, dye**

leaves 2, **gall** n[1], **gallberry, gallbush 1, gall ring berry, mammybush, snakeberry, winterberry**

1765 (1942) Bartram *Diary of a Journey* 11 Oct **nFL,** Little & poor grass[,] mixed with dwarf mirtle[,] . . ink berries[,] & chinkapin. **1858** Warder *Hedges* 275, The *Prinos glaber,* or Winter-Berry, is a handsome shrub, growing three or four feet high, and bearing black berries, called ink-berries. **1901** Mohr *Plant Life AL* 604, *Ilex coriacea. . . Tall Inkberry. . .* Fruit . . shining black. . . *Ilex glabra. . . Inkberry.* **1908** Britton *N. Amer. Trees* 621, *Ilex verticillata. . .* Also called Inkberry. **1960** Vines *Trees SW* 652, *Ilex glabra. . .* The vernacular names are Gallberry, because of the bitter taste, and Inkberry which refers to the black fruit. **1968** McPhee *Pine Barrens* 46 **NJ,** In December, . . shiploads of holly, laurel, mistletoe, ground pine, greenbriar, inkberry, plume grass, and boughs of pitch pine were sent to New York for sale as Christmas decorations. **1968** *DARE* (Qu. I44, *What kinds of berries grow wild around here?*) Inf **PA**100, Inkberry. **1974** Morton *Folk Remedies* 77 **SC,** *Inkberry. . . Ilex glabra. . .* Dried leaves have been commonly used as a substitute for tea in the past.

2 also *inkberry bush,* ~ *weed, inkbush*: A **pokeweed** (here: *Phytolacca americana*).

[**1888** *Century Illustr. Mag.* 36.765 **Sth,** The juice of poke-berries, compounded with vinegar, . . usurped the place of ink.] **1889** *Century Dict.* 3103, *Inkberry-weed. . .* The pokeweed, *Phytolacca decandra.* **1897** *Jrl. Amer. Folkl.* 10.54 **Long Is. NY,** *Phytolacca decandra. . .* Ink bush, ink-berry bush. **1910** Graves *Flowering Plants* 171 **CT,** Ink Berry. . . The berries are sometimes employed to color vinegar. **1936** IL Nat. Hist. Surv. *Wildflowers* 80, *Phytolacca americana. . .* This species . . is variously called Pokeweed, . . and Inkberry. . . The inedible fruits are dark purple, very juicy berries. **1974** Morton *Folk Remedies* 109 **SC,** *Ink berry. . . Phytolacca americana. . .* Juice of berries has been commonly used to color foods and wine.

3 A plant of the genus *Randia.* [*DJE* 1864 →]

1889 *Century Dict.* 3103, *Inkberry. . .* The plant *Randia aculeata.* **1900** Lyons *Plant Names* 315, *R[andia] aculeata. . .* Ink-berry. *Fruit* yields a blue dye.

4 =**bearberry honeysuckle.** [See quot 1937]

1931 U.S. Dept. Ag. *Misc. Pub.* 101.146, *Bearberry honeysuckle . . ,* known also as . . inkberry, . . is a freely branching, large-leaved shrub, about 3 to 6 feet high. **1937** U.S. Forest Serv. *Range Plant Hdbk.* B95, Bearberry honeysuckle. . . The glossy, dark, almost black fruits, with their unpleasant taste, give rise to the common names of inkberry and skunkberry. **1960** Vines *Trees SW* 955, *Lonicera involucrata. . .* is also known under the vernacular names of Twinberry, . . Pigeonberry, and Inkberry.

5 =**rouge plant.**

1937 Stemen–Myers *OK Flora* 128, *Rivina humilis. . . Ink-berry.* Shrubby herb. . . Berries subglobose, mostly red.

6 =**beachberry.**

1982 *Naples Now* May 36 **sFL,** Walking along stretches of beach, one might notice the *inkberry* or *beach berry,* a succulent plant that can reach four feet. It has sprawling stems that spread under the sand to form extensive colonies.

inkberry bush, inkberry weed See **inkberry 2**

inkbottle n

=**butter-and-eggs 1.**

1967 *DARE* (Qu. S11, . . *Other names . . for . . wild snapdragon*) Inf **IL**25, Inkbottles.

inkbush See **inkberry 2**

ink cap See **inky cap**

inkle n

1 See quot. [*EDD inkle* sb.[2] 3 "A notion, hint, suspicion, 'inkling.' "]

1953 Randolph–Wilson *Down in Holler* 256 **Ozarks,** *Inkle. . .* A hint, a tip, a bit of secret information. A woman once told me, "I got a inkle that gal of mine is fixin' to run off with Tommy Sturgis."

2 A small amount; hence adj *inkling* paltry, measly.

1954 *Harder Coll.* **cwTN,** Inkle—a small amount. **1969** *DARE* (Qu. LL2, . . *Too small to be worth much: "I don't want that little _____ potato."*) Inf **KY**53, Inkling.

inkle v

See quot 1944.

1939 in 1944 *ADD* **WV,** I'm going over to the party & inkle in. **1944** *ADD, Inkle.* . . To attend (a party, &c.) without invitation.

inkling n [Engl, Scots dial; cf *EDD inklin(g* sb.1]

A desire, inclination.

1978 Dance *Shuckin' & Jivin'* 218, These white guys . . got this Black guy . . and they just started to shooting around his feet. . . So when they got through he said . . "You use *all* your bullets?" They say, "Yeah." He pulled out that *blade;* he say, "You ever kiss a mule?" The white guys say, "Naw, but I always had a inklin'." **1991** *NADS Letters,* My family in N.W. S.C. used that term [=*inkling*] as 'urge, desire' as in 'I've got an inkling to go, since it's my birthday.' *Ibid* **wPA,** The commander had recommended her though she hadn't the slightest inkling to do it at first. *Ibid,* I have, ever since childhood heard and used *inkling* . . [meaning 'A desire to do something']. I . . hail originally from WI (Wausau . .) but have lived in all points west (Seattle, Portland, SF, LA) Nevada, Arizona, NM & TX. I recall quite vividly that *inkling* = 'desire to do s.t.' was/is used on some of those locales.

inkling adj See **inkle** n 2

‡**inkpot** n Cf **inkbottle**

1966 *DARE* (Qu. S26e, *Other wildflowers not yet mentioned;* not asked in early QRs) Inf **WA**15, Inkpot—poison.

inkroot n [See quot 1830]

A **sea lavender** (here: *Limonium carolinianum*).

1830 Rafinesque *Med. Flora* 2.93, *Statice caroliniana. . .* Inkroot. [*Ibid* 94, The root is the officinal part; it is . . equal to Galls, since an equal quantity of both makes ink equally black.] **1869** Porcher *Resources* 479 **Sth,** Ink Root. . . The root is employed in infusion, decoction, or tincture. **1901** Lounsberry *S. Wild Flowers* 411, Ink Root. . . grows in salt marshes along the coast. **1910** Graves *Flowering Plants* 314 **CT,** *Limonium carolinianum. . .* Ink-root. . . The root has long been used in medicine. **1974** Morton *Folk Remedies* 89 **SC,** Ink Root. . . Some people merely chew the raw root to halt diarrhea.

inkslinger n [By ext from *inkslinger* a writer] **Nth** Cf **alphabet slinger**

Among loggers: a camp clerk or timekeeper; see quots.

1913 *DN* 4.3 **ME, Gt Lakes,** *Pencil-pusher.* . . A clerk in a lumber camp. Also called *ink slinger.* **1925** *AmSp* 1.136 **Pacific NW,** The "ink-slinger" . . keeps the camp's records and conducts the commisary [sic]. **1941** *AmSp* 16.233 **MT** [Logger talk], *Inkslinger.* Any office worker but usually the timekeeper. **1958** McCulloch *Woods Words* 95 **Pacific NW,** *Inkslinger*—The camp timekeeper. **1964** Hargreaves–Foehl *Story of Logging* 59 **MI,** [Glossary:] *Ink slinger*—The clerk who kept time and production records in the logging camp. He sometimes doubled as a scaler. **1966** *DARE* Tape **MI**10, In the office [of the lumber camp] the clerk was nicknamed a inkslinger.

ink spot See **ink B**

inkweed n

1 =**pickleweed.**

1938 Van Dersal *Native Woody Plants* 45, *Allenrolfea occidentalis. . .* Inkweed. . . A small to large, succulent, almost leafless shrub.

2 A **sea blite**, usu *Suaeda torreyana.* [See quot 1941]

1941 Jaeger *Wildflowers* 48 **Desert SW,** Inkweed. . . *Suaeda Torreyana ramosissima.* . . The name "inkweed" was given because a poor sort of black ink can be made from the herbage. **1985** Dodge *Flowers SW Deserts* 14, Inkweed. . . *Suaeda suffrutescens. . . Suaeda torreyana. . .* Coahuila Indians extracted from the plants a black dye which they used in artwork.

3 A drymary (here: *Drymaria pachyphylla*).

1964 Kingsbury *Poisonous Plants U.S.* 247, *Drymaria pachyphylla. . .* Inkweed, drymary. . . A purplish juice may be squeezed from the immature capsules (hence the common name, inkweed). . . Western Texas, southern New Mexico to southeast Arizona. **1968** Schmutz et al. *Livestock-Poisoning Plants AZ* 137, Inkweed. . . This prostrate, annual forb is highly toxic.

inkwood n

1 A small tree *(Exothea paniculata)* native to southern Florida. [See quot 1961] **FL** Also called **ironwood c(1)**

1884 Sargent *Forests of N. Amer.* 45, *Hypelate paniculata. . . Ink Wood. . .* Wood very heavy, exceedingly hard, very strong . . ; color, bright reddish-brown. **1897** Sudworth *Arborescent Flora* 296 **FL,** *Exothea paniculata. . . Common names.* Inkwood. **1908** Britton *N.*

Amer. Trees 666, Inkwood. . . is used in boat-building, for dock-piles, and for tool-handles. **1946** West–Arnold *Native Trees FL* 133, *Inkwood*. . . is found along the East Coast. . . The fruits are quite conspicuous. . . becoming juicy and dark purple in the fall. **1961** Douglas *My Wilderness* 148 **Everglades FL,** The inkwood tree, whose berries were used to make a dye, serves a unique role. Its wood is so hard, it can be used for bearings. **1971** Craighead *Trees S. FL* 201.

2 =white ironwood.

   1962 Harrar–Harrar *Guide S. Trees* 490, *Inkwood. Hypelate trifoliata*. . . A shrub or small tree, occasionally 30′ to 40′ in height and 12″ to 18″ in diameter. . . Florida Keys and West Indies.

inky cap n Also *ink cap, inky, inky(-cap) mushroom* [See quot 1981] Cf **desert inky cap**

A fungus of the genus *Coprinus.* Also called **black-top mushroom.** For other names of var spp see **mica cap, shaggy-mane**

   [**1908** Hard *Mushroom Edible* 333, *Coprinus atramentarius.* . . The Inky Coprinus.] **1911** *Century Dict. Suppl.,* Ink-cap. . . A mushroom of the genus *Coprinus.* **1943** Fernald–Kinsey *Edible Wild Plants E. N. Amer.* 382, Ink-cap, Inky Mushroom, *Coprinus atramentarius. Ibid* 385, The *Ink-cap* is one of the most familiar of mushrooms. . . *Early Inky Mushroom . . Coprinus micaceus.* . . is highly appreciated by lovers of mushrooms. . . The baked Inkys are delicious. **1949** Palmer *Nat. Hist.* 66, *Inky-cap Mushroom.* . . If cooked immediately after harvesting, it is excellent or can be made into a catsup that is delicious. **1966–68** *DARE* (Qu. S18, *A kind of mushroom*) Inf **MI**120, Inkies—umbrella with blue underneath cap; (Qu. I37, *Small plants shaped like an umbrella that grow in woods and fields—which are safe to eat*) Inf **NY**48, Inky caps—nickname [for] mushrooms; (Qu. S26e) Inf **WA**15, Inky caps. **1974** (1977) Coon *Useful Plants* 274, *Coprinus micaceus*—Inky mushroom, . . ink-cap. . . There is another species again commonly known as the inkcap, (*C. stramentarius* [sic]) which will be found on old manure heaps, on rubbish, or rich fields. **1981** Lincoff *Audubon Field Guide Mushrooms* 596, *Coprinus* is the genus of the inky caps; all but a few have gills that liquefy, or deliquesce, on maturing, dissolving the cap into a black inky fluid.

inky-dink(y) See **ink B**

inky egg n
=**shaggymane.**
   1980 Marteka *Mushrooms* 180, *Shaggy-Mane.* . . *Common Names* . . inky egg. . . *Cap:* 2 to 4 inches long; like narrow egg at first. . . *Gills:* . . white, tinged with pink before becoming black with spores and melting with deliquescence.

inky mushroom See **inky cap**

inland alewife n Cf **alewife**

A **skipjack** (here: *Alosa chrysochloris*).
   1884 Goode *Fisheries U.S.* 1.594 **FL,** The Inland Alewife or Skipjack . . which is found in many parts of the Mississippi Valley, has recently been found . . in the salt water off Pensacola—a surprising circumstance, since the species was thought to be an inhabitant of fresh water exclusively.

in mind See **in reason**

inmortal n [Span] **Desert SW**

A **spider milkweed** (here: *Asclepias asperula*).
   1947 Curtin *Healing Herbs* 36 **NM,** Ground seeds [of anise] may be mixed with the grated room [sic] of *inmortal,* strained and drunk with hot water for pneumonia. *Ibid* 265, Inmortal. *Asclepiodora decumbens* [=*Asclepias asperula*]. **1987** Bowers *100 Roadside Wildflowers* 5, In parts of New Mexico, antelope horns is known as *inmortal* and is used for congested lungs and to ease childbirth. **1988** Schoenhals *Span.-Engl. Gloss.* 62, *Inmortal.* . . The term is applied especially to spider milkweed. White flowers and thin leaves; many medicinal uses.

innards See **inwards**

innding See **inning**

inner-rested See **interest**

inners n pl¹ See **inwards**

inners n pl² Also *one-inner, two-inner*
   1967 *DARE* (Qu. EE11, *Bat-and-ball games for just a few players [when there aren't enough for a regular game]*) Inf **TX**10, Inners—one base; **TX**5, One-inner—one base, two-inner—two bases.

innfare See **infare**

inning n Pronc-spp *ending, in(n)ding* Cf Intro "Language Changes" I.8

Std sense, var forms.
   1946 *PADS* 6.18 **eNC** (as of 1900–10), *Innding. . . Inning,* in baseball. Heard among ball players. **1954** *Harder Coll.* **cwTN,** *Inding.* . . Inning. *Ibid, Ending* . . inning.

innit See **isn't it**

innocence n

1 also *innocents:* =**bluet 2.** chiefly **NEng**
   1821 Barton *Flora* 1.119, Fairy-flax. Bluett. Innocence. Venus' Pride. **1838** *Boston Weekly Mag.* 22 Sept 17, I must not omit a passing notice of that most exquisite little flower, known by the name of "Venus' Pride" and "Innocence", and called by botanists the *Houstonia Coerulea.* **1893** *Outing* 22.286 **swNH, nMA,** We see a little brook of clear water . . with a tangle of blackberry vines, and a small patch of "innocents" growing beside it. **1907** *DN* 3.245 **eME,** Innocence. . . Houstonia caerulea. **1941** Percy *Lanterns* 97 **nwMS,** We call our bluets "innocence," for that's what they are. **1954** Forbes *Rainbow* 86 **MA** (as of early 19th cent), One green pasture maybe sprinkled with innocence. **1966–70** *DARE* (Qu. S11, . . *Other names . . for . .* bluets) Infs **MA**5, 6, 42, 67, 68, 78, **TN**11, Innocence. [All Infs old] **1967** Borland *Hill Country* 120 **nwCT,** In the meadow that sloped down to the bog were a few patches of bluets . . which some call Quaker Ladies and some call Innocence.

2 =**blue-eyed Mary 1,** esp *Collinsia heterophylla* and *C. verna.*
   1861 Wood *Class-Book* 521, *Collinsia.* . . Innocence. **1897** Parsons *Wild Flowers CA* 294, *Innocence. Collinsia.* . . They vary much in color, from the typical rose-purple and white or lilac to all white. **1900** Lyons *Plant Names* 111, *C[ollinsia] verna.* . . New York to Wisconsin and Indian Territory. Blue-eyed Mary. Innocence. **1934** Haskin *Wild Flowers Pacific Coast* 321, *Collinsia grandiflora.* . . The name blue lips it shares with other species of *Collinsia,* as also that of innocence. **1949** Moldenke *Amer. Wild Flowers* 276, *Collinsia verna.* . . Its common names—*innocence* and *blue-eyed-mary*—somehow, fit it perfectly. **1961** Thomas *Flora Santa Cruz* 309 **cwCA,** *C[ollinsia] heterophylla.* . . Innocence, Purple-and-white Chinese Houses.

innocents See **innocence 1**

in one's See **in** prep **B5**

in pocket See **pocket**

inquirement See **-ment**

in reason adv phr Also *in mind* **sAppalachians**

As a reasonable assumption; with certainty—usu in phr *know in reason.*
   1887 (1967) Harris *Free Joe* 125 **nGA,** I know in reason they must be somep'n 'nother wrong when a great big grown man kin work hisself up to holdin' spite. **1891** Harris *Balaam* 142 **nGA,** He did not really see the negro clearly, but knew "in reason" that it must be Ananias. **1901** Harben *Westerfelt* 293 **nGA,** I know in reason 'at you won't close yore eyes till—till we see some way out of the difficulty. **1913** Kephart *Highlanders* 297 **sAppalachians,** I knowed in reason she'd have the mullygrubs over them doin's. **1931** *PMLA* 46.1305 **sAppalachians,** I know in reason he's right about it. **1939** *Hall Coll.* **wNC,** I know in reason the house was built by Uncle Tom Bradley. **1952** Brown *NC Folkl.* 1.556 **c,eNC,** *Know in mind.* . . To be certain or relatively certain. "I didn't see him take that gun, but I know in mind he did." *Ibid, Know in reason.* . . Same as *know in mind.* **c1960** *Wilson Coll.* **csKY,** *Know in reason:* Be certain about. **1974** Fink *Mountain Speech* 13 **wNC, eTN,** *In reason* . . beyond doubt. "I knowed in reason he'd go." **1976** Garber *Mountain-ese* 46 **sAppalachians,** I know, in reason, that the cow is already with calf.

in room of See **room**

ins and withs n Also *ins and outs*

A bat-and-ball game; see quots.
   1957 *Sat. Eve. Post Letters* **sePA** (as of 1930s), We used to play "ins and withs" when I was a boy in . . a suburb of Philadelphia. I was very much surprised to find later that this name is unknown in the other places I have lived (Long Island, northern New Jersey, and Los Angeles). . . It is baseball, when there aren't enough players for two teams. The first player to holler "In!" is "in" and bats first. The first to holler "With!"

is "with," and tries to drive the other home if he gets on base. The positions of catcher, pitcher, first base, second base, third base, and outfielders, if any, are also filled by hollering, and advance to "with" in that order as the in or with are put out. **1968** *DARE* (Qu. EE11, *Bat-and-ball games for just a few players [when there aren't enough for a regular game]*) Inf **WI**50, Ins and outs.

insane adj Usu |ɪn'sen|; also |'ɪnse(ɪ)n| Cf Intro "Language Changes" IV.2

Std sense, var form.

1928 *AmSp* 3.407 **Ozarks,** The hillman usually places a strong emphasis upon the first syllable of . . *insane.* **1940** in 1944 *ADD* **nWV,** *In*sane asylum. **c1960** *Wilson Coll.* **csKY,** Recessive accent . . insane. **1965–70** *DARE* (Qu. HH6) Infs **AL**25, **CT**37, **IN**61, **KY**53, **MI**116, **NY**70, 234, **SC**32, **TX**36, ['ɪnse(ɪ)n]. **1981** Pederson *LAGS Basic Materials* **cAR, cwLA, cwMS,** [3 infs use proncs of the type ['ɪn,seɪn].]

insect n Cf *DS* Z12

1952 Brown *NC Folkl.* 1.554, *Insect.* . . A crawling baby.—Hatteras Island. Reported.

insho(r)ance See **insurance**

inshore adv, adj Cf **off-island**

From the perspective of an offshore island: to or on the mainland.

1968 *Courier-Gaz.* (Rockland ME) 19 Mar **Monhegan Is. ME,** Mr. and Mrs. Vernon Burton were inshore for two days. . . His Dad took him inshore Sunday. . . He went inshore. . . Doug Odom has returned from a trip inshore.

inshow(a)nce See **insurance**

inside n **AK** Cf **inside** adv **2, outside** n **1**

Alaska, esp the interior part of the state.

1902 London *Daughter of Snows* 21 **AK,** And then you went away, over the Pass, to the Inside, and we never heard a word of you. [**1904** Lynch *3 Yrs. Klondike* 76, One might have been a prince or a peasant in the 'inside'; here in the 'inside' we were all equal.] **1916** Smith *Under N. Lights* 6 **AK,** *Inside*—Refers always to the northern country with the exception of the coast towns. **1934** *Anchorage Daily Times* (AK) 24 Feb 2/1, The ocean lines serve well the traveler for his comfort in covering the 2,000 miles between Seattle and all points north of the Panhandle. Hence travelers between the outside and the inside stick to the ocean lines as much as possible. **1944** Williamson *Far North* 209 **AK,** When an Alaskan says Inside, he is referring to residence or sojourn within the country, while Outside is either the States or some other place beyond the confines of Alaska. A strange distinction; it conveys the abruptness of a door, separating completely the life within and the life without.

inside adv Cf **down below**

1 To a more populated area; see quots.

1877 (1878) Hinton *Hdbk. AZ* 168, A genuine Arizona pioneer always speaks of going "inside" if he is about to visit California. **1967** *DARE* Tape **CA**4, [FW:] When I was out in the Mohave Desert . . people would talk about coming to San Bernardino . . They had an expression for going there. . . They would say they're going inside. [Inf:] Inside usually means to a city. That's the expression. **1967** *DARE* FW Addit **sCA,** When people of the Mohave Desert east of San Bernardino go to San Bern[ardino] or L[os] A[ngeles] or, so it seems, anywhere west to southwest of the San Bern[ardino] Mountains, they are going "down below" or, less frequently, "inside."

2 To or in Alaska, esp the sparsely settled interior. **AK** Cf **in** adv **C, inside** n, **outside** adv

1905 McLain *Alaska* 8, Those who are going to the interior of Alaska are "going inside" and those who leave the country are going "outside." **1909** Rickard *Through Yukon & AK* 281, On the coast there is trouble making hay. . . 'Inside,' within the vast interior of the country, the light precipitation may necessitate the aid of irrigation. **1922** *Anchorage Daily Times* (AK) 4 Dec 6, No notice or information had been given to the boys inside about the new trail. **1923** *Ibid* 5 Jan 8 (Tabbert *Dict. Alaskan Engl.*), [Headline:] Operator Goes Inside. Tom Aitken and Mrs. Aitken departed on yesterday's train for the Interior. **1939** Franck *Lure of AK* 32, A mere boy from Brooklyn . . who came "inside" a year ago and has been driving a taxicab in Fairbanks ever since, can get a resident license. **1958** *Anchorage Daily Times* (AK) 28 Aug 8, The impact of statehood has been more obvious and spectacular Outside than it has been Inside.

3 See quot 1966; hence adj *inside.*

1966 *DARE* Tape **SC**18, [Inf:] State laws prohibit the taking of shrimp in creeks. The only place they can shrimp is in the ocean proper. . . Shrimping is getting to be a big-time industry. There used to be small boats here before they cracked down on inside shrimping. [FW:] What do you mean, "inside shrimping"? [Inf:] Not in the ocean, in the creeks—inside, as opposed to outside, in the ocean. **1968** *Times-Picayune* (New Orleans LA) 7 Mar 11/1, There was some fishing activity both offshore and inside; but entries were few in the log.

4 See quot. [*EDD inside* adv. "in an inner room, in the next room"]

1972 *NYT Article Letters* **NY,** The other expression is the use of "inside" to mean a room other than the one you're in. Ex: "I'm going to take this inside", which means, if you are in the kitchen, that you are going to take it into the livingroom; but if you are in the livingroom, it means you are going to take it into the kitchen.

inside adj See **inside** adv **3**

inside horse n

=**near horse.**

1956 Ker *Vocab. W. TX* 218, Horse on left side in plowing or hauling. . . *inside horse* [2 of 67 infs].

inside-out flower n [See quot 1934]

A plant of the genus *Vancouveria* native to the Pacific coast. For other names of var spp see **redwood ivy.**

1901 Jepson *Flora CA* 204, *V[ancouveria] chrysantha* . . var. *parviflora. Inside-out Flower.* . . Coast Ranges, in the shade of forests. **1934** Haskin *Wild Flowers Pacific Coast* 121, *Inside-out Flower. Vancouveria hexandra.* . . The petals and sepals are turned abruptly backward until the flower is truly inside out. **1949** Moldenke *Amer. Wild Flowers* 21, The only other genus . . in our area is *Vancouveria,* with . . species known as *insideoutflowers.* **1961** Thomas *Flora Santa Cruz* 172 **cwCA,** *V[ancouveria] planipetala.* . . Inside-out Flower. . . Usually growing in redwood forests. **1973** Hitchcock–Cronquist *Flora Pacific NW* 143.

inso interrog exclam |,ɪn'so| Pronc-sp *enso* [Contr of *isn't it so*] **WI** Cf *ain't so* (at **ain't** v²)

=**ainna.**

1949 *WELS Suppl.* **seWI,** "Inso" . . is commonly used in Sheboygan, . . but many people from other communities are unfamiliar with it. **1950** *WELS* (*Words and expressions meaning "Don't you agree?":* "*She's a nice-looking woman, _____?*") 1 Inf, **ceWI,** Enso—common. **1974** *WI Trails* 15 **seWI,** And English teachers shake their heads at "Ja" and "inso?" (the latter meaning "isn't it?"—a classier version of the "aina?" of Milwaukeeans). **1986** *DARE* File **seWI,** A woman in her eighties who has lived her entire life in Watertown, Wisconsin, said to her neighbor, "You're going to the church supper Saturday, inso?" After some discussion, the neighbor added, "I saw the new pastor yesterday, inso?" The term is in common use. **1990** *Ibid* **ceWI,** Basically, the meaning of *inso* [,ɪn'so] is "It's true, isn't it?" or, "Say that it's so." It's often heard in arguments among children when they try to get someone to back their opinion or confirm some fact. For example, "He hit me, inso! He hit me, inso!" means "Didn't he, didn't he?" Sometimes one will hear *inso* repeated, as in, "He hit me!" "No, I didn't!" "Inso! Inso!" **1994** *Ibid* **ceWI,** There is a tag-question in east central Wisconsin. . . The tag is . . [ɛnso]. **1995** *Ibid* **ceWI** (as of 1930s), When I was growing up in Manitowoc, everybody used to say [ɪn'so] after a question, meaning 'Don't you agree?' As far as I know, people there still say it.

in someone See **in** prep **B6**

inspector n Cf **camp inspector**

Esp among loggers: an itinerant worker or hobo.

[**1896** Farmer–Henley *Slang* 4.12, *Inspector of pavements.* . . (common).—A man out of work.] **1942** Berrey–Van den Bark *Amer. Slang* 456.5, *Migratory laborer.* . . inspector (one who goes from job to job, seemingly only to see what it is like). **1944** Nute *Lake Superior* 210 **MI, MN, WI,** The camps had "inspectors," too. This was the lumberjack's name for hoboes. **1958** McCulloch *Woods Words* 95 **Pacific NW,** *Inspector.* . . A nosey guy. . . A logger who stays in camp just long enough to take one look. **1969** Sorden *Lumberjack Lingo* 61 **NEng, Gt Lakes,** *Inspectors*—Hobos.

instant n [*OED instant* sb. 5 "*Obs.*"; perh back-formation from *instance* understood as *instants*] Cf **incidence**

An instance.

1966 *Gilchrist Co. Jrl.* (Trenton FL) 31 Mar 4/6, He reported fer instant, we had just finished up one $57 million Boondoggle operation. **1967** *DARE* Tape **MA6**, I just remember that one thing, for instant, but there were other places; they didn't care.

instead adv Usu |ɪn'stɛd, ən-|; also **chiefly Sth, S Midl, NEast** |ɪn'stɪd| Pronc-spp *insteed, (in)stid, sted;* in phr *instead of: steada,* also **chiefly Sth, S Midl** *esp freq among Black speakers, stedder, stidder;* for addit pronc and sp varr see quots
Std senses, var forms.

   1829 in 1956 Eliason *Tarheel Talk* 313 **NC**, Insteed. **1857** *Ibid*, In stid. **1867** Lowell *Biglow* xxvii 'Upcountry' **MA**, While the New-Englander cannot be brought to say *instead* for *instid* (commonly *'stid* where not the last word in a sentence), he changes the *i* to *e* in *red* for *rid*. **1871** Eggleston *Hoosier Schoolmaster* 39 **sIN**, A poar Yankee schoolmaster, that said 'pail' instid of bucket. **1871** (1892) Johnston *Dukesborough Tales* 71 **GA**, Instid of her, you may give it . . to *me*. **1884** *Anglia* 7.255 **Sth, S Midl** [Black], Stidder (stead of), instidder (instead of). **1884** Murfree *TN Mts.* 262, Ye mought hev brought him hyar ter eat . . stiddier a-leavin' him a-grievin' over his dead wife. **1887** (1967) Harris *Free Joe* 82 **GA** [Black], Fum dat day down ter dis, stedder Flew Ellen, I'm bin name Fountain. **1891** *DN* 1.133 **cNY**, [ɪn'stɪd]. **1893** Shands *MS Speech* 39, Instid. . . Negro and illiterate white for *instead*. **1899** (1967) Chesnutt *Wife of Youth* 65, He oughter be burnt, stidier bein' hung. **1899** Garland *Boy Life* 163 **nwIA** (as of c1870s), I wanted to hear old Plunket 'stid of all that stuff about nothin'. **1907** *DN* 3.245 **csME**, Instid. **1908** *DN* 3.323 **eAL, wGA**, Instid. . . Sted is also commonly heard. **1922** *DN* 5.184 **GA**, Stidder. . . Instead of. **1922** Gonzales *Black Border* 329 **sSC, GA coasts** [Gullah glossary], 'Stead'uh— (also 'stidduh) instead of. **1936** *AmSp* 11.15 **eTX**, Among the less literate. . . *instead* . . is usually . . [stɪd]. **1943** *LANE* Map 726, [The pronc [ɪnstɪd] is widespread throughout **NEng**, but is more freq in **ME**.] **1948** Manfred *Chokecherry* 14 **nwIA**, T'ud been better if you'd a gone off to a barber's school 'steada that Comus Seminary. **1955** *PADS* 23.43 **e,cSC, eNC, seGA**, /-stɪd/ in *instead* (also New England and upstate New York). **1968** *DARE* Tape **NY43**, Instead [ɪn'stɪd]. **1989** Pederson *LAGS Tech. Index* 332 **Gulf Region**, [Proncs of the type [ɪn'stɛd, ən-] occur most frequently; somewhat less frequent are those of the types [ɪn'stɪd, ən-; ɪn'sted, ən-; ən'stʌd]; aphetic forms [stɛd, stɪd] occur occasionally; recessive stress in ['ɪnstɛd] occurs infrequently.]

instefy v Also sp *instify*
   1899 (1912) Green *VA Folk-Speech* 240, Instefy. . . Instify. To show; testify; set forth.

instid See **instead**

instify See **instefy**

insurance n Usu |ɪn'ʃurən(t)s, -'ʃɚ-|; freq **Sth, S Midl** |'ɪn-, -ˌʃo(r)əns| Pronc-spp *insho(r)ance, onsurance;* for addit pronc and sp varr see quots Cf Intro "Language Changes" IV.2, **sure**
A Forms.

   1893 [see **B** below]. **1927** Kennedy *Gritny* 143 **sLA** [Black], You goin' take charge de in-sho-ince money. **1930** in 1944 *ADD* **eVA** [Black], Insu'ance [ɪn'ʃuəns]. **1933** *AmSp* 8.1.32 **wTX**, In many words, the West Texan moves the accent to the first syllable . . *insurance*. **1944** *PADS* 2.15 **AL, GA, LA, nSC, TN**, Insurance ['ɪnʃurəns]: Frequent pronunciation of many standard speakers, especially in black belt. **1949** *New Yorker* 3 Dec 44 **TN** [Black], He's an onsurance man, ain't he? **1955** in 1958 Brewer *Dog Ghosts* 121 **TX** [Black], A ten thousan' dolluh insu'ance pol'cy. **c1960** *Wilson Coll.* **csKY**, Recessive stress. . . Insurance. **1967** *DARE* Tape **TX5**, Insurance ['ɪnˌʃoɚəns]. **1967** *DARE* FW Addit **eTN**, Insurance ['ɪnˌsjuɚɪnts]. . . Common [among] people with high school education or less. **1970** *Thompson Coll.* **cnAL** (as of 1920s), Insurance. . . pronounced inshow(a)nce, esp. by Negroes. **1976** Garber *Mountain-ese* 46 **sAppalachians**, Inshorance. **1977** Smitherman *Talkin* 249 [Black], In-sho-ance. **1981** Pederson *LAGS Basic Materials* **Gulf Region**, [31 infs had proncs of the type ['ɪnˌʃu(ə)ənts, -ˌʃɚ̩ɪnts]; 1 inf, **seGA**, [ˌɪnˈʃoˆʊənts]; 1 inf, **cwAL**, [ī̃<n̩ˈʃuˆ-ənts]; 1 inf, **cwTN**, ['ī̃·nˌšənts].] [5 of 34 infs Black] **1983** *Reinecke Coll.* 7 **LA**, *Insurance oil.* . . ['ɪnʃuəns]. . . Black folk etym. "shoo-ants oil." Obsolescent. **1995** *DARE* File **csWI** (as of 1948), We must be sure to get this in our inventory so our ['ɪnˌʃɚ̩ənts] will cover it.

B Sense.
See quots.

   1893 Shands *MS Speech* 39, Inshoance [ɪnʃoəns]. A corruption of *insurance.* Used by negroes and illiterate whites to mean *assurance* in

the sense of *boldness, impudence.* They would say: "He had the inshoance to ask me to give him my last dollar." **1899** (1912) Green *VA Folk-Speech* 240, Insurance. . . For *assurance.* Great boldness; impudence.

insurance oil n [See quot 1983] **esp LA**
Kerosene.

   1916 *DN* 4.269 **New Orleans LA**, Insurance oil. . . coal-oil. **1968** *DARE* (Qu. F45, . . *Fuel that's used in an ordinary lamp*) Inf **LA43**, Insurance oil—called this because people used to use it to burn down their houses for insurance. **1971** *Yankee* Nov 34, Insurance oil—A term for kerosene. . . Devious characters found kerosene was very helpful if they wanted to collect insurance. Some of 'em even went so far as to heave a bucket of kerosene on the fire instead of water. **1983** *Reinecke Coll.* 6 **LA**, Insurance oil. ['ɪnʃuəns]. Kerosene, probably because it was less flammable than gasoline, and qualified one for better rates on fire insurance. **1986** Pederson *LAGS Concordance* **New Orleans LA** (*Kerosene*) 1 inf, Insurance oil; 1 inf, Insurance oil—better insurance rates than gas.

insure v Usu |ɪn'ʃu(ə)r, -ʃuə, -ʃur, -ʃɚ|; for addit varr see quots
A Forms.
   1902 [see **B** below]. **1967** *DARE* FW Addit **eTN**, Insure ['ɪnˌsjuɚ]. **1981** Pederson *LAGS Basic Materials*, 1 inf, **neGA**, ['ɪˑnˌʃuˀ̞əd].
B Sense.
See quots. [Cf *OED insure* v. 2 "Obs."]
   1902 *DN* 2.237 **sIL**, Insure [ɪnšur, ɪnšor]. . . To assure. . . To guarantee. **1906** *DN* 3.120 **sIN**, Insure. . . "I'll insure you it will rain to-night." **1907** *DN* 3.223 **nwAR**, Insure. . . To assure. . . To guarantee.

int See **a-aint**

intend v [*OED intend* v. 21 "Obs.";* cf also *EDD intend* v. 1]
See quot.
   1914 *DN* 4.158 **ce,sePA**, Intend. . . To expect. "They intend my grandmom to die any day."

intentioned adj
Intending; having the intention.
   1939 *Hall Coll.* **wNC**, Intentioned. . . Having designs. . . Hit was intentioned to bite me. I never heerd a snake sing so vigrous.

inter See **into**

interduce, interduction See **introduce** v

interels See **entrails**

interest n, v, hence adjs *interested, interesting* Usu |'ɪntrɪst|; also |'ɪntrəst, 'ɪntərəst|; for addit varr see quots Pronc-spp *innerrested, intrust*
Std senses, var forms.

   1837 Sherwood *Gaz.* **GA** 70, Intrust, for interest. **1861** Holmes *Venner* 1.44 **NEng**, This, however, made him look more interesting, or, as the young ladies at Major Bush's said, "interéstin'." **1887** *Scribner's Mag.* 2.479 **AR**, Ain't ye got no natchell motherlike feelin's 'bout the po' little trick's own intrusts? **1890** *DN* 1.68 **KY**, Intrust: for *interest* on money. Old persons, white and black, say, "What is the intrust on that amount?" **1891** *DN* 1.134 **cNY**, [ɪntrɪst]. **1891** *PMLA* 6.172 **TN**, They also say *intrust;* as, 6% intrust, putting considerable stress of voice on each syllable. **1893** Shands *MS Speech* 39, Intrust [ɪntrəs]. Negro for *interest.* . . "When I makes a bargain, I always looks after my own intrusts." **1899** (1912) Green *VA Folk-Speech* 240, Interest'ing. . . The third syllable long. **1909** *DN* 3.399 **nwAR**, Intrust. . . Interest on money. **1912** Green *VA Folk-Speech* 241, Intrust-money. . . For *interest-money.* **1929** *AmSp* 5.120 **eME**, A man might be said to have . . "got money out at intrust." **1940** in 1944 *ADD* **AR**, ['ɪn'trɛstɪn]. Radio. **1941** *LANE* Map 404, 1 inf, **ceCT**, [ɪntrɛstəd]; 3 infs, **eRI, eMA**, [ɪntərɛstɪd]; 1 inf, **neMA**, [ɪntr̩'ɛstɪd]; 1 inf, **eMA**, [ɪntə'rɛstɪd]; 1 inf, **csNH**, ['ɪntərɛstɪd]. **1942** Hall *Smoky Mt. Speech* 64 **wNC, eTN**, It is difficult to say whether *interest* is more commonly ['ɪntrəst] or ['ɪntɚst]. **1967–70** *DARE* (Qu. AA12) Inf **NY167**, [He] lost ['ɪntrɛst]; **PA163**, [He] lost ['ɪnt̩,rəst]; **VA81**, [He] lost [ɪnə·ɪst]; (Qu. HH27a) Inf **LA8**, [ˌɪntə'rɛstɪd] in their work; (Qu. KK29, . . *"He was slow at first but now he's really _____."*) Inf **IL131**, [ɪntɚ·stɪd]; **MO5**, ['ɪnɚˌɛstɪd]. **1981** Pederson *LAGS Basic Materials* [For *interest* used as noun: 1 inf, **cLA**, ['ɛ̃·nrəst]; 1 inf, **swMS**, ['ɪ·nrrɪst] [both infs Black]; for *interest* used as verb: 1 inf, **nwTN**, ['ɪntərɛˀst]; for *interested:* proncs of the type ['ɪnərɛsˌtɪd] occur frequently, as do proncs of the type [ˌɪnə'rɛstɪd]; 1 inf, **cwAR**, ['ɪˑnɚ·stɪd]; for *interesting:* proncs of the type ['ɪn(t)ərɛstɪŋ] occur frequently; 1 inf, **neAL**, [ˈɪˈnɚ-stn].] **1984** Burns *Cold Sassy* 99 **nGA** (as of 1906), I can forgive a fool, but I ain't inner-rested in coddlin' hypocrites.

interpretate v, hence n *interpretater* [Back-formation from *interpretation*]
To interpret.
c1938 in 1970 Hyatt *Hoodoo* 1.745 **ceVA** [Black], They's very good girls—they are very good *interpretaters*. They had a mental capacity— all those girls did. **1970** Rosenberg *Art Amer. Preacher* 158, Brought him on up there / And get him to interpretate the king's dream.

interrupted fern n [See quot 1952]
A **flowering fern** (here: *Osmunda claytoniana*).
1824 Bigelow *Florula Bostoniensis* 388, Interrupted Fern. . . A pretty large, smooth fern. . . The divisions of the frond are principally opposite, . . and subdivided into segments. **1910** Graves *Flowering Plants* 26 **CT**, Interrupted Fern. Frequent or common. Old pastures, along fence-rows and in open wood-lands. **1938** Small *Ferns SE States* 344, The interrupted-fern . . has a wide geographic distribution, which lies mainly east of the Mississippi River and north of Georgia. **1952** Strausbaugh–Core *Flora WV* 12, Interrupted Fern. . . The fertile pinnae . . [are] borne in the middle of the sterile leaf so that its normal pattern seems to be interrupted, hence the common name. **1963** Zimmerman–Olson *Forest* 141 **WI**, Interrupted Fern. . . The first fern to appear in the spring with stout fuzzy "fiddleheads"—the unrolling leaves. **1976** Bailey–Bailey *Hortus Third* 803.

intervale n Also sp *interval* **chiefly NEng** Cf **bottom** n **1a**
An area of low-lying land, usu along a stream or river.
1647 in 1880 Suffolk Co. MA *Deeds* 1.85, Fifty Acres of Interval. **1653** in 1884 Lancaster MA *Early Rec.* 27, Thirty acors of vppland and fortie acors of Entervale Land. **1792** Belknap *Hist. NH* 3.6, Another word, . . intervale. . . is well understood in all parts of New-England to distinguish the low-land adjacent to the fresh rivers, which is frequently overflowed by the freshets; and which is accounted some of our most valuable soil, because it is rendered permanently fertile, by the bountiful hand of nature, without the labour of man. **1870** Pollard *VA Tourist* 224 **wVA**, The fountain issues from the foot of a gentle slope, terminating in the low interval upon a small and beautiful stream. **1885** Howells *Rise Lapham* 18 **NEng**, A sightly bit of nature—a smooth piece of interval with half a dozen . . wine-glass elms in it. **1914** *DN* 4.74 **ME, nNH**, Interval. . . A narrow river-valley. **1946** Attwood *Length ME* 14, Intervale—A low tract of land between hills or along a stream. Generally the soil is alluvial. **1949** Kurath *Word Geog.* 22 **NEng**, Other "Down East" expressions are . . intervale, interval . . for a river bottom (from Massachusetts Bay to Maine and westward to Lake Champlain and the northern Berkshires, with relics on Cape Cod and in eastern Connecticut). **1966–69** *DARE* (Qu. C9, *Water from a river that comes up and covers low land when the river is high*) Inf **CT25**, Interval—it comes and goes; (Qu. C15, *A place in mountains or high hills where you can get through without climbing over the top*) Inf **MA30**, [ˈɪntɚvəl]—narrow, low, moist; (Qu. C29, *A good-sized stretch of level land with practically no trees*) Inf **NH10**, Interval. **1971** Wood *Vocab. Change* 143, *Low ground in a river valley*, 2 infs, **MS**, Intervale. Ibid 147, *A low grassland*, 3 infs, **GA, TN**, Intervale. **1982** *Smithsonian Letters* **ME**, Interval, a fertile stretch along a river. My neighbor always plants his corn on his interval. **1992** *DARE* File **nwMA**, An interval [ˈɪntɚvəl] is a valley between mountains. Well, it makes sense, an interval is a space between objects or points in time. There's Intervale [ˈɪntɚˈvel], New Hampshire, you know, in the White Mountains.

‡**intestinals** n pl [Prob blend of *intestines* + *internals*] Cf **inwards**
1968 *DARE* (Qu. X8, . . *General words . . for the organs inside the body*) Inf **MI75**, Intestinals.

in the circle n Cf **in the fat**
In marble play: a ring game; see quot.
1957 *Sat. Eve. Post Letters* **WI**, In the circle. . . A marble game in which marbles are placed inside a circle and have to be knocked out of it.

in the family way See **family way, in a**

in the fat n [**fat** n¹ **2**] Cf **in the circle**
In marble play: a ring game; see quot 1899.
1899 Champlin–Bostwick *Young Folks' Games* 484, *Ring game*. A ring is drawn. . . The players in turn now shoot at the marbles in the ring. . .

The form of the ring, the number of marbles placed in it . . vary in different places, and the game is often given some fanciful name in allusion to the changed shape of the ring. Thus, forms of the game played in New York City are called "In the Fat," and "In the Soup." **1940** *Recreation* (NY) 34.110, Games of marbles played throughout the country. . . In the fat.

in the floor See **in** prep **B3b**

in the grass See **grass** n **4**

in the gum See **in** prep **B7**

in the head of prep phr Also *in head of*
Ahead of.
1954 *Harder Coll.* **cwTN**, [Letter:] Me & C. are in the head of you we know how to jitterbug. **1990** Brown *Big Bad Love* 85 **MS**, Dorothea had gotten that promotion and her boss liked her, took her out to lunch so she wouldn't have to spend her own money. She had a real future in head of her.

in the hole See **hole** n **5a**

in the jaw (or lip) See **in** prep **B7**

in the mad(s) See **mad** n

in the manner of See **manner** n **2**

in the room of See **room** n

in the street(s) See **street**

inti-inti-i-over See **indi-i-over**

intimate gate n
Prob a gate at the rear of a residence reserved for use by one's friends or relatives.
1937 (1977) Hurston *Their Eyes* 14 **FL**, When she arrived at the place, Pheoby Watson didn't go in by the front gate and down the palm walk to the front door. She walked around the fence corner and went in the intimate gate with her heaping plate of mulatto rice.

in time See **time**

intment See **ointment**

into prep Usu |ˈɪntu|; also |ˈɪntə| Pronc-sp *inter* (representing |ˈɪntə| in r-less areas, when not foll by a vowel); for addit varr see quots
A Forms.
1848 Lowell *Biglow* 144 'Upcountry' **MA**, Inter, intu, *into*. **1857** *Putnam's Mag.* 10.347 **CT**, I sed nothin', but stept along inter the bedroom. **1871** (1892) Johnston *Dukesborough Tales* 68 **GA**, I was a-goin' right outen your school intoo Dukesborough. **1884** *Anglia* 7.255 **Sth, S Midl** [Black], Intow, eentow, inter. **1911** Wharton *Ethan Frome* 14 **wMA**, It eats inter him. **1926** *DN* 5.399 **Ozarks**, Feather into. . . "Ol' Cap Morgan he out 'ith his weepon an' feathered inter them fellers."
B Senses.
1 In; inside. [Scots and Engl dial; cf *SND* intae prep. 1; cf *EDD* into prep. 3] **chiefly NEast, S Atl**
1814 in 1816 Pickering *Vocab.* 112 **NY**, We get in the *stage*, and have the rheumatism *into* our knees. **1874** (1895) Eggleston *Circuit Rider* 120 **IN** (as of early 1800s), He must have the very devil into him! **1878** *Appletons' Jrl.* 5.413 **PA**, The word *into* is much used for *in* in Pennsylvania. A horse will be said to have a white spot *into* his forehead, or a field to have a fine spring of water *into* it. **1893** *KS Univ. Qrly.* 1.140 **NJ**, Is there any milk *into* that pail? **1903** Wasson *Cap'n Simeon's Store* 157 **ME**, Rowin' round and round the Cove into one o' them hotel let-bo'ts. **1918** *DN* 5.16 **eMA**, There was mor'n two tons of hay into that mow. **1923** Parsons *Folk-lore Sea Islands* 7 **csSC** [Black], They put the butter up into the kag and buried it into a woods. **1933** Rawlings *South Moon* 27 **FL**, I never seed that much corn liquor into him, to make him sociable. **1969–70** *DARE* FW Addit **ceNY**, No truth into it at all; a maple [seed] has a pit into it; **ceNC**, She lives into the apartment house; **cNC**, A house with one room into it; **NJ**, He took a bath into it. **1975** Allen *LAUM* 2.66 **Upper MW** (as of c1950), Burn coal *in* the stove. A suspected contrast between *in* and *into* in this context did not turn up in the U[pper] M[idwest]. Only two infs. have *into*, both using it in free conversation. . . [Another inf] terms it "old-fashioned," and [another] reports having heard it from others. [All 4 infs **MN**]
2 See quots. [Cf *EDD* into prep. 4] *arch*
1889 (1971) Farmer *Americanisms* 317, Into.—With the exception of;

short of—a qualifying contraction used in Connecticut of number or quantity. Thus, a given distance may be referred to as six miles *into* a quarter; or one might be willing to give a dollar *into* ten cents for a particular article. **1896** Farmer–Henley *Slang* 4.13, *Into.* . . (American).—'Short of'; wanting: *e.g.* 'I thought I did pretty well delivering all the load into one box[*]' (*i.e.,* all but one box). **1950** *AmSp* 25.176 **CT** (as of c1870), *Into.* Used as denoting a number or quantity, &c., deficient; as, 'I had enough (money) into six cents;' 'It was wide enough into an inch.'

3 See **in** prep **B7.**

into the jaw (or lip) See **in** prep **B7**

into, want See **want**

intown adv, adj, n

A As adv.

In, to, or toward the central or business section of a city; to a larger city.

1941 in 1966 Stevens *Letters* 25 Mar 388 **CT,** Today, as I walked in-town, I heard . . song sparrows. **1958** *AmSp* 33.75, In the community in which I live (Newark, Delaware), there is the expression *in town,* as in the question 'Are you going in town?'—that is, to a larger city, such as Wilmington. **1967** *DARE* Tape **MA**8, When I was living on the other part of Roxbury, people would say. . . "I'm going intown [ɪn'taʊn]; do you want me to bring you back something?" They meant they were coming down . . to Dudley Street, which is just about a block or so from . . the church. Now since I've been over here I don't say "I'm going intown" when I go to Dudley Street. . . If I say "I'm going intown [from this part of Roxbury]" I usually mean downtown Boston, where the . . big stores are. **1968–70** *DARE* (Qu. MM23, . . '*Uptown*' and '*downtown*') Inf **LA**40, Here we say "We're going intown," even if they live right in town; **PA**242, To Harrisburg [from Elizabethtown] is intown [FW: stress on first syllable].

B As adj.

Of the central city; by ext, urbane or sophisticated; acceptable. [By analogy with *uptown*]

1942 *Sun* (Baltimore MD) 9 Apr 26/8, Two of Goucher's in-town buildings . . are being considered as quarters for a regional office. **1957** *Ibid* 2 Feb 9/7, The two left for an intown hotel, after posing affably for photographers in the car window. **1967** *Boston Herald* 1 Apr. 22/1 (*OEDS*), Three intown congregations . . will join in worship here at 11 a.m. Sunday. **1967** *DARE* Tape **MA**8, People would say, "I'm going intown [ɪn'taʊn]." They didn't mean intown ['ɪn,taʊn] from Boston, but they meant intown to Dudley Street. **1969** *Current Slang* 3.3.8 **OH,** *In town.* . . Acceptable; okay.—College males, Negro. **1986** Pederson *LAGS Concordance,* 1 inf, **cAL,** "Pantry" is an intown word.

C As noun.

The central or business section of a town or city; by ext, sophistication, urbanity.

1967–68 *DARE* (Qu. C35, . . *Different parts of your town or city*) Inf **PA**171, Intown—center city—business district [of Philadelphia]; (Qu. MM23, . . '*Uptown*' and '*downtown*') Inf **MA**45, Intown—Boston proper. **1969** Emmons *Deep Rivers* 60 **TX** [Black], About the smoothest compounded term I ever heard was uttered, apparently impromptu, by a Negro man who was likewise smooth. . . "Well, they certainly ruined a good plowhand when they rounded up that boy and put shoes on him and brought him to college." "Well, I don't know, Mrs. Dix," came softly and gently from the young Negro. "Don't you think that boy need some *intown*?" (Heavy accent on the *in*.) . . Suppose we had recognized the proper treatment of the boy's lack of urbanity, who of us could have expressed it so aptly? [**1992** *DARE* File **csWI,** A motel close to a hospital and not far from the center of the city is punningly called the Inntowner.]

intrils See **entrails**

introduce v Usu |ɪntrə'dus, -'djus|; also |ɪntə(r)'dus, -'djus| Pronc-sp *interduce* Similarly n *interduction*

Std senses, var forms.

1843 [see **introducing to (the) king and queen**]. **1891** *DN* 1.163 **NY,** [ɪntə'dus] 'introduce.' **1905** *DN* 3.58 **eNE,** A sort of metathesis . . is very frequent in *counterdict, interduce.* **1908** *DN* 3.323 **eAL, wGA,** *Interduce, interduction.* . . Introduce, introduction. **1923** (1946) Greer-Petrie *Angeline Steppin'* 36 **csKY,** He reshes up and interduces hisse'f. **1928** *AmSp* 3.406 **Ozarks,** Some consonants, particularly *l* and *r*, are frequently shifted about by a kind of metathesis, producing such mon-

strosities as *interduce, hunderd, childern.* **1936** *AmSp* 11.155 **eTX,** *Introduce* . . [ˌɪntrə'djus], [ˌɪntəˈdjus], [ˌɪntə'djus]. **1942** Hall *Smoky Mt. Speech* 98 **eTN, wNC,** Introduce [ˌɪntə'djus]. **c1960** *Wilson Coll.* **csKY,** *Introduce* is often [ˌɪntə'djus].

introduce n Cf **invite**

An introduction.

1857 in 1912 Thornton *Amer. Gloss.* 1.484, I kind of froze to her right off, and got better very fast, after having had an *introduce.* **1858** Hammett *Piney Woods Tavern* 135 **eTX,** Some of the boys come up, and I give 'em a sorter introduce. **1957** in 1958 Brewer *Dog Ghosts* 119 **TX** [Black], Ah has to go wid de deacon so's he kin show me de chu'ch house an' gib me a introduce to some of t'othuh membuhs of de chu'ch.

introducing to (the) king and queen n Also *introduction to the king and queen*

See quot 1952.

1843 Thompson *Major Jones' Courtship* 58 **GA,** She told him bout a new play. . . called "Interduction to the King and Queen." **1952** Brown *NC Folkl.* 1.42 **cNC** (as of 1927), *Introducing to King and Queen.* . . A boy and girl are chosen as king and queen. Their "thrones" are draped with a sheet or some other large covering, with a vacant space left between the two, presumably an empty chair. Sometimes a pan of water is put under the sheet at this spot. A player is brought into the room to be introduced. . . As he sits down, the king and the queen rise from their "thrones," letting him take a seat in the pan of water. **1953** Brewster *Amer. Nonsinging Games* 121 **IN,** [Practical jokes:] *Introducing to the King and Queen.*

intrust See **interest**

intwuds See **inwards**

in-ty adv [Etym uncert: cf *EDD* in-ty(e) "not I," used after a negative assertion] *obs*

See quots.

1889 (1971) Farmer *Americanisms* 317, *In-ty.*—An obsolete corruption (of the French *entier*), meaning certainly, indeed. **1950** *AmSp* 25.176 **MA, NH,** *In-ty.* Certainly, indeed. 'Yes; in-ty.' Salem, Mass., about 1820. By aged persons. 'No; in-ty.' Stoddard, N.H., about 1820. . . The word is . . used much as the English-speaking Irish now use *entirely.* . . 'Yes, in-ty,' 'No, in-ty,' were formerly used in vicinity of Roxbury and of Newton, Mass., said Prof. C.E. Stowe, D.D., to me, Dec. 22, 1862. [*AmSp* Ed: Probably similar to 'indeedy.']

in under prep phr Also aphet *nunder* [Engl dial; prob var of earlier *anunder*]

Underneath; below.

1795 Dearborn *Columbian Grammar* 137, *List of Improprieties.* . . Nunder for Under. **1887** (1895) Robinson *Uncle Lisha* 54 **wVT,** Ye ain't no sociabler 'n a passel o' snails holdin' a meetin' 'n under a cabbage leaf! **1896** *DN* 1.419 **wCT, NY, nOH,** *In under:* for *under.* **1909** *Atlantic Mth.* 104.137 **N Cent,** "In under," "onto," are composites for which there is no Southern demand. **1930** Shoemaker *1300 Words* 32 **cPA Mts** (as of c1900), *In-under*—Underneath, below. **1964** *Mt. Life* 40.1.54 **sAppalachians,** Telescoped clusters of prepositions are discernible in . . *nunder (in under),* [etc].

invite n |'ɪnvaɪt| (cf Intro "Language Changes" IV.2) [*OED* 1659 →; *EDD*]

An invitation.

1834 Caruthers *Kentuckian* 1.29, The whole company stared at me as if I had come without an invite. **1874** (1895) Eggleston *Circuit Rider* 100 **sOH** (as of early 19th cent), Those who got "invites" danced cotillions and reels nearly all night. **1884** *Anglia* 7.268 **Sth, S Midl** [Black], *An invite* . . an invitation. **1902** *DN* 2.237 **sIL,** Invite (with strong accent on first syllable.) . . 'Did you git a invite to the dance?' **1903** *DN* 2.318 **seMO.** **1907** *DN* 3.223 **sIL, nwAR.** **1908** *DN* 3.323 **eAL, wGA.** **1941** *LANE* Map 414, 1 inf, **cwVT,** I had [ən 'ɪnvæt] to a sociable. **1950** *WELS* ("Did you get a(n) _____ to the party?") 12 Infs, **WI,** Invite. **c1960** *Wilson Coll.* **csKY,** *Invite.* . . An invitation; usually humorous. **1965–70** *DARE* (Qu. FF6) 224 Infs, **widespread,** Invite.

in, want See **want**

inwards n pl Usu |'ɪnə(r)dz|; also **esp Nth** |'ɪnwə(r)dz| (See Map on p. 52) Pronc-spp *in'ards, innards, inners, intwuds* Note: The sp *innards* is now virtually std, but until recently was appar felt by many to be a pronc-sp. [*OED* inward sb. 1.b a1300 →. The loss of *w* is not attested before the 19th cent *(OEDS innards),* but appears to be widespread in Engl dial *(EDD inwards* sb. 4).] Std senses, var forms.

1713 (1901) Hempstead *Diary* 27 **seCT,** Mr Hutton had 1 Sheep 33 lb & he had ye Inwards as formerly. **1825** Neal *Brother Jonathan* 1.77 **CT,** Miriam stood stirring up the "innards." **1872** White *Words & Uses* 387, The simple English word [=*guts*] for which some New England "females" elegantly substitute *in'ards,* would shock many. **1897** Johnston *Old Times GA* 179, It appears like the fool in Dan Hickson have growed to be so big that it ockepy all his in'ards. **1899** (1912) Green *VA Folk-Speech* 241, Inwards. . . In'ards. The inner parts of an animal. **1903** *DN* 2.291 **Cape Cod MA** (as of a1857), *Innards = inwards.* **1907** *DN* 3.191 **seNH,** Innards. **1910** *DN* 3.458 **FL, GA,** Innards. **1916** *DN* 4.341 **seOH,** Innards. **1927** Kennedy *Gritny* 150 **sLA** [Black], Dey sho is good w'en somh'n be wrong wid yo' intwuds. **1932** Farrell *Young Lonigan* 29 **Chicago IL,** His innards made slight noises, as they diligently furthered the process of digesting a juicy beefsteak. **1939** *LANE* Map 209 *(Pluck, haslet)* **NEng,** [15 infs gave resps of the type ['ɪnwədz, 'ɪnwrdz], 6 of the type ['ɪnədz, 'ɪnrdz].] *Ibid* Map 216 *(Giblets),* [15 infs gave resps of the type ['ɪnwədz, 'ɪnwrdz]; 12 of the type ['ɪnədz, 'ɪnrdz].] **1940** *Ibid* Map 304, 1 inf, **seMA,** [ɪnwədz]; 1 inf, **cwVT,** [ɪnwrdz]. **1941** *Time* 28 Apr 19, The B-19 [airplane]. . . has ten miles of wire in her innards. **1950** *WELS WI (The organs inside the body)* 19 Infs, Innards; 6 Infs, Inwards; 1 Inf, Inners (occasional). **c1960** *Wilson Coll.* **csKY,** Innards (or *inwards*). . . One's body cavity and its contents. **1965–70** *DARE* (Qu. X8, . . *General words . . for the organs inside the body)* 215 Infs, **widespread,** Innards; 22 Infs, **esp Nth,** Inwards; **NJ3,** Inners; (Qu. H43) Inf **FL30,** Innards; (Qu. BB18, *To vomit a great deal at once)* Inf **MI56,** Heaved up my innards; **MN33,** Throw up your innards; **OH57,** Upchuck your innards; **WA17,** Lost his innards; (Qu. JJ10b) Inf **PA76,** Innards. [Of 23 Infs responding with *inwards,* 18 were old, 5 mid-aged, 18 comm type 4 or 5.] **1966** *DARE* Tape **ME26,** He kicked her [=a bear's] innards right out; **MI21,** The inwards, or the guts of the fish. [Both Infs old]

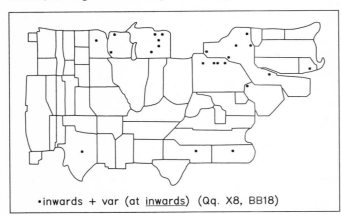

•inwards + var (at <u>inwards</u>) (Qq. X8, BB18)

inyan, inyin, inyon See **onion** n

io n [Haw *'io*] **HI**
The Hawaiian hawk *(Buteo solitarius).*
1933 Bryan *Hawaiian Nature* 263, Io, the Hawaiian hawk. . . makes its large nests of dry twigs high in the forks of trees. **1944** Munro *Birds HI* 48, The io is endemic to the island of Hawaii and is well distributed over the island from about 2,000 to 5,000 feet elevation. . . The io is a useful bird and does little harm. **1972** Berger *Hawaiian Birdlife* 83, The Io or Hawaiian Hawk. . . The Io has two color phases. **1992** *DARE* File **HI,** There's a hawk here called an *io* ['io].

iodeodonda See **hediondilla**

iodine n Usu |'aɪə,daɪn|; also |-,dɪn, -,dın|; for addit varr see quots
A Forms.
1943 *LANE* Map 516, [Pronunciations of the type ['aɪə,daɪn] are widespread throughout **NEng,** but somewhat more frequent in **eNEng;** pronunciations of the type [-dɪn] are chiefly **MA, s,cCT, wVT, sNH;** pronunciations of the type [-dın] are scattered in **s,wNEng,** esp **RI.**] **1961** Kurath–McDavid *Pronc. Engl.* 165, Iodine. . . [aɪ] predominates in the North and North Midland, including all of West Virginia, on Delmarva, in North Carolina, and in Georgia; it is nearly universal in Eastern New England, in Pennsylvania (except for Philadelphia and

vicinity), and in West Virginia. . . The [i] of *dean* is nearly universal in South Carolina, except for the cities on the coast, and predominates decisively in Virginia. In North Carolina . . [i] occurs as a minority pronunciation with varying frequency. . . *Iodine* riming with *din* occurs in scattered instances in New England (especially Rhode Island) and the New England settlement area, rarely elsewhere. It is usually a prestige pronunciation. **1965–70** *DARE* (Qu. BB50c) Infs **AL39, 59, AR47, NY73, PA**185, 205, **TX**95, **WI**62, ['aɪ(ə),daɪn]; **AL**10, **KY**86, ['aɪ,dɪn]; **CA**97, **PA**188, ['aɪ(j)ə,dɪn]; (Qu. BB50b) Inf **OH**45, ['aɪədɪn]; (Qu. BB51a) Inf **GA**3, ['ɑrədaɪn] [sic]; **PA**90, ['aɪ,dɪn]. **1973** *PADS* 60.54 **seNC,** Iodine. . . the last syllable of this word in North Carolina is given the vowel /aɪ/ of *sight.* . . most of our informants pronounced it [ɑɪ] or [ɒɪ] . . two . . said [a·]. **1989** Pederson *LAGS Tech. Index* 286 **Gulf Region,** [Of the numerous proncs recorded, those of the type ['aɪədaɪn] occur most frequently; those of the type ['aɪdaɪn] and ['aɪ(ə)dɪn] also occur frequently; among the less frequent proncs are [aɪ(ə)'daɪn], [aɪ'dɪn], and ['aɪədn].]
B Senses.
1 Among loggers: see quot. Cf **epsom salts**
1958 McCulloch *Woods Words* 95 **Pacific NW,** Iodine. . . A first aid man.
2 See quots. Cf *DS* H74a
1942 Berrey–Van den Bark *Amer. Slang* 92.4, *Coffee.* . . iodine. **1958** McCulloch *Woods Words* 95 **Pacific NW,** Iodine. . . Strong coffee.

iodine bush n Also *iodine weed* **SW**
1 =**pickleweed.** [See quot 1944]
1931 U.S. Dept. Ag. *Misc. Pub.* 101.36, Pickleweed *(Allenrolfea occidentalis),* known also as iodine-weed . . , will endure a soil alkali content of 1.2 per cent. **1940** Writers' Program *Guide NV* 13, The desert plants are the salt bushes, grease wood, seep weed, iodine bush. **1944** *AZ Univ. Biol. Sci. Bulletin* 6.128, *Allenrolfea occidentalis.* . . *Iodine Bush.* . . The name iodine bush is derived from the color of the dried sap of the crushed stems. **1981** Benson–Darrow *Trees SW Deserts* 174, *Iodine Bush.* . . tolerates more alkali than any other desert shrub.
2 A **sea blite.**
1941 Jaeger *Wildflowers* 48 **Desert SW,** *Iodine Weed. Suaeda Torreyana ramosissima.* . . Although it is strong in tannic acid, which acts as an astringent, the plant produces dysentery in animals occasionally feeding upon it. **1985** Dodge *Flowers SW Deserts* 14, Iodinebush. . . *Suaeda suffrutescens.* . . *Suaeda torreyana.*

i'on See **iron**

ione bush n [Perh for **iodine bush**]
A **ceanothus** (here: *Ceanothus tomentosus).*
1938 Van Dersal *Native Woody Plants* 91, *Ceanothus tomentosus.* . . *Ione bush.* . . A large, loosely-branched shrub. . . Of slight importance as browse for mule deer.

Iowa n Usu |'aɪəwə, 'aɪowə|; also |-we(ɪ)|; for addit varr see quots
Pronc-spp *Eyeway, Ioway, Iowuh, Iowy*
Std senses, var forms.
1835 (1927) Evans *Exped. Rocky Mts.* 14.198 **IN,** The Ioways & Nemahaws meet us here in council. **1891** *DN* 1.143 **cNY,** [aɪ'o-ɪ] < *Iowa.* **1899** Garland *Prairie Folks* 100 **IA,** Why, they ain't a harder-workin' woman in the hull State of Ioway. **1931** *PMLA* 46.1315 **sAppalachians,** Iowy. **1936** (1947) Mencken *Amer. Lang.* 541, In the early days the pronunciation of *Iowa* was always *Ioway,* but the schoolmarm has brought in *Iowuh,* with the accent on the first syllable. **1941** in 1944 *ADD* **sWV,** Ioway ['aɪə,we]. **c1960** *Wilson Coll.* **csKY,** *Iowa* is sometimes ['aɪowə] among elderly, otherwise ['aɪ,owe] or ['aɪə,we]. **1966–68** *DARE* FW Addit **sKY,** *Iowa* is very often [,aɪ'owə]; **ME**16, Iowa [aɪ'jowə]. **1976** Allen *LAUM* 3.350 (as of c1950), The medial [o] ranges from a full [o] to [ə]. Although the regional average places [ə] in a slight majority, its frequency in Iowa itself is much higher. . . Nine infs. . . have dropped the medial vowel completely . . [aɪwə]. . . Although one-third of the U[pper] M[idwest] infs. cling to the historical pronunciation of *Iowa* with final [e] that bears secondary stress, this variant is clearly moving toward obsolescence. . . It is somewhat curious that ['aɪə,we] is actually most frequent in South Dakota and not in Iowa. **1976** Garber *Mountain-ese* 27 **sAppalachians,** They live in the state uv Eyeway. **1981** Pederson *LAGS Basic Materials* **Gulf Region,** 8 infs, [a(ɪ)owe(ɪ)]; 6 infs, [a(ɪ)owə]; 2 infs, [a(ɪ)owe]; 2 infs, [a(ɪ)owə(ɪ)]; 1 inf, [aɛwe]; 1 inf, [aɪəwɨ].

‡I packed my grandfather's trunk n
A children's game; see quot.

1968 *DARE* (Qu. EE3, *Games in which you hide an object and then look for it*) Inf **PA**112, Hide-the-thimble; I spy; treasure hunt; button, button; I packed my grandfather's trunk.

ipo n [See quot 1937]
=yampah.

1929 *Nature Mag.* 14.171 **OR,** A woman of the Klamath tribe. . . gutturally demanded: *"I shanahuli kash?"* . . In broken English she interpreted herself: "You wan' ipo?" **1937** *U.S. Forest Serv. Range Plant Hdbk.* W48, Yampa. . . Although the Klamath Indians originally called the plant kash, contemporary members of the tribe and white men know it as ipo. . . Klamath Indians say that the word ipo comes from the south and was the Shasta's tribal name for the plant. However, it is probably not of Shastan origin, but a corruption of the Spanish-Californian apio, meaning celery. **1964** Jackman–Long *OR Desert* 299, *Food from Roots and Tubers,* Wild onion, mariposa, . . Ipo (squawroot). **1970** Kirk *Wild Edible Plants W. U.S.* 120, *Perideridia* species. . . Yampa, Squawroot, Ipo. . . The raw roots have a pleasant, sweet, nutty flavor when eaten raw and resemble carrots when cooked.

Ipswich sparrow n [See quot 1917]

A brownish-gray sparrow (*Passerculus princeps*) found on the Atlantic coast. Also called **gray bird c, sand sparrow**

1892 Torrey *Foot-Path Way* 54 **seMA,** The Ipswich sparrow, a very retiring but not peculiarly timid creature, I have now seen at Nahant in every one of our seven colder months . . though it is unquestionably rare upon the Massachusetts coast between the fall and spring migrations. **1910** Wayne *Birds SC* 117, The Ipswich Sparrow frequents the coast islands during the winter and early spring, where it is found among the low sand hills upon which the wild oats (*Zizania miliacea*) grow, which appear to be its chief food. **1917** (1923) *Birds Amer.* 3.24, *Ipswich Sparrow.* . . is a songless Sparrow which . . seems to have been first discovered near Ipswich, Mass., in 1868. **1946** Hausman *Eastern Birds* 589, *Ipswich Sparrow.* . . A chunky-bodied, pale gray and white sparrow, the color of dry sand. **1969** *DARE* (Qu. Q21, . . *Kinds of sparrows*) Inf **IN**69, Ipswich.

IQ n *joc*

One's signature.

1967–70 *DARE* (Qu. JJ13, . . *Joking words . . for a name signed to a paper: "I'll put my _____ on that."*) Infs **IA**9, **NJ**68, IQ.

Irelandish adj

Irish; of Irish background and manners.

1924 Raine *Land of Saddle-Bags* 33 **sAppalachians,** Hit were Virginia they moved from, but the McKee generation was Irelandish. I reckon they come from 'cross the water.

Ireland mallard n

A **Florida duck** (here: *Anas fulvigula maculosa*).

1911 *Forest & Stream* 77.172, *Anas fulvigula.* . . Ireland Mallard, Chef Menteur, La. **1957** *AmSp* 32.183 **LA,** Ireland mallard. Mottled duck. . . This may be a corruption of *island mallard.*

iris n Usu |'aɪrɪs|; also |'ɑ(ɪ)rɪš|; for addit varr see quots Pronc-sp *Irish*

A Forms.

1943 in 1944 *ADD* **nWV,** Iris. . . [ɒr(ɪ)s]. **c1960** *Wilson Coll.* **csKY,** *Iris* is often ['aɪrɪš] or ['ɑrɪs] or even [arš]. **1965–70** *DARE* (Qu. S24, *A wild flower that grows in swamps and marshes and looks like a small blue iris*) 14 Infs, **scattered,** Wild Irish; **GA**65, **KY**9, **MI**95, Irish; **GA**35, Blue flag Irish; **KY**24, Blue flag Irish; **NY**200, Swamp Irish; (Qu. S11) 12 Infs, 7 **GA,** Irish; **GA**3, Irish flower; (Qu. S26a, . . *Roadside flowers*) Inf **MI**96, Irish—same as flags—old-fashioned, no more along roads; **NJ**1, Wild Irish.

B Senses.

1 Std: a plant of the genus *Iris.* Also called **flag** n[1]. For other names of var spp see **blue flag, ~ lily, ~ Lucy 2, crocus** n[1] **2b, cube-seed iris, flag flower, flag lily, fleur-de-lis, flower-de-luce, French iris, lily 2b, poison flagroot, snake lily, swamp lily, violet** Cf **mountain lily 5**

2 =wild calla.

1966 *DARE* Wildfl QR Pl.4 Inf **WI**35, Called iris but it isn't.

irisette n

=blue-eyed grass 1.

1933 Small *Manual SE Flora* 327, *Sisyrinchium.* . . Blue-eyed grasses.

Fever-grasses. Irisettes. **1949** Moldenke *Amer. Wild Flowers* 362, A winsome group of low, tufted, grasslike herbs with small . . flowers, starlike in shape, bears the name of. . . *irisette.*

Irish n[1], adj Usu |'aɪrɪš|; also **esp S Midl** |ɑrš|; **esp Sth** |a(ɪ)š| Pronc-spp *Ar(ri)sh, Ash, I'(i)sh, Orsh;* for addit pronc and sp varr see quots

A Forms.

1858 in 1956 Eliason *Tarheel Talk* 313 **cnNC,** Arrish. **1891** *DN* 1.156 **cNY,** ['ɑrɪš] < Irish. **1924** (1946) Greer–Petrie *Angeline Gits an Eyeful* 13 **KY,** Fanchette would begin snatchin' the grub right out from under Mis' Clark's nose—*Orsh* 'taters and cream and sugar. **1930** *DN* 6.81 **cSC,** I'sh potato. . . Irish potato. . . The pronunciation is common. **1936** *AmSp* 11.243 **eTX,** Irish (potatoes). . . *Plantation-Type,* ['aɪrɪš]. *Hill-Type,* [aɪ:š], [ɒrš]. *Negro,* [a:š]. **1940** Harris *Folk Plays* 91 **NC,** Course sometimes we help shell the peas, and peel the I'sh 'taters. **1940** *Qrly. Jrl. Speech* 26.265 **VA,** Among the country people. . . *Irish potatoes* may be "ash potatoes." **1941** *LANE* Map 257, 1 inf, **ceMA,** [aerɪʃ plʌmz], jocular name for onions. *Ibid* Map 299, 1 inf, **seNH,** Irish [eerɪʃ]. **1942** Hall *Smoky Mt. Speech* 44 **wNC, eTN,** *Irish* is commonly [aˑš] in the expression *Irish potatoes.* **1952** in 1958 Brewer *Dog Ghosts* 105 **TX** [Black], I'ish 'taters. **1952** Brown *NC Folkl.* 1.516 **cn,swNC,** Ash potato. . . Illiterate. Rare. **1954** Harder *Coll.* **cwTN,** Irish [ɑrš] potatoes. **1955** Roberts *S. from Hell-fer-Sartin* 5 **seKY,** Delbert . . gave out with two or three of the many "Arshman" jokes that he knew. **1956** Ker *Vocab. W. TX* 368 **nwTX,** Awrish [1 inf]. **1965–70** *DARE* (Qu. I9) Infs **SC**7, 26, 34, [aɪš]; **AR**56, [ɔɚš]; **LA**6, ['aɪš]; **NC**55, [ɑɚš]; **SC**39, [aɚɚš]; **SC**46, [ɑɚɚš]; **SC**57, [aɪɚš]; **VA**40, Irishes ['aɪɚ,šɪz]; (Qu. H47) Inf **TX**99, [aɚš]; **VA**35, ['aɪɚˑš]; (Qu. H49) Inf **AL**15, [aš]; (Qu. I4) Inf **NC**50, [æˑš]. **1966–69** *DARE* FW Addit swNC, ['aɚš ,tetəz] Irish potatoes—common pronc among older folks; ceNC, ['aɚš pə,tedəz] Irish potatoes—common, old-fashioned; NC, I have heard [aɚˑš] and [aš] for *Irish.*

B As noun.

1 Temper, anger; fighting spirit—usu in phr *get one's Irish up.* [*OEDS Irish* sb. B.5 "orig. *U.S.* and *dial.*" Cf *EDD Irish* sb.[2]]

1834 Crockett *Narrative* 30 **TN,** I thought she ought to cool off. But her Irish was up too high to do any thing with her, and so I quit trying. **1856** (1928) Twain *Advent. Snodgrass* 22, She'd got her Irish up now, and din't keer a scratch for bars and nothin else. **1905** *DN* 3.12 **cCT,** Irish. . . Temper. 'He's getting his Irish up.' **1906** *DN* 3.142 **nwAR,** Irish. . . Temper. "To get one's Irish up," to get into a passion. **1908** *DN* 3.323 **eAL, wGA,** Irish. . . "By that time I got my Irish up, and I was ready to fight." **1941** Smith *Going to God's Country* 133 **MO** (as of 1896), Then he said, "Well it's just up to you." He saw that I was getting my Irish up. **1942** Warnick *Garrett Co. MD* 9 **nwMD** (as of 1900–18), Irish. . . temper. "He's got his Irish up this morning." **c1960** *Wilson Coll.* **csKY,** Irish. . . temper; hot-headedness. **1968–69** *DARE* (Qu. GG4, *Stirred up, angry: "When he saw them coming he got _____.")* Inf **MI**101, His Irish up; (Qu. HH30) Inf **NY**42, Irish up—temper; **NY**54, Irish up—mad, angry.

2 in phr *black Irish:*

a A person of Irish descent having black hair; see quots. [*OEDS* 1888 →]

1967–69 *DARE* (Qu. HH28, *Names and nicknames . . for people of foreign background*) Infs **CA**14, **NY**217, Black Irish. [*DARE* Ed: These Infs may refer instead to **2c** below.] **1983** *NADS Letters* **WI,** With regard to the term "black Irish" . . my mother, who grew up in an Irish settlement in Wisconsin, used the term to denote a dark haired, dark eyed Irishman, but with no reference to a "dark temper". *Ibid* **NJ,** Black Irish: This describes a specific combination of physical traits among the Irish, to wit, blue eyes, a fair skin and coal black hair, often tending to premature greying. . . [It is] used between the Hudson and York Rivers along the East Coast. **1985** *WI Alumnus Letters* **csWI,** Some Irish are dark complected, have dark hair and facial features. . . I heard once that the "black Irish" are de[s]cendents of intermarriage between ancestors of the Spanish Queen Isabella's . . armada that tried unsuccessfully to invade England. . . Since many of the . . troops in the armada were Moors, this would explain the dark features. *Ibid* **seWI,** The only use of the term *black Irish* I've heard was by a dark haired Irish friend who was born in Union Grove (near Racine). . . Over twenty years ago . . it meant "Irish of Roman blood." *Ibid* **IA** (as of c1900), My niece, from Iowa, knew the term "black Irish" as meaning *Irish* with black hair as opposed to red hair.

b An Irish Protestant.

1983 *NADS Letters* **GA,** Her folks always referred to themselves as black Irish, meaning Irish Protestants. Someone else in the crowd agreed that such had always been his idea of its meaning also. **1985** *WI Alumnus Letters* **KY** (as of c1950), The Irish side of the family remarked that he was "black Irish," & explained to me & my brothers that he was a Trinity College man & a Protestant.

c See quots—often considered derog. Cf *lace-curtain Irish* (at **lace curtain 2**)

1969 *DARE* (Qu. HH28, *Names and nicknames . . for people of foreign background*) Inf **IN**60, Black Irish—Irish person with a terrible temper. **1985** *DARE* File **CA,** Black Irish—used as a term of social snobbery and opprobrium. . . used to indicate Irish families of lower social orders, usually Catholic . . often used in conjunction with "shanty," such as "that Shanty Black Irishman." . . that term is grounds for a punch in the nose. **1985** *WI Alumnus Letters* **nwIL** (as of c1900), *Black Irish* to me as a child meant somebody new come from the old country, Ireland, not yet familiar with our local ways, meaning "wild", uncivilized, hard drinking, probably dirty in personal habits. *Ibid* **UT,** The term "Black Irish" is familiar to me from my childhood in Salt Lake City and Ogden, Utah. My father used the term to describe a man of Irish descent who was a rogue, someone not to be trusted, one who was capable of almost any kind of dastardly, dishonest or unlawful deed.

d See quot.

1985 *WI Alumnus Letters,* Some former slaves took the family names of their owners after the Civil War and . . in some sections there were many white families of Irish origin. Therefore, the descendants of these former slaves gave rise to the term "black Irish".

3 See **Irish potato.**

C As adj.

See quot. Cf *DS* U33–35

1968–70 *DARE* (Qu. HH30) Inf **MD**28, Irish—a joking synonym for tight—disinclined to spend money; **PA**245, Irish—tighter than a Jew; tight; also "worse than a Scotchman."

Irish n[2] See **iris**

Irish apple n Also *Irish grape,* ~ *lemon joc* Cf **Irish potato**
=**white potato.**

[**1891** Maitland *Amer. Slang Dict.* 150, *Irish apricots* or *Irish lemons,* potatoes.] **1942** Berrey–Van den Bark *Amer. Slang* 91.76, *Potato. . . Irish apple . . or lemon.* **1950** *WELS* (*Nicknames or other names for potatoes*) 2 Infs, **WI,** Irish lemons; 1 Inf, Irish apples. **1958** McCulloch *Woods Words* 95 **Pacific NW,** *Irish apples*—Potatoes. **1967** *DARE* (Qu. I9) Inf **OR**3, Irish apples. **1967** *DARE* FW Addit **CO**4, Irish lemons—another name for potatoes. **1977** Churchill *Don't Call* 44 **nwOR** (as of c1918), The only camp item Mother accepted readily was "Irish apples," sometimes used for potatoes. **1979** *Amer. Heritage Soc. Americana* Mar/Apr 70 [Glossary of military food during World War II], *Irish grapes.* White potatoes.

Irish baby buggy See **Irish buggy**

Irish banjo n Also *Irish fan,* ~ *spoon joc* Cf **banjo B2**
A shovel.

1862 in 1903 Norton *Army Letters* 73 **VA,** One company just passed armed with "Irish spoons," going out to work in the trenches. **1922** *DN* 5.181 **nID,** *Irish fan. . . A shovel.* Miners. **1941** *Rotarian* July 48/2 **neOH,** "Guess we'll set you to strumming an 'Irish banjo' ". . . They handed me a shovel! **1962** *Western Folkl.* 21.30 **Los Angeles CA,** *Irish banjo*—a shovel. **1967** *DARE* (Qu. HH30, *Things that are nicknamed for different nationalities*) Inf **IL**11, Irish banjo—for a shovel.

Irish brawl See **Irish fight**

Irish buggy n Also *Irish baby buggy,* ~ *man-o'-war,* ~ *pluggy,* ~ *wagon, Irishman's automobile,* ~ *buggy,* ~ *car,* ~ *locomotive;* for addit varr see quots **chiefly West** See Map
A wheelbarrow.

1929 *AmSp* 4.341 [Vagabond lingo], *Irish buggie*—A wheelbarrow. **1930** Irwin *Amer. Tramp* 107, *Irish buggy.*—A wheelbarrow, another of the many popular references to the Irish worker, always an object of mirth to the public. **1934** (1940) Weseen *Dict. Amer. Slang* 81 [Logger and miner talk], *Irish baby buggy*—A wheelbarrow. **1937** *AmSp* 12.74 [Among workers in the Civilian Conservation Corps], *Irish pluggy* or *Irish buggy*—wheelbarrow. **1938** Stuart *Dark Hills* 181 **neTN,** We dynamited the limestone rocks . . , beat them with sledge hammers . . , and . . wheeled them in Irish-buggies to a crusher. **1939** *LANE* Map 163 *(Wheelbarrow),* 1 inf, **nwCT,** An Irishman's locomotive; 1 inf,

cwVT, Irishman's buggy. **1949** Chisholm *Brewery Gulch* 42 **AZ** (as of 1880s), He could put a loaded Irish-man-o'-war, as the miners called a wheelbarrow, on his hard head and walk off with it. **1960** *AmSp* 35.270 **San Francisco CA,** *Irish buggy.* **1966–70** *DARE* (Qu. L41, *A device for moving dirt and other loads, with one wheel in front and handles to lift and push it behind*) 14 Infs, **chiefly West,** Irish buggy; **CA**124, **CO**19, Irishman buggy; **CO**19, Irishman cart; **MT**4, Irish wagon; **PA**211, Irishman's automobile; **KS**5, Irishman's car; (Qu. HH30) Inf **IL**11, Irish baby carriage; **TX**5, Irish buggy. [16 of 21 Infs old, 5 mid-aged] **1969** Sorden *Lumberjack Lingo* 61 **NEng, Gt Lakes,** Irish baby buggy.

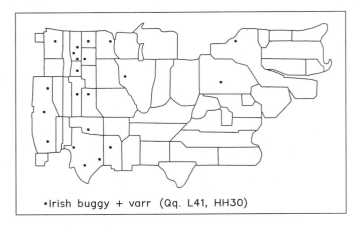

•Irish buggy + varr (Qq. L41, HH30)

Irish cabbage n

1 =**skunk cabbage** (here: *Symplocarpus foetidus*).

1958 Jacobs–Burlage *Index Plants NC* 17, *Symplocarpus foetidus. . . Irish cabbage. . .* It has been reported to be the main ingredient of an old patent remedy called "Shookum". A salve has been used locally for ringworm and inflammatory rheumatism.

2 See quot. Cf **Irish turkey**

1968 *DARE* (Qu. HH30, *Things that are nicknamed for different nationalities*) Inf **LA**46, Irish cabbage—corned beef, cabbage, and Irish potatoes. It is eaten on St. Patrick's Day.

Irish canvasback n
A **merganser.**

1923 U.S. Dept. Ag. *Misc. Circular* 13.5, *American Merganser. . . Vernacular Names. . . In local use. . .* Irish canvasback (Delaware Valley). **1956** *AmSp* 31.181, Irish canvasback. . . Mergansers . . Delaware Valley.

Irish cheese n Cf **clabber cheese, Dutch cheese**

1941 *LANE* Map 299 *(Cottage cheese)* 1 inf, **seNH,** Irish ch[eese].

Irish cobbler See **cobbler** n[2]

Irish confetti n
Bricks, stones, or fragments thereof, esp when thrown in a fight.

1935 Pollock *Underworld Speaks* np, *Irish confetti,* bricks. **1945** Saxon *Gumbo Ya-Ya* 50 **New Orleans LA,** There will be those who agree and those who will not, and, even at this late date, Irish confetti may fly. **1957** in 1962 *Western Folkl.* 21.31 **Los Angeles CA,** Irish confetti—bricks or cobblestones (formerly, now less definite) thrown in a street fight. . . (. . from a trade union organizer.) [*Ibid* 28, The term seemingly originated with the anti-Catholic rioting promoted by the Know-nothings in 1852.] **1960** *AmSp* 35.270 **San Francisco CA,** Phrases . . I have heard in actual usage in San Francisco building construction and waterfront employment are . . *Irish buggy, Irish confetti.* **1965** *DARE* FW Addit **OK,** Irish confetti—Part of a brick, either broken or cut in half to fill in ends of a wall. Also called brickbat. **1967–68** *DARE* (Qu. HH30) Inf **IL**11, Irish confetti—brickbats; **IN**49, Irish fight: with brickbats—Irish confetti.

Irish coupling n Cf **Irish measurement**
Among loggers: see quot.

1958 McCulloch *Woods Words* 95 **Pacific NW,** *Irish coupling*—Logs not completely bucked [=cut] through.

Irish curtain See **Irish lace**

Irish daisy n [*EDD* 1876]
=dandelion 1.
   1900 Lyons *Plant Names* 364, T[*araxacum*] *Taraxacum*. . . Irish Daisy. **1904** Henkel *Weeds Used in Med.* 13, Dandelion. . . *Other common names.*—Blow-ball, . . Irish daisy. **1930** Sievers *Amer. Med. Plants* 26. **1959** Carleton *Index Herb. Plants* 66, *Irish daisy:* Taraxacum officinalis. **1967** *DARE* (Qu. S11, . . *Other names . . for . . dandelion*) Inf **CO**37, Irish daisy.

Irish dividend n
   An assessment; see quots.
   1867 Richardson *Beyond the Mississippi* 375 **NV**, Many [mining] companies after immense expenditure reap only assessments, which in this region are termed 'Irish dividends.' **1881** *Harper's New Mth. Mag.* 62.805 **NYC**, Members [of the NY Philharmonic Society] found themselves in debt, and obliged to declare an "Irish dividend" to make the accounts balance. **1934** (1940) Weseen *Dict. Amer. Slang* 355, *Irish dividend*—An assessment. **1967** *Western Folkl.* 26.189, *Irish dividends*—a stock assessment. . . Used in Gerry Pratt's financial column, *The Oregonian* (Portland), early 1966.

Irish drapery See **Irish lace**

Irisher n
   A person who is Irish or of Irish descent.
   1807 in 1810 Schultz *Travels* 1.8 **ceNY**, The inhabitants are mostly of German descent, and still, in a great measure, retain their national prejudices, and consider all who do not speak their own language either as *Yankees* or *Irishers*. . . I was an *outlandish man,* or an *Irisher.* **1827** *Western Mth. Rev.* 1.385 **wPA**, He could flog, in a fair fist fight, any Dutchman, Irisher, or Yankee in the place. *Ibid* 386, Jacob Barndollar . . [asked] the fair Irisher, if she would marry him? **1907** *DN* 3.191 **seNH**, *Irisher*. . . "What did she want to marry an Irisher for?" **1942** *Sat. Eve. Post* 7 Nov 40/2 **sCA**, His before-breakfast ritual includes a romp with the kids. He [=Bing Crosby] calls them "the Irishers." **1945** Saxon *Gumbo Ya-Ya* 50 **New Orleans LA**, To think I am the last Irisher left in the Irish Channel! **1956** Gold *The Man Who* 90, I'm a Wop Irisher from Boston. **1968** *DARE* (Qu. HH28, *Names and nicknames . . for . . Irish*) Inf **NJ**12, Irishers. [*DARE* Ed: Inf is of Irish descent.]

Irish fair See **Irish fight**

Irish fan See **Irish banjo**

Irish fight n Also *Irish brawl, ~ fair* somewhat old-fash Cf **Irish confetti**
   A brawl, donnybrook.
   1965–70 *DARE* (Qu. HH30, *Things that are nicknamed for different nationalities*) Infs **AL**5, 6, 10, 20, **PA**24, 208, **NY**105, Irish fight; **IN**30, 45, **NY**105, Irish fight—a donnybrook; **DC**1, Irish fight—no holds barred; **IA**34, Irish fight—a *real* fight; **IN**32, **TN**43, Irish fight—a free-for-all; **IN**35, Irish fight—brawl; **IN**49, Irish fight—with brickbats (Irish confetti); **MI**113, Irish fight—a free-for-all or brouhaha; **NY**32, Irish fight [FW sugg]; **NY**57, Irish fight [FW: Inf doesn't know what it is]; **NY**50, Irish brawl—good fight; **SC**69, Irish brawl—big fight; (Qu. Y13, *A fist fight with several people in it*) Inf **FL**15, Free-for-all, Irish fair, donnybrook. [17 of 21 Infs old]

Irish flag n
   A diaper.
   1967 *DARE* (Qu. W19, *Names and nicknames for the folded cloth worn by a baby in place of pants*) Inf **TX**9, Irish flag.

Irish frank n Cf **Irish turkey**
   See quots.
   1967 *Chagrin Valley Herald* (Chagrin Falls OH) 21 Sept sec A 12, [Advt:] *Irish Franks*—corned beef wieners. **1978** *DARE* File **Cleveland OH** (as of c1970), Irish franks were available at meat counters. These were frankfurters made with corned beef.

Irish funnies n pl
   See quots.
   1971 Seaburg *Boston Observed* 246, The obituary columns of local newspapers have long been known as the "Irish funnies." **1979** *DARE* File **eMA**, In the Boston area, *Irish funnies* means the obituary columns in the newspapers.

Irish goose n [See quot 1938]
=double-crested cormorant.
   1938 Oberholser *Bird Life LA* 37, Double-crested Cormorant. . . On

the wing it flies much like a goose. . . This similarity undoubtedly accounts for its name 'nigger goose,' or 'Irish goose'. **1956** *AmSp* 31.181 **MS**, Irish goose. . . Double-crested cormorant.

Irish grape See **Irish apple**

Irish gray watermelon n Also *Irish green melon, Irish (gray) melon*
   A cultivar of the watermelon (*Citrullus lanatus*).
   1966–70 *DARE* (Qu. I26, . . *Kinds of melons*) Inf **NE**3, Irish gray melons; **OK**43, Irish gray melons—watermelons; **SC**7, Irish gray watermelons; **VA**46, Irish green—light; **OK**18, Irish melons—gray, plain watermelons. **1986** Pederson *LAGS Concordance* **Gulf Region** (*Watermelons*) 12 infs, Irish gray; 2 infs, Irish gray—white (thin) rind; [1 inf, Ice [a⸳ɛs] gray—long, green].

Irish hint n
   A very broad hint.
   1769 in 1962 Madison *Papers* 1.43 **NJ**, I believe there will not be [the] least danger of my getting an Irish hint as they call it. **1834** Nott *Novellettes* 1.8 **SC**, Various young men, that prowled about when honest people should be at home, a-bed, and asleep, intimated, in what might be called Irish hints, that they had espied the worthy Mr. Hunt at irregular places and at irregular hours. **1842** Kirkland *Forest Life* 1.115, As Butts was one of those who cannot take the broadest hint—even an irish one—he only talked the more. **1989** *NADS Letters* **sePA**, My husband attended a Jesuit high school in Philadelphia from 1960–64. He recalls two instances of the term [=*Irish hint*] there. In one, a teacher, having stumped a student with a question, rephrased it in such a way as to make the answer obvious, adding, "An Irish hint." On another occasion, another teacher (both were priests) recalled the wandering attention of a student by administering a painful twist to a handful of his hair. "Just an Irish hint," he explained.

Irish hurricane See **Irishman's hurricane**

Irish lace n Also *Irish curtain, ~ drapery* Cf *lace-curtain Irish* (at **lace curtain 2**)
   Cobwebs.
   [**1909** Ware *Passing Engl.* 148, *Irish draperies*. . . Cobwebs.] **1950** *WELS Suppl.* **ceWI**, Irish lace—cobwebs in the house. **1968–70** *DARE* (Qu. R29a, . . *The thing that a spider spins and lives in—if it is indoors*) Inf **PA**176, Irish lace; **TX**85, Irish curtains—web that hangs down from ceiling, inside [the] house. **1975** Gould *ME Lingo* 142, *Irish* draperies are cobwebs, perhaps a bit of one-upmanship with "lace-curtain" *Irish.*

Irish lemon See **Irish apple**

Irish lord n esp **AK**
   A Pacific sculpin of the genus *Hemilepidotus*. For other names of var spp see **red sculpin**
   1898 U.S. Natl. Museum *Bulletin* 47.1934, Hemilepidotus. . . *Irish Lords*. . . North Pacific, in shallow water. **1928** Pan-Pacific Research Inst. *Jrl.* 3.3.14 **OR, WA**, *Hemilepidotus hemilepidotus*. . . Irish Lord. **1946** Dufresne *AK's Animals* 287, Enormously wide of mouth are these "Irish Lords," all head and spines and dagger-sharp points. No two of them are colored alike. **1960** Amer. Fisheries Soc. *List Fishes* 39, Red Irish lord. . . P[acific]. . . *Hemilepidotus hemilepidotus*. . . Brown Irish lord. . . P[acific]. . . *Hemilepidotus spinosus*. **1968** *DARE* (Qu. P4, *Saltwater fish that are not good to eat*) Inf **AK**1, Irish lord—hundreds of species of sculpins—very colorful; **AK**9, Irish lord—sculpin. **1978** *AK Fishing Guide* 89, Sculpin, or Irish lord, has a large head with eyes placed high.

Irish mail n Also *Irish mailcar, ~ rover, ~ wagon* [Prob ironic ref to *mail* a (usu fast) conveyance for transporting mail]
   A child's wheeled vehicle propelled by pushing a handle forward and backward.
   [**1900** *DN* 2.45 **OH** [College lingo], *Irish local* . . a hand-car.] **1927** (1970) Sears *Catalogue* 602, *Genuine Irish Mails*—Adjustable for Boys and Girls 3 to 12 Years—They sail along quietly. . . Cog wheels covered to prevent any possible injury to rider or clothing. **1967** *DARE* FW Addit **AR**, *Irish mailcar*—a toy wagon propelled by pumping the handlebars handcar fashion. **1992** *DARE* File **NYC**, *Irish mail*—A childsize four wheel vehicle for use on the sidewalks of New York City propelled by a handle pulled back and pushed forward, steered by the feet resting on the front axle. *Ibid* **Louisville KY** (as of c1946), Irish mail. . . It was hand pumped with handlebars, which drove the back wheels. My wife, upon reflection, remembers something called an Irish wagon, but it was a vehicle large enough to carry two people, somewhere between a riding

lawn mower and a golf cart. It was also propelled by pumping front handle bar type cranks. If my memory serves, I also used Irish wagon as well as Irish mail for the child's vehicle that I rode. *Ibid* **nKY,** Damned if my buddy . . who grew up right across the river from me didn't have an Irish Rover when he was a kid! . . A note from his wife, another local, suggests, however, that the Irish Rover may have been hand-cranked rather than pedal-driven.

Irish mallard n

Any of three ducks: **Florida duck, mallard 1,** or **shoveler.**

1923 U.S. Dept. Ag. *Misc. Circular* 13.8 **LA,** Mallard *(Anas platyrhynchos)*. . . *Vernacular Names.* . . *In local use.* . . Irish mallard. *Ibid* 10, *Anas fulvigula*. . . Irish mallard. **1956** *AmSp* 31.181 **CA,** Irish mallard. . . Shoveler.

Irishman See **Irish potato**

Irish man-o'-war See **Irish buggy**

Irishman's automobile (or buggy, car) See **Irish buggy**

Irishman's hurricane n Also *Irish hurricane*

Esp among sailors: a calm; see quots.

1827 Cooper *Red Rover* 3.118 **N Atl,** We had the wind at east-with-southing, the first day out, and then it chopp'd in the night, and blew great guns at north-west, where it held for the matter of a week. After which there was an Irishman's hurricane, right up and down, for a day; then we got into these here trades. **1840** (1841) Dana *2 Yrs.* 364, We were . . within five degrees of the line, to which two days of good breeze would take us; but we had, for the most part, what the sailors call 'an Irishman's hurricane—right up and down.' This day it rained nearly all day. **1942** ME Univ. *Studies* 56.57, An Irishman's hurricane,—a dead calm. **1945** Colcord *Sea Language* 47 **ME, Cape Cod, Long Island,** Other names for a calm are Irish hurricane and Paddy's hurricane. **1975** Gould *ME Lingo* 142, An "Irish hurricane" is a *flat-arse calm.*

Irishman's locomotive See **Irish buggy**

Irishman's potato See **Irish potato**

Irishman's sidewalk n

See quots.

1907 *DN* 3.191 **seNH,** Irishman's sidewalk. . . The street. "I am going to take the Irishman's sidewalk." **1931–33** *LANE Worksheets* **seMA,** Irishman's sidewalk—center of the street.

Irishman's turkey See **Irish turkey**

Irish measurement n Cf **Irish coupling**

Among loggers: see quot.

1946 *CA Folkl. Qrly.* 5.167 **MT** [Timbermen's terms], An "Irish measurement" is a timber either too long or too short.

Irish melon See **Irish gray watermelon**

Irish moss n

1 An edible red alga *(Chondrus crispus)* found on the North Atlantic coast. [*OED* 1845 →] Also called **carrageen, sea moss**

1853 (1982) Lea *Domestic Cookery* 104, Carrageen or Irish Moss Blancmange. Wash in three waters half an ounce of Carrageen moss; drain and put it in two quarts of new milk, let it boil for a few minutes, strain it in a pitcher, wet the moulds, and pour it in while hot; let it stand till it becomes thick. **1854** King *Amer. Eclectic Dispensatory* 340, *Chondrus crispus.* Irish Moss. . . This plant . . [is] said also to be a native of the United States. **1876** Hobbs *Bot. Hdbk.* 20, Carrageen moss, Irish moss, Chondrus crispus. **1884** U.S. Natl. Museum *Bulletin* 27.1037, An estimate . . of the comparative value of the products of some of the fisheries . . credits the cod fishery with $4,000,000; . . seaweed industry, $19,000; and the Irish moss industry, $16,000. *Ibid* 1144, Irish moss *(Chondrus crispus).* **1901** Arnold *Sea-Beach* 80, Carrageen or Irish moss. . . is an edible alga, and was formerly used very generally for culinary purposes. At Hingham, Massachusetts, large quantities are gathered as an article of commerce. **1948** Pearson *Sea Flavor* 37 **NH,** *Irish moss.* . . clings tenaciously to rocks from the low-water mark to a depth of about 14 feet at ebb tide. **1975** Gould *ME Lingo* 142, *Irish moss* is carrageen, a marine plant harvested along the Maine coast. . . After processing, it is used as a stabilizer in food. Early coastal housewives knew it could be boiled to make a pudding of the blanc-mange type, and along in the 1930s the dairy industry began using it to smooth out ice cream. . . Today *Irish moss* is included under one name or another in almost all packaged and pre-packaged foods where it suits.

2 =**cypress spurge.**

[**1892** *Jrl. Amer. Folkl.* 5.102, *Euphorbia cyparissias*. Irish moss. N[ew] B[runswick].] **1959** Carleton *Index Herb. Plants* 66, *Irish moss:* Chondrus crispa; Euphorbia cyparissias; Helxine solieroli; Portulaca (v).

Irish nightingale n [See quot 1976] *joc* Cf **Dutch nightingale** =**bullfrog 1.**

1901 *DN* 2.142, *Irish nightingale.* . . Bull frog. Newburgh, N.Y. **1942** Berrey–Van den Bark *Amer. Slang* 120.33, Irish nightingale, *a bull frog.* **1976** Flexner *America Talking* 136, In the 1850s . . humorous terms mocking the Irish began to multiply, as . . *Irish nightingale,* a bullfrog (based on *the Swedish nightingale* Jenny Lind, who made a highly publicized concert tour of America 1850–52).

Irish nose n Also *Irish snub*

A turned-up nose.

1966–70 *DARE* (Qu. X15, . . *Kinds of noses*) Inf **CT**40, Irish [nose]; **FL**27, Tip-tilted—Irish; tip comes up; **MA**5, Irish snub—tip-tilted; **OH**98, Turned-up Irish nose.

Irish pennant n Also *Irish pendant* [Orig naut]

A loose or frayed end; something that hangs loose or flaps untidily.

1840 (1841) Dana *2 Yrs.* 221 **MA,** There was no rust, no dirt, no rigging hanging slack, no fag ends of ropes and "Irish pendants" aloft. **1942** ME Univ. *Studies* 56.29 [Nautical terms], A rope was at loose ends if the strands at the end had become loose. . . That was called the *fag end* . . if it was hanging dangling it was called an *Irish pennant.* **1945** Colcord *Sea Language* 107 **ME, Cape Cod, Long Island,** *Irish pennant.* A loose, dangling end of rope. Alongshore, a rag, or anything frayed out and fluttering untidily, is likely to be called by this name. Also called Irish pendant. **1962** *Western Folkl.* 21.31 **CA** (as of c1945), Irish pennants—rags or laundry hung up to dry on board ship. **1975** Gould *ME Lingo* 142, "Irish" pennants are loose strands on the ends of lines. **1982** *Smithsonian Letters* **neVA,** "There was Irish pennants all over it [=a badly installed awning]". . . Irish pennants—ragged edges, untrimmed ravelings.

Irish pluggy See **Irish buggy**

Irish plum n

1 A **horse nettle 1** (here: *Solanum carolinense*).

1819 Thomas *Travels W. Country* 224, *Solanum carolinense*—horse nettle, or Irish plumb. **1940** Clute *Amer. Plant Names* 272, *Solanum Carolinense.* . . Irish plum.

2 See quot. *joc* Cf **French lozenger**

1941 *LANE* Map 257, 1 inf, **ceMA,** *Irish plums,* jocular name for onions.

Irish pompano n

A **mojarra 1** of the Florida east coast (here: *Diapterus olisthostomus*). Also called **hogfish f, muttonfish 3**

1882 U.S. Natl. Museum *Proc.* 5.423 **FL,** *Gerres olisthostoma.* . . Mr. R. E. Earll . . obtained at Indian River six specimens. . . They are known as the "Irish pompano." **1896** Jordan–Evermann *Check List Fishes* 392, Irish Pompano. . . West Indies, north to southern Florida. **1955** Carr-Goin *Guide Reptiles* 106 **FL,** Irish Pompano. . . Recorded in fresh water from Florida only in the St. Johns River. **1973** Knight *Cook's Fish Guide* 387.

Irish potato n Also *Irish, Irishman, Irishman's potato* [See quot 1901; *OED* 1664 →, "now U.S."] **scattered, but more freq Sth, S Midl** See Map and Map Section Cf **Irish apple, Mick 3, murphy**

=**white potato,** esp as contrasted with a **sweet potato** (here: *Ipomoea batatas*). Also called **ice potato**

1685 in 1687 Blome *Present State* 123 **sePA,** I have planted the *Irish Potatoes,* and hope to have a brave encrease to transplant next year. **1750** (1916) Birket *Cursory Remarks* 9 **ME,** They have. . . abundance of Garden Culture as Beans, . . Asparagus, English or whats commonly called Irish Potatoes also the Sweete Potatoe. **1851** *De Bow's Rev.* 11.58 **LA,** The *Irish Potatoe* grows very luxuriantly, but is never reared for shipment. Seldom kept through winter. **1899** (1912) Green *VA Folk-Speech* 241, *Irish potato.* . . The well known potato so called to distinguish it from the *sweet-potato.* **1901** *Boston Morning Jrl.* 8/1 *(OED),* Irish potatoes . . are called Irish from the Irish, who came in 1719, settled Londonderry, N.H., and were required to pay quit rent to the amount of a peck of potatoes. . . The white potato, called Irish, . . did not become general until after 1800. **1905** *DN* 3.83 **nwAR,** *Irish potato.* . . Common white potato. The expression 'white potato' is never used and is not understood. **1908** *DN* 3.323 **eAL, wGA,** *Irishman's (po)tato.* . . Irish potato. **1916** *DN* 4.269 **IA, IL, LA, NC, TN, VA,** *Irish potatoes.* **1930** *DN* 6.88 **cWV,** *Irishman* . . an Irish potato; one of many facetious names for food. **1954** *Harder Coll.* **cwTN,** Irish potatoes. . . Never white potatoes. **1964** *PADS* 42.19 **csKY,** *Irish potatoes.* Formerly regular, to distinguish them from *sweet potatoes.* The general usage now is *potatoes,* with no prefix. **1965–70** *DARE* (Qu. HH30) 44 Infs, **scattered,** Irish potato; **NY234,** Irish potato digger, Irish potato eater; **SC3,** Irish potatoes—white potatoes; (Qu. I9) 37 Infs, **chiefly Sth,** Irish potatoes; **CA77, SC7, VA40,** Irish(es); **AL15,** "Potatoes" are really sweet potatoes; otherwise Irish potatoes; **SC4,** "Potato" means yam here; the white kinds must be designated specifically: white potato, Irish potato; **SC29,** Irish potatoes—white ones; (Qu. H47) 12 Infs, **esp Sth, S Midl,** (Fried) Irish potatoes; **NC44, OK21,** Irish; (Qu. H17) Inf **AR26,** Hops and Irish potatoes; (Qu. H36) Inf **MS85,** Irish potato soup; (Qu. H49) Inf **LA6,** Boiled Irish potatoes; **SC3,** Irish potato dumplings; (Qu. H65) Inf **LA20,** Irish potatoes; (Qu. I4) Infs **NC50, 76, TX6,** Irish potatoes; (Qu. L22) Infs **OK20, 43,** Plant Irish potatoes; (Qu. L34) Inf **AL31,** Irish potatoes; (Qu. R30) Inf **NC49,** Irish potato bug; (Qu. S26e) Inf **DC5,** Wild Irish potato; (Qu. BB50c) Inf **SC11,** Irish potato poultice; (Qu. BB51a) Inf **AL43,** Sliced Irish potato; **MS59,** Rub with an Irish potato. **1981** *DARE* File **NC** (as of 1910–25), Irish potato meant white potato, as distinguished from sweet potato (which has a brownish color).

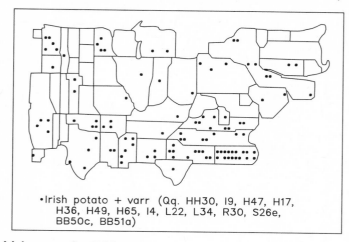

•Irish potato + varr (Qq. HH30, I9, H47, H17, H36, H49, H65, I4, L22, L34, R30, S26e, BB50c, BB51a)

Irish rover See **Irish mail**

Irish snipe n

1 =bluestocking 2. [See quot 1956]
1916 *Times–Picayune* (New Orleans LA) 2 Apr mag sec 5, *American Avocet.* . . Irish Snipe; Blue Stockings. **1918** Grinnell *Game Birds CA* 337, *Avocet.* . . *Other Names* . . Irish Snipe; Blue-stocking. **1953** Jewett *Birds WA* 283, Irish Snipe. . . with its large size, pale coloration, black wing, and long upturned bill is always conspicuous about the lakes where it makes its home. **1956** *AmSp* 31.185 **CA, LA, TX,** Irish snipe. . . Avocet. . . In allusion to its upturned beak or 'nose.'

2 =sandhill crane.
1956 *AmSp* 31.183, In *gandersnipe* (great blue heron, Pa.), the fun is in the second part; for so large a bird to be called a snipe . . , a modifier indicating its large size is necessary. . . *Irish snipe* for the almost equally tall sandhill crane is a name of the same sort (seen on the label of a bird in a Minnesota market in 1894).

Irish snowstorm n Cf **Norwegian snowstorm**
Among loggers: see quot.
1969 Sorden *Lumberjack Lingo* 61 **NEng, Gt Lakes,** *Irish snowstorm*—Putting snow on bare spots of logging roads to get out the last of the logs in spring breakup. The shovel had a five- to six-foot handle.

Irish snub See **Irish nose**

Irish spoon See **Irish banjo**

Irish tea n [By analogy with *Irish coffee*]
A drink made of tea laced with whiskey.
1967–69 *DARE* (Qu. HH30, *Things that are nicknamed for different nationalities*) Infs **NJ57, WA20,** Irish tea; **NY76,** Irish tea—tea with [a] shot of whiskey.

Irish trick n Also *dirty Irish trick*
See quots.
1966 *Oregonian* (Portland OR) 17 Mar 9/8 **Chicago IL,** It seems like a dirty Irish trick that an individual would say this [=that St. Patrick was really two persons] just two days before St. Patrick's Day. **1967** *Western Folkl.* 26.189 **cKS** (as of c1900), *Irish trick, dirty*—always, to the best of my recollection, used jocularly. A "dirty trick" was a scurvy act, but "Irish" as a modifier carried with it an implication of unwilling amusement or admiration and removed most or much of the sting. **1967–68** *DARE* (Qu. HH30) Infs **NE9, VA33A,** Irish trick; **MI67,** Dirty Irish trick; **IL5,** Irish trick—a fast one.

Irish trot n
A type of round dance; see quot 1936, 1940.
1824 Doddridge *Notes Indian Wars* 158 **wVA, PA,** I remember to have seen once or twice, a dance which was called "the Irish Trot" but I have long since forgotten its figure. **1936** Owens *Swing & Turn* 51 **TX,** *Irish trot.* . . Partners . . join hands to form a ring. They march around to the right while singing the first stanza. . . While singing the last stanza the couples . . march around the circle, one couple in line behind another. **1940** *Handy Play Party Book* 87 **neTX,** *Irish trot.* . . Join hands high in a single circle, with girls facing out, boys facing in, and go around clockwise. . . Circle counter-clockwise. . . Partners face and do the grand right and left until they met [sic]. . . Double L swing. **1966** *DARE* (Qu. FF5a, . . *Different steps and figures in dancing—in past years*) Inf **MS6,** Irish trot.

Irish turkey n Also *Irishman's turkey* joc Cf **Cape Cod turkey, Irish cabbage 2, ~ frank, New York turkey**
Corned beef, often with cabbage.
1926 *AmSp* 1.651 [Hobo lingo], *Irish turkey*—corned beef and cabbage. **1927** *WI News* (Milwaukee) 16 Nov 20 *(Zwilling Coll.),* [Cartoon:] I'm gonna play the old C.B. and C. I can eat Irish turkey 4 times a day. **1927** *DN* 5.451 **cnNC** [Underworld jargon], *Irish turkey.* . . corned beef and cabbage. **1929** *AmSp* 4.341 [Vagabond lingo], *Irish turkey*—Corn beef and cabbage. **1936** *AmSp* 11.43 [Soda jerker jargon], *Irish turkey.* Corned beef and cabbage. **1945** *AN&Q* 5.88/2, Irish turkey—corned beef. **1966** *Western Folkl.* 25.38, *Irishman's turkey.* Corned beef and cabbage. **1994** *DARE* File **CA,** In San Francisco at Eighth and Bryant Streets, a large green turkey revolves over the door of a corned beef maker. The origin? A century ago beef was cheap and turkey expensive. The immigrant Irish could not afford anything expensive, so corned beef was "Irish turkey."

Irish twin n
One of two siblings born within a year of each other.
1966 *DARE* File **csWI,** Irish twins—two children born within or in less than one year of each other in a family. (Heard from a doctor in Waunakee.) **1979** *Ibid* **neNJ,** They couldn't have children, so they adopted a foreign baby. Then, within a month of the adoption, she was pregnant. It was just like the Irish twins—you know, one was conceived right after the other was born. **1985** Greeley *Happy Meek* 194 **neIL,** Margaret and Wolfe Junior were Irish twins, born eleven months apart. **1990** *DARE* File **ceWI,** When I was a little girl—about 1920—I heard my Aunt Minnie refer to a neighbor's babies as "Irish twins." Because I wasn't quite sure of how long it took to have a baby, I was very interested to find out that, as Aunt Minnie explained "Irish twins" to me, you could have two babies within twelve months!

Irish wagon n
1 See **Irish buggy.**
2 See **Irish mail.**

Irish wash n joc Cf **French dry clean**
See quot.
1966–70 *DARE* (Qu. HH30, *Things that are nicknamed for different nationalities*) Inf **KY50,** Irish wash—give it the Irish wash—turning the garment or whatever around so the dust doesn't show; **MI17,** Irish wash—give it an Irish wash—turn the tablecloth over, put the dirty side down; (Qu. KK49) Inf **PA234,** Give it an Irish wash—you just turn the tablecloth over. [All Infs old]

Irish whisper n
An instance of saying something out loud when silence or a true whisper would be more appropriate.
1985 Wilkinson *Moonshine* 117 **neNC,** I went ahead of Garland, and when I came to the fence and saw an insulator on the post and realized it was electrified, I slid under it on my back, so I could watch it, and

when I did I gave Garland an Irish whisper. I didn't want to say it too loud, because we were right behind West's house. **1989** *NADS Letters,* I . . have heard *Irish whisper,* which refers to saying something aloud when whispering would have been more appropriate (e.g., blurting out a secret). The only two people from whom I have heard this expression are my mother and late aunt (both Irish). I clearly remember the first time I met with the term: I was about 8 or 10 years old at the time and had to ask my aunt to define the expression, which she had used spontaneously.

iris lily See **lily 2b**

iron n, v, adj Usu |'aɪə(r)n|; also **chiefly S Midl** |ɑrn|; occas by metath |'aɪrən|; for addit varr see quots Pronc-spp *ah(r)n, ahun, a(i)rn, i'(o)n, i'u(r)n, orn*

A Forms.

1862 (1864) Browne *Artemus Ward Book* 194, I was carrid to Montgomry in iuns. **1867** Lowell *Biglow* lxxxix **'Upcountry' MA,** She is sprinklin' cl'oes / Agin to-morrer's i'nin. **1891** *DN* 1.152 **cNY,** ['aɪən] . . 'iron.' *Ibid* 156, Diphthongs become monophthongs. . . especially before *r:* . . [ɑrn] < iron. **1894** Riley *Armazindy* 47 **IN,** Th'ough the iurnweeds. **1901** *DN* 2.182 **neKY** [Black], *Iron*—i'on. **1915** *DN* 4.180 **swVA,** *Arn.* **1916** *DN* 4.276 **NE,** *Iron.* . . Occasionally . . *orn.* [Footnote:] In Kan. the sound â is used, as *iron* [ɑrn]. **1917** *DN* 4.407 **wNC,** *Arn.* **1922** Gonzales *Black Border* 307 **sSC, GA coasts** [Gullah Glossary], *I'on, I'un.* . . iron, irons, ironed, ironing. **1927** Kennedy *Gritny* 159 **sLA** [Black], Workin' so heavy on dat i'nin-board. **1929** (1931) Faulkner *Sound & Fury* 5 **MS,** Holding on to that ahun gate. **1933** *AmSp* 8.1.32 **nwTX,** I warshed this mornin' and arned this evenin'. **1936** *AmSp* 11.33 **eTX,** *Hired, iron,* are also often pronounced with [a:], [ɑ:], [ɒ:], or in illiterate speech even [ɔ:]. **1937** *AmSp* 12.288 **nwVA,** [ɑrn] for *iron.* **1939** *LANE* Map 154 *(Crowbar),* [Throughout **NEng,** *iron* occurs as [aɪən, ajən, aɪn] in the phrase *iron bar;* in **wNEng,** it occas occurs as [aɪrn, aɛrn].] **1941** *Ibid* Map 244 *(Sycamore)* 1 inf, **neMA,** [aɪənwʊd]. **1941** *AmSp* 16.9 **eTX** [Black], Iron [ãɔn]. **1941** in 1944 *ADD* **ncWV,** Airn [ern]. **1942** Hall *Smoky Mt. Speech* 44 **wNC, eTN,** *Iron* is [ɑən]. In the speech of those who have been but little exposed to classroom influences, the sound is frequently [ɒ] or [ɔ] before *r: iron* [ɔən]. **1952** Brown *NC Folkl.* 1.516 **wNC,** *Arn.* **1953** *New Yorker* 12 Dec 97 **Baltimore MD,** "He was a prisoner of the Japs. . . And they had him in irons." She pronounced it "ahns." **1959** Faulkner *Mansion* 414 **MS,** I got to find a stick of stovewood or a piece of ahrn somewhere. **c1960** *Wilson Coll.* **csKY,** Iron [ɑrn] is widely used, by people on many educational levels. **1965–70** *DARE* (Qu. D32) Infs **CT39, NY233, PA5, 234,** ['æd₁aɪrən(z)], Add-iron(s); **MD35, 41,** ['æd₁ɑ·nz]; **MO4,** ['æd₁ɑɚnz]; (Qu. F1) Inf **MS55,** [ɑɚn]; **MO7,** [ɑ·ɚn·]; **TN23,** [aɚn]; (Qu. F29) Inf **DC1,** ['aˑɚnz]; **IL61,** ['sædɑɚn]; **IN7,** [ɑɚn]; **LA12,** ['koʊl₁daən] cold iron or ['koʊl₁aən] coal iron; **TN37,** [ɑɪɚən]. **1989** *DARE* File **Upstate NY,** For i-r-o-n I say ['aɪ·rən]. Always have said it that way. My mother says it ['aɪ·rən], but my younger siblings all say ['aɪ₁ɚn]. **1990** Amory *Cat & Curmudgeon* 192 **eTX,** On the way to our first pasture I kept thinking about that East Texas accent. . . of "all" for oil . . "are" for hair . . "arn" for iron.

B As noun.

1 also pl: A livestock brand. [Transf from *iron* a branding iron] Cf **C** below

1907 White *AZ Nights* 84, Finally, one day, we run on a four-months' calf all by himself, with the T O iron onto him. **1934** (1940) Weseen *Dict. Amer. Slang* 100 [Western terms], *Iron*—A branding iron; a brand made with such a tool. **1936** McCarthy *Lang. Mosshorn* np **West** [Range term], *Irons.* . . Another term for brand. **c1937** in 1970 Yetman *Voices* 43 **TX** [Black], De captain say, "Iffen de cow got iron burns de rancher gwine to shoot hisself a nigger scout." But de cow ain't got no iron, it's. . . Maverick.

2 =**andiron.** Cf **dog iron 1, fire iron 1, log iron**

1949 *AmSp* 24.110 **cSC,** *Irons.* . . Andirons. **1956** Ker *Vocab. W. TX* 120, The literary term *andirons* has equal currency with the Southern *dog irons.* . . One informant . . responded with *irons.* **1965** Carmony *Speech Terre Haute* 16 **sIN,** *Andirons.* . . *irons* [offered by 1 young, well-educ inf]. **1965–70** *DARE* (Qu. D32, *The metal stands in a fireplace that the logs are laid on*) 13 Infs, **scattered,** Irons. **1966** Dakin *Dial. Vocab. Ohio R. Valley* 2.36 **sIL, KY,** *Andirons.* . . [6 of 207 infs] *irons.* **1972** *PADS* 58.11 **cwAL,** *Andirons.* Southern and Midland *fire dogs* (7), *dog irons* (7), *fire irons* (1), *irons* (1), and *dogs* (1) occur more frequently than the general term *andirons* (10). **1973** Allen *LAUM* 1.162 (as of c1950), 1 inf, **nwIA,** *Irons.* **1986** Pederson *LAGS Concordance,* 1 inf, **swAL,** Iron—used to put logs on.

3 Pots and pans.

1924 Raine *Land of Saddle-Bags* 81 **sAppalachians,** Commonly we jest bring in some iron and delft, a leetle coffee, some indigo, and alum for dyein'. **1944** *PADS* 2.19 **sAppalachians,** *Iron and deft* [sic]. . . Pots, pans, and dishes.

4 See **iron man 1.**

C As verb.

To brand livestock. Cf **B1** above

1942 Berrey–Van den Bark *Amer. Slang* 918.4 [Western terms], *Brand. Flank, iron.* **1956** Almirall *From College* 44 **CO,** My lessons in this art had commenced by learning to read Dad's brand, which was Bar LA, or as ironed upon the left hips of his critters— –LA. **1961** Adams *Old-Time Cowhand* 255 **SW,** The reg'lar "calf brandin' " occurred in the spring, and this was called "ironin' the calf crop," because it was the brandin' of the season's calves.

iron ball (hickory nut) n Cf **hard-shell hickory**

Prob a **pignut** (here: *Carya glabra*).

1969–70 *DARE* (Qu. I43, *What kinds of nuts grow wild around here?*) Inf **KY75,** Iron-ball hickory nut; (Qu. T16, . . *Kinds of trees* . . *'special'*) Inf **KY11,** Iron ball—type of hickory nut, shells ¼ to ½ inches thick—last thing a squirrel will eat.

iron bar n [*EDD* (at *iron* sb. 1.(3)) 1886] **chiefly NEng**

A crowbar or other metal lever.

1939 *LANE* Map 154 *(Crowbar; lever),* Iron bar is often used, like *bar,* as a general term including all kinds of metal levers (even those made of steel, according to [two infs.]). Less commonly it denotes a particular kind of lever, defined as between four and eight feet long . . , as having one sharp end . . or as pointed at both ends. . . Iron bar is described as being the usual term by [4 infs]; as modern by [1 inf]; and as older though still in use by [2 infs]. . . 122 infs, **chiefly MA, NH, RI, VT,** Iron bar. **1966–70** *DARE* (Qu. L40, *A long iron bar used to move rocks and other heavy things*) 13 Infs, 9 **NEng,** Iron bar. [10 Infs old, 3 mid-aged]

iron bender n

1 Among loggers and railroad workers: see quots.

1958 McCulloch *Woods Words* 95 **Pacific NW,** *Iron bender.* . . A railroad brakeman. **1962** *AmSp* 37.133 **nwCA** [Logging railroad terms], *Iron bender.* . . A railroad brakeman.

2 Among loggers: see quot. Cf **iron burner**

1958 McCulloch *Woods Words* 95 **Pacific NW,** *Iron bender.* . . A camp blacksmith.

iron blood n

1 Prob iron-rich blood.

1967 Fetterman *Stinking Creek* 70 **seKY,** Hit's a weed around here—we call it niggerweed or sometimes iron blood. Dig the roots. It makes your iron blood. If you ain't got enough iron blood and get run down, you may have enough of the other blood but no iron blood. Brother, this niggerweed will put it in you.

2 A **boneset 1** (here: *Eupatorium purpureum*).

1967 [see **1** above].

iron burner n

Among loggers: see quots. Cf **iron bender 2**

1938 (1939) Holbrook *Holy Mackinaw* 262, *Iron burner.* Camp blacksmith. **1956** *Western Folkl.* 15.203 **West** [Loggers' lingo], *Iron burner*—the blacksmith. **1958** McCulloch *Woods Words* 95 **Pacific NW.** **1969** Sorden *Lumberjack Lingo* 61 **NEng, Gt Lakes.**

iron bush n

A **hardhack 1** (here: *Spiraea tomentosa*).

1898 *Jrl. Amer. Folkl.* 11.226, *Spiraea tomentosa,* . . iron bush, South Berwick, Me.

iron chink n [**chink** n[3] 1] **AK, WA**

A machine for cleaning and dressing fish; see quots.

1913 Underwood *Alaska* 189, The fish pass into the clutches of a machine known as the "Iron Chink," an indescribably intricate mixture of clanking wheels and shafts and whirling knives, that works with almost human ingenuity. When the salmon leave the machine, they are cleaned of every speck of blood and viscera and every fin has been eliminated. **1919** *DN* 5.57 **WA,** *Iron chink.* A machine for cleaning fish, a substitute for Chinese (Chink) hand labor. **1933** *Natl. Geogr. Mag.* 63.146/2 **nwWA,** The fish come in fresh from the waters of Puget Sound

[and] pass through the "iron chink" which cleans them at the rate of 60 to the minute. **1939** FWP *Guide AK* xl, *Iron chink.* **1944** Williamson *Far North* 125 **AK,** The fish were now subjected to a mechanical monster known as the "iron chink," which beheaded, untailed, and degutted them with slam-bang efficiency. **1959** Hart *McKay's AK* 32, [Glossary:], *Iron chink:* An automatic device for splitting and cleaning fish which may be seen when visiting the canneries; it is an expression coined as a result of automation when the machines replaced the Chinese workers and made the "China gang" obsolete in Alaska. **1967** *DARE* Tape **WA**11, In Alaska. . . years ago they . . imported . . Chinese working in the fish canneries. . . Then they developed what was called an "iron Chink," . . this machine which would clean the fish. **1967** VanStone *Eskimos* 77 **seAK,** The most significant of these improvements was a remarkable machine called the "Iron Chink," first used in 1903, which beheaded, split, and cleaned the fish. Its name, of course, derives from the fact that it replaced Chinese labor. The "Iron Chink" was introduced on a large scale between 1911 and 1913.

iron dishcloth n Also *iron dishrag* [Cf *OED* iron-cloth (at *iron* sb.¹ 12) "chain-mail, *esp.* as made in modern times for cleansing greasy vessels"] *old-fash*
A pad of interlocking metal rings used to scour pots.
    1950 *WELS* (*A ball or pad of rough metal used to scour pots and pans*) 1 Inf, **WI,** Iron dishrag—The old ring-mesh ones—old-fashioned. **1967–68** *DARE* (Qu. G14) Inf **NY**105, Iron dishrag or iron dishcloth—made of metal rings; **OH**8, Iron dishcloth—old-fashioned; **PA**29, Iron dishrag. [All Infs old]

iron dog n
1 =andiron. **Sth, S Midl** Cf **dog iron 1, iron B2,** *DS* D32
    1782 in a1972 *Hench Coll.* **ceVA,** I give to my son. . . all the axes and Hoes . . , one pr. of Iron Dogs. **1903** Murrie *White Castle LA* 224, A small log was slowly burning, one end on the homely iron dog, the other resting on the hearth of the great brick fireplace. **1966** Dakin *Dial. Vocab. Ohio R. Valley* 2.36, Andirons. . . [2 of 207 infs] iron dogs. **1967** Faries *Word Geog. MO* 72, There are five write-in expressions: *iron dogs, fire place irons, fire irons, irons,* and *log rests.* **c1970** Pederson *Dial. Surv. Rural GA* **seGA,** *Iron dogs*—used for andirons by 2 of 64 informants. **1986** Pederson *LAGS Concordance,* 2 infs, **cTN,** Iron dogs; 1 inf, **neGA,** Iron dogs—older name; 1 inf, **seMS,** Two iron dogs.
2 A snowmobile. [By analogy with *iron horse* a locomotive] **AK**
    1960 *AK Sportsman* June 20/3, Three "iron dogs" were making a demonstration trek that may push flesh-and-blood dogs even further into the background as freighters in the bush. The "iron dogs" [are] known commercially as Snow-Travelers. . . The Snow-Traveler is a ski-equipped sled powered by a one-cylinder, air-cooled Kohler engine driving endless cleated track. **1978** *Fairbanks Daily News–Miner* (AK) 28 Feb (Tabbert *Dict. Alaskan Engl.*), Wood cutting and hauling quite a job now—too many Iron Dogs out of commission. **1988** *Fairbanks Daily News–Miner* (AK) 2 Mar 25 (Tabbert *Dict. Alaskan Engl.*), Routing the Quest through here has seen the beginning of a local mushers group, . . an interesting combination of dog owners, iron-dog owners (snowmachiners), and cross-country skiers.

iron dollar n Cf **iron man 1,** *DS* U 27
A silver dollar.
    1909 *DN* 3.399 **nwAR,** Iron dollar. . . Silver dollar. **1914** *DN* 4.109 **KS,** Iron dollar. . . A silver dollar.

iron flower See **iron plant**

iron glass n [Folk-etym for *isinglass*]
    1896 *DN* 1.419 **swNC,** Iron-glass: mica.

iron grass n
1 A knotgrass 1 (here: *Polygonum aviculare*). Cf **wire grass**
    1900 Lyons *Plant Names* 300, P[olygonum] aviculare. . . Iron-grass. **1940** Clute *Amer. Plant Names* 228, Polygonum aviculare. Iron grass.
2 A sedge (here: *Carex caryophyllea*).
    1940 Clute *Amer. Plant Names* 155, C[arex] caryophyllea. . . Iron-grass.

iron hat n
=gossan.
    1881 Raymond *Gloss. Mining* 50, Iron hat. See *Gossan.* [Ibid 44, *Gossan.* . . Hydrated oxide of iron, usually found at the decomposed outcrop of a mineral vein.] **1952** FWP *Guide SD* 274, Iron Mountain

is estimated to have 55 percent iron content. Such a deposit is known as "Iron Hat." **1968** Adams *Western Words* 162, *Iron hat*—In mining, the outcrop of a lode, usually colored by the decomposition of the iron.

ironhead n
1 A goldeneye 1 (here: *Bucephala clangula*).
    1888 Trumbull *Names of Birds* 79, Golden-eye. . . At Havre de Grace, Md., *Bull-head;* at Morehead, N.C., *Iron-head.* **1917** (1923) *Birds Amer.* 1.138, Golden-eye. . . Other Names. . . Iron-head. **1946** Hausman *Eastern Birds* 157. . . Iron-head. **1970** *DARE* (Qu. Q5, . . *Kinds of wild ducks*) Inf **VA**79, Ironhead—dull-colored body, rust brown head, not a red-headed duck. **1982** Elman *Hunter's Field Guide* 218, American Goldeneye. . . Common & regional names . . ironhead. [Ibid 219, Goldeneyes. . . are recognized by their big, round, dark heads.]
2 also *ironhead crane:* =wood ibis. **FL, GA, esp Okefenokee GA** Cf **mulehead** n¹
    1913 *Auk* 30.491 **Okefenokee GA,** *Mycteria americana.* . . 'Ironhead'. . . This species is considered a game bird, and is eaten whenever it can be secured. **1917** (1923) *Birds Amer.* 1.179 **Okefenokee GA,** "Gourd Head," "Iron Head," and "Gannet" are the appellations given to these birds by many swamp-dwellers to whom the name Wood Ibis is unknown. **1950** *PADS* 14.76 **FL,** Iron-head. . . The gannet. **1968** *DARE* (Qu. Q10, . . *Water birds and marsh birds*) Inf **GA**20, Ironhead—nickname for wood ibis. **1968** *DARE* FW Addit **GA**25, Ironhead—nickname for wood ibis. **1968** *DARE* Tape **GA**30, This big wood ibis, they all called him a ironhead . . he's got a head that looks like rubber, no feathers or anything on his head. **1975** Newell *If Nothin' Don't Happen* 122 **nwFL,** A heap of them old ironhead cranes come into Corkscrew Swamp to nest—them big old white fellers with black tips on their wings and black heads and curved bills. The Yankees call them wood ibexes, I believe, but they're just ironheads to me. **1988** Van Meter *Florida's Wood Storks* 2, Because of the appearance of the head and upper neck, the wood stork is sometimes called . . "ironhead."
3 A knapweed (here: *Centaurea nigra*). [See quot 1889]
    1889 *Century Dict.* 3184, Ironheads. . . The knapweed, *Centaurea nigra:* so called in reference to the knobbed involucres. **1900** Lyons *Plant Names* 89, C[entaurea] nigra. . . Iron-head. **1940** Clute *Amer. Plant Names* 220, Centaurea nigra. Iron-head.

ironhead crane See **ironhead 2**

iron hull pea n Also *iron pea*
    1967–68 *DARE* (Qu. I20, . . *Kinds of beans*) Inf **NC**81, Iron hull pea; **SC**38, Iron peas.

iron-jawed adj
Having a very strong or prominent jaw; hence n *iron jaw* a prominent jaw.
    1883 Twain *Life on Missip.* (Boston) 45 **AR,** I'm the old original iron-jawed, brass-mounted, copper-bellied corpse maker from the wilds of Arkansaw. **1926** (1939) Hemingway *Torrents* 6 **MI,** The foreman was a short iron-jawed man. **1968–70** *DARE* (Qu. X6, *If a person's lower jaw sticks out prominently*) Infs **CA**94, **NY**144, **OH**44, **PA**216, 243, Iron-jawed; **OH**65, Iron jaw; **IL**47A, Iron jaw—that's what Frank Lloyd Wright called his.

iron man n
1 also *iron (wheel):* A dollar, esp a silver dollar. *somewhat old-fash* Cf **iron dollar**
    1906 *NY Eve. Jrl.* (NY) 5 Feb 8 (Zwilling Coll.), [In column "The Fable Of The Sailor":] Once upon a time there was a deck scrubber named Tom Sharkey who had a drag on Uncle Sam's roll for about nine irons a month. **1908** Green *Maison de Shine* 45 **NYC,** A feller who shells out his six iron men every week . . he's got to go shy. **1918** *DN* 5.25 **NW,** Iron-man. . . A silver dollar. General. **1929** *AmSp* 4.358, "Dollar," . . iron man (. . usually in the plural). **1950** *WELS* (*Joking names and nicknames for a silver dollar*) 2 Infs, **csWI,** Iron man; ("Dollars": "It cost 100 _____.") 1 Inf, **csWI,** Iron men. **1952** Brown *NC Folkl.* 1.554, Iron man. . . A silver dollar. **1963** Wright *Lawd Today* 133 **Chicago IL** [Black], It cost me five hundred iron men. **1966** Barnes–Jensen *Dict. UT Slang* 26, Iron man . . dollar. **1966–68** *DARE* (Qu. U20, . . *Dollars* . . "It cost a hundred _____.") Inf **MI**24, Iron men; **NJ**43, Iron men—old-fashioned; (Qu. U27, . . *A silver dollar*) Inf **CO**46, Iron men—old fashioned; **IL**7, Iron wheel; (Qu. U28b, . . *A ten-dollar bill*) Inf **MN**1, Ten iron men—used to call 'em this at the sawmill. [4 of 5 Infs old]
2 also *iron tender:* The cowboy responsible for tending or handling the branding irons; see quots.

1933 (1950) Allen *Cowboy Lore* 59, *Iron man,* one who keeps the branding irons hot at branding time. **1961** Adams *Old-Time Cowhand* 256 **SW,** The "brander" or "iron man," was the one whose immediate duty it was to place the brand on the animal. . . The "iron tender," the man who heated and attended to the brandin' irons, came on the trot from the fire with the brandin' iron wanted as it glowed a cherry red.

iron mule n Also *iron ox* [By analogy with *iron horse*]
Among loggers and railroad workers: a donkey engine or other piece of equipment; see quots.
   1942 Berrey–Van den Bark *Amer. Slang* 512.10 [Logger talk], *Iron mule* . . a donkey engine. *Ibid* 774.20 [Railroad terms]. **1958** McCulloch *Woods Words* 95 **Pacific NW,** *Iron mule*—A dirt moving machine. *Ibid, Iron ox*—In some early day camps big logs were skidded down the ties behind a locie or iron ox. This was done at the Bridal Veil Lumber Company in Oregon before the turn of the century. **1968** Adams *Western Words* 162, *Iron mule*—A logger's name for the donkey engine. In mining, a small dump cart with caterpillar drive.

iron oak n [From their dense, strong woods]
Any of several American oaks, as:
a A **post oak** (here: *Quercus stellata*).
   1814 Pursh *Flora Americae* 2.632, The *Upland White Oak* or *Iron Oak* is a spreading tree about fifty or sixty feet high; its timber is of great value in ship-building. **1860** Curtis *Cat. Plants NC* 32, *Post Oak.* . . is . . sometimes called *Iron Oak* and *Box White Oak.* . . It cannot be employed for all the purposes for which the *White Oak* is used, although in fineness of grain, strength and elasticity, it is superior to it. **1897** IN Dept. Geol. & Nat. Resources *Rept. for 1896* 617, Iron Oak. . . Dry, sandy soil. **1910** Graves *Flowering Plants* 150 **CT,** Iron Oak. . . The wood is very hard, heavy and strong. **1966–70** *DARE* (Qu. T10, . . *Kinds of oak trees*) Infs **IL**143, **SC**28, Iron oak; (Qu. T16, . . *Kinds of trees . . 'special'*) Inf **IL**143, Iron oak. **1979** Little *Checklist U.S. Trees* 228, *Quercus douglasii.* . . Iron oak. *Ibid* 242, *Quercus stellata.* . . Iron oak.
b A **blackjack oak** (here: *Quercus marilandica*).
   1861 Wood *Class-Book* 644, *Barren Oak. Black Jack. Iron Oak.* . . The wood is very valuable for fuel. (Q. ferruginea Mx.) **1897** Sudworth *Arborescent Flora* 154, *Quercus stellata.* . . Iron Oak (Del., Miss., Nebr.) *Ibid* 164, *Quercus chrysolepis.* . . Iron Oak (Cal.) *Ibid* 174, *Quercus marilandica.* . . Iron Oak (Tenn.) **1933** Small *Manual SE Flora* 430, *Q. marilandica.* . . Iron-oak. **1960** Vines *Trees SW* 183, *Quercus marilandica.* . . Also known by the vernacular names of Iron Oak, Black Oak. . . The wood is used mostly for posts, fuel, and charcoal.
c =**canyon oak 1.**
   1897 [see **b** above]. **1910** Jepson *Silva CA* 223, "Iron Oak," . . and "Hickory Oak" are names which . . speak the respect of the ranch man for its wood. . . *Quercus chrysolepis.* **1938** Van Dersal *Native Woody Plants* 346, Oak . . Iron (*Quercus chrysolepis, Quercus stellata*).
d =**blue oak 2.**
   1910 Jepson *Silva CA* 216, Blue Oak. . . In felling trees one occasionally finds sections of wood which are black, so extremely dense and hard that they will turn the edge of an axe; whence the folk-name, "Iron Oak." **1925** Jepson *Manual Plants CA* 273, *Q[uercus] douglasii.* . . Often called Mountain Oak and Iron Oak by settlers. **1979** [see **a** above].

iron out v phr Cf **let the hammer down**
To ride (a restive horse) until it is calm enough to work; similarly phr *iron out the humps*
   1936 Adams *Cowboy Lingo* 102, After the 'buster' had ridden a bronc a few times, he turned him over to the riders as 'gentled' or 'broken,' but it would be a long time before the rider who inherited him could ride him on duty without first riding him long enough to take the kinks out of his back which the cowboy spoke of as 'topping off,' 'uncorkin',' . . or 'ironin' him out.' **1944** Adams *Western Words* 84, *Ironing him out*—Taking the rough edges off a bucking horse. *Ibid, Ironing out the humps*—Another expression for the above.

iron ox See **iron mule**

iron pea See **iron hull pea**

iron plant n Also *iron flower*
A **goldenweed 1** (here: *Haplopappus spinulosus*).
   1932 Rydberg *Flora Prairies* 789, Iron Plant. . . *S[ideranthus] spinulosus.* **1936** Whitehouse *TX Flowers* 161, Iron Flower (*Sideranthus spinulosus*). . . Very abundant on prairies and hills in the western part

of the state. **1968** Barkley *Plants KS* 347, Haplopappus spinulosus. . . Iron Plant. Prairies and plains.

iron-plated possum n Cf **hardshelled possum**
An armadillo (*Dasypus* spp).
   1960 Williams *Walk Egypt* 203 **GA,** "Mr. Harl is hunting armydillos." "Iron-plated possums? There's none around. They're just hearsay."

iron pot n Also *old iron pot* [See quot 1956]
A **scoter.**
   1888 Trumbull *Names of Birds* 96, The . . "scoters". . . are referred to collectively, and facetiously, at Pleasantville (Atlantic Co.), N.J., as "iron pots," or "old iron pots." **1956** *AmSp* 31.182 **NJ,** The scoters . . have names referring to their black color, hardiness, and inedibility, all in one combination, such as *iron pot* and *old iron pot.* **1982** Elman *Hunter's Field Guide* 237, *American Scoter.* . . Common & Regional Names . . iron pot. *Ibid* 240, *Surf Scoter.* . . Iron pot. *Ibid* 250, *White-winged Scoter.* . . Iron pot.

iron ragweed n
   1968 *DARE* (Qu. S26a, . . *Roadside flowers*) Inf **CT**12, Iron ragweed.

ironroot n Cf **iron blood 2**
   1940 in 1968 Haun *Hawk's Done Gone* 29 **eTN,** I give her bone-set tea and iron-root tea.

ironside n Also *ironsides* old-fash Cf **hard-shell** adj 2
A member of a very conservative religious denomination, or the denomination itself; hence adj *ironside(s)* having characteristics of such a denomination.
   1891 *PMLA* 6.168 **WV,** One minister, a hard-shell Baptist, or Ironsides as they call this sect there, spoke of the *texes* from which he preached his sermon. *Ibid* 169, The most amusing expressions . . were those heard in an Ironside sermon. **1901** *Scribner's Mag.* 29.398/2 **sAppalachians,** Mountaineers. . . are for the most part Methodists and Baptists—sometimes, Ironsides feet-washing Baptists. **1926** *WV Legislative Hdbk.* 561 **WV** (as of 1861), I concluded old Jack [=Stonewall Jackson] must be a fatalist sure enough when he put an Ironside Presbyterian parson as his chief of staff.

ironsides n
1 =**scup.**
   1939 Natl. Geogr. Soc. *Fishes* 68, Scup (Stenotomus chrysops). . . This species . . has several local names. It is . . the maiden, fair maid, and ironsides in Chesapeake Bay. **1975** Evanoff *Catch More Fish* 208, The northern porgy . . is also called . . ironsides.
2 See **ironside.**

iron tag n [Cf *OED tag* sb.[2] quot 1738] Cf **wood tag**
A variation of the children's game of tag; see quots 1953, 1980.
   1883 Newell *Games & Songs* 158, *Tag.* . . The original form of this game seems to have been "Iron Tag," or "Tag on Iron," once universal in the United States, and still here and there played. **1952** Brown *NC Folkl.* 1.74, *Iron Tag.* **1953** Brewster *Amer. Nonsinging Games* 66 **IN,** *Iron Tag.* . . This game is played exactly like Wood Tag, except that players can escape capture only by touching some object made of iron. **1957** *Sat. Eve. Post Letters* **NYC** (as of c1945–1951), *Iron Tag*—immune if you touched iron. **1980** *DARE* File **NYC** (as of c1925), *Iron tag* . . anyone in contact with an iron lamppost, hydrant, railing, manhole cover, etc., could not be [tagged] out.

iron tender See **iron man 2**

iron water n
Water impregnated with iron salts.
   1939 FWP *Guide TN* 311, *Galbraith Springs.* . . It has been believed locally that the chalybeate water, commonly called "iron water," has medicinal properties.

ironweed n
1 A plant of the genus *Vernonia.* Also called **ironwood a(6), ox-joint.** For other names of var spp see **devil's bit f, flattop, Joe-Pye weed 3, queen of the meadow**
   1819 Thomas *Travels W. Country* 231 **swPA,** The *iron-weed,* which I first saw above Pittsburgh, extends on clayey lands all the way to the Wabash. **1859** (1968) Bartlett *Americanisms* 218, *Iron Weed.* (*Vernonia noveboracensis*) . . almost the only tall weed found in the beautiful "woods pastures" of Kentucky and Tennessee. Western. **1871** Hay *Pike Co. Ballads* 97, And widely weaves the Iron-Weed / A woof of purple

dyes. **1948** Manfred *Chokecherry* 107 **nwIA,** In the striding forenoon sunlight, the shadows in the roots of the ironweeds were green-black. **1965–70** *DARE* (Qu. S21, . . *Weeds . . that are a trouble in gardens and fields*) 33 Infs, **chiefly N Midl, S Atl,** Ironweed(s); (Qu. S26a, . . *Roadside flowers*) 14 Infs, **chiefly N Midl,** Ironweed; (Qu. S25, . . *The small wild chrysanthemum-like flowers . . that bloom in fields late in the fall*) Infs **GA**70, **MI**31, **OH**6, Ironweed; (Qu. S26b, *Wildflowers that grow in water or wet places*) Infs **PA**142, **VA**101, **WI**12, Ironweed; (Qu. S26c, *Wildflowers that grow in woods*) Inf **PA**234, Ironweed; (Qu. S26d, *Wildflowers that grow in meadows*; not asked in early QRs) Infs **KY**28, 74, **OH**78, 95, **PA**95, **TN**11, Ironweed; (Qu. S26e, *Other wildflowers . .*; not asked in early QRs) Infs **DC**2, **IN**32, **OH**2, 72, Ironweed. **1976** Bruce *How to Grow Wildflowers* 272, A wet meadow. . . was bright all summer long with hardhack and meadowsweet, milkweed, asters, ironweed. **1990** *Plants SW* (Catalog) 40, *Verbena missurica.* Ironweed. . . This is a striking plant in the fall when it . . blooms with clusters of purple thistlelike flowers.

2 A **hemp nettle** (here: *Galeopsis tetrahit*).

1835 Audubon *Ornith. Biog.* 3.56 **KY,** Locusts . . were gathered by boys from the trunks of trees and the "iron weeds," a species of wild hemp very abundant in that portion of the country. **1935** (1943) Muenscher *Weeds* 391, *Galeopsis Tetrahit.* . . Hemp nettle . . Wild hemp . . Ironweed. . . Locally common in Canada and the northeastern United States.

3 A **vervain** (here: *Verbena hastata*).

1894 *Jrl. Amer. Folkl.* 7.96, *Verbena hastata* . . iron-weed, Jones Co., Iowa. **1930** Sievers *Amer. Med. Plants* 15, *Blue Vervain.* . . *Other common names.* . . Ironweed. **1940** Clute *Amer. Plant Names* 69, *V[erbena] hastata.* . . Ironweed. **1974** (1977) Coon *Useful Plants* 264, Iron weed. . . A tall-growing perennial with violet-blue flowers, this plant is found wide widely in this country.

4 A **knapweed** (here: *Centaurea nigra*).

1900 Lyons *Plant Names* 89, *C[entaurea] nigra.* . . Iron-weed. **1959** Carleton *Index Herb. Plants* 66, *Iron-weed:* Centaurea nigra; Verbena hastata; Vernonia (v). **1968** *DARE* (Qu. S15, . . *Weed seeds that cling to clothing*) Inf **UT**4, Ironweed.

5 usu with modifier: A **crownbeard** (here: *Verbesina alternifolia*).

1914 Georgia *Manual Weeds* 468, *Winged Ironweed.* . . *Other names:* Yellow Ironweed. . . A tall, unsightly weed. . . Stem . . very hard and woody when mature and therefore troublesome to harvesting machines. **1959** Carleton *Index Herb. Plants* 54, *Golden-ironweed:* Actinomeria [sic] alternifolia. *Ibid* 126, *Winged-ironweed:* Actinomeris alternifolia. **1967–69** *DARE* (Qu. S7, *A kind of daisy, bright yellow with a dark center, that grows along roadsides in late summer*) Inf **IL**62, Ironweed; (Qu. S26e, *Other wildflowers . .*; not asked in early QRs) Inf **IA**7, Ironweed—has a yellow flower. **1976** Bailey–Bailey *Hortus Third* 1150, *Yellow ironweed.* . . E[astern] U[nited] S[tates].

6 A **bitterweed** (here: *Hymenoxys acaulis*).

1937 U.S. Forest Serv. *Range Plant Hdbk.* W6, Stemless actinea . . is known by a great variety of (and often misapplied) local names, such as . . ironweed.

7 A **boneset 1.** Cf **ironroot**

1966 *DARE* Wildfl QR Pl.230 Inf **WI**35, Ironweed—mother's name; boneset.

8 A **teaweed** (here: *Sida rhombifolia*).

1974 Morton *Folk Remedies* 143 **SC,** Ironweed; Tea Fever Weed. . . Sida rhombifolia. . . A decoction of the plant is taken for indigestion and to regulate menstruation.

ironweed aster n

1913 Eaton *Barn Doors* 259 **NEng,** They held little blue asters, sometimes called iron weed asters.

iron wheel See **iron man 1**

ironwood n Cf **red ironwood, white ironwood**

Any of numerous plants, usu trees or shrubs noted for their hard, durable wood, as:

a Any of several plants native generally to the eastern half of the US, spec:

(1) A **hop hornbeam 1** (here: *Ostrya virginiana*). Cf **d(3)** below

1762 Gronovius *Flora Virginica* 151, *Carpinus squamis strobilorum inflatis.* . . Nostratibus Iron-wood. [=*Carpinus* with the scales of the

nutlets inflated. . . Among us, Iron-wood.] **1831** Audubon *Ornith. Biog.* 1.204, *The Virginian Hornbeam, or Iron-wood Tree.* . . The common name in America is *Iron-wood,* which it receives on account of the great hardness of the wood. **1851** (1976) Melville *Moby-Dick* 476, Perth was standing between his forge and anvil, the latter placed upon an iron-wood log. **1921** Deam *Trees IN* 80, *Ironwood.* . . is 30 per cent stronger than white oak, and 46 per cent more elastic. **1965–70** *DARE* (Qu. T16, . . *Kinds of trees . . 'special'*) 20 Infs, **chiefly Inland Nth, Midl,** Ironwood. **1966** *DARE* FW Addit **cnME,** Ironwood—a very tough wood—tree looks like an ash, but leaves are like birch. No grain to the wood. **1967** *DARE* Tape **MI**47, [The skid was] made from hardwood, . . either white ash, ironwood, or hard maple.

(2) =**hornbeam 1.**

1860 Curtis *Cat. Plants NC* 75, Hornbeam. Ironwood. (Carpinus Americana . .). The wood is white, exceedingly hard, compact and fine grained. **1901** Lounsberry *S. Wild Flowers* 115, *Ironwood.* . . is . . often seen . . hung with its long graceful clusters of fruit. **1932** Rydberg *Flora Prairies* 262, *Ironwood.* . . A small tree or shrub, 5–15 m. high. **1967–70** *DARE* (Qu. T15, . . *Kinds of swamp trees*) Infs **AR**56, **CT**6, **GA**84, **LA**7, **NY**123, **WV**14, 16, Ironwood; **MA**5, Ironwood—grows in rocky places. **1973** Wharton–Barbour *Trees KY* 508, *Ironwood.* . . Pioneers used its hard strong wood in hand-wrought tools, such as rake teeth, mallets, cogs, and handles, but since the tree is small and usually crooked, it is not used today.

(3) A **flowering dogwood** (here: *Cornus florida*).

1913 Torreya 13.233, *Cornus florida.* . . Ironwood, Lake Pearl, La. **1970** *DARE* (Qu. T13) Inf **PA**242, Dogwood is ironwood.

(4) A **sycamore** (here: *Platanus occidentalis*).

1941 *LANE* Map 244, 1 inf, **neMA,** [aɪənwʊd], thought to be the same as *buttonwood.* **1966** *DARE* (Qu. T13, . . *Other names . . for . . sycamore*) Inf **MA**6, Ironwood.

(5) =**Osage orange.**

1941 Writers' Program *Guide AR* 314, *Bois d'arc,* known variously as ironwood, . . and rabbit hedge.

(6) =**ironweed 1.**

1959 Carleton *Index Herb. Plants* 66, *Iron-wood:* Vernonia (v).

(7) A **hackberry.**

1966–69 *DARE* (Qu. T13, . . *Other names . . for . . hackberry*) Infs **IN**49, **MI**100, **SC**4, Ironwood; **MS**21, Hackberry, ironwood.

(8) =**box elder.**

1969 *DARE* (Qu. T13, . . *Other names . . for . . box elder*) Inf **NY**183, Ironwood.

b Any of var trees native generally to the Southeast:

(1) also *swamp ironwood:* =**he-huckleberry 1.**

1785 Marshall *Arbustrum* 9, *Andromeda plumata.* Plumed Andromeda, or Carolinian Iron-wood Tree. . . This and the last mentioned, grow naturally by the sides of ponds, and swamps, in Carolina and Florida. **1884** Sargent *Forests of N. Amer.* 37, *Cyrilla racemiflora.* . . Iron Wood. . . Wood heavy, weak, hard, close-grained, compact. **1897** Sudworth *Arborescent Flora* 277 **FL, GA, LA, MS, NC, SC,** *Cyrilla racemiflora.* . . Common Names. Ironwood. **1940** Clute *Amer. Plant Names* 126, *Leatherwood.* . . Iron-wood, he-huckleberry. *Ibid* 257, *Cyrilla racemiflora.* . . Swamp ironwood. **1968** *DARE* FW Addit **GA**25, Ironwood—old-fashioned nickname for the summer ty-ty [=titi] tree. **1979** Little *Checklist U.S. Trees* 122, *Cyrilla racemiflora.* . . Other common names . . "swamp-ironwood", he-huckleberry.

(2) A plant of the genus *Bumelia:* **southern buckthorn** or *B. tenax.*

1830 Rafinesque *Med. Flora* 2.263, *Sideroxylon.* . . Ironwood, Turlbay. Very hard wood, berries sweetish astringent, useful in diarrhea. **1869** Porcher *Resources* 423 **Sth,** Ironwood, (Bumelia lycioides . .). **1892** Coulter *Botany W. TX* 257, *B[umelia] lycioides.* . . Known as "ironwood" and "southern buckthorn." . . Wood tough and compact, making excellent axe handles. **1933** Small *Manual SE Flora* 1034, *B[umelia] lycioides.* . . Ironwood. . . B. tenax. . . Ironwood. **1960** Vines *Trees SW* 834, *Bumelia lycioides.* . . Vernacular names are Buckthorn, . . Ironwood, Chittamwood. **1979** Little *Checklist U.S. Trees* 66, *Bumelia lycioides.* . . "Ironwood." . . *Bumelia tenax.* . . "Ironwood."

(3) =**buckwheat tree.**

1884 Sargent *Forests of N. Amer.* 38, *Cliftonia ligustrina.* . . Titi. Iron Wood. Buckwheat Tree. . . Wood heavy, soft, not strong, close-grained, compact. **1897** Sudworth *Arborescent Flora* 277, *Cliftonia monophylla.* . . Ironwood. **1933** Small *Manual SE Flora* 812, *C. monophylla.* . . Ironwood. . . The brown and red-tinged heart-wood is close-grained and heavy, but brittle. **1953** Greene–Blomquist *Flowers South* 68, *Ironwood*. . . Another excellent source of honey, this small evergreen tree is distinguished . . by its terminal . . panicles and by its winged nut-like drupes. **1976** Bailey–Bailey *Hortus Third* 287, *Ironwood*. To 24 ft. or more; . . fl[ower]s white, fragrant. A bee plant.

c Any of var trees native to southern Florida and the Keys:

(1) =**inkwood 1.**

1884 Sargent *Forests of N. Amer.* 45, *Hypelate paniculata*. . . *Ink Wood. Iron Wood*. . . Wood very heavy, exceedingly hard, very strong, close-grained. **1897** Sudworth *Arborescent Flora* 296, *Exothea panicu-lata*. . . *Ironwood*. **1908** Rogers *Tree Book* 387, The *Ironwood*. . . is a small tree whose hard red wood is used for piles and boats, because it seems to be immune from the attacks of the ship-worm. **1933** Small *Manual SE Flora* 829, *Ironwood*. . . Has been carried far up the coast [of Florida] and planted on kitchenmiddens by birds. **1979** Little *Checklist U.S. Trees* 130, *Inkwood*. . . Other common names—butterbough, "ironwood."

(2) A **lignum vitae B** (here: *Guaiacum sanctum*).

1897 Sudworth *Arborescent Flora* 264 **FL**, *Guajacum sanctum*. . . *Common Names*. Lignum Vitae. . . Ironwood. **1908** Britton *N. Amer. Trees* 564, *G[uaiacum] sanctum* inhabits southern Florida, growing on several of the Keys. . . It is sometimes called Ironwood.

(3) A **stopper** (here: *Eugenia confusa*).

1933 Small *Manual SE Flora* 936, *E[ugenia] confusa*. . . *Ironwood*. . . The red-brown heart-wood, close-grained, heavy, and very hard, is used locally for cabinet work. **1976** Bailey–Bailey *Hortus Third* 458, *Iron-wood*. Tree, with scaly bark. . Fla. and W. Indies.

d Any of var trees native generally to the Southwest:

(1) =**desert ironwood.**

1871 U.S. Dept. Ag. *Rept. of Secy. for 1870* 411, *Iron-wood, (Olneya tesota)*, . . grows in the most desolate and rocky places of Arizona and Sonora. The seeds are produced in bean-like pods. . . When care is taken to parch them they equal peanuts, with no perceptible difference in taste. **1908** Sudworth *Forest Trees Pacific* 378, *Olnea* [sic] *tesota* is commonly called "ironwood" in the United States on account of its cross-grained, exceedingly heavy, hard wood. . . "Ironwood" was applied to several eastern hard-wooded trees long before this species was discovered. **1923** Davidson–Moxley *Flora S. CA* 199, *Ironwood*. A small tree often armed with spines below the leaves. **1957** Jaeger *N. Amer. Deserts* 73, Iron-woods . . are plentiful along the margins of many of the dry water-courses. **1981** Benson–Darrow *Trees SW Deserts* 256, The ironwood is one of the most characteristic trees of the desert, and it is a useful one. The wood, so heavy it sinks in water, makes excellent fuel.

(2) A **mesquite B1** (here: *Prosopis glandulosa* or *P. juliflora*).

1897 Sudworth *Arborescent Flora* 252 **TX**, *Prosopis juliflora*. . . Iron-wood. **1938** Van Dersal *Native Woody Plants* 340, Ironwood, (*Bumelia lycioides, Bumelia tenax, Carpinus caroliniana, Cliftonia monophylla, Ostrya knowltonii, Ostrya virginiana, Prosopis chilensis*).

(3) A **hop hornbeam 1** (here: *Ostrya knowltonii*). Cf **a(1)** above

1922 Sargent *Manual Trees* 204, *Ostrya Knowltonii*. . . *Ironwood*. . . Wood light reddish brown, with thin sapwood. **1938** [see **d(2)** above]. **1960** Vines *Trees SW* 145, *Ostrya knowltonii*. . . *Wood*. . . Hard, tough, durable, used for fuel or posts occasionally. . . Some vernacular names are Western Hornbeam and Ironwood. **1979** Little *Checklist U.S. Trees* 181, *Knowlton hophornbeam*. . . Other common names . . "ironwood."

(4) A **forestiera** (here: *Forestiera acuminata* var *parvifolia*, also known as *F. neomexicana*).

1923 Davidson–Moxley *Flora S. CA* 275, *Ironwood*. . . *F[orestiera] neomexicana*. . . Common in the desert foothills near Big Rock Creek. **1931** U.S. Dept. Ag. *Misc. Pub.* 101.137, New Mexican adelia (*Forestiera neomexicana*), called also . . ironwood. . . is usually a smooth shrub 4 to 12 feet high but sometimes a small tree 20 feet tall.

(5) A **mountain mahogany 2** (here: *Cercocarpus betuloides*).

1925 Jepson *Manual Plants CA* 502, *C[ercocarpus] betuloides*. . . *Hard Tack*. . . Also called Sweet Brush, Ironwood, and Birch-leaf Ma-hogany. **1976** Elmore *Shrubs & Trees SW* 63, *Birchleaf mountain-mahogany* . . Ironwood. . . "Ironwood" is a catch-all name for any shrub whose wood is "as hard as iron," and birchleaf mountain-mahogany is no exception. Its wood is exceptionally hard and heavy, and when green will sink in water.

e A small tree (*Lyonothamnus floribundus*) native to the California islands.

1897 Sudworth *Arborescent Flora* 204, *Lyonothamnus floribundus*.

Santa Cruz Ironwood. **1908** Sudworth *Forest Trees Pacific* 331, The name ironwood was doubtless given because of the hardness of the wood. **1910** Jepson *Silva CA* 254, The Catalina Ironwood is an insular species found only on the islands of Santa Catalina, San Clemente, Santa Rosa, and Santa Cruz. . . On account of its great strength it is used for fish-poles and also for canes and similar articles. **1965** Teale *Wandering Through Winter* 23 **CA**, It [=sunlight] touched the tops of the ironwoods. **1987** *Nature Conserv. News* 37.3.10 **CA**, Nearly 1,000 different stands of "ironwood" (*Lyonothamnus floribundus* spp. *asplenifolius*) flourished. *Ibid* 13, Deep in the ironwood and oak groves, shoots emerged around the base of long standing adult trees.

f The casuarina (*Casuarina equisetifolia*), naturalized in Hawaii.

1900 Lyons *Plant Names* 86, *C[asuarina] equisetifolia*. . . Iron-wood (South Sea Islands). **1908** Britton *N. Amer. Trees* 162, *Casuarina*. . . is reported to attain a height of 45 meters in the Polynesian region, and is variously known as Ironwood, . . and Swamp Oak. **1928** Pan-Pacific Research Inst. *Jrl.* 3.2.5 **HI**, Casuarina, . . "ironwood"; leafless trees resembling pines. **1965** Neal *Gardens HI* 289, How long ironwoods live is not known. **1982** Perry–Hay *Field Guide Plants* 18, South sea iron-wood. . . They make good timber trees, the hard wood taking a fine polish.

ironwood elm n

A **rock elm** (here: *Ulmus thomasii*).

1966 *DARE* (Qu. T11, . . *Kinds of elm trees*) Inf **AR**16, Ironwood elm—same as rock elm.

Iroquois n

=**Mohawk.**

1968 *DARE* (Qu. X5, . . *Different kinds of men's haircuts*) Inf **NY**107, [ˈɪrəˌkwoi]; **NY**123, [ˈɪrɪkwojz]; **WV**10, [ˈɪrəkwɔɪ].

irrigate v Usu |ˈɪrəge(ɪ)t|; also |ˈɑr-, ˈær-| Pronc-sp *arragate*

A Forms.

1911 *DN* 3.550 **WY**, *Arragate*, irrigate. "arragated land," "arragation ditch," etc. **1942** Hall *Smoky Mt. Speech* 16 **wNC, eTN**, *Irrigate* was pronounced [ˈɑrəgeɪt] by a CCC foreman of Cades Cove (Blount Co., Tenn.), [ˈærəgeɪt] by older speakers of the White Oak (Haywood Co., N.C.)

B Sense.

Also in phr *irrigate the ulcers*: To take a drink of liquor; to drink to excess; also n *irrigation* the provision or consumption of alcoholic beverages. **esp West** *somewhat old-fash*

1856 Derby *Phoenixiana* 104 **swCA**, His Reverence . . was invited by the urbane proprietor to *irrigate*. *Ibid* 162, Being naturally of an arid disposition, and perhaps requiring irrigation at that particular moment, you unguardedly invite Brown . . to step over to Parry and Batten's, and imbibe. **1880** Hayes *New CO* 120, This person taking out a large flask, asked, "Stranger, do you irrigate?" **1900** *DN* 2.42 **NY, OH, AL, MO, CT** [College slang], *Irrigate*. . . To drink to excess. **1905** (1970) Adams *Outlet* 298 **TX**, Sponsilier . . called every one to the bar to irrigate. **1909** *Denver Republican* Feb. (*DN* 6.380), We've cut out the type of rancher . ./ Who thinks that irrigatin' means a-quenchin' of his thirst. **1951** *Western Folkl.* 10.81 **NM** [Barroom slang], *The Act of Drinking* . . to irrigate the ulcers.

is conj, pron, prep, adv See **as**

-is suff See **-es** suff[1] 1

Isaac n Also *Isey* [Transf from the common Jewish name] *derog*

=**Ikey** n **1.**

1941 *LANE* Map 455 (*Nicknames for a Jew*) **NEng**, 4 infs, Isaac; 1 inf, Sheeny Isaacs; 1 inf, Isey [aɪzɪ]. **1950** *WELS* (*Names and nicknames for people of foreign background: Jewish*) 1 Inf, **WI**, Isaac.

Isabella-wood n [Prob for *Isabella* of Borbon, Queen of Spain 1833–68]

A **red bay** (here: *Persea borbonia*).

1900 Lyons *Plant Names* 281, *P[ersea] Borbonia*. . . Isabella-wood. **1901** Lounsberry *S. Wild Flowers* 192, *Isabella-wood*. . . The rose coloured wood . . is very beautiful, as it takes a most brilliant polish. **1940** Clute *Amer. Plant Names* 118, *P. Borbonica* [sic]. . . Isabella-wood. **1960** Vines *Trees SW* 296, *Persea borbonia*. . . Vernacular names are . . Laurel-tree, and Isabella-wood.

I send n

A type of tag game; see quot.

1950 *WELS* (*Other outdoor games*) 1 Inf, **WI**, I send—two sides with captains [who each] choose one from [their] side [and say, for example,] "I send John after Mary." He [=John] goes over, just so far up near [the] other line, then she [=Mary] tries to catch him.

Isey See **Isaac**

ish intj Also *isham(a)y* [Norw *isj,* Dan, Sw *isch*] **esp MN, WI** Cf **ishy**

Used as an expression of disgust.

1948 Sandburg *Remembrance* 727 **IL,** She snorted, "Seat of learning!" Then she let out a syllable she had picked up from a Swede who worked at the sawmill, "Ish!" It was a spewing syllable. She repeated it before walking on. "Ish!" **1966–68** *DARE* (Qu. NN23, *Exclamations when people smell a very bad odor*) Infs **ND2, WI65,** Ish; **MN16,** Ishamay, [or] ishamy. **1979** [see **ishy**]. **1980** *Children's Folkl. Newsl.* Winter 3 **seMN,** Ish. . . Exclamation of disgust. **1981** [see **ishy**]. **1985** Keillor *Lake Wobegon* 166 **MN,** *Ish,* his clothes smell like a cesspool, but she washes them anyway. **1992** *DARE* File **MN,** The second word is one which I had never heard in Oregon but hear quite often in Minnesota—the word "ish", pronounced [ɪʃ]. It's a term showing disgust. If, for example, you were to step on a banana while barefoot, you might say "Ooh, ish!"

I'sh See **Irish** n¹, adj

isham(a)y See **ish** intj

ishic(k)le See **icicle**

ish kabibble phr, adj Also sp *ish kabibbul, ish ki bibble* [Etym unknown] Cf **Abie Kabibble, I should worry**

It's of no importance to me, I couldn't care less; of no importance or concern.

1913 *NY Eve. Jrl.* (NY) 23 May home ed 22 *(Zwilling Coll.),* [Cartoon:] Ish ki bibble. **1924** *DN* 5.271 [Exclams], Ishkabibble (=I should worry, or nothing doing). **1926** *AmSp* 2.92, We next read on the sport's arm ban[d] and the flapper's pennant "Ish Kabibbul" or "Ishkabibble"—or "I Should Worry." We not only read it, we heard it also. Through that expression all youth declared its independence. **1938** FWP NYC *NY Panorama* 156, Heard each day are countless similar expressions, some going strong . . , others quickly discarded *(ish kabibble, so's your old man).* **1963** North *Rascal* 18 **WI** (as of 1918), "You'll get a licking when you get home." "Ishkabibble, I should worry!" Oscar said, a happy grin spreading across his wide face. **1968–70** *DARE* (Qu. KK26, *Something that makes no difference at all to you: "He can think what he likes, it _____ me."*) Inf **CT42,** It's ish kabibble; **MI68,** Ish kabibble [ɪš kəbɪbl]; (Qu. GG21a, *If you don't care what a person does*) Inf **MI68,** Ish kabibble. **1978** *Blair & Ketchum's Country Jrl.* Aug 61 **Cape Cod MA,** He's outlived three electric refrigerators . . and a succession of dogs and remembers when you said Twenty-three Skidoo and Ish kabibble. [**1992** *DARE* File, Merwyn Bogue, a trumpet player and comedian with Kay Kyser's band during the 1940s, as well as a radio personality in his own right, performed under the name "Ish Kabibble," which was also the title of a song with which he was associated. During World War II he was a big hit on USO tours.]

I should worry phr Also *I should care* [Prob ult from a Yiddish phr] **orig NYC** old-fash Cf **ish kabibble**

I don't care; it's no concern of mine.

1912 *NY Eve. Jrl.* (NY) 9 Aug 8th ed 8 *(Zwilling Coll.),* [Cartoon of man standing before a judge:] I should worry. **1913** *Ibid* 16 May home ed 20 *(Zwilling Coll.),* [Cartoon:] What is that I should worry thing—Gee it gets my goat worse than that What d'ye mean—you lost your dog—gag. **1919** Mencken *Amer. Lang.* 151, *I should worry,* in its way, is correct English, but in essence it is as completely Yiddish as *kosher, ganof,* . . or *mazuma.* [Footnote:] All of which, of course, are coming into American, along with many other Yiddish words. **1924** [see **ish kabibble**]. **1928** *AmSp* 4.157 **sTX,** The popular "I should worry" is often thought to be derived from the Yiddish "Ish-ka-bibble." **1930** *Forum* 84.376, Within the last decade, we tongued *I should worry* into merciful oblivion. **1937** *New Yorker* 13 Nov 32 **NYC,** [Children's rhyme:] I should worry, I should care,/ I should marry a millionaire. **1963** [see **ish kabibble**]. **1966–70** *DARE* (Qu. GG21a, *If you don't care what a person does*) Infs **NY130, OH5, VA58, WA3,** I should worry; **CA115,** I should care; (Qu. KK26, *Something that makes no difference at all to you*) Inf **IL36,** I should worry. [5 of 6 Infs old] **1970** Feinsilver *Yiddish* 338, "Should"—ironic. This Yiddish influence is seen in popular ironies like "I should worry". . . Sources are the ironic *hob ich a dayge* (I've got a worry) and *mayn dayge.*

ishter See **oyster**

ishy adj [**ish** intj] **esp MN, WI**
=**icky.**

1950 *WELS* **WI** (A dark, unattractive brownish color: "They painted the house a(n) _____ color.") 2 Infs, Ishy; (When you are only a little bit sick) 1 Inf, I feel ishy; (If somebody's food did not agree with him, he might feel _____) 1 Inf, Ishy. **1967–68** *DARE* (Qu. H25, . . *Fried cornmeal*) Inf **MI94,** Fried cornmeal—and ishy! Boy! (Qu. BB5, *A general feeling of discomfort or illness*) Infs **MN1, 28,** Ishy feeling. **1975** *DARE* File **neMN,** *Ishy*—naturalized (foreign source not generally recognized). **1979** *Ibid* **MN,** In Toledo if something was gross or vulgar it was "icky". . . In Minneapolis such an item or thought was described as "ishy" and one would exclaim, "Oh, ish!" **1981** *Ibid* **MN, WI,** My mother first heard "ish" and "ishy" when she visited Minneapolis in 1935. When Mother moved to Racine, Wisconsin, in 1938, both words were in common use in her neighborhood of Danish descendants. I grew up in Racine and knew these as everyday words, even among local people with no Scandinavian antecedents. **1992** *Ibid* **MN,** A mother might tell her child "Don't eat that, it's ishy!"

is it exclam Cf **isn't it**

Used to express interest or concern.

1982 *DARE* File **seWI,** "So-and-so got married last week." "Is it?" "The De Boers bought a new car." "Is it?" Often it is hardly spoken as a question, . . especially if the news is bad: "Uncle George had an accident and is in the hospital." "Is it!" The expression is used frequently by people in the Oostburg–Cedar Grove area.

island n Usu |ˈaɪlənd|; also **chiefly Sth, S Midl** |ˈaɪlənt| Pronc-spp *i(s)lant;* for addit pronc and sp varr see quots
A Forms.

1902 *DN* 2.237 **sIL,** [aɪlənt]. **1907** *DN* 3.223 **nwAR,** [ˈaɪlənt]. **1909** *S. Atl. Qrly.* 8.45 **eSC** [Gullah], An' w'en 'e die eh neahly kill de whole i-lant fuh laff [=with laughing], eh gone so sweet an' easy! **1918** *DN* 5.16 **Martha's Vineyard MA,** *Island.* . . Frequently pronounced as if *ile-dand.* Very common among older people. **1926** *AmSp* 1.415 **Okefenokee GA,** That happened on Black Jack Islant. **1927** *AmSp* 2.358 **WV,** Islant. **1930** Woofter *Black Yeomanry* 50 **seSC** [Gullah], *Islant* for island. **1939** Griswold *Sea Is. Lady* 788 **csSC** (as of 1920) [Gullah], An' de people 'pon dis oilan' is too sinful. **1942** Hall *Smoky Mt. Speech* 98 **wNC, eTN,** [ˈaɪlənt]. **c1960** *Wilson Coll.* **csKY,** Island is very often [ˈaɪlənt]. **1965** *Dict. Queen's English* 4 **NC,** Oisland (for island) (pronounced oy-land). **1966** *Wilson Coll.* **csKY,** Island [ˈaɪənt].
B Senses.

1 also *islet:* A peninsula.

1608 Smith *True Relation* [29] **VA,** I . . chased them out of the Iland [on which Jamestown stood]. **1654** in 1940 *AmSp* 15.276 **VA,** Thirteen hundred Acres . . in Northampton County at ye Sea board Side being a Neck or Iland. **1965–70** *DARE* (Qu. C13, *A piece of land that sticks out noticeably into a body of water*) 37 Infs, **scattered,** Island; **TX26, 54,** Islet; **IL71,** Bay island—not really an island, though; sticks out from land; **LA3,** Island—sometimes but not always surrounded by water; **LA15,** Island—connected to main body of land; **LA20,** Little island—doesn't have to be exactly surrounded by water; **NC37,** Island—sometimes not surrounded by water; **TN37,** Island [FW: Inf was quite positive when questioned. Actually, the only major lakes around here are man-made and quite new, and people simply don't call these features anything.]; **OK23,** Peninsula, but many old settlers would call it an island. [*DARE* Ed: 3 Infs corrected resp to "point"; comments and other resps of other Infs suggest that some Infs took the Qu. to refer to land completely surrounded by water or broadly to any landform connected with water.]

2 also *i(s)le:* A grove or clump of trees surrounded by prairie or scrub. **scattered, but esp Gulf States** Cf **motte**

1770 Washington in 1985 Lederer *Colonial Amer. Engl.* 122, Large Planes 30 Miles in length without a Tree except little Islands of Wood. **1834** *Visit to TX* 41, These groves are called islands, from the striking resemblance they present to small tracts of land surrounded by water. **1859** (1968) Bartlett *Americanisms* 218, *Island.* In prairie regions, the same terms are used as if the timber were land, and the prairie water. A cluster of trees is called an *island.* **1870** *Overland Mth.* Feb 148, Sons of the Forest, still they sought the shelter of the bordering groves for their dwellings, or else in the shade of those singular, but beautiful "islands"—or groves in the midst of the prairie—dense and dark within, but bending their graceful boughs over the pure sward of grass all around. **1938** Rawlings *Yearling* 18 **nFL,** He had bought . . high good land in the center of a pine island. The island was called by such a name, in an arid forest, because it was literally an island of long-leaf pines, lifted high, a landmark, in the rolling sea that was the scrub. **1962** Atwood *Vocab. TX* 42, Of the nine occurrences [among c270 infs] of *island* with this meaning [=a grove of trees], eight are found in the southeastern corner of the state. **1966–68** *DARE* (Qu. T1, . . *A bunch of trees growing together in open country, especially on a hill*) Infs **LA**31, **MI**2, **PA**73, Island; **FL**4, A hammock or island (in saw grass); **FL**32, Oak island, pine island; **AR**32, Grove—we call them islands; (Qu. T2a, . . *A piece of land covered with trees . . only a few acres*) Inf **AR**32, Island; **FL**32, Hammock—large area; island—small area, named for kind of timber on it. **1966** *DARE* Tape **AR**32, Island. . . A thick group of trees on lower land. **1972** *S. Folkl. Qrly.* 36.121 **TX,** *Island* as a synonym for grove. . . is confined to the southeastern corner of Texas. . . There is little doubt that *island* is an inheritance from "Cajun" French. An expert on Louisiana place name generics writes that "the terms 'island', 'isle', and 'ile' are in common use in southwestern Louisiana to signify an isolated stand of timber on the prairies."

island duck n Also *island mallard*

=Florida duck.

1921 LA Dept. of Conserv. *Bulletin* 10.53 **LA,** A variety of French and English names are applied to the summer mallard, among which are . . "Mexican mallard," . . and "island duck." **1923** U.S. Dept. Ag. *Misc. Circular* 13.10 **LA,** *Anas fulvigula.* . . *Vernacular Names.* . . *In local use.* . . Island duck, island mallard.

island fever n Cf **cabin fever**

Irritability or depression caused by living on an isolated island.

1945 Hatcher *Lake Erie* 269 **Gt Lakes,** They know that if "island fever" hits them they can board Hersberger's plane, go to the mainland towns and see a moving picture.

island mallard See **island duck**

island myrtle n Cf **myrtle** n[1] **B6**

A **ceanothus** (here: *Ceanothus arboreus*) native to the California islands.

1937 U.S. Forest Serv. *Range Plant Hdbk.* B39, A few others, including island myrtle (*C[eanothus] arboreus*), . . become small trees under favorable conditions. **1938** Van Dersal *Native Woody Plants* 86, *Island myrtle.* . . A large shrub to small tree. **1979** Little *Checklist U.S. Trees* 79, *Feltleaf ceanothus.* . . Island myrtle.

Islang See **Isleño**

islant See **island**

islay n [AmSpan]

1 also *islaya:* A shrub or small tree (*Prunus ilicifolia*) with evergreen, spiny-toothed leaves, that is native to California. Also called **evergreen cherry 2, holly** n[1] **2, hollyleaf cherry, mountain holly 5, Spanish wild cherry**

1857 (1929) Hayes *Pioneer Notes* 230 (*DA*), Somebody has gathered for Miss Schiller the branches of the *islaya*, now in bloom and very pretty. **1893** *Jrl. Amer. Folkl.* 6.140, *Prunus ilicifolia*, islay, S. Cal. and W. Arizona. **1910** Jepson *Silva CA* 253, Islay grows in the Southern Coast Ranges from San Diego to the San Jacinto River. **1959** Munz–Keck *CA Flora* 790, *Islay.* . . Fr[uit] red, rarely yellow, . . with plum sweetish pulp. . . Common on dry slopes and fans. **1970** Kirk *Wild Edible Plants W. U.S.* 248, Islay. . . The fruit is pleasant tasting, and the large pit may be used after proper preparation to remove the cyanide. **1979** Little *Checklist U.S. Trees* 213.

2 A liqueur or similar beverage made from the fruit of *Prunus ilicifolia.*

1867 Cozzens *Sayings Dr. Bushwhacker* 5.33 **NY,** A little more of the Islay; thank you.

islaya See **islay 1**

isle See **island B2**

Isleño n Also *Islang, Islingue* [See quot 1983] **LA**

A member of an ethnic group living in southeastern Louisiana and descended primarily from immigrants from the Canary Islands.

1891 Sweetser *King's Hdbk. U.S.* 295, The Spanish settlers [in Louisiana] were mainly Catalans, and Islingues, as the Canary-Islanders were called. **1941** Writers' Program *Guide LA* 87, In St. Bernard Parish are to be found the "Isleños," Canary Islanders brought to Louisiana by

Governor Galvez in the 1770's. . . They have retained the Spanish language and many of their native customs. **1983** *Reinecke Coll.* 6 **LA,** *Isleno* [ɪsˈlenjo] rarely *Islang* [islæŋ]. . . Descendent of Spanish-speaking Canary Islanders who settled in St. Bernard, Plaquemines and Ascencion Parishes in late 18th c. Some still preserve their Spanish. First form is directly from Spanish for "Islander"; second form has passed through La. French "Islingue". **1990** Lipski *Lang. Isleños* 11, At present, perhaps only 1,000 to 2,000 isleños of all ages still adhere to the cultural practices and way of life that have defined this community since its inception, and the number of fluent and semifluent Spanish speakers is probably well below 500.

islet n

1 See **island B1.**

2 also sp *ilet:* A city block. [Fr *îlet* little island, block of buildings] **LA, esp New Orleans**

[**1931** Read *LA French* 46, Îlet. . . A city square; a square of ground. . . Îlet is still used in this sense by the Creoles of New Orleans.] [**1932** Ditchy *Acadiens* 131, *Ilet*, espace compris entre quatre rues en général se coupant à angles droits. Toute la Nouvelle-Orleans est divisée en îlets. [=*Ilet*, space included within four streets, usually being cut off at right angles. All of New Orleans is divided into îlets.]] **1941** Writers' Program *Guide LA* 689, Îlet—a city square or block. **1976** Dillard *Amer. Talk* 46, What are *blocks* in New York City may be *ilets* ('little islands') in New Orleans. **1981** Pederson *LAGS Basic Materials,* 1 inf, seLA, [ɪˈəˈleˠ] = islet, French . . city block, called islet[,] small "island"—each block surrounded by gutter.

Islingue See **Isleño**

isn't it interrog exclam Pronc-sp *innit* Cf **inso, is it**

=ainna.

1940 *AmSp* 15.82 **swMI, neOH,** *Isn't it?* Commonly used as an enclitic. 'You are going, isn't it?' From Dutch *is't niet?*—'is it not (so)?'[ˈ] **1950** *WELS* ("She's a nice looking woman, _____?" "We ought to come back here again, _____?") 1 Inf, **WI,** Isn't it. **1965–70** *DARE* (Qu. NN3, . . *'Don't you agree?'*) Infs **CT**42, **GA**15, **MN**6, **MO**32, **OK**14, 31, **PA**69, 142, Isn't it. **1993** *DARE* File **csWI,** The Wisconsinism that most strikes me . . is the monosyllabic d-less pronunciation of *shouldn't, wouldn't, couldn't.* I have a similar . . pronunciation of *isn't it.* I say [ɪn:ɪʔ], stress on first syllable, and use it as a universal tag. "You must be hungry, innit?" **1994** *Ibid,* "Innit" is . . the favorite, all-purpose tag-question in the Cheyenne [Amer Ind] dialect of English. . . You can get statements such as "you're goin' up north, innit?" or even "we're going tomorrow night, innit?" **1995** *Ibid* **csOK,** I have recorded numerous instances of [ˈɪnɪt] . . as an invariant (but not exclamatory) tag following sentences with any subject, mood, or negation, from speakers in and from south-central Oklahoma. Many of these people were original native speakers of American Indian languages, but others were not. To my knowledge they don't have German or black influences.

I spy n

1 also *I-spy-hi:* **=hide-and-seek A.** Cf **hide-and-spy 1, hy spy** n **1, I spy exclam**

[**1883** Newell *Games & Songs* 160, I Spy. [Footnote: Pronounced *Hie Spy.*]] **1891** *Jrl. Amer. Folkl.* 4.226 **Brooklyn NYC,** *I spy*, or hide and seek. . . A lamp-post or tree is taken as the "home" or "hunk;" the one who is "it" must stand there with his eyes closed, and count five hundred by fives . . while the others go hide. . . When "it" discovers a player in hiding, he cries out, "I spy so and so," calling the person by name, and runs to "hunk," for if the one spied should get in to "hunk" first, he would relieve himself. The players run in to the "hunk" when they have a good chance, and cry *relievo!* and if they get in first, they are free. . . If the one who is "it" mistakes one player for another . . and calls out the wrong name, both boys cry, "False alarm!" and are permitted, according to custom, to come in free. **1892** *DN* 1.236 **NEng,** In New England the game . . is variously called *I spy, hi spy, hi-spry* (Cape Cod); *hide and (go) seek, hide and whoop.* **1893** Shands *MS Speech* 72, *Hi-Spy.* . . is applied to both out-door and in-door hide-and-go-seek. *I spy* is also used. **1899** Champlin–Bostwick *Young Folks' Games* 442, *I spy*, an out-door hiding game. . . [T]he others hide, . . and when the player at the goal has finished counting, he goes out in search of them. When he sees one he names him, saying, "I spy James Smith," or whoever it may be. Both now run for the goal. If the hider touch it first, without being touched himself, he is safe. **1899** (1912) Green *VA Folk-Speech* 241, *I-spy.* . . So called from the exclamation of the seeker "I-spy" so-and-so, when he discovers a hidden player. **1906** Lovett *Old Boston Boys* 10, The games played by the boys of Chestnut and the adjacent streets are most pleasantly recalled; among which "I Spy," "The Red Lion," and "Punk" stand out prominently. **1940** Kennedy–Harlow *Schoolmaster* 227 **IN**, There were other games which the boys and girls began playing together—Hide and Seek or I Spy. **1952** Brown *NC Folkl.* 1.38, I Spy. **1957** *Sat. Eve. Post Letters* **cwCA** (as of 1915–19), I spy (a form of hide-and-seek started at dusk and played until too dark to see). *Ibid* **swCA**, We played "I Spy" where we stood at Home Base and said "I spy so and so" and told where they were hidden if questioned. **1968–70** *DARE* (Qu. EE13a, *Games in which every player hides except one, and that one must try to find the others*) Infs **AL**52, **IL**107, **MA**14, 24, **PA**115, **TN**37, 43, **WI**52, I spy. **1970** *AmSp* 45.207, Other names for this game included *I-spy, hi-spy, I-spy-hi, whoop-* or *hoop-and-hide,* and *hide-and-coop.*

2 A game in which an object is hidden and one or more players look for it. Cf **hide-and-spy 2**

1950 *WELS* (Games in which you hide an object and look for it) 7 Infs, **WI**, I spy. **1953** Brewster *Amer. Nonsinging Games* 46 **IN**, *I-spy.* . . This is an indoor game known also as Hide the Button, Huckle Buckle Beanstalk, Hunt the Thimble, Thimble in Sight. . . All the players except the one who is to be "It" leave the room. The latter puts the thimble in some out-of-the-way place . . always in plain view. He then calls back the other players, and they begin to hunt for the thimble. **1965–70** *DARE* (Qu. EE3) 131 Infs, **widespread exc NEng,** I spy.

3 A children's game in which players guess the name of a visible object chosen by a player who is "it."

[**1957** *Sat. Eve. Post Letters* **nwManitoba Canada,** Some of the games played by my playmates and me when we were children. . . "I spy with my little eye."] [**1970** *AmSp* 45.207, [The term] *I-spy* . . survives in a children's parlor game: "I spy with my little eye something that begins with. . . (a letter of the alphabet)."] **1990** *DARE* File **cwCA** (as of c1950), When I was a child, we played *I spy* just by saying "I spy" and having someone else guess what we were looking at. My children, who grew up in Wisconsin, learned the game from friends; they say "I spy with my little eye something that begins with (a particular letter)."

I spy exclam Also *I spy (someone);* for addit varr see quots Cf **bushel of wheat, bushel of rye; hy spy** exclam

Used as a call in children's hiding games, usu when "it" discovers a hiding player.

1891 [see **I spy** n 1]. **1899** Champlin–Bostwick [see **I spy** n 1]. **1899** Green [see **I spy** n 1]. **1965–70** *DARE* (Qu. EE15, *When he has caught the first of those that were hiding what does the player who is 'it' call out to the others?*) Infs **DC**11, **MD**39, **NJ**6, 35, **NY**69, 205, **OH**70, **TX**40, 43, I spy; **IA**92, **LA**11, **NJ**28, **TN**24, **VA**50, I spy [followed by name of person discovered]; **IA**29, I spy one-two-three on [name]. **1966** *DARE* Tape **AL**6, [FW:] How about I spy? [Aux Inf:] That's hide-and-go-seek, isn't it? . . One person's "it" and they count to a hundred, . . and then "I spy, all not hid, holler 'I,' " and everybody hid, and they holler "I," and they count again. And then this person has to go find them. But if they can beat home to base, they're home free. **1970** *AmSp* 45.207, *I-spy* has remained in the twentieth century as a signal of discovery in the game of hide-and-seek ("I spy Bill Jones").

I-spy-hi See **I spy** n 1

isse'f See **hisself**

issue n, v Usu |ˈɪš(j)u|; also |ˈɪšu, ˈɪšə|; rarely |ˈɪšɪ| Pronc-sp *isshy*

A Forms.

1940 in 1944 *ADD* 323 **WV,** [Radio:] Issue. . . [ˈɪšə], n. **1941** *Ibid,* /ˈɪšud/, ptc. **1952** Brown *NC Folkl.* 1.554, Isshy [ˈɪšɪ].

B As noun.

1 A person of racially mixed ancestry (White, Black, and American Indian), esp one of a group living in central Virginia. [**free issue**] **Mid Atl, esp VA** *usu considered derog*

1908 *S. Churchman* 4 Jan 6 **cVA,** There are several settlements of Indians in Virginia, but this will concern only the Amherst county group. . . They are known among the neighboring whites as "Issues," a name that has clung to them from ante-bellum days. Negroes who were not slaves were called "free issue," and these Indians, being neither whites nor slaves, were classed with the "free issue niggers." They dislike the name very much, and they call themselves "Indian Men" and "Indian Women." **1927** Adams *Congaree* 57 **cSC** [Black], Wuh de ole Issue do? . . I axe Saber and he say he look and he seen all dem Issue walkin' off through de swamp. **1946** *Social Forces* 24.442 **VA,** Issues of Virginia. . . Amherst and Rockbridge Counties. Name is derived from

term applied to free Negroes prior to the Civil War. *Numbers.* Said to be around 500 in 1926. . . A highland folk of the Blue Ridge foothills they are mostly renters who cultivate tobacco in shares. Chief stronghold on Tobacco Row Mountain. *Physique.* A mixture of White, Indian, and Negro types. . . *Cultural Peculiarities.* Traditions of Indian descent. . . Ancestors of these people were in this area as far back as 1790. **1963** Berry *Almost White* 27, Virginia, in addition to its Ramps and Melungeons, is the home of Issues. *Ibid* 34, Almost as bad is the term "Issues," which is applied to a group long known in Amherst County, Virginia, and whose counterparts are found up and down the Blue Ridge region of that state. Issue is a shortened form of Free Issue. **1968–70** *DARE* (Qu. HH28, *Names and nicknames . . for people of foreign background: Indian*) Inf **VA**101, Issues; (Qu. HH29a, *. . People of mixed blood—part Indian*) Inf **VA**25, Issue—claim Indian descent, but it is believed they are descendants of free issue niggers who came in 1618 or 1619 [sic]; **VA**101, Issues [ˈɪšuz] are Indians of very mixed blood who live near Lynchburg.

2 See **free issue 1.**

issueberry n

=Chinaberry 1.

1949 *AmSp* 24.110 **seSC,** Issueberries. . . Chinaberries.

issue free See **free issue 2**

issue-free Negro See **free issue 1**

ist See **just 7**

-ist See **-est**

iste See **istle**

ister See **oyster**

istle n Also *iste, ixtle, ystle* [See quot 1938] **chiefly TX**

A fiber obtained from any of var **agaves.**

1834 (1847) Lundy *Life & Travels* 96 **swTX,** The men set themselves at work, in making ropes out of "iste," a kind of stuff much used in this country, for ropes and bagging. It consists of the fibres of a plant, called "letchugia." **1892** *DN* 1.190 **TX,** Istle, ixtle: very strong fiber from which sisal hemp is made. It is taken by decortication from the long leaves of *Agave rigida,* var. *sisaleana.* **1938** *AmSp* 13.120 **TX,** Much employed in making sisal hemp, 'Mexican fiber'—the strong fibrous material obtained from agaves—bears the Texan names of *istle* (or *ystle*) and *ixtle.* These forms have been borrowed from Mexican-Spanish *ixtle, iztle,* which in turn derives from Nahuatl *ichtli.*

Is your finger sore? See **finger B1c**

it pron Usu |ɪt|; for varr see **A** below

A Forms.

1 |hɪt|; pronc-sp *hit.* Note: *Hit* and *it* often alternate in the same dialect; the evidence for the rules governing the choice between them is contradictory and may reflect regional or idiolectal as well as contextual variation. [Scots, nEngl dial] **chiefly Sth, S Midl**

1837 Sherwood *Gaz. GA* 70, *Provincialisms. . . Hit,* for it. **1853** in 1956 Eliason *Tarheel Talk* 313 **NC,** Hit. **1887** (1967) Harris *Free Joe* 104 **GA,** That's who I 'lowed hit wuz. **1890** *DN* 1.8 **sePA,** The rural districts about Philadelphia were interesting. He mentioned the old Anglo-Saxon *hit* (=it) as still existing. *Ibid* 68 **KY,** Hit's. . . said by children. **1891** Page *Elsket* 125 **VA** [Black], Hit all growed out of a tunament, suh. **1893** Shands *MS Speech* 36, *Hit.* . . Very frequently used by negroes and illiterate whites. **1895** *DN* 1.376 **seKY, eTN, wNC,** Hit. **1902** *DN* 2.236 **sIL,** Hit. . . It. So pronounced in emphatic, while *it* is used in unemphatic position. **1903** *DN* 2.316 **seMO,** Hit. . . It (emphatic, or when used at the beginning of a clause in speaking). Dialect writers in general throw in *hit* as if used invariably for 'it' which is by no means the case. Both pronunciations are often heard in one sentence. 'Hit's a hard bargain and you know it!' No Southerner would ever say 'You know hit's so.' **1907** Wright *Shepherd* 11 **Ozarks,** When God looked upon th' work of his hands an' called hit good, he war sure a lookin' at this here Ozark country. Rough? Law yes! Hit war made that a way on purpose. **1907** *DN* 3.223 **nwAR,** Hit. . . So pronounced in emphatic . . position. **1908** *DN* 3.320 **eAL, wGA,** Hit. . . It: chiefly for emphasis. **1909** *DN* 3.412 **nME,** Hit. **1915** *DN* 4.242 **eTN,** Hit. **1923** *DN* 5.210 **swMO,** Hit. **1927** *AmSp* 2.285 **Ozarks,** Wright [=1907 Wright *Shepherd*] also falls into the common error of supposing that *it* is nearly always turned into *hit,* while as a matter of fact the initial aspirate is used only at the beginning of a clause, or when some unusual emphasis is required—and not always even then. **1936** *AmSp* 11.239 **eTX,** Pronunciations in . . illiterate or low colloquial speech. . . *It:* [hɪt]. **1942** Hall *Smoky Mt. Speech* 86 **wNC, eTN,** The pronoun *it* [hɪt] . . preserves its initial historical [h], except when unstressed. . . Even unstressed *hit* often occurs without initial loss. **1952** Brown *NC Folkl.* 1.551, *Hit. . . It.* A number of writers on the use of *hit* and *it* . . say that *hit* is the emphatic form and *it* the unemphatic. I have been unable to detect any such distinction in Southern use. Our dialect speakers will use, without distinction, both *hit* and *it* in the same sentence. . . Very common in west [NC]; heard even among educated. Elsewhere rare except among those of no education or but little. **1965–70** *DARE* FW Addits **NC, KY,** Hit—it; **swAR,** Hit—stressed form of "it" [FW: [Inf] is in his 80s, but I heard this from younger speakers, too, though not from children.]; **csLA,** Hit eats some good; **seGA,** Hit don't make no nevernminds; **wNC,** I don't know what to do with hit; **ceTN,** Hit [=a cow] knowed his name; **seTN,** Hit can just rain anytime. **1967–68** *DARE* (Qu. KK42a) Inf **TN13,** Hit'd be easy for him; (Qu. OO38a) Inf **GA44,** Hit sho' do fit you good. **1968–69** *DARE* Tape **GA25,** Hit's a terrible wet swamp; **TN15,** Hit was the nicest looking one I'd made in all; **TN31,** Hit was a mule; **VA9,** Hit was about three miles from our house; **VA27,** Hit was a very difficult job. **1976** Wolfram–Christian *Appalachian Speech* 58, *H* is still retained by a number of the older residents of the area. . . When the winter set in, *hit* set in, *hit's* just like in a western. . . The retention of the initial *h* in these forms is most likely to be found in the more stressed items in a sentence, and occurs rarely, if at all, in unstressed items.

2 |ɛt, ət|; pronc-sp *et.* Cf *if*

1852 in 1956 Eliason *Tarheel Talk* 313 **NC,** Et. **1880** (1886) Woolson *Rodman* 258 **SC** [Black], Somehow et's rusty, sah. **1897** Lummis *King of Broncos* 39 **NM,** Et'll shore be a job to round 'em up. **1934** *AmSp* 9.38 **Sth,** The substitution of [ə] for [ɪ] in the unstressed syllables of such words as *pocket, palace, goodness,* and especially in unstressed *it* and *him* is unpleasant to the Southern ear. **1939** in 1944 *ADD* 323 **csIN,** To do [ət] will require. *Ibid* **neTX,** [ɛts] so nice 'n' snug here.

B Gram form.

Possessive: usu *its;* also rarely *(h)it.* [*OED* 13 . . →; "Now *dial.*"; for quot 1909 cf **he** pron **2**]

1896 *DN* 1.419 **cNY,** It: occasionally for possessive *its.* . . A curious Elizabethan survival. **1909** *S. Atl. Qrly.* 8.49 **sSC coast** [Gullah], W'en yo' is come intuh de choche yo' mus' 'bey hit' gubberners. [=When you have come into the church you must obey its governors.]

C Syntax.

1 esp with existential *be:* Used in place of std *there* to anticipate a postponed subject. [*OED* a1300–a1617] **scattered, but chiefly Sth, S Midl**

1800 (1898) Hunt *Diary* 3 **sePA,** In the afternoon it came on a severe storm of wind & snow. **1866** in 1983 *PADS* 70.39 **sePA,** To meet the Boat on Lake Cayuga a small one it was not many passengers. **1930** Faulkner *As I Lay Dying* 29 **MS,** I told Anse it likely wont be no need. **1935** Hurston *Mules & Men* 126 **FL** [Black], And it's so many weeds in dis yard, Ah'm liable to git snake bit at my own door. **1937** *Engl. Studies* (Amsterdam) 19.209, The expression *it is,* familiar to students of Old and Middle English . . still survives among negroes and less educated whites of the Southern section of the United States. A note just received from a negro wash-woman . . began: " . . it was'nt [sic] but one Dollar in the Basket Monday morning." I had once heard a white store-clerk say, "It's some wool in that box." **1941** Smith *Going to God's Country* 142 **MO** (as of 1896), It came a big rain and killed it. **1941** *Hench Coll.* **seVA,** [A student from Portsmouth VA] used *it is* only with singulars, not plurals. E.g. "It's a man at the door, mother." **1944** *PADS* 2.34 **NC,** It is a book in the French room that might be yours. **1958** Humphrey *Home from the Hill* 7 **TX,** It may be some out there now. **1963** Wright *Lawd Today* 119 **Chicago IL** [Black], Aw, it's some strange folks in the world. **1966** *Wilson Coll.* **csKY,** Squirrels gits what few it is. **1966–68** *DARE* FW Addit **OK41,** It was (a tank over there, etc)—used quite often for "there was. . ."; **LA2,** It's a good many of 'em drink buttermilk and won't drink sweet milk; **ceVA,** "It's time enough to go." He means: "Stay, you've plenty of time"; **LA6,** Hit was a man living in that house. **1967** *DARE* Tape **MN4,** [FW:] Would you ever consider going into growing potatoes? [Inf:] No, not unless it'd be a different, altogether different, trend in weather. **1968** *DARE* (Qu. B36) Inf **LA15,** It'll fog up, but it won't be any ice. **1976** Wolfram–Christian *Appalachian Speech* 126, King Cobra 'posed to be 'bout the deadliest snake *it* is. . . *It's* too much murder. . . *It's* a lotta them that does. . . The use of *it* as a correspondence for expletive *there* is a pattern that appears to be fairly extensive. . . in vernacular Black English. It is also found in White non-mainstream varieties spoken in the North and

South. **1977** Smitherman *Talkin* 31 [Black], It ain nobody I can trust. *Ibid* 250, It's five kid in my family. **1986** Pederson *LAGS Concordance Gulf Region,* [Examples include] 1 inf, **seGA,** It ain't a damn thing to it; 1 inf, **nwMS,** It ain't anything meaner; 1 inf, **csGA,** It ain't but three sisters; 1 inf, **seAL,** It ain't but two classes [of people]; 1 inf, **seLA,** It ain't going to be no people; nothing but machines; 1 inf, **cwMS,** It ain't none; 1 inf, **swAL,** It ain't nobody worth that much; 1 inf, **nwFL,** It ain't nobody really here to hurt nobody; 1 inf, **nwFL,** (I)t ain't never been.

2 Used redundantly immediately following a noun subject. [*OED* c1430 →] Cf **he** pron **1**

1849 (1850) Poe *Works* 2.28, Our love it was stronger by far than the love / Of those who were older than we. **1857** in 1983 *PADS* 70.39 **ce,sePA,** The water it was up to the horses bodys. **1923** in 1983 Taft *Blues Lyric Poetry* 111, This northern country : it make you choose / But it will never cure : the Mason-Dixon blues. **1935** *Ibid* 72, My tires ain't going to fail me : and my motor it is good and strong.

D Sense.

He—usu derog or in ref to a child. [*EDD*]

1851 Hooper *Widow Rugby's Husband* 128 **AL,** "Hit'll fight!" . . "Hit!" he exclaimed; "who dars to call me *hit?*" **1924** (1946) Greer-Petrie *Angeline Gits an Eyeful* 24 **csKY,** I spied that tryflin' Lum [=the speaker's husband] a-standin' thar with his bar' laigs a-shinin', and I hope to my die if *hit* didn't have *hits* arms locked around that thar Reno widder's waist and *hit* was a-holdin' her hand as they div' off'n a high plank into the warter! **1938** *AmSp* 13.237, Still another extension of meaning for the pronoun *it* . . is pointed out by . . others. If a person wishes to scoff at or subordinate some one, he may do so by saying to him something like 'Well, what's it thinking now?' or 'Well, what's it doing now?' **1967** *DARE* FW Addit, [Inf **TN17:**] Where's Johnny [=a boy of 11 or 12]? [Inf **TN17A:**] Hit went home. [Inf **TN17:**] When's hit a-comin' back?

it n

1 A person one considers stupid or worthless. *derog* Cf **it** pron **D**

1896 *DN* 1.419 **cNY, nOH,** It: A worthless fellow. "An awful it." **1900** *DN* 2.42 [College slang], It. . . A word of contempt expressing that one is something less than a human being; hence an idiot, a dolt. **1903** *Pedagogical Seminary* 10.371, You big it. **1916** *DN* 4.276 **NE, MA,** It. . . Idiot. "What an It that man is." "He's a perfect It." In writing or print, usually capitalized. **1919** *DN* 5.66 **NM,** It, a term of disparagement used in disgust or contempt. "Her brother is a perfect It, mother won't have him on the place." **1925** *AmSp* 1.103, In . . slang usage *it* means simpleton or booby.

2 A homosexual.

1942 Berrey–Van den Bark *Amer. Slang* 405.1, Homosexual. . . it. **1968** *DARE* (Qu. HH39, *A homosexual man*) Inf **NJ12,** An it.

3 also *i.t., it-taggers:* Any of var children's games of tag.

1965 *DARE* File **ceTX** (as of c1920), It—the child's game of tag. **1968** *DARE* (Qu. EE28, *Games played in the water*) Inf **OH46,** It; **PA76,** It-taggers—tag; **PA94,** I.t.—if you say the word "it," you're still "it"; (Qu. EE33, . . *Outdoor games . . that children play*) Inf **LA43,** It—a simple tag game.

it ain't done it phr Also *ain't done (it);* for addit varr see quots chiefly Sth, S Midl *esp freq among children*

That isn't so!

1915 *DN* 4.229 **wTX,** 'T ain't done it. . . Universal among children and common (in facetious use) among adults. "He hit me." " 'T ain't done it!" (*i.e.,* "I didn't.") **1923** *DN* 5.200 **swMO,** Ain't done. . . A form of denial commonly used by children or by facetiously inclined adults. **1953** *PADS* 19.10 **ceKY,** When one is unjustly accused of wrong-doing, one may answer, "It ain't done it." **1954** *Harder Coll.* **cwTN,** " 'E left 'at car outta shed?" "Ain't done it." "Ye're red in the face." "Ain't done it." **1969** *DARE* FW Addit **seNC,** It ain't done it. Used by kids to mean "that's not so." [**1976** Garber *Mountain-ese* 45 **sAppalachians,** *I ain't dunnit* . . I am not—She thinks I'm gonna marry her but I ain't dunnit.] **1978** *NADS Letters* **AR** (as of 1950s), It ain't done it! I remember this expression from . . Cale, Arkansas . . It often came in a more emphatic form: *It ain't done it no such of a thing.* . . I recall it from children my own age and younger as well as adults, so I assume it is still current there. My wife, who grew up in Brinkley, Arkansas . . says the expression was and is in use there too. *Ibid* **neTX,** Regarding "It ain't done it". . . My colleague, from Bonham, Texas, and his wife, from Wood County, Texas, both have used the expression. They state, and I agree, that the expression is predominantly used among non-adults. . . The heaviest stress comes on *done,* the next to heaviest on *ain't,* the least stress on the last *it. Ibid* **ceTX** [Black], In a recent dialect survey of the Huntsville Area, we found that the expression "It ain't done it!" appears here in Black English, meaning, "You don't mean it," or "It has not happened." *Ibid* **ceMS** (as of 1940s), *It ain't done it!* was a common expression . . in the western part of Neshoba County, Mississippi . . in the 1940's. (My wife says that I still use this expression.) . . Examples: "The bus is coming!" "It ain't done it!" . . "My car is eleven years old." "It ain't done no such a thing." **1978** *DARE* File **cnGA** (as of 1920s), "It ain't done it!" meaning "It isn't so! That's not true!" was common among children, white and probably also black. **1979** *NADS Letters* **ceAL**, *It ain't done it,* it isn't true. I remember this as common in my childhood in Talledega, Ala. I don't associate it with adult English, and I don't recall hearing it recently. The emphatic form was *It ain't so done it. Ibid* **OK** (as of 1922–40), "It ain't done it" was a commonplace way of saying something was not true. . . That was early childhood's way of disagreeing vehemently without saying "That's not so" or "That's a lie." **1986** Pederson *LAGS Concordance,* 1 inf, **cAL**, It ain't done it.

Italian adj, n Usu |ɪˈtæljən, ə-|; also |aɪˈtæljən| Pronc-spp *Eyetalian, Eyetallion;* for addit pronc and sp varr see quots Cf **Itie**

A Forms.

1838 (1843) Haliburton *Clockmaker* (2d ser) 304 **NEng**, The *Eye*talian is too lazy, the French too smirky. **1887** Francis *Saddle & Mocassin* 141 **swNM**, He always laughingly denies the nationality which his unmistakable brogue betrays, and declares that he is an "*I*-talian." **1896** *DN* 1.419, *Italian:* variously pron[ounced] [ɪˈtæljən], [əˈtæljən], [aɪˈtɑljən], [raɪˈtæljən], [ræˈtæljən]. **1899** Garland *Boy Life* 138 **nwIA** (as of c1870s), Right *here* you'll find your Eyetallion species. **1903** *DN* 2.292 **Cape Cod MA** (as of a1857), [ˈaɪtæljən]. **1905** *DN* 3.101 **nwAR**, [aɪtæljən]. **1910** *DN* 3.444 **wNY**, *Italian*. . . Pronounced *Aitalian.* **1919** Kyne *Capt. Scraggs* 285 **CA**, This syndicate ain't a-goin' to come rampin' home to Gawd's country lookin' like a lot o' Eyetalian peddlers. **1931** Hannum *Thursday April* 92 **wNC**, Hit's a right smart lot of furriners, French and Eyetalians and what not. **1936** *AmSp* 11.152 **eTX**, *Italian* is also frequently pronounced with [aɪ], [aɪˈtæljən], as well as with [ɪ] and [ə]. *Ibid* 308 **Upstate NY**, *Italian* occurs occasionally as [ˌaɪˈtæljən]. **1941** *LANE* Map 453 *(Italian),* [Proncs of the type [aɪˈtæljən] (sometimes with secondary stress on the first syllable, and in two cases with equal stress on the first two syllables) are common throughout NEng.] **1942** Hall *Smoky Mt. Speech* 56 **wTN**, [aɪ] . . appears . . usually in *Italian. c1960* Wilson *Coll.* **csKY**, *Italian* is often /ˌaɪˈtæljən/. **1965–70** *DARE* (Qu. HH28) Infs **AR47, LA16, 28, NY73, PA82, SC31**, [aɪˈtæljən(z)]; **MI101, WI22, 44**, [aɪˈtælɪən]; **WV3, 7**, [aəˈtæljən]; **IL46**, [aɪˈtæˑjən]; **NY123, RI11**, Eyetalians. **1968–69** *DARE* Tape **CA123**, My folks were [ˈaɪˌtæljən]; **CA103**, Italians [ˌaɪˈtæljənz].

B As noun.

1 See **Italian sandwich**.

2 =**Irish** n[1] **B1**.

1991 *Capital Times* (Madison WI) 31 July sec D 1, Fraboni said Wisconsin Bell owes him . . a service just as he owes his patrons the service of a coin phone. . . Fraboni still has his Italian up. . . "I'm teed off" [he said].

Italian bean n Also *Italian green bean, Italian pole ~, Italian string ~*

Either of two **snap beans:** a bush variety or a pole variety; see quots.

1965–70 *DARE* (Qu. I20, . . *Kinds of beans*) Infs **PA74, 248, WA6, WI52**, Italian beans; **CA132**, Italian string beans—also called [bəˈč́ičə]; **CO27**, Italian beans—broad, flat; **IA30**, Italian green beans; **NJ26**, Italian beans—like a string bean; **NC36**, Flat Italian beans; **WI20**, Italian beans—similar to a green bean; (Qu. I4) Inf **MI88**, Italian green beans; (Qu. I14, *Kinds of beans that you eat in the pod before they're dry*) Inf **CA32**, Italian beans—wide-podded; **MI68**, Italian beans—Italian string beans—you don't often hear that term; **NY106**, Italian green beans; **OR1**, Italian beans; (Qu. I16, *The large flat beans that are not eaten in the pod*) Inf **CA170**, Italian beans—eaten in pod; **IL29**, Italian beans—white with purple spots on it; **NY2**, Italian beans; **PA248**, Italian string beans. **1974** *Burpee Seeds* 78, *Romano (Italian Pole).* . . The distinctive flavor and heavy yield of this pole bean makes it excellent for small home gardens. The vines are loaded with long, wide-podded green beans that are perfectly stringless and exceptionally tender and meaty. **1978** *Wanigan Catalog* 11 **MA**, *Italian Pole.* Known in California as Speckled Cranberry. Romano is the commercial catalog name. *Italian String Bean.* A . . black seed with a prominent white eye area. Pods are 8″ long, flat green, and mature in mid-season in Michigan, as here. **1990** *Seed Savers*

Yearbook 49, *[Bean/snap/bush]—Berrier's Italian* . . large green shell beans, 4–5″ broad flat pod, putty-colored seed turns pale-tan when dry. *Ibid* 61, *[Bean/snap/pole]—Italian* . . Romano-type, vigorous, drought res[istant], lima bean-shaped beige seed with brown marks like finger-prints, brought from Italy in 1909.

Italian bell pepper See **Italian pepper**

Italian daisy n

=**orange hawkweed**.

1900 *Plant World* 3.132, While on a botanical trip this summer in northeastern Pennsylvania, I noted the following common names in use . . *Italian Daisy* . . for *Hieracium aurantiacum* [etc].

Italian green bean See **Italian bean**

Italian grinder See **grinder 3**

Italian ice n esp **NYC** area

A confection of crushed ice infused with fruit-flavored syrup.

1968 *Burlington Co. Herald* (Mount Holly NJ) 8 Aug sec B 18/2, [Advt:] Italian ice . . ½ gal. 39¢. **1980** *DARE* File **neNJ** (as of 1960s), Italian ices were something between sherbet and snowcones. We bought them from a vendor who sold nothing else. They came in small paper cups, and in lemon, orange, or cherry flavor. And they were much more refreshing than a popsicle or an ice-cream cone on a hot summer day. **1980** *NADS Letters* **NYC** (as of 1950s), We used *ice,* but in most cases *ices* were Italian ices, i.e., soft and served in a cup. *Ibid* **NYC**, We used to eat "Italian ices" (frozen fruit-flavored water) in accordian-pleated wax cups. **1981** *DARE* File **Buffalo NY**, They've got the best beef on weck and Italian ices available around here. **1991** *Ibid* **sePA**, In the fifties in Philadelphia, my childhood friends and I enjoyed Italian ice daily in the summer. This treat, which peaked about three inches out of a paper cone, consisted of ice crushed to the size of raw sugar, over which was poured a fake fruit syrup. *Ibid* **NYC** (as of 1950s), Italian ices were very finely ground, flavored ice. The consistency of the ices was very smooth. I remember it being sold out of a pushcart-like affair. You'd ask the man for the flavor you wanted and he'd open the hatch on top of the cart, scoop out what you wanted from a cardboard tub, and serve it in a small paper cup.

Italian pepper n Also *Italian bell pepper*

A pepper (*Capsicum annuum* Longum Group), usu hot and red. chiefly **NEast** See Map

1952 Tracy *Coast Cookery* 25 **San Francisco CA**, Pickled Italian Bell Peppers. . . Serve these peppers as an appetizer, by cutting them into strips. **1965–70** *DARE* (Qu. I22a, . . *Peppers—small hot*) 10 Infs, **chiefly NEast**, Italian peppers; **CT11**, All hot ones [are] Italian peppers; **MD41**, Italian peppers—red, round, somewhat hot; **NJ11**, Italian peppers—four inches long, red; **NJ24**, Hot or Italian; (Qu. I22b, . . *Peppers—large hot*) Infs **CT11, MA122**, Italian peppers; (Qu. I22c, . . *Peppers—small sweet*) Inf **NY123**, Italian peppers.

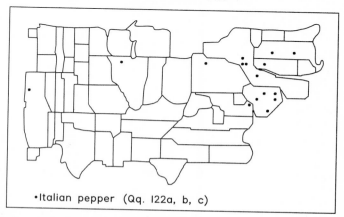

•Italian pepper (Qq. I22a, b, c)

Italian pole bean See **Italian bean**

Italian sandwich n Also *Italian* **NEast, esp ME** See Map on p. 68 Cf **grinder 3, hero**

=**submarine sandwich**.

1952 *Reading Eagle* 7 Sep. 1/3 *(Mathews Coll.)* **PA**, Canned music of all descriptions was drifting across the fairground last night with the aroma of frying hamburgers and Italian sandwiches. **1964** *Reading Times* 30 May 9/4 *(Mathews Coll.)* **PA**, The Italian sandwich has many aliases. . . Andrew Galantuomo, a friendly paisano, began manufacturing them in 1933, and during the Depression sold them for 15 cents apiece. **1965–70** *DARE* (Qu. H42, . . *[A sandwich] . . in a much larger, longer bun, that's a meal in itself*) Infs **ME**7, 9, 11, 16, 19, 23, **PA**159, **MA**34, **NH**15, Italian sandwich; **FL**37, Italian; (Qu. H65, *Foreign foods favored by people around here*) Infs **ME**16, 19, Italian sandwiches. **1967** *AmSp* 42.282, Italian Sandwich [used for submarine sandwich in] Louisville [KY], Reading [PA], Allentown [PA]. [*DARE* Ed: This article is based on a survey of classified advt in the telephone directories of 100 cities.] **1971** *Today Show Letters* s**ME**, An Italian sandwich . . is a loaf of Italian bread sliced lengthwise and filled with ham or salami, cheese, onion, green peppers, tomatoes and sometimes pickled black olives and sprinkled liberally with salt and olive oil. **1975** Gould *ME Lingo* 143, *Italian sandwich*—Originated as such by an Italian–American restaurateur in Portland, *Italian sandwich* is the Maine term for the submarine, grinder, etc. **1988** *DARE* File, [A map by Wm. Labov of regional terms for "submarine sandwich" shows three instances of *Italian sandwich* in ne**MA**.]

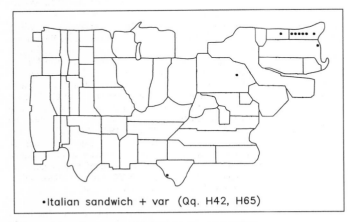

•Italian sandwich + var (Qq. H42, H65)

Italian squash n scattered, but esp CA, SW

A zucchini squash (*Cucurbita pepo* var *melopepo* cv *Zucchini*).

1926 *Ladies' Home Jrl.* Nov 149, Italian squash which is found in many markets at present is most satisfactory. **1965–70** *DARE* (Qu. I23, . . *Kinds of squash*) 11 Infs, 7 **CA, AZ, TX**, Italian (squash); **CA**182, Italian—long, green, same as zucchini; **CT**12, Italian squash—twelve inches long, green with light stripes; **MI**63, Zucchini—that's Italian squash, only it's smaller and nicer quality; **TX**67, Italian squash—long, green; (Qu. I4) Inf **CT**12, Italian squash. **1967–69** *DARE* FW Addit **San Francisco CA**, Italian squash—small, green; also called zucchini; cs**AZ**, [Sign in supermarket at zucchini:] Italian squash.

Italian string bean See Italian bean

italic period n Also *italic space*

A nonexistent item used as the basis of a practical joke.

1921 *DN* 5.94, Italic period. Printer sends apprentice for. **1923** *DN* 5.241 **Cleveland OH**, Italic periods. **1968** *DARE* (Qu. HH14, *Ways of teasing a beginner or inexperienced person—for example, by sending him for a 'left-handed monkey wrench'*: "Go get me _____.") Inf **PA**104, Italic spaces (printing office).

Italy n

A children's ball game; see quot.

1970 *DARE* (QR, near Qu. EE1) Inf **MA**128, [Aux Inf:] Italy—bounce a ball in ten different ways. [FW: offered by the Inf's fourteen-year-old]

itch n, v Usu |ɪč|; also chiefly Sth, S Midl |ič|; rarely |ɛč| Pronc-spp *ea(t)ch, ee(t)ch, etch* Similarly adj *eachy* Cf Pronc Intro 3.I.5.a

A Forms.

1795 in 1944 *ADD* 324 **NC**, The People . . mostly have the Each. **1867** Harris *Sut Lovingood Yarns* 116 **TN**, Hit pester'd em ni ontu es bad as the eatch. **1899** (1912) Green *VA Folk-Speech* 161, Each. . . Eachy. **1903** *DN* 2.292 **Cape Cod MA** (as of a1857), Vowels are pronounced long in . . itch *(eetch)*. Ibid 318 se**MO**, [ič]. **1906** *DN* 3.142 nw**AR**, [ič]. **1908** *DN* 3.323 e**AL**, w**GA**, [ič]. **1915** *DN* 4.184 sw**VA**, [ič]. **1917** *DN* 4.411 w**NC**, **LA**, **IL**, **SC**, **KS**, **KY**, Eetch. **1923** [see **B**1 below]. **1923** Parsons *Folk-lore Sea Islands* 210 cs**SC**, If you' right hand eatches, you' money comin'; lef' hand, you' money goin'. **1927** *AmSp* 2.353 **WV**, The children got the eetch at school. **1929** Sale *Tree Named John* 104 **MS**, Don'chu see he jes eechin' fer it? **1933**

Rawlings *South Moon* 117 **FL**, He'll eetch and eetch. **1934** *AmSp* 9.210 **Sth**, A great many words having standard [ɪ] before [g], [n], [ŋ], and possibly [č], change [ɪ] to [i]. . . *itch* (also [ič], [ɛč]). [Footnote:] This word is perhaps exceptional, for other words in -*itch* have [ɪ]: *bitch, flitch* [etc]. **1937** in 1976 *Weevils in the Wheat* 248 **VA** [Black], Ef your nose etch, somebody coming to your house. If it's the right side etches, the visitor will be a man. **1942** Hall *Smoky Mt. Speech* 15 w**NC**, e**TN**, There is a tendency in some speakers to use . . /i/ in *fish, itch, little, stick, wick.* **1954** [see **B**1 below]. c**1960** [see **B**1 below]. **1963** [see **B**1 below]. **1966–70** *DARE* (Qu. A20) Inf **VA**1, Hurry up, you're as slow as seven-year [ioč]; (Qu. AA4a) Inf **VA**65, [ičɪn]; (Qu. BB25) Inf **IN**13, Two-year [ič]; **SC**27, [ič]; (Qu. GG13b) Inf **GA**77, [i·č]. c**1970** [see **B**1 below].

B As noun.

Usu with *the*:

1 Any of var diseases, esp scabies, that cause chronic itching. **widespread, but esp Sth, S Midl** See Map Cf **dew poison, ground itch, seven-year ~, toe ~**

1795 [see **A** above]. **1867** [see **A** above]. **1923** *DN* 5.206 sw**MO**, *Eetch.* . . the itch. **1927** [see **A** above]. **1954** *Harder Coll.* cw**TN**, [Letter:] The school children all have the Eatch so they tell. **1958** *VT Hist.* 26.276, Don't need it any more than I need the itch. Worse than the (seven year) itch. c**1960** *Wilson Coll.* cs**KY**, It's no disgrace to catch the eetch, but it's a disgrace to keep it. **1963** Watkins–Watkins *Yesterday Hills* 129 cn**GA**, You ought to have the each jist one time. **1965–70** *DARE* (Qu. BB25, . . *Common skin diseases around here*) 175 Infs, **widespread exc Pacific, but esp Sth, S Midl,** (The) itch; **IL**35, The winter itch—we haven't had it for years—not since long underwear; **KY**40, The itch—caused by itch bug—a small black bug; **MO**2, Itch—you catch it from other people; you break out between your fingers mostly; **OK**13, The itch—skin or blood disease; something in blood causes it; **SC**2, The itch—called scabbies [sic—FW sp] now; **SC**11, The itch—takes in a whole lot; **TX**98, The itch—now called "allergy"; (Qu. A18, . . *A very slow person*: "What's keeping him? He certainly is _____!") Infs **NC**48, **KY**74, **PA**92, (As) slow as the itch; **KY**28, Slow as itch; **CA**107, Slower than the itch; **OK**42, Too slow to catch the itch; **TX**102, The itch; (Qu. X59, . . *The small infected pimples that form usually on the face*) Inf **VA**9, Itch; (Qu. BB28, *Joking names . . for imaginary diseases*: "He must have the _____.") Infs **NE**3, **NC**50, **PA**126, Itch; **MO**17, Little itch; (Qu. HH22b, . . *A very mean person* . . "He's meaner than _____ .") Inf **NC**76, The itch; (Qu. KK42b) Inf **RI**3, He's like a one-armed paperhanger with the itch. c**1970** Pederson *Dial. Surv. Rural GA* (*What do you call an itching soreness between the toes?*) 1 inf, se**GA**, Itch [ɪ^·ʃ]. **1990** Cavender *Folk Med. Lexicon* 25 s**Appalachians**, (The) itch—scabies.

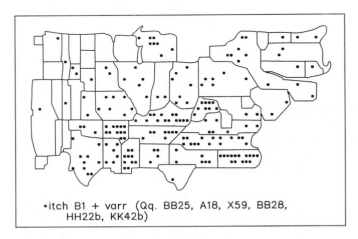

•itch B1 + varr (Qq. BB25, A18, X59, BB28, HH22b, KK42b)

2 A feeling of nervousness or uneasiness.

1966–70 *DARE* (Qu. GG13a, *When something keeps bothering a person and makes him nervous*) Inf **NJ**35, He's got the itch; (Qu. GG13b, *When something keeps bothering a person and makes him nervous* . . "It gives me the _____.") Infs **CT**28, **FL**19, **MS**80, **NY**38, Itch; **GA**77, Nervous itch; Qu. II29b, . . *To explain the unpleasant effect that person has on you*: "He just _____.") Inf **CA**107, Gives me the itch.

‡**itchety** adj [Var of *itchy*, perh infl by *fidgety*]

1930 *AmSp* 6.98 c**NY**, *Itchety*: Uneasy. "I always feel itchety until I know who people are."

itchweed n

1 also *itching plant*; pronc-spp *eetch(-weed):* An **Indian poke 1** (here: *Veratrum viride*).

1822 Eaton *Botany* 506, *Veratrum. . . viride . .* itch-weed, indian poke. . . Useful in rheumatism and many cutaneous eruptions. 1840 *MA Zool. & Bot. Surv. Herb. Plants & Quadrupeds* 205, *V[eratrum] viride.* . . Itch-weed. . . The pulverized root, when snuffed into the nose, produces violent . . sneezing, and. . . boys sometimes make dangerous experiments with it. 1869 Porcher *Resources* 606 **Sth,** *Itch-weed. . . Veratrum viride.* . . It has been externally employed, in the form of ointment, in many cutaneous affections. 1917 *DN* 4.411 **wNC,** *Eetch.* . . That's eetch-weed; it's good for the eetch. 1930 Sievers *Amer. Med. Plants* 6, Itchweed. . . The plant is very poisonous. 1967–70 *DARE* (Qu. S17, . . *Kinds of plants . . that . . cause itching and swelling)* Infs **IN3, 14, KY21, 53, MI102, NY183, OH80, PA73, WI50,** Itchweed; **KY75,** Itchweed—a plant two feet high; **KY83,** Itchweed—leaves are fuzzy; **VA46,** Itchweed—1 to 1½ feet high, white flower, grows in sandy soil; **NY28,** Itching plant—little white flowers. 1976 Bailey–Bailey *Hortus Third* 1148, Itchweed.

2 A **valerian** (here: *Valeriana officinalis*).

1940 Clute *Amer. Plant Names* 274, *Valeriana officinalis.* . . Itch-weed.

3 also *itchy plant:* =**poison ivy 1.**

1967–69 *DARE* (Qu. S16, *A three-leaved plant that grows in woods and countryside and makes people's skin itch and swell)* Inf **MO3,** The old itchweed; **PA213,** Itchy plant.

4 A **smartweed.**

1969 *DARE* (Qu. S17, . . *Kinds of plants . . that . . cause itching and swelling)* Inf **IL80,** Itchweed—same as smartweed.

‡**itchy** v Pronc-sp *eetchy*

To itch, desire.

1893 Shands *MS Speech* 28, *Eetchy.* . . A negro once told me that on a cold morning he felt more like working, but that he never did *eetchy* for work.

itchy plant See **itchweed 3**

item n *old-fash*

A hint, inkling; information.

1816 Pickering *Vocab.* 118, *Item.* An intimation, a hint. *Ex.* I had an item of his designs. This is a low word, and is used here only by the illiterate. 1818 Fearon *Sketches* 124 **ceMA,** *Q.* What is her sickness? *A.* Consumption. *Q.* I had an item (a supposition) of that. 1853 Hammett *Stray Yankee in TX* 129, The minute you get item that I'm back, catch up your horses, meet me at the cross-roads. 1859 (1968) Bartlett *Americanisms* 218, *Item.* Information; as "I got item of his being in town." This word is used among Southern gamblers to imply information of what cards may be in their partner's or opponent's hands; this is called "giving item." 1899 (1912) Green *VA Folk-Speech* 241, *Item.* . . A hint. 1905 *DN* 3.12 **neCT,** *Item.* . . Information. 'I got an item of his being in town.'

it gives See **give B1a**

ith See **with**

ither adj[1], adv, pron[1], conj[1] See **either**

ither adj[2], n, pron[2], conj[2] See **other**

ithur See **either**

Ithuriel's spear n [See quot 1889]

A **brodiaea** (here: *Triteleia* [formerly *Brodiaea*] *laxa*). Also called **grass lily, grassnut 2, harvest lily, highland potato 1, Indian potato e, triplet lily, wallybasket**

1889 *Century Dict.* 3203, *Ithuriel's spear.* . . [*Century* Ed: So called in allusion to the spear of Ithuriel (Milton, P[aradise] L[ost], iv. 810), which caused everything it touched to assume its true form.] The California liliaceous plant *Brodiæa (Triteleia) laxa.* 1897 Parsons *Wild Flowers CA* 302, Ithuriel's spear. . . there is something commanding about this tall blossom-crowned shaft. It will perhaps be remembered that the angel Ithuriel possessed a truth-compelling spear. 1915 (1926) Armstrong–Thornber *Western Wild Flowers* 24, Ithuriel's Spear. . . is common on hillsides and in adobe fields. 1949 Moldenke *Amer. Wild Flowers* 355, In the . . Ithuriels-spear, . . the funnel-form flowers are violet-purple in color. 1961 Thomas *Flora Santa Cruz* 125 **cwCA,** Ithuriel's Spear. . . Common, especially on the eastern slopes of the Santa Cruz Mountains in grasslands and on serpentine slopes. 1974 Munz *Flora S. CA* 882, *T[riteleia] laxa.* . . Ithuriel's Spear.

Itie n Usu |ˈaɪti|; for addit varr see quots Pronc-spp *Ey(e)tie* [Dimin of **Italian**] *derog* Cf **Ikey 2**

An Italian; something Italian.

1925 Fraser–Gibbons *Soldier & Sailor Words* 90, *Eyeties:* Italians. 1941 *LANE* Map 453 *(Italian)* 1 inf, **cnME,** [ɪtᵻˈˆ]; 1 inf, **seVT,** [ɐˈtʰᵻˀ]. 1947 Berrey–Van den Bark *Amer. Slang Suppl.* 39.2 [Military slang], *Eye Tie,* any Italian plane. 1960 Wentworth–Flexner *Slang* 175, *Eytie*[ᵻ] *Eyetie* n. An Italian. *Common W.W.II Army use, though the term is much earlier in origin.* 1968–69 *DARE* (Qu. HH28, *Names and nicknames . . for people of foreign background: Italian)* Infs **IN39,** [ˈɑiti]; **MA58,** [ˈɑiti]; **IL97,** [ˈaɪtaɪz].

-itis suff *usu joc*

Used to form names for real or imagined diseases.

1915 *Lincoln Daily News* (NE) 17 Apr 1/8, London and east coast towns suffered from "Zeppelinitis" today. In the excited minds of the Essex villagers every cloud concealed a German dirigible. 1917 *Sat. Eve. Post* 3 Nov 85, He had even talked golf to his wife—which is the last stage of incurable golfitis. 1918 *DN* 5.8, *Philippinitis.* Name used colloquially, or jocularly, with reference to the state of relative relaxation or inertia felt by Americans who have remained for a time in the Philippine Islands. 1927 *AmSp* 2.245, The coinages are mainly nonce-words; and the list below, chance-gathered, epitomizes in an astonishing way the American scene of the moment. *Aint-supposed-to-itis, blueitis, bookitis, Charlestonitis, conventionitis, crosswordpuzzleitis, danceitis, flapperitis, flunkitis* [etc]. 1942 Berrey–Van den Bark *Amer. Slang* 230.1, *Anditis, adjectivitis &c., the habit of the over use of ands, adjectives &c.* 1950 *WELS WI (Joking or fantastic names for imaginary diseases)* 2 Infs, Imaginitis; 1 Inf, Sickitis. 1965–70 *DARE* (Qu. P36, *When a hunter sees a deer . . and gets so excited he can't shoot, he has _____)* Infs **GA77, MS1, OH60,** Buckitis; (Qu. X38, *Joking names for unusually big or clumsy feet)* Inf **WA22,** Elephantitis; (Qu. BB8, *When a person's joints and muscles ache . . he may have _____)* Inf **AZ2,** Awfulitis [ˌɔfəlˈaɪtɪs]; (Qu. BB9, *A sickness in which you have a severe cough and difficult breathing . . and lasts a week or two)* Inf **AR47,** Lungitis; (Qu. BB19, *Joking names for looseness of the bowels)* Inf **LA14,** Bathroomitis; (Qu. BB20, *Joking names or expressions for overactive kidneys)* Infs **AL61, KY60, MN42, MS29, NY23, OH103, PA115, TX37, 54, VA26, WA30,** Pissitis; (Qu. BB23, *The disease where the skin becomes a yellowish color)* Inf **PA66,** Janitis; **IL4,** Longitis; **LA37,** Yellow jitis; **NY215,** Yellownitis; (Qu. BB28, . . *Imaginary diseases: "He must have the _____."*) Inf **MD28,** Barnitis—or any kind of word ending in -itis, the first element naming the work or place that the malingerer is trying to avoid; **MO25,** Doctoritis; **MA9,** Fakitis; **CO14,** Goof-offitis; **KS7,** Imaginitis; [**PA79,** It is of some kind of -itis;] **NC88, NJ21, OR13,** Lazyitis; **NY69,** Maginitis; **MO18,** Sickitis; **MD39,** Stomachitis; **IL11,** Whiskyitis; **MD24,** Workitis hyderphoggia.

it's four o'clock See **four-o'clock 7**

it's one's (own) funeral See **funeral B4b**

it-taggers See **it** n **2**

itty-itty-it n Cf **it** n **2,** DS **EE12**

1957 Battaglia *Resp. to PADS 20* **eMD** *(Games in which one captain hides his team and the other team tries to find it)* Itty-itty-it.

i'u(r)n See **iron**

iver See **ever** adv

ivis n [Var of *ibis;* cf Pronc Intro 3.I.17]

1968 *DARE* (Qu. Q10, . . *Water birds and marsh birds)* Inf **GA35,** White ivis [ˈavɪs], wood ivis, glossy ivis.

ivory n[1]

1a usu pl: Teeth, esp prominent ones; rarely, false teeth. **scattered, but less freq Sth, nNEng** See Map on p. 70

1841 *Spirit of Times* 13 Feb 596 **nNEng,** The old wolf smiled quite pleasant, and . . his ivories appeared quite distinct. 1848 Lowell *Biglow* 137 **'Upcountry' MA,** He showed his ivory some, I guess, an' sez, "You're fairly pinned." 1871 (1882) Stowe *Fireside Stories* 117 **NEng,** And then he showed all his ivories from ear to ear. 1950 *WELS (Large front teeth that stick out of the mouth)* 1 Inf, **WI,** Ivories. 1951 Johnson *Resp. to PADS 20* **DE** *(Joking names for teeth)* Ivories. 1953 *New Yorker* 25 Apr 21 **NYC,** Beaming at each other, with as fine a display of ivories as we've seen in our time. 1965–70 *DARE* (Qu. X13a, . . *Joking names . . for teeth)* 43 Infs, **scattered, but less freq Sth, nNEng,** Ivories; (Qu. X13b, *Joking names for false teeth)* Infs **CA87, CT5, 11, 12, MI47, NY136,** Ivories; (Qu. X12) Inf **CA12,** Ivories.

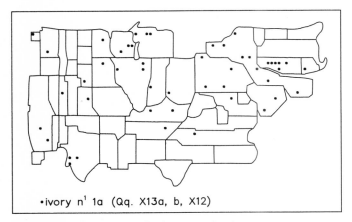

•ivory n¹ 1a (Qq. X13a, b, X12)

b Used in var combs referring to a dentist.

1942 Berrey–Van den Bark *Amer. Slang* 529.10, *Dentist.* . . Ivory carpenter, jaw smith, tooth carpenter. **1950** *WELS (Joking and nicknames for a dentist)* 1 Inf, **WI**, Ivory-snatcher. **1967–69** DARE (Qu. BB52) Inf **NY**183, Ivory-puller; **TX**33, Ivory-picker.

2 In marble play: a marble, esp a white one. Cf **creamy**

1942 Berrey–Van den Bark *Amer. Slang* 665.2, *Marble.* Ivory. **1963** *KY Folkl. Rec.* 9.3.59 **eKY**, *White colored marble:* ivory [reported from six counties].

ivory n² Also sp **ivry** [Folk-etym for **ivy**] **scattered, but more freq Sth, S Midl, NEast** See Map

1770 *Boston News–Letter* (MA) 7 June 4/1, [They] found the Child picking of Ivory leaves. **1891** *Jrl. Amer. Folkl.* [see **ivy 6**]. **1892** *Ibid* 5.100 **NH**, *Gaultheria procumbens.* . . Young ivories. **1903** *DN* 2.318 **seMO**, *Ivory.* . . Ivy. 'He ran into a poison-ivory vine.' **1931–33** *LANE Worksheets* **csRI**, Ivory [aɪvɚɪ]—children's word for ivy, but inf uses it herself. **1941** *LANE* Map 249 (*Mountain laurel*) 3 infs, **wCT, wMA**, [ɪvɪɹɪ]. **1943** Fernald–Kinsey *Edible Wild Plants E. N. Amer.* 309, "Ivry"-leaves. **1965–70** DARE (Qu. S16, *A three-leaved plant that grows in woods and countryside and makes people's skin itch and swell*) 35 Infs, **scattered, but more freq Sth, S Midl, NEast**, Poison ivory; **DC**5, Poisonous ivory; **VA**46, Ivory vine—same as poison ivory; (Qu. S26c, *Wildflowers that grow in woods*) Infs **VA**75, 77, Mountain ivory; (Qu. S26e, *Other wildflowers . . ; not asked in early QRs*) Inf **VA**57, Ivory . . shrub that kills sheep; (Qu. BB25, . . *Common skin diseases around here*) Inf **MO**1, Poison ivory. **1971** Wood *Vocab. Change* 303 **Sth**, 39 [infs], Poison ivory. *Ibid* 34, *Poison vine* . . competes equally with *poison ivory. **1973** Allen *LAUM* 1.334 **Upper MW** (as of c1950), *Poison ivory,* a form produced by folk etymology . . , is used by four older speakers in the Dakotas and by one in Iowa. It seems to be declining. *Ibid,* Ivory [1 inf, **seIA**].

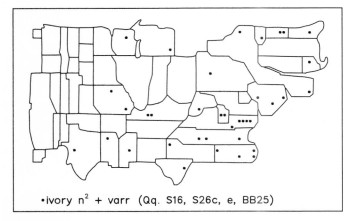

•ivory n² + varr (Qq. S16, S26c, e, BB25)

ivorybill n

1 See **ivory-billed coot.**

2 See **ivory-billed woodpecker.**

ivory-billed coot n Also *ivorybill*

A **coot** n¹ **1** (here: *Fulica americana*).

[**1888** Trumbull *Names of Birds* 118, March, in his Notes on the Birds of Jamaica (1863–64), calls it [=*Fulica americana*] *ivory-billed coot.*]

1917 (1923) *Birds Amer.* 1.214, *Coot.* . . *Other Names* . . Pond Hen; Mud Coot; Ivory-billed Coot. **1963** Gromme *Birds WI* 215, Ivorybill.

ivory-billed woodpecker n Also *ivorybill, ivory-billed whicker, ivorybill woodcock, ~ woodpecker* [See quot 1784]

A large woodpecker *(Camphephilus principalis),* formerly found chiefly in the S Atl and Gulf States, but now extinct in the US. Also called **gollybird, Indian hen 3, logcock 2, log god 1, lord god 2, nigger guinea, pait, pique bois, poule d'bois, white-billed woodpecker, woodchuck, woodcock**

1784 (1929) Filson *Kentucke* 26, The ivory-bill wood-cock, of a whitish colour with a white plume, flies screaming exceeding sharp. It is asserted, that the bill of this bird is pure ivory. **1787** *Ellicott Alman. 1788* (Winchester, Va.) B2ʳ *(DA),* The land fowls [of Ky.] are turkeys, pheasants, . . the perraquet, ivory-bill, woodcock, and the great owl. **1811** Wilson *Amer. Ornith.* 4.20 **GA, NC, SC,** *Ivory-billed Woodpecker. Picus principalis* . . [has] a distinguished characteristic in the superb carmine crest and bill of polished ivory. **1911** Howell *Birds AR* 45, *Ivory-billed Woodpecker.* . . Formerly common in the heavy swamps of the Mississippi Valley as well as the Southeastern States generally. **1938** Matschat *Suwannee R.* 32 **Okefenokee GA,** The ivory-billed woodpecker . . lived recently on Minnie Islands, and is doubtless still somewhere in the wild interior. **1955** Lowery *LA Birds* 354, On the rainy Christmas morning of 1935. . . we . . beheld not one but *four* Ivory-bills feeding on a tall dead snag. . . in search, no doubt, for "betsy-bugs." **1966–70** DARE (Qu. Q17, . . *Kinds of woodpeckers*) Inf **FL**4, Ivorybills; **LA**3, Ivorybill woodpecker—I've never seen one myself; **VA**43, Ivory-billed whicker; **SC**4, Ivory-billed. **1968** DARE Tape **GA**30, We had ivory-billed woodpeckers in this swamp. None of these birds remained after the Hubbard Cypress Company finished their operations.

ivory dome See **dome 2**

ivory leaf n [**ivory** n²]

A **wintergreen** (here: *Gaultheria procumbens*).

1892 *Jrl. Amer. Folkl.* 5.100, *Gaultheria procumbens.* . . Ivory leaves. . . Ipswich, Mass.; Me. **1903** *DN* 3.191 **seNH**, *Ivory leaf.* . . Checkerberry. *Ibid* 245 **eME. 1943** Fernald–Kinsey *Edible Wild Plants E. N. Amer.* 309, "Ivry"-leaves . . *Gaultheria procumbens.* . . The young leaves in the spring while still red are tender and highly flavored with oil of checkerberry, but in mid-summer become tough and less palatable.

ivory plum n [**ivory** n²] **chiefly NEng**

A **wintergreen:** usu *Gaultheria procumbens,* but also *G. hispidula.*

1828 Neal *Rachel Dyer* 55 **MA,** The more brilliant ivory-plumbs [sic] or clustered bunch-berries rattled among the withered herbage. **1891** [see **ivyberry**]. **1891** *Jrl. Amer. Folkl.* 4.149, Gaultheria procumbens seems to have an almost endless variety of epithets. . In South Berwick, Me., and many other places, the berries are called *Ivory plums.* **1892** *Ibid* 5.99, *Chiogenes serpyllifolia,* ivory plums. Washington Co., Me. *Ibid* 100, *Gaultheria procumbens.* . . Ivory plums. N.H. . . Ipswich, Mass.; Me. **1907** *DN* 3.245 **eME,** *Ivory plum.* . . Checkerberry. **1929** *Torreya* 29.150 **ME,** Gaultheria procumbens always was "Ivory Plum." **1959** Carleton *Index Herb. Plants* 66, *Ivory-plum:* Chiogenes hispidula. **1971** Krochmal *Appalachia Med. Plants* 128.

ivry See **ivory** n²

ivy n Cf **ivory** n²

1 Std: any of a number of woody vines often planted for ornament, such as Boston ivy *(Parthenocissus tricuspidata),* English ivy *(Hedera helix),* or grape ivy *(Cissus* spp).

2 now usu in comb *American ivy:* =**Virginia creeper.**

1629 Parkinson *Paradisi* 612, *Vitis, seu potius Hedera Virginensis.* The Virginia Vine, or rather Iuie. **1784** in 1785 Amer. Acad. Arts & Sci. *Memoirs* 1.423 **neMA,** *Hedera.* . . Woodbine. Ivy. . . It is planted by walls and buildings, upon which it will ascend. **1837** Darlington *Flora Cestrica* 153, *Ivy-like Ampelopsis.* . . Virginian Creeper. American Ivy. . . *Stem* 10 to 30 or 40 feet long, . . climbing trees and walls, clinging to them by adhesive expansions of the points of the tendrils. **1860** Curtis *Cat. Plants NC* 115, The rapidity of its growth renders this Creeper useful for covering old walls, &c. . . It is, indeed, sometimes called *American Ivy.* **1901** Lounsberry *S. Wild Flowers* 332, Virginia creeper, American, or five-leaved ivy, designates the noble vine so abundantly seen throughout the south. **1960** Vines *Trees SW* 712, *Parthenocissus quinquefolia.* . . Vernacular names for the vine are Woodbine . . and

American Ivy. **1976** Bailey–Bailey *Hortus Third* 824, *American ivy*. . . Ne. U.S. to Fla., Tex., and Mex.

3 A **rhododendron** (here: *Rhododendron minus*).
1739 (1946) Gronovius *Flora Virginica* 21, *Azalea*. . . Ivy. **1964** Batson *Wild Flowers SC* 82, *Ivy: Rhododendron minus*. . . Straggling evergreen shrub up to 8 ft. tall. Leaves . . elliptic, dark green above, paler and resinous-dotted beneath. Flowers . . pink to rose and with greenish dots on the upper petal.

4 =**mountain laurel 1. chiefly Appalachians, sNEng**
1743 (1946) Gronovius *Flora Virginica* 160, The common Laurel / vulgarly called Ivy. **1832** Williamson *Hist. ME* 1.116, The *Lamb-kill*. . . has been called *Mountain Laurel, Spoonwood, Ivy* and *Calico Bush*. **1915** *DN* 4.184 swVA, *Ivy*. . Mountain laurel. **1937** Hall *Coll.* eTN, *Ivy* . . local term for laurel. "Ivy pizens them [=cattle]." **1941** *LANE* Map 249 *(Mountain laurel)* 24 infs, **chiefly wMA, w,sCT,** Ivy; 1 inf, **cwCT,** They call it ivy, but that's wrong. Ivy is a vine; 1 inf, **nwCT,** Ivy, usually. You can't kill ivy; it's a damn nuisance; 1 inf, **csCT,** My father still calls it ivy; 1 inf, **seCT,** Ivy isn't the pretty, fashionable name. My wife and daughter always call it *mountain laurel;* 1 inf, **cwMA,** Ivy, older term. **1944** *PADS* 2.34 wNC. **1953** *PADS* 19.12 sAppalachians. c1960 Wilson *Coll.* csKY, *Ivy*. . . Mountain laurel . . is most often meant by older people. **1966–70** *DARE* (Qu. T5, . . *Kinds of evergreens*) Infs **GA**70, **NC**37, 41, Ivy; **KY**39, Ivy [FW: =laurel], laurel [FW: = rhododendron]; (Qu. T15, . . *Kinds of swamp trees*) Inf **KY**24, Ivy; (Qu. T16, . . *Kinds of trees* . . *'special'*) Inf **KY**16, Ivy [FW: =mountain laurel]; (Qu. S26e, *Other wildflowers*) Infs **GA**70, **SC**70, Ivy. **1969** *DARE* Tape **KY**16, Fox's way ahead of him. I seen him way down below him in what we call the ivy here. Laurel. **1982** Ginns *Snowbird Gravy* 130 nwNC, The rhododendron, they call it now, we used to call it "laurel"; and the other, they call it "laurel" now, we called it "ivy."

5 =**poison ivy 1. esp NEast**
1788 in 1873 May *Jrl.* 65 NEng, I have been clearing land for eight days, and now begin to feel the effects of poison—from ivy, doubtless. **1848** *Knickerbocker* 31.4 NEng, In the morning Shaw found himself poisoned by ivy. **1966–69** *DARE* (Qu. S16, *A three-leaved plant that grows in woods and countryside and makes people's skin itch and swell*) 18 Infs, 11 **NEast,** Ivy.

6 A **wintergreen** (here: *Gaultheria procumbens*).
1891 *Jrl. Amer. Folkl.* 4.149, Gaultheria procumbens seems to have an almost endless variety of epithets. . In South Berwick, Me., and many other places, . . the young shoots [are called] *Ivory*, often contracted to *Ivy*. **1891** in 1946 *PADS* 11.33 **ME,** She then brought on some ivy leaves / Just picked near Deacon Howse's;/ We sat and sat, and ate the best. **1949** *PADS* 11.33 **ME,** When as children we spoke of *ivy* leaves . . we recognized the error for *ivory*.

7 =**arbutus.**
1924 *Amer. Botanist* 30.57, *Epigaea repens*. . . another instance of low evergreen being called "ivy."

8 =**dog hobble 1.**
1933 Small *Manual SE Flora* 1001, *L[eucothoe] Catesbaei*. . . *Ivy*. . . *Dog-hobble*. . . Piedmont to Appalachian Plateau, Ga. to Ala., Tenn., and Va. **1942** Van Dersal *Ornamental Amer. Shrubs* 257 (DA), There it is variously known as fetterbush, switch-ivy, dog-hobble, and ivy, no one of which seems to be a particularly apt common name.

ivyberry n Also *ivy plum*

A **wintergreen** (here: *Gaultheria procumbens*).
1840 *S. Lit. Messenger* 6.518 **ME,** There were the fringed polygala, the butter-cup, wild geranium, bunch-plum, ivy-berry. **1890** *AN&Q* 6.95, The aromatic and toothsome berries [of the checkerberry] were called "ivy plums" in New Hampshire. **1891** *Ibid* 118, In Essex county, Mass., I have heard the berries of [checkerberry] called "ivy plums," and even "ivory plums." **1900** Lyons *Plant Names* 169, *G[aultheria] procumbens*. . . Ivy-berry. **1911** Henkel *Amer. Med. Leaves* 19, *Wintergreen*. . . *Other common names*. . . Ivyberry. . . Evergreen leaves. . . are alternate, shining dark green above, lighter colored underneath, spicy, thick and leathery, oval. **1949** *PADS* 11.33 **ME,** When as children we spoke of . . *ivy* plums we recognized the error for *ivory*.

ivy bindweed n
=**black bindweed.**
1900 Lyons *Plant Names* 300, *P[olygonum] Convolvulus*. . . Ivy . . Bindweed. **1940** Clute *Amer. Plant Names* 139. **1973** Hitchcock–Cronquist *Flora Pacific NW* 85, *L[ea]f bl[ade]* sagittate-ovate. . . Ivy bindweed. *P. convolvulus*.

ivybush n Also *ivywood* Cf **ivy 4**
=**calico bush 1.**
1897 Sudworth *Arborescent Flora* 315 SC, *Kalmia latifolia*. . . Ivywood. **1900** Lyons *Plant Names* 209, *K[almia] latifolia*. . . Ivy-bush. **1940** Clute *Amer. Plant Names* 41, *K[almia] latifolia*. . . Ivy-bush. **1964** Kingsbury *Poisonous Plants U.S.* 252, Ivybush. . . Rocky wooded areas, sometimes in clearings, eastern United States.

ivy duckweed See **ivy-leaved duckweed**

ivyleaf n
A **wintergreen** (here: *Gaultheria procumbens*).
1907 *DN* 3.245 eME, *Ivory leaf*. . . Checkerberry. Corruption of *ivy leaf*.

ivyleaf duckweed See **ivy-leaved duckweed**

ivyleaf laurel n
=**calico bush 1.**
1960 Vines *Trees SW* 828, *Kalmia latifolia*. . . Vernacular names are Big-leaf Ivy, Ivy-leaf-laurel.

ivy-leaved duckweed n Also *ivy(leaf) duckweed, ivy-leaved duckmeat*
A **duckweed 1** (here: *Lemna trisulca*).
1847 Wood *Class-Book* 670, *L[emna] trisulca*. . . *Ivy-leaved Duckmeat*. . . Floating in ponds and pools of clear water. **1923** in 1925 Jepson *Manual Plants CA* 195, *Ivy-leaf Duckweed*. Fronds forming dense masses. . . Cold springs and running water, Sierra Nevada. **1936** Winter *Plants NE* 19, Ivy-leaved Duckweed. **1959** Anderson *Flora AK* 143, Ivy-leaved Duckweed. Fronds usually submerged with several generations attached to each other. **1970** Correll *Plants TX* 345, *Ivy duckweed*. Often forming dense masses, usually floating just beneath the surface except when flowering. **1973** Hitchcock–Cronquist *Flora Pacific NW* 677, Fronds oblong to lanceolate, . . finely serrulate toward the tip. . . Ivy d[uckweed].

ivy plum See **ivyberry**

ivy poison n esp PA
=**poison ivy 1** or the rash produced by it.
1967–70 *DARE* (Qu. S16, *A three-leaved plant that grows in woods and countryside and makes people's skin itch and swell*) Infs **IN**3, **OH**56, **PA**22, 206, 211, Ivy poison; **PA**242, Ivy poison—same as poison ivy; (Qu. BB25, . . *Common skin diseases*) Infs **MA**73, **OH**56, **PA**147, Ivy poison.

ivy treebine n
A **possum grape** (here: *Cissus incisa*).
1942 Amer. Joint Comm. Horticult. Nomenclature *Std. Plant Names* 127, *Cissus*. . . *incisa* . . Ivy t[reebine]. **1948** Stevens *KS Wild Flowers* 328, *Ivy Treebine*. . . Leaves somewhat succulent. . . Fruit borne on recurved pedicels and becoming nearly black. **1960** Vines *Trees SW* 709, *Ivy Treebine*. . . *Fruit*. . . berry . . , shiny black, . . not edible. *Leaves*. . . Very fetid when crushed. **1970** Correll *Plants TX* 1022, *Cissus incisa*. . . *Ivy treebine*. . . A stout heavy vine with warty tight-barked stems. **1976** Bailey–Bailey *Hortus Third* 273.

ivywood See **ivybush**

I went to Paris n
A type of parlor game; see quots.
1919 Elsom–Trilling *Social Games* 78, *I went to Paris* . . justifies itself only by the laughter it provokes on account of its absurd movements. The company, seated around the room, imagines that it has taken a journey to Paris in order to purchase certain necessary commodities. The first player says "I went to Paris." The second . . "What did you buy?" The first . . "A pair of shoes," and moves his feet about slightly, to indicate the nature of his purchase. He must continue the movement throughout the whole game. . . When the game [reaches its conclusion], the whole company is patting its feet, opening and closing the fingers of the left hand, fanning with the right, winking fast with the eyes, and opening and closing the mouth! **1992** *NADS Letters*, I remember playing "I went to Paris" in Shreveport, Louisiana . . [about] 1939 to 1944 . . both at school and at church socials. . . You said, "I went to Paris and I bought a pony." The next person had to repeat and add another item . . whose name started with a "p." . . The next person repeated and added another "p" item. The winner was the person who remembered the longest sentence with the most "p" words. The game started up again with . . "I went to London and I bought a lamb, etc."

ixcuse See **excuse**

ixpect See **expect**

ixperance See **experience**

ixtle See **istle**

iz v See **be** A3

iz conj, pron, prep, adv See **as**

izard See **izzard**

izickity intj [Var of **ziggety**] Cf *DS* NN6a, b

    1906 *DN* 3.142 **nwAR,** *Izickity* [ɪˈzɪkɪtɪ]. . . An exclamation.

izzard n Also sp *izard*

The letter *z*—used in var fig phrr, as:

a *A and izzard:* The beginning and end, the epitome of (something).

    1835 Nicklin *Virginia Springs* 19 *(DAE),* That celebrated spot which is . . the Ay and Izzard of a tour to the Virginia Springs.

b *from A to izzard:* From beginning to end; thoroughly; in every detail.

    [**1839** (1969) Briggs *Advent. Franco* 1.4 **eNY,** She read the dictionary through from *A* to *izzard.*] **1888** *Harper's New Mth. Mag.* 76.783 **eKS,** [He] knows "from a to izzard" every detail of a soldier's needs. **1899** (1912) Green *VA Folk-Speech* 242, "From *a* to *izzard.*" From beginning to end; from first to last. **1907** Mulford *Bar-20* 137 **West,** One man who don't know nothin' about prospectin' goes an' stumbles over a fortune an' those who know it from A to Izzard goes 'round pullin' in their belts. **1908** *DN* 3.313 **eAL, wGA,** I know this town from A to izzard. **1949** *PADS* 11.3 **wTX,** "He knows the Bible from A to izzard." Rare. Old-fashioned. **1952** Brown *NC Folkl.* 1.554 **c,eNC. c1960** *Wilson Coll.* **csKY,** He told me everything about his family, from a to izzard. **1966–68** *DARE* Tape **MS15,** Then I went on and told him from A to izzard; **NJ15,** [Aux Inf:] His mother was a lady from A to izzard. **1968** *DARE* (QR p189) Inf **CA59,** Read him the riot act from A to izzard.

c *know* (or *learn*) *A from izzard:* To know (or learn) the most rudimentary thing.

    1914 Furman *Sight* 42 **KY,** I . . never had no chance to l'arn 'a' from 'izard.' **1965–69** *DARE* (Qu. JJ15b, *Sayings about a person who seems . . very stupid: "He doesn't know _____ ."*) Infs **CA59, FL18, IN30, LA12, NC52, PA7,** A from izzard. [5 of 6 Infs old, 1 mid-aged]

J See **jay** v²

‡**jab** v [Perh abbr for *jabber* to talk rapidly or foolishly; perh infl by *gab*] Cf **jib-jab**
   1969 *DARE* (Qu. HH7b, *Someone who talks too much* . . "*He's always* _____.") Inf **GA**77, Jabbing.

‡**jab** n [Perh var of *jamb*]
   1952 Brown *NC Folkl.* 1.554 **wNC**, *Jab*. . . A chimney corner.

jabalina n Also *havalena, jabalí, javalina, javelin(a)* [Span *jabalí* wild boar, *jabalina* wild sow] **esp TX**
   The collared peccary (*Dicotyles tajacu*). Also called **Mexican hog 1, musk hog, pig, wild hog, wild pig**
   1822 in 1858 Dewees *Letters TX* 25 **ceTX**, Bears are very plenty, but we are obliged to use great care when hunting for them, lest the *havalenas* (meaning the peccary) kill our dogs. **1892** Duval *Young Explorers* 96, Cudjo came rushing out with half a dozen Mexican hogs or "javalinas" in hot pursuit of him. **1892** *DN* 1.191 **TX**, *Jabalí:* wild boar, peccary. **1923** U.S. Dept. Ag. *Farmers' Bulletin* 1375.11 **AZ**, *No open season:* . . peccary or javalina (wild hog), bobwhite, grouse, . . and all shore birds. **1940** Writers' Program *Guide TX* 26, The muskhog or collared peccary, a vicious wild hog locally called javelina, is numerous from the Edwards Plateau to the Rio Grande, and also in the Big Bend. **1966** *DARE* (Qu. P32, . . *Other kinds of wild animals*) Infs **TX**11, 19, **NM**13, [ˌhævəˈlinə]; **TX**29, [ˈhævəlinəz]; **TX**3, [ˌhævɑˈlinɑ]; **TX**101, [ˌhævɑˈlinə]; **TX**27, [ˌhɑvəˈlinə]; **TX**28, 42, Javelinas; **TX**31, Javelin; (QR, near Qu. K27) Inf **CO**22, [ˈhævəlinəz]—wild pigs—terrible tusks. **1967–69** *DARE* Tape **TX**24, The first [ˈhævəˌlinz] I began to see on this place here was along in the thirties; **TX**68, Jabalina [hævəlinə]—it's a small wild hog and they have great big teeth. They're really not very aggressive. . . They get up to about 50 pounds. **1982** Elman *Hunter's Field Guide* 437, The name javelina . . [is] more current than peccary in the Southwest. **1988** *DARE* File **cwTX**, Among those whose pronunciation I considered uncontaminated, I got [havəlˈinə] as the winner. . . Evidently the spelling hasn't affected the pronunciation among the natives. **1990** Pederson *LAGS Regional Matrix* 445, [The map shows 23 exx of *jabalina(s)*, 16 in **seTX**, 4 in **ceTX**, and 3 in **wLA**.]

jabber n¹ See **jab stick**

jabber n² [*jabber* to talk rapidly or foolishly]
   A gabfest.
   1969 *DARE* (Qu. KK12, *A meeting where there's a lot of talking:* "*They got together* . . *and had a real* _____.") Inf **RI**17, Jabber.

jabberbox n [*jabber* to talk rapidly or foolishly + **box** n **5a**]
   1966–68 *DARE* (Qu. HH7a, *Someone who talks too much*) Infs **ID**5, **IL**50, **MN**42, Jabberbox.

jabble v Also with *up* [Prob Scots, Ir, nEngl dial *jabble* to agitate or splash a liquid; cf *EDD jabble* sb.¹ 6 "*fig.* turmoil, confusion"] Cf **jamble, jambled**
   To shake, mix together; fig: to confuse, befuddle.
   1760 in 1889 Washington *Writings* 2.163 **VA**, All mix'd . . by . . jabling them well together in a Cloth. **1967** *DARE* (Qu. GG2, . . '*Confused, mixed up'*: "*So many things were going on at the same time that he got completely* _____.") Inf **OH**33, Jabbled up.

jabees intj [Euphem for *Jesus*, perh from the name *Jabez*, or a form of *bejabbers*]
   1950 *WELS* (*Exclamations beginning with the sound of "J"*) 1 Inf, **cWI**, Jabees [ˈjebiz].

jabfest n Also *jab session* Cf **feast** n, **jab** v
   A gabfest.
   1967–70 *DARE* (Qu. KK12, *A meeting where there's a lot of talking*) Infs **MI**68, **VA**72, Jabfest; **NC**51, Jab session.

Jabib n Also *Jabip, Japip;* rarely *Jaboot* **NJ**, **sePA**
   Also in comb *Fifth and Japip:* An imaginary, extremely remote place.
   1983 *Lutz Coll.* **neNJ**, It was in the 1950s that I heard Ramsey High School pupils say such things as, "She lives way back of Jabib," and, "You have to go way out in Jabib." I heard one of the teachers use the word in 1973. . . It obviously meant "the boondocks" or "back of beyond." **1984** *NADS Letters* **sePA**, Jabib—My wife and her relatives in West Chester, Pennsylvania, use this term. It is pronounced [jəbɪp]. It is commonly used to describe a long and drawn-out shopping trip for a hard-to-get item: "I had to go all the way to Jabip and back to get this one." *Ibid* **Philadelphia PA**, My boss is a 35-year-old white man from Philadelphia. He has mentioned the phrase "Fifth and Japip" as a phrase that he used in his youth. "Fifth and Japip" was a mythical intersection supposed to be out in the middle of nowhere. *Ibid* **sePA**, She doesn't live near here, she lives past Fifth and Japip [jəˈpɪp]. *Ibid* **cnNJ**, We used it only as East Jabib (pronounced [jəˈbɪb]), and it meant—still means—"way-out-who-knows-where." **1986** *DSNA Letters* **neNJ**, Jabib. . . My family and I used this word and the word jaboot . . to refer to a place remote by distance or from amenities, as in "from here to jabib;" "from here to jaboot;" "from jabib to jaboot" (or vice versa); or "He lives way out in jabib (or jaboot)." **1991** *DARE* File **sNJ**, **sePA**, "To go from here to Japip" means to take forever to get somewhere or do something. The expression has been used in the Philadelphia, southern New Jersey, and Delaware Valley area since about 1900, and is still common there. **1992** *NADS Letters* **Philadelphia PA**, My Philly friends say *by Fifth and Japip*. *Ibid* **sePA**, I am from Philadelphia. . . The expression I've mostly heard is "he lives at Fifth and Japip", meaning: out of the way, or "God knows where". **1992** *DARE* File **Philadelphia PA**, Have heard of "You can go to 'Japip' as far as I am concerned"—in other words, the land of nowhere! Just a slang expression of dislike. *Ibid* **nNJ** (as of 1960s), He lives way out in East Jabib—in the middle of nowhere.

‡**jabo** n
   1969 *DARE* (Qu. EE41, *A hobgoblin* . . *used to threaten children and make them behave*) Inf **GA**77, [ˌjæˈbou].

jaboney See **jabronie**

Jaboot See **Jabib**

jabronie n Also *jab(r)oney, jarboni, jiboney, jumbloney;* for addit varr see quots [Etym unknown]
   An inept, stupid, or inexperienced person; a guy or fellow.
   1931 *AmSp* 6.439 **NY** [Prison slang], *Jaboney*. . . A greenhorn; a newly-arrived foreigner. **1952** *Esquire* June 84 **NYC**, He had a couple of his jiboneys with him. . . I never saw Nicky alone. **1959** *VT Hist.* 27.144, Like a flying jarboni: . . In a state of confusion. Occasional. **1982** *Smithsonian Letters*, Jabronie . . as in "that god-damned fumbled-thumbed jabronie could cause a malfunction in a rolling pin" as the name for an inept, incompetent, clumsy person, inept particularly in the physical sphere, and in the operation of any mechanical device. Whether I had this from dad, who had worked among what *he* called Hunkies and Slovenes in the tractor factory, or I picked it up myself through service with similar ethnic groups during WWII I am not sure. **1984** *NADS Letters,* I use the above [=jabroney] (which I always assumed was spelled *gibroney*) often in informal speech in the sense given in NADS 16.1 [=an inept, incompetent, clumsy person], but also in the

vaguer sense of "guy" or "fellow". I suppose I adopted it years ago in upstate New York, but can't be sure. *Ibid* **Detroit MI,** My father . . knew the term *jabroney* (although he pronounced it as 'jumbloney'). He said that he had heard it from Polish workers at the factory where he worked. . . As a sample sentence, he offered "Here comes that jumbloney"—namely a worker whom the speaker considers either inefficient or incompetent. He thinks that the term is rather coarse and suggested that the English equivalent (or euphemism?) might be "that joker." *Ibid* **sCA,** In 1980 . . I worked on a film . . called *The Escape Artist.* The properties man used the term "jaboney" regularly. **1985** Kidder *House* 106 **wMA,** In Apple Corps parlance, a carpenter gone sloppy is "a beaver," "a jabronie," or "a Hoople." **1991** *DARE* File, Joe Bohbee. . . They recall their mother using this term from the time they were youngsters. We are of Austria, Hungary, Czech descent. There is also a *jabonee*—(slob, no gooder) used but my one cousin has also heard [the] expression who is of French descent. **1992** *Ibid* **csWI,** I learned *jabronie,* probably in New Jersey, in the 1950s. Now I generally use it in the context of driving: "Look what that blankety-blank jabronie just did!"

jab session See **jabfest**

jab stick n Also *jabber*
1967–68 *DARE* (Qu. K27, . . *The sharp-pointed stick used to get oxen to move*) Inf **KS**17, Jab stick; **NV**1, Jabber.

jacal n Usu |hæˈkæl, hɑˈkɑl|, but see also quots 1932, 1970 Also sp *jacel, jackall, jeccal;* dimin *jacalito;* pronc-sp *hackel* [Mex-Span < Nahuatl *xacalli* hut] **SW**
A hut, esp one of vertical poles plastered with mud and roofed with thatch; the material or method used to build such a hut.
1838 Ganilh *Mexico Versus TX* 249 **csTX,** His house. . . was a little *Jacal,* or cabin, built with large unburnt bricks, called *adobes,* . . and thatched over with *tule,* a kind of rushes. **1844** (1954) Gregg *Commerce* 198 **NM,** They [=Navajo Indians] mostly live in rude *jacales,* somewhat resembling the wigwams of the Pawnees. **1850** (1906) Audubon *Western Jrl.* 230 **CA,** A comfortable . . log and jacal built house. **1877** McDanield–Taylor *Coming Empire* 124 **TX,** Here [=San Antonio] the houses are of straight cedar posts, stuck upright into the ground, and covered with roofs of grass. The cracks between the poles are daubed with mud. They generally have but one room. . . Some of them have chimneys, . . and none, I believe, have floors. . . These edifices are called *jacels.* **1885** *Santa Fe Wkly. N. Mexican* 10 Dec. 2/6 *(DA),* A very miserable shanty of jackall. **1886** *Outing* 9.111 **AZ,** An old *hackel,* or Mexican hut. **1889** Ripley *Flag to Flag* 81 **TX,** Mexican *jeccals* (huts). **1892** *DN* 1.191 **TX,** *Jacál:* a hut, cabin. **1925** White *Them Was* 214 **cwTX** (as of 1913), *Jacalito.* **1932** Bentley *Spanish Terms* 148, *Jacal* (Spanish, [hɑˈkɑːl]; English, [hæˈkæl, hɑːˈkɑːl, jæˈkæl and ˈjækəl]). . . *Jacal* is used frequently in writing and in speaking. It is, however, usually restricted to contexts relating to the life or habitations of Mexicans. **1967** *DARE* (Qu. D21, *A small, poorly-built house, or one in rundown condition*) Inf **TX**5, Jacal [ˌhæˈkæl]; **TX**28, Jacal. **1970** *DARE* Tape **TX**102, One time we stayed three weeks in a Mexican jacal [haˈkeɪəl]. . . They are made out of wood and daubed with mud and have a straw roof over 'em. **1981** Pederson *LAGS Basic Materials,* 1 inf, **csTX,** [hæˈˈkæ·ət]—it's some kind of building with a thatched roof; 1 inf, **csTX,** A [haˈkaˈl]—same [as a *puerto*], but smaller; sometimes = outside kitchen for workmen.

jack n[1], often cap
1 A man or boy—used as a form of address. Cf **Jackson** n, **jake** n[1] **2, jim** n **2**
1854 (1932) Bell *Log TX-CA Trail* 35.233, The Mexicans . . were discussing whether thay wou'd be considered white people, or not, in California. One settled the discussion by saying thay would be considered negros and whistled about, called Jack! as is the custom among the Southern States. **1897** Barrère–Leland *Slang* 1.463, *Jack* (American). It is common among schoolboys in Philadelphia to address a stranger as *Jack.* **1904** Number 1500 *Life in Sing Sing* 17, "Jack",—all convicts are Jack—"do you smoke?" **1930** Irwin *Amer. Tramp* 108, *Jack.*—A generic term for any tramp or other man. **1930** Williams *Logger-Talk* 25 **Pacific NW,** *Jack:* A logger might say to a stranger, *H'are yuh, Jack?* **1942** *AmSp* 17.222 [Loggers' talk], *Jack.* Any man. **1943** Shulman *Barefoot Boy* 90 **MN,** Man, he's murder, Jack. **1958** *PADS* 30.42 [Language of jazz musicians], *Man,* as direct address, has, in the last 15 years, almost completely replaced *Jack* of the swing period and seems likely to remain in the language for some time. **1965–70** *DARE* (Qu. II10b, . . *When you don't know his name—what you'd say to a man: "Say, _____, how far is it to the next town?"*) Infs **CT**23, **FL**48, **MA**35, **NJ**28, **NY**211, **UT**3, Jack; (Qu. II10a, . . *To a boy*) Inf **IL**96, Jack; (Qu.

GG23c) Inf **WA**22, Relax, Jack; (QR, near Qu. II1) Inf **LA**32, Friends call each other (boys) hoss, stone, jake, stud, jack. **1980** Folb *Runnin' Down* 137 **Los Angeles CA** [Black], When we get married, what dey gon' do, Jack?

2 in phr *free jack:* A person of mixed black and white ancestry. **esp LA** Cf **free issue 1, Jackson White**
1986 Pederson *LAGS Concordance,* 3 infs, **ceLA,** Free jacks; 1 inf, **csMS,** Free jack—half white, half black; in Cajun country; 1 inf, **csMS,** Free jack—light-skinned black; 1 inf, **ceLA,** Free jack—mulatto? 1 inf, **ceLA,** Free jack—a little black blood; heard; 1 inf, **ceLA,** Free jack—Negro, if black at all; 1 inf, **seLA,** Free jack—not locally; 1 inf, **ceLA,** Free jacks—half black and half white; 1 inf, **ceLA,** Free jacks—in the country before us; 1 inf, **ceLA,** Free jacks—in Lower LA; dark; not considered black; 1 inf, **cLA,** Free jacks—around one half white or so.

3 A lumberjack. **esp Gt Lakes**
a1900 in 1926 Rickaby *Ballads Shanty-Boy* 97 **cnMN,** Every jack's a cant-hook man. . . They do some heavy loggin'. **1913** *Collier's* 18 Jan 21 **MN,** The breaking up of the lumber camps and the streaming southward of thousands of "jacks." **1950** *WELS,* 2 Infs, **WI,** Lumberjack, jack. **1958** McCulloch *Woods Words* 97 **Pacific NW,** *Jack.* . . A lumberjack (more used inland than on the Coast). **1966–68** *DARE* Tape **MI**10, They met this big jack going into camp; **WI**59, The real old lumberjack. . . The old jack, as we called him [around 1900]. **1968** *DARE* FW Addit **WI**59, Jack—nickname for a lumberjack. **1969** Sorden *Lumberjack Lingo* 62 **NEng, Gt Lakes,** *Jack.* . . Lumberjack. **1976** Maclean *River Runs Through* 115 **wMT** (as of 1927), If he doesn't like a jack because the jack has the bad manners to talk at meal time, the cook goes to the woods foreman and the jack goes down the road.

4 also *country jack:* A rustic. Cf **clumsy-jack, country B2a, jake** n[1] **1**
1930 Shoemaker *1300 Words* 33 **cPA Mts** (as of c1900), *Jack*—A simple fellow, a yokel. **1951** *AmSp* 26.26 **HI,** Some pidgin words have an archaic English flavor: *humbug, country jack* (jake), and *rascal.* **1967–68** *DARE* (Qu. HH1, . . *A rustic or countrified person*) Infs **HI**6, 13, **VA**25, Country jack; (Qu. II21, . . *Somebody . . without manners*) Inf **HI**13, Country jack.

5a Orig a device for carrying and casting a light, esp one used for hunting or fishing by night; the light itself; later, any powerful, portable light; hence n *jack-hunter,* vbl n *jack-hunting.* Cf **jack** v **1, jacklight** v
1785 in 1956 Eliason *Tarheel Talk* 301 **neNC,** 2 Tin jacks. **1859** *Harper's New Mth. Mag.* 19.175 **NY,** "A jack" composed of a bit of tin, acting as a reflector on one side and as a shade on the other, is bent round a piece of wood holding a candle. **1881** *Ibid* 63.690 **neNY,** It is the only way to get venison in that season of the year that intervenes between jack-hunting and still-hunting. **1888** *Ibid* 77.510 **wMN,** The jack-hunter hears them [=caribou] prowling among the bushes. **1895** *Outing* Apr 61, Standing with my eyes below the level of the flaming jack, I could scan every foot of the shallow waters, and readily detect the skulking fish. **1896** Robinson *In New Engl. Fields* 77, The boat of the spearers, its bow and the intent figure of the spearman aglow in the light of the jack which flares a backward flame with its steady progress. **1899** *Contemp. Rev.* (London) 75.669 **nNY,** I went out after dark to kill a deer by the unsportsmanlike method of jack-hunting. **1902** White *Blazed Trail* 61 **eMI,** They stole about in the evening with a bull's-eye lantern fastened on the head of one of them for a "jack." **1939** (1962) Thompson *Body & Britches* 292 **neNY** (as of a1910), The light fell off my head, but that didn't bother me none; I just reached up and poked the cat into the water. Then I lit up the jack and shot the deer.
b By ext: a deer killed with the aid of such a light. Cf **jack** v **1**
1967–69 *DARE* (Qu. P35a, . . *Deer shot illegally*) Inf **NY**132, Jack deer; **IA**45, **MA**72, Jack.

6 also *jack frame, jack horse, jack rack:* An X- or occas A-shaped frame to hold wood for sawing. [*OED jack* sb.[1] 9, 1573 →] Cf **sawjack, straddle jack, wood jack**
1872 (1876) Knight *Amer. Mech. Dict.* 2.1208, *Jack.* . . A saw-horse or saw-buck. Two X-shaped frames united by a round or rundle. **1949** Kurath *Word Geog.* 59, In the Alleghenies the saw horse is sometimes called a *(wood) jack.* **1965–70** *DARE* (Qu. L59, *An implement with an X-frame . . to hold firewood for sawing*) 15 Infs, *scattered, but esp* IN, KY, OH, PA, Jack; (Qu. L58, *An implement with an A-shaped frame . . that you put boards on*) Infs **CA**72, **KY**27, Jack. **1969** *DARE* FW Addit **cKY,** An implement to hold boards for sawing is a jack rack. **1970** Tarpley *Blinky* 136 **neTX,** *Wooden rack for sawing planks.* . . jacks [3 of 200 infs]. *Ibid,* Jack horse [2 of 200 infs]. **1971** Wood *Vocab.*

Change 50 **Sth,** If the wood to be sawed is firewood, the supports of the frame are shaped like an X. . . *Buck, jack, saw jack, trestle,* and *wood buck* occur in scattered distributions. If the piece of wood is a board, the appropriate equipment has the form of an A. . . Scattered terms—*jack, rack, sawbuck, saw jack,* and *trestle*—do not exceed one-tenth of the choices made in any state [covered in the survey]. **1973** Allen *LAUM* 1.221 (as of c1950), *Sawbuck. . . Jack* occurs nine times in Midland territory. **1986** Pederson *LAGS Concordance* **Gulf Region,** 6 infs, Jack—X-frame; 2 infs, Jack-horses—A-frame; 1 inf, Jack frame—sawhorse; A-frame.

7 See quot. [Perh transf from preceding sense]

1917 *DN* 4.394 **neOH,** *Jack. . .* An upright post or frame at the front and back ends of a hayrack.

‡8 pl: Stilts. Cf **jake walkers**

1968 *DARE* (Qu. EE35, *Long wooden poles with a footpiece that children walk around on to make them tall*) Inf **GA**23, Jacks.

‡9 A crowbar.

1968 *DARE* (Qu. L39, *An iron bar with a bent end, used for pulling nails, opening boxes, and so on*) Inf **MD**3, Jack.

10 A locomotive. [Perh transf from **19** below; see quot 1968] Cf **ball the jack 1**

1930 *RR Man's Mag.* June 471, *Jack*—Locomotive. **1937** *Sat. Eve. Post* 21 Aug 51, In comparison with that [=a steam locomotive], the silent rush of an electric "jack" . . is tame. **1945** Hubbard *Railroad Ave.* 349, *Jack*—Locomotive. (A term often confused with the lifting device, hence seldom used). **1958** McCulloch *Woods Words* 97 **Pacific NW,** *Jack. . .* A locie. **1968** Stearns–Stearns *Jazz Dance* 98, *Jack* is the name given to the locomotive by the Negro folk, on the analogy of the indestructible donkey or jackass.

11 also *jack pie:* =**applejack 4.** *obs* Cf **flapjack 3**

1832 Kennedy *Swallow Barn* 1.57 **VA,** She was usually occupied in paring apples to be baked up into tough jacks for our provender. **1857** *Harper's New Mth. Mag.* 15.446 **VA,** The groom went out and presently returned with ten or twelve turnovers, or Jack-pies.

12 =**flapjack 2.** *obs* Cf **slapjack**

1850 Ryan *Personal Advent.* 1.238 **CA,** We agreed to convert a portion of our flour into "slap-jacks." This primitive substitute for bread is manufactured by mixing up some flour and water in a tin, seasoning with salt, and frying in a pan of grease. . . Frederic, Halliday, and myself, set to work upon the "jacks," and soon tossed up a sufficiency for our purpose.

13 Any of several alcoholic drinks, as:

a Spec: =**applejack 1. NJ**

1894 *DN* 1.331 **NJ,** In Salem, Sussex, and Burlington counties, where apple whiskey is made, it is commonly called "jack." **1940** Weygandt *Down Jersey* 94 **sNJ,** Jerseymen truncate "applejack" to just "jack." **1946** *Reader's Digest* Aug 160 **sNJ,** A New Year party for me and you with a side of beef and a gallon of jack to wash it down. **1968** McPhee *Pine Barrens* 59 **NJ,** Applejack is the laureate liquid of the pines. It is known as jack, and its effects are known as apple palsy.

b in combs denoting var home-brewed drinks: See quots.

1930 *DN* 6.89 **cWV** [Logger talk], *Tater jack,* variety of fermented liquor, made in camp from potatoes. **1940** Writers' Program *Guide PA* 67, Steve's wife made an extra supply of prune-jack, and Steve ordered two barrels of beer. **1966** *DARE* (Qu. DD28b, *. . Fermented drinks . . made at home*) Inf **OK**25, Raisin jack. **1972** Shafer *Dict. Prison Slang* [31] **TX,** *Raisin jack*—homebrew. **1986** Pederson *LAGS Concordance,* 1 inf, **nwAR,** Grape jack—distilled homemade wine; 1 inf, **ceTX,** White jack—made in a still; quality varies.

14 High spirits—usu in phrr *tear up* (or *cut up, kick up*) *jack* and varr: to be noisy or rowdy; to cause a disturbance. **chiefly Sth, Midl** Cf **molly** n[1] **3**

1845 *Lowell Offering* 5.104 **MA,** The mill has been started on sometime now, and the girls always tear up Jack, in my absence. **1867** in 1919 Hale *Letters* 23 **MA,** The street is narrow, so it looks quite deep,—and full of Arabs raising Jack all the time. **1872** *Ibid* 96 **MA,** Mr. Holmes. . . and James Lowell were full of Jack, chaffing each other and going on. **1906** *DN* 3.161 **nwAR,** *Tear up jack. . .* To raise a commotion. "He just tore up jack when he found out he was fired." **1908** *DN* 3.327 **eAL, wGA,** *Kick up jack. . .* To raise a disturbance, cause a commotion, disarrange things. **1909** *DN* 3.380 **eAL, wGA,** They pulled down the blinds and tore up jack generally. **1912** *DN* 3.580 **wIN,** They are goin' over to the school-house to-night and will just kick up high jack. **1915** *DN* 4.191 **swVA,** The boys were just tearin' up Jack when the teacher come. **1930** *DN* 6.80 **eSC,** Cut up Jack and kill

Jinny. . . To raise a commotion in anger. "Cut up Jack" is sometimes heard, but the fuller expression is the more usual. "Tear up Jack" . . is never said. **1940** Richter *Trees* 201 **OH** (as of early 19th cent), The young ones were making high jack all over the place, wrestling and fighting, racing and wading, swinging on creepers, every last one yelling at the other and none listening. **1942** *AmSp* 17.130 **IN,** Tear up Jack (to be rowdy). **c1960** *Wilson Coll.* **csKY,** Tear up jack. . . Cause a disturbance, raise hell. **1967–68** *DARE* (Qu. FF18, *. . A noisy . . celebration . . "They certainly _____ last night."*) Inf **SC**46, Cut up jack; (Qu. KK11, *To make . . a big fuss about something*) Inf **SC**59, Cut up jack. **1971** *DARE* File **NC,** Tear up jacks—to act rambunctiously. **1985** Attebery *ID Folklife* xvi, Have you ever heard your mother . . say . . "You kids quit messin' and gommin' and tearin' up Jack!"?

15 A charm or **hand** n B4; a device for divination. **chiefly Sth** *among Black speakers*

1938 FWP *Guide MS* 27 [Black], If the trouble be insanity, boils, or constipation, the verdict is that a secret enemy has "fixed" him and nothing in the world but a powerful "toby" or "jack" (charm) can dispel this conjuration. **c1938** in 1970 Hyatt *Hoodoo* 1.191 **VA,** I used to go to an old man's house and *he had a bag and he called that bag Jack.* It was long and big at one end and kinda small at the other end. . . And then when you would ask him any questions he would take this bag and hold it up. . . If you asked him if this person was *hurt,* this bag would spin around . . ; if he wasn't *hurt,* it would stand still. *Ibid* 915 **MD,** This *jack* is a magnet, a magnet *jack. Magnets dey called jacks them days.* . . He'd tell you git him a magnet, an' he'd take this hair . . , an' this magnet, an' gits de—I'm sure he had other things put with it, you know. But anyhow, that was fixed up in a bag [as a charm to ensure a woman's fidelity]. **1947** (1964) Randolph *Ozark Superstitions* 170, Negroes in Arkansas make and sell charms to keep husbands constant, to bring back wandering lovers, to help in seducing girls, and so on. They are little cloth bags containing feathers, hair, blood, graveyard dirt, salt, and sometimes human bones. . . They are called *charms, conjures, hands, jacks* or *jujus.*

16 freq cap; in phr *make one's jack:* To make one's fortune; to succeed in an undertaking. **esp Sth, S Midl** *old-fash*

1778 in 1928 *Hist. KY* 1.153 **KY,** [Footnote:] My greatest Pleasure here is thinking I shall make my Jack here if I can preserve my Night-Cap. **1807** in 1956 Eliason *Tarheel Talk* 279 **NC,** She said . . he'd make his Jack for a few years and then the mill would be done. **1817** in 1830 Royall *Letters AL* 95, "Mine host" and hostess, who I dare say, expect to make their Jack out of me. **1853** in 1942 *MO Hist. Rev.* 36.257, We are inclined to think now is the time for them to make their "jack." **1877** Bartlett *Americanisms* 378, *Made his Jack.* Carried his point; was fortunate in his undertaking. **1896** Farmer–Henley *Slang* 4.23, *To make one's jack.* . . (American.)—To succeed; to gain one's point. [Farmer–Henley: From the game of faro]

17 See **jack Mormon.**

18 See **jackleg** adj **1.**

19 The male donkey *(Equus asinus),* sometimes distinguished from the smaller **burro 1.** [Abbr for *jackass*] Cf **American jack, jack** v **3, jenny 1**

1785 (1925) Washington *Diaries* 2.458 **VA,** Dispatched at his own reqt. the Spaniard who had the charge of my Jack from Spain. **1800** (1907) Thornton *Diary* 10.107 **PA,** A young Jack Mr Young has taken—three Jennies at the Farm. **1906** *DN* 3.142 **nwAR. 1908** *DN* 3.323 **eAL, wGA. 1937** Hall *Coll.* **eTN,** *Jack . .* jack ass. "Captain Frye was riding an old jack." **1949** Webber *Backwoods Teacher* 134 **Ozarks,** If a lady must speak or be spoken to of a stallion or breeding jack, all sorts of circumlocutions are used. **1954** *Harder Coll.* **cwTN. c1960** *Wilson Coll.* **csKY. 1966–70** *DARE* (Qu. K50) Inf **IL**114, Jack—breeds a mare; **IL**134, Jack and jennies—donkeys; **MD**29, Jackass, jack—these are donkeys, not mules; **OK**27, Jackass or jack—not a mule, a donkey; **OK**52, A male donkey is a jack; **PA**147, Jack—a breeding mule; **TX**71, 94, Jack—donkey. **1967–69** *DARE* Tape **IA**8, [Inf:] Well, an old jack—I don't think he's got any brains at all. . . [FW:] What sort of animal is this jack? [Inf:] You know what a burro is—you've seen the burros? . . Well, they're . . a bigger breed of the burros—they look just like 'em; **MO**16, He had good jack over there, and we'd take 'em [=mares] over there and git 'em bred; **TX**24, Those Missoura jacks, they had a white nose, you know—these Spanish burros, they haven't got that mealy nose; **TX**26, A jack'll cover a mare.

20 also *jack mule;* Transf: a male mule; often used as a quasi-proper name. Cf **buck** n[1] **1d, jake** n[1] **4, jenny 1, joe** n[2] **1, john 1, molly** n[1] **1**

1884 Baldwin *Yankee School-Teacher* 38 **VA,** Git up now, you mule!

git up strong! you Jack! **1950** *WELS* **WI** (*Joking names for mules*) 4 Infs, Jack(s); 1 Inf, Long-eared jacks; 1 Inf, Jacks and jennies. **1963** Watkins–Watkins *Yesterday Hills* 22 **cnGA,** I had an old mule, and his name was Jack./ Tied him on the railroad track. **1965–70** *DARE* (Qu. K50, *Joking nicknames for mules*) 84 Infs, **scattered exc NEng, NW,** Jack; **AL34,** Jack—large mule; **LA15,** Jack—this is the most common given name for horse-mules; **OK18,** Mare mule is "Molly," male mule is "Jack"; **CO44,** Jack mule and mare mule; **LA22,** Jack mule; **LA44,** Jack mule—a mule that won't work. **1967** *DARE* Tape **AZ2,** And a pair of mules we called Jack and Jenny. **1984** *Smithsonian* Jan 16 **NE,** My dad, a Nebrasky farmer, owned a jack and a jenny in the 1920s. Jack was one of a kind. . . He was an expert at lifting a latch or two to get into the garden. . . For some mulish reason of his own, he always closed the latches behind him.

‡21 See quot.

1950 *PADS* 14.76 **FL,** *Jack.* . . A Brahman cow.

22 =jackrabbit 1.

1864 in 1938 *KS Hist. Qrly.* 7.9 **wNE,** Went to the bluffs hunting. . . Started one "jack" and a flock of chickens. **1911** *N.Y. Evening Post* 21 Dec 7/2 (1939 Thornton *Amer. Gloss.*), They were bagged in a big rabbit round-up of the sort now popular in western Kansas, where the "jacks" have been causing much trouble for farmers. **1936** *Sun* (Baltimore MD) 31 July 9/7 (*Hench Coll.*), We saw hundreds of jack rabbits . . coming to the water-hole area. In regions where there is no water, the "jacks" are dying in large numbers. **1948** *Life* 23 Aug 101 **NE,** Now this was corn, he was exclaiming as the jack went lolloping off. **1966–69** *DARE* (Qu. P30, . . *Wild rabbits*) 11 Infs, **esp SW, Nth,** Jack. **1967–69** *DARE* Tape **CA89,** That's the highest up I've ever seen a jack; **MA32,** The club stocks 'em . . white rabbits, jacks. . . They're wild. **1980** Whitaker *Audubon Field Guide Mammals* 363, The long ears play an important role in regulating body temperature: in hot weather, they stand erect, and their dilated blood vessels give off heat, thus cooling the jack.

23 Any of several birds, as:

a =Hudsonian curlew.

1880 *Forest & Stream* 15.4, Hudsonian curlew. . . The Long Island baymen term this bird the Jack. **1888** Trumbull *Names of Birds* 200, *Hudsonian curlew.* . . On Long Island at Shinnecock Bay, Bellport, and Seaford, *Jack.* . . Not Jack-*curlew* be it understood, . . ever . . in that locality. **1895** Elliot *N. Amer. Shore Birds* 156, This species [=*Numenius phaeopus*] bears many names among the gunners in various parts of our country, among which . . Horse-foot Marlin, and Jack. **1923** U.S. Dept. Ag. *Misc. Circular* 13.66 **AL, IN, MA, ME, MD, NY, RI,** *Hudsonian Curlew.* . . *Vernacular Names.* . . *In local use.* . . Jack. **1925** (1928) Forbush *Birds MA* 1.455, *Hudsonian Curlew.* . . *Other names:* Jack curlew; Jack; foolish curlew; blue-legs.

b =pectoral sandpiper.

1895 Elliot *N. Amer. Shore Birds* 76, *Pectoral Sandpiper.* . . Known by many names in the various parts of our country, some of which are . . Jack, . . Brown Bird, . . Cow Snipe, etc.

c =red-breasted merganser.

1917 *Wilson Bulletin* 29.2.76, *Mergus serrator.* . . Jack, Hickman, Ky. **1932** Bennitt *Check-list* 21 **MO,** *Red-breasted merganser.* . . Jack. **1982** Elman *Hunter's Field Guide* 230, *Red-breasted merganser* . . *Common & regional names* . . jack.

d =Canada jay. Cf lumberjack, whiskey jack

1917 (1923) *Birds Amer.* 2.226, There are only black, white, and gray . . in his [=the Canada jay's] plumage, which furthermore presents an unkempt appearance, so that withal "Jack" looks a good deal like an exaggerated and much disheveled Chicadee. Also "Jack" has a distinctly uncanny air about him. . . As a vocalist, "Jack" is considerably more versatile . . than the Blue Jay.

e =Wilson's snipe.

1923 U.S. Dept. Ag. *Misc. Circular* 13.50, *Wilson Snipe.* . . *Vernacular Names.* . . *In general use.* . . Jacksnipe, often abridged to snipe, and rather rarely heard as common snipe or jack.

24 Any of var fishes; see below. Cf **jackfish**

a A freshwater fish, as:

(1) A fish of the genus *Esox,* such as **redfin pickerel** or **muskellunge 1,** but esp **northern pike 1** (here: *E. lucius*) and **chain pickerel. chiefly S Atl** See Map

1709 (1967) Lawson *New Voyage* 162 **NC, SC,** The Jack, Pike, or Pickerel. . . very plentiful with us in *Carolina.* **1820** Rafinesque *Ohio R. Fishes* 70, This fish [=*Esox lucius*] is rare in the Ohio. . . It is

sometimes called Jack or Jackfish. **1884** Goode *Fisheries U.S.* 1.464, *The Common Pickerel—Esox reticulatus.* . . in the Southern States . . is usually the "Jack." **1911** U.S. Bur. Census *Fisheries 1908* 311, *Jack.*—A name applied to the common pickerel *(Esox reticulatus)* in the South, to the bocaccio *(Sebastodes paucispinis)* on the Pacific coast, and to the wall-eyed pike *(Stizostedion vitreum)* in the South. **1920** Packard *Old Plymouth* 330 **seMA,** Esox reticulatus . . [is] known sometimes as green pike or jack, but more often as pond pickerel. **1927** Weed *Pike* 42, *Esox americanus.* . . Jack; North Carolina. *Ibid* 43, *Esox lucius.* . . Jack; Chicago Fish Markets. *Ibid* 45, *Esox niger.* . . Jack; North Carolina to Florida. . . *Esox ohioensis.* . . Jack; North Carolina. **1958** Babcock *I Don't Want* 155, The lithesome chained pickerel is always stigmatized as "jack." **1965–70** *DARE* (Qu. P1, . . *Freshwater fish . . good to eat*) 10 Infs, **chiefly S Atl,** Jack(s); **AR51,** Jack, sometimes jack pike or jackfish; **GA25,** Eastern pickerel, jack the same; (Qu. P3, *Freshwater fish . . not good to eat*) Inf **FL27,** Jack—a pike; **GA65,** Pike, jack—not very good eating; **NC10,** Jack. **1972** Sparano *Outdoors Encycl.* 366, *Muskellunge. Common Names* . . jack. *Ibid* 367, *Northern Pike. Common Names* . . jack. . . *Chain Pickerel. Common Names* . . jack. **1983** Becker *Fishes WI* 398, *Esox lucius.* . . Jack.

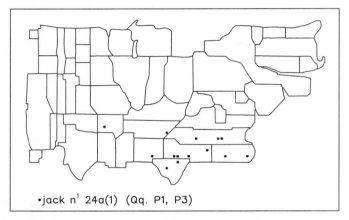

•jack n¹ 24a(1) (Qq. P1, P3)

(2) A fish of the genus *Stizostedion:* usu **walleye,** but also a **sauger** (here: *S. canadense*).

1884 Goode *Fisheries U.S.* 1.418, Southward the name 'Jack' is applied to this species [=*Stizostedion vitreum*] as well as to the Pike. **1911** [see **24a(1)** above]. **1927** Weed *Pike* 46, [*Stizostedion* spp:] Jack; Ohio Valley and western North Carolina. **1933** LA Dept. of Conserv. *Fishes* 367, *The Walleyed Pike . . Stizostedion vitreum.* . . The name, Jack, is also erroneously applied in Louisiana. **1949** Caine *N. Amer. Sport Fish* 115, The walleye is blessed—or cursed—with an abundance of aliases. . . The most common are: Blue Pike, . . Jack [etc]. *Ibid* 117, Frequently confused with the walleye it [=*Stizostedion canadense*] is also known as Eastern Sauger, . . Jack [etc]. **1983** Becker *Fishes WI* 871, *Stizostedion vitreum vitreum.* . . Jack.

b A saltwater fish, as:

(1) Any of several fishes of the family Carangidae, as:

(a) =crevalle a, esp *Caranx hippos* or **hardtail 1.**

1873 in 1878 Smithsonian Inst. *Misc. Coll.* 14.2.25, *Paratractus pisquetos.* . . Yellow crevallé; . . Jack. **1884** U.S. Natl. Museum *Bulletin* 27.438, *Caranx chrysus.* . . Jack, Buffalo Jack. . . Atlantic coast of the United States north to Cape Ann. . . The fish is abundant, but has little commercial importance. **1897** *Outing* 29.331, Other game fishes of Florida are the "jack," or crevallé, also called carvalho. **1935** Caine *Game Fish* 59, *Caranx hippos.* . . The crevalle or jack may well be called the bull-dog of the sea, for its stubborn fighting tactics possess all of the qualities for which a bull-dog is noted. **1946** LaMonte *N. Amer. Game Fishes* 34, The *Jacks* (Genus *Caranx*) form a group which contains a number of rather similar fishes. . . *Caranx crysos.* . . *Names* . . Hardtailed Jack, Jack. *Ibid* 37, *Caranx latus.* . . Jack. **1955** Zim–Shoemaker *Fishes* 94, Jacks and their kin prefer warm waters, though in summer some may be found all along the Atlantic Coast. **1966** *DARE* (Qu. P4, *Saltwater fish that are not good to eat*) Infs **FL4, 29,** Jack(s). **1994** Stone–Pratt *Hawai'i's Plants* 81, Fishes such as kūpīpī . . and . . crevalle or jack . . were probably introduced into the pools from the ocean by humans, for use as food.

(b) An **amberfish,** usu *Seriola dumerili* or **California yellowtail.**

1889 *Century Dict.* 3208, *Jack.* . . A name of several different fishes. . .

as. . . *Seriola carolinensis.* **1946** LaMonte *N. Amer. Game Fishes* 40, *Seriola dorsalis.* . . *Names* . . Jack, California Yellowtail. **1947** Caine *Salt Water* 5, Amberjack. *Seriola lalandi.* . . is also known as amberfish, . . and jack. *Ibid* 34, California Yellowtail. *Seriola dorsalis.* . . Also known as pacific yellowtail, . . and jack. **1966** *Fishing World* 13.6.48 **AL**, A big 'jack' came too close. Captain Tom gave a quick lunge, a mighty heave, and forty-nine pounds of surprised amberjack suddenly found itself on the deck of the *Sun Circle!* **1968** *DARE* (Qu. P2, . . *Kinds of saltwater fish . . good to eat*) Inf **NC82**, Jack—not too valuable, like a herring; **NC49**, Sea jack; (Qu. P4, *Saltwater fish . . not good to eat*) Inf **NC82**, Jack(s); (Qu. P14, . . *What do the fishermen go out after?*) Inf **NC49**, Jacks.

(2) A **rockfish** (here: *Sebastodes paucispinis*).

  1882 *U.S. Natl. Museum Bulletin* 16.656, *S[ebastodes] paucispinis.* . . *Jack.* . . Coast of California; abundant in rather deep water. **1887** Goode *Amer. Fishes* 268, About Monterey and San Francisco, the Boccacio [sic], *Sebastodes paucispinis*, is known as . . "Mérou" . . to the Portuguese. American fishermen use the name "Jack." . . "Jack" comes from the species of *Esox* and *Stizostedium* [sic], which in the Southern States are called by that name. **1898** *U.S. Natl. Museum Bulletin* 47.1780. **1911** [see **24a(1)** above].

(3) A **shad** (here: *Alosa sapidissima*).

  1905 NJ State Museum *Annual Rept. for 1904* 99, *Alosa sapidissima.* . . Shad. Jack. Brass Back. [*Ibid* 101, This well-known fish is perhaps the most important of Delaware River food-fishes.]

(4) An early-maturing male salmon; see quots. Cf **jack salmon 3**

  [**1975** *Names* 64 [Salmon fishing terms], *Coho, chinook,* and *sockeye* also produce *jacks*, precocious males that have matured in their second or third years. While the term *jack* has been in use since the sixteenth century to refer to the males of other kinds of fish . . , this specific usage referring only to early-maturing male salmon is peculiar to British Columbia.] **1978** *AK Fishing Guide* 46, Jack kings—male fish that have matured sexually after a year at sea—may return at 3 or 4 pounds. They are capable of breeding. Jacks may be more numerous in some years and in some river systems. *Ibid* 53, Like king salmon, male silver salmon occasionally mature sexually after a year at sea and return to spawn as 2 to 3 pound "jacks."

25 also *jackworm:* Prob a **doodlebug 2**. Cf **Jack-come-up-the-world**

  1908 *DN* 3.323 **eAL, wGA**, *Jack.* . . A sort of worm which lives in the earth in a small bored hole. Children amuse themselves fishing for *jacks*. The worms will seize a straw poked into their holes, and they may be jerked out as a fish. Also called *jack-worm*. **1934** (1943) *W2, Jack worm.* The larva of a tiger beetle. Colloq., U.S. **c1960** Mathews *Coll.* **AL** (as of c1900), We fished for "jacks."

26 See **jack snapper 1**.

27 A **yellow jacket**. Cf **jack daubler**

  1944 Howard *Walkin' Preacher* 1 **IA**, A violent yellow jacket . . circled . . near the mules. . . The jack . . buzzed off into the fragrant air.

28 A **jack-in-the-pulpit 1** or its spadix.

  1925 *Book of Rural Life* 2975 **NY**, *Jack-in-the-pulpit.* . . The "Jack" is a novel preacher, seemingly well equipped with a handsome pulpit and sounding board. **1929** Burgess *Wild Flowers* 3, The real flowers . . are tiny, greenish yellow and are around the base of the slender green spadix, which is what the children call "Jack." **1967–69** *DARE* (Qu. S1, . . *Jack-in-the-pulpit*) Infs **NY28, WI**12, Jack. **1975** Duncan–Foote *Wildflowers SE* 238, *Arisaema triphyllum.* . . Flowers unisexual, sessile on the fleshy axis (the spadix or "Jack").

29 See **jack-o'-lantern 3**.

30 See **jackrock 3**.

jack *v*

1 To hunt or fish at night with a **jack** n[1] **5a**; hence ppl adj *jacked*; vbl n *jacking*; n *jacker.* **chiefly NEast** See Map and Map Section Cf **jacklight** *v*

  1842 Hawes *Sporting Scenes* 1.219 **seNY**, Not a man on Long Island can clam, crab, jack, shoot, or draw a net for bony fish with the skill and success of those who have inherited the honorable name of "Smith." **1881** *Harper's New Mth. Mag.* 63.692 **neNY**, Gad went out "jacking" with him, and jumped right over the bow of the boat to catch a deer. **1885** (1891) Roosevelt *Hunting* 168, The streams are not suited to the floating or jacking with a lantern in the bow of the canoe, as practised in the Adirondacks. **1889** *Century Dict.* 3210, *Jacker.* . . One who hunts

game with a jack. **1939** (1962) Thompson *Body & Britches* 291 **neNY** (as of a1910), It was in the days when "jacking" deer at night with a light was still legal; but even this dubious practice did not avail the two tenderfoot hunters. **1959** *Washington Post & Times Herald* (DC) 17 Nov sec C 5/6, Although they view with horror the idea of jacking deer . . some people feel waterfowl are their special property. **1965–70** *DARE* (Qu. P35b, *Illegal methods of shooting deer;* not asked in early QRs) 85 Infs, **chiefly NEast**, Jacking; **MA**62, They jack 'em; **NY**164, Jack; (Qu. P35a, . . *Deer shot illegally*) Infs **FL**35, **NY**87, Jacking deer; **CT**31, **NY**151, 156, 209, Jacked deer; (Qu. P13, . . *Ways of fishing*) Inf **NY**44, Jacking—at night, use spears for eels and crabs. **1965** *DARE* FW Addit **ME**, To jack nightwalkers—to gather nightcrawlers at night with a flashlight. **1968** McPhee *Pine Barrens* 140 **NJ**, The state police told me of one deerjacker who used to kill over three hundred deer a year. **1975** Gould *ME Lingo* 145, *Jack.* . . To shine a light into the eyes of game at night, with special Maine reference to deer. . . *Jacking* carries stiff penalties. . . One who *jacks* is a *jacker.* **1990** *Yankee* May 144 **NEng**, Whenever we dumped our trash at dusk, our headlights invariably spotlighted him—startled, momentarily frozen like a jacked deer.

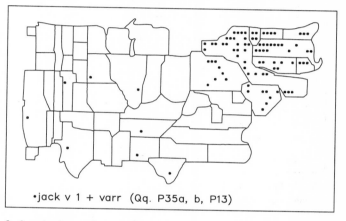

•jack v 1 + varr (Qq. P35a, b, P13)

2 See **jack up 1**.

3 See quot. [Cf **jack** n[1] **19**, **jack up 4**]

  1954 *Harder Coll.* **cwTN**, *Jack.* . . As a verb, in the sense of breeding. "I am goint [sic] to have the mare jacked."

4 also with *out:* To fight.

  1970 *DARE* (Qu. EE21b, *When boys were fighting very actively*) Inf **TN**46, They was jacking—were jacking out; common expression.

5 See quot. [**jack** n[1] **13a**]

  1992 *DARE* File **OH**, Another word "jack" meaning "to be[come] fermented"—apple juice will "jack" and turn into cider. I learned this from a man in his thirties raised on a farm in Ohio.

jack *adj* See **jackleg 1**

jack n[2]

1 A playing piece in the game of **jackstone 1**; pl: the game itself. [Folk-etym for Scots *chack* (*SND* at *chuck* n[2])] Cf **bob jack, check** n[1] **2**, **jackrock 2**

  1899 Champlin–Bostwick *Young Folks' Games* 443, The Jack-stones are held in the hand, and one, called the "Jack," is thrown into the air. **1903** (1963) Newell *Games & Songs* 191, Instead of pebbles, little double tripods of iron . . are generally in use; and the fifth stone, or "jack," is often replaced by a ball or marble. **1908** *DN* 3.323 **eAL, wGA**, *Jack.* . . A piece of metal with five tines or protuberances, used in the game of jacks. *Ibid, Jacks.* . . An indoor catching game. **1933** *Sun* (Baltimore MD) 28 June 22/3 (Hench Coll.), Catherine Remming . . was playing "jacks" in the front room of her home when a bolt struck a . . trolley pole in front of the house, glanced off and struck a jack she was holding. The jack became so hot she dropped it. **1965–70** *DARE* (Qu. EE33, . . *Outdoor games . . that children play*) 38 Infs, **scattered, but esp Nth, N Midl**, Jacks; (Qu. EE7, . . *Kinds of marble games*) Inf **OK**14, They play jacks with marbles—pick up marbles (as many as one can) when ball is in air; **UT**10, My mother played jacks with marbles; **TX**69, Jacks; **KS**7, You toss up the jacks and try to pick up marbles, as many as you can before you have to catch the jacks; **PA**221, Jacks and marbles.

2a freq pl: The game of tick-tack-toe. [Either transf from **1** above, from an earlier use of pebble markers, or from Scots and Engl dial *chack,* var of *check* pattern of differently colored squares] **esp N Midl**

1967–70 *DARE* (Qu. EE38a, *A game played with pencil and paper where the players try to get three X's or three O's in a row*) Infs **GA**86, **IN**32, **SC**58, Jack; **IL**80, 143, **IN**30, **PA**16, 28, 29, 71, Jacks; (Qu. EE39, . . *Games played on paper*) Inf **IN**16, Jack = tit-tat-toe.

b An imaginary person credited with the win when a game of tick-tack-toe results in a tie; a tie game. **esp N Midl** See Map Cf **cat's game, old cat 2**

1966–70 *DARE* (Qu. EE38b, *If the game of tick-tack-toe . . comes out so that neither X nor O wins, you call that _____*) 12 Infs, **chiefly N Midl**, Jack's game; **MD**46, Jack; **KY**74, A jack—Old Jack won the game; **NY**220, A jack—Jack wins; **PA**26, 71, Jack's (win); **WI**24, Jack wins; **OH**97, It went to Jack; **KY**62, Jack got it; **MO**11, Jack got it; Jack got that game; **IL**143, **IA**36, Jack got the game.

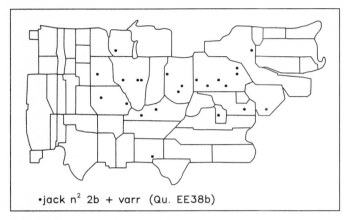

•jack n² 2b + varr (Qu. EE38b)

‡3 pl: The game of hopscotch.

1968 *DARE* (Qu. EE19, *The game in which children mark a 'court' on the ground or sidewalk, throw a flat stone in one section, then go on one foot and try to kick it or carry it out*) Inf **PA**71, Jacks.

jack n³ Cf **chankings**

1968 *DARE* FW Addit **CA**101, Jacks—potato peelings.

jack-a-lite See **jack-o'-lantern 1**

jackall See **jacal**

jackalope n [Blend of **jackrabbit 1** + *antelope*]
An imaginary animal.

1955 *Lincoln Star* (Lincoln, Neb.) 11 Jan. *(Mathews Coll.),* However, if the Kansas searchers are interested, the mounted head of a "jackalope" can be viewed at Mullen. **1965** *Natl. Observer* (Silver Spring MD) 6/1 **WY,** The jackalope is the rarest of all North-American animals. . . It seems some sort of mixture of large jackrabbit and small antelope. Of course the jackalope doesn't exist. He is a sort of perennial joke Westerners and Northerners play on the tourists who are always interested in seeing wild and unusual animals. *Ibid* 10/5 **CO,** Any Coloradoan will assure you that the animal pictured is the rather common buckbunny, and not the jackalope at all. **1968–69** *DARE* (Qu. CC17, *Imaginary animals or monsters*) Inf **MN**30, Jackalope—a jackrabbit with antlers—doesn't do anything; **AZ**11, Jackalope—antelope-sized jackrabbit. **1990** *DARE* File **ID, NV,** I remember seeing postcards with pictures of jackalopes—huge jackrabbits with large antlers. Along with the postcards with a single huge Idaho potato filling a flatbed railroad car, they were part of the bragging stock of the West.

Jack and Jill n attrib
Of social gatherings: attended by both sexes.

1968–69 *DARE* (Qu. FF3, . . *'Showers' or 'gift parties'*) Inf **CT**23, Jack and Jill shower; **CT**19, Jack and Jill showers—lately: men and women go; (Qu. FF2, . . *Kinds of parties*) Inf **MA**38, New Year's Eve parties—called Jack and Jill parties.

Jack and Jim n Also *fly away, Jack* Cf **Peter and Paul**
A children's game; see quots.

1909 *DN* 3.420 **Cape Cod MA** (as of a1857), *Fly away, Jack.* . . A trick to amuse children. A person sticks pieces of white paper to the nails of his forefingers. He places his forefingers on the edge of a table with the other fingers closed. He raises his right hand and brings it back, with the middle finger substituted for the forefinger, crying *fly away, Jack.* He does the same with the left and cries *fly away, Gill.* He then

restores his forefingers in the same way, crying *come again, Jack; come again, Gill.* **1953** Brewster *Amer. Nonsinging Games* 166 **IN,** *Jack and Jim.* . . The leader sticks a bit of black paper on the nail of the index finger of each hand . . [and] recites . . : *Two little blackbirds / Sitting on a limb,/ One named Jack / And one named Jim./ Fly away, Jack!/ Fly away, Jim!/ Come back, Jack!/ Come back, Jim!* **1961** Sackett–Koch *KS Folkl.* 225, Our mother taught us a finger game called "Jack and Jim." Stick a small piece of white paper on the first finger of each hand. Put these two fingers on the edge of a table and say, "Here's Jack and Jim. Fly away, Jack; fly Jim," and raise hands above shoulders. By changing to middle finger the birds fly away. By changing again they can come back.

jack and pole fence, jack and rail fence See **jack fence**

Jack-and-the-beanstalk n

1 =**kudzu.**
1959 Carleton *Index Herb. Plants* 67, *Jack-and-the-beanstalk:* Pueraria thunbergiana.

2 =**butter-and-eggs 1.**
1970 *DARE* (Qu. S11, . . *Other names . . for . . wild snapdragon*) Inf **TN**52, Jack-and-the-beanstalk.

jackass See **jackass brandy**

jackass bat n [See quot 1917]
=**spotted bat.**
1917 Anthony *Mammals Amer.* 315, *Spotted Bat,* or *Jackass Bat.* . . Ears even larger than those of Big-eared Bat, about 1.5 inches high by nearly an inch wide. . . Scattered localities in the Southwest; California, New Mexico and Arizona. **1980** Whitaker *Audubon Field Guide Mammals* 327, "Jackass Bat" *(Euderma maculatum).* . . It emerges late, carrying its huge ears forward during flight and giving a loud, high-pitched call.

jackass brandy n Also *jackass* [From the "kick"] **scattered, but esp CA** Cf **gray mule 1, white mule**
A homemade, illegal, or poor quality liquor.
1921 *DN* 5.109 **CA,** *Jackass brandy.* . . A home-made brandy with a powerful 'kick.' **1922** *Federal Reporter* 278.42 **cwCA,** Intoxicating liquor, to wit, one pint bottle of jackass brandy. **1923** *San Francisco Examiner* 18 Feb. 16/7 *(OEDS),* A still in operation and a stock of jackass brandy close by. **1924** Henderson *Keys to Crookdom* 289, The "jackass-brandy" hound will boil up anything from grapes to prunes. *Ibid* 290, The maker of jackass . . uses potato, corn, prune or raisin mash. **1968–70** *DARE* (Qu. DD21b, *General words . . for bad liquor*) Inf **CA**136, Jackass; (Qu. DD21c, *Nicknames for whiskey, especially illegally made whiskey*) Infs **CA**136, 160, 197, Jackass; (Qu. DD28b, . . *Fermented drinks . . made at home*) Inf **VT**4, Jackass brandy. **1974** Dabney *Mountain Spirits* 107 (as of 1920s), "Jackass brandy," made of peaches, created a stir in some sections of Virginia, causing intestinal pains and internal bleeding—all for a mere four dollars a quart.

jackass cheese n [Cf *jack cheese* a soft, moist whole-milk cheese]
1941 *LANE* Map 299 (*Cottage cheese*) 1 inf, **cCT,** Jackass cheese, 'the regular old New England name for it'.

jackass clover n [See quots 1911, 1985]
A rank-smelling plant *(Wislizenia refracta)* native from west Texas to southern California. Also called **stinking mustard, stinkweed**
1911 CA Ag. Exper. Sta. Berkeley *Bulletin* 217.992, *Wislizenia refracta.* . . Jackass Clover. . . will be one of the greatest honey-producing plants of this State. . . It was Henry T. Chrisman of Coalinga, who first became aware of its value as a honey plant, and gave it its present name. **1925** Jepson *Manual Plants CA* 409, *Jackass-Clover.* . . A bee plant in the San Joaquin. **1949** Moldenke *Amer. Wild Flowers* 36, Another rank-scented southwesterner is . . the jackass-clover. **1970** Kirk *Wild Edible Plants W. U.S.* 225, Jackass Clover is found in sandy, often rather alkaline, soil. **1985** Dodge *Flowers SW Deserts* 77, Since the leaves somewhat resemble the tri-foliate leaves of clover, the plant is commonly called jackass-clover.

jackass rabbit n Also *jackass hare* [See quots 1946, 1982]
=**jackrabbit 1.**
1845 in 1847 Henry *Campaign Sketches* 61 **TX,** We . . started any number of hares (called jackass rabbits), and had no little amusement in witnessing some animated runs; their speed is wonderful. **1872** Twain *Roughing It* 32 **NE,** We saw the first specimen of an animal known

familiarly . . —from Kansas clear to the Pacific Ocean—as the "jackass rabbit." . . He is just like any other rabbit, except that he is from one third to twice as large, has longer legs in proportion to his size, and has the most preposterous ears that ever were mounted on any creature *but* a jackass. **1882** *Ornith. & Oologist* 7.98 **swCA,** I have often found, in its burrows, portions of the large Jackass Hare (Lepus californicus) or "Narrow Gauged Mule,"—as popularly known in California. **1946** Peattie *Pacific Coast* 92 **nCA,** Undoubtedly those spiring ears account for the name, given by the pioneers, jackass rabbit. Some, however, have fancied that it may have been bestowed because "the kick of his powerful hind legs is like that of a mule." **1982** Elman *Hunter's Field Guide* 383, Originally named "jackass rabbits" by settlers who were understandably impressed by their long ears, jacks are not rabbits but hares.

jack bean n

1 A plant of the genus *Canavalia,* esp *C. ensiformis.* Also called **horsebean 4.** For other names of var spp see **June bean, wild hop, wonder bean**

1885 Murfree *Prophet of Smoky Mts.* 280 **eTN,** He sat upon the cabin porch beneath the yellow gourds and the purple blooms of the Jack-bean. **1911** *Century Dict. Suppl., Bean. . . Jack bean,* the sword-bean, *Canavali ensiforme,* growing well in the southern United States, but not much eaten by animals. **1964** Kingsbury *Poisonous Plants U.S.* 313, *Canavalia ensiformis. . .* Jack bean. . . Occasionally . . grown in the southern United States or . . imported for livestock feed. **1970** Correll *Plants TX* 883, *Canavalia. . .* Jackbean. . . In addition to the species below [=*C. maritima*], . . *C. ensiformis* . . has been cultivated in Texas. **1985** *Seed Savers Exchange* Winter 77, Jack Bean. . . Swordbean [=*Canavalia ensiformis*] has larger longer reddish seed & very tough wide pod.

2 =**hyacinth bean.**

1940 Clute *Amer. Plant Names* 18, *D[olichos] Lablab. . .* Jack-bean. **1959** Carleton *Index Herb. Plants* 67, *Jack-bean:* Canavalia ensiformis; Dolichos lablab.

jack bite n [Prob folk-etym for Scots, Ir, nEngl dial *chack* a snack + *bite*] Cf **check** n[2]

A snack.

1949 Kurath *Word Geog.* 36 **wWV,** On the Kanawha we find *check* and *jack-bite. . .* beside the Southern *snack* for a bite between meals. **1968** *DARE* (Qu. H5, . . *A small amount of food eaten between regular meals*) Inf **WV3,** Jack bite.

jack brush n Cf **jim brush**

A **ceanothus** (here: *Ceanothus oliganthus*).

1921 Hall *Hdbk. Yosemite* 251 **ceCA,** An allied species is the Jack Brush *(Ceanothus divaricatus).*

jack bump n Also *j-bump, jacky bump* [Prob *jack off* to masturbate + **bump** n 1] Cf **fuck bump, jerk ~, love ~ 1, passion pimple**

A pimple; pl: acne.

1967–69 *DARE* (Qu. X59, . . *The small infected pimples that form usually on the face*) Inf **OR3,** Jack bumps, j-bumps; **WA30,** Jacky bumps. **1990** Cavender *Folk Med. Lexicon* 25 **sAppalachians,** *Jack bumps*—acne.

jack cavally See **jack crevalle**

jack chain n Cf **bull chain**

In logging: see quots.

1905 U.S. Forest Serv. *Bulletin* 61.40 [Logging terms], *Jack chain.* An endless spiked chain, which moves logs from one point to another, usually from the mill pond into the sawmill. **1969** Sorden *Lumberjack Lingo* 63 **NEng, Gt Lakes,** *Jack chain*—An endless chain used for bringing logs from the hot pond into the sawmill. Same as bull chain.

Jack-come-up-the-world n Cf **jack** n[1] **25**

An ant lion (Myrmeleontidae).

1899 Bergen *Animal Lore* 62 **eOH,** Jack-come-up-the-world, ant-lion.

jack crevalle n Also *jack cavally, crevalle jack*

=**crevalle a,** esp *Caranx hippos.*

1882 U.S. Natl. Museum *Proc.* 5.594, *Caranx chrysus. . .* Jack-Crevalle. *Ibid* 595 **SC,** *Caranx chrysus* is the only species of *Caranx* brought in much abundance to the market of Charleston, during the summer months. The name *Jack-Crevalle* is there applied to all species of Caranx without distinction. **1935** Caine *Game Fish* 59, *Caranx hippos. . .* Jack Cavally . . Jack Crevalle. **1946** LaMonte *N. Amer. Game Fishes* 34, *Caranx crysos. . .* Names . . Crevalle Jack. **1972** Sparano

Outdoors Encycl. 377, *Caranx hippos. . .* Probably the best-known member of a very large family, the jack crevalle is considered a fine gamefish by some anglers but a pest by others. **1975** Newell *If Nothin' Don't Happen* 81 **FL,** I had a lot of fun with a shark line too, baitin' with a jack crevalle and slashin' it to make it bleed and them old sharks couldn't let it alone.

jack curlew n [See quot 1955]

=**Hudsonian curlew.**

1805 (1905) Lewis *Orig. Jrls. Lewis & Clark Exped.* 6.133, It is about the size of the yellow leged plover common to the U'States, and called the jack curloo by some. **1876** *Forest & Stream* 7.68, I have just returned from the Jersey coast . . and herewith give you the names of the bay-birds . . as they are known along that beach: . . *Numenius hudsonicus,* Jack curlew. *Ibid* 149, Description given to the *Sun* by an old Long Island sportsman of thirty-three years experience: . . Jack curlew has a bowed bill four or five inches long, a body a little bigger than a pigeon, and is of a light brown color. **1881** *Ibid* 17.226 **Cape Cod MA. 1909** Field Museum Nat. Hist. *Zool. Ser.* 9.423 **IL, WI,** *Hudsonian Curlew. Local name:* Jack Curlew. **1921** LA Dept. of Conserv. *Bulletin* 10.81. **1955** MA Audubon Soc. *Bulletin* 39.446, *Hudsonian Curlew. . .* Jack Curlew (General; the term "jack" in such combinations means small.) **1962** Imhof *AL Birds* 237, Jack Curlew. . . is a large, brown shorebird with a long, down-curved bill. . . It frequents mudflats and sandbars, but it often feeds in short grass or on plowed fields.

jack daubler n Cf **jack** n[1] **27**

A **mud dauber 1.**

1968 *DARE* (Qu. R20, *Wasps that build their nests of mud*) Inf **MD15,** Jack daubler ['dɔblə]—nest round, size of grapefruit. Insect looks like a big fly—brown, stings.

jackdaw n

1 also *daw, jackjaw;* A **grackle B:** esp **boat-tailed grackle,** but also **great-tailed grackle** and **purple grackle.** [See quot 1917] **chiefly S Atl, Gulf States** See Map

1731 Catesby *Nat. Hist. Carolina* 1.12 **SE,** *Monedula purpurea.* The Purple Jack-Daw. . . At a distance they seem all black, but at nearer view, they appear purple. **1832** Nuttall *Manual Ornith.* 1.192, *Quiscalus major. . .* This large and Crow-like species, sometimes called the Jack-daw, inhabits the southern parts of the Union only, particularly the states of Georgia and Florida. **1858** Baird *Birds* 555, *Quiscalus major. . . Jackdaw. . .* Southern Atlantic and Gulf coast. **1917** (1923) *Birds Amer.* 2.267, *Purple Grackle. . .* Other names. . . New England Jackdaw; . . Purple Jackdaw. *Ibid* 270, *Boat-tailed Grackle. . .* This is the "Jackdaw" of the South. . . It got its popular name from the early settlers of the country on account of its superficial resemblance to the European Jackdaw, which, of course, is a totally different bird. **1928** Bailey *Birds NM* 659, The large, Great-tailed Grackles, known as Jackdaws . . , have strikingly long, keeled, and graduated tails. **1938** Oberholser *Bird Life LA* 598 **LA, TX,** *Boat-tailed Grackle. . .* 'jackdaw.' **1965–70** *DARE* (Qu. Q11, . . *Kinds of blackbirds*) 22 Infs, **chiefly S Atl, TX,** Jackdaw; **FL32,** Black jackdaw; **VA52,** Jackdaw; **NY11, 66,** Daw; (Qu. Q12, . . *Kinds of crows;* total Infs questioned, 75) Inf **FL17,** Old jackdaws. **1969** Longstreet *Birds FL* 143, *Boat-tailed Grackle.* Other names: *Jackdaw. . .* The largest blackbird in Florida.

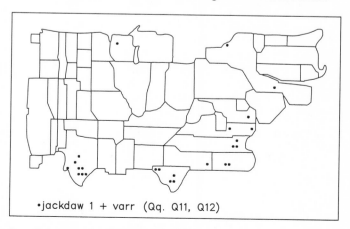

•jackdaw 1 + varr (Qq. Q11, Q12)

2 =**fish crow 1.** [See quot 1955]

1926 *AmSp* 1.416 **Okefenokee GA,** The Jackdaw [Footnote: Fish Crow (*Corvus ossifragus*)], the Raccoon, an' the Bear will eat the [turtle]

aigs. They shore love a aig. **1955** *Oriole* 20.1.11 **GA,** *Fish Crow.*
Jackdaw (by transfer of the name of a small European crow ally).

‡3 also pl: See quot. [Perh var of **jackknife** n **1**] Cf **mumblety-peg**
  1968–69 *DARE* (Qu. EE5, *Games where you try to make a jackknife
stick in the ground*) Inf **CT5,** Jackdaws; **IN76,** Jackdaw [FW: Inf
doubtful].

Jack Dempsey n
A small fish *(Cichlasoma octofasciatum)* naturalized in Florida.
  1991 Amer. Fisheries Soc. *Common Names Fishes* 101, *Cichlasoma
octofasciatum*—[Common name:] Jack Dempsey [Where established:]
Florida.

jacked See **jack** v **1**

jacked up See **jack up 4**

jacker See **jack** v **1**

jacker-mer-lantern See **jack-o'-lantern 1**

jacket n
1 A man's sleeveless garment, usu worn over a shirt; a vest.
chiefly Midl
  1705 *Boston News–Letter* (MA) 10 Dec 4/2 **ME,** [Advt:] Ran away
from his Master . . , a Negro Man-Slave named Peter, . . has on a mixt
gray home-spun Coat, white home spun Jacket and Breeches. **c1770** in
1833 Boucher *Glossary* xlix **MD, VA,** A *Jacket;* a waistcoat. **1899**
(1912) Green *VA Folk-Speech* 242, *Jacket.* . . A short coat or body
garment; any garment for the body coming not lower than the hips. **1907**
German Amer. Annals 9.380 sePA, *Jacket*—Vest; waistcoat. **1946** *PADS*
5.26 **VA,** *Jacket* . . *:* A vest; fairly common among older people in the
southern part of the Blue Ridge. **1949** Kurath *Word Geog.* 60, *Jacket*
[for *vest*] is common in the piedmont and the Blue Ridge of North
Carolina and in adjoining parts of South Carolina, Virginia, and West
Virginia. Scattered instances of *jacket* in central Pennsylvania and its
common use along the upper reaches of the Potomac in West Virginia
make it highly probable that the term is of Pennsylvania origin. **1983**
MJLF 9.45 ceKY, *Jacket* . . a vest. **1986** Pederson *LAGS Concordance
(Vest)* 28 infs, **chiefly TN,** Jacket. [*DARE* Ed: Some infs indicate that
jacket is old-fashioned or obsolete.]

2 See **hatching jacket.**

3 See quots.
  1967–69 *DARE* (Qu. I12, *The outside covering of dry beans*) Inf
CA170, Jacket; (Qu. I39, . . *The thick outside covering of a walnut*) Inf
OH3, Jacket. **1970** *DARE* FW Addit **VA46,** Jacket . . outside covering—bean or pea inside.

4 Appar a **yellow jacket** (here: *Vespula* spp.). Cf **jack** n¹ **27**
  1966 *DARE* (Qu. R21, . . *Other kinds of stinging insects*) Inf **FL26,**
Jacket, hornet, wasps, bumble bees. **1969** Gt. Smoky Mt. Nat. Park
Recordings 27:8 *(Montgomery Coll.),* They would find an old jacket nest
or bumblebee nest.

5 The skin of a dead lamb put over another lamb to induce
the mother of the dead one to accept it.
  1967 [see **jacket** v]. **1978** [see **jacket** v]. **1992** Attebury *Sheep* 40
swID, eOR, "When you graft. . . a lamb onto a ewe that's lost hers, do
you have to skin the dead one . . ?" "We do that often. They skin the
dead one more so down at the shed than they do out on the range, but
they do that out on the range, too. . . slip that jacket right over and use
some of the afterbirth on the lamb they're grafting on."

jacket v, hence ppl adj *jacketed,* vbl n *jacketing* **West**
To wrap (a lamb) in the skin of a dead lamb to induce the
mother of the dead one to accept it; to wrap a lamb in this
way; with *onto:* to introduce (a lamb) to (a ewe) by this means.
  1967 *DARE* Tape **OR**18, [Inf:] If a lamb dies you take another ewe's
lamb if she got a twin and skin it [=the dead one] and put it [=the skin]
on this other lamb and fool the ewe until she gets to sucking for several
days. [FW:] Why do you have to skin it? [Inf:] So she'll retain the smell
of her own lamb. . . Then you just jacket, you put it right over the top
of him. . . It's just like putting a coat on yourself, you take the other
lamb's skin and put it over the top of the other one, the one that's alive.
You put a jacket on. **1968** Adams *Western Words* 163, *Jacketing*—Skinning a dead lamb and placing its pelt upon the body of an orphan so
that the mother of the dead lamb will nurse it. Ewes recognize their
offspring by smell and refuse to nurse lambs not their own. **1978** Doig
This House 163 **MT** (as of c1955), The . . lamb is a goner, I'm gonna

have to jacket a fresh one onto that ewe. . . Who says I couldn't jacket
day onto night if I wanted to, now-I-ask-ye? *Ibid,* Jacketing was a ruse
played on a ewe whose lamb had died. A substitute lamb quickly would
be singled out, most likely from a set of twins. . . Dad would skin the
dead lamb, and into the tiny pelt carefully snip four small leg holes and
a head hole. Then the stand-in lamb would have the skin fitted onto it
like a snug jacket. . . The next step . . was to cut out the dead lamb's
liver and smear it several times across the jacket of pelt. In its borrowed . . skin, the new lamb was then presented to the ewe. She would
sniff . . , distrustful but pulled by the blood-smell of her own. When in
a few days she made up her dim sheep's mind to accept the lamb, Dad
snipped away the jacket. **1985** Ehrlich *Solace* 19 **WY,** Some [of the
dead lambs] they skinned, dressing an orphaned lamb with the hide in
hopes that the ewe who had just lost her lamb would think the "jacketed"
lamb was hers.

jacket-and-breeches n
A **wild columbine** (here: *Aquilegia canadensis*).
  1896 *Jrl. Amer. Folkl.* 9.179, *Aquilegia Canadensis.* . . Jacket-and-
breeches.

jacketed See **jacket** v

jacketing n [*OED jacketing* sb. 3 1851 →] Cf *dust one's jacket*
(at **dust** v)
A beating; a tongue-lashing.
  1891 Maitland *Amer. Slang Dict.* 152, *Jacketing,* a thrashing. **1903**
(1931) Adams *Log Cowboy* 253, Explaining the jacketing I had got
from Priest, and the partial promise I had made not to bet, [I] gave
him my forty dollars. **1912** Green *VA Folk-Speech* 242, *Jacketing.* . . A
thrashing.

jacketing vbl n See **jacket** v

jack fence n Also *jack (and) pole fence, jack and rail* ~ [**jack**
n¹ **6**] esp **NW** Cf **stake-and-rider fence**
See quots.
  1938 *Rotarian* Sept 55 **ID,** The "jack and pole" fence used on the
eastern slope of the Rocky Mountains is constructed with all portions
of wood being placed above ground because formerly portions placed
in the ground soon rotted. **1942** Giese *Farm Fence Hdbk.* 11, [Captions:]
Jack pole fence, supplemented with wire, in Idaho. . . Jack pole fence
in Montana. **1951** *S. Folkl. Qrly.* 16.125 **ID,** *Jack and pole.* Mr. R.F.
Flint [=author of 1938 quot] published . . a photograph of this style of
fence, . . which shows the economical use of wood. Crossed stakes
support a pole on top, with another horizontal row of poles secured to
one side of the stakes midway to the ground. . . Mr. Flint wrote: "The
'jack' fence is distinctly a dry area type, the only distinctively western
rail fence of which I have knowledge." **1968** *DARE* (Qu. L62, *A fence
made of split logs*) Inf **VA24,** Jack fence—same as stake-and-rider fence.
1991 *DARE* File c**ID,** A jack and pole fence, or jack fence, is one made
with bucks or jacks (logs fastened together in an X-shape) spaced about
eight feet apart, with poles (usually of lodgepole pine) laid between the
crossed pieces of the bucks. Sometimes there's a strand of barbed wire
along the top, sometimes both along the top and the bottom. These are
good fences for country with heavy snowfall because they withstand the
weight and movement of snow deposits. Poles are sometimes attached
to the bucks at angles to the ground for added stability. *Ibid* eOR, A
jack and rail (or buck and rail) fence is like a jack and pole fence except
that the poles have been split into rails.

jackfish n Cf **jack** n¹ **24**
1 Any of several freshwater fishes, as:
a A fish of the genus *Esox,* usu **northern pike 1** (here: *E.
lucius*) or **chain pickerel. chiefly Sth** See Map
  1820 Rafinesque *Ohio R. Fishes* 70, This fish [=*Esox lucius*] is rare
in the Ohio. . . It is sometimes called Jack or Jackfish. **1855** Simms
Forayers 277 **SC,** I've caught. . . three fine cat, seven perch and, two
jackfish, in an hour. **1904** *Sun* (NY NY) 23 Aug 9/1, The Rev. Isaac
W. Johnson to-day vouched for the truth of a fish story in Gates county,
N.C., to the effect that . . a jack fish, eighteen inches long, jumped into
the buggy and was cooked for supper. **1917** Kephart *Camping & Woodcraft* 2.410, Here in the Carolina mountains the natives call it [*sc.*
mascalonge] the "jack fish"—yes, we have the real mascalonge. **1930**
DN 6.82 c**SC,** Men go out at night in a bateau . . with a flambeau . .
and the jack-fish, attracted by the light, jump into the boat. **1953**
Chicago Nat. Hist. Museum *Bulletin* Feb 6, In northern waters, where
northern pike or jack-fish, as they're called in the north, abound in
duck-nesting waters, pike are accused of eating so many ducklings as

to affect the survival of the broods. **1960** Williams *Walk Egypt* 251 **GA,** Jacks whistled when they were caught. That was a cool sound, too, jackfish whistling. **1965–70** *DARE* (Qu. P1, . . *Kinds of freshwater fish . . caught around here . . good to eat)* Infs **FL**48, **GA**28, **LA**12, **NC**15, 49, **SC**26, Jackfish; **AR**51, Jack, sometimes jack pike or jackfish; **FL**4, Grass pickerel or jackfish; **GA**19, Jackfish, northern pike the same; **GA**34, Jackfish—real name is northern pike; **LA**15, Pike—they are called this "up the road," [but] we call them jackfish; **MN**38, Northern jackfish; **SC**40, Jackfish—pike family; **VA**43, Jackfish—same as pike; (Qu. P3, *Freshwater fish that are not good to eat)* Infs **AL**7, **FL**34, **SC**7, 45, 63, Jackfish; **AL**31, Jackfish—too many bones; **LA**14, Jackfish—that's a southern pike. **1973** Knight *Cook's Fish Guide* 383, Jackfish—Walleye or see Gar, Alligator or see Pickerel, Chain or see Pike, Northern. **1983** Becker *Fishes WI* 398, *Esox lucius.* . . Jackfish. *Ibid* 880, *Stizostedion canadense.* . . Jackfish.

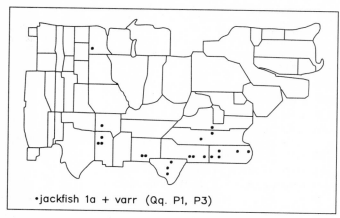

•jackfish 1a + varr (Qq. P1, P3)

b A fish of the genus *Stizostedion:* usu **walleye,** but also a **sauger** *(S. canadense).*

   1935 Caine *Game Fish* 31, *Wall-eyed Pike. Stizostedion vitreum.* . . Jackfish. **1940** *Collier's* 6 Apr 16 **Missip Valley,** You can try for wall-eyed pike, known locally as jackfish. **1956** Harlan–Speaker *IA Fish* 142, *Sauger. Stizostedion canadense.* . . *Other Names* . . jack fish. *Ibid* 143, *Walleye. Stizostedion vitreum vitreum.* . . jack fish. **1972** Sparano *Outdoors Encycl.* 363, *Walleye. Common Names* . . jackfish. *Ibid* 364, *Sauger.* . . Jack fish. **1973** [see **1a** above]. **1983** [see **1a** above].

c =**alligator gar.**

   1820 Rafinesque *Ohio R. Fishes* 77, It [=*Lepisosteus spatula*] is a voracious fish: Its vulgar names are . . Jack fish, Garjack, &c. **1973** [see **1a** above].

2 Any of several saltwater fishes, as:

a =**crevalle a,** esp *Caranx hippos.*

   1882 U.S. Natl. Museum *Proc.* 5.269, *Caranx hippus.* . . Jack-fish; Crevallé. . . Specimens of enormous size, weighing more than 25 pounds, were seen in the markets of New Orleans. **1884** U.S. Natl. Museum *Bulletin* 27.439, *Caranx hippus.* . . Jack-fish. . . This species sometimes exceeds 25 pounds in weight; it is occasionally taken at Wood's Holl [sic], where it is readily sold. **1884** Goode *Fisheries U.S.* 1.324, *Caranx pisquetus.* This fish, known . . along the Florida coast as "Jack-fish," . . is found in the Western Atlantic. **1933** LA Dept. of Conserv. *Fishes* 169, *The Common Jack. Caranx hippos.* . . is a fine Louisiana game fish. . . Other Jack Fishes which are edible occur commonly in Louisiana and provide spirited sport for the angler. **1935** Caine *Game Fish* 48, *Caranx crysos.* . . Jackfish. *Ibid* 59, *Caranx hippos.* . . Jackfish. **1946** Stilwell *Hunting in TX* 31, Along the coast of Texas you will encounter one fish that those of us who know the ropes consider a prime nuisance. . . This fish is the jackfish, or crevallé. . . He is practically unfit for human consumption. **1966–68** *DARE* (Qu. P4, *Saltwater fish that are not good to eat)* Infs **FL**39, **TX**14, Jackfish; **LA**26, Jackfish [FW: =jack crevalle].

b An **amberfish:** esp a **rudderfish** (here: *Seriola zonata),* but also *S. dumerili.*

   1882 U.S. Natl. Museum *Proc.* 5.596 **seSC,** *Seriola carolinensis.* . . Jack-fish; Amber-jack. . . Two young specimens, each about 1 foot long, were obtained in the market, and many very young (3 or 4 inches long) were seen swimming on the surface, on the fishing grounds outside the harbor. **1884** Goode *Fisheries U.S.* 1.331, *The Amber-fish—Seriola carolinensis.* . . is . . rather common on the Carolina coast, where it is known as the "Jack-fish." **1911** U.S. Bur. Census *Fisheries 1908*

307, *Amber-fish (Seriola).*—A food fish found from Cape Cod to Cape Hatteras. It is known as "jack-fish" on the Carolina coast. **1935** Caine *Game Fish* 35, *Seriola lalandi* [=*S. dumerili*]. . . Jackfish.

jackfish farmer n Cf **jackpine savage**
   A rustic.
   1973 Allen *LAUM* 1.351 **ND** (as of c1950), *Jackfish farmer:* "They live on fish from the [Red] river here" [1 inf].

jack-fool n
   A great fool.
   1944 Wellman *Bowl* 190 **KS,** Yes, you jack-fool! Whiskey's the one thing that's good for snake-bite.

jack frame See **jack** n[1] 6

jack frost n, freq cap [*OED* "frost or frosty weather personified" 1826 → (at *jack* sb.[1] 35)]
1 also attrib, freq in phrr: The ice crystals that form on windows in cold weather; the agent, freq personified, that causes them. **widespread, but chiefly Nth, N Midl** See Map
   1942 Berrey–Van den Bark *Amer. Slang* 71.4, *Jack Frost,* personification of frost. **1950** *WELS* **WI** *(Patterns inside a window glass in winter)* 5 Infs, Jack Frost; 4 Infs, Jack Frost patterns *(or paintings, pictures)*; 1 Inf, Paintings by Jack Frost; 1 Inf, Jack Frost's painting; 1 Inf, Jack Frost painted windows; 2 Infs, Trimmed *(or decorated)* by Jack Frost; 1 Inf, Jack Frost has been here. [**1956** Almirall *From College* 302 **CO,** Hidden mountain lakes would show their shimmering blue surfaces instead of their Jack Frosted black frowns. . . spring was in the air.] c1960 *Wilson Coll.* **csKY,** Jack Frost. . . Ice on the inside of a window. **1965–70** *DARE* (Qu. B36, *Patterns formed by ice inside a window glass in winter)* 112 Infs, **widespread, but chiefly Nth, N Midl,** Jack Frost; 70 Infs, **widespread, but chiefly Nth, N Midl,** Jack Frost pictures; 31 Infs, **scattered, but esp PA,** Jack Frost paintings; 16 Infs, **scattered,** Jack Frost patterns *(or designs, fingers, markings, paint-pictures, picture-paintings, portraits)*; **PA**128, Jack Frost with fairy pictures; **MI**100, **NJ**5, **PA**66, 220, **WI**47, Jack Frost was here (last night); **GA**89, **MD**35, **VA**71, Jack Frost on the window(panes); **MD**21, **NY**3, Jack Frost was *(or is)* on the window; **CT**6, **SC**26, Jack Frost has been here; **NJ**42, Jack Frost came in the night; **NJ**4, Jack Frost is around; **MN**2, **PA**146, Jack Frost has painted; **MD**1, 8, **NY**23, Jack Frost painted the window-panes *(or on the window, on it)*; **ME**20, Jack Frost has been painting; **MI**63, **WA**19, Jack Frost has been working (here last night); **VT**16, What Jack Frost did; **NM**11, **PA**165, Jack Frost's work *(or paintbrush)*; **NY**88, Where Jack Frost paints pictures.

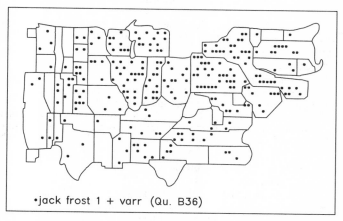

•jack frost 1 + varr (Qu. B36)

2 Occas personified, also *Jack Frost's son:* a frost, esp a severe one. **chiefly Sth, S Midl** See Map on p. 82
   1899 (1912) Green *VA Folk-Speech* 242, *Jack-frost.* . . Frost. "Jack-frost is about this morning;" a cold morning when the ground is white. **1950** *WELS (A frost that does not kill plants)* 1 Inf, **swWI,** Jack frost. **1965–70** *DARE* (Qu. B30, *A frost that kills plants)* 26 Infs, **chiefly Sth, S Midl,** Jack frost; **AR**1, A big frost is a jack frost; **LA**7, Jack Frost—he's white everywhere, kills everything; (Qu. B29, *A frost that does not kill plants)* Infs **AL**1, **CA**105, **GA**77, **MS**17, **MO**36, **NC**70, **OK**13, **SC**11, Jack frost; **NC**83, Jack frost—little old light frost that comes in the fall; **CA**15, Jack Frost was here last night; **MS**60, Jack Frost's son. [13 of 38 total Infs Black] **1983** *MJLF* 9.45 ceKY (as of 1956), *Jack frost.* . . A killing frost. **1986** Pederson *LAGS Concordance (Frost)* 23 infs, **chiefly inland Gulf Region,** (A) Jack frost. [11 infs describe a Jack

frost as a severe, heavy, or killing frost; 4 describe it as not severe or as a general term for frost.]

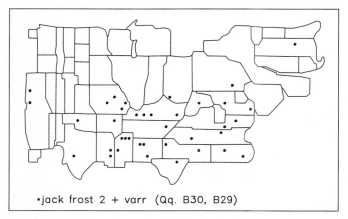

•jack frost 2 + varr (Qq. B30, B29)

3 A type of ice; see quots. Cf **fox frost 2**

c1960 *Wilson Coll.* **csKY**, *Jack Frost*. . . Not rime but the ice that spews up around dittany stalks in early heavy freezes. Known elsewhere as rabbit-ice. Once regarded as aphrodisiac. **1966** *DARE* (Qu. B30) Inf **SC**19, Jack frost—spews up out of sandy land. **1966–67** *DARE* FW Addit **nwSC**, Jack frost—the kind of ice that springs up out of the ground—especially on road banks—also on level ground; **SC**, A jack frost—ice that comes up out of the ground on ditch banks—looks like icicles.

4 Personified: the agent that causes trees to turn color in the fall.

1994 *DARE* File [In resp to the query "Who or what do you consider to be responsible for the leaves turning red or yellow in the fall?"] **ceTX**, My mother . . told me that Jack Frost was responsible for the change. *Ibid* **ID** (as of c1940), "Jack Frost" made the leaves turn. *Ibid* **MI**, Jack Frost colors the leave[s] in fall. *Ibid* **eWA** (as of 1930s), Jack Frost did it.

Jack Frost's son See **jack frost 2**

jack grindle n

1 A **bittern** (here: *Botaurus lentiginosus*).

1955 *Oriole* 20.1.2 **GA**, American Bittern. . . Jack Grindle (a "pet" name, or perhaps a recollection of a sonic term heard elsewhere).

2 pronc-sp *jack grinner:* =**bowfin.** Cf **grindle** n[1]

1967 *DARE* (Qu. P3, *Freshwater fish that are not good to eat*) Inf **SC**40, Jack grindle—usually called mudfish here—scavenger. **1986** Pederson *LAGS Concordance (Freshwater fish)* 1 inf, **swMS**, Jack grindles; 1 inf, **swMS**, Jack grinner—can't be eaten; too bony.

jack gull n

The black-legged **kittiwake.**

1925 (1928) Forbush *Birds MA* 1.62, *Rissa tridactyla tridactyla*. . . Jack gull. . . Smaller than Herring Gull or Ring-billed Gull. **1946** Hausman *Eastern Birds* 318, Jack Gull. . . While with us in winter it is found mostly at sea, not often approaching the shore. **1955** Forbush–May *Birds* 225, Jack Gull. . . Winters from the Gulf of St. Lawrence south to New Jersey.

jack hammer n Cf **hammerhead 6, woodchuck**

A **woodpecker.**

1958 McCulloch *Woods Words* 97 **Pacific NW**, *Jack hammer*—A particularly big or busy woodpecker; taken from the jack hammer used in rock pits to prepare holes for shooting.

jack honeysuckle n Cf **honeysuckle 3**

Perh a **rhododendron.**

1945 Saxon *Gumbo Ya-Ya* 540 **LA**, *Prostitute's lure*—Essences of vanilla, verbena, Jack honeysuckle, wintergreen, rosebud, and 'follow-me-boy' water. **1946** Tallant *Voodoo* 178 **New Orleans LA** [Black], Rub your body good with bay rum when you get through, then with verbena essence and jack honeysuckle.

jack horse See **jack** n[1] **6**

jack-house n [*SND jack* n.[2] "Sc. variant of Eng. *jakes*, a privy"] **esp VA**

A privy.

1935 *Hench Coll.* **cVA**, *Jack-house*—Fred N. Knoblock, of Crozet,

Albemarle County, Virginia mentioned to me . . the existence of this word in the speech of Albemarle farmers and mountaineers. He says it is the most common word for privy and that he has heard it as long as he can remember. He is . . somewhere in his 20's. **1949** Kurath *Word Geog.* 53, *Privy* and *back-house* are current everywhere for the old-fashioned outdoor toilet. The more common regional terms are: . . *johnny (house), jack house,* in Virginia. **1952** Brown *NC Folkl.* 1.554, *Jack-house.* . . A privy. **1967** Faries *Word Geog. MO* 145, Jack house . . *(Privy).* [1 inf] **1970** *DARE* (Qu. M21b, *Joking names for an outside toilet building*) Inf **VA**43, Jack-house.

jack-hunter, jack-hunting See **jack** n[1] **5a**

Jackie n Cf **blackjack 1c**

A **black duck 1** (here: *Anas rubripes*).

1940 Trautman *Birds Buckeye Lake* 176 **OH**, *Anas rubripes*. . . The former market hunters and the sportsmen were united in their opinion that from 1860 to 1885 the "black mallard" or "Jackie" was a decidedly uncommon duck and that few were shot for sport or for the market. . . All agreed that the "black mallard" became a most numerous and conspicuous species several years before 1915. **1951** *AmSp* 26.275, Big winter Jackie . . the black duck in Ohio.

jacking See **jack** v **1**

jacking up See **jack up 1**

jack-in-the-box n

=**jack-in-the-pulpit 1.**

1966–69 *DARE* (Qu. S1, . . *Jack-in-the-pulpit*) Infs **DE**3, **KY**18, **MI**67, **NC**44, Jack-in-the-box.

Jack-in-the-bush n

1 =**fennel-flower.** Cf **devil-in-the-bush 1**

1896 *Jrl. Amer. Folkl.* 9.180, *Nigella Damascena* . . Jack-in-the-bush, Worcester, Mass.

2 also *Jack-up-a-bush, Jacky-in-the-bush:* A guessing game similar to **hull-gull;** see quots. **esp Mid and S Atl** Cf **eggs in the basket 2, snake in the grass, old gray mare**

1908 *DN* 3.323 **eAL, wGA,** *Jack-in-the-bush.* . . A guessing game. The following is the formula for the game: "*First player.* Jack in the bush. *Second player.* Cut him down. *First p.* How many licks? *Second p.* Five (his guess)." **1915** *DN* 4.184 **swVA,** Jack-in-the-bush. **1952** Brown *NC Folkl.* 1.60 **cnNC** (as of 1922), The first player holds out a number of chinquapins in his closed hands and says, "Jack in the bush." The second player replies, "Cut him down." "How many licks?" demands the other, and the second player must guess the number. **1957** *Sat. Eve. Post Letters* **IA,** Jack in the bush—two persons. Each has ten matches. Guessing how many the other has in his hand. If guess is correct, those in the hand are given to the guesser. If guesser is wrong, he gives either the amount over or the amount under to you. **1966** *DARE* (Qu. DD37, . . *Table games played a lot by adults*) Inf **SC**3, Jack-in-the-bush—played with grains of corn: you take a few in one hand and hold hand up, saying "Jack-in-the-bush"; somebody says, "Cut him down." Everwho's got the corn says, "How many?" Everybody makes a guess and he's to make up the difference, if there is any, to the holder. When somebody gets the right number, the holder gives him the corn. A record is kept of the guesses and when all have failed or someone has guessed right, then the guessers have to pay off their debts. As each person goes broke he drops out. Last man left wins; (Qu. EE33, . . *Outdoor games . . that children play*) Inf **FL**33, Jack-in-the-bush—grab a handful of peanuts, say "how far?" Other guy says three or four—if he's wrong he pays. **1968–70** *DARE* Tape **VA**9, Chinquapin games. . . We used to play "Jacky-in-the-bush, cut him down, how many lick." Well, I didn't know how many he had in his hand and of course I couldn't get it, so Poppy got all the chinquapins; **FL**50, I loved to play . . Jack-in-the-bush. **1980** *Foxfire 6* 292 **nwNC,** One person puts some marbles (or none) in his hand and says, "Jack up a bush." A second person says, "Cut it down." The first person says, "How many licks?" Then the second person guesses how many marbles the first person has. If he gets it right, he gets all of them, and if he doesn't, he has to give the first person the difference.

jack in the dark where are you n [**jack** n[1] **3**]

1969 Sorden *Lumberjack Lingo* 62 **NEng, Gt Lakes,** *Jack in the dark where are you?:* A robust, roughhouse game played in the bunkhouse. Two jacks are blindfolded; one is "jack in the dark," and the other jack is searching for him. On the query "Jack in the dark where are you?" both jacks would attempt to swat each other with long stockings stuffed with a couple of pair of water-soaked socks. Real swatting resulted.

jack-in-the-lantern See **jack-o'-lantern 1**

jack-in-the-pulpit n

1 also *Jill-in-the-pulpit, Jock-in-the-pulpit*: A plant of the genus *Arisaema*, usu *A. triphyllum*. [See quot 1975] Also called **Adam's apple 1, bitey root, dragon arum, dragonroot 1, dragon turnip, grandmother's thimble, guinea turnip, hood flower, Indian horseradish, ~ potato** n, **~ turnip 1, jack** n[l] **28, jack-in-the-box, Jack-jump-up, Jack-the-preacher, jenny 10, johnny-jump-up 2a, lady's slipper 9, minister-of-the-woods, parson plant, pepper turnip, preacher, ~ flower, ~ Jack, preacher-in-the-pulpit, preacher plant, preacher's box, Robin Adair, swamp lily, turkey tongue, wake-robin, wild artichoke, ~ turnip.** For other names of *A. triphyllum* see **bog onion 2, cooter wampee 3, cuckoo plant, devil's ear, ~ lily, Indian cherry 3, ~ cradle, ~ jack-in-the-pulpit, lady-in-a-chaise 1, marsh turnip, meadow bugle, ~ turnip, memory root, one-berry 3, starchwort, swamp cherry, ~ turnip, wild pepper.** For other names of var spp see **five-leaved jack, green dragon, parson-in-the-pulpit**

1837 (1966) Martineau *Soc. in America* 1.284 neMA, Fine specimens of Jack-in-the-pulpit, and moccasin-flower. **1876** Hobbs *Bot. Hdbk.* 59, Jack in the pulpit, Dragon root, Arum triphyllum. **1880** *Harper's New Mth. Mag.* 61.75 NEng, That grotesque Jack-in-the-pulpit, rising above that crumbling log, is named more to my mind. **1919** (1923) House *Wild Flowers NY* 39, Jack-in-the-pulpit . . *Arisaema triphyllum*. . . A common plant . . flowering from early spring to June. **1936** Winter *Plants NE* 20, *Arisaema*. . . Jack-in-the-pulpit. . . Nebr. is on the western limit of the range. **1952** Strausbaugh–Core *Flora WV* 204, *Jack-in-the-pulpit*. . . Corms eaten by black bears in spring. **1965–70** DARE (Qu. S1, . . *Other names . . for the jack-in-the-pulpit*) 124 Infs, **widespread**, Jack-in-the-pulpit; **CT**30, Jill-in-the-pulpit; **IL**104, Jock-in-the-pulpit; (Qu. S26c, *Wildflowers that grow in woods*) 10 Infs, **scattered**, Jack-in-the-pulpit(s); (Qu. S26a, . . *Roadside flowers*) Inf **WV**4, Jack-in-the-pulpit; (Qu. S26b, *Wildflowers that grow in water or wet places*) Infs **CT**31, **NJ**48, **VA**11, Jack-in-the-pulpit. [DARE Ed: Some of these Infs may refer instead to other senses below.] **1975** Duncan–Foote *Wildflowers SE* 238, Jack-in-the-pulpit . . *Arisaema triphyllum*. . . Flowers . . sessile on the fleshy axis (the spadix or "Jack"). . . The spathe (the "pulpit") with a tube and a hood which arches over the spadix.

2 Any of several other plants; see below.

a =**wild calla.** Cf **false jack-in-the-pulpit**

1869 Fuller *Uncle John* 36, Little *bluets*, great broadleaf *trilliums* and *waterarum* and the jack-in-the-pulpit we called it then).

b =**fennel-flower.**

1896 *Jrl. Amer. Folkl.* 9.180 cMA, Nigella Damascena. . . Jack-in-the-pulpit.

c A **trillium** such as *Trillium recurvatum.*

1897 *Jrl. Amer. Folkl.* 10.145 cIL, Trillium recurvatum. . . Jack-in-the-pulpit. **1967–68** DARE [(Qu. S1, . . *Jack-in-the-pulpit*) Inf **IL**16, Trillium;] (Qu. S2, . . *The flower that comes up in the woods early in spring, with three white petals that turn pink as the flower grows older*) Inf **NY**84, Jack-in-the-pulpit.

d A **Turk's-cap lily** (here: *Lilium superbum*).

1898 *Jrl. Amer. Folkl.* 11.281 cPA, Lilium superbum . . Jack-in-the-pulpit.

e =**pitcher plant.**

1941 Writers' Program *Guide SC* 326 eGA, On closer inspection the gold turns to a sickly green as the apparent lily is found to be a fly catcher, pitcher plant, side-saddle flower, or jack-in-the-pulpit—all local names for the *Sarracenia flava*. **1966–70** DARE (Qu. S1, . . *Jack-in-the-pulpit*) Infs **FL**16, **NC**3, Jack-in-the-pulpit or pitcher plant; [**AL**15, **GA**35, **NC**41, **PA**245, Pitcher plant].

f =**California bee plant.**

1934 (1943) *W2*, Jack-in-the-pulpit. . . A figwort (*Scrophularia californica*) of western N[orth] A[merica] with dull-red flowers.

g A **calla lily** (*Zanthedeschia* spp).

1966–68 DARE (Qu. S1) Inf **CA**70, Jack-in-the-pulpit—species of calla lily; **FL**11, Jack-in-the-pulpit, calla lily.

h =**shooting star.**

1967–69 DARE (Qu. S1, . . *Jack-in-the-pulpit*) Inf **AK**1, Jack-in-the-pulpit—white with pink, grows in shady places; **CA**7, Jack-in-the-pulpit—in mountains, very small; [**CA**126, Johnny jumpers, shooting star].

i A **violet** such as *Viola nuttallii.* Cf **johnny-jump-up 1**

1966–67 DARE [(Qu. S1, . . *Jack-in-the-pulpit*) Inf **WA**30, Same as yellow violet—johnny-jump-up;] (Qu. S3, *A flower like a large violet with a yellow center and small ragged leaves—it comes up early in spring on open, stony hilltops*) Infs **MO**1, **WA**30, Jack-in-the-pulpit.

j Appar a **flag** n[1].

1968 DARE (Qu. S24, *A wild flower that grows in swamps and marshes and looks like a small blue iris*) Inf **NY**83, Jack-in-pulpit [sic].

Jack-in-trousers n

A **wild columbine** (here: *Aquilegia canadensis*).

1896 *Jrl. Amer. Folkl.* 9.179 ceMA, Aquilegia Canadensis. . . Jack-in-trousers. . . Children's name. **1951** Teale *North with Spring* 170 NC, The white Dutchman's breeches and the red columbine—the Jack-in-trousers—these, each in turn, attracted our attention.

jackjaw See **jackdaw 1**

jack jump(er) See **jumper 7c**

Jack-jump-up n Cf **johnny-jump-up**

A **jack-in-the-pulpit 1.**

1967 DARE (Qu. S1, . . *Jack-in-the-pulpit*) Inf **MI**67, Jack-jump-up.

jackknife n

1 also *jackknife throw*: See quot. Cf **mumblety-peg**

1965–70 DARE (Qu. EE5, *Games where you try to make a jackknife stick in the ground*) 62 Infs, **chiefly NEast, N Cent, Mid and S Atl**, Jackknife; **MN**28, Jackknife throw.

2 also *jackknife jump*: A handspring.

1965–68 DARE (Qu. EE9b, *If children jump forward, land on the hands, and turn over*) Inf **FL**18, Jackknife; **PA**130, Jackknife jump.

‡3 See quot.

1968 DARE (Qu. EE32, *A homemade merry-go-round*) Inf **PA**163, Jackknife.

jackknife v, hence vbl n *jackknifing* [*jackknife* to double up like a *jackknife*]

1 See quots. Cf **crowhop v 2, fold up 1**

1929 *AmSp* 5.65 NE [Cattle country talk], "Jack-knifing" is a clipping together of the front and rear legs sometimes as part of a "straight buck." **1954** *Julian Apple Day* [21] csCA, Around the big pole corral they went, with that cayuse [=horse] doin' everything in the book, sunfishin', jack-knifin', and just plain hard stiff-legged buckin'.

2 See quot. Cf **coon v 2**

1966 DARE (Qu. EE36, *To climb the trunk of a tree by holding on with your legs while you pull yourself up with your hands*) Inf **MI**34, Jackknifing.

jackknife carpenter n Cf **jackleg adj 1**

An incompetent carpenter.

1950 *Western Folkl.* 9.121 nwOR [Sawmill workers' speech], Jackknife carpenter. An inept or inefficient millwright. **1959** *VT Hist.* 27.144, Jack-knife carpenter. . . A carpenter without much skill. Occasional.

jackknife clam n [From the long, narrow shape]

1 A **razor clam** (here: *Tagelus californianus*).

1920 CA Fish & Game Comm. *Fish Bulletin* 4.22, The firmer flats of relatively undisturbed fine, dark, muddy sand are also the home of an interesting small species of razor clam, *Tagelus*, the jackknife clam. **1949** Palmer *Nat. Hist.* 358, California Razor Clam, Jackknife Clam. Tagelus californianus. . . Favored food of ducks and eaten by human beings. **1981** Rehder *Audubon Field Guide Seashells* 789, *Californian Tagelus*. . . This species is known as the California Jackknife Clam on the Pacific Coast.

2 A **razor clam** of the family Solenidae, usu of the genus *Ensis* or *Solen.*

1920 CA Fish & Game Comm. *Fish Bulletin* 4.50, *Solen sicarius*. . . Jackknife clam. . . A species of sheltered bays, . . it is said to form burrows somewhat similar to *Tagelus*. **1954** Abbott *Amer. Seashells* 443, Genus *Ensis*. . . The Jackknife Clams closely resemble *Solen*. **1981** Rehder *Audubon Field Guide Seashells* 762, *Atlantic Jackknife Clam (Ensis directus)*. . . Common on tidal flats in New England, . . they make good eating and are frequently sold in local markets. The related Minor Jackknife Clam (*E. minor*) is smaller. . . Green Jackknife Clam (*Solen viridis*). . . Rhode Island to Florida and Louisiana. Ibid 763, *Rosy Jackknife Clam (Solen rosaceus)*. . . Santa Barbara, California to central Mexico.

jackknife face n Cf **hatchet B3a**

[1844 Stephens *High Life in NY* 2.57 **CT**, A sneaking critter with a face like a jack-knife.] **1968** *DARE* (Qu. X29) Inf **NY96**, Jackknife face—thin and pointed.

jackknife gull n

The **least tern**.

1889 *Century Dict.* 3211 **NEng**, *Jack-knife gull,* the least tern, *Sterna antillarum.* **1956** MA Audubon Soc. *Bulletin* 40.22 **MA**, *Least Tern. . . Jack-knife Gull* (. . . From its small size.)

jackknife jump See **jackknife** n 2

jackknife throw See **jackknife** n 1

jackknifing See **jackknife** v

jack lamp n Also *jack lantern*

=**jacklight** n.

1884 Knight *New Mech. Dict.* 510, *Jack Lamp. . .* One for still-hunting, *weequashing* or fire-fishing, and general camp use. It is sometimes carried on the hat or helmet, but is preferably supported by standard from the belt. . . It burns kerosene without a chimney. **1888** *Harper's New Mth. Mag.* 77.510 **wMN**, Occasionally a caribou is killed at night by the light of a jack-lamp. **1896** *DN* 1.419 **eNY**, *Jack light:* same as *jack lantern . . ,* used in hunting.

jack lantern n

1 See **jack lamp.**

2 A fool. [Prob because his head is hollow like a *jack-o'-lantern*] Cf **pumpkin head**

1896 *DN* 1.419 **wNY**, *Jack lantern. . .* A dull, stupid fellow.

jack-lantern v Cf **jack lamp**

=**jacklight** v.

1967 *DARE* (Qu. P35b, *Illegal methods of shooting deer;* not asked in early QRs) Inf **IA4**, Jack-lantern 'em. Shine a light at deer at night, deer's eyes reflect light and provide a target.

jackleg adj

1 also *jack;* usu of a member of an occupational group: Inept, untrained, unprofessional; dishonest; hence n *jack(leg)* an inexpert, incompetent, or disreputable professional or worker. **chiefly Sth, S Midl** See Map

1850 *Amer. Whig Rev.* 9.465 **TX**, A party of some twenty of the most notorious rode up, headed by what is there known as a "jack-leg" lawyer, who acted as leader and speaker for the party. **1853** Hammett *Stray Yankee in TX* 284, In the Texan vocabulary, all men who have a mere inkling of any trade or profession, are called "jack-legs." *Ibid,* You will hear of "jack-leg" lawyers, "jack-leg" preachers, and "jack-leg" doctors. These men were "jack-leg" carpenters. **1894** Twain *Pudd'nhead Wilson* 311, He has been told many a time how the born-and-trained novelist works; won't he let me round and complete his knowledge by telling him how the jack-leg does it? **1899** (1912) Green *VA Folk-Speech* 242, *Jack-leg. . .* Used to signify a poor specimen in any trade or profession: "a jack-leg carpenter;" "a jack-leg doctor." **1908** *DN* 3.323 **eAL, wGA**, *Jack-leg. . .* A bungling workman, a cheat. **1915** *DN* 4.184 **swVA**, *Jack-leg. . .* (One) poor in quality; as, a *jackleg* lawyer. **1950** in 1977 Randolph *Pissing in the Snow* 88 **nwAR**, That young jackleg [=a lawyer] ain't no good! **c1960** Wilson Coll. **csKY**, *Jackleg. . .* A sorry or weak professional. Used also as an adj. **1965** Brown *Manchild* 24 **NYC** [Black], Mrs. Rogers . . was also a jackleg preacher. **1965–70** *DARE* (Qu. CC10, . . *An unprofessional, part-time lay preacher*) 116 Infs, **chiefly Sth, S Midl**, Jackleg (preacher); **OR1A**, Jack preacher; (Qu. HH44, *Joking or uncomplimentary names for lawyers*) 42 Infs, **chiefly Sth, S Midl**, Jackleg (lawyer); (Qu. BB53b, . . *A doctor who is not very capable or doesn't have a very good reputation*) 26 Infs, **chiefly Sth, S Midl**, Jackleg (doctor); (Qu. V10c, . . *Joking names for a constable*) Inf **NC33**, Jackleg; [(Qu. Z12, *Nicknames and joking words meaning 'a small child': "He's a healthy little _____."*) Inf **SC34**, Booger [laughter]; jackleg; cooter;] (Qu. HH1) Inf **LA32**, Jackleg—someone who doesn't do anything well but can do a lot of little things; (Qu. HH15, *A very inexperienced person, one who is just learning how to do a new thing*) Inf **FL48**, Jackleg; (Qu. HH21, *A very awkward, clumsy person*) Infs **FL22, IL11, NC40, 51, 69, SC24, 31, TX65**, Jackleg; (Qu. HH43b, *The assistant to the top person in charge of a group of workmen*) Inf **GA84**, Straw boss—he is a jackleg boss. **1967–69** *DARE* FW Addit **nwSC**, Jackleg—one who knows just enough to

impress a greenhorn, but has a long way to go toward becoming an expert himself; **KY60**, Jackleg—a mechanic who does poor work. **1986** Pederson *LAGS Concordance* **Gulf Region** *(Untrained; part-time)* 2 infs, (Old) jack carpenter; 1 inf, A jack—preacher or anyone; not quite professional; 1 inf, Jack—not too good; mostly just beginning; 1 inf, He's a jack. [*Jackleg* in reference to carpenters, lawyers, preachers, teachers, etc, is found throughout the region.]

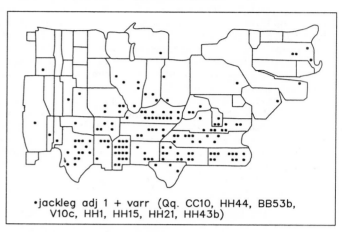

•jackleg adj 1 + varr (Qq. CC10, HH44, BB53b, V10c, HH1, HH15, HH21, HH43b)

2 By ext: shoddy, makeshift.

1942 *Daily Progress* (Charlottesville VA) 26 Nov 14/6, I write news, editorials, advertisements . . repair presses and linotype (jackleg repairing), splice belts. **1966–70** *DARE* (Qu. KK63, *To do a clumsy or hurried job of repairing something*) Infs **SC5, VA50**, (Did a) jackleg job; (Qu. N37, *Joking names for a branch railroad that is not very important or gives poor service*) Inf **MO35**, Jackleg road.

jackleg n See **jackleg** adj 1

jackleg adv [**jackleg** adj]

1967 *DARE* (Qu. KK48, *When you work something out as you go, without having a plan or pattern to follow: "I didn't have anything to go by, so I just did it _____."*) Inf **TX33**, Jackleg.

jack-legged adj

1 =**jackleg** adj **1.**

1839 U.S. Congress *Congressional Globe* (App.) 19 Jan 127, That party contains no *jack-legged pettifogging lawyers.* **1870** Nowland *Early Indianapolis* 37 **IN** (as of 1825), About that time there was a kind of "Jack-legged lawyer" (as they were then called) here. **1892** *Congressional Record* 27 May 4777 **WV**, He goes away, and a jack-legged officer could do nothing except to mark him as a deserter. **1894** Twain *Tom Sawyer Abroad* 125 **MO**, Jim was a kind of jack-legged tailor. **1937** in 1972 *Amer. Slave* 250 **SC**, Asked about marriages among the slaves, he said the ceremony was performed by some "jack-legged" colored preacher who pronounced a few words and said they were man and wife. **1967–69** *DARE* (Qu. CC10, . . *An unprofessional, part-time lay preacher*) Infs **AR52, KY10**, Jack-legged preacher. **1986** Pederson *LAGS Concordance*, 15 infs, **Gulf Region**, Jacklegged (carpenter, lawyer, preacher, teacher).

‡2 See quot. Cf **knee-jacked**

1967 *DARE* (Qu. X37, . . *Words . . to describe people's legs if they're noticeably bent, or uneven, or not right*) Inf **TX3**, Jack-legged.

jacklegging vbl n [**jackleg** adj]

Working inexpertly; fiddling.

1918 Lincoln *Shavings* 133 **Cape Cod MA**, He took the refractory timepiece in his arms and, after an hour of what he called "putterin' and jackleggin'," hung it up again.

jacklight n Also sp *jacklite* [**jack** n[1] **5a**] Cf **fire jack, jack lamp**

Orig a light carried in a cresset; now any powerful, portable light, esp one used for hunting or fishing by night.

1842 Hawes *Sporting Scenes* 1.228 **seNY**, A stranger . . presented in the glare of the jack-light an object of fear and admiration. **1883** *Advance* (Chicago IL) 30 Aug 579 **neNY**, Once after that in a jack-light hunt. **1896** *DN* 1.419 **eNY**, *Jack light.* **1920** *DN* 5.82 **WA**, It shall be unlawful to hunt deer with a jacklite . . or any other form of artificial light. **1931** Faulkner *Sanctuary* 30 **MS**, It was a long, low roadster, with a jacklight. **c1937** in 1970 Yetman *Voices* 314 **AL** (as of 1850s) [Black], Dey had jacklights in de cotton patch for us to see by. De lights was made on a forked stick and moved from place to place whilst we picked. **1949** *Pacific Discovery* Jan/Feb 11, We never saw them during the day and had to collect specimens at night with a jack-light. **1967** *Natl. Geogr. Mag.* Jan 144 **FL**, "Nearly all poaching used to be done at night with a jacklight and rifle," Ross said, "or by locating dens and dragging the alligator out with a long pole with a hook at the end." **1975** Gould *ME Lingo* 145, Any many-celled flashlight is called a "jacklight" in Maine, whether used for *jacking* or not. **1994** Guterson *Snow Falling* 212 **nwWA**, From a distance a gill net appeared as a line of cork with the stern of the boat at one end and a warning jacklight at the other.

jacklight v, hence vbl n *jacklighting,* n *jacklighter* **scattered, but chiefly NEast** See Map Cf **jack** v 1, **lamp-lighting, light** v[1]
To hunt or fish with a **jacklight** n.

   1883 *Advance* (Chicago IL) 30 Aug 579 **neNY**, By night, it is called "jacklighting" the deer. **1895** *Outing* 26.63, Dark banks so suggestive of jacklighting experiences. **1942** U.S. Natl. Park Serv. *Fading Trails* 30, We have come a long way since the days of market hunting, . . of legal jack lighting, and of using snares and many-barreled guns. **1959** *Washington Post & Times Herald* (DC) 6 Jan sec A 16/5 **eWV**, We were riding the back roads late one night . . trying to look like jacklighters and hoping to spot another car doing the same. **1965–70** *DARE* (Qu. P35b, *Illegal methods of shooting deer;* not asked in early QRs) 42 Infs, **scattered, but chiefly NEast**, Jacklighting; **NY**207, Jacklighting them; **NY**122, **RI**12, Jacklight; **IL**27, Jacklight—shine a light on a deer and then kill it; **NJ**31, Jacklight—still watch, go out in field and sit (out of season); **NY**132, Jacklight—shine a strong flashlight or headlight in their eyes; **TX**5, Jacklight—hunt at night with a light; **NJ**16, Jacklighter. **1983** Glimm *Flatlanders* 140 **cnPA**, One time he an' his drunken gang jacklighted a deer, drug it into the house, an' gutted an' butchered it on the kitchen table. **1983** *Isthmus* (Madison WI) 7 Oct 16 **NY**, To rationalize this kind of behavior [=the snagging of salmon] . . makes as much sense as proposing the jacklighting of deer in areas where hunters don't expect to kill as many as natural density would allow. **1993** *DARE* File **Upstate NY**, Jacklighting is the only term [for *shining*] I recall. [Inf 50 years old, Ulster County]

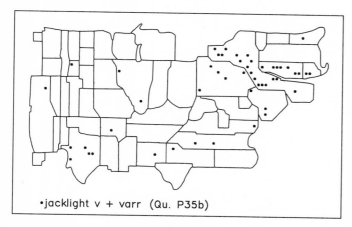

•jacklight v + varr (Qu. P35b)

jack line n [Perh var of **checkline 2**]
   1968 *DARE* (Qu. L51, *The leathers or ropes that a driver holds to guide a horse*) Inf **PA**158, Two horses—jack line.

jacklite See **jacklight** n

jack mackerel n
1 =**bluefish 1.**
   1882 Eggleston *Wreck Red Bird* 18 **eSC**, They call them blue fish up North, I believe, but we call them skip-jacks or jack mackerel.
2 A food fish (*Trachurus symmetricus*) of the California coast. Also called **horse mackerel 3, Spanish mackerel, saurel**
   1953 Roedel *Common Fishes CA* 82, *Pacific Jack Mackerel. Trachurus symmetricus. . .* Fished chiefly in Southern California and landed for the most part at Los Angeles. **1955** Zim–Shoemaker *Fishes* 95, Pacific jack mackerel is an important commercial fish in southern California. **1960** Amer. Fisheries Soc. *List Fishes* 30, Jack mackerel. P[acific]. *Trachurus symmetricus*.

jack-ma-lantern See **jack-o'-lantern 1**
Jack Mariddle n Cf **John Mariggle 1**
=**ten-pounder.**
   1882 U.S. Natl. Museum *Proc.* 5.584 **SC**, *Elops saurus. . . Jack Mariddle.* Common in the harbor, but not eaten, the flesh is said to be tasteless. **1960** Amer. Fisheries Soc. *List Fishes* 60, Jack-ma-riddle— see ladyfish. **1973** Knight *Cook's Fish Guide* 383, Jack-ma-riddle—Ladyfish.

Jack-married-a-widow n Also *Jack-marry-the-widow* [See quot 1955] Cf **Dick-married-a-widow**
=**chuck-will's-widow.**
   1955 *Oriole* 20.1.9 **GA**, *Chuck-wills-widow.*—All names are sonic unless otherwise explained. . . *Jack-married-a-widow.* **1966** *DARE* (Qu. Q3, . . *Birds that come out only after dark*) Inf **GA**11, Jack-marry-the-widow.

jack-mer-lant'en, jack-m'lantern See **jack-o'-lantern 1**
jack Mormon n, freq cap Also *Jack* **esp West**

1 A non-Mormon with Mormon sympathies; hence n *jack Mormonism.* **derog, old-fash**
   1845 *Niles' Natl. Reg.* 4 Oct 70/1, *Jack Mormon* is the appellation by which the anti-Mormons designate every man that is suspected of taking sides with the Mormons against their lawless measures. **1845** *Quincy* (Ill.) *Whig* 30 Oct. 2/1 *(DA)*, Jack Mormons, and sympathizers abroad may croak and groan over the poor Mormons to their heart's content, but their sympathies will not shield the scoundrels collected at Nauvoo from the just indignation of the people of Illinois. *Ibid* 25 Nov. 2/1 *(DA)*, The Mormons and Jacks, will doubtless create the impression that the contrary is the case. **1870** J.H. Beadle *Life in Utah* 197 *(DA)*, From 1850 to 1862, 'jack-Mormonism' ruled at Washington. **1886** *Congressional Record* 7 Jan 514 **CO**, I will bear testimony to their virtues and I will condemn their vice. I am not to be deterred because somebody says "You must be a Jack Mormon." **1890** *Ibid* 2 Apr 2941 **ID**, In our country you have a *genus homo* called "Jack-Mormon," . . [a] class of individuals who do not belong to the Mormon church, . . yet who are ever found doing the bidding of Mormon priests. **1900** *Ibid* 24 Jan 1129 **IN**, A "Jack-Mormon" county attorney overruling the supreme court of Utah. **1947** Morgan *Great Salt Lake* 401, During the turbulent months in 1846 before the Saints finally evacuated Illinois, "Jack Mormon" was a term opprobriously applied by the anti-Mormons to a gentile exhibiting Mormon sympathies. But in the new vocabulary it describes a nonpracticing member of the church.

2 An apostate Mormon. *often derog*
   1944 (1967) McNichols *Crazy Weather* 113 **SW**, Strange to say, . . although he swore that his life was devoted to a perpetual feud against all Mormons, he ran away every time one of them confronted him. The man who ran him out of Needles said that this was because the trapper was a Jack-Mormon, an apostate who had come to hate his own kind but couldn't make himself raise a hand against one of them. **1947** *Time* 21 July 21, The number of backsliding "jack-Mormons" is increasing. **1947** [see **1** above]. **1950** *PADS* 14.40 **SC**, *Jack Mormon. . .* A person born a Mormon but who does not live up to the rules of the church, especially as regards drinking, smoking, etc. **1955** in 1965 *DARE* File **cnUT**, Jack Mormon—a person born into the L.D.S. [=Latter Day Saints] church but not following its tenets. **1965–70** *DARE* (Qu. CC7, . . *A person who goes to church very seldom or not at all*) 10 Infs, **West, HI**, Jack Mormon; [(Qu. CC4, . . *Nicknames . . for various religions or religious groups*) Inf **CA**169, Jack Mormon]. **1966** Barnes–Jensen *Dict. UT Slang* 26, *Jack Mormon* . . a member of the Mormon Church who only half heartedly adheres to it, and who rarely attends its services. One never hears it applied to a mere Mormon sympathizer . . , although it once had that meaning. **1969** O'Connor *Horse & Buggy West* 261 **AZ** (as of early 20th cent), Even when I was growing up some of the younger Mormons did not adhere strictly to the Mormon law. They smoked, drank hard liquor, and gambled. These were known as Jack Mormons.

jack mosquito n [Cf Nfld, Engl dial *jacky longlegs* crane fly] Cf **blind mosquito**
Appar a **crane fly.**
   1892 *KS Univ. Qrly.* 1.97 **KS**, *Jack mosquito,* a large insect of the mosquito family, three times the size of the pestiferous kind; this one does not bite.

jack-muh-lantum, jack mulatta See **jack-o'-lantern 1**

jack mule See **jack** n[1] 20

jacko n Also *jacko bush*

A **marsh elder 1** (here: *Iva frutescens*).

    1916 *Torreya* 16.240, *Iva frutescens*. . . Jacko bush, Cat I[slan]d, S.C.; jacko, Waccamaw Plantation and Kinloch Club, S.C.

jack oak n

Any of var **oaks,** as:

a =**shingle oak.**

    1812 Michaux *Histoire des Arbres* 2.78, A l'ouest de ces montagnes [=Alleghany Mts] . . elle est désignée . . *Jack oak, Black Jack oak,* et quelquefois . . *Laurel oak.* [=West of these mountains it is called . . *Jack oak, Black Jack oak,* and sometimes *Laurel oak.*] **1847** Wood *Class-Book* 495, Shingle Oak. . . In Indiana it is called *Jack Oak.* **1860** Curtis *Cat. Plants NC* 36, Q[uercus] imbricaria. . . is more common in the Western States, as far north as Illinois, and is there known by the names of *Jack Oak* . . and *Shingle Oak.* **1901** Lounsberry *S. Wild Flowers* 128, *Shingle Oak.* . . Through its western range it is called Jack oak or black Jack although mostly we associate these names with Quercus Marylandica. **1960** Vines *Trees SW* 179, Jack Oak. . . is considered valuable as a shade tree in the North because of its dense, lustrous, dark green foliage. **1967–69** *DARE* (Qu. T10, . . *Kinds of oak trees*) Infs **IN**17, 26, 35, 40, **IA**11, **OH**41, 89, Jack oak. [*DARE* Ed: Some of these Infs may refer instead to other senses below.]

b A **blackjack oak** (here: *Quercus marilandica*).

    1816 in 1915 *MD Hist. Mag.* 10.266 sePA, Jack Oaks and other Scrub Wood. **1884** Sargent *Forests of N. Amer.* 150, Q[uercus] Marylandica. . . *Jack Oak.* . . Dry, barren uplands, or often on heavy clay soils. **1900** (1927) Keeler *Our Native Trees* 372, Since very early times Jack has, in certain ways, been used as a word of opprobrium. . . What more likely, than that the first settlers of this country finding this worthless oak [=*Quercus marilandica*] upon worthless land should name it in opprobrium the Jack Oak. **1906** *DN* 3.142 nwAR, *Jack oak.* . . Black oak, black jack oak. **1950** Moore *Trees AR* 55, Blackjack Oak (*Quercus marilandica* . .) Local Names: Jack . . Oak. . . Probably the poorest of all Arkansas oaks. . . Most common on dry, stony exposed ridges and slopes of the mountainous sections; considered an indicator of dry or poor soil. **1965–68** *DARE* (Qu. T10, . . *Kinds of oak trees*) Infs **NC**1, 81, **OK**1, 7, 52, Jack oak. **1979** Little *Checklist U.S. Trees* 236, *Quercus marilandica.* . . *Other common names* . . jack oak.

c =**blue oak 2.**

    1910 Jepson *Silva CA* 216, Blue Oak has many common names. . . One of the ranchmen's names is Jack Oak.

d An oak *(Quercus ellipsoidalis)* native chiefly to the Upper Midwest and north central US. Also called **black oak, black-jack ~, pin ~, yellow ~**

    1938 Van Dersal *Native Woody Plants* 215, *Quercus ellipsoidalis.* . . *Jack Oak.* . . A small to large shrub or small to large tree; often occurs on clay soils. **1938** Brown *Trees NE U.S.* 225, *Jack Oak.* . . ranges from northwestern Ohio and central Michigan westward to southeastern Minnesota and eastern Iowa. **1951** Martin *Amer. Wildlife & Plants* 309, Some of the species of oaks of particular importance to wildlife in different regions of the country are: . . Northeast: . . jack (*ellipsoidalis*), . . bur (*macrocarpa*). **1979** Little *Checklist U.S. Trees* 229, *Northern pin oak.* . . *Other common names* . . jack oak.

e A **black oak** (here: *Quercus velutina*).

    1906 [see **b** above]. **1940** Clute *Amer. Plant Names* 269, *Quercus velutina.* . . Jack oak.

jacko bush See **jacko**

Jack of the rocks n

An **alumroot 1** (here: *Heuchera rubescens*).

    1984 Niehaus *Field Guide SW & TX Wildflowers* 54, *Jack o' the rocks. Heuchera rubescens.* . . Dry rocky slopes. N. Ariz., w. Tex., R[ocky] Mts.

Jack of war n

Prob =**conquer John.**

    1935 Hurston *Mules & Men* 342 **Gulf States,** Medicine to Purge. Jack of War tea, one tablespoon to a cup of water with a pinch of soda after it is ready to drink.

jack-o'-lantern n [*OED* 1673 →]

1 often *jack-ma-lantern;* for addit varr see quots: =**will-o'-the-wisp;** in folklore, sometimes said to be a spirit that leads travelers astray; see quots. **chiefly Sth, Midl** See Map Cf **foxfire 2, mineral light, money light**

    1828 Willis *Legendary* 2.194 **CT,** It was said that she had so bewitched him by her arts . . that he could do nothing but follow her about like a Jack-o'lantern. **1859** Taliaferro *Fisher's R.* 155 **nwNC** (as of 1820s), I . . got lost—led out'n my way by a stinkin' jacker-mer-lantern. **1883** (1971) Harris *Nights with Remus* 157 **GA** [Black], Dish yer Jacky-ma-Lantun is a sho' nuff sperit. *Ibid,* 'E skeer dem Jack-me-Lantun. **1899** (1912) Green *VA Folk-Speech* 242, *Jack-m'lantern.* . . A light that goes about at night to mislead people, carrying them who follow through briars and swamps. **1922** Gonzales *Black Border* 307 **sSC, GA coasts** [Gullah glossary], *Jacky-lantu'n*—Jack-o'-lantern—will-o'-the-wisp. **1927** Adams *Congaree* 80 **cSC** [Black], A Jack-ma-lantern is a . . evil sperrit. . . It is folks wuh ain't 'lowed in heben and can't git in hell, and dey punishment is to wander in de bad places . . and dey business is enticing mens to follow 'em. **c1938** in 1970 Hyatt *Hoodoo* 1.40 seSC, Well, dat's whut yo' call a *jack mulatta* an' it'll go in jes' lak a hag would. **c1939** in 1977 *Amer. Slave Suppl. 1* 1.59 **AL,** You sho' will git los' ef yer follow er Jack-mer-Lant'en. **1945** Saxon *Gumbo Ya-Ya* 265 **sLA,** In this section of the State 'Jack o'Lanterns' . . are common and are here believed to lead to buried pirate gold. **1950** *WELS* **WI** (*A small light that seems to dance over a swamp or marsh by night*) 1 Inf, Jack-a-lite; 1 Inf, Jack-o'-lantern. **1955** Warren *Angels* 12 **KY** (as of c1850), Gonna tell you how Jack-muh-Lantum got him, got him in the swamp. **1965–70** *DARE* (Qu. CC16, *A small light that seems to dance or flicker over a marsh or swamp at night*) 76 Infs, **chiefly Sth, Midl,** Jack-o'-lantern; **VA**69, ['jæko'lænən]—had one the other week that stopped a train—think maybe someone got killed there a long time ago and it's a haint [hent]; **GA**19, **TN**15, ['jækɪˌlæntɚn]; **GA**5, **KY**6, **SC**26, ['jækəməˌlæntɚn, -ən]; **MS**1, Jack-o-my-lantern; **NC**49, ['jækəməˌladə]; **OK**13, **VA**87, ['jækməˈlæntɚn]; **IL**69, Jack-in-the-lantern; (Qu. CC17, *Imaginary . . monsters*) Inf **VA**83, ['jækəˌlænən]. **1967** Williams *Greenbones* 52 **GA** (as of c1910), His mother had told him jacky-my-lanterns lived in swamps, ghosts that had slits in their necks so they could turn themselves inside out. **1981** Harper–Presley *Okefinokee* 141 **Okefenokee GA** (as of a1951), *Jack-o-my-lantern.* . . Inman Smith spoke of seeing one . . , and it was small enough to "light" on a fence post.

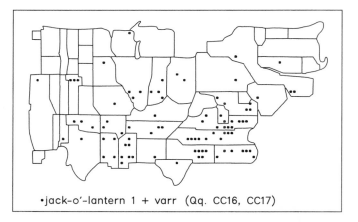

•jack-o'-lantern 1 + varr (Qq. CC16, CC17)

2 also *jack-o-my-lantern:* =**firefly 1.**

    1966–67 *DARE* (Qu. R1, . . *The small insect that flies at night and flashes a light at its tail*) Inf **AR**5, Jack-o-my-lantern; **VA**73, Jack-o'-lantern. **1968** *DARE* Tape **GA**30, You can see lights at night [in the Okefenokee swamp] . . , but I always thought it was lightnin' bugs—jack-o'-lanterns ['jækəˌlænɚnz]—you know, they'll ball up sometime, git three or four in a ball, make a big light.

3 also *jack, jack-o'-lantern mushroom:* An orange to yellowish-orange mushroom *(Omphalotus illudens).* [See quot 1971] Also called **false chanterelle 2** Cf **fox fire 1a**

    1908 Hard *Mushroom Edible* 91, *Clitocybe illudens.* . . It will be interesting . . to show its phosphorescence. . . by putting it in a dark room. . . It is frequently called "Jack-'o-lantern." **1943** Fernald–Kinsey *Edible Wild Plants E. N. Amer.* 378, Avoid the beautiful saffron-yellow or yellowish-orange large mushroom, often occurring in late summer and autumn. . . This very handsome species is *Jack-o'-lantern, Clitocybe illudens.* **1950** *WELS* (*A large round mushroom*) 1 Inf, **cWI,** Jack-o'-lantern—brightly colored. **1966–70** *DARE* (Qu. S18, *A kind of mushroom that grows like a globe*) 10 Infs, **esp sIL,** Jack-o'-lantern. **1971**

Living Museum 33.38 **IL,** When a fresh, young specimen is taken into a dark place, its gills give off an eerie, greenish glow, not noticeable in the light. This unusual phosphorescence has given the jack-o-lantern mushroom its common name. **1981** Lincoff *Audubon Field Guide Mushrooms* 788, Also called the "False Chanterelle." . . the eastern Jack is more properly called *O[mphalotus] illudens.* . . When this species is gathered fresh and taken into a dark room, the gills give off an eerie green glow. **1987** McKnight–McKnight *Mushrooms* 178, Jack O'Lantern.

jack-o'-lantern mushroom See **jack-o'-lantern 3**

jack-o-my-lantern See **jack-o'-lantern 1, 2**

jack out See **jack** v 4

Jack-over-the-ground n
  =**ground ivy 1.**
    1892 *Jrl. Amer. Folkl.* 5.102 **eMA,** *Nepeta Glechoma.* . . Jack-over-the-ground.

jack owly n
  =**old-squaw.**
    1936 Roberts *MN Birds* 1.272, Old-Squaw. . . Other names . . "Jack Owly" (Chippewa Indian name). **1982** Elman *Hunter's Field Guide* 232, Oldsquaw. . . Common & Regional Names . . jack-owly, old-wife [etc].

jack perch n Cf **jack** n¹ 24a
  A **yellow perch** (here: *Perca flavescens*).
    1849 Howitt *Our Cousins in OH* 221, We fish in the Miami. . . I have caught plenty of great Jack perch myself. [*DARE* Ed: This may be a different fish, perh =**walleye.**] **1949** Caine *N. Amer. Sport Fish* 112, *Colloquial Names* [of *Perca flavescens*] . . Jack Perch. **1972** Sparano *Outdoors Encycl.* 363, *Yellow Perch. Common Names* . . jack perch. . . Predominately a fish of lakes large and small, though it is also found in rivers.

jack pie See **jack** n¹ 11

jack pike n Cf **jack** n¹ 24a(1)
  Either of two related fishes: **muskellunge 1** or **northern pike 1** (here: *Esox lucius*).
    1818 *Amer. Monthly Mag. & Crit. Rev.* 3.447, Erox [sic] vittatus. . . Jack pike. **1819** Thomas *Travels W. Country* 212 **IN,** The *Jack pike* or *pickerel* is an excellent fish, and weighs from six to twenty pounds. **1949** *Esquire* Mar 88 **NC,** A four-pound jack pike struck his lure. **1949** Caine *N. Amer. Sport Fish* 98, Muskellunge. . . *Colloquial Names* . . Jack Pike. **1949** Palmer *Nat. Hist.* 444, *Pike, Jack Pike. Esox lucius.* **1967** *DARE* (Qu. P1, . . *Kinds of freshwater fish . . caught around here . . good to eat*) Inf **AR**51, Jack, sometimes jack pike or jack fish.

jack pine n [*jack* often in ref to something smaller than the norm]

1 A **pine** (here: *Pinus banksiana*) native chiefly to the Great Lakes and northern New England areas, but also introduced outside of its natural range. Also called **blackjack pine 1, black pine 1b, cypress 2b, gray pine a, juniper 2f, Labrador pine, paperwood pine, prince's pine, rock pine, scrub pine, shore pine, unlucky tree**
    1883 Shields *Hunting* 285 **neMI,** This [country] is now grown up with scattering dwarf-pines, or as the settlers call them, "jack-pines." **1888** in 1942 Beck *Songs MI Lumberjacks* 186 **MI,** We are swamping out the jack pines,/ And I'll tell you it's no fun. **1894** *Jrl. Amer. Folkl.* 7.100 **MI, MN,** *Pinus Banksiana* . . jack-pine. **1908** Rogers *Tree Book* 22, "Jack pines," used locally for ties and timbers, but not in the regular lumber trade, are small or medium-sized trees: *P[inus] rigida, P. Virginiana* and *P. divaricata* in the East and North; *P. contorta,* var. *Murrayana,* one in the West. *Ibid* 51 **MI,** The Grey or Scrub Pine (*P. divaricata* [=*P. banksiana*] . .) . . dips down to the southern point of the lake, . . clothing the barren stretches of the lower peninsula . . known as the "Jack Pine Plains." **1940** Gates *Flora KS* 106, Of the several conifers planted, especially in eastern Kansas, occasional local escapes have been found of *Pinus banksiana* . . , Jack-pine. **1966–70** *DARE* (Qu. T17, . . *Kinds of pine trees; not asked in early QRs*) 69 Infs, **chiefly Gt Lakes, nNEng,** Jack pine; (Qu. T15, . . *Kinds of swamp trees*) Infs **IL**82, **MI**36, Jack pine; (Qu. T16, . . *Kinds of trees . . 'special'*) Inf **MI**104, Jack pine—it grows where nothing else will. **1966** *DARE* Tape **MI**26, There's more of Coney Island than the jack pine around the bridge, but . . I think the thing that will save the peninsula is . . what I love about it. **1979** Little *Checklist U.S. Trees* 190, Jack

pine. . . *Range* . . Maine . . w[est] to . . Minn., Wis., extreme nw. Ind., Mich., . . n. N.Y., and N.H. Also extinct in n. Vt. and n. Ill.
2 Any of var other **pines,** as: See below. Note: In some of the quots below it is not possible to determine the precise subsense.
  a =**Jersey pine.**
    1908 [see **1** above]. **1932** *Sun* (Baltimore MD) 26 Apr 22/5 **cnMD** (*Hench Coll.*), The only damage done consisted of the loss of some jack pine on the area burned over. **1966–68** *DARE* (Qu. T17, . . *Kinds of pine trees; not asked in early QRs*) Infs **AL**4, **SC**4, Jack pine; **MD**29, Jack pine—same as nigger pine; **NC**37, Jack or nigger pine.
  b A **pitch pine** (here: *Pinus rigida*).
    1908 [see **1** above]. **1966–70** *DARE* (Qu. T17, . . *Kinds of pine trees; not asked in early QRs*) 35 Infs, **chiefly Appalachians,** Jack pine; **MA**15, Jack pine—same as yellow; **MA**74, Jack pine—hard splintery kind.
  c =**lodgepole pine.**
    1908 [see **1** above]. **1966–67** *DARE* (Qu. T17, . . *Kinds of pine trees; not asked in early QRs*) Infs **CO**3, 37, 47, **ID**4, 5, **MT**1, 2, 3, **WY**4, Jack pine. **1976** Maclean *River Runs Through* 139 **wMT** (as of 1919), In a thicket on top of a jack pine, I found the skeleton of a deer. **1991** *DARE* File **cOR,** In the area southwest of Bend, the terms *jack pine, lodgepole pine,* and *black pine* were all used of *Pinus contorta.* This fairly scrubby tree was used for corral fences, firewood, and pulp.
  d =**ponderosa pine.** Cf **blackjack pine 2**
    1910 Jepson *Silva CA* 79, The bark of *Pinus ponderosa* is exceedingly variable. . . The quality of the wood varies also in different individuals and in the view of many woodsmen this difference corresponds to differences in the bark, all of which indicates the significance of their local names, "Black Pine," "Bull Pine," "Jack Pine," and "Yellow Pine." [**1929** Pool *Hdbk. NE Trees* 25, *Pinus ponderosa.* . . Younger trees, up to 2 feet in diameter, are often unlike older ones in having dark reddish-brown or blackish, narrowly furrowed bark, the "black jack" of lumbermen.] **1966–69** *DARE* (Qu. T17, . . *Kinds of pine trees;* not asked in early QRs) 22 Infs, **chiefly Pacific, Black Hills SD,** Jack pine; **CA**130, Jack pine—same as bull pine. **1967** Gilkey–Dennis *Hdbk. NW Plants* 29, *Pinus ponderosa.* . . Jack pine. . . Cascades, sometimes along high coast ranges, and scattered through Willamette Valley.

jack-pine bird n Also *jack-pine warbler*
  Kirtland's warbler (*Dendroica kirtlandi*).
    1917 (1923) *Birds Amer.* 3.146, Kirtland's Warbler. . . *Other Names.* Jack-pine Warbler; Jack-pine Bird. *Ibid* 147, In Michigan. . . The bird is a frequenter of high, sandy jack-pine plains; makes its home in jack-pine and scrub oak. . . It is called by the natives Jack-pine Bird. **1955** Forbush–May *Birds* 438, Jack-pine Warbler. . . In Michigan. . it is very locally distributed in those counties . . grown up to the jack pine, *Pinus banksiana.*

jackpine savage n Also *jackpine farmer* [**jack pine**] esp **MN, WI** *joc* or *derog* Cf **cedar savage 2**
  A woods-dweller, esp one thought to be ignorant or uncultivated.
    1957 *WELS Suppl.* **nwWI,** "Jack pine savage." We picked it up from a bartender at Gordon, Wisconsin. He spoke of the residents who spent the entire year up north as such. Possibly he learned it in Minnesota. We have heard it in the state many times since. **1968** *DARE* (Qu. HH1, *Names and nicknames for a rustic or countrified person*) Inf **OH**72, Jackpine savage; **MN**36, Jackpine savage—the shiftless people up north. **1968** Adams *Western Words* 163, *Jack-pine savage*—A cowboy's name for a man from the timber country. **1971** Wood *Vocab. Change* 38, A *rustic.* . . [A] few instances of *jackpine savage* occur east of the Mississippi [in TN and AL]. **1973** Allen *LAUM* 1.349 **Upper MW** (as of c1950), In the cutover timberland of northern Minnesota appear *cedar savage* and *jackpine farmer* as derogatory epithets [for a rustic]. *Ibid* 350, Jackpine savage [7 infs, **MN**]. *Ibid* 351, Jackpine farmer [2 infs, **MN;** term for someone from n**MN**]. *Jackpine savage* [1 inf, **MN;** term for someone from n**MN;** 1 inf, **IA;** Heard by inf in **MN**]. **1990** *DARE* File (as of 1969), I heard the expression *jackpine savage* from my Milwaukee friends when I first came to Wisconsin. They used it to refer to the permanent residents of the northern part of the state, all of whom were considered to be crude and ignorant.

jack-pine warbler See **jack-pine bird**

jack poke n [By analogy with **jill poke** n 3; cf **jack** n¹ 1]
    1942 Berrey–Van den Bark *Amer. Slang* 414.3, Listless or slow person. . . *Jack poke.*

jack pole fence See **jack fence**

jackpot n

1 A predicament, tight spot; a muddle; hence ppl adj *jackpotted*. [*DCan* 1887 →; the relation to *jackpot* a large pot in poker is unclear] **esp West**

1887 Devol *40 Yrs. Gambler* 117 **Missip Valley**, We devoted ourselves to studying how to get out of the "jack-pot" we had got into, without losing our stake. **1902** McKee *Land of Nome* 123 **AK**, I was flattered to know that on the occasion of his getting into a "jack-pot" (some trouble) he had hunted Nome after me for legal advice. **1905** [see **2a** below]. **1914** Jackson *Criminal Slang* 48 **OR**, *Jackpot.* . . General currency. A dilemma; a difficult strait; a retribution; trouble; an arrest. . . "Where's Joe? He pulled a raw-jaw stunt and made a jackpot." **1922** Rollins *Cowboy* 79, Many gambling terms were used in a figurative way. . . poker's "jack-pot" signified either a general smash-up or else a perplexing situation. **1946** *NYT Mag.* 20 Oct 35 [Rodeo lingo], *Jackpotted:* tangled up with fallen steer or horse. **1948** *NE Hist.* 29.14 **Rocky Mts, NE**, Maybe you'll catch me in a jack-pot some day when I'll need help. **1961** Adams *Old-Time Cowhand* 79 **West**, Which reminds me of a story John Hendrix told me 'bout the jackpot a pair of chaps got one old wagon cook into. **1967** *DARE* (Qu. DD22, . . *Delirium tremens*) Inf **NY**10, In the jackpot. **1967** *DARE* FW Addit **cnNY**, In the jackpot—to be in trouble, in the doghouse. **1970** *Current Slang* 5.1.6 [Railroad jargon], *Get in a jackpot.* . . To be involved in an accident or dangerous situation with a train. *Ibid* 5.1.7, *Get in a jackpot.* . . To get in trouble with the company management. **1987** Hiaasen *Double Whammy* 213 **FL**, You're probably already in the jackpot for taking a duty car out of Dade County.

2 Spec: a tangled pile, as:

a An irregular pile of logs or brush.

1905 U.S. Forest Serv. *Bulletin* 61.40, *Jackpot* . . 1. A contemptuous expression applied to an unskillful piece of work in logging. (N[orthern] F[orest]). 2. An irregular pile of logs. (App[alachian Forest]). **1939** Pinkerton *Wilderness Wife* 301, And in the bush they jerked the toboggan over jackpots of wind-downed balsam that were ten feet high. **1956** Sorden–Ebert *Logger's Words* 19 **Gt Lakes**, *Jack-pot.* . . A bad slash. . . Lodging of more than one tree in felling. **1958** McCulloch *Woods Words* 97 **Pacific NW**, *Jackpot*—A bunch of logs criss-crossed and messed up in a bunch instead of lying straight. Used to describe a pile-up either on land, or where dumped in the water. Also logs felled every which way by a green faller. **1967** Parris *Mountain Bred* 133 **wNC**, A jackpot is an irregular pile of logs.

b See quot.

1945 Hubbard *Railroad Ave.* 349, *Jackpot*—Miscellaneous assortment of mail and parcels piled in the aisle of a baggage car and requiring removal before the mail in the stalls can be "worked."

3 In marble play: =**potty**.

1966 *DARE* (Qu. EE7, . . *Kinds of marble games*) Inf **ND**3, Jackpot—dig hole; whoever throws his marble in gets others.

jackpot cattle n Also *jackpot herd*

Cattle yielding a good profit, esp where there is a minimal outlay of money and labor.

1948 Hanna–Hanna *Lake Okeechobee* 278 **FL**, Cattle were turned loose on the open range. . . Taxes were light; the labor required, small; the returns, gratifying. . . jackpot herds, . . they were called. **1969** Green *Wild Cow Tales* 10 **TX**, It was mid-July and all the country cattle had gotten fat on summer grass; and now was the time to start ridin' the rivers and the ridges to buy what was commonly referred to as "jackpot" cattle.

jackpot herd See **jackpot cattle**

jackrabbit n

1 A hare of the genus *Lepus*. [Abbr for **jackass rabbit**] Also called **jack** n[1] **22, jackass rabbit, mule-eared rabbit, narrow-gauge(d) mule, small mule.** For other names of var spp see **antelope jackrabbit, mountain hare, mule rabbit, prairie hare, varying hare**

1863 in 1940 *Colorado Mag.* 17.69 **CO**, We saw wolves, buffalos, antelopes, jack-rabbits, prairie-dogs innumerable, deer, and birds of various kinds. **1879** U.S. Natl. Museum *Bulletin* 14.19 **SW**, *Lepus callotis.* . . *Jack Rabbit.* **1931** *Durant* (Okla.) *D. Democrat* 26 Jan. 1/6 *(DA)*, Huntsmen gathered here today for a jack rabbit drive near Cam-

bridge. **1947** Cahalane *Mammals* 601, As the jack rabbit bobs off across the plains in great easy bounds, the ears stand up like twin busbys on a hop-skipping grenadier. **1965–70** *DARE* (Qu. P30, . . *Wild rabbits*) 291 Infs, **widespread, but chiefly West**, Jackrabbit. **1967–68** *DARE* Tape CA89, A great big old jackrabbit—my, he was the biggest thing—a great big overgrown clumsy thing—took off across the road; TX19, I have known of 'em [=rattlesnakes] swallowing a half-grown jackrabbit. **1982** Elman *Hunter's Field Guide* 388, A jack rabbit is silent unless injured or caught by a predator, in which event it shrieks piercingly.

2 also *jackrabbit mule*: A mule (or, occas, a horse), esp a small one.

1940 Faulkner *Hamlet* 329 **TX**, Whoa you blare-eyed jack rabbit [=a pony], whoa!. . . The pony shot free in mad, staglike bounds. *Ibid* 330 **TX**, Every jack rabbit one of them [=ponies] will be . . tame. **1950** *WELS (Joking names for mules)* 1 Inf, **nWI**, Jackrabbits. **1966** *Wilson Coll.* **csKY**, Jackrabbit mule—a small mule. "Little old jackrabbit mule." **1967–69** *DARE* (Qu. K50, *Joking nicknames for mules*) Infs **AL**52, **IN**67, **KS**1, **OH**81, **PA**27, **WV**3, Jackrabbit; **IN**4, Jackrabbit, if it's a little one.

3 See quots. [Cf *Jack Robinson*]

1966–67 *DARE* (Qu. A14, . . *A very short period of time* . . *"It won't take any longer than _____."*) Inf **OH**23, Jackrabbit; **SC**3, To say jackrabbit. **1986** Pederson *LAGS Concordance*, 1 inf, **AR**, Before you could say jackrabbit.

‡4 See quot. Cf **jack Mormon 2**

1969 *DARE* (Qu. CC4, . . *Nicknames* . . *for various religions or religious groups*) Inf **CA**169, Jackrabbits (Latter Day Saints).

jackrabbit mule See **jackrabbit 2**

jack rack See **jack** n[1] **6**

jack rake n Cf **loafer rake**

1967 *Amer. Agric. & Rural New Yorker* 164.6.30 **ME**, [In a list of old words not now commonly known:] Jack or loafer rake—a rake for raking scatterings.

jackrock n [Var of **jackstone**; cf **rock**]

1 A small, rounded stone, esp one suitable for throwing. Cf **jackstone 2, river jack**

1920 Thomas–Thomas *KY Superstitions* 263, A "bullrock," also called a "jackrock" (as small round rock), in the ashes keeps hawks away from chickens. **c1960** *Wilson Coll.* **csKY**, *Jackrock.* . . A throwing rock. **1965** *DARE* (Qu. C25, . . *Kinds of stone* . . *about* . . *size of a person's head* . . *smooth and hard*) Inf **OK**4, Jackrock—smaller, but smooth and round—like David slew Goliath with.

2 =**jackstone 1**.

1965 *DARE* (Qu. EE7, . . *Kinds of marble games*) Inf **NC**16, Jackrocks—with five marbles—had to throw one up and pick one up, then next time pick two up, then three, etc. **1980** *Foxfire 6* 292 **nwNC**, Jack Rocks. . . You have five round rocks 'cause flat ones were much harder to pick up, and one rubber ball. You throw up the ball and reach down and get one rock while the ball is in the air, then catch the ball before it hits. Then you put the first rock back and throw up the ball again and this time pick up two rocks. . . and so on until you get all five. **1986** Pederson *LAGS Concordance (Jacks games)* 2 infs, **eTN, wFL**, Jack rocks.

3 also *jack*: Waste rock associated with coal, as shale or limonite. [Cf *EDD jack* sb. 30 "a portion of stone in the roof of a mine"; *SND jack* n[1] 3 "a large piece of rock in a coal seam" and *jock* 3 "lumps of stone in coal"]

1940 (1978) Still *River of Earth* 66 **KY**, Mothercoal Mine put fifty men to hauling fallen jackrock and setting new timbers. *Ibid* 194, By grabbies if he didn't put them to snagging jackrock. *Ibid* 198, Father kicked at a finger of jackrock hanging from the grate basket. **1949** Arnow *Hunter's Horn* 48 **KY**, When he'd worked in the company mines, a coal car had broken loose . . and run backward; he'd heard the man scream . . and he had gone with his miner's cap on his head and spotlighted the man's eyes— . . and then they were not man's eyes, but only something glittering like glass or ice or a bit of jack. **1969** *DARE* (QR, near Qu. C26) Inf **KY**41, Jackrock—round, small, white, slick; about one to two inches in diameter; found along the roads—found in mines. Also called kidney rock.

jack saddle n

1909 *DN* 3.413 **nME**, *Jack saddle.* . . The saddle of a horse's harness.

jack salmon n

1 Either of two related fish: esp a **walleye** (here: *Stizostedion vitreum vitreum*), but also a **sauger** (here: *S. canadense*).

1870 McClung *MN in 1870* 180, *Varieties* [of fish] . . chubb or jack salmon. **1902** Jordan–Evermann *Amer. Fishes* 361, *Wall-eyed Pike*. . . In the Susquehanna and Juniata rivers, and in the small lakes of northern Indiana, it is known as . . jack salmon, [a name] absurd and wholly without excuse. **1920** *Outing* 76.118 swMO, We always hope . . to catch a few jack salmon, which is the local name for wall-eyed pike (pike perch). **1953** Randolph–Wilson *Down in Holler* 256 **Ozarks,** Jacksalmon. . . The walleyed pike (*Stizostedion vitreum),* or the sauger (*Stizostedion canadense).* **1965–70** *DARE* (Qu. P1, . . *Kinds of freshwater fish . . caught around here . . good to eat*) Infs **AR**36, 56, **IN**45, **MS**58, **MO**10, 32, **TN**36, Jack salmon(s). **1966** *DARE* Tape **AR**36, [FW:] What's a jack salmon? [Inf:] Well . . it's built . . just like a salmon, but they have teeth here in front, sharp teeth . . they get up to weighin' ten, twelve pounds. **1983** Becker *Fishes WI* 871, *Stizostedion vitreum vitreum.* . . Jack salmon. *Ibid* 880, *Stizostedion canadense.* . . Jack salmon.

2 =**muskellunge 1.**

1939 Writers' Program *Guide KY* 14, Of the game fishes, the one most closely identified with Kentucky (particularly the Barren and Green River section) is the muskallonge, known locally as jackfish or jack salmon.

3 =**coho salmon,** usu the male. Cf **jack** n[1] **24b(4)**

1944 (1945) Helmericks *We Live in AK* 34 c**AK,** The other day I heard about another salmon called the jack salmon, which some people think is the young king before he reaches maturity, for a young king has never been found. They don't know whether this jack salmon is a young king or another species. **1946** Dufresne *AK's Animals* 267, A strange offshoot of the Coho is the so-called "jack salmon." This name . . in southeastern Alaska is applied only to precocious 2-year-old silver salmon which have returned to fresh water one year ahead of normal time. . . These 2-year-olds are generally 15 to 18 inches in length, black-spotted, trout-like in appearance, and every one of them is a male fish! **1953** Roedel *Common Fishes CA* 42, *Silver Salmon. Oncorhynchus kisutch.* . . *Unauthorized Names:* Coho salmon, . . jack salmon. **1967** *DARE* (Qu. P1, . . *Kinds of freshwater fish . . caught around here . . good to eat*) Inf **WA**30, Jack salmon.

Jacks, by intj Also *i Jacks* [Euphems for *by Jesus*] esp Midl Cf **i** prep

Used as a mild oath; see quots.

1894 Riley *Armazindy* 45 **IN,** It haint no *dream* / 'At I'm wantin',— but *the fac's* / . . i jacks! **1931** *AmSp* 7.121 e**ID,** By Jacks is a favorite byword. *By* is used to intensify imprecations. **1937** Sandoz *Slogum* 195 **NE,** By jacks, but there was a noise in that courtroom—like a bunch of old hens. **1944** *PADS* 2.57 cs**MO,** Jacks, by. . . An expression of surprise, seldom heated enough to represent swearing, but occasionally used for *by God.* Douglas Co. Rural. Rare. **1964** *Mt. Life* Spring 55 s**Appalachians,** That possum's hide is wuth a round dollar if hits wuth ary red pinny under the sun, by Jacks! **1966–70** *DARE* (Qu. NN30, *Exclamations beginning with the sound of 'j'*) Infs **IN**13, 19, 31, 40, **WV**14, 16, **OK**52, By Jacks. **1968** *DARE* Tape **IN**13, And so—by Jacks he come back and I says to him, I says, "Old George," I says, "has treed the coon round there."

jackscrew-root n

=**Oconee bells.**

1964 Batson *Wild Flowers SC* 89, Oconee-bells, Jackscrew-root: *Shortia galacifolia.* . . Perennial evergreen spreading by short runners to form colonies.

Jack's game See **jack** n[2] **2b**

jack shad n

A **gizzard shad 1** (here: *Dorosoma cepedianum*).

1983 Becker *Fishes WI* 273, *Gizzard Shad.* . . Other common names . . jack shad [etc].

jack shirt n [Prob **jack** n[1] **3,** or *jack* abbr for *jacket*]

1950 *WELS* **WI** (*Men's outdoor coats and jackets . . short*) 1 Inf, Jack shirt—wool; 1 Inf, Jack shirt.

Jacks, i See **Jacks, by**

jack smelt n

A **silversides** (here: *Atherinopsis californiensis*).

1953 Roedel *Common Fishes CA* 76, *Atherinopsis californiensis.* . . Most jacksmelt mature when two years old and about six inches long. **1955** Zim–Shoemaker *Fishes* 82, Jacksmelts are taken by anglers and also form a major part of the California "smelt" fisheries. **1968–69** *DARE* (Qu. P2, . . *Kinds of saltwater fish caught around here . . good to eat*) Infs **CA**65, 168, Jack smelt.

jack snapper n

1 also *jack:* A **click beetle.** esp Sth

1908 *DN* 3.323 e**AL,** w**GA,** Jack. . . Same as *jack-snapper. Ibid* 324, *Jacksnapper.* . . The click beetle. **1938** Brimley *Insects NC* 164, Family Elateridae, *The Click Beetles.* . . Locally called "jack-snappers." **1966–68** *DARE* (Qu. R8, . . *Kinds of creatures that make a clicking or shrilling or chirping kind of sound*) Infs **NC**6, **VA**38, Jack snapper. **1982** Slone *How We Talked* 45 e**KY** (as of c1950), "Jack snapper"—a long, black beetle that made a loud snapping sound when it snapped its head. We children loved to play with them and make them snap their heads.

2 A bedbug.

1929 *KY Folkl. & Poetry Mag.* 4.1.12, From Eastern Kentucky a boy tells me that they call the bed bugs Jack-Snappers.

3 See quot.

1967 *DARE* (Qu. P3, *Freshwater fish that are not good to eat*) Inf **TX**32, Jack snapper.

jacksnipe n

1 =**pectoral sandpiper.** [See quot 1956]

1844 Giraud *Birds Long Is.* 235 se**NY,** Mr. Baird has informed me that it [=*Calidris melanotos*] occurs in Pennsylvania, in which section it has received the appellation of "Jack Snipe." I have occasionally seen it in our location during the month of July. **1858** Baird *Birds* 720, *Jack Snipe.* . . Of rather frequent occurrence on the coast of the Atlantic, and rearing its young in the northern States of the Union. . . This species has been ascertained to breed abundantly in Wisconsin. **1881** *Forest & Stream* 17.225 **Cape Cod MA,** A pectoral sandpiper in our section is "jack snipe." **1907** Anderson *Birds IA* 217, The Pectoral Sandpiper, . . or jack-snipe, . . is an abundant migrant in nearly all parts of the state. **1936** Roberts *MN Birds* 1.502. **1956** MA Audubon Soc. *Bulletin* 40.19, *Pectoral Sandpiper.* . . Jack Snipe (General. Meaning a small snipe.)

2 =**solitary sandpiper.** obs

1844 DeKay *Zool. NY* 2.249, *The Solitary Tatler.* . . is called the *Green-rump Tatler,* . . and the *Jack Snipe,* in various places in the interior.

3 =**Wilson's snipe.**

1846 *Spirit of Times* 25 Apr 97/1 cs**TX,** The jack snipe in the low grounds were found in flocks. **1887** *Forest & Stream* 28.248 **WY,** I can verify . . the hardiness of the jack snipe. I procured a specimen on the 1st of January this year in a small spring on the ranch, and have noticed them quite frequently for the last three winters. **1916** *Times-Picayune* (New Orleans LA) 2 Apr mag sec 5, *Wilson Snipe (Gallinago delicata).* Jack Snipe. . . Snipe are found in the open places along the coastal portions of Louisiana, in "snipe marshes." **1933** *Daily Progress* (Charlottesville VA) 9 Aug 7/3 c**VA,** Wilson Snipe or Jacksnipe. **1939** FWP *Guide CA* 582 cw**CA,** The Wilson snipe, called hereabout the Jacksnipe, is abundant. **1950** *WELS* (*Water and marsh birds*) 1 Inf, ce**WI,** Snipe or Jacksnipe. **1965–69** *DARE* (Qu. Q10, . . *Water birds and marsh birds*) 15 Infs, **scattered, but esp West,** Jacksnipe; (Qu. Q7, *Names and nicknames for . . game birds*) Infs **CA**105, **IA**3, 11, **IL**32, **KS**12, **LA**31, **MI**71, **NY**71, Jacksnipe; (Qu. Q9, *The bird that looks like a small, dull-colored duck and is commonly found on ponds and lakes*) Infs **MO**16, **WI**32, Jacksnipe; (Qu. P32, . . *Other kinds of wild animals*) Inf **IA**5, Jacksnipe; (Qu. X37, . . *Words . . to describe people's legs if they're noticeably bent, or uneven, or not right*) Inf **LA**31, Legs like a jacksnipe. [*DARE* Ed: Some of these Infs may refer instead to other senses.] **1982** Elman *Hunter's Field Guide* 328, *Wilson's Snipe* . . Common & regional names . . jacksnipe.

4 also *Jackson snipe:* A **dowitcher,** usu *Limnodromus scolopaceus.*

1888 Trumbull *Names of Birds* 162, *Macrorhamphus scolopaceus.* . . In the markets of Los Angeles, according to Dr. Cooper, Jack Snipe. **1895** Elliot *N. Amer. Shore Birds* 57, The Long-billed Dowitcher, also called . . Jack Snipe at Los Angeles, . . is . . a somewhat larger bird than its relative, the Dowitcher of the Atlantic Coast, and with a longer bill. **1918** Grinnell *Game Birds CA* 360, The Long-billed Dowitcher is the "Jack Snipe" of the seashore. **1923** U.S. Dept. Ag. *Misc. Circular* 13.51, *Dowitcher (Limnodromus griseus).* . . The vernacular names for the subspecies [=*L. g. g.* and *L. g. scolopaceus*] are hardly separable. . . Jacksnipe (B.C., Calif.) Jackson snipe (N.J.)

5 =black-necked stilt. CA

1913 *Pacific Coast Avifauna* 9.28 **sCA,** Among the farmers the name "jack snipe" is usually applied to this species [=*Himantopus mexicanus*]. **1918** Grinnell *Game Birds CA* 344, *Black-necked Stilt . . Other names . .* Jack Snipe (in San Joaquin Valley). **1923** U.S. Dept. Ag. *Misc. Circular* 13.48, *Black-necked Stilt. . . Vernacular Names. . . In local use. . .* Jacksnipe (Calif.)

6 =least sandpiper. CA

1913 *Pacific Coast Avifauna* 9.29 **sCA,** *Least Sandpiper. . .* I was greatly surprised on one occasion to hear a farm hand refer to these tiny waders as "jack snipes." I had always supposed that the Stilts held undisputed possession of that name. **1923** U.S. Dept. Ag. *Misc. Circular* 13.55 **CA,** *Least Sandpiper. . . Vernacular Names. . . In local use. . .* Jacksnipe.

7 =killdeer.

1950 *WELS (Other names for killdeer)* 1 Inf, **WI,** Jacksnipe.

jacksnipe hunt See **snipe hunt**

Jackson n

=jack n[1] **1.**

1941 *AmSp* 16.166 [Army slang], *Jackson.* Form of address for any soldier. **1970** Major *Dict. Afro-Amer. Slang* 70, *Jack, Jackson:* (1930's– 40's) term of address by one male to another.

jackson v, hence ppl adj *jacksoned*

See quots.

[**1867** Smyth *Sailor's Word Book* 408, *Jammed in a clinch like Jackson,* involved in a difficulty of a secondary degree, as when Jackson, after feeding for a week in the bread-room, could not escape through the scuttle.] **1903** *DN* 2.294 **Cape Cod MA** (as of a1857), *Jackson. . .* To block in either direction; properly applied to a ship which will not come in stays nor fill away again, and figuratively of a person or animal. 'That calf's jacksoned now; he can't move one way nor tother.' [**1925** Fraser-Gibbons *Soldier & Sailor Words* 130, *Jammed like Jackson:* A Navy phrase, used when something goes seriously wrong, or leads to a disaster. (In allusion to John Jackson, Master of the frigate *Leander* in 1787 who refused to listen to the pilot and nearly wrecked his ship in consequence).] **1942** ME Univ. *Studies* 56.46, If she would not pay off she would be *in stays,* or, as it was called on square riggers, *in irons,* or by a less common term, *jacksoned.* To *jackson* also meant to contrive to get out of difficulty. **1945** Colcord *Sea Language* 108 **ME, Cape Cod, Long Island,** *Jacksoned.* In irons . . or figuratively, in difficulties; from the phrase "hard up (or jammed) in a clinch, like Jackson," the origin of which is not known. Sometimes he was further hampered by having "no knife to cut the seizing." There are other and less seemly phrases about Jackson.

Jackson ball n esp **NY**

A round hard candy.

1889 Mellick *Story Old Farm* 9 **NJ,** Dusty jars tempt the school children to barter eggs for sticks of peppermint and wintergreen, or the succulent Jackson-ball. **1894** Frederic *Marsena* 209 **nNY,** The grocer's hired man gave me a Jackson ball and two molasses cookies the very first time I saw him. **1902** (1969) Sears *Catalogue* 20, *Candy. . .* 5-pound box. . . *Jackson Balls* . . \$.59. **1967–69** *DARE* (Qu. H82a, *Cheap candies sold especially for schoolchildren*) Inf **NY**2, Jackson balls— round hard candies; old-fashioned; (Qu. H82b, *Kinds of cheap candy that used to be sold years ago*) Inf **NY**5, Jackson balls—a hard sucking candy; **NY**199, Jacks and balls [sic].

Jackson brier n

A **greenbrier** (here: *Smilax lanceolata* or *S. smallii*).

1933 Small *Manual SE Flora* 313, *S[milax] lanceolata. . . Jackson-brier. . .* The leaves are evergreen. Much used for winter decorations, large quantities being shipped from the Gulf States. **1952** Blackburn *Trees* 266, *S[milax] lanceolata* (se United States and to Texas) *Jackson-brier.* **1966** Grimm *Recognizing Native Shrubs* 75, *Lanceleaf Greenbrier. Smilax smallii. . .* Also known as Jacksonbrier. Often gathered and sold to florists where abundant. **1976** Bailey–Bailey *Hortus Third* 1050, *[Smilax] lanceolata. . . Jackson brier.* Climbing, evergreen, woody vine.

Jackson cracker n [Perh named for Andrew *Jackson* (1767– 1845)]

A kind of firecracker.

1877 Bartlett *Americanisms* 319, *Jackson crackers.* Fire crackers. South-

western. **1950** *WELS (Fire-crackers: different kinds)* 1 Inf, **cWI,** Jackson crackers—old-fashioned. [Both of the Inf's parents are from **KY.**]

jacksoned See **jackson** v

Jackson fork n **West** Cf **Jenkins derrick**

A steel-tined fork suspended from a derrick or system of pulleys and cables, used for loading loose hay onto a stack or into a mow; see quot 1985.

1968 Adams *Western Words* 163, *Jackson fork*—A large steel fork operated by horses or by pulleys and used to move quantities of loose hay; used on latter-day ranches. **1968–69** *DARE* (QR, near Qu. M2) Inf **CA**161, Jackson fork—for storing loose hay, gave ventilation; (QR, near Qu. L15) Inf **CA**87, Use a Jackson fork to put hay in—four tines hung on a hook suspended from a pulley arrangement. **1976** Wells *Barns U.S.A.* n.p. **ID,** The barn [built in 1914] had . . a hay loft in the upper level. A Jackson fork was used to elevate hay into the loft. **1985** Attebery *ID Folklife* 3 **sID, wWY, UT, nwAZ,** Hay derricks of the alfalfa-growing districts of the Great Basin and upper Snake River Valley . . use the Jackson fork . . to carry the hay from load to stack. This fork grasps a sixth to an eighth of a wagonload at a time. It is carried from load to stack by a cable which travels over pulleys at appropriate points on the derrick and is pulled by a single horse, a team, or a tractor. When the hay has been raised to a point above . . the stack . . the fork is tripped and the hay falls on the stack. *Ibid* 5, The earlier four-tined Jackson fork . . the six-tined Jackson fork.

Jackson press n [Perh named for Andrew *Jackson* (1767– 1845)]

A kind of sideboard.

1952 Drepperd *Dict. Amer. Antiques* 207, *Jackson press:* A dining-room piece now often called a hunt board, which it is not. The styling is of the early Empire period, and it is a cabinet-piece sideboard with bottle, silver, and linen drawers or cupboards. Date is from 1820s, and many were used from Louisiana to Georgia in both town and plantation homes. **1969–70** *DARE* (Qu. E5, *A piece of furniture with a flat top for keeping tablecloths, dishes, and such*) Inf **KY**61, I call mine a Jackson press [FW: Word used by other local residents as well]; **KY**63, Jackson press; **IL**122, Jackson press—fancy name.

Jackson snipe See **jack snipe 4**

Jackson vine n

1 A **matrimony vine** (here: *Lycium halimifolium*).

1892 *Jrl. Amer. Folkl.* 5.101, *Lycium vulgare . .* Jackson vine; jasmine. Mansfield, O[hio]. **1931** U.S. Dept. Ag. *Misc. Pub.* 101.142, Matrimony-vine (*L. halimifolium,* syn. *L. vulgare*), known also as . . Jackson vine, . . occurs in waste places, about settlements, along watercourses, etc. **1940** [see **2** below]. **1960** Vines *Trees SW* 914, *Lycium halimifolium. . .* Also known by the local names of Matrimony-vine . . and Jackson-vine.

2 A **greenbrier** (here: *Smilax lanceolata* or *S. smallii*).

1940 Clute *Amer. Plant Names* 15, *S[milax] lanceolata.* Jackson-vine. *Ibid* 50, *L[ycium] halimifolium. . .* Jackson-vine. **1959** Carleton *Index Herb. Plants* 67, *Jackson-vine:* Smilax lanceolata. **1967** *DARE* (Qu. T5, . . *Kinds of evergreens, other than pine*) Inf **AL**37, Jackson vine.

Jackson White n [Etym uncert; see quot 1946; cf **jack** n[1] **2**]

A person of racially mixed ancestry in northeast New Jersey and adjacent parts of New York; also a White person living in the mountains of the same region.

1878 in 1974 Cohen *Ramapo Mt. People* 21 **seNY,** The two Degroots, and Wm. Robinson, alias "Cock Robin," the "Jackson Whites," who broke into the office of Hutton Bro's, at Nanuet, . . were indicted for Burglary. **1900** *Ibid* 12, The Ramapo Indians sometimes visited the settlements in the township of Franklin. They were known formerly as the Hackensack Indians, but are more properly described as the "Jackson Whites." They bear little resemblance to the Indians, yet as tradition gives it they are descendants of Hessians, Indians, and negroes, but know nothing of their ancestry, so ignorant have they become. **1911** S. Workman 40.105 **seNY,** As to the actual history of this community and the origin of the name Jackson-White, little is definitely known. Some claim that the term is the corruption of a contemptuous title, Jack-and-whites; others that it is from the common surnames among Negroes, Jackson and White, although they are not common in these mountains. In no sense of the word do the people themselves recognize the community name, being known by it only among their neighbours. **1946** *Social Forces* 24.443, *Jackson Whites of New Jersey and New York. . .* Orange and Rockland Counties in New York; Bergen, Morris, and Passaic counties, New Jersey. Name said to be derived from "Jackson and White" which are common surnames. Another derivation is from "Jacks" and "Whites," the terms for Negroes and Caucasians. Still another idea is that Jackson was a man who imported some of the ancestors of these people during the Revolutionary War. In one part of this area are the so-called "Blue-eyed Negroes" who are said to be a race apart from the rest. **1968** *DARE* (Qu. HH29b, . . *People of mixed blood—part Negro*) Inf **NY**66, Jackson Whites. **1974** Cohen *Ramapo Mt. People* 22, The name always seems to be applied to someone else. People in Ringwood, New Jersey, say that the Jackson Whites are in Mahwah. People in Hillburn say that the Jackson Whites are the white mountaineers who used to live behind Ladentown, New York, in the northeast section of the Ramapo Mountains. **1983** *Lutz Coll.* **nNJ,** Years ago a school bus driver told me of a remark made by one of the mountain children in the Ramapos—one of the dark-skinned folk sometimes called Jackson Whites.

jack-sparrow n Cf **jickie**
Prob =**English sparrow.**
    1966 *DARE* (Qu. Q21, . . *Kinds of sparrows*) Inf **DC**4, Jack-sparrow—similar to English sparrow.

jackstand n [**jack** n[1] **5a**] Cf **fire stand, jacklight** n
    1922 Gonzales *Black Border* 307 **sSC, GA coasts** [Gullah glossary], *Jackstan'* . . stands on which fires are kept at night in summer settlements for protection against mosquitoes and other insects.

jack-stick n Cf **jap-stick**
    1966–68 *DARE* (Qu. EE10, *A game in which a short stick lying on the ground is flipped into the air and then hit with a longer stick*) Infs **MA**27, **NJ**8, **PA**1, Jack-stick.

jackstone n [Folk-etym for Engl *chackestone* (*OED* at *check-stone* sb.[1])]
1 A small pebble or specially made metal object used in play; in pl, the game in which they are used, consisting of various exercises in dexterity. Cf **bob jack, check** n[1] **3, jack** n[2] **1, jackrock 2**
    1811 in 1814 Brackenridge *Views of LA* 251, The women . . amuse themselves with a game something like jack-stones: five pebbles are tossed up in a small basket, with which they endeavor to catch them again as they fall. **1854** Shillaber *Life Partington* 61 **MA,** Ike, unwatched, was weighing his knife and five Jackstones. **1877** Bartlett *Americanisms* 787, [Addenda:] Jack-Stone. A metal toy, consisting of several arms with globular termini. It is so tossed and caught that the player may keep as many of the toys as possible in motion at the same time. **1899** Champlin-Bostwick *Young Folks' Games* 443, Jack-stones, a game played by one or more persons with five small pebbles, or little pieces of iron. **1937** *Sun* (Baltimore MD) 22 May 8/8 (Hench Coll.), There were boys that could outplay the gals at jackstones ten to one. **1966–70** *DARE* (Qu. EE33) Inf **MA**69, Jackstones—threw up a ball; had to pick up the stones before catching the ball; **FL**30, **GA**18, **IL**55, **OH**65, **SC**68, Jackstones; (QR p230) Inf **AL**10, Jackstones—the game of jacks [FW adds drawing of a six-pointed metal jack]. **1967** *DARE* Tape **IN**1, Jacks, or sometimes called jackstones.
2 A medium size, rounded stone. Cf **jackrock 1, river jack**
    1936 *Hench Coll.* **cWV,** Uncle Sam spoke of his hiring a lot of men in Marlinton, W. Va., to protect the bank of the Greenbrier river with logs and jack stones, big round stones from the stream. **1968** *DARE* (Qu. C25, . . *Kinds of stone . . about . . [. . size of a person's head], smooth and hard*) Inf **MD**31, Jackstone.

jackswift n Also *swiftjack*
The five-lined **skink** (*Eumeces fasciatus*).
    1959 McAtee *Oddments* 6 **cnNC,** Jackswift . . swiftjack, the striped lizard (*Eumeces fasciatus*).

jack the dog v phr Cf **fuck the dog**
To loaf, shirk work.
    1988 Lincoln *Avenue* 209 **wNC** (as of c1940) [Black], Po' Boy made a whole lot of money for Jelus. He could cut more wood than two or three men, and he didn't lay around on the job or jack the dog like Jelus had expected he would when he had to be away on business.

Jack-the-preacher n Also *Johnny-the-preacher* Cf **preacher Jack**
A **jack-in-the-pulpit 1.**

1950 *WELS* **WI** (*Other names for the Jack-in-the-pulpit*) 1 Inf, Jack the preacher; 1 Inf, Johnny the preacher.

jack up v phr
1 rarely *jack*: To call to account, rebuke; to "light a fire under" (someone); to irritate; hence vbl n *jacking up.*
    1896 (1898) Ade *Artie* 107 **Chicago IL,** He was goin' to clean the streets and jack up the coppers. **1897** *KS Univ. Qrly.* (ser B) 6.54 **KS,** *Jack-me-up:* 'poke' me up, give me a reminder. **1905** *DN* 3.83 **nwAR,** *Jack up. . .* To reprove severely. 'If he doesn't quit cutting, he'll get jacked up mighty suddenly.' *Ibid, Jacking up. . .* 'He gave him a good jacking up.' Common. **1908** *DN* 3.324 **eAL, wGA,** *Jack-up. . .* To reprimand, reprove severely. *Ibid* 323, *Jacking-up. . .* **1912** *DN* 3.579 **wIN,** The boss will jack him up if he isn't careful. *Ibid,* That ditcher needs a jacking up. **1914** Adams *Clarion* 100, I think I'll jack up our boys in the city room by hinting that there may be a shake-up coming under the new owner. **1916** *DN* 4.324 **KS, MA, NY, NE,** *Jack up. . .* To urge, incite; sometimes, to scold. . . "They get careless and need to be jacked up every so often." **1939** Hall *Coll.* **ceTN,** *Jack up. . .* To find fault with. **1950** *WELS* (*To urge somebody to do something: "He's a week late: I'm going to _____!"*) 3 Infs, **WI,** Jack him up. **1965–70** *DARE* (Qu. Y6, . . *To put pressure on somebody to do something he ought to have done but hasn't: "He's a whole week late. I'm going to _____."*) 82 Infs, *scattered,* Jack him up; **NJ**15, Jack him; **CA**15, Jack up; **IN**3, **MS**63, Give him a jacking up; (Qu. Y7, *When one person never misses a chance to be mean to another or to annoy another: "I don't know why she keeps _____ me all the time!"*) Inf **IA**34, Jacking me up; (Qu. II27, *If somebody gives you a very sharp scolding . . "I certainly got a _____ for that."*) Infs **GA**9, **KY**33, **MS**71, Jacking up; **VT**12, He jacked me up.
2 Spec: to bring legal charges against; to take to court.
    1967 *DARE* FW Addit **AR**55, Jacked up for—charged with. "A man jacked up for murder." **1968** *DARE* Tape **CA**100, I read an article in my last magazine today—somebody's jacked up this attorney general that we have . . and he denied the whole thing—they hadn't done anything. This paper jumped him, don't you see, and he's trying to crawl out of it.
3 To beat up; to rob. [Cf *EDD jack* v.[1] **4** to beat] *esp freq among Black speakers*
    1971 Roberts *Third Ear* np [Black], *Jack up . .* to rob; to steal; to hold up and beat up. **1972** Claerbaut *Black Jargon* 69, *Jack up . .* 1. to rob or hold up someone. 2. to beat someone up: *I'll jack up the dude.* **1980** Folb *Runnin' Down* 48 **Los Angeles CA** [Black], One night, this dude jacked me up for my leather piece. We got to thumpin', and I pulled out my knife and stabbed him. *Ibid* 80, Then, he come back an' tell them and they go back and jack up some Businessmen [=a gang]. *Ibid* 106, Like you and some brothers swoop on dis dude, jack 'im up, righteously jam him fo' his money.
4 To have sexual intercourse with; hence ppl adj *jacked up* pregnant. Cf *heisted* (at **hoist** C2), **jack** v **3**
    1970 *DARE* (Qu. AA28, . . *Joking or sly expressions . . women use to say that another is going to have a baby . . "She['s] _____."*) Inf **NY**241, Jacked up [Inf Black]. **1980** Folb *Runnin' Down* 152 **Los Angeles CA** [Black], And some of the same terms used to characterize physical assault are also used to connote sexual intercourse—voluntary or otherwise—such as *rip off/on someone,* to *jam,* to *jack up,* to *throw.*
5 To bungle (something); to foul up. [Cf *fuck up*]
    1963 *AmSp* 38.44 **RI** [Truckers' language], *Jack up. . .* To wreck a truck or to make a sudden stop. **1970** *DARE* (Qu. JJ42, *To make an error in judgment and get something quite wrong: "He usually handles things well, but this time he certainly _____."*) Inf **PA**236, Jacked it up.

Jack-up-a-bush See **Jack-in-the-bush 2**

jack vine n Pronc-sp *jack wine* Cf Pronc Intro 3.I.19, **Jackson vine 2**
Prob a **greenbrier.**
    1913 Morley *Carolina Mts.* 249 **cwNC,** Just beyond here you get some one to guide you a mile or two along a wild ravine where the jack-vine grows, to the upper falls of the Tuckasegee. **1924** (1969) Gonzales *With Aesop* 84 **SC coast** [Gullah], De man mek uh trap wid rope en' jackwine en' t'ing. **1930** Stoney-Shelby *Black Genesis* 187 **seSC,** Den he twis' roun' for git out, an' he tangle up bad in dat jackwine an' briar. **1945** Saxon *Gumbo Ya-Ya* 526 **LA,** Jack Vine tea is the best blood purify you can get. . . We allus made tea out of it when we would be in the swamps.

jack wax n

1 A confection made by pouring boiled-down maple syrup onto snow. **esp NY** Cf **cackany, maple wax, wax**

1904 *DN* 2.398 seNY, *Jack-wax.* . . The same as *cany.* **1953** Van Wagenen *Golden Age* 174 ceNY (as of 19th cent), Syrup cooked down to the point where it cools to sugar and then poured on snow becomes the "jack wax" of blessed memory. **1967–68** *DARE* (Qu. H80, *Kinds of candy . . made at home*) Infs NY1, 12, 92, Jack wax; (Qu. FF2) Inf NY1, Jack-wax parties. **1967–69** *DARE* Tape NY1, We used to wait for what we called a sugar snow, which would be a nice fresh-fall snow, . . and they'd go out and get . . large pans full of the snow—pack it down. And you boil . . the maple syrup down until it shows stringy when you dip the spoon in it. . . When it gets about right . . you let it drip or pour from the spoon onto the snow and it . . forms a little disk . . of this sticky, taffy-like material, which you eat. . . From time to time you take a little swig of maybe diluted vinegar to offset the sweetness of the sugar. And that's called jack wax; NY223, Jack wax. . . You put it on snow and then roll it on a fork. . . It sticks your teeth together. **1967** *DARE* FW Addit neNY, Jack-wax party. **1970** *NY Times* (NY) 19 Apr sec 10 10/5, The tradition of "sugaring off," which takes place at the end of the season, when the last of the hot and slightly thickened syrup is poured on snow, has been taken indoors. Today, many sugarhouses serve "sugar-on-snow," "sugar patties," or "jackwax." **1988** *Yankee* June 19, Why do good New Englanders . . call what I was brought up on as "Jack Wax" various variations such as "maple syrup on snow". . . It seems a shame to have that fun name die out. Jack Wax was no simple syrup on snow, but rather had to be carefully boiled down to just the right stage, then trickled over pans of fresh snow. It was wonderfully chewy.

2 =**black wax.** Cf **gumbo 6a, waxy**

1968–69 *DARE* (Qu. C31, . . *Heavy, sticky soil*) Inf OH69, Jack wax; OH89, Jack wax—it's thick mud and dries slow and gets hard.

Jack White n Cf Mr. White is out of jail

A shirttail; hence phr *Jack White is out of jail*—used as a warning that a man's pants are torn.

1909 *DN* 3.420 Cape Cod MA (as of a1857), *Jack White.* . . A shirt tail. Jack White is out of jail means that there is a hole in the seat of one's trousers. **1965–70** *DARE* (Qu. W24b, *Sayings to warn a man that his pants are torn or split*) 11 Infs, **scattered**, Jack White is out of jail.

jack wine See **jack vine**

jackworm See **jack** n¹ 25

jacky bump See **jack bump**

Jacky-in-the-bush See **Jack-in-the-bush 2**

jacky(-ma)-lantun, jacky-my-lantern See **jack-o'-lantern 1**

jacob n, v

A lie; a liar; to lie.

1908 *DN* 3.324 eAL, wGA, *Jacob.* . . A false statement, a lie; also a liar. A euphemism. "Thats a Jacob." "You're a Jacob." . . To tell a falsehood, lie. "You're a-Jacobin."

Jacob and Rachel n Also *Jacob and Ruth, Ruth and Jacob*; for addit varr see quots [In allusion to the deception of Jacob in Genesis 29:16–25]

A version of the game of blindman's buff; see quots 1909, 1945.

1909 (1923) Bancroft *Games* 115, *Jacob and Rachel.* . . All of the players but two form a circle with clasped hands. The two odd players are placed in the center, one of them, "Jacob," being blindfolded. The object of the game is for Jacob to catch the other player, "Rachel," by the sound of her voice; but Rachel is supposed to be rather coy, and to do all in her power to avoid being caught by Jacob, even though she answer his questions. **1923** Acker *400 Games* 27, *Ruth and Jacob* (Jacob and Rachael)—The players form a circle with two in the center; one is Ruth, the other Jacob. Jacob is blindfolded and must try to catch Ruth. He calls "Ruth!" and she must answer "Jacob!" **1945** Boyd *Hdbk. Games* 78, *Jacob and Rachel.* . . The players stand with their hands joined in a circle to prevent the two in the center from running outside the circle. Jacob, who is blindfolded, tries to catch Rachel, who has a string of sleigh bells . . hung around her neck. **1950** *WELS* (Games in which one player's eyes are covered and he has to catch the others and guess who they are) 3 Infs, WI, Ruth and Jacob. **1953** Brewster *Amer. Nonsinging Games* 69 NE, *Jacob and Rachel.* **1957** *Sat. Eve. Post Letters* neKS (as of c1907), "Ruth and Jacob". . . "Jacob" was blind, so was blindfolded. He was in the middle of the ring, with "Ruth," his

"wife," who might be anyone, man, woman, or child. All the other players joined hands to form a large ring. Jacob tried to catch Ruth. Everytime he called "Ruth," she must answer "Jacob" at once. This continued until he touched her. Then Ruth became Jacob, etc. and another player became "Ruth." *Ibid* cwPA (as of c1900), [In a list of games played:] Ruth and Jacob. **1966–69** *DARE* (Qu. EE4, *Games in which one player's eyes are bandaged and he has to catch the others and guess who they are*) Inf AR52, Jacob and Rachel—Jacob is blindfolded, tries to touch Rachel, locating her by sound—she has to answer "Jacob" when he says "Rachel." [Illustr in text: "Jacob" stands within, and "Rachel" without, a ring of children holding hands]; MA24, Jacob and Rachel and Isaac and Rebecca—A circle was formed—Isaac has to find Rebecca and Jacob has to find Rachel (one or other of couple is blinded); IA3, Rachel and Jacob; ND9, Ruth and Jacob—one blindfolded and one not in the ring—Jacob who is blindfolded calls Ruth—he tries to catch her.

Jacob bird n

A **starling** (here: *Sternus vulgaris*).

1928 Ritchie *Forty-Niners* 25 CA, Jacob birds squawking from the tips of the Digger pines.

Jacob Evertzens n Also *Jacob Evers* [After *Jacob Evertsen*, 17th-cent Du sea captain; *OEDS* 1727 →]

A **coney** n² **a** or similar fish.

1772 in 1924 Phillips *Notes B. Romans* 123 FL, It Abounds here in fish of all kinds, that are Usually found in those Latitudes, Principally the Jacob Evers, or Jew Fish, the Tarpom [sic], the Mangrove Snapper [etc]. **1933** John G. Shedd Aquarium *Guide* 97, *Cephalopholis fulvus punctatus.* . . These fishes are sometimes called Jacob Evertzens after a Dutch pilot. . . It is said that on account of his pock-marked face, his fellow sailors gave his name to these spotted fishes.

Jacob ladder n

1 See **Jacob's ladder 1.**
2 See **Jacob's staff 2.**

Jacob's cat n

=**Job's turkey 1.**

1966 *DARE* (Qu. U41b, *Somebody who has lost everything and is very poor: "He's poor as _____.")* Inf MA6, Jacob's cat.

Jacob's cattle bean n Also *cattle bean, Jacob's cattle, Jacob's ladder bean* [From its spotted appearance, in allusion to Genesis 30:39] esp ME

A cultivated red-and-white splotched or speckled bean (*Phaseolus vulgaris* var).

1946 Gould *Yankee Storekeeper* 171 cwME, Where can I buy a barrel of Jacob's cattle beans? . . The Bible says Jacob's cattle were ring-streaked and speckled. So were the beans. **1959** Carleton *Index Herb. Plants* 67, *Jacob's cattle:* Applied to many old varieties of snap beans. **1964** Gould *Parables of Peter* 144 ME, You take Jacob's Cattle Beans. They are the finest baking bean available to the yearning palate of man, and three cups of them in a pot with the proper assistance and attention will become the pleasantest supper anybody ever stuck a tooth in. **1966–69** *DARE* (Qu. I20, . . *Kinds of beans*) Infs ME12, 20, Jacob's cattle; NH16, Jacob's cattle—from Maine; NH6, Jacob's ladder bean—same as cattle bean. **1976** *Wanigan Catalog* 11, *Jacob's Cattle.* . . Beautiful and unusual color. . . White, with red solids and spots over half the surface. Found in Southwest Indian sites, (1200 A D), but now a Maine Heirloom. Early dry baking bean. **1989** *Yankee* Apr 105 scME, Up-north baked beans—1 pound (2 cups) dried Jacob's Cattle (or Great Northern) beans. **1990** *Seed Savers Yearbook* 39, Pike [seed company owner] said Jacob's Cattle strain was heirloom in Pike and Clark families in Lubec [ME], came as gift of Passamaquoddy Indians to Joseph Clark, first white child born in Lubec.

Jacob's coat n Also *Jacob's coat-of-many-colors* [Prob in allusion to Genesis 37:3]

A **copperleaf** such as *Acalypha wilkesiana*, or similar plant with variously colored or variegated leaves.

1948 Neal *In Gardens HI* 445, *Copper leaf, Jacobs coat. Acalypha wilkesiana.* . . The numerous, attractively colored leaves are bronze-green spotted with red. **1970** *DARE* Tape MI112, I have a lot of things—oddities. . . I have the one they call Jacob's coat-of-many-colors. **1976** Bailey–Bailey *Hortus Third* 8, [*Acalypha*] *Wilkesiana.* . . *Jacob's-coat.* . . There are many c[ulti]v[ar]s in the trades, with l[ea]v[e]s variously colored. **1982** Perry-Hay *Field Guide Plants* 42, *Acalypha* *wilkesiana.* . . Jacob's coat. . . is widely grown as a garden ornamental, or as a small pot plant in cool climates.

Jacob's coffin n

1978 Massey *Bittersweet Country* 382 **Ozarks,** The mountain dulcimer, also known as the Indian walking cane or Jacob's coffin. . . is a long, narrow, stringed instrument, sometimes rather resembling an elongated guitar without the neck.

Jacob's ladder n

1 also *Jacob ladder:* A plant of the genus *Polemonium.* [In allusion to Genesis 28:12; *OED* 1733 →] Also called **bluebell 1b, Greek valerian, skunkweed, sky pilot.** For other names of *P. reptans* see **abscess (root), forget-me-not 6, snakeroot, sweatroot**

1791 in 1793 *Amer. Philos. Soc. Trans.* 3.163 **sePA,** Polemonium, Jacobs-Ladder. reptans. **1876** Hobbs *Bot. Hdbk.* 59, Jacob's ladder. Smilax peduncularis. Jacob's ladder. American Greek valerian, Polemonium reptans. **1906** Rydberg *Flora CO* 280, *Jacob's Ladder.* . . On hills from Mont. and Wash. to Colo. and Calif. **1960** Williams *Walk Egypt* 15 **GA,** Most of all Aunt Baptist liked to toll out the names of plants. "Adam's-flannel, Aaron's-rod, Noah's-ark, Jacob's-ladder, apple of Sodom." **1966** *DARE* Wildfl QR Pl.179 [=*Polemonium caeruleum*] Infs **OH**14, **WA**30, Jacob's ladder. **1968–69** *DARE* (Qu. S23) Inf **IL**52, Jacob's ladder; (Qu. S26b) Inf **PA**99, Jacob's ladder; (Qu. S26c) Inf **IN**17, Jacob's ladder; (Qu. S26e) Inf **IL**37, Jacob's ladder. **1969** *SC Market Bulletin* 11 Sept 4, Star of Bethlehem, Jacob Ladder. . . 35c doz.

2 =**bellwort.**

1784 in 1785 *Amer. Acad. Arts & Sci. Memoirs* 1.434, *Uvularia.* . . Bellwort, Sweet-smelling Solomon's Seal, Jacob's Ladder. . . The young shoots may be eaten as asparagus. The roots are nutritious, and are used in diet-drinks. **1967** *Ozark Visitor* (Point Lookout MO) Feb 6/2, There, over a patch of green moss, bent the seeding Jacob's Ladder known as a remedy against hoarseness.

3 A **carrion flower 1,** usu *Smilax herbacea.*

1817 Eaton *Botany* 116, *Smilax . . peduncularis,* (Jacob's ladder). **1840** MA Zool. & Bot. Surv. *Herb. Plants & Quadrupeds* 210, *Smilax.* . . Jacob's Ladder. . . *S. peduncularis.* . . Jacob's Ladder. Unarmed, and distinguished by its acuminate, 9-nerved leaves, offensive, greenish flowers, and bluish berries. **1876** [see **1** above]. **1939** Medsger *Edible Wild Plants* 88, Carrion Flower, or Jacob's Ladder, . . ranges from New Brunswick to Manitoba, south to Florida and Oklahoma. **1943** Fernald–Kinsey *Edible Wild Plants E. N. Amer.* 138, Carrion-flower, Jacob's-ladder, *Smilax . . herbacea.* Ibid 140, Bryony-leaved Jacob's-ladder, *Smilax tamnifolia.* . . Whereas the conspicuous over-wintering long-stalked globes of blue-black berries of the wide-ranging *Carrion-flower* are disagreeable in taste and very rubbery, the very similar ones of *Bryony-leaved Jacob's-ladder* are delicious—sweet and date-like. **1970** Kirk *Wild Edible Plants W. U.S.* 295, *Smilax herbacea* . . Jacob's Ladder. . . The young shoots, tendrils and all, may be cooked like asparagus.

4 A **bittersweet** (here: *Celastrus scandens*).

1835 (1906) Bradley *Jrl.* 235 **NH,** It [=a poisonous vine] much resembled, except in its larger size, a vine that flourishes between Exeter and Newmarket and which we used to call Jacob's Ladder. **1892** *Jrl. Amer. Folkl.* 5.94, *Celastrus scandens.* . . Jacob's ladder. Stratham, N.H. **1930** Sievers *Amer. Med. Plants* 4, *American Bittersweet.* . . *Other common names.* . . Jacob's-ladder. . . A woody and shrubby climber. **1960** Vines *Trees SW* 660, *Celastrus scandens.* . . Known also by the vernacular names of False Bitter-sweet, . . Jacob's Ladder.

5 =**butter-and-eggs 1.**

1892 *Jrl. Amer. Folkl.* 5.101 **NEng,** *Linaria vulgaris,* Jacob's ladder. **1897** *Ibid* 10.52 **NY,** *Linaria vulgaris,* . . Jacob's ladder, Long Island. **1935** (1943) Muenscher *Weeds* 418, *Linaria vulgaris.* . . Jacobs-ladder. . . Common throughout eastern North America; also local on the Pacific Coast. **1949** Moldenke *Amer. Wild Flowers* 272, The common name of *butter-and-eggs* for this plant [=*Linaria vulgaris*] seems appropriate because of the colors of the corolla, but the names . . *Jacobsladder,* . . *brideweed* . . are a bit more obscure in their application. **1959** Carleton *Index Herb. Plants* 67, *Jacob's ladder:* Dioda virginiana; Linaria vulgaris; Polemonium (v). **1967** *DARE* (Qu. S26a, . . *Roadside flowers*) Inf **NY**30, Butter-and-eggs—same as Jacob's ladder—because there is a spur revealed when blossom is removed which can be stuck in another flower ad infinitum.

6 A **twisted-stalk** (here: *Streptopus* spp).

1897 *Jrl. Amer. Folkl.* 10.145, *Streptopus roseus,* . . Jacob's ladder, Paris, Me.

7 =**celandine.**

1900 Lyons *Plant Names* 94, C[*helidonium*] *majus.* . . Jacob's-ladder. **1930** Sievers *Amer. Med. Plants* 22, *Celandine.* . . *Other common names.* . . Jacob's-ladder. . . Leaves . . are deeply and variously cleft.

8 A **buttonweed 1** (here: *Diodia virginiana*).

1920 *Torreya* 20.25, *Diodia virginiana.* . . Jacob's-ladder, Savannah, Ga. **1959** [see **5** above].

9 =**jewbush.**

1955 *S. Folkl. Qrly.* 19.234 **FL,** Pedalanthus [sic]. All varieties are commonly called *Devil's Backbone* or *Jacob's Ladder,* perhaps from the jointed, angular, and branching stem. **1976** Bailey–Bailey *Hortus Third* 832 **FL,** [*Pedilanthus*] *tithymaloides.* . . Subsp. *Smallii.* . . Jacob's-ladder. St[em]s zig-zag. **1982** Perry–Hay *Field Guide Plants* 70, *Pedilanthus tithymaloides* . . Jacob's ladder. . . Fleshy, cylindrical, zig-zag stems containing milky sap.

10 A **false Solomon's seal** (here: *Smilacina racemosa*).

1966 *DARE* Wildfl QR Pl.18 [=*Smilacina racemosa*] Inf **CO**7, Jacob's ladder.

11 Any of var other plants; see quots.

1894 *Jrl. Amer. Folkl.* 7.101, *Gladiolus,* sp. . . Jacob's ladder, Lincolnton, N.C. *Ibid* 102, *Hyacinthus orientalis,* . . Jacob's ladder, No. Ohio. **1897** *Ibid* 10.146, *Tradescantia crassifolia* (green), Jacob's ladder, Wandering Jew, Sulphur Grove, Ohio. **1940** Clute *Amer. Plant Names* 256, *Convallaria majalis.* . . Jacob's ladder. **1970** *DARE* (Qu. S6, . . *Queen Anne's lace:* [*Summertime roadside weed two feet high or so with a lacy white top*]) Inf **KY**93, Jacob's ladder.

12 See quots. Cf **Job's coffin 2**

1908 *DN* 3.324 **eAL, wGA,** *Jacob's ladder.* . . A form made on the fingers with string. **1968** Haun *Hawk's Done Gone* 310 **eTN,** My feet hurt—tote me—me like you tote me. Make me Jacob's ladder. **1986** Pederson *LAGS Concordance* (Games) 1 inf, **cnAL,** Jacob's ladder.

Jacob's ladder bean See **Jacob's cattle bean**

Jacob's lantern n Cf **devil's lantern, frog lantern 1**
=**jack-o'-lantern 1.**

1967 *DARE* (Qu. CC16, *A small light that seems to dance or flicker over a marsh or swamp at night*) Inf **SC**34, Jacob's ['ĵeikəps] lantern.

Jacob's onion n

A **green onion 1**; see quot.

1975 Purkey *Home in Madison Co.* 106 **cwNC** (as of 1915), I will never forget the endless bundles of crisp spring onions with their long white heads and their tender green blades, which my mother prepared for market. Mama called them "Jacob's Onions." I don't know why unless it was because they were so prolific.

Jacob's rake n [Cf *Cent. D.* Jacob's staff]
Prob =**ellenyard.**

1930 Shoemaker *1300 Words* 33 **cPA Mts** (as of c1900), *Jacob's rake*—The three kings, a constellation.

Jacob's staff n [In allusion to St. James *(Jacob),* symbolized in religious art by a pilgrim's staff]

1 =**ocotillo.**

1891 Coulter *Botany W. TX* 33, F[*ouquieria*] *splendens.* . . Known as "Jacob's staff" or "ocotillo." **1903** Small *Flora SE U.S.* 784, *Fouquiera* [sic] *splendens.* . . A shrub or a tree, . . the gray ridges of some of the branches terminating in spines. . . *Jacob's staff.* **1960** Vines *Trees SW* 762, Vernacular names for the plant are Coachwhip-cactus, . . Jacob's Staff. . . The slender stems are used for walking sticks, and are planted close together to make fences and hut walls, often sprouting from the barren stem. **1976** Bailey–Bailey *Hortus Third* 484, [*Fouquieria*] *splendens.* . . Jacob's-staff. . . New Mex. and Tex. to s. Calif.

2 also *Jacob ladder,* ~ *staff,* ~ *stick, Jake staff:* Any of var bars, staves, or poles; see quots.

1937 (1963) Hyatt *Kiverlid* 20 **KY,** Git the jacob stick and start turnin' slow. **1958** McCulloch *Woods Words* 98 **Pacific NW,** *Jacob's staff*—a. A stout bar attached to the axle of a big-wheel log carrier at right angles to the tongue; when the driver pulled on the staff the tongue of the tongue was forced into the ground, acting as a brake. b. A pointed steel staff used as a support for a staff compass. . . *Jake staff*—Another name for a Jacob's staff. **1967** *DARE* FW Addit **seOR,** Jacob's staff—the pole in front of hayrack. **1969** Sorden *Lumberjack Lingo* 63 **NEng, Gt Lakes,** *Jacob's staff*—1. A heavy bar attached to the axle of big wheels to raise logs. 2. A staff used to support a staff compass. **1992** Attebery *Sheep* 13 **swID,** The bottom part [of a door on a sheepherder's wagon] could be closed, keeping some wind out, while the upper part opened onto the Jacob staff (or ladder) behind which the driver stood.

Jacob's tears n Cf **wild Job's tears**

Prob **Job's tears 1.**

1945 Saxon *Gumbo Ya-Ya* 534 **LA,** Negro teether: A cow tooth, or a string of Jacob's Tears (a kind of seed).

Jacob stick See **Jacob's staff 2**

jade v [*OED jade* v. 3 "To befool; to jape. *Obs.*"]

See quot 1906.

1906 *DN* 3.142 **nwAR,** *Jade.* . . To tantalize, tease. "Don't let 'em jade you." [**1925** *DN* 5.334 **Nfld,** *Jade* . . =*moider* [i.e. pester, bother]. "We don't want to be jaded about de princess."]

jaded adj Also with *out* [*OED* 1693 →] **chiefly S Atl, Gulf States**

Tired; exhausted.

1828 Webster *Amer. Dict.* np, *Jaded.* . . Tired; wearied; fatigued. **1960** Williams *Walk Egypt* 274 **GA,** I mean, betwixt the store and Jack and my daddy, I'm jaded out. **1966–68** *DARE* (Qu. X47, . . *"I'm very tired, at the end of my strength"*) Inf **NC49,** Jaded; (Qu. BB5, *A general feeling of discomfort or illness that isn't any one place in particular*) Inf **NC7,** Feels jaded all over; (Qu. KK30, *Feeling slowed up or without energy: "I certainly feel _____."*) Inf **NC82,** Jaded out. **1986** Pederson *LAGS Concordance* (*Drowsy, sleepy*) 4 infs, **GA, MS,** Jaded; (*Worn out*) 1 inf, **AL,** Jaded—very tired, fatigued; old people said; 1 inf, **GA,** A little jaded; 1 inf, **MS,** I'm jaded; (*Tired, exhausted*) 1 inf, **MS,** Jaded out.

jade flower n

The flower of the jade vine (*Strongylodon macrobotrys*).

[**1965** Neal *Gardens HI* 461, *Jade vine.* . . A vigorous vine from the Philippines is popular in Hawaii for its . . flowers, which are used for decorations and leis. The flowers are blue-green and about 3.5 inches long.] **1967** *DARE* (Qu. S26a, . . *Wildflowers.* . . *Roadside flowers*) Inf **HI11,** To make leis . . jade flowers.

jadehopper n

1916 Macy–Hussey *Nantucket Scrap Basket* 137 **seMA,** "Jadehopper"—A curious old word applied to a lewd or vicious woman, or sometimes to one who is only mischievous and lively.

jaeger n[1]

Std: a predatory seabird of the genus *Stercorarius.* Also called **gull hunter, jiddy hawk, marlinspike 1, sea hawk, turdeater.** For other names of var spp see **long-tailed jaeger, parasitic jaeger, pomarine jaeger**

jaeger n[2] See **jagger** n[1] c

jaeger gull n

=**pomarine jaeger.**

1917 (1923) *Birds Amer.* 1.33, *Pomarine Jaeger.* . . *Other Names.* . . Jaeger Gull. [*Ibid* 34, When no victims are available for a hold-up, the Jaeger turns scavenger and picks up dead marine life like a true Gull.] **1946** Hausman *Eastern Birds* 300, Jaeger Gull. . . *Habits*—Similar to those of other jaegers, except that this species is said to be less bold, daring, and fierce. **1963** Gromme *Birds WI* 215, Gull, . . Jaeger (Pomarine Jaeger).

jag n[1] [*OED jag* sb.[1] 2 "A shred of cloth; in *pl.* Rags, tatters." 1555 →]

1 See quot.

1899 (1912) Green *VA Folk-Speech* 243, *Jags.* . . Tatters. "Rags and jags."

2 See quot.

1967–69 *DARE* (Qu. W27, . . *A three-cornered tear in a piece of clothing from catching it on something sharp*) Infs **IL**72, **NY**70, **OH**27, 43, **WI**56, Jag.

jag n[2]

1 An approximate measure of quantity; see below. Note: It is not always possible to distinguish among the following subsenses.

a A load, esp a small or partial one, usu of hay or wood. [*OED jag* sb.[2] "A load . . of hay, wood, etc." 1597 →] **chiefly Nth, N Midl, West** See Map

1636 in 1855 New Plymouth Colony *Records* 1.40 **MA,** The quan-

tity of two loade or jaggs of hey at the Iland Creeke. **1721** (1901) Hempstead *Diary* 17 Oct 115 **seCT,** Wee Carted 2 Jaggs of hay from mothers. **1890** *DN* 1.76 **MD.** **1892** *DN* 1.213 **NEng.** **1892** *AN&Q* [see **2** below]. **1894** *DN* 1.331 **NJ.** *Ibid* 341 **wCT.** **1903** *DN* 2.298 **Cape Cod MA** (as of a1857). **1907** *German Amer. Annals* 9.380 **sePA.** **1909** *DN* 3.399 **nwAR,** *Jag.* . . A small amount of hay, wood, corn, or other commodity hauled on a wagon. **1910** *DN* 3.444 **wNY.** *Ibid* 454 **seVT.** **1912** *DN* 3.568 **cNY.** **1923** *DN* 5.211 **swMO.** **1940** *AmSp* 15.453 **KS,** In my Kansas farm days the word [=*jag*] had become modified to mean a small load, less than a full load. 'Is there a load of hay out in the field?' 'No, just a jag.' A *jag,* however, was considerably more than a *shirt-tail.* **1949** Kurath *Word Geog.* 57, The quantity of corn a farmer has (or had) ground at one time at the gristmill is (or was) called a *grist of corn,* a *turn of corn,* or a *jag of corn.* . . *Jag of corn* is current in all of Pennsylvania, on Delaware Bay, in Maryland, and on the upper reaches of the Potomac in West Virginia. In Delaware and Maryland, where *grist* is not current, *jag* means a *grist.* But in Pennsylvania and southern New Jersey a *jag* is less than a *grist;* here *jag* is applied to a part load of anything carried on a wagon. **1950** *WELS* **WI** (*If the wagon was only partly full* [*of wood*], *you say he has a _____*) 31 Infs, Jag; 6 Infs, Jag of wood; 1 Inf, Half jag; 1 Inf, Occasionally you hear jag load. **1953** Randolph–Wilson *Down in Holler* 162 **Ozarks,** In the Ozarks a jag. . . means a light load, a comparatively small quantity. . . I think *jag* is more often used with reference to hay and firewood than anything else. **1964** (1965) Gould *You Should Start* 183 **ME,** The size of the load depended on the size of the cart. Sometimes the load was a "jag," which is all you can haul without having any slide off. **1965–70** *DARE* (Qu. L55, *If the wagon was only partly full . . he had a _____*) 138 Infs, **chiefly Nth, N Midl, West,** Jag; 14 Infs, **chiefly Nth, N Midl, West,** Little (*or* small) jag; **CT**10, **MI**38, **NH**14, **NY**206, **UT**4, **WI**6, 24, 30, Jag on; **IA**6, **MI**101, **NY**13, **VT**16, Half a jag; **CT**7, **IN**42, Jag load; **AR**4, **IL**116, Jag of a load; **MI**56, Just a jag. **1971** Tak *Truck Talk* 91, *Jag:* a small cargo or pay load.

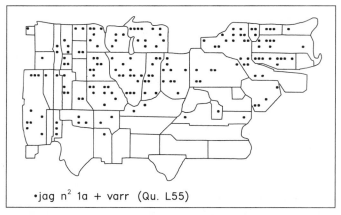

•jag n[2] 1a + varr (Qu. L55)

b also *big* (or *good,* etc) *jag:* An indefinite but large quantity or amount.

1818 Fearon *Sketches* 93 **NY,** What a *jag* (a load) there is of them 'ere salt-water fish lately come into the States. **1834** Davis *Letters Downing* 168 **MA,** As there was a very little rale mony in the country, the Bank went and bo't a good jag on't in Europe. **1899** (1912) Green *VA Folk-Speech* 243, *Jag.* . . A lot; parcel. **1905** *DN* 3.12 **cCT,** *Jag.* . . A great deal. 'He had a jag of work to do.' **1907** *DN* 3.214 **nwAR,** *Jag.* . . A great deal. **1935** Sandoz *Jules* 210 **wNE** (as of 1880–1930), The outfit's been . . putting up a big jag of hay on them wet flats. **1943** Hench *Coll.* **cVA,** He said to the boy: "Whenever you get a jag of them [flower orders], let me know." I asked him what a jag was and he answered "A good number." **1950** *WELS Suppl.* **ceWI,** (A) whole jag—a large amount. **1965** Will *Okeechobee Boats* 23 **FL,** They takened on a right good jag of cypress shingles piled high on her decks for to finish up the load. **1967** *DARE* (QR, near Qu. L55) Inf **CO**38, A good jag is 100–125 bales—a jag is a lot here.

c also *little jag:* An indefinite but small quantity or amount. **chiefly Midl, esp sAppalachians**

a1862 (1865) Thoreau *Cape Cod* 57 **MA,** A few piles of driftwood . . proved to be insignificant little "jags" of wood. **1892** *KS Univ. Qrly.* 1.97 **KS,** *Jag:* a bit of anything. **1913** Johnson *Highways St. Lawrence to VA* 186 **cwNJ,** People were cutting up firewood. . . Practically all of them brought a little jag at a time from the mountain . . and cut it up as needed. **1937** (1963) Hyatt *Kiverlid* 29 **KY,** Tell Jason . . to slip old

Dorie's bridle and fling her a leetle jag o' roughness. **1937** Sandoz *Slogum* 216 **NE,** She was just doing a jag of contract work for some homesteaders . . , giving a little work to some poor devils that needed it bad. **1949** Arnow *Hunter's Horn* 288 **eKY,** She bought a little jag a beans. **1953** Randolph–Wilson *Down in Holler* 163 **Ozarks,** William R. Lighton, who used to live near Fayetteville, Arkansas, spoke of "a little jag of potatoes," and a man in Carroll County, Arkansas, told me that his wife wanted "a jag of rich dirt" to put in a flower bed. **1974** Fink *Mountain Speech* 13 **wNC, eTN,** *Jag* . . a small amount. *"A jag o' corn."* **1983** *MJLF* 9.1.45 **ceKY,** *Jag* . . small, indefinite amount. **1985** *DARE* File **Appalachians,** *Jag:* In Appalachia, it's just a little.

d Spec: a catch or load of oysters. **esp MD, VA**

1881 Ingersoll *Oyster-Industry* 245 **Atl coast,** *Jag.*—A lot, parcel, or quantity of oysters of indefinite size: *e.g.,* "I sold a jag of 75 bushels to A, B, & Co." **1939** *Sun* (Baltimore MD) 10 Nov 8/5 *(Hench Coll.),* You'll see close-ups of Maryland's disappearing oyster industry, showing how the tongers and the dredgers work, the "jags" they bring in, and the inspection the oysters undergo. **1976** Ryland *Richmond Co. VA* 372, *Jag*—load, as in "a jag of oysters." **1976** Warner *Beautiful Swimmers* 256 **eMD,** They could tow their dredges more smoothly and gently with power, they claim, and still make their jags in a shorter time. **1991** *DARE* File **Chesapeake Bay,** When the oystermen go out in their boats, there's also a bigger boat out there, called the buy boat, where there's a buyer for the oysters. When they've made their day's catch, the oystermen will say, "I'll have to take my jag in to the buy boat."

2 An amount of alcohol sufficient to produce intoxication; a state of alcohol (or less freq drug) intoxication—esp in phrr *have* (or *get*) *a jag (on)* to be (or get) drunk. [*OED* 1678 →] **chiefly Nth** See Map

1887 *Courier–Jrl.* (Louisville KY) 27 Jan 2/6, The three respectable ladies had "jags" on last night and attempted to "do up" the police. **1892** *AN&Q* 8.150 **NY,** When I was a boy in the country, any fraction of a load of hay was called a 'jag;' that is, a small load. By an easy transition, one heated with wine was said to have a load or be loaded, but nowadays it is common to hear him described as 'having a frightful old jag on,' meaning the biggest kind of a load. **1892** *DN* 1.216 **eMA,** *Jag.* . . The sense "a load of drink" . . has been known in Boston for only a very few years. **1896** *Congressional Record* 15 Apr 4024 **MI,** It is, then, the policy of the Board to run a saloon at one of the institutions and a "jag cure" at the other? **1909** *DN* 3.399 **nwAR,** *Jag.* . . In the phrase, "to have a jag on," to be drunk. **1910** *DN* 3.454 **seVT,** *Jag.* . . Too much whisky. "He had a jag on." **1912** *DN* 3.568 **cNY,** *Jag.* . . humorously for intoxication. **1946** (1972) Mezzrow–Wolfe *Really Blues* 334 **Chicago IL,** *Jag,* a state of extreme stimulation, produced by marihuana or some other stimulant. **1965–70** *DARE* (Qu. DD13, *When a drinker is just beginning to show the effects of the liquor . . he's _____*) Infs **IL4, WI26,** Getting a jag on; **OH76,** Got a jag; (Qu. DD14, *When a person is partly drunk, "He's _____."*) Infs **ME9, PA230,** Got a jag on; **WI30,** Getting a jag on; **NY163,** Got a good jag on; **MI10,** Got a little jag on; (Qu. DD15, *A person who is thoroughly drunk*) Inf **MA62,** Got a good jag on; **CO4,** Got a jag; (Qu. DD22, *. . Delirium tremens*) Inf **MI92,** They have a jag on; **MA123,** Jag; (Qu. L55) Inf **NH14,** [He had a] jag on—also used for someone partly drunk; (QR, near Qu. L55) Inf **CA23,** A jag on—a fellow who had too much to drink. **1989** *DARE* File **neWI** (as of c1958), To "have a jag going," or to "have half a jag," etc., meant to be totally or somewhat drunk, as in: "Her husband came home with half a jag on and couldn't get the car in the garage," or, "She really had a jag going at the Christmas party."

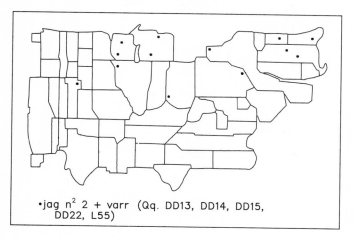

•jag n² 2 + varr (Qq. DD13, DD14, DD15, DD22, L55)

3 A drunken spree; a drinking binge.

1892 *KS Univ. Qrly.* 1.97 **KS,** *Jag:* . . a spree, a brief drunk. **1926** *Chicago Daily Tribune* (IL) 4 Apr sec 1 18/2, [Headline:] Dry Finland on 4 Days' Jag to Observe Easter. **1942** McAtee *Dial. Grant Co. IN* 36 (as of 1890s), *Jag* . . "on a _____", drunk. **1950** *WELS* (To have a drinking bout and get drunk: go on a _____) 2 Infs **WI,** Jag. **c1960** Wilson *Coll.* **csKY,** *Jag.* . . A drunken spree, a bender. **1966–70** *DARE* (Qu. DD16) Infs **FL16, IL37, 144, MN29, OH37,** Jag; **VA43,** Drinking jag; (QR, near Qu. DD24) Inf **FL27,** Jag—four or five days' drinking.

4 Transf: a bout of irrational or compulsive behavior.

1913 London *Valley of Moon* 119 **CA,** "Aw, it's only one of his cryin' jags," Mary said. **1920** *DN* 5.82 **cwWA,** *Jag, Crying.* "Crying jag has good reason to weep." **1924** Marks *Plastic Age* 254 **N Atl,** A girl got a "laughing jag" and shrieked with idiotic laughter. **1945** Lewis *Cass Timberlane* 361 **MN,** Now you're beginning to get over your love-jag, maybe you can see that Jinny is as . . tricky and grabbing as a monkey. **1962** *AmSp* 37.30, Our employment of it in such expressions as *crying jag,* which is still in use, and such inventive variants as *buying jag, eating jag,* and others, still current, suggests that even if the word is not exclusively an Americanism we are tending to use it more widely in slang and in colloquial speech than do the English. *Jag* used alone . . , seems to occur relatively infrequently today. **1970** *DARE* (Qu. GG31, *To laugh very hard: "I thought I'd _____."*) Inf **NY249,** Throw a fit, laughing jad [sic]. **1972** *New Yorker* 26 Aug 38, A neurotic habit . . may be overt, like a temper tantrum or a crying jag.

jag v[1] [Scots, Ir, nEngl dial] **esp PA**

A Forms. Note: The strong past and past participial forms appear to be an American innovation.

1 past: usu *jagged;* also *jug;* occas pleonastic *jugged.*

1953 [see **B1** below]. **1967–69** [see **B1** below]. **1978** [see **B1** below]. **1982** [see **B1** below]. **1986** [see **B1** below].

2 past pple: usu *jagged;* also *jug.*

1967–69 [see **B1** below]. **1978** [see **B1** below].

B Senses.

1 To prick, stab, jab.

1876 Clark *Elbow Room* 24 **PA,** He went up and jagged a pin into the baby's leg. **1884** *Amer. Philol. Assoc. Trans. for 1883* 14.50 **Sth, esp SC,** *Jag,* 'to prick or pierce with a thorn or any sharp-pointed thing.' Common in various parts of the South. So in South Carolina, a man in swimming was said to have been "jagged by a snag." **1953** *AmSp* 28.250 **csPA,** The verb . . appears in Bedford subarea folk speech with the past tense *jug* ('I jug my finger'). **1967–69** *DARE* (Qu. Y46a, *. . "He _____ a thorn into his hand."*) Inf **PA148,** Jug; **PA72,** Jug, got jug, jagged; **PA199,** Jugged, stuck; (Qu. Y46b, *. . "She _____ herself with a needle."*) Infs **PA29, 152,** Jagged; **PA18,** Jug [ǰʌg]; **PA142,** Jug; **PA72,** Jug, jagged; **PA164,** Jugged, jabbed. **1978** *AP Letters* **swPA,** Also used as a verb—*jag, jug, jug,* both transitive and intransitive. **1982** *Barrick Coll.* **csPA,** *Jag*—jab, pierce. . . *Jug*—past tense of *jag:* "He jug his finger on the locust tree." **1986** Pederson *LAGS Concordance* *(Stabbed)* 1 inf, **eLA,** Jug it; 1 inf, **swGA,** Jugged him in the belly.

2 also with *off;* By ext: to annoy, irritate, play tricks on; to disparage; to reject. [Perh infl by *jack (someone) off* to tease, harass]

1968 *DARE* (Qu. Y3, *To say uncomplimentary things about somebody*) Inf **PA94,** Jag him off; (Qu. Y7, *When one person never misses a chance to be mean to another or to annoy another: "I don't know why she keeps _____ me all the time!"*) Infs **PA76,** Jagging; (Qu. AA11, *If a man asks a girl to marry him and she refuses, . . she _____*) Inf **PA94,** Jagged him off; (Qu. GG32a, *To habitually play tricks or jokes on people: "He's always _____."*) Inf **PA94,** Jagging people off.

3 intr; with *around:* See quots. [Perh infl by *jack around* to idle around]

1968 *DARE* (Qu. GG32a, *To habitually play tricks or jokes on people: "He's always _____."*) Inf **PA76,** Jagging around; (Qu. KK31, *. . "He doesn't have anything to do, so he's just _____ around."*) Inf **PA94,** Jagging. [Both Infs young White male coll students in Pittsburgh]

jag v[2]

To make a jog or change in direction.

1970 *DARE* FW Addit **VA43,** Jag—turn. "Jag back a little": turn a little while backing up a car or truck.

jag n[3] See **jagasee**

jag around See **jag** v[1] **B3**

jagasee n Also abbr *jag* [AmPort *jagacida;* see quot 1981] **MA**
See quot 1939.

1939 Berolzheimer *U.S. Cookbook* 102, Jagasee (A Cape Cod Dish). . .
Lima beans . . salt pork . . onions . . celery . . green pepper . . rice.
1940 Brown *Amer. Cooks* 372 **MA,** Jagasee. **1947** Bowles–Towle *New
Engl. Cooking* 109, Jagasee—1 cup dried lima beans, 3 slices salt pork,
1 onion, minced, ½ cup diced celery, 1 green pepper, minced, Salt and
pepper, 1 tablespoon rice. **1970** *DARE* (Qu. H50, *Dishes made with
beans, peas, or corn that everybody around here knows, but people in
other places might not*) Inf **MA**122, Jag—Portuguese, with onions, lima
beans. **1979** Flagg *Cape Cod Cooking* 160 **seMA,** Jagasida—This dish
originated in Cape Verde and is popular in many Cape Cod homes,
where it is called "Jag". [**1981** Pap *Port.–Americans* 215 **Cape Cod
MA,** Frequently the family also ate *jagacida* (which was made with
lima beans, onion, and rice).]

jagety See **jaggedy 1**

jagga See **jagger** n¹ **a**

jagged adj¹ Cf **jaggedy 2**
Exhausted.

1968 *DARE* (Qu. X47, . . *"I'm very tired, at the end of my strength"*)
Inf **NY**59, Jagged.

jagged adj² |jǽgd| [**jag** n² **2**]
Intoxicated with liquor or drugs.

1745 in 1887 Franklin *Complete Wks.* 2.24 **PA,** He's. . . Jagg'd. **1907**
Porter *Trimmed Lamp* 162 **NYC,** What I want is a masterful man that
slugs you when he's jagged and hugs you when he ain't jagged. **1915**
DN 4.212, Jagged, drunk. "That poor man is pretty well jagged." **1926**
Finerty *Criminalese* 32, Jagged—Intoxicated. **1938** in 1973 Himes *Black
on Black* 175, She made him smoke pot and when he got jagged . . she
put him out on the street. **1946** Gould *Yankee Storekeeper* 139 **cwME,**
Uncle Dave continued to drink alone, and was pretty well jagged when
the horse stopped at a depression in the road.

jagged chickweed See **chickweed 1d**

jaggedy adj
1 also sp *jagety:* Having a jagged edge; see quot 1899. [Cf
Intro "Language Changes" III.1] **Sth, S Midl** Cf **fadedy**
1899 (1912) Green *VA Folk-Speech* 243, Jagged. . . Having notches
or teeth, or ragged edges; cleft; divided. Jaggedy. Jagety. **1943** *New
Yorker* 20 Mar 42 **Sth,** A jaggedy piece of shrapnel went right through
one of the tires. **c1960** *Wilson Coll.* **csKY,** Jaggedy. . . Jagged, irregular.
1967 *Mt. Life* 43.1.15 **sAppalachians,** He could see the jaggedy aidge
of a great big rock. **1986** Pederson *LAGS Concordance,* 1 inf, **cnLA,**
Jaggedy edges.
2 See quot. Cf **jagged** adj¹
1986 Pederson *LAGS Concordance* (*Someone's been sick a while; he's
up and about now, but still looks a bit _____*) 1 inf, **ceAL,** Jaggedy.

jagger n¹
Something that pricks or jags; spec:
a also *jaggerknife;* pronc-sp *jagga:* A jagging wheel; see quot
1872. *old-fash* Cf **jiggering iron**
1853 Webster *Amer. Dict.* 629, Jagger. . . A brass wheel for cutting cakes. . . See jagging-iron. **1872** (1876) Knight *Amer. Mech. Dict.*
2.1210, Jagger. . . A small wheel mounted in a handle and used for
crimping or ornamenting edges of pies, cakes, etc., or cutting them into
ornamental shapes. A *jagging-iron.* **1892** *NY Voice* (NY) 15 Sept 6/2
cOH, Mix the eggs with flour . . cut them the shape of a long narrow
leaf . . cut them with a jagger so they will be notched. **1896** (c1973)
Farmer *Orig. Cook Book* 388 **NEng,** The pastry-jagger, a simple device
for cutting paste, makes rims with fluted edges. **1902** (1969) Sears
Catalogue 597, Paste Jagger. Made of boxwood with corrugated wheel
for pressing down crust at rim of pies, etc. **1944** Holton *Yankees Were
Like This* 215 **Cape Cod MA** (as of c1890), If you know what a
jaggaknife is you. . . might even qualify as an honorary Cape Codder. . .
It is carved from a flat piece of whale ivory . . in the semblance of a
sea horse. . . Between his hoofs he holds a little wheel. . . It isn't an
ordinary wheel, it's a jagga, for the horse himself is nothing but a handle
and this . . pivoted . . fluted bit of ivory is the business end of the
jaggaknife. . . The jaggaknife is the most exclusive of kitchen implements and essentially a pie-making gadget. *Ibid* 217, She worked out
designs in squirls and twizzles of jagga crust that made you wobble
between the urge to bite into their crispness and the desire to keep them
whole to feast your eyes upon.

b A thorn or burr. [**jag** v¹ **B1;** cf *DSL jagger* "A prickle"]
chiefly PA
1923 *DN* 5.211 **swMO,** Jagger. . . Any small, sharp-pointed object or
implement. Applicable chiefly to thorns or briars. **1935** *AmSp* 10.171
sePA, [Footnote:] The term *jaggers* is regularly used instead of thorns,
prickles, or the mid-western folk term 'stickers.' 'Don't go in there.
There are jaggers.' **1953** *AmSp* 28.250 **csPA,** Jagger. . . A sharp point,
particularly and almost exclusively of a thorn or brier. 'Look out for that
branch, it's all over jaggers.' In general use. **1968–69** *DARE* (Qu. S13, . .
*A common wild bush with bunches of round, prickly seeds; when they
get dry they stick to your clothing*) Infs **PA**77, 216, Jaggers; **PA**152,
Jaggers [čægaᵊz]—also called this in Kutztown. **1978** *AP Letters* **swPA,**
A jagger is a small thorn as from berry briars or barberry hedge. **1982**
McCool *Sam McCool's Pittsburghese* 19 **PA,** Jaggers: thorns—"Watch,
there's jaggers on that plant!"

c also *jaeger, jigger;* In logging: a frayed strand protruding
from a worn wire rope.
1919 *DN* 5.57 **swWA,** Jaeger. . . Jack Morvee was layed off Tuesday
with a sore hand caused by a jaeger from the line. Kalama Bulletin.
1938 (1939) Holbrook *Holy Mackinaw* 262 **MI,** Jagger. A sliver of wire
rope. **1950** *Western Folkl.* 9.118 **nwOR** (as of c1892) [Logger speech],
Jaggers. Frayed bits of wire sticking out from a line. **1958** McCulloch
Woods Words 98 **Pacific NW,** Jagger—A broken strand on worn cable,
sticking out to tear hands or clothes. *Ibid, Jigger*—Same as jagger. **1969**
Sorden *Lumberjack Lingo* 63 **NEng, Gt Lakes,** Jagger—A sliver from
a wire rope or cable.

jagger n² [Pronc-sp for *jaguar*]
1906 Casey *Parson's Boys* 126 **sIL** (as of c1860), There came from
the roof a loud, hoarse "Hoo, hoo hoo, hoo hooahh!" which died away
in a growl. "Oh, Pa, it's a jagger!" chattered William. . . William did
not know that jaguars did not inhabit Illinois; but he had read about
them, and knew that they screamed. *Ibid* 127, They slept soundly,
forgetful of nightly terrors until aroused by the Apostle's joking call:
"It's time ye was a-gittin' out of here, 'fore some kind of a jagger or
night-bird gits holt of ye!" The sun was up.

jaggerknife See **jagger** n¹ **a**

jagger up v phr [**jag** to cut unevenly] Cf **jaggle 1**
To cut raggedly.
1966 *DARE* Tape **OK**27, You'd whet your knife and then you would
take your steel and get your fine edge on it and that's where you
wouldn't jagger your meat up.

jagger wagon n Also *jogger (wagon)* [See quot 1911; but perh
< **jag** n² **1**] esp **NJ and adjoining areas** *old-fash* Cf **jig-
ger** n¹ **2**
A plain light wagon, orig one having the body unsprung and
the seat supported on longitudinal wooden springs.
1858 *NY Coach-Maker's Mag.* 1.28 **NY,** New Rochelle, or Jagger
Wagon. . . This is a very plain wagon, which appears to have sprung
into existence, in this vicinity, from the exigencies of the times. . . One
reason for this popularity, no doubt, is. . . that we, . . in order to cure
the dyspepsia in our stomachs, have adopted the best remedy extant—a
vehicle without springs—and gone back to the old-fashioned "bolster."
[**1884** Knight *New Mech. Dict.* 4.511, Jagger Spring. . . A spring beneath a seat and resting by its ends upon blocks or cleats, in the bed or
body of the vehicle.] **1895** *DN* 1.383 **cNJ,** Jagger-wagon: light, open
farm-wagon used on the roads for light work, such as carting small truck
and going for the mails. Central Burlington Co. **1911** *Century Dict.
Suppl., Wagon.* . . Jagger wagon, a buggy with bolsters like a farm
wagon and a seat supported by two wooden springs running the full
length of the body, the ends resting upon the ends of the corner posts.
It takes its name from the original builder and was the first light wagon
to use wooden springs of the side-bar type. Used chiefly by farmers in
New Jersey. **1940** *Sun* (Baltimore MD) 24 May 26/4 *(Hench Coll.)* **MD,**
A chestnut and bay pranced in front of a fifty-year-old jagger wagon as
Messrs. Borland and Biggins were assisted into its rear seat. **1968** *DARE*
(Qu. N41c, *Horse-drawn vehicles to carry light loads*) Inf **NJ**50, Jag-
ger wagon ['jægə]; **NJ**51, Jogger wagon [jɑ·gə]—like topless carryall;
PA126, Jogger—took the place of a small pickup truck. **1977** Berkebile
Amer. Carriages pl. 56, Jagger Wagon. . . Later models featured improved
suspension and canopy tops. By 1900 the name had become almost
synonymous with "spring wagon" in some areas. Useful as family
carriages, they were also extensively used as light business wagons.

jaggle v [Engl dial; cf *EDD*]
1 See quot. Cf **haggle** v, **jagger up**

1930 Shoemaker *1300 Words* 33 **cPA Mts** (as of c1900), *Jaggle—*To cut unevenly.

‡2 vbl n *jaggling:* See quot.
1966 *DARE* (Qu. KK13, . . *Arguing:* "They stood there for an hour ———.") Inf **DC**8, Jaggling.

jag-off n [**jag** v¹ **B2, 3**] esp **PA**
Used as a general term of disparagement; see quots.
1968 *DARE* (Qu. GG42, *A reckless person, one who takes foolish chances*) Inf **PA**94, Jag-off; (Qu. HH3, *A dull and stupid person*) Inf **PA**94, Jag-off; (Qu. HH16, *Uncomplimentary words with no definite meaning—just used when you want to show that you don't think much of a person: "Don't invite him. He's a ———."*) Infs **PA**76, 94, Jag-off; (Qu. HH21, *A very awkward, clumsy person*) Inf **PA**133, Jag-off; (Qu. II7, *Somebody who doesn't seem to 'fit in' or to get along very well . . "He's kind of a ———."*) Inf **PA**76, Jag-off. [All three Infs young White male coll or hs students] **1971** Landy *Underground Dict.* 111, *Jag off.* . . Inept or stupid person. **1987** Turow *Presumed Innocent* 16, He thinks it would help my chances a lot if we arrested Carolyn's murderer before Election Day. Can you believe that jagoff? And he said it with a straight face.

jag off v phr See **jag** v¹ **B2**
jag wire fence n [**jag** v¹ **B1**]
A barbed wire fence.
1956 Ker *Vocab. W. TX* 157, Fence made of wire with spikes on it . . jag wire [1 inf]. **1967–68** *DARE* (Qu. L63, *Kinds of fences made with wire*) Inf **AR**21, Jag wire; **VA**2A, Jag wire [FW: same as bob wire fence, but older term].

Jahnywary See **January**
‡jahoo n¹ Cf **jewlarker 1**
1939 *AmSp* 14.91 **eTN,** *Jahoo.* A courting boy. 'He's my jahoo.'

jahoo n² [Perh blend of **Jehu 1** + *yahoo*]
1965 Carmony *Speech Terre Haute* 41 **IN,** *Hick.* . . The expression *jahoo* (2 [infs]) . . appears to be an older form, being given by informants 1 and 7, the oldest members of their respective groups.

jail n
Any of var children's games; the place of "confinement" in such games.
1946 TN *Folk Lore Soc. Bulletin* 12.1.17, "Jail" was a splendid game. Here certain rules and bounds were set up and recognized. Drunkenness and fighting were the two principal offenses. **1967** Jacobs *Rejoicing* 129 **cIN** (as of c1930), Jail was played this way: A square was drawn on the ground and designated as the jail; two or three persons were chosen sheriff and his deputies, the remainder of those playing—both boys and girls—scattered out on the school grounds. Sheriff and deputies set out to catch whomever they could. When they made their catch, the sheriff could make up whatever charge he wished. "You are wanted for murder in Blue River County," he would say. . . The wilder the charge, the better the game. Once in jail, the culprits had to be kept there by brute force. When the jail got four or five husky ones in it, they often turned on the sheriff's crew and escaped. **1967–70** *DARE* [(Qu. EE2, *Games that have one extra player—when a signal is given, the players change places, and the extra one tries to get a place*) Inf **TN**1, Jail-breaker—old-fashioned;] (Qu. EE14, . . *The place where the player who is 'it' has to wait and count while the others hide*) Inf **LA**37, Pole, base, jail; (Qu. EE33, . . *Outdoor games . . that children play*) Inf **GA**80, Jail—prisoners try to get something from others; a circle is the jail; **KY**89, Jail—variation of cops and robbers. **1975** Ferretti *Gt. Amer. Book Sidewalk Games* 142, A centrally located stoop is chosen as both the Hunters' home base and as the Jail. . . [T]he Hunted must . . allow himself to be taken back to the stoop and put in Jail. **1986** Pederson *LAGS Concordance*, 1 inf, **swAL,** Jail—hit person with ball—he has to go to jail—he can escape while you chase others. Object to get everyone in jail—never worked.

jailhouse n [Redund; cf Intro "Language Changes" I.4] **scattered, but somewhat more freq Sth, S Midl** See Map
A jail.
1812 (1821) Asbury *Jrl.* 3.337 **KY,** We left our lodging in the jail-house, and came away to Green Hill's. **1904** *DN* 2.419 **nwAR,** *Jailhouse.* . . Jail. 'I can find my way when I get past the jail-house.' **1930** Irwin *Amer. Tramp* 108, *Jailhouse.—*A city or county jail, never applied to a penitentiary. No doubt adopted from the negro, who loves to use a big word. **1942** Rawlings *Cross Creek* 102 **cnFL,** I aimed to put you in the jailhouse. **1942** *Time* 2 Mar 74 **Chicago IL,** She hires the town's best criminal lawyer . . ,—enjoys the run of her jailhouse. **1943** *New*

Yorker 23 Oct 65 **cTX,** The penalties of evil-doing . . did not always lead to the jail house. **1952** Brown *NC Folkl.* 1.554, *Jail-house:* . . Jail, the building. **c1960** Wilson *Coll.* **csKY,** *Jailhouse.* . . Jail. **1962** Atwood *Vocab. TX* 71, *Local prison.* . . [Other expressions] of less frequency are *jailhouse, cooler, pokey, lock-up, brig* and *can.* **1965–70** *DARE* (Qu. V11, . . *Joking names . . for a county or city jail*) 31 Infs, **scattered, but somewhat more freq Sth, S Midl,** Jailhouse.

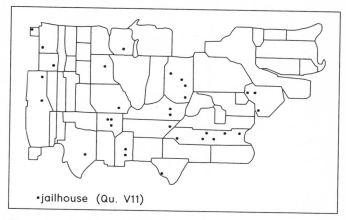

•jailhouse (Qu. V11)

jail wagon n Also *jailhouse wagon*
A patrol wagon.
1868 *Harper's New Mth. Mag.* 37.515 **NJ,** To secure this we have brought with us the jail-wagon, and we must request you to put the sick man into it. **1968–70** *DARE* (Qu. N3, *The car or wagon that takes arrested people to the police station or to jail*) Infs **NC**79, **VA**73, Jail wagon; **NJ**67, Jailhouse wagon.

jair v See **jar** v¹
jair n See **jar** n
jaist See **joist 1**
jajoba See **jojoba**

jake n¹ [Prob abbr for *Jacob*]
1 also *farmer jake:* A rustic, uncouth, or inexperienced person; a lout. **esp S Midl** *derog* Cf *country jake* (at **country** n **B2a**)
1884 (1890) Peck *Peck's Boss Book* 68 **Milwaukee WI,** A masher, like many of the Jakes of the present day. **1895** *DN* 1.389 **KS, MO, NC, TN,** *Jake:* a rough, uncouth country fellow. **1901** Harben *Westerfelt* 243 **nGA,** Mrs. Floyd laughed slyly as she turned away. "You leave them two Jakes to me." **1906** *DN* 3.120 **sIN,** *Jake.* . . Country fellow; inexperienced person. **1955** Faulkner *Big Woods* 194 **MS,** It was jest fine . . without no women to worry us or take off in the middle of the night with a durn Vicksburg roadhouse jake without even waiting to cook breakfast. **c1960** Wilson *Coll.* **csKY,** *Jake* (or *country jake*). . . A corny, awkward, green fellow, no matter where he lives. **1966–70** *DARE* (Qu. HH1, *Names and nicknames for a rustic or countrified person*) Inf **AR**22, Jake; **MO**12, Farmer jake; (Qu. U17) Inf **MS**80, Jake.
2 Used as a form of address; see quot. Cf **jack** n¹ **1**
1968 *DARE* (QR, near Qu. II1) Inf **LA**32, Friends call each other (boys) hoss, stone, jake, stud, jack.
3 A large marble.
1963 *KY Folkl. Rec.* 9.58 **eKY,** *Large marbles* . . jake. **1968** *DARE* (Qu. EE6d) Inf **WV**5, Jake—large marble in center of ring that you try to knock out.
4 See quot. Cf **john** n **1**
1967 *DARE* (Qu. K22, *Words used for a bull*) Inf **PA**23, Bull, mostly—when a kid on the farm, he called them "Jake."

jake n² [Abbr for *Jamaica* (ginger)]
1 also *jakers, jakey:* An alcoholic extract of Jamaica ginger used as a beverage during Prohibition.
1926 Finerty *Criminalese* 32, *Jake—*Jamaica ginger. *Ibid* 31, *Jake par*—Paralysis caused from Jamaica ginger. **1929** *AmSp* 4.341 [Vagabond lingo], *Jake—*Jamaica ginger. **1930** Irwin *Amer. Tramp* 108, *Jake.—*Jamaica ginger, used as a beverage and much favoured by the older tramp and more hardened drinker, but practically impossible for the average man to stomach. **1939** Steinbeck *Grapes* 131 **OK,** He would drink jake or whisky until he was a shaken paralytic. **1958** McCulloch

Woods Words 98 **Pacific NW,** *Jakey*—Jamaica ginger flavoring, much favored during Prohibition times because of its high alcoholic content. **1965–70** [see **jake leg 1**]. **1967–70** *DARE* (Qu. DD21b, *General words . . for bad liquor*) Inf **LA**2, Jake—not intended for drinking, it had alcohol and ginger in it—a cold remedy called Jamaica ginger, with wood alcohol; **VA**39, [ǰeɪŋk]. **1974** Dabney *Mountain Spirits* 108 (as of 1920s), Just about the most horrible drink appearing during the Noble Experiment was "jake," an almost ninety per cent alcohol fluid extract of Jamaica ginger with wood alcohol added, which literally paralyzed its victims in the hands and feet. "Jake paralysis" victims walked with a goose step, their feet flopping around out of control. **1976** Brown *Gloss. Faulkner* 110, During Prohibition, *Jamaica ginger,* known as "jake," "jakey," "jakers," etc., was widely used as a beverage among alcoholics. Jakeleg was a form of paralysis attributed to its habitual use.

2 See **jake leg** n¹ **1.**

jake arm, jake foot See **jake leg** n¹ 1

Jake Gould See **Jay Gould**

jake leg n¹

1 also pl; also *jake:* Paralysis of the leg(s), caused by drinking **jake** n² **1** or other contaminated liquor; the limb(s) so affected; similarly nouns *jake arm, ~ foot.* **chiefly S Midl, wGulf States** See Map

1931 Reeves *Ol' Rum River* 374 **NJ,** Much of the present liquor [is] being poisoned as a result of the Government's own acts, and thus directly responsible for thousands of cases of blindness, paralysis, "jake," and death. **1933** *Sun* (Baltimore MD) 10 Nov 9/8 *(Hench Coll.)* **cOK,** He was one of the victims of the "Jakefoot" epidemic of 1930. **1940** Stuart *Trees of Heaven* 182 **neKY,** The Lord ain't kind to moonshiners nohow. Look what happens to 'em. . . I never saw so many men walkin on canes with the jakeleg. **1954** *Harder Coll.* **cwTN,** Jake leg. . . A condition caused after many years of drinking. The legs become stiffened. *Jake arm.* . . The arms become stiffened. *Jake leg whiskey.* . . "Makes ye walk curious." **c1960** *Wilson Coll.* **csKY,** Jakeleg. . . A condition resulting from drinking bad liquor; a very modern word. *Give the jakeleg*—poison with bad whiskey. **1965–70** *DARE* (Qu. DD22, . . *Delirium tremens*) 11 Infs, **chiefly S Midl, neTX,** (The) jake legs; **KY**60, The jake legs—Prohibition era; **AR**13, 22, **LA**15, **MS**6, 16, **NC**52, **TX**38, (The) jake leg; **KY**65, Jake leg—caused by rotgut; **KY**84, Jake leg—from drinking jake, a fiery and hot alcohol; **NC**72, Having the jake walk—caused by Jamaica ginger loaded into bad liquor; **CA**65, Jake foot—from Jamaica ginger; they drag one leg; (Qu. BB1, *When a person has been injured so that when he walks he steps more heavily on one foot than the other: "He _____."*) Inf **VA**11, Has a jake leg—because he drank white lightning; **TN**12, Has the jake leg—caused by drinking Jamaica ginger; (Qu. DD21b, *General words . . for bad liquor*) Inf **OH**57, Jake-leg liquor; **KS**2, Jake-leg whiskey; (Qu. DD24, . . *Diseases that come from continual drinking*) Infs **GA**59, **TX**37, Jake leg; **KY**59, Jake leg—from bad whiskey or canned heat; **LA**2, Jake leg—from drinking jake; it was a kind of paralysis; **OK**25, Jake leg—caused from bad whiskey; leg gets kinda stiff. **1976** Garber *Mountainese* 47 **sAppalachians,** Jake-leg. . . "Jeems kaint walk very fast since he's had the jake-leg." **1976** [see **jake** n² **1**].

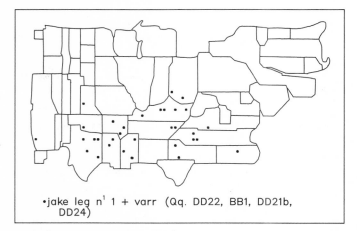

•jake leg n¹ 1 + varr (Qq. DD22, BB1, DD21b, DD24)

‡**2** See quot. Cf **buck fever 1**
1967 *DARE* (Qu. P36, *When a hunter sees a deer or other game*

animal and gets so excited he can't shoot, he has _____) Inf **TX**32, Jake leg.

jakeleg adj, n² [Var of **jackleg** adj, infl by **jake leg** n¹] **Gulf States, TN**
=**jackleg** adj.
1969–70 *DARE* (Qu. BB53b, . . *A doctor who is not very capable or doesn't have a very good reputation*) Inf **TN**30, Jakeleg doctor; (Qu. CC10, . . *An unprofessional, part-time lay preacher*) Inf **TN**30, Jakeleg preacher; (Qu. HH44, *Joking or uncomplimentary names for lawyers*) Infs **TN**30, 66, Jakeleg lawyer; **TN**62, Jakeleg. **1986** Pederson *LAGS Concordance* **Gulf Region,** 1 inf, Jake leg—anyone not professional; uncomplimentary; 1 inf, Jake leg—has same meaning as "cobbler"; 1 inf, Jake leg—preacher; not other professions; old term; 1 inf, Jake leg—it's supposed to be jack leg; jake-leg preacher—just kindly [sic] preaches; 1 inf, Jake leg—not a finished carpenter; 1 inf, Jake leg, jake-leg mechanic—heard from her husband, from Missouri; 1 inf, Jake leg—mechanic or carpenter; not very good; 1 inf, Jake leg—not good at trade; carpenter; 1 inf, Jake-leg carpenter—good for rough work.

jakers See **jake** n² 1

Jake staff See **Jacob's staff 2**

jake-walk v [*jake* (at **jake leg** n¹ 1)]
1968 *DARE* (Qu. BB1, *When a person has been injured so that when he walks he steps more heavily on one foot than the other: "He _____."*) Inf **OH**57, Jake-walks.

jake walkers n pl [Prob by analogy with **johnny walkers, tom walkers,** but perh infl by **jake-walk,** in ref to the stiff gait of one who has **jake leg** n¹ 1]
=**tom walkers.**
1969 *DARE* (Qu. EE35, *Long wooden poles with a footpiece that children walk around on to make them tall*) Inf **KY**6, Jake walkers.

jakey adj
Like or characteristic of a **jake** n¹ **1.**
1891 *PMLA* 6.173 **TN,** If his clothes are *tacky* and he appears to be from the backwoods, he is called a *country-jake,* and is said to look *jakey.* **1953** Randolph–Wilson *Down in Holler* 256 **Ozarks,** *Jakey.* . . Countrified, old-fashioned, uncouth. **c1960** *Wilson Coll.* **csKY,** *Jakey.* . . Acting like a jake or greenhorn. **1964** *AmSp* 39.235 **KS** [Student slang], *Jakey.* . . Peculiar or odd in appearance. **1968–69** *DARE* (Qu. HH1, *Names and nicknames for a rustic or countrified person*) Inf **MD**24, Jakey; (Qu. W29, . . *Expressions . . for things that are sewn carelessly*) Inf **IL**63, Jakey.

jakey n
1 See **jake** n² **1.**
2 Perh by ext: see quot. [Etym uncert; perh in ref to one with **jake leg** n¹ 1]
1967 *DARE* (Qu. EE41, *A hobgoblin that is used to threaten children and make them behave*) Inf **PA**22, [My mother said] the jakies were coming—the children would not know what they were, but would remain still.

jalap n Also *cancer jalap* Cf **wild jalap**
A **pokeweed** (here: *Phytolacca americana*).
1847 Wood *Class-Book* 478, *P[hytolacca] decandra.* . . *Jalap.* . . A common, well-known plant. . . The juice of the berries stains paper and linen a beautiful purple color. **1876** Hobbs *Bot. Hdbk.* 59, Jalap, cancer . . Phytolacca decandra. **1892** (1974) Millspaugh *Amer. Med. Plants* 139-1, *Poke Weed.* . . *Com[mon] names.* . . *Jalap.* . . The young shoots . . make an excellent substitute for asparagus, and I much prefer them, if gathered early and discriminately. **1930** Sievers *Amer. Med. Plants* 46, Cancer jalap. . . The root, collected in late autumn, is sliced and dried. **1940** Clute *Amer. Plant Names* 266, *Phytolacca decandra.* . . Jalap. **1971** Krochmal *Appalachia Med. Plants* 190, *Phytolacca americana.* . . *Common Names* . . jalap. . . In Appalachia, pokeberry wine is thought to help alleviate rheumatism. **1973** *Foxfire 2* 67 **sAppalachians,** Cancer jalap. . . Drooping white flowers are followed by shiny, wine-red berries on bright red stems. **1974** (1977) Coon *Useful Plants* 205, *Phytolacca americana* . . jalap. . . The roots are prepared . . and sold in the drug trade as an emetic and an "alternative" in chronic rheumatism.

jalapeño n Usu |ˌhɑləˈpeɪnjo|; also |ˌhæləˈpino, -ə|; for addit varr see quot 1967–70 Also *chili jalapeno, jalapeña, jalapena, jalapeno (chili), jap(aleeno)* [MexSpan < *jalapeño* pertaining to Jalapa Enríquez, Veracruz, Mexico] **orig chiefly TX, but now widely recognized** See Map

A cultivated hot pepper (*Capsicum annuum* var); by ext, any small chili pepper.

1960 *Washington Post & Times Herald* (DC) 17 Nov sec B 7/1 **TX,** The visitors' first taste of Texas food started the meal off with a zesty zing as they nibbled hot, hot noches [sic]—which are tiny tortillas topped with cheese and a scorching green pepper called jalapenas. **1965–70** *DARE* (Qu. I22b, . . *Peppers—large hot*) Infs **TX**3, 29, 43, Jalapeño(s); **TX**9, [ˌhælə'pino]; **TX**97, [ˌhɔlə'pino]; **TX**11, Jalapeña; **TX**26, ['hælə,pinə]; **TX**73, [ˌhælə'pinə]; **IL**17, [ˌhælə'piniə]; (Qu. I22a, . . *Peppers—small hot*) Infs **TX**4, 28, 54, Jalapeño(s); **CA**87, Chili jalapeno ['hɑləpino]; **TX**16, [ˌhælə'pinə]; **CA**175, [ˌhɔlə'pinjə]; (Qu. H14) Inf **TX**11, Jalapeña corn bread; (Qu. H18) Inf **TX**3, Jalapeño corn bread; (Qu. I4, . . *Vegetables . . less commonly grown around here*) Inf **TX**4, Jalapeno peppers. **1966** *Deming Graphic* (NM) 21 Mar 5, [Advt:] Jalapeno *chili* yellow hot 2 lbs. 39¢. **1967** *DARE* FW Addit **neCO,** Jalapeño and bell peppers in local supermarket. **1970** GA Dept. Ag. *Farmers Market Bulletin* 12 Aug 5/4, [Advt:] Jalapeno Chili hot pepper, 25 seed, 40¢. **1981** Pederson *LAGS Basic Materials,* 4 infs, **TX,** Jalapeno (peppers); 1 inf, **seGA,** Red ones [=peppers] he calls ['dʒæˑpə,linə] or ['ɐppɨˑli˂nə]. **1983** *Kerr Home Canning Book* 37, *Jalapeno Jelly—*3 Jalapeno peppers, 4 Bell peppers. **1987** *NADS Letters* **cOK,** At fast-food places around here, the workers call jalapeño peppers *japaleenos* or *japs.* **1990** *Seed Savers Yearbook* 170, *Jalapeno.* . . thick flesh, green → red, blunt nose, to 2.5″, . . use fresh or pickled . . good in dips and chili. . . *Jalapeno, Miniature.* . . plant bears abundant supply of . . jalapeno shape peppers, hotter . . than regular jalapenos. **1994** *DARE* File **NM,** For many Anglos in Albuquerque there is a shift in meaning going on: all small chilis are called jalapeños now—or pequeños simply.

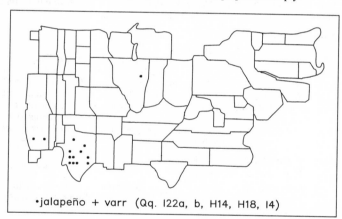

•jalapeño + varr (Qq. I22a, b, H14, H18, I4)

jallus adj, n¹ [Var of *jealous(y)*]
   1922 Gonzales *Black Border* 307 **sSC, GA coasts** [Gullah glossary], *Jallus—*jealous, jealousy.

jallus n² [Cf *EDD gallus* (at *gallows* sb. 4) "The devil, deuce, used as an exclamation or mild oath" and *OED gallows* a. 2 "As an intensive"] Cf **i** prep
Used as a mild oath; see quot.
   1935 Sheppard *Cabins* 299 **cwNC,** When we got back to Hector's, aye jallus, he'd done gone. *Ibid* 300, He didn't say a word about a drink for us, so I thought, 'Aye jallus, I'll look around a little.'

jalousie n Also *jealousy* [Fr *jalousie* jealousy, fig: a blind or shutter that ensures privacy (*OEDS* 1766 →); the form *jealousy* (*OED* 1834) is either a calque or folk-etym]
A blind or shutter of slanted opaque horizontal slats; now also a window made with a similar arrangement of glass slats that can be tilted for ventilation.
   1832 Trollope *Domestic Manners* (NY) 125 **swOH,** At length . . the summer burst upon us full blown, and the icehouse, the piazza, and the jalousies were again in full requisition. **1872** (1876) Knight *Amer. Mech. Dict.* 2.1210, *Jalousie.* A *louvre* or *Venetian* shutter. **1932** Stribling *Store* 348 **AL,** An old brick manor with green jalousies, a colonnaded piazza, an observatory on top; and he went on describing the sort of manor one saw anywhere in the South. **1941** Writers' Program *Guide LA* 689, *Jalousie.* . . A two-battened outdoor window blind. **1965–70** *DARE* (Qu. E14, *Wooden slats built into a window frame that shut out the sun*

but let in light and air) 22 Infs, **scattered,** Jalousies; **AL**15, Jalousies—are glass; **FL**23, Jalousies are the glass windows that open and close; **IL**9, Jalousies—these are glass; **MN**16, Jalousies—in the South; a few ornamental ones here; **NJ**11, Jalousies—they don't shut out light; they are set in a door or porch and made of glass that tilts; **WI**76, Jalousies—now of glass; not here (seen in Florida); **FL**11, Jalousie windows—the glass ones that you crank; **IL**43, I can't do a thing with those darn jalousie windows; **MI**69, Jealousies—but the ones I've seen are of opaque glass, not of wood; **WI**47, Jealousies—a special kind of window with built-in glass louvers; **WI**50, Jealousies—just coming in from Florida; **WI**52, Jealousies. **1966** *DARE* Tape **AL**11, [FW:] Did you have a smokehouse on your place? [Inf:] No, we'd hang 'em up to the jalousies of the house. **1968** *State* (Columbia SC) 1 May sec B 12/6, [Advt:] Jalousies for 12x8 porch, good condition. **1968** *DARE* FW Addit **NJ,** On a sign, permanent, in New Jersey, just across from New York City, at a lumber company: "Wood doors and jalousies." I suppose many know what jalousies are; none of my informants have used the term, however.

jam n See **jamb**

jam v

1 To injure or damage by crushing or striking. [*OED jam* v.¹ 1.d 1832 →] **scattered, but chiefly NEast, N Cent** See Map and Map Section Cf **mash** v¹ **1**
   1838 [see **mash** v¹ 1]. **1899** (1912) Green *VA Folk-Speech* 243, *Jam.* . . To press; squeeze; to thrust or press down or in with force or violence. **1934** (1943) *W2, Jam.* . . To crush or bruise; as, to *jam* a finger in a door. **1965–70** *DARE* (Qu. Y33, . . *Squeezing or crushing something* . . "I _____ my finger in the door.") 79 Infs, **scattered, but chiefly NEast, N Cent,** Jam(med); (Qu. KK21, *When something hollow is crushed by a heavy weight, or by a fall:* "They ran the wagon over the coffee pot and _____.") Infs **DC**3, **MA**68, **VT**16, Jammed it (all to hell). **1967** *DARE* FW Addit **LA,** Jam the finger—to mash the finger from the end, as when a baseball hits the end and pushes it straight back toward the knuckle.

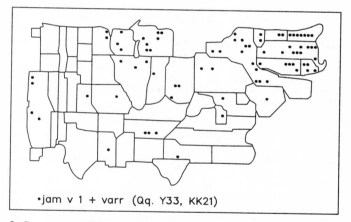

•jam v 1 + varr (Qq. Y33, KK21)

2 See quot. Cf **jam up** adv phr **2**
   1969 *DARE* (Qu. KK53, *When one thing suddenly hits hard against something else:* "He ran _____ into a car.") Inf **VT**12, Jammed into it.

jam adv See **jam up** adv phr **1, 2, 3**

jam adj See **jam up** adj phr

Jamaica apple n
   A **custard apple 1.**
   1966 *DARE* (Qu. I53, . . *Fruits grown around here . . special varieties*) Inf **FL**23, Jamaica apples.

Jamaica dogwood n
   A tree (*Piscidia piscipula*) native to southern Florida. Also called **fishfuddle tree, fish poison 3**
   1876 Hobbs *Bot. Hdbk.* 59, Jamaica dogwood, Piscidia erythrina. **1884** Sargent *Forests of N. Amer.* 57, *Jamaica Dogwood.* . . The bark, especially of the root, narcotic, occasionally administered in the form of tinctures, or used, as well as the young branches and leaves, to poison or stupefy fish. **1908** Britton *N. Amer. Trees* 560, Jamaica dogwood is quite abundant on the sandy coastal lands of southern peninsular Florida and the Keys. **1933** Small *Manual SE Flora* 712, *Jamaica-dogwood.* . .

The hard durable wood is valued for boat-building. **1979** Little *Checklist U.S. Trees* 200, *Piscidia piscipula.* . . Jamaica dogwood.

jamb n Also sp *jam* [Cf *OED jamb* sb. 6 "An angular turn or corner in a street or way. *Obs.*" and *EDD jamb* sb. 4 "A corner made by a projection"] **S Atl** Cf **jamb of the fence**

The angle where two sections of fence meet.

1937 in 1977 *Amer. Slave Suppl. 1* 11.144 **SC**, Sam Watson come dere en make dat fellow lay down on uh plank in de fence jam en he take dat cat o' nine tail . . en strak John 75 times. **1940** Harris *Folk Plays* 154 **eNC**, I see . . a little place, green truck growin' 'round it . . yeller flowers growin' in the jam's o' the fences. **1968** *DARE* FW Addit **GA**33, Fence jambs—the intersecting points on a rail fence. **1981** Harper–Presley *Okefinokee* 141 **seGA** (as of a1948), *Jam*—Corner. "There was a big palmetter patch growing in the jam of his fence." **1986** Pederson *LAGS Concordance,* 1 inf, **neFL**, Fence jamb—where rails come together; 1 inf, **nwFL**, Fence jamb—joint in rail-fence construction.

jamb adv See **jam up** adv phr **2**

jambalaya n Usu |ˌʤʌmbə'laɪə|; for varr see quot 1965–70 Also sp *jambalayah, jambolaya, jumbal(l)aya* [LaFr]

1 A spicy stew of rice usu cooked with sausage, ham, chicken, or shellfish. **chiefly Gulf States, esp LA; becoming more widely recognized** See Map

1872 *N.O. Times* 28 June *(DA)*, Those who brought victuals, such as gumbo, jambalaya, etc., all began eating and drinking. **1885** Cable *Dr. Sevier* 201 **LA**, On one of Mrs. Riley's large hands there rested a blue-edged soup-plate, heaping full of the food that goes nearest to the Creole heart—*jambolaya.* There it was, steaming and smelling,—a delicious confusion of rice and red pepper, chicken legs, ham, and tomatoes. **1896** *Daily News Cook Book* 97 **SD**, Jambalaya. . . Chicken, oysters or shrimps may be substituted for the sausage. **1903** Eustis *Cooking Creole* 14, *Jumballaya*—A Spanish Creole dish. **1916** [see **2** below]. **1945** Saxon *Gumbo Ya-Ya* 203 **swLA**, What happen we have no more oyster, hein? Then maybe we have no more shrimps and no more crab, how we gon' make *gumbo* or *jambalaya?* And if we don't have no more *gumbo* and no more *jambalaya,* what hell Cajun gon' eat that's any good, hein? **1950** *WELS Suppl.* **IA**, Jumballaya—A party dish. To a large cooked hen should be added various seasonings, ham, onions, tomatoes, etc. **1954** Armstrong *Satchmo* 85 **LA**, Her jumbalaya was delicious. It is a concoction of diced Bologna sausage, shrimp, oysters, hard-shell crabs mixed with rice and flavored with tomato sauce. **1965** Little *Autobiog. Malcolm X* 96 **NYC** [Black], And Bill sold plates of his spicy, delicious Creole dishes—gumbo, jambalaya. **c1965** Randle *Cookbooks* (Ask Neighbor) 3.26 **OH**, *Jambalayah.* . . Mix together chicken, rice and tomatoes. . . chop and add the onion, Green pepper, and celery. **1965–70** *DARE* (Qu. H45, *Dishes made with meat, fish, or poultry that everybody around here would know, but that people in other places might not*) Inf **AR**8, ['jumbə,laɪə]—rice, tomatoes, and any meat; **FL**17, [ˌʤəmbə'laɪʤə]—seafoods all mixed together; **FL**21, ['ʤəmbəlaɪ]—conglomeration of seafood; **LA**19, [ˌʤəmbə'laɪə]—made with vegetables and meats; **LA**28, [ˌʤəmbə'laɚ]—made either with chicken, pork, or shrimp; **LA**31, ['ʤəmbə'laɪə]—with chicken, duck, pork, shrimp, or oysters; **LA**3, 23, 41, **TX**9, 15, [ˌʤʌmbə'laɪ(j)ə]; **IL**113, [ʤæmbə'laɪʤə]; **LA**20, [ˌʤæmbə'laɪə]; **NY**181, [ʤæmbə'leə]; **CA**101, [ˌʤamə'laɪə]; **MA**122, [ʤæmbə'le,jə]; **TX**33, [ˌʤʌmbo'laɪʤə]; **MS**2, ['ʤʌmbə,laɪ]; **MS**73, ['ʤʌmbə,laɪə]; (Qu. H50) Inf **LA**20, Peas jambalaya; (Qu. H55, . . *Kinds of stew; total* Infs questioned, 75) Inf **FL**17, Crab [ʤəmbələ^]. **1968**

DARE Tape **LA**25, French people use jambalaya [ˌʤʌmbə'laɪə] a whole lot—oyster jambalaya or shrimp jambalaya. **1983** *Reinecke Coll.* 6 **LA**, *Jambalaya* [ˌʤʌmbə'lɑjɑ] or [ʤæm-] . . rice, cooked in a heavy iron pot until solid, with tomato, meats, or sausage, or shrimp, or chicken, eaten either as a main or side dish. . . Universally used. Dish widely served and eaten. **1986** Pederson *LAGS Concordance,* 2 infs, **seLA**, Jambalaya; 1 inf, **seLA**, Jambalaya—dish with meat and rice; 1 inf, **cwMS**, Jambalay [sic]—Red rice, Spanish rice, onions, tomato; 1 inf, **seMS**, Shrimp jambalaya.

2 Fig: a mixture of heterogeneous elements.

1916 *DN* 4.268 **New Orleans LA**, *Jambalaya.* . . A hash containing rice and ham. Also used figuratively, like 'potpourri.' "The show was a regular jambalaya of stunts." **1945** *Democrat* 25 Oct. 2/2 *(DA)* **AL**, The above might very well be called typesetter's hash, or compositor's jumbalaya. **1951** *Times-Picayune* (New Orleans LA) 4 Feb mag sec 8/3, A Creole beauty, a murder in a fashionable French home, an illicit love affair . . —these are the ingredients of the movies' latest jambalaya.

jamberry n [See quot 1977]

A **ground-cherry** (here: *Physalis ixocarpa*).

1976 Bailey–Bailey *Hortus Third* 868, [*Physalis*] *ixocarpa.* . . *Jamberry.* . . Mature calyx . . frequently split by the enlarging fr[uit]. . . Naturalized in e. N. Amer. [**1977** Freitus *Wild Preserves* 95, *Ground Cherry.* . . There are two widely used species, . . *P[hysalis] ixocarpa* . . and . . *P. heterophylla.* . . *Ground Cherry Jam.* 2 quarts of fruit. Juice of 1 lemon [etc]. . . Use fully ripened ground cherries.]

jamb-ke-dab See **jam-ke-dab**

jamble n [Prob var of *jumble,* but cf *EDD jabble* sb.¹ 6 "*fig.* turmoil, confusion"] Cf **jambled**

1965 *DARE* (Qu. Y38, *Mixed together, confused: "The things in the drawer are all _____."*) Inf **FL**17, In a jamble.

jambled adj Also with *up* Cf **jabble**

Confused, jumbled, befuddled; awry.

1745 in 1887 Franklin *Complete Wks.* 2.24 **PA**, [Drinker's dictionary], He's Jolly./ Jagg'd / Jambl'd./ Going to Jerusalem./ Jocular./ Been to Jericho / Juicy. **1896** Twain in *Harper's New Mth. Mag.* 93.537 **MO**, He preached them the blamedest, jambledest, idiotic sermons you ever struck. **1967–69** *DARE* (Qu. Y38, *Mixed together, confused: "The things in the drawer are all _____."*) Inf **WY**4, Jambled up; (Qu. KK70, *Something that has got out of proper shape: "That house is all _____."*) Inf **IN**75, Jambled.

jamb of the fence n Cf **jamb** n

Prob homegrown tobacco.

1969 *State* (Raleigh, N.C.) 1 Aug. 40/3 *(Mathews Coll.),* Next time you're down in Eastern Carolina, ask one of the old-time tobacconists or farmers about "jam o' the fence."

jambolaya See **jambalaya**

jamb-rock n Also sp *jam(m)-rock* [Cf *EDD jamb-stone* (at *jamb* sb. 2.(3)), *SND jam-stane* (at *jamb* n. 1.(2))] **S Midl**

A stone forming one of the side pieces of a fireplace.

1927 *DN* 5.475 **Ozarks**, *Jam rock.* . . One of the side stones in the fireplace. "Jeff he sets up t' thet 'ar gal like a sick kitten t' a jam rock." **1941** Stuart *Men of Mts.* 95 **neKY**, She reached in her apron pocket and got a match. She struck it on the jamm-rock above the fireplace. **c1960** *Wilson Coll.* **csKY**, *Jam* (or *jamb*)-*rock.* . . One of the two sides of a fireplace. **1986** Pederson *LAGS Concordance,* 1 inf, **cnAR**, Jamb rocks—at the side of the fireplace.

jam cake n **chiefly S Midl, esp KY** See Map

A kind of spice cake flavored with jam.

1932 (1946) Hibben *Amer. Regional Cookery* 302 **GA**, *Blackberry Jam Cake.* **1940** Brown *Amer. Cooks* 482 **MO**, Jam cake. Ibid 879 **WV**, *Blackberry jam cake.* **1964** *Favorite Recipes Virginias* 158 **WV**, Jam Cake. **c1965** Randle *Cookbooks* (Ask Neighbor) 1.71 **KY**, *Blackberry Jam Cake.* **1968–70** *DARE* (Qu. H63, *Kinds of desserts*) Infs **KY**57, 63, 71, 74, 79, 84, 85, 90, **TX**99, Jam cake(s); **OH**61, Jam cake—made with blackberries. **1968** *DARE* FW Addit **neKY**, Jam cake. **1970** *DARE* Tape **TX**99, [Inf:] This is called a jam cake . . and this has been in the family for years. . . [FW:] It must be very spicy. [Inf:] It is spicy, but it is good. **1979** Flagg *Cape Cod Cooking* 119 **MA**, *Strawberry Jam Cake*—This is a classic recipe which at one time was served everywhere, from the humble Cape Cod cottage to the White House. **1986** Pederson *LAGS Concordance,* 1 inf, **nwTN**, Blackberry jam cakes.

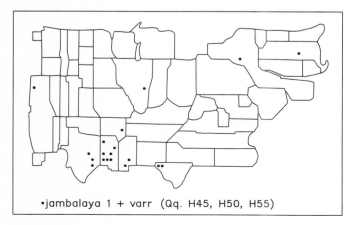
•jambalaya 1 + varr (Qq. H45, H50, H55)

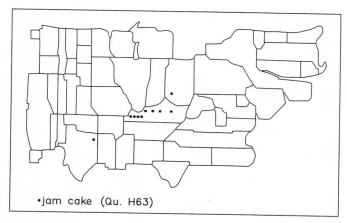

•jam cake (Qu. H63)

jam cracker n

In logging: one who breaks up logjams.

1905 U.S. Forest Serv. *Bulletin* 61.40 [Logging terms], *Jam cracker.* See Head driver. [*Ibid* 39, *Head driver.* An expert river driver who . . is stationed at a point where a jam is feared.] **1930** Shoemaker *1300 Words* 33 **cPA Mts** (as of c1900), *Jam-cracker*—One who breaks a log-jam by loosening the key log. **1969** Sorden *Lumberjack Lingo* 63 **NEng, Gt Lakes,** *Jam cracker*—A riverman expert in breaking log jams.

James Brown n *among Black speakers*

A dance step.

1970 Major *Dict. Afro-Amer. Slang* 70, *James Brown, the:* a dance originated by James Brown, singer. **1970** *DARE* (Qu. FF5b, *More recent dance steps*) Infs **FL**51, **MS**84, **PA**247, **VA**41, James Brown. [All Infs Black]

Jamestown lily n

A **jimson weed** (here: *Datura stramonium*).

1894 *Jrl. Amer. Folkl.* 7.95, *Datura Stramonium.* . . Jamestown lily, Lincolnton, N.C.

Jamestown weed n [*Jamestown* VA, where the plant was appar first introduced or observed] Note: This form prob survives only as a literary term or as a hypercorrect sp for the pronc ['ǰɪmsən].

=jimson weed.

1687 in 1744 Royal Soc. London *Philos. Trans. for 1739* 41.160 **eVA,** Several of them went to gather a Sallad . . and lighting in great Quantities on an Herb called *James-town-weed,* they gathered it; and by eating thereof in plenty, were rendered apish and foolish, as if they had been drunk, or were become Idiots. **1709** (1967) Lawson *New Voyage* 84, *James-Town-*Weed, . . the Seed it bears is very like that of an Onion; it is excellent for curing Burns, and asswaging Inflammations. **1832** Kennedy *Swallow Barn* 1.180 **eVA,** A rank crop of Jamestown weed grew up within. **1885** Thompson *By-Ways* 74, I have known a quail to swallow the seeds of the Jamestown weed with no bad result. **1904** Glasgow *Deliverance* 273 **VA,** Well, you must persuade her to use a liniment of Jamestown weed steeped in whisky. There is positively nothing like it for rheumatism. **1970** *NC Folkl.* 18.7, Jamestown or jimson weed is beaten and given to child to strengthen its memory and character. **1974** (1977) Coon *Useful Plants* 249, Jamestown weed. . . is extremely poisonous. . . In Appalachia, poultices made of the leaves have been used to treat wounds and kill pains while in the Southwest it has been used as an hallucinogenic.

‡jamfest n [Perh blend of *gabfest* and *jam session;* cf **jabfest**]

1967 *DARE* (Qu. KK12, *A meeting where there's a lot of talking: "They got together yesterday and had a real _____."*) Inf **MI**68, Jamfest.

jam-ke-dab adj, adv Also sp *jamb-ke-dab* [*jam* (at **jam up** adv phr **2**) + *ke-dab* (cf **ker-**); cf **smack-dab**]

1944 *PADS* 2.45 **NC,** *Jam(b)-ke-dab* ['ǰæmkə,dæb]: *adj.* and *adv.* Close up, completely. "I rid jamb-ke-dab up agin that house." . . also elsewhere in South.

jammer n

A derrick for loading logs onto a vehicle.

1905 U.S. Forest Serv. *Bulletin* 61.40, *Jammer.* . . An improved form of gin, mounted on a movable framework, and used to load logs on sleds and cars by horsepower. (N[orthern] F[orest]). **1938** (1939) Holbrook

Holy Mackinaw 262, *Jammer.* A steam engine for loading logs onto cars. Western pine country. **1940–41** Cassidy *WI Atlas* **ceWI,** Jammer—in the logging camps, a pole with a block and chain, the chain running to a crotched chain with a hook at the end of each piece. To lift logs from skidway to sleigh, put one hook, into each end of log—lift with block and chain, swing into position, drop and detach hooks. Supersedes hand-loading. **1956** *Seattle Daily Times* (WA) 22 Apr pictorial sec 34 **ID,** [Caption:] Logs ready to go into the flume were piled up at right by a "jammer"—cables, pulleys, boom. **1958** McCulloch *Woods Words* 98 **Pacific NW,** *Jammer*—Used now to mean a loading rig of almost any kind, in the pine country. Originally it was a huge machine used in railroad logging in the pinery of the south-eastern states, and from there moved to the pine of the west. **1967–68** *DARE* Tape **MI**47, The jammer was . . two upright timbers, thirty feet long, . . and they was a block, or pulley, on the top and one on the crotch of the hooks where you loaded the logs and . . they picked the log right up and the log didn't roll—it picked it up and put it on the sleigh; **MI**56, The jammer had two hooks, and you hooked the log on the end, double purchase; and there was no log that come into Moran that one team couldn't raise up . . fifty to seventy-five feet; **MI**96, Later they had what they called a "jammer" that did that work, but that wasn't until . . after the nineteen-tens; **WI**59, The top-loader, the man who was on top of the pile as the logs were hoisted up to him by what they called the "jammer"—that required a lot of dexterity. **1984** *MJLF* 10.152 **ME, WI.**

jam(m)-rock See **jamb-rock**

jam up adj phr Also *jam* chiefly **Sth, S Midl**

Excellent; first-rate.

1832 *Boston Eve. Transcript* (MA) 6 Aug 1/1, Do you like jam spruce beer, Miss. **1838** *Lexington Observer* 2 June *(DAE)*, There was something jam about Nance, that they couldn't hold a candle to. **1841** *S. Lit. Messenger* 7.54/2 **TX,** Introduced him to "the jam-/ Up little company" in his command. **1843** *Brother Jonathan* (NY NY) 5.495/2 **MD,** "And I sows till I got them to look considerable jam again." A Maryland phrase that. **1847** Hurd *Grammatical Corrector* 45, *Jam up,* used *adjectively;* a low barbarous phrase . . signifying *good, very excellent;* as, "His credit is jam up." "These apples are jam up." **1905** *DN* 3.12 **CT,** *Jam up.* . . First rate. **1932** *Santa Fe Mag.* Jan 66/1, Here's an original newspaper story of a Texas Negro, whom we will have to admit was jam-up on his geography. **1940** *Sat. Eve. Post* 24 Feb 77 **TX** [Black], I gwan have one jam-up buryin'. **1946** (1972) Mezzrow-Wolfe *Really Blues* 2, I got my first chance to play in a real man size band, with jam-up instruments. **1949** *PADS* 11.7 **wTX.** **1954** *Harder Coll.* **cwTN.** **c1960** *Wilson Coll.* **csKY,** *Jam-up.* . . Good, satisfactory, all that could be expected. **1966–70** *DARE* (Qu. BB47, *Feeling in the best of health and spirits: "I'm feeling _____!"*) Inf **SC**40, Jam up; (Qu. GG29, *To be in a good or pleasant mood: "This morning he seems to be feeling _____."*) Inf **SC**40, Jam up; (Qu. KK1a, . . *Very good—for example, food: "That pie was _____."*) Inf **SC**40, Jam up; (Qu. KK1b, . . *'In the very best condition': "His farm is _____."*) Infs **GA**84, **SC**40, Jam up; (Qu. KK4, *When things turn out just right . . "Everything is _____ now."*) Infs **GA**3, 84, **SC**40, Jam up; (Qu. KK18, *If something is in good running order: "This sewing machine is _____.";* total Infs questioned, 75) Inf **MS**69, Jam up.

jam up adv phr chiefly **Sth, S Midl**

1 also *jam:* Completely, fully; all the way.

1835 Crockett *Account* 192 **TN,** Andrew Jackson. . . went jam up for war; but the cabinet got him down to half heat. **1874** (1895) Eggleston *Circuit Rider* 141 **sOH** (as of early 1800s), [He was now full sixty or seventy miles from home.] *Ibid* 142, "How far you rid her to-day?" . . "Jam up fifty miles, and over tough roads." **1905** *DN* 3.83 **nwAR,** *Jam.* . . Completely. 'The room was filled jam up to the door.' **1946** *PADS* 5.27 **VA,** *Jam (across).* . . Entirely across. **1949** Kurath *Word Geog.* 61, Instead of, or by the side of, the common expression *clear across* (the bed), we encounter in the Southern area . . *jam across* between the Rappahannock and the James. **c1960** *Wilson Coll.* **csKY,** *Jam.* . . Completely, entirely. **1967–70** *DARE* (Qu. LL26a, . . *'All the way': "He drove _____ to the end of the road."*) Infs **SC**11, 26, 40, Jam; **SC**56, Jam up. **1986** Pederson *LAGS Concordance* (A large pillow; it goes _____ across the bed) 1 inf, **swGA,** Jam up; 1 inf, **seGA,** Jam up in the back.

2 also *jam(b):* Squarely; smack-dab.

1842 *Amer. Pioneer* 1.184 **DE,** The next moment the sloop ran jamb against it. **1932** *K.C. Star* 24 May 18 *(DA),* His Chevrolet. . . [ran] jam up against a house on a neighboring lot. **1966–70** *DARE* (Qu. KK53,

When one thing suddenly hits hard against something else: "He ran —— into a car.") Infs **SC**11, 24, 26, 40, Jam.

3 also *jam:* Very near, close; hard up against.

1837 in 1912 Thornton *Amer. Gloss.* 1.488 **MD,** I was standing by the doctor jam up to him. **1843** *Brother Jonathan* (NY NY) 5.495/2, All along the eastern shores of Virginia. . . [t]hey say *jam up,* for close up[,] very near. **1851** (1852) Stowe *Uncle Tom's Cabin* 1.49 **KY,** "It'll stand, if it only keeps jam up agin the wall!" said Mose. **1884** *Anglia* 7.274 **Sth, S Midl** [Black], To git right jam up 'mungs' de feelin's er = to be loved by. **1912** Green *VA Folk-Speech* 243, *Jam.* . . Close to: "wait until you get jam up to him before you speak." **1952** Brown *NC Folkl.* 1.554, *Jam by.* . . Near by. "He went jam by me and didn't see me." **1954** *Harder Coll.* **cwTN,** *Jam up* . . close against. "He's jam up agin'er." **1967** *DARE* Tape **TX**26, They probably had time [sic] getting this horse to stay jam up to this other horse's tail.

4 In a first-rate manner; excellently. Cf **jam up** adj phr

1845 *Quincy* (Ill.) *Whig* 4 Nov. 1/5 *(DA),* I am glad, girl, that you have this time made choice of a man who knows how to pettifog, jam-up, without being too lazy to work on a farm. **1847** Hurd *Grammatical Corrector* 45, *Jam up.* . . Adverbially, it is supposed to mean *promptly, punctually, well,* &c.; as, He pays jam up. He was there jam up. He does his work jam up, &c. **1866** Smith *Bill Arp* 61 **GA,** Linton played his part of the programme jam up. **1955** in 1958 Brewer *Dog Ghosts* 20 **TX** [Black], Dey don' wan' no woman teachuh . . hit tecks a man to do de job jam up. **1966** *DARE* (Qu. KK3b, *Something done perfectly—for example, a piece of work: "It's done to _____."*) Inf **GA**9, Done jam up. **1970** Green *Ely* 561 **Sth** [Black], Now most of my people was doing the job they had been taught jam up.

5 Extremely.

1874 (1895) Eggleston *Circuit Rider* 36 **sOH** (as of early 1800s), She used to . . tell me . . stories . that she'd read about in grandfather's books when she was a girl—jam up good stories, too. **1966** Medford *Gt. Smoky Mt. Stories* 83 **swNC,** 'Cordin' to the book, Washington was awful good gen'ral an' jam-up smart man. **1966** *DARE* (Qu. FF17, . . *A very good or enjoyable time: "We all had a _____ last night."*) Inf **AR**15, Jam up good time. **1966** *DARE* Tape **AL**3, He was very deaf, and he was kind of an old nigger, but he was a jam up good carpenter.

Janary See **January**

jander See **jaundice B**

janders, jandice See **jaundice**

jane See **jean**

jangle v

To quarrel; to engage in (an argument).

1847 *Yankee Doodle* 25 Sept 242, *The Katy-did's Jangle.*—Two Katy-dids perched on a tree./ Jangled the following colloquy/. . . 1st—Katy-did. 2nd—Katy *didn't,* Katy *didn't,* Katy *didn't.* **1899** (1912) Green *VA Folk-Speech* 243, *Jangle.* . . To quarrel; altercate; wrangle. **1966–69** *DARE* (Qu. KK13, . . *Arguing: "They stood there for an hour _____."*) Infs **CA**145, 157, **IA**45, **ID**1, **NY**131, **PA**130, 177, Jangling. **1989** Mosher *Stranger* 331 **nVT,** "These voices were coming from the parsonage porch. It was a fella and a woman. Jangling." "Jangling?" "Yes. Back and forth." "Could you please explain the term 'jangling,' Mr. Kinneson?" "Jangling," Elijah said impatiently. "Like these." He half rose and gave his key ring a great clangorous jerk. "Arguing," he said.

jangle n

1 A quarrel, altercation.

1847 [see **jangle** v]. **1898** Westcott *Harum* 342 **NY,** "Did I ever tell you," said David . . "how Lawyer Staples come to switch round in that there railroad jangle last spring?" **1966–69** *DARE* (Qu. Y12a, *A fight between two people, mostly with words*) Infs **MA**30, **WI**27, 33, Jangle; (Qu. KK12, *A meeting where there's a lot of talking*) Inf **ID**1, Jangle.

2 A musical session.

1938 Matschat *Suwannee R.* 111 **neFL, seGA,** He's a right smart hand with a banjo, so I brung him for a little jangle.

‡Janie n Cf **Betsy 1, Jenny 9**

1967 *DARE* (Qu. P37b, *Nicknames for a shotgun*) Inf **PA**27, Janie.

Jannery, Jan'ry See **January**

jant See **jaunt**

janted up adj phr Cf **gant** v, **gantered**

Worn out.

1937 (1963) Hyatt *Kiverlid* 14 **KY,** She ha'n't never been ja'nted up. Jeems don't put up with over-workin' and strainin' his horse-stock.

janty See **jaunt**

January n Usu |ˈjænjəˌwɛri, -juˌɛri|; also |jɛn(j)uɛri, jɛnəwɛri, jinəwɛri| Pronc-spp *Jahnywary, Jan'ry, Jenooary, Jinnywerry;* for addit pronc and sp varr see quots

Std sense, var forms.

1768 in 1956 Eliason *Tarheel Talk* 313 **c,csNC,** January—Jenary. **1817** *Ibid* **nw,cnNC,** January. . . Janary. **1828** New York *Enquirer* 22 April 2/1 *(AmSp* 38.25), [Dateline:] Konstanty Nople, Jennywerry, 1828. **1847** Hurd *Grammatical Corrector* 84, *January* ["incorrect" pronc = [ˈjinɚweri]]. **1867** Lowell *Biglow* lxxx **'Upcountry' MA,** Jenooary. **1884** *Anglia* 7.277 **Sth, S Midl** [Black], 'Twix dis an' nex' Jinawerry = indefinite period. **1884** Murfree *TN Mts.* 249, I went up there, one Jan'ry day, a-lookin' fur my cow. **1893** Shands *MS Speech* 41, *Jinerwary* [jinəweri]. Negro for January. **1903** *DN* 2.291 **Cape Cod MA** (as of a1857), *January, February* were Jenoowery, Feboowery, with mutual analogical rapprochement. **1911** *DN* 3.545 **NE,** January. . . Occasional pronunciation. **1912** Green *VA Folk-Speech* 244, Jeneway. **1915** *DN* 4.184 **swVA,** Jineway. **1921** Haswell *Daughter Ozarks* 107 (as of 1880s), My son Jeemes is a'wantin' to move back onto Turtle, come Jannery. **1922** Gonzales *Black Border* 308 **sSC, GA coasts** [Gullah glossary], Jinnywerry. **1937** *AmSp* 12.126 **NY,** Rensselaer County and the city of Troy are said to have a local preference for [ŋ] before [j] in such words as *january* and *onion,* but my records show the variation occurring in scattered regions, albeit infrequently, throughout the state. **1939** *LANE* Map 64, [Throughout **NEng** proncs of the types [ˈdʒænjuɛrɪ] and [ˈdʒɛnjuɛrɪ] are about equally common; there is a scattering of the types [ˈdʒɛnəwɛrɪ] and [ˈdʒɪnəwɛrɪ], esp in **nNEng,** but even there they are frequently regarded as obsolete or old-fashioned.] **1942** Hall *Smoky Mt. Speech* 68 **eTN, wNC,** In *January* also there is variation: in the speech of a few old people it is still the early modern [ˈdʒɪnəwɛrɪ], but in the current pronunciation it is [ˈdʒænjəwɛrɪ] or [ˈdʒænju-]. One old man's [ˈdʒɪnjuɛrɪ] suggests reaction against the form with variation [ə]. **c1960** *Wilson Coll.* **csKY,** *January* is almost always /ˈdʒænjəˌwɛri/. **1963** Carson *Social Hist. Bourbon* 111 **TN,** I just made . . one run of peppermint in Jahnywary.

Jan van Gent n [Cf *EDD gant* sb.³ "The gannet or solon-goose, *Sula bassana.*"]

A **gannet 1** (here: *Morus bassanus*).

1917 (1923) *Birds Amer.* 1.91, Gannet. Sula bassana. . . Other Names. . . Jan van Gent.

Jap n¹ See **Jap flap**

‡jap v [Prob var of *jab*]

1968 *DARE* (Qu. Y46a, *To get hurt with something sharp . . "He _____ a thorn into his hand."*) Inf **PA**115, Japped.

jap n², **japaleeno** See **jalapeño**

‡Japan chili n

1950 *WELS (Small hot peppers grown in your neighborhood)* 1 Inf, **cWI,** Japan chili.

Japanese artichoke n

An introduced **hedgenettle** (here: *Stachys affinis*).

1902 Bailey *Cyclop. Horticult.* 4.1714, Chorogi. Chinese or Japanese Artichoke. Knotroot. **1942** Amer. Joint Comm. Horticult. Nomenclature *Std. Plant Names* 24, *Japanese A[rtichoke].* . . Betony. . . *Stachys sieboldi.* **1950** Gray–Fernald *Manual of Botany* 1233, *Stachys sieboldii.* . . Japanese . . Artichoke . . cult. for its edible tubers. **1976** Bailey–Bailey *Hortus Third* 1067, *S[tachys] affinis.* . . *Japanese a[rtichoke].* . . Slender, knotty, white tubers abundantly produced just below the soil surface. . . Sometimes grown in U.S. in garden collections of economic plants.

Japanese hill robin See **hill robin**

Japanese hornet n esp **VA**

A wasp (family Vespidae).

1968–70 *DARE* (Qu. R21, . . *Other kinds of stinging insects*) Infs **NC**67, **VA**40, 79, Japanese hornet; **VA**15, Japanese hornet—new, yellow with black stripes, larger than regular hornet; **VA**75, Japanese hornet—

yellow with stripes, very long, deadly. **1986** Pederson *LAGS Concordance,* 1 inf, **cnGA,** Japanese hornets.

Japanese lantern n

1 A **ground-cherry,** usu *Physalis alkekengi.* Cf **Chinese lantern 1**

  1959 Carleton *Index Herb. Plants* 68, *Japanese lanterns:* Physalis (v). *Japanese lanterns:* Platycodon (v). **1969** *DARE* (Qu. S26d, *Wildflowers that grow in meadows;* not asked in early QRs) Inf **RI**10, Japanese lanterns (cultivated?). **1976** Bailey–Bailey *Hortus Third* 868, *[Physalis] Alkekengi. . .* Japanese-lantern. . . Mature calyx nearly globose, vermillion-red. **1982** *Barrick Coll.* **csPA,** Japanese lanterns—winter cherry—Physalis Alkengi [sic].

2 The balloonflower (*Platycodon* spp).

  1959 [see **1** above].

Japanese needles n

A **beggar ticks 1.**

  1970 *DARE* (Qu. S14, *. . Prickly seeds, small and flat, with two prongs at one end, that cling to clothing*) Inf **VA**52, Sticktights, Japanese needles.

Japanese poinsettia n

1 A **spurge** (here: *Euphorbia heterophylla*).

  1976 Bailey–Bailey *Hortus Third* 463, *[Euphorbia] heterophylla . . Japanese poinsettia. . .* From Ariz. s. throughout trop. Amer.; naturalized in La. and Tex.

2 =**jewbush.**

  1976 Bailey–Bailey *Hortus Third* 832, *[Pedilanthus] tithymaloides. . . Japanese poinsettia. . .* Fla., W. Indies, Mex. to n. S. Amer.

Japan pea n

The soybean *(Glycine max).*

  1853 *Amer. Inst. NYC Annual Rept. for 1852* 388, The thanks of the Club were voted . . to Mr. Ernst, of Cincinnati, for his great present of the Japan peas—a plant whose height is nearly five feet. . . The crew of a Japan vessel in distress was relieved by an American ship, and carried into San Francisco, with some of the stores among which was found what resembled a pea. A few of these were brought to Alton, in Illinois, last year (1851). **1855** *Amer. Inst. NYC Annual Rept. for 1854* 597, *Japan pea . .* has been since cultivated with remarkable success. **1946** *PADS* 6.18 **eNC** (as of 1900–10), *Japan peas. . .* Soy beans . . Obsolete.

jape v [*OED* "Obs."] esp **sAppalachians**

To copulate; to copulate with.

  1917 *DN* 4.413 **wNC,** *Jape. . .* To copulate. **1927** *AmSp* 2.358 **cwWV** (as of c1925), *Jape . .* to have sexual intercourse. "He said that he would jape that woman before another week." **1944** *PADS* 2.19 **sAppalachians,** *Jape. . .* To cohabit, copulate. *Ibid* 45 **eNC, sVA,** *Jape. . .* To copulate.

Jap flap n Also *Jap (slap)*

=**flip-flop 6.**

  1967 *DARE* (Qu. W21, *Soft shoes that people wear only inside the house*) Inf **OH**2, Japs—like rubber sandals. **1982** *Barrick Coll.* **csPA** (as of 1970s), *Jap flaps*—Japanese flipflops. **1986** Pederson *LAGS Concordance (Shoes)* 1 inf, **nwFL,** Jap slaps—straw; made in Japan.

Japip See **Jabib**

japon See **yaupon**

Jap slap See **Jap flap**

jap-stick n Cf **jack-stick, jippy-stick**

=**cricket** n².

  1966–69 *DARE* (Qu. EE10, *A game in which a short stick lying on the ground is flipped into the air and then hit with a longer stick*) Infs **AL**3, **IA**46, **ID**5, **IN**1, **WA**18, **WI**12, **WV**18, Jap-stick.

jar v¹ Usu |jɑr|; for varr see **A** below Pronc-sp *jair*

A Forms. Cf **jar** v¹

  1890 [see **B1** below]. **1942** Hall *Smoky Mt. Speech* 30 **eTN, wNC,** In a few words, [æ] appeared before r: *. . jarred* (past tense; once). **1966–68** [see **B1** below]. **1972** Cooper *NC Mt. Folkl.* 93, *Jair . .* to jar.

B Senses.

1 To quarrel, argue, bicker; hence vbl n *jarring* (pronc-sp *jaring*). **esp S Midl** Cf **jower** v

  1890 Holley *Samantha among Brethren* 4 **NY,** To say nothin' of the jarin' that would take place and ensue. **1923** *DN* 5.212 **swMO,** *Jar. . .* To wrangle, to quarrel, to argue. Also *Jower.* **1941** Cleaveland *No Life* 290 **NM,** It was all idyllic—except for one circumstance. Two of the men had been 'jarring at each other' from the beginning—some old feud fanned to flame by the exasperations of life in camp. **1962** *Mt. Life* 38.4.12 **sAppalachians,** If the stubborn wife persists in her "jarrin' and mouthin'," the irate husband is "like to commence a-foulin' one hock and a-rubbin' it on t'other." **1966–68** *DARE* (Qu. KK13, *. . Arguing: "They stood there for an hour _____."*) Infs **MO**11, **SC**19, Jarring; **VA**5 ['jæərɨn].

2 To surprise, upset.

  1897 *KS Univ. Qrly.* (ser B) 6.54, *Jar . .* to surprise or shock: as, "Doesn't that jar you?" **1899** (1977) Norris *McTeague* 158 **CA,** Whoever thinks of buying Nottingham's lace now-a-days? Say, don't that *jar* you? **1965–70** *DARE* (Qu. Y2, *. . Upsetting or disturbing somebody: "Losing all that money didn't seem to _____ him a bit."*) 8 Infs, **scattered,** Jar; (Qu. GG9, *To suddenly embarrass somebody and throw him off balance: "When they told him what she had said about him, it certainly did _____ him."*) Infs **IL**29, **MA**14, **NY**35, **OH**44, **TX**10, Jar; (Qu. GG13a, *When something keeps bothering a person and makes him nervous . . "It _____ me."*) Inf **NJ**6, Jars; (Qu. GG27b, *To get somebody out of an unhappy mood . . "Don't _____."*) Inf **NY**93, Let it jar you; (Qu. II29b, *. . To explain the unpleasant effect that person has on you: "He just _____."*) Inf **MN**3, Jars me; (Qu. NN7, *Exclamations of surprise: "They're getting married next week? Well, _____."*) Inf **OR**4, Wouldn't that jar you.

jar n Usu |jɑr|; for varr see **A** below (cf Pronc Intro 3.I.1.c) Pronc-sp *jair*

A Forms. Cf **jar** v¹

  1968 *DARE* (Qu. DD1) Inf **MD**4, One pound jar [ǰɔə]. **1969** *DARE* FW Addit **cwIL,** Jars—['ǰaʊəz] or [ǰɑrz]. **1972** Cooper *NC Mt. Folkl.* 93, *Jair*—a jar. **1976** Garber *Mountain-ese* 47 **sAppalachians,** *Jair . .* jar. We put up forty jairs uv green beans.

B Senses.

1 Any of var containers, spec:

a A crock.

  1929 *AmSp* 5.127 **ME,** Crocks were "jars," and glass jars were "cans."

b See quot.

  1974 Dabney *Mountain Spirits* xxii **sAppalachians,** Jars: A moonshiner term for whiskey containers, be they made of glass, tin, plastic, or ceramic.

c A chamber pot. [Prob abbr for **slop jar** or *night jar* (at **night glass**)]

  1965–69 *DARE* (Qu. F38, *Utensil kept under the bed for use at night*) Infs **IL**61, **UT**3, Jar; **PA**26, The jar.

2 A culvert.

  1961 *PADS* 36.12 **sLA,** The special Louisiana additions to the questionnaire produced a considerably longer list of terms which are almost surely confined to the area. . . That they could be generally current in other areas is extremely doubtful. . . *jar* (culvert)—32.8 [% of 70 infs]. . . Sometimes we may . . say that . . certain usages are confined to the rural parishes as against New Orleans. Among these are *jar* [etc].

3 A jail. [Cf *jug* jail, prison]

  1969 *DARE* (Qu. V11, *. . Joking names . . for a county or city jail*) Inf **IN**66, Jar.

jar v² Also with *up*

To preserve (fruit, etc) in jars.

  1952 Brown *NC Folkl.* 1.274, Put out into hot sunlight daily for ten days, then jar it and the fruit will keep solid. **1965–70** *DARE* (Qu. H75, *When a housewife is going to preserve fruit in jars, she says she's going to _____ some fruit*) Infs **CA**157, **MD**27, **ME**23, **OH**78, **PA**92, 159, 203, **SC**67, Jar; **FL**36, 37, Jar (it) up. **1966** *DARE* Tape **FL**41, Then we jar up our fruits and things. **1972** *Atlanta Letters, Jar up*—To can foods in season. The women (and men) called it "jarring up." **1986** Pederson *LAGS Concordance,* 1 inf, **seLA,** Jar some fruit; 1 inf, **neFL,** That's what she done jarred—put up in jars.

jarboni See **jabronie**

jar bug See **jarfly 1**

jarby See **job** n¹, v¹

jarfish n [Perh for *garfish* (at **gar**)]

See quot.

1966 *DARE* (Qu. P2, . . *Kinds of saltwater fish caught around here . . good to eat*) Inf **SC9,** Jarfish.

jarfly n

1 also *jar bug:* **=cicada.** [Echoic; cf *chirr*] **chiefly S Midl**
See Map

1880 Allan–Olney *New Virginians* 1.110 **VA,** There is the thing they call the "jar-fly," for instance. . . It makes a noise like a watchman's rattle. **1897** Glasgow *Descendant* 10 **VA,** The low chirping of insects began in the hedges, the treble of the cricket piercing shrilly above the base [sic] of the jar-fly. **1940** Stuart *Trees of Heaven* 48 **KY,** There is the singing from the jarflies among the soapy poplar trees. **1942** Hall *Smoky Mt. Speech* 30 **eTN, wNC,** ['dʒæɚˌflaˑ⁹]. **1949** Webber *Backwoods Teacher* 103 **Ozarks,** Our great trees with the katydids fiddling and the jarflies snarling their loud, long song. **c1960** *Wilson Coll.* **csKY,** *Jarfly.* . . A common summer cicada, not the seventeen-year locust. **1965–70** *DARE* (Qu. R7, *Insects that sit in trees or bushes in hot weather and make a sharp, buzzing sound*) 69 Infs, **chiefly S Midl,** Jarfly; **VA2,** ['jɔrflaɪ [sic]; **VA15,** ['jɛrflæɪ]; **OK11,** Jarfly—not a real fly; comes from a cocoon; makes a jarring sound; **VA89,** Jar bug; (Qu. R4) Inf **TN42,** Jarfly; (Qu. R5, *A big brown beetle that comes out in large numbers in spring and early summer, and flies with a buzzing sound*) Inf **MO15A,** Jarfly; (Qu. R8, . . *Kinds of creatures that make a clicking or shrilling or chirping kind of sound*) Inf **MO3,** ['jɑrˌflaɪ]; **VA96,** [jɑ]-fly; (Qu. R12, . . *Other kinds of flies*) Infs **AL12, MO27,** Jarfly; (Qu. R30, . . *Kinds of beetles; not asked in early QRs*) Inf **VA15,** Jarfly. **1966** *PADS* 46.26 **cnAR,** Jar fly. . . Locust. **1976** Garber *Mountain-ese* 47 **sAppalachians,** *Jar-fly* . . cicada, locust.

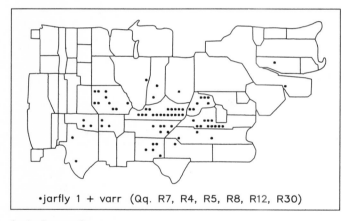

•jarfly 1 + varr (Qq. R7, R4, R5, R8, R12, R30)

2 A **dragonfly.**

1956 Ker *Vocab. W. TX* 230, Dragonfly—jar fly. **1968** *DARE* (Qu. R2, . . *The dragonfly*) Inf **VA7,** Jarfly.

jarhead n Cf **jughead**

1 A mule. **chiefly SE** See Map

1918 *DN* 5.18 **NC,** *Jarhead,* a mule. **1939** *AmSp* 14.91 **eTN,** *Jar head.* A mule. 'He rides the jar head to town.' **1939** McGuire *FL Cracker Dial.* 177. **1941** Nixon *Possum Trot* 89 **neAL,** Steel mules are . .

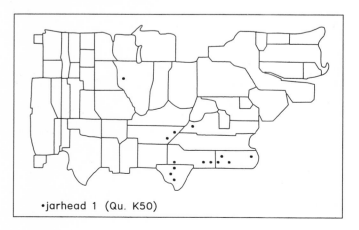

•jarhead 1 (Qu. K50)

displacing the 'hard-tail,' or 'jar-head,' variety. **1946** Sierra Club *Bulletin* Dec 50, Few of our motor-minded city-bred soldiers knew the fuel consumption, rated-load capacity, and first echelon maintenance of a jarhead. **1950** *PADS* 14.40 **SC.** Ibid 72 **FL. c1960** *Wilson Coll.* **csKY,** Jar-head. . . Facetious name for mule. **1965–70** *DARE* (Qu. K50, *Joking nicknames for mules*) 14 Infs, **chiefly SE,** Jarhead; [**NC73, VA43,** Jawhead [*DARE* Ed: prob pronc-sp for *jarhead*]].

2 Used as a derog epithet; see quots.

1942 *Amer. Mercury* 55.95 **NYC** [Harlem slang], *Jar head*—Negro man. **1942** Berrey–Van den Bark *Amer. Slang* 516.13, Oil field worker. . . *Spec.* . . jarhead . . , *a cable-tool driller.* [*DARE* Ed: with pun on *jar* part of a cable drilling rig] **1947** Berrey–Van den Bark *Amer. Slang Suppl.* 43.1, Bellhop, jarhead, a Marine. **1962** *AmSp* 37.288, Jarhead. . . A Marine; used affectionately by the Marines themselves, but by an outsider at his own peril. **1969** *DARE* (Qu. X28, *Joking words . . for a person's head*) Inf **NC72,** Jarhead; (Qu. HH3, *A dull and stupid person*) Inf **IN75,** Jarhead.

jarring See **jar** v¹ **B1**

jar up See **jar** v²

jasack See **jassack**

jasamer See **jasmine 2a**

jasm n Cf **jism 1**

Energy, vitality.

1860 Holland *Miss Gilbert* 350 **CT,** If you'll take thunder and lightning, and a steamboat and a buzz-saw, and mix 'em up, and put 'em into a woman, that's jasm. **1871** *Scribner's Mth.* 2.433, When a man has genuine "jasm" and irrepressibility, a way of carrying out big enterprises to brilliant and successful issues . . we are apt to wink at his processes and praise his pluck. **1886** *Harper's New Mth. Mag.* 73.579 **NY,** The most shif'less creeter I ever see. Willin', but hain't no more jas'm than a dead corn-stalk.

jasmine n Also *jessamine*

1 Std: a plant of the genus *Jasminum.*

2 A plant thought to resemble **jasmine 1** in some way, as:

a also *jasamer, jassmine, jessamy wine:* **=Carolina jasmine.** esp **SE**

1709 (1967) Lawson *New Voyage* 70 **NC,** Myrtles, Jessamines, Woodbines . . interweave themselves with the loftiest Timbers. **1802** Drayton *View of SC* 6, Their undergrowth is covered with a profusion of shrubbery; and jassmines *(bignonia sempervirens)* are abundantly strewed along the ground; or clasp the trees above them, in beautiful festoons. **1853** Simms *Sword & Distaff* 269 **SC,** Myrtle and cane, the honeysuckle and jessamine, . . grew. **1872** *Atlantic Mth.* 29.548 **MS,** They got among tangled jasmine-vines and green brier. **1901** Lounsberry *S. Wild Flowers* 424, Interwoven . . with the beauty and sentiment of the southern lowlands is the "Jasamer," as it is called by the natives. . . Before, or just after, it has flowered, the people collect its rhizomes which if taken with wisdom has been known to cure rheumatism. **1950** *PADS* 14.41 **SC,** *Jessamy wine.* . . The jessamine vine. In Negro speech, *v* is often sounded like *w*, especially in lower S.C. **1960** Vines *Trees SW* 871, *Gelsemium sempervirens.* . . Some vernacular names in use are . . Jasmine . . and Evening Trumpet Flower. This native vine is not to be confused with the cultivated jessamines and jasmines, which belong to the genera *Jasminum* and *Cestrum.* **1966–70** *DARE* (Qu. S10, *A shrub that gets covered with bright yellow, spicy-smelling flowers early in spring;* total Infs questioned, 75) Infs **FL6, 20, 29,** Jasmine; (Qu. S26a, . . *Wildflowers . . Roadside flowers*) Inf **SC67,** Jasmine; (Qu. S26c, *Wildflowers that grow in woods*) Infs **MS8, SC70,** Jasmine; **LA15,** ['jæsmən]; **NC24,** ['jɛsmən]. **1974** (1977) Coon *Useful Plants* 180, Jasmine, jessamine. . . The beautiful vines which grow in the wild in our southern states with yellow blooms seem a far cry from . . the buddleias, and yet they too belong to this . . family.

b also *bastard jasmine, ~ jessamine:* A **matrimony vine** (here: *Lycium halimifolium*).

1837 Darlington *Flora Cestrica* 135, *L[ycium] barbarum.* . . Matrimony vine. Bastard Jasmine. . . This straggling, limber-branched, half-vine kind of shrub . . is something of a nuisance, in many places. **1892** *Jrl. Amer. Folkl.* 5.101, *Lycium vulgare* . . Jasmine. Mansfield, O[hio]. Jessamine. Stratham, N.H. **1894** Ibid 7.95 **IA,** *Lycium vulgare* . . bastard jasmine. **1898** Ibid 11.275, *Lycium vulgare* . . , jessamine, Monroe, Wis. **1931** U.S. Dept. Ag. *Misc. Pub.* 101.142, Matrimony-vine *(L[ycium] halimifolium,* syn. *L. vulgare)* . . bastard jessamine (or jasmine). **1969** *DARE* (Qu. S26a, . . *Wildflowers* . . *Roadside flowers*) Inf **IN**83, Jasmine.

c =**cypress vine 1**. Cf **red jasmine**

   1847 Wood *Class-Book* 443, *Q[uamoclit] vulgaris*. . . Jasmine. . . *Cypress Vine*. . . Flowers much smaller than those of the common morning glory, scarlet, varying to crimson and rose-color. **1900** Lyons *Plant Names* 313, *Q[uamoclit] coccinea*. . . American Jasmine. **1940** Clute *Amer. Plant Names* 92, *I[pomoea] coccinea*. . . American jasmine. **1959** Carleton *Index Herb. Plants* 3, *American jasmine:* Ipomaea coccinea.

d A low shrub (*Macrosiphonia macrosiphon*) native to the Southwest.

   1894 *Jrl. Amer. Folkl.* 7.94 **AZ**, Macrosiphonia brachysiphon . . , jessamine.

e A **forsythia** (here: *Forsythia viridissima*).

   1898 *Jrl. Amer. Folkl.* 11.274 **sKY**, Forsythia viridissima . . , jessamine.

f =**star jasmine**. Cf **Confederate jasmine**

   1953 [see **2g** below]. **1960** Vines *Trees SW* 878, *Trachelospermum difforme*. . . Also known under vernacular names of Dogbane, Doublepod, and Southern Jasmine.

g often with qualifier: Any of var other plants; see quot.

   1953 Greene–Blomquist *Flowers South* 169, Many call any shrub or vine bearing fragrant, white, star-shaped flowers a "jasmine." . . A few non-jasmines are . . illustrated here so their flowers may be compared with the hope that they will no longer be confused with jasmines or called by that name. . . Not Jasmines! . . *Gelsemium sempervirens*[·], *Trachelospermum*[·] *Tabernaemontana*[·] *Gardenia florida*[·], *Cestrum diurnum*[·] *Cestrum nocturnum* . . *Cestrum elegans*[·] *Stephanotis*[·] Others often confused with jasmines are: tail-grape (*Artabotrys odoratissimus*), not cinnamon-jasmine; potato vine (*Solanum jasminoides*); *Murraya paniculata*, not orange-jasmine; *Cestrum Parqui*, not willow-leaved jasmine; *Mandevilla laxa*, not Chilean or star jasmine; Androsaces, not rock-jasmines. *Ibid* 172, (*Ervatamia coronaria*) This white-flowered shrub . . is often confused with jasmines because it is called "crepe-jasmine." *Ibid* 173, *Stephanotis floribunda*. . . Delicately fragrant. . . This fragrance wrongly wins for it the name "jasmine." *Ibid* 179, (*Cestrum nocturnum*) Few plants have been so often confused with jasmines, for it is habitually called "night-blooming jasmine."

jasper n[1]

A type of playing marble.

   1906 Lovett *Old Boston Boys* 42, A boy's stock of marbles was usually carried in a bag with a running string, and consisted of "Alleys," "Jaspers," "Chinees," "Pewees," "Agates," "Bulls' Eyes," and several other kinds.

jasper n[2] [From the proper name]

1 A fellow, guy, esp a rustic, stranger, or one who behaves unacceptably. *often derog*

   1896 Blossom *Checkers* 229 **KS**, After supper . . I went over to the only shanty in the place that looked like a store, and opened the door. There were a lot of 'Jaspers' sitting around the stove, chewing Tobacco and swapping lies. **1897** *KS Univ. Qrly.* (ser B) 6.88, *Jasper:* farmer.—General. **1912** (1914) Sinclair *Flying U Ranch* 174, Some uh you boys help me rope him—like him and that other jasper over there done to Andy. **1966–68** *DARE* (Qu. HH1, *Names and nicknames for a rustic or countrified person*) Inf **OH**61, Jasper; (Qu. HH22a, *A mean or disagreeable person;* total Infs questioned, 75) Inf **FL**28, Jasper. **1980** *DARE* File **DC**, The first time I saw it [=the word *humongous*] in print was in the *Washington Post* 2–3 years ago, when some jasper had been ticketed for using some city-owned sand to get his car out of a predicament. **1981** *NADS Letters* **swIN**, Jasper. . . Those of us who grew up in town (Mt. Vernon, Ind., pop. approx. 5,600 at the time) used the term . . as a synonym for a country bumpkin or in reference to a naive young man who had grown up on a farm. *Ibid* **swIN**, Jasper is used to mean a stranger, but in Posey County, Indiana, if the term is applied to a stranger, the implication is that the stranger is of questionable character. . . But *jasper* is also applied to non-strangers in a kind of quasi-pejorative manner, as in . . , "that jasper beat me out of two dollars." *Ibid* **KY, NC, GA**, On *jasper*—3 'sightings" all from people in their early 40s who heard it from parents now in 70s. Always in context of derogatory nature, as in, "Well, that jasper just don' know what he's doing." A jasper is not necessarily from out of town, or a stranger, but *he* (not she) is unfamiliar with culturally prescribed ways of doing things. *Ibid* **sMN**, My father used it frequently. . . He always preceded the term

with adjectival modifiers—a curious jasper, an out of town jasper—and always gave jasper slightly pejorative connotations. A forty-eight-year-old colleague of mine here, who grew up in Central Illinois, also found the phrase "out of town jasper" a legitimate use of the term. As he explained it, a *jasper* could be someone you know but don't see very much . . , but it could also refer to someone you don't know. . . In either event, a *jasper* behaves peculiarly or does something which, for the moment, seems bizarre to the speaker. **1984** Doig *English Creek* 259 **nMT**, After supper I got to go to town for some sickle heads for the mowers, and I can take two of you jaspers in with me in the pickup. **1985** *WI Alumnus Letters*, An older brother, born in 1884, used to refer to a person as a *Jasper* all his life from the time he returned from . . Colorado. . . My niece, who grew up in . . Iowa, also had heard the term *Jasper* used impersonally as a person all her youth. **1991** Still *Wolfpen Notebooks* 55 **sAppalachians**, That town-raised jasper moved up in the head of the hollow and tried to farm. Naturally he starved out. He didn't even know what makes a pig's tail curl.

2 See quot 1981.

   1926 *Univ. of Va. Mag.* Oct., 17 (*DAS*), Jasper. . . A term originating in Richmond . . from John Jasper . . the eminent colored divine. **1981** *McDavid Coll.* **NC** (as of c1900), About the turn of the century, there was a black preacher in Richmond, Va., the Rev. John Jasper, who was very popular on the black evangelistic circuit, and in fact often drew large white audiences. . . He flourished during my father's undergraduate days at Davidson College, NC, . . and he was much talked about on the campus . . , so much so that the ministerial students were known as *jaspers.*

jassack n Also sp *jasack;* abbr *jass*, hence joc *jass-ass*, *jass-onkey* [*jas(s)ack* by metath] **scattered, but esp WV** See Map A mule or jackass.

   1845 in 1930 Meine *Tall Tales* 55 **TN**, They say that he lied a jassack to death in two hours! **1867** Harris *Sut Lovingood Yarns* 80 **TN**, Es solemn es a jasack in a snow storm, when the fodder gin out. **1906** Casey *Parson's Boys* 199 **sIL** (as of c1860), At breakfast he had a droll story to tell about "the father of all rabbits" which he had seen in the lot. The narrative had proceeded some time before William suddenly saw the joke and exclaimed laughingly: "Why, that's our jassack, Uncle!" **1950** *WELS* (*Joking names for mules*) 1 Inf, **csWI**, Jassack. **1951** Johnson *Resp. to PADS 20* **DE** (*Joking names for mules*) Jass-ack. **c1960** Wilson *Coll.* **csKY**, Jassack. . . Humorous name for mule. **1965–70** *DARE* (Qu. K50, *Joking nicknames for mules*) 39 Infs, **scattered, but esp WV**, Jassack; **AL**26, **NY**198, **PA**29, Jass-ass; **AZ**5, **ID**3, Jass-onkey; **TX**6, Jass.

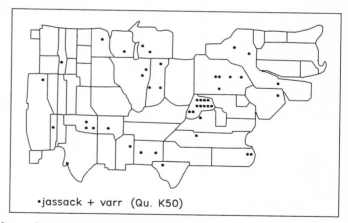

•jassack + varr (Qu. K50)

jassmine See **jasmine 2a**

jass-onkey See **jassack**

jaundeez See **jaundice**

jaunder See **jaundice B**

jaundice n Usu |ˈjɔndɪs, ˈjɑ-, -əs|; also **esp Sth, S Midl, ME,** |ˈjɔndə(r)z, ˈjɑ-|; **esp Sth, S Midl,** |ˈjændə(r)z|; for addit varr see quots 1952, 1965–70 Pronc-spp *janders, jandice, jaunders, jaundeez, jindice, johndice*

A Pronc varr.

   1827 in 1956 Eliason *Tarheel Talk* 313 **NC**, Jandice. **1847** Hurd *Grammatical Corrector* 84, Jaundice ["incorrect" pronc = [ˈjændəɹz]]. **1892** *DN* 1.212 **NEng**, Jaundice: [jandɪs]. **1893** Shands *MS Speech* 72,

Janders [ˈdʒændəz]. A form of the word *jaundice*. . . *jaunders* . . also is heard in Mississippi. **1899** (1912) Green *VA Folk-Speech* 243, *Janders*. . . For jaundice. "Yallerjanders." . . *Jaunders*. . . A form of jaundice. **1907** *DN* 3.232 **nwAR, seMO**, *Jaundice*. . . Pronounced janders. There are "yaller janders" and "black janders." **1908** *DN* 3.324 **eAL, wGA**, *Janders*. . . Not common. **1912** *DN* 3.579 **wIN**, *Janders*. **1916** *DN* 4.341 **eOH, NY, LA**, *Janders*. **1923** *DN* 5.211 **swMO**, *Janders*. . . Yaller janders. **1928** *AmSp* 3.404 **Ozarks**, Vowel substitution is frequent. . . *Gaunt* and *jaundice* become . . *gant* and *janders*. **1941** Faulkner *Men Working* 154 **MS**, I believe the doctor called hit the yellow johndice. **1942** McAtee *Dial. Grant Co. IN* 7 (as of 1890s), *Janders*. **1952** Brown *NC Folkl.* 1.554 **c,eNC**, *Jindice* [ˈdʒaɪndɪs]. **c1955** Reed–Person *Ling. Atlas Pacific NW*, 1 inf, *Jaundeez*. **c1960** *Wilson Coll.* **csKY**, Jaundice appears in three forms: /ˈdʒɔndɪs/, /ˈdʒændɪs/, /ˈdʒændɚs/ (now largely humorous). **1965–70** *DARE* (Qu. BB23, *The disease where the skin becomes a yellowish color*) 852 Infs, **widespread**, (Yellow) jaundice [usu pronc [ˈjɔndɪs, jɑ-, -əs]]; **NH16**, The [ˈjɔndəs; **MS88, MO22**, Yellow [ˈjɑndɪs]; **AL4, NJ54, PA36**, 124, 139, (Yellow [ˈjɔnɪs]; **MO16**, [ˈjɑnɪs]; **OH63**, [ˈjɛlə ˈjɑdɪs]; **OH103**, [jɛlə ˈjɔdɪs]; **VA13, WA9**, [ˈjɔntɪs]; **IL21**, [ˈjɑntɪs]; **MI2**, [jɛlo ˈjɑndus] [FW: sic]; **SC55**, [jɛlə jɔndaɪs]; **IL88, IN3, OH47, SC11, TN30, TX62**, 65, (Yellow) [ˈjɑundɪs, -əs]; **AR52, NY250**, (Yellow) [ˈjɔundɪs]; 47 Infs, **scattered, but esp KY, ME**, (Yellow) jaunders [usu pronc [ˈjɔndə(r)z, jɑ-]]; **CA15**, The yellow [ˈjɔndɚz]; 48 Infs, **scattered, but esp Sth, S Midl**, (Yellow) janders [ˈjændə(r)z]; **PA115**, The [ˈjændɚz]; **GA72, LA3, MD20, MA69, MO37, NY61, OH56, TX9**, (Yellow) jandice [ˈjændɪs, -əs]; **MO12**, Yellow [ˈjæntɪs]; **SC3**, Yellow [ˈjædɪs]; **TN27**, [jɛlɚ ˈjændɪsɪz]; **LA37**, [ˌjɛlə ˈjaɪtɪs] [Inf doubtful]; **PA66**, [ˈjænɑɪtɪs]; (Qu. BB49, . . *Other kinds of diseases*) Infs **IL113, RI1**, Jaundice; **LA18**, Yellow jaundice; **TX62**, Black jaundice, yellow jaundice; **NC50**, Yellow [ˈjeɪnjɪs]; **ME9**, Janders; (Qu. DD24, . . *Diseases that come from continual drinking*) Infs **KY35, MA4, NH18, NY241, WI60**, (Yellow) jaundice; (Qu. K47, . . *Diseases . . horses or mules commonly get*) Inf **LA31**, Jaundice; **NJ53**, Janders. **1976** Allen *LAUM* 3.261 (as of c1950), As in the eastern states the two principal pronunciation types are that with a rounded vowel ranging from /ɔ/ to /ɒ/ and that with an unround vowel ranging from /ɑ/ to /ɑ/. The incidence of the unrounded type is higher in the U[pper] M[idwest] than in the eastern states. . . Also in the East *jaundice* contrasts with *haunted* because of its greater retention of an earlier minority pronunciation with /æ/. Particularly, the slightly higher incidence of /æ/ in Pennsylvania than in New England is reflected in a higher incidence in the Midland speech territory of the UM. But it clearly is a dying form. . . A curious correlation is that between the pronunciation with /æ/ and a final syllable containing . . /ɚ/. This correlation is noticeable in New England, where most of the 47 instances are in the pronunciation /ˈjændɚz/. More than one-half are in southwestern New England. . . But presumably this pronunciation is even more frequent in the Midland area, since most of the 19 UM examples are in Midland speech territory. . . All of the UM instances with /ɚ/ in the second syllable are from the least educated infs., . . and all but one . . of the instances of /æ/ are from the same group.

B Gram forms.

Occas treated as pl; hence also sg *jander* or *jaunder*.

1903 *DN* 2.318 **seMO**, *Jaundice*. . . Pronounced janders. Two varieties of this disease are recognized by old-fashioned people, 'yaller janders' and 'black janders.' Always spoken of in the plural: 'I was down with yaller janders and haven't got over them yet, as you can see.' **1965–70** *DARE* (Qu. BB23) Inf **MA6**, [ˈjɔndɪs] [FW: pl]; **MO39**, [ˈjɔndɚ]; **GA42**, [ˌjɛlə ˈjændə]; **SC10**, [jɛlə gjændə].

jaundice root n [See quot 1869]
=**goldenseal 1**.

[**1869** Porcher *Resources* 16, It [=*Hydrastis canadensis*] has been employed . . in jaundice and other functional disorders of the liver.] **1876** Hobbs *Bot. Hdbk.* 59, Jaundice root, Goldenseal root, Hydrastis Canadensis. **1930** Sievers *Amer. Med. Plants* 31, *Goldenseal*. . . Other common names. . . Jaundice root. . . In reasonably constant demand. **1968** *Foxfire* 2.2.15 **nGA**, Best known as sang-sign is the "little brother of the ginseng", the golden seal. . . Other names . . include . . jaundice-root. **1974** (1977) Coon *Useful Plants* 220, Jaundice root. . . The roots are the parts used, either as a source for a yellow dye, or in reputable medical practice as an alterative and bitter tonic.

jaunt n, v Usu |jɔnt, jɑnt| Also esp Sth, S Midl |jænt| Pronc-sp *jant;* similarly adj *janty*
Std senses, var forms.

1806 (1970) Webster *Compendious Dict.* 167, *Janty* or *Jaunty*. [*DARE* Ed: This entry was carried over from Webster's English model.] **1828** Webster *Amer. Dict.* np, *Jaunt*. [See *Jant*.] **1891** *PMLA* 6.163 **WV**, [In] words like *gaunt, haunt, jaunt*, . . Sweet's low-front-wide (=*a* in *man*) is commonly heard. . . Occasionally one hears the mid-back-wide (=*a* in *father*). . . I have never heard Sweet's low-back-narrow-round (=*aw* in *law* . .). **1892** *DN* 1.239 **cwMO**, *Jaunt* is [jænt]. **1901** Harben *Westerfelt* 166 **nGA**, He's got a-plenty [of horses], an' he won't need 'em atter our ja'nt. **1908** *DN* 3.324 **eAL, wGA**, *Jant* [jænt]. . . Jaunt, trip. **1922** (1926) Cady *Rhymes VT* 124, Them jants that tickled girls and boys / And went by steam, alloyed with noise. **1929** *AmSp* 4.56 **Ozarks**, *Jaunt* . . pronounced so as to rhyme with *rant*. **1933** Rawlings *South Moon* 134 **FL**, You goes off on them j'ants and stays off. **1952** Brown *NC Folkl.* 1.554 **wNC**, *Jant* [dʒænt]. . . Jaunt. **c1960** *Wilson Coll.* **csKY**, *Jaunt* is sometimes /dʒænt/, now largely humorous.

javalina, javelin(a) See jabalina

javelina bush n Also *javelin(a) brush*
A **crucillo 1** (here: *Condalia ericoides*).

1938 Van Dersal *Native Woody Plants* 168, *Javelin brush*. . . A small to large, spiny evergreen shrub with minute leaves. **1970** Correll *Plants TX* 1014, *Condalia ericoides*. . . Javelina bush. . . Fruit . . when fully mature and juicy reddish-black or purplish-black. . . Locally abundant. **1975** Lamb *Woody Plants SW* 28, Javelina-brush. . . has no wildlife significance except that it makes fine escape cover for quail and small mammals.

jaw n
In var phrr indicating that one is very angry: See quots. *among Black speakers*

1970 *DARE* (Qu. LL37, *To make a statement as strong as you can:* "I could have wrung her neck, I was so _____ *mad.*") Inf **NY241**, My jaw was hard. [Inf Black] **1970** *DARE* FW Addit **TN50**, Man, his jaws were so tight when he found out that his woman had run out on him. [FW: young Black street talk] **1971** Landy *Underground Dict.* 137, *My jaws are tight* (B[lacks]) Expression meaning I'm angry. **1972** Claerbaut *Black Jargon* 83, *Tight jaws* . . furious; very angry: *I'm getting some tight jaws now.*

jaw v Cf jawbone v
To talk a seller into lowering his price.

1954 *Harder Coll.* **cwTN**, *Jaw*. . . Same as *jew (down)*.

jaw at the jibs See jib n¹ 1b

jaw back v phr esp Sth, S Midl Cf back-jaw
To retort, talk back.

1885 Green *Memoir Otey* 9 **VA**, The services of the Church were something so strange to them [=Tennessee backwoodsmen], that the Bishop would afterwards illustrate it by telling what one of these rude sons of the forest was once heard to say to another: "Come, let us go and hear that man preach, and his wife jaw back at him,"—alluding to the responses made by Mrs. Otey, who was oftentimes the only respondent. **1906** *DN* 3.142 **nwAR**, *Jaw back*. . . To retort indignantly. "He jawed back at him." **1908** *DN* 3.324 **eAL, wGA**, *Jaw-back*. . . To retort saucily. **1923** (1946) Greer–Petrie *Angeline Steppin'* 42 **csKY**, She ought to a jaw'd him back. **1969** *DARE* (Qu. KK13, . . *Arguing:* "They stood there for an hour _____.") Inf **GA77**, Jawing back at each other.

jawbone n

1 The dried jawbone (with the teeth) of a horse or similar animal used as a percussion instrument esp by Black slaves; see quot 1962. Cf *DJE* 1837 →, *DBE*

1869 Dumont *Benedict's Cong. Songster* 50 (*DA*), I can play the old jawbone, and can use the fiddlebow. **1931** Randolph *Ozarks* 206, The slaves frequently used the jawbone of a horse or mule as a musical instrument, played by drawing a bit of metal across the teeth. Several country dance melodies are still known vaguely as "jawbone tunes." **1942** (1965) Parrish *Slave Songs* 16 **GA coast**, Those who can . . play upon the well-seasoned and polished "old jawbone" of some ox, horse, or mule with the aid of a blacksmith's rasp or a large key [a rhythmic tooth-rattling performance]. **1952** Ulanov *Hist. Jazz* 46 **LA**, By the end of the 1880s New Orleans Negro musicians were no longer playing jawbones, hide-covered casks, or bamboo tubes. **1960** in 1984 Gilmore *Ozark Baptizings* 190 **MO**, This jawbone of the mule is the underjaw of an old dead mule, been dead for years and years, and you can beat a rhythm on that just the same as you can on a drum. **1962** Nathan *Dan*

Emmett 149 (as of 1840s), The jawbone was taken from a horse, ox, ass, or sheep. . . Its teeth were rattled, scraped, or struck, producing what someone called a "tremolo"—a quick succession of dry staccato clicks not dissimilar to those of the bones. *Ibid* 151, At times smaller combinations of instruments were favored, such as. . . fiddle, jawbone, and tambourine; . . and accordion and bones.

2 in var phrr, esp *walk jawbone,* referring to Black or minstrel dance steps, routines, or tunes: See quots. Cf **pat juba**

    1826 *Constitutional Advocate* (Frankfort, Ky.) 3 Feb. 3/3 *(DA),* They then toasted Massa, . . after which they all patted *Jawbone* very *soft* and slow. **1832** *Polit. Examiner* (Shelbyville, Ky.) 7 July 3/1 *(DA),* Tune, Walk jaw-bone. **1833** *Sketches D. Crockett* 39 **TN,** I started off from Tennessee,/ My old horse wouldn't pull for me./ *(Ben cries out—"Now, back step an' heel an' toe.")*/ He began to fret an' slip,/ An' I begin to cus [sic] an' whip;/ Walk jawbone from Tennessee;/ Walk jawbone from Tennessee./ *("Now, weed corn, kiver taters, an' double shuffle.")* **1839** *Observer & Reporter* 24 Aug. *(DA),* No more shall he enliven the negro quarters on Saturday nights . . or sing 'jaw bone' at the corn shucking. [**1919** *Jrl. Amer. Folkl.* 32.359 **VA,** Jaw-bone walk-a, jaw-bone talk,/ Jaw-bone cat-er [*DARE* Ed: perh rel to *DJE cotta* a drum] wid a knife an' fork.] **1962** Nathan *Dan Emmett* 91, There is equally sparse data available on "turkey trot" and "walking jawbone." . . "Walking jaw-bone" must have been a very strenuous step. It is likely that it consisted of quick taps reminiscent of the rattle of the teeth of a jawbone when used as an instrument. *Ibid* 88, Dey all got drunk, but me alone / I make ole Tucker walk jaw-bone [from an 1843 version of "Old Dan Tucker"]. An when old master goes from home,/ My missus make me walk jaw bone [from an 1840's version of "Walk Jawbone, Original Verses by Dan Emmitt [sic]"].

3 Empty talk; a promise or claim, esp one that is exaggerated or unrealistic.

    1898 *NY Voice* (NY) 24 Mar 41, Jawbone is cheap, and there is plenty of it; backbone is something rare and all the reputed riches of the Klondike can not buy it. **1939** (1973) FWP *Guide MT* 92, From Harlowton to Lombard and to Lewistown it [=the Chicago, Milwaukee, St. Paul & Pacific Railroad] used the tracks of the old Central Montana Railroad, known as the "Jawbone Line." The history of this now important part of the system is diverting. Not only was it promoted by the generous use of "jawbone" (promises or talk), but its builders seemed to have little basis for their hopes. **1942** Henry *High Border* 209 **nRocky Mts,** On the upper Missouri the Jawbone Railroad thrust a steel trail across the prairie—"jawbone" because it was financed mainly on verbal promises. **1958** McCulloch *Woods Words* 98 **Pacific NW,** *Jawbone.* . . A deal cooked up by talk instead of good sense.

4 Credit; hence adv *jawbone* on credit. Cf **jawbone** v

    1862 *Times* (London) 21 Oct 9/4 **CA,** Individuals who, in digger's parlance, live on jawbone (credit). **1900** *Nation* 4 Oct 270, A common slang among American soldiers for the word "credit" is "jawbone." . . The soldier asks . . the native keeper . . to sell him a bottle of beer "on jawbone." **1926** *AmSp* 1.564, To buy something which is to be paid for on pay day is to "buy jawbone." The term was picked up by our soldiers from the Filipinos in the "Days of the Empire." It is even yet common among the Filipinos. They distinguish between buying for cash and "buying jawbone" by charging more when the purchase is of the second type. . . From its origin in Filipino dealings the term spread until it is now used in the United States by civilians as well as by ex-servicemen. **1941** Smiley *Hash House Lingo* 33, *Jawbone*—credit. **1941** [see **jawbone** v]. **1944** Adams *Western Words* 84, *Jawbone*—Credit. A cowboy who lives on his credit until next payday is said to "live on his jawbone." **1947** *AmSp* 22.55 [Pacific war language], *Jawbone.* Credit. **1967–70** *DARE* (Qu. U11, *If you buy something but don't pay cash for it . . "I _____."*) Inf **CA**197, Put it on the cuff; jawbone—answer to question "How d'you get that so 'n' so?"; **WA**20, [Got it] on jawbone.

5 See quot.

    1983 *McDavid Coll.* **SC,** Duke's Mixture and other types of jawbone (as we used to call home-rolled cigarettes and the tobacco used for making them) constituted a small part of the tobacco business.

jawbone v Cf **face, run one's**

To talk someone into extending credit; to buy (something) on credit.

    1941 *AmSp* 16.166 [Army slang], *Jawbone.* Credit. To buy without money. **1942** Berrey-Van den Bark *Amer. Slang* 895.2, Jawbone, *to buy on credit.* **1950** *WELS* (If you buy something but don't pay cash for it, you might say, "I _____.") 1 Inf, **csWI,** Jawboned it.

jawbone breaker n

1 See quot. [Var of *jawbreaker* a large, round hard candy; cf *DBE*]

    1966–70 *DARE* (Qu. H82a, *Cheap candies sold especially for schoolchildren*) Infs **SC**26, 70, Jawbone breakers. [Both Infs Black]

2 See **jawbreaker 1.**

jawbone doctor See **jawbreaker 1**

jawbone talk n

See quot.

    1895 *Chicago Times-Herald* (IL) 10 Nov 35/1 **Sth,** The jawbone talk was a droning song game, in which those engaged sat in a ring and made a rhyme to the prevailing tune by turns. But if one hesitated when his time came the next one took up the measure and the failing one was ruled out.

jawbreaker n

1 also *jawbone breaker,* ~ *doctor,* ~ *jaw cracker,* ~ *puller,* ~ *smith:* A dentist. joc

    1942 Berrey-Van den Bark *Amer. Slang* 529.10, Dentist . . jawsmith. **1944** Adams *Western Words* 84, *Jaw cracker*—A traveling dentist who goes from place to place over the range to relieve cowboys of their pain, teeth, and money. **1954** Harder *Coll.* **cwTN,** Jaw breaker. . . Dentist. **1965–70** *DARE* (Qu. BB52, . . *Joking words . . for a dentist*) 73 Infs, **widespread,** Jawbreaker; **SC**27, Jawbone breaker; **WA**30, Jawbone doctor; **MO**5, Old jaw puller.

2 In marble play: a shooter. [Cf *jawbreaker* a large, round hard candy]

    1966–67 *DARE* (Qu. EE6a, . . *Different kinds of marbles—the big one that's used to knock others out of the ring*) Infs **FL**35, **MO**21, Jawbreaker.

jaw cracker See **jawbreaker 1**

‡jawer n Cf **jower** n

    1966 *DARE* (Qu. II36a, *Somebody who talks back or gives rude answers: "Did you ever see such a _____?"*) Inf **MS**6, Jawer.

jaw harp See **jaw's harp**

jaw lap n [*lap* flap, fold] Cf **dewlap** n

    1929 *AmSp* 5.70 **NE,** Cattle are frequently given not only a "scorch" but a "mark," often called a "jaw lap" if the skin on the jaw is cut.

jawlock n [Reversed compound; cf *lockjaw* and Intro "Language Changes" I.1]

Tetanus.

    1892 (1969) Christensen *Afro-Amer. Folk Lore* 43, You aint yerry [=heard] 'bout ole Coon son dead wid de jaw-lock?

jaw puller See **jawbreaker 1**

jaws are hard (or tight), one's See **jaw** n

jaw's harp n Also *jaw harp* [Prob euphem or folk-etym for *Jew's harp*]

    [**1927** *Melody Maker* Aug 811/1 *(OEDS),* When I tune my 'Jaws Harp' as a 'Jujulele', I do not seem to get the *full* banjolic effect.] **1958** Gammond *Decca Book* 23, Cheap guitars, jaw's harps and harmonicas became available in greater numbers in the 'nineties. **1986** Pederson *LAGS Concordance,* 1 inf, **seTN,** Jaw harp; 1 inf, **cnGA,** Jaw harp—has been "corrupted" to Jew's harp; 1 inf, **cnTN,** Jaw harp—some say—if "Jew's harp" is offensive. **1988** *DARE* File, What we used to call a Jews Harp in New York City now goes by the name of Jaw Harp on the radio (Prairie Home Companion).

jaw smith See **jawbreaker 1**

jaw tooth n

A molar tooth.

    1815 (1922) Valpey *Jrl.* 25 **MA,** I . . had three of my Jaw teeth taken out by a fellow prisoner. **1859** Taliaferro *Fisher's R.* 90 **nwNC** (as of 1820s), He drawed and drawed, wusser nur a man drawin' jaw teeth. **1924** (1969) Gonzales *With Aesop* 83 **SC coast** [Gullah], Uh po' leely creetuh lukkuh me, wuh yent big 'nuf fuh full de holluh een you jaw teet'. [=A poor little creature like me, which ain't big enough to fill the hollow in your jaw teeth.] **1965–68** *DARE* (Qu. X13a, . . *Teeth*) Inf **NC**49, Front teeth, eye teeth, stomach teeth, jaw teeth, ['wɪzbən] teeth; **OK**1, Eye teeth, jaw teeth, stomach teeth; (Qu. BB20, *Joking names or* *expressions for overactive kidneys*) Inf **IN**13, Jaw teeth's a-floatin'. **1968** *DARE* Tape **IL**29, He had a double row of teeth, upper and lower, and he never had a tooth pulled up till the day he died. . . He had a double row clear around, jaw teeth and all. **1986** Pederson *LAGS Concordance* **Gulf Region** (*Tooth, teeth*) 6 infs, Jaw tooth; 2 infs, Jaw tooth = molar.

jay n

A person or fellow, esp a rustic or one considered otherwise ignorant, awkward, or unsophisticated.

   1890 Hall *Turnover Club* 49 **Chicago IL**, The next summer I played in a 'snap' stock company in a small town. The 'jays' continued to make me very weary, and the populace of twelve hundred souls united in giving me a cramp in the scarf-pin. **1892** *Congressional Record* 28 May 4795 **IL**, No Joshua, that is not necessary and appropriate for an old jay like you. **1892** *KS Univ. Qrly.* 1.97, *Jay:* a green, conceited fellow. **1894** *Life* 23.256 **NYC**, People of taste and refinement. . . haven't any 'pull,' and the jay vote is the one to consider in matters of an artistic nature. **1896** *Chicago Daily Tribune* (IL) 27 July 7/1 **Chicago IL**, To the "city jay" the twelve-hour day is a severe strain. **1904** (1972) Harben *Georgians* 189 **GA**, I acknowledge I felt like a plumb jay from the backwoods. **1915** *DN* 4.197, *Jay.* . . Also used in about the same meaning as "hayseed." **1919** *DN* 5.70 **NM**, *Jay,* a gawky person. "Who is that jay across the street?" **1923** *Nation* 12 Dec 688 **MA**, The Holstein is the cow to raise for producing milk to be sold to the city jay. **1931–33** *LANE Worksheets,* 1 inf, neMA, Jays—nickname for a rustic—old fashioned. **1936** Fellows–Freeman *This Way* 119, "Rube" was not the only word by which circus folk stigmatized the townsmen. They were also called "gillipins" or "gills," "jays," and "saps." **1942** Berrey–Van den Bark *Amer. Slang* 914.4, [Western terms:] Cultivated land. . . *jay country.* **1966** *DARE* (Qu. HH1, *Names and nicknames for a rustic or countrified person*) Inf **MS**49, Jay; (Qu. HH3, *A dull and stupid person*) Inf **MI**4, Jay.

jay adj [**jay** n]

Rustic, ignorant, unsophisticated.

   1889 *Daily Eve. Bulletin* (San Francisco CA) 13 July 1/6, Smith has a poor opinion . . of St Joseph, which he alludes to as a "jay" town of the worst description. **1890** (1891) Bunner *Short Sixes* 91 **NY**, 'T ain't neuralogy, you jay pill-box, she's cooked! **1890** in 1937 Moses *Repr. Amer. Dramas* 28 **TX**, When I fixed myself all up to please him, he thought I looked jay,—and . . wouldn't let me go down to dinner. **1912** Nicholson *Hoosier Chron.* 268 **IN**, He's only a state senator from the jayest county in Indiana. **1916** Wilson *Somewhere* 348 **West**, He puts it up with the press agent of this big hotel to have the poor things sleep up on the roof, . . so them jay New York newspapers would fall for it, and print articles about these hardy sons of the forest. **1931** Faulkner *Sanctuary* 322 **MS**, So dont you be sending no jay cops up here with no letters for nobody. **1951** Porter *Ragged Roads* 134 **OK**, We . . got out, measured the solid outer rim of the road and found that with a feather-edge drive we could make it around; but there was no room for jay-driving, no monkey work.

‡**jay** v[1] Cf **jaybird** n 4, **hootenkack**

To harass, pester (someone) until a desired result is obtained.

   1927 *AmSp* 2.358 **cwWV**, Jay . . , to get a job. "I went up to the office and jayed the superintendent."

jay v[2], hence vbl n *jaying* Also with *off, out* Also sp **J** **Appalachians** Cf **jay grab, jay hole, jay path**

In skidding logs: to step out of the skid road and let the logs continue downhill under their own weight; to cause (a team of animals) to do this; to cause (logs) to slide in this way; also fig.

   1932 Strong *Behind Gt. Smokies* 32, Hit takes low gear to pull us up, an' low, high, *an'* reverse ter hold us back when we go a-jayin' down. **1939** *Hall Coll.* **wNC, eTN**, Bus Carpenter has heard loggers yell "Jay!" at their horses; "a good team of horses will know what to do." **1964** Clarkson *Tumult* 365 **WV**, Jay-off—When a team steps aside to allow running logs to pass by. *Ibid* [see **jay grab**]. **1968** *DARE* Tape **VA**27, We had jay grabs. We had to jay them there horses offen a trail of logs. We couldn't let the logs run into the horses. We had to jay 'em and let the logs pass by the horses. **1977** *Foxfire 4* 275 **wNC**, You jay your steers off and let the logs go on by theirselves. And whenever you go to jay, you just turn your spread hook over and put it in that grab and your spread hook turns loose and it just goes right on by. I've jayed off eighteen and twenty of them, and the cracker [=the last log in the string] would go past and he'd be a foot off the ground when he passed. *Ibid* 276, It was a long time before they ever done that jaying with steers. . .

Then they got to learning steers to where they'd jay. **1994** *Jrl.–Patriot* (N. Wilkesboro NC) 25 Aug sec D 7/1 [Logging terms], Hendrix said the horses he worked with were trained to "J-out" to safety to the left or right when they felt slack while pulling a load down a slope.

jaybird n [Prob from Engl dial *jay-bird* (applied to the European jay, *Garrulus glandarius*); though attested in Britain only from the late 19th cent, this folk-name is prob considerably older (cf *OED, EDD* **jay** sb.)]

1a A jay of the family Corvidae, usu **blue jay 1.** **scattered, but chiefly Sth, S Midl** See Map

   1661 in 1894 Dedham MA *Early Rec.* 4.41 **MA**, En Dani Fisher is creditor to the Towne for his sonne catching of Jaybirds: the sume of one shiling twoopenc. **1805** (1904) Lewis *Orig. Jrls. Lewis & Clark Exped.* 2.295, I also saw . . a blue bird about the size of the common robbin. it's action and form is somewhat that of the jay bird. **1832** Kennedy *Swallow Barn* 2.55 **VA**, A scream of jay-birds, heard at intervals. **1899** (1912) Green *VA Folk-Speech* 244, *Jay-bird.* . . The common blue jay. This bird is said to go to hell every Friday to carry the devil a grain of corn. **1903** *DN* 2.318 **seMO**, Jay-bird. **1905** *DN* 3.84 **nwAR**, *Jay-bird.* . . Blue jay. **1908** *DN* 3.324 **eAL, wGA**, Jay-bird. **1942** Rawlings *Cross Creek* 222 **nFL**, I am obliged to . . pick them a trifle green, for the 'coons and 'possums and jay-birds are likely to be ahead of me. **c1960** *Wilson Coll.* **csKY**, Jaybird. **1965–70** *DARE* (Qu. Q16, . . *Kinds of jays*) 106 Infs, **scattered, but chiefly Sth, S Midl**, Jaybird; (Qu. Q14) Infs **AL**6, **MO**15, Jaybird. **1986** Pederson *LAGS Concordance,* 28 infs, **Gulf Region**, Jaybird(s).

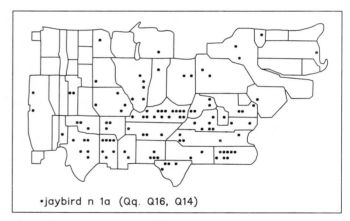

•jaybird n 1a (Qq. Q16, Q14)

b Used in var proverbial comparisons, esp *naked as a jaybird* and varr. **scattered, but chiefly Sth, S Midl** See Map

   1847 (1962) Robb *Squatter Life* 98 **MO**, As enticin' as a jay bird. **1884** *Anglia* 7.267 **Sth, S Midl** [Black], To be ez sassy ez er jay-bird = to be extremely saucy. **1897** Johnston *Old Times GA* 48, They'll even take holt of their hand, and be as proud as a jay-bird when they do it. **1917** *DN* 4.407 **wNC**, He's as antic as a jaybird. **1922** Gonzales *Black Border* 222 **sSC, GA coasts** [Gullah], I gwi' strip nakit ez a jaybu'd befo' 'e fedduh' grow! **1950** *PADS* 14.80 **FL**, *Naked* as a jaybird. Suwannee backwoods simile. **1952** Brown *NC Folkl.* 1.431, As happy as a jaybird. . . As naked as a picked jaybird. . . As naked as a jaybird's

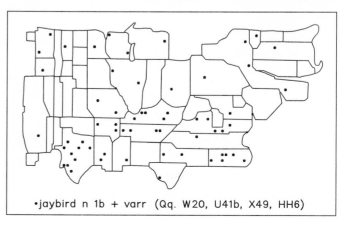

•jaybird n 1b + varr (Qq. W20, U41b, X49, HH6)

ass. . . As saucy as a jaybird. . . Git along about as well as a jaybird does with a sparrer hawk. . . As spry as a jaybird in wild cherry time. **1965–70** *DARE* (Qu. W20, *If somebody has no clothes on at all—for example, "There was Johnny, _____." or, "They went in swimming _____.")* 56 Infs, **scattered, but chiefly Sth, S Midl,** (As) naked as a jaybird; **KY**84, Naked as a picked jaybird; **NY**35, Bare as a jaybird; (Qu. U41b, "He's poor as _____.") Inf **SC**68, A jaybird; [(Qu. X5, . . *Different kinds of men's haircuts*) Inf **FL**33, Jaybird;] (Qu. X49, *Expressions . . about a person who is very thin*) Inf **TX**76, Poor as a jaybird; (Qu. HH6, *Someone who is out of his mind*) Inf **WI**47, Loony as a jaybird; [(Qu. HH20c, . . "He isn't worth _____.")] Inf **LA**2, A gill of jaybird gravy]. **1970** *DARE* Tape **FL**50, She was just as happy as a jaybird.

2 =killdeer.
1967 *DARE* (Qu. Q14, . . *Names . . for . . birds*) Inf **MI**69, Killdeer—sometimes called a "jaybird," but I think people do it with an I-know-I'm-wrong-but-I-like-the-sound-of-the-term attitude.

3 =jay n. Cf **jayhawk** n 1
1886 in 1939 Thornton *Amer. Gloss.* 1.382, From the land of logs and peaches / Came a callow jay-bird dressed / In homespun coat and breeches / And a gaudy yellow vest. **1930** *AmSp* 10.80 **MO,** With its hills, hollows, and swamps, southeast Missouri is well adapted to propagation of the *Podunk* idea. . . Closely allied to the *Toonerville* concept is the satirical reference made to that nondescript neighborhood on the outskirts of a town. . . Others heard occasionally are *Skintown, Bugtown,* and *Jaybirdtown.* **c1960** *Wilson Coll.* **csKY,** *Jaybird.* . . A rustic; a term of reproach, usually humorous. **1981** *NADS Letters,* [In response to a query about "out of town Jasper" used of a stranger:] In the South, and in Indiana, he would be called a "jaybird."

4 A saucy or impudent person.
[**1880** (1881) Harris *Uncle Remus Songs* 24 **GA** [Black], Dez ez sassy ez a jay-bird.] **1927** *AmSp* 2.358 **cwWV,** *Jay bird* . . an impudent fellow. "We have no use here for such a jay bird."

5 attrib: Misshapen, scrawny; inferior; see quots. [Cf *EDD jay-legged* "Small or feeble in the legs"]
1887 *Courier-Jrl.* (Louisville KY) 2 May 6/5, The man who has one or more good mares to breed can . . make a very ridiculous ass of himself . . in using some jay-bird stallion to breed them to. **1960** Williams *Walk Egypt* 208 **GA,** Calla was sixteen, with a bullet head and jaybird heels. **1967** *DARE* (Qu. X37, . . *Words . . to describe people's legs if they're noticeably bent, or uneven, or not right*) Inf **SC**32, Jaybird legs—real skinny. **1992** *NADS Letters,* When I was a small boy in Decatur, Georgia, in the early 1920s, I wore long black stockings on schooldays in the wintertime. My mother often helped me get them on. When she had trouble getting them over my heel and on to my ankle and calf, she would jokingly complain that I had jaybird heels—big heels which combined with a high instep to make the job difficult. I suppose the comparison was to the back claw on a blue jay's foot.

‡6 A kind of haircut.
1966 *DARE* (Qu. X5, . . *Different kinds of men's haircuts*) Inf **FL**33, Jaybird.

jaybird intj [Euphem for *Jesus*]
See quots.
1939 *Sat. Eve. Post* 25 Nov 60 **FL,** My heart lept like a mullet jumping. I thought, "Merciful jay bird, now's the time." **1966** *DARE* (Qu. NN30, *Exclamations beginning with the sound of 'j'*) Infs **MI**28, **OK**27, Jaybird.

jaybird bath n Cf **cat bath**
c1950 *Halpert Coll.* 3 **wKY,** To take a jaybird bath = [one] confined to parts that show, usually the face and hands.

jaybird gossip n
1950 *PADS* 14.40 **SC,** *Jaybird gossip.* . . The petty scandal of the backyard, malicious and amusing like the raucous chatter of the jays.

jaybird it v phr
To mope.
1935 Davis *Honey* 153 **OR,** It [=a song] was about a lonesome *vaquero* jaybirding it out on the corral gate with his head on his brisket, and how the foreman came along and told him not to be so down in the mouth.

Jay Gould n Also *Jake Gould* [*Jay Gould* Amer financier, 1836–1892] **esp Sth, S Midl**
One who is rich or important.

1965–70 *DARE* (Qu. U41b) Inf **MS**1, Rich as Jay Gould; (Qu. GG19b, *When you can see from the way a person acts that he's feeling important or independent: "He seems to think he's _____.")* Inf **VA**21, (Mrs.) Jay Gould; (Qu. II21, *When somebody behaves unpleasantly or without manners: "The way he behaves, you'd think he was _____.")* Inf **MO**25, Jay Gould; (Qu. II26, *Joking ways of saying that you would not know who somebody is: "I wouldn't know him from _____.")* Inf **KY**85, Jay Gould; **TX**95, Jake Gould.

jay grab n Also *J-grab, J-hook* [From its resemblance to the letter *J*] **Appalachians** Cf **jay** v[2], **jay hole**
In skidding logs: an open hook affixed to one of the logs, by which the team is attached, but from which it may be quickly disengaged when the logs begin sliding under their own weight.
1913 Bryant *Logging* 239, The process is repeated until a turn is made up, when a team is attached to the rear end of the last log by a chain or rope from 30 feet to 50 feet long, to which is fastened an "L" hook, swamp hook, grab hook, or "jay grab." . . If the logs start to run in the slide the teamster can readily detach the hook and free the team. **1930** *DN* 6.88 **cWV,** Jay grab, a hook used only on the header. [*Ibid,* Header, the first log in a line of them to be dragged down a mountain side.] **1964** Clarkson *Tumult* 365 **WV,** J-grab—Special type of grab or coupler used on steep slopes. This type of grab permits the skidding team to step aside (jay off), become disengaged and stand while the logs continue down the slope. Syn J-hook. **1968** *DARE* Tape **VA**27, I worked . . for the Moore Lumber company—drove horses for 'em in the woods. . . It was steep ground. We had jay grabs. We had to jay them there horses offen a trail of logs. **1977** *Foxfire 4* 275 **wNC,** We used a J-grab on that header log. Put your J-grab on that. See, if you fix your road right, they'll be a lot of places where you can let [the line of logs] run. **1994** [see **jay hole**].

jayhawk n [*jay* a bird of the family Corvidae + *hawk* n]
1 also *jayhawker:* **=jay** n.
1907 Stewart *Partners* 269 **Lower Missip Valley,** We was just jay-hawks and greenhorns that had been picked up everywhere and did n't [sic] know nothing about war. **1911** *Sun* (NY NY) 10 Aug 7/1 **NYC** (as of 1861), These too were farmers' boys and hillbillies and jayhawk-ers. **1917** Garland *Son Middle Border* 291, We sank upon the benches along with the other "rubes" and "jay-hawkers." **c1955** Reed–Person *Ling. Atlas Pacific NW* (A rustic) 1 inf, Jayhawks. **c1960** *Wilson Coll.* **csKY,** *Jayhawker.* . . A rustic, with no reference to Kansas and earlier times. **1960** *PADS* 34.52 **eCO,** A more credible example of folk speech, probably also jocular, is the eastern Colorado *jayhawk* 'a rustic,' especially meaningful along the main routes of communication with Kansas. **1967–68** *DARE* (Qu. HH1, *Names and nicknames for a rustic or countrified person*) Infs **WI**13, **OR**13, (Country) jayhawk; **CA**36, Jayhawker.

2 A jay of the family Corvidae, such as **blue jay 1.** Cf **jaybird** n 1
1966 *DARE* (Qu. Q16, . . *Kinds of jays*) Inf **GA**3, Blue jay = jayhawk. **1984** *DARE* File **cCA,** Kinds of jays: jayhawk.

3 See quot.
1968 *DARE* (Qu. R15a, . . *Names or nicknames . . for mosquitoes*) Inf **LA**20, Jayhawk [laughter].

jayhawk v
1 See quots. [Transf < *jayhawk* to make a predatory attack]
1905 U.S. Forest Serv. *Bulletin* 61.40 [Logging terms], *Jay hawk, to.* To strip one 4-foot length of bark from a tanbark oak, leaving the tree standing. (P[acific] C[oast] F[orest]) **1958** McCulloch *Woods Words* 98 **Pacific NW,** *Jayhawk*—To peel bark from a small tanoak as high as can be reached with a long handled bark spud without falling the tree.

‡2 See quot. [Infl by *hawk* to peddle]
1966 *DARE* (Qu. U5, *Someone who sells small articles on a street corner*) Inf **MS**15, [He] jayhawks.

3 To go on a diagonal course; hence ppl adj *jayhawked* out of square.
1967–68 *DARE* (Qu. MM16, *If you're walking with somebody to the other corner of a square, and you want to save steps . . "It'll be shorter if we _____.")* Inf **TX**10, Jayhawg [sic; *DARE* Ed: cf *jaywalk*]; (Qu. MM13, *The table was nice and straight until he came along and knocked it _____*) Inf **PA**138, Jayhawked.

4 vbl n *jayhawking:* Clumsy or inept dancing.
1966 *DARE* (Qu. FF5a, . . *Different steps and figures in dancing—in*

past years) Inf **GA**1, Jayhawking—stumbling around or poor dancing. **1966** *DARE* FW Addit neGA, *Jayhawking*—in square dancing (Georgia breakdown style), stumbling about and dancing very poorly or clumsily.

jayhawked See **jayhawk** v 3

jayhawker n
1 See **jayhawk** n **1.**
2 See quot.
    1889 *Century Dict.* 3223 **West,** *Jayhawker.* . . A large spider or tarantula, as species of *Mygale.*
3 See quot. [Transf < *jayhawker* a predatory raider]
    1968 *DARE* FW Addit **eMD** [Among watermen], *Jayhawker* [ˈjeˌhɔkɚ] = pistol:—an explosive sort of person who is accustomed to getting what he wants by any means available, violent or otherwise.

jayhawking See **jayhawk** v 4

jay hole n Also *J-hole, J-pit* [**jay** v²] **Appalachians**
In skidding logs: a place prepared beside a skid road to allow a team to get out of the way when the logs begin to slide under their own weight; hence, a passing place in a narrow road.
    1932 Strong *Behind Gt. Smokies* 164, About a hundred feet down, a jay-hole, a piece of level ground, was cut in the hillside, to one side of the jay-path. The horses stepped aside into this jay-hole and allowed the log to continue downhill. **1939** *Hall Coll.* **wNC,** On a steep place on a skid road, you'd have a jay hole for your team to run into so as not to be injured by the logs. **1952** Brown *NC Folkl.* 1.554 **wNC,** *Jay-hole.* . . Space on a mountain road where a vehicle or a team may pass another. **1964** Clarkson *Tumult* 365 **WV,** *Jay-hole*—Space prepared along a skidway to permit a team to jay-off while logs run by. **a1975** Lunsford *It Used to Be* 165 **sAppalachians,** "Jayhole" is a wide place, or a place that's trimmed out of the side of a mountain road, wide enough to hold a wagon and team or to hold a car or any vehicle that might be going along the road, in order to get the main traffic by. **1977** *Foxfire* 4 276 **wNC,** But if the ground's not level enough for a team to get out of the way when you jay off, you've got to dig that J-hole into the road bank for them to get into 'cause when those logs run, they've got to get in that so the logs can pass them up. **1983** Aiken *Mountain Ways* 165 **wNC, eTN,** The horses got the log to going real fast, when they got out of the way the horses were trained to step aside into the "J" pit and the log released by the "J" hook went "ball hooting" down the mountain. **1994** *Jrl.–Patriot* (N. Wilkesboro NC) 25 Aug sec D 5/5 [Logging terms], On skidding trails, a "jay-hole" was a cleared place for the team of horses or other draft animals to go when the turn of logs had attained high speed and was so-called because of the use of the "J-hook." Hendrix called this a "J-grab." The J-hook had a re-curved head, to each end of which a grab was attached by a short chain. The J-hook was attached to the top of the forward log of a turn of logs and served as the point of attachment to the team of horses. If logs started to move too fast down a slope while the horses were pulling them, the animals could be automatically freed and saved from harm by turning them at right angles into the jay hole.

jaying, jay off, jay out See **jay** v²

jay path n [**jay** v²]
A steep skid road down which logs will slide under their own weight.
    1932 Strong *Behind Gt. Smokies* 164, When the log was in place at the top of the jay-path, the horses started downhill at a gallop, the log thundering after them.

jay walkers n pl Cf **jake walkers, johnny walkers**
Stilts.
    1969 *DARE* (Qu. EE35, *Long wooden poles with a footpiece that children walk around on to make them tall*) Inf **GA**86, Jay walkers.

jayweed n Cf **mayweed 1**
=**dog fennel 1.**
    1900 Lyons *Plant Names* 37, *A[nthemis] Cotula.* . . Jay-weed. **1940** Clute *Amer. Plant Names* 251, *Anthemis cotula.* . . Jay-weed.

jaywhacker n
=**blue jay 1.**
    1966 *DARE* (Qu. Q16, . . *Kinds of jays*) Inf **OK**42, Blue jay, also called jaywhackers.

jazzbo n [Etym uncert, but perh transf < *jazzbo* slapstick comedy; cf *OEDS;* also perh infl by the association of Blacks with *jazz* + **bo**] *derog*
A person, esp a Black person; see quots.
    [**1919** *Greenwich Village Quill* June 9, Have you heard Jazzbo the chocolate syncopated Hobohemian at the Moulin Rouge Cave?] **1923** Witwer *Fighting Blood* 272 *(OEDS),* I merely commence to stutter an apology, when the old jazzbo [=fellow] shuts me off kind of angrily. **1942** Berrey–Van den Bark *Amer. Slang* 385.14, *Negro.* . . jazz-bo. *Ibid* 438.1, *Dissolute person.* . . jazz-bo. *Ibid* 583.18, Jazz-bo, jazzbo, *a negro performer, esp in a minstrel show.* **1944** *AmSp* 19.174, Such vulgar synonyms for *Negro* as . . *jazzbo, jigabo,* . . *zigaboo.* **1957** Kerouac *On Road* 113, He dodged a mule wagon; in it sat an old Negro plodding along. . . He slowed down the car for all of us to turn and look at the old jazzbo moaning along. **1960** Wentworth–Flexner *Slang* 288, *Jazz-bo.* . . A fancily dresesd, hep, sharp person; a stud. **1964** *PADS* 42.29 **Chicago IL,** *Spook, spade,* and *jazzbo* were also elicited [as terms of abuse for Blacks] only from Negroes in this survey, but these three, especially the first two, are common in the speech of Caucasian Chicagoans. **1983** Allen *Lang. Ethnic Conflict* 49 [Terms for Blacks], *Jazzbo.*

j-bump See **jack bump**

jealousy See **jalousie** n¹

jean n, freq pl Usu |jin|; also *old-fash* |jeɪn| Pronc-spp *jane, jeam*
A Forms.
    1828 Webster *Amer. Dict.* np, *Jane.* . . A kind of fustian. **1845** in 1943 Carleton *Prairie Logbooks* 181, Most of them wore loose blouses of Kentucky jane. **1908** *DN* 3.324 **eAL, wGA,** *Jeams.* . . Jeans. **1935** Sheppard *Cabins* 47 **nwNC,** Four suits of clothes, two of which should be good "janes." **1942** Hall *Smoky Mt. Speech* 13 **eTN, wNC,** *Jeans* . . pronounced [jeɪnz] . . by many old people. **1943** in 1944 *ADD* **wPA,** *Jeans.* . . Janes. . . |jenz|. . . Not |jinz|. **1966** Dakin *Dial. Vocab. Ohio R. Valley* 2.190 **nOhio Valley,** Jeans (occasionally pronounced [jenz]).
B Sense.
Pl: See **long jeans.**

Jeans See **Jeems**

jeas(e)ly See **jeezly**

jeberdees n pl Cf **dribbies**
Men's undershorts.
    1965–70 *DARE* (Qu. W14, *Names for underwear, including joking names. Men's . . short*) Inf **MS**63, Jeberdees [ˈjɛbərˌdiz]; **VA**69, Jeberdees—old folks said this.

jeccal See **jacal**

jeck See **jerk** n¹, v¹

jedge See **judge**

jedg(e)matically See **judgmatically**

jedgment See **judge**

Jedus n [Var of *Jesus;* cf Pronc Intro 3.I.17] *Gullah*
    1922 Gonzales *Black Border* 308 **sSC, GA coasts** [Gullah glossary], *Jedus*—Jesus. **1925** *DN* 5.359 **seGA** [Gullah], Lawdy Jedus [jidəs]. **1928** Peterkin *Scarlet Sister Mary* 35 **SC** [Gullah], Satan knowed you b'longed to him an' not to Jedus. **1939** Griswold *Sea Is. Lady* 788 **csSC** (as of c1918) [Gullah], We gotta come fuh res' 'pon Jedus bosom, I know dat, Miss Em'ly.

jeebers (creepers) See **jeepers** intj

Jeehosaphat See **Jehoshaphat**

Jeehu See **Jehu**

jeekers intj [Prob euphem for *Jesus (Christ)*] **esp MA** Cf **jeepers** intj, **juckers**
    1967–68 *DARE* (Qu. NN30, *Exclamations beginning with the sound of 'j'*) Infs **MA**8, 9, 28, 33, 54, Jeekers. [All Infs young or mid-aged]

jeelico See **jellico weed**

jeemanently, jeemanetty See **jiminetty**

Jeemes See **Jeems**

jeemies See **jimmies** n pl¹ **1, 2**

Jeemima See **Jemima**

jeeminee See **jiminy**

jeeminoley See **jiminetty**

jeeminy fit See **jiminy fit**

Jeems intj Also *Jeans, Jeemes* [Euphems for *Jesus;* prob infl by [jĭmz], pronc of *James*]

In var combs: Used as a mild oath.

1863 in 1962 Nathan *Dan Emmett* 392 [Black], Jeemeses Ribber Massa Greely, O! **1914** *DN* 4.75 **ME, nNH,** *Jeems Rice!* Common ejaculation, probably corrupted from "Jesus Christ!" **1923** (1946) Greer–Petrie *Angeline Doin' Society* 8 **csKY,** Jeemses River! How them young folks could dance! **1923** *DN* 5.212 **swMO,** *Jeem's river,* an exclamation indicating great surprise. **1924** *DN* 5.271 **ME** [Exclams], Jeans Rice . . , my Jeans. **1950** (1965) Richter *Town* 249 **OH** (as of c1900), By Jeems' cousin! **1959** *VT Hist.* 27.144, *By Jeems Rice! . .* Rare.

jeeper n Cf **cheeper, spring peeper**

A tree frog.

1968 *DARE* (Qu. P21, *Small frogs that sing or chirp loudly in spring*) Inf **IN**18, Jeepers.

jeepers intj Also *jeepers creepers, jeebers (creepers);* for addit varr see quots [Euphems for *Jesus (Christ)*]

Also in combs: Used as a mild oath.

1929 Edmonds *Rome Haul* 24 **NY,** Jeepers! A cat would n't stand no show at all. *Ibid* 30, Spinning swore. "I'll bet that's right. Jeepers cripus!" **1930** *AmSp* 6.98 **cNY,** An expression of astonishment. "By Jeepers!" **1939** (1962) Thompson *Body & Britches* 134 **NY,** I thought I'd see whether I could dive right down to the floor of the Pond out in the middle. Well, by Jeepers, I dove like a fish. **1950** *WELS (Exclamations beginning with the sound of 'j')* 19 Infs, **WI,** Jeepers; 10 Infs, Jeepers creepers; 1 Inf, Jumping jeepers; *(Exclamations of joy: for example, when somebody gets a pleasant surprise)* 1 Inf, Jeepers creepers. **1956** Ker *Vocab. W. TX* 385, [Expressions of mild disgust:] Jeepers. **1959** *VT Hist.* 27.144, *By jeepers! . .* Rare. *Jeepers! . .* Common. **1965–70** *DARE* (Qu. NN30, *Exclamations beginning with the sound of 'j'*) 138 Infs, **widespread,** Jeepers; 41 Infs, **scattered,** Jeepers creepers; **CT**25, Jeebers creepers; **GA**9, **LA**15, Jumpin(g) jeepers; **GA**28, Good jeepers; **IN**19, Great jeepers; **PA**216, Jeepers pelts; (Qu. NN31, *Exclamations beginning with the sound of 'cr-'*) Infs **CT**12, **DC**13, **FL**2, **ME**16, **MI**28, **NC**15, **WI**13, 26, Jeepers creepers; **AR**3, Creepers jeepers; (Qu. NN6b, *Expressions of joy used mostly by children*) Infs **OH**84, **VA**2, (Great) jeepers; (Qu. NN27b, *Weakened substitutes for 'god': "For _____ sakes!"*) Inf **CT**25, Jeebers; (Qu. NN29c, *Exclamations beginning with 'holy': "Holy _____!"*) Inf **MN**10, Jeebers. **1967** *DARE* FW Addit **cnNY,** Jeepers cripes.

jeepers n pl Cf **heebie-jeebies 1, jibbies**

1968 *DARE* (Qu. GG13b, *When something keeps bothering a person and makes him nervous . . "It gives me the _____."*) Inf **GA**28, Jeepers.

jeepers creepers See **jeepers** intj

jeep stick n

=**gee-haw whimm(e)y-diddle.**

1980 *Foxfire 6* 252 **nGA,** First one I ever saw was about twenty-five years ago. . . When I first started making jeep sticks I told everybody I could tell their fortunes with them. The idea is to put your thumbnail up against the stick and it [=a propeller] will go one way. If you want it to go the other way, put your thumbnail under the stick. *Ibid* 253, I've always called them "jeep sticks," that's all I ever call them.

jeeroosl(e)y adj [Perh emphatic var of *Jerusalem*]

See quot 1914.

1904 Day *Kin o' Ktaadn* 212 **ME,** He gave a most jeeroosly bound. **1914** *DN* 4.75 **nNH, ME,** Jeeroosely. . . Mighty, big, enormous.

Jeerus(a)lem See **Jerusalem**

jees(h) See **jeez**

jeesum crow See **jeezum crow**

jee whilikens, ~ whillikins, ~ whilligins, ~ wooligans See **gee whillikers**

jeez intj Also *geez, jees(h), jeeze, jez* [Euphems for *Jesus*] **scattered, but chiefly Nth, N Midl** See Map

Also in combs: Used as a mild oath.

1920 Lewis *Main Street* 104 **MN,** Other evening when I was coming over here, she'd forgot to pull down the curtain, and I watched her for ten minutes. Jeeze, you'd 'a' died laughing. **1930** Dos Passos *42nd Parallel* 73, Jez we got to get us women. Them dreams weaken a guy. **1932** *AmSp* 7.399, "Jesus" (almost always contracted to "Jeez") was the principal [profane] word current among the boys [in an orphanage]. **1932** Golding *Magnolia St.* 472 **NYC,** "Jeeze!" he said. "It's going to be a swell party!" **1965–70** *DARE* (Qu. NN30, *Exclamations beginning with the sound of 'j'*) 80 Infs, **scattered, but chiefly Nth, N Midl,** Jeez [Of all Infs responding to the question, 13% were young; of those giving this response, 25% were young.]; **MA**14, **OH**40, Jeesh; **MI**72, Jees [jis]; **NJ**64, By jeez; (Qu. NN6b, *Expressions of joy used mostly by children*) Inf **MN**2, Jeez; (Qu. NN20a, *Exclamations caused by sudden pain—a blow on the thumb*) Inf **PA**175, Jees, that hurt; (Qu. NN21a) Inf **NY**80, Oh jeez [o jiz]; (Qu. NN24, *Humorous substitutes for stronger exclamations: "Why the son of a _____!"*) Inf **MN**2, Jeez. **1967–69** *DARE* Tape **CA**168, That was a beautiful spot. Oh man, jeez; **MI**42, Jeez, I had the biggest brownie [=brown trout] you ever saw. **1968** Hailey *Airport* 32, At an adjoining table, a woman said loudly, "Geez! Lookit the time!"

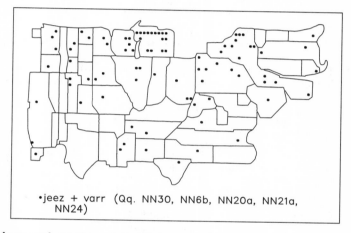

•jeez + varr (Qq. NN30, NN6b, NN20a, NN21a, NN24)

jeez and crackers intj Cf **cheese and crackers**

1968 *DARE* (Qu. NN30, *Exclamations beginning with the sound of 'j'*) Inf **PA**133, Jeez and crackers.

jeeze See **jeez**

jeezer n [Prob var of *geezer*]

See quot 1975.

1975 Gould *ME Lingo* 146, Jeezer—A chap, fellow, guy, joker, etc. Used chiefly in Aroostook County, it has the muted tone of blasphemy, but there is none in its usage. A quotation from the Fort Fairfield *Review* of February 23, 1972: " . . the poor jeezer hardly got a word in edgewise." **1978** *UpCountry* May 46 **csME** (as of c1910), A young jeezer with a tendency to spread himself around [hanging May baskets] would get an awful lot of popcorn and cocoa.

jeezly adj, adv Also *jeas(e)ly, jeezless, jo-jeezly* [Prob from **jeez**] **ME** Cf **jesusly**

Damned; contrary; measly; extremely, very.

1930 *Amer. Mercury* 21.236 **ME,** Tell him . . that here is his jeasely ol' pie and biscuit irons. **1950** Moore *Candlemas Bay* 20 **ME,** You're lucky I don't tear this jeasly trunks off you and make you go in your hide. **1965** *DARE* FW Addit **neME,** Jeezly—cuss word, used as adj. **1975** Gould *ME Lingo* 146, *Jeezly* is a long accepted Maine adjective and adverb without relevancy to Jeez or Jesus: "Don't be so jeezly hard to get along with!" Small biscuits can be jeezly biscuits and jeezly small biscuits. "I never saw such jeezly poor fishing!" **1979** Lewis *How to Talk Yankee* [16] **nNEng,** He will modify the phrase from time to time with the unblasphemous adjectives "jeezly" or "jeezless" for variety. *Ibid* [19], *Jo-jeezly. Adj.* and *Adv.,* ornery or cussed. "I never see anything so jo-jeezly hard to split as that dry oak." **1980** (1987) Syatt *Like We Say* 163 **ME,** It's jeezly cold. **1982** *DARE* File **coastal ME,** Jo jeezly: contrary, ornery. **1986** *DARE* File **ME,** I've often heard sentences like: "That jeezly hunting dog is the most independent bird-bouncer I've ever seen."

jeezum crow intj Also *jeesum crow, jeezun ~* [Euphems for *Jesus Christ*] **VT, nNY**

1959 *VT Hist.* 27.144, *Jeesum Crow!* . . Rare. **1965** *DARE* File **VT** (as of 1959), Jeezun crow ['jizṇ 'kro]. **1969** *DARE* (Qu. NN30, *Exclamations beginning with the sound of 'j'*) Inf **VT**16, Jeezum [jizəm] crow. **1993** *DARE* File **nNY**, In the North Country we say Jeezum Crow instead of taking an important name in vain. Children everywhere—from K-Mart to corner stores can be heard lamenting, "But Mom. . . Jeezum Crow!" **1994** Moore *Who Will Run* 15 **nNY** (as of c1970), In a town where everyone said things like "Jeesum Crow" and "sheesh," we said "fuck"—but in a daring, private way.

jeez-wax intj Also sp *jeswax* [Prob blend of **jeez** and **beeswax**] Also in combs: Used as a mild oath.

1895 *DN* 1.397 **NYC**, Jeswax: [jizwæks]: an oath. "Jeswax," "By Jeswax," "Holy Jeswax," etc. Sometimes "Jeswax Christmas." **1969** *DARE* (Qu. NN25a, *Weakened substitutes for 'damn' or 'damned'*: "_____ it all!") Inf **NY**163, Jeez-wax.

jeezy-peezy intj [Redup euphem for *Jesus (Christ)*] Used as a mild oath.

1960 Wentworth–Flexner *Slang* 289, *Jeezy-peezy*. . . An expression of surprise or disgust. **1966** *DARE* (Qu. NN30, *Exclamations beginning with the sound of 'j'*) Inf **SC**8, Jeezy-peezy.

jeff n [*Jef*ferson Davis, president of the Confederate States of America 1861–65]

1 also *Jeff Davis, jeffer:* An ignorant, unsophisticated, or boring person; any White person. *chiefly among Black speakers; derog*

1938 C. Calloway *Hi De Ho* 16 (OEDS) [Black], *Jeff*, a pest, a bore, an icky. **1946** (1972) Mezzrow–Wolfe *Really Blues* 335, *Jeff Davis:* an unenlightened person, a hick from down South; sometimes shortened to *jeff.* **1960** Wentworth–Flexner *Slang* 289, *Jeff*. . . A boring person; a square. *Negro use.* **1969** *PADS* 51.29 **IL**, Names used exclusively by Negroes . . jeff, jeffer, jeff davis, jeff artist. [*DARE* Ed: used by Black prisoners in referring to Whites] **1970** Major *Dict. Afro–Amer. Slang* 70, *Jeff:* (1930s) a white person. **1973** *Black World* 22.6.57, He wears a jeff hat and a light raincoat.

2 in phr *name oneself Jeff:* See quots.

1967 *DARE* (Qu. Y19, *To begin to go away from a place:* "It's about time for me to _____.") Inf **LA**3, Name myself Jeff. That means you gonna [gō] get going. **1986** *NADS Letters, Name myself Jeff.* Orig. Negro. Legend has it that when Union Troops surrounded Richmond, Jeff Davis disguised himself as a woman and slipped away.

jeff v [**jeff** n] *among Black speakers*

1 See quot.

1970 Major *Dict. Afro–Amer. Slang* 70, *Jeff:* (1930s) . . to inform on someone.

2 vbl n *jeffing;* Of Blacks: behaving in a servile or ingratiating manner towards White people.

1972 Kochman *Rappin'* 246, The terms used by the black to describe the role he played before white folks in the South was [sic] "tomming" or "jeffing." **1976** *Harper's Weekly* 26 Jan 18 **TN** [Black], White people in our neighborhood are called "boojums." If you try to become friendly with the "boojums," you are accused of "jeffing."

Jeff Davis, jeffer See **jeff** n 1

Jeff Davis pie n Also *Jefferson Davis (chess) pie* Cf **chess pie** A rich custard pie.

1940 Brown *Amer. Cooks* 483 **MO**, The origin of the recipe for Jeff Davis Pie has caused perh as much controversy as the real beginning of the cocktail. . . *1 cup butter / 1 cup cream / 2 cups sugar / 6 eggs.* **1946** Rombauer *Joy of Cooking* 515, *Jefferson Davis Pie.* . . butter . . sugar . . egg yolks . . flour . . cinnamon . . nutmeg . . allspice . . cream . . dates . . raisins . . pecan meats. **1964** *Favorite Recipes Virginias* 173 **VA**, Jefferson Davis chess pie—½ c. butter or margarine / 2 c. sugar / 1½ c. cream / 3 eggs / Juice of 2 lemons. **c1965** Randle *Cookbooks* (Plain Cookery) 3.12 **cnOH**, *Jeff Davis pie*—1 c. sugar / 1 c. cream / 1 T. flour / 1 t. vanilla / 1 egg yolk / ½ t. vanilla / Bake this in a crust, then spread with jelly, put on meringue and brown. **c1965** Randle *Cookbooks* (Ask Neighbor) 4.90, *Jefferson Davis pie.*

1977 Anderson *Grass Roots Cookbook* 134 **cwAL**, This has to be the richest pie in all creation. There's nothing here to adulterate the rich, honest flavor of butter, sugar, eggs and cream—not even vanilla. Jeff Davis Pie is said to have been invented about the time of the Civil War by a talented Southern plantation cook, who when pressed for the name of the superlative pie, answered simply, "Why, I calls it Jeff Davis Pie" (because she was purported to be an admirer of Jefferson Davis).

Jefferson pine n [Prob for **Jeffrey pine**]

1967–70 *DARE* (Qu. T17, . . *Kinds of pine trees;* not asked in early QRs) Infs **CA**7, 207, Jefferson pine.

jeffing See **jeff** v 2

Jeff, name oneself See **jeff** n 2

Jeffrey pine n

Std: a long-needled **pine** (here: *Pinus jeffreyi*) native to the western US, esp California. Also called **black pine 2b, bull ~ 1b, hard ~ 3, ponderosa ~, redbark ~, sapwood ~, Truckee ~, yellow ~**

Jehoshaphat n Pronc-spp *Je(e)hosaphat, Jehosophat, Geehosofat* [The Biblical name used as a euphem for *Jesus*] Used in exclams or mild oaths; see quots.

1857 S.A. Hammett *Sam Slick in Texas* xxiv.161 (OEDS), 'Jehoso-phat!' . . 'Easy over the stones, Joe,' ses I. **1866** (1869) Reid *Headless Horseman* 39, Geehosofat! what a putty beest it air! *Ibid* 100, By the jumpin' Geehosofat, what a gurl she air sure enuf! **1876** Besant & Rice *Gold. Butterfly* II.xiii.195 (OED at *great* a. III.12.c), Great Jehoshaphat! . . can't you see when a gentleman is on the stump? **1905** *DN* 3.62 **NE**, Jehoshaphat, it's hot. **1908** *DN* 3.324 **eAL, wGA**, Jehosaphat Jenkins. **1924** *DN* 5.271 [Exclams], Holy jumping Jehosophat. **1950** *WELS* **WI** (*Exclamations beginning with the sound of 'j'*) 10 Infs, (Jumping) Jehoshaphat; 3 Infs, (Jumping) Jehoshaphat. **1952** in 1953 Botkin–Harlow *Treas. Railroad Folkl.* 516, The Vanderbilts cannot run me if they run the rest of the country, by Jehosaphat. **1965–70** *DARE* (Qu. NN30, *Exclamations beginning with the sound of 'j'*) 136 Infs, **widespread**, Jumping Jehosaphat; 45 Infs, **chiefly Nth, N Midl**, Jehosaphat; **MI**112, **NC**79, **NV**7, **SC**54, **VA**58, Great (jumping) Jehosaphat; **FL**38, **MD**25, Jehosaphats; **IA**5, Jiminy Jehosaphat; **KY**21, Gee jumping Jehosaphat; **CT**16, **MD**22, **MA**5, **NY**69, 105, [ji'hasəfæt]; **NY**123, ['ji,hasəfæt]; **MI**13, [ji'hasəfət]; **CT**9, [ji'asəfæt]; **MD**49, [jɪ'hosɪfæt]; **OK**42, **DE**7, [jɪ'ho(ʊ)səfæt]; **PA**242, Jeehosaphat; **NY**69, [jɪ'ho(ʊ)səfæt]; **MN**2, Jehoshaphat [-'houzɪfæt]; **SC**2, 3, [ji'hosɪfæt]; (Qu. NN29a, *Exclamations beginning with 'great':* "Great _____!") 23 Infs, **scattered**, (Jumping) Jehosaphat; **PA**134, Jehosaphat gentleman; **DE**1, **SC**54, [ji'hasəfæt]; **OH**72, [ji'hasɪfæt]; **NY**126, **DE**7, [ji'ho(ʊ)səfæt]; **NC**8, [ji'hosɪfæt]; (Qu. NN29c, *Exclamations beginning with 'holy':* "Holy _____!") 10 Infs, **scattered**, (Jumpin') Jehosaphat; (Qu. GG13b, *When something keeps bothering a person and makes him nervous*) Inf **NY**42, Jump Jehasophat; (Qu. NN6a, *Exclamations of joy . . when somebody gets a pleasant surprise, he might shout* "_____.") Inf **GA**72, Jumping Jehosaphat; (Qu. NN27a, *Weakened substitutes for 'god':* "My _____!") Inf **VA**31, Great Jehosaphat.

Jehu n Also sp *Jeehu* [Cf 2 Kings 9:2, 20]

1 See quot. [Prob infl by **jay** n] Cf **nimshi, yahoo**

1906 *DN* 3.120 **sIN**, Jehu. . . A greenhorn; country fellow. "That Jehu's silly."

2 also *Jehu Nimshi:* Used as an exclam.

1859 Taliaferro *Fisher's R.* 53 **nwNC** (as of 1820s), Jehu Nimshi! thar he [=a snake] were right dab at my heels. **1967** *DARE* (Qu. NN30, *Exclamations beginning with the sound of 'j'*) Inf **OH**11, Jumping Jeehu.

‡jelapidated adj [Pronc-sp for **dilapidated**]

1969 *DARE* (Qu. KK20a, *Something that looks as if it might collapse any minute:* "That old shed is certainly _____.") Inf **IN**80, Jelapidated; (Qu. KK70, *Something that has got out of proper shape:* "That house is all _____.") Inf **IN**80, Jelapidated.

jeld v, hence ppl adj *jelded*, n *jelding* [Pronc-spp for *geld(ed), gelding*]

1967 *DARE* (Qu. K24, *What does the word 'ox' mean?*) Inf **LA**14, A [jeldɪd] bull—everybody says jelding, not gelding; (Qu. K70, *Words used . . for castrating an animal*) Inf **LA**14, [jeld].

jell v

1 To be compatible, get along.

1965–70 *DARE* (Qu. II11a, *If two people don't get along well together* . . *"They don't _____."*) Infs **CA**147, **CO**27, **MA**28, **MI**4, **PA**151, 245, **SC**44, **WA**1, Jell; (Qu. II29b, . . *To explain the unpleasant effect that person has on you: "He just _____."*) Inf **MA**28, Doesn't jell with me; **SC**45, Doesn't jell.

2 Of a statement: to be consistent, hold together.

1967–68 *DARE* (Qu. KK58, *An excuse that looks as if it would not stand up under questioning: "His story won't _____."*) Infs **NJ**30, **PA**11, Jell; **PA**108, Doesn't jell.

3 See **jelly** v.

jell n *chiefly Nth old-fash*

Jelly.

1870 Parton *Ginger Snaps* 262 **neMA,** My excellent country friends put up pounds and quarts of *"jell"* every fall. **1890** *DN* 1.78, A noun *jell = jelly* is also known in Massachusetts. **1895** *DN* 1.397 **IL, MN, NY,** *Jell:* jelly. **1909** *DN* 3.399 **nwAR,** *Jell.* . . Try some of the plum jell. (Common.) **1910** *DN* 3.444 **cwNY,** *Jell.* . . Jelly. "We had some jell for dinner." **1914** *DN* 4.75 **ME, nNH,** *Jell.* . . Jelly. **1914** Dickinson *WI Plays* 35, I could take her in a cup o' jell, or somethin'. **1947** Bowles–Towle *New Engl. Cooking* 258, Currant "jell" was indispensable in all New England homes: it was used to tempt the appetite of invalids, served to the family in puddings and gravies, and used as an accompaniment for partridge and other wild game. **1981** *DARE* File **cnMA** (as of c1915), *Jell* meant 'jelly,' but was considered a vulgar word, like *drapes* for 'draperies.'

jellico weed n Also *jeelico* [Aphet forms of *angelica*]

=**angelica 1a.**

1900 Lyons *Plant Names* 35, A[ngelica] *Archangelica.* . . (Jeelico, Aunt Jerichos). **1917** *DN* 4.413 **wNC,** *Jellico weed.* Angelica.

jell poke See **jill poke** n

jelly n

1 also in phr *bowl of jelly* and combs *jelly belly, ~ fat:* A fat person; an oversize stomach. **esp Sth, S Midl** *esp freq among Black speakers*

[**1896** Farmer–Henley *Slang, Jelly-belly.* . . A fat man or woman.] **1934** (1940) Weseen *Dict. Amer. Slang* 357, *Jelly belly*—A very corpulent person. **1965–70** *DARE* (Qu. X50, *Names or nicknames for a person who is very fat*) Infs **AL**61, **KY**94, **MS**1, 80, **SC**32, **VA**69, Bowl of jelly; **FL**48, Jelly belly; **TN**52, Jelly fat; **FL**15, Jelly; (Qu. X53a, . . *An oversize stomach*) Inf **FL**48, Jelly belly. [6 of 9 total Infs Black]

2 =**jelly roll 2.** *esp freq among Black speakers*

1927 in 1961 Oliver *Blues Fell* 123 [Black], Jelly roll, jelly roll ain't so hard to find,/ There's a baker shop in town bakes it brown like mine,/ I got a sweet jelly, a lovin' sweet jelly roll,/ If you taste my jelly it'll satisfy your worried soul. **1929** in 1983 Taft *Blues Lyric Poetry* 139, You never miss your jelly : till your jellyroller's gone. [*DARE* Ed: Singer is female.] **1930** *Ibid* 275, I'm not a cheap woman : I sell about every day / My jelly too expensive : you know I can't give it away. **1942** *Amer. Mercury* 55.223.84 **Harlem NYC** [Black], [His mama named him Marvel, but after a month on Lenox Avenue, he changed all that to Jelly. How come? Well, he put it in the street that when it came to filling that long-felt need, sugar-curing the ladies' feelings, he was in a class by himself. . . "It must be Jelly, 'cause jam don't shake."] *Ibid* 95, *Jelly*—sex. **1980** Folb *Runnin' Down* 150 **Los Angeles CA** [Black], Expressions like "I'm gonna get me some *jellyroll, jelly, jam, sweet potato*" reflect a sense of sweet-tasting sex, of nourishment, of being fed.

3 A close friend, esp one's girl friend or boyfriend. [Prob from **2** above, but cf *OEDS jelly* sb.[1] 2.e quot 1889 "a buxom, good looking girl." The sense "boyfriend" has prob been infl by **jelly bean 2.**]

1931 Faulkner *Sanctuary* 28 **MS,** Gowan goes to Oxford a lot. . . He's got a jelly there. He takes her to the dances. *Ibid* 43, [Man speaking to woman:] Dont think I spent last night with a couple of your barber-shop jellies [=boyfriends] for nothing. **1968** *DARE* FW Addit **PA**66, Jelly. . . Boyfriend. **1993** *Atlanta Jrl.–Constitution* (GA) 22 Sept sec B 1, When I came to Atlanta in the 1940s I . . heard about "pinks" as that group of teenage girls who gathered at the Palace of Sweets on Broad Street when they changed streetcars on their way home from Girls High after school. Other writers have essayed to discuss pinks and their male opposites, "jellies," but I don't think anybody ever knew where or why the names originated.

‡**4** A foolishly generous person; a soft touch.

1968 *DARE* (Qu. U32, . . *A very generous person: "He's _____."*) Inf **PA**66, [A] jelly. **1968** *DARE* FW Addit **PA**66, Jelly. . . A person so generous he can easily be made to appear foolish.

5 =**toe jam.**

1970 *DARE* FW Addit **ceAR,** Jelly—gummy substance that forms under and between the toes when feet go unwashed for a long time.

jelly v Also *jell;* also with *around* [Cf **jelly** n 3]

To loaf about, esp at a drugstore or other informal eating place; hence v *jelly-date* to go on a date to such a place; n *jelly date* a date at such a place; one's date.

1931 *AmSp* 6.205 **MO** [Univ slang], *Jelly:* loiter for idle conversation in university buildings, or join friends to pass the time of day at a café or drug-store near the campus. Distinctively a University of Missouri expression. **1934** (1940) Weseen *Dict. Amer. Slang* 187 [College slang], *Jell*—To loaf in a lunch room. **1942** Berrey–Van den Bark *Amer. Slang* 354.5, Bean-, cake-, coke-, *or* jelly-date, jelly, *to take a girl to a soda fountain, or the like, to sit and chat.* *Ibid* 443.12, Cake *or* jelly date, *a person with whom a date is made to go to a soda fountain.* *Ibid* 847.2, Cake *or* jelly date, *a "date" to idle in a soda fountain or similar place.* **1966–70** *DARE* (Qu. Y27, *To go about aimlessly, with nothing to do: "He's always _____ around the drugstore."*) Inf **NC**36, Jellying; (Qu. KK31, *To go about aimlessly looking for distraction: "He doesn't have anything to do, so he's just _____ around."*) Inf **AL**62, Jellying. **1982** Mason *Shiloh* 41 **seMI,** She was away . . , out on "jelly dates." A jelly date was a Coke date. She had jelly dates with Bob and Jim and Sam all on the same day.

jelly around See **jelly** v

jelly bean n

1 A silly, weak, inexperienced, or effeminate person—used as a generalized epithet. *derog*

1919 *DN* 5.65 **NM,** Mary is such a jelly-bean that she never gets her lessons. **1927** *AmSp* 3.132 [College slang], Upper classmen subordinate the freshmen in true traditional fashion. A talkative freshman will be told: "pipe down," [etc]. . . His inferiority is further emphasized when he is called: "a de-rail," "a dumb-bell," "a dumb-rock," "a jelly-bean," "a sissy," "a rookie," or "a woozy upstart." **1929** (1951) Faulkner *Sartoris* 154 **MS,** And so when the negroes first blended their instruments beneath the window she paid them only the most perfunctory notice. "Why in the world are those jelly-beans serenading me?" **1934** (1940) Weseen *Dict. Amer. Slang* 187 [College slang], *Jelly bean*—A person disliked. **1942** Berrey–Van den Bark *Amer. Slang* 404.1, *Weakling; coward.* . . Jelly bean. *Ibid* 405.2, *Effeminate man.* . . Jelly bean. *Ibid* 456.1, *Inexperienced person.* . . Jelly bean. **1943** *AmSp* 18.108 [Baseball jargon], *Jelly beans* (raw rookies). **1950** Bissell *Stretch on River* 8 **eIA** (as of c1935), If Honest Abe had met some of the jelly beans I went to school with down there he would have called off the war and spent the money on a wall instead. **1979** in 1987 *NADS Letters* **cwMS** [Black], "He was a—he'd mess around—he's kinda jellybean. . ." When I asked him to tell me what he meant by a jellybean, he continued, "Well, you see, it's just like a man got a lot of money and maybe a young girl pull at him. And he will fall for it." **1986** Pederson *LAGS Concordance* **Gulf Region,** [8 infs indicate that a *jelly bean* is an effeminate or homosexual man; 4 of them equate *jelly bean* with *sissy.*]

2 A fashionably dressed young man; a ladies' man, dude—sometimes used as a term of address. *sometimes derog*

1921 *Capital Times* (Madison WI) 5 Apr 8, [Cartoon:] Those jelly beans give me a pain. [*DARE* Ed: The jelly bean is portrayed as an overdressed, supercilious young man.] **1923** *Chicago Herald & Examiner* (IL) 27 May sec 4 5, [Cartoon:] The judge fined the man $50 for flirting. Those jelly beans make me sick. **1935** *AmSp* 10.52 [English of the cartoons], Facetious epithets (often affectionate) . . Jellybeans. **1937** (1958) Levin *Old Bunch* 22, It made them all feel glowingly united, not just flappers and jellybeans, but a new young generation capable of facing the serious things of life. **1967** *DARE* (Qu. AA6a, . . *A man who is fond of being with women and tries to attract their attention—if he's nice about it*) Inf **TX**37, Jelly bean. **1970** Major *Dict. Afro–Amer. Slang* 70, *Jellybean:* (1930's–50's) a term of address. **1971** *Today Show Letters* **cnAL** (as of a1940), A dandy in that day was to them at that time a "jellybean." **1986** Pederson *LAGS Concordance* **Gulf Region,** [50 infs indicate that a *jelly bean* is a man who is fond of dressing up or overly proud of his looks; many say or imply that it is a derog or joc term, though a few regard it as complimentary.]

jelly belly See **jelly** n 1

jellybread n [By analogy with Ger *Butterbrot* bread and butter] **esp PaGer area** Cf **butterbread**

Bread, or a slice of bread, spread with jelly or other preserves.

1923 Watts *L. Nichols* 33 *(DAE)*, I bet she eats her meals that same way—cup of coffee once, an' mebbe another time a slice of jelly-bread, standin' up somewhere. **1934** *Language* 10.4 **cPA**, Bread and butter is a *butterbread* (German *Butterbrot*); they likewise say *jellybread*. **1935** *AmSp* 10.171 **sePA**, Jellybread. Bread and jelly. **1950** Klees *PA Dutch* 282, Butterbread and jellybread and applebutterbread are descriptive compounds. **c1960** *Wilson Coll.* **csKY**, Jelly-bread, an afternoon snack. **1968** *Helen Adolf Festschrift* 38, Jellybread (Pennsylvania German *Tschellibrot*) for 'bread and jelly.' **1970** *DARE* FW Addit **ceIN**, Give me a jellybread, a slice of bread with jelly, jam, or preserves spread on it.

jelly bun n

=**jelly doughnut.**

1950 *WELS Suppl.* (*A round cake cooked the same way* [=in deep fat] *but with jelly inside*) 1 Inf, **WI**, Jelly bun or bismarck. **1966–70** *DARE* (Qu. H29, *A round cake, cooked in deep fat, with jelly inside*) Infs **FL**1, **MI**61, 108, **NY**80, 199, **VA**94, Jelly bun; (Qu. H32, . . *Fancy rolls and pastries*) Infs **KY**74, **NJ**67, Jelly buns.

jelly cake n

=**jelly doughnut.**

1965–70 *DARE* (Qu. H29, *A round cake, cooked in deep fat, with jelly inside*) 41 Infs, **scattered, but esp Sth, S Midl,** Jelly cake; (Qu. H30, *An oblong cake, cooked in deep fat*) 18 Infs, **scattered,** Jelly cake. [45 of 52 Infs old] [*DARE* Ed: Some Infs may be referring instead to a rolled or layered cake with jelly filling.]

jellycoat n Cf **jerry coat**

=**red-headed woodpecker.**

1917 (1923) *Birds Amer.* 2.155, Red-headed Woodpecker. . . *Other Names*. . . Jellycoat. . . *Head, neck, and upper chest, uniform bright crimson.*

jelly-date See **jelly** v

jelly doughnut n **widespread, but esp freq NEast, S Atl, CA** See Map Cf **bismarck**

A deep-fried cake filled with jelly.

1902 *Bulletin* (San Francisco CA) 29 Jun mag sec 12 *(Zwilling Coll.),* When de wind blows it's fierce. Make [sic] a feller feel like de inside of a jelly doughnut. **1948** *WELS Suppl.* **Detroit MI**, We always referred to these items of confection [=bismarcks and long johns] as *jelly doughnuts* and *lunch buns* respectively. **1960** Criswell *Resp. to PADS 20* **Ozarks**, Jelly doughnut—this is rare and very recent. **c1960** *Wilson Coll.* **csKY**, Jelly doughnuts are very modern; all doughnuts are modern. **1965–70** *DARE* (Qu. H29, *A round cake, cooked in deep fat, with jelly inside*) 432 Infs, **widespread, but esp freq NEast, S Atl, CA,** Jelly doughnut; [16 Infs, **chiefly Atl exc N Atl,** Jelly-filled doughnut; **IA**24, Jellied doughnut;] (Qu. H28, *Different shapes or types of doughnuts*) 20 Infs, **scattered, but esp NEast,** Jelly doughnut; [**IL**84, **WV**16, Jelly-filled doughnut;] (Qu. H30, *An oblong cake, cooked in deep fat*) 14 Infs, **esp Atlantic,** Jelly doughnut; [**OH**52, Jelly-filled doughnut;] (Qu. H26) Inf **PA**239, Jelly doughnut. **1985** *Parents Mag.* Oct 136 **PA**, *Grandma's Jelly Doughnuts.* . . How I looked forward to visiting Grandma and eating her version of jelly doughnuts.

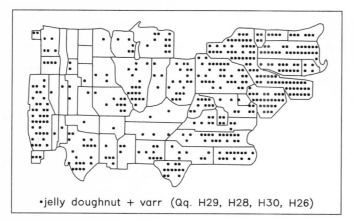

•jelly doughnut + varr (Qq. H29, H28, H30, H26)

jelly drops n pl [See quot]

Either of two related mushrooms: *Ascocoryne sarcoides* or *Bulgaria inquinans.*

1981 Lincoff *Audubon Field Guide Mushrooms* 362, *Purple Jelly Drops. Ascocoryne sarcoides.* . . This species may resemble jelly fungi. *Ibid* 363, *Black Jelly Drops. Bulgaria inquinans.* . . As the common name suggests, this mushroom looks like jelly drops or licorice drops.

jelly false tooth See **jelly tooth**

jelly fat See **jelly** n 1

jelly fungus n Also *jelly mushroom*

Any of var mushrooms which in some way suggest jelly, esp those of the order Tremellales, but also those of such genera as *Auricularia* and *Dacrymyces*. For other names of var of these mushrooms see **jelly leaf 2, jelly roll 3, jelly tooth, orange jelly, silver ear, sulfur butter, witches' butter, wood ear**

1972 Miller *Mushrooms* 210, Tremellales. . . All of the species of jelly fungi have a gelatinous flesh and most of them are yellow, orange, red to brown, or colorless. *Ibid* 212, *Pseudohydnum gelatinosum.* . . There is no other jelly fungus with teeth like this. **1980** Smith–Weber *Mushroom Hunter* 56, *Jelly Fungi.* . . The fruiting body is more or less jellylike in consistency when fresh. **1981** Lincoff *Audubon Field Guide Mushrooms* 379, Jelly fungi can be soft and gelatinous or stiff and rubbery. . . Some jelly fungi usually distinguished from the Tremellales. . . may took similar to *Tremella* and its allies. **1985** Weber–Smith *Field Guide S. Mushrooms* 42, *Tremella fuciformis.* . . Another common name for it is white jelly mushroom.

jelly leaf n

1 also *jelly plant:* A **teaweed** (here: *Sida rhombifolia*).

1911 *Century Dict. Suppl., Jelly-leaf.* . . The Queensland hemp. **1958** Jacobs–Burlage *Index Plants NC* 146, *Sida rhombifolia.* . . jelly plant. . . This plant grows in North Carolina and other southern states. . . It contains a *mucilage* and has been used as a vermifuge. **1974** Morton *Folk Remedies* 143 **SC**, "*Jelly leaf*". . . *Sida rhombifolia.* . . Common in coastal plain of South Carolina and North Carolina. . . *South Carolina (Current use):* Plant is boiled for "tea," drunk as a beverage. . . The plant is mucilaginous and emollient and has various medicinal uses.

2 also *leaf jelly:* A **jelly fungus** (here: either *Tremella foliacea* or *T. frondosa*).

1981 Lincoff *Audubon Field Guide Mushrooms* 384, *Jelly Leaf. Tremella foliacea.* . . Broadly leafy or wavy. . . Flesh gelatinous, thin to thick. . . Yellow Jelly Leaf *(T. frondosa),* a yellowish-buff but otherwise similar mushroom. **1987** McKnight–McKnight *Mushrooms* 67, Leaf Jelly *Tremella foliacea* . . *gelatinous* but *firm. Ibid* 68, Yellow Leaf Jelly *(T. frondosa* . . *)* is larger, lighter (straw-colored), and has more leaf-like lobes.

jelly mushroom See **jelly fungus**

jelly palm n [See quot 1960]

An introduced palm *(Butia capitata).*

1960 McGeachy *Hdbk. FL Palms* 36, *Jelly Palm.* . . A delicious clear jelly is often made from the fruit of this tree in its native habitat, South America. In North America the tree is used . . to give variety to ornamental planting. It is so hardy that it may be found . . as far north as South Georgia. **1966** *Vero Beach Press–Jrl.* (FL) 31 Mar sec B 4/3, A very hardy and stately palm is the Pindo, or Jelly Palm, Butia Capita [sic], with a stout, single trunk.

jelly plant See **jelly leaf 1**

jelly roll n

1 =**jelly doughnut.** Cf **bismarck**

1957 Battaglia *Resp. to PADS 20* **eMD** (*A cake cooked the same way* [=in deep fat] *but with jelly inside*) Jelly roll. **1965–70** *DARE* (Qu. H29, *A round cake, cooked in deep fat, with jelly inside*) 153 Infs, **widespread, but less freq N Atl,** Jelly roll; (Qu. H30, *An oblong cake, cooked in deep fat*) 52 Infs, **scattered, but somewhat more freq Gulf States, S Atl,** Jelly roll; (Qu. H28, *Different shapes or types of doughnuts*) Inf **MI**94, Jelly roll. [*DARE* Ed: Of the 193 total Infs, 5 Infs subsequently corrected this response and 2 were doubtful about it; FWs recorded comments from 13 Infs which show or indicate that they were referring to a rolled, jelly-filled cake. It is impossible to guess how many of the other Infs understood the questions in this way.] **1986** Pederson *LAGS Concordance* **Gulf Region** *(Bismarck)* 18 infs, Jelly roll(s) [3 other infs offered *jelly roll* but indicated that it was a kind of cake, not a bismarck.]; *(Doughnut)* 1 inf, Jelly roll—jelly-filled doughnut; 1 inf, Jelly roll—filled doughnuts; 1 inf, Jelly roll—round or long, jelly in center; *(Sweet roll)* 1 inf, Jelly rolls; *(Frosted doughnut)* 1 inf, Jelly roll. **1990** *DARE* File **Chicago IL,** A jelly roll? That's a square or round of deep-fried raised dough, with jelly in the center—which is often seeping out through a navel-like hole in the side—and with a coating usually of large, sticky sugar crystals or of powdered sugar.

2 Fig: a lover; the vagina; sexual intercourse. *among Black speakers* Cf **jelly** n **2**

1914 Handy *St. Louis Blues* [Black], Cause I'm most wile 'bout my Jelly Roll. **1926** in 1961 Oliver *Blues Fell* 114 [Black], Some are young, some are old,/ My man says sissy's [=a homosexual's] got good jelly roll. **1927** *Jrl. Abnormal Psych.* 22.13, Relatively few symbols for the sex organs are found in the blues. . . By far the most common of these terms is *jelly roll*. As used by the lower class Negro it stands for the vagina, or for the female genitalia in general, and sometimes for sexual intercourse. **1927** [see **jelly** n **2**]. **1929** Wolfe *Look Homeward* 304 **NC** [Black], "What's he going to give you a dollar for?" he muttered, barely audible. "Jelly Roll," said Ella Corpening. **1936** *Amer. Caravan* 130 **MS** [Black], "Ol man Harveys too doggone ol t think erbout jelly-roll," said Big Boy. "Hes dried up; all the saps done lef im," said Bobo. **1967** *DARE* FW Addit **AL**14, I noticed much embarrassment from this response [=*jelly roll* for a dessert]. Jelly roll also (among Negroes) means visiting and having intercourse with a woman. "I'm going to get some jelly roll tonight." **1970** Major *Dict. Afro–Amer. Slang,* Jelly-roll: (1890's–1900's) one's lover, spouse; (1920's–40's) a term for the vagina. **1980** [see **jelly** n **2**].

3 A **jelly fungus** of the genus *Exidia.*

1981 Lincoff *Audubon Field Guide Mushrooms* 382, *Black Jelly Roll. Exidia glandulosa.* . . Blisterlike, fusing with others to form a long, narrow row. . . Flesh gelatinous, thin. *Ibid* 383, There are several species of *Exidia,* all beginning as more or less translucent blisters. The Granular Jelly Roll *(E. nucleata)* turns a reddish-brown and contains granular material. The Pale Jelly Roll *(E. alba)* is white. The Amber Jelly Roll *(E. recisa)* has a small stalk and becomes yellowish-brown.

jelly tooth n Also *jelly false tooth*

A **jelly fungus** (here: *Pseudohydnum gelatinosum*).

1981 Lincoff *Audubon Field Guide Mushrooms* 384, Also called "Jelly False Tooth," this is the only toothed jelly fungus. . . Like some other jelly fungi, the Jelly Tooth is edible, although it has little or no flavor.

jellywhopper n

=**golly-whopper.**

1993 *Coast Watch* Sept/Oct 12 **Outer Banks NC,** Jellywhopper—something large.

Jemima n Pronc-spp *Gee-mi-my, Jeemima, Jemimy* [The Biblical name used as a euphem for *Jesus*]

Used in exclams and mild oaths.

1847 in 1930 Meine *Tall Tales* 382 **GA,** Then thar's Pete! *Gee-mi-my!* jest to think o' Pete. **1887** *Century Illustr. Mag.* 34.713 **GA,** Well, the great Jemimy! What's her name, maw? **1888** *Outing* May 108 **MI,** After which I advanced to "Great Caesar!" "Jemima!" "Jerusalem!" (prolonging the *je* in both cases). **1905** *DN* 3.62 **eNE,** *Jemimy,* interj. Used like Jehoshaphat. **1950** *WELS* (*Exclamations beginning with the sound of 'j'*) 1 Inf, **WI,** Jeemima. **1959** *VT Hist.* 27.139, Great Jemima! interj. Rare. **1966–68** *DARE* (Qu. NN30) Inf **NM**11, [jɪˈmaɪmɪz] little kitten; **WI**26, Jumpin' Jemima Jane.

jemmison See jemson

jemmy john n

1969 Sorden *Lumberjack Lingo* 63 **NEng, Gt Lakes,** *Jemmy John*—The handcar on a railroad track. A pede or velocipede.

jempson weed See jimson weed

jemson n Also *jemmison* [Etym uncert]

The penis.

1939 in 1977 Randolph *Pissing in the Snow* 154 **Ozarks,** One time there was some fellows hanging around the store, and they got to talking about which one had the longest tool. So finally Jim Henson. . . out with his old jemson, and it sure was a dandy. **1953** Randolph–Wilson *Down in Holler* 100 **Ozarks,** In several parts of the Ozark region I have heard a term for penis, which sounds like *jemson* or *jemmison.* . . Few of the younger people seem to be familiar with it. Uncle Jack Short, Galena, Missouri, told me that in the eighteen seventies . . *jemmison* was the common term, used by everybody. It has been suggested that

this derives somehow from . . Jimson weed . . , a plant which is said to carry some esoteric sexual significance.

Jenary, Jenewary See January

Jenkins Creeker n Also *Jenkins Creek catboat* =**crab scraper.**

1976 Warner *Beautiful Swimmers* 204 **Chesapeake Bay,** The boat was small. . . Its freeboard amidships was . . not more than eighteen inches. . . "Funny looking things, ain't they?" . . "They're crab scrapers. Here we call them 'Jenkins creekers'." *Ibid* 208, I asked about the origins of the crab scrapers. Yes, he had heard them called Jenkins Creekers and thought the name came from the locality where they may have been first built, over near Crisfield [MD]. **1984** *DARE* File **Chesapeake Bay** [Watermen's vocab], Jenkins Creeker (Jenkins Creek catboat).

Jenkins derrick n Also *Jenkins stacker (derrick)* Cf **Jackson fork**

A device for piling loose hay on a stack; see quots.

1967 *DARE* FW Addit **csID,** Jenkins derrick—The boom is counterbalanced with the butt end up. Loose hay is piled upon the fork. The fork is then swung up in the air and pivoted in a 90° arc over the stack and is tripped as it passes over the stack, depositing its load of hay. This machine is still used to move horses in their farming. *Ibid* **seOR,** A Jenkin [ˈjɪnkən] [sic] stacker derrick—like a buck rake; a team lifted it till it throwed it over on the stack. **1991** *DARE* File **cwID** (as of 1930s), My father was concerned about two sorts of haystackers—those for which no patents existed and were thus in the public domain, and those for which patents existed and which could not be constructed by farmers without paying the legal fee. My father thus built two Mormon derricks and one A-derrick; but he never built a Jenkins stacker because it was patented. The Jenkins stacker was kind of an overshot stacker, which tossed hay up, over, and onto the stack instead of lifting it up and dropping it down.

Jenkins up, Jenks up See up Jenkins

jenk, spread one's v phr [Cf *SND jink* n.[1] III.3 "A (playful) trick or frolic"]

1935 Hurston *Mules & Men* 91 **nFL,** "Ah'll play it if you sing it," he countered. So he played and I started to sing the verses I knew. They put me on the table and everybody urged me to spread my jenk [Footnote: Have a good time], so I did the best I could.

jenny n Also *jennie, jinnie, jinny*

1 A female ass or mule; hence n *jenny mule* a female mule. Cf **jack** n[1] **20, Maud, molly** n[1] **1**

1786 in 1963 Lamb *Mule in S. Ag.* 6 **VA,** A Jack Ass of the first race in the kingdom of Spain will cover mares and jennies (the asses) at Mount Vernon the ensuing spring. **1800** (1907) Columbia Hist. Soc. *Records* 10.107 **PA,** A young Jack Mr Young has taken—three Jennies at the Farm. **1851** *California Laws* 515 (*DAE* at *judge*), Whenever any dispute arises respecting the ownership . . of any horse, mule, jack, jenny, . . it shall be the duty of the Judges . . to decide on such dispute. **1893** Shands *MS Speech* 40, *Jenny* [ˈjɛnɪ]. Used by all classes for *jennet.* I don't think I ever heard a dozen people say *jennet.* It is almost without exception *jenny,* or, if not that, *jinny* [ˈjɪnɪ]. **1902** *DN* 2.237 **sIL,** *Jinny.* . . The female ass. **1903** *DN* 2.318 **seMO,** *Jinny.* . . Jennet; a female ass. **1906** *DN* 3.143 **nwAR,** *Jinny.* . . A she-ass. **1908** *DN* 3.325 **eAL, wGA,** *Jinny.* . . A she-ass. **1928** Ruppenthal *Coll.* **KS,** The farmer had a jack and a jennie. **1950** *WELS* **WI** (*A female donkey*) 30 Infs, Jenny; 6 Infs, Jinny; (*Joking names for mules*) 3 Infs, Jenny. **c1960** Wilson *Coll.* **csKY,** *Jenny.* . . The female donkey [ˈjɪnɪ]. **1965–70** *DARE* (Qu. K50, *Joking nicknames for mules*) 46 Infs, **scattered,** Jenny; **CT**6, Jenny mule; 9 Infs, **scattered,** Jinny; **CA**210, **KS**1, [ˈjɪni]; **IL**31, [ˈjɪni(z)]; **MS**58, [ˈjɪni]; **NJ**22, Jinny mule; (QR, near Qu. K43) Inf **CA**105, Jinny—female jackass. **1967** *DARE* Tape **TX**26, These big jacks will breed another jack—a female—and they get what you call a jenny if she's a mare. **1969** *State* (Raleigh, N.C.) 15 March 28/3 (*Mathews Coll.*), We really have come a long way from first doing the plowing with an oxen or a Jenny mule and now to see plowing done with a tractor.

2 See **jenny wren 1.**

3 as *jinny:* =**ruddy turnstone.**

1888 Trumbull *Names of Birds* 186 **NY,** [*Arenaria interpres*] At Amityville, *Jinny.* **1917** (1923) *Birds Amer.* 1.268, *Ruddy Turnstone.* . . Other Names. . . Jinny; Bishop Plover. **1944** Hausman *Amer. Birds* 518, Jinny—see Turnstone, Ruddy.

4 also *jinny-woman:* See quots. [Cf *SND jennie* n. 2 "A man who meddles with or assists in a housewife's work . . ; a man with effeminate habits"]

1917 *DN* 4.421 **LA,** *Jinny-woman.* . . A mollycoddle. **1971** Dwyer *Dict. for Yankees* 28 **Sth, S Midl,** *Jenny*—A man busied with women's affairs.

5 See quot.

1969 Sorden *Lumberjack Lingo* 64 **NEng, Gt Lakes,** *Jinnie*—A drag used to haul logs from woods to skidway. Same as travois, crazy drag, go-devil, snow snake.

6 also *jenny-go-round:* =**flying jenny 1. Sth, S Midl**

[**1906** *DN* 3.136 **nwAR,** *Flying jinny.* . . A merry-go-round. Originally the propelling power was furnished by a mule.] **1966** *AmSp* 41.281, *Jennie.* . . A merry-go-round. **1968–70** *DARE* (Qu. EE32, *A homemade merry-go-round*) Inf **MS**84, Jenny; **VA**18, Jenny-go-round. **c1970** Pederson *Dial. Surv. Rural GA* (*A home-made merry-go-round*) 1 inf, **seGA,** Jenny; flying jenny. **1975** McDonough *Garden Sass* 294 **AR,** Both the Fourth of July picnic and the Old Soldiers usually had a jenny-ride. "Jennie" is a gypsy word meaning merry-go-round and that is about what a jenny-ride was. . . They'd give you a stick and as you'd go by if you could hook a ring you'd get a free ride. Ever so often they changed mules because the mule going round and round got dizzy. **1986** Pederson *LAGS Concordance* (*Flying jenny*) 8 infs, **chiefly AL, GA,** Jenny (or *jennies*); [1 inf, **cwMS,** Jenny stripe].

7 See quot.

1966 *DARE* FW Addit **SC,** *Jenny*—a self-propelled child's toy with pedals, a sort of old-fashioned tricycle—wooden, with the front in the shape of a horse.

8 See quot.

1968 *DARE* (Qu. AA27, . . *A woman's menstruation*) Inf **NY**83, I've got jenny.

9 See quot. Cf **Betsy 1, Janie**

1968 *DARE* (Qu. P37a, *Nicknames for a rifle*) Inf **NJ**6, Jenny.

10 A **jack-in-the-pulpit 1.**

1969 *DARE* (Qu. S1, . . *Jack-in-the-pulpit*) Inf **RI**12, A light-colored, all-green one is called Jenny.

jennyass n [By analogy with *jackass* a fool]

1940 Stong *Hawkeyes* 200 **IA,** She made forty-nine kinds of a Jenny-ass of herself all over the region.

jenny creeper n Also *jenny weed* Cf **creeping Jennie 5** A **bindweed 1.**

1968 *DARE* (Qu. S5, . . *Wild morning glory*) Infs **IN**26, 41, Jenny creeper; **IL**29, Jenny weed; (Qu. S26e) Inf **IN**3, Jenny creeper.

jenny-go-round See **jenny 6**

jenny horse n Cf **jenny 6, 7**

1986 Pederson *LAGS Concordance* (*A seesaw*) 1 inf, **cwLA,** Jenny horses—old-fashioned term.

jenny-in-the-wood n

Perh =**jack-o'-lantern 3.**

1930 Shoemaker *1300 Words* 34 **cPA Mts** (as of c1900), *Jenny-in-the-wood*—The "Jack o' Lanthorn."

jenny-jump-up See **johnny-jump-up 1**

Jenny Lind n Also *Jenny Lind carriage* [*Jenny Lind* (1820–87) Swedish soprano, whose US tour in 1850 inspired a wide variety of things to be named in her honor; cf *DA*] **esp PA**
See quot 1948.

1854 *Penna. Agric. Rep.* 128 (*DAE*), To S. P. Hamilton, . . for a Jenny Lind Carriage. **1901** Churchill *Crisis* 267 **ceMO,** A "Jenny Lind" passed them. Miss Belle recognized the carriage immediately. **1930** Shoemaker *1300 Words* 33 **cPA Mts** (as of c1900), *Jenny Lind*—A small covered vehicle like a buggy. **1948** Rittenhouse *Amer. Horse-Drawn Vehicles* 11, A 'Jenny Lind' was an early type of buggy with a fixed top. . . Usually of elaborate design and painting. Body 30 inches wide; wheels 47 and 50 inches. **1966–70** *DARE* (Qu. N41a, . . *Horse-drawn vehicles . . to carry people*) Inf **PA**3, Jenny Lind—had tassels; **PA**136, Jenny Lind—like a surrey, only one seat; **PA**242, Jenny Lind.

jenny mule See **jenny 1**

jenny weed See **jenny creeper**

Jennywerry See **January**

jenny wren n

1 also *jenny:* A wren (Troglodytidae), usu **house wren 1.** [*OED* 1648 →]

1895 (1907) Wright *Birdcraft* 83, The House Wren is a bird who has allowed the word *male* to be obliterated from its *social* constitution at least. We always speak of Jenny Wren. **1903** Dawson *Birds OH* 260, Arriving about the middle of April, the House Wren—or Jenny Wren, as it is fondly called—proceeds immediately to renovate last year's quarters. **1945** Eifert *Birds* 128, Sometimes, however, even the finest and most elaborate of houses does not suit the finicky, tilt-tailed, spluttering Jenny. Off it goes, flipping about, bright eyes looking everywhere for a better place. **1950** *WELS,* 12 Infs, **WI,** Jenny wren. **1954** Sprunt *FL Bird Life* 330, Wrens. . . Small, but very vocal, with voices out of proportion to their size, the whole tribe is usually lumped together under the blanket name of "Jenny Wren." **1968–70** *DARE* (Qu. Q14) Infs **PA**245, **VA**22, Jenny wren; (Qu. Q21) Inf **MD**20, Jenny wren; (Qu. Q23) Inf **WI**50, Jenny wren; **OH**98, Little jenny wren. **1982** *Barrick Coll.* **csPA,** *Jenny wren*—house wren.

2 =**herb Robert.**

1889 *Century Dict.* 3225, *Jenny-wren.* . . Herb-robert, *Geranium Robertianum.* **1900** Lyons *Plant Names* 172, *G[eranium] Robertianum.* . . Jenny-wren.

Jenooary See **January**

jensang See **ginseng 1**

jensen n Also *jenson* [Pronc-spp for **gentian**]

1967 *DARE* (Qu. S26c, *Wildflowers that grow in woods*) Inf **PA**53, Blue jensen, bottle jensen. **1983** *MJLF* 9.1.45 **ceKY,** *Jenson* . . a medicinal herb; "for heart dropsy."

January See **January**

Jerdan, Jerden, Jerdon See **Jordan**

jerdge See **judge**

Jerewsalem See **Jerusalem**

jergment See **judge**

jerk n[1], v[1] Usu |jǝ(r)k|; also |jĕk, jʌk, jɔık, jɜık| Cf Pronc Intro 3.II.12, **joog** Pronc-spp *jeck, joik, juck, ju'k, jurk*

A Forms.

1815 Humphreys *Yankey in England* 106, *Jurk,* jerk. **1884** *Anglia* 7.275 **Sth, S Midl** [Black], *To gin er big juk* = to give a big jerk. **1908** *DN* 3.324 **eAL, wGA,** *Jeck.* **1922** Gonzales *Black Border* 308 **sSC, GA coasts** [Gullah glossary], *Ju'k*—jerk, jerks, jerked, jerking. **1930** Stoney-Shelby *Black Genesis* 104 **seSC,** He hold only slack up a leetle bit, but dat's jis' enough for Br' Rabbit to juck loose an' gone! **1950** *PADS* 14.41 **NC,** Jerk is often pronounced *jeck,* and on the coast, *juck* [dzʌk]. **1967–70** *DARE* (Qu. HH3) Inf **PA**39, Jeck; (Qu. HH16) Inf **NJ**69, Stupid jerk [jĕk]; (Qu. GG32b) Inf **NJ**69, [jĕk]; (Qu. GG38) Inf **NJ**69, [jĕk]. **1986** *DARE* File **NYC** (as of 1965), Joik [jɔık, jɜık]. **1986** [see C5 below].

B As noun.

1 pl; often with *the; also jerking exercise, jerking(s):* A manifestation of religious ecstasy involving vigorous (apparently involuntary) movement, esp of the head. **chiefly S Midl, Sth** Cf **barking exercise, C1 below**

1805 in 1851 Mayo *On Pop. Superstition* 131 **TN,** I have seen all denominations of religion exercised by the jerks. . . I passed a meeting house, where I observed the undergrowth had been cut done [sic] for camp-meetings, and from fifty to a hundred saplings were left for the people who were jerked to hold by. **1805** in 1956 Eliason *Tarheel Talk* 125 **TN,** First they took what they call the Jurkin exercise. **1842** Buckingham *E. & W. States* 2.427, At a great Camp-Meeting in Kentucky . . the women were seized with convulsions, called at that time "jerkings." **1847** Howe *Hist. Coll. OH* 46 (as of 1803), The phenomena of "*bodily exercises,*" then common in the west. . . have been classified by a clerical writer as 1st, the *Falling* exercise; 2d, the *Jerking* exercise. . . It was familiarly called the Jerks. **1930** Shoemaker *1300 Words* 33 **cPA Mts** (as of c1900), *Jerks*—A nervous affliction, common and infectious at mountain camp-meetings and revivals. **1945** Saxon *Gumbo Ya-Ya* 407 **LA,** As she mentioned Jesus, she was afflicted with an attack of the 'jerks' and she shuddered and jerked until she had to be assisted back into her chair. **1949** in 1984 Gilmore *Ozark Baptizings* 80 **MO,** Exhorters by the dozen would shout in unison. A young girl in the front row would get the jerks, swishing her head back and forth in vigorous, rhythmic motion.

2 pl; also with *the:* Any of various conditions resulting in spasmodic involuntary movement.

1968–69 *DARE* (Qu. P36, *When a hunter sees a deer or other game animal and gets so excited he can't shoot, he has* _____) Inf **GA**77, Nervous jerks; (Qu. BB19, *Joking names for looseness of the bowels*) Inf **MD**5, Got the jerks; (Qu. DD22, *. . Delirium tremens*) Inf **KY**21, The jerks.

3 Fig: a short period of time—usu in phr *two jerks of a lamb's tail* and varr. [Cf *EDD* in two claps of a lamb's tail (at *lamb* sb. 3. (1))]

1901 *DN* 2.142 **csNY**, *Jerk of a lamb's tail*. . . Very short time. "I'll do it in three jerks of a lamb's tail," i.e., very quickly. **1922** *DN* 5.178 **AL, AR, KY, MA, NE**, *Jerk of a lamb's tail*. . . A very short time, a trice. **1965–70** *DARE* (Qu. A14, *. . A very short period of time: "I'll be ready in* _____." *or "It won't take any longer than* _____.") Infs **NY**206, **VT**7, Two jerks of a lamb's tail; **NJ**39, Couple jerks of a cow's tail; **NC**53, Three jerks of a sheep's tail; **WI**5, A jerk; **WI**75, Two jerks of a dead lamb's tail; **NC**78, Two jerks of a dog's tail.

4 usu in combs *jerk line, ~ (rail)road, ~ train:* See quot 1927.

1907 *London Road* 26, By mistake I had missed the main line and come over a small "jerk" with only two locals a day on it. **1927** *DN* 5.451 [Underworld jargon], *Jerk road*. . . A small, branch railway. **1950** *WELS* **WI** (*Joking names for a branch railroad that is not very important or does not give the best of service*) 3 Infs, Jerk train (*or* line); (*Names for a train that stops at every station along the way*) 1 Inf, Jerk train. **1965–70** *DARE* (Qu. N37) 9 Infs, **scattered**, Jerk line; **NC**41, **NY**214, **PA**235, Jerk road; **NJ**25, Jerk railroad.

5 also *jerk town* (or *place, village*): An insignificant place. Cf **jerkwater** adj **2**

1950 *WELS* **WI** (*Joking names for an out-of-the-way place or an unimportant village*) 4 Infs, Jerk town; 3 Infs, Jerk; 1 Inf, Jerk in the road. **1967–68** *DARE* (Qu. C33) Infs **CT**68, **NC**41, Jerk town; **MN**15, Jerk of a town; **NY**23, Jerk place. **1967** *DARE* FW Addit **cnNY**, Jerk village—a wide spot in the road.

6 A reprimand. Cf **jack up 1, C2** below

1913 *DN* 4.11 **MN**, *Jerk*. . . A notice of being deficient in school work. "The old man sent me a jerk three times before he conned [*DN* Ed: i.e., 'conditioned'] me."

C As verb.

1 To experience a paroxysm of religious excitement; to cause to experience such a paroxysm; hence vbl n *jerking.* Cf **B1** above

1805 in 1851 Mayo [see **B1** above]. **1805** in 1956 Eliason *Tarheel Talk* 125 **TN**, Their was a terable uproar amongst the Baptists. . . they will begin to Jurk and to twitch and to Jump and stamp until you would think they would run mad. **1843** (1916) Hall *New Purchase* 370 **IN**, The camp was furnished with several stands for preaching, exhorting, jumping and jerking. **1984** Wilder *You All Spoken Here* 181 **Sth**, Jerkin' poles are stout anchors for those caught in the undertow of religious frenzy, something for them to grab a-holt of, to jerk on.

2 with *up;* Fig: to call to account, reprimand; to harass; see quots. Cf **jack up 1, B6** above

1843 *Spirit of Times* 22 July 241/1, The Association having delegated a Commission to investigate the charges, . . the Commissioners "made no bones" of jerking us up "under the 7th Section." **1901** Merwin–Webster *Calumet "K"* 222, He'll probably try to make out a case of criminal carelessness against me, and get me jerked up. **1910** McCutcheon *Rose* 122, The cops. . . jerk up a circus man on the slightest excuse. **1968** *DARE* (Qu. Y6, *. . To put pressure on somebody to do something he ought to have done but hasn't: "He's a whole week late. I'm going to* _____.") Inf **OH**82, Jerk him up. **1981** Harper–Presley *Okefinokee* 141 **seGA** (as of a1948), *Jerk up*—Discipline imposed by the Primitive Baptist church, an admonition for wrong-doing. "Old man Jack went to church that day, and they jerked him up for cussing chickens in the garden."

3a To serve, draw, or dispense; see quots.

1883 (1890) Peck *Peck's Bad Boy No. 2* 126 **Milwaukee WI**, Well, I must go down to the sweetened wind factory, and jerk soda. **1884** Miller *Memorie* 20, They stared at me, but went on jerking beer behind the counter. **1967** *AmSp* 42.62 **ceKS**, An order for four chocolate sodas is *jerk a bridge.* **1969** Sorden *Lumberjack Lingo* 64 **NEng, Gt Lakes**, *Jerk the hash*—Serve the food.

b also *jerk soup* (or *a drink*); spec, in railroading: See quot 1938. Cf **jerkwater** adj **1**

1931 *Writer's Digest* 11.42 [Railroad terms], *Jerk Soup or Jerk a Drink*—To take water from a track pan without stopping the train. **1938** Beebe *High Iron* 222 [Railroad terms], *Jerk, to:* To take up water for a locomotive from a track pan without stopping.

4 also with *off:* To milk—usu in phrr *jerk the cow(s), jerk (the) tits. joc*

1965–70 *DARE* (Qu. K8, *Joking terms for milking a cow: A farmer might say, "Well, it's time to go out and* _____.") Infs **CT**2, **MI**113, 120, **NY**198, Jerk the cow(s); **CA**36, **NY**109, **OH**50, **TX**11, Jerk (the) tits; **LA**44, Jerk her off; **NY**123, Jerk; **PA**235, Jerk 'em off.

5 with *up;* =**drag up 1.**

1941 *AmSp* 16.22 **sIN**, He wasn't raised: he was jerked up by the hair of the head. **1950** *PADS* 14.41 **SC**, *Jerked up*. . . Grown up without breeding, rearing, training. **1965–68** *DARE* (Qu. Z17, *To take care of or bring up a child: "All her children were* _____ [on the farm].") Inf **VA**5, Jerked up; (Qu. II21, *When somebody behaves unpleasantly or without manners: "The way he behaves, you'd think he was* _____.") Infs **AZ**6, **SC**32, 34, **VT**3, Jerked up. **1981** Pederson *LAGS Basic Materials*, 1 inf, **swAL**, Sort of got 'em by the hair of the head and ['dʒɝ˧kt əm ʌ<ᵊp]; 1 inf, **ceMS**, I was ['dʒɝ˧ᵻkt ɝˇp]—heard a man say once.

jerk v² [Back-formation from **jerky** n², or directly from AmSpan *charquear* < *charqui*]

To preserve (meat) by drying, esp by cutting it into strips and exposing it to air; occas to cut (meat) into strips in preparation for drying; hence ppl adj *jerked,* by assim *jerk,* preserved in this way; vbl n *jerking.*

c1770 in 1953 Woodmason *Carolina Backcountry* 196 **SC**, If any Beef, they jerk it and dry it in the Sun—So that You may as well eat a Deal Board. **1775** in 1835 Hall *Sketches West* 2.263, We . . fixed Mr. Cocke off with a good Queen Ann's musket . . and no small quantity of jerked beef. **1835** (1955) *Crockett Almanacks* 24 **wTN**, To preserve the flesh for future use, the hunters and Indians cut it into thin slices and dry it in the open air which is called *jerking.* **1882** Chase *Editor's Run* 204, Fresh meat is cured by hanging it out doors, "jerked," as they say, into strips. **1916** Thoburn *Std. Hist. OK* 1.262, Every well-appointed plantation and farm had its smoke-house, which hung full of cured pork and "jerked" beef. **1941** *LANE* Map 303, 1 inf, **cRI**, Jerked [beef], not a local term; 1 inf, **ceMA**, Jerked [beef], in large pieces; 1 inf, **csNH**, Jerked [beef], not locally; 1 inf, **ceME**, Jerked [beef], sun dried. **1965–70** *DARE* (Qu. H44) 24 Infs, **scattered, but esp TX**, Jerked beef; **TX**39, 40, Jerked meat; **AL**11, **AK**8, **FL**6, **ID**1, **WV**1, Jerk beef; **MI**108, Jerk beef—in the logging camps; **MA**40, Jerk beef—old Indian name for it; **LA**16, Jerk meat; **HI**6, Jerk meat—slice, salt and hang to dry. [32 of 35 Infs old] **1969** *DARE* Tape **AZ**11, They would often jerk the beef. **1973** Allen *LAUM* 1.286 (as of c1950), Beef that has been cut into long strips and dried in the open air is known by the Americanisms *jerked beef, jerky,* or, once, *jerk.* Because the process itself is characteristic of pioneer life and hence is old-fashioned, the terms themselves often are considered obsolete. Although remembered here in New England as early expressions, in the U[pper] M[idwest] they survive principally in South Dakota and Nebraska, where some infs. associate them with Indians. . . A Nebraskan inf. says that one can have *jerked venison* as well as *jerked beef.*

jerk n² Also sp *jirk*

1 also *jerk beef:* =**jerky** n².

1799 Smith *Acct. Travels* 65, This we kept to stew with our jirk as we needed it. **1831** in 1904 Thwaites *Early W. Travels* 8.64 **Inland Sth**, The venison, for want of salt to preserve it, is cut in slices, dried and smoked, which makes what they call jerk. **1869** (1921) Haycraft *Hist. Elizabethtown KY* 16, The dried venison, called "jirk," was the bread. **1967** *DARE* (Qu. H44, *Beef that has been dried to preserve it*) Infs **TX**35, **WA**19, Jerk. **1973** Allen *LAUM* 1.287 (as of c1950), Jerk: "The Sioux have that; they eat their 'jerk.' " [1 inf, **cSD**] **1986** Pederson *LAGS Concordance*, 1 inf, **csTX**, Jerk beef = beef jerky; we used to make it.

2 A slab of preserved meat.

1948 Manfred *Chokecherry* 94 **nwIA**, Kaes cut a hunk three inches by six from a jerk of bacon.

jerk a drink See **jerk** v¹ **C3b**

jerk beef See **jerk** n² **1**

jerk-bird n [From its habit of bobbing its head and tail]
=**spotted sandpiper.**
  1917 *Wilson Bulletin* 29.2.80, *Actitis macularia*. . . Jerk-. . bird, Wallops I[slan]d, Va.

jerk bump n Also *jerk pimple* [Prob < *jerk off* to masturbate]
=**jack bump.**
  1936 *Hench Coll.* [Prison language], *Jerk bumps*—acne vulgaris. **1969** *DARE* (Qu. X59, . . *The small infected pimples that form usually on the face*) Inf **NY**197, Jerk pimples.

jerk coffee See **jerkwater** n 2

jerked See **jerk** v²

jerker n
=**hornyhead c.**
  1882 *U.S. Natl. Museum Bulletin* 16.212, *C[eratichthys] biguttatus*. . . Jerker. . . The most widely diffused of our *Cyprinidae*. **1902** Jordan–Evermann *Amer. Fishes* 71, In different parts of its ranges it [=*Nocomis biguttatus*] is known as the hornyhead, . . or jerker. **1943** Eddy–Surber *N. Fishes* 131, *Hornyhead Chub* (Jerker). . . is one of the best live-bait minnows for bass, pickerel and other game fishes. **1983** Becker *Fishes WI* 485, *Hornyhead Chub*. . . Other common names . . jerker.

jerkey See **jerky** n¹

jerk frog n
An unidentified frog (Ranidae).
  1926 (1949) McQueen–Mizell *Hist. Okefenokee* 177 **seGA**, Another good time to fish is when the birds are singing, and the "jerk frogs" are hollering.

jerkin n¹ [*OED* "*Obs.*"]
=**jerky** n².
  [**1612** Smith *Map VA* 17, As drie as their ierkin beefe in the west Indies.] **1954** *Harder Coll.* **cwTN**, Jerkin—beef preserved by drying. A term seldom used, although known to all informants. **1968** *DARE* (Qu. H44, *Beef that has been dried to preserve it*) Infs **GA**29, **KS**11, Jerkin.

jerkin n² [Pronc-sp for *gherkin*]
  1954 *Harder Coll.* **cwTN**, A jerkin' cucumber is as big as a goose egg. **1965–70** *DARE* (Qu. H56, *Names for . . pickles*) 36 Infs, **scattered, but esp WV**, (Sweet) jerkin(s). [32 Infs old]

jerking n, vbl n¹ See **jerk** n¹, v¹ **B1, C1**

jerking vbl n² See **jerk** v²

jerking exercise See **jerk** n¹ **B1**

jerkings See **jerk** n¹ **B1**

jerk knife n Cf **tomahawk knife**
  1967 Key *Tobacco Vocab.* **TN**, Jerk knife. A tomahawk-shaped knife used to harvest tobacco. Archaic.

jerk line n
  1 also *jerk rein*: A single rope or strap used to control a large team of horses or mules; also fig; see quot 1964. **chiefly West old-fash** Cf **line** n¹ **1, long line**
  1888 Grigsby *Smoked Yank* 156 **WI**, The driver rode on the nigh wheel mule, and drove the leader with a jerk-line. **1895** *Forum* June 475 **West**, The big freight-wagon, with its six or eight mules guided by a single jerk-rein. **1904** Steedman *Bucking Sagebrush* 22 **UT**, They were driven with a "jerk line" manipulated by the "mule skinner" who rode the nigh wheeler. **1907** White *AZ Nights* 287, I bet that Sang would get a wiggle on him with his little old cleaning duds if he had a woman ahold of his jerk line. **1910** Hart *Vigilante Girl* 140 **nCA**, They were drawn by strings of twelve to twenty animals, usually mules. This train of animals was driven by a "jerk line" instead of reins. A long line of braided rawhide ran from the bit of the near landing mule through the turrets of the harness to the succeeding animals until it reached the driver. **1922** Rollins *Cowboy* 194, Or else the wagons were drawn by a "jerk-line string," a string of horses or mules harnessed either in single file or in a series of spans, and, in either case, following a highly trained leader controlled by a "jerk line." **1964** Jackman–Long *OR Desert* 277, The jerk-line teams usually ran from ten to twenty horses. The driver rode the "near" or left wheel horse, with a long, small, hard-twist rope running along the entire team and ending in the bit ring of the left leader. A steady pull on this rope meant a left turn, a few sharp jerks, a right turn—hence, the name jerk line. **1967** *DARE* FW Addit **seOR**, Jerk line—line to lead team in series of teams of horses; **neOR**, Jerk line—one line to lead pair of mules in sixteen-mule line.

2 See **jerk** n¹ **B4**.

jerk of a lamb's tail See **jerk** n¹ **B3**

jerk off See **jerk** v¹ **C4**

jerk pimple See **jerk bump**

jerk place See **jerk** n¹ **B5**

jerk railroad See **jerk** n¹ **B4**

jerk rein See **jerk line** 1

jerk road See **jerk** n¹ **B4**

jerk soup See **jerk** v **C3b**

jerk town See **jerk** n¹ **B5**

jerk train See **jerk** n¹ **B4**

jerk up See **jerk** v¹ **C2, 5**

jerk village See **jerk** n¹ **B5**

jerkwater adj
  1 Of or pertaining to a small local railway; also n *jerkwater* a branch line, a local train; by ext, a small town. [See quot 1941; cf **jerk** v¹ **C3b**] **scattered exc NEng; infreq Sth, Inland Sth** See Map *joc* or *derog; somewhat old-fash*
  1878 Hart *Sazerac Lying Club* 16 *(DA)*, I wish I may be run over by a two-horse jerk-water. **1905** *DN* 3.84 **nwAR**, Jerkwater railroad. . . Insignificant branch railway. 'The St. Paul branch is a jerkwater railroad.' Common. *Jerkwater (train)*. . . Train on a branch railway. 'Has the jerkwater come in yet?' Common. **1925** in 1953 Botkin–Harlow *Treas. Railroad Folkl.* 428, Down in Arkansas in the old days there was a jerk-water railroad with a reputation. The reputation was that it never adhered to its schedule. **1929** *Ruppenthal Coll.* **KS**, Jerkwater . . a small, short or insignificant line of railroad. **1941** *Sun* (Baltimore) 7 Mar. 12/7 *(OEDS)*, In the early days of railroads the small boilers of the locomotives required frequent refilling, and water tanks were very few. Every train crew carried a leather bucket on a long rope with which they 'jerked water' from the streams along their track. As locomotives increased in size the small 'jerk-water' engines were relegated to branch-line service. Today no train crew carries a bucket, but the name 'jerk-water' still sticks and has become part of our national heritage of American slang. **1945** Hubbard *Railroad Ave.* 349, *Jerk a drink*—Take water from track pan without stopping train. From this came the word *jerkwater*, which usually means a locality serving only to supply water to the engines of passing trains; a place other than a regular stop, hence of minor importance as *jerkwater* town, *jerkwater* college, etc. **1950** *WELS* (*Joking names for a branch railroad that is not very important or does not give the best of service*) 8 Infs, **WI**, Jerkwater (line). **1960** Criswell *Resp. to PADS* 20 **Ozarks**, Jerkwater . . a short line of a railroad with small trains and few accommodations. Once common. **1965–70** *DARE* (Qu. N37) 85 Infs, **scattered exc NEast; infreq Sth, Inland Sth**, Jerkwater (express, line, road, railroad, outfit, *or* train). [Of all Infs responding to the question, 70% were old; of those giving these responses, 85% were old.]

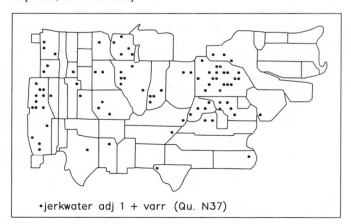

•jerkwater adj 1 + varr (Qu. N37)

2 Insignificant; backwoodsy—used esp of places.
  1897 *Chicago Tribune* (IL) 25 July 15/2, Jerkwater—insignificant—John J. Ingalls regards the Swiss mission as a jerkwater job, and would not take it if it were offered to him. **1901** in 1953 Botkin–Harlow *Treas. Railroad Folkl.* 375, Mrs. Catt had been speaking at a jerkwater town in the mountains and was due in another berg of the same dimensions

down in the valley the same evening. **1911** Harrison *Queed* 225, The spring found West stronger and more contented with his lot as president of a jerkwater college. **1945** [see **1** above]. **1945** Street *Gauntlet* 131 **MO** (as of 1920s), The Milford supporters cheered and jeered and Linden was called a jerkwater dump and a tank town and other names, none of them complimentary. **1950** *WELS* (. . *Joking names or nicknames* . . *for an out-of-the-way place or an unimportant village*) 9 Infs, **WI**, Jerkwater (town, place, stop *or* station). **1965–70** *DARE* (Qu. C33, . . *Joking names* . . *for an out-of-the-way place, or a very small or unimportant place*) 18 Infs, **scattered,** Jerkwater (town, place, *or* joint); **CA**11, **GA**31, Little jerkwater town. **1968** *DARE* Tape **CA**104, But there's a lotta little jerkwater sawmills was in operation.

jerkwater n

1 See **jerkwater** adj **1.**

2 also *jerk coffee:* See quots.

1941 Writers' Program *Guide WV* 403 **csWV**, Although changed in other respects, the West Virginia logger has retained his jargon. Cooks are still 'stomick robbers'; their helpers are 'cookees'; coffee is 'jerkwater'; prunes, 'log berries'; biscuits, 'cat-heads'; and milk is 'cow.' **1964** Clarkson *Tumult* 365 **WV** (as of 1920) [Logger lingo], Jerk water—Coffee. **1968** *DARE* (Qu. H74b, . . *Coffee* . . *very weak*) Inf **IN**30, Jerkwater. **1982** Ginns *Snowbird Gravy* 25 **nwNC**, He took coffee beans, and he dried 'em in the stove. . . Then he took a string and put a hole through several beans of the coffee, put the string through it. . . Then he'd hold the coffeepot lid up and hold these beans down in here on this string and let it stay so long. Then he'd jerk it out. Hang it up, let it dry, and use it again. And that's what's called "jerk coffee." I'd call it water.

jerk wire n

In logging: a wire attached to a whistle and pulled to sound a signal; hence v phr *jerk wire* to operate such a whistle system.

1938 (1939) Holbrook *Holy Mackinaw* 262, *Jerk wire.* Wire attached to whistle on yarding donkey [=**donkey 1**], by which the punk [=the boy who blows whistles for a yarding crew] blows starting and stopping signals. **1950** *Western Folkl.* 9.118 **nwOR** [Logger speech], *Jerk wire.* A signal wire fastened to the whistle on a donkey. **1958** McCulloch *Woods Words* 98 **Pacific NW**, *Jerk wire*—a. The old style whistle punk signal system, a wire tied directly to the donkey whistle and pulled by the punk. Electrically operated whistles appeared in the woods around 1914. All the punk had to do then was to squeeze a switch. . . b. To work as a whistle punk.

jerky n[1] Also sp *jerkey, jirky* chiefly MT

A springless horse-drawn vehicle used esp to carry passengers.

1869 *New No. West* (Deer Lodge, Mont.) 3 Sep. 3/5 *(DA)*, Hon. Simon Estes is carrying the United States mails between Virginia and Bannock—per 'jerkies.' **1871** in 1909 Roe *Army Letters* 2 **seCO**, We came all that distance in a funny looking stage coach called a "jerkey," and a good name for it, too. **1882** *Century Illustr. Mag.* Oct 864 **cwMT**, The "jerky" is a sort of cross between a coach proper and a common wagon. **1884** Shepherd *Prairie Exper.* 108 **wMT**, The liveliest travelling was by jerky, the ordinary American farm-waggon without springs. You sat on a board laid across the waggon-box; that is, you tried to sit, for truly half the time you spent in the air. **1911** Strahorn *15000 Miles* 127 **wMT**, The valley varies from six to ten miles in width and is sixty miles in length. The "jerky" stage made tri-weekly trips carrying mail and other commodities and an occasional passenger. It was expected soon to have the road opened to Bannock City and then regular freight traffic would open up and give the farmers a choice of two ways to ship out their products. **1925** Stuart *40 Yrs.* 2.103 **ceMT**, Here we changed for a covered jirky. **1939** (1973) FWP *Guide MT* 90, For a time the stage-coach was the frontier's best answer to the problem of swifter travel. . . Concord coaches replaced the early vehicles, to be replaced in turn by the "jerky," an unpleasant contrivance without springs or thoroughbraces. **1977** Dunlop *Wheels West* 143, For short distances some stage lines carried their passengers in a jerky, which an Army wife on a trip from Kit Carson, Colorado, to Fort Lyon called "a funny looking stage coach." It was a light, two-seat conveyance with roll-up canvas sides. The jerky was springless, and nobody ever claimed that the ride it gave was smooth.

jerky n[2] Also *jerky beef* [AmSpan *charqui* < Quechua *ch'arki*] scattered, but chiefly West See Map

Meat, esp beef, preserved by drying, esp in strips in the open air.

1848 (1850) Colton *3 Yrs.* 298 **CA**, A tin cup of coffee, a junk of bread, and a piece of the stewed jerky. **1919** in 1942 *Colorado Mag.*

19.96, He lived just like a coyote. If he found a dead horse he would take a quarter or a half and make jerky out of it. **1942** Perry *Texas* 139, Dried beef to us is "jerky." **1958** *PADS* 30.6 **Upper MW**, *Jerky.* . . Mostly it is older . . speakers who recall the expression, but even then only 25% in South Dakota and 20% in Nebraska. In Iowa only one old-timer remembered the word; it did not turn up at all in North Dakota or Minnesota. The distribution suggests the spreading influence of the northward-traveling cattlemen from the Spanish-speaking southwest. **1965–70** *DARE* (Qu. H44, *Beef that has been dried to preserve it*) 172 Infs, **scattered, but chiefly West,** Jerky; **AR**55, **CA**105, 118, 184, **IL**45, **MT**1, Beef jerky; **AZ**8, **CO**20, **HI**1, **MS**1, Jerky beef; **CA**105, Venison jerky.

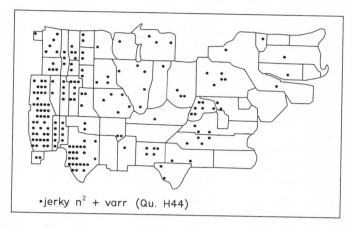

•jerky n[2] + varr (Qu. H44)

jerky adj

Nervous, impatient.

1899 (1912) Green *VA Folk-Speech* 244, *Jerky.* . . impatient. **1933** Williamson *Woods Colt* 253 **Ozarks**, He's plumb out of chawin' [tobacco], an' gittin' jerky about it.

jerky beef See jerky n[2]

jerl n

1994 NC Lang. & Life Project *Harkers Is. Vocab.* 7 **eNC**, *Jerl.* . . A quiver or slight motion (usually of fish) just below the surface of the water. *We saw a jerl of minnows by the dock.*

jernt See joint

Jerome n [Echoic] Cf jugarum

A **bullfrog 1.**

1950 *WELS* (*Names or nicknames for a very large frog that makes a deep, loud sound*) 1 Inf, **WI**, Jerome.

jerp n [Cf *EDD jirt* "A dram or small quantity of drink"]

1927 *DN* 5.475 **Ozarks**, *Jerp.* . . A small quantity. This word is most often used with reference to sweets. "She shore does like a leetle jerp o' sugar on her bread."

jerps, by intj [Prob euphem for *by Jesus*]

1927 *DN* 5.473 **Ozarks**, *By jerps!* . . A common expression of astonishment.

jerry n Cf snipe n

In railroading: a section worker or other laborer; a section foreman.

1916 *DN* 4.356, *Jerry* . . = snipe: used in the East. **1927** *DN* 5.451 [Underworld jargon], *Jerry.* . . A railway section worker. **1932** *Santa Fe Employes' Mag.* Jan 34, A foreman of a section gang is a *Jerry* or a *king;* a section laborer is a *snipe.* **1940** Cottrell *Railroader* 130, *Jerry*— A section worker; sometimes applied to any laborer. **1958** McCulloch *Woods Words* 98 **Pacific NW**, *Jerry gang*—A section crew.

jerry coat n [Prob *jerry* of poor material or workmanship; cf *jerry-built*] Cf half-a-shirt, jellycoat =red-headed woodpecker.

1913 *Auk* 30.497 **Okefenokee GA**, *Melanerpes erythrocephalus.* . . 'Jerry Coat'. **1956** *AmSp* 31.184, The redheaded woodpecker, . . [has] its lower back and rump (as well as matching parts of the wings) white. . . The back above this white marking is black, suggesting a skimpy coat, not long enough to cover the shirttail, whence the name *jerry coat* in Georgia.

jerry walkers n pl Cf **johnny walkers**
=**tom walkers.**
   1966 *DARE* (Qu. EE35, *Long wooden poles with a footpiece that children walk around on to make them tall*) Infs **GA**1, 9, Jerry walkers.

Jerry Wringle n Cf **chickamy chickamy craney crow**
A children's ring game; see quot.
   1957 *Sat. Eve. Post Letters* **cwPA**, *Jerry Wringle*—All but two players joined hands to form a circle, with one player in the center of the circle and one outside. The one in the center would say "Who's going around my house this dark night?" and the one outside, walking around the circle, would answer "Only me and Jerry Wringle." Center one, "Don't take any of my sheep." "I won't, come along my Jerry Wringle," and he would tap someone on the back (the nearest at the time). That one would follow and the circle would join again. This would go on until there were no sheep left. Then each sheep would put his arms around the one in front, the leader would stretch out his arms wide, and the one who had been in the center would have to catch his sheep, the leader having to try and stop him without touching him, just by twisting the line of sheep behind him and keeping his arms out. And the shepherd could only catch the one on the end and then that one would drop out and he could try for the next.

Jersey n
1 See **Jersey wagon.**
2 See **Jersey mosquito 1.**

Jersey bird, Jersey bomber See **Jersey mosquito 1**

Jersey devil n Also *Jersey monster* **NJ** Cf **Leeds devil**
An imaginary monster; a hobgoblin.
   1909 *NY Eve. Jrl.* (NY) 1 Feb 2 *(Zwilling Coll.)*, [Cartoon title:] The Jersey Devil and Some Others. [Cartoon caption:] The Jersey devil *now* has eye in middle of head, green feathers and feet like man. [*DARE* Ed: Cartoon was prompted by a number of reports emanating from New Jersey of sightings of a monster.] **1939** *FWP Guide NJ* 584, The Jersey Devil, it should be noted, conventionally appears as a sort of winged creature with no more illumination than is provided by an occasional fiery snort. **1965–70** *DARE* (Qu. CC17, *Imaginary animals or monsters that people . . tell tales about—especially to tease greenhorns*) 10 Infs, **NJ**, Jersey devil; **NJ**2, Jersey monster; (Qu. EE41, *A hobgoblin that is used to threaten children and make them behave*) Infs **NJ**16, 22, Jersey devil. **1968** McPhee *Pine Barrens* 75 **NJ**, The Pine Barrens also have their own monster. This creature has been feared in the woods—on a somewhat diminishing scale—from the seventeen–thirties to the present. It is known as Leeds' Devil, or the Jersey Devil. *Ibid* 76, The Jersey Devil is real. . . A woman named Leeds. . . had her thirteenth child, and it growed, and one day it flew away. It's haunted the earth ever since. It's took pigs right out of pens. And little lambs. . . The Leeds Devil is a crooked-faced thing, with wings. **1968** *DARE* Tape **NJ**62, [Inf:] The Pineys [=residents of central New Jersey] . . believe in the Jersey devil. . . Some say they saw one but, as I say, I think it was more fiction than fact. [FW:] Was he supposed to have done certain things? [Inf:] Just frighten—that's all—people.

Jersey dory n
   1970 *DARE* FW Addits **VA**47, 52, *Jersey dory*—a vee-type ocean-going fishing boat, seaworthy, rowed; old-fashioned.

Jersey Dutch n
See quot 1910.
   1896 (1897) Haswell *Reminiscences* 91 **NJ** (as of 1818), A well-known and intelligent citizen of Hackensack being asked if the language he spoke (now known as Jersey Dutch) was alike to that of the Germans, he replied he did not know. **1910** *DN* 3.459, "Jersey" or "Bergen County Dutch" is the usual name for the vernacular of the descendants of the original Netherland settlers in old Bergen County, N.J., now subdivided into Bergen and Passaic Counties. . . The Jersey Dutch was originally the South Holland or Flemish language, which, in the course of centuries (ca. 1630–1880), became mixed with and partially influenced by English, having borrowed also from the Minsi (Lenâpe-Delaware) Indian language a few animal and plant names. **a1949** (1964) Storms *Jersey Du. Vocab.* np, As a small boy at home I never attempted to reply in Jersey Dutch, as my parents frowned upon it . . , yet I understood everything they said in it. . . Later in life . . my mother and I when alone held converse in the strange tongue. [*DARE* Ed: Writer born 1860] **1974** Cohen *Ramapo Mt. People* 143, Today the Jersey Dutch dialect is no longer spoken as such by the Ramapo Mountain People. Survivals of this dialect, however, still exist in their speech. In many cases those who use such words and expressions are unaware that they are Jersey Dutch and not English.

Jersey eagle See **Jersey mosquito 1**

Jersey glider n
=**turkey vulture.**
   1956 *AmSp* 31.186 **NJ**, Jersey glider—Turkey vulture . . —For its wonderful soaring ability.

Jersey goose n
A **phalarope:** either *Phalaropus fulicarius* or *P. lobatus.*
   1917 *Wilson Bulletin* 29.2.79, [*Phalaropus fulicarius*. . . Jersey geese, coast of Nova Scotia]. *Ibid, Lobipes lobatus*. . . Jersey geese, coast of Maine. **1925** (1928) Forbush *Birds MA* 1.372, *Red Phalarope*. . . Other names . . *Jersey-goose.* **1946** Hausman *Eastern Birds* 296, *Red Phalarope*. . . Jersey Goose. . . Along the Atlantic coast.

Jersey lightning n Cf **lightning n[1]**
=**applejack 1;** also whiskey, esp bad or illegal whiskey.
   1852 *Alta California* (S.F.) 23 Aug. 2/5 *(DA)*, The rumsellers dealt out Jersey lightning by the gallon. **1860** in 1939 FWP *Guide KS* 466, A muleteer. . . can do nothing without whiskey, which he loves to call tarantula juice, strychnine, red-eye, corn juice, Jersey lightning, . . and many other hard and grotesque names. **1894** *DN* 1.331 **NJ**, In Salem, Sussex, and Burlington counties, where apple whiskey is made, it is commonly called "jack." "Jersey Lightning" is hardly used by natives for this article. **1926** Finerty *Criminalese* 32, *Jersey lightning*—Bad whiskey. *Ibid* 33, *Jersey-lightning*—Apple brandy. **1945** Beck *Jersey Genesis* 101 **NJ**, "How much cider makes how much 'Jersey Lightning'?" I asked. "Ten gallons of apple whiskey should come from about one hundred gallons of cider," Mr. Ewan said. **1966** *DARE* (Qu. DD21c, *Nicknames for whiskey, especially illegally made whiskey*) Inf **MA**11, Jersey lightning.

Jersey monster See **Jersey devil**

Jersey mosquito n
1 also *Jersey, Jersey bird, ~ bomber, ~ eagle, ~ robin, New Jersey (mosquito);* pronc-sp *Joisy mosquito:* A large **mosquito n[1] B1,** esp a salt-marsh mosquito (here: *Aedes sollicitans*). chiefly **NEast** See Map
   1897 *Congressional Record* 18 May 1137, I have never been in New Jersey [laughter], but I know the reputation of the New Jersey mosquito. **1906** McHugh *Skiddoo* 53 *(Hench Coll.)*, When the Jersey mosquito makes you forget the politeness due to your host . . rush hither to your happy little home. **1909** *NY Eve. Jrl.* (NY) 20 July 10 *(Zwilling Coll.)*, [Cartoon of a man with a swarm of mosquitoes buzzing around his head, labeled:] Jersey eagles. **1931** *Atlantic City Press* 3 Aug. *(DA)*, Has the Mosquito Commission gone on a strike, or are the 'Jersey Birds' breeding so fast they can't cope with them? **1950** *WELS* **WI** (*Nicknames for a mosquito . . [or] for an extra big mosquito*) 5 Infs, Jersey mosquito; 1 Inf, Jersey bomber; 1 Inf, Jersey skeeter; 2 Infs, New Jersey mosquito; 1 Inf, New Jersey. **1965–70** *DARE* (Qu. R15b, . . *An extra-big mosquito*) 34 Infs, chiefly **NEast,** Jersey mosquito; 23 Infs, chiefly **NEast,** Jersey bomber; 13 Infs, chiefly **NEast,** Jersey skeeter; 11 Infs, chiefly **NEast,** Jersey; **NJ**31, Jersey robin; **RI**12, Jersey skeeto; **PA**44, Jersies; **CA**65, **CT**23, **MA**74, **NY**233, New Jersey mosquito; **CA**41, New Jersey one; **MI**109, Joisy mosquito. **1972** Swan–Papp *Insects* 592, *Salt-marsh mosquito: Aedes sollicitans*. . . This is the notorious "New Jersey mosquito." . . Fierce biters and strong fliers, they . . attack in full sunlight.

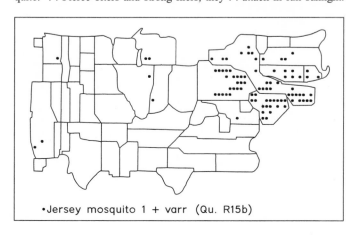

•Jersey mosquito 1 + varr (Qu. R15b)

2 A children's game; see quot.

1960 Korson *Black Rock* 325 **cePA,** [He] recalled memories of his youth in Trevorton, when "Jersey Mosquito" was played there. "In Jersey Mosquito," he explained, "you pick your intended victim, take him into a room, turn out the light, and then give him the works. Now the 'works' may mean pushing him around or slapping him, but did not go so far as bruising him or breaking any bones."

Jersey pine n Also *New Jersey pine* [See quot 1832]

A **pine** (here: *Pinus virginiana*) with short needles, native to the eastern US. Also called **cedar pine 2, jack ~ 2a, nigger ~ 1, poverty ~, river ~, scrub ~, shortleaf ~, shortshat ~, shortshucks, spruce pine, Virginia ~**

1743 (1946) Gronovius *Flora Virginica* 190, Pinus Virginiana. . . *The common Yersay-Pine.* **1785** Marshall *Arbustrum* 102, *Jersey Pine.* This is generally of but low growth, but divided into many branches. **1832** Browne *Sylva* 234, *New Jersey Pine.* . . The Jersey Pine has probably been so named from its abounding in the lower part of New Jersey, where the soil is meagre and sandy. **1860** Curtis *Cat. Plants NC* 20, *Jersey Pine.* . . is too small, often crooked, and generally with too much sap-wood, to be of any value. **1908** Britton *N. Amer. Trees* 46, *Jersey Pine.* . . grows . . from southern New York to Indiana, southward to Georgia and Alabama. *Ibid* 47, It is also called by many other names, as . . New Jersey pine. **1979** Little *Checklist U.S. Trees* 199, *Virginia pine.* . . *Other common names*—scrub pine, Jersey pine.

Jersey robin See **Jersey mosquito 1**

Jersey tea n [See quot 1863]
=**New Jersey tea.**

1808 in 1930 Dunbar *Life* 203 **sePA,** Red Root or Jersey Tea we call the Ceanothus. americanus a little shrub with white Flowers, cordate leaves—Some times the sanguinaria is called so. **1864** Acad. Nat. Sci. Philadelphia *Proc. for 1863* 276, No botanist will ever . . unfold the leaves of the American tea, without easily recognizing . . *Ceanothus Americanus,*—very common in our woods, and popularly known by the name of *Jersey tea,* under which it was used during the Revolutionary War. **1870** *Amer. Naturalist* 4.583 **nIL, IA,** The *Ceanothus,* or Jersey tea, is a frequent inhabitant of the prairies. **1939** FWP *Guide NJ* 19, Jersey-tea, a shrub with plumy white flowers seen in dry open woodlands and along gravel banks (used by Colonial housewives as a substitute during the British boycott). **1942** Tehon *Fieldbook IL Shrubs* 181, *Ceanothus.* . . *The Jersey-Teas. Ibid* 182, *Ceanothus americanus.* . . The Jersey-Tea prefers dry situations and often is found on slopes with black oak, as well as occasionally in prairie regions. *Ibid* 184, *Ceanothus ovatus.* . . *Inland Jersey-Tea.* . . The fruit matures in autumn and is similar to that of the Jersey-Tea. **1965** *Native Plants PA* 57, Ceanothus americanus. Jersey-tea.

Jersey wagon n Also *Jersey old-fash* Cf **dearborn**
A light horse- or mule-drawn wagon.

[**1778** *Boston Gaz.* 25 Aug. 373 *(OEDS),* Handy, light, Jersey made waggon.] **1818** Hall *Travels* 206, At Queenston I commenced a new, and infinitely more convenient mode of travelling, viz. in my own carriage; this being a light Jersey waggon, (a machine I have already described, by the name of a Dearborn). **1834** Simms *Guy Rivers* 2.308 **nGA,** A small *Jersey*—a light waggon in free use in that section. **1843** (1916) Hall *New Purchase* 163 **IN,** Meanwhile uncle John carried in brush enough to make a Jersey load of oven faggots. **1883** Johnston *Dukesborough Tales* 83 (Zeigler *Lexicon Middle GA*), A Jersey wagon, drawn by horses reeking with sweat, drove rapidly to the church. **1916** DN 4.343 **MD,** *Jersey wagon.* A 'spring wagon' with a top. **1935** Truett *Trade & Travel* 133 **sAppalachians** (as of c1820), Another type, similar to the heavy wagon, in that it was used to transfer goods, was the little Jersey wagon. This wagon was much lighter in construction than the Conestoga and was suitable primarily for local traveling. . . The Jersey wagon was sometimes called a "dearborn" and other times a "carry all." **1961** Eggenhofer *Wagons* 130, A Jersey wagon. . . had roll-up side curtains . . an open seat for the driver in front, with an outside footboard. . . drawn by either two or four animals. . . used well into the twentieth century. **1965–70** DARE (Qu. L13, *The kind of wagon used for carrying hay*) Inf **GA28,** Jersey ['jɛzɪ] wagon—old-fashioned—one mule; (Qu. N41a, . . *Horse-drawn vehicles . . to carry people*) Inf **FL17,** Jersey wagon; (Qu. N41c, *Horse-drawn vehicles to carry light loads*) Infs **FL17, NJ16, 56, SC40, VA87,** Jersey wagon. [5 of 6 total Infs old]

Jerusalem n Pronc-spp *Jeerus(a)lem, Jerewsalem* [The Biblical name used as a euphem for *Jesus*]
Used in exclams and mild oaths; see quots.

1840 *Spirit of Times* 8 Aug. 276/2 *(OEDS),* By Jerusalem! **1862** Newell *Orpheus C. Kerr* 234 **TX,** Jerewsalem crickets! I'm like a fellow jist out of a feather bed. **1888** [see **Jemima**]. **1891** Cooke *Huckleberries* 44, Oh, Jeerus'lem! **1903** DN 2.298 **Cape Cod MA** (as of a1857), *Jerusalem crickets! Jerusalem cherry tree!* . . 'Jerusalem crickets, isn't it cold!' **1905** DN 3.62 **eNE,** Je ru salem, Jerusalem crickets, Jerusalem June-bugs. . . Pronounced with strong stress on both first and second syllables. "Jerusalem June-bugs! You'll not get me to believe that." **1906** DN 3.143 **nwAR,** Jerusalem [jɪˈruzələm] [jɪrusəˈlɛm], *interj.* It is interesting to note that the *s* in this word is voiced when the principal accent immediately precedes, but voiceless when the principal stress is on the ultimate. **1908** DN 3.324 **eAL, wGA,** Jerusalem crickets. **1950** WELS **WI** (*Exclamations beginning with the sound of 'j'*) 3 Infs, Jerusalem; 2 Infs, Jumping Jerusalem; (*Exclamations of joy*) 1 Inf, Jerusalem. **1959** VT Hist. 27.139, Great Jerusalem! . . Rare. **1965–70** DARE (Qu. NN30) 19 Infs, **scattered,** Jerusalem; **AR52,** [jɪˈruzələm]; **DE3,** [ˌjɪˈruzələm]; **IL7, MA11,** Jeerusalem; **NY219,** [ˈjɪˌrusələm]; 14 Infs, **scattered,** Jumping Jerusalem; **FL6,** Great Jerusalem; (Qu. NN7, *Exclamations of surprise*) Inf **VA21,** Oh, Jerusalem; (Qu. NN26b, *Weakened substitutes for 'hell':* "Go to _____!") Inf **WI26,** Jerusalem; (Qu. NN29a, *Exclamations beginning with 'great':* "Great _____!") Inf **AR55,** Jerusalem; (Qu. NN31, *Exclamations beginning with the sound of 'cr-'*) Inf **MA6,** Christopher Jerusalem.

Jerusalem artichoke n [*OED* 1620 →; ult folk-etym for Ital *girasole*] Cf **artichoke pickle, artichoke relish**
An American **sunflower** (*Helianthus tuberosus*) cultivated for its edible tuber; the tuber itself. Also called **fishweed 2, ground artichoke, groundnut B3, Indian potato b, pignut.** Cf **artichoke potato, choke-tater, Jerusalem root**

1705 Beverley *Hist. VA* 4.57, The poorer Sort brew their Beer with . . *Jerusalem Artichoke,* which some People plant purposely for that use. **1792** Pope *Tour U.S.* 8 **VA,** I observed about an Acre of Ground well beset with *Jerusalem* Artichokes. . . To this Vegetable, Swine and horned Cattle of every Description, particularly Sheep, are surprisingly attached. **1814** in 1815 Lit. & Philos. Soc. NY *Trans.* 1.163, The Jerusalem artichoke, or helianthus tuberosus, grows spontaneously over the country, is sometimes brought to our markets for sale, and is a wholesome, agreeable vegetable. **1912** Blatchley *IN Weed Book* 173, The Jerusalem artichoke. . . in many places . . grows rankly as a weed. **1943** Fernald-Kinsey *Edible Wild Plants E. N. Amer.* 357, The *Jerusalem Artichoke* . . is indigenous in the central part of North America and was cultivated by the Indians who introduced it to the Europeans. **1965–70** DARE (Qu. I4, . . *Vegetables . . less commonly grown around here*) 36 Infs, **scattered,** Jerusalem artichoke. **1970** Kirk *Wild Edible Plants W. U.S.* 133, Jerusalem Artichoke.

Jerusalem artichoke relish See **artichoke relish**

Jerusalem bean n
Prob =**Job's tears 1.**

c1938 in 1970 Hyatt *Hoodoo* 2.934 **VA,** [In ref to objects used in conjuration:] "What's that round thing?" . . "That's a Jerusalem bean. That's for luck in gambling."

Jerusalem brush weed See **Jerusalem weed**

Jerusalem candy n Cf **Jerusalem tea**
A sweet made from **Jerusalem oak 1** and used as a vermifuge.

[**1869** see **Jerusalem oak 1.**] **c1937** in 1970 Yetman *Voices* 39 **AL** [Black], Dey made Jerusalem candy full ob seeds and gib ter de chillun' ter eat so dey cud git rid ob de worms. [**1968** Foxfire Spring 14 **GA,** For worms. . . Mix Jerusalem Oak seeds with any kind of syrup to make a candy. Feed this to the afflicted person.]

Jerusalem cherry n

1 A **nightshade 1** (here: *Solanum pseudo-capsicum* or *S. capsicastrum*) cultivated for the beauty of the inedible red berries.

1788 (1888) Cutler *Life* 1.428 **sePA,** Landlady gave me Jerusalem cherries, and Vandaver's Apple, fine summer Sweetings. [DARE Ed: This may instead refer to **2** below.] **1840** MA Zool. & Bot. Surv. *Herb. Plants & Quadrupeds* 167, *S[olanum] pseudo-capsicum.* . . Jerusalem Cherry. . . A small ornamental shrub, beautiful in form and color, and bearing a few large cherry-looking berries. **1881** Vanderbilt *Social Flatbush* 290 **seNY,** There were other plants which were transplanted to the garden after being sheltered during the winter, such as . . Cape jessamine, a glossy-leaved plant bearing a bright-red fruit known as "Jerusalem cherry," and wax-plant. **1941** *Yankee* Dec. 33/2 *(DA),* Jerusalem cherries and Christmas peppers, old-fashioned favorites are very intolerant of illuminating and coal gas. **1969** *Oregonian* (Portland OR) 14 Dec mag sec 19/3, Christmas potted plants are just as important a part of the scene. Poinsettias, cyclamens, chrysanthemums, Christmas peppers, Jerusalem cherries, . . and others are among them. **1970** GA Dept. Ag. *Farmers Market Bulletin* 16 Dec 8/1 **GA,** Jerusalem cherry—Solanum Pseudo-capsicum, also called Christmas cherry, is a small shrubby relative of the egg-plant, potato and bittersweet. . . The berries of some species are thought to be deadly poisonous while in others they are edible. **1976** Bailey–Bailey *Hortus Third* 1055, *Jerusalem cherry.* . . Pot plant, popular for showy fr[uit], which is poisonous if eaten. **1994** Stone–Pratt *Hawai'i's Plants* 259, Jerusalem cherry has been in the [Hawaii Volcanoes National] Park more than 50 years and was probably spread by fruit-eating birds from nearby ornamental plantings.

2 =ground-cherry.

1933 Small *Manual SE Flora* 1107, *Physalis.* . . Berry globular, enclosed in the papery calyx. . . *Jerusalem-cherries.*

Jerusalem corn n

A **sorghum** (here: *Sorghum bicolor*).

1894 Coulter *Botany W. TX* 494, S[orghum] *vulgare* is widely introduced in cultivation. This species includes the many varieties cultivated as . . Jerusalem corn, and broom corn. **1911** *Century Dict. Suppl.,* *Kafir-corn.* . . Some varieties . . are adapted for use as forage; others, particularly that known as *Jerusalem-corn,* furnish grain. **1933** Small *Manual SE Flora* 47, *H[olcus] Sorghum.* . . *Jerusalem-corn.* . . Its sweet juice . . is made into sirup.

Jerusalem cricket n

A **grasshopper 1** (here: *Stenopelmatus fuscus*) native to much of the western US. Also called **potato bug, sand cricket** Cf **man-faced spider**

1905 Kellogg *Amer. Insects* 157, On the Pacific Coast occurs a large, awkward, thick-legged, transversely striped form . . called . . Jerusalem cricket. . . It . . has a large, smooth head with "baby-face." **1947** *Desert Mag.* Jan. 22/3 *(DA),* It appears that the Babyface is actually our old friend the yellow-and-black striped Jerusalem-cricket or sand-cricket. **1968** Abbey *Desert Solitaire* 31 **seUT,** Watch out for . . Jerusalem crickets. **1980** Milne–Milne *Audubon Field Guide Insects* 437, *Jerusalem Cricket.* . . Humpbacked. Very long antennae. Shiny amber-brown with darker brown crossbands on abdomen. Wingless. Head large with wide space between small compound eyes and jaws. **1986** *Yankee* May 163 **swCA,** Stepping on a "potato bug," or Jerusalem cricket as they are also known, is quite an experience while going from bedroom to bathroom in the middle of the night.

Jerusalem, going to n

1 also *marching to Jerusalem, walking ~, journey ~, going to Bethlehem,* and varr: **=musical chairs. scattered, but esp NEast; infreq West** See Map

1899 Champlin–Bostwick *Young Folks' Games* 375, Going to Jerusalem, a game in which the players sit at first in two rows of chairs placed closely back to back in the middle of a room. . . As soon as the music begins, all rise and march in line around the chairs. While they are marching, some one . . takes away one chair from the end of the line. The music stops suddenly, and all who can do so, sit down. Of course one player is left standing, . . and that player is out of the game. The music begins again . . a new chair being taken away each time until only one player is left. He is said to "get to Jerusalem." **1950** *WELS* **WI** *(Games with an extra player: At a signal the other players change places, and the extra tries to get a place)* 7 Infs, Going to Jerusalem; 3 Infs, Marching to Jerusalem. **1953** Brewster *Amer. Nonsinging Games* 98 **IN,** *Marching to Jerusalem.* . . All the players but one are seated in chairs. . . While someone plays the piano, the leader, carrying a cane, walks around the row of seated players, saying, "I'm going to Jerusalem." Every few minutes he stops in front of one of the other players and taps his cane upon the floor. This player immediately rises and follows him. This continues until all are marching. Then the music suddenly stops, and all scramble for seats. The one who fails to get a chair drops out of the game, and one chair is taken from the row. The game goes on until only one player is left, who becomes leader for the next game. **1957** *Sat. Eve. Post Letters* **swIN** (as of c1900), At parties and indoor socials we played a musical game we called "Going To Jerusalem" . . but now I understand the same game is called Musical Chairs. *Ibid* **ceWI** (as of 1890s), Going to Jerusalem (Musical Chairs). **c1960** *Wilson Coll.* **csKY,** *Going to Jerusalem* . . an indoor group game. **1965–70** *DARE* (Qu. EE2) 89 Infs, **scattered, but esp NEast,** Going to Jerusalem; **GA**19, 33, **MA**11, **NY**88, **NC**23, Marching to Jerusalem;

MI103, Marching around Jerusalem; **AR**3, Walking to Jerusalem; **CT**16, Journey to Jerusalem; **MI**81, Jerusalem chairs; **WA**6, Jerusalem; **PA**16, Going to Bethlehem.

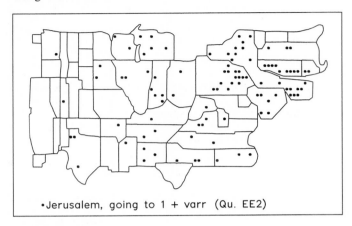

•Jerusalem, going to 1 + varr (Qu. EE2)

2 =go-to-mill.

1968 *DARE* (Qu. EE39) Inf **KS**7, Going to Jerusalem. Draw two parallel lines for each individual and then box it off. You put in diagonal lines to show how far a person has travelled. In order to travel you must guess which hand the other player is holding an object in; (Qu. EE40, . . *Table games . . using dice*) Inf **IL**47, Going to Jerusalem [Inf doubtful].

Jerusalem haddock n

=opah.

1889 *Century Dict.* 2677, *Jerusalem haddock,* the opah, or king of the herrings. **1896** U.S. Natl. Museum *Bulletin* 47.954, *Opah . . Jerusalem Haddock.* . . One of the choicest of fishes, the flesh rich, firm, and of delicate flavor. **1902** Jordan–Evermann *Amer. Fishes* 326, The opah. . . is called . . Jerusalem haddock. . . It is a fish of most gorgeous colouration.

Jerusalem huckleberry n

=box huckleberry.

1933 Small *Manual SE Flora* 1010, *Gaylussacia brachycera.* . . *Jerusalem-huckleberry.* . . Where abundant the berries are made into a preserve. **1991** *Sentinel* (Carlisle PA) 3 July sec D 1 **swPA,** The box huckleberry, known locally as . . Jerusalem huckleberry, is sometimes confused with the blueberry because of its fruit.

Jerusalem oak n

1 also *oak (of) Jerusalem:* Either of two **goosefoots:** *Chenopodium botrys* or *C. ambrosioides.* **widespread, but esp freq Sth** Also called **ambrosia 1, drizzle oak, droozly-make, Jerusalem tea, Jerusalem weed, Jesuit tea, jewsly moke, wormseed.** For other names of *C. ambrosioides* see **fishweed 1, Jerusalem parsley, Mexican tea 1, pigweed, sowbane, Spanish tea, stickweed, stinkweed, terrywuk;** for other names of *C. botrys* see **feather geranium, hind-heal 1, turnpike geranium** Cf **Jerusalem candy**

1672 Josselyn *New-Englands Rarities* 178, Oak of Hierusalem for . . colds . . and the ptisick. **1759** in 1910 Commons *Doc. Hist. Amer. Industrial Soc.* 1.109 **VA,** The Breeding wenches [=slaves] more particularly you must Instruct the Overseers to be Kind and Indulgent to. . . Give them, every Spring & Fall the Jerusalem Oak seed for a week together. **1775** (1962) Romans *Nat. Hist. FL* 254, The stincking weed which is known by the name of Jerusalem Oak, and in those provinces is the most efficacious vermifuge, and the safest medicine especially for children. **1817** Eaton *Botany* 30, *Chenopodium botrys* (oak-of-Jerusalem . .) leaves sinuate-pinnatifid. **1869** Porcher *Resources* 399 **Sth,** *Jerusalem Oak . . (Chenopodium anthelminticum . .).* It is well known as "one of our most efficient indigenous anthelmintics," adapted to the expulsion of lumbrici in children. . . These plants are much employed on the plantations in South Carolina and Georgia for their anthelmintic properties, the seeds being collected in the fall. *Ibid* 400, *Jerusalem Oak of some, (Chenopodium botrys . .).* The expressed juice of this species is given in doses of a tablespoonful, in molasses, to children affected with worms, or the seeds are reduced to a powder, and made into an electuary with syrup. **c1873** in 1976 Miller *Shaker Herbs* 255, *Chenopodium ambrosioides.* Oak Jerusalem Seed. Goose-Foot. Valuable to expel worms from children. **1894** Coulter *Botany W. TX* 368, *C[henopodium]*

Botrys. . . Jerusalem oak. . . Across the continent, but not common in the West. **1937** in 1977 *Amer. Slave Suppl. 1* 1.174 **AL,** Mah man also used Jerusalem Oak seed, for worms. **1960** Criswell *Resp. to PADS 20* **Ozarks,** Jerusalem oak—common, bitter, tough barnyard weed which ruins the taste of cow's milk. **1966–68** *DARE* (Qu. S21, . . *Weeds . . that are a trouble in gardens and fields*) Infs **FL7, GA35, NC27, SC43,** Jerusalem oak; **NC81,** Oak of Jerusalem. **1968** *Foxfire* Spring 14 **GA,** For worms. . . Mix Jerusalem Oak seeds with any kind of syrup to make a candy. Feed this to the afflicted person. **1986** Pederson *LAGS Concordance,* 1 inf, **cnGA,** Jerusalem oak—for roundworm tonic; grows by barn; 1 inf, **nwMS,** Jerusalem oak—provided worm remedy for children; 1 inf, **cwAR,** Jerusalem oak—weed; 1 inf, **cwLA,** Jerusalem oak—seed used for medicine; 1 inf, **cnLA,** Jerusalem-oak weed—in yard; root used for worms.

2 A **mountain misery 1** (here: *Chamaebatia foliosa*).

1925 Jepson *Manual Plants CA* 500, C[hamaebatia] foliosa. . . Mountain Misery. . . Also called . . Jerusalem Oak.

Jerusalem parsley n

A **Jerusalem oak 1** (here: *Chenopodium ambrosioides*).

1974 Morton *Folk Remedies* 43 **SC,** Jerusalem Parsley. . . Chenopodium ambrosioides. . . Leaves alternate, . . more or less irregularly lobed and toothed.

Jerusalem root n

The root of the **Jerusalem artichoke.**

1970 Hyatt *Hoodoo* 1.244 **ceNC** (as of c1935), Anothah certin sort of a *root* dey call *Jerusalem root.* **1970** Anderson *TX Folk Med.* 73 **csTX,** Teething. . . Cut up some Jerusalem root [Anderson: Jerusalem artichoke, a perennial American sunflower] and put it on a string around the neck.

Jerusalem star n [See quot 1914]

A **goatsbeard 1** (here: *Tragopogon porrifolius*).

1876 Hobbs *Bot. Hdbk.* 60, Jerusalem star, Vegetable oyster, Tragopogon porrifolia [sic]. **1914** Georgia *Manual Weeds* 533, *Tragopogon porrifolius. . .* The heads . . are purple, often three inches broad, the long, green points of the involucral bracts extending for about half their length beyond the rays, making an eight- to ten-pointed green star with a purple center, whence the name "Jerusalem Star." **1935** (1943) Muenscher *Weeds* 523, Jerusalem star. . . Widespread throughout the United States and eastern Canada; locally common.

Jerusalem tea n

A **Jerusalem oak 1,** usu *Chenopodium ambrosioides*.

c1873 in 1976 Miller *Shaker Herbs* 211, Oak of Jerusalem. Chenopodium botrys and Chenopodium anthelminticum. . . Jerusalem Tea. **1914** Georgia *Manual Weeds* 108, Chenopodium ambrosioides. . . Jerusalem Tea. . . A strong-scented, unpleasant weed, rejected by all grazing animals, even goats. **1935** (1943) Muenscher *Weeds* 206, Chenopodium ambrosioides. . . Jerusalem-tea. . . Grown in Maryland and South Dakota for the volatile oil which is distilled from the tops of the plant. **1971** Krochmal *Appalachia Med. Plants* 86, Chenopodium ambrosioides. . . Common names . . Jerusalem tea. . . Used as an infusion. **1974** Morton *Folk Remedies* 43 **SC,** Jerusalem tea. . . Chenopodium ambrosioides. . . Plant juice or infusion valued as a vermifuge for children. . . Some people beat the leaves in a cup until juicy, add milk, strain, and give the liquid daily to expel worms.

Jerusalem thorn n

A **paloverde:** usu *Parkinsonia aculeata.* [*DJE* 1756 →] For other names of this species see **horsebean 2, retama**

1897 Sudworth *Arborescent Flora* 255, Parkinsonia microphylla . . Common Names. . . Jerusalem Thorn. **1900** Lyons *Plant Names* 275, Parkinsonia. . . Jerusalem Thorn. . . Bark febrifuge. **1931** U.S. Dept. Ag. *Misc. Pub.* 101.79, Jerusalem-thorn (P. aculeata) . . ranges from Florida to California and south into South America, and is frequently cultivated in border towns. **1949** Curtin *By the Prophet* 90 **AZ,** Cercidium floridum. . . Jerusalem Thorn. . . When covered with yellow blossoms it is highly decorative. **1990** *Seed Savers Yearbook* 269, Jerusalem Thorn. . . Parkinsonia aculeata, legume, long-drooping mesquite-like foliage, golden blossoms, bee plant, thorns, determined survivor of city ills and desertification, gathered seed in '88 on vacant lot in Brady Texas and farm near Pear Valley Texas.

Jerusalem weed n Also *Jerusalem brush weed, old Jerusalem weed*

=**Jerusalem oak 1.**

c1937 in 1970 Yetman *Voices* 57 **AL** [Black], Dey only had homemade medicines. . . Jerusalem brush weed to get rid of worms. **1968–70** *DARE* (Qu. S21, . . *Weeds . . that are a trouble in gardens and fields*) Infs **FL48, SC3,** Jerusalem weed; **NC80,** Old Jerusalem weed; (Qu. BB50d, *Favorite spring tonics*) Inf **SC40,** Jerusalem weed.

Jerusely-moke See jewsly moke

Jerush(e)y intj [Pronc-spp for the Biblical name *Jerusha* used as euphems for *Jesus;* cf Intro "Language Changes" IV.1.b, -y] Also in comb *Jerushey mighty:* Used as a mild oath.

1864 (1868) Trowbridge *3 Scouts* 23 **TN,** Bime-by I got mad. 'Jerushey mighty, Tildy!' says I. **1908** Lincoln *Cy Whittaker* 25 **eMA,** "Jerushy!" he exclaimed.

jes(s) See just 1b

jessamine See jasmine

jessamy wine See jasmine 2a

jesse n Also *jessie, jessy* [Cf Isaiah 11:1]

1 rarely *hesse:* A punishment, scolding; a bad or painful time—used esp in phr *give one jesse.* Cf **gowdy, hissy**

1839 *Spirit of Times* 19 Oct 396/3 **NY,** If I thought he had been shot and creesed in that savigerous sorta fashion, I'd give him jessy with my butcher knife. **1847** (1962) Robb *Squatter Life* 59 *(DAE),* The afarr [affair] raised jessy in Nettle Bottom. **1859** Vielé *Following* 172 **sTX,** General Harney . . had come down from Northern Texas, to administer *"jesse"* generally to all delinquents. **1863** *Rocky Mountain News,* Denver, April 2 (1912 Thornton *Amer. Gloss.*), Wherever we go [after vaccination] we are sure to catch jesse on our sore arm. **1899** (1912) Green *VA Folk-Speech* 244, To give one Jesse, to give one a good scolding or dressing; punish one severely. **1907** *DN* 3.244 **eME,** Give one Hes-se. . . To reprimand sternly. **1930** Shoemaker *1300 Words* 34 **cPA Mts** (as of c1900), Jesse—To give a person a severe scolding, "give her jesse". **1939** Aurand *Quaint Idioms* 24 [PaGer], The girl came home late at night and got *jesse* (a severe scolding; literally "hell"). **1944** *ADD* **cwWV** (?as of 1890), 'My arm is just givin' me Jessie' = paining greatly. **1949** *PADS* 11.14 **wTX,** To give one Jessie. (To curse one; to tell one how bad he is.) **1952** Brown *NC Folkl.* 1.431, Give him Jessy (punish). **1991** Heat Moon *PrairyErth* 510 **ceKS,** Not long ago I received a letter from a stranger who gave me jessie for several failures in my writing.

2 in phr *go jesse:* To be energetic or skillful; to go great guns. Note: The phr *a going jesse* has also been understood as a n phr; see quot c1970.

c1950 *Halpert Coll.* 34 **wKY, nwTN,** He's a goin' Jessie. . . Cf. the term "a going concern" for a successful business. **1967–70** *DARE* (Qu. HH27a, *A very able and energetic person who gets things done*) Inf **TX80,** Goin' jesse; (Qu. KK5, *A very skilled or expert person—for example, at woodworking: "He's a _____."*) Inf **TX19,** Goin' jessie; (Qu. KK27, *A very lively, active old person: "For his age, he's _____."*) Inf **IL115,** Goin' jessie. **1968** *DARE* FW Addit **cAR,** Going jessie: an ameliorative term for an automobile that runs well, especially smooth and fast. "Boy, she's a going jessie, ain't she?" **1970** *DARE* Tape **IL115,** He married a 60-year-old lady . . he's eighty years old, never had a sick day in his life, he's really goin' jesse.

3 See quot.

1968 *DARE* (Qu. KK49, *When you don't have the time or ambition to do something thoroughly: "I'm not going to give the place a real cleaning, I'll just _____."*) Inf **PA173,** Give it a jesse.

4 A critter, varmint, or disagreeable person.

1933 Rawlings *South Moon* 29 **nFL,** Them fightin' jessies come jest to stir up a ruckus. *Ibid* 123, He was sure they would be fox-squirrels. "They're piney-woods jessies," he told his cousin. **1938** Rawlings *Yearling* 223 **nFL,** Them ocean jessies don't belong to be crossin' Floridy. *Ibid* 286, I had me a good go-round with them jessies [=disagreeable neighbors].

jess-ellif n

=**hog sucker.**

1929 *AmSp* 5.19 **Ozarks,** Jess-ellif. . . A fish, also known as the *hog-molly* or *hog-sucker.* It is said that the name was originally used in derision of a man named Ellif, supposed to have resembled this fish in appearance or habits. It is now used by many people who have no notion of its origin.

jessie, jessy See jesse

jest See **just 1a**

jester n [Prob aphet for *digester;* cf *OED* digester sb. 4, *DJE* digester, jesta]

    1966 *DARE* FW Addit **SC,** *Jester* [jĕstə]—a small pot used when people cooked in the chimney; **SC,** *Jester* [jĕstə]—like a small washpot, usually for rice; same as a skillet but bigger—built just alike.

jestes, jestice, jestiss, jestuss See **justice**

Jesuit's bark n Also *(bastard) Jesuit bark, false ~* [From its resemblance in appearance or medicinal properties to *Jesuit's bark* cinchona bark]

A **marsh elder 1** (here: *Iva frutescens*).

    1830 Rafinesque *Med. Flora* 2.233, *Iva frutescens. . . Bastard Jesuit bark. . .* Bark smelling like Elder flowers, tonic, eq[uivalent] of *Sambucus.* Leaves fragrant, may be pickled. **1894** *Jrl. Amer. Folkl.* 7.92 **NY,** *Iva frutescens, . .* Jesuit's bark. **1960** Vines *Trees SW* 997, *Iva frutescens. . .* Vernacular names are . . Jesuit Bark, and False Jesuit Bark.

Jesuit tea n

A **Jerusalem oak 1,** usu *Chenopodium ambrosioides.*

    c**1873** in 1976 Miller *Shaker Herbs* 211, *Oak of Jerusalem. Chenopodium botrys* and *Chenopodium anthelminticum. . .* Jesuit Tea. **1914** Georgia *Manual Weeds* 108, *Chenopodium ambrosioides. . .* Jesuit Tea. . . A strong-scented, unpleasant weed, rejected by all grazing animals, even goats. **1974** (1977) Coon *Useful Plants* 95, *Chenopodium ambrosioides* var. *anthelminticum . . .* Jesuit tea. . . In our Southwest a tea is made of the leaves to encourage milk flow and to relieve post-delivery pains. Although from the South, it has spread widely in the states.

Jesus bug n [In allusion to Matthew 14:25]

A **water strider** (family Gerridae).

    1945 *Amer. Mercury* 60.621, In areas of unsubdued Christian idiom, a popular name has long attached to the curious insects called *Gerridae.* Because of their eerie ease in walking on the water, the people call them Jesus-bugs. **1949** Palmer *Nat. Hist.* 392, *Water Strider, Jesus Bug. Gerris* sp. . . On surface of fresh or salt water, often crowded together in flocks. **1967** Williams *Greenbones* 21 **GA** (as of c1910), Two-Hearted Pond, where yellow spatterdock bloomed and Jesus-bugs walked the water. **1967** *DARE* (Qu. R28) Inf **TN**22, Jesus bug—walks on water. **1980** Milne–Milne *Audubon Field Guide Insects* 469, These insects [=*Gerris remigis*] are called "Jesus Bugs" in Texas because they "walk" on the water. **1988** Kingsolver *Bean Trees* 2 **KY,** You could . . watch the Jesus bugs walk on the water, their four little feet making dents in the surface but never falling through.

Jesus Christ bird n [In allusion to Matthew 14:25] Cf **bonnet walker, Jesus bug**

The jacana *(Jacana spinosa).*

    1923 U.S. Dept. Ag. *Misc. Circular* 73 **TX,** *Jacana spinosa. . . Vernacular Names:* Jacana, Jesus Christ bird. [**1951** Pough *Audubon Water Bird* 207, *Jaçana. . .* These curious birds live and nest on the open blanket of water lettuce and other floating plants that often completely cover small ponds, lakes, and old river channels. . . Their extraordinarily long toes enable them to run over the leaves to catch the insects and other small animals that appear to be their chief food.]

Jesus H. Christ n For varr see quots [Prob joc interpretation of *IHC,* var of *IHS,* monogram for *Jesus*]

Used in exclams or oaths.

    a1910 (1924) Twain *Autobiog.* 2.282 **MO** (as of c1850), In that day the common swearers of the region had a way of their own of *emphasizing* the Saviour's name when they were using it profanely, and this fact intruded itself into Wales's incorrigible mind. . . He enlarged the offending J.C. into Jesus H. Christ. **1924** *DN* 5.264 [Exclams], Oh Jesus Christ, Jesus H. Christ, holy jumping Jesus Christ. **1927** (1955) Faulkner *Mosquitoes* 202 **New Orleans LA,** Jesus H, if I ever get out of this alive. **1936** (1947) Mencken *Amer. Lang.* 316, The insertion of infixes into *Jesus Christ* also seems to be an American invention. The common form is *Jesus H. Christ,* but for special emphasis *Jesus H. Particular Christ.* **1938** (1939) Holbrook *Holy Mackinaw* 7 **ME,** He never used . . vulgar and shopworn phrases like "blue-eyed, bandy-legged, jumped-up ol' whistlin' Jesus H. Mackinaw Christ." **1951** *PADS* 15.58 **neIN** (as of 1890s), *Oaths:* Holy smoke; Jesus H. Christ. **1969** *DARE* (Qu. NN30, *Exclamations beginning with the sound of 'j'*) Inf **IL**97, Jesus H. Christ. **1994** *AmSp* 69.332, Occasionally, men (always men, in my experience) swear with an *H* in *Jesus Christ* to give it extra heft and punch, sometimes drawing it out yet more with *Jesus Henry Christ.*

    1995 *DARE* File (as of c1960) **Milwaukee WI,** My father, when an oath was required, would sometimes shout, "Jesus H. Christ!" If more was needed, he would yell, "Jesus H. Cockeyed Christ!" Even more ornate versions were sometimes used.

jesusly adv Cf **jeezly**

Extremely, very.

    1935 Davis *Honey* 28 **OR,** It was jesusly hard work, waist-deep in mud.

Jesus to Jesus and four hands round intj Also *Jesus to Jesus and eight hands around*

See quot 1975.

    1968 *DARE* (Qu. NN30, *Exclamations beginning with the sound of 'j'*) Inf **AK**5, Jesus to Jesus and four hands round. **1975** Gould *ME Lingo* 146, *Jesus to Jesus and eight hands around!* An exclamation of complete astonishment and utter disbelief; sometimes sheer exuberance. Probably an enthusiastic imitation of a square-dance call, although some say it was the way woodsmen described a very big tree—earth to heaven and eight reaches in circumference.

jet v, hence ppl adj *jetting* [Prob var of *jut* but cf *OED* jet v.[2] 1 "to project, protrude, jut. . . *Obs.*"]

To project or protrude prominently.

    1947 Santee *Apache Land* 4 **AZ,** Two Apache riders had been running a yearling the day before. . . We had dismounted for a smoke when, by accident, I saw what had happened to the yearling. Under a jetting rock was what had been inside the paunch. **1967–69** *DARE* (Qu. C13, *A piece of land that sticks out noticeably into a body of water*) Inf **AR**55, Where the land jets out; **NJ**28, Jet, jetty . . because it jets out; (Qu. X6, *If a person's lower jaw sticks out prominently*) Inf **VT**16, Chin jets out.

jet n [Cf *OED* jet sb.[3] 1 "A projection, protruding part. . . *Obs.*" and *jut* sb.[2] 1 "A . . protruding point"]

1 A piece of land projecting into a body of water.

    1967–68 *DARE* (Qu. C13, *A piece of land that sticks out noticeably into a body of water*) Inf **NJ**28, Jet, jetty—in lake, because it jets out; **OH**26, Jet—none here. **1969** *DARE* Tape **CA**154, Did you see the peninsula? A jet of rocks sticking out here and there?

2 See quot.

    1969 *DARE* (Qu. D28, *What hangs below the edge of the roof to carry off rain-water?*) Inf **RI**5, Jet.

jet-jawed adj [**jet** n]

Having a protruding jaw; jut-jawed.

    1968 *DARE* (Qu. X6, *If a person's lower jaw sticks out prominently . . he's _____*) Inf **OH**80, Jet-jawed.

jet-out n [**jet** v]

    1981 Pederson *LAGS Basic Materials,* 1 inf, **csAL,** A jet-out—a place on his old house that jutted out from the rest of the house.

jetting See **jet** v

jew See **due**

jewberry See **dewberry 1**

jewbird n [See quot 1921] Cf **Ikey n 3**

An ani (here: *Crotophaga ani* or *C. sulcirostris*).

    1916 in 1917 *DN* 4.426 **LA,** Groove-billed ani. . . Jew bird. **1917** (1923) *Birds Amer.* 2.125, Groove-billed Ani. . . Other Names. . . Jew Bird. **1921** LA Dept. of Conserv. *Bulletin* 10.97, Ani, or Jew-bird. . . They may be distinguished readily [from grackles] by their heavy aquiline bills. **1932** Howell *FL Bird Life* 290, Groove-billed Ani. . . Other Name: Jewbird.

Jew bread See **Jewish bread**

jewbush n [*OED* 1830 →]

A red-flowered succulent shrub *(Pedilanthus tithymaloides)* native to Florida. Also called **angel's slipper, devil's backbone, Jacob's ladder 9, Japanese poinsettia 2, Joseph's coat, niggermouth, redbird cactus, redbird flower, ribbon cactus, slipper plant, snow-on-the-mountain**

    1876 Hobbs *Bot. Hdbk.* 60, Jew bush, Pedilanthus tithymaloides. **1892** (1974) Millspaugh *Amer. Med. Plants* 147–3, Jew-bush . . is used in venereal complaints, amenorrhoea, and in lieu of Ipecacuanha. **1933** Small *Manual SE Flora* 804, Jew-bush. . . Hammocks and pinelands, Everglade Keys, pen[insular] Fla. and Florida Keys. . . Used medicinally. **1982** Perry–Hay *Field Guide Plants* 70, Jewbush. . . flowers mainly in summer, but intermittently throughout the year.

jew claw See **dewclaws**

jew duck n [From the prominent beaks]
1 A puffin (family Alcidae). Cf **ikey** n **3**
  1917 *Wilson Bulletin* 29.2.75, *Lunda cirrhata*. . . Jew duck (in recognition of the Semitic profile), Willapa Harbor, Wash. **1956** *AmSp* 30.185, Jew duck. . . Puffins. Alaska, North Pacific.
2 =**surf scoter.**
  1923 U.S. Dept. Ag. *Misc. Circular* 13.30 **OR,** Surf Scoter. . . Vernacular Names. . . In local use. . . Jew duck.
3 also *Jewish mallard:* =**shoveler.**
  1956 *AmSp* 30.185, Jew duck. Shoveler. Ill. . . Jewish mallard. Shoveler. N. Dak., La., Calif. From its prominent beak or 'nose'.

jewee See **jo-wheet**

jewel box n
1 A mollusk of the family Chamidae. For other names of *Chama arcana* see **rock oyster**
  1954 Abbott *Amer. Seashells* 392, *Chama macerophylla* . . Leafy Jewel Box. . . This is the most common and most brightly hued Atlantic species. *Ibid* 393, *Chama pellucida* . . Clear Jewel Box. **1981** Rehder *Audubon Field Guide Seashells* 728, Jewel Box Family (Chamidae). . . These shells are commonly found firmly cemented to rocks of reef flats, intertidally or in shallow water. . . The edges of the mantle lobes often have vividly colored projections. . . Kitchen middens contain many large jewel box shells, proof that . . they were used as food. **1981** Meinkoth *Audubon Field Guide Seashore* 554, *Arcinella cornuta*. . . This jewel box. . . begins as a swimming larva, settles and attaches to a solid object as the Leafy Jewel Box does, but later in life becomes free again.
2 A **burning bush 1** (here: *Euonymus americanus*).
  1937 Thornburgh *Gt. Smoky Mts.* 25, One of the showiest shrubs in the Great Smokies [is] . . wahoo or spindlebush. . . [It is] especially lovely in October when its seed-pod bursts open displaying orange-colored seeds in its glowing red heart. It has many descriptive local names . . catspaw, jewel-box.

jewel flower n
1 A **twist flower** (here: *Streptanthus glandulosus*).
  1901 Jepson *Flora CA* 182, *S[treptanthus] glandulosus* . . Jewel Flower. . . Petals purple, or white with conspicuous purple veins. **1961** Thomas *Flora Santa Cruz* 180 **cwCA,** *S. glandulosus* var. *glandulosus*. . . Common Jewel Flower. Rocky slopes. . . April–June.
2 See **jewelweed 1.**

jewelhead n Cf **eyestone 2, lucky stone**
=**freshwater drum.**
  1884 Goode *Fisheries U.S.* 1.370, The Fresh-water Drum. . . Another name used in the Southwest is "Jewel-head." **1903** [see **lucky stone**]. **1972** Sparano *Outdoors Encycl.* 369, Freshwater Drum. Common names . . jewelhead. . . The otoliths, or ear bones, of freshwater drum were used as wampum by Indians, as lucky pieces, and to prevent sicknesses.

jewelry n
In logging: see quots.
  1950 *Western Folkl.* 9.118 **nwOR** [Logger speech], *Jewelry.* The blocks, lines, hardware, and other material used in logging. **1958** McCulloch *Woods Words* 98 **Pacific NW,** *Jewelry*—a. Various kinds of fancy gadgets put on logging engines, supposed to save coal, make more steam at less cost, etc. b. Odds and ends of small logging gear, particularly a small block.

jewelry chest n Cf **jewelry, jockey box**
  1944 Adams *Western Words* 85, *Jewelry chest*—An outside box on the front of the chuck wagon in which were stored hobbles, extra cartridges, and anything else that might be needed in a hurry in an emergency.

jewelry rock n Also *jewelry(-store) ore*
See quots.
  1940 Writers' Program *Guide NV* 58, *Jewelry-store ore* and *jewelry-ore* mean about the same—exposures of rich ore beautiful in color and high in metal content. **1970** Wilhelm *Last Rig* 171 **West,** Dad never paid much attention to pioneer shacks, trails or relics that we found in our travels. What he wanted was to get to the next range of hills so he could look or dig a hole in the ground looking for jewelry rock. That's what they call ore that's chock-full of gold.

jewels-of-Opar n [Perh var of *Ophir* an ancient land rich in gold; cf 1 Kings 9:27-28]
A **fameflower** (here: *Talinum paniculatum*).
  1970 GA Dept. Ag. *Farmers Market Bulletin* 5 Aug, Jewels-of-Opar. **1976** Bailey–Bailey *Hortus Third* 1095, [Talinum] paniculatum. . . Jewels-of-Opar. . . Fl[ower]s red to yellowish, in a panicle to 10 in. long. S. U.S. . . A form with white-edged l[ea]v[e]s is a tub or pot plant.

jewel wasp n
=**cuckoo wasp.**
  1949 Swain *Insect Guide* 172, Cuckoo Wasps. . . These beautiful insects often are called "jewel wasps" because of the brilliant green, blue, red, or purple of their bodies.

jewelweed n
1 also *jewel flower:* A plant of the genus *Impatiens*. [See quot 1889] Also called **balsam 2, balsamweed 1, lady's slipper 2, quick-in-the-hand, slippers, snapweed, touch-me-not, waterweed, weathercock, wild celandine.** For other names of var spp see **ear jewel, kicking-colt, lady's eardrop 3, lady's pocket, policeman's helmet, shining grass, silverleaf, silverweed, slipperweed, snapdragon, speckled jewels**
  1817 Eaton *Botany* 28, *Impatiens*. . . *noli-me-tangere* (jewel weed) peduncles many-flowered. **1889** *Century Dict.* 3231, Jewel-weed. . . So called from the earring-like shape of the flowers, and the silver sheen of the under surface of the leaf in water. **1911** (1916) Porter *Harvester* 228 **IN,** Rank jewel flower poured gold from dainty cornucopias. **1937** Thornburgh *Gt. Smoky Mts.* 22, Flowers. . . most frequently encountered are . . turtlehead . . and jewelweed or wild touch-me-not, with its showy blossoms of lemon yellow or deep orange. **1965** *Bee* (Phillips WI) 19 Aug [3/3], There are still brown-eyed susans, and the jewel-weed (I call them) are yellow orange. **1965–70** *DARE* (Qu. S21, . . *Weeds . . that are a trouble in gardens and fields*) Inf **PA**89, Jewelweed; (Qu. S26b, *Wildflowers that grow in water or wet places*) Infs **NJ**45, **NC**36, **PA**169, **TN**11, Jewelweed; (Qu. S26c, *Wildflowers that grow in woods*) Inf **VA**52, Jewelweed; (Qu. S26d, *Wildflowers that grow in meadows; not asked in early QRs*) Infs **NC**36, **RI**15, Jewelweed; (Qu. BB51a, . . *Cures for corns or warts*) Inf **CT**3, Jewelweed. **1966** *DARE* Wildfl QR Pl.122A Infs **MI**57, **MN**14, **NH**4, **WA**10, **WI**35, Jewelweed; Pl.122B Inf **MI**57, Jewelweed. **1970** Anderson *TX Folk Med.* 55, Poison Ivy—Use jewel weed or touch-me-not. Rub the sap on the rash. *Dallas.*
2 =**butterfly weed 1.**
  1959 Carleton *Index Herb. Plants* 68, Jewel-weed: Asclepias tuberosa; Impatiens (v).

jewfish n
1 A **grouper 1** or other fish of the family Serranidae, as:
a also *spotted jewfish:* A **grouper 1a** (here: *Epinephelus itajara*). [*OEDS* 1679 →] S Atl, Gulf States Also called **black grouper 2, ~ snapper 2, giant sea bass 2, Junefish, spotted grouper, warsaw**
  1775 (1962) Romans *Nat. Hist. FL* xix, A little to the north hereof is a small reef . . where vast quantites [sic] of groopers, snappers, . . Jew-fish, &c. may be taken. **1837** (1962) Williams *Territory FL* 42 **swFL,** Highly prized . . are the Jew-fish, porgy, hog-fish, and bass. **1890** *Boston* (Mass.) *Jrnl.* 13 Apr. 2/3 (OED), The largest jewfish ever caught on the Gulf coast . . weighed 348 pounds, was 6 feet in length and 8 feet in circumference just back of the gills. **1909** Holder–Jordan *Fish Stories* 200, Why these huge creatures are called jewfishes no one knows. It may be from their aquiline noses, or it may be that they are chosen people among fishes. **1933** John G. Shedd Aquarium *Guide* 98, *Promicrops itaiara*—Spotted Jewfish. The jewfishes are the largest of the groupers, reaching a length of six or seven feet. The Spotted Jewfish. . . is common around Key West. **1966–70** *DARE* (Qu. P2, . . *Kinds of saltwater fish caught around here . . good to eat*) Infs **FL**24, **TX**14, 19, Jewfish; (Qu. P4, *Saltwater fish that are not good to eat*) Infs **MS**73, **TX**9, 17, Jewfish. **1968** *DARE* FW Addit **csLA,** Jewfish, an alternate term for the giant grouper. **1975** Evanoff *Catch More Fish* 106, The groupers. . . such as the Warsaw grouper and Jewfish.
b A **warsaw** (here: *Epinephelus nigritus*). S Atl, Gulf States
  1882 U.S. Natl. Museum *Bulletin* 16.540, E[pinephelus] nigritus. . . Black Grouper; Jew-fish. . . Gulf of Mexico, north to South Carolina. **1911** U.S. Bur. Census *Fisheries 1908* 311, Jewfish (Stereolepis gigas).—The largest food fish found on the Pacific coast, sometimes reaching a weight of 500 pounds. . . The name is also applied to the black grouper (Garrupa nigrita) in Florida and Texas, and to the tarpon (Tarpon

atlanticus) in Georgia and Florida. **1933** LA Dept. of Conserv. *Fishes* 207, *Garrupa nigrita.* . . Jewfishes are especially fond of haunting the vicinity of submerged wrecks. **1973** Knight *Cook's Fish Guide* 383, Jewfish . . Black see Grouper, Warsaw; california [sic] see Bass, Giant Sea; . . Spotted.

c =black grouper 1.

1935 Caine *Game Fish* 71, *Mycteroperca bonaci.* . . Jewfish. . . Caught mostly on outside reefs and offshore banks. . . Abundant around the Florida Keys. **1946** LaMonte *N. Amer. Game Fishes* 49, *Mycteroperca bonaci.* . . Jewfish. . . Maximum about 50 pounds, usually runs from 5 to 10.

d =giant sea bass 1. CA

1880 *Lib. Universal Knowl.* VIII.299 (DAE), *Jew-fish,* a common name of several species of the serranidae. . . The jew-fish of California is the *stereolepis gigas.* **1902** Jordan–Evermann *Amer. Fishes* 380, Imagine . . a small-mouthed black bass lengthened out to 6 feet, bulky in proportion, . . and you have the jewfish, . . or *Stereolepis gigas,* of the Pacific coast. **1909** Holder–Jordan *Fish Stories* 200, The California jewfish is common . . principally about rocky offshore banks. *Ibid* 201, The jewfish . . is olive-green in color, dark above but nearly plain. Its flesh is white, firm and well flavored, and it has a good repute as a market fish. **1911** [see **1b** above]. **1953** Roedel *Common Fishes CA* 72, *Stereolepis gigas.* . . *Unauthorized Name:* Jewfish. **1968–70** DARE (Qu. P2, . . *Kinds of saltwater fish caught around here . . good to eat)* Infs **CA**65, 191, Jewfish.

2 =tarpon.

1873 in 1878 Smithsonian Inst. *Misc. Coll.* 14.2.32, *Megalops thrissoides.* . . Jew-fish; tarpum. . . Cape Cod to Florida. **1884** Goode *Fisheries U.S.* 1.611, "Tarpon." In Georgia and Florida it is commonly called the "Jew-fish." **1911** [see **1b** above]. **1935** Caine *Game Fish* 134, *Tarpon atlanticus.* . . Jewfish.

3 =summer flounder.

1889 *Century Dict.* 3231 **CT,** *Jewfish.* . . A flat-fish, *Paralichthys dentatus,* the wide-mouthed flounder.

Jew flag See **Jewish flag**

Jew harp See **Jew's harp**

jewhilliken, jewhillikin See **gee whillikers**

jew-huff See **dew-hoof**

Jewish bread n Also *Jewish rye (bread), Jew bread* **chiefly Nth, esp NEast** See Map

Usu rye bread, but see quots.

1965–70 DARE (Qu. HH30, *Things that are nicknamed for different nationalities)* 10 Infs, **chiefly Nth,** Jewish bread; 9 Infs, **chiefly Nth,** Jewish rye (bread); **CO**7, Jew bread (pumpernickel); **GA**44, Jew bread; (Qu. H18, . . *Special kinds of bread)* Infs **MA**3, **NY**83, 86, 126, 237, Jewish rye bread; **PA**171, Jewish rye bread (Jewish braided bread); **IA**22, Jewish bread. **1991** DARE File **Cleveland OH,** Jewish rye bread is a medium-light rye, sliced pretty thin, with a hard thin crust. You can't get a good Jewish rye in Iowa, but you can in Cleveland. *Ibid* **swCA,** I've heard uninformed non-Jews call rye bread, any kind of rye bread, "Jewish bread." I've also heard "Jewish bread" used for matzoh. [Inf Jewish]

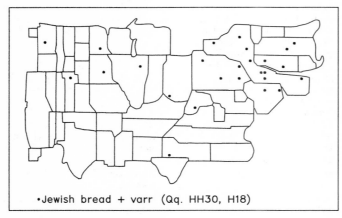

•Jewish bread + varr (Qq. HH30, H18)

Jewish dill See **Jewish pickle**

Jewish flag n Also *Jew flag* **esp West** Cf **flag** n[2] **4**

A dollar bill or other piece of paper money.

1929 AmSp 4.341 [Vagabond lingo], *Jewish flag*—A one dollar bill. **1930** Irwin *Amer. Tramp* 109, *Jew flag.* . . A dollar bill; any paper money. **1941** AmSp 16.23 **sIN,** *Jew flag.* A dollar bill. **1965** *Western Folkl.* 24.198 **Los Angeles CA** (as of c1950), *Jewish flag*—a dollar bill. **1967–70** DARE (Qu. U26, *Names or nicknames . . for a paper dollar)* Infs **CA**59, **TX**43, 89, **UT**4, Jew flag; **CO**22, **IL**58, **MO**11, **TX**13, Jewish flag.

Jewish harp See **Jew's harp**

Jewish mallard See **jew duck 3**

Jewish penicillin n

Chicken soup.

1968 DARE (Qu. HH30, *Things that are nicknamed for different nationalities)* Inf **NJ**30, Jewish penicillin (chicken soup). **1986** Chapman *New Dict. Amer. Slang* 235, *Jewish penicillin.* . . Chicken soup. **1986** DARE File **NYC,** I remember hearing *Jewish penicillin* used for chicken soup in the mid 1950s; **wMA** (as of 1960s), When you're sick you eat chicken soup because it's Jewish penicillin; **swMI** (as of c1965), Well, you better take some Jewish penicillin for that cold; **csWI,** I recall first hearing *Jewish penicillin* used for chicken soup in the early 1970s; **csWI,** I first heard *Jewish penicillin* meaning chicken soup about 1980 from a guy from Chicago.

Jewish pickle n Also *Jewish dill, Jew pickle* **esp PA, NJ, NY** See Map

A kosher-style dill pickle; see quots.

[**1949** (1986) Leonard *Jewish Cookery* 423, *Dill Pickles* (Kosher Style) [Recipe includes: cucumbers, pickling solution, bay leaves, celery or mustard seed, mixed spice, vinegar, garlic, dill, grape leaves.]] **1965–70** DARE (Qu. H56, *Names for . . pickles)* Infs **NJ**56, 59, 64, **PA**96, 245, 248, Jewish (pickle); **NJ**54, Jew pickle (half sour); **PA**66, Jewish—Jewish is more bitter [than kosher]; **PA**171, Jewish pickles—term only used by non-Jews; **PA**239, Jewish pickles (kosher)—these are sour; **MA**125, Jewish pickle or kosher pickle; **NY**79, Jewish dill; **NY**130, Jewish dill is the best; (Qu. HH30) Infs **NJ**43, **PA**242, 247, Jewish pickles; **NJ**57, Jew pickle. **1991** DARE File **Philadelphia PA** (as of 1950s), When I was a child, my mother and I ate Jewish pickles like bananas—these dill pickles were at least five inches long, two to three inches in diameter, and very garlicky. We were permitted to lift the pickles of our choice out of a wooden barrel near the meat counter at the grocery store. *Ibid* **Cleveland OH,** A Jewish pickle is a kosher dill out of the barrel. Jews don't call such a pickle a "Jewish pickle," of course; they call it a kosher dill.

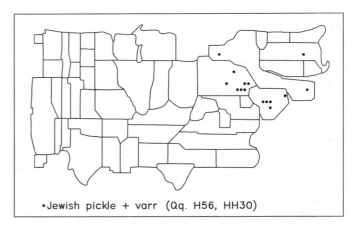

•Jewish pickle + varr (Qq. H56, HH30)

‡**Jewish piece** n

1968 DARE (Qu. H71, . . *The last piece of food left on a plate)* Inf **OH**84, The Jewish piece. I don't know where that came from.

Jewish rye (bread) See **Jewish bread**

Jewish time n Also *Jewish Standard Time,* abbr *J.S.T.* Cf **Alaska time, colored people's ~, farmers' ~, Indian ~** See quots.

1952 in 1962 *Western Folkl.* 21.31 **Los Angeles CA,** Jewish time—refers to the supposed habit of Jews of being compulsively late for appointments. Usually used as a taunt: "Do you mean regular or Jewish time?" **1979** DARE File **Madison WI,** [In a group of Jewish people:] I should have known that when they called the meeting for 8:00, they meant "Jewish time." It's now 8:20 and not everyone is even here yet. **1991** *Ibid* **Los Angeles CA** (as of 1960s), You hear "J.S.T." all the time.

I used it a lot as a teenager. It means "Jewish Standard Time," but we always said "J.S.T." You'd say, "Meet you at 9:30 J.S.T." and that meant people could show up 15 minutes to half an hour late. It didn't allow you more than a half hour and it never meant earlier than the time stated. Before we were dating but during the time boys and girls went around together in groups, a common situation was that the girls would say, "We'll be there at 7:30" and the boys would mutter cynically, "Right, J.S.T." That was because no one wanted to be first at a party, so everyone agreed to a time, and then came a little later. [Inf Jewish]

jewlacky See **jewlarker**

jewlark v, hence vbl n *jewlarking* Also sp *julark* [Cf *gill, jill* a girl, sweetheart, and *EDD lark* v. "To flirt"] **esp Sth, S Midl**
To flirt or court.

   1851 Hooper *Widow Rugby's Husband* 59 **AL,** Wonder if I'll ketch that rascal Jim Sparks jewlarkin' round Betsy, down at old Bob's. **c1960** *Wilson Coll.* **csKY,** Jewlarking. . . To go courting. **1984** Wilder *You All Spoken Here* 93 **Sth,** Jularkin': Courtin'.

jewlarker n Also *jewlark(y)* Also sp *jularker, jularky;* pronc-sp *jewlacky* [**jewlark**] **Sth, S Midl**
1 A sweetheart; a beau. Cf **joe** n[1]
   c1862 in 1943 Wiley *Life Johnny Reb* 163 **TX,** The boys all thought that it [=a letter] was from my jularky. **1892** *DN* 1.230 **KY,** Jewlarky [ˈjulɑkɪ]: sweetheart. "I'm going to see my jewlarky." **1893** Shands *MS Speech* 40, *Jew-Larky* [ˈjjuˈlɑrkɪ]. Sometimes used by negroes and illiterate whites for *sweet-heart*. This word is generally applied to the female sex, but it sometimes has reference also to the male. **1908** *DN* 3.324 **eAL, wGA,** Jewlarker. . . a beau, a lover. **1934** Vines *Green Thicket* 164 **cnAL,** They always have been settin' on their jewlarkies' knees. . . and their jewlarkies had rather die than not to have the sweet things there. **1939** *AmSp* 14.91 **eTN,** Jew larker. Beau. 'Susie's jew larker bussed her.' **1950** *PADS* 14.41 **SC,** Jewlark. . . A sweetheart. **1952** Brown *NC Folkl.* 1.555 **nwNC,** Jularker. . . A beau. **1956** McAtee *Some Dialect NC* 24, *Jularky*: . . . Beau. **c1960** *Wilson Coll.* **csKY,** Jewlark (or jewlarky). . . One's sweetheart. **1966–70** *DARE* (Qu. AA15b, . . . *Joking ways . . of saying that a man is getting married. . . "He _____."*) Inf **SC26,** Got him a jewlacky; (Qu. AA23, *Joking names that a woman may use to refer to her husband: "It's time to go and get supper for my _____."*) Inf **NC88,** Jewlarky [ˈjuləkɪ] [FW: Inf's mother's word]. **1987** *NADS Letters* **SC,** The term *jewlarker* [for a male sweetheart] . . has primary stress on the first syllable and secondary stress on the second syllable. This is at least according to my experience; I've heard the term a couple of times.
2 A citified person; a dandy.
   1884 Harris *Mingo* 166 **nGA,** The folks, they 'ud come an' stan' an' star' [at the mountain woman who had been brought to Atlanta to demonstrate how to card cotton], an' then they 'ud go some'r's else; an' then new folks 'ud come. . . They wuz jewlarkers thar frum ever'where's, an' they lookt like they wuz too brazen to live skacely. *Ibid* 167, Who else but Sis wuz a-gwine to grab me an' gimme a buss right here on the jaw a-frontin' of all them jewlarkers? **1908** *DN* 3.324 **eAL, wGA,** Jewlarker. . . A person of fine dress, manners, etc. . . Also *jewlarky*.

jewlarking See **jewlark**

jewlarky See **jewlarker**

Jew pickle See **Jewish pickle**

Jew's harp n Also *Jew(ish) harp* Pronc-sp **esp Sth, S Midl** *juice harp;* rarely *chews harp, jusarp* Cf **bruce harp, jupe harp**
A Forms.
   1843 (1916) Hall *New Purchase* 262 **IN,** I'm sentimentally of opinion it's [=a piano is] as fur afore a fiddle, as a fiddle's afore a jusarp. **1915** *DN* 4.227 **wTX,** Juice-harp. . . The Jew's harp. **1919** Kyne *Capt. Scraggs* 116 **CA,** We took five thousand dollars in trade-beads, an' mouth organs, an' calico, an' juice harps. **1919** *DN* 5.34 **seKY,** Juice harp. . . Jew's harp. **1937** in 1972 *Amer. Slave* 3.3.66 **SC,** All de use we had fer money was to buy fish hooks, barlows, juice harps and marbles. **1965–70** *DARE* (Qu. FF8, . . *Small instrument that you hold between the teeth and pluck on*) 644 Infs, **widespread,** Jew's harp; 199 Infs, **widespread, but more freq Sth, S Midl,** Juice harp [Of all Infs responding to the question, 31% were comm type 5, 33% coll educ; of those giving the response *juice harp*, 42% were comm type 5, 21% coll educ.]; 10 Infs, **scattered exc Sth, S Midl,** Jewish harp; **NJ**6, 46, **OH**56, **PA**130, 245, **TX**31, Jew harp; **OH**81, Chews harp; (Qu. FF7, *A small musical instrument that you blow on, and move from side to side in your mouth*) 25 Infs, **chiefly Sth, Missip Valley, West,** Jew's harp; 24 Infs, **scattered, but esp Sth,**

S Midl, Juice harp; **AL**10, Jew harp. **1971** Bright *Word Geog. CA & NV* 158, *Jew's harp* 60% . . *juice harp* 19%. **1973** Gawthrop *Dial. Calumet* 71 **nwIN,** [Results of mail survey:] *Instrument held between teeth and picked:* Jew's harp 44 [of 125 infs], juice harp 22, mouth harp 9. **1973** Allen *LAUM* 1.207 (as of c1950), The small musical instrument played by being plucked while held against the teeth is called a *jew's harp* by two-thirds of the U[pper] M[idwest] infs and *juice harp* by the remaining third. No geographical pattern emerges. *Juice harp,* however, clearly correlates with informant types, as its highest frequency (40%) is with Type I speakers [=old, with little educ]. Only 18% of the Type II speakers [=mid-aged, with approx hs educ] use it, and 13% of the college graduates. [Two of the checklist respondents offered *jew harp* and one offered *jewish harp*.]
B Senses.
1 See quots. [From the shape; cf *OED Jew's harp* sb. 2 1750 →]
   1872 (1876) Knight *Amer. Mech. Dict.* 2.1213, *Jew's-harp.* . . *(Nautical.)* The shackle by which a cable is bent to the anchor-ring. **1956** Sorden–Ebert *Logger's Words* 20 **Gt Lakes,** *Jews-harp,* A ring used to hold the draft-chain on an ox yoke. **1958** McCulloch *Woods Words* 98 **Pacific NW,** *Jew's harp.* . . A ring in an ox yoke shaped like a jew's harp, used to shorten or lengthen the skidding chain. Also called *bitch link.*
2 also *Jew's-harp plant:* A **trillium,** usu *Trillium cernuum.* [Perh from the shape of the leaf]
   1830 Rafinesque *Med. Flora* 2.96, *Trillium latifolium.* Names. . . Jews Harp. *Ibid* 2.103, *Trillium.* . . The sessile species are called *Jewsharp* in Kentucky, and used for sores and ulcers. **1876** Hobbs *Bot. Hdbk.* 60, *Jews' harp plant,* Beth root, Trillium pendulum. **1900** Lyons *Plant Names* 378, *T[rillium] pendulum* . . . Jew's-harp plant. **1959** Carleton *Index Herb. Plants* 68, *Jew's-harp-plant:* Trillium cernuum.
3 A harmonica. [By ext from or confusion with std sense: a small, lyre-shaped instrument with a flexible metal tongue] **chiefly Sth, S Midl, Missip Valley, West**
   1941 *LANE* Map 413 *(Harmonica),* Many informants offered the terms *harp, mouth harp,* and *Jew's harp* (. . *juice harp*). . . These terms probably always denote a different instrument from the harmonica, namely one consisting of a bent tongue set in a lyre-shaped metal frame. . . Even those informants who identify the term (mouth ~, jew's-~) with the harmonica may do so because only one type of instrument or the other happens to be familiar to them. **1965–70** *DARE* (Qu. FF7, *A small musical instrument that you blow on, and move from side to side in your mouth*) 24 Infs, **chiefly Sth, Missip Valley, West,** Jew's harp; 20 Infs, **scattered, but esp Sth, S Midl,** Juice harp; **AL**10, Jew harp; **SC**3, Harmonica—new name, juice harp, mouth organ; **SC**32, Harp, juice harp—a lot of people use this, though it's really one you pluck; **VA**6, French harp—a lot of people call it a juice harp even though it isn't correct; **VA**31, Juice harp, harmonica—right name, Jew's harp. [17 of 64 total Infs also responded *Jew's* (or *juice*) *harp* to Qu. FF8.] **c1970** Pederson *Dial. Surv. Rural GA* (*A small musical instrument that you hold up to your mouth and blow on*) 2 infs, **seGA,** Juice harp; 1 inf, Jew's harp. [The first 2 infs also responded with *juice harp* for "a small musical instrument that is made out of metal and held between the teeth and picked."] **1973** Allen *LAUM* 1.207 (as of c1950), Two uncertain responses of *juice harp* [for *harmonica*] come from Nebraska. . . The mailed information also adds 82 instances (9%) of *jew's harp.* **1986** Pederson *LAGS Concordance Gulf Region,* [38 infs gave *Jew's* (or *juice*) *harp* in response to a description of a harmonica or stated that *Jew's* (or *juice*) *harp* and *harmonica* are synonymous. A number of infs were doubtful or confused.]
4 =**mouth bow.**
   1989 *DARE* File **cnNC,** Otis in 1986 yakked to me about the "juice harp," and he meant the song-bow. . . Otis knew a Danbury man who played it, and Otis thinx that the name came from the fact that since the player had tobacco in his mouth, the playing released the juice!

Jew's-harp plant See **Jew's harp B2**

jewsly moke n Also *Jerusely-moke, jewsly mose*
=**Jerusalem oak 1.**
   1951 *PADS* 15.10 **nwNC,** *Chenopodium botrys.* . . Jewsly Mose, corruption of Jerusalem oak, Mitchell County, N.C. **1953** *PADS* 19.12 **nwNC,** *Jewsly moke:* . . Jerusalem oak. Mitchell Co., N.C. **1982** Powers *Cataloochee* 256 **cwNC,** Worm medicine: Get seeds off Jerusely-moke (Jerusalem Oak) plant in fall.

jez See **jeez**

J-grab See **jay grab**

J-hole See **jay hole**

J-hook See **jay grab**

jib n¹

1a also *jip:* The face, nose, lip, or mouth. [*EDD jib* sb.² 1]
1938 *Collier's* 14 May 55 **neKY,** If Pa put his jib in I would tell him to stay out of my love affair. **1942** Berrey–Van den Bark *Amer. Slang* 121.25, *Face. . . jib.* **1969–70** *DARE* (Qu. X9, *Joking or uncomplimentary words for a person's mouth . .* "I wish he'd shut his _____.") Infs **IL**96, **MI**103, Jib; **NY**241, Jibs; **VA**9, Jip; (Qu. GG23a, *If you speak sharply to somebody to make him be patient . .* "Now just keep your _____.") Inf **IL**96, Jib out of this. **1970** Young *Snakes* 29 **ceMS** [Black], I think you probly saved the cat from a awful beatin splittin him in his jibs right quick like that. **1970** Major *Dict. Afro–Amer. Slang* 71, *Jib:* mouth. **1972** Claerbaut *Black Jargon* 70, *Jibs. . .* lips: It hit him in the jibs.

b in phrr *jaw at the jibs, run off (at) the jibs:* To talk foolishly or excessively.
1980 Folb *Runnin' Down* 44 **Los Angeles CA** [Black], Like a lotta people run off at the jibs when they runnin' offa whites. They cain't control they mouth. *Ibid* 128, Like some dudes jus' run off d'jibs. Talkin' lotta jive, jus' always talkin'. *Ibid* 243, *Jibs, jaw at the / run off at the* l. Talk too much. 2. Engage in foolish or irrelevant talk.

2 The rump or buttocks.
1970 *DARE* (Qu. K73, *. . Names . . for the rump of a cooked chicken*) Inf **VA**38, Jib. **1972** Claerbaut *Black Jargon* 70, *Jibs. . .* buttocks.

jib v [**jib** n¹ **1b**]
To talk foolishly or excessively.
1980 Folb *Runnin' Down* 44 **Los Angeles CA** [Black], Jibbin' too damn much! Cons'anly talkin' bout nuthin. *Ibid* 118, Like some sucker frontin' off like a pimp—be jibbin' 'bout his 'hos [=whores].

jib n² Also sp *gib* Cf **pee-jib**
See quots.
1967 *DARE* (Qu. EE6b, *Small marbles or marbles in general*) Inf **OH**11, Mibs, gibs. **1983** *MJLF* 9.1.45 **ceKY,** *Jibs . .* another name for marbles, the game as well as the marbles themselves.

jibagoo See **jigaboo**

jibberjawed See **jimberjawed**

jibbers n¹ [Perh var of *bejabbers*]
Used in exclams and mild oaths.
1924 *DN* 5.271 [Exclams], By jibbers. **1967** *DARE* (Qu. NN25b, *Weakened substitutes for 'damn' or 'damned':* "Well, I'll be _____!") Inf **MN**10, Jibbers.

jibbers n² [Perh var of **jibbies**, or perh assoc with *gibbers* gib-berings]
1963 Watkins–Watkins *Yesterday Hills* 156 **cnGA,** St. Vitus's dance, "the jibbers," was caused, the people believed, when a child was conceived while his father was drunk.

jibbies n Cf **heebie-jeebies 1, jibbers** n²
=**all-overs** n pl **1.**
1967 *DARE* (Qu. GG13b, *When something keeps bothering a person and makes him nervous . .* "It gives me the _____.") Inf **NC**48, Jibbies. **1968** Moody *Coming of Age MS* 302 [Black], I was thinking maybe a little fresh air might even cure Doris of the jibbies.

jibble v [Cf *EDD gibbles* sb. pl. "Sc. . . odds and ends" and *jibbly* "A fragment, odd piece"]
To reduce to small pieces.
1953 Randolph–Wilson *Down in Holler* 256 **Ozarks,** *Jibble. . .* To cut into small pieces. Asked how to cook squash, a woman answered, "You just take an' jibble 'em up, an' then bile 'em." Another cook was talking about hash. "Sometimes I grind the meat, but mostly I just jibble it." **1954** *Harder Coll.* **cwTN,** *Jibble*—To mash up or squeeze up. **1983** *MJLF* 9.1.45 **ceKY,** *Jibble . .* to cut cloth, food, etc. into small pieces.

‡**jibbucrew** n
1930 Stoney–Shelby *Black Genesis* 162 **seSC,** He been in a strange country, for true, nothin' but red mud an' red ribber an' jibbucrew (low brush), an' not so much as a lightwood stump for to git a little kindlin'.

jibe v Rarely with *up* Also sp *gibe, gybe* **chiefly Nth, N Midl, West** See Map Cf **gee** v², **jive** v²
To harmonize, agree, get along; to be in accord with—often in neg constrs.
1844 Stephens *High Life in NY* 2.40 **NYC,** The streaked mittens marm knit for me when my yaller gloves wore out, they didn't exactly gibe with my other fix up. **1857** *Jrl. of Discourses* 5.251, But now the thread is cut between us and them, and we will never gybe again; no, never, worlds without end. **1892** Harte *Col. Starbottle* 11 **CA,** This here name . . did n't seem to jibe with it. **1899** (1912) Green *VA Folk-Speech* 244, *Jibe. . .* To agree; being in harmony or accord; work together. **1905** *DN* 3.12 **cCT,** *Jibe. . .* To agree. **1907** *DN* 3.214 **nwAR,** *Jibe. . .* To agree. Always in negative. "They don't jibe." **1910** *DN* 3.444 **wNY,** They don't jibe very well. **1912** *DN* 3.579 **wIN,** Henry and his second wife don't seem to jibe very well. **1928** Ruppenthal *Coll.* **KS,** *Jibe*—to fit accurately, to agree, to harmonize. The testimony of all witnesses jibes with that of the defendant. The stones in the wall don't jibe. **1965–70** *DARE* (Qu. II11a, *If two people don't get along well together . .* "They don't _____.") 118 Infs, **chiefly Nth, N Midl, West,** Jibe; **PA**142, Jibe together; **IL**126, Jibe up; **GA**53, Their ideas don't jibe with each other; **SC**10, Jibe one another; (Qu. KK67, *When people think alike about something:* "On that particular thing, we _____.") 17 Infs, **scattered, but esp Nth,** Jibe; **MI**108, Our minds jibe; (Qu. KK58, *An excuse that looks as if it would not stand up under questioning:* "His story won't _____.") 11 Infs, **scattered,** Jibe; **IA**15, Doesn't jibe; **NC**13, Jibe with the facts; (Qu. KK68, *When people don't think alike about something:* "We agree on most things, but on politics we're _____.") Inf **IL**96, Don't jibe. **1982** *Barrick Coll.* **csPA,** *Jibe*—agree, meet; esp. in carpentry, etc., to line up. "I can't get these pieces to jibe."

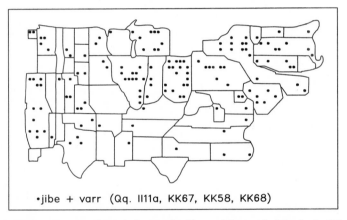

•jibe + varr (Qq. II11a, KK67, KK58, KK68)

jib-jab v [Perh clipped form of *jibber-jabber*; cf *chit-chat*] Cf **jab** v
To talk or chat.
1968 *DARE* (Qu. II12, *Talking about meeting somebody on the street and speaking only a few words with him:* "We just _____.") Inf **LA**46, Jib-jabbed.

jib-job lot n [Perh redup of *job lot;* cf *EDD jibs* "Small, waste pieces of cloth"]
1964 Jackman–Long *OR Desert* 333, Odds and ends were gathered into boxes, baskets or barrels, and sold as "jib-job lots."

jiboney See **jabronie**

jib-rag n [Cf *EDD jibs* "Small, waste pieces of cloth"]
1899 (1912) Green *VA Folk-Speech* 245, *Jib-rags. . .* Torn into strips or small pieces.

jice See **joist 1**

jick n Also *jickey, jicki(e)* [Etym unknown] **sNEng** Cf **jickie bird**
See quots.
1936 (1947) Mencken *Amer. Lang.* 216, In Bristol County, Massachusetts, where there are many Portuguese immigrants, a number of Portuguese loan-words are encountered, e.g., . . *jick* or *jickie* (Englishman). **1960** *WELS Suppl.* **seMA,** Jick—Lower-class English immigrant, usually one with a strong regional accent and little education. (Used c1930–40 at least of millworkers in New Bedford.) **1969** *DARE* (Qu. HH28, *Names and nicknames . . for people of foreign background: English*) Infs **CT**21, **RI**4, 6, 11, 13, Jickey. **1987** *DARE* File, The term "jicki"

has been in use at least since I was a child. In fact, it is still used by my mother-in-law (whose parents were English) and the members of her family. I was born in Cumberland, Rhode Island in 1932. Everybody knew and used the word in the 1930s and '40s. I doubt very much that the term is, *pace* Mencken, a Portuguese loan-word. My other informants were a native of New Bedford, Mass., and another Luso-American who grew up in Providence, Rhode Island. They all belong to the same generation and recognized the word immediately.

jickhead n Also *jig head* [Perh abbr for *jigger* a measure of liquor + **head** n **C1c**] *esp freq among Black speakers*
A drunkard.
    1928 in 1983 Taft *Blues Lyric Poetry* 270, [Song title:] Jig Head Blues. **1938** *AmSp* 13.316 **NE** [Black], A habitual drunkard is a *jickhead*. **1941** *AmSp* 16.70, Drunken person (or Habitual Drunkard) . . *jickhead*. **1970** Major *Dict. Afro-Amer. Slang* 71, *Jick head:* a drunk. **1970** *DARE* (Qu. DD12, . . *A person who drinks steadily or a great deal*) Inf **MO**24, Jickhead.

jicki(e) See **jick**

jickie bird n Also *jickie, jickie sparrow* [**jick**]
=**English sparrow.**
    1956 **MA** Audubon Soc. *Bulletin* 40.130, *House Sparrow.* . . Jickie, Jickie Bird, Jickie Sparrow (Mass. From a slang term, meaning Englishman.)

jiddy hawk n [Etym unknown]
=**jaeger** n¹.
    [**1918** Macmillan *4 Yrs.* 404, *Stercorarius parasiticus*. Parasitic jaeger. Bosun bird. Teaser. Jiddy hawk. Skua gull. . . I saw this species when sledging along the eastern shore of Grant Land in latitude 82° N.] **1925** (1928) Forbush *Birds MA* 1.52, *Pomarine Jaeger. Other names:* jiddy hawk. *Ibid* 55, *Parasitic Jaeger.* . . Jiddy hawk. **1946** Hausman *Eastern Birds* 300, *Pomarine Jaeger.* . . Jiddy Hawk. . . Said to be less bold, daring, and fierce in its relations with other jaegers. *Ibid* 301, *Parasitic Jaeger.* . . Jiddy Hawk. . . This species seems to victimize the Kittiwake Gull on the fishing banks more often than the others. **1951** Pough *Audubon Water Bird* 334, Jiddy hawk. See Jaegers.

jidge See **judge**

jiffin(g) n [Scots varr of *jiffy; DSL jiffie, jiffin* 1788, 1802; *EDD* "Obs."]
An instant or moment.
    [**1776** Leacock *Brit. Tyranny* 44, He'll hoist his sheet-anchor presently, he'll be up in a jiffin.] **1815** Humphreys *Yankey in England* 53, "Deliver it, and bring an answer—quick—quick—" "In a jiffing." *Ibid* 106, Jiffing, or *jiffin*. **1891** in 1949 *PADS* 11.29 **ME**, Threw me at the backs and the arms'-end;/ But then I tried a different lug / And took him at the old side-hug,/ And whooped and laid him on his mug / In just a half a "jiffin."

jig n¹ Also sp *gig* [*jig* a sprightly dance in triple time]
1 in phrr *(the) jig is up* (or *over*): See quot 1928.
    1777 *MD Jrl. & Baltimore Advt.* (MD) 17 June 3/1 **seRI**, Mr. John Miller, who came in and said, "The jig is over with us." **1800** *Aurora* (Phila.) 27 Dec. *(DAE)*, As the Baltimore paper says 'The jig's up, Paddy.' **1844** (1846) Kendall *Santa Fé Exped.* 1.62, Time was . . when I could cut pigeon-wings and extras, and perform the double shuffle with no inconsiderable precision and activity; but those days are over now—the "jig is up." **1894** *Harper's New Mth. Mag.* 88.380 **ceMA**, The die is cast, the jig is up, the fat's in the fire, the milk's spilt. **1905** *DN* 3.12 **cCT**, Jig. . . Game. 'The jig is up.' **1908** *DN* 3.324 **eAL, wGA**, Jig. . . In the expression 'the jig's up,' meaning all is over, the plan is discovered, etc. **1928** Ruppenthal *Coll.* **KS**, The jig is up—an admission that a plan, ruse, trick, pretense, etc. can no longer be maintained. **1969** *DARE* (Qu. NN30, *Exclamations beginning with the sound of 'j'*) Inf **CA**155, Jig's up.
2 in phrr *in jig('s) time:* Rapidly; in a very short period of time.
    1916 Wilson *Somewhere* 314, Kate has about four more of 'em licked to a standstill in jigtime. **1949** *Time* 7 Mar 12, [Advt:] Well, I fixed up that car in jig-time. **1963** Burroughs *Head-First* 139 **CO**, If we had other business lined up, or if a storm threatened, we turned to and got the job done in jig time. **1967–69** *DARE* (Qu. A22, . . *'To start working hard':* "She had only ten minutes to clean the room, but she _____.") Inf **MA**50, Did it in jig time; (Qu. KK42b, *Expressions about a person who does something very easily:* "He could do that _____.") Infs **IL**96, **NY**86, In jig time; **NY**185, In jig's time. **1968** Robinson *Assassin*

203, If I was you, I'd see Gracie Hutchinson. . . She'd solve your problem in jig time.
3 also *jigg(s)*, rarely *jigwalker, jigwawk:* A Black person—usu considered offensive. [Prob from the close association in the 1830s–1850s of Blacks with *jig dancing* or minstrel dancing and with the banjo, the tunes for which were known as *jigs*] Cf **jigaboo**
    1924 F.J. Wilstach *Slang Dict. Stage* (Typescript in N.Y. Public Libr.) (OEDS), Jiggs, Negro actor. **1926** Finerty *Criminalese* 33, Jig show—Colored minstrel show. **1926** Van Vechten *Nigger Heaven* 13 **Harlem NYC**, Blues, smokes, dinges, charcoals, chocolate browns, shines, and jigs. *Ibid* 286, *Jig-chaser:* a white person who seeks the company of Negroes. **1928** Fisher *Walls Jericho* 301 **NYC** [Black], Jig, jigaboo, jigwalker, see *boogy*. [*Ibid* 297, *Boogy*—Negro.] c**1930** Swann *Lang. Circus Lot* 11, *Gig show:* Minstrel show. **1932** Farrell *Young Lonigan* 113 **Chicago IL**, Janitor's jobs were for jiggs. **1942** *Amer. Mercury* 55.91 **Harlem NYC** [Black], Free schools and dumb jigs! Man, how you going to put Delaware in Georgy? **1942** Handy *Father of Blues* 117 **Memphis TN** (as of c1912) [Black], A white person was always "ofay," a Negro "jigwawk." The terms . . were also extended to cover fine distinctions. Thus if the girl you were sparking at the moment was light colored, you might describe her as ofay jigwawk. If she was the stove-pipe variety, you might have to hear her called a jig-wawk-jigwawk. **1949** *PADS* 11.7 **wTX**, Jig. . . A Negro. Low colloquial. **1950** Blesh-Janis *Ragtime* 23, Up to that time [=1897] ragtime piano was called "jig piano," and the syncopating bands, like Joplin's, were called "jig bands." This term, taken from jig dances, even came a little later to be a designation for the Negro himself. **1962** [see **jigaboo**] **1965–70** *DARE* (Qu. HH28, *Names and nicknames . . for people of foreign background:* Negro) 25 Infs, **scattered**, Jig; (Qu. C35, *Nicknames for the different parts of your town or city*) Infs **GA**13, **NE**7, Jig town; (Qu. D40, *Names and nicknames . . for the upper balcony in a theater*) Inf **GA**13, Jig gallery; (Qu. II25, *Names or nicknames for the part of a town where the poorer people, special groups, or foreign groups live*) Infs **GA**13, **IL**50, **NY**131, **OK**27, Jig town. **1982** Barrick *Coll.* **csPA**, Jig, jigg—nigger, from *jigaboo*.
4 in phr *get a jig on:* See quot. Cf **jiggle** n
    1970 *DARE* (Qu. A19, *Other ways of saying "I'll have to hurry":* "I'm late, I'll have to _____.") Inf **PA**244, Get a jig on.

jig v
1 To snag (a fish) by jerking or dragging an unbaited hook (or hooks) through the water; to fish in this way; to fish by working a baited hook (or hooks) up and down in the water; hence vbl n *jigging;* also *jig fishing;* n *jigger* the set of tackle used in fishing in this way. Cf **jiggering, jug** v¹
    1872 (1876) Knight *Amer. Mech. Dict.* 2.1214, *Jigger.* . . A weighted line with several hooks, set back to back, dropped into the water, and suddenly jerked upward to catch fish. **1877** Hallock *Sportsman's Gaz.* 243, Keep the line constantly in motion, and half the time you will "jig" them in the belly, tail or side, as the finny mass moves over the hook. **1902** Jordan-Evermann *Amer. Fishes* 500 **AK**, The usual method of taking it [=the Atka mackerel] is by "jigging." . . We used 3 hooks tied together in a bunch, just above which was tied a piece of white muslin. The line was weighted so that the hooks would descend quickly. When they had reached the bottom, or near it, they would be jerked up and down and the fish, striking at the muslin, would be hooked or would catch the hooks in their mouths. **1920** *DN* 5.82 **NW**, Jig, to. To catch fish by drawing naked hooks through the water where the fish are passing in schools. *Jigger.* A hook used for "jigging" fish, or the pole and other apparatus. **1957** McMeekin *Old KY Country* 205, You may see fishermen "jigging" along the banks of creeks. This is done with a long pole and a short line equipped with some jingling spinners and a worm for bait. Jiggled in the crevasses along a rocky bank, the spinners attract and the worm is snapped up by lunkers along the shore. **1965–70** *DARE* (Qu. P17, . . *When . . people fish by lowering a line and sinker close to the bottom of the water*) 16 Infs, **scattered, but infreq Sth, S Midl**, Jigging; **OH**79, Jig fishing—you work the line up and down; (Qu. P13, . . *Other ways of fishing*) Infs **CT**31, **MI**32, **NY**6, 142, 164, **WA**30, Jigging; **AK**1, Jigging—a cluster of 3 or 4 hooks back to back—gang hooks; **CA**65, Jig—[with] a line pulled through the water rhythmically; **IA**28, Jigging—two or three hooks on and you jerk so as to snag a running fish—illegal; [**IL**41, Bottle-fishing—also called jigging; you tie a hook and line to a bottle and let it float;] **KY**60, Jig fishing—you take a gob of nightcrawlers, go along the banks dropping the line, and you jerk the fish out; **KY**65, Jig fishing—you use a short pole, a short line,

a sinker, and a bunch of worms on a hook; you fish from a slowly moving boat, jerking the pole a little as you go; when the fish bites, you jerk him in the boat quickly; **MA**55, Jigging—keep your hand goin' up and down; you don't have no bait on the line but it has a piece of stainless steel with lots of hooks on it; **NY**200, Jigging—a short pole with the line moved up and down; **NY**207, Jig; **NC**60, Jig fishing; **SC**11, Jigging—trying to snag a fish; **SC**63, Jig fishing—you use a short line on a pole with a lure and you jiggle it in the water; **VA**47, Jig—you drag a line with lots of hooks through the water and the hooks grab the fish anywhere in their bodies; an old practice; (Qu. P15, . . *Fishing that's done from a slowly moving boat*) Infs **FL**13, **NY**6, Jigging. **1967** *DARE* Tape **WA**30, We used to go jigging . . at nights, you know. . . There was a big pool there and they [=the fish] would just lay in there. And we'd use maybe eight or nine ounces of lead with a triple hook below it and we'd throw it out there, you know, and reel it in. **1984** *MJLF* 10.152 **WI**, Jig fish. To fish with a hand-held line. . . "To jig" means "to snag" fish in Maine.

2 To bother or annoy. Cf **bug** v **4**, **jag** v[1] **B2**

    1970 *DARE* (Qu. Y7, *When one person never misses a chance to be mean to another or to annoy another: "I don't know why she keeps _____ me all the time!"*) Inf **NY**249, Jigging.

3 with *around*: To putter around, dally. Cf *jag around* (at **jag** v[1] **B3**)

    1906 *DN* 3.143 **nwAR**, Jig. . . To jog. "If we could get this race pulled off under the shelter inside this building, perhaps the Senator would jig around on the corners and let me beat him." **1968** *DARE* (Qu. A10, . . *Doing little unimportant things: . . "What are you doing?" . . "Nothing in particular—I'm just _____."*) Inf **NH**14, Jigging around; (Qu. A12, *When somebody keeps you waiting . . "Hurry up! I don't have all day to _____ you!"*) Inf **NH**14, Jig around with—I can't jig around with you all day.

4 with *around*: To strut, prance, or swagger.

    1966 *DARE* (Qu. Y22, *To move around in a way to make people take notice of you: "Look at him _____."*) Inf **MS**6, Jig around.

jig n[2]

    1944 *PADS* 2.29 **eKY**, Jig. . . Pudenda muliebria. . . Common.

jig n[3] Also *jigger* Cf **gig** n[2] **2**

An oxgoad.

    1968 *DARE* (Qu. K27, . . *The sharp-pointed stick used to get oxen to move*) Inf **LA**44, Jigger. **1969** *DARE* FW Addit **cwNJ**, Jig [jɪg]—a prod or stick for prodding an ox with; a goad.

jig n[4] [Var of **jag** n[2] **1a**]

    1939 *AmSp* 14.91 **eTN**, Little jig of wood. A small amount of wood. 'I sold a little jig of wood.'

jigaboo n Also *chickaboo, jibagoo, jigabo, jiggaboo, jiggerboo* [Prob from **jig** n[1] **3** by analogy with **bugaboo**] Cf **zigaboo**

A Black person; rarely, an Asian—usu considered offensive.

    [**1909** Barnes–Weston *I've Got Rings* 5, [Song lyrics:] So come to your na-bob, and next Pat-rick's Day, Be Mis-tress Mum-bo Jum-bo Jij-ji-boo J. O'Shea.] [*DARE* Ed: Although the song was not published until 1909, it first appeared in the show *The Yankee Girl*, which opened in New York on Feb. 2, 1907. The locale of the song is India.] **1926** Finerty *Criminalese* 32, Jiggaboo—A negro or yellow race chauffeur. **1930** *AmSp* 6.133 [Underworld jargon], Jigaboo. . . Negro. **1936** (1947) Mencken *Amer. Lang.* 296, [In a list of racial epithets:] For Negro: jigabo, jigaboo. **1954** *PADS* 21.31 **SC**, Jiggerboo. . . A Negro. Only in a derogatory sense. Not often heard, and evidently imported into South Carolina from other states. Returning servicemen report having heard it from various outside quarters. **1961** (1962) Griffin *Black Like Me* 47 **TX**, Hearing himself referred to as nigger, coon, jigaboo. **1962** Atwood *Vocab.* **TX** 74, The presumably Northern words *jigaboo* and *jig* show only nine occurrences between them. **1964** *PADS* 42.27 **Chicago IL**, Terms most popular [for Blacks] among young Caucasians are *jigaboo, booboo, blacky,* and *jungle bunny*. **1965** Little *Autobiog. Malcolm X* 106, Some others had that vinegary "worst kind of nigger" look. And a few were amused, seeing me as the "Harlem jigaboo" archetype. **1965–70** *DARE* (Qu. HH28, *Names and nicknames . . for people of foreign background: Negro*) 18 Infs, **esp Sth, S Midl**, Jigaboo; **CA**94, Chickaboo. **1982** *Barrick Coll.* **csPA**, Jigaboo—nigger.

jigamaree n Also *gigamaree, jigamafloocus, jigamahoo, jiggermaree*

A gadget, contrivance, thingamajig; a gewgaw.

    1824 *Old Colony Mem.* (Plymouth MA) 6 Mar 180/1 **NEng**, O, the

wonderation, what a nation sight of jiggermarees! **1851** (1969) Burke *Polly Peablossom* 71 **GA**, One day one uv them ar all-fired yankee pedlars come er long with er outlandish kind uv er jigamaree to make the wimmin's coat sorter stick out in the t'other eend. **1872** (1973) Thompson *Major Jones's Courtship* 106 **GA**, Mary was sowin something mighty fine and white, with ruffles and jigamarees all round it. *Ibid* 233, All round the room, was all sorts of fineries and gigamarees, more'n anybody know'd what to do with. **1908** *DN* 3.324 **eAL, wGA**, Jigamaree. . . A gewgaw, a thingumabob. . . Common. **1974** in 1982 *Barrick Coll.* **csPA**, Jigamafloocus—whatchamacallit. **1979** *Ibid*, Jigamahoo—whatchamacallit.

jig around See **jig** v **3, 4**

jigarum See **jugarum**

jiger See **jigger** n[1] **1**

jig fishing See **jig** v **1**

jigg See **jig** n[1] **3**

jiggaboo See **jigaboo**

jiggamy n [*EDD jiggamy* "A name given to any implement, tool, &c., the proper name of which cannot be recalled at the moment"; cf **jigamaree**]

    1899 (1912) Green *VA Folk-Speech* 245, Jiggamy. . . Any implement or tool.

jigged, I'll be See **jiggered, I'll be**

jigger n[1]

1 also *jiger*: A fishing vessel. **coastal NEng** *obs*

    1819 (1914) Bentley *Diary* 4.570 **neMA**, Every Jiger takes out several dories. **1842** Buckingham *E. & W. States* 1.107 **seME**, Vessels collectively he calls *craft*, and subdivides them into *Pinkies, Pogies, Jiggers,* &c. **1859** (1968) Bartlett *Americanisms* 221, Jigger. . . A small fishing vessel. New England. **1860** Babson *Hist. Gloucester* **neMA** 572, At that time [c1820], the size of the Chebacco boats was increased; and it began to be common to furnish them with a bowsprit, and call them "jiggers." **1880** *Harper's New Mth. Mag.* 61.350 **coastal ME**, The jigger, . . a small schooner of perhaps forty feet long by ten feet beam, with a considerable hold, and a cabin with four bunks. **1932** Wasson *Sailing Days* 114 **cME coast**, Smaller schooners . . sometimes used seines, but with the . . "porgy catchers," they generally drew single fish over the side upon lead-weighted hooks, called "jigs," and so were known, the coast over, as "jiggers."

2 also *jigger wagon*: A low-slung wagon; a dray. [Cf *EDD jigger* sb.[4] "An open vehicle for carrying trees from the forest"] **esp NEng** Cf **jagger wagon**

    1872 (1873) Drake *Old Landmarks* 177, While in the neighborhood of the prominent wharves, we may appropriately refer to the long trucks once used in Boston for conveying heavy merchandise. . . The long jiggers now used are scarcely less objectionable than the old trucks. **1907** *DN* 3.245 **eME**, Jigger. . . A dray, with the body hung under the axles. **1966** *DARE* (Qu. N41b, *Horse-drawn vehicles to carry heavy loads*) Inf **ME**9, Jigger wagon; **ME**22, Jigger—a low one. **1973** Allen *LAUM* 1.219 (as of c1950), Jigger: On four wheels, but set close to the ground [1 inf, **csMN**, in response to the *stone boat* question]. **1975** Gould *ME Lingo* 147, Jigger—A four-wheeled wagon peculiar to the Bangor waterfront in the old days and said to have been designed there. Low-slung, it would probably be a dray in other places. **1976** *Yankee* Sept 134 **Cape Cod MA**, Nobody in the [1902] photo is working except the straw-hatted horse and its driver. The "jigger" behind them, low slung for carting barrels of fish from Railroad Wharf, was often used to carry baggage from the Boston steamer *Cape Cod*, which had docked at Provincetown at 12:30 p.m.

3 also *jiggie, jiggus*: =**doohickey 1**; a device, contraption. Cf **doojigger**

    1890 *DN* 1.74 **sePA**, Jigger: thing (very vague), "thingemajig." **1900** Day *Up in ME* 39, Some new folderinos come 'long every day,/ All sorts of new jiggers to git yer hay. **1914** *DN* 4.158 **PA**, Jigger. . . Thing. **1923** *DN* 5.205 **swMO**, Dinkus. . . Thing. Also . . Jigger. **1926** *AmSp* 1.628, Jigger. . . The term *jigger* has long been used of small mechanical devices. . . [It] is often used as an indefinite name, not too dignified, of the same order as *thingumbob, doodad,* or *dingus*. **1931** *AmSp* 6.258 [American Indefinite Names], Jigger, jiggie, jiggus. **1968** *DARE* Tape **CA**100, [It was] not exactly a tractor but a big, powerful jigger. . . Others have a big jigger. **1982** *Barrick Coll.* **csPA**, Jigger—handle; knob; any unidentified object, whatchamacallit.

4 An odd or amusing person; a guy, fellow—occas used in ref to an animal. [*EDD jigger* sb.¹ 1 "A contemptuous term applied to a human being"]

1921 *Harper's Mth. Mag.* 144.121 **ceMA,** A goon is a person with a heavy touch as distinguished from a jigger, who has a light touch. While jiggers look on life with a genial eye, goons take a more stolid and literal view. It is reported that George Washington was a goon, whereas Lincoln was a jigger. **1950** *WELS (Uncomplimentary words for an old man)* 1 Inf, **WI,** Jigger. **1950** *WELS Suppl.* **WI,** Crazy Frank used to foretell the weather from the sun, moon, and stars—he was a queer old jigger. **1961** Adams *Old-Time Cowhand* 20 **West,** Our man was as full of verbal lather as a soap peddler. . . Them two old jiggers jes' jabbered at each other like a couple of honkers on a new feed ground. **1967–68** *DARE* (Qu. Z12, *Nicknames and joking words meaning 'a small child': "He's a healthy little _____."*) Infs **NY**7, 96, Jigger; (Qu. HH5, *Someone who is queer but harmless*) Inf **WI**13, Odd jigger; (Qu. KK27, *A very lively, active old person: "For his age, he's _____."*) Inf **TX**31, Quite a jigger. **1967** *DARE* Tape **MI**42, I set a trap an' eventually I caught that jigger [=a mink]. **1969** *DARE* FW Addit **MA**15, Comical old jiggers—characters; likable old-timers whose words and actions were amusing, though not always intended to be. **1973** Allen *LAUM* 1.349 (as of c1950), Several additional terms of limited use [for a rustic] appear in the detailed list below. . . country boy . . ~ jigger [1 inf, **cwMN;** inf showed amusement].

5 See quot.

1935 Sandoz *Jules* 25 **wNE** (as of 1880–1930), But they listened eagerly enough when he talked of preëmptions and timber claims and read the Homestead Act to them from the bulletin that was only a mess of little black jiggers on white paper to them.

6 =long john 2.

1970 *DARE* (Qu. H28, *Different shapes or types of doughnuts*) Inf **MI**119, Jiggers—same as long-johns.

7 A jail. Cf **digger 3**

1942 Berrey–Van den Bark *Amer. Slang* 466.11, Jail . . jigger.

8 See **jagger** n¹ **c.**

9 See **jig** v **1.**

10 See **jig** n³.

jigger n² Cf **chigger**

1 also *jigger flea:* =chigger 2. [*OED* 1756 →]

1827 Williams *View W. FL* 29 **nwFL,** Of these [=insects] the jigger is the most troublesome; it enters the skin, most usually of the feet, and produces an excessive itching and inflammation. **1859** (1968) Bartlett *Americanisms* 77, Chigoe, spelt also *chigre, chigger, jigger,* etc. *(Pulex penetrans.)* Sand-fleas, which penetrate under the skin of the feet, particularly the toes. **1869** *Amer. Naturalist* 3.386, As I was not in the habit of going entirely barefooted, I cannot say whether I would have been more troubled by the nigua (Spanish)—or jigger (Florida), or chigoe or chique (French) . . —than with shoes. **1903** *DN* 2.318 **seMO,** Jigger or *chigger.* . . Chigoe; a minute flea. **1905** Kellogg *Amer. Insects* 356, The male jigger-fleas hop on or off the host as other fleas do, but the females . . burrow into the skin, especially that of the feet. **1949** *PADS* 11.19 **CO,** Chigger, jigger. . . A flea that burrows under the skin. **1954** Borror–DeLong *Intro. Insects* 652, The chigoe flea or jigger, *Tunga penetrans.* **1972** Swan–Papp *Insects* 659, *Tunga penetrans.* . . Jiggers (not to be confused with chiggers—mites which cause reddish welts on the human skin).

2 =harvest mite. **chiefly Nth, N Midl** See Map

1873 *Amer. Naturalist* 7.17, We have, however, in the southwestern States, two other mites which cause great annoyance from harvest time till into October. . . Both of them are six-legged, reddish, microscopic specks, and both are popularly termed jiggers. **1874** MO State Entomol. Annual Rept. 122, "Jiggers" or Harvest-mites: *Leptus irritans,* . . and *L. Americanus.* **1892** KS Univ. Qrly. 1.97, *Jigger or chigger:* a minute red mite, which frequents weeds and lawns, burrows beneath the human skin and causes excruciating itching. **1906** Johnson *Highways Missip. Valley* 137 **Ozarks,** "You're bound to get acquainted with them ticks in summer," explained the man; "and there's a little kind of a bug we call jiggers that's worse still." **1916** Kephart *Camping & Woodcraft* 1.253, *Northern Chiggers.*—The *moquim* mentioned above answers the description of our own chigger, jigger, red-bug, as she is variously called, which is an entirely different beast from the real chigger or chigoe of the tropics. I do not know what may be the northern limit of these diabolic creatures, but have made their acquaintance on Swatara Creek in Pennsylvania. They are quite at home on the prairies of southern Illinois,

exist in myriads on the Ozarks, and throughout the lowlands of the South, and are perhaps worst of all in some parts of Texas. **1950** *WELS* **WI** (*Very small red bugs . . that get under your skin and cause itching*) 14 Infs, Jigger; (*A very tiny fly that you can hardly see but that stings sharply*) 1 Inf, Chigger, jigger. **c1960** *Wilson Coll.* **csKY,** *Trombicula irritans.* . . Farther north it is a *jigger.* **1965–70** *DARE* (Qu. R22, *Very small red insects, almost too small to see, that get under your skin and cause itching*) 155 Infs, **chiefly Nth, N Midl,** Jiggers; **MO**38, Grass jiggers; **MI**112, Sand jiggers; (Qu. R11, *A very tiny fly that you can hardly see, but that stings*) Infs **NY**148, **PA**29, 242, Jigger; (Qu. R12, . . *Flies . . that fly around animals*) Inf **MD**3, Jigger; (Qu. R21, . . *Other kinds of stinging insects*) Infs **IL**29, 30, Jigger.

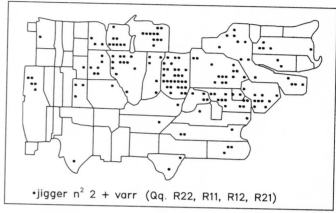

•jigger n² 2 + varr (Qq. R22, R11, R12, R21)

3 =wiggler.

1967–69 *DARE* (Qu. R14, *Small worm-like things [seen in rain barrels or standing water] that hatch into mosquitoes*) Infs **MI**101, **OH**12, **PA**115, Jiggers.

jigger v¹

1905 U.S. Forest Serv. *Bulletin* 61.40 [Logging terms], *Jigger.* . . To pull a log by horsepower over a level place in a slide. (Gen.) Syn.: lazy haul, to.

jigger v², hence ppl adj *jiggered* [Cf *EDD jiggered* exhausted, tired]

To tire, exhaust.

1900 Willard *Tramping* 394, [Glossary:] *Jiggered:* "done," beaten. **1936** McCarthy *Lang. Mosshorn* np **West** [Range terms], *Jiggered,* adj. [Of] An overrun horse or cow. **1944** Adams *Western Words* 84, *Jigger*—To overrun a horse.

jigger exclam Also *jiggeroo, jiggers*

Used as an exclamation of warning; also in phrr *give jiggs* (or *jiggers*) to signal a warning.

1911 *DN* 3.545 **NE,** *Jigger.* . . Look out; be careful. "Jigger, kids, the teacher's coming." **1919** *DN* 5.41 [Hobo cant], *Jiggeroo.* . . Cheese it: a warning to be careful or escape. **1927** *DN* 5.452 [Underworld jargon], *Jiggeroo.* . . A warning that the police are coming. **1932** *AmSp* 7.402 [Orphans' home argot], *Jiggers.* . . Look out! Run! (A word of warning.) "Jiggers, the stick[=night watchman or discipline officer]'s coming." **1932** Farrell *Young Lonigan* 267 **Chicago IL,** Johnny O'Brien hung outside in the alley to give jiggs. *Ibid* 268, Benny Taite suddenly gave jiggers. The janitor from the O'Connell building, and the one from the building they looted were coming across the prairie after them. [**1972** Shafer *Dict. Prison Slang* 23 **TX,** Jigger—a lookout to warn others by relay.]

jiggerboo See **jigaboo**

jiggered adj Also *jiggery* [Prob < *jigger* to jerk up and down] Mentally disordered.

1895 *DN* 1.389 **seMA,** *Jiggery, jiggered* . . not sound minded; having a "screw loose."

jiggered ppl adj See **jigger** v²

jiggered, I'll be phr Also *I'll be jigged,* ~ *jiggerooed* **chiefly Nth, N Midl, West** See Map on p. 132 Cf **dog** v **6**

Used as a mild oath or exclam.

1886 Burnett *Little Lord Fauntleroy* 18 **NYC,** "Well," said Mr. Hobbs, "I'll be—jiggered!" This was an exclamation he always used when he was very much astonished or excited. **1905** *DN* 3.62 **NE**, *Jiggered, I'll be*. . . Confounded. "I'll be jiggered if I do what he says." **1905** *DN* 3.84 **nwAR**, *Jiggered*. . . In the exclamation of surprise, 'I'll be jiggered!' Common. **1908** *DN* 3.325 **eAL, wGA**, *Jigg(er)ed*. . . In the exclamatory phrase [*"*]"I'll be jiggered." **1912** *DN* 3.579 **wIN**, *Jiggered*. . . Used only in the exclamation, "Well, I'll be jiggered!" **1913** London *Valley of Moon* 108 **CA**, I'll be everlastingly jiggerooed if I put up for a wigwam I can't be boss of. **1950** *WELS* **WI** (*Weakened substitutes for "damn" and "damned": "Well, I'll be _____!"*) 3 Infs, Jiggered; 1 Inf, Jigged; (*Exclamations of surprise*. . . *"Well, _____."*) 2 Infs, I'll be jiggered. **1956** McAtee *Some Dialect NC* 24, *Jiggered, I'll be*: saying of surprise or amazement. **1965–70** *DARE* (Qu. NN25b, *Weakened substitutes for 'damn' or 'damned': "Well, I'll be _____!"*) 16 Infs, esp **Nth, N Midl, West**, Jiggered; (Qu. NN7, *Exclamations of surprise: "They're getting married next week? Well, _____."*) Infs **CA**53, 136, **IA**41, **ME**19, **NY**7, **OH**15, I'll be jiggered; (Qu. NN32, *Exclamations like 'I swear' or 'I vow'*) Infs **MD**49, **MT**4, I'll be jiggered.

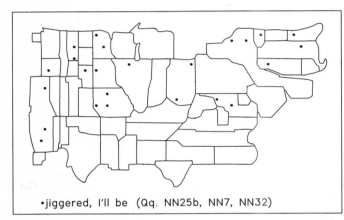

•jiggered, I'll be (Qq. NN25b, NN7, NN32)

jigger fishing See **jiggering**

jigger flea See **jigger** n² **1**

jigger-head n [Prob < *jigger* to jerk up and down] Cf **head** n **C1a**

One who is **jiggered** adj.

  1895 *DN* 1.389 **seMA**, *Jigger-head*: not sound minded; having a "screw loose."

jiggering vbl n Also *jigger (pole) fishing, jiggerpoling* esp **S Atl** Cf **jig** v **1**

Fishing by creating a disturbance at the surface of the water; see quots.

  1930 *DN* 6.82 **cSC**, *Jiggering*, a method of fishing, in which the bait, a long thin strip of pork rind, is attached to the end of a short line. The bait is shaken very close to the surface of the water. **1966–68** *DARE* (Qu. P13, . . *Other ways of fishing*) Inf **FL**32, Jigger pole fishing—you use a long pole, a short line, and you shake the line in the water; **FL**34, Jigger fishing—you put several hooks on a line and fish at night; **NY**101, Jiggering—a cane pole used to hold the bait just above the surface of the water; **SC**19, Jiggering—using a short line, you splash the bait to make the fish come to the top; (Qu. P15, . . *Fishing that's done from a slowly moving boat*) Infs **AL**17, **GA**7, Jigger fishing. **1982** Sternberg *Fishing* 77, Jiggerpoling is an unusual technique for fishing big bass. Fishermen tie a short length of heavy line to a cane pole, then add a treble hook gobbed with worms. To attract bass, they slap the rod tip on the surface. Jiggerpoling is usually done in shallow water choked with timber, weeds or other cover.

jiggering iron n

=**jagger** n¹ **a.**

  [**1776** in 1985 Lederer *Colonial Amer. Engl.* 125 **NY**, 1 hang iron, 2 toasters, 2 jiggin irons, 1 baking pot.] **1903** *DN* 2.352 **sCT**, *Jiggering iron*. . . A kitchen utensil to cut out cakes. Heard in New Haven, Conn. from an old lady.

jiggerjawed See **jimberjawed**

jiggermaree See **jigamaree**

jiggeroo See **jigger** exclam

jiggerooed, I'll be See **jiggered, I'll be**

---

jigger pole fishing, jiggerpoling See **jiggering**

jiggers n¹

=**heebie-jeebies 1.**

  1966–69 *DARE* (Qu. P36, *When a hunter sees a deer or other game animal and gets so excited he can't shoot, he has _____*) Inf **MS**72, Jiggers; (Qu. GG13b, *When something keeps bothering a person and makes him nervous* . . *"It gives me the _____."*) Infs **CO**4, **DC**3, **MI**101, Jiggers.

jiggers n² [Euphem for *Jesus*] Cf **jiggered, I'll be**

Used in exclams and mild oaths.

  1924 *DN* 5.271 [Exclams], Jigger, holy jigger, by jiggers, oh jiggers. **1968** Moody *Horse* 21 **nwKS** (as of c1920), Well, by jiggers, they sure are in nice flesh. **1969** *DARE* (Qu. NN8a, *Exclamations of annoyance or disgust: "Oh _____. I've lost my glasses again."*) Inf **CA**137, Jiggers.

jiggers exclam See **jigger** exclam

jigger wagon See **jigger** n¹ **2**

jiggerweed n

A **spiderling** (here: *Boerhaavia erecta*).

  1897 *Jrl. Amer. Folkl.* 10.53, *Boerhaavia erecta*, . . jigger weed, Florida keys.

jiggery See **jiggered** adj

jiggie See **jigger** n¹ **3**

jigging See **jig** v **1**

jiggle n

A slow, steady trot; hence v *jiggle* to ride at this pace; vbl n *jiggling*.

  1934 (1940) Weseen *Dict. Amer. Slang* 100 [Cowboys and westerners], *Jiggle*—The ordinary gait of about five miles an hour; to ride at this gait. **1936** Adams *Cowboy Lingo* 104, Ordinary riding was known as 'rackin',' or 'jiggling.'

jiggle board See **jiggling board 1**

jiggle-o n Cf **jiggling board, joggling board**

  1943 *LANE* Map 577 (*Seesaw*), Several informants mention a different kind of plaything, consisting of a flexible plank supported at each end by a trestle or the like, used by one child standing in the center to bounce up and down. . . 1 inf, **seMA**, ['dʒɪgəloᵛᵁ], 'a nice boughten one' (perhaps a trade name).

jiggling See **jiggle**

jiggling board n

1 also *jiggle board*: =**joggling board.**

  1859 (1968) Bartlett *Americanisms* 221, *Jiggling-board*. A board the ends of which are placed upon frames or stools, upon which a person stands and springs up. **1968** *DARE* (Qu. EE31, *Playground equipment with a long board for two children to sit on and go up and down in turn*) Inf **GA**58, Jiggle board—one you jump on.

2 See quot.

  1889 (1971) Farmer *Americanisms* 325, *Jiggling-board*.—A springboard, such as is used for diving and athletics.

jiggs See **jig** n¹ **3**

jiggs, give See **jigger** exclam

jiggumbob n *obs* Cf **thingamabob**

See quot 1899.

  1859 (1968) Bartlett *Americanisms* 221, *Jigamaree*. A trivial or nonsensical thing. A factitious word, equivalent to "jiggumbob" and "thingumbob." **1899** (1912) Green *VA Folk-Speech* 245, *Jiggumbob*. . . Something strange, peculiar, or unknown; a thingumbob. **1934** (1943) *W2*, *Jiggumbob*. . . Colloq.

jiggus See **jigger** n¹ **3**

jig head See **jickhead**

jig is up (or over) See **jig** n¹ **1**

jig, jag, jinny, and the game n

=**high-low-jack.**

  1906 *DN* 3.143 **nwAR**, *Jig, jag, jinny, and the game*. . . High, low, jack, game.

jig juice See **jig water**

jig leg n [Cf **jake leg** n[1] **1**]

1967 DARE (Qu. DD21b, *General words . . for bad liquor*) Inf **OH**37, Jig leg.

jig load n [Var of **jag** n[2] **1a** + redund *load*]

1966 DARE (Qu. L55, *If the wagon was only partly full . . he had a ———*) Inf **FL**12, Jig load, half load, piece load.

jig on, get a See **jig** n[1] **4**

jig-stick n Cf **sand jigger**

1970 DARE (Qu. L18, *Kinds of plows*) Inf **TX**78, Jig-stick . . shaft with rotating teeth to turn up wet dirt.

jig('s) time, in See **jig** n[1] **2**

jigwalker See **jig** n[1] **3**

jig water n Also *jig juice*

Liquor; an alcoholic beverage, esp of bad quality.

1888 in 1971 Farmer *Americanisms* 325, A middle-aged countryman had just tottered away from the counter, over which fusil oil (jig-water) is dispensed. **1897** Lewis *Wolfville* 70 **AZ**, I s'pose this yere bein' married is a heap habit, same as tobacco an' jig-juice. **1901** DN 2.142 **MI**, Jig-water. . . A drink made from a mixture of alcohol, sugar, water and wintergreen. **1908** McGaffey *Sorrows* 121 *(DA)*, We had to force the only jig juice in the crowd between his clinched teeth before he could be revived. **1931–33** LANE Worksheets **MA**, Jig juice—A kind of cider. **1968** Adams *Western Words* 165, Jig juice—A freighter's name for whisky. Also called *jig water*.

‡**jilfer** v Cf **gillflirt** n

To jilt.

1966 DARE (Qu. AA11, *If a man asks a girl to marry him and she refuses, . . she ———*) Inf **MS**21, Jilfered him.

jillflirt See **gillflirt** n

jillflirted See **gillflirted**

jillikens n

1953 Randolph-Wilson *Down in Holler* 256 **Ozarks**, Jillikens. . . Backwoods. "Them folks live away back in the jillikens; don't come to town but twice a year."

Jill-in-the-pulpit See **jack-in-the-pulpit 1**

Jill-o'er-the-ground See **Gill-over-the-ground**

jill poke n Also *gill poke, jell poke* **Nth**

1 A log stuck so as to threaten to cause a logjam; a limb overhanging a river; transf: a limb or plank on a road that threatens to snag a passing vehicle.

1914 DN 4.75 **ME, nNH**, Jill-poke. . . A log stuck in the mud or along the banks of a lake or stream (Jell-poke.) **1942** Beck *Songs MI Lumberjacks* 86, Logger Parmentier, of Rose City, says that a jill-poke is a snag. . . Now a jill-poke in the alders / Is a mighty measly thing;/ It can tie a lot of timber in a knot. **1958** McCulloch *Woods Words* 70 **Pacific NW**, Gill poke. . . A loose plank on a plank road or bridge which flies up and spears a car or truck; or a branch lying in a road which does the same thing. *Ibid* 98, Jill poke. . . A loosely balanced timber on a plank road which may fly up and spear a car passing over it. **1969** Sorden *Lumberjack Lingo* 56 **NEng, Gt Lakes**, Hit a Gill poke—On a log drive, to go ashore on the limb of a tree that overhangs the river. *Ibid* 64, Jill poke. . . A log stuck in the bank of a stream where it could cause a jam. **1975** [see **3** below].

2 By ext: see quot.

1914 DN 4.152 **csME**, Jillpoke. . . A blow given to a boat or canoe by a log floating down stream. Used also figuratively for a kick.

3 A slow or awkward person—also used as a vague term of abuse.

[**1914** DN 4.80 **ME, nNH**, *Slower'n a jill-poke.* Extremely slow.] **1942** Berrey-Van den Bark *Amer. Slang* 414.3, Listless or slow person. . . Jill Poke. **1968** DARE (Qu. HH16, *Uncomplimentary words with no definite meaning—just used when you want to show that you don't think much of a person: "Don't invite him. He's a ———."*) Inf **NH**14, Gink, jill poke—may be joking or mildly uncomplimentary. **1969** Sorden *Lumberjack Lingo* 64 **NEng, Gt Lakes**, Jill poke. . . An awkward person. **1975** Gould *ME Lingo* 147, Jillpoke—A long log on a river drive which gets one end stuck somehow and swings to start a jam. Thus, an awkward person likely to do something foolish or start trouble.

4 also *jill pole*; In logging and railroading: a lever, prop, or pole used to move or restrain heavy objects; any such lever that unintentionally impedes movement. Cf **jill poke** v **2**

1950 [see **jill poke** v **2**]. **1956** AmSp 31.151 **nwCA**, Jill poke. . . A lever used to dump logs from flat cars into a pond. **1958** McCulloch *Woods Words* 70 **Pacific NW**, Gill poke—a. A horizontal stiff-arm or swinging boom used to poke logs off cars at a log dump. b. A pole or plank used to shove something. *Ibid* 98, Jill poke. . . A stout pole used in shoving cars out of a siding when the engine is working on the main line and cannot head in to pick up the cars. *Ibid* 99, Jill pole—Same as jill poke. **1961** Labbe-Goe *Railroads* 166 **Pacific NW**, [Caption:] Jill-poke as used by the Wisconsin Logging and Lumber Company. The end of the beam was placed against the load, and as the train moved ahead it swung around, forcing the logs off the car. *Ibid* 258, Jillpoke: A rod, or pole, used as a lever to prevent movement in one direction, as a prop. Also any such lever, or prop, inadvertently interfering with movement. **1969** Sorden *Lumberjack Lingo* 64 **NEng, Gt Lakes**, Jill poke. . . A wood prop to hold the sleigh [=logging sled] in place while loading logs.

5 An oxgoad.

1967 DARE (Qu. K27, . . *The sharp-pointed stick used to get oxen to move*) Inf **OR**1, Jill poke.

jill poke v Also sp *gill poke* [**jill poke** n] **Pacific NW**

1 To hit an obstruction; to puncture, poke, or knock down; also fig; hence ppl adj *jill poked*.

1950 *Western Folkl.* 9.118 **nwOR** [Logger speech], Jill-poke. To run into an obstruction. **1958** McCulloch *Woods Words* 70 **Pacific NW**, Gill poked—a. Stuck, or hung up. b. Hit in the stomach. c. Shoved off, as a logger knocked off a car by a swinging log. *Ibid* 99, Jill poked—a. A cat radiator punctured by a sharp stick or branch. b. To be stuck, or caught foul, or hung up on a job of any kind. **1963** *Western Folkl.* 22.266 **nwCA**, A jill poke is now a horizontal pole or lever used to dump logs from flat cars into a log pond. To be jill-poked is to be hit or to be shoved off any object. It is also used in popular speech [meaning] to be treated unfairly: "The mill owners have been jill-poking him."

2 To move by leverage with a **jill poke** n **4**.

1950 *Western Folkl.* 9.118 **nwOR** [Logger speech], Jill poke. . . To move an object that cannot be reached by ordinary methods by placing a timber or bar between the object and moving force; the timber or bar so used.

jill poked See **jill poke** v **1**

jill pole See **jill poke** n **4**

jillyflirt See **gillflirted 1**

jilote n Also *helote, hilote* [MexSpan]

An ear of **green corn 2.**

1892 DN 1.248 **TX**, Jilóte: a "roasting ear," an immature ear of corn. Also *helote*, or *hilote*. From Mexican *xilotl*. **1938** AmSp 13.117, An ear of green corn, or 'roasting ear,' bears the Texan name *jilote*, derived from the Nahuatl *xilotl* in a similar sense.

jim n

1 Used in exclams and mild oaths; see quots.

1866 Devens *Pictorial Book* 444, By Jim! Major, you got out of *that* snarl completely—slick! **1897** Stuart *Simpkinsville* 56 **AR**, I'd give every doggone cent . . ef I'd 'a' been raised to swear—I'll be . . jim-blasted ef I wouldn't! **1911** Saunders *Col. Todhunter* 7 **MO**, I'll be jim-swizzled if I don't. **1914** DN 4.75 **ME, nNH**, Jim Hill, or Jim Whittiker! Ejaculations. **1924** DN 5.271 [Exclams], I'll be jim-swiggled. **1934** Hanley Disks **swME**, By the Jim Hill. Old-fashioned. **1959** VT Hist. 27.144, *By Jim Whiz!*. . . Rare. *Ibid*, Jim Cracky!. . . Rare. **1970** DARE (Qu. NN30, *Exclamations beginning with the sound of 'j'*) Inf **WV**21, By jim; **IL**115, Jim.

2 Used as a term of address for a man. Cf **jack** n[1] **1**

1970 Major *Dict. Afro-Amer. Slang* 71, Jim: (1940's) term of address to a man. **1970** Young *Snakes* 16 **ceMS** [Black], I just wanna knock out chicks and show these other dudes they aint hittin on doodleysquat when it comes to talkin trash. I got it down, jim! *Ibid* 34, I didn't know where the hell I was. I mean I was out there, jim.

3 =**great blue heron.**

1917 *Wilson Bulletin* 29.2.78, *Ardea herodias*. . . Jim, Hamburg, La.

jim v

1 also with *around*: To do odd jobs; to loaf about; hence n *jim-around* an odd-job man. **esp WV** Cf **gin** v[1] **4**, **jim-hand**, **jim work**

1912 *DN* 3.579 **wIN,** *Jim.* . . To potter, to trifle. "He just jims around all the time." **1920** Fay *Gloss. Mining* 370 **WV,** Jim-around. . . A man who does miscellaneous work at mines. **1927** *AmSp* 2.358 **cwWV,** *Jim* . . to work at odd jobs. "I jimmed after the ox team last week." **1939** *AmSp* 14.156 **WV,** 'To gin (or jim) around' . . means 'just to dabble around, to fool around, to fiddle around.' 'Well, what have you been doing during the holidays?' Answer: 'Oh, just ginning (or jimming) around.' **1942** Berrey–Van den Bark *Amer. Slang* 245.9, Jim, jim around, *to do odd jobs. Ibid* 456.6, *Handy man; "Jack-of-all-trades."* . . jim-around, jim-hand. **1971** *AN&Q* Apr 121, The small farmers of Jesse Stuart's W-Hollow area of Kentucky. . . go "ginning" around town, meaning to wander around looking for amusement without anything specific in mind. The farmers of the central counties of West Virginia . . go "Jimming."
2 also with *up:* To spoil, ruin, damage; also fig; hence ppl adj phr *jimmed up.*
1913 *DN* 4.27 **NW,** *Jim.* . . To spoil. **1942** in 1944 *ADD,* If some . . executive had got this job there might have been so much envy . . in rubber circles as to jim the rubber conservation program. N.Y. *Daily News.* **1953** Randolph–Wilson *Down in Holler* 256 **Ozarks,** *Jim.* . . To damage, to mar, to deface. The Lamar, Mo., *Democrat* (September 5, 1939) describes a motor wreck on the highway: "Williams said it turned his Chevrolet over and sprang the frame, besides jimming it up." **1954** *Harder Coll.* **cwTN,** *Jim.* . . To damage, to mar, to deface. **1967** *DARE* (QR, near Qu. Y38) Inf **MI55,** Jimmed up—With a piece of machinery we might say 'It's all jimmed up.'

jim around See **jim** v 1

jimberjaw n Also *gimberjaw, jipperjaw* [Cf **jimberjawed**]
1 A protruding lower jaw.
1889 (1971) Farmer *Americanisms* 325, *Jimberjaw.* . . A protruding lower jaw. **1899** (1912) Green *VA Folk-Speech* 245, *Jimber-jaw.* . . A projecting lower jaw. **1934** (1943) *W2, Jimberjaw.* . . Colloq. **1958** Baker *Friend in Power* 66 **NJ,** Jim Sloane leaned forward, his jipper-jaw protruding.
2 Back talk, verbal show of resistance.
1834 *Life Andrew Jackson* 36 **TN,** Now my lads, said the gineral, if they give you any jimber jaw be at 'em flugens, and make them scamper. **1950** (1965) Richter *Town* 3 **OH,** Then Guerdon with his Yankee gimber jaw, always a scheming to get out of work like his Grandpappy Luckett.

jimberjawed adj Also *gimberjawed, jibberjawed, jiggerjawed, jim(mer)jawed, jimmiejawed, jimmyjawed, jip(per)jawed* [Prob varr of **gimbal-jawed**] chiefly **Sth, S Midl** Cf **wapper-jawed**
1 Having a protruding, loose, or crooked lower jaw.
1830 *N.Y. Constellation* 11 Sep. 2/5 (*DA*), You jimber-jawed rascal. **1834** Carruthers *Kentuckian* I.195 (*DAE*), Some. . . pushed out the under jaw, like a person who (to use a Southern term) is jimberjawed. **1885** Murfree *Prophet of Smoky Mts.* 74 **eTN,** His long chin, of the style familiarly denominated jimber-jawed, was still smooth and boyish. **1890** *DN* 1.74 **Philadelphia PA,** *Jimber-jawed:* with lower jaw projecting. A bull-dog is "jimber-jawed." **1892** Harris *Uncle Remus & Friends* 172 **GA,** You'll be jimber-jaw'd long 'fo' you gnyaw thoo my hide! **1893** Shands *MS Speech* 72, *Jimmy-jawed.* . . This expression is very common. **1899** (1912) Green *VA Folk-Speech* 196, *Gimber-jawed.* . . Having the lower jaw apparently out of joint, projecting beyond the upper, and moving with unusual freedom. Jimber-jawed. **1942** Faulkner *Go Down* 40 **MS,** A jimber-jawed clown who could not even learn to make whiskey. **1946** *PADS* 6.18 **cwVA** (as of 1900–10), *Jimmy-jawed.* . . Prognathous. . . Reported as occasional, 1942. **1950** *PADS* 14.41 **SC,** Jimmie-jawed. **1952** Brown *NC Folkl.* 1.555, *Jip-jawed.* . . Having jaws that do not meet. **1958** Baker *Friend in Power* 60 **NJ,** It's our jipper-jawed friend. **c1960** *Wilson Coll.* **csKY,** *Jimmer* (or *jimber*)*-jawed.* Prognathous, lantern jawed. **1965–70** *DARE* (Qu. X6, *If a person's lower jaw sticks out prominently . . he's* _____) Infs **CT30, IL96, MA47, NC14, 18, SC2, 4, VA13,** Jimberjawed; **KY40, MS23, MO25, VA42,** Jimmyjawed; **NC48,** Jibberjawed; **TN3,** Jimmerjawed. **a1975** Lunsford *It Used to Be* 166 **sAppalachians,** "Jipjawed" is a term that has reference to an animal or mule whose upper jaw and lower jaw do not meet.
2 Transf: crooked, lopsided.
1904 Clay–Clopton *Belle* 256 **AL** (as of c1860), They were a guard, flanking on each side an old "jimber-jawed, wobble-sided" barouche, drawn by two raw-boned horses. **1960** Williams *Walk Egypt* 190 **GA,** You got to keep her quiet if you don't want her arm setting jibber-jawed. **1968** *DARE* (Qu. KK70, *Something that has got out of proper shape:*

"That house is all _____.") Inf **OH70,** Jiggerjawed; (Qu. MM13, *The table was nice and straight until he came along and knocked it* _____) Inf **VA15,** Jibberjawed.

jimble-jawed See **gimbal-jawed**

jimbo n[1] [Perh var of **gumbo 2**]
1966 *DARE* (Qu. H36, *Kinds of soup*) Inf **SC26,** Jimbo [ˈjɪmbo]—butterbeans, corn, tomatoes, okra, sweet peas, carrots.

jimbo n[2] Cf **flambeau 2**
1982 *McDavid Coll.* **nwSC,** *Jimbo*—a lantern improvised out of a long neck bottle with a rag wick, filled with kerosene.

Jim Brannigan See **brannigan 2**

jim brush n Also *jim bush*
A **ceanothus** (here: *Ceanothus sorediatus*) native to California.
1925 Jepson *Manual Plants CA* 621, *C[eanothus] sorediatus.* . . *Jim Brush.* . . It often forms extensive thickets. **1938** Van Dersal *Native Woody Plants* 90, *Jim brush.* . . coppices vigorously after cutting or burning. **1961** Thomas *Flora Santa Cruz* 235 **cwCA,** Jim Bush. Common in chaparral and along the edges of woods from northern San Mateo County southward.

jim climber n
A **trumpet creeper** (here: *Campsis radicans*).
1968 *DARE* (Qu. S26c, *Wildflowers that grow in woods*) Inf **DE3,** Jim climbers (=trumpet vine).

jim crab See **jimmy** n 3

jimcrack n
1 See **jimcracker.**
2 A fool, nincompoop. [Cf *OED gimcrack* sb. 3 "An affected showy person, a fop. . . *Obs.*"]
1908 *DN* 3.325 **eAL, wGA,** *Jim-crack.* . . A sorry sort of person, a ninny. "He's a regular jim-crack." **1956** Settle *Beulah Land* 186 **WV** (as of 1754–74), He . . thought with contempt of the jimcrack he had been—that posturing, ridiculous boy who had stumbled into a transported hell for the price of a watch.
3 See quot.
1908 *DN* 3.325 **eAL, wGA,** *Jim-crack.* . . A lie. "He told me a jim-crack."

jimcracker n Also *jimcrack(y)* Cf **jim-dandy** n 1
=**cracker 4.**
1834 *Bastinado* 49 **SC,** Beauty Billy had been a great man in his day—that is, a great man on a small scale, and delivered himself as fast as he conceived. He was a thorough bred jim-crack, at beating the devil round the stump, and was addicted to spinning mighty yarns, which took the congress a long time to unravel. **1937** *AmSp* 12.239 **MN,** 'He's a jimcracker!' is frequent in Minnesota to indicate that the person commented upon has exceptional skill; it is especially applied to persons excelling in games. **1970** *DARE* (Qu. KK1b, . . *'In the very best condition': "His farm is* _____.") Inf **NY234,** A jimcracky.

jim crow n
1 See quots. [Perh infl by *jimmy* a short crowbar + *crow* abbr for *crowbar*]
1872 (1876) Knight *Amer. Mech. Dict.* 2.1215, *Jim-crow.* . . An implement for bending or straightening rails. **1945** *CA Folkl. Qrly.* 4.322 **CO** [Mining terms], *Jim Crow:* Crow bar with a hook on it for curving straight ore car tracks in a tunnel. **1960** Climax Molybdenum Co. *Manual* 47 [Mine terms], *Jim-crow*—A railroad rail bender.
2 In logging: see quot.
1931 *AmSp* 7.48 **Sth, SW** [Lumberjack lingo], "Tie men" are known as "Jim Crow men." Their boss is called "Captain Jim Crow." These names are derived from the "jim crows," the small unsalable [railroad] ties which they make.
3 attrib: Incompetent; small-time; fraudulent.
1838 *N.Y. Advt. & Exp.* 18 April 2/1 (*DA*), Gov. Marcy's message, Mr. Secretary Woodbury's Letter . . are Jim Crow performances. **1885** Siringo *TX Cowboy* 161, Some mexican thieves, who robbed Mr. Pitcher of everything he had in his little Jim Crow store. **1890** *Stock Grower & Farmer* 11 Jan. 3/4 (*DA*) **NM,** The *Stock Grower* has refused to puff a fraudulent jim crow ditch scheme whose projectors have handled a big profit before the 'preliminary survey' was made. **1893** James *Cow-Boy Life in TX* 27, And my advice to the Jim Crow counterfeiter . . is for him to stick just as close to the piney woods of east Texas and Arkansaw

as possible. *Ibid* 180, There came a "Jim Crow" circus to a little town in the West and of course everybody went. **1903** (1965) Adams *Log Cowboy* 203 **West,** When they cut them into car lots and shipped them, they were a hundred and eighteen short. They wanted to come back on me to make them good, but, shucks! I wasn't responsible if their Jim Crow outfit lost the cattle.

4 See **jim crow card.**

5 =**black vulture.**

    1955 Forbush–May *Birds* 95, *Black Vulture. . . Other names:* Carrion Crow; . . Jim Crow. . . In the South, especially near the coast, the Black Vulture is often a very common bird.

jim-crow card n Also *jim crow* [*jim crow* a Black person + **card** n²] S Atl

An implement similar to a wool card, esp as used by a Black person to comb the hair.

    1883 (1971) Harris *Nights with Remus* 75 **GA** [Black], You better go git yo' Jim Crow kyard en straighten out dem wraps in yo' ha'r. I allers year w'ite folks say you better keep yo' eye on niggers w'at got der ha'r wrop up in strings. **1885** in 1976 Rose *Doc. Hist. Slavery* 399 **SC,** The unsuccessful attempt was made to straighten out our unruly wools with some small cards, or Jim-crows as we called them. **1899** Chesnutt *Conjure Woman* 22 **csNC** [Black], He wuk at it [=his hair] ha'f de night wid er Jim Crow, en think he git it straighten' out. **1908** *DN* 3.325 **eAL, wGA,** *Jim-crow card. . .* A currycomb: so called because the negroes sometimes use it for combing the kinks out of their hair. **1950** *PADS* 14.41 **Charleston SC,** *Jimcrow cards. . .* Small wool cards used by Negroes to comb out their hair. "A familiar article in trade forty years ago, but little sold today."

jim-dandy n Pronc-sp *chim-dandy*

1 A superior or excellent person or thing. Cf **joe-dandy**

    1887 *Courier–Jrl.* (Louisville KY) 12 Jan 2/1, Dear Sir: Though a stranger to you (yet a Democrat), let me say, you are a "Jim Dandy." **1895** (1969) Crane *Red Badge* 100, He was reg'lar jim-dandy fer nerve. **1895** Townsend *Chimmie Fadden* 100 **NYC,** Say, did ye ever hear such langwudge like dat? Ain't 'e er chim-dandy? **1905** *DN* 3.62 **NE,** *Jim dandy. . .* Intensive of *dandy,* as term of approbation or admiration. "Your knife is a jim dandy." **1909** *DN* 3.399 **nwAR,** *Jim-dandy. . .* Term of approbation. "He's a jim-dandy." **1914** Atherton *Perch of the Devil* 242 **MT,** I've got a . . jim dandy of a limousine. **1950** *WELS Suppl.* **WI,** Jim-dandies. Fine ones, great ones. (Sarcastic.) "You're jim-dandies, you are." **1954** *Harder Coll.* **cwTN,** *Jim-dandy.* One who feels that he is important. **1966–69** *DARE* (Qu. KK1b, . . *'In the very best condition':* "*His farm is _____.*") 14 Infs, **scattered,** A jim-dandy; (Qu. KK2, . . *'Very likeable or popular':* "*He's _____.*"; total Infs questioned, 75) Inf **MS**1, A jim-dandy; (Qu. KK5, A very skilled or expert person . . "*He's a _____.*") Inf **AR**31, Jim-dandy; (Qu. LL5, *Something impressively big:* "*That cabbage is really a _____.*") Inf **LA**17, Jim-dandy—this also means outstandingly good in other respects. **a1975** Lunsford *It Used to Be* 169 **sAppalachians,** "Jim dandy" means a very good one. Whatever it is, it's a jim dandy. **1976** Garber *Mountain-ese* 48 **sAppalachians,** Jim-dandy . . [a] fine specimen.

2 See quots.

    1954 *Harder Coll.* **cwTN,** *Jim-dandy.* A person who dresses to look his best. " 'E's jist a nold Jim-dandy, a-struttin' lak banty rooster." **1967** *DARE* (Qu. HH2, *Names and nicknames for a citified person*) Inf **TX**31, Jim-dandy.

jim-dandy adj, adv

Excellent; excellently.

    1888 in 1971 Farmer *Americanisms* 325, George C. Ball came upon the floor yesterday arrayed in a jim-dandy suit of clothes. **1902** Wister *Virginian* 346 **WV,** He cert'nly must have been a jim-dandy boy. **1908** *DN* 3.325 **eAL, wGA,** *Jim-dandy. . .* "He has a jim-dandy crop of melons." **1913** *DN* 4.23 **AK,** *Jim-dandy. . .* Usage widespread in Alaska. . . "This pie tastes jim-dandy." "You did jim-dandy." **1923** *DN* 5.212 **swMO,** *Jim dandy. . .* "That was a jim dandy meal." **1941** Stuart *Men of Mts.* 154 **neKY,** He said the blue-tick hound was a jim-dandy possum dog. **1942** Perry *Texas* 143, Old folks in general . . are just jim-dandy. **1967–69** *DARE* (Qu. KK1b, . . *'In the very best condition':* "*His farm is _____.*") Infs **AL**16, **LA**28, **NC**72, Jim-dandy; (Qu. KK4, *When things turn out just right* . . "*Everything is _____ now.*") Infs **MN**28, **NY**213, **VA**15, Jim-dandy. **1979** *Comments on Etym.* 8.15.18, *Jim-Dandy* (=Super, Peachy). . . She . . suggested that *jim-* here may be derived not from the nickname *Jim* but rather from English dialectal *gim* (=natty, spruce) [*DARE* Ed: Cf **jimpsecute**].

jim-hand n Cf **jim** v 1, **jim work**

An odd-job man.

    1927 *AmSp* 2.358 **cwWV,** *Jim-hand . .* one who works at all the odd jobs. "The jim-hand has to keep the camp clean." **1968** *DARE* (Qu. L1, *A man who is employed to help with work on a farm*) Inf **WV**3, Jim-hand.

Jim Hill mustard n [After James J. Hill (1838–1916), American railway promoter: see quots 1937, 1968 at **2** below] NW

1 A **wallflower** (here: *Erysimum inconspicuum*).

    1913 *Torreya* 13.230, *Erysimum inconspicuum. . .* Jim Hill Mustard, Missoula Mont. (according to Prof. D.E. Lantz, Aug 23, 1912). This term insinuates that the Northern Pacific Railroad is responsible for the dissemination of this weed.

2 A **hedge mustard 1** (here: *Sisymbrium altissimum*).

    1923 *Amer. Botanist* 29.153, Among other mustards may be mentioned . . the "tumble mustard" (*Sisymbrium altissimum*) also known as "Jim Hill mustard" from its appearance along the railroad promoted by the person named. **1935** (1943) Muenscher *Weeds* 279, *Sisymbrium altissimum. . .* Jim Hill mustard. . . Most common and troublesome in the Northwest and on the Pacific Coast. **1937** U.S. Forest Serv. *Range Plant Hdbk.* W135, Tumblemustard. . . The common name most generally used in the northern part of the United States is Jim Hill mustard, referring to James J. Hill, the late capitalist and railroad builder, whose Great Northern Railroad transporting the seed of tumblemustard, incidental to the movement of hay, grain, and livestock, greatly assisted in the distribution of this weed pest. **1941** Writers' Program *Guide WA* 325, Barbed-wire fences, against which winds have piled the skeletons of last year's tumbleweeds, Russian thistles, and Jim Hill mustard. **1956** St. John *Flora SE WA* 177, *Sisymbrium altissimum. . .* Jim Hill Mustard. . . The mature plant breaks loose and is tumbled along by strong winds, scattering seeds as it bounces. **1966** *DARE* (Qu. S21, . . *Weeds . . that are a trouble in gardens and fields*) Inf **WA**6, Jim Hill mustard. **1968** Adams *Western Words* 165, *Jim Hill mustard*—Wild mustard, discovered in the early nineties, when Jim Hill built the Great Northern Railroad to Seattle. It dries and blows, forming a tumbleweed as common as the Russian thistle. The term is used exclusively in the Northwest. **1973** Hitchcock–Cronquist *Flora Pacific NW* 176, Jim Hill mustard. . . *S[isymbrium] altissimum.*

3 also *Jim Hill weed:* A **pennycress** (here: *Thlaspi arvense*).

    1923 *Amer. Botanist* 29.154, In these pages Prof. Nelson has recently noted that in our Northwest the plant [=*Thlaspi arvense*] is known as "Jim Hill weed" because introduced along the railroad sponsored by Hill. **1937** U.S. Forest Serv. *Range Plant Hdbk.* W187, From an economic standpoint, field pennycress . . , known locally . . and erroneously as Jim Hill mustard, is now well distributed throughout the United States. **1940** Clute *Amer. Plant Names* 38, *T[hlaspi] arvense. . .* Jim Hill weed.

jiminetty intj Also *geemenetti, geminetti, jeemanently, jeemanetty;* for addit varr see quots [Varr of **jiminy**] Cf **crimanetly**

Used as an expression of surprise, anger, annoyance, etc.

    1901 *DN* 2.142 **cNY, swNY, IN,** *Jiminetty. . .* Used in surprise, anger, etc. *Ibid* **swOH,** *Jiminetties.* **1924** *DN* 5.267 [Exclams], *Geminetti, geemenetti, geemenety,* or *geminettae* (all surp[rise] or vex[ation] in South of U.S.) **1941** *Sat. Eve. Post* 6 Dec 13/1 **MS,** Gee m'netty, Uncle Jess, I ain't never had nothing like this before. **1965–70** *DARE* (Qu. NN30, *Exclamations beginning with the sound of 'j'*) Infs **NY**250, **NC**88, **SC**21, 40, Jeemanetty; **DC**11, Jeemonettimay; **FL**22, Jeemanitty; **MD**9, Jiminetty [jɪmɪˈnɛti]; **NJ**7, Jiminy eddies; **NJ**44, Jiminy netties; **OR**1, Jeeminoley. **1987** *DARE* File **neOH** (as of c1920), Jee-ma-nently. A strong protest among boys.

jiminy n Also *geeminy, gemenee, jeeminee, jeminy, jimmety, jiminy;* for addit varr see quots [Varr of *gemini;* perh also infl by *Jesus,* as in many other minced oaths]

a Used in exclams and mild oaths.

    1836 Simms *Mellichampe* 1.54 **SC,** "Gimini!" exclaimed Thumbscrew, as he beheld . . their irregular approach. "Gimini! if the major was only here now." **1846** (1973) Porter *Quarter Race* 121 **OH,** But oh! Jeminy! see Dick run! **1867** Harris *Sut Lovingood Yarns* 30 **TN,** Nara wun, by geminy! **1874** (1895) Eggleston *Circuit Rider* 150 **sOH** (as of early 1800s), They warn't nothin' in the nex' world too bad fer a hoss-thief, by jeminy hoe-cakes. **1875** (1876) Twain *Tom Sawyer* 21 **MO,** I wish to geeminy she'd stick to one or t'other. **1885** Twain *Huck. Finn* 97 **MO,** By Jimminy, away down through the texas-hall we see a light!

1899 (1912) Green *VA Folk-Speech* 193, *Geemany.* . . A mild oath. **1906** *DN* 3.143 **nwAR,** *Jeeminee* [ˈjiminı]. . . Heavens! **1908** *DN* 3.324 **eAL, wGA,** *Jeeminy.* **1914** *DN* 4.75 **ME, nNH,** *Jimmety whiskers!* **1915** *DN* 4.183 **VA,** *Gee-miny.* **1924** *DN* 5.264 **CO** [Exclams], Jiminy whizzle cat. *Ibid* 267, *Gemini, gemminy, gemenee . . gemini whiz, gemini whiz-zle cats.* **1950** *WELS* **WI** (*Exclamations beginning with the sound of "j"*) 11 Infs, Jiminy gosh (*or* jeepers, jehosephat, jinks, moses, whig, whiskers, whiz); 4 Infs, Jumping jiminy; 1 Inf, Jiminy; 1 Inf, By jimini. **1965–70** *DARE* (Qu. NN30, *Exclamations beginning with the sound of 'j'*) 69 Infs, **scattered, but esp freq PA, WV,** Jeeminy; 50 Infs, **scattered, but esp Nth, N Midl, West,** Jiminy; 19 Infs, **scattered,** Jumpin(g) jiminy; 15 Infs, **scattered,** Jiminy goodness (*or* gosh, gracious, jehos-aphat, john, master, pete, pots, whillikers, whiskers, whiz); **MD**49, **MI**112, **MO**36, **NH**5, **OK**52, By jiminy; **MO**35, Jeeminy sakes; **TX**104, Good jiminy; **NC**72, Great jiminy; **TN**23, Jeemineezer; (Qu. NN20a, *Exclamations caused by sudden pain—a blow on the thumb*) Inf **CA**164, Jiminy; (Qu. NN20b, *Exclamations caused by sudden pain—a slight burn*) Inf **KS**5, Oo jiminy; **NC**82, O jiminy master; (Qu. NN27b, *Weakened substitutes for 'god': "For _____ sakes!"*) Inf **CA**145, Jiminy's; **VT**16, Jiminy; (Qu. NN29c, *Exclamations beginning with 'holy': "Holy _____!"*) Inf **VA**11, Jumpin' jiminy. **1984** *Lutz Coll.* **seNY,** [He], a woodsman and carpenter, did not swear, but he would exclaim, "By Jiminy Spruce!"

b esp in combs *jiminy Christmas,* ∼ *crickets,* ∼ *criminy* and varr. [Euphems for *Jesus Christ*]

1848 in 1935 *AmSp* 10.40 **Nantucket MA,** *By Jiminy Cricket.* An exclamation of surprise. **1859** Taliaferro *Fisher's R.* 238 **nwNC** (as of 1820s), Jeeminny O Jeeminny! what shall I do? . . Jeeminny Crimony! O Jeeminny Crimony! have massy on me, a poor misuble cuss of a sinner! **1887** (1967) Harris *Free Joe* 66 **GA,** "Great Jiminy Craminy!" Major Jimmy Bass would exclaim. **1905** *DN* 3.62 **NE,** *Jimminy Christ-mas, or crickets, or criminy.* . . "Jimminy Christmas, it's cold." **1906** *DN* 3.143 **nwAR,** *Jeeminy Chris'mas.* . . "Jeeminy Chris'mas! That hurts." **1908** *DN* 3.324 **eAL, wGA,** *Jeeminy crickets, jeeminy Chris(t)mas.* **1909** *DN* 3.399 **nwAR,** *Jiminy crickets.* **1910** Hart *Vigi-lante Girl* 305 **nCA,** She's going to try and separate Salem's heirs from some of Salem's money, and by jimminy crick, Yarrow, I think she'll make it go. **1912** *DN* 3.568 **CT, MO, cNY, PA, VT,** *Jimminy crickets.* . . Mild oath. **1930** Dos Passos *42nd Parallel* 147 **DC,** Jimminy criskets what I couldn't do to a watermelon, Joe. **1931** *PMLA* 46.1308 **sAp-palachians,** Gee-miny-crimminy! **1950** *WELS* **WI** (*Exclamations be-ginning with the sound of "j"*) 46 Infs, Jiminy cricket(s); 8 Infs, Jiminy Christmas; 3 Infs, Jiminy crackers; 2 Infs, Jiminy kraut; 1 Inf, Jiminy cripes; (*Exclamations caused by sudden pain*) 1 Inf, Jiminy kraut. **1965–70** *DARE* (Qu. NN30, *Exclamations beginning with the sound of 'j'*) 214 Infs, **widespread,** Jiminy crickets; **KS**15, Jeeminy crickets; 97 Infs, **widespread, but esp freq WV,** Jiminy Christmas; 10 Infs, **scat-tered, but esp Sth, S Midl,** Jiminy cricket; **CA**99, **MD**13, 26, **PA**223, **VA**11, 50, Jiminy criminy; **KY**24, **WI**48, **WV**1, Jeeminy criminy; **GA**73, **IA**4, **ND**2, **NY**84, **OR**10, Jiminy crackers; **MD**34, Jeeminy crackers; **MD**42, **ME**16, **NC**52, Jiminy Christ; **FL**19, **KY**75, Jiminy creepers; **LA**17, **PA**28, Jeeminy creepers; **IL**100, Jiminy christopher; **MD**5, Jiminy cracket; (Qu. NN31, *Exclamations beginning with the sound of 'cr-'*) Infs **ME**6, 12, **PA**82, Jiminy crickets; **OK**11, **WI**44, Jiminy creepers; **IL**82, Jiminy cricket; **TX**76, Jiminy criminy; **VA**8, Jiminy criminy, criminy crow; **OH**74, Jeeminy cripes; (Qu. NN6a, *Exclamations of joy . . when somebody gets a pleasant surprise, he might shout "_____."*) Inf **DE**1, Jiminy crickets; **MD**37, Jeeminy Christmas; (Qu. NN7, *Exclamations of surprise: "They're getting mar-ried next week? Well, _____."*) Inf **OH**72, Jeeminy krauts.

jiminy Christmas See **jiminy b**

jiminy eddies See **jiminetty**

jiminy fit n Also *geminy fit, jeeminy* ∼*, jimmy* ∼
An outburst of excitement, agitation, or nervousness.

1906 *DN* 3.143 **nwAR,** *Jeeminy-fit.* . . Fit of excitement. "I like to have had a jeeminy-fit when he told me that." **1927** *Ruppenthal Coll.* **KS,** *Jiminy fit* (sarcastic, etc.) Much agitation, especially over trifles. **1960** Carpenter *Tales Manchaca* 148 **cTX,** I just threw a jiminy fit, however, when the children were ill. I suppose having lost my first three offspring made me unduly nervous. **c1960** *Wilson Coll.* **csKY,** *Geminy fits . .* unnecessary nervousness, heebie jeebies. *Ibid,* *Jimmy fit,* a big fuss made about something. **1966** *DARE* (Qu. GG13b, *When something keeps bothering a person and makes him nervous . . "It gives me the _____."*) Inf **OK**31, Jiminy fits.

jiminy netties See **jiminetty**

jimjammed, I'll be phr Also *I'll be jimjohnned*
Used as an exclam; see quots.

1905 *DN* 3.84 **nwAR,** *Jimjohned.* . . In the exclamation of surprise, 'I'll be jimjohnned!' **1912** *DN* 3.579 **wIN,** *I'll be jimjammed!* An exclamation of surprise.

jimjams n

1 =**all overs** n pl **1, 2.** Cf **collywobbles 1**
1896 Twain in *Harper's New Mth. Mag.* 93.537 **MO,** They give me the jimjams and the fantods and caked up what brains I had. **1908** *DN* 3.325 **eAL, wGA,** *Jim-jams.* . . A fit of nervous jerking, a spell of the blues. **1911** Ferber *Dawn O'Hara* 29 **Milwaukee WI,** You'll give your-selves nervous jim-jams and then you'll have to go home to be patched up. **1911** *DN* 3.545 **NE,** *Jimjams.* . . A violently upset or disturbed feeling. "Her talking so so [sic] long gave me the jimjams." **1950** *WELS* **WI** (*A dislike that you can't explain . . "He gives me the _____."*) 4 Infs, Jimjams; (*When something is upsetting, or makes a person nervous: "It gives me the _____."*) 1 Inf, Jimjams. **1956** McAtee *Some Dialect NC* 24, *Jimjams . .* severe fits, hysteria. **c1960** *Wilson Coll.* **csKY,** *Jimjams.* A fit of nervousness. **1965–70** *DARE* (Qu. GG13b, *When something keeps bothering a person and makes him nervous . . "It gives me the _____."*) 10 Infs, **scattered,** Jimjams; (Qu. BB28, *Joking names . . for imaginary diseases: "He must have the _____."*) Infs **MA**24, **NY**14, **OH**15, Jimjams; (Qu. GG34a, *To feel depressed or in a gloomy mood: "He has the _____ today."*) Infs **CT**15, **NY**75, Jimjams. **1989** Mosher *Stranger* 212 **nVT,** I don't like that quarry much. . . It gives me the jim-jams, like the cemetery at night.

2 Delirium tremens.
1877 Bartlett *Americanisms* 323 **KY,** *Jim-jams.* Delirium tremens. **1877** [see **katzenjammer**]. **1888** in 1971 Farmer *Americanisms* 325, Burbridge . . began to drink very excessively. . . He had the jim-jams yesterday evening, and last night he raved like a madman. **1889** (1971) Farmer *Americanisms* 325, *Jim-jams.* . . Delirium tremens. This term, said to have originated in Kentucky, is now common everywhere. **1893** *KS Univ. Qrly.* 1.140, *Jim-jams:* delirium tremens. **1893** Shands *MS Speech* 41, *Jim-jams* [jɪm-ˈjæmz]. Bartlett says that this word is used for *delirium tremens* in Kentucky. It is the common name for that disease in Mississippi. **1899** (1912) Green *VA Folk-Speech* 245, *Jimjams.* . . Delirium tremens. **1908** *DN* 3.325 **eAL, wGA,** *Jim-jams.* . . Delirium tremens. **1910** Hart *Vigilante Girl* 31 **nCA,** You don't drink, and I do. I don't get howling drunk, nor get arrested, nor have jim-jams. But I drink. **1969** *DARE* (Qu. DD22, . . *Delirium tremens*) Inf **MA**68, Jimjams.

3 See quot.
1968 *DARE* (Qu. BB19, *Joking names for looseness of the bowels*) Inf **PA**150, Jimjams.

jimjawed See **jimberjawed**

jim-john See **jimmy-john 3**

jimjohnned, I'll be See **jimjammed, I'll be**

jim-kay v
1953 Randolph–Wilson *Down in Holler* 256 **Ozarks,** *Jim-kay.* . . To stuff with food. Somewhere near Joplin, Mo., a pioneer family had a pet pig, named James K. Polk, and the story goes that they fed the animal till it busted wide open. Since that time, if a guest is urged to eat more of this or that, he says, "Don't you jim-kay me, now!"

jimmed up See **jim** v **2**

jimmerjawed See **jimberjawed**

jimmety See **jiminy**

jimmie-dick See **jimmy** n **3**

jimmiejawed See **jimberjawed**

jimmie-john See **jimmy-john**

jimmies n pl[1] Also *jeemies* [Perh var of **jimjams**]

1 =**all overs** n pl **1, 2.** esp **Sth, S Midl, West** Cf **collywob-bles 1, willies**
1905 *DN* 3.84 **nwAR,** *Jimmies.* . . blues. **1928** *New Yorker* 22 Dec 18 **NYC,** Him Popping down the chimney—well, frankly it gives me the jimmies. **1965–70** *DARE* (Qu. GG13b, *When something keeps both-ering a person and makes him nervous . . "It gives me the _____."*) 30 Infs, **esp Sth, S Midl, West,** Jimmies; **AR**31, Jeemies. **1972** *Atlanta Letters* **GA,** [To have the] jimmies, to be real nervous.

2 Delirium tremens.
1899 (1900) Harris *On the Wing* 42 **NYC,** Take 'im to the hospital,

Tim; 'tis the only way to clear the jimmies from his [=a drunk man's] head. **1905** *DN* 3.84 **nwAR**, *Jimmies*. . . Delirium tremens. . . 'We had a friend once who had a bad case of jimmies, and he got it into his head he was bleeding to death.' **1908** *DN* 3.325 **eAL, wGA**, *Jimmies*. . . The delirium tremens. **1967–69** *DARE* (Qu. DD22, . . *Delirium tremens*) Infs **KY6, SC31**, Jimmies. **1980** Banks *First-Person America* 81 **OR** (as of 1938), Most assayers were drunkards and had the jimmies so bad that they didn't know what they were doing.

3 A disease of livestock marked by trembling, seizures, etc, caused by var poisonous plants. Cf **jimmy fern, jimmyweed**

1949 Curtin *By the Prophet* 101 **AZ**, *[Isocoma heterophylla]* is called "jimmyweed" by cowmen because, when eaten by horses or cattle, it gives them the "jimmies.". . The effects are still more serious because if a cow eats the plant in quantity the calf gets "milk sickness" or the "trembles" and the disease is transmissible through the milk to human beings. **1964** Kingsbury *Poisonous Plants U.S.* 102, The nervous syndrome produced by this fern [=*Notholaena sinuata* var *cochisensis*] is popularly termed "jimmies." [*Ibid* 103, Jimmy fern remains green and succulent after frost eliminates most other forage. . . Jimmy fern poisoning in cattle is rare . . because the range where the plant grows is more suited to sheep than cattle.]

jimmies n pl[2] [Trademark] **esp NEast** Cf **ant** n B, **log** n 2, **sprinkles**

Tiny balls or rod-shaped bits of candy used as a topping for ice cream, cakes, and other sweets.

1963 *Sat. Review* 13 Apr 51/1 **neMA** (as of 1941), We could buy a generous ice cream cone, dipped in chocolate "jimmies," as we called them. **1967** *Harvard Alumni Bulletin* 22 Apr (*W3* File), Why is it traditional to order your Harvard Square cone with jimmies, so that Brigham's goes through 25–40 pounds of them on a normally brisk day? Why are jimmies called jimmies? **1973** *Esquire* Apr 130, The mystery manuscript was as sprinkled with details as an ice cream cone dipped in chocolate jimmies. **1977–78** Foster *Lexical Variation* 25 **NJ**, Among the newer words, the distribution of *jimmies* and *sprinkles* 'little candy bits put on a sundae' . . provides another indication of the North–Midland boundary. In this case, Mercer County is divided, with Trenton and its near suburbs using the Midland *jimmies* or the local *ice cream mints* and northern Mercer preferring the Northern *sprinkles*. The fact that far more informants in the pure *sprinkles* areas of North and Northwest Jersey deny *jimmies* than *jimmies* users in South Jersey deny *sprinkles* . . suggests that *sprinkles* is the older or more general term; the *jimmies* enclave in Essex and Union Counties may be the vanguard of a northern movement of the newer term. **1981** *DARE* File Milwaukee WI (as of c1947), *Jimmies:* small bits of chocolate—spherical, lozenge shaped, and such—used to decorate cakes, sprinkle on ice cream cones, etc. *Ibid* (as of 1963), [On a jar lid:] barq & foster's *Rainbow Jimmies*—perfect for cookies, cakes, salads and desserts. [*DARE* Ed: Purchased by a woman in Portage, WI, who describes rainbow jimmies as oblong, multicolored candies.] **1982** *NY Times* (NY) 25 Nov sec A 22, What do you call the tiny multicolored flecks of candy that are . . scattered on . . cakes, or into which ice cream cones are dipped? . . "Jimmies," say people from Massachusetts confidently. **1982** Chaika *Speaking RI* [7], *Jimmies* = chocolate bits on ice cream cones. **1991** *DARE* File, The small chocolate slivers . . used as a topping for ice cream are called jimmies. We always used them on vanilla ice cream cones. I was in New Orleans 15 years ago and asked for jimmies on my ice cream cone and the lady behind me squealed that she hadn't hear [sic] that word since she left Philadelphia.

jimmi-john See **jimmy-john**

jimminy See **jiminy**

jimmy adj [Engl dial] Cf **jim-dandy** adj, adv

1899 (1912) Green *VA Folk-Speech* 245, *Jimmy*. . . Spruce; neat; smart; handy; dextrous.

jimmy n

1 In railroading: a small coal or ore car.

1880 Fisk & Hatch *Descr. Chesapeake & Ohio Ry.* 15 (*Mathews Coll.*), The present equipment of the road is as follows, viz: . . Jimmies, 241; Gondolas, plain, 290. **1887** in 1889 *Century Dict.* 3233, The express train. . . ran into a freight. . . The second car on the freight was lifted from the rails and carried on top of two jimmies loaded with coal. **1938** (1964) Korson *Minstrels Mine Patch* 315 **nePA**, *Jimmy:* A small railroad car in which anthracite was hauled in early days. **1940** *RR Mag.* Apr 47, *Jimmies*—Four-wheeled ore or coal cars.

2 A **pinfish** (here: *Diplodus holbrooki*).

1902 Jordan–Evermann *Amer. Fishes* 444 **NC**, *Diplodus holbrooki*. . . is frequent also at Lake Worth, where it is called jimmy.

3 also *jim crab, jimmie-dick:* A mature male blue crab *(Callinectes sapindus).* **Chesapeake Bay, VA and NC coasts** Cf **jimmy-and-his-wife**

1905 U.S. Bur. Fisheries *Rept. for 1904* 427, A "channeler," or any large male hard crab, is called a "Jimmy" or "Jim crab." **1942** Chesapeake Biol. Lab. *Pub.* 53.8, When a big 'Jimmy' gets into the pot, the little crabs . . keep their distance. **1952** *Sun* (Baltimore MD) 23 June 14/5 **Chesapeake Bay**, *Jimmy Or Chandler Or Channeler*—A mature male crab, one that has reached maximum growth and will not shed again. **1968–70** *DARE* FW Addit **MD43**, Jimmy crab—a male hard crab; **ceVA**, Jimmy or big jimmy—a large male crab. The term is in common use. **1970** *DARE* (Qu. P18) Inf **VA55**, Jimmy—a male crab. **1970** *DARE* Tape **VA47**, When they're catchin' peeler crabs, they usually put out a jimmy crab, which is the male crab, in pots [as bait]. **1976** Warner *Beautiful Swimmers* 17 **eMD**, Male or "Jimmy". . . Atlantic blue crab. *Ibid* 136, Jimmy potting is a seasonal method of taking large peelers. . . Two or three large Jimmies are placed in the upstairs section of the pot. The virginal females . . are attracted by the encaged males. **1982** Heat Moon *Blue Highways* 60 **NC**, A jimmy reached up and clamped onto my pant leg and slid back and forth across the floor with me. **1984** *DARE* File Chesapeake Bay [Watermen's vocab], Jimmies; jimmie-dicks.

4 See quot. [Perh trademark] Cf **jimmy-slinger, josie** 2

1968 *DARE* (Qu. W4, . . *Men's coats or jackets for work and outdoor wear*) Inf **PA130**, Jimmy—a denim jacket worn with a jumper (bib pants).

5 Used as an exclam; see quot. [Perh var of **jiminy**]

1970 *DARE* (Qu. NN30, *Exclamations beginning with the sound of 'j'*) Inf **IL115**, Jimmy.

jimmy v [Cf *jimmy* to pry open]

1892 *KS Univ. Qrly.* 1.97, *Jimmy:* to meddle, as, to jimmy with a thing or person, to 'fool with.'

jimmy-and-his-wife n [**jimmy** n 3] Cf **doubler** 4

A pair of mating blue crabs *(Sapindus callinectes).*

1984 *DARE* File Chesapeake Bay [Watermen's vocab], Jimmie-and-his-wife.

jimmy cane n [Prob joc var of *hurricane;* cf the pronc-sp *harrycane* at **hurricane** A5]

A strong wind; see quots.

1905 *DN* 3.62 **NE**, *Jimmycane*. . . Hurricane. (Reported by several.) "The air feels like we might have a jimmycane to-day." **1912** *DN* 3.579 **wIN**, *Jimmy-cane*. . . A cyclone. **1967** *DARE* (Qu. B17, *A destructive wind that blows straight*) Inf **CO11**, Jimmy cane ['jɪmɪkən]; (Qu. B18, . . *Special kinds of wind*) Inf **NY2**, Jimmy cane ['jɪmɪkən]—Like a hurricane in the woods; it blows down an area of trees. **1967** *DARE* FW Addit **ceNY**, Jimmy cane ['jɪmɪkən]—a gale or other strong wind in the woods capable of clearing bushes and trees; **cnNY**, Jimmy cane ['jɪmɪkən]—a small twister, a dust devil.

jimmy-dancer n

1979 *DARE* File **eKY**, The *jimmy-dancer* [is] a simple top made by whittling in two a wooden spool for sewing thread, driving a stick through the spool and whittling it to a point, leaving enough stem to flip the toy with the thumb and middle finger.

jimmy fern n [**jimmies** n pl[1] 3]

A cloak fern (here: *Notholaena sinuata* var *cochisensis*).

1964 Kingsbury *Poisonous Plants U.S.* 101, *Notholaena sinuata* . . var. *cochisensis*. . . Jimmy fern. . . Knowledge of the poisonous properties of jimmy fern is based on . . investigations . . in Texas. **1967** *Merck Vet. Manual* 1060, Jimmy fern. . . Affected animals [include] sheep, also goats and cattle. . . After exercise by walking, will have arched back, stilted movement of hind legs, and usually increased respiration. Continued walking induces violent trembling and death if not allowed to rest.

jimmy fit See **jiminy fit**

jimmyjawed See **jimberjawed**

jimmy-john n Also sp *jimmi(e)-john* [Varr of *demijohn*]

1 A demijohn; a liquor jug. **chiefly Sth, S Midl**

1884 Harris *Mingo* 28 **cGA**, Ole Marster he ain't say nothin', but he tuck a fresh grip on de jimmy-john. **1889** Murfree *Despot* 200 **eTN**,

Jes' ketch a-holt o' the handle o' that thar jimmy-john [=liquor container] in the corner. **1890** *DN* 1.65 **KY,** *Jimmie john:* a demijohn. **1899** (1912) Green *VA Folk-Speech* 245, *Jimmy-john.* . . A form of *demijohn.* **1922** *DN* 5.189 [Black], *Jimmy-john.* . . Demijohn. **1941** Writers' Program *Guide AL* 317, Many a family has its still and store of "Jimmijohns" full of corn-likker. **1945** *CA Folkl. Qrly.* 4.322 **CO** [Mining terms], *Jimmy-John:* Crockery gallon jug. **1952** Brown *NC Folkl.* 1.554, *Jimmie-john.* . . Demijohn.—General. Illiterate. **1960** Criswell *Resp. to PADS 20* **Ozarks,** [Referring to liquor containers:] *Jimmy-john* for *demijohn.* Once common. **1966** *DARE* (Qu. DD29, *Common containers for liquor [now and in the past];* total Infs questioned, 75) Inf **MS**43, Jimmy-john. **1971** Evans *Tommy Johnson* 62 **MS** (as of 1930) [Black], They had a five gallon jimmyjohn of liquor.

2 Transf: whiskey.

1968 *DARE* (Qu. DD21c, *Nicknames for whiskey, especially illegally made whiskey*) Inf **MO**9, Jimmy-john.

3 also *jim-john:* A chamber pot.

1967–69 *DARE* (Qu. F38, *Utensil kept under the bed for use at night*) Inf **KY**48, Jim-john; **MI**43, Jimmy-john.

jimmy-jug n
=**jimmy-john 1.**

1986 Pederson *LAGS Concordance,* 1 inf, **nwFL,** Jimmy jug—large jar for bootleg whiskey.

jimmy longlegs n
=**walkingstick.**

1967 *DARE* (Qu. R9a, *An insect from two to four inches long that lives in bushes and looks like a dead twig*) Inf **TX**32, Jimmy longlegs.

jimmy-slinger n [Prob var of **jimswinger 1**] Cf **jimmy** n **4, wamus**

1912 *DN* 3.579 **wIN,** *Jimmy-slinger.* . . A coat-like jacket; a *wammus.*

Jimmy square-foot n

1969 *DARE* (Qu. CC8, . . *The devil*) Inf **IN**79, Jimmy square-foot.

jimmy swinger n Cf **flying jenny 1a**

1966 *DARE* (Qu. EE32, *A homemade merry-go-round*) Inf **NC**33, Jimmy swinger.

jimmyweed n [**jimmies** n pl¹ **3**] **West**

A **goldenweed 1:** usu *Haplopappus heterophyllus,* but also *H. gracilis.*

1931 U.S. Dept. Ag. *Misc. Pub.* 101.156, *Jimmyweed.* . . Its taste is bitter-resinous, and under normal conditions livestock do not relish it. If forced to graze it, cattle, horses, and sheep are liable to be poisoned. **1945** Benson–Darrow *Manual SW Trees* 322, Jimmyweed, like the closely related burroweed, is an aggressive invader of depleted grassland ranges. **1945** Pickard–Buley *Midwest Pioneer* 21, Among the chief offenders were white snakeroot and jimmyweed or rayless goldenrod. **1949** Curtin *By the Prophet* 101 **AZ,** [*Haplopappus heterophyllus*] is called "jimmyweed" by cowmen because, when eaten by horses or cattle, it gives them the "jimmies." **1967** Dodge *Roadside Wildflowers* 75, Slender goldenbush and jimmyweed are other names applied to. . . *Haplopappus gracilis.* **1970** Correll *Plants TX* 1579, *Jimmy-weed.* . . Locally abundant, often in open alkaline places, Trans-Pecos and Plains Country. **1985** Dodge *Flowers SW Deserts* 91, Jimmyweed. . . often takes over heavily grazed rangeland since it is generally unpalatable to livestock and replaces vegetation destroyed by overgrazing. **1995** Brako et al. *Scientific & Common Names Plants* 168, Jimmy-weed—*Haplopappus heterophyllus.*

Jim Narrowface n

A snake.

1967 in 1982 *Barrick Coll.* **csPA,** *Jim Narrowface*—snake. **1991** *DARE* File, [Letter from author of 1967 quot:] The only dated occurrence I have is October 22, 1967. The informant, my aunt . . , used it in the plural: "The Jim Narrowfaces are still out." I remember her using it in such situations as whenever they went out to pick strawberries or huckleberries, they had to watch out for Jim Narrowfaces. . . This is the only person I ever heard use it, but she used it so frequently that everyone understood the reference. She was not sufficiently inventive to have created the term.

jimplecute n Also *jimplicute* Cf **jimpsecute**

1 Used as the name of a pamphlet or newspaper.

1982 *Ayer Directory Pub.* 859, Jefferson [TX], *Jimplecute* . . Estab. 1865. **1983** Tarpley *Jefferson* 71 **ceTX,** [The] county clerk of Harrison

County in 1845 . . had used the name *Jimplecute* for a little leaflet he published. *Ibid* 79, The curious name of Jefferson's newspaper spawned namesakes in Illmo, Missouri [in 1914], where the *Jimplicute* is still being published, and in Spring Place, Georgia. . . [where the] *Jimplecute* was established in . . 1879. . . By 1911, the paper had . . ceased publication.

2 An imaginary monster. **esp AR, MS, MO, TX**

1867 in 1983 Tarpley *Jefferson* 77 **ceTX,** We saw that terrible picture of the Jimplecute [used as an illustration on the masthead of the newspaper of the same name] that so frightened our friend . . some time since. It is a compound of the alligator, the lion, the snake, the whale, the tiger, the eagle, and divers other brutes. It is a whole menagerie in epitome. . . How so . . refined a gentleman as Ward Taylor [=publisher of the *Jimplicute*] ever conceived such a picture, we cannot well imagine. **1926** *Sat. Review* 2 Oct 164, The xanthus joshed the jimplecute / The aardvark hugged the auk / The woozle woggled in and out / To snare the stubenrauch. **1950** *AR Hist. Qrly.* 9.69 **Ozarks,** There are men still living who remember stories of the jimplicute, a kind of ghostly dragon or dinosaur supposed to walk the roads at night, grab travelers by the throat and suck their blood. Some say this creature was invented near Argenta, Arkansas, in the 1870's, to frighten superstitious Negroes. **1966** *DARE* (Qu. CC17, *Imaginary animals or monsters that people . . tell tales about—especially to tease greenhorns*) Inf **MS**33, Jimplecute. **1981** *AR Gaz.* (Little Rock) 16 Aug sec F 3, Jerry Jones is from Missouri. . . "I know that the Illmo, Mo., newspaper is called the *Jimplicute*," he said. He doesn't know what *Jimplicute* means, however. . . For that matter, the staff of the *Jimplicute* isn't entirely sure. A *Jimplicute* employe said by telephone that there were two stories. . . One has it that a *Jimplicute* is a mythical animal of great ferocity. The other story is that a printer dropped some type and the letters spelled out *jimplicute* on their own.

3 See **jimpsecute.**

jim pole n [Var of **gin pole 1**]

See quots.

1966 *DARE* Tape **SD**4A, A jim pole . . was a pipe, just an ordinary piece of two-inch pipe, as a rule . . high pressure pipe, about a seven-foot piece of that. They would stick one end of it into the rock pile and let the other end lay over against the wall an' they'd just hook this snatch block into this jim pole and that would hold it up there so they could hoist . . whatever they wanted up there. **1984** *MJLF* 10.152 **cnWI,** *Jim pole.* A pole rigged up with a pulley for getting timbers or other heavy objects in place.

jimpsecute n Also *jimplecute, jimpsycute* [Orig uncert but cf *EDD jimpsey* (at *jimp* adj.) "neat, smart" + *cute; SND jimp* adj. **1** "Of persons: slender, small, graceful, neat, dainty"] **MS, SW, esp TX** *obs*

A sweetheart.

1869 *Overland Mth.* 3.131 **TX,** When a Texan goes forth on a sparking errand, he does not go to pay his devoirs to his Amaryllis . . but his "jimpsecute." **1870** in 1896 Farmer–Henley *Slang* 58, The *Jimplecute* of Texas changed her name, and now has a good thing to do—*Jimplecute* being Texas vernacular for sweetheart. **1890** *AN&Q* 5.6, In some of the South-western States a young man's sweetheart is his *jimpsecute.* **1891** *Ibid* 8.60, In the State of Mississippi, I several times heard the word *jimpsycute* used in the sense of "sweetheart," it being always, so far as I remember, applied to the young lady in the case.

jimpson weed See **jimson weed**

jimption n [Cf *gumption*]

Heat, fire.

1887 *Amer. Field* 27.62, The slang of the fraternity [of cowboys] is highly amusing to a stranger. . . For instance, when they brand an animal they put the "jimption" to him; when they want a hot drink they say "put some jimption in it."

jim-slicker n Cf **dingclicker, jimswinger 2**
=**jim-dandy** n **1**

1914 *DN* 4.75 **nNH, ME,** *Jim-slicker.* . . Dingclicker.

jimson weed n Also *gimson weed, gympson* ~, *jempson* ~, *jimpson* ~, *jimson,* ~ *grass,* ~ *root;* for addit varr see quots [Varr of **Jamestown weed**] chiefly **Sth, Midl** See Map

A **thorn apple:** usu *Datura stramonium,* but also *D. innoxia.* For other names of *D. stramonium* see **angel's trumpet 1, apple (of) Peru 2, devil's apple 1, devil's trumpet, fire-**

weed f, gypsyweed 3, gypsum weed, Jamestown lily, Jamestown weed, stink apple, stinkweed. For other names of *D. innoxia* see **angel's trumpet 1, devil's trumpet, Gabriel's trumpet, Jamestown weed, wild trumpet**

1812 *Cramer's Pittsburgh Almanack for 1813* 26, James'-town weed, from James'-town, on James' River, in Virginia, where the plant seems to have first attracted notice. It is also known by the name of Jimson, and Thorn-apple. **1832** in 1854 Benton *30 Yrs. View* 1.256, An eagle. . [was] by a pig under a jimpson weed . . caught and whipt. **1848** in 1850 Cooper *Rural Hours* 107 **cNY**, The gimson weed, or Datura, is an Abyssinian plant. **1855** *Knickerbocker* Dec 600, The schooners . . are manned by a primitive race of people who live . . [on] crabs, shrimps, and a species of gympson (Jamestown) weed. **1876** Hobbs *Bot. Hdbk.* 60, Jimpson seed, . . Jimpson weed, . . Jimson weed, Thorn apple seed, Datura Stramonium. **1903** *Atlantic Mth.* July 82, The smell of jimson-weed was heavy on the evening air. **1922** Gonzales *Black Border* 308 **sSC, GA coasts** [Gullah glossary], *Jimpsin-weed, Jimsin-weed*—Jimpson or Jamestown-weed. **1937** Thornburgh *Gt. Smoky Mts.* 32, Then there's jimpson weed. Hit's tall, grows as high as my head, sort o' sprangly, with big spiked leaves. . . If ye ever have a felon, git ye some . . jimpson weed. **1951** *PADS* 15.39 **TX**, *Datura meteloides* [=*D. innoxia*]. . . Jimson weed. **1965–70** *DARE* (Qu. S21, . . *Weeds . . that are a trouble in gardens and fields*) 191 Infs, **chiefly Sth, Midl**, Jimson weed(s); **IL**80, **NC**6, **OH**25, 69, **PA**162, **VA**24, Jimson; **AL**42, Jimson grass; **PA**60, Jimson root; (Qu. K14, *Milk that has a taste from something the cow ate in the pasture . . "That milk is _____."*) Inf **MO**24, Jimson-weed milk; (Qu. S8) Inf **CA**101, Jimson grass; (Qu. S9) Inf **AR**33, Jimson weed; (Qu. S13) Inf **NC**49, Jimson; **GA**46, Jimson weed; (Qu. S15) Inf **VA**24, Jimson; **IL**95, **MS**47, **MO**13, **WA**8, Jimson weed; (Qu. S17, . . *Kinds of plants . . that . . cause itching and swelling*) Inf **OK**52, Jimson weed; (Qu. S20) Infs **MS**47, **MO**22, **OK**58, Jimson weed; (Qu. S23) Inf **PA**35, Jimson; (Qu. S26a, . . *Wildflowers. . . Roadside flowers*) Infs **CA**60, **NJ**69, Jimson weed; (Qu. S26d, *Wildflowers that grow in meadows;* not asked in early QRs) Infs **NY**35, **UT**13, Jimson weed; (Qu. S26e, *Other wildflowers not yet mentioned;* not asked in early QRs) Infs **AR**49, **OH**86, Jimson weed; (Qu. BB34b, *What is a poultice made with?* total Infs questioned, 75) Inf **OK**50, Jimson-weed leaves; (Qu. BB50c, *Remedies for infections*) Inf **KY**74, Jimson leaf; **NC**88, Jimson weed and salt; **IL**39, Jimson-leaf poultice; **IN**38, Jimson-weed seed and lard. **1982** Slone *How We Talked* 107 **eKY** (as of c1950), Cure [for pinkeye]: wash the eyes with tea made from catnip, peach tree bark, Jempson weed (this will change the color of your eyes for a few hours). **1985** Dodge *Flowers SW Deserts* 17, Western-Jimson, Thornapple, Giant-Jimson. . . *Datura meteloides*. . . All portions of this coarse, bushlike herb are poisonous, and are used by some Indians as a narcotic to induce visions. **1992** *USA Today* (Arlington VA) 6 Nov sec A 11 **KS**, *Topeka*—State residents are being cautioned by police against using jimson weed as a hallucinogen.

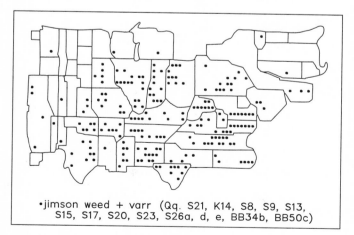

•jimson weed + varr (Qq. S21, K14, S8, S9, S13, S15, S17, S20, S23, S26a, d, e, BB34b, BB50c)

jimson-weed preacher n Cf *DS* CC10

A **jackleg** preacher.

1953 Randolph–Wilson *Down in Holler* 26 **Ozarks**, I once knew a jimson-weed preacher . . who . . pronounced heaven as if it were spelled *heving*. **1958** Randolph *Sticks* 33 **Ozarks**, A big camp meeting, where one of them jimsonweed preachers was hollering about the second coming of Christ.

jim-sweetener n Cf **jim-slicker**

1946 *PADS* 6.18 **swVA** (as of 1900–10), *Jim sweetener*. . . A fine specimen. A jocular expression. Salem.

jimswigger See **jimswinger 1**

jim-swiggled See **jim** n 1

jimswinger n

1 also *jimswigger, jimswing(er) coat*: A long-tailed coat. [Perh *Jim* given name common among Black men + *swinger* in ref to the motion of the coattails] **Sth** *old-fash; esp freq among Black speakers* Cf **jim** n 2

1893 Shands *MS Speech* 41, Jim-swinger. . . The common negro name for a *Prince Albert* coat. **1895** *DN* 1.389, *Jim-swinger:* long-tailed coat, especially a "Prince Albert." O[ld]. **1898** Dunbar *Folks from Dixie* 52 [Black], He walked to church, flanked on one side by Aunt Caroline . . and on the other by her husband stately in the magnificence of an antiquated "Jim-swinger." **1908** *DN* 3.325 **eAL, wGA**, *Jim-swinger*. . . A long-tailed coat. . . Also *jim-swigger*. **1927** Adams *Congaree* 98 **cSC** [Black], De white folks come down to Congaree wid striped pants on an' a jim swinger coat. **1929** Sale *Tree Named John* 104 **MS** [Black], Harnesses jes nach'ly don' fit on a mule . . no mo' 'n a jimswinger coat fits on a nigger. *Ibid* 111, He 'uz w'arin' a jimswinger coat 'ca'se you know he 'uz allus a mighty stylish gent'mun. **1947** Ballowe *The Lawd* 122 **LA** [Black], Scott Garner whipped off his long jimswinger coat and wrapped it around Lilly. **1950** *PADS* 14.75 **nwFL**, Cutaway and Jim Swinger: . . Formal clothes. **1972** Cooper *NC Mt. Folkl.* 93, Jim-swinger—a frock or long-tailed coat. **1984** Burns *Cold Sassy* 82 **nGA** (as of 1906), Hot as he was from running, he kept on the long black jim-swing coat till he saw me shivering, and then he put it around me. *Ibid* 227, Then a Negro sermon by Loomis, all dressed up in his dingy white vest, black pants, jim-swing black tailcoat, and beaver hat.

2 =**jim-dandy** n 1. Cf **jim-slicker**

1956 McAtee *Some Dialect NC* 24, Jim-swinger: . . Something remarkable of its kind. "A jim-swinger of a dress."

jimswinger coat See **jimswinger 1**

jim-swizzled See **jim** n 1

jim town n [Perh clipped form of *jimcrack* shoddy, flimsy + *town*, but cf *Jim* given name used as a generic for a Black man] A shantytown—also used as a nickname for a neighborhood or settlement, esp a poor one.

1946 McWilliams *S. CA Country* 218, While a few of the large commercial growers maintain camps for their employees, the typical citrus worker settlement is the Mexican town or, in the parlance of the region, the "jim-town". From Santa Barbara to San Diego, one can find these jim-towns, with their clusters of bizarre shacks, usually located in an out-of-the-way place on the outskirts of an established citrus-belt town. **1967–69** *DARE* (Qu. C34, *Nicknames for nearby settlements, villages, or districts*) Inf **CA**55, Jim town—old-fashioned; **DE**1, Jim town—another colored section; **IL**17, Jim town; **IN**76, Jim town—nicknamed for man who settled it; (Qu. II25, *Names or nicknames for the part of a town where the poorer people, special groups, or foreign groups live*) Inf **DE**1, Jim town—name for part of Georgetown.

jim up See **jim** v 2

jim-winder n Cf **jim work, stem-winder**

1954 *Harder Coll.* **cwTN**, *Jim-winder:* a hard worker.

jim work n [Prob folk-etym for **gin work**, but see quot] Cf **jim** v 1, **jim-hand**

1971 *AN&Q* Apr 121, The origins of the West Virginia expression, "Jim Work" can be traced. In Salem . . there are older persons who were told as children that the expression was brought in by people from the Valley of Virginia. In that region before the Civil War, male slaves who became too old or feeble to work in the fields were known generically as the "Jims". They were brought into the plantation house and given lighter work, "Jim Work".

jin See **gin** v[1]

jindice See **jaundice**

jine(en) See **join**

jinely See **generally**

jiner See **join**

Jine(r)wary See **January**

jinete n [Span]

See quots.

1932 Bentley *Spanish Terms* 150, *Jinete* (*Spanish*, [hi'ne:te:]; *English*, [hɪn'ɛti:]) A horse-rider. *Jinete* is often used in conjunction with the Spanish word *muy* as in "that man is muy jinete," signifying that so and so is an excellent rider, i.e., bronco buster. Likewise colloquially: "He is some jinete." **1934** (1940) Weseen *Dict. Amer. Slang* 100, *Jinete*—A bronco buster. **1944** Adams *Western Words* 85, *Jinete* [hi'nete]—Modern Spanish, meaning *a rider* or *a horseman*. Used in the cattle country in referring to a bronc buster, or a man who is an excellent rider.

jing n Also *jings* [Scots, Engl dial]

Used in exclams or mild oaths—usu in phrr *by jing(s)*.

1808 Barker *Tears & Smiles* 39, Ma'am!—ha—no—yes—it is, by jing! How d'ye do, ma'am. **1815** [see *jingo*]. **1889** (1971) Farmer *Americanisms* 111, *By jings!*—A corruption of "by jingo," a phrase which, as used by most people, possesses no significance beyond that of a vulgar expletive. **1924** *DN* 5.271 [Exclams], By jing, jing jang, I jing.

jingeroo n [Cf *OED jink* v.[1] 4 "To trick, cheat, diddle, swindle," *OED* quot 1832, and **-eroo**]

A Gypsy.

1953 Johnson *Sullivan* 56 seME, "Some said he were a Jingeroo, but I always thought him a pure-bred." "What's a Jingeroo, Aunt Nebbie?" "You outlanders call 'em Gypsies," she explained.

jingle v, hence vbl n *jingling*

To round up (horses).

1944 Adams *Western Words* 85, *Jingling*—Rounding up the horse herd. **1969** *DARE* (Qu. L43a, . . *To get horses ready to work* . . "I'll _____ *the horses.*") Inf **TX**66, Jingle—round them up and bring them in.

jingle n

1 See **jingle shell**.

2 Money; scrip. Cf **chink** n[2], **jink money**

1968 *DARE* (Qu. U19a, . . *Money in general:* "He's certainly got the _____.") Inf **IN**31, Jingle. **1973** *PADS* 59.40 [Bituminous coal mining vocab], *Jingle* . . = scrip.

jinglebob n

1 A cattle-mark made by cutting the ear or the dewlap so that a piece hangs down; an animal so marked. **West** Also called **dinglebob 2** Cf **dewlap** n, **earmark** n

1890 *Stock Grower & Farmer* 11 Jan. 11/2 *(DAE)*, Ear marks, double jinglebob left ear. **1913** (1979) Barnes *Western Grazing* 382, *Jingle Bob*. . . An ear-mark made by cutting the ear on the upper side, so as to break the back of the ear. This allows it to hang down along the side of the face much as do the long ears of the Angora goat. **1920** Hunter *Trail Drivers TX* 15, In about the late 60's or early 70's, Mr. Charles Goodnight went the western route up the Pecos . . trailing the "Jingle Bobs" or the John Chissum cattle. *Ibid* 298, A "jingle-bob" is to split the ear to the head and let the pieces flap. **1933** *AmSp* 8.1.29 **TX**, *Jingle-bob*. An identification mark on an animal made by slashing the ear and letting a piece of it dangle, or a similar mark on the dewlap. **1966–68** *DARE* (Qu. K18, . . *Kind of mark* . . *to identify a cow*) Inf **CA**87, Jinglebob—the dewlap is cut a little and let dangle; a jinglebob cow is a cow marked by cutting the dewlap and letting it dangle; **NM**13, Jinglebob—the skin on the lower jaw is cut on one or both sides so that it hangs down; not used anymore.

2 See quots. Cf **jingler 2**

1926 Branch *Cowboy* 24, Spurs might have "jingle-bobs" to tinkle as the cowboy walked. **1936** Adams *Cowboy Lingo* 36, The little pear-shaped pendants which hung loosely from the end of the axle of the spur rowel, and whose sole function was to make the music that the cowboy loved to hear, were called 'danglers' or 'jingle-bobs.' **1946** Mora *Trail Dust* 64 **West,** "Cascabel" is the Spanish word for a certain kind of bell, a jingle-bob.

3 =**doohickey 1.**

1960 Williams *Walk Egypt* 89 **GA,** Boxes of doodads and jinglebobs.

jingled ppl adj Cf *DS* DD13–15

Intoxicated, drunk.

1906 (1908) Lorimer *Jack Spurlock* 315, Old Mr. Corliss was purple with pleasure at having so plausible a pretext for getting comfortably jingled. **1919** Kyne *Capt. Scraggs* 6 **CA,** If I was you, skipper, I'd hold my temper until I got to port; then I'd git jingled an' forgit my troubles inexpensively. **1930** *New Outlook* 155.580, A man who drank immoderately, . . who permitted himself to become pleasantly jingled, was sure to be talked about.

jingler n

1 A goldeneye 1 (here: *Bucephala clangula*). [*OED* 1829 →]

1888 Trumbull *Names of Birds* 79 **NJ**, *Golden-eye*. . . At Pleasantville . . , *Jingler*. **1923** U.S. Dept. Ag. *Misc. Circular* 13.22 **MD, NJ**, *Goldeneye*. . . *Vernacular Names*. . . *In local use*. . . Jingler. **1982** Elman *Hunter's Field Guide* 218, *American Goldeneye* . . *Common & Regional Names* . . whistle duck, . . jingler. . . A shrill of whistling wings identifies them.

2 See quot. Cf **jinglebob 2**

1930 Shoemaker *1300 Words* 33 **cPA Mts** (as of c1900), *Jinglers*—Ornaments on the bridle or saddle of a harness; a swinging disk, which rattled when horse was in motion.

3 A horse wrangler.

1936 Adams *Cowboy Lingo* 25, The day 'wrangler' was a . . 'jingler,' and the 'night-herder' was called a 'night-hawk'. **1936** McCarthy *Lang. Mosshorn* np [Range term], *Wrangler*. . . Sometimes called a jingler. **1941** Writers' Program *Guide WY* 463, *Jingler*—Man who takes care of cavvy [=a string of horses used in ranch work]. **1942** Berrey–Van den Bark *Amer. Slang* 913.11, *Horse wrangler*. Horse jingler.

jingles n

1 See quot.

1967 *DARE* (Qu. V10a, . . *Joking names* . . *for a sheriff*) Inf **WY**3, Jingles.

2 in phr *by jingles*: Used as an exclam. [Cf **jingo**]

1970 *DARE* Tape **CA**208, By golly . . by jingles, there was a limb in the road.

jingle shell n Also *jingle* [From the noise produced by shaking the dried valves]

A shell of the family Anomiidae. For other names of var of these shells see **gingle, gold shell, rock oyster**

1881 Ingersoll *Oyster-Industry* 245 **NY**, *Jingle*. Any species of *Anomia*. (Long Island sound.) **1935** Pratt *Manual Invertebrate Animals* 660, *Anomia*. . . Jingle-shells. . . Outer surface scaly and dark colored, but in dead shells often worn off, exposing the glistening greenish or golden mother-of-pearl. **1949** Palmer *Nat. Hist.* 356, *Jingle Shell*. . . *Pododesmus macroschisma*. . . Rough outside but pearly inside, with purple and green tints. Flesh bright orange, edible, commercially important. **1981** Meinkoth *Audubon Field Guide Seashore* 546, *Common Jingle Shell*. . . When strung on a cord and suspended in the wind, these shells make a fine jingling sound.

jingling See **jingle** v

jingo n Also *gingo, jingoes* [Perh euphem for *Jesus; OED* 1694 →] Cf **Neddy-jingo**

Used in exclams and mild oaths—esp in phr *by jingo*.

1815 Humphreys *Yankey in England* 106, *Jumping jings, jingoes,* expletives indicative of confirmation. **1858** (1929) Taylor *Life on a Whaler* 14 **NEng**, If I was only by the side of my old gal tonight and anyone should urge me to go to sea again, I would knock him down, by gingo. **1864** (1868) Trowbridge *3 Scouts* 21, Then, by jingoes, we will be! **1872** Schele de Vere *Americanisms* 612, *Jingo, by,* a favorite oath imported from England. **1924** *DN* 5.271 **cnNY** [Exclams], By jingo, oh jingo, jingo putty. **1959** *VT Hist.* 27.144, *By Jingo!* . . Common. **1968** *DARE* [(Qu. KK48, *When you work something out as you go, without having a plan or pattern to follow:* "I didn't have anything to go by, so I just did it _____.") Inf **OH**42, By guess and by jingo;] (Qu. NN2, *Exclamations of very strong agreement*) Inf **NC**82, By jingo, you're right. **1969** *DARE* Tape **IN**79A, We sent it [=a check to Disabled Veterans] and by jingo, next thing that came in the mail was that. **1986** Pederson *LAGS Concordance*, 1 inf, **cLA**, By jingo; 1 inf, **cwFL**, By Jingoes.

jings See **jing**

‡jink n[1] [Perh infl by *clink* a jail]

1956 Ker *Vocab. W. TX* 406, [In a list of jocular terms for a jail:] Jink [given by 1 of 67 infs].

jink n[2] [Perh from *jinks* pranks, frolics, but cf **chink** n[3] 1]

See quot.

1962 Salisbury *Quoth the Raven* 75 **seAK**, They [=Amer Indian children] are the oddest little jinks imaginable. They speak their native language at home and of course they have very little of our language to go on, so she [=the teacher] is at her wits' end sometimes to get her ideas across to them.

jink n³ [Perh back-formation from *jinx*]
    1968 *DARE* (Qu. HH3, *A dull and stupid person*) Inf **WI**44, Jink.

jink v
    1 See quot. [Cf *SND jink* v.¹ 5 "*tr.* To evade, dodge, elude, escape the notice of"]
    1969 *DARE* (Qu. Y51, . . *Ways of saying 'to avoid' things or people* . . *"He's not your kind—you'd better _____ him."*) Inf **CA**157, Jink.
    2 To afflict with misfortune; to cheat. [Cf *SND jink* v.¹ 5 "to cheat, trick"; but perh back-formation from *jinx* to bring bad luck upon]
    1965–70 *DARE* (Qu. CC12a, . . *Bad luck* . . *"Poor Joe. He's really been having _____."*) Inf **MA**1, He is jinked; (Qu. CC12b, . . *If a person has a lot of bad luck* . . *"He's been _____."*) Infs **IN**19, **KS**18, **MA**6, **MS**80, **TN**6, 48, **WI**52, Jinked; (Qu. LL23, *Cheated, treated dishonestly: "These apples are wormy, I think you got _____."*) Inf **KS**18, Jinked.

jinked ppl adj [Perh Scots *jink* to trick, cheat, but perh back-formation from *jinx* to bring bad luck upon]
    1966–68 *DARE* (Qu. CC12b, . . *If a person has a lot of bad luck* . . *"He's been _____."*) Inf **KS**18, Jinked [jɪŋt]; **MS**1, Jinked; (Qu. LL23, *Cheated, treated dishonestly: "These apples are wormy, I think you got _____."*) Inf **KS**18, Jinked [jɪŋt].

jink money n [Cf *SND jink* v.¹ 5 "*tr* . . to cheat, trick," but cf also **chink** n²] Cf **jingle** n 2
    1967 *DARE* FW Addit **ceTN**, Jink [jɪŋk] money means counterfeit money—among country people.

jinks n¹ [Prob varr of *jings* (at **jing**)]
    Used in exclams or mild oaths—usu in phr *by jinks*.
    a1870 Chipman *Notes on Bartlett* 221 (*DAE*), Jinks. . . By Jinks! An expletive in N[ew] E[ngland]. **1902** Wister *Virginian* 276 **WY**, "My jinks!" said Scipio, quietly, and he shut the door. **1908** *DN* 3.325 **eAL**, **wGA**, Jinks. . . In the mild imprecation 'by jinks.' **1959** *VT Hist.* 27.144, By Jinks! . . Rare. **1968** *DARE* (Qu. NN9a, *Exclamations showing great annoyance: "_____. The electric power is off again."*) Inf **WI**62, Oh, jinks [jeŋks]; (Qu. NN30, *Exclamations beginning with the sound of 'j'*) Inf **MO**36, By jinks. **1970** *DARE* FW Addit **seMA**, By jinks. Exclamation, recalled from North Shore area. **1978** *DARE* File **cNY**, Jinks, it's hot today! [Speaker a 90-year-old woman] **1986** Pederson *LAGS Concordance*, 1 inf, **nwFL**, By jinks—they wanted so much for it.

jinks n² [Var of **chinks 1**]
    A **wintergreen** (here: *Gaultheria procumbens*).
    1892 *Jrl. Amer. Folkl.* 5.100 **MA**, **NH**, *Gaultheria procumbens*. . . Jinks.

jinks n³ Cf **jimjams**
    =**collywobbles 1.**
    1966 *DARE* (Qu. GG13a, *When something keeps bothering a person and makes him nervous*) Inf **WA**18, [It] gives me the jinks.

jinky adj
    Jinxed; likely to jinx someone.
    1967–68 *DARE* (Qu. CC12b, . . *If a person has a lot of bad luck* . . *"He's been _____."*) Inf **TX**26, Jinky [jĭᵛŋki]; (Qu. II28, *An unexplainable dislike that you feel from the first moment you meet a person*) Inf **GA**44, He's jinky.

jinky-whistle n Cf **whimmy-diddle**
    1912 *DN* 3.579 **wIN**, *Jinky-whistle*. . . A small or insignificant inanimate object of any kind.

jinnie, jinny See **jenny**

Jinnywerry See **January**

jinny-woman See **jenny 4**

jinshang, jinshard See **ginseng 1**

jint See **joint**

jin-whacker n Cf **jim** v 1
    One who does **gin work.**
    1976 Garber *Mountain-ese* 48 **sAppalachians**, *Jin-whacker* . . handyman. Moe ain't worth much money, he's jist a sort uv jinwhacker.

jip n¹ See **gyp** n¹

jip n² See **gyp** n²

jip n³ See **jib** n¹ **1a**

jipjawed See **jimberjawed**

jipperjaw See **jimberjaw**

jipperjawed See **jimberjawed**

jippy-stick n Cf **jap-stick, knick-knock**
    =**cricket** n².
    1950 *WELS Suppl.* **csWI**, Jippy-stick = nick-nock. So in Stoughton.

jirk See **jerk** n²

jirky See **jerky** n¹

jis See **just 2**

jism n Also sp *chism, chis(s)um, gism, gissum, jizum, jizz(um)* [Etym uncert, but cf *EDD chissom* sb. and v. "A shoot, budding out," "To sprout, bud, germinate." 1757 →]
    1 Energy, vim; ability. Cf **jasm**
    1842 *Spirit of Times* 29 Oct. 409/3 (*OEDS*), At the drawgate Spicer tried it on again, but his horse was knocked up—'the gism' and the starch was effectively taken out of him. **1848** in 1935 *DN* 6.453 **RI**, *Gism*. Strength, talent, Genius, ability. **1937** (1959) Weidman *I Can Get It* 263 **NYC**, "Step on it, will you?" "Sure. . ." "All right . . but put a little jism into it, will you?" **1942** Morley *Thorofare* 178, One of the same fields that the Major said had had the jizzum leached out of it by tobacco. **1951** West *Witch Diggers* 381 **sIN**, If nobody'd ever told me my age, he'd thought, I could be twenty-three now not sixty-three. Same old gism, same old piss and vinegar. **1969** *DARE* (Qu. KK28, *Feeling ambitious and eager to work*) Inf **NY**174, Full of jism ['jɪzəm]. **1984** Wilder *You All Spoken Here* 96 **Sth**, To "put a little jism to it" means apply extra effort.
    2 Semen; seminal fluid.
    1899 (1912) Green *VA Folk-Speech* 113, Chism. . . Chissum. Seminal fluid. **1927** *Ruppenthal Coll.* **KS**, Chisum, jizum—semen. **1935** [see **3** below]. **1942** McAtee *Dial. Grant Co. IN Suppl.* 1 5, *Gism* . . semen. **1944** *PADS* 2.19 **sAppalachians**, *Gism* ['jɪzəm]. . . Semen. [*PADS* Ed: Also Va., N.C., upper S.C.] **1945** *PADS* 3.10 **CT**, *Gism* [=semen]. . . Common among boys in Conn. in my childhood. **c1960** *Wilson Coll.* **csKY**, *Gism*. . . Semen. Not too common. **1968** Updike *Couples* 311 **seMA**, Georgene would wash herself before and after. Said his jizz ran down her leg. **1969** Roth *Portnoy* 132 **NJ**, You've got to . . walk around downtown Newark dripping gissum down your forehead. **1984** Wilder *You All Spoken Here* 96 **Sth**, Jism; gism: Dog water; crotch oil; a by-product of foreplay.
    3 See quot. Cf *DS* H37, **bull fuck**
    1935 *DN* 6.453, *Gism*. . . In various parts of the South, *gism* has the meaning "gravy[₅] . . cream sauce." In the North, it is commonly used to mean "semen." In Maine and eastern New England the word is commonly pronounced *chism*.
    4 See quot.
    1943 *LANE* Map 513 *(Pus)* 1 inf, **eCT**, [dʒɪzm], sometimes used for pus. 'Gism is any soft liquid that runs from a sore, or the juice from a rotten apple.'

jisslem n Cf **jism 3**
    1957 *Sat. Eve. Post Letters* **neTN**, *Jisslem*—heard while visiting in Ozark, Ala. and a favorite word to describe a sticky frosting on commercially baked pastries.

jist adv See **just 2**

jist(e) n See **joist 1**

jit n¹ [Prob abbr for **illegitimate**]
    1930 Shoemaker *1300 Words* 34 **cPA Mts** (as of c1900), *Jit*—An illigitimate [sic] child.

jit n² [Clipped form of **jitney** n 1]
    A five-cent piece.
    1914 *DN* 4.120 **NE** (as of 1913), *Jit*, from jitney. "We went to the

second jit show." **1915** *Chicago Herald* (IL) 13 Dec 18/4, "How comes
it," asked Evelyn, "that you're as clean as this here—strapped for a jit
for transportation on a snowy night like this here?" **1915** *DN* 4.236
neOH, *Jit.* Jitney: meaning 'a five-cent piece.' **1926** Black *You Can't
Win* 318 [Black], A "jit," as the Southern negro affectionately calls his
nickel. **1929** *AmSp* 4.341 [Vagabond lingo], *Jit*—A five cent piece.
1938 Farrell *No Star* 6 IL, I get 'em for two cents and sell 'em for a
jit. Made nearly half a buck yesterday. **1944** *PADS* 2.34 **wNC,** *Jit.* .
A nickel. **1950** *WELS* (Nicknames for: *$.05*) 3 Infs, **WI,** Jit. **1965–70**
DARE (Qu. U22, . . *A five-cent piece*) 13 Infs, **esp Atlantic exc NEng,**
Jit. **1979** *NYT Article Letters* ceMA, As a boy growing up in Boston
we kids had slang words for money. A nickle was called a "jit."

jit n³

A Black person; see quot 1983.

   1930 Irwin *Amer. Tramp* 110, *Jit.* . . A negro or, more usually, a
negress, and seemingly a term of derision. **1936** (1947) Mencken *Amer.
Lang.* 296, For Negro . . *jit.* **1983** Allen *Lang. Ethnic Conflict* 50, [In
a list of epithets for Blacks indicating status diminution:] Jit [Allen:
especially, fem. . .]

jit v [Perh var of *jet* to spout, emit]

To urinate, wet with urine.

   1948 Manfred *Chokecherry* 257 **nwIA,** Hippy started across the highway, . . sniffed at a weed . . , lifted his leg and jitted it with a few
drops. . . And the dog continued to jit.

jitlins See **chitterlings**

jitneur n [Prob blend of *jitney* + *chauffeur*]

A driver of a **jitney** n 2 or 3.

   1922 *Funk & Wagnalls College Std. Dict.* 623, *Jitneur.* . . One who
drives a jitney. **1934** *AmSp* 9.74 **seNJ,** An ordinance of 1922 . . compelled the word *jitney* to be placed on an illuminated sign on the bus,
and referred to the driver as a *jitneur.* **1934** (1940) Weseen *Dict. Amer.
Slang* 357, *Jitneur*—The driver of a small or cheap automobile. **1946**
Sun (Baltimore MD) 31 May 12/3 **neMD** *(Hench Coll.),* In looking over
the *Cecil Whig,* of Elkton, [I] . . find that a description of an auto
accident in the streets there referred to the driver of an offending taxi
as a "jitnour [sic]." References made in several places in the paper
convince me that jitnour has become a common term there for the cab
drivers that haul romantic couples to the homes of the marrying parsons
of that fair town. Thus the language grows.

jitney n Also sp *chitney, gitney, jittany* [Etym unknown]

1 A five-cent piece.

   1903 *Cincinnati Enquirer* 2 May 11/5 *(OEDS),* [In St. Louis] . . a
'gitney' is a nickel. **1915** *Nation* 4 Feb 142, The word "jitney." It is the
Jewish slang term for a nickel; so that "jitney 'bus" means simply a 'bus
charging a fare of five cents. **1915** *DN* 4.233 **neOH,** *Jitney.* . . A
five-cent piece. **1917** *DN* 4.413 **wNC,** *Jittany.* . . Variant of *jitney.* **1936**
(1947) Mencken *Amer. Lang.* 189, [Commenting on quot 1915 *Nation*
above:] I recall hearing it [=*jitney*] to designate a five-cent piece long
before there was any considerable immigration of Eastern Jews. It began
to be used to designate a cheap automobile bus in 1914. **1943** *CA Folkl.
Qrly.* 2.41, *Jitney* is supposed to be California's verbal gift to the nation,
but in the East a jitney is a nickel and here a jitney is an ordinary
automobile that runs on a regular route and carries passengers for small
fares. **1947** Saroyan *Jim Dandy* 11 **CA,** Call that money? A jitney? A
nickel? **1949** *Sun* (Baltimore MD) 22 Aug 10/2 *(Hench Coll.),* A "jitney," of course was a nickel. . . As far as Baltimore was concerned, it
was a Western term and came with the bus. **c1960** *Wilson Coll.* **csKY,**
Jitney, a nickel; very modern. **1965–70** *DARE* (Qu. U22, . . *A five-cent
piece*) 63 Infs, **scattered, but esp Missip-Ohio Valleys,** Jitney. **1983**
DARE File **seMS,** My 94-year-old friend tells me that about 1900 the
City of Biloxi . . put in operation a horse-drawn tram, a jitney. The fare
was five cents to ride the jitney. Soon, people in Biloxi began calling a
nickel a jitney and the practice was observed throughout the city for
about ten years when the jitney service was discontinued and, so far as
he recalls, the use of the word for the coin was also discontinued.

2 also *jitney bus:* Any of var forms of cheap, often makeshift,
public transportation, esp an old car used to provide unofficial
bus service.

   1914 in 1915 *Nation* 14 Jan 50 **Los Angeles CA,** This autumn
automobiles, mostly of the Ford variety, have begun to run in competition with the street cars in this city. The newspapers call them "Jitney
'buses." **1915** *KS Rept.* 96.827, The city of Huntington [WV] . . passed
an ordinance for the regulation and licensing of "jitney busses." *Ibid*

831, [Quoting a decision of the Louisiana Supreme Court of June 29,
1915:] The jitneys are automobiles . . but they are automobiles used in
a peculiar way, which sets them apart in a class by themselves—a fact
well recognized the country over. **1916** *SW Reporter* (1st ser) 182.276
nwAR, Section 5 defines the term "jitney" to include any and all
self-propelled vehicles operating for hire between fixed points or places
along designated or advertised routes. *Ibid* 276, The jitney bus service,
transporting people for hire, for a uniform five-cent fare, in low priced
or second hand automobiles, over definite routes in cities or towns, is
of but recent origin. **1921** Tucker *Amer. Engl.* 271, *Jitney* . . bus on
which the fare is 5 cents, 1912. **1928** *Ruppenthal Coll.* **KS,** *Jitney*—a
local railroad train, whether steam or gasoline motor; a slow train. The
jitney stops at every station and even at crossings out in the country
when people want to get on or off the train. **1943** [see **1** above]. **1949**
Sun (Baltimore MD) 22 Aug 10/2 *(Hench Coll.),* In 1914 a battered car
had appeared on the streets of Oakland, Cal., bearing a placard offering
to carry passengers "anywhere for a jitney." The idea swept the country. . . Thousands of men and women who had cars or could rent one
set themselves up as "jitney" transit companies. **1967–70** *DARE* (Qu.
N37, *Joking names for a branch railroad that is not very important or
gives poor service*) Infs **KS**15, **MN**2, **PA**74, Jitney; (Qu. N41a, . .
Horse-drawn vehicles . . to carry people) Infs **IN**39, **PA**199, **SC**69,
Jitney; **IN**56, Jitney—a big wagon with several seats pulled by four
horses. **1967** *DARE* Tape **MI**41, We brought this car back and we'd rent
it—we had a jitney, see, back and forth around town and to these other
towns that had no other means of transportation. **1983** [see **1** above].

3 An automobile, esp one that is old or broken down.

   [**1916** see **2** above.] **1917** in 1954 Weingarten *Amer. Dict. Slang* 208.
1930 *AmSp* 6.85, So most of the Ford jokes originated in the self-con-
sciousness of the Ford owner . . out of the need of . . averting criticism.
Half-contemptuously, half-affectionately, he dubs his car . . a *jitney*
(nickel-cheap). **1965–70** *DARE* (Qu. N5, *Nicknames for an automobile,
especially an old or broken-down car*) 40 Infs, **scattered, but esp Sth,
S Midl,** Jitney; **MT**1, Chitney [čɪtnɪ]; **VA**75, Old jitney; (Qu. N6, *An
old car that has been fixed up to make it go fast or make a lot of noise*)
Inf **NC**49, Souped-up jitney.

4 Any of var small vehicles used for moving loads within a
limited area.

   1939 FWP *Guide AK* 112, Longshoremen endanger shins with bull
jitneys and push-pull jitneys. **1945** Hubbard *Railroad Ave.* 349, *Jitney*—
Four-wheel electric truck that carries baggage around inside a terminal.
1950 *Western Folkl.* 9.121 **nwOR** [Sawmill workers' speech], *Jitney.* A
motor vehicle that straddles a load of lumber and picks up the load by
means of flanges which slide under the ends of the blocks. [**1970** *DARE*
(Qu. N41c, *Horse-drawn vehicles to carry light loads*) Inf **SC**69, Jitney.]

5 See quot.

   1992 *DARE* File **csAK,** A jitney looks like a large rowboat and is
towed behind the fishing boat until it is needed to pull the purse seine
net into the closed "purse" shape to trap the fish. It has no oars or
oarlocks, and the gunwales are smooth to facilitate hauling the net over
them.

6 in phr *jitney dance:* A dancing party at which a small
fee is paid for each dance; hence n *jitney dance hall* a taxi
dance hall.

   1918 *Capital Times* (Madison WI) 12 Sept 5, [Advt:] Good entertainment for the soldiers at the Jitney Dance. **1925** *AmSp* 1.152 **West,** That
bastard word "jitney" is still used in outlying places, where a "jitney
dance" means a nickel dance. **1933** *Amer. Mercury* Aug 490, Also about
the little unpleasantness I had with the wife when I fallen for a little
"dame" in a jitney dance hall. **1934** (1940) Weseen *Dict. Amer. Slang*
100, *Jitney dance*—A public dance in which a charge is made for each
dance. [**1958** Charters *Jazz* 167 **New Orleans LA,** Jitney: a "dime-a-
dance" hall. Also known as "taxi dance hall."] **1968** *DARE* [(Qu. DD30,
*Joking names for a place where liquor is [or was] sold and consumed
illegally]* Inf **LA**45, Jitney;] (Qu. FF4, *Names and joking names for different kinds of dancing parties*) Inf **OH**52, Jitney dance—costs a nickel.

7 in phr *jitney supper:* See quots. Cf **dime-a-dip dinner**

   1968 *DARE* (Qu. FF1, . . *A kind of group meeting called a 'social' or
'sociable'. . . [What goes on?]*) Inf **OH**47, Jitney supper—kind of a
potluck where you pay five cents for each dish. It's to raise money. **1970**
DARE FW Addit **OH,** Jitney supper—a fundraising dinner of donated
food, held especially at schools.

8 =**flying jenny 1a.**

   1966–68 *DARE* (Qu. EE32, *A homemade merry-go-round*) Inf **MS**1,
Jitney [ˈjɪtnɪ]; **NY**64, Jitney [FW: Inf has heard].

jitney adj Cf **two-bit**

Cheap, shoddy; incompetent, inferior.

1916 Wilson *Somewhere* 59, He . . sells these jitney pianos and phonographs and truck like that. **1920** Fitzgerald *This Side of Paradise* 120 **NYC,** Here's the old jitney waiter. **1933** *NY Herald Tribune* (NY) 5 Dec 17/3, We refer to the jitney economists, the boys who play the money tunes only by ear. **1935** *Amer. Mercury* 35.472 **neNJ,** The prolificity of these jitney St. Georges [=newspaper editors] . . has been . . amazing. **1937** *AmSp* 12.4, [Pejorative terms applied to Pres. Franklin D. Roosevelt's group of advisors known as the Brain Trust:] Jitney Marxes, academic theorists, The Order of Inferior Pedagogues. **1946** O'Neill *Iceman Cometh* 36 **NYC,** He never worries in hard times because there's always old friends from the days when he was a jitney Tammany politician.

jitney v Also with *it*

To travel or transport in or as if in a **jitney** n **2** or **3.**

1915 *Amer. Mag.* Dec 21, Four masked men held up an omnibus in which seventeen men were jitneying to Salem, New Jersey, with their pay envelopes in their pockets. *Ibid* 18 **VA,** It is the experience of a lifetime to "jitney" over that tortuous, deep-gullied whirligig of a City Point road. **1942** Berrey–Van den Bark *Amer. Slang* 767.2, Travel by bus. . . Jitney (it). **1956** *Sun* (Baltimore MD) 23 May sec B 1/6 *(Hench Coll.),* Freeman described in some detail . . the control mechanism for the . . rocket that will jitney the satellite into a globe-encircling path. **1969** *DARE* FW Addit **MA**48, Jitney—transport, especially a person, by automobile. "He'd have to jitney me."

jitney dance (hall) See **jitney** n **6**

jitney supper See **jitney** n **7**

jittany See **jitney** n

jitterbug n

1 See quots. *chiefly among Black speakers*

1970 Young *Snakes* 71 **ceMS** [Black], All you wanna do lately is run around these old so-called hip niggers, these little jitterbugs. **1970** *DARE* (Qu. HH2, *Names and nicknames for a citified person*) Infs **FL**48, **NJ**69, **SC**69, Jitterbug. [All Infs Black] **1972** Shafer *Dict. Prison Slang* 23 **TX,** Jitterbug—someone who is trying to impress others. **1977** Smitherman *Talkin* 251 [Black], *Jitterbug,* a superhip, streetified black, often used with just a touch of scorn. **1980** Folb *Runnin' Down* 243 **cwCA** [Black], *Jitterbug.* . . One who talks too much or talks nonsense.

2 See quot.

1970 *Western Folkl.* 29.231 **MS** [Black], On 25 March 1969, I recorded Napoleon Strickland of Como, Mississippi, singing blues and playing a one-stringed instrument. . . It consists of a strand of broom wire about four feet long strung horizontally along a wall between two metal staples with two bottles for bridges. . . The index finger of the right hand beats the string, while the left hand holds the snuff bottle which is slid along the string. Strickland also uses the free fingers of his left hand to stop the string. He has played this instrument, which he calls a "jitterbug," since childhood in Como. At present he is forty-five years old.

jive n Also sp *gieve* [Etym unknown] *chiefly among Black speakers*

Deceptive, insincere, or foolish talk; by ext, anything false, pretentious, or trifling; nonsense.

1928 Fisher *Walls Jericho* 301 **Harlem NYC** [Black], *Jive*—1. Pursuit in love or any device thereof. Usually flattery with intent to win. 2. Capture. In either sense this word implies passing fancy, hence, deceit. **1934** *AmSp* 9.26 [Black prison parlance], *Gieve.* . . Conversation; misleading talk. **1946** (1972) Mezzrow–Wolfe *Really Blues* 334, *Jive* . . confusing doubletalk, pretentious conversation, anything false or phony. **1950** Bissell *Stretch on River* 224, You got quite a line of jive, ain't you? **1954** Armstrong *Satchmo* 150 [Black], There was lots of just plain common shooting and cutting. But somehow all of that jive didn't faze me at all. *Ibid* 193, I bought a lot of cheap jive at the five and ten cents store to give to the kids in my neighborhood when I got back to New Orleans. **1968–70** *DARE* (Qu. JJ17, *When you know that somebody has been trying to deceive you . . "He's not fooling me one bit, I'm _____ [him]."*) Inf **TN**53, Hip to his jive; **GA**45, On to his jive; (Qu. NN13, *When you think that the thing somebody has just said is silly or untrue: "Oh, that's a lot of _____."*) Infs **TN**46, **VA**39, Jive. [All Infs Black] **1970** Young *Snakes* 55 **ceMS** [Black], Aw, man, it's just some jive they had us studyin last semester at school. **1973** *Black World* Oct. 36/2

(OEDS), Everything that we do must be aimed toward the total liberation . . of Afrika. . . Anything short of that is jive.

jive v[1] Also with *around* Also sp *gieve* [**jive** n] *chiefly among Black speakers*

1 To tease, put (someone) on; to mislead, con; to pretend; to lie, cheat; hence n *jiver.*

1928 Armstrong *Don't Jive Me* (Phonodisc) [title]. **1929** in 1983 Taft *Blues Lyric Poetry* 95, You can jive me baby : but I don't believe a thing you say / You just a confidencing woman : and wants to have your way. **1934** *AmSp* 9.26 [Black prison parlance], *Gieve.* . . To mislead with words; to take into one's confidence. **1946** (1972) Mezzrow–Wolfe *Really Blues* 334, *Jive.* . . to kid, to talk insincerely or without meaning, to use an elaborate and misleading line. **1950** Lomax *Mr. Jelly Roll* 172 [Black], I . . jived the expressman to haul my trunks to the station by telling him my money was uptown. **1968–70** *DARE* (Qu. BB27, *When somebody pretends to be sick . . he's _____*) Infs **NY**241, **OH**103, Jiving; (Qu. BB53b, . . *A doctor who is not very capable or doesn't have a very good reputation*) Inf **NJ**67, Nothing but a jiver; (Qu. II20b, *A person who tries too hard to gain somebody else's favor: "He's always trying to _____ the boss."*) Infs **DC**13, **SC**68, Jive; (Qu. II33, *To get an advantage over somebody by tricky means: "I don't trust him, he's always trying to _____."*) Inf **SC**68, Jive you; (Qu. JJ36, *To work out a plan, especially a secret plan: "Mary knows more about that, you and she can _____ together."*) Inf **LA**46, Jive. [5 of 6 total Infs Black] **1970** Bullins *Electronic* 85 **sCA,** You're accusing my wife of jivin' around on me. **1970** Young *Snakes* 54 **ceMS** [Black], Two joints—and finally the third. "You mean to tell me you still dont feel nothin, MC?" Shakes said. "You jivin, nigger!" *Ibid* 56, Naw, you cant jive the jiver, I aint goin for that. **1973** *Black World* Mar. 57 *(OEDS),* Lawd, don't jive Miz Jackson, . . Ride on King Jesus. *Ibid* May 84/1 *(OEDS),* He comes down hard on white racists, but he also attacks Black 'jivers' who seek to exploit their brethren under the guise of blackness.

2 also *bull-jive:* To idle, loaf about.

1938 *AmSp* 13.317 **NE** [Black], To jive around. . . Used with a rather indefinite meaning, perhaps 'to fool around.' **1969–70** *DARE* (Qu. A10, . . *Doing little unimportant things: . . "What are you doing?" . . "Nothing in particular—I'm just _____."*) Inf **NC**70, Bull-jiving; (Qu. KK31, *To go about aimlessly looking for distraction: "He doesn't have anything to do, so he's just _____ around."*) Infs **FL**52, **NJ**70, Jiving. [All Infs Black]

jive adj Also *jive-ass, jive-time, jive-town* [**jive** n] *chiefly among Black speakers*

Deceitful, pretentious, insincere; confused, ignorant.

[**1959** *Esquire* Nov 70J [sic *OEDS*—quot not found], *Jive,* to fool, to kid. The adjective is bogus.] **1964** Gold *Jazz Lexicon* 169, *Jive-ass mother-fucker* . . in the sense of flattering, practicing deceit, "kidding"; *-ass* is an emphasis suffix here. **1969** Brown *Life & Loves* 31 [Black], You jiveass nigger, Reb said, laughing. No, I'm telling the truth. **1969–70** *DARE* (Qu. V7, *A person who sets out to cheat others while pretending to be honest*) Inf **TN**50, Jive-time artist; (Qu. AA6b, . . *A man who is fond of being with women and tries to attract their attention—if he's rude or not respectful*) Inf **TN**46, Jive-time nigger; (Qu. HH2, *Names and nicknames for a citified person*) Inf **GA**83, Jive [ʤɑɪv] man. [All Infs Black] **1970** *DARE* Tape **WV**21, We was havin' this pep assembly. . . Before we have a game . . we . . say cheers an' all that other jive-town stuff. [Inf Black] **1970** Bullins *Electronic* 85 **sCA** [Black], That little jive-ass square gettin' next to your woman. **1970** Young *Snakes* 79 **ceMS** [Black], "She was kinda, you know—jive." "Jive?" "Yeah. She couldnt dig what I was into and went for all this old hippy-dippy shit." **1972** Claerbaut *Black Jargon* 70, *Jive.* . . stupid. *Ibid, Jivetime.* . . 1. insincere; not serious: *This is a jivetime place.* . . 2. dishonest; deceptive: *a jivetime dude.* 3. ignorant; dull-witted. **1973** *Black World* June 61 *(OEDS),* Awh, Sistuh, u sho is jive. *Ibid* 79/1 *(OEDS),* The hero . . is 'hip', but not 'jive'. *Ibid* Aug. 55/2 *(OEDS),* Silly-ass so-called hangups of jive-ass white folks. **1979** Gillespie–Fraser *To Be Or Not To Bop* 298 [Black], The publishing company would give you one of them jive contracts, where you'd never get no royalties on it. So this was a rip-off.

jive v[2] [Prob var of **jibe**]

To agree, get along; to make sense—usu used in neg constrs.

1943 *AmSp* 18.153, Doesn't jive. 'Doesn't make sense.' **1950** *WELS* *(If two people don't get along well together: "They don't _____.")* 1 Inf, **WI,** Jive together. **1965–70** *DARE* (Qu. II11a) 48 Infs, **scattered,** Jive; **AR**55, Jive in with one another; **KY**72, Jive together; **NY**239, Jive too well; (Qu. KK67, *When people think alike about something: "On that particular thing, we _____."*) 18 Infs, **scattered**, Jive; **SC**26, Jive together; **GA**19, Our opinions jive; (Qu. II29a, *An unexplainable dislike that you feel from the first moment you meet a person: "I don't know why, but I just can't _____ him."*) Inf **TX**95, Jive with; (Qu. II29b, . . *To explain the unpleasant effect that person has on you: "He just _____."*) Inf **LA**40, Doesn't jive with me; (Qu. KK58, *An excuse that looks as if it would not stand up under questioning: "His story won't _____."*) Infs **IA**22, **LA**45, **MO**17, **NY**131, Jive; (Qu. KK68, *When people don't think alike about something: "We agree on most things, but on politics we're _____."*) Inf **IN**83, Don't jive. **1966** *DARE* FW Addit **SC**, Jive [ʤɑɪv]—to be in accord, agree with respect to facts or figures, but not people.

jive-ass See **jive** adj

jiver See **jive** v[1] **1**

jive-time, jive-town See **jive** adj

jiwampused adj Cf **catawampus** adj **1**, **gee-hawed**, *DS* MM13, 14, 15

     1969 *DARE* (Qu. MM3, *When someone does something the wrong way round . . "This is the front, you've got the whole thing turned _____."*) Inf **CA**136, All jiwampused [ʤɪˈwɑmpəst].

jizibee n
     A **nuthatch**.
     1969 *DARE* (Qu. Q23, *The insect-eating bird that goes headfirst down a tree trunk*) Inf **CA**136, Jizibee [ˈʤɪzibi]. I've seen 'em, but don't know the name.

jizum, jizz See **jism**

jizzicked adj Cf *DS* KK20b [Perh infl by **tizzicky**]
     1975 Gould *ME Lingo* 147, *Jizzicked* . . so far gone that repairs are pointless: "That washing machine is so jizzicked you might's well buy a new one."

jizzum See **jism**

jizzywig See **chizzywink**

jo n
     1 See **joe** n[2].
     2 See **poor joe**.

joan v, hence vbl n *joaning* (also sp *joning*) *among Black speakers* Cf **dozen** n **B1**
To engage in a ritualized exchange of insults.
     1939 *Amer. Imago* 1.15 **Sth** [Black], In this city [*DARE* Ed: city unspecified] there is another name for the Dozens, "joaning." . . "Joaning" is reported by children from middle and upper-class families. . . "Keep on joanin' / You'll make me mad./ I'll tell you the trouble / Your grandmaw had." **1971** Roberts *Third Ear* np [Black], Signifying, sig-gin(g) . . language behavior that makes direct or indirect implications of baiting or boasting, the essence of which is making fun of another's appearance, relatives, or situation. Variations include joning, playing the dozens, screaming on, sounding. **1972** Kochman *Rappin'* 274, Terms for the game of exchanging ritualized insults. . . "Woofing" is common in Philadelphia and elsewhere, "joning" in Washington. **1981** Pederson *LAGS Basic Materials*, 1 inf, **Atlanta GA**, Joaning—talking about somebody's mama. **1992** *DARE* File **cnGA**, *Joning on somebody*—making a joke about somebody; identified as Atlanta Black slang.

job n[1], v[1] Also *jarby* [*EDD* job sb.[1] 4, v.[1] 9] Cf **do one's business** (at **do** v **D4**)
A bowel movement; to defecate—usu in phr *do (a) job*.
     1899 (1912) Green *VA Folk-Speech* 215, *Job* . . Do a job, to go to stool. **1910** in 1944 *ADD* **cNY**, 'Do job.' Child's wd. **1930** Shoemaker *1300 Words* 33 **cPA Mts** (as of c1900), *Job*—Human excrement. **1970** *Foxfire* Spring–Summer 85 **nGA**, He hadn't done his mornin' job, an' he just pulled his britches down an' set down in th'trail. **1971** *Today Show Letters* **RI** (as of c1930), [Child's postcard from camp:] I did a jarby in my pants last night when I couldn't get into the washhouse. **1975** *DARE* File **cnMA** (as of c1915), When I was a small child, a boy about my age told me, "If you eat green green apples you'll job and job and job till you die." **1975** *AmSp* 50.62 **AR** (as of c1970), *Job* . . Bowel movement—"He did a job in his pants." **1994** *DARE* File **csWI**, Back in the 1930s, the [neighbor] kids called a bowel movement a *big job*.

job v[2] [*OED* job v.[1] 2 1573 →] **chiefly Sth, S Midl** Cf **stob**
     1 To strike, poke, or thrust sharply; also fig.
     1773 (1865) Jones *Jrl.* 66 **NJ**, He took some tobacco, and with violence jobbed it to my mouth, saying *tobaac*. **1846** U.S. Congress *Congressional Globe* 16 June 983 **IL**, Delivered into the hands of the Philistines, and his eyes jobbed out. **1884** Smith *Bill Arp's Scrap Book* 57 **nwGA**, Is every man what can write a paragraph to consider us bars [=bears] in a cage, and be always a-jobbin at us to hear us growl? **1899** (1912) Green *VA Folk-Speech* 245, *Job* . . To strike, stab, or punch. **1903** *DN* 2.291 **Cape Cod MA** (as of a1857), Don't job your fork into it so. *Ibid* 318 **seMO**. **1906** *DN* 3.120 **cwIN**, He jobbed me with a fork. *Ibid* 143 **nwAR**. **1908** *DN* 3.325 **eAL, wGA**. **1915** *DN* 4.184 **swVA**. **1917** *DN* 4.413 **IA, IL, wNC**. **1923** *DN* 5.212 **swMO**. **1938** Rawlings *Yearling* 84 **nFL**, I takened a piece o' meat and I jobbed it on a long stick. **1939** *Hall Coll.* **eTN**, He . . jobbed his knife in 'im, and the old bear jumped. **1959** Lomax *Rainbow Sign* 66 **AL** [Black], He jobs straight in. Then he rips down with the end of his knife. **1967** *DARE* (Qu. Y46a, *To get hurt with something sharp . . "He _____ a thorn into his hand."*) Infs **KY**33, **LA**6, Jobbed; (Qu. Y46b, *To get hurt with something sharp . . "She _____ herself with a needle."*) Inf **LA**6, Jobbed. **1986** Pederson *LAGS Concordance (Stabbed)* 2 infs, **FL, MS**, Jobbed him; 1 inf, **ceLA**, Job (=jabbed). **1990** Cavender *Folk Med. Lexicon* 26 **sAppalachians**, *Job* . . used to refer to a sharp, stabbing pain: "The pain in my neck jobbed me all day."
     2 Spec: to thrust (a **jobber**) into the ground to make a hole for planting or staking a crop; to make (such a hole); to plant (a crop) using a **jobber**.
     1965 *DARE* Tape **OK**1, They'd break a little sod every year. . . Sometime they'd take a—what they call a job planter . . you job it down between those two sods . . plant your corn and stuff in there that way the first year, then afterward you could break it up. **1966** *PADS* 45.16 **cnKY**, You really have to bend your back to job tobacco. **1967** Key *Tobacco Vocab.* **NC**, You job the planter down in the dirt and throw a plant in it, and turn it. *Ibid* **GA**, One would go along and job [ʤɪb] the hole and another'd come along and put the plant in. *Ibid* **TN**, You job it [=a cone-shaped hand setter] down in the ground. **1967** *DARE* FW Addit **LA**1, I use that bar for sticking beans, just job it down in the ground.
     3 Fig: to tease, razz, make fun of.
     1961 Adams *Old-Time Cowhand* 321, But when dawn came and still no snipe drivers, he began to realize he'd been jobbed. **1971** Jennings *Cowboys* 205 **MT, WY** (as of 1877), She had a quick little tongue that drew howls of laughter when she began jobbing somebody. **1976** Sublette Co. Artist Guild *More Tales* 308 **WY** (as of c1900), Cowboys are pretty bad to pull jokes on one another. . . I never saw one that was as bad for jobbin' somebody as my good old friend, Everett Curtis.

job n[2] [**job** v[2] **1**] **chiefly Sth, S Midl**
A stab or blow.
     1899 (1912) Green *VA Folk-Speech* 245, *Job* . . A sudden stab, prick, or thrust, as with anything pointed. **1906** *DN* 3.143 **nwAR**, He gave me a job in the ribs. **1908** *DN* 3.325 **eAL, wGA**, *Job*, n. and v. Jab. Common. **1915** *DN* 4.184 **swVA**, *Job*. Variant of jab, n. and v. **1954** *Harder Coll.* **cwTN**, Job (a stab).

Job n[3]
See quot.
     c1938 in 1970 Hyatt *Hoodoo* 2.942 **Richmond VA**, Then we has a 'erb that grows that they call *Job*. [Hyatt: The preceding *Job* is perhaps Job's-tears, seed from an Asiatic grass often strung in a necklace and formerly worn as a common teething remedy.]

jobber n Also *corn jabber, job planter, jobber* ~, *jobbing* ~ [**job** v[2] **2**; cf Engl dial *jobber* small spade (*EDD* job v.[2] 2)] **chiefly S Midl** Cf **corn stabber, peg**
A tool for making holes in the ground, esp for planting; a dibble.
     1923 *DN* 5.212 **swMO**, *Jobber* . . Anything that may be used for 'jobbing' or jabbing. A pointed steel bar used in punching holes in the ground for posts, or a 'post hole jobber.' **1947** Steed *KY Tobacco Patch* 88, The mountain country where most corn planting is done with a jobber. **1965** [see **job** v[2] **2**]. **1966** *PADS* 45.16 **cnKY**, You use a jobber to make a hole for each plant. **1967** Key *Tobacco Vocab.* **MO**, Jobber. **1967–68** *DARE* (Qu. L23, . . *Machinery . . used . . in putting in the seed*) Inf **PA**135, Planter—[for] corn, also known as jobber; **OH**10, Corn

jabber. **1967** *DARE* FW Addit **CO,** Jobbing or jobber planter—a two-handled thing resembling a post-hole shovel—it had a bucket to hold the grain and as you pulled the handles apart the seed dropped into the hole you'd made with the same tool. **1983** Montell *Don't Go Up* 47 **csKY, cnTN,** The job-planters preceded by many years the mechanized one-row planters such as those made by Oliver and John Deere. Operated by hand, the job-planter was jabbed into the soil and then triggered so that one or two grains were released. This new device was not much faster than dropping seed by hand, but it was a back-saver and therefore highly prized. It was later used during replanting sessions, following the introduction of one-row planters. **1986** Pederson *LAGS Concordance,* 1 inf, **nwAR,** Post-hole jobber.

jobbernowl n Pronc-sp *jobbermow* [EDD *jobbernowl* sb. 2; OED *jobbernowl* sb. 2 "A stupid person, a blockhead" 1592 →]
Used as a vague term of derogation; see quots.

1955 Adams *Grandfather* 261 **NY** (as of 1830s), I'll talk that cheap jobbermow right out of his trick and that purse right into my pants pocket. **1982** *Smithsonian Letters, Jobbernowl,* as in "damned, mumbling, bald-headed ol' jobbernowl," apparently, in the usage I have heard it, some sort of pejorative noun for an old fudderer. . . Dad probably picked it up in the Ozarks where, before WWI, he was a traveling bill collector for the Rumely [sic for *Rumley*] tractor company.

jobber planter See **jobber**

jobber's sun n [*jobber* a contractor]
In logging: a source of nighttime illumination allowing longer hours to be worked; spec, the moon or a kerosene lantern.

1905 U.S. Forest Serv. *Bulletin* 61.40 **NW, Gt Lakes** [Logging terms], *Jobber's sun.* A term applied to the moon in a jobber's or contractor's logging camp, on account of the early and late hours of commencing and ending work. **1964** Hargreaves–Foehl *Story of Logging* 59 **MI,** [Glossary:] *Jobber's suns*—Kerosene torches used for night work in the woods.

jobbing planter See **jobber**

Job in his coffin See **Job's coffin 2**

job lot n [Transf from *job lot* a group of usu miscellaneous, inferior, or nonstandard articles sold at a discount]

1915 *DN* 4.209 **NE,** *Job-lot,* poorest of anything. "You're nothing but a job-lot." Common.

job planter See **jobber**

Job's coffin n
1 A constellation; see quots.

1883 Wilder *Sister Ridnour* 133 *(DA),* I chanced to get a glimpse of the stars in 'Job's coffin.' **1896** *DN* 1.419 **nOH,** *Job's Coffin:* for *Pleiades.* **1912** Green *VA Folk-Speech* 245, *Job's-coffin.* . . A group of four stars in the shape of a coffin not far to the eastward of the seven stars. The constellation Dolphin. **1930** Shoemaker *1300 Words* 33 **cPA Mts** (as of c1900), *Job's coffin*—A heavenly constellation, the seven stars. **1931** *Randolph Enterprise* (Elkins, W.Va.) 12 Nov. 2/2 *(DA),* We watch the Great Dipper, the Seven Stars, Jobs coffin and several others. [c1938 in 1970 Hyatt *Hoodoo* 2.942 **ceVA,** Then we have a star . . that is called Job, repisent Job in his coffin. It's complete—you kin see the shape of the coffin an' you kin [see] the form of Job.] **1943** Weslager *DE Forgotten Folk* 177, The Big Dipper and Little Dipper are known to all. Constellations known as Job's Coffin, Four Runners, and Milkmaid's Path could also be readily recognized.

2 also *Job in his coffin:* A figure in a string game such as cat's cradle; the game itself. Cf **Jacob's ladder 12**

1908 *DN* 3.325 **eAL, wGA,** *Job's coffin.* . . A form made on the fingers with a string. **1909** *DN* 3.399 **nwAR,** *Job's coffin.* . . A game. **1968** Haun *Hawk's Done Gone* 310 **TN,** Jamie I miss. . . Always talking his baby talk. . . "Make me Job in his coffin," he'd say. " . . Make me Jacob's ladder."

job shark See **shark**

Job's heads n
=**Job's tears 1.**

1954 *Harder Coll.* **cwTN,** *Job's heads:* Small seeds that grow on grass. Take goiter out of neck.

Job's lantern n Cf *DS* CC16
=**will-o'-the-wisp.**

1950 *WELS* (A small light that seems to dance over a swamp or marsh by night) 1 Inf, **cWI,** Job's lantern.

Job's mouse See **Job's turkey 1**

Job's off-ox n Also *Job's ox* Cf **Adam's off-ox 2, Job's turkey 1**
Used in compar phrr as an intensive; see quots.

1908 Lincoln *Cy Whittaker* 120 **MA,** Even if her folks was poorer'n Job's off ox I'd spend a little on my own account and trust to getting it back some time. **1966–70** *DARE* (Qu. U41b, *Somebody who has lost everything and is very poor:* "He's poor as _____.") Inf **DE4,** Job's off-ox; **MA37,** Job's ox; (Qu. HH4, *Someone who has odd or peculiar ideas or notions*) Inf **MI116,** Odder than Job's off-ox; (Qu. HH21, *A very awkward, clumsy person*) Inf **MA35,** Awkward as Job's off-ox.

Job's tears n
1 Std: an Asiatic grass (*Coix lacryma-jobi*) cultivated for its hard whitish seeds. Also called **corn bead (seed), Job's heads, Job's teeth, tear grass**
2 See **wild Job's tears.**
3 A **false Solomon's seal** (here: *Smilacina racemosa*).

1894 *Jrl. Amer. Folkl.* 7.102 **NY,** *Smilacina racemosa* . . Job's tears. **1940** Clute *Amer. Plant Names* 14, *S[milacina] racemosa.* . . Job's tears.

4 =**spiderwort.** [See quot 1949]

1910 Graves *Flowering Plants* 113 **CT,** *Tradescantia virginiana.* . . Job's Tears. . . Sometimes in river meadows. **1940** Clute *Amer. Plant Names* 273, *Tradescantia Virginiana.* . . Job's tears. **1949** Moldenke *Amer. Wild Flowers* 307, All these spiderworts are often called *jobs-tears* . . because the handsome flowers early in the afternoon transform themselves into "tears"—about noon the petals begin to contract in size, shrivel up, and deliquesce into a fluid jelly, which trickles away like a tear if touched. **1966** *DARE* Wildfl QR Pl.7 Inf **NH4,** Job's tears. **1968** *DARE* (Qu. S26b, *Wildflowers that grow in water or wet places*) Inf **AL42,** Job's tears—grows in wet places—glossy leaves, bunch of purple blooms at top.

Job's teeth n
=**Job's tears 1.**

1946 *PADS* 6.18 **swVA** (as of 1940), *Job's teeth.* . . Small, hard beans on a string for a teething child. **1983** *MJLF* 9.1.45 **ceKY,** *Job's teeth.*

Job's turkey n
1 in var compar phrr such as *poor* (or *mean,* etc) *as Job's turkey* (or *mouse,* etc): Very poor (or mean, etc). [*Job,* the Old Testament patriarch, proverbial for his poverty] **widespread, but more freq Sth, Midl** See Map on p. 146

[**1817** Scott *Blue Lights* 76 **CT,** Art thou as that turkey poor, Which at Uz, by famine died.] [**1830** Ames *Mariner's Sketches* 184 **MA,** The skipper of the Boston ship . . went to sea and carried all my clothes with him, leaving me in the situation of Job's turkey, without a feather to fly with.] **1830** *VA Lit. Museum* 496, I am left by my new house,/ Poor as Job's turkey, or a starv'd church mouse. **1853** Haliburton *Sam Slick's Wise Saws* 2.252, He is as mean as Job's turkey. **1853** Simms *Sword & Distaff* 143 **SC,** He's dead now as Job's turkey. **1854** Smith *'Way Down East* 184 **swME,** I should rather be as poor as Job's cat all the days of my life. **1871** Eggleston *Hoosier Schoolmaster* 39 **IN,** I remember when he was poarer nor Job's turkey. **1909** *DN* 3.358 **eAL, wGA,** Poor as Job's turkey. . . Very lean, emaciated. *Ibid* 414 **nME,** Poor as Job's turkey. . . Poor in purse or in flesh. **1912** *DN* 3.586 **wIN,** Poor as Job's turkey. . . 1. Very lean or thin. 2. Poverty-stricken. **1927** *AmSp* 2.362 **cwWV,** Poor as Job's turkey . . very poor. **1954** *Harder Coll.* **cwTN,** Slow as old Job's turkey. **1960** Criswell *Resp. to PADS* 20 **Ozarks,** Poor as Job's turkey refers to someone with no money; the commonest term. **1965–70** *DARE* (Qu. U41b, *Somebody who has lost everything and is very poor:* "He's poor as _____.") 388 Infs, **widespread, but esp Sth, Midl,** (Old) Job's turkey; 7 Infs, **esp S Midl,** (Old) Job's turkey hen; **CT20, LA11, VA41,** Job's old turkey (hen); **MO11, MT4,** Job's (church) mouse; **VA63,** Job's hen; **OH16,** Job's kite; **PA100,** Job's turkeys; **NY143,** Poor Job's turkey; (Qu. U41a, *Somebody who has lost everything and is very poor:* "He's _____.") Infs **TN14, 15,** Poor as Job's turkey; (Qu. X49, *Expressions . . about a person who is very thin*) Infs **SC3, TX35,** Poor as Job's turkey; (Qu. FF21a, *A joke that is so old it doesn't seem funny any more:* "His jokes are all _____.") Infs **GA77, SC32,** Old as Job's turkey; **NJ33,** Older than Job's turkey.

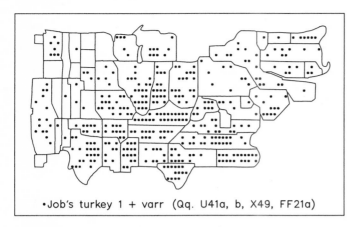

•Job's turkey 1 + varr (Qq. U41a, b, X49, FF21a)

2 in phr *not to know one from Job's turkey:* Not to know or even recognize one. Cf **Adam's off-ox 1**

1967–70 *DARE* (Qu. II26, *Joking ways of saying that you would not know who somebody is: "I wouldn't know him from _____."*) Infs **MS**88, **TN**12, Job's turkey.

Job weed n
See quot.

c1938 in 1970 Hyatt *Hoodoo* 2.942 **Richmond VA,** We has a flower that grows tha' choo call *Job weed,* see, an' on it it has de pictures—jis' a[s] complete a face on it as you [ever] seed growin' on a wall, if you take notice to the 'erbs. [Hyatt: *Job's weed,* if it exists, I do not know.]

jo cake n Cf hoecake, johnnycake
Prob an **ashcake 1.**

1956 *Hall Coll.* **neTN,** Ma called it a jo cake. She took some lard and put it in the middle of some dough, then put the dough in the ashes, and laid the fire over it.

jock n
1 A bull. [*EDD jock* sb.[1] 4]

1949 Kurath *Word Geog.* 62, [Expressions for *bull:*] West Virginia . . contributes *Durham, jock,* and *major.* **1966–68** *DARE* (Qu. K22, *Words used for a bull*) Infs **NC**33, **VA**24, Jock; (Qu. K23, *Words used by women or in mixed company for a bull*) Inf **VA**24, Jock.

2 See **jocks.**

jock, by See jocks

jockey n
1 also *horse jockey:* A dealer in horses; transf: *cow jockey* a dealer in cows. [*OED jockey* sb. 3 "One who deals in horses. *Obs* or *dial.*"; *W3* "archaic"]

1774 (1900) Fithian *Jrl.* 1.138 **NJ,** My Horse seems (as jockeys say) in good Flesh. **1842** Kirkland *Forest Life* 1.241 **MI,** He buys and sells horses, (he is a born horse-jockey). **1855** Simms *Forayers* 71 **seSC,** His horse . . was unfavorably marked, in the estimation of the jockeys, by four white feet. **1865** *Atlantic Mth.* June 667 **cCT,** His father's tavern [was] a great resort for horse-jockeys, cattle dealers [etc]. **1905** Lincoln *Partners* 145 **seMA,** His brother Sol . . would skin the eye-teeth out of a Down-East horse jockey. **1930** Shoemaker *1300 Words* 34 **cPA Mts** (as of c1900), *Jockey*—One who deals in horses. **1935** *AmSp* 10.172 **sePA,** Other terms more rarely used [among the Pennsylvania Germans] include the following: . . *jockey* for a horse-trader, and even for a cow-buyer, the *cow-jockey.* **1939** *AmSp* 14.91 **eTN,** *Jockey.* A horse or mule trader. **c1960** *Wilson Coll.* **csKY,** *Jockey.* . . Horse trader, usually a word that is hardly complimentary.

2 A sheep herder.

1940 Writers' Program *Guide NV* 78, The *herder* or *jockey* is the man who cares for the sheep.

3 A leather flap on a saddle; see quot 1936.

1936 Adams *Cowboy Lingo* 44, Fitting closely around the base of the 'horn' and 'cantle' on top of the 'skirt' were the 'front jockeys' and the 'back' or 'rear jockeys.' . . The leather side extensions of the 'seat' of a saddle were called 'side jockeys.' *Ibid* 46, A flat leather plate, overlaying the stirrup leather when the latter issued from the saddle's side, was known as the 'seat jockey' or 'leg jockey.' **1946** Mora *Trail Dust*

106 **West,** Another mighty handy gadget [on a saddle] is a snap placed at the rear jockey button, for hanging the quirt or spurs when not in use.

4 See quot.

1969 *DARE* (Qu. K50, *Joking nicknames for mules*) Inf **MA**46, Jockey.

jockey bar See jockey stick

jockey box n chiefly NW
Orig a box in a wagon, usu beneath the driver's seat, in which small articles were carried; later, the glove compartment of an automobile.

1889 *Century Dict.* 3236, *Jockey-box.* . . A box in a wagon, underneath the driver's seat, for carrying small articles. **1935** Davis *Honey* 147 **OR,** The gun's in the jockey-box on the front of the wagon. **1979–80** *NYT Article Letters,* As a 'westerner' born in Montana and raised in Nevada, I have become keenly aware of inter-regional differences in the American language. What Rhode Islanders call the glove compartment I call the jockey box. *Ibid* **cnWY,** My husband, who hails from Sheridan, Wyoming, grew up using the expression *"jockey box"* for the more commonly used *"glove compartment."* **1980** *DARE* File **cOR,** Jockey box . . in cars . . comes from the wagon day's before automobiles. It is a small box on the front end gate of a wagon. . . They were about 2 in. wide on the bottom and sloped out for about 14 inches high about the same in length but about 6 inches wide on top with a cover. Used to carry axel grease and tools handy. Also to put what every small trinket along the road it made a good ketchal like the glove compartment in the cars. *Ibid* **OR,** *Jockey box*—a glove compartment in a car. *Ibid* (as of c1960), My Idaho cousins called it a jockey box instead of a glove compartment or glove box. **1983** *DARE* File **cwID,** *Jockey box*—Glove compartment in a motor vehicle. **1991** *Ibid* **seID, nwWY, cnUT,** Another term . . is "jockey box" for glove compartment of a car. This term is used in the region of southeastern Idaho, a little corner of Wyoming, and the northern valley of Utah called Cache Valley. It is the only term we use for that part of a car! **1992** Volk *MT Women* 192 **wMT** (as of 1950s), "I swear he wore the same hat all his life." "Hell, yes. And when it got hot, he'd squash that old thing up and put it in the jockey box."

Jockey Day n [jockey 1] Cf jockey lot
See quots.

1939 Writers' Program *Guide KY* 416, The open field behind the courthouse is the scene of old-time horse trading each Jockey Day which is the first day of the circuit court term in January, April, and September. **1991** Still *Wolfpen Notebooks* 162 **sAppalachians,** *Jockey Day:* first day of Circuit Court.

jockey horse n
The horse guided by the **jockey stick.**

1968 *DARE* (Qu. K32b, *The horse on the left side in plowing or hauling*) Inf **IN**32, Jockey horse. **1976** Sublette Co. Artist Guild *More Tales* 159 **cwWY** (as of c1900), The horse on the right in lead was the "Jockey Horse". There was an iron rod from the curb strap in his bridle bit to the hame ring of the line horse. Thereby the line horse would use such a "Jockey Bar" or "Jockey Stick" to jockey or push his teammate wherever he wanted them to go.

jockey lot n [jockey 1] Cf first Monday, Jockey Day
A flea market; the place where such a market is held.

1939 Writers' Program *Guide KY* 271, County court day here is the second Monday of each month, and at this time every man in the county who can comes in to "Jockey Lot" to talk and trade. . . Guns, watches, knives, harness, wagons, horses, mules, dogs—anything and everything that can be "swapped" or sold is "fetched in." **1984** Wilder *You All Spoken Here* 37 **Sth,** *Jockey lot:* Flea market. Originally an open space near the courthouse where, on Tuesdays of court week, horses were swapped. Horse traders were known as jockeys.

jockey stick n Also jockey bar Cf gee stick
A rod used to keep a pair of draft animals in a team at a fixed distance from each other; see quots.

1872 (1876) Knight *Amer. Mech. Dict.* 2.1216, *Jockey-stick.* A stick five or six feet long, which is connected at one end to the hame of the *near* horse of a pair, and at the other end to the bit of the off-horse, to keep him at a distance. Used in connection with a single line, the favorite mode of driving a team in most parts of the West, many parts of the South, and worthy of adoption by all. **1887** Custer *Tenting* 352, [In driving a prairie schooner] a small hickory stick, about five feet long, called the jockey-stick, not unlike a rake handle, is stretched between a pilot [mule] and his mate. **1910** Hart *Vigilante Girl* 140 **nCA,** They were drawn by strings of twelve to twenty animals, usually mules. This train of animals was driven by a "jerk line" instead of reins. . . An iron "jockey-stick" ran from the near leader's hames to the off leader's bit—this pushed or pulled his head as his mate moved in answer to the "jerk line." **1942** Warnick *Garrett Co. MD* 9 **nwMD** (as of 1900–18), *Jockey-stick . .* a stick fastened to the bridles of a team of horses to prevent crowding. **1942** McAtee *Dial. Grant Co. IN* 37 (as of 1890s), *Jockey stick . .* a stick, the ends of which were fastened to the bits of a team of horses to keep them the proper distance apart when cultivating row crops. **1968–69** *DARE* (Qu. K27) Inf **CA**152, Jockey stick or a rod that fastened on its hames and goes to the off-horse so that when you jerk him gee (to right) he shoves the right-hand horse over; [(Qu. L45, *The long piece of wood that sticks out in front of a wagon, and you put a horse on each side*) Infs **IN**32, **MD**24, Jockey stick. [*DARE* Ed: These Infs appar misunderstood the question.]] **1976** *PA Folklife* Spring 26 (as of 1925), *Public Sale. . . Farming Implements. . .* 3 jockey sticks, spreaders, bag wagon, bag holder, double extension ladder. **1976** [see **jockey horse**].

jock-in-the-pulpit See **jack-in-the-pulpit 1**

jocks n Also *jock* Cf **juckers**
Used as a mild oath—usu in phrr *by jock(s), I jocks.*
1896 *DN* 1.419 **cNY,** Jocks . . "By jocks!" **1903** *DN* 2.318 **seMO,** *Jocks* or *by jocks.* . . A mild imprecation. **1904** in 1944 *ADD* **cNY,** By jock! **1906** *DN* 3.143 **nwAR,** Jocks. . . In the mild imprecation, "by jocks." **1929** Sale *Specialist* 7 **ceIL,** All mixed up with hollyhocks—/ Everything! . . I jocks.

jo-dandy See **joe-dandy**

jo darter See **joe darter**

joe n[1] [Scots *jo(e),* varr of *joy;* cf Robert Burns's poem "John Anderson My Jo" 1792]
A sweetheart.
1930 Shoemaker *1300 Words* 33 **cPA Mts** (as of c1900), *Joe*—A term of endearment, a darling. **1937** NE Univ. *Studies* 37.241 **AR,** I went up on the mountain,/ To give my horn a blow./ I thought I heard my Liza say,/ "There comes my Joe."

joe n[2] Also sp *jo*
1 attrib; Of an animal: male. Cf **jack** n[1] **20, Maud**
1935 (1944) Rawlings *Golden Apples* 332 **Sth,** Is it a Maud mule or a Jo-mule? **1960** Williams *Walk Egypt* 91 **GA,** One white Joe-mule had his teeth laid over the neck of a little roan horse.
2 attrib: Very strong, powerful, or exceptional; see quots. Cf **joe-dandy, joe darter**
1955 *Western Folkl.* 14.135 **CA** [San Quentin prison slang], *Joe hog.* A heavy eater. **1967** *Times–Crescent–Charles Co. Leaf* (La Plata MD) 27 July 1/3, A joe-bolter—The shattered condition of this locust tree resulted from a bolt of lightning which zoomed in on it last Thursday. **1968** *DARE* FW Addit **LA**22, *Joe heaver*—a stout pole from twelve to sixteen feet long with a crosspiece near one end used for prying large, heavy objects, e.g. lengths of sewer pipe in the ground.
3 also *joe house:* A privy. Cf **john 2a, Mrs. Jones**
1847 in 1946 *AN&Q* 6.61 [Amherst College slang], Feeling quite lively after my return, disguised myself, and went down and nailed up all the South College joe-doors! **1851** Hall *College Words* 175, A name given at Yale and Hamilton Colleges to a privy. The following account of *Joe-burning* is by a correspondent from Hamilton College. **1923** *DN* 5.240 **swWI,** *Jo.* . . A privy. **1966–70** *DARE* (Qu. M21b, *Joking names for an outside toilet building*) Infs **FL**12, **KY**72, Joe; **AZ**15, Joe house. [All Infs old]
4 See **Nava-Joe.**

jo'e See **joree** n **1**

joe bacon n Also *joe hide* [Prob assim form of *jowl*]
See quots.
1968 *DARE* (Qu. H38, *. . Words for bacon [including joking ones]*) Inf **OH**40, Joe bacon; **NJ**21, Joe hide (colored). **1992** *NADS Letters* **cwIN,** I called a local butcher shop, and the woman who answered said they use all these terms: *Joe bacon* or *jowl bacon* the bacon cut from the jowl of the pig. *Joe hide* or *jowl hide* is the hide or rind cut from this same area.

Joe Bell flower n
A **gaillardia B**; see quot.
1969 *DARE* File **Hatteras Is. NC,** Joe Bell flower. Plant common on Hatteras Island. Also called "blanket flower." Joe Bell is supposed to be the name of the person who introduced this flower to the Banks.

joe blade n
1965 *DARE* (Qu. L35, *Hand tools used for cutting underbrush and digging out roots*) Infs **MS**1, 60, Joe blade.

joeboat n chiefly Ohio Valley, esp KY See Map Cf **johnboat 1**
A small rowboat.
1874 Collins *Hist. Sketches KY* 1.238, 5 persons, while crossing the Big Sandy river in Floyd co, in a joe boat, caught in the ice and drowned. **1887** *Courier–Jrl.* (Louisville KY) 15 Feb 6/4, The Noise of the Midnight Hammer Is Heard in the Land, Building "Joe Boats" To Be Used in the Second-story of High Houses. **1953** (1977) Hubbard *Shantyboat* 47 **Missip-Ohio Valleys,** As we drifted from one section [of river] to another our johnboat was called flatboat, joeboat, footboat, dinkyboat, paddleboat, and on the Lower Mississippi, bateau. **1957** in 1958 *KY Folkl. Rec.* 4.111 **KY,** *Joeboat.* . . a small rowboat. It is flat at both ends, or perhaps I should say square. **c1960** Wilson *Coll.* **csKY,** A small rowboat or fishing boat . . *joe boat . . john* or *johnny boat.* **1965–70** *DARE* (Qu. O1, *. . A small rowboat, not big enough to hold more than two people*) Infs **IN**3, 45, **KY**6, 11, 16, 43, 47, **MO**27, Joeboat; (Qu. O2, *Nicknames . . for an old, clumsy boat*) Infs **IN**45, **KY**11, **MO**3, **OH**50, Joeboat. **1986** Pederson *LAGS Concordance (Rowboat)* 3 infs, **LA,** Joe boat; 1 inf, **nwTN,** Joe boat—aluminum boat, one end flat.

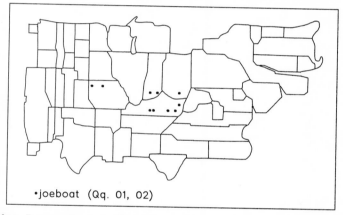

•joeboat (Qq. O1, O2)

Joe Brown frog n [See quot; perh in allusion to *Joseph E. Brown,* governor of Georgia 1857–65]
=**pig frog.**
1932 Wright *Life-Hist. Frogs* 364 **Okefenokee GA,** Rana grylio. . . *Common Names . .* Joe Brown Frog. *Ibid* 372, Some of the residents call this species the "Joe Brown" frog because of a fancied resemblance of the grunt to this name. The croak can be heard at a considerable distance and a midnight chorus might be pronounced "loud."

joe buckety geiss n [Cf *buckety buck* (at **buck buck 1**) and Ger *Geiss* goat]
Prob =**Johnny-on-the-pony.**
1970 *DARE* (Qu. EE33, *. . Outdoor games . . that children play*) Inf **PA**245, Joe buckety geiss. [FW: My name for it is *Johnny-on-the-pony.*]

joe bucks n
=**tomato worm.**
1966 *DARE* (Qu. R27, *. . Kinds of caterpillars or similar worms*) Inf **SC**3, Joe bucks ['jo,bʌks] = tomato worm.

joe cat n
=**gaff-topsail catfish.**
1973 Knight *Cook's Fish Guide* 383, Joe cat—Catfish, Gafftopsail.

joe-dandy n Also *jo-dandy*
=**jim-dandy** n **1.**
1890 *Juliaetta Gem* (ID) 9 Aug 1/2 **cwID,** Ben is what is conmonly [sic] termed a "Joe dandy," and undoubtedly knows how to build grades in a rapid and workman like manner. **1893** *KS Univ. Qrly.* 1.140 **KS,** *Jo-dandy:* intensified form of 'dandy.' **1905** *DN* 3.62 **NE,** *Jim dandy,*

joe dandy. **1914** *DN* 4.109 **KS,** *Jo-dandy.* . . A superlative of excellence. "This pie is a jo-dandy."

joe darter n Also sp *jo darter;* pronc-spp *(joe) dodder, joe dotter*

1 also *joe driver:* A powerful blow. **esp Gulf States, Lower Missip Valley** See Map

1851 Burke *Polly Peablossom* 151 **MS,** Soon as I got close 'nuff to him, so as I could hit him a jo-darter, sez he, "Hole on er minit." **1859** Taliaferro *Fisher's R.* 106 **nwNC** (as of 1820s), Sam J—was a little too hard for Dick in discussion, and Dick turned upon him with a "jodarter," and smote him thus: "Sam, you's chock full uv yer grandaddy's blood." **1895** *DN* 1.390, *Joe-darter:* = jim-slinger [=a hard blow]. **1965–67** *DARE* (Qu. Y11, . . *A very hard blow: "You should have seen Bill go down. Joe really hit him a _____."*) Infs **KY**90, **MS**71, **TX**26, 37, Joe dotter; **AL**3, **GA**72, 77, Joe darter; **MS**1, Joe dodder; **TX**32, Dodder; **AR**51, Joe driver; (Qu. Y14a) Inf **AR**55, Joe darter.

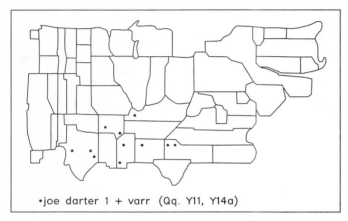

•joe darter 1 + varr (Qq. Y11, Y14a)

2 Transf: an outstanding example of its kind; see quots; a **jim-dandy** n **1. esp Gulf States, S Midl**

1893 Shands *MS Speech* 41, *Jodarter.* . . Negroes and illiterate whites frequently use this word to express something unsurpassed in its way; as, "That man is a jodarter"; i.e. in some way he is unsurpassable. A negro, speaking to me of a chill that he had, said, "It sho was a jodarter," meaning that it was one of the very worst kind. **1905** *DN* 3.84 **nwAR,** *Joe Darter.* . . Monster. 'It's a Joe Darter of an elephant.' Rare. **1908** *DN* 3.325 **eAL, wGA,** *Joe darter.* . . A very fine or excellent thing, a shrewd or smart person. "He's a joe darter when it comes to trading." **1927** in 1944 *ADD* **WV,** *Joe-darter.* . . A high-flying fellow. **c1960** *Wilson Coll.* **csKY,** *Joe* (or *jo-*) *darter.* . . An excellent thing of its kind, humdinger. **1965–67** *DARE* (Qu. B25, . . *Joking names . . for a very heavy rain. . . "It's a regular _____."*) Inf **AL**36, Joe darter; (Qu. LL5, *Something impressively big: "That cabbage is really a _____."*) Inf **MS**1, Joe dotter. **1971** Dwyer *Dict. for Yankees* 28 **Sth, S Midl,** *Joe-darter*—An unsurpassed person or thing.

‡joe-dock to go on a gumfudgeon n

1967 *DARE* (Qu. NN12b, *Things that people say to put off a child when he asks, "What are you making?"*) Inf **TX**43, Joe-dock to go on a gumfudgeon.

joe dodder, joe dotter See **joe darter**

joe driver See **joe darter 1**

joe-fired adj, adv Also sp *jo-fired* Cf **all-fired** adj, adv

Darned—used as an intensifier.

1824 *Woodstock* (Vt.) *Observer* 24 Feb (1912 Thornton *Amer. Gloss.*), Whate'er joe fir'd racket they keep up. **1833** Greene *Yankee Among Nullifiers* 29, He's a jo-fired smart horse for all that. **1835** Thompson *Advent. Peacock* 168, I have lately found out a most Jo-fired discovery. **1858** Hammett *Piney Woods Tavern* 42, My friend wanted to pick up a nigger to pilot us about the streets, but I was too jofired smart for that. *Ibid* 61, The Yankees war the jofiredest fellers agoin' for whittlin' and axin' questions. **1977** in 1993 Major *Calling the Wind* 389 **sIL,** I'm going to school you myself. Teach you everything I know, son, which ain't so joe-fired much—just common sense.

joe flogger n **coastal MA, ME**

1 also *jo flogger:* A type of pancake; see quots.

1852 U.S. Congress *Serial Set* 676 Doc 23 260, [The boatfisherman

of the Bay of Fundy] is kind and hospitable in his way; and the visitor . . is treated to *fresh smother, duff,* and *jo-floggers.* [Note:] Potpie of sea-birds, pudding and pancakes. **1889** Munroe *Dorymates* 47 **seMA,** The cook made them [=the crew] a great dish of Joe-floggers (peculiar pancakes stuffed with plums) for breakfast. **1902** (1904) Rowe *Maid of Bar Harbor* 180 **ME,** [Mandy tossed a flapjack into the air and dextrously caught it. . . in the long-handled iron skillet.] *Ibid* 183, These jo-floggers air prime, an' make about the best ballast that a man c'n have f'r a night's cruise.

2 also *joe frog(ger):* A doughnut-like pastry; see quots.

1941 *LANE* Map 284 *(Doughnut)* 1 inf, **eME coast,** Frog, Joe Flogger, puffs up when dropped in deep fat; 1 inf, **eME coast,** Joe Frog; puff ball. **1969** *DARE* (Qu. H28) Inf **MA**57, Used to make Joe froggers— also called horse-turd doughnuts—made out of biscuit dough, cut in squares, cooked in hot lard, dropped into kettle of hot molasses.

3 usu as *joe frogger:* A type of molasses cookie; see quots.

1954 *This Week Mag.* 1 May 27 (Mathews Coll.), The place I loved best [at Old Sturbridge Village] was Minor Grant's store. . . Cookies were baking, the old time favorites: hobnails, lumberjacks, pine-tree shillings and these big Joe Froggers. Black Uncle Joe who lived by the frog pond in Marblehead, Mass., originally baked these spicy sweets for the local fishermen. . . The big flat cookies were remindful of the big fat frogs that sat on the lily pads in Uncle Joe's pond. **1975** *Parade* 13 July 7, "Joe Froggers"—big, delicious molasses cookies. They're made from a recipe that is over 100 years old—the pride of one man, "Uncle Joe," as he was known to the people of Marblehead, Mass. Since he lived on the edge of a frog pond, the cookies soon became known as "Joe Froggers." **1977** *Yankee* Jan 73 **csME,** *Joe flogger* is a rock-hard molasses cookie whose keeping qualities made it especially desirable to take to sea. *Ibid* Feb 21 **ceMA,** Joe Froggers . . are another oldtime favorite. These are large, molasses-flavored cookies. The recipe for which is supposed to date back to colonial times having been invented by a fiddle-playing half-black Gay Head Indian known as Black Joe. **1978** *Ibid* Mar 31, *Joe Froggers* . . became known throughout Massachusetts as "froggers" for they were as plump as the frogs in Joe's pond.

joe frog See **joe flogger 2**

joe frogger See **joe flogger 2, 3**

Joe harrow n Also *little Joe (harrow)* Cf **gee whiz** n

A type of harrow; see quot.

1986 Pederson *LAGS Concordance,* 9 infs, **chiefly coastal Gulf Region,** Joe harrow(s); 1 inf, Joe harrow—for pulverizing, digs with spikes; 1 inf, Joe harrow—for one horse; 1 inf, Joe harrow—one mule or horse; 1 inf, Joe harrow = spring tooth; 1 inf, Joe harrow—with little pegs that tore ground up; 1 inf, Joe harrow—three rows of teeth, handles; 1 inf, Joe harrow—smaller; 1 inf, Gee whiz Joe harrow—a small harrow; 2 infs, Little Joe harrow; 1 inf, A little Joe harrow—straight teeth go into ground; 1 inf, A little Joe harrow—teeth go straight down; 1 inf, Little Joe—a drag harrow.

joe hide See **joe bacon**

Joe Hookered, I'll be phr [*Joseph Hooker* (1814–1879) Union general in the Civil War] Cf **John Brown**

1967 *DARE* (Qu. NN25b, *Weakened substitutes for 'damn' or 'damned': "Well, I'll be _____!"*) Inf **OH**18, Joe Hookered.

joe house See **joe** n² 3

joe-lee n [Echoic; cf **joree** n 1]

=rufous-sided towhee.

[**1977** Bull–Farrand *Audubon Field Guide Birds* 577, Towhees often feed on the ground, scratching noisily in the dry leaves.] **1980** in 1982 *Barrick Coll.* **csPA,** Joe Leaf [sic]—small bird that hunts insects under dead leaves. **1991** *DARE* File, [Letter from author of quot 1980:] I . . talked to the informant who gave me the name Joe Leaf. . . It is indeed the rufous-sided towhee, but apparently I misheard him. The bird is called *joe lee,* from the sound the bird makes. He said, "My dad used to call it joe lee. It'd be diggin' around under the leaves, throwing the leaves up, and the next thing you know, it'd be settin' up on a limb, going 'Joe lee, joe lee.' "

Joe Louis n [*Joe Louis* heavyweight boxing champion 1937– 49; from the "punch" of the liquor] *esp freq among Black speakers*

Bad or homemade liquor.

1967–70 *DARE* (Qu. DD21b, *General words . . for bad liquor*) Infs **AL**59, **TX**26, Joe Louis. [Both Infs Black] **1986** Pederson *LAGS Con-*

cordance (*Cheap whiskey... home made* [or] *poor quality*) 4 infs, **AL**, Joe Louis. [3 of 4 infs Black] **1987** *DARE* File **nwMS** (as of 1960s) [Black], *Joe Louis*—homemade liquor.

Joe McGee n attrib

Haphazard; makeshift.

1943 *AN&Q* 3.57, In a late issue of *Publishers' Weekly* I found a reference to the "Joe McGee system of packing books." I assume that "Joe McGee" means "haphazard." **1969** *AmSp* 44.18 **Pacific NW** [Painter jargon], *Joe McGee rig...* 1. Any makeshift item of gear... 2. A poor or unsafe rigging.

Joe Moore See **jomo**

Joe-Pye See **Joe-Pye weed 3**

Joe-Pye weed n

1 also *Joe-Pye('s weed), jopiroot, jopiweed, Jo-Pye weed:* =**boneset 1**, esp *Eupatorium purpureum*. [See quots 1822, 1843] **chiefly NEast, Mid Atl** See Map

1822 Eaton *Botany* 278, [*Eupatorium*] *purpureum*... joe-pye... [*E.*] *verticillatum*... joe-pye's weed... The two species, called joe-pye (from the name of an Indian) are in common use in the western counties of Massachusetts as diaphoretics, &c. in typhus fever. **1843** Torrey *Flora NY* 1.326, *Eupatorium purpureum... Joe Pye Weed*. [*Ibid* 327, The popular name is said to be that of an Indian who recommended it to the whites.] **1892** Coulter *Botany W. TX* 177, *E. purpureum... Joe-Pye weed*... Stout and tall simple stems, 6 to 36 dm. high... Var. *maculatum*... is 9 to 12 dm. high. **1912** Blatchley *IN Weed Book* 156, *Eupatorium purpureum... Jo-pye-weed*. **1937** Thornburgh *Gt. Smoky Mts.* 23, In late summer or early fall one sees... the purple iron-weed and lavender Joe-pye-weed or Queen-of-the-meadow. **1966–70** *DARE* (Qu. S26a, ... *Wildflowers... Roadside flowers*) 19 Infs, **chiefly NEast, Mid Atl**, Joe-Pye weed; (Qu. S21, ... *Weeds... that are a trouble in gardens and fields*) Infs **CT**11, **KY**24, **PA**176, Joe-Pye weed; (Qu. S26b, *Wildflowers that grow in water or wet places*) Infs **MA**68, 100, **SC**2, **VA**101, Joe-Pye weed; **DE**3, Joe-Pye; (Qu. S26d, *Wildflowers that grow in meadows; not asked in early QRs*) Infs **CT**30, **KY**28, **NJ**45, **PA**95, 169, **VA**52, Joe-Pye weed. **1970** *NC Folkl.* 18.32, Typhus was treated with the herb joe-pye. **1971** Krochmal *Appalachia Med. Plants* 120, *Eupatorium purpureum... Common names*... Joe-pyeweed, jopiroot, jopiweed. **1982** *Greenfield Recorder* (MA) 11 Sep 4/2, Recently I noticed some unusually tall, big flowers of Jo Pye weed, with its soft lavender colored flowers, and was told they were very large everywhere this year.

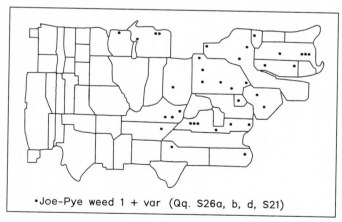

•Joe-Pye weed 1 + var (Qq. S26a, b, d, S21)

2 =**butterfly weed 1**.

1966 *DARE* Wildfl QR Pl.171 Inf **NH**4, Joe-Pye weed.

3 also *Joe-Pye:* An **ironweed 1**; see quots.

1969 *DARE* (Qu. S26a, ... *Wildflowers... Roadside flowers*) Inf **KY**47, Queen-of-the-meadow = ox-joint (Joe-Pye). **1990** *Plants SW* (Catalog) 40, *Vernonia missurica—Joe Pye Weed, Ironweed*... A striking plant in the fall when it.. blooms with clusters of purple, thistlelike flowers.

joe rick, joerigger See **joree** n **1**

joe rocker n **seMA**

The green crab (*Carcinus maenas*).

1884 Goode *Fisheries U.S.* 1.774, In Vineyard Sound and Buzzard's Bay it [=*Carcinus maenas*] is known to the fishermen as the "Joe

Rocker." **1965** *PADS* 43.37 **seMA**, The response.. revealed a local term which probably is restricted to the Buzzards Bay area of the Massachusetts coast. The name *Joe rockers* for the small spotted crabs (probably a type of green crab) found around docks was known by five of the [nine] informants, including the three Portuguese informants and two of the Yankees, who are in close contact every day with the sea and with people of Portuguese origin. It seems likely that this name is related to the Portuguese, but the exact connection is unknown.

joe-wheat See **jo-wheat**

joewood n

A small tree (*Jacquinia keyensis*) native to southern Florida. Also called **cudjoe-wood, myrtle** n[1] **B7, sea myrtle**

1884 Sargent *Forests of N. Amer.* 100, Joe Wood... The saponaceous leaves sometimes used as a substitute for soap. **1897** Sudworth *Arborescent Flora* 317 **FL**, *Jacquinia armillaris... Common Name*. Joewood. **1933** Small *Manual SE Flora* 1028, *Joe-wood*... Hammocks along the coast, S pen. Fla., Everglade Keys, Fla. and Florida Keys. **1946** West–Arnold *Native Trees FL* 169, *Joewood*... The hard, close-grained wood has a distinctive grain, but pieces of workable size are rarely found. **1971** Craighead *Trees S. FL* 94, Some of the more characteristic trees and shrubs of the beaches and coastal ridges are randia, buttonwood,.. joewood,.. and saffron plum.

jo-fired See **joe-fired**

joffy-stick n Cf **jippy-stick**

1969 *DARE* (Qu. EE10, *A game in which a short stick lying on the ground is flipped into the air and then hit with a longer stick*) Inf **NY**219, Joffy [ʤɑfi]-stick.

jo flogger See **joe flogger 1**

jog v, hence vbl n *jogging* Cf **jig** v **1, joog**

1 See quot.

1915 (1916) Johnson *Highways New Engl.* 209, We spear a good many eels in the holes on the ma'sh and in the cricks that make up around there. Sometimes we ketch 'em almost as fast as we can jog. We fellers around here call it joggin'.

2 as vbl n: Bottom fishing.

1966 *DARE* (Qu. P17, ... *When... people fish by lowering a line and sinker close to the bottom of the water*) Inf **ME**20, Jogging.

jog n[1]

1975 Gould *ME Lingo* 147, A *jog* is also an irregularly shaped field or piece of timberland, which probably explains *jog* of pie: a piece of pie, not too large, not too small, "just a *jog*."

jog n[2] [Var of **jag** n[2] **1a**]

1968 *DARE* (Qu. L55, *If the wagon was only partly full.. he had a ———*) Inf **OH**45, Jog.

jog board See **joggling board**

jogger (wagon) See **jagger wagon**

jogging See **jog** v

jogging board See **joggling board**

joggle n See **joggling board**

joggle v [*OED joggle* v.[1] 2 "intr. To move to and fro with a succession of short jerky movements; to shake or rock about...; dial. to jog *along*"; 1683 →]

1 also *jog:* To bounce up and down on a **joggling board;** hence vbl n *joggling*. **chiefly SC**

1859 [see **joggling board**]. **1884** *Amer. Philol. Assoc. Trans. for 1883* 14.50, *Joggle*, 'to shake up and down *or* move up and down on a plank suspended between supports at each end.' From this we have the word *joggling board* to indicate the contrivance itself. *Joggling* is a favorite amusement of children in South Carolina, and the joggling board on the front piazza is a common sight. **1930** [see **joggling board**]. **1966** *DARE* (Qu. EE31) Inf **SC**19, Joggling board—plank fastened at both ends and you sit between the horses and joggle; **SC**24, Joggling board— in the past, anchored at both ends and you joggle on the plank. **1966** [see **joggling board**]. **1967** *State* (Raleigh, N.C.) 1 Oct. 5/1 (*Mathews Coll.*), One or more persons could joggle while seated on the board, but the up-and-down movement required more effort than the back-and-forth movement of a swing. The board was the right height for adults to sit on with their feet touching the ground. *Ibid* 15 Nov. 6/2 (*Mathews Coll.*), Joggling was enjoyed from infancy to adulthood, and in a fashion appropriate to each age. **1986** Pederson *LAGS Concordance,* 1 inf, **cnGA,** Joggle on—verb; 1 inf, **cwMS,** Joggled; 1 inf, **nwLA,** I don't think we joggled; 1 inf, **cGA,** Jogging board—you jog up and down.

2 To travel slowly or aimlessly; to drift.

1944 *PADS* 2.19 **sAppalachians,** *Joggle. . .* To walk along slowly and aimlessly. Variant of jog. **1967** Williams *Greenbones* 91 **GA** (as of c1910), They joggled southeast, following the bend of the coastline, putting on shows.

joggling board n Also *jog(ging) board, joggle (board), joggler* [**joggle** v **1,** but cf quot 1949; perh an instance of "multiple etymology," with coalescence of forms and overlap of meaning] **chiefly SC, GA** Also called **jiggle-o, jiggling board 1, jolly board, limber jack 4** Cf **jump board, jumping jack 7**
A thick but flexible board, supported at each end by uprights, upon which one sits and bounces.

1859 Turnbull–Turnbull *Amer. Photographs* 2.101 **Charleston SC** (as of 1854), Out . . on the Piazza . . we saw ladies and gentlemen, in full dress, sitting in a row, bobbing up and down . . on a very long wooden plank, each end of which was passed through a slit near the tops of two upright pieces of wood, and secured from slipping through by a cross piece. This, we at once divined, was the "joggling board," and we were correct, for we were invited to "joggle," which invitation we positively declined. **1882** Eggleston *Wreck Red Bird* 14 **SC coast,** The best way to get acquainted with a joggling board . . is to get on it. **c1885** in 1981 Woodward *Mary Chesnut's Civil War* 391 **SC** (as of 1862), Another visit she sat on the joggle board and bounced up and down between every sentence. All that was not joggle was jiggle. **1905** Dixon *Clansman* 206 **SC,** He took his seat on the joggle-board beside the door and awaited her return. **1905** Chesnutt *Col.'s Dream* 81 **GA,** The long wooden porch bench or "jogging board" on which the lady sat. **1930** *DN* 6.82 **cSC,** *Joggling board. . .* A thick, resilient plank, about twelve feet long, resting on two uprights, on which one sits and "joggles" up and down. Formerly, everyone had a joggling board on his piazza. A few may still be seen, but they are not as popular as they once were. **1933** Rawlings *South Moon* 60 **FL,** Le's go yonder to the timberin' and see kin we ketch Pa workin' on a jog-board. **1949** Turner *Africanisms* 195 [Gullah], [Words used in conversation:] ['ɟɔgal, 'ɟɔglɔ] 'to rise' (used in the compound ['ɟɔgal-bod, 'ɟɔglɔ-bod] 'rise-up board, seesaw'[)]. W[olof] [ɟɔgal, ɟɔglɔ, ɟugal] 'to rise'; 'to cause to rise.' **1965–70** *DARE* Qu. EE31, *Playground equipment with a long board for two children to sit on and go up and down in turn*] Inf **GA**44, Jogging board; **SC**7, 11, 40, 44, 54, Joggling board; **SC**19, Joggling board—plank fastened at both ends and you sit between the horses and joggle; **SC**24, Joggling board—in the past; anchored at both ends and you joggle on the plank; (Qu. EE33, . . *Outdoor games . . that children play*) Inf **VA**33, Joggling board—sat on it and bounced. **1966** *DARE* File **SC,** *Joggling board*—two stands with a limber board (had to be cut a special way—thin at the center, thicker at the ends) suspended by them. You joggle on it; **SC,** *Joggle*—another name for joggling board. **1967** *State* (Raleigh, N.C.) 15 Nov 6/3 (*Mathews Coll.*), The joggling board at her old home was built before the Civil War. . . O.W. Avant . . also reported the joggler at Oliver's Lodge, said it was "much more than 100 years old." **1986** Pederson *LAGS Concordance* (Limber plank suspended at both ends) 31 infs, **chiefly GA,** Joggling board; 1 inf, **ceGA,** Joggle board; 2 infs, **GA,** Jogging board. [*DARE* Ed: A number of these infs were doubtful or appar knew the object or word only by hearsay.]

joggly adj [*OED* "dial. or colloq."]
Shaky; unsteady.

1899 (1912) Green *VA Folk-Speech* 246, *Joggly. . .* Unsteady; shaky. **1968** *DARE* (Qu. KK23, *Weak or unsteady:* "I think the footbridge will hold but it is a bit _____.") Inf **VA**21, Joggly [jagli].

john n, often cap
1 also *johnny;* usu attrib: The male of a species. Cf **jake** n[1] **4, jack** n[1] **20**

1859 Taliaferro *Fisher's R.* 234 **nwNC,** Some one passed the road with a long-eared animal, politely called a John Donkey. **1934** (1943) *W2, Johnny. . .* Local, U.S. The male of any animal. **1966** Dakin *Dial. Vocab. Ohio R. Valley* 2.242, Boar (polite terms where tabu is noted), 2 infs, **IN,** John hog. **1969** *DARE* (Qu. K22, *Words used for a bull*) Inf **IL**31, Johnny cow; **NY**216, Sire; John. **1984** Wilder *You All Spoken Here* 155 **Sth,** *John donkey:* Jackass.

2a also *john('s) house;* for addit combs see quots: A toilet; an outhouse. **widespread, but somewhat less freq Sth** See Map Cf **johnny house**

[**1735** in 1953 Bentinck-Smith *Harvard Book* 146, No freshman shall

mingo against the College wall or go into the fellows' cuzjohn.] **1933** *AmSp* 7.333 [Johns Hopkins jargon], *John . . a* lavatory. **1950** *WELS Suppl.* **cwWI,** *John*—privy is more dignified. **1951** Johnson *Resp. to PADS 20* **DE,** (An indoor toilet) John; (An outside toilet building) John. **1965–70** *DARE* (Qu. F37, . . *An indoor toilet*) 197 Infs, **widespread, but less freq Sth, S Midl,** John; **VA**2, Private john; (Qu. M21b, *Joking names for an outside toilet building*) 93 Infs, **scattered,** John; **NY**80, 109, **WV**7, Big John; **CT**24, **PA**204, **WV**4, John house; **IA**12, John Henry; **MI**12, John's house; **MS**81, Lil' John; **WA**5, Mr. John; **NY**84, Outside john; **KY**49, Uncle John; (Qu. M21a, *An outside toilet building*) 9 Infs, **scattered,** John; **NY**80, Big John; **MI**74, Outdoor john; (Qu. F37b, *Joking names for an indoor toilet;* total Infs questioned, 75) Infs **FL**1, 8, 15, 27, 37, **MS**37, **OK**51, John. **1966** Barnes–Jensen *Dict. UT Slang* 26, *John. . .* a toilet. **1967** *Times Herald Rec.* (Middletown NY) 15 Aug 42/5, [Classified advt:] Cellar with john.

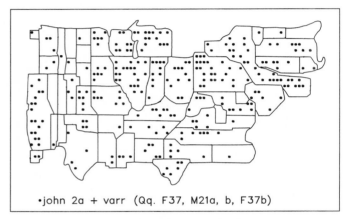

•john 2a + varr (Qq. F37, M21a, b, F37b)

b See quot. Cf **jimmy-john 3, johnny pot**
1970 *DARE* (Qu. F38, *Utensil kept under the bed for use at night*) Inf **IL**117, John.

3 in combs *Long John, Old John:* See quot.
1966–70 *DARE* (Qu. P37b, *Nicknames for a shotgun*) Infs **NC**6, **TN**53, Long John; **AL**35, Old John.

4 cap; in var combs as a joking word for one's signature: **=John Hancock.**
1965–70 *DARE* (Qu. JJ13, . . *Joking words . . for a name signed to a paper:* "I'll put my _____ on that.") Inf **HI**6, John D.; **MO**11, John Esquire; **KY**11, John Handle; **SC**3, John Q.; **WI**52, John Rogers; **WI**34, John Smith; **MS**6, John Willy; **VA**69, John Brown. **1971** *DARE* File **cnGA,** If you'll just put your John H. here . . [=on a work order].

5 See **John Chinaman 1.**

6 pl: See **long john 1.**

John A. Grindle n Also *Johnny Grindle* Cf **grindle** n[1] **=bowfin.**
1882 U.S. Natl. Museum *Bulletin* 16.94, *A[mia] calva. . .* "John A. Grindle." . . A voracious fish of remarkable tenacity of life. **1884** Goode *Fisheries U.S.* 1.659, The Bowfin . . is also abundant. . . in all parts of the Mississippi Valley, where it is variously called the 'Johnny Grindle,' 'Bowfin,' and 'Dogfish.' **1896** U.S. Natl. Museum *Bulletin* 47.113, "John A. Grindle." . . Great Lakes and sluggish waters from Minnesota to Virginia, Florida, and Texas; abundant. **1933** LA Dept. of Conserv. *Fishes* 383, Throughout the rest of its range [i.e., outside of **LA**], the Grindle is known as the John A. Grindle, . . the Mudfish, . . and . . the Dogfish. **1943** U.S. Dept. Interior *Conserv. Bulletin* 34.28, Despite the fact that it is not widely used as a food, the bowfin is a well-known fish bearing a variety of local names; Virginians give it the dignified name of John A. Grindle, which in the central Mississippi Valley is shortened to Grindle. **1943** *Richmond Times-Dispatch* (VA) 26 Dec sec B 2/1 (*Hench Coll.*), Bowfin. . . John-a-grindle, John A. Grindle. . . Found in Virginia waters and . . a most underrated piscatorial specimen. **1983** Becker *Fishes WI* 251, *Bowfin. . .* Other common names . . John A. Grindle.

John B n [From Philadelphia hatter *John B.* Stetson (1830–1906)] **West**
A cowboy hat.
1933 *AmSp* 8.1.31 **nwTX,** *John B.* A hat. No hat was worthy of the name unless it was a Stetson. **1936** Adams *Cowboy Lingo* 35, His hat. . . might slangily be called 'Stetson' or 'John B.' after this maker's name,

whether it was 'genuwine' or not. **1980** *AZ Highways* Feb 7, The cowboy's most distinguishable feature was his wide-brimmed Stetson, sometimes called his "John B" in honor of the manufacturer. [**1986** Pederson *LAGS Concordance,* 1 inf, **neTX**, John B. Stetson hat.]

johnboat n

1 also *johnny boat, jonboat:* A narrow, flat-bottomed, square-ended boat usu used for fishing. **chiefly Missip-Ohio Valleys** See Map Cf **joeboat**

    1905 *Eve. Post* (NY NY) 2 Sept 3/1, Two men came down the Mississippi in an Illinois Jon-boat, paddling slowly with rough-whittled boards. **1917** Kephart *Camping & Woodcraft* 134 **wNC**, We conceived . . a brilliant scheme for transporting a gallon of whiskey inconspicuously in our John-boat. **1937** *Esquire* 36/2 **KY**, We'd run down to the river and Hilton would take it [=a fox-horn] out to Pop in a john-boat. **1953** (1977) Hubbard *Shantyboat* 46 **Missip-Ohio Valleys,** A johnboat is a rowboat usually fourteen or sixteen feet long, square at both ends, and flat-bottomed. With this fundamental design, it may be little more than a box or trough. Some of them are just about that. On the other hand, if it is built by a craftsman who has a feeling for good design, a johnboat is a beautiful, easy-running boat. It is to be found the length of the river, and in every tributary and creek big enough to float one. **c1960** *Wilson Coll.* **csKY,** Johnboat (or johnnyboat). . . A flat-bottomed fishing or row boat. **1965–70** *DARE* (Qu. O1, . . *A small rowboat, not big enough to hold more than two people*) 36 Infs, **chiefly Missip-Ohio Valleys,** Johnboat; **VA8,** Johnny boat; (Qu. O2, *Nicknames . . for an old, clumsy boat*) 19 Infs, **Missip-Ohio Valleys,** (Old) johnboat; (Qu. O10, . . *Kinds of boats*) 13 Infs, **chiefly Missip-Ohio Valleys,** Johnboats. **1968** *Milford Chron.* (DE) 2 May 19/1, For Sale—aluminum 10′ jon boat and home-built trailer for same. Boat will take up to 5 ½ h.p. motor. **1969** *Cape Cod Std.-Times* (Hyannis MA) 22 Jan 3, The wind soon shifted and increased to about 50 knots in gusts. We thought we could return in our John boat on low tide by mostly walking the boat back on the edge of the creek. **1978** Massey *Bittersweet Country* 286 **Ozarks,** One of the most interesting indigenous products of the Ozarks is the johnboat. . . a long, narrow, flat-bottomed wooden boat designed for fishing the pools (called eddies) of the Ozark rivers and floating over the swift shallow riffles. It floats downstream with the current and is paddled by one person in the back using a lightweight paddle. . . [I]t is generally agreed that it was first designed by a man named John for float trips on the White River.

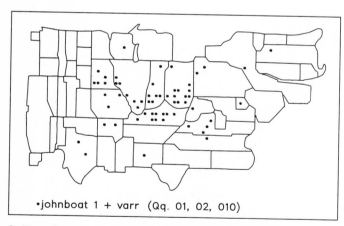

•johnboat 1 + varr (Qq. O1, O2, O10)

2 Transf: a man's square-toed shoe. Cf **canal boat**

    1968 *DARE* (Qu. W42b, . . *Nicknames for men's square-toed shoes*) Inf **DE3,** Johnboats.

John Brown v phr, hence ppl adj phr *John Browned* (pronc-sp *John Brown;* cf Pronc Intro 3.I.22), also *Johnny Browned* [*John Brown* (1800–1859) American abolitionist, hanged for leading the attack on Harpers Ferry, West Virginia, in 1859; cf phr *I'll be hanged*] **chiefly Sth**

Fig: used as a euphem for *damn*—usu in phr *I'll be John Browned.*

    1905 *DN* 3.84 **nwAR,** John(ny) Browned. . . In the exclamation, 'I'll be John(ny) Browned.' Rare. **1942** (1954) Rosborough *Don't You Cry* 9 **FL,** I'll be John-Browned. **1952** Brown *NC Folkl.* 1.555, John Brown, I'll be. . . A mild imprecation. . . Rare now. **1966** *DARE* (Qu. NN7, *Exclamations of surprise:* "*They're getting married next week? Well, _____.*") Inf **GA**1, I'll be John Browned; (Qu. NN8b, . . *Expressions of annoyance:* "*This jar won't come open, _____ it.*") Inf **GA**7, John

Brown. **1975** Newell *If Nothin' Don't Happen* 59 **FL,** Well, I'll be John Browned, Uncle said. Who'd ever of thought Jim Drigger's boy would be chickenhearted? **1978** *DARE* File (as of 1960s), A friend of mine (b.1880) from a Confederate family in Charleston, South Carolina used to say to indicate great surprise, "Well, I'll be John-Browned." **1982** *Ibid* **NC**, From a 30-ish woman, Black, from Winterville, N.C. . . I was so John Brown weak (also used with other adjectives—sick, tired, and maybe others). **1986** Pederson *LAGS Concordance,* 1 inf, **ceAL**, One of those John Brown things. (Invective)

John Bull n Also freq *Johnny Bull* **chiefly Nth, esp NEast** See Map Cf **limey**

An Englishman; hence adj *John(ny) Bull* English.

    1778 (1925) *MA Hist. Soc. Coll.* 73.40, I never was however much of John Bull. I was John Yankee and such I shall live and die. **1849** in 1956 Eliason *Tarheel Talk* 279 **seNC,** William is the Lion just now . . his round-tailed coat is altogether *John Bull.* **1942** Berrey–Van den Bark *Amer. Slang* 385.7, Englishman. . . *John* or *Johnny Bull.* **1965–70** *DARE* (Qu. HH28, *Names and nicknames . . for people of foreign background—English*) 26 Infs, **chiefly Nth, N Midl, esp NEast,** Johnny Bull; 13 Infs, **esp Nth,** John Bull. **1968** *DARE* FW Addit **IA**30, A Johnny Bull dish—an English recipe or specialty.

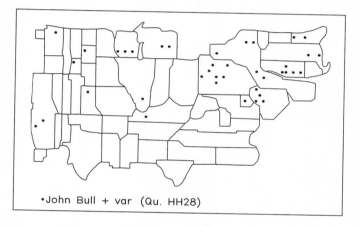

•John Bull + var (Qu. HH28)

johncake See **johnnycake**

John Canoe n, also attrib Also *John Cunner, Johnkannau, (John) Kuner* [Folk-etym from W Afr source; cf *DJE,* 1774 →, and *AmSp* 41.45-51] **NC** Cf **coonah, coonering**

One of a band of costumed Black revellers who go about on Christmas Day singing and soliciting contributions; hence n *John Canoeing, John Kunering* participation in such a celebration.

    1844 in 1956 Eliason *Tarheel Talk* 279 **ce,neNC,** On Christmas day we had real fine fun; four young fellows blacked themselves & dressed up in negro clothes & went nearly all over town, one with a fiddle under his arm & they would stop before the doors of the houses & the fiddler would play & the rest dance. They acted the part of "John Cunners" very well. **1861** Jacobs *Incidents Slave Girl* 179, Every child rises early on Christmas morning to see the Johnkannaus. . . These companies, of a hundred each, turn out early in the morning, and are allowed to go round till twelve o'clock, begging for contributions. **1922** *Jrl. Amer. Folkl.* 39.54 **NC** (as of c1850), The John Kuners were negroes. . . dressed in "tatters", strips of cloth of gay colors sewn to their usual garments. . . [and wearing] masks known as kuner faces. . . The band of Kuners . . drew up in the street . . and began their show. The leader stood out in front of his group and sang the verses of his song, the others joining in the refrain while they rattled their bones, made of beef ribs, and made noises upon the cows' horns, triangles, and jew's-harps. . . After the song, one of the dancers . . would approach the spectators with his hat held out. Having collected large copper pennies, the Kuners danced off down the street to the next house. **1937** Johnson *Ante-Bellum NC* 552, One of the diversions of the slaves on Christmas day was called "John Canoeing" in Edenton and "John Kunering" in Wilmington. The Negroes arose early Christmas morning, singing their John Canoe songs and shouting "Christmas gif'" at their masters' doors. *Ibid* 553, With the rattling of bones, the blowing of cows' horns, and the tinkling of tambourines, the singing slaves, grotesque in their "Kuner" costumes, would halt wherever an appreciative crowd gathered. **1952** Brown *NC Folkl.* 1.224, The John Kuners are definitely a North Carolina institution, and have no counterpart outside the ceremonies of the Bahamas, where they are said to have originated.

John Chinaman n chiefly West

1 also *John, Johnny:* A Chinese person; used as a term of address for a Chinese.

1834 *Amer. Railroad Jrl.* 3.189, They are required to twirl the Tee-To-tum and ascertain the height of John Chinaman in a breath. **1855** Helper *Land of Gold* 91 **CA,** The Americans salute them all indiscriminately by the easy and euphonious appellation of "John." **1855** in 1942 *CA Folkl. Qrly.* 1.277 **CA,** John Chinaman, John Chinaman,/ But five short years ago,/ I welcomed you from Canton, John—/ But I wish I hadn't, though. **1884** Shepherd *Prairie Exper.* 140 **CA,** The American atmosphere of independence . . has breathed into Johnny the spirit of equality. **1889** *Woodburn* (Wash.) *Independent* 7 Sep. 1/4 *(DA),* It will only be a matter of time when the demand for 'John' will be little or nothing. **1913** London *Valley of Moon* III.v. *(DAE)* **cCA,** There are . . apple canneries and cider and vinegar factories. And Mr. John Chinaman owns them. **1950** *WELS (Names and nicknames for people of foreign background: Chinese)* 1 Inf, **ceWI,** John Chinaman. **1951** Morgan *Skid Road* 85 **WA,** The Chinese, one and all, were called "John," and the stories of John's prowess as a construction worker almost reached the status of folk legend. **1968** *DARE (Qu. U6, Someone who sells vegetables or other articles from a wagon or truck, going from house to house)* Inf **NV7,** John Chinaman.

2 Transf: a dish made with rice.

1936 Adams *Cowboy Lingo* 149, 'John Chinaman' was boiled rice with raisins—sometimes called 'hoss thief's special.' **1939** Rollins *Gone Haywire* 137 **MT** (as of 1886), The only feasible menu . . seemed at the moment to be beans, "sow belly . . ," . . "saddle blankets" (griddle cakes), and "john chinaman" (boiled rice with raisins). **1950** *Trail Riders Bul.* Nov. 18/2 *(Mathews Coll.),* 'John Chinaman' was plain boiled 'swamp seed,' or rice.

john constant n Also *johnny constant* obs Cf **Christ-dust**

Cornmeal or corn bread.

1884 Baldwin *Yankee School-Teacher* 49 **VA** [Black], "John Constant" or corn-meal is the usual week-day "staff of life." *Ibid* 50, "I don't see how dey could live 'thout John Constant". **1896** (1897) Hughes *30 Yrs. a Slave* 15 **MS** (as of 1844), The next attraction for me was the farm hands getting their Christmas rations. Each was given a pint of flour of which they made biscuit, which were called "Billy Seldom," because biscuit were very rare with them. Their daily food was corn bread, which they called "Johnny Constant," as they had it constantly.

john crow n [*DJE* 1826 →]

=**turkey vulture.**

1955 Forbush-May *Birds* 94, *Turkey Vulture. . . Other names . .* John Crow.

John Cunner See **John Canoe**

John D n [*John D.* Rockefeller (1839–1937) founder of the Standard Oil Company]

1 Kerosene oil; transf: an oil bottle; see quots.

1958 McCulloch *Woods Words* 99 **Pacific NW,** John D.—An old time name for a logger's oil bottle. **1975** Gould *ME Lingo* 147, John D—Maine woods term for kerosene oil, after Mr. Rockefeller. "Put the John D to her!" means to kindle a fire. Maine guides early invented "kerodust," a bottle of sawdust impregnated with *John D.* A tablespoon of it will start a fire in a rainstorm.

2 See **john 4.**

John Demon n

The white **crappie** *(Pomoxis annularis).*

1887 Goode *Amer. Fishes* 71, *Pomoxys* [sic] *annularis. . .* has other names of local application as . . "John Demon." **1902** Jordan–Evermann *Amer. Fishes* 334, The crappie. . . is known as bridge perch, . . and John Demon, the last name being heard in northeastern Indiana. **1933** LA Dept. of Conserv. *Fishes* 333, *Pomoxis annularis. . .* Popularity is very well attested by the variety of names . . : Crappie, . . Goldring, John Demon. **1947** Dalrymple *Panfish* 85, Here . . are the various names by which you may address . . the Crappie . . : Bachelor, . . Grass Bass, John Demon. **1983** Becker *Fishes WI* 857, *White Crappie. . .* Other common names . . John Demon.

johndice See **jaundice**

John Doe n Cf **John Hancock**

One's signature.

1950 *WELS (When you sign your name to a check or a contract, you call it your _____. Joking names)* 1 Inf, **csWI,** John Doe. **1965–70** *DARE (Qu. JJ13, . . Joking words . . for a name signed to a paper: "I'll put my _____ on that.")* 43 Infs, **scattered,** John Doe.

John Hancock n Also *Hancock* [In ref to the bold signature of *John Hancock* on the Declaration of Independence] **widespread, but more freq NEast, N Cent** See Map and Map Section Cf **john 4, John Henry 1, John Doe**

One's signature.

[**1846** in 1898 Griswold *Corresp.* 221, Avoiding . . the pretentious boldness of John Hancock . . I subscribe myself Yours very truly.] **1903** Ade *People* 150, After he got through filling the Blank Spaces with his John Hancock, he didn't have a Window to hoist or a Fence to lean on. **1914** [see **John Henry 1**]. **1922** Lewis *Babbitt* 69, Put your John Hancock on that line. **1923** *DN* 5.212 **swMO,** *John Hancock. . .* Signature. **1937** *N&Q* 6 Mar 178, There is also a popular phrase for signature, "John Hancock," as in, "Go ahead. Put down your John Hancock." **1965–70** *DARE (Qu. JJ13, . . Joking words . . for a name signed to a paper: "I'll put my _____ on that.")* 337 Infs, **widespread, but chiefly NEast,** John Hancock; **NY75, OH8, WI51,** Hancock. **1982** *Barrick Coll.* **csPA,** John Hancock—signature. "Put your John Hancock on here."

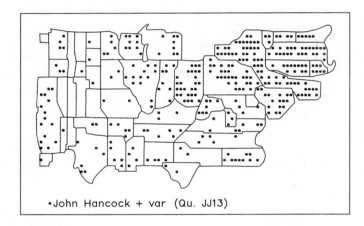

•John Hancock + var (Qu. JJ13)

John Henry n

1 for addit varr see quot 1965–70: =**John Hancock;** by ext, one's handwriting. **widespread, but less freq NEast, OH** See Map and Map Section

1914 *DN* 4.109 **cKS,** John Henry or John Hancock. Autograph. [From Hancock's first signing the Declaration of Independence?] **1950** *PADS* 13.18 **TX,** *John Henry. . .* A fairly common humorous name for a signature. "Put your John Henry to that." **1951** *PADS* 15.56 **neIN** (as of 1890s), *John Henry. . .* Signature; our substitute for "John Hancock." Put your John Henry on that. **1952** Brown *NC Folkl.* 1.555, *John Henry. . .* Handwriting.—Central and east. Jocular. **1965–70** *DARE (Qu. JJ13, . . Joking words . . for a name signed to a paper: "I'll put my _____ on that.")* 595 Infs, **widespread, but less freq NEast, OH,** John Henry; **PA236, WI12,** O. Henry; **MN12,** John T. Henry; **OK9,** Paul Henry; **TX62,** Sam Henry. **1986** Pederson *LAGS Concordance,* 1 inf, **seMS,** Sign their John Henry—= John Hancock.

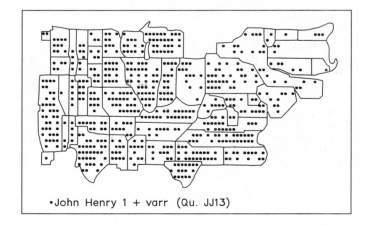

•John Henry 1 + varr (Qu. JJ13)

2 See **john** n **2a.**

3 =**great blue heron.**

1951 Teale *North with Spring* 36, A great blue heron—a 'Poor Joe', a 'John Henry' of the South—sailed in followed by a Louisiana heron and an anhinga.

john house See **john 2a**

John is dead phr

=**Charlie's dead.**

1970 DARE (Qu. W24a, . . *Expressions . . to warn a woman slyly that her slip is showing*) Inf **CA208,** John is dead.

john-jumper n

1 See quot. Cf **jumper 6, long john 7**

1989 NYT Mag. 19 Nov 50/2, Seldom do you hear a worm called a john-jumper any more.

2 See **johnny-jump-up 2b.**

Johnkannau, John Kuner(ing) See **John Canoe**

John Mariggle n

1 =**ten-pounder.** [DJE 1892 →] Cf **Jack Mariddle**

1896 U.S. Natl. Museum *Bulletin* 47.410, *Elops saurus.* . . *John-Mariggle.* . . Common in America, north to Carolina and the Gulf of California. **1902** Jordan–Evermann *Amer. Fishes* 87, The bony-fish rejoices in a multiplicity of vernacular names, among which are big-eyed herring, . . and John Mariggle. **1935** Caine *Game Fish* 98, *Elops saurus.* . . John Mariggle. . . In the past this fish was frequently confused with . . *Albula vulpes,* but it is an entirely different fish, belonging to a different family and found in different waters. **1946** LaMonte *N. Amer. Game Fishes* 14, Ten-Pounder. . . Names: Chiro, John Mariggle.

2 A **bonefish 1** (here: *Albula vulpes*).

1935 Caine *Game Fish* 50, *Albula vulpes.* . . John Mariggle. . . It is considered by many to be the fastest fish that swims.

John Marzetti See **Johnny Marzetti**

johnnied, I'll be phr Also *I'll be johnny-jump-up* Cf **John Brown**

1906 DN 3.143 nwAR, *Johnnied.* . . In the exclamation, "I'll be Johnnied." **1968** DARE (Qu. NN25b, *Weakened substitutes for 'damn' or 'damned'*: "Well, I'll be _____!") Inf **TX51,** Johnny-jump-up.

johnnie walkers See **johnny walkers**

johnny n

1 Any of var Pacific **sculpins,** but usu *Oligocottus maculosus.*

1882 U.S. Natl. Museum *Bulletin* 16.718, *O[ligocottus] maculosus.* . . *Johnny.* . . One of the smallest of marine *Cottidae.* **1884** Goode *Fisheries U.S.* 1.259, *Sculpins of the Pacific Coast.* . . "Johnny" is applied only to very little Sculpins along the shore, notably *Oligocottus maculosus.* **1887** Goode *Amer. Fishes* 302, The Cottidae . . are represented on the Pacific coast by about eighteen separate species, known by such names as "Sculpin," . . "Johnny." . . Only one of these species, *Scorpaenichthys marmoratus,* has any sort of economic importance. **1898** U.S. Natl. Museum *Bulletin* 47.2013, *Oligocottus maculosus.* . . *Johnny.* . . A bright-colored inhabitant of rock pools. **1933** John G. Shedd Aquarium *Guide* 132, The Rock-pool Johnny is . . rarely . . over three inches long. **1960** Amer. Fisheries Soc. *List Fishes* 60, Johnny, tidepool—see sculpin, tidepool.

2 A **darter 1** (here: *Etheostoma* spp). Cf **johnny darter**

1884 Goode *Fisheries U.S.* 1.259, "Johnny." . . The . . name is given in the Ohio Valley to fishes of precisely similar habits [i.e., to those of the sculpins], the *Etheostomatinae.* **1887** (1888) Jordan *Sci. Sketches* 21, The realistic dwellers in the Ohio Valley call some of them "Hog-fish," and the boys call them [=*Etheostoma* spp] "Johnnies." Certainly the boys ought to know,—and Johnnies they are. **1896** U.S. Natl. Museum *Bulletin* 47.1057, We never grew tired of watching the little Johnny (*Boleosoma nigrum* . .). **1903** NY State Museum & Sci. Serv. *Bulletin* 60.518, The blue darter, blue Johnny, rainbow darter, or soldier fish, is found in the Ohio valley and in some parts of the Mississippi valley. **1957** Trautman *Fishes* 567, The Johnny was present in all waters capable of sustaining fish life, from the deep waters of western Lake Erie to the shallowest of small brooks. . . In high-gradient streams the Johnny was restricted largely to the quiet waters in the pools.

3 =**violet.** Cf **johnny-jump-up 1, little johnny 2**

1892 DN 1.236 cwMO, *Johnnies.* A popular name for violets. Also used in Michigan. **1929** Burgess *Wild Flowers* 10, *Viola pedata.* . . In some places where they grow in numbers, and are much loved, [they]

are called] Velvet Johnnies, or Velvet Johnny-jump-ups. **1968** DARE (Qu. S3) Inf **IN49,** Johnny.

4 See **johnny house.**

5 Used in var phrases as a warning that one's fly is open; prob by ext, as a warning that one's slip is showing. [Cf *johnny* the penis] Cf **Mr. White is out of jail**

1967–68 DARE (Qu. W24a, . . *Expressions . . to warn a woman slyly that her slip is showing*) Inf **IN30,** Johnny's out of jail; (Qu. W24c, . . *To warn a man that his trouser-fly is open*) Inf **IA8,** Johnny's about to show; **CA80,** Johnny's out.

6 See **john 1.**

7 See **John Chinaman 1.**

8 See **johnny crook 2.**

9 See quot. [Cf *Johnny Navajo* "A familiar name for the Navahos" (DAE 1863–65)]

1990 DARE File cnAZ, [Letter:] A Navajo (traditional backwoods Johnny) sees "tree" in branch or root or leaf—just the gestalt totality, not parts. *Ibid,* "Johnny" is used for a remote Rez [=reservation] Navajo and for the pidgin s/he speaks.

Johnny Appleseed's weed n

=**dog fennel 1.**

1959 Carleton *Index Herb. Plants* 68, *Johnny-Appleseed's-weed:* Anthemis cotula.

johnny-at-the-rat-hole, play v phr

1911 DN 3.545 NE, *Johnny-at-the-rat-hole, to play.* . . To pry into other people's affairs; to eavesdrop. "He's always playing Johnny-at-the-rat-hole."

johnny board See **johnnycake board**

johnny boat n

1 See **johnboat 1.**

2 also *johnnywood boat:* See quot.

1975 Gould *ME Lingo* 148, *Johnnywood boats, Johnny boats*—Small boats that specialized in bringing firewood for Maine's lime kilns. The name derives from the St. John River, where most of these boats were built. It took 30 cords of wood to fire a single burning of lime, so *Johnnywood boats* were numerous in and out of Rockport, Rockland, and Thomaston. *Johnnywood boats* were also known as kiln-wooders, kiln-coasters, and lime-wooders.

johnnyboy n Cf **johnnycake 2**

1959 VT Hist. 27.145 neVT, *Johnnyboy.* . . A small piece of uncooked bread broken from dough and fried on a griddle. Common.

johnny bread See **johnnycake**

Johnny Bull n

1 See **John Bull.**

2 =**ruddy duck.**

1938 Oberholser *Bird Life LA* 140, Ruddy Duck. . . Probably no duck has so many different names as this well-known bird. Some of those commonly heard are 'butterball', 'dipper', . . and 'Johnny bull'.

3 A **bullfrog 1.**

1967 DARE (Qu. P22, *Names or nicknames for a very large frog that makes a deep, loud sound*) Inf **PA58,** Johnny Bull.

4 =**English sparrow.**

1968 DARE (Qu. Q22, *Joking names or nicknames for the common sparrow*) Infs **PA75, 135,** Johnny Bull.

johnnycake n Also *johncake, johnny bread* Also sp *jonnycake* [Etym uncert; cf note in DA]

1 A bread consisting primarily of cornmeal, and either baked in a pan or cooked in cakes on a griddle; rarely, boiled cornmeal. **scattered, but chiefly Nth** See Map on p. 154 Cf **corn cake, journey cake**

1739 SC Gaz. (Charleston) 15 Dec 4/2, New Iron Plates to bake Johnny Cakes or gridel Bread on. **1836** (1955) Crockett Almanacks 52 wTN, I didn't care the fag end of a johnny cake for him. **1856** in 1862 Colt *Went to KS* 44 **NY,** Supper . . consists of hominy, not soft Johnny-cake, (or corn bread, as it is called here,) stewed apple, and tea. **1893** Earle *Customs in Old New Engl.* 67, One [wife], owing to her spouse's stinginess, had to use "Indian branne for Jonne bred," and never tasted good food. **1908** DN 3.325 eAL, wGA, *Johnny-cake.* . . A small corn meal cake fried in lard. **1910** DN 3.444 wNY, *Johnny-cake.* . . A cake made of corn meal; corn bread. The latter term not heard. **1915** Hazard

Jonny-Cake Papers 52 **RI** (as of c1880), The huckleberry jonny-cake . . to be first-rate, must be made half and half of meal and fresh gathered ripe berries. **1923** in 1931 McCorrison *Letters Fraternity* 50 **NEng,** One little sparrow just got a piece of Johnny bread the dogs had left, and it was amusing to see him struggle to swallow it. **1939** Wolcott *Yankee Cook Book* 132, Rhode Island Jonnycake. . . A true Rhode Islander would not dream of using an "h" in jonnycake. **c1940** Eliason *Word Lists FL* 9 **wFL,** *Johnny cake: Johncake* is similar to *hoecake,* but is made from a mixture of corn meal and flour. It is usually baked inside the oven instead of on top of the stove. **1965–70** *DARE* (Qu. H14, *Bread that's made with cornmeal*) 166 Infs, **scattered, but chiefly Nth,** Johnnycake(s); **CT**39, Johnnycake bread; **CA**15, Johnny bread or johnnycake; **CA**87, Johnny bread is original cornbread; **CA**167, Johnny bread, but that's not used out here much; **ME**7, Johnny bread; **MI**68, Johnny bread same as johnnycake; **NY**130, **PA**131, Johnny bread—lighter than southern cornbread; (Qu. H25, . . *Names or nicknames . . for fried cornmeal*) 21 Infs, **scattered, but esp CT, RI,** Johnnycake(s); **MA**83, Fried johnnycakes; **NY**83, Johnny bread; (Qu. H20b, . . *Names . . for pancakes*) 10 Infs, **scattered,** Johnnycakes; (Qu. C34, *Nicknames for nearby settlements, villages, or districts*) Inf **MA**42, Johnnycake Hollow; (Qu. C35, *Nicknames for the different parts of your town or city*) Inf **MA**40, Johnnycake Hill; (Qu. F1) Inf **RI**3, Griddle for johnnycakes; (Qu. F3) Inf **CT**39, Johnnycake turner; (Qu. H18) Inf **RI**1, Johnnycakes; (Qu. H19) Inf **OR**3, Johnnycake biscuit; (Qu. H24, . . *Names or nicknames . . for boiled cornmeal*) Infs **CT**39, **IA**47, Johnnycake. **1981** *Yankee* Apr 68, Rhode Islanders have come to blows over jonnycakes for any number of reasons . . over how to spell them . . over which kind of corn to grind for jonnycake meal . . and even over how to grind that corn. **1983** *MJLF* 9.1.45 **ceKY,** *Johnny cake . .* a corn griddle cake, a hoe cake. **1986** Pederson *LAGS Concordance* **Gulf Region,** [59 infs indicated that they were familiar with the term *johnnycake,* though some could not describe it; 10 indicated that it was made with cornmeal, 10 said it was made with flour; 1 inf, Johnnycake bread—with flour; made by grandparents; 1 inf, Johnny bread—made in frying pan with wheat flour; 1 inf, Johnny bread—corn bread with beaten eggs.]

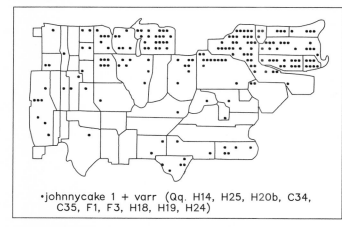

•johnnycake 1 + varr (Qq. H14, H25, H20b, C34, C35, F1, F3, H18, H19, H24)

2 A similar bread or cake made with wheat flour.

1938 FWP *Ocean Highway* xxvii **NC,** *Johnny Bread:* pastry of white flour, lard, and sweet milk, spread an inch thick in a biscuit pan and baked in a quick oven, split and buttered while hot, and cut into squares when served. **1967** *DARE* (Qu. H32, . . *Fancy rolls and pastries*) Inf **SC**43, Johnnycake—made with wheat flour sweetened with sugar, molasses, or honey; like a cookie. **1986** [see **1** above].

johnnycake board n Also *johnny board* hist

A board on which to bake **johnnycake 1.**

1841 *Daily Picayune* (New Orleans LA) 16 Jan 1/6, She's got *every thing* that ever was perduced for sich pupposes. . . kittels, pots, a jonny-cake board, troth to mix rine-injin bread in. **1907** Cockrum *Pioneer IN* 322 (as of c1800), A Johnny-cake board. . . about ten inches wide and fifteen inches long and rounding at the top end. The corn dough was made thick and put on the board which was placed against a chunk of wood near the fire. After one side was baked to a nice brown, it was turned over and the other side was baked in the same way. **1915** Hazard *Jonny-Cake Papers* 29 **RI** (as of c1880), The red oak jonny-cake board was always the middle portion of a flour barrel from five to six inches wide. **1918** Waller *IL Pioneer Days* 76, Johnny-board, a smooth board to put dough on before the fire to bake bread. **1931** Randolph *Ozarks* 27, The so-called johnny-cake is baked slowly on a grease-soaked "johnny board" set up before the fire. **1943** Weslager *DE For-*

gotten Folk 192, The Johnny cake board was an indispensable device in the preparation of this old-time favorite. These Johnny cake boards are still found in the old homes. It is said that the wood of the board imparted a rare flavor to the cake.

johnny cat n
=**flathead catfish 1.**
1983 Becker *Fishes WI* 728, Flathead Catfish. . . Other common names: flathead, . . Johnny cat.

johnny chuck n [Prob in ref to character in *Mother West Wind's Children* by Thornton W. Burgess]
A **woodchuck** (here: *Marmota monax*).
1938 FWP *Guide CT* 421 **nwCT,** Canned woodchuck is a favorite dish along the lower slopes of Mt. Riga. A local woman has taught the people to 'put up' the meat of Johnny Chuck.

johnny cock n
=**pileated woodpecker.**
1953 *AmSp* 28.284 **SC,** Pileated woodpeckers. . . *Johnny cock.*

johnny cockhorse n Also *johnny cockaw, johnny crook(horse)* **SC**
=**praying mantis.**
1888 *Nature* (London) 26 July 303 **SC,** [The hummingbird] was in the clutches of an insect, which he identified as a mantis, popularly known in those parts as "Johnny-cock-horse." **1950** *PADS* 14.41 **SC,** *Johnny cockhorse, Johnny cockaw, Johnny crookhorse. . .* The praying mantis. **1954** *PADS* 21.25 **SC,** *Devil's riding horse. . .* The praying mantis. Also Johnny cockhorse. **1967** *DARE* (Qu. R9b, *An insect that holds up its front feet as if saying a prayer; not asked in early QRs*) Inf **SC**43, Johnny crook.

‡**johnny-come-lately** n
=**thank-you-ma'am.**
1967 *DARE* (Qu. N30, . . *A sudden short dip in a road*) Inf **PA**55, Johnny-come-lately.

johnny constant See **john constant**

Johnny Corn n [Prob var of *John Barleycorn*] Cf **corn** n **B1**
Whiskey personified.
1984 Gilmore *Ozark Baptizings* 116 **MO,** "There was no whiskey on the ground nor was a drunken man to be seen," and in almost every instance of disturbance at such affairs "Johnny Corn" was in some way involved.

johnny cracker n Cf **johnnycake**
1978 *DARE* File **neSC,** Johnny cracker—a plain cracker, good with cheese, about 3 inches.

johnny crook n
1 See **johnny cockhorse.**
2 also *johnny:* Any of var kinds of candy; see quot. **LA**
1968 *DARE* (Qu. H82b, *Kinds of cheap candy that used to be sold years ago*) Inf **LA**24, Johnny crook—like a pull candy; you can't bite it, you just have to wait till it comes a-loose; **LA**40, Johnny crook—oblong, as thick as your finger, made with coconut; **LA**16, Syrup candy usually called johnny.

johnny crookhorse See **johnny cockhorse**

johnny-cut-me-down n
An unidentified plant; see quot.
1943 Weslager *DE Forgotten Folk* 163, The following record of Cheswold herbs represents an ethnobotanical study of hitherto unformulated cures and applies only to the Cheswold Moors. . . *Common Name*—Johnny-cut-me-down. . . *Use*—A tea for babies; general tonic.

johnny darter n chiefly Upper Missip Valley Cf **johnny 2**
A **darter 1,** usu *Etheostoma nigrum*.
1887 (1888) Jordan *Sci. Sketches* 20, Any one who has ever been a boy . . will recall an experience like this: You tried some time to put your finger on a little fish that was lying, apparently asleep, on the bottom of the stream. . . When your finger came near the spot where he was lying, . . you saw the fish again resting, head up-stream, a few feet away, leaving you puzzled to know whether you had seen the movement or not. You were trying to catch a Johnny Darter. **1896** U.S. Natl. Museum *Bulletin* 47.1057, Johnny Darter. . . We may know him by his short fins, . . and by the absence of all color save a soft yellowish brown, which is freckled with darker markings. **1908** Forbes–Richardson *Fishes of IL* 295. **1943** Eddy–Surber *N. Fishes* 199, The Johnny

darter reaches a length of 2½ inches. . . It is more common in and more widely distributed over Minnesota than any of the other darters. **1956** Harlan–Speaker *IA Fish* 151, The Johnny darter. . . has an ecological preference for riffles and gravelly runs in streams. **1967** Cross *Hdbk. Fishes KS* 300. **1983** Becker *Fishes WI* 921, The johnny darter occurs in the Mississippi River, Lake Michigan, and Lake Superior drainage basins in Wisconsin. *Ibid* 923, When establishing a territory, the male johnny darter assumes an inverted position. . . When a female johnny darter enters the territory, the male usually darts out at her as he would at any other intruder.

johnny gaugghy n Also *johnny gonkers, johnny woggins* **NC** Cf **John Henry 3, johnny gongle**

A bird of the family Ardeidae; see quots.

1946 *PADS* 6.18 **eNC** (as of 1900–10), Johnny Gaugghy ['gɔgɪ]. . . A long-legged bird sometimes seen wading in shallow water of creeks and ponds. Probably a member of the heron family. *(Arcidae.)* **1947** [see **johnny gongle**]. **1966** *DARE* (Qu. Q10, . . *Water birds and marsh birds*) Inf **NC21**, Herons—scoggins or scouts or johnny gonkers ['gɔŋkɚz].

johnny gongle n

A **bittern** (here: *Botaurus lentiginosus*).

1947 *PADS* 8.17, I have heard this [=*johnny gaugghy*] from N.C. in the forms: *Johnny Gongle* and *Johnny Woggins,* applied to the bittern and the great blue heron, respectively.

johnny gonkers See **johnny gaugghy**

Johnny Grindle See **John A. Grindle**

johnny house n Also *johnny* chiefly **Sth, S Midl, esp Mid and S Atl** See Map Cf **john 2a**

An outhouse; a toilet.

[**1855** see **Mrs. Jones**]. **1889** *Century Dict.* 3215, Jakes. . . [*Century* Ed: The occurrence of dial. *johnny,* a jakes . . suggests that *jakes* was orig. *Jake's* or *Jack's,* a humorous euphemism.] **1933** *AmSp* 7.333 [Johns Hopkins jargon], *Johnny* . . . a lavatory. **1936** (1938) Ferber–Kaufman *Stage Door* 35, Then a peremptory voice shouts from upstairs: "Judy! You going to stay in the johnny all night?" **1946** *PADS* 5.27 **VA,** Johnny house. . . Privy; fairly common in the James Valley and the southern part of the Blue Ridge. *Ibid* 6.18 **cwVA** (as of 1900–10), Johnny house. . . A privy. **1952** Brown *NC Folkl.* 1.555, Johnny-house. . . A privy. **1954** Harder *Coll.* **cwTN,** Johnny house—Outhouse . . in Virginia. . . Johnny also. Never used at home, usually "outdoors." **c1960** Wilson *Coll.* **csKY,** Johnny-house. . . A privy. **1965–70** *DARE* (Qu. M21b, *Joking names for an outside toilet building*) 104 Infs, **chiefly Sth, S Midl, esp Mid and S Atl,** Johnny (house); **TX**37, 38, Outside johnny; **FL**6, Outdoor johnny; **KY**86, Poor johnny; (Qu. F37, . . *An indoor toilet*) 28 Infs, **scattered, but esp Appalachians, GA, SC,** Johnny; (Qu. M21a, *An outside toilet building*) 12 Infs, **Sth, S Midl,** Johnny (house); (Qu. F37b, *Joking names for an indoor toilet; total Infs questioned, 75*) 10 Infs, **esp Sth,** Johnny (house); (Qu. V2b, *About a deceiving person, or somebody that you can't trust . . "I wouldn't trust him _____";* not asked in early QRs) Inf **VA**16, In a johnny house; (Qu. BB20, *Joking names or expressions for overactive kidneys*) Inf **FL**19, Running to the johnny. **1976** Garber *Mountain-ese* 48 **sAppalachians,** They turned over our johnnyhouse on Halloween night.

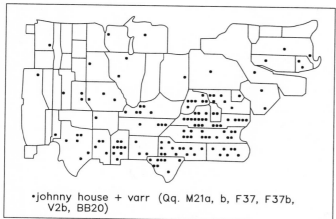

•johnny house + varr (Qq. M21a, b, F37, F37b, V2b, BB20)

johnny-humpback n Cf **john-jumper 1**
See quot.

1940 (1978) Still *River of Earth* 59 **KY** [Author from **AL**], "Looks

like a johnny-humpback," he said. It did look like a worm. *Ibid* 172, There was no getting away from Fletch. We fished dirt holes for johnny-humpbacks. If I caught one first he spat down the hole for spite.

johnny-in-a-rag n

A bag pudding; see quot.

1969 *DARE* (Qu. H63, *Kinds of desserts*) Inf **IN**60, Johnny-in-a-rag: suet pudding boiled in cloth. Cloth, pie dough covered with suet, sugar, raisins, boiled 3 hours.

johnny is about to show, johnny is out (of jail) See **johnny 5**

johnny-jump n

A **shooting star** (here: *Dodecatheon meadia*).

1894 *Jrl. Amer. Folkl.* 7.94 **sCA,** Dodecatheon Meadia. . . Johnny jump. **1940** Clute *Amer. Plant Names* 112, D[odecatheon] meadia. . . Johnny-jump. **1959** Carleton *Index Herb. Plants* 68, Johnny-jump: Dodecatheon meadia.

johnny-jumper n

1 See **johnny-jump-up 1, 2b.**

2 See **jumper 7a.**

johnny-jump-up n

1 also *jenny-jump-up, johnny-jumper;* for addit varr see quots: =**violet.** Cf **jump-up-johnny** For other names of *Viola tricolor* see **biddy's eyes, bird bill 2, bird's-foot violet 1, black-eyed Susan 5, cat's face 1, come-tickle-me, Cupid's delight, ~ flower 2, field pansy, forget-me-not 3, heartsease 1, kisses 1, ladies' delight, none-so-pretty 2, pansy, pansy violet, three-faces-under-a-hood, tickle-my-fancy, wild pansy**

1842 *Knickerbocker* 19.115 **sePA,** Mr. Ketchup had now kissed little Chip and stuck a johnny-jump-up in his cap. **1858** U.S. Congress *Congressional Globe* 19 May 2244 **KY,** You stand here, and, with smiling faces, spend $60,000 a year for morning-glories and johnny jump-ups! **1859** (1968) Bartlett *Americanisms* 221, *Johnny Jump up and Kiss me. Johnny Jump up. Johnny Jumper.* Names given to the Heart's Ease, or Violet. **1895** *DN* 1.390, *Johnny-jump-ups:* violets. Springdale, Pa. **1905** *DN* 3.84 **nwAR,** Johnny-jumper. . . Johnny-jump-up. . . Wild violet, wild pansy. Common. **1909** *DN* 3.413 **nME,** Johnny jump up. **1934** Haskin *Wild Flowers Pacific Coast* 219, Johnny-jump-up. . . On the Pacific slope I have found this name most frequently coupled with the yellow flowers of *Viola nuttallii* . . , although . . many will differ with me, and claim the name for some other species. **1950** *WELS Suppl.,* 6 Infs, **WI,** Johnny-jump-up; 1 Inf, Bird's-foot violet, johnny-jump-up— because of the way the blossoms seem to just jump up out of the bare ground. **1965–70** *DARE* (Qu. S3, *A flower like a large violet with a yellow center and small ragged leaves—it comes up early in spring on open, stony hilltops*) 342 Infs, **widespread,** Johnny-jump-up; **AR**55, Uncle Johnny-jump-up; **MD**23, **SC**57, Johnny-jumper; (Qu. S11, . . *Blue violet*) 50 Infs, **chiefly N Midl,** Johnny-jump-up; **GA**70, Johnny-jump-your-head-off; (Qu. S1) Inf **WA**30, Yellow violet—same as johnny-jump-up; (Qu. S23) Infs **GA**80, **PA**73, **WA**28, Johnny-jump-up; (Qu. S26a, . . *Wildflowers . . Roadside flowers*) Infs **CA**101, **WV**4, Johnny-jump-up; (Qu. S26c, *Wildflowers that grow in woods*) Inf **MI**80, Johnny-jump-up; (Qu. S26e, *Other wildflowers not yet mentioned;* not asked in early QRs) Infs **CA**20, 195, 204, **MD**30, **MA**58, **OH**74, Johnny-jump-up(s). **1969** *DARE* Tape **PA**203, Lady slippers, jenny-jump-ups, and those kind of things. **1973** *Foxfire 2* 82, *Viola papilionacea* . . johnny-jump-up. . . Violet leaves and flowers are both edible. **1977** Churchill *Don't Call* 73 **nwOR** (as of c1918), In April the bright yellow Johnny-jump-ups dotted the greening expanse of the land.

2 Any of var other plants, as:

a also *john(ny)-jumper:* A **jack-in-the-pulpit 1.**

1950 *WELS* (Other names for the jack-in-the-pulpit) 4 Infs, **WI,** Johnny-jump-up. **1965–70** *DARE* (Qu. S1, . . *Jack-in-the-pulpit*) 16 Infs, **scattered, but esp N Midl,** Johnny-jump-up; **CA**126, Johnny-jumpers; **CA**127, Johnny-jumper, john-jumper. **1969** *DARE* FW Addit **CA**133, Jack-in-the-pulpit—johnny-jump-up.

b =**trillium.**

1967–69 *DARE* (Qu. S2, . . *The flower that comes up in the woods early in spring, with three white petals that turn pink as the flower grows older*) Infs **MO**6, 13, 15, 39, **WV**8, Johnny-jump-up.

c See quots.

1907 Obenchain *Aunt Jane* 274 **KY,** I used to call 'em Johnny-jump-ups, till Henrietta told me that their right name was daffydil. **1966** Barnes–Jensen *Dict. UT Slang* 26, *Johnny-jump-up* . . a local name given the Phacelia (*Phacelia linearis*). **1966** *DARE* Wildfl QR (Wills–

Irwin, Pl.44C [=*Maurandya antirrhiniflora*] Inf **TX**34, Johnny-jump-up. **1967–68** *DARE* (Qu. S5, . . *Wild morning glory*) Inf **OH**57, Johnny-jump-up; (Qu. S11, . . *Bluets*) Inf **LA**12, Johnny-jump-up; (Qu. S24, *A wild flower that grows in swamps and marshes and looks like a small blue iris*) Inf **MO**10, Johnny-jump-up.

3 in phr *I'll be johnny-jump-up:* See **johnnied, I'll be.**

johnny-jump-up-and-kiss-me, johnny-jump-your-head-off See **johnny-jump-up 1**

Johnny-know-it-all n
  1968–69 *DARE* (Qu. II35, *A person who is disliked because he seems to think he knows everything*) Infs **OH**45, **RI**15, Johnny-know-it-all.

Johnny Marzetti n Also *(John) Marzetti, Jo Mazzotti, Tony Marzetti, ya-ma-zetta;* for addit varr see quots [See quot 1967 *DARE*] **scattered, but esp OH, N Cent**
  A dish consisting primarily of ground meat, noodles, and canned soup.
  1946 Farmer *Boston Cook Book* 96, *Jo Mazzotti.* . . Celery . . onions . . green peppers . . ground pork . . lemon . . tomato soup . . sharp cheese . . broad noodles. . . Cover closely and cook slowly 1 hour on top of the stove or in a moderate oven. **c1965** Randle *Cookbooks* (Plain Cookery) 1.[3] **ceOH**, *Yumzetti.* Ibid [4], *Yum-e-setti.* . . *Yum setta.* . . *Yumma setti.* Ibid [5], *Yumezetti.* . . *Ya-ma-zetta casserole.* Ibid [6], *Yum zetti.* . . *Yuma zetta.* Ibid [7], *Yum zetta.* Ibid [17], *Marzetti.* [*DARE* Ed: All recipes contain ground beef, noodles, and canned soup as primary ingredients.] **c1965** Randle *Cookbooks* (Ask Neighbor) 1.58, *John Marzetti.* Ibid 59, *John Maszume.* **1967** *Weston Chron.* (MO) 8 Sept 6/4, School Menu[:] John Marzetti[,] Apple Sauce[,] Cole Slaw and Green Peppers [,] Bread and Butter[,] ½ pt. milk. **1967** *DARE* (Qu. H45, *Dishes made with meat, fish, or poultry that everybody around here would know, but that people in other places might not*) Inf **OH**45, Johnny Marzetti: at restaurant in Columbus called Marzetti's. The recipe took on the name of it. It has ground beef, tomatoes, garlic. **1968** *Favorite Recipes Univ. Women* 135 **MD**, Johnny Marzetti. Ibid 172 **NH**, John Marzetti. Ibid 316 **IL**, Johnny Marzetti. **1974** *DARE* File **MI**, *Tony Marzetti*—Johnny Marzetti; recipe from Ludington, Michigan.

Johnny Miller See **miller boy**

johnny-nip n **esp CA** Cf **johnny-tuck**
  An **owl's clover** (here: *Orthocarpus castillejoides*).
  1925 Jepson *Manual Plants CA* 943, *O[rthocarpus] castilloides.* . . *Johnny-Nip.* . . Commonly 6 to 11 in. high. **1949** Moldenke *Amer. Wild Flowers* 275, In the *johnnynip, O. castilloides,* the bracts are white- or yellow-tipped, and the corolla is variegated white, purple, yellow, and rose. **1964** Munz *Shore Wildflowers* 19, Another member of the Figwort Family is a native plant, *Johnny Nip* . . , which grows in low saline places and on sea bluffs from British Columbia to Monterey County, California.

Johnny-on-the-pony n Also *Johnny on a pony, Johnny-ride-a* (or *the*)-*pony* **chiefly NYC** Cf **bumbay**
  =**buck buck 2.**
  1953 Brewster *Amer. Nonsinging Games* 116 **NY**, *Johnny on the Pony.* **1957** *Sat. Eve. Post Letters* **cCT** (as of c1880), [In a list of games:] Johnny ride a pony. **1968–70** *DARE* (Qu. EE33, . . *Outdoor games . . that children play*) Inf **NY**51, Johnny-ride-a-pony—one boy starts with hands on wall, others jump on him; **NY**235, Johnny-ride-a-pony—made up of teams; five to six people line up, the last one tries to get on; the others try to shake him off; **NY**119, Johnny-on-the-pony—two teams; one guy starts against the wall—he's the pillow—and his team faces him one behind each other; they all bend over with hands on each other's waists; the other team jumps on them and tries to break them; **NY**44, Johnny-ride-the-pony—leap onto a team to knock it down. [All Infs from **NYC**] **1975** Ferretti *Gt. Amer. Book Sidewalk Games* 156 **NYC**, *Johnny on a pony.* . . There are two teams, usually of five or six boys each. The first team is the Pony, and the second is Johnny. The Pony team lines up this way: One member stands upright with his back braced against a tree; then the second player bends down, thrusts his head into the first person's stomach, and grabs him tightly around the waist. The next bends down, placing his head between the legs of player 2 and grabbing him tightly around the thighs. Players 4, 5, and 6 repeat what number 3 did. The whole team then braces. The Johnny team . . races at them, one at a time, and vaults atop the row of backs as far forward as he can, shouting, "Johnny on a Pony, one, two, three!" The . . object is to cave in the backs of the Pony team. If the jumping team can do that, the others must brace themselves again for the onslaught. If they hold and

support all six members of the other team, then that team becomes the Pony and the jumpers have to bend over. **1986** *DARE* File **NYC** (as of 1930s), *Johnny on a pony*—a boys' game. One player bends over, supporting himself by holding on to a wall, etc.; others leap straddling on to his back and try to weigh him down until he loses his grip and falls. **1990** Ibid **Bronx NYC** (as of c1955), In the Bronx this game was known as Johnny on a pony. . . We played it bracing ourselves against a wall and the first member of the pony team was called the "pillow." Before we leaped we called out "Johnny on a pony one two three!" Sometimes we'd have 10 or more kids on a side. If the pony team was able to support all the Johnny team, the latter would then all start swaying back and forth on the backs of the ponies to bring them down, which it always did. **1991** Ibid **Brooklyn NYC** (as of 1940s), You had to be older to play Johnny on the pony. There were two teams, equal numbers. . . One team made a train out into the gutter, an L-shaped train. The other team ran and jumped on the backs of the first team. If the first team couldn't hold them, the second got to run and jump on again. If they could hold them, then the first team had to guess how many fingers the leader of the second team was holding up. If they guessed correctly, they got to be the jumpers.

Johnny-on-the-spot n Cf **Charlie-on-the-spot**
  A person who is ready and willing to undertake the task at hand; a competent and enthusiastic person—sometimes used ironically.
  1896 (1898) Ade *Artie* 24 **Chicago IL**, I could see that a Johnny-on-the-spot, with a big badge, marked 'Committee,' was tryin' to keep cases on her. **1912** (1914) Sinclair *Flying U Ranch* 106, When it arrives I'm sure Johnny-on-the-spot. **1916** *DN* 4.324 **KS**, *Johnny on the spot.* . . Fully prepared for such occasion as arises; 'there[,]' Not local. "They needed a man to run the engine and he was Johnny on the spot." **1927** *AmSp* 2.358 **cwWV**, *Johnny on the spot* . . one who is always on hand. "He has always been Johnny on the spot when there is a hard job to be done." **1929** *AmSp* 5.127 **ME**, Someone who was industrious was "steady to work," "right on deck," "Johnny on the spot." **1942** Perry *Texas* 115, There is a merry historian . . who is always Johnny-on-the-spot with his recording machine. **1966** *DARE* (Qu. GG19b, *When you can see from the way a person acts that he's feeling important or independent: "He seems to think he's _____."*) Inf **MA**6, Johnny-on-the-spot; (Qu. HH27a, *A very able and energetic person who gets things done*) Inf **GA**7, Johnny-on-the-spot. **1988** Palmer *Lang. W. Cent.* **MA** 36, You'd better be johnny-on-the-spot when it's time to take [the syrup off the fire] because you can lose it all just like that.

johnny owl n
  =**burrowing owl.**
  1944 (1967) McNichols *Crazy Weather* 148 **AZ**, Havek, his head going around like a Johnny-owl's, was staring in bewilderment. **1955** Forbush–May *Birds* 271, *Florida Burrowing Owl.* . . *Other names:* Johnny Owl; Ground Owl. **1970** *DARE* (Qu. Q2) Inf **CA**191, Johnny owl.

johnny pot n Cf **john 2b, johnny house**
  1966 *DARE* (Qu. F38, *Utensil kept under the bed for use at night*) Infs **MD**17, **MI**18, Johnny pot.

johnny pump n
  A fireplug.
  1985 *DARE* File **NYC**, *Johnny pump.* . . In the area of Brooklyn NY, where I was brought up, the word[s] "fire hydrant" or "fire plug" were never used and for all practical purposes unknown. . . The areas of NYC which used "fire hydrant" never used the word Johnny pump and in fact didn't know what it meant.

johnnyquil See **jonquil**

Johnny-ride-a (or **the**)-**pony** See **Johnny-on-the-pony**

johnny roach n Cf **roach**
  A **sunfish** (*Lepomis* spp).
  1968 *DARE* (Qu. P1, . . *Kinds of freshwater fish . . caught around here . . good to eat*) Inf **CT**13, Johnny roach = sunfish; **CT**17, Roach or johnny roach or sunfish.

johnny smokers n Also *johnny smoker* [See quot 1893]
  A **prairie smoke** (here: *Geum triflorum* var *ciliatum*).
  1893 *Jrl. Amer. Folkl.* 6.141, *Geum triflorum,* Johnny smokers. Rockford, Ill. . . Applied at time of fruiting, when conspicuous with plumose styles. **1940** Clute *Amer. Plant Names* 6, *G[eum] ciliatum.* . . Johnny smokers. **1959** Carleton *Index Herb. Plants* 68, *Johnny smoker: Geum ciliatum.*

Johnny the Conqueror See **conquer John**

Johnny-the-preacher See **Jack-the-preacher**

johnny trots n Cf *johnny* (at **johnny house**)

See quots.

1970 *DARE* (Qu. BB19, *Joking names for looseness of the bowels*) Inf **VA**94, Johnny trots. **1990** Cavender *Folk Med. Lexicon* 26 **sAppalachians**, *Johnny trots*—diarrhea.

johnny-tuck n chiefly **CA** Cf **johnny-nip**

An **owl's clover** (here: *Orthocarpus erianthus*).

1911 Jepson *Flora CA* 386, *O[rthocarpus] erianthus. . . Johnny-Tuck. . .* Very abundant on the plains of the Sacramento and San Joaquin valleys and on the low hills of the Coast Ranges. **1915** (1926) Armstrong–Thornber *Western Wild Flowers* 498, *Johnny-Tuck. Orthocarpus erianthus. . .* The sulphur-yellow flowers are usually an inch long, with a magenta "beak" and a very slender, white tube. . . *Pink Johnny-Tuck . . Orthocarpus erianthus* var. *roseus. . .* Very pretty little flowers . . varying from almost white to bright pink, . . and a maroon-colored "beak." **1937** U.S. Forest Serv. *Range Plant Hdbk.* W136, Johnny-tuck. . . is very abundant in the foothills of California, frequently coloring wide stretches . . with gold-tinted streamlike bands. **1961** Thomas *Flora Santa Cruz* 318 **cwCA**, Johnny-Tuck. Open fields and grassy slopes. **1973** Hitchcock–Cronquist *Flora Pacific NW* 429, Butter-and-eggs, Johnny-turk [sic] owl-clover. . . *O[rthocarpus] erianthus.*

Johnny verde n **CA**

A **rock bass** (here: *Paralabrax* spp, usu *P. nebulifer*).

1882 U.S. Natl. Museum *Bulletin* 16.536, *S[erranus] nebulifer. . . Johnny Verde.* Greenish with irregular pale and dark mottlings and traces of dark oblique cross-bars, the colors having a washed or faded appearance. **1884** Goode *Fisheries U.S.* 1.413 **swCA**, The Johnny Verde—*Serranus nebulifer. . .* The distinctive Spanish name of "Johnny (Juan) Verde" is also in frequent use, especially at San Pedro. **1902** Jordan–Evermann *Amer. Fishes* 395, The johnny-verde occurs on our Pacific coast from Monterey to Lower California. **1911** U.S. Bur. Census *Fisheries 1908* 308, Cabrilla. A name applied indiscriminately to several serranoid fishes of the southern coast of California. They are also called "rock bass," . . "Johnny Verde," . . etc. **1946** LaMonte *N. Amer. Game Fishes* 48, *Paralabrax nebulifer. . .* Johnny Verde. . . The species of *Paralabrax* are considerably confused by fishermen.

johnny walkers n pl Also *johnnie walkers* **S Midl**, esp **TN** Cf **long john 4**

=**tom walkers.**

1940 *Amer. Mercury* June 210 **sAppalachians**, Leaf was stalking the calf lot on johnny-walkers Grandpa had chopped for him. . . I'll make you a pair o' johnny-walkers. **1952** *The State* (Columbia, S.C.) 31 Aug. (*Mathews Coll.*), Another correspondent reports that in Spartanburg [SC] they [=stilts] are also called Johnnie Walkers. **1965–70** *DARE* (Qu. EE35, *Long wooden poles with a footpiece that children walk around on to make them tall*) Infs **KY**34, **MD**15, **NC**53, **TN**32, 33, 34, 35, 36, Johnny walkers.

johnny woggins See **johnny gaugghy**

johnny-wonny berry n Cf **wintergreen**

See quot.

1968 *DARE* (Qu. I44, *What kinds of berries grow wild around here?*) Inf **NY**97, Johnny-wonny [ˌʤɑnɪˈwɑnɪ] berries—similar to wintergreen berries.

johnnywood boat See **johnny boat 2**

john-paw n

A **grouper 1a** (here: *Epinephelus drummondhayi*).

1879 U.S. Natl. Museum *Bulletin* 14.50, *Epinephelus Drummond-Hayi.* — Star Snapper; Hind; John Paw. **1896** *Ibid* 47.1159 **FL**, John Paw. . . Common on the Snapper Banks off Pensacola, where it is a valued food-fish; the most beautiful in color of all the groupers. **1902** Jordan–Evermann *Amer. Fishes* 385, The speckled hind or john-paw. . . attains a weight of 30 pounds, and is an important food-fish in the Pensacola market.

John Rogers n [Perh in allusion to *John Rogers* (d1555) English Protestant martyr] Cf **Jehoshaphat**

Used in exclams or mild oaths; see quots.

1949 *WELS Suppl.* **csWI**, By the Holy Jumping John Rogers—exclamation used by an old neighbor lady. **1959** *VT Hist.* 27.145, By John

Rogers! . . Occasional. **1968–70** *DARE* (Qu. NN26c, *Weakened substitutes for 'hell': "What the _____!"*) Inf **WI**44, John Rogers; (Qu. NN29c, *Exclamations beginning with 'holy': "Holy _____!"*) Inf **CA**200, Jumped-up John Rogers; (Qu. NN30, *Exclamations beginning with the sound of 'j'*) Inf **MA**14, By the jumped-up John Rogers.

John's cabbage n

A **waterleaf** (here: either *Hydrophyllum canadense* or *H. virginianum*).

1843 Torrey *Flora NY* 2.92, The young leaves [of *Hydrophyllum virginianum*] are said to be eaten as a potherb, under the name of *John's Cabbage.* **1943** Fernald–Kinsey *Edible Wild Plants E. N. Amer.* 326, *John's Cabbage, Hydrophyllum virginianum* and *H. canadense. . .* Kephart records the commendable virtue, that the plants stand repicking and that the leaves do not quickly become woody. **1959** Gillespie *Compilation Edible Wild Plants WV* 102, Water Leaf and John's Cabbage (*Hydrophyllum virginianum* . . and *H. canadense* . .). Both fairly common throughout the state. . . The young, smooth leaves are used as a potherb. **1976** Bailey–Bailey *Hortus Third* 580, *[Hydrophyllum] virginianum. . .* Shawnee-salad, Indian-salad, John's cabbage. . . Fl[ower]s white or violet-purple, in loose cymes. . . The tender shoots were eaten by the Amer. Indians.

john's house See **john 2a**

Johnson grass n

1 also *Johnson's grass, Johnson weed*: A naturalized **sorghum** (here: *Sorghum halapense*) introduced for hay and forage. chiefly **Sth, West, W Midl** Also called **Egyptian grass 2, evergreen millet, guinea grass 2, mange ~, Means ~, Morocco millet**

1884 Vasey *Ag. Grasses* 51, *Sorghum halapense.* (Cuba grass, Johnson grass, Means grass, False Guinea grass, Evergreen millet, Arabian millet.) **1894** *Jrl. Amer. Folkl.* 7.104 **sNE**, *Andropogon sorghum, . .* Johnson-grass. **1898** *Ibid* 11.283 **WY**, *Sorghum halapensis, . .* Johnson grass. **1906** *DN* 3.143 **nwAR**, Johnson grass. . . A kind of grass usually regarded as undesirable. "If allowed to mature seed, Johnson grass hay is coarse and lacking in nourishment." **1908** *DN* 3.325 **eAL, wGA**, Johnson grass. **1946** Driscoll *Country Jake* 148 **csKS**, He had called upon God to damn the horses and cattle, the cockleburs, the Johnson grass, the politicians and the botts that annoyed the horses. **1954** *Harder Coll.* **cwTN**, Johnson grass. . . A parasitic grass, almost impossible to root out of the soil. **1965–70** *DARE* (Qu. S9, . . *Kinds of grass that are hard to get rid of*) 232 Infs, chiefly **Sth, West, W Midl**, Johnson grass; **CA**94, Johnston [sic] grass; **WI**20, Johnson's grass; (Qu. S8, *A common kind of wild grass that grows in fields: it spreads by sending out long underground roots, and it's hard to get rid of*) 94 Infs, chiefly **Sth, SW, W Midl**, Johnson grass; **CA**94, Johnston [sic] grass; (Qu. L9a, . . *Kinds of grass . . grown for hay*) 81 Infs, chiefly **Sth, SW, W Midl**, Johnson grass; (Qu. S21, . . *Weeds . . that are a trouble in gardens and fields*) 10 Infs, **Sth, SW, W Midl**, Johnson grass; **SC**63, Johnson weed; (Qu. L8, *Hay that grows naturally in damp places*) Infs **AR**21, **GA**19, 80, **IN**3, **MO**16, **SC**40, **TN**62, Johnson grass; (Qu. L9b, *Hay from other kinds of plants [not grass]; not asked in early QRs*) Infs **AR**4, **MO**16, Johnson grass; (Qu. S15, . . *Weed seeds that cling to clothing*) Infs **OR**14, **VA**15, Johnson grass. [*DARE* Ed: Some of the Infs from **LA** and **TX** may refer instead to **2** below.] **1976** Bailey–Bailey *Hortus Third* 1061, *[Sorghum] halapense. . .* Johnson grass. . . Cult. for forage and naturalized in many parts of the U.S.; often a troublesome weed.

2 A **panic grass**: usu *Panicum repens*, but also *P. virgatum*. chiefly **LA**

1910 *Auk* 27.338 **seLA**, In the Mississippi Delta the. . . flats are covered by a dense growth of . . "Johnson grass" (*Panicum repens*), and cat-tails. **1913** *Torreya* 13.227, *Panicum repens. . .* Johnson grass, Mississippi Delta, La., Belle Isle, La. **1926** *Ibid* 26.4, *Panicum virgatum. . .* Johnson Grass, Mississippi Delta, La. . . At this same locality the writer had *Panicum repens* . . pointed out as Johnson grass; probably the name is applied to almost any robust grass resembling the cultivated bearer of this name, that is *Sorghum halapense.* **1947** *Jrl. Wildlife Management* 2.51 **Gulf coast**, When early spring floods deeply inundate the flats and interior marshes, geese feed on rhizomes of dog-tooth grass (*Panicum repens*; locally called "Johnson grass") along the banks of old bayous.

Johnson's grass See **Johnson grass 1**

Johnson's spanks n Also *Johnson spanks*

A small, deep-fried cake; see quots.

1941 *LANE* Map 284 (*Doughnut*) 1 inf, **ceRI**, Keech cake, wholly of 'Indian meal' (instead of meal and rye flour) with egg and milk, shaped between the hands and fried in deep fat; also called Johnson's spanks. **1969** *Yankee* May 26 **NEng,** My aged mother recalls her mother serving a food item called "Johnson Spanks"—a flat cake fried in deep fat. Could you tell me where this recipe can be obtained? . . *Answer: Old Dutch delicacy—any dough will do if you serve it with sweet sauce.*

Johnson weed See **Johnson grass 1**

John's weed n
=Mexican clover.
   1933 *Torreya* 33.84, *Richardsonia scabra.* . . Alabama clover, John's weed.

John's-wort n [*OEDS* 1753 →] **NEng**
=St. John's wort.
   1818 in 1826 MA Hist. Soc. *Coll.* 2d ser 8.170, In July the lover of plants is gratified with . . two species of pyrala, the small geranium, several species of hypericum or John's wort. **1836** in 1957 Old Farmer's *Almanac Sampler* 98, A nosegay of buttercup, hog lily, and john's-wort. **1864** *Catalogue of Herbs* **swME,** John's wort—Hypericum perforatum. **1874** VT State Bd. Ag. *Rept. for 1873–74* 2.390, It is very desirable that the dairyman's pastures should be well stocked with good nutritious grasses, not wild grass of the low boggy pasture, or johnswort, or daisies, but June or blue grass and clover. **1900** Lyons *Plant Names* 197, H[ypericum] perforatum. . . John's-wort. **1959** Carleton *Index Herb. Plants* 68, John's wort: Hypericum (v).

John the Baptist n Cf **doughboy** n[1] **3**
=Baptist cake.
   1975 Gould *ME Lingo* 148, John the Baptists—Small bits of yeast-bread dough snitched before the batch is put in pans for baking, and fried as a breakfast hotbread. Bacon or pork fat gives them a crisp outside. Well buttered, they are delicious with jam, molasses, maple syrup, and honey.

John the Conqueror See **conquer John**

johnyquil See **jonquil**

joice See **joist 1**

joik See **jerk** n[1], v[1]

join v Usu |ǰɔɪn|; freq |ǰaɪn| Pronc-sp *jine* Similarly vbl n *jineen,* n *jiner* Cf Pronc Intro 3.I.11
A Forms.
   1834 Caruthers *Kentuckian* 1.20 **KY,** O! as to *jine*en the army to the north, . . I was afraid the blasted tories would sell me to the British. **1837** Sherwood *Gaz.* GA 70, *Jine,* for join. **1848** Lowell *Biglow* 145 **'Upcountry' MA,** Jine. **1851** in 1956 Eliason *Tarheel Talk* 33 **NC,** Jined. **1884** *Anglia* 7.265 **Sth, S Midl** [Black], To done jine de chu'ch = to have joined the church. **1890** *DN* 1.68 **KY,** Jine: for join. . . jiners. . . "How many jiners did they have?" *Ibid* 71 **LA,** Jine. **1893** Frederic *Copperhead* 87 **nNY,** He sneaked off behind our backs to jine Lincoln's nigger-worshippers. **1893** Shands *MS Speech* 41, Jine [ǰaɪn]. Negro and illiterate white for join. Common throughout the South. **1905** *DN* 3.57 **eNE,** For *oi, ai* is very common; . . join. **1908** *DN* 3.325 **eAL, wGA,** Jine. **1914** *DN* 4.75 **ME, nNH,** J'iner. **1917** *DN* 4.394 **neOH,** Jiner. **1923** *DN* 5.212 **swMO,** Jine. **1926** *DN* 5.387 **ME,** Jiner. **1928** *AmSp* 3.404 **Ozarks** (as of 1916–27), In such words as . . join the *oi* takes the sound of long *i* . . jine. **1935** *AmSp* 10.165 **PA** [Engl of PA Germans], Regularly in the Deitsch [aɪ] corresponds to the [ɔy] of High German. . . There was thus an additional impetus given to the tendency already present among the English-speaking neighbors of the German settlers to say *jine* instead of *join, biler* instead of *boiler,* and *jice* instead of *joist.* . . It is heard among the illiterate, but among the educated classes and among the younger speakers of all classes it has disappeared. **1936** *AmSp* 11.35 **eTX,** Another group of words . . are still occasionally heard with [aɪ] in more illiterate speech and in jocular usage . . : join. **1942** Hall *Smoky Mt. Speech* 46 **wNC, eTN,** A number of people retain the archaic [aɪ] in words like . . join. **1969** *DARE* FW Addit **KY**31, Join [ǰaɪn], point [paɪnt]—typical of mountain speech of older and illiterate speakers. **1982** *Barrick Coll.* **csPA,** Join—pron. [ǰaɪn]. Now rare.
B Senses.
1 To be contiguous; also with *on, to, up with:* to be contiguous to; hence ppl adj *joining.* [*OED* join v[1] 8 c1325 →; v[1] 16.b 1837 →] **chiefly Sth, S Midl**

1781 Peters *Genl. Hist.* CT 164, The houses are . . well built, but, as I have observed in general of the towns in Connecticut, do not join. **1796** Morse *Amer. Universal Geog.* 1.443, It joins to the sea on the east side of the island. **1884** *Anglia* 7.265 **Sth, S Midl** [Black], *Jinin' on* = next to. **1899** (1912) Green *VA Folk-Speech* 246, *Join.* . . Two pieces of land lying alongside of each other "joined." A man was said to want all the land that "joined" his own. **1922** Gonzales *Black Border* 308 **sSC, GA coasts** [Gullah glossary], *Jinin'* . . adjoining. **1942** Rawlings *Cross Creek* 13 **FL,** Old Boss' grove joins up with mine. **1967** *DARE* FW Addit **AR**47, Joining—adjoining. **1968** *DARE* (Qu. MM6, . . *'Very close' or 'only a short distance away':* "The house is _____ the park.") Inf **VA**5, Joining. **1976** Ryland *Richmond Co.* VA 372, *Joins*—is adjacent to; "His land joins ours." **1986** Pederson *LAGS Concordance* **cwAR,** 1 inf, Joining (or "adjoining"?); 1 inf, Joins—one lot meets or adjoins another.
2 To start (an activity). [*EDD* join v. II.2]
   1882 (1971) Gibbons *PA Dutch* 390, Said a tavern-keeper's wife, "Don't jine sweeping." "It's time to jine sweeping," was the reply.
3 with *out:* To drop out.
   1959 *VT Hist.* 27.145, Join out. . . To drop out of membership. Occasional.
4 with *back:* To rejoin.
   1966 *PADS* 46.26 **cnAR,** Join back. . . Rejoin.—"The army wanted him to, so he joined back."

joiner snake See **joint snake**

joining, join on See **join B1**

join out See **join B3**

joint n Usu |ǰɔɪnt|; also esp **Sth, S Midl** |ǰaɪnt|; infreq |ǰʌɪnt, ǰɚnt| Pronc-spp *gint, jernt, jint, jynt* Cf **joist**
Std senses, var forms.
   1847 Hurd *Grammatical Corrector* 84, Joint ["incorrect" pronc = [ǰaɪnt]; "correct" pronc = [ǰɔɪnt]]. **1851** Burke *Polly Peablossom* 95 **GA,** By this time, they began to be considerable tired and limber in the gints. **1867** Lowell *Biglow* xxiv **'Upcountry' MA,** Thus for *joint* . . we have *jynt.* **1890** *DN* 1.68 **KY,** Joint. Often pronounced [ǰaɪnt]. **1891** *PMLA* 6.166 **WV,** [oɪ] often becomes [aɪ], as *joint.* **1899** (1912) Green *VA Folk-Speech* 245, *Jint.* **1908** *DN* 3.325 **eAL, wGA,** Joint. . . Often pronounced *jint.* **1915** *DN* 4.184 **swVA,** Jint [ǰaɪnt]. **1923** *DN* 5.212 **swMO,** J'int o'meat. **1936** *AmSp* 11.35 **eTX,** Words . . pronounced with [ɔɪ] . . occasionally heard with [aɪ] in more illiterate speech and in jocular usage . . *join, joint, joist.* **1940** *AmSp* 15.376 **NYC,** The variation in pronunciation here discussed is characteristic only of that type of New York City speech which is farthest removed from Standard English. . . [It includes] [dʒɔɪnt]. **1941** in 1944 *ADD,* [dʒɚnt]. I bet he'll wreck the jernt. Radio song. **1941** *AmSp* 16.7 **eTX** [Black], Joint [has] [aɪ]. **1942** *New Yorker* 11 July 17, She's got about as much talent in her bones as the first jernt of my pinky. **1961** Kurath–McDavid *Pronc. Engl.* 167, The word *joint* . . has the vowel /ɔi/ of *boy* in cultivated and in common speech. Except for parts of New Hampshire and Maine, this pronunciation predominates in the North and the North Midland also in folk speech. . . Joint with the vowel /ai/ of *five* predominates in folk speech (1) in the coastal plane [sic] from Chesapeake Bay to the Pee Dee in South Carolina and (2) in the Appalachians and the Blue Ridge; it is much less frequent in the intervening area, the piedmont of Virginia and North Carolina, and rather rare in the Lower South. In the North Midland and the North, the /ai/ of *five* is rather rare in *joint,* except for parts of New Hampshire and Maine. Scattered instances of this pronunciation survive in the Hudson Valley and in the New England settlements of northeastern Pennsylvania; elsewhere it has been eliminated. **1967** *DARE* (Qu. DD30, *Joking names for a place where liquor is [or was] sold and consumed illegally*) Inf **LA**6, Joint [ǰaɪnt]. **1976** Allen *LAUM* 3.27 **Upper MW** (as of c1950), A . . minority subtype [of /ɔi/] is that with an unround beginning, ranging from [ai] to [ʌi]. . . In the U[pper] M[idwest] it persists in 21 instances in *[boiled, poison, joint].* . . All but one of the instances appear in the first settled eastern portion of the five states.

jointed rush See **joint rush**

jointed snake n
1 See **joint snake.**
2 =coral snake 1a.
   1928 Baylor Univ. Museum *Contrib.* 16.19 **TX,** *Micrurus fulvius.* . . is known on account of its brilliant annulated bands as . . *Jointed Snake.*

joint fir n [*OED* 1866 →] Cf **joint pine**
=**Mormon tea 1.**

  1889 *Century Dict.* 3239, Joint-fir. . . A general name of the species of the natural order *Gnetaceæ*. **1906** Rydberg *Flora CO* 10, *Ephedra*. . . Joint-firs. . . On desert lands. **1937** U.S. Forest Serv. *Range Plant Hdbk.* B73, The jointfirs, with jointed branches resembling those of horsetails (*Equisetum* spp.), are distinctive shrubs or small trees. . . Jointfir, the . . common name, is rather descriptive, but as yet only limitedly employed in the range country. **1951** Martin *Amer. Wildlife & Plants* 295, Ten or eleven species of jointfir are found in the arid parts of the Southwest, from Wyoming and Texas to Southern California. **1976** Elmore *Shrubs & Trees SW* 92, Joint-fir. . . From its dried stems the early pioneers brewed a hot drink, though the Navajo roasted the stems first, claiming that it improved the flavor. **1985** Dodge *Flowers SW Deserts* 70, Jointfir. . . Apparently leafless, these common Southwestern shrubs do have leaves, although they are reduced to tiny scales.

joint grass n

  1 A **bullgrass 1** (here: *Paspalum distichum*). **scattered, but esp Mid and S Atl**

  1853 (1890) Simms *Partisan* 55 seSC, Rebellion grows like joint-grass when it once takes root. **1857** Gray *Manual of Botany* 576, *P[aspalum] distichum*. . . Joint-grass. . . Wet fields, Virginia and southward. **1894** Coulter *Botany W. TX* 499, Joint grass. . . Moist places throughout Texas and across the continent. **1923** in 1925 Jepson *Manual Plants CA* 137, Joint Grass. . . Along the seacoast and interior irrigation ditches. **1947** *Jrl. Wildlife Management* 2.72 **Gulf coast,** Cattle graze on the foliage of cordgrass, . . "joint grass" (*Paspalum distichum*), . . and to a lesser extent on almost all marsh vegetation. **1966–70** *DARE* (Qu. S8, *A common kind of wild grass that grows in fields: it spreads by sending out long underground roots, and it's hard to get rid of*) 14 Infs, **chiefly Mid Atl,** Joint grass; (Qu. S9, *. . Kinds of grass that are hard to get rid of*) 10 Infs, **chiefly S Atl,** Joint grass; (Qu. S21, *. . Weeds . . that are a trouble in gardens and fields*) Inf **IN26,** Joint grass.

  2 See **joint tail.**

join-the-dots See **dot 2**

joint mouse n Cf **mouse** n **B2**

  1970 Rogers *Grandma's Is.* 31 seME, The tennis court has been mentioned and its slipperiness if not thoroughly dry. I went down on it on one occasion and I still have a couple of little pieces of torn cartilage in my right knee as a result. . . They are known as "joint mice."

join to See **join B1**

joint pine n Cf **joint fir**
=**Mormon tea 1.**

  1903 (1950) Austin *Land of Little Rain* 84 seCA, Who taught them [=Paiutes] that the essence of joint pine (*Ephedra nevadensis*), which looks to have no juice in it of any sort, is efficacious in stomachic disorders[?] **1923** in 1925 Jepson *Manual Plants CA* 60, *Ephedra*. . . Joint Pine. . . Shrubs with slender long-jointed stems. **1937** U.S. Forest Serv. *Range Plant Hdbk.* B73, Other local names [for *Ephedra*] include . . jointpine. **1967** Harrington *Edible Plants Rocky Mts.* 356, Jointpine. Several species grow in the western part of the Rocky Mountains. They are quite similar in general appearance.

joint plant n
A cultivated **spiderwort.**

  1892 *Jrl. Amer. Folkl.* 5.104, *Tradescantia crassifolia*. . . Joint-plant. Cambridge, Mass. **1948** Bean *Yankee Auctioneer* 234 wMA, Fill it [=a beer stein] with joint plant. (At least that's what we call those trailing plants up here in the country.)

jointpod n [See quot]
=**sweet vetch.**

  1937 U.S. Forest Serv. *Range Plant Hdbk.* W87, *Hedysarum*. . . "Jointpod" is sometimes applied as a common name, because of the peculiar jointed pods (loments).

joint rush n Also *jointed rush*
A **rush** (here: *Juncus articulatus*).

  1859 in 1942 Hafen *Overland Routes* 11.118 **NE,** There are islands in the Platte covered with dense undergrowth, and containing immense patches of the sand rush (or joint rush), which keeps green all winter, affording excellent fodder for cattle. **1940** Clute *Amer. Plant Names* 149, *J[uncus] articulatus*. Jointed Rush. **1967** *DARE* (Qu. L8, *Hay that*

grows naturally in damp places*) Inf **WY1,** Joint rush. **1973** Hitchcock– Cronquist *Flora Pacific NW* 572, Jointed r[ush]. . . *J[uncus] articulatus*.

joint snake n Also *joiner snake, jointed ~* **chiefly Sth** See Map
=**glass snake.**

  1789 Morse *Amer. Geog.* 61, The Joint Snake is a great curiosity. Its skin is as hard as parchment, and as smooth as glass. . . When it is struck, it breaks like a pipe stem; and you may . . break it from the tail to the bowels into pieces not an inch long. **1892** Duval *Early Times in TX* 113, To-day I came across a specimen of the jointed snake, the first I had ever seen. **1929** Sale *Tree Named John* 55 **MS,** J'inted snakes er chicken snakes er *all* uv 'em. **1961** Sackett–Koch *KS Folkl.* 75, It is thought by some people that if one strikes a joint snake, he will break in two and then if he is left alone, the two parts will come back together and the whole snake will go on his way. The truth is, only the tail can be broken off so easily. It will not join back on the snake but the snake will grow a new tail in time. **1965–70** *DARE* (Qu. P25, *. . Kinds of snakes*) 22 Infs, **chiefly Sth,** Joint snake; **AR55, LA15,** Jointed snake; (Qu. CC17, *Imaginary animals or monsters that people . . tell tales about—especially to tease greenhorns*) Infs **KY76, TX11,** Joint snake; **TX61,** Joiner snake—a snake which if cut into four pieces before sundown will put itself back together. **1972** *Foxfire Book* 293 nGA, Well, y'take them there joint snakes now. Why, y'can hit one and it'll fly all t'pieces. . . And you'll go on and leave him, and if you'll turn back and watch him, that head hit'll just take back'erds and hunt ever' piece, by grannys, and he'll go right back t'gether. **1974** Cohen *Ramapo Mt. People* 149 neNJ, They used to talk about a snake—a joint snake, too. You'd see a head over here, a part of a body here, part of a body there. They said then when you come up by him, they'd jump right together and come after you. **1981** Vogt *Nat. Hist. WI* 117, Folk tales of the joint snake may have originated with this genus [=*Ophisaurus*]; they claimed that the snake would break into several pieces and then grow back together again. The breaking apart is true, but the pieces never become attached again.

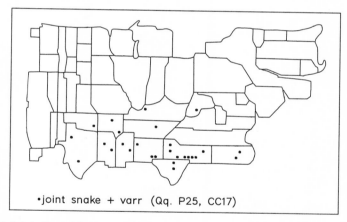

•joint snake + varr (Qq. P25, CC17)

joint tail n Also *joint grass*
A grass of the genus *Manisurus*. Also called **rat-tail grass**

  1968 Radford et al. *Manual Flora Carolinas* 159, *Manisurus*. . . Joint Grass. Perennials from short rhizomes or hardened bases, nodes and internodes glabrous. **1968** Barkley *Plants KS* 50, Manisurus cylindrica. . . Carolina Jointtail. **1970** Correll *Plants TX* 202, *Manisurus*. . . Joint-tail.

joint vetch n [From the jointed seed pod; *OEDS* 1829 →] **esp TX**
A plant of the genus *Aeschynomene*. For other names of var spp see **indigo 2d**

  1868 (1870) Gray *Field Botany* 105, *Æschynomene, Sensitive Joint-vetch*. . . Pod resembling that of Desmodium. **1900** Lyons *Plant Names* 17, *Aeschynomene*. . . Joint-Vetch. . . Herbs or shrubs with yellow flowers. **1939** Tharp *Vegetation TX* 58, Joint Vetch (*Aeschynomene*) westward. **1970** Correll *Plants TX* 853, Joint Vetch. . . Fruit a loment, of 2 to 12 1-seeded joints. **1979** Ajilvsgi *Wild Flowers* 170 **TX,** Joint vetch. *Aeschynomene indica*. . . Fruit: . . constricted between joints and falling apart when mature into 1-seeded sections.

jointweed n

  1 A plant of the genus *Polygonella*. [See quots 1822, 1938] Also called **salt-cedar weed, wireweed.** For other names of var spp see **October flower 1, sand grass**

1822 Eaton *Botany* 401, *[Polygonum] articulatum. . . Joint-weed. . .* About a foot high, terminated by delicate racemes; to which the bracts give a jointed appearance. **1892** Torrey *Foot-Path Way* 60 **MA,** Two kinds of groundsel, fall dandelion, and jointweed. **1901** Lounsberry *S. Wild Flowers* 156, *P[olygonella] Americana,* southern jointweed . . hardly occurs further northward than Georgia. . . About the growth of the plant there is a wiryness and its fine, linear-spatulate stem leaves seldom more than half an inch long, produce the effect of a pine-like, graceful foliage. **1938** Madison *Wild Flowers OH* 60, *Jointweed. . .* St[em]s noticeably jointed. . . July-Oct. Sandy shores, Great Lakes. **1966** *DARE* Wildfl QR Pl.49A Inf **OR9,** Jointweed. **1976** Bailey–Bailey *Hortus Third* 895, *Polygonella. . . Jointweed. . .* Nine spp. of ann[ual] or per[ennial] herbs with jointed st[em]s, native to e. U.S. and se. Canada.

2 A **smartweed** (here: *Polygonum longistylum*).

1930 OK Univ. Biol. Surv. *Pub.* 2.59, *Polygonum longistylum. . .* Long-styled Joint-weed. **1951** *PADS* 15.30 **TX,** *Persicaria longistyla. . .* Knotweed; jointweed.

jointworm n [See quot 1882]
The larva of any of var chalcid insects of the genus *Tetramesa*.

1851 *Cultivator* 8.322/1, I first observe, lying upon the infested stalk, the insect to which you allude in your letter, as perhaps having been hatched from the joint-worm. **1852** Harris *Treatise Insects* 443, The ravages of the joint-worm in the wheat-fields of Virginia are said to have been first observed in Albemarle county, about four or five years ago. **1882** (1903) Treat *Injurious Insects* 124, *Isosoma hordei. . .* In certain years and in particular States the crops of wheat, of barley, or of rye are greatly injured by a minute maggot, popularly known as the "Joint-worm." . . These galls. . . are apt to elude observation, because, being almost always situated just above the joint or knot on that stem—whence comes the popular name "Joint-worms"—they are enwrapped and hidden by the sheath of the blade. **1938** Brimley *Insects NC* 422, *H[armolita] tritici. . .* Wheat Joint Worm. . . Probably all the wheat growing sections of the state. **1972** Swan–Papp *Insects* 537, *Wheat Jointworm. . .* Several larvae form a hard woody gall, each in its individual cell just above the second or third joint, causing the stem to bend or break.

join up with See **join B1**

joist n
Std senses, var forms.

1 sg: usu |jɔɪst|; also |jɔɪs|; also **esp Sth, S Midl** |jaɪs(t)|; infreq |jʌɪst| Pronc-spp *gice, giste, jaist, jice, jist(e), joice, jois, joyce, juh-ist*

1818 in 1956 Eliason *Tarheel Talk* 313 **NC,** Gice. **1844** Thompson *Major Jones's Courtship* 97 **GA,** Thar . . was a grate big meal-bag hangin to the jice. **1899** (1912) Green *VA Folk-Speech* 196, *Giste. . .* A joist. Jiste. **1903** *DN* 2.291 **Cape Cod MA** (as of a1857), *Jaist* for joist. **1903** *DN* 2.318 **seMO,** *Joist. . .* Pronounced joice [jɔɪs]. **1905** *DN* 3.57 **eNE,** For *oi, ai* is very common; . . joist. **1906** *DN* 3.120 **cwIN,** *Joist. . .* Regularly called *jaist*. Ibid 143 **nwAR,** *Jois. . .* Joist. **1908** *DN* 3.324 **eAL, wGA,** *Jice* or *jist. . .* Joist. . . Joice. Often pronounced [jais]. **1915** *DN* 4.184 **swVA,** *Jice* [jaɪs]. . . Also *jiste*. **1917** *DN* 4.413 **wNC,** *Jiste.* **1923** *DN* 5.212 **swMO,** *J'ist.* **1927** Shewmake *Engl. Pronc. VA* 31, Perfectly familiar to Virginia ears is the pronunciation of . . *joist* . . with *i* as in . . light [=lʌɪt]. . . *juh-ist* would be heard regularly. **1930** Shoemaker *1300 Words* 33 **cPA Mts** (as of c1900), *Jice*—A joist. **1935** [see **join A**]. **1942** Hall *Smoky Mt. Speech* 46 **wNC, eTN,** A number of people retain the archaic [aɪ] in words like . . joist. **1984** [see **2** below].

2 pl: usu |jɔɪsts|; also |jɔɪs(əz)|; for addit pronc and sp varr see quots. Cf **fist** n[1]

1703 (1879) S. Sewall *Diary* 2.89 **MA,** The Beams and Joyce of the old Hall Floor are laid. **1847** Hurd *Grammatical Corrector* 84, *Joist. . .* The log was sawed into jice. **1867** Harris *Sut Lovingood Yarns* 34 **TN,** I . . jump'd thru tu the groun' floor, jis' thuteen foot wun inch clear ove jists. **1899** (1912) Green *VA Folk-Speech* 245, *Jices. . .* Joists; joist. Ibid 246, *Joices. . .* For joists. **1912** *DN* 3.579 **wIN,** The joice are all rotten in that house. **1931** *AmSp* 7.91 **eKY,** She's raised in a log-house with the peppers 'n' beans hung up to the jistes to dry. **1942** Hall *Smoky Mt. Speech* 82 **wNC, eTN,** Joists ['jɔɪsəz] (once on a disc; also [jɔɪs:]). **1969–70** *DARE* Tapes **KY50, VA43,** [jɔɪs]. **1976** Ryland *Richmond Co. VA* 372, *Joyces*—joists. **1981** Pederson *LAGS Basic Materials,* 1 inf, **swTN,** ['dʒɔ·ɪsɪz]; 1 inf, **ceAR,** [dʒɐˑˈʃɪz, dʒa·ɪsɪz]; 1 inf, **cLA,** [dʒɔɪs] [plural]. **1984** *WI State Jrl.* (Madison) 19 Apr sec C 3/8, *Wood* . . ideal for floor joyces, $100.

Joisy mosquito See **Jersey mosquito 1**

jo-jeezly See **jeezly**

jojoba n |ˌhoˈhobə| Also *jajoba* Pronc-sp *hohoba* [See quot 1962] A shrub *(Simmondsia chinensis)* of the Southwest, having oily, edible seeds. Also called **bucknut, bushnut, coffeeberry 2b, coffeebush, deer nut, goatberry, goat nut, nutbrush, pignut, shampoo bean, sheepnut, wild hazel**

1920 Saunders *Useful Wild Plants* 80, The oily, chocolate-brown seeds, which are of about the size and appearance of hazelnut kernels. . . [are called] jojobas. Ibid 160, Much more appealing to the average taste is a drink that Mexicans sometimes make from the oily kernels of the *jojoba* nut of Southern California and northern Mexico. **1925** Jepson *Manual Plants CA* 607, *Jajoba. . .* Rigid much-branched shrub 2 to 4 or 7 ft. high. . . Arid hills. **1941** Jaeger *Wildflowers* 139 **Desert SW,** *Jojoba. . .* The little white-tailed antelope ground squirrels . . store the fresh seeds and thus aid in dissemination. **1961** Douglas *My Wilderness* 82 **AZ,** The jojoba grows here in five-foot bushes. This plant, related to the common box family, has thick leathery leaves that stay all winter. They are browse for cattle, and their seeds, once eaten by Indians, produce an oil used in hair tonics. **1962** Balls *Early Uses CA Plants* 89, The large, edible nuts of Jojoba have received almost more attention from investigators and chemists than any other plant of the Southwest. The name Jojoba comes from the original Indian Hohohwi. **1985** Dodge *Flowers SW Deserts* 10, Jojoba (ho-HO-ba) is another of the desert plants which is noticeable not because of its flowers, but due to its leathery gray-green foliage which persists throughout the year. **1993** Kingsolver *Pigs in Heaven* 112, In the store we sell these shampoos they make with ho-hoba. . . A fellow come in today and says he's all set up down in Arizona to grow ho-hoba beans on his farm.

jo-jumper n [See quot 1941] Cf **jumping cholla**
A **prickly pear** (here: *Opuntia fragilis*).

1926 *Torreya* 26.6, *Opuntia pes-corvi. . .* Jo-jumper, Jekyl [sic] I[slan]d, Ga. **1941** Ibid 41.50, Aided by their minutely barbed and promptly clinging spines, the joints of chollas become detached at the slightest contact of animal or man. . . Similar qualities of an eastern cactus, *Opuntia pes-corvi*[s] have also inspired the fancy that the joints jump, as implied by the name jo-jumper recorded in . . 1926.

joke v **esp Sth, S Midl** Cf **fun** v **1**
To tease, kid, make fun of (someone).

1859 Taliaferro *Fisher's R.* 111 **nwNC** (as of 1820s), Dick was a rough hand to joke people. **1927** Kennedy *Gritny* 8 **sLA** [Black], Please suh, doctor, don' joke me in my mis'ry. **1934** Carmer *Stars Fell on AL* 139, The news of his capture spread and the townspeople came to the jail to peer through the bars at the notorious bandit and joke him over his plight. **1940** (1942) Clark *Ox-Bow* 94 **NV** (as of 1885), They didn't mind Smith joking Sparks, but that offended their present sense of indecision and secrecy. **1945** FWP *Lay My Burden Down* 82 **GA,** He was just as gay as they was, and joked the boys. **1986** Pederson *LAGS Concordance,* 1 inf, **cAL,** He can joke you = he can play a joke on you; 1 inf, **ceAR,** She was just joking him = kidding him.

joke-box n
1969 *DARE* (Qu. GG32b, *To habitually play tricks or jokes on people: "He's an awful _____."*) Inf **KY40,** Joke-box.

joker n
1 See quot.
1967 *DARE* (Qu. L18, *Kinds of plows*) Inf **OH35,** Joker—a cultivator.
2 See quot.
1967 *DARE* (Qu. L42, *Do you use the word 'rig' around here? What kind of thing do you call a 'rig'?*) Inf **MN2,** Joker—tractor or old car used off highway on farm, beat up, stripped down, usually has oversized wheels.

jokey adj, also used absol Also sp *joky* **esp Sth, S Midl**
Humorous; inclined to humor—often in comb *jokey fellow;* freq used euphem of a feebleminded person.

1923 *DN* 5.212 **swMO,** *Jokey. . .* Jocular, fun loving, given to practical jokes. **1928** *AmSp* 4.116 **Ozarks,** A *jokey feller* is not exactly an *eediot* or *nateral*, but he is certainly not normal—perhaps what the outside world would call a high-grade imbecile. Ibid 117, The *jokey feller* is usually the butt of all sorts of rustic humor; he is always imitated to perfection by the local comedians, and his most striking peculiarities of speech are used facetiously by . . people in the neighborhood. **1930** *VA Qrly. Rev.* 6.250 **S Midl,** Occasionally one runs upon . . such waning linguistic forms as . . jokey, a harmless imbecile. **1953** Randolph–Wilson *Down in Holler* 257 **Ozarks,** *Joky fellow. . .* A clown, a mental defective of a lively disposition. "Hank ain't no idiot; he's just a joky feller." **1954** *Harder Coll.* **cwTN,** *Jokey fellow.* **1955** Ritchie *Singing Family* 62 **seKY,** He's allus a right jokey kind of feller. Going across the Duane Mountain he got to showing off what a good rider he was. **1965–68** *DARE* (QR, near Qu. BB54) Inf **OK**13, In kind of a jokey way; (Qu. GG32a, *To habitually play tricks or jokes on people: "He's always _____."*) Inf **VT**5, Jokey; (Qu. GG32b, *To habitually play tricks or jokes on people: "He's an awful _____."*) Infs **GA**7, **SC**26, Jokey fellow. **1976** Maclean *River Runs Through* 158 **wMT** (as of 1919), I worked with a lot of crews in the woods, and day in and day out we weren't jokey. . . For one thing, we worked too hard and too long to be left bubbling over with the comic spirit. **1986** Pederson *LAGS Concordance,* 1 inf, **neTN,** A jokey old fellow; 1 inf, **neFL,** A jokey way (=say it jokingly).

jokeyfied adj [**jokey** + **-ified**]
 1929 *AmSp* 5.19 **Ozarks,** *Jokeyfied. . .* Jocular, clownish. Sometimes used in the sense of feebleminded.

joky See **jokey**

jole, joll See **jowl** n

jollies See **jolly** exclam

jollop n [Cf *EDD jollop* sb. "A semi-fluid mess of anything; a big mess of food"] Cf **gollop** n
 1968 *DARE* (Qu. FF2, *. . Kinds of parties*) Inf **GA**44, Jollop [ˈjɑləp] supper; jollop—a type of creamed chicken . . [served over] hot rolls or toasted buns.

jolly exclam Also *jollies* [Prob var of *golly*]
 Used in var exclam phrr or as a mild oath; see quots.
 1824 *Old Colony Mem.* (Plymouth MA) 6 Mar 180, "By jolly," said Zachary Diggins, "I insign to see the nail works." **1896** *DN* 1.419 **cwNY,** By *jolly!* . . Also [nOH] "Jolly!" **1905** *DN* 3.62 **NE,** *Jolly. . .* "Jolly, I wonder what he meant?" **1915** (1916) Johnson *Highways New Engl.* 51, "This is hot weather," he remarked. "By jolly! I was pretty near petered today." **1924** *DN* 5.271 [Exclams], By jolly. **c1940** *Hall Coll.* **wNC, eTN,** By jollies! . . An exclamation expressing various emotions. I noted it down from the speech of a forty year old man. **1959** *VT Hist.* 27.145 **nwVT,** By faith and by jolly, Sir! . . Obsolete. *Ibid,* My Jolly! . . Obsolete. **1966–69** *DARE* (Qu. NN30, *Exclamations beginning with the sound of 'j'*) Inf **NY**206, By jolly tar—old-fashioned; **FL**16, Jolly, jolly; (Qu. NN32, *Exclamations like 'I swear' or 'I vow'*) Inf **NY**206, By jolly tar.

jolly board n Cf **jiggling board**
 =**joggling board.**
 1859 (1968) Bartlett *Americanisms* 221, *Jiggling-board.* A board the ends of which are placed upon frames or stools, upon which a person stands and springs up—also called a *jolly-board.*

jolly boy n **NEng**
 =**drop cake 1.**
 1896 *Daily News Cook Book* 25 **nIL,** Jolly Boys—Mix together . . one and a half pints of ryemeal, half a pint of flour, half a teacupful of cornmeal, two pinches of cinnamon, a little salt and small teaspoonfuls of baking powder. Add one egg, well beaten, two tablespoonfuls each of molasses and sugar, and cold water enough to make a thick batter. Fry in hot lard, a heaping teaspoonful at a time. **1934** *Harwich Port Lib. Assoc. From Cape Cod* 103 **seMA,** *Jolly Boys:* 3 heaping tb. cornmeal, 2 heaping tb. bread flour, 1 heaping tb. sugar, 1 level t. baking powder, salt. Beat 1 egg, add milk enough to make the batter soft, add to dry mixture. Beat all well and drop by small spoonfulls into hot fat. (If too large they will not cook quickly). **1939** Wolcott *Yankee Cook Book* 136 **VT,** *Jolly Boys* [Wolcott: Also called *Rye Meal Drop Cakes*]. **1940** Brown *Amer. Cooks* 321 **ME,** *Jolly Boys. . .* Whip everything together and drop big spoonfuls into fat which has been heated.

jolly is the miller See **miller boy**

jolly, jolly butcher boy n
 A children's game: =**lemonade.**
 1968 *DARE* File **seID,** Jolly, jolly butcher boy. . . Divide into two sides. The first decides something to act out. . . and . . comes over chanting "Jolly, jolly butcher boy seeking for a tray [sic for *trade*]." Second side: "What's your tray?" First side: "Sweet lemonade." Second side: "Get to work and show us if you're not afraid." The first side then

acts out their activity. . . Side two calls out what they think the activity is. . . Side two chases side one.

jolly jumper See **jumper 15**

jolly (old) miller, the See **miller boy**

jolt wagon n **S Midl,** esp **KY** See Map
 A type of springless farm wagon.
 1931 Hannum *Thursday April* 79 **wNC,** The wheels of Joe's jolt wagon would not sink much over their hubs in mud. **1939** Writers' Program *Guide KY* 236, Traveling through the mountains, sometimes in a jolt wagon, sometimes on foot, she made a study of the legends, ballads, and dances of the Kentucky mountaineer. **1942** (1971) Campbell *Cloud-Walking* 7 **seKY,** Like I were a-saying—I heared a jolt wagon lumbering up Piney Creek. **1949** (1958) Stuart *Thread* 24 **KY,** The joltwagon-wheel of yellow moon was rolling not too high above the green hills under heaven. **1953** (1977) Hubbard *Shantyboat* 319 **Missip-Ohio Valleys,** We had considered the sunken road impassable except for a jolt wagon, but these boys drove ten trucks down into Tom's field and back up again. **1957** *Sat. Eve. Post Letters* **swVA** (as of 1880s), Families came to town in "jolt wagons"; **OK,** Jolt wagons—pioneer wagons. **c1960** *Wilson Coll.* **csKY,** *Jolt-wagon. . .* A springless wagon, like a typical farm wagon. **1963** Edwards *Gravel* 168 **eTN** (as of 1920s), What some people refer to as the horse-and-buggy days but Speedwellians call the jolt-wagon days. **1965–70** *DARE* (Qu. L13, *The kind of wagon used for carrying hay*) Inf **KY**16, Put a hay frame on a jolt wagon; (Qu. N41a, *. . Horse-drawn vehicles . . to carry people*) Inf **IN**35, Jolt wagon—same as farm wagon; [**CO**33, Jolties—a buggy name or nickname on a rough road;] (Qu. N41b, *Horse-drawn vehicles to carry heavy loads*) Infs **IN**13, 45, **KY**17, Jolt wagon; **MD**22, Jolt wagon—four wheels, no springs, two horses for a small one, four for large one; (Qu. N41c, *Horse-drawn vehicles to carry light loads*) Infs **KY**17, 26, 39, 42, **OH**50, Jolt wagon.

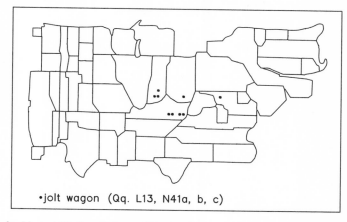

•jolt wagon (Qq. L13, N41a, b, c)

Jo Mazzotti See **Johnny Marzetti**

jomo n Also *jo(o)moo;* by folk-etym *Joe Moore* [By metath from **mojo** n] **Sth, S Midl** *esp freq among Black speakers* Cf **hand** n B4
 An amulet, charm, or spell; hence v phr *jomo work* to cast a spell on (someone).
 1935 Hurston *Mules & Men* 190 **FL,** Ah got my Joe Moore in my hair. [Footnote:] A piece of gamblers [sic] lucky hoodoo. **c1935** in 1970 Hyatt *Hoodoo* 1.72 **seGA,** During de time dey [=the police] supposed to travel dat beat, jes' *roll mah jomoo* an' dey'd pass on by. *Ibid* 482 **ceNC,** Ah heard dat chew take yore ole shoes an' burn 'em so no one kin *jomo work* yo'. *Ibid* 595 **seGA,** [Go] to de fo'ks of de road 'bout twelve or one a'clock in de night an' git some sand . . an' put it in a bag . . an' put it ovah yore mantlepiece [sic]. Go tuh de graveyard . . an' git some dirt an' sew it up wit dat. An' dat'ud . . make yo' lucky—good a *jomo* as yo' want. . . Yo' kin take *graveyard dirt* for gamblin'. . . [E]ver' time yo' go tuh fix up anything, or tuh give a person a *joomoo,* jes' take some of dat an' put in it. **c1938** *Ibid* 2.1334 **seGA,** Tuh make 'em move—git 'em out from livin' so close to yo' . . dat's de *jomoo work.* Dat's de *jomoo work* do dat. . . He do dat wit snake charms. *Ibid* 1335 **seGA,** An' if yo' got a wife an' anothah fellah wants her . . he goes to de *jomoo man.* **1962** *Jrl. Amer. Folkl.* 75.314 **NC,** Local names for amulets are "mojo," "monjo," . . and "jomo." **1964** Will *Hist. Okeechobee* 205 **FL,** His lucky Jomo must have failed, for he lost his

farm land, his city property, and most everything that he had. **1968** *DARE* (Qu. CC14, . . *Where one person supposedly casts a spell over another*) Infs **GA**19, 31, Put the jomo on; **GA**26, Jomo. [All Infs White]

Jonah n, v Usu |'jonə|; also |'jonɚ, -ɪ| Pronc-spp *Joner, Joney* Cf Intro "Language Changes" I.8, IV.1.b

A Forms.

1916 *DN* 4.324 **KS**, *Joner*. . . A Jonah. General. **1942** Hall *Smoky Mt. Speech* 76 **eTN, wNC**, Words ending in *-a*. . . show the old-fashioned [ɪ]. . . The words in which [ɪ] was heard . . Jonah (the Biblical figure). **1942** McAtee *Dial. Grant Co. IN* 37 (as of 1890s), *Jonah*, v., pronounced joner. **1950** *WELS Suppl.* [see **B2** below]. **1954** *Harder Coll.* **cwTN**, *Joney's gourd vine*. **1967–68** [see **B2** below]. **1968** *DARE* FW Addit **NY**69, Jonah ['jonɚ].

B As noun.

1 in phr *heave up Jonah* and varr: To vomit copiously and violently. [From the Old Testament story of Jonah and the whale; cf Jonah 1:17; 2:10] **scattered, but esp Nth, N Midl** See Map

1915 (1916) Johnson *Highways New Engl.* 238 **RI**, When I got home I was taken sick, and didn't I heave up Jonah! Yes, I did heave up Jonah terribly. **1917** *DN* 4.393 **KS, NEng, neOH**, Heave up Jonah. . . To vomit violently. **1922** *DN* 5.178 **ME, NH**, Throw up Jonah. . . To be extremely nauseated. **1940–41** Cassidy *WI Atlas*, 1 inf, **ceWI**, Heave Jonah—Vomit. **1942** McAtee *Dial. Grant Co. IN* 33 (as of 1890s), Heave up Jonah . . vomit copiously. **1943** *LANE* Map 504, Vomit. . . 1 inf, **cnVT**, Heave up Jonah; 1 inf, **nwVT**, Throw up Jonah. **1960** Bailey *Resp. to PADS 20* **KS**, Heave up Jonah (turn yourself inside out, do the old heave-ho.) **1965–70** *DARE* (Qu. BB18, *To vomit a great deal at once*) 27 Infs, **scattered, but esp Nth, N Midl**, Heave up Jonah; **MN**6, **OH**45, Heave Jonah; **OH**40, Heave up Jonah and the whale; **MN**3, Heaved Jonah; **AR**37, Heaved up Jonah; **OH**15, Vomit up Jonah; **MS**15, Whale up Jonah. [28 of 33 Infs old] **1973** Allen *LAUM* 1.369 (as of c1950), 3 infs, **SD, NE**, Heave up Jonah.

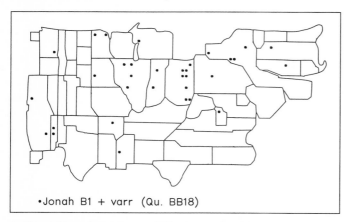

•Jonah B1 + varr (Qu. BB18)

2 Something that causes difficulty or is difficult to do. [By ext from *Jonah* someone believed to bring misfortune]

1887 *Amer. Field* 27.159 **MA**, Cartwright was well pleased with the result, as the Chicopee Falls range has always been his "Jonah," he having never made a decent score on the range yet. [**1905** *DN* 3.84 **nwAR**, Jonah. . . Surprise. 'That was a Jonah.'] **1950** *WELS* ("I managed to do it, but it was _____.") 1 Inf, **seWI**, A Jonah. **1950** *WELS Suppl.*, 1 Inf, **csWI**, Joner—the one most likely to give trouble; used in speaking of a spring on a rototiller. "It's this one right here—that's the Joner." **1965–68** *DARE* FW Addit **seNY**, Sometimes in a whole pack of cars one will be a Joner; **OK**52, That's always been a Jonah to me [FW: an insurmountable obstacle]; **WV**4, He chose brick siding (imitation brick) for a house and it turned out to be "A Jonah of a choice." **1967–68** *DARE* (Qu. C22, *A piece of stone too big for one person to move easily*) Inf **AL**49, Joner ['jonɚ]; (Qu. KK41, . . *"I managed to get through with it, but it was _____."*) Inf **OH**24, A Jonah [laughter]; **KS**18, **NE**10, A Joner; **NY**123, A real Jonah.

3 also *Jonah pie*: See quots. Cf **crybaby**

1919 ME Writers Research Club *ME My State* 289 (as of 1860s), One forenoon . . we coaxed Theodora and Ellen to fry a batch of three dozen pies, and two "Jonahs". . . They would not let us see what they filled the "Jonahs" with, but we knew it was a fearful load. Generally, it was something shockingly sour, or bitter. The "Jonahs" looked precisely like

the others and were mixed with the others on the platter. . . The rule was that whoever got the "Jonah pie" must either eat it, or crawl under the table for a foot-stool for the others during the rest of the meal! What they actually put in the two "Jonahs," this time, was wheat bran mixed with cayenne pepper—an awful dose. **1975** Gould *ME Lingo* 148, *Jonah*. . . In Maine cookery a *jonah* is a *crybaby* cookie filled with red pepper or something other than sweets. When it was mixed with the good cookies at table, the one who got it became the *jonah* and was expected to pay a forfeit.

4 See **Jonah crab.**

C As verb.

See quot. [By ext from *Jonah* to bring bad luck to]

1960 *AmSp* 35.239 **cwCA** [Black], Jonah ['dʒonə], 'to pester, keep after, or bother [some one]': 'I've got to go home, Man, or my wife will Jonah me till I do.' The origin of the word in the proverbial meaning of Jonah as the bringer of bad luck is obvious. I have only heard this sense of *Jonah* in the dialect of one speaker . . from West Texas, but others from the same general area have told me that it was current in that part of the country a few years back.

Jonah crab n Also *Jonah*

A large reddish crab *(Cancer borealis)* of the Atlantic coast.

1883 U.S. Natl. Museum *Bulletin* 27.110, The . . Jonah Crabs (Cancer . . borealis) are eaten only to a slight extent, probably for the reason that their range is coextensive with that of the lobster, which is much more favorably regarded as an article of food. **1884** Goode *Fisheries U.S.* 1.767, There is no reason why the Rock Crab, as well as the "Jonah," should not be utilized to a very great extent. *Ibid* 770, The term "Jonah crab" . . is the one by which it is commonly known in and about Narragansett Bay, Rhode Island, and to some extent also about Vineyard Sound, Massachusetts, but not apparently elsewhere. The origin of the name we have not been able to ascertain. **1901** Arnold *Sea-Beach* 277, The Jonah crab. . . resembles, and is frequently taken for, C[ancer] *irroratus*. **1976** Warner *Beautiful Swimmers* 10, Perhaps almost as tasty . . are . . the rock and Jonah crabs of Maine. **1981** Meinkoth *Audubon Field Guide Seashore* 642, Jonah Crab (Cancer borealis). . . This crab is a common species among seaweeds along the open rocky coast of northern New England, but it seldom moves into brackish estuaries.

Jonah pie See **Jonah B3**

Jonah's gourd n Also *Jonah's gourd vine* [Cf Jonah 4:6–10] The castor bean *(Ricinus communis);* also used fig of a person.

1934 Hurston *Jonah's Gourd Vine* 230 **FL** [Black], Iss uh shame, Sister. Ah'd cut down dat Jonah's gourd vine [=her husband] in uh minute, if Ah had all de say-so. You know Ah would, but de majority of 'em don't keer whut he do, some uh dese people stands in wid it. *Ibid* 241, Ah been sorta feelin' 'round 'mong some de members and b'lieve de time done come when we kin chop down dis Jonah's gourd vine. **1954** *Harder Coll.* **cwTN**, Jonah's gourd vine. . . Sticker vine which grows on cornstalks. *Ibid*, Joney's gourd vine. . . A plant that causes itching and swelling: "Gits in ye shirt, jis burns ye up, sticky." **1959** Carleton *Index Herb. Plants* 69, Jonah's gourd: Ricinus communis.

jonboat See **johnboat 1**

Joner See **Jonah**

Jones' house See **Mrs. Jones**

Jones' place n Also *Jones's place*

1 See **Mrs. Jones.**

2 A **line camp.**

1942 Berrey–Van den Bark *Amer. Slang* 914.8, Ranch buildings. . . *Jones' place, line camp* . . an outpost cabin or camp where "line riders" are stationed. **1961** Adams *Old-Time Cowhand* 201 **West**, In the early days before fences, cow outfits employed line riders and maintained line camps 'long the borders of their range. . . Them camps were ordinarily small, one- or two-room shacks, or maybe a dugout. . . They were called "hoodens," "sign camps," or often referred to as "Jones's place."

Jones's, lean toward See **lean v B3**

Jones's place See **Jones' place**

Joney See **Jonah**

joning See **joan**

jonny-cake See **johnnycake**

jonquil n Also *john(n)yquil*

A Forms.

1908 *DN* 3.325 **eAL, wGA**, *Johny-quil*. . . The jonquil. Common. **1934** (1943) *W2*, *Jonquil*. . . *formerly, and still by some*, ['jʌŋkwɪl]. **1970** *DARE* (Qu. S22, . . *The bright yellow flowers that bloom in clusters in marshes in early springtime*) Inf **MS**82, Johnnyquils. **1971** Dwyer *Dict. for Yankees* 28 **Sth, S Midl**, *Johnnyquil*—Jonquil.

B Sense.

Any of var flowers other than those of the genus *Narcissus*; see quots.

1897 *Jrl. Amer. Folkl.* 10.145 **ME**, *Erythronium Americanum*. . . Jonquil, . . Oxford County. **1968–70** *DARE* (Qu. S1, . . *Jack-in-the-pulpit*) Inf **NY**49, Jonquil; (Qu. S22, . . *The bright yellow flowers that bloom in clusters in marshes in early springtime*) Inf **TN**49, Buttercup, jonquil; **MS**82, Johnnyquils.

joog v |jug, jŭg, jŭk, juk, jʌk| Also *jook, joug, jug, juke* [Prob of Afr origin (cf *DJE juk, DBE jook*), but cf also *SND joog, joug, jugg, jowg* (at *jog* v., n.) "To prick, pierce with a sharp instrument". . . "A prick, a jab with something sharp". Perh an instance of "multiple etymology," with coalescence of forms and some overlap of meaning.] **chiefly SE, esp SC** Cf **chug** v **1, jag** v[1] **B1**

To poke, jab, stick; to shake, wiggle (something); hence n *joug* a punch, jab.

1884 *Amer. Philol. Assoc. Trans. for 1883* 14.50, The form often heard in South Carolina and elsewhere is *jōog* which means rather 'to punch,' and may be the same as *jag*. **1893** Shands *MS Speech* 41, Joog [jug]. Used by negroes and illiterate whites to mean *to punch* or *poke*; as, "I jooged the hornet-nest with a pole." **1922** Gonzales *Black Border* 308 **sSC, GA coasts** [Gullah glossary], *Jook*—jab. **1930** *DN* 6.82 **cSC**, *Joog* [jŭg]. . . means something between punch and gouge, and always implies the use of a blunt instrument. "Stop jooging me with your elbow." "She almost jooged my eye out with her umbrella." A very common word in everyone's vocabulary. **1930** Stoney-Shelby *Black Genesis* 106 **seSC**, An' he gib Br' Wolf a joug (punch) wid de pin. **1950** *PADS* 14.41 **SC**, *Joog* [dʒug]. . . To prod, to punch. "If I go to sleep in church, you joog me in the side." **1966–68** *DARE* (Qu. Y46a, *To get hurt with something sharp* . . "He _____ a thorn into his hand.") Infs **SC**40, 58, Jooged; **SC**44, Jooged [jugd]—children's word; **SC**46, Jooged [jugd]—occasionally; **SC**55, Joog [jug] [FW: suggested; very common]; (Qu. Y46b, *To get hurt with something sharp* . . "She _____ herself with a needle.") Inf **SC**21, [jʌk]—to stab, stick, poke; Negro. **1966–67** *DARE* FW Addit **cwAL**, *Joug* [jug]—to manipulate with the hand; to wiggle (something) about. "He jouged it around till he made it fit"; **cLA**, *Joog* [jug]—to probe or punch. "That wiring wouldn't work till he jooged it with a stick"—Negro usage passed over to White; **SC**, *Joog* [jug] (once [jung])—to poke or punch with a sharp or pointed object; to stab [FW: common in some areas, less freq than formerly in others]; **SC**, *Jook* [juk]—punch, stick with something sharp. **1975** Newell *If Nothin' Don't Happen* 121 **FL**, "And by grannies," he told us, "I just jooged that cat to death." He did, too, because I remember seein' the hide when I was just a little feller and it was full of holes. **1976** *DARE* File **Baton Rouge LA** [Black], Don't joog me with that. **1981** Harper-Presley *Okefinokee* 141 **seGA** (as of a1951), *Joog*—To dig or push. . . "I went and jooged my foot down and scratched him [=a rat in a molehill] out." **1981** Pederson *LAGS Basic Materials*, 1 inf, **cwTN**, After hog is killed, you "put him down in that barrel and just joog ['dʒʊˢug] him up and down" in the water; (Stabbed) 1 inf, **seLA**, ['dʒugd ɪm] (pret + him)—black usage, now spreading among young whites; 1 inf, **csLA**, ['dʒʌgɪt] = stick it, of a knife; 1 inf, **swGA**, ['dʒʊˢgdɪˀm] in the belly = stabbed him; 1 inf, **cwMS**, Juke it [dʒʊuk ɪˀt] down (using a fishing pole, pushed up and down a chimney to remove soot); 1 inf, **cGA**, [dʒʊuk ɪˀt] down in a bottle; 1 inf, **swGA**, Every time the old folks get a headache, somebody wants to [dʒuk əm] in the old folks home. **1987** Kytle *Voices* 160 **NC** [Black], She jugged herself way back in a straight chair and held herself real erect. **1991** *NADS Letters* **cLA** (as of c1940), To prick or stab. People in my neighborhood used [dʒug] for this action. . . This term was often applied to warnings ("Don't run with that stick; you'll [dʒug] your eye out if you fall.") and complaints ("Make him stop [dʒugɪŋ] me with that stick.")

joogle v Also with *up* Also sp *juggle* [Scots, Engl dial; *EDD* (at *juggle* v.[2]), pronc both ['jugl] and ['jʌgl]] Cf **joog**

To poke (something) repeatedly; to shake (something).

1908 *DN* 3.325 **eAL, wGA**, *Juggle* [jugl]. . . To punch or poke

repeatedly as with a stick, shake or move repeatedly as for mixing, etc. "We juggled the rabbit out of his hole." "Juggle the jug up and down to make the sugar come out." **1962** Faulkner *Reivers* 71 **MS**, Waiting for that gasoline . . to get all joogled up to where it would decide to blow up too.

joogle n [Perh < **joogle** v] Cf **goozle** n **1, juger**

1981 Pederson *LAGS Basic Materials*, 1 inf, **swAL**, Joogle ['dʒʊugɫ] (=Adam's apple); [inf] rejects *goozle*; 1 inf, **cGA**, Joogles ['dʒʊˢuˢgləz] (=Adam's apple).

joogle up See **joogle** v

jook v[1] See **jouk** v[1]

jook v[2] See **joog**

jook n Also sp *jouk, juck, juke* [Cf *SND jouk* n. II.4 "A shelter of any kind from a storm or a blow . . ; a sheltered spot, nook, winding passage"]

1 A hidden or sheltered place; an isolated stand of trees.

1941 Writers' Program *SC Folk Tales* 61 **Edisto Is. SC**, Dem day I been courtin uh gal who stay way down in one o' dem juck [Footnote: A hidden, or out-of-the-way, spot] on torrer [=the other] side of Zion Church. **1948** *Studies Ling.* 6.36, About 1900 in South Georgia the term *jook* [dʒuk] was commonly applied to a nook in the woods or to a small stand of timber, generally a rather isolated group of trees on one of the small ridges of comparatively high land between one of the bays of a swamp. A member of a surveying party would call the attention of the surveyor to 'a little *jook* [dʒuk] of pine' that had been overlooked. Or the whereabouts of a missing member of the party might be explained by saying, 'He's way back down yonder in the jook.' **1967** *DARE* (Qu. D7, *A small space anywhere in a house where you can hide things or get them out of the way*) Inf **SC**62, Jook [juk].

2 also *jook house, ~ joint*: A place where prostitutes ply their trade; an establishment, usu in a rural location, providing liquor, music, entertainment, and often prostitutes; a roadhouse. [Perh by ext from **1** above, but see quot 1949. Perh an instance of "multiple etymology," with coalescence of forms and some overlap of meaning.] **orig FL, later chiefly Gulf States, S Atl** See Map on p. 164 *orig among Black speakers; often derog*

1934 Hurston *Jonah's Gourd Vine* 314 **AL**, *Jook*, the pleasure houses near industrial work. A combination of bawdy, gaming, and dance hall. Incidentally the cradle of the "blues." **1935** Hurston *Mules & Men* 93 **nFL** [Black], What does he do when he gets to the jook and the longhouse? . . He raps on the floor of the porch with a stick and says: "Ah ha! What make de rooster crow every morning at sun-up? Dat's to let the pimps and rounders know de workin' man is on his way." **1937** in 1938 *FL Rev.* Spring 28, There were negro jook-joints as far back as I can remember. **1939** FWP *Guide FL* 114, Least known are the Negro 'jooks', primitive rural counterparts of resort night clubs, where turpentine workers take their evening relaxation deep in the pine forests. **1941** *AmSp* 16.319 **sGA**, What jouk-joint do you want to go to? **1941** Faulkner *Men Working* 162 **MS**, Go back to your beer and your jook houses and your girls. **1942** Kennedy *Palmetto Country* 183 **NC**, Altogether the jook is a democratizing influence—a place where the "best people" and "reliefers" can drink away their inhibitions in neighboring booths. **1942** in 1959 Lomax *Rainbow Sign* 185 **nMS** [Black], The young devils slip off to the country jooks and dance to the blues. **1948** *Studies Ling.* 6.36 **sGA**, By 1912–14 the application of the word had shifted from the stand of timber to the wash-house and cabins located there, and *jook* was generally applied to the quarters in which the camp-followers of the turpentine industry plied their ancient profession. **1948** *Sat. Eve. Post* 9 Oct 136 **MS**, Here on the "Gold Coast," a squalid collection of jooks and honky-tonks, liquor may be bought openly by the case. **1949** Turner *Africanisms* 195 [Gullah], [jug (juk)] 'infamous, disorderly' . . used in the compound [jug hʊus (juk hʊus)] 'a disorderly house, a house of ill repute'—W[olof], [jug (jɔg)] 'to lead a disorderly life, to misconduct oneself.' Cf B[ambara], [jugu] 'wicked, violent'; 'a naughty person.' **1965–70** *DARE* (Qu. DD30, *Joking names for a place where liquor is [or was] sold and consumed illegally*) Infs **AL**16, 24, **GA**36, 59, 89, **MS**16, 64, **SC**32, Jook joint; **GA**59, [jʌk]; **LA**6, [juk]; (Qu. D39, . . *Nicknames . . for a small eating place where the food is not especially good*) Infs **FL**15, 27, Jook joint. **1967** *DARE* FW Addit **SC**, *Juke joint* [juk jaɪnt]—a place for drinking, carousing, etc. **1974** Opdyke *Alachua Co.* 42 **cnFL**, Some time in the twenties and thirties, an institution known as the "jook" began to appear. A jook was generally out of the city limits, with something like a filling station in front of a two-story building, often with cabins out back. . . Tales were told of other attractions being available, including alcoholic beverages. **1981** Pederson *LAGS Basic Materials,* 1 inf, **swGA,** "The Nigras' " . . [dʒʊʌˑəkˑs] . . bars . . pool halls; 1 inf, **nwFL,** [dʒʊᵊks] = a place where they have a piano and woman, and whisky; 1 inf, **neFL,** [ˈdʒʊᵊk ˌhaˑʊᶜzɪz]. **1990** Burke *Morning for Flamingos* 26 **seLA,** On the corner was a clapboard juke joint, . . and because it was Friday afternoon the oyster-shell parking lot was already full of cars, and the roar of the jukebox inside was so loud it vibrated the front window.

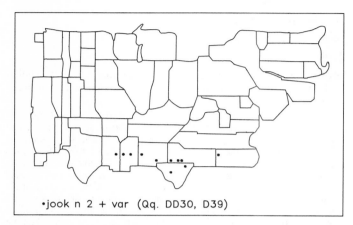

•jook n 2 + var (Qq. DD30, D39)

3 in comb *jook organ:* A jukebox; rarely, a player piano. **esp FL, GA**

1937 in 1938 *FL Rev.* Spring 25, The screeching of the "jook" organ. **1939** FWP *Guide FL* 5, To attract patronage he installed a 'jook organ' that would dispense Bronx-composed records of hillbilly laments at the drop of a nickel. **1939** *Time* 25 Dec 3 **cnFL,** [Letter:] To the Florida Man such an instrument is a jook-organ and nothing else. **1940** *Sat. Eve. Post* 13 Jan 17 **Gulf States,** A jook is any place that sells beer and has a nickel phonograph. . . The jook organ was cold going at it. [**1941** *Ibid* 26 Apr 20 **FL,** The term "jook" was coined in the turpentine camps of Northern Florida. It means a coin-operated magazine phonograph, usually called an "organ" in Florida.] **1941** *AmSp* 16.319 **sGA,** Feed the jouk-organ (nickelodeon). **1948** *Studies Ling.* 6.37 **sGA,** The player-piano, which was one of the common furnishings of such an establishment, became known as a *jook-organ.* **1981** Pederson *LAGS Basic Materials,* 1 inf, **swGA,** Juke organs [ˈdʒɹuᶜk ˌɔˑᵊgn̩z] = jukeboxes.

4 A night on the town.

1938 *FL Rev.* Spring 25/2 *(Mathews Coll.),* We had a swell jook Saturday night, went all over Jacksonville.

jook v³, hence vbl n *jooking* |ǰuk, ǰʊk, ǰʌk| Also sp *jouk, juke* **chiefly S Atl, esp FL** *esp freq among Black speakers*

1 To play (music) in the style typical of a **jook** n **2.**

1933 in 1968 *Bessie Jackson & Walter Roland* (Phonodisc), [Song title:] Jookit Jookit; [Lyrics:] Ah, jookit [jukɪt]! [*DARE* Ed: Pianist Walter Roland's style is characterized by rapid and percussive repetition of single notes, sixths, and octaves in the right hand over a steady bass in the left.] **1935** Hurston *Mules & Men* 185 **nFL** [Black], The jook was in full play when we walked in. The piano was throbbing like a stringed drum and the couples slow-dragging about the floor were urging the player on to new lows. "Jook, Johnnie, Ah know you kin spank dat ole pe-anner." "Jook it Johnnie!" [Footnote:] Play the piano in the manner of the jook or "blues." **1941** *AmSp* 16.319 **FL,** Mr. Lomax found Floridian Negroes applying *jouk* to a certain style of guitar playing in which the player, 'using a pattern of bass runs, played the melody on the tenor strings with a bottle neck on his little finger—Hawaiian fashion.' Characteristic expressions were 'jouk it boy,' 'I'm joukin' it now.' **1942** *Amer. Mercury* 55.95 **NYC** [Harlem slang], *Jooking*—playing the piano, guitar, or any musical instrument in the manner of the Jooks (pronounced like "took").

2 To dance, esp at a **jook** n **2;** to make the rounds (of **jooks**).

1937 in 1977 *Amer. Slave Suppl. 1* 1.234 **AL,** Young generation done gone, Satan got them, too much 'juking' these days, have no time to study 'bout the Lord . . , all they do is juke, juke, juke! *Ibid* 235, By "juking" Aunt Ellen meant rough dancing, perpetrated by the generation of tod[a]y. **1939** FWP *Guide FL* 133, Now to go 'jooking' means to attend any night club. **1941** *AmSp* 16.319 **sGA,** *Jouk* is defined by a South Georgia high school girl as 'dancing to *boogie-woogie* or *jive*

rhythm' of the *jouk* numbers. . . 'Let's jouk' is an invitation to dance, but 'let's go joukin' ' is a request for a date. **1958** Williams *Orpheus Descending* 22 **Sth,** I'd like to go out jooking with you tonight. . . That's where you get in a car and drink a little and drive a little and stop and dance a little to a juke-box. **1966** *DARE* (Qu. FF18, *Joking words . . about a noisy or boisterous celebration or party: "They certainly _____ last night."*) Inf **SC26,** Jooked it up, went jooking [ǰuk]; [had a [ǰuk] time;] (Qu. FF4, *Names and joking names for different kinds of dancing parties*) Inf **FL14,** Going jooking [ǰukɪn]; **FL28,** Going jooking [ǰukn̩]—going dancing to several different places in one evening—old-fashioned; **GA12,** Jooking [ǰukɪn]. **1969** Kantor *MO Bittersweet* 253, "Why do you call this jooking?" "That's because of what these cafes are called. Jooks. Or jook joints." "In England they'd call it pub-crawling." **1975** *AmSp* 50.62 **AR** [Juke . . 1: Dance. 2: Have a good time, especially at a party—"Let's juke; I don't feel like staying here to study." **1981** Pederson *LAGS Basic Materials,* 1 inf, **csAL,** Didn't want to go [əˈdʒɝᵊkn̩] (a-juking, honky-tonking, barhopping); *(A dance)* 1 inf, **neFL,** Juking [ˈdʒʌᵊkn̩]; 1 inf, **nwFL,** Juking [ˈdʒʊᵊkn̩]; 1 inf, **cwFL,** Go out juking [ˈdʒɹukɪn]. **1984** *WI State Jrl.* (Madison) 20 Dec sec 4 1 **cFL,** When I was a kid in Central Florida people said, "Let's go jookin." My own folks said it. They meant "Let's go dancing and partying at the roadhouse just outside the county line." The road-house was called a jook joint. In it was a jook box. It was spelled j-o-o-k and pronounced to rhyme with hook or book. I know this for a fact. But somehow, Yankees appropriated the word, corrupted it to "juke" and rhymed it with "duke."

jook house See **jook** n **2**

jooking See **jook** v³

jook joint See **jook** n **2**

jook organ See **jook** n **3**

joomoo See **jomo**

jopardy n [Pronc-sp for *jeopardy*]

1903 *DN* 2.318 **seMO,** Jeopardy. . . Pronounced jopardy. 'I want to get my land out of jopardy as soon as possible.' Said by a man whose farm was mortgaged.

jopiroot, jopiweed, Jo-Pye weed See **Joe-Pye weed**

Jordan n Usu |ˈjɔrdn̩, ˈjɔədn̩|; also **chiefly Sth, S Midl** |ˈjɝ(r)dn̩|; for addit varr see quots Pronc-spp *Jerdan, Jerden, Jerdon, Jurdan, Jurdin, Jurdon*

A Forms.

1800 in 1956 Eliason *Tarheel Talk* 313 **cnNC,** Jordan—Jurdin. **1928** *AmSp* 3.403 **Ozarks,** The proper name *Jordan,* which is rather common in the hill country, is always pronounced *Jerdan* or *Jurdan.* **1931** (1991) Hughes–Hurston *Mule Bone* 81 **cFL** [Black], I wouldn't give a poor consumpted cripple crab a crutch to cross the River Jurdon. **1931** *PMLA* 46.1316 **sAppalachians,** Jerdan. **1942** Hall *Smoky Mt. Speech* 34 **eTN, wNC,** Jordan [ǰɝdn̩]. **1951** *PADS* 15.56 **neIN** (as of 1890s), *Jerdon.* . . Jordan River. **1954** Harder Coll. **cwTN,** *Jerdon*—Jordan River. **c1960** Wilson Coll. **csKY,** Jordan is almost universally [ǰɝdən]. **1968** *DARE* (Qu. M16) Inf **GA68,** [ǰɝdn̩]. **1976** Garber *Mountain-ese* 47 **sAppalachians,** *Jerden* . . Jordan—John was baptized in the river Jerden.

B Sense.

See quot. [Euphem for *Jesus*]

1966 *Wilson Coll.* **csKY,** "Cold enough to freeze Jordan [ǰɝdən] off the cross." Often used by women.

joree n [Echoic]

1 also *jo-e, joree bird, ~ sparrow, joreeper, joe reed, ~ rick, joerigger; juree:* =rufous-sided towhee. **chiefly Sth, S Midl** Cf **joe-lee, joritte**

1851 *De Bow's Rev.* 11.54 **LA,** Joree—A kind of thrush, partly dark and yellow, living in the thickest briars; called *joree* from its song. **1884** Harris *Mingo* 179 **cGA,** We seem to agree, Brother Brannum, like the jay-bird and the joree,—the one in the tree and t'other on the ground. **1890** Warren *Birds PA* 244, The several terms, Towhee, Chewink, Juree and Shewink, by which this bird is known, are applied in imitation of its sharp, quick and rather petulant cry. **1908** *DN* 3.325 **eAL, wGA,** *Joree.* . . A small swamp bird; the swamp robin; so called from its song. Universal. **1913** *Auk* 30.499 **Okefenokee GA,** *Pipilo erythroph-thalmus.* . . 'Jo-e.' Fairly common among the saw-palmettos on the islands. **1919** Pearson et al. *Birds NC* 251, The towhee . . , most commonly known in this state as "Joree," "Joreeper," or "Joerigger," is found throughout the mountain region. **1926** *DN* 5.400 **Ozarks,** *Joree-bird.* . .

The Chewink or ground robin. **1940** (1941) Bell *Swamp Water* 32 **Okefenokee GA,** A joree ran along the leaf-littered sandbank, chirping with absent-minded friendliness and twisting his black-hooded head. **1944** *PADS* 2.19 **sAppalachians,** *Joree-bird* ['dʒorī-]. . . The chewink, of the towhee or sparrow family. **1966–68** *DARE* FW Addit **GA,** Joree ['jo͜ri] or [ˌjo͜'ri]—common south Georgia name for the towhee; **FL26,** Once in a while we get the jorees [ju'riz] at the feeder, but not often. **1967–69** *DARE* (Qu. Q14) Inf **LA2,** Joree [jo͜u'ri]; (Qu. Q16) Inf **NC49,** Joe ricks [jo rĭks]; (Qu. Q21, . . *Kinds of sparrows*) Inf **GA77,** Joree sparrow. **1968** *DARE* Tape **GA30,** This little bird, the towhee, we call him a joree [ˌjo'rī]. **1971** in 1983 Johnson *I Declare* 115 **nwFL,** With some affection, Gov. Marvin Griffin of Georgia called the fawners "jorees," after the friendly little birds that twitch their tails as they scratch and dip in the leaves for crumbs and grubs. **1982** Slone *How We Talked* 46 **eKY** (as of c1950), *Joe reed*—I don't know the real name for this bird, but it made a sound as if it was saying, "Joe Read."

2 A **loggerhead shrike** (here: *Lanius ludovicianus migrans*).
   1956 MA Audubon Soc. *Bulletin* 40.129 **ME,** Southern Shrike. . . Joree. . . Sonic.

joree v, hence vbl n *joree(n)ing*

1 To make fun of, tease; to insult.
   1941 Street *In Father's House* 25 **seMS,** Papa joreed Woody about the way he asked for things. *Ibid* 208, Ever'body was in a joreeing humor. **1965** *DARE* FW Addit **MS,** Joreening [jo'rinin]—joking or spoofing. Never heard use by anyone except Negroes. **1971** Dwyer *Dict. for Yankees* 28 **Sth, S Midl,** Joree—To make fun of, jest with or at, "Ever'body joreed him 'bout his long hair." **1984** Wilder *You All Spoken Here* 78 **Sth,** *Jawin' an' joreein':* Exchanging harsh words such as "You make my ass want to chew tobacco" and "You make my ass want to bite corn cobs."

2 with *around:* See quot.
   1965 *DARE* FW Addit **ceMS,** Joreening around—hurrying about.

joree bird See **joree** n 1

joree-grasel See **grasset 1**

joree(n)ing See **joree** v

joreeper, joree sparrow See **joree** n 1

joritte n Also *joreetz* [Prob LaFr varr of **joree** n 1]
=rufous-sided towhee.
   1916 *Times–Picayune* (New Orleans LA) 23 Apr mag sec 5, Towhee . . Joritte. . . This black and white and brown plumaged bird is a common inhabitant. **1921** LA Dept. of Conserv. *Bulletin* 10.106, The towhee is known under the names of chewink, joree, joritte, and ground robin. **1969** Longstreet *Birds FL* 148, Towhee. . . Other names . . Joreetz.

Joseph's coat n Also *Joseph coat* [In allusion to the patriarch Joseph and his coat of many colors; cf Genesis 37:3] **chiefly Sth**
Any of several plants with variegated leaves or flowers, as coleus (*Coleus* spp), a **goosefoot** (here: *Chenopodium amaranticolor*), **jewbush**, or an **amaranth** such as *Amaranthus tricolor*.
   1866 Lindley–Moore *Treas. Botany* 1.48, In the gardens of the Southern United States these hues are so richly developed as to have procured for it [=*Amaranthus tricolor*] the appellation of Joseph's Coat. **1894** *Jrl. Amer. Folkl.* 7.96, *Coleus Blumei,* Joseph's coat. General. **1897** *Ibid* 10.146, *Tradescantia crassifolia* . . (striped), Joseph's coat, Sulphur Grove, Ohio. **1929** Pope *Plants HI* 58, *Amaranthus.* . . the lasting color character of the flower . . is well represented in . . "Joseph's Coat" (*A. gangeticus*). **1946** Reeves–Bain *Flora TX* 112, C[henopodium] amaranticolor. . . Joseph's Coat. . . Leaf-blades . . bright red when young, becoming normal or pale (mealy) green. **1955** *S. Folkl. Qrly.* 19.234 **FL,** Pedalanthus [sic]. . . The variegated, white-flowered variety is called Joseph's Coat. **1966–70** *DARE* (Qu. S2) Inf **GA2,** Joseph's coat; (Qu. S26e) Inf **MS82,** Joseph's coat. **1969** *SC Market Bulletin* 11 Sept 4/5, Dutchmans pipe, Joseph coat, 35c doz. **1976** Bailey–Bailey *Hortus Third* 63, Alternanthera. . . Joseph's-coat. . . L[ea]v[e]s opp[osite], entire, green, or variously colored or variegated. *Ibid* 65, [Amaranthus] tricolor. . . In cult[ivation], plants usually have l[ea]v[e]s blotched and colored, and are then known as Joseph's-coat. **1990** Inter-State Nurseries *Roses* Spring 20, *Joseph's Coat.* This unusual multi-color variety [of rose] is appropriately named. . . Its tight buds are cardinal red, changing to marigold orange, then opening into flowers of bright yellow splashed with crimson, and finally turning cardinal red.

Joseph's staff n [Prob in allusion to the legend of St. Joseph's flowering staff] Cf **Jacob's staff 1**
=ocotillo.
   1949 Curtin *By the Prophet* 89 **AZ,** *Fouquieria splendens.* . . Common name . . Joseph's Staff. . . This spiny shrub with wand-like stems . . [has] bright scarlet flowers [which] decorate the sword-like tips during April and May.

Joses n [Minced form of *Jesus,* perh infl by *Moses* or *Joseph*] Cf **Jehoshaphat, jumping** adj 1
In phr *jumping Joses:* Used as a mild oath.
   1960 Bailey *Resp. to PADS 20* **KS,** Jumping Joses. **1966–68** *DARE* (Qu. NN30, *Exclamations beginning with the sound of 'j'*) Infs **IN42, MN26, MS1, 16, WA9, WV3, WI66,** Jumping Joses.

josey See **josie**

josh v Also with *around* [Cf *EDD joss* v. 1 "To crowd; to squeeze; to jostle" and 4 "To bump, jolt, shake"]
To jounce, jostle (something).
   1960 *AmSp* 35.238 **cwCA,** *Josh* [dʒɔʃ], 'to shake, jostle': 'Don't josh the baby around'; 'Josh it up and down in the bottle.' I have heard this term a number of times from . . Negroes. My own mother, originally a North Texan . . , makes frequent use of it. While most Negroes are familiar with this word in its meaning 'to tease or kid,' they have also heard it used in this other sense.

josh pear See **juice pear**

Joshua n Also *Joshua palm, ~ tree, ~ yucca* [See quot 1942]
A **yucca** (here: *Yucca brevifolia*) native to desert regions of the western US. Also called **tree yucca**
   1867 (1959) Jackson *Diaries* 15 Feb 1.134 **sCA,** Sage brush is used for cooking and the cactus or Joshuas, as I hear them called, for other fires. **1897** Sudworth *Arborescent Flora* 106, *Yucca arborescens.* . . Joshua Yucca. . . *Common Names.* . . The Joshua (Utah). Joshua Tree (Utah, Ariz., N. Mex.) **1929** Ellis *Ordinary Woman* 251 **CO** (as of early 20th cent), This is all desert country, covered with tufts of yucca, Joshua palms, and in the spring, beautiful flowers. **1942** Whipple *Joshua* 50 **UT** (as of c1860), Nearby grew a stunted, cactus-like tree with spiny branches; it looked like a gnarled dwarf with weird, extended arms. 'That's a Joshua tree,' explained Abijah. *Ibid* 51, Giant Joshuas. The Saints called 'em that because their twisted branches made 'em look like Joshua with his arms outstretched pointing the Israelites toward the Promised Land. **1966–70** *DARE* (Qu. S26a, . . *Wildflowers.* . . *Roadside flowers*) Inf **CA4,** Joshua; (Qu. S26e) Inf **CA60,** Joshua tree; **CA207,** Joshua tree bloom; (Qu. T16, . . *Kinds of trees . . 'special'*) Infs **CA1, 2, 4, 10, 62,** Joshua tree. **1976** Bruce *How to Grow Wildflowers* 165, The famous Joshua Tree of the Southwest is *Yucca brevifolia.* **1985** Dodge *Flowers SW Deserts* 24, *Joshua-tree.* . . Giant Joshua. . . The Joshua-tree is outstanding among the many species of yucca because of its short leaves growing in dense bunches or clusters, and because the plant has a definite trunk with numerous branches forming a crown.

josie n Also sp *josey* [Prob varr of *jersey,* but cf *joseph* a long cloak]

1 Any of several women's garments, esp a jacket; see quots. **chiefly Sth, S Midl**
   1844 in 1965 *AmSp* 40.130, De Boston gals got a new fashion: Little cloaks dey call dem Joseys. **1848** Bartlett *Americanisms* 192, A garment made of Scotch plaid, for an outside coat or habit, was worn in New England about the year 1830, called . . by some a Josey. **1853** in 1976 Rose *Doc. Hist. Slavery* 504 **LA,** Who's been here since I've been gone?/ Pretty little gal wid a josey on. **1859** Taliaferro *Fisher's R.* 19 **nwNC,** I visited them in 1857, and found "sacks" and "joseys" in full fashion. **1886** *Harper's New Mth. Mag.* 73.297 **LA,** And I hope to gracious you 'ain't made the josie too tight! I busts my josies awful. **1899** (1912) Green *VA Folk-Speech* 246, *Josey.* . . A little jacket, part of a girl's dress. **1927** Kennedy *Gritny* 12 **sLA** [Black], Her dress was a guinea blue, of plain make, the "josey" very close-fitting. **1945** Saxon *Gumbo Ya-Ya* 163 **LA,** The servants . . were given bright *tignons,* wide cotton aprons . . and checked calico 'josies.' **1953** Randolph–Wilson *Down in Holler* 257 **Ozarks,** *Josie.* . . A woman's garment, something like a long undershirt. The old-timers say it is derived from *joe-sack,* an old word for chemise or "shimmy." **1954** Harder *Coll.* **cwTN,** Josie.

2 A man's garment; see quots. Cf **jimmy** n 4
   1909 *DN* 3.413 **nME,** Josey. . . A garment worn by men. **1968** *DARE* (Qu. W4, . . *Men's coats or jackets for work and outdoor wear*) Inf **NJ7,** Josies—denim, like overalls.

joskin n [Engl dial]
1899 (1912) Green *VA Folk-Speech* 246, *Joskin*. . . A clownish fellow; a countryman.

jot n
A length or piece of plug tobacco.
1966–67 *DARE* (Qu. DD1, . . *Forms* . . *[of] chewing tobacco*) Inf **MI**2, Long bar, ready to be broken up into jots [jɑts]; **MI**54, Jot—plug used to be, but no more, used to press it in what were called jots [jɑts], maybe 14, 15 inches long. Cut a length off for you.

jota n |'hotə| Also sp *jotah* [Span] **esp CA, sID, eOR**
A Spanish dance.
1846 Robinson *Life in CA* 23, Singing or whistling the air of some favorite "*jota*". **1850** Buffum *6 Months* 143 **CA**, Often have I seen little girls . . dancing with great skill their favorite *jotah*. **1910** Hart *Vigilante Girl* 157 **nCA**, The *jota,* from Aragon, was a favorite; the *cuadrilla* and the *contra-danza* were very similar to the quadrilles and contra-dances of you Americans—these three were the decorous dances of the better classes. **1967** *DARE* (Qu. FF5a, . . *Different steps and figures in dancing—in past years*) Inf **OR**10, Jota ['hotə]—Basque. **1985** Attebery *ID Folklife* 98 **swID, eOR,** Among their [=Basque-American dancers'] repertoire is the *jota,* long considered the traditional Basque dance in Boise, Ontario, and Jordan Valley. *Ibid* 100, [Footnote:] A *fandango,* the *jota* is thought to have originated in Aragon rather than the Basque provinces.

jot-'em-down n
1968 *DARE* (Qu. C33, . . *Joking names* . . *for an out-of-the-way place, or a very small or unimportant place*) Inf **VA**13, Jot-'em-down.

joug See **joog**

jouk v¹ Also sp *jook, juke* [Scots, nEngl dial] **esp PA**
1 To duck, dodge; by ext: to evade; to hide. Cf **duke** v
1834 *Life Andrew Jackson* 230, They say *three hundred thousand dollars* was drawn from the Nashvil Bank tu aid your election, that there is positive proof of this, and that there isn't any way tu jouk it. **1890** *DN* 1.74 **ePA**, Jook [jŭk]: to avoid a blow by dodging. **1896** *DN* 1.419 **nOH**, Juke. . . To hide quickly. **1944** *PADS* 2.29 **eKY**, Djuke [sic] [dʒuk]. . . To incline or duck. "He djuked his head and looked right at the ground." . . Common. **1953** *AmSp* 28.250 **csPA**, Jouk. . . To duck, to dodge. Popular speech. **1966** *DARE* File **cwPA**, That's a low beam. Juke! **1968** *DARE* (Qu. JJ6, *To stay away from school without an excuse*) Inf **PA**104, Jouk school—old term. **1969** *DARE* File **seOH**, Juke—to jerk, esp the body or upper body. **1973** *Ibid* **swPA** (as of 1920s), Juke down. . . Bend when passing under something low. **1982** Barrick Coll. **csPA**, Juke—duck, dodge. **1982** Heat Moon *Blue Highways* 99 **AL** [Black], On the basketball court, Walker was alone, juking and shooting.
2 with *around:*
a To skulk.
1904 (1913) Johnson *Highways South* 252 **WV**, Brown [=John Brown] didn't molest nobody exceptin' those that carried weapons, or that was jukin' round whar they had no business.
b See quot.
1913 Johnson *Highways St. Lawrence to VA* 165 **csPA**, He was about three parts in whiskey or perhaps he would n't have been so loud about it. He juked around in the crowd makin' his brag.

jouk v² See **jook** v³

jouk n See **jook** n

jouk around See **jouk** v¹ **2**

jounce v [Cf *EDD* jounce v. 2 "To use some violent action by which the shape of a thing is altered"]
1952 Brown *NC Folkl.* 1.555, Jounce. . . To whip, beat.—West.

jour See **jower** v

journeycake n Also *journey (bread)* [Prob folk-etym for *johnnycake*]
=johnnycake 1.
1754 in 1925 Fries *Rec. Moravians* 2.531 **NC**, We kept a Lovefeast with the Journey Cakes, and afterwards a blessed Communion. **1775** (1962) Romans *Nat. Hist. FL* 125, It [=rice] is (for our use) only fit for puddings, and to put in soops, or to make the wafer-like bread called journey cakes in Carolina. **1835** in 1956 Eliason *Tarheel Talk* 279 **NC**, I have been trying to instruct our cook in the practical parts of breakfast

operations—as making biscuit & Journey cake. **1852** Reynolds *Pioneer Hist. IL* 265, The bread used at these frolics . . was baked generally on jonny, or *journey*-cake boards. **1868** Channing *Recollections* 25 **RI** (as of c1800), The "journey-cake," vulgarly called *Johnny-cake*—how can I sufficiently extol it? **1896** *DN* 1.419 **NY**, Journey cake . . for johnny cake. **1915** *DN* 4.239 [Colonial cookery terms], *Journey bread.* Johnny bread:—originally so called because Indian corn bread was often carried by travelers. **1968** *DARE* (Qu. H14, *Bread that's made with cornmeal*) Inf **CT**5, Journeycake—you could take corn and grind it as you needed it; now johnnycake. **1969** Sorden *Lumberjack Lingo* 64 **NEng, Gt Lakes,** *Journey* or *journey cake*—A corn pone bread baked in a reflector oven. A johnny cake.

journey-proud adj **chiefly Sth, S Midl**
1 Excited and restless at the prospect of a trip. [*EDD* (at journey sb. 6)] Cf **proud**
1891 *AN&Q* 8.27, I have heard New Englanders speak of a person as *journey-proud,* meaning that one is so elated on the eve of a journey as to care nothing for food. **1952** Brown *NC Folkl.* 1.555 **nwNC,** Journey-proud. . . So excited over the prospect of a journey that one cannot eat or sleep. . . Old people. Rare. **1969** Emmons *Deep Rivers* 59 **eTX** [Black], Journey-proud. . . But who ever did so well describe the sleeplessness, loss of appetite, and general excitement which one experiences on the eve of a trip? **1969** *Tennessean* (Nashville TN) 2 Nov sec E 1, Journey-proud. . . Southerners, brought up with the phrase, will understand what I mean. . . There's a delicious complex of emotions and activity centered around getting ready to go on a trip. *Ibid* 6/1, Being journey-proud is wrapping all these vague, unspelled-out, and nameless but genuine elements around one's shoulders. **1972** *DARE* File, *Journey-proud*—pleased and excited over a journey. Said to be "Old South." Used by a woman of 55–60 years, born and lived in Arkansas, with family background from Virginia. **1973** *Patrick Coll.* **cAL,** *Journey proud*—fussily eager to start going.
2 Conceited because one has traveled.
1952 Brown *NC Folkl.* 1.555 **seNC**, Journey-proud. . . Acting in a superior manner because one has travelled. . . Common. **1965** *Dict. Queen's English* 8 **NC**, She was so journey proud when she returned from the city she couldn't stop talking about her trip.

Jove's fruit n
1 A **spicebush** (here: *Lindera melissifolia*).
1866 Lindley–Moore *Treas. Botany* 2.639, Jove's-fruit. *Lindera melissaefolia.* **1889** *Century Dict.* 3243, *Jove's-fruit.* . . A shrub, *Lindera melissæfolius,* native in the United States, and related to wild allspice. **1933** Small *Manual SE Flora* 924, *B[enzoin] melissaefolium.* . . *Jove's-fruit.* . . Bushes make a brilliant show in early spring. **1953** Greene-Blomquist *Flowers South* 78, "Jove's-fruit" . . is more showy with larger flowers. **1976** Bailey–Bailey *Hortus Third* 667, *Jove's fruit.* . . Wet places, very local, N.C. and s.Mo., s. to Fla. and La.
2 =**persimmon.**
1876 Hobbs *Bot. Hdbk.* 60, Jove's fruit, Persimmon, Diospyros [sic] Virginiana. **1900** Lyons *Plant Names* 137, *D[iospyros] Virginiana.* . . Jove's-fruit. **1960** Vines *Trees SW* 838, Persimmon. . . Vernacular names are Jove's-fruit . . and Possum-wood.

jow v |jaʊ| [Cf *EDD* jow v.³ "To talk loud"] Cf **jar** v¹ **B1, jower** v, **jowl** v
To jaw; to argue; to banter.
1880 *Atlantic Mth.* Jan 101 **Allegheny Mts,** But law, I can't stand hyar all day jowin' 'bout Rufus Chadd! **1908** *DN* 3.325 **eAL, wGA,** Jow. . . To jaw, talk in a scolding manner. "We jowed for 'bout an hour." **1952** Brown *NC Folkl.* 1.555, Jow [dʒaʊ]. . . To talk loud and angrily.—General. **1968** Haun *Hawk's Done Gone* 209 **eTN,** There wasn't any sense to gals jowing and carrying on with every stinking boy that come along. He didn't aim for her to ever spark anybody.

jower v, hence vbl n *jowering* |'jaʊə(r)| Also with *around* Also sp *jour* [*OED* "dial. and local U.S." 1628 →] **chiefly Sth, S Midl** *somewhat old-fash*
To quarrel loudly, scold; to growl, grumble; to jaw; hence adj *jowery.*
1767 *Boston Eve.–Post* (MA) 23 Nov [4/1] **MA**, [The dog] snarls and jowers at friends as well as foes. **1883** (1971) Harris *Nights with Remus* 32 **GA** [Black], W'en dey git der h'ar smoove down, dey 'gun ter jower 'mongs deyse'f. **1891** Johnston *Primes & Neighbors* 124 **GA**, He ain't a-pesterin' hisself about how much them lawyers palavvers, and jaws, and jowers 'ith one 'nother and the jury. **1892** *DN* 1.230 **KY**, Jower

[ĵauə]: to quarrel. **1899** (1912) Green *VA Folk-Speech* 246, *Jower.* . . To quarrel with much confused talk; all talking together. *Ibid*, *Jowery.* . . Given to scolding; growling; grumbling. **1903** *DN* 2.318 **seMO**, *Jower* . . to discuss in a wordy manner. **1905** *DN* 3.84 **nwAR**, *Jower.* . . To quarrel. **1908** *DN* 3.325 **eAL, wGA**, *Jower.* . . To quarrel, talk in a loud, scolding tone. **1912** *DN* 3.579 **wIN**, Stop jowering around now and go to bed. **1923** *DN* 5.212 **swMO**, *Jar.* . . To wrangle, to quarrel, to argue. Also *Jower.* **1927** *DN* 5.475 **Ozarks**, *Jower.* . . To argue, to quarrel, to complain. **1942** Thomas *Blue Ridge Country* 25 **Appalachians**, Instead of jowering, she would give him a good scrubbing. **1952** Brown *NC Folkl.* 1.555, *Jower, jour* ['dʒauə, -ɚ]. . . Quarreling, incessant talking; to quarrel, to talk constantly. *c1960* Wilson *Coll.* **csKY**, *Jower.* . . To quarrel, chew the rag, argue. **1968** *DARE* (Qu. KK13, . . *Arguing: "They stood there for an hour _____."*) Inf **IN40**, They jowered ['jawɚd] around.

jower n [jower v] Sth, S Midl

A quarrel, noisy argument.

1891 *PMLA* 6.175 **TN**, Jower is a word in common use for a quarrel in which noise plays the principal part. "I got into a jower with him." **1903** *DN* 2.318 **seMO**, A quarrel. **1908** *DN* 3.325 **eAL, wGA**, *Jower.* . . A wordy quarrel. "We got up a big jower." **1913** Kephart *Highlanders* 294 **sAppalachians**, If he and his neighbor dislike each other, there is a hardness between them; if they quarrel, it is a ruction, a rippit, a jower, or an upscuddle. **1927** *DN* 5.475 **Ozarks**, *Jower.* . . The word is also used as a noun: "They done had a little jower, 'pears like." **1952** [see **jower** v]. **1954** *Harder Coll.* **cwTN**. **1966** *DARE* (Qu. Y12a, *A fight between two people, mostly with words*) Inf **AL3**, Jower [ĵɔwɚ]. **1981** Harper–Presley *Okefinokee* 142 (as of a1951), *Jower—* Quarrel. . . "Look like they had a jower."

jower around, jowering See jower v

jowery See jower v

jo-wheet n Also *jewee, joe-wheat, jo-wink* [Echoic]
=rufous-sided towhee.

1822 Latham *Genl. Hist. Birds* 5.343, [The towhe bunting] is found in Georgia, and called chew-wink, or Joe wheat. **1932** Bennitt *Check-list* 61 **MO**, *Red-eyed towhee.* . . Jewee, ground robin. **1936** *Sun* (Baltimore MD) 17 Feb 7/2 (*Hench Coll.*), One side asserts it has seen "robins" hopping about in the snow; the opponents are scornful—they're not robins, but "go-wanks," or if that name fails to strike a responsive chord, they're towhees, bush-birds, chewinks, go-winks, jo-winks, or just plain swamp robins. **1955** *Oriole* 20.1.13 **GA**, *Eastern Towhee.* . . Jo-wheet (sonic). **1956** MA Audubon Soc. *Bulletin* 40.254, *Towhee.* . . Jo-wheet (Mass. Sonic.)

jowl n Usu |ĵoul, ĵɔl|; also |ĵaul|; for addit varr see quots Pronc-spp *jole, joll, jual* Often in combs *hog('s) jowl* **chiefly Sth, S Midl** See Map

The cheek meat of a hog prepared as food; see quots.

1859 Taliaferro *Fisher's R.* 220 **nwNC** (as of 1820s), Mose Cackerham ate up the back-bones of several hogs, and their joles. **1898** Dunbar *Folks from Dixie* 103 **KY**, There was hog jole and cold cabbage. **1899** (1912) Green *VA Folk-Speech* 246, *Jowl.* . . The lower jaw of a hog, prepared for the table: as, "jowl and turnip sallet." **1931** *Durant Daily Democrat* (OK) 14 Jan 1/7, Boiled turnips and hog jowl will be the principal items on the menu. **1942** McAtee *Dial. Grant Co. IN* 37 (as of 1890s), *Jowl* . . disk-shaped muscle from the cheek of a pig, regarded as a delicacy. **1952** Tracy *Coast Cookery* 229 **TN**, *Hog's Jowl and Turnip Greens with Potlikker.* . . The jowl must have that special smoke and cured flavor about it. **1956** Ker *Vocab. W. TX* 270, [Salt pork; home-cured bacon:] *Jowl meat* . . one old-timer . . and *joll* by one. **1965–70** *DARE* (Qu. H38, . . *Words for bacon [including joking ones]*) Infs **IN76, KY62, 79, 81, 84**, Jowl bacon; **IN82**, Jowl; **KY37**, [ĵoəl] meat; **MI88**, [ĵɔl]—chunky bacon you slice yourself; it's spelled *joll;* **OH42**, Jowl meat is fresh pork; **SC22**, [ĵɔⱽlz]; **VA72**, [ĵol]; **VA98**, Hog [ĵowl]; (Qu. H43, *Foods made from parts of the head and inner organs of an animal*) Infs **GA11, OR1**, Hog jowl(s); **NY92**, Hog [ĵaulz]; **NC82**, Hog's jowl; **SC51**, [ĵolz]; **TN5**, Hog [ĵoul]; **VA48**, Jowl; (Qu. H45, *Dishes made with meat, fish, or poultry that everybody around here would know, but that people in other places might not*) Inf **FL30**, Hog's [ĵoulz] and black-eyed peas; always served on New Year's Day for good luck; (Qu. H50) Inf **SC21**, [ĵɔwl]—required eating for New Year's Day; **TN64**, Hog jowl and black-eyed peas. **1966** *DARE* Tape **FL31**, We get the dried black-eyed peas from the store and the hog jowl [ĵo:l] comes smoked and already packaged up and I always cook it every New Year's for dinner; **MS75**, [FW:] Didn't you say you had hog jowl instead

of hog head? [Inf:] Hog jowl, either one is the head. . . the jowls of the head. **1967** Faries *Word Geog. MO* 124, Terms [for *scrapple*] . . occurring only occasionally . . *jowl bacon, jowls.* **1969** *Weakley Co. Press* (Martin TN) 2 Oct 8, [Advt:] Sugar Cured Sliced Jowls lb. 49¢. **1972** *Atlanta Letters* **csGA**, Hog jowl. . . To eat hog jowl and peas on New Year [is traditional]. Rhymes with bowl, soul. *Ibid* **nwGA**, Hogs jual.

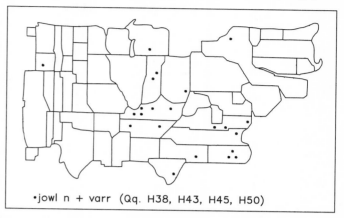

•jowl n + varr (Qq. H38, H43, H45, H50)

jowl v, hence vbl n *jowling* [*OED* jowl v.2 "*Obs. exc. dial.*"] Cf jower v
See quots.

1902 *DN* 2.237 **sIL**, *Jowling.* . . Talking together privately. **1906** *DN* 3.143 **nwAR**, *Jowl* [ĵaul]. . . To quarrel (used of dogs and children). "The dogs were jowling around there." "Can't those children quit their infernal jowling?"

joyce See joist 1

joy jumper See jumper 15

joy-killer n [Var of *killjoy;* cf Intro "Language Changes" I.1]
See quots.

1927 *Ruppenthal Coll.* **KS**, *Joy killer*—a pessimist; one who always sees the reverse side of any good thing. **1966–69** *DARE* (Qu. GG14, *Names and nicknames for someone who fusses or worries a lot, especially about little things*) Inf **AR31**, Joy-killer; (Qu. HH16, *Uncomplimentary words with no definite meaning—just used when you want to show that you don't think much of a person: "Don't invite him. He's a _____."*) Infs **IA9, KY65, MO15, NH10, UT5**, Joy-killer.

joy-leaf n
A **rattlesnake root** (here: *Prenanthes alba* or *P. altissima*).

1940 Clute *Amer. Plant Names* 71, *P[renanthes] alba.* . . Joy-leaf. . . *P. altissimus.* . . Joy-leaf. **1959** Carleton *Index Herb. Plants* 69, *Joy-leaf:* Prenanthes alba (Nabalus albus).

joy-of-the-mountain n
Trailing **arbutus.**

1928 Chapman *Happy Mt.* 20 **TN**, Times past, joy-o'-the-mountain would grow so thick you'd scarce have to stir a leaf to find it. *Ibid* 312, *Joy o' the Mountain*—trailing arbutus.

J-pit See jay hole

jual See jowl n

juba n Also sp *joober, jubah, juber* [Perh Afr; cf *DJE* Juba, day-name in Twi for women born on Monday] **chiefly Sth**
1 A dance of plantation Blacks involving rhythmic hand clapping and body patting—freq in phrr *dance juba, pat juba;* hence n *juba-pat, juba-patting;* also fig. *hist*

1834 Caruthers *Kentuckian* 1.113, A man looks so unromantic with his teeth, and his hands, and his feet all in motion like a negro dancing 'Juba.' **1837** Raleigh (N.C.) *Standard* 25 Oct. 3/4 (1939 Thornton *Amer. Gloss.*), Your last potato is "*dancing Juba*" to the melancholy music of a tea kettle. **1899** (1912) Green *VA Folk-Speech* 247, *Juba.* . . A negro dance. One sang, patting his hands together, and on his thighs, keeping time with his foot, while one or more danced to the music. *Ibid*, *Juba-patting.* . . The patting on the knee or thigh practiced by negroes in keeping time to the juba-dance. **1899** Garland *Boy Life* 152 **nwIA** (as of c1870s), Jack, the first hired man, was a most amazing dancer of negro breakdowns, and the boys delighted to get him at it of an evening in the kitchen, and patted "juber" for him, while he shuffled and double-shuffled and hoed-down and side-stepped, and drummed with heel and toe on the floor. **1903** *DN* 2.324 **seMO**, *Pat juba*. . . To pat the knees for singing or dancing. A negro custom. **1930** *Copeia* 97 **ceNC** (as of 1878), Very soon young negro boys began to bring us specimens. . . Dr. Jordan began to make a study of these boys. In a note-book, he wrote each boy's name, his age, color (whether black, dark, yellow or tan), kind of hair (whether simply black and wooly, kinky, or pepper-corn), and what his specialty was—whether singing, dancing, patting jubah, or what. **c1937** in 1972 *Amer. Slave* 2.242 **SC**, We had what was called a 'Juber' game. He would dance a jig and sing, 'Juber this, Juber that, Juber killed a yellow cat'. **1955** Warren *Angels* 116 **LA** (as of 1850s), Some eighty or ninety Negroes were there. . . When we came over the levee, they yelled and clapped hands and patted their feet, yelling, "Massa, Massa—Massa, high-juba." *Ibid* 121, The most feared punishment, past things like short pork rations or banishment from the Saturday night juba-pat, was the "finger-pointing." **1968** Stearns–Stearns *Jazz Dance* 28 **Sth** [Black] (as of a1860), The Juba step itself is described as going around in a circle with one foot raised—a sort of eccentric shuffle—and it is danced by the surrounding circle of men before and after each performance of the two men in the center. Both the words and the steps are in call-and-response form, and the words must ring out as rhythmically as a drummer's solo. The two men in the center start the performance with the Juba step while the surrounding men clap, and then switch to whatever new step is named in the call.

2 By ext; in phr *dance juba*: To move or jump about violently, esp as a result of a whipping.
1890 *DN* 1.65 **KY**, *Joober*. . . "To make a child *dance joober*" is to whip him. **1929** *AmSp* 5.17 **Ozarks**, *Dance juber*. . . To leap about wildly, as one in pain. "Th' ol' man he cut him a good hick'ry, an' he shore did make them boys dance juber!" **1954** *Harder Coll.* **cwTN**, *Dance juber*. . . To dance or jump violently.

Juba bush See **Juba's bush**

jubah See **juba**

jubajawed adj [Var of **jimberjawed 1**]
1969 *DARE* (Qu. X6, *If a person's lower jaw sticks out prominently . . he's _____*) Inf **AL56**, Jubajawed.

juba-pat(ting) See **juba 1**

Juba's bush n Also *Juba bush, Juba's brush*
A **bloodleaf** (here: *Iresine celosia*).
1889 *Century Dict.* 3245, *Juba's-bush, Juba's-brush*. . . The plant *Iresine celosioides*. **1914** Georgia *Manual Weeds* 126, *Juba's Bush*. . . A very conspicuous weed because of its white flowers and the red color which the foliage often assumes. **1930** *OK Univ. Biol. Surv. Pub.* 2.60, *Iresine paniculata*. . . Blood-leaf. Juba's Bush. **1935** (1943) Muenscher *Weeds* 218, Jubas bush. . . A weed . . in the southern states. It has opposite leaves and large showy panicles of small silvery-white flowers. **1959** Carleton *Index Herb. Plants* 69, *Juba-bush*: Iresine paniculata. **1970** Correll *Plants TX* 564, *Juba's bush*. . . Mostly along the coast, N.C. to Fla., w. to Tex.

jubbers See **dubious A3**

juber See **juba**

juberous, jubers See **dubious A3**

jubersome See **dubious A4**

juberus See **dubious A3**

jubilee n
An episode during which shallow bays in the Gulf of Mexico teem with fish and shellfish that are easily caught; see quots.
1956 Rayford *Whistlin' Woman* 145 **AL**, Some men say that even the jubilees are caused when fish eat in these polluted areas. Jubilees are mysterious things. It is said that they occur nowhere in the world except on the eastern shore of Mobile Bay. . . The fish get drunk at nip (neap) tide. Nobody understands it. Crabs and flounders and other fish come into the shallowest water and people gather them in by the tub full. **1967** *DARE* Tape **AL9**, The thing we call jubilees—this only occurs in Mobile and another place somewhere on the Mediterranean. . . It's an occurrence . . that no one can explain, usually happens late at night, early in the morning. . . It's when the fish and crabs, shrimp, eels, stingrays, and flounder come into the shore in a sort of a dazed state, and you can pick 'em up with scoop nets, stab your flounders with a . . gig . . you can pick the crabs up with your hands, but you have to be very careful because of the eels and the stingrays, . . lots of people step on 'em and get hurt. People catch as many as 250 pounds. . . Make crab gumbo and

everybody hollers "Jubilee" and from miles around people on the beach come down screaming in their pajamas. *Ibid* **AL22A**, Just on the eastern shore of Mobile Bay. . . A jubilee usually happens in August or September . . and . . can be predicted by some old-timers on the basis of these precedents, by a wind off the shore, a very calm day the day before, a land breeze, and a tide which will . . begin to come in after midnight . . and the jubilee more or less comes in with the tide. . . They [=jubilees] begin in calm water ninety-nine times out of a hundred and it affects mainly the fish that live closest to the bottom: flounder, eel, stingray, crab, shrimp, and it also affects mullet a great deal. . . You do have some jubilees that affect only one species; for some reason you have what you call a crab jubilee, where maybe there are only five flounders taken and just tubful after tubful of crabs. . . And then you have a shrimp jubilee and a flounder jubilee, but you never have anything like an eel or a stingray jubilee, although . . there's a little bit of everything in every jubilee. . . As soon as daylight comes it [=the jubilee] begins to wane. . . Sometimes . . it'll be a big jubilee as far as the quantity of fish but it won't cover more than a half a mile of beach . . and at other times . . there'll be a jubilee from . . a distance of . . close to twenty-five miles. . . Some of the old people believe that the moon has something to do with it. **1992** *NADS Letters*, My daddy was born in 1891 and talked about going to the beach for a "jubilee" when he was a boy in Mobile, Alabama. . . [W]hen heavy rains have the rivers . . emptying an unusual amount of fresh water into the bay, the salinity level drops below what the fish and shellfish can tolerate. . . For some reason, jubilees occur most often at night. . . [I]f anyone . . saw the jubilee, he . . passed the word along the shore. People got up and ran down to the water's edge with torches and . . lanterns and started gathering the bounty. . . [P]eople frequently started bonfires and cooked and ate right then and there. . . As late as the 1950's this was still happening on the east side of the bay. . . There are some other bays along the Mississippi and Florida coasts where I have heard the term used.

Jubilee Day n
=**Juneteenth**.
1976 *WI State Jrl.* (Madison) 21 June 29, Jubilee Day or Juneteenth Day was originally celebrated in the Southwest and is still celebrated in places like Texas.

jubious See **dubious A1**

jub(o)us See **dubious A2**

juck n[1], v See **jerk** n[1], v[1]

juck n[2] See **jook** n

juckers n Also *juck(ie)s* [Prob euphem for *Jesus*] *old-fash* Cf **jocks**
Used as a mild oath—usu in phr *by juckers* and varr.
1859 Taliaferro *Fisher's R.* 36 **nwNC** (as of 1820s), No, by juckers! **1894** Riley *Armazindy* 1 **IN**, Name ain't down in *History*,—But, i jucks! it *ort* to be! **1927** *DN* 5.473 **Ozarks**, *By juckies!* . . An exclamation denoting surprise or excitement. **1931** *PMLA* 46.1308 **sAppalachians**, By juckers! **1933** Williamson *Woods Colt* 3 **Ozarks**, By juckies you're bound to take a journey in the same direction what you heerd it [=the sound of a turtle dove] from. **1934** (1943) *W2*, *Juckies*. . . An exclamation expressing excitement, surprise, etc.

Judas n Pronc-sp *Judast* [Minced form of *Jesus*] **chiefly Nth, N Midl, esp NEast** See Map
Used as a mild oath—often in phrr *Judas priest, by Judas, jumping Judas*, and varr.
1901 *DN* 2.142 **cNY**, *Jumping Judas*. . . Used in an oath. "By the jumping Judas." **1907** Lincoln *Cape Cod* 31 **MA**, "Judas!" says Jonadab, "there's somebody *coming!*" **1916** Lincoln *Mary-'Gusta* 121 **MA**, By the jumpin' Judas! **1922** Lewis *Babbitt* 126, Judas Priest, I could write poetry myself if I had a whole year for it. **1924** *DN* 5.271 **ME** [Exclams], Judas Priest. **1950** *WELS* (*Exclamations beginning with the sound of 'j'*) 7 Infs **WI**, Judas priest; **1959** *VT Hist.* 27.145, By Judas! . . Rare. *Ibid*, Judas Priest! . . Common. **1965–70** *DARE* (Qu. NN30) 26 Infs, **chiefly Nth, N Midl, esp NEast**, Judas priest; **ME22, NY22, 92, RI8, WI55**, Judas; **OR10, VT16**, Jumped-up Judas; **ME22**, By Judas; **IL25**, Jumping Judas; **NY9**, Holy Judas priest; **NY234**, By Judast; (Qu. NN8a) Inf **CT36**, Judas; Judas priest; (Qu. NN9a) Inf **CT36**, Judas priest; **MA20**, Oh Judas; (Qu. NN20a) Inf **CT36**, Judas priest; (Qu. NN23) Inf **CT36**, Judas priest; (Qu. NN27a) Inf **UT6**, Judas; (Qu. NN29c) Inf **MO7**, Judas priest. **1966** Barnes–Jensen *Dict. UT Slang* 21, *Great jumping Judas!*: an exclamation of astonishment. **1966–67** *DARE* FW Addit **ME22**, Judas priest—exclamation similar to "I'll be

damned"; by Judas—exclamation like "by God"; **neNY,** Judas priest—an exclamation; by Judas; **seOR,** Judas priest—Jesus Christ.

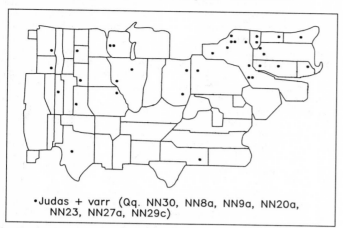

•Judas + varr (Qq. NN30, NN8a, NN9a, NN20a,
NN23, NN27a, NN29c)

Judas bird n [See quot 1874]
=**dickcissel.**

1874 Coues *Birds NW* 166, In Illinois, Mr. Ridgway tells me, it is called "Judas-bird" . . in allusion to its song. **1898** (1900) Davie *Nests N. Amer. Birds* 406, *Dickcissel.* . . Known as the Black-throated Bunting, "Little Field Lark," and "Judas-bird." **1910** Wayne *Birds SC* 135, The Black-throated Bunting or "Judas-bird" breeds at Augusta, Georgia, as well as in Aiken and Fairfield counties, South Carolina. **1950** *PADS* 14.42 **SC,** Judas bird. . . The dickcissel, the black-throated bunting.

Judas goat n Similarly nouns *Judas buffalo,* ~ *bull,* ~ *ewe,* ~ *steer* [In ref to *Judas* Iscariot, apostle who betrayed Jesus]
A goat (or other animal) used to lead sheep (or other animals) to slaughter; fig, of persons: one who leads others to their destruction; one who serves as a decoy or lure.

1939 FWP *Guide IL* 295 **neIL,** "Judas goats," trained rams, are still used to lead lambs from their pens to the slaughter. **1941** *AmSp* 16.236 **NE** [Stockyard and packing house lingo], Sheep are led to the shackling pen by a *Tony* or *Judas* goat. The *Judas* goats are trained to know the paths from the sheep pens to the slaughter houses. **1944** Adams *Western Words* 85, *Judas steer*—One used at slaughterhouses and so trained that he leads others to slaughter. He is then returned to lead others. **1958** in 1977 Kornbluth *Best* 326, "Forward march, boys," she shrilled at them. "Wouldn't y'all just like to follow me?" Seductive smile and a wiggle of the rump; a Judas ewe. She strutted off in time to the music. . . They shuffled after her. **1965** Liberty Lobby *J. William Fulbright: Freedom's Judas-Goat.* **1978** MN Div. Parks *Blue Mounds State Park* np **swMN,** A brave served as a "judas buffalo." Wrapped in a buffalo robe, he lured the herd to the cliff edge where hunters lay hidden in the rocks. The Indians leaped from their hiding places screaming and waving scare-robes. Then, forming a human corral, they stampeded the herd over the edge. **1979** *DARE* File **SD,** "Part of the operation [at a packing plant in Sioux Falls] included killing of sheep. The animals had to walk up a ramp to the door of the killing area. . . Apparently it is hard to chase sheep, but they will follow quite readily. . . So they had trained a goat to lead the way up the ramp and the sheep would follow." . . When he . . first described this critter to me, he called it a "Judas goat." . . A 60-year old Madison [WI] friend tells me about what he calls a "Judas bull". . . who's used to lead other cattle to the slaughter house. **1982** Del Vecchio *13th Valley* 366, "We bein Judas Goats fo a whiteman's operation," Jax said. "They sendin' us down here ta git slaughtered so they know right where ta drop the bombs."

Judas priest See **Judas**

Judas steer See **Judas goat**

Judast See **Judas**

Judas tree n Also *flowering Judas* [*OED* 1668 →; see quots 1850, 1961]
=**redbud.**

1785 Marshall *Arbustrum* 32, *Red-bud, or Judas Tree.* . . This grows naturally in several parts of North-America. . . The flowers . . are of a fine red colour and coming out before the leaves, make a beautiful appearance. **1849** Howitt *Our Cousins in OH* 70, The . . trees were also beginning to be very beautiful in the woods; . . here and there the purplish pink of the red-bud, shining out from the margin of the forest

and on the hill sides. The red-bud was the name given by the Indians. It was also called the Judas-tree, from the circumstance that bees were said to fall down dead beneath its shade, from the poisonous quality of the honey. **1850** *New Engl. Farmer* 2.411, The American Judas-tree, sometimes called the Red Bud, is an early flowering, small tree. . . It received the appellation of Judas-tree from the supposition that it was the one on which the traitor hung himself. **1897** Parsons *Wild Flowers CA* 198, By April, or earlier, our interior hills and valleys begin to show the rosy blossoms of the Judas-tree. **1901** Lounsberry *S. Wild Flowers* 259, About our American plants, we find very frequently that it has been through their similarity to European ones that the early settlers of this country bestowed on them certain common names. So this beautiful plant [=*Cercis canadensis*] is called Judas-tree, as is the European species, . . although it could never have been the traditionary one from which the Apostle is said to have hung himself. **1930** (1935) Porter *Flowering Judas* 160 **TX,** From the Judas tree he stripped the warm bleeding flowers. **1937** Thornburgh *Gt. Smoky Mts.* 20, There is the rose tint of redbud, or Judas tree; the white of service, . . silver bell . . ; the fragrant blossoms of . . the mountain magnolia or cucumber tree. **1961** Douglas *My Wilderness* 191 **MD,** The redbud. . . is sometimes called the Judas tree, from the legend that it is the tree on which Judas Iscariot hanged himself. Its flowers, once said to be white, turned red with blood; and they grow right out of the branches. **1965–70** *DARE* (Qu. T16, . . *Kinds of trees . . 'special'*) 12 Infs, **esp Sth, S Midl,** Judas tree; **TX40,** Flowering Judas; (Qu. S26e) Inf **CA**87, Judas tree; (Qu. T9) Infs **GA**18, **OH**37, Judas tree. **1981** Benson–Darrow *Trees SW Deserts* 250, *Judas Tree.* . . Distinguished readily . . by its simple, kidney- or bean-shaped leaves. . . [and] pink and lavender flowers, which superficially resemble those of the sweet pea.

judge n, v |jʌj|; also **esp Sth, S Midl** |jɛj|; for addit varr see quots Pronc-spp *je(r)dge, jidge* Similarly nouns *jedgment, jergment*
A Forms.

1832 in 1956 Eliason *Tarheel Talk* 313 **neNC,** Judge—jidge. **1848** Lowell *Biglow* 145 'Upcountry' **MA,** Jedge, judge. **1894** Frederic *Marsena* 145 **nNY,** I tell you the War's a jedgment on this country for its wickedness. **1899** Chesnutt *Conjure Woman* 191 **csNC** [Black], Ole missis 'lowed [=supposed] it was a jedgment on 'im fer sump'n he'd done. **1903** *DN* 2.318 **seMO,** Judge. . . Pronounced jedge. **1907** *DN* 3.232 **nwAR, seMO,** Judge, n. and v. Pronounced jedge. **1908** *DN* 3.324 **eAL, wGA,** Jedge, n. and v. Judge. A common illiterate pronunciation. *Jedgment.* . . Judgment. **1914** *DN* 4.75 **nNH, ME,** Jedgment. **1915** [see **B1** below]. **1921** Haswell *Daughter Ozarks* 28 (as of 1880s), Farmer, doctor, parson, jedge. **1952** Brown *NC Folkl.* 1.554, Jedge [dʒɛdʒ]: pronc. Judge.—General. Illiterate. **c1970** Pederson *Dial. Surv. Rural GA,* [In rural southeast Georgia, *judge* is most frequently pronounced [dʒʌˑdʒ] or [dʒʌ·ɪdʒ]; infrequently it occurs as [dʒɛdʒ], [dʒʊdʒ], or [dʒɝ·dʒ].] **1972** *Atlanta Letters,* Tell it to the jerdge. **1976** Garber *Mountain-ese* 47 **sAppalachians,** Jedgment-day. **1986** *DARE* File **Ozarks,** Jergment (judgement).

B As noun.

1 Used as a form of address to, or a courtesy title for, a lawyer or justice of the peace.

1869 Browne *Adventures* 394 **NV,** My friend was called the Judge, though I believe he claimed to be no higher rank than an attorney at law. All popular lawyers . . are judges in Nevada, whether they practice at the bar or sit upon the bench. **1905** *Eve. Post* (NY NY) 18 Mar [2/1] **TX,** The title of "Judge" stuck to him from the time he was a justice of the peace. **1915** *DN* 4.227 **wTX,** Jedge. The title gratuitously bestowed on any lawyer. **1929** *Ruppenthal Coll.* **KS,** Judge—term frequently used of and more often in address to any old lawyer. **1936** Drury *Ed. on the Comstock* 21 **NV** (as of 1870s), All lawyers . . were also Colonels, excepting those called Judge. **c1960** *Wilson Coll.* **csKY,** Judge—Often a prominent lawyer was called by this title, whether he had ever sat as a judge or not.

2 A fool or clown.

1923 *DN* 5.212 **swMO,** Jedge. . . Judge. Also, a droll person. "He shore is a jedge" (or clown). "I made a jedge o' m'se'f," *i.e.,* made a fool of myself. **1931** Randolph *Ozarks* 71, The noun judge or jedge, by the way, is regularly used to mean a fool or a clown.

judgmatically adv Pronc-spp *jedg(e)matically* [By ext from *judgmatically* judiciously, gravely (*OED* 1814 →)] **sAppalachians**
In one's considered opinion—used to qualify a following statement.

1913 Kephart *Highlanders* 117 **sAppalachians,** "Do you suppose that

Tom is running a still up there at the head of that little cove?" The man's face hardened. . . "Jedgmatically, I don't know." **1928** Chapman *Happy Mt.* 289 **seTN,** Judgmatically, I'd say the rope broke by a mistake. **1974** Fink *Mountain Speech* 13 **wNC, eTN,** *Jedgematically* . . in my judgment. "Jedgematically, he'll come tomorrow." **1976** Garber *Mountainese* 47 **sAppalachians,** *Jedgematically* . . in my opinion—Jedgmatically, I'd say they's ten acres in that field.

‡**judicule** n [Perh blend of *judy* (cf **judy bag**) + *reticule*]
   1957 *Sat. Eve. Post Letters* **cnKY,** Ridicule [sic] or judicule (big bag) used by my grandmother.

‡**Judith priest** intj [Var of *Judas priest* (at **Judas**)]
   1967 *DARE* (Qu. NN30, *Exclamations beginning with the sound of 'j'*) Inf **OR10,** Judith priest.

judy adj, adv [Etym uncert, but cf *judy* a girl or woman]
   See quot.
   1968 *DARE* (Qu. II3, *Expressions to say that people are very friendly toward each other: "They're _____."*) Inf **NY83,** Judy friendly; **NY54,** Very judy.

judy bag n [Etym uncert] Cf **judicule**
   1940 *AmSp* 15.447 **eTN,** *Judy bag.* Travelling bag. 'Minnie bought a new judy bag.'

judy-coon n
   See quot.
   1956 Sorden–Ebert *Logger's Words* 20 **Gt Lakes,** *Judy-coon,* A raft with a capstan for floating logs across the lake.

judy pot n Cf *DS* F38
   1967 *DARE* FW Addit **CO21,** Judy pot—the chamber pot; heard by Inf in area.

jue See **due**

jug n
1 The flower of **wild ginger.** [From the shape] Cf **jug plant, little brown jug, monkey jugs**
   1908 *DN* 3.325 **eAL, wGA,** *Jug.* . . The brownish purple, jug-shaped flower of the plant called 'heart-leaf.' **1964** Campbell et al. *Gt. Smoky Wildflowers* 36, *Asarum arifolium.* . . Its . . fleshy jug-shaped calyx—a flower without petals—give[s] this plant a unique appeal. . . Often hidden by the leaves, the interesting jugs occur at ground level, in May, and are purplish-brown and less than an inch long.
2 A playing marble; see quots. Cf **agate 3.**
   1908 *DN* 3.285 **eAL, wGA,** *Agate.* . . A marble made of glazed clay. Also called *jug.* **1955** *PADS* 23.21 **KY,** *Jug.* . . An agate marble. **1969** *DARE* (Qu. EE6c, *Cheap marbles*) Inf **GA86,** Jugs—large glazed clay marbles.
3 The head or mouth. Cf **jughead 2,** *DS* X9, 28
   1933 Williamson *Woods Colt* 64 **Ozarks,** I didn't do nothin' except bust that Prather's jug for him. It was jest a scrap, that's all. **1942** Berrey–Van den Bark *Amer. Slang* 121.65, *Mouth.* . . jug. **c1960** Wilson *Coll.* **csKY,** *Jug*—Mouth or head. "Don't open your jug, or I'll. . ."
4 A sheep's udder.
   1973 *Foxfire 2* 177 **neGA,** They take those old mountain sheep and improve 'em so they have more wool and mutton, and now they're not as good mothers. . . Those old sheep would hold their jug up for 'em and push the baby to it and just tell 'em, 'you either get it or you die.'
5 A woman's breast. Cf **can** n **3b**
   1965–70 *DARE* (Qu. X31, *. . A woman's breasts*) 13 Infs, **scattered,** Jugs; **GA89, MS86, MO29, TN52,** Ninny jugs; **GA77,** Milk jugs. **1983** De Vries *Slouching* 234 **ND,** With the other [hand] she secured her bathrobe lapels about a pair of jugs on which I certainly had no designs.
6 A sheep pen. [Transf from *jug* a jail]
   1939 (1973) FWP *Guide MT* 197, At shearing time—late May and early June—the big sheds on sheep ranches are busy places. In preparation for the shearing, the rancher builds jugs (pens) of boards wired together, and arranges a runway through which a few sheep at a time are passed on their way to and from the pens. . . As the sheep enter the jug, each shearer catches a ewe by a hindleg and hauls her to a sitting position. **1978** Doig *This House* 162 **MT** (as of c1955), Then she was strongarmed into one of the jugs, and her lamb put in after.

jug v[1], hence vbl n *jugging* **chiefly Missip Valley** Cf **jig** v **1, jug fishing**
   To fish, esp for catfish, with a baited line attached to a floating jug or bottle; to catch (fish) in this manner.

1872 *KS Mag.* Feb 178, Jugging for catfish in the chutes of the Missouri and the Kaw. **1893** *KS Univ. Qrly.* 1.140 **MO,** *Jug:* to catch fish by a certain method. **1941** Writers' Program *Guide MO* 128, Catfish are frequently caught . . by "jugging." . . Large sealed jugs or cans with lines attached are set afloat; the jug bobs when a fish is hooked. **1947** *Life* 15 Sept 155 **MO,** The boys go jugging for catfish. They tie their fishing lines to jugs and haul them in when the jug bobs in the water. **1953** (1977) Hubbard *Shantyboat* 313 **Missip–Ohio Valleys,** It was Ohio River jugging on a grand scale. The fisherman sets adrift in midstream fifty or seventy-five blocks, which might be tin cans, jugs, or pieces of lightweight cypress root, each with a short piece of line and a single baited hook attached. He drifts along in his boat, watching all the blocks. When a fish takes one of them he chases after it. **1957** Trautman *Fishes* 413, Before the Ohio River was impounded, jugging was the usual method of fishing for this catfish. . . An earthen jug, or gallon tin can, was tied to one end of 9 to 15 feet of No. 30 twine. A No. 10 hook was tied to the other end and was baited with a piece of raw beef larger than a baseball, a sucker or bullhead of a pound in weight, a chicken less than 1/3 grown, or a small kitten. Between five and ten jugs with lines and hooks attached were floated down the chutes, the fishermen following behind in a boat. **1966–69** *DARE* (Qu. P13, *. . Ways of fishing . . besides the ordinary hook and line*) Infs **MS6, MO**19, Jug; **MO**16, Jug fish; **IN42, MO7, 17, 36, TX**19, Jugging. **1970** *DARE* File **sIN,** Jugging for fiddlers—Catching catfish (small, 8–10″) with baited hook attached to empty jug (once pottery—now plastic). When the jug starts to move, it is pursued in a boat by the fisherman. (Ohio River.)

jug v[2] See **jag** v[1] **A1, 2**

jug v[3] See **joog**

jugarum n Also *chugarum, jigarum, jugarum frog, jug o' rum* [Echoic] **chiefly NEast** See Map
   =**bullfrog 1;** also the sound made by such a frog.
   1928 Pope–Dickinson *Amphibians* 41 **WI,** Bullfrog. *Rana catesbiana.* . . Other common names are Jug-o-rum and Cow Frog. **1939** *LANE* Map 231, Names of the large croaking frog. . . Several of the fieldworkers asked their informants, 'What does the bullfrog . . say?' The responses to this question, consisting of imitations of the frog's croak . . , are given in the commentary. . . 1 inf, **cwCT,** [tʃʌgəˈrʌmz], nickname for frogs, from the sound of their cry; 6 infs, **cCT, sw,ceMA,** The bullfrog says [ˌdʒʌgəˈrʌm]; 1 inf, **ceMA,** The bullfrog says [tʃʌgəˈrʌᵊm]. **1941** *Nature Mag.* 34.139, The "song" of the bullfrog . . has been worded in a variety of ways, the most familiar of which is "jug-o'-rum." **1944** Howard *Walkin' Preacher* 218 **Ozarks,** He has learned his music from the orchestration of the many familiar sounds of nature: the calls of birds, . . the "chugarum" of frogs, the chirping of crickets. **1963** *PADS* 39.13 **MA,** For the bullfrog, *jug-o-rum* and *jig-a-rum* appear to be innovations in Easthampton and Worcester. **1965** *PADS* 43.21 **seMA,** A big, deep-voiced bullfrog . . jugarum [1 inf]. **1965–70** *DARE* (Qu. P22, *Names or nicknames for a very large frog that makes a deep, loud sound*) 25 Infs, **chiefly NEast,** Jugarum; **CT23,** Old jugarum; **VT4,** Jugarum frog; **CT2, 10, 13, MA13, PA1, 83,** Chugarum.

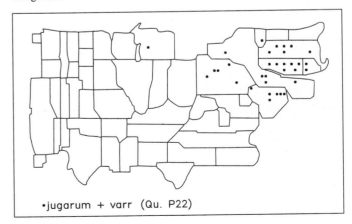

•jugarum + varr (Qu. P22)

juger n Cf **joogle** n
   1970 *DARE* (Qu. X7, *. . The throat: "Some food got stuck in his _____."*) Inf **KY75,** Juger [ˈjugɚ].

jugfish n
   A **puffer** (here: *Lagocephalus pachycephalus*).
   1898 U.S. Natl. Museum *Bulletin* 47.1728, *Jug-fish.* . . Body heavy,

tapering from middle of head backward. **1960** *Amer. Fisheries Soc. List Fishes* 49, Jugfish. . . *Lagocephalus pachycephalus.*

jug fishing vbl n **chiefly Missip Valley** See Map Cf **bottle fishing, jug** v[1]

Fishing with a baited line attached to a floating jug or bottle.

  1889 *Century Dict.* 3249, *Jug-fishing.* . . fishing with empty jugs or bottles, which are corked and thrown overboard to serve as buoys, carrying a line, at the end of which is the hook. **1965–70** *DARE* (Qu. P13, . . *Ways of fishing . . besides the ordinary hook and line*) 31 Infs, **chiefly Missip Valley,** Jug fishing; (Qu. P15, . . *Fishing that's done from a slowly moving boat*) Inf **IL**69, Jug fishing. **1982** Sternberg *Fishing* 72, In the South, jug-fishing for catfish is popular on reservoirs and slow-moving rivers. Fishermen suspend nightcrawlers, shad, chicken livers or other baits from bleach jugs or 2-liter plastic soft drink bottles. Paint the bottoms fluorescent orange to signal a strike.

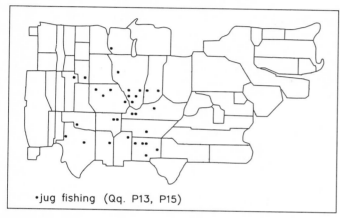

•jug fishing (Qq. P13, P15)

jugful(l), not by a adv phr *old-fash*

Fig: by no means; absolutely not.

  1831 *Boston Eve. Transcript* (MA) 14 Nov 2/1, "Vote on your side!" says another; "Not by a jug full." [**1840** Haliburton *Clockmaker* (3d ser) 248, The last mile . . took the longest [time] to do it in by a jug full.] **1893** *Congressional Record* 2 Oct 2048 **MO**, Take the Republicans one at a time and they are very clever sort of gentlemen . . but take them en masse and they will not do to tie to, by a jugful. **1899** (1912) Green *VA Folk-Speech* 247, *Not by a jugfull,* not by a great deal; by no means. **1907** *DN* 3.214 **cCT, nwAR**, "Not by a jug full," by no means. **1908** *DN* 3.325 **eAL, wGA**, Not by a jugfull. **1910** *DN* 3.444 **wNY**, "Not by a jug full," not by any means. **1912** *DN* 3.580 **wIN**, He can't do it,—not by a jugfull. **1927** *AmSp* 2.358 **cwWV**, He was not ready by a jug-full. **1965–70** *DARE* (Qu. KK55a, *To deny something very firmly: "No, not by a _____."*) 96 Infs, **widespread**, Jugful [Of all Infs responding to the question, 63% were old; of those giving this response, 87% were old.]; (Qu. KK55c, . . *Expressions of strong denial*) Infs **CT**29, **MA**58, **MI**27, **NJ**55, **NY**42, 105, 136, **OH**44, Not by a jugful [All Infs old]; (Qu. NN4, . . *Ways of answering 'no': "Would you lend him ten dollars?" "_____."*) Infs **GA**5, 15, **KS**7, **VA**5, 15, **WA**3, Not by a jugful [All Infs old].

jugged See **jag** v[1] A1

jugging See **jug** v[1]

juggle n [Var of *joggle* a notch in a piece of building material into which another piece is fitted]

1 See quot.

  1930 Shoemaker *1300 Words* 34 **cPA Mts** (as of c1900), *Juggle*—The straight cut into the heart of a tree when felling.

2 A large chip hewn from a log, esp in the making of railroad ties. **S Midl** Cf **juggle** v[1]

  1902 *DN* 2.237 **sIL**, *Juggle.* . . Chip or block scored from timber. **1953** Randolph–Wilson *Down in Holler* 257 **Ozarks**, *Juggles.* . . Very large chips, seen about the camps of woodsmen who make railroad ties. To *box the juggles* is to cut these big chips loose from a tie that has been notched, after which it is smoothed up with the broadaxe. **1954** *Harder Coll.* **cwTN**, *Juggles*—Large chips cut off logs. **c1960** *Wilson Coll.* **csKY**, *Juggles.* . . Large chips and slabs from making crossties. **1973** *DARE* File **Ozarks** (as of c1910), The chips left when hewing ties were juggles. **1987** *Foxfire* Winter 210 **neGA**, He [=a hewer of crossties] works his way down the length of the log knocking off the sections between the notches. These sections are called juggles. He remembers

when his parents would send the smaller kids to pick these up for firewood.

juggle v[1], hence vbl n *juggling*

To score or hew timber, esp in the making of railroad ties.

  1902 *DN* 2.237 **sIL**, *Juggle.* . . To score timber before hewing. **1986** Pederson *LAGS Concordance,* 1 inf, **csTN**, Juggling—in making crossties. **1988** *DARE* File **cwNC**, Peter Gott, a master log cabin builder from Marshall County, N.C., has told me that the hewing process was sometimes called "juggling" around there.

juggle v[2] See **joogle** v

juggle boat n

A small tug used for moving log rafts.

  1956 *Seattle Daily Times* (WA) 10 June 16 **wWA**, Sea Hag, a "juggle boat," is used to tow log rafts and to push them around.

juggling See **juggle** v[1]

jug handle n [From the shape]

1 A traffic intersection that facilitates left-hand turns; see quots; hence n *jug-handle (turn)* a turn in such an intersection. **esp NJ** Cf **cup turn**

  1961 Mumford *City in Hist.* 506, To ensure the continuous flow of traffic . . immense clover leaves and jug-handles are designed. **1968** *DARE* FW Addit **cNJ**, Jug handle—a method for making a left turn when none is permitted. Not too well known a term; used along Route 22 and in communities bordering on it; term not used in official signs. **1969–70** *DARE* (Qu. N20, . . *A circular arrangement on one level at a big intersection, where cars can go around till they come to the road they want*) Inf **NJ**55, Jug handle; (Qu. N28, *A road that connects a big highway with stores and business places set back from it*) Inf **NJ**67, Jug handle. **1971** Tak *Truck Talk* 93, *Jughandle:* a type of intersection found in New Jersey formed by a lane from the right-hand side of the road that curves away from the highway and then crosses it at right angles. A jughandle, named for its appearance, enables traffic to make a left-hand turn or a U-turn without blocking the left-hand lane of traffic on the highway. **1980** *NYT Article Letters* **neNJ**, Jug handle—Design of crossing approach at highway intersection, where left turns are forbidden, to enable motorists to turn right out of the stream of traffic and get in line for a traffic light change (New Jersey Highway Department). **1981** *DARE* File **seVT**, To make a left turn into a cross road—a jug-handle turn—you keep right, then swing around to face into the cross road, and when the traffic permits, you go ahead into the cross road.

2 A mark of identification made on the dewlap of cattle; also adj *jug-handled*; see quots. **West**

  1913 (1979) Barnes *Western Grazing* 382, *Jug Handle.* . . A mark made in cattle by slitting the dew lap about 4 inches so that the outside strip hangs free from the animal. **1920** Hunter *Trail Drivers TX* 298, A jud [sic] handled "dewlap" is a cut in the fleshy part of the throat, also used sometimes as a mark of distinction. **1936** Adams *Cowboy Lingo* 132, The 'jughandle' was made by cutting a long slash on the skin of the brisket and not cutting out at either end, which, when healed, looked similar to the handle of a suitcase. **1941** Writers' Program *Guide WY* 463, *Jug handle*—Slit in loose hide under animal's throat sometimes made for identification.

3 See quots.

  1956 McAtee *Some Dialect NC* 24, *Jug-handle* . . a hair-do, including a loop on top of the head. **1969** *DARE* (Qu. X3, *When a woman puts her hair up on her head in a bunch*) Inf **IN**70, Jug handle.

jug-handle adj See **jug-handled 1**

jug-handle v [**jug-handled** adj]

To treat in a disproportionate or unequal way.

  1912 *DN* 3.580 **wIN**, *Jug-handle.* . . To want everything one's own way in a transaction. "I was willing to do what was right in the matter, but he wanted to jug-handle me."

jug-handle corner n

A sharp curve.

  1948 Manfred *Chokecherry* 2 **nwIA**, The big cross-country truck sped down the . . [h]ighway. . . On jug-handle corners it teetered on two wheels; slowly righted itself.

jug-handled adj

1 also *jug-handle:* One-sided; disproportionate.

  1881 *Congressional Record* 8 Dec 60 **VT**, English reciprocity in pleasure travel, . . like their often proposed commercial reciprocity, is comparatively jug-handled. [**1899** (1912) Green *VA Folk-Speech* 34, Like a jug-handle, all on one side.] **1904** *Boston Herald* 28 Sep. 6 *(DA)*, The trade between Canada and the United States is distinctly jug-handled, with the handle altogether on the side of our people. **1914** *DN* 4.109 **KS**, *Jug-handle, adj.* One-sided.

2 See **jug handle** n **2**.

jug-handle turn n See **jug handle** n **1**

jughead n, hence adj *jugheaded* [From the shape] **chiefly S Midl, West**

1 A mule or horse with a large, chunky head; by ext, a stupid or stubborn one—less freq used of other animals. Cf **hammerhead 3, jarhead 1, longhead 2**

    1924 James *Cowboys N. & S.* 43, There's a difference in horses' nature and very few can be handled alike. . . [T]here's what we call the "jug-head"; he's got to be pulled around a heap, and it takes a lot of elbow grease to get him lined out for anything. **1926** Branch *Cowboy* 40 **West**, When the cowpuncher's loop spreads over the mustang's head and draws up, he's fighting the same as he would with the cougar. . . The "jug-head" seemed never to remember his hazing of the day before. **1936** McCarthy *Lang. Mosshorn* np **West** [Rodeo terms], *Jughead.* A horse which seemingly has no brains. **1948** Baumann *Old Man Crow's Boy* 63 **ID**, The Old Man had captured wild horses . . and he knew that any we caught there would be fairly good, not jug-headed runts such as might have been taken in some of the Snake River country closer at hand. **1949** *PADS* 11.23 **CO**, *Jughead.* . . A horse or mule with a large, long head. **1950** WELS *(Joking names for mules)* 1 Inf, **cWI**, Jughead. **1954** *Harder Coll.* **cwTN**, Jughead—A horse or mule with a large, long head. **1956** Moody *Home Ranch* 53 **CO** (as of 1911), He's [=a horse is] bay, and he's a little bit jugheaded, and not very pretty. **1959** Robertson *Ram* 288 **ID** (as of c1875), He had roped a jug-headed colt. **c1960** *Wilson Coll.* **csKY**, *Jughead.* . . Contemptuous name for colt, ox, mule, or calf; sometimes applied to a stupid-looking boy. **1960** Criswell *Resp. to PADS 20* **Ozarks**, *Jug-head*: Used both of people and animals because of certain shapes of people's heads and perhaps also of animals like mules which were frequently called that. Also, a stupid horse. **1965–70** *DARE* (Qu. K50, *Joking nicknames for mules*) 9 Infs, **scattered**, Jughead. **1984** Smith *SW Vocab.* 127, *Jughead*: A stupid horse. A horse with a long, clumsy, jug-like head, and a horse which shows little or no spirit. The word was applied to mules as well as horses, and sometimes, unkindly, to humans.

2 Transf: a person's head; a slow or stupid person.

    1926 Nason *Chevrons* 86, Unload everything. . . you jugheads. **1927** *DN* 5.452 [Underworld jargon], *Jug head.* . . A numbskull. **1949** *PADS* 11.23 **CO**, *Jughead.* . . A stupid or slow person. **1954** *Harder Coll.* **cwTN**, *Jughead.* . . A stupid or slow person. **c1960** *Wilson Coll.* [see **1** above]. **1960** Criswell [see **1** above]. **1965–70** *DARE* (Qu. X28, *Joking words . . for a person's head*) Infs **AR**18, **MS**30, **NC**62, 72, Jughead; (Qu. HH3, *A dull and stupid person*) Infs **CA**154, **CO**3, **IN**75, **NJ**53, **SC**31, Jughead; (Qu. HH16, *Uncomplimentary words with no definite meaning—just used when you want to show that you don't think much of a person: "Don't invite him. He's a ____."*) Infs **GA**3, **WA**30, Jughead. **1967** *DARE* Tape **WA**30, Some jughead sent back east [for women]. . . They didn't have enough women out here for the men. **1984** [see **1** above]. **1984** Doig *English Creek* 248 **nMT**, He seemed to take particular pleasure in any evidence that jugheaded behavior wasn't a monopoly of the Forest Service.

3 Perh a **flathead catfish 1.**

    1965 *DARE* (Qu. P1, *. . Kinds of freshwater fish . . caught around here . . good to eat*) Inf **MS**60, Jughead.

‡**jug-legged** adj [From the shape]

    1966 *DARE* (Qu. X37, *. . Words . . to describe people's legs if they're noticeably bent, or uneven, or not right*) Inf **FL**19, Jug-legged: big ankles.

jug-maker n

A **potter wasp** (here: *Eumenes fraternus*).

    1971 *Living Museum* 33.4 **IL**, The jug-makers or potter wasps (*Eumenes fraternus . .*) are outstanding artists of the clay-working wasps. *Ibid* 5, The jug-maker, Eumenes, however, is the finest potter of all and builds a diminutive "Grecian urn."

jugmouth n

A **warmouth** (here: *Lepomis gulosus*).

    1933 LA Dept. of Conserv. *Fishes* 342, The Warmouth Bass has come to bear many confusing popular names. These are: Warmouth, Goggle-

eye, . . Jugmouth [etc]. **1935** Caine *Game Fish* 33 **Sth**, *Warmouth. . . Synonyms . .* Indianfish. Jugmouth.

jug o' rum See **jugarum**

jug plant n [From the shape of the flowers] Cf **jug** n **1**

=**wild ginger.**

    1940 Clute *Amer. Plant Names* 137, *A[sarum] arifolium.* Jug-plant. **1959** Carleton *Index Herb. Plants* 69, *Jug-plant*: Asarum arifolium. **1972** Brown *Wildflowers LA* 46, *Wild-ginger, Jug-plant. Hexastylis arifolia. . .* Calyx jug-shaped, about 1 inch long, . . just peeping out of the leaf duff.

jug stack n

A type of haystack; see quot.

    1966 Dakin *Dial. Vocab. Ohio R. Valley* 2.74, Other terms for hay stacks were each used once: . . jug-stack (Allen Cty., Ky.— built around a pole and "shaped like a jug"—thus *jug-stack*).

jug swallow n [From the shape of the mud or clay nest]

=**cliff swallow.**

    1868 *Amer. Naturalist* 2.217 **cwNY**, I had nailed a board . . under the eaves of a barn to form a resting-place for the nests of the Cliff, or Jug-swallow. **1917** (1923) *Birds Amer.* 3.84, *Cliff Swallow. . . Other Names.* Eave Swallow; Jug Swallow. . . *Nest:* A cleverly constructed retort-shaped structure. **1946** Hausman *Eastern Birds* 416, Jug Swallow. . . They nest in colonies and attach their flask-shaped nests, composed of regularly sized pellets of mud or clay, in rows under the eaves of barns, or under hanging ledges and cliffs.

juh-ist See **joist 1**

juice v, hence vbl n *juicing* **chiefly Sth, S Midl, West** See Map

To milk—usu in phr *juice the cow* and varr.

    1915 *DN* 4.227 **wTX**, *Juice.* . . To milk. Formerly very common, this verb is now chiefly used facetiously (as "Juice, the heifer") and has been largely displaced by *pail*. **1939** FWP *Guide NE* 111, Peculiarly expressive are the terms describing the sandhill region: . . to juice or pail a cow. **1941** Writers' Program *Guide WY* 463, *Juice.* . . To milk. **1944** *PADS* 2.57 **cwMO**, *Juice, to juice a cow. . .* To milk. . . Rather common. **1954** *Harder Coll.* **cwTN**, *Juice.* . . to milk. "Got to go juice old cow." **c1960** *Wilson Coll.* **csKY**, *Juicing.* . . Humorous term for milking. **1965–70** *DARE* (Qu. K8, *Joking terms for milking a cow: A farmer might say, "Well, it's time to go out and ____."*) 178 Infs, **chiefly Sth, S Midl, West**, Juice the cow(s); 48 Infs, **chiefly Sth, S Midl, West**, Juice; 30 Infs, **chiefly Sth, S Midl, West**, Juice the jersey(s) (*or the bossies, the heifer, etc*); [**IA**14, **SC**19, Pull the juice; **VA**43, Get cow juice].

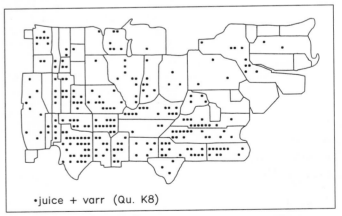

• juice + varr (Qu. K8)

juice harp See **Jew's harp**

juice pear n Also *josh pear, juicy pear*

A **serviceberry** (here: *Amelanchier canadensis* or *A. arborea*).

    a1862 (1865) Thoreau *Cape Cod* 188 **seMA**, The fruit of the shadbush or *Amelanchier*, which the inhabitants call Josh-pears (some think from juicy?), is very abundant on the hills. **1892** *Jrl. Amer. Folkl.* 5.95, *Amelanchier Canadensis.* . . Juice-pear or juicy pear. Provincetown, Mass. **1960** Vines *Trees SW* 416, *Amelanchier arborea.* . . Vernacular names are . . Indian-cherry, . . Juice-pear. . . It is occasionally cultivated in gardens for the showy white flowers.

juice the cow, juicing See **juice**

juicy pear See **juice pear**

jujang n
A testicle.
    1968 DARE (Qu. K70, *Words used . . for castrating an animal*) Inf **VA**7, Cut their jujangs.

jujube n
Std: a plant of the genus *Ziziphus*. For other names of *Z. jujuba* see **Chinese date;** for other names of spp native to the US see **lotebush**

ju'k See **jerk** n[1], v[1]

juke v[1] See **jouk** v[1]

juke v[2] See **joog**

juke v[3] See **jook** v[3]

juke n See **jook** n

jukey adj [Cf **jouk** v[1] **1,** EDD *jouk* v. 3 "To bow, bend, make obeisance."]
    1930 Shoemaker *1300 Words* 33 **cPA Mts** (as of c1900), *Jukey*—Tall, but of not erect carriage.

juksie n
See quot.
    1945 FWP *Lay My Burden Down* 85 **AL,** My grandmammy was a juksie, 'cause her mammy was a nigger and her daddy a Choctaw Indian.

julark See **jewlark**

jularker, jularky See **jewlarker**

julebukk n |ˈjuləˈbʊk, -ˈbuk, -ˈbʌk| Also sp *julebokk;* pl *julebokke, julebukker(s)* [Norw *julebukk* masked and costumed person who goes from door to door between Christmas and New Year's seeking treats of food and drink] **WI, MN, ND in Norw settlement areas** *somewhat old-fash*
= **Christmas fool;** also n *julebukking* going from house to house in costume.
    1938 FWP *Guide ND* 79, In many Norwegian towns, Jule Bokke or Christmas Fools still make the rounds of the homes between Christmas and New Year. They are young people dressed in costume and masked, who call on neighbors and are given food and drink at each home visited. **1968** DARE (Qu. FF9, *A Christmas gathering*) Inf **MN**12, During Christmas fortnight went [ˈjuləˌbukɪŋ] . . dressed in disguise and went visiting (Norwegian). **1976** *Capital Times* (Madison WI) 28 Dec 39/1 **cwWI** (as of c1920), You are . . falling asleep when your mother . . whispers: "Do you want to see the Christmas Fools?" You have heard . . about these funny costumed people called "Julebukker" by your grand-parents and others who speak Norwegian. . . You become very fright-ened, for all are wearing horrible masks and clothes that are just as wild. . . The visitors lift their masks, however, to partake of the coffee and Christmas goodies later served them. . . This was your introduction to "Julebukking." . . Older folks had their get-togethers, but for the young people this was the time of the "Julebukk." **1981** Bly *Letters* 54 **cwMN,** Why are we frenetic and miserable at Christmas then? and why is the suicide rate so high at Christmas? . . julebokking isn't an accident! We "horse around" during the days of Christmas; it is the season of horses and mischief. [Footnote to *julebokking:*] Christmas joking, the Norwegian equivalent of the horsing around with fools' masses, etc. **1991** DARE File **csWI,** People in Stoughton still go julebukking [ˈjuləˈbʌʃkɪŋ] before Christmas. The first time julebukkers came to our door, I had no idea what was going on. Several people wearing ragged old clothes and rubber masks that covered their faces pushed their way into the living room and silently pointed to the mugs, shot glasses, and plates they were carrying. They wouldn't speak or identify themselves. I didn't realize they were expecting cookies and a cup of Christ-mas cheer—I almost called the police! *Ibid* **csWI,** People still go [ˈjuləˈbukɪŋ] between Christmas and New Year's, but not as much as they used to.

julekake n Also *julekage, julicokki* [From one or more Scan languages; cf Norw *julekake* bread containing raisins, citron, cardamom, etc] *esp in Scan settlement areas*
A sweetened bread usu including dried or candied fruits, traditionally served at Christmastime; see also quot 1991.
    1940 Tufford *Scandinavian Recipes* 8 **MN,** *Julekage* (Christmas Bread) . . Add eggs . . beating thoroughly, add fruit, cardamom and enough flour to make a soft dough . . knead and let rise. . . Brush tops with egg yolk and milk mixture. . . After removing from oven brush tops with melted butter and sprinkle with sugar and cinnamon. **1952** Tracy *Coast Cookery* 172 **ND,** Norwegian Julekake. **1968** DARE (Qu. H18, . . *Special kinds of bread*) Inf **MN**30, Julekake—a fruit bread, same as Christmas bread; **OR**4, Julicokki—Finnish bread. **1991** *Star Shopper* (Stoughton WI) 19 Nov 4, [Advt:] Let Us Help With Your Christmas Baking. . . Try These Norwegian Specialties. . . *Fattigman . . Krumkake . . Julekake.* . . Fos-dal Home Bakery. **1991** DARE File **csWI,** Julekake [ˈjuləˌkɑkə] is a rather dry Christmas bread made with cinnamon and topped with white icing and candied fruit. A few older people of my acquaintance refer to Scandinavian cookies or pastries (such as spritz or rosettes) as "julekakes" if they are served at Christmastime.

julie n Cf *DS* L41
    1963 Edwards *Gravel* 165 **eTN** (as of 1920s), One Monday morning he was given the job of hustling a Julie (wheelbarrow).

juliet n Cf **romeo**
A style of girls' or women's slipper.
    1927 (1970) Sears *Catalogue* 312, [Slippers:] Restful Juliet for Chil-dren. . . Red felt Juliet trimmed with black fur. **1950** *WELS* (Soft shoes, *worn only inside the house [describe different kinds]*) 1 Inf, **cWI,** Juliets are slippers built up around the ankle. **1968–69** DARE (Qu. W21), Inf **NJ**24, Juliets—soft leather slippers with elastic V in sides, and a loop to pull them on; **NJ**56, Juliets.

juliper n
    1936 *AmSp* 11.315 **Ozarks,** Juliper. . . The juice from a fowl, or other meat. 'I jest baste th' turkey, an' save th' juliper.'

July See **July hound**

July fly n
1 also *July beetle:* = **cicada. chiefly SE** See Map
    1939 FWP *Guide TN* 135, The old weather signs have vital meaning in the lives of rural people and farmers watch them closely. . . Frost will come as sure as judgement just six weeks after you hear the first July fly. **1956** McAtee *Some Dialect NC* 24, *July-fly.* . . Cicada of the genus *Tibicen.* **1965–70** DARE (Qu. R7, *Insects that sit in trees or bushes in hot weather and make a sharp, buzzing sound*) 20 Infs, **chiefly SE,** July fly; (Qu. R4) Inf **GA**3, July fly; (Qu. R5) Inf **NC**87, June bug . . different from July fly; (Qu. R8, . . *Kinds of creatures that make a clicking or shrilling or chirping kind of sound*) Infs **GA**9, **NC**16, **SC**40, July fly; (Qu. R12) Inf **MI**2, Dog fly or July fly; (Qu. R30) Inf **KY**53, July beetle. **1984** DARE File **NC,** We called the cicada *July fly.*

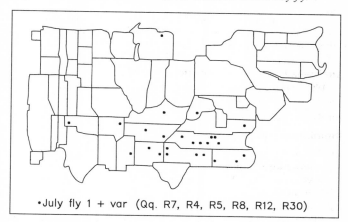

•July fly 1 + var (Qq. R7, R4, R5, R8, R12, R30)

2 A **dragonfly.**
    1969 DARE (Qu. R2, . . *The dragonfly*) Inf **GA**80, July fly.
3 = **mayfly 1.**
    1966 DARE (Qu. R4, *A large winged insect that hatches in summer in great numbers around lakes or rivers, crowds around lights, lives only a day or so, and is good fish bait*) Inf **GA**3, July fly.

July grape n [From the time of its ripening]
A **sand grape** (here: *Vitis rupestris*).
    1960 Vines *Trees SW* 729, *Vitis rupestris.* . . Vernacular names are Sand Beach Grape, July Grape [etc].

July hound n Also *July* [See quot 1948]
A type of hound of US origin; see quots.
    1947 *Clarke Co. Democrat* (Grove Hill AL) 30 Oct 4/3, A hound is

a hound, regardless of whether he is July, Red Bone, Walker, potlicker, or just plain hush-puppy. **1948** Camp *Hunter's Encycl.* 154, Generations of careful breeding [of foxhounds in the US] produced. . . the Walkers, . . the Triggs, . . the Julys, Trumbos, and a few others. [*Ibid* 843, Mr. Miles G. Harris secured a very fine hound from . . Maryland and brought him to Georgia. The dog came to him on the first day of July and, for this reason, was named July. . . In 1861, July was crossed on the Birdsong dogs.] *Ibid* 844, As their fame spread through Georgia and the surrounding states, . . after the infusion of July blood, they were called by many "July" hounds. **1949** Arnow *Hunter's Horn* 42 **eKY**, Newt Taylor, from the other side of Bear Creek, with his two fine spotted July hounds. *Ibid* 216, Pinkney . . talked of his own four hounds—not such great hunters—two Trigs and two Julys—but they had the prettiest tongues. **1966–67** *DARE* Tape **AR**15, July, we usually think of them as a solid color . . some calls 'em light red and some calls 'em brown; **DC**9, Night-hunters . . hunt hounds that are known . . as July hounds, and Trig hounds, and different breeds. **1967** *DARE* FW Addit **AR**51, July—a breed of hound for fast-trailing deer, foxes, wolves. No uniform color pattern.

jumbalaya See **jambalaya**

jumball See **jumble**

jumballaya See **jambalaya**

jumble n Also *jumball, jumber, jumblie* [*OED* 1615 →]
Any of var confections, esp a thin, sweet cake baked in the shape of a ring.
1827 Leslie *75 Receipts* 70, [Recipe for] Jumbles. . . Roll . . into long thin rolls . . curled up into rings. **1853** (1982) Lea *Domestic Cookery* 119, *Jumbles for Delicate Persons.* **1861** Holmes *Venner* 1.141 **NEng**, There were brown cakes and yellow cakes . . and *jumbles,* which playful youth slip over the forefinger before spoiling their annular outline. **1911** Shute *Plupy* 211 **NH**, Every train thet came through Exeter found her at the station with a basket of cookies 'n jumbles 'n things for the soldiers. **1915** *DN* 4.239 [Colonial cookery terms], *Jumballs.* Variant of *jumbles.* **1922** (1926) Cady *Rhymes VT* 205, A twelve-pound ham jest fades away,/ Like Johnny's sugared jumble. **1947** Bowles–Towle *New Engl. Cooking* 210, Jumbles [=Spice cookies rolled thin in sugar and cut with a doughnut cutter]. **1967** *DARE* (Qu. H32, . . *Fancy rolls and pastries*) Inf **SC**29, Jumbles—tea cakes, a cookie, fancy one. **1967** *DARE* FW Addit **SC**, Jumbers, sweet jumbers, or jumbers biscuit—flour, flavoring, egg, sugar, milk, water. Roll it, cut it in shapes, bake it. **1979** Solomon–Solomon *Cracklin Bread & Asfidity* 29 **AL**, Jumblies—Cream together . . sugar . . butter, add . . eggs . . milk . . baking powder . . flour . . break off pieces about the size of a walnut and make into a ring. . . Put them in pans to bake. **1982** *DARE* File **cMA**, Jumbles—soft drop cookies, usu with some brown sugar or maple syrup and with raisins, sometimes nuts or other small candied fruit.

jumble-jawed adj [Var of **jimberjawed**]
1965 *DARE* (Qu. X6, *If a person's lower jaw sticks out prominently . . he's _____*) Inf **MS**30, Jumble-jawed; [**NY**48, Jumbled jaw].

jumblie See **jumble**

jumbloney See **jabronie**

jumbo n
1 =**dogtooth violet.**
1968 *DARE* (Qu. S11, . . *Other names . . for . . dog-tooth violet*) Inf **NY**79, Jumbos.
2 =**bluefish 1.**
1972 Sparano *Outdoors Encycl.* 378, Bluefish. Common Names: Bluefish, chopper, . . jumbo. . . Once hooked, the bluefish makes an angler fervently thankful that these fish don't reach the size of tuna, for blues are among the most powerful fighters in the sea.
3 Bologna sausage. **swPA**
1973 *DARE* File **swPA**, Jumbo—bologna sausage. [2 Infs] **1978** *New Haven Reg.* (CT) 30 Nov [np], How do you recognize a Pittsburgher? Where else but here does one . . serve "jumbo" (bologna) . . for lunch? **1982** McCool *Sam McCool's Pittsburghese* 20 **PA**, Jumbo: bologna. When a Pittsburgher orders a jumbo sandwich, he is not ordering a large sandwich. **1986** *DARE* File **Pittsburgh PA**, [She] might stop at the five 'n' ten . . before she gets a pound of jumbo at Isaly's.

jump v, hence vbl n *jumping*
1 To catch (fish), esp by attracting them with a light and

startling them so that they jump into a net or boat; to catch fish in this way. [Transf from *jump* to flush or start game] **esp Sth, S Midl**
1839 *S. Lit. Messenger* 5.377 **seGA**, I would go, but I am *a* going to jump mullet to-night. **1930** *DN* 6.82 **cSC**, *Jack jumping,* the method of catching jack-fish. Men go out at night in a bateau . . with a flambeau . . and jack-fish, attracted by the light, jump into the boat. **1931** Randolph *Ozarks* 254, Sure you can jump bass, if the water's murky enough; I've often seen it done on the White River in Arkansas. **1941** Writers' Program *Guide MO* 128, "Jumping" and "bumping" bass is practiced at night, or in the day time when a rapid rise muddies the stream. . . In night "jumping," the boat, with a light in it, is allowed to drift along the edge of the weeds. The feeding bass and "skip-jacks," believing themselves trapped between boat and bank, may jump into the boat. **1966–70** *DARE* (Qu. P13, . . *Ways of fishing . . besides the ordinary hook and line*) Inf **CA**211, Jumping smelt; **FL**7, Light jumping—net and light.
2 also with *out, up:* To confront; to admonish; to question with severity.
1905 *DN* 3.84 **nwAR**, *Jump up.* . . To censure. 'He got jumped up for that.' Common. **1914** *DN* 4.109 **cKS**, *Jump.* . . To address with an unexpected inquiry, especially in taking to task. "They heard that he told yarns about them; so they jumped him for it." **1923** *DN* 5.212 **swMO**, *Jump out.* . . To take to task, to call to account. "I jumped 'im out fer talkin' about me." **1927** *AmSp* 2.358 **cwWV**, *Jump* . . to inquire about a happening, with the inference of attempting to verify a suspicion. "The principal jumped me about throwing the snowballs as soon as I got back to school." **1947** *True* 32.102 **New Orleans LA** [Black], Only one youngster had nerve enough to jump him up. **1954** Armstrong *Satchmo* 212 **LA**, I did not like the way he cut under me. But I did not want to jump him up about it. **1968–70** *DARE* (Qu. Y6, . . *To put pressure on somebody to do something he ought to have done but hasn't: "He's a whole week late. I'm going to _____."*) Infs **IL**82A, **NY**109, **TX**86, Jump him. **1968** *DARE* Tape **CA**100, This paper jumped him, don't you see, and he's trying to crawl out of it. **1975** Gainer *Witches* 12 **sAppalachians**, He jumped me about spending too much.

jump n
1 in phr *from the jump* and varr: From the very beginning; at the start.
1831 *Maysville* (Ky.) *Eagle* 12 July *(DA)*, I'll give you a history of Henry Clay, from the *first jump* of him. **1848** in 1968 Bartlett *Americanisms* 223, A whole string of Democrats, all of whom had been going the whole hog for Cass from the jump. **1852** in 1956 Eliason *Tarheel Talk* 280 **se,csNC**, I will give time [Eliason: credit], but Interest from the Jump [Eliason: i.e. beginning immediately]. **1856** Simms *Charlemont* 224 **KY**, The great desire which he felt . . to make him display the qualities of both from the very jump. **1887** (1967) Harris *Free Joe* 82 **nwGA** [Black], You bin mighty fur ways, suh, kaze we all bin knowin' 'bout it fum de jump. **1911** Ferber *Dawn O'Hara* 32 **MI**, Asked for you, right from the jump. **1916** *Out West Mag.* Sept 102, He said he hadn't met a fellow for a coon's age he liked so much right from the jump.
2 also *jump-up:* A loft or half-story in a house. [Prob from *jump* a short distance] **S Atl**
1930 Woofter *Black Yeomanry* 214 **seSC**, The next type was the two-room house with a "jump up." The "jump up" corresponds, on a smaller scale, to the second story rooms placed under a bungalow roof. Sometimes it is approached by stair and sometimes by ladder. Here the children are given separate quarters. **1942** Hurston *Dust Tracks* 27 **FL** [Black], We called it a two-story house; but later on I learned it was really one story and a jump. The big boys all slept up there, and it was a good place to hide and shirk from sweeping off the front porch or raking up the back yard. **1986** Pederson *LAGS Concordance,* 1 inf, **seGA**, A-story-and-a-jump—a one-and-a-half-story-house.
3 See **jumper 8.**
4 pl; also *jumping exercise:* A convulsive movement occasioned by religious excitement. Cf **jerk** n[1] **B1, jumper 15**
1834 *Biblical Repertory* 6.349 **swVA**, We saw another who had, what was termed the "jumping exercise;" which resembled that of the jumpers in Wales. **1946** Tallant *Voodoo* 170 **New Orleans LA**, They [=members of spiritualist churches] sing Baptist and Methodist hymns and the congregation "testifies" and suffers attacks of the "jumps" and the "jerks," such as are common to all cults of the revivalist type.

jump a twig See **hop the twig**

jump board n Also *jumping board* esp Gulf States Cf **jog-gling board**

See quots.

1966 *DARE* (Qu. EE31, *Playground equipment with a long board for two children to sit on and go up and down in turn*) Inf **FL10**, Jump board—they jump on it at each end; **FL33**, Jumping board; (Qu. EE33, . . *Outdoor games . . that children play*) Inf **FL2**, Jump board—like a seesaw but they jump on it. **1986** Pederson *LAGS Concordance* **chiefly coastal Gulf Region** *(Joggling board/limber plank suspended at both ends)* 44 infs, Jump board; 36 infs, Jumping board. [*DARE* Ed: Comments by infs indicate that the term refers variously to a joggling board, see-saw, diving board, or other piece of play equipment involving a flexible board.]

jump butt n Cf **catface 1a, long butt**

The lower end of a tree trunk discarded by loggers because of a defect.

1942 *Democrat* 1 Oct. 1/2 *(DA)* swAL, Three colored men . . overturned the jumpbutt of an old poplar log and found underneath 22 rattlesnakes. **1966** *DARE* FW Addit AL, Jump butt—that part of the tree on which is the catface. When the lumberers come through to cut trees for wood, they leave the part with the catface on it. After it's cut, it's called a jump butt. People in turpentine collecting areas use it for firewood. It burns very well and long. **1992** *NADS Letters* sGA, Jump butt for 'the base of a tree trunk having a defect that makes it unsuitable as a saw log,' . . is still known and used in Georgia. My father, age 81, from South Georgia and a forester all his adult life, says it is still current, especially indicating to those felling the tree to cut above the jump butt, usually where it has been marred by earlier turpentining.

jumped up adj phr Also *junked-up*
=**jumping** adj **1.**

1905 *DN* 3.84 nwAR, Jumped up. . . In the exclamation of surprise, . . 'Well, I'll be jumped up.' **1908** *DN* 3.290 eAL, wGA, Be jumped up. . . Used in exclamations as the preceding [=*I'll be jiggered*]. **1938** [see **Jesus H. Christ**]. **1939** FWP *ID Lore* 243, Some Mild Profanity. . . Holy jumped-up Moses!—Moses often yields to members of the Trinity. **1966–70** *DARE* (Qu. NN9a, *Exclamations showing great annoyance: "_____. The electric power is off again."*) Inf **GA7**, I'll be jumped up; (Qu. NN29c, *Exclamations beginning with 'holy': "Holy _____!"*) Inf **IN56**, Jumped-up Jesus Christ; **CA200**, Jumped-up John Rogers; (Qu. NN30, *Exclamations beginning with the sound of 'j'*) Inf **MA14**, By the jumped-up John Rogers; **VT16**, Jumped-up Christmas; **NM11**, Junked-up Jesus. **1971** Brunvand *Guide Folkl.* UT 31, The [sham swear] phrases include . . "Holy jumped-up cheese and rice."

jumped up ppl adj phr See **jump up** v phr **1**

jumped-up song See **jump-up song**

jumper n

1 A **grasshopper 1** or similar saltatorial insect.

1852 Harris *Treatise Insects* 126, Jumpers (Orthoptera saltatoria), such as crickets, grasshoppers, and locusts . . the thighs of the hind legs are much larger than the others, and are filled and moved with powerful muscles, which enable these insects to leap with facility. **1889** *Century Dict.* 3252, Jumper. . . Any saltatorial insect, as a . . grasshopper. **1965** *DARE* (Qu. R6, . . *Names . . for grasshoppers*) Inf **FL22**, Jumpers.

2 A **black bass 1**: usu **largemouth bass** or **smallmouth bass**, but also **spotted bass**. [See quot 1908] esp Sth, S Midl

1877 NY Acad. Sci. *Annals Lyceum Nat. Hist.* 11.375 GA, Jumper. Jumping Pearch [sic]. Micropterus sps. **1884** Goode *Fisheries U.S.* 1.401, The Big-Mouth Black Bass. . . in Kentucky . . is called "Jumper." . . The Small-mouth shares with the Large mouth in the Southern States the names "Jumper," "Perch," and "Trout." **1908** Forbes-Richardson *Fishes of IL* 268, It [=*Micropterus salmoides*] will, however, leap five or six feet out of the water to escape a net, and is for that reason called the "jumper" in some localities. **1933** LA Dept. of Conserv. *Fishes* 313, None of our other fresh water fishes has been given so many popular names as our Black Bass. . . These often confusing designations . . are . . Trout, Jumper [etc]. **1935** Caine *Game Fish* 3 Sth, *Large-mouthed Black Bass*. . . Synonyms . . Jumper. *Ibid* 7, *Small-mouthed Black Bass*. . . Jumper. *Ibid* 9, *Spotted . . Bass*. . . Jumper. **1949** Caine *N. Amer. Sport Fish* 20, Although sometimes confused with the large-mouth bass because of the similarity in general characteristics, the smallmouth is generally conceded a superiority in dash, stamina and acrobatics. *Colloquial Names* . . Jumper.

3 See **jumping mullet 1.**

4 See **jumping spider.**

5 See **jumping mouse 1.**

6 also *long jumper*: An earthworm. Cf **john-jumper 1, jumping jack 4**

c1970 Pederson *Dial. Surv. Rural GA* seGA (*Ordinary worms used for bait*) 2 infs, Jumpers. [Both infs Black] **1986** Pederson *LAGS Concordance (Earthworm)* 1 inf, swMS, Long jumpers. [Inf Black]

7 Any of var types of sleds or sleighs; spec:

a also *johnny jumper*: A roughly made sled used for hauling heavy loads, often over bare or partially bare ground. **Nth, esp NEast** See Map Cf **lumber sleigh**

[**1812** in 1967 *Dict. Canadianisms* 396, They had not gone far when the Indian drew their attention to the tracks of a jumper in the snow.] **1823** Cooper *Pioneers* 2.145 cNY, They frequently make these jumpers to convey their game home. **1893** Leland *Memoirs* 278 PA (as of 1865), A *jumper*. . . is the roughest form of a sledge, consisting of two saplings with the ends turned up, fastened by cross-pieces. **1901** *DN* 2.142 seNY, Jumper. . . A large home-made sled. **1901** [see **lumber sleigh**]. **1905** U.S. Forest Serv. *Bulletin* 61.40 [Logging terms], *Jumper*. . . A sled shod with wood, used for hauling supplies over bare ground into a logging camp. (N[orthern] F[orest]) **1907** *DN* 3.245 eME, *Jumper*. . . A woodsman's sled. **1909** *DN* 3.413 nME, *Jumper*. . . An unshod sled consisting only of a frame used on bare ground in the woods for hauling supplies. **1911** (1913) Johnson *Highways Gt. Lakes* 149, That's a road . . just wide enough to go through with an old jumper, which is a kind of rough sled that has runners made of small trees with a natural crook in 'em. **1943** *LANE* Map 573–74 (*Sled; sleigh*) 1 inf, nRI, *Jumper*, 'for drawing logs'. **1950** *WELS* (*A low wooden platform used for hauling stones or heavy things out of the fields*) 1 inf, cwWI, Jumper. **1958** McCulloch *Woods Words* 99 **Pacific NW**, Jumper—A small wooden sled like a farmer's stone boat, used in hauling short length pulpwood. **1965–70** *DARE* (Qu. N40a, . . *Sleighs . . for hauling loads*) Inf **CT26**, Jumper—used to haul logs and timber out of woods—sled, but no pole; just hitch on with a chain; **CT29**, Jumper—wooden sled with wooden runners, used in woods; **CT36**, Jumper—wooden shod; **ME10**, Jumper—one set [of runners]; **MI40**, Jumper—built somewhat like the cutter; floor about a foot from the ground, runners eight feet in length; **NJ1**, Jumper—one set of runners, unpredictable over uneven ground; **NY23**, Jumper, for part-bare land; **NY88**, Jumper—a short affair; **PA82**, Jumper—coal, one sleigh, no sections, runners pointed front and back so he could back up; **RI6**, Jumper—wood and stuff; **NY82**, Johnny jumper; (Qu. L57, *A low wooden platform used for bringing stones or heavy things out of the fields*) Inf **MI47**, Jumper. **1981** *PADS* 67.26 **Mesabi Iron Range MN**, *Jumper . . stone buggy . .* and *rock boat . .* are infrequent Range terms not recorded for the other Minnesota informants [for a stoneboat].

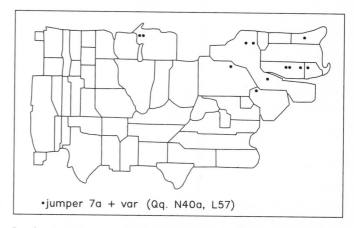

•jumper 7a + var (Qq. N40a, L57)

b also *jumper sleigh*: A sleigh used for carrying people.

1833 in 1835 Hoffman *Winter in West* (NY) 1.166, Did you ever see a *jumper*? . . It is a primitive kind of sledge or *traineau*. A couple of hickory poles are so bent as to serve for both shafts and runners; on these is placed a crate, supported by four props. . . The crate being filled with hay, and the driver well wrapped up in a buffalo robe, the turn-out is complete, and by no means uncomfortable. **1872** (1876) Knight *Amer. Mech. Dict.* 2.1220, Jumper. . . A cheaply formed sled . . , in which supple pieces of wood form the shafts and runners, and support a box or trestle in or on which the person rides. **1944** Duncan *Mentor Graham* 154 **IL** (as of 1830s), Many New Salem folk had jumpers (sleighs) that might be borrowed by an ingratiating young man or rented in exchange for a day's work. **1966** *DARE* (Qu. N40b, . . *Sleighs for carrying people*) Inf **ND3**, Open ones called jumpers. **1975** in 1982 *Barrick Coll.* **csPA**, *Jumper sleigh*—type of sleigh with a buckboard bed.

c also *jack jump(er):* A child's single-runner coasting sled; see quots. **wNEng, nNY, MI**

1898 *New Engl. Mag.* June 455 **ceMA** (as of 1820s), My pulse quickens as I recall the glorious times with our "jumper," and the hair-breadth escapes from posts and barberry bushes, in our swift descent upon the ice. **1901** *DN* 2.142 **cnNY**, *Jumper.* . . A small sled with a high seat. **1943** *LANE* Map 573–74 *(Sled; sleigh)* 20 infs, **chiefly VT, wMA**, *Jumper;* 1 inf, **eCT**, *Jumper,* 'long, for 3–4 children'; 1 inf, **cwVT**, *Jumper,* 'barrel-stave runner'; 1 inf, **nwVT**, *Jumper, barrel-stave jumper;* 1 inf, **cnVT**, *Jumper,* 'a barrel-stave with a post nailed onto it and a seat on top for that'; 1 inf, **swVT**, *Jack jumper;* 1 inf, **swVT**, *Jack-jump,* 'barrel-stave runner, post and seat'. **1969** *DARE* (Qu. EE24a, *When there's snow, children go down the hill on a _____*) Inf **MA21**, *Jumper*—sliding stick (runner) with an upright, usually a two-by-four about 18 inches high, and also a piece to sit on parallel to the slider; **MA58**, *Jumper*—not a sled; runner on bottom, cross seat on top; **MI108**, *Jumper*—a ski runner with a seat on top; **NY205**, *Jumper*—stool on a barrel stave; **NY213A**, *Jumper* or *skipper*—barrel stave and a post and a seat on a top, bear grease on bottom; **VT12**, *Jumper*—barrel stave, with seat up on it. **1975** Gould *ME Lingo* 149, *Jumper* is a small child's sled, perhaps because he jumps on it to ride. Sometimes a barrel stave rigged with a small seat for coasting. **1977** *Blair & Ketchum's Country Jrl.* Dec 63 **VT**, Jack-jumpers were sit-down ski sleds where the user perched precariously and skillfully on a little ski up above an old cut-down ski. **1984** *DARE* File **nMI** (as of 1960s), A jumper is something we used for sledding when we stayed at my grandmother's in northern Michigan. It has one runner, and a foot above that is a narrow seat. You sit down, hang on to either side of the seat with your hands, lift up your legs, and steer by leaning. No one in northern Illinois . . had ever heard of one. **1988** Palmer *Lang. W. Cent. MA* 59, *Jumper.* . . You'd take a barrel stave, nail a 4 x 4 onto it and put a crossboard on top of it with a seat. You'd get onto that thing and go down the hill like lickety-split.

8 also *jump:* A light, two-wheeled cart drawn by a single horse. **esp LA** Cf **gully jumper 2**

1871 Eggleston *Hoosier Schoolmaster* 224 **IN**, Driving Martha to a wedding in a "jumper" was the one opportunity Bud needed. [*DARE* Ed: It is possible that some other type of vehicle is meant.] **1946** Driscoll *Country Jake* 67 **KS**, He would put the sack in his "jump," or two-wheeled cart, and tote it home to Knight. **1967–70** *DARE* (Qu. N41a, . . *Horse-drawn vehicles . . to carry people*) Inf **LA3**, *Jumper*—one-horse vehicle with single seat, no top; **LA7**, *Jumper*—had a seat and body, no top; big enough for two people; two wheels; made like a gig used in horse races; **LA10**, *Jumper*—two-wheeled vehicle; **LA12**, *Jumper*—just had two wheels; **VA41**, *Jumper*—two-wheeled sulky-like vehicle.

9 A type of heavy wagon; see quot. *obs*

1938 *FWP Guide ND* 192 (as of 1870s), Teamsters hauling freight overland . . in their heavy, eight-horse, high-wheeled "jumpers", and trappers and Indians with their catches, here boarded the Hudson's Bay Co. steamer.

10 See quots. Cf **jumping adj 2**

1872 (1876) Knight *Amer. Mech. Dict.* 2.1220, *Jumper.* . . A plow having an upturned cutter in front of its share, and which, going below the share, prevents its being caught on roots, etc. **1889** *Century Dict.* 3252, *Jumper.* . . A special form of plowshare for rough soil, or soil filled with roots.

11 also *jumping Frenchman:* A person (usu believed to be a French Canadian) who exhibits an exaggerated response to being startled. **ME** Cf **jumps 1**

1878 *Jrl. of Nervous & Mental Disease* 5.526, Dr. Beard then made some remarks upon the "Jumpers, or jumping Frenchmen," who are to be found in the northern part of Maine, among the French Canadians and lumbermen of that region, and who have for a long time been known for jumping or striking on sudden excitation. **1880** Beard in *Pop. Sci. Mth.* 18.170 **nME**, These people were called in the language of that region "Jumpers" or "Jumping Frenchmen." It was claimed that all, or most of them were of French descent and of Canadian birth,

and that their occupation was mainly that of lumbering in the Maine woods. **1902** Day *Pine Tree Ballads* 251 **ME**, *The Jumper*—Ba gor! J [sic] jomp an' jomp all tam'/ Bot jos' can't help dat—dere she am!/ Cos' w'en som' fellaire he say "Boo!"/ Morgee! I jomp an' holler, too. **1907** *DN* 3.245 **eME**, *Jumping Frenchman.* . . A nervously weak French Canadian who is easily caused to jump. **1967** *Yankee* Oct 127 **nME, nNH**, In some towns and hamlets one may hear of a "Killer Jumper," an otherwise well-mannered, mild, and agreeable individual who will haul off and soundly sock the nearest bystander when startled or shouted at. **1975** Gould *ME Lingo* 149, *Jumper.* . . In Maine, this is usually "jumping Frenchman." . . For some time medical authorities erroneously believed it was peculiar to Canadian-Frenchmen working in the Maine woods. In recent years a Portland neurologist, Dr. E. Charles Kunkle, has spent much time studying these people, and he now says he believes it seemed indigenous to Maine only because it was first noticed here and gained attention through lumber-camp horseplay. It has always seemed great fun to jump a *jumper.*

12 also *jumper bull:* A bull; see quots. **esp WI**

1950 *WELS* (Words used for a bull) 1 Inf, **ceWI**, *Jumper.* **1968** *DARE* (Qu. K22) Inf **WI63**, *Jumper.* **1984** *MJLF* 10.152 **cnWI**, *Jumper bull.* A young bull of no particular heritage pastured with heifers to get them with calf for the first time.

13 A light marble; see quot.

c1970 Wiersma *Marbles Terms* **WA** (as of 1959), *Jumper*—lighter marble, used to try and break up knots of marbles; **swMI**, *Jumpers*—light marbles used for arc-shots.

14 A ridge for drawing water off a road. Cf **breaker 2, thank-you-ma'am**

1901 *DN* 2.142 **csNY**, *Jumper.* . . The same as thank-you-ma'am.

15 also *jolly jumper, joy ~:* =**Holy Jumper.** [*OED jumper* sb.¹ 2] Cf **bench-jumper 1, jerk** n¹ **B1, v¹ C1, jump n 4**

1889 *Pop. Sci. Mth.* June 148, Examples of this [=religious excitement] in America are seen in the "Jumpers," "Jerkers," and various revival extravagances, especially among the negroes and "poor whites" of the Southern States. **1966–70** *DARE* (Qu. CC4, . . *Nicknames . . for various religions or religious groups*) Inf **TX37**, Jolly jumpers—Roly Holers; **VA105**, Holy Rollers; joy jumpers; **NC22**, Jumpers—Holy Rollers. **1986** Pederson *LAGS Concordance*, 1 inf, **seFL**, The big jumper church [where] people jump, shout, [and] roll.

jumper bull See **jumper 12**

jumper sled n Also *log jumper* Cf **jumper 7a**
See quots.

1904 *DN* 2.398 [Lumber words], *Log-jumper.* . . A sled on which one end of the log is placed, the other end dragging behind. **1907** *DN* 3.245 **eME**, *Jumper sled.* . . A woodsman's sled with an elevated crosspiece on which the end of a log rests when dragged from the stump to the "yard."

jumper sleigh See **jumper 7b**

jump-for-down n Cf **high-back 3**
A var of the children's game of leapfrog; see quot 1957.

1957 *Sat. Eve. Post Letters* **cwWA** (as of c1900), *Jump-for-Down.* The players each made a standing jump for distance. The one who jumped the farthest was chosen 'leader.' The one who jumped the least distance was 'it.' He 'made a back' by bending over. . . The leader went first vaulting over the bent back and calling the stunt to be performed. . . [He] might call for 'Jump' or 'Hop' . . or even 'Hop, Skip and Jump.' Where he finished he toed a line in the dirt and all following him had to exceed that distance. . . The next man vaulted over . . and then joined them. . . It is obvious that the last . . had a lot of backs to clear. *Ibid* **Joplin MO** (as of c1914), We also played Jump for Down. **1967** Williams *Greenbones* 13 **GA** (as of c1910), He ate and looked; he couldn't look enough at the Maypole dancers . . at the smaller children playing jump-for-down. **1970** *DARE* (Qu. EE33, . . *Outdoor games . . that children play*) Inf **KY84**, Jump-for-down: see who could jump the farthest.

jumping adj

1 Used as one element of var exclams or mild oaths; see quots. Cf **Jehoshaphat, Jehu 2, Jerusalem, jiminy, John Rogers, Joses, Judas, Jupiter**

1815 Humphreys *Yankey in England* 106, *Jumping jings, jingoes,* expletives indicative of confirmation. **1914** *DN* 4.75 **ME, nNH**, *Jumpin' jewsharps!* Exclamation, usually of surprise. **1916** Lincoln *Mary-'Gusta*

146 **MA**, A habit of his wife's which irritated the Captain extremely. "Jumpin' fire!" said the latter on one occasion. **1923** *DN* 5.212 swMO, *Jumpin' Jesus,* an exclamation of great surprise. **1924** *DN* 5.271 [Exclams], Jumping geraniums, holy jumping Jesus Christ, holy jumping jellybeans, jumping Joseph, . . jumping juleps, . . (all, surp[rise] or vex[ation]), jumping Moses on a blue raft, in the mountains, in a benzine buggy, etc. (New York). **1939** FWP *ID Lore* 243, *Jumpun* [sic] *blue blazes!*—a meaningless expletive. **1942** McAtee *Dial. Grant Co.* IN 37 (as of 1890s), *Jumping Jesus* . . sometimes preceded by "holy", exclamation of surprise. **1950** *WELS* WI (*Exclamations beginning with the sound of "J"*) 7 Infs, Jumping Jehoshaphat; 6 Infs, Jumping Jiminy (Cricket); 5 Infs, Jumping Jupiter; 3 Infs, Jumping Jerusalem; 2 Infs, Jumping juniper; 2 Infs, Jumping catfish; 7 Infs, Jumping Jenny (*or* jeppers [sic], Jeremiah, Jerush, Jesus, jitterbug, Jonah). **1960** Criswell *Resp. to PADS 20* **Ozarks**, Jumpin' Jesus. **1965–70** *DARE* (Qu. NN30, *Exclamations beginning with the sound of 'j'*) 196 Infs, **widespread**, Jumpin(g) beans (*or* catfish, gee whillikers, grasshoppers, hyenas, jack(s), jeepers, Jehosaphat, Jehovah, Jehu, Jemima Jane, Jenny, Jerusalem, Jesu, Jews, jiminy, John(ny), Joseph, Joses, Judas, juniper(s), Jupiter); **KY**21, Gee jumping Jehosaphat; **MI**112, Great jumping Jehosaphat; (Qu. NN6a, *Exclamations of joy*) Inf **GA**72, Jumping Jehosaphat; jumping jelly beans; (Qu. NN29a, *Exclamations beginning with 'great':* "*Great _____!*") Infs **AR**41, **CA**120, **HI**1, **NJ**57, **NY**42, Jumping Jehosaphat; **CA**120, Jumping Jupiter; **TN**65, Jumping ploppies; (Qu. NN29c, *Exclamations beginning with 'holy':* "*Holy _____!*") Inf **PA**69, Jumping.

2 Of a plow or cultivating blade: capable of cutting through small roots but passing over large ones. Cf **jumper 10**

1921 in 1942 McAtee *Dial. Grant Co.* IN 79, *Jumping shovel plow.* **1981** Hardeman *Shucks* 61, Southerners and many farmers of the West preferred the jumping-shovel plow. *Ibid* 62, The jumping shovel plow was remarkably well adapted to loosening root-infested soil in deadenings and new clearings. The coulter blade in front of the shovel, which could cut roots up to three to four inches in diameter, jumped over larger roots. **1983** *MJLF* 9.1.45 ceKY, *Jumping coulter* . . a cutting coulter.

3 Of a pain: throbbing. *old-fash*

1884 Lewis *Sawed-Off Sketches* 53, The wife of the man next to the corner had the jumping-toothache the day she spit out her criticism. **1904** Day *Kin o' Ktaadn* 153 **ME**, Has got the jumpin' roomatiz most awful, so he says. **1942** McAtee *Dial. Grant Co.* IN 37 (as of 1890s), *Jumping toothache* . . a throbbing one. **1956** McAtee *Some Dialect NC* 25, *Jumping toothache* . . a throbbing toothache. **c1960** Wilson *Coll.* csKY, *Jumping.* . . Throbbing, like a jumping toothache. **1973** Van Noppen–Van Noppen *Western NC* 105 (as of 1880s), Other well-known diseases of the area, in the vernacular, were "pneumony fever," "side pleurisy," "joint rheumatism[,]" "jumpin' toothache," the "bloody flux" (dysentery), and "gallopin' consumption."

jumping *vbl n* See **jump** *v*

jumping beetle *n*
Prob a flea beetle (family Chrysomelidae).
[**1911** *Century Dict. Suppl.,* Jumping-beetle. . . The flea-beetle; specifically, the turnip flea-beetle of England, *Phyllotreta nemorum.*] **1968** *DARE* (Qu. R30, . . *Kinds of beetles; not asked in early QRs*) Inf **GA**25, Jumping beetle.

jumping board See **jump board**

jumping cholla *n* Also *jumping cactus* [See quot 1941]
A **prickly pear,** usu *Opuntia bigelovii* or *O. fulgida.*
1939 Pickwell *Deserts* 65, So notorious is Cholla that in the desert it is known by many different names: "Silver Cactus" (the new stems at the top are silvery in color . .); "Jumping Cactus" (when the loose stems on the ground are touched, their needles may cause the whole stem to leap . .) [etc]. **1940** (1966) Writers' Program *Guide AZ* 295, The cholla (pronounced CHO-yah) is conspicuous because of its stout trunk and short branches covered so thickly with glistening white or yellow spines that they appear fuzzy. The loosely attached joints readily fasten themselves to passing objects, hence its nickname, jumping cactus. **1941** *Torreya* 41.50, *Opuntia* spp. . . Aided by their minutely barbed and promptly clinging spines, the joints of chollas become detached at the slightest contact of animal or man, earning for the plants the popular name of jumping cactus. . . The name jumping cholla is also used. **1949** Moldenke *Amer. Wild Flowers* 103, The famous *jumping cholla* or *teddybear cactus,* C[ylindropuntia] *bigelovii*) . . [is] common on warm talus slopes of desert mountains. . . Riders will often swear that they did not touch the plant in passing, but that the joints "jumped" on to

them. **1967** *DARE* (Qu. S15, . . *Weed seeds that cling to clothing*) Inf **CA**4, Jumping cholla. **1985** Dodge *Flowers SW Deserts* 65, *Opuntia bigelovii.* . . Because the joints are so easily detached, they actually seem to jump at a passerby, this characteristic giving the plant the name jumping cactus. *Ibid* 126, The tree-sized, Sonora jumping cholla (*Opuntia fulgida*) . . is the largest of the branching, cylindrical-jointed cactuses and is very common in restricted portions of the desert.

jumping exercise See **jump** *n* 4

jumping Frenchman See **jumper 11**

jumping horse *n*
A type of play equipment for children.
1967 *Smith Co. Pioneer* (Smith Center KS) 26 Oct 4/1, Community Auction. . . cedar chest; 3 mantle [sic] clocks; ¾ size upright piano; child's jumping horse. **1986** Pederson *LAGS Concordance* (Joggling board) 2 infs, **csTN, neGA**, Jumping horse.

jumping jack *n*

1 A **click beetle.** Cf **jack snapper 1, skipjack**
1861 in 1865 IL State Ag. Soc. *Trans.* 5.416, There is scarcely an individual . . to be found who is unacquainted with the "Spring-beetles," or as they are often termed, "Jumping-Jacks." **1966** *DARE* (Qu. R8, . . *Kinds of creatures that make a clicking or shrilling or chirping kind of sound*) Inf **NC**24, Click beetle, jumping jack.

2 A **grasshopper 1.** Cf **jumper 1**
1968 *DARE* (Qu. R6, . . *Names . . for grasshoppers*) Inf **IL**27, Jumping jacks.

3 A **jumping mouse 1** (here: *Zapus hudsonicus*).
1961 Jackson *Mammals WI* 262, *Zapus hudsonicus hudsonicus.* . . In Wisconsin usually called jumping mouse or jumping jack.

4 An **earthworm.** Cf **jumper 6**
c1970 Pederson *Dial. Surv. Rural GA* seGA (*Large worms used for bait*) 1 inf, Jumping jacks. **1986** Pederson *LAGS Concordance* (Earthworm) 1 inf, ceLA, Worms, earthworm, redworm, night crawler, jumping jack.

5 A jointed doll that can be made to "dance" by means of strings, a sliding stick, a rhythmically tapped wood splint, etc. Also called **limber jack 3, supplejack**
1883 *Harper's New Mth. Mag.* 66.277 **NY**, Barley-candy statuettes, jumping-jacks, and other . . toys. **1888** *Century Illustr. Mag.* Sept 771 **Sth**, Jumping-jacks, or "supple sawneys," were made of pasteboard, and worked their arms and legs through the medium of a cotton string. **1896** Harris *Sister Jane* 351 **GA**, You're setting there acting for all the world like a jumping-jack! Have you got the fidgets? **1959** *MI Hist.* 43.390 (as of 1880s), It was a beautiful, handmade jumping jack, about nine inches long. Gus firmly held the figure by means of a short peg on the back of it between his right forefinger and thumb. In a moment he caught up the rhythm of the tune, while the Jack danced up and down, its head and arms flopping around in perfect time. [**1968** *DARE* (Qu. NN12b, *Things that people say to put off a child when he asks,* "*What are you making?*") Inf **IN**13, A jumping jack.] **1986** Pederson *LAGS Concordance,* 1 inf, ceMS, Jumping jack—homemade toy.

6 See quot.
1980 *Foxfire 6* 293 nwNC, Jumping Jack. . . We'd draw a line on the ground and then just see who could jump the furtherest. Whoever did, won. It was a simple game, but we'd play it.

7 See quot. Cf **jump board**
1986 Pederson *LAGS Concordance* (Joggling board) 1 inf, **csMS**, Seesaw, jumping jack, merry-go-round.

jumping Joses See **Joses**

jumping Judas See **Judas**

jumping mouse *n*

1 also *jumper:* A mouse of the family Zapodidae. Also called **kangaroo mouse 1.** For other names of *Zapus hudsonius* see **jumping jack 3, long-legged mouse, wood mouse**
1818 *Amer. Monthly Mag. & Crit. Rev.* 3.446 **KY**, *Gerbillus megalops.* . . Big-eye jumping mouse. . . Tail longer than the body, black with a white tuft at the end. **1842** DeKay *Zool. NY* 1.72, *Dipus hudsonius.* . . Its leaps of ten to twelve feet at a time are truly remarkable, and have occasioned it to be called the *Jumping Mouse.* In these leaps, it is of course aided by its long tail. **1849** Howitt *Our Cousins in OH* 24, It was a little mouse;—one of the kind which is called in America jumping mice, and which are extremely pretty little creatures.

It is with propriety that they are called *jumping* mice, for they can leap many yards at a bound. They might, however, with equal justice be called kangaroo mice, for they are formed very much like that animal, with short fore legs and very long hind ones. **1917** Anthony *Mammals Amer.* 264, (Zapodidae) Jumping Mice have several strong marks of distinction. . . They are slender and graceful Mice with exceptionally long tails, short fore legs, extremely long hind legs . . , and cheek pouches. . . The family is widely distributed over North America. **1961** Jackson *Mammals WI* 262, *Zapus hudsonius hudsonius.* . . In Wisconsin usually called jumping mouse. . . Other names include . . jumper [etc]. **1980** Whitaker *Audubon Field Guide Mammals* 522, Jumping mice are beautiful yellowish or reddish mice . . with deeply grooved orange incisors.

2 A **white-footed mouse**, usu *Peromyscus leucopus.*

1842 DeKay *Zool. NY* 1.82, The Jumping Mouse. *Mus leucopus. Ibid* 83, This little mouse. . . is very agile, jumping in the manner of the deer-mouse [=*Zapus hudsonius*], and is called, in common with that animal, the *jumping mouse.* . . The Jumping Mouse is found in every part of the State, and is said to build its nest in trees. **1857** U.S. Patent Office *Annual Rept. for 1856: Ag.* 90 **IL**, *Common White-footed Wood-Mouse . . Mus leucopus.* . . is known . . in common with the Wood Mouse *(Jaculus labradorius,)* . . [as] "Jumping Mouse." **1961** Jackson *Mammals WI* 216, *Peromyscus leucopus noveboracensis.* . . In Wisconsin often called deer mouse, white-footed mouse, or wood mouse. Other names include jumping mouse [etc].

jumping mullet n

1 also *jumper:* =**striped mullet.** [See quot 1933] **chiefly Mid Atl, esp NC**

1766 (1942) Bartram *Diary of a Journey* 42 **FL**, Saw a mullet jump three times in a minute or two, which they generally do before they rest, so are called jumping-mullets. **1884** Goode *Fisheries U.S.* 1.449 **NC**, The Striped Mullet, *Mugil albula.* . . About Cape Hatteras the names "Jumping Mullet" and "Sand Mullet" occur. **1899** (1912) Green *VA Folk-Speech* 247, *Jumping-mullet.* . . A small fish that jumps out of the water when startled. **1933** LA Dept. of Conserv. *Fishes* 200, The Striped Mullet, *Mugil cephalus.* . . Other popular names for the species are Callifavor . . and Jumping Mullet. [*Ibid* 201, This species usually tends to jump clear of the water whereas the White Mullet ordinarily only flips its tail above the surface.] **1939** Natl. Geogr. Soc. *Fishes* 91, Striped Mullet. . . Two of its several common names, jumping mullet and jumper, it has acquired because of its leaping habit. **1966-69** *DARE* (Qu. P2, . . *Kinds of saltwater fish caught around here . . good to eat*) Infs **NC**12, 27, Jumping mullet; **MD**36, Fatback or jumping mullet ['mʌli]—attracted to light, will jump into boat if a light is there—very oily; (Qu. P7, *Small fish used as bait for bigger fish*) Inf **NC**78, Jumping mullet. **1966** *DARE* Tapes **NC**25, 65, Jumpin' mullet. **1984** *DARE* File **Chesapeake Bay** [Watermen's vocab], Jumping mullet.

2 A **redhorse:** usu *Moxostoma cervinum,* rarely *M. erythrurum.*

1877 NY Acad. Sci. *Annals Lyceum Nat. Hist.* 10.349 **GA**, One of the "natives" "reckoned it was a Jumping Mullet," but no one else remembered having seen it before. **1878** U.S. Natl. Museum *Bulletin* 12.129, *Myxostoma* [sic for *Moxostoma*] *cervinum.* . . *Jump-rocks. Jumping Mullet.* . . It occurs in the greatest abundance in the swift streams of the South, frequenting especially the rapids or "shoals", and often throwing itself from the water in its endeavors to reach some higher rock-pool. **1896** *Ibid* 47.197, *Moxostoma cervinum.* . . *Jumping Mullet.* . . Rivers of the South Atlantic States from the James to the Neuse. **1902** Jordan-Evermann *Amer. Fishes* 61, Jumping mullet (*M[oxostoma] cervinum*).

jumping spider n Also *jumper* [*OED* 1813 →]

A spider of the family Salticidae.

1889 *Century Dict.* 3252, *Jumping-spider.* . . A spider of the family *Attidæ,* which spins no web, but captures its prey by leaping upon it. **1913** Comstock *Spider Book* 661, The jumping spiders. . . are apt to attract attention by their peculiar appearance; their short, stout legs, bright colours, conspicuous eyes, quick jumping movements being very different from those of other spiders. **1950** *WELS* (Other kinds of spiders found in your neighborhood) 2 Infs, **ceWI**, Jumping spider. **1965-70** *DARE* (Qu. R28, . . *Kinds of spiders*) 17 Infs, **scattered, but esp Sth, S Midl,** Jumping spider; **GA**20, Gray jumper. **1971** GA Dept. Ag. *Farmers Market Bulletin* 26 May 1/2, The spider was a jumping spider of the attidae family. It is not harmful and chases its prey instead of making webs. **1980** Milne-Milne *Audubon Field Guide Insects* 910, *Jumping Spiders*—(Family Salticidae). This large family gets its name from the spectacular leaps the spiders make pouncing on prey.

jumping toothache See **jumping** adj 3

jump jacket n [Prob abbr for *jumper jacket,* but cf Engl dial *jump* a man's loose jacket] **S Midl, esp KY**

A man's denim work jacket.

1941 *Sat. Eve. Post* 10 May 36 **eKY**, Buttoning jump jacket and spying to see what was in the skillet. **c1960** *Wilson Coll.* **csKY**, Jump jacket—short work coat for men. Usually jumper jacket. **1965-70** *DARE* (Qu. W4, . . *Men's coats or jackets for work and outdoor wear*) Infs **KY**42, **VA**2, Jump jacket; **KY**24, Jump jacket—same as jumper or overall jacket; **KY**30, Jump jacket—made of denim; **KY**37, Jump jacket—denim, lined with flannel; **KY**40, Denim jacket same as jump jacket; **KY**44, Jump jacket—denim with flannelette lining, waist-length; **VA**45, Jump jacket—denim. **1974** Fink *Mountain Speech* 13 **wNC, eTN**, Jump-jacket . . overall jacket. **1986** Pederson *LAGS Concordance,* 1 inf, **neTN**, Jump jacket—of denim material.

jump Josie v phr

To step lively, get going.

1937 NE Univ. *Studies* 37.104 **OK** [Terms from play-party songs], Big foot guy and can't jump Josie. . . Big-footed nigger and can't jump Josey. *Ibid* 111, Once and a half if you can't jump Josey. **1992** *DARE* File **NC** (as of c1915), I remember the phrase "to jump Josie," used by my mother. It apparently meant 'to make an extraordinary effort to get something done.' She would have said, "I've waited so long to do that job that I'm really going to have to jump Josie."

jump, jump, how many fingers up n [Var of *buck, buck, how many . . up* (at **buck buck 1**)]

1971 *AmSp* 46.84 **Chicago IL**, Crude games involving . . brutality . . *jump-jump-how-many-fingers-up.*

jump meat n

1969 *DARE* (Qu. P35a, *Names or nicknames for any deer shot illegally*) Inf **WI**77A, Jump meat.

jump off the deep end v phr Also *jump off the bridge,* ~ *overboard joc* Cf **jump the broom**

To get married.

1968-69 *DARE* (Qu. AA15a, . . *Joking ways . . of saying that people got married . . "They _____."*) Inf **PA**189, Jumped off the deep end; (Qu. AA15b, . . *Joking ways . . of saying that a man is getting married . . "He _____."*) Inf **CT**7, Jumped off the deep end; **NJ**39, Jumped overboard; **PA**167, Jumped off the bridge.

jump out See **jump** v 2

jumpover n Cf **flopover**

1905 *DN* 3.84 **nwAR**, *Jump-over.* . . Griddle-cake. 'Jumpovers and 'lasses are larrupin' good.' Rare.

jump overboard See **jump off the deep end**

jump over the broom(stick) See **jump the broom**

jump over the doorstep (or hoop, traces) See **jump the bucket**

jump plant n [Perh from the seed's sticking to clothing] Cf **jumping cholla**

=**lopseed.**

1940 Clute *Amer. Plant Names* 266, *Phryma leptostachys.* Lop-seed, jump-plant.

jump-rock n Also *jump-rocks* [See quot 1878]

Any of several **redhorses** (here: *Moxostoma* spp).

1878 U.S. Natl. Museum *Bulletin* 12.26 **SC**, *Myxostoma* [sic] *cervinum.* . . This little Sucker. . . abounds in rapids and rocky shoals, and is popularly known as "Jump-rocks", from its habit of leaping from the water. It is not much valued, except by negroes, small boys, and naturalists. **1896** *Ibid* 47.196, *Moxostoma rupiscartes.* . . *Jump-rocks.* . . Rivers of Carolina and Georgia from the Catawba to the Chattahoochee. **1902** Jordan-Evermann *Amer. Fishes* 61, Jump-rocks (*M[oxostoma] rupiscartes*) . . abundant about rapids and rocky pools. **1957** Blair et al. *Vertebrates U.S.* 82, *Moxostoma lachneri.* . . Greater jumprock. . . *Moxostoma rupiscartes.* . . Striped jumprock. . . *Moxostoma cervinum.* . . Black jumprock. **1960** Amer. Fisheries Soc. *List Fishes* 17, Bigeye jumprock . . *Moxostoma ariommum.*

jumps n pl

1 often with *the:* Feelings of nervousness or apprehension; exaggerated startle responses; delirium tremens. Cf **fidget** n 1

1912 Green *VA Folk-Speech* 247, *Jumps.* . . Fidgets; nervous starts. **1928** Wharton *Squad* 63, I can't blue tag every fellow who's got the jumps. I've got 'em myself. We'd all have to go to the rear. **1934** (1940) Weseen *Dict. Amer. Slang* 278, *Jumps*—Delirium tremens. **1942** Berrey–Van den Bark *Amer. Slang* 130.9, *Delirium tremens.* . . the jumps. *Ibid* 267.1, *Nervousness.* . . jumps. **1958** Latham *Meskin Hound* 11 **cTX**, "Shut up!" Cleever lurched toward him swinging the carbine, but it was false pretense. There was more on his mind than beating up his stepson. . . The big black jumps were riding him, scratching him with mortal terror. **1965** *DARE* (Qu. P36, *When a hunter sees a deer or other game animal and gets so excited he can't shoot, he has* _____) Inf **OK**11, The jumps. **1967** *Yankee* Oct 85 **nME**, Ever heard of "the jumps?" If not, ask someone from northern Maine sometime.

2 in phr *by jumps:* Used as an exclam or mild oath.
    1959 *VT Hist.* 27.145, *By Jumps!* . . Obsolete.

3 also *jumpsies, jump shot;* In marble play: see quot.
    c1970 Wiersma *Marbles Terms, Jumps.* . . Type of shot in which the shooter flips the marble over his opponent['s marble] into the hole using the thumb-forefinger shooting technique. *Ibid, Jumpsies*—a marble is thumped and jumped over another marble. *Ibid, Jump shot*—making the shooter jump one marble (player's own) to hit another one (opponent's) in the circle.

jump salty v phr *esp freq among Black speakers* Cf **salty**
To get angry; to respond (to someone or something) in an extreme or unexpected manner.
    1938 *NY Amsterdam News* (NY) 26 Feb 17/2, Let's sound a high C on the postoffice man whose Girl Friday is "jumpin' salty" 'cause he won't Reno the wife who thinks but isn't sure. **1938** *AmSp* 13.314 [Black], *Jump salty.* Implies an unexpected change in a person's attitude or knowledge. The person may become suddenly angry, or an unhipped person may become hipped. **1941** in 1983 Taft *Blues Lyric Poetry* 284, [Title:] My Feet Jumped Salty. . . [Lyrics:] The little game rooster : told the little guinea hen / If I ever catch you squatting : around my nest again / I will have to jump salty. . . One [woman] found out : the other one had a man / Then that woman jumped salty. . . A man cocked a pistol : right in my face / Then my feet jumped salty. **1942** *Amer. Mercury* 55.89 **Harlem NYC** [Black], If you trying to jump salty, Jelly, that's your mammy. *Ibid* 95, [Glossary:] *Jump salty*—get angry. **1965** Bradford *Born with the Blues* 91 **Sth** [Black], "My Man Jumped Salty on Me" [and three other songs] . . have become collectors' items already. *Ibid* 93, I jumped salty and told him in front [=to his face] these historical facts. **1970** Major *Dict. Afro–Amer. Slang* 72, *Jump salty:* (1930's–40's) to suddenly become angry. **1974** Baldwin *If Beale St. Could Talk* 82 **NYC** [Black], He warned me if I didn't take my hands off him we might never get uptown and then my Daddy might jump salty.

jumpseed n [See quots 1931, 1933]
A **knotweed 1** (here: *Polygonum virginianum*).
    1931 Clute *Common Plants* 137, The New Jersey tea . . propels its seeds . . , but . . one must watch and wait to see the explosion. Not so the jump-seed (*Tovaria Virginica*). This has a trigger arrangement which needs only a touch to set things going. **1933** Small *Manual SE Flora* 454, *Jump-seed.* . . The common name refers to the surprising distance the ripe achenes fly when pressed under the thumb nail. **1950** Gray–Fernald *Manual of Botany* 571, *Jumpseed.* . . Tall perennials of e. N[orth] Am[erica]. **1970** Correll *Plants TX* 522, *Polygonum virginianum.* . . *Jump seed.* . . Local in rich woodlands.

jump shot, jumpsies See **jumps 3**

jump sticks n pl
Stilts.
    1967 *DARE* (Qu. EE35, *Long wooden poles with a footpiece that children walk around on to make them tall*) Inf **NJ**3, Jump sticks.

jump-sturdy n
    1941 *AmSp* 16.16 **eTX** [Black], In the winter . . go in the woods and get you a bush-bacon. That's a rabbit. Some of them calls them a jump-sturdy.

jump the broom v phr Also *jump over the broom,* ~ *(over) the broomstick;* for addit varr see quots **scattered, but chiefly Sth, S Midl, TX** See Map
Of a man and a woman: to step over a broomstick together as a ceremony symbolizing marriage or common-law marriage; to get married.
    [**1828** Cooper *Prairie* 2.157, An honest woman is no better in his eyes than one of your broomstick jumpers.] **1856** Kelly *Humors* 422 **cwNY**,

Let's make up a wedding-party—*let's jump the broomstick!* **1899** (1912) Green *VA Folk-Speech* 247, *Jump over the broom.* . . Phrase for an irregular marriage. **1918** *DN* 5.20 **NC**, *Jump the broom,* to get married (facetious). c1937 in 1977 *Amer. Slave Suppl. 1* 1.167 **AL**, Dey jus jumped over de broom, den atter slavery wus over she had to remarry. **1941** Stuart *Men of Mts.* 107 **neKY**, We walked five miles to town and got our license. We walked six miles back to Brother Tobbie Bostick's and jumped the broom. **1944** *PADS* 2.25 **cwNC**, *Broom-stick, to jump over the.* . . To get married. (In some sections: common-law marriage.) **1945** Saxon *Gumbo Ya-Ya* 239 **LA**, Elizabeth Ross Hite said, 'My master would say to two peoples what wanted to get married, "Come on, darky, jump over this here broom and call yourself man and wife." ' **1950** *PADS* 13.16 **cTX**, *Broomstick, to jump over the.* . . To get married. Often shortened to *jump the broom.* **1952** Brown *NC Folkl.* 1.236, An old slave custom was to "jump the broom" instead of having a marriage ceremony. [*Ibid* 237, [Footnote:] Another suggestion is that the broomstick was probably originally a branch of a sacred tree and that the jumping over it was intended to promote the fertility of the bride. It is possible also that the jumping may originally have been a virginity or chastity test (cf. the dancing in some of the English and Scottish popular ballads).] **1953** Randolph–Wilson *Down in Holler* 257 **Ozarks**, *Jump the broomstick.* . . To marry. Sometimes perhaps it means to propose marriage. **1960** Hall *Smoky Mt. Folks* 65, *To jump the broom:* to get married, referring to an old protection against witches. . . Mrs. Polly Grooms, of Newport, Tennessee, said, "Lay a broom across the door, and no witches won't step over that, they say." **1965–70** *DARE* (Qu. AA15a, . . *Joking ways* . . *of saying that people got married* . . "They _____.") 52 Infs, **chiefly Sth, S Midl, TX**, Jumped the broom(stick); 16 Infs, **scattered,** Jumped the broom handle; **MO**3, **NY**162, Jumped over the broomstick; **IN**38, Hopped the broomstick; **MO**8, Stepped over the broomstick; (Qu. AA4a, . . *A man who is very eager to get married* . . "He's _____.") Inf **KY**19, Dying to jump the broom; **NC**37, Trying to jump the broom; **NY**76, Getting ready to go over the broom; (Qu. AA15b, . . *Joking ways* . . *of saying that a man is getting married* . . "He _____.") Inf **VA**2, Jumped a broomstick; **KS**18, Jumped over a broomstick; **KY**19, Jumped the broom; **AR**37, 39, **MO**23, Jumped the broomstick; (Qu. AA15c, . . *Joking ways* . . *of saying that a woman is getting married* . . "She _____.") Infs **AR**39, **KY**28, **MI**115, **VA**2, Jumped the (*or* a) broomstick; **TX**10, Jumped over the broomstick; **KY**19, Jumped the broom; (Qu. AA20, *A marriage that takes place because a baby is on the way*) Inf **VA**31, She jumped the broomstick. **1968** *DARE* FW Addit **LA**32, *Jump the broom*—to get married. There was a custom when the priest came around only every so often that a couple would jump over a broom to indicate that they were married; the official ceremony would then be held when the priest arrived. **1984** Wilder *You All Spoken Here* 99 **Sth**, *Jump the broomstick; jump the twig; jump the stick:* Common law or simulated marriage ceremony; nuptials without benefit of clergy or justice of the peace.

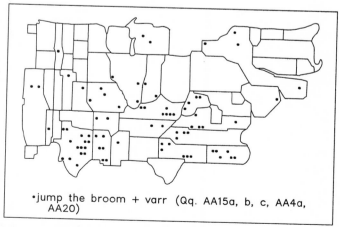

•jump the broom + varr (Qq. AA15a, b, c, AA4a, AA20)

jump the bucket v phr Also *jump the ditch,* ~ *fence,* ~ *puddle, jump over the doorstep,* ~ *hoop,* ~ *traces* joc
=**jump the broom.**
    1967–70 *DARE* (Qu. AA15a, . . *Joking ways* . . *of saying that people got married* . . "They _____.") Inf **AK**8, Jumped the puddle; **MS**21, Jumped the bucket; **NY**92, Jumped the ditch; **VA**41, Jumped the fence; (Qu. AA15b, . . *Joking ways* . . *of saying that a man is getting married* . . "He _____.") Inf **MS**21, Jumped the bucket; **IN**54, Jumped over the doorstep; **CA**36, Jumped over the hoop; **CA**17, Jumped over

the traces; (Qu. AA15c, . . *Joking ways . . of saying that a woman is getting married. . . "She _____."*) Inf **IN**54, Jumped over the doorstep; **KY**44, Jumped the fence. **1986** Pederson *LAGS Concordance (Married)* 1 inf, **cTN**, Jumped the bucket.

jump the buckeye log See **buckeye log**

jump the ditch (or fence, puddle) See **jump the bucket**

jump the rope v phr **esp Sth, S Midl**
=**jump the broom.**
    1966–69 DARE (Qu. AA15a, . . *Joking ways . . of saying that people got married . . "They _____."*) Infs **AL4, KY28, MO9, NM5**, Jumped the rope. **1986** Pederson *LAGS Concordance (Married)* 3 infs, **cwGA, neFL, cTN**, Jump the rope.

jump-the-rope n **chiefly Sth, S Midl** See Map
The game of jump rope.
    1957 *Sat. Eve. Post Letters* **MA**, Jump the rope—a version of regular skip rope. **1965–70** DARE (Qu. EE33, . . *Outdoor games . . that children play*) 14 Infs, **Sth, S Midl**, Jump-the-rope. **1967** DARE File **swOR**, Jump-the-rope. [DARE FW: what I call jump rope or jumping rope (children's game)]

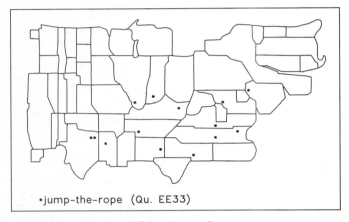

•jump-the-rope (Qu. EE33)

jump the track v phr Cf **fly the track**
    c1960 *Wilson Coll.* **csKY**, Jump the track. . . Violently quit something, blow up, change sides.

jump up v phr
1 To assemble or arrange hastily; hence ppl adj phr *jumped up.* Cf EDD *jumped-up do* (at *jumped-up* ppl. adj. 3) "an incident that has been suddenly developed or brought about"]
    1848 in 1973 Thompson *Major Jones's Courtship* 260 **GA**, The company was jest about as good a one as could be jumped up for sich a occasion. **1908** DN 3.326 **eAL, wGA**, Jumped-up. . . Sudden, quickly and thoughtlessly arranged. "It was a jumped-up affair." **1943** *AmSp* 18.237 **cwMS** [Black], A colored woman born about 1870 in Louisiana near Vicksburg, Mississippi, raised there, and having little formal education, used the following expressions: . . *Jumped up,* . . hurriedly organized, extemporized. 'I don't like dese jumped-up churches.' **1958** McCulloch *Woods Words* 99 **Pacific NW**, *Jump-up landing*—One where the loading is done by means of a gin pole raised or jumped up on the spot.
2 See **jump** v 2.

jump-up n
1 A **violet.** Cf **johnny-jump-up 1**
    1942 *Sat. Eve. Post* 5 Sept 53, Ma was in her chair, fresh as a jump-up. **1967** DARE (Qu. S26e, *Other wildflowers not yet mentioned; not asked in early QRs*) Inf **OR**10, Yellow jump-up.
2 See quot.
    1953 Randolph–Wilson *Down in Holler* 257 **Ozarks**, Jump-up. . . A meeting at which extemporaneous speeches are delivered. I have heard the exercises on the "last day" of school called a *jump-up.*
3 See **jump** n 2.
4 See **jump-up song.**

jump-up-johnny n Cf **johnny-jump-up 1**
=**violet.**
    1844 *New Mirror* (NY NY) 9 Mar 354/1 **NEng**, As you peep through

the branches of the tall, white lilac . . you will probably see Aunt Nancy weeding among the beet and onion beds, or looking with a pleased eye upon the clusters of "china-pinks," *"jump-up-johnnies,"* and *"none-so-pretty's."* **1881** Vanderbilt *Social Flatbush* 287 **seNY**, Pansies were abundant, but they were very small, and, under the common name of "jump-up Johnnies," crept out from the garden-bed to the grass-plot. **1888** *Century Illustr. Mag.* 35.947 **cKY**, Beds of jump-up-Johnnies, sweet-williams, daffodils. **1963** Edwards *Gravel* 85 **eTN** (as of 1920s), Children romped barefoot . . close to the foot of Cumberland Mountain, picking bunches of jump-up-johnnies from along the bases of old rotten logs, where they were wont to grow in profusion.

jump-up song n Also *jump-up, jumped-up song* **chiefly Sth** *chiefly among Black speakers* Cf **jump up** v phr **1**
Appar a lively song with simple, partly extemporized lyrics.
    1939 FWP *Guide TN* 144, "Note singing" and "book singing" are rapidly replacing the "jump-up" songs among the Negroes. **1947** Lomax *Advent. Ballad Hunter* 148 **AR** (as of 1930s) [Black], "Can you sing axe-cutting songs like the ones I heard in Mississippi? *Stewball, Rosie* and songs like that?" "Them's old common songs," Kelly said. "We'll give you some old Arkansas, jumped-up songs." *Ibid* 165 **TX** (as of 1933) [Black], I know lots of jumped-up, sinful songs—more than any of these niggers. **1953** Randolph–Wilson *Down in Holler* 257 **Ozarks**, Certain wild chants popular in Holy Roller circles are known as *jump-up* songs. **1959** Lomax *Rainbow Sign* 62 **AL** [Black], Then sometimes he sing songs of olden times like "Boll Weevil," "Stagolee," . . and all such jump-up songs. **1960** (1961) Oliver *Blues Fell* 132, The old-time religion of the Southern churches does not permit the singing of 'devil songs' and 'jumped-up' songs as the blues are commonly termed. **1971** Evans *Tommy Johnson* 18 **MS**, LeDell Johnson recalls that the Wilsons played 'love songs' and 'jump ups', such as *I Want Somebody To Love Me.* **1981** Palmer *Deep Blues* 41, If they [=Black musicians of the Reconstruction era] performed blueslike material, it was almost certainly either narrative ballads with a melodic flavor that approximated what later became known as blues, or songs called jump-ups that strung together more or less unrelated lines, most of them of a proverbial nature, over a simple chorded accompaniment. **1995** DARE File, "Jumped-up" is a generic term for a song with few words, usually in short phrases, accompanied by body movement.

junco n[1] [See quot 1917]
A small gray to gray-brown bird (*Junco* spp) with white abdomen. Also called **snowbird;** for other names of the eastern race of *J. hyemalis* formerly designated as the "slate-colored junco" see **blue snowbird, rainbird, skeet, white-tailed sparrow;** for other names of var western races see **Oregon junco**
    1887 Ridgway *N. Amer. Birds* 422, J[unco] aikeni. . . White-winged Junco. . . *J. hyemalis.* . . Slate-colored Junco [etc]. **1917** (1923) *Birds Amer.* 3.46, Coues says that it is derived from the Latin *juncus* meaning a seed [sic for *reed*]. It was after 1830 that the word "Junco" was first brought into scientific use. **1938** Oberholser *Bird Life LA* 662, The Junco is a familiar visitor around houses, in both country and town. **1949** Leopold *Sand Co. Almanac* 55 **WI**, The tamaracks change from green to yellow when the first frosts have brought woodcock, fox sparrows, and juncos out of the north. **1966–69** DARE (Qu. Q14) Infs **NY**126, **VT**4, Junco; (Qu. Q20) Inf **CA**6, Junco; (Qu. Q21) Infs **ME**8, 22, Junco; **OR**4, Oregon junco; **TN**11, Slate-colored junco; (Qu. Q23) Inf **CA**24, Junco. **1977** Udvardy *Audubon Field Guide Birds* 731, In appearance this junco [=*Junco caniceps*] seems to be an intermediate form between the Dark-eyed and Yellow-eyed juncos. Its plumage is similar to that of the Yellow-eyed, but it has dark eyes.

junco n[2] [Span *junco* rush]
1 pronc-sp *honco:* =**allthorn 1. chiefly SW**
    1849 in 1932 *Amer. Antiq. Soc. Proc.* 41.382, You speak of a "dry berry" which I send you as seed of the *junco* (green-thorn-shrub). **1871** *Overland Mth.* 6.555 **cwTX**, The *junco* has absolutely no foliage, except immense, horrid, green thorns. **1903** Small *Flora SE U.S.* 672, *Koeberlinia. . . Junco.* . . An intricately branched almost leafless shrub or small tree . ., the branches all ending in firm thorns, clothed with a bright green puberulent bark. **1929** Dobie *Vaquero* 202 **West**, The *junco* (the all-thorn), . . naked of leaves, was, according to Mexican belief, woven into Christ's crown of thorns, and, as a result, has ever since been shunned by all birds of the air save one—the butcher bird, who alone will alight upon it. **1951** PADS 15.36 **TX**, *Koeberlinia spinosa.* . .

Crown-of-thorns; junco; honco. **1970** Correll *Plants TX* 1074, *Koeberlinia*. . . Junco. Allthorn.

2 A low, dense shrub *(Adolphia infesta)* native to Texas. Also called **allthorn 3**

    1960 Vines *Trees SW* 687, Texas Adolphia *(Adolphia infesta)*. . . Also known under the names of Junco, or Allthorn, but these names also apply to *Koeberlinia spinosa,* which this shrub somewhat resembles. **1970** Correll *Plants TX* 1011, *Adolphia*. . . Junco. . . The roots have an anise- or licorice-like odor.

jundy v [Cf *EDD jundy* v. "Sc. Irel." 1. "to jostle" 2. "of a vessel containing liquid: to rock from side to side"]

    1903 *DN* 2.352, *Jundy*. . . To topple over.

June n See **June apple 1**

june v [Prob echoic] **chiefly Sth, S Midl**

1 also with *along, around:* To hasten, hurry; to bustle. Cf **zoon**

    1869 *Overland Mth.* 3.127 **TX,** A trig, smirk little horse is a "lace-horse," and he often has to "june" . . or "get up and dust." [*Overland Mth.* Ed: There is a large colony of Germans in Western Texas, and "june" is said to be corrupted from their *gehen.*] **1892** *DN* 1.230 **KY,** *June-in'* [ˈjunɪn]: running fast. "She came a-june-in'." An onomatopoetic word, from the humming noise made by what we call *June-bugs.* They are the bronze-coated beetles that children catch to tie long strings to their legs to hold them while they hum in their efforts to fly away. **1893** Shands *MS Speech* 41, *June*. . . A word used by all classes to mean *to get along, to progress;* as, "He made that horse june." **1903** (1965) Adams *Log Cowboy* 228 **West,** Now, we thought, if the herd could be brought up slowly, and this bridgeful let off in their lead, they might follow. To june a herd of cattle across in this manner would have been shameful. **1905** *DN* 3.84 **nwAR,** *June*. . . To hurry. 'It made him june (with what he was doing).' 'We went just a-junin'.' 'He kept me a-junin' ' (used by a stenographer of an employer). Not uncommon. **1923** *DN* 5.212 **swMO,** *June along*. . . To hasten. *To come a-junin'* = to come hastily. **1940** (1978) Still *River of Earth* 199 **KY,** This time o' year the mining business ought to be juning. **1984** Burns *Cold Sassy* 154 **nGA** (as of 1906), I really juned around when I got home that evening. I needed to lay in a store of good feelings as well as stovewood before asking permission to go camping.

2 also with *around:* To make a humming or rasping sound; to buzz. Cf **June bird**

    1893 Shands *MS Speech* 41, *June*. . . To make a humming noise, as is made by a body moving or revolving swiftly; . . a nail when thrown through the air, is said to *june.* **c1960** Wilson *Coll.* **csKY,** *June bug*. . . Children . . would tie a thread to one of its legs and let the insect "June" around.

3 with *around:* To putter; to loaf or idle (about).

    1895 *Inlander* Nov 61, *June around.* To be busy but not accomplish anything. **1948** *AmSp* 23.305 **Ozarks,** You stay here and I'll go down and june around awhile. (Gossip with loafers on streets of the town.) [**1968** Adams *Western Words* 167, *Junin' 'round*—A cowboy's expression meaning *restless.*] **1975** *DARE* File **eVA,** June around—take it easy; used in the Virginia counties of Delmarva Peninsula. **1984** Wilder *You All Spoken Here* 17 **Sth,** *Juneing around:* Flitting leisurely.

4 To pay court to. Cf **junesey**

    1948 Manfred *Chokecherry* 27 **nwIA,** He's been junin' Gert Hansen. **1953** Randolph–Wilson *Down in Holler* 258 **Ozarks,** *June*. . . Sometimes it seems to mean courting or sparking: "They tell me Jim Burke's a-junin' Sally Randall here lately."

june along See **june v 1**

June apple n

1 also *June (Harvest):* A yellow transparent or similar early-ripening apple; see quots. **chiefly S Midl, esp KY**

    1853 *S. Lit. Messenger* 19.221 **KY,** She was painted up like a doll; her withered old face streaked like a June apple. **1856** U.S. Patent Office *Annual Rept. for 1855: Ag.* 291 **swIL,** The "Red" and "Yellow June Harvest," and other kinds of summer apples, are drugs in the market. **1906** *DN* 3.137 **nwAR,** How much are June apples a gallon? **1954** Harder *Coll.* **cwTN,** *Apple:* Varieties: . . June, sweet apple. **1960** Criswell *Resp. to PADS 20* **Ozarks,** June apple, or red June. **c1960** Wilson *Coll.* **KY,** June apple. An old-time favorite . . because of its being so early to ripen. **1968–70** *DARE* (Qu. I53, . . *Fruits grown around here . . special varieties)* Infs **KY42, 50, NC55,** June apples; **IA22,** June apple—a red apple like a Delicious—matures early; **KY71,** June apple [same as] Transparent; **KY74,** Early June apples (Transparent); (Qu.

T13) Inf **NC49,** June apple. **1985** *NC Folkl. Jrl.* 33.37 **wNC** (as of c1920), After wild strawberries ripened it wasn't long until the early transparent and striped June apples came along.

2 A **pinxter flower** (here: prob *Rhododendron nudiflorum*). Cf **swamp apple**

    1969 *DARE* (Qu. S4) Inf **NY205,** June apple, swamp apple.

3 =**mayapple 1** (here: *Podophyllum peltatum*).

    1970 *DARE* (Qu. S4, . . *Mayapple:* [Woodside plant, not a tree, with two large spreading leaves; they grow in patches and have a small yellow fruit late in summer]) Inf **VA111,** June apple.

june around See **june v 1, 2, 3**

June bean n

A **jack bean 1** (here: *Canavalia maritima*).

    1933 Small *Manual SE Flora* 727, *C[anavalia] lineata*. . . *June-bean*. . . Coastal sand-dunes, Fla. and Tex. and sandy shores of Lake Okeechobee, Fla. **1953** Greene–Blomquist *Flowers South* 61, *Bay-bean, June-bean (Canavalia lineata)*. . . This extensively trailing vine . . grows in the coastal sand dunes of the Gulf states from Fla. to Tex. and the W[est] I[ndies]. . . The pods are from 3½″–4″ long.

June beetle See **June bug 1**

Juneberry n

1 =**serviceberry.** [See quot 1973] **chiefly MI, MN, WI; also PA** See Map

    1813 Michaux *Histoire des Arbres* 3.32, Mespilus arborea. *June berry,* nom donné à cet arbre dans tous les Etats du milieu. [=Mespilus arborea. *June berry,* name given to this tree in all the middle States.] **1821** *Jrnl. Science* III.275 *(DA),* Found the apple . . trees, the iron-wood, june-berry [etc]. **1844** Lapham *Geogr. Descr. WI* 79, Amelanchier Canadensis, . . June berry, shad berry, service tree, &c. **1892** *Jrl. Amer. Folkl.* 5.95, *Amelanchier Canadensis,* June berry. Various parts of N.E. and Central States. **1905** *DN* 3.84 **nwAR,** *June berry*. . . Service berry. 'June berries are bigger than huckleberries.' **1935** Sandoz *Jules* 180 **wNE** (as of 1880–1930), He sent samples of the dark berries, delicious and heavily sweet. . . [T]hey were Juneberries, rare in Nebraska. **1950** *WELS* (*Kinds of berries . . wild*) 9 Infs, **WI,** Juneberries. **1961** Douglas *My Wilderness* 192, Early to bloom is a tree which in the Far West we call juneberry. **1965–70** *DARE* (Qu. I44, *What kinds of berries grow wild around here?*) 26 Infs, **chiefly MI, MN, WI,** Juneberries; (Qu. H63, *Kinds of desserts*) Infs **MI104, MN16,** Juneberry pie; (Qu. I46, . . *Kinds of fruits that grow wild around here*) Inf **WI64,** Juneberries; (Qu. I53, . . *Fruits grown around here . . special varieties*) Inf **MN29,** Juneberries; (Qu. S26c, *Wildflowers that grow in woods*) Inf **PA198,** Juneberries; (Qu. T15, . . *Kinds of swamp trees*) Inf **MI96,** Juneberry; (Qu. T16, . . *Kinds of trees . . 'special'*) Inf **PA206,** Juneberry. **1966** *DARE* Tape **MI36,** There was a nice sugar plum tree there or Juneberries. **1973** Wharton–Barbour *Trees KY* 528, *Amelanchier*. . . In many places it is known as Juneberry because its fruits mature earlier than most edible fruits.

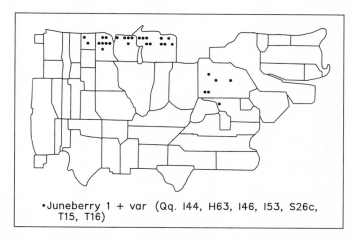

•Juneberry 1 + var (Qq. I44, H63, I46, I53, S26c, T15, T16)

2 A **wolfberry** (here: *Symphoricarpos occidentalis*).

    1924 *Amer. Botanist* 30.32 **West,** *Symphoricarpos occidentalis* is known variously, and often incorrectly, of course, as . . "June-berry" and "partridge-berry." **1940** Clute *Amer. Plant Names* 167, June-berry. *Symphoricarpos occidentalis.*

3 Appar a **dewberry 1** or similar blackberry of the genus *Rubus;* see quot. **esp SC Cf mayberry 1**

1966–67 *DARE* (Qu. I44, *What kinds of berries grow wild around here?*) Inf **SC**4, Juneberries—on a bush and come sooner than blackberries—otherwise blackberries = Juneberries; **SC**9, Juneberries—high-bush; Juneberries, mayberries—both are blackberries; **SC**43, Juneberries—grows [sic] up on a sticky vine; blackberries = Juneberries; blackberries—runs [sic] on the ground; **SC**62, Juneberries—a highbush blackberry.

June bird n¹ [Prob **june** v **2**; uppercase *J* in *June* is prob by folk-etym]

A **hummingbird 1.**

1933 Rawlings *South Moon* 180 **nFL,** Humming-birds darted at the coral honeysuckle on the fence. Piety said, "The June-birds is early."

June bird n² [*June* from its appearance in that month]

A **goldfinch 1** (here: *Carduelis tristis*).

1951 *AmSp* 26.271 **TN,** A few names particularize individual months, as . . *June bird* for the familiar goldfinch.

Junebud n

A **redbud** (here: *Cercis canadensis*).

1908 Britton *N. Amer. Trees* 535, *Cercis canadensis*. . . This beautiful tree, which is also called . . Junebud, occurs from Ontario and New Jersey to Florida, and westwardly to Minnesota and Arkansas. **1938** Van Dersal *Native Woody Plants* 340, Junebud *(Cercis canadensis).* **1940** Clute *Amer. Plant Names* 17, Junebud.

June bug n [From its appearance in late spring (cf Ger *Maikäfer* "May chafer" for *cockchafer*); but cf **june** v **2**] Cf **June fly**

1 also *June beetle, Juney bug, Juny (bug):* Any of var scarab beetles of the genus *Phyllophaga* or var related genera. Also called **dorbug, fish bug, hard-shell beetle, horn bug 3, June fly 2, May bee, May beetle, May bug 1, mayfly 2, white grub.** For other names of *Cotinus nitidus* see **figeater 1** See also **brownback 4, dinapaddy, dry fly 2**

1829 in 1965 *AmSp* 40.132, Snake. . . Dere's possum up de gumtree, An Raccoon in de hollow, Wake Snakes for June Bugs Stole my half a dollar. **1857** Strother *VA Illustr.* 110, [A Negro] dressed in his holiday suit, with a ruffled shirt of red calico, a June-bug breast-pin, a brass-headed cane [etc]. **a1883** (1911) Bagby *VA Gentleman* 45, The humming-birds and the bumble-bees and Juney-bugs, which knew them [=flowers] once, shall know them no more forever. **1893** Shands *MS Speech* 41, There is a certain kind of bugs called *june-bugs,* because they make a peculiar humming noise with their wings when they are tied with a string. These bugs form one of the favorite playthings of Mississippi children. **1905** Kellogg *Amer. Insects* 275, The June-beetle, *Lachnosterna fusca.* **1906** Churchill *Coniston* 189 **NEng,** June-bugs hummed in at the high windows. **1908** *DN* 3.326 **eAL, wGA,** June-bug. . . A large greenish scarabaeid: common from early May until August. . . Also called . . *juny-bug.* **1956** McAtee *Some Dialect NC* 25, *June bug:* the Scarabaeid beetle *Phanaeus vindex.* **c1960** *Wilson Coll.* **csKY,** June bug. . . The beetle *Cotinis nitida,* beloved of children, who would tie a thread to one of its legs and let the insect "June" around. **1965–70** *DARE* (Qu. R5, *A big brown beetle that comes out in large numbers in spring and early summer, and flies with a buzzing sound: [Note: some are green.]*) 767 Infs, **widespread,** June bug; **IA**11, **IL**135, **KY**53, **NE**3, **NJ**55, June beetle; **IL**25, **VA**96, Juny; **TN**52, Juny bug; (Qu. R30, . . *Kinds of beetles;* not asked in early QRs) Infs **IL**58, **KY**11, **NJ**3, **NY**22, 165, **OH**79, **PA**9, **TX**38, **VA**26, June bug; **PA**26, June beetle; (Qu. P6, . . *Kinds of worms . . used for bait*) Infs **MI**65, June bug; **TX**19, June bug larva; (Qu. HH6, *Someone who is out of his mind*) Inf **VA**101, Crazy as a June bug. **1976** Ryland *Richmond Co. VA* 372, *Juny-bug*—a large green beetle.

2a =**firefly 1.**

1931–33 *LANE Worksheets* **cMA,** They're called June bugs, but we always called them lightning bugs. **1939** *LANE* Map 238 *(Lightning bug)* 5 infs, **CT, MA,** June bug(s). **1948** Davis *Word Atlas Gt. Lakes* 167, *Insect that glows at night.* . . June bug fairly common [in northern section of **OH**]. **1966** Dakin *Dial. Vocab. Ohio R. Valley* 2.406, Two Ohio informants in widely separated communities (Clermont and Jefferson Counties) say June bug. In both cases the term unquestionably = *lightning bug* and not the large hard-shelled flying beetle (*Phyllophoga fasca* [sic]) usually called "June bug." **1967–69** *DARE* (Qu. R1, . . *The small insect that flies at night and flashes a light at its tail*) Infs **KS**18, **MN**29, **MO**7, **NJ**30, June bug; **MA**26, Firebug, firefly—same as June

bug; **OH**22, Lightning bug, June bug—that's not the proper name; **PA**70, Lightning bug, June bug. **1971** Wood *Vocab. Change* 35 **Sth,** *A glowing insect.* . . Three-fourths or more of the choices are *lightning bug.* . . Instances of *June bug* are reported. **1973** Allen *LAUM* 1.328 (as of c1950), *June bug,* generally accepted as the name of a kind of beetle, is firmly accepted by several infs. as their term for a firefly. This confusion—if that is what it is—appears in all the U[pper] M[idwest] states except Iowa. **1981** Pederson *LAGS Basic Materials* **Gulf Region** *(Firefly)* 18 infs, June bug(s); 1 inf, Lightning bug, June bugs—many call them this because they show up in June or late May.

b Transf: a lantern.

1956 Sorden–Ebert *Logger's Words* 20 **Gt Lakes,** June-bug, A lantern set on the booms while loading logs at night.

3 =**mayfly 1** (here: Ephemeroptera). **esp N Cent**

1950 *WELS* **WI** (*Large winged insect that hatches in summer in great numbers around lakes or rivers, crowds around lights, lives only a day or so, and is good fish bait*) 1 Inf, Mayfly often but wrongly called June bugs; 1 Inf, Mayfly or June bug; 1 Inf, June bugs [or] mayflies; 1 Inf, June bug. **1950** *WELS Suppl.* **cnOH** (as of 1905), On a visit to Sandusky, Ohio, in 1905, I found them [=mayflies] called "June bugs," which seemed odd to me, since a June bug in my experience was a very different creature. **1960** Teale *Journey into Summer* 37 **cnOH,** They are allergic to mayflies. With eyes swollen, red and watering, they are miserable with "Junebug fever" as long as the fluttering hosts remain. **1967–69** *DARE* (Qu. R4) Infs **IL**56, **IN**58, **MO**27, **OH**27, 67, **VT**10, June bug; **MI**80, Mayfly, fishfly (more common)—some people (strangers) call it a June bug; **OH**33, June bug, June fly; **WI**54, Mayfly, June bug.

4 in phrr *like a duck* (or *chicken, hen, nighthawk) on a June bug* and varr: Eagerly, rapaciously. **chiefly Sth**

1835 Longstreet *GA Scenes* 78, Soon as they seize him, you'll see me down upon him like a duck upon a June-bug. **1836** Smith *Col. Crockett's Exploits* 154 (Taylor–Whiting *Dict. Amer. Proverbs*), He was down upon me like a night-hawk upon a June bug. **1836** U.S. Congress *Congressional Globe* 24th Cong 1st Sess 5 May 3.349 **KY,** They hopped upon it, to use a homely phrase, like a duck on a June-bug. **1840** Haliburton *Clockmaker* (3d ser) 40 **CT,** He walked 'em into him as a duck does a June bug. *Ibid* 182, I'd come down on him like a duck on a June bug. [**1862** *Standard* 12 Dec. *(OED),* He has lighted upon [General] Scott as a hawk lights upon a June bug.] [**c1870** in 1904 *Ala. Hist. Soc. Trans.* IV.484 *(DA),* Why a hog has no more chance to live among these thieving negro farmers than a juney bug in a gang of puddle ducks.] **1909** *DN* 3.346 **eAL, wGA,** Like a chicken (hen) on a June-bug. **1922** *DN* 5.169 **AL,** "He jumped on him like a chicken on a June bug." Eagerly. **1949** *PADS* 11.13 **wTX,** Like a duck on a June bug. (Quickly.) Common. **1968** *DARE* FW Addit **LA**17, He jumped on it like a duck on a June bug = he accepted eagerly; or, more literally, he pounced on it. Both literal and figurative meanings used. **1980** Safire *On Language* 144 **LA,** The President [=Carter]. . . warned that an oil lobby "would be all over Capitol Hill like a chicken on a June bug." . . A Virginia farmer reports: "June bugs are too large and too tough for a chicken to make a meal of easily, so the chicken will run around pecking and scratching at it for quite a while, sometimes to no avail."

June corn n **esp Gulf States**

Early **Indian corn 1** suitable for table use.

1943 *Clarke Co. Democrat* (Grove Hill AL) 3 June 2/6, Some June corn planted in the garden now will give some roasting ears later on. **1965–67** *DARE* (Qu. I34, *If you don't have sweet corn, you can always eat young* _____) Infs **FL**18, **LA**6, June corn. **1986** Pederson *LAGS Concordance* (*Sweet corn*) 2 infs, **cGA, seAL,** June corn.

June daisy n

=**oxeye daisy 1.**

1968 *DARE* (Qu. S26a, . . *Wildflowers.* . . *Roadside flowers*) Inf **NY**123, Field daisies = June daisy.

Junefish n [*DJE* 1873 →]

=**jewfish 1a.**

1935 Caine *Game Fish* 94 **Sth,** Jewfish (*Promicrops itaiara*). . . Junefish. . . *Largest on record.* . . caught with rod and reel . . at Miami, Florida, during 1925. **1946** LaMonte *N. Amer. Game Fishes* 45, Spotted Jewfish. . . Names . . Junefish. . . Present most of the year off rocky shores and often around pilings, etc. A rather sluggish fish.

June flower n

1 =**Canadian wood violet.**

1892 *Jrl. Amer. Folkl.* 5.92, *Viola Canadensis,* June flower. . . Houlton, Me. **1940** Clute *Amer. Plant Names* 233, *Viola Canadensis.* June-flower.
2 See quot.
1968 *DARE* (Qu. S26a, . . *Wildflowers. . . Roadside flowers*) Inf **MN**19, June flower—a large rose-colored flower.

June fly n Cf June bug

1 =mayfly 1 (here: Ephemeroptera).
1945 Hatcher *Lake Erie* 99, He exclaimed over the "millions of flies (called May flies in England, but here June flies) along the lake shore, and to half a mile distance, smothering everything." **1950** *WELS Suppl.,* 1 Inf, **csWI,** June fly—for May fly. **1960** Teale *Journey into Summer* 38, Other names [for *Ephemeroptera*] we encountered along the way were: lake flies, fish flies, June flies [etc.]. **1967–68** *DARE* (Qu. R4, *A large winged insect that hatches in summer in great numbers around lakes or rivers, crowds around lights, lives only a day or so, and is good fish bait*) Infs **MI**54, 82, June fly; **NC**52, June fly—long, slim, four wings, long things from tail; **OH**33, June bug, June fly.
2 =June bug 1.
1966 *DARE* (Qu. R5, *A big brown beetle that comes out in large numbers in spring and early summer, and flies with a buzzing sound: [Note: some are green.]*) Inf **AR**42, June fly.
3 =deerfly 1.
1968 *DARE* (Qu. R12, . . *Other kinds of flies*) Infs **GA**35, **MD**3, June fly—mottled wing, clear and black, bites people and animals; **MD**9, June fly—come around water, brown, size of housefly, bite and stick to you like leeches; **NY**113, June fly—bad for painters.

June grape n

A **riverbank grape** (here: *Vitis riparia*) or similar **grape.**
1819 (1821) Nuttall *Jrl.* 98 **AR,** A species of *Vitis,* called the June grape, from its ripening at that early period, was also nearly in blossom. **1950** Gray–Fernald *Manual of Botany* 998, *V[itis] riparia.* . . Var. *Praecox.* . . June-G[rape]. . . Grapes 6–7 mm. in diameter, without bloom, sweet. . . *Fr[uit]* June.

June grass n

1 Any of var grasses, as:
a =Kentucky bluegrass.
1855 MI State Ag. Soc. *Trans. for 1854* 6.160, One tree of the damson variety, standing in a stiff June grass sod plat. **1892** IN Dept. Geol. & Nat. Resources *Rept. for 1891* 158 **neIN,** *P[oa] pratensis.* . . June Grass. . . Kentucky Blue-Grass. **1912** Baker *Book of Grasses* 197, June Grass. . . flowers bloom in June, before the summer grasses. **1919** ME Writers Research Club *ME My State* 336, How fair her fields when June-grass waves! **1945** Wodehouse *Hayfever Plants* 41, June grass . . (*P. pratensis . .*) is one of the most important hayfever grasses of the United States. . . It flowers in May and June. **1950** *WELS* (*Grass . . grown for hay*) 3 Infs, **WI,** June grass. **1966–69** *DARE* (Qu. L8, *Hay that grows naturally in damp places*) Infs **MN**33, **NH**5, 14, June grass; (Qu. L9a, . . *Kinds of grass . . grown for hay*) Infs **CT**14, **MI**2, 83, **MN**4, **VT**12, June grass; **ME**19, There is a wild June grass; **MN**16, June grass—same as Kentucky bluegrass. **1976** Bailey–Bailey *Hortus Third* 890, June grass. . . Commonly cult. for lawns and pastures in the humid n. regions where soils are limy.
b A grass of the genus *Koeleria,* usu *K. cristata.* **chiefly West** Also called **prairie grass.** For other names of *K. cristata* see **prairie June grass**
1889 Vasey *Ag. Grasses* 60, *Koeleria cristata.* . . In Montana it is sometimes called June grass. It is an early grass, ripening about the first of July. **1894** *Jrl. Amer. Folkl.* 7.104, **NE,** *Koeleria cristata . . ,* June grass. **1912** Wooton–Standley *Grasses NM* 119, June Grass (*Koeleria cristata*) is one of the most widely distributed grasses in the mountains of this and adjoining States where it forms a considerable part of the summer forage. **1932** Rydberg *Flora Prairies* 108. **1961** Thomas *Flora Santa Cruz* 92 **cwCA,** *K[oeleria] macrantha.* . . June Grass. **1966–68** *DARE* (Qu. L8, *Hay that grows naturally in damp places*) Inf **CO**38, June grass—needs some care; (Qu. L9a, . . *Kinds of grass . . grown for hay*) Infs **UT**4, **WA**1, June grass. **1974** Welsh *Anderson's Flora AK* 582, *Junegrass.* . . Open hillsides; in southern Yukon; southward to Mexico and Texas and eastward to Maine.
c An **oat grass c** (here: *Danthonia spicata*). **esp NEast, Gt Lakes**
1891 Jesup *Plants Hanover NH* 54, D[anthonia] spicata. . . Sometimes called "June Grass," a name that belongs to Poa pratensis. **1894** *Jrl. Amer. Folkl.* 7.104, *Danthonia spicata,* . . June-grass, Penobscot Co.,

Me. **1950** *WELS* (*Other kinds of grass that are hard to get rid of*) 12 Infs, **WI,** June grass. **1950** Gray–Fernald *Manual of Botany* 149, *D[anthonia] spicata.* . . Junegrass. . . Dry to damp and peaty soil or in thin woodland. . . May–July. **1966–70** *DARE* (Qu. S9, . . *Kinds of grass that are hard to get rid of*) Infs **MI**2, 9, **NY**233, **WI**37, June grass; **MI**92, June grass—has a spike of seeds on the top; (Qu. S21, . . *Weeds . . that are a trouble in gardens and fields*) Inf **NY**207, June grass.
d A **bromegrass** (here: *Bromus tectorum*). **West**
1922 *Amer. Botanist* 28.84 **ID,** In June . . the lower gravel hills are red from the ripening *Bromus tectorum,* locally called June grass. **1937** U.S. Forest Serv. *Range Plant Hdbk.* G38, Downy chess, also known as . . junegrass, . . attains a height up to about two feet, and is either an annual or summer annual. . . It is ready to graze early in March . . and remains tender and palatable until about the middle of May. . . On the higher foothills it is grazed from April to early June. **1952** Davis *Flora ID* 95, *B[romus] tectorum.* . . Downy Chess, June Grass. . . is one of the most abundant grasses in Idaho. . . This is good feed for stock when it is young, but the awns become harmful when they are mature. It is sometimes cut for hay. **1966** Barnes–Jensen *Dict. UT Slang* 26, *June grass:* . . a local name for an annoying brome grass with penetrating awns (*Bromus tectorum*). It grows on foothills and plains, and it is said to have been introduced by early Mexicans intentionally against pioneers. **1967–68** *DARE* (Qu. S9, . . *Kinds of grass that are hard to get rid of*) Inf **UT**7, June or cheat grass; (Qu. S15, . . *Weed seeds that cling to clothing*) Inf **CO**15, June grass—beautiful in spring, but [they] dry up and have stickers, fan out like bearded wheat.
2 A **hornwort 1** (here: *Ceratophyllum demersum*).
1913 *Torreya* 13.230 **NY,** *Ceratophyllum demersum.* . . June grass, Centre Moriches, L.I.

June Harvest See June apple 1

June hog n

=chinook salmon.
1989 Lesley *River Song* 169 **cnOR** [Amer Ind speaker], "What do you think he saw?" "I don't know," Danny said. "Salmon, maybe." Willis nodded. "Thousands of them. June Hogs. Those big Chinooks that used to go a hundred pounds." **1993** *Amer. Rivers* Summer 8, "June hogs"— upper-Columbia River summer chinook weighing in the 100-pound range . . —were prized by settlers and Native Americans. That stock was displaced to the mid-Columbia, however, because Grand Coulee Dam didn't have a fish ladder. Now the descendants of June hogs need special help.

June pea n Also early June pea Cf May pea

An early-maturing **garden pea.**
1966–70 *DARE* (Qu. H49, *Dishes made by boiling potatoes with other foods*) Inf **VA**78, Potatoes and June peas; (Qu. I4, . . *Vegetables . . less commonly grown around here*) Inf **VA**78, June pea; (Qu. I14, *Kinds of beans that you eat in the pod before they're dry*) Inf **NC**12, June peas or May peas. **1986** Pederson *LAGS Concordance,* 1 inf, **swTN,** Early June peas.

June pink n esp NEng

A **rhododendron** (here: *Rhododendron nudiflorum* or *R. viscosum*).
1897 *Jrl. Amer. Folkl.* 10.49 **NH,** *Azalea viscosa,* . . June pink. **1948** Peattie *Berkshires* 46 **wMA,** Sometimes called June pinks or Pinxters, this shrub [=*Rhododendron nudiflorum*] is quite common throughout the region. **1969** *DARE* (Qu. S26c, *Wildflowers that grow in woods*) Inf **NY**183, June pinks. **1979** *DARE* File **cnMA** (as of c1915), We always called wild azalea "June pink" though I've heard it referred to as "swamp pink." I don't recall that we had any name for the little green growths (gall?) that were always on the stems.

June plum n

=serviceberry.
1896 *Jrl. Amer. Folkl.* 9.186 **West,** *Amelanchier Canadensis.* . . June plum. **1960** Vines *Trees SW* 416, *Amelanchier arborea.* . . Vernacular names are . . June-plum [etc.]. . . The berries may be eaten uncooked or made into pies.

June rise n Eye-dial sp Joone rise West

Increased flow of a river in early summer caused by the melting of snow in the mountains.
1847 Robb *Squatter Life* 134 *(DA),* The varmint's [a rival's] countenance looked as riled as the old Missouri in a June rise. **1880** McElrath *Yellowstone Valley* 33 **MT,** The satisfaction of the journey is materially

enhanced by availing one's self of that season of high water known technically as the "June rise." **1901** *Land of Sunshine* 14.203 **West,** Nearly every family plants a garden after the June rise of the Colorado river. **1904** *Technical World* 1.665 **West, SW,** In the case of mountain rivers, the heaviest flow, known as the "June rise," is caused by melting snows. **1910** *Cosmopolitan* Feb 305, Me? I'm twenty-six the last Joone rise of the old Missouri. **1931** Allhands *Gringo Builders* 214 **TX,** The June rise scoured the channel to a greater depth exposing the shore piers with the sloughing off of the river bank.

junesey n [Cf **june** v 4]
A sweetheart; also vbl n *juneseying,* visiting one's sweetheart, courting.

1899 Chesnutt *Conjure Woman* 71 **csNC** [Black], Mars Jeems didn' 'low no co'tin' er juneseyin' roun' his plantation,—said he wanted his niggers ter . . not be wastin' dey time wid no sech foolis'ness. *Ibid* 74, Mars Jeems wuz so tuk up wid his own junesey dat he didn' paid no 'tention . . ter w'at wuz gwine on 'twix' Solomon en his junesey. *Ibid* 99, Dey all tuk ter sweethea'tin' en juneseyin' en singin' en dancin'.

June sucker n

1 A white sucker (here: *Catostomus commersoni*). [From its time of spawning]

1886 Mather *Memoranda* 35, *The June sucker.* . . This fish was found in masses in the swift cold mountain streams which tumble rapidly over rocks in the latter part of June, depositing their eggs, thereby showing that they are adult fish. **1902** Jordan–Evermann *Amer. Fishes* 52, In the spring of the year, as the spawning season approaches, they [=*Catostomus commersoni*] run up the streams in great number and spawn upon the riffles. This is, in most parts of its range, in May or June, and the fish is called the "June Sucker." **1983** Becker *Fishes WI* 682, *White Sucker.* . . Other common names . . June sucker. [*Ibid* 683, In Wisconsin, the white sucker generally spawns from April to early May. In northern Wisconsin, spawning has been observed in late May and early June . . , and it may possibly occur in late June.]

2 A sucker (here: *Chasmistes liorus*) native to Utah.

1896 U.S. Natl. Museum *Bulletin* 47.183, *Chasmistes liorus.* . . *June Sucker of Utah Lake.* . . L[ength] 18 inches. Utah Lake; very abundant. **1957** Blair et al. *Vertebrates U.S.* 87, *Chasmistes liorus.* . . June sucker. . . Formerly abundant in Utah Lake, Utah, but now believed to be extinct. **1963** Sigler–Miller *Fishes UT* 93, The June sucker . . , in common with other species of this type that inhabit certain lakes of Nevada and Oregon, has a terminal and rather oblique mouth, with thin lips and almost no papillae.

Juneteenth n Also *Juneteenth Day, June the teenth* **chiefly OK, TX** Cf **Emancipation (Proclamation) Day**
June 19th, celebrated by Blacks as the anniversary of the emancipation of the slaves in Texas on that date in 1865.

1936 *AmSp* 11.275, *Juneteenth* day at the Dallas Centennial Exposition was given over to the colored race. It came on June 19th, the day of the proclamation of Negro emancipation in Texas. **1940** Writers' Program *Guide TX* 276 **seTX,** On June 19, 1865, Major General Gordon Granger unwittingly established an annual holiday that has endured ever since, when he took over the city [=Galveston] and proclaimed that all slaves in the state were free. "Juneteenth," as it is commonly called, is Emancipation Day in Texas, the greatest Negro day of celebration. **1958** Humphrey *Home from the Hill* 98 **neTX,** It was the barbecue sauce, Chauncey's recipe, famous at every Juneteenth, as the Negroes call Emancipation Day. **1966–67** *DARE* (Qu. FF16, . . *Local contests or celebrations*) Infs **OK**28, **TX**11, 33, Juneteenth. **1967–69** *DARE* FW Addit **ceOK,** Juneteenth—old Texas and southern Oklahoma custom for June 19th of each year. All of the time I was growing up, every June 19th the Negroes would celebrate. The City Park was turned over to them, the merchants would donate food, beer, water. There would be no arrests, plenty of preaching and singing. That was their day. *Ibid* **TX,** June the teenth called nigger day by Whites. 19th of June. Negro emancipation day. Big celebration by Galveston Negro population. **1976** *WI State Jrl.* (Madison) 21 June 29, Juneteenth Day was originally celebrated in the Southwest and is still celebrated in places like Texas. . . But to the best of our knowledge Milwaukee is still the only city that celebrates it in the North. **1986** Pederson *LAGS Concordance,* 1 inf, **cTX,** Juneteenth—6 months to day of Emancipation.

Juney bug See **June bug 1**

jungle bunny n *derog*
A Black person.

1964 *PADS* 42.27 **Chicago IL,** Terms most popular among young Caucasians are *jigaboo, booboo, blacky,* and *jungle bunny;* both middle-aged informants giving *jungle bunny* . . work with adolescents. **1965–70** *DARE* (Qu. HH28, *Names and nicknames . . for people of foreign background: Negro*) 10 Infs, **scattered,** Jungle bunny. **1970** Tarpley *Blinky* 265 **neTX,** Derogatory names for Negroes. . . *jungle bunnies.* **1980** *Children's Folkl. Newsl.* Winter 3 **RI,** Jungle bunny—Black American. **1986** Pederson *LAGS Concordance (Negro)* 10 infs, **Gulf Region,** Jungle bunny (*or* bunnies). [*DARE* Ed: 10 other infs offered "jungle bunny" (or "bunnies") in response to other questions about racial background, but the referents were not clear. 12 of the 20 infs noted that the term is derogatory, pejorative, or insulting.] **1993** *DARE* File **NYC** (as of mid 1950s), "Jungle bunny" was commonly used by White teens for a Black person.

juniper n

1 Std: a plant of the genus *Juniperus.* Also called **cedar 1, red cedar.** For other names of var spp and for related terms see **alligator juniper, brake** n[2] c, **cedar apple, cherrystone juniper, creeping ~, fairy circle, gin juniper, ground cedar 1, ground juniper, hackmatack 1b, horse savin, juniper cedar, mountain cedar, ~ juniper, mule pine, pencil cedar, redberry juniper, red ~, sand cedar, weeping ~, weeping juniper, white cedar, ~ juniper, yellow cedar**

2 Any of var other plants, as:

a A tamarack (here: *Larix laricina*). **chiefly ME**
[**1748** Ellis *Voyage* 138 **Canada,** They are commonly of Fir, or Larch, which the *English* there call Juniper.] a**1862** (1864) Thoreau *ME Woods* 213, The Indian called these [=larch trees] juniper. **1891** *Jrl. Amer. Folkl.* 4.140, In South Berwick, Maine, and I think some other places, I found *Juniper* used for Larix Americana. **1894** *Ibid* 7.99, *Larix Americana.* . . Juniper, Penobscot Co., Me., Grand Lake region of Penobscot River, Me. . . Hardly ever called by any other name. **1897** *Ibid* 10.144 **West,** *Larix Americana,* . . juniper. **1909** *DN* 3.413 **nME,** Juniper. . . The hackmatack. **1944** Hyland–Steinmetz *Woody Plants ME* 1, L[arix] laricina. . . Locally, but misappropriately, called "Juniper." **1966** *DARE* (Qu. T5, . . *Kinds of evergreens, other than pine*) Inf **ME**12, Juniper—also called hackmatack; (Qu. T13, . . *Names . . for these trees: . . tamarack*) Inf **ME**3, Juniper. **1985** Clark *From Mailbox* 202 **ME,** In some parts of Maine, people call the tamarack the "juniper tree." The Maine Forestry Department lists it as the eastern larch.

b also *juniper cypress:* A white cedar (here: *Chamaecyparis thyoides*). **Sth, esp Mid Atl**
1630 Higginson *Nevv Englands Plantation* sig B3ᵛ, There is also good Ash, Elme, Willow, Birch, Beech, Saxafras, Iuniper Cipres, Cedar, Spruce, Pines & Firre. **1773** in 1940 *AmSp* 15.278 **VA,** A Tract of Land . . well timbered with White Oak and old Pine, and joins a Juniper Swamp. **1813** Michaux *Histoire des Arbres* 3.20, Dans le Maryland, la Virginie et la Caroline du Nord, il [=*Chamaecyparis thyoides*] porte celui [=le nom] de *Juniper.* [=In Maryland, Virginia and North Carolina, it bears that [=the name] of *Juniper.*] **1860** Curtis *Cat. Plants NC* 28, *White Cedar.* . . In North-Carolina and some other portions of the South, this seems to be known only under the name of *Juniper.* . . The shingles made of it are, in some places, preferred over all others, and last from 30 to 35 years. **1897** Sudworth *Arborescent Flora* 77, *Chamaecyparis thyoides.* . . Juniper (Ala., N.C., Va.) **1950** Peattie *Nat. Hist. Trees* 71, *Southern White Cedar.* . . The living tree is . . "Juniper" to many of the folks who live in the lonely swamp country where it grows. **1960** Vines *Trees SW* 9, White Cedar. . . Other vernacular names are . . Swamp Cedar, Swamp Juniper, Juniper-tree, and White Cypress. **1966–70** *DARE* (Qu. T15, . . *Kinds of swamp trees*) Infs **NC**3, 18, 21, 41, **RI**15, **VA**47, Juniper; **NC**81, Juniper or white cedar (they're the same); (Qu. T16, . . *Kinds of trees . . 'special'*) Inf **NC**49, Juniper—for boats, light as cork. **1974** Morton *Folk Remedies* 41 **SC,** Juniper. *Chamaecyparis thyoides.* . . South Carolinians occasionally chew the twigs, just as a "nibble."

c =**black spruce 1. esp NC**
1860 Curtis *Cat. Plants NC* 27, *Black Spruce* (A[bies] nigra . .). In our mountains, it is sometimes very improperly called *Juniper,* and it is, I believe, what is most commonly and absurdly called *He Balsam.* **1897** Sudworth *Arborescent Flora* 34 **NC,** *Picea mariana.* . . Common Names. . . Juniper. **1900** Lyons *Plant Names* 288, P[icea] Mariana. . . Juniper.

d also *creeping juniper:* A yew (here: *Taxus canadensis*).
1891 *Jrl. Amer. Folkl.* 4.140 **MA,** We called . . Taxus Canadensis,

Juniper. **1900** Lyons *Plant Names* 365, *T[axus] minor.* . . Creeping Juniper. **1911** *Century Dict. Suppl.*, *Juniper.* . . *Creeping juniper.* . . The ground-hemlock, *Taxus Canadensis.*

e =**incense cedar.**

1897 Sudworth *Arborescent Flora* 64 **NV**, *Libocedrus decurrens.* . . *Common Names.* . . Juniper. **1908** Britton *N. Amer. Trees* 94, This tree [=*Libocedrus decurrens*] is also called Bastard cedar . . and Juniper.

f =**jack pine 1.**

1908 Britton *N. Amer. Trees* 44, It [=*Pinus banksiana*] is also known as Labrador pine, Jack pine, . . and erroneously as Juniper and Cypress.

g =**box huckleberry.** Cf **he-juniper**

1922 *Torreya* 22.17 **WV**, He asked if I had ever eaten "Juniper" pie. . . I suspected that it might be the box huckleberry, *Gaylussacia brachycera.* . . Juniper . . is the only name I have been able to find for this plant, although other plants are also called "Junipers." **1933** Small *Manual SE Flora* 1010, *Gaylussacia brachycera.* . . Juniper. . . Where abundant the berries are made into a preserve.

3 A rustic. Cf *DS* HH1

1944 Adams *Western Words* 86, *Juniper*—The western equivalent of *hayseed.*

juniper berry n

=**box huckleberry.**

1922 *Torreya* 22.17 **WV**, In a few days I set to work . . to try and discover the extent of . . *Gaylussacia brachycera* in this section. . . This could never have been done without the common name "Juniper Berry." **1924** *Amer. Botanist* 30.12, *G[aylussacia] brachycera* . . in the localities where it grows . . is known as "juniper berry."

juniper cedar n Cf cedar 1

A **juniper 1**; see quots.

1897 Sudworth *Arborescent Flora* 97 **TX**, *Juniperus occidentalis conjugens.* . . *Common Names.* Juniper Cedar. **1908** Britton *N. Amer. Trees* 116, *Juniperus mexicana* [=*J. ashei*]. . . is also called Juniper cedar [etc]. **1968** *DARE* (Qu. T5, . . *Kinds of evergreens, other than pine*) Inf **NJ**31, Juniper cedar.

juniper jay n

Prob Steller's jay (*Cyanocitta stelleri*).

1967 *DARE* (Qu. Q16, . . *Kinds of jays*) Inf **OR**1, Juniper jay (a blue jay).

juniper juice n Also juniper squeezing

See quots.

1929 *AmSp* 4.386 **KS** [Wet words], *Gin* does not seem to be much in favor here, but I take it that *Gordon water* and *juniper juice* are names for this beverage. **1930** Williams *Logger-Talk* 25 **Pacific NW**, *Juniper juice*: Gin. **1967** *DARE* (Qu. DD21c, *Nicknames for whiskey*) Inf **NY**1, Bathtub gin, bootleg, hooch, juniper juice, juniper squeezing.

juniper-leaf n

A low-growing plant (*Polypremum procumbens*) with leaves resembling those of **juniper 1**.

1979 Ajilvsgi *Wild Flowers* 225 **eTX**, *Juniper-leaf* . . *Polypremum procumbens.* . . *Leaves*: opposite, sessile, . . often with small leaves clustered in axils. . . *Flower*: white, about ¼ in. across.

juniper squeezing See juniper juice

juniper tree n

1 A **hackberry** (here: *Celtis occidentalis*).

1897 Sudworth *Arborescent Flora* 185 **NJ**, *Celtis occidentalis.* . . Juniper Tree. **1940** Clute *Amer. Plant Names* 164, *C[eltis] occidentalis.* . . Juniper-tree. **1960** Vines *Trees SW* 206, *Celtis occidentalis.* . . Vernacular names are . . Beaverwood, Juniper-tree [etc].

2 See quot.

1934 (1970) Wilson *Backwoods Amer.* 81 **AR, MO**, There is another good play-party game called "The Juniper Tree." This is a ring game, too, but the central sitter is a girl. A circle is formed . . and an old hat tossed up for snatch-grab. Whoever of the masculine portion gets hold of the hat is reckoned . . lucky. . . The participators march around in the circle singing. . . At the lyric command of "Keep your hat on," the lucky man puts the hat upon the head of the central female and claims his kiss.

junk n

1 A chunk, hunk, or piece, esp of firewood. [*OED junk sb.²* 2 1726 →] **chiefly NEng, esp ME** Cf **chunk n 1**

1848 Lowell *Biglow* 145 'Upcountry' **MA**, *Junk*, a fragment of any solid substance. **1848** (1850) Colton *3 Yrs.* 298 **NEng**, A tin cup of coffee, a junk of bread. **1899** (1912) Green *VA Folk-Speech* 248, *Junk.* . . A thick piece; a lump; a chunk. **1922** Gonzales *Black Border* 308 **sSC, GA coasts** [Gullah glossary], *Junk*—chunk, chunks, as of lightwood. **1926** *AmSp* 2.81 **ME**, Sticks of wood or other ungainly units are called "junks." **1926** *DN* 5.387 **ME**, *Junk.* . . Chunk or large portion. Similar in use to hunk; a junk of wood for the stove; a junk of bread. Common. **1941** *LANE* Map 330 (*Log*), Pieces of wood used for fuel are . . called . . *junks* [by 3 infs, **ME**]. **1946** Gould *Yankee Storekeeper* 130 **cwME**, A West Athenite came in and asked, "Bill, what are you getting for salt pork?" Bill said, "Seven cents." The man said, "I want a junk." **1967** *DARE* FW Addit **MA**101, One of his tales concerned the moving of Plymouth Rock—he said, "I've still got a few [jʌŋks] of it sitting in a coffee can over to the house." **1971** *Down East* Nov 24 **ME**, I announced that I was going to put an all-night *junk* in the stove and was surprised that my children never had heard the term. **1975** Gould *ME Lingo* 150, *Junk.* . . *A junk* of wood for the stove, meat for a pot-roast, pie for a dinner pail. A fairish-sized piece; a hunk. **1982** *DARE* File **coastal ME**, A junk of pork.

2 pl: Miscellaneous discarded items or personal belongings; see quots. Cf **accoutrements, clatterment**

1899 (1977) Norris *McTeague* 20 **San Francisco CA**, She was collecting junks, bits of iron, stone jugs, glass bottles, old sacks, and cast-off garments. **1972** Carr *Da Kine Talk* 134 **HI**, "I was so shame! All da junks wen fall [=fell] down from my purse!" In Hawaii, *junks* is used much more frequently to mean small personal possessions than to mean old automobiles. **1981** *Pidgin To Da Max* np **HI**, *Junks*—1. What girls carry in their purses. 2. What guys carry in their car trunks.

junk v¹ Also with up [junk n 1] ME

To cut (wood) to length; to cut into pieces.

a1890 (1944) Robinson *Hist. Morrill* 106 **csME**, By September the trees would be dry, . . then junked, that is; chopped up about ten feet long, and piled. **1909** *DN* 3.413 **nME**, *Junk.* . . To cut up into convenient lengths for piling and burning the logs that are left after a piece of land has been burned over. **1971** *DARE* File **swME**, When you have a down tree you ask a man with a chain saw to "junk it up" for you . . [to] fit your fireplace or Franklin stove. In my experience this did not include splitting. **1975** Gould *ME Lingo* 150, *Junk.* . . Wood which has been sawn to stove-length but not yet split . . is *junked.* **1979** Lewis *How to Talk Yankee* [19], *Junk.* . . To divide into pieces. "He junked up one hindquarter of that deer." *Ibid* [39], Well, I was junking up that old sugar maple that got blowed down last weekend.

‡junk v² Cf joog

To jab, punch.

c1938 in 1970 Hyatt *Hoodoo* 2.1121 **swTN**, An' in de middle of yore gate, yo' take a can of lye, an' . . *junk* three holes in it an' turn it bottom upwards in de earth.

junk bottle n Also chunk bottle [Prob junk n 1] arch

A bottle made from thick, dark glass.

1786 *CT Courant & Weekly Intelligencer* (Hartford) 29 May 3/3, *Drugs, Medicines and Groceries* . . Junk Bottles, Corks. **1819** Schoolcraft *Lead Mines MO* 81, The principal kinds are the *black junk bottle*, and the *common green bottle.* **1824** (1925) Bagley *Diary* 16 **MA**, A junk bottle of some kind of liquid preparation cures them all. **1845** (1852) Simms *Wigwam & Cabin* (2d ser) 146 **SC**, Mingo brought with him a "chunk-bottle" of whiskey. **1852** in 1927 Jones *FL Plantation Rec.* 70, Poor of a Chunck [Jones: sic] bottle full of the solution and drench your Mule with it. **1899** (1912) Green *VA Folk-Speech* 248, *Junk-bottle.* . . The ordinary black, glass bottle, low and big round.

junked-up See jumped-up

junker n scattered, but chiefly N Cent, NEast See Map on p. 186 usu joc

An old or dilapidated vehicle or other piece of machinery considered ready to be discarded.

1948 *AN&Q* 8.120 **Detroit MI**, Used-car Jargon: . . "junker" (car so decrepit that it cannot be economically repaired). **1954** *AmSp* 29.99 **swCA**, *Junk car* or *junker.* . . A car in poor condition that has been made to look like a hot rod. Usually used sarcastically of any car ready for the junk yard. **1961** *AmSp* 36.273 **NW, West**, *Junker.* . . An old truck. **1965–70** *DARE* (Qu. N5, *Nicknames for an automobile, especially an old or broken-down car*) 92 Infs, **chiefly Inland Nth, Midl, West**, Junker; **CO**20, Old junker; (Qu. O2, *Nicknames . . for an old, clumsy* *boat*) Infs **KY**6, **MI**49, **OH**67, Junker. **1986** Chapman *New Dict. Amer. Slang* 241, *Junker. . .* A car or other machine that is worn out and ready to be discarded.

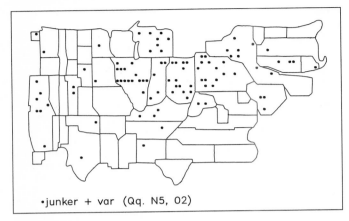

•junker + var (Qq. N5, O2)

junket n Also *junketing (party)* [*OED junket* sb. 4 "A feast . . ; a merrymaking accompanied with feasting;" 1530 →] NEng *old-fash* Cf **kitchen dance**

A party; a dance.

    1806 (1970) Webster *Compendious Dict.* 168, *Junket. . .* a private entertainment. [*DARE* Ed: This entry was carried over from Webster's English model.] **1820** Irving *Sketch Book Crayon* 2.158, Snug junket-ting parties at which I have been present; where we played . . choice old games; and where we sometimes had a good old English country dance. **1835** Mahony *6 Months* 57 **MA,** I indulged my love of retire-ment at Catholic dances and junkettings. **1937** FWP *Guide VT* 244, Lacking in major or distinctive attractions of sophisticated appeal, this fair is truly festive in a kitchen junket way, a real community celebration. **1941** LANE Map 410 (*A dance*), Terms for the old kitchen dance (a private dance held on the farm or in the village) were incidentally recorded by some of the fieldworkers. . . [28 infs] (Kitchen) junket. [Comments include the following:] 2 infs, *(Kitchen) junket*, private party; 1 inf, *Junket*, a party; 1 inf, *Junket . . a regular junket*, a party; 1 inf, *Junket*, an informal party; 1 inf, *Junket*, a party where you have a good time; 1 inf, *Hoedown*, a special dance in a kitchen junket; 1 inf, *Kitchen junket*, private; 1 inf, *Kitchen junket*, a dance on a small scale; 1 inf, *Kitchen junket*, rural; 1 inf, *Kitchen junket*, ~ *tunk*, a small neighborhood dance; 1 inf, *Junketing*, among laboring people. **1953–54** *VT Life* Winter 40, When the farm kitchen frequently was the setting for a country dance or "junket."

junk pickle See **chunk pickle**

junk room n Cf **lumber room, plunder ~**

A room or other space in a house used for storage.

    1949 Kurath *Word Geog.* 52, *Store room* appears to be the usual term in the Philadelphia area, *junk room* from the Susquehanna westward. *Junk room* is in use also in the Pennsylvania settlements of the piedmont of North Carolina and on the Cape Fear River by the side of *plunder room*. **1957** *Sat. Eve. Post Letters* **IN,** Junk room (store room). **c1960** *Wilson Coll.* **csKY,** *Junkroom* and *storeroom* both appear; but the terms are not used regularly. **1962** Atwood *Vocab. TX* 43, A room where disused articles are stored is generally a store room . . , but is also frequently called a *junk room*. **1965–70** DARE (Qu. D7, *A small space anywhere in a house where you can hide things or get them out of the way*) 16 Infs, **scattered,** Junk room; (Qu. D4, *The space up under the roof, usually used for storing things*) Infs **SC**42, 56, Junk room. **1971** Bright *Word Geog. CA & NV* 146, *Store room. . . junk room* 9% [of 300 infs]. **1973** Allen *LAUM* 1.170 **Upper MW** (as of c1950), The minor variant *junk room* [for *storeroom*], . . reported by nearly 9% of the infs., may have Midland orientation, but the evidence is not conclu-sive. **1981** *KS Qrly.* 13.68 **nNY,** *Junk room . . .* room in bunkhouse or ranch house for storage of miscellaneous gear. **1986** Pederson *LAGS Concordance* (*What would you call a room that is used to store odds and ends in?*) 378 infs, **Gulf Region,** A (or the) junk room (or junk rooms).

junk up See **junk** v¹

junky adj [Cf *EDD junky* (at *junk* sb.¹ 1) "thick" and **junk** n **1**] Cf *DNE, DJE, SND*

1941 LANE Map 458 (*Stout, paunchy*) 1 inf, **swME,** [dʒʌˑŋkɨ].

juntleman See **gentleman**

Juny (bug) See **June bug 1**

jupe harp n [Var of **jew's harp**]

    1968–70 DARE (Qu. FF8, . . *Small instrument that you hold between the teeth and pluck on*) Inf **NY**70, Jupe harp; **VA**50, [jup] harp. **1981** Pederson *LAGS Basic Materials* (*Jew's harp*) 3 infs, **TX,** Jupe harp.

Jupiter n

Used in var exclams or mild oaths.

    1924 DN 5.272 [Exclams], (Oh) Jupiter, by Jupiter, holy Jupiter, jumping Jupiter. **1950** WELS (*Exclamations beginning with the sound of "J"*) 5 Infs, **WI,** Jumping Jupiter. **1965–70** DARE (Qu. NN30) 11 Infs, **scattered,** Jumping Jupiter; **NY**92, Jupiter; **RI**13, Jupiter Amon; (Qu. NN29a, *Exclamations beginning with 'great': "Great _____!"*) Inf **CA**120, Jumping Jupiter; **ID**5, **TN**65, Jupiter; **MO**19, Jupiters; (Qu. NN29c, *Exclamations beginning with 'holy': "Holy _____!"*) Infs **KS**8, **ME**12, **VT**12, Jupiter.

Jurdan, Jurdin, Jurdon See **Jordan**

juree See **joree** n **1**

jurel n

=**crevalle a,** usu *Caranx caballus, C. crysos,* or *C. latus.*

    [**1760** Juan–Ulloa *Voyage to S. Amer.* 2.224, The chief kinds are cod, berrugates, the spur fish, sole, turbet, jureles, and lobsters.] **1884** Goode *Fisheries U.S.* 1.324 **FL,** The *Jurel—Caranx pisquetus* [=*C. crysos*]. This fish, known about Pensacola as the "Jurel," . . and "Hard-tail". . . is. . . especially abundant in the Gulf of Mexico. **1896** U.S. Natl. Museum *Bulletin* 47.921, *Caranx crysos. . .* Jurel. . . *Caranx caballus. . .* Jurel. *Ibid* 923, *Caranx latus. . .* Jurel. **1905** NJ State Mu-seum *Annual Rept. for 1904* 258, *Caranx latus. . .* Jurel. . . Body deep, compressed. **1911** U.S. Bur. Census *Fisheries 1908* 311, *Jurel (Caranx crysos).*—A food fish found along the Atlantic and Gulf coasts. . . They measure from 12 to 18 inches in length, and are caught in seines. **1933** LA Dept. of Conserv. *Fishes* 168, This family . . also embraces the Horse-eyed Jack or Jurel, *Xurel lata* [=*Caranx latus*]. **1973** Knight *Cook's Fish Guide* 383, Jurel—Jack, Horse-eye.

jurk See **jerk** n¹, v¹

jusarp See **Jew's harp**

jusem-sweet n Cf **jewlarker 1**

See quots.

    1952 Brown *NC Folkl.* 1.555, *Jusem-sweet. . .* A beau.—Avery county. **1972** Cooper *NC Mt. Folkl.* 91, *Everyday gal*—steady sweetheart; jusem sweet.

jussel See **justle**

just adv Usu |jʌst|; also freq |jʌs|; for addit varr see below For many of the forms below cf *EDD just* adv.

Std senses, var forms.

1a |jɛst|; pronc-spp *gest(e), jest.*

    1775 in 1915 *New Engl. Hist. & Geneal. Reg.* 69.122 **MA,** Jest at Night when I come home I found my Brother Abijah Parker at my house. **1815** Humphreys *Yankey in England* 106, *Jest*, just. **1837** Sherwood *Gaz. GA* 70, *Jest* for just. **1848** Lowell *Biglow* 145 'Upcountry' **MA,** *Jest*, just. **1854** in 1956 Eliason *Tarheel Talk* 313 **cnNC,** *Just. . .* gest, geste. **1860** Holmes *Professor* 86 **eMA,** Jest a little spell ago. **1899** Garland *Boy Life* 4 **nwIA** (as of c1870s), I'd jest about give you up. **1899** (1912) Green *VA Folk-Speech* 244, *Jest.* **1901** DN 2.142 **NEng, cNY,** *Just*, pron. [jɪst] and [jɛst] frequently. **1906** DN 3.120 **sIN,** *Just. . .* Always pronounced jest. **1908** DN 3.324 **eAL, wGA,** *Jes(t).* **1910** DN 3.444 **cNY,** *Just. . .* Often pronounced jest and jes. **1923** DN 5.212 **swMO,** *Jest.* **c1960** *Wilson Coll.* **csKY,** *Just. . .* Often [jɛst], [jɛs], [jɪst]. **1976** Garber *Mountain-ese* 48 **sAppalachians,** *Jest.*

b |jɛs|; pronc-spp *ges, jes(s).* **chiefly Sth, S Midl** Cf *Pronc Intro* 3.I.22

    1854 in 1956 Eliason *Tarheel Talk* 313 **cnNC,** *Just. . .* ges. **1861** Holmes *Venner* 2.189 **wMA,** Waäl, I calc'late I sh'll jes' holt on to 'em myself. **1871** Eggleston *Hoosier Schoolmaster* 140 **sIN,** He wants to bind out that boy jes' to spite . . me. **1887** (1967) Harris *Free Joe* 32 **GA,** If they'll jess but lemme keep the ginny-wine ole Whig docterin'. **1890** DN 1.68 **KY,** *Just. . .* [jɛs]. **1893** Shands *MS Speech* 41, *Jes* . . [jɛs]. . . used by negroes and illiterate whites. . . Sometimes heard in the conversation of educated people. **1908** [see **1a** above]. **1909** DN

3.399 **nwAR,** *Jes so. . .* Just so. **1910** [see **1a** above]. **1915** *DN* 4.227 **wTX,** *Jes' tolable.* **1916** *DN* 4.341 **seOH,** *Jesso.* Contraction of *just so.* General. **1931** Randolph *Ozarks* 69, They never did have nothin' on'y jes' a heap o' poke sallat. **1936** *AmSp* 11.355 **eTX,** They jes' don't come up. **1958** Humphrey *Home from the Hill* 51 **neTX,** Cooked till all you got to do is je suck the meat off the bones. **c1960** [see **1a** above].

2 |jɪs(t)|; pronc-spp *jis(t).* **scattered, but esp freq Sth, S Midl**

  c1820 in **1944** *ADD* **NYC,** *Jist.* **1830** in **1956** Eliason *Tarheel Talk* 313 **cs,seNC,** *Just—jist.* **1871** Eggleston *Hoosier Schoolmaster* 216 **sIN,** Dr. Small warn't jist the sort to tie to. **1890** *DN* 1.59, *Just* is sometimes pronounced *jist* in Charleston, S.C. **1891** *DN* 1.165 **cNY,** [jɪs] < *Just.* **1893** Shands *MS Speech* 41, *Just. . .* jis . . [jɪs]. **1901** [see **1a** above]. **1906** Casey *Parson's Boys* 19 **sIL** (as of c1860), Jist you wait. **1922** Gonzales *Black Border* 308 **sSC, GA coasts** [Gullah glossary], *Jis'—just.* **1923** *DN* 5.212 **swMO,** *Jist.* **1927** *AmSp* 2.358 **cwWV,** *Jist.* **1952** Brown *NC Folkl.* 1.555, *Jist. . . Just.—Illiterate.* **1958** Humphrey *Home from the Hill* 55 **neTX,** That great big ole hawg jist about this far from yo papa. **c1960** [see **1a** above]. **1982** *Barrick Coll.* **csPA,** *Just—pron. jist.*

3 |dɛs|; pronc-sp *des.* **chiefly Sth** *esp freq among Black speakers*

  1887 (1967) Harris *Free Joe* 58 **GA** [Black], I des went en hitch up de hoss. **1893** Shands *MS Speech* 41, *Just. . .* des . . [dɛs]. *Des* is used almost exclusively by negroes. **1899** Edwards *Defense* 32 **GA** [Black], Lor'! but you got yo' pa's walk—carry yo' head des lak 'im. **1899** Chesnutt *Conjure Woman* 13 **csNC** [Black], De grapes begin ter swivel [=shrivel] up des a little. **1908** *DN* 3.304 **eAL, wGA,** *Des. . . Just.* Chiefly a negroism. **1922** Gonzales *Black Border* 297 **sSC, GA coasts** [Gullah glossary], *Des'—just,* as "des' so," just so. **1927** Kennedy *Gritny* 9 **sLA** [Black], An' Susan goin' look aft' you des like she did befo'. **1968** *DARE* FW Addit **TN24,** He just [dɛs] had one eye looking.

4 |dɪs(t)|; pronc-spp *dis(t).* **chiefly Sth, S Midl**

  1888 Jones *Negro Myths* 98 **GA coast,** Buh Rabbit duh seddown een de big road, dist es content es ef nuttne bin happne. **1917** in **1944** *ADD* **sWV,** I dist does as good as anybody. *Ibid,* I dis' can't believe it's true. **1922** Gonzales *Black Border* 297 **sSC, GA coasts** [Gullah glossary], *Disso—just so.* **1940** *Sat. Eve. Post* 24 Feb 78 **TX,** If it's all de same to you, I dist as soon collec' de five dollahs now. **1940** in **1944** *ADD* **nWV,** [dɪs]. **1942** Hall *Smoky Mt. Speech* 76 **wNC, eTN,** [dɪst]. **1949** Turner *Africanisms* 266 **seSC** [Gullah], [dɪs]. **1976** Garber *Mountain-ese* 23 **sAppalachians,** We dist made it to the depot afore the train pulled out.

5 pronc-sp *thes.*

  1887 (1967) Harris *Free Joe* 107 **GA,** Go right along wi' me thes ez neighborly ez you please. *Ibid* 121, Why, bless your soul an' body! he thes natchally dribbles at the mouth when he gits a whiff from the dinner-pot. **1890** *DN* 1.68 **KY,** *Just. . .* Children say, "Thes let me tell you."

6 pronc-spp *this(t).*

  1890 (1895) Riley *Rhymes of Childhood* 86 **IN,** An' thist as she kicked her heels, an' turn't to run an' hide,/ They was two great Black Things a-standin' by her side. **1919** *DN* 5.35 **seKY,** *This. . . Just,* or "jist." Intensive, in "I this know hit is so!"

7 pronc-sp *ist.*

  1890 (1895) Riley *Rhymes of Childhood* 62 **IN,** When our baby died—/ My Ma she ist cried and cried! **1974** Fink *Mountain Speech* 13 **wNC, eTN,** *'Ist . . . just.* "Hit's 'ist right." **1976** Garber *Mountain-ese* 46 **sAppalachians,** There wuz ist one way to go, back.

8 pronc-sp *chust.* Cf Pronc Intro 3.I.15

  1985 *DARE* File **sePA,** Now you chust sit still.

just as adv phr [Prob ellip for *just as _____ as can be* or similar constr]

Extremely.

  1943 McAtee *Dial. Grant Co. IN Suppl.* 2 9 (as of 1890s), *Just as . .* very; "I'll be just as good." **1956** McAtee *Some Dialect NC* 25, I'll be just as good. **1992** *NADS Letters,* *Just as:* in the meaning "extremely". Several [students in Indiana] who worked with young children said they had heard it there, but not among adults.

just as well adv phr Also *just as good* **esp Sth, S Midl**

Used as a quasi-modal; foll by infin (with or without *to*): Might as well.

1933 Rawlings *South Moon* 220 **nFL,** Jest about here is where a feller got to hurry. The buck goes flat in no time, and you jest as good to pitch the mash in the creek, for you'll get no more alcohol. [**1956** *Hall Coll.* **wNC,** We'd just as well to quit.] **1960** Williams *Walk Egypt* 257 **GA,** We just as good eat. [**1967** Green *Horse Tradin'* 115 **TX,** You'd just as well buy you a leather strap and buckle it real tight around that horse's neck at the throat latch, because then he can't swell his neck to bite and suck wind.] **1967** *DARE* Tape **AZ4,** You jus' as well to make up your mind right here and now.

justice n Pronc-spp *jestes, jestice, jestiss, jestuss* **chiefly S Midl** Cf **just 1a, b**

Std senses, var forms.

  1825 in **1956** Eliason *Tarheel Talk* 313 **cwNC,** Jestice. **1851** Hooper *Widow Rugby's Husband* 82 **AL,** Maybe, he's *the Jestes of the Pease* for the Town Beat. **1884** Murfree *TN Mts.* 281, It always did 'pear ter me ez thar war mighty little jestice in that. **1908** *DN* 3.324 **eAL, wGA,** *Jestiss of the peace* is commonly heard. **1921** Haswell *Daughter Ozarks* 28 (as of 1880s), I am Jestice of the Peace. **1922** Gonzales *Black Border* 308 **sSC, GA coasts** [Gullah glossary], *Jestuss—justice.* **1976** Garber *Mountain-ese* 48 **sAppalachians,** *Jestice . . justice.*

justice weed n Also *justice's weed* [See quot 1854]

A **boneset 1** (here: *Eupatorium hyssopifolium* or *E. leucolepis*).

  1854 King *Amer. Eclectic Dispensatory* 460, The *Eupatorium hyssopifolium* and *Eupatorium Leucolepsis* [sic], both called "Justice's Weed," have been used with success for curing the bites of snakes and other poisonous animals; they were employed for this purpose by John Justice of South Carolina in 1800, who received a premium for disclosing his remedy. **1876** Hobbs *Bot. Hdbk.* 61, Justices' weed. Eupatorium Hyssopifolium. . . Eupatorium leucolepis [sic]. **1900** Lyons *Plant Names* 155, *E[upatorium] leucolepis. . .* New Jersey to Florida and Louisiana. Justice-weed. . . The name Justice-weed is applied also to . . *E. hyssopifolium . . ,* Massachusetts to Texas. **1940** Clute *Amer. Plant Names* 82, *E[upatorium] leucolepis.* Justice-weed. **1974** Morton *Folk Remedies* 59 **SC,** *Justice's weed. Eupatorium hyssopifolium. . . South Carolina* (Current use): The whole plant is pulled up, root and all, folded over and boiled. The very bitter decoction is commonly taken as a remedy for colds. **1979** Ajilvsgi *Wild Flowers* 289 **eTX,** *Justice-weed . . Eupatorium leucolepis. . .* Uncommon in the Big Thicket.

justle n, v Also *jussel* [Varr of *jostle; OED jostle, justle* v. "*Justle* was usual in the 17th c.; and the main form in the 18th"] *old-fash*

  1806 (1970) Webster *Compendious Dict.* 169, *Justle . .* to run against, push about, jostle. [*DARE* Ed: This entry does not appear in Webster's English model.] **1869** Whitney *Hitherto* 117 **NEng,** Grandon began again the little bantering with Allard. . . There was such a charm to me in this little sportive justle and antagonism. **1899** Garland *Boy Life* 236 **nwIA,** In such wise does practical middle age justle the elbow of the dreaming boy. **1912** Green *VA Folk-Speech* 248, *Jussel. . .* For *jostle.* "Don't jussel me when you pass."

juty n [Pronc var of *duty*] Cf **due**

  1887 *Scribner's Mag.* 2.479 **AR,** She's got the law on her side and I have to do my juty. **1894** in **1941** Warfel–Orians *Local-Color Stories* 738 **sAR** [Black], I wants ter do my juty. **1899** (1912) Green *VA Folk-Speech* 248, *Juty. . .* For *duty.* **1927** Adams *Congaree* 31 **cSC** [Black], Dat been he juty and dat been he pleasure.

juvember n [Blend of *June + November*]

1 in phr *from now to Juvember:* A long time; forever.

  1980 *NADS Letters* **NC,** "It would take me from now to Juvember to finish all that work." This means 'an impossible or unreasonable amount of time.'

2 A slingshot.

  1980 *NADS Letters* **seNC,** The Lumbees use the word *juvember* (juvimber?) with the meaning 'slingshot.' A juvember is a forked stick to which a strip of innertube is tied; it is used to shoot rocks at birds, windows, lights, and other assorted things. **1984** Wilder *You All Spoken Here* 150 **Sth,** Gravel flipper, juvember: Beanshooter. **1994** NC Lang. & Life Project *Dial. Dict. Lumbee Engl.* 7 **seNC,** *Juvember. . .* Slingshot. *Daddy said he used to make juvembers all the time when he was a boy.*

jynt See **joint**

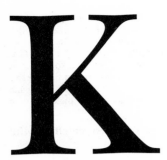

k', ka- prefix See **ker-**

ka adv [See quot 1972] **HI**
How; see quots.
    1938 Reinecke *Hawaiian Loanwords* 16, *Ka* . . adj. The definite article, used with rather facetious intent in such expressions as "Oh, *ka* cute!", especially by schoolchildren. In the Island dialect, the use of the article *the* for emphatic indication is common: *e.g.,* "Oh, the noisy!" [**1972** Carr *Da Kine Talk* 153 **HI**, It is quite possible that "Oh, the pretty!" derives from the Hawaiian phrase *Auwē ka nani!,* in which *ka* is 'the' and *nani* is 'pretty'. Translated literally the phrase means "Oh, the pretty!" and more freely, "Oh, how pretty!"]

ka intj See **ki** intj

kaa v [Haw *kā* to turn a rope for children to jump; also *ka'a* to turn, revolve; the forms coalesce in English] **HI**
See quots.
    1938 Reinecke *Hawaiian Loanwords* 16, *Ka'a.* . . To turn a rope for jumping. V[ery] F[requent] among children. **1968** *Jrl. Engl. Ling.* 2.81 **HI** [Common Hawaiian loanwords], *Kaa.* . . To turn a rope for jumping.

kabola n [Prob *ka-* (at **ker-**) + pronc-sp for **bowler**]
    1990 *WI State Jrl.* (Madison) 13 June "Neighbors: West" sec 2/3, American children know their marbles as kabolas, steelies, jumbos, milkies and peewees in decending [sic] order of size.

kabush adj [Perh *ka-* (at **ker-**) + *bushed* exhausted, infl by **kaput** adj **B1**]
    1970 *DARE* (Qu. X47, . . *"I'm very tired, at the end of my strength"*) Inf **MI**120, I'm [kə'bʌš]—not a Polish word, just slang.

kabushka n Also *kabuska, kapushka* [Varr of **babushka**]
See quot 1968.
    1950 *WELS Suppl.* se**WI**, *Kapushka* [kə'puškə]—head scarf. **1968** *DARE* (Qu. W3, *A piece of cloth that a woman folds over her head and ties under her chin*) Inf **MD**9, Kabushka [kə'buškə]; **WI**74, Kabuska [kə'buskə].

kace See **scarce**

kacely See **scarcely**

kack n[1] See **cack** n[1]

kack n[2] See **cack** n[2]

kacky See **cacky** v, n

kadabble n Also *kadoodle* [Varr of **caboodle**]
See quot.
    1967 *DARE* (Qu. LL10, *A whole group of people: "They made too much noise, so he sent the whole _____ home."*) Inf **SC**45, Kadabble; **LA**40, Kadoodle [corr to *caboodle* on sugg of wife].

ka dai See **co-day**

Kadiak bear See **Kodiak bear**

kadifter n [*ka-* (at **ker-**) + **dift**]
    1930 Shoemaker *1300 Words* 35 c**PA Mts** (as of c1900), *Kadifter*—A hard blow on the head.

‡**kadoo** n [Perh *ka-* (at **ker-**) + **do** n[1] **1**]
A to-do.
    1968 *DARE* (Qu. KK11, *To make great objections or a big fuss about something: "When we asked him to do that, he _____."*) Inf **VA**15, Made a big [kə'du].

kadoodle v [Prob *ka-* (at **ker-**) + **doodle** v[1] **2**]
    1875 Holland *Sevenoaks* 232 **N Atl**, I never seen but one [pauper] in the woods, an' he come here one night tootin' on a tin horn, an' blowin' about bein' the angel Gabrel [sic]. . . I skeered 'im, and he went off into the woods pertendin' he was tryin' to catch a bullet. That's the kind o' ball I allers use when I have a little game with a rovin' angel that comes kadoodlin' round me.

kadoodle n See **kadabble**

‡**kadoowy** n Cf **doohickey 1**
    1916 *DN* 4.276 **NE**, *Ka'doowy.* . . Indefinite term, used, for example, of a dish of some undefined nature at table. "Pass me that there kadoowy, please."

kady See **cady**

kaffee klatch See **klatch** n

kaffir (corn), kafir See **kafir corn**

kafir ant n [See quots]
=**thief ant.**
    1916 *Jrl. Economic Entomology* 9.30 **KS**, Locally, this species [=*Solenopsis molesta*] is known as the "kafir ant." . . The colonies are numerous. . . Nests have also been found in kafir, wheat, rye, oats, and alfalfa fields. **1926** Essig *Insects N. Amer.* 858, *The thief ant* . . is known as the kafir ant in Kansas and destroys kafir and Indian corn.

kafir corn n Also *kafir, kaffir (corn)* [See quot 1925; *OEDS* 1785 →]
A **sorghum** (here: *Sorghum bicolor* Caffrorum Group).
    1889 Vasey *Ag. Grasses* 37, *Sorghum vulgare.* This name as at present applied includes. . . millo maize, Kaffir corn, dourra, and broom corn. **1901** Mohr *Plant Life AL* 135, Various kinds of sorghum, known as durrha or kafir corn, millo maize, and pearl millet . . furnish green forage and hay crops throughout the summer. **1925** *Book of Rural Life* 3026, *Kafir,* . . perhaps the most important group of grain sorghums. The Kafirs originated in South Africa, and the name is taken from that of the tribe native in that region. This group of sorghums was introduced into the United States about 1876, and has been known very largely as *Kafir corn* in the grain trade and among farmers. . . Kafir is classed as a grain sorghum, but it is fully as important as a forage crop. **1938** Rawlings *Yearling* 214 n**FL**, The Kaffir corn for the chickens was ripening, its long heads like sorghum. **1941** Ward *Holding Hills* 85 **IA** (as of early 20th cent), This man knows soybeans and kaffir corn. **1944** Wellman *Bowl* 39 **KS** (as of c1890), I'll let you try your hand at the kaffir-corn in the mornin'. **1945** FWP *Lay My Burden Down* 198 **AL** (as of 1860s) [Black], But 'stead of eating corn bread, us eats bread out of kaffir corn and maize. **1948** Wolfe *Farm Gloss.* 181, *Kafir*—also spelled *kaffir.* A grain sorghum with juicy but not sweet stalks. **1953** (1977) Hubbard *Shantyboat* 323 **Missip-Ohio Valleys**, As another source of whole grain we began using hen scratch, a mixed feed for chickens, composed of cracked corn, wheat, sorghum seeds, kafir corn, and maize. **1966** *DARE* (Qu. L21, . . *Kinds of grain grown around here*; total Infs questioned, 75) Infs **NM**6, **OK**18, 52, Kaffir corn. **1976** Bailey–Bailey *Hortus Third* 1060, [*Sorghum*] Caffrorum Group. . . *Kafir corn, kafir.* . . Grown in s. Great Plains.

kag See **keg A1**

kagy See **cadgy**

kah See **ki** intj

kahala n [Haw] **HI**
An **amberjack 2** (here: *Seriola dumerili*).

1960 Gosline–Brock *Hawaiian Fishes* 170, The kahala is one of the two species of *Seriola* reported from Hawaiian waters. **1967** *DARE* (Qu. P2, . . *Kinds of saltwater fish caught around here . . good to eat*) Inf **HI**14, [kɑˈhɑlɑ]. **1967** *Honolulu Star-Bulletin* (HI) 31 May sec F 1/4, *Kahala*—Amber Fish or Yellow Tail.

kahili n Arch spp *kahile, kahiri* [Haw] Note: Haw has only one liquid consonant, which early writers often represented with *r* rather than *l*. **HI**
See quot 1826.

1823 (1970) Stewart *Jrl. Sandwich Is.* 118 **HI**, There is something approaching the *sublime* in the lofty noddings of the kahiles of state, as they tower far above the heads of the group whose distinction they proclaim. **1826** Ellis *Narrative HI* 75, A servant . . stood behind his chair, holding a . . handsome *kahiri*, an elastic rod, three or four feet long, having the shining feathers of the tropic-bird tastefully fastened round the upper end, with which he fanned away the flies. *Ibid* 341, Though the Kahiris were usually small, . . they were sometimes upwards of twenty feet high; the handle twelve or fifteen feet long, beautifully covered with tortoise shell and the ivory of whales' teeth; and the upper part formed with red, yellow, or black feathers, fastened on a kind of wicker work, and resembling a cylinder twelve or thirteen inches in diameter. These, however, are only used on state occasions, when they are carried in processions. **1866** in 1938 Twain *Letters Sandwich Is.* 125 **HI**, A dozen or more of these gaudy kahilis were upheld by pall-bearers. **1873** in 1966 Bishop *Sandwich Is.* 18 **HI**, We . . passed the tasteful mausoleum, with two tall Kahilis, or feather plumes, at the door of the tomb. **1938** Reinecke *Hawaiian Loanwords* 17, *Kahili*. . . A large feather brush used as a symbol of *ali'i* rank, and later of royalty. *Kahilis* are displayed on state occasions, as recently as at the funeral of a mayor of Honolulu . . ; also in pageants. F[requent]. **1972** Carr *Da Kine Talk* 87 **HI**, *Hawaiian Words Commonly Heard In Hawaii's English. . . Kāhili.* Feather standard of royalty.

kahili ginger n [See quot 1948] **HI**
A **ginger lily** (here: *Hedychium gardneranum*).

1929 Pope *Plants HI* 49, Another species [of *Hedychium*] occasionally found in cultivation in Hawaii is the kahili ginger, *H. gardenerianum* [sic]. . . The common name, ginger, is freely applied to these species. **1948** Neal *In Gardens HI* 215, In many ways, the kahili ginger resembles the white and yellow gingers and, like them, has fragrant flowers. . . At stem tips . . develop open inflorescences about 1 foot long which look like Hawaiian kahilis. **1967** *DARE* (Qu. S11) Infs **HI**6, 8, Kahili ginger—(on mountains) grows like a kahili, around stalk; (Qu. S26a, . . *Wildflowers. . . Roadside flowers*) Inf **HI**11, Ginger (not for leis)—kahili—yellow, tiny flowers, used by royal family. **1976** Bailey-Bailey *Hortus Third* 546, [*Hedychium*] *Gardneranum*. . . Kahili ginger. **1982** Perry-Hay *Field Guide Plants* 120, Kahili ginger; ginger lily. . . Noted for their showy flowers and fragrance. **1994** Stone-Pratt *Hawai'i's Plants* 197, Unlike many other ginger species in Hawai'i, kāhili ginger is a prolific producer of fruits and seeds.

kahiri See **kahili**

kahuna n Also sp *kahoona* [Haw] **chiefly HI**
1 A priest of the native Hawaiian religion; now esp a sorcerer.

1873 in 1966 Bishop *Sandwich Is.* 254 **HI**, Several other instances have been told me of persons who have actually died under the influence of the terror and despair produced by being told that the *kahuna* was "praying them to death." **1886** in 1892 Gowen *Paradise Pacific* 85 **HI**, The King had dreamed that he would die on a certain day, and the *Kahunas* advised him to stave off the calamity by getting rid of the *white power*. **1915** Bryan *Nat. Hist. HI* 54, Besides the regular order of priests there was a numerous class of more irregular priests or kahunas, that were little more than sorcerers. **1938** Reinecke *Hawaiian Loanwords* 17, *Kahuna*. . . Originally, one of a class of experts, including priests and sorcerers; now applied chiefly to the *kahuna anaana,* or sorcerer, a person of great importance among Hawaiians. . . V[ery] F[requent]. **1967** *DARE* (Qu. CC14, . . *Where one person supposedly casts a spell over another*) Inf **CA**10, Kahuna [ˌkəˈhunə]—Hawaiian; **HI**1, A medicine man/witch doctor is a kahuna; still [are] people of Hawaiian blood who believe in this; **HI**4, Kahuna [FW: noun and verb]; **HI**9, Kahuna; (QR, near Qu. CC17) Inf **HI**4, Kahuna (witch doctor)—could stop the wind blowing. **1967** *DARE* Tape **HI**4, The kahuna . . feed the idol so he get power. . . If you have sick, they cure you. . . Or they make you sick. **1984** *Isthmus* (Madison WI) 3 Aug 18/4, [Radio schedule:] Talk about the Big Kahoona . . Hawaiian "Master of Secrets," discusses native Hawaiian culture and medicine and . . the actual meaning of the hula dance.

2 A spell or curse. Cf **hoodoo** n **1c**
1938 Reinecke *Hawaiian Loanwords* 17, *Kahuna*. . . A spell: "To put a kahuna on" someone. . . V[ery] F[requent]. **1954–60** Hance et al. *Hawaiian Sugar* 3, *Kahuna*. . . A curse.
3 See quot.
1954–60 Hance et al. *Hawaiian Sugar* 3, *Kahuna*. . . ghost.

kahuna v, hence ppl adj *kahuna'(e)d* [**kahuna** n] **HI**
To practice sorcery; to cast a spell.

1938 Reinecke *Hawaiian Loanwords* 17, *Kahuna*. . . To practice the art of a *kahuna;* to practice Hawaiian sorcery or white magic; to place a spell on one, as, "K kahuna-ed M." **1942** *CA Folkl. Qrly.* 1.320 **HI** (as of 1926), [A version of the "vanishing hitchhiker" legend:] A number of times . . friends of Mr. _____ have picked up a girl pushing a smashed bike along the road. . . She gives the governor's mansion as her address. . . The driver looks over to discover that she has disappeared. Upon returning the bike to the governor's mansion, they learn that she is dead. (Everyone knows that she has been *kahuna*'ed, i.e., bewitched.) **1951** *AmSp* 26.20 **HI**, Terms drawn from Hawaiian anthropology and folklore include . . *kahuna.* . . As a verb it means to practice magic or cast a spell. **1967** *DARE* (Qu. CC12b, . . *If a person has a lot of bad luck . . "He's been _____."*) Inf **HI**9A, Kahuna'd; (Qu. CC14, . . *Where one person supposedly casts a spell over another*) Inf **HI**4, Kahuna [FW: noun and verb]; **HI**1, He's kahuna'd [ˌkəˈhunəd]—Hawaiian.

kahysene See **kerosene**

kai n, adv [Haw] **HI** Cf **makai, moana** n[1], **wai**
See quots.

1938 Reinecke *Hawaiian Loanwords* 17, *Kai*. . . The sea. **1951** *AmSp* 26.23 **HI**, Other common Hawaiian words are . . *kai* (sea, salt water). *Ibid* 24, *Wai* (fresh water) and *kai* (salt water). **1954–60** Hance et al. *Hawaiian Sugar* 3 **HI**, *Kai*. . . Sea water, ocean. [*Ibid* 4, *Makai* . . (Abbrev. *Kai*). . . Towards the ocean.] **1984** *Sunset HI Guide* 85, *Kai*—sea.

kai intj See **ki** intj

kaidge See **kedge**

kaig See **keg** A2

kain't See **can** v[1] **1b**

Kaintock See **Kentuck** 2a

Kaintuc See **Kentucky**

Kaintuck n
1 See **Kentucky**.
2 See **Kentuck** 2a.

Kaintuck(e)y See **Kentucky**

kaiser blade n Also *kaiser hook* [Prob < *Kaiser Bill*, nickname of Wilhelm II, Emperor of Germany during WWI] **chiefly Lower Missip Valley, esp MS** See Map on p. 190 Cf **blade** n **3, brier hook, bush hook**
A hooked blade usu fixed to a wooden handle and used to cut brush and weeds; a billhook.

1965–70 *DARE* (Qu. L35, *Hand tools used for cutting underbrush and digging out roots*) 9 Infs, 7 **MS**, Kaiser blade; **TN**26, Kaiser blade or bush blade; **AL**2, Kaiser blade—3½' to 4' handle, made with a hook on the end; **AR**56, Kaiser blade [FW: similar to brush hook]; (Qu. L37, *A hand tool used for cutting weeds and grass*) Infs **MS**81, **TN**26, Kaiser blade. **1984** *NADS Letters* neAR, I grew up in northeast Arkansas with "hands-on" familiarity with Kaiser blades (and the blisters and calluses to prove it). They were heavy, wicked tools with sharp double blades and hooked tips for pulling out the brush after you had whacked it off. *Ibid* wTN, Kaiser blades are so called in Tipton County, Tennessee. At least, they were so called in the 40's and 50's. . . Other names for the tool: bushblade, weed hook, brush hook. . . Negroes who worked with it did *not* use "K[aiser] B[lade]." **1984** *DARE* File csMS, In World War I, the American GIs . . were . . cleaning up the roadsides in Germany. . . These guys, these American prisoners, termed their brier blade—what we call a brier blade today—they termed them "Kaiser blades" because the old Kaiser Wilhelm had them out there using them. . . You know what it is—simply a blade on the end of a handle you cut briers and stuff with. **1986** Pederson *LAGS Concordance*, 1 inf, seMS, Kaiser blade—used for chopping cane; 1 inf, cMS, A cradle with a Kaiser blade on it. **1991** *DARE* File AR, This Christmas I was visiting a friend's grandfather, and he has his kaiser hook hanging in a shed in back. He's using it. It's a mean-looking thing . . with a big hook on the end.

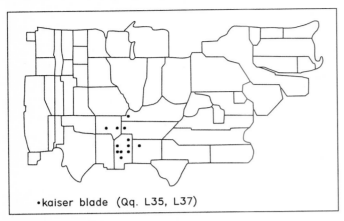

•kaiser blade (Qq. L35, L37)

Kaiser's buttonhole flower n Also *Kaiser's flower*
=**cornflower 1.**

[**1884** *Harper's New Mth. Mag.* 68.861, The Emperor . . is a great friend of the corn-flower (the bachelor's-button).] **1967–68** *DARE* (Qu. S11, . . *Bachelor's button*) Inf **MN**36, Kaiser's flower—from the German *Kaiser's blumen;* **NY**10, Kaiser's buttonhole flower.

kak See **cack** n²

kakio n [Haw *kāki'o* impetigo, itch] **HI**
See quots.

1938 Reinecke *Hawaiian Loanwords* 17, *Kaki'o.* . . Tiny itching sores; the itch. (A children's word, especially.) **1967** Reinecke–Tsuzaki *Hawaiian Loanwords* 99, Kakio. **1981** *Pidgin To Da Max* np **HI**, *Kaki'o.* . . Scab.

kala n¹ [Haw] **HI**

A **surgeonfish:** usu *Naso unicornis,* but also *N. brevirostris.*

1926 Pan-Pacific Research Inst. *Jrl.* 1.1.11 **HI**, Naso unicornis. . . Kala. **1933** Bryan *Hawaiian Nature* 241, The unicorn fish, or *kala* . . is olive gray . . with blue spines, and blue on the fins. **1960** Gosline–Brock *Hawaiian Fishes* 251, Although the Hawaiian name "Kala" appears to be applied most specifically to this species, it is often used for the other species of *Naso. N. unicornis* is light olive drab in color. **1967** *DARE* (Qu. P2, . . *Kinds of saltwater fish caught around here* . . *good to eat*) Inf **HI**4, Kala—unicorn fish. **1967** *DARE* Tape **HI**9, They have kala in there [=in a fishing net] too. . . Kala fish. Hawaiians like that fish.

kala n² [Haw pronc-sp for *dollar*] **HI**

A dollar; money.

1955 Day *HI People* 310, Kala (English): dollar. **1967** Reinecke–Tsuzaki *Hawaiian Loanwords* 99, Kala. . . [Eng. *dollar.*] Money. V[ery] F[requent]. **1967** *DARE* (Qu. U19a, . . *Money in general: "He's certainly got the _____."*) Inf **HI**1, [,ka·'la]; **HI**4, ['ka·'la:] = money; (Qu. U28a, . . *A five-dollar bill*) Inf **HI**6, Kala-pepa [FW: =money-paper]; (Qu. U28b, . . *A ten-dollar bill*) Inf **HI**6, Umi-kala-pepa. **1990** *DARE* File **Honolulu HI**, I have heard *kala* meaning "money" or "dollar" but I never used it myself.

kalaber, kalabrìas See **clabber** n²

kalakoa adj, n [Haw pronc-sp for *calico*] **HI**

1938 Reinecke *Hawaiian Loanwords* 18, *Kalakoa.* . . 1. "Calico," piebald or variegated, referring to the color pattern primarily of a horse, but sometimes to that of a pig or other animal, a fish, or a dress. 2. Scars left after impetigo or other sores have healed—forming a pattern on one's skin. **1968** *Jrl. Engl. Ling.* 2.81 **HI** [Common Hawaiian loanwords], *Halakoa* [sic]; adj., n. [Eng. *calico.*] Calico, piebald, or variegated, with reference to color patterns.

kalikali n **HI**

A **snapper:** either *Pristipomoides sieboldii* or *Rooseveltia brighami.*

1926 Pan-Pacific Research Inst. *Jrl.* 1.9, Rooseveltia brighami. . . Kalikali. **1960** Gosline–Brock *Hawaiian Fishes* 182, The lutjanids form one of the most important groups of Hawaiian market fishes, including . . the onaga, kalikali, and 'opakapaka. [*Ibid* 184, *Rooseveltia brighami* . .

The fish is brought into the market from time to time along with catches of other species of the family.] *Ibid* 186, *Pristipomoides sieboldii* (*Kalikali*). . . In the kalikali the mouth is both smaller and more oblique than in the 'opakapaka.

kalkerlate, kalkilate, kal'late See **calculate**

kallyope See **calliope**

kalua v, hence ppl adj *kalua'd* [Haw *kālua* to bake in an underground oven] **HI**

To bake in an **imu** or underground oven; hence adj *kalua* baked in such a manner; employing this method.

1938 Reinecke *Hawaiian Loanwords* 18, Kalua. . . 1. To bake in an underground oven, or *imu.* . . V[ery] F[requent]. *Ibid,* Kalua'd . . Baked underground in Hawaiian style. F[requent]. [**1940** Bazore *Hawaiian Foods* 40, Characteristic Hawaiian Dishes. . Kalua Puaa—cleaned pig, rubbed with seasonings, has the abdominal cavity filled with hot stones; then the pig is placed in a pit containing hot stones. The pig is covered with leaves and damp burlap sacks and allowed to cook for several hours. *Ibid* 177, Barbecued Pig (Kalua Puaa).] **1951** *AmSp* 26.21 **HI**, At a 'luau,' or Hawaiian feast . . food is wrapped in 'ki' or 'ti' leaves and baked in an 'imu' or underground oven in the steam rising from heated and drenched lava rocks. A whole pig is baked in this way, 'kalua' style. [**1967** *DARE* (QR, near Qu. H38) Inf **HI**6, Kalua—method [for cooking] pig in imu.] **1972** Carr *Da Kine Talk* 87 **HI**, *Hawaiian Words Commonly Heard In Hawaii's English.* . . *Kālua.* To bake in the ground oven. *Ibid* 114, *Kālua pig.* . . A pig that is roasted in an *imu* 'underground oven'; the principal dish at a *lū'au* 'Hawaiian feast'. **1981** *Pidgin To Da Max* np **HI**, *Kalua pig.* . . This is what you get when you put the pua'a [=pig] inside the imu and let 'em cook.

kamaaina n, also attrib Also *kamaina* [Haw *kama'āina* native-born; literally "child of the land"] **HI** Cf **haole, malihini**

In Hawaii: a native-born or fully assimilated resident; a well-established person or institution.

1875 in 1966 Bishop *Sandwich Is.* vii **HI**, I had so completely lived the island life, and acquainted myself with the existing state of the country, as to be rather a kamaina than a stranger. **1938** Reinecke *Hawaiian Loanwords* 18, Kamaaina. . . 1. "A native born in any place and continuing to live in that place." 2. A resident of long standing, especially one who has fitted into the local culture and point of view. . . 3. Characteristic of old-timers, as, *kamaaina* ways. V[ery] F[requent]. **1951** *AmSp* 26.20 **HI**, A newcomer to the islands is a 'malihini,' a guest or stranger. An old-timer in Hawaii, or one born there, is a 'kamaaina,' meaning 'child of the land.' **1969** *DARE* File **Honolulu HI**, *Kamaaina*—an old-timer, established person, e.g. you might speak of a long established business as a kamaaina firm. **1972** Carr *Da Kine Talk* 87 **HI**, *Hawaiian Words Commonly Heard In Hawaii's English.* . . *Kama'āina.* A person born in Hawaii. [**1984** Sunset *HI Guide* 85, *Kama'aina*—native born.]

kamaboko n Also *kamaboku* [Japanese *kamaboko*] **HI**

A type of fish cake; see quot 1940.

1940 Bazore *Hawaiian Foods* 64, *Kamaboko* . . is a cooked fish cake made of finely chopped flesh of shark or swordfish. . . The cake is molded into varied shapes; steamed or broiled. . . One finds kamaboko in steamed custards, noodle soup, and in rice or vegetable dishes. A feast on a holiday or served at a wedding or birthday is not complete without sliced kamaboko. **1972** Carr *Da Kine Talk* 91 **HI**, *Kamaboko* 'boiled fish paste' is well known in Hawaii as 'fishcake'. **1989** *DARE* File **Honolulu HI**, Kamaboku—those are fishcakes. By the way, it's "kamaboku" not "boko". Lots of people say "kamaboku"—not just Japanese-Americans. **1992** *Ibid,* Kamaboko is a common food item in the [Hawaiian] Islands—most people know it since the Japanese culture is so pervasive. It's a combination of ground up seafoods that are then steamed and put in molds. The most common shape is that of a long log, split down the middle. It's sliced and served cold.

kamaina See **kamaaina**

kamani n [Haw] **HI**

A slow-growing tree *(Calophyllum inophyllum)* native to Hawaii.

1850 Cheever *Whale & Captors* 39, Overgrown with huge roots of the Kamani and Koa trees. **1873** in 1966 Bishop *Sandwich Is.* 43 **HI**, I cannot convey to you any idea of the greenness and lavish luxuriance of this place. . . It presents a bewildering maze of lilies . . gardenias . . *kamani* trees . . and quantities of other trees and flowers. **1929** Neal *Honolulu Gardens* 211, The true *kamani.* . . is a tall, handsome, smooth-barked tree, which in flowering time generously spreads fragrance . . from snowy clusters of many small flowers. . . The *kamani* is mentioned in old chants of Hawaii. **1965** Krauss–Alexander *Grove Farm* 307 **HI,** One morning a new attendant brought George's horse to the kamani tree.

kamas (root) See **camas**

Kamchatka lily n AK

A **fritillary** (here: *Fritillaria camschatcensis*).

1955 U.S. Arctic Info. Center *Gloss.* 45, Kamchatka lily. A perennial herb, *Fritillaria camschatcensis,* . . bearing a bell-like, dark red flower. Also called 'black lily,' 'saranna.' **1963** Craighead *Rocky Mt. Wildflowers* 26, Other species [of *Fritillaria*], such as the Kamchatka Lily (or Indian Rice), are regularly gathered and eaten by Eskimos. **1966** Heller *Wild Flowers AK* 93, Kamchatka Lily. . . Flowers chocolate colored. **1987** Hughes–Blackwell *Wildflowers SE AK* 74, Kamchatka Lily. . . The large, nodding and bell-like flowers have a strong, unpleasant odor.

kamfire See **camphor**

kamleika n Also *camley, comleka, kamláyka, kamley* AK [Perh Chukchi *kemlilyun*]

A waterproof garment usu made from animal intestines; see quots.

1866 in 1942 James *First Scientific Explor.* 206 **AK,** Bought a comleka to-day. **1870** Dall *Alaska* 532, Kamláyka.—A water-proof shirt, made of the intestines of the seal or sea-lion, and used while travelling in their kyaks, or in rainy weather, by the Aleuts and Esquimaux. **1893** Barnum *Life AK Mission* 14, In wet weather the natives wear a splendid water-proof which is called an emaranetik. The Russians termed it Kamleika. It is an over-parki composed of narrow strips of membrane dextrously sewn together with a peculiar water-tight stitch. **1939** FWP *Guide AK* 335, In wet weather, or when out at sea, they [=Aleuts] wear a camley . . formed of the intestines of sea animals: the bladder of the halibut, or the skin off the tongue of the whale. It has a hood to cover the head and ties close around the neck and wrists; so that no water can penetrate. **1949** *AK Sportsman* Apr 39, Kamleika making was almost a lost art in Old Harbor at one time, but two of the women . . have mastered the intricate stitching. **1959** *Ibid* Nov 13, In early Alaskan writings about the Aleuts and southern Alaskan Eskimos this garment is known as the *kamleika,* or the *kamley.* It was called *ingmangnituk* by the northern Eskimos.

kamloops trout n [*Kamloops*, British Columbia] =**rainbow trout.**

1896 U.S. Natl. Museum *Bulletin* 47.499, *Salmo gairdneri kamloops.* . . Kamloops Trout. . . Kamloops Lake, Okanogan Lake, Kootenay Lake, and other lakes tributary to Fraser River or to the Upper Columbia. . . Somewhat different in appearance from the ordinary "Steelhead," but not distinguished by any technical character of any importance, and doubtless intergrading fully with the latter. **1904** *Salmon & Trout* 245, The Kamloops trout has a large eye, a rounded snout, and a rather large mouth. **1947** *Field & Stream* June 19/1 *(DA),* He makes his favorites, the sea-run steelheads and the Kamloops trout, which he knows well, appear to be magnificent fish. **1972** Sparano *Outdoors Encycl.* 356, Common names: Rainbow trout, . . Kamloops trout. **1991** Amer. Fisheries Soc. *Common Names Fishes* 180, Trout, . . Kamloops—see rainbow trout.

kamsh See **camas**

kanaka n For varr see quots [Haw] **chiefly HI** *often derog* Cf **Canuck**

A Hawaiian native, esp a man—formerly applied to other Polynesian islanders; the Hawaiian language.

1820 (1931) Holman *Jrl.* 21 **HI,** All the fresh water used by the natives. . . is all brought on the kahnahka's (men) shoulders in calabashes. *Ibid* 22, The crowd began to scatter . . as we approached the King's house, which was surrounded by kahnahkas (men) which are his life-guard. **1833** in 1934 Frear *Lowell & Abigail* 75 **HI,** One of the Chiefs recently departed this life. The kanakas assembled about 9 A.M. and commenced digging a vault. **1840** (1841) Dana *2 Yrs.* 180, The long name of Sandwich Islanders is dropped, and they are called by the whites, all over the Pacific ocean, "Kanákas," from a word in their own language which they apply to themselves, and to all South Sea Islanders, in distinction from whites, whom they call "Haole." *Ibid* 182, New Zealand Kanaka eat white man;—Sandwich Island Kanaka,—no. Sand-wich Island Kanaka *ua like na haole*—all 'e same a' you! **1847** Melville *Typee* 81 **HI,** [Footnote:] The word "Kannaka" is at the present day

universally used in the South Seas by Europeans to designate the Islanders. In the various dialects of the principal groups it is simply a sexual designation applied to the males; but it is now used by the natives in their intercourse with foreigners in the same sense in which the latter employ it. **1866** in 1938 Twain *Letters Sandwich Is.* 85, A white Chief Clerk . . handed the document to Bill Ragsdale . . who translated and clattered it off in Kanaka. **1889** (1890) Harte *Heritage* 33 **CA,** You'll go out among the hounds ez allowed your mother was a Spanish nigger or a kanaka. **1938** Reinecke *Hawaiian Loanwords* 18, Kanaka ['kɑˈnɑkɑ] [ˌkəˈnækə], sometimes facetiously [kəˈnæk]. . . A native Ha-waiian. As used in Hawaiian speech, with the proper pronunciation, the word is acceptable; but as used in English speech, with the [æ], it is taken in a somewhat derogatory sense by the Hawaiians. . . V[ery] F[requent]. **1967** *DARE* (Qu. HH28, *Names and nicknames . . for peo-ple of foreign background*) Inf **HI**4, [kɑˈnɑkɑ]—Hawaiian [Inf of Haw ancestry]; **HI**13, [kəˈnækə]—Hawaiian [Inf of Japanese ancestry]. **1972** Carr *Da Kine Talk* 87 **HI,** *Hawaiian Words Commonly Heard In Ha-waii's English. . . Kanaka.* Human being, man, individual; as a loanword used by non-Hawaiians, the meaning is sometimes 'native' or 'fellow'. **1980** Bushnell *Water of Kane* 447 **HI,** There they stood, dozens of 'em—Kanakas, Chinks, Japs, haole trash fallen even lower while con-sortin' with the heathen.

ka-nanny See **co-nan(nie)**

kane n Usu |'kɑne, 'kɑni|; for var see quot 1967 [Haw] **HI** Cf **kanaka, wahine**

A male; spec: a man; a husband.

1938 Reinecke *Hawaiian Loanwords* 18, Kane ['kâˌne]. . . 1. The male of any species, particularly the human, but sometimes applied even to plants. . . 2. Husband, one's "man." . . V[ery] F[requent]. **1951** *AmSp* 26.20 **HI,** *Kane* for 'man' or 'husband' and *wahine* for 'woman' or 'wife' are often heard, and seen as well on the doors of rest rooms; the terms are also used to denote sex (*pipi kane,* bull). **1967** *DARE* (Qu. K22, 23, *Words . . for a bull*) Inf **HI**2, Kane ['kʌni] cow. **1969** *DARE* File Honolulu **HI,** Kane ['kɑni]—a man, common. **1972** Carr *Da Kine Talk* 87 **HI,** *Hawaiian Words Commonly Heard In Hawaii's English. . . Kāne.* Male, husband.

kangaroo mouse n

1 A **jumping mouse 1,** usu *Zapus hudsonicus.* [See quot 1917]

1838 Geol. Surv. OH *Second Annual Rept.* 160, Meriones Canaden-sis . . Kangaroo Mouse. **1857** U.S. Patent Office *Annual Rept. for 1856: Ag.* 96, This animal is known as the "Long-tailed Deer Mouse," "Fob-tailed Mouse," "Kangaroo Mouse." **1917** Anthony *Mammals Amer.* 264, *(Zapodidae)* Jumping Mice. . . are slender and graceful Mice with exceptionally long tails, short fore legs, extremely long hind legs which have given them their other name of Kangaroo Mice. . . Like the Kangaroo, their muscular hind legs give them remarkable jumping powers, while their tails aid to balance them and give them direction. *Ibid, Zapus hudsonicus . . Other Name.*—Kangaroo Mouse. **1955** U.S. Arctic Info. Center *Gloss.* 45, *Kangaroo mouse.* The jumping mouse. **1966** *DARE* (Qu. P32, . . *Other kinds of wild animals*) Inf **MI**32, Kangaroo mouse.

2 Any of var small rodents with external cheek pouches; see below. **West**

a =**kangaroo rat 1.**

1867 *Amer. Naturalist* 1.394, They are known in the vernacular as "Kangaroo" or "Jumping" Rats and Mice, and are entirely confined to Transmississippian regions. **1874** Coues *Birds NW* 366, In the stomachs of those [buzzards] examined I found the remains of burrowing pouched-rats, . . kangaroo-mice (*Dipodomys ordii*) and some *Arvicolae.* **1876** Miller *First Fam'lies* 243 **ceCA,** Wood-rats, . . had gone into winter-quarters under the great logs. **1967** *DARE* (Qu. P32, . . *Other kinds of wild animals*) Inf **WY**1, Kangaroo mouse.

b =**pocket mouse** (here: *Perognathus* spp).

1889 *Century Dict.* 3265, Kangaroo-mouse. . . An American rodent mammal of the family *Saccomyidae* and genus *Perognathus;* a pocket mouse. The kangaroo-mice are closely related to the species of *Dipo-domys* . . but are smaller. They inhabit the same parts of the United States.

c A mouse-sized rodent of the genus *Microdipodops.* [See quot 1980] Also called **kangaroo rat 2, pocket rat**

1925 *Jrl. Mammalogy* 6.57 **CA,** About two miles east of Eagleville, it was my good fortune to encounter colonies of . . the Oregon kanga-roo mouse, *Microdipodops megacephalus oregonus.* **1935** Pratt *Manual*

Vertebrate Animals 323, *Microdipodops*. . . Kangaroo mice. Size very small. **1957** Jaeger *N. Amer. Deserts* 150 **West,** Two kangaroo rats . . and the tiny black or brownish, large-headed kangaroo mouse *(Microdipodops megalocephalus),* with tail peculiarly swollen in the middle, occur on the Sagebrush Desert. **1980** Whitaker *Audubon Field Guide Mammals* 436, Kangaroo mice (*Microdipodops*), smaller editions of the Kangaroo rats, also have long hindlegs for jumping, but their tails are quite different, being broadest in the middle and without a terminal crest or tuft. *Ibid* 447, *Dark Kangaroo Mouse* (*Microdipodops megacephalus*). . . This species apparently stores no food in its burrow. . . *Pale Kangaroo Mouse* (*Microdipodops pallidus*). . . The "kangaroo" tail stores fat, . . and also helps maintain balance during jumps.

kangaroo rat n West

1 A rodent of the genus *Dipodomys*. [See quots 1957, 1980] Also called **gopher** n[1] **2e, kangaroo mouse 2a, pocket rat**

1854 (1932) Bell *Log TX–CA Trail* 35.234, Killed an animal that somewhat resembled a medium sized rat. . . teeth like a squirrel . . a pocket on each side the mouth lined in the inside with fur . . and what is most remarkable is the hind legs are about 3 times the length of the fore ones, giving it the appearance of a Kangeroo; in fact by some in camp it is called the Kangeroo Rat. **1867** [see **kangaroo mouse 2a**] **1889** *Century Dict.* 3265, *Kangaroo-rat*. . . An American rodent of the family *Saccomyidæ* and subfamily *Dipodomyinæ,* as *Dipodomys phillipsi* or *D. ordi.* They resemble jerboas rather than kangaroos, and are common in the southwestern parts of the United States and Mexico. **1890** *Stock Grower & Farmer* 4 Jan. 7/2 (*DAE*), I also found a queer sort of kangaroo rat, a mouse with jackass ears, and another kind of a mouse with pockets in its cheeks . . in the Grand Canon [*sic*]. **1917** Anthony *Mammals Amer.* 259, Pocket Rat—*Perodipus agilis* Gambel—Other Name.—Kangaroo Rat. *Ibid* 260, It is unfortunate that the name "Kangaroo Rat" has become attached to this group [=*Dipodomys* and *Microdipodops*] of beautiful rodents; for . . "they are as unratlike as they are widely removed from the Marsupials." **1948** *Pacific Discovery* Mar/Apr 9 **csCA,** On those nights our delight was to watch the kangaroo rats, those long-tailed elves of the great sand wastes, at their play and fighting. **1957** Barnes *Nat. Hist. Wasatch Summer* 57 **UT,** The Utah kangaroo rat . . , being neither kangaroo nor rat, . . is closely related to the pocket mice. It does have short forelegs, strong hind legs for jumping and a long tail for balancing, hence the name "kangaroo." **1967** *DARE* (Qu. P29) Inf **CO22,** [Gophers are] blue, like a kangaroo rat; (Qu. P32, . . *Other kinds of wild animals*) Inf **TX5,** Kangaroo rat. **1980** Whitaker *Audubon Field Guide Mammals* 436, Kangaroo rats . . when alarmed, . . use their springlike hindlegs to make spectacular hops; some of the larger species can leap almost 9′, thus suggesting their common name. . . They also use their hindlegs when fighting and to make a drumming sound.

2 =**kangaroo mouse 2c.**

1917 Anthony *Mammals Amer.* 263, The *Pygmy Kangaroo Rat* [=*Microdipodops megacephalus*] is, as its name indicates, a very much smaller animal than either of the two other genera mentioned above. The hind feet are densely covered with fur to the tips of the toes, and. . . it is an inhabitant of Central Nevada. **1947** Cahalane *Mammals* 442, *Kangaroo Rat*—*Dipodomys* and *Microdipodops* sp. *Ibid* 451, The dwarf kangaroo rat (genus *Microdipodops*), only 6 to 7 inches in total length, looks like a good-sized pocket mouse with large head and heavy body. Its range is limited almost entirely to the Great Basin of Nevada, southeastern Oregon, and extreme eastern California.

Kankakee bar plover n
=**golden plover.**

1877 *Forest & Stream* 8.49, From the regularity of the visits of these birds, in former years, to the sand bars of the upper Illinois and Kankakee they have been called by the resident shooters Kankakee Bar Plover. **1923** U.S. Dept. Ag. *Misc. Circular* 13.69, *Golden Plover*. . . *Vernacular Names*. . . *In local use*. . . Kankakee-bar plover (Ind., Ill.)

‡kanozzle n [Perh *ka-* (var of **ker-**) + *nozzle* nose]

1969 *DARE* (Qu. X14, *Joking words for the nose*) Inf **MI103,** Kanozzle [ˌkəˈnazəl].

Kansas banana See **banana B1**

Kansas City fish n Cf **Albany beef, Arkansas chicken, Boston woodcock, Cincinnati B1, Florida chicken**

1944 Adams *Western Words* 86, *Kansas City fish*—Fried salt pork.

Kansas thistle n
=**buffalo burr.**

1897 *Jrl. Amer. Folkl.* 10.52 **swMO,** *Solanum rostratum*. . . Kansas thistle. **1950** Gray-Fernald *Manual of Botany* 1254, *S[olanum] rostratum*. . . Buffalo-bur, Kansas-thistle. . . Native on the Plains, w. of our range, now an aggressive weed. **1970** Correll *Plants TX* 1397, *Solanum rostratum*. . . Kansas-thistle. . . An aggressive weedy plant of overgrazed land, flats and waste places, generally throughout Tex.

Kanu(c)k See **Canuck**

kanyon See **canyon**

kapa See **tapa**

kapakahi adj [Haw] HI
See quots.

1938 Reinecke *Hawaiian Loanwords* 19, *Kapakahi*. . . One-sided; uneven; crooked; upside down. . . Sometimes applied figuratively. . . F[requent]. **1951** *AmSp* 26.23 **HI,** Common Hawaiian words are . . *kapakahi* (crooked, uneven, biased). **1967** *DARE* (Qu. B15, *When the wind suddenly begins to blow in a different direction* . . *it* _____) Inf **HI9,** Kapakahi—inside out; (Qu. MM3, *When someone does something the wrong way round* . . *"This is the front, you've got the whole thing turned* _____.") Inf **HI13,** [ˌkɑpəˈkɑhi]. **1969** *DARE* FW Addit Honolulu **HI,** *Kapakahi* [ˌkɑpəˈkɑhi]—crooked, e.g., "His eyes are kapakahi." **1972** Carr *Da Kine Talk* 87 **HI,** *Hawaiian Words Commonly Heard In Hawaii's English*. . . *Kapakahi.* One-sided, crooked. **1981** *Pidgin To Da Max* np **HI,** *Kapakahi*. . . All mix up; all mess up. [Cartoon:] Chee, Mona. . . Yo' files all kapakahi!

kapoodle See **caboodle**

kapoop See **kaput** adj

kapu adj Also *tabu* [Haw "sacred, inviolable; prohibited"; cf *taboo*]
Forbidden, off limits—often used as a warning to deter trespassing.

1826 Ellis *Narrative HI* 365, This [="sacred"] appears to be the legitimate meaning of the word tabu, though the natives, when talking with foreigners, use it more extensively, applying it to everything prohibited or improper. This, however, is only to accommodate the latter. **1930** Degener *Ferns of HI* 111, Of this entire complex system the only relic that has survived to the present day may be seen in wayside warnings. Instead of reading "No Trespassing," they usually read *Kapu*. **1938** Reinecke *Hawaiian Loanwords* 19, *Kapu*. . . Tabu; forbidden. Keep out!—commonly seen on signboards. . . V[ery] F[requent]. **1954** *Ellery Queen's Mystery Mag.* 4.27 **HI,** "I saw his studio. . . That's where the man really lives." "Was the party given there?" "Oh, no. That room is *kapu*. Definitely not the background for the sort of shindig his wife throws." [Both speakers are mainlanders.] **1954–60** Hance et al. *Hawaiian Sugar* 3 **HI,** *Kapu*. . . Taboo, forbidden, keep out, danger. **1969** *DARE* FW Addit Honolulu **HI,** *Kapu* [kɑˈpu]—Keep out (common). **1972** Carr *Da Kine Talk* 87 **HI,** *Hawaiian Words Commonly Heard In Hawaii's English*. . . *Kapu.* Taboo, forbidden.

kapulu adj, adv [Haw] HI
See quots.

1938 Reinecke *Hawaiian Loanwords* 19, *Kapulu*. . . 1. Dirty; slovenly; carelessly done. . . 2. Unfaithful in one's work. . . 3. Foolish; sottish. . . F[requent]. **1954–60** Hance et al. *Hawaiian Sugar* 3 **HI,** *Kapulu* . . careless, slovenly, dirty. **1967** *DARE* (Qu. W29, . . *Expressions* . . *for things that are sewn carelessly* . . *"They're* _____.") Inf **HI9,** Kapulu [kɑˈpulu]—sloppy, half-done; (Qu. KK63, *To do a clumsy or hurried job of repairing something: "It will never last—he just* _____.") Inf **HI13,** Kapulu [kɑˈpulu]—poorly done. Made it kapulu.

kapushka See **kabushka**

kaput adj Usu |kɑˈput, -ˈput|; also |kəˈpʌt|; for addit varr see quot 1965–70 at **A** Also *kaputs(t)* Pronc-spp *gabut, gaput, kapoop* [Ger *kaputt*; cf *EDD Suppl.* go capooch (at **capooch**) "to collapse, die." *OEDS* 1895 →]

A Forms.

1939 Aurand *Quaint Idioms* 14 [PaGer], I'm nearly *gabut* (exhausted; very tired). **1965–70** *DARE* (Qu. Y35) Infs **CT1, 8, KS3, OR1,** [kəˈput]; **CO27,** [ˈkʌput]; **WA3,** [kəˈput]; **MI108,** [kɑˈput]; **PA223,** [ˈkʌput]; **IL9, MI116,** [kəˈpʌt]; **PA115,** [gəˈput]; **WI19,** [giˈput]; (Qu. KK20b) Inf **CA140,** [kɑˈput]; **IL35,** [keˈput]; **NY136,** [kɑˈput]; **TX53,** [kəˈput]; **IA4, MI123, PA165, RI15, 17,** [kəˈput]; **IN1, MI116,** [kəˈpʌt]; (Qu. KK19) Infs **IL64, KY11, 25, MI92, NY18, WA1,** [kəˈput]; **CT21,** [kæˈput]; **CA114, CT3, MN2,** [kəˈput]; (Qu. U39) Inf **WA28,** Went [kə'put]; **OR**1, Went [kə'pup]; (Qu. KK10) Infs **IN**22, **PA**167, [kə'put]; **WI**77, [kɐ'put]; **NY**190, [kə'put]; (Qu. KK20a) Inf **AK**8, [kə'put]; (Qu. LL17) Inf **MO**2, [kɑ'puᵛut]; **NJ**16, [kə'put]; **NY**7, [kə'putst]; [**WI**48, Ganz kaput ['gɑns kə'put];] (Qu. LL25) Inf **MA**4, [kə'put].

B Sense.

Completely ruined or useless; exhausted, used up, failed—often in phr *go kaput.* **chiefly Nth, N Midl, West** See Map Cf **ker-**

   1926 O'Brien *Wine Women & War* 204 (as of a1918), Found one man sharing optimism about war—N—, British I.O. Bases theory on experience in business with German character. . . The Hun on the ropes and groggy. Bulgaria gone under and Turkey soon with her. Austria hurrying to get warm seat on mourner's bench, and then—*kaput!* **1939** [see **A** above]. **1950** *WELS* **WI** (*Out of order:* "My sewing machine is _____.") 2 Infs, Kaput; 1 Inf, Kaput—no good; 1 Inf, Kaput—not working. **1964** *Time* 9 Oct 110, Once compromised, the cellist collapses, corporeally and artistically *kaput.* **1965–70** *DARE* (Qu. KK20b, *Something that looks as if it might collapse any minute:* "Our old washing machine is _____.") 66 Infs, **chiefly Nth, N Midl, West,** Kaput; **MD**30, Kaput—fairly new word; **MI**123, **VT**16, Kaput [FW sugg]; **MI**46, Kaput—common [FW sugg]; **MN**36, Kaput—occasional, the French used it in World War I [FW sugg]; **CA**39, Gone kaput; **IL**50, About kaput; (Qu. KK19, *If a machine or appliance is temporarily out of order:* "My sewing machine _____.") 14 Infs, **Nth, N Midl, West,** Is kaput; **KY**11, **WA**1, Is (*or has*) gone kaput; **HI**6, **MN**42, Went kaput; **CT**3, Is kaput—picked it up in Germany; **MD**8, Kaputst; (Qu. Y35, *To spoil something so that it can't be used . .* "My new coffee pot—it's completely _____.") 11 Infs, **esp Nth, N Midl, West,** Kaput; **CO**27, Kaput—World War II; **CT**8, Kaput—i.e., useless; **MI**108, Kaputs; **PA**115, Gaput; (Qu. LL17, *. . There's no more of something:* "The potatoes are _____.") Infs **CA**121, 155, **CT**42, **MO**27, **NJ**16, **NY**89, **PA**138, Kaput; **WA**6, Kaput, all kaput if you're German; **NY**7, Kaputst; (Qu. U39, *Somebody who has lost all his money:* "During the depression he _____.") Infs **GA**82, **WA**28, Went kaput; **OR**1, Went kapoop; (Qu. BB15, *Somebody who is unconscious from a hard blow:* "He's been _____ for ten minutes.") Inf **CA**36, Kaput; (Qu. KK10, *. . Words for something failing . .* "He didn't work it out carefully enough, and his plan _____.") Infs **IN**22, **NY**190, 241, **PA**50, 167, **WI**77, (Went) kaput; (Qu. KK20a) Inf **AK**8, Going kaput; (Qu. KK22, *. . Completely shattered:* "The jug fell out of the window and was _____.") Infs **NY**224, **PA**130, **WA**28, Kaput; (Qu. KK30, *Feeling slowed up or without energy:* "I certainly feel _____.") Inf **MN**26, Kaput [laughter]; (Qu. LL14, *None at all, not even one:* "This pond used to be full of fish but now there's _____ left.") Inf **NY**109, It's kaput; (Qu. LL25) Inf **MA**4, Kaput.

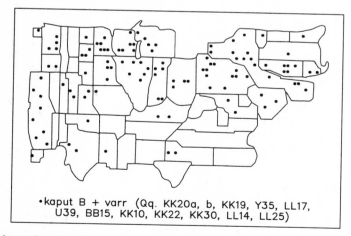

•kaput B + varr (Qq. KK20a, b, KK19, Y35, LL17, U39, BB15, KK10, KK22, KK30, LL14, LL25)

karosine See **kerosene**

kase, kasin See **because** conj

Kate n Also *Katycock, old Kate, wood cady,* ~ *Kate* [See quot 1955] **S Atl**
=**pileated woodpecker.**
   1913 *Auk* 30.496 Okefenokee **GA,** *Phloeotomus pileatus pileatus.* Pileated Woodpecker; 'Kate'; 'Wood Kate'. . . An unsuspecting pair of 'Kates' in a swampy thicket is a glorious spectacle. **1949** Sprunt–Chamberlain *SC Bird Life* 331, Southern Pileated Woodpecker. . . Local Names: Log-cock; Kate; Woodcock. **1950** *PADS* 14.42 **SC,** *Kate.* . .

The southern pileated woodpecker. **1953** *AmSp* 28.284 **FL,** This species [=pileated woodpecker] has more *cock* names than any other North American bird. . . Its simple *cock* titles include . . *katycock.* **1954** Sprunt *FL Bird Life* 273, Southern Pileated Woodpecker. . . Wood-cady. **1955** *Oriole* 20.1.9, Pileated Woodpecker. . . Kate (apparently by transfer from the Ivory-billed Woodpecker, whose almost exclusive utterance has been syllabilized as *kient* or *kent*). . . Old Kate. . . Wood Kate. **1967** *DARE* (Qu. Q17, *. . Kinds of woodpeckers*) Inf **SC**43, Wood Kate.

katiedid See **katydid**

katish See **catish**

katonk See **kotonk**

katooch See **katush**

katter-kornered See **catercorner** adj, adv

kattydid See **katydid**

katush n Also *katooch*
   See quots.
   1968 *DARE* (Qu. K73, *. . Names . . for the rump of a cooked chicken*) Inf **MI**78, Katush [ˌkə'tuš]. **1979** *NYT Article Letters* **MI,** Dad always ate the "katooch" of the chicken—the part that went over the fence last.

katy n¹ See **katydid**

katy n² See **cady**

Katycock See **Kate**

katydid n Usu |'keti,dɪd|; also |'kætidɪd, 'kiti,dɪd| Also *kattydid, katy(dee), katydiddle, kittydid;* for addit pron and sp varr see quots
A Forms.
   [**1743** (1751) Bartram *Observations* 70 **PA, NY,** It was fair and pleasant, and the great green grass-hopper began to sing (*Catedidist*) these were the first I observed this year.] **1806** in 1815 Sutcliff *Travels N. Amer.* 268 **PA,** I was entertained with the harmony . . of the bull frogs, tree frogs, kittydids, and a variety of other animals. **1825** Paulding *John Bull* 35 **GA,** The caty-dids, caty-didded it. **1827** *Western Mth. Rev.* 1.451 **nIN,** Not the slightest noise was heard, but the never ending creakings of the catadeds. **1832** Trollope *Domestic Manners* (NY) 91 **OH,** Locusts, katiedids, beetles, and hornets. **1832** Kennedy *Swallow Barn* 1.311 **VA,** The little catadid pierced the air with his shrill music. **1965–70** [see **B**1 below].
B Senses.

1 Any of var, usu green, **grasshoppers 1** of the family Tettigoniidae, but esp *Pterophylla camellifolia.* [Echoic] Also called **cha-cha 1, chitterdiddle, frost bug, katydidn't, kittledee 1, locust B5, night-did, sniddydid**
   [**1743** see **A** above.] **1784** Smyth *Tour U.S.A.* 2.387 **NY,** There is a very singular insect in this island [=Long Island], which I do not remember to have observed in any other part of America. They are named by the inhabitants here *Katy did's.* **1816** in 1824 Knight *Letters* 62 **PA,** The tops of the trees are vociferous with sawyers, other larger insects of the locust tribe, called also *katy dids.* **1856** in 1862 Colt *Went to KS* 58 **NY,** All the crickets and katy-dids are finishing up . . their last autumnal songs. **1896** Robinson *In New Engl. Fields* 133, In the cool dusk the katydids call and answer one to another out of their leafy tents. **1901** Howard *Insect Book* 337, Our commonest katydids ordinarily call "Katy," or say "She did," rather than "Katy did." That is to say, they rasp their fore wings twice oftener than three times. **1950** *WELS* **WI** (*Creatures that make a clicking, shrilling, or chirring sound*) 13 Infs, Katydid; (*Insects that sit in trees or bushes and make a sharp buzzing sound in hot weather*) 5 Infs, Katydid; (*Grasshopper*) 1 Inf, Katydid. **c1960** Wilson *Coll.* **csKY,** *Katydid.* . . An insect known to everybody, esp. since it is a prophet of frost. **1965–70** *DARE* (Qu. R8, *. . Kinds of creatures that make a clicking or shrilling or chirping kind of sound*) 407 Infs, **widespread,** Katydid; **CT**2, Katydid, katydidn't—little green things, both the same but say different things; **CT**6, Katydid—male, deeper green [than the female katydidn't]; **FL**4, Katy; **KY**34, Katydiddle is green; **MD**32, Katydid—after the first appears, it's six weeks until frost; **SC**40, Katydates—loves Johnson grass or dog fennel, good bream bait, green all over; **MO**8, Katydays; **MO**38, **NC**31, Kittydid; (Qu. R7, *Insects that sit in trees or bushes in hot weather and make a sharp, buzzing sound*) 54 Infs, **scattered,** Katydid; **AL**25, Katydid; **CT**2, Katydids—when you hear them scratching their wings, you'll have frost in six weeks; big green bugs; **DC**4, Katydid—looks like giant grasshopper; **IL**69, Kittydids; **IN**3, Katydids or kittydids;

MA42, Katydid, katydidn't; **NC54,** Katydid—day or night; jarfly—just in the day; **NC67,** Katydiddle; (Qu. R6, . . *Names . . for grasshoppers*) Infs **CT11, IN49, 76, MI112, MO5, NC44,** Katydid; **AL25,** Kattydid; **GA28,** Katydee—a big grasshopper; **CA3,** Kittydid; (Qu. R5) Inf **DC11,** Katydid. **1980** Milne–Milne *Audubon Field Guide Insects* 429, Most katydids are green. Many members of this large family [=Tettigoniiidae] are known for their songs, especially the katydid with its shrill *katy-DID-katy-DIDN'T.*

2 =cicada. Cf **jarfly 1, locust B3**
   1965–70 *DARE* (Qu. R6, . . *Names . . for grasshoppers*) Inf **AL25,** Locust—a different insect; [it's] also called kattydid; (Qu. R7, *Insects that sit in trees or bushes in hot weather and make a sharp, buzzing sound*) Inf **LA31,** Katydid—local name for 17-year locust; **MO6,** Jarflies and katydids are the same insect; **OK25,** Cicadas—a katydid.

3 A night-calling bird such as a **screech owl** or **whippoorwill.** Cf **cat owl, kittenhead**
   1957 Battaglia *Resp. to PADS 20* eMD (*Other names for the whippoorwill*) Katty-did. **1969** *DARE* (Qu. Q3, . . *Birds that come out only after dark*) Inf **IL38,** Katydid. [FW: Both Inf and wife agreed that a katydid was a bird, not an insect.] **1986** Pederson *LAGS Concordance* (*Hoot owl*) 1 inf, csTN, Katydid.

4 A **tree frog** or similar frog. Cf **rain frog**
   1968 McDavid *Coll.* nGA, Katydid—for 'tree frog.' **1986** Pederson *LAGS Concordance* (*Spring frogs*) 1 inf, neMS, When a katydid sings, it's going to rain; (*Bullfrog*) 1 inf, cTN, Katydid—makes noise around pond; 1 inf, nwLA, Katydid.

5 In logging: see quots. Cf **big wheels, galamander**
   1905 U.S. Forest Serv. *Bulletin* 61.40 [Logging terms], Katydid. . . See Logging wheels. [*Ibid* 42, Logging wheels. A pair of wheels, usually about 10 feet in diameter, for transporting logs.] **1941** Writers' Program *Guide MI* 59 (as of c1890), [Caption:] A "katydid"—a contrivance used for hauling logs. **1958** McCulloch *Woods Words* 101 **Pacific NW,** *Katydid*—An old name for a set of big wheels in the pine country. **1967** Parris *Mountain Bred* 133 **wNC,** A katydid is a pair of wheels from 7 to 12 feet in diameter for transporting logs.

6 See quot.
   1970 *DARE* (Qu. N37, *Joking names for a branch railroad that is not very important or gives poor service*) Inf **KY80,** The katydid.

katydidn't n
=katydid B1.
   1846 in 1850 Colman *European Life* 2.116, We landed amidst . . a jabbering of voices which can only be rivalled among the Katydids and the Katydidn'ts of Connecticut. [**1909** *Springfield Republican* (MA) 16 Sept 1/5, All around the globe people are like katydids, saying he did and he didn't in an endless reiteration.] **1965–70** *DARE* (Qu. R8, . . *Kinds of creatures that make a clicking or shrilling or chirping kind of sound*) 11 Infs, **chiefly east of Missip R,** Katydid, katydidn't; **CT2,** Katydid, katydidn't—little green things, both the same but say different things; **CT6,** Katydidn't—female, green; katydid—male, deeper green; **MD3,** Katydid, katydidn't—same thing; **MD32,** Katydidn't—joking name for katydid; (Qu. R7, *Insects that sit in trees or bushes in hot weather and make a sharp, buzzing sound*) Inf **MA42,** Katydid, katydidn't. [14 of 16 Infs old]

katykiller n
=cicada killer.
   1970 *DARE* (Qu. R21, . . *Other kinds of stinging insects*) Inf **IL119,** Katykiller—kill locusts.

katynipper n Cf **gallinipper**
1 =dragonfly.
   1953 Randolph–Wilson *Down in Holler* 258 **Ozarks,** Katynipper. . . Dragonfly, snake feeder. Any of the larger *Odonata*, particularly *Anax junius*. This term used to be common in Reynolds County, Mo.

2 A **mosquito** n¹ **B1.**
   1954 Harder *Coll.* cwTN, Katynipper—A mosquito.

katzenjammer n [Ger]
A hangover; a symptom of a hangover.
   1849 U.S. Congress *Serial Set* 571.733, Some of Mr. Hale's men had kept up a drunken frolic all night—general kakenjammer [sic], therefore, all day. **1877** Burdette *Rise & Fall* 291, This 'Centennial Cordial and American Indian Aboriginal Invigorator' . . has positively no equal for the cure of . . jim-jams, katzenjammer, tight boots, bad breath. **1906**

Peck *Peck's Bad Boy with Circus* 103 **WI,** The colonel . . invited the whole crowd to go to his distillery and help themselves. When we got to the next town every man in the show had . . a Katzenjammer. **1942** Berrey–Van den Bark *Amer. Slang* 107.1, *Aftereffects of drinking.* . . katzenjammers, *low spirits after drinking.* **1950** *WELS* (*Sickness the day after a drinking bout*) 2 Infs, **WI,** Katzenjammer. [**1954** *WELS Suppl.,* If Grandmother saw a drunkard she would remark in German, "he's got one sitting," and for anyone suffering from a hangover she would come up with, "that's a real katzenjammer."] **1965** De Vries *Let Me Count* 125, The symptoms classic to hangover persist. Dizziness, nausea, headache—you know that katzenjammer just above the eyes.

kauka n [Haw pronc-sp for *doctor*] **HI**
   1951 *AmSp* 26.23 **HI,** Common Hawaiian words are . . *kauka* (doctor). **1967** Reinecke–Tsuzaki *Hawaiian Loanwords* 100, *Kauka.* . . Doctor; physician.

kaukau n, v Also sp *cow-cow* [See quot 1972] **HI**
Food; to eat or drink.
   1820 (1931) Holman *Jrl.* 19 **HI,** The larger and fatter the women in Owhyhee [=Hawaii], the better. One of the old Queens weighs 350. She got me into her lap, and felt me from head to foot and said I must cow-cow and be nooe-nooe, i.e., I must eat more and grow larger. **1826** Ellis *Narrative* HI 365, They [=natives] use *kaukau* (a word of Chinese origin) instead of the native word for eat, and *pikaninny,* for small, supposing they are thereby better understood [by foreigners]. **1938** Reinecke *Hawaiian Loanwords* 19, Kaukau. . . 1. Food. 2. To eat; to eat and drink; to drink. . . V[ery] F[requent]. **1954** *Ellery Queen's Mystery Mag.* 4.34 **HI,** "I've got to fix *kaukau* for Keoni—he wants to start back as soon as he eats?" . . "Suppose we *kaukau* too? Fish and poi?" **1954–60** Hance et al. *Hawaiian Sugar* 3, *Kaukau.* . . To eat or drink, food. *Kaukau-tin.* . . Metal container for food, usually carried in a cloth. **1972** Carr *Da Kine Talk* 98 **HI,** Manuel Quimper, making his glossary of Hawaiian words in 1791, set down a word which he spelled *caucao,* assuming it to be a native term. It was the Hawaiianized form of the Chinese pidgin *chowchow* 'food' or 'to eat'—the present-day popular term *kaukau*—which had already found its way to the Islands. *Ibid* 135, *Kaukau* vs. *food, eat*—[Pidgin:] "Come! Get plenty kaukau!" [Std English:] 'Come along, there's plenty of food.' [Pidgin:] "When dey go kaukau, anybody crash da party!" [Std English:] 'When they begin to eat, everybody comes in.' *Kaukau* passes for a Hawaiian word to many residents of the Islands and to visitors. **1989** *DARE* File **Honolulu HI,** *Kaukau* is very common. It means "food." You'd say "have some more kaukau." You'd also say "Let's kaukau." That's very common.

kawakawa n [Haw] **HI**
A **tuna** (*Euthynnus affinis*) of Hawaiian waters. Also called **bonito 1, little tunny 1, skipjack**
   1926 Pan-Pacific Research Inst. *Jrl.* 1.1.8, Euthynnus yaito. . . Kawakawa. Reef[,] c[ommon]. **1933** Bryan *Hawaiian Nature* 226, The name "tuna" is loosely applied to several species of mackerel-like fishes. In Hawaiian waters these include . . the little tunny or *kawa-kawa.* **1960** Gosline–Brock *Hawaiian Fishes* 258, The kawakawa is an inshore pelagic species not taken remote from land. . . A large portion of the food animals are reef- or bottom-dwelling species, indicating that kawakawa does forage for food away from the surface. **1991** Amer. Fisheries Soc. *Common Names Fishes* 65, *Euthynnus affinis* . . P[acific] kawakawa.

kawan See **caouane**

kayak See **kyack** n¹

‡**kazeetch kazotch** adj phr [Cf Fr *comme ci comme ça*]
   1968 *DARE* Tape NY118, Other terms we used [when growing up] were like "kazeetch kazotch," [kəˈzič kəˈzač] which meant like, you know, "neither here nor there," something like that. "It's kazeetch kazotch," it's like neuter, kind of a neuter.

kazen See **cazen**

ke- See **ker-**

keandle See **candle A**

kear n¹ See **car** n¹

kear v, n² See **care**

kearb See **curb**

keard See **card** n¹

kearf See **kerf**

kearnel See **kernel**

kearry See **carry A1**

keat See **guinea keet 1**

keawe See **kiawe**

kebbidge See **cabbage**

keboodle See **caboodle**

kedge v, n Pronc-spp **NEng** *cage, kaidge* See Pronc Intro 3.I.5.b
A Forms.

1903 *DN* 2.293 **Cape Cod MA** (as of a1857), *Kedge* [pronounced:] *(cage)*. **1905** [see **B** below]. **1942** *ME Univ. Studies* 56.27, A light kedge (pronounced cage) anchor was used when a vessel was too near a lee shore or was lightly aground. It could be carried in a boat to its cable length. It was then cast and the vessel hove up to it.
B Sense.
Of a ship: to move, drift, as a result of dragging anchor.

1905 Wasson *Green Shay* 189 **NEng**, That 'ere schooner is commencin' to kaidge in [Footnote: To drag] a grain, sure's ever you live! *Ibid*, That vessel is kaidgin' to loo'ard every secont now, and no rubbin' of it out! *Ibid* 190, I can see her kaidge astern on every sea now.

kedgeree n [Var of Hindi *kitcheri* a dish of rice and var kinds of legumes cooked with spices] **chiefly NEng**
A dish consisting of boiled rice mixed with hard-boiled eggs, usu fish, and other ingredients; see quots.

1916 Kephart *Camping & Woodcraft* 1.369, *Kedgeree.*—Soak 1 pint split peas overnight; drain them, add 1 pound rice, some salt, pepper, and ½ teaspoonful ginger. Stir, and cover with 1 quart water. Stir and cook slowly until done and almost dry. Make into a mound, garnished with fried onions and sliced hard-boiled eggs. **1932** (1946) Hibben *Amer. Regional Cookery* 172 **MA**, *Kedgeree* . . onion . . cream . . eggs . . cooked fish . . curry powder . . cooked rice. **1939** Wolcott *Yankee Cook Book* 38, *Connecticut Kedgeree* . . cooked rice . . cooked flaked fish . . hard-cooked eggs . . top milk. . . This recipe . . in its present form was handed down in the family of Mrs. Evan J. David, Westport, Conn., since the days of Clipper ships. **1940** Brown *Amer. Cooks* 470 **MO**, *Kedgeree. Ibid* 736 **RI**, *Old-time Rhode Island Kedgeree*. **1947** Bowles–Towle *New Engl. Cooking* 16, Kedgeree is not strictly a New England dish, but it was very popular on Beacon Hill tables in the 1850s. [*Ibid* 27, Take some fish. . . hard-boiled eggs . . and as much rice . . as you require to fill your dish. . . The dish must be served up very hot.]

kedidoes See **dido 1**

keebo v
=**cubbie**.
1986 Pederson *LAGS Concordance* (Calls to calves) 1 inf, **csLA**, Keebo—three times.

keech cake n [Cf *EDD keech* sb.[1] "A kind of cake or pasty"] Cf **keekling**
1941 *LANE* Map 284 (*Doughnut*) 1 inf, **ceRI**, [kitʃ] cake, wholly of 'Indian meal' (instead of meal and rye flour) with egg and milk, shaped between the hands and fried in deep fat; 1 inf, **cwRI**, [kitʃ] cake, of 'rye and Indian', fried in lard; 'like a doughnut but not raised.'

keeck See **kick** v

keehee n
A **goldfinch 1** (here: *Carduelis tristis*).
1955 *Oriole* 20.1.13, *Goldfinch.* . . Keehee (sonic).

‡**kee kee** exclam phr
Used as a reproach; see quot.
1948 *AN&Q* 7.170, "Kee, kee," with Gesture. In country school we used to try to shame or embarrass a pupil who had committed some gaucherie by pointing the left forefinger at him, briskly rubbing the right forefinger across it (in the direction of the left) and repeating over and over again the words "kee, kee."

keekling n Also *keekel, kinkling* [Cf Ger *Küchlein*, PaGer *kichli* little cake] Cf **keech cake**
Any of several types of pastries; see quots.

c1965 Randle *Cookbooks* (Ask Neighbor) 4.79 **OH**, *Apple Keekels.* . . Core . . apples, leaving apple whole. Cut in slices so you have a circle with a hole in center. . . Put . . an apple ring [in hot oil] and add . . batter over each circle. Fry until golden brown. . . Dip in granulated sugar. Eat while warm. **1968** *DARE* (Qu. H28, *Different shapes or types of doughnuts*) Inf **MD**19, Keekling [kiklɪn]—doughnut without a hole; [**MI**93, Kuechle [kʊklə]—square, hollow inside]. **1991** *DARE* File **nwMD**, I wonder if you have "kinkling," which is, so far as I know, confined to the area around Frederick, Maryland. It is simply a square raised donut, with a hole, covered with powdered sugar. February, for some reason unknown to me, is Kinkling Month, with large signs on local donut shops, often to the puzzlement of tourists, who wonder what exactly is going on inside.

keel n See **kiln** n

keel v See **kill** v **A**

keelapi See **killapie**

keel a somersault See **keel over**

keeled up See **keel up**

keeleg See **killick**

keeler n Also *keeler-tub* **chiefly NEast, Mid Atl** Cf **losset, piggin**
A broad, often shallow, wooden vessel used for catching or holding liquids.

1646 in 1916 **MA** (Colony) Probate Court (Essex Co.) *Records* 1.55, One barrell & keeler. **1662** in 1906 Essex Inst. *Coll.* 42.133 **MA**, One tub two keelirs. . . 2 beere vessels & pails. **1758** in 1905 Franklin *Writings* 3.464, A shallow tray, or keeler, should be under the frame, to receive any water that might drip from the wetted cloths. **1867** Lowell *Biglow* lviii 'Upcountry' **MA**, *Keeler-tub*: one in which dishes are washed. **1909** *DN* 3.413 **nME**, *Keeler.* . . A small wooden tub holding about a bucketful and used as a dish pan, etc. **1930** Shoemaker *1300 Words* 36 **cPA Mts** (as of c1900), *Keeler*—A small tub used to receive maple sap, a "sugarkeeler". **1935** Sheppard *Cabins* 262 **NC Mts**, Uncle Milt is an expert at making wooden keelers, piggins, and buckets, the distinction being that a keeler is a wooden measure of peck size or less without a handle; a piggin has a straight handle on one side only . . and the bucket has a complete bail. **1939** Wolcott *Yankee Cook Book* 367, *Losset:* wooden container for holding milk. *Keeler:* similar to losset. **1942** Warnick *Garrett Co. MD* 9 **nwMD** (as of 1900–18), *Keeler* . . container for catching sugar water. It was a coopered tub about 15 inches high, the sides straight up and down; probably held four or five gallons. **1944** *PADS* 2.45 **NC**, *Keeler* ['kilɚ, -ə]. . . A wooden tub-like vessel five or six inches deep and eighteen or twenty inches in diameter, used to put milk or other warm liquids into to cool. Yancey and Gaston cos., N.C. Rare. **1966** Dakin *Dial. Vocab. Ohio R. Valley* 2.112, *Keeler* = "a wooden tub" also survives in the speech of some speakers in southeastern Kentucky, and was attested once in Washington County, Ohio. **1970** *Mod. Maturity* June/July 61 **PA**, What Mr. Wolkomir calls a bucket, we call a keeler; what he describes as sap, we call sugar-water. **1983** *Lutz Coll.* **NY**, Silas Van Orden . . spent some time as a boy watching his grandfather make . . barrels and other wooden containers. . . [such as] keelers, which were broad, shallow tubs in which milk was cooled till the cream could be skimmed to make butter.

keeling over See **keel over**

keel out adj phr Cf **fin out, keel up**
Incapacitated because of illness.
1916 Macy–Hussey *Nantucket Scrap Basket* 137 **seMA**, "Keel Out"—Literally, of course, upside down, but used to express illness, as "I've been keel out for a week with the grip."

keel over v phr Also *keel (a) somersault* **esp NEast**
To turn a **somersault**; hence vbl n *keeling over*, n *keely-over* a somersault.

1910 *DN* 3.444 **wNY**, *Keel.* . . To turn (a somersault). Used by boys. "Let's keel somersets." *Ibid* 449, Can you keel a somerset? **1917** *DN* 4.394 **neOH**, *Keel (over).* . . To turn a somersault. . . "Come on, boys, let's keel over." "Let's keel summersets." Also Vt. **1943** *LANE* Map 578 (*Somersault*), 1 inf, **cMA**, He keels over = he turns a somersault; 1 inf, **wMA**, I've heard children say, "Let's play keely-over." **1967–69** *DARE* (Qu. EE9a, *The children's trick of turning over rapidly straight forward* close to the ground) Inf **MA**5, Keeling over; **NY**205, Somersault, keeling over—same thing; **NY**219, **WY**1, Keelin' over. [All Infs old] **1986** Pederson *LAGS Concordance,* 1 inf, **seGA,** Keel over—somersault.

keel up v phr, hence ppl adj phr *keeled up* [keel up, ~ over to overturn; cf quot 1942] **esp coastal NEng** Cf **keel out**
To incapacitate, esp by illness or age; to kill, deprive of life.
1856 Stowe *Dred* 1.116, "Now, *if there is* any such place as heaven, I should like to have them get to it." "Ah! bah! Don't bother about that! When we get keeled up, that will be the last of us!" **1873** *Cincinnati Commercial* (OH) 3 Mar 3/3 **seND,** The wind is what kills people. . . A few hours in the wind at such a temperature would keel a man up. **1899** (1912) Green *VA Folk-Speech* 248, *Keeled up.* . . Laid up or worn out from sickness or old age. "He's been keeled up for more than a year." **1903** *DN* 2.294 **Cape Cod MA** (as of a1857), He's keeled up with rheumatis. **1942** ME Univ. *Studies* 56.23 **NEng,** If she [=a vessel] . . was *stranded* on her side, she was *keeled up.* [Footnote: Fig. Laid up; sick.] **1968** *DARE* (Qu. BB42, *If a person is very sick . . he's* _____) Inf **NH**14, Keeled up.

keely-eyely-over See **keely-over 2**

keely-over n
1 See **keel over.**
2 also as exclam; also *keely-eyely-over, kelly-(kelly-)over, killy-over:* =**Antony over.** Cf **eevy-ivy-over, hilly-over, tilly-I-over**
1968–69 *DARE* (Qu. EE22, . . *The game in which they throw a ball over a building . . to a player on the other side*) Inf **MA**14, Killy ['kɪˌli]-over; **NY**73, Keely-eyely ['kɪlɪˈaɪlɪ]-over; **NY**209, Keely [kili]-over; (Qu. EE23a, *In the game of andy-over . . what . . you call out when you throw the ball*) Inf **MA**14, Keely-over; **NY**73, Keely-eyely-over. **1990** *DARE* File **seWI** (as of 1920s), As a child in West Bend, Wisconsin, I played "Kelly-over" with my friends. We would shout "Kelly-kelly-over!" and then throw a ball over the woodshed behind the Washington House [=a hotel]. Those on the other side of the shed had to catch the ball, give the same call, and return the ball over the shed.

keen adj
1 also in combs; Of something not designed for cutting or piercing: sharp, pointed. **scattered, but esp Sth, S Midl** See Map *esp freq among Black speakers*
1966–70 *DARE* (Qu. W42a, . . *Nicknames . . for men's sharp-pointed shoes*) Infs **MI**89, **MO**29, **TX**106, Keen-toed; **GA**8, **VA**39, Keen-toe(s); **LA**8, Keen-toe shoes; **VA**42, Keen-pointed shoes; **WA**20, Keen-pointed—you could kick a snake in the tail with 'em; **FL**51, She'd get some very, very keen ones there; (Qu. X15, . . *Kinds of noses, according to shape or size*) Infs **KY**94, **LA**8, **OK**13, **VA**39, Keen (nose); **NC**49, Keen—pointed; (Qu. X29, *Joking or uncomplimentary words for a person's face*) Inf **MS**86, Keen face. [9 of 13 total Infs Black, 1 Amer Ind] **1986** Pederson *LAGS Concordance,* 1 inf, **seMS,** Keen on the end; (Picket fence) 1 inf, **nwFL,** Keen—pointed, of pickets. [Both infs Black]

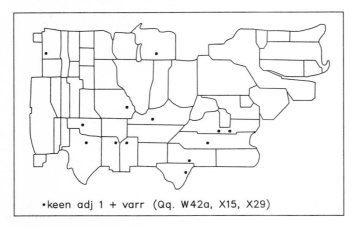
•keen adj 1 + varr (Qq. W42a, X15, X29)

2 Of the eyes: sharp, piercing; hence adj *keen-eyed.* **scattered, but chiefly Sth, S Midl** See Map
1965–70 *DARE* (Qu. X21b, *If the eyes are very sharp or piercing*) 60 Infs, **scattered, but chiefly Sth, Midl,** Keen-eyed; 34 Infs, **chiefly Sth, S Midl,** Keen eye(s).

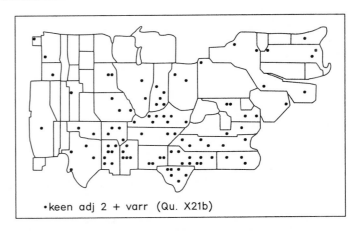
•keen adj 2 + varr (Qu. X21b)

keen v [Prob from *keen* sharp; but cf *ken* to discern] Cf **keen adj 1**
To scan; to direct (one's eyes) sharply.
1941 Still in *Sat. Eve. Post* 10 May 114 **KY,** He keened eyes at mother, beginning to laugh. **1973** Garfield *Tripwire* 157, Boag saw him stop the horse a hundred feet away and scan the forest with patient care, gun up. . . The horseman was taking his time, moving forward a few yards and stopping to keen the forest, then walking the horse a few paces and stopping again to search. **1991** Still *Wolfpen Notebooks* 147 **sAppalachians,** Then he keened his eyes at Mother. "You hain't said what you want. All's had their say except you."

keen-eyed See **keen adj 2**

keep v
A Forms.
1 infin: usu *keep;* rarely *kept.*
1950 Faulkner *Stories* 756, He rid all de way to Washn'ton in de carriage, wid two niggers . . to heat de bricks to kept he foots warm.
2 pres (exc 3rd pers sg): usu *keep;* also *esp freq among Black speakers, keeps.*
1965 *DARE* Tape **MS**61, I keeps that all the time. [Inf Black] **1986** Pederson *LAGS Concordance* **chiefly AR, LA,** 2 infs, I keeps them; 1 inf, I keeps them going; 1 inf, I keeps it covered up; 1 inf, I keeps it; 1 inf, I keeps up with it; 1 inf, I keeps my milk up in the icebox; 1 inf, People keeps them in toolboxes; 1 inf, Most of them keeps them; 1 inf, The children keeps you young; 1 inf, That's why lot of people keeps dogs; 1 inf, They keeps good. [7 of 12 infs Black]
3 pres 3rd pers sg: usu *keeps;* esp freq among Black speakers, *keep.*
1986 Pederson *LAGS Concordance* **Gulf Region,** 1 inf, A boy keep a-going; 1 inf, A farm what always keep cows; 1 inf, I guess he just keep doing them same things over and over; 1 inf, My son keep me supplied; 1 inf, As long as that plane keep moving; 1 inf, One that keep on doing; 1 inf, He keep on; 1 inf, He just keep on popping it to you; 1 inf, I don't know if it keep snakes out or not. [7 of 9 infs Black]
4 past: usu *kept,* pronc-sp *kep;* also *cope, keeped.* Cf Pronc Intro 3.I.22
1848 Lowell *Biglow* 57 **'Upcountry' MA,** [He] come an' kep' school here. **1858** Hammett *Piney Woods Tavern* 62, Thar war Sime Jorrocks, that kep store. **1893** *DN* 1.277 **nwCT,** The preterit and past participle are . . alike. . . *kep.* **1899** Chesnutt *Conjure Woman* 27 **csNC** [Black], He kep' dat sellin' business up for five year er mo'. **1899** (1912) Green *VA Folk-Speech* 249, *Kep.* . . Past tense of *keep; kept.* **1908** *DN* 3.326 **eAL, wGA,** *Kep,* pret. and pp. of *keep.* **1927** *DN* 5.478 **Ozarks,** He kep' a-swiddlin' his finger in th' puddin'. **1943** *LANE* Map 643 **eCT, MA, VT,** The following preterites of *keep* . . were incidentally noted from the informants' conversation: [kɛp] [15 infs]. **1951** *PADS* 15.69 **nLA,** *Cope.* . . Kept; past tense of keep. **1955** Roberts *S. from Hell-fer-Sartin* 169 **seKY,** He keeped working his hands till finally he got them loose. **1975** Allen *LAUM* 2.79 **NE, ND, SD** (as of c1950), *Keep.* The loss of the second member of the /pt/ consonant cluster of *kept* in the speech of some infs. has led to their accepting the vowel change from /kip/ to /kɛp/ as signaling the preterit tense. . . *Kep* /kɛp/ was heard in the speech of [8 infs].
5 past pple: usu *kept,* pronc-sp *kep;* also *keep.*
1848 Lowell *Biglow* 101 **MA,** I haint kep' no account on 'em. **1871**

Eggleston *Hoosier Schoolmaster* 118 **sIN,** Ef you'd jest kep off of my ground I wouldn't a-touched you. **1893** [see **A4** above]. **1908** [see **A4** above]. **1986** Pederson *LAGS Concordance,* 1 inf, **seLA,** Must have keep people pretty busy.

B Senses.

1a Usu of school: to be in session; to commence.

1845 *Knickerbocker* 26.277, One afternoon, when 'school didn't keep,' some one got into the house. **1903** Eggleston *First of Hoosiers* 31, The bound girl or bound boy always went to school with the other children of the family, . . whenever "school kept," as the phrase went—that is to say, whenever there was a school open in the neighborhood. **1942** (1971) Campbell *Cloud-Walking* 26 **seKY,** A few other folks made their younguns go over on Elk what time school kept, but they weren't no plumb good school noways nigh. **1943** *LANE* Map 539 *(When does school begin?),* 1 inf, **seMA,** *Keep,* the regular term for 'begin' in the given context [=in ref to the date on which vacation ends]. **1967** *DARE* FW Addit **OK,** If school don't keep—if there is no school (because of snow). **1974** Fink *Mountain Speech* 14 **wNC, eTN,** *Keep* . . remain in session. "Will school keep next week?" **1975** Gould *ME Lingo* 151, *Keep*—The Maine term for the operation of the public school system; school *keeps.* School does not *keep* during vacation. The word is important in a derived Maine expression to show intense happiness and indifference to consequences: "He was so full of Nell's lobster stew he didn't care if school keeps or not!" One time a summercater walked down on Sim Coombs's wharf and said to Sim, "Folks around here don't seem too friendly!" Sim said, "Oh, them kind'll all be gone soon's school keeps." **1976** Garber *Mountain-ese* 49 **sAppalachians,** *Keep* . . continue, hold. The revival will keep another week.

b in phr *not to care whether school keeps or not* and var; Fig: not to care what happens; to go one's own way. *somewhat old-fash*

1852 *Yankee Notions* 1.354, I was aout on a time, marm, and I didn't care a darn whether school kept or not, as the boy said to his boss. **1872** Twain *Roughing It* 280, I was worth a million dollars, and did not care "whether school kept or not!" **1913** London *Valley of Moon* 312 **cwCA,** We're not in a hurry, and we don't care whether school keeps or not. **1930s** in **1944** *ADD* **eUS,** *Keep.* . . Common in 'He doesn't care whether school keeps or not.' Used fig. **1968** *DARE* Tape **PA**135, When I worked I kept my house, and my yard. It looks it but I've been out here in the back doin' things and I'm just not carin' whether school keeps or not! **1975** [see **B1a** above]. **1981** *NADS Letters* **Detroit MI,** "He doesn't care if school keeps" . . means 'He does what he wants to and doesn't care what anyone else does.' My father uses this phrase.

2 To persevere in, carry on with, maintain. [*OED keep* v. 36 c1425 →; cf *SND, EDD*]

1935 Davis *Honey* 283 **OR,** "Now take it easy," he advised for the last time. "Them hounds can't keep that lick, and there's no use wearin' your horse out." **1963** Wright *Lawd Today* 97 **Chicago IL** [Black], They kept so much noise that passengers turned and stared.

3 To take temporary care of (a child); hence vbl n *keeping children* babysitting. [Cf *OED keep* v. 16.a] **scattered, but esp Sth, Midl** See Map

1965–70 *DARE* (Qu. Z13, *If a mother has to leave her baby for a little while, she might ask a neighbor, "While I'm gone, will you _____ the baby for me?"*) 64 Infs, **chiefly Sth, Midl,** Keep; **GA**33, Keep the baby—old-fashioned; **LA**6, Keep my baby; **LA**11, 15, **TX**98, Keep—old-fashioned; **MD**19, 24, 31, Keep [FW: used in conv]; **NH**14,

Keep the kids. **1967** *Charlotte Observer* (NC) 8 May 7/3, [Classified advt:] *Will keep* child my home days. . . Keep child my home days or by hour. **1976** Ryland *Richmond Co. VA* 373, *Keep*—tend; as in "keep the baby." **1984** *DARE* File, The southern equivalent of babysitting is said to be "keeping" children. **1986** Pederson *LAGS Concordance,* 1 inf, **cnAL,** A grandbaby here that I keep. **1993** *DARE* File **wMA,** When Ruthie and Martha were little we would always keep them after school.

4 with *up:*

To detain, hold up. [Calque of PaGer *uf(f)halde*]

1935 *AmSp* 10.167 [Engl of PA Germans], Such expressions . . are the accepted currency of daily speech. . . Don't let me keep you up (don't let me detain you). **1968** *Helen Adolf Festschrift* 38, Keep up . . for 'detain'; for example, "Don't let me keep you up." **1987** *Jrl. Engl. Ling.* 20.2.171 **ePA,** *Keep up* 'to detain'. . . [12 of 100 informants], ages 20 to 101.

5 in var phrr:

a *keep house* (or *one's bed*) and varr: To remain indoors or in bed. *old-fash*

1770 in 1915 *New Engl. Hist. & Geneal. Reg.* 69.9 **MA,** I was very Poorly so that I keep house the greatest part of ye Day. **1856** in 1862 Colt *Went to KS* 195 **NY,** I have been obliged to keep my bed all day. **1864** in 1983 *PADS* 70.39 **ce,sePA,** I have had plenty of sewing to do sence I have come so I had to keep purty close house closter than I did when we went down to look in Charley's window. **1879** in *Ibid,* This has been a very stormy day we kept house most of the day. **1943** *LANE* Map 495 *(In bed)* 1 inf, **seCT,** She still keeps her bed; 1 inf, **swMA,** He kept his bed.

b *keep company (with), keep one company:* To act as sweethearts; to associate with as a lover; to court. [Cf *OED to keep company (with)* (at *company* sb. 1.c) "to associate *with* . . esp. (*vulgar* and *dial.*) to associate as lovers or as a lover, to 'court'" 1715–25 →]

1842 Kirkland *Forest Life* 2.200 **MI,** Be it known that the term [=keeping company] has with us a sort of technical sense, which it would be difficult for me to explain. Suffice it to say that it implies a regular Sunday evening visit from the gentleman; and that it is considered only part of the etiquette of "keeping company" if the sitting is prolonged far into the small hours, or even until daylight. **1848** Bartlett *Americanisms* 193, *To keep company.* To court. A common term in the interior parts of New England, applied to a man whose visits to a lady are frequent, with the intention of gaining her hand. 'He keeps company with her,' i.e. he is courting her, or 'They are keeping company,' i.e. are courting. **1905** *DN* 3.12 **cCT,** *Keep company.* . . To court. **1907** *DN* 3.214, **nwAR,** *Keep company with.* **1909** *DN* 3.413 **nME,** *Keep company with.* **1910** *DN* 3.444 **wNY,** *Keep company with.* **1941** *LANE* Map 405 *(Keeping company with her),* [This phr, varr such as *keeping her company, keeping regular* (or *steady*) *company,* and the phr *keeping company* used absolutely, are **widespread throughout NEng.**] **1954** *Harder Coll.* **cwTN,** *Keep solid company*—To woo or court seriously. **c1955** Reed–Person *Ling. Atlas Pacific NW,* 3 infs, Keeping company (with her); 1 inf, Keep her company. **1962** Atwood *Vocab. TX* 67, *Courting.* . . terms . . declining in frequency, are *sparking* . . and *keeping company (with).* **1965–70** *DARE* (Qu. AA1, *When a man goes to see a girl often and seems to want to marry her, he's _____ her*) 30 Infs, **scattered,** Keeping company with; **NY**76, Keeping steady company. **1986** Pederson *LAGS Concordance* **Gulf Region** *(Courting her)* 8 infs, Keeping company; 2 infs, Keeping her company; 1 inf, They're keeping company; 1 inf, Keeping her.

c *keep close to the willows:* See **willow.**

d *keep one's skillet* (or *smokehouse*) *greasy:* To make a living; to live well.

1942 Perry *Texas* 134, One who is determined to make a living claims, "I'm gonna keep my skillet greasy." **1984** Wilder *You All Spoken Here* 126 **Sth,** He keeps his smokehouse greasy: He provides a good table.

keep n

1 also *keeping;* used as a pl count noun rather than a mass noun: Provisions.

1941 Stuart *Men of Mts.* 305 **neKY,** The regular price fer clearin land in Elliot County is six dollar an acre and you keep yourself. I'll give you ten dollars an acre and your keeps. *Ibid* 307, I went out to find a place to work fer my clothes and keeps. **1966** *DARE* (Qu. GG34b, *To feel depressed or in a gloomy mood: "She's feeling _____ today."*) Inf **AR**22, Her keeps; (Qu. KK28, *Feeling ambitious and eager to work*) Inf **AR**31, Feeling his keepin's.

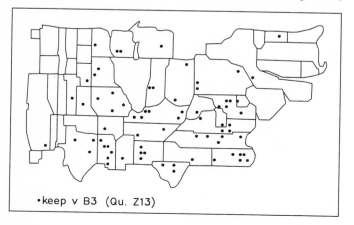

•keep v B3 (Qu. Z13)

2 Notice; care. [*W3 keep* n 1 *"archaic: Heed, notice*—usu. used in the phrases *give keep, take keep"*]

1975 Gainer *Witches* 12 **sAppalachians**, *Keep*. . . caution, care. "Take keep you don't get hurt."

keep-away n Also *keep ball* Cf **saluggi**

Any of several games that involve keeping a ball or other object out of reach; by ext, a type of teasing that involves withholding a personal object.

1932 (1953) Smith *Games* 246, *Keep away*. . . (Keep Ball, Chase Ball). . . Boys are so fond of the game that they use a cap if no ball is available. **1953** Brewster *Amer. Nonsinging Games* 83 **IN**, *Keep Ball*. . . Two selected captains choose their teams. . . Players of the team in possession of the ball throw it back and forth to each other, while those of the opposing team attempt to intercept the throws or to recover the ball first in case it is dropped. **1965–70** *DARE* (Qu. EE28, *Games played in the water*) Infs **CA**14, **CT**21, 23, **IL**126, **IA**27, **LA**32, **MO**18, **TX**27, Keep-away; **CA**1, Water keep-away; **CA**37, Keep-away—keep an object away from someone else by throwing it; **GA**11, Keep-away—a ball is kept from "it" in water; **KS**15, Keep-away—played with a ball and one team tries to keep the ball away from the other team; **MO**19, 26, Keep-away—keep a ball (*or* some object) away from one person (or another team); **NY**161, Keep-away—two teams, like in water polo—each team tries to keep the ball away from the other; **SC**54, Keep-away—keep a ball away from another; **TN**30, Keep-away—a ball or other floatable object is tossed back and forth. The aim is to keep members of the opposing team from getting the object; **WI**68, Keep-away—with beach balls; (Qu. EE11, *Bat-and-ball games for just a few players [when there aren't enough for a regular game]*) Inf **NE**10, Keep-away; (Qu. EE27, *Games played on the ice*) Inf **CT**21, Keep-away—one team gets a hockey puck or tin can and tries to keep it from the other side; **CT**23, Keep-away [FW: sugg]—scrub game, not enough for regular game; (Qu. EE33, . . *Outdoor games . . that children play*) Infs **DC**8, **MN**21, Keep-away; **CA**87, Keep-away—a ball is kept from a few players; **CT**23, Keep-away—with football, basketball—scrub game in any sport; **IL**16, Keep-away—try to keep the basketball away from other players; **LA**32, Keep-away—played with a ball on water or on land. **1976** Knapp-Knapp *One Potato* 266, [The school bus] is a good place for bawdy songs, jeers . . and scapegoating versions of Keep-away (a spontaneous game in which a glove, shoe, or other object belonging to the victim is tossed from child to child, just out of its owner's reach). **1986** Pederson *LAGS Concordance* **Gulf Region**, 1 inf, Keep away—game; (*Ball, puck, and tin-can games*) 2 infs, Keep away; (*Rough games*) 1 inf, Keep away = passe. **1991** *DARE* File **cIA** (as of 1960s), In my Des Moines neighborhood, keep-away was a "game" only from the keeper's point of view. It involved the unwilling participation of the one from whom some personal object had been taken, usually by force. The "fun" increased in proportion to the unhappiness or frenzy of the victim.

keep company (with) See **keep** v **B5b**

keeped See **keep** v **A4**

keeper n

1 =**backlog 1.**

1968 *DARE* (Qu. D33, *When you build a fire in the fireplace . . the big log that goes behind the others*) Inf **CT**2A, Keeper.

2 also *keepie*: See quot.

c1970 Wiersma *Marbles Terms*, Keepers—marbles won in a game. *Ibid* **swMI** (as of c1935), Keepies—The marbles belonging to the winner after playing "for keeps." E.g. "All my keepies show how good a shot I am."

3 pl, but sg in constr: =**keeps 1.** Cf **for keeps, keepsies 2**

1965–70 *DARE* (Qu. EE7, . . *Kinds of marble games*) Infs **AL**41, **CA**154, **KY**70, **PA**126, Keepers; **CA**161, Keepers—gambled to win each others' marbles and keep them; **IL**76, Keepers—they bet the marbles they won; **MI**108, Marbles were rolled towards a line, the game was called "keepers"; **TX**97, Keepers—you keep marbles shot out of ring; **MO**27, No special games except "keepers." **c1970** Wiersma *Marbles Terms*, 1 inf, Keepers—A type of game . . where those who win will retain the marbles won from the original owner; 1 inf, **swMI**, Keepers—shooter keeps all marbles he hits—"he got 15 on keepers!" **1986** Pederson *LAGS Concordance* (*Marble . . games*) 1 inf, **nwTN**, Keepers—played with marbles.

keep house (or one's bed) See **keep** v **B5a**

keepie See **keeper 2**

keepies See **keepsies 2**

keeping See **keep** n **1**

keeping children See **keep** v **B3**

keeping room n [Cf *EDD keeping-room* (at *keeping* ppl. adj. 2.(4)) "the room gen. sat in by the family"] **chiefly NEng old-fash**

A sitting room or parlor intended for family use, as distinct from a **front** room, reserved for company.

1771 in 1914 Copley-Pelham *Letters* 141 **MA**, I forget weither or not there was to be a Clossit in the Keeping Room. **1791** in 1912 Ford *Notes N. Webster* 1.351 **NEng**, Altered my keeping-room Chimney. **1809** Kendall *Travels* 3.264 **VT**, The latter spent his evening in the parlour, or, as it is called, the *keeping-room*. **1848** Bartlett *Americanisms* 193, *Keeping-room*. A common sitting-room; the parlor, in New England. The term is chiefly used in the interior, although it may sometimes be heard in the sea-port towns. **1857** Goodrich *Recollections* 1.74 **swCT**, Carpets were then only known in a few families, and were confined to the keeping-room and parlor. **1875** (1886) Woolson *Castle Nowhere* 263 **ceOH**, Breakfast was awaiting us in the keeping-room, and our hostess said that an ox-team from the Community would come for us before nine. **1941** *LANE* Map 323 (*Parlor, sitting room*) 4 infs, **sCT**, **cnRI**, **neMA**, Keeping room. [3 of 4 infs regard this as old or old-fashioned.] **1955** Taber *Stillmeadow Daybook* 114 **swCT**, Jill's bedroom is across the landing from the keeping room.

keep one company See **keep** v **B5b**

keep one's skillet (or smokehouse) greasy See **keep** v **B5d**

keeps n pl but sg in constr

1 Any of var marble games played with the understanding that any marbles won are to be kept. [Perh Scots; cf *SND keep* n. 2] **scattered, but chiefly West, W Midl** See Map Cf **for keeps**

1875 (1876) Twain *Tom Sawyer* 135 **MO**, Next they got their marbles and played "knucks" and "ring-taw" and "keeps." **1906** Casey *Parson's Boys* 25 **sIL** (as of c1860), They came across Dick Patterson, one of their schoolmates with whom William played a game of "keeps." Dick was a past master at that kind of sport, and quickly won every marble William had. **1915** *DN* 4.227 **wTX**, Keeps. . . A game of marbles, in which the player who knocks his opponent's marble out of a certain figure retains the marble. **1922** *DN* 5.187, Keeps. . . A game [of marbles] played for the stakes. The stakes are placed in the center of the ring, and the "taw," "go," or starting place is the circumference. **1950** *WELS* **WI** (*Marble games*) 1 Inf, Keeps; 1 Inf, Keeps—throw marbles at each others', one who hits the marble keeps it; 1 Inf, Keeps—each player puts in so many marbles, then each takes his turn and all the marbles he knocks out are his. **1963** *KY Folkl. Rec.* 9.3.60 **eKY**, When marbles being played for change owners as they are won: keeps: [in 18 counties]—keepsies: [in 2 counties]. **1965–70** *DARE* (Qu. EE7, . . *Kinds of marble games*) 73 Infs, **scattered, but chiefly West, W Midl**, Keeps; **TX**99, Tennessee keeps; **CA**105, Breaks and keeps—each takes all his marbles and tries to break the other's with his agate; [**CO**35, Keep marbles—in a ring]. [61 of 75 Infs comm type 4 or 5] **1966** *DARE* Tape **AL**3, [Inf:] You've played keeps, haven't you? [FW:] Playing for keeps? [Inf:] Yeah. [FW:] Now, when we played it we put a whole bunch of marbles in the center and . . you continued to shoot as long as you knocked one [marble] out of the ring. [Inf:] And you got that. . . And then if you broke the other fellow, you just had all the marbles. *Ibid*

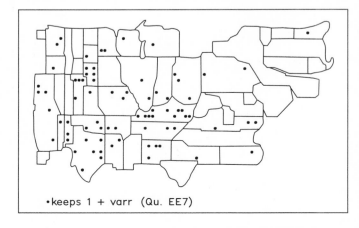

•keeps 1 + varr (Qu. EE7)

WA7, You would have two ways of playing this game, before you started you would say, what did we call that? Keeps? [**WA6**:] Oh, yes, keeps, we played for keeps. [**WA7**:] If you shot for keeps, when you hit it with the marble you launched at it, you kept that if you played for keeps. **c1970** Wiersma *Marbles Terms, Keepsies, keeps:* Playing so that the winner gets to keep whatever marbles are wagered on a game. *Ibid* **csCA** (as of c1958), *Keeps*—A game played for "blood." All marbles captured are gone forever into the opponent's bag. *Ibid* **swMI** (as of c1960), *Keeps*—game in marbles where the winner keeps all the marbles.

2 used as an exclam to stake a claim: See quot.
    1956 [see **keepsies 1**].

keepses, keepsie See **keepsies 2**

keepsies n pl but sg in constr [Blend of **keeps** + **-ies 2**]

1 A claim; first rights (to something). Cf **dib** n[1] **2, honey** v[2]
    1956 *AmSp* 31.37, There is the *I've got keepsies*—or *wholsies* or *checks* or *beans* or *ducks* or *benches*—*on your seat* pattern. And there are its shortened forms, *Honies for me!* . . *Keeps on the money!*

2 also *keepses, keepies, keepsie:* Usu a marble game played **for keeps** (but cf quot c1970)—also used as an exclam to stipulate that the game will be so played. Cf **keeps**
    1963 [see **keeps**]. **1966–68** *DARE* (Qu. EE7, . . *Kinds of marble games*) Inf **AZ**8, Keepies; **ME**11, Keepses; [**NC**9, Play for keepses;] **WI**68A, Keepsies—drop in hole. **1968** *DARE* Tape **IA**37, The one that got the most marbles out of the center of the ring won the game, and if you were playing for keeps—he kept the marbles. Many times the last shooter wouldn't even get a shot. Then, when the ring was empty, each one would enter some more and repeat the process. [FW:] I think that that's keepsies. [Inf:] Oh that was called keepsies. **c1970** Wiersma *Marbles Terms* **WA** (as of 1960), Keepsies. . . Keep marbles you win. Sometimes keep marbles you lose. *Ibid* **swMI** (as of 1973), Keepsie— when one player knocks out the majority of marbles from the circle he wins, gets to keep opponent's marbles. *Ibid,* Keepsies—a game where one kept all the marbles that he won. *Ibid, Keepies*—a stipulation that the marbles won or lost are to remain with the winner as opposed to merely keeping score to determine a theoretical winner. *Ibid, Keepsies, keeps:* Playing so that the winner gets to keep whatever marbles are wagered on a game. **1982** Slone *How We Talked* 92 **eKY** (as of c1950), Some expressions used in the game of marbles. . . *Keepsies*—a game where all the marbles were placed in a ring (a line drawn in a circle on the ground). Each player took turns trying to knock them out by hitting them with another marble flipped with the thumb lying against the closed fist. Each player got to keep all the marbles he knocked outside the sides of the ring.

keep up See **keep** v **B4**

keer See **care**

keerd See **card** n[1]

keerless weed See **careless weed 1**

kees See **kish**

keeshka See **kishka**

keet See **Guinea keet**

keg n, v Usu |kɛg|; for addit proncs and pronc-spp, see **A** below
A Forms.

1 |kæg|; pronc-spp *cag(g), kag.* [*OED cag* 15th cent →; *keg* 17th cent →] **chiefly NEast, S Midl, Sth** *somewhat old-fash* Cf Pronc Intro 3.I.6.a Note: *kag* dominated as the std pronc through the 18th cent, and competed with *keg* as the std into the 19th. Cf **beg**
    1653 in 1855 New Plymouth Colony *Records* 3.28, Wee present Richard Templer, of Yarmouth, for stealing certaine caggs of oysters. **1725** in 1916 Mereness *Travels* 184 **GA**, Two Caggs of Spanish [sic] Brandy. **1748** in 1904 Thwaites *Early W. Travels* 1.32 **PA**, 8 Gallon Cag of Liquor. **1777** in 1856 Moore *Songs & Ballads* 171 **NY**, I. . . will. . . spoil your feathering and your tarring;/ And cagg you up for pickled herring. **1781** (1910) *MD Hist. Mag.* 5.124 **ceMA**, Our cag had no water in it. **1818** Fessenden *Ladies Monitor* 172 **VT**, Some provincial words and phrases, which ought to be avoided by all who aspire to speak or write the English language correctly. . . *kag* for keg. **1828** Webster *Amer. Dict.* np, *Keg*. . . Written more correctly *cag.* **1892** *DN* 1.239 **cwMO**, *Keg.* Often pronounced [kæg] and [kɛg] in Kansas City. *Ibid,* Both [kæg] and [kɛg] or [kɛɪg] are common in New England. **1899** (1912) Green *VA Folk-Speech* 104, *Cag.* . . Kag. **1903** *DN* 2.292 **Cape Cod MA** (as of a1857), *Keg* [kæg]. **1908** *DN* 3.326 **eAL, wGA**, *Kag*

[kæg]. **1912** *DN* 3.580 **wIN**, *Kag.* . . Very common. "They bought a kag of beer at Terre Haute." **1917** *DN* 4.409 **wNC**, *Cag.* **1923** *DN* 5.212 **swMO**, *Kag* or *kaig.* **1929** *AmSp* 5.131 **ME**, *Kag.* **1930s** in 1944 *ADD* **eWV**, *Kag*, never *keg.* **1954** Harder *Coll.* **cwTN**, *Keg*—[kæɪg]. **1961** Kurath–McDavid *Pronc. Engl.* 133, *Keg* rimes either with *bag, beg,* or *plague.* The /æ/ of *bag* occurs nearly everywhere in the Eastern States, but varies greatly in frequency, both regionally and by social groups. In the South Midland . . in Delmarva and Southern New Jersey, and in North Carolina it is in rather general use, except among cultured speakers. It is somewhat less common in Virginia, South Carolina . . and Georgia, where it competes both with /kɛg/ and /kɛg/. In the North, /kɛg/ is the predominant variant in folk speech . . even some cultured speakers still use it in New England. It is rare in . . Metropolitan New York and in large parts of Pennsylvania, and no longer current in New York City, Philadelphia, and other cities in this section. **1965–70** *DARE* (Qu. F13; total Infs questioned, 75) Infs **AR**17, 26, **FL**9, 37, **GA**1, **MS**72, **OK**3, 18, 42, (Nail) kag; **AR**38, **MS**55, [kæg]; [**FL**26, Keg [FW: about half-way between [kɛg] and [kæg]]]; (Qu. V2b) Inf **MD**43, Keg [kæg] of nails; (Qu. DD29) Inf **MS**16, Kags; (Qu. HH22c) Inf **NC**76, [kæg]. **1967–70** *DARE* Tape **KY**85, A nail [kæ·g]; **NC**54, Thump [kæʌɪg]; **TN**9, [kæ·ɛg]; **TX**49, I had [kæg] beer. You tap a [kæg] a beer; **VA**27, A twenty gallon [kæɪg]. **1968–69** *DARE* FW Addit **ceDE, swMA, c,csNC,** [kæg]. **1976** Allen *LAUM* 3.272 (as of c1950), All three of the eastern pronunciations of *keg* were carried into the U[pper] M[idwest], but the clear trend was toward the general adoption of standard /kɛg/. . . The form with /æ/ . . is represented in the UM by. . . [21 infs] most of whom are in the Midland territory in Iowa and Nebraska. **1989** Pederson *LAGS Tech. Index* 78 **Gulf Region,** [474 infs gave proncs of the type [kɛg]; 269 infs gave proncs of the type [kæg].]

2 |ke(ɪ)g, kɛɪg| and varr; pronc-sp *kaig.* [From mod StdE [kɛg]] Cf Pronc Intro 3.I.6.a, **egg** v[1] **A**
    1892 [see **A1** above]. **1899** Garland *Boy Life* 169 **nwIA**, Pull out that brandy kaig. **1923** [see **A1** above]. **1939** *LANE* Map 146 (*Keg*), [51 infs, **scattered NEng exc ME**, gave proncs of the type [kɛg, kɛɪg]; 2 infs, **seNH**, gave proncs of the type [kejg].] **1944** Kenyon–Knott *Pronc. Dict.* 242, *Keg* [kɛg]—L[inguistic] A[tlas] shows that [kɛg] & less freq. [kæg] are used by cultured informants. **1961** Kurath–McDavid *Pronc. Engl.* 133, *Keg.* . . A variant riming with *plague* . . occurs not infrequently in three separate areas: New England, Virginia, and South Carolina. . . it is sometimes hard to decide whether the upgliding phones . . before fronted /g/ are to be assigned to the checked vowel /ɛ/ or to the free vowel /e/. **1965** Carmony *Speech Terre Haute* 110 **sIN**, In the pronunciation of *keg*, /e/ is clearly a minority feature, occurring 5 times [among 16 infs]. **1965–66** *DARE* (Qu. F13) Infs **MS**27, **UT**3, [kɛɪg]. **1969** *DARE* Tape **GA**74, [kɛɪg]. **1976** Allen *LAUM* 3.272 (as of c1950), All three of the eastern pronunciations of *keg* were carried into the U[pper] M[idwest], but the clear trend is toward the general adoption of standard /kɛg/. . . The form with /e/ . . is unmistakably used by only 17 UM infs . . all but three are in Northern speech territory. [*DARE* Ed: 2 infs **Canada**] **1989** Pederson *LAGS Tech. Index* 78 **Gulf Region,** [82 infs gave proncs of the type [kɛg].]

3 |kjæg, kjɛg|; for addit varr see quots; pronc-sp *kyag.* **esp S Atl, Gulf States** Cf Pronc Intro 3.I.16
    1922 Gonzales *Black Border* 309 **sSC, GA coasts** [Gullah glossary], *Kyag*—keg, kegs. **c1940** *LAMSAS Materials,* [24 of 1216 infs in the Middle and South Atlantic states gave proncs with a palatal glide, of the types [kjæg, kjɛg, kjag]; of these, 11 were in SC, 7 in NC, 4 in GA, and 2 in VA.] **1989** Pederson *LAGS Tech. Index* 78 **Gulf Region,** [5 infs gave proncs of the type [kjɛg]; 1 inf, [kjæg]; 1 inf, [kjɪg].]

4 |kag|; for addit varr see quot c1940. *esp Gullah*
    c1940 *LAMSAS Materials,* [Four infs offered proncs of the type [k(j)ag]; two (one Black) were natives of Charleston SC, the other (both Black) of the Sea Islands (Hilton Head Is., SC, and Sapelo Is., GA). Another inf, from csSC, had heard this pronc from others.] [**1949** Turner *Africanisms* 16 [Gullah], [a] . . is the sound used regularly in positions where in General American [æ] and [ɑ] are usually heard.] **1961** Kurath–McDavid *Pronc. Engl.* 133, *Keg.* . . Along the South Carolina-Georgia coast (Charleston to Brunswick), three elderly Negroes and one uneducated white offered /kag/, the Gullah variant corresponding to /kæg/.

B As noun.

1 The stomach; in comb *beer keg*: a "beer belly."
    1877 Wright *Big Bonanza* 366, His "keg" was evidently "full" to overflowing, yet he was still athirst. **1887** Francis *Saddle and Moccasin* 270 (Farmer-Henley *Slang*), We'd been having a time and my keg was pretty full too. **1966–69** *DARE* (Qu. X53b, *An oversize stomach that*

results from drinking) Infs **AR**28, **KY**24, **NC**18, 41, **PA**34, Beer keg. [4 of 5 Infs male]

2 in phr *taste of the keg;* Fig: to be stale, seem monotonous.
 1923 *DN* 5.212 **swMO,** *To taste o' the kag* = to become monotonous. [**1984** Wilder *You All Spoken Here* 191 **Sth,** *Fill:* A sufficiency, as in "I had my fill of that teacher." *A taste of the keg:* Same as above.]

C As verb.
With *up;* Fig: see quots.
 1958 McCulloch *Woods Words* 101 **Pacific NW,** *Keg up*—a. To hide stuff away for a rainy day. b. To collect material ready for a job. c. To stay put in one place, as in a hunting shack in rough weather. **1984** Lesley *Winterkill* 13 **neOR,** This time of the year, the unfenced stock might range as far as Wildhorse, kegging up in the cool of the high timber and sticking close to water.

keiki n, also attrib [Haw] **HI**
A child; an immature plant or animal; a plant shoot.
 1938 Reinecke *Hawaiian Loanwords* 19, *Keiki* . . 1. Offspring; young; child. . . . 2. Shoot of a plant, especially of taro or pineapple. . . V[ery] F[requent] *Keiki kane* [*DARE* Ed: literally "young male"] and *keiki wahine* [*DARE* Ed: literally "young female"] are terms occasionally heard. **1965** Krauss-Alexander *Grove Farm* xv **HI,** *Keiki*—child. **1967** *DARE* (Qu. Z12, *Nicknames and joking words meaning 'a small child':* "*He's a healthy little _____.*") Inf **HI**1, Keiki—Hawaiian [for] young child. **1969** *DARE* FW Addit **Honolulu HI,** *Keiki* [ˈkeki]—child, small one. **1973** *AmSp* 48.122, Common Hawaiian loanwords . . *keiki* 'child, immature plant or animal.'

keint See **can** v[1] **1b**

kelleck(e), kelleg, kellock See **killick**

kelly n[1] Cf **benny 1**
A man's hat.
 1908 *NY Eve. Jrl.* (NY) 16 Sept 12 (*Zwilling Coll.*), [Cartoon:] Hey, douse the kelly. I can't see third [base] at all. **1915** *Recruiter's Bulletin* (U.S.) Dec. 33/2 (*OEDS*), Say, old top, when you go home tonight, Pull your old brown Kelly down real tight. **1922** *Collier's* 4 Mar 8, I have got to wear a brass Kelly on my head which weighs at the least ten pounds. **1922** Lewis *Babbitt* 121, I tip my benny to him. [*DARE* Ed: In the "Fourth Printing, November, 1922" *benny* was changed to *kelly*.] **1926** *AmSp* 1.652 [Hobo lingo], *Kelly*—hat. **1948** *Dly. Ardmoreite* (Ardmore, Okla.) 25 April 1/1 (*DA*), A ring was drawn and some brawny gent who felt his strength, would toss his kelly into the circle.

kelly n[2] See **killifish 1**

kelly fisher n [See quot 1955]
=**green heron.**
 1946 Hausman *Eastern Birds* 107, Eastern Green Heron *Butorides virescens virescens.* . . Other Names . . Minnow Fisher, Kelly Fisher. **1955** MA Audubon Soc. *Bulletin* 39.312 **CT,** *Green Heron.* . . Kelly Fisher. . . As feeding on killifishes, called kellies.

kelly-(kelly-)over See **keely-over 2**

Kelly slide n [In ref to 1889 comic song "Slide, Kelly, Slide!" by J.W. Kelly, in ref to Amer baseball player Michael J. Kelly]
A playground slide.
 1950 *WELS Suppl.* **cnWI,** I have always called the slide for children you described a "kelly slide"—that's what it was called at home (Montreal, Iron County, Wis.) when I was a child. [*Ibid* **IL,** You were discussing Kelly slide. That was a familiar phrase in my youth. My father often said "Slide Kelly Slide" and it was my impression that it came from baseball games.]

kelly weed n
=**quelite.**
 1981 Pederson *LAGS Basic Materials,* 1 inf, **csTX,** [ˈkɛli wid] (Eng.) Same as [kʼɛˈli,te] (Span.); 1 inf, **cwMS,** Kelly weed.

kelp bass n Also *kelp salmon*
A **rock bass:** usu *Paralabrax clathratus,* but also *P. nebulifer,* native to the California coast.
 1884 Goode *Fisheries U.S.* 1.413 **cwCA,** This species [=*Serranus clathratus*] is called at Monterey, where it is not common, the "Kelp Salmon"; farther South it is known to the "Americans" usually as "Rock Bass." **1933** John G. Shedd Aquarium *Guide* 102, The Kelp Bass is the most common species of the genus [=*Paralabrax*] on the California coast, where it attains a weight of five pounds and is an excellent food fish. **1953** Roedel *Common Fishes CA* 73, Both kelp and sand bass

appear to spawn in the summer and to mature when about 10 inches long. **1967–70** *DARE* (Qu. P2, . . *Kinds of saltwater fish caught around here . . good to eat*) Infs **CA**23, 181, Kelp bass. **1991** Amer. Fisheries Soc. *Common Names Fishes* 46. *Paralabrax clathratus* . . kelp bass.

kelp cod n
A **greenling** (here: *Hexagrammos decagrammus* or *H. superciliosus*).
 1928 Pan-Pacific Research Inst. *Jrl.* 3.3.13, *Decagrammus decagrammus* . . Kelp-cod. *Ibid,* *Lebius serperciliosus* [sic] . . Kelp-cod.

kelpfish n
Any of several fishes of the Pacific coast which are commonly found in kelp beds, as:
a A **greenling** (here: *Pleurogrammus monopterygius*). **AK**
 1882 Petroff *Report on the Population, Industries, and Resources of Alaska* (1880 census) 72 (Tabbert *Dict. Alaskan Engl.*), This fish (. . . known at present as *Pleurogrammus monopterygius*) is found about the whole of the Aleutian chain, and also among the Shumagin islands, congregating in large schools. At Attoo it is known as the kelp-fish, on the Shumagins as the yellow or striped fish, and from Oonalashka to Atkha as the Atkha mackerel. **1907** U.S. Dept. Commerce Bur. Fisheries *Document* 618.60 **AK,** *Atka mackerel (Pleurogrammus monopterygius).*—This species, which is also known locally as kelp-fish and yellow or striped fish, is found about the whole of the Aleutian chain and among the Shumagin Islands.
b A **wrasse** (here: *Halichoeres semicinctus*). **CA**
 1882 U.S. Natl. Museum *Bulletin* 16.603, *P[latyglossus] semicinctus* . . Kelp-fish. **1884** Goode *Fisheries U.S.* 1.275 **CA,** The species, *Platyglossus semicinctus,* bears in company with *Heterostichus rostratus,* and perhaps others, the name of "Kelp-fish." It . . . is found in the kelp about Santa Catalina Island and southward, and is not very abundant. **1933** John G. Shedd Aquarium *Guide* 145, *Iridio semicinctus*—California Kelpfish. The California Kelpfish is common on the southern California coast. **1968** *DARE* (Qu. P4, *Saltwater fish that are not good to eat*) Inf **CA**36, Kelpfish—a long slender yellow fish.
c A fish of the family Clinidae: usu *Heterostichus rostratus* or a fish of the genus *Gibbonsia.*
 1884 [see **b** above]. **1898** U.S. Natl. Museum *Bulletin* 47.2351, *Heterostichus rostratus* . . Kelpfish. **1928** Pan-Pacific Research Inst. *Jrl.* 3.3.15, *Heterostichus rostratus* . . Kelpfish. Recorded north of California only from British Columbia. **1953** Roedel *Common Fishes CA* 145, Kelpfish—*Heterostichus rostratus.* . . Those in kelp are usually kelp-colored, those in eelgrass bright green with brilliant silvery stripes. **1955** Zim-Shoemaker *Fishes* 142, *Kelpfishes.* . . Most species are found all along the coast and rocky shores and in kelp beds. Most are small fishes (4 to 8 in. long) which. . . are related to the blennies. **1991** Amer. Fisheries Soc. *Common Names Fishes* 62, *Gibbonsia elegans* . . spotted kelpfish. *Gibbonsia metzi* . . striped kelpfish. *Gibbonsia montereyensis* . . crevice kelpfish. . . *Heterostichus rostratus* . . giant kelpfish.

kelp heron n
=**great blue heron.**
 1923 Dawson *Birds CA* 1891, We dwellers by the southern sea oftenest descry this bird [=great blue heron] as a lone watcher far out in the kelp-beds, and we are moved to call him the Kelp Heron. . . The bird will stand by the hour on a sinking raft of kelp-fronds, though it leave him submerged to the belly.

kelp perch n
1 A **surfperch** (here: *Brachyistius frenatus*).
 1953 Roedel *Common Fishes CA* 113, Kelp Perch—*Brachyistius frenatus.* **1983** *Audubon Field Guide N. Amer. Fishes* 638, Kelp Perches breed in the fall and give birth to fully developed young in the spring. **1991** Amer. Fisheries Soc. *Common Names Fishes* 56, *Brachyistius frenatus* . . kelp perch.
2 A **demoiselle 1** (here: *Chromis punctipinnis*).
 1953 Roedel *Common Fishes CA* 114, Blacksmith—*Chromis punctipinnis.* . . Common in the kelp and around rocks. . . Unauthorized Names: Black perch, blue perch, kelp perch.

kelp plover n [See quot 1956]
=**dowitcher.**
 1923 U.S. Dept. Ag. *Misc. Circular* 13.52 **ME,** Dowitcher (*Limnodromus griseus*). . . In local use . . kelp plover. **1955** Forbush–May *Birds* 201, Eastern Dowitcher *Limnodromus griseus griseus.* . . Kelp Plover. **1956** MA Audubon Soc. *Bulletin* 40.20 **ME, MA,** Kelp Plover. . . From feeding among cast-up seaweed.

kelp salmon See **kelp bass**

kem See **come A3**

kemmilwick See **kimmelweck**

ken See **can** v[1] **1a**

kennebecker See **kennebunker**

Kennebec turkey n Cf **bloater 1, 2, Cape Cod turkey, mackerel 1**

See quot.

1975 Gould *ME Lingo* 152, *Kennebec turkey*—A bloater. [*Ibid* 15, *Bloater*—A smoked herring or alewife, and sometimes a mackerel.]

kennebunker n Also *kennebecker* [From assoc with *Kennebunk* ME, or with the *Kennebec* river] **NEng, esp ME**
Orig among loggers: a type of pack or valise.

1895 *DN* 1.390 ME, *Kennebunker:* valise in which clothes are put by lumbermen when they go into camp for a "winter operation." **1902** *Jrl. Amer. Folkl.* 15.245, *Kennebunker,* a word of comparatively recent origin used to denote "the valise (for clothes) which Maine lumbermen take with them to the woods." **1926** *AmSp* 1.395, *Kennebecker* (or *kennebunker*): an extension-valise (named from Kennebunk, Maine). **1938** (1939) Holbrook *Holy Mackinaw* 262, *Kennebecker.* In New England any sort of knapsack. **1969** Sorden *Lumberjack Lingo* 67, *Kennebecker*—A knapsack, or packsack—generally a carpet bag. It was most an eastern term. **1975** Gould *ME Lingo* 152, *Kennebecker*—A Maine woodsman's knapsack or packsack, and now including the packbasket.

kennedy See **Canada honker**

keno exclam [Transf from *keno* a type of bingo game; also the call used to signal that a player has won] *old-fash*
1 Used to signify that something is successfully completed.

[**1868** *Territorial Enterprise* (VA City NV) 30 Sept 3/2, When they thus got three beans in a row they were to call out "Keno!" and rake in the pot.] **1890** Jefferson *Autobiog.* 65 **TX** (as of c1845), In the death scene, just as *Richard* expired, a voice, signifying that the game was over, shouted "Keno!" **1907** Mulford *Bar-20* 290 **TX**, When Buck says anything, she goes. He wants to know where th' cards are stacked an' why he can't holler 'Keno,' an' I'm goin' to find out if I can. **1920** Hunter *Trail Drivers TX* 205, [Square dance call:] Promenade like skeery cattle—/ Balance all an' swing yer sweets!/ Shake yer spurs an' make 'em rattle!/ Keno! Promenade to seats. **1936** Adams *Cowboy Lingo* 230, Gambling terms are used in a figurative way by the cowboy. . . Keno lent its name to the cowboy for exclamatory use when heralding the end of any act. The conquering of a horse, the throwing of a steer, anything might evoke 'keno!'

2 Used as a tag question; see quot.

1940 White *Wild Geese* 69 **NW** (as of 1890s), I want you to ride herd on my talk a little. . . more'n half the time I'm talkin' like a man who didn't know such a thing as grammar was ever invented. . . Now what I want: when you catch me sailing off the reservation that away, I want you should stop me right there and mend my speech. Keno?

kensington n, often attrib [Perh < *kensington stitch* an embroidery stitch]
1 also *kensinger:* A women's sewing club; a women's social club.

1909 in 1993 *W3* File **ceIA**, [Correspondence:] I . . do not find . . listed in your latest dictionaries: *Kensington,* meaning a kind of sewing circle. **1950** *WELS* (*A group of women that meet to sew together*) 1 Inf, **eWI**, Kensington Club. **1967–68** *DARE* (Qu. W32, . . *A group of women that meet to sew together*) Inf **IL5**, Kensinger Club; **NE8, 9, UT9**, Kensington (Club); **NE6, WY5**, Kensington Club—years ago; (Qu. FF22a, . . *Clubs and societies . . for women*) Inf **IA3**, Social kensingtons. **1994** *DARE* File **NE**, There were the ladies of the Kensington Circle. . . The gatherings are a sense of community as well as an act of charity. . . Quilters have been meeting here for generations. . . The love and pride of Trinity [Church]'s Kensington Circle.

2 also *kenson;* Prob by ext: a social gathering; a **potluck** meal.

1931 in 1993 *W3* File **neWA**, Kensington (A social p.m.) **1947** *WELS Suppl.* **cwWI**, *Kensington*—about fifty years ago there was an informal club of elderly women. . . They had a kensington . . every other week with each member bringing her chef d'oeuvre . . for a hot supper. . . Somehow the word "kensington" became used in the church social evening meals and if potluck was ever used, it became completely replaced. . . We feel that kensington food is superior to potluck. **1948**

Ibid **cwWI**, Did you know that Lord Kensington . . once invited guests to dinner, but asked them to bring their own food? [Also] my aunt, who lived forty years in Rhode Island, says that "Kensington" is used there. *Ibid* **cwWI**, In northeastern Monroe County [what we called a "kensington" is] called a "kenson". . . "Let's have a kenson feed" . . was a typical use. **1950** *WELS* (*When people bring hot dishes to a meeting place and share*) 1 Inf, **cwWI**, Kensington potluck. *Ibid (Parties)* 1 Inf, **cwWI**, Kensingtons. **1977** *DARE* File **cwWI**, [Newspaper column:] Mrs. Romayne Hanson was guest of honor at a Kensington Party.

kentry See **country**

Kentuck n
1 See **Kentucky A.**
2a pronc-spp *Kaintock, Kaintuck:* A Kentuckian; one who is or is assumed to be of Kentucky origin. *often derog*

1826 Flint *Recollections* 15, You learn the received opinion, that a "Kentuck" is the best man at a pole. **1830** *Western Mth. Rev.* 3.357, His captain had deported, like a real Kentuck. **1835** Ingraham *South-West* 1.105, Here are congregated the primitive navies of Indiana, Ohio, and the adjoining states, manned . . by "real Kentucks." **1942** in 1944 *ADD, Kentuck.* . . A Kentuckian. . . The Kaintucks have spared a feud with the N.Y.C. police. Assoc. Press, July 24. **1946** Roberts *Lake Pontchartrain* 159 **sLA** (as of c1805), The keelboatmen and flatboatmen of the middle frontier came down the Mississippi. . . The Creoles called them Kaintocks on the assumption that they were all from Kentucky. **1968** *DARE* (Qu. HH18, *Very insignificant or low-grade people*) Inf **IN32**, Kentucks.

b spec: A person of Kentucky origin residing in one of the northeastern counties of Wisconsin.

1950 *WELS Suppl.* **cwWI**, The Kentuck settlement in Forest and Langlade counties. . . was a delightful spot to us before W[orld] W[ar] 2 . . when the mountaineer speech was still new to us. . . There seemed to be no carry-over from the Kentucks to the others [living in the area] except the overwhelming prevalence of the double negative. **1969** Sorden *Lumberjack Lingo* 67 **NEng, Gt Lakes**, *Kentucks*—People imported to Forest County, Wisconsin, from Kentucky. They settled throughout the woods and were a great help in logging. **1976** *Green Bay Press–Gaz.* (WI) 31 Oct sec B 6/4 **WI**, Ingram is a "Kentuck." He came to Langlade county as a young boy with his parents in 1910.

Kentucky n Usu |kən'tʌkɪ, kɛn-|; also **chiefly Sth, S Midl** |kɛn'tʌk(ɪ); kɪn-|; also with recessive stress |'kɛntəkɪ|; for addit varr see quots Pronc-spp *Caintuck(y), Kaintuc(k), Kaintuck(e)y, Kaintuck(e)* Cf **Kentuck**
A Forms.

1775 (1971) Calk *Jrl.* 34 **VA**, I set out from prince wm. to travel to caintuck on tuesday Night. **1784** (1929) Filson *Kentucke* 8, John Finley . . travelled over the fertile region, now called Kentucke. **1802** in 1920 *TN Hist. Mag.* 6.35, Caintucky line. **1813** in 1912 Thornton *Amer. Gloss.* 1.511, In a few years more, those of us who are alive will have to move off to Kaintuck or the Mississippi, where corn can be had for sixpence a bushel. **1826** Flint *Recollections* 64, Heaven is a Kentuck of a place. **1827** (1939) Sherwood *Gaz.* GA 139, *Provincialisms.* . . *Kaintuc,* for Kentucky. **1843** (1916) Hall *New Purchase* 282 **IN**, Some customers from Kaintuck stopped me. *Ibid* 331, Mr. Harwood of Kaintuckey. **1903** *DN* 2.318 **seMO**, *Kentucky.* . . Pronounced Kaintucky. **1940** in 1944 *ADD*, [Radio:] *Kentucky.* . . Kentuck'. **1941** *Ibid* **Sth**, [Radio:] *Kentucky* ['kɛntʌkɪ]. **1942** Hall *Smoky Mt. Speech* 54 **wNC, eTN**, *Kentucky,* usually [kən'tʌkɪ] (not [kɛn-]), is frequently ['kɛn,tʌkɪ] in the speech of old-timers. **1943** in 1944 *ADD*, [Radio:] ['kɛn,tʌki] Club tobacco. **c1960** Wilson *Coll.* **csKY**, *Kentucky*—[,kɪn'tʌkɪ]—regular; [,kɛn'tʌkɪ, ,kɛn'tʌk]—humorous. **1989** Pederson *LAGS Tech. Index* 320 **Gulf Region**, [For *Kentucky,* the Index shows 417 pronunciations of the type [kən'tʌkɪ], 203 of the type [kɪn'tʌkɪ], 57 of the type [kɛn'tʌkɪ], 10 of the type ['kɛntʌkɪ], 6 of the type [ken'tʌkɪ], 2 of the type [kæn'tʌkɪ], 1 [kjən'tʌkɪ], 1 [kjɪntəkɪ].]

B Sense.

In the name of var ring games: see quot. Cf **I went to Paris, Old Kentucky girl**

1968–69 *DARE* (Qu. EE1, . . *Games . . children play . . in which they form a ring, and either sing or recite a rhyme*) Inf **GA72B**, I went to old Kentucky; **NJ13**, We're going to Kentucky, we're going to a fair.

Kentucky bass n Also *Kentucky black bass,* ~ *spotted bass*
A spotted bass (here: *Micropterus punctulatus*).

1932 OH Bur. Scientific Research *Bulletin* 1.29.1, [Title:] *The Spotted or Kentucky Black Bass in Ohio.* Ibid 3, Their description of this variation is undoubtedly that of the Spotted or Kentucky Bass. **1933** LA Dept. of Conserv. *Fishes* 320, *The Kentucky or Spotted Bass.* . . ranks as the most valuable of the three Black Basses for purpose of propagation. **1935** Caine *Game Fish* 9, *Micropterus pseudoplites.* . . Kentucky Bass—Kentucky Black Bass. **1943** Eddy–Surber *N. Fishes* 207, The other two [species of *Micropterus*], including the spotted or Kentucky bass, . . are southern. **1946** *Richmond Times–Dispatch* (VA) 16 June sec B 12/1 *(Hench Coll.)*, When a largemouth bass grows big enough to be clearly seen, he will have a broad dark band along his sides. . . The smallmouth is not thus marked, nor is the close relative, the Kentucky or Southern smallmouth bass, both of which species occur in this State. **1966–69** *DARE* (Qu. P1, . . *Kinds of freshwater fish . . caught around here . . good to eat*) Infs **AL**2, **MO**20, Kentucky bass. **1972** Sparano *Outdoors Encycl.* 360, Spotted Bass, Kentucky bass, Kentucky spotted bass. . . *Micropterus punctulatus.* **1991** Amer. Fisheries Soc. *Common Names Fishes* 116, [Bass,] Kentucky—see spotted bass.

Kentucky bluegrass n [See quot 1889]

A **bluegrass 1** (here: *Poa pratensis*). Also called **green grass, June ~ 1a, meadow ~ 2a, spear grass**

1849 Emmons *Agriculture NY* 2.68, An earlier kind of grass than timothy, is the Spear grass, Meadow grass, or Kentucky blue grass. **1889** Vasey *Ag. Grasses* 66, *Poa pratensis.* . . From the unexampled success its cultivation has met with in Kentucky it has acquired the name of Kentucky blue grass. **1912** Baker *Book of Grasses* 205, *Kentucky bluegrass.* . . Although well known by name at least, few seem acquainted with the fact that this is one of our most common grasses from the Atlantic to the Pacific. Its most luxuriant growth is attained in the far-noted blue-grass region of Kentucky, on limestone soils in the counties about Lexington. **1937** U.S. Forest Serv. *Range Plant Hdbk.* G103, Kentucky bluegrass usually produces an abundance of nutritious forage and lush herbage. **1952** Strausbaugh–Core *Flora WV* 134, *Kentucky bluegrass.* . . An important pasture grass in West Virginia. **1968–70** *DARE* (Qu. L8, *Hay that grows naturally in damp places*) Inf **CT**32, Kentucky bluegrass; (Qu. L9a, . . *Kinds of grass . . grown for hay*) Infs **MN**16, **PA**174, Kentucky bluegrass; (Qu. S15, . . *Weed seeds that cling to clothing*) Inf **IL**58, Kentucky bluegrass. **1976** Bailey–Bailey *Hortus Third* 890, *P[oa] pratensis.* . . Kentucky bluegrass.

Kentucky board fence See **Kentucky fence**

Kentucky breakfast n esp KY

A "meal" which includes or consists of liquor, usu bourbon; see quots.

1882 *Century Illustr. Mag.* Apr 884, [The] typical Southerner. . . traveled with a dusky valet, a silver-headed cane, two ruffled shirts, and a case of hair-triggers. His morning meal was a simple Kentucky breakfast—"three cocktails and a chaw of terbacker." **1907** White *AZ Nights* 136, He staked me to a Kentucky breakfast. What's a Kentucky breakfast? Why, a Kentucky breakfast is a three-pound steak, a bottle of whisky, and a setter dog. What's the dog for? Why, to eat the steak, of course. **1932** Stieff *Eat in MD* 298, [Caption to drawing of Southern-style gentleman with bottle and whiskey glass:] *Kentucky breakfast.* **1968** Harris S. *Home Remedies* 9 **NC**, One treatment for the cold commends itself to me. . . That is known as a "Kentucky Breakfast," the ingredients of which are a bottle of bourbon, a beefsteak, and a dog. The dog, of course, is to eat the beefsteak.

Kentucky coffee tree n Also *Kentucky coffee bean (tree)*

A tree (*Gymnocladus dioicus*) of the family Leguminosae, with large pods having seeds that can be used as a coffee substitute. Also called **coffee bean 1, coffeeberry 1, coffee nut, ~ tree 1, luck bean, mahogany 2a, nicker tree, stump tree**

1785 (1925) Washington *Diaries* 2.360, Eight Nuts from a tree called the Kentucke Coffee tree. **1848** Gray *Manual of Botany* 111, *G[ymnocladus] Canadensis* . . Kentucky Coffee-bean Tree. **1872** Schele de Vere *Americanisms* 416, The *Coffee-tree* (Gymnocladus canadensis), often called *Kentucky Coffee-tree,* or *Kentucky locust,* derives its name from the fact that in the days of early settlements the seeds were frequently used as a substitute for coffee, a practice renewed during the late Civil War. **1876** Hobbs *Bot. Hdbk.* 25, Kentucky coffee bean, Gymnocladus Canadensis. **1897** Sudworth *Arborescent Flora* 255, *Gymnocladus dioicus.* . . *Common Names.* Kentucky Coffee Tree (Mass., R.I. . . , N.Y., Pa. . . , Del., Va., W.Va., N.C., Miss., Ark., Mo., Ill., Kans., Mich.) **1939** Medsger *Edible Wild Plants* 210, Kentucky Coffee Tree, or Chicot, or American Coffee Bean. **1968** *DARE* (Qu. T15, . . *Kinds of swamp trees*) Inf **PA**89, Kentucky coffee bean. **1973** Wharton–Bar-

bour *Trees KY* 537, Kentucky Coffee-tree. . . The coffee-tree, occurring in open woods and grassy areas in all limestone sections of Kentucky, is common only in the Inner Bluegrass. The early settlers used the roasted seed as a somewhat unpalatable coffee substitute. **1980** Little *Audubon Guide N. Amer. Trees E. Region* 524, Kentucky Coffeetree. . . The roasted seeds were once used as a coffee substitute; raw seeds, however, are poisonous.

Kentucky colonel n Cf **Georgia major, major 1**

A Kentuckian called by the unofficial title **colonel B1;** one who resembles such a person; one given this honorary designation by the governor of Kentucky.

[1825 in **1947** *N&Q* Apr 4/1, In the Blue Grass region / A "Paradox" was born,/ The corn was full of kernels / And the "colonels" full of corn.] **[1920** U.S. Patent Office *Official Gaz.* 276.750, *Kentucky Colonel*—No claim being made to the exclusive use of the word "Kentucky" apart from the mark as shown in the drawing [*DARE* Ed: representing a man's head with white hair, moustache, and goatee, and wearing a hat and bow tie]. . . *Particular description of goods.*—Smoking-Tobacco.] **1940** *The Honorable Order of Kentucky Colonels* (title). **1942** Berrey–Van den Bark *Amer. Slang* 184.1, Alabama Joe, Arizona Pete. . . Kentucky Colonel . . *nicknames for persons from Alabama, Arizona &c.* **1947** *N&Q* April 8, No Kentucky colonel, in our time, takes his title seriously. **1962** Fuller *Untitled Epic* 40, Engineers,/ who . . / together with lawyer vice-presidents / were fast being substituted / for the Kentucky colonels / as executive heads of industry. **1986** Pederson *LAGS Concordance* (Colonel *Sanders*) 5 infs, **GA, swAL, csTX,** Kentucky Colonel. **1989** *Encycl. S. Culture* 750, By 1949 Sanders had received from Governor Lawrence Wetherby his second Kentucky colonel's commission, an honor typically bestowed for outstanding community service or as a political favor. . . He began signing his name "Colonel Harland Sanders," grew a moustache and a goatee, and allowed his nearly white hair to lengthen. Later he added the white suit and string tie to complete the Kentucky colonel image traditionally caricatured in popular films and literature. **1991** *DARE* File **KY,** I've heard "Kentucky colonel" used informally to indicate something about a man's personality. I assumed it meant the person was extroverted. In Kentucky, the governor can make someone a "Kentucky colonel." It doesn't mean the person receives a military commission, but it's an honor the governor can officially bestow.

Kentucky fence n Also *Kentucky board fence, ~ plank fence, ~ white wooden fence*

Any of var types of rail or slat fences; see quots.

1837 (1848) Peck *New Guide* 318 **IL**, Fencing it into four fields, with a Kentucky fence of eight rails high, with cross stakes. **1966–67** *DARE* (Qu. L64, *The kind of wooden fence that's built around a garden or near a house*) Inf **MS**4, Kentucky plank fence—these have network of wood; (Qu. L65) Inf **AL**20, Kentucky fence—boards running horizontal. **1986** Pederson *LAGS Concordance* (Rail fence) 1 inf, **cnGA,** Kentucky board fence—cross pieces stacked, zigzag; 1 inf, **cwGA,** Kentucky fences—long slats, straight, white; 1 inf, **ceTN,** Kentucky white wooden fence.

Kentucky girl See **Old Kentucky girl**

Kentucky hunter n

=**hedge bindweed 1.**

1897 *Jrl. Amer. Folkl.* 10.51, *Convolvulus sepium* . . Kentucky hunter, . . Sulphur Grove, Ohio.

Kentucky mahogany See **mahogany 2a**

Kentucky mockingbird See **mockingbird 5**

Kentucky oysters n pl esp KY

=**chitterlings 1.**

1898 Dunbar *Folks from Dixie* 103 **Sth** [Black], There was hog jole and cold cabbage, ham and Kentucky oysters, more widely known as chittlings. **1939** Writers' Program *Guide KY* 406, Commonly known in this State as Kentucky oysters, chitterlings (hog intestines) may be prepared in several different ways. **1970** *DARE* (Qu. H43, *Foods made from parts of the head and inner organs of an animal*) Inf **KY**94, Kentucky oysters—people use this term for chitterlings. [Inf Black] **1986** Pederson *LAGS Concordance* (Chitterlings) 1 inf, **cMS,** Some people call them Kentucky oysters, up north. [Inf Black] **1990** *Atlanta Constitution* (GA) 5 Apr sec E 3/1, Health authorities said the outbreak [of diarrhea among infants in Atlanta] was due, in part, to lapses in household sanitation during the preparation of chitterlings, better known to generations of Southerners as chitlins or "Kentucky oysters."

Kentucky pill n [In ref to Kentuckians' reputation as sharp-shooters]
A bullet.
1861 in 1912 Thornton *Amer. Gloss.* 1.511, Phillips gave a Kentucky pill, and brought the wasps about our ears.—*Harper's Weekly,* Sept. 21. **1932** *WV Review* June 378, It is rather common in the southern part of West Virginia to hear mention of "Kentucky pills."

Kentucky plank fence See **Kentucky fence**

Kentucky spotted bass See **Kentucky bass**

Kentucky treat n Cf **arkansaw** adv, *Dutch treat* (at **Dutch** adv)
1917 *DN* 4.420 New Orleans LA, *Kentucky treat.* . . Same as *Dutch treat.*

Kentucky white wooden fence See **Kentucky fence**

kenyon See **canyon**

keounty See **county**

keow See **cow**

kep See **keep** v A4, 5

kepp'n See **captain**

ker- pref, rarely infix Also *ca-, che-, co-, com-, con-, cor-, cul-, cur-, ga-, k'-, ka-, ke-, ki-, ko-* [See 1983 *AmSp* 58.291–302 for summary of suggested etyms] Note: The quots illustrate only a small selection of words containing this element; for further exx see 1942 Berrey–Van den Bark *Amer. Slang* 60.1, 4, 140.2, 3, 13, 14, 1973 *Comments on Etym.* 6.3–4.2–8, 1983 *AmSp* 58.291–302. See also **caboodle, kit 2b**
Used as an intensifier, often with an imitative second element, to form words (esp advs and verbs) expressive of sudden or great force, speed, bewilderment, etc.
1758 in 1909 Essex Inst. *Coll.* 45.343, They came within a Mile and ½ of this Stockade, where lay in Ambush near 50 of the Enemy, who cahoop'd. **1832** *Political Examiner* (Shelbyville KY) 8 Dec 4/1, By gum, if I dident sit plump cowallish right down on Deby's aunt's cat. **1834** *Life Andrew Jackson* 65, Gets so . . cornubbled, he was amost laid under hatches. *Ibid* 93, Give those chaps a curnubblin. **1836** *Pub. Ledger* (Philadelphia PA) 27 July [4/2], Down I came chewallop . . and overset the chair. **1843** (1847) Field *Drama Pokerville* 27, Down he went—"K'chuck!" as an excited auditor exclaimed, in a half-suppressed tone of sympathy! **1843** (1916) Hall *New Purchase* 227 IN, In he splasht'd kerslush. **1844** 'J. Slick' *High Life N.Y.* II.88 *(OEDS),* We drew up co-wallop right afore Jase's house. *Ibid* 154, Ca-smash went the chair. **1848** *S. Lit. Messenger* 14.686, He "Kawallups" the fish. **1858** Hammett *Piney Woods Tavern* 127, The Major made a grab at Pond's head-riggin', and away went the Major and Pond's bandanna down stairs, kolumpus, inter the cabin. **1859** (1968) Bartlett *Americanisms* 63, *Cachunk!* A word like *thump!* describing the sound produced by the fall of a heavy body. Also written *kerchunk!* A number of fanciful onomatopoetic words of this sort are used in the South and West; in all of which the first syllable, which is unaccented, is subject to the same variety of spelling. These words are of recent origin. **1893** Russell *Americanisms* 49 *(DA)*, Chewallop (or Kerwallop). A bow-wow word . . to express the sound of a falling body. **1908** *DN* 3.326 eAL, wGA, *Kerspang, kerspank.* . . Intensive forms of *spang, spank.* **1912** Green *VA Folk-Speech* 137, *Cullumpus.* . . In imitation of the sound. . . "He slipped and fell, coming down cullumpus." **1924** *DN* 5.257 [Onomatopoetic exclams], *Plink-plank-plunk, ker-plunk, galunk. Ibid* 258, *Whack, che-whack, ke-whack* (blow). **1938** FWP *Guide DE* 509, If you don't know how to travel the old swamp, you'll likely go ka-sow-jup, head and years! **1942** Berrey–Van den Bark *Amer. Slang* 173.3, *Bewilder.* . . *Comfoozle, conflummox.* **1942** Hurston *Dust Tracks* 230 sFL [Black], Ker-blam-er-lam-er-lam! **1943** *LANE* Map 576 (Belly-bump) 1 inf, **seCT,** Belly-[kəbʌmp]; 2 infs, **seCT,** Belly-[kətʃʌŋk]; 1 inf, **swNH,** Belly-[kəhuwt]. **1944** [see **jam-ke-dab**]. **1959** McAtee *Odd-ments* 4 cNC, Catty-ker-wampus. **1965–70** DARE (Qu. KK53, *When one thing suddenly hits hard against something else: "He ran _____ into a car."*) 12 Infs, **scattered,** Kerplunk; **AL40, CA136, NY30, 200, VT16,** Kerbang; **MA24,** Kerbunk; kerflop; **OH44, VT16,** Kersmash; **ME16,** Kerslap; **NC7,** Kerwham; **SC34,** Kerdab; **NH14,** Kaboom, kaplow; **NY69,** Kabang; **VT10,** Kawallop; (Qu. KK19, *If a machine or appliance is temporarily out of order: "My sewing machine _____."*) Inf **PA19,** Went kerflooey; **WV1,** Has gone kerplunk; **KS18, MI25, PA28, 165, SC11, WI61,** Went (*or* [has] gone) kaflooey; **IN83,** Went kaflop; **LA25, MS30,** (Has) gone kaflunk; **AL3, NC69, TN4,** Has

gone kafloonk; **MI18,** Went kaplooey; **NC84, ND3, SD2,** Went (*or* has gone) kaplunk; **MI68,** Is geflummoxed; (Qu. KK10, . . *Words for something failing* . . "*He didn't work it out carefully enough, and his plan _____.*") Infs **AL3, KY60, MS30, ND3, PA150,** Went kaflunk; **FL6, IA41, IN32, SC21, TX95,** Went kaflooey; **OK27,** Went kaplunk; **PA193,** Went kapook; **VA31,** Kaflopped—most common (a cake doesn't go flat, it kaflops); **WI62,** Went kerplunk; (Qu. F38) Inf **NY111,** Ker-thunder mug; (Qu. Y1, . . *Expressions* . . *for a person suddenly falling down:* "*He slipped on the steps and took quite a _____.*") Inf **MI100,** Kaboom; (QR, near Qu. Y30a) Inf **MA76,** To put it down—he ker-plunked it; (Qu. Y35) Inf **PA234,** Kerplooey; (Qu. EE25) Inf **NY232,** Belly kabonk; (Qu. EE29) Inf **WA28,** Kersplash; (Qu. HH35) Infs **IN60, NM4, NY232, TN6,** High-kaflutin; **MI101,** High-konflukin; (Qu. JJ42) Inf **IL96,** Kaflummoxed; (Qu. KK11) Inf **MA38,** Made a great catouse about it; **MA73,** Made a big catouse; (Qu. KK16) Inf **MA79,** Catouse; (Qu. KK20b, *Something that looks as if it might collapse any minute:* "*Our old washing machine is _____.*") Inf **WI73,** Kaflooey; **NJ16, WI70,** Kaplunk; (Qu. KK70, *Something that has got out of proper shape:* "*That house is all _____.*") Inf **IA41,** Kitty-kiwampus; (Qu. LL10, *A whole group of people:* "*They made too much noise, so he sent the whole _____ home.*") Infs **CA61, IL4, NJ28,** (Shootin') kabang; (Qu. LL17, . . *There's no more of something:* "*The potatoes are _____.*") Inf **PA234,** All gaflooey; (Qu. MM12a, . . '*In all directions*' . . "*He shot into a flock of birds and they went _____.*") Infs **AL30, AR47, WV8, 14,** Kerflooey; **IN35, NC14, 15,** Kaflooey; **TX27,** Kerflooey—Inf's cousin uses (from New Mexico); (Qu. MM12b, . . '*In all directions*' . . "*When she was out on the dance floor, she broke her beads and they went _____.*") Infs **AL6, 30, AR47, TX102,** Kerflooey; **MI24,** Kerfloo; **CA14,** Kapow; **GA31,** Kaflooey; (Qu. MM13, *The table was nice and straight until he came along and knocked it _____*) Infs **CA170, MI24,** Kerflooey; **DC1, NM12,** Kaflooey; (Qu. NN2, *Exclamations of very strong agreement: Somebody says,* "*I think Smith is absolutely right,*" *and you reply,* "*_____.*") Inf **WI48,** You're dang ka-tootin'; (Qu. NN8b, . . *Expressions of annoyance: "This jar won't come open, _____ it.*") Inf **IL4,** Kabang [FW: without "it"]; (Qu. NN29c, . . "*Holy _____!*") Inf **TX81,** Kamoley. **1986** Pederson *LAGS Concordance* (To dive in the water and land on your stomach) 1 inf, **nwTN,** He did a belly buster, kawhop.

kerbase See **cabeza**

ker'd See **carry** A2

kere See **care**

kerf n Also *carp* Pronc-spp *calf, carf(e), curf, kearf* Cf **scarf** A Forms. Cf Pronc Intro 3.I.1.f
1636 in 1892 Dedham MA *Early Rec.* 3.25 MA, Yf any man hence-forth from this day shall fell any Tree of six Inches thicknes in the Carfe. **1897** Howells *Landlord* 31 nAtl, He lifted his axe, and struck it into the carf on the tree. **1898** [see **B** below]. **1899** (1912) Green *VA Folk-Speech* 249, *Kerf.* . . *Kearf.* A channel or cut made in wood by a saw or other cutting instrument. A cut in a tree with an axe for felling. **1930** Shoemaker *1300 Words* 14 cPA Mts (as of c1900), *Carf.* **1933** Karns *Hist. Sketches* 3 PA, A skilled axeman could notch a log as perfect as if the carp had been sawed in. **1945** Le Sueur *North Star Country* 247 MN, The teamsters and choppers felled the trees, cutting a notch or "calf" in the side toward which they wished it to fall.
B Sense.
Fig; in phr *cut a curf*: See quot.
1898 Lloyd *Country Life* 136 AL, The trouble with a heap of men is that they sail in to make money and cut a big curf and don't have time to make a livin.

kerflommix, kerflummux v See **flummox** v

kerflummux adv See **flummox** adv

ker-inch See **co-wench**

Kerliny See **Carolina**

kermis(s) n Also *kermes, kirmes(s)* [Du *kermis,* BelgianFr *ker-messe,* Ger *Kirmes* a fair] **chiefly ceWI**
A community festival usu held in the fall and sponsored by a local church. Note: For an earlier and appar independent bor-rowing of this word, see *DAE* at *kirmess.*
1931 *WI Mag. Hist.* 14.339 ceWI There is no current holiday so distinctly Belgian as the "kirmess". . . In our neighborhood these harvest festivals are a tradition. They begin in late August at Grandlez now Lincoln and spread from community to community—Brussels, Walhain, Rosière, Thiry Daems, Duvall, Sansouver, Tonet, Dyckesville, Namur.

Ibid 341, *The First Kirmess* . . August . . 1858. **1949** *WELS Suppl.*
ceWI, The [Door] peninsula Belgians . . pronounce it ['kɜ·məs]. The
most usual spelling on posters announcing the event is *kirmes; kirmess,
kermis,* and *kermiss,* are also seen. These feasts are still held every year
and are very popular. . . and each town has its own kirmes week-end. . .
Most of the people who participate are farmers from the surrounding
area. In fact every place large enough to have a church and two saloons
has a kirmes of its own. . . The drinking is public; no invitation is
necessary. . . The dancing begins in the afternoon. *Ibid* ceWI, [Near]
New Holstein, which was a Protestant '48er community, there was a
small Catholic village St. Anna. Every summer, a festival known as
"Kermes" was regularly held there in connection with the church. **1950**
WELS (*Local . . church suppers . . fairs*) 1 Inf, **ceWI,** Catholic
church—kermis—all-day celebration with suppers; 1 Inf, **ceWI,** Kermiss; 1 Inf, **ceWI,** Kermiss and Schut—popular in Holland communities. Kermiss was a two-day dance, now obsolete. **1968–69** *DARE* (Qu.
FF16, . . *Local contests or celebrations*) Inf **WI**61, Kermis—starts last
Sunday in September after last mass, there's a brass band waiting outside
the church [and] all people march to the dance hall and dancing continues Sunday, Monday, and Tuesday—a kind of homecoming; free dinner
and free beer; serve chicken, beef booya, and Belgian pie; . . a harvest
festival, no longer three days, just on Sunday now; (Qu. FF18, *Joking
words . . about a noisy or boisterous celebration or party: "They certainly _____ last night."*) Inf **MI**103, [FW: Inf recalls his mother
saying a party was a real ['kɜ·məs]—a Dutch word]. **1968** *DARE* Tape
WI61, Every locality, every crossroad has its own name, and each has
its weekend allocated for their kermis, which is perpetuated from year
to years [sic]. Of course, some of these people make sport of that day.
They claim that instead of a kermis, which to most of us is a harvest
festival and thanksgiving for good crops and so on, some call it mating
season. **1989** *DARE* File ceWI, Each of the Catholic churches had
kermis. Kermis was held on that church's saint's feast day. . . First
there'd be mass, then a potluck—a big dinner—and then people played
cards and danced. We haven't had kermis here for awhile though; it kind
of petered out.

kern See **kernel**

ker·nanny See **co·nan(nie)**

kernel n Also sp *kearnel;* rarely abbr *kern*

1 The hard seed of a peach, plum, or cherry. [*OED kernel*
sb.[1] "A seed; esp the seed contained within any fruit. . . *Obs.
exc. dial.*"; c1000 →] **chiefly C and S Atl; also Gulf States**
See Map and Map Section Cf **pit, seed, stone**
1939 *LANE* Map 268 (*Peach pit*) 1 inf, **seCT,** Peach kernel. **1955**
PADS 23.45 e,cSC, eNC, seGA, Cherry kernel—'seed' (also Delmarva).
1965–70 *DARE* (Qu. I50, . . *The hard center of a peach*) 59 Infs, **chiefly
C and S Atl,** Kernel; (Qu. I49, . . *The hard center of a plum*) 12 Infs,
chiefly C and S Atl, Kernel; (Qu. I48, *The hard center of a cherry*) 11
Infs, **chiefly C and S Atl,** Kernel. [26 of 62 Infs gs educ or less] **1966**
DARE Tape **NC**25, She threw the kernels out when she was preservin'
peaches one summer—and she just dumped the kernels down in the
hole . . and two trees come up. **c1970** Pederson *Dial. Surv. Rural GA*
(*The hard thing in the middle of a cherry*) 11 [of 64] infs, **seGA,** Kernel;
(*The center of a peach*) 39 infs, **seGA,** (Peach) kernel. **1973** Allen
LAUM 1.304 **MN, SD** (as of c1950), Seed (of a cherry). . Kernel [2
infs]. **1986** Pederson *LAGS Concordance* **Gulf Region** (*Seed . . of a
peach*) 110 infs, Kernel; 1 inf, Kern[el]; 1 inf, Used to, we called them
kernels; (*Seed . . of a cherry*) 33 infs, Kernel; 1 inf, Cherry kernel.

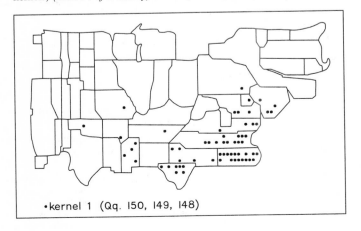

•kernel 1 (Qq. I50, 149, 148)

2 By ext:

a The core of an apple. *esp freq among Black speakers*
1986 Pederson *LAGS Concordance* (*Core . . of an apple*) 15 infs, **Gulf
States, GA,** Kernel; 1 inf, **seGA,** Kern[el]; 1 inf, **neFL,** Kernel—part
of an apple you throw away; [1 inf, **csGA,** Kernel—individual apple
seed, perhaps; 1 inf, **cnTN,** Kernels]. [14 of 17 infs Black]
b The hard shell of a walnut.
1986 Pederson *LAGS Concordance* **Gulf Region** (*Walnut shell*), [8
infs used *kernel* to refer to the hard shell of a walnut.]

3 The **meat** n 1 of a nut; the soft, often edible, part within
the hard seed of a fruit. **widespread, but more freq Midl**
See Map [*OED kernel* sb.[1] 2 c1000 →]
1689 in 1892 *MA Hist. Soc. Coll.* 6th ser 5.24, I hope my friends . .
will overlook, & not cast away a good kernel for som spots that may
be on ye outside of ye nut. **1879** (1965) Tyree *Housekeeping in Old VA*
459, On each bit of candy thus dropped, lay half the kernel of an English
walnut. **1899** (1912) Green *VA Folk-Speech* 248, *Kearnel*. . . Kernel.
Edible substance contained in the shell of a nut or the stone of a fruit.
1941 *LANE* Map 268 (*Peach pit*) 1 inf, **RI,** Kernel = peach meat, inside
the stone. **1950** *WELS* **WI** (*The part of the nut that you eat*) 22 Infs,
Kernel; 1 inf, Meat, as in hickory nuts; kernel, as in peanuts. **1954**
Harder Coll. cwTN, Kernel—the part of a nut that is eaten. **c1960**
Wilson Coll. csKY, Kernel. . . The edible part of a nut. Also the inner
part of a peach, cherry, or plum seed. **1960** Criswell *Resp. to PADS 20*
Ozarks, Kernel. A possibly recent term might be *meat,* especially when
the kernels are put in cookies and cakes. **1965–70** *DARE* (Qu. I41, *The
part of the nut that you eat*) 375 Infs, **widespread, but more freq Midl,**
Kernel; **MI**68, Nut kernel [Of all Infs responding to the question, 70%
were old; of those giving these responses, 82% were old.]; (Qu. I50, . .
The hard center of a peach) Inf **FL**26, Seed, kernel inside that; **LA**15,
40, Kernel—inside the seed. **1986** Pederson *LAGS Concordance* **Gulf
Region** (*Seed of a peach*), [90 infs indicated that the kernel was the soft
inner part of the seed; 8 of them said or implied that it is edible]; (*Walnut
shell*) [13 infs indicated that the *kernel* was the meat of the walnut];
(*Colonel*) 1 inf, The kernel = the meat of a nut; (*Peanut*) 1 inf, Goober
has only one kernel; 1 inf, Kernel—inside nut; (*Seed of a cherry*) 2 infs,
Kernel—inside the seed; 1 inf, Kernel—inside cherry or peach seed.
1989 Whealy *Fruit Inventory* 104, Lisa Sweet-Pit—Freestone fruit [=an
apricot] with edible kernel in the pit. A high percentage of the fruits
yield double kernels.

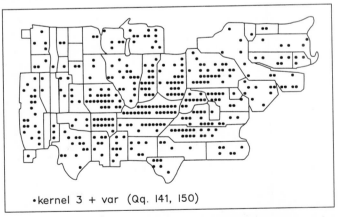

•kernel 3 + var (Qq. I41, I50)

4 also *waxing* (or *waxen*) *kernel:* A lump or swelling under
the skin; a gland, esp a swollen lymph gland. [*OED kernel*
sb.[1] 4 c1000 →] **esp Sth, S Midl**
1899 (1912) Green *VA Folk-Speech* 248, *Kearnel*. . . Enlarged lym-
phatic glands, in the groins, or about the neck; *waxen kearnels.* **1916**
Kephart *Camping & Woodcraft* 1.314 **sAppalachians,** Cut the leetle red
kernels out from under their forelegs; then bile 'em, fust—all the strong
is left in the water. **1935** Hyatt *Folkl. Adams Co. IL* 286, Cure a kernel
by making a cross over it with soot. **1944** *Jrl. Amer. Folkl.* 5.46 **SC,**
The swellings known as "kernels" . . result from a bruise on some part
of the body. *Ibid* 47, To cure a kernel. If you find a piece of flint, rub
it on the swelling and leave it in the woods. **1958** Browne *Pop. Beliefs
AL* 75, For kernels under the arms or on the groins, put your finger
behind the chimney and make a cross and put your sooty finger on the
kernels and they will get well. **1966–70** *DARE* (Qu. X60, . . *A lump
that comes up on your head when you get a sharp blow or knock;* not
asked in early QRs) Inf **DC**8, Waxing kernel; (Qu. BB30, . . *A hard,*

painful swelling [often on a finger] that seems to come from deep under the skin) Infs **IL75, NY235, SC67,** Kernel; (Qu. BB33a, . . *A swelling under the skin, bigger than a pimple, that comes to a head*) Inf **MD37,** Kernel—smaller than a boil and hard. **1974** Fink *Mountain Speech* 14 **wNC, eTN,** Kernels . . small glands in neck, armpits, groin, etc. These in some game animals must be removed if the meat is to be edible. **1976** Garber *Mountain-ese* 49 **sAppalachians,** Kernels . . swellings— James got kernels under his arm ater he stuck a rusty nail in his foot. **1986** Pederson *LAGS Concordance,* 1 inf, **cwFL,** Kernel—the result of a wasp sting; *(Boil)* 1 inf, **ceLA,** Kernel—in sore; 3 infs, **AL, GA,** (A) kernel. **1990** Cavender *Folk Med. Lexicon* 26 **sAppalachians,** Kernels— swollen lymph nodes under the arms, on the neck or groin.

5 An animal's testicle. [*SND kirnel* n. 3 "A gland in an animal's body used as food . . lamb's testicles"] Cf **nut** testicle

    1986 Pederson *LAGS Concordance (Chitterlings)* 1 inf, **neAR,** Kernels—hog testicles, eaten by some.

kerosene n Pronc-spp *kahysene, karosine, kirsene, kuracene, kyarrysene*

Std sense; var forms.

    1884 Barber *Diary* **MA,** Bot cheese & kuracene. **1908** *DN* 3.326 **eAL, wGA,** *Karosine(-oil).* . . Kerosene. **1912** *DN* 3.568 **cNY,** Kirsene. **1922** Gonzales *Black Border* 309 **sSC, GA coasts** [Gullah glossary], *Kyarrysene*—kerosene. **1932** Faulkner in *Sat. Eve. Post* 3 Dec 39 **MS** [Black], "Where does yawl keep that there Tennessee spring water? . . That there drinking kahysene." "Kahysene?" "That there light-colored lamp oil what yawl drinks. . ." "Oh. . . You mean corn."

kerosene oil n Also sp *kerosine oil* **scattered, but esp SE, NEast** See Map and Map Section *old-fash* Cf **coal oil, K oil, lamp oil**

Kerosene.

    1856 *Amer. Railway Times* 26 June [3], *Kerosene Lubricating Oil.* This Oil has the same fluidity as best Sperm Oil. . . *Austens, Agents of Kerosine Oil Company.* **1858** *Boston Directory* 114, Downer, Samuel, kerosene oil, 76 Water. **1867** *Atlantic Mth.* Feb 156 **PA,** Sharpley trimmed the kerosene-oil lamps freshly. **1908** [see **kerosene**]. **1930** Dobie *Coronado* 102 **SW,** He did not have to raise many cattle in order to keep himself and family supplied with such necessities as Bull Durham, frijoles, salt pork, kerosene oil, calico, and a good buggy. **1937** in 1958 Brewer *Dog Ghosts* 89 **TX** [Black], So he stoops down an' picks up a Coca Cola bottle what layin' on de groun' side de wagon he been settin' in an' goes down to de groce'y sto' . . , an' buys 'im 'nuff kerosene oil to fill up de bottle. **1944** Clark *Pills* 41 **Sth, S Midl,** The back half of the store was devoted to heavy barreled goods. . . of whisky, molasses. . . kerosene. . . Kerosene oil was forever getting into the sugar or the lard or the meat box. **1965–70** *DARE* (Qu. F45, . . *Fuel that's used in an ordinary lamp*) 30 Infs, **scattered, but esp SE, NEast,** Kerosene oil; (Qu. BB50c, *Remedies for infections*) Infs **NC82, VA105,** Kerosene oil; **GA74,** Kerosene oil—on infection; **TX11,** Kerosene-oil poultice; (Qu. BB51b) Inf **TX62,** Rub it with kerosene oil. [29 of 33 Infs old] **1991** Pederson *LAGS Social Matrix* 66 **Gulf Region,** Kerosene oil [42 of 49 infs age 66 or older].

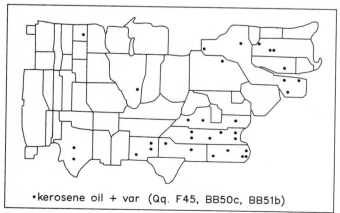
•kerosene oil + var (Qq. F45, BB50c, BB51b)

kerp See **curp**

kerry See **carry A1**

Kerry chicken See **Mother Carey's chicken 1**

ker-winch See **co-wench**

keskatomas See **kiskitomas**

keskydee n Also *kiskeedee* [Var of Fr *Qu'est-ce qu'il dit?* What is he saying?]

See quots.

    1945 Saxon *Gumbo Ya-Ya* 175 **LA,** Creole children . . refused even to speak French because the others taunted them with the appellation of 'Kis-kee-dee!' when they did so. **1971** Carter *Ghost Towns* 21 **CA** (as of 1850s), The English, Scotch, Irish, and Welsh were accepted . . ; but the French were disliked because they kept to themselves, and became known as "Keskydees" because they kept asking "Qu'est-ce qu'il dit?"

ketch v See **catch v A1, 2, 3**

ketch n See **catch n**

ketch colt See **catch colt**

ketch dog See **catch dog**

ketched, ketcht See **catch v A3**

ketchy See **catchy**

kettle n Usu **chiefly Nth, N Midl, West** (See Map) |'kɛtl̩, 'kɛdl̩|; also **chiefly S Midl, also NEast** (See Map) |'kɪtl̩|; for addit varr see quots 1965–70, 1989 Pronc-spp *cattel, kittle* Cf Pronc Intro 3.I.15, 16, 3.II.19 [*OED* cites forms with *i* from c1000 →]

A Forms.

    1633 in 1867 NH *Prov. & State Papers* 1.75, 4 kittles. **1677** in 1896 Hempstead NY *Records* 1.312 **seNY,** He saw . . two Greate Cattels. **1785–99** in 1967 *PADS* 48.40 **NC,** Kittle. **1815** Humphreys *Yankey in England* 106, *Kittle,* kettle. **1823** in 1956 Eliason *Tarheel Talk* 313 **cwNC,** Kittle. **1847** Hurd *Grammatical Corrector* 85, Kettle ["incorrect" pronc = ['kɪtl]; "correct" pronc = ['kɛtl]]. **1903** *DN* 2.291 **Cape Cod MA** (as of a1857), *Kittle.* **1907** *DN* 3.192 **seNH,** Kittle. **1908** *DN* 3.327 **eAL, wGA,** Kittle. . . Common pronunciation. **1910** *DN* 3.444 **wNY,** Now I'll fill the tea-kittle and get supper. **1912** *DN* 3.580 **wIN,** Kittle. . . Very common. **1917** *DN* 4.413 **wNC,** Kittle. **1950** *WELS* (A deep metal container used to boil food) 1 Inf, **WI,** Kettle—occas; kittle—old-fash. **1960** Criswell *Resp. to PADS 20* **Ozarks,** Kittle for kettle, common years ago. About obsolete now. **1961** Kurath–McDavid *Pronc. Engl.* 133 **Atlantic,** With few exceptions, cultured speakers have the vowel /ɛ/ of

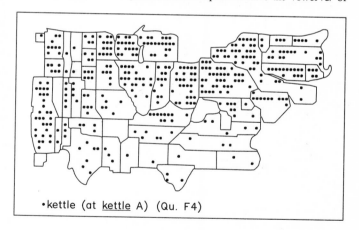
•kettle (at kettle A) (Qu. F4)

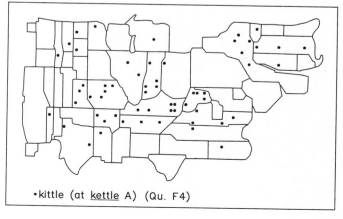
•kittle (at kettle A) (Qu. F4)

bet in kettle. . . [T]he /ɪ/ of *bit* is rather regular in folk speech, except for highly urbanized areas. The usage of the middle group varies, /ɪ/ being common in rural areas, as in northern New England, central Pennsylvania, the Appalachians, and the greater part of North Carolina, /ɛ/ elsewhere. **1965–70** *DARE* (Qu. F4) 402 Infs, **chiefly Nth, N Midl, West,** [proncs of the types [ˈkɛt(ə)l, ˈkɛd(ə)l]]; 59 Infs, **chiefly S Midl, also NEast,** [proncs of the types [ˈkɪt(ə)l, ˈkɪd(ə)l, ˈkɪʔl]]] [29 of 59 Infs comm type 5, 27 gs educ or less]; **MA**44, 50, **RI**12, 14, **VA**53, [ˈkɛʔl]; **OH**11, [ˈkʌt̬l]; **OH**36, [ˈkʌdl]; **MI**115, [ˈkedəl]. **1976** Allen *LAUM* 3.272 **Upper MW** (as of c1950), *Kettle*. . . Of . . 157 infs. . . only 39, or 25%, have the [ɪ] pronunciation; and 30 of those are in the oldest and least educated group. . . The higher frequency in Iowa may reflect a strong Midland background derived from the common occurrence of [ɪ] in central Pennsylvania. **1989** Pederson *LAGS Tech. Index* 68 **Gulf Region,** [504 infs gave proncs of the types [ˈkɛt(ə)l, ˈkɛd(ə)l]; 235 infs, [ˈkɪt(ə)l, ˈkɪd(ə)l]; 25 infs, [ˈkjɪt(ə)l, ˈkjɛt(ə)l]; 6 infs, [ˈkæt(ə)l]].

B Senses.

1 also in combs: A deep metal cooking vessel, usu having a bail handle. **widespread, but less freq Sth** See Map and Map Section Cf **boiler** n[1] **1, dinner kettle 2, pot** Note: Some of the quots at **A** may also refer to this sense.

1843 (1916) Hall *New Purchase* 433 **IN,** As round as a sugar kittle. **1902** (1969) Sears *Catalogue* 582, *Imperial All Enameled Cast Kettle*. . . Diameter at top in. 9½[.] 10⅝[.] 11½[.] Depth, inches . . 6½[.] 7⅛[.] 8. **1950** *WELS* **WI** (*A deep metal container used to boil food*) 42 Infs, Kettle; 1 Inf, A kettle has a handle across the top, a saucepan at the side; 1 Inf, Kettle—with handle like a pail; 1 Inf, A kettle—with a bail; 1 Inf, Cooking kettle. **1951** Johnson *Resp. to PADS 20* **DE,** A deep metal container used to boil food—kettle. **1954** *Harder Coll.* **cwTN,** Kettle—a deep metal container used to cook beans. **1960** [see **kettle cousin**]. **1965–70** *DARE* (Qu. F4, . . *The deep metal container used to boil foods*) 475 Infs, **widespread, but less freq Sth,** Kettle; **MI**68, Kettle, pot—cast iron, three-legged, rounded at bottom and sides, smaller at the top; 11 Infs, **scattered,** Stew(ing) kettle; **MI**68, Stewing pan or kettle—deeper than a frying pan, maybe larger in diameter; **NC**43, Aluminum kettle; **IA**18, Berlin [ˈbɝlɪn] [=boiling] kettle—the large one to boil a ham in; **KY**85, Dinner kettle; **MA**69, Iron kettle; **NY**72, Potato kettle; **IA**25, Scotch kettle—stood on tripod legs; old-fashioned; **MI**69, Soup kettle. **1990** Pederson *LAGS Regional Matrix* 48 **widespread Gulf Region, but less freq coastal Gulf, GA,** 355 infs, Kettle.

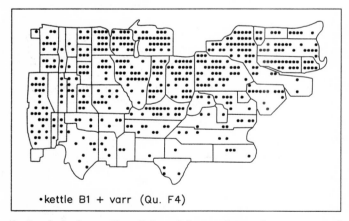

•kettle B1 + varr (Qu. F4)

2 A relatively small or lightweight metal vessel, esp one used for carrying food. **Nth** Cf **dinner kettle 1**

1871 Eggleston *Hoosier Schoolmaster* 110 **IN,** He'll . . make us both as 'shamed of ourselves as dogs with tin-kittles to their tails. **1877** Bartlett *Americanisms* 331, *Kettle*. . . a dinner-pail. **1907** *DN* 3.243 **eME,** *Dinner kettle*. . . Dinner pail. *Ibid* 250, *Tin kettle*. . . A tin pail, particularly a dinner pail. **1923** *DN* 5.235 **swWI,** *Kettle*. . . A tin pail. **1939** *LANE* Map 130 **seME,** Various covered containers, usually . . made of tin, in which farmers and laborers carry the food for their midday meal. . . [5 infs] *dinner kettle.* **1960** Korson *Black Rock* 202 **PA,** In the West End a miner carried his underground dinner in a two-quart round container termed a "kettle." **1969** *DARE* (Qu. F22b, . . *"He had his lunch in a _____."*) Inf **RI**1, Used to take lunch in a lard kettle to school.

3 also *mill kettle, teakettle:* A steam engine, esp a steam locomotive. Cf **coffeepot 1, teapot**

1926 *AmSp* 1.250 **PA** [Railroading terms], Locomotives are "mills" or "kettles." **1931** *Writer's Digest* 11.40 [Railroad terms], *Tea Kettle or Teapot*—Locomotive. **1932** *Santa Fe Employes' Mag.* Jan 34, A locomotive is known as a *mill kettle.* **1932** *RR Mag.* Oct 368, *Kettle*—Locomotive. *Ibid* 370, *Teakettle*—Leaky, old locomotive; any small engine. **1958** McCulloch *Woods Words* 101 **Pacific NW,** *Kettle*—Most any steam equipment, a donkey or locie or other engine, especially if it leaked steam. *Ibid* 191, *Tea kettle.* **1962** *AmSp* 37.134 **nwCA,** *Kettle*. . . A locomotive which leaked steam. **1969** Sorden *Lumberjack Lingo* 128 **NEng, Gt Lakes,** *Tea kettle outfit*—A small mill crew.

4 The boiler of a still; a still.

1942 Faulkner *Go Down* 60 **MS,** He's running a kettle in that gully. . . If you want the whiskey too, look under his kitchen floor. **1957** Faulkner *Town* 317 **MS,** They now called the pots "kettles" though the drink (even I can remember this) was still usquebaugh. **1968** *Foxfire* Fall/Winter 49 **nGA,** *Still*—the container into which the beer is placed for boiling. Also called the . . Kettle. **1974** Dabney *Mountain Spirits* xxi [Corn whiskey glossary], *Copper Pot:* Sometimes called a "copper," or kettle, this still . . was a favorite along the Appalachians and can still be found in isolated spots in the hills. . . Also called the buccaneer, the blockade still, and mountain teapot.

kettle band n Cf **callithumpian** n b, **horning** n 1, **tin-panning**
A group of people using kettles and other makeshift instruments to make a loud racket.
    1967 *DARE* (Qu. AA18, . . *A noisy neighborhood celebration after a wedding, where the married couple is expected to give a treat*) Inf **PA**42, Kettle band.

kettle cousin n
    1960 Williams *Walk Egypt* 76 **GA,** When he was eight years old, a tornado had bellowed out of the . . west. It . . took . . the house . . and Wick's family with it. . . He [=the only survivor] had become a kettle-cousin, living around from relative to relative, licking the kettle for his supper.

kettle-de-bender See **kittly-bender**

kettle halyard n Also *kitchen halyard* [**kettle B1** + *halyard* tackle for hoisting and lowering]
    1916 Macy–Hussey *Nantucket Scrap Basket* 137 **seMA,** "Kettle Halyards," or sometimes "Kitchen Halyards"—refers to domestic duties, especially of a culinary nature or work in the kitchen. In the absence of the mother, a child was often left to "tend the kettle halyards."

kettle meal n [**kettle B1**]
=**boiled dinner.**
    1967 *DARE* (Qu. H49, *Dishes made by boiling potatoes with other foods*) Inf **PA**22, Kettle meal—everything boiled.

kettle meat n [**kettle B1**]
    1968 *DARE* (Qu. H43, *Foods made from parts of the head and inner organs of an animal*) Inf **PA**136, Heart, liver, head are kettle meat.

kettlepot n [Folk-etym; cf **skillpot**] Cf **killpot, steelpot**
=**mud turtle 2b(1).**
    1970 *DARE* (Qu. P24, . . *Kinds of turtles*) Inf **VA**38, Kettle[ˈkɪd]pot.

kettle-stretcher See **stretcher**

kettle tea n [Cf *EDD* kettle-broth (at *kettle* sb.[1] 1.(4))] **esp S Midl** Cf **cambric tea, hot-water tea, milk tea**
A drink made of hot water, usu with milk and sugar.
    1906 *DN* 3.144 **nwAR,** *Kittle tea*. . . Hot water with an admixture of milk and sugar. **1908** *DN* 3.324 **eAL, wGA,** *Kettle-tea*. . . Tea made of hot water, milk and sugar. Also called *hot-water tea.* **1950** *PADS* 14.42 **SC,** *Kettle tea*. . . 1. Cambric tea, tea made of hot water, milk and sugar. 2. Plain hot water, with or without sugar, which some people drink, usually before breakfast, for their health. **1956** McAtee *Some Dialect NC* 25, *Kettle tea:* . . drink made from hot water, milk, and sugar.

kever See **cover**

kewcumber See **cucumber**

kewrus See **curious** adj

kewster n [Cf obs Engl *coistrel, custrel* a knight's page; a knave, base fellow; cf *SND custril* n. "A fool, a foolish person"] Cf **cooster** n 1, **cooter** n 7, **skeester**
    1967 *DARE* (Qu. Z16, *A small child who is rough, misbehaves, and*

doesn't obey, you'd call him a _____) Inf **TN**2, Kewster [ˈkjustɚ]—
old-fashioned.

key n

1 Used in var phrr and combs for a nonexistent item used as
the basis of a practical joke. *joc*

1942 Berrey–Van den Bark *Amer. Slang* 281.8, *Fictitious objects used
in practical jokes. . .* key to the compass *(sailor).* **1965–70** *DARE* (Qu.
HH14, *Ways of teasing a beginner or inexperienced person—for example, by sending him for a 'left-handed monkey wrench': "Go get me
_____."*) Infs **MA**11, **MI**110, A (*or* the) key for a (*or* to) keelson;
NY141, **PA**219, A (*or* the) key(s) to the oarlocks; **GA**3, Stove key—for
electric heater; **IL**71, The key to the flagpole—Army term; **TX**11, Key
to the flagpole; **CA**15, The key to the situation; **NJ**18, Key to the
sundial; **NJ**39, Key to the johnny box; **NC**52, A cupalo key—a cupalo
is an iron-melting furnace; **SD**8, Key to the curtains; **TN**1, Breakthrough
keys—in coal mines; **TN**14, Parade key—Army, World War I; **TX**43,
A key to the clearinghouse—banking business; **VA**5, A key to the drill
ground—learned this in the Navy; **WA**22, The key to the pitcher's box.
1980 Banks *First-Person America* 84 **IL** (as of 1939), Every drift mine
has a hole called the "sump" dug at its lowest point for the seepage to
drain into. Every greenhorn in a mine is sent all around the place looking
for "the key to the sump."

2 The winged fruit of a **maple** or similar tree. [*OED* 1523 →]
Cf **hanger 4, maplewings, monkey** n¹ **7, pollynose, whirly-
bird**

1714 (1860) Lawson *Hist. Carolina* 166, It [=the sycamore] bears no
keys but a bur like the sweet gum. **1906** (1907) Dickerson *Frog Book*
64, We stand at the edge of a pond, under a maple brilliant with its
fringes of red keys. **1960** Teale *Journey into Summer* 3 **NH,** As we
stood . . listening to whitethroats and wood thrushes in the dawn, watching a red squirrel gathering maple keys from the topmost twigs below
us, the coming of the second season was ushering in the longest day of
the year. **1966** Grimm *Recognizing Native Shrubs* 179, Maple fruits,
called "keys," have a seed-bearing portion tipped with a broad flat wing.
1995 *NADS Letters* **csMA,** My kids called the keys or samaras "propellers" for a time—until the Frisbee took their attention.

3 freq in combs, esp *stove key:* =**hook** n **4. chiefly S Atl,
AL** See Map and Map Section Cf **cap** n¹ **2a, eye** n¹ **1**

1965–70 *DARE* (Qu. F11, *The thing you use to remove the lids . .
from a wood-burning stove when it is hot*) 24 Infs, **esp S Atl, AL,** Stove
key; 16 Infs, **esp S Atl, AL,** Key; **GA**1, **SC**38, Eye key; **GA**8, Cap key.

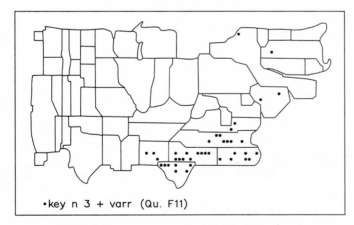

•key n 3 + varr (Qu. F11)

4 in comb *key bundle:* The top bundle of a stack of grain or
hay; hence v *key* to finish off a stack with such a bundle. Cf
cap n¹ **1**

1966 *DARE* (Qu. L31, . . *The top bundle of a shock*) Inf **WA**31, Key
bundle—it held the others together; **OK**52, Capping out the top, keying
the top.

5 See **key log.**

6 The fruitlet of a screw pine (here: *Pandanus tectorius*);
see quot.

1994 Stone–Pratt *Hawai'i's Plants* 61, *Hala or Screwpine. . .* is a tree
characteristic of wet to moist coastal forests in windward Hawai'i. . .
Tiny female flowers occur in round clusters at branch tips; these later
develop into large, globose, collective fruits containing many (perhaps

50) fruitlets or "keys". . . When ripe, these keys are brightly variegated
yellow, orange, or red and may be strung into colorful leis.

key v, key bundle See **key** n **4**

keyhole n

A marble game; see quot.

c1970 Wiersma *Marbles Terms* **MS,** *Keyhole . .* a game of marbles; a
hole is dug in the ground in the shape of a key-hole, and small "toar
[*DARE* Ed: prob =taw] balls" . . are placed around the outside; the first
man to knock one of the "toar balls" into the "keyhole" from a three-foot
distance (approx.) wins the other marbles lined up around the "keyhole"
(each player puts one or two "toars" around, depending on the number
of players.)

key log n Also *key*

In a logjam: a log that must be dislodged to release the other
logs.

1851 (1856) Springer *Forest Life* 166 **ME,** It may be thought best to
cut off the key-log, or that which appears to be the principal barrier.
1860 *Harper's New Mth. Mag.* 20.452 **ME,** The most vulnerable point—
the "key-log" of the jam—is sought. **1873** Beadle *Undeveloped West*
719 **csMN,** There is generally what is called a "key-log," and by
attaching a rope thereto the whole mass is loosened. Climbing over the
"jam," hunting for this "key-log," and loosening it, is a most perilous
business. **1902** White *Blazed Trail* 226 **MI,** This had to be done by
pulling out or chopping through certain "key" logs which locked the
whole mass. **1905** U.S. Forest Serv. *Bulletin* 61.40 [Logging terms], Key
log. In river driving, a log which is so caught or wedged that a jam is
formed and held. **1930** Shoemaker *1300 Words* 36 **cPA Mts** (as of
c1900), *Key*—A log which if struck loose, releases a "jam." **1932**
Wasson *Sailing Days* 86 **cME coast,** Expert river-drivers from up-
stream, lithe active men accustomed to singling out and destroying the
"key-logs" of log jams, would try their hands on this ice barrier with
varying success. **1968** *DARE* Tape **WI**59, When the ice started melting
out, you'd have what was known as a logjam—could be 2000 logs . .
maybe 40 feet high. . . An expert, he'd look them over, study it. There's
always a key log or a couple of key logs; if you could find this particular
log or logs and loosen it up, you probably would solve your problem;
WI67, Somebody would have to go out and pull the key log, and that
would break the jam, and they'd float on down the river.

key western crooked adj phr Cf **hell-west and crooked; high,
west, and crooked**

=**sky, west, and crooked.**

1908 *DN* 3.326 **eAL, wGA,** *Key weste(r)n crooked. . .* Completely
out of shape, position, business, etc. "He knocked him key-western
crooked."

keywinding adj Cf **key western crooked**

1951 Rayford *Child Snapping Turtle* 2 (as of c1820s), Andy fired at
the cup on Mike's [=Mike Fink's] head. . . [T]he bullet . . knocked the
cup key-winding.

k'flummux See **flummox** v

ki- pref See **ker-**

ki n See **ti**

ki intj Also *ka(h), kai, kih, kwi, kwoy* [W Afr; cf 1949 Turner
Africanisms 196] esp **sSC, GA coast** *Gullah* Cf *DJE*

Used as an expression of amazement, denial, consternation,
etc; see quots.

1835 Longstreet *GA Scenes* 47 [Black], Ki, massa! how gwine cut live
chicken in two? **1864** (1868) Trowbridge *Cudjo's Cave* 56 **TN** [Black],
Ki! How fat he ar! **1872** (1973) Thompson *Major Jones's Courtship*
170 **GA** [Black], Kih! . . dat mus be ole Santa-claus heself. **1883** (1971)
Harris *Nights with Remus* 142 **GA** [Black], Ki, B'er Rabbit! wut dis is
mek you blow so? Wut mekky you' bre't' come so? **1922** Gonzales
Black Border 309 **sSC, GA coasts** [Gullah glossary], Ki—an exclamation. (Sometimes "kwi" or "kwoy"). **1926** Smith *Gullah* 32 **sSC, GA
coasts,** There are curiously few survivals of native African words in
Gullah. . . The commonest are the exclamation *ki* (or *kai*) to express
wonder or to add emphasis to a statement, and *buckra* for white man.
1928 Peterkin *Scarlet Sister Mary* 129 **SC** [Gullah], But Ki! Dat ain'
reason fo cry! **1942** *Sat. Eve. Post* 14 Feb 20 [Black], Kah-ka-ka! *Ibid*
50, Kah-ka-ka! Boy, you's foolin.

kiack See **kyack** n¹

kiawe n Also sp *keawe* [Haw] **HI**
=honey mesquite.

1916 HI Ag. Exper. Sta. *Press Bulletin* 26.1, The algaroba, or keawe *(Prosopis juliflora),* is commonly recognized as the most valuable tree which has thus far been introduced into the Territory of Hawaii. **1929** Neal *Honolulu Gardens* 136, *Kiawe, algaroba, mesquite [Prosopis juliflora].* . . The algaroba, locally known as the *kiawe,* is a fairly large tree . . with sinewy trunk and branches and widespreading crown. **1955** Day *HI People* 263, [They] plunged their [air]craft into a clump of keawe trees on Molokai. **1967** *DARE* (Qu. T16, . . *Kinds of trees* . . *'special'*) Inf **HI**11, Algiroba—kiawe. **1967** *DARE* Tape **HI**2, He brought in the . . kiawe or algaroba, which is called a mesquite. **1972** Carr *Da Kine Talk* 87 **HI,** *Hawaiian Words Commonly Heard In Hawaii's English.* . . *Kiawe.* Algaroba or mesquite tree. **1980** Bushnell *Water of Kane* 395 **HI,** Looks like I must wear the crown of kiawe thorns.

kib n
1975 Gould *ME Lingo* 153, *Kib*—An invention of Maine woodsmen to keep black flies at bay while sleeping. A box-like frame was covered with netting to permit breathing, and one side was open for the communicant to stick in his head. The loose end of the netting about the neck was tucked under the blanket or jacket collar. The *kib* amounted to a screened-in porch just big enough for one man's head.

kibby n[1] See **kivver**

kibby n[2] [Cf *EDD kib* sb.[1] "A small bone in a sheep's foot, used in playing the game of 'Bobber and kibbs' . . also a small cube of earthenware, used in the same game"]
A marble; see quot.

1967–68 *DARE* (Qu. EE6a, . . *Different kinds of marbles—the big one that's used to knock others out of the ring*) Inf **OH**66, Kibby; (Qu. EE6b, *Small marbles or marbles in general*) Inf **OH**20, Kibbies.

kibby v See **cubbie**

kick v, hence ppl adj *kicked* Usu |kɪk|; also |kik| Pronc-sp *keeck*
A Form. [*SND kick* v. "Also *kik, keek*"]
1917 *DN* 4.413 **wNC,** *Keeck.* . . Variant of *kick.*

B Senses.
1 also with *out;* rarely with *off:* To reject or jilt (a suitor); to turn (someone) down. **chiefly sAppalachians, S Atl** See Map Cf **mitten** v **1**

1809 Mrs. Ann Simons in *Singleton P.* in *So. Hist. Coll.* (at U. of N.C.) 1 Sep. *(DA),* A lady whom I met. . . affirmed that poor Ashby had been kicked by you. . . She insisted upon the fact and concluded by saying, he still wished to renew his suit. **1845** in 1956 Eliason *Tarheel Talk* 280 **cnNC,** I am fearful. . . that I would be fool enough to make a speech to [a girl], and if so I would get kicked so far I would hardly get back in a coons age. **1865** Byrn *Advent. Fudge Fumble* 169 **TN,** I found out I was not the only one who had been "kicked," for she was a most notorious coquette, having rejected . . twenty-three chances. **1881** Pierson *In the Brush* 8, They did not say the lady rejected or "mittened" her suitor, but, "She kicked him." The first time I ever heard that figure used was at a social gathering in Richmond, Virginia, in 1843. **1895** *Outing* 27.74 **VA,** Some years ago, when a Suffolk gal kicked me. **1908** *DN* 3.326 **eAL, wGA,** *Kick.* . . To jilt, reject as a suitor. **1941** *LANE* Map 407A, *She refused him.* . . meaning . . She rejected his proposal of marriage. . . 10 infs, **nNEng,** Kicked him; 3 infs, **eNEng,** Kicked him

out; 1 inf, **swME,** Kicked him off; 2 infs, **eME,** Kicked him = 'refused to walk home with him from a party.' **1946** *PADS* 5.27 **VA,** *Kick.* . . Jilt (someone); common. **1950** *PADS* 14.42 **SC,** *Kick.* . . To jilt. **1966–70** *DARE* (Qu. AA11, *If a man asks a girl to marry him and she refuses,* . . *she* _____) Infs **GA**57, **NC**48, **TX**35, **VA**18, Kicked him; **SC**24, Kicked him—*very old, never hear it now* [FW sugg]; (Qu. AA12, *If a man loses interest in a girl and stops seeing her* . . *he* _____) Infs **GA**8, **NC**45, Kicked her; **VA**90, Kicked her—used by older people. **1986** Pederson *LAGS Concordance (She turned him down)* 10 infs, **chiefly GA, nFL,** (She *or* she's) kicked him; 1 inf, **seGA,** Kicked him = stopped seeing him; 1 inf, **swGA,** She kicked him = refused proposal or broke up; 1 inf, **csGA,** She kicked him—they used to say this; 1 inf, **nwFL,** She kicked him—stopped courting, or at proposal; 3 infs, **AL, TN, TX,** (She) kicked him out.

2 usu with *off;* also with *in, over, out,* or *up:* To die. **scattered, but chiefly west of Appalachians** See Map

1912 *NY Eve. Jrl.* (NY) 8 April 14 *(Zwilling Coll.),* [Cartoon:] He told a friend that his sweetheart had kicked off and he was in mourning. **1920** Lewis *Main Street* 175 **cwMN,** Not that I care a whoop what they say, after I've kicked in and can't hear 'em. **1921** Dos Passos *3 Soldiers* 61, Another kid's kicked off with that—what d'they call it?—menegitis. **1927** *Ruppenthal Coll.* **KS,** *Kick off*—to die. "I thought for a while he'd kick off." **1943** *LANE* Map 521 *(Kicked the bucket)* NEng, 5 infs, Kicked out; 4 infs, Kicked off; 1 inf, Kicked up; 1 inf, Kicked in. **1950** *WELS* **WI** *(Ways [serious or joking]* . . *for saying someone died)* 4 Infs, Kicked off; 1 Inf, Kicked in. **1965–70** *DARE* (Qu. BB56, *Joking expressions for dying: "He* _____.") 58 Infs, **scattered, but chiefly west of Appalachians,** Kicked off; 13 Infs, **esp S Midl,** Kicked out; **CA**144, **MO**11, 25, **PA**147, Kicked in; **MO**15, Kicking up; (Qu. BB54, *When a sick person is past hope of recovery* . . *he's [a]* _____) Inf **OK**7, About to kick off. **1986** Pederson *LAGS Concordance* **Gulf Region** *(Died)* 21 infs, Kicked off; 15 infs, (He) kicked out; 3 infs, Kicked; 1 inf, Kicked over. **1992** *DARE* File, Kick in—die, kick the bucket.

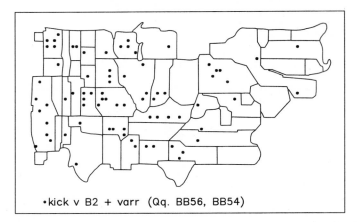

•kick v B2 + varr (Qq. BB56, BB54)

3 with *out* or *up:* To flush (an animal) from cover. **esp C Atl, Gt Lakes** See Map

1948 *WELS Suppl.* **cwWI,** He is a York State descendent. Also, he speaks of "kicking up" a deer instead of starting one, in going through the woods. **1960** Criswell *Resp. to PADS 20* **Ozarks** *(Making a hunted animal run)* Usually, one *kicked out* a rabbit when snow was deep. **1964** Babcock *Jaybirds* 69 **VA,** To our surprise the birds held so snugly that we had to kick them up. **1965–70** *DARE* (Qu. P39a, *When a hunter or a dog finds a game animal and makes it start running* . . *he* _____ *it*) Infs **PA**35, 38, 47, 155, Kicked (*or* kick) it out; **MI**32, Kicks him out; **MD**31, **MI**71, **NC**48, **NJ**60, **OH**6, Kicked it up; **TN**11, Kicked up; (Qu. P39b, *If a hunter or a dog makes a bird or a covey fly*) Inf **TN**11, Kicked up. [10 of 11 Infs male] **1966–68** *DARE* Tape **IN**36, When you see him pointing, why, you know he's got 'em and you just walk over and kick 'em up. And off they go, and you're expecting 'em then; **NC**24, You can't make one go in the direction you want him to go. A dog will have a bird pointed and you'll say, "Well, I'm gonna make him go out into this open place," and you walk up there and try to kick him out, kick him up, make him fly to that open place where you can get an open shot at him and he'll fly right straight in your face. **1991** *DARE* File **NEast, WI,** The term 'to kick up' game is well known and commonly used by everyone I've ever hunted with. I might say, "I think I'll go out and see if I can kick up some rabbits." 'Kick up' can be used with any game, birds or animals, that will flush.

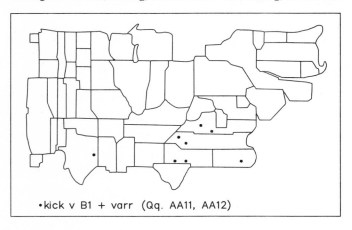

•kick v B1 + varr (Qq. AA11, AA12)

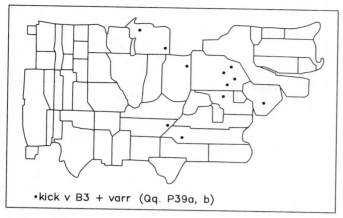

•kick v B3 + varr (Qq. P39a, b)

4 also with *up:* To toss (hay) with a tedder or other implement to speed drying. Cf **kicker** n **4b**

1925 *Book of Rural Life* 4.2533, This machine [=a hay tedder] is designed to kick up the newly mown hay so that it will cure more quickly and evenly. **1966** *DARE* File **WV**, *"Ted" the hay*—stir or "kick" the hay to loosen or turn it for drying. Done with a machine called a "tedder". **1969–70** *DARE* (Qu. L11, *What do you do to hay in the field after it's cut?*) Inf **KY**80, Kick it—old-fashioned—a machine . . kicked the hay into the air to fluff it up; **IN**77, Kick it up in piles. [Both Infs old]

5 with *through:* To pay up. **Pacific NW** See Map Cf **come through 3**

1965–70 *DARE* (Qu. U18, *If you force somebody to pay money that he owes you, but that he did not want to pay* ___.") Infs **OR**2, 17, **WA**1, 11, 30, Kick through; **WA**13, Kick out [corr to] kick through; (Qu. U8b, . . *"I paid ten dollars for it."*) Inf **CA**137, Kicked through. [6 of 7 total Infs male, 6 old]

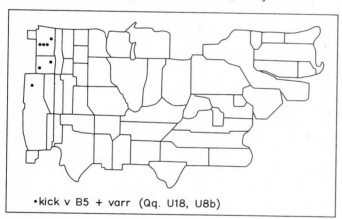

•kick v B5 + varr (Qq. U18, U8b)

6 in phrr *I'll be kicked (by a mule):* See quot. Cf **cow-kicked, I'll be**

1969–70 *DARE* (Qu. NN25b, *Weakened substitutes for 'damn' or 'damned': "Well, I'll be* ___!") Inf **CT**25, Kicked [laughter]; (Qu. NN7, *Exclamations of surprise: "They're getting married next week? Well,* ___.") Inf **PA**234, I'll be kicked by a mule.

kick n

1 See quot. Cf **boot** n[1] **1a, lagniappe**

1967–69 *DARE* (Qu. U15, *When you're buying something, if the seller puts in a little extra to make you feel that you're getting a good bargain*) Inf **TX**68, Kick.

2 in phr *not to give a kick:* Not to care at all. *euphem*

1965–70 *DARE* (Qu. GG21b, *If you don't care what a person does . . "Go ahead—I don't give a* ___.") Infs **OK**1, **VA**69, Kick.

Kickapoojian n Also sp *Kickapoojan* [*Kickapoo* R, in southwestern Wisconsin] Cf **amarugian, hoojin, Kentuck 2b** See quots.

1950 *WELS Suppl.* **cwWI**, Kickapoojan—A resident of the Kickapoo Valley. Descendant of Georgia mountaineers who settled in Richland County. Somewhat derogatory. Used in Sandy Plains, Jackson County, by neighbors of Kickapoojans who lived there. **1993** *DARE* File **cwWI**

(as of 1940s), In Black River Falls and the nearby area, settlers from the American South in the Kickapoo River Valley are called Kickapoojians [ˌkɪkəˈpuʤənz]. The name is jocular or lightly disdainful.

kickboard n
A baseboard.
1969 *DARE* (Qu. D37, *The strip of wood about eight inches high along the bottom of the wall [inside a room] joining to the floor*) Inf **GA**80, Kickboard—some people say. [Inf is a builder and carpenter.]

kick-can See **kick the can 3**

kicked, I'll be See **kick v B6**

kicker n[1]

1 A device to prevent a cow from kicking when being milked.
[**1923** Sears *Catalogue* 838, *Anti-cow kicker.* . . A satisfactory device for hobbling a cow to prevent kicking while milking.] **1969** *DARE* Tape **MO**32, He's almost got killed a few times up there at the barn. We had some really mean cows, even with kickers on their feet. . . If she has a sore udder . . and you go to put these milkers on there . . she'd just haul off. **1986** Pederson *LAGS Concordance*, 1 inf, **neTX**, Kickers—chain for cow's back leg, prevent kicking.

2 A shoe or boot, esp one with a sharp toe; see quots. Cf **ass-kicker, shit-kicker**
1942 Berrey–Van den Bark *Amer. Slang* 87.33, *Shoes.* . . Kickers, kicks. [*Ibid* 121.29, *Feet.* . . Kickers, kicks.] **1950** *WELS (Canvas top shoes with rubber soles)* 1 Inf, **WI**, Kickers; **1965–70** *DARE* (Qu. W11, *Men's low, rough work shoes*) Inf **OR**1, Kickers; (Qu. W42a, . . *Nicknames . . for men's sharp-pointed shoes*) Infs **AR**47, **ID**4, **ND**3, **TN**31, **UT**12, Kickers; **TX**37, Kickers—boots, I think; **MO**15, Sharp-toed kickers; [**IL**68, Kicking shoes;] (Qu. W42b, . . *Nicknames for men's square-toed shoes*) Inf **CA**122, Kickers; **IL**88, Kickers [FW: Inf unsure]. **1975** *AmSp* 50.62 **AR** (as of c1970), [University slang:] Kickers . . Shoes, especially canvas shoes with rubber soles. **1991** *DARE* File **wNE, Dallas TX**, There are two kinds of boots, both of which have pointed toes: kickers and shit-kickers. Men wore kickers for dancing. Kickers have an inch, inch-and-a-half heel and are made out of rare, reptilian leathers—alligator, different kinds of snake, even armadillo. . . People go dancing to Western music and most of these dances involved stomping, so you need a hard heel; kickers are just what you want. . . Shit-kickers are your everyday work boots, and that's what they're called, "shit-kickers." They're made out of horse hide or ordinary leather. People wore shit-kickers in western Nebraska too but out there nobody had kickers.

3 Any of var mechanical devices imparting quick movement, as:
a An outboard motor for a small boat; a boat having such a motor; an inboard auxiliary motor.
1911 *Century Dict. Suppl.*, *Kicker.* . . *Naut.*, the propeller of a small launch. **1942** Rawlings *Cross Creek* 125 **FL**, We want to borrow your outboard motor. We've all paddled until we're give out. . . We'll cover the lake with the kicker. **1943** *AK Sportsman* Oct 10 (Tabbert *Dict. Alaskan Engl.*) **seAK**, Here anyone living within a few hours' travel by row-boat, "kicker," or gasboat is our neighbor. **1948** *AK Sportsman* Jan 31 **cAK**, Sometimes on the Tanana it was necessary to tie up to some cottonwood trees on the bank while the kicker, Yukon terminology for outboard motor boat, went ahead to find the channel. **1954** *Living Wilderness* 19.50.4 **seGA**, We started . . all of us in a good-sized bateau, using a kicker and towing three dugouts. We proceeded by motor up the old . . canal. **1965–70** *DARE* (Qu. O11, . . *An outboard motor*) 144 Infs, **widespread exc W Midl**, Kicker; **FL**13, **LA**40, **SC**69, Stern kicker. **1966–68** *DARE* Tape **DE**1, The outboard motor is come [sic] from the little kicker, as they call it . . ; they have seventy-five and hundred horsepower; **FL**16, We have our own boat, and we have a small kicker. **1986** Pederson *LAGS Concordance*, 1 inf, **nwFL**, Kicker—in bow of bird-dog boat; 1 inf, **nwFL**, Kicker—motor on a small boat; 1 inf, **ceFL**, A kicker—an outboard motor. **1987** *AK Mag.* Aug A-6 [sic Tabbert *Dict. Alaskan Engl.*—quot not found], We might go a thousand miles and not see another vessel. Just a local kicker-boat. **1990** *DARE* File **Gulf coast FL**, With a motor boat, a kicker is used to mean a small auxiliary motor. I call it an "outboard," but other Florida people say "kicker." The "small" is relative too: a ten-horse motor on a very large boat is a kicker, but the same motor on a small rowboat is a real *engine.* With sailing it's a little different. For a sailboat, the primary source of power is the wind, and your secondary source is your kicker, your motor.
b also *hay kicker:* A **tedder.** Cf **kick v B4**
[**1925** *Book of Rural Life* 2532, Hay Tedder. . . This machine consists

of a number of forks which give a kicking motion to the rear as the machine passes over the hay, thereby lifting the hay and leaving it lying loosely on the stubble.] **1950** *WELS (Machines used . . in handling hay)* 1 Inf, **WI,** Hay kicker. **1965–70** *DARE* (Qu. L16, *Machines used . . in handling hay)* Infs **MA**75, **NJ**17, Hay kicker—(official name is a) tedder; **PA**169, Hay kicker; **RI**4, Hay kicker—takes it and tosses it up so it dries on all sides; **IN**35, Kicker—lifts it up so the sun can get at it; **IN**77, **NY**9, Kicker; **NC**30, Kicker—stirs it to dry it; **OH**35, Kicker—to cure it [FW: Used by Inf in conv].

c A machine that throws baled hay from the baler to the accompanying wagon.

1968–69 *DARE* (Qu. L16, *Machines used . . in handling hay)* Inf **MD**20, Kicker—attached to baler, throws hay back on wagon; (Qu. L13, *The kind of wagon used for carrying hay: [. . special wagon, or frame put on ordinary wagon]*) Inf **NY**160, Kicker wagon—in current use.

4 A **red-neck;** a cowboy or would-be cowboy. Cf **shit-kicker**

1986 Pederson *LAGS Concordance* **ce,csTX,** 1 inf, Kicker—runs around in cowboy hat, pickup truck; 1 inf, Kicker = a cowboy?; 1 inf, Kicker shirt—cowboy wears, Western, pearl snaps; *(A rustic)* 1 inf, Kicker—same as "red-neck," in rodeo, wears boots; I'm not a kicker— why he avoids Western clothes; 1 inf, Kicker—a cowboy or Westerner; 1 inf, Kicker—likes Western clothes and music; 1 inf, Kicker—short for "shit kicker"; 1 inf, Cow kicker—cowboy; *(Poor Whites)* 1 inf, Kicker, shit kicker, wears boots, a dude—pejorative; kicker music—country and western; *(A dance)* 1 inf, Kicker dance—could be square dancing or rock; 1 inf, Kicker dancing—same as Western dancing; *(Music)* 1 inf, Kicker music—country and western, slow dance.

kicker n² See **krieker**

kicker n³ [Echoic]
Either the black **rail** (here: *Laterallus jamaicensis*) or the **yellow rail;** see quots.

1901 *Auk* 18.321 **MA** (as of 1889), As his song invariably began with a series of *kick-kicks* we christened him the 'Kicker' by which name he has since been known among the Cambridge ornithologists. *Ibid* 326, The habits, haunts and especially the voice of the 'Kicker' indicate that he is a Rail of some kind. **1910** Eaton *Birds NY* 281, Nuttall describes the note of the Yellow crake as "an abrupt, cackling cry *'krek, 'krek, 'krek, 'krek, 'kuk, 'k, 'kh.*" Mr J.H. Ames of Toronto describes its note as a scolding *kik-kik-kik-kik-queah.* When much surprised his specimen uttered a longer call *kik-kik-kik-kik-kik-kik-kik-kik-ki-queah,* like the famous Kicker of the Massachusetts marshes. *Ibid* 283, The Kicker . . is supposed to be the Black rail, but may possibly refer to the Yellow rail whose notes are doubtless similar. The commonest Kicker notes are as follows: *Kik-kik-kik, queeah; Kik-kik-kik, ki-queeah.* **1955** MA Audubon Soc. *Bulletin* 39.443 **MA, CT,** Yellow Rail. Kicker . . From a cry which embodies repeatedly a sound like the syllable, *kik.*

kick high v phr
To feel in good health and spirits.

1986 Pederson *LAGS Concordance (How are you?)* 1 inf, **neTX,** I'm not kicking very high = feeling bad; 1 inf, **swAL,** Kicking, but not so high.

kick in v phr
1 See **kick** v **B2.**
2 See quot. [Var of *turn in*]
1968 *DARE* (Qu. X40, *. . Ways . . of saying, "I'm going to bed")* Inf **MO**10, I think I'll kick in.

kicking-colt n Also *kicking-horses* [See quot 1896]
A **jewelweed 1,** usu *Impatiens capensis.*
1892 *Jrl. Amer. Folkl.* 5.93 **eMA,** *Impatiens fulva* . . kicking colt. **1896** *Ibid* 9.184 **cME,** *Impatiens fulva* . . kicking horses . . From the manner in which the ripe seed-vessel bursts open when touched. **1940** Clute *Amer. Plant Names* 130, *I[mpatiens] biflora.* . . Kicking horses, kicking colt.

kicking the can See **kick the can 1**

kick off See **kick** v **B1, 2**

kick one's north end to going south v phr Cf **north end of a chicken flying south**
1970 *DARE* (Qu. Y6, *. . To put pressure on somebody to do something he ought to have done but hasn't: "He's a whole week late. I'm going to _____.")* Inf **TX**104, Kick his north end to goin' south.

kick out See **kick** v **B1, 2, 3**

kick over See **kick the can 3**

kicks exclam, n Cf **bases-out**
In marble play: used to claim the right to move or kick a marble, esp one's shooter when it has been stopped by an obstruction; the privilege so claimed.

1908 *DN* 3.326 **eAL, wGA,** Kicks. . . A term used in marbles as a penalty for the accidental stopping of a taw, as by the feet. **1915** *DN* 4.184 **swVA,** Kicks. . . In game of marbles for the accidental stopping of a "man," especially by an opponent, the player cries out *"kicks"! "kicks"!* and thus wins the right to have his "man" go on to the place, where it presumably would have gone, had it not been interfered with. **1922** *DN* 5.187 **KY,** Kicks. . . A case of one's "taw" hitting some person or animal. If the opponent calls out "kicks," the "taw" must be placed where it presumably would have rolled. This is not necessary if the player first cried out, "Vence ye kicks." **1950** *WELS (Cries or calls used in playing marbles: To stop another player from doing something)* 1 Inf, **WI,** No kicks. **1958** *PADS* 29.35 **WI** [Marbles terms], Kicks. . . In the game of *chase,* a call permitting the player who makes it to drive away his opponent's shooter which he has hit: he places one foot next to the shooter and touching it, then swings the other foot sidewise against his first foot, imparting through it a kick (whence the name) which drives the shooter away (very much as in croquet). **1962** *PADS* 37.2 **cKS** [Marbles terms], Kicks. . . A call used to claim the following advantage: when one's marble hits an object, one may put the outside of his foot against the marble and bring the other foot up sharply against the first so as to make the marble roll. *Ibid, Save my kicks.* A call used to claim the advantage of not taking kicks when the situation occurs in order to take it at some later time.

kick-stick See **kick the stick**

kick Sue in the side v phr For varr see quot [Cf **kick** v **B2, susanside**] Cf **sideways**
To commit suicide.

1966–69 *DARE* (Qu. BB57, *If someone committed suicide . . he _____)* Infs **NY**209, **PA**214, Kicked Suzy in the side; **SC**10, Kick Sue in he side; **SC**27, Kicked Sue in the side—schoolboy's remark of about thirty-five years ago.

kick the ball (or bar, block) See **kick the can 2**

kick the bottle See **kick the can 3**

kick the bucket See **kick the can 1, 3**

kick the can n

1 also *kick the bucket, picket, kicking the can:* A hide-and-seek game that involves sending out or freeing players by kicking a can or other object. [Cf *SND kick the block, ~ bucket, ~ can(nie)* (at *kick* v. 3(6))] Also called **lurky, nurky** Cf **kick the stick, knock the can**

1950 *WELS* **WI** *(Hiding games that start with some . . elaborate way of sending the players out to hide)* 2 Infs, Kick the can; 1 Inf, Kick the can (Tin Can Alley); 1 Inf, Kick the can—"it" would give the can a kick from goal line, then go after it and bring it back to goal; meantime the rest of players find a hiding place. **1952** Brown *NC Folkl.* 1.39, Kicking the Can. . . This is a variant of 'Hide and Seek.' The player who is "It" kicks a can some distance from the base. While he is recovering it, the others hide. **1957** *Sat. Eve. Post Letters* **nwMI** (as of c1900), Kick the can. . . Someone would draw a circle about 2 feet in diameter. . . Someone . . would kick the can that had been placed in the center of the circle. The one who was 'it' had to get it and put it back . . before he could start looking for the others. *Ibid* **OH,** The game is called kick the can. . . While the person who was it was looking for the hidden players, the ones who were not in the penalty box could come out of hiding and kick the can, thus freeing the ones in the penalty box. **1965–70** *DARE* (Qu. EE16, *Hiding games that start with a special, elaborate method of sending the players out to hide)* Infs **NY**130, 172, **OH**8, 15, 37, 42, 63, 65, 82, 84, Kick the can; **NY**250, Kick the can—put the can on the floor. Kick it. The person who's "it" has to get the can and walk backwards to home base. Then he has to find everybody. When I see he's away, I go kick the can; **NY**161, Kick the bucket; (Qu. EE13a, *Games in which every player hides except one, and that one must try to find the others)* Infs **AL**41, **CA**133, **MT**1, 4, **NY**184, **UT**10, Kick the can; **AK**5, Kick the can—this was a can set up by "it" in a hiding game; when "it" left goal to look for hidden players, they tried to sneak in and kick the can. He had to replace it before he could go looking again; **NM**9, Kick the can—player kicks a can instead of counting, otherwise similar [to hide-and-seek]; **SD**3, Kick the picket—if the picket is kicked by someone, those who have been caught can rehide; **TX**68, Hide-and-(go-)seek or "kick the bucket"—to come in free, you kick the bucket; (Qu. EE12, *Games in which one captain hides his team and the other team tries to find it*) Inf **CA**32, Hide-and-go-seek; kick the can; **IN**39, Kick the can—same as run sheep run; (Qu. EE18) Inf **CT**11, Kick the can—you have to kick the can without the person who is "it" catching you, then you hide again; **ID**1, Kick the can—similar to hide-and-go-seek, kick a can instead of touching a home base; **MD**20, Kick the can—hiding and kicking a can were involved; **MI**69, Kick the can—somebody trying to guard the can, somebody kicks it, everybody goes and hides while the man who was "it" went and got it; **RI**15, Kick the can—don't try to knock it down, count to ten and others hide; **VT**16, Kick the can [Inf unsure]—a form of hide-and-seek; (Qu. EE33) Inf **CA**59, Kick the can—a base where object put, kicked by one person; "it" had to go after it, returned to base, counted to ten before catching [others]; if one of those out could kick it again, you had to start over; **NC**30, Kick the can—hit can with broom during game of hide-and-seek; **NY**40, Kick the can—like hide-and-seek but before everyone hides, someone kicks the can. "It" must carry the can to the base, walking backwards, before he starts looking. While he is looking, anyone may run out and kick the can and then he must start again. If he finds someone hiding, "it" must run back and tap the can and call "tap tap so-and-so.". . But if anyone kicks the can, everybody is free. This game is still played in this area. **1968** *Chicago Tribune* (IL) 15 Sept mag sec 78 **Chicago IL,** We'll play kick the can and ringalevio. Don't need to know anything except where to hide or how to run so your sides won't hurt. **1986** Pederson *LAGS Concordance* **Gulf Region,** *(Hiding games)* 1 inf, Kick the can; *(Tin-can games)* 2 infs, Kick the can—a hiding game; 1 inf, Kick the can—a hiding game played in the house; 1 inf, Kick the can—hiding game, last kicker was "it"; 1 inf, Kick the can—used a coffee can; 1 inf, Kick the can—kick can without being caught; 1 inf, Kick the can—kick it, hiding players retrieve it; *(Goal—in children's game)* 1 inf, Kick the can.

2 also *kick the ball, ~ bar, ~ block, ~ rubber:* Any of var games played somewhat like baseball or field hockey. Note: It is not always possible to determine what game is meant by a particular response; some responses may belong at **1** above. Cf **knock the can**

1891 *Jrl. Amer. Folkl.* 4.230 **Brooklyn NYC,** *Kick the Can.* This game is identical with "kick the wicket," except that an empty tin can . . mounted on a rock, is substituted for the wicket. **1966** *DARE* File **Boston MA,** *Kick the rubber.* 14-inch piece of garden hose leaning against post at an angle. Game started with kick of hose and from then on continued as a regular ball game with runners, bases, etc., using hose instead of ball. **1966–70** *DARE* (QR, near Qu. EE16) Inf **NY**36, Kick the can—played on a corner; each of four corners was used for a base, the can was kicked and the players ran as in baseball; (Qu. EE27, *Games played on the ice*) Inf **TX**5, Shinny—not on ice; tin can and sticks, played on schoolyard; also kick the can with no sticks; (Qu. EE33, . . *Outdoor games . . that children play*) Inf **KY**85, Kick the can—a rough game between two teams, old-fashioned; **ME**11, Kick the can—kick can as far as possible, all run and try to kick it; **MI**108, Kick the can—a stick or can was leaned against a curb and the object was to kick it [FW: Inf can't recall the rules]; **CA**32, Kick the ball—like kick the can; **MA**27, Kick the bar—a piece of rubber hose about a foot long is placed on the curb and is kicked; the kicker would run to a base, game played like scrub. Kick the block. . . A board would extend about four or five inches over the curb—a small block is placed on the other end. . . The player strikes the board with his foot and propels the block on the other end. Played like scrub or at intersections the four corners would make four bases; **MA**45, Kick the bar—get a piece of a bicycle tire, cut about a foot off of it; place it on the curbstone and kick it. **1986** Pederson *LAGS Concordance (Tin-can games)* 1 inf, **cnTN,** Kick the can—something like hockey.

3 also *kick-can, kick over, ~ the bucket;* for addit varr see quots: Any of var games that involve kicking an object. Note: Qu. EE18 was intended to elicit names for games like **duck on a rock;** some of these responses may belong at **1** above. **1954** *Harder Coll.* **cwTN,** *Kick over the can*—A children's game. **1965–70** *DARE* (Qu. EE18, *Games in which the players set up a stone, a tin can, or something similar, and then try to knock it down*) 124 Infs, **widespread,** Kick the can; **CA**102, **TX**33, 41, Kick the bucket; **DC**8, Kick the tin can; **PA**190, Kick the pan; **RI**6, Kick the bottle; **MO**26, Kick-can—what is often called kick the can; **SC**26, Kick over; (Qu. EE33, . . *Outdoor games . . that children play*) 26 Infs, **scattered,** Kick

the can; **MO**14, Kick the can—one type is to just kick a can around; **PA**72, Kick the can, kick the old man; **TX**42, Old sow—kick the can. **1986** Pederson *LAGS Concordance* **Gulf Region** *(Tin-can games)* 14 infs, Kick the can; 1 inf, Kick the cans; *(Line and running games)* 2 infs, Kick the can; *(Ring games)* 2 infs, Kick the can; *(Rough games)* 1 inf, Kick the can.

kick the picket n
1 See **kick the can 1.**
2 See quot.
1970 *DARE* (Qu. EE3, *Games in which you hide an object and then look for it*) Inf **CA**197, Kick the picket.

kick the rubber See **kick the can 2**

kick the stick n Also *kick-stick* esp NEast Cf **kick the can, whipstick, wicket**
Any of several games; see quots.
1901 *DN* 2.142 **csNY,** Kick the stick. . . The name of a game somewhat like hide and seek. **1907** *DN* 3.245 **eME,** Kick the stick. . . An outdoor game played after the season for marbles as soon as there is dry ground enough. **1950** *WELS (Games [other than regular football] where you kick a ball or some other object)* 1 Inf, **seWI,** Kick the stick. **1957** *Sat. Eve. Post Letters* **CT** (as of c1890), Kick the stick. *Ibid* **cwNY** (as of c1947), Kick the stick. *Ibid* **neNJ** (as of c1920), Kick the stick—form of baseball. **1968–69** *DARE* (Qu. EE10, *A game in which a short stick lying on the ground is flipped into the air and then hit with a longer stick*) Inf **MN**15, Kick-stick; **PA**206, Kick the stick; (Qu. EE33, . . *Outdoor games . . that children play*) Inf **NY**73, Kick the stick—lean a stick on the wall, try to kick it down and get out of sight before the child watching could put the stick back; **PA**94, 234, Kick the stick. **1986** Pederson *LAGS Concordance (Tin-can games)* 1 inf, **seLA,** Kick the stick.

kick the tin can See **kick the can 3**

kick the wicket (or wickie) See **wicket**

kick through See **kick v B5**

kick up v phr See **kick v B2, 3, 4**

kickup n
1 A social gathering with games and dancing. *old-fash*
1778 in 1908 *MD Hist. Mag.* 3.116, We Collected the Girls in the neighbourhood and had a kick up in the Evening. **1804** Fessenden *Poems* 17, See what lasses we can pick up / For our famous village kick up. **1910** 'G.B. Lancaster' *Jim of Ranges* vi.126 *(OEDS),* 'What d'yer do at a kick-up, Jim?' 'Oh, hide-an'-seek . . an' kiss-in-the-ring,' explained Jim.
2 A fight or argument; a disturbance. *old-fash*
1843 (1916) Hall *New Purchase* 333, Our venerable Congress at Washington sometimes gets into a row, and even breaks up in a riot. . . Whether we, the New Purchase people . . followed the example, need not be determined; but we certainly adjourned to-day in a grand kick-up. **1891** Maitland *Amer. Slang Dict.* 159, Kick up, a noise or disturbance. **1912** Green *VA Folk-Speech* 250, Kick-up. . . A row; falling out: "They had a regular kick-up."

kick up jack See **jack** n[1] 14

kicky adj [Cf *EDD* kickish (at **kick** v.[1] 6) "irritable"]
1930 Shoemaker *1300 Words* 35 **cPA Mts** (as of c1900), Kicky—Disagreeable, contrary.

kid n[1] chiefly NEng
A wooden tub, spec:
a A container for meat on shipboard. *obs*
1840 (1841) Dana *2 Yrs.* 225, The cook scraped his kids (wooden tubs out of which the sailors eat). **1846** (1968) Browne *Etchings Whaling* 141, The cook, in order to see fair play, generally watched his opportunity, and, when the hands were scattered around the forecastle, he would pitch the meat kid down on the deck, and sing out, at the top of his voice, "Meat! meat! fall to, all hands!" **1847** Melville *Typee* 38, Just as I was about to ascend to the deck my eye happened to light on the bread-barge and beef-kid, which contained the remnants of our last hasty meal. **1980** *Yankee* Jan 90 (as of 19th cent), The boiled salt horse or salt junk was served to the foremast hands by dumping it into a wooden tub, or "kid". . . A crewman would be appointed daily in turn to sit with his back to the kid while another would select, at random, a piece of meat and ask, "Whose piece is this?"

b A container on the deck of a fishing vessel into which fish are thrown. *old-fash*

1848 Bartlett *Americanisms* 194 **NEng,** *Kid.* A large box in fishing vessels into which fish are thrown as they are caught. **1889** *Century Dict.* 3283, *Kid.* . . A box or wooden pen built on the deck of a fishing-vessel to receive fish as they are caught. **1975** Gould *ME Lingo* 153, *Kids*—Pens on the deck of a fishing boat for holding the catch as it comes aboard. Each man hove into his own *kid,* and later would call out his tally to the skipper as he moved them into the main *kid.*

kid n[2] Cf Intro "Language Changes" II.7
Used as a plural.

1986 Pederson *LAGS Concordance,* 1 inf, **cGA,** Eight kid; 1 inf, **seFL,** Five head of kid; 1 inf, **neMS,** Mama used to make it for us kid.

kiday See **co-day**

kiddledee-bender, kiddly bender See **kittly-bender**

kiddy See **kitty** exclam

kiddy-corner See **kitty-corner** n

kid hack See **kid wagon**

kidney-bender See **kittly-bender**

kidney colic n [Transf from *kidney colic* any of var problems associated with the kidneys] Cf **floating kidney**

1970 *DARE* (Qu. BB20, *Joking names or expressions for overactive kidneys*) Inf **VA**52, Kidney colic.

kidney foot n, hence adj *kidney-footed*
A large or clumsy foot.

1905 Chesnutt *Col.'s Dream* 194 **GA,** What gentleman here would want his daughter to marry a blubber-lipped, cocoanut-headed, kidney-footed . . nigger? **1968** *DARE* (Qu. X38, *Joking names for unusually big or clumsy feet*) Inf **OH**43, Kidney feet; [**TX**26, Bear kidneys].

kidneyroot n

1 also *kidney weed, kidneywort:* A **boneset 1** (here: *Eupatorium purpureum*).

1876 Hobbs *Bot. Hdbk.* 61, Kidney root,—Queen of the meadow root,—Eupatorium purpureum. **1914** Georgia *Manual Weeds* 416, Joe-Pye Weed. . . Gravel-root, Kidney-root. **1959** Carleton *Index Herb. Plants* 70, *Kidney-root:* Eupatorium purpureum. . . *Kidney-wort* . . Eupatorium purpureum, Hepatica triloba. **1971** Krochmal *Appalachia Med. Plants* 120, *Eupatorium purpureum.* . . kidneyweed. . . This plant is used for urinary disorders. **1974** (1977) Coon *Useful Plants* 108, Kidney root. . . Among herbalists it is claimed to be of value as a diuretic and tonic.

2 =**chaparral broom.**

1900 Lyons *Plant Names* 56, Kidney-root. Plant, diuretic. **1931** U.S. Dept. Ag. *Misc. Pub.* 101.160, Kidney-root.

3 See **kidneywort 1.**

kidney vine n [See quot 1929]
A **bedstraw** (here: *Galium asprellum*).

1929 *Torreya* 29.151, Gallium asprellum, . . "Kidney vine," used in kidney troubles by the country people. **1935** (1943) Muenscher *Weeds* 434, *Galium asprellum* . . Kidney-vine. **1940** Clute *Amer. Plant Names* 259, *Galium asprellum.* Kidney vine, hay-ruff, mutton chops.

kidney weed n

1 A **false foxglove** (here: *Agalinis tenuifolia*).

1974 Morton *Folk Remedies* 63 **SC,** Kidney weed. . . *Gerardia tenuifolia.* . . hung up in long bundles under porch roof. . . Decoction is taken as a diuretic.

2 See **kidneyroot 1.**

kidneywood n [From its diuretic properties]
Std: a small tree or shrub of the genus *Eysenhardtia,* esp *E. polystachya,* native to Arizona, New Mexico, and Texas. For other names of var spp see **mountain locust, palo dulce, rock brush**

kidneywort n

1 also *kidneyroot:* A **hepatica** (here: *Hepatica nobilis obtusa*).
1892 (1974) Millspaugh *Amer. Med. Plants* 2-1, [*Anemone*] *hepatica.* . . trefoil, herb trinity, kidney-wort. **1931** Clute *Common Plants* 124, Kidney-root (*Hepatica triloba*). **1959** Carleton *Index Herb. Plants* 70, *Kidney-wort:* Baccarhis [sic] pilularis; . . Hepatica triloba.

2 =**chaparral broom.**

1931 U.S. Dept. Ag. *Misc. Pub.* 101.160, Kidneywort . . is typically a coastal or seashore plant. **1937** U.S. Forest Serv. *Range Plant Hdbk.* B33, Kidneywort . . a common prostrate-spreading or erect shrub, which ranges from Oregon to southern California, is useful in preventing wind erosion of sand dunes. **1938** Van Dersal *Native Woody Plants* 68, *Baccharis pilularis* . . Kidneywort. **1959** [see **1** above].

3 See **kidneyroot 1.**

kidoodle See **canoodle** v

kid wagon n Also *kid hack*
A vehicle used to transport children to school.

1917 *DN* 4.395 **neOH,** *Kid-wagon.* . . A conveyance for carrying pupils to a centralized school. Now often in serious use. Recent. **1918** *DN* 5.26 **NW,** *Kid-wagon.* . . A carry-all which gathers in the children to the rural district schools. General. **1976** Sublette Co. Artist Guild *More Tales* 304 **cwWY** (as of c1926), I had to walk from there to catch the kid wagon, as we called it. Mr. Wolfenberger drove it. He had a black team. **1980** *DARE* File **nOH** (as of c1925), A friend of mine from . . just south of the Western Reserve . . says she knew "kid-wagon" as a child. **1982** *Smithsonian Letters* **OH,** The older people in Burton consistently refer to the horsedrawn vehicles that served as "school buses" in their youth as *kidhacks.*

kielbasa n Usu |ˌkɪlˈbɑsə|; for varr see quots Also *kielbassi, kielbasy, kielbusa, ko(l)basa, kolbasy* [Pol *kiełbasa;* Russ *kolbasá*] **chiefly NEast, Gt Lakes, esp in Polish settlement areas**
Pork sausage.

1950 *WELS* (Sausage) 1 Inf, **seWI,** Polish-style sausage called kielbasa. **1953** Bellow *Advent. Augie March* 435 **Chicago IL,** All these poor punks . . with immigrant blood and washday smells and kielbasa and home-brew beer. **1965** Brown *Manchild* 218 **NYC,** I sat down on my bed and started to eat a sandwich, a kielbasy sandwich. **c1965** Randle *Cookbooks* (Ask Neighbor) 1.33, *Smoked Kobasa and Sauerkraut. Ibid* 3.14, *Smoked Kielbusa Soup. Ibid* 18, *Busha's Kraut and Kielbasa.* . . dutch oven . . sauerkraut . . fresh kielbasa (never use smoked). *Ibid* 72, *Polish Kolbasa. Ibid* 73, *Kobasa* (Homemade Easter Sausage). . . pork butts . . garlic . . salt . . Casings. . . If you have no smokehouse, you can make one from a large tin drum. **1967–69** *DARE* (Qu. H41, *Kinds of roll or bun sandwiches . . in a round bun or roll*) Inf **PA**167, Kolbasy; (Qu. H45) Inf **NY**49, Kielbasy—Polish sausage; (Qu. H49, *Dishes made by boiling potatoes with other foods*) Inf **RI**3, Potatoes with [kɪˈbɑsə]—Polish sausage; (Qu. H65, *Foreign foods favored by people around here*) Inf **MD**8, Kielbasa—spicy Polish sausage; **MA**1, Kielbasa [kɪlˈbɑsə]—Polish (meat); **MA**43, Kielbasa [kɪlˈbɛsə]—a Polish dish; **NY**49, Kielbasy—Polish sausage; **OH**68, Kielbasy [kɪlˈbɑsi]—a sausage; **PA**167, Kolbasy and sauerkraut. **1968** *Tunkhannock Republican & New Age* (PA) 18 July sec A 4, Store-made *Fresh Kielbassi* 79¢ lb. **1970** [see **mettwurst**]. **1986** Pederson *LAGS Concordance* (Sausage) 1 inf, **Miami FL,** Kielbasa. **1988** *DARE* File **Milwaukee WI** (as of 1970s), When I worked for the circus we traveled out to Pittsburgh. Bunch of guys and I went looking for kielbasa—that's one of my favorite foods—it's kind of a spicy Polish sausage. We eat it all the time in my part of Milwaukee [=Polish settlement area]. So we're in Pittsburgh and we look all over where there's supposed to be real Polish food, but the *only* thing we ever find is something called kielbasy [kɪlbɑsˈi] and it's something else completely and it's terrible—bland, no flavor. Just bad. Kielbasy's available all over Pittsburgh. **1989** *Ibid* **Madison WI,** Kielbasa [ˌkɪlˈbɑsə] or Polish sausage—it's seasoned, spiced. Some places, theirs is fresh, but ours is cooked. I don't think there's fresh available anywhere in this area.

kieye See **kiyi**

kif exclam [Prob var of *calf;* cf **calf** n[1] **A**]
1968 *DARE* (Qu. K83, *To call a calf to you at feeding time*) Inf **CT**14, [kɪf kɪf].

kife See **kipe**

kih See **ki** intj

kike n [Etym unknown] **widespread, but more freq NEast, N Cent, West** See Map *derog* Cf **yid**
A Jew, esp one considered greedy, miserly, dishonest, or shrewd; by ext, any person thought to have such characteristics.

1904 McCardell *Show Girl & Friends* 49 **NYC,** He had the impudence to tell me that Louie Zinsheimer was a kike! **1917** (1951) Cahan *Rise David Levinsky* 407, You know who Mr. Levinsky is, don't you? It isn't some kike. It's David Levinsky, the cloak-manufacturer. **1940** R. Stout *Over My Dead Body* vi.84 *(OEDS),* I don't care if the background is wop or mick or kike . . so long as it's American. **1941** *LANE* Map 455 *(Nicknames for a Jew)* 11 infs, **scattered NEng exc NH,** Kike; 1 inf, **cwCT,** A kike is a Jew who won't keep his word; that's the worst word you can use; 1 inf, **swCT,** Kike, the lower strata of Jews; 1 inf, **cCT,** *Kike,* especially of 'little East-Side dealers' in New York; 1 inf, **sRI,** [kɔɪk], heard in Hartford, Conn.; 1 inf, **seMA,** [keɪk], heard in New York; 1 inf, **neMA,** *Kike,* a cheap Jew; 1 inf, **cMA,** [kʰaʒjk], rare, not restricted to Jews; 1 inf, **wME,** *Kike,* term learned at the academy in Hebron. **1950** *WELS* **WI** *(Jewish)* 21 Infs, Kike; *(People living in nearby settlements)* 1 Inf, Kike. **1950** Bracke *Wheat Country* 298 **KS,** In any discussion a Jew is likely to be immediately labeled as such although his Gentile neighbors may admit that he is no "kike." **1964** *PADS* 42.32 **Chicago IL** [Terms of abuse], The most popular of these pejoratives [for Jews] is *kike.* **1965–70** *DARE* (Qu. HH28, *Names and nicknames . . for people of foreign background*) 174 Infs, **widespread, but less freq Sth, S Midl,** Kike; (Qu. U33, *Names or nicknames for a stingy person*) Inf **IN75,** Kike; **LA23,** Kike [laughter]—said without regard to person's race in this meaning—also used as a nickname for Jew; (Qu. U36b, . . *A person who saves in a mean way or is greedy in money matters: "She certainly is _____."*) Inf **CA136,** A kike; (Qu. V2a, . . *A deceiving person, or somebody that you can't trust*) Inf **IN75,** Kike; (Qu. V7, *A person who sets out to cheat others while pretending to be honest*) Inf **IN75,** Kike; (Qu. CC4, *Nicknames . . for various religions or religious groups*) Inf **CA213,** Kike—Jew; **MO26,** Kikes; (Qu. FF23, . . *Joking names . . for . . clubs or lodges*) Inf **NJ37,** K. of C. = Knights of Cincinnati = Kikes of Cincinnati; (Qu. HH40, *Uncomplimentary words for an old man*) Inf **MA35,** Old kike. **1968** Rosten *Yiddish* 180, Dr. Shlomo Noble informs me that the miners of northeastern Pennsylvania would say, "I bought it from the kike man," or "The kike man will be coming around soon." **1986** Pederson *LAGS Concordance,* 9 infs, **scattered, Gulf Region,** Kike(s); 1 inf, **swAL,** Kike—has heard, never used; 1 inf, **cAR,** Kike—low bred Jew; 1 inf, **cAR,** Kike—seldom used here; 1 inf, **cTX,** Kike—abusive; 1 inf, **cTX,** Kike—horrible term, it's so harsh; 1 inf, **csTX,** Dirty Kike; 1 inf, **cnTN,** Kikes—Jews call each other [Inf Jewish]; 1 inf, **ceAL,** Kikes—any white person; 1 inf, **swAL,** Kikes—general; 1 inf, **seLA,** Kikes—very insulting; 1 inf, **ceTX,** Kikes—old term, but not obsolete; 1 inf, **ceTX,** Kikes—powerful, anti-Semitic feeling in Houston; 1 inf, **seFL,** Goddamn kikes or sheenies—heard others say. **1989** *NY Times* (NY) 13 Dec 31/1 **cnMD** (as of 1930s–40s), [Newspaper column:] Mencken's diary avoids most of these dreary words, but it is startling indeed to find him writing "kikes," a word that even the street-corner crowd considered too vile to be spoken without the strongest justification.

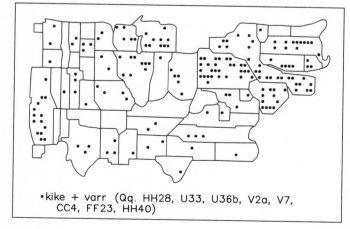

     •kike + varr (Qq. HH28, U33, U36b, V2a, V7,   CC4, FF23, HH40)

ki-ki hen n
=Florida gallinule.
   1953 *AmSp* 28.281 **WI,** Ki-ki hen—Common gallinule.

Kilby n [SwissGer *chilbi, kilbi* dial varr of Ger *Kirchweih*] **csWI, in Swiss settlement area** Cf **kermis(s)**
A celebration marking the end of summer; see quots.
   1950 *WELS (A party where the main entertainment is dancing)* 1 Inf, **csWI,** *Kilby*—a celebration of thanksgiving at the close of the har-

vest season among the Swiss. Kilby is more than a dancing party. It starts with religious services and ends in dances. [Inf of Swiss background] **1992** *DARE* File **csWI** [Swiss community], We have Kilby Sunday every year. It's a confirmation reunion, the last Sunday in September. *Ibid,* Kilby celebrates bringing the cattle down from the mountains in Switzerland at the end of summer. Years ago Kilby here was three days, we had tug-of-war, baseball. The Kilby dance was Monday night, always had dances, bands. So many people came both dance halls were full. Now . . it's just one day, when roll call of the confirmed church members is taken. Each year is called out, and we see who is the oldest member. That's Kilby Sunday. **1994** *Ibid* **csWI,** The Kilby Fest in Switzerland commemorated bringing the cows down from the mountain pastures at the end of the summer. . . Here in New Glarus it's a harvest festival around the end of September. We celebrate with a Church supper—a community get-together—with lots of Swiss food.

kildea(r), kildee(r) See **killdeer 1**

kilfliggin adj
   1895 *DN* 1.390 **eKY,** *Kilfliggin* . . lazy.

kilgubbin n [Cf *EDD gobbin* sb.[1] "A receptacle for any kind of waste goods" and *gubbin(g)s* "offal, refuse"]
   1910 *DN* 3.458 **Chicago IL** [Expressions heard from Chicago people of New England antecedents], *Kilgubbin.* . . A low or poor neighborhood.

kilhig n Also *killig (pole)* [Prob var of **killhag**]
In logging: see quots.
   1905 U.S. Forest Serv. *Bulletin* 61.41 **nNEng, nNY** [Logging terms], *Kilhig.* . . A short, stout pole used as a lever or brace to direct the fall of a tree. **1913** Bryant *Logging* 83, *Kilhig or Sampson.* . . It consists of a pole . . from 8 to 16 feet long, either sharpened or armed on one end with a spike. In operation the pointed end of the pole is placed in a notch in the tree trunk from 5 to 8 feet above ground. The free end projects downward to a point 10 or 12 inches above the ground where it is supported on a peavey handle or a pole the lower end of which is firmly planted in the ground. A laborer grasps the free end of the peavey handle and by pressing forward is able to exert a very strong pressure against the bole of the tree. Kilhigs are frequently made as needed by the saw crew. **1969** Sorden *Lumberjack Lingo* 67 **NEng, Gt Lakes,** *Killig pole.* **1975** Gould *ME Lingo* 154, *Killig pole*—About the same as the *Samson pole.* . . Both are leverage devices.

kiljackums n pl
   1944 *PADS* 2.19 **sAppalachians,** *Kiljackums.* . . Slang for sorghum molasses.

kill v
A Pronc varr.
Usu |kɪl|; also **Sth, S Midl** |kjɪl, kɪəl, kɪɪl|; pronc-sp *keel.*
   1936 *AmSp* 11.247 **eTX,** [ˈkjɪl ɪm]. . . [ˈkjɪəl]. *Ibid* 338, [ʃid ə kjɪldm]. **1942** Hall *Smoky Mt. Speech* 15 **wNC, eTN,** Kill [kɪɪl]. **1943** in 1944 *ADD* **nWV,** [Radio:] *Kill.* . . It [kɪəlz] rats. **1981** Pederson *LAGS Basic Materials* **Gulf Region,** [In phrases such as "kill him" and "killed me," pronunciations of the type [kɪəl] and [kɪəld] predominated.] **1989** Nicholson *Field Guide S. Speech* 9, *Keel:* to inflict grievous bodily harm, even unto death.

B Gram forms.
Past, past pple, ppl adj: usu *killed;* also, **Sth, S Midl,** *kilt;* rarely *kilted.* [*OED kilt* pple. (at *kill* v. 2.a.β) c1400 →]
   1884 *Anglia* 7.261 **Sth, S Midl** [Black], To git kilt = to be killed. **1890** *DN* 1.68 **KY,** Kilt: for killed. Frequently used. "He kilt him dead." **1899** (1912) Green *VA Folk-Speech* 250, *Kilt.* . . Past tense of *kill.* **1909** *DN* 3.399 **nwAR,** *Kilt* . . pret. and pp. Killed. **1928** *AmSp* 3.404 **Ozarks,** *T* replaces the final *d* in words like *salad, ballad, killed* . . so that these words are best rendered *salat, ballat, kilt.* **1931** (1991) Hughes–Hurston *Mule Bone* 52 **cFL** [Black], Look lak you done kilt a cow. **1937** in 1976 *Weevils in the Wheat* 121 **VA** [Black], Dat blessed chile was kilt. **1966** Maddux *Spring Rain* 91 **WV,** I kilt mine for you. **1969** *DARE* (Qu. X47) Inf **KY46,** I'm plumb kilt. **1986** Pederson *LAGS Concordance* **Gulf Region,** 8 infs, Kilt; 6 infs, Kilt; Got (*or* gotten) kilt; 1 inf, Got kilt—was killed, literal; 1 inf, Got kilt—joking; 1 inf, Your son just got kilt—insulting, crude; 3 infs, Was kilt; 3 infs, Kilt her (*or* him, one boy); 1 inf, I don't know why we didn't get kilt; 1 inf, Kilt—heard people say it; 1 inf, Done kilt—already killed; 1 inf, The dry weather kilt everything; 1 inf, I have kilt hogs; 1 inf, How many mens they kilt; 1 inf, Kind of kilt it out; 1 inf, I ain't never kilt us; 1 inf, I kilted him. **1991** [see C4 below].

C Senses.

1 used with redundant or emphatic adverbs, esp *out, up:* To kill, exterminate, butcher. **chiefly Sth, S Midl**

1834 Crockett *Narrative* 52, His [battalion] and the one Russell was now appointed to command, composed a regiment, which . . was . . to kill up the Indians on the Scamby river. **1866** Smith *Bill Arp* 29 **nwGA,** You will have all the scum of your population killed up. **1887** *Scribner's Mag.* 2.481 **AR,** She'll shore git killed up! **1889** Edwards *Runaways* 107 **GA** [Black], De Cass'ls used ter live heah tell de war cummed on, den dey uz mos'ly killed up. **1924** *Qrly. Jrl. Speech* 10.235 **sAppalachians,** *Kill up.* The Mountain man uses *kill up* as Shakespeare does. **1931** *AmSp* 7.93 **eKY,** *Kill-up.* . . "We're aimin' to kill-up a lot o' meat this fall." **1935** Hurston *Mules & Men* 128 **FL,** He useter rob and steal and he was always in a fight and killin' up people. **1939** *Hall Coll.* **wNC, eTN,** *Kill down*—addition of an intensive adverb is a noteworthy characteristic of Gt. Smokies speech. "I shot the bear in the mouth and killed him down." *Ibid* **eTN,** We was so interested in gettin' that brute [=a bear] that was a-killin' our cattle up. **1944** *AmSp* 19.309, A cattleman . . wrote to the New York *Times* . . about butchering cattle, legally and illegally. He used *kill out* and explained its meaning in parentheses: 'A cattleman here secured a permit to kill out (butcher) a few steers at the rate of twenty-five a week.' **1952** *AmSp* 27.235 **cKY,** In 1836 my grandmother's grandmother . . applied for a revolutionary pension. . . Among other things, she says that at one time a large part of the company of which her husband was captain was 'killed up.' . . [In 1951, in the same town, a man said] 'It is too bad . . that so many of our boys are going over there and getting killed up.' **1960** (1962) Eichenlaub *Minnesota Dr.* 111, Home laundry or helpy-selfy machines do not use hot enough water to kill out crabs. **1966** *DARE* Tape **MA6,** Every place a leaf stands, it has a root come on it, so it just kills out everything it can get to; **SC24,** They used to burn the soil . . to kill out all the seed. **1986** Pederson *LAGS Concordance,* 1 inf, **neTN,** To kill out—to destroy . . poison oak; 1 inf, **cFL,** Now they're killed out—depleted by hunters; 1 inf, **neFL,** You can't hardly keep them killed out—of roaches; 1 inf, **cnTN,** Exterminators will kill them out—of termites; 1 inf, **nwFL,** Kind of kilt it out; [1 inf, **csGA,** They don't let you kill them out here now no more;] 1 inf, **seAR,** Killed them back—reduced the number of insects; 1 inf, **csGA,** Shooting and killing up one another and cutting up one another.

2 in phr *kill dead* and varr: To kill completely—often fig. [Redund; cf Intro "Language Changes" I.4] **esp Sth, S Midl** Cf *dead as four-o'clock* (at **four-o'clock 5**)

1834 *Life Andrew Jackson* 62, In this battel 557 were kill'd dead on the peninsula. **1851** Burke *Polly Peablossom* 125 **AR,** I was just about *killed dead* for a few minutes, and it required considerable vinegar and *whiskey* to resuscitate me. **1956** *Hall Coll.* **eTN,** My legs just seemed like they was killin' me to death. **1986** Pederson *LAGS Concordance,* 3 infs, **nwLA, cw,nwMS,** Killed her (*or* him) dead; 1 inf, **ceTN,** Killed her deader than four o'clock; 1 inf, **cTN,** Kill it dead as four o'clock—the hull on ringworm. **1994** *DARE* File **WI,** [Television advt:] Orkin kills bugs dead.

3 In cooking: to cause (greens) to wilt; hence ppl adj *kilt,* wilted.

1939 *Hall Coll.* **eTN,** Take small lettuce leaves and small green onions with stems and mustard. Take a hot pan of grease and pour over. This is called "killin' with grease." **1976** Garber *Mountain-ese* 50 **sAppalachians,** Ma allers kills the lettuce with grease and vinegar jist afore dinner. **1991** Still *Wolfpen Notebooks* 79 **sAppalachians,** Kilt lettuce—Chop green onions . . into a bowl along with broken-up leaf lettuce. . . Dump into an iron skillet over a low fire and add bacon grease and stir like crazy until the lettuce is kilt. My mother, she always called it kilt.

4 In var phrr:

a *kill one's own snakes:* To mind one's own business.

1928 Nason *Sergeant Eadie* 315, First come, first served, and let every man kill his own snakes. A whole skin beats a hero's death six ways. **1932** Randolph *Ozark Mt. Folks* 95, Whut do them fellers over t' Durgenville know 'bout how things is a-goin' up hyar in th' Holler? Let 'em stay home an' kill their own snakes! **1954** *Harder Coll.* **cwTN,** *Kill your own snakes*—mind one's own business.

b *kill another skunk:* See quot.

1984 Wilder *You All Spoken Here* 21 **Sth,** *Kill another skunk:* Create a diversion.

c *like killing (black) snakes:* See quots.

1906 *DN* 3.145 **nwAR,** *Like killing black snakes.* . . Very industriously. "I've been working today like killing black snakes." **1956** McAtee *Some Dialect NC* 27, *Like killing snakes* . . intensively. "He works like killing snakes."

d *like a dog killing snakes:* See quot.

1984 Wilder *You All Spoken Here* 113 **Sth,** *Like a dog killing snakes:* With a violent shaking of the head.

e *I be killed:* See **I be.**

kill n[1] [Du *kil*] **esp NY, in Du settlement areas** Cf **killifish**

A natural waterway, esp a stream, creek, or channel.

1639 in 1912 Jenkins *Story of Bronx* 177, The Kil which runs behind the Island of Manhattan, mostly east and west. **1669** in 1877 *Documents Colonial Hist. NY* 12.464, Upon ye request of Mr. William Tom that some Familyes from Maryland may haue liberty to come and settle upon ye Kill below Apoquenimi . . I doe hereby graunt ye said request upon condition that . . a Draught be taken of ye Land lying in ye said Kill & a returne thereof be made unto me. **1705** in 1882 Taylor *Hist. Gt. Barrington MA* 3, Northerly to a Creek or Kill that comes out of the woods called Wata-pick-aak. **1890** *AN&Q* 5.54, *Kill* . . a Dutch word denoting any tidal channel or backset water. Haarlem river is a *kill.* **1937** Gardner *Folkl. Schoharie* 24 **ceNY,** Nearly every body of running water smaller than a river is called a "kill." **c1940** *LAMSAS Materials* **NY,** *LAMSAS* has two occurrences of 'kill' to mean simply creek. [One inf of] Saratoga Co. . . notes it is "½ [size of a] river." [One inf of] Monroe Co. comments "in Delaware." **1942** *New Yorker* 19 Sept 11 **nNJ,** Northern [New Jersey rivers], like the Paulins Kill, flow through mountains. **1955** Assoc. Amer. Geogr. *Annals* 45.329, The limitation of the term *kill* to the Hudson Valley, Catskills, and upper Delaware Valley . . can be accounted for quite readily. This Dutch equivalent of *brook* or *run* is almost exactly coterminous with the region of significant, or even transient, Dutch settlement. **1981** *AmSp* 56.117 **ceNY,** In the vicinity of Schenectady, New York, where such streams abound, it is common to speak of "a kill" or "the kill." In fact . . I have never heard another generic term used for these small streams. **1993** *DARE* File **ceNY** (as of 1950s–60s), My husband, who grew up in Catskill, always thought that kill meant valley, so never thought of the name Cauterskill Creek as being redundant.

kill n[2] See **kiln** n

kill another skunk See **kill** v C4b

killapie adj, n Also *keelapi* [Chinook Jargon] **Pacific NW** See quots.

[**1863** Gibbs *Chinook Jargon* 8, *Kel'-a-pi,* or *Ká-la-pi,* v. Chinook, *Kelapai. To turn; return; overturn; upset.*] **1930** Williams *Logger-Talk* 25 **Pacific NW,** *Keelapi:* Tipped over; from the Chinook jargon. **1958** McCulloch *Woods Words* 101 **Pacific NW,** *Killapie*—The mess which results when the dipper stick of a shovel flops back over the cab. [**1970** Thomas *Chinook* 72, *Killapi* or keelapi. . . To turn, return, overturn, upset, reverse, retreat, capsize, and often to denote crooked or twisted deformities.]

kill back See **kill** v C1

killblazes n Cf **blazes, blue blazes b** Hell.

1905 *DN* 3.62 **eNE,** *Killblazes.* . . ["]It's hotter than killblazes," "That beats killblazes." Always used in plural.

kill-calf n Also *calfkill* Cf **kill-kid, lambkill** A **sheep laurel** (here: *Kalmia angustifolia*).

1821 Cobbett *Amer. Gardener* 361, *Kill-calf.* . . It is a dwarf shrub, and . . is very pretty. When in bloom it resembles a large clump of Sweet Williams. [**1830** Rafinesque *Med. Flora* 2.17, It [=*Kalmia latifolia*] is certainly deleterious to horses, calves, and sheep feeding on it in winter, because indigestible to them. Sheep, if not soon relieved by oil, will swell and die.] **1900** Lyons *Plant Names* 209, *K[almia] angustifolia.* . . Calf-kill, Lamb-kill, Kill-kid. **1924** *Amer. Botanist* 30.58, *Kalmia angustifolia* . . is disparaged by such names as . . "calf kill," "kill kid" and "sheep poison." **1964** Kingsbury *Poisonous Plants U.S.* 251, *Kalmia angustifolia.* . . Lambkill, sheepkill, calfkill.

kill cow n [See quot 1952] A **spike rush** (here: *Eleocharis tenuis*).

1894 *Jrl. Amer. Folkl.* 7.103 **WV,** *Eleocharis tenuis,* . . poverty-grass, kill cow. **1952** Strausbaugh–Core *Flora WV* 160, *E[leocharis] tenuis.* . . *Kill cow.* . . In places it occupies large areas, but cattle will not thrive on it, hence the name Kill Cow.

kill-dad n

1 also *kill-dead twist:* Homecured tobacco.

1939 *Hall Coll.* **wNC,** Kill-dead twist, home-made chewin' tobacco

locally grown and cured. **1950** *WELS (Home-grown and home-cured tobacco)* 1 Inf, **WI**, Homespun kill-dad.
2 By ext: see quot.
1956 Sorden–Ebert *Logger's Words* 20 **Gt Lakes**, *Kill-dad*, An empty tin pail where all lumber-jacks threw old or odd pieces of chewing or smoking tobacco. Anyone could borrow from it for his pipe.

killdare See **killdeer 1**

kill dead See **kill v C2**

kill-dead twist See **kill-dad 1**

killdeer n

1 also chiefly **Sth, S Midl, SW, Pacific** (See Map) *kil(l)dee*; also *chilldee, kildea(r), kildeer, killdare, killdee(r) plover, killdill, killee:* A **plover** (here: *Charadrius vociferus*). [Echoic] Also called **bobble-ass, chattering plover, cheweeka 1, cold-weather bird, cotton bird, cou collier, cracker-ass 2, dot-terel, geek, jack snipe 7, jaybird 2, meadow plover 1, noisy plover, old-field snipe, ringneck, ringneck plover, shit-ass, snipe, teeter-ass snipe, telltale, upland plover**
1733 Royal Soc. London *Philos. Trans. for 1731* 37.176 **VA**, The Chattering Plover. In *Virginia* they are called *Kildeers,* from some Resemblance of their Noise to the Sound of that Word. **a1782** (1788) Jefferson *Notes VA* 74 **VA**, Charadrius vociferus . . Pluvialis vociferus . . Chattering plover, kildee. **1791** Bartram *Travels* 296, Charadrus [sic] vociferus, the kildea or chattering plover. **1835** Crockett *Account* 90, That's a poor country down yander; it makes the tears come into the kildear's eyes when they fly over it the old fields. **1844** Giraud *Birds Long Is.* 219, To most persons residing in the country, this species of Plover is familiar by the name of "Kildeer"—so called from the semblance its notes have to those syllables. **1898** (1900) Davie *Nests N. Amer. Birds* 155, Killdeer. . . This familiar bird whose notes *kil-deer, kil-deer,* are heard in the daytime, and often in moonlight nights . . is very abundant in North America. **1909** Porter *Options* 204 **eTX**, They was going to give us the biggest blow-out, complimentary, alimentary, and elementary, that ever disturbed the kildees on the sand-flats. **1923** Dawson *Birds CA* 1299, *Killdeer.* . . Synonyms.—*Kildeer. Killdee Plover. Killdee.* **1929** Dobie *Vaquero* 290 **SW**, At times the water is so strong with alkali that it is almost undrinkable. "It would give a killdee that flew over it the diarrhoea," so an old timer described its alkaline effect. **1941** LANE Map 474, 1 inf, **RI**, [He ran like a] killdeer. **1950** *WELS* **WI**, 36 Infs, Killdeer; 1 Inf, Killdee; 1 Inf, Killdee, killdeer. **1954** *Harder Coll.* **cwTN**, Killdeer. **1955** Forbush–May *Birds* 173, Killdeer. . . *Other names:* Killdeer Plover; Kildee; Meadow Plover. . . A noisy bird, often calling *kill-dee, kill-dee* shrilly. *Ibid* 174, The Killdeer is an exceedingly swift and graceful bird on the ground or in the air. To 'run like a Killdeer' is a common saying in the South. **1965–70** DARE (Qu. Q14, . . *Names . . for . . killdeer*) 274 Infs, **widespread, but less freq Sth, S Midl**, Killdeer; 259 Infs, **chiefly Sth, S Midl, SW, Pacific**, Killdee; **KY**11, **NC**54, Chilldee [čɪldi]; **AR**42, **CO**22, **NY**109, Killdare; **CO**22, Killdill; **MS**47, Killee; (Qu. Q10, . . *Water birds and marsh birds*) 29 Infs, **scattered**, Killdeer; 20 Infs, **chiefly Sth, SW**, Killdee; **CO**22, Killdill wades in water and fools around; (Qu. Q7, *Names and nicknames for . . game birds*) Infs **CT**5, **RI**17, Killdeer; **MA**42, Killdeer will come in on new-plowed land; **LA**20, Killdee; (Qu. Q8) Infs **FL**22, **OR**3, Killdee; **WA**3, Killdeer; (Qu. Q3) Infs **VA**30, **WA**24, Killdeer; (Qu. Q9) Inf **MO**1, Killdeer; (Qu. Q15) Inf **MA**46, Killdeer. **1986** Pederson *LAGS Concordance,* 1 inf, **cwMS**, Killdee; 3 infs, **cwAL, cnLA, swMS**, Killdeer.

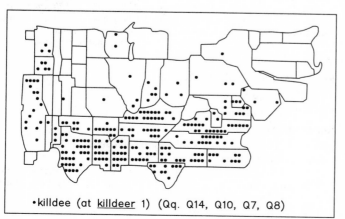

•killdee (at killdeer 1) (Qq. Q14, Q10, Q7, Q8)

2 =black-bellied plover. Cf **black-bellied killdeer**
1955 **MA** Audubon Soc. *Bulletin* 39.445, *Black-bellied Plover.* . . Killdeer (Mass. In full, this name is Black-bellied Killdeer, the latter term not having its usual sonic significance, but meaning a bird of general alliance to that commonly called Killdeer).

killdeer hawk See **killy hawk**

killdeer plover See **killdeer 1**

kill-devil n

1 Rum; liquor, esp that of poor quality.
1639 in 1674 Josselyn *Two Voyages* 26, Captain *Thomas Wannerton* . . drank to me a pint of kill-devil *alias* Rhum at a draught. **1654** in 1850 CT (Colony) *Pub. Rec.* 1.255, Berbados Liquors, commonly called Rum, Kill Devil, or the like. **c1738** (1929) Byrd *Histories* 92, Most of the Rum they get in this Country comes from New England, and is so bad and unwholesome, that it is not improperly call'd "Kill-Devil." **1885** *Century Illustr. Mag.* 29.884, Rum, or "kill-devil," as it was everywhere called, was rendered plentiful by the trade with the West Indies and by the New England stills. **1911** *Century Dict. Suppl.,* Kill-devil . . 3. Among sailors, etc., alcoholic spirits of bad quality; a strong raw liquor. **1953** Randolph–Wilson *Down in Holler* 258 **Ozarks**, Kill-devil . . High-proof whiskey of poor quality. "Kill-devil don't do a feller's stummick no good, but it ain't so bad as this here limber-leg applejack." **c1960** Wilson Coll. **csKY**, Kill-devil—bad, strong whiskey.
2 See quot. Cf **kill-dad 1**
1953 Randolph–Wilson *Down in Holler* 258 **Ozarks**, The term kill-devil is sometimes applied to very strong tobacco.

killdill See **killdeer 1**

kill down See **kill v C1**

killeck See **killick**

killee See **killdeer 1**

killegenico See **kinnikinnick**

kill 'em Polly See **killing-peter**

killfish See **killifish 1**

killhag n Also *culheag* [Of Algonquian orig; see quot 1907] **ME, NH** obs Cf **kilhig**
A wooden deadfall trap.
1784 in 1876 Belknap *Jrl.* 13 **NH**, Along this road yesterday and this morning we saw the culheags, or log-traps, which the hunters set for sables. **1792** Belknap *Hist. NH* 3.90, The *culheag* or log-trap, is used for taking wolves, bears and martins. Its size varies, according to the bulk or strength of the animal. It is a forceps, composed of two long sticks, one lying on the other, connected at one end, and open at the other. Near the open end is made a semicircular, covered enclosure, with short stakes, driven into the ground on one side of the logs, which are firmly secured by another stake, on the opposite side. In this enclosure is placed the bait, fastened to a round stick, which lies across the lower log, the upper log resting on the end of a perpendicular pointed stick, the other end of which is set on the round stick. **1848** Bartlett *Americanisms* 194, *Killhag.* (Indian.) A wooden trap, used by the hunters in Maine. **1864** in 1872 Schele de Vere *Americanisms* 21 **ME**, The first furs were brought into town yesterday, and already a number of *Killhags* have been put up everywhere. **1907** Hodge *Hdbk. Amer. Indians* 1.688, *Killhag.* A sort of trap . . ; from *kilhigan* in the Malecite dialect of Algonquian, signifying 'trap', from the radical *kilh,* 'to catch or keep caught', and the suffix radical *igan,* 'instrument.'

kill-house n
1901 *DN* 2.143 **ceNY**, *Kill-house.* . . Used of a building in which farm utensils are stored. Origin < kiln-house? (There had been no hop-yard near.)

killicanic See **kinnikinnick**

killick n Also sp *keeleg, kelleg, kellock, killock;* for addit varr see quots [Appar of Gaelic origin; cf Manx (and ManxEngl) *killagh* a wooden anchor with a stone in it; *killick* is also reported from Dorset, England. Cf also Ir *cailleach* a stone weight for a rope or net (literally "old woman")] **chiefly NEng** Cf *DNE* (and suppl), *AND*; cf also **humdurgan**
A wooden anchor weighted with a stone; a small or makeshift anchor; also fig.
1630 (1790) Winthrop *Jrl.* 22, The wind overblew so much at N.W. as they were forced to come to a hillock [sic] at twenty fathom. **1631**

in 1846 Young *Chron. MA Bay* 327, They . . let down their killock, that they might drive the more slowly. . . But the stone slipping out of the killock, . . they found themselves out of sight of land. **1637** (1972) Morton *New Engl. Canaan* 262, The inconstant windes shiftinge at night did force the kellecke home, and billedge the boat. **1663** in 1881 Boston Registry Dept. *Records* 7.16, If any . . doe drop any ancor, Grapnell or Kelleck upon the flatts . . theay ar to pay tenn shillings. **1776** in 1954 Colonial Soc. MA *Pub.* 36.414, Upon which the fleet immediately up Killeck and stood out to sea. **1840** (1841) Dana *2 Yrs.* 109, We . . wade out with them [=hides] and throw them into the boat, which . . we usually kept anchored by a small hedge [sic for *kedge*], or keeleg, just outside of the surf. **1865** Essex Inst. *Coll.* 7.35 **NEng coast,** The killick (usually so pronounced) . . is an implement of very ancient and very common use on our New England sea-board; and . . the word is familiar to all our mariners and to every boy that sails a "dory." The name is properly applied to a peculiarly constructed anchor used for small boats. The anchor consists of a wooden frame enclosing a weight, usually a stone. The bottom of the killick is composed of one or more bars of wood. . . A few inches from the extremities of these bars strong wooden rods two or three feet in length are made secure to the bars perpendicularly and are brought together around the stone previously placed within them. **1894** *DN* 1.332 **NJ,** *Killick:* small anchor. (Very common on coast.) **1896** *DN* 1.419 **neMA,** *Killick (killock, kellock):* a stone enclosed in a wooden crate or frame, used as an anchor. **1899** (1912) Green *VA Folk-Speech* 250, *Killick.* **1909** *S. Atl. Qrly.* 8.40 **seSC** [Gullah], The fisherman *drops killick* on a *whiting drop.* [**1925** *DN* 5.337, *Old granny.* . . A kellock anchor (made of sticks and stones lashed together).] **1945** Colcord *Sea Language* 111 **ME, Cape Cod, Long Island,** *Killick.* . . Used alongshore in the phrase "up killick," meaning to start off in a hurry. **1975** Gould *ME Lingo* 153, A *killick* is a small anchor, usually homemade and sometimes from a rock. . . To put down a *killick* means to settle in, almost to take root. A select-man said, "We watch these newcomers to town, and if they look's-if they're going to drop their killicks, we charge 'em back to the place they came from." This means that if they look as if they might go on welfare, their residence is carefully established in town of origin before the time limit that would make them "settled" and the responsibility of the new town.

killickinnic See **kinnikinnick**

killifish n [Var of **kill** n[1] + *fish*]

1 also *kelly, killfish, killie(fish), killy(fish):* A fish of the family Cyprinodontidae. **chiefly seNY** See Map Also called **minnow B2b, topminnow, mummichog.** For other names of var genera and spp see **flagfish, gudgeon 1, hardhead 2g, mayfish, pupfish, pursy minnow, rainwater fish, rockfish, sheepshead killifish, sac-a-lait, starhead topminnow, studfish, yellowtail**

1787 Gesellschaft Naturforschender Freunde *Schriften* 8.172, Diese beyde Fische, der Yellow bellied Cobler und Killfish, halten sich um Neuyork, in Kriken [sic] und Teichen . . auf. [=Both these fishes, the Yellow bellied Cobbler and Killfish, are found in creeks and ponds about New York.] **1814** in 1815 Lit. & Philos. Soc. NY *Trans.* 1.441, *Sheep's-Head Killifish. (Esox ovinus.)* . . Length about an inch and a half; and remarkably large in the girth. **1842** DeKay *Zool. NY* 4.216, *The Striped Killifish. Ibid* 217, Its [=the striped killifish's] popular name is de-rived from its abundance in creeks and estuaries, which our Dutch ancestors termed "kills." *Ibid* 218, This fish [=*Fundulus heteroclitus*] is known under the names of *Minny* (minnow), and more generally of *Big Killie.* **1856** *Porter's Spirit of Times* 27 Dec 274 **NY,** The young shad are hauled ashore, without thought, and left to perish, high and dry, by thousands, the destroyers, probably, not distinguishing them from ordinary small-fry, killy-fish, shiners, and the like. **1860** *Harper's New Mth. Mag.* 20.489, Our minnow—or, as it is called around New York, killie-fish—is not the same as the English fish which goes by that name. **1897** NY Forest Fish & Game Comm. *Annual Rept. for 1896* 232, *Fundulus majalis.* . . Killifish.—This large killifish is found all the year in Gravesend Bay. **1898** (1970) Hamblen *Genl. Manager* 243 **neNJ,** Frank had remained for a bit seated on a stone behind me, watching the 'killies' swimming in the shallow water. **1906** NJ State Museum *Annual Rept. for 1905* 185, *Fundulus majalis.* . . Minnow. Killi Fish. *Ibid* 188, *Fundulus heteroclitus macrolepidotus.* . . Killy. Killie. Killy Fish. *Ibid* 193, *Fundulus diaphanus.* . . Killy. Killie Fish. **1913** [see 2 below]. **1955** MA Audubon Soc. *Bulletin* 39.312 **CT,** *Green Heron.* . . Kelly Fisher. . . As feeding on killifishes, called kellies. **1968** *DARE* (Qu. P7, *Small fish used as bait for bigger fish*) Infs **NY**36, 37, 44, 47, 51, 57, 63, 89, Killie. **1993** *DARE* File **seNY** (as of 1940s), I

don't use *kill* as a small stream but the minnows that live in them ever were *killies!* I was raised on southern Long Island.

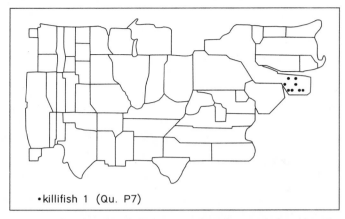

•killifish 1 (Qu. P7)

2 Usu a live-bearing fish *(Heterandria formosa),* but also the related oviparous **mosquito fish. Sth**

1907 NJ State Museum *Annual Rept. for 1906* 163, *Heterandria formosa.* . . Least Killifish. Introduced by the New Jersey Agricultural College Experiment Station, with *Gambusia,* during November of 1905. **1913** *Auk* 30.488 **Okefenokee GA,** Among the water-lilies abound ribbon snakes . . , killifishes (*Fundulus* and *Gambusia*), and several species of frogs. **1955** Carr–Goin *Guide Reptiles* 78 **FL,** *Heterandria formosa* . . Least Killifish. . . Tiniest of fishes, with a spot on the dorsal fin. . . South Carolina to Florida. . . Swamps, ditches, and the margins of nearly any body of water. **1991** Amer. Fisheries Soc. *Common Names Fishes* 35, *Heterandria formosa* . . least killifish.

killig (pole) See **kilhig**

killikinnick, killinick See **kinnikinnick**

killing-peter n Also *kill peter, kill 'em Polly* [Prob echoic] **esp FL**

=least tern.

1925 Bailey *Birds FL* 9, Least tern. . . *Sterna albifrons antillarum* Sand peter, Kill peter, Sea swallow, Little striker. **1932** Howell *FL Bird Life* 266, *Least Tern.* . . *Other Names:* Little Striker, Killing-peter. **1951** Pough *Audubon Water Bird* 334, Kill 'em Polly. . . Killing-peter. *See* Least tern. **1969** Longstreet *Birds FL* 68, *Killing-peter.* . . The least tern . . is the smallest . . member of the tern family living in the United States.

kill-kid n Cf **kill-calf, lambkill**

A **sheep laurel** (here: *Kalmia angustifolia*).

1900 Lyons *Plant Names* 209, *K[almia] angustifolia.* . . Calf-kill, Lamb-kill, Kill-kid. **1924** *Amer. Botanist* 30.58, *Kalmia angustifolia* . . is disparaged by such names as . . "calf kill," "kill kid" and "sheep poison." **1941** *LANE* Map 249, 1 inf, **seMA,** Low laurel = kill kid = lamb kill.

kill-kit'n kaboodle See **kit** n 2b

kill-lamb n

1 See **lambkill.**

2 A **staggerbush** (here: *Lyonia mariana*).

1843 Torrey *Flora NY* 1.435, *Andromeda Mariana.* . . *Kill-lamb. Stag-gerbush.* . . It is supposed to be poisonous to lambs and calves, produc-ing a disease called the *staggers.* **1958** Jacobs–Burlage *Index Plants NC* 85, *Lyonia mariana.* . . Kill lamb. . . It is also said to be poisonous.

killock See **killick**

kill one's own snakes See **kill** v C4a

killorill See **quillaree**

kill out See **kill** v C1

kill peter See **killing-peter**

killpot n [Folk-etym; cf **skillpot**] Cf **kettlepot**

=mud turtle 2b(1).

1952 Brown *NC Folkl.* 1.555 **cnNC,** *Kill-pot.* . . A water-terrapin. **1970** *DARE* (Qu. P24, . . *Kinds of turtles*) Inf **VA**38, Killpot—small, 6–8 inches long.

kill the dog See **dog** n B5a

kill up See **kill** v C1

killy bird See **killy hawk**

killy(fish) See **killifish 1**

killy hawk n Also *killdeer hawk, killy bird, kitty hawk* [Echoic]
chiefly Sth Cf **billy hawk, chilly ~**
=**sparrow hawk.**

  1904 (1910) Wheelock *Birds CA* 162, Desert Sparrow Hawk. . . *Cerchneis sparveria phalaena.* . . His call is a sharp, high "killy-killy-killy," uttered as he flies over his prey, and has given him the nickname of "Killy Hawk." **1917** (1923) *Birds Amer.* 2.90, Sparrow Hawk. . . Mouse Hawk; Kitty Hawk; Windhover. **1918** (1927) Chapman *Our Winter Birds* 128, The Sparrow Hawk's call is a high, rapidly repeated "Killy, killy, killy," which in the south gives it the name of "Killy Hawk." **1928** Skinner *Guide Winter Birds NC* 113, Sometimes while flying, and while perching too . . , Sparrow Hawks give their call of "killy, killy." This is rapidly repeated and so characteristic that these birds are often known as "Killy Birds" or "Killy Hawks." **1946** Hausman *Eastern Birds* 205, Eastern Sparrow Hawk. . . Other Names—Killy Hawk, Kitty Hawk. **1955** Lowery *LA Birds* 212, The call is a *killy-killy-killy,* from which the local name "killy-hawk" is derived. **1955** MA Audubon Soc. *Bulletin* 39.442 **ME, MA,** *Sparrow Hawk.* Killy Hawk. . . First term sonic. **1966–69** DARE (Qu. Q4, . . *Kinds of hawks*) Inf **FL**27, Killy hawk—small; **GA**46, Killy hawk ['kɪlɪ hɔk]; **GA**65, Kitty hawk; **MO**19, Killdeer hawk.

killyloo (bird) n Cf **chilly-lou**
=**filliloo bird.**

  1967 DARE FW Addit **TN**22, Killyloo ['kɪlɪ,lu]—joking name for a bird that can't be identified. "What's that?" "It must be a killyloo." Used in conversation. **1969** DARE (Qu. CC17, *Imaginary animals or monsters that people . . tell tales about—especially to tease greenhorns*) Inf **NJ**58, Killyloo ['kɪlɪ,lu] bird—common.

kiln n Usu |kɪl|; also |ki(ə)l|; for addit varr see quots Pronc-spp *keel, kill* **esp C Atl, Lower Missip Valley** See Map *esp freq among speakers with little formal educ* Cf **bank** n¹ **1, dry house, hill** n **2, hole** n **3**

A place for storing root vegetables consisting of a mound or pit covered with earth, or a shed; hence v *kiln* to preserve in such a place.

  1966–70 DARE (Qu. M19, *A place for keeping carrots, turnips, potatoes, and so on over the winter*) Inf **AR**40, Keel or a cellar; **DC**5, [kɪ^əl]—dirt over potatoes, now done to keep them over winter; **DE**3, [kɪl]—dig a hole, put straw in it, cover them with board and earth; **LA**12, These days they don't use banks, they have dry [kɪlz]—a wooden house that keeps these things dry—they keep all winter; **LA**22, [kɪl]—you make a pit like and line it with pine straw and put your potatoes in it and cover it—also called "pine-straw kill"; **MD**15, **VA**57, Kiln; **VA**77, Kill; **MD**38, [kɪl]—a foot of straw placed on ground, vegetables piled on, several inches of dirt piled over this; **MD**43, [kɪəl]—small building, half in ground, dark, no windows—used to have here, not now; **MS**87, Potato (or turnip) keel; **TN**24, [kɪl]—just like the roof of a house—two gable ends—made of lumber—like shiplap covered with dirt; **TN**26, [kɪl]—pour potatoes on the ground and cover them with cornstalks or grass, then dirt; **TX**26, Kills; **VA**38, [kɪlz]—old-fashioned; **VA**68, [kɪɪl]; **VA**105, Potato [kɪɪl]—mound of straw and dirt covering potatoes and other root vegetables. [13 of 17 Infs gs educ or less] **1986** Pederson *LAGS Concordance* **Gulf Region, esp MS, LA,**

TX, AR, 1 inf, Kiln—where potatoes were kept; they would kiln their turnips and apples; 1 inf, Make a kiln—to take care of potatoes; 1 inf, Kiln—sweet potatoes kept here in winter; 1 inf, Those kilns—potatoes; potato kiln—shed with rafters, straw bed; 1 inf, Dirt kiln—for potatoes; 4 infs, Potato kiln; 1 inf, (Po)tato kiln—dug in ground; makeshift building; 1 inf, Potato kiln—just dirt pile or separate building; 1 inf, Potato kiln—potatoes kept—walled, roof, straw; 1 inf, Potato kiln—shed or covered hill [Inf unsure]; 1 inf, Potato kiln, turnip kiln. [12 of 14 infs old, 11 gs educ or less; all proncs of the type [kɪʌ^əl]]

kilt adj See **kill** v C3

kilt(ed) v See **kill** v B

kim See **come** A3

kimmelweck n Pronc-spp *kemmilwick, kimmilwick* [Ger *Kümmel* caraway + *Weck* roll] **wNY, esp Buffalo** Cf **beef on weck**
A caraway roll, used esp for a beef sandwich.

  1952 Tracy *Coast Cookery* 141 **wNY,** There's only one food that seems to be pretty much Buffalo's own—the Kimmel Weck. This is a hard-crusted roll with a cross in the center dividing it so it may be easily broken in fours. Each roll is glazed to hold a generous sprinkling of coarse salt and caraway seeds. The rolls were developed, we are told, to accompany beer. . . They are too difficult to make at home. **1969** DARE (Qu. H41, . . *Kinds of roll or bun sandwiches . . in a round bun or roll*) Inf **NY**135, Kimmelwick ['kɛmɪl,wɪk] [FW: I think this is just in western NY]. **1977** DARE File **wNY,** Kimmelweck—a bun or roll, sometimes cloverleaf in shape, frequently with seeds on top, that's used especially for beef sandwiches. Common in restaurants. **1982** *Smithsonian Letters* **wNY,** *Beef on weck.* Weck is short for the German Kummelweck (pronounced "kimmelwick"). . . Kummelweck is a crusty roll topped with a sprinkling of *caraway* seeds and coarse salt.

kimmie See **commie**

kin n [By ext from *kin* family, relations]
  1 in phr *kin to:* A relative (or relatives) of; a relationship to; similarity to; often becoming adjectival: related to; resembling. **chiefly Sth, S Midl**
  1884 Smith *Bill Arp's Scrap Book* 72 **GA,** Then there is . . snakes, which are my eternal horror, and I shall always believe are sum kin to the devil himself. **1902** DN 2.237 **sIL** [Pioneer dialect], *Kin.* . . Relative. The latter or relation are not used. Negatively and ironically, 'I don't claim any kin to' = I don't identify myself with. **1903** DN 2.298 **Cape Cod MA** (as of a1857), *Kin.* . . In expression 'no kin to me,' of no resemblance in disposition. **1905** DN 3.85 **nwAR,** *Kin, adj.* Related. 'Is he kin to you?' Universal. **1906** DN 3.120 **sIN,** *Kin.* . . Relative. "I'm no kin to him." **1923** DN 5.212 **swMO,** *Kin,* adj. or noun. Related to. "Is he kin t' you-all?" [**1936** *Esquire* Sept 32 **neKY,** He wasn't no akin to us.] *Ibid,* Them boys ain't no kin to me. [**1940** in 1944 ADD, 'He's no akin to her.' Very common in W.Va.] **1941** Nixon *Possum Trot* 146 **neAL,** Regionalism. . . is akin to folklore. **1951** *New Yorker* 31 Mar 26 **TN,** She was only going for another stay with some of that Tolliver family she was kin to. **c1960** Wilson Coll. **csKY,** *Kin.* . . "He is kin to me." **1970** Thompson Coll. **Birmingham AL** (as of 1920s), They got you kin to 'em pretty good since they talked you into buying that old wreck of a car, ain't they. **1986** Pederson *LAGS Concordance* **Gulf Region,** 88 infs, Kin to; 72 infs, No kin to; 26 infs, Not (any) kin to. [DARE Ed: LAGS fieldworkers may have included the phrase "kin to" in eliciting a response.] **1988** Lehrer *Kick the Can* 208 **TX,** "I'm no sinner." "You're kin to a few."

  2 in phr *out of kin:* See quot.
  1913 DN 4.5 **ME,** *Out of kin.* . . Not related.

kin v See **can** v¹ **1a**

kind adj
  1 See quot. [OED *kind* a. 4.b "Now only *dial.*"]
  1899 (1912) Green *VA Folk-Speech* 250, *Kind.* . . Easy to work; gentle; easily managed; a horse is recommended as, "A good saddle-horse, and kind in harness."
  2 See quot. [OED *kind* a. 6 "Now *rare* exc. *dial.*"]
  1899 (1912) Green *VA Folk-Speech* 250, *Kind.* . . Intimate; friendly.

kindle See **kindle wood**

kindler n
A piece of kindling.
  1845 Judd *Margaret* 6 **NEng,** Put some kindlers under the pot. **1884** (1885) McCook *Tenants* 380 **PA,** "Now, Dan," I said, "get a few kindlers and we shall make a little bonfire." **1927** *AmSp* 2.358 **cwWV,** Kin-

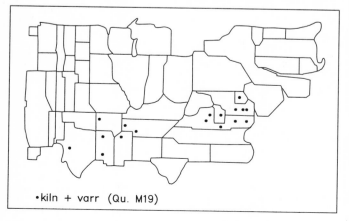

•kiln + varr (Qu. M19)

dlers . . kindling wood. "Have the children brought in kindlers for morning?" **1941** *LANE* Map 330 *(Log)* 1 inf, **cCT,** Kindlers [kɪnlr̩z] = *kindling.* **1986** Pederson *LAGS Concordance (Wood you use to start a fire)* 1 inf, **swGA,** Kindler.

kindle wood n Also *kindle* Cf **kindling wood**

Wood used to light a fire.

c1955 Reed–Person *Ling. Atlas Pacific NW,* 1 inf, Kindlewood. **1968** *DARE* (Qu. D34, . . *The small pieces of wood and other stuff that are used to start a fire*) Inf **FL**51, Kindle wood [FW: corr to kindling]; **IL**57A, Kindle wood; **LA**20, Kindle [kɪn]. **1986** Pederson *LAGS Concordance (Wood you use to start a fire)* 3 infs, **seMS, seTN,** Kindle wood; 1 inf, **cnAL,** Kindle wood—split pine.

kindling n esp N and C′Atl Cf Intro "Language Changes" II.6 Gram form.

Used as a count noun.

1839 Kirkland *New Home* 73, I guess they'll do better for kindlin's than any thing else. **1871** (1882) Stowe *Fireside Stories* 112 **MA,** I see him goin' by as I was out a splittin' kindlin's. **1877** Habberton *Jericho Road* 69 **NY,** He . . industriously devoted himself to the preparation of kindlings for the morning's fire. **1911** Shute *Plupy* 14 **NH,** When he was a man he would never make his boy split kindlings, but would buy them all split. **1941** *LANE* Map 330 *(Log),* Pieces of wood for fuel are usually called . . collectively *kindling(s)* or *kin(d)lers.* . . 1 inf, **swCT,** Kindlings to build the fire; 1 inf, **cCT,** Rubble = kindlings; 3 infs, **CT, ceMA,** Kindlings; 1 inf, **ceMA,** When you put the kindlings in you call it basting the fire. **1965–70** *DARE* (Qu. D34, . . *The small pieces of wood and other stuff that are used to start a fire*) 16 Infs, **scattered, but esp N and C Atl,** (Wood) kindlings. **c1970** Pederson *Dial. Surv. Rural GA,* 1 inf, **seGA,** Kindlings. [Inf old] **1986** Pederson *LAGS Concordance (Lightwood)* 11 infs, **GA, TN, AR, AL, LA,** Kindlings.

kindling weed n [See quot]

A **snakeweed** (here: *Gutierrezia dracunculoides*).

1936 Whitehouse *TX Flowers* 157, *Kindling-weed (Amphiachyris dracunculoides)* is a pasture pest in the southern part of the Great Plains region. . . The resinous foliage of the dried plants was also highly valued for kindling fires.

kindling wood n Pronc-sp *kin'lin-wood* scattered, but more freq Atl See Map Cf **fatwood, lightwood** n[1] Note: The term *kindling* is found throughout the US.

Small pieces of wood used for lighting a fire; also fig.

1833 in 1834 Smith *Letters Jack Downing* 177, Gineral, I'm afraid we'll git a stumper from Philadelphy one of these days, that will nock us all into kindlin wood. **1876** Clark *Elbow Room* 54, Keyser, if you want any supper, you'd better get me some kin'lin-wood pretty quick. **1904** *NY Post* (NY) 30 Sept 6/3, His calm verdict upon the struggle for the gold standard makes kindling wood of the Republican platform. **1927** [see **kindler**]. **1962** Atwood *Vocab. TX* 48, *Wood to start the fire.* The small pieces of wood used to kindle a fire are usually referred to as . . *kindlin(g) wood* [20% of 273 infs]. **1965–70** *DARE* (Qu. D34, . . *The small pieces of wood and other stuff that are used to start a fire*) 60 Infs, **scattered, but more freq Atl,** Kindling (or kindlin') wood; (Qu. T8, *Joints of pine wood that burn easily and make good fuel*) Inf **PA**70, Kindling wood. **1990** Pederson *LAGS Regional Matrix* 23 **Gulf Region,** 52 Infs, Kindling wood.

kindly adv [Cf *EDD* kindly adv. 9 "Rather, somewhat"] chiefly Sth, S Midl, esp sAppalachians

Kind of, somewhat; rather; to some degree.

1892 (1958) Wister *Out West* 146, Both these men are simple and pleasant natures, and I grew to kindly like them in the four days. **1910** *DN* 3.456 **KY,** *Kindly.* . . Kind of. Very common. "He was kindly angry at me." **1931** *PMLA* 46.1306 **sAppalachians,** Kindly crazy-like; he ain't nothin' above his eyes. **1937** *Hall Coll.* **eTN,** "I feel kindly tough [=sick] today." "Eddie Conner seemed to have kindly stayed at the Enloe place." "It's kindly poison." "We killed him [a bear] and rolled him down the mountain to where we could kindly dress him." **1954** *Harder Coll.* **cwTN,** We have all been sick but are kindly straight now. **1954** Roberts *I Bought Dog* 9 **seKY,** And his brother got kindly uneasy about him and he went to see about him because he hadn't been to work. **1966** *PADS* 46.24 **cnAR** (as of 1952), It got me kindly agured. **1967** *DARE* FW Addit **NC,** "I'd kindly ['kaɪnli] like to do that." Kind of ['kaɪnə] is also used but is not as warm. **1968–69** *DARE* Tape **GA**50, During the fall of the year when the water's kindly low, you would just see them old water moccasins; **NC**53, I polished two or three rubies myself, but it takes diamond dust to polish it and I can't afford it so mine's kindly rough but they're shaped. **1986** Pederson *LAGS Concordance,* 1 inf, **neTN,** Kindly runs in our family—sort of; 1 inf, **ceTN,** It was kindly funny how things would go up right quick; 1 inf, **swTN,** Jake-leg preacher—just kindly preaches. **1988** Tyler *Breathing Lessons* 142 **sePA** [Black], I reckon it must've hit you-all the same way—kindly like you half glimpsed it out of the corner of your vision. **1993** Offutt *Same River Twice* 63 **wTX,** "I told him that if we fought, all we'd do was rip our clothes, and women didn't favor men wearing tore-up shirts. I said there was nothing wrong with fighting but I didn't feel like it today." "That's all it took?" "No," Bill said. "I kindly had hold of his balls the whole time, squeezing tighter and tighter."

kindry, kinery See **kinnery**

kinfolk n pl Also *kinfolks;* rarely *kinsfolk(s), kinfolkses* widespread, but chiefly Sth, S Midl, Cent, TX See Map Cf folk B2, kinlin, kinnery, kinpeople, relation

Relatives, kin.

1873 Twain–Warner *Gilded Age* 33, No father, no mother, no kin folks of no kind. **1893** Shands *MS Speech* 42, *Kinfolks* is the common term for kindred (noun) used by all classes in Mississippi. **1902** *DN* 2.237 **sIL,** *Kinfolks.* . . Never kinsfolk. Kinsman and kinswoman not used; but 'He is kin to me'—'They're some o my kin,' and the like expressions. **1903** *DN* 2.318 **seMO,** *Kinfolks* or often *kin.* **1907** *DN* 3.237 **nwAR,** *Kin-folks.* . . The words 'relatives' and 'relations' are rarely used. Universal. **1908** *DN* 3.327 **eAL, wGA,** *Kin-folks.* . . Common. **1931** *AmSp* 7.93 **eKY,** But maybe Clevie has gone to some of his kin-folks. **1941** *LANE* Map 388 *(Relatives),* 1 inf, **cCT,** Kin folks; 1 inf, **ceCT,** *Kin folks,* heard in Maine; 1 inf, **cVT,** Kin folks; 1 inf, **sME coast,** *Kin folks* [regarded as old-fashioned]; 1 inf, **cME,** Kin folks; 1 inf, **NH,** Kinsfolk. **1950** *WELS* **WI** *(Relatives)* 1 Inf, Kinfolk; *(People that are related to you)* 3 Infs, Kinfolk; 1 Inf, Kinfolk—old-fashioned; 1 inf, Kinfolks. **1964** in 1970 Johnson *White House Diary* 103 **TX,** I had asked Mrs. MacArthur and her son, and the Ambassador and all the kinfolks. **1965–70** *DARE* (Qu. Z9, *General word for others related to you by blood*) 156 Infs, **widespread, but chiefly Sth, S Midl, Cent, TX,** (My) kinfolks; 33 Infs, **scattered,** (My) kinfolk; (Qu. Z8) Infs **CO**20, **GA**54, **AL**26, **DC**8, **MI**89, **OH**56, **PA**42, **TX**61, (My) kinfolks; **FL**18, **NY**159, (My) kinfolk; (Qu. Z7) Inf **DC**8, Kinfolks; (Qu. AA17) Infs **CO**33,

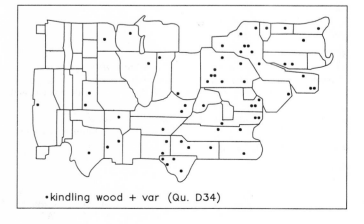
•kindling wood + var (Qu. D34)

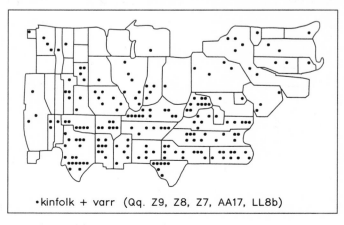
•kinfolk + varr (Qq. Z9, Z8, Z7, AA17, LL8b)

TX103, Kinfolks; (Qu. LL8b) Inf **MA**58, Plenty kinfolks. **1986** Pederson *LAGS Concordance* **Gulf Region,** 360 infs, Kinfolks; 3 infs, Kinfolks—extended family; 1 inf, Kinfolks—more distant; 1 inf, Kinfolks—more distant than parents, grandparents; 1 inf, Kinfolks—other than parents, grandparents; 1 inf, Kinfolks—usually other than immediate family; 84 infs, Kinfolk; 2 infs, Kinsfolks; 1 inf, Kinfolkses.

king n

1 also *queen:* The chief or key player in var children's games; see quots.

1907 *DN* 3.245 **eME,** *King. . .* the player who is *it* in the game of *king's land.* **1965–70** *DARE* (Qu. EE1, *. . Games . . children play . . in which they form a ring, and either sing or recite a rhyme*) Inf **TN**62, "It" [said]: "King king cannico." Others [said]: "You go nannico"; then "it" or "king" caught others; (Qu. EE13b, *In games in which all the others hide, the one who must try to find them, he's _____*) Inf **OK**16, King or queen.

2 A large playing marble, esp a **shooter** or **middleman 1;** one's most valuable or best marble. **esp N and C Atl** See Map

1957 *Sat. Eve. Post Letters* **WI,** King—a shooter. **1957** Battaglia *Resp. to PADS* 20 **eMD** (*Kinds of marbles—large ones*) King. **1965–70** *DARE* (Qu. EE6a, *. . Different kinds of marbles—the big one that's used to knock others out of the ring*) Infs **MD**38, **MA**15, NJ16, 53, **NY**200, NC33, King (marble); FL33, **KY**70, NJ3, **NY**75, King (marble) [Infs unsure]; **HI**1, King—kinged the smaller ones; NJ69, King—larger than vents; VA30, The king; WV3, King—center marble; (QR, near Qu. EE6a) RI12, Flipper—could be an agate or a steelie or a China king—a white China marble; (Qu. EE6d, *Special marbles*) Inf **CT**12, King marbles—boys had them; **MD**31, King—large marble placed in center of ring—only after knocking this one out can player keep the other marbles he's shot out of ring; NC33, The king; RI12, Kings. [16 of 17 total Infs old] **1968** *DARE* Tape **SC**58, [FW:] You put one [marble] in each corner of the ring. . . and one in the middle. [Inf:] And one in the middle. . . If I hit your marble—if I went in and busted that ring—we always said "get the king," in the middle, the king—we'd shoot and try to get him out, and then we'd start and try to get the rest out. **c1970** Wiersma *Marbles Terms* **MI,** King marble—the most valuable marble that one possesses.

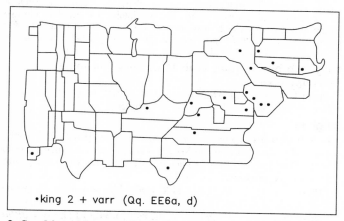

•king 2 + varr (Qq. EE6a, d)

3 See **king, king can I go.**
4 See **king's ex.**
5 See **king salmon.**
6 See **kingfish 1, 2.**
7 See **king mackerel.**

king and queen, King Arthur was King William's son See King William was King George's son

king bee n esp Sth, S Midl See Map Cf queen bee

A man in a position of authority or dominance.

1875 Lewis *Quad's Odds* 434, Daniel Webster was a king bee in his time. He could get up at a moment's notice and speak on any topic, from free trade to the best cure for poll-evil. **1965** Will *Okeechobee Boats* 55 **FL,** Them was the days of steamboats on the river, my boy, and the king bees of this river was the brothers, J. Fred and Conrad Menge. **1965–70** *DARE* (Qu. HH17, *A person who tries to appear important, or who tries to lay down the law in his community: "He'd like to be the _____ around here."*) 36 Infs, **esp Sth, S Midl,** King

bee; (Qu. V10a, *. . Joking names . . for a sheriff*) Inf **IA**22, King bee; (Qu. GG19b, *When you can see from the way a person acts that he's feeling important or independent: "He seems to think he's _____."*) Inf **AL**6, King bee; (Qu. HH43a, *The top person in charge of a group of workmen*) Inf **CO**34, King bee. **1986** Pederson *LAGS Concordance (Master)* 1 inf, **csTX,** King bee.

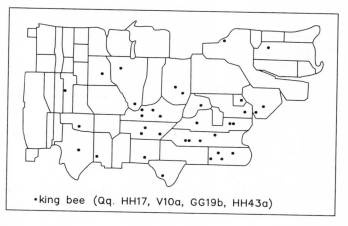

•king bee (Qq. HH17, V10a, GG19b, HH43a)

kingbilly n

A **croaker** n[1] **1a(1)** (here: *Micropogon undulatus*).

1984 *DARE* File **Chesapeake Bay** [Watermen's vocab], Croaker, grumbler, growler, hard head, kingbilly.

kingbird n Cf yellow kingbird

1 A bird of the genus *Tyrannus,* esp *T. tyrannus.* [See quots 1895, 1956] Also called **bee bird 1, ~ martin 1, flycatcher 1a.** For other names of *T. tyrannus* see **bee catcher 2, billy martin, black grasset, buddy bee martin, crow snatcher, dishwasher 2, fence-post bird, field martin, grasset 4, king martin, ~ priest;** for other names of *T. verticalis* see **catbird 3 Cf martin**

1778 Carver *Travels N. Amer.* 475, The King Bird is like a swallow, and seems to be of the same species as the black martin or swift. **1801** *Thomas' MA Spy or Worcester Gaz.* (MA) 25 Nov 1/2, Now he has a number of them picking at him. Just as a parcel of King birds will pick at a Crow. **1895** Minot *Land-Birds New Engl.* 284, The King-birds feed almost exclusively on winged insects, which they seize with a click of the bill. . . Their notes are shrill twitters. . . Among them may be heard the syllable *king,* which constantly recurs. *Ibid* 282, The Gray King-bird (*T. dominicensis*) is about nine inches long. **1913** *Pacific Coast Avifauna* 9.59 **cwCA,** Western Kingbird. *Tyrannus verticalis.* . . This valley supports a very large population of kingbirds. **1932** Howell *FL Bird Life* 316, Kingbirds are rather noisy and restless, and not at all shy. Their common name was given to them because of their habit of driving other birds away from their territory. *Ibid* 319, Arkansas Kingbird: *Tyrannus verticalis.* **1940** Todd *Birds W. PA* 340, The Kingbird is well named. . . Nervous, irritable, and truculent in disposition, always intolerant when it fancies that its proprietary rights have been invaded, and brooking no interference with its domestic arrangements, this tyrant compels the respect of its feathered neighbors. **1956** MA Audubon Soc. *Bulletin* 40.83, Kingbird. . . In allusion to its dominating habit of driving other, and often larger, birds away from its nesting territory. **1965–70** *DARE* (Qu. Q14) 123 Infs, **widespread,** Kingbird; AL2, IL25, MD3, TX40, Kingbird—bee martin; IL32, Kingbird—bee bird; NM13, Also have a bee martin or a kingbird—not really a martin; CA115, Western kingbird; CO7, Kingbird—eastern and western; IL143, KS15, Kingbird—catbird; MA21, Kingbird—they are crow chasers; MA30, Kingbird—fence-post bird; MA40, Kingbird—they'll fight a hawk or crow; MA68, Kingbird—fight crows; NY227, Kingbird—go after the crows; PA121, Kingbird—has a topknot; WA12, Arkansas kingbird; (Qu. Q23) Inf **ME**14, Kingbird—size of a robin—black and many other colors mixed in. **1977** Udvardy *Audubon Field Guide Birds* 550, Eastern Kingbird (*Tyrannus tyrannus*).

2 =**scissor-tailed flycatcher. esp LA**

1911 *Forest & Stream* 77.174 **seLA,** *Muscivora forficata.*—Kingbird. **1916** *Times–Picayune* (New Orleans LA) 16 Apr mag sec 1/3, *Scissor-tailed flycatcher* (Muscivora forficata), "Kingbird;" Texan Bird of Paradise; Swallow-tailed Flycatcher. [**1964** Phillips *Birds AZ* 80, The Scissor-tailed Flycatcher is nothing but a Western Kingbird with pinkish belly and long tail streaming behind. Even the call note is similar.]

3 =**golden-crowned kinglet.** [See quot 1956]

1917 *Wilson Bulletin* 29.2.85 **cME coast,** *Regulus satrapa*—Kingbird. **1956** MA Audubon Soc. *Bulletin* 40.129, Golden-crowned kinglet. King Bird (Maine. The ornamentation of the head suggests a crown.)

4 A **kingfisher** (here: *Megaceryle alcyon*).

1968 *DARE* (Qu. Q14, . . *Names* . . *for* . . *kingbird*) Inf **IA**29, King-bird [same as] kingfisher.

king buzzard n

1 =**caracara.**

1951 Teale *North with Spring* 43 **cFL,** In the aristocracy of carrion feeders, the caracara ranks first. It justifies its local name of king buzzard. **1955** Forbush–May *Birds* 123, Audubon's Caracara *Polyborus cheriway auduboni*. . . King Buzzard.

2 =**turkey vulture.**

1968 *DARE* (Qu. Q13, *Names* . . *for the vulture*) Inf **LA**20, Buzzard—has a black head; red-headed one is called the king buzzard.

king cake n esp New Orleans LA

A party cake, usu made for Mardi Gras season, containing an object used to determine the "king" or host of a succeeding party.

[**1889** (1971) Farmer *Americanisms* 333, *King Cake Day.*—A Mexican equivalent for the English Twelfth Cake Day, the 6th of January. It is customary then to invite one's friends to dinner, and for dessert a large cake resembling a crown is served. It is cut into as many slices as there are persons at the table. In the cake, before baking, a large bean is placed, and whoever gets the slice containing the bean has to give a party within a few weeks. There is always much merriment at the cutting of the *king cake.*] **1916** *DN* 4.269 **seLA,** *King-cake.* . . A kind of cake containing a single nut or bean, used to determine who shall be king at the next series of balls. **1968** *DARE* (Qu. FF2, . . *Kinds of parties*) Inf **LA**46, King cake parties—a round cake is made with a bean in it; whoever gets the bean in his piece of cake gives the next party. **1983** *Reinecke Coll.* 6 **LA,** *King Cake.* . . a ring or crown-shaped cake of yeast bread, sweetened and decorated with citron, colored sugar, etc. It conceals a nut, bean, or, generally now, china or plastic baby doll. . . Beginning of King Cake season in N[ew] O[rleans] is Twelfth Night. Participant who gets "bean" . . must give next party. He is "King" or "Queen" of evening. . . Twelfth Day is "Kings' Day" and the concealed baby is revealed, undergoes an epiphany. **1984** Stall *Proud New Orleans* 7, Food has been used for hundreds of years in France and New Orleans to help celebrate Mardi Gras. One of these foods is called the King Cake. The shape has always been in the form of a huge ring, size depending upon the number of people who were to attend the balls that were held weekly from January 6 (Little Christmas) until Mardi Gras. **1991** *DARE* File **csMS,** [Advt:] *Paul's Pastry Shop King Cakes.* We now offer 20 different flavors to customize your favorite King Cake. . . Be sure to watch for our "Super Bowl" and Valentines Day King Cakes! . . Our family King Cake recipe has 20 years of baking experience. . . Our King Cakes have been shipped to all 50 states. *Ibid,* Starting the twelfth day after Christmas, King Cake Parties continue until the first day of lent, ending on Fat Tuesday, Mardi Gras! King Cakes were originally a simple ring of dough with little decoration. The New Orleans style King Cake is brightly decorated with Mardi Gras colored sugars and fruit. **1992** *Ibid* **Baton Rouge LA,** [Catalog:] *Mardi Gras King Cake.* A cinnamon-flavored confection that's the center of parties during carnival season in New Orleans.

king calico See **king, king can I go**

king coal-oil See **king's cure-all 1**

king coot n

Either the **surf scoter** or the American **scoter** (*Melanitta nigra*).

1923 U.S. Dept. Ag. *Misc. Circular* 13.30 **ME,** *Surf Scoter.* . . *Vernacular Names.* . . *In local use.* . . King coot. **1925** (1928) Forbush *Birds MA* 1.277, *Oidemia perspicillata.* . . King coot. **1955** MA Audubon Soc. *Bulletin* 39.377 **ME,** *American Scoter.* . . King Coot.

king crab n

1 A crablike marine arthropod (*Limulus polyphemus*) of the Atlantic and Gulf coasts. Also called **horsefoot, horseshoe crab**

c1612 (1849) Strachey *Hist. VA Britannia* 127, There be twoo sorts of sea crabbs, and the one our people call a king crabb . . of a foote in

length and half a foote in bredth. **1775** (1962) Romans *Nat. Hist. FL* 302, It was no other than a crab of the kind called in the southern province a king crab, and to the northward a horse-shoe. **1792** Belknap *Hist. NH* 3.183, King crab, or Horse shoe—*Monoculus polyphemus.* **1844** DeKay *Zool. NY* 6.56, This common species [=*Polyphemus occidentalis*] on our shores is known here under the popular name of *Horse-foot,* on account of its shape, and still retains in some districts the name given to it by the early English colonists, of *King Crab,* in allusion to its size. **1884** Goode *Fisheries U.S.* 1.829, The King Crab is sluggish in its movements, and spends much of its time more or less buried in the mud and sand of shallow water, coming up occasionally to high-water mark. **1901** Arnold *Sea-Beach* 295, The horseshoe-crab, also called king-crab, is especially interesting. **1946** Kopman *Wild Acres* 57 **LA,** On the wide, beveled slope of the outer beach. . . were such stranded curiosities as medusas, king crabs, and strange shells. **1968** *DARE* FW Addit **DE**3, *King crabs*—local name for horseshoe crabs.

2 also with modifier: A large edible Pacific crab, usu *Paralithodes camtschatica.* **chiefly AK** For other names of *P. camtschatica* see **devil crab**

1923 *Anchorage Daily Times* (AK) 14 Sept 7, The Alaska All-Year-Round cannery of Seldovia will probably begin packing the huge Japanese spider crab, also called the Alaska king crab, sometime in October. **1942** *Alaska Sportsman* Nov 21 (Tabbert *Dict. Alaskan Engl.*), King crab are found in the North Pacific from Southeastern Alaska to Japan. **1965** Bowen *Alaskan Dict.* 20, *King Crab*—A spider crab spanning several feet across the spread of its legs. The king crab is the basis of Alaska's great crab fishery. **1968–69** *DARE* (Qu. P2) Inf **CA**111, King crab; (Qu. P14) Inf **CA**111, King crab; (Qu. P18) Inf **AK**1, King crab—commercial name for spider crab; **AK**9, King crab—name in use for 60 years or more. **1978** *AK Fishing Guide* 93, The king crab. . . Found from Southeastern Alaska to the Bering Sea, this huge crab (spreads to 6 feet, weights to more than 20 pounds) can be taken with pots and ring nets. **1989** Mickelson *Nat. Hist.* 27 **sAK,** Even larger [than tanner crabs], but far less abundant, are king crabs. The blue king crab occurs in northern P[rince] W[illiam] S[ound], whereas some brown king crabs occur in southern and eastern P[rince] W[illiam] S[ound], and in deeper waters of the Gulf of Alaska. **1991** Tabbert *Dict. Alaskan Engl.* 153, Three species of anomuran crabs found in Alaskan waters are now referred to with the name *king crab.* The largest is *Paralithodes camtschatica,* called *red king crab* to distinguish it from the others. . . Because the catch of *P. camtschatica* has varied so dramatically, interest has developed in two other crab species which also now are usually referred to as *(Alaska) king crab: Paralithodes platypus,* called *blue king crab,* and *Lithodes aequispina,* called *brown king crab.*

king-crab bird n [**king crab 1**] Cf **horsefoot snipe** =**ruddy turnstone.**

1923 U.S. Dept. Ag. *Misc. Circular* 13.71 **NC,** *Ruddy Turnstone.* . . *Vernacular Names.* . . *In local use.* . . King-crab bird.

kingcup n

1 A **buttercup 1** (here: *Ranunculus acris*). [OED 1538 →]

1896 *Jrl. Amer. Folkl.* 9.180 **ME,** *Ranunculus acris* . . kingcup. **1900** Lyons *Plant Names* 316, *R[anunculus] acris.* . . Guilty-cup, King-cup.

2 =**poppy mallow.**

1898 *Jrl. Amer. Folkl.* 11.223 **cTX,** *Callirhoë* (sp.), king-cup, poppy mallow.

3 also *king's cup, kingcups:* A **marsh marigold** (here: *Caltha palustris*).

1900 Lyons *Plant Names* 77, *C[altha] palustris.* . . King-cups. **1933** Small *Manual SE Flora* 511, *C[altha] palustris.* . . King-cup. **1959** Carleton *Index Herb. Plants* 70, King Cup: *Caltha palustris.* . . King's Cup: *C. palustris.* **1976** Bailey–Bailey *Hortus Third* 206, *Caltha palustris.* . . kingcup.

king devil n Also *king devil weed, king of devils* [See quot 1889] Cf **devil's-weed 2c**

Any of several **hawkweeds;** see quots.

1889 *Bot. Gaz.* 14.13 **cnNY,** There was a hawkweed growing there on all the farms which was a terrible pest to the country and had gained the name of Devil-weed, King of Devils, or, more briefly, the King-Devil. . . One hour after arriving there I satisfied myself that the King-Devil was none other than Hieracium præaltum. *Ibid* 14, The King-Devil. . . forms a continuous mat of pale green leaves lying flat on the ground and preventing any other form of vegetation from taking root. **1891** *AN&Q* 6.162, There is a rather rare and curious weed growing in Northern New York, which is locally known as *king-devil.* It is a

European nuisance, not much known in this country. . . I have been told it is *Hieracium praealtum.* **1898** *Jrl. Amer. Folkl.* 11.230, *Hieracium proealtum* [sic] . . devil's paint-brush, devil's weed, king devil weed. **1914** Georgia *Manual Weeds* 556, Field Hawkweed—*Hieracium pratense.* . . King Devil. *Ibid* 558, Two other species of Hawkweed are becoming abundant. . . Both are promptly named "King Devils" by the farmers whom they victimize. *Hieracium floribundum,* increasing by numerous stolons and also by flowering branches at the base. . . [and] *Hieracium florentinum.* **1949** Moldenke *Amer. Wild Flowers* 181, The *kingdevil, H[ieracium] floribundum,* . . grows to 3 feet in height. Its popular name is derived, like that of the devilspaintbrush [=*H. aurantiacum*] from allusions to its weedy nature. **1966** *DARE* Wildfl QR Pl.223A Inf **MI**31, Yellow hawkweed—some call it king devil. **1970** *DARE* (Qu. S26d, *Wildflowers that grow in meadows; not asked in early QRs*) Inf **MA**78, King devil. **1973** Hitchcock–Cronquist *Flora Pacific NW* 530, King devil. . . *H[ieracium] aurantiacum.*

king diver n

A **goldeneye 1** (here: *Bucephala clangula*).

1888 Trumbull *Names of Birds* 79 **seMD,** At Crisfield . . [the American Golden-eye is called] *King diver.*

kingdom n

1 also with *the;* also in combs: A neighborhood; an area of town.

1969 *DARE* (Qu. C34, *Nicknames for nearby settlements, villages, or districts*) Inf **KY**37, Possum Kingdom [FW: these are real names for real places though very small places]; (Qu. C35, *Nicknames for the different parts of your town or city*) Inf **KY**21, The Kingdom—local niggertown [FW: Inf also used in conv]; (Qu. II25) Inf **KY**21, The Kingdom. **1993** *DARE* File **nNY,** I'm sure I've heard *kingdom* applied to locales elsewhere [=other than those labeled *Northeast kingdom*] in Vermont or northern New York.

2 See **Northeast Kingdom.**

Kingdom Come n [From "thy kingdom come" in the Lord's Prayer, an allusion to the Christian concept of the millenium, the "Second Coming"]

1 The hereafter—often used as euphem for hell, perdition.

1867 Harris *Sut Lovingood Yarns* 212 **TN,** Now, a yung doctor what hed help'd Seize over the fence, twixt this an' kingdum cum, wanted his cackus tu chop up. **1869** Twain *Innocents* 2.171, Other pitiful nobodies between Kingdom Come and Baalbec. **1907** *DN* 3.245 **eME,** *Kingdom-come.* . . Destruction, ruin, hell. "If you don't look out, you'll go to kingdom-come before your time." **1908** *DN* 3.327 **eAL, wGA,** *Kingdom-come.* . . "Where in the kingdom come did you come from?" **1912** *DN* 3.580 **wIN,** *Kingdom-come.* . . Hell. An attempt at euphemism. "Where in the kingdom-come has that horse gone?" **1939** Coffin *Capt. Abby* 232 **ME** (as of c1860s), On March 14, a veteran sailor went to Kingdom Come. **1954** *Harder* Coll. **cwTN,** Go to kingdom come. **1965–70** *DARE* (Qu. HH20c, *Of an idle, worthless person* . . "He isn't worth ___.") 11 Infs, **scattered,** The powder to blow him to Kingdom Come; **FL**16, **WV**4, The powder and lead it'd take to blow him to Kingdom Come; (Qu. CC9, . . *Words or expressions for hell:* "That man is headed straight for ___.") Inf **CT**21, Kingdom Come.

2 An indefinitely remote time or place.

1908 *DN* 3.327 **eAL, wGA,** *Kingdom-come.* . . The end of time, a long period. "That'll hold till kingdom-come." **1928** *Ruppenthal Coll.* **KS,** *Kingdom come*—long delayed; slow. "That will never happen till kingdom come." "I am waiting but he's slower than kingdom come." **1942** McAtee *Dial. Grant Co. IN* 66 (as of 1890s), Till *kingdom come.* . . Pending a long or indefinite time. **1950** *WELS* **WI** (*A very long period of time* . . *You could wait from now until ___*) 4 Infs, Kingdom Come. **1960** Criswell *Resp. to PADS 20* **Ozarks,** *Kingdom come*—a piece, a long way off. "Knock him to kingdom come." Still common. **1966–70** *DARE* (Qu. A16, *A very long period of time:* "I haven't seen him ___.") Inf **TX**102, Since Kingdom Come; (Qu. A18, . . *A very slow person:* "What's keeping him? He certainly is ___!") Inf **MI**106, Slower than Kingdom Come; [**OK**18, Slower than Kingdom to come]; (QR, near Qu. C33) Inf **CA**166, Out in Kingdom Come [Inf laughs]; (Qu. MM12b, . . *'In all directions'* . . "When she was out on the dance floor, she broke her beads and they went ___.") Inf **CA**61, Flew to Kingdom Come.

kingdoodle n Cf gowrow

A fictitious monster of great size.

1950 *AR Hist. Qrly.* 9.69 **swMO,** The kingdoodle is another big reptile, doubtless related to the gowrow, the jimplicute and the high-behind. One of my old neighbors in McDonald County, Missouri, told his children that the kingdoodle looks like an ordinary mountain boomer, except. . . the mountain boomer or collared lizard seldom attains a length of more than ten inches, while the kingdoodle is "longer'n a wellrope, an' fourteen hands high." It is strong enough to tear down fences and pull up saplings, but is not bloodthirsty. Near Jane [MO, we] . . stopped to look at a small building which had fallen off its stone foundation and rolled into a ditch. . . A little boy who lived nearby. . . [said] "I reckon the old kingdoodle must have throwed it down, in the night."

king eider n Also *king duck* [Perh from the prominent gold-colored processes at the base of the bill] Cf **eider duck**

An arctic duck (*Somateria spectabilis*).

1858 Baird *Birds* 810, *Somateria spectabilis* . . King Eider. **1889** *Century Dict.* 3290, *King-eider.* . . Same as *king-duck. Ibid, King-duck.* . . A kind of eider-duck, *Somateria spectabilis* . . common on the northerly coasts of Europe and America. **1917** (1923) *Birds Amer.* 1.148, The King Eider is an arctic species. . . The raised frontal processes at the base of the bill, which adorn the head, develop immensely in the breeding season, bulging high above the rest of the bill. **1955** MA Audubon Soc. *Bulletin* 39.376, King Eider. . . The enlarged base of bill and pearl-gray crown may have kingly suggestions. **1977** Bull–Farrand *Audubon Field Guide Birds* 353, King Eider (*Somateria spectabilis*). . . Male has a *black back* and a conspicuous orange-yellow bill and "shield" on forehead.

king eveque n [From its resemblance to the indigo bunting, in LaFr *évêque*]

The blue **grosbeak** (*Guiraca caerulea*).

1921 LA Dept. of Conserv. *Bulletin* 10.117, An interesting and at most times a rather uncommon species visiting Louisiana is the blue grosbeak (*Guiraca caerulea*), resembling a large indigo-bird or "blue pop", and known locally as the "king eveque", or "blue ricebird".

kingfish n

1 also *king:* A saltwater fish of the genus *Menticirrhus,* usu *M. americanus* or *M. saxatilis.* Also called **whiting.** For other names of var spp see **barb, black mullet 1, Carolina whiting, channel mullet, hake 4, hogfish h, mullet** n[1] **4, roundhead, sand mullet, sea mink, ~ mullet, ~ smelt, ~ trout, tomcod**

1743 Catesby *Nat. Hist. Carolina* 2 [app] xliii, King fish. **1814** in 1815 Lit. & Philos. Soc. NY *Trans.* 1.408, King-fish (*Sciaena nebulosa*). **1849** (1851) Herbert *Frank Forester's Fish & Fishing* 210, The King-Fish.—Bermuda Whiting. . . The angler regards the King-Fish in his basket much as the sportsman looks upon the Woodcock in his bag—as worth a dozen of the more easily captured and less worthy fry. **1887** Goode *Amer. Fishes* 124, Its great gaminess, its beauty of color and form, and its excellent flavor . . caused the loyal citizens of New York in colonial days to call this species the "King-fish." **1942** Chesapeake Biol. Lab. *Pub.* 53.17, One specimen of the kingfish, *Menticirrhus americanus,* was obtained off Punch Island Creek. **1965–70** *DARE* (Qu. P2, . . *Kinds of saltwater fish caught around here . . good to eat*) 13 Infs, **Atlantic, FL, TX,** Kingfish; **DE**3, Kingfish (book name is king whiting); **MD**36, Sandmullet or kingfish; **NC**80, Sea mullet = kingfish; (Qu. H45, *Dishes made with meat, fish, or poultry that everybody around here would know, but that people in other places might not*) Inf **FL**23, Pickled kingfish (Cuban); (Qu. P14, . . *Commercial fishing . . what do the fishermen go out after?*) Infs **NJ**39, **TX**101, **VA**47, Kingfish; **FL**4, Kingfish—lined. [*DARE* Ed: Some of these Infs may refer instead to 2 below] **1966** *Carteret Co. News–Times* (Morehead City & Beaufort NC) 16 Aug 2/4, Roy Honnycutt . . pulled aboard 23 kings. **1975** Evanoff *Catch More Fish* 127, The whitings (called "kingfish" in northern waters) are often plentiful in the surf along the Atlantic Coast, Florida, and in our Gulf Coast States. **1986** Pederson *LAGS Concordance* **FL, c,csTX,** 7 infs, Kingfish; 1 inf, Kingfish—saltwater, head was eaten; 1 inf, Kingfish—sea food.

2 also *king:* A **Spanish mackerel** (here: either *Scomberomorus cavalla* or *S. regalis*). Cf **king mackerel**

[**1775** (1962) Romans *Nat. Hist. FL* app 7, *Groopers* are in great plenty, *king-fish, Spanish mackerel* and *Barrows* are also often caught towing.] **1787** Gesellschaft Naturforschender Freunde *Schriften* 8.142, *Blennius.* Kingfish in Neu-York. *Ibid* 143, Dieser King-Fisch hält sich in den wärmeren Monaten an der Küste auf, und beißt an der Angel. Das Fleisch ist nicht besonders gut. [=This King-Fish is found off the coast in the warmer months, and it takes the hook. The flesh is not particularly good.] **1884** Goode *Fisheries U.S.* 1.316, The Cero or King-fish—*Scomberomorus caballa. Ibid,* The King Cero or Spotted Cero—*Scomberomorus regalis.* . . It is more than likely that this and the preceding species are both included by the Key West fishermen under the name "King-fish," the differences in general appearance being so slight that it is hardly likely that they would be noticed by ordinary observers. **1902** Jordan-Evermann *Amer. Fishes* 286, Sierra; Pintado; Kingfish—*Scomberomorus regalis.* . . found on the south Florida Coast. *Ibid* 287, Kingfish; Cero; Cavalla—*Scomberomorus cavalla.* . . Of all the host of Florida game-fishes that are used as food this is the greatest. **1935** Caine *Game Fish* 96, Kingfish—*Scomberomorus cavalla.* . . Florida Kingfish, Great Kingfish. . . This fish should not be confused with the northern kingfish, which while bearing the same name is not related to it and never reaches a weight of more than several pounds. **1966** *DARE* (Qu. P2, . . *Kinds of saltwater fish caught around here . . good to eat*) Inf **FL13**, Kingfish—a mackerel; **FL4**, King. **1973** Knight *Cook's Fish Guide* 383, Kingfish . . Gulf; Northern . . or see Croaker, White or see Mackerel, King or see Cero.

3 Either of two related fish: a **queenfish** (here: *Seriphus politus*) or the **little roncador. CA**
  1882 *U.S. Natl. Museum Bulletin* 16.582 **CA,** *S[eriphus] politus* . . Queen-fish; King-fish. **1887** Goode *Amer. Fishes* 128, The Queen-fish, *Seriphus politus,* is also known as "Kingfish" in California. **1898** U.S. Natl. Museum *Bulletin* 47.1460 **CA,** *Genyonemus lineatus* . . Little Roncador; Kingfish; Croaker. **1946** LaMonte *N. Amer. Game Fishes* 82, Kingfish. . . California Kingfish. **1973** Knight *Cook's Fish Guide* 383, Kingfish . . see Croaker, White.

4 also *Pacific kingfish;* A **wahoo** (here: *Acanthocybium solandri*).
  1935 Caine *Game Fish* 142, Wahoo—*Acanthocybium solandri.* . . Kingfish . . Pacific Kingfish. **1946** LaMonte *N. Amer. Game Fishes* 25, Wahoo. . . Queenfish, Pacific Kingfish. **1947** Caine *Salt Water* 32, The wahoo is one of the great game fish of the world and is considered, by those who have caught it, to be the fastest fish of its size in the water. It is also known as guarapucu, Pacific kingfish, queenfish [etc.].

5 A **kingfisher** (here: *Megaceryle alcyon*).
  1966–70 *DARE* (Qu. Q10, . . *Water birds and marsh birds*) Infs **KY28, 86, LA44, OH66,** Kingfish; (Qu. Q14) Infs **MI27, NJ3, TX37,** Kingfish.

kingfisher n
Std: any of three birds of the family Alcedinidae: *Megaceryle alcyon, M. torquata,* or *Chloroceryle americana.* [*OED* c1440 →] For other names of *M. alcyon* see **fisher 2, king-bird 4, kingfish 5, kingfisherman, lazybird 2;** for other names of *Chloroceryle americana* see **Texas kingfisher**

kingfisher fly n
  A **dragonfly.**
  1967 *DARE* (Qu. R2, . . *The dragonfly*) Inf **CA6,** Kingfisher flies.

kingfisherman n Also *kingfishman*
  A **kingfisher** (here: *Megaceryle alcyon*).
  1968 *DARE* (Qu. Q14) Inf **NC49,** Kingfishman; **NC80,** King fisherman.

kinghead n [See quot 1922]
  =**giant ragweed.**
  1912 Blatchley *IN Weed Book* 149, *Ambrosia trifidia* [sic]. . . Great Ragweed. . . Kinghead. **1922** *Amer. Botanist* 28.41, The last time I was in northern Minnesota I found that the Scandinavian settlers had begun to call it [=*Ambrosia trifida*] "king-head," from a fancied resemblance of the akene with its sharp points to a crown. **1924** *Ibid* 30.32, Have you omitted the name kinghead from the list of appellations of *Ambrosia trifida?* I have seen this used a great deal. **1950** Stevens *ND Plants* 282, *Ambrosia trifida.* . . Kinghead is the common name here, referring to the seed, but Giant Ragweed is used in other regions.

‡King Henry n
  A chamber pot.
  1969 *DARE* (Qu. F38, *Utensil kept under the bed for use at night*) Inf **PA194,** The King Henry.

king hornet n
  =**cicada killer.**
  1938 Brimley *Insects NC* 447, *S[phecius] speciosus.* . . King Hornet, . . Cicada Killer. . . The largest of our wasps.

king, king can I go n Also *king; king (king) calico; king kangalo; king, king can do;* for addit varr see quots Cf **black man 2, Dixie** n[1]
A children's chasing game, esp one similar to **pom-pom-pull-away;** also used as a phr in the game.
  1882 Watkins *1861 vs. 1862* 24 **TN,** The earth and hills and trees were covered with snow, and the lightnings seemed to be playing "King, King Canico" along its crusted surface. **1895** *DN* 1.398, *King.* A common game among boys is known variously as *king* and *king calico* [cNY] . . *pom-pom-pull-away* [IA, MN, NY] . . *dixie* [eNY] . . *king kangalo* [neNY]. **1966** *DARE* Tape **AL4,** We had king king calico, you come and I'll go. . . [FW:] How did you play that? [Inf:] Well, there's king king calico, just like calico dress. . . That was more or less like what . . we referred to as old stinkbase. . . You'd start out with two, would break the other crowd up. You'd have a tree over here and a tree over here and all of the crowd would get over here . . and every time you'd touch one he'd have to come on the other side. **1968–70** *DARE* (Qu. EE1, . . *Games . . children play . . in which they form a ring, and either sing or recite a rhyme*) Inf **TN62,** We played a game in which this was said: "It": "King king cannico." Others: "You go nannico"; then "it" or "king" caught others; (Qu. EE33, . . *Outdoor games . . that children play*) Inf **VA26,** King candy go—"King candy go, here I come and there I go." **1981** Pederson *LAGS Basic Materials,* 1 inf, **seMS,** ['kʻɛŋ kʻɛŋ ˌkʻæᶜn ɐˁ 'goˁʊ]—children's game; 1 inf, **swGA,** Used to play [kʻɪˆŋ kʻɪˆŋ 'kʻæ·n doˆʊ]—like "drop the handkerchief." [*DARE* Ed: interpreted as "king, king can I go" and "king, king can do" in the 1986 *Concordance*]

king log n
  =**key log.**
  1904 Day *Kin o' Ktaadn* 113 **ME,** He had chopped the binding king-log and he cracked Seboomook jam.

king mackerel n Also *king* **S Atl, Gulf States**
  A **Spanish mackerel:** usu *Scomberomorus cavalla,* but also *S. regalis.*
  1935 Caine *Game Fish* 96, Kingfish—*Scomberomorus cavalla.* . . Synonyms . . King Mackerel. **1946** LaMonte *N. Amer. Game Fishes* 26, *Scomberomorus cavalla.* . . King Mackerel. . . Inshore in the Gulf Stream; offshore in winter. *Ibid* 28, *Scomberomorus regalis.* . . King mackerel. . . Fairly common around the Florida Keys. **1965** McClane *McClane's Std. Fishing Encycl.* 448, King mackerel reach a much larger size than any other American Spanish mackerels. **1966–68** *DARE* (Qu. P2, . . *Kinds of saltwater fish caught around here . . good to eat*) Infs **LA26, 31, NC12, SC21,** King mackerel. **1973** Knight *Cook's Fish Guide* 383, King—Mackerel, King. **1986** Pederson *LAGS Concordance,* 9 infs, **AL, FL, csGA, seMS,** King mackerel; 1 inf, **seMS,** King mackerel—out by the oil rigs. **1991** Amer. Fisheries Soc. *Common Names Fishes* 66, *Scomberomorus cavalla* . . king mackerel.

king martin n
  A **kingbird 1** (here: *Tyrannus tyrannus*).
  1967 *DARE* (Qu. Q14, . . *Names . . for these birds: . . martin*) Inf **LA14,** Martin—sometimes called king martin.

king mosquito n
  Prob a **crane fly.**
  1967–68 *DARE* (Qu. R15b, . . *An extra-big mosquito*) Infs **MN2, MO25,** King mosquito.

kingnut n chiefly **Sth, S Midl**
  Either **shellbark hickory** or **mockernut hickory.**
  1884 Sargent *Forests of N. Amer.* 134, *Mocker Nut. . . King Nut.* . . Very common in the Gulf states, and throughout the south the most widely distributed species of the genus. **1894** *Bot. Gaz.* 19.438, *Carya alba,* Nutt. . . king-nut, West Va. **1894** Coulter *Botany W. TX* 3.411, *Big shell-bark. King-nut.* . . The hull [of the fruit] very thick: nut large (3 to 5 cm. long). **1897** Sudworth *Arborescent Flora* 114 **TN,** *Hicoria laciniosa.* . . *Common Names.* . . King Nut. **1931** Mattoon *Forest Trees Okla.* 32 (*DA*), The king nut hickory becomes a very large tree and is found in the rich bottom land forests of the eastern part of the State. **1945** MI Ag. Exper. Sta. *Technical Bulletin* 201.25, Some of these are not at all common such as blue ash . . king-nut (*Carya laciniosa*). **1980** Little *Audubon Guide N. Amer. Trees E. Region* 350, "Kingnut"—*Carya laciniosa.* . . This . . species is distinguished from other hickories by the large leaves, large nuts, and orange twigs.

king of devils See **king devil**

king of the castle, king of the hill See **king of the mountain 1**

king-of-the-meadow n

1 A **meadow rue** (here: *Thalictrum pubescens*).

1891 *Jrl. Amer. Folkl.* 4.147 **swNH**, Thalictrum polygamum . . my father called *King of the Meadow.* **1950** Gray–Fernald *Manual of Botany* 659, T[halictrum] polygamum . . *King-of-the-meadow.* . . Meadows, low thickets, and swamps. **1976** Bailey–Bailey *Hortus Third* 1105, *King-of-the-meadow.* . . Fl[ower]s mostly white.

2 also *king-of-the-prairie:* A **boneset 1** (here: *Eupatorium purpureum*).

1896 *Jrl. Amer. Folkl.* 9.192 **NH**, Eupatorium purpureum . . king of the meadow. **1899** *Plant World* 2.199, King of the Meadow for *Eupatorium purpureum.* . . Probably because of the great purple heads of bloom, which tower over the other meadow plants. **1940** Clute *Amer. Plant Names* 82, King-of-the-prairie. **1966** *DARE* FW Addit **cMA**, *King-of-the-meadow.* . . Joe-Pye weed. **1971** Krochmal *Appalachia Med. Plants* 120, Eupatorium Purpureum. . . Common Names: . . king-of-the-meadow.

king of the mountain n

1 also *king of the castle,* ~ *hill, king's castle;* for addit varr see quots; similarly n *queen of the mountain:* A game in which each player or team attempts to gain and hold a high point (or rarely, some area) against the attempts of others to seize it. Cf **old man on the mountain**

1899 Champlin–Bostwick *Young Folks' Games* 447, *King's Castle,* a game in which several players try to dislodge one from some position he has chosen. . . In Pennsylvania the defender of the castle says: "Hally, hally, hastle,/ Come into my new castle." **1940** Harbin *Fun Encycl.* 173, *King of the castle.*—One player is chosen by lot to be King. He assumes a position on a mound, or tub, or box, or stump. He bids defiance to all his foes by shouting: "I'm King of the Castle;/ Get out you cowardly rascal." **1950** *WELS* **WI** *(Games played in the snow)* 2 Infs, King of (*or* on) the hill; 1 Inf, King of the hill—choose sides and each tries to keep other from advancing to top of snow hill. **1958** *Sat. Eve. Post Letters* **MA**, King of the Hill; **PA**, King of the Mountain. **1965–70** *DARE* (Qu. EE33, . . *Outdoor games . . that children play*) Infs **CA**190, **CO**14, **IN**35, **MI**8, **WI**50, King of (*or* on) the hill; **MO**26, King on the hill—2 teams; one teamon would try to hold the top of the hill against the others coming up; **NY**40, King on a hill—someone stands on a little hill and others try to push him off; whoever wins is king; **AR**18, **CA**80, 174, **MI**123, **TX**27, King of the mountain; **IL**47, **MI**8, King of the castle—"I'm (the) king of the castle, (and) you're the dirty rascal;" (Qu. EE26, . . *Games . . children play in the snow*) Infs **MN**16, **SD**2, King of (*or* on) the hill; **WV**10, King of the hill—snow piled up and packed; one person becomes king; the others try to knock him off the hill; one who knocks him off becomes king; **OH**84, **PA**165, King of the mountain; (Qu. EE28, *Games played in the water*) [Infs **AL**20, **WI**47, King of (*or* on) the raft]; **KY**73, King on the mountain—one person takes a corner of the pool and guards it; the others attack him, trying to get his place. **1968** *Wall St. Jrl.* (NY NY) 13 Feb 1 **cnMN**, On 40-below days, the kids play king of the hill on seven-foot piles of snow. **1969** Opie–Opie *Children's Games* 234, 'King of the Castle'—in the United States generally known as 'King of the Mountain' or 'King of the Hill.' **1986** Pederson *LAGS Concordance* (*Line and running . . rough games;* this question was asked chiefly in urban areas) 3 infs, King of the mountain; 1 inf, King of the hill. [All infs urban, less than 35 years old] **1993** *DARE* File **IA, IN, KY, NC, PA, SD, VT,** King of the mountain; **IL, IN, NYC, OR, SD, TX, VA, WY,** King of the hill; **IN,** King on the hill; **IN, MA,** King or Queen of the mountain; **VA,** King of the castle—"I'm king of the castle and you're the dirty rascal!"

2 See quot.

1966 *DARE* (Qu. EE33, . . *Outdoor games . . that children play*) Inf **MI**19, King of the mountain—Four or five on their knees on the bottom, then three on top, then two, then one. If the one on top could stay up with the ones on the bottom wiggling, he was King of the Mountain. Two broken arms in school from that one year.

king-of-the-prairie See **king-of-the-meadow 2**

king of the woods n Also *master of the woods*

A **spikenard** (here: *Aralia racemosa*).

1926 Puckett *Folk Beliefs S. Negro* 246, King of the Woods (*Aralia racemosa*)—(Three leaves representing the Trinity)—Fine for making any sort of conquering "hands." Mix with sarsaparilla and coon-root and steep into a tea. Will cure almost anything. **c1938** in 1970 Hyatt *Hoodoo* 1.596 **seNC**, If yo' got some enemies an' they worry yo' an' yo' wanta be friends with them, yo' take dis heah de *King of de Woods.* Dey call it *King of de Woods* an' put it in a bag an' take an' put some *John de Conker* in de bag with it. *Ibid* 1.608 **seGA**, Git a root dat chew call *master of de woods*—dat's a common root, an' yo' kin tote dat an' yo' anoint it with *Heartshorn Cologne,* an' yo' be successful winning money in games.

king ortolan n Cf **ortolan 1**

=**Florida gallinule.**

1888 Trumbull *Names of Birds* 122, At Washington, D.C., [the Florida gallinule is called] *King-ortolan.* **1923** U.S. Dept. Ag. *Misc. Circular* 13.44 **MD, DC**, Florida Gallinule. . . Vernacular names. . . king ortolan.

king owl n

=**great horned owl.**

1955 *Oriole* 20.1.8, Great Horned Owl. . . *King Owl* (from its large size).

king priest n

A **kingbird 1** (here: *Tyrannus tyrannus*).

1927 Forbush *Birds MA* 2.328, Among the people of Mashpee, one of the last two Indian villages in Massachusetts, it [=*Tyrannus tyrannus*] is known as the King Priest, a name which bears its resemblance to little chief, but has a somewhat similar meaning. **1956** MA Audubon Soc. *Bulletin* 40.83, Eastern Kingbird. . . King Priest (Mass. . . "Priest" probably from its black and white coloration.)

king-queen n Also *kings* **NYC**

=**Chinese handball;** see quot 1991.

1968–70 *DARE* (Qu. EE33, . . *Outdoor games . . that children play*) Inf **NY**118, King-queen—Chinese handball; **NY**241, King-queen or Chinese handball—each player gets cement block and section of sidewalk, first is king, then queen, jack, etc. **1968** *DARE* Tape **NY**118, There was king-queen. That was . . where everybody would line up. The person who'd be king would serve. It was sort of like handball, except you'd have to bounce it [=the ball] before it hit the wall and bounce it into somebody else's box, and you got points out if you were anything but the king. The king could never lose any points. He'd rotate. Sometimes they'd call that Chinese handball. **1975** Ferretti *Gt. Amer. Book Sidewalk Games* 79 **Brooklyn NYC**, Requiring more agility and concentration is the version of Chinese Handball called *Kings,* played out in the Bay Ridge section of Brooklyn. Kings is Chinese Handball expanded to five players and . . to five sidewalk squares. **1991** *DARE* File **Brooklyn NYC**, Kings was best played in an alley. Each sidewalk square was a box, one player per box. The server was "king" and that's who you had to get out. We had hundreds of variations of kings. You always used a spaldeen; only wimps used a tennis ball. *Ibid* **Bronx NYC** (as of 1950s), King-queen, which we also called Chinese handball, was played with a spaldeen against a convenient wall with the lines separating the blocks of the sidewalk determining each player's space. The server, called the "ace," was on the extreme left, and followed to his right by the "king," then the "queen," the "jack" and so forth. . . The server hits the ball against the wall (the ball first bouncing before hitting the wall) which must be returned by the player in whose space the ball bounces. The game is one of rotation and elimination. **1995** *Ibid* **Brooklyn NYC** (as of c1960), Kings—throw the spaldeen at a flat wall . . (actually a little more complicated than that).

king rail n

1 A long-billed **rail** (here: *Rallus elegans*). Also called **bull rail, double ~, freshwater marsh hen, ~ meadow hen, Indian pullet 4, king sora 2, marsh hen 1a, meadow ~ 1, mud ~ 1a, prairie chicken, ~ hen, red-breasted rail, rice hen, sedge ~, swamp chicken, water hen**

1835 Audubon *Ornith. Biog.* 3.28 **S Atl**, Hunters. . . now and then obtained a few of these birds, which they considered as very rare, and knew only by the name of "King Rails." **1898** (1900) Davie *Nests N. Amer. Birds* 123, The King Rail, . . or Red-breasted Rail, is distributed in summer from New York southward, breeding throughout the inland marshes. **1900** LA Soc. Naturalists *Proc.* 93, *Rallus Elegans.* . . King Rail. An abundant winter resident, and much esteemed as a game bird. **1947** Ballowe *The Lawd* 252 **LA**, I walked out to a pond in the field to hear the chant of the king rails to the sinking sun. **1950** *WELS* (*Water and marsh birds*) 1 Inf, **ceWI**, King rail. **1955** MA Audubon Soc. *Bulletin* 39.443, King Rail. . . From its large size and bright coloration. **1968** *DARE* (Qu. Q10, . . *Water birds and marsh birds*) Inf **GA**20, Marsh hen—I believe it's a king rail; **NJ**52, King rail. **1986** Pederson *LAGS Concordance,* 1 inf, **seLA**, King rail—a game bird.

2 =**Florida gallinule.**

1879 *Forest & Stream* 13.684, While rail shooting on the meadows of the Housatonic River in Connecticut . . the Natural History editor took a specimen of the Florida gallinule *(Gallinula galeata),* or, as it is usually called in that State, the king rail. **1888** Trumbull *Names of Birds* 122, In Connecticut, at East Haddam and Essex, at Havre de Grace, Md., and to many at Enterprise, Fla., [the Florida Gallinule is known as] King Rail. **1955** Forbush–May *Birds* 166, Florida Gallinule. . . *Other names* . . King Rail [etc.].

3 =**clapper rail.**

1918 Grinnell *Game Birds CA* 283, California Clapper Rail. . . Other names . . King Rail. **1923** U.S. Dept. Ag. *Misc. Circular* 13.41, California Clapper Rail. . . Clapper rail, king rail, San Mateo rail. **1967** *Weston Chron.* (MO) 8 Sept 5/6, There will be no open season on king or clapper rails, but . . Virginia and yellow rails may be hunted in Missouri from September 1 to November 9.

kings n

1 also as exclam: See **king's ex.**

2 See **king-queen.**

3 in phr *have kings on:* =**dib** n[1] **2.**

1977–78 Foster *Lexical Variation* 87 **NJ,** *(Claim Calls)* I've got kings on that (1 [inf], evidently a fusion of *dibs* and the truce term *King's X*). **1993** DARE File **cwCA** (as of 1950s), When I was a child I said I had "dibs" on something I wanted, but some of my friends said they had "kings" on it.

king salmon n Also king Pacific, AK

=**chinook salmon.**

1870 Dall *Alaska* 201, Early in June the king salmon *(Kahthl'* of the Ingaliks, or *chowichee* of the Russians) begin to ascend the river. **1882** U.S. Natl. Museum *Bulletin* 16.306, *O[ncorhynchus] chouicha.* . . King Salmon. **1944** (1945) Helmericks *We Live in AK* 34 **cAK,** The other day I heard about another salmon . . which some people think is the young king before he reaches maturity, for a young king has never been found. **1962** Salisbury *Quoth the Raven* 121 **seAK,** The *King* salmon, also called the *Tyee,* which means king in the Chinook jargon, and also the *Chinook,* are largely caught by trolling, and as that precedes the run of the other species, it fills the gap between the early halibut season and the later canning season. **1966–68** DARE (Qu. P1, . . *Kinds of freshwater fish . . caught around here . . good to eat)* Inf **CA31,** King salmon; **WA24,** Kings; (Qu. P2, . . *Kinds of saltwater fish caught around here . . good to eat)* Infs **AK9, WA18, 22,** King salmon; **WA24,** Kings. **1968** DARE Tape **CA104,** King salmon. **1977** *New Yorker* 2 May 65 **AK,** Athapaskan Indians, harvesting from the Yukon, put king salmon on their own tables and feed chum salmon to their dogs. **1989** Mickelson *Nat. Hist.* 161 **AK,** King salmon anglers use 20 or 30 lb. test line to "mooch" by drifting or casting a small, whole herring or cut plug herring. Anglers catch kings by trolling. **1991** Tabbert *Dict. Alaskan Engl.* 131, In Alaskan English, the most common name for the fish is *king salmon,* often shortened to *king,* especially in the plural. . . most newspaper, magazine, and other general writing reflects the popular preference for *king.* **1994** Guterson *Snow Falling* 119 **nwWA,** Rafts of seabirds rose off the water, making way . . [for] the *Islander* bound for home . . , half a thousand kings in her hold, the whine of wind in her rigging.

king's arrow pine See **king's pine**

king sax See **king's ex**

king's crown n West

=**roseroot.**

1938 (1958) Sharples *AK Wild Flowers* 121, *R[hodiola] integrifolia.* "King's Crown." **1953** Nelson *Plants Rocky Mt. Park* 83, *King's crown, Sedum integrifolium.* . . A fleshy plant . . with a crowded terminal cluster of very dark red or purplish, dioecious blossoms. **1961** Douglas *My Wilderness* 19 **CO,** King's crown *(Sedum integrifolium)* has a flat head of maroon flowers. While their blooming period usually comes in Summer, I have found the king's crown resplendent in September. Even after the flowers have passed, the plant turns with the early frosts and weaves a red pattern into the brilliant carpets that Fall brings to the alpine basins. **1973** Hitchcock–Cronquist *Flora Pacific NW* 183, King's crown. . . *S[edum] roseum.* **1979** Spellenberg *Audubon Guide N. Amer. Wildflowers W. Region* 470, *King's Crown.* . . Across northern North America; south in the mountains to southern California, Nevada, Utah, and northern New Mexico.

king's cruse See **king's ex**

king's cup See **kingcup 3**

king's cure n

A **pipsissewa:** usu *Chimaphila umbellata,* but also *C. maculata.*

1876 Hobbs *Bot. Hdbk.* 61, Kings' cure, Wintergreen, Chimaphila umbellata. Kings' cure, Spotted wintergreen, Chimaphila maculata. **1924** *Amer. Botanist* 30.55, *Chimaphila umbellata.* . . really has medicinal qualities as its name [sic] "rheumatism-weed" and "king's cure" attest. **1971** Krochmal *Appalachia Med. Plants* 90, *Chimaphila umbellata.* . . King's cure. . . The dried leaves are reportedly used as a diuretic, astringent, tonic, and antirheumatic.

king's cure-all n

1 also, by folk-etym, *king coal-oil:* An **evening primrose a** (here: *Oenothera biennis);* also a remedy made from this plant. Cf **coal oil, cure-all 2**

1893 *Jrl. Amer. Folk.* 6.142, *Oenothera biennis* . . king's cure-all. Southern States. **1911** Henkel *Amer. Med. Leaves* 14, Evening Primrose. . . *Other common names* . . king's cure-all. [Footnote:] A misleading name. **1912** Blatchley *IN Weed Book* 100, In the East and South the young roots [of the evening-primrose] are also grated fine and mixed with fresh lard, butter or tallow to form a salve for burns, scalds, bunions, boils, felons, erysipelas, cuts, bruises, etc. In the South this salve is known as "King's cure-all" and by the negroes is used even for snake bites. **1969** DARE (Qu. I28b, *Kinds of greens that are cooked)* Inf **KY42,** Speckle britches [same as] king coal-oil. **1974** (1977) Coon *Useful Plants* 197, *Oenothera biennis* . . King's cure-all. . . The one name above should indicate great values medicinally, but it seems little recommended except for coughs and as a possible cure for skin eruptions.

2 =**starry campion.**

1901 Lounsberry *S. Wild Flowers* 158, *Starry Campion. King's Cure All.* . . Perhaps there is no other tradition which so indiscriminately clings to certain plants as that they are efficacious in curing snake-bites.

king's ex exclam, n Also king('s), king('s) sax, king's (s)cruse;

for addit varr see quots [Cf *EDD king's,* ~ *cruise,* ~ *ground,* ~ *speech* (at *king* sb. 10, 1.[13], [23], [45]). According to 1959 (1967) Opie–Opie *Lore Schoolchildren* 141–53, *kings* and *crosses* are common truce terms in ceEngl; *(s)cruce(s)* and *exes* are also attested. Although *ex* is often assumed to be an abbr for *excuse,* it seems more likely that it, as well as *(s)cruce(s)* and *crosses,* refers to the act of crossing the fingers, often an essential part of claiming a truce or time out.] **chiefly west of Missip R, Gulf States, Ohio Valley** See Map and Map Section Cf **fins 2, time out**

Used to demand a pause, exemption, or truce during a fight or game; the momentary truce or state of immunity so demanded.

1856 Watson *Men & Times* 60 **VA** (as of 1778), My attention was attracted by a fight between two very unwieldy, fat men . . until one succeeding . . in the act of thrusting . . his thumb into the latter's eye, he bawled out "king's cruse," equivalent, in technical language, to "enough." **1889** *MLN* 4.121, I have sought in vain for the origin of this old phrase, variously pronounced in various localities: King's cruse, King's truce, King's 'scuse (excuse), King's ex (short for excuse). **1890** *DN* 1.61 **swOH,** King: (like *barley)* a child's word, to intermit play, for a rest. The opposite is *king out.* Ibid 65 **KY,** *King's excuse.* . . Abbreviated to *king's ex.* In playing base, when a boy falls down, to keep from being caught he says, "King's ex." **1892** *DN* 1.217 **NC,** *King's excuse.* . . Lieutenant Darnall reports the North Carolina phrase as *king's crew.* **1893** Shands *MS Speech* 72, *King's ex* or *King's excuse.* Used in Mississippi as in Missouri for the purpose of stopping children's games—as *tag* or *base.* **1899** (1912) Green *VA Folk-Speech* 250, *King's cruse.* . . A cry to stop a game; or a fight; enough! King's truce? Scruse. **1903** (1963) Newell *Games & Songs* 186, [In marble play:] If any accident happens, and the opponent's play is to be checked, a Georgia lad will say "King's excuse." That this is an ancient phrase is shown by the corruption of the same cry in Pennsylvania, "King's scruse." **1905** *DN* 3.62 **NE,** *King's ex.* **1906** *DN* 3.144 **nwAR,** *King's ax, king's ex(cuse).* **1908** *DN* 3.327 **eAL, wGA,** *King's ex(cuse).* **1916** *DN* 4.346 **New Orleans LA,** *King's X.* . . An exclamation in playing tag, to indicate that a player is temporarily out of the game. **1920** *Topeka Daily Capital* (KS) 24 Jan 4/2, Has the time come when there is no "King's ex" any more on the globe? **1946** in 1969 Frost *Poetry* 399, [Title:] *U.S. 1946 King's X,* [Poem:] Having invented a new Holocaust,/ And been the first with it to win a war,/ How they make haste to cry with fingers crossed,/ King's X—no fairs to use it anymore! **1950** *WELS Suppl.* **WI,** 6 Infs, King's ex; 3 Infs, King's ex—had to have (or show) fingers, etc. crossed. [**1959** (1967) Opie–Opie *Lore School-children* 143, In England and Wales the usual way a child shows that he wants to drop out of a game is by crossing fingers. *Ibid* 150, *Exes.* . . Probably a form of 'crosses'.] **1965–70** *DARE* (Qu. EE17, *In a game of tag, if a player wants to rest, what does he call out so that he can't be tagged?*) 265 Infs, **chiefly west of Missip R, Gulf States, Ohio Valley,** King's ex; 23 Infs, **scattered,** King's; NJ4, SC26, King; **AR28, IN10, MO11, OH72,** King's ax (*or* hex, rest); [IA27, I'm kings;] **MN42, TX101,** King('s) sax; **TX54,** King sets; **TX38,** King's excuse; **IL7,** King's out; **IN35,** King's sick; (Qu. EE20, *When two boys are fighting, and the one who is losing wants to stop, he calls out, "_____.*") 45 Infs, **chiefly Missip-Ohio Valleys, West,** King's ex; **IN35,** King's; **MS1,** King's sax. **1973** *Jrl. Amer. Folkl.* 86.132 IN, Only five children [out of 351] reported what appear to be traditional terms: "Kings" (2), "I've got Kings X" (1), "Black-outs" (1), and "Queens" (1).

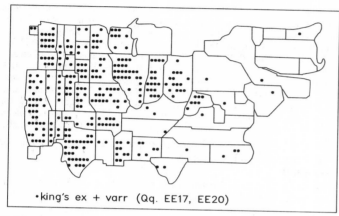

•king's ex + varr (Qq. EE17, EE20)

king's free *exclam*
=**all (in) free.**
1967 *DARE* (Qu. EE15, *When he has caught the first of those that were hiding what does the player who is 'it' call out to the others?*) Inf **CO3,** King's free.

king six *n* Cf **king's ex**
1966 *DARE* (Qu. EE2, *Games that have one extra player—when a signal is given, the players change places, and the extra one tries to get a place*) Inf **MS21,** King six.

king snake *n*
1 A snake of the genus *Lampropeltis.* Also called **chicken snake 2, corral ~, egg ~. chiefly Sth, SW** For other names of var spp see **chain snake, coral ~ 2a, cow ~ 2, cowsucker 2, dotted black snake, guinea ~, milk ~ 1, mole ~, rattlesnake pilot, salt-and-pepper snake, speckled ~, swamp wamper, thunder snake** Cf **first-and-last snake,** *house kingsnake* (at **house snake 2**)
1709 (1967) Lawson *New Voyage* 137, The King-Snake is the longest of all others, and not common. **1827** Williams *View W. FL* 28, The king snake kills them [=poisonous snakes] whenever they cross his path. **1848** *Santa Fe Republican* 29 Jan. 4/1 *(DAE),* There is a species of snake commonly called in the southern states the king snake, perhaps because he is the most formidable enemy of the rattlesnake. **1894** U.S. Natl. Museum *Proc.* 17.324, Rather common in south Florida, where it is sometimes known under the name of "king snake," and is then said to kill and devour the rattlesnake. **1909** *DN* 3.399, *King-snake.* . . A kind of snake found in N.W. Arkansas. **1949** *Scientific Mth.* 68.55, When pursued by an enemy such as a king snake or some mammal, the lizard attempts to slip away. **1965–70** *DARE* (Qu. P25, . . *Kinds of snakes*) 148 Infs, **chiefly Sth, SW,** King snake [*DARE* Ed: Some of these Infs may refer instead to **2** below.]; **AR55,** Chicken snake or king snake; **CA101,** King snake—kills rattlesnake; **CA111,** King snakes—devour the rattlesnakes; **DE3,** King snake . . or cowsucker; **FL13,** King snake— kills rattlers; **SC19,** King snake—same as thunder snake; **SC66,** King snake or chicken snake; **TX1,** King snake (rattlesnake pilot). **1968** *DARE* Tape **CA89,** A rattler does have enemies too, you know. There's different things that kill rattlers. I guess these king snakes, they call 'em, I guess they'll kill rattlesnakes. **1974** Shaw-

Campbell *Snakes West* 115, Some people seem to believe that king-snakes have a warm spot in their hearts for mankind and kill rattlesnakes as a sort of gallant gesture. **1986** Pederson *LAGS Concordance* **Gulf Region,** 51 infs, King snake(s) [*DARE* Ed: Some of these infs may refer instead to **2** below.]; 5 infs, King snake(s)—kill(s) other snakes; 1 inf, King snake—kills other snakes, harmless to people; 2 infs, King snake(s)—eat(s) snakes; 2 infs, King snake—can whip (*or* catches these other) snakes; 1 inf, King snakes—kill other snakes by choking; 3 infs, King snake(s)—not (*or* non)poisonous; 1 inf, King snake—immune to poison; 1 inf, King snake—speckled like a guinea; 1 inf, Now them king snakes is hard on poisonous snakes.

2 =**coral snake 1a.**
1926 *TX Folkl. Soc. Pub.* 5.67, In some sections the beautiful coral snake (red, yellow, and black in accumulated bands) is called the king snake. **1928** Baylor Univ. Museum *Contrib.* 16.18, On account of its brilliant coloring, this serpent enjoys a variety of names, many of which are also applied to very different reptiles. Many persons fail to distinguish the differences between this species and the red snakes of the genus *Lampropeltis* and call it the *King Snake.* **1986** Pederson *LAGS Concordance,* 1 inf, **csLA,** King snake—poisonous.

king snipe See **snipe**

king sora *n*
1 =**Florida gallinule.**
1888 Trumbull *Names of Birds* 122, At Alexandria, Va., [the Florida gallinule is called] king-sora.
2 =**king rail 1.**
1913 Bailey *Birds VA* 54, *Rallus elegans.* . . Marsh Hen. King sora.

king's pine *n* Also *king's arrow pine* [Because in colonial times such trees were reserved as crown property and were often marked as such with the broad arrow] Cf **mast pine**
An especially tall, straight **white pine** (here: *Pinus strobus*); the wood of such a tree.
[**1795** Winterbotham *Amer. U.S.* 3.386, Before the revolution, all white pines, excepting those growing in any township granted before the twenty-first of September, 1722, were accounted the king's property, and heavy penalties were annexed to the cutting of them, without leave from the king's surveyor.] **1992** *DARE* File **ME** (as of late 1970s), Mast pine, also called the king's pine, were the tallest, straightest white pines, reserved, by decree, for masts for the king's ships. I don't think any are left now. **1995** *Fine Woodworking* Nov–Dec 36, [Letter:] Recently, I learned that I am to receive some King's Arrow pine from my father's trust. It is old-growth clear pine.

king's sax, king's scruse See **king's ex**

king's taste, to the See **queen's taste, to the**

king's x See **king's ex**

king-toe *n* Also *king-toed shoe* Cf **keen** *adj* **1**
A pointed shoe.
1968–70 *DARE* (Qu. W42a, . . *Nicknames . . for men's sharp-pointed shoes*) Infs **IL137, KY82, VA2,** King-toes; **KY40, 94,** King-toed shoes.

king turtle *n* esp NJ
A **soft-shell turtle** (here: *Trionyx spiniferus*).
1937 Cahn *Turtles IL* 182, *Amyda mutica* is much less vicious than is *Amyda spinifera.* . . It is this fact of relative tempers of the two species which has won for . . [*Amyda spinifera*] the local name of . . "king" turtle. **1968** *DARE* (Qu. P24, . . *Kinds of turtles*) Infs **NJ39, 53,** King turtle; **NJ31,** King turtle—yellow belly.

King Tut's tomb *n*
1968 *DARE* (Qu. M21b, *Joking names for an outside toilet building*) Inf **NY79,** King Tut's tomb.

King William was King George's son *n* Also *King Arthur was King William's son, King William(s), King and Queen;* for addit varr see quots
A ring game; see quots.
1883 Newell *Games & Songs* 73, King Arthur was King William's Son. A row of hats of various sizes, and belonging to both sexes, are placed on the floor. The leader picks up the first hat, and puts it on his own head, marching and singing the verse. . . King Arthur was King William's son,/ And when the battle he had won,/ Upon his breast he wore a star,/ And it was called the sign of war. *Orange, New Jersey.* The following rhyme is exceedingly familiar, throughout the Middle and

Southern States, as a kissing-round: King William was King James's son, [Footnote: Or, "King *George's* son."]/ And all the royal race he run [etc]. **1888** *Amer. Anthropologist* 1.247 **DC,** *King William Was King James's Son,* as played among us, is chiefly notable for a curious corruption in the fourth line, where an aboriginal reminiscence sometimes takes the place of the time-honored "sign of war." . . King William was King James's son,/ Upon a royal race he run,/ Upon his breast he wore a star,/ Which was called *the diamond squaw.* **1903** (1963) Newell *Games & Songs* 246 **CT** (as of 1865), *King William was King George's Son.* . . King William was King George's son,/ And from the royal blood he sprung;/ Upon his breast he wore a stowe,/ Which denotes the sign of woe. *Ibid* 247 **eIA,** King Charles he was King James's son. *Ibid* **DC,** King William was King James's son. **1916** Wolford *Play-Party IN* 62 **swIN,** *King William Was King Jamie's Son.* . . All, excepting one boy, join hands and form a circle. The boy in the center . . chooses his favorite girl, kneels, . . salutes her and kisses her hand, then takes a place in the ring beside her. The game known in Oregon, New Jersey is played with hats and is entirely unlike this simple marriage game. **1951** West *Witch Diggers* 35 **IN,** Christie lost track of the dances. . . He cast up, cast down, whirled his partner . . and at one point on an inspiration of his own flapped his arms and crowed like a rooster. They were singing, "King William was King James' son,/ Up from the royal race did come," when Uncle Wes beckoned to him from the kitchen. **1952** Brown *NC Folkl.* 1.113, *King William Was King James's Son.* . . Nearly fifty texts of this popular game were sent in by contributors. . . There is considerable disagreement as to the identity of William's parent, the honor being ascribed to King George, King Simon, and King James respectively. *Ibid* (as of c1927), King William was King George's son;/ Round the royal race he run,/ Wore a star upon his breast / First to the East and then to the West./ Go choose you East, go choose you West;/ Choose the one that you love best./ If she's not here to take your part,/ Choose another with all your heart. *Ibid* 114, *King William. Ibid* 115, *King and Queen.* . . Has "King Simon's son." **1969** *DARE* (Qu. EE1, . . *Games . . children play . . in which they form a ring, and either sing or recite a rhyme*) Inf **NC72,** King Williams.

kini n |'kini] Also redup *kinikini* [Haw pronc-sp for *tin*] **HI**
A playing marble.
 1938 Reinecke *Hawaiian Loanwords* 20, *Kini* . . [kini] . . [Engl. *tin*] 1. A small steel marble, like a ball bearing. 2. Any kind of marble, a steel marble being distinguished as an "iron *kini.*" **1967** *DARE* (Qu. EE6b, *Small marbles or marbles in general*) Inf **HI4,** Kinikini ['kini'kini].

kinick n Also *canick* [Prob < Du *knikker* or Ger *Knicker;* cf **nick** n[1], **nicker** n[2]]
A playing marble; see quots.
 1957 *Sat. Eve. Post Letters* **IN,** Kinick—a five cent shooter for playing marbles. *Kineelia*—a large-sized shooter costing possibly twenty cents or more. (Machined and polished stone.) **1958** *PADS* 29.31 **IL** [Marbles terms], *Canick* . . "real agate marble, 30¢ to $1.50 apiece." **1967** *DARE* (Qu. EE6c, *Cheap marbles*) Inf **WY5,** Kinicks [kə'nɪks]—made out of colored stone, agate.

kinikaneck See **kinnikinnick**

kinikini See **kini**

kinikinik See **kinnikinnick**

kinipopo, on the adj phr [Haw *kinipōpō* ball, baseball] **HI**
On target; on the ball.
 1967 Reinecke–Tsuzaki *Hawaiian Loanwords* 101, *Kinipopo* [kinipo:po:] . . [Literally, ball or baseball.] Used in the phrase "right on the kinipopo," meaning "right on the nose (or button)" or "on the ball." **1967** *DARE* (Qu. KK29, *To start working very hard: "He was slow at first but now he's really _____."*) Inf **HI4,** On the kinipopo; (Qu. NN2, *Exclamations of very strong agreement: Somebody says, "I think Smith is absolutely right," and you reply, "_____."*) Inf **HI13,** Right on the kinipopo.

‡kink n
The heel of a loaf of bread.
 1991 *DARE* File **seMI,** My husband's family is from Saginaw, MI., and they have always called it [=end slice of bread] the 'kink'.

kink-bush See **kinks-bush**

kinkling See **keekling**

kinks-bush n Also *kink-bush*
=**groundsel tree.**

 1916 *Torreya* 16.240 **VA,** *Baccharia* [sic] *halimifolia* . . Staminate plants are called salt-water bush, and the pistillate kinks-bushes at Revels [Island], Va.; the latter name is also used at Wallops [Island], Va. **1937** *Torreya* 37.101 *Baccharis* spp. . . the appellation kink-bush [is] similarly misused near Ocean City, Md. **1940** Clute *Amer. Plant Names* 77, *B[accharis] halimifolia.* Groundsel-bush . . kinks-bushes.

kinky adj *esp* **nNEng** Cf **gimpy**
Lively, high-spirited.
 1903 Wasson *Cap'n Simeon's Store* 107 **ME,** He ain't over and above kinky, though, I s'pose likely? **1913** *DN* 4.4 **ME,** *Kinky.* . . In high spirits. "You seem to be feeling pretty kinky to-day." **1914** *DN* 4.75 **ME, nNH,** *Kinky.* . . Lively, strong, energetic. **1926** James *Smoky* 110 **West,** After riding and lining out nine head of rough and kinky broncs, [he] went to where Smoky was picketed. **1958** *VT Hist.* 26.261, As kinky as a bobcat.

kinky-head n *derog* Cf **head** n **C1b,** *nappy-head* (at **nappy** adj)
A Black person.
 1944 *AmSp* 19.173 [Designations for colored folk], When, in 1936, Cab Calloway, the Negro musician, used *kinky-head* in a broadcast, he was violently belabored by the radio critic of one of the Negro weeklies. **1964** *PADS* 42.30 **Chicago IL,** Negro . . kinkyhead [1 inf]. **1966** Dakin *Dial. Vocab. Ohio R. Valley* 2.449, Other miscellaneous terms, all clearly derogatory . . are . . *burr head, wooly* ~, *kinky* ~ (Ky.) **1966–68** *DARE* (Qu. HH28, *Names and nicknames . . for people of foreign background: Negro*) Infs **MD9, MI67, MS71,** Kinky-head; **SC32,** Kinky-head—old. **1970** Tarpley *Blinky* 265 **neTX,** Teasing and derogatory names for Negroes . . [include] *chocolate drops . . kinky heads . . night creepers.* **1986** Pederson *LAGS Concordance (Negro)* 1 inf, **csTX,** Kinky heads.

kinlin n [Prob *kin* + *lin,* pronc-sp for *-ling,* used as dimin or familiarizing suff] Cf **kinnery**
=**kinfolk.**
 1966 *DARE* (Qu. Z9, *General word for others related to you by blood*) Inf **AR27,** My kinlin, my kinfolks.

kin'lin-wood See **kindling wood**

kinnekinaick See **kinnikinnick**

kinnery n Also *kindry, kintry* Also sp *kin(e)ry* **Sth, S Midl** *sometimes joc*
=**kinfolk.**
 1890 *DN* 1.70 **LA,** *Kinry:* relatives, kindred. This word I have heard several times, used with a somewhat contemptuous or jocular force. **1893** Shands *MS Speech* 42, *Kinnery.* . . Used by negroes and illiterate whites for the whole number of one's kindred or relations; as, "I hates my kinnery, dey is all low down trash." **1905** *DN* 3.85 **nwAR,** *Kinery.* . . Relatives. 'All our kinery will be home for Christmas.' Jocose. **1908** *DN* 3.327 **eAL, wGA,** *Kinnery.* . . "I've got so much poor kinnery I can't count 'em." **1952** Brown *NC Folkl.* 1.556, *Kinnery.* . . Kinfolk. **1966–67** *DARE* (Qu. Z9, *General word for others related to you by blood*) Inf **LA8,** My kintry ['kɪntrɪ]; **SC26,** My kinry [kɪnrɪ]. [Both Infs Black] **1986** Pederson *LAGS Concordance,* 1 inf, **swGA,** Any kindry at all; *(Relatives)* 2 infs, **csFL, cAL,** Kinnery; 1 inf, **cwMS,** Kinnery—kindred, biblical; 1 inf, **swMS,** My kinnery—to about fourth generation. [4 of 5 infs Black]

kinnikinnick n Also *killikinnick;* for addit varr see quots [Algonquian; see quot 1902 at **1** below]
1 A mixture made of the dried leaves or bark of var plants, often including tobacco, for smoking. *hist* Also called **Indian tobacco 14**
 1805 (1965) Ordway *Jrls.* 199, Some Indian had hung up. . . a Scraper a paint bag . . kinikaneck bags, flints &c. **1809** (1817) Bradbury *Travels* 91, They did not make use of tobacco, but the bark of *Cornus sanguinea,* or red dog wood, mixed with the leaves of *Rhus glabra,* or smooth sumach. This mixture they call kinnikineck. **1812** Henry *Campaign Against Quebec* 223, A half part of Red-willow bark, added to as much of the dried sumach forms the killekinic. **1835** in 1847 Featherstonhaugh *Canoe Voyage* 1.265 **MN,** He only smoked the *kinnekinnic,* which is a mild preparation of the inner bark of the willow, mixed with a little tobacco. **1839** (1974) Murray *Travels* 1.452, We . . smoked our pipe of Kinnekinnik, and . . spread our clothes and skins to dry. [Footnote: Kĭnnĕkĭnnĭck . . , which is smoked by all the Indians of the western regions, is usually composed of the dried leaves of the shumack and the inner bark of the red willow.] **1859** in 1942 Hafen *Overland Routes* 11.139, I was received with cordial greeting by an elderly [Sioux]

Indian, who was quietly and meditatively smoking his kinnekinaick. **1884** Smith *Bill Arp's Scrap Book* 37 **nwGA,** Calmly and coolly we smoked our killikinick. **1890** Custer *Following* 101 **West,** Kinni-kin-nic. . . is a mixture of willow bark, sumach leaves, sage leaf, and tobacco, and this is thoroughly mingled with marrow from buffalo bones. **1892** (1974) Millspaugh *Amer. Med. Plants* 100–3, The American Aborigines smoke the dried leaves [of the bearberry] with tobacco, making a mixture called . . *Kinikinik* among the Western tribes. **1902** *Jrl. Amer. Folkl.* 15.246, *Kinnikinnick.* A mixture of tobacco with leaves and bark of sumac, red-willow *(bois-rouge),* etc., used by Indians, half-breeds, and early white settlers in the region of the Great Lakes and the Northwest. The name is also applied to various shrubs and plants whose leaves or bark was thus employed: Red osier *(Cornus stolonifera);* bear berry *(Arctostaphylos uva-ursi);* silky cornel *(Cornus sericea);* ground dogwood *(Cornus Canadensis),* etc. The word *kinnikinnick* (the variants are quite numerous, *killikinnick, k'nick-k'neck,* etc.) is derived from one of the dialects of the country about the Great Lakes, in all probability Ojibwa, and signifies "what is mixed, mixture" (Ojibwa *kinikinige,* "he mixes,"—the radical is *kinika,* "mixed, pell-mell"). **1928** Buffalo Child Long Lance 241 **nMT** [Indian speaker], He dispatched a runner to the Crow Chief, who was coming with his band more than one hundred miles away, with a present of Indian tobacco—*kinikinik.* . . Six days later the runner returned with a present of "Eastern Indian tobacco"—tobacco like that used by the white man today. **1948** *NW Ohio Qrly.* 20.40, The council fire was lighted and the calumet of *kinnekanick* (tobacco) was passed from chief to chief. **1956** Settle *Beulah Land* 110 **WV** (as of 1754–74), "Ye got to take some of the Injun's killinick and smoke it." He wanted to see the English boy gag over the tobacco. **1968** Adams *Western Words* 170, *Kinnikinnick.* . . emits a delightful odor. Also called *killickinnic.*

2 Any of var plants, or plant parts, included in the mixture above, spec:

a A **sumac,** usu *Rhus microphylla* or *R. virens;* also the dried leaves of such a plant. Cf **tobacco sumac**

1792 Pope *Tour U.S.* 63 **S Atl,** *Killicanic* or *Sumac* Leaves, which when mixed with Tobacco, emit a most delightful Odour from the Pipe. **1799** Smith *Acct. Travels* 11, [A] pouch, which . . contained tobacco, *killegenico,* or dry sumach leaves, which they mix with their tobacco. **1960** Vines *Trees SW* 631, *Rhus virens.* . . Vernacular names . . are . . Tobacco Sumac, . . Kinnikinick. . . Tamaichia was the name given by the Comanche Indians, who gathered the leaves in the fall, sun-cured them, and mixed them with tobacco for smoking.

b Any of var **dogwoods 1;** also the bark of such a plant. Cf **Indian tobacco 1 3**

1848 (1855) Ruxton *Life Far West* 116 **Rocky Mts,** There are also certain creeks where the Indians resort to lay in a store of kinnik-kinnik (the inner bark of the red willow), which they use as a substitute for tobacco, and which has an aromatic and very pungent flavor. **1853** Bond *Minnesota* 303, Some dry Kinne-kin-nick bark is generally carried along, cut very fine for the purpose of smoking. **1902** [see **1** above]. **1936** *Torreya* 36.38, The silky dogwood called Kinnikinnick grows with thickets of witch hazel in Pennsylvania. **1940** Clute *Amer. Plant Names* 97, *C[ornus] amomum.* . . Kinnikinnik. *Ibid* 257, *Cornus suecica.* Kinnikinnik. **1950** *WELS Suppl.* **csWI,** Kinnickinnic. Swamp bush—branches grow deep crimson as spring approaches—color fades when bush leafs out. **1966** Barnes–Jensen *Dict. UT Slang* 27, *Kinnikinnick* . . this name is sometimes given to the Dogwood or Cornel *(Cornus stolonifera)* although it properly describes the Bearberry. **1980** Little *Audubon Guide N. Amer. Trees E. Region* 617, Red-osier Dogwood—"Kinnikinnik"—"Red Dogwood"—*Cornus stolonifera.*

c A **bearberry 2,** usu *Arctostaphylos uva-ursi;* also the dried leaves of such a plant. Cf **Indian tobacco 2**

1824 Eaton *Botany* 208, [*Arbutus*] *uva-ursi* . . bear-berry, kinnikinnick . . Dry barren sand-plains, &c. Very abundant about the great lakes. **1878** Meehan *Native Flowers* 1st ser 1.78, The Bear-Berry has, however, an association with Indian history, as it is the "Kinnikinnick" of the Western races, who smoke it, and believe the practice secures them from malarial fevers. **1878** (1887) Jackson *Bits of Travel* 289 **CO,** The ground was gay with yellow lupines, daisies, and great mats of killikinnick vines (the bear-berry). **1902** [see **1** above]. **1924** *Amer. Botanist* 30.13, The term "kinnikinik," applied to this plant [=*Arctostaphylos uva-ursi*] is of Indian origin. **1929** Ellis *Ordinary Woman* 62 **CO** (as of early 20th cent), Here, too, kinnikinnic grew all the year, creeping and spreading, such a soft carpet for tired bare feet. **1933** Cannell *Signs* 13 **NE,** Many berries on kinnikinic portend a hard winter; few berries indicate a mild winter. **1950** *WELS Suppl.* **nWI,** Kinikinik. There is a trailing plant with

thick glossy leaves and red berries that grows in Oneida Co[unty] where we go in the summer. The name given for it in the flower book is bearberry. **1966** [see **2b** above]. **1966–67** *DARE* FW Addit **CO7,** Kinnikinnick (bearberry); **WA**12, ['kɪnɪ,kɪn'ɪk] or bearberry—blooms in spring, heather family, blooms pink bell shaped, grows low over ground, bright red berries in fall; **WA**30, Indian tea—kinnikinnick; shiny, green-leafed vine; tea is purgative. **1967** *DARE* (Qu. S26c, *Wildflowers that grow in woods*) Inf **MI**53, Kinnikinnick—its leaves were the Indian smoking tobacco; (Qu. T5, . . *Kinds of evergreens, other than pine*) Inf **ID**5, Kinnikinnick. **1979** Spellenberg *Audubon Guide N. Amer. Wildflowers W. Region* 479, Kinnikinnick, an Indian word for many tobacco substitutes, is most frequently applied to this species [=*Arctostaphylos uva-ursi*], which also had many medicinal uses.

d Any of var other plants, or the dried leaves or bark of such plants; see quots. Cf **Indian tobacco 1, 3**

1841 Steele *Summer Journey* 108 **MI,** Our friends kindly gathered for me a variety of these, among which was a fine scarlet lilium superbum, blue bells, and kinni kanic, or Indian tobacco. **1931** Clute *Common Plants* 28, One of the kinnikinniks is still known as Indian tobacco *(Lobelis* [sic] *inflata).* **1940** Clute *Amer. Plant Names* 258, *Euonymus atropurpureus.* . . kinnikinnik. **1967** *DARE* FW Addit **ND,** Kinnikinnick [ˌkɪnɪkə'nɪk]. In the Great Plains area of North Dakota this word designates an Indian tobacco substitute which is obtained from the willow. The inner bark is scraped off and dried. It was then usually mixed with tobacco and smoked in stone pipes. Early white Alsatian settlers in the Walhalla area of Pembina County also used this in lieu of tobacco. **1969** *DARE* (Qu. S20, *A common weed that grows on open hillsides: It has velvety green leaves close to the ground, and a tall stalk with small yellow flowers on a spike at the top*) Inf **MI**108, Mullein; Indian tobacco; kinnikinnick—Indian name.

kinpeople n Also *kinpeoples* [Varr of *kinspeople*] **Sth, S Midl** Cf **people**
=**kinfolk.**

1965–70 *DARE* (Qu. Z9, *General word for others related to you by blood*) 21 Infs, **AL, GA, KY, NC, SC,** (My) kinpeople. **1966–69** *DARE* Tape **FL**34, I have kinpeople in Missouri; **GA**82, Even among your kinpeople who don't live within your household, you would say "Christmas gift"; **VA**9, My father, he moved out, and he swum across the creek to my kinpeople. **1970** Tarpley *Blinky* 202 **neTX,** People who are related to you . . kin-people [1 of 200 infs]. **1986** Pederson *LAGS Concordance* **Gulf Region** *(Relatives)* 52 infs, (My) kin people; 4 infs, Kin peoples; 2 infs, Her (older) kin people; 1 inf, Kin people—includes third cousin; 1 inf, Kin people—[corrects to "kinfolk"]; 1 inf, Kin people—includes parents and grandparents; 1 inf, I've got close kin people; 1 inf, They were kin people.

kinry See **kinnery**

kinsfolk(s) See **kinfolk**

kin to See **kin 1**

kintry See **kinnery**

kiote See **coyote** n

kip n [Du *kip* hen, fowl, chicken] **chiefly NJ, NY** *esp in Dutch settlement areas*

A young chicken—often used as a call to chickens.

1895 *DN* 1.383 **NJ,** *Kip:* young chicken. (Used also as call—"kip, kip.") **1940–41** Cassidy *WI Atlas (Calls to chickens)* 1 inf, Kip kip. [Dutch settlement area; inf of Dutch background] **1949** Kurath *Word Geog.* 24, The chicken call *kip!* . . has survived all the way from Bergen County, New Jersey, to the Mohawk Valley. None of these calls [=*kip!, kees!, kish!*] occurs outside the Dutch settlement area, and they are, therefore, presumably of Dutch or Flemish origin. **1967–69** *DARE* (Qu. K79, *How do you call the chickens to you at feeding time?*) Infs **NJ**1, **NY**62, 70, 209, 220, (Here) kip kip [sometimes repeated]. **1986** Pederson *LAGS Concordance,* 1 inf, **ceAL,** Kip (x2) chicky (x2).

kipe v, hence vbl n *kiping* Also sp *kife, kipp, kype* [Etym uncert; cf *EDD kip* v. 4 "To take the property of another by fraud or violence"; *OED kip* v. "Obs."] **scattered, but esp West** See Map on p. 228

To steal or pilfer; see quots.

1934 Minehan *Boy & Girl Tramps* 199, Three long butts I kipped right in front of the entrance. *Ibid* 265, *Kipp*—seize. **1938** *AmSp* 13.151 **IN** [Black], *Chip.* To steal, kipe. **1960** Wentworth–Flexner *Slang* 305, *Kife.* . . To steal. *Ibid* 306, *Kipe* . . To steal, usu. something of small value. **1965–70** *DARE* (Qu. V4, . . *Words for stealing something valuable . . "Yesterday somebody* _____ *my watch."*) 10 Infs, **esp West,** Kiped [kaɪpt] (*or* [kaɪpt]); **CA93,** Kiped—occasionally; **CO36,** Kiped—young people say; (Qu. V5a, *To take something of small value that doesn't belong to you—for example, a child taking cookies: "Who's been* _____ *the cookies?"*) Infs **OR**1, **WA**22, Kiping [ˈkaɪpɪŋ]. [7 of 13 total Infs young] **1967** *DARE* FW Addit **WA,** Kipe [kaɪp]—nonpejorative for stealing. [FW: used by high school students] **1968** *Sat. Eve. Post* 18 May 25, This typical teen-age shoplifter will brag to her friends about what she has "bagged," "hocked," "kyped" or "snitched," using the particular word that is common to the vernacular of her region. **1989** *Isthmus* (Madison WI) 6 Oct 20, [Comic strip:] Someone stole her rock with the eyes painted on it . . that said "smile" and it was on her desk and someone kyped it. [*DARE* Ed: Strip creator is a Seattle native.] **1990** *DARE* File **sCA** (as of 1950s), I know the word *kipe* as the usual term at school (grammar and high school) for "steal" or "swipe". "He was always kiping something; and now he's kiped a car and will probably do time for it." **1991** *Ibid* **cIA** (as of c1965), We used *kipe* as the term for what was considered nonserious stealing by children or adolescents. *Ibid* **nwKS** (as of 1960s), Kyping was petty stealing or shoplifting. One kyped earrings from the local drugstore. **1994** *Ibid* **csWI,** When I was about 19 in 1969, I remember hearing a guy of about my age say that he had *kifed* something, meaning that he had swiped it.

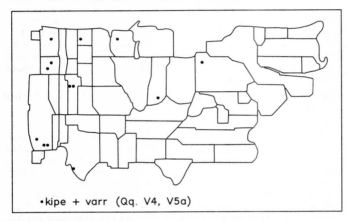

•kipe + varr (Qq. V4, V5a)

kipper adj [*EDD kipper* adj. 1 "Lively, in good spirits"] Chipper.
  1977 *Yankee* Jan 73 **cME coast,** Aside from that [=arthritis], winter is an exhilarating time when folks feel pretty kipper.

kippy woodpecker n
=**flicker** n[2] **1.**
  1956 MA Audubon Soc. *Bulletin* 40.82 **NH,** Yellow-shafted Flicker. . . Kippy Woodpecker. . . Kippy is a slang term meaning smart, attractive; this is a "dressy" bird.

kirmes(s) See **kermis(s)**

kirry See **carry A1**

kirsene See **kerosene**

kiscatoma See **kiskitomas**

kish exclam Also *kees, kissy* [Prob Du *koetje,* dimin of *koe* cow] Cf **cossie, cush** v
Used as a call to cows or calves.
  1949 Kurath *Word Geog.* 24, Kees! or kish! . . is occasionally heard on the upper Delaware and in the Catskills. . . None of these calls [to cows] occurs outside the Dutch settlement area, and they are, therefore, presumably of Dutch or Flemish origin. **1967** Faries *Word Geog. MO* 135, *(Call to calves)* Kees!—1 [inf]; Kish!—1 [inf]. **1973** Allen *LAUM* 1.260 **ND** (as of c1950), *Calls to calves. . . kissy* is the term of a North Dakota inf. both of whose parents came from The Netherlands.

kishka n
1 also *keeshka, kiszka*: A blood sausage. [Pol *kiszka*] *esp in Polish communities* Cf **kishke**
  1950 *WELS* (*Sausage most eaten in your neighborhood*) 1 Inf, **Milwaukee WI,** Kishka—Polish kind of a sausage. [Inf of Polish background] **1963** Yankovic *Who Stole the Keeshka* (Phonodisc). **1968–69** *DARE* (Qu. H43, *Foods made from parts of the head and inner organs of an animal*) Inf **PA**167, Beef blood and barley: kishka [kɪškə] or blood pudding; (Qu. H45, *Dishes made with meat, fish, or poultry that every-*

body around here would know, but that people in other places might not) Inf **NY**130, Kishka [ˈkɪškə]—Polish or Jewish sausage. **1989** *Valley Advocate* (Hatfield MA) 10 Apr 33/3, Such Polish rarities as white and red borsch, flaczki (pork stew) and kiszka (a blood sausage dish). **1991** *DARE* File **Milwaukee WI,** Kishka [ˈkɪškə]—I love that sausage. It's a blood sausage. There's a lot of liver in it, like a liver sausage, and blood. It's not smoked, it's a fresh sausage. I like them fried, or you bake it. It turns black when you cook it, because of the blood. It's pork. In my neighborhood [=Polish area of town] and family, it's definitely not what's meant by Jewish sausage—kishke [ˈkɪškɛ]—that's big, looks like a stuffed sock. The filling is chopped up meat and meal.
2 See **kishke.**

kishke n Also sp *kishka* [Yiddish, ult of Slavic origin; cf **kishka**] *esp among speakers of Jewish background*
1 The stomach, gut.
  1902 *Bulletin* (San Francisco CA) 18 May 12 (*Zwilling Coll.*), [Cartoon entitled "Johnny Wise Had A Dream At A Fight Where Sam Pruitt Was Winnin 'Hands Down' ":] In his kishkus [sic] [=hit him in his stomach or gut]. **1936** (1947) Mencken *Amer. Lang.* 217, In New York City the high density of Eastern Jews in the population has made almost every New Yorker familiar with a long list of Yiddish words, *e.g., kosher* . . and many non-Jewish New Yorkers have added others that are not generally familiar . . *blintzes* . . *dokus* . . *kishkes.* **1968** Rosten *Yiddish* 181, *Kishka*—Pronounced *kish-keh.* 1. Intestines. 2. A sausagelike comestible of meat, flour, and spices stuffed into intestine casing, and baked. . . Aside from food, the words *kishka* and *kishkas* are used to mean intestine, "innards," belly. Genteel Jews hesitate to do so. My father and mother never would use, or approve, the following: "His accusation hit me right in the *kishka.*" "I laughed until my *kishkas* were sore.". . 4. Plural: *kishkas*—even though the same intestine is being described. To hit someone "in the *kishkas*" means to hit him in the stomach, or, in indelicate parlance, "in the guts." **1989** *DARE* File **cIA** (as of 1964), At B'nai Brith Youth basketball games, the cheers from the stands were based on screaming dirty words in Yiddish. One cheer went something like "Ishkes, pishkes, hit 'em in the kishkes." **1993** Isaacs *After All* 269 **Long Is. NY,** "Oh, Rosie, aren't you afraid?" "Of course I am. I've been afraid ever since I tripped over a big, lumpy thing on my kitchen floor and it turned out to be my husband. I've been living with my *kishkes* in a knot ever since then."
2 Beef casing usu stuffed with meal, chopped meat, onion, and spices.
  1949 (1986) Leonard *Jewish Cookery* 189, *Stuffed Kishke* (Beef Casings—also called Stuffed Derma). *Ibid* 190, It is ready to be tucked into the midst of a Tzimmes. . . Stuffed Kishke may be roasted with chicken . . goose or turkey. Or, it may be roasted independently on a bed of sliced onions to which schmaltz and grebenes have been added. . . Stuffed Kishke is sometimes added to Cholent. **1968** [see **1** above]. **1968–69** *DARE* (Qu. H45, *Dishes made with meat, fish, or poultry that everybody around here would know, but that people in other places might not*) Inf **NY**130, [ˈkɪškə]—Polish or Jewish sausage; **PA**110, Kiski [sic] . . in casings, cook in oven. **1970** Feinsilver *Yiddish* 293, Gentiles are learning to enjoy and pronounce such typical dishes as *kishke* and *tsimmes.* **1981** *AmSp* 56.7 [Jewish English], The plural inflection of many Yiddish nouns is *-s,* as it is in English (for example, *kishke* 'gut, stuffed derma,' plural *kishkes*). **1991** [see **kishka 1**].

kiskadee n Also *kiskadee flycatcher* [Echoic; *OEDS* 1891 →] Cf **keskydee**
A **flycatcher 1a** (here: *Pitangus sulphuratus*).
  1960 Peterson *Field Guide Birds TX* 154, *Kiskadee Flycatcher—Pitangus sulphuratus. . . Voice:* A loud *get-ter-heck* . . ; also *wheep!* . . *Resident* of lower Rio Grande Valley. **1965** Teale *Wandering Through Winter* 129 **TX,** We were seeing . . the kiskadee or Derby flycatcher. . . The first hoarse "weeeep!" was followed by a loud, far-carrying "kiskadee!" or "git-a-here!" **1977** Bull-Farrand *Audubon Field Guide Birds* 607, *Kiskadee Flycatcher (Pitangus sulphuratus). . .* Extreme southern Texas (lower Rio Grande Valley) to South America. This large and striking bird, also called the Derby Flycatcher, is numerous throughout Latin America.

kiskatoma See **kiskitomas**

kiskeedee See **keskydee**

kiskitomas n Also *keskatomas, kiscatoma, kiskatoma, kisskatomass, kiskythomas, kiskytom* [Of Algonquian origin; see quot 1902] **chiefly NY, NJ** *prob obs*

A **shagbark hickory** (here: *Carya ovata*); also the nut of such a tree.

1750 in 1968 Earle *Colonial NY* 144, The printer hereof . . has been obliged to provide for the Winter Evening Diversion . . a Parcel of the Nuts commonly called Keskatomas Nuts. **1809** Ritson *Poetical Picture* 161 *(DA)*, Their nuts, black walnuts, persimins, Kiscatoma nuts, and Chinquapins. **1810** Michaux *Histoire des Arbres* 1.190 **nNJ**, Les descendans des Hollandois, qui habitent cette partie du New-Jersey qui avoisine la ville de New-York, lui donnent encore fréquemment le nom de *Kiskythomas nut*. [=The descendants of the Dutch, who live in the part of New Jersey neighboring the city of New York, still frequently give it [=the shagbark hickory] the name of *Kiskythomas nut*.] **a1817** (1822) Dwight *Travels* 4.58 **cwNY**, On these grounds, . . grow the chestnut, the shag-bark, or kiskatoma, and several other trees. **1836** Dunlap *30 Years Ago* 1.48 **VT**, While the rustic jest, or the tale of . . wars . . mingle with the cracking of the *kisskatomasses* . . and walnuts. **1850** in 1968 Bartlett *Americanisms* 230, Hickory, shell-bark, *kiskitomas* nut!/ Or whatsoever thou art called, thy praise / Has ne'er been sounded yet in poet's lays. **1894** *Jrl. Amer. Folkl.* 7.98, *Carya alba*, kiskytom, Otsego Co., N.Y. **1902** *Ibid* 15.246, *Kiskitómas*. A name for the . . hickory, formerly common in New Jersey, Long Island, etc. . . The radical is seen in the Ojibwa *nin kishkibidon*, "I tear or rend with the teeth," Cree *kiskisikâtew*, "it is cut *or* gnawed," Abnaki *nese kouskadámen*, "I crack with the teeth." The chief root seems to be the Algonkian radical *kisk*, "to gnaw." The word is derived from one of the Algonkian dialects southeast of the Great Lakes.

kispel n [Prob Scan; cf Sw *kisse* cat, *spel* game]
=**cat** n **3a**.

1950 *WELS Suppl.*, Besides two common stones or bricks for the base of the short sticks for the game kispel, we often simply dug a small depression in the ground and put the stick across that.

kiss v

Of a marble or other game piece: to touch lightly; to come to rest against or on top of; hence n *kiss, kissie*, often pl *kiss(i)es*, an instance of this; also used as exclam.

1942 Berrey–Van den Bark *Amer. Slang* 665.1, *Marbles*. . . *Kissie, kissies, the act of touching another's "lagger" when throwing to the "lag line," which entitles the one whose marble "kisses" to shoot first.* *Ibid* 665.4, *Play marbles*. . . *kiss, of the "shooter" or "lagger," to touch another marble.* **1968** *DARE* File, Kissies—When jacks are thrown and one stacks on top of the other. Other player could pop the two jacks. **c1970** Wiersma *Marbles Terms* **swMI**, Kiss—To touch (marbles) while at rest. "My cateye and his boulder were kissing." "My cateye kissed his boulder." *Ibid* **swMI**, Kisses—marbles hit each other and break apart. *Ibid* **swMI** (as of c1965), Kisses—shooting at a marble and it just touches it—it is then thrown into the air and played from where it lands; e.g. you kissed it so you get to toss it. *Ibid*, Kiss—two marbles which come together after a *taw*. *Ibid* **MI** (as of 1955), Kisses—A player shoots at an opponent's marble and just touches it. The play is completed by retrieving the shot marble, throwing it in an arc, and continuing the game from where it lands. . . "Kisses, fix it up." *Ibid* **swMI** (as of c1965), Kissies in the pot—two marbles hit together while entering the pot. *Ibid*, Kissies, kisses: 1. When two marbles hit; 2. When a rolled marble stops beside another without moving it; synonym: nick. *Ibid* **seFL**, Kisses—the slightest degree of contact between marbles. "He lost it by kisses." *Ibid* **swMI** (as of 1973), Kissies: two marbles touching each other. **1973** Ferretti *Marble Book* 83, Nucks. . . A player can keep shooting as long as he's landing his marble in the saucers. When he misses, the next player gets his turn. The second has the option of shooting for a saucer or "kissing" his opponent off the track, for which he wins an extra shot. **1975** Ferretti *Gt. Amer. Book Sidewalk Games* 101, *[Jacks:]* "Easies" also permits the separation of "kissies" (two jacks touching after being thrown). . . Upon calling "kissies," . . the player can pick up the touching jacks and drop them again. *Ibid* 218, *[Jump Rope:]* You can also play with two ropes. In Double Dutch, great stress is placed on the Ender to prevent the rope from "kissing" (slapping together) and thus ruining the flow of the jumps and the rhymes.

kiss apple n Cf **apple of Sodom, love apple 1**
Prob a **nightshade 1** such as *Solanum aculeatissimum*.

1968 *DARE* (Qu. S15, . . *Weed seeds that cling to clothing*) Inf **GA25**, Kiss apple—a thorny plant.

kiss bug See **kissing bug**

kisses n

1 also *kiss-me*: A **johnny-jump-up 1** (here: *Viola tricolor*).

1889 *Century Dict.* 3294, Kiss-me. . . The wild form of *Viola tricolor*, the pansy. Also called *kisses*.

2 =**red maids**. CA
1911 Jepson *Flora CA* 159, C[alandrinia] caulescens . . var. *menziesii*. . . Called "Kisses" in Solano Co. **1920** Saunders *Useful Wild Plants* 131, Also of California is . . the pretty wild flower known as Red Maids or Kisses (*Calandrinia caulescens Menziesii* . .), whose crimson blossoms . . make sheets of vivid color over considerable areas in the spring.

3 A **butterfly weed 2** (here: either *Gaura lindheimeri* or *G. suffulta*). TX
1936 Whitehouse *TX Flowers* 84, Large-flowered or Lindheimer's Gaura (*Gaura lindheimeri*) is, like other members of this group, called kisses . . because of its sweet fragrance. **1961** Wills–Irwin *Flowers TX* 30, The *Gauras* are a distinctive group of plants. . . *[Gaura suffulta]*, also known as Bee-blossom and Kisses, grows mainly in limestone soils. **1970** Correll *Plants TX* 1126, *Gaura suffulta*. . . Bee blossom, kisses.

kissie See **kiss**

kissing ball n Also *kissing bell*
A Christmas decoration made of mistletoe.

1980 *Amer. Heritage Soc. Americana* Nov–Dec 38 **Columbia SC**, "At the Mills house, we portray an English Christmas as it was celebrated here in the states. . . The South retained its ties with England longer than the North, and this is reflected in the decorations." Before the Christmas tree, the kissing ball was the center of merrymaking. . . Kissing balls were made by sticking boxwood or other evergreens into a potato and tying mistletoe to the bottom. . . Legend has it that when a man claimed a kiss from a woman under the kissing ball, he plucked one of the white berries from the mistletoe. *Ibid* 78 **NY**, On *December 26–28* Van Cortland Manor will celebrate Twelfth Night. A kissing bell made of fruit, holly, and mistletoe will hang in the front hall. **1993** *DARE* File **cwCA** (as of c1968), One year when I had more time than usual at Christmas, I made lots of decorations, including kissing balls. These were styrofoam balls about four inches in diameter that were then decorated with velvet ribbon, sequins, beads, stars, etc. The most important part was the sprig of mistletoe hanging from the bottom.

kissing bridge n
A covered bridge.

[**1783** *Polite Traveller* 62 *(DA)*, In the way is a bridge, distant about three miles from New York, which . . is called the Kissing-Bridge, where it is part of the etiquette, for the gentleman to salute the lady who has put herself under his protection.] [**1807** Irving *Salmagundi* 22 **NYC**, He particularly noticed a worthy old gentleman of his acquaintance, who had been somewhat a beau in his day, whose eyes brightened at the bare mention of Kissing-bridge.] **1946** Congdon *Covered Bridge* 18, Various fanciful names have been applied to covered bridges; the most popular seems to be "kissing bridge" and in the horse-and-buggy days it was a bashful swain indeed, who failed to take advantage of the custom. **1966** *Lake Winnipesaukee News* (Pittsfield NH) 7 July 4/1, North, south, east and west of Winnipesaukee and her sister lakes . . are three-score covered or "kissing" bridges. **1969** *DARE* FW Addit **NC**, The *Charlotte Observer* used "kissing bridge" to refer to "the covered bridges of years gone by." **1992** *USA Today* (Arlington VA) 27 Nov sec A 9, It is one of only 12 "kissing bridges" left in Alabama. **1993** *DARE* File **nwMA**, When I asked my grandmother and great aunt if they knew any other names for covered bridges, they both said, "Why, kissing bridges, of course."

kissing bug n Also *kiss bug* [See quot 1911]
=**assassin bug**.

1899 *Pop. Sci. Mth.* Nov 33 **DC**, Several persons suffering from swollen faces visited the Emergency Hospital in Washington and complained that they had been bitten by some insect while asleep. . . Thus began the "kissing-bug" scare. **1901** Howard *Insect Book* 293, Other species [of assassin bugs], especially *Melanolestes picipes* and *Reduvius personatus*, were especially abundant in the eastern states in the summer of 1898, and their bites were responsible for the extraordinary so-called "kissing bug" scare which was greatly advertised by the newspapers. . . Of these "kissing bugs," *Reduvius personatus*, is a cosmopolitan form which, in the northern states, is found in basements and cellars of dirty houses and preys upon bed-bugs and cockroaches. **1911** *Century Dict. Suppl.*, Kissing-bug. . . Any one of several species of predatory bugs of the family Reduviidae. Applied notably to *Opsicoetes personatus*, *Melanolestes picipes*, *Rasahus biguttatus*, and *Conorhinus sanguisugus*. The name *kissing-bug* originated in the newspapers in June, 1899, many persons being bitten that summer and often on the lip. **1936** *AZ Univ. Genl. Bulletin* 7.3.113, When houses are built in the desert these kissing bugs transfer their affections to people. **1947** Dodge *Poisonous Dwellers* 19 **SW,** Although not limited to the deserts of the Southwest, the Kissing bug, of which there are many species, is commonly associated with subtropical climates. **1966** *Sumter Co. Times* (Bushnel FL) 31 Mar 8/6, Several cases of fatal reaction to the sting [sic] of the Mexican kissing bug have been reported. **1967–68** *DARE* (Qu. R7) Inf **NY**10, Kiss bug; (Qu. R21) Inf **NY**66, Kissing bug; (Qu. R22) Inf **CA**9, Kissing bug; (Qu. R30) Inf **CA**62, Kissing bug. **1969** *DARE* FW Addit **CA**138, Chiny bugs are now called kissing bugs by her daughter and grandchildren. **1989** Entomol. Soc. Amer. *Common Names Insects* 150, *Onocephalus pacificus* . . Pacific kissing bug. *Ibid,* Triatoma rubrofasciata . . large kissing bug.

kiss-in-the-ring n Also *kiss ring* [*OEDS* 1801 →] Cf **drop the hat**

A game similar to drop-the-handkerchief.

1817 (1914) Gallatin *Gt. Peace Maker* 117, We were allowed to play kiss-in-the-ring, suppressing the kiss; it was like 'Hamlet' minus the Prince of Denmark. **1910** 'G. B. Lancaster' *Jim of Ranges* vi.126 *(OEDS),* 'What d'yer do at a kick-up, Jim?' 'Oh, hide-an'-seek . . an' kiss-in-the-ring,' explained Jim. **1960** Korson *Black Rock* 242 **PA** (as of c1900), The teen-age boys and girls were in a mood to play the game they had been waiting for impatiently all day—the ring game, also known as "kiss ring," and "ring tag." *Ibid* 243, [One girl becomes "it." She walks around the ring. . . [S]he finally taps the boy of her choice lightly on the shoulder. . . He chases her around the ring. . . Finally, . . she stops with her hands up and palms out. He touches her palms lightly as, across the barrier, they kiss.]

kisskatomass See **kiskitomas**

kiss-me n
1 See **kisses 1.**
2 See **kiss-me-quick 3.**

kiss-me-and-I'll-tell-you n
1 A **fleabane** (here: *Erigeron annuus*). **chiefly TX, Gulf States**
1931 Clute *Common Plants* 131, "Kiss-me-and-I'll-tell-you" replied an attractive native of the Southern States when asked the name of that plant which people of colder climes know as the daisy fleabane (*Erigeron anuus* [sic]). **1936** Whitehouse *TX Flowers* 162, Kiss-me-and-I'll-tell-you *(Erigeron annuus)* is a taller daisy and is very abundant in East Texas. **1965–70** *DARE* (Qu. S26a, . . *Wildflowers. . . Roadside flowers)* Infs **AL**11, **NY**28, **TX**3, 39, 40, 45, Kiss-me-and-I'll-tell-you; **AL**30, Kiss-me-and-I'll-tell-you [FW: Inf tells about taking one to a friend who didn't know the name; obvious joke]; **FL**18, Kiss-me-and-I'll-tell-you; have a very strong, bad smell; (Qu. S23) Inf **NC**16, Kiss-me-and-I'll-tell-you; small blue [sic] flowers.
2 A **honeysuckle 2** (here: *Lonicera fragrantissima*). Cf **kiss-me-over-the-gate**
1955 *S. Folkl. Qrly.* 19.232 **FL,** A child would offer his flower to a friend to smell, and the friend would inevitably ask, "What is it?" The answer was always, "Kiss me and I'll tell you," whereupon he would be rewarded with a kiss and the demand, "Now, tell me." Again the answer was "Kiss me and I'll tell you." Thus the flower came to be called "Kiss me and I'll tell you" as often as "Breath of Spring."

kiss-me-at-the-gate See **kiss-me-over-the-gate**

kiss-me-ma'am See **kiss-me-quick 3**

kiss-me-over-the-fence n Also *kiss-me-over-the-garden-gate,* ~*-wall* [See quot 1913]

A **prince's-feather** (here: *Polygonum orientale*).
1897 *Jrl. Amer. Folkl.* 10.54, *Polygonum orientale.* . . Kiss-me-over-the-fence, Sulphur Grove, Ohio. **1910** Graves *Flowering Plants* 162 **CT,** *Polygonum orientale.* . . Kiss-me-over-the-Fence. . . An old-fashioned plant still frequent in cultivation. **1913** (1980) Hardy *OH Schoolmistress* 14 **swOH,** He had allowed to remain among his turnips two or three plants. . . sometimes called Kiss-me-over-the-fence, alluding to its habit of swaying in the least wind and touching you on the cheek as you went by. Its common bookname is Prince's Feather. **1953** Greene–Blomquist *Flowers South* 28, One species *(P[olygonum] orientale),* a tall, hairy annual, known as . . "kiss-me-over-the-garden-gate," . . is spreading to some extent from cultivation. **1968** *DARE* (Qu. S26a, . . *Wildflowers. . . Roadside flowers)* Inf **WI**8, Kiss-me-over-the-garden-gate; (Qu. S26e) Inf **WI**50, Kiss-me-over-the-garden-gate—tall with tiny red flowers. **1968** *DARE* FW Addit **NY**91, Kiss-me-over-the-garden-wall or princess

feather. **1976** Bailey–Bailey *Hortus Third* 897, *Kiss-me-over-the-garden-gate.* . . Naturalized in N. Amer.

kiss-me-over-the-gate n Also *kiss-me-at-the-gate* Cf **mountain honeysuckle**

Either a **honeysuckle 2** (here: *Lonicera fragrantissima*) or a **rhododendron;** see quots.
1956 McAtee *Some Dialect NC* 56, Kiss-me-over-the-gate . . the bush honeysuckle *(Lonicera fragrantissima).* Chapel Hill. **1967** *DARE* (Qu. S26a, . . *Wildflowers. . . Roadside flowers)* Inf **AL**27, Kiss-me-at-the-gate (a bush). **1984** Wilder *You All Spoken Here* 176 **Sth,** Kiss-me-over-the-gate; bush honeysuckle, mountain honeysuckle: Azalea.

kiss-me-quick n
1 Any of var plants such as **bladder campion,** a **bedstraw** (here: *Galium aparine*), a **burdock 1** (here: *Arctium lappa*), or a **meadowsweet 2** (here: *Filipendula ulmaria*). [Cf *EDD, OED*]
1959 Carleton *Index Herb. Plants* 70, Kiss-me-quick: Arctium lappa; . . Filipendula ulmaria (Spirea ulmaria); Galium aparine; . . Silene cucubalus.
2 A type of bonnet. *old-fash*
1845 *Knickerbocker* 25.375, Seen from the Bowery, it [=a church] looks like a barn with a 'kiss-me-quick' hood on. **1848** Bartlett *Americanisms* 403, *Kiss-me-quick.* A homemade quilted bonnet which does not extend beyond the face. They are chiefly used to cover the head by ladies when going to parties, or the theatre. **1855** Haliburton *Nature* 2.287, She has a new bonnet on. . . It has a horrid name, it is called a kiss-me-quick. **1891** Maitland *Amer. Slang Dict.* 160, *Kiss-me-quick,* a short veil; a bonnet not now in fashion. **1966–68** *DARE* (Qu. W2, . . *A cloth bonnet worn by women for protection from the sun)* Inf **VA**25, Kiss-me-quick [drawing shows a bonnet that leaves the face exposed]; (Qu. W3) Inf **MA**6, Kiss-me-quick—knit or crocheted. [Both Infs old]
3 also *kiss-me(-ma'am):* A sudden dip or rise in the road; a sudden jolt to a vehicle. Cf **duck-and-dip, love-hole, thank-you-ma'am**
a1877 in 1950 *AmSp* 25.176 **NEng,** Kiss-me. Used, as is 'Thank-you-Ma'am,' for a ridge or hollow place across a roadway; a jolting obstruction to vehicles. **1945** *AmSp* 20.156 **SC, GA,** Although *kiss-me-quick* does not seem to appear in the dictionaries with the meaning of ridge or depression in a roadway, it does have that meaning . . in the southeastern part of the United States. I recently asked one hundred young people of high school age in South Carolina what name they used for such a jolting obstruction to vehicles. Fifty-seven named *kiss-me-quick;* one named *thank-you-ma'am.* . . In Georgia many young people and adults told me they had never known any term except *kiss-me-quick.* **1950** *WELS* **WI** (A sudden, short dip in the road) 1 Inf, Kiss-me-quick—occasional; 1 Inf, Kiss-me-quick—old-fashioned. **1966–68** *DARE* (Qu. N30) Infs **OH**34, 78, **SC**26, Kiss-me-quick. **1971** Bright *Word Geog. CA & NV* 113, (Chuck hole) 1 inf, Kiss-me-mams—jocular. **1981** *NADS Letters* **NY,** "Kiss-me-quick" [provided] an opportunity for courting couples to "have a chance" when the wagon/buggy lurched. My source is lore from Westfield, NY—the plank road tradition. **1985** *WI Alumnus Letters* **wMA, NY,** Kiss-me-quick. My mother . . always heard that term applied to a rise in the road (not a dip . .) of the kind that nearly (or actually) bumped auto passengers' heads on the car ceiling. She learned it from my father, who grew up in the Hudson River Valley . . of parents from there and neighboring Western Massachusetts.

kiss ring See **kiss-in-the-ring**

kiss the cook v phr *old-fash* Cf **manner n 3, old maid 4**
Used in allusion to the custom that the one who takes the last bit of food must kiss the cook; see quots.
1908 *DN* 3.327 **eAL, wGA,** Kiss the cook. . . At table when one takes the last piece on a dish he must be willing to kiss the cook. **1928** Ruppenthal Coll. **KS,** When the food at a meal or lunch has all been eaten, a favorite phrase is, "Everything is eaten, now we'll have to kiss the cook." **1935** Hyatt *Folkl. Adams Co. IL* 388, The person who takes the last biscuit must kiss the cook. **1954** *WELS Suppl.* **WI,** One says, "I'll kiss the cook!"—as he helps himself to . . the last of any dish. It means the food was so good that the cook deserves a kiss. **1966–70** *DARE* (Qu. H71, . . *The last piece of food left on a plate)* Infs **IL**124, **MA**6, **NC**23, **SC**11, (Gets to) kiss the cook; **NC**10, Have to kiss the cook; **ND**3, Custom that the one who takes the last piece must kiss the cook—no real name [for this custom]. [All Infs old]

kiss the pillow See **pillow**

kissy See **kish**

kisutch See **quisutsch**

kit n

1 A small tub or barrel. Cf **kid** n[1], **lunch kit**

1899 (1912) Green *VA Folk-Speech* 251, *Kit.* . . A small tub, pail . . containing or holding particular commodities or articles: as, a *kit* of mackerel. **1904** *DN* 2.426 **Cape Cod MA** (as of a1857), *Kit.* . . A small firkin, a kid. **1942** McAtee *Dial. Grant Co. IN* 38, *Kit.* . . a small coopered tub; kits of salt mackerel were sold by the stores. **c1960** *Wilson Coll.* **csKY**, *Kit.* . . A small tub. **1969** *DARE* Tape **GA84**, Those fish came from the Great Lakes up around Michigan and Wisconsin. A kit of fish had six pounds of fish in it packed in brine. *Ibid* **MA56**, We tied these [lobster] pots on the . . line. . . Then we had a buoy—"kit" we called it, 'cause we didn't have the buoys they have now.

2 A group or collection of people, animals, or objects viewed as a whole: see below. [*OED kit* sb.[1] 3 1785 →]

a usu in phr *the whole kit:* See quots.

1848 Bartlett *Americanisms* 403, *The whole kit.* An expression common in various parts of the country. [Quoting *Poetical Epistle from a Volunteer:*] The clymit seems to me jest like a teapot made o' pewter / Our Prudence had, that wouldn't pour (all she could do) to suit her;/ Fust place the leaves would choke the spout, so's not a drop would dreen out,/ Then Prude would tip, and tip, and tip till the whole *kit* bust clean out. **1859** Elwyn *Glossary* 65, "The whole *kit* of them" is a frequent expression, and partaking somewhat of the contemptuous. **1859** Taliaferro *Fisher's R.* 151 **nwNC** (as of 1820s), He cotch the fox . . a mile ahead uv the whole kit uv 'um [=fox hounds]. **1899** (1912) Green *VA Folk-Speech* 251, *Kit.* . . A family; a brood; *the whole kit,* the whole lot or assembly; every one: used with reference to persons in contempt: as, "I defy the whole kit of them." **1941** *LANE* Map 415 *(The whole crowd)* **NEng**, Collective terms applied to a group of persons whom the speaker dislikes or of whom he disapproves. . . 17 infs, Kit; 14 infs, The whole kit of 'em (*or* you); 1 inf, Kit o' 'em. **1967** *DARE* (Qu. LL10, *A whole group of people: "They made too much noise, so he sent the whole _____ home."*) Inf **NY30**, Kit.

b in phr *whole kit and (ca)boodle* (sometimes abbr to *kit(c)aboodle*) and varr: See quots. **widespread, but somewhat more freq Nth, N Midl** See Map Cf **boodle 1, caboodle**

1862 Winthrop *John Brent* 28.296 **OR**, I motioned we shove the hul kit an boodle of the gamblers ashore on logs. **1888** *Boston Daily Globe* (MA) 5 Feb 1/3, If any "railroad lobbyist" cast reflections on his character he would wipe out the whole kit and caboodle of them. **1890** *DN* 1.74 **sePA**, *Kit and caboodle:* the same as *kit and boodle.* **1891** *Jrl. Amer. Folk.* 4.70, *Kitcaboodle.*—Used in New England, in the same sense as . . [*kerhoot* 'crowd, assembly']. "The whole kitcaboodle." **1894** *DN* 1.341 **wCT**, *Koboodle.* . . the hull koboodle is commonest; *kit and boodle* is also heard. **1899** (1912) Green *VA Folk-Speech* 251, The whole kit and boodle. **1941** *LANE* Map 415 **NEng** *(The whole crowd)* 55 infs, Kit and (ca)boodle; 1 inf, Kit a caboodle [kɪt ə budl]; 1 inf, Not [kɪt ænd budl] but [kɪt ə budl]; 1 inf, Kit and caboose; 1 inf, Kit and caboozle. **1949** *Time* 18 July 13/2, There was no longer any point to the whole kit & caboodle of anti-inflation controls which he had been demanding. **1963** Edwards *Gravel* 26 **eTN** (as of 1920s), Come when you can, the whole kill-kit'n kaboodle of you. **1965–70** *DARE* Qu. LL10, *A whole group of people: "They made too much noise, so he sent the whole _____ home."*) 89 Infs, **widespread, but more freq Nth, N Midl,** Kit and caboodle; **LA2, MI78, NY136, WI65,** Kit and caboodle [laughter]; **MS69,** Kit and caboodle—not used much; **TX3,** Kit and caboodle—old-fashioned [laughter]; **OH1,** Kit and caboodle—old-fashioned; **CT4,** Kit and boodle; **MN30,** Kit and caboodle; **TX102,** Kit and caboodlement [laughter]; (Qu. LL25, *. . Entirely, completely: "He sold out the whole place, _____."*) 75 Infs, **widespread, but more freq Nth, N Midl,** Kit and caboodle; **IL53, MN1,** Kit and boodle; **GA68,** All kit 'n boodle [laughter]; **IL92,** Kit, cat, and caboodle; **IN68,** Kit and capoodle; **TN65,** Kit, dang, and caboodle; (Qu. Z8) Inf **IL113,** Kit 'n caboodle. **1966** Dakin *Dial. Vocab. Ohio R. Valley* 2.504, *The whole crowd.* . . comments made seem to indicate that some . . (*gang, kit and kaboodle,* etc.) are usually deprecative. *Ibid,* The words *kit; kaboodle* . . and the compounds *kit 'n kaboodle* (~ ~ *boodle,* ~ ~ *poodle,* ~ ~ *kapoodle,* ~ ~ *taboodle*) . . and *kit 'n kapoose*—are common throughout Ohio and Indiana. **1973** Allen *LAUM* 1.376 **Upper MW, esp MN** (as of c1950), The whole *crowd.* . . (deprecative). . . *kit and caboodle* [33 infs]. **1986** Pederson *LAGS Concordance* **Gulf Region** *(The whole crowd)* 6 infs, Kit and caboodle; 7 infs, (The) whole kit and caboodle; 1 inf, Kit and caboose.

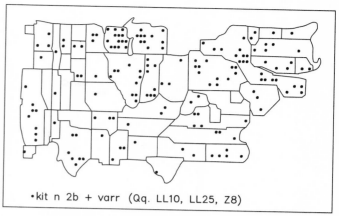

•kit n 2b + varr (Qq. LL10, LL25, Z8)

c in phrr *kit(tle) and biling* and varr: See quots. [**boiling** n; the later var *kittle and biling* is prob by folk-etym] **chiefly Sth, S Midl; also NEng**

1859 (1968) Bartlett *Americanisms* 32, *Biling.* . . The phrase *the whole* (or more commonly *hull*) *kit and bilin,* means the whole lot, applied to persons or things. **1885** Twain *Huck. Finn* 319 **MO**, Give a body a rest! Go 'long now, the whole kit and biling of ye. **1887** (1967) Harris *Free Joe* 191 **GA**, They're all proud—the whole kit and b'ilin'. **1899** (1912) Green *VA Folk-Speech* 251, The whole kit and biling. **1905** *DN* 3.85 **nwAR**, *Kit an' bilin'.* . . All of a number. **1908** *DN* 3.327 **eAL, wGA**, *Kit an(d) bilin.* . . The crowd. Usually in the expression 'the whole kit an bilin.' **1916** *Scribner's Mag.* 59.356 **VA**, De whole kit'n'bile uv 'em. **1920** Lewis *Main Street* 50 **MN**, The whole kit and bilin' of 'em are nothing in God's world but socialism in disguise. **1927** *AmSp* 3.139 **eME**, The older people spoke of. . . "whole kit and bilin'," whole being pronounced as if spelled "hull." **1933** Williamson *Woods Colt* 107 **Ozarks**, He knows the hull kit an' b'ilin' of 'em, an' most of 'em he don't like. **1939** Writers' Program *Guide KY* 89, The mountaineer. . . says, "All I ask is to be let alone. I was doin' middlin' well. The hull kit and bilin' can go to the devil." **1941** *LANE* Map 415 *(The whole crowd)* 14 infs, **esp ME**, Kit and biling; 3 infs, **ME, NH**, Kittle and biling; 1 inf, **swME**, Kit and biler—rare. **1952** Brown *NC Folkl.* 1.433 **NC**, Kit and biling. **1953** Randolph–Wilson *Down in Holler* 258 **Ozarks**, *Kittle an' bilin'.* . . Sometimes it is shortened to *kit an' bilin'.* . . May Kennedy McCord . . says "the whole *kit an' bile of us.*" **1959** Faulkner *Mansion* 165 **MS**, Congress refused to honor the terms of surrender and banished the whole kit-and-biling of them. **c1960** *Wilson Coll.* **csKY**, *Kit and bilin'.* **1966** Dakin *Dial. Vocab. Ohio R. Valley* 2.504, *Kit 'n bilin'* . . common throughout Ohio and Indiana. **1967–69** *DARE* (Qu. LL10, *A whole group of people: "They made too much noise, so he sent the whole _____ home."*) Infs **MD30, MA58, NC38**, Kit and bilin'; (Qu. LL25, *. . Entirely, completely: "He sold out the whole place, _____."*) Inf **MA58**, Kit and bilin'.

d in var other phrr: See quots.

1856 Whitcher *Bedott Papers* 257 **cNY**, The hull kit and cargo on 'em had conspired together. **1871** Eggleston *Hoosier Schoolmaster* 50 **sIN**, He'll beat the whole kit and tuck of 'em. **1932** *DN* 6.283 **swCT**, *Kit-an-tolic.* All of a group of rollicking children or young people. **1941** *LANE* Map 415 **NEng** *(The whole crowd)* 5 infs, Kit and posse; 3 infs, Kit and passel; 1 inf, Kit and parcel; 1 inf, Kit and crew; 1 inf, Kit and pack. **1944** *AmSp* 19.206 **IN**, Whole kit 'n bustle. **1966–68** *DARE* (Qu. LL10, *A whole group of people: "They made too much noise, so he sent the whole _____ home."*) Inf **IA17**, Kit and posse—old-fashioned; **MS15**, Kit and parcel; (Qu. LL25, *. . Entirely, completely: "He sold out the whole place, _____."*) Inf **KS19**, Kit and killybang. **1973** Allen *LAUM* 1.376 (as of c1950), The whole *crowd.* . . *kit and posse* [1 inf, **ND**].

kit exclam See **kitty** exclam

kitaboodle See **kit** n **2b**

kit and biling See **kit** n **2c**

kit and (ca)boodle See **kit** n **2b**

kitarber, kitarby See **catawba A**

kitash See **catish**

kitawber See **catawba A**

kitcaboodle See **kit** n **2b**

kitch n [PaGer *kitsch*]

1907 Wayland *Ger. Element* 198 **nwVA**, The coals and ashes had been removed [from the hearth] with the "kitch," or scraper. [1924 Lambert *PA Ger. Dict.* 94, *Kitsch* . . rake, scraper (for removing ashes).]

kitchen n[1]

1 In railroading:

a The cab or fireman's shelter of a locomotive.

1940 *RR Mag.* Apr 47, *Kitchen*—Engine cab. Firebox is *kitchen stove.*
1945 in 1953 Botkin–Harlow *Treas. Railroad Folkl.* 471 (as of c1850), The fireman's shelter was grimly called "the kitchen" because of the number of men roasted alive there in collisions. When the fireman was not in the kitchen he was on the roof of it, furiously shoveling coal into the top firing chutes.

b A caboose.

1940 Cottrell *Railroader* 131, *Kitchen*—Caboose. Sometimes it is equipped for light housekeeping and used by the crew on the foreign end of their run. 1945 in 1953 Botkin–Harlow *Treas. Railroad Folkl.* 344, It is a caboose, crummy, way car . . kitchen.

2 The section of a lobster trap that holds the bait. **ME** Cf **head B10, parlor**

1957 Beck *Folkl. ME* 126, Some [lobster pots] had two openings or "heads" at opposite ends, others one "head" into a "parlor" and thence into the "kitchen" where the lobster was finally caught. 1966 *DARE* Tape **ME**17, [A lobster trap has] two heads in one end and a bedroom head in the other. . . That's the kitchen where you keep the bait. **ME**22, [FW:] Do you have any name for the front part of the trap? [Inf:] I guess we call that the kitchen. Yeah, the kitchen and the bedroom. We call the bedroom what they go in through. 1978 Merriam *Illustr. Lobstering* 52 **ME**, *Kitchen*—The first chamber in the lobster trap. The lobster enters the kitchen through the heads.

kitchen n[2] [Perh < Scots, Engl, Ir dial *kinch,* by metath from pl ['kɪnčəz] to ['kɪčənz]; see below]

1 See quot. [Cf *EDD kinch* sb.[1] 1 "A loop, twist, noose of a rope, &c., a hitch" and *SND kinch* n.[1] 2 "A cross rope twisted round another so as to tighten it."]

1949 *PADS* 11.8 **wTX** (as of 1911–29), *Kitchen.* . . A rope tied around the flanks of a horse to make him buck.

2 The nape of the neck; the hair at the nape of the neck, esp when knotted or kinky; a knot or tangle of hair, esp at the nape of the neck. [Cf *SND kinch* n.[1] 1 "A twist or doubling in a rope, a kink"] *esp freq among Black speakers*

1974 Baldwin *If Beale St. Could Talk* 27 **NYC** [Black], Her hair is turning gray, but only way down on the nape of her neck, in what her generation called the "kitchen." 1977 Smitherman *Talkin* 64 [Black], *Kitchen* refers to the hair at the nape of the neck, which is inclined to be very kinky. . . In the old days of whiteomania, black women, especially, were extremely self-conscious about their kitchens. . . Many refused to wear upsweep hairdos because it would expose the kitchen. If you were one of the "lucky" ones who had a straight, silky kitchen, you bragged about it and were often complimented for it. 1991 *DARE* File **seGA** (as of c1950) [Black], My hair was so dry and kinky it took four of my sisters to comb the kitchens out of my hair before church on Sunday morning. They didn't have any kitchens—I was the only one of the females in our family who had them. Other women have different kitchens—not necessarily so knotty. Men never do have them. 1991 *NADS Letters* **swMS**, My daughters are the only White students in their school; they don't have kitchens [=knots], but all their Black friends do. *Ibid* **NC** [Black], When your grandmother is straightening your hair and she doesn't do a very good job of it, then you'll get kitchens. 1992 *Ibid* **NJ**, Among the Black population which I grew up with, the "kitchen" was the hair that grew along the nape of the neck. You might say, "I want to get the knots out of your kitchen." It's the area where the hair has knotted up and gotten kinky. It's also the kinky hair itself. *Ibid* **Los Angeles CA** (as of 1950s) [Black], We used to call the hair at the nape of a woman's neck the "kitchen." My parents were from Arkansas. 1992 Morrison *Jazz* 206 **NYC** (as of c1926) [Black], Her husband must have done her kitchen for her. Who else? She never stepped foot in a beauty shop. . . I could picture her husband doing her neckline for her.

kitchen breakdown See **kitchen dance**

kitchen broom n **scattered, but less freq C and Mid Atl, SE** See Map
A long-handled household broom.

1965–70 *DARE* (Qu. F36, . . *Kinds of brooms*) 45 Infs, **scattered, but**

less freq C and Mid Atl, SE, Kitchen broom(s); **CO**47, **WA**8, Regular kitchen broom(s); **CA**87, Kitchen broom; parlor broom—smaller and lighter than a kitchen broom; **CT**7, Regular broom = kitchen broom; fireplace broom (smaller than regular broom); **DE**3, Long-handled brooms are sometimes called kitchen brooms; **IA**36, Kitchen broom; scrubbing broom—an old kitchen broom used for scrubbing; **IN**76, Kitchen brooms cover a multitude of sins; **KY**52, Straw broom = kitchen broom; **MN**1, Kitchen broom—corn broom made of straw; **MO**27, Kitchen broom—on the job, he calls a kitchen broom a straight broom; **NV**7, Floor broom or kitchen broom or regular broom; **NY**68, Kitchen broom or house broom. 1986 Pederson *LAGS Concordance,* 1 inf, **cAR**, Kitchen broom.

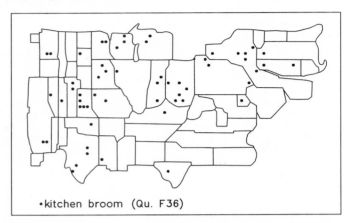

• kitchen broom (Qu. F36)

kitchen chamber n Also *kitchen parlor* **NEast, esp NEng** *old-fash*
A room, usu a bedroom, above or connected to the kitchen.

1649 in 1850 CT (Colony) *Pub. Rec.* 1.497, *An Inventory of the Estate of Mr. William Whiting. . . In the kitching chamber* . . a bed. 1780 (1899) Parkman *Diary* 227 **cMA**, Ye kindled in ye Kitchen Chamber. 1865 (1889) Whitney *Gayworthys* 346 **NEng**, The kitchen-chamber at the head of the 'end staircase,' was what had been Joanna's room. 1930 Shoemaker *1300 Words* 35 **cPA Mts** (as of c1900), *Kitchen parlor*—A bedroom over the kitchen. 1941 *LANE* Map 337 *(Bedroom)* 1 inf, **cwCT**, *Kitchen chamber;* 1 inf, **nwCT**, *Kitchen chamber,* a room over the kitchen, not used as a bedroom; 1 inf, **neMA**, *Kitchen chamber* [any upstairs room or the upstairs undivided]. 1991 *DARE* File **seNY**, The kitchen chamber was the little room over the kitchen.

kitchen closet n [Cf *closet* a cabinet or recess for china or household utensils]
A **closet 1** or kitchen pantry; a cabinet or cupboard.

1889 Jewett *Betty Leicester* 222 **ceMA**, I heard a clacketing in the kitchen closet. . . [T]here was y'r father with both his hands full o' somethin' he'd collected to stay himself with. 1941 *LANE* Map 344 *(Pantry)* 7 infs, **eCT, eMA, RI**, Kitchen closet; 1 inf, **swCT**, *Kitchen closet,* a small pantry . . daughter's term; 1 inf, **sRI**, *Kitchen closet,* a recess in the kitchen. 1966–68 *DARE* (Qu. D8, *The small room next to the kitchen [in older houses] where dishes and sometimes foods are kept*) Infs **FL**11, **TX**51, Kitchen closet; **LA**37A, Closet or kitchen closet. 1986 Pederson *LAGS Concordance* **Gulf Region** *(Pantry)* 20 infs, Kitchen closet(s); 1 inf, Kitchen closet—shelves, doors, not a walk-in closet; 1 inf, Kitchen closet—moveable piece of furniture; 1 inf, Kitchen closet—for pots, pans, glasses; 1 inf, Kitchen closet—grandmother had one; 1 inf, A kitchen closet—kitchen utensils, canned goods; 1 inf, Kitchen closet—has heard.

kitchen dance n Also *kitchen breakdown, ~ dig, ~ frolic, ~ sweat;* for addit varr see quots **chiefly Nth, N Midl** *somewhat old-fash* Cf **breakdown, frolic** n **1, kitchen game**
An informal or private dancing party, usu held in the kitchen.

1880 *Harper's New Mth. Mag.* 62.89 **NEng**, The younger people had their berrying frolics, sleigh-rides, kitchen dances, nuttings, and the like. 1927 *AmSp* 3.24 **eTX** [Sawmill talk], A dance is a "struggle," "wrastle," or "kitchen sweat," and it is attended by men who consider themselves "free, white, twenty-one, and hairy chested." Henry Ford who professes to be fond of old time "fiddlin' " would appreciate one of these "kitchen sweats." 1941 *LANE* Map 410 *(A dance)* **NEng**, Terms for the old kitchen dance (a private dance held on the farm or in the village) were incidentally recorded. . . kitchen dance . . [18 infs]; (kitchen) junket . . [22 infs]; (kitchen) breakdown . . [30 infs]; . . kitchen scrape . . [1 inf];

kitchen tunk . . [7 infs]; kitchen jig . . [5 infs]; kitchen dig . . [4 infs]; kitchen spree . . [1 inf]; (kitchen) frolic . . [1 inf]. **1941** *Language* 17.338 **WI** [*LANCS* fieldwork], *Kitchen sweat*—1 [of 50 infs]. . . Said with laughter. . . Kitchen dancing has almost disappeared, and the terms with it. **1950** *WELS (Different kinds of dancing parties)* 1 Inf, **cwWI**, Kitchen sweat—old-fashioned. **1953** Randolph-Wilson *Down in Holler* 258 **Ozarks**, *Kitchen-sweat:* . . A country dance. "We was a-goin' to a kitchen-sweat over on Bear Creek." **1959** *VT Hist.* 27.146, *Kitchen hop* . . var. kitchen junket; kitchen tonk; kitchen tunk; kitchen tunket. A good time; a dance; a party. Formerly, a dance held in the kitchen of a private house, with music furnished by one fiddler who was usually seated in a chair placed on the top of the kitchen stove, in order to keep the floor clear for dancing. Common among older people; occasional among younger. **1966–69** *DARE* (Qu. FF2, . . *Kinds of parties*) Inf **MA58**, Kitchen dances—square dancing—also kitchen digs; **NY1**, Kitchen hop—square dance, when kitchen was biggest room in cabin; (Qu. FF4, *Names and joking names for different kinds of dancing parties*) Inf **IA30**, Kitchen dance—move all the things out of the kitchen and really go to it; **MA5**, Kitchen digs—not in very good repute—harmonica, violin, etc; **MA58**, Kitchen dance; **NY1**, Kitchen hop; **SD8**, **WY5**, Kitchen sweats. [All Infs comm type 4 or 5; 5 of 6 Infs old] **1967** *DARE* Tape **OH6**, It's a matter of help and getting things organized to give bobsled rides—things of that sort, old-time kitchen parties, just small groups. . . We'd . . go to some person's home and there they would have a—they'd play kitchen games. *Ibid,* [FW:] Did they ever have any other kinds of parties other than a kitchen party? [Inf:] Now that was strictly farm folk, of course . . they've always had dances. **1973** Allen *LAUM* 1.377 **csNE, nwSD** (as of c1950), A dance. . . Colorful *kitchen sweat* . . names specifically a progressive dance, one with a change in location from one house to another. [2 infs] **1977** Jones *OR Folkl.* 101 **eOR** (as of 1949), *Kitchen sweat:* a country dance at a farmhouse.

kitchen ell See **ell** n¹ 2

kitchen fried potatoes n pl Cf **cottage fried potatoes, shanty fried potatoes**

=**home fried potatoes.**

    1968 *DARE* (Qu. H47, *Kinds of fried potatoes*) Inf **CT6**, Kitchen fried—country style fried—potatoes cut up after they are cooked and fried in grease.

kitchen frolic See **kitchen dance**

kitchen furniture n Also *change kitchen furniture, moving ~* esp **Sth**

A game similar to **musical chairs**—also used as a call initiating movement in the game.

    1965–68 *DARE* (Qu. EE2, *Games that have one extra player—when a signal is given, the players change places, and the extra one tries to get a place*) Infs **AL20, MS30, PA28**, Moving kitchen furniture; **GA68**, Change kitchen furniture; **LA11**, Kitchen furniture. [All Infs old, female] **1967** *DARE* Tape **LA11**, We play kitchen furniture inside the school and we do that with little chairs. And there might be about twenty in little chairs and one standin' up, you see, and we say "kitchen furniture" and everybody's to move and somebody's not gonna get a chair. And that's what we do to that each time. We just keep sayin' "kitchen furniture" and they keep movin' and somebody's up all the time without a chair.

kitchen game n Cf **fancy four, kitchen dance, play-party**

Any of var singing games, usu with dance-like steps, played at parties.

    1967 *DARE* Tape **OH6**, Well, years ago we'd get up a bobsled ride, a load or two, and go to some person's home and there they would have a—they'd play kitchen games. . . They'd sing and have certain steps to the music; they provided their own music by singing—folk dances, really. . . They didn't call it dancing, really, they just called it playing games, but that's what it was; "Skip to My Lou," . . that was one, and games similar to that. . . The Virginia Reel is a song, a kitchen game, that can be played that way.

kitchen garden n **scattered, but esp Nth, N Midl** See Map Cf **house garden**

A garden in which vegetables and fruits are cultivated for domestic use; a **truck garden** in which produce is grown for market; hence vbl n *kitchen gardening* the growing of produce for market.

    1634 Wood *New Engl. Prospect* 37, *Dorchester.* . . is the greatest Towne in *New England;* well woodded and watered . . faire Corne-fields and pleasant Gardens, with Kitchin-gardens. **1776** in 1901 *Documents*

Revol. Hist. NJ 1.32, A plantation in . . Hunterdon County, West New-Jersey, containing . . a good kitchen garden. **1867** De Voe *Market Asst.* 320, By the progress of the science brought to bear upon that branch we now term "kitchen-gardening," markets are supplied with the asparagenous plants, spinaceous plants. **1939** *LANE* Map 121 *(Vegetable garden)* 24 infs, **NEng**, Kitchen garden. [Commentary:] 1 inf, **swCT**, Kitchen garden, read in seed catalogues; 1 inf **cnCT**, Kitchen garden, read in the newspapers; 1 inf, **seRI**, Kitchen garden, older term; 2 infs, **ceMA**, Kitchen garden, rare term; 1 inf, **seMA**, Kitchen garden, formerly very common; 1 inf, **ceMA**, Kitchen garden, specific term; 1 inf, **ceMA**, Kitchen garden, to grow herbs and parsley. **1950** *WELS* **WI** *(The garden where carrots, beans, etc. are grown to eat at home)* 9 Infs, Kitchen garden. c**1960** *Wilson Coll.* **csKY**, Kitchen garden is rarely used to mean the garden rather than the truck patch. **1965–70** *DARE* (Qu. I1) 46 Infs, **scattered, but esp Nth, N Midl**, Kitchen garden; **CT2**, Kitchen garden = small garden; **VT16**, Kitchen garden; truck garden—that's bigger. **1966** Dakin *Dial. Vocab. Ohio R. Valley* 2.353, *Vegetable garden*—The home garden cultivated . . for family use in the kitchen is known by a variety of names of single occurrence. . . *kitchen garden* . . *home garden.* **1973** Allen *LAUM* 1.303 **IA, MN** (as of c1950), *Vegetable garden* (for home use). . . kitchen garden [3 infs]. **1986** Pederson *LAGS Concordance (Vegetable garden)* 2 infs, **FL**, (A) kitchen garden; 1 inf, **cTN**, Kitchen garden—heard of; 1 inf, **seMS**, Kitchen garden—very small; 1 inf, **cnGA**, A little kitchen garden.

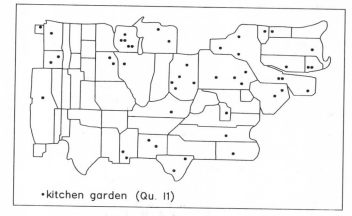

• kitchen garden (Qu. I1)

kitchen halyard See **kettle halyard**

kitchen house n Cf **house B1a**

A kitchen set apart from the main residence; a **summer kitchen.**

    1986 Pederson *LAGS Concordance (Kitchen)* 1 inf, **cGA**, Kitchen house; 1 inf, **neAL**, Maybe out in the kitchen house; [1 inf, **cnFL**, House kitchen]. [*DARE* Ed: 151 infs reported familiarity with an old-fashioned kitchen separated from the main structure, often connected by a walkway, breezeway, or porch.]

kitchen parlor See **kitchen chamber**

kitchen physic n [*OED* 1592 →] *old-fash*

Food, esp nourishing, healthful, or substantial food.

    1889 (1971) Farmer *Americanisms* 333, *Kitchen physic* (Cant).—Victuals; food of any kind. **1899** (1912) Green *VA Folk-Speech* 251, *Kitchen physic.* . . Nourishing diet for a patient; good living; substantial fare.

‡**kitchen rattlesnake** n

    1977 Jones *OR Folkl.* 101 (as of 1925), *Kitchen rattlesnake:* a rattlesnake with only one button.

kitchen sweat See **kitchen dance**

kitchen town n

    1957 *Sat. Eve. Post Letters* **cIN**, He lived in "Kitchen-town"—a part of town where the poor lived, *not trashy,* the one or two room house is built, then a "lean-to" is built on, the lean-to is a kitchen, therefore, "Kitchen town."

kitchen wood n

Firewood cut in stove lengths.

    1897 (1902) Moore *Songs & Stories* 15 **TN**, I ain't got nuffin' ter do but to tote de kitchin wood in fer mammy. **1986** Pederson *LAGS Concordance (Lightwood)* 1 inf, **cwGA**, Kitchen wood.

kitchen yard n Cf **dooryard**

See quots.

1969 *DARE* FW Addit **csKY,** *Kitchen yard*—front yard, between house and road. [FW: used in conv] **1992** *NADS Letters,* My mother who also grew up in Central Illinois use[d] the term "kitchen yard" but it was the yard near the kitchen door or back door. She grew up on a farm where the front door was used only by visitors to enter the parlor. In country homes, the back door was the normal entry into the house via the kitchen.

kitcht See **catch** v A3

kite n

1 Either the **loggerhead shrike** or the **northern shrike.**

1956 MA Audubon Soc. *Bulletin* 40.129 **ME,** *Northern Shrike.* . . Kite. . . from its predatory habits. . . *Southern Shrike.* . . Kite.

2 See quot.

1950 *Western Folkl.* 9.123 **nwOR** [Team-logging terms], *Kite.* A sled which was attached to the end of a turn and which carried the extra dogs, peavies, and skid grease.

kite v Also in phr *kite it*

To move or go quickly or energetically; to hurry; hence adv *(a)kiting* rapidly; hurriedly.

1854 Adams *In Doors & Out* 99, You did not use to be fond of 'kiting' round in this manner. **1857** *Lawrence Republican* (KS) 18 June np, The team is hitched to the plow, and on it goes, kiting along the surface. **1859** in 1942 Hafen *Overland Routes* 67 **VA,** Tonight the wind is blowing a gale from the north, and the snow is just "kiting" it. **1877** in 1882 Harte *Condensed Novels & Stories* 324 **CA,** The other way is to whip up and yell, and send the whole six kiting by like h-ll! **1892** *DN* 1.230 **KY,** *Kitin'* . . moving rapidly. "To go a-kitin." [*kite,* v., in this sense is known also in New England and Michigan.] **1893** Shands *MS Speech* 33, Go a kitin. . . This, as noted by Dr. Brown, means about the same thing as to *go a gilpin;* i.e. to go fast. **1903** *DN* 2.298 *Cape Cod MA* (as of a1857), *Kite.* . . To run fast. 'I turned the horse out in the pasture and you ought to see him kite it.' **1907** *DN* 3.205 **nwAR,** *Kite it.* . . To run fast. **1908** *DN* 3.327 **eAL, wGA,** *Kite.* . . To run fast. **1912** *DN* 3.580 **wIN,** *Kite.* . . "You kite down to the pasture and get the cows." **1945** FWP *Lay My Burden Down* 105 **AR** (as of c1860) [Black], He just job the spurs in his hoss and go kiting off down the road after that white man. **1947** Ballowe *The Lawd* 206 **LA** [Black], Looker yonder; Neal kitin' out. **c1960** *Wilson Coll.* **csKY,** *Kiting.* . . Hurrying or hurriedly. "He went kiting down the road in his new buggy." **1969** *DARE* (Qu. Y20, *To run fast: "You should have seen him _____!"*) Inf **IN61,** Kite. **1977** in 1982 *Barrick Coll.* **csPA,** *Kitin'*—rapidly. "To go a-kitin'." "She'll take you around through the house a-kitin'." **1983** *Lutz Coll.* **Philadelphia PA,** *Kite.* Mother used this to mean to go fast, to dash. . . My recollection of it is of someone scooting on foot as fast as possible.

kite-tailed widgeon n Also *kitetail (widgeon)*

=**pintail 1.**

1888 Trumbull *Names of Birds* 39, *Dafila acuta.* . . At St. Augustine the full-feathered drake is the kite-tailed widgeon. **1917** (1923) *Birds Amer.* 1.128, *Pintail—Dafila acuta.* . . Kite-tail. **1955** *AmSp* 30.182 **FL,** The elongated tail feathers of the pintail duck have stimulated the invention of numerous names, some of which carry comparisons with other birds. Thus, *kite-tailed widgeon* . . seems to allude to the conspicuous tail of the swallow-tailed kite. **1982** Elman *Hunter's Field Guide* 156, *Pintail (Anas acuta)*—Common & Regional Names . . kitetail, kitetail widgeon.

kit fox n Also *kitt* [From *kit* the young of any of various small, fur-bearing animals, in allusion to its size]

Either of two small, closely related foxes (*Vulpes macrotis* or *V. velox*) native to much of the western US. Also called **desert fox, prairie fox, swift fox** Note: Some taxonomists consider *Vulpes macrotis* a subspecies of *V. velox.*

1805 (1904) Lewis *Orig. Jrls. Lewis & Clark Exped.* 2.216, The party who were down with Capt. Clark also killed a small fox. . . [I]t is so much like the comm[on] small fox of this country commonly called the kit fox that I should have taken it for a young one of that species. **1812** Cutler *Topog. Descr.* 139, The . . Cree Indians . . traffic in beaver, otter, lynx, . . small fox or kitts, . . and moose deer skins. **1879** U.S. Natl. Museum *Bulletin* 14.2, *Vulpes velox.* . . Kit Fox or Swift Fox.—Western States. **1928** Anthony *N. Amer. Mammals* 142, The Kit Fox is much smaller than the Red Fox and is a plains or prairie dweller, spending rather more of its time in burrows and is less cunning than its red relative. **1965** Teale *Wandering Through Winter* 32 **CA,** Beside a dead

paloverde tree . . we discovered the used burrow of a kit fox. **1967–68** *DARE* (Qu. P32, . . *Other kinds of wild animals*) Inf **CA9,** Kit fox—red fox; **CA62,** Desert fox—also called a swift—weigh 5 or 6 pounds—also called kit fox. **1980** Whitaker *Audubon Field Guide Mammals* 548, *Vulpes macrotis* . . [is] found mainly in the Southwest but also north to southeastern Oregon and southwestern Idaho . . The names Kit Fox and Swift Fox are used interchangeably for both species [=*Vulpes macrotis* and *V. velox*]. **1982** Elman *Hunter's Field Guide* 353, The southwestern part of the range is shared with the kit fox, or desert fox *(Vulpes macrotis),* smallest and fastest of American foxes but no more capable than the gray of sustaining its speed over long distances.

kiting See **kite** v

kitney n [Pronc-sp for *kidney;* cf Pronc Intro 3.I.15]

1899 (1912) Green *VA Folk-Speech* 251, *Kitney* . . Form of *kidney.*

kitra-corner See **kitty-corner** adv, adj

kitron(ways) See **kittering**

kitsie n [Cf Ger *Kitz* the young of var hoofed quadrupeds] Cf **spatzie**

=**English sparrow.**

1967 *DARE* (Qu. Q21, . . *Kinds of sparrows*) Inf **PA29,** ['kɪtsɪ].

kitt See **kit fox**

kittacorner(ed) See **kitty-corner** adv, adj

kitten n

1 also *dust kitten, kitten fur, (dust) kitty;* for addit varr see quots: A roll of dust under furniture. **chiefly Nth, N Midl, esp NEast** See Map Cf **dust bunny, pussy**

1932 *DN* 6.283 **swCT,** *Kittens.* The rolls of dust that come under rugs, beds, and bureaus in the corners of the room. "There are plenty of kittens under that bed." *Ibid,* Kitten traps. Before the days of vacuum cleaners, a rolled-up rug would be put across an open doorway or at an angle to keep the kittens from the cleaned portion. "Don't fall over my kitten trap." **1934** in 1935 *AmSp* 10.236, [Newspaper article:] It was Mary who told me that, in hospital vernacular, the gray fluffy balls of dust which gather in every corner are called *kittens.* **1949** *WELS Suppl.* **seWI,** Dust under beds is "kittens" to our family, from Polish nurse. *Ibid* **PA, CT,** Dust kitties—friend from Penna. . . Kitties—Conn. *Ibid* **cWI,** The same person, in describing how she cleaned up the kittens said she had angel-fluffs to clean up too. *Ibid* **csWI,** Fluffs of dust under the bed I have heard called "little kittens." **1950** *WELS* **WI,** 5 Infs, (Dust) kittens; 5 Infs, Kitties; 1 Inf, Kitty-fuzzes; 1 Inf, Kitten and curls. **1954** *WELS Suppl.* **ceWI,** Rolls of dust that gather under beds are known as *kittens* or *kitties. Ibid* **seWI,** Kitten farms are the woolies under a bed. **1965–70** *DARE* (Qu. E20, *Soft rolls of dust that collect on the floor under beds or other furniture*) 49 Infs, **chiefly Nth, N Midl, esp NEast,** (Dust) kittens; **WI35,** Kittens—old-fashioned; **IL31,** Cats and kittens; **DE2,** Gray kittens; **IA7,** Kitten fur; 32 Infs, **chiefly Nth, N Midl, esp NEast,** (Dust) kitties; **MA63,** Gray kitties.

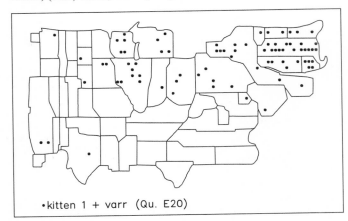

·kitten 1 + varr (Qu. E20)

2 See **kitty** n **1.**

kittenball n Also *kittyball* **IA, MN, WI** Cf *cat ball* (at **cat** n 3c), **pussyball**

The game of softball.

[**1938** FWP *Guide MN* 130 **csMN,** When Lewis Rober, a member of the Minneapolis Fire Department, introduced the "Kitten League

Game" . . in 1893, no one imagined it might become the recreational park's most popular sport for people of all ages. Yet today diamondball, or softball, as it is often called, is played throughout the State and other States as well.] **1940** Harbin *Fun Encycl.* 403, Softball (playground ball, kittenball, indoor baseball). **1942** Berrey–Van den Bark *Amer. Slang* 675.1, Kittenball, kittyball . . *softball.* **1948** Manfred *Chokecherry* 104 **nwIA,** "Say," Elof said, suddenly understanding that the green clothes both were wearing were softball uniforms, "say, you're talking about kittenball, ain't you? . . Then I'm not playing for sure. I'm a hard-ball man myself. . . no kid's game for me." **1950** *WELS (Outdoor amusements)* 1 Inf, **swWI,** Kittenball. **1968** *DARE* (Qu. EE11, *Bat-and-ball games for just a few players [when there aren't enough for a regular game]*) Inf **IA22,** Kittenball. [FW: very common name here for softball] **1985** Keillor *Lake Wobegon* 171 **MN,** The little sliver of tree was so frail; it didn't last the spring. Bill had dug the hole in left field and the tree got stomped in a kittenball game at the All-School Picnic. **1989** Dickson *Dickson Baseball Dict.* 234, Kittenball/kitten ball. . . One of the early names for softball. After Chicago, Minneapolis was the second city to embrace the new game created in Chicago in 1887. It was introduced in Minneapolis in 1895 by Lt. Lewis Rober of Fire Company #11 as a form of exercise. The first team took the Kittens as their nickname and set up a small diamond in the vacant lot next to the station. The game soon took off in Minneapolis and, in honor of the first team, was called kitten ball. **1993** *DARE* File **ceIA,** Kittenball as I remember it from Cedar Rapids, Iowa, in the 1940s was softball played with a ball which was larger than a normal softball. My memory is that this was a game for girls. [*Ibid* **csWI** (as of c1968), We never had enough kids in our neighborhood (or enough grassy space) to play a real game of softball, so we modified the rules. If you hit the ball past a certain landmark, it was an automatic home run. To make things fair, there were two home run landmarks—one for the bigger kids and one for the smaller kids. Some of the older boys would complain, "That's kittenball—it's baby stuff," but they always played anyway.]

kitten breeches n
=**Dutchman's breeches 1.**

1896 *Jrl. Amer. Folkl.* 9.181, *Dicentra cucullaria* . . kitten breeches, Sulphur Grove, Ohio. **1903** Small *Flora SE U.S.* 550, *B[icuculla] Cucullaria.* . . Kitten-breeches. **1903** Small *Flora SE U.S.* 550, *B[icuculla] Cucullaria.* . . Kitten-breeches. **1910** Graves *Flowering Plants* 198 **CT,** *Dicentra Cucullaria.* . . Kitten Breeches. **1959** Carleton *Index Herb. Plants* 71, Kitten britches—Dicentra cucullaria.

kitten fur See **kitten 1**

kittenhead n Also *kitty owl* Cf **cat owl**
=**screech owl.**

1955 *AmSp* 30.178 **TX,** Derived terms [from cat owl] are *kitten-head* for the screech owl. **1962** Imhof *AL Birds* 306, *Otus asio.* . . Kitty Owl. . . A *small, chunky* owl with *eartufts.*

kittens had hair, before adv phr Cf **hair n C13**
1967 *DARE* (Qu. FF21b, . . *About old jokes people say: "The first time I heard that one _____."*) Inf **IL11,** Was before kittens had hair.

kittens, have v phr Also *get kittens, have a kitten, pass kittens* esp Nth See Map Cf **cat fit**

To lose one's composure; to become agitated; to become angry.

1900 *DN* 2.44 [College slang], *Kitten.* . . In phrases 'get kittens', 'have kittens'. 1. To get angry. 2. To be in great anxiety, or to be afraid. [**1903** *DN* 2.298 **Cape Cod MA** (as of a1857), *Kitten.* . . To become unduly excited, also to have a *chicken flutter.*] **1931** *AmSp* 6.206 **MO** [Univ slang], *To have kittens:* to be angry. **1942** Berrey–Van den Bark *Amer. Slang* 284.4, *Fly into a rage.* . . have *or* pass kittens . . *or* a cow . . *or* throw a cat fit. **1950** *WELS* **WI** (*Nervously annoyed, upset: "When they didn't get there on time, she was all _____."*) 2 Infs, Having kittens; (*When a person becomes over-excited, and loses control: "I thought I was going to _____!"*) 2 Infs, Have kittens; (*To laugh very hard."*) 1 Inf, Having kittens. **1959** *VT Hist.* 27.146 **cn,cVT,** Have a kitten with a calico tail. . . To be worried or disturbed over something. Rare. **c1960** Wilson Coll. **csKY,** Have kittens. . . Raise great objections; throw a fit. **1965–70** *DARE* (Qu. KK11, *To make great objections or a big fuss about something: "When we asked him to do that, he _____."*) 11 Infs, **esp Nth,** Had kittens; **MI15,** Had kittens [FW sugg]; **VT16,** Had cat fits, had kittens; (Qu. LL37, *To make a statement as strong as you can: "I could have wrung her neck, I was so _____ mad."*) Inf **AZ12,** I could have had kittens. [7 of 14 Infs young] **1993** *DARE* File **cwCA** (as of 1950s), When I was a child, if another child got overly excited

about some slight or insult, we would say, "Don't have a kitten." If he got *really* excited, we'd say, "Don't have a cat."

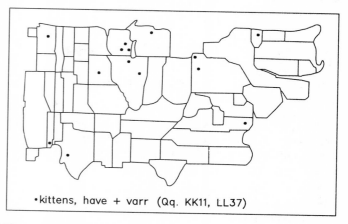

•kittens, have + varr (Qq. KK11, LL37)

kittentails n [See quot 1979]

A plant of either of two related genera—*Besseya* or *Synthyris*—native to the western US. For other names of *S. reniformis* see **dolly-flower, grouse flower, mowitch 2, spring queen, snow ~**

1932 Rydberg *Flora Prairies* 720, *Besseya.* . . Kitten-tails. **1936** McDougall–Baggley *Plants of Yellowstone* 109, Kittentails (*Synthyris wyomingensis*). **1949** Moldenke *Amer. Wild Flowers* 276, A small group of midwestern and far western plants known as kittentails, *Synthyris,* contains some handsome members. **1953** Nelson *Plants Rocky Mt. Park* 145, Kittentails, *Besseya plantaginea.* . . A plant usually having several erect stems bearing dense spikes of lavender or pinkish flowers. . . There are numerous sessile, oblong, or round bracts along the stem. These bracts and the leaves are at first woolly, but become smooth with age. *Ibid* 146, Alpine kittentails, *Besseya alpina.* . . Similar to the above. **1959** Anderson *Flora AK* 415, *S[yntheris] borealis.* . . Kitten tails. Stems woolly with brown hairs. **1979** Spellenberg *Audubon Guide N. Amer. Wildflowers W. Region* 780, Mountain Kittentails. . . Description: *Dense racemes of bilaterally symmetrical flowers with deep blue-violet corollas* bloom above basal leaves on generally low, erect plants.

kitter v Also *kittern* [Var of **cater**; *kittern* is prob infl by **kittering**]

To move diagonally.

1905 *DN* 3.62 **eNE,** Kitter. . . See *catter* [=move diagonally]. "He kittered across the campus." Not very common. **1982** Brooks *Quicksand* 195 **swUT** (as of c1916), Kittern, to cut diagonally cross-lot.

kitter-corner(ed) See **kitty-corner** adv, adj

kittering adv, adj Also *kittern-cornered, kitronways;* pronc-spp *kitter(i)n, kitron* [Varr of **catering**] scattered, but esp NY, NEng Cf **caterway, quartering**
=**kitty-corner** adv, adj **1.**

1891 *PMLA* 6.168 **WV,** Kittering means *topling* [sic]. **1894** *Century Illustr. Mag.* 47.854 **ceNY,** Our people, in sawing or nailing anything at an angle other than a right angle, do not place it or cut it "quartering,"—which is the recognized technical term,—but "cattering." . . For "cattering" there is a ludicrous diminutive much oftener used in my neighborhood—namely, "kittering"—that is, somewhat cattering; for is not a kit a little cat? **1895** *DN* 1.398 **cNY,** Kitron-ways. . . kitty-cornered. **1896** *DN* 1.419 **cNY,** Kitter-, kittern-cornered: for *cater-cornered.* **1912** *DN* 3.568 **cNY,** Kitterin', adv. Diagonally. **1914** *DN* 4.154 **NH,** Kitterin. . . Diagonally. **1936** *AmSp* 11.191 **swWY,** Kittern. Cornerwise, or across the corner of a room. 'She placed the piano kittern.' **1943** *LANE* Map 547 *(Cater-cornered)* 6 infs, **VT, wMA,** Kittering. **1968** *DARE* (Qu. MM16, *If you're walking with somebody to the other corner of a square, and you want to save steps . . "It'll be shorter if we _____."*) Inf **WI21,** Go [kɪtrən]. **1982** Brooks *Quicksand* 145 **swUT** (as of c1908), His place in town was just across the street and "kittern" from ours—that is, we were on the northeast corner of our block and he was on the southwest corner of his. *Ibid* 330 (as of 1933), His family took lodging on the same block with us, just around the corner and down the sidewalk, and "kittern" through by a shorter trail from his door to mine.

kittern v See **kitter** v

kittern adv, adj, **kittern-cornered** See **kittering**

kittikit n
=mountain misery 1.
　1906 (1918) Parsons *Wild Flowers CA* 94, *Chamaebatia foliolosa.* . . Another common name for the plant among our mountaineers is "kit-tikit," possibly taken from the Indians. **1915** (1926) Armstrong–Thornber *Western Wild Flowers* 222, *Mountain Misery.* . . The smell and foliage attract attention and the shrub has many names, such as Bear-mat and Kittikit, or Kit-kit-dizze, so-called by the Indians.

kittiwake n Also *kittiwake gull*
Std: a **gull** of the genus *Rissa*, esp the black-legged *R. tridactyla.* For other names of this bird see **frostbird 2, frost gull, haddock ~, jack ~, mackerel ~ 3, pick-me-up, pinyole, snow gull, squaretail, winter bird, ~ gull**

kittle See **kettle**

kittle and biling See **kit** n **2c**

kittledee n Sth *esp freq among Black speakers*
1 =katydid B1.
　1965–70 DARE (Qu. R8, . . *Kinds of creatures that make a clicking or shrilling or chirping kind of sound*) Infs **MS**60, **NC**40, 64, 85, **VA**70, 73, Kittledee. [5 of 6 Infs Black] **1981** Pederson *LAGS Basic Materials*, 1 inf, **cwMS**, ['kɪˀt̻ł, diᵛi]—Informant disagrees with friend as to whether this is a bird (=chickadee?) or a bug. [Inf Black]
2 An unidentified bird. Cf **katydid B3**, *killdee* (at **killdeer 1**)
　1970 DARE (Qu. Q9, . . *Bird* . . *commonly found on ponds and lakes*) Inf **SC**69, Sandpiper or kittledee also fit description; (Qu. R8, . . *Kinds of creatures that make a clicking or shrilling or chirping kind of sound*) Inf **FL**48, Kittledee—a bird. [Both Infs Black] **1981** [see **1** above].

kittle-ding n Cf **kit** n **2**
See quot.
　1941 LANE Map 415, Collective terms applied to a group of persons whom the speaker dislikes or of whom he disapproves. . . 1 inf, **neMA**, The whole [kɪtł'dɪŋ] of 'em [is] also used.

kittly-bender n, usu pl Also *kettle-de-bender, kiddledee-bender, kiddly-~, kitty-bendler;* by folk-etym, *kidney-bender* [Cf SND *kittlie* adj. 3 "difficult, dangerous . . precarious"] **esp MA, PA** *old-fash* Cf **bender 1, tiddly-bender**
Flexible ice that is barely strong enough to support a person's weight, **rubber ice**; the act of walking on such ice; also fig.
　1831 Finn *Amer. Comic Annual* 138 **MA**, The boys . . glided over the 'kiddledee-benders,' and chased some poor bow-legged nigger from their skating ground. **1854** (1969) Thoreau *Walden* 353 **ceMA**, Let us not play at kittlybenders. **1858** in 1870 Dallas *Letters* 2.39 **sePA**, This will enable our ministers here to walk, on this treacherous element of dress, as on thick ice, not as heretofore on what boys call "kiddly benders." **1871** Hale *How to Do It* 46 **ceMA**, You will, with unfaltering step, move quickly over the kettle-de-benders of this broken essay. **1911** *Century Dict. Suppl., Kiddly-benders.* . . Same as *kittly-benders.* Also *tiddly-benders* and *tids.* **1968** DARE (Qu. B35, *Ice that will bend when you step on it, but not break*) Inf **DE**3, Kitty-bendler [kɪtɪ'bɛndlɚ]; **PA**78, Kidney-bender. [Both Infs old]

kitty n
1 also *kitten, kitty-cat;* usu with modifier: **=skunk.** Cf **civet cat 2, polecat, pussy**
　1921 DN 5.114 **CA**, Sachet kitten, sachet pussy. . . Pole cat. **1941** Writers' Program *Guide WY* 463, Nice kitty—A skunk. **1965–70** DARE (Qu. P26, *Names and nicknames . . for a skunk*) Infs **MD**29, **OH**42, **PA**128, 234, **TX**9, 11, Sachet kitten (*or* kitty); **ID**5, **IL**108, **IN**35, **KS**10, **OH**48, Striped kitty (*or* kitten); **AR**28, **DE**1, **IN**58, **OH**3, Kitty; **AZ**11, **CA**87, Black-and-white kitty; **FL**16, **VA**8, Pole-kitty; **OH**33, **PA**73, Woods kitty; **CA**62, **MA**15, Pew (*or* piss) kitty; **CA**91, Civet kitty; **IL**115, Fluid-drive kitty [laughter]; **LA**15, House kitty, pretty kitty—joking; **DE**1, Little black kitty; **GA**18, Perfume kitty—not common; **IL**32, Smell kitty; **NH**5, Smelling kitten; **CT**7, Kitty-cat; **MI**120, Kitten. [23 of 31 Infs old] **1969** LAUM *AUM* 1.321 (as of c1950), *Skunk* . . striped kitty [2 infs, 1 **IA**, 1 **SD**, the latter indicated amusement]. **1986** Pederson *LAGS Concordance* (Skunk) 2 infs, **neAL**, **cnFL**, Pole kitty; 2 infs, **ceFL**, **cnTN**, Sachet kitten; 1 inf, **cnFL**, Black-and-white kitty; 1 inf, **cwFL**, Stink kitties; 1 inf, **swAR**, Striped kitty; 1 inf, **nwFL**, Wild kitty—some kind of kitty; 1 inf, **csAR**, Wood kitty; 1 inf, **cnGA**, Kitten with fluid drive—facetious.

2 See **kitten 1.**
3 in phr *not to give a kitty:* Not to care at all. **esp KY, MD, VA** See Map *euphem; esp freq among women* Cf **dog** n **B7**
　1950 WELS ("I don't give _____") 1 Inf, **cWI**, A kitty what you do. [Inf female] **1965–70** DARE (Qu. GG21b, *If you don't care what a person does . . "Go ahead—I don't give a _____.")* 11 Infs, **esp KY, MD, VA**, Kitty. [9 of 11 Infs female] **1989** *Black Amer. Lit. Forum* 23.323, I simply don't need all those cameras up in my face while I'm trying to watch the game, especially when I can't give a kitty who wins.

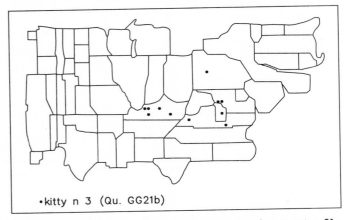
•*kitty* n 3 (Qu. GG21b)

4 also *kitty-cat(ty):* A game similar to **cat** n **3a;** a **cat** n **3b;** also used as a call in the game. [Cf OED *kit-cat* sb.¹ "Now dial. . . The game of tip-cat"; 1664 →] Cf **cricket** n²
　1901 DN 2.143, Kitty. . . The same as cat. [DARE Ed: cat = "pussy: a game played with a small bat . . and a small block 1″ by 4″, which is also termed a *pussy.* Ithaca, N.Y."] **1957** *Sat. Eve. Post Letters* **MA**, Kitty—played with a wooden plug pointed at both ends. . . You hit the kitty a smart blow on the end which raised it in the air, then batted as far as possible in the direction you wished to travel. If we were headed for the river, the plan was to choose a course which would keep on good solid ground. If the kitty fell into the "rough," the fellows would call "kitty, kitty, kitty." You were sworn to stay with the kitty till you had knocked it out where you could travel—"No hands!" . . Of course, each member had his kitty and stick. **1966–70** DARE (Qu. EE10, *A game in which a short stick lying on the ground is flipped into the air and then hit with a longer stick*) Inf **NY**40, Catty—short for kitty-cat; 30 years ago; **OK**52, Kitty-cat—short stick is squared and has one pointed end (to be hit); each side had a different number of points—1, 2, 3, or 4; **TN**43, Kitty-cat; **IN**35, Kitty-catty.
5 in phr *kitty's game:* **=cat's game.**
　1966–69 DARE (Qu. EE38b, *If the game of tick-tack-toe . . comes out so that neither X nor O wins, you call that _____)* Inf **MN**12, Kitty's game; [**RI**15, It goes to the cat or kitty; **WA**16, Kitty gets it.]

kitty exclam Also *kiddy, kit* [Cf SND *kit* int. "Also *kittie.* . . used in calling hens."] **esp LA** Cf **biddy** n¹ **1, kip**
Used as a call to chickens.
　1968 DARE (Qu. K79, *How do you call the chickens to you at feeding time?*) Inf **LA**20, Kitty, kitty, kitty. **1971** Wood *Vocab. Change* 184 **LA**, (A call to chickens). . . Kit, kit [3 infs]. **1986** Pederson *LAGS Concordance* (Calls to chickens) 4 infs, **LA**, Kitty [repeated]; 1 inf, **csAL**, Kiddy—x2.

kittyball See **kittenball**

kitty-bendler See **kittly-bender**

kitty-cat See **kitty** n **1**

kitty-cat(ty) See **kitty** n **4**

kitty-corner adv, adj Also *kittacorner(ed), kitter-corner(ed), kitty-cornered;* for addit varr see quots [Prob folk-etym for *catty-corner* (at **catercorner** adj, adv)] Note: It is not always possible to distinguish adv from adj uses.
1 Diagonally, obliquely, crooked, askew; hence prep (phrr) *kitty-corner (from), ~ (to)* diagonally across from. **chiefly Nth, N Midl, West** See Map and Map Section Cf **kittering, kitty-cross, ~-wampus**
　1890 DN 1.8, *Kittycornered* . . would be an easy development from

cattycornered. **1896** *DN* 1.419 **NY,** *Kitter-. . cornered.* **1905** *DN* 3.62 **eNE,** *Kittercorner(ed), kittacorner(ed), kittycorner(ed). . .* See *cattercornered.* [*Ibid* 60, The building is cattacorner(ed) from the court house.] **1910** *DN* 3.444 **wNY,** *Kittacornered, kittycornered. . .* See *catacornered.* [*Ibid* 438, *Catacornered. . .* Diagonally across from.] **1912** *DN* 3.580 **wIN,** *Kitty-cornered.* **1942** Berrey–Van den Bark *Amer. Slang* 42.4, *Diagonal(ly); cater-cornered. . . kitty-catty-corner, kitty-catty-cornered, kitty-corner, kitty-cornered.* **1943** *LANE* Map 547 (*Cater-cornered*), [The forms *kitty-corner(ed)* are common throughout NEng in reference to diagonal motion; 4 infs gave the form *kitty-corners* and 2 *kitter-corner(ed).* c25 infs used *kitty-corner(ed)* in reference to something oriented at an angle to something else or (rarely) to the vertical.] 1 inf, *Kitty-corner,* of two buildings on opposite corners; 1 inf, *Kitty-corner,* of two buildings facing each other across a street (not at a corner) but not exactly opposite; 1 inf, *Kitty-cornered,* of a house front not parallel with the street; 1 inf, *Kitty-cornered,* of something intentionally set at an angle; 1 inf, A bench is kitter-cornered if it's [kə'rɪlɪn 'ouvə] (i.e. about to fall). **1950** *WELS* **WI** (*On the opposite corner of a square, diagonally:* "The drug store is _____ the gas station.") 25 Infs, Kitty-corner from; 3 Infs, Kitty-cornered from; 1 Inf, Kitter-corner from; 9 Infs, Kitty-corner; 3 Infs, Kitty-corner to; ("He nailed the boards on _____") 2 Infs, Kitty-corner; 1 Inf, Kitty-cornered; (*To go across at an angle:* "If we have to walk, let's _____; it's shorter.") 5 Infs, Go kitty-corner; 1 Inf, Cut kitty-corner. **1954** *Harder Coll.* **cwTN,** *Kitty-corner (catty-corner), to go . .* to cross at an angle. . . "He cut kitty-cornered 'cross the field." **1965–70** *DARE* (Qu. MM14, *If a drugstore is on one corner of a square and a gas station is on the far corner . .* "The drugstore is _____ the gas station.") 142 Infs, **chiefly Nth, N Midl, West,** Kitty-corner from; 56 Infs, **chiefly Nth, N Midl, CA,** Kitty-corner to; 44 Infs, **chiefly Nth, N Midl, West,** Kitty-corner; **FL**31, 38, **IA**27, **MN**26, 33, **MS**42, **SC**5, **UT**4, Kitty-cornered from; **CA**80, **MA**73, **NY**68, 217, **VA**11, Kitty-cornered to; **CO**17, **ME**19, **MO**37, **OH**78, Kitty-cornered; [**MA**5, 6, Kitty-cornering;] **MI**2, Kitty-cornered across the block; **MI**54, Kitty-corner of; **NY**30, Kitter-corner; **NY**123, Kitter-corner from; **OH**18, Kitra-corner from; (Qu. MM16, *If you're walking with somebody to the other corner of a square, and you want to save steps . .* "It'll be shorter if we _____.") 27 Infs, **esp Nth, N Midl, CA,** Go kitty-corner; **MN**26, Go kitty-cornered; **CA**80, Walk kitty-corner; **MN**12, Went kitty-corner; (Qu. KK70, *Something that has got out of proper shape:* "That house is all _____.") Inf **MI**9, Kitty-cornered; (Qu. MM1, . . '*Opposite to*'. . "The shed is _____ the barn.") Inf **CA**74, Kitty-corner to; **CA**122, **NY**163, Kitty-corner; **WI**34, Kitty-cornered; (Qu. MM13, *The table was nice and straight until he came along and knocked it _____*) Infs **OH**5, **VA**99, Kitty-corner; **NY**123, Kitter-corner; (Qu. MM15, *If a carpenter nails a board crossing another board at an angle . .* "He nailed the board on _____.") Infs **MN**40, **MA**5, Kitty-corner; **VA**11, Kitty-cornered. **1965** *DARE* FW Addit **cwWI,** *Kitty-corner*—Diagonally across an intersection. "The post office is across the street, kitty-corner." *Ibid* **ME,** *Kitty-corner*—of furniture: set in a corner, facing the center of the room. **1967** *DARE* Tape **CA**13, They all lived over near the hot springs, they're just kitty-corner from the Historical Society house. **1973** Allen *LAUM* 1.402 **SD** (as of c1950), *Kitty-corner:* diagonally [1 inf].

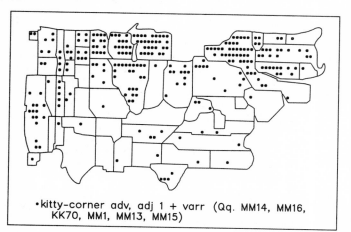

•kitty-corner adv, adj 1 + varr (Qq. MM14, MM16, KK70, MM1, MM13, MM15)

2 also *kitty-katty:* Triangular; zigzag. **esp NEng**
1890 *DN* 1.78 **TN,** In this [the Seguachee] valley [Tennessee] *cattycornered,* for zigzag, is sometimes called *kitty-catty-cornered.* **1892** *DN* 1.217 **MA,** *Kitty-cornered* [in reference to *zigzag*] . . Familiar to an

elderly lady of Springfield, Mass., a native of Chicopee. **1943** *LANE* Map 547 (*Cater-cornered* [triangular(ly) or on the bias]) 2 infs, **MA,** Kitty-corner; 2 infs, **ME, VT,** Kitty-cornered; 1 inf, **wCT,** Kitty-corner, of a triangular piece of land; 1 inf, **cCT,** A kitty-cornered place is one quick turn and then another; 1 inf, **cMA,** Kitty-corner, of two walls or fences built zigzag or intersecting at an angle of less than 90°; 1 inf, **swNH,** Kitty-katty = zigzag. **1969** *DARE* (Qu. W27, . . *A three-cornered tear in a piece of clothing from catching it on something sharp*) Infs **MA**48, **RI**6, Kitty-corner tear.

kitty-corner v [Var of **catercorner** v]
To go on the diagonal; to cut diagonally across.
1892 *DN* 1.236 **cwMO,** *Kitty-corner . .* to cut off a corner by going across lots. **1942** Berrey–Van den Bark *Amer. Slang* 42.2, Catty-corner, kitty-corner . . , *to become or go diagonally.* **1944** Howard *Walkin' Preacher* 123 **IA,** I veered from the creek and kitty-cornered the Andrews farm to follow the shortest route to Mulberry School. **1950** *WELS* (*To go across at an angle:* "If we have to walk, let's _____") 1 Inf, **seWI,** Kitty-corner. **1965–69** *DARE* (Qu. MM16, *If you're walking with somebody to the other corner of a square, and you want to save steps . .* "It'll be shorter if we _____.") Infs **MI**76, **MA**46, **SC**5, **UT**3, Kitty-corner.

kitty-corner n Pronc-sp *kiddy-corner* [By ext from **kitty-corner** adv, adj]
A corner circumvented by going on the diagonal; a triangular space.
1950 *WELS* (*To go across at an angle:* "If we have to walk, let's _____; it's shorter.") 1 Inf, **csWI,** Cut a kitty-corner. **1968** *DARE* FW Addit **NY,** When something fits in the corner of the room, we say it fits in the kitty-corner. **1992** *DARE* File, Kiddycorner—kitty corner, diagonal corner.

kitty-cornered See **kitty-corner** adv, adj

kitty-corner from (or to) See **kitty-corner** adv, adj 1

kitty-cross adv, adj Also *kitty-ma-crossways, kittyways*
=**kitty-corner** adv, adj 1.
1943 *LANE* Map 547, [Diagonally, obliquely, aslant] 1 inf, **swCT,** Kitty-cross; 1 inf, **csMA,** Kittyways. **1968** *DARE* (Qu. MM14, *If a drugstore is on one corner of a square and a gas station is on the far corner . .* "The drugstore is _____ the gas station.") Inf **PA**138, Kitty-cross from; **PA**134, Kitty-ma-crossways ['kɪtɪmə-] [laughter].

kittydid See **katydid**

kitty hawk See **killy hawk**

kitty-katty See **kitty-corner** adv, adj 2

kitty-ki-slaunch adj Cf *kitty-ki-wampus* (at **kitty-wampus**), **slaunchwise**
1968 *DARE* (Qu. MM15, *If a carpenter nails a board crossing another board at an angle . .* "He nailed the board on _____.") Inf **IL**29, Kitty-ki-slaunch [kɪtɪkɨ'slɑnč].

kitty-kitty-corner See **kitty wants a corner**

kitty-ki-wampus See **kitty-wampus**

kitty-macbias See **catabias**

kitty-ma-crossways See **kitty-cross**

‡**kitty-nine-tails** n Cf **cat-o'-nine-tails 1**
=**cattail 1.**
1968 *DARE* (Qu. S26e, *Other wildflowers not yet mentioned;* not asked in early QRs) Inf **MD**23, Kitty-nine-tails—grow in damp places, on long stalk, brown cylinders on end. [*DARE* Ed: Illustr shows a cattail.]

kitty on a broomstick n
A ring game; see quot.
1950 *WELS,* 1 Inf, **WI,** *Kitty on a broomstick*—blindfold "it" and he touches someone in circle with broomstick and yowls; they must yowl in answer as "it" guesses the name. [Inf old]

kitty owl See **kittenhead**

kitty paw n Cf **cat's-paw 1**
=**ground ivy 1.**
1959 *VT Hist.* 27.146 **cwVT,** *Kitty paw. . .* Ground ivy. Occasional.

kitty's game See **kitty** n 5

kitty-wamp adj [Abbr for **kitty-wampus**]

Disordered, mixed-up.

1980 *DARE* File **Madison WI,** If the box is dropped, the problem is that the papers all get kitty-wamp ['kɪtɪˌwaˤmp] in the machine.

kitty-wampus adv, adj Also *kitty-ki-wampus* Also sp *kitty-wumpus* [Prob blend of **kitty-corner** adv, adj + **wampus**] Note: It is not always possible to distinguish adj from adv senses. Cf **catawampus** adj, adv, **catercorner** adj, adv =**kitty-corner** adv, adj **1.**

1942 McAtee *Dial. Grant Co. IN* 37 (as of 1890s), *Kittywampus . .* oblique. **1957** *Sat. Eve. Post Letters* ceIL, *Kitty-wampus* (diagonal). **1965–70** *DARE* (Qu. W23, *When a collar or other clothing works itself up out of place . . "It's _____.";* total Infs questioned, 75) Inf **MS37,** Kitty-wampus; (Qu. KK70, *Something that has got out of proper shape: "That house is all _____.")* Inf **IA**41, Kitty-ki-wampus [kɪtɪˈkiwampəs]; **ID5, OH**75, Kitty-wampus; (Qu. MM3, *When someone does something the wrong way round . . "This is the front, you've got the whole thing turned _____.")* Inf **IL**28, Kitty-wampus; (Qu. MM13, *The table was nice and straight until he came along and knocked it _____)* Infs **FL**28, **MD**49, **NC**36, Kitty-wampus ['kɪtɪwɔmpəs]; **MN**15, Kitty-wampus ['kɪti wɑmpəs]; **ID**5, Key-wampus [ˌki'wɑmpəs]; [corr to] ski-wampus [ˌski'wɑmpəs;] (Qu. MM14, *If a drugstore is on one corner of a square and a gas station is on the far corner . . "The drugstore is _____ the gas station.")* Infs **CA**14, **IL**39, **WI**27, Kitty-wampus (from); **IA**41, Kitty-ki-wampus [kɪti'kɪwɑmpəs]. **1967** *DARE* File **WI,** *Kittywumpus*—at an oblique angle; askew. "The house is set kittywumpus to the street." "The house is set kittywumpus on the lot." **1973** Allen *LAUM* 1.402 **ND, SD** (as of c1950), *Askew* or *diagonal. . . kittywampus:* [4 infs]. *Ibid, Kittywampus:* Diagonally [1 inf].

kitty wants a corner n Also *kitty-kitty-corner* **scattered, but esp Sth, S Midl** See Map

=**pussy wants a corner** or a similar game with an extra player.

1896 *DN* 1.420 **c,nNY,** *Kitty-kitty-corner:* same as *puss-in-the-corner.* **1906** *DN* 3.144 **nwAR,** *Kitty wants a corner. .* The same game as "Pussy wants a corner." **1965–70** *DARE* (Qu. EE2, *Games that have one extra player—when a signal is given, the players change places, and the extra one tries to get a place)* Infs **AL**6, **GA**6, **KY**29, **NC**30, 53, **PA**1, **UT**3, Kitty wants a corner; **KY**25, Kitty wants a corner, [corr to] pussy wants a corner [FW: Inf unsure of corr]; **SC**3, Kitty wants a corner—used to call it; now, fruit basket upset; **SC**54, Kitty wants a corner—[same as] turn over the fruit basket. **1966** *DARE* Tape **AL**6, That's kitty wants a corner. It's just a certain number of corners in a room and when they say "change" then somebody's left out and that's the one in the middle. **1986** Pederson *LAGS Concordance,* 1 inf, **ceTN,** Kitty wants a corner—a game with 4 bases.

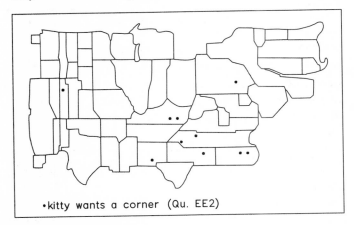

•kitty wants a corner (Qu. EE2)

kittyways See **kitty-cross**

kitty-wumpus See **kitty-wampus**

kit whale n [Perh < *kit* a young or undersized specimen of var fur-bearing animals]

The killer whale (*Orcinus orca*).

1962 Salisbury *Quoth the Raven* 223 **seAK,** In front of the little house stood a broken shaft of gray marble, with the figure of a "kit whale," or killer-whale lying in the grass at the base.

kiva n [Hopi] **chiefly SW** Cf **estufa 1**

A Pueblo Indian structure, built wholly or partly underground, used by men for religious and fraternal purposes; the fraternal group associated with a specific structure.

[**1871** in **1939** *UT Hist. Qrly.* 7.54 **seUT,** Found pieces of pottery and arrowheads. . . Also saw a "kiver" or underground "clan room."] [**1875** *Scribner's Mth.* Dec 205 **cnAZ,** This kiva, as it is called in their own tongue, is called "Estufa" by the Spaniards, and is spoken of by writers in English as the "Sweat House."] [**1893** Donaldson in U.S. Census Office *Moqui Pueblo Indians* 55, An estufa is a large room under ground, called by the Indians "kiva" [Donaldson: keva or keevah] meaning "man house", a place where men hold their private councils.] **1910** Hodge *Hdbk. Amer. Indians* 2.321, In the ancient pueblos the fireplace was generally in the form of a shallow box or pit in the middle of the floor, the smoke finding egress through the hatchway as in some of the kivas to-day. **1964** Nida *Toward Sci. Transl.* 169, For the Zuñis, uttering *melika* in a kiva ceremony would be as out of place as bringing a radio into such a meeting. **1979** *New Yorker* 5 Mar 98 **NM,** Kiva ladder in distance over flat roofs. **1993** Hillerman *Sacred Clowns* 41 **AZ,** Neither the boy nor any other citizen of the pueblo would ever discuss the business of his particular religious society with anyone not initiated into its kiva. Not even with his mother. *Ibid* 46, You keep the secrets of your fraternity—your kiva—because only the people who have to know these secrets to perform their duties are supposed to know them.

kiver n

1 See **cover.**

2 See **kivver.**

kiverlet, kiverlid See **coverlet**

kivver n Also *kiver;* pronc-spp *kibby, kiv(v)y, quiver* For other varr see quots **chiefly NEng** Cf **coverclip**

A **sunfish** of the genus *Lepomis,* esp **bluegill 1, pumpkinseed,** or **redbreast sunfish.**

1903 *Ill. Sport. News* 20 June 21/1 (*Mathews Coll.*), The big brother of this little 'kiver' (so-called because he looks like a lid of a stew-kettle) is among us. **1907** *DN* 3.192 **seNH,** *Kivy* ['kɪvi]. . . Sunfish. "Pumpkin seed" is a book word. "How many kivies do you think we caught?" **1911** *Century Dict. Suppl., Kiver.* . . A sunfish or pumpkin-seed. . . Also *kivy.* [*Century* Ed: Local, U.S.] **1911** Shute *Plupy* 36 **NH,** A string of kivers and small perch. **1945** McAtee *Nomina Abitera* 20, When I first went to Washington, D.C. (1903), I heard the name "Kiver" for sunfishes and before long learned it was short for "cunt-kiver," these fishes being deemed of about the right size and shape to serve in that role. One of my mentors of the period . . said that this appellation was employed at Lake George, N.Y., and another . . reported it in the form Kiver-cunt from Massachusetts. A younger friend . . had heard it as Kippy-cunt in New England. Shortened and derived forms are recorded as follows: Kiver (Maine, New York and Ohio); Kivy (New Hampshire); and quiver (Maine and New York). **1954** McAtee *Suppl. to Nomina Abitera* [6] **NH,** Sunfishes (*Eupomotis gibbosus* and *Lepomis auritus*)—Kibbec is recorded in fishes of New Hampshire, by R.G. Carpenter and H.R. Siegler (1947: 68, 69). **1968–69** *DARE* (Qu. P1, . . *Kinds of freshwater fish . . caught around here . . good to eat)* Inf **MA**15, Kivvers; (Qu. P3, *Freshwater fish that are not good to eat)* Infs **MA**35, 74, ['kɪvəz]; **MA**68, ['kɪvəz]; (Qu. P7, *Small fish used as bait for bigger fish)* Inf **MA**62, ['kɪvəz]—small flatfish. **1969** *DARE* File **csMA** (as of 1940s–50s), Kivver—the name by which we knew the small trashy, spiny fish that one catches nine times out of ten in lake fishing; I think they are also called sunfish. *Ibid* **ceMA,** Kibby—a sunfish. *Ibid* **cnMA,** Kivvy—a sunfish. **1982** *Ibid* **ceMA,** ['kɪbɪz]—small fish—up to 8″ long, flat, in freshwater pond. Same as *bluegill.* **1986** *Ibid* **eMA** (as of 1950s), Since childhood I've known the word kibby to be used for what other people call pumpkinseeds. **1993** *Ibid* **csWI** (as of c1920), My friend Ralph and I used to go fishing for kivvers in Lake Mendota and Lake Monona. Kivvers were a kind of sunfish, somewhat smaller and more silvery than a bluegill. We caught pumpkinseeds, too.

kiyi n Also sp *kieye* **Gt Lakes**

A **cisco:** usu *Coregonus kiyi,* but also *C. hoyi.* For other names of the former see **mooneye 2, paperbelly, waterbelly**

1896 U.S. Natl. Museum *Bulletin* 47.469, *Argyrosomus Hoyi.* . . Kieye of Lake Michigan. **1957** Blair et al. *Vertebrates U.S.* 69, *Coregonus kiyi.* . . Kiyi. Lakes Superior, Michigan, Huron, and Ontario. **1983** Becker *Fishes WI* 361, *Coregonus kiyi* . . *kiyi*—name used by commercial fishermen of Lake Michigan. . . The kiyi occurs in Lakes Superior and Michigan.

kiyoodle, kiyutle See **kyoodle**

klab See **clabber** n²

Klamath weed n [See quot 1937] **chiefly CA**

A **St. John's wort** (here: *Hypericum perforatum*).

1922 Smiley *Weeds of Calif.* 54 *(DA)*, (Hypericum perforatum L.) English names: . . Klamath Weed. **1937** U.S. Forest Serv. *Range Plant Hdbk.* W99, Common St. Johnswort *(Hypericum perforatum) . .* is commonly known in California and Oregon as Klamath weed, as the original infestation came from the Klamath River country near the Oregon line. **1961** Thomas *Flora Santa Cruz* 239 **cwCA,** *H[ypericum] perforatum. . .* Klamath Weed, Common St. John's Wort. **1970** *DARE* (Qu. S21, *. . Weeds . . that are a trouble in gardens and fields)* Inf **CA204,** Klamath weed. **1974** Munz *Flora S. CA* 519, *H[ypericum] perforatum. . .* Klamath Weed.

klap door See **klop door**

klatch n Usu |klɑč|; also |klæč, klʌč| Also sp *clatch, clotch, clutch, glutch, klatsch, klot(s)ch, klutch* [Ger *Klatsch* gossip] **scattered, but chiefly Upper Missip Valley, Gt Lakes** See Map

An informal social gathering for talking and refreshment—often in combs *coffee klatch, kaffeeklatch,* and *-kaf.*

1888 Randall-Diehl *2000 Words* 122, Kaffe Klatsch, A festival or other informal gathering at which a light repast is served. **1895** *Amer. Jrl. Psychology* 7.216, Coffee-clatches, where the members [=men] dress themselves with aprons, etc., and knit, gossip and crochet. [**1940** *AmSp* 15.83, [Dutch survivals in Michigan:] *Koffie Kletz* [kɔfi klɛts]. The most common Dutch term, the English equivalent 'chatter over coffee.'] **1941** *Time* 13 Oct 83, Of all the civic beefing-fests and subcontracting-klatches caused by . . priorities unemployment. **1944** *Sun* (Baltimore MD) 17 Jan 18/7, There was a time when the Canton Market. . . boasted of aisles sufficiently wide to permit Mrs. Schultz to hold comfortably her market-day *klotsch* with Mrs. O'Brien and other neighbors. **1950** *WELS* **WI** (*Joking words for a meeting where there is a lot of talking)* 4 Infs, Coffee klatch (or clatch, clotch, klotch); 3 Infs, Coffee clutch; 1 Inf, Coffee glutch; 1 Inf, Kaffee klatch; [1 Inf, Kaffe Klätch;] *(A group of women that meet to sew together)* 4 Infs, Kaffee klatch (or klotch); 1 Inf, Kaffee klutch; 1 Inf, Kuffy klutch; *(Nicknames for local clubs)* 4 Infs, Kaffee klatch(es); 2 Infs, Coffee clutch; 1 Inf, Klotch-fests. **1965–70** *DARE* (Qu. W32, *. . A group of women that meet to sew together)* 9 Infs, **esp Gt Lakes,** Coffee klatch; **NY34,** Monday klatch; **PA230,** Sewing klatch; **NY92,** Ladies' Aid—password is [ˈkɑfi ˈklæč] Club is meeting today; (Qu. O21, *When men out in seagoing boats get together for a visit and a cup of hot coffee . . a _____)* Infs **IL9, IN58, NJ28,** Coffee klatch; **MI65,** (Coffee) [klæč]; **OH99,** [klæč]; (Qu. FF1, *. . A kind of group meeting called a 'social' or 'sociable'. . . [What goes on?])* Infs **IA7, MI69,** Coffee clutch(es); **MI93,** Coffee klatch—to sew or talk; **PA81,** Kuchen klatches—coffee and cake and talk; (Qu. FF2, *. . Kinds of parties)* Inf **CT27,** Coffee klatch; **NM5,** Coffee klatch—German people; (Qu. FF23, *. . Joking names . . for . . clubs)* Inf **CA133,** Coffee klatch—a breakfast club; **WI61,** Coffee clutch; (Qu. HH30, *Things that are nicknamed for different nationalities)* Inf **CT19,** Swedish coffee clutch [klʌč]—Swedes gather for sewing and coffee; (Qu. KK12, *A meeting where there's a lot of talking: "They got together yesterday and had a real _____.")* Infs **IA21, NV9, PA175,** Coffee klatch; **MI108,** Coffee klatch—informal gathering; **NY100,** Klatch; **MI18, WI21,** Coffee clutch. **1973** Allen *LAUM* 1.379 **Upper MW** (as of c1950),

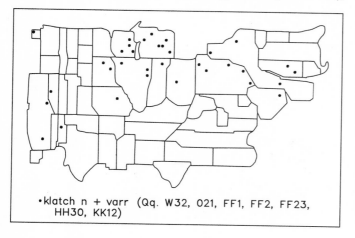

•klatch n + varr (Qq. W32, O21, FF1, FF2, FF23, HH30, KK12)

Kaffeeklatch . . an informal daytime party, usually for women and usually with coffee. . . The *kaffee-* (sometimes *coffee*) forms are all immediately derived from the first language of U[pper] M[idwest] immigrants, particularly from Germany but also from The Netherlands, Norway, and Sweden. They are used in an English language context. . . They characterize especially the most recent German settlement areas of Nebraska and Minnesota. The forms with *klatch* /ɑ/ and those with *klutch* /ʌ/ are phonetic variants but are treated separately here because several infs. insist upon their distinctiveness. [*Ibid, Kaffe(e)-kalas* is from colloquial Swedish, *kaffe(e)-klat* and *kaffe(e)-lag* are from Norwegian, and *kaffee-klets* is from Dutch.] **1995** *DARE* File **csWI,** A local church sponsors a men's Bible study and discussion group called Men in Christian Community (MCC). Since the meetings always take place over breakfast in a restaurant, it's a long-standing town joke that MCC really stands for "Men's Coffee Clutch."

klatch v Also *coffee-klatch* Also sp *clutch, klatsch, klotch*

To take part in a **klatch** n; hence n *klatcher, klutcher* one who takes part in such a gathering.

1932 Fitzsimmons *No Witness* 145 *(AmSp* 10.236), She'll have me down klotching with her if I'm not careful. **1956** Whyte *Organization Man* 286 **nIL,** Dot will be *Kaffeeklatsching* and sun-bathing with the girls. **1968** *DARE* (Qu. W32, *. . A group of women that meet to sew together)* Inf **MO36,** Coffee clutching [ˈkɑfi ˌklʌčn̩]—German expression; **OH76,** Coffee klatchers. **1973** Allen *LAUM* 1.379 **MN** (as of c1950), Two male infs. volunteer names for a woman who regularly goes to coffee parties. "She's a gadder," reports one Minnesotan . . ; she's an "old klutcher," reports another. **1979** *Jerusalem Post* 6 May 11 (*Barnhart Dict. Companion* 1.1.3) **CA,** Wives spend their days shopping, coffee-klatching, and carpooling their offspring to school, dancing, swimming, . . and art lessons.

klatcher, klatsch v See **klatch** v

klatsch n See **klatch** n

klediment See **clatterment**

kliekies n pl Also *klikkes* [Du *kliekjes* leftovers] Leftovers.

1969 *DARE* (Qu. H67, *Food that was not finished at one meal but saved for another)* Inf **MI102,** Kliekies [ˈklikiz]—a neighbor used to use this term; never heard it elsewhere. **1993** *DARE* File, Ken . . says that his mother-in-law, from Peoria, Iowa (near Pella [=a Dutch-settled community]), said "klikkes" [for "leftovers"] during the 60s and on into the 70s in his hearing, but that it was probably a home or regional dialect word all her life.

klim See **climb** 2b

klob See **clabber** n²

klooch(man) See **klootchman**

klook-klook n Cf **clook-clook**

A **yellowlegs** (here: either *Totanus flavipes* or *T. melanoleucus*).

1916 *Times-Picayune* (New Orleans LA) 2 Apr mag sec 8/1, Greater yellow-legs (Totanus melanoleucus). Klook-klook. Pied Jaune. . . *Lesser yellow-legs* (Totanus flavipes). Klook-klook. Pied Jaune.—Very similar in form, color and markings to the preceding.

klootchman n Also abbr *klootch* Also sp *clootchman, klooch(man), klutchman* [Chinook Jargon "woman, female"] **chiefly Pacific NW, AK** *often derog*

An American Indian woman; by ext: any woman.

1865 (1973) Stuart *Montana as it Is* 83, Oregon is the place to hear the "Chinnook" in all its glory; it has "played" the English language "square out" in that land of rain, fir-trees, "cloochmans," and "camus." **1896** Pike *Through Subarctic Forest* 39, Here [=on the Stikine River above the Little Cañon] there was no difficulty; indeed, it is known, in derision, as the Klootchman Cañon—"Klootchman" being the name for woman in the Chinook jargon universally employed between whites and Indians on the Pacific coast. **1900** Spurr *Through Yukon Diggings* 54, It was a native and his "klutchman" or squaw. **1911** Clayson *Hist. Narr.* 13 **wWA** (as of 1868), At length a canoe, paddled by two Siwashes and a klootchman, came along. **1930** Williams *Logger-Talk* 25 **Pacific NW,** *Klootchman:* Woman, squaw; from the Chinook jargon. **1938** (1939) Holbrook *Holy Mackinaw* 265, *Kloochman,* or *klooch.* A woman. **1966–68** *DARE* (Qu. U5, *Someone who sells small articles on a street corner)* Inf **AK1,** Klootch [kluč] = Tlingit or Chinook for "woman"; Indian women do it; (Qu. HH28, *Names and nicknames . . for people of* *foreign background)* Inf **AK**8, Klooch [kluč]—Indian mama—unfavorable; [(Qu. HH29a, . . *People of mixed blood—part Indian)* Inf **WA**16, Klootchman ['klučmən];] (Qu. HH34, *General words . . for a woman, not necessarily uncomplimentary)* Inf **AK**5, Klooch [kluč]—used to be common for Indian woman. **1976** Hobbs-Specht *Tisha* 222 **AK**, "Take a slant at her [=an Indian]," he said, jerking a thumb towards the corner. "See what a good klooch looks like." "There's no need for that kinda talk, Arnold," Maggie said.

klop door n Also sp *klap door, klopp* ~ [Ger *Klapptür* spring-action door, trap door; Du *klapdeur* swing door] Cf **bulkhead 1, cellarway, hatchway, louk**

1967–68 *DARE* (Qu. D20, *Names for a sloping outside cellar door)* Infs **NY**34, **NY**116, Klop door; **WI**12, **WI**50, Klap [klæp] door. [3 Infs from communities of predominantly Ger background; 4th Inf's family of Du origin]

klotch n See **klatch** n

klotch v See **klatch** v

klotsch See **klatch** n

kluck See **cluck** n

klutch See **klatch** n

klutcher See **klatch** v

klutchman See **klootchman**

klutz n |klʌts| Pronc-sp *glutz* [Yiddish, cognate with Ger *Klotz* a block of wood] *esp in urban areas; esp freq among young speakers*

One who is physically or socially awkward; a fool; hence adj *klutzy* awkward, foolish.

1965 *Sat. Review* 28 Aug 51, The dancers look good and the artists look a little *klutzy.* **1965–70** *DARE* (Qu. HH21, *A very awkward, clumsy person)* Infs **IA**32, **MI**123, **MA**2, **NY**81, 119, 211, **PA**94, Klutz; **NY**89, Klutz—very common New York City expression; (Qu. HH3, *A dull and stupid person)* Infs **IA**32, **NY**241, Klutz; (Qu. HH16, *Uncomplimentary words with no definite meaning—just used when you want to show that you don't think much of a person: "Don't invite him. He's a _____.")* Inf **PA**133, Klutz. [8 of 10 total Infs young, 7 comm type 1 or 2] **1967** *DARE* FW Addit **PA**162, The word *klutz* is "glutz" in Kutztown, Pa., area. **1970** *Time* 2 Nov 83, Candice [Bergen] is generally hailed as heiress apparent to Grace Kelly, but the princess role does not quite fit. Says she: "Basically I'm the klutz who makes a terrific entrance to the party and then trips and falls and walks around with food in her hair." **1972** *DARE* File **Salt Lake City UT**, Klutz [klʌts]—stupid person, clod. "I'm just being a klutz." **1975** Ferretti *Gt. Amer. Book Sidewalk Games* 38 **NYC**, One without balance is always a *Klutz* and is a much-sought-after opponent. **1980** *Children's Folkl. Newsl.* Winter 3 **seMN**, Klutz. . . Uncoordinated awkward boy (adj Klutzy). **1986** Pederson *LAGS Concordance* (*He's so . . awkward . . referring to physical appearance)* 5 infs, **AL, FL**, Klutz; 1 inf, **nwMS**, He's a klutz—acts strangely, does odd things; 2 infs, **FL**, Klutzy; *(That fool)* 4 infs, **AL, FL, TN**, (A) klutz. [All infs young; 11 of 12 infs urban] **1988** Tyler *Breathing Lessons* 36 **eMD**, Ira thought she was a klutz. Everybody did. She had developed a sort of clownish, pratfalling reputation.

kmass See **camas**

knabbler n Cf **gnabble** [*EDD* nabbler (at *nabble* v.²) "a gossip; a mischief-maker; an argumentative, captious person"]

1930 Shoemaker *1300 Words* 36 **cPA Mts** (as of c1900), Knabbler—A person who talks much to little purpose.

knack n [Prob abbr for **knickknack** n¹, but cf *OED* knack sb.² 3.b "A choice dish; a delicacy, a dainty. *Obs.*"]

=**knickknack** n¹; also *knacking* snacking.

1986 Pederson *LAGS Concordance* (*A bite . . food taken between regular meals)* 1 inf, **cwLA**, Knack; 1 inf, **swLA**, Knacking—from "knickknack"?

knackaway See **anaqua**

knacking See **knack**

knackwurst n Pronc-sp *knockwurst* [Ger *Knackwurst*] **esp in Ger and Jewish settlement areas**

A short, thick, highly spiced sausage.

1939 Brinig *Anne Minton's Life* 241 (*OEDS*), This very second, with us full of beer and knackwurst and sauerkraut . . , there's nothing to worry about. **1950** *WELS* (*Kinds of sausage most eaten in your neigh-*

borhood) 1 Inf, **seWI**, Knauckwurst [sic]. **c1965** Randle *Cookbooks* (Ask Neighbor) 4.31 **OH**, *Knockwurst in Beer with Sauerkraut.* **1968** *Washington Post* (DC) 5 July sec A 19/3, [Advt:] Foremost knockwurst, kosher style. **1968–70** *DARE* (Qu. H65, *Foreign foods favored by people around here)* Infs **NJ**64, **PA**88, Knockwurst. **1968** *DARE* FW Addit **cwNY**, Knockwurst on a toasted roll—sign in Geneseo, NY, soda fountain. **1975** *Studies in Honor of Kasten* 30 **swIL**, Knockwurst [< *knackwurst*]—a thick brown sausage. **1986** Pederson *LAGS Concordance,* 1 inf, **Tampa FL**, Knockwurst—made of pork sausage; 1 inf, **Tampa FL**, Knockwurst; 1 inf, **Miami FL**, Knockwurst—German; 1 inf, **Miami FL**, Knockwurst—served with sauerkraut; 1 inf, **Miami FL**, Knockwurst. [This question was asked chiefly in urban areas.]

knapweed n

Std: any of var **star thistles**, but esp *Centaurea nigra,* which is also called **bullweed 1, buttonweed 3, drumstick 2, hardhead 6a, horse knobs, hurtsickle, ironhead 3, ironweed 4, Spanish buttons.**

knawel n [*OED* 1578 →; < Ger *Knäuel,* literally "knot, tangle"] A naturalized weedy plant *(Scleranthus annuus).* Also called **chickweed 1f**

1739 (1946) Gronovius *Flora Virginica* 14, Knawel sive Polygono affinis erecta ramosa. [=Knawel, an erect branching relative of Polygonum.] **1813** Muhlenberg *Catalogus Plantarum* 44, Scleranthus annuus—*Knawel.* **1900** Lyons *Plant Names* 338, S[cleranthus] annuus. . . Nat. in eastern U.S. Knawel. **1925** *Book of Rural Life* 5.3083, Knawel, . . or German knotgrass . . (Scleranthus annuus). . . The plant may be recognized by the characteristic short, awl-shaped leaves and the low-spreading habit of growth. In sections of Virginia the knawel grows in such profusion as to form large masses of vegetation. **1973** Hitchcock-Cronquist *Flora Pacific NW* 117, S[cleranthus] annuus. . . knawel.

knead v

Std sense, var form.

Past, past pple: usu *kneaded;* also *kned.* [Perh independent formation by analogy with *bleed/bled, meet/met;* also in Engl dial; cf *EDD* kned, ned (at *knead* v. I.2(3), 3(4), (8))]

1909 *DN* 3.420 **Cape Cod MA** (as of a1857), Kned. . . Past of knead. **1982** *Barrick Coll.* **csPA**, Kned—p.t. and p.p. of knead.

knee n Cf **nine-pin**

Usu =**cypress knee;** rarely a similar woody projection on a **tupelo gum** (here: *Nyssa aquatica*).

1823 Vignoles *Observations Floridas* 91, The *cypress galls* have firm sandy bottoms, and are only troublesome from the multitude of the sprouting knees. **1827** Williams *View W. FL* 89, These swamps, when covered with small coast cypress trees and knees, are usually, but improperly, termed cypress galls. Cypress knees are hollow cones, which rise from roots of the cypress tree, from one to six feet high, and terminate in a blunt point. **1856** *Harper's New Mth. Mag.* 13.444 **VA**, Pools of black, slimy water, from which rose the broad-based cypress, and grouped around those strange contorted roots, called knees, gnarled and knotted like stalagmites in a cave. **1889** *Science* 13.176 **KY**, Inquiries concerning the knees of the swamp cypress . . led me to the supposition that these peculiar processes from the roots served in some manner to aerate the sap. *Ibid* 177 **VA**, At this stage . . if the crown be permanently wet, the knees [of *Nyssa aquatica*] become an extremely conspicuous feature. **1938** Matschat *Suwannee R.* 12 **neFL, seGA**, Their attention was fixed on a big cottonmouth basking on a cypress root—knee, the swampers call it—which protruded above the water. **1962** Kurz–Godfrey *Trees N. FL* 19, The "knees" of the bald-cypress are sharp at their tips; those of the pond-cypress are rounded and blunt at their tips. **1975** Natl. Audubon Soc. *Corkscrew* 17 **FL**, Growing through the water, up from the roots of the cypress trees, are many short, conical, bark-covered projections called "knees." . . The knees do not produce foliage or grow into trees themselves. **1980** Little *Audubon Guide N. Amer. Trees E. Region* 302, Baldcypress. . . Large, needle-leaf, aquatic, deciduous tree often with cone-shaped *"knees"* projecting from submerged roots.

knee baby n Also *knee child* [Cf *SND* knee-bairn "a child that sits on the knee, as not yet able to walk"; also cf *EDD* knee-bairn] **Sth, S Midl, esp NC** *now esp freq among Black speakers* Cf **apron child**

A child old enough to stand unaided, a toddler; a child who is no longer the youngest in a family; see quots.

1939 FWP *Guide NC* 98, The boy, or "chap" may be called a little "shirttailed boy" to distinguish him from her "arm baby and her knee baby." **1944** *PADS* 2.45 **NC,** *Knee-baby.* . . A walking baby—one that stands by one's knee; a second child. "My parents had nineteen children; I'm the knee-baby."—A man, 40. **1953** *PADS* 19.12 **wNC,** *Knee baby.* . . A child, barely able to toddle, who can stand at his mother's knee. Used in and around Fayetteville, N.C. **1968** Harris *S. Home Remedies* 50 **NC,** Jennie was my knee-baby and had to find something to substitute for the usual maternal attention while I cared for the newborn. **1968** *DARE* FW Addit **LA,** *Knee baby*—oldest baby of the series—comes up to your knee. Negroes sometimes carry this designation into later life, e.g., "He's my knee baby." *Ibid* **NC,** *Knee baby*—second youngest child. **1970** *DARE* File **St. Louis MO** [Black], *Knee child*—Toddler, child from ages 1 to 2. "You should have your knee child toilet-trained by now." **1974** (1975) Shaw *All God's Dangers* 9 **AL** [Black], She taken them two baby boys at the death of *her* mother and raised em until they got to be grown men—Grandma Jane's two babies, the knee-baby, Uncle Sherman Culver, and the real baby, Uncle John Culver. **1986** Pederson *LAGS Concordance,* 1 inf, **nwLA,** I'm the knee baby—next to the youngest. [Inf Black] **1989** *DARE* File **cAR,** Kids are called different things—"lap child" or "yard child"—depending on their size. We used those in my family. I know "knee baby" too, but that's Black.

knee-deep n Also *knee-deeper* esp **NEast, N Cent** See Map
Usu a **tree frog,** but also a **bullfrog 1.**
    [**1898** Lloyd *Country Life* 72 **AL,** The bull frog in the mill pond sounds the bass and hollers "kneedeep."] **1938** Sullivan *Educ. Amer.* 15 **PA,** We called them "knee-deeps." For that name we had two explanations: one that the frogs were still knee-deep in the swamp, the other that their cry sounded like *knee-deep.* [**1939** *LANE* Map 231 *(Frog)* 1 inf, **swMA,** The bullfrog says [ˈdʒʌgə ˈrʌm]; the peeper says [ˌnɪi ˈdɹip, ˌnɪi ˈdɹip, ˈbɛtʃ go ˈɹaõn]; 1 inf, **cVT,** The bullfrog says [gə ˈrɑond, ɨts tu^ ˈdɹip].] **1955** Parris *Roaming the Mountains* 232 **cwNC,** And then there are "knee-deeps," which are really only bull-frogs. **1965–70** *DARE* (Qu. P21, *Small frogs that sing or chirp loudly in spring*) Infs **NJ**2, 3, **PA**35, 58, Knee-deeps; **IN**35, **MS**81, **MA**125, Knee-deeps [FW sugg]; **IN**33, Knee-deepers; **MI**47, You can hear them little knee-deeps around here in the spring—never see 'em, though; **VT**16, Knee-deeps or just frogs.

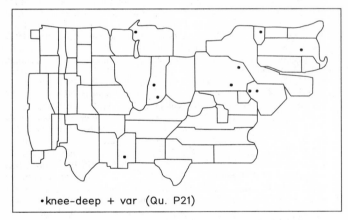

•knee-deep + var (Qu. P21)

knee drop n Also *knee drops(ies)* Cf **drop C7a, eye-drop a**
In marble play: a shot dropped either from knee height or from a kneeling position; a game in which such a shot is used; also used as a call claiming the right to such a shot.
    1958 *PADS* 29.35 **WI,** *Knee-drops.* . . A call claiming the right to drop one's marble from one's knee. **c1970** Wiersma *Marbles Terms* **swMI** (as of c1955), *Knee-dropsies* . . game where the player drops a marble from knee height in attempting to hit another marble. *Ibid* **MI** (as of 1960), *Knee drops* . . when the player drops his marble from a kneeling position. . . "Try knee drops." *Ibid* (as of c1965), *Knee drops*—same . . as above [=*drops*] only the marble is dropped while on your knees. *Ibid* (as of c1972), *Knee drop.* . . A shot which consists of falling to the knees, then dropping your marble upon your opponent's marble from eye level. . . "If you get to do knee drops, then I get to do regulars."

knee farmer n
A farmer who must work on his knees; a truck gardener.
    1941 Writers' Program *Guide IN* 434 **n,cIN,** Throughout this section dairy farms are frequent, and over large areas Dutch, Swedes, and Hungarians, who call themselves 'knee farmers,' raise truck produce.

knee-high to a grasshopper adj phr Also **chiefly Sth, S Midl**
knee high to a duck; for addit varr see quots
Very short or small; by ext, very young; also fig—often in neg constrs.
    1814 *Portsmouth Oracle* (NH) 2 Apr np, One . . who, as farmer Joe would say, is "about knee high to a toad." **1833** Neal *Down-Easters* 78, A bit of a rogue he was too, when he want more 'n knee high to a bumbly-bee. **1856** Simms *Eutaw* 530 **SC,** Knee-high to a cock-sparrow. **1892** *DN* 1.230 **KY,** *Knee high to a duck:* very short. **1905** *DN* 3.12 **cCT,** *Knee-high to a grasshopper.* . . Short in stature. *Ibid* 63 **eNE,** *Knee-high to a grasshopper.* . . Very small. "The child never was more than knee-high to a grasshopper." *Ibid* 85 **nwAR,** *Knee-high to a duck / knee-high to a June-bug.* . . Short of stature. 'He ain't more'n knee-high to a duck / June-bug.' Common. **1908** *DN* 3.327 **eAL, wGA,** *Knee-high to a duck.* . . Very small or short. Usually in negative expressions. "He ain't knee-high to a duck." **1909** *DN* 3.413 **nME,** *Knee high to a grasshopper.* . . Used to describe a very short person. **1910** *DN* 3.444 **wNY,** *Knee-high to a grasshopper.* **1912** *DN* 3.580 **wIN,** *Knee high to a duck.* . . Very short or small. Applied chiefly to the small stature of childhood. "I knew your father before you were knee high to a duck." **1915** *DN* 4.184 **swVA,** *Knee high to a duck.* **1927** *AmSp* 2.358 **WV,** *Knee high to a duck* . . of little value or importance. "The people won't consider him knee high to a duck when they hear how he treated his mother." *Ibid* 359, *Knee high to a grasshopper* . . of no value or importance. "He doesn't stand knee high to a grasshopper in his own county." **1940** *AmSp* 15.219 **wVT,** I am not sure whether I had 'knee-high to a duck' from my environment or my mother or from print; my father's form (western Vermont), which he felt to be amusing, was 'knee-high to a grasshopper.' . . [A] lady from Maine. . . comments 'Knee-high to a grasshopper is everybody's form as far as I know; I never heard *knee-high to a duck.*' **1947** *Harper's Mag.* 195.133 **CO,** Fatigue was gone forever when, knee-high to nothing, I caught my first trout. **1965–70** *DARE* (Qu. FF21b, . . *About old jokes people say: "The first time I heard that one _____."*) 26 Infs, **scattered,** I was knee-high to a grasshopper; **NY**45, I was knee-high to a grasshopper [FW sugg]; **IL**29, **KY**70, **MS**8, **TX**91, **WV**1, 4, 7, I was knee-high to a duck; **DC**11, **OH**63, (Since) I was knee-high to a pup; **TX**41, Since I was knee-high to a jackrabbit; (Qu. A24, . . *Someone who has always been the same way: "He's been hot-tempered from _____."*) Infs **IL**124, **IN**68, **NJ**39, **NY**1, 34, 88, **UT**8, **WI**75, (He was *or* time he was *or* since he was) knee-high to a grasshopper; **TN**4, **TX**37, (Time he was *or* since he was) knee-high to a duck. **1986** Pederson *LAGS Concordance,* 1 inf, **cnAL,** When I was knee-high to a duck; 1 inf, **ceTX,** Ever since they was knee-high to a duck.

knee-jacked adj Cf **buck-kneed, jack-legged 2,** *knee-sprung* (at **sprung**)
    1969 *DARE* (Qu. X37, . . *Words . . to describe people's legs if they're noticeably bent, or uneven, or not right*) Inf **CT**36, If his knees stick out, he's knee-jacked.

knee jump See **kneel jump**

kneel v
Std sense, var forms.
Past, past pple: usu |nild, nɛlt|; for varr see quots.
    1981 *PADS* 67.44 **neMN,** Kneel (pret.) . . kneld /nɛld/ [1 inf]. **1989** Pederson *LAGS Tech. Index* 351 **Gulf Region,** (Kneel) [For the past and past participle, 315 infs responded with *knelt* [nɛlt], and 157 infs with *kneeled* [nild]; 68 infs, [nil]; 7 infs, [nɪld]; 4 infs, [nɪlt]; 4 infs, [njɛlt]; 1 inf, [nelt]; 1 inf, [nilt]; 1 inf, [nɪl]; 1 inf, [nʌl].]

kneelie See **neelie**

kneelies n, exclam
In marble play: see quot.
    c1970 Wiersma *Marbles Terms* **seMI** (as of 1960), *Kneelies*—a move by a player when he sees that his shot has missed. He places a knee on the playing surface and retrieves the marble. This is a form of cheating. *Ibid, Kneelies*—same as *stoops.* [*Ibid, Stoops*—a call which allows a player to shoot at the opponent's piece from a squatting or stooped position rather than the standard full upright stance.]

kneel jump n Also *knee jump* **AK** Cf **ear weight contest**
See quots.
    1973 *Theata* 1.11 **cAK,** For example, one team may choose to do the knee jump. In this game, the person has to kneel on the floor, lift his whole body up and try to jump as far as he can. . . [T]hey have to land on only the feet without the help of their hands or arms. **1983** in 1991 Tabbert *Dict. Alaskan Engl.* 241, *Kneel jump*—Contestants kneel behind

a line, sitting on their heels, with their toes pointed out behind them. The contestants then leap forward . . , land on both feet simultaneously, and remain in that position without moving their feet or using their hands to retain balance. **1986** *Ibid* 241, The Kneel Jump is another Eskimo game used to develop agility and dexterity.

knee patch n

A deep-fried pastry.

1957 Showalter *Mennonite Cookbook* 344 **KS, OH,** *Knee Patches or Swiss Crumpets*—eggs . . flour . . cream. . . Take a piece of dough the size of a large marble and roll as thin as possible. (The Swiss used to cover the knee with a tea towel and then stretch the dough over knee until very thin.) Fry in deep fat. . . Makes 24–30 patches. **c1965** Randle *Cookbooks* (Plain Cookery) 3.15 **OH,** *Knee blatz (knee patches)*—1 egg . . sour cream . . salt . . flour, knead well. . . roll paper thin, fry in deep fat like doughnuts. Put on dinner plate one on top of the other, sprinkling each one with sugar.

knee-sprung See **sprung**

knee work n

Prayer.

1975 Thomas *Hear the Lambs* 97 **nwAL,** I say truthfully that without the Lord answering my prayers I would have been helpless in the face of so many obstacles. Many times have I told you that it would take knee work to accomplish great things.

kneffli n Also *knefler, knepplie, knofli* [Ger *Knöpfle* (or corresponding dial form), dimin of *Knopf* knob, dumpling; cf **knepp**] **Ger settlement areas**

A small dumpling.

1945 Saxon *Gumbo Ya-Ya* 417 **New Orleans LA,** "Mudder" Hecht. . . was the best cook in the world. She could make the best Sviebel Cougan. . . She made Kneflers, too, and Dompfernoodles to eat with chicken stew or Hassenpfeffer. **1957** Showalter *Mennonite Cookbook* 316 **OH,** *Cherry Knepplies. Ibid* 317, Tilt bowl containing batter at an angle. . . As it is about to drop off into salt water, cut it off with the side of a spoon so that about ½ teaspoon of batter drops at once. . . In former times this dish was used as a main course. . . The old folks used to say that "as long as it gives knepplies and cabbage the Dutchman will not die!" **1981** Hachten *Flavor WI* 249 **ceWI,** A thin batter made with eggs and flour and then cooked in boiling liquid was another way to fill out a meal. Called spatzen, spaetzle, egg dumplings, knofli, etc., they could be cooked and eaten in soup, or as a side dish with meat, or embellished with cheese, or with sugar and vanilla as a pudding for dessert. The batter could be dropped from a spoon or pushed through a colander. **1994** *DARE* File **seWI,** My mother used to make a sort of dumpling to serve with sauerkraut and sausage. These were made with flour and eggs; the batter was cut into boiling water and cooked for a few minutes. Kneffli was the only word we used for these.

knepp n pl, rarely sg Now usu |nɛp| Also sp *(k)nep* [PaGer *gnepp* dumplings, pl of *gnopp, knopp* button, lump] **chiefly PA** See Map

Dumplings, often served with **schnitz**; rarely, a dumpling.

1869 *Atlantic Mth.* 24.484 **sePA,** "Schnitz and knep" is said to be made of dried apples, fat pork, and dough dumplings, cooked together. **1872** Haldeman *PA Dutch* 57 [English influenced by German], German forms of food have furnished the vicinal English with . . *knep* (G. *Knöpfe,* the *k* usually pronounced). **1929** *Sat. Eve. Post* 23 Mar 166 **PA,** "What are you havin' for supper, mom?" . . "Schnitz and knepp," said Mrs. Holzoppel heavily. **1957** Showalter *Mennonite Cookbook* 79 **PA,** *Snitz and Knepp.* . . For knepp or dumplings: flour . . egg, beaten . . baking powder . . butter . . salt. . . milk. . . make a batter. . . Drop batter by spoonfuls into boiling ham and apples. . . cook dumplings 10 to 12 minutes. **c1965** Randle *Cookbooks* (Plain Cookery) 1.[24] **New Holland PA,** *Knepp.* . . [B]oil 20 min. & put on top of sourkraut. **1965–70** *DARE* (Qu. H45, *Dishes made with meat, fish, or poultry that everybody around here would know, but that people in other places might not*) Infs **PA**2, 22, 52, Snitz (*or* schnitz) and knepp; **MD**27, Snits and knepp [nɛp]—pot pie dough containing dried apple slices cooked in ham broth—a Pennsylvania Dutch dish; **PA**1, Schnitz and knepp ['snɪtz ˌən 'nɛp]; **PA**9, Knepp [nɛp]—flour, egg, salt, milk—drop in boiling water—is a type of dumpling; **PA**72, Knepp—a dough product; **PA**242, Schnitz and knepp [šnɪts ənɛp]—dried apple and ham dumpling; (Qu. H50) Inf **PA**159, Schnitz and knepp. **1967** *DARE* Tape **PA**29, Well, the schneedles is nothing more than the knepp [nep], but that's . . the old German; they called 'em schneedles over there, we call 'em knepp

here. . . Knepp's a sort of a doughball. . . It's cooked in water, and then they'll put brown butter over top of 'em. **1982** *Barrick Coll.* **csPA,** *Nep*—doughy filling, as in "snitz and nep."

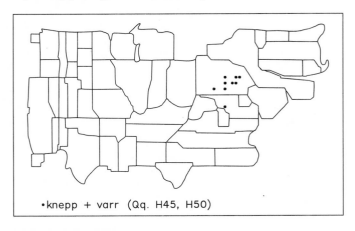

•knepp + varr (Qq. H45, H50)

knepplie See **kneffli**

knet See **knit**

knewed, knewn See **know B3b, 4b**

knicker See **nicker** n[2]

knickknack n[1] Also sp *nick(y)nack, nic-nac;* rarely *nicnacry,* as mass or count noun [By ext from *knickknack* a trifle; *OED knick-knack* sb. 2 1725 →; cf *OED knickknackery* 1813] **esp Sth, Missip Valley** See Map Cf **knack**

A delicacy, tidbit; a snack.

1843 (1916) Hall *New Purchase* 41 **PA,** The stores laid in at Pittsburgh were smoked meats, sausages, flour, cornmeal, tea, coffee, sugar, salt, spices[,] sweatmeats [sic], some fruits, and many other things unknown to Noah. . . From our nicnacries we often supplied the captain's table with a desert [sic]. *Ibid* 247, She was . . mistress of . . the most elegant cookery, either as regards substantial dishes or nicnacry. **1912** Green *VA Folk-Speech* 298, *Nick-nacks.* . . Nice things to eat; delicacies. **1922** Gonzales *Black Border* 76 **sSC, GA coasts** [Gullah], Dem gone tuh de Jew' sto' fuh buy gunjuh en' nickynack en' t'ing. *Ibid* 315 [Gullah glossary], *Nickynack*—"nic-nac" crackers, biscuit. **1957** *Sat. Eve. Post Letters* **cIN,** Nic-nacs—sweet stuff as pie and cake. **1965–70** *DARE* (Qu. H5, . . *A small amount of food eaten between regular meals*) 12 Infs, **esp S Atl, Missip Valley,** Knickknack(s); **IL**45, Knickknacks—a Southern friend says; (Qu. H6, *Words for food in general: "He certainly enjoys his _____."*) Inf **MO**9, Knickknacks. **1966** *DARE* FW Addit **eNC,** Knickknacks—snacks. "Let's get us a knickknack." Common. **1967** Fetterman *Stinking Creek* 152 **seKY,** They won't buy good food, just knickknacks, pop, ice cream—such as that. **1986** Pederson *LAGS Concordance* **Gulf Region, esp AL, LA,** (*A bite . . food taken between regular meals*) 14 infs, Knickknack(s); 1 inf, Knickknack—a bite of this and a bite of that; 1 inf, Knickknack—snack; 1 inf, Knickknack snack; 1 inf, Knickknacks—candy, crackers, grandfather's term; 1 inf, We're having knickknacks—snacks; 1 inf, Knickknacks—food for snacking; 1 inf, Knickknacks—children's term.

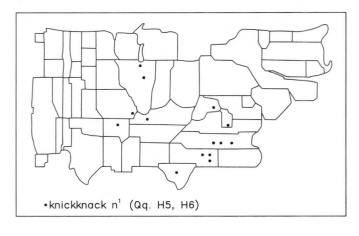

•knickknack n[1] (Qq. H5, H6)

knickknack v, hence vbl n *knickknacking* Also with *around* [**knickknack** n[1]]

To eat a snack.

1966 Dakin *Dial. Vocab. Ohio R. Valley* 2.349, The verb usages *piecing, snacking* = "eating between meals" are commonly noted. A Kentucky speaker says this is *knick-knacking.* **1968** *DARE* FW Addit **eTX,** We knickknack around in the evening. **1986** Pederson *LAGS Concordance (A bite . . food taken between regular meals)* 1 inf, **seAL,** He'd just knickknack; 1 inf, **cwLA,** Knickknacking.

knick-knack n[2] See **knick-knock**

knickknack around See **knickknack** v

k'nick-k'neck See **kinnikinnick**

knick-knock n Also sp *knick-knack, nick-knock* **esp N Cent** =**cricket** n[2].

1947 *WELS Suppl.* **seWI,** *Nick-knock* ['nɪk,nɑk]—child's game: dig a trench in the ground about 3″ wide, 8″ long; place a short stick in it, about 6–8″ long; with a longer stick—a yard or so—flip it out, then hit it as far as possible. Measure the distance with the longer stick. Longest distance attained wins. Name: you "nick" it, then "knock" it. **1968–70** *DARE* (Qu. EE10, *A game in which a short stick lying on the ground is flipped into the air and then hit with a longer stick*) Infs **IL**83, **OH**103, **PA**216, **WV**1, Knick-knock; **IL**86, Knick-knock [FW: Inf unsure]. **1993** *DARE* File **WI,** We played it, called it knick-knack ['nɪk,næk] in English. The pitcher stood 20–25 feet away and threw the short stick to the batter. If you could hit it as far as the pitcher that was considered a good hit. The short stick was about 6 inches long, the long one 2½–3 feet.

knife n [Cf *OEDS knifey, knifie* "Chiefly *Sc.* . . (a) = *mumble-the-peg*" 1896 →] **esp Nth** See Map and Map Section Cf **mumblety-peg**

See quot 1957.

1932 Farrell *Young Lonigan* 167 **Chicago IL** (as of 1916), He could have such a swell time by himself, playing some goofy baseball game or other, or just sitting down playing knife. Danny was such a crack knife player, that no one would play pull the peg with him. **1957** *Sat. Eve. Post Letters* **Chicago IL,** "Pull the peg" or "knife" was played with a jack knife. The one who lost the game must pull a wooden peg out of the ground with his teeth. The winners first drove the peg into the ground by so many allotted blows with the back or side of the knife handle. The farther into the ground it could be driven, the more dirt the loser got into his teeth or mouth. *Ibid* **NJ** (as of 1920–25), We referred to most knife games as just plain "knife." **1965–70** *DARE* (Qu. EE5, *Games where you try to make a jackknife stick in the ground*) 16 Infs, **chiefly Nth,** Knife; **MI**14, Knife—called it "knife" mostly; **MI**34, Knife, [corr to] jackknife; **RI**3, Jackknife or knife; **NY**80, Game of knife; **MI**67, Knives; [**MA**6, **TN**14, Throwing the knife; **HI**6, Knife-playing; **VA**75, Flipping the knife]. **1966** *DARE* File, *Knife* (mumfe[sic]-peg)—south shore of Lake Superior.

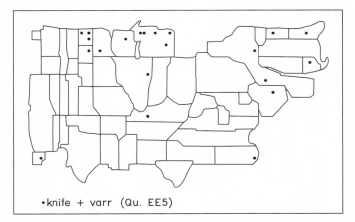

• knife + varr (Qu. EE5)

knife-and-fork club n

See quots.

1949 VA Univ. Div. Extension *Bulletin* 104.1, The "knife-and-fork" clubs are a familiar phenomenon of the American scene. . . [E]very American town has its quota of luncheon and dinner clubs mixing food, good-fellowship, and discussion. **1968** *WI State Jrl.* (Madison) 21 July sec 4 8/3, There was a knife and fork club known as the Forty Thou-

sand Club. **1968** *DARE* (Qu. FF23, . . *Joking names . . for . . clubs or lodges*) Inf **NJ**6, Knife-and-fork clubs—like Kiwanis—because every time [they] meet [they] have [a] meal; **OH**74, Knife-and-fork club—they meet and eat. **1986** Pederson *LAGS Concordance,* 1 inf, **csTX,** Knife-and-fork clubs that just meet and eat.

knife rock n

A whetstone.

1956 Ker *Vocab. W. TX* 168, *Flat piece of stone to sharpen knives . .* knife rock [1 inf]. . . *whet rock* is the common locution; *whet stone* is used, however, by about one-third of all [=67] informants. **1986** Pederson *LAGS Concordance (Whetstone)* 2 infs, **ne,nwLA,** Knife rock; 1 inf, **swMS,** Knife rock—larger than whetrock. [All infs Black]

knip n Also sp *knipp* [See quot 1981; < Ger *knipsen,* dial *knippen* to snip] Cf **liver nip** =**headcheese 1.**

1968 *DARE* (Qu. H43, *Foods made from parts of the head and inner organs of an animal*) Inf **WI**24, Knip [knɪp]. [Inf of Ger background] **1973** Allen *LAUM* 1.288 (as of c1950), *(Head cheese). . . knip* [1 inf, **NE,** of Ger background]. **1981** Hachten *Flavor WI* 246, *Knipp (German)*—4 pounds scrap meat from pig when butchering, for example cheeks, jowls, and neck . . salt . . onions . . oats . . [spices]. In a kettle combine meat, salt, and onions; add water to cover. Simmer. . . To the broth add oats. . . Add meat . . [and spices]. Simmer. . . consistency should be like cooked oatmeal. Pour into pans or molds. [Footnote:] A modern version . . calls for substituting for the pork scraps 3 pounds of pork shoulder roast and 1 or 1½ pounds of beef chuck roast. . . *Knipp,* incidentally, means "snips" in German.

knit v

Std sense, var forms.

1 past: usu *knit, knitted;* also *knet.* [*EDD* (at knit v. I.2)]

1899 (1912) Green *VA Folk-Speech* 252, *Knet. . .* Past tense of *knit.*

2 past pple, ppl adj: usu *knit, knitted;* also *knet, knitten.* [*EDD* (at knit v. I.3)]

1895 (1969) Crane *Red Badge* 9, I've knet yeh eight pair of socks, Henry. **1945** FWP *Lay My Burden Down* 112 **LA** (as of c1860) [Black], They kept warm with the bedclothes and the knitten clothes they had.

knitting pain n Cf **drop a stitch**

A cramp, stitch.

1949 Webber *Backwoods Teacher* 38 **Ozarks,** I had a knitting pain in my side this mornin' till I couldn't hardly stand up. **1995** *NADS Letters* **cWI,** *Knitting pain:* I heard this when I lived in Wisconsin during the 50s. It was mainly used by the elderly and mothers and was limited to the side of the rib cage.

knob n

1 An isolated, usu rounded, rise, hill, or mountain peak; a prominence on a hill—often in combs in place names. [*OED* 1650 →] **widespread, but more freq N Cent, Appalachians** See Map on p. 244 Cf **knoll B**

1750 (1892) Washington *Jrl. Journey* 109, On ye Mouth of Wiggan's Run & opposite to a nob of ye Mountains in Maryland. **1791** Bartram *Travels* 338, The surface of the land . . is . . uneven, occasioned by natural mounds or rocky knobs. **1814** Brackenridge *Views of LA* 106, Flint knobs present themselves, strewed with rude masses of horn stone. *Ibid* 108, Those dividing ridges of streams, which in Kentucky, are called *knobs.* **1859** (1968) Bartlett *Americanisms* 231, *Knob.* In Kentucky, round hills or knolls are called *knobs.* These hills are formed by the weathering of the soft sandstones and shales composing them. The approach to this "*knob* formation" from the rich land is very characteristic, and the sudden change in soil is accompanied by a corresponding change in the inhabitants. The word, however, has extended its meaning, and in Kentucky, as well as other parts of the West, is used simply for hill. In Maryland and Virginia the term *knob* is applied to the highest peaks of the Blue Ridge, and other irregular mountains. **1939** *LANE* Map 38 *(Hill; knoll)* 1 inf, **swCT,** Knoll, little knob; 1 inf, **csCT,** Knob, pointed; 1 inf, **eMA,** Knob; 1 inf, **cMA,** Knob, a peak or projection on a mountain. **1943** Peattie *Great Smokies* 40, The word peak is found on our maps and might be understood in this region but it is not really native to it. The equivalent is top, or knob; high top and high knob indicate lofty peaks. **1950** *WELS (A small, rounded hill)* 7 Infs, **WI,** Knob. **1965–70** *DARE* (Qu. C17, . . *A small, rounded hill*) 68 Infs, **scattered, but esp N Cent, Appalachians,** Knob [*DARE* Ed: 17 of these Infs indicated that a knob is "not very big," or that it could be up to

100 feet high; 6 Infs indicated that it is higher than 100 feet.]; **CA**62, Knob—heard Southern people say; **IN**3, Knob—higher than a knoll; **KY**65, Knob—higher [than a knoll], knoll can be part of a knob; **KY**68, Knob—half a mile to two miles across; **KY**72, Knob—bigger than knoll; parts of Nelson County are in "the knobs"; **KY**83, Knob—one to two acres, some smaller; **MN**15, Knob—if of rock; **MN**36, Mound, 15 feet high or so; knob—much higher than a mound; **NE**2, Knob—here, it's "sandhill"; **NC**62, Knob—up to several acres; **NY**59, Knob—much smaller than mountain, more symmetrical than a hill; **OH**44, Knob—can be any height, calling it a knob depends on the shape; it's round; **OH**61, Knob—25 to 50 feet high, could be an Indian mound; **PA**205, Knoll—small knob; knob—two by three miles in diameter, 700–800 feet high; **SC**32, Knob—about same size as knoll, definitely smaller than a mountain; **TN**11, Knoll—just a little rise; knob—bigger, or bump on high mountain; **VA**8, Knob—any size or a small ridge or on a mountain—rounded off is the most important characteristic; **WI**58, Knob—50 feet high, evenly contoured all around; (Qu. II24, *Names or nicknames for the part of a town where the well-off people live*) Infs **MS**1, **NC**72, **PA**185, Hob's Knob; **AZ**15, **NY**156, Hob's Knob [FW sugg]; **CA**81, **OH**63, **VA**5, 26, Snob('s) Knob; **IL**7, Quality Knob; **MI**106, Mortgage Knob; (Qu. C33, *. . Joking names . . for an out-of-the-way place, or a very small or unimportant place*) Inf **OH**79, Gobbler's Knob; (Qu. C34, *Nicknames for nearby settlements, villages, or districts*) Inf **IN**48, The Knobs; **PA**134, Pine Knob; **PA**205, Gobbler's Knob; (Qu. C35, *Nicknames for the different parts of your town or city*) Inf **IL**11, Bald Knob; **NY**92, Gobbler's Knob; **VA**26, Snob's Knob—where the 500 live. **1968** *DARE* Tape **IN**9, My great-grandmother told about coming up the knobs out north of us, that it was a pole road, an old mud pole road. **1986** Pederson *LAGS Concordance* **Gulf Region** *(Hill)* 86 infs, Knob; 8 infs, Knob [in reference to a formation larger or higher than a hill, or a particularly large or high hill]; 4 infs, (The) bald knob; 1 inf, Bald Knob—a hill in this area; 1 inf, Knob—knoll, maybe between a hill and a knoll; 1 inf, Knob = knoll, a small rise in a low place; 1 inf, Canyon's around a bald knob—some north of Natchez; 1 inf, Knob—a bald hill; 1 inf, A hick comes "out of the knobs"; *(Mountain)* 1 inf, Knob; *(Poor whites . . white . . terms)* 1 inf, I've heard people say "you come out of the knobs."

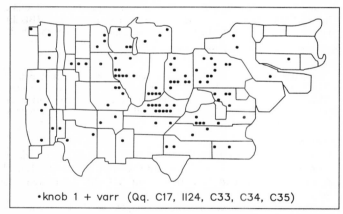

•knob 1 + varr (Qq. C17, II24, C33, C34, C35)

2 A lump on the head. **scattered, but chiefly Nth** See Map Cf **knot** n¹ **2a**

1965–70 *DARE* (Qu. X60, *. . A lump that comes up on your head when you get a sharp blow or knock;* not asked in early QRs) 32 Infs, **scattered, but chiefly Nth,** Knob.

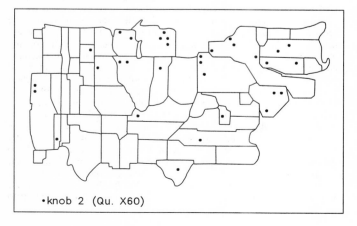

•knob 2 (Qu. X60)

3 Hair worn up in a bun. **scattered, but esp Nth** See Map Cf **hobnob** n³

1965–70 *DARE* (Qu. X3, *When a woman puts her hair up on her head in a bunch*) 10 Infs, **scattered, but esp Nth,** Knob; **NY**69, Knob [FW: Inf unsure]; **CA**151, Knob—old-fashioned; (Qu. X1b, *False hair worn by women*) Inf **CT**1, A big coil of hair, or a very showy knob. [12 of 13 total Infs old]

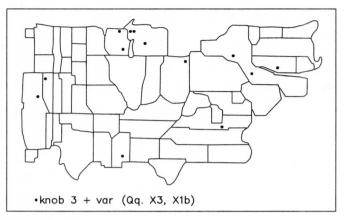

•knob 3 + var (Qq. X3, X1b)

4 See quot.

1989 *NADS Letters* **seLA** (as of 1920s), My brother-in-law . . , a Cajun from the Irish Channel section of New Orleans, tells me that in the early 1920's, the end slice of a loaf of French bread was the "knob." It was considered a treat and was much vied for. It was customary to remove the soft interior and to pour Eagle Brand milk into the crust.

knobcone pine n [See quot 1911]

A **pine** (here: *Pinus attenuata*) native to the Pacific coast.

1884 Sargent *Forests of N. Amer.* 196, Knob-cone Pine. . . Valley of the Mackenzie River, Oregon, south along the western slope of the Cascade and Sierra Nevada mountains, and in the California Coast ranges. **1897** Sudworth *Arborescent Flora* 25 **CA, ID, OR,** *Pinus attenuata*. . . Knobcone Pine. **1911** Jepson *Flora CA* 19, *Knob-cone Pine.* . . Scales moderately thickened at tip, except on the outside towards the base where they are raised into conspicuous rounded or pointed knobs. **1947** Peattie *Sierra Nevada* 141, The knobcone pine. . . Clusters of cones . . surround its main stem, usually remaining on the tree, still closed, until a fire forces them open and gives their seeds a chance in the cleared but ashy soil. **1967–69** *DARE* (Qu. T17, *. . Kinds of pine trees;* not asked in early QRs) Infs **CA**7, 97, 150, Knobcone (pine). **1980** Little *Audubon Guide N. Amer. Trees W. Region* 271, *Knobcone Pine.* . . Since the cones may become imbedded within the wood of the expanding trunk, this species has been called "the tree that swallows its cones."

knob grass n

1 also *knobroot, knobweed:* A **horse balm** (here: *Collinsonia canadensis*). Cf **knotroot 1**

1876 Hobbs *Bot. Hdbk.* 61, Knob grass, . . Knob root, Collinsonia Canadensis. **1900** Lyons *Plant Names* 111, *C[ollinsonia] Canadensis.* . . Knob-root, Knob-grass, Knob-weed. **1930** Sievers *Amer. Med. Plants* 23, Citronella horsebalm—*Collinsonia canadensis.* . . Knob-root, knob grass, knobweed. . . The root . . is . . woody, the upper side rough, knotty, and irregularly branched. **1971** Krochmal *Appalachia Med. Plants* 100, *Collinsonia canadensis* . . knob grass, knobroot. **1974** (1977) Coon *Useful Plants* 156, *Collinsonia canadensis* . . knob-grass.

2 A **knotgrass 1** (here: *Polygonum aviculare*).

1892 (1974) Millspaugh *Amer. Med. Plants* 141-2, The fruit of the Knob Grass (*P[olygonum] aviculare . .)* is said to be emetic and cathartic.

knob-rabbit n [knob 1]

1968 *DARE* (Qu. HH18, *Very insignificant or low-grade people*) Inf **VA**5, Knob-rabbits—people who live on the foothills of the mountains. They are not considered mountaineers because they don't have the bloodlines. [FW: Inf used in conv]

knobroot, knobweed See knob grass 1

knock v

1 also with *out, up:* To hit (a baseball, usu a fly ball)—usu used in combs and phrr referring to an informal bat-and-ball game. **scattered exc N Cent, Upper MW** See Map Cf **flies and grounders, knocker 7c**

1866 in 1989 Dickson *Dickson Baseball Dict.* 236, *Knock.* [Dickson: To hit the ball. 1st [use] 1866. (Constitution and By-Laws of the Olympic Base Ball Club, Philadelphia.)] **1927** *AmSp* 2.255 [Baseball slang], When Babe Ruth was said to "knock the orange over the fence for a home run" every fan understood that the "orange" was the ball. **1942** Berrey–Van den Bark *Amer. Slang* 677.25, [Baseball:] *Knock a fly. . . to knock an easy fly . . to knock a "pop fly"* with the handle of a bat. *Ibid* 677.26, *Knock a foul. Ibid* 677.27, *Knock a grounder.* **1954** *PA Dutchman* 15 Feb 13/1 (Mathews Coll.) (as of c1860), *Knock-Out*— Knock-out ball was knocking or striking the ball with a bat. The bat was made of pine wood, and in dimensions was about 2½ feet long, 4 inches broad and 1 inch thick, with a handle at one end nicely rounded. Any number could play at this game. One player would strike the ball as far and high as he could, and the out-player who caught it was entitled to be the striker until his ball was caught. **1965–70** *DARE* (Qu. EE11, *Bat-and-ball games for just a few players [when there aren't enough for a regular game]*) Infs **CO**3, 7, **KY**50, **LA**15, 40, Knocking up flies; **GA**1, Knock-ups; **ME**19, No real name, knocking up flies; **MO**3, Knock-up—flies and grounders type; **MT**1, Knock-up and roll-in; **NJ**1, Knock up flies; **MD**38, Knock-up and catch; **PA**35, Knocking up—one hits for the others to catch; **SC**3, Knocking (up) flies—hit a fly to the fielders—whoever catches it knocks (up) flies to the others; **VA**1, Knock-up and catch-out; **CA**133, **MO**27, **VA**18, Knocking flies; **KY**23, Knock fly balls; **MA**40, Knocking flies—same as scrub; **OK**1, They just knock flies, bat flies; **OR**1A, Knocking flies—not a name; **GA**72B, Knocking out flies; **NY**82, **TN**43, Knock-out; **WY**4, Knock out flies. **1966** *DARE* Tape **AL**4, This man would pitch and if he knocked this ball or if he ducked the ball and crossed you—threw it in front of you—you were out. **1986** Pederson *LAGS Concordance,* 1 inf, **cnAR,** Knock skinners = flies and skinners; baseball game. **1992** *DARE* File **TX** (as of 1950s), When I was a kid we would "knock some flies." We would say, "Let's go knock some flies" or "Wanna go knock some flies?" I don't think we had a name that would serve as the complement of the verb *play.* We had variants of rules that we would use depending on how many of us there were.

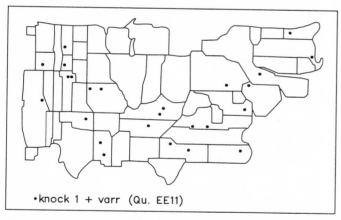

•knock 1 + varr (Qu. EE11)

2 also with *it (off):* To fight with the fists; hence n *knocker.* **esp Sth** See Map Cf **knock-fight**

1913 [see **knock-fight**]. **1923** in 1952 Mathes *Tall Tales* 8 **sAp-**

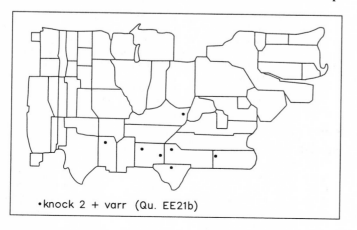

•knock 2 + varr (Qu. EE21b)

palachians, Those who remembered Wesley Shelton as a young man told thrilling tales of his prowess in the arts that consititute the pentathlon of the mountain youth—running, lifting, wrestling, boxing ("knocking") and swimming. **1966–69** *DARE* (Qu. EE21b, *When boys were fighting very actively . . "For a while those fellows really _____."*) Inf **AL**3, Knocking it; **AL**32, Knocked it off; **FL**6, Were knocking it off; **GA**75, **LA**12, Were knocking; **KY**44, Knocked it; **SC**32, Was knocking. **1986** Pederson *LAGS Concordance (Fight)* 1 inf, **csAL,** Knock.

3 fig; in var phrr referring to snoring: See quots.

1966–70 *DARE* (Qu. X45, . . *Joking expressions . . about snoring*) Infs **MN**42, **MO**35, **SC**11, **VA**74, Knocking it (or her, them) off; **NC**61, Knocking the roof in; knocking shingles.

4 To dance (a particular dance step); to play (a particular tune); hence vbl n *knocking it* playing an instrument in a strongly rhythmic style.

1972 Jones–Hawes *Step it Down* 55 **eGA,** "Jim Crow" thus developed from a dance imitating the motions of birds and hunters, and quite possibly magical in nature, into a commercial caricature. . . The [Sea] Islanders, however, clearly regard this as a pleasurable dance, probably about birds, and "knock Jim Crow" with enthusiasm and alacrity. **1981** Howell *Surv. Folklife* 199, Nineteenth-century methods of playing the banjo were quite different and have recently gained renewed interest among fans of old-time music. The old minstrel show "frailing" or "clawhammer" style called "knocking it" by Big South Fork musicians was probably derived from the Afro-American banjo tradition. **1986** Pederson *LAGS Concordance,* 1 inf, **cwFL,** Some of them could sure knock "Sugar in the Gourd" on them things—of people playing Jew's harps.

knockaway See **anaqua**

knock down v phr

1 To introduce (someone). **now chiefly Sth, S Midl** See Map *somewhat old-fash* Cf **knockdown** n

1897 Barrère–Leland *Slang* 1.497, *Knock one down, to* (American society), to introduce. "Knock me down to that daisy," *i.e.,* "Introduce me to that fine girl." **1908** *DN* 3.327 **eAL, wGA,** *Knock-down. . .* To introduce. "I'll knock you down to that girl." Also as noun. **1916** *DN* 4.325 **KS, MA,** *Knock down. . .* To introduce (one person to another). Also Pa. as early as 1890, both *v.* and *n.* (an introduction). "I was knocked down to about a dozen girls at the dance." **1946** *PADS* 6.19 **ceNC** (as of 1900–10), *Knock down to. . .* To introduce one person to another. **1950** *WELS* **WI** (*When you ask to be introduced:* "I'd like to _____ John Smith.") 1 Inf, I'd like to get knocked down to John Smith; 1 Inf, Knock down. **1965–70** *DARE* (Qu. II4, *When people . . ask to be introduced to someone—for example:* "I'd like to _____ John Smith.") Infs **TN**1, 12, **TX**43, Be knocked down to; **TN**13, **TX**40, 42, Get knocked down to; **GA**7, 19, How about knocking me down to (So-and-so); **OH**95, **SC**34, Knock me down to (this chap); **AR**41, Knock me down; **MO**39, They'd usually be knocked down; So-and-so knocked me down to So-and-so; **SC**3, Be knocked down to—don't say it much anymore, common in her childhood; **SC**31, Be knocked down to [FW sugg]—Inf hasn't heard it in a long time; **SC**19, Knock me down to that gal there [laughter]; **TX**1, I'd like for you to knock me down to So-and-so; **TX**18, Be knock-downed to. [15 of 17 Infs old] **1966** *DARE* FW Addit **MS**1, "How about knocking one down to her?"— used when one wishes to be introduced to someone else. **1986** Pederson *LAGS Concordance,* 1 inf, **neTN,** Knock you down—introduce you; **cnGA,** Knock you down—introduce you, strictly slang.

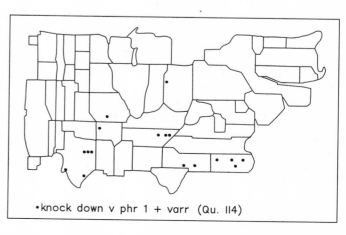

•knock down v phr 1 + varr (Qu. II4)

2 To plow (land) so as to turn under any residual plant matter or raised rows.

1946 *PADS* 6.19 **ceNC** (as of 1900–10), *Knock down ground. . . To plow down (flatten out) last year's rows. The plowing is down [sic] with two furrows.* **1967** *DARE* Tape **HI**2, *They no longer let the field lie fallow, so they'd knock down a field which had finished fruiting and would chop up the . . plant material into small pieces and turn this under, plow this under. . . This is what they do now.*

knockdown n *somewhat old-fash* Cf **knock down** v phr **1**
An introduction.

1865 Byrn *Advent. Fudge Fumble* 61, *I asked the young man if he would go down some night and give me a "knock down" to the family, and Miss Kate, more especially.* **1897** *KS Univ. Qrly.* (ser B) 6.54 **KS**, *Knock-down . . an introduction.* **1905** *DN* 3.12 **cCT. 1907** *DN* 3.214 **nwAR. 1908** [see **knock down** v phr **1**]. **1912** *DN* 3.580 **wIN**, *Have you had a knock-down to that girl?* **1916** [see **knock down** v phr **1**]. **1950** *WELS* **WI** (*When you ask to be introduced: "I'd like to _____ John Smith." Someone introduces you: "_____ John Smith.")* 2 Infs, *Get a knockdown to;* 2 Infs, *Give me (or her) a knockdown (to);* 1 Inf, *A knockdown;* 1 Inf, *Have a knockdown to;* 1 Inf, *Will you give me a knockdown to him?* 1 Inf, *I got a knockdown to.* **1960** Criswell *Resp. to PADS 20* **Ozarks**, *"Say, give me a knockdown to that purty girl over there." Once very common. May not now be current. Slang.* **1965–70** *DARE* (Qu. II4, *When people . . ask to be introduced to someone—for example: "I'd like to _____ John Smith.")* 35 Infs, *scattered,* (Get *or* have a) knockdown to; **CO**17, 27, Get a knockdown to—heard; **CT**37, **NY**231, **SC**7, **TX**3, 4, Get a knockdown to—old-fashioned; **SC**19, 21, 24, 26, 34, **TN**44, Get a knockdown to [FW sugg]; **MI**93, Have you give me a knockdown to; **NM**4, Give me a knockdown to—was used a lot years ago, but not used anymore; **NY**88, A knockdown to—old-fashioned, slang; **NY**213, Get a knockdown to—with a girl; **OH**56, Get a knockdown with; **OH**95, Get a knockdown to—old-fashioned; knock me down to this chap; **PA**130, Get a knockdown to [laughter]; **PA**175, Have a knockdown—obsolete; **WY**2, Get a knockdown to [FW: Inf used in conv]; [**ID**4, Heard a man in town say "I'd like to have a knock-me-down with So-and-so"]. [42 of 57 Infs old] **1986** Pederson *LAGS Concordance* **ne,ceTN**, 3 infs, Give you a knockdown—introduce you; 1 inf, He gave me a knockdown to so-and-so—introduced.

knocked in adj phr
1966 *PADS* 46.27 **cnAR** (as of 1952), *Knocked in. . . Infirm with age.—"Old man Smith's gettin' pretty knocked in, ain't he?"*

knocker n

1 usu in combs, esp *wood-knocker:* A **woodpecker** such as the **hairy woodpecker.**

1929 *Wilson Bulletin* 29.2.81, *Dryobates villosus. . . Wood-knocker,* Hickman, Ky. **1967–70** *DARE* (Qu. Q17, . . *Kinds of woodpeckers*) Inf **IN**19, Red-headed knocker; (Qu. Q18, *Joking names and nicknames for woodpeckers*) Infs **GA**72, **LA**40, **MI**67, **OH**56, Wood-knocker; **NY**198, Knocker; **NY**183, **VA**57, Tree-knocker. **1986** Pederson *LAGS Concordance (Woodpecker)* 1 inf, nwFL, Wood knocker—has heard, not often; 1 inf, nwMS, They call it [=ivory-billed bird] wood knocker; 1 inf, ceTX, Wood knocker; 1 inf, swGA, Hammer knocker.

2 also *hammer knocker:* A rustic; someone considered uncouth or of low quality. Cf **appleknocker 3, clodknocker 1**

1967 Will *Dredgeman* 31 **FL**, *There ain't no tellin' what them crazy knockers might have done to him.* **1986** Pederson *LAGS Concordance (Poor whites—white man's terms)* 1 inf, nwFL, A lazy hammer knocker.

3 also *hammer knocker:* A child; see quots.

1954 *PADS* 21.31 **SC**, *Knocker. . . A small boy. Usually a little knocker. Sometimes depreciatory.* **1967** *DARE* (Qu. Z12, *Nicknames and joking words meaning 'a small child': "He's a healthy little _____."*) Inf **SC**40, Knocker. **1986** Pederson *LAGS Concordance,* 1 inf, cwFL, Hammer knockers—calls her children, an endearment.

4 A large marble. Cf **clodknocker 3**

1950 *WELS* (*Marbles . . large ones*) 1 Inf, **WI**, Knockers. **1968** *DARE* (Qu. EE6a, . . *Different kinds of marbles—the big one that's used to knock others out of the ring*) Inf **NY**81, Knocker.

5 A children's game; see quot.

1968 *DARE* (Qu. EE18, *Games in which the players set up a stone, a tin can, or something similar, and then try to knock it down*) Inf **IA**22, Knocker—set up brickbats and knocked them off with brickbats.

6 See **knock 2.**

7 in var combs:

a usu in comb *head knocker;* also *top knocker:* Someone in a position of authority. **Sth, S Midl**

[**1942** Berrey–Van den Bark *Amer. Slang* 432.2, *Capable person; expert. . . knocker.*] **1953** Brewer *Word Brazos* 29 **eTX** [Black], *One Sunday de haid-knocker of de Baptist convention comed to visit Elduh Freeman's chu'ch to spy on 'im an' see how he feedin' de sheep in his flock.* **1967–70** *DARE* (Qu. HH17, *A person who tries to appear important, or who tries to lay down the law in his community: "He'd like to be the _____ around here."*) Infs **AL**8, **GA**53, **VA**86, Head knocker; **GA**89, Top knocker; (Qu. HH43a, *The top person in charge of a group of workmen*) Inf **KY**94, Head knocker. **1967** *DARE* Tape **AR**52, *I have a son, by the way, that's one of the head knockers* [ˌhɛd ˈnɑkɚz] *at Firestone.* **1967** *DARE* FW Addit **cnLA**, *The head knocker* [ˌhɛd ˈnɑkɚ]—top person in charge of a group (applied to a nurse in charge of a nursing home).

b *apple knocker, dumpling ~:* The throat; the Adam's apple. Cf **goozle** n **1**

1986 Pederson *LAGS Concordance (Neck; throat)* 1 inf, neTN, Apple knocker—throat, swallow, goozle; 1 inf, seGA, Dumpling knocker—same as goozle?

c *one-knocker, two-knockers:* An informal type of baseball; see quot. [Prob **knock** v **1**] **DC**

1966–70 *DARE* (Qu. EE11, *Bat-and-ball games for just a few players [when there aren't enough for a regular game]*) Infs **DC**2, 11, One-knocker; **DC**8, Two-knockers—baseball with one base; batter may get "home run"—to base and back; if stuck on base, shouts "two-knockers" and may then be brought home by next batter if he makes a hit; rotation of position; "outs" go in field and work up; **DC**12, One-knocker, two-knockers.

knocker-bill n Cf **bill** n[1] **2**
The nose.

1969 *DARE* (Qu. X14, *Joking words for the nose*) Inf **KY**40, Knocker-bill [laughter].

knock-fight n [*knock* to strike; cf **knock** v **2**]
A fistfight.

1913 Kephart *Highlanders* 141 **sAppalachians**, *He was what a mountaineer described to me as "a practiced knocker." This phrase . . was interpreted to me as denoting "a master hand in a knock-fight." Pugilism, as distinguished from shooting or stabbing, was an unknown art in the mountains until Jack introduced it.* **1974** Fink *Mountain Speech* 14 **wNC, eTN**, *Knock-fight . . fist fight. "Them boys had a big knock-fight."* **1976** Garber *Mountain-ese* 50 **sAppalachians**, *Knock-fight . . fist brawl—They had a real knock-fight at the ballgame Saturday night.*

knock galley-west See **galley-west**

knocking it See **knock 4**

knocking on wood n
=**wood tag.**

1969 *DARE* (Qu. EE33, . . *Outdoor games . . that children play*) Inf **KY**6, War-ball, bull-pen, needle's eye, knocking on wood. **1969** *DARE* Tape **KY**6, [FW:] *You also talked about a game that was called something like knockin' on wood.* [Inf:] *Oh, yeah, they had a game that they would . . run from one place to the other, you know, and if they caught you before you got there—caught you off of wood—why, you was "it," you had to be the runner then.*

knock in the head with a churn dasher v phr
To stunt (a calf) by depriving it of milk.

1941 Dobie *Longhorns* 169, *It was a custom among ranchers to allow poor squatters to catch up range cows, provided the borrowers would not "knock the calf in the head with a churn dasher"—would leave it a fair share of milk.* **a1975** Lunsford *It Used to Be* 170 **sAppalachians**, *The expression "knocked in the head with a churn dasher" is used a good deal in speaking of a calf that has been weaned too early because the family needed the milk. . . The calf never did grow.*

knock it (off) See **knock 2**

knock-knock n

1 =**heavy, heavy, what hangs over.**

1968 *DARE* (Qu. EE33, . . *Outdoor games . . that children play*) Inf **IL**29, Knock-knock—players sit in circle, one player stomps on the floor and holds his hand over someone's head and says "heavy, heavy hangs over thy head." Then the person he stands behind must guess what he has in his hand. If he fails to guess, he has to pay a penalty.

2 pl: =**water chinquapin.** [Perh from the rattling seed pod]

1941 *Torreya* 41.47, *Nelumbo lutea.* . . Knock-knocks, Oakley, S.C.

knock Molly n Cf old Molly

=**old-squaw.**

1911 *Forest & Stream* 7.453 **NC,** Long-tailed Duck.—Knock Molly. Cape Hatteras and nearby waters of Pamlico Sound. **1923** U.S. Dept. Ag. *Misc. Circular* 13.24 **NC,** Old-squaw. . . *Vernacular Names.* . . *In local use.* . . Knock-molly.

knock one off the Christmas tree See Christmas tree 4

knock out v phr See knock 1

knockout n

1 A marble game; see quots.

1958 *PADS* 29.35 **WI,** *Knockout.* . . A marble game in which marbles are thrown against a wall to bounce back and hit others placed on the ground. **1967–70** *DARE* (Qu. EE7, . . *Kinds of marble games*) Inf **GA**93, Knockout; **MN**2, Knockout—knock marbles out of ring.

2 A children's game; see quot.

1969 *DARE* (Qu. EE18, *Games in which the players set up a stone, a tin can, or something similar, and then try to knock it down*) Inf **NC**60, Knockout.

knocks-kneed adj

Knock-kneed.

1967 *DARE* (Qu. X37, . . *Words* . . *to describe people's legs if they're noticeably bent, or uneven, or not right*) Inf **TN**24, Knocks-kneed.

knock the camas out See camas 3

knock the can n For varr see quots Cf kick the can

Any of several children's games; see quots.

1954 *Harder Coll.* **cwTN,** *Knock over the can.* . . Same as *kick over the can.* **1968–70** *DARE* (Qu. EE13a, *Games in which every player hides except one, and that one must try to find the others*) Inf **GA**86, Knocking the tin can—like hiding but instead of counting one would kick the tin can and bring it back; (Qu. EE18, *Games in which the players set up a stone, a tin can, or something similar, and then try to knock it down*) Inf **MD**42, Knocking the can off; **TN**59, Knock the can; (Qu. EE33, . . *Outdoor games . . that children play*) Inf **KY**54, Knocking the tin can; **VA**35, Knock the can [is the same as] kick the can. [**1986** Pederson *LAGS Concordance* (Tin-can games) 1 inf, **swTN,** Knocking a can with a stick.]

knock up See knock 1

knockwurst See knackwurst

knofli See kneffli

knoll n Usu |no(ʊ)l|; for varr see A below Also sp (k)nole, knowl(e); pronc-sp know (cf Pronc Intro 3.II.27) [SND know "Sc. form of Eng. knoll"]

A Forms.

1910 Univ. NC *Mag.* 40.3.8 **Hatteras Is. NC,** Know (knoll). *Ibid* 9, In the broadest part of the island near Buxton there are *knows* of sand covered with tall pines. **1939** *LANE* Map 38 (Knoll), [Proncs of the type [noʊl, nowl, nol] predominate throughout **NEng;** 9 infs, **scattered,** proncs of the type [noʊl], [nowl, nɔol]; 3 infs, proncs of the type [nʌʊl, nɐl];] 1 inf, **sVT,** [nɒˑl]; 1 inf, **RI,** Some say [nɒl].

B Sense.

A small, rounded hill. **widespread, but somewhat less freq Sth Cf knob 1**

1656 *Boston Rec.* 130 *(DAE),* Itt is ordered that the gallowes shall bee removed to the next knole of land. **1691** in 1889 *Plymouth MA Records* 203, Where as A knowle of land was . . graunted to William Harlow. **1788** (1925) Washington *Diaries* 3.406, Were taking out dung to spread on the poor knowls in this field. **1834** Davis *Letters Downing* 21 **NY,** Jest as we got on the nole on tother side the brook, we come in sight of Downingville. **1859** [see **knob 1**]. **1932** *DN* 6.230 **West,** Knoll. This word is heard now and then, apparently with no local limitation, as in the East. **1942** ME Univ. *Studies* 57.38 [Pulpwood terms] **nwME** (as of 1935–40), It may be necessary [in road construction] to grub out stumps or knolls which are too high, and conversely it may be necessary to fill in depressions between knolls with material removed. **1950** *WELS* (*A small, rounded hill*) 25 Infs, **WI,** Knoll.

1965–70 *DARE* (Qu. C17, . . *A small, rounded hill*) 417 Infs, **widespread, but somewhat less freq Sth,** Knoll; **IN**3, A knob's higher than a knoll; **IN**65, Knob—higher [than a knoll], knoll can be part of a knob; **IN**72, Knob—bigger than knoll; **KY**84, Big knoll; little knoll; **MI**122, Knob [or] knoll—almost ten feet high; **MO**39, Knob, knoll—thirty feet high is the upper limit; **NM**1, Knob [or] knoll—up to 100 feet high, usually flat on top; **NY**75, Gravel knoll; **NY**92, Cradle knoll; **PA**205, Knoll—small knob; **SC**32, Knob—about same size as knoll; **TN**11, Knoll—just a little rise; (Qu. C3, *A place in a swift stream where the surface of the water is broken*) Inf **OK**18, Knoll; sand knoll—where water is shallow; (Qu. C13) Infs **GA**36, **TN**52, Knoll; **MS**11, Peninsula; knoll of land; (Qu. MM5, *When you're pointing out a house that's not far away: "The house is over _____."*) Inf **NY**75, Just over the knoll; **CT**22, The knoll. **1966–69** *DARE* Tape **MI**20, With their very huge wheels at least eight, maybe ten, feet high . . why, small knolls and so forth, they'd roll over those; **VT**15, And it's the nature of a fox to climb up on a knoll to look the situation over. **1973** Allen *LAUM* 1.237 **IA, MN, ND** (as of c1950), (Butte). . . variation in the question may have caused the eliciting of *hill, knoll, cliff,* and *bluff* as well as the likely *butte.* *Ibid,* Knoll [5 infs].

knot n[1]

1 The excrescence caused by a fungus of the genus *Gymnosporangium;* a **cedar apple.**

1880 Farlow *Gymnosporangia* 14, The common "cedar apple" of the Atlantic States. . . is very abundant along the seaboard. . . The knots together with the sporiferous masses, often measure three inches across when swollen. *Ibid* 38, *Gymnosporangium macropus* . . in a dry condition showing the knot or cedar-apple. **1932** Felt–Rankin *Insects & Diseases Trees* 276, Abrupt swellings of the stems of junipers are often caused by species of Gymnosporangium. . . Small knots . . as large as 1 inch in diameter and 1½ inches long are formed on the small branches. *Ibid,* In addition to cedar-apples and . . knots, several rust-fungi cause long spindle-shaped swellings of the branches of juniper.

2 A protuberance or raised area on the body, esp:

a A lump raised by a blow, esp one on the head; hence v *knot* to cause such a lump. **widespread, but less freq Nth** See Map Cf **knob 2** See also **bump knot, hump knot, pumpknot, punk knot**

1942 Hurston *Dust Tracks* 133 **FL** [Black], This was not just another escapade which Mama would knot his head for in private and smooth out publicly. **1945** FWP *Lay My Burden Down* 125 **LA** [Black], I mind the time her husband, Uncle Jim, git mad and hit her over the head with the poker. A big knot raise up on Aunt Rachel's head. **c1950** Halpert *Coll.* 36 **wKY, nwTN,** The blow will raise a knot on your arm. **1963** Edwards *Gravel* 20 **eTN,** If you don't shut up you're gonna have a purty knot on your head. **1965–70** *DARE* (Qu. X60, . . *A lump that comes up on your head when you get a sharp blow or knock;* not asked in early QRs) 278 Infs, **widespread, but less freq Nth,** Knot; **NC**79, Knot on the head. **1985** *Commercial Appeal* (Memphis TN) 19 Mar np **KY,** I'll knock a knot on your head 'til you can't get your shirt off.

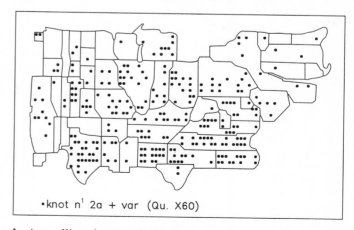

•knot n[1] 2a + var (Qu. X60)

b A swelling, lump; a boil.

1965–70 *DARE* (Qu. BB30, . . *A hard, painful swelling [often on a finger] that seems to come from deep under the skin*) Infs **CA**178, **FL**28, **GA**17, 54, 72, **IL**140, **MD**9, **NE**10, **NC**82, **OH**2, Knot; (Qu. BB33b, . . *A swelling under the skin—if it is very big or serious*) Infs **IL**4, **PA**247, Knot. **1982** Heat Moon *Blue Highways* 136 **TX,** He . . pointed to a tiny lump. "Got nipped there last year by a far [=fire] ant. If you don't pick the poison out, it leaves a knot for two or three years." **1986** Pederson *LAGS Concordance*, 1 inf, **neTN**, My hands broke out with little knots—of illness; *(Boil)* 1 inf, **cwAL**, A knot—rising caused by tick; 1 inf, **cwGA**, A knot on your arm. **1990** Cavender *Folk Med. Lexicon* 26 **sAppalachians**, *Knot*—can refer to a tumor, lump, or tightened muscle.

3 also *muscle knot:* The head; the face. **chiefly Sth, Midl, Cent** See Map Cf **knothead 1, topknot**

[**1942** Berrey–Van den Bark *Amer. Slang* 121.56, *Head . . . knot in the spinal cord.*] **1950** *WELS (Joking names for a person's head)* 1 Inf, **cwWI**, Muscle knot. **1954** *Harder Coll.* **cwTN**, *Knot . . .* head. **c1960** *Wilson Coll.* **csKY**, *Knot*—Humorous word for the head. **1965–70** *DARE* (Qu. X28, *Joking words . . for a person's head*) 34 Infs, **esp Sth, Midl, Cent**, Knot; [**AR40**, Knot on the end of the backbone;] (Qu. X29, *Joking or uncomplimentary words for a person's face*) Infs **GA**44, 54, **KS**2, Knot.

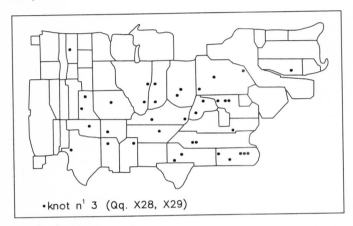

•knot n[1] 3 (Qq. X28, X29)

4 =**knothead 2.**

1935 Davis *Honey* 78 **OR**, Even the possession of a deadly weapon wasn't enough to overcome his deep-set timidity of that thick-headed old knot whose very lack of intelligence and sensitiveness made him impossible to be argued with or scared.

5 in phr *hit a knot* and varr: To make a noise characteristic of interrupted snoring. [In ref to a sawyer's hitting a knot while sawing a log] Cf **saw wood**

1965–70 *DARE* (Qu. X45, *. . Joking expressions . . about snoring*) Inf **MD**9, Cut a knot; **CO**20, **MN**34, Sawing logs (*or cutting trees*) and hit a knot; **CA**4, Hit a snag or knot; **CA**196, He really hit a knot; **MI**67, Hit a knot; **NJ**56, Strike a knot—if snoring is interrupted; **MO**11, You struck a knot; sounds like a dull saw in pine knots.

6 A small or insignificant fruit or vegetable; hence adj *knotty* tiny.

1966–69 *DARE* (Qu. LL2, *. . Too small to be worth much: "I don't want that little _____ potato."*) Infs **GA**80, **KY**19, Knot; **AR**51, Knot—it ain't worth a penny; **NC**7, Dinky, knotty; **SC**32, Dinky [FW sugg], knotty [FW: Inf unsure]; **TN**1, Tiny, knotty—of a potato. **1986** Pederson *LAGS Concordance*, 1 inf, **cwLA**, Knots—very small melon, ripe; 1 inf, **cwFL**, Knots—small watermelons; 1 inf, **ceMS**, Knot—a little melon; 1 inf, **csAL**, Knots—last of tomatoes, dying out.

7 in adv phr *on the knot:* Exactly.

1983 *MJLF* 9.1.49 **ceKY** (as of 1956), *On the knot . . on the dot,* exactly.

knot n[2]

Std: a shorebird (*Calidris canutus*). Also called **beach quail, ~ robin, blue plover, brownbird 1, grayback 1a, gray plover 3, ~ snipe 2, horsefoot snipe 2, maybird 3, redbreast, red-breasted robin, ~ sandpiper, ~ snipe, redbreast plover, red sandpiper, robin, robin-breast, robin plover, ~ snipe, silverback, silver plover, stib, white robin snipe, whiting**

knot v

1 To remove knots or limbs from a log; hence vbl n *knotting;* n *knotter* one who trims knots and limbs. Cf **limb v 1**

1905 U.S. Forest Serv. *Bulletin* 61.41, *Limber . . .* One who cuts the limbs from felled trees. (Gen[eral use]) Syn[onym]: knotter (P[acific] C[oast] F[orest]). **1920** *DN* 5.82 **NW**, *Knotter.* A knot sawyer. Sawmill

term. **1930** *DN* 6.88 **cWV**, *Log knotter,* a trimmer of branches. **1958** McCulloch *Woods Words* 102 **Pacific NW**, *Knot*—To knock the knots or limbs off pine logs. *Ibid, Knotter*—A knot bumper. **1969** Sorden *Lumberjack Lingo* 67 **NEng, Gt Lakes**, *Knotting*—Smoothing the branch stubs close to the trunk of a fallen tree.

2 See **knot n[1] 2a.**

knot bindweed n Also *bind knotweed* [From the swollen nodes of the stem, which resemble knots; cf **knotweed 1**]

=**black bindweed.**

1822 Eaton *Botany* 402, *[Polygonum] convolvulus . . .* bind knotweed. *. . Stem twining.* **1847** Wood *Class-Book* 476, *P[olygonum] convolvulus. Knot Bindweed. . . .* A common climbing species, in fields and waste grounds. **1914** Georgia *Manual Weeds* 104, *Polygonum Convolvulus . . .* Knot Bindweed. *. .* Not very troublesome in ground requiring close tillage, but a special nuisance in grain fields. **1935** (1943) Muenscher *Weeds* 192, *Polygonum Convolvulus. . .* Knot bindweed. **1973** Hitchcock–Cronquist *Flora Pacific NW* 85, *Knot . . bindweed . . P. convolvulus.*

knot bumper n Cf **knot v 1**, *limber* (at **limb v 1**)

In logging: one who removes knots and limbs from logs.

1905 U.S. Forest Serv. *Bulletin* 61.41 **Appalachians** [Logging terms], *Limber. . .* One who cuts the limbs from felled trees. *. . .* knot bumper. **1950** *Western Folkl.* 9.381 **neCA** [Lumberjack language], *Knot bumper.* An ax man who chops limbs and knots off logs. **1956** Sorden–Ebert *Logger's Words* 20 **Gt Lakes**, *Knot-bumper,* A man who works on the landing and unhooks chokers, and chops off limbs missed by the buckers. Same as knotter, limber, or tailing down. **1958** McCulloch *Woods Words* 102 **Pacific NW**, *Knot bumper*—In the pine country, a man who knocks the knots off logs before they are loaded on truck or car at the landing. **1971** Kline *Pitch Pine* 143 (as of c1920), An axe man to remove the limbs . . was frequently called a "Knot bumper."

knotgrass n

1 =**knotweed 1**, usu *Polygonum aviculare.* [See quot 1840; *OED* 1538 →] For other names of *P. aviculare* see **carpetweed 3, crabgrass 3, dogtail 2, door grass, dooryard knotweed, iron grass 1, knob grass 1, matgrass 3, pinkweed, sidewalk weed, wire grass, yard grass**

1769 in 1909 Earle *Child Life* 8 **CT**, Give it several times a Day ye following Syrup made of Comfry, Hartshorn, Red Roses, Hog-brake roots, knot-grass, petty-moral roots, sweeten ye Syrup with Melosses. **1784** in 1785 Amer. Acad. Arts & Sci. *Memoirs* 1.440, *Polygonum. . .* Knotgrass. Blossoms reddish white. Common by the road sides. June-September. **1814** Bigelow *Florula Bostoniensis* 93, *Knot grass. . .* A hardy weed growing every where. **1840** MA Zool. & Bot. Surv. *Herb. Plants & Quadrupeds* 101, *P[olygonum] aviculare. . .* Although unlike the grasses, yet, because its stem is jointed or knotted, and it is eaten by cattle, it is called Knotgrass. **1860** Holmes *Professor* 206 **MA**, The wiry, jointed stems of that iron creeping plant which we call "knotgrass," *. .* loves its life so dearly that it is next to impossible to murder it with a hoe, as it clings to the cracks of the pavement. **1891** Jesup *Plants Hanover NH* 35, *P[olygonum] aviculare. . .* (Knotgrass.) Roadsides, dooryards, etc. Common. **1912** Blatchley *IN Weed Book* 67, *Polygonum aviculare. . .* Knot-grass. *. .* Very common, forming mats of spreading, wiry, jointed stems in yards and along pathways and roadsides where the ground is much trodden. *. .* The erect knot-grass (*P. erectum . .*) is often also found with the common form. **1937** U.S. Forest Serv. *Range Plant Hdbk.* W154, Knotweeds, also known as doorweeds and knotgrasses, compose a fairly large and widely distributed genus. *. . .* The generic name *Polygonum* is from the Greek *. . ,* referring to the swollen stem joints characteristic of many species. This knotted appearance of the stem is also emphasized in the common name. **1974** (1977) Coon *Useful Plants* 212, *Polygonum aviculare*—Knot-grass. *. .* This is just one of a number of *Polygonums* which grow very widely and are persistent weeds.

2 =**quack grass.**

1843 (1844) Johnson *Farmer's Encycl.* 360, *Couch . . Grass. . .* Sometimes called dog-grass and knot-grass. **1876** Hobbs *Bot. Hdbk.* 45, *Grass, Knot, . . Triticum repens* [=*Agropyron repens*]. **1910** Graves *Flowering Plants* 79 **CT**, *Agropyron repens. . .* Knot Grass. *. .* A bad weed, very troublesome in cultivated ground.

3 A **bullgrass 1** (here: *Paspalum distichum*). **West** Cf **joint grass 1**

1901 Jepson *Flora CA* 30, *P[aspalum] distichum . . Knot-grass. . .*

Somewhat resembling Bermuda-grass. **1950** Hitchcock–Chase *Manual Grasses* 603, *Knot-grass.* . . Ditches and wet, rarely brackish places. **1961** Thomas *Flora Santa Cruz* 102 **cwCA**, *P. distichum.* . . Knot Grass. . . Often growing in water to about 1½ feet deep. **1970** Correll *Plants TX* 162, *Paspalum distichum.* . . *Knotgrass.* . . Frequent in e., s.e. and n.-cen. Tex. **1973** Hitchcock–Cronquist *Flora Pacific NW* 654, Knotgrass. . . Always where the soil is moist at least part of the season.

knothead n

1 The head. Cf **knot** n[1] **3**

c1960 *Wilson Coll.* **csKY**, *Knothead.* . . Joking name for head. **1965–70** *DARE* (Qu. X28, *Joking words . . for a person's head*) 15 Infs, **scattered**, Knothead. [12 of 15 Infs old, 12 male]

2 A stupid, obstinate, or intractable person or animal; hence adj *knotheaded* unreasoning, contrary, stubborn.

1920 *DN* 5.82 **NW**, *Knot head.* A bucking horse. **1929** *AmSp* 5.57 **NE** [Cattle country talk], "Green riders" and "rookies" are the newly enlisted but uninitiated "ranch hands." If these prospective "he-men" never attain skill in their riding and work, they are "knotheads." **1935** Sandoz *Jules* 410 **NE** (as of 1880–1930), Unable to turn the knot-head, Jule, hazing for his brother, pulled the rider from his horse. **1940** *AmSp* 15.447 **eTN**, *Knot head.* Low intelligence. 'Bob was a knot head when he went to school.' **1950** Reeves *Man from SD* 104, Them *ewes* was worth two strings apiece, I could shear two good sheep easy in the time it took me to skin one of them knotheads. **1965–70** *DARE* (Qu. HH3, *A dull and stupid person*) 10 Infs, **scattered**, Knothead; **CO34**, Knothead—most common; (Qu. K44, *A bony or poor-looking horse*) Inf **IL87**, Knotheads [laughter]; (Qu. K50, *Joking nicknames for mules*) Inf **IN46**, Knothead; (Qu. X28) Inf **AR18**, Knothead—just uncomplimentary term; **CT30**, Knothead—stupid fellow; **VA31**, Knothead—not very bright; (Qu. GG18, . . *'Obstinate': "Why does he have to be so _____."*) Infs **MA58**, **SC58**, Knotheaded; (Qu. GG42, *A reckless person, one who takes foolish chances*) Infs **MT3**, **NH17**, Knothead; (Qu. HH2, *Names and nicknames for a citified person*) Inf **AK8**, Knothead; (Qu. HH16, *Uncomplimentary words with no definite meaning—just used when you want to show that you don't think much of a person: "Don't invite him. He's a _____."*) Inf **GA12**, Knothead. **1967–68** *DARE* Tape **IA8**, They [=mules] can be the dumbest damn creatures in the world. . . They're just knotheaded, I guess, or something. They can be the contrariest thing that ever was; **IN36**, I tell you, a good dog is worth something for coon hunting. You gotta have it. If you just got a knothead out there, you might as well be out there by yourself trying to catch them. **1978** Doig *This House* 31 **MT**, I remember Charlie could spiel with the best of us knotheads, . . had a story ready whenever he remembered to look up from his work. **1986** Pederson *LAGS Concordance,* 1 inf, **cwFL**, A knothead—of a person; **cwLA**, Knothead—slow thinker; *(Poor white)* 1 inf, **neMS**, Knothead; *(Don't be so . . obstinate)* 1 inf, **ceTX**, Knotheaded.

3 =scrapple.

1970 *DARE* (Qu. H43, *Foods made from parts of the head and inner organs of an animal*) Inf **KY74**, Knothead—broth plus cornmeal, eaten fried and sliced.

4 also *(k)nottyhead*, abbr *notty*: A **stone roller** (here: *Campostoma anomalum*).

1965 McClane *McClane's Std. Fishing Encycl.* 891, Stoneroller *Campostoma anomalum*—Also known as hornyhead and knottyhead. **1970** *DARE* (Qu. P1, . . *Kinds of freshwater fish . . caught around here . . good to eat*) Inf **VA43**, Knothead—small, bony, 6 inches; catch in branches; sweet eating. **1988** Russell *It Happened in the Smokies* 122 **sAppalachians** (as of 1920s), An exciting bit of fishing was to catch the "notty-heads" when they fluttered each spring at the mouth of Two-Mile Branch. . . We sometimes dammed up the branch . . and caught the "notties" by hand.

5 A woodpecker. Cf **hammerhead 6, hardhead 5b**

1969 *DARE* (Qu. Q18, *Joking names and nicknames for woodpeckers*) Inf **MI101**, Knothead.

knotheaded See **knothead 2**

knothole n

1 in phr *be dragged through a knothole* and varr: To suffer an exhausting, painful, or humiliating experience. **esp Nth**

1833 in 1834 Smith *Life Jack Downing* 219 **ME**, It's worse than being dragged through forty knot holes. **1859** Smith *30 Yrs.* 250 **ME**, Looking as tired as a rat that had been drawed through forty knot-holes. **1907** *DN* 3.186 **seNH**, *Dragged through a knot-hole.* . . Exhausted, worn out. "He looks as though he'd been dragged through a knot-hole." **1922** *DN*

5.161 **NE, NH**, Dragged through a knot-hole. **1927** *AmSp* 2.353 **WV**, *Drag through a knothole* . . to undergo a humiliating experience. "You look like something had drug you through the knothole lately." **1929** *AmSp* 4.470 **NEast, Gt Lakes**, Looked as if he had been drawn through a knothole. **1956** McAtee *Some Dialect NC* 13, "I feel like I've been drug through a knot-hole," i.e., fatigued or worn out. **1966–69** *DARE* (Qu. X52, . . *A person . . who had been sick was looking _____*) Inf **NY103**, As if he'd been dragged through a knothole; **MI55, 107**, Like he was drawn (*or* drawed) through a knothole; (Qu. BB38, *When a person doesn't look healthy, or looks as if he hadn't been well for some time . . "He looks _____."*) Inf **WA3**, Drawn through a knothole; **IL52, MN15**, Like he's been pulled through a knothole; (Qu. KK30, *Feeling slowed up or without energy: "I certainly feel _____."*) Inf **MO27**, Like I'd been drug through a knothole; **PA175**, As though I'd been pulled through a knothole. **1970** *DARE* FW Addit **nwPA**, Looks as if she were pulled down a knothole, and the knothole pulled in after. **1979** *DARE* File **cnMA** (as of c1915), My mother and women of her generation used to speak of feeling as if they'd been dragged through a knothole—tired, worn out. They didn't have to do a day's work to reach this state: they woke up feeling dragged through a knothole sometimes.

‡2 The most insignificant thing; see quot.

1967 *DARE* (Qu. GG21b, *If you don't care what a person does . . "Go ahead—I don't give a _____."*) Inf **TX36**, Knothole.

knot-on-the-tree n

=green heron.

1955 *AmSp* 30.185 **OH**, An interesting term that may well be appended here is *knot-on-the-tree* (green heron . .), which apparently refers to the inanimate appearance of the bird, in its 'freezing' posture.

knotroot n

1 A **horse balm** (here: *Collinsonia canadensis*). Cf **knob grass 1**

1828 [see **knotweed 2**]. **1837** Darlington *Flora Cestrica* 349, *C[ol-linsonia] canadensis.* . . The infusion of the *root* was formerly a popular febrifuge. **1900** Lyons *Plant Names* 111, *C[ollin-sonia] Canadensis.* . . Knot-root. **1930** Sievers *Amer. Med. Plants* 23, Citronella Horsebalm *Collinsonia canadensis* . . knotroot. **1959** Carleton *Index Herb. Plants* 71, Knot-root: *Collinsonia canadensis.*

2 An introduced **hedgenettle** (here: *Stachys sieboldi*).

1902 Bailey *Cyclop. Horticult.* 4.1714, Chorogi. Chinese or Japanese Artichoke. Knotroot. **1976** Bailey–Bailey *Hortus Third* 1067, *[Stachys] affinis.* . . *Knotroot.* . . Erect herb . . with slender, knotty, white tubers abundantly produced just beneath the soil surface.

3 A **boneset 1** (here: *Eupatorium purpureum*).

1941 *Torreya* 41.52 **DC**, *Eupatorium purpureum.* . . Knot-root.

knotroot grass n

A **muhly (grass)** (here: *Muhlenbergia mexicana*).

1895 U.S. Dept. Ag. *Yearbook for 1894* 434, *Knot-root grass* is very common along river banks, usually where the soil is somewhat sandy. **1910** Graves *Flowering Plants* 61 **CT**, *Muhlenbergia mexicana.* . . Knot-root Grass. Frequent or common. . . Sometimes troublesome as a weed in gardens and lawns. **1914** Georgia *Manual Weeds* 43, Knot-root Grass. . . The strong, creeping, knotted, and scaly rootstocks of this grass are often of much service in binding the soil and preserving it from washing. . . If cut or grazed while very young, it makes good hay and forage. **1935** (1943) Muenscher *Weeds* 163, Knot-root-grass. . . Common in eastern North America. Native.

knotter, knotting See **knot** v **1**

knotty n See **pine knot**

knotty adj See **knot** n[1] **6**

knottyhead See **knothead 4**

knotweed n

1 Any of var plants of the genus *Polygonum*. Also called **bindweed 3, bird's-tongue 1, birdweed 1, doorweed, gander grass 1, knotgrass 1**. For other names of the common *P. aviculare* see **knotgrass 1**; for other names of var spp see **beggarweed 2, Eskimo rhubarb, goosegrass 1b, hearts-ease 2, jumpseed, pokeweed, wild rhubarb** Cf **lady's thumb, smartweed, tearthumb, water pepper**

1822 Eaton *Botany* 401, *[Polygonum] pensylvanicum* [sic] . . knee knotweed . . stem with swelling knee-joints. . . *[P.] sagittatum* . . prickly knotweed. . . *[P.] arifolium* . . halbert knotweed. **1830** Rafinesque *Med. Flora* 2.65, *Polygonum aviculare.* . . Common Knotweed. *Ibid* 66, *Polygonum* means with many knots. This species is found every where . . , in fields, blossoming all the year round. **1876** Hobbs *Bot. Hdbk.* 61, Knot weed, Heartsease, Polygonum Persicaria. **1901** Lounsberry *S. Wild Flowers* 154, The genus Polygonum is one which is very large and we see it abundantly represented by such plants as the . . knotweeds. **1937** U.S. Forest Serv. *Range Plant Hdbk.* W154, Knotweeds often mantle denuded areas with a fairly dense cover, which provides some protection. **1961** Douglas *My Wilderness* 20 **CO,** Before timber line is reached, gooseberries and currants are thick. . . Here too are shooting stars and knotweed and the snowball saxifrage. **1979** Niering–Olmstead *Audubon Guide N. Amer. Wildflowers E. Region* 705, Polygonaceae. . . This group includes . . the Knotweeds, with flower clusters in the leaf axils. **1987** Hughes–Blackwell *Wildflowers SE AK* 51, Fowler Knotweed. . . Sandy seashores.

2 A **horse balm** (here: *Collinsonia canadensis*). *obs* Cf **knotroot 1**

   1828 Rafinesque *Med. Flora* 1.111, *Collinsonia canadensis.* . . Knotroot, Stone-root, Knot-weed, &c. . . Root perennial, knotty, depressed, hard with many slender fibers. **1869** Porcher *Resources* 486 **Sth,** *Gravel root; Horseweed; Knotweed, (Collinsonia Canadensis.)* Grows in the mountains of the Carolinas. . . The root is used in colic from lochial discharge.

3 also *knotweed spurge:* A **spurge** (here: *Euphorbia polygonifolia*).

   1938 Madison *Wild Flowers OH* 40, Seaside Spurge. Knotweed. Euphorbia polygonifolia. . . Sandy shores. **1940** Clute *Amer. Plant Names* 99, E[uphorbia] polygonifolia. . . Knotweed spurge.

know v

A Pronc varr.

1 pres: usu |no(ʊ)|; rarely |nɑʊ|.

   1934 *AmSp* 9.212 **Sth,** With some speakers the first element of the diphthong [=[oʊ]] is so low as to seem to be [ɑ], making the diphthong [ɑʊ]. . . *Know.*

2 past: usu |nu|; also |nju|, |nɪu|. See Pronc Intro 3.I.10 Cf **new**

   1942 Hall *Smoky Mt. Speech* 38 **wNC, eTN,** In the following words, [u] is unusually tense and fronted and is always preceded by the palatal glide [j]: . . dew . . knew, new. **1942** *AmSp* 17.40 **seNY,** *Knew* [proncs with [u], 21 infs; proncs with [ɪu], 2 infs; proncs with [ju], 4 infs].

3 past pple, ppl adj: usu |no(ʊ)n|; also |ˈnoən|; pronc-sp *knowen.*

   1928 *Ruppenthal Coll.* **KS,** *Knowen* (for known). It was knowen who stole the horses. Heard, illit[erate] speech. **1934** *Language* 10.2 **sePA,** ōn > owen in *known, grown,* [etc]. . . These words, however, . . are used only by the 'educated': in popular speech the participles are *knew* or *knowed, throwed,* etc. **1942** in 1944 *ADD* **WV,** [Radio:] The cause of tuberculosis is [ˈnoən]. **1993** *DARE File,* A friend who grew up in east central Idaho in the 1920s–30s always pronounced *known* [ˈnoən], *thrown* [θroən], and *Joan* [joən].

B Gram forms.

1 infin: usu *know;* also, following aux verb, *know(e)d.*

   1937 (1977) Hurston *Their Eyes* 266 **FL** [Black], Ah don't know, Tea Cake. Didn't even knowed he wuz back. **c1937** in 1976 *Weevils in the Wheat* 163 **VA** [Black], Now don't ax me no mo' 'bout dat. I ain't knowd [=don't know] no mo' dan dat. **1986** Pederson *LAGS Concordance,* 1 inf, **nwMS,** I ain't knowed of none.

2a pres (exc 3rd pers sg): usu *know;* also *knows.*

   1843 (1916) Hall *New Purchase* 133 **IN,** That's your idee; but I knows better nor that comes to. **1893** Shands *MS Speech* 42, Illiterate white and negro. . . "Not as I knows on." **1894** Riley *Armazindy* 1 **IN,** 'Specially the ones 'at knows / Fac's o' how her story goes. **1958** Humphrey *Home from the Hill* 129 **neTX,** I knows em about all. **1966–70** *DARE* Tape **AL**1, None that I knows of; **TN**51, I knows if I quit eating sweets . . I would be a whole lot better off; **GA**8, He said, the Lord's called you to preach. I said, I knew it. I knows it. He did. [2 of 3 Infs old, Black] **1986** Pederson *LAGS Concordance* **Gulf Region,** [25 infs used *knows* as the present tense form in situations where *know* is standard.] [21 infs 60 years old or older, 17 Black]

b pres 3rd pers sing: usu *knows;* also *know.*

   1901 *DN* 2.143 **NY,** He know what he is about. **1960** Williams *Walk Egypt* 24 **GA,** Dear Lord know what will happen to the poor creatures. **1986** Pederson *LAGS Concordance,* 1 inf, **csLA,** If you scared of him,

he know it; He know his stuff though; He know it; Cause he know me personally; 1 inf, **seFL,** She know about them; He act like he know; 1 inf, **cMS,** Each one know; 1 inf, **cGA,** She know everything happen in Lamar County; 1 inf, **cnGA,** He know; 1 inf, **seGA,** Somebody that know how to do it; 1 inf, **cLA,** Everybody know it; 1 inf, **swGA,** I don't care if the world know it; 1 inf, **swAL,** He know me; 1 inf, **swMS,** She know me; 1 inf, **swGA,** Everybody round here know my mother-in-law; 1 inf, **csLA,** Somebody know; 1 inf, **cwMS,** That old man know; 1 inf, **csGA,** The Lord always know what to do; 1 inf, **seLA,** She know where they at; 1 inf, **neFL,** He know which way he supposed to go. [10 of 16 infs Black]

3 past: usu *knew;* also: See below. *esp freq among speakers with little formal educ*

a *knowed;* pronc-sp *node* **scattered, but chiefly Sth, S Midl** See Map Cf **grow 1, throw**

   1781 *PA Jrl. & Weekly Advt.* (Philadelphia) 16 May [1]/2, [In list of vulgarisms common to England and America but more frequent in America:] I *know'd* him perfectly well, for I *knew* him. **1815** Humphreys *Yankey in England* 106, *Know'd,* knew. **1836** (1955) *Crockett Almanacks* 41 **wTN,** I'le be shot if I *node* how to calculate the time of the moon's rising and setting. **1837** Sherwood *Gaz. GA* 70, *Knowed,* for knew. **1862** in 1983 *PADS* 70.40 **ce,sePA,** I liked him as well as eny boy i knowd. **1872** U.S. Congress *Serial Set* 1494 Rept 41.11.484 **ceMS** [Black], Of course I knowed him. **1884** *Anglia* 7.252 [Black], To the regular forms of the Irregular verbs as used by the whites, the Negro adds the following forms of his own. . . Past. knowed, knewed. **1893** Shands *MS Speech* 42, *Knowed.* . . Negro and illiterate white for *knew.* **1893** *DN* 1.277 **nwCT,** *Know.* [Past, past pple:] *knowed* (knew). **1902** *DN* 2.237 **sIL,** *Knowed.* Pret. and pp. of know. **1903** *DN* 2.318 **seMO,** *Knowed,* pret. and *pp.* Knew. (Very common.) **1907** *DN* 3.233 **nwAR,** *Knowed.* . . Knew, known. **1908** *DN* 3.327 **eAL, wGA,** *Knowed,* pret. and *pp.* of *know.* Common among the uneducated. **1934** *WV Review* Dec 79 **WV,** Our *betted* for *bet* is not local with us, neither is our *knowed* for *knew* and *known.* **1942** Hall *Smoky Mt. Speech* 38 **wNC, eTN,** In uneducated speech, the preterites *blew* and *knew* are replaced by [bloud], [noud]. **1950** *WELS WI* (When we were in school, I _____ him well) 10 Infs, Knowed. **1954** *Harder Coll.* **cwTN,** [Pres:] know—[past:] knowed—[past pple:] knowed. **c1960** *Wilson Coll.* **csKY,** *Know—knowed—p[ast]—p[ast] p[article].* Rather common still. **1965–70** *DARE* (Qu. OO22a, *About knowing people: "He used to live next door. At that time I _____ [him well].")* 74 Infs, **chiefly Sth, S Midl,** Knowed; (Qu. A24, . . *Someone who has always been the same way: "He's been hot-tempered from _____.")* Infs **NC**37, **OK**25, (Ever) since I knowed him; **VA**1, When I knowed him; (Qu. GG12) Infs **NY**70, **VA**1, 73, Knowed; (Qu. JJ45) Inf **TN**26, What he knowed to hisself. [49 of 80 total Infs gs educ or less, 49 male, 71 comm type 4 or 5] **1966–70** *DARE* Tapes **GA**1, 25, 30, **KY**16A, 21, 23, **LA**7, **PA**14, 17, **SC**7, **VA**2, 9, 27, 38, Knowed [=knew]. **1989** Pederson *LAGS Tech. Index* 360 **Gulf Region,** [192 of 914 infs gave [nod] as the past tense of *know.*]

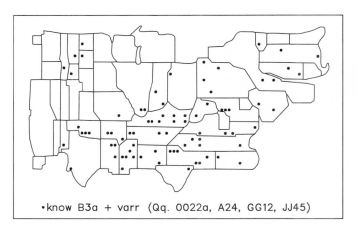

·know B3a + varr (Qq. OO22a, A24, GG12, JJ45)

b *knewed, knewn.*

   1884 [see **B3a** above]. **1969** *DARE* (Qu. OO22a, *About knowing people: "He used to live next door. At that time I _____ [him well].")* Inf **MO**32, Knewn. **1986** Pederson *LAGS Concordance* **se,csLA,** 1 inf, A lady that I knewed well; *(I knew it)* 2 infs, Knewed; 1 inf, I knewed it was going to happen; 1 inf, He knew it (e)nough—or "knewed enough"? [All infs gs educ or less]

c *know, known.*

1911 Wharton *Ethan Frome* 138 **wMA,** I always known it. **1965–70** *DARE* (Qu. A24, . . *Someone who has always been the same way: "He's been hot-tempered from _____.")* Infs **GA4, LA20,** Ever(y) since I know him; **NJ25, OR14,** (For) as long as I know him; **PA157,** Ever I know him; (Qu. GG12, *To have an inner feeling that something is about to happen: "There she comes now, I _____ she would.")* Inf **SC26,** Know; had a good mind; (Qu. OO22a, *About knowing people: "He used to live next door. At that time I _____ [him well].")* Infs **SC10, 26,** Know. **1976** Tyler *Searching for Caleb* 236 **cnMD** [Black], Make certain you put in that Sulie known the answer all along. **1986** Pederson *LAGS Concordance,* 2 infs, **cnMS, csTX,** Know [*DARE* Ed: marked as preterite]; 1 inf, **cwMS,** He made out, he act like he know everything; 1 inf, **cwFL,** I never know nobody eat none of them.

4 past pple: usu *known;* also:

a *knowed;* sometimes *know.* **scattered, but chiefly Sth, S Midl** See Map Cf **grow 2**

1853 Simms *Sword & Distaff* 500 **SC,** Ef I'd ha' knowed it! **1893** *DN* [see **B3a** above]. **1899** Chesnutt *Conjure Woman* 24 **csNC** [Black], Ef you'd 'a' knowed . . [him], you'd 'a' knowed dat. **1902** [see **B3a** above]. **1903** [see **B3a** above]. **1907** [see **B3a** above]. **1908** [see **B3a** above]. **1932** Randolph *Ozark Mt. Folks* 24, I've knowed 'em t' be wrote thataway. **1934** *Language* [see **A3** above]. **1934** [see **B3a** above]. **1954** [see **B3a** above]. **c1960** [see **B3a** above]. **1965–70** *DARE* (Qu. OO22b, *About knowing people: "For the past twenty years I've _____ [him well].")* 59 Infs, **scattered, but more freq Sth, S Midl,** Knowed; 8 Infs, **scattered,** Knowed [FW: used in conv]; **FL26, NY219, PA236, TX104,** Knowed; known; **KY94, LA2, NY209,** Knew; knowed; **AR18,** Knew; knowed—this is heard frequently; **AR55,** Known; knowed—lower class; **GA73,** Known; knowed—lot of people say; **IL76,** Known; country people said knowed; **MD17,** Known; knowed—most people would say; **MD24,** Known; knowed—some people say—usually old; **MS69,** Knowed; knowed (Negro); **MO11,** Known; knowed—frequently used here; **MA5,** Known; knowed—old-fashioned; **PA234,** Known; knowed [FW sugg]; **TN12,** Known; knowed—country; **TX1,** Known; knowed—old-timers; **MO1, SC10,** Know. [Of 86 Infs who responded with *knowed,* 54 were gs educ or less, 55 male, 73 comm type 4 or 5.] **1967** *DARE* FW Addit **nwLA,** Man, I'd a went if I'd a knowed it 'uz a-gonna be like this. **1968** [see **B4b** below]. **1969** *DARE* Tape **GA30,** He had knowed 'em to tote water fer a hunderd yards; **GA72,** I never had knowed of a man even going on trial in this county for shooting a revenuer; **VA27,** Had you not knowed that? **1986** Pederson *LAGS Concordance* **Gulf Region,** [32 infs used *knowed* as the past pple]; 1 inf, **nwFL,** I have know; 1 inf, **ceGA,** No, I ain't never know nobody eaten any.

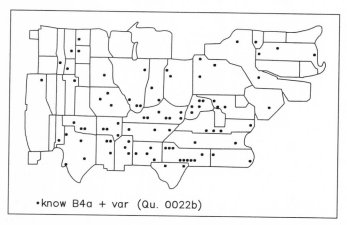

• know B4a + var (Qu. OO22b)

b *(a-)knew, knewed, knewn.* [Cf *EDD* kneawn, knew (at *know* v. 3.(6), (7))]

1847 Hurd *Grammatical Corrector* 46, Knew, for *known;* as, "I have knew him these twenty years; and I must say, I have never knew an honester man." **1934** *Language* [see **A3** above]. **1950** *WELS* **WI** (*I have _____ him for many years*) 2 Infs, Known; knew; 1 Inf, Known; knew, knowed; 1 Inf, Knew, known, knowed. **1965–70** *DARE* (Qu. OO22b, *About knowing people: "For the past twenty years I've _____ [him well].")* 40 Infs, **scattered,** Knew; **AR27, MS1, ND2, SC7,** Knew, known; **AR41, TN6,** Known, knew; **KY94, LA2,** Knew, knowed; **DC3,** Knew—now and then heard; known; **FL19,** Knowed, known; if I had a-knew [FW: used in conv]; **MI33,** Known; you'll also

hear "I've knew"; **NY75,** Known; knew [FW: used in conv]; **NC76,** Knew, [corr to] known; **MO21,** Knewn; **SC32,** Knew; knowed [FW: used in conv]; (Qu. A24, . . *Someone who has always been the same way: "He's been hot-tempered from _____.")* Inf **OK4,** Ever since I've knew him. [Of 55 Infs who responded with *knew,* 30 were female, 30 gs educ or less, 47 comm type 4 or 5.] **1968** *DARE* File **cWI,** Speaker [=an elderly farmer] changed "If I'd have knowed" . . to "If I'd have knowed" . . when conscious of speaking to [a] professor. **1986** Pederson *LAGS Concordance,* 1 inf, **cTX,** He'd have knew; 1 inf, **neTX,** I ought to have knew; 1 inf, **nwLA,** Must have knew; 1 inf, **swAL,** I'd have knew; 1 inf, **cnAL,** I wouldn't have knew; 1 inf, **swGA,** He might have knew it; 1 inf, **cnFL,** She probably would have knew.

5 ppl adj: usu *known;* also *knowed, knowned.* Cf grow 2

1932 Randolph *Ozark Mt. Folks* 124, Most people go primarily to visit and gossip, and to enjoy the wit of the auctioneer, who is usually a "knowed character" and a good speaker. **1962** *Mt. Life* 38.1.17 **sAppalachians,** Past participles used as direct adjectives are often given *-en* or *-ed* endings: . . a knowed fact.

C Syntax.

Used in perfect progressive rather than perfect tenses, and progressive rather than present or past tenses; see quots. **esp Gulf States** Cf be **B7c**

1887 (1967) Harris *Free Joe* 8 **GA** [Black], We all bin knowin' 'bout it fum de jump. **1927** Kennedy *Gritny* 14 **sLA** [Black], I'm knowin' Miss Mimi ever since she was a baby-chile. **1966–67** *DARE* (Qu. II2b, *When two people have become friendly . . "It's been quite a while that Mary and Jane have been _____.")* Inf **TX11,** Knowing; (Qu. OO22b, *About knowing people: "For the past twenty years I've _____ [him well].")* Inf **GA5,** Been knowing; **LA6,** Knowed; been knowing [FW: used in conv; this is the almost universal expression among Negroes here]. **1967** *DARE* Tape **LA12,** I've been knowing him 30 years. **1967** *DARE* FW Addit **AL,** "I've been knowing him for years." People from rural areas or from small towns invariably use [this]. **1971** Mitchell *Blow My Blues Away* 110 **nwMS** [Black], I's been knowing all the time we is all peoples, but we was separated. **1972** Cooper *NC Mt. Folkl.* 93, I'm a knowing—I know. **1986** Pederson *LAGS Concordance* **Gulf Region,** 8 infs, I been knowing him (*or* her, that, *etc.*); 1 inf, I'd been knowing for years; 1 inf, How long you been knowing?; 1 inf, I wasn't knowing = I didn't know; 1 inf, Some of them be knowing better.

D In var phrr.

1 *(I) want to know:* Used as an exclam to express surprise. **NEng**

1833 Neal *Down-Easters* 45 **NEng,** I *want* to know! exclaimed the other down-easter. Well you *do* know, replied the southerner, in perfect good faith, mistaking a northern exclamation for a formal interrogatory. **1888** *Harper's New Mth. Mag.* 77.530 **NEng,** "Why, Jered Hopkins!" she said, looking up at him; "I want to know!" **1905** *DN* 3.23 **cCT,** Want to know. . . Used in exclamations of surprise, as 'I want to know!' **1907** *DN* 3.203 **seNH,** Want to know. . . Really? Polite exclamation in the way of appreciation of a person's remarks. **1923** Paine *Comrades* 169 **ME,** And you come from North Dakoty? I want to know. That's where you find farmin' on a grand scale. **1926** *AmSp* 2.81 **ME,** If they think you expect them to manifest an interest in your remarks they will be polite enough to say, "I want t' know!" or "Do tell!" **1943** *LANE* Map 601–602 *(For goodness sake)* 3 infs, **cnMA, seME, cRI,** I want to know. **1954** Forbes *Rainbow* 67 **CT,** We just sat in the best parlor . . and he talked and they shook their heads and said, "Tut, tut" and that they "wanted to know." **1959** *VT Hist.* 27.146, *I want to know!* . . (with emphasis on the word *want.)* Common. **1966** *DARE* (Qu. NN7, *Exclamations of surprise: "They're getting married next week? Well, _____.")* Inf **NH5,** I want to know!—not to know when or anything in particular, just to show surprise. **1968** Coatsworth *ME Memories* 155, They exclaim, "Want to know!" at a piece of news. **1969** *DARE* File **cnMA** (as of c1915), I suspected when grownups said in response to one of my childish pronouncements, "Well, I want to know!" that they were really saying that they didn't believe a word of it.

2 *I do know:* Used as an exclam to express surprise.

1926 Roberts *Time of Man* 27 **KY,** "If Davie was here he'd be sixteen now." "Well I do know!" **1940–42** in 1944 *ADD* **AR,** [Radio broadcasts:] Well, I do know! **1941** Faulkner *Men Working* 181 **MS,** "Well, I do know," said Maw. "I would never have thought of that." **1969** *DARE* (Qu. NN7, *Exclamations of surprise: "They're getting married next week? Well, _____.")* Inf **PA206,** I do know.

3 *know in reason* (or *mind*): See **in reason.**

knowance See **knowing** n 1

know cow v phr Also *savvy cow*
To understand the nature of cows.

1967 Green *Horse Tradin'* 241 **TX**, This kind of operation took a lot of cowboyin' which could not be done without some good, stout, hard, usable horses. They didn't have to be pretty, but they had to savvy a lot of cow. **1980** *AZ Highways* Feb 6, This "broomtail" [=a horse] possessed a great amount of "cowsense," or, in the Southwest vernacular, "knew cow."

know(e)d See **know** B1, 3a, 4a, 5

knowen See **know** A3

knowing n
1 also pl; also *knowance:* Knowledge. **chiefly sAppalachians, Ozarks**

1927 *DN* 5.475 **Ozarks**, *Knowance.* . . Knowledge. "Wal, hit mout be so, but I sure aint got no knowance of hit." **1929** *WV Review* 7.1.9, Many dialetical [sic] words that were formerly widely used among us are seldom heard today. . . [O]ne rarely hears *knowance* for *knowledge of.* **1941** Stuart *Men of Mts.* 298 **neKY**, Not to my knowings. **1942** Thomas *Blue Ridge Country* 135 **sAppalachians**, It's more satisfaction to let a body's knowing fall on fresh ears. **1956** *Hall Coll.* **eTN**, "That's all the houses they was in my knowin'." As far as I know. **1986** Pederson *LAGS Concordance,* 1 inf, **nwLA**, Not of my knowing; 1 inf, **cGA**, Not to my knowing. **1991** Still *Wolfpen Notebooks* 162 **sAppalachians**, *Knowance:* knowledge.
2 A hunch.

1970 *DARE* (Qu. GG12, *To have an inner feeling that something is about to happen: "There she comes now, I _____ she would."*) Inf **VA46**, Had a knowing.

knowing adj Pronc-sp *known*
With *to:* Knowledgeable about, aware of, familiar with.

1841 Catlin *Letters Indians* 2.187, I must be supposed to be knowing to and familiar with the whole circumstances. **1858** Hammett *Piney Woods Tavern* 28, Dern my skin, ef they ain't all pretty well knowin' to your ways here. **1871** (1882) Stowe *Fireside Stories* 28 **MA**, Yer Aunt Lois was knowin' to all this 'ere about Ruth. *Ibid* 109, I didn't railly have no hand in't, though I was knowin' to 't, as I be to most things that goes on round here. **1877** Still *Early Recoll.* 76 **cwNJ** (as of 1844), I made up some tinctures for my own family, and one of the neighbors was known to it. One of the daughters of this neighbor developed scrofula, and he had me visit her. **1906** *DN* 3.144 **nwAR**, Knowing to. . . Aware of, acquainted with, informed of. "I'm knowing to that; you're wrong." **1931** *PMLA* 46.1304 **sAppalachians**, I suspect Hence wuz knowin' to the sarcumstance?

knowings See **knowing** n 1

knowing to See **knowing** adj

know in mind (or reason) See **in reason**

knowl(e) See **knoll**

knowledge box n [*OED* 1796 (at *knowledge* sb. III.16)] Cf **box** n 5b, **think box**
The head; the skull.

1831 Finn *Amer. Comic Annual* 100, The muse *Melpomene*—/ Inspired by 'possum fat and hominy,'/ Resolved to break into her knowledge-box./ And, like a thief nefarious,/ At work burglarious,/ She did not wait to *pick* her patent-*locks*./ Her hands were hunting after hairs,/ She was more partial to a *wig* than tory / In her upper story,/ To which, her eyes appeared a *pair* of stares. **1859** Taliaferro *Fisher's R.* 134 **nwNC** (as of 1820s), After wavin', brandisherin', and gleameratin' thar tommyhocks over my knowledge-box for a long spell, and then thar butcher-knives in the same threatnin' aspex, they helt a council over my case. **1899** (1912) Green *VA Folk-Speech* 253, *Knowledge-box.* . . The skull. **1934** (1940) Weseen *Dict. Amer. Slang* 237 [Boxing and prizefighting slang], *Knowledge box*—The head.

knowledge bump n Also *bump of knowledge* [In allusion to the *bumps* of phrenological theory; cf *OED bump* sb.[1] 4] joc
See quot.

1966–68 *DARE* (Qu. X60, . . *A lump that comes up on your head when you get a sharp blow or knock;* not asked in early QRs) Inf **OH**47,

Knowledge bump—you're supposed to learn from it; **WA**11, Knowledge bump; **MN**18, Bump of knowledge [laughter].

knowledge man n
A smart, shrewd, or astute man.

1944 in 1958 Brewer *Dog Ghosts* 60 **TX** [Black], He come to be a knowledge man 'bout cattle, an' dey raisin', an' de prices dey brung. So, li'l by li'l, he buy a bunch of cattle of his own 'till he done rech de place whar he hab a putty good herd. **1956** *Ibid* 50 **TX** [Black], Ole Brothuh Rabbit de smaa'tes' thing. . . Dere's lots of peoples . . dat begrudges Brothuh Rabbit de mother-wit he got to help 'im meck his way thoo de worl'. Evuhbody'd lack to be a knowledge man lack Brothuh Rabbit, but dey ain't got dem Judas ways lack Brothuh Rabbit nachul bawn got.

known adj See **knowing** adj

knowned See **know** B5

knuck n[1] [Abbr for *knuckle*]
1 A knuckle; hence n *knuck-bone* a bone with a rounded or knuckle-like end. Cf **knuckle** n 1

1908 *DN* 3.327 **eAL, wGA**, Knucks. . . The knuckles. "He hit me on the knucks." **1942** Berrey–Van den Bark *Amer. Slang* 121.32, Knuck, *a knuckle.* **1944** *PADS* 2.45 **nwNC**, *Knuck-bone.* . . A bone having a rounded end or "ball." "The knuck-bone came out of my uncle's hip."— A woman, 90. . . Rare. **1957** *Sat. Eve. Post Letters* **eMA**, Then there was the standard circle game with "knucks down tight." **1970** [see **2a** below]. **1973** Ferretti *Marble Book* 52, *Shot.* Snapping the marble from the hand with the thumb from where it is held against the ball of the first finger. Knucks, of course, must be down.
2 In marble play:
a pl; also *nucks, knugs:* A game in which players shoot at a series of holes or at the knuckles of another player. [Cf *EDD knuck* sb.[1] 2 "*pl.* A game of marbles" and *nags* (at *nag* sb.[5] 3(2)) "a game of marbles, in which the loser has his knuckles struck . . with the marbles of the other players"] **esp W Midl** See Map Cf **knuckle** n 3

1840 *S. Lit. Messenger* 6.386, [In] the game of marbles he . . is counted a proficient particularly in knucks and five in the ring. **1857** in 1956 Eliason *Tarheel Talk* 281 **NC**, The gentlemen played knucks all day. **1890** *DN* 1.65 **KY**, Knucks . . a game at marbles in which the winner shoots at his adversary's knuckles. **1892** *DN* 1.217 **MA**, *Knucks.* . . In Chicopee, Mass., this game is called *knugs* . . and the process of shooting the marbles at the knuckles of the defeated one is called *giving him the knugs.* **1893** [see **2d(1)** below]. **1899** (1912) Green *VA Folk-Speech* 253, *Knucks.* . . A boy's game played with marbles. The winner having the right to shoot his taw so many times at the knuckles of the loser. **1908** *DN* 3.327 **eAL, wGA**, *Knucks.* . . A game at marbles. **1915** *DN* 4.184 **swVA**, *Knucks.* . . a game at marbles. **1922** *DN* 5.187 **KY** [Marbles terms], *Knucks.* . . A game, so called from the winner being allowed to shoot his taw at the taw of the loser, placed in the loser's knuckle. **1965–70** *DARE* (Qu. EE7, . . *Kinds of marble games*) Infs **GA**9, 18, **KY**21, 75, **LA**8, **TN**65, Knucks; **KY**66, Knucks—winner shot at your knuckles; **TN**62, Knucks—holes in ground; **TX**37, Knucks—if you lose, the other guy shoots into your knuckles. **1969** *DARE* FW Addit **KY**21, Knucks—a marble game in a rectangle 9' x 15' called a marble yard. It contained three holes. Players worked as partners going from hole to hole. This [was] done three times. . . Old-fashioned. **1969** *DARE* Tape **KY**21, [Inf:] There was four of us playing—partners. We'd make three rounds in this game. The two that got in this first hole that was shot from first is the ones that won. [FW:] What did you call this game? [Inf:] Knucks or marbles. **1970** *Ibid* **KY**75, Knucks—you would double your fist up and lay it on the ground and you would put a marble between the two middle fingers and kind of let it stick out, and the guy that was shooting at your knucks, if he missed your knucks and hit the marble, then it was your turn to get a whack at his knucks. **1976** Sublette Co. Artist Guild *More Tales* 115 **WY** (as of c1910), Marbles was a popular game and a few of us boys played a game we called "Nucks". We would close our hand and put it on the ground, then shoot each others knuckles. **1985** Runyan *Knuckles Down* 9, *Three Holes* (Also called Knucks). . . Players take alternate turns shooting for the first hole, not being able to advance to the next until he lands a marble in the target. If a player is the first one to hit a hole, he gets to collect one marble from each of the other players. The game is over when every one has hit all three holes and marbles are counted to determine the winner. **1986** Pederson *LAGS Concordance*, 2 infs, **ceAL, cLA,** Knucks—marble game.

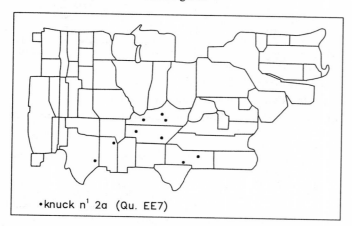

•knuck n¹ 2a (Qu. EE7)

b as *(k)nug:* A penalty inflicted by shooting a marble at an opponent's knuckles. [Cf **2a** above and *EDD nag* sb.⁵ 10 "A stroke in the game of 'nags.' "]

1892 [see **2a** above]. **1922** *DN* 5.187 **MA,** The one who came in last had to put down his closed fist on the ground and let the others drive their marbles at his knuckles. . . Hard shooters could give very painful *nugs.* **1966** *DARE* Tape **GA**13, The man who won would get to shoot. . . He'd won the game and then the other boys had to pay off in knugs. . . They'd all get the knugs from one guy.

c A shooter.

1942 Berrey–Van den Bark *Amer. Slang* 665.2, Knuck, *a marble used in "knuckling."* **1970** *DARE* (Qu. EE6a, . . *Different kinds of marbles— the big one that's used to knock others out of the ring*) Inf **VA**65, Knuck.

d Used in var calls:

(1) *knucks (down):* Used to require or allow the knuckles of the shooting hand to touch the ground. Cf **knuckle** n **2a**

1893 Shands *MS Speech* 73, Knucks. . . A game of marbles in which the defeated player must allow the other players to have one "plump" apiece at his knuckles from a distance of eight or ten feet. The word *knucks* is also cried out in a game of marbles in order to make the player who is shooting, keep his hand on the ground. **1935** *AmSp* 10.159 **seNE** [Marbles terms], *Knucks down.* **1942** Berrey–Van den Bark *Amer. Slang* 665.6, Knuckles down!, knucks!, *said to a player who has lifted his hand off the ground to shoot.* **1957** *Sat. Eve. Post Letters* **OK** (as of 1891–97), All shooting was from a knuckle contacting the ground position, and held that way until the marble was shot or released. We simply called the whole thing knux [sic], or to make it plainer or more emphatic, "knux down." **1958** *Ibid* **GA,** I have a particularly hard shot to make. It would be easier to make it with the shooting hand a few inches above the ground. However, if my opponent said "knucks," I must make my shot with my shooting fist held motionless and close to the ground. If I beat him to the punch by saying "vince knucks," I could shoot the easier way. **1963** *KY Folkl. Rec.* 9.3.66 **eKY,** *Command to keep shooting hand on the ground when shooting* . . knucks-down. **1967** *DARE* Tape **AZ**8, As the game [=purg] proceeds, each of the players may call his own rulings. They may have any number of rulings as they go through the game . . and as these rulings are called out, the other players have to abide these rulings, such as "no knucks," which means they can't put their knuckles on the ground.

(2) *knucks (up):* Used to claim the right to raise the shooting hand on the other hand. Cf **knuckle** n **2b**

1958 *Resp. to PADS 29,* Here are a few more marble terms. . . Knucks Up—Player allowed to rest shooting hand on the other or on knee. **1963** *KY Folkl. Rec.* 9.3.66 **eKY,** *To ask for permission to elevate shooting hand with shooter to a position on top of the free hand:* . . knucks. . . *Command to keep shooting hand on the ground when shooting:* . . no-knucks. **1966** *DARE* Tape **NC**22, If it was a bad shot, a close shot, you could say "knucks up" and that would mean put your fist down and hold the other hand on that fist. . . and shoot that way.

3 pl: A card game; see quots.

1968 *DARE* (Qu. DD35, . . *Card games*) Inf **LA**45, Fish, knucks, battle—these are children's card games. **1994** *DARE* File **Bronx NYC** (as of early 1950s), Knucks—A popular card game played by young

boys. The object was to divest oneself of the cards in one's hand, the loser being struck on the knuckles with the deck by each player as many times as there were cards remaining in his hand. The severity of the blow was determined by the loser cutting the cards—a red card meant hard blows, a black card, soft ones.

4 pl: See quot. Cf **noogie**

1957 *Sat. Eve. Post Letters* **Seattle WA** (as of c1900), 'Bombay'. . . was a 'catch' game. This usually started with some such simple operations like 'Knucks.' You dug your knuckles into the 'down' man's spine as you vaulted over.

knuck v See **knuckle** v **a**

knuck n² See **Canuck**

knuck-bone See **knuck** n¹ **1**

knuckle n

1 also *knucklebone:* The protuberant part of a joint.

1965–70 *DARE* (Qu. X33, *The place in the elbow that gives you a strange feeling if you hit it against something*) Inf **FL**18, Knuckle; **SC**10, 70, Knucklebone. **1986** Pederson *LAGS Concordance,* 1 inf, **cAL,** All them joints your knuckles; *(Joint)* 1 inf, **seAL,** Knucklebone—at knee, ankle, elbow, etc.

2 In marble play; used in var calls:

a *knuckles (down):* Used to require that the knuckles of the shooting hand touch the ground; hence adv phr *knuckles down* with the hand in this position. Cf **knuck** n¹ **2d(1), knuckle-down** n

1958 *Resp. to PADS 29* **cnOK,** Advantage could be gained by being the first to cry. . . Knuckles down and three fingers flat to make an easy shot more difficult for your opponent. **1963** *KY Folkl. Rec.* 9.3.66 **eKY,** *Command to keep shooting hand on the ground when shooting* . . knuckles-down. **c1970** Wiersma *Marbles Terms, Knuckle(s)-down.* . . Rule; keeping the hand stationary and knuckles to the ground while shooting with the thumb. *Ibid* **neOH** (as of c1965), The knuckles position describes a position for shooting. The player almost makes a fist so that his knuckles are almost resting on the ground. . . The player then shoots with his thumb. . . "Hey, no cheatin'. We called knuckles." *Ibid* **neIL** (as of c1953), Knucklesdown: a type of shot in which the fist contacts the ground at the first joint as the marble is snapped off the forefinger by the thumb. Noun. Ex: "Let's say this game is knuckles down." **1976** *WI Acad. Rev.* Mar 9 (as of 1920s), If an opponent shouted "knuckles down" before you shouted "fernanz," you had to shoot with the knuckles of the ring and little finger on the ground.

b *knuckles up:* Used to claim the right to shoot with the knuckles raised; hence adv phr *knuckles up* with the hand in this position; n *knuckles-up* a shot made in this way. Cf **knuck** n¹ **2d(2)**

1963 *KY Folkl. Rec.* 9.3.64 **eKY,** *The act of lifting the shooter to a shooting position above the ground* . . knuckles-up. *Ibid* 66, *To ask for permission to elevate shooting hand with shooter to a position on top of the free hand* . . knuckles-up. **c1970** Wiersma *Marbles Terms* **neIL** (as of c1953), Knuckles up: a type of shot in which the second joint is the fist's point of contact as the marble is snapped. The higher position may give more speed and distance. Noun. Also may be Adv. noun. Ex: "Let's play this one knuckles up."

3 pl: A marble game; see quots. [Cf *EDD knuckle* sb. 4 "pl: A game of marbles"] Cf **knuck** n¹ **2a**

1957–58 *Sat. Eve. Post Letters* **cwCA** (as of c1915), We played such games as: . . Miggs or knuckles. . . Knuckles is just a regular game of marbles except that every and all shots are made with the knuckles of the shooting hand on the playing surface. **1965–68** *DARE* (Qu. EE7, . . *Kinds of marble games*) Inf **FL**22, Knuckles—put knuckles on table (or ground), put four marbles in front of four knuckles; opponent shoots for knuckles; if he hits marble then you shoot at him. You try to hit and hurt the other guy's knuckles without hitting the marbles; **LA**11, Knuckles—the one that wins shoots the other one's knuckles; **LA**20, Knuckles.

4 pl: See **knuckle shot.**

5 A rise of ground; a **knob 1.**

1962 Fox *Southern Fried* 142 **SC,** Buried him out on that hill knuckle in front.

knuckle v

In marble play:

a usu with *down*, rarely with *in;* also *knuck, knucks down:* To hold one or more knuckles on the ground while shooting; hence vbl n *knuckling (down);* ppl adj *knuckled down* having the hand in this position. [*OED knuckle* v. 1 1740 →] Cf **knuckle** n **2a.**

1843 (1916) Hall *New Purchase* 42 **IN,** Colonel Wilmar proposed marbles. . . And at it we went with the zest of boyhood. . . Clearings!—'fen!—knuckle-down! **1890** *DN* 1.76 **NJ, NYC,** "Fen histing" means that it is not permitted to raise the knuckles from the ground in "shooting," or, as it is often expressed, "You knuckle down." **1899** (1912) Green *VA Folk-Speech* 253, *Knuckle.* . . To hold the knuckles close to the ground, in playing marbles; usually with *down.* A player is required to *knuckle down* in order to keep him from gaining undue advantage by "pudging" nearer the mark. **1906** Lovett *Old Boston Boys* 41, To shoot an "alley" with force and precision, "knuckling down," that is, with the knuckles resting upon the ground, is not so easy and requires much practice. **1922** *DN* 5.187 **KY** [Marbles terms], *Knuckle down.* . . To shoot (the taw) without lifting the knuckle from the ground. **1927** *88 Successful Play Activities* 29, *"Knuckle Down"*—Knuckling—Grounding—To rest back of hand or little finger of shooting hand on ground when shooting. **1942** Berrey–Van den Bark *Amer. Slang* 665.4, Knuck, knuckle (down), *to rest the knuckles on the ground in shooting.* **1957** *Sat. Eve. Post Letters* **WV** (as of c1920), The first boy there would sing out "First in the ring, Any old thing." Then when other players joined him, he would sing out again, "Knuckle down, Bony tight." **1963** *KY Folkl. Rec.* 9.3.66 **eKY,** Command to keep shooting hand on the ground when shooting . . knuckle-down. **1966–67** *DARE* Tape **TX**1, 'Course when you were shootin', you had to knucks down, they call it, hold your knuckles on the ground. *Ibid* **WA**7, [Inf:] You didn't knuckle down as you did in the ring game. . . [FW:] Can you explain "knuckle down"? [Inf:] Just put your knuckle on the ground and shoot from there; . . if you fail to knuckle down they tell you in no uncertain terms. **1968** *DARE* (Qu. EE7, . . *Kinds of marble games*) Inf **CT**16, Call out to each other "Knuckle down, shoot hard"; **NJ**53, Knuckle down tight—get your hand down on the ground; **PA**104, Would say "knuckle down"—knuckles had to be down. **c1970** Wiersma *Marbles Terms* **neIL** (as of c1928), Putting your knuckles down on the pavement in order to steady your shooting arm is called knuckling down. *Ibid* **swMI** (as of c1930), *Knuckle down.* . . E.g. You better knuckle down or it's my turn! *Ibid* **csIA** (as of c1935), *Knuckle in, knuckle down*—A rule requiring the player who is shooting to put his hand flat on the ground. . . Why "knuckle in" is used . . [is] not known. *Ibid* **swMI,** *Knuckle down. Ibid, Knuckling down*—position taken by player when shooting. *Ibid, Knuckling down.* **1983** Santiago *Famous All Over Town* 55 **Los Angeles CA,** I set up a glassie on the linoleum and knuckle down with my faithful shooter. **1985** Runyan *Knuckles Down* 4, Players do not need to "knuckle down" when lagging. This brings us to the most important rule in marble playing, the "knuckling down" or shooting technique. The correct way to fire a shooter marble is to place all of the knuckles (excepting the thumb) on the ground behind the ring line. . . The important thing to remember when shooting is that you keep at least one knuckle down until the shooter marble has left your hand. . . Anything from squatting, kneeling and crouching to a stomach or side lie is permissible, as long as you are "knuckled down."

b with *down:* To place one's knuckles on the ground for an opponent to shoot at; hence vbl n *knuckling down.* [*EDD* (at *knuckle* v. 8)]

1968 *DARE* Tape **NJ**18, [Inf:] So I'd say "knuckle down tight," and if you lost the game, you had to put your fist down and the other boys would shoot at your knuckles with a shooter. [FW:] How far? [Inf:] Well, I'm telling you, you didn't want to lose. [FW:] And that's knuckling down? [Inf:] That's knuckling down.

knucklebone See **knuckle** n **1**

knuckle-buster n

1 In marble play:

a =**knuck** n¹ **2a.**

1968 *DARE* (Qu. EE7, . . *Kinds of marble games*) Inf **VA**5, Knucklebuster—same as roly-hole—if you missed, you put your fist by the hole, and your opponent hit your knuckles with his marble.

b See quots. Cf **knuckler**

1970 *DARE* (Qu. EE6d, *Special marbles*) Inf **NY**236A, Knuckle-busters. **c1970** Wiersma *Marbles Terms* **swMI** (as of 1960), *Knuckle busters*—big marbles.

2 A wrench, esp an adjustable one.

1941 *AmSp* 16.166 [Army slang], *Knuckle buster.* Crescent wrench. **1960** Criswell *Resp. to PADS 20* **Ozarks,** *Knuckle-buster*—a wrench. Have heard for years. **1965** *DARE* FW Addit **MA,** *Knuckle-buster*—an adjustable wrench (liable to slip). A good mechanic does not use this type of wrench because it tends to round corners on nuts and bolt heads. **1969** *AmSp* 44.19 **Pacific NW** [Painter jargon], *Knucklebuster.* . . 1. A crescent wrench. . . 2. The old-time monkey wrench which would often slip and cause one skinned knuckles.

knuckled down See **knuckle** v **a**

knuckle down v phr See **knuckle** v **a, b**

knuckle-down n Also *knuckles-down* Cf **knuckle** n **2a,** **knuckle** v **a**

In marble play:

a also *knuckle-downer:* A shot made with the knuckles resting on the ground.

1949 *NY Herald Tribune* (NY) 1 Aug 13/1 **NYC,** Any kid who knows a heist-shot from a knuckle-down can tell you. **c1970** Wiersma *Marbles Terms* **swMI** (as of c1960), *Knuckle-downer*—a type of shot in which at least one knuckle must rest on the ground. *Ibid* **neIL** (as of c1953), *Knuckles down*—a type of shot in which the fist contacts the ground at the first joint as the marble is snapped off the forefinger by the thumb.

b also *knuckle(s)-down-tight:* A marble game.

1957 *Sat. Eve. Post Letters* **CT** (as of 1890s), Here are a few games I remember as a boy. . . Knuckle down (Mibs). **1967–70** *DARE* (Qu. EE7, . . *Kinds of marble games*) Infs **PA**196, 245, Knuckle-down; **IL**26, Knuckles-down—played in ring; **MI**65, Knuckle-down-tight—the marbles in a ring, had to get right down on the ground and shoot them out; **MN**21, Knuckles-down-tight—a ring marble [game].

knuckle-downer See **knuckle-down** n **a**

knuckle-down-tight See **knuckle-down** n **b**

knucklehead pea n Also *knucklehead, knucklehull (pea), knuckle purple hull* [See quot 1988] Cf **crowder**

A cultivated **cowpea.**

1965–67 *DARE* (Qu. I20, . . *Kinds of beans*) Inf **AL**15, Knucklehull peas—market peas; **FL**18, Knucklehead peas—hard as rocks. **1986** Pederson *LAGS Concordance,* 1 inf, **cAL,** Knucklehead—crowder peas; 1 inf, **seAL,** Knuckle purple hull—type of field pea. **1988** Whealy *Garden Seed Inventory* (2d ed) 163, *Cowpeas.* . . *Knuckle Purple Hull* (Knucklehull Purple Hull, Purple Hull Knucklehull, Purple Hull Brown Crowder). . . Brown sugar crowder with purple hull when mature . . bush plant . . big plump dark-brown dry peas form knuckles along the pod, fine flavor.

knuckle hop n

An Eskimo contest; see quot 1973.

1965 *AK Sportsman* Jan 7 (Tabbert *Dict. Alaskan Engl.*), [Caption:] It not only takes strong knuckles, but a stout heart in the knuckle hop. **1973** *Theata* 1.1.8 **cAK,** The object of the knuckle-hop is for the competitor to lift his whole body by only the tip of his toes and knuckles. He has to hop on only these two parts of his body and try to go as many feet as he can. His knuckles get cuts, start bleeding and will be sore for a long period of time. **1985** *Tundra Times* (Fairbanks AK) 1 July 8 (Tabbert *Dict. Alaskan Engl.*), Some of the events seen will be the knuckle-hop, which is the most grueling sport during the four-day event.

knuckle in See **knuckle** v **a**

knuckle kneeling n

1963 Watkins–Watkins *Yesterday Hills* 17 **cnGA,** In knuckle kneelings, two boys faced each other and locked their fingers with their arms extended high over their heads, and each tried to force the other to kneel.

knuckle purple hull See **knucklehead pea**

knuckler n [*EDD knuckler* (at *knuckle* sb. 7)] Cf **knuck** n¹ **2c**

A playing marble; see quot.

1968–70 *DARE* (Qu. EE6a, . . *Different kinds of marbles—the big one that's used to knock others out of the ring*) Inf **PA**81, 138, Knuckler; (Qu. EE6d, *Special marbles*) Inf **PA**138, Glass knuckler.

knuckles exclam See **knuckle** n **2a**

knuckles n See **knuckle shot**

knuckles down exclam phr, adv phr See **knuckle** n **2a**

knuckles-down n See **knuckle-down** n

knuckles-down-tight See **knuckle-down** n b

knuckle shot n Also *knuckles*

In marble play: see quot.

c1970 Wiersma *Marbles Terms, Knuckles*. . . Type of shot in which knuckles must be kept on the ground and marble is shot with the thumb. *Ibid* **WA** (as of 1960), *Knuckle shot*. . . Tuck thumb in behind index finger and flip out against marble.

knuckles up See **knuckle** n 2b

knuckle-up line n [Cf **knuckle** v]

c1955 Reed–Person *Ling. Atlas Pacific NW* (Starting line in marbles) 1 inf, Knuckle up line.

knuckling (down) See **knuckle** v a, b

knucks See **knuck** n¹ 2d(1), (2)

knucks down n See **knuck** n¹ 2d(1)

knucks down v See **knuckle** v a

knucks up See **knuck** n¹ 2d(2)

knug See **knuck** n¹ 2b

knugs See **knuck** n¹ 2a

knull See **null** n, v¹

knurl n Also sp *gnurl* [Cf *EDD knurly* (at *knurl* sb. 2(2)) "fig. ill-tempered, sulky"] **scattered, but esp NEng**

A burl or knot on a tree or other plant; hence adj *(k)nurly, nirly* knotty, tough; also fig: irritable, ill-tempered; coarse, unrefined.

1804 Fessenden *Poems* 32, He's tall, like swamp cedar . . / But shrub-oak was never so *nurly*. [Footnote:] A *yankeyism*, for knotty, or gnarled. **1848** Bartlett *Americanisms* 237, *Nurly*. A corrupt pronunciation of *gnarly*, i.e. gnarled. **1872** Schele de Vere *Americanisms* 620, *Nurly*, a vulgar corruption of *gnarly*, and thus applied to persons, who are said to be *nurly* when they are ill-tempered and cross-grained. **1887** (1895) Robinson *Uncle Lisha* 170 **wVT**, Hain't I tougher 'n a ellum gnurl? **1904** *DN* 2.427 **Cape Cod MA** (as of a1857), *Nurly*. . . Gnarly, rough. 'See these little nurly apples.' **1923** *DN* 5.215 **swMO**, *Nurly*. . . Gnarled, twisted, tough, cross-grained, ill tempered, viciously inclined, irritable. **1928** Chapman *Happy Mt.* 312 **seTN**, *Nirly*—good-humored, but rough-spoken. **1966–68** *DARE* Tape **MA**86, They were the [ˈnɝ·liəst] dang things; **WI**7, [Inf:] The pickle gets very hard and white and knurly, and they're bitter. [FW:] What do you mean by "knurly"? [Inf:] You know what an ordinary cucumber looks like, got a little wart. These look like a knot on the side of a tree, they're knurly . . they're not edible. **1969** Sorden *Lumberjack Lingo* 67 **NEng, Gt Lakes**, *Knurl*—A live protuberance, like a huge wart, that grew on some hardwood trees. It might be a foot or two in diameter and project six inches out from the foot of a tree. Because the grain ran in every direction, one made an excellent head for a large wooden maul because it would not split like straight-grain wood.

ko- pref See **ker-**

ko v See **co** v

ko n [Haw] **HI**

Sugar cane *(Saccharum officinarum)*.

1929 Neal *Honolulu Gardens* 23, Sugar cane, ko *(Saccharum officinarum)*. **1951** *AmSp* 26.23 **HI**, Common Hawaiian words are . . *ko* (sugar cane). **1954–60** Hance et al. *Hawaiian Sugar* 3 **HI**, *Ko*. . . Sugar cane.

koa n [Haw]

A tree *(Acacia koa)* native to Hawaii; also the wood of this tree.

1836 *Sandwich Is. Gaz. & Jrl. of Commerce* (Honolulu HI) 22 Oct [4], Koa Wood, resembles mahogany and is excellent for furniture. **1873** in 1966 Bishop *Sandwich Is.* 71 **HI**, I notice that the foreigners never use the English or botanical names of trees or plants, but speak of *ohias, ohelos, kukui* (candle-nut), *lauhala* (pandanus), *pulu* (tree fern), *mamané, koa,* &c. **1887** *Science* 10.115 **HI**, The remarkable boards of koa-wood . . standing on which they rode through the surf. **1928** Pan-Pacific Research Inst. *Jrl.* 3.2.6, Some of the more important . . in Hawaii are . . koa. . . kiawe. . . mamani. **1955** Day *HI People* 207, A pair of elephant tusks on a koa-wood stand. **1967** *DARE* (Qu. T16, . . *Kinds of trees . . 'special'*) Inf **HI**2, Acacia koa. **1967** *DARE* Tape **HI**7, [Inf:] The canoes that the Hawaiians use, koa. [FW:] Koa wood. [Inf:] It's pretty heavy;

it's way heavier than the fiberglass canoes. **1972** Carr *Da Kine Talk* 87 **HI**, *Hawaiian Words Commonly Heard In Hawaii's English*. . . *Koa*. . . largest of the native forest trees. **1991** Saiki *From the Lanai* 41 **HI**, Shiz [=a servant] slipped into the room to gather dishes in a koa tray. **1995** *NY Times* (NY) 16 Feb sec B 4/4, He hopes someday to have an adjustable [piano] bench of koa wood, which Hawaiians use for canoes and surfboards.

koa haole See **haole koa**

kobasa See **kielbasa**

koboodle See **caboodle**

kochcase See **cook cheese**

Kodiak bear n Also *Kadiak bear*

A **grizzly bear** (here: *Ursus arctos middendorffi*).

1899 Ward *Records* 474, Even more gigantic is the Kadiak bear . . of Kadiak Island, Alaska. **1917** Anthony *Mammals Amer.* 94, Alaska Brown Bear—*Ursus middendorffi*. . . Other Names.—Kodiak, or Kadiak Bear. . . The habitat of this interesting Bear extends along the coast of southeastern Alaska and most of the large islands adjacent thereto. Kodiak Island and the Alaskan Peninsula seem especially adapted to their liking. **1930** *Sat. Eve. Post* 13 Dec 11, A Kodiak bear looks as big as an elephant as he ambles . . through vegetation that comes only to his stomach. [**1936** in 1967 *Dict. Canadianisms* 409, After we had taken care of all the stations around Cook Inlet we went over to Kodiak Island where are found the famous Kodiak brown bears, the largest in the world.] **1955** U.S. Arctic Info. Center *Gloss.* 47, *Kodiak bear.* The world's largest carnivore, *Ursus middendorfi* [sic], occasionally weighing 1,500 pounds, yellowish to dark brown in color. **1982** Elman *Hunter's Field Guide* 570, Alaskan Brown Bear *(Ursus arctos middendorffi)*—Common & Regional Names: . . For Alaskan brown bear—brown bear . . Kodiak bear . . coastal grizzly.

kohee See **cohee**

K oil n **FL, sGA**

=**kerosene oil.**

c1970 Pederson *Dial. Surv. Rural GA* **seGA** (What do you call the liquid burned in lamps?) 6 [of 64] infs, K oil; 1 inf, Used to say kerosene, now say K oil. **1986** Pederson *LAGS Concordance (Kerosene)* 1 inf, **seGA**, K oil; 1 inf, **seGA**, K oil—now; 1 inf, **seGA**, Other people call it K oil, "K" for kerosene; 1 inf, **seGA**, K oil—abbreviation for kerosene; 1 inf, **seGA**, Some people call it K oil, but I call it "kerosene"; 1 inf, **nwFL**, K oil—she has heard, unsure; 1 inf, **nwFL**, K oil—old term.

kokanee (salmon) n [Prob < *Kokanee* Creek, in southeastern British Columbia] **West, esp AK, NW, Rocky Mts** Cf *DCan*

The lake-dwelling **sockeye salmon.** Cf **landlocked salmon** 2

1961 *Today's Health* July 53 **ID**, Priest Lake . . is well stocked with native cutthroat trout and kokanee, the land-locked sockeye salmon. **1963** Sigler–Miller *Fishes UT* 157, Kokanee (freshwater form). This member [=*Oncorhynchus nerka*] of the true salmons . . was first brought to Utah from Washington in 1922 and was introduced into Bear Lake in 1923. **1964** *AK Sportsman* July 57 (Tabbert *Dict. Alaskan Engl.*), A term with which many anglers in the Pacific Northwest are familiar is "kokanee"; these are landlocked red salmon which grow to be only fifteen or sixteen inches maximum length. **1965** McClane *McClane's Std. Fishing Encycl.* 457, The kokanee was originally found in Oregon, Idaho, Washington, British Columbia, and northward into Alaska. . . Morphologically the sockeye and sockeye are identical. **1965–70** *DARE* (Qu. P1, . . *Kinds of freshwater fish . . caught around here . . good to eat*) Infs **NM**6, **WY**1, Kokanee; **CA**195, Kokanee [ˈkokæni]—freshwater salmon; **CO**12, Kokanees—a few planted; **ID**4, Blueback—kokanee—this is a landlocked salmon, called silvers around Spokane; **CA**130, Kokanee salmon—a landlocked salmon, they plant them; actually, they're a sockeye; **CO**47, Kokanee salmon; (Qu. P13, . . *Ways of fishing . . besides the ordinary hook and line*) Inf **CO**12, Snare kokanee—with large treble hook dragged through water. **1966** *Flathead Courier Vacation Guide* (Polson MT) Summer sec B 3/2, Silver Salmon—Silvers or kokanee tend to average around 12–14 inches with the top being in the 3¼ pound bracket. **1971** Brown *Fishes MT* 49, Kokanee is the name applied to the landlocked stock of the sockeye salmon—those that go to sea are sockeye, the remainder are kokanee. **1987** *AK Fish & Game* 19.2.6, Trophy class fish are found in large landlocked lakes that have populations of kokanee (landlocked red salmon . .) which serve as forage. **1991** Amer. Fisheries Soc. *Common Names Fishes* 28, Lacustrine stocks of sockeye salmon are known as kokanee.

kokua v, n [Haw] **HI**

See quot 1938.

1938 Reinecke *Hawaiian Loanwords* 20, *Kokua* . . v., n. 1. To help in any way. 2. Aid. 3. One who aids . . V[ery] F[requent] in these three senses. 4. One who accompanies a person afflicted with leprosy (nearly always a husband or wife) to the settlement at Kalaupapa, Molokai. (A legal as well as a popular term.) **1954–60** Hance et al. *Hawaiian Sugar* 3, *Kokua*. . . Help, aid. **1969** *DARE* FW Addit **Honolulu HI**, *Kokua* [kouˈkuə]—to help, cooperate. E.g., "We appreciate your kokua." Common. **1972** Carr *Da Kine Talk* 87 **HI**, *Hawaiian Words Commonly Heard In Hawaii's English*. . . *Kokua*. Help. **1984** Sunset *HI Guide* 85, *Kokua*—help.

kokus sheldrake n

=**hooded merganser.**

1925 (1928) Forbush *Birds MA* 1.187, *Lophodytes cucullatus*. . . Hooded Merganser. . . Kokus sheldrake.

kolacky n Usu |koˈlač(k)i, koˈlač; ˈko-, kə-| Also freq *kolach(e)*, *kolachky*; pl *kolacky, kolache(s), kolatchen;* for addit pronc and sp varr see quots Note: It is not always possible to distinguish sg and pl forms in the quots. [Czech *koláč* < *kolo* wheel, circle] **chiefly WI, Upper MW** See Map

A pastry of sweetened yeast dough with a sweet filling; a pastry of rich pie dough with a sweet topping.

1919 Cather *My Antonia* 381 **NE**, Show him the spiced plums, mother. Americans don't have those. . . Mother uses them to make *kolaches*. **1920** Kander *Settlement Cook Book* 358, *Bohemian Kolatchen*—Make Kuchen Dough. . . Add a little cinnamon and mace and 1 teaspoon anise seed. . . Let rise till very light, then . . roll out to about half inch. Cut in rounds, . . pressing down the centre of each so as to raise a ridge around the edge. **1938** FWP *Guide MN* 77, The Czechs still raise poppies in their gardens that they may have seeds for the sweet turn-over rolls, filled with citron, which they call *kolacky*. **1940** Brown *Amer. Cooks* 224 **cIA**, *Bohemian Kolaches*. Ibid 509 **NE**, *Plain Kolach*. . . These excellent Bohemian cakes referred to as kolaches in the plural . . arrived in Omaha by covered wagon and the Bohemians who brought them are now sturdy old American stock in our Midwest. **1948** *WELS Suppl.* **cwWI**, [One of the only] Bohemian word[s] in our locality [is] kolače. *Ibid,* At our centennial celebration, there was an especially delectable koláče, which was fried like a doughnut, then dabbed with prune filling *and* whipped cream. Of course, you are familiar with the Bohemian kolache, as it is Englished? It is riz dough cast in rounds, first raised, then dented in the middle and baked, and filled with mashed prunes, or grated apple fried in butter, or poppy-seed pounded in a mortar and cooked in cream, with "sugar to the taste." . . But the fried one is a variation. **1952** FWP *Guide SD* 323, Tabor . . is the center of a Bohemian, or Czech, settlement. . . Their best known food is the kolach, a small biscuit filled with fruit or with poppyseed. **1952** Tracy *Coast Cookery* 67 **Chicago IL**, *Quick Kolacky*—This is a Bohemian recipe. **1955** (1956) Clark *Best Cookery Middle West* 176 **ND**, *Kolachky or Kolaches*. . . from a Bohemian community in North Dakota. **c1965** Randle *Cookbooks* (Ask Neighbor) 3.59 **OH**, *Quick Kolaczki*. **1965–70** *DARE* (Qu. H32, . . *Fancy rolls and pastries*) Inf **MN**11, Kolaches [koˈlačɨs]; **MN**28, Kolache [ˈkolači]—doughnut-like dough, shaped like a long john with pudding inside, glaze on outside; **NE**2, Kolache [ˈkolači]; **WI**13, Kolache [koˈlači]—like a turnover, prune filling; **WI**47, Kolache [kəˈlači]; **WI**49, Kolache [kəˈlači] [FW: Inf unsure of pronc]; **WI**58, Kolaches—Czech—dough with a depression in it filled with fruit mixture, poppy seeds or sweetened cottage cheese mixture; **WI**60, Bohemian kolaches are sold in the bakery here; **WI**70, 71, Kolaches; (Qu. H29, *A round cake, cooked in deep fat, with jelly inside*) Inf **KS**18, [kəˈlæči]—Bohemian roll with fruit filling which is put in before the roll is baked; (Qu. H65, *Foreign foods favored by people around here*) Inf **OH**78, Kolaches [kəˈlačiz]—Bohemian pastry [FW: used by Inf in conv]. **1967** *DARE* Tape **MN**11, [FW:] You mentioned kolaches. [Inf:] They're made of a rich pie dough and they're cut in squares about four, five inches and slit from the corners in, . . [with] cooked prunes or apples or peaches—any kind of fruit that you want to put inside—and then the corners turned in so they sort of look like a star, but you can see the fruit from the top of it too. **1971** *AmSp* 46.79 **Chicago IL** [Urban word geography], Various breakfast pastries: 1. small cakes: *kolacky, kolaks.* **1973** Allen *LAUM* 1.277 **Upper MW exc IA** (as of c1950), *Kolachy* . . [5 infs]. *The Minneapolis Star* . . 1959, reported: "Some 50,000 kolacky (Bohemian buns) are being baked for distribution . . at the annual Kolacky Dairy celebration Sunday." **1989** *DARE* File **Chicago IL**, *Kolachky* [ˌkɔˈlački]—Czech term for pastries made from sweet, rich, leavened dough—round and flat with fruit preserves,

or cheese or poppyseed filling in a depression in the center. My parents, second-generation Czech-Americans, use "kolachky" and "kolach" as both singular and plural terms. They pronounce it [ˈkɔˈlački] or [ˈkɔˈlač]. *Ibid* **Omaha NE**, My Aunt Elsie—whom my mother refers to as "my Bohunk sister-in-law"—brought kolache to every family event. . . Peach are best. One piece or one pan—is [koˈlačɛ]; plural is [koˈlačɨz]. **1991** *Ibid* **cIA**, A teacher brought a pan of kolachy. The dough was rich, yeasted, and filled with mashed fruit.

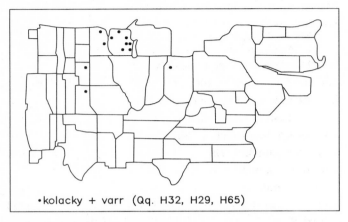

• kolacky + varr (Qq. H32, H29, H65)

kolbasa, kolbasy See **kielbasa**

kol'-breaking See **col'-bucking**

kolumpki, kolupki See **golumpki A**

kona n Also *kona wind* [Haw < *kona* leeward side of the islands (because it blows in the opposite direction to the prevailing trade winds)] **HI**

A strong, humid, southerly or southwesterly wind, often accompanied by heavy rain.

1866 in 1947 Frear *Mark Twain & HI* 272, In the stormy season—in the season of the terrible *Kona*. **1873** in 1966 Bishop *Sandwich Is.* 145, The sun was fierce and bright, the ocean had a metallic glint, the hot breath of the *kona* was scorching. *Ibid* 173, The trade winds have set in, and though they may yet yield once or twice to the *kona*, they will soon be firmly established for nine months. **1892** Stevenson–Osbourne *Wrecker* 9, It was blowing a kona, hard. **1934** Frear *Lowell & Abigail* xiv **HI**, But by night . . how the Kona wind moaned and drove the rain up from the sea. **1955** Day *HI People* 12, A sudden kona storm hit them at midnight four days later. *Ibid* 311, [Glossary:] *Kona:* west or southwest; a muggy wind. **1967** *DARE* (Qu. B16, *A destructive wind that comes with a funnel-shaped cloud*) Inf **HI**4, Kona—south wind and storm, punishing; (Qu. B18, . . *Special kinds of wind*) Inf **HI**1, Kona storm—one with wind coming from the south, muggy, hot; kona weather; **HI**9, Kona wind—brings rain, comes from south, it's warm. **1972** Carr *Da Kine Talk* 114 **HI**, *Kona weather*. . . The muggy weather that comes when the northeast trade winds are replaced by the *Kona wind* from the south or southwest. A *Kona storm* brings with it heavy rains from the south or leeward side of the islands. **1980** Bushnell *Water of Kane* 162 **HI**, And always there was the mud, even on days of kona weather, when the winds blew from the south and no rain at all descended upon the ditch country.

konck See **conch**

konks n pl

=**chitterlings 1.**

1969 *Foxfire* Winter 59 **nGA**, Chitlin's—"konks". Clean all the fat off the pig's intestines. . . Boil in salt water until tender . . then cut into one-inch pieces. Sprinkle with corn meal and brown in hot fat.

konkus See **conk** n[2] **1**

koonta, koontie See **coontie**

kootznehoo See **hoochinoo**

kopasetee See **copacetic**

kope See **cope** v[2]

kosha grass n

See quot.

1985 Ehrlich *Solace* 17 **WY**, When he became too old or infirm to work, he might live in the ranch yard and feed the dogs or clear the kosha grass from the pens in the spring.

kotation See **quote**

kotch v See **catch** v A1, 3

kotch n See **cotch** n

kotched See **catch** v A3

kote See **quote**

kotonk n Also *katonk* [Perh echoic; see quot 1953] **HI** Cf **buddhahead**

A Japanese-American from the mainland rather than from Hawaii.

1953 in 1966 Morimoto *Hawaiian Dial. Engl.* 111, 'Kotonk' is an appellation fixed on the Mainland Nisei's by their Hawaiian brethren. Its origin is attributed to a wise-acre from Hawaii who claimed if one tapped on the skull of a Mainland Nisei, the resulting sound would be hollow 'kotonk' like that of a coconut. **1954** *Ibid* 97, Discord between buddhaheads and kotonks gradually died out. Mainland and Island AJAs [=assimilated Japanese-Americans], living and working together, came to know each other as individuals, which led to better understanding. **1966** *Ibid* 111, A mainland girl of Japanese ancestry related. . . When I first started going to this high school, I wondered why the boy I sat next to never spoke to me. We have since become friends so I asked why he wasn't friendly, and he jokingly replied, 'I didn't want to be caught talking to a stupid "kotonk." ' **1967** *DARE* (Qu. HH28, *Names and nicknames . . for people of foreign background*) Inf **HI**13, [ka'tɔŋk]—mainland U.S. Japanese. **1972** Carr *Da Kine Talk* 93 **HI**, Two humorous terms used during World War II were *Buddhahead* . . for Japanese-Americans born in Hawaii, and *Kotonk*, for those born on the mainland of the United States. **1981** *Pidgin To Da Max* np **HI**, *Kotonk*. . . Japanese person from the U.S. mainland. Hollow-head buddhahead. **1995** *NY Times* (NY) 19 June sec A 6/4, The Hawaiians called the mainlanders "Katonks," meaning hollowheads, Mr. Oka said, and they in turn were called "Buddhaheads" as ridicule for their pidgin English and more traditional ways.

kotz v Pronc-sp *kutz* [Colloq Ger *kotzen*, PaGer *kotze*] **Ger and PaGer settlement areas**

To vomit.

1967–68 *DARE* (Qu. BB17, . . *Vomiting*) Inf **IA**32, Kutzing [kʊtsɪŋ]—German, used a lot; **PA**18, Throw up; he kutzed [kʌtst]—**PA**139, Kutz [kʌts]. [All Infs from Ger or PaGer settlement areas] **1968** *Helen Adolf Festschrift* 36 **cs,sePA**, The verb to kotz (Pennsylvania German *kotze*), meaning 'to vomit,' is used quite widely, even in the upper strata of society. **1987** *Jrl. Engl. Ling.* 20.2.171 **ePA**, *Kotz* 'to vomit'. . . 6 [of 100 infs]. *Ibid*, Buffinton's remark [in 1968 *Helen Adolf Festschrift*] that *kotz* "is used quite widely, even in the upper strata of society" seems untrue today. . . Five informants marked alternates to *kotz* in responding to the question. **1991** *DARE* File **ceWI**, To kutz—to throw up.

kou n [Haw]

A tree (*Cordia subcordata*) naturalized to Hawaii.

1825 Ellis *Jrl. HI* 27, The houses, which are neat, are generally built on the sea-shore, shaded with cocoanut and *kou* trees. **1866** in 1966 Twain *Letters HI* 128, It [=a coffin] is made of those two superb species of native wood, kou and koa. The former is nearly as dark as ebony. **1873** in 1966 Bishop *Sandwich Is.* 197 **HI**, The calabashes . . were of highly polished *kou* wood. **1886** in 1892 Gowen *Paradise Pacific* 85 **HI**, The king has been for some time engaged in receiving presents, and large calabashes of *kou* wood have been presented to him from 300 native communities. **1930** Degener *Ferns of HI* 175, The Hawaiians made their calabashes . . from the *kou* tree and practically never from the *koa* because . . it imparted a disagreeable flavor to food stored within it. **1965** Neal *Gardens HI* 714, The kou was probably brought to Hawaii by early Polynesian immigrants. . . In Hawaii, at Ewa, Oahu, a legend tells of a chiefess who saw an old woman stringing a lei of kou blossoms.

kouse See **cous**

kow-bird See **cowbird** 2

kow-kow See **cow-cow** 2

kram n |krɑm| Also sp *crom* [Ger *kram* rubbish, junk; Norw *kram* junk, trifles] **esp WI** Cf **crawm**

A jumble of articles of little value; junk.

1947 *WELS Suppl.* **cWI**, There is another queer word used by some

here. It is *crom*. It is used as a noun to mean trash or junk. **1948** *Ibid* **ceWI**, The word [=*kram*] was used in my family 50 years ago and no doubt much longer than that. I'm quite sure it is of low german origin, spoken by the people who came from Mecklenburg. It means "trash." My mother would speak of the "Kram-kammer," also calling the same room a "Rumple-kammer." This was a room used in place of an attic. If we played with a lot of different things and left them all helter skelter we were told to clean up our *Kramerei*. Also, when we looked for something, as in a dresser drawer and got it all upset, we were told we got everything "umgekramt." *Ibid* **csWI**, "Kram." My mother used that word. She was born in Wisconsin, but her parents were from Norway. *Ibid* **csWI**, *Kram* for junk, etc., is also used. *Ibid* **seWI**, The word "kram," as a verb, was always used in our family, also meaning aimless searching. But we also used the noun forms, "Kramerei" and "Kram" frequently. [*Ibid* **ceWI**, I think I can enlighten you on one of the words. . . sent in by one of your listeners. It was the word *crumb* or *cromb*. This is not an English word; it is decidedly *German*. As a child, I can remember hearing my mother say, "Now that you're through playing, clear your 'kraam' (cromb) away." Meaning: "clear your *junk* away." *Ibid* **seWI**, The lady in Wausau may have heard the word "Kram" which we use in the German language to designate what we call "junk" in the English language, meaning something of small marketable value, or any jumble of articles of little or no value.] **1992** *DARE* File **cWI**, *Kram* [krɑm]—as a noun means junk, a whole jumble of stuff. It's a verb too, and means a disorganized search for something.

kram v |krɑm| Also sp *crom, krom* [Ger *kramen*; cf **kram** n] **esp WI**

To rummage around; to search haphazardly.

1947 *WELS Suppl.* **cWI**, There is another queer word used by some here. It is *crom*. . . It is used . . as a verb [to mean] to mess around or search confusedly. **1948** *Ibid* **seWI**, The word "kram," as a verb, was always used in our family, . . meaning aimless searching. *Ibid* **cWI**, I pronounce it Kr(om) as in (Com)merce. . . For instance, . . I wanted to use a certain pattern that I knew was somewhere upstairs in a certain box, but which box? I started to "krom" through all my patch and pattern boxes until I found that pattern. **1992** [see **kram** n].

krapfen n Also *krapfel, kroepfle* [sGer dial *Krapfen*, dimin *Kräpfel*] **Ger settlement areas** Cf **krebbel**

A type of **friedcake 1** or a **bismarck 2.**

1871 (1975) Levy *Jewish Cookery* 79, *Krapfen*, or German Puffs. . . [W]hen they have risen then fry them a light color; as soon as they are done, drain them on a napkin and strew cinnamon, orange and sugar on the top. **1920** Kander *Settlement Cook Book* 291 **Milwaukee WI**, *Spritz Krapfen* . . flour . . water . . butter . . lemon . . rind . . yolks . . whole eggs. . . Drop by spoonfuls or through Spritz Krapfen tube into deep, hot fat and bake a nice brown. [**1935** Frederick *PA Dutch* 228, *Dutch Puffs (Krapfen)* . . flour . . butter . . sugar . . eggs . . yeast . . cream. . . Let rise. . . knead it. . . Cut into about 30 pieces of equal size, knead these into balls. . . Then immerse in hot Crisco or lard until golden brown. . . sprinkle over them cinnamon.] **1948** *AmSp* 23.107 **swIL**, German names having to do with foods and cooking are sufficiently numerous in the local vocabulary to give a decided German atmosphere. The following names are frequently heard . . *krapfel*. **1954** *WELS Suppl.* **csWI**, Did you ever hear the word "*Kroepfle*" to designate something like a filled doughnut or a Berliner? **1986** Pederson *LAGS Concordance*, 1 inf, **cTX**, *Krapfen*—doughnut dough, square.

kraut n Also sp *krout* [Ger *Kraut*]

1 =**sauerkraut**; occas, fresh cabbage. **chiefly Midl** See Map on p. 258

1830 Ames *Mariner's Sketches* 8 **MA**, Indeed, the whole Dutch nation have entered into the argument, with such zeal, that on board both men of war and merchant-men, the bell is rung, not only at "krout time," but not a single glass of "schnaps" can be served out, without due tintinnabulary notice being given thereof. **1836** (1837) Goodrich *Universal Traveller* 39 **Mid Atl**, There are many other *festivals and occasions* of recreation observed in the Middle States, such as St. Patrick's day, Pasche, Krout feasts, and Target firing. **1867** Harris *Sut Lovingood Yarns* 73 **TN**, Thar a-lyin es cold es krout. **1905** *DN* 3.85 **nwAR**, *Kraut*. . . Sauerkraut. 'We've got good can kraut.' General. **1950** *PADS* 14.42 **SC**, Kraut. . . Cabbage. Dutch Fork. **1956** McAtee *Some Dialect NC* 26, *Kraut* . . cabbage. **1960** Criswell *Resp. to PADS 20* **Ozarks**, Kraut, sometimes called *sauerkraut*, made from long ago. No nicknames for *cabbage*. *Kraut*, used only for cabbage cut up and put down in salt brine, never for fresh cabbage. **1960** Hall *Smoky Mt. Folks* 60, *Krout*: Sauerkraut. **1965–70** *DARE* (Qu. H52, *Dishes made with fresh cabbage*) 10 Infs, **esp Midl**, Kraut; **IL**134, Kraut—let it sour, salt it, get juice, make in a jar; **NC**33, Fresh kraut; (Qu. H41, . . *Kinds of roll or bun sandwiches . . in a round bun or roll*) Inf **CO**7, Krautburger; (Qu. H45) Inf **VA**9, Kraut dumplings; (Qu. H51, *Dishes made with cooked cabbage;* total Infs questioned, 75) Inf **OK**19, Kraut; (Qu. H57, *Tasty or spicy side-dishes served with meats*) Inf **CA**113, Kraut salad, sauerkraut salad—kraut, peppers, onions; **IN**48, Kraut; **NC**33, In kraut season, kraut is eaten with lots of meats. **1968** Pochmann *Triple Ridge* 63 **cWI**, The big wooden kraut bowl and a smaller salad bowl . . hang on the white wall. **1968** *DARE* Tape **IN**3, [When I was a child] they put a lot of stuff up in barrels, like barrels of kraut, and pickles; **IN**35, And we make sauerkraut too, with an old-fashioned kraut-cutter. **1986** Pederson *LAGS Concordance (Cabbage)* 3 infs, **nwGA, AR**, Kraut; 3 infs, **cTN, neAL, neMS**, Kraut—sauerkraut; 2 infs, **neMS, neAR**, Homemade kraut; 1 inf, **neTN**, Make kraut of cabbage; 1 inf, **nwGA**, Kraut—stored in churns; 1 inf, **cTN**, Kraut—of cabbage; 1 inf, **ceAR**, Kraut—made from cabbage; 1 inf, **neAR**, Raw kraut; 1 inf, **seAR**, Kraut ain't bad—sauerkraut is quite good; 1 inf, **cwTN**, Big-old bowl of green kraut; 1 inf, **cTX**, Cold as kraut; 1 inf, **seAR**, Cooked kraut; 1 inf, **cwTN**, He eat like a pig on that green kraut; [1 inf, **ceTN**, Turnip kraut—turnip tops instead of cabbage].

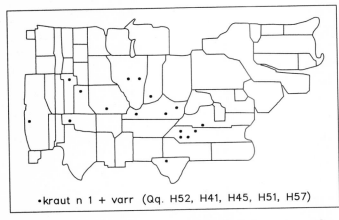

•kraut n 1 + varr (Qq. H52, H41, H45, H51, H57)

2 also *krauthead, ~-eater, ~-stomper:* A German, esp a German soldier; someone of German background. [Transf from **1** above] **widespread, but less freq Mid and S Atl, Lower Missip Valley** See Map *derog* Cf **sauerkraut**

1918 Griffin *Ballads Regiment* 34, But he always loved a soldier be he . . "Krout" or "Mick." **1926** Nason *Chevrons* 139, I ain't had much to do with krauts in France, but I've had some truck with 'em in Wisconsin. **1929** Scanlon *God Have Mercy* 4, What gives me a pain in the neck is all the time we wasted up at Verdun in the old trenches when we might have been killing Krautheads. **1936** *Our Army* Feb 14, We and the kraut-eaters were mixing it up . . to make the world safe for bigger and better wars. **1950** Hemingway *Across the River* 224, Therefore they bombed us the same as they had bombed the Krauts. **1960** Criswell *Resp. to PADS 20* **Ozarks**, *Kraut*, for a German, very common; *Dutchman* always used for German. **1965–70** *DARE* (Qu. HH28, *Names and nicknames . . for people of foreign background*) 200 Infs, **widespread, but less freq Mid and S Atl**, Kraut; **CO**47, **IL**25, 116, **NY**34, **OH**47, **WA**33, Krauthead; **CA**36, **CO**34, **IN**45, Kraut-eater; **IL**80, Kraut-stomper [Of all Infs responding to the question, 63% were old;

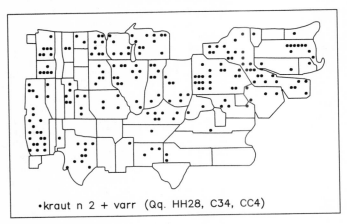

•kraut n 2 + varr (Qq. HH28, C34, CC4)

of those giving these responses, 51% were old.]; (Qu. C34, *Nicknames for nearby settlements, villages, or districts*) Inf **MO**32, Kraut Town; (Qu. CC4, . . *Nicknames . . for various religions or religious groups*) Inf **MD**34, Kraut; **NY**83, Kraut Church. **1983** Allen *Lang. Ethnic Conflict* 57 [Ethnic epithets], *Germans. . . sauerkraut. . .* Also *kraut* (WWI), *krauthead* (WWII). **1986** Pederson *LAGS Concordance* **Gulf Region** *(German)* 39 infs, Kraut(s); 2 infs, Kraut—derogatory; 1 inf, Kraut—on TV; Germans not recognized as a group; 1 inf, Kraut—from World War II; 1 inf, Kraut—heard on television; 1 inf, Kraut—heard in the service; 1 inf, Kraut—father's term; 3 infs, Kraut heads; 1 inf, Kraut eaters.

kraut *v*, hence ppl adj *krauted*
To pickle in the manner of **sauerkraut**.
   1917 *DN* 4.413 **wNC**, I don't do like old Mis' Posey, kraut my cabbage whole. **1940** Brown *Amer. Cooks* 475 **MO**, All it is is a chopped up mess of green peppers, cabbages, green tomatoes, packed in a stone jar, and 'krauted.' No vinegar, no sugar, no spice. *Ibid* 634 **NC**, *Krauted Beans*—Put down green string beans with salt, like sauerkraut.

kraut-eater See **kraut** n 2

krauted See **kraut** v

krauthead, kraut-stomper See **kraut** n 2

kraut stone *n*
   1968 *DARE* (Qu. C25, . . *Kinds of stone . . about . . [. . size of a person's head], smooth and hard*) Inf **OH**66, Dornick, kraut stone.

krawm *n* See **crawm**

krebbel *n* Also *grebble* [Ger dial *Kräppel*, dimin of *Krapfen*] Cf **krapfen**
=**cruller.**
   1961 Sackett–Koch *KS Folkl.* 232, Krebbel. . . Beat 4 eggs well, then add . . sugar . . shortening . . sweet milk . . Flour enough to make a rather stiff dough. . . Roll out thin and cut in strips. . . cut a slit lengthwise down the center of each strip . . stretch, and twist into different shapes and bake in deep hot grease. **1962** Atwood *Vocab. TX* 63, *Doughnut.* For the sweetish, doughy, fried pastry with a hole. . . Some five informants of German-speaking background use *krebbel. Ibid* 94, Examples of German influence . . *krebbel* for doughnut. **1991** Kirlin–Kirlin *Smithsonian Folklife Cookbook* 229 **NEast**, Grebble (Fried Pastries) . . buttermilk . . sour cream . . eggs . . baking powder . . baking soda . . sugar . . flour . . dry yeast . . oil for frying. Pinch off small amounts of dough. Roll out . . cut into . . squares, and twist. Fry in deep fat.

krechs, krechts See **krex**

kreeker See **krieker**

kreistle *v*
=**greissel.**
   1921 in **1944** *ADD*, Kreistle. . . 'If that wouldn't kreistle a body . .' = bother.

krewe *n* [See quot 1951] **New Orleans LA**
A private social club that sponsors festivities such as parades and balls at **Mardi Gras 1.**
   1900 *Collier's* 10 Mar 19 **New Orleans LA**, The Krewe of Proteus gave a fine presentation from the most noted fairy tales of childhood. **1951** *AmSp* 26.110 **New Orleans LA**, Although the custom of masquerading on Mardi Gras was popular in New Orleans as early as the 1830s the first formal masked parade did not take place until 1857. It was presented by an organization which called itself "The Mistick Krewe of Comus." . . The 'theme' or motif which the New Orleans group selected for their parade and ball was Milton's *Paradise Lost.* Apparently, the name of the organization was suggested by Milton's mask, 'Comus,' and the line from 'L'Allegro' in which the poet calls upon Mirth to 'admit me of thy crew.' *Ibid* 111, *Krewe:* . . now a generic term for any carnival organization. **1960** (1966) Percy *Moviegoer* 17 **New Orleans LA**, It is still a week before Mardi Gras and this is a new parade, a women's krewe from Gentilly [Louisiana]. A krewe is a group of people who get together at carnival time and put on a parade and a ball. . . The other day a group of Syrians from Algiers formed a krewe named Isis. *Ibid* 29, He's krewe captain. **1984** Stall *Proud New Orleans* 7, The Twelfth Night Revelers are a Mardi Gras krewe which take their name from the twelfth night after Christmas, or January 6, the night the three kings visited the Christ child. The Revelers have been in existence since 1870. **1992** *San Francisco Chron.* (CA) 2 Jan sec A 4/5 **New Orleans LA**, Historically, many of the largest Mardi Gras clubs—or krewes—have not allowed Jews, blacks, Italians or women to join.

krex v Also *crex, grex, gretch, krech(t)s, kretz* [Ger *krächzen* to caw, croak; to complain; PaGer *greckse*, Yiddish *krekhts(e)n* to groan, grumble, complain] **esp in Ger, PaGer, and Jewish settlement areas** Cf **kvetch** v, n

To complain, grumble; to fret, whine; hence n *krex* a complaint; *krexer* a complainer, whiner; adj *krexy* fretful, whiny.

  1939 Aurand *Quaint Idioms* 15 [PaGer], You needn't *grex* (grunt) so; it ain't that heavy. **1950** *PADS* 14.42 **SC,** *Krex.* . . To fret. "The baby is krexin'." **1950** *WELS* (*A person who complains a great deal*) 1 Inf, **ceWI,** Krexer. **1950** *WELS Suppl.* **Milwaukee WI,** My mother remembers her grandmother often using the word "krechs." I don't know how to spell it, but it was always said with the "k" sound, never with a "g" sound. "I'm a krechser." If the children were ill and someone inquired for them, she would say, "They've been krexing all morning." *Ibid* **seWI,** My husband's grandmother . . had a chronic "hexenschuss" . . and she was wont to give the symptoms in detail. . . Then she'd conclude thusly: "I know I'm grexing, but . . it *does* hurt *so!*" [Another West Bend resident] says her husband is hard to live with: "He's always grexing about something." *Ibid* **seWI,** You spoke of the word *grex*, as meaning complaining. I too have heard that term used in Sheboygan County, rural communities, with that same meaning, but I always heard it pronounced kivecks [sic]. *Ibid* **csWI,** Our family is very well acquainted with the use of the word *crex* meaning to complain. *Ibid* **csWI,** Gretch. **1967** *DARE* (Qu. GG16, . . *Finding fault, or complaining: "You just can't please him—he's always _____."*) Inf **PA28,** Grexing [grɛksɪŋ]. **1970** Feinsilver *Yiddish* 364, *Krechtsing . . krechts* sessions. . . statements I heard in recent months are typical of second- and third-generation American Jewish speech: "When he doesn't feel well, he won't go to bed, but he walks around krechtsing" (i.e. groaning); . . "They just meet for krechts sessions" (of oldsters who have not found outside interests and merely exchange accounts of their aches and pains). **1987** *Jrl. Engl. Ling.* 20.2.170 **ePA,** *Grex* 'to groan, to complain' [actively used by 13 of 100 infs]. . . Although six of the informants are under 30, four of them are residents of Lebanon or Berks County. **1992** *DARE* File **Milwaukee WI,** My mother remembers her mother gossiping with friends—all of them Jewish. One person would name a name, and then others would give that name a label. For some names, her mother would say ['krɛksɚ] or she'd say "He's always ['krɛksɪn]." She said it didn't mean "complain" so much as "whine." . . Her group were speaking English, although Grandma knew Yiddish. *Ibid* **cIA,** My father knows *kretz* as a Yiddish word used in English. Adults said someone was a *kretzer* meaning a nag, a complainer, that someone was always *kretzing*. His was a family where everyone slipped Yiddish words into their English. *Ibid* **cWI,** *Krex* means to moan or complain about something. **1993** *Ibid* **Milwaukee WI** (as of c1960), I remember my mother, of German-Bohemian background, saying of a complaining child, "He's krexy; he needs a nap."

krick See **creek** n¹

krieker n Also sp *creaker, creeker, kreeker;* also *kicker, krinker* [Etym uncert; see quots 1888, 1977]
=pectoral sandpiper.

  1866 Roosevelt *Game-Birds N. States* 160, *Krieker.* Meadow Snipe, Fat Bird, Short Neck, Jack Snipe. . . *Tringa Pectoralis.* **1876** *Forest & Stream* 7.68, *Tringa pectoralis.* Creaker; meadow-snipe. **1880** *Ibid* 15.4, Pectoral sandpiper (*Tringa maculata*); krieker. **1881** *Ibid* 17.226 **NEng,** There is another beautiful plump little bird (*Tringa maculata . .*) well-known on our coast in summer and autumn under various cognomens, as "Jack snipe," . . "krieker." **1886** *Ibid* 27.287 **Cape Cod MA,** The "grass bird" is the "jacksnipe," "kicker," or pectoral sandpiper (*Tringa maculata*). **1888** Trumbull *Names of Birds* 176, *Tringa maculata.* . . At Newport, R.I., on Long Island at Shinnecock Bay, Moriches, and Bellport, and at Barnegat, N.J., *Krieker.* I write this name as it is usually spelled. It was not applied, as popularly believed, because of the bird's creaking note, but because of its crouching or squatting habit—German *Kriecher,* a cringing person. **1923** U.S. Dept. Ag. *Misc. Circular* 13.54, Pectoral Sandpiper (*Pisobia maculata*). . . In local use . . creaker (also spelled creeker, and krieker) (R.I., Long Id., N.Y., N.J., Pa., N.C.) **1956** MA Audubon Soc. *Bulletin* 40.19 **MA, RI,** Pectoral Sandpiper. . . Krieker. . . other theories are reflected in the spellings, "Creaker, Kreeker, and Krinker," supposed to be imitative of its notes; and "Creeker" from its frequenting creeks or channels in marshes. **1977** Bull–Farrand *Audubon Field Guide Birds* 429, Hunters called this species [=*Calidris melanotos*] the "Grass Snipe," referring to its liking for grassy meadows, or "Krieker" because of its grating snipe-like call when in flight.

kringle n Usu |'krɪŋ(g)l|; also |'krɪŋglə| Pronc-sp *kringla;* pl *kringle(s), kringler* [Prob primarily < Dan *kringle* (also dial or arch *kringel*), pl *kringler,* literally "ring, loop"; however, cognate terms are found in all Scan languages and Ger, applied to var baked goods in ring, pretzel, or figure-eight shapes.] **Scan settlement areas, esp WI**

A usu sweet, flaky pastry, often with fruit or nut filling, that is usu formed into a ring or a pretzel-like shape.

  1950 *WELS* **WI** (*Fancy home-baked rolls*) 1 Inf, Kringle; 1 Inf, Kringle ['krɪŋglə]—made with string of sweetened bread dough, glazed. **1951** Tufford *Scandinavian Recipes* 29, *Kringle* . . yeast . . salt . . milk . . butter . . sugar . . flour . . eggs . . anise seed. . . Take small pieces of dough and roll into long strips, forming them into figures of 8. *Ibid* 30, *Danish Kringle.* . . Roll each piece into strip about 9 inches wide. Spread each piece with stiffly beaten egg whites, then brown sugar, then a layer of raisins and apples or dates and sprinkle with nuts. Fold ⅓ of dough over crosswise, then fold remainder of dough to the fold, making 3 layers. Place on a well greased baking sheet and shape into a kringle. **1967–69** *DARE* (Qu. H32, . . *Fancy rolls and pastries*) Inf **IL49,** [Inf:] Kringle—Danish, get them in Racine WI. [FW:] Racine Danish kringles are large, round pastries with different fruit fillings and icing on top—tremendously good; **MA44,** Kringler; **MN6,** Kringler ['krɪŋlɚ]. **1967** *Geauga Times Leader* (Chardon OH) 2 Oct 4/3, She was the guest of honor for coffee and kingle [sic]. **1992** *DARE* File **seWI,** [Advt:] Send a Heart Shaped Kringle To Someone Special. . . A Treat In Any Flavor! Fillings That Travel Best: Almond, Apricot, Date, Pecan, Raspberry, Walnut. Lehmann's Bakery, Racine. *Ibid* **Minneapolis MN,** *Kringler* is the plural (in Norwegian, at least) of kringle. *Ibid,* I asked . . where their kringler are produced. The clerk responded "At our bakery in New Hope Minnesota." *Ibid* **seOR,** My mother's best friend used to bring us a Danish kringle for Christmas. It was an oblong pastry filled with a hazelnut mixture that was swirled throughout, frosted lightly then topped off with a lighter dusting of nuts. **1994** *Ibid* **Racine WI,** I say ['krɪŋl], everyone in my family says it that way—like "sing," no "g". *Ibid,* ['krɪŋl] is a pastry shaped into an oval ring. Often the ends are overlapped a bit and give it a form somewhat like an open pretzel. *Ibid* **csWI,** Around here, people say ['krɪŋgl] for the special pastry from Racine. *Ibid* **cIA,** The "kringla" I'm talking about is the pastry popular in Story City. . . There I encountered what they were calling and selling [as] "kringla." It reminded me a lot of the Dutch letter pastry. The kringla there was one "cookie" (about three by four inches in size) and in the contorted shape of a pretzel (though not exactly).

krinker See **krieker**

Kris Kringle v See **Christkindle**

Kris(s) Kringle n Also *Chriskingle, Christ Kindel, Christ-kinkle;* for addit varr see quots [Ger *Christkindlein*] **chiefly PaGer area, but more widely recognized** Cf **Belsnickel**

A folklore character supposed to bring gifts to good children at Christmas, orig identified with the Christ child, but later with St. Nicholas or Santa Claus; occas a person representing this character; hence rarely n *Christ-kindly* a Christmas present.

  1827 in **1954** *PA Dutchman* Winter 34 **sePA,** Our readers are perhaps aware this Mr. Bellschniggle is a visible personage Ebony in appearance, but Topax [sic] in spirit. He is the precursor of the jolly old elf "Christkindle," or "St. . . Nicholas." . . Christkindle, or St. Nicholas, is never seen. He slips down the chimney, at the fairy hour of midnight, and deposits his presents quietly in the prepared stocking. **1830** Watson *Annals Philadelphia* 242 **sePA,** Every father in his turn remembers the excitements of his youth in Belsh-nichel and Christ-kinkle nights. **1842** in **1954** *PA Dutchman* Winter 34 **sePA,** Christmas Eve—a few "belsnickels" or "kriskinckles" were prowling about this evening frightening the women and children, with their uncouth appearance—made up of cast-off garments made parti-colored with patches, a false face, a shaggy head of tow, or rather wig, falling profusely over the shoulders and finished by a most patriarchal beard. **1849** Rees *Mysteries City Life* 93 **PA,** Do you think *Kris Kringle* will come down the chimney to-night? . . How can such a huge figure as he is represented get down our *poor* chimney? **1872** Haldeman *PA Dutch* 58, *Crìstkintly* . . the Christ Child who is supposed to load the chrìstmas trees and bring presents at christmas. Perverted in the Philadelphia newspapers to *Kriss Kringle, Kriss Kingle,* and *Kriss Kinkle.* **1874** in **1954** *PA Dutchman* Winter 34 **sePA,** "Does he [=Belsnickel] always go along with Krist Kindle?" "Yes, he is always with his master, whom he assists in many ways. He carries the black book, the birchen rods, and the 'bad filling' for naughty children's stockings." **1876** in 1969 *PADS* 52.53 **seIL**, Up early and Pearl and Florence was delighted beyond measure at the sight Kris Kringle left there last night. **1881** in 1950 *PA Dutchman* 15 Dec 3 (as of 1823), Its [=a Christmas tree's] base was garnished by the Christ-kindlies of the children, which consisted of "henshing" or mittens, stockings, ear-warmers, shoes . . and such like articles. **1890** Howells *Boy's Town* 17 **sePA**, His mother had told him how the Peltsnickel used to come with a bundle of rods for the bad children when the Chriskingle brought the presents of the good ones, among his grandmother's Pennsylvania German kindred. **1928** in 1973 Ade *Letters* 136 **IN**, We really believed that Kris Kringle could . . go down chimneys which were not large enough to take care of a nest of barn swallows in the summer time. **1935** *AmSp* 10.170 [Engl of PA Germans], Other German words used in English are . . *Kriss Kringle* or *Grishtkind'l* (< *Krist Kindlein*) and *Belsnik'l* (< *Pelz Nicker*), names for Santa Claus. **1964** Smith *PA Germans* 122, As early as the eighteenth century the Pennsylvania Germans also had a *Christ-Kindel* or Christ-child who brought gifts to good children. Christ-Kindel became Kriss Kringle sometime during the first half of the nineteenth century, and a century ago merged into the popular Santa Claus of today.

kroepfle See **krapfen**

krom n See **crawm**

krom v See **kram**

kronky n Cf **cranky** n
=**sandhill crane.**
   1949 Sprunt–Chamberlain *SC Bird Life* 191, Sandhill Crane: *Grus canadensis tabida.* . . *Local Names:* Kronky; Whooping Crane. **1950** *PADS* 14.42 **SC**, *Kronky.* . . The sandhill crane.

kroton See **croton bug**

krout See **kraut** n

krumkake n Usu |ˈkrum͟ˌkɑkə, ˈkrʌm-| Also *krumkaka, krumkakke, krum kage;* pl *krumkaker, krum kager* [Norw *krumkake* < *krum* curved, bowed + *kake* cake, cookie; Sw *krumkaka;* Dan *krumkage*] **chiefly MN, WI** Cf **julekake, ostkaka**
A thin cookie baked in a hinged iron and formed into a cone or cylinder while still warm.
   1950 *WELS* (Fancy home-baked rolls) 1 Inf, **WI**, Krumkaka. **1951** Tufford *Scandinavian Recipes* 48 **MN**, *Krum Kager.* . . Spread [batter] as thin as possible on Krum Kage iron [*DARE* Ed: Illustr shows a round, hinged appliance similar to a waffle iron, with nearly flat plates imprinted with a shallow design.] and bake until light brown. Roll on cone while warm to shape. **1952** Tracy *Coast Cookery* 117 **MN**, *Krumkake.* . . *You must have a krumkake iron to bake these Scandinavian goodies.* . . Drop a large teaspoonful [of batter] on the krumkake iron and bake to a light brown. Roll quickly into the shape of an ice-cream cone. **1966** *Stoughton Courier* (WI) 1 Dec sec 2 [12/3], When freshly baked Krum Kake are warm off the iron they are quickly rolled on a stick or shaped into a cone. Sometimes these crisp, flavorful cookies are filled with whipped cream or a fruit filling. **1967** *DARE* (Qu. H32, . . *Fancy rolls and pastries*) Inf **MN6**, Krumkake [ˈkrumˌkɑkə]—a cylindrical cookie. **1967** *DARE* Tape **MN6**, Krumkaker [ˈkrumkɑkɚ] is [sic] made on an iron and they're made real, real thin, of course, and then rolled after you get it off. They're made out of whipping cream and eggs and sugar, flour, salt, and vanilla. We found that the recipe with whipping cream is more satisfactory than those used with butter. The iron doesn't smoke up and they get thinner and more tasty. **1983** *Capital Times* (Madison WI) 11 May "PM" sec 19/2, Passing culinary heritage from generation to generation prompts the Sons of Norway Mandt Lodge, Stoughton, to host a smorgasbord. . . Pastries include . . krumkake. **1991** [see **julekake**]. **1992** *DARE* File **csWI**, [Advt at ice-cream shop:] Come in for krumkake—a delicious Swedish cookie. *Ibid,* [ˈkrʌmˌkɑkə]. *Ibid* **cwCA**, My mother makes [ˈkrumˌkɑkə] with a Norwegian friend from Minnesota. **1994** *Capital Times* (Madison WI) 1 July sec A 3/4 **csWI**, A member of the Country Corners 4-H Club . . won a blue ribbon for her krumkakke, the delicate cone-shaped Norwegian cookies.

ku See **co** v

kuchen n Usu |ˈkukə(n), ˈkux(ɨ)n|; for addit varr see quot 1965–70 Also *kucha, kuche* [Ger, Yiddish *Kuchen* cake; PaGer *kuche* cake, cookie] **Ger settlement areas, esp N Cent, PA** See Map Cf **lebkuchen**

Often in combs: any of var cakes, cookies, or pastries, but esp a coffee cake.
   1901 Kander *Settlement Cook Book* 311 **Milwaukee WI**, *Kuchen Dough.* . . Crumble the yeast in a cup with a teaspoon of sugar, and one-half cup of the scalded, cooled milk. . . To the rest of the scalded milk add the butter, sugar, salt, nutmeg. . . Cover closely and let rise. *Ibid* 352, Filling for pie or kuchen. *Ibid* 356, Kuchen tarts. **1912** in 1914 Stewart *Letters* 181 **WY**, Dear Mrs. Louderer, with her goose-grease, her bread, and her delicious "kuchens." **1935** *AmSp* 10.170 **PA** [Engl of PA Germans], Other German words used in English are . . *Fawsnocht (fastnacht) kucha,* molasses or honey doughnuts. [**1948** Hutchison *PA Du. Cook Book* 20, *Kaffee Kuche* (Coffee Cake). *Ibid* 21, *Ebbel Kuche* (Apple Cake). *Ibid* 130, *Ebbel Kuche* (Apple Tart). *Ibid* 142, *Blitz Kuchen* (Lightning Cakes).] **1948** *AmSp* 23.107 **swIL**, German names having to do with foods and cooking are sufficiently numerous in the local vocabulary to give a decided German atmosphere. . . blitz kuchen . . käse kuchen . . obst kuchen . . bundkuchen. **1949** (1986) Leonard *Jewish Cookery* 309, *Kuchen* (Basic Recipe) . . yeast . . flour . . eggs . . melted shortening mixed with . . scalded milk . . sugar . . vanilla. . . Divide [dough] into 12 equal parts. . . Yields 12 kuchen. **1950** *WELS* **WI** (*Different words for bread according to the shape and texture of the loaf*) 1 Inf, Kuchen; (*Special kinds of bread made now or in past years*) 1 Inf, Kaffee kuchen; (*Names for different kinds of biscuits*) 1 Inf, Kuchen biscuits; (*Kinds of fancy home-baked rolls*) 1 Inf, Apple kuchen; 1 Inf, Kaffee kuchen; 1 Inf, Kuchen tart. **1965–70** *DARE* (Qu. H32, . . *Fancy rolls and pastries*) Inf **IL113**, Kuchen [ˈkukn]—yeast bread and sour cream; **IL131**, Kuche [ˈkukə]—German orig; **IN41**, Kuchen—sweetened bread dough; **MO25**, Coffee kuchen [kukxɨn]; **PA167**, Kuchen [ˈkukn]; **MN13**, Coffee kuchen—a coffee cake, German name; **OH93**, Coffee kuchen [ˈkikən]; **MN23**, Butter kuchen [ˈkɔkən]—a coffee cake, German; currants, cinnamon, sugar on top; did not raise high; had a bread dough base; **WI24**, Apple kuchen; (Qu. H18, *Inf* **MO25**, [kuxɨn]; **NY130**, Kuchen; (Qu. H65, *Foreign foods favored by people around here*) Inf **IL70**, Apple kuchen—coffee cake with apples in it; **OH4**, Kuchen—made out of bread dough sprinkled with sugar and cinnamon; **WV1**, Murberbiskuit kuchen; (Qu. FF1) Inf **PA81**, Kuchen klatches—coffee and cake and talk. **1973** Allen *LAUM* 1.277 **MN, SD** (as of c1950), *Kuchen,* a kind of sweetened bread with bits of candied fruit, sometimes baked in a round tin, reflects German settlement [and was offered incidentally by 5 infs]. **1991** *DARE* File **Milwaukee WI**, Kuchen [ˈkuxən] is coffee cake made of a butter dough, not sweet.

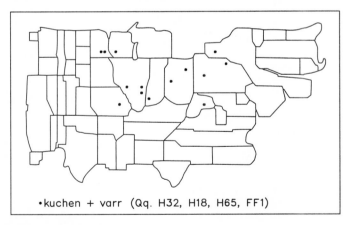

•kuchen + varr (Qq. H32, H18, H65, FF1)

kudack See **co-dack**

kuday See **co-day**

kudge v
=**co-jack.**
   1969 *DARE* (Qu. K82, *The call used . . to get horses in from the pasture*) Inf **RI**16, Kudge kudge kudge [kʌj].

kudzu n Usu |ˈkʌd͟ˌzu|; for addit varr see quots 1966–69, 1967 Also *kudzu vine* [Japanese *kuzu*] **chiefly Sth** Cf **Arkansas traveler 2, foot-a-night, overnight weed**
An introduced, fast-growing, weedy vine (*Pueraria lobata*). Also called **jack-and-the-beanstalk 1, mile-a-minute 1, porch vine, yard-a-night**
   1893 *Garden and Forest* 6.504, In Japan, the Kudzu, for so this plant [=*Pueraria lobata*] is called, has some economic value. . . It is probably

as an ornamental plant only that Pueraria will be used in this country. **1901** Bailey *Cyclop. Horticult.* 3.1465, *Kudzu Vine.* Perennial with large tuberous starchy roots . . fl[ower]s pea-shaped, purple in axillary spikes late in the season, not showy: pod large and flat. **1948** *Atlantic Mth.* 182.5.60 **Sth,** Kudzu, a coarse, rapidly growing legume of incredible efficiency in checking gullies, restoring drainage, and storing nitrogen, came from Japan. **1960** Williams *Walk Egypt* 202 **GA,** Kudzu crowns. County agent says, 'Plant them along the gully.' **1966–69** *DARE* (Qu. K14, *Milk that has a taste from something the cow ate in the pasture*) Inf **AL2,** Kudzu vines or foot-a-night; (Qu. L9a, . . *Kinds of grass* . . *grown for hay*) Inf **NY213,** Kudzu ['kʌdsu]; (Qu. L9b, *Hay from other kinds of plants [not grass];* not asked in early QRs) Inf **GA**84, Kudzu; **GA**80, Kudzu ['kʌdzu]—a pea; **KY**43, ['kʌjju]; **SC**43, Kudzu ['kʌdzu] clover; (Qu. S21, . . *Weeds* . . *that are a trouble in gardens and fields*) Inf **AL**25, ['kʌtsu] vines; **SC**53, Kudzu ['kʌtsɪ] vines. **1967** *DARE* Wildfl QR Pl.110 Inf **AR**46, Leaf like a kudzu ['kʌd,žu]. **1976** *Smithsonian* 7.93, Kudzu is a vine. It is lush. It is fast-growing. It is engulfing the South. **1987** Kytle *Voices* 212 **NC,** The day I found I'd stayed too long, when Momma and all the rest of it had swarmed all over me like kudzu . . , that would be the day I would die.

kugali See **kugeli**

kugel n [Yiddish]

1 also sp *coogle:* A sweet or savory casserole or pudding; see quot 1949.
1871 (1975) Levy *Jewish Cookery* 58, *Coogle, or pudding, and peas and beans.* . . get a pint of Spanish beans . . and a pint of Spanish peas. . . Make the coogle . . : currants . . raisins . . sugar . . bread crumbs and suet . . eggs . . flour. . . Mix well together; put the coogle (or pudding) in a basin, place it in the pan with the peas and beans, and cover the pudding basin with a plate. Let it cook a day and night. **1901** Kander *Settlement Cook Book* 254 **Milwaukee WI,** Kugel. . . Soak rolls in water, then press the bread quite dry. Knead it with suet, sugar, molasses, cinnamon, and lemon rind. . . Line an iron pot with alternate layers of above dough, and stewed and stoned prunes. Bake two hours. **1949** (1986) Leonard *Jewish Cookery* 355, A *Kugel* in Jewish cuisine is a pudding. There are two types of kugels—those which may be served as a side-dish with the meal (generally made of vegetables), and those which may be served as desserts (sweet kugels). Puddings or kugels may be served either hot or cold. **1967–69** *DARE* (Qu. H48, *Baked dishes made of potatoes cut up with meat or cheese*) Inf **NY**119, Kugel—baked noodle pudding with cottage cheese or raisins; potato kugel—baked potato pudding—no meat or cheese; (Qu. H57, *Tasty or spicy side-dishes served with meats*) Inf **IL**99, Kugel; Luchsen kugel. [Both Infs Jewish] **1983** *WI State Jrl.* (Madison) 6 Nov sec 7 6/5, She also follows some of her mother's traditional recipes. . . Her apple noodle kugel recipe is a combination of a couple of recipes. **1992** *DARE* File **Cincinnati OH,** My mother makes potato kugel and noodle kugel. *Ibid* **NYC,** My former mother-in-law always made . . noodle kugel when we came to visit. Her noodle kugel was a casserole made of egg noodles and butter and poppy seeds. **1993** *Good Housekeeping* Dec 228, Deborah's Hanukkah dinner menu . . [includes] *Spinach-Noodle Kugel.*

2 See quots.
1967 *DARE* (Qu. H65, *Foreign foods favored by people around here*) Inf **KS**4, ['kʊgə]—a mixture of flour, sugar, and butter—then you work it into fruit and bake it. **1973** Allen *LAUM* 1.279 **ND** (as of c1950), *Kugels:* Bischits [*sic*] of sweet dough and raisins; made by inf.'s mother.

kugeli n Also *kugali* [Lithuanian *kugeli* potato dish < **kugel**]
A potato casserole; see quots.
c1965 Randle *Cookbooks* (Ask Neighbor) 3.25 **nOH,** *Grandma's Kugali* (Potato Loaf)—Grate 4 to 6 potatoes . . and 1 onion. (or chop onion fine and brown in 1 or 2 strips of bacon—cut fine) Add . . eggs . . salt . . pepper . . flour . . melted bacon grease. . . Mix all of above thoroughly and place . . in greased baking dish in . . oven for about 45 minutes. *Ibid* 78, *Potato Kugeli.* **1969** *DARE* (Qu. H65, *Foreign foods favored by people around here*) Inf **IL**98, Kugeli ['kugli]—bacon pieces, onion, potatoes—baked. **1981** Hachten *Flavor WI* 240, *Kugelis* (Lithuanian) . . bacon . . potatoes. . . Cut in squares and serve with sour cream.

kukae n, v Also sp *kukai* [Haw] **HI**
Excrement, dung; manure; to have a bowel movement.
1938 Reinecke *Hawaiian Loanwords* 20, *Kukae* ['ku'kɑe], n., v. 1. Excrements; dung; dung used as manure. 2. To move the bowels. . . F[requent]. **1954–60** Hance et al. *Hawaiian Sugar* 3, *Kukai* . . ['ku'kɑ-i] —Animal excrement, manure. **1967** *DARE* (Qu. L17, . . *Names* . .

for manure used in the fields: [Also joking names]) Inf **HI**2, Kukai ['ku,kaɪ]—Hawaiian; (Qu. BB21, . . *Being constipated*) Inf **HI**4, Kukai paa ['kukaɪ 'paa]—bowelnut; hard. **1981** *Pidgin To Da Max* np **HI,** *Kukae.* . . What the neighborhood dogs deposit on your lawn if you don't put out the water jars.

kukui n [Haw] **HI**
The candlenut tree *(Aleurites moluccana).*
1825 Ellis *Jrl.* **HI** 167, Along the narrow and verdant border of the lake at the bottom, the bread-fruit, the *kukui,* and the *ohia* trees, appeared. **1866** in 1938 Twain *Letters Sandwich Is.* 74, These trees were principally of two kinds—the *koa* and the *kukui*—the one with a very light green leaf and the other with a dark green. **1886** in 1892 Gowen *Paradise Pacific* 47 **HI,** Wild mountains, serrated with watercourses and dark with guava bushes and *kukui* trees. **1916** HI Ag. Exper. Sta. *Press Bulletin* 39.1, In Hawaii kukui is common on all the islands, . . and easily recognized at a distance by the pale color of its leaves. *Ibid 2,* Everyone knows that the ground under kukui trees is literally covered with nuts of which few are used for any purpose at present, except in the preparation of a native relish and occasionally for fuel. **1954** *Ellery Queen's Mystery Mag.* 4.33 **HI,** On the northern coast of Kauai. . . people . . spear fish at night with *kukui* torches flaring orange over black waters. **1965** Krauss–Alexander *Grove Farm* 54 **HI,** Ahead he saw a thick grove of grey-trunked kukui trees with silvery-green leaves. **1967** *DARE* (Qu. I43, *What kinds of nuts grow wild around here?*) Inf **HI**1, Kukui—highly cathartic; **HI**3, Kukui—oil nut formerly used for light; **HI**11, Kukui—not eaten; (Qu. S26e, *Other wildflowers not yet mentioned;* not asked in early QRs) Inf **HI**4, Kukui—used against mouth ulcers; milky liquid where nut breaks off, rub around gums, teeth, tongue. **1991** Saiki *From the Lanai* 82 **HI,** Grandma Sayegusa stood quietly in the shadow of a kukui nut tree.

kuleana n |'kule'ɑnɑ, 'kuli'ænɑ| [Haw] **HI**
Orig, a freehold, homestead; by ext, a bailiwick, sphere of responsibility.
1873 in 1966 Bishop *Sandwich Is.* 70, The people of Hawaii-nei are clothed and civilized in their habits; they have equal rights; 6500 of them have kuleanas or freeholds. **1938** Reinecke *Hawaiian Loanwords* 21, *Kuleana* ['kule'ɑ:na] ['ku:li'ænɑ] n. A small land claim inside another's land; the small land holding of a Hawaiian of commoner stock, which has been inherited from the Great Mahele or division of lands in 1848. F[requently used]. **1954–60** Hance et al. *Hawaiian Sugar* 3, *Kuleana* . . ['kule'ɑnɑ]—A small land claim, area of resp[onsibility] e.g. irrigation contract. **1955** Day *HI People* 126, The revolution was complete when the *kuleanas*—lands lived on and cultivated by the common people—were taken from the holdings of king, chief, or government and given outright to the occupants. **1967** Reinecke–Tsuzaki *Hawaiian Loanwords* 102, *Kuleana.* . . 2. Sphere or bailiwick, as in the phrase "That's your kuleana." F[requent]. **1972** Carr *Da Kine Talk* 87 **HI,** *Hawaiian Words Commonly Heard In Hawaii's English.* . . *Kuleana.* Private property; responsibility, jurisdiction. **1981** *Pidgin To Da Max* np **HI,** *Kuleana.* . . Responsibility, job. "I no like do dat—da garbage yo' kuleana!"

kulikuli v [Haw; redup of *kuli* noise] **HI**
To be quiet—used in imper.
1938 Reinecke *Hawaiian Loanwords* 21, *Kulikuli* . . v. Shut up! Be quiet! F[requent]. **1951** *AmSp* 26.21 **HI,** [How to talk in Hawaii:] Handy phrases include *wikiwiki* (hurry up) . . [and] *kulikuli* (keep quiet).

kulolo n [Haw] **HI**
A steamed or baked pudding usu made of taro and coconut.
1938 Reinecke *Hawaiian Loanwords* 21, *Kulolo* ['ku:'lolo]. . . Pudding made of taro and coconut, or sometimes of breadfruit and coconut. V[ery] F[requent]. **1940** Bazore *Hawaiian Foods* 41, [Characteristic Hawaiian Dishes:] *Kulolo*—A pudding made of grated raw taro mixed with coconut milk and brown sugar, then cooked in an imu or steamed over boiling water. Kulolo is cut into cubes and served cold. **1973** *AmSp* 48.122, Common Hawaiian loanwords . . *kulolo* 'pudding made of baked or steamed grated taro and coconut cream.'

kultus See **cultus**

kump n

1 See quot.
1914 *DN* 4.109 **cKS,** *Kump.* . . A kind of dish, usually deep, as for soup.

2 A playing marble. Cf **cumbo, gumbee**
c1955 Reed-Person *Ling. Atlas Pacific NW (Marbles)* 1 inf, Kumps.

kumu n [Haw] **HI**
    A **goatfish 1** (here: *Parupeneus porphyreus*).
    1926 Pan-Pacific Research Inst. *Jrl.* 1.1.10 **HI,** *Upeneus porphyreus. . .* Kumu. **1933** John G. Shedd Aquarium *Guide* 114, The Kumu is another goatfish abundant at Hawaii. It is one of the best food fishes, ranking with the Red Mullet of Europe. **1960** Gosline-Brock *Hawaiian Fishes* 191, Kumu. . . This fish is usually greenish, but sometimes reddish, in coloration. In either color phase there is a prominent white saddle just behind the dorsal fin. **1967** *Honolulu Star–Bulletin* (HI) 31 May sec F 1/4, Kumu—Goatfish.

Kuner See **John Canoe**

kunger See **conjure** v, n

kunjine See **coonjine** n 3

kunnel See **colonel**

kup See **cope** v²

kupipi n [Haw] **HI**
    A **demoiselle 1** (here: *Abudefduf sordidus*).
    1926 Pan-Pacific Research Inst. *Jrl.* 1.1.11 **HI,** Abudefduf sordidus. . . Kupipi. **1960** Gosline-Brock *Hawaiian Fishes* 208, Family Pomacentridae (Damselfishes). . . *Abudefduf sordidus* (Kupipi). . . The kupipi can readily be distinguished from the maomao by the black spot at the front of the caudal peduncle. **1994** Stone-Pratt *Hawai'i's Plants* 81, Fishes such as kupipi . . and . . crevalle or jack . . were probably introduced into the pools from the ocean by humans, for use as food.

kuracene See **kerosene**

kurnal, kurnel See **colonel**

kurrup v
    =**curp.**
    1967 *DARE* (Qu. K82, *The call used . . to get horses in from the pasture*) Inf **TN**1, Whistle and [ˌkɚˈʌp ˌkɚˈʌp]; **TN**10, [ˈkɝˑəp]—repeated.

kuse adj See **curious** adj

kuse adv See **curious** adv

kush(ie) See **cush** v

kusk See **cusk** 2

kutch See **catch** v A3

kutsie See **cutsie**

kutz See **kotz**

kuyui See **cui-ui**

ku'yus See **curious** adj

kvetch v, hence vbl n *kvetching* [Yiddish *kvetchen*] **esp in Jewish settlement areas** Cf **krex**
    To complain, gripe, esp chronically; hence n *kvetcher* a complainer.
    1950 *WELS Suppl.,* Kvetch—Meaning: To complain. Used by mother (New Britain, Conn., native). Reports *kvetching* as very common in New York, where she now lives. **1968** *Atlantic Mth.* 222.4.70, He is an amiable one, not given to angry kvetching. **1968** Rosten *Yiddish* 200, Pronounced *kvetch,* to rhyme with "fetch"; *kvetch*-er, to rhyme with "stretcher". . . *Kvetch* is a verb and a noun; *kvetcher* is a man who *kvetches. Ibid,* As a noun. Kvetch, kvetcher, or *kvetcherkeh.* . . Anyone . . who complains, frets, gripes. . . A chronic complainer. . . To be strictly grammatical, a female *kvetcher* should certainly be called a *kvetcherkeh.* **1969** *DARE* (Qu. GG16, . . *Finding fault, or complaining: "You just can't please him—he's always _____."*) Inf **IL**99, Kvetching. [Inf Jewish] **1971** *Harper's Mag.* Feb 111, After listening to Kashouk *kvetch* for a couple of hours, Sol Hurok . . put the question direct. "Tell me, Kashouk," Hurok wanted to know. "If you always lose so much money, why do you stay in business?" **1992** *DARE* File **Des Moines IA,** Both my parents use *kvetch* to refer to what my father calls "a real irritant," "a nag." They also use it to refer to the act of nagging. They use *kvetch* where their parents would have said *krex. Ibid* **csWI,** I had friends in graduate school . . who, when making fun of themselves for going on and on with complaints, would say, slowly and emphatically, [kəˈvɛč, kəˈvɛč, kəˈvɛč]. Part of what made it funny was that they weren't Jewish and knew no Yiddish. *Ibid* **NYC** (as of 1950s), No matter what was said, my mother heard most everything as kvetching.

kvetch n Also sp *kvets(c)h* [**kvetch** v]
    A habitual complainer; a nag; a worrier; a complaint.
    1964 Bellow *Herzog* 61, She's got a disgusting father and a *kvetsch* of a mother. **1967** *DARE* (Qu. GG14, *Names and nicknames for someone who fusses or worries a lot, especially about little things*) Inf **MA**2, Kvetch [kəˈvɛč]. [Inf Jewish] **1968** Rosten [see **kvetch** v]. **1970** Feinsilver *Yiddish* 112, Kvetsh—Whiner, complainer, pickle-puss. This showed up on TV several years ago with Soupy Sales's "The Adventures of Philo Kvetsh." **1972** *Los Angeles Times* (CA) 21 May mag sec 8, Tradition Types— . . Shmendrik . . A.K. . . Kvetch. **1992** [see **kvetch** v]. **1994** *DARE* File **csWI** (as of c1975), One of the members of our school orchestra always seemed to have a complaint about something. "What's your kvetch now?" our director would bellow in mock exasperation. "What's the kvetch of the day?"

kvetcher, kvetching See **kvetch** v

kvets(c)h See **kvetch** n

kwee-wee See **cui-ui**

kwi See **ki** intj

kwirl See **curl** n, v

kwoip, kwope, kworp See **cope** v²

kwoy See **ki** intj

kyack n¹ Also *kayak, kiack, kyach, kyauk* [Prob Algonquian; see quot 1965] **esp ME**
    Usu the **glut herring,** but also an **alewife** (here: *Alosa pseudoharengus*).
    [**1849** Gesner *Ind. Resources N.S.* 121 (*DCan*), Sometimes a hundred men, among whom is a sprinkling of Indians, are engaged in taking the "kiacks" from the stream.] **1873** in 1878 Smithsonian Inst. *Misc. Coll.* 14.2.33 **sME coast,** *Pomolobus pseudoharengus.* . . kyack, blueback, alewife. **1887** Goode *Amer. Fishes* 394, Around the Gulf of Maine this species [=*Clupea aestivalis*] is also known by the names "Kyack" or "Kyauk," "Saw-belly," and "Cat-thrasher." **1902** Jordan-Evermann *Amer. Fishes* 104, Glut Herring; Summer Herring. . . Other names . . are blueback, black-belly, saw-belly and kyach. **1911** U.S. Bur. Census *Fisheries 1908* 307, P[omolobus] aestivalis is. . . also known as "black-belly," "saw-belly," and "kyack." [**1965** *Cdn Geog. Jnl* June 209/1 (*DCan*), "Alewives" is the common name used in Britain and New England, while the MicMac Indians [=an Algonquian tribe of eCanada] called the fish "kayaks."] **1966** *DARE* (Qu. P1, . . *Kinds of freshwater fish . . caught around here . . good to eat*) Inf **ME**16, Kayak [ˈkaɪˌjæk]—both fresh and salt. **1976** Tryckare et al. *Lore of Sportfishing* 70, *Alosa pseudoharengus*—Other common names . . kyak or kiack.

kyack n² Also sp *kyak* [Cf **cack** n²] **West**
    A packsack for a saddle; a packsaddle.
    1901 *Sunset* 6.138 **CA,** Our camp now lay in perfect chaos—blankets, kyacks, saddle-bags, and cooking utensils in a jumble. **1907** White *AZ Nights* 17, We skirmished around and found a condemned army pack saddle with aparejos, and a sawbuck saddle with kyacks. **1913** (1979) Barnes *Western Grazing* 370, With . . a lot of bedding, cooking utensils and grub, one must either have them done up into bundles, tied in sacks or packed in "kyaks" or pack pockets. *Ibid* 374, [Caption:] Kyaks . . or Pack Pockets. The Loops Hook over the Tops of the Pack Saddle. **1936** Adams *Cowboy Lingo* 48, Special saddles used for carrying camp equipment, etc., were 'pack-saddles,' 'kyacks,' 'cross-bucks,' or 'aparejos.' **1948** Sierra Club *Bulletin* Dec 2, He must therefore plod on trails engineered for stock that don't like a steep ascent and don't mind getting wet up to the kyacks at a stream crossing.

kyag See **keg** A3

kyak See **kyack** n²

kyar v See **carry** A1

kyar n See **car** n¹

kyard See **card** n¹

kyare See **care**

kyarn(y) See **carrion**

kyarrysene See **kerosene**

kyar'yin' See **carry** A3

kyauk See **kyack** n¹

kyiver See **cover**

kyo See **cure**

kyoodle n Also *cayoodle, kiyutle, kiyoodle;* abbrs *kiyoo, kyood* [Cf *kyoodle* to holler, yap] **scattered, but esp LA** *derog or joc* Cf *ki-yi*

A dog, esp one of mixed breed or little value; a mutt.

  1906 Kildare *My Old Bailiwick* 136 **NYC,** So you was going to have me arrested for finishing that kyoodle o' your'n? **1908** *NY Eve. Jrl.* (NY) 4 Nov 20 *(Zwilling Coll.),* A foolish kyoodle named bunk / Whose eyesight was wretchedly punk / Attempted to chat / With a black and white cat / And found that the cat was / A _____. **1923** *DN* 5.244 **LA,** *Kiyutle. . .* A small dog. **1942** Berrey–Van den Bark *Amer. Slang* 120.11, *Dog. . .* kiyoodle, kyoodle. **1961** *PADS* 36.11 **sLA,** A small group of words that are positively confined to the informants of southern Louisiana. . . *pirogue . . Memere . . kiyoodle* (worthless dog). **1967** Le-Compte *Word Atlas* 194 **seLA,** *A worthless dog . .* cayoodle [1 of

21 infs]. **1968** *DARE* (Qu. J1, . . *A dog of mixed breed*) Inf **LA20,** Kyoodle [kəˈjudl] [laughter]; **LA44,** Kiyoo [kaɪju]; (Qu. J2, . . *Joking or uncomplimentary words . . for dogs*) Inf **LA44,** Kiyoo; **WA**12, Kyoodle [ˌkɑˈjudəl]. **1986** Pederson *LAGS Concordance* **chiefly seLA** *(Mongrel)* 2 infs, (A) kyoodle; 1 inf, Kyoodle = a "mix-breed" dog, worthless; 1 inf, Kyoodle—mixed breed; 1 inf, Kyoodle—fifty-seven varieties; 1 inf, Kyoodle—no breed; 1 inf, Kyoodle—street dog, has heard term; 1 inf, Kyoodle—not used commonly; 1 inf, Kyoodle—joking name for any old dog; 1 inf, Kyoodle—rough, worthless dog, eats anything; 1 inf, Kyoodle—old local name for mixed-breed dog; 1 inf, Kyoodles—mixed breeds; 1 inf, Kyood; [1 inf, Kyoodle—not for dog, possibly "coyote"].

kyore See **cure**

kyount See **count** v

kyounty See **county**

kype See **kipe**

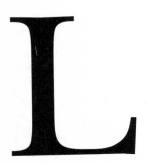

L See **ell** n¹, n²

l' See **let** v A2a

la See **law** n², intj

laa'n See **learn** v A

laather See **ladder**

lab, labatory See **lavatory**

labber(ed) See **lobber**

labbersided See **lapsided**

label n, v Pronc-spp *lay-bell, laybill*
  Std sense, var forms.
  1876 in 1969 *PADS* 52.53 **seIL,** I was laybilling by cabinet articles. **1923** *DN* 5.213 **swMO,** *Lay-bell.* . . To label, "I lay-belled all o' my canned fruit." **1925** in 1944 *ADD* **cNY,** ['le₁bɛl] [sic], n. Habitual with one person.

lab one's mouth v phr [Cf *EDD* lab v.³; *SND* lab(b) (at *laib* v. I.3) to chatter, talk incessantly; cf also *DJE* laba, labrish to chatter] Cf **crack one's teeth**
  To chatter, blab.
  1966 *DARE* (Qu. HH7b, *Someone who talks too much, or too loud*) Inf **SC10,** He lab [læb] he mouth [mɑʊt]. [Gullah speaker]

labor n, v *hist*
  Among Shakers: an energetic dance or exercise performed as part of worship ceremonies; to move or shake in performing such a dance; to perform (a song or dance).
  1832 Williamson *Hist. ME* 2.699, The Shakers live in families, having. . . a house of public worship, which they call their *Temple.* Here both sexes join in acts and exercises of devotion, which they denominate 'labor.' **1838** *Knickerbocker* 11.535 **eNY,** The suggestion 'let us begin to labor' is made, and the brethren proceed to divest themselves of their drab frock-coats. . . At a signal, the 'music' strikes up, to a wild, irregular chant, and the 'labor' begins. The first movement . . consisting of a lively dancing march by the whole company. . . Wilder and louder swells the music; quicker and more intricate becomes the 'labor.' Now all are prancing around the room . . now they perform a series of dexterous but indescribable manoeuvres; now they balance; now whirl one another round. . . At length, what was a measured dance becomes a wild, discordant frenzy. **1968** *Filson Club Hist. Qrly.* 42.158 **KY,** In the accounts of the Shaker services [between 1807 and 1922] it was often written that the songs *were labored;* that is, the singing Shakers *labored* or *worked* at shaking out their evil spirits.

laboratory See **lavatory**

Labrador See **Labrador tea**

Labrador duck n
  =**black duck 1.**
  1955 MA Audubon Soc. *Bulletin* 39.314 **ME,** *Black Duck.* . . Labrador Duck.

Labrador herring n
  An Atlantic **herring** n¹ **1** (here: *Clupea harengus*).
  1976 Warner *Beautiful Swimmers* 126 **Chesapeake Bay,** First to come by a few days is what the watermen call the Labrador herring. Sleek and firm-bodied, it is the sea herring of northern waters.

Labrador pine n
  =**jack pine 1.**

  1803 Lambert *Descr. Pinus* 1.7, *Pinus Banksiana.* Labrador Pine. . . Habitat in Americâ septentrionali. [=It lives in northern America.] **a1862** (1864) Thoreau *ME Woods* 275, A peculiar evergreen overhung our fire, . . the *Pinus Banksiana,*—"Banks's, or the Labrador Pine," also called Scrub Pine, Gray Pine, &c., a new tree to us. . . Richardson found it forty feet high and upward, and states that the porcupine feeds on its bark. **1890** *Century Dict.* 4496, *Labrador pine.* Same as *gray pine* [=*Pinus Banksiana,* a species ranging from the northern borders of the United States northward, of an ashen color, varying in size from 60 feet high down to a straggling bush. Its wood serves for fuel, railway-ties, etc. Also called *Hudson's Bay* or *Labrador pine, northern scrub-pine,* and *prince's-pine*]. **1908** Britton *N. Amer. Trees* 43, [*Gray Pine—Pinus Banksiana.* . . A northern tree, ranging from Nova Scotia to the North-west Territory and south to Maine, northern New York and the southern shores of the great lakes to central Minnesota.] *Ibid* 44, It is also known as Labrador pine, Jack pine, Scrub pine, [etc.] **1916** Kephart *Camping & Woodcraft* 1.239, The gray (Labrador) pine or jack pine is considered good fuel in the far North.

Labrador tea n Also *Labrador*
  A plant of the genus *Ledum,* esp *L. groenlandicum;* also an infusion made from such a plant. Also called **Alaska tea, marsh tea 1, swamp tea.** For other names of var spp see **Hudson Bay tea, trapper's tea, wild rosemary**
  1766 in 1852 Buckingham *Specimens Newsp. Lit.* 1.34 **MA,** Throw aside your Bohea and your Green Hyson tea,/. . . / Procure a good store of the choice Labradore. **1767** in 1985 Lederer *Colonial Amer. Engl.* 131 **MA,** There is a certain herb, lately favoured in this province, which begins already to take Place in the Room of Green tea and Bohea tea. . . It is called Labrador. **1784** (1888) Cutler *Life* 1.103 **NH,** There were large beds of what is called the Labrador tea, of a very aromatic taste and smell. **1830** Rafinesque *Med. Flora* 2.236, Ledum. . . *Marsh tea, Labrador tea.* . . in strong decoction, kills lice and insects. **1859** (1968) Bartlett *Americanisms* 234, *Labrador Tea. (Ledum palustre.)* A plant used far in the North-west as a substitute for tea. **1938** (1958) Sharples *AK Wild Flowers* 76, *L[edum] groenlandicum.* Leaves are said to have been used during the Revolutionary War as a substitute for tea. Hence the common name, "Labrador Tea." **1955** U.S. Arctic Info. Center *Gloss.* 47, Labrador tea. . . Any shrub of the genus *Ledum.* . . The infusion made from the leaves of *Ledum* and used as a tea substitute. **1966–68** *DARE* Wildfl QR Pl.155A Infs **MI**7, 31, **NY**91, **OH**14, Labrador tea; Pl.114 Inf **MN**14, Labrador tea—a brush [sic] here, an evergreen. **1977** *New Yorker* 9 May 94 **AK,** The trails would go along, well cut and stamped out through moss campion, reindeer moss, . . lichens, Labrador tea; then, abruptly, and for no apparent reason, the trails would disappear.

Labrador twister n
  A **woodcock** (here: *Philohela minor*).
  1895 Minot *Land-Birds New Engl.* 424, Those very small, wiry, compactly feathered, weather-tanned birds [=woodcocks]. . . are called, perhaps locally, "Labrador twisters." **1917** (1923) *Birds Amer.* 1.225, *Philohela minor.* . . American Woodcock; . . Labrador Twister; Bog-sucker. **1955** MA Audubon Soc. *Bulletin* 39.446, *American Woodcock.* . . Labrador Twister (Mass. In reference to the erratic flight of late-staying birds which are deemed hardy, as if from Labrador.)

labrick See **laverick**

labsided See **lapsided**

lace v
  1 also with *into:* To hit or thrash; to scold or criticize harshly; hence vbl n *lacing (down)* a whipping, dressing down. [Cf *OED* lace v. 7 1599–1867] **chiefly NEast** See Map

1836 (1838) Haliburton *Clockmaker* (1st ser) 117 **NEng,** He would . . throw all the blame on him, and order him to have an everlastin lacin with the cowskin. **1866** *Galaxy* 2.272, So all our common street expressions . . are found in old English Provincial works, as "I'll lick you," or "larrup," or "pummel," . . or give you a good "dressing," or "trimming," or "lacing," or "currying," or "drubbing." **1899** (1912) Green *VA Folk-Speech* 254, *Lace.* . . To beat; to thrash. **1923** Witwer *Fighting Blood* 292 **seNY,** They laced into me with a gusto! **1940** *Sun* (Baltimore MD) 2 Feb 5/4 **DC,** Committeemen registered surprise at this blast . . but he was not yet finished lacing the one-time professor. **1941** *LANE* Map 397 *(A whipping)* 3 infs, **seNEng,** Terms for a severe beating . . *lacing.* **1966–70** *DARE* (Qu. Y14a, *To hit somebody hard with the fist*) Inf **NH**14, He laced him a good one [FW: used by Inf in conv]; (Qu. Y16, *A thorough beating: "He gave the bully an awful _____."*) Infs **CT**35, **NH**14, **NY**114, 201, **PA**244, **RI**6, 8, **WA**3, Lacing; (Qu. II27, *If somebody gives you a very sharp scolding . . "I certainly got a _____ for that."*) Infs **CT**15, 35, **MN**2, **NJ**25, **NY**120, 234, Lacing; **NY**38, Lacing down. **1967** *DARE* Tape **MI**42, I always liked horses, and I never used a whip, but that time I used a whip, and I laced him.

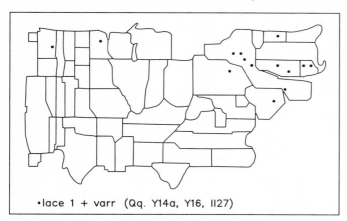

•lace 1 + varr (Qq. Y14a, Y16, II27)

2 with *out:* To walk or go rapidly. [Cf *EDD lace* v.[2] "To go along at great speed"]
1936 Smiley *Gloss. New Paltz* **seNY,** On seeing Mr. Hamilton walking up the hill very fast, F. Purcell comments: "He is lacing right out this morning."

laceaway n
1966 *DARE* (Qu. W11, *Men's low, rough work shoes*) Inf **OK**32, Just work shoes—they're laceaways (any shoe with three to five lace holes on a side).

lacebacks n pl
1976 Garber *Mountain-ese* 51 **sAppalachians,** *Lace-backs* . . overall pants—Cleve wore his new lace-backs to school this morning. .

lace bread See lace corn bread

lace-button n
A **sweet scabious** (here: *Erigeron annuus*).
1900 Lyons *Plant Names* 148, *E[rigeron] annuus.* . . Sweet Scabious (U.S.), Daisy-Fleabane, Lace-button. **1959** Carleton *Index Herb. Plants* 71, *Lace-button:* Erigeron annuus.

lace cactus n Also *frilled lace cactus, white ~*
A **hedgehog cactus 3** (here: *Echinocereus reichenbachii*).
1936 Shiner Cactus Nursery *Illustr. Catalog* 26, Third is an unusually fine specimen of Echinocereus reichenbachii var. caespitosus or the "White Lace" cactus, Texas. A very attractive species with large, fragrant pink blooms. **1942** Hylander *Plant Life* 324, The delicately spined Lace Cactus is a . . little plant, varying in height from one to ten inches, unusual in the flat clusters of spines which spread comb-like back over the ribs. **1976** Bailey–Bailey *Hortus Third* 413, *E[chinocereus] Reichenbachii* . . Lace cactus. . . *E. Fitchii* . . Frilled lace cactus.

lace corn bread n Also *lace bread, lacy ~*
A thin, crisp, corn bread made lacelike by air bubbles.
1966 *State* (Raleigh, N.C.) 15 Dec. 27/1 *(Mathews Coll.),* We had something they called 'lace bread' at a little restaurant. I think it was The Oasis, on Roanoke Island. (Mrs. Zoeller was almost right—location on Nags Head Causeway). The bread had the appearance of a large, flat, crisp, very thin flower—the Queene [sic] Anne's Lace—and had a slight onion flavor. *Ibid,* My lace corn bread is not a secret, and you have my

permission to publish it. **1968** *DARE* (Qu. H25, . . *Names or nicknames . . for fried cornmeal*) Inf **NC**82, Lace corn bread. **1986** Pederson *LAGS Concordance,* 1 inf, **swGA,** Lacy bread—very thin hoecake; "holes" in batter; 1 inf, **csGA,** Her oldest son calls hoecake bread lacy bread; 1 inf, **ceAL,** Lacy bread—thin hush puppy; fried, holes.

lace curtain n
1 A window curtain as distinguished from a window shade; see quots. Cf **curtain B1**
1926 *AmSp* 2.79 **ME,** "Lace-curtains." Irrespective of material all window hangings are so designated. If you spoke of "curtains" simply, you would be understood to refer to the window *shades.* **1941** *LANE* Map 327, Some informants use *curtain* both of a roller shade and of a draped curtain. When it is necessary to specify which kind of curtain is meant, the former is called *roller curtain* or *window curtain,* the latter *lace curtain* [by 5 infs, **sNEng**], *sash curtain,* or *inside curtain.* **1946** *PADS* 6.19 **eNC** (as of 1900–10), *Lace curtains.* . . Window curtains. Used to distinguish curtains from shades, which are also called curtains. . . Obsolescent. **1954** *Harder Coll.* **cwTN,** *Lace curtains.* . . Window curtains. **c1960** *Wilson Coll.* **csKY,** *Lace curtains.* . . Window curtains, lace to distinguish them from shades, also called curtains by older people.
2 n attrib, also used absol: Having social or economic pretensions, esp to middle- or upper-class status; genteel; well-to-do, newly prosperous—usu in phr *lace-curtain Irish.* Cf **shanty Irish**
1934 Farrell *Young Manhood* 282 **Chicago IL,** They were all trying to put on the dog, show that they were lace-curtain Irish, and lived in steam-heat. **1947** *PADS* 8.22, In Cleveland, Ohio, I hear *lace curtain Irish* as distinguished from *shanty Irish.* . . The term is obsolescent. **1947** *AmSp* 22.23, The Irish who came into America in the nineteenth century were, as immigrants, on the lower levels of society. As they moved across the tracks and into the lace-curtain class, they shed . . most of the Gaelicisms which marked their dialect. **1949** *Sat. Review* 25 June 33 **NYC,** Mrs. Ruskay's folks were lace-curtain Jews; they had a piano and a Polish maid. **1950** *WELS (People of foreign background: Irish)* 2 Infs, **WI,** Lace-curtain Irish. **1951** Longstreet *Pedlocks* 141 **ceMA,** Came from an Irish family, oh, no shanty or lace-curtain Irish. Rich, well-brought-up family. Rigid Catholics, of course. **1967–69** *DARE* (Qu. HH28, *Names and nicknames . . for people of foreign background*) Infs **PA**199, 227, Lace-curtains; **WI**71, Lace-curtain [Irish]; (Qu. II24, *Names or nicknames for the part of a town where the well-off people live*) Inf **MA**28, Up where the lace-curtain Irish are. **1967** *DARE* FW Addit **cwOR,** Lace-curtain Irish. Fancy Irish. **1967** *DARE* File **csMA** (as of c1947), *Lace-curtain Irish*—upper-class Irish. Sometimes called venetian-blind Irish. This is common in Boston and perhaps wherever there is an Irish population. I have heard variations on it, too. **1978** *New Yorker* 6 Nov 51 **NEng,** My nesting and my neatening were compulsions in me that Theron looked on as plebian, anti-intellectual, lace-curtain Irish. **1995** *DARE* File **csWI** (as of 1930s), My grandmother was "shanty Irish" by her own declaration, as opposed to cousin Grover's wife Stella, who "put on airs" and acted like "lace-curtain Irish."

lace fern n Also *lace lip-fern*
A **lip fern** (here: *Cheilanthes gracillima*) or a related fern (*Aspidotis californica*) native to the Pacific Northwest or to California (respectively).
1889 *Century Dict.* 3321, *Lace-fern.* . . A small elegant fern, *Cheilanthes gracillima,* in which the under side of the bipinnate frond is densely covered with matted wool. It is found in California, Oregon, and British Columbia. **1900** Lyons *Plant Names* 94, *C[heilanthes] gracillima* . . Pacific slope of U.S. Lace Fern, a name applied also to the species of Hymenophyllum and to other finely cut ferns. **1923** Abrams *Flora Pacific States* 1.25, *Cheilanthes californica.* . . California Lace-fern. . . Base of cliffs, . . chiefly in the coast ranges. **1937** St. John *Flora SE WA & ID* 3, *Cheilanthes gracillima* . . Lace Fern. . . Common in rock crevices in the mountains, and open woods. **1973** Hitchcock–Cronquist *Flora Pacific NW* 50, Lace l[ip-fern] *C[heilanthes] gracillima.*

lace flower n
1 also *lace plant, ~ stalk:* =**wild carrot.** Cf **Queen Anne's lace**
1894 *Jrl. Amer. Folkl.* 7.89 **sePA,** *Daucus Carota* . . lace-flower, Philadelphia, Pa. . . Evidently a city-born name. **1899** Going *Flowers* 349 (*DAE* at *wild carrot*), There are places west of the Mississippi where wild-carrot . . is cosseted and extolled under the appropriate alias of 'lace flower'. **1923** Pellett *Amer. Honey Plants* 76, The wild carrot, also

called Queen Anne's lace, . . and sometimes lace flower, is a common weed . . in the northeastern states. **1954** *Harder Coll.* **cwTN,** *Lace Stalk* . . Queen Anne's lace (Daucus carota). **1966–68** *DARE* (Qu. S6, . . *Queen Anne's lace: [Summertime roadside weed two feet high or so with a lacy white top])* Infs **IN**35, **NC**36, Lace flower; **OH**28, Lace plant; (Qu. S26a, . . *Wildflowers ... Roadside flowers)* Inf **OH**57, Lace flower.

2 A **foamflower,** usu *Tiarella trifoliata.* **Pacific NW, AK**

    1944 Abrams *Flora Pacific States* 2.371, *Tiarella trifoliata* . . Lace-flower. **1968** Hultén *Flora AK* 583, *Tiarella trifoliata.* . . Lace Flower. **1973** Hitchcock–Cronquist *Flora Pacific NW* 199, *Tiarella.* . . Foam-flower. . . Laceflower. **1987** Hughes–Blackwell *Wildflowers SE AK* 100, Trifoliate Foam-flower, lace flower *(Tiarella trifoliata).*

lace grass n

A **love grass** (here: *Eragrostis capillaris).*

    1901 Mohr *Plant Life AL* 382, *Eragrostis capillaris.* . . Lace Grass. . . Dry sandy hills, borders of fields and roadsides. **1930** OK Univ. Biol. Surv. *Pub.* 2.50, Lace-grass. Tiny Love-grass. **1952** Strausbaugh–Core *Flora WV* 128, *Lacegrass.* . . In autumn the mature panicles break off and are blown about by the wind. **1968** Barkley *Plants KS* 46, Lace-grass. . . Open, dry places. **1970** Correll *Plants TX* 208, *Lacegrass.* Loosely tufted annual. . . E. U.S. w. to Wisc., Ia., Kan., Okla. and Tex.

lace into See **lace 1**

lace lip-fern See **lace fern**

lace-necked dove n Also *laceneck dove* [See quot 1972] **HI** =**spotted dove.**

    1944 Munro *Birds HI* 158, *Lace-neck* . . *Dove.* . . A fine game bird in its flights. **1972** Berger *Hawaiian Birdlife* 199, *Streptopelia chinensis chinensis.* . . This is a large (12 inches), grayish brown dove with a rosy tinge on the upper breast feathers and a band of black with discrete white spots on the back and sides of the neck, hence the name Lace-necked Dove. **1994** Stone–Pratt *Hawai'i's Plants* 116, Spotted or lace-necked doves . . somewhat resemble, and are the same size (12 in.) as, the mourning dove of the U.S.

lace one's coat with gold v phr

To embellish one's reputation.

    1960 Williams *Walk Egypt* 114 **GA,** "You know nothing. You don't know I'm the best guitar-player from Limus to Leon County, Florida. . . You don't know I can take a piece of glass and out-chord a feller with a five-dollar pick. . . The fiddling-and-picking contest. I figured to take first prize. I figured to head to Nashville where the dollars is—" "You sure lacing your coat with gold."

lace out See **lace 2**

lace parsnip n Cf **wild parsnip**

A **biscuit root 1** (here: *Lomatium dasycarpum).*

    1961 Thomas *Flora Santa Cruz* 261 **cwCA,** *L[omatium] dasycar-pum* . . Woolly-fruited Lomatium, Lace Parsnip.

lace plant See **lace flower 1**

lacepod n

=**fringepod.**

    1891 *Century Dict.* 6326, A variety of *T[hysanocarpus] curvipes* with perforated wing is known as *lace-pod;* and a fringed variety of *T. laciniatus,* as *fringepod.* **1901** Jepson *Flora CA* 225, *T[hysanocar-pus] elegans* . . Lace-pod. . . Middle North Coast Ranges. . . Sierra foothills. **1956** St. John *Flora SE WA* 180, *Thysanocarpus curvipes* . . Lace Pod. **1973** Hitchcock–Cronquist *Flora Pacific NW* 180, *Thysano-carpus.* . . Lacepod.

lace stalk See **lace flower 1**

Lacey oak n

Std: a western **oak** (here: *Quercus glaucoides).* Also called **bastard oak 2, canyon ~ 2, mountain ~ c, rock ~, smoky ~**

lacing (down) See **lace 1**

lack v[1] Usu |læk|; also esp **Sth, S Midl** |laɪk| Pronc-sp *like* Std sense, var form.

    1857 in 1956 Eliason *Tarheel Talk* 313 **cnNC,** Like [for *lack*]. **1905** *DN* 3.86 **nwAR,** *Like.* . . To lack. 'I like two dollars.' 'It liked two minutes of ten.' **1909** *DN* 3.346 **eAL, wGA,** We just liked a little of bein' through. **1942** Faulkner *Go Down* 77 **MS,** That porch and well money liked two dollars of being enough. **1948** *AmSp* 23.264 **Ozarks,** *Like* and *likin'* (derived from *lack*) were indispensable words in my vocabulary. . . We would say, 'I got it all likin' a bushel,' or, 'I liked a

bushel gittin' it all.' **1957** *Sat. Eve. Post Letters* **ceNM,** "Like" for "lack," as in "I just like two credits of having my degree." **c1960** *Wilson Coll.* **csKY,** *Lack* is often sounded *like.* **1965–70** *DARE* (Qu. LL12) 36 Infs, **scattered,** Lack(ing) [læk(ɪŋ)]; **MS**7, 71, ['laɪkɪŋ]; **GA**61, ['laɪkɪŋ]; **GA**77, [laɪkɪn]; **MS**60, [laɪk]; **OK**18, ['laɪkɪn]; **VA**37, ['laɪkən]. **1982** Mason *Shiloh* 160 **wKY,** "You would go to a rest home and leave me by myself?" he asked, with a little whine. "I've a good mind to," she said. She measured an inch off her index finger. "I like about this much from it," she said. **1984** Burns *Cold Sassy* 104 **nGA,** You need to understand that in Cold Sassy. . . [w]e . . say . . *like* for lack, as in "Do you like much of bein' th'ew?"

lack v[2] See **like** v[1], adj, vbl aux, n, adv, prep, conj

lackadaisical adj Pronc-spp *lacksadaisi(c)al, lapsadazical;* also, perh by folk-etym, *lackadaisy* [Cf Pronc Intro 3.I.23] Std sense, var forms.

    1913 (1919) *WNID, Lackadaisy.* . . Lackadaisical. . . *Rare.* **1941** in 1944 *ADD,* [Radio song:] With a lazy lackadaisy melody. **1967–70** *DARE* (Qu. KK46, . . *Taking things as they come and not worrying:* "*The whole family was sort of _____.")* Infs **CA**9, **NJ**54, **NC**63, **OH**63, **PA**94, 242, Lacksadaisical; **NJ**4, **VA**31, Lackadaisy; **NY**2, Lack-sadaisial; **TX**102, Lapsadazical; (Qu. A18, . . *A very slow person:* "*What's keeping him? He certainly is _____!")* Inf **NY**63, Lack-sadaisial; (Qu. Y21, *To move about slowly and without energy)* Inf **IL**34, Lacksadaisical ['læksə'dezə,kəl]; **MN**15, Lackadaisy; (Qu. KK30, *Feeling slowed up or without energy:* "*I certainly feel _____.")* Inf **OH**57, Lacksadaisical; (Qu. W29, . . *Expressions . . for things that are sewn carelessly* . . "*They're _____.")* Inf **OR**10, Lackadaisy. **1974** *ME Sunday Telegram* (Portland) 21 July sec D 1, They [=Brooklynites] were sometimes lacksadaisical.

lackaday intj [*OED* "Obs. or arch."] *relic* Used as an expression of surprise, dismay, or regret.

    1828 Webster *Amer. Dict., Lack-a-day,* exclam. of sorrow or regret; alas. **1859** Taliaferro *Fisher's R.* 59 **nwNC** (as of 1820s), Nur did I—lack-a-day!—know what were to befall me that dreadful, dreadful day. **1968** *DARE* (Qu. NN20a, *Exclamations caused by sudden pain—a blow on the thumb)* Inf **VA**15, Lackaday, lackaday. [Inf old]

lacken See **liken** conj

lackey bug n =**whirligig beetle.**

    1941 *Nature Mag.* 34.138, I will not try to explain the names lackey bug and eel bug, which are given to the whirligigs in Massachusetts and North Carolina, respectively.

lacking prep

With the exception of, save.

    1950 *WELS* **WI** (One person has not come: "They're all here now, _____ John.") 1 Inf, Lacking; 1 Inf, Only lacking. **1960** Bailey *Resp. to PADS 20* **KS,** Lacking. **1968–70** *DARE* (Qu. LL31) Infs **NH**16, **NY**219, **TN**26, **TX**104, **VT**12, 16, Lacking.

lackly See **likely**

Lack o' mercy See **Lord** n[1] **B1**

lacksadaisi(c)al See **lackadaisical**

lacuite See **cuite**

lacy bread See **lace corn bread**

lad n [Cf *EDD* *lad-bairn, lad-lass* (at *lad* sb.[1] 1)] Cf **chap** n, **fellow 3**

A young person or animal—usu in phr *lad of a boy* (or *girl,* etc).

    1966 *PADS* 46.27 **cnAR** (as of c1952), *Lad.* . . This term carries with it the idea of youthfulness, as in "Lad of a boy," "Lad of a pup," or "my lads" when speaking of both sons and daughters. **1967** *DARE* FW Addit **LA**2, *A lad of a girl, a lad of a boy* used of a young girl or boy; old-fashioned. **1986** Pederson *LAGS Concordance,* 1 inf, **ceAR,** A lad of a boy—a young boy. [Inf old]

ladder n Pronc-spp *la(a)ther* [Cf *OED* *lather* 16th–17th cent (at *ladder* sb. Forms); *EDD* *lather* (at *ladder* sb. I.(6))] Std sense, var forms.

    1837 Sherwood *Gaz.* **GA** 70, *Lather,* for ladder. **1899** (1912) Green *VA Folk-Speech* 257, *Lather.* . . Laather. Ladder. **1922** *DN* 5.184 **GA** [Black], *Lather.* . . Ladder. "An' dese yer flags an' Jacob's lathers, I ain't seed dem, nudder."

ladderback See **ladder-backed woodpecker 1, 2**

ladder-backed See **ladder-backed woodpecker 1**

ladder-backed three-toed woodpecker See **ladder-backed woodpecker 2**

ladder-backed woodpecker n [From the black and white markings on the back]

1 also *ladderback, ladder-backed, ladder woodpecker*: A **woodpecker** (here: *Picoides scalaris*) native to the southwestern US. Also called **Mexican woodpecker 2, speckle-cheek ~, Texas ~**

    1869 *Amer. Naturalist* 3.474, The resident species not found westward of this valley [=the Colorado Valley in Calif.] were the Ladder Woodpecker *(Picus scalaris)* [etc]. **1898** (1900) Davie *Nests N. Amer. Birds* 265, Texan Woodpecker. *Dryobates scalaris bairdi.* . . This bird is called the Ladder-backed Woodpecker, from the black and white cross-bars on the back. **1928** Bailey *Birds NM* 410, These attractive little barred, or "Ladder-backed Woodpeckers" of the lowlands and river bottoms . . differ from some of their relatives. . . He had a list of pairs of the Ladder-backed along the San Pedro River. **1948** *Ecological Monogr.* 18.171 swUT, Typical nesting residents include . . the Yuma ladder-backed woodpecker, *Dryobates scalaris yumanensis.* **1961** Ligon *NM Birds* 172, Ladder-Backed Woodpecker *Dendrocopos scalaris* . . The little Ladder-backed is common . . over the more arid parts of the state. **1964** Wetmore et al. *Song & Garden Birds* 93, Ladder-backed Woodpecker—*Dendrocopos scalaris*—Vast stretches of hot, treeless desert seem a curious habitat for a woodpecker. Yet to the ladderback such country is home. **1977** Bull–Farrand *Audubon Field Guide Birds* 605, Ladder-backed Woodpecker *(Picoides scalaris).*

2 also *ladderback (woodpecker), ladder-backed three-toed woodpecker*: The northern **three-toed woodpecker** *(Picoides tridactylus).*

    1884 Coues *Key to N. Amer. Birds* 485, *P[icoides] americanus.* . . Ladder-backed Three-toed Woodpecker. **1898** (1900) Davie *Nests N. Amer. Birds* 268, *Picoides americanus.* . . The . . Ladder-backed Three-toed Woodpecker is found in the spruce and fir regions of Northern North America. **1917** (1923) *Birds Amer.* 2.149, The Ladder-back Woodpeckers are divisible into three regional varieties. **1936** Roberts *MN Birds* 1.690, *Picoides tridactylus.* . . "Ladder-back". . . The American Three-toed, or Ladder-backed, Woodpecker is a permanent resident in most of the evergreen forests of the state. **1946** Hausman *Eastern Birds* 392, *Picoides tridactylus.* . . Ladderback. . . Similar to the Arctic Three-toed Woodpecker but with a "ladder back"—that is, a back barred black and white. **1963** Gromme *Birds WI* 215, Ladder-back (Northern Three-toed Woodpecker).

3 =**red-bellied woodpecker.**

    1930 OK Univ. Biol. Surv. *Pub.* 2.146, *Centurus carolinus.* . . Red-bellied Woodpecker. . . Local Names: Big "sapsucker" . . "ladder-backed" woodpecker.

ladderback woodpecker See **ladder-backed woodpecker 2**

ladder wagon See **hay ladder**

ladder woodpecker See **ladder-backed woodpecker 1**

laddle See **ladle**

laden n

1 A dipper, ladle; also v *laden* to dip, ladle. [Prob abbr for *ladin' can, laden tin;* cf EDD lade v.[1] 2(7),(9)]

    1936 *AmSp* 11.191 swWY, Laden. A dipper, cup, or spoon for transferring liquids from one vessel to another. Also verb, to dip, as liquids. 'She drank from the laden.' 'Laden it with this cup.'

‡**2** A food turner, spatula. Cf **ladle**

    1970 *DARE* (Qu. F3, *When you're frying things—for example, eggs—you turn them over with a* _____) Inf VA36, Laden ['ledn̩].

laden v See **laden** n **1**

ladies' bedstraw See **lady's bedstraw**

ladies' chewing tobacco See **ladies'-tobacco a, d**

ladies' cigar See **lady cigar**

ladies' delight n Also *lady's delight* NEng

A **johnny-jump-up 1** (here: *Viola tricolor*).

    1841 (1843) Child *Letters from NY* 2, I am like the Lady's Delight, ever prone to take root. **1861** Holmes *Venner* 1.82 NEng, Marigolds, and flower-de-luces, and lady's-delights, and peonies. **1884** Jewett

Country Dr. 237 ME, She . . had made friends with the disorderly company of ladies-delights and periwinkles which had cropped up everywhere. **1892** *Jrl. Amer. Folkl.* 5.92 MA, *Viola tricolor* . . lady's delight. **1899** (1909) Earle *Child Life* 383 NEng, The flowers chosen to sail in these tiny crafts were those most human of all flowers, pansies, or their smaller garden sisters, the "ladies'-delights" that turned their laughing, happy faces to us from every nook and corner of our garden. **1909** *DN* 3.413 nME, Ladies' delight. . . The pansy. **1966** *DARE* FW Addit MA6, Lady's delight—wild pansy—often come in grass seed. **1985** Clark *From Mailbox* 54 ME, The Johnny-jump-ups are blooming in every corner. . . Also known as ladies' delights, heartease and wild pansy, these hardy violas resemble miniature pansies.

ladies' dresses See **ladies' tresses**

ladies' eardrop(s) See **lady's eardrop 1, 3, 5**

ladies' grass n Also *lady grass* [EDD 1837 →]
=**ribbon grass.**

    1909 *DN* 3.413 nME, Ladies' grass. . . Ribbon grass. **1959** Carleton *Index Herb. Plants* 71, Lady-grass: Phalaris arundinacea var.

ladies' nightcap See **lady's nightcap**

ladies' pocket See **lady's pocket**

ladies' slipper See **lady's slipper**

ladies' sorrel See **lady's sorrel**

ladies'-streamer n Also *lady's streamer* [Folk-etym for *Lagerstroemia*] Cf **laggerstreamer**
=**crape myrtle.**

    1913 *Auk* 30.497 Okefenokee GA, A few birds were observed . . , especially at the crape myrtle ('lady's-streamer') bushes in one of the yards. **1933** Small *Manual SE Flora* 930, *Lagerstroemia indica.* . . Crape-myrtle. Ladies' streamer. **1944** AL Geol. Surv. *Bulletin* 53.159, *L[agerstroemia] Indica.* . . In some parts of Georgia it is called "ladies' streamer," evidently a corruption of the generic name. **1960** Vines *Trees SW* 787, Common Crapemyrtle. . . Another vernacular name is Ladies' Streamer.

ladies' thimble See **lady's thimble 2**

ladies' thumb See **lady's thumb**

ladies'-tobacco n Also *lady's tobacco*

Any of var plants, parts of which are chewed, as:

a also *ladies' chewing tobacco, woman's ~*: =**pussytoes**, esp *Antennaria plantaginifolia.*

    1892 *Jrl. Amer. Folkl.* 5.98, *Antennaria plantaginifolia* . . woman's tobacco. Boston, Mass. . . ladies chewing tobacco. Wisconsin. **1914** Georgia *Manual Weeds* 441, Plantain-leaved everlasting—*Antennaria plantaginifolia.* . . Ladies-Tobacco, Pussy-toes. . . Labrador to Nebraska, southward to Georgia and Texas. **1933** Small *Manual SE Flora* 1401, *Antennaria* [spp] . . Ladies'-tobaccos. **1938** (1958) Sharples *AK Wild Flowers* 12, *Antennaria* [spp]. . . Ladies' Tobacco. **1940** Steyermark *Flora MO* 530, Pussy Toes, Ladies' Tobacco . . *Antennaria* [spp]. *Ibid*, Ladies' Tobacco . . (*Antennaria plantaginifolia*). *Ibid*, Ladies' Tobacco . . (*Antennaria fallax*). *Ibid* 531, Ladies' Tobacco . . (*Antennaria neglecta*). **1959** Carleton *Index Herb. Plants* 72, Lady's-tobacco: *Anaphalis margitacea; Antemmaria* [sic] *plantaginifolia.* **1963** Craighead *Rocky Mt. Wildflowers* 190, *Antennaria rosea.* . . Catspaws, Everlasting, Ladies-tobacco. . . Gum prepared from the stalks of some species of *Antennaria* was chewed by western Indians.

b also *old lady's tobacco*: A **pearly everlasting** (here: *Anaphalis margaritacea*). NEast

    1896 *Jrl. Amer. Folkl.* 9.191 cME, *Anaphalis margaritacea* . . ladies' tobacco. **1898** *Ibid* 11.229, *Anaphalis margaritacea* . . ladies' tobacco, New Durham, N.H. **1931** Harned *Wild Flowers Alleghanies* 565, A number of household names cling to it [=*Anaphalis margaritacea*], among them are Silver-leaf . . and Ladies'-tobacco. **1938** Damon *Grandma* 191 CT (as of late 19th cent), The small white cottony flowers called ladies'-tobacco—on Sundays we mustn't pick and chew that. **1955** *Moosehead Gazette* (Dexter ME) Feb 17/4 *(Hench Coll.)*, Locally . . Pearly Everlasting is Old Lady's Tobacco. **1959** [see **a** above].

c =**cudweed 1.**

    1896 *Jrl. Amer. Folkl.* 9.192, *Gnaphalium* [spp], ladies' tobacco, Madison, Wis. **1906** (1918) Parsons *Wild Flowers CA* 63, Everlasting Flower. Lady's Tobacco. *Gnaphalium decurrens.* . . In our rural districts it is believed that sleeping upon a pillow made of these flowers will cure catarrhal affections.

d also *ladies' chewing tobacco, lady's ~:* =**sweet fennel.**

1914 Saunders *With Flowers in CA* 61, [A tall umbellifer with . . flat-topped masses of yellow flowers, the whole plant abounding in the fragrance of licorice. . . is really fennel *(Foeniculum vulgare).*] *Ibid* 62, The pleasant flavor of the plant has long made it attractive to California children, who find enjoyment in chewing the buds and young leaves. This use of the herb . . gained for it among the young folk of San Francisco the polite name of "ladies' chewing tobacco." **1947** (1976) Curtin *Healing Herbs* 99 **NM**, *Lady's Chewing Tobacco.* [*Ibid* 100, For young girls who suffer from a lapse of catamenia, the leaves are chewed and swallowed.] **1968** *DARE* (Qu. S20, *A common weed that grows on open hillsides: It has velvety green leaves close to the ground, and a tall stalk with small yellow flowers on a spike at the top*) Inf **CA53**, Lady's tobacco—had a licorice taste.

ladies' torn dress n
=**farewell-to-spring.**

1970 Conkling *Steens Mt.* 120 **nwMT**, Where I grew up . . our local name for this beautiful flower [=Clarkia] was "ladies torn dress," and the petals do look torn.

ladies' tresses n pl Also *ladies' dresses, ~ traces, lady's tresses;* rarely sg *ladies' tress* [From the spiral arrangement of the flowers; for *traces* see *OED trace* sb.³, v.³] **scattered, but chiefly NEast**

A plant of the genus *Spiranthes.* Also called **pearl-twist, tresses.** For other names of var spp see **corkscrew plant, hens' toes, screw auger, twisted-stalk**

1814 Bigelow *Florula Bostoniensis* 207, *Neottia cernua.* Drooping Neottia. Ladies traces. **1832** *MA Hist. Soc. Coll.* 2d ser 9.152 **cwVT**, *Neottia cernua,* . . Ladies' tresses. [*Neottia*] *pubescens,* Blood-vein ladies' tresses. **1840** *MA Zool. & Bot. Surv. Herb. Plants & Quadrupeds* 200, *N[eottia] tortilis* . . Ladies' Tresses. Has finely twisted flowers, white and ringent, on a stem a foot high, and leafy towards the base. **1887** Jackson *Between Whiles* 158 **sePA**, A curious little white flower called "Ladies'-Tress" grew there in great abundance. **1894** *Jrl. Amer. Folkl.* 7.100, *Spiranthes,* sp., ladies' tresses, ladies' dresses, ladies' traces (the latter two corruptions). **1938** Matschat *Suwannee R.* 216 **neFL, seGA**, Thousands upon thousands of "lady's-tresses" were spread in great clumps of fifty or more over the drowned floor of the savanna. **1966–68** *DARE* Wildfl QR Pl.16 Inf **NH4**, One of the ladies' tresses—an orchid; **SC41**, Ladies' tresses; Plates 36, 37A Inf **SC41**, Ladies' tresses; Pl.41B Inf **NH4**, One of the ladies' tresses; **NY91**, Ladies' tresses or rattlesnake plantain; Pl.42A Inf **MI7**, Hooded ladies' tresses common. . but wide-leaved variety not around here; **MI57**, Ladies' tresses. **1969** *DARE* (Qu. S26d, *Wildflowers that grow in meadows;* not asked in early QRs) Inf **VT13**, Lady's tresses—little, many orchid-like [flowers] on spike, in wet ground. **1979** *Greenfield Recorder* (MA) 24 Nov sec A 4/1, They . . often have for companions those little sweet-scented green orchids, named "Ladies Tresses." **1987** Case *Orchids* 162, The genus name *Spiranthes* is derived from the Greek words meaning "coiled flowers"—an allusion to the spiraled arrangement of the blossoms, most strikingly evident in such single-ranked forms as the slender ladies'-tresses *(S. lacera).*

ladies' twist n Also *lady's twist* arch Cf **pigtail**
Tobacco twisted into small ropes or coils.

1789 in 1960 Heimann *Tobacco* 190, [Advt:] Tobacco & Snuff of the best quality & flavor . . Where may be had as follows . . Ladies twist do, Pigtail do. in small rolls, Plug do. Hogtail do. **1821** *Turner's NY Shipping & Commercial List* [4]/3 **NYC**, *Tobacco,* Richmond. . . Kentucky. . . Ladies Twist. . . Cavendish. . . Sweet scent. **1843** in 1844 Lumsden *Amer. Memoranda* 14, My next communication will probably contain full details of the methods adopted by the Virginian planters in the manufacturing of the nigger-head, ladies'-twist, cavendish, plug, pig-tail, honey-dew, and other varieties of the stimulating and soothing herb. **1864** Burritt *Walk from London* 290 **cCT**, An American tobacco-chewer, of fifty years' standing, would not have asked a cut from a neighbor's "lady's twist," or "pig-tail." **1884** Baldwin *Yankee School-Teacher* 104 **VA**, As for the Virginia weed alluded to, a generous "lady's twist" was always beside her red clay Powhatan pipe. . . she also "chewed" the seductive staple, but this was an universal custom among the colored women of her acquaintance.

ladigo See **latigo**

ladino adj, also used absol [AmSpan < Span *ladino* cunning, crafty] esp **TX**
Of a horse or cow: vicious, unmanageable, wild.

1892 *DN* 1.191 **TX**, *Ladino.* . . In Texas . . a vicious, unmanageable horse, full of cunning and tricks. **1904** Adams *TX Matchmaker* 154, There are a lot of big *ladino* beeves in those brushy hills to the south and west. *Ibid* 298, We rode away merrily to declare war on the *ladino* stallion. **1929** Dobie *Vaquero* 14 **swTX**, They were all outlaws, *ladinos,* as wild as bucks, cunning, and ready to fight anything that got in front of them. . . Among them were wrinkle-necked maverick cows and bulls that had never had a loop tossed over their heads.

ladino (clover) n
=**white Dutch clover.** Cf **dana clover**

1925 *Book of Rural Life* 2.1148, There is one special variety [of white clover], the Ladino, cultivated in the Valley of the Po in Italy, which is much larger than the common sort. **1960** Criswell *Resp. to PADS* 20 **Ozarks**, In late years lespedeza, alsike and ladino clover, alfalfa. . . have come in. **1967** *News Reporter* (Whiteville NC) 7 Aug 13/6, If ladino clover, a legume, is to thrive and fix adequate nitrogen for the crop, the soil should be limed. **1967–70** *DARE* (Qu. L9b, *Hay from other kinds of plants [not grass];* not asked in early QRs) Infs **CA28, CT2, KY84, OH10, PA103, VA77, WI77,** Ladino clover; **IN80, PA116,** Ladino; (Qu. L8, *Hay that grows naturally in damp places*) Inf **WI63**, [ləˈdinəl] clover; (Qu. L9a, *. . Kinds of grass . . grown for hay*) Inf **IN67**, Ladino; **CT9**, Ladino clover. **1972** Brown *Wildflowers LA* 92, White Dutch Clover, Ladino Clover—*Trifolium repens.* . . Widely distributed in Louisiana, making best growth on the floodplain soils. Also Texas, Arkansas, and Mississippi.

ladle n Pronc-sp *laddle* **chiefly west of Appalachians** See Map *old-fash*

A food turner or spatula.

1965–70 *DARE* (Qu. F3, *When you're frying things—for example, eggs—you turn them over with a _____*) 12 Infs, **chiefly west of Appalachians,** Ladle; **CA105**, Pancake ladle; **MI68**, Pancake ladle or pancake turner; **TX94**, Laddle [ˈlædəl] [All Infs old]; (Qu. G6, *. . Dishes that you might have on the table for a big dinner or special occasion—for example, Thanksgiving*) Inf **AZ8**, Pie ladle; **MN33**, Butter ladle—the flat knife. **1986** Pederson *LAGS Concordance,* 1 inf, **cwLA**, Ladle—flat device for cooking eggs. [Inf old]

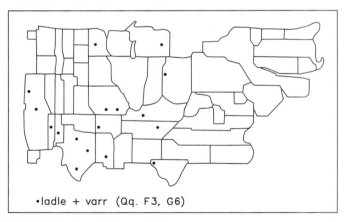

•ladle + varr (Qq. F3, G6)

lad of a boy (or girl) See **lad**

ladrone n Also *ladron* [Span *ladrón*] **SW** arch
A thief, robber.

[**1838** *NY Mirror* 6 Jan 217 **SW**, For some time their conversation ran on robbers. . . "Carramba! . . " exclaimed a [Mexican] soldier; "no ladrone in Mejico dare attack a party guarded by myself and brother soldiers."] **1844** (1846) Kendall *Santa Fé Exped.* 2.70 **SW**, The ladrones, or common thieves, could now reap a rich harvest of plunder. **1867** *New Mexican* (Santa Fe NM) 6 Apr 1/4, The soldiers would not be able to discriminate the good Indian from the ladrone, (thief). **1930** Dobie *Coronado* 363 **SW** (as of c1860) [Glossary], *Ladron,* robber. **1947** Westerners Los Angeles Corral *Brand Book* 99 **sAZ** (as of a1914), The thieves had a good start, but the pursuers tracked them, finding every place where the ladrones stopped signs of other offenses against the law—the killing of beef.

lad's love See **boy's love**

lady n **Sth, S Midl** *old-fash*
A wife.

1872 Schele de Vere *Americanisms* 478, The vulgarity of entering a traveller's name on the register of the hotel, as "Mr. _____ and lady," is only surpassed by placing the same words on visiting-cards. **1905** *DN* 3.85 **nwAR**, *Lady*. . . Wife. 'Bring your lady and the children.' Common. **1909** *DN* 3.343 **eAL, wGA**, *Lady*. . . Wife. "Did you bring your lady along?" *The madam* is used in the same sense. **1934–44** in 1944 *ADD* **nWV**, [*Lady*—A wife] Common in newspapers. **c1960** *Wilson Coll.* **csKY**, *Lady*. . . One's wife.

lady-at-the-gate n
A **speedwell.**
   1950 *WELS Suppl.* **csWI**, Lady-at-the-gate *(Veronica).*

lady beetle n
=**ladybug.**
   1868 MI State Bd. Ag. *Annual Rept.* 7.175, Quite a number of lady-beetles have been noticed on the vines. **1938** Brimley *Insects NC* 185, The Lady Beetles are . . usually either black with red, yellow or white spots, or red or yellow with black spots, some however are solid colored, not spotted. **1949** Palmer *Nat. Hist.* 401, On Pacific Coast, convergent lady beetles are collected in great numbers and distributed in crop areas. **1970** *DARE* (Qu. R30, . . *Kinds of beetles;* not asked in early QRs) Inf **PA**246, Lady bug [or] beetle. **1989** Entomol. Soc. Amer. *Common Names Insects* 192, Coccinellidae—lady beetles.

Lady Birch n Also *Lady Quince* Cf **peach-tree tea**
A switch used to punish children; see quots.
   1932 *DN* 6.283 **swCT**, *Lady Quince.* A switch made of quince wood, very hard. "You're going to get Lady Quince." **1941** *LANE* Map 398 *(Switch)* 1 inf, **swME**, Terms for an implement used in whipping children. . . *Lady Birch,* a switch of birch.

ladybird n
1 also *ladybird beetle:* =**ladybug.** [*OED* 1704 →]
   1737 (1911) Brickell *Nat. Hist. NC* 158, The *Lady Bird* is a beautiful small Insect (with red Wings and black spots thereon) which . . is to be met with in *Carolina* in the *Summer* time, and is a wonderful Cordial, curing all Fevers. **1849** Howitt *Our Cousins in OH* 100, They found some golden lady-birds upon a young vine. . . They were indeed beautiful insects, as bright and metallic as if they had been made of the finest gold, and their wings when they were spread for flight, appeared to be made of silver net-work. **1854** Emmons *Agriculture NY* 5.161, Plant-lice have numerous foes . . among these foes we may rank the numerous species of *Coccinella,* or *ladybirds.* **1868** MO State Entomol. *Annual Rept.* 16, The next most efficient aid we have is the Twice-stabbed lady-bird (*Chilocorus bivulnerus,* Muls.) This good friend is readily recognized by its polished black color, and the blood-red spot on each wing-case. **1909** Smith *Insect Friends* 102, Among the *Coccinellidae* popularly known as "ladybirds," "ladybird beetles" or simply "ladybugs," we find a very decided specialization as to the character of the prey. **c1930** Brown *Amer. Folkl. Insect Lore* 4, To kill a lady-bird is to bring bad luck. **1967–69** *DARE* (Qu. R30, . . *Kinds of beetles;* not asked in early QRs) Infs **MO**5, **RI**15, Ladybird; **MD**30, **NY**155, **WI**43, Ladybird beetle.
2 =**fringed polygala.** Cf **bird-on-the-wing**
   1970 *DARE* (Qu. S26e, *Other wildflowers not yet mentioned;* not asked in early QRs) Inf **MA**78, Ladybirds = fringed polygala.

ladybird beetle See **ladybird 1**

lady bleeding See **love-lies-bleeding 1**

lady bloom n Also *lady bush*
A **ceanothus** (here: *Ceanothus parryi*).
   1923 in 1925 Jepson *Manual Plants CA* 618, *C[eanothus] parryi.* . . Lady-bloom. **1938** Van Dersal *Native Woody Plants* 89, *Ceanothus parryi.* . . Lady-bloom. . . flowers April–June. **1951** Abrams *Flora Pacific States* 3.68, *Ceanothus Parryi* . . Parry's Ceanothus or Lady-bush.

lady bonnet n Cf **Quaker bonnet**
Perh a **bluet 2** such as *Houstonia caerulea.*
   1967 *DARE* (Qu. S23, *Pale blue flowers with downy leaves and cups that come up on open, stony hillsides in March or early April*) Inf **MI**65, A lady bonnet.

lady britches n
=**Dutchman's breeches 1.**
   1968–70 *DARE* (Qu. S26a, . . *Wildflowers . . Roadside flowers*) Inf **IA**29, Lady britches [FW: The Dutchman's britches]; (Qu. S26e, *Other wildflowers not yet mentioned;* not asked in early QRs) Inf **MI**120, Lady britches = bleeding heart.

lady-broke adj Cf **cowboy-broke, green broke, Indian-broke**
Of a horse: well-trained, gentle.
   1944 Adams *Western Words* 88, *Lady broke*—Said of a horse when he is thoroughly gentle.

ladybug n
Std: a round, usu brightly colored and spotted beetle of the family Coccinellidae. Also called **lady beetle, ladybird 1, lady cow.** For other names of var of these beetles see **Mexican bean beetle**

lady bush See **lady bloom**

lady-by-the-gate n
=**bouncing Bet 1.**
   1896 *Jrl. Amer. Folkl.* 9.182 **NC**, *Saponaria officinalis* . . lady-by-the-gate. **1900** Lyons *Plant Names* 334, *S[aponaria] officinalis* . . Lady-by-the-gate. **1958** Jacobs–Burlage *Index Plants NC* 35, *Saponaria officinalis.* . . Lady-by-the-gate. . . The herb . . is common . . in all parts of North Carolina.

lady-by-the-lake n
1 A **false dragonhead 1** (here: *Physostegia virginiana*).
   1940 Clute *Amer. Plant Names* 266, *Physostegia Virginiana.* Lady-by-the-lake.
2 A **blue-eyed Mary 1** (here: *Collinsia verna*).
   1940 Clute *Amer. Plant Names* 221, *Collinsia verna.* . . blue eye, lady-by-the-lake.

lady cat n
A **channel catfish** (here: *Ictalurus punctatus*).
   1889 *Century Dict.* 3328, *Lady-cat.* . . The large channel catfish of the United States, *Ictalurus punctatus.* It attains a weight of 5 to 15 pounds, and is much esteemed for food. **1957** Trautman *Fishes* 415 **OH**, Young [of the channel catfish] less than 14.0″ long (colloquially called . . ladycats . .) are bluish- or olivaceous-silvery dorsally. **1983** Becker *Fishes WI* 712, *Channel Catfish.* . . Other common names: . . blue cat, lady cat, chucklehead cat [etc].

lady cigar n Also *ladies' cigar* Cf **Indian cigar, ladyfinger 8**
The pod of **catalpa B1;** hence n *lady cigar tree* = **catalpa B1.**
   1957 *Sat. Eve. Post Letters* **swIL**, "Lady cigars" grew on catalpa trees. **1966–70** *DARE* (Qu. T9, *The common shade tree with large heart-shaped leaves, clusters of white blossoms, and long thin seed pods or 'beans'*) Infs **CT**28, **MO**21, 25, **WA**33, Lady cigar tree; **IL**143, Ladies' cigar—the pods [of this tree]. **1967** *DARE* FW Addit **cMO**, Lady cigar—a catalpa tree bean.

lady cigar tree See **lady cigar**

lady cow n [*OED* 1606 →]
=**ladybug.**
   1967 *DARE* FW Addit **neNY**, Lady cow—a ladybug.

lady crab n
A common crab *(Ovalipes ocellatus)* of the Atlantic coast. Also called **sand crab**
   1844 DeKay *Zool. NY* 6.10, Although occasionally eaten, it [=*Ovalipes ocellatus*] is not much esteemed as an article of food. By the shore-dwellers, it is often designated as the *Lady Crab,* from the beauty of its colors. **1884** U.S. Natl. Museum *Bulletin* 27.111, The Lady Crab . . is occasionally taken for food on the Atlantic coast, . . but is rarely seen in the markets. . . On the New England coast it is used as bait. **1901** Arnold *Sea-Beach* 276, The lady-crab. . . is found among the loose sands at low-water mark, . . and also is abundant on sandy bottoms offshore. **1933** John G. Shedd Aquarium *Guide* 201, The *Lady Crab* . . and the *Blue Crab* . . are more plentiful along the sandy shores of the Middle Atlantic States. **1981** Meinkoth *Audubon Field Guide Seashore* 638, *Lady Crab.* . . This handsome crab is known for its aggressive disposition and sharp pincers.

lady cracker n Also *lady firecracker*
=**ladyfinger 1.**
   1950 *WELS (Other names for firecrackers)* 3 Infs, **WI**, Lady crackers. **1967** Borland *Hill Country* 210 **NE** (as of c1915), Firecrackers came in all sizes, from the tiny "lady crackers," not much bigger around than the lead in a pencil, to "giant crackers" that could blow up a barn. **1967–69** *DARE* (Qu. FF14, . . *Kinds of firecrackers*) Infs **CT**27, 30, **LA**17, **MI**44, **PA**29, 49, **WI**13, Lady crackers; **CA**53, **NV**7, Lady firecrackers. **1967** *DARE* FW Addit **nwLA**, *Lady crackers*—firecrackers,

smaller than the usual. **1978** *Capital Times* (Madison WI) 3 July 13/4, I always went to my girl friend's house to shoot my lady crackers. These were a very small firecracker, which we lit with punk since we weren't allowed to light matches. It was more fun at her house because she didn't have an older brother and sister to tease her about the "baby" crackers.

lady cream pea See **cream pea**

Lady Estherbilt n Abbr *Lady Esther* [Var of **Astorbilt**, prob infl by name *Esther*]

A pretentious or self-important woman.

    1966–67 *DARE* (Qu. HH35, *A woman who puts on a lot of airs*) Inf **AZ**6, Lady Estherbilt; **OK**45, She's a Lady Esther.

lady fart n

Prob =**ladyfinger 1.**

    1967 *DARE* (Qu. FF14, . . *Kinds of firecrackers*) Inf **IL**11, Lady farts.

lady-fashion adv [In ref to riding sidesaddle] Cf **belly-buster 1**

In sledding: see quot.

    1892 *DN* 1.235 **cwMO,** Boys always use this word [=belly-buster] for coasting face downwards on their sleds. To coast sidewise, with the left leg slightly folded under the body, is called *lady-fashion.*

lady fern n

1 A fern of the genus *Athyrium,* esp *A. filix-femina.* [OED 1825 →] For other names of *A. filix-femina* see **backache brake, female fern, spring ~**

    1868 (1870) Gray *Field Botany* 367, A[splenium] filix-foemina. Lady-fern. Common in moist woods. **1878** Williamson *Ferns KY* 73, The Lady Fern is by no means uncommon in Kentucky, having been collected by myself in many localities. **1889** *Century Dict.* 3328, *Lady-fern.* . . An elegant fern, *Asplenium Filix-fœmina,* widely diffused, in numerous varieties, throughout the northern temperate zone. **1923** Davidson–Moxley *Flora S. CA* 17, *Lady Fern.* . . Occasional about springs and streams and in bogs. **1950** Stevens *ND Plants* 43, *Athyrium angustum* . . Lady Fern. . . In a wooded swamp. **1951** Graham *My Window* 46 **ME,** She is familiar with ferns. . . she finds lady fern. **1967** *DARE* (Qu. S26a, . . *Wildflowers* . . *Roadside flowers*) Inf **MA**5, Lady fern. **1973** Hitchcock–Cronquist *Flora Pacific NW* 48, *Athyrium* [spp]. Lady-fern. *Ibid* 49, Alpine l[ady-fern]. . . *A. distentifolium.* **1994** Guterson *Snow Falling* 153 **nwWA,** She knew where lady fern grew and phantom orchids and warted giant puffballs.

2 =**maidenhair fern.**

    1954 Harrington *Manual Plants CO* 18, *Adiantum* [spp]. . . Lady fern.

ladyfinger n

1 A small firecracker. Cf **lady cracker, ~ fart**

    1944 *Sun* (Baltimore MD) 5 July 10/7, A man I know bought himself several packages of firecrackers—not cannon crackers, nor what, in our youth, we used to call "lady fingers," but ordinary medium-sized Chinese firecrackers. **1950** *WELS* **WI** (*Other names for firecrackers*) 7 Infs, Ladyfingers; 1 Inf, Ladyfingers—tiny firecrackers. **1965–70** *DARE* (Qu. FF14, . . *Kinds of firecrackers*) 114 Infs, **scattered,** Ladyfingers; **CO**17, **FL**51, **MT**1, Ladyfingers—small ones; **CA**22, Ladyfingers—the little bitty ones; **CO**9, Ladyfingers—twenty small ones in a row; **CO**13, Ladyfingers—small ones on a string; **MN**2, Ladyfingers—long and thin. **1967** *DARE* FW Addit **swAR** (as of early 1950s), During my three year residence in southern Arkansas, around Cale, in Nevada County, these [=lady crackers] were called ladyfingers. **1989** Mosher *Stranger* 363 **nVT,** On the common, kids raced here and there setting off lady fingers left over from the Old Home Day celebration.

2 A type of candy; see quot.

    1967–68 *DARE* (Qu. H82b, *Kinds of cheap candy that used to be sold years ago*) Infs **IN**3, **PA**159, Ladyfingers; **PA**22, Ladyfingers—long, chocolate-covered, creamy. [All Infs old]

3 also *lady's finger:* Okra *(Abelmoschus esculentus).*

    1905 *U.S. Dept. Ag. Farmers' Bulletin* 232.12, There are three general types of okra, viz, tall green, dwarf green, and lady finger. **1976** Bailey-Bailey *Hortus Third* 1, *[Abelmoschus] esculentus.* . . Okra, gumbo, gobo, gombo, lady's finger.

4 also *lady's finger:* Either of two related plants: **prince's-feather** or a **lady's thumb** (here: *Polygonum persicaria*).

    1913 (1980) Hardy *OH Schoolmistress* 14 **swOH,** He had allowed to remain among his turnips two or three plants, known to us as the Lady-fingers, which he carefully hoed along with his vegetables, evidently cherishing the common belief that the plant kept out weeds. . .

It was sometimes called Kiss-me-over-the-fence, alluding to its habit of swaying in the least wind and touching you on the cheek as you went by. Its common bookname is Prince's Feather. **1930** OK Univ. Biol. Surv. *Pub.* 2.59, *Polygonum persicaria.* . . Lady's Thumb. Lady's Finger. Heartsease. **1938** Stuart *Dark Hills* 209 **eKY,** That smell of crab-apple blossoms was sure sweeter than the smell of the snowballs in the back yard, the bleeding heart or the lady's finger.

5 A **milkvetch** (here: *Astragalus utahensis*). Cf **lady's slipper 8**

    1915 (1926) Armstrong–Thornber *Western Wild Flowers* 258, *Pink Lady-fingers* . . *Astragalus Utahensis.* . . The pale leaves are symmetrically arranged in neat clusters and ornamented at intervals with pink flowers.

6 A small hot pepper *(Capsicum* spp).

    1967 *DARE* (Qu. I22a, . . *Peppers—small hot*) Inf **SC**29, Ladyfinger—finger-sized and shaped; **SC**62, Ladyfinger.

7 See **lady pea.**

8 =**catalpa B1.** Cf **lady cigar**

    1968 *DARE* (Qu. T9) Inf **OH**77, Ladyfinger is the nickname for [catalpa].

9 A freshwater clam (here: *Elliptio dilatata*).

    1941 *AmSp* 16.155, The following list gives the common names [of freshwater clams] as applied by the cutter and fisher of shells. . . Ladyfinger [etc]. **1979** *WI Week-End* 6 Apr 6/3, Such shellfish as the . . lady fingers and pig's foot go right on living their private lives in the quiet waterways of the Mississippi. **1982** U.S. Fish & Wildlife Serv. *Fresh-Water Mussels* [Wall chart], *Spike.* Ladyfinger. Historically widespread, uncommon.

ladyfinger cactus n

A **hedgehog cactus 3** (here: *Echinocereus pentalophus*).

    1942 Hylander *Plant Life* 324, Lady Finger Cactus of southern Texas is a prostrate plant with stems which grow erect at their extremities, forming extended clumps of four- to six-angled stems with spine-bearing tubercles.

ladyfinger pea See **lady pea**

lady firecracker See **lady cracker**

ladyfish n esp FL

1 A **bonefish 1** (here: *Albula vulpes*).

    1873 in 1878 Smithsonian Inst. *Misc. Coll.* 14.2.32, *Albula conorhynchus* . . Lady-fish. Cape Cod to Florida. **1884** Goode *Fisheries U.S.* 1.612, With us it [=*Albula vulpes*] is usually called the "Lady-fish." **1926** Pan-Pacific Research Inst. *Jrl.* 1.1.5 **HI,** *Albula virgata.* . . Lady-fish. **1968** *DARE* (Qu. P4, *Saltwater fish that are not good to eat*) Inf **LA**37, Banana fish—this is the same fish called skipjack in south Texas, horse mackerel farther north and east in Texas—maybe same as ladyfish in Florida. **1975** Newell *If Nothin' Don't Happen* 83 **wFL,** Once in a while we'd make a strike with our gill nets, thinkin' we'd surrounded a big school of mullet, only to find out that we had us a slew of ladyfish. Them ladyfish will gill just like mullets, but they're full of bones and fit for nothin'.

2 A **hogfish a** of the genus *Bodianus,* usu *B. rufus.*

    1882 U.S. Natl. Museum *Bulletin* 16.601, *Harpe* [spp] . . Lady-fishes. . . Coarse, brightly-colored fishes, inhabiting tropical seas. *Ibid, H. rufa* . . Lady-fish. **1896** *Ibid* 47.1583 **sFL,** *Harpe rufa* . . Lady-fish; Spanish Lady-fish. **1933** John G. Shedd Aquarium *Guide* 141, *Bodianus rufus*—Spanish Hogfish; Ladyfish. This handsomely colored Hogfish reaches a length of two feet.

3 A **ten-pounder** (here: *Elops saurus*).

    1882 U.S. Natl. Museum *Proc.* 5.246, *Elops saurus* . . Lady-fish. . . Very abundant in summer; at Pensacola, largely salted as bait for the Red Snapper. Not used as food. **1935** Caine *Game Fish* 99, Large schools of ladyfish can be seen feeding out in the ocean, and when the tide turns and starts to come in, they will come with it and then one may expect plenty of action. **1944** *Richmond Times–Dispatch* (VA) 20 Oct 18/1 **ceFL,** I wish you could see those ladyfish. . . They are shaped something like a pike, look a lot like a bonefish and must be kin to a tarpon, for they really are acrobats. **1966** *DARE* (Qu. P4, *Saltwater fish that are not good to eat*) Inf **FL**4, Ladyfish; **FL**24, Ladyfish, ten-pounder; too boney. **1991** Amer. Fisheries Soc. *Common Names Fishes* 16, *Elops saurus* . . ladyfish.

4 =**pinfish.**

    1897 *Outing* 29.331 **FL,** The "bony fish," or "lady fish" . . abounds in all Florida rivers, and has been malignantly christened by some bilious scientist a *Lagodon rhomboides.*

lady grass n

1 A **blue-eyed grass 1** (here: *Sisyrinchium angustifolium*).
    1966 *DARE* Wildfl QR Pl.28A, Inf **WA**15, Lady grass.

2 See **ladies' grass.**

lady gum n *old-fash*

A type of candy; see quot.
    1969–70 *DARE* (Qu. H82b, *Kinds of cheap candy that used to be sold years ago*) Inf **MI**108, Lady gum—white paraffin stick with a ring on it; **MI**119, Lady gum; **WI**76, Lady gum—flat, with picture, mostly heart-shaped, [sold] long ago when I was young. [All Infs old]

Lady Haley n [Etym unknown]
    1904 *DN* 2.426 **Cape Cod MA** (as of a1857), *Lady Haley.* . . A well behaved, obliging, little girl. 'That's a little lady Haley.'

lady-hearted adj

Soft-hearted, disposed to help people.
    c1938 in 1970 Hyatt *Hoodoo* 1.197 **seNC**, Ah tell yo' de kinda man he are. He's a *lady-hearted* man. He won't do nuthin' tuh harm anybody, he'll take it [=any hoodoo harm from which one suffers] off yo'.

lady-in-a-chaise n

1 A **jack-in-the-pulpit 1** (here: *Arisaema triphyllum*).
    1891 *Jrl. Amer. Folkl.* 4.148 **NEng**, Arisaema triphyllum was always *Dragon Root,* or *Lady in a Chaise.*

2 =**fennel-flower.**
    1892 *Jrl. Amer. Folkl.* 5.91 **NH**, *Nigella Damascena* . . lady-in-a-chaise.

lady-in-the-green n

=**fennel-flower.**
    1836 (1840) Phelps *Lectures on Botany* 119, [*Nigella*] damascena . . fennel-flower, lady-in-the-green. **1891** *Jrl. Amer. Folkl.* 4.148 **NEng**, When children, we knew Nigella damascena only as *Lady in the Green.* **1892** *Ibid* 5.91, *Nigella Damascena* . . Lady-in-the-green. N.E. and Westward.

lady-in-white n

A **pearly everlasting** (here: *Anaphalis margaritacea*).
    1966 *DARE* Wildfl QR Pl.211B Inf **WA**15, Lady-in-white.

lady legs n Also *lady's leg* [From the smooth, pinkish bark]

A **madrone** (here: *Arbutus texana*).
    1960 Vines *Trees SW* 805, *Arbutus texana.* . . Also known under the vernacular names of Texas Arbutus, Madroño, . . Lady Legs. **1970** Correll *Plants TX* 1174, *Lady's leg.* Small evergreen tree . . ; bark pinkish to red-brown, peeling off in large papery sheets. **1980** Little *Audubon Guide N. Amer. Trees W. Region* 579, The local names [for *Arbutus texana*], "Naked Indian" and "Lady's Leg," refer to the smooth flesh-colored bark.

lady lock n [From similarity in shape to a lock of hair]

A cream-filled, spiral-shaped pastry.
    1920 Kander *Settlement Cook Book* 363 **seWI**, Lady Locks—Cut Puff or other Rich Pastry . . into strips. . . Wind this around cone shaped wooden forms or lady lock sticks, having edges overlap, but keeping the space between the paste quite narrow. . . bake in a moderate oven. Remove the pastry from the sticks, and fill the hollow centers with heavy cream, sweetened and flavored before whipping. **1942** *AN&Q* 2.55, Regional Pastries. . . The eastern "lady-lock [*"*]" is a "cornucopia." **c1965** Randle *Cookbooks* (Ask Neighbor) 3.57, *Little Lady Locks.* . . Roll [rich pastry] dough out about ¼″ and cut into strips. Wrap around clothes pins. (round ones). . . Bake until dried and turn brown. When warm, slide off clothes pin and fill [with mixture of egg white, sugar, boiling water, and marshmallow cream]. **1978** *New Haven Reg.* (CT) 30 Nov 68/1 **Pittsburgh PA**, How do you recognize a Pittsburgher? Where else but here does one . . serve . . "lady locks" (cream pastries) for lunch? **1986** Pederson *LAGS Concordance,* 1 inf, **neGA**, Lady lock—twisted; cream in center.

lady lord See **lord** n[1] **B2**

lady lupine n

A **lupine** (here: *Lupinus villosus*).
    1933 Small *Manual SE Flora* 681, *L[upinus] villosus.* . . (Lady-lupine). Dry pinelands and shady barrens. **1949** Moldenke *Amer. Wild Flowers* 134, From North Carolina to Florida and Louisiana grows the

lovely *lady lupine.* **1953** Greene-Blomquist *Flowers South* 55, Lady-lupine . . [is] a remarkable species with deep-lilac to purple corollas with a red spot in the center of the standard. **1972** Brown *Wildflowers LA* 81, *Lady Lupine.* . . Flower cluster terminal, . . with many pea-shaped blossoms.

lady of the waters n Cf **demoiselle 2**

=**Louisiana heron.**
    1916 *Times–Picayune* (New Orleans LA) 2 Apr mag sec 1, *Louisiana Heron.* . . Lady of the Waters. . . The most stately of the herons. **1932** Howell *FL Bird Life* 104, *Hydranassa tricolor ruficollis.* . . Lady-of-the-waters. **1946** Hausman *Eastern Birds* 105, *Louisiana Heron.* . . Its names Demoiselle and Lady-of-the-Waters suggest that it is considered the most graceful of all the heron tribe. **1955** Forbush–May *Birds* 32, Lady of the Waters.

lady pea n Also *ladyfinger (pea)* **chiefly Sth, sS Midl** See Map Cf **cowpea, cream pea**

A var or cultivar of a **black-eyed pea** (here: *Vigna unguiculata* subsp *unguiculata*).
    1788 (1925) Washington *Diaries* 3.324 **VA**, Below, were sowed, or rather planted, the everlasting (or Lady Pease) sent me by the Honble. James Mercer. **1837** (1962) Williams *Territory FL* 112, The cow pea, lady pea, and chickasaw pea, produce excellent crops during the heat of summer. **1906** *DN* 3.144 **nwAR**, *Lady pea.* . . A small pea, raised, as a usual thing, to fertilize land. **1909** *DN* 3.343 **eAL, wGA**, *Lady-pea.* . . A small white pea, considered very desirable as a table vegetable. **1912** Cobb *Back Home* 78 **wKY**, He overturned a little wooden measure that held a nickel's worth of dried lady-peas. **1953** (1977) Hubbard *Shantyboat* 308 **Missip-Ohio Valleys**, There were some vegetables, however, which seemed to thrive in the heat. One was field peas. Of the many varieties, we planted black eye and crowder peas. Tom brought us some of his own seed, white lady peas of delicate flavor, and an earlier, darker kind which he called gentleman peas. **1954** Harder *Coll.* **cwTN**, *Peas.* . . various names: crowders . . lady peas. *Ibid,* Lady pea hay. **1965–70** *DARE* (Qu. I20, . . *Kinds of beans*) Infs **LA**15, **MS**54, 59, **SC**26, **TN**24, 52, Lady pea(s); **NC**44, Lady peas—pale yellow; **NJ**39, Lady peas—small, black-eyed pea; **OK**1, Lady pea—small, white pea; **FL**18, 33, 49, **SC**38, Ladyfinger peas; **GA**6, Ladyfinger—very small pea, yellow; **GA**11, Ladyfingers; (Qu. I15, *Some of the beans that you eat in the pod have yellow pods; you call these _____*) Inf **TX**73, Lady peas; (Qu. I18, *The smaller beans that are white when they are dry*) Infs **AL**6, 25, **GA**9, 90, **TX**73, Lady peas; **AR**55, Lady pea—a small white pea called table pea (new fangled); (Qu. I19, *Small white beans with a black spot where they were joined to the pod*) Inf **MS**35, Lady peas; **MS**87, Lady peas—resemble black-eyed beans but are smaller. **1970–76** *DARE* File **swTN**, *Lady peas,* a very small bean, white—seen at a seed store in Jackson, TN; **sGA**, An Inf from southern Georgia says the older generation call them [=field peas] lady peas, but they are known by younger people, and in SC, as acre peas. **1988** Whealy *Garden Seed Inventory* (2d ed) 163, *Lady* (Lady Finger). . . Tiny fine-flavored peas, bunch type, very prolific.

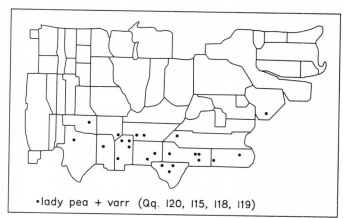

•lady pea + varr (Qq. I20, I15, I18, I19)

Lady Quince See **Lady Birch**

lady rain n
    1993 *DARE* File, A term used by a Virginian: "lady rain" for a gentle rain.

lady rue n

A **meadow rue** (here: *Thalictrum clavatum*).

1933 Small *Manual SE Flora* 524, *T[halictrum] clavatum. . . Lady-rue. . .* Ga. to Ala., W. Va., and Va. **1950** Gray–Fernald *Manual of Botany* 658, *Lady-Rue. . .* Brooksides, mts. **1975** Duncan–Foote *Wildflowers SE* 46, *Lady-rue. . .* Inconspicuous but easily recognized by its stalked, curved (scimitar-shaped) fruits. . . Moist places, often in deep shade but occasionally in the open.

lady's bedstraw n Also *ladies' bedstraw, Our Lady's ~* [See quot 1943]

A **bedstraw,** usu the naturalized *Galium verum.*

1837 Darlington *Flora Cestrica* 99, *G[alium] trifidum. . .* Three-cleft Galium . . Ladies Bed-straw. **1938** (1958) Sharples *AK Wild Flowers* 60, *Galium* [spp]. . . "Ladies' Bedstraw," so called because of the legend that one of these plants was in the hay on which the mother of Jesus rested. **1943** Fernald–Kinsey *Edible Wild Plants E. N. Amer.* 343, Yellow Bedstraw or Our-Lady's Bedstraw, *Galium verum,* is fragrant upon drying and was very early designated as the plant which filled the manger at Bethlehem, with the result that, being thus blessed and having a pleasing aroma when dry, it was for many centuries used in mattresses. **1976** Bailey–Bailey *Hortus Third* 493, *[Galium] verum . .* Our-Lady's b[edstraw] . . naturalized and weedy in N. Amer.

lady's chewing tobacco See **ladies'-tobacco d**

lady's delight See **ladies' delight**

lady's eardrop n

1 also *ladies' eardrop(s), lady's eardrops:* A plant of the genus *Fuchsia.* Cf **eardrop 2**

1829 Phelps *Familiar Lect.* 145, The Ladies'-ear-drop, (*Fuschia* [sic],) is a beautiful exotic. It has a funnel-form calyx, of a brilliant red colour. **1868** (1870) Gray *Field Botany* 147, Short-flowered Fuchsias, or Ladies' Eardrops. **1889** *Century Dict.* 1816, *Ear-drop. . . Lady's ear-drops,* the common garden fuchsia: so called from the formation and pendency of its flowers. **1976** Bailey–Bailey *Hortus Third* 489, *Fuchsia . .* Lady's-eardrops, ladies'-eardrops.

2 also *lady's eardrops:* =**bleeding heart 1. NEng**

1887 Freeman *Humble Romance* 195 **NEng,** He cut lavishly sprays of dioletra [=*Dielytra,* now *Dicentra*], or lady's ear-drop, snowballs, daffodils. **1893** *Jrl. Amer. Folkl.* 6.137, *Dicentra spectabilis,* lady's eardrops. Concord, Mass. **1899** (1909) Earle *Child Life* 383 **MA,** The "dielytra" (bleeding-heart, or lady's-eardrops we called it) had long, gracefully dropping racemes of bright red-pink flowers, which when pulled apart and straightened out made fairy gondolas, or which might be twisted into a harp and bottle.

3 also *ladies' eardrop, lady's earrings:* A **jewelweed 1** (here: *Impatiens capensis*).

1891 *Jrl. Amer. Folkl.* 4.151, Lady's eardrop . . for *Impatiens.* **1892** *Ibid* 5.94 **OH,** *Impatiens fulva* [now = *I. capensis*] . . lady's eardrop. Mansfield, O. **1900** Lyons *Plant Names* 201, *I[mpatiens] biflora* [now =*I. capensis*] . . Ladies'-eardrop. **1931** Clute *Common Plants* 74, Lady's ear-drop (*Impatiens biflora*), lady's purse . . and many others have a more mundane origin, though some may have been named because of their blooming at Lady-tide. **1950** Gray–Fernald *Manual of Botany* 991, *I[mpatiens] capensis . .* Lady's-earrings. **1974** (1977) Coon *Useful Plants* 72, *Impatiens biflora . .* lady's ear-rings.

4 A **delphinium** (here: *Delphinium nudicaule*).

1891 Victor *Atlantis Arisen* 226 **NW,** Bending over springs may be found the lady's-ear-drop (*Delphinium nudicaule*), red.

5 also *ladies' eardrops:* The buckwheat vine (*Brunnichia ovata*). Cf **eardrop 4**

1901 Mohr *Plant Life AL* 487, *Brunnichia cirrhosa. . .* Ladies' Ear Drops. **1940** Steyermark *Flora MO* 169, *Ladies' Ear-drops. . .* Flowers greenish, in long slender spreading sprays at the ends of the branches. **1950** Gray–Fernald *Manual of Botany* 590, *B[runnichia] cirrhosa . .* Ladies'-eardrops. **1959** Carleton *Index Herb. Plants* 72, *Lady's Eardrop:* Brunnichia cirrhosa.

lady's eardrops See **lady's eardrop 1, 2**

lady's earrings See **lady's eardrop 3**

lady's finger See **ladyfinger 3, 4**

lady shovel n Cf **boy's ax**

A small, lightweight shovel; see quot.

1984 Doig *English Creek* 123 **nwMT,** An old short-handled lady shovel Toussaint Rennie had given my father. . . The lady shovel I was using was perfect for this finishing-off work of dabbing dirt into the

bucket. To make it handy in his ditch-riding Toussaint always shortened the handle and then ground off about four inches of the shovel blade, cutting it down into a light implement about two thirds of a normal shovel.

lady's keys n

A **gromwell** (here: *Lithospermum canescens*).

1959 Carleton *Index Herb. Plants* 72, Lady's keys: Lithospermum canescens.

lady's lace n Cf **lace flower 1, Queen Anne's lace**

A **wild carrot** (here: *Daucus carota*).

1950 *WELS Suppl.* **csWI,** Lady's lace—Queen Anne's lace.

lady's leek n

A **wild onion** (here: *Allium cernuum*).

1933 Small *Manual SE Flora* 288, *A[llium] cernuum. . . Wild-onion. Lady's-leek. . .* Rocky hillsides and prairies, various provinces N of Coastal Plain, S.C. to Tex., Sask., and N.Y. **1949** Moldenke *Amer. Wild Flowers* 356, The *Lady's-leek, A. cernuum. . .* has nodding clusters of white or rose blossoms. **1976** Bailey–Bailey *Hortus Third* 49, *Lady's-leek. . .* Rocky slopes and dry hillsides.

lady's leg See **lady legs**

lady slipper See **lady's slipper**

‡**lady's monthly journal** n [Prob alluding to *The Ladies' Home Journal*] joc, euphem

Menstruation.

1966 *DARE* (Qu. AA27, . . *A woman's menstruation*) Inf **MI**19, The lady's monthly journal [*DARE* Ed: used by Inf's father].

lady's-nightcap n Also *ladies' nightcap* [*EDD* 1825 →]

=**hedge bindweed 1.**

1900 Lyons *Plant Names* 115, *C[onvolvulus] Sepium . .* Ladies'-night-cap. **1959** Carleton *Index Herb. Plants* 72, Lady's nightcap . . *Convolvulus sepium.* **1973** Hitchcock–Cronquist *Flora Pacific NW* 364, Lady's-nightcap . . *C[alystegia] sepium.*

lady's pocket n Also *ladies' pocket* [See quot 1911]

A **jewelweed 1** (here: *Impatiens capensis*).

1892 *Jrl. Amer. Folkl.* 5.94 **OH,** *Impatiens fulva . .* lady's pocket. Mansfield, O. **1900** Lyons *Plant Names* 201, *I[mpatiens] biflora . .* Ladies'-pocket. **1911** *Century Dict. Suppl.,* Lady's pocket. . . The spotted touch-me-not, *Impatiens biflora:* so called from the saccate sepal of the flower.

lady's slipper n Also *ladies' slipper, lady ~* [So called from the shape of the flower] Cf **false lady's slipper**

1 A plant of the genus *Cypripedium.* [*OED* 1597 →] Also called **ducks** n¹ **2, foxglove 6, Indian shoe, moccasin flower, old goose, pitcher plant, nerveroot, nervine, Noah's ark 1, slipper, squirrel shoes, umbil, valerian, whippoorwill's shoe.** For other names of var spp see **bull bag, dainty cups, dog's ballocks, golden slipper 1, hare's lip, monkey flower 2, pussy plant, ram's-head, steeple-cap**

1743 Catesby *Nat. Hist. Carolina* 2.72, The Lady's Slipper of Pensilvania. . . The Flower . . resembles more a slipper than any other of this Tribe that I have seen. . . The Slipper is of a greenish Yellow, with a Tincture of Red. *Ibid* 73, *Calceolus. . .* The Yellow *Lady's Slipper. . .* They grow on the sandy Banks of Rivers in *Carolina, Virginia* and *Pensilvania.* **1806** (1905) Lewis *Orig. Jrls. Lewis & Clark Exped.* 5.173, I also met with the plant in blume which is sometimes called the lady's slipper or mockerson flower. **1822** Eaton *Botany* 261, *Cypripedium candidum . .* (white ladies' slipper . .) stem leafy. . . *[Cypripedium] spectabile . .* (gay ladies' slipper . .). **1860** in 1986 *This State of Wonders* 84 **cIA,** They came home tired enough and laden down with Lady Slippers and other wild flowers. **1928** in 1931 McCorrison *Letters Fraternity* 177 **NEng,** The ground was covered with wild flowers. . . There were two kinds of trilliums . . ladies slipper, . . and numerous other kinds of a dwarf nature that I can not name. **1941** Percy *Lanterns* 97 **nwMS,** Our orchids we try to make respectable by christening them "lady-slippers," but they still look as if they had been designed by D.H. Lawrence—only they're rose- and canary-colored. **1965–70** *DARE* (Qu. S26c) 53 Infs, **chiefly Nth,** Lady('s) slipper(s); **MA**58, **MN**36, **NM**6, **NC**44, **PA**1, 99, **VT**4, **WI**58, Pink (*or* wild, yellow) lady('s) slipper; (Qu. S26e) 15 Infs, **chiefly Nth,** Lady('s) slipper(s); **CT**17, **MA**6, **NJ**4, Pink (*or* purple, showy, white, yellow) lady('s) slipper(s); (Qu. S26b) 16

Infs, **chiefly Nth,** Lady('s) slipper(s); **GA**35, Lady slipper orchid; (Qu. S17) Inf **WI**8, Lady slippers; (Qu. S22) Inf **WA**8, Lady slippers; (Qu. S24) Infs **IL**50, **MN**6, **NY**142, **NC**38, Lady slipper; **OH**61, Lady slipper, moccasin; (Qu. S26a) Infs **ID**1, 5, **MN**19, **NJ**12, **NM**9, **RI**15, **VA**11, Lady('s) slipper(s); (Qu. S26d) Infs **IN**30, **MA**29, 39, **NY**28, **VA**30, Lady slipper(s); **NC**44, Pink (*or* yellow) lady slipper. **1965–70** *DARE* Wildfl QR Plates 29, 30, 31, 32B, 33, 34 [=*Cypripedium* spp.] 63 Infs, **chiefly Nth,** Lady('s) (*or* ladies') slipper(s); Plates 29, 30, 31, 33 [=*Cypripedium* spp] 24 Infs, **chiefly Nth,** White (*or* yellow, pink *or* showy) lady('s) (*or* ladies') slipper(s); (Craighead) Pl.4.2 Inf **CO**29, Lady slipper. **1967** *Hall Coll.* eTN, Lady slipper. . . One of the orchids. It has a pink blossom and a broad leaf. **1989** Mosher *Stranger* 63 nVT (as of 1952), Besides painted and red trillium, wild ginger, hepaticas, trout lilies, white and Canada violets, and golden thread, we discovered a good-sized bed of rare yellow lady slippers.
2 =**jewelweed 1,** esp *Impatiens balsamina.*
    1836 (1840) Phelps *Lectures on Botany* 101, The *Impatiens* of the garden is sometimes called *Ladies-slipper,* sometimes *Balsamine.* **1848** Gray *Manual of Botany* 76, I[*mpatiens*] *balsamina,* the Garden Balsam or Ladies' Slippers, is becoming spontaneous about gardens. **1863** *Horticulturist & Jrl. Rural Art* 18.127, Lady Slippers, (*Balsamina hortensis.*) . . are very beautiful. **1892** *Jrl. Amer. Folkl.* 5.93, *Impatiens fulva* . . lady's slipper. Plattsburg, N.Y.; Mansfield, O[hio]. . . *Impatiens balsamina,* lady's slipper. Mansfield, O[hio]. **1959** Carleton *Index Herb. Plants* 72, *Lady's slipper.* . . Lady slipper . . Cyprepedium [*sic*] (v); Impatiens (v); . . Polygala pauciflora.
3 =**fringed polygala.**
    1896 *Jrl. Amer. Folkl.* 9.182, *Polygala paucifolia* . . ladies' slipper, Gardiner, Me. **1959** [see **2** above].
4 =**butter-and-eggs 1.**
    1897 *Jrl. Amer. Folkl.* 10.52 **MA,** *Linaria vulgaris* . . ladies' slipper. **1950** *WELS* (Other names for . . wild snapdragon) 1 Inf, ceWI, Lady's slipper; butter-and-eggs. **1967–70** *DARE* (Qu. S11, . . Wild snapdragon) Infs **IL**47, **MI**120, **OH**2, **UT**10, Lady slipper; **OH**80, Golden slipper, lady slipper. **1967** *DARE* Wildfl QR Pl.196 Inf **NY**17, Lady slippers.
5 A **fairy slipper** (here: *Calypso bulbosa*).
    1898 *Jrl. Amer. Folkl.* 11.280, *Calypso borealis,* . . lady's slipper, Pierce Co., Wash. **1934** Haskin *Wild Flowers Pacific Coast* 67, The fir woods of Oregon were a revelation to me. . . I saw a numberless host of tiny, rose-colored, slipper-like blooms, nodding in the breeze. . . The name lady's slipper so often given to this species [=*Calypso bulbosa*] does not properly belong to it, . . and the more specific name of "Chinese lady's slipper," sometimes used, seems to me to be an unnatural affectation and, moreover, suggests the untrue idea of an Asiatic origin. **1967** *DARE* Wildfl QR Pl.43A Inf **OR**9, Lady slipper.
6 A **wild columbine** (here: *Aquilegia canadensis*).
    1898 *Jrl. Amer. Folkl.* 11.221, *Aquilegia Canadensis,* . . lady's slipper, Newton, Mass.
7 A **shooting star** (here: *Dodecatheon meadia*).
    1898 *Jrl. Amer. Folkl.* 11.274 **WY,** *Dodecatheon pauciflorum,* . . lady-slipper.
8 A **milkvetch** (here: either *Astragalus cibarius* or *A. utahensis*).
    1957 Barnes *Nat. Hist. Wasatch Spring* 37 **UT,** We find . . a little further down among the oak trees, lady slippers or milk vetch (*Astragalus cibarius*) already showing its whitish purple bloom. *Ibid* 38, On the same south-facing slopes is blooming one of the most beautiful flowers in Utah, the sheep-pod, lady slipper or wild sweet pea (*Astragalus utahensis*). *Ibid* 40, A flower half hidden in the snow catches our eye. By its woolly white, tomentose, rounded leaflets and other characteristics we know it to be the lady's slipper (*Astragalus utahensis*).
9 A **jack-in-the-pulpit 1.**
    1966–70 *DARE* (Qu. S1, . . Jack-in-the-pulpit) Infs **AL**30, **MD**34, **NC**37, **OH**52, Lady slipper(s); **NY**75, Lady's slipper; **KY**40, Lady's slipper—old-fashioned; jack-in-the-pulpit—present usage; **MD**42, Jack-in-the-pulpit, lady slipper; **VA**77, Lady slipper—some people erroneously call them this.

lady's sorrel n Also *ladies' sorrel, lady's wood-sorrel*
=**wood sorrel** (here: *Oxalis* spp.)
    1832 *MA Hist. Soc. Coll.* 2d ser 9.153 cwVT, [*Oxalis*] *dillenii,* Ladies' sorrel. **1833** Eaton *Botany* 244, [*Oxalis*] *corniculata,* (lady's wood-sorrel . .). **1892** *Jrl. Amer. Folkl.* 5.93, *Oxalis stricta,* ladies' sorrel, Allston, Mass.; Stratham, N.H. **1931** Harned *Wild Flowers Alleghanies* 266, *Lady's Sorrel (O. corniculata).* . . When the flowering season is over, thickened, erect, tipped pods appear. **1950** Stevens *ND Plants* 194,

Lady's Sorrel. . . Common in open ground or in partial shade. **1969** *DARE* (Qu. S26d, *Wildflowers that grow in meadows;* not asked in early QRs) Inf **VT**16, Lady's sorrel—3 leaves and yellow blossoms and sour flavor. **1970** Correll *Plants TX* 896, *Oxalis* . . Lady's-sorrel. . . *O. corniculata* . . Creeping lady's-sorrel.

lady's streamer See **ladies'-streamer**

lady's tail n
    A thatch of matted hair on a newborn child; see quot.
    1981 Puckett *Pop. Beliefs* 1.54 **nOH** (as of 1950), [Item 1303:] Some children are born with a thatch of hair that is stuck together. This is called a "lady's tail" and it is not to be touched, but allowed to fall out of its own accord. Otherwise it will bring misfortune.

lady's thimble n [*OED* 1853 →]
    1 A **harebell 1** (here: *Campanula rotundifolia*).
    1900 Lyons *Plant Names* 77, C[*ampanula*] *rotundifolia* . . Lady's-thimble. **1973** Hitchcock–Cronquist *Flora Pacific NW* 459, Lady's-thimble . . C[*ampanula*] *rotundifolia.*
    2 also *ladies' thimble, lady ~:* A **foxglove 1** (here: *Digitalis purpurea*).
    1900 Lyons *Plant Names* 136, *Digitalis purpurea* . . Ladies'-thimble. **1949** Moldenke *Amer. Wild Flowers* 272, The long, tubular, drooping flowers resemble fingers of a glove, and this fact is the basis for many of its names, including its scientific one (*Digitalis*) and . . ladythimble . . It is interesting . . that our present American name of foxglove is a corruption of the original English *folk's-glove.*

lady's thumb n Also *ladies' thumb* [See quot 1931]
    Any of var **smartweeds** of the genus *Polygonum,* but usu *P. persicaria.* For other names of this sp see **black heart 4, crab's claws, doorweed, guinea grass 3, heart's-ear, heartsease 2, heart-spot knotweed, heartweed 1, knotweed 1, ladyfinger 4, lover's pride, peachwort;** for other names of var spp see **ass-smart, curage** Cf **knotweed 1, tearthumb, water pepper**
    1822 Eaton *Botany* 401, [*Polygonum*] *persicaria* (ladies' thumb . .). **1848** in 1850 Cooper *Rural Hours* 106 **NY,** A very large proportion of the most common weeds in our fields and gardens . . are strangers to the soil. It will be easy to name a number of these: . . the lady's thumb and May-weed. **a1862** (1864) Thoreau *ME Woods* 319, *Polygonum Persicaria* (lady's-thumb). **1931** Clute *Common Plants* 74, Lady's thumb (*Polygonum persicaria*) is so named to explain the dark markings on the leaves which are reputed to be the marks of Our Lady's thumb. **1941** Writers' Program *Guide WY* 427, Lady's thumb, starwort, and other aquatic plants grow out in the deep waters. **1966–67** *DARE* Wildfl QR Plates 47A, B Inf **MI**7, Lady's thumb; **OR**12, Ladies thumb. **1975** Duncan–Foote *Wildflowers SE* 26, Lady's-thumb—*Polygonum pennsylvanicum.* . . The ocreae are thin and have no cilia. **1979** Spellenberg *Audubon Guide N. Amer. Wildflowers W. Region* 677, Water Lady's Thumb (*Polygonum amphibium*). . . In mud or floating on still fresh water. . . The pink flower masses are very attractive, but since the plants grow quickly, they can become an unwelcome weed.

lady's tobacco See **ladies'-tobacco**

lady's toes n
    Appar a **mullein.**
    1968 *DARE* (Qu. S20, *A common weed that grows on open hillsides: It has velvety green leaves close to the ground, and a tall stalk with small yellow flowers on a spike at the top*) Inf **PA**89, Lady's toes.

lady's tresses See **ladies' tresses**

lady's twist See **ladies' twist**

lady's wood-sorrel See **lady's sorrel**

lady terrapin n Also *lady turtle*
    A **red-bellied turtle** (here: *Chrysemus scripta*).
    1879 Smith *Catalogue Reptilia MI* 7, *Chrysemus marginata* [=*C. picta*]. . . Lady Turtle. *Chrysemus picta.* . . Painted Lady Turtle. **1909** *Biol. Soc. DC Proc.* 22.136 **NC,** *Pseudemys scripta.* Lady Terrapin. Common; specimens seen and taken in all three years. **1968** *DARE* (Qu. P24, . . Kinds of turtles) Inf **LA**31, Lady turtle—smaller than the black turtle; a little striped turtle, a yellow stripe down the neck.

lady thimble See **lady's thimble 2**

lady turtle See **lady terrapin**

Lady Washington lily See **Washington lily**

lady wasp n

1969 *DARE* (Qu. R21, . . *Other kinds of stinging insects*) Inf **GA**76, Lady wasp—a small wasp.

lady wine n

A sweet wine.

1968 *DARE* Tape **CA**98, I gave myself my little glass of port . . and gave you one of . . Malvasia, which is a very nice after-dinner or any kind of a lady wine.

lae n

A Hawaiian fish of the genus *Scomberoides.* For other names of *S. sancti-petri* see **leatherback 6, runner**

1926 Pan-Pacific Research Inst. *Jrl.* 1.1.8 **HI**, Scomberoides tolooparah. . . Lae. **1960** Gosline–Brock *Hawaiian Fishes* 169, *Scomberoides sancti-petri.* . . The lae is distinguished . . by its leathery skin imbedded with tiny, needle-like scales. . . The lae is a good game fish, but is locally considered of poor quality as food.

laer See **law** n[1]

Lafayette n

1 also *Lafayette fish:* A **spot** (here: *Leiostomus xanthurus*). [See quot 1842] esp **NY**

1842 DeKay *Zool. NY* 4.69, *The Lafayette.* . . This beautiful little fish . . is usually rare in our waters, but visits us in almost incredible numbers at irregular and generally distant intervals. One of these visits happened to coincide with the arrival of the great and good La Fayette at New-York, in the summer of 1824. His name was unanimously given to a fish, which was considered as entirely new, and this name it still retains. **1843** (1971) Mathews *Writings* 266 **NYC**, He had caught . . a small carful of striped-bass and Lafayette fish. **1862** Acad. Nat. Sci. Philadelphia *Proc. for 1861* 33 **NY**, *Liostomus xanthurus.* . . "Lafayette." **1903** *Sun* (NY NY) 15 Nov *(DAE)*, The fish are small—something like Lafayettes. **1910** *Sat. Eve. Post* 13 Aug 7 **NYC**, On another [day] I'd stroll down to the dock . . and try my luck on the tomcods and lafayettes. **1933** John G. Shedd Aquarium *Guide* 115, *Leiostomus xanthurus*—Spot; Lafayette. **1973** Knight *Cook's Fish Guide* 383, Lafayette—Spot.

2 A **butterfish 1** (here: *Peprilus triacanthus*).

1882 U.S. Natl. Museum *Bulletin* 16.451, *S[tromateus] triacanthus* . . Dollar-fish; Harvest-fish; Butter-fish; La Fayette. **1889** *Century Dict.* 3329, *Lafayette.* . . A stromateoid fish, *Stromateus triacanthus.* **1903** NY State Museum & Sci. Serv. *Bulletin* 60.458, This [=*Peprilus triacanthus*] is known as the dollarfish, harvestfish and lafayette.

3 =**mademoiselle.**

1903 NY State Museum & Sci. Serv. *Bulletin* 60.577, In Great South bay [NY] we heard the name Lafayette given it [=*Bairdiella chrysura*], but this belongs more properly to the spot Liostomus xanthurus.

Lafayette fish See **Lafayette 1**

laff See **laugh**

laffsa See **lobster**

Lafitte skiff n Also *Lafitte's skiff* [See quot 1978] **cs,seLA**

A type of boat used esp for trawling; see quots.

1968 *DARE* (Qu. O10, . . *Kinds of boats*) Inf **LA**45, Lafitte's skiff—used for trawling; may be from eighteen to twenty foot, you could row it or it could have a motor. **1978** *DARE* File **cs,seLA**, The Lafitte skiff is a folk boat indigenous to the bayou country of South Central Louisiana (from Vermillion Bay to the Chandeleur Islands). It is said that it evolved in the community of Lafitte on Bayou Barataria, about 30 miles southwest of New Orleans. Traditionally the Lafitte skiff is a flat-bottom, shallow-draft boat from 14–16 feet long and made of cypress. Nowadays, however, Spanish cedar is used and a V-bottom variant has evolved. **1979** Hallowell *People Bayou* 129 **seLA**, Most of the boats are Lafitte skiffs, a graceful design whose lines are adapted to the local ecology. It was first used in the early years of the century by shrimp fishermen from the small bayou settlement of Lafitte, whose work in the open-water shallows of Barataria Bay required a craft that could withstand swells driven by a south wind. **1986** Pederson *LAGS Concordance,* 1 inf, **seLA**, Lafitte skiff—fast boat; they trawl with them; 1 inf, **csLA**, Lafitte skiff—used by shrimpers; [has] low sides; 1 inf, **seLA**, Lafitte skiffs—for shrimping; pointed at front.

lag v[1], hence vbl n *lagging* Pronc-sp *leg* [Appar Brit dial; cf *OED lag* sb.[1] and a., A.1.a,b, B.1.b and *EDD lag* sb.[3], *laggy* adj. 2, sb. 4]

1 also with *up;* In marble play:

a To toss, throw; to throw toward (a line); spec, to toss or roll a marble toward a goal, esp to determine order of play. Cf **dib** n[1] **2, go** n **3, lag** n[1] **1b, lagger, lag line**

1893 Shands *MS Speech* 73, *Leg* or *Lag.* . . The word is pronounced in both ways indicated, and is used as an intransitive verb. It belongs to the vernacular of marble-players. In *legging* or *lagging* each player endeavors to so roll a marble as to make it stop on a horizontal line drawn about five or six feet from the players. This is the method generally adopted of determining who shall have the "first go"—the player whose "taw" stops nearest the line being entitled to that privilege. The word may be, and probably is, connected with the verb *to lag,* meaning to fall behind, as the order in which the players shall shoot is determined by the distance that they fall behind one another. **1895** *DN* 1.390 ceKY, "*Lag* for goes" = to roll up from taw to see who could come nearest to the middleman, and so win the first play. **1899** Champlin–Bostwick *Young Folks' Games* 484, A ring is drawn on hard ground. . . A line is drawn six or seven feet distant, and each player shoots a marble from it toward the ring, he who comes nearest to the centre being allowed the first turn. This is sometimes called "lagging." **1909** *DN* 3.399 nwAR, "*Lag* for goes." **1922** *DN* 5.187 KY, *Lag.* . . To drop up [=to shoot or roll a marble to a more advantageous position] near the ring with a taw, after winning the "goes" [=the right to be the first to shoot]; also, to shoot at the ring for the "goes." Also *lag up.* **1957** *Sat. Eve. Post Letters* wKY (as of c1930), We lagged for first, i.e. tossed the marbles from waist height at a line about ten feet away. **1958** *PADS* 29.36 KY, OR, WI, Lag. **1963** *KY Folkl. Rec.* 9.3.63 eKY, *When a marble is tossed by a player toward a line to decide the order of play* . . lag . . lag-up . . lag-to-line. **1966** *DARE* FW Addit SC, Lagging—in marbles refers to tossing a marble or a quarter towards a line drawn in the dirt to determine which player should shoot first. **1967–70** *DARE* (Qu. EE7, . . *Kinds of marble games*) Inf **CA**169, Lagging game—try to reach a line; **FL**48, Lagging game; **WA**6, Lag the line—to see who shoots first; (QR, near Qu. EE7) Inf **MO**13, [One game is] where you knock 'em out of the ring; the other where you lag for a line; (QR, near Qu. EE8) Inf **CA**133, You lag for the line; **LA**3, They would lag to the line—that means throwing to the line; **OK**52, Pitched from one side of the ring to another—called lagging; **UT**4, We'd lag to see who got first shot. **1967–70** *DARE* Tape **AZ**8, They stand back of the three holes and lag a taw, or a marble, toward the lag line, and the person whose marble rests closest to the lag line becomes the first player; **CA**190, You lag to see who starts first toward a line, any line; **IA**37, You draw a line, in the dirt, and you'd toss your marble toward the line, see who could get the closest. That would be called "lagging" for the order of the shooters; **IL**2, They would draw a line and then lag for the line; **NJ**18, We would lag to see who came closest to the line, and the one that came closest, he shot and then the next and so forth. . . We'd draw a small ring . . and then we'd get off so far and lag. . . [FW:] When you lag do you shoot along the ground or toss it? [Inf:] No, we'd just roll it; **WY**1, Cincinnati was a game that 2 or 3 boys could play. The ring was 18 inches long and oval in shape. Out about 15 feet was the lag line. . . Each player put in 2, 3, or 4 marbles. . . Then they lagged to the lag line . . and the one got nearest there was the first one to lag back and he lagged back to the ring. . . Purgatory . . series of holes . . just like golf. We lagged; you lagged the first time and if you didn't get the hole, then you shot. **c1970** Wiersma *Marbles Terms* swMI (as of c1930), The four boys were lagging for dibs. **1983** *MJLF* 9.1.46 ceKY, *Lag* . . to shoot or toss the taw to see who goes first. . . *Lag up* . . to lag. **1986** Pederson *LAGS Concordance,* 1 inf, **swGA**, Lag for the line—in marbles; 1 inf, **swGA**, Lag the line—when starting marble game; 1 inf, **swGA**, Lagging—in marbles; 1 inf, **seFL**, Lagged—roll marbles at line [to] see who goes first.

b =**lay up** v phr **7.** [Cf *EDD lig up* (at *lag* sb.[3])]

1922 [see **1a** above].

2 By ext: to throw or toss a small object as part of a game; to toss (such an object); see quots.

1938 Farrell *No Star* 417 **Chicago IL**, "Pretty soon we can lag buttons," Perc said. . . "Wilson buttons are hard to get now. Kids think they're valuable. But I had a lot when Wilson was running for President. That's when we was in second grade," Danny said. "I can't lag buttons good. And I ain't got any now. But I'm sure my father can get me a lot when kids start lagging buttons." **1947** Baldridge *Time & Chance* 39 (as of 1900), In the vacant lot on Forty-fourth Street [Chicago], the "Forty-third Street kids" were gambling with Bryan and McKinley campaign buttons, "lagging" at a line. **1957** *Sat. Eve. Post Letters* **wKY** (as of c1930), In back alleys we lagged for pennies too. **1969** *DARE* (Qu. EE33, . . *Outdoor games . . that children play*) Inf **IL**84, Lagging pennies.

lag n[1]

1 In marble play:

a See quot. [Cf *OED lag* sb.[1] A.1 "The last . . person (in a . . game . .). Now *rare* exc. in schoolboy use"] Cf *laggard*

   1899 (1912) Green *VA Folk-Speech* 254, *Lag.* . . A player who comes in last at a game of marbles.

b A toss of a marble; spec, a toss toward a goal, often used to determine order of play; a game involving such a toss. [Cf *EDD lag* sb.[3] "A game of marbles"]

   1935 *AmSp* 10.159 **seNE** (as of c1920) [Marbles terms], When all have lagged, the nearest *shooter* is entitled to the first shot of the game. *Last lag* is usually considered a privilege and must be called for. **1937** (1947) Bancroft *Games* 158, The lag is the first operation in Ringer. To lag, the players stand toeing the pitch line or knuckling down upon it, and toss or shoot their shooters to the lag line across the ring. The player whose shooter comes nearest the lag line, on either side, wins the lag. **1940** *Recreation* (NY) 34.110, Games of marbles played throughout the country . . *Lag.* **1950** *WELS* **WI** (*Kinds of marble games*) 1 Inf, Lag; 1 Inf, Lag—you have to knuckle down with this game. **1966–68** *DARE* (Qu. EE7) Infs **CO**28, **GA**42, **IL**7, **OR**1, **WA**13, Lag. **1967–68** *DARE* Tape **NJ**18, If you knocked a marble out on a lag, then you'd shoot until you missed; **WY**1, Lag was . . make two lines about 12 or 16 feet apart. All line up there and lag. The one that got closest to the line took the marbles. . . [FW:] Your first shot from the hole was always a lag? [Inf:] Was a lag. **c1970** Wiersma *Marbles Terms* **neIL** (as of c1953), *Lag* . . a type of game where the object is to throw your marble as close to a line as you can without touching it. . . The shot used in the game. . . "Let's play lag." *Ibid* **csIA** (as of 1935), *No lag.* . . this refers to following through with your arm while shooting the marble. It is not allowed because it would enable you, if at close range, to almost reach out and throw the marble where you want. Instead you must shoot the marble with the knuckle down. **1976** *WI Acad. Rev.* June 20/2 (as of 1920s), When we made the initial toss toward the ring on the ground, or a pot scooped into the soil, it was a "lag."

c See **lagger 1.**

d See **lag line.**

2 A tossing game; see quot. [**lag** v[1] **2**]

   1978 *DARE* File (as of 1950s), *Lag.* Played to a wall with pennies using an underhand toss. Whoever's coin is closest to the wall wins.

3 A shot—used in a game of tops; see quot.

   1916 *DN* 4.346 **seLA**, *Lag.* . . A shot at. Used in playing tops. New Orleans. "Don't take a lag at my top."

lag v[2] See **leg** v[1]

lag n[2] See **leg** n

lag-along n Also *lag-behind*

   A tagalong.

   1966–67 *DARE* (Qu. Y9, *Somebody who always follows along behind others: "His little brother is an awful _____."*) Infs **NV**5, **NM**9, Lag-behind; **AL**3, Lag-along.

lagger n [**lag** v[1] **1a**]

1 also *lag(gie)*: A playing marble, esp a large one for shooting or for tossing to the **lag line**; see quots.

   1942 Berrey–Van den Bark *Amer. Slang* 665.2, Lagger, *a large marble used in "lagging."* **1949** *PADS* 11.23 **CO**, *Lagger.* . . A shooter in marbles. **1955** *PADS* 23.23 **cwTN, cwAL**, *Lagger.* . . The marble used for rolling toward the lag line. **1967–70** *DARE* (Qu. EE6a, . . *Different kinds of marbles—the big one that's used to knock others out of the ring*) Inf **CA**14, Laggie; **LA**23, Lagger [FW: Inf queries]; (Qu. EE6d, *Special marbles*) Inf **SC**68, Lag—the one you shot to the taw line. **c1970** Wiersma *Marbles Terms* **IL** (as of 1960), *Lag*—a marble dropped on to an opponent's marble. . . "Drop a lag."

2 In the game of hopscotch: see quots.

   1957 *Sat. Eve. Post Letters* **Chicago IL** (as of 1930s), When we jumped at hopscotch, we used "laggers" (or stones) to throw on the squares. **1981** *AmSp* 56.21 **cw,swCA** (as of 1950s), The game was called *hopscotch* and the object thrown a *lagger*.

laggerstreamer n Also sp *leggerstreamer* [Folk-etym for *Lagerstroemia*] Cf **ladies'-streamer**

=crape myrtle.

   1909 *DN* 3.343 **eAL, wGA**, *Laggerstreamer*[,] leggerstreamer . . The crepe-myrtle. This is a sort of popularized form of *Lagerstræmia*, the botanical family name, from Magnus N. *Lagerstrœm* . . a Swede and friend of Linnæus.

laggie See **lagger 1**

lagging vbl n See **lag** v[1]

lagging n See **lagging line**

lagging horse n Cf **lead horse**

=near horse.

   1969 *DARE* (Qu. K32b, *The horse on the left side in plowing or hauling*) Inf **GA**77, Laggin' horse; [(Qu. K32a, *With a team of horses, . . the horse on the driver's right hand*) Inf **GA**77, Leadin' horse].

lagging line n Also *lagging* **chiefly West, Gulf States, W Midl, esp sIL** See Map

=lag line; see also quot c1970.

   1949 *PADS* 11.23 **CO**, *Lagging line.* . . The line drawn about ten feet away from the circle in marble games. **c1955** Reed–Person *Ling. Atlas Pacific NW*, 1 inf, Lagging line. **1965–70** *DARE* (Qu. EE8, *The line toward which the players roll their marbles before beginning a game, to determine the order of shooting*) 34 Infs, **chiefly West, Gulf States, W Midl, esp sIL**, Lagging line; **AK**5, **MO**13, **UT**3, Lagging; **DC**11, Lagging [FW: Inf queries]. **c1970** Wiersma *Marbles Terms* **Pacific NW**, *Lagging line* . . line behind which one must stand to legally shoot at marbles. **1973** Allen *LAUM* 1.404 **IA, NE, SD** (as of c1950), *Lagging line* [6 infs].

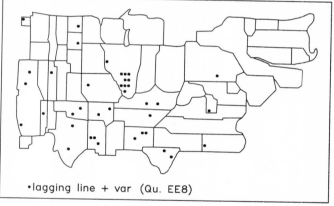

•lagging line + var (Qu. EE8)

laggy adj [Engl dial; cf *EDD laggy* 1; *SND laggie* (at *lag* adj. I.1)] **esp nNJ** *somewhat old-fash* Cf **do-less**

Slow, lethargic.

   1942 Berrey–Van den Bark *Amer. Slang* 54.5, *Slow.* . . laggy. **1950** *WELS* (*Very slow: "Where can he be? He certainly is _____."*) 1 Inf, **csWI**, Laggy. **1967–68** *DARE* (Qu. KK30, *Feeling slowed up or without energy: "I certainly feel _____."*) Infs **NJ**1, 11, 47, Laggy.

lag leg n

   1959 *VT Hist.* 27.146 **nVT**, *Lag leg.* . . A lazy person. Occasional.

lag line n Also *lag*; for addit varr see quots [**lag** v[1] **1a**] **chiefly West, Missip Valley, sNJ** See Map on p. 276 Cf **dragline 2, draw line, lagging ~, taw ~**

In marble play: the line toward which players roll or toss marbles to determine the order of shooting.

   1937 (1947) Bancroft *Games* 158, To lag, the players stand toeing the pitch line or knuckling down upon it, and toss or shoot their shooters to the lag line across the ring. The player whose shooter comes nearest the lag line, on either side, wins the lag. **1949** *PADS* 11.23 **CO**, *Lag line, lagging line.* . . The line drawn about ten feet away from the circle in marble games. **1950** *WELS Suppl.* **WI**, *Lag*—a term used in playing for position or order of playing marbles. The lag is a line drawn about fifteen feet from the circle holding the marbles. Players stand at the circle and toss their shooters to the lag. The nearest has first shot at the marbles. **c1955** Reed–Person *Ling. Atlas Pacific NW*, 8 infs, Lag line. **1958** *PADS* 29.36 **OK**, *Lag line.* **1965–70** *DARE* (Qu. EE8, *The line* *toward which the players roll their marbles before beginning a game, to determine the order of shooting)* 62 Infs, **chiefly West, Missip Valley, sNJ**, Lag line; 17 Infs, **chiefly west of Missip R**, Lag; **LA**20, Lag mark; **TX**26, Lagger line. **1966–67** *DARE* Tape **AZ**8, They stand back of the three holes and lag a taw, or a marble, toward the lag line; **WA**6, We had what we called a lag line; **WY**1, Then out about 15 feet was the lag line. Each player put in 2, 3, or 4 marbles . . and then they lagged to the lag line. **1984** *WI State Jrl.* (Madison) 8 Apr sec 9 1/3 **csWI** (as of c1923), Players lag for turns by tossing or shooting their shooter marble from the pitch line to the lag line.

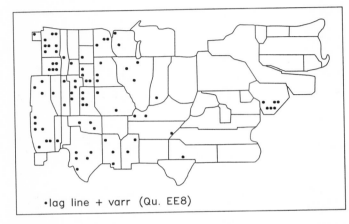

•lag line + varr (Qu. EE8)

lagniappe n Usu |ˈlænˌjæp|; also |ˌlænˈjæp| Pronc-spp *lagnappe, laniappe, lan(ny)-yap, lanyope;* abbr *nap;* for addit pronc and sp varr see quots [See quot 1931] **chiefly Gulf States, esp LA** See Map and Map Section Cf **boot** n[1] **1a, broadus**

A small gratuity or bonus included with a purchase; by ext, anything extra thrown in for good measure.

1849 *Knickerbocker* 34.407, Ime sum pumpkins in that line; but he's a huckleberry above my persimmon, and right smart lanyope too, as them creole darkies say. **1853** Hammett *Stray Yankee in TX* 47, When he lost [at poker], if the money were not absolutely staked, he would usually put off the winner with . . a dubious note that he had received as "lanyappe," (*Anglice,* boot money.) **1883** Twain *Life on Missip.* (Boston) 450 **LA**, We picked up one excellent word—a word worth travelling to New Orleans to get; a nice limber, expressive, handy word—"Lagniappe." They pronounce it lanny-*yap*. It is Spanish—so they said. . . It is something thrown in, gratis, for good measure. **1884** Cable *Creoles of LA* 114, *Ñapa*—the petty gratuity added, by the retailer, to anything bought . . [was] drawn out into Gallicized *lagnappe.* **1892** *KS Univ. Qrly.* 1.97 **LA**, *Lagniap.* **1893** *Harper's New Mth. Mag.* 86.380 **New Orleans LA**, "Take that for a lagniappe" (pronounced lan-yap), says a storekeeper as he folds a pretty calendar into the bundle of stationery you have purchased. **1897** Lewis *Wolfville* 267 **AZ**, She'd swap the whole Mexican outfit for a word from Mace, an' throw herse'f in for laniyap. **1903** Murrie *White Castle LA* 256, Little Liza received a banana for "laniappe." **1909** *DN* 3.351 **sAL**, *Nap.* . . Something given as a gratuity to a purchaser. Used in and around Mobile in south Alabama. Compare *lagniappe* in the same sense in Louisiana. [**1931** Read *LA French* 142, *Lagniappe.* . . A trifling gift presented to a customer by a merchant, or, by extension, any kind of gratuity that may be regarded as thrown in for good measure. . . *Lagniappe* is composed of the French *la,* "the," and a French adaptation of Spanish *ñapa,* which is taken in turn from Kechuan *yapa,* "a present made to a customer."] **1954** Armstrong *Satchmo* 178 **New Orleans LA**, For every name she called me I called her the same, and I hit her with a few real hard ones for lagniappe. **1961** *PADS* 36.12 **sLA**, *Lagniappe* [appears] as [laˈŋap], [lænˈjæp], and [ˈlænˌjæp]—there is even a taped occurrence of [ˌlanˈjæp]. **1962** Atwood *Vocab. TX* 68, In the Southwest, the West, and part of Central Texas *pilón* . . is very well known and widely used. . . The Louisiana word *lagniappe* has invaded Southeast Texas, particularly the Beaumont and Galveston areas. **1965–70** *DARE* (Qu. U15, *When you're buying something, if the seller puts in a little extra to make you feel that you're getting a good bargain*) 12 Infs, **esp LA, MS, TX**, [ˈlænˌjæ(ə)p]; **FL**17, **LA**14, 15, 20, 31, [ˌlænˈjæp]; **LA**33, 37, [ˌlanˈjap]; **CA**15, [ˈlanˌjeɪp]; **CA**185, [ˈlɔnˌjap]; **LA**25, [ˈlanˌjæp]; **LA**28, [ˈlænɪˌnæp]; **LA**40, [ˌlæniˈæp]; **MS**12, [ˈlæniˌæp]; **MS**73, [ˈlænˌjəup]; [**TN**11, It's *not* lagniappe, that's New Orleans]. **1983** Reinecke Coll. 7 **LA**, *Lagniappe*—[ˈlanjap] or [ˈlænjæp] or [lanˈjap] a bonus expected by

the purchaser and given by storekeeper. The expectation no longer exists, but still often used for promotion extras or anything thrown in. **1990** Pederson *LAGS Regional Matrix* 467, [*Lagniappe*—something extra, chiefly **wLA, sMS, swAL**; less freq **eTX**.]

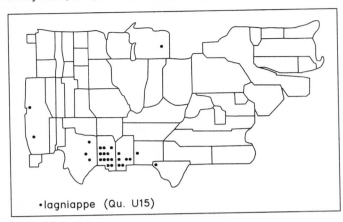

•lagniappe (Qu. U15)

lagoona See **laguna**

lagoonberry n [Folk-etym for **nagoonberry**] **AK** =**nagoonberry.**

1934 *Anchorage Daily Times* 11 Aug 3 (Tabbert *Dict. Alaskan Engl.*), Highbush cranberries, currants, blueberries, gooseberries, cranberries, lagoon berries. **1938** (1958) Sharples *AK Wild Flowers* 128, *R[ubus] stellatus.* "Nagoon or Lagoon Berry." **1952** Williams *AK Wildfl. Glimpses* 39, *Lagoonberry.* . . Grows in wet places such as muskeg or tundra but will also grow in drier ground. **1961** *AK Sportsman* Sept 20, Sometimes it [=nagoon berry] is misnamed "lagoon" colloquially, probably because it is found in muskeg or swamp.

lagoon frog n =**pig frog.**

1966 LA Wild Life Comm. *Hunting Fishing Regulations 1967–68* 6, Closed season on taking of Bullfrogs and Lagoon Frogs each year during the months of April and May.

la grippe n Also with *the* (cf Intro "Language Changes" I.4) [Fr "the grippe"] *old-fash*

Grippe, influenza.

1915 *DN* 4.229 **wTX**, The la grippe. Ordinary tautological phrase. **1932** Stribling *Store* 271 **AL**, The bitter weather would give you the la grippe. **1966–70** *DARE* (Qu. BB9, *A sickness in which you have a severe cough and difficult breathing—it often starts with a cold, and lasts a week or two*) Infs **CA**144, 202, **IL**82, **SC**11, 24, **TX**65, La grippe; (Qu. BB13, . . *Chills and fever*) Infs **CA**202, **TX**40, **WA**9, La grippe; (Qu. BB49, . . *Other kinds of diseases*) Infs **IN**28, **MS**68, **WA**30, La grippe; **WA**18, The la grippe. [11 of 12 total Infs old] **1986** Pederson *LAGS Concordance,* 1 inf, **cwMS**, *La grippe*—the flu, influenza. [Inf old]

laguna n Also sp *lagoona* [Span] **chiefly TX, CA**

A pool or pond of salt or fresh water, often alongside a larger body of water.

[**1811** Humboldt *Political Essay* (transl. Black) 2.275, The shore of the provinces of Santander and Texas, from the 21° to the 29° of latitude . . presents a succession of interior basins. . . They go by the name of *lagunas,* or salt-water lakes.] **1838** Ganilh *Mexico Versus TX* 163 **TX**, The whole company spread themselves about, following the banks of the *laguna,* and looking for the *track.* **1853** (1854) Bartlett *Personal Narr.* 2.532 **TX**, The navigation here is carried on with boats of light burden through the shallow bays or lagunas, which line the west and north-west shores of the Gulf of Mexico. **1854** (1932) Bell *Log TX–CA Trail* 36.52 **sAZ**, Found good cool water in a *Lagoona* by the roadside. . . Toward noon had a bath in the *Lagoona.* **1892** *DN* 1.191 **TX**, *Lagúna:* a lagoon, shallow lake without outlet, or an arm of the sea, a sound, a bay. **1927** Cather *Death Comes* 90 **Santa Fé NM**, Jacinto got firewood and good water from the Lagunas. **1967–68** *DARE* (Qu. C4b) Inf **CA**87, Lagoon—smaller than a lake, but shallower, also called laguna; **TX**5, Laguna—old riverbed with seepage water in it; (Qu. C14, *A stretch of still water going off to the side from a river or lake*) Inf **CA**87, Laguna—a lake, the Spanish word for lake or pond; **TX**5, Laguna; (Qu. C34, *Nicknames for nearby settlements, villages, or districts*) Inf **TX**4,

Laguna; (Qu. C35, *Nicknames for the different parts of your town or city*) Inf **CA**30, Laguna Lake District.

lag up See **lag** v[1] **1**

lahf See **laugh**

laid by ppl adj
1 See **lay by** v phr **1**.
2 See **lay up** v phr **1**.

laig See **leg** n

lair n [Perh for *layer*]
A considerable quantity.
   1944 *PADS* 2.30 **eKY**, Lairs [lɑrz]. . . Plenty. "They wuz lairs of poplar timber in these here woods when I wuz a boy." Rare.

lak v[1], adj, vbl aux, n, adv, prep, conj See **like** v[1], adj, vbl aux, n, adv, prep, conj

-lak suff See **-like** suff

lake Atlantic salmon See **lake salmon 2**

lake bass n Cf **striped lake bass**
1 =**black bass 1.**
   1795 Scott *U.S. Gaz.* np (at *Vermont*), The rivers are stored with a great variety of fish, as . . a species of fish called lake bass. **1817** *Amer. Monthly Mag. & Crit. Rev.* 2.120, *Bodianus Achigan* . . Black-bass, Lake-bass, Big-bass, Oswego bass, Spotted-bass, &c. **1858** *Harper's New Mth. Mag.* 17.621 **NEng**, I should not forget to mention a fine brace of lake bass, which Eliphalet . . had hauled in. **1935** Caine *Game Fish* 3, Large-Mouthed Black Bass—*Micropterus salmoides*. . . Lake Bass. *Ibid* 7, Small-Mouthed Black Bass—*Micropterus dolomieu*. . . Lake Bass. *Ibid* 9, Spotted Small-Mouthed Black Bass—*Micropterus pseudoplites*. . . Lake Bass. **1983** Becker *Fishes WI* 809, Largemouth Bass—*Micropterus salmoides* . . Other common names: . . line side . . lake bass.
2 A **rock bass** (here: *Ambloplites rupestris*).
   1935 Caine *Game Fish* 24, Rock Bass. . . Lake Bass. **1973** Knight *Cook's Fish Guide* 375, Lake [bass]—Rock [bass].

lake buffalo n
=**bigmouth buffalo.**
   1956 Harlan-Speaker *IA Fish* 59, Bigmouth Buffalo—*Ictiobus cyprinellus* . . Other Names . . lake buffalo. **1983** Becker *Fishes WI* 615, Bigmouth Buffalo—*Ictiobus cyprinellus*. . . Other common names: redmouth buffalo . . lake buffalo.

lake bug See **lake fly 1**

lake chub n
A **minnow B1** (here: *Couesius plumbeus*).
   1886 Mather *Memoranda* 30 **NY**, Lake Chub. *Couesius prosthemius*. **1943** Eddy-Surber *N. Fishes* 129, The lake chub ranges from the Rocky Mountains eastward through Wyoming and Nebraska to Maine and northward. **1950** Everhart *Fishes ME* 35, Lake Chub. . . Barbel on lower edge of maxillary. **1966** *DARE* (Qu. P3, *Freshwater fish that are not good to eat*) Inf **MI**14, Inland lake chub. **1971** Brown *Fishes MT* 92, The lake chub favors the creek type habitat, mostly at lower elevations. **1991** Amer. Fisheries Soc. *Common Names Fishes* 19, *Couesius plumbeus* . . lake chub.

lake duck n Cf **laker 2**
=**lesser scaup.**
   1911 *Forest & Stream* 77.173, *Marila affinis*. . . Lake duck, Cameron, La. **1982** Elman *Hunter's Field Guide* 209, Lesser Scaup. . . lake duck. [*Ibid* 210, The lesser [scaup], fundamentally an inland bird, visits coastal marshes, but prefers smaller lakes, ponds, streams, and freshwater marshes.]

Lake Erie gull n Cf **lake gull**
The common **tern** (*Sterna hirundo*).
   1917 (1923) *Birds Amer.* 1.60, *Common Tern*. . . *Common Names*. . . Lake Erie Gull. **1946** Hausman *Eastern Birds* 321, *Sterna hirundo hirundo*. . . Lake Erie Gull. . . Habitat—Islands and shores of either large lakes or the sea. **1951** Pough *Audubon Water Bird* 334, Lake Erie gull. See Common tern.

Lake Erie trout See **lake trout 1**

Lake Erie whitefish See **lake whitefish**

lake fly n chiefly Gt Lakes
1 also *lake bug*: =**mayfly 1.** Cf **bay fly, Green Bay fly**
   1889 *Century Dict.* 3333, *Lake-fly*. . . An ephemerid, *Ephemera simulans*, which swarms on the Great Lakes late in July. **1905** Kellogg *Amer. Insects* 65, May-flies, lake-flies, or shad-flies, common names for the insects of the order Ephemerida, are familiar to people who live on the shores of lakes or large rivers, but are among the unknown insects to most high-and-dry dwellers. **1926** Essig *Insects N. Amer.* 139, The mayflies, shadflies, or lakeflies, as the adults are called, are active, fragile insects which dance about the lights at night and rest quietly on some convenient object during the day. **1950** WELS WI (*Large winged insect that hatches in summer in great numbers around lakes or rivers, crowds around lights, lives only a day or so, and is good fish bait*) Lake fly (*or flies*); 2 Infs, Lake fly, Green Bay fly; 1 Inf, May fly, Green Bay fly, lake fly—have heard them called by these names, but they are all the same fly; 1 Inf, Shad fly, lake fly, May fly; 1 Inf, We have lots of lake flies that . . come around Decoration Day and again in August; 1 Inf, Lake fly—like miller, no sting, gray brown, one-half inch; 1 Inf, Lake fly—every locality has a different name. I have been seeking the name for a long time. **1950** WELS Suppl. ceWI, Lake bugs—scobolotches. **1960** Teale *Journey into Summer* 38, Other names [for *Ephemeroptera*] we encountered along the way were: lake flies, fish flies, June flies [etc]. **1967–69** *DARE* (Qu. R4) Infs **NY**217, **PA**182, Lake fly; **OH**20, Lake fly—Canadian soldier; (Qu. R10), Inf **MN**42, Lake fly—like a great big mosquito.
2 A **midge 1**; see quots.
   1950 WELS, 1 Inf, cWI, Lake fly smaller [than miller]; comes in clouds, buzzes. **1967–70** *DARE* (Qu. R10, *Very small flies that don't sting, often seen hovering in large groups or bunches outdoors in summer*) Infs **NY**100, 198, 217, 231, **OH**20, **PA**182, **WI**52, Lake fly. **1994** *DARE* File csWI (as of 1962), The small flies that gathered in clouds and sometimes got into your mouth or nose were called "lake flies."

lake gull n Cf **Lake Erie gull**
1 =**herring gull.**
   1917 (1923) *Birds Amer.* 1.42, Herring Gull—*Larus argentatus*. . . Lake Gull. **1946** Goodrich *Birds in KS* 315, Gull, lake—gull, herring. **1946** Hausman *Eastern Birds* 312, Herring Gull—*Larus argentatus smithsonianus* . . Other Names—Sea Gull . . Lake Gull.
2 =**ring-billed gull.**
   1917 (1923) *Birds Amer.* 1.46, Ring-billed Gull—*Larus delawarensis*. . . Common Gull; Lake Gull. **1953** Jewett *Birds WA* 301, Ring-billed Gull. *Larus delawarensis*. . . Lake Gull.

lake herring n
A **cisco**, usu *Coregonus artedi*.
   1875 *Amer. Naturalist* 9.135 **IN**, I received . . a collection of deep-water "Siscoes". . . Compared with Coregonus most of the species have a more slender form; hence their popular name of "lake herrings," although their resemblance to the sea herring is quite superficial. **1896** Jordan-Evermann *Check List Fishes* 289, *Argyrosomus artedi* . . Cisco; Lake Herring; Michigan Herring. Great Lakes and neighboring waters, and northward into Labrador. **1935** Pratt *Manual Vertebrate Animals* 39, *Leucichthys* [spp] . . Ciscoes; lake herrings. *Ibid* 40, L[eucichthys] artedi . . Common lake herring. . . the most important of the lake herrings commercially. **1949** Caine *N. Amer. Sport Fish* 165, The cisco (or lake herring) is closely related to the Great Lakes whitefish and is a moderately important food fish. **1955** U.S. Arctic Info. Center *Gloss.* 48, *Lake herring*, Any of various whitefish of the genus *Leucichthys*, caught in great numbers in circumpolar fresh waters. Also called 'cisco.' **1982** Sternberg *Fishing* 23, Ciscoes have a sleek body and an adipose fin. . . Also called *lake herring* or *tullibees*, they inhabit large, deep lakes of the northern states and Canada. **1991** Amer. Fisheries Soc. *Common Names Fishes* 27, *Coregonus artedi*. . . cisco or lake herring.

lake lawyer n Cf **lawyer B4, 5**
1 =**bowfin.**
   1838 Geol. Surv. OH *Second Annual Rept.* 196, *A[mia] calva*. The dog-fish is found in Lake Erie, where it is frequently called by the fishermen, "the Lake Lawyer." It is distinguished by its ferocious looks and voracious habits. **1933** LA Dept. of Conserv. *Fishes* 383, Throughout the rest of its range, the Grindle (*Amia calva*) is known as the John A. Grindle, Poisson marais . . the Lake Lawyer. **1946** LaMonte *N. Amer. Game Fishes* 102, Bowfin—*Amia calva* . . Fresh-water Dogfish . . Lake Lawyer. **1983** Becker *Fishes WI* 251, Bowfin—*Amia calva* . . . Other common names: dogfish . . lake lawyer.

2 =**burbot.**

1882 U.S. Natl. Museum *Bulletin* 16.802, *L[ota] maculosa* . . Burbot; Lake Lawyer. **1905** U.S. Bur. Fisheries *Rept. for 1904* 579, The only Lake Erie fishes on which I observed leeches at all commonly were the lake lawyer (*Lota maculosa*) and some of the cat-fishes (especially *Ictalurus*). **1946** LaMonte *N. Amer. Game Fishes* 166, Burbot—*Lota maculosa*. . . Lake Lawyer. **1983** Becker *Fishes WI* 747, *Lota lota*. . . Other common names: lawyer, lake lawyer.

lake perch n

A **yellow perch** (here: *Perca flavescens*).

1933 John G. Shedd Aquarium *Guide* 85, The Yellow Perch is one of the best known fresh water fishes in the eastern half of the United States. . . It is the well known Lake Perch of the Chicago water front. **1956** Harlan-Speaker *IA Fish* 145, Yellow Perch—*Perca flavescens* . . Other Names . . ringed perch, ring-tailed perch, lake perch. **1969** DARE Tape **MI**102, We heard that they were catching lake perch, Lake Michigan perch, on the pier here. **1983** Becker *Fishes WI* 886, Yellow Perch—*Perca flavescens* . . Other common names: . . lake perch . . striped perch.

lake pickerel n Also *lake pike*

1 =**northern pike 1.**

1884 U.S. Natl. Museum *Bulletin* 27.469, *Esox lucius*. . . Pike; Lake Pike; Grass Pike. . . . This is a well-known game fish and very important commercially. The supply for the Washington markets is brought mostly from the Great Lakes. **1927** Weed *Pike* 43, [*Esox lucius*] Lake Pickerel; Northern Ohio. Lake Pike; Western Pennsylvania. **1949** Caine *N. Amer. Sport Fish* 107, Northern Pike—*Colloquial Names*. . . Lake Pickerel.

2 =**chain pickerel.**

1927 Weed *Pike* 45, [*Esox niger*] Lake Pickerel; Lake Pike. **1946** LaMonte *N. Amer. Game Fishes* 128, Eastern Pickerel—*Esox niger* . . (Also listed in many books as *Esox reticulatus*.) . . Names: Chain Pickerel . . Lake Pickerel . . Chain Pike.

laker n

1 =**lake trout 1.**

1823 Cooper *Pioneers* 2.76, I see a laker there, that has run out of the school. **1864** Lowell *Fireside Travels* 151 **NEng**, Telemachus caught a *laker* of thirteen pounds and a half. **1884** Goode *Fisheries U.S.* 1.488, The Lake Trout has other appellatives, such as . . "Tyrant of the Lake," "Laker" . . and "Lake Salmon." **1937** FWP *Guide ME* 411 **cME**, The thoroughfare between Sugar Island and the eastern shore of the lake is good trolling ground for 'lakers' (togue). . . 'Lakers' are taken by deep trolling. **1968** DARE (Qu. P1, . . *Kinds of freshwater fish . . caught around here . . good to eat*) Inf **NH**14, Lakers—lake trout. **1972** Sparano *Outdoors Encycl.* 356, The lake trout is distributed throughout Canada and in the northern U.S., principally in New England, New York's Finger Lakes, the Great Lakes, and many large western lakes. Stockings have widened the laker's range considerably. **1983** Becker *Fishes WI* 323, Lake Trout—*Salvelinus namaycush namaycush* . . Other common names: . . mackinaw trout . . laker . . forktail trout.

2 =**greater scaup.**

1923 U.S. Dept. Ag. *Misc. Circular* 13.20 **NY**, Greater Scaup Duck (*Fulix marila*). . . laker. **1982** Elman *Hunter's Field Guide* 206, *Greater Scaup*. . . laker, lake bluebill.

lake salmon n

1 =**lake trout 1.**

[**1822** Gourlay *Upper Canada* I 177 (*DCan*), I think the proper name of this fish is the *lake salmon.*] **1842** DeKay *Zool. NY* 4.239, This [=*Salmo confinis*] is the well known *Lake Salmon, Lake Trout* or *Salmon Trout* of the State of New-York. **1856** *Porter's Spirit of Times* 20 Dec 253, Dr. Unzicker . . was confident . . that the Ohio fish called salmon is identical with the lake salmon. **1884** Goode *Fisheries U.S.* 1.487, In the lakes of Northern New York the same species [=*Salvelinus namaycush*] occurs, being known by the names "Lake Salmon," "Lake Trout," and "Salmon Trout." **1904** *Salmon & Trout* 287, In the northern part of New York it [=*Cristivomer namaycush*] is sometimes called "lake salmon." **1940** Smith *Puyallup-Nisqually* 236 **wWA**, These smoked lake salmon would keep as well as any smoked salmon.

2 also *lake Atlantic salmon*: The lake-dwelling Atlantic **salmon** (*Salmo salar*). Cf **landlocked salmon 1**

1886 Mather *Memoranda* 18, Under the title of "Lake Salmon," Mr. Everett Smith, a well-informed gentleman of Maine, writes as follows:. . . I have caught the lake salmon (variety *Sebago*) in the west branch of the Penobscot river. **1946** LaMonte *N. Amer. Game Fishes* 111, *Salmo salar sebago*. . . a famous landlocked form of the Atlantic

Salmon . . Names: Sebago Salmon . . Lake Salmon. **1949** Caine *N. Amer. Sport Fish* 62, Originally described from Sebago Lake, Maine, it was known for years as Sebago salmon. . . *Colloquial Names* . . Lake Trout . . Lake Salmon. **1975** Evanoff *Catch More Fish* 77, The landlocked salmon (*Salmo salar sebago*) is also called the Sebago salmon, Sebago trout, Schoodic salmon, lake salmon [etc]. **1991** Amer. Fisheries Soc. *Common Names Fishes* 28, Lake populations of Atlantic salmon are variously known as ouananiche, lake Atlantic salmon, landlocked salmon, and Sebago salmon.

lake sculpin n

=**mottled sculpin.**

1983 Becker *Fishes WI* 969, *Cottus bairdi*. . . Lake sculpin. . . In headwater streams and large lakes.

lake shad n

1 A **gizzard shad 1** (here: *Dorosoma cepedianum*).

1884 Goode *Fisheries U.S.* 1.610, In the Great Lake regions the Gizzard Shad is sometimes split and salted as "Lake Shad," but it probably meets with little sale, owing to the inferior quality of the flesh and the presence of the vast number of small bones that make up the skeleton. It is usually thrown away by the fishermen, and when brought to market it is only bought by the poor or the ignorant. [**1889** *Century Dict.* 3333, *Lake-shad.* . . One of several different inferior fishes, as suckers, etc.: a commercial name under which the prepared fish are sold. [*Century Dict.* Ed: Lake region, U.S.]] **1897** *Outing* 30.435, Most abundant . . was the "sheepshead" (freshwater drum), a good-looking silvery fish, somewhat like the lake shad. **1908** Forbes-Richardson *Fishes of IL* 47, *Dorosoma cepedianum* . . gizzard-shad; hickory-shad. . . In the Great Lake region this species is often caught and offered for sale under the name of "lake shad."

2 A **redhorse** (here: *Moxostoma macrolepidotum*).

1887 Goode *Amer. Fishes* 438, Philadelphia receives a large supply [of *Moxostoma aureolus*, now = *M. macrolepidotum*] from the Susquehanna and the Delaware. It is sometimes called the "Lake Shad."

lake sheepshead n Also *sheepshead of the lake*

=**freshwater drum.**

1838 Geol. Surv. OH *Second Annual Rept.* 168, *Scioena oscula* . . Sheep's Head of the Lake. **1842** DeKay *Zool. NY* 4.73, The Lake Sheepshead. *Corvina oscula*, . . is a very common fish in Lake Erie. . . Unlike the Sheepshead of the ocean (*Sargus ovis*), it is a poor, dry and tasteless fish. **1898** U.S. Natl. Museum *Bulletin* 47.1484, *Aplodinotus grunniens* . . Lake Sheepshead. . . Great Lakes to Texas; abundant in all lakes and large streams west of the Alleghanies and east of the plains, reaching a weight of 50 to 60 pounds. Its flesh is not of high quality.

lake shiner n

1 A **shiner** (here: *Notropis atherinoides* or *N. hudsonius*).

1929 OK Univ. Biol. Surv. *Pub.* 1.83, *Notropis atherinoides* . . Lake shiner. **1968** DARE (Qu. P7, *Small fish used as bait for bigger fish*) Inf **MN**42, Lake shiner—hard to keep alive, also called spot-tails. **1983** Becker *Fishes WI* 505, Emerald Shiner—*Notropis atherinoides* . . Other common names: lake shiner.

2 A **cisco** (here: *Coregonus hoyi*).

1903 NY State Museum & Sci. Serv. *Bulletin* 60.236, *Argyrosomus hoyi*—Mooneye Cisco; Shiner. . . Mr. Annin wrote me that the people at Canandaigua lake told him that there were large quantities of small lake shiners, as they are called, in the lake.

lake sturgeon n

Std: a **sturgeon** (here: *Acipenser fulvescens*). Also called **rockfish, red sturgeon, rock ~, rubber-nose ~, shellback ~, smoothback, stone sturgeon**

Lake Superior whitefish See lake whitefish

lake teal n

=**green-winged teal.**

1923 U.S. Dept. Ag. *Misc. Circular* 13.13 **UT**, Green-winged Teal (*Nettion carolinense*). . . lake teal. **1982** Elman *Hunter's Field Guide* 178, Green-winged Teal (*Anas crecca carolinensis*)—Common & Regional Names: greenwing . . lake teal.

lake thunder n

1983 *Isthmus* (Madison WI) 7 Jan 5 **csWI**, The expansion and contraction of the ice will produce the lake thunder you hear rumbling across the ice every winter. Magnuson is confident that lake thunder will be heard across Mendota this year.

lake trout n

1 also *Lake Erie trout:* A salmonid fish (*Salvelinus namay-cush*). **chiefly Gt Lakes, Upstate NY** See Map Also called **bear trout, buckskin 4, forktail trout, gray ~ 2, Great Lake(s) ~, laker 1, lake salmon 1, landlocked ~ 3, lean trout, lunge n[1], Mackinaw trout, mountain ~ 1, namay-cush, paperbelly, racer, red trout, reef ~, salmon, ~ trout, shoalwater trout, siscowet, togue, trout, tuladi** Cf **humper n[1]**

1830 *Cabinet Nat. Hist.* 1.147 **PA,** In the outlet, or stream from the lake, none of the lake trout were ever found. **1839** Hoffman *Wild Scenes* 1.38 **seNY,** Storing our canoe with a good supply of brook and lake trout. **a1862** (1864) Thoreau *ME Woods* 271, In the midst of our dreams of giant lake-trout, . . our fisherman drew up a diminutive red perch. **1887** Goode *Amer. Fishes* 1.463, The angling authorities still refuse to admit that the Lake Trout of the East is identical with the Mackinaw Trout, or Namaycush, supporting their views by accounts of their very different habits. **1904** *Salmon & Trout* 287, It is, in addition to the name of Great Lake trout, called Mackinaw trout in the region of the Great Lakes. . . At Green Bay, Wisconsin, those that have salmon-colored flesh and black bodies are called "black trout"; those with white flesh, "lake trout." **1965–70** *DARE* (Qu. P1, . . *Kinds of freshwater fish . . caught around here . . good to eat*) 32 Infs, **chiefly Nth, esp Gt Lakes, Upstate NY,** Lake trout; **ME**10, Lake trout or togue; **OH**3, Lake Erie trout; (Qu. P14, . . *Commercial fishing . . what do the fishermen go out after?*) 21 Infs, **chiefly Gt Lakes,** Lake trout; **MI**101, Lake trout—former times; **MI**103, Lake trout—which they don't get; **MI**123, For whitefish and lake trout on Lake Michigan; **MN**2, Lake trout—in Lake Superior; (Qu. H45, *Dishes made with meat, fish, or poultry that everybody around here would know, but that people in other places might not*) Inf **WI**60, Fish boil; start potatoes boiling, add fish; the liquid must boil over three times before it's finished; use lake trout. I think this originated in Algoma. **1966–69** *DARE* Tape **MI**21, The only fish [on Lake Superior] that amounted to anything for the past forty years or so is your lake trout, and when you can't get them, you can't do much in the fishing business; **MI**22, Down at Lake Superior when you go out trout fishing there, for lake trout, you're allowed one fish, certain amount of pounds, and then one extra, and that's it for the day. . . I prefer . . brook trout . . because they're nice and pink. . . They're not . . as fat as lake trout would be; **MI**29, My son always went with us . . and he did the trawling on Lake Superior for lake trout; **MI**32, Quite a few inland lakes have been stocked with [what] . . they call a splake . . a cross between a speckled trout and a lake trout; **MI**109, The lake trout are starting to come back. They're catching a lot of lake trout out here trolling, or did this year. **1991** Amer. Fisheries Soc. *Common Names Fishes* 28, *Salvelinus namaycush* . . lake trout.

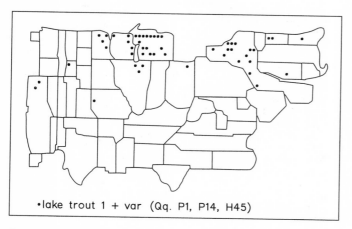

•lake trout 1 + var (Qq. P1, P14, H45)

2 =**cutthroat trout.**

1882 U.S. Natl. Museum *Bulletin* 16.314, *S[almo] purpuratus* . . Rocky Mountain Brook Trout; Lake Trout. **1889** *Century Dict.* 3333, *Lake-trout.* . . The common salmon-trout of western North America, *Salmo purpuratus.* . . It may be generally recognized by the profusion of small round black spots on most of the body, and a red blotch on the lower jaw. . . It abounds in the rivers of Alaska, Oregon, and Washington. **1968** *DARE* (Qu. P1, . . *Kinds of freshwater fish . . caught around here . . good to eat*) Inf **KS**15, Lake trout—a species of steelhead.

3 =**Dolly Varden 1.**

1884 Goode *Fisheries U.S.* 504, The Dolly Varden Trout—*Salvelinus malma.* . . This species is known in the mountains as "Lake Trout" [etc]. **4** The lake-dwelling Atlantic **salmon** (*Salmo salar*). **1949** [see **lake salmon 2**].

lake whitefish n Also *Lake Erie whitefish, Lake Superior ~*

A **whitefish** (here: *Coregonus clupeaformis*).

1863 U.S. Dept. Ag. *Rept. of Secy. for 1862* 55, The fishes of Maine . . which are known to spawn in fresh water. They are: . . lake trout, *Salmo confinis;* lake white fish, *Ceregonus albus* [etc]. **1870** McClung *MN in 1870* 180, *Varieties* . . Lake Superior white fish. **1903** NY State Museum & Sci. Serv. *Bulletin* 60.225, The name whitefish is . . seldom varied except by means of the prefix "common" or "lake." **1920** Lewis *Main Street* 414 **MN,** He was the guest of honor at the Commercial Club Banquet . . an occasion for . . soft damp slabs of Lake Superior whitefish served as fillet of sole. **1969** *DARE* (Qu. P14, . . *Commercial fishing . . what do the fishermen go out after?*) Inf **NY**132, Lake Erie whitefish—they used to fish commercially, but no more. **1983** Becker *Fishes WI* 333, The lake whitefish (*Coregonus clupeaformis*) is easily identified but the other *Coregonus* species are not. **1991** Amer. Fisheries Soc. *Common Names Fishes* 27, Lake whitefish.

lakted See like v[1] B

l'aky See leaky

lalapalooza n Also sp *lallapaloosa;* pronc-sp *lollypaloozer;* for addit varr see quots [Etym unknown]

1 An exceptionally fine, remarkable, or unusual person or thing. **chiefly Nth, N Midl**

1896 (1898) Ade *Artie* 8 **Chicago IL,** "But the girls—wow!" "Beauties, eh?" "Lollypaloozers!" **1904** Hobart *I'm from MO* 89 **seNY,** Saturday night we had our final parade with the fireworks finish, and it was a lallapalootza! **1907** Mulford *Bar-20* 371, Johnny Nelson blew a cloud of smoke at the ceiling and paused with a pleased expression on his face: "This is a lalapoloosa of a cigar," he cried. **1908** (1915) Calhoun *Miss Minerva* 204 **TN,** You sho' is genoowine corn-fed, sterlin' silver, all-wool-an'-a-yard-wide, pure leaf, Green-River Lollapaloosas. **1911** *DN* 3.545 **NE,** Lallapaloosa. . . Something fine or grand; term of approbation. "You have a lallapaloosa of a hat," "That's a lallapaloosa." **1912** *DN* 3.582 **wIN,** "Isn't John's new buggy a lolly-paloozer?" **1913** *DN* 4.17 **NE, WY,** Lallapalooser. . . "That horse is a lallapalooser." **1916** *DN* 4.341 **seOH,** Lollypaloozer. **1918** *DN* 5.26 **NW,** Lollopalouser. **1946** McAtee *Dial. Grant Co. IN Suppl.* 3 7 (as of 1890s), Lollypaloozer. **1947** in 1966 Stevens *Letters* 547, I think that the book, as a book, is a lollapalooza. **1960** Criswell *Resp. to PADS 20* **Ozarks,** Lollie-palooser . . lolapalooza. **1966–70** *DARE* (Qu. B25, . . *Joking names . . for a very heavy rain.* . . "It's a regular _____.") Inf **IL**26, [ˌlaləpəˈlusə]; **PA**244, Lalapaloozer; (Qu. Y11, . . *A very hard blow:* "You should have seen Bill go down. Joe really hit him a _____.") Inf **AR**11, Lalapoozer; **MN**24, [ˈlaləpəluzə]; **SD**2, [ˈlaləpəˌlusə]; (Qu. KK41, *Something that is very difficult to do:* "I managed to get through with it, but it was _____.") Inf **MA**58, [A] lalapaloozer; (Qu. LL5, *Something impressively big:* "That cabbage is really a _____.") Inf **ME**13, Lalapalooza. **1980** Ciardi *Browser's Dict.* 224, *Lalapalooza / lallapalooza / lolapalooza / lollapalooza*—An outstanding person, thing, creature. A oner. **1991** *Chicago Tribune* (IL) 4 Aug sec 2 2/4, As many as 30,000 concertgoers came for the seven rap and rock acts of the Lollapalooza Festival.

2 Spec: an extremely tall tale; a lie.

1918 *DN* 5.26 **NW,** Lollopalouser. . . A great lie. **c1960** *Wilson Coll.* **csKY,** Lallypalucy (sp?) . . A mild word for lie.

3 In the game of poker: a special hand or game usu employed to deceive an inexperienced player; see quot 1949; also fig. Also called **looloo**

1934 *Sun* (Baltimore MD) 10 Jan 1/8 (*Hench Coll.*) **OK,** He [=a man who had gone to Washington DC in hopes of landing a government contract] asserted he encountered the old lallapaloosa game in which the rules are changed to fit the occasion and other indirect methods of arriving at desired results. **1939** MacDougall–Furnas *Gamblers Don't Gamble* 149 **West,** But I got a lalapalooza. Out here we call a deuce, four, six, eight and ten a lalapalooza and that beats everything, even a royal flush. Ain't that right, boys? **1949** *San Diego Union* (CA) 7 Nov sec B 1/2, They would scorn to use the classical old lalapaloozer which was once the favorite California device for taking a tenderfoot. . . Here is an account of it. A stranger playing in the early days of Sacramento found himself holding four aces. . . The pot grew and grew. Finally came the showdown. The stranger spread his hand, and reached for the pot . . "Not so fast," barked a native son. "I've got a lalapaloozer." He laid down a 3, 5, 7, 9 and 10. . . "Under the rules we play here that hand is a lalapaloozer and it beats any other hand," said the native son as he collected the chips. . . Several hours later the tenderfoot was dealt a hand from 3 to 10 without a pair. . . When the showdown came the other man laid down a King full and . . started to take the chips . . "Not so fast," cried the visitor. "I've got a lalapaloozer." "I'm sorry, stranger," retorted the other. "Under the rules here a lalapaloozer is good only once a night." **1949** (1976) Coffin *Secrets of Poker* 180, *Lalapalooza*—A freak hand, a special hand allowed only once in one session. **1974** Gibson *Hoyle* 254, *Lalapalooza:* A [poker] game in which an odd but fairly common hand is given top rating—above a royal flush—for the first player who is dealt one; but from then on, it reverts to its usual rank, during the remainder of that session.

lalla adj [Cf *OED* la-la " 'So-so', not so good as it might be, poor." 1800–a1849]
  1950 *PADS* 14.43 **eSC**, *Lalla.* . . Careless, indifferent. "He acted in a lalla manner." Coastal.

lallapaloosa See **lalapalooza**

lalla shop n Also *lally's* [**lalla** adj]
  See quot 1950.
  1950 *PADS* 14.43 **SC**, *Lalla shop* ['lælə]. . . A small, perhaps disreputable shop catering to a low grade patronage, dealing in cheap miscellany, second-hand wares and clothing. **1954** *PADS* 21.31 **seSC**, *Lally's.* . . Same as *lalla shop.* . . Charleston.

lalligag See **lollygag**

lallop See **lollop**

lallygag, lallylag See **lollygag**

la loche See **lush**

lalock See **lilac**

lam v, hence vbl n *lamming*
  1 To strike, beat; to shoot; to throw; also fig. [*OED* lam v. 1. "Now *colloq.* or *vulgar.*"] *old-fash*
  1848 Bartlett *Americanisms* 198, *To lam.* . . To beat soundly; to drub. Colloquial in some of the Northern States. **1859** (1968) Bartlett *Americanisms* 236, *Lamming.* A beating. **1859** Taliaferro *Fisher's R.* 67 **nwNC** (as of 1820s), I lammed away at him [=a buck] and away he went round the mounting, and the bullet arter him. **1884** *Anglia* 7.274 **Sth, S Midl** [Black], *To gib or give er lammin'* = to chastise. *Ibid* 278, *To lam, ef it's de las' ack* = to flog if it costs one's life. **1887** (1967) Harris *Free Joe* 172 **GA** [Black], Dat nigger man tuck'n lam me side de head. **1892** *DN* 1.236 **swMO, MI**, *Lam.* "Lam him one over the head," ["Give him a lam," = hit him once.] Kansas City. [*DN* Ed: So in Michigan. . . The verb is well known.] **1905** *DN* 3.63 **eNE**, *Lam.* **1909** *DN* 3.343 **eAL, wGA**, *Lam.* *Ibid* 413 **nME**, *Lam.* **1910** *DN* 3.454 **seVT**, *Lam.* . . "He lammed him one in the jaw." *Lamming.* A beating. **1921** *DN* 5.116 **seKY**, *Lam.* **1929** *AmSp* 5.121 **ME**, Elders would say . . "I will lam you, you imp or limb of Satan," or "I will wear out a stick on you." **1945** FWP *Lay My Burden Down* 68 **SC** [Black], Somebody lam on the door. **1950** *WELS*, 1 Inf, **cwWI**, Lamming, thrashing, whipping. **c1960** Wilson *Coll.* **csKY**, *Lam.* . . To hit, strike, slap; also used figuratively. **1968–69** *DARE* (Qu. Y10, *To throw something* . . "*The dog came at him, so he picked up a stone and _____ it at him.*") Inf **IL105**, Lammed; (Qu. Y11) Inf **CT1**, He lammed him one; (Qu. Y14a, *To hit somebody hard with the fist*) Inf **CT1**, Lam.
  2 also with *it, out*: To leave in a hurry, run, make a fast getaway—freq used in imper. [Cf *EDD* lam v. 4. "To run quickly"]
  1886 Pinkerton *30 Yrs.* 41 **Chicago IL**, After he [=a pickpocket] has secured the wallet he will . . utter the word "lam!" This means to let the man go, and to get out of the way as soon as possible. This word is also used in case the money cannot be taken, and further attempts are useless. **1919** *DN* 5.41 [Hobo cant], *Lam.* . . To run. **1927** *DN* 5.453 [Underworld jargon], *Lam.* **1928** *AmSp* 3.255 [Crook argot], *Lam*—to escape. **1966–69** *DARE* (Qu. Y18, *To leave in a hurry:* "*Before they find this out, we'd better _____!*") Infs **GA84, MA27, NC36**, Lam; **IL97**, Lam outa here; (Qu. Y20, *To run fast:* "*You should have seen him _____!*") Inf **SC55**, Lam it out of here; (Qu. JJ6, *To stay away from school without an excuse*) Inf **MS6**, Played hookey, lammed out. **1985** *DARE* File **WV**, Let's lam out of here before they start askin' for volunteers.

3 with *on* or *away*: See quots.
  1848 in 1935 *AmSp* 10.40 **Nantucket MA**, *Lam on.* Work fast. **1884** *Anglia* 7.270 **Sth, S Midl** [Black], *To lam away at* = to make an attempt to.
  4 also with *on to*: See quots. Cf **glom** v[1] **2**
  1934 Minehan *Boy & Girl Tramps* 266, *Lammed*—left; struck; stole. **1950** *WELS* (*To take something of small value that does not belong to you:* "*I'm going to _____ this before somebody else does.*") 1 Inf, **ceWI**, Lam on to.

lam away See **lam 3**

lamb n
  1 also *lamb fuzz:* =**dust bunny.** Cf **lamb's tail 1**
  1950 *WELS* **WI** (*Soft rolls of dust that collect on the floor under beds or other furniture*) 1 Inf, Lambs; 1 Inf, Lamb fuzz. **1968** *DARE* (Qu. E20) Inf **MN30**, Little lambs.
  2 See **lamb without horns.**

lamb bush n
  =**chaste tree.**
  c1938 in 1970 Hyatt *Hoodoo* 2.942 **VA**, Well, we has a bush. . . Well, it's called a *lamb bush.* . . On one side of this bush, on the—would be on the wes' side, we has a brownish leaf an' twig. An also dere's bark on the bush. On this side we has a re'l pale green, dark green. [*Ibid* 943, You kin git dose leaves an' . . rub 'em an' place 'em to your head, your headache'll soon go 'way. You'll find it draw out the fever, it'll soon leave you. You kin have a pain in your side or your wris' an' . . no need no liniment an' no medicine.]

lamb fry See **fry 4**

lamb fuzz See **lamb 1**

lambkill n Rarely *kill-lamb* [See quot 1830] **scattered, but esp NEng** Cf **kill-calf, kill-kid**
  A **mountain laurel 1**, usu **sheep laurel** (here: *Kalmia angustifolia*).
  1790 Castiglioni *Viaggio* 2.271, K[almia] Angustifolia. . . Sheep-poison, Ivy, Dwarf-Laurell, Lamb-kill. **1824** Bigelow *Florula Bostoniensis* 170, A low shrub with rose coloured flowers, very common in low grounds, and known by the names *sheep poison, lambkill, low laurel,* &c. **1830** Rafinesque *Med. Flora* 2.16, *Kalmia latifolia* . . Lambkill, Sheep-poison [etc]. [*Ibid* 17, It is certainly deleterious to horses, calves, and sheep feeding on it in winter, because indigestible to them. Sheep, if not soon relieved by oil, will swell and die.] **1832** Williamson *Hist. ME* 1.116, *Lamb-kill* [Footnote: Kalmia Latifolia]. . . has been called *mountain Laurel, Spoonwood, Ivy* and *Calico Bush.* Its wood is dense and hard. **1845** Judd *Margaret* 90 **NEng**, She proceeded to collect such as grew near her, calico bush, Solomon's seal, lambkill and others. **1869** Fuller *Uncle John* 65 **NY**, One of the Andromedas, with deciduous or falling leaves, has acquired the bad name of 'Kill-lamb,' because it is thought to poison sheep if they eat it. It has smooth oval leaves, pale and downy on the under surface [etc]. **a1870** Chipman *Notes on Bartlett* 228 *(DAE)*, *Kill-lamb,* C[onnecticu]t Usage. See Lamb-Kill. **1907** *DN* 3.192 **seNH**, *Lambkill.* . . Sheep laurel; poisonous to sheep. **1941** *LANE* Map 249, 3 infs, **c,eME**, Lamb kill; 1 inf, **cME**, Laurel = lamb kill; 1 inf **sME coast**, Lamb kill, nanny kill; 1 inf, **nwVT**, Sheep laurel, lamb kill; 1 inf, **csCT**, Lamb kill, thought to be the old name for the laurel; 1 inf, **csRI**, Lamb kill = sheep laurel, common here; 1 inf, **seMA**, Low laurel = kill kid = lamb kill. **1953** Greene-Blomquist *Flowers South* 90, *Sheep-laurels, Lamb-kills, Wickys (Kalmia)*—The smaller species of *Kalmia* have smaller flowers and leaves than mountain-laurel [=K. latifolia]. **1967** *DARE* (Qu. T16, . . *Kinds of trees* . . 'special') Inf **MA5**, Lambkill—sheep laurel. **1979** Niering-Olmstead *Audubon Guide N. Amer. Wildflowers E. Region* 500, Sometimes called Lambkill, this small shrub is poisonous to livestock.

lam black See **lampblack**

lamb leg See **lamb's leg**

lamb lettuce See **lamb's lettuce**

lamb licker n [See quot 1939] **chiefly MT** *derog*
  A sheepherder or lamber.
  1936 McCarthy *Lang. Mosshorn* np **MT** [Range term], *Lamb Licker.* . . A pretentious term for a sheepherder. **1938** FWP *Guide SD* 87, *Lamblicker:* derisive term for lamber. **1939** (1973) FWP *Guide MT* 414, *Lamb licker*—Sheepman (derisive), from a ewe's habit of licking a newborn

lamb. **1984** Doig *English Creek* 140 **nMT**, Lamb lickers (as guys who worked in lambing sheds were known).

lamb lily n [*SND* 1886]

A false asphodel of the genus *Tofieldia*.

1938 (1958) Sharples *AK Wild Flowers* 145, *Tofieldia*. . . "Lamb Lily." A plant with fibrous roots and leaves like a small German Iris.

lamb quarter(s), lamb shoulders See **lamb's quarter(s) 1**

lamb's leg n Also *lamb leg, lamb's quarters, ~ tail* [Engl dial; cf *EDD* [lamb]'s-leg, lambs'-legs (at *lamb* 1.(13)) nasal excrement] Cf **cheap tail**

Nasal mucus; a bit of mucus hanging from the nostrils.

1950 *WELS* **WI** (*Sticky mucus that forms in the nose*) 1 Inf, Lamb's quarters [old-fashioned]; 1 Inf, Lamb's leg—when it's hanging out. **1965** *DARE* File **nMA, sNH** (as of c1915), Said by my grandmother to a child with a runny nose, "Let's wipe off that lamb's tail." **1967–68** *DARE* (Qu. X16) Inf **MA5**, Lamb's legs—kid's word for runny nose; **MO9**, Lamb's leg; **OH43**, Lamb leg—hangs out of the nose; **OH74**, Lamb leg—when it hangs down. **1979** Stegner *Recapitulation* 34 **UT** (as of 1922), Thirteen years old and running around with a lamb's leg under your nose, making mud pies.

lamb's lettuce n Also *lamb lettuce* [*OED* 1597 →]

An edible plant of the genus *Valerianella*, usu *V. locusta*. Also called **fetticus, Pawnee lettuce.** For other names of *V. amarella* see **feverweed 4**

1817 Eaton *Botany* 10, [*Fedia*] *radiata*, (lamb lettuce). **1848** Gray *Manual of Botany* 183, *F[edia] olitoria*. . . Also called, like the other species, *Lamb-lettuce*. **1914** Georgia *Manual Weeds* 402, Corn Salad—*Valerianella Locusta*. . . Lamb's Lettuce, Milk Grass. **1939** FWP *Guide TN* 22 **cTN**, Wild flowers common to much of Middle Tennessee are the spring-beauty, . . lamb's lettuce, . . and the flameflower. **1953** Piercy *Shaker Cook Book* 210, Lamb's lettuce, a blunt-leafed, clumpy little salad plant which lasts late into the fall and can be covered with straw and used throughout the winter. **1969** *DARE* (Qu. I28a, . . *Kinds of things . . you call 'greens' . . [Those that are eaten raw]*) Inf **PA203**, Lamb's lettuce ("greens"); (Qu. S26e, *Other wildflowers not yet mentioned;* not asked in early QRs) Inf **TN35**, Lamb's lettuce. **1973** *Foxfire 2* 86, Corn salad (*Valerianella radiate* [sic]) . . (lamb's lettuce)—A common plant of early spring. . . Young leaves are edible "used any way you'd use lettuce." **1976** Bailey–Bailey *Hortus Third* 1144, *Valerianella* [spp] . . Corn-salad, lamb's lettuce. . . Two species are grown as pot herbs or salad plants and others as ornamentals.

lamb's quarter(s) n

1 also *lamb quarter(s), lamb('s) shoulders:* A **goosefoot,** usu *Chenopodium album.* [Etym unknown; *OED* 1773 →; see quot 1920]

1804 (1904) Clark *Orig. Jrls. Lewis & Clark Exped.* 1.79, In those small Praries or Glades I saw wild Timothy, lambs-quarter, Cuckle burs, & rich weed. **1837** (1962) Williams *Territory FL* 86, [Upland herbs include:] Lamb's Quarter. C[henopodium] alleum [sic]. C. botrys. C. ambrossoides. **1849** Howitt *Our Cousins in OH* 82, They brought . . a basket full of what is called lamb-quarter, a species of wild spinach, which is a favorite vegetable at this season. **1899** (1912) Green *VA Folk-Speech* 254, *Lamb's quarter.* . . A weed; *chenopodium album;* used as a sallet for cooking in the spring. **1920** Saunders *Useful Wild Plants* 119, Another old-fashioned pot-herb that may be gathered freely in spring is the early growth of that familiar weed of gardens and waste places . . the homely Pigweed . . or Lamb's quarters. This latter queer name, by the way, like the plant itself, is a waif from England, and according to Prior is a corruption of "Lammas quarter," an ancient festival in the English calendar with which a kindred plant (*Atriplex patula*), of identical popular name and usage, had some association. **1922** *DN* 5.184 **GA**, *Lam's* [sic] *quarter*. . . A plant cooked as "greens." **1950** *WELS* **WI** (*Weeds common in your locality*) 7 Infs, Lamb's quarters; 1 Inf, Lamb quarters; 1 Inf, Lamb's quarter; (*Greens*) 2 Infs, Lamb's quarter(s); 1 Inf, Lamb quarters; (*Weed with furry green leaves close to the ground and a tall stalk with small yellow flowers*) 1 Inf, Lamb's quarters. **c1960** Wilson *Coll.* **csKY**, Lamb's quarter(s). **1965–70** *DARE* (Qu. S21, . . *Weeds . . that are a trouble in gardens and fields*) 124 Infs, **widespread exc Gulf States, S Atl**, Lamb's quarter(s); **DC5, PA21**, Lamb quarters; **MO19**, Lamb's-quarter weed; **MA100**, Lamb shoulders; (Qu. I28b, *Kinds of greens that are cooked*) 44 Infs, **chiefly Cent, Midl**, Lamb's quarter(s); **MO16, 38**, Lamb quarters; (Qu. I28a, . . *Kinds of things . . you call 'greens' . . [Those that are eaten raw]*) 35

Infs, **chiefly Cent, Midl**, Lamb's quarter(s); **VA71**, Lamb quarters; **CA210**, Lamb's shoulders; (Qu. H54, *Dishes made with greens: [. . kinds of 'greens' . . eaten];* total Infs questioned, 75) Infs **OK1, 3, 19**, Lamb's quarter; (Qu. S9) Inf **AR33**, Lamb's quarter; (Qu. BB50d, *Favorite spring tonics*) Inf **KS5**, Lamb's-quarter greens. **1967–69** *DARE* Tape **CO1**, [FW:] What kind of weeds are those. . . [Inf:] Oh I don't know, lamb's quarter I guess. . . Lamb's quarter or red roots; **KY44**, You take plantain and dock and lamb's quarter and dandelion; it makes a very good green salad in spring; **WI30**, [FW:] You remember that weed you showed me today? What were some of the names for that? [Inf:] Well, lamb's quarter, silver leaf, and pigweed, as it was called. **1986** Pederson *LAGS Concordance*, 1 inf, **cnAR**, Lamb's quarter; 1 inf, **nwLA**, Lamb quarter—herb that Indians eat; 1 inf, **neTN**, Lamb's quarter—a weed, used as a green. **1991** Still *Wolfpen Notebooks* 77 **sAppalachians**, What I look forward to in the spring hain't garden sass—hit's wild greens. . . What you want to look for is plantain, . . lamb's quarter, . . and blue thistle. And don't spare the seasoning.

2 A **trillium** (here: *T. cernuum* or *T. erectum*).

1854 King *Amer. Eclectic Dispensatory* 932, *Trillium pendulum*. Beth-root. . . is one of an extensive genus of North American . . plants, which are variously known under the names of *Wake-robin*, . . *Lamb's Quarter*, . . etc. **1892** (1974) Millspaugh *Amer. Med. Plants* 175–1, *Trillium erectum*. . . lamb's quarter. **1940** Clute *Amer. Plant Names* 14, *T[rillium] erectum*. . . [misapplied names:] Lamb's quarters, herb Paris, true-love. **1971** Krochmal *Appalachia Med. Plants* 256, *Trillium erectum*. . . lamb's quarters.

3 See **lamb's leg.**

lamb's shoulders See **lamb's quarter(s) 1**

lamb's tail n

1 =**dust bunny.** Cf **bunny tail, lamb 1**

1966 *DARE* (Qu. E20, *Soft rolls of dust that collect on the floor under beds or other furniture*) Inf **NC34**, Lamb's tails.

2 A cirrus cloud; see quot. Cf **cow's tail 4, mare's tail 1**

1969 *DARE* (Qu. B10, . . *Long trailing clouds high in the sky*) Inf **MI100**, Lamb's tails.

3 A tagalong. Cf **cow's tail 2**

1967 *DARE* (Qu. Y9, *Somebody who always follows along behind others: "His little brother is an awful _____."*) Infs **IL12, TX3**, Lamb's tail.

4 See **lamb's leg.**

5 =**blazing star 2.**

1931 Harned *Wild Flowers Alleghanies* 102, Lamb's tail: Blazing star. . . Flowers feathery, white, fragrant, in a nodding raceme 3 to 9 in. long. **1968** *DARE* (Qu. S26a, . . *Wildflowers . . Roadside flowers*) Inf **NJ8**, Lamb's tails—white flower six inches long, comes up about one foot and curves over.

lamb's tongue n [*OED* 1578 →; "A name given to species of plantain . . and other plants"]

1 also *lamb tongue:* =**dogtooth violet. chiefly Pacific NW**

1873 Miller *Modocs* 128 **cnCA**, He [=winter] cut down the banners of the spring that night, lamb-tongue, Indian turnip and catella. **1894** *Jrl. Amer. Folkl.* 7.102, *Erythronium Americanum*, lamb's tongues, Banner Elk, N.C. **1922** *Amer. Botanist* 28.81, *Erythronium giganteum* is known universally in Oregon as "lamb's-tongue"—probably from the shape of the leaves. **1935** Davis *Honey* 221 **OR**, The tall cream-colored wild lilies known in that country as lamb-tongues clustered in the undergrowth like grass-heads in a hay-field. **1937** FWP *Guide ID* 110, Named horrendously avalanche lily by some, lamb's tongue by others, Easter bells in Utah, dog-toothed violet in the East. **1949** Peattie *Cascades* 252 **Pacific NW**, The yellow glacier lily, Erythronium grandiflorum, is called fawn lily and lamb's-tongue. **1966–68** *DARE* (Qu. S2) Infs **OR3, 5**, Lamb('s) tongue; (Qu. S11, . . *Dog-tooth violet*) Infs **ID5, IN14, 38, OR3, WA30**, Lamb's tongue; (Qu. S22, . . *The bright yellow flowers that bloom in clusters in marshes in early springtime*) Inf **WA3**, Lamb's tongue, but not in marshes, more on hillsides; (Qu. S26c, *Wildflowers that grow in woods*) Inf **OR4**, Early spring—lamb's tongue—like a wild bleeding heart, moist shady places.

2 =**hart's tongue 1.** [*EDD* 1886]

1890 *Century Dict.* 5404, The plant [=*Phyllitis Scolopendrium*] is commonly called *hart's-tongue*, but has also such provincial names as *adder's tongue, buttonhole, fox-tongue, lamb's-tongue, snake-leaves*, etc. **1900** Lyons *Plant Names* 338, *S[colopendrium] scolopendrium* . . Lamb's-tongue.

3 A **mullein** (here: *Verbascum thapsus*). Cf **sheep mullein**
1898 *Jrl. Amer. Folkl.* 11.276, *Verbascum Thapsus* . . lamb's tongue, South Berwick, Me.
4 =**goosefoot**. [*EDD* 1879 →] Cf **lamb's quarter(s) 1**
1950 *WELS (Other weeds)* 1 Inf, **cWI**, Lamb's tongue. **1968–70** *DARE* (Qu. I28b, *Kinds of greens that are cooked*) Infs **IA**30, **KY**24, Lamb's tongue; (Qu. S21, . . *Weeds . . that are a trouble in gardens and fields*) Inf **VA**43, Lamb's tongue.

lambstongue groundsel n Also *lambstongue ragwort*
A **ragwort** (here: *Senecio integerrimus*).
1937 *U.S. Forest Serv. Range Plant Hdbk.* W168, Broom groundsel . . and lambstongue groundsel (*S[enecio] integerrimus*) . . are definitely known to be poisonous. **1950** Stevens *ND Plants* 292, *Lambstongue ragwort*. . . Fairly common, especially in coulees. **1968** Barkley *Plants KS* 373, Lambs Tongue Groundsel. Wet prairies and plains.

lamb's wool n Cf **cottonweed 6, flannel leaf, sheep mullein**
A woolly or hairy plant; see quot.
1959 Carleton *Index Herb. Plants* 73, *Lamb's wool*: Anemone cylindrica; Stachys lanata; Verbascum thapsus.

lamb tongue See **lamb's tongue 1**

lamb weed n Cf **lamb's quarter(s) 1**
A **goosefoot**.
c1938 in 1970 Hyatt *Hoodoo* 2.942 **VA**, Also we has a weed. . . It zalso [sic] called a *lamb weed*. [Hyatt: this is the lamb's-quarters.] **1969** *DARE* (Qu. I28a, . . *Kinds of things . . you call 'greens' . . [Those that are eaten raw]*) Inf **MO**32, Lamb weeds.

lamb without horns n Also *lamb* Cf *DS* P35a
=**mountain lamb**.
1954 White *Adirondack Country* 40 **nNY**, Game is still killed out of season and a doe may be dragged out of the woods at night to be cut up quickly and put in the freezer—hoping a warden won't call and ask to look in it. "Lamb without horns" or "Adirondack goat" turns up at Sunday dinner in back country homes now and then, but the penalty, when infraction is discovered, is steep. **1975** Gould *ME Lingo* 157, *Lamb*—Out-of-season venison. . . A gentleman who poaches a deer will package the meat neatly and put it in his freezer marked *Lamb*.

lame n [Cf *EDD* lame sb.¹ 5. "A hurt, injury"; *OED* lame sb.² "*Obs*. . . Lameness; infirmity."]
Lameness.
1926 Roberts *Time of Man* 171 **cKY**, The filly had a lame shoulder and seems like Shine knowed it but traded when the filly was all rested up and the lame didn't show.

lame duck n
=**ducks and drakes 1**.
1968 *DARE* (Qu. EE30, *Throwing a flat stone over the surface of water so that it jumps several times*) Inf **WI**5, Skimming or lame duck—it is now called skimming.

lamentate v [Back-formation from *lamentation*; cf Intro "Language Changes" III.3]
1936 *AmSp* 11.316 **Ozarks**, *Lamentate*. . . To complain, to lament. 'He was in hyar a-lamentatin' 'bout how his barn burnt up.'

lameta See **lemita**

lam it See **lam 2**

lamming vbl n See **lam**

lamming adj [Cf *EDD* lamming (2) (at **lam 1**) "huge, great, violent"; cf **lam 1**] Cf **larruping adj 1**
Large, prodigious; also adv *lamming* very, exceptionally.
1950 *PADS* 14.76 **FL**, *Lammin' load*. . . A large amount of food taken into the body through gluttony. **1956** McAtee *Some Dialect NC* 26, *Lammin' big*: . . very large.

lammux v Cf **lam v 1**
To beat, thrash.
1925 Dargan *Highland Annals* 90 **cwNC**, He was a friend o' yorn, stayin' in yore barn, an' I couldn't go over there an' lammux him. I'm a peaceable man anyhow.

lam on See **lam 3**

lam on to See **lam 4**

lam out See **lam 2**

lampblack n Pronc-sp, by assim, *lam black*
A very dark-skinned Black person; see quot.
1942 *Amer. Mercury* 55.89 **Harlem NYC** [Black], You [are] trying to get your hips up on your shoulders [=get angry] 'cause I said you was with a beat broad. One of them lam Blacks. *Ibid* 94, *Dark black*—a casually black person. Superlatives: *low black*, a blacker person; *lam black*, still blacker; and *damn black*, blackest man.

lamp bug n
1 A large beetle such as a **giant water bug** or **June bug 1**. Cf **electric light bug**
1967–68 *DARE* (Qu. R5, *A big brown beetle that comes out in large numbers in spring and early summer, and flies with a buzzing sound*) Infs **LA**8, **MO**17, Lamp bug(s).
2 also *lamp fly*: =**firefly 1**.
1968 *DARE* (Qu. R1, . . *The small insect that flies at night and flashes a light at its tail*) Inf **MO**17, Lamp bugs; **WI**50, Lamp fly. **1986** Pederson *LAGS Concordance (Firefly)* 1 inf, **nwLA**, Lamp bug.
3 also *lamp fly*: A moth.
1986 Pederson *LAGS Concordance (Moth)* 3 infs, **LA, TX**, Lamp bug(s); 1 inf, **cwMS**, Lamp bug—looks "like a little butterfly"; 2 infs, **GA, TN**, Lamp fly.

lamp-chimney n
=**sand collar**.
[**1891** *Century Dict.* 5332, *Sand-saucer*. . . A popular name for the egg-mass of a naticoid gastropod, as *Lunatia heros*, commonly found on beaches, resembling the rim of a saucer or lamp-shade broken at one place and covered with sand.] **1914** *DN* 4.155 **Cape Cod MA**, *Lamp-chimney*. . . Sand-saucer. "Them summer folks ha' been dryin' lamp-chimneys they found on the flats an' keepin' 'em for ornaments."

lamp eel n
1 Usu the **congo snake 1**, but also a related amphiuma (*Amphiuma tridactylum*). esp **LA** Cf **lamper eel 3**
1927 Kennedy *Gritny* 161 **sLA** [Black], I jus' as soon eat lamp-eel, as eat dat nasty slimy mud feesh. **1953** [see **lamper eel 3**]. **1967** LeCompte *Word Atlas* 217 **seLA**, A snake like creature with four tiny legs, usually found in ditches after a heavy rain. . . Lamp eel [4 of 21 infs]. **1981** Pederson *LAGS Basic Materials*, 1 inf, **cwMS**, Lamp eel—not an insect.
2 See **lamprey eel 1**.

lamper eel n
1 also *lamper;* rarely *lampeer:* =**lamprey**. [Engl dial] chiefly **NEng, Gt Lakes**
1704 in 1832 *NH Hist. Soc. Coll.* 3.53, Edward Taylor was slain by the Indians at Lamper-eel river. **1828** in 1918 Dale *Ashley–Smith Explor.* 240, Some Inds. . . gave me a lamper eel dryed, but I could not eat it. **1833** in 1834 Davis *Letters Downing* 23, Mr. Van Buren hung on like a lamper-eel. **1842** DeKay *Zool. NY* 4.384, This species [=*Ammocœtes unicolor*], which is common in most of the muddy streams of the northern and western districts, varies in thickness from that of a common earth-worm to the size of a swan's quill. . . Its popular name in this state is *Lamper Eel*. I am not aware that it is used for any other purpose than as bait for other fishes. **1848** Bartlett *Americanisms* 198, *Lamper-eel*. The lamprey. A common name for lampreys in New England. **1897** *Outing* 30.440, The lamprey, or lamper-eel, may once have been considered a delicacy, but the boys would have none of him. **1905** U.S. Bur. Fisheries *Rept. for 1904* 579 **OH**, The fishermen told me that "lamper eels" were "common" up the Portage River, and I often found them among the fish brought to the wholesale house from both the river and the lake. This was the so-called silvery lamprey, *Ichthyomyzon concolor. Ibid* 580, On the 10th of August, 1902, I was assisting in making a seine haul of carp in the Sandusky River when one of the fishermen noticed a lamper "about 5 inches long" attached to one of the fish. **1943** Eddy–Surber *N. Fishes* 49, The lampreys, or lamper eels, are characterized by circular funnellike "mouth," or buccal, cavities armed with toothlike horny spines. **1956** Harlan–Speaker *IA Fish* 43, *Ichthyomyzon unicuspis*. . . Lamprey eel, lamper. *Ibid* 44, *Ichthyomyzon castaneus*. . . Lamprey eel, . . lamper. **1966–69** *DARE* (Qu. P3, *Freshwater fish that are not good to eat*) Infs **ME**6, **MI**80, Lamper eels; **WI**78, Lampeer [læmpiɚ] (=lamprey), also . . ['læmpɚ]; (Qu. P7, *Small fish used as bait for bigger fish*) Inf **NY**223, Lamper eel. **1983** [see **lamprey eel 1**].

2 =**eelpout 1.**

1873 in 1878 Smithsonian Inst. *Misc. Coll.* 14.2.19, *Zoarces anguillaris* . . lamper-eel (Eastport) [*DARE* Ed: Prob Eastport ME]. **1884** Goode *Fisheries U.S.* 1.247, The Mutton-fish, *Zoarces anguillaris,* called Congo Eel and Ling, and also Lamper Eel, especially by the Maine fishermen, is often seen near the shore north of Cape Cod. **1889** *Century Dict.* 3339, *Lamper-eel.* . . The mutton-fish or eel-pout, *Zoarces anguillaris* . . inhabiting the Atlantic coast of North America from Labrador to Delaware.

3 Esp the **congo snake 1** or a related amphiuma *(Amphiuma tridactylum),* but also a **siren. esp Gulf States**

1925 TX Folkl. Soc. *Pub.* 4.51, Throughout the bayou regions of eastern Texas and Louisiana the bite of the "lamper . . eel" is thought to be deadly. . . The innocent subject of this myth is the so-called great siren *(Siren lacertina).* **1953** Schmidt *N. Amer. Amphibians* 27, *Amphiuma means.* . . Lamp or lamper eel. *Ibid* 28, *Amphiuma means tridactylum.* . . Lamp eel, lamper eel [Louisiana] . . three-toed amphiuma. **1958** Conant *Reptiles & Amphibians* 205, *Amphiuma means.* . . is the "congo (conger) eel," "lamper eel," or "ditch eel" of fishermen and country folk. (The same names are often applied to both species of *Siren.*) **1966** *DARE* (Qu. P3) Inf **MS**16, Lamper eel. **1969** *DARE* File **Okefenokee GA,** Lamper eel, or eel . . a round-bodied creature, about 5′ long [sic], with little black pieces sticking out behind the head.

lamperina n

A **hagfish 1** (here: *Polistotrema stouti*).

1896 U.S. Bur. Fisheries *Rept. for 1895* 211, *Polistotrema stouti* . . California Hagfish; Lamperina. Coast of California; Monterey. **1911** *Century Dict. Suppl., Lamperina.* . . [Amer. Sp.] A common name of *Polistotrema stouti,* one of the eel-like lower vertebrates found on the California coast and north to Cape Flattery. **1933** John G. Shedd Aquarium *Guide* 18, The hagfishes. . . *Polistotrema stoutii*—California Hagfish; Lamperina.

lamp fly See **lamp bug 2, 3**

lamp globe n Also *lantern globe*

See quots.

1905 *DN* 3.85 **nwAR,** *Lamp-globe.* . . Lamp-chimney. 'That kind of a lamp-globe breaks easy.' *Ibid* 86 **nwAR,** *Lantern-globe.* . . Glass chimney of a lantern. **1942** McAtee *Dial. Grant Co. IN* 39 **ceIN, AR, FL** (as of 1890s), *Lamp-globe.* . . lamp chimney. **1956** McAtee *Some Dialect NC* 26, *Lamp globe.* . . lamp chimney. **c1960** *Wilson Coll.* **csKY,** *Lamp-globe.* . . Lamp chimney.

lamplighter n

1 A strip of paper rolled into a spill and used to light lamps or pipes. **chiefly NEast** *old-fash*

1833 Neal *Down-Easters* 2.115 **NEng,** One side [of a sheet of writing paper] is clean, said she—and it will do for lamplighters. **1859** *Harper's New Mth. Mag.* 18.342 **NYC,** Mr. Beebe tore off the margin of the newspaper and commenced rolling a lamp-lighter after the most approved pattern. **1907** *DN* 3.192 **seNH,** *Lamplighter.* . . A narrow strip of paper rolled to form a taper. **1909** *DN* 3.343 **eAL, wGA,** *Lamplighter.* . . A paper spill. Also called *pipe-lighter.* **1910** *DN* 3.444 **wNY,** *Lamplighter.* . . A strip of paper rolled into a taper. Used to save matches. Older generation. **1912** *DN* 3.581 **wIN,** *Lamp-lighter.* . . A twisted paper used for lighting lamps and pipes. **1938** Damon *Grandma* 25 **CT** (as of late 19th cent), On every mantelpiece stood a vase filled with "lamplighters." These were cunningly twisted papers (no envelope fell to the floor that Grandma did not take notice of it), the making of which was one of the daily stents for us children.

2 in phr *like a lamplighter:* Fast, quickly. [Cf *EDD* (at *lamp* sb.¹ 1.(2)), and *OED* (at *lamplighter* 1)] **NEast** *old-fash*

1838 Neal *Charcoal Sketches* 193 **Philadelphia PA,** Make me spry and jump about like a lamp-lighter. **1843** (1916) Hall *New Purchase* 69 **PA,** The little bodies did climb up and down like lamp-lighters. **1848** in 1935 *AmSp* 10.42 **Nantucket MA,** Go like a lamplighter. Go quickly. **1903** *DN* 2.299 **Cape Cod MA** (as of a1857), *Lamp-lighter.* . . In expression 'go like a *lamplighter.*' To walk fast. **1904** *DN* 2.426 **Cape Cod MA** (as of a1857), *Like a lamplighter.* With long rapid strides. 'She went like a lamplighter.' **1941** *LANE* Map 474, 2 infs, **cVT, swNH,** When a person runs very fast he is said to run like . . *a lamplighter.*

3 =**crappie.**

1877 OH Comm. Fisheries *First Annual Rept.* 77, *P[omoxys] hexacanthus.* . . Strawberry Bass; . . Lamp-lighter, of Portsmouth; Grass Bass, of Kirtland. **1884** Goode *Fisheries U.S.* 1.336, This species [=*Po-*

moxys sparoides] is known by a variety of names. . . In Lake Erie, and in Ohio generally, it is the "Strawberry Bass," or "Grass Bass." The names "Bitter Head" and "Lamplighter" are also ascribed to it. **1892** Lummis *Tramp* 33, For three years I had been fairly starving for a bout with those beauties—a hunger which the catfish and "lamplighters" of Ohio had utterly failed to satisfy. **1947** Dalrymple *Panfish* 84, Here, my friend, are the various names by which you would address that little gamester, the Crappie, depending on where you happened to be at the moment: . . Lake Bass—Lake Erie Bass—Lamplighter. **1975** Evanoff *Catch More Fish* 90, The white crappie has been called . . lamplighter, and many other names. **1983** Becker *Fishes WI* 863, Black Crappie. . . lamplighter.

lamp-lighting vbl n Cf **jacklight** v

Hunting at night with a spotlight.

1968 *DARE* (Qu. P35b, *Illegal methods of shooting deer;* not asked in early QRs) Infs **PA**168, Lamp-lighting—using a spotlight out of season.

lamp oil n

1 Kerosene. [*OED* oil for burning in lamps; 1581 →] **scattered, but esp Appalachians** See Map Cf **carbon oil, coal oil**

c1937 in 1972 *Amer. Slave* 2.1.115 **SC** [Black], We 'lamp-oil chillun'; they 'lectric light' chillun now! We call our wedding 'lamp-oil wedding.' **1946** *PADS* 5.28 **VA,** *Lamp oil* . . Kerosene oil; in the southern parts of the Blue Ridge and the Piedmont. **1949** Kurath *Word Geog.* 60, *Lamp oil* [occurs] in Pennsylvania west of the Alleghenies, in West Virginia, and in the Virginia Piedmont. . . The present spread of *coal oil* and *lamp oil* must be connected somehow with the marketing areas of this product of Pennsylvania and northern West Virginia. **1954** Harder *Coll.* **cwTN,** *Lamp oil.* . . Kerosene. **1960** Hall *Smoky Mt. Folks* 52 **wNC, eTN,** For a remedy her sisters put "lamp oil" (kerosene) on a woolen cloth and placed the cloth on the chest. **1965–70** *DARE* (Qu. F45, . . *Fuel that's used in an ordinary lamp*) 34 Infs, **scattered, but esp Appalachians,** Lamp oil; (Qu. BB50a, . . *Favorite remedies . . for a cough*) Inf **KY**21, Lamp oil, turpentine, vinegar and grease—mixed and put on the chest and throat; (Qu. BB50c, *Remedies for infections*) Inf **VA**35, Lamp oil; **VA**42, Turpentine and lamp oil. **1966** Dakin *Dial. Vocab. Ohio R. Valley* 2.182, *Lamp oil.* . . is common along the Ohio River from the Big Sandy to Pennsylvania (and farther north in eastern Ohio) and in the Muskingum Valley. *Lamp oil* is almost unknown as far west as the Scioto River, however . . [and] is rare in Kentucky. **1990** Pederson *LAGS Regional Matrix* 66, [*Lamp oil*—21 of 31 infs giving this response are in **eTN** and **nGA.**]

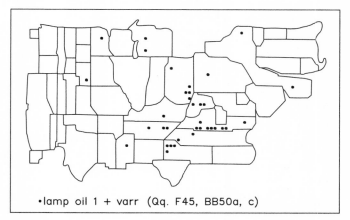

•lamp oil 1 + varr (Qq. F45, BB50a, c)

2 Whiskey.

1944 Adams *Western Words* 88, *Lamp oil*—A slang name for whisky. **1950** Faulkner *Stories* 757 **MS** [Black], "Where does yawl keep dat ere Tennessee spring water. . . Dat ere light colored lamp oil whut yawl drinks. Aint you got a little of it hid back here somewhere?" "Oh," the girl said, "You mean corn."

lamppost v

1959 *VT Hist.* 27.146, *Lamppost.* . . To talk. Rare.

lamprey n

Std: an eel-like creature of the family Petromyzontidae. Also called **lamper eel 1, lamprey ~ 1.** For other names of *Petromyzon marinus* see **eelpout 3, sea lamprey;** for other names of var freshwater genera and spp see **fish leech, mud eel 2, river lamprey, silver ~**

lamprey eel n

1 also *lamp eel:* =**lamprey.**

1704 in 1824 NH Hist. Soc. *Coll.* 1.31, Next day, they kill'd Edward Taylor near Lamprey-Eel River. **1789** Morse *Amer. Geog.* 208, About four miles northeast of Providence lies a small village . . famous for lamprey eels. **1844** Lee–Frost *10 Yrs. OR* 156, A fire was struck, some dried salmon and lamprey-eels roasted; and we sat down and made a good hearty Indian supper. **1885** *Amer. Naturalist* 19.922, The lamprey eel of Kansas . . proves to be usually the *chestnut* lamprey. **1903** NY State Museum & Sci. Serv. *Bulletin* 60.11, *Petromyzon marinus* . . Great Sea Lamprey; Lamprey Eel. **1947** Hubbs–Lagler *Fishes Gt. Lakes* 26, There is some confusion of lampreys with the eel, and lampreys are often called "lamprey eels." **1966–70** DARE (Qu. P3, *Freshwater fish that are not good to eat*) Inf **KY**93, Lamprey eel; **MI**120, [læmfri] eel; **TN**24, Lamp eel; (Qu. P4, *Saltwater fish that are not good to eat*) Inf **GA**12, Lamprey eel; (Qu. P6, . . *Kinds of worms . . used for bait*) Inf **NY**74, Lamprey eels—for bass. **1966–70** DARE Tape **MI**15, [FW:] You said trout streams are closed because of the weirs. What are those? [Inf:] The weirs are the things that they use to cut down the lamprey eel population. . . They're replanting Lake Superior with trout; **MI**109, Between the fishermen, the lamprey eel, and the shad, they just cleaned 'em up; **MI**120, One of those lamprey eels. . . They're like a big bloodsucker; they just stick onto a fish, and they kill fish that way; **WI**75, The eel that we have here is the lamprey eel. He's the fellow that sucks onto the fish and draws the blood of it. **1983** Becker *Fishes WI* 201, Silver Lamprey—*Ichthyomyzon unicuspis.* . . lamprey eel, lamper eel. *Ibid* 208, Chestnut Lamprey—*Ichthyomyzon castaneus.* . . lamprey eel, river lamprey, lamper. *Ibid* 211, Sea Lamprey—*Petromyzon marinus.* . . lamprey eel, lamper eel, lamper. *Ibid* 216, American Brook Lamprey—*Lampetra appendix.* . . lamprey eel.

2 The great **siren** (*Siren lacertina*). Cf **lamper eel 3**

1928 Baylor Univ. Museum *Contrib.* 16.9, Lamprey Eel. . . is the name the Siren assumes when it becomes the dreaded animal whose bite is considered to produce instant death. In common use throughout Louisiana and Texas east of the Trinity River. (The true Lamprey Eel is found in the same sections of country, but is known as the "Fish Leech").

lampshade n

1 See quots. Cf **lamp globe**

1946 PADS 6.19 **eNC** (as of 1900–10), Lamp shade. . . A lamp chimney. Pamlico. Common. **1954** *Harder Coll.* **cwTN**, Lampshade. . . a lamp chimney. **c1960** *Wilson Coll.* **csKY**, Lampshade. . . Lamp chimney, whether shaded or not.

2 also *lampshade plant:* Prob =**jimson weed.** Cf **nightshade 1**

1967 DARE (Qu. S17, . . *Kinds of plants . . that . . cause itching and swelling*) Inf **PA**26, Lampshade. **1995** NADS Letters **cwCA**, Could this be the plant that is called *floripondio* in Spanish? Some people here in California call a certain flowering plant a *lampshade plant,* because the white blossoms like [sic] much like the (glass?) protective covering for the bulb of a reading lamp.

lan' See land

lanai n Orig |ˈlɑnɑ-i|, now usu |laˈnaɪ, lə-|; for addit varr see quots [Haw] **chiefly HI** Note: Haw has only one liquid consonant, which early writers often represented with *r* rather than *l.*

A roofed structure with open sides built near or onto a house; a porch, veranda, or patio.

1823 (1970) Stewart *Jrl. Sandwich Is.* 97, The chiefs were all under one *ranai,* or rude bower. **1825** Ellis *Jrl. HI* 223, About 800 people . . assembled under a large *ranai,* (a place sheltered from the sun,) formed by two large canvas awnings, and a number of platted cocoanut leaves, spread over the place, from posts fixed in the fence which encloses the courtyard. **1838** in 1934 Frear *Lowell & Abigail* 124 **HI,** We soon found that the school house did not accomodate [sic] one half of the congregation; and we built a large *lanai* in the front yard and covered it with rushes to keep off the sun. **1897** Twain *Following Equator* 3.61 **HI,** Nearly every house [in Honolulu] has what is called a *lanai.* It is a large apartment, roofed, floored, open on three sides, with a door or a draped archway opening into the drawing-room. **1938** Reinecke *Hawaiian Loanwords* 21, Lanai [ˈlɑːˈnɑː-i]. . . A porch. V[ery] F[requent]. **1954–60** Hance et al. *Hawaiian Sugar* 4, Lanai [ˈlɑnɑ-i]—Veranda, porch. **1967–68** DARE (Qu. D17, . . *The platform, sometimes with a roof, that's built on the front or the side of a house*) Inf **CA**82, [ˈlʌnaɪ]—can be screened with roof; secluded area; **HI**1, Lanai—very common; **HI**4, [lɑˈnaɪ]; **HI**9, Lanai—small terrace or balcony to get the air. **1969** DARE File **Honolulu HI,** Lanai [ləˈnaɪ]—patio. *Lanai sale—*

what is commonly called a garage sale in Wisconsin. **1969** *New Yorker* 31 May 95, [Advt for a Boston hotel:] 1000 air-conditioned rooms, tower suites and lanais surrounding the . . swimming pool. **1971** Bright *Word Geog. CA & NV* 111, Lanai. . 'patio.' "Fancy, with chairs." "Glassed in, snazzy." . . "Outdoor living room." **1982** DARE File **cwFL,** "Lanai" . . is also used in Sun City Center, Florida. . . I believe this use was started by the developer. . . In cities . . which surround Sun City Center, the term isn't used.

lance v[1] Usu |læn(t)s|; also |lænč|; for addit varr see quots Pronc-spp *la(u)nch* [Cf OED launch v. 1.b "To cut with a lancet. . . Obs.," Pronc Intro 3.I.18] Cf **launch v[1], rinse**

Std sense, var forms.

1795 Dearborn *Columbian Grammar* 136, *List of Improprieties.* . . Launch'd for Lanced *(laid open).* **1810** (1912) Bell *Journey to OH* 3 **MA,** [She] has been ill five months with a swelling & she had come that afternoon to see it *launch'd* by the Physicians. **1899** (1912) Green *VA Folk-Speech* 255, Lanch. . . To lance. "I had a big gethering, the doctor lanched it, and all the stuff came out." **1954** *Harder Coll.* **cwTN,** Lanch [lænč] . . lance. . . "I'm a-gonna git t'at bone fellern lanched today." **1981** Pederson *LAGS Basic Materials* **Gulf Region,** 1 inf, [læ·ᶦntʃ]; 1 inf, [læ·ᵋnts]; 1 inf, Lanced [læ·ᵋntʃt]; 1 inf, Lanced [leᵊᵼntʃt].

lance v[2] See launch v[1]

lancewood n

A tree (*Ocotea coriacea*) native to southern Florida.

1884 Sargent *Forests of N. Amer.* 119, Lance Wood. . . Wood heavy, hard, close-grained, checking in drying, containing many small, regularly-distributed, open ducts. **1897** Sudworth *Arborescent Flora* 202 **FL,** *Ocotea catesbyana.* . . Lance Wood. **1933** Small *Manual SE Flora* 922, Lancewood. . . The dark-brown heartwood, hard and heavy, is used locally for cabinet-work. **1946** West–Arnold *Native Trees FL* 145, Lancewood. . . The dark-green, pleasantly aromatic leaves nearly all point downward, while both the fragrance of the flowers and the size of the fruits are conspicuous. **1961** Douglas *My Wilderness* 147 **Everglades FL,** The woods that fringe this hammock are strange to most of us. Lancewood, ironwood, inkwood, gumbo limbo—these were all new to me. **1979** Little *Checklist U.S. Trees* 176, *Nectandra coriacea* . . Florida nectandra. . . Other common names—Jamaica nectandra, lancewood.

lanch v[1] See lance v[1]

lanch n, v[2] See launch v[1]

land n Pronc-sp *lan'* [Orig euphem for *Lord;* now often understood in literal sense] Cf **landy**

In var exclam phrr: See quots.

1834 Davis *Letters Downing* 232, 'For the land's sake,' says I, 'jist look at it.' **1848** Cooper *Oak-Openings* 1.82 **MI,** Land's sake! I've forgotten all about them barrels! **1850** (1852) Warner *Wide World* 1.167 **NY,** "But what are they called turnpikes for?" "The land knows!—I don't." **1865** (1889) Whitney *Gayworthys* 324 **NEng,** Land alive! Why, Grace, child, what's happened [sic] you? **1880** *Harper's New Mth. Mag.* 62.91 **NEng,** Land! ef I was to set sail on them seas o' divinity, I should be. . drownded right off. **1885** Howells *Rise Lapham* 315, What in the land *did* he want? **1885** Jackson *Zeph* 17, Land o' the livin'! What a hole! **1886** Stapleton *Major's Christmas* 95 (DA), Good land a mercy, she's been gone to New York these three months! **1889** Twain *CT Yankee* 132, Good land! a man can't keep his functions regular on spring chickens thirteen hundred years old. **1894** Twain *Pudd'nhead Wilson* 98 **eMO** [Black], My lan', what de reason 't ain't enough? **1903** DN 2.299 **Cape Cod MA** (as of a1857), 'Land! I could do that in five minutes.' . . 'For the land sakes, stop that racket.' **1904** Day *Kin o' Ktaadn* 52 **ME,** Land o' Goshen how things bother! **1906** DN 3.144 **nwAR,** Land's aliving. **1907** DN 3.427 **eME,** My land. . . Common oath among women for *My Lord.* **1909** DN 3.343 **eAL, wGA,** Land-sakes (alive). . . Sometimes *land sakes a livin(g).* **1914** DN 4.75 **nNH, ME,** Lan' sakes! *Lansy sake-a-Peter!* Common exclamations with women. *Ibid* 77, My land o' livin'! Exclamation of surprise among women. **1917** DN 4.395 **neOH,** Land! good land! my land! (for) (the) land sake(s). . . *Land-a-massy!* **1931** PMLA 46.1308 **sAppalachians,** Land warm it! **1957** VT Hist. 27.146, Land of Goshen!: interj. Occasional. *Land of Liberty!* . . Occasional. *Land of Love!* . . Rare. *Land sakes!* . . Common. *Land sakes alive!* . . Common. **1965–70** DARE (Qu. NN29b, *Exclamations beginning with 'land':* "Land _____!") 810 Infs, **widespread,** Sake(s) [and var phrr: see DS]; 151 Infs, **widespread,** O'Goshen [and var phrr: see DS]; 58 Infs, **scattered,** O' livin' [and var phrr: see DS]; 42 Infs, scattered, O' mercy [and var phrr: see *DS*]; 31 Infs, scattered, Alive [and var phrr: see *DS*]; 23 Infs, scattered, O' goodness [and var phrr: see *DS*]; 20 Infs, scattered, O' heaven (*or* love, Moses, shuckin', etc); 14 Infs, scattered, O' mighty [and var phrr: see *DS*]; **AR**51, **CO**33, **NY**92, **WI**52, My land; **IN**49, **MD**34, **NC**51, Knows; **MD**25, Above; **OH**49, Good land; (Qq. NN1, 2, 7, 9a, 27a, 28a, 29a, c) 34 Infs, scattered, but more freq Midl, Lands [and var phrr: see *DS*]; 27 Infs, scattered, but more freq Midl, Land [and var phrr: see *DS*]; 7 Infs, Land o' Goshen; 4 Infs, Land sakes [and var phrr: see *DS*]; **CA**15, Land of good; **MO**37, Land o' living; **GA**77, Lands of livin'; **VA**69, Land of Moses; (Qu. NN27b, *Weakened substitutes for 'god'*: "For _____ sakes!") 29 Infs, scattered, Land; 16 Infs, scattered, Lands. **1986** Pederson *LAGS Concordance* Gulf Region, 26 infs, Land sake(s); 2 infs, Land's sake(s); 2 inf, Land of Goshen; 2 inf, Oh, (good) land; 1 inf, Oh land of rest; 1 inf, Oh, my, land.

land-baist v [Folk-etym for *lambaste*]
    1975 Gould *ME Lingo* 158, *Land-baisted*—Maine variant of lambasted.

land chicken n Cf **gopher** n¹ **1a, land turtle**
=chicken turtle.
    1966 *DARE* (Qu. P29, . . '*Gophers*' . . *other name . . or what other animal are they most like*) Inf **FL**1, Hard-shell, land turtles, or land chickens.

land cress See **cress**

land doctor n
    1950 *PADS* 14.43 **seSC** [Black], *Land doctor*. . . An engineer or surveyor. He is supposed to cut up the land, as a doctor cuts up people. . . Charleston.

land dressing See **dressing 5**

lander n¹ [*EDD* *lander* sb. "A heavy blow"]
    1966 *DARE* (Qu. Y11, . . *A very hard blow*: "*You should have seen Bill go down. Joe really hit him a _____.*") Inf **NM**12, Lander.

lander n² [Cf quot 1975]
A downspout.
    1941 *Language* 17.333 **WI** [*LANCS* fieldwork], *Gutter*. . *Landers* 1 [of 50 infs]. . . He says it was his mother's word. [*DARE* Ed: Inf's mother was from Wales.] Several other informants use this to mean downspout. [**1975** Mather-Speitel *Ling. Atlas Scotl.* 1.245, *Gutter (the kind running along the side of a paved street)*. . . Lander [1 inf, **nEng**]. *Ibid* 251, *Gutter (the kind running along the edge of a roof)*. . . Lander [1 inf, **nEng**].]

land frog n chiefly Midl, C Atl See Map Cf **frog** n **B1, dry-land frog, highland frog, land toad**
A **toad,** esp *Bufo americanus*.
    1743 Catesby *Nat. Hist. Carolina* 2.69, *Rana terrestris*. The Land Frog. . . Their Bodies are large, resembling more a Toad than a Frog, yet they do not crawl as Toads do, but leap. **1791** Bartram *Travels* 195 **eFL**, They [=snakes] prey on rats, land frogs, young rabbits, birds, &c. **1896** IL Ag. Exper. Sta. Urbana *Bulletin* 3.337, The entire build of these two specimens [of *Bufo lentiginosus* var *lentiginosus*] is suggestive of the appropriateness of the name "land frog." **1965–70** *DARE* (Qu. P23, *Names for the animal similar to the frog that lives away from water*) Infs **IL**89, **MD**40, **NY**198, 220, **PA**240, **TN**34, **VA**73, **WV**10, 12, 13, 14, Land frog; **MD**31, Toad frog, land frog; **TN**36, Toad, land frog;

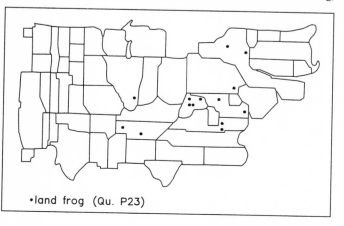
•land frog (Qu. P23)

VA70, Land frog, toad frog—no difference. **1966** Dakin *Dial. Vocab. Ohio R. Valley* 2.391, A speaker in Cincinnati and another in the northern American Bottom say *land frog* [for *toad*]. It may be only coincidence, but both instances of this usage are from areas of heavy German settlement. **1981** Pederson *LAGS Basic Materials*, 2 infs, nwLA, cTX, Land frogs.

land-horse n [Engl, Scots dial; cf *EDD* (at *land* sb.¹ 1.(24)), *SND* (at *land* I.2.(1)(v))] Cf **furrow horse, lead horse**
In plowing: the horse that treads on the unplowed ground.
    1966–67 *DARE* (Qu. K32b, *The horse on the left side in plowing or hauling*) Inf **MI**2, In plowing, the land-horse (as opposed to the furrow horse); **OH**22, 30, Land-horse. **1967** Faries *Word Geog. MO* 96, To distinguish the left from the right horse in a team, the Missouri informants use a variety of regional expressions, the most prevalent of which are *lead horse* . . (291 occurrences) and *near horse* (195 occurrences). . . substitute expressions . . are *off horse* (18 occurrences) . . *land horse* [2 occurrences].

landing n
1 In logging: an area or platform where logs are collected in preparation for loading and transport; the logs so collected; see quots. **chiefly Nth**
    1851 (1856) Springer *Forest Life* 156 **neME**, In forming a landing on the margin of such streams, the trees and bushes are cut and cleared out of the way for several rods back, and a considerable distance up and down, according to the number of logs to be hauled into it. **1905** U.S. Forest Serv. *Bulletin* 61.41 [Logging terms], *Landing*. . . *1*. A place to which logs are hauled or skidded preparatory to transportation by water or rail. A *rough and tumble landing* is one in which no attempt is made to pile the logs regularly. . . *2*. A platform, usually at the foot of a skid road, where logs are collected and loaded on cars. A *lightning landing* is one having such an incline that the logs may roll upon the cars without assistance. **1907** *DN* 3.246 **eME**, *Landing*. . . A heap of logs beside a stream or on its ice, ready to be floated down stream. **1925** *AmSp* 1.135 **ME, MI, MN**, "Choppers" go out in the winter to fell and trim the trees. The trees are hauled over iced roads to "landings" by the rivers. **1958** McCulloch *Woods Words* 103 **Pacific NW**, *Landing*—Supposedly flat ground to which logs are yarded, to be loaded on cars or trucks; a collecting point for logs. **1966–67** *DARE* Tape **ME**26, When we did come down and come out into main river, we went back up to what they call the big run. . . that's where the big landing was. There was 9,000 cords of pulp there. *Ibid* **OR**1, The landing man unhooks the chokers, paints the logs, and knocks the bolts and the knots off. **1968** *DARE* FW Addit **WI**59, *Landing*—A place where logs are piled during the winter; located near a river; logs enter the river from this point in the spring. Used in the logging camps in and around Antigo. **1975** Gould *ME Lingo* 158, *Landing* . . a timberland term for a place to unload and store logs, a *brow*.
2 A porch; see quots.
    1964 O'Hare *Ling. Geog. E. MT* 69, A raised platform at the front or back door of a house. . . landing [without roof]. **1967–70** *DARE* (Qu. D17, . . *The platform, sometimes with a roof, that's built on the front or the side of a house*) Infs **GA**23, **OH**81, **PA**235, Landing; **AL**14, Front landing—without a top or roof. **1971** Wood *Vocab. Change* 382 **LA**, *Landing* . . : small porch. **1973** Allen *LAUM* 1.174 **MN** (as of c1950), *Porch*. . . landing [2 infs]. **1981** *PADS* 67.20 **neMN**, *Porch*. . . The usual term for Iron Range informants . . is the general *porch*, which is also used by all the other Minnesota informants. . . Infrequent Mesabi variants are *entrance* (2 occ[urrences]), *landing* (1 occ[urrence]). **1986** Pederson *LAGS Concordance*, 1 inf, **ceAL**, A landing—a small porch; 1 inf, **neFL**, A landing—like [a] porch, but halfway up the house.

land locator See **locator**

landlocked salmon n
1 also *landlock (salmon)*: The lake-dwelling Atlantic **salmon** (*Salmo salar*). **NEast, esp NEng**
    1869 U.S. Dept. Ag. *Rept. of Secy. for 1868* 324 **MA**, The taking of trout and land-locked salmon by any other means than by hook and hand-line is prohibited. **1886** Mather *Memoranda* 32 **NY**, Difference in size is commonly very great, land-locked salmon in general being but one-fourth or one-fifth the size of the river or sea salmon. **1901** Thompson *In Maine Woods* 7 (*DA*), Nowhere in Maine can the land-locked salmon . . be found more plentiful than at Sebec and Onama Lakes. **1904** *Salmon & Trout* [facing p75], [Caption:] Head of landlock salmon in spawning season. **1935** Perry *And Gladly Teach* 151 **MA**, The lake was perfect for bathing and boating. There were big 'square-

tails' in it then, and plenty of landlocked salmon and 'lakers.' **1966–70** *DARE* (Qu. P1, . . *Kinds of freshwater fish . . caught around here . . good to eat*) Infs **CT9, ME10, MA97, NY1, 10, 92, 93,** Landlocked salmon. **1972** Sparano *Outdoors Encycl.* 352, *Common Names:* Land-locked salmon, landlock. . . *Salmo salar sebago.* . . The landlocked salmon is very similar in coloration and general appearance to the Atlantic salmon of which the landlock is a subspecies. **1989** Mosher *Stranger* 295 **nVT** (as of 1952), I'd troll a big red-and-white spoon slowly . . , sometimes picking up a smallmouth bass or a land-locked salmon or two.

2 The lake-dwelling **sockeye salmon.** Cf **kokanee (salmon)**
    [**1939** Natl. Geogr. Soc. *Fishes* 287, Some of the red salmon are landlocked in lakes, never going to sea, although they could. These landlocked red salmon, or redfish, may be caught in Lake Washington, at Seattle. . . While in the lake they pass under the name of "silver trout."] **1967** *DARE* (Qu. P1, . . *Kinds of freshwater fish . . caught around here . . good to eat*) Inf **CO9,** Kokanee—landlocked salmon; **OR13,** Landlocked salmon.

3 =**lake trout 1.**
    1943 Eddy–Surber *N. Fishes* 93, The lake trout . . is frequently called a "landlocked salmon" by anglers, but it is a misnomer, for this name properly belongs to the landlocked variety of the Atlantic salmon. . . The color of the flesh also varies from almost white in some inland lakes to a deep pink in Lake Superior. **1949** Caine *N. Amer. Sport Fish* 66, *Lake Trout.* . . *Colloquial Names* . . Landlocked Salmon. **1983** Becker *Fishes WI* 323, *Salvelinus namaycush namaycush.* . . Great Lakes trout . . salmon trout . . landlocked salmon . . forktail trout.

landlock salmon See **landlocked salmon 1**

landlooker n
1 A land agent or speculator.
    1840 *Knickerbocker* 16.206 **MI,** Another class of operators . . became popularly known as 'land-lookers.' These meet you at every turn, ready to furnish 'water-power,' 'pine-lots,' 'choice farming tracts,' or any thing else, at a moment's notice. **1887** *Courier–Jrl.* (Louisville KY) 2 Feb 5/4, The country [=Summertown TN] is full of land prospectors, most of whom are buying. . . Most of these land-lookers come from the great Northwest, the rich and beautiful state of Iowa contributing her full share. **1929** *AmSp* 5.152 **cNY,** The landlookers of Hamilton were Quakers. **1958** [see **2** below].
2 =**cruiser 1.**
    1891 *Voice* 15 Oct. (*DAE*), I took what woodsmen call a 'land-looker,' i.e. a timber expert whose business it is to locate pine timber land in Michigan. **1900** Bruncken *N. Amer. Forests* 81, This [=the absence of pine timber in accessible places] has given rise to a peculiar class of people variously known as woodsmen, cruisers, landlookers, whose business it is to give information as to the existence of pine timber, its location, amount, value. **1911** (1913) Johnson *Highways Gt. Lakes* 265, I must tell you about the land-lookers or timber-cruisers. **1957** Steuber *Landlooker* 273 **nIL** (as of c1870), "Up in the pine country [of WI] is a special trade. Strong men that walk alone in the woods to only look and decide. You know, Emil, the name of the trade?" "Sure, Pa, that's the landlooker. He goes into the timber ahead of any crews or even before it's been bought and makes up his mind what it amounts to and whether they should go after it or not." **1958** McCulloch *Woods Words* 103 **Pacific NW,** *Land looker.* . . A timber cruiser. . . An appraiser. . . A real estate man buying timber land on commission. **1969** Sorden *Lumberjack Lingo* 69 **NEng, Gt Lakes,** *Land looker*—A man who estimates standing timber. Same as cruiser, estimator, valuer.

landlooking vbl n Cf **look** v **B1a**
Inspecting and evaluating land, esp for its suitability for settlement or timber harvest.
    1839 Thompson *Green Mt. Boys* 2.146 **VT,** Remington seemed suddenly to become convinced that it would not be prudent to proceed any farther in the land-looking excursion, which he stated was his business to the north. **1902** Hulbert *Forest Neighbors* xiii **nMI,** Some thirty years ago, while out on one of his landlooking trips in the woods of Northern Michigan, my father came upon a little lake. **1948** Dick *Dixie Frontier* 64 **MS** (as of c1820–30), Several hundred persons were engaged in this business, known as land-hunting or land-looking.

land otter n [*DCan* 1828 →] esp **AK, Pacific NW**
=**river otter.**
    1844 Lee–Frost *10 Yrs. OR* 71 **Pacific NW,** Beaver was valued at two dollars per skin, . . land otter at fifty cents. **1899** U.S. Bur. Amer. Ethnology *Annual Rept. for 1896–97* 232 **AK,** In very early days, . . the skin of the full-grown land otter was considered the unit of value.

Equaling it was the skin of the large hair seal. Of late years the skin of the beaver has replaced the otter skin as the unit of trade value. **1947** Cahalane *Mammals* 200, The river or land otter has the outline of a small seal or a very big weasel. **1961** Jackson *Mammals WI* 382, *Lutra canadensis.* . . In Wisconsin, commonly called otter; other vernacular names include American otter, common otter . . fisher . . land otter . . river otter, and waterdog. **1962** Salisbury *Quoth the Raven* 214 **seAK,** The spirit of the drowned was supposed to be caught and dragged into a hole in the bottom of the sea by a land otter, where it became a goosh-ta-kah (hobgoblin), which was never warm. **1968** *DARE* Tape **AK11,** The natives from . . the Canadian side. . . would come down the river into Juneau and bring the furs. . . They had very beautiful furs: white fox, silver fox, blue fox, black fox, lynx and land otter and mink and marten and sable.

land pike n
A hog such as a **razorback hog;** see quots.
    1840 *Cultivator* 7.82 **IA,** I am a most sincere hater of alligators and landpikes [=wood hogs]. **1842** *Ibid* 10.37, Hogs, Landpike variety, are so cheap that stealing them is no longer petit larceny. **1879** U.S. Dept. Ag. *Special Rept.* 12.189 **FL,** I have not learned of a single person having an improved breed of pigs. All depend on the "razorback" or "land pike." **1890** *AN&Q* 5.21, I think the term *land-pike* more frequently designates a thin, lank, half-wild swine. **1972** Hilliard *Hog Meat* 102, The actual reproduction of the semiwild "land pike" will never be known accurately, but it is possible to get some idea of litter size and survival rates by examples extracted from the periodical literature and plantation documents.

land plow See **landside plow**

land rain n [Calque of Ger *Landregen* (PaGer *landrejje, landregge*) a steady rain] *old-fash*
A rainfall; see quots.
    1950 *WELS* (*A light rain*) 1 Inf, **cWI,** Land rain—old-fashioned, used by Germans. **1967–68** *DARE* (Qu. B23, . . *A light rain that doesn't last . . it's just a* _____) Inf **PA63,** Land rain; (Qu. B25, . . *Joking names . . for a very heavy rain.* . . "*It's a regular* _____.") Inf **PA146,** Land rain—one that lasts two or three days. [Both Infs old]

land's end n [By ext from std sense]
See quot 1950.
    1950 *WELS* (*Joking names or nicknames for an out-of-the-way place or an unimportant village*) 1 Inf, **csWI,** Land's end. **1951** Johnson *Resp. to PADS 20* **DE,** Land's end.

landside plow n Also *land plow* [*landside* the part of a plow that presses against the unplowed ground and resists the sideward pressure on the moldboard] esp **NEng, TN, KY** Cf **turning plow**
Prob a moldboard plow.
    1968–70 *DARE* (Qu. L18, *Kinds of plows*) Infs **MA66, 75,** Landside plow; **KY27, NY68,** Land plow; **CT29,** Landside plow—only plowed one way, turned sod in set direction; **MA74,** Landside [plow]—a walking plow that went round and round the field; **KY49,** Land plow—same as turning plow. [All Infs old] **1986** Pederson *LAGS Concordance (Plows)* 1 inf, **cnTN,** Landside [plow]; 2 infs, **neTN,** Landside plow(s). [2 infs old, 1 mid-aged]

land-soaker See **sod-soaker**

land terrapin See **land turtle**

land toad n Cf **land frog, tree toad**
=**toad** (here: *Bufo* spp).
    1939 *LANE* Map 232 (*Toad*) 1 inf, **seCT,** Land toad. **1950** *WELS* (*The animal like a frog that lives away from water*) 1 Inf, **cWI,** Land toad—common. **1968** *DARE* (Qu. P23) Inf **IA22,** Toads—tree toads, land toads.

land turtle n Also *land terrapin,* ~ *tortoise* **scattered, but chiefly N Midl, C Atl** See Map Cf **dry-land turtle**
Usu a **box turtle** (here: *Terrapene* spp), but occas also other turtles such as a **gopher** n[1] **1a**; see quots.
    1607 (1910) Smith *Travels & Wks.* 1.xlix **VA,** He made ready a land turtle which we eate. **1688** in 1695 Royal Soc. London *Philos. Trans. for 1694* 18.125 **VA,** They have great store both of Land and Water Tortoises. **1709** (1967) Lawson *New Voyage* 138 **NC, SC,** The Land-Terebin is of several Sizes, but generally Round-Mouth'd, and not Hawks-Bill'd. **1838** Geol. Surv. OH *Second Annual Rept.* 188, C[*hely*-dra] *serpentina.* It is universally known as the *snapping turtle, the mud*

turtle, or the land turtle. **1842** DeKay *Zool. NY* 3.25, This beautiful species [=*Cistuda carolina*], which is designated in this State under the names of *Box Tortoise* and *Land Turtle,* and in the west by the name of *Lock Tortoise,* is a very gentle and timid animal. **1928** Baylor Univ. Museum *Contrib.* 16.21 **TX,** Painted Box Tortoise . . Three-toed Box Tortoise. . Both of the above box tortoises are known as *Land Terrapins* and *Box Turtles.* **1935** Pratt *Manual Vertebrate Animals* 239, *Gopherus* [spp] . . Land tortoises. . all herbivorous and strictly terrestrial. **1938** Rawlings *Yearling* 91 **nFL,** The small dusty land turtles whose deep burrows were an indication of the poorest soil, were the last food most inhabitants of the scrub considered edible. **1951** Johnson *Resp. to PADS* 20 **DE** (*Kinds of turtles*) Land turtles, lower Delaware. **1957** Battaglia *Resp. to PADS* 20 **eMD** (*Kinds of turtles*) Land turtle. **1958** Conant *Reptiles & Amphibians* 43, Both other "land turtles" occurring within the range of Wood Turtle (Blanding's and Eastern Box) have strongly hinged plastrons. **1965–70** *DARE* (Qu. P24, . . *Kinds of turtles*) 111 Infs, **scattered, but chiefly N Midl, C Atl,** Land turtle; **MA**15, Land turtle—little, spotted; **MA**58, Small land turtle; **MA**68, Land turtle—black with yellow speckles; **NJ**8, Land turtle—like box turtle, but with a higher shell; **NJ**13, Woods turtle—also called land turtle; **NJ**17, 53, **PA**28, Land turtle [same as] box turtle; **NY**233, Black and yellow land turtle; **IL**17, **IN**83, **MD**29, 34, **VA**55, Land terrapin; **DE**3, **MD**45, Land terrapin [same as] box terrapin; **FL**34, **IN**27, **OH**56, Land tortoise; **OH**58, Land tarpin; [(Qu. P29, . . *'Gophers' . . other name . . or what other animal are they most like*) Infs **FL**34, **GA**3, 7, 11, 12, 16, 34, 47, 91, **NY**101, Land tortoise; **AL**17, Land tortoise—a turtle that doesn't live in water; **AL**22, Gopher = land tortoise; they don't use the term; **FL**51, Land tortoise [FW sugg]—don't say here, though that is right name; **FL**18, Land tortoise—has hard shell; like turtles, but live on land; **NC**72, Land tortoise—gopher here = tarrypin; **FL**1, 4, 6, 20, 24, 29, **GA**19, Land turtle]. **1971** Bright *Word Geog. CA & NV* 187, *Terrapin—turtle* 63% [of 300 infs]. . *tortoise* 16%. . *land turtle* 15%. **1982** *Barrick Coll.* **csPA,** Land turtle—any of several varieties, including box turtle, wood turtle and spotted turtle. **1986** Pederson *LAGS Concordance* (*Something like a turtle only it lives on dry land*) 39 infs, **Gulf Region,** Land turtle(s); 1 inf, **cnAL,** Land turtle = terrapin; smaller, eats bugs; 1 inf, **cwFL,** Land turtle = freshwater turtle; 2 infs, **cnLA, cTN,** Land terrapin; 2 infs, **csTN, neFL,** Land tortoise; 1 inf, **csTX,** Land turtles—can't be eaten.

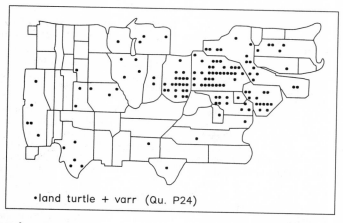

•land turtle + varr (Qu. P24)

land worm n
=**earthworm.**

1967–69 *DARE* (Qu. P5, . . *The common worm used as bait*) Infs **MO**38, **RI**1, Land worm.

landy n Pronc-sp *lansy* [Euphem for *Lordy;* cf **land**]
In var exclam phrr: See quots.

1877 Jewett *Deephaven* 194 **NEng,** 'Landy!' said she, 'if it ain't old Parson Lorimer!' **1909** Porter *Girl Limberlost* 70 **IL,** 'Landy, ain't I a queen?' she murmured. **1914** *DN* 4.75 **ME, nNH,** Lansy sake-a-Peter! Common exclamations with women. **1966** *DARE* (Qu. NN29b, *Exclamations beginning with 'land':* "Land _____!") Inf **NM**11, Landy sakes.

Lane cake n [Etym uncert, but see quot 1985] **Sth, esp AL, GA**
A layer cake with a rich filling often including nuts, raisins, and brandy.

1951 Brown *Southern Cook Book* 249, Mrs. Merrill's Lane Cake—Four layers—Many Southern states claim the famous Lane Cake, which is similar to the "Rocky Mountain Cake," made extensively in the

Carolinas. The difference is in the filling. The Lane Cake has a rich egg-yolk filling with coconut, raisins, and nuts, while the filling for the Rocky Mountain Cake is generally white. It is said that this cake originated in Eufaula, Alabama. **1952** Tracy *Coast Cookery* 51 **GA,** Lane Cake. **1960** (1962) Lee *Mockingbird* 78 **AL,** I'll make him a Lane cake. That Stephanie's been after my recipe for thirty years. **1979** *DARE* File **GA** (as of 1970), After telling me of a "fantastic" dessert called "Aunt Lottie's Lane Cake," my roommate returned from her home in New Orleans with a sample. It was indeed a treat—an extremely rich cake made with layers of pecan filling and flavored with brandy. It was apparently traditional in her community, and other Southern friends were familiar with it. **1980** *DARE* File **Nashville TN,** Lane cake recipe. **1985** *WI Alumnus Letters,* [Quoting *Chicago Tribune* article c1960:] Who really did invent Lane Cake and what is the original recipe? Emma Rylander Lane who lived in Clayton, Ala. wrote a cookbook called "A Few Good Things to Eat," published in 1898, which included Mrs. Lane's "prize recipe." . . Lane Cake was served at holiday teas when guests came visiting. [*DARE* Ed: Recipe is for a rich white cake with boiled white frosting and a filling of egg yolks, sugar, butter, raisins, bourbon or brandy, and vanilla.] *Ibid* **cAL,** Lane cake is a traditional holiday dessert down here. . Although I have eaten lane cake all my life, I have never heard the origin of the name. In fact, I've never even thought about it! By the way, it should be made with *homemade* brandy—peach or apple. **1986** Pederson *LAGS Concordance,* 1 inf, **swAL,** Lane cake—layer cake.

lane daisy n
A **black-eyed Susan 2.**

1969 *DARE* (Qu. S7, *A kind of daisy, bright yellow with a dark center, that grows along roadsides in late summer*) Inf **KY**21, Lane daisy.

lane drop n
See quots.

1989 *DARE* File **swMA,** While driving near Stockbridge . . I encountered a road sign: "Lane Drop Ahead." . . It referred to a lane ending, narrowing from two lanes to one. Subsequently, I saw the same sign on another road in this area. **1991** *Ibid* **nwMA** (as of c1960–91), A frequently seen road sign in the hilly parts of Mass. reads "Lane Drop Ahead." As all Mass. residents know, this is a warning that the climbing lane will merge in with the traveling lane shortly. This has been a common and official State road sign, used whenever the road will be narrowed, hilly section or not, for as long as I can remember.

langijer See **languager**

lang(th) See **lank**

languager n Pronc-sp *langijer* [*OED* "Obs. rare."]
=**linguister.**

1928 Chapman *Happy Mt.* 312 **seTN,** Linkster—interpreter, letter-reader for the illiterate (languager). **1940** *AmSp* 15.46 **sAppalachians,** The obsolete *linkister,* usually pronounced *link'ster,* sometimes *lingister* or *ling'ster,* is an interpreter in the Great Smokies and Cumberlands, while in the Blue Ridge you may hear him called a *langijer.*

langue de boeuf n Cf **bull tongue 2**
An **arrowhead 1** (here: *Sagittaria lancifolia*).

1942 *Torreya* 42.157 **LA,** *Sagittaria lancifolia* . . Bull-tongue, langue du [sic] boeuf.

languid lady n
=**bluebell 1g.**

1915 (1926) Armstrong–Thornber *Western Wild Flowers* 430, Languid Lady, Lungwort—*Mertensia sibirica*. . . The flowers are in handsome loose clusters, most of them drooping. **1937** [see **lungwort 1**]. **1949** Moldenke *Amer. Wild Flowers* 257, The languidlady, *M. foliosa,* is a smooth thick-leaved species of the hills and canyons from the Dakotas to Utah. **1957** Roberts–Nelson *Wildflowers CO* 40, It [=*Mertensia lanceolata*] is eight to ten inches high and seems to be walking in a droopy fashion, hence its name "languid lady." **1966** Barnes–Jensen *Dict. UT Slang* 28, Languid lady . . a local name given the Mertensia (*Mertensia foliosa*).

languister See **linguister**

laniappe, laniyap See **lagniappe**

lank adj Also *lang(th), lanky* [By ext from std *lank* gaunt, meager]
Hungry.

1968 Adams *Western Words* 172, *Lank inside*—A logger's expression meaning that he is hungry. **1977** in 1982 *Barrick Coll.* **csPA,** *Lank—hungry*[·] "I was feelin' a little lank. I didn't have no breakfast." **1982**

Smithsonian Letters **cwWV** (as of c1930), For the past five or six years I have secretly recorded some of the unusual phrases that continually pop up in my mother's conversation. She is seventy years old, grew up in Doddridge County, W.Va. . . getting lēngth = becoming hungry. **1992** *DARE* File **WV,** [From writer of quot 1982:] My stepmother . . was born (1919) and grew up in the same neighborhood in Doddridge County, West Virginia. . . My stepmother told me, "Ever since I was a kid, I've heard 'lank' or 'lang' or 'lanky' meaning 'my stomach's empty.' Back when I was young, it meant your stomach was weak or you was weak because your stomach was empty." My father (who was born in 1910 in Barbour County, West Virginia . .) told me . . : "That just means you're getting hungry." He . . says he has only heard it pronounced "lank" and never "length." I spoke to an elderly West Virginia man . . who was familiar with the term "length" and told me he had used it since his youth to signify being hungry.

lank down v phr [Cf *OED* lank v. 2 "To become lank or shrunken"; 1606]
To become sparing or frugal.
1935 Davis *Honey* 2 **OR,** The old people . . went right on living at their ordinary clip, neither able to put on any extra dog in the good times nor obliged to lank down and live frugal in the bad ones.

lanky See **lank**

lannon stone n **WI**
A limestone originally associated with quarries in Lannon, Wisconsin.
1950 *WELS* **WI** (*Kinds of stones*) 3 Infs, Lannon stone; 1 Inf, Lannon stone—a building stone that comes from quarries in a range from Fond du Lac to Lannon, Wisconsin. **1968** *DARE* (Qu. C26, . . *Special kinds of stone or rock*) Infs **WI**35, 47, 50, 62, Lannon stone. **1994** *DARE* File **seWI,** I would have liked to use the well-known lannon stone for the new house we built in Racine in 1941, but couldn't afford it; instead, I used fieldstone collected on a local farm over two or three generations.

lanny-yap See **lagniappe**

lansy See **landy**

lant n [Prob back-formation from *lance,* interpreted as *lants; DNE* 1620 →]
=sand lance.
1884 U.S. Natl. Museum *Bulletin* 27.415, *Ammodytes personatus.* . . Sand Launce; Lant. Monterey Bay and Puget Sound . . ; entire coast of Alaska north to Point Belcher. . . This little fish plays a very important part in the cod fishery, because of its great abundance and the greediness with which cod feed upon it. **1884** Goode *Fisheries U.S.* 1.244, Of all the small species of fishes occurring in the North Atlantic there is probably none more important to man than the Lant—Launce, as it is called in Europe, frequently also the Sand-eel both in Europe and America. **1897** NY Forest Fish & Game Comm. *Annual Rept. for 1896* 235, *Ammodytes americanus.* . . Sand Launce, Sand Eel; Lant.—The species appears in Gravesend Bay in July, but is more plentiful in Maine. **1911** U.S. Bur. Census *Fisheries 1908* 311, *Lant (Ammodytes americanus).*—A small fish found on the north Atlantic coast, probably as far south as Maryland, and *A. personatus* in California and Alaska.

lantana n
Std: a plant of the genus *Lantana.* For other names of var spp see **polecat geranium, tea plant, Texas lantana**

lantern n Also, by metath, *lantrun, lattren* [Cf *OED* lantren "obs."; cf Intro "Language Changes" I.1]
Std sense, var forms.
1913 *DN* 4.4 **cME,** *Lantrun.* . . Lantern. **1970** Hyatt *Hoodoo* 1.35 **neFL** (as of c1935) [Black], He [=a railroad night watchman] disappeared—dey found his lattren [Hyatt: lantern] an' all by a hole dere.

lanterned-jawed See **lantern-jawed**

lantern flower n
=desert fivespot.
1941 Jaeger *Wildflowers* 142, *Malvastrum rotundifolium.* . . The globular corolla, with its fine [sic] red spots on the inner bases of the petals, suggested its local names of "lantern flower" and "five-spot."

lantern globe See **lamp globe**

lantern-jawed adj Rarely *lanterned-jawed* [*OED* (at lantern jaws) a1700–1865]

Having long, thin jaws or a prominent lower jaw.
1899 (1912) Green *VA Folk-Speech* 255, *Lantern-jawed.* . . Having lantern jaws [=long, thin jaws]; having a long, thin face. **1919** *DN* 5.72 **NM,** *Lanterned-jawed,* a long faced person. "They are all lanterned jawed." **1930** Shoemaker *1300 Words* 38 **cPA Mts** (as of c1900), *Lantern-jawed*—Projecting jaws. **1936** (1972) Ise *Sod & Stubble* 233 **KS** (as of c1890s), One of the teachers, a tall, angular, lantern-jawed tyrant, affectionately nicknamed "Slats" by the boys, was more than commonly rigorous in her discipline. **1950** *PADS* 14.43 **SC,** *Lantern-jawed.* . . Having long thin jaws and hollow cheeks. **1950** *WELS* (*If a person's lower jaw sticks out, you say he is _____*) 22 Infs, **WI,** Lantern-jawed. **c1960** Wilson *Coll.* **csKY,** Lantern-jawed. . . With the lower jaw protruding. **1965–70** *DARE* (Qu. X6) 261 Infs, **widespread,** Lantern-jawed; [SC42, Lantern-jaw].

lantern leaves n
A **buttercup 1** (here: *Ranunculus repens*).
1900 Lyons *Plant Names* 316, *R[anunculus] repens* . . Lantern-leaves. **1959** Carleton *Index Herb. Plants* 73, Lantern-leaves: *Ranunculus repens.*

lantern of the fairies See **fairy lantern 1**

lantrun See **lantern**

lan-yap, lanyappe, lanyope See **lagniappe**

lap v¹
1 To wrap; to fold. [*OED* lap v.² a1300 →]
1902 *Centreville Press* (AL) 19 June [2]/2, You may shake all feet loose, and he [=an opossum] laps his tail around the limb, and he clings and he clings urever, ah! **1916** *DN* 4.277 **NE,** *Lap.* . . Wrap. "Let me lap that bundle for you." **1926** Roberts *Time of Man* 71 **KY,** She rolled up her quilts and lapped her clothes into the bundle. **1930s** in 1944 *ADD* **eWV,** Lap up the groceries. **1951** West *Witch Diggers* 307 **IN,** The minute you lap your arms about a man and go to bed with him, you lay yourself open to word of this kind, you invite it.
2 also with *up*: See quot.
1970 *DARE* (Qu. AA8, *When people make too much of a show of affection in a public place . . "There they were at the church supper _____ [with each other]."*) Inf **NC**86, Lapping; **TN**46, Lapping up. [Both Infs Black]

lap n Also *lapwood* [Var of *lop* branches trimmed from a tree; cf *EDD* lap sb.³ 2 "The lopped-off branches of trees"] **esp S Midl**
The top or branches of a tree, esp a felled or fallen tree.
1851 *S. Lit. Messenger* 17.45 **wVA,** The glancing of a squirrel in a fallen lap, attracts your attention. **1881** [see **lap** v²]. **1902** *DN* 2.237 **sIL,** *Laps.* . . 1. Branches and limbs of a tree. 2. The entire tree top. A wood-chopper's term. **1903** *DN* 2.318 **seMO,** *Laps.* . . Tops of trees after same have been felled and the trunks removed. 'He gave me the laps for firewood.' **1905** U.S. Forest Serv. *Bulletin* 61.41 [Logging terms], *Lap* . . *Lapwood.* . . Tops left in the woods in logging. **1913** Kephart *Highlanders* 296 **sAppalachians,** A treetop left on the ground after logging is called the lap. **1939** *Hall Coll.* **wNC,** The dogs they wouldn't run into it—the lap of it [i.e. the bushy branches of a felled tree]. **1951** Giles *Harbin's Ridge* 74 **eKY,** By the light we could tell we were in a blowdown, with tree laps all around us. **1968** *Foxfire* Mar 76 **nGA,** Along the craggy hillsides where ginseng might grow in the rich mould behind fallen chestnut laps, or under grapevine shade. **1985** Wilkinson *Moonshine* 103 **neNC,** Logging had removed a number of trees and left piles of brush. People called them laps because the tree tops lap down over one another in the piles.

lap v², hence vbl n *lapping,* pronc-sp *lopping* [Prob < **lap** n; cf *EDD* lap v.⁴ "To lop off branches of trees"] **esp sAppalachians, TX** Cf **lapped**
Esp of a bear: to pull at or tear down branches of a tree or vine to obtain the fruit, nuts, etc; to strip the fruit from (a tree).
1853 Hammett *Stray Yankee in TX* 18, Just you sight that muscadine vine, whar one of the varmint's [=a bear] been a lappin'. **1868** *Amer. Naturalist* 2.122 **TX,** [Bears] climb in order to "lap," as the hunter says, described by Mr. Clapp as drawing in branches to get the fruit. **1881** *Scribner's Mth.* 22.858 **nwMS,** This is called the lapping season, as he [=a bear] ensconces himself in a tree-lap and breaks the limbs to pieces, in gathering nuts and fruits. **1907** Cockrum *Pioneer IN* 434, Bears. . . in early autumn . . will climb the oak and beech trees and pull the limbs to secure the nuts. This the old hunters called "lopping." **1939** *Hall Coll.*

wNC, Me an' one of my first cousins found a 'coon lappin' a chestnut tree an' we killed hit. **1960** Hall *Smoky Mt. Folks* 17, We heerd a bear a-lappin' (tearing down branches of a tree to obtain fruit or nuts) and shined our light in his eyes. Then we tuck a bead right in his eye and shot him. **1966** *DARE* Tape NC30, The bear will . . climb a tree and do what we call lappin' the tree. They'll pull the limb in with his paw and take the acorns off before they get ripe and eat them that way.

lap v[3], hence vbl n *lapping* [*EDD lap* v.[3] 1 "To flog, beat." Cf *lick* to beat, whip] Cf **lapjack**
To punish by whipping.
   1927 *AmSp* 2.359 cwWV, *Lap* . . to whip with a stick. "The teacher lapped four of the scholars yesterday." *Lapping* . . a whipping. "That girl needs a good lapping." **1975** Gainer *Witches* 12 sAppalachians, *Lappin'* . . whipping. "The teacher gave Harry a lappin'."

lap alum See **lap salt**

lap child n Also *lap baby* [*OED lap-child* (at *lap* sb.[1] 7) "*Obs.*"] **Sth, S Midl** Cf **apron child, yard child**
An infant or child still small enough to be held on the lap; the youngest child in a family; by ext, a spoiled child.
   1944 *PADS* 2.45 eNC, *Lap-baby.* . . A baby or child small enough to sit on one's lap. **1945** *PADS* 3.10 cSC, She's got one *lap-chile*, one po'ch chile, and three *ya'd chillen*. **1952** Brown *NC Folkl.* 1.556, *Lap child.* . . A child small enough to sit on one's lap; a spoilt child of any size; a child that likes to sit on one's lap. **1953** *PADS* 19.12 sAppalachians, *Lap baby.* . . A child not able to walk. **1968–69** *DARE* FW Addit csNC (as of c1920), Lap baby—the youngest child; nwLA [Black], Lap baby—a very young baby. **1973** *Patrick Coll.* cAL, *Lap child*—infant. **1986** Pederson *LAGS Concordance,* 1 inf, cnGA, Lap baby—very small; 1 inf, ceGA, Lap children. **1989** *DARE* File cAR, Kids are called different things—"lap child" or "yard child"—depending on their size. We used those in my family. I know "knee baby" too, but that's . . something Blacks would use. That's not in my family. In my family you were a lap child or a yard child. That was for most White families.

lapjack n Also *lap-jacket* [Cf **lap** v[3]] *old-fash* Also called **lickety-cut**
A children's whipping game; see quots; hence v *lapjack* to play this game.
   1897 *KS Univ. Qrly.* (ser B) 6.55 KS, *Lapjack.* . . to play lapjack = to switch. **1912** *DN* 3.581 wIN, *Lap-jack.* . . A game in which the two contestants whip each other with keen switches until one of them says "Enough." *Lap-jacket.* . . The same as *lap-jack*. **1927** *AmSp* 2.359 cwWV, *Lapjack* . . a game which is played by two persons striking each other with a switch, to see which one will cry enough the sooner. "The teacher does not allow us to play lapjack." **1968** *DARE* (Qu. EE33, . . *Outdoor games . . that children play*) Inf VA5, Lapjack—where everybody got a switch and try [sic] to corner somebody. [Inf old]

lap-legged adv [Cf **lapsided**]
In a lopsided or wobbly fashion—also in phr *lap-legged drunk* thoroughly drunk.
   1938 in 1983 Taft *Blues Lyric Poetry* 143 [Black], You know when I found myself / I was lap-legged drunk again / Love will make a-many man drink and gamble / and stay out all night long. **1948** Hurston *Seraph* 217 FL [Black], Them . . hogs didn't gain none, but they lost a'plenty. They got to walking kind of lap-legged and squealing.

lap-love n [*EDD* 1796]
A **bindweed 1** (here: *Convolvulus arvensis*).
   1900 Lyons *Plant Names* 115, *C[onvolvulus] arvensis* . . Lap-love. **1949** Moldenke *Amer. Wild Flowers* 270, The field bindweed, *Strophocaulos arvensis*. . . possesses scores of common names including such picturesque ones as hedgebells, cornlily . . laplove and sheepbine. **1959** Carleton *Index Herb. Plants* 73, Lap love: *Convolvulus arvensis.*

lap lunch n Also *lap supper, ~ tea*
A light meal eaten from a plate on one's lap rather than at a table; similarly n *lap party* an occasion at which food is served in this way.
   1867 Lowell *Biglow* lviii 'Upcountry' MA, A few phrases not in Mr. Bartlett's book which I have heard [include]. . *Laptea:* where the guests are too many to sit at table. **1889** *Century Illustr. Mag.* 37.853 CO, [As the] last act of this woful tragedy [of overeating], which, till now, had been what is innocently called in the Colorado vernacular a "lap-

party"—the guests were summoned to "a *full* supper." **1920** Lewis *Main Street* 12, They made a specialty of sandwich-salad-coffee lap suppers. **1928** *Ruppenthal Coll.* KS, When there is quite a crowd and tables are not handy, or it is desired to reduce the work to a minimum, a lap supper may be given. The food is handed to guests who hold the plate, often of paper, in their laps and eat from it. **1960** Williams *Walk Egypt* 182 GA, She had meant to pack a lap-lunch. *Ibid* 302, Toy looked down at the greasy hamburger and wished she had brought a lap lunch . . fried chicken and pound cake. **1973** *Patrick Coll.* cAL, Lap lunch—a lunch eaten on one's lap (rather than a table).

lap organ n
1 An accordion. *old-fash*
   1892 *Jrl. Amer. Folkl.* 5.330, It involves neither deadly sin nor any spiritual risk whatever to play the accordeon [sic] or the 'lap organ,' as they call it. **1955** Adams *Grandfather* 189 NY (as of 19th cent), Micajah Wembley was a notable performer on the lap-organ. *Ibid* 191, Micajah sat beside him, the lap-organ ready on his knees. **1960** Wentworth–Flexner *Slang* 312, Lap organ—An accordion. *Not common.*
2 A baby. *joc*
   1939 *AmSp* 14.91 eTN, Lap organ. A baby. 'His lap organ's playing.'

lap party See **lap lunch**

lapped ppl adj [Cf **lap** n, **lap** v[2]]
Of a tree: having the top or branches broken off.
   1951 Giles *Harbin's Ridge* 74 eKY, The trees were lapped so bad that in places there wasn't anything to do but get down and crawl.

lapping vbl n[1] See **lap** v[2]

lapping vbl n[2] See **lap** v[3]

lapping good adj phr [Cf *lap* to lick; by analogy with *licking* adv exceedingly as in phr *licking good*] Cf *larruping good* (at **larruping** adj **1**), **licking good**
Of food: exceptionally good.
   1965–69 *DARE* (Qu. LL35, *Words used to make a statement stronger: "This cake tastes _____ good."*) Infs ME16, MS60, NY1, Lapping; MA71, Lapping—old-timers said that; NY214, Lapping [FW sugg]. **1986** Pederson *LAGS Concordance,* 1 inf, neTX, Lord, it was lapping good—of syrup.

lapsadazical See **lackadaisical**

lap salt v phr Also *lap alum*
To do the most rudimentary or commonsensical thing.
   1914 *DN* 4.75 ME, nNH, Lap salt, know enough to. . . To have common sense. "He don't know enough to lap salt." He is thoroughly stupid. **1969** *DARE* (Qu. JJ15a, *Sayings about a person who seems to you very stupid: "He hasn't sense enough to _____."*) Inf VT16, Lap alum and drool.

lapsided adj Also *lab(ber)sided* [Varr of *lopsided;* cf *OED lapsided* (at *lop-sided*) 18th–19th cent; cf also *EDD lapsided, SND lab-sided* (at *lab-* adj.)]
   1806 (1970) Webster *Compendious Dict.* 172, *Lapsided.* . . having one side heavier than the other. [*DARE* Ed: This entry does not appear in Webster's English model.] **1835** Crockett *Account* 90, If you were to see their hounds! Lean, lank, labber-sided pups, that are so poor they have to prop up agin a post-and-rail fence, 'fore they can raise a bark. **1899** (1912) Green *VA Folk-Speech* 256, *Lapsided.* . . One-sided; leaning more to one side. "That gate is not straight, it's lapsided." **1968–69** *DARE* (Qu. KK70, *Something that has got out of proper shape: "That house is all _____."*) Inf MD36, Lapsided ['læp,saɪdɪd]; (Qu. MM13, *The table was nice and straight until he came along and knocked it _____*) Inf KY21, Labsided ['læb,saɪdɪd].

lap supper, lap tea See **lap lunch**

lap up See **lap** v[1] **2**

lapwood See **lap** n

‡**larafamedlus** n [Prob var of *layovers for meddlers;* cf *larofamedlers* (at **layover(s) to catch meddlers** quot 1892)]
   1950 *WELS* (*A dish made of several foods mixed together*) 1 Inf, cwWI, Larafamedlus—from Holland, great-grandmother near Scranton, Pennsylvania.

‡**lara-hoopin** adj [Perh blend of **larruping** adj **1** + *whooping*]
   1935 *Sun* (Baltimore MD) 11 Nov 4/5 cnMD, The Mint Julep Association, lured by the balmy weather Saturday, turned out en masse at the

edge of the meadow by the side of Grumbine's pond and had a regular lara-hoopin' time over three sprigs of mint.

larapen, laraping See **larruping** adj

larb n [Perh < Fr *l'herbe*]
A **bearberry 2** (here: *Arctostaphylos uva-ursi*).
1846 Sage *Scenes Rocky Mts.* 232, Frequent clusters of larb, richly laden with its deep red berry. [Footnote:] The larb-berry is of a deep red color, and somewhat larger than the common currant. **1871** U.S. Dept. Ag. *Rept. of Secy. for 1870* 413 **West**, Bearberry, (*Arctostaphylos uva-ursi.*)—This plant is the killikinick of the Indians and larb of hunters. **1878** (1880) Stanley *Rambles* 143 **WY**, The moose feeds upon willows, "larb," and various other shrubs and branches of trees. **1892** (1974) Millspaugh *Amer. Med. Plants* 100-3, The American Aborigines smoke the dried leaves [of *Arctostaphylos uva-ursi*] with tobacco . . this is the *Larb* of the Western hunters.

larbo n [Etym unknown] **NH** *old-fash* Cf **larrup** n **2, maple wax**
See quots.
1874 (1969) Coffin *Caleb Krinkle* 144 **cNH**, "It is done enough for larbo!" shouted Dan. The word "larbo" will not be found in the dictionary, but everybody in Millbrook knew what it meant,—that the molasses was boiled just enough to be cooled into candy on the snow. **1890** *AN&Q* 4.283, In Central New Hampshire the name of "larbo" is applied to maple candy, *i.e.,* maple syrup boiled to the right consistency and ladled out upon pans of snow. I have never known the origin of this word, and have never heard it used by any people but the natives of the region I have named. **1941** *LANE* Map 307, 1 inf, **csNH**, ['la·bow], thick maple syrup.

larch n
1 =**tamarack** (here: *Larix* spp). **chiefly Nth, N Midl** See Map
1792 Belknap *Hist. NH* 3.109, The *Larch (pinus larix)* is the only tree of the terebinthine quality which sheds its leaves in autumn. Its turpentine is said to be the same with the Burgundy pitch. **1824** Bigelow *Florula Bostoniensis* 360, The Larch is a fine tree, differing remarkably from the Pines . . in its leaves, which fall at the approach of winter. . . It frequents a low, moist soil. **a1862** (1864) Thoreau *ME Woods* 214, We continued along through the most extensive larch wood which I had seen. **1897** Sudworth *Arborescent Flora* 32, *Larix laricina.* . . *Common Names.* Larch (Vt., Mass., R.I., Conn., N.Y., N.J., Pa., Del., Wis., Minn., Ohio, Ont.) **1950** *WELS (Kinds of evergreens)* 3 Infs **WI**, Larch. **1965–70** *DARE* (Qu. T13, . . *Names . . for . . tamarack*) 33 Infs, **Nth, N Midl**, Larch; **CT**23, Larch tree; **NY**22, American larch; **GA**91, **IL**11, **IN**58, **NY**101, 105, 113, **NC**48, **PA**99, **VA**73, **WI**72, **WV**17, Swamp larch; **ID**5, Western larch; **WI**23, Outside of Belmont there is a farm called "the Larch Grove" with a large number of tamaracks growing around the barn and farmhouse; (Qu. T5, . . *Kinds of evergreens, other than pine*) 22 Infs, **Nth, N Midl**, Larch; **MA**78, American larch; (Qu. T6) Inf **PA**29, Larch; (Qu. T15, . . *Kinds of swamp trees*) Infs **NY**142, **PA**242, Larch; (Qu. T16, . . *Kinds of trees . . 'special'*) Infs **NC**36, **WI**58, Larch; (Qu. T17, . . *Kinds of pine trees;* not asked in early QRs) Infs **PA**29, 70, Larch. **1985** Clark *From Mailbox* 202 **ME**, Only in November does that tamarack really show forth glowing dusky gold before its winter rest. Down in Rockland County, New York, along the Hudson River, this conifer [=the tamarack] is referred to as the larch. Frequently as the American larch.

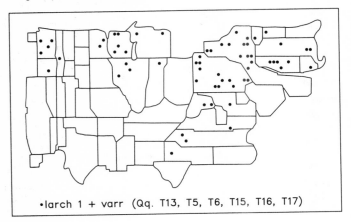
•larch 1 + varr (Qq. T13, T5, T6, T15, T16, T17)

2 =**noble fir. Pacific NW**
1897 Sudworth *Arborescent Flora* 57, *Abies nobilis* . . Noble Fir. . . "Larch" (Oreg. lumbermen). **1910** Jepson *Silva CA* 123, The Noble Fir [=*Abies nobilis*], or "Larch" of the Washington lumbermen, inhabits the Cascades and Coast Range of Washington and Oregon. **1949** Peattie *Cascades* 202 **Pacific NW**, Lumbermen have been guilty of a botanical libel in the naming of noble fir. Years ago an enterprising lumber dealer found that he could sell larch when he couldn't sell balsam fir, so noble fir promptly became larch. It is still "larch" to Northwest loggers, and the misnomer is perpetuated in Larch Mountain, east of Portland. There are no larches within many miles of the mountain, and the top is wholly covered with noble fir. **1967** *DARE* (Qu. T5, . . *Kinds of evergreens, other than pine*) Inf **WA**20, Larch or white fir.

lard n¹, v Pronc-sp *lord* Cf Pronc Intro 3.I.1.c
A Forms.
1856 in 1956 Eliason *Tarheel Talk* 313 **cnNC**, Lord [for *lard*]. **1919** *DN* 5.34 **seKY**, Lord. . . Lard. **1936** *AmSp* 11.241 **eTX** [Black], They [=Black speakers] sometimes compensate for . . omission [of final and preconsonantal *r*] by substituting [ə], as in lard [lɑːəd], but often this word is [lɑːd] (and also [lɔɪˆd]) in their speech.
B As verb.
1 with *up:* To eat heartily; to gain weight; hence ppl adj phr *larded up* fat. [Cf *OED* *larding* ppl. a. "Fattening" (intr) 1612]
1930 Shoemaker *1300 Words* 38 **cPA Mts** (as of c1900), *Lard-up*—To take on flesh. **1966** *DARE* (Qu. X50, *Names or nicknames for a person who is very fat*) Inf **WA**13, Larded up [laughter]. **1986** Pederson *LAGS Concordance (Invitation to sit down at the table)* 1 inf, **neTX**, Hunker down to the table and lard up—sit down and eat.
2 with *down;* as vbl n: Preserving in lard; see quot. [Cf *OED lard* v. 5 "To smear or cover with lard. . . *rare.*"]
1975 McDonough *Garden Sass* 73 **AR**, Her mother-in-law used to fry the sausage and then put it in a churn and pour the grease over it. This was called "lardin' it down" and meat fixed that way would keep all winter.

Lard n² See **Lord** n¹

lard bucket See **bucket of lard**

lard down See **lard B2**

larded up See **lard B1**

larder beetle n [Folk-etym for the species name *lardarius*, literally "of bacon"]
A dermestid beetle (*Dermestes lardarius*). Also called **bacon beetle**
1868 (1869) *Amer. Naturalist* 2.165, *Ptinus fur* . . is destructive to cloth, furs, etc., resembling the Larder-beetle (*Dermestes*) in its habits. **1895** Comstock–Comstock *Manual Insects* 539, The Larder Beetle, *Dermestes lardarius.* . . This pest of the larder is the most common of all the larger members of this family [=Dermestidae]. **1905** Kellogg *Amer. Insects* 264, The larder or bacon-beetle . . is about ⅓ inch long. **1969** *DARE* (Qu. R30, . . *Kinds of beetles;* not asked in early QRs) Inf **MI**108, Larder beetle. **1989** Entomol. Soc. Amer. *Common Names Insects* 36, Larder beetle—*Dermestes lardarius.*

larding down See **lard B2**

lard up See **lard B1**

Larence See **Lawrence**

larepin See **larruping** adj

larf See **laugh**

large adj *old-fash*
1 Fine, pleasant, enjoyable, lively.
1896 *DN* 1.420 **c,seNY, nOH**, "A large evening," a fine evening. **1928** Ruppenthal *Coll.* **KS**, Fine, large morning—phrase used to comment on bright, pleasing, fair weather, or as a greeting. **1930** *AmSp* 5.239 **NY** [College slang], *Large:* very active. "That was a large evening." **1930s** in 1944 *ADD* **cNY**, Large. . . Fine. . . Humorous. Common. **1967–68** *DARE* (Qu. FF17, . . *A very good or enjoyable time:* "We all had a _____ last night.") Infs **MI**67, 78, (Fine) large time. [Both Infs old] **1970** Major *Dict. Afro-Amer. Slang* 75, Large: (1930's–40's) successful, thrilling, well-to-do. **1986** Pederson *LAGS Concordance*, 1 inf, **neGA**, [It's] a nice, large day. [Inf old]
2 also as adv: Much; see quots.

1895 *DN* 1.390 **swOH,** *Large:* much. "He has large money." **1968** *DARE* (Qu. II39, . . '*Thank you*') Inf **KS**18, Thanks very large. [Inf old]

largemouth bass n Also *largemouth (black bass), largemouthed (black) bass*

Std: a **black bass 1** (here: *Micropterus salmoides*). Also called **bayou bass, bigmouth 3, bigmouth trout, black perch 1a, ~ trout 1, grass bass 2, gray ~ 1, green ~, green perch 1, ~ trout, growler n¹ 1, hookbill 1, Huron, jumper 2, lake bass 1, linesides, marsh bass, mossback 2, moss bass, mountain trout 2, mud bass 2, Oswego ~, painted tail, perch, redeye, river bass, rock ~, salmon, slough bass, speckled hen, spotted bass, straw ~, striped ~, swamp ~, tiger ~, trout, welshman, white bass, ~ salmon, ~ trout, widemouth bass, yellow bass, ~ perch**

largemouth black bass See **largemouth bass**

large rampion n

An **evening primrose a** (here: *Oenothera biennis*).

1900 Lyons *Plant Names* 265, O[*enothera*] *biennis* . . Large Rampion. **1911** Henkel *Amer. Med. Leaves* 14, Evening Primrose—*Oenothera biennis* . . Other common names . . large rampion . . scabish.

large water n [Var of *high water*]

High tide.

1920 CA Fish & Game Comm. *Fish Bulletin* 4.71, Every person who takes, catches or gathers in any manner any razor clam (*Siliqua patula*), except during a period of forty-eight hours beginning at the first low tide after the first high tide (large water) of the full moon of each month and for a period of forty-eight hours beginning at the first mean low tide after the first high tide (large water) of the new moon of each month, . . is guilty of a misdemeanor.

lariat n Pronc-spp *lariet(te);* rarely *lariat rope;* for addit varr see quots [AmSpan *la reata* the rope, lasso] **chiefly West** Cf **lasso**

A long rope, often with a running noose, used for catching or tethering livestock.

1832 (1937) Ellsworth *W. Irving* 84 **OK,** The Lariat is [a] long braided leather thong made of strips of Buffaloe hide of sufficent [sic] strength to hold the strongest horse. **1835** (1927) Evans *Exped. Rocky Mts.* 14.201 **IN,** Having to . . picket them [=horses] with larreyettes attached to their necks and to a stake in the ground. **1843** in 1917 Pelzer *Marches* 199 **Plains States,** *This morning* several horses were missing and evidence of foul play shown by the lariettes being cut. **1844** Gregg *Commerce* 2.170 **SW,** Spurs, lareats and other scraps of equipage, were found. **1848** Emory *Notes Reconnoissance* 532 **neNM,** The "laryettoes" of the living [=mules] were entangled about the dead. **1850** Garrard *Wah-to-yah* 9 **SW,** The lariat noose is sure to fall on their unwilling necks. **1864** *New Mexican* (Santa Fe NM) 21 Oct 2/3, Indians. . . cut the lariat that held two horses to the picket rope. **1897** Hough *Story Cowboy* 62, The rope in the Spanish country is called *reata* (*la reata*), and even to-day is often made of rawhide, with an eye re-enforced with that durable material. Such a hide rope is called a "lariat" in the South. . . The "lariat" is in the North used sometimes as another term in place of *rope,* more especially to describe the picket rope by which the horse is tied out. **1929** *AmSp* 5.63 **NE** [Cattle country talk], "Lariat," a contraction of the Spanish *la reata,* and "lasso," Spanish *lazo,* a snare or slip-knot, are little used except by the uninitiated and at the rodeos. **1939** (1973) FWP *Guide MT* 414, *Lariat*—Light, strong rope with a running noose, used for catching and tying livestock. **1940** *Cattleman* May 17 **West,** Nowadays most boys will say "rope." If there is any doubt they will say "lariat rope." **1961** Folk *Word Atlas N. LA* map 609, Lariat [56% of 275 responses]. **1967** *DARE* FW Addit ceTX, [ˈlɛrɹɪt]. **1971** Bright *Word Geog. CA & NV* 174, Rope with a loop; rawhide or hemp. . . *lariat* 54% [of 300 informants]. **1973** Allen *LAUM* 1.407 **ND, SD, NE** (as of c1950), The long rope that, noosed at one end, is used in roping horses or cattle. . . Most commonly reported is *lariat,* with redundant *lariat rope.* **1986** Pederson *LAGS Concordance,* 5 infs, 3 **TX,** Lariat (rope).

lariat v Also with *out* Also sp *larriet* **chiefly West**

To catch, fasten, or tether with a **lariat** n; also fig.

1846 *Spirit of Times* 4 July 222/2 **SW,** [The horse] has never been backed or before *lariated.* . . He was caught in the following manner. . . from the tree top the young brave succeeded in passing the fatal rope around his neck and bringing him thus into captivity. **1849** in 1930 Page *Wagons West* 125 **KS,** When we stop early enough, for the cattle to fill

themselves before night, . . we larriet (tie with long ropes to stakes) them till just at daylight when they are turned loose. **1869** *Overland Mth.* 3.127, I have even heard a Texan speak of land which he "lariated out," meaning thereby that he had just bought it from Government, but not occupied it yet. **1886** *Outing* 9.104 **wWY,** A mustang was lariated, saddled, and. . . we were *en route* for the mountains. **1888** *Red Man* (Carlisle, Pa.) Sept. (*DAE*), Two [Indian] women took our mules and lariated them out. **1927** *Ruppenthal Coll.* **KS,** *To lariat.* . . to catch or fasten with a lariat. We lariated his stick on the land. **1936** Adams *Cowboy Lingo* 58, 'Lariat' may be used as a verb, as 'to fasten' or 'catch' with a lariat.

lariat rope, lariet(te) See **lariat** n

larigan See **larrigan**

lark n¹ [From the resemblance to a bird of the family Alaudidae; cf **horned lark**] Cf **skylark, titlark**

1 =**meadowlark 1. scattered, but chiefly C and S Atl**

1709 (1967) Lawson *New Voyage* 148 **NC, SC,** The Lark with us resorts to the Savannas, or natural Meads, and green Marshes. **1731** Catesby *Nat. Hist. Carolina* 1.33, *Alauda magna.* The Large Lark. . . They feed mostly on the Ground on the seed of Grasses: Their flesh is good Meat. They inhabit *Carolina, Virginia* and most of the Northern Continent of *America.* **1851** *De Bow's Rev.* 11.54 **LA,** Lark, *Alauda Magna,* or *A. Alpestris,* is a good deal seen here, and is indigenous. **1851** (1874) Glisan *Jrl. Army Life* 88 **OK,** The birds . . most common to this country, that are good for food, are teal, . . plover, lark, robin [etc]. **1858** Baird *Birds* 537 **West,** *Sturnella neglecta.* . . *Western Lark.* . . This species is so very closely related to the *S. magna* as to render it difficult to distinguish them. **1890** Warren *Birds PA* 214, Although larks frequently alight on trees, they never, I think, are seen to feed in such places, their food is collected from the ground. . . In the Carolinas, Audubon says, many planters agree in denouncing the lark as a depredator, "alleging that it scratches up oat seeds, when sown early in spring, and is fond of plucking up the young corn, wheat, rye or rice." **1910** Wayne *Birds SC* 109, *Sturnella magna.* . . The Lark, as it is called in this state, is a permanent resident, exceedingly numerous in autumn and winter. **1913** *Auk* 30.498 Okefenokee **GA,** *Sturnella magna.* . . 'Lark.' . . On Honey Island we found young on the wing by June 1. **1919** Pearson et al. *Birds NC* 210, The birds most commonly called "larks" in this State, namely the Meadowlark . . (*Sturnella magna*), and the Pipit . . (*Anthus rubescens*) . . are not true larks. **1923** WV State Ornith. *Birds WV* 46, Sometimes a few larks spend the winter north. . . At such times the Meadowlark has to change his diet . . , but no farmer should begrudge him a little grain. **1955** *Oriole* 20.1.12 **GA,** *Meadowlark.* . . Lark. **1956** MA Audubon Soc. *Bulletin* 40.130 **MA,** *Meadowlark.* . . Lark. **1966–69** *DARE* (Qu. Q7, *Names and nicknames for . . game birds*) Infs **FL**20, **NC**13, 21, Lark; (Qu. Q15, . . *Kinds of larks*) Infs **CA**137, **GA**3, **MD**3, 29, **NC**78, **TX**12, Lark; **SC**4, Meadowlark—generally called lark; **NV**6, Western lark. [*DARE* Ed: Some of the Infs at Qu. Q15 may refer instead to other senses of *lark.*]

2 A **pipit:** usu *Anthus spinoletta,* but also *A. spragueii.*

1874 Coues *Birds NW* 43, These wheel-tracks . . seemed to be their favorite resorts. . . These were the only circumstances under which the Larks [=*Anthus spragueii*] could be procured without the great quickness and dexterity required to take them on the wing. . . On making a camp at Turtle Mountain, a pair of Larks . . circled about in such evident and painful agitation, that I knew they had a nest somewhere near by. **1883** Nuttall Ornith. Club *Bulletin* 8.78, In my long list of local American names for this species [=*Anthus spinoletta*] occur the following: Titlark, . . Lark [etc]. **1891** Goss *Hist. Birds KS* 594, This Lark [=*Anthus spinoletta*] is a bird of easy and beautiful flight, passing and repassing through the air with graceful evolutions. **1919** [see **1** above].

lark n² Also dimins *larkie, larky* [EDD *lark* sb.² 3 "A wild fellow, a 'rattlepate.' "]

A person, esp a young and mischievous one; also fig.

1833 *New Engl. Mag.* 4.205, "I say, my larkie," thundered he, reaching over and grasping the unconscious object of his anger, in the midst of a pigeon-wing (which he was executing to show that he could dance,) and drawing him with a kind of bear's hug out of the reel; "I say, my honey, a'n't you a doctor?" **1835** Longstreet *GA Scenes* 22, Fetch up your nag, my old cock; you're jist the lark I wanted to get hold of. **1839** (1840) Simms *Border Beagles* 1.169, The other lark told Betsy a different story. **1851** Hooper *Widow Rugby's Husband* 71 **AL,** The courthouse town of Randolph . . had its dozens of wild youngsters—clerks, overgrown school-boys, and other larks, who were always ready for any deviltry that might turn up. **1859** Cary *Pictures Country Life* 12 **OH,** Old Wolverton's . . was a moughty hard place for the gal, whatever kind of a lark she mought be. **1950** *WELS Suppl. Lark*—used for younger sons. Father concluding a lecture said "Now watch it m'lark." Used by man (B. 1813, N.Y.) (Rare. Old-fashioned.) **1960** Criswell *Resp. to PADS 20* **Ozarks,** *Larky*—Of course, a housewife talked to her chickens. Finally, she would biff one of them which was trying to crawl over the others and get to the choicest feed, and say, "I'll crack your head, you young larky".)

lark bunting n

Std: a sparrow-sized bird *(Calamospiza melanocorys).* Also called **buffalo bird 2, prairie bobolink, ~ reed-bird, white-wing, white-winged blackbird**

lark finch n

=**lark sparrow.**

1825 Bonaparte *Amer. Ornith.* 1.47, [The] Lark Finch. *Fringilla Grammaca. . .* frequent the prairies, and very seldom, if ever, alight on trees. **1877** *Field & Forest* 3.51 **DC,** A pair of lark finches were seen and identified by Mr. Ridgway. **1910** KY Hist. Soc. *Register* 8.23, Lark Finch. . . An abundant summer resident; arrives about April 22d. **1936** Roberts *MN Birds* 2.401, Eastern Lark Sparrow: *Chondestes grammacus grammacus . .* Other name: Lark Finch. **1940** Todd *Birds W. PA* 706, Lark Finch.

lark sparrow n [Appar from its song]

A sparrow *(Chondestes grammacus)* native chiefly to the Mississippi-Ohio Valleys and westward. Also called **lark finch, little meadowlark 2, Mexican lark, potato bird, quailhead, road-bird, snakebird**

1887 Ridgway *N. Amer. Birds* 414, *C[hondestes] grammacus. . .* Lark Sparrow. **1898** (1900) Davie *Nests N. Amer. Birds* 375, *Lark Sparrow. . .* It is one of the sweetest songsters among our Sparrows. **1916** *Times-Picayune* (New Orleans LA) 23 Apr mag sec 1, *Lark Sparrow. . .* Handsome little sparrows found in the state in some numbers, having the sweetest song of any of the sparrows found here. **1936** Roberts *MN Birds* 2.403, The Lark Sparrow. . . often chooses to build its nest beneath a canopy of silky, waving, pasque-flower plumes. **1955** Taber *Still-meadow Daybook* 24 **swCT,** This winter we had our first lark sparrows, and we are waiting to see whether they stay or go in summer. They are odd looking birds with white markings as if they had gone too close to a can of white paint, and they are aggressive. **1964** Phillips *Birds AZ* 195, The Lark Sparrow's melodious notes are interspersed with throaty gurgles. **1966–70** *DARE* (Qu. Q15, . . *Kinds of larks*) Inf **IA3,** Lark sparrow; (Qu. Q21, . . *Kinds of sparrows*) Infs **CO7, NM13, TX84,** Lark sparrow; **WI58,** Lark. **1977** Bull-Farrand *Audubon Field Guide Birds* 521, The easiest way to find Lark Sparrows is to drive through grasslands and watch for the birds to fly up into the trees along the road.

larkspur n [*OED* 1578 →] chiefly West, S Midl See Map

=**delphinium.**

1737 (1911) Brickell *Nat. Hist. NC* 22, *Prickly Bind-Weed, Larks-Spur, Hops, Flax* and *Hemp,* the best and finest in the known World groweth in *North Carolina.* **1819** (1821) Nuttall *Jrl.* 148, These vast plains . . were now enamelled with innumerable flowers, among the most splendid of which were the azure Larkspur, gilded Coreopsides [etc]. **1849** Howitt *Our Cousins in OH* 79, They found the purple spikes of the wild larkspur in full bloom, as fine as ever grew in a garden. **1852** Stansbury *Expedition* 26 **seNE,** In the bottom of the creek a species of larkspur and wild-onion abound. **1925** Stuart *40 Yrs.* 2.227 **MT,** There were . . several varieties of larkspurs and lobelia. **1965–70** *DARE* (Qu. S26e) 11 Infs, **chiefly West,** Larkspur; **WY5,** Larkspur ['lark,spar]—poisonweed (poisonous to cattle); (Qu. K28, . . *Chief diseases that cows have*) Infs **CO33, WY1,** Larkspur poison; (Qu. S11) Inf **OH95,** Larkspur; (Qu. S15) Inf **FL48,** Larkspur; **SC19,** Larkspurs—used to didn't have them; (Qu. S17) Inf **WY3,** Larkspur; (Qu. S20) Inf **NM9,** Larkspur—fuzzy, violet color; (Qu. S21) Infs **UT10, VA24,** Larkspur; **CO22,** Larkspur—kills cattle; (Qu. S26a) Infs **CA53, KY49, TN39, WA1,** Larkspur; **KY71, NV8,** Wild larkspur; (Qu. S26b) Inf **KY74,** Larkspur; (Qu. S26c) Infs **CA126, ID5, VA24,** Larkspur; **CA31,** Larkspurs; **PA99,** Spring larkspur; **KY63,** Wild larkspur; (Qu. S26d) Infs **IN17, KY35,** 49, 63, **NC52,** Larkspur; **CA22, GA80,** Wild larkspur. **1966–67** *DARE* FW Addit **CO29,** Larkspur *(Delphinium nelsoni);* **WA10,** Delphinium—larkspur. **1968** *DARE* Tape **IN14,** I do have some wild flowers set out. . . I have the larkspur . . that is very beautiful pink and purple and white. **1979** Ajilvsgi *Wild Flowers* 140 **eTX, wLA,** Blue larkspur—*Delphinium carolinianum.*

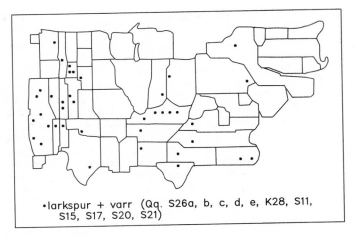

•larkspur + varr (Qq. S26a, b, c, d, e, K28, S11, S15, S17, S20, S21)

larkspur lettuce n

A **wild lettuce** (here: *Lactuca pulchella).*

1936 McDougall-Baggley *Plants of Yellowstone* 138, *Larkspur lettuce. . .* The flowers are blue or violet. **1963** Craighead *Rocky Mt. Wildflowers* 223, *Lactuca pulchella. . .* Larkspur Lettuce. . . When injured, plant exudes a milky juice.

lark woodpecker See **woodpecker-lark**

larn(ed) See **learn**

larnicks See **larnyx**

larning, larnt See **learn**

larnyx n Also sp *larnicks* [By metath from *larynx*]

1914 *DN* 4.109 **cKS,** *Larnyx. . .* Larynx. **1916** *DN* 4.277 **NE, KS,** *Larnyx. . .* Frequent for *larynx.* "The vocal chords are situated in the larnyx." **1930** Shoemaker *1300 Words* 38 **cPA Mts** (as of c1900), *Larnicks*—The larynx. **1934** *AmSp* 9.213 **TX,** Examples of metathesis which occur very frequently . . and which are so well established as to be called "old-fashioned" are . . *larnyx* for *larynx.* **1967–69** *DARE* (Qu. X7, . . *The throat:* "Some food got stuck in his _____.") Infs **CO22, IL57, LA40, NY33,** 88, 221, **PA195,** Larnyx. **1973** *DARE* File **swPA,** *Larnyx. . .* Larynx.

laro(ver)s to catch meddlers See **layover(s) to catch meddlers**

larp See **larrup** n 2

larpin See **larruping** adj

Larrans See **Lawrence**

larreyette See **lariat** n

‡larricky adj [Cf *EDD larruping* ppl. adj. (2) (at *larrup* v. 2) "ungainly, thin, tall"]

1941 *LANE* Map 463, 'Tall and thin,' usually without any implication of awkwardness . . 1 inf, **swME,** *larricky . .* [læ⸱ᵊrəkɪ̵ꞈ].

larriet See **lariat** v

larrigan n Also sp *larigan, larrigin* esp ME

A type of long-legged moccasin or boot; see quots; also adj *larriganed* larrigan-clad.

1889 *AN&Q* 3.308 **ME,** A *larigan,* or *larrigin,* in Maine and New Brunswick, is a kind of boot or moccasin of yellow leather, having a long leg reaching above the knee. It is worn by lumbermen in the deep snows of winter. **1904** Day *Kin o' Ktaadn* 105 **ME,** Smoke wreaths curl into the steam from the leggings, larrigans, and jackets. **1909** *DN* 3.413 **nME,** Larrigan. . . A long-legged moccasin. **1915** *Outing* 67.27, A "shoe-pac" or "larrigan" is a beef-hide moccasin with eight to ten-inch top, and with or without a light, flexible sole. **1922** *Short Stories* Feb. 129/1 *(DA),* [The dogs] clipped fangs at Cherriman's larriganed legs. **1969** Sorden *Lumberjack Lingo* 69 **NEng, Gt Lakes,** *Larrigans*—An oil-tanned moccasin with legs used by lumbermen. Both lake states and Canadian lumberjacks wore them. **1975** Gould *ME Lingo* 159, *Larrigans*—The old felt boots and rubbers of the Maine woodsman; warm, comfortable footwear for the climate. The rubber bottom (originally detachable for evening wear) on a felt or leather boot gave L.L. Bean his idea for the famous Maine Hunting Shoe.

larripin See **larruping** adj

larripy-dope See **larrup** n 2

larrows catch meddlers See **layover(s) to catch meddlers**

larrup v

1 To strike, thrash, whip; hence vbl n *larruping* a whipping, thrashing; a tongue-lashing. [*OED larrup* v. "dial. and colloq."; perh ult < Du *larpen* to whip.]

1824 Peake *Americans Abroad* 5 **VT,** I'll larrup you till you can't stand. **1838** Neal *Charcoal Sketches* 188 **PA,** I'll larrup you like ten thousand, if you'll only come a little nearer. *Ibid* 190, Larrupings don't do any good as I see. **1851** Burke *Polly Peablossom* 83 **GA,** Well, you have got a whaling to submit to, then; I'll larrup you like blazes! **1866** [see **lace** v 1]. **1899** (1912) Green *VA Folk-Speech* 256, *Larrup*. . . To whip; flog; thrash. *Larruping*. . . A thrashing. **1903** *DN* 2.318 **seMO,** *Larrup*. . . To whip; to thrash. **1905** *DN* 3.63 **eNE,** *Larrup*. . . Whip, or thrash. "He larruped his horses." **1907** *DN* 3.214 **nwAR, cCT,** *Larrup*. . . To beat thoroughly by way of punishment. [lærəp]—[lɑrəp]—both pronunciations. *Larruping*. . . A beating. *Ibid* 232 **nwAR, seMO,** *Larrup*. . . To whip. **1918** *DN* 5.18 **NC,** *Larrup*, to whip. **1929** *AmSp* 5.121 **ME,** Children. . . might be . . "larruped," "walloped," "lambasted," if disobedient. **1939** (1973) FWP *Guide MT* 414, *Larrup*—To strike, thrash. **1950** Stuart *Hie Hunters* 168 **eKY,** If ye take another step, I'll larrup ye with this ear of corn right betwixt the eyes. **1950** *WELS* (He gave his horse an awful _____) 2 Infs, **WI,** Larruping. **1967–68** *DARE* (Qu. Y15, *To beat somebody thoroughly: "John really _____ that fellow!"*) Inf **WI64,** Larruped; (Qu. II27, *If somebody gives you a very sharp scolding . . "I certainly got a _____ for that."*) Inf **OH16,** Larruping. **1975** Gould *ME Lingo* 159, Maine people use . . *larruping* for a spanking or even a downright thrashin'. **1986** Pederson *LAGS Concordance (A whipping)* 1 inf, **swAL,** Larruping—he has heard; 1 inf, **nwFL,** I'll get my larruping pole.

2 also with *along* or *around*: To thrash around, move noisily; to hurtle along. [Cf *EDD larrup* v. 2 "To walk in a heavy, shambling manner"] **esp ME**

a1874 in 1949 *PADS* 11.33 **cME,** Then told me that he always waked/ From any little noise or sound,/ He wanted me to feel at home—/ But hoped I wouldn't "larrup 'round." **1949** *PADS* 11.23 **CO,** Larrup along. . . To go fast. *Ibid* 33 **cME,** *Larrup*. . . Move in an awkward, noisy fashion; still in use. **1975** Gould *ME Lingo* 159, Maine people use *larrup around* for reckless speed.

3 See quot. [Cf *EDD lerrup(s* "A lazy, slovenly fellow; a slut. . . Hence *lirripy, adj.* slouching"]

1903 *DN* 2.299 **Cape Cod MA** (as of a1857), *Larrup*. . . To slouch, of a woman.

4 with *into*: See quot.

1983 *DARE* File **ceWI,** Larrup into—pitch in and do.

larrup n Also sp *larup*

1 A switch; whip. [**larrup** v 1]

1938 in 1944 *ADD* **neKY,** She'd use the larrup on us—right around the bare legs too. **1968–69** *DARE* FW Addit **csNC,** Larrup ['lɛrəp]—an old scolding switch with a leather strap at the end for added sting.

2 also *larrupy-*(or *larripy-*)*dope;* pronc-spp *larp, lerp:* Syrup, molasses. [Cf **larruping** adj 2] **chiefly West** Cf **lick** n 7

1895 *DN* 1.390 **West,** Larrup: molasses. **1904** White *Mountains* 184 **CA,** Larrupy-dope. . . Camp-lingo for any kind of syrup. *Ibid* 189, The batter [to make a flapjack] is rather thin, is poured into the piping hot greased pan, "flipped" when brown on one side, and eaten with larrupy-dope or brown gravy. **1916** *DN* 4.325 **NE,** *Larrup*. . . Syrup of any kind—molasses, sorghum, etc. "The children wanted some kind of larrup to eat on their bread." *Ibid* 277 **NE, MA, KS,** *Larrup*. . . 1. Thick syrup. . . 2. Molasses. **1925** *AmSp* 1.139 **Pacific NW** [Logger talk], He goes forth to eat . . a "string of flats," and "larup (pancakes and sirup)." **1967** *DARE* (Qu. H21, *. . The sweet stuff that's poured over these [pan]cakes*) Inf **CA22,** [lærəp]—the harvesters' term for syrup; **MI51,** Some people call it lerp [lɝp]—I don't hear it anymore, except as a joke. **1968** Adams *Western Words* 173, *Larripy dope*—A cowboy's name for any kind of sirup. **1973** Allen *LAUM* 1.408 (as of c1950), 1 inf, **swSD,** *Larrup*. Any kind of syrup.

larrup along (or around) See **larrup** v 2

larruping adj Pronc-spp *larapen, larepin, lar(ri)pin;* for addit varr see quots

1 also *tad-larruping;* Esp of food: delicious, excellent; hence adv *larruping* extremely—usu in comb *larruping good.* [**larrup** v 1, by analogy with *whopping, thumping;* cf *EDD lar-*

ruping (2) (at *larrup* v. 1)] **esp W Midl, TX, OK** See Map Cf **lamming** adj

1905 *DN* 3.86 **nwAR,** Larrupin'. . . Good. 'I've got something larrupin' for you.' **1921** *DN* 5.113 **CA,** Larapen, laraping. . . Accent first syllable. . . very good; . . exceedingly. Of southern origin. Widely current in California. **1923** *DN* 5.213 **swMO,** Larrupin'. . . Exceeding pleasant to taste. **1929** *AmSp* 4.330 **TX,** Larripin. . . seems to be complimentary in its nature as one hears of "larripin good" pie or soup. **1939** (1973) FWP *Guide MT* 414, *Larrupin' truck*—"Great stuff." **1939** FWP *Guide TN* 458 **cwTN,** "They" (sorghum is never referred to as "it") are "larrupin good truck" for the table. **1942** Perry *Texas* 138, A tasty dish is "larrupin'," which could have come from the use of the same word meaning a "beating," thus developing a connotation of superiority. **1943** (1970) Guthrie *Bound for Glory* 48 **cOK,** Anything you like real good an' ain't got fer a long time, an' then you call it, that's larepin'. **1949** *PADS* 11.23 **CO,** Larrupin'. . . Extremely. "Larrupin' good food." **1959** *VT Hist.* 27.147, Larruping. . . Slang. Extremely. Occasional. **1960** Criswell *Resp. to PADS* 20 **Ozarks,** Larrupin—exceedingly good to the taste; first rate, top-notch; plenty good. **1965–70** *DARE* (Qu. KK1a, *. . Very good—for example, food: "That pie was _____."*) Infs **IL25, NE11, OK9, 27, 31, TN26, TX1, 81,** Larruping; **IL96, TN23, 31, TX35,** Larruping good; **MS1,** Ain't that tad-larruping; **NM9,** Larrupin' dope—cowboy used to say; **TN36,** Larruping good truck; (Qu. DD15, *A person who is thoroughly drunk*) Inf **LA14,** Larruping drunk; (Qu. LL35, *Words used to make a statement stronger: "This cake tastes _____ good."*) Infs **IL135, LA28, MO7, OK25, TN31, TX98,** Larrupin(g). **1975** Gainer *Witches* 13 **sAppalachians,** Larpin'. . . very, exceedingly. "This pie is larpin' good." **1976** *Harper's Weekly* 26 Jan 19 **cKS,** If the pecan pie at the family reunion was delicious, people . . proclaimed, "This pie is absolutely larapin." **1986** Pederson *LAGS Concordance,* 1 inf, **nwLA,** Larruping—really good; 1 inf, **cwFL,** Larruping good.

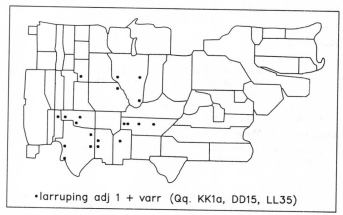

•larruping adj 1 + varr (Qq. KK1a, DD15, LL35)

2 By ext: see quot. Cf **larrup** n 2

c1968 *DARE* FW Addit **swOK,** Larruping ['lærpɪn]—Too sweet to be good eating; cloying.

larruping vbl n See **larrup** v 1

larruping adv See **larruping** adj 1

larruping good See **larruping** adj 1

larrup into See **larrup** v 4

larrupy-dope See **larrup** n 2

Larry See **Lawrence**

larup See **larrup** n

lary adj [Prob var of *leery*]

1906 *DN* 3.144 **nwAR,** Lary ['lærɪ]. . . Shy, distrustful. "He's lary of me."

lash n Cf **backlog 1, forestick**

Prob firewood or kindling; see quot.

1968 *DARE* (Qu. D33, *When you build a fire in the fireplace . . the big log that goes behind the others*) Inf **OH49,** Backlog; forestick goes in front; lash goes in the middle.

lashhorn n Also *lashhorn tree, lashorn* **Appalachians** =Fraser fir.

1878 Coale *Life & Advent.* 19 **swVA,** The field . . is bordered by . . a growth of timber known in that region by the name of Lashorn. . . It is a species of and very much resembles Norway Spruce. . . The lashorn of White Top is peculiar to that locality, and of the thousands that have been transplanted, not one has ever been known to grow, though some have lived several years. **1889** *Auk* 6.51 **swVA**, The extreme summit [of White Top Mountain] is covered with a thick growth of a species of balsam known locally as the lash-horn. **1903** Small *Flora SE U.S.* 30, *Abies Fraseri*. . . On mountain peaks, southern Virginia to Tennessee and North Carolina . . Silver Fir. She Balsam. Lash Horn. **1908** Britton *N. Amer. Trees* 76, This southern fir, also called . . Lashhorn, occurs in the higher mountains of Virginia and West Virginia to North Carolina and Tennessee. **1937** *Torreya* 37.94, *Abies Fraseri*. Years ago in North Carolina I was told about the lash-horn or lash-horn tree as being peculiar to the high mountains. **1943** Peattie *Great Smokies* 197, The "heath balds," as botanists call them . . , can only be compared to . . the *Krummholz* of the Alps or the "lashorn thickets" of dwarf spruce on the high mountains of Virginia, all of which are practically impenetrable growths of scrub.

lashings n pl Pronc-spp *lashins, lashuns* [Engl dial; cf *EDD lashin(g)s* and *lavins* (at *lashing* 1)] **esp Sth, S Midl** *old-fash*
An abundance, a great plenty.
 1894 *DN* 1.332 **NJ**, *Lashin(g)s:* plenty; abundance. "Lashins o' money." **1927** [see **lavins**]. **1939** FWP *Guide TN* 458, "Lashings" or "slathers" (liberal quantities) of sorghum served with yellow butter on brown biscuits, batter cakes, or flapjacks is the "best eatin' ever intended to man." **1941** Hench *Coll.* **cVA**, "And there are lashuns of perch." "How many did you say?" I asked. "Lashuns and lashuns of perch," he answered. **1945** *AmSp* 20.167, According to Kathryn McEuen, *loads and lashings,* meaning a large quantity of anything, is now taking its place in colloquial currency, at least in eastern states, alongside the familiar 'gobs,' 'heaps,' . . *et al.* **1984** [see **lavins**].

lashings and lavins See **lavins**

lashins See **lashings**

lashorn See **lashhorn**

lash pole n
In logging: see quots.
 1905 U.S. Forest Serv. *Bulletin* 61.41 [Logging terms], *Lash pole.* A cross pole which holds logs together in a raft. **1951** Swetnam *Pittsylvania Country* 84, Loggers held their rafts together by an ingenious arrangement of "lash poles," which spanned the logs or timbers and were held to them by wood bows pegged into holes in the timber.

lash rope n **West**
A rope used to secure a load on a pack animal.
 1806 (1905) Lewis *Orig. Jrls. Lewis & Clark Exped.* 5.114 **West**, Sergt. Gass, McNeal, Whitehouse and Goodrich accompanyed them [=Amer Indians] with a view to procure some pack or lash ropes. **1882** Baillie-Grohman *Camps* 45 **Rocky Mts**, The "cinche" . . and the lash-rope that is thrown over the load and round the animal are as taut as a strong man's arms can make them. **1893** Roosevelt *Wilderness Hunter* 178 **WY**, A skilful professional packer . . adjusts the doubles and turns of the lash-rope so accurately, that everything stays in place. **1946** Sierra Club *Bulletin* Dec 5 **West** (as of 1884), Tying a loop on a lash rope, I made a throw.

lashuns See **lashings**

laskit See **elastic (band)**

laso See **lasso**

lassengers n [Cf *lasses* (at **molasses**)] *joc* Cf **lozenger**
Molasses.
 1917 in **1944** *ADD* **sWV**, Lassengers. **c1960** Wilson *Coll.* **csKY**, Lassengers. . . Humorous nickname for molasses.

lasses, lassie(s) See **molasses**

lasso n, v Usu |'læˌso, 'læˌsu|; also |ˌlæˈsu| Also sp *laso;* proncsp *lassoo;* for addit pronc and sp varr see **A** below [Span *lazo*] **chiefly West**
A Forms.
 1819 [see **B** below]. **1837** Irving *Rocky Mts.* 2.142, The vaqueros, or Indian cattle-drivers, have . . learnt the use of the laso from the Spaniards. **1920s** in **1944** *ADD* **cNY**, [læˈsu] lassoo usual among boys playing cowboy. **1937** *DN* 6.621 **swTX** [Cowboy lingo], Wherever writers of Western thrillers found the corrupt *lassoo* for "lasso," it certainly was not West of the Pecos. **1941** in **1944** *ADD*, [ˌlæˈsuː]. While

I go out in the corral & practice my lassoo lessons. Radio. *Ibid* **NY**, ['læsu]. **c1960** Wilson *Coll.* **csKY**, Lasso ['læsˌo] is the regular form; ['læˌsu] is older usage. **1970** [see **C** below]. **1976** Allen *LAUM* 3.288 **NE** (as of c1950), Three different stress patterns appear in *lasso.* Fourteen infs. have initial stress. Twelve of them have strong enough secondary stress on the second syllable so that the vowel quality is retained, either as /o/ (typically [oᵁ] or [ou]) by [5 infs] . . or as /u/ by [7 infs] . . For two infs., however, a weakened stress is indicated by their final vowels [uˠ] . . and [ʌ]. . . One inf. is recorded as having even stress in ['læˈsu]. . . Four infs. reflect the Spanish origin of the term with their stress on the second syllable. In that syllable three have /u/ . . , and one has /o/ [a total of 19 infs gave the response *lasso*].
B As noun.
A long rope with a running noose used esp for catching livestock. Cf **lariat** n, **lass-rope**
 1819 *Petersburg* (Va.) *Republican* 5 Oct. 3/1 (*DA*), He was equipt with a *lassau,* a long Knife, and sword; mounted on a high pummeled saddle. **1841** Catlin *Letters Indians* 1.142, These horses. . . are taken with the *laso,* which is a long halter or thong, made of raw-hide, of some fifteen or twenty yards in length, and which the Indians throw with great dexterity; with a noose at one end of it, which drops over the head of the animal they wish to catch. **1897** Hough *Story Cowboy* 62, The term "lasso," which we read about in books, is never heard, unless in California, nor is the common term of the Mexican, *"reata."* **1910** Hart *Vigilante Girl* 196 **nCA**, But the riata, or lasso, at her pommel is probably purely for ornament. **1929** [see **lariat** n]. **1956** Ker *Vocab. W. TX* 164, A rope with loop for catching animals. . . *lasso* [is reported] by twenty-two or one-third of the sixty-seven West Texans interviewed. **1958** *Resp. to PADS 29* **ceNM**, Our local speech is complicated by all the Spanish words that we have picked up from the Mexicans. I list only a few: . . lasso—a rope for use with cattle. **1961** Folk *Word Atlas N. LA* map 609, Rope with loop for catching animals . . lasso [38% of 275 responses]. **1962** Atwood *Vocab. TX* 50, Rope used with cattle. . . lasso occurs throughout the area. **1973** Allen *LAUM* 1.407 **Upper MW** (as of c1950), *Lasso* [22 infs, **chiefly NE**]. **1986** Pederson *LAGS Concordance*, 3 infs, **ceGA, csTN, ceTX**, Lasso.
C As verb.
To catch with, or as with, a **lasso**; also fig, to snare; hence n *lassoer,* vbl n *lassoing.* Cf **lariat** v
 1831 Beechey *Narrative* 2.62 **cwCA**, Two or three men are dispatched for a wild bull, which they lasso in an equally dexterous manner. **1838** Ganilh *Mexico Versus TX* 48, The men were collecting the mules, and when these were driven together, the *lassoing* began. **1860** Holmes *Professor* 40 **ceMA**, A country-boy, lassoed when he was a half-grown colt. Just as good as a city-boy, and in some way, perhaps better. **1883** Sweet–Knox *Mexican Mustang* 584 **TX**, Juan Gonzales . . is said to be the champion lassoer of the world. **1897** Hough *Story Cowboy* 62, The common name gives the verb form, and the cowpuncher never speaks of "lassoing" an animal, but of "roping" it. **1907** *St. Nicholas* May 589, Jo . . had just come in stealthily from behind, and now by a dexterous twist had Peace safely lassoed with a bath towel. **1939** (1973) FWP *Guide MT* 415, Lasso . . to catch with a lariat. **1966–68** *DARE* (Qu. AA15b, . . *Joking ways . . of saying that a man is getting married.* . . "He _____.") Inf **FL28**, Lassoed her; **IN49**, Got lassoed; **PA55**, Lassoed. **1970** *DARE* Tape **CA192**, Their jobs would be . . to bring out a little calf, and they would lassoo [læˈsu] him around his legs.

lasso trade n [Folk-etym for **last-go-trade**]
 1968 *DARE* (Qu. KK35, *When someone wants to pass on a compliment about you, in exchange for one about himself* . . "I have a _____ for you.") Inf **GA28**, Lasso trade ['læso ˌtred].

lass-rope n **West**
A **lariat** n or **lasso B.**
 1940 (1942) Clark *Ox-Bow* 194 **NV** (as of 1885), The two punchers were tying the prisoners on one lass rope. **1940** (1966) Writers' Program *Guide AZ* 64, By holding a lass-rope in each hand the men made a rope corral while their ponies were roped out. **1946** Mora *Trail Dust* 105 **West**, It isn't every rider that knows how to tie a real good knot that will hold a heavy coil of rope. . . Many a good lass rope was dropped and lost. **1958** *AmSp* 33.271 **eWA**, Rope; lass; lass-rope; throw rope; twine. The usual words by which the 'lasso' (this term is never used) is known. **1971** Bright *Word Geog. CA & NV* 174, Lariat . . lass rope 26 [of 300 infs]. **1977** Jones *OR Folkl.* 101 (as of c1912), Lassrope: lariat.

lassy See **molasses**

last-bloom-of-summer See **last-rose-of-summer 1**

last button on Gabe's coat n

1 also *last button of Jacob's coat;* for addit varr see quots: The last thing, piece, or bit, esp of food; see quots. **chiefly Sth, S Midl** See Map *old-fash* Cf **last pea in the dish, last-rose-of-summer 3**

1909 *DN* 3.344 **eAL, wGA,** *Last button on Jacob's coat, the...* The last thing. Also *the last pea in the dish.* **1912** Green *VA Folk-Speech* 41, The last button off Gabe's coat. **1915** *DN* 4.184 **swVA,** *Last button on Gabe's coat...* The last of anything. **1953** Randolph–Wilson *Down in Holler* 259 **Ozarks,** Last button on Gabe's coat... The very last bit of anything; usually refers to meal, bacon, whiskey, sugar or some other household commodity. If there is only one piece of meat left in the smokehouse, the hillman says: "Well, fetch out the *last button on Gabe's coat,* an' let's have at it." . . *Last shingle on the barn* is sometimes used with the same meaning. **1965–70** *DARE* (Qu. H71, . . *The last piece of food left on a plate*) Infs **GA3, IL122, IN52, NC72, 88, VA9, 69,** Last button of Jacob's coat; **KY25, MD17, NJ21, VA104,** Last button on Gabe's (or Job's) coat; **MS60,** Last button off Gabriel's coat; **AR17,** Last button on Job's shirt. [10 of 13 Infs old, 3 mid-aged] **1984** Wilder *You All Spoken Here* 209 **Sth,** That's the last button off Gabe's britches.

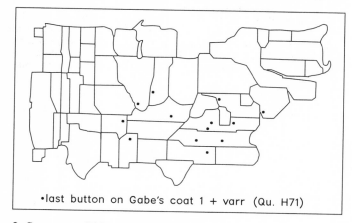

•last button on Gabe's coat 1 + varr (Qu. H71)

2 See quot. Cf **last run of shad 1**

1972 *NYT Article Letters* **KY** (as of c1920), [To] our colored cook, in Kentucky, whenever. . . we children were not well dressed, or looked untidy in her opinion, we looked like "the last button on Gabe's coat."

3 The last straw, the limit; see quot. Cf **last pea in the dish, DS GG22a**

1956 McAtee *Some Dialect NC* 7, The last button on Gabe's coat. . . the limit of one's patience.

last chance n

1 A dish made with cooked ham bones and scraps; see quot. Cf **scrapple**

1942 *Daily Progress* (Charlottesville VA) 31 Oct 4/1, Philadelphia scrapple is a very inferior imitation of "last chance" which is what frugal housewives in the back country prepare from the remains of well-eaten hams by cooking the bones in pots of corn meal mush.

2 An out-of-the-way or unimportant place. *joc* Cf **end of nowhere(s)**

1968–70 *DARE* (Qu. C33) Infs **NC87, OH67,** Last chance; (Qu. C35) Inf **IN49,** Last chance.

3 See quot. *joc*

1966 *DARE* (Qu. M21b, *Joking names for an outside toilet building*) Inf **NC12,** Last chance.

last couple out n [See quot 1919] **esp Upper MW, KS** See Map

A children's chasing game; see quots 1919, 1966–68.

1909 (1923) Bancroft *Games* 125, *Last Couple Out...* In the Scotch and Swedish forms of this game, the title is "Widow" or "Widower," the catcher supposedly taking the part of the bereaved one and trying to get a mate. It has been suggested that the game has descended from old methods of marriage by capture. **1919** Elsom–Trilling *Social Games* 58, *Last Couple Out...* is said to be an old Swedish game, a survival of some of the ancient wedding games of that country. . . Any number of couples may play . . odd player stands . . in front of the rest . . [and] calls, "Last couple out!" . . the couple at the rear . . endeavor to pass

the player at the head of the line without being tagged by him. **1929** (1982) Rölvaag *Peder Victorious* 143 **SD,** The smaller children were playing "Last Couple Out"; two groups of the larger girls were . . playing jacks. **1950** *WELS* (Games with an extra player) 1 Inf, **ceWI,** Last couple out. **1957** *Sat. Eve. Post Letters* **swMN** (as of c1910), Last couple out. **1966–68** *DARE* (Qu. EE2, *Games that have one extra player*) Inf **IA7,** Last couple out; (Qu. EE33, . . *Outdoor games . . that children play*) Infs **IA13, KS8, MN33, ND2,** Last couple out; **ID5,** Last couple out—line of couples; one single [player] who tried to catch a partner from the last couple before it reached the front of the line; **KS7,** Last couple out—[players] form in couples and make a long line; the one who is "it" must stand with his back to the line and say "last couple out." Then the last couple must run to the front and join hands before "it" catches them.

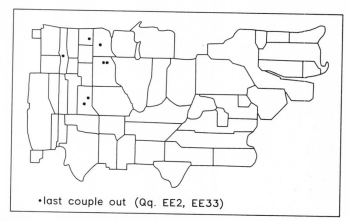

•last couple out (Qq. EE2, EE33)

last dog is hung, until the adv phr For varr see quots [Cf *OED dog* sb. 15.h *"Give a dog an ill name and hang him"*] **esp Inland Nth, N Midl**

Until the very last, to the end.

1902 White *Blazed Trail* 251 **MI,** They were loyal. It was a point of honor with them to stay "until the last dog was hung." **1943** McAtee *Dial. Grant Co. IN Suppl.* 2 10 (as of 1890s), Last dog's dead," "till the . . to the end. **1946** *Western Folkl.* 5.230 **wOR,** He'll stay till the last dog's hung. He never leaves until there is no longer a pretext for staying. **1966** Barnes–Jensen *Dict. UT Slang* 40, Stay until the last dog is hung . . remain until the last. [**1968** *DARE* (Qu. H71, . . *The last piece of food left on a plate*) Inf **IA22,** Last dog hung.] **1985–87** *DARE* File **ceNY** (as of 1932), He who promises to "stay until the last cat's hung" and "work his fingers to the bone" may "clear out" "at the first frost" without "wondering where his summer's wages have gone." *Ibid* **neOH,** Staying until [the] last dog is hung. **1992** *NYT Mag.* 12 Apr 14, [Clinton] said on Feb. 15 that he wanted people to see him "working hard, reaching out to them and fighting *until the last dog dies.*" Philip J. Bergan of New York recalls that his father, the grandson of Irish immigrants in the hard-coal region of northeastern Pennsylvania, would say of neighbors who had been the last to leave a late-night party that "they'd stay *till the last dog was hung.*"

last drop n Also *last drop in the bucket* **esp Sth**

The last straw, the limit; see quot.

1966–67 *DARE* (Qu. GG22a, *When you have come to the end of your patience . . "Well that's the _____."*) Infs **SC24, TN12, TX35,** Last drop; **AL6, FL26, SC19,** Last drop in the bucket. [All Infs old]

last-flower-of-summer See **last-rose-of-summer 1**

last gone adj phr Cf **gone adj 6**

With a time word: last, just past.

1871 (1892) Johnston *Dukesborough Tales* 56-b (Zeigler *Lexicon Middle GA*), I knowed the very day he was born, and that ain't but nineteen year last gone August [=nineteen years ago last August]. **1887** (1967) Harris *Free Joe* 118 **cGA,** I hearn 'im a-quollin' . . las' Sunday gone wuz a week [=a week ago last Sunday].

last-go-trade n Also *last-go-swap;* for addit varr see quots [Var of **trade-last**] **chiefly Mid and S Atl, WV** See Map on p. 296 Cf **Alaskan trade, lasso trade**

=trade-last.

1930 *DN* 6.82 **cSC,** Last-go-trade. . . A "trade-last." **1950** *PADS* 14.68 **SC,** Trade. . . Compliment. "I have a good *trade* for you." Usually in the phrase *last-go-trade,* whereby the speaker demands a compliment in prepayment. Confined mostly to teen-agers. **1956** McAtee *Some Dialect NC* 26, *Last-go-trade:* . . trade-last in Indiana dialect; a compliment which will be imparted in return for one for the speaker. **1965–70** *DARE* (Qu. KK35, *When someone wants to pass on a compliment about you, in exchange for one about himself, . . "I have a _____ for you."*) 37 Infs, **chiefly Mid and S Atl, WV,** Last-go-trade; **GA**1, [læsko]-trade; **FL**25, **MD**33, 34, Last-go(-swap); **WV**1, Last trade.

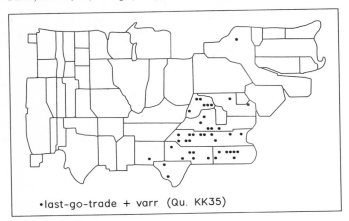

•last-go-trade + varr (Qu. KK35)

lastic (band) See **elastic (band)**

lasting log n
=**backlog 1.**
    1969 *DARE* (Qu. D33, *When you build a fire in the fireplace . . the big log that goes behind the others*) Inf **MA**15, Lasting log.

lastly adv [*OED lastly* adv. 1 "*Obs.* or *arch.* exc. as used to indicate the last point or conclusion of a discourse."]
Finally, at long last.
    1939 in 1944 *ADD* **WV,** [You hunt & hunt] & lastly you see it.

last of pea-time(s) n Also *last of pea-picking(s)* **esp Sth, S Midl, NEng** Cf **last run of shad 1**
The time when peas have almost ceased bearing; hence fig, a state of decline, exhaustion, or poverty; someone or something in this state.
    1834 Caruthers *Kentuckian* 190, He [=our parson] whines it out to us like an old woman in the last of pea-time. [**1867** Lowell *Biglow* 11 'Upcountry' **MA,** Ther' 's ollers chaps a-hangin' roun' thet can't see pea-time's past.] **1872** Schele de Vere *Americanisms* 623, *Peatime,* the season of pease, is of sufficient importance in the New England States to give a number of phrases to their speech. The *last of peatime,* represents the era in a man's life when he is in great trouble, perhaps at his wit's ends. **1889** (1971) Farmer *Americanisms* 413, *The last of pea-time or pea-picking.*—A familiar phrase drawn from the decline in fruitfulness, which characterizes the later crops of this staple of food. Metaphorically, when a man is said to be in *the last of pea-time,* it is meant that he is in the decline of years, or that his opportunities of usefulness to himself, or to his fellows, are passing away, or that he is "hard-up." . . She looks like *the last of pea-picking, i.e.,* sickly, faded; passée. **1893** Owen *Voodoo Tales* 199 **MO** [Black], 'Deed my gyarden am a-lookin' mighty bad. Hit look mo' lak de las' o' pea-time den de fust o' truck-time. **1909** *DN* 3.344 **eAL, wGA,** *Last of pea pickin(g)s.* . . The last choice: used to indicate the worthlessness or unimportance of a person or thing. **1911** Saunders *Col. Todhunter* 108 **MO,** What on earth's the matter, Bill. . . You look like the last of pea-times. **1923** *DN* 5.238 **swWI,** *Pea-time, like the last of.* . . Utterly worn out. "He looks like the last o' pea-time.["] **1946** Hench Coll. **cVA,** Last of pea time. . . Continually in Charlottesville this proverbial phrase is used to describe something poor or bad or "shacklin'," particularly people. "She's the last of pea time," i.e. she's no good in any way. **1947** Bowles–Towle *New Engl. Cooking* 107, Then at "the last of pea time"—the New England expression for being hard up . . there were two special dishes . . peas and dumplings, and pea fritters. **1967** *DARE* (Qu. HH18, *Very insignificant or low-grade people*) Inf **OH**37, Last of pea-time. **1976** Ryland *Richmond Co. VA* 374, "The last of pea-time," quite inferior, poor, sickly.

last-of-the-garden n Cf **end-of-the-garden pickle**
A kind of relish or pickle; see quots.
    1968 Kellner *Aunt Serena* 88 **cIN** (as of c1920), "Well, I reckon it's

time to start on the Last-of-the-Garden," which was a delicious relish made from everything left in the Truck Patch. **1968–70** *DARE* (Qu. H50, *Dishes made with beans, peas, or corn that everybody around here knows, but people in other places might not*) Inf **MO**39, Last-o'-the-garden; (Qu. H56, *Names for . . pickles*) Inf **IL**113, Last-o'-the-garden; **IN**30, Last-of-the-garden.

last-one-squats-shall-tell-his-name n
A children's game; see quot.
    1981 Mebane *Mary* 45 **cnNC** (as of c1940) [Black], I liked a game called last-one-squats-shall-tell-his-name. We formed a circle, held hands, and sang, "Last one squats [etc] . . so early in the morning." At the last word, you sat down fast. The last one down was "it" and had to tell the name of the one he loved.

last part through the fence See **part that went over the fence last**

last pea in the dish n Also *last pea in the pot* **chiefly SE** See Map Cf **last button on Gabe's coat 1, 3**
The last one, last thing, esp the last piece of food left on a plate; the last straw, the limit.
    1909 *DN* 3.344 **eAL, wGA,** The last thing. . . the last pea in the dish. **1965–70** *DARE* (Qu. H71, . . *The last piece of food left on a plate*) Infs **AL**52, **GA**8, **MS**63, **NC**84, Last pea in the dish; **AL**14, Last pea in the pot; (Qu. GG22a, *When you have come to the end of your patience . . "Well that's the _____."*) Infs **GA**9, **TX**98, Last pea in the dish. **1986** Pederson *LAGS Concordance,* 1 inf, **nwFL,** Last pea in the dish— youngest child.

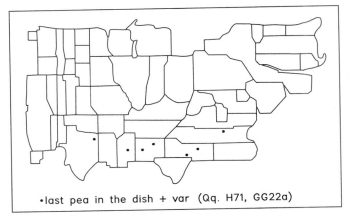

•last pea in the dish + var (Qq. H71, GG22a)

last-rose-of-summer n
1 also *last-bloom-of-summer,* ~*-flower-*~: An aster such as *Aster nova-angliae.* Cf **fall rose, farewell-summer 1**
    1931 Clute *Common Plants* 140, The New England aster (*Aster Nova Angliae*), which lingers long in the fields and fence corners, is further distinguished as last-rose-of-summer. **1966–69** *DARE* (Qu. S25, . . *The small wild chrysanthemum-like flowers . . that bloom in fields late in the fall*) Inf **KY**43, Last-bloom-of-summer; **IN**14, Last-flower-of-summer; **KY**56, Last-rose-of-summer; (Qu. S26e, *Other wildflowers not yet mentioned; not asked in early QRs*) Inf **VA**24, Last-rose-of-summer.
2 Fig: someone or something whose scent or vitality is spent. Cf **last of pea time(s), last run of shad 1**
    1872 Twain *Roughing It* 443 **MO,** We remained as centless [sic] as the last rose of summer. **1915** *San Francisco Call & Post* 18 Feb 10 (Zwilling Coll.), He swore off [smoking, drinking and gambling] and now he looks like the last rose of summer. **1941** *LANE* Map 482 (*Exhausted*) 1 inf, **ceVT,** I feel like the last rose of summer. **1952** Brown *NC Folkl.* 1.469, Looks like the last rose of summer. **1966** *DARE* (Qu. BB5, *A general feeling of discomfort or illness that isn't any one place in particular*) Inf **SD**5, Feel like the last-rose-of-summer.
3 See quot. Cf **last button on Gabe's coat 1**
    1968 *DARE* (Qu. H71, . . *The last piece of food left on a plate*) Inf **NJ**53, Last-rose-of-summer [laughter]. [Inf old]

last run of shad n **chiefly NEast, esp NEng**
1 also *last run of smelt;* Fig: someone or something weakened by time or ill health; someone or something weak, inferior, undesirable. Cf **last of pea time(s)**
    1876 Burroughs *Winter Sunshine* 187 **NY,** Small, spiritless, inferior-looking men all of them. They were like Number Three mackerel or the

last run of shad, as doubtless they were—the last pickings and resiftings of the population. **1929** *AmSp* 5.125 **ME,** The children might . . "look like an object of charity," . . or "the last run of shad." **1941** *LANE* Map 482 *(Exhausted)* 1 inf, **ceMA,** She looks like the last run of shad. **1946** *CA Folkl. Qrly.* 5.232 **wOR,** It looks like the last run of shad. It looks battered and thin, inadequate, umpromising. (Oregonians sometimes say "the last run of *smelt,*" which is a more appropriate term for them . .). **1965** *DARE* File **cMA** (as of c1915), My mother used to say of a person who had recently had an illness and only partially recovered, "Why she looked like the last run of shad," meaning washed out, peaked, pale. **1968** *DARE* (Qu. X52, *A person . . who had been sick was looking* ———) Inf **PA104,** Like the last run of shad—eggs are all out and [the fish] are all weak. **1979** *AmSp* 54.100 **swME** (as of 1899–1910), Them rusticators look like the las' run o' shad.

2 See quot.

    1985 *DARE* File **ME,** Last run of shad, the: In Maine, it's the end of a project.

last run of smelt See **last run of shad 1**

lasts n Cf **firsties 1**

In marble play: see quot.

    c1970 Wiersma *Marbles Terms* **swMI** (as of c1965), *Lasts* . . throwing marble toward the pot last—this give him an advantage . . Dave, you get lasts this game.

last tag n Cf **face tag**

A children's game of tag; a children's leave-taking game; see quots.

    1891 *Jrl. Amer. Folkl.* 4.223 **Brooklyn NY,** Last tag. When a company of children are about dispersing to their homes after their play, one will start up the cry of "Last tag," and endeavor to touch one of the others, and retreat into the house. Each will then try to tag and run, until at last there will be two left, and one of them, getting the advantage, will tag the other, and escape to the refuge of his own doorway. From this point of vantage he will exultingly cry, *"Last tag, last tag!"* **1901** *DN* 2.139 **cNY,** *Face tag.* . . The name of a game; the same as *last tag.* **1940** Marran *Games Outdoors* 140, *Last Tag.* A player tries to tag all of the other players in the group by touching them on the arm or shoulder and yelling, "last tag!" Then he runs out of reach as fast as he can to prevent being tagged himself. **1957** *Sat. Eve. Post Letters* **swMN** (as of c1910), [Children played] Wood tag, Tree tag, Squat tag and Last tag. **1965** *DARE* File **cnMA** (as of c1915), *Last Tag*—This is defined as a children's game sometimes. I suppose it is a game, but as I know it, not *really* a game. It was what we said as we gave a friend a quick poke just before we left him/her. Perhaps you were walking home from school with another little girl. As you came to the spot where you turned off you poked her, said "Las' tag" and took off as fast as you could run. It meant nothing more than "Goodbye—I thought of tagging you before you tagged me."

last trade See **last-go-trade**

lasty adj [nEngl, Scots dial; cf *EDD lasty, SND* (at *lest* v., n. I)] **chiefly Appalachians, S Midl**

Durable; long lasting, enduring.

    1882 (1971) Gibbons *PA Dutch* 12 **sePA,** In the county of Lancaster [PA]. . . Those who speak English use uncommon expressions, as,—"That's a werry *lasty* basket" (meaning durable). **1887** *Amer. Philol. Assoc. Trans. for 1886* 17.38 **wNC, eTN,** I heard myself last summer a "foot-washing" Baptist preacher in Craddock's Great Smoky Mountains say, "Stone is the most *lastiest,* the most *endurablest* material there is." **1895** *DN* 1.372 **seKY, eTN, wNC,** *Lasty:* enduring. "They's the lastiest blossoms in the gyarden." **1903** *DN* 2.318 **seMO,** It's a good lasty wagon. **1923** *DN* 5.213 **swMO,** *Lasty.* . . Durable, substantial, permanent. **1927** *DN* 5.469 **Appalachians,** *Lasty.* . . Prolonged. "It's a lasty winter." **1930** in 1952 Mathes *Tall Tales* 159 **sAppalachians,** Made of genuwine walnut, the solidest, lastiest wood they is! **1937** in 1968 Haun *Hawk's Done Gone* xii **eTN,** And that store-bought cloth never was very lasty anyhow. **1942** (1971) Campbell *Cloud-Walking* 62 **seKY,** Some things she reckoned learning would make different but a heap more things would turn out too lasty to get changed. **1953** *AmSp* 28.251 **csPA,** *Lasty.* . . Lasting, durable. Popular speech. **1954** *Harder Coll.* **cwTN,** *Lasty* . . Hardy, existing a long time. **1985** *NYT Mag.* 13 Jan 9 **sAppalachians,** The spring never went dry in summer; it was *lasty.*

last year's bird's nest n Usu with *a* Also *last year's crow's* (or *wasp*) *nest;* for addit varr see quots

Fig: something utterly worthless, senseless, outmoded, or untidy.

    1905 *DN* 3.86 **nwAR,** *Last year's bird's-nest.* . . In the expression,

'He hasn't any more sense than a last year's bird's-nest,' i.e., his head is as empty as a last year's bird-nest. **1927** *AmSp* 2.359 **cwWV,** *Last year's birds' nests* . . things of very little value. "Those old clothes are not worth any more than a last year's bird's nest." **1929** *AmSp* 5.125 **ME,** [A slovenly woman's] hair might look like a "last years robin's nest." **1946** *Western Folkl.* 5.230 **wOR,** That looks like a last year's bird's nest. Said of an old hat or something much out of style. **1950** *WELS* (*If a house is untidy and everything is upset, . . it looks like* ———) 1 Inf, **cwWI,** Last year's crow's nest. **1966** *DARE* (Qu. JJ15b, *Sayings about a person who seems to you very stupid: "He doesn't know* ———.") Inf **OK18,** As much as a last year's bird nest. **1986** Pederson *LAGS Concordance,* 1 inf, **cwTN,** He's got as much sense as last year's wasp nest.

latanier n Also *latania* [Fr *latanier,* ult of Carib origin] **LA =cabbage palm;** also the fan-shaped leaf of this palm.

    [**1714** (1906) Joutel *Joutel's Jrl.* 64, I could see from the Ships . . [an] Abundance of that Sort of Palm-Trees, in French call'd *Lataniers,* fit for nothing but making of Brooms, or scarce any other use.] **1799** in 1810 Cuming *Sketches* 336 **New Orleans LA,** Some . . cabins [were] covered over with a shrub like a large fan, called latania. **1819** Dana *Geog. Sketches* 238 **cLA,** On the. . . outer margin of the cane, the palmetto, or latania, fill the slope between the cane and the inundated lands. **1827** *Western Mth. Rev.* 1.315 **seLA,** Palmetto, or latanier, peet, and long moss, add an aspect of novelty to the view in the eye of strangers. **1868** *Putnam's Mag.* new ser 1.594 **seLA,** Here and there. . . is a "latanier hut," with adobe walls and a roof thatched with. . . palmetto. **1898** Sudworth *Forest Trees* 104 **LA,** *Sabal palmetto* . . Cabbage Palmetto. . . Latanier. **1958** Grau *Hard Blue Sky* 153 **sLA,** He wasn't thinking of anything in particular, just fanning himself slowly with a latanier. **1967** LeCompte *Word Atlas* 231 **seLA,** Plant with fan shaped leaves . . latanier [9 of 21 infs].

latched, get v phr [Cf *get hitched*]

To get married.

    [**1942** Berrey–Van den Bark *Amer. Slang* 359.4, *Marry.* . . latch.] **1944** in 1958 Brewer *Dog Ghosts* 60 **TX** [Black], He ast de girl to ma'ie 'im one Saddy night, an' dey gits latched an' buy 'em a li'l' spot of lan'.

latch pin n **chiefly S Midl** *old-fash*

A safety pin.

    1940 (1978) Still *River of Earth* 72 **KY,** The men wore white shirts, with collars buttoned. One had a latch-pin at his throat, for the button was gone. **1946** *AmSp* 21.190 **seKY,** *Latch-pin.* . . safety pin. 'I lost the button off 'n my coat. You got a latch-pin?' **1952** Brown *NC Folkl.* 1.556 **w,cnNC.** **1953** *PADS* 19.12 **sAppalachians.** **1954** *PADS* 21.32 **SC.** **1978** *AP Letters* **neGA,** "Latch pin" safety pin. This comes from . . my uncle . . [who] was raised in Habersham County. **1986** Pederson *LAGS Concordance,* 2 infs, **ce,cnTN,** Latch pin. [Both infs old]

late on the tide adj phr Also *late in the tide*

Fig: see quots.

    1916 Macy–Hussey *Nantucket Scrap Basket* 137, *"Late On the Tide"*—Delayed, belated. **1927** *AmSp* 3.135 **eME,** A man or woman who was inefficient but not vicious was often called "a poor tool." Some were "always late in the tide," had "reached the puttering stage," or just "fudged." **1942** ME Univ. *Studies* 56.69 [Sea terms come ashore], If he was *late on the tide* [Footnote: Fig. Missing an opportunity] he would better . . wait *through slack water* [Footnote: Fig. Dull times].

later exclam Also *later on* [Shortened form of *I'll see you later*] *esp freq among Black speakers*

Good-bye!—used as an informal expression of farewell.

    1954 *Time* 8 Nov 70 [Jazz jargon], *Later.* . . Catchall word for "I'll be seeing you"; also used at the end of letters, *e.g.,* "Later. . . Dave." **1970** *DARE* (Qu. NN11, *Informal ways of saying 'good-bye' to people you know quite well*) Infs **CA177, 188, GA91, IL139, MO30, NJ70, NY236, OH103, WV21,** Later; **MO30, TN54,** Later on. [9 of 10 total Infs young, 8 Black, 6 coll educ] **1970** Major *Dict. Afro-Amer. Slang* 75 (as of 1950s), *Later* . . a manner of saying goodbye, short for "see you later." **1972** Claerbaut *Black Jargon* 71, *Later.* . . farewell; goodby. **1972** Kochman *Rappin'* 214 [Black], The players all started heading for the door, stating, "Peace," "Later," "Hat Time," "I'm in the wind," etc. **1974** Baldwin *If Beale St. Could Talk* 111 **NYC** [Black], "Oh, baby, get me out of here." "I will. Hold on." "I promise.—Later." "Later."

late years adv phr Also *later years*

Recently, nowadays.

    1967–70 *DARE* Tape **CA164,** And . . late years, I think the sleighs are practically all out of the country; **TX24,** Late years, why, they don't hold water; **TX**30, You mean, late years, or way back there? **TX**100, Later years, I've got off of all my games. **1969** *DARE* FW Addit **neNY**, Late years—i.e. in late years—lately.

lather n See **ladder**

latherbush n Also *latherleaf* [See quot 1938]

=sweet pepperbush.

  1927 Boston Soc. Nat. Hist. *Proc.* 38.213 **Okefenokee GA**, *Clethra alnifolia* 'Lather-bush'; 'lather-leaf'. **1938** Matschat *Suwannee R.* 285 **Okefenokee GA**, *Clethra*, the common sweet pepperbush of the East, is called . . latherleaf in the swamp, . . because the leaves make a lather when scrubbed in water.

lather down, keep one's v phr [*Lather* foam or froth from profuse sweating, esp of horses; fig: an agitated state] **esp WV** See Map

  1965–70 *DARE* (Qu. GG23a, *If you speak sharply to somebody to make him be patient . . "Now just keep your _____."*) Infs **MS**25, **NC**69, **WV**4, 8, 13, 14, 16, 18, Lather down. [All Infs male]

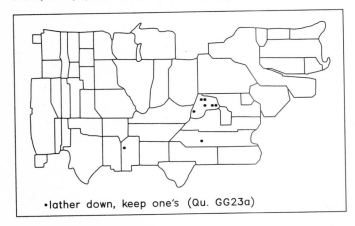

•lather down, keep one's (Qu. GG23a)

latherleaf See **latherbush**

latherwort n Cf **soapwort**

=bouncing Bet 1.

  1900 Lyons *Plant Names* 334, *S[aponaria] officinalis* . . Latherwort.

lath-open bread n

  1913 Kephart *Highlanders* 293 **sAppalachians**, Lath-open bread is made from biscuit dough, with soda and buttermilk, in the usual way, except that the shortening is worked in last. It is then baked in flat cakes, and has the peculiar property of parting readily into thin flakes when broken edgewise. I suppose that . . lath-open bread denotes that it opens into lath-like strips.

lathy adj

Of a person: tall and thin; gangling.

  1941 *LANE* Map 463 (*Awkward, clumsy*), The following adjectives . . mean 'tall and thin,' usually without any implication of awkwardness: . . 1 inf, **sNH**, Long and lathy; 1 inf, **swME**, Lathy. **1973** *McDavid Coll.* **FL**, Lathy—gangling, gawky.

latigo n |ˈlætɪˌgo, ˈlæd-| Also *latigo strap* Pronc-sp *ladigo* [Span] **West**

A leather strap on a saddle, esp one used to attach the cinch.

  1874 Evans *A la CA* 331, The wide band of woven horsehair, known as the cinch, is drawn up by the powerful purchase on the *látigo* strap until it deeply imbeds itself in the animal's belly. **1887** *Scribner's Mag.* 2.510 **West**, The two ends of the tough cordage which constitute the "cinch" terminate in long, narrow strips of leather, called *látigos* (Sp., thongs), which connect the "cinches" with the saddle and are run through an iron ring, called . . the *larigo* ring. **1929** (1978) Watt *Mule Train* 42 **eWA** (as of 1860s), The "ladigo" strap or cinch strap was 2 inches wide, and it was well greased so as to slip easily in tightening. **1956** Moody *Home Ranch* 173 **CO**, Her braids flapped like latigo strings on the saddle of a bucking horse. **1958** *AmSp* 33.271 **eWA** [Ranching terms], Latigo [ˈlætəgo]. The strap, attached to the left side of the saddle, looped through the ring of the cinch. **1966** *DARE* (Qu. L53a, *The band that goes under a horse's middle to hold a saddle on*) Inf **MT**3, Latigo [ˈlætɪgo]; **NM**13, Latigo [lædɪgo]—there's a double and a single—used to tighten girth. **1967** *DARE* Tape **TX**25, Latigo? That's just a strip of

leather with holes in it, and it wraps around these rings . . . It's just a long piece of leather. . . it just goes around and around, then you pull it up like, you know, cinch it up. . . just like a belt. **1973** Allen *LAUM* 1.408 (as of c1950), 1 inf, **ND**, Latigo /lætɪgo/. A strap attaching the cinch to the saddle. **1976** Maclean *River Runs Through* 129 **wMT** (as of 1919), You can't even talk to a packer unless you know what a cinch (*cincha*) is, a latigo, and a manty (*manta*).

latke n [Yiddish] **chiefly in Jewish settlement areas**

A potato pancake.

  1927 *Amer. Mercury* 10.206, Luscious potato *latkes*—pancakes made of grated, raw potatoes, [etc.] **1967–69** *DARE* (Qu. H20b) Inf **MA**4, Latke [ˈlʌtki]; **PA**171, Latkes [lɑtkəz]—potato pancakes; (Qu. H47) Inf **NY**119, Potato latkes—potato pancakes—[potatoes] mixed with flour and onions; (Qu. H57) Inf **IL**99, Latke. [**1970** Feinsilver *Yiddish* 193, *Latkes* . . This usually means potato pancakes, made from grated raw potatoes and traditionally served on Chanuka.] **1989** *Village Voice* (NY NY) 17 Oct 27, What about the sitcom that never got on the air—the one about my family being attended by a British butler? ("The *latkes*, Jeeves.")

lattercrop n Cf **lattermath**

=aftermath.

  1939 *LANE* Map 125 (*Second crop*) 2 infs, **eME coast**, Lattercrop. **1949** Kurath *Word Geog.* fig 112 **nPA**, Second crop . . lattercrop [5 infs]. **1967** Faries *Word Geog. MO* 97, The customary Missouri expression for a second growth of hay or clover seems to be *second crop* (90 percent). . . The New England settlement area relic . . *lattercrop* (20 occurrences [from a total of c700 infs]) . . [is] obviously not well known to the Missouri informants.

latter days adv phr Cf **late years**

Recently; nowadays.

  1976 Warner *Beautiful Swimmers* 221 **eMD**, Latter days state's passed a law you can't have a dog aboard when you're out arstering [=oystering]. *Ibid* 286, We use to run the crabs . . right on the dirt. . . Well, we moved to the Somer's Cove Marina seven or eight years ago and put up this board track. You seen how we do it latter days, I guess.

lattermath n [*OED* 1530 →; "*dial.*"; *EDD* (at *latter* adj. (8))] *old-fash* Cf **lattercrop**

=aftermath.

  1828 Webster *Amer. Dict.* np, Lattermath. . . The latter mowing; that which is mowed after a former mowing. **1925** *Book of Rural Life* 3141, Lattermath, the growth of grass appearing in a meadow after the main crop has been cut for hay. It is usually called *aftermath*. **1939** *LANE* Map 125, The second crop of grass or clover . . *lattermath* and *lattercrop* have initial stress. [*DARE* Ed: no exx included on the map or in the commentary.] **1981** Pederson *LAGS Basic Materials*, 1 inf, **seGA**, Lattermath [inf old]; [1 inf, **neFL**, Has never heard of 2d cutting or lattermath—father has, calls it [ˈlætəˌmæs]].

lattice leaf n

=rattlesnake plantain.

  1961 Smith *MI Wildflowers* 85, Lattice-leaf . . *Goodyera repens* . . var. *ophioides*. . . Leaves . . with about 5 parallel veins, . . the fine veins netted. **1976** Bailey-Bailey *Hortus Third* 517, *Goodyera*. . . Rattlesnake plantain, latticeleaf.

latticework jam See **lattwaerrick**

‡lattle n

  1914 *DN* 4.109 **cKS**, Lattle. . . Lath.

lattren See **lantern**

lattwaerrick n Also *lattwerk, lotwaer(r)ick*; by folk-etym, *latticework jam*; for addit forms see quots [PaGer < Ger *Latwerge* electuary]

Apple butter.

  1858 in 1951 *PA Dutchman* 1 Oct 2, "In de dembel of solymon, syx meil from redding . . Will dack blayse A grate lott-waerg frolix. . . " The term "lotterwaerg," which occurs in the above classical effusion, is the Bushwacker appellation for that cooling relish known as apple-butter. **1930** Shoemaker *1300 Words* 38 **cPA Mts** (as of c1900), *Lotta warrick*—Apple butter. **1935** Frederick *PA Dutch* 219, Dutch Applebutter (Lot waerick). **1938** *Amer.-German Rev.* 5.1.41 [PaGer foods], *Lattwaerrick* is a sort of apple jam cooked until fine and dark, sometimes with pears and spices added, the name coming from the German *Latwerge*, which was an herb mixture serving as a stomach tonic. **1948**

Hutchison *PA Du. Cook Book* 105, *Lattwerk* (Apple-Butter). **1951** *Reading* (Pa.) *Times* 15 Aug. 15/1 *(Mathews Coll.)*, There were Shoofly and Montgomery pie . . Schmier Kase un Lodworrick. **1954** *Ibid* 3 Sep. 16/1 *(Mathews Coll.)*, No self-respecting countryman, however, would get up from his breakfast table . . without topping off the meal with a huge slice of bread, thickly spread with applebutter (which he calls "lotwaerrick") and the kind of cottage cheese that is called "schmierkase." **1992** *DARE* File **ceIA** (as of c1970), My aunt used to receive gifts of homemade "latticework jam" from her neighbor, an elderly woman of German descent. This "jam" looked and tasted like apple butter. I don't know whether "latticework jam" was the neighbor's term or my aunt's attempt at pronouncing a German word or phrase.

laugh n, v Usu |læf|; also **esp NEng** |laf, lɑf|; also |lɑrf| Pronc-spp *lahf, larf;* for addit pronc and sp varr see **A** below

A Forms. Note: Proncs of both the types [læf] and [lɑf] have been current in std Brit Engl since at least the 18th cent. The sp *laff* may be a pronc-sp for [læf] by writers who consider [lɑf] std.

   1840 Haliburton *Clockmaker* (3d ser) 91 **NEng**, And then he bust out a-larfin'. **1843** (1916) Hall *New Purchase* 174 **IN**, Some folks laff in meetin. **1851** [see **mouse** n A1]. **1884** *Anglia* 7.268 **Sth, S Midl** [Black], *To larf fit ter kill* = laugh immoderately. **1899** (1912) Green *VA Folk-Speech* 254, *Laff.* . . A form of *laugh*. **1910** *Univ. NC Mag.* 40.3.8 **Hatteras Is. NC**, Others of unusual pronunciation, as . . leuch (laugh). **1926** *AmSp* 2.77 **ME**, You would be "larfed" at. **1931** *AmSp* 7.19 **swPA**, The true Western Pennsylvanian pronounces a decidedly flat *a*, which he regards as more normal than the broad *a* of the East. . . "Ant Marsh" and "laff." **1938** *AmSp* 13.52 **Boston MA**, [hi 'bfən laft]. *Ibid* **eVA**, [lɑft]. **1938** in 1944 *ADD* **eVA**, [lɑf]. *Ibid* **eMA**, [laft]. **1942** *AmSp* 17.33 **seNY**, *Laugh.* . . [æ] 18 [occurrences]—[ɑ] 9—[a] 1. **1943** in 1944 *ADD* **sME coast**, [lɑf] lahf. **1958** Humphrey *Home from the Hill* 127 **neTX**, Damndest funniest sight you ever saw in your life. Laff, I thought I'd die. **1959** *VT Hist.* 27.147 **sVT**, *Laugh* [lɑrf]. . . The [ɑ] sound is followed by a faint voicing of the [r] sound. Common. **c1960** *Wilson Coll.* **csKY**, Laugh is generally [læɪf].

B As noun.

1 Laughter—usu in phr *full of laugh. old-fash*

   1851 (1969) Burke *Polly Peablossom* 70 **MS**, When he hearn what had been goin' on, he was so full er larf his face turned wrong side out'ards. **1871** (1882) Stowe *Fireside Stories* 65 **MA**, Huldy came behind jist chokin' with laugh, and afraid the minister would look 'round and see her. **1875** Twain in *Atlantic Mth.* May 572, He would be "so full of laugh" that he could hardly begin. **1901** *DN* 2.143 **cNY**, *Laugh.* . . Laughter. "I was full of laugh." **1909** *DN* 3.344 **eAL, wGA**, I was so full of laugh I couldn't hold in. **1912** Green *VA Folk-Speech* 257, *Laugh.* . . "He was so full of laugh he couldn't talk."

2 See quots. [Cf PaGer *lache* to laugh, whinny < Ger *lachen* to laugh] **chiefly sePA** *somewhat old-fash* Cf **snicker**

   1949 Kurath *Word Geog.* 63 **ePA**, *Laugh* [=the gentle noise made by horses], a Germanism, is still current in the Great Valley of Pennsylvania, but it is being replaced by *whinny*. **1967** Faries *Word Geog. MO* 90, The current expression throughout Missouri . . is the South and Midland *nicker.* . . The Germanism *laugh* (Pennsylvania Valley) appears once in Montgomery and once in Osage Counties [out of c700 infs]. **1971** Wood *Vocab. Change* 46 **TN, FL**, For the gentle sound that a horse makes. . . *laugh* [4 of c1000 infs]. **1981** *PADS* 67.30 **neMN**, *Whinny.* . . *Laugh* is used by an informant of Swedish parentage [1 of 17 infs]. **1985** *AmSp* 60.232 **sePA**, *Whinny* seems now to have replaced *laugh* in the Pennsylvania German area, although the latter term is still remembered by the oldest informants. **1986** Pederson *LAGS Concordance*, 2 infs, **cnAL, cGA**, Laugh; 1 inf, **cnGA**, Laughs [*DARE* Ed: It is not possible to determine whether this is a noun or verb.]; [1 inf, **neFL**, A gentle laughing noise]. [3 of 4 infs Black]

C As verb.

1 in phrr *laugh on the other side of one's face* (or *mouth*) and varr: To cry; to experience unexpected failure, defeat, or regret. [Cf *OED laugh* v. I.b 1779 →; *EDD laugh* v. II.1.(5)] **chiefly Sth, S Midl**

   1843 (1916) Hall *New Purchase* 174 **IN**, Some folks laff in meetin, but wait till they gits to h—l, and maybe they'll laff tother side of their mouth. **1899** (1912) Green *VA Folk-Speech* 34, Laugh on the wrong side of your mouth, that is, cry. **1909** *DN* 3.344 **eAL, wGA**, *Laugh on the other side of the mouth.* . . To cry. **1912** *DN* 3.581 **wIN**, *Laugh out of the other corner of one's mouth.* . . To cry. **1942** McAtee *Dial.*

Grant Co. IN 39 (as of 1890s), *Laugh on the wrong side of the face* . . cry. **1946** *PADS* 6.39 **eNC** (as of 1900–10), I'll make you *laugh* on the other side of your face. (That is, make you cry.) **1947** *PADS* 8.16 **sIN** (as of c1910), *Laugh* [in phr *I'll make you laugh on the other side of your face*]. **1950** *PADS* 13.20 **cTX**, I'll make you laugh on the other side of your face. **1960** Wentworth–Flexner *Slang* 313, *Laugh on the other side of [one's] face*—To cry; to change one's mood from happy to sad; to become a failure or be defeated after having expected or experienced success. Colloq. **c1960** *Wilson Coll.* **csKY**, Laugh on the wrong side (or other side) of the face. . . Cry or regret one's former conduct.

2 in phr *laugh all over oneself*: To laugh hard. [Cf *EDD laugh all over the face* (at *laugh* v. II.1.(3))]

   c1960 *Wilson Coll.* **csKY**, Laugh all over oneself—laugh unrestrainedly. [**1967** *DARE* (Qu. GG30, *To suddenly break out laughing: "When he told her that, she just _____."*) Inf **TX29**, Laughed all over.]

laugh and go foot   See **grin-go-foot**

laughing goose   n [See quot 1982]
=white-fronted goose.

   [**1772** Royal Soc. London *Philos. Trans.* 62.415 **nOntario Canada**, The laughing goose is of the size of the Canada or small grey goose.] **1791** Bartram *Travels* 294, A[nser] fuscus maculatus, the laughing goose. **1828** NY Acad. Sci. *Annals Lyceum Nat. Hist.* 2.376, *White-fronted Goose.* . . *Laughing Goose.* . . *Anas albifrons.* . . rare and accidental in the middle states. **1834** Nuttall *Manual Ornith.* 2.346, White-fronted, or Laughing Goose. [*Ibid* 347, The Indians imitate its call by patting the mouth with their hand, while they repeat the syllable *wah;* and the resemblance of this note to the laugh of a man has given rise to the trivial name.] **1898** Elliot *Wild Fowl* 47, Although the name by which this species is generally known to the gunners of the west is Brant, it has also various others in different parts of its dispersion [including] Laughing Goose,—on account of its cry, supposed to resemble the sound a man makes when laughing. **1918** Grinnell *Game Birds CA* 218, American White-fronted Goose. . . Laughing Goose. **1936** Roberts *MN Birds* 1.212, White-fronted Goose. . . Laughing Goose, Gray Wavie. **1982** Elman *Hunter's Field Guide* 298, Hunters on some of the western marshes call the white-front the "laughing goose." Its cries are like hysterical laughter or the eerie hooting of loons. . . No mechanical call reproduces the laughter, and few hunters learn to mimic it.

laughing gull   n [See quot 1969]
A gull (here: *Larus atricilla*). Also called **black-headed gull, mackerel ~ 1, molly ~, summer ~**

   [**1731** Catesby *Nat. Hist. Carolina* 1.89, *Larus major.* The Laughing Gull. . . These birds are numerous in most of the *Bahama* Islands. The noise they make has some resemblance to laughing, from which they seem to take their name.] **1789** Morse *Amer. Geog.* 59, American Birds. . . Laughing Gull / Goose / Canada Goose [etc]. **1844** Giraud *Birds Long Is.* 359, This handsome fowl. . . is quite a common species, and well known by the name of Laughing Gull, so called from its notes resembling the coarse laugh of a human being. **1883** U.S. Natl. Museum *Bulletin* 27.169, *Larus atricilla* . . Laughing Gull. . . Atlantic coast, from Maine (casually) to mouth of the Amazon. **1924** Howell *Birds AL* 25, The laughing gull nests abundantly on the Louisiana coast. **1966–70** *DARE* (Qu. Q10, . . *Water birds and marsh birds*) Infs **CO7, RI17, VA47**, Laughing gull; **FL13**, Laughing gulls. **1969** Longstreet *Birds FL* 67, The laughing gull is abundant in Florida. [*Ibid* 68, The birds receive their name from their high, clear notes of *Hah-ha-ha-hah-hah-hah*, the final syllable a long sustained chuckle.]

laughing jackass   n obs Cf **dragon's-mouth 1**
A **swamp pink** (here: *Arethusa bulbosa*).

   1894 *Jrl. Amer. Folkl.* 7.100, *Arethusa bulbosa* . . laughing jackass.

laughing owl   n Cf **barking owl**
An owl such as the barred owl (*Strix varia*) or a **screech owl**.

   1848 *S. Lit. Messenger* 14.531, The free open shout of the large laughing owl, so abundant in South Florida. **c1940** *LAMSAS Materials*, 4 infs, **NC, VA**, Laughin' owl; 1 inf, **NC**, Cat head owl—'a laughing owl.' **1966** Dakin *Dial. Vocab. Ohio R. Valley* 2.387, Another name [for *screech owl*] . . is *laughing owl*. This name is known in the eastern Knobs [of KY] and in the Pennyroyal south and west of the Knobs, but is unused north of the Ohio. **1967–68** *DARE* (Qu. Q2, . . *Kinds of owls*) Inf **GA46**, Laughing owl—have a mournful sound; **OK52**, Laughing owl—big, laughs like two drunken Scotchmen; **TN22**, Laughing owl; **WI22**, Laughing owl [same as] barred owl. **1969** *DARE* Tape **KY16**,

Back then we had all kind of owl. We had . . barking owl and laughing owl. **1986** Pederson *LAGS Concordance (Hoot owl)* 2 infs, **AR,** Laughing owl.

laughing woodpecker n
=pileated woodpecker.

1956 MA Audubon Soc. *Bulletin* 40.83, *Pileated Woodpecker.* . . Laughing Woodpecker (Maine. Ordinary call, *cack, cack, cack,* may be likened to laughter.)

laugh on the other side of one's face (or mouth) See **laugh C1**

lauhala n [Haw "pandanus leaf" < *lau* leaf + *hala* pandanus] **HI**
A screw pine (here: *Pandanus tectorius*); also the leaf of this tree.

1826 *Voyage H.M.S. Blonde* 108 **HI,** A church . . has lately been erected here: its walls are of reeds, lined with the woven leaves of the lauhala. **1866** in 1938 Twain *Letters Sandwich Is.* 75, Shady groves of forest trees . . the bread-fruit, the *lau hala,* the orange, lime. **1873** in 1966 Bishop *Sandwich Is.* 71 **HI,** I notice that the foreigners never use the English or botanical names of trees or plants, but speak of *ohias, ohelos, kukui* (candle-nut), lauhala (pandanus), *pulu* (tree fern), *mamané, koa,* &c. **1938** Reinecke *Hawaiian Loanwords* 22, Lauhala. . . 1. The leaf of the pandanus, much used in manufacture of mats, hats, baskets, etc. 2. The pandanus tree. V[ery] F[requent]. **1954** *Ellery Queen's Mystery Mag.* 4.42 **HI,** With *lauhala* mats and some reed furniture . . it will be quite charming. **1967** *DARE* (Qu. T16, . . *Kinds of trees . . 'special'*) Inf **HI**11, Lauhala = pandanus.

laulau n [Haw] **HI**
A dish consisting of meat or fish wrapped and cooked in leaves.

1938 Reinecke *Hawaiian Loanwords* 22, Laulau [ˈlau-ˈlau]. . . V[ery] F[requent]. **1940** Bazore *Hawaiian Foods* 38, For special occasions . . *laulaus* are prepared. They may be steamed or cooked in the imu. At serving time each guest unwraps the laulau set before him. **1967** *DARE* (Qu. H45, *Dishes made with meat, fish, or poultry that everybody around here would know, but that people in other places might not*) Inf **HI**1, [ˈlau͵lau]—little packet of food, wrapped in ti leaves: pork, fat, butterfish enclosed in taro leaves; **HI**9A, Laulau—fish and pork and taro leaf, wrapped in ti leaf. **1972** Carr *Da Kine Talk* 47 **HI,** Laulau. . . [ˈlau͵lau]. *Ibid* 87 **HI,** *Hawaiian Words Commonly Heard In Hawaii's English.* . . Laulau . . ti or banana leaves containing pork, beef . . fish. **1981** *Pidgin To Da Max* np **HI,** Laulau.

launch v[1] Usu |lɔnč, lɑnč|; also |lænč|; for addit varr see quots Pronc-spp *lance, lanch* [Cf *EDD lanch, lonch,* etc. (at *launch* v. and sb.); cf also *OED lanch* "obs. form of *launch,*" and *lance* v. 3 "To launch (a boat). . . To launch forth. *Obs.*"] Cf **calm, haunt** n, v **A, lance** v[1]
Std senses, var forms.

1805 (1904) Clark *Orig. Jrls. Lewis & Clark Exped.* 2.220 **KY,** Lanced [launched] the Leather boat, and found that it leaked a little; corked Lanced & loaded the Canoes. **1806** (1970) Webster *Compendious Dict.* 173, Launch . . lanch. [*DARE* Ed: This entry does not appear in Webster's English model.] **1891** *DN* 1.122 **cNY,** [læːnč] . . launch. **1893** Shands *MS Speech* 6, [In] the dialects of the negroes and the illiterate whites. . . the [æ] sound is given also to the vowels in *launch, haunch* . . and nearly all similar words. **1939** *LANE* Map 182 *(Launch),* [Proncs of the type [læntʃ] are found throughout **NEng,** but are esp freq in **sNEng;** proncs of the type [lɑntʃ, lantʃ, lɒntʃ] are found throughout the region; proncs of the type [lɔntʃ] are more freq in **sNEng.**] **1989** Pederson *LAGS Tech. Index* 93 **Gulf Region,** [345 infs responded with proncs of the type [lɔnč]; 166 infs, of the type [lɑnč]; 21 infs, [lɒnč]; 5 infs, [lʌnč]; 2 infs, [lænč]; 2 infs, [lončˑ]; 2 infs, [launč]; 2 infs, [lɔɪnč]; 2 infs, [lɔnš]; 2 infs, [lɑnts]; 1 inf, [lɔnj]; 1 inf, [ˈlančɪŋ]; 1 inf, [lɑɪnč]; 1 inf, [læntʃ]; 1 inf, [lons].]

launch v[2] See **lance** v[1]

laundry v
To launder.

1880 *American Mail Order Fashions* (1961) 14 *(OEDS),* The wires can be taken out . . so that the entire bustle can be laundried with the greatest care. **1930s** in 1944 *ADD* **eWV,** Laundry. . . To launder. . . But *wash* is the usual word. **1960** Criswell *Resp. to PADS 20* **Ozarks,** *Laundry* for *launder.* Very common in the past. **1986** Pederson *LAGS*

Concordance, 1 inf, **cnAR,** A lot of them wants to laundry on Monday; 1 inf, **seAL,** Laundry = launder.

laundry tray n esp Pacific
A permanently installed laundry tub; a set tub.

1885 *Century Illustr. Mag.* 29.266, *Laundry Trays* . . are hardly to be regarded as a conspicuous element of the sanitary works of a house. **1925** *AmSp* 1.152, Western speech is full of differences from Eastern speech. . . What is the difference between a "set tub" and a "laundry tray?" **1943** *CA Folkl. Qrly.* 2.41, I asked my landlord to install a washtub. He thought I was asking him to buy me a wash boiler, and it turned out that in his strictly San Franciscan vocabulary a washtub is a *laundry tray.* **1980** *DARE* File **nwOR,** A friend from Portland used the term "laundry tray" for what I would call a set tub. **1995** *Ibid* **cwCA,** We first heard the term *laundry tray* for the sink next to the washing machine when we moved here in 1948. All the houses in the new subdivision had them.

laurel n
1 also *laurel tree:* **=magnolia 1.** Cf **laurel magnolia**

1637 (1972) Morton *New Engl. Canaan* 92, There are divers arematicall herbes . . , Balme, Lawrell, Hunnisuckles, and the like. [*DARE* Ed: This quot may refer instead to a sense below.] **1682** (1836) Ash *Carolina* 64, There are many other Fragrant smelling trees, the Myrtle, Bay and Lawrel, several Others to us wholly unknown. **1709** (1967) Lawson *New Voyage* 97 **NC,** Laurel-Trees, in Height equalizing the lofty Oaks; the Berries and Leaves of this Tree dyes a Yellow. *Ibid* 101, Bay and Laurel generally delight in a low, swampy Ground. **1791** Bartram *Travels* 6 **S Atl,** The natural produce of these testaceous ridges, besides many of less note, are, the great Laurel Tree, (Magnolia grandiflora) Pinus taeda [etc]. **1830** Rafinesque *Med. Flora* 2.32, The genus *Magnolia.* . . includes about ten American species. . . chiefly found in the Southern States, but the *M. glauca* extends to New England. They are promiscuously called Laurels, . . Umbrella Tree, &c. **1897** Sudworth *Arborescent Flora* 193 **SC,** *Magnolia foetida* [=*M. grandiflora*]. . . *Common Names.* . . Laurel. **1933** Small *Manual SE Flora* 535, *M[agnolia] grandiflora.* . . Laurel. . . Hammocks, bluffs, sand-dunes, and sandy bottoms. **1950** Gray–Fernald *Manual of Botany* 676, *M[agnolia] virginiana.* . . Laurel. . . Swamps and low woods, Fla. to Miss., n. to Pa., N.J. and locally to e. Mass. and Tenn. **1966–70** *DARE* (Qu. T5, . . *Kinds of evergreens, other than pine*) Inf **TX**38, Laurel; (Qu. T15, . . *Kinds of swamp trees*) Infs **FL**34, **KY**24, **NC**81, **VA**82, Laurel.

2 **=mountain laurel 1.** chiefly Atlantic, Appalachians

1743 (1946) Gronovius *Flora Virginica* 160, *Andromeda foliis ovatis obtusis, corollis corymbosis infundibuliformibus* [=*Andromeda* with blunt oval leaves, corollas corymbose, funnel-shaped] . . The common Laurel / vulgarly called Ivy. Ovium præsentaneum venenum [=A quickacting poison to sheep]. **1765** (1942) Bartram *Diary of a Journey* 28 **seGA,** Wee observed our north[ern] laurel of Kallmia grow[ing] plentifully near ye falls. **1802** Drayton *View of SC* 69, *Calico flower, wild ivy, or laurel* whose flowers of red and white, grow in such large clusters together; as to give the whole plant at a small distance, the appearance of having a bit of calico thrown over it. **1852** Ellet *Pioneer Women* 206 **wPA,** "Laurel ridge," . . is so named from the profusion of . . kalmia latifolia, or laurel, which cluster along its rocky sides. **1884** Sargent *Forests of N. Amer.* 98, *Kalmia latifolia.* . . *Laurel.* . . Most common and reaching its greatest development in the southern Alleghany mountains, here often forming dense, impenetrable thickets. **1941** *LANE* Map 249 *(Mountain laurel),* [For *Kalmia latifolia* the response *laurel* is common throughout **sNEng,** where the plant grows wild. Three infs offered *laurel* as a term for the sheep laurel *(Kalmia angustifolia).*] **1965–70** *DARE* (Qu. T5, . . *Kinds of evergreens, other than pine*) 18 Infs, **chiefly Appalachians, Atlantic,** Laurel; (Qu. S26a, . . *Roadside flowers*) 14 Infs, **esp PA,** Laurel; (Qu. S26c, *Wildflowers that grow in woods*) Infs **CT**8, **NJ**16, 17, **NY**183, **PA**3, **VA**30, Laurel; (Qu. S26e, *Other wildflowers not yet mentioned;* not asked in early QRs) Infs **GA**70, **NC**52, **PA**73, **TN**22, Laurel; (Qu. T12) Inf **SC**67, Laurel. [*DARE* Ed: Some of these Infs may refer instead to **3** below.] **1966–69** *DARE* Wildfl QR Pl.156A Infs **MI**31, 57, Laurel; Pl.156B Inf **MI**31, Laurel; Pl.160A Inf **OR**12, Laurel—not here; **WI**80, Laurel. **1976** Bailey–Bailey *Hortus Third* 623, *Kalmia.* . . *Laurel.* . . About 6 spp. of evergreen or rarely deciduous shrubs . . ; fl[ower]s white, pink to purple. . . Foliage is poisonous if eaten.

3 **=rhododendron;** also a thicket of this plant. **chiefly sAppalachians, esp NC** Cf **mountain laurel 2**

1859 Taliaferro *Fisher's R.* 165 **nwNC** (as of 1857), In a little cabin on the side of a steep laurel-hill . . , lives my friend John Senter. **1860**

Curtis *Cat. Plants NC* 97, Laurel. (Rhododendron maximum . .). This is rare north of Pennsylvania, but becomes abundant southward in the Alleghanies, . . where it often forms impenetrable thickets, many acres in extent. . . The leaves and flowers are reputed poisonous. **1894** *Jrl. Amer. Folkl.* 7.93 **NC,** *Rhododendron,* all species, laurel. **1897** *Ibid* 10.49 **ME,** *Rhododendron Rhodora,* . . laurel, Paris, Me. **1922** (1926) Kephart *Highlanders* 369 **sAppalachians,** Rhododendron is laurel. **1924** *Amer. Botanist* 30.123, In North Carolina however the people never by any chance call *Rhododendron Catawbiense* anything but rhododendron. . *Rhododendron maximum* they call "laurel." . . They call *Kalmia* "ivy." **1939** *Hall Coll.* **wNC,** We went right up here on Walkers Creek Laurel one time. **1950** Peattie *Nat. Hist. Trees* 518, The mountain folk of the southern Appalachians and the visitors from the north will never agree on the proper name for this shrub [=*Rhododendron maximum*]. . . To the mountaineer it is Laurel (with or without adjectives). **1953** *Hall Coll.* **wNC,** [He] stayed up there and had him a camp right in the middle of a big laurel, under a rock clift, and lived in that for four years through the war. **1964** Campbell et al. *Gt. Smoky Wildflowers* 48, Early settlers knew laurel [=*Kalmia latifolia*] as ivy, and rhododendron as laurel. . . Flower-clad ridges of these two shrubs are known to mountain people as laurel slicks. **1969** *DARE* (Qu. T5, . . *Kinds of evergreens, other than pine*) Inf **KY6,** Laurel—poison; **KY3,** Ivy (laurel), laurel (rhododendron); (Qu. T16, . . *Kinds of trees . . 'special'*) Inf **KY16,** Laurel [FW: rhododendron]. **1982** Ginns *Snowbird Gravy* 130 **nwNC,** The rhododendron, they call it now, we used to call it "laurel"; and the other, they call it "laurel" now, we called it "ivy."

4 also *laurel tree:* =**California laurel. Cf mountain laurel 3**
  1888 Lindley–Widney *CA of South* 171, The California bay, or laurel, which may be called a tree from its size, though usually growing in bushy form, is beautiful in color, and is a favorite because of its fragrance. **1906** (1918) Parsons *Wild Flowers CA* 378, *Umbellularia Californica.* . . The wood of the laurel is one of the most beautiful employed by the cabinet-maker. **1968–69** *DARE* (Qu. T15, . . *Kinds of swamp trees*) Inf **CA65,** Bay or laurel tree (same tree); (Qu. T16, . . *Kinds of trees . . 'special'*) Inf **CA107,** Laurel—also called California bay.

5 also *laurel tree, laurelwood:* A **madrone** (here: *Arbutus menziesii* or *A. texana*). **esp OR, CA**
  1897 Sudworth *Arborescent Flora* 312, *Arbutus menziesii.* . . Common Names. . . Laurelwood (Oreg.) . . Laurel (Oreg.) *Ibid* 313, *Arbutus xalapensis.* . . Common Names. . . Laurel. **1908** Britton *N. Amer. Trees* 758, *Arbutus Menziesii* . . A large evergreen tree extending from British Columbia to southern California. . . It is also called . . Laurelwood, and Laurel. *Ibid* 759, *Arbutus texana* . . A small evergreen tree or shrub, entering southwestern Texas . . , where it is quite abundant. . . It is also called . . Laurel. **1910** Jepson *Silva CA* 275, About Ashland, Oregon, adult trees [of *Arbutus menziesii*] are remarkably symmetrical and are called "Laurel." **1925** Stuart *40 Yrs.* 1.59 **cCA,** There were also . . some beautiful madrona or laurel trees. **1931** U.S. Dept. Ag. *Misc. Pub.* 101.123, *Pacific madrone (A. menziesii),* often but incorrectly called California-laurel, . . produces tanbark and is a famous bee plant.

laurel cherry See **cherry laurel**

laurel-leaf oak See **laurel oak 2**

laurel-leaved magnolia See **laurel magnolia**

laurel-leaved oak See **laurel oak 2**

laurelly adj Also sp *laurely*
Laurel-covered.
  1913 Kephart *Highlanders* 79 **sAppalachians,** The Tennessee side of the mountain is powerful steep and laurely, so 't man nor dog cain't git over it in lots o' places. **1953** *Hall Coll.* **swNC,** Laurely. . . Of terrain covered with rhododendron. . . "It was so awful rough and laurely and not much open woods on that side of the mountain."

laurel magnolia n Also *laurel-leaved magnolia* Cf **laurel 1**
Either **southern magnolia** or a **sweet bay** (here: *Magnolia virginiana*).
  1791 Bartram *Travels* 85 **S Atl,** The Laurel Magnolia, which grows on this river is the most beautiful and tall, that I have anywhere seen. . . The flowers are on the extremities of the subdivisions of the branches, in the center of a coronet of dark green, shining, ovate pointed entire leaves: they are large, perfectly white, and expanded like a full blown Rose. **1806** Wakefield *Excursions N. Amer.* 93, The laurel magnolia reaches to the height of an hundred feet. **1826** Flint *Recollections* 294 **LA,** You begin to discover the ever-verdant laurel magnolia, with its beautiful foliage of the thickness and the feeling of leather. **1897** Sud-

worth *Arborescent Flora* 193, *Magnolia foetida* [=*M. grandiflora*]. . . Common Names. . . Great Laurel Magnolia (Ala.) . . Laurel-leaved Magnolia (Tenn.) **1908** Britton *N. Amer. Trees* 387, The Bull bay, or Great laurel magnolia, is the largest leaved evergreen tree of our flora, and grows naturally . . from eastern North Carolina to central Florida, westward through the Gulf States to Texas and Arkansas. *Ibid* 388, The Sweet bay, . . or Laurel magnolia, . . grows in swamps from eastern Massachusetts to southern Florida, extending westward to Lebanon county, Pennsylvania, central North Carolina, and westward through the Gulf States to Texas and southern Arkansas. **1939** Medsger *Edible Wild Plants* 221, Laurel Magnolia, Magnolia virginiana. . . It is said that the leaves give flavor to roasts and gravy and perfume is made from the very fragrant flowers. **1960** Vines *Trees SW* 281, *Magnolia grandiflora.* . . Vernacular names are Bull-bay, Great Laurel Magnolia, and Loblolly Magnolia.

laurel oak n

1 =**shingle oak.**
  1810 Michaux *Histoire des Arbres* 1.23, Laurel oak. **1812** *Ibid* 2.78, *Quercus imbricaria.* . . Cette espèce de Chêne, assez rare à l'est des monts Alléghanys, n'y est connue . . sons aucun nom particulier; tandis qu'à l'ouest de ces montagnes, où elle est plus multipliée . . elle est désignée sous ceux de *Jack oak, Black Jack oak,* et quelquefois de *Laurel oak* . . d'après la forme de ses feuilles. [=This species of oak, rather rare east of the Alleghanies, . . is not known there by any special name; but west of these mountains, where it is more widespread, it is known as *Jack oak, Black Jack oak,* and sometimes *Laurel oak,* . . after the shape of its leaves.] **1900** (1927) Keeler *Our Native Trees* 372, Shingle Oak. Laurel Oak. . . A tree of the mid-continent; rare in the east, abundant in the lower Ohio valley. **1950** Moore *Trees AR* 58, Shingle Oak. . . Local Name: Laurel Oak. **1970** *DARE* (Qu. T10, . . *Kinds of oak trees*) Inf **PA234,** Laurel oak. **1980** Little *Audubon Guide N. Amer. Trees E. Region* 391, *Shingle Oak* "Laurel Oak". . . A handsome tree with a symmetrical, conical to rounded crown.

2 also *laurel-leaf* (or *-leaved*) *oak, swamp laurel ~:* An **oak** (here: *Quercus laurifolia*) native chiefly to the South Atlantic and Gulf States. [See quot 1980] Also called **diamond-leaf oak, evergreen ~ a, live ~ 1, pin ~, pine ~, red ~, spotted ~, water ~, willow ~**
  1830 Rafinesque *Med. Flora* 2.255, Wood of Q[uercus] virens and Q. laurifolia (Live Oak, Laurel Oak) as heavy as Guayac, cannot split, nails driven in cannot be taken off, hardens by age, strong, compact, durable, our best timber. **1884** Sargent *Forests of N. Amer.* 153, Laurel Oak. . . most common and reaching its greatest development on the rich hummocks of the Florida coast. **1938** Van Dersal *Native Woody Plants* 217, Laurel oak. *Ibid* 346, Laurelleaf [Oak] (*Quercus laurifolia*). **1960** Vines *Trees SW* 182, [The Diamond-leaf Oak] is also known as . . Swamp Laurel Oak, Pine Oak, Spotted Oak, and Laurel-leaved Oak. **1966** *DARE* Tape **FL5,** There's another type of oak that grows around here too called holly oak, laurel, excuse me, no it's a laurel oak. **1969** *DARE* FW Addit **Hatteras Is. NC,** Laurel oak. **1970** *DARE* (Qu. T5, . . *Kinds of evergreens, other than pine*) Inf **FL49,** Only two varieties of oak are evergreen—laurel oak and live oak; (Qu. T10, . . *Kinds of oak trees*) Infs **FL49, 51,** Laurel oak. **1980** Little *Audubon Guide N. Amer. Trees E. Region* 394, *Laurel Oak . . Quercus laurifolia.* . . Common and Latin species names refer to the resemblance of the foliage to Grecian Laurel (*Laurus nobilis* . .), of the Mediterranean region.

3 =**canyon oak 1.**
  1910 Jepson *Silva CA* 223, On account of the pollen-like powder on the under side of the younger leaves it [=*Quercus chrysolepis*] is famed as Gold-leaf Oak or Golden Oak, while certain shapes of the leaves explain the term "Laurel Oak."

4 A **willow oak** (here: *Quercus phellos*).
  1938 Van Dersal *Native Woody Plants* 346, Laurel [Oak] (*Quercus phellos*). **1940** Clute *Amer. Plant Names* 163, Q[uercus] phellos. . . Willow Oak. Laurel oak.

laurel sumac n [See quot 1980]
A **sumac** (here: *Rhus laurina*).
  1910 Jepson *Silva CA* 28, A number of species, which are typically shrubs, develop arborescent individuals most frequently southward. . . Under this head may be noted . . Laurel Sumac (*Rhus laurina*). **1911** CA Ag. Exper. Sta. Berkeley *Bulletin* 217.1005, Laurel Sumac. . . Amber honey with a marked odor, but of a fine flavor. Many southern apiaries get one or more extractings from this source. **1938** Van Dersal *Native Woody Plants* 230, *Laurel sumac.* . . A large evergreen shrub . . ;

produces a very dense shade. **1959** Munz–Keck *CA Flora* 998, *Laurel Sumac.* . . Dry slopes, below 3000 ft. **1980** Little *Audubon Guide N. Amer. Trees W. Region* 521, *Laurel Sumac.* . . Glossy foliage and odor of bitter almonds. [*Ibid* 522, The common and scientific names refer to the resemblance of the foliage to that of Laurel (*Laurus nobilis* . .), an unrelated small tree of the Mediterranean region.]

laurel tree n
1 See **laurel 1**.
2 See **laurel 4**.
3 See **laurel 5**.
4 A **red bay** (here: *Persea borbonia*).
1897 Sudworth *Arborescent Flora* 201 **LA**, *Persea borbonia.* . . *Common Names.* . . Laurel Tree. **1908** Britton *N. Amer. Trees* 399, The Red bay . . , known also as . . Laurel tree, inhabits moist soil from Virginia to Florida, Texas, and southern Arkansas. **1933** Small *Manual SE Flora* 922, *Laurel-tree.* . . The bright-red heart-wood, close-grained, heavy, and strong, is used for cabinet-work and construction. **1976** Bailey–Bailey *Hortus Third* 848, *Laurel tree.* . . Tree, 30–40 ft.

laurelwood See **laurel 5**

laurely See **laurelly**

Laurence See **Lawrence**

laury mundy n Also *lauria mundi, laurii amande* [Varr of LaFr *laurier (a)mande* (= *Prunus caroliniana*) < Fr *laurier-amandier* (= *P. laurocerasus*)]
=**Carolina cherry.**
1854 Wailes *Rept. on Ag. & Geol. MS* 342, Lauria mundi, *Cerasus Carolinensis.* **1897** Sudworth *Arborescent Flora* 246 **LA**, *Prunus caroliniana.* . . Laury Mundy (La.). Laurii amande (La.).

laus-a-day, lausyday See **lawsy**

lava bowl n [Folk-etym for *lavabo*]
1979 *AmSp* 54.290 **cwAL**, A local couple are reported to "have built some personal, special features in their home. One of her favorite places is their patio where they enjoy sitting by themselves or entertaining guests. She has a lava bowl with running water affixed to one of the walls." . . I have heard [this] . . form frequently during the past ten years, but never before found it in print.

‡**lavadated** adj [Perh var of *dilapidated*]
1927 Kennedy *Gritny* 110 **sLA** [Black], Wa't I want wid anybody comin' hyuh to talk to me, all lavadated like I is . . ? *Ibid* 227, De ole house so rickety an' lavadated.

lavatory n Pronc-spp *labatory* and (perh infl by folk-etym) *laboratory;* abbr *lab* Cf Pronc Intro 3.I.17 *esp freq among Black speakers*
Std sense, var forms.
1962 in a1972 Hench *Coll.* **MD** [Black], Laboratory—Negro modification of lavatory (=bathroom). . . Our cleaning woman . . , while in my downstairs study, asked me about a little walled-off room: "Is that a laboratory in there?" "No," I said. "It would be nice to have a laboratory there. You wouldn't have to run upstairs." **1967–70** *DARE* (Qu. F37, . . *An indoor toilet*) Inf **DC**12, Labatory; **MA**27, Lab; **GA**90, Laboratory ['læbrətori]. [2 of 3 Infs Black] **1986** Pederson *LAGS Concordance* (*An outdoor toilet*) 1 inf, **ceAL**, Laboratory. [Inf Black]

lavendar Jesus See **lavender Jesus**

lavender n
1 A **groundsel tree** (here: *Baccharis halimifolia*).
1913 *Torreya* 13.234 **SC**, *Baccharis halimifolia* . . Lavender, Santee Club, S.C.
2 A **marsh elder 1** (here: *Iva frutescens*).
1913 *Torreya* 13.234 **SC**, *Iva frutescens* . . Lavender, Santee Club, S.C.
3 A **lupine** (here: *Lupinus diffusus*).
1913 *Torreya* 13.231 **FL**, *Lupinus diffusus* . . Lavender, St. Vincent [Island], Fla.

lavender Jesus n Also sp *lavendar Jesus*
See quots.
1930 *AmSp* 5.391 [Language of N Atl fishermen], *Lavendar Jesus.* . . A choice bit of profanity, probably a variation of 'blue Jesus.' **1957** Beck *Folkl. ME* 168, An angry man . . swore like "lavender Jeasus [sic]," fiercely.

laverick n Also *labrick*
A fool, dolt; a greenhorn—often used as a mild term of abuse.
1889 Twain *CT Yankee* 382, As a rule, a knight is a lummox and sometimes even a labrick, and hence open to pretty poor arguments when they come glibly from a superstition-monger. **1894** Twain *Pudd'nhead Wilson* 25 **seMO**, "That's what he is," said No. 4, "he's a labrick—just a Simon-pure labrick, if ever there was one." "Yes, sir, he's a damn fool, that's the way I put him up," said No. 5. **1895** *DN* 1.390 **West**, *Laverick:* slightly contemptuous term for a man, usually a stranger. **1911** *Century Dict. Suppl.* np, *Laverick.* . . In the western United States, a contemptuous term for a greenhorn or stranger; a tenderfoot. **1966** *DARE* (Qu. HH3, *A dull and stupid person*) Inf **MI**26, Laverick ['læv,rɪk]—Irish.

lavins n pl [Ir dial var of *leavings;* cf *EDD* leavin(g sb., lashin(g sb. 1] Cf **lashings**
In phr *lashings and lavins:* A great plenty.
1927 *DN* 5.475 **Ozarks**, *Lashins and lavins.* . . A great quantity. "Shore them Hawkinses hev got money—lashins an' lavins of hit." **1984** Wilder *You All Spoken Here* 71 **Sth**, *Lashin's an' lavin's:* An abundance; plenty and some to spare; more than you can shake a stick at in a whole week.

lavish n [*OED* lavish sb. "*Obs.* . . Profusion, excessive abundance . . ; prodigality, lavishness."; 1483–1597]
1 An abundance, plenty. **chiefly S Midl**
1913 Kephart *Highlanders* 283 **sAppalachians**, If anybody wanted a history of this county for fifty years he'd git a lavish of it by reading that mine-suit testimony. **1926** *DN* 5.401 **Ozarks**, Ef them Hammonses is-a-lookin' fer trouble, they'll shore git a lavish of it. **1926** Roberts *Time of Man* 245 **KY**, He'll maybe see trouble and a lavish of it too. **1937** (1977) Hurston *Their Eyes* 58 **FL** [Black], It takes money tuh feed pretty women. Dey gits uh lavish uh talk. **1940** *AmSp* 15.52 **sAppalachians**, We shore got a lavish o' onions this year. **1944** *PADS* 2.45 **NC**, We have a lavish of fruit this year. **1960** Williams *Walk Egypt* 233 **GA**, I got a lavish of jars left over. **1976** Garber *Mountain-ese* 52 **sAppalachians**, *Lavish* . . abundance—Our trees had a lavish uv apples on them this year.
2 See quot. *obs*
1899 (1912) Green *VA Folk-Speech* 257, *Lavish, n.* Waste; squandering.

law n[1] Usu |lɔ|; also |lɒ, lɑ|; also esp **NEast** |lɔr| See Pronc Intro 3.II.9, 26 Pronc-spp *laer, law(e)r, lor*
A Forms.
1795 Dearborn *Columbian Grammar* 136, *List of Improprieties,* commonly called *Vulgarisms,* which should never be used in *Speaking, Reading, or Writing.* . . Lor for Law. **1931** *AmSp* 6.400 **eME coast,** [ɒ] final as in *law, flaw, saw,* has the tendency to acquire a final [ɹ], becoming [lɒɹ], etc. **1932** *AmSp* 7.324, The addition of an [r] to such words as *idea* and *law,* especially when the following word begins with a vowel . . is not, of course, limited to New York City, but is also encountered in New England. **1936** *AmSp* 11.190 **swWY,** There is some use of *r* after a final vowel, *law* being sometimes pronounced *lawer* or even *laer.* **1941** *AmSp* 16.157 **NYC** [New York dialect], *Lor*—law. **1942** *New Yorker* 11 July 20 **NY,** The rope king's son-in-lawr. **1943** *LANE* Map 550 *(Law and Order),* [In **NEng** [lɔr ən ɔdə] is common though not universal.] **1950** Hubbell *Pronc. NYC* 48, The pronunciation of /r/ as a word-final in *law* . . occurs sometimes before a pause . . *Obey the law* . . or before a following initial consonant . . *law school.* **1959** *PADS* 32.117, [Table shows the distribution of low-central and low-back vowels in the Eastern US. In *law, salt, brought,* the usual phoneme is /ɔ/ in **wVT, NYC, sePA, wNC, eVA, and eSC;** the usual phoneme is /ɒ/ in **coastal ME, seNH, and wPA.**] **1961** Kurath–McDavid *Pronc. Engl.* 106, The Vowel in *law, salt, dog.* . . Three major phonic types are widely current in the Eastern States: a well-rounded monophthongal raised low-back [ɔ], usually prolonged; a slightly rounded low-back [ɒ]; and an upgliding diphthong [ɒə], with progressive lip rounding. *Ibid* 172, Positional allomorphs ending in /r/ are often created in Eastern New England and Metropolitan New York for words that historically end in the vowels /ɒ~ɔ, a~ɑ, ə/, as *law, ma, Martha.* Thus one hears *law and order* /lɔr ənd ɒdə, lɔr ənd ɔdə/. **1976** Allen *LAUM* 3.23 **Upper MW** (as of c1950), The fully rounded [ɔ] . . expectedly dominates the U[pper] M[idwest]. . . [I]n *law,* . . [ɔ] or [ɔ·] is strong in all the states but Iowa. *Ibid* 24, The weakly rounded low-back [ɒ] . . consistently appears also in both Northern and Midland speech areas of the UM. . . [T]he tendency toward unrounding historic [ɔ] in such words as *law,* the tendency that then yields the unrounded [ɑ], may actually be strengthened in the UM. . . [A]n apparently rather rapid and highly noticeable

development in the UM. . . [is evidenced by the] steadily increasing proportion of students who have no low-back rounded vowel except before /r/. Annually, more and more students have only [ɑ] or even [ɑ] in *law, jaw, fall*.

B Senses.

1 often with *the:* A law-enforcement officer; the police. **widespread, but more freq Sth, S Midl** See Map

1835 *Vade Mecum* (Phila.) 17 Jan. 3/6 *(DA),* A dreadful uproar is heard in the domicile of the Simpkinses. The law opens the house and the belligerent couple are extracted like an oyster from its shell. **1923** *DN* 5.213 **swMO,** *Law.* . . An officer. "Yander comes the law." **1937** *Hall Coll.* **eTN,** *Law.* . . State or federal liquor control officers. "The law never raided many times." **c1938** in 1970 Hyatt *Hoodoo* 1.699 **seLA** [Black], If you running a place of business and you don't want the laws to bother you. *Ibid* 700, You take the law's name— . . you take his name and you write it nine times. **1938** Stuart *Dark Hills* 258 **neKY,** The Law and his deputies part the crowd. **1942** Thomas *Blue Ridge Country* 256 **sAppalachians,** The revenooer (mountain folk usually call him the law). **1945** *AmSp* 20.83 **TX,** Sooner or later . . somebody will call 'the laws.' **1955** in 1958 Brewer *Dog Ghosts* 38 **TX** [Black], De p'liceman pulls back de lapel of his coat an' shows de Nigguh his badge. So de Nigguh say, "You ain't de law, is you?" "Ah sho ain't de preachuh," 'low de p'liceman. **c1960** *Wilson Coll.* **csKY,** *Law,* esp. *The Law* . . Authority, often the sheriff or other arresting officer. **1965–70** *DARE* (Qu. V10a, . . *Joking names . . for a sheriff*) 159 Infs, **scattered, but more freq Sth, S Midl,** Law; **CO**5, **IN**3, **KS**18, **NC**22, **SC**21, 45, **TX**39, The law; (Qu. V9, . . *Nicknames . . for a policeman*) 60 Infs, **scattered, but more freq Sth, S Midl, esp SC,** Law; 11 Infs, **scattered,** The law; **MO**39, High law; (Qu. V10b, . . *[Joking names] for a marshal*) 19 Infs, **scattered,** Law; **MS**1, 80, **NY**100, **TX**94, City law; (Qu. V10c, . . *A constable*) 16 Infs, **scattered,** Law; **LA**28, **NC**18, The law; **TX**32, Big law; **AZ**7, Town law. **1986** Pederson *LAGS Concordance* **Gulf Region,** 6 infs, The law—the police; 3 infs, The law—policeman; 1 inf, The law—law officer or officers; 1 inf, They looked like policemen or deputies; 1 inf, Law; 1 inf, I ain't going wait till the law get over here; [1 inf, The law—fireman; 1 inf, The law—of fireman as well as policeman].

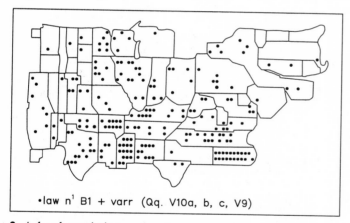

•law n¹ B1 + varr (Qq. V10a, b, c, V9)

2 A legal restriction on hunting; see quots.

1929 *AmSp* 5.71 **NE** [Cowboy talk], The Cowboys . . shoot crows . . black tailed rabbits, or any other small animals . . often not caring whether or not "the law is open," meaning that it is hunting or "open" season. **1960** *DE Folkl. Bulletin* 1.36, The law's off (open season on ducks, etc.) **1966** *DARE* FW Addit **ME**14, The law is on 'em—They're protected by law (referring to a species of woodpecker). **1975** Gould *ME Lingo* 159, With reference to hunting and fishing, the Maine *law* is either on or off. Instead of "open season," the *law* is on or off. When the season closes, the *law* goes on. When moose were well-nigh extinct in Maine, the state "put on" a *law;* now that moose have increased, there is agitation to "take the *law* off."

law v, hence vbl n *lawing* **scattered, but more freq Sth, S Midl**

1 To go to law, engage in litigation; hence n *lawing* litigation, a lawsuit. [*OED law* v. 2.[a]; a1550 →]

1859 (1968) Bartlett *Americanisms* 237, *Lawing.* Going to law. "I got my debt of him by lawing." Western. **1923** *DN* 5.213 **swMO,** *Law.* . . To enter into litigation. "They're a-lawin' over the will." **a1930** in 1991 Hughes–Hurston *Mule Bone* 36 **cFL** [Black], Ah done been to de cot-house at Orlando an' set under de voice of dem lawyers an' heard

'em law from mornin' tell night. **1935** Sandoz *Jules* 147 **wNE,** The county was in debt $5000 for its three years of lawing. **1937** Thornburgh *Gt. Smoky Mts.* 94, Thar was a barn o' his'n burnt up. Thar wuz lawin' about it. **1939** (1962) Thompson *Body & Britches* 492 **NY,** We are also somewhat cynical about the law, though many farmers still enjoy a "lawing". **1942** Hurston *Dust Tracks* 112 **FL** [Black], She "lawed" for a divorce and he let it slide. **1943** Stuart *Taps* 252 **eKY,** A-lawin over the last remains of Brother Kim would've looked bad. **1960** (1962) Lee *Mockingbird* 107 **AL,** Not only a Finch waiting on tables but one in the courthouse lawing for niggers!

2 To take legal action against; to sue, prosecute (someone); to obtain by legal action. [*OED law* v. 2.b; 1647 →]

1859 Taliaferro *Fisher's R.* 185 **nwNC** (as of 1820s), Now the rest of the acts of John Senter, . . how he lawed the people at the justice's courts, how he loved apple brandy, and danced the "double shuffle," etc., are they not written in the memory of all who know him? **1903** (1965) Adams *Log Cowboy* 81 **West,** They'd have lawed me if I had, but I ought to have shot him. **1914** *DN* 4.75 **ME, nNH,** *Law.* . . To sue or prosecute. **1931** (1991) Hughes–Hurston *Mule Bone* 101 **cFL** [Black], But we all know how come he so hot to law Jim outa town. *Ibid* 102, I'm goin' to law 'em from Genesis to Revelation. **1957** Faulkner *Town* 243 **MS,** Sue me? . . If she was fixing to try to law something out of me about that fire, do you reckon she would a hunted me up and offered to pay me for it? **1960** Hall *Smoky Mt. Folks* 16 **wNC,** Over in Swain County a man named Calhoun was lawed fer killin' a bear that was breakin' into his chicken house. **1967** *DARE* (Qu. U18, *If you force somebody to pay money that he owes you, but that he did not want to pay . . "I finally made him _____."*) Inf **TN**11, I lawed him. **1976** Garber *Mountain-ese* 52 **sAppalachians,** I got the debt Lackey owed me but I had to law him for it. **1977** Norman *Kinfolks* 70 **eKY,** "If Mommy had taken Daddy to the hospital when I told her to, he'd be living yet," she whimpered. "We ought to of lawed the bastards for every cent they had," said Evelyn.

law n², intj Also *la, laws* [Appar by convergence of *la* (var of *lo*) with proncs of **Lord** n¹ (cf *OED la* int., *law* int.)] **now chiefly Sth, S Midl,** formerly also **NEast** *esp freq among women* See also *Law mercy, Laws-a-mercy* (at **Lord** n¹ **B1**) Used, often in phrr, to express surprise, annoyance, or dismay.

1789 Dunlap *Father* 2.1 **NY,** Law souls! I protest I can't think, nor guess ni'ther. **1830** Ames *Mariner's Sketches* 239 **MA,** The Vermont lady . . exclaimed with some disappointment, 'Why law you, he has not got the least bit of a tail.' **1843** (1916) Hall *New Purchase* 70 **IN,** Law! bless you, no! *Ibid* 295, La! me!—good gracious! *Ibid* 312, Laws! bless you, stranger! **1845** Kirkland *Western Clearings* 78 **MI,** Law sakes alive! . . I'm clear tuckered out with these young'uns. **1861** Holmes *Venner* 1.118 **NEng,** Law! it's nothin' but the Cranes' folks! **1872** [see **lawks**]. **1890** *DN* 1.74 **NEng,** La [lɔ]. . . My aunt in Chicopee, who died fifteen years ago, used it constantly, either alone or 'Oh, la!' usually expressing disgust, disapproval, or to show the absurdity of some remark. It is familiar to Connecticut people also, and is still frequent in New England. **1892** *DN* 1.217 **VA, NC, TN,** La. **1892** *KS Univ. Qrly.* 1.99 **KS,** Suz. . . Dear suz, and Law suz. **1899** Chesnutt *Conjure Woman* 136 **NC** [Black], Law, suh! you doan hafter prove 'bout de rabbit foot! **1903** (1965) Adams *Log Cowboy* 77 **West,** 'Law me,' said this woman. **1903** *DN* 2.299 **Cape Cod MA** (as of a1857), La! la suz! la me suz! suz a day! Ejaculations of women. **1905** *DN* 3.13 **cCT,** Law sakes! or law sakes alive! **1913** Kephart *Highlanders* 85 **sAppalachians,** "Good la!" exclaimed four men in chorus; "you hadn't orter a-told." **1942** Hall *Smoky Mt. Speech* 32 **eTN, wNC,** Law (in the interjection [oˈlɔᵒ]). . . There is occasional unrounding to . . [ɑ] in . . *Law me!* [ˈlɑːˌmi] (used by women). **1943** *LANE* Map 601–602 *(For goodness sake)* 1 inf, **ceMA,** Law sakes [inf indicates that this is used only or chiefly by women]. **1944** *PADS* 2.45 **NC, VA,** La [lɔ, lɒ, lɑ]. . . Oh, ah, lo. (From *Lord*?). . . Most Southern states. Common. **1956** McAtee *Some Dialect NC* 26, Law, Oh! . . Really "Oh! Lord." Often used to pass off something embarrassing. *Archaic & Dial.* **1965** *DARE* FW Addit **MS,** Law, law me . . expressions heard frequently. **1966–70** *DARE* (Qu. NN2, *Exclamations of very strong agreement: Somebody says, "I think Smith is absolutely right," and you reply, "_____."*) Inf **KY**78, Laws, yes! [FW: used by Inf in conv]; (Qu. NN7, *Exclamations of surprise: "They're getting married next week? Well, _____."*) Inf **NM**6, Law, go on!; **KY**36, Oh law! [FW: used by Inf in conv]; **KY**37, Law me! [ˈlɔːmi]; (Qu. NN8a, *Exclamations of annoyance or disgust: "Oh _____. I've lost my glasses again."*) Inf **KY**44, Law!; **KY**65, Law! [FW: used by Inf in conv]; (Qu. NN27a, *Weakened substitutes for 'god': "My _____!"*) Inf **MI**51, Laws!—probably substitute for Lord;

TN24, Law! [FW: used by Inf in conv]; (Qu. NN27b, *Weakened substitutes for 'god': "For _____ sakes!"*) Inf **VA**34, Law's; (Qu. NN28a, *Exclamations beginning with 'good': "Good _____!"*) Inf **GA**45, [Good] law! [8 of 10 Infs old, 2 mid-aged; 8 of 10 Infs female] **1966–68** *DARE* Tape **GA**11, Oh! law, yes; **NY**43, Oh, my laws, at that time it took about 1 hour. **1986** Pederson *LAGS Concordance* **Gulf Region exc FL** *(Exclamations of surprise)* 22 infs, (Oh *or* my) law; 9 infs, Law me (*or* yes, yeah, shucks); 1 inf, Laws. [27 of 32 infs old, 21 women]

Lawd See **Lord** n[1]

lawd god See **lord god 1**

law dog n [**law** n[1] **B1**]
A sheriff or deputy sheriff.
  1944 Adams *Western Words* 89, *Lawdog*—A sheriff or deputy. **1966–70** *DARE* (Qu. V10a, *. . Joking names . . for a sheriff*) Inf **MS**1, Law dog; **TN**53, Law dog [FW sugg].

Lawdy See **Lordy**

lawer See **law** n[1]

lawing vbl n See **law** v

lawing n See **law** v **1**

Lawk' a' mercy See **Lord** n[1] **B1**

lawks intj [*OED* 1768–74 →] *arch* Cf *Lack o' mercy* (at **Lord** n[1] **B1**), **law** n[2], intj, **lawsy**
Used to express surprise, annoyance, or dismay.
  1856 Neal *Misfortunes* 58, Lawks!—do tell!—and is that Stiggins? **1872** Schele de Vere *Americanisms* 613, *La*, for Lord! is generally pronounced *law*, and often so written. Even *laws* and *lawks* are heard in these contemptible efforts to avoid the charge of profanity, and yet to yield to the temptation. **1886** *The Pioneer* (New York), Oct. *(Century Dict.)*, "Lawks!" exclaimed Mrs. Partington, "what monsters these master-builders must be!"

lawr See **law** n[1]

Lawrence n Also *lazy Lawrence* Also sp *Larence, Larrans, Laurence*; nickname *Larry* [Cf *EDD* **lawrence** sb. 2 "idleness personified; laziness, indolence"]
Used as a nickname for a lazy person; the personification of laziness, sometimes identified with the shimmering of the air observed on hot days.
  1824 Doddridge *Notes Indian Wars* 69 **WV, PA,** A person who did not perform his share of labour. . . was designated by the epithet of "*Lawrence*" or some other title still more opprobrious [sic]. **1869** Alcott *Little Women* 2.243, "Flo and I have got a new name for you [=Theodore Lawrence]; it's 'Lazy Laurence'; how do you like it?" . . "Because with every chance for being good, useful and happy, you are faulty, lazy and miserable." **1899** (1912) Green *VA Folk-Speech* 256, *Larrans. . . Larence*. Lawrence, patron saint of idlers. When the summer air is seen vibrating with heat it is called "larrans," and the lazy feeling of that time is said to be caused by " 'lazy larrans' having hold of you." **1907** Cockrum *Pioneer IN* 189 (as of 19th cent), [Lazy children were told that] they were in danger of being caught by the Laurences, meaning the little heat waves caused by the heat from the earth on a very hot day. Such days would add much to the child's disposition to rest. **1941** Ward *Holding Hills* 102 **IA** (as of early 20th cent), He went from job to job, and was slow to settle down; people claimed that he was affected by what we know as Larry in the back[woods]. **1952** Brown *NC Folkl.* 1.435, *Lazy Lawrence*. If ye don't watch ole Lazy Lawrence, 'e'll git ye. (This expression is generally used to urge lazy children.) **1953** Randolph–Wilson *Down in Holler* 259 **Ozarks,** *Lawrence. . .* A lazy moocher, a loafer, a parasite. Of a man named Dixon McGee a woman said: "I reckon the old lawrence is hangin' round the pool-hall."

laws See **law** n[2], intj

lawsy n, intj Also *lawzee;* for addit varr see quots [Cf *laws* (at **law** n[2], intj)] **scattered, but more freq Sth, S Midl**
Used, often in phrr, to express surprise, annoyance, or dismay; rarely in phrr formulaic phrr as a euphem for *Lord.*
  1859 Taliaferro *Fisher's* 103 **nwNC** (as of 1820s), Laus-a-day, I'm 'most dade. *Ibid* 167 **nwNC** (as of 1857), Lausyday, Hardy! is that you? **1880** in 1917 Twain *Letters* 1.383, A kind-hearted, well-meaning corpse was the Boston young man, but lawsy bless me, horribly dull company. **1894** Riley *Armazindy* 142 **IN,** Lawsy! but they're pore!

1906 *DN* 3.144 **nwAR,** *Lawsee* ['lɔzi]. . . Goodness! *Lawsy mercy*. . . A woman's exclamation. *Lawsy's sakes.* **1909** *DN* 3.420 **Cape Cod MA** (as of a1857), *La zee!* . . Expresses mild admiration or surprise. **1914** *DN* 4.75 **ME, nNH,** *Lawzee!* or *lawzee me!* or *lossyme!* Common ejaculations with women. Probable corruption of "Lord have mercy on me!" **1934** Stribling *Unfinished Cathedral* 116 **AL,** Lawzee, what you got against Brother Catlin? **1935** Davis *Honey* 244 **OR,** The elderly woman said, wistfully, that she hadn't seen a real funeral with mourners since the lawsy knew when. **1940** in 1976 *Weevils in the Wheat* 335 **VA** [Black], Why, I kin tell you all 'bout that there battle. Lawsy, I should say so. **1942** McAtee *Dial. Grant Co. IN* 39 (as of 1890s), *Lawsy daisy . .* woman's exclamation. **1965–67** *DARE* FW Addit **MS,** *Lawsy me . .* heard frequently; **wNC,** Lawsy me. Common; **TN**13, "Oh lawsy ['lɔzɪ]!" used as an exclamation of surprise or amusement. **1968–69** *DARE* (Qu. NN7, *Exclamations of surprise: "They're getting married next week? Well, _____."*) Inf **CA**127, Lawsy [lɔsi] me! Lawsy sakes!—old-fashioned; (Qu. NN27a, *Weakened substitutes for 'god': "My _____!"*) Inf **IA**41, Lawsy ['lɔzi]. **1986** Pederson *LAGS Concordance (Exclamations of surprise)* 1 inf, **ceTX,** Lawsy.

Lawsy mercy See **Lord** n[1] **B1**

lawyer n Usu |'lɔɪ(j)ə(r)|; also |'lɑjə(r), 'lɔ-|; also (often facetiously) |'laɪjə(r)|; for addit varr see quots Pronc-spp *la'yer, liar, li-yer*

A Forms.
  1891 Page *Elsket* 140 **VA** [Black], I had a some sort of a la'yer, but not much of a one. **1942** in 1944 *ADD* **PA,** *Lawyer. . . liar.* Common in folk speech. **1951** Johnson *Resp. to PADS 20* **DE** *(Joking . . names for lawyers)* Li-yers. **1965–70** *DARE* (Qu. HH44, *Joking or uncomplimentary names for lawyers*) Inf **ID**1, ['lajə]; **LA**8, ['lɑjə] [FW: Pronounced to be ambiguous with *liar*]; **MT**1, ['lɔjə]; **ND**5, **PA**163, **SD**1, 3, ['lɔɪ(j)ə-]; **TN**30, Jakeleg ['lɑˑujə-]; **TN**66, Jakeleg ['lɑujə-]. **1991** *DARE* File **Madison WI,** The pronunciation "liar" for "lawyer" is commonly heard from clients at the Veterans Hospital here. When I first encountered it, I thought it was just being used facetiously, but after a while I realized that was just the way some people pronounced it. And after my ear had gotten attuned to it, I found, when visiting a friend in Topeka, Kansas, that people said "liar" for "lawyer" there also.

B Senses.
1 also *lawyer bird:* =**bluestocking 2**.
  1813 (1824) Wilson *Amer. Ornith.* 7.132, American Avocet: *Recurvirostra Americana*. . . from its perpetual clamour and flippancy of tongue, is called, by the inhabitants of Cape May, the Lawyer. **1918** Grinnell *Game Birds CA* 340, Together with the Black-necked Stilt, this bird is sometimes known as the "lawyer bird" because of its long bill and its oft-repeated vociferations! **1923** U.S. Dept. Ag. *Misc. Circular* 13.48, Avocet *(Recurvirostra americana)*. . . Blue-stocking (N.J.; La.); lawyer (N.J.); lawyer-bird (Calif.)

2 also *lawyer bird:* =**black-necked stilt**.
  1844 DeKay *Zool. NY* 2.266, It [=*Himantopus nigricollis*] is known under the various popular names of *Tilt, Stilt, Longshanks* and *Lawyer.* The origin of this last popular name (which is most in use), I have not been able to discover: there appears to be nothing unusual in the length of its *bill.* **1872** Coues *Key to N. Amer. Birds* 247, Stilt. Longshanks. Lawyer. **1916** *Times–Picayune* (New Orleans LA) 2 Apr mag sec 5/7, *Black-necked stilt* (Himantopus mexicanus). Soldat; Beccasine du Marais; Lawyer.—The extremely long and bright-red legs; the long and slender neck and bill, identify this peculiar summer resident of Louisiana. **1923** U.S. Dept. Ag. *Misc. Circular* 13.48, Black-necked Stilt *(Himantopus mexicanus)*. . . Daddy-long-legs (Wash.); jacksnipe (Calif.), lawyer (N.Y., Tex., Calif.), lawyer-bird (Calif.) **1925** (1928) Forbush *Birds MA* 1.384, The Black-necked Stilt is known in parts of its range as the "Lawyer" because of its vociferousness. **1955** Forbush–May *Birds* 209, Black-Necked Stilt—*Himantopus mexicanus*. . . Other names: Longshanks; Lawyer Bird; Daddy-long-legs.

3 =**double-crested cormorant**.
  1917 (1923) *Birds Amer.* 1.97, Double-Crested Cormorant—*Phalacrocorax auritus auritus*. . . Other Names.—Crow Duck . . Lawyer; Nigger Goose. **1946** Hausman *Eastern Birds* 90, Double-Crested Cormorant—*Phalacrocorax auritus auritus*. . . Other Names—Shag . . Lawyer.

4 =**burbot. esp MI, MN, WI** See Map Cf **lake lawyer 2**
  1857 Hammond *Wild N. Scenes* 45 **Upstate NY,** "That . . is a species of ling; we call it in these parts a lawyer." "A lawyer!" said I; "why, pray?" "I don't know, . . unless it's because he ain't of much use, and is the slipriest fish that swims." **1884** Goode *Fisheries U.S.* 1.236, The

Burbot *[Lota maculosa]* . . is the "Lawyer" of Lake Michigan, according to Earll. **1911** (1913) Johnson *Highways Gt. Lakes* 222 **cnMI,** These lawyers, or bullheads as they're called by some, are ugly lookin' fish—too much like a lizard, and the taste is nothing extra, but the flesh is white, and there's not many bones. One time a fellow down here at Munising went to skinning 'em and calling 'em "fresh water cod." **1936** *Copeia* 3.164 **MN,** On the night of February 12. . . a dark shadow was noted at the edge of the ice. . . Eventually this . . was seen to be . . a ball—a tangled, nearly globular mass of moving, writhing lawyers. **1950** *WELS* **ceWI** (*Kinds of fish not commonly eaten*) 1 Inf, Lawyer; 1 Inf, Lawyers—sucker family, scaleless, eat spawn. **1966–69** *DARE* (Qu. P1, . . *Kinds of freshwater fish . . caught around here . . good to eat*) Infs **MI**20, 32, **MN**2, Lawyer(s); **MN**15, Lake Superior. . . Lawyer—no backbone, an eel; (Qu. P3, *Freshwater fish that are not good to eat*) Infs **MI**103, **MN**10, **WI**72, Lawyers; **MI**14, Lawyer, or dogfish; **WI**78, Lawyer—look like cod—good eating, but people won't eat 'em—throw 'em away now; **MN**5, Eel pout, burbot, lawyers; (Qu. P14, . . *Commercial fishing . . what do the fishermen go out after?*) Inf **MN**5, Lawyers—used for mink feed. **1968** *DARE* Tape **WI**75, The reason they call them a lawyer . . is because his heart is in his ass . . his heart is just above his bunghole. **1971** *WI Conserv. Bulletin* 36.6.23 **WI,** Burbot is more commonly referred to as eelpout, lawyer, or ling. **1991** Amer. Fisheries Soc. *Common Names Fishes* 145, Lawyer . . burbot.

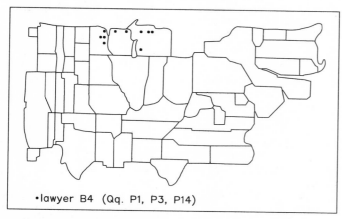

•lawyer B4 (Qq. P1, P3, P14)

5 **=bowfin.** Cf **lake lawyer 1**

1882 U.S. Natl. Museum *Bulletin* 16.94, *A[mia] calva*. . . Lawyer. . . A voracious fish of remarkable tenacity of life. The flesh is peculiarly soft and pasty, and is of no value for food. **1896** U.S. Natl. Museum *Bulletin* 47.113, *Amia calva*. . . Mudfish; Dogfish; Bowfin; Grindle; "John A. Grindle;" Lawyer; Poisson de Marais. **1946** LaMonte *N. Amer. Game Fishes* 102, Lawyer, Lake Lawyer, Cottonfish. **1983** Becker *Fishes WI* 251, Bowfin . . Other Common names: . . John A. Grindle, grinnel, lake lawyer, lawyer.

6 also *sea lawyer:* Usu the **gray snapper** but also the **schoolmaster.**

1882 U.S. Natl. Museum *Proc.* 5.275, *Lutjanus caxis*. . . Black Snapper; Lawyer. **1884** Goode *Fisheries U.S.* 1.397, *Lutjanus caxis*. . . known as the 'Gray Snapper,' and also, on account of its sly, cunning habits, the 'Sea Lawyer.' **1911** U.S. Bur. Census *Fisheries 1908* 316, The gray snapper or mangrove snapper (*L[utianus] griseus*), also known in Florida as "Lawyer," is a most common species. **1935** Caine *Game Fish* 130, Mangrove Snapper—*Lutianus griseus* . . Synonyms: Bastard Snapper . . Lawyer. **1946** LaMonte *N. Amer. Game Fishes* 59, Schoolmaster—*Lutianus apodus* . . Names: Caji, Sea Lawyer . . Dog Snapper.

lawyer bird See **lawyer 1, 2**

lawzee See **lawsy**

lax n [Cf *OED lax* sb.² 2 1540–1877; "Obs. exc. dial."] *arch* Cf **flux**

See quots.

1805 (1905) Clark *Orig. Jrls. Lewis & Clark Exped.* 3.86, All Complain of a *Lax* & heaviness at the stomack. **1806** (1970) Webster *Compendious Dict.* 173, Lax . . a looseness. [*DARE* Ed: This entry was carried over from Webster's English model.] **1899** (1912) Green *VA Folk-Speech* 257, Lax . . Diarrhœa.

laxed ppl adj [*OED* (at *lax* v.) 1623–1718; here perh a relic, but perh erron for *prolapsed* or aphet form of *relaxed*]

1990 Cavender *Folk Med. Lexicon* 26 **sAppalachians,** Laxed privates—a prolapsed uterus; See *fallen womb.*

laxflower n [See quot 1941]

A **desert marigold** (here: *Baileya pauciradiata*).

1941 Jaeger *Wildflowers* 290, Lax-flower. . . The rays, at first narrow and lying horizontally, become broad-ovoid and lax and turn down as the flowers age. **1960** Abrams *Flora Pacific States* 4.196, *Baileya pauciradiata* . . Colorado Desert Marigold. . . Type locality: California . . Laxflower.

lay v Note: The use of *lay* as an intransitive verb in place of *lie* is very common in US folk and colloq speech; senses and combs in which *lay* is the only or preponderant form in our evidence are entered under **lay** or its compounds.

1 also with *down:* =**lie** v¹ **1.** chiefly **S Midl, Sth** See Map and Map Section Cf **go down** v phr **1**

1902 *DN* 2.237 **sIL,** When the wind lays, it'll rain. **1906** *DN* 3.120 **sIN,** Lay. . . To cease; be still. "The rain is over and the wind has laid." **1907** *DN* 3.223 **nwAR, sIL,** Lay. . . To cease blowing (used of the wind). **1909** *DN* 3.399 **nwAR,** The wind has laid. **1919** *DN* 5.34 **seKY,** Wait till the wind lays. **1939** *Atlantic Mth.* Oct 535 **eKY,** The stars were leavin' the sky now. The wind laid. **1946** *PADS* 5.28 **VA,** (Be) laying. . . Of the wind, subside; fairly common. **1953** (1977) Hubbard *Shantyboat* 346 **Missip-Ohio Valleys,** If the wind should lay before dark, we would go on. **1960** Criswell *Resp. to PADS* 20 **Ozarks,** Wind is laying. **1965–70** *DARE* (Qu. B13, *When the wind begins to decrease . . it's _____*) 38 Infs, **chiefly S Midl, Sth,** Laying; **AR**56, **IL**114, 134, **MS**45, **TN**30, **TX**4, **VA**8, Beginning to lay; **IN**3, **KY**39, **OK**42, **TX**104, A-laying; **KY**28, 72, **SC**34, Laid; **MD**19, **TX**39, Starting to lay; **AR**38, **GA**84, **OH**31, The wind(s) laid; **AR**47, **IN**82, Laying down (with the sun); **MS**55, Looks like the wind's begin to lay; **MO**19, Gonna lay; **PA**242, Laying itself—old-fashioned. **1967** *Good Old Days* Jan 9 **nwAR** (as of c1900), En-route the storm continously got worse and on his arrival the midwife frankly informed him—I "am not budgin" till this storm "lays"! **1969** *DARE* FW Addit **se,csKY,** "I wish that wind would lay some." Common. **1986** Pederson *LAGS Concordance* **Gulf Region,** 57 infs, (A-)laying; 15 infs, Laid; 14 infs, (About to, *or* beginning to, etc) lay; 3 infs, Laying down; 2 infs, (If) the wind lays.

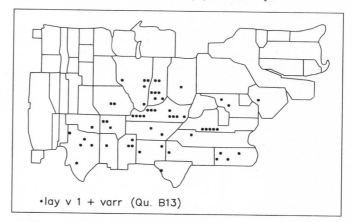

•lay v 1 + varr (Qu. B13)

2a foll by n clause: To vow, declare; to figure, bet, be sure—usu used in emphatic assertions. [*OED lay* v.¹ 12.b c1380 →] chiefly **Sth, S Midl** *old-fash* Cf **allow 2, bound** v **1**

1835 Longstreet *GA Scenes* 141, You Rose! if you do not quiet that child, I lay I make you. **1875** (1876) Twain *Tom Sawyer* 97 **MO,** But if ever I get off this time, I lay I'll just *waller* in Sunday-schools. **1887** (1967) Harris *Free Joe* 109 **GA,** I don't reckon he's right slam bang at home, but I lay he ain't fur off. *Ibid* 119, Well, I lay a man that works is boun' ter eat. **1892** *DN* 1.230 **KY,** Lay. "I lay you'll catch it," same as "I 'low you'll catch it" and "I'll be bound you'll catch it." **1899** (1912) Green *VA Folk-Speech* 257, Lay. . . I'll lay he'll come tomorrow. **1909** *DN* 3.344 **eAL, wGA,** Lay. . . To bet: used in emphatic asseverations. . . Common, especially among the illiterate. **1911** *DN* 3.538 **eKY,** I'll lay he won't do that again. **1935** Davis *Honey* 16 **OR,** There was some buzzards circulatin' around. . . I laid somebody had been killin' a deer out of season.

b with *to:* To bet on, be sure of.

1933 Rawlings *South Moon* 8 **nFL,** "You kin lay to it, they's a reason," Lantry said. "You jest don't know the reason yit." **1958** Babcock *I Don't*

Want 23 **eSC**, One thing is certain: a dog, a boy, and a wife can learn exactly how far they can go, and you can lay to that.

3 To lie in wait; to await an opportunity (to do something). Cf **lay for**

1884 *Anglia* 7.263 **Sth, S Midl** [Black], *I lay an' fetch you!* = I'll catch you! **1895** *DN* 1.372 **seKY, eTN, wNC,** *Layin'*: lying in ambuscade. "He's a layin' to kill him." **1896** *Boston* (Mass.) *Jrnl.* 3 Dec. 4/3 *(OED),* Fitzsimmons evidently laying to get in right on jaw. **1969** *Hall Coll.* **wNC** *(Montgomery Coll.),* How long did you lay to kill him?

4 See quot 1899. [*OED lay* v.¹ 36 1472–3 →; "dial."]

1806 (1904) Roe *Diary* 26 **NY,** Austin is gon to Isaac Homons to git an ax Layd. **1837** in 1956 Eliason *Tarheel Talk* 281 **NC,** 25¢ for laying a bul tung. 40¢ for laying a shovel. **1899** (1912) Green *VA Folk-Speech* 257, To *lay* an axe, or grubbing-hoe is to weld a new piece of steel into the body of the old axe or hoe that had been worn out.

5 in phrr *lay it on (one)*:

a also *lay one on (one)*: To strike a blow or blows, fight vigorously; to strike or beat someone severely.

1960 Wentworth–Flexner *Slang* 314, *Lay one on [a person]*—To strike or hit. **1965–70** *DARE* (Qu. Y11, . . *A very hard blow*: "You should have seen Bill go down. Joe really hit him a _____.") Infs **CA87, TN1, WA30,** Laid one on (him); (Qu. Y12a, *A fight between two people, mostly with words*) Inf **VA26,** They laid it on; (Qu. Y14a, *To hit somebody hard with the fist*) Infs **LA3, PA199,** Lay one on him; **GA77,** Laid it on him; (Qu. Y15, *To beat somebody thoroughly*: "John really _____ that fellow!") Infs **CA113, GA84, LA8, MD29, TX37,** Laid it on; **GA89,** Laid one on him; (Qu. EE21b, *When boys were fighting very actively . . "For a while those fellows really _____."*) Inf **KY94,** [Were] laying it on ; **IN35, KY59, OH41, 98,** Laid it on; **NY250,** Laid it on each other. **1984** [see **5b** below].

b To chastise; to reprimand someone severely.

1942 Berrey–Van den Bark *Amer. Slang* 322.4, *Chastise. . .* Lay it on . . let have it . . light into. **1967–68** *DARE* (Qu. Y6, . . *To put pressure on somebody to do something he ought to have done but hasn't*: "He's a whole week late. I'm going to _____.") Inf **IA32,** Lay it on; **WA22,** Really lay it on him. **1984** Wilder *You All Spoken Here* 185 **Sth,** *Lay it on*: Give one a cussin'; tell it straight out; frail one.

6 in phrr *lay (it) on*: To do something with vigor and enthusiasm.

1942 Berrey–Van den Bark *Amer. Slang* 243.3 *Do efficiently or well. . .* go great guns . . hit on all six . . cylinders . . lay it on. **1968–70** *DARE* (Qu. FF18, *Joking words . . about a noisy or boisterous celebration or party*: "They certainly _____ last night.") Inf **VA18,** Laid it on; (Qu. KK29, *To start working very hard*: "He was slow at first but now he's really _____.") Infs **CA87, TX79,** Laying it on. **1987** Childress *Out of the Ozarks* 16, Dad didn't really lay on, and in his homely way he was teaching a lesson that everyone must learn: Life isn't fair, and you gotta get along, little dogie.

7 See **lie** v¹ **2.**

8 See **lie** v¹ **3.**

lay n¹

1 The terms of a bargain or contract; a rate of purchase; broadly, a situation, opportunity. *old-fash*

1703 in 1880 *New Engl. Hist. & Geneal. Reg.* 34.92, So soon as wee delivered him the particulars wisht for, wee supplyed the Indians at a very moderate lay. **1772** (1925) Washington *Diaries* 2.81 **VA,** Agreed with my Overseer. . . to continue another year on the same lay as the last. **1816** Pickering *Vocab.* 121, *Lay. . .* Terms or conditions of a bargain; price. . . I bought the articles at a good lay; he bought his goods on the same lay that I did mine. *A low word. New England.* **1902** *DN* 2.238 **sIL,** *Lay. . .* Advantage afforded by a contract, situation or employment, as 'A good lay'—'A poor lay.' **1903** *DN* 2.318 **seMO,** *Lay. . .* Prospect; opportunity. 'He has a good lay if he will only improve it.'

2 Esp in ref to work done on shares; spec:

a In fishing, whaling, etc: a specified share of the proceeds of a voyage; broadly, a share in any venture; an agreement to work on shares. **esp NEast**

1848 Bartlett *Americanisms* 199, *Lay.* A word used colloquially in New York and New England in relation to labor or contracts performed upon shares; as, when a man ships for a whaling voyage, he agrees for a certain *lay,* i.e. a share of the proceeds of the voyage. **1849** Cooper *Sea Lions* 55 **seNY,** Yes, ship a goodly number of green hands [for a sealing voyage]. . . They work at cheap 'lays,' and leave the owners the greater profits. **1851** (1976) Melville *Moby-Dick* 76, I was already aware that

in the whaling business they paid no wages; but all hands, including the captain, received certain shares of the profits called *lays,* and that these lays were proportioned to the degree of importance pertaining to the respective duties of the ship's company. **1872** *Harper's New Mth. Mag.* 44.256 **AK,** The whale and cod fishermen make their voyages on a "lay," or share of the profits. **1916** Macy–Hussey *Nantucket Scrap Basket* 137, "*Lay*"—A share, a percentage. All whaling voyages were conducted on the profit-sharing basis, each man interested, from the owners and captain down to the greenhorn and boy, getting a proportionate part of the proceeds. The word has lingered in common use in the island speech. **1930** *AmSp* 5.391 [Language of N Atl fishermen], *Lay. . .* The relationship or agreement between vessel-owners and fishermen with regard to the proportionate share of each in the catch. The *lays* of every type of vessel are different. **1945** Colcord *Sea Language* 115 **ME, Cape Cod, Long Island,** *Lay. . .* A share in a fishing or whaling voyage. In this sense, it is used alongshore in connection with raffles, etc.

b In mining: a (specified) share in the proceeds of a mining venture; a lease (of a mine claim) granted on this basis. **AK**

1870 *Overland Mth.* 4.236 [North Pacific whaling fleet], Who is going to dig gold on the one-hundredth or two-hundredth lay? **1897** Harris *Alaska* 139, Several men worked on an interest, or what is termed a "lay," and during the winter realized $5000 to $10,000 each. **1901** Grinnell *Gold Hunting* 90 **AK,** A 'lay' is a lease given by a claim owner to a party to work a claim for a certain percentage of the outcome. **1935** *Anchorage Daily Times* Oct 4 (Tabbert *Dict. Alaskan Engl.*), Several other properties in the district also are worked under the lay or lease system. **1986** Cruikshank *Life* 75 **AK,** They're old-timers in the country and they had a lay on that ground there, deep underground mining.

3 In marble play: the act of placing the shooter in an advantageous position—used in exclams *lays, no lay.* Cf **lay up** v phr **7**

1963 *KY Folkl. Rec.* 9.3.64 **ceKY,** Request to toss marble into ring in order to be closer for next shot. The turn to shoot is forfeited when this is done and permission is granted: . . lays. c**1970** Wiersma *Marbles Terms* **csIA** (as of 1935), *No lay*—The players cannot "lay" the target marbles where they want them—they must leave them where they are.

lay n² [Scots dial] **S Midl** *somewhat old-fash*
A lathe.

1933 *AmSp* 8.1.50 **Ozarks,** *Lay. . .* A turning lathe. This pronunciation seems to be almost universal among the old-timers. **1937** Eaton *Handicrafts* 158 **ceTN,** I use a foot lay. **1941** Smith *Going to God's Country* 36 **MO** (as of 1890), One man had what they caled a turning lay and he made furnature for the people that could aford it. **1960** Criswell *Resp. to PADS 20* **Ozarks,** *Lay. . .* Used by many older people for *lathe.* "Turning lay." Once common . . not now. **1981** Pederson *LAGS Basic Materials,* 2 infs, **ceTN, cTX,** Turning [lɛɪ]. **1982** Slone *How We Talked* 7 **eKY** (as of c1950), In making a chair the post was formed on a turning lay.

lay a corpse v phr Also *lay corpse* **S Midl**
To lie dead; to be laid out for burial.

1927 *DN* 5.475 **Ozarks,** When anybody's a-dyin', or a-layin' a corpse, th' chickens crows day an' night. **1944** *PADS* 2.30 **eKY, wSC,** *Lay a corpse. . .* "All the fam'bly gathered in when he lay a corpse." . . Common. **1950** *Hall Coll.* **eTN,** *Lay a corpse. . .* "They started running and run on to their grandmaw's . . where she was a-layin' a corpse." **1954** *Harder Coll.* **cwTN,** *Lay a corpse.* c**1960** *Wilson Coll.* **csKY,** *Lay a corpse. . .* To be a corpse laid out. "When Grandma laid a corpse, she looked so peaceful and rested." **1981** Pederson *LAGS Basic Materials,* 1 inf, **nwMS,** He laid corpse in two days—in two days he was dead.

lay away v phr *euphem*

1 To bury.

1885 *Harper's New Mth. Mag.* 70.594 **NEng,** It was hardly six months since my poor sister was laid away. **1911** (1916) Porter *Harvester* 205 **IN,** Trying to lay away poor Aunt Molly decently. **1929** [see **2** below]. **1939** FWP *Guide TN* 141, Many a Negro will pay dues to a lodge all his life so that he and his relatives may be "laid away" in style. **1950** *WELS,* 1 Inf, **csWI,** He's laid away. c**1960** *Wilson Coll.* **csKY,** *Lay away. . .* Bury (euphemistic). **1960** Criswell *Resp. to PADS 20* **Ozarks,** "She was laid away in Sinking Creek Cemetery." Very common still. **1966** Barnes–Jensen *Dict. UT Slang* 28, *Lay away . .* bury. "Poor soul, they had laid her away at last."

2 To destroy, put down (an animal).

1929 *AmSp* 5.129 **ME,** One hoped to be "laid away" before he "failed as so and so has." Or a dog is "so old he ought to be laid away." **1975**

Gould *ME Lingo* 159, *Lay away*—Kindly term for destroying an animal: "We had to lay old Tige away."

layaway v See **layway**

lay back v phr

To put aside, save.

1940 Stuart *Trees of Heaven* 143 **KY**, Ma will lay back a few pennies from every dozen of eggs she sells. **c1960** *Wilson Coll.* **csKY**, *Lay back*. . . Hoard. **1979** *Smokies Heritage* 259 (*Montgomery Coll.*), And thus, in this lull before winter, mountain folk began to "lay back" stores for the certain winter ahead.

lay-bell, laybill See **label**

lay by v phr

1 To leave (a crop) to mature without further attention; to work (a crop) for the last time; to perform a final cultivation; hence ppl adj *laid by*; n, also attrib *lay(ing) by* the last working of a crop; the period between the last working and harvest. **chiefly Sth, S Midl** See also **laying-by time**

1759 in 1902 *William & Mary Qrly.* 11.106 **ceVA**, [Journal entry for 12 July:] Mowing oats & laying by corn. **1800** Tatham *Communications* 56 (sic *DA* (at *laying by*)—quot not found), What is termed the *laying by* of the crop in autumn; that is, the last ploughing and hoeing which it requires before it is suffered to remain at rest and ripen like other fruits of the earth. **1854** in 1910 Commons *Doc. Hist. Amer. Industrial Soc.* 1.262 **SC coast**, This is called the lay-by flow. Up to the time of this flow, is about ninety days for Rice sown the first week in April. **1859** *Harper's New Mth. Mag.* 19.728, The "lay-by water" . . is kept on until the rice is fully headed and the blossoms have dropped. **1868** *IA State Ag. Soc. Rept. for 1867* 158 **seIA**, The ground should then be thoroughly rolled; . . then lay by with barshear plow. **1887** *Century Illustr. Mag.* 35.111 **LA**, There is constant cultivation [of sugar cane] with the plow till about the 1st of July, when the crop is "laid by." No more work is done on it till the cutting begins in September. **1899** (1912) Green *VA Folk-Speech* 258, After all the plowing and hoeing was done, it was said: "I'm done working my corn, it is ready to lay by." "I'm laying by my corn." **1902** *DN* 2.238 **sIL**, *Lay by*. . . To plough a crop for the last time. **1903** *DN* 2.319 **seMO**, His craps [sic] are all laid by. **1905** *DN* 3.63 **eNE**, To-morrow we lay by our corn. **1906** *DN* 3.120 **sIN**, He's layin' his corn by. **1907** *DN* 3.232 **nwAR**, *Lay by, v. phr. tr.* **1909** *DN* 3.344 **eAL, wGA**, *Lay-by, v. phr.* **1911** *DN* 3.538 **eKY**, *Lay-by*. To finish the cultivation of any crop, especially maize. **1915** *DN* 4.184 **swVA**, *Lay by, v. phr.* **1923** *DN* 5.213 **swMO**, *Lay by, v. phr.* **1933** *Sun* (Baltimore MD) 24 June 6/7 (*Hench Coll.*) **cMD**, And the cantaloupe patches "laid by" as they say in Anne Arundel when they have been given the last working. **1937** *Natl. Geogr. Mag.* 72.278 **MS**, Come plantin' time and I needs my rations. Come layin-by and I's got to buy shoes for the family. **1940** Coulter *Thomas Spalding* 77 **LA** (as of c1840), In the last flowing, called the lay-by, the water was kept on the field until the rice stalks had borne their fruits. **1941** Writers' Program *Guide SC* 95, Special schools have been developed in the campaign against illiteracy . . 'Lay-by' schools, organized in summer after the crops have been 'laid by' and farm workers are at leisure. **1966–67** *DARE* (QR, near Qu. L23) Inf **CO22**, Corn [is] laid by in July; (Qu. L26, *Sayings about corn and other important crops around here*; total Infs questioned, 75) Inf **MS4**, Lay corn by when you can bring roasting ears in for dinner. **1966–70** *DARE* Tape **IN45**, [FW:] "Laying it by"—what does that mean? [Inf:] That means that you're through plowing it [=tobacco]; you won't go into it any more with a plow; **IA1**, I laid my corn by the 26th of June this year; **SC24**, And then you wait till what you call lay by. When it [=cotton] gets too large to get the plow in, it's laid by; **TX107**, About July, June . . is what you call lay it by, you don't have to fool with it [=cotton] no more. **1986** Pederson *LAGS Concordance* **esp wGulf Region**, 31 infs, Lay(ing) it (*or* the cotton, corn, crops, etc) by; 16 infs, Lay(ing) by (cotton, *or* crops, etc); 1 inf, Lay by—operation with a turning plow; 22 infs, Laid by (corn, or crops, etc); 11 infs, Laid it (*or* cotton, crops, etc) by.

2 To intend, decide. Cf **lay off** v phr **3**, **~ out** v phr **3**

1887 *Scribner's Mag.* 2.478 **AR**, Ye wunt never dance at *my* weddin' . . an' iz ter Bulah, she have laid by ter stay single. **1972** Cooper *NC Mt. Folkl.* 93, *Laid by*—had intended.

lay by n[1] See **lay by** v phr **1**

lay-by n[2]

1975 Gould *ME Lingo* 160, A *lay-by* is a turn-out on a log-haul where one vehicle *lays by* until another passes. The original state highway from Eustis to Coburn Gore, completed in 1928, was described as "a one-lane gravel road with lay-bys."

lay-by season (or time) See **laying-by time**

laycorn See **leghorn**

lay corpse See **lay a corpse**

lay down v phr[1] See **lie down** v phr **1**

lay down v phr[2]

1 See **lay** v **1**.

2 To jilt (someone).

c1955 Reed–Person *Ling. Atlas Pacific NW*, She turned him down, broke off with him, gave him the sack. . . Laid him down [1 inf].

la'yer See **lawyer**

lay for v phr [Cf *OED lay* v.[1] 18.b; 1494 →] **esp Sth, S Midl**

To lie in wait for; to plan revenge against, be out to get. Cf **lay** v **3**

1865 in 1926 Twain *Sketches* 196, He was always ready and laying for a chance. **1879** Peck *Peck's Fun* 85 **Milwaukee WI**, Since we told the story about Hanscom stealing the bell off of his own cow . . he has been laying for us. **1903** *DN* 2.319 **seMO**, *Lay for*. . . To lie in wait for. **1906** *DN* 3.120 **sIN**, *Lay for*. . . "I'll lay fer you." **1907** *DN* 3.232 **nwAR**, *Lay for.* **1909** *DN* 3.344 **eAL, wGA**, *Lay for*. . . To lie in wait for; to plan an opportunity to get even with. *Ibid* 399 **nwAR**, I'm layin' for him and I'll get him yet. **1912** Green *VA Folk-Speech* 258, *Lay for*. . . To waylay: "To lay for a thief." To lie in wait. **1933** Rawlings *South Moon* 83 **nFL**, Something had been digging at the grave. . . She said, "Don't say nothin' to nobody. We'll come tonight and lay for it." **1960** Criswell *Resp. to PADS 20* **Ozarks**, *Lay for*—To wait in hiding for. "I'll lay for Blair and shoot him." Still common. **c1960** *Wilson Coll.* **csKY**, *Lay for*. . . Try to catch, waylay. **1966–69** *DARE* (Qu. AA5, *If a woman seems to be going after one certain man that she wants to marry: "She's _____ him."*) Infs **IL47, WA3**, Laying for. [Both Infs old] **1967** *DARE* Tape **TX49**, Old man John Bradley got the news of whar that Joel Gooden was layin' for him in Logansport. **1981** Pederson *LAGS Basic Materials*, 1 inf, **csTX**, They laid for a man—to kill him; 1 inf, **cLA**, Laying for one another—looking for opportunities to shoot each other.

lay heavy (or hard) on one's stomach See **lie** v[1] **3**

lay in v phr

1 To exert oneself, work hard—also used as an expression of encouragement; see quots. [Scots, Engl dial]

1929 Dobie *Vaquero* 257 **West**, Straightedge [=a horse] was as shy as a rabbit, but Peckerwood finally got him to lay in after the clanging, smoking object [=the smokestack of a locomotive, which the cowboy was trying to rope]. **c1950** Hall Coll. **wNC, eTN**, *Lay in there!* Good-natured exhortation to keep at something at which one is straining hard, e.g., wrestling, chopping wood, pushing a car. Usually followed by the person's name: "Lay in there, Joe!" . . Common. **1959** *VT Hist.* 27.147, *Lay in*. . . To apply oneself well. . . To pull well, as in a horse drawing contest. Common. **1967** Green *Horse Tradin'* 201 **TX**, A pair of good pulling horses, they go down in front with their heads and necks and lay their weight against the collars. . . Those big mares laid in there and you could hear them grunt a little bit. They just kept laying and getting closer to the ground and closer to the ground, and directly that wagon began to move.

2 See **lie in**.

laying by See **lay by** v phr **1**

laying-by time n Also *lay-by time*, *~ season* [**lay by** v phr **1**] **chiefly S Atl**

The time of year when the cultivation of crops is finished; the lull in farm work between the last cultivation and harvest time.

1909 *DN* 3.344 **eAL, wGA**, *Laying-by time*. . . The time when crops are laid by; also the season of rest after the crops are laid by. "We're goin on a camp-fish in the layin-by time." **1939** FWP *These are Our Lives* 76 **NC**, At layin'-by time in July we gen'ly has some time off but since we been makin' 'backer dis is not always de case. **1945** *AmSp* 20.306 **SC**, Some time toward the end of July, on the plantations and one- and two-hoss farms of the South Carolina Low Country, all cultivation of cotton and corn is completed—the crops are *laid-by*. . . This prized interim . . [is] called by all classes and colors *lay-by time*. **1950** *PADS* 14.43 **SC**, *Lay-by time* . . Fourth of July to Labor Day, when cotton crops are too mature to be cultivated and are not ready for picking.

1966 *DARE* Tape **GA**1, I done sawmilling in the lay-by time and through the winter months, when it wasn't in the farming season. . . We call that a lay-by time between the growing time and gathering time. **1986** Pederson *LAGS Concordance* **chiefly GA**, 7 infs, Lay(ing)-by time; 1 inf, Lay-by season.

laying-off plow n Also *layoff plow* [lay off v phr 2] **esp KY, TN** Cf **bull tongue 1**
A type of plow used esp to make furrows for planting; see quots.
1960 Criswell *Resp. to PADS 20* **Ozarks**, A laying-off plow with one blade, to make a straight furrow for planting corn. **1966–70** *DARE* (Qu. L18, *Kinds of plows*) Inf **IN**19, Laying-off plow; **KY**9, Laying-off plow—to make a row to put the corn in; **NC**37, Layoff or single foot [plow]; **VA**3, Layoff plow—same as bull-tongue plow, made a furrow in which beans or corn was planted; (Qu. L25) Inf **KY**84, Laying-off plow—for "laying off" and "bursting middle," [has] one shovel, old-fashioned. **1967** Key *Tobacco Vocab.* 178 **TN**, They used to lay the rows off with a mule . . [using] a layoff plow. **1969** *SC Market Bulletin* 11 Sept 3/5, Sears 2 wheel Garden Tractor with . . Cultivator, turn plow, lay off plow, spike and spring tooth harrows $165. **1970** *DARE* Tape **KY**84, We also made layin' off plows complete. . . That was for layin' off ground . . for the tobacco hills. . . Just with the one point, it throws the ground both ways, move the dirt both ways. **1986** Pederson *LAGS Concordance* **chiefly TN, esp neTN**, 5 infs, Lay-off plow(s); 1 inf, Lay-off plow—bull tongue, with one point on it; 4 infs, Laying-off plow; 1 inf, Laying-off plow—bull tongue.

laying-out vbl n See **lay out** v phr **2a**

laying out n See **layout** n **4**

lay it all over See **lay over 1**

lay it on See **lay** v **6**

lay it on (one) See **lay** v **5**

lay it over See **lay over 1**

laylark, laylock See **lilac**

lay low sheepie n Also *lay sheepie lay;* for addit varr see quots **esp PA, NJ** See Map
The children's game **run sheep run;** also used as a call in this game.
1957 *Sat. Eve. Post Letters* **csPA** (as of 1924–32), The children of our neighborhood . . used to play . . Lay Low Sheepie, Watch-the-Moon (This, I believe, would be similar to Run Sheep Run). **1966–69** *DARE* (Qu. EE12, *Games in which one captain hides his team and the other team tries to find it*) Infs **PA**1, 49, Lay low sheepie; **NJ**55, 57, Lay sheepie lay; **MI**81, Lay low; (Qu. EE15, *When he has caught the first of those that were hiding what does the player who is 'it' call out to the others?*) Inf **PA**98, Low sheepie lay [FW: Inf queries]; (Qu. EE16, *Hiding games that start with a special, elaborate method of sending the players out to hide*) Inf **NJ**55, Lay sheepie lay; **PA**7, Lay low sheepie, lay low; (Qu. EE33, . . *Outdoor games . . that children play*) Inf **NJ**18, Lie low sheepie—group hides, if one is caught, he warns others by calling when "it" is near; [**TX**9, Lay low, keep up—can't think how it was played.] **1967–69** *DARE* Tape **PA**49, [Inf:] Lay low sheepie. . . [Aux Inf:] There are two teams, one's hunting the other continually. [Inf:] And we would play it on bicycles so that you really ran the whole town. . . they had to call—Lay low sheepie! [Aux Inf:] I think spies were appointed to do that, go around and shout—Lay low sheepie!—

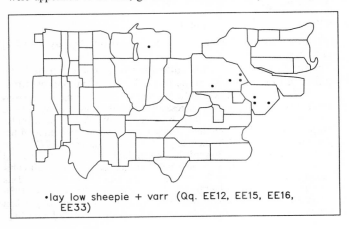

•lay low sheepie + varr (Qq. EE12, EE15, EE16, EE33)

when the other team was approaching. [FW:] And if you ever called—Run sheep run!—you'd go to what? [Inf:] . . There was a base and you had to get to it. You would be hidden. And the other team would be looking for you. . . the idea was . . [to] get back to safety before they caught you in your hiding place. And I think that's what the lay low sheepie was. *Ibid* **NY**199, Lie still sheep. . . Lie still my sheep. . . there are two groups and there's a leader for each group. . . the first group would go and hide. And then there would be colors given. For instance the color yellow was that they [=the seekers] were not very near. . . And then green they were getting closer and red they were almost on top and purple you better run for the goal.

layman n [lay n[1] 2b] **AK**
A miner who works for a share of the proceeds in a mining venture.
1899 *Harper's Weekly* 8 Apr 344 **AK**, The laymen struck it the first hole, and out of thirty burnings took out $40,000. **1909** Rickard *Through Yukon & AK* 274, The mines are worked mainly by lessees; fully three quarters of the gold extracted in the Fairbanks district is taken out of the ground by 'lay-men', who pay the owners of the claims a royalty of 25 to 50 per cent on the gross output. **1924** Mertie–Harrington *Ruby–Kuskokwim Reg. AK* 107, Active mining was begun on a four-claim association by the owners in 1914 and continued by laymen the following year.

lay off v phr
1 To take off (an article of clothing). [*OED* (at *lay* v.[1] 54.a) "*Obs.*"]
1865 Byrn *Advent. Fudge Fumble* 214 **TN**, I . . laid off my coat. **1871** Eggleston *Hoosier Schoolmaster* 118 **sIN**, The master took off his coat and showed his slender arms. Bud laid his off. **1890** Howells *Boy's Town* 140 **sOH** (as of 1840s), That day they all laid off their bonnets on the hall-table. **1894** Twain *Pudd'nhead Wilson* 250 **seMO**, He laid off his coat and hat and began his preparations. **1917** Garland *Son Middle Border* 4 **WI**, The soldier laid off his heavy army shoes. **1929** *AmSp* 5.126 **ME**, Hospitable remarks were . . "Won't you step in and lay off your things." **1937** Hall Coll. **eTN** (*Montgomery Coll.*), I laid off my linen and swum across the river. **1967** *DARE* FW Addit **swMA**, "Just lay your coat off and try this on." "Lay off your coat and stay awhile."

2 To mark out (a field, rows, etc) with a plow for planting; to mark out land for planting. [A specific use of std *lay off* to mark or measure off] **Sth, S Midl** Cf **laying-off plow**
1787 (1925) Washington *Diaries* 3.187 **VA**, Brought another of the Muddy hole plows home from French's, and set it to laying off the 20 acre cut designed. . . for Carrots. **1847** in 1927 Jones *FL Plantation Rec.* 223, 2 [slaves] laying off cotton land in Redoak field. **1909** *DN* 3.344 **eAL, wGA**, Lay off. . . In plowing, to plow single furrows at certain distances. "I've been layin off cotton rows all day." **1915** *DN* 4.184 **swVA**, Lay off. . . To make furrows for planting grain in. **1923** *DN* 5.213 **swMO**, [Lay] off. **1940** Hall Coll. **wNC, eTN**, Lay off. . . [To] make little rows through the field with a bull tongue. . . lay off to plant it so you can have straight rows to hoe it by. **1949** *PADS* 11.8 **wTX** (as of 1911–29), Lay off. c1960 Wilson Coll. **csKY**, Lay off rows. **1966–70** *DARE* Tape **GA**1, Go in the first thing in the spring of the year and plow up your land, break it, tear it up good, and lay it off, list it, bed it. *Ibid* **GA**69, After we . . get our nursery stock . . rows are laid off in a check, principally twenty by twenty. *Ibid* **KY**84, After you got your tobacco ground prepared, you broke your ground and worked it down and laid it off two ways, made crosses about, oh, three and a half to four feet apart. . . and where these fur [=furrow] lines crossed, that's where you made your tobacco hill. **1985** *NC Folkl. Jrl.* 33.32 **wNC** (as of c1912), To plant [corn] by the old method, Did would hitch his gentlest horse to a bull tongue plow and "lay off" the field. This meant that the plow opened a straight furrow about five inches deep in rows about five feet apart. **1986** Pederson *LAGS Concordance* **Gulf Region, esp AL, GA, TN**, 6 infs, Laying off (the rows, the furrow, etc); 3 infs, Lay it off (in a furrow); 2 infs, Lay the rows off (with a scooter plow); 2 infs, Lay off the rows (with a cultivator); 1 inf, Where you couldn't lay off—in sandy soil; 1 inf, A plow that you laid the ground off with; 1 inf, Laid our rows off—early stage of cotton planting.

3 foll by infin: To plan, intend. **chiefly Sth, S Midl** Cf **lay by** v phr **2, lay out** v phr **3**
1843 Thompson *Major Jones' Courtship* 22 **GA**, I's been layin off to go to see Miss Mary, but my nose wasn't well whar I blazed it on that dratted grape vine. **1892** *DN* 1.230 **KY**, I laid off to tell him. **1893** Shands *MS Speech* 43, Lay off. . . to intend; used by all classes; as, "I lay off to go away to-morrow." Bartlett gives *lay out* this meaning, but

it is not so used in Mississippi, at least to any great extent. *Lay off* is used in Tennessee. **1899** (1912) Green *VA Folk-Speech* 258, *Lay off.* . . I laid off to go to town last week but couldn't get there. **1905** *DN* 3.86 **nwAR,** I laid off to plow that field next week. **1909** *DN* 3.344 **eAL, wGA,** I laid off to do that next week. **1915** *DN* 4.184 **swVA,** I've been a layin' off all summer to come to see you. **1917** *DN* 4.414 **wNC, IL, KY,** *Lay off.* . . To purpose without attempting. "I've laid off and laid off to do that, an' I've never got it done." **1928** in 1952 Mathes *Tall Tales* 43 **sAppalachians,** "I'm afeared yer pappy's tomb rock's goin' to blow clear down in the fust big wind, Honey," quavered the old woman. "I've been layin' off fer me an' you to git out thar an' h'ist it up." **1938** FWP *Guide DE* 500 **cDE,** We're layin' off to have supper by and by. **1939** McGuire *FL Cracker Dial.* 177, I lay off to do it next week. [Used by 2 of 3 infs.] **c1950** *Hall Coll.* **wNC,** I've been layin' off to go up there for a long while. **1960** Criswell *Resp. to PADS 20* **Ozarks,** I laid off to tell him but never did. **1976** Garber *Mountain-ese* 52 **sAppalachians,** I've been layin' off to quit smokin'.

4 To stay away from work or school without an adequate excuse; to play hookey. [By ext from *lay off* to take a break from work, be idle] Cf **lie out 2**

1966 Dakin *Dial. Vocab. Ohio R. Valley* 2.512, In all of southern Kentucky, in the Mountains south of the upper Kentucky and Licking Rivers, and among older speakers in the southern Knobs the expression of the Carolinas and western Virginia *lay out (of school)* is usual. *Lay off* is occasional in the area. **1966–68** *DARE* (Qu. BB27, *When somebody pretends to be sick . . he's _____*) Infs **CO33, KS18, TX39,** Laying off; (Qu. JJ6, *To stay away from school without an excuse*) Inf **SC19,** Layin' off from school. [All Infs old] **1986** Pederson *LAGS Concordance (Skipped class)* 1 inf, **cTN,** Laid off.

5 foll by vbl n: To delay, put off; see quot.

1975 Gainer *Witches* 13 **sAppalachians,** Lay off . . to procrastinate. "I've laid off goin' to town for a week."

layoff n old-fash

A stopover, layover.

1942 Berrey–Van den Bark *Amer. Slang* 62.3, Stopover. . . Lay-off. **1950** *WELS (When making a long trip, if you have to change trains and wait a while between them, you might say, "I have a two-hour _____ in Chicago.")* 1 Inf, **cWI,** Layoff. [Inf old] **1966–69** *DARE* (Qu. N38) Infs **KS5, ME1, MD20, NY12, RI17, VA27,** Layoff. [All Infs old]

layoff plow See **laying-off plow**

lay on See **lay** v **6**

lay one on (one) See **lay** v **5a**

lay one's tongue to v phr Also *lay tongue to* [Scots, Engl dial]

To think of to say—usu in phrr *call someone everything one can lay (one's) tongue to* and varr.

1884 Twain *Huck. Finn* 185 **MO,** And so he went on, calling Sherburn everything he could lay his tongue to. **1943** McAtee *Dial. Grant Co. IN Suppl.* 2 10 (as of 1890s), *Lay tongue to* . . speak; "She called him everything she could _____." **1960** Criswell *Resp. to PADS 20* **Ozarks,** *Lay tongue to* . . To utter. "[He] called the lawyer everything he could lay tongue to." Common. **1970** *Thompson Coll.* **cnAL** (as of 1930s), I cussed him to everything I could lay my tongue to.

layo(s) to catch meddlers See **layover(s) to catch meddlers**

lay out v phr

1 To prepare (a corpse) for burial. [*OED lay out* (at *lay* v.[1] 56.b) 1595 →] **chiefly Midl, Sth**

1804 (1965) Ordway *Jrls.* 112, Sergt Charles Floyd Expired. . . He was laid out in the Best Manner possable. **1828** Webster *Amer. Dict.* np, *To lay out.* . . To dress in grave clothes and place in a decent posture; as, to *lay out* a corpse. **1899** (1912) Green *VA Folk-Speech* 254, *Laid out.* . . A body is said to be laid out, when it is clad in burial garments ready to be put into the coffin. **1928** Ruppenthal *Coll.* **KS,** *Lay out,* to prepare for burial. "He was laid out in his best suit." **1933** Rawlings *South Moon* 333 **FL,** I'll git somebody to come lay her out and I'll see the preacher for the buryin'. **1960** Criswell *Resp. to PADS 20* **Ozarks,** When I was a child neighbors came in and laid out the body of the dead. **1968** *DARE* (Qu. BB60) Inf **MO16,** Laid out. **1969** *DARE* Tape **KY6,** What they call lay him out, they washed him clean, and dressed him; **KY24,** What they called laying 'em out. That's what they called preparing 'em for a burial. There was no embalming or anything of that sort . . they were buried naturally. **1972** Hall *Sayings Old Smoky* 92 **eTN** (as of 1953), Uncle Proctor would never be any whiter when he

was laid out than he was then. **1976** Garber *Mountain-ese* 52 **sAppalachians,** Zack went over to help lay-out Mr. Brown, who died last night. **1986** Pederson *LAGS Concordance,* 1 inf, **cnGA,** I've help lay out several for burial.

2a To scold severely, berate; hence vbl n *laying-out.* [Fig from *lay out* to knock down]

1942 McAtee *Dial. Grant Co. IN* 39 (as of 1890s), *Lay out* . . denounce or scold severely. **1960** Criswell *Resp. to PADS 20* **Ozarks,** He laid me out, read the riot act to me. **c1960** *Wilson Coll.* **csKY,** *Lay out* (or *lay out cold*). . . Scold severely. **1965–70** *DARE* (Qu. II27, *If somebody gives you a very sharp scolding* . . "*I certainly got a _____ for that.*") 10 Infs, **esp Atlantic,** Laying-out; **NY27,** Laid out; (Qu. Y6, . . *To put pressure on somebody to do something he ought to have done but hasn't:* "*He's a whole week late. I'm going to _____.*") Infs **MI50, WA6,** Lay him out; (Qu. Y12a, *A fight between two people, mostly with words*) Inf **NC62,** They really laid each other out. **1967** *DARE* FW Addit **swAR,** "I laid that fellow out about his plumbers." = I told him off, let him know they didn't do satisfactory work.

b in phr *lay out in lavender:* = **2a** above. [By ext from *lay up in lavender* to store (in dried lavender leaves) for future use; to put out of circulation; also infl by *lay out* to beat, knock out] **esp NEast**

1948 Bean *Yankee Auctioneer* 185 **wMA,** I moved over in front of the troublemakers and laid them out in lavender. The staid old hall where I was holding this sale never before heard the English language reeled off in the style I rendered right then. **1965–70** *DARE* (Qu. Y12a, *A fight between two people, mostly with words*) Inf **NY233,** Laid him out in lavender; (Qu. II27, *If somebody gives you a very sharp scolding* . . "*I certainly got a _____ for that.*") Infs **CT39, NY88, 108, PA46,** Laid out in lavender; **RI13,** He laid me out in lavender; (Qu. JJ35b) Inf **CA59,** Lay him out in lavender. **1970** *DARE* FW Addit **cNY,** Laid out in lavender—bawled out. **1976** *Harper's Weekly* 26 Jan 19 **PA** (as of c1950), "I'll lay you out in lavender" (I'll scold you severely).

3 foll by infin: To intend, plan. [Cf *OED* (at *lay* v.[1] 56.f) "to take measures to win or get. Also, to scheme, plan *to effect some purpose*"] **scattered, but esp S Midl** Cf **lay by** v phr **2, lay off** v phr **3**

1828 Webster *Amer. Dict.* np, *To lay out,* to purpose; to intend. He lays out to make a journey. **1867** Howells *Ital. Journeys* 57 **sOH,** He laid out to go ashore the next time he came to Venice. **1884** *Anglia* 7.268 **Sth, S Midl** [Black], *To lay out fer ter* = to intend to. **1899** (1912) Green *VA Folk-Speech* 258, *Lay out.* . . To arrange; to plan. "I laid out to do that tomorrow." **1909** *DN* 3.413 **nME,** *Lay out.* . . To plan. **1926** *DN* 5.401 **Ozarks,** *Lay out.* . . To plan, to purpose. **1928** Ruppenthal *Coll.* **KS,** I had laid out to do that. **1946** *AmSp* 21.98 **sIL,** *Layin' out to do,* intending to do. **c1960** *Wilson Coll.* **csKY,** *Lay out.* . . To plan something that is to be done.

4 See quot 1917. Cf **draw** v **C6**

1899 Garland *Boy Life* 185 **nwIA** (as of c1870s), When the stacker wishes to "carry the stack up straight," he lays the sheaves sidewise. When he wishes to "lay out" his bulge, he turns the long point of the "slanch" upward. When he wishes to "draw in," he reverses them, putting the point down and the slant upward. **1917** *DN* 4.395 **neOH, IL, NEng,** *Lay out.* . . To extend the edge of a load or stack of hay or sheaves; opposite of *draw in.* . . "You can lay out that corner a little."[?] "You can lay out yet for another tier." **1927** *AmSp* 2.359 **cwWV,** *Lay out* . . to extend the side of a hay stack. "Have I laid out the stack enough?"

5 To haul off, "let loose"; see quot. [Cf *let out* to lash out]

1966 *PADS* 46.27 **cnAR** (as of 1952), That kid jist laid out and cut him down.

6 To avoid, refrain from; see quots.

1956 *Hall Coll.* **eTN,** I was falling a chestnut tree and it struck a dead locust which fell against me, and I had to lay out doing anything for two or three weeks. **1970** Major *Dict. Afro-Amer. Slang* 76, *Lay out:* to avoid.

7 See **lie out.**

layout n

1 A plan, scheme. [Transf from std *layout* a plan or arrangement of physical objects]

1867 in 1942 *AmSp* 17.71 **NW,** A 'lay-out' is any proposed enterprise, from organizing a State to digging out a prairie-dog. **1901** White *Westerners* 292, I'm sorry that I have this to do, Billy. . . I don't want to. It's none of my lay-out. **1904** Smith *Promoters* 53, There isn't a single move in this whole lay-out that we can't justify by history. **1928** *Sat. Eve. Post* 4 Feb 81, Here's the layout. The bonds bear 6 per cent.

2 An expedition or company of people, "gang"; an organization, operation, "outfit." **chiefly Sth, S Midl, West**

1867 in 1887 Custer *Tenting* 529, One of our officers dined with me to-day, and complained that their mess [=commissary unit] was an 'awfully poor lay-out.' **1869** *Overland Mth.* 3.128 **NM**, Several persons in our "lay-out" (*i.e.,* our company) in New Mexico "swapped" good American horses for mustangs. **1884** Murfree *TN Mts.* 143, He went thar one day when all them Peels, the whole lay-out, war gone down ter the Settlemint. **1891** *AN&Q* 8.75 **TN**, *Lay-out,* a noun, seems to mean *crowd* in such expressions as, 'he is big enough to whip the whole *lay-out,*' that is, to whip the whole shebang, or whole number of them. **1903** (1965) Adams *Log Cowboy* 100, Surround this layout [=a gang of cattle-thieves], lads, and let's examine them more closely. **1909** *DN* 3.344 **eAL, wGA**, *Lay-out.* . . Crowd. "The whole lay-out got drunk." **1927** (1944) Russell *Trails Plowed Under* xiii **West**, I tell you they was a pretty sad looking outfit. They sho was a lonesome layout. **1930** Williams *Logger-Talk* 26 **Pacific NW**, *Lay-out:* A logging concern might be called either an *outfit* or a *lay-out.* **1933** Rawlings *South Moon* 218 **FL**, They's a risk, I know that. I'm jest natchelly countin' on nary snooper gittin' in to this lay-out [=a moonshining operation]. **1936** Adams *Cowboy Lingo* 13, The ranch, together with its buildings, cattle, and employees, was spoken of as the 'spread,' 'layout,' or 'outfit.' **1958** McCulloch *Woods Words* 104 **Pacific NW**, *Layout.* . . The company for which a man works. **1966** Dakin *Dial. Vocab. Ohio R. Valley* 2.505, Single occurrences of . . [the whole] company, flock, layout, mess, pile . . (="group of people") . . are recorded.

3 In logging: an area prepared to receive the fall of a large tree. Cf **bed** n **B3**

1936 in 1949 Powers *Redwood Country* 116 **nCA, sOR**, After determining the direction of the fall [of a redwood tree], smaller trees, called 'bedding,' are felled into the layout to build up the low spots. **1968** *DARE* Tape **CA**104, You have to make a layout, . . so you don't have a pocket that the log will spring down and if it does these redwoods all shatter, you see. You got to get in there with a bulldozer . . and work several days to fix the layout, so when the tree falls it wants [to] lay down flat. You can't have any spring to it.

4 also *laying out:* See quot. Cf **viewing, visitation**

1966–68 *DARE* (Qu. BB60, *When friends and relatives gather together at the place where the body is, usually the night before the funeral*) Infs **OH**76, **PA**97, (A) layout; **DE**2, Layout—colored people around here call it this; **MI**10, Set up at the layin' out—used to be.

lay out in lavender See **lay out** v phr **2b**

lay out with the dry cattle See **lie out 1b**

lay over v phr

1 also *lay it (all) over:* To surpass, outdo; to excel. *old-fash*
1853 (1930) Buck *Yankee Trader* 128, These Chinese. . . lay over the genuine Yankee even in buying and selling. **1879** (1880) Twain *Tramp Abroad* 37 **MO**, In the one little particular of scolding . . a blue-jay can lay over anything, human or divine. **1892** *KS Univ. Qrly.* 1.97 **KS**, That lays over anything I know. **1911** Wilson *Land Claimers* 179 **nwOR**, He let on as how anybody with grit and gumption could lay it all over you. **1923** Watts *Luther Nichols* 210 **OH**, In Luther's own language, she laid over the whole bunch. **1942** Berrey–Van den Bark *Amer. Slang* 22.3, *Surpass; excel.* . . Lay it (all) over, lay over.

2 To move aside; see quot.
1938 Stuart *Dark Hills* 32 **neKY**, A yoke of oxen pulled the sled with everything we had loaded on it. . . Cattle are powerful things . . watch old Berrey get down there and pull. Lay over there, Buck, and quit that a-crowdin' Berry.

layover(s) to catch meddlers n Also *larovers to catch meddlers, laros ~, layo(s) ~, lee rows ~, lie low(s) ~, layovers for meddlers;* phrr *larrows catch meddlers, lay rows to catch meddlers;* for addit varr see quots [*OED* layer-over (in the earliest quots sp *lare-over(s)*) a1700 →; *EDD* lay-overs (varr include *lare-overs, layers, layo(r)s, leeoze*). The original form of the first element is prob unrecoverable; the wide variety of forms suggests that its sense was lost long ago.] **chiefly Sth, S Midl** See Map Cf **aloes to catch meddlers, cat's fur to make kitten britches, fool's fumbling ball, Pharaoh for meddlers**

Used as an evasive answer to a question, esp "What's that?"

1848 Bartlett *Americanisms* 200, *Lay-overs for meddlers.* A reply to a troublesome question on the part of a child, in answer to 'What's that?' . . I have never heard it except in New York. **1886** (1887) Murfree *In the Clouds* 406 **eTN**, But when asked what she was talking about she would only reply in enigmatical phrase, "Laros to ketch meddlers!" and shake her head unutterably. **1892** *KS Univ. Qrly.* 1.97 **MD, PA, OH, AR**, *Larofamedlers* . . used generally as equivalent to, It's none of your business. **1895** *DN* 1.383 **NJ**, "What's that, ma? Do tell, won't you?" "Why, didn't I say it's lay-overs for meddlers?" **1899** (1912) Green *VA Folk-Speech* 33, Larovers to catch meddlers. *Ibid* 256, "A lareover to catch meddlers." As when children are over inquisitive as to the meaning or use of any articles, it is some times the custom to rebuke them by saying they are "lareovers for meddlers." **1905** *DN* 3.86 **nwAR**, 'What's that?' 'O, that's layover to catch meddlers.' **1909** *DN* 3.344 **eAL, wGA**, *Layo(vers) to catch meddlers.* . . "What's that?" "Layos to ketch meddlers; you better watch out or hit 'ill ketch you." **1917** *DN* 4.414 **wNC, LA**, *Lay-over.* . . Trap; dead-fall. "That's a lay-over to catch meddlers." In La., *laroes catch meddlers.* **1926** *Amer. Mercury* 7.241, The saying, "Lay rows to catch meddlers," is still used in Mississippi, Alabama and Louisiana to nonplus inquisitive childhood's annoying questions. It is simply a way of evading an answer. **1927** *AmSp* 2.408 **Sth, S Midl**, When I was a small boy in the mountains of North Carolina. . . *Lay overs to catch meddlers* is the style of the rebuke as I always heard it. . . The following phrases . . have been reported to me as having been heard in various sections of the South . . *Larrows are traps for meddlers*—Georgia. *Larrows to catch meddlers*—North Carolina and Louisiana. *Larrows to catch meddloes*—North Carolina. *Layers to catch meddlers*—Georgia. *Lay holes to catch meddlers*—Georgia. *Layo to catch meddlers*—Georgia. *Layoes to catch meddlers*—Georgia and South Carolina. *Layoes to catch meddloes*—Georgia. *Layoles to catch meddlers*—Georgia. *Lay overs catch meddlers*—Georgia. *Lay overs to catch meddlers*—Georgia, Florida, North Carolina, and South Carolina. *Lay rows to catch meddlers*—Georgia, South Carolina, and Mississippi. *Lee oters to catch meddlers*—Georgia and South Carolina. *Lee rows to catch meddlers*—Georgia and South Carolina. *Lee roys to catch meddlers*—Georgia. *Leodables to catch meddlers*—Georgia. *Leoes catch meddlers*—Georgia. *Leoes to catch meddlers*—Georgia. **1935** *AmSp* 10.282, Children and other inquisitive persons asking 'What is that?' are often silenced with the answer, 'Oh, it's a so-and-so for meddlers.' And the so-and-so is called variously either a *laro,* a *lareo,* a *faro,* a *Pharaoh,* or a *marrow.* **1936** Greene *Death Deep South* 99, This Yankee with . . his alien inability to understand such plain English as *larrers catch maddlers.* **1939** Hench Coll. **swVA**, Lariat to catch meddlars, lassoes . . , lay-overs . . , larruss . . , English teacher at Roanoke College, Salem, Va. has heard all these forms of the expression. **1944** *PADS* 2.45 **NC, VA**, Lay-over or lay-overs to catch meddlers; larus ['læras] . . ; *la rose* ['laroz, 'læroz] catch meddlers; larrows or laroes . . ; lay rows to catch meddlers; ledlow . . ; lay-o's. . . Some form of this expression seems to appear in most Southern states. I have not observed two or more forms in the same community. **1950** *PADS* 14.43 **SC**, Layover to catch meddlers. . . has been corrupted in popular speech into: laros, naro, lairs, larovus. **1952** Brown *NC Folkl.* 1.557, Lay-overs to catch meddlers. . . some of the variant forms for the first word . . are. . . larrus, Va. . . lie rose—Tenn.; lorries—N.C. **1954** *PADS* 21.32 **SC**, A lie-low to catch meddlers. **1960** (1966) Percy *Moviegoer* 124 **nMS**, "Well I can tell you one thing, son." "What's that?" "You're surely not gon find out from me." "Why not?" "Larroes catch medloes." **1965–70** *DARE* (Qu. NN12a, *Things that people say to put a child off when he asks too many questions: "What's that for?"*) Infs **CA**97, **DC**8, **GA**77, **KY**11,

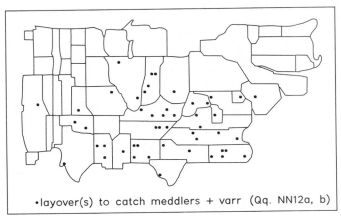

•layover(s) to catch meddlers + varr (Qq. NN12a, b)

SC39, (That's a) layover to catch meddlers; **IN**56, Layover to catch meddlers, and you're the first one caught; **MD**17, **NJ**57, Layovers to catch (*or* for) meddlers; **IL**29, Layover for a meddler; (Qu. NN12b, *Things that people say to put off a child when he asks, "What are you making?"*) 28 Infs, **chiefly Sth, S Midl**, Layover to catch meddlers; **DE**1, **MD**17, **MS**64, **SC**44, 59, **VA**11, Layovers to catch meddlers; **KY**77, **TN**1, 12, Layover; **IL**29, **IN**76, Layover for a meddler (*or* for meddlers); **KY**59, **NC**84, Layover to catch meddlers (and) caught you, the first one; [**KY**70, **OH**59, Something to catch meddlers (with);] **MO**38, Laying on and making layovers to catch meddlers; **GA**1, ['lɑro] to catch meddlers; **LA**14, [lærɔuz] to catch meddlers—old-fashioned, Negro; **OK**14, Laying rope to catch a meddler. **1968** Kellner *Aunt Serena* 44 **IN**, If I asked Aunt Serena what was in one of these sacred periodicals, she turned the key and tartly replied, "Layovers [Kellner: leftovers] for meddlers!" **1983** *DARE* File neNJ (as of c1910–20), When Mother had something that we were not to open or even to ask about, she'd tell us that the box contained "lay overs for meddlers." *Ibid* **neNJ** (as of c1950), Ralph L. Woods in a newspaper item said that his mother's phrase was "Lielows to catch meddlers."

lays See **lay** n[1] 3

lay sheepie lay See **lay low sheepie**

lay (something) up against See **lay up** v phr **2**

lay to See **lay** v **2b**

lay tongue to See **lay one's tongue to**

lay under hatches See **hatch** n[1] **2**

lay up v phr

1 To store, save, reserve, stash away; hence ppl adj *laid up*. [*OED lay up* (at *lay* v.[1] 60.c) ?a1366 →] Cf **lay back**
1753 in 1961 Franklin *Papers* 4.482, I should think the Poor would be more careful. . . and lay up something for themselves against a rainy day. **1863** in a1972 Hench *Coll.*, I suppose the fear of scarcity, combined with the plethora of money induces people to "lay up" a stack, with this they enhance the price of provisions. **1912** Green *VA Folk-Speech* 254, *Laid up*. . . Something to be done at another time, as in the phrase: "I have a whipping laid up for you." **1933** Hanley *Disks* **ceMA**, He wasn't a practical man, you know; he never could lay up any money. [Inf old] **1954** Harder *Coll.* **cwTN**, Lay away. . . hide. "He's got 'er laid away so's nobody'll never find 'er." Also *laid up*. **1958** McCulloch *Woods Words* 104 **Pacific NW**, Lay up. . . To take a machine out of work and store it. **1963** Adamson *Household Hints* 90 **NEng** (as of late 19th cent), In laying up furs for summer, lay a tallow candle in or near them, and danger from worms will be obviated. **1965–69** *DARE* (Qu. Y47, *To hide something away for future use: "I know he's got it _____ somewhere."*) Infs **AL**56, **GA**84, **IL**14, **MI**95, **OK**15, **SC**55, **WV**5, Laid up. [All Infs old]

2 in phr *lay (something) up against*: To hold (something) against; to blame for (something). *old-fash*
1856 Whitcher *Bedott Papers* 49, I felt dretful hurt about it, but I never laid it up agin him, 'cause I know'd he dident know no better. **1887** Wilkins *Humble Romance* 35 (*DAE*), You don't lay up anything agin me, Maria? **1913** Kephart *Highlanders* 123 **sAppalachians**, Oh, we-uns don't lay *that* up agin the Government! **1916** Lincoln *Mary-'Gusta* 62 **MA**, Goody-by. I'll try not to lay it up against you. **1942** McAtee *Dial. Grant Co.* **IN** 39 (as of 1890s), Lay up against . . blame; "I don't lay that up against him."

3 also *lie up*: To remain in one's bed, lair, nest, or hiding place.
1883 Twain *Life on Missip.* (Boston) 53, A man that was running aft stumbled and fell and sprained his ankle so that he had to lay up. **1938** Rawlings *Yearling* 31 **nFL**, He [=a bear] ain't full weight right now, account of his stomach bein' shrunk up from layin' up, and empty. *Ibid* 105, She's learned the fawn to lay up so still hit'll not git noticed. **1966–69** *DARE* (Qu. P33, *When an animal goes into its hole to sleep all winter, it _____;* total Infs questioned, 75) Inf **NM**3, Lays up in his den—a wolf; (Qu. X43b, *If you sleep later than usual one day on purpose . . "I _____."*) Inf **GA**72, We lay up; (Qu. BB41, *Not seriously ill, but sick enough to be in bed: "He's been _____ for a week."*) Infs **LA**2, 15, Laying up; **SC**19, Lying up. **1968** *DARE* Tape **IN**36, *Lay up.* They'll lay up all day and come out at night [of raccoons]. **1986** Pederson *LAGS Concordance* (He lay in bed all day) 1 inf, **cwAL**, Lay up in bed all day; 1 inf, **cnTN**, Lay up; 1 inf, **neGA**, He laid up—stayed in bed.

4 To make a forced stop in traveling or itinerant labor; hence n *lay-up*.
1839 Ga., Western & Atlantic RR. Comm. 15 (*Mathews Coll.*), I made . . two trips to Kingston, and three to White's Creek, where we 'lay up' again, or stopped running. **1860** (1936) Hawley *Diary* 19.326 **WI**, We can not lay up for bad weather this near home. **1864** *Santa Fe Wkly. New Mexican* 25 Nov. 3/2 (*DA*), Large trains have been compelled to 'lay up' on the road. **1922** Rollins *Cowboy* 197, Such compulsory stoppings were termed "lay ups." **1939** FWP *Guide CA* 251 **nCA**, Migratory farm refugees, dust bowl refugees, and itinerants "lay up" in Sacramento between harvests. **1942** [see **5** below].

5 also *lie up*: To rest, loaf, take it easy.
1858 Hammett *Piney Woods Tavern* 134, He . . cal'lated to sell off lock, stock and barrel, and lay up for life. **1942** Berrey–Van den Bark *Amer. Slang* 62.3, [A] stopover. . . lay-up. *Ibid* 248.2, Idle spell. Lay-up. *Ibid* 248.3, Idle; loaf; loiter. . . lie up. *Ibid* 250.1, [A] rest. . . Lay-up. *Ibid* 250.3, [To] rest. Lay up. **1958** McCulloch *Woods Words* 104 **Pacific NW**, Lay up. . . To stop work and take it easy. **1971** Roberts *Third Ear* np [Black], *Lay up* . . to relax. **1984** Wilder *You All Spoken Here* 205 **Sth**, Layin' up: Malingering; loafing. **1986** Pederson *LAGS Concordance*, 1 inf, **nwFL**, Lay up on your money—rest on what you've made.

6 To cohabit.
1928 Ruppenthal *Coll.* **KS**, Lay up with, to have sexual relations with, esp. illicit—always implies disparagement. "The man on trial had laid up with one of the witnesses at a house near the edge of town."; *To lay up*—to cohabit with, esp. illicitly. **1958** McCulloch *Woods Words* 104 **Pacific NW**, Lay up. . . To take up with a momentarily unattached female. **1970** *DARE* (Qu. AA19, . . . *A man and woman who are not married but live together as if they were*) Inf **MO**23, Laying up together. **1977** Randolph *Pissing in the Snow* 207 **MO** (as of 1920s), One time there was a pretty widow-woman that lived all by herself. Lots of the country boys wanted to lay up with her. *Ibid* 180 **MO** (as of 1951), She thought it was terrible how the town girls laid up with the boys. **1980** Folb *Runnin' Down* 244 **Los Angeles CA** [Black], *Lay . . up*. . . Engage in sexual intercourse.

7 also *lie up*; In marble play: see quots. [Cf *EDD lay up* "to lie close to the ring at marbles" and *lig up* (at *lag* sb.[3])] Cf **lag** v[1] **1a, b, lay** n[1] **3**
1922 *DN* 5.187, *Lie up* . . =lag up. [*Ibid*, Lag . . To drop up [=to shoot a marble to a more advantageous position] near the ring with a taw, after winning the "goes;" also, to shoot at the ring for the "goes." Also *lag up*.] **1955** *PADS* 23.24 **cwTN, cwAL**, Lay up. . . To place the taw as near the ring as possible in order to have a favorable position for the next shot. *Ibid* **cwTN**, Lie up. . . Var. of *lay up*.

8 See quot. Cf **lay out** v phr **3**
1952 Brown *NC Folkl.* 1.558, *Lay up*. . . To intend.—Central and east.

lay-up n See **lay up** v phr **4**

layway v, hence vbl n *laywaying* Also *layaway* [Reversed compound; cf Intro "Language Changes" I.1] **chiefly S Midl**
To waylay.
1913 Kephart *Highlanders* 339 **sAppalachians**, He . . is likely to be . . "laywayed." *Ibid* 347, A real mountain feud. . . is marked by suave treachery, "double-teaming," "laywaying," "blind-shooting," and general heartlessness and brutality. **1923** *DN* 5.213 **swMO**, [Lay]way. . . To waylay, to attack from ambush. **1930** *Herald-Advt.* (Huntington WV) 30 Nov sec 3 6/7 **KY, WV**, Contrary to popular opinion, he is not likely to be waylaid. Almost invariably, if he should be shot from ambush . . , he will be "lay-wayed." In other words, he will be laid in wait for. **1936** *AmSp* 11.316 **Ozarks**, Layway. . . To waylay, to ambush. The noun *laywayin'* is common. **1952** Brown *NC Folkl.* 1.558, Layaway. . . Waylay.—Central and east. . . Illiterate. **1954** Harder *Coll.* **cwTN**, Layway. c1960 *Wilson Coll.* **csKY**, Layway.

lay whip v phr
To ride or drive fast.
1936 *AmSp* 11.316 **Ozarks**. **1953** Randolph–Wilson *Down in Holler* 259 **Ozarks**, Lay whip. . . To drive rapidly. I have heard it used seriously, in a moment of stress, in urging the driver of a motorcar to speed up. **1983** *MJLF* 9.1.46 **ceKY** (as of 1956), Lay whip . . to drive a buggy or ride a horse fast.

lay with v phr
To hold tight to, keep at, stick with—often in phr *lay with it*.
1954 Harder *Coll.* **cwTN**, Lay with. . . Hold tight to. "Lay with that pry pole, so's it won't whack ye in the face." **1965** *DARE* FW Addit

MS, *Lay with it*—stick with a task or a project or continue to work hard. **1967–70** *DARE* (QR, near Qu. JJ8) Inf **GA**77, I've got to lay with it tonight—work hard; (Qu. KK8, . . *Succeeding, especially in spite of difficulty: "He had a hard time, but at last he _____."*) Inf **LA**8, Laid with it; went through with it; (Qu. KK47, *Something that is left undecided or unfinished: "Perhaps we'd better just _____."*) Inf **NY**241, Lay with it.

lazy adj esp West Cf **flying**
Esp of a livestock brand, but also of any letter or figure: lying on its side rather than standing upright; also transf.

1887 *Scribner's Mag.* 2.508, Words used in connection with . . life on the plains: . . *flying-brand; lazy-brand.* **1907** White *AZ Nights* 76, I didn't see them any more after that until I'd hit the Lazy Y [ranch]. **1927** *Ruppenthal Coll.* **KS,** *Lazy brand*—a brand (for cattle, etc.) wherein the figure is made sideways, instead of upright, as to its appearance. Thus, a lazy N brand looks like a Z, when the N is turned on its side. **1936** Adams *Cowboy Lingo* 122 **West,** Any letter or figure 'too tired to stand up' and lying on its side was called a 'lazy brand,' as 'Lazy Y.' **1938** FWP *Guide DE* 362, An avenue of trees and "lazy-X" fences, painted white, led past the coach house. **1959** Martin *Gunbarrel* 68 **WY,** Against the end wall and beneath a lazy window (so called because it was laid down instead of standing) there was a table for working space.

lazybed n [*SND lazy-bed* (at *lazy* adj. I.1) 1743 →; *EDD lazy-bed* (at *lazy* adj. 1.(4))]
In potato growing: see quots.

1822 (1972) Deane *New Engl. Farmer* 347, The lazy bed method, or trenching, is most practised in Ireland. I have tried it several times, and am convinced, that a greater quantity on the same ground may be raised in this way, than in almost any other. But the labour is so great, as it must be performed with the spade, that I dare not recommend it, unless in particular cases, or to those who have but little land. **1952** Brown *NC Folkl.* 1.558, *Lazy-bed.* . . A patch of land in which Irish potatoes are planted and covered with straw, leaves, etc., to make work after the crop is planted unnecessary; hence "*lazy-bed*."—Granville county. **1959** *Hench Coll.* **cVA,** I planted them in a lazy bed. . . you put your potato eyes into the ground down just about two inches. Then you cover the eyes with straw. It gets packed down & rots as the summer goes by and keeps away weeds. When you want potatoes, you just push the straw away and there they are. **1965** *Daily Progress* (Charlottesville VA) 6 Jan 11/1, Lazy bed . . is a method of . . raising . . Irish potatoes. . . [A] two or three-inch layer of wheat . . or other straw should be spread over the plot. . . Pieces [of potato] are laid on the straw. . . A layer of straw about eight or ten inches thick is spread over the entire bed. . . The bed requires no cultivation. . . The potatoes do not have to be dug . . [and] the harvested potatoes are clean. *Ibid,* It may be that whoever first devised the lazy bed was allergic to labor in its many forms.

lazybird n
1 **=cowbird 1.** [See quot 1956]
1899 Howe–Sturtevant *Birds RI* 67, *Molothrus ater* . . Cowbird. Lazybird. **1917** *Wilson Bulletin* 29.2.83, *Molothrus ater* . . Lazy-bird, Hickman, Ky. **1950** *WELS,* 1 Inf, **csWI,** Lazybird—cowbird. **1956** MA Audubon Soc. *Bulletin* 40.253, Common Cowbird. . . Lazy Bird (Mass., Conn., R.I. From foisting its young upon other birds to rear.)

2 A **kingfisher** (here: *Megaceryle alcyon*). [See quot 1946]
1927 Forbush *Birds MA* 2.248, Belted Kingfisher . . Kingfisher; Lazybird. **1946** Hausman *Eastern Birds* 376, Kingfisher, Halcyon, Lazybird. . . Kingfishers are seen sitting motionless on an exposed perch over the water.

lazy blood See **tired blood**

lazy board n
1 A board on the left side of a wagon that can be extended for the driver to sit on; see quots. *old-fash*
1889 *Century Dict.* 3383, *Lazyboard.* . . A short board used by teamsters to ride on. It is placed on the left of the wagon-bed, between the front and rear wheels. **1930** Omwake *Conestoga Teams* 18 **PA** (as of early 18th cent), The driver, instead of having a seat inside, rode on the lazy board, a sliding board of strong white oak that was pulled out on the left-hand side of the wagon body. **1959** Tallman *Dict. Amer. Folkl.* 174, *Lazy board*—On all the great Conestoga wagons there was a place on the left-hand side of the wagon for a board to be pulled out. As this was intended as a place for the driver to rest when he was not riding the left wheel horse or walking by the side of the wagon, it gained the designation of "lazy" board. It was usually of white oak and had to be

strong enough to support the weight of an unusually big man. **1976** Sublette Co. Artist Guild *More Tales* 161 **WY** (as of c1900), Just behind the front wheels of the lead wagon was a "Lazy Board". This was a two inch board about twelve inches wide. It hung under the wagon on the clevises. When everything was going well and the trail was good the lazy board could be pulled out far enough so that the driver could sit on it and ride.

2 Transf: see quots.
1935 *Yachting* Nov. 45/1 (*Mathews Coll.*), By standing on the "lazy-board" placed across the outer ends of these davits, the reef points can be reached. **1948** *Sat. Eve. Post* 25 Dec 69, Then, warmed and comfortable, Kemp [=the train brakeman] pulls himself up into the cupola [=observation tower in a caboose] and stretches out on the lazy boards in the darkness.

lazy boy n
1 also *lazy daisy, lazy lad:* A grass-cutting tool; see quots.
esp S Atl, Inland Sth Cf **lively lad**
1948 Hurston *Seraph* 236 **FL,** There was Jeff standing with a "lazy boy" in one of his big brawny hands. . . He . . began to slash at the weeds viciously with the lazy boy. **1950** *PADS* 14.44 **SC,** *Lazy boy.* . . A hand-operated blade for cutting weeds and grass. It has a very long handle and doesn't require stooping. **c1960** *Wilson Coll.* **csKY,** *Lazy boy.* . . Any device that a lazy boy would use to avoid work; a blade for cutting weeds is often so called. **1966–70** *DARE* (Qu. L35, *Hand tools used for cutting underbrush and digging out roots*) Inf **FL**15, Lazy boy—handle with a bow [at the end] and a blade across [the] bottom [of the open end of the bow]; swing it back and forth; **TN**58, Lazy daisy; (Qu. L37, *A hand tool used for cutting weeds and grass*) Inf **FL**15, Lazy boy [FW illustr: a long handle attached to the apex of a triangle-shaped piece, the bottom of which is a blade]; **NY**92, Lazy lad [FW illustr: a long handle attached to a bow-shaped curve, the ends of which are connected by a blade]; **TN**58, Sling blade, slinging blade—same as lazy daisy [FW illustr: a long handle which attaches at the bottom to two spreading prongs, the ends of which are connected by a blade].

2 See quot.
1967 *Amer. Agric. & Rural New Yorker* 164.8.30, [In a list of old words not now commonly known:] Lazy-boy. . . a stout iron bar attached to the front axle of a farm wagon so one end drags on the ground. When the team stops on a hill, it engages the ground and helps hold the wagon.

lazy bread n
1966 *DARE* (Qu. H18, . . *Special kinds of bread*) Inf **ME**23, Lazy bread—add more milk to dough and spoon into pan, saves kneading.

lazy chair n Also *lazy man's chair*
A comfortable chair suitable for resting or relaxing; an easy chair.

1948 *AmSp* 23.51 **VT** (as of c1870–1900), *Lazy-chair* was Vermont vernacular for an easy-chair (not a rocking-chair) in the latter half of the nineteenth century; whether throughout the whole half-century, or throughout all Vermont, I cannot say. There was a time when the typical farmhouse had several rocking-chairs for the comfort of the family, and one lazy-chair for a guest, though some member of the family might develop a fondness for taking the lazy-chair when no guest was present. **1951** Craig *Singing Hills* 136 **sAppalachians,** I never have worked in the field . . and I never will. But I'll sit in the lazy chair and rock, and wait for you. **1966** *DARE* (Qu. E7, *The piece of upholstered furniture that you can stretch out on to rest*) Inf **MT**5, Lazy chair; **OK**23, Lazy chair—chair that tips back. [Both Infs old] **1986** Pederson *LAGS Concordance,* 1 inf, **csTX,** Lazy chair, lazy man's chair. [Inf old]

lazy daisy n
1 A plant of the genus *Aphanostephus,* esp *A. skirrhobasis.* [See quot 1936] **esp TX**
1936 Whitehouse *TX Flowers* 226, The rays of the Lazy Daisy [=*Aphanostephus skirrhobasis*] behave like those of the Sleepy Daisy, opening in late morning to about 1½ in. across and becoming erect in late afternoon. **1965** Teale *Wandering Through Winter* 150 **TX,** All across Texas . . picturesque names have been bestowed on the wild plants of the state . . they run from angel's trumpet . . to . . lazy daisy. **1967** *DARE* Wildfl QR (Wills–Irwin) Plates 55A.1, 55A.2 Inf **TX**44, Lazy daisy. **1972** Correll *Plants TX* 1612, *Aphanostephus* . . Lazy Daisy. **1972** Brown *Wildflowers LA* 185, Lazy Daisy—*Aphanostephus skirrobasis* [sic]. **1979** Ajilvsgi *Wild Flowers* 299, Arkansas lazy daisy. . . Erect to sprawling perennial to 20 in. tall, with dense fine soft gray pubescence mostly throughout.

2 A **black-eyed Susan 2** or similar flower. Cf **lazy Susan**

1970 *DARE* (Qu. S7, *A kind of daisy, bright yellow with a dark center, that grows along roadsides in late summer*) Inf **NC**83, Lazy daisy.

3 See **lazy boy 1**.

lazy daisy pickle n Also *lazy wives' pickle*

A type of pickle requiring very little preparation.

1967–69 *DARE* (Qu. H56, *Names for . . pickles*) Inf **OR**1, Lazy daisy pickles—twenty-four-hour pickles; **CA**165, Lazy wives' pickles—one quart vinegar, one cup sugar, one half cup mustard.

lazy gal n Also *lazy wife*

1944 *PADS* 2.34 **wNC**, Lazy gal, lazy wife. . . A bucket operated by ropes passing through pulleys, used to bring water from a distant spring.

lazy housewife bean See **lazy wife (bean)**

lazy jack n [Cf *EDD* lazy-back (at *lazy* 1.(I)(c)) a hangnail]

1905 *DN* 3.86 **nwAR**, Lazy-jack. . . Hangnail. 'A lazy-jack is a sign of laziness.' Common.

lazy John See **lazy Tom**

lazy lad See **lazy boy 1**

lazy Lawrence See **Lawrence**

lazy line n

In shrimping: a rope used to assist in emptying the net; see quot.

1966–67 *DARE* Tape **SC**18, There's a rope running from the inside door on each net . . back to the top part of the bag called the lazy line. It saves 'em trouble. They don't have to take the whole net in to empty it if they're gonna put the net over again; **TX**14, Then we got what we call a lazy line, which is . . just ahead of the tail portion of the net. And we pick the tail portion of the net up with that till we can put a block and tackle on the tail portion of the net and . . swing it on deck with a little boom.

lazy man's burden See **lazy man's load 1**

lazy man's chair See **lazy chair**

lazy man's fence n Cf **snake fence**

1972 *Old Farmer's Almanac for 1973* 162, Snake fences are also known as . . lazy man's . . fences. Place rails, split medium-sized logs, or saplings at an angle—one on top of another. Then lay their ends in one panel in zigzag fashion. Intersect them alternately with the ends of the next panel. Now drive a pair of strong stakes into the ground at the end of each intersection to hold the fence upright.

lazy man's gate n

See quot 1992.

1948 Manfred *Chokecherry* 44 **nwIA**, He noticed that a steer had jumped the fence. . . He studied a moment; then saw a lazy man's gate at the end of the lane near the barnyard. . . He would let the jumping critter go through that. . . [H]e went up to the gate, opened it, chased the steer through, and closed it. **1992** *DARE* File **swMN**, [Communication from author of quot 1948:] A lazy man's gate is a temporary gate in a post-and-wire fence. It's made of three horizontal strands of wire attached to a stationary fencepost on one side and a movable post on the other. To close the gate, you put the bottom of the movable post in a wire loop attached to the bottom of the fencepost on the other side of the opening. This stationary post has a thick stick attached near the top as a lever that can be used to pull the temporary post tight so that a wire loop can be slipped over the top. *Ibid*, I often did it with my long arms and skipped the lever. But using the lever means you're a bit lazy or weak and so you use the lazy man's gate lever.

lazy man's grass n

=**centipede grass**.

1976 Bailey–Bailey *Hortus Third* 434, [Eremochloa] ophiuroides . . Centipede grass, lazy man's grass.

lazy man's load n

1 also *lazy man's burden*: An awkwardly large load carried to avoid making two trips; also fig.

[**1811** in 1896 Farmer–Henley *Slang* 167, Lazy-man's load. Lazy people frequently take up more than they can safely carry, to save the trouble of coming a second time.] **1913** *DN* 4.56 **seMA**, Lazy man's load. . . A burden inconveniently large. "He'd rather take a lazy man's load than go twice." **1928** Ruppenthal *Coll.* **KS**, Lazy man's load. You have to make up your mind whether to make two trips with a small load each time, or to go once with a lazy man's load. **1941** *AmSp* 16.23 **sIN**,

MO, Lazy man's load. One who carries a heavy load in order to avoid making two trips is carrying 'a lazy man's load.' **1946** *CA Folkl. Qrly.* 5.241 **wOR**, Don't try to carry a lazy man's burden (*or* load). **1957** *Sat. Eve. Post Letters* **cIN**, Carry a lazy man's load—meaning to attempt to complete a job too soon. **1963** in 1982 *Barrick Coll.* **csPA**, Lazy man's load—Trying to take everything at one time (to save trips). **1967** *DARE* (Qu. L55, *If the wagon was only partly full . . he had a _____*) Inf **MI**67, Half load, part load; lazy man's load—and this also has another meaning, pejorative: when you carry too much, to save a trip, and drop something as a consequence.

‡**2** A half or partial load.

1967 [see **1** above].

lazy man's rake n Cf **bull rake, drag rake**

1909 *DN* 3.420 **Cape Cod MA** (as of a1857), Lazy man's rake. . . A large drag rake.

lazy man's sheep n Cf **lamb's tail 1, lazy rat,** *DS* E20

1950 *WELS* (Soft rolls of dust that collect on the floor under beds or other furniture) 1 Inf, **ceWI**, Lazy man's sheep.

lazy man's wood n

A **hackberry**.

1968 *DARE* (Qu. T13, . . *Names . . for . . hackberry*) Inf **LA**15, Hackberry—used to call it "lazy man's wood" because it don't throw any heat.

lazy Mary n

A children's ring game; see quots.

1883 Newell *Games & Songs* 96 **NY**, Lazy Mary. A mother and daughter in the centre of a ring. . . Mother[:]. . . "Lazy Mary, will you get up. . ." [daughter:] "What will you give me for my breakfast. . ." The reply is, "A slice of bread and a cup of tea," whereon Mary answers, "No . . I won't get up," . . but for supper the mother offers "a nice young man with rosy cheeks," which is accepted . . whereon the ring clap their hands. The round is familiar in New York streets. **1942** *S. Folkl. Qrly.* 6.240, Lazy Mary. . . Children join hands and march . . and sing the mother's answers to Lazy Mary's questions. At the end of the song, when the children say "Then hurry!" Lazy Mary catches one of the girls, who is Lazy Mary for the next singing of the song. **1950** *WELS* (Games in which the players form a ring and either sing or recite a rhyme) 1 Inf, **swWI**, Lazy Mary; (Ring Games) 1 Inf, **seWI**, Lazy Mary. **1952** Brown *NC Folkl.* 1.55 (as of c1927), Lazy Mary. . . The players form a circle with Lazy Mary in the center, seated in a chair. One speaks as the mother; this one and all the others march around Mary, singing. The players select the boy Mary is to be given for getting up. **1957** *Sat. Eve. Post Letters* **Chicago IL** (as of c1898–1900), Girls singing ring games, always played in a circle . . "Lazy Mary will you get up." *Ibid* **sePA**, When I was a child . . we played singing games [such as] . . "Lazy Mary will you get up."

lazy rat n Cf **lazy man's sheep**

1967 *DARE* (Qu. E20, *Soft rolls of dust that collect on the floor under beds or other furniture*) Inf **LA**2, Lazy rats. [Inf old]

lazy Susan n Also *lazy Sue*

=**black-eyed Susan 2**. Cf **lazy daisy 2**

1966–69 *DARE* (Qu. S7, *A kind of daisy, bright yellow with a dark center, that grows along roadsides in late summer*) Infs **AL**6, **IL**83, **LA**41, **MA**5, **MS**8, **MO**20, **WA**24, Lazy Susan; **ND**3, Lazy Sue; (Qu. S26a, . . *Wildflowers . . Roadside flowers*) Inf **VA**2, Lazy Susans.

lazy Tom n Also *lazy John*

A type of water-powered mill; see quots.

1920 *Outing* 75.220, Fifteen years ago, when I first came into the southern mountains, I heard at times of a mysterious machine whereby a pestle was worked up and down by water-power. This was called a pounding-mill, or, facetiously, a "lazy John" or "tri-weekly." **1952** Brown *NC Folkl.* 1.558 **wNC**, Lazy-tom. . . A water-run hominy beater. **1953** Randolph–Wilson *Down in Holler* 260 **Ozarks**, Lazy Tom. . . A rude water mill for grinding corn.

lazy wife See **lazy gal**

lazy wife (bean) n Also *lazy housewife bean* [See quot 1988] **scattered, but esp PA**

Usu a cultivated, round white bean (*Phaseolus vulgaris* var), but see quots.

1967–70 *DARE* (Qu. I19, *Small white beans with a black spot where they were joined to the pod*) Inf **PA**203, Lazy wife [beans]; (Qu. I20, . . *Kinds of beans*) Infs **MD**17, **PA**2, 9, 136, Lazy wife beans; **PA**242, Lazy wives; **MO**38, Lazy housewife beans. **1978** *Wanigan Catalog* 12, *Lazy Housewife.* From South Africa, this red kidney with pink blossoms, runs to 3′ here. Flat, green, 8″ pods. Late. *Lazy Wife.* . . Dates back to 1810. Seed is round, white, with a very faint gray veiling. 5″ flat green pods slow to start and very late to mature here. **1979** *UpCountry* Jan 20 **neMA,** The commodity is beans—Goose Cranberry, Lazy Wife, . . and hundreds of other varieties of shell beans. **1988** Whealy *Garden Seed Inventory* (2d ed) 38, *Lazy Wife* . . Probably introduced by German immigrants, may have been grown here as early as 1810 as White Cranberry Pole, named Lazy Wife because they were the first snap beans that did not need de-stringing. *Ibid* 39, *Lazy Wife, Red.* . . Snap or dry, drought tolerant. **1990** *Seed Savers Yearbook* 46, *Lazy Housewife. Ibid, Lazy Wife.* . . Large round white seeds, best used as shell or dry.

lazy wife biscuit n Cf **drop biscuit, lazy bread**

  1950 *WELS (Kinds of biscuits)* 1 Inf, **cwWI,** Lazy wife biscuit—drop biscuit.

lazy wives' pickle See **lazy daisy pickle**

lazy woman's quilt n

  1983 *MJLF* 9.1.46 **ceKY** (as of 1956), *Lazy woman's quilt* . . a quilt with large pieces of cloth in it making it easy to put together.

le See **let A2a**

lea n Cf **bottom** n **1a, intervale, meadow B1**

  An area of grassland or pastureland.

  1705 in 1940 *AmSp* 15.279 **VA,** Likewise my interest of ye Land I have in ye Green Lea to my Son Jonathan. **1939** *LANE* Map 28 *(Lowland)* 1 inf, **nME,** *Lea,* not as low as a meadow. **1966** Dakin *Dial. Vocab. Ohio R. Valley* 2.202 **OH,** *Meadow* is used everywhere in the Ohio Valley [for *bottomland*]. . . Simple *grasslands* and scattered use of *lea* [1 inf], . . *grazing land,* . . *glade,* and *swale* . . are also noted. **1969** *DARE* (Qu. L7, *A piece of land with a hay crop planted on it*) Inf **TX**63, Meadow, lea. **1973** Allen *LAUM* 1.234 (as of c1950), *(Swampy ground with small stream running through it)* 1 inf, **nwMN,** *Lea:* Heard used by itinerant workers. **1986** Pederson *LAGS Concordance (Meadow)* 1 inf, **ceAL,** Lea—of the pasture.

leab See **leave** v **A1**

leabe v See **leave** v **A1, 3**

leabe n See **leaf** n¹

lead n |lid|

  1 A path, trail. [*OED lead* sb.² 3.c "A path" 1590; *DNE lead* n² 2 "an animal trail"]

  1926 *AmSp* 1.413 **Okefenokee GA,** So I got ter wind'ard uv 'em where they were, an' got on the lead where they always run—on the Deer lead where they always traveled. . . I stayed on the lead an' watched fer 'im.

  2 also *water lead:* A navigable channel through an area of swampy or obstructed water. [Cf *lead* a channel through an ice field (*OED lead* sb.² 3.b 1835 →)]

  1898 (1910) Willoughby *Across Everglades* 114 **sFL,** Several very good leads were met, in which the boats made good progress, and the water was in all places clear, even where the grass was thick. *Ibid* 117, We struck a good water-lead and made very good headway at first, but the difficulties of Everglade travel soon made themselves apparent. The good water-leads came to an end, many of them heading up in big saw-grass, beyond which we could see nothing that could float a canoe. **1964** Will *Hist. Okeechobee* 16 **FL,** Except in the lower Glades you couldn't cross the Everglades in a boat. To be sure, there were open channels, "leads" as they were called, where water flowed deep and swift . . but most leads just twisted here and there, ending at nowhere in particular. **1968** *DARE* (Qu. C1, . . *A small stream of water not big enough to be a river*) Inf **DE**4, Lead [lid]—where muskrats run.

  3 A mountain spur; a steep ridge. **sAppalachians**

  1913 Kephart *Highlanders* 20 **sAppalachians,** Beyond lie steep and narrow ridges. . . There are few "leads" rising gradually to their crests. Each and every one of these ridges is a Chinese wall magnified to altitudes of from a thousand to two thousand feet, and covered with thicket. **1937** Thornburgh *Gt. Smoky Mts.* 91 **eTN,** Brushy in reality is a "lead" off from Le Conte, part of the same mountain formation. . . Brushy is one of the heath balds, elevation 4,911 feet. **1939** *Hall Coll.* **wNC,** A lead, as for example, between Big Creek and Mt. Sterling, with ridges running up to the lead. [Hall: The informant gave this explanation to explain the place name Twenty Mile Lead.] **1956** *Ibid* **eTN,** He told

us children that he wanted to be buried in that old bear trail, on the lead out from Low Gap. **1956** (1964) Fink *That's Why* 4 **wNC, eTN,** Ridges, particularly those running down from a high peak or standing out like buttresses from the main divide, have various designations. . . *Lead* is sometimes used for a long ridge or one connecting two prominent points, and generally bears the name of one of these, as *Chapman Lead,* on the north flank of Mt. Chapman.

  4 See **lead trough.**

lead a goose to water See **goose** n **B4**

leadback n

  1 =**red-backed sandpiper.** [From its grayed winter plumage]

  1888 Trumbull *Names of Birds* 181 **NY,** *Tringa alpina pacifica. Red-backed Sandpiper* . . at Shinnecock Bay, *Leadback.* **1917** (1923) *Birds Amer.* 1.237, *Red-Backed Sandpiper—Pelidna alpina sakhalina.* . . Lead-back. **1932** Howell *FL Bird Life* 241. **1944** Hausman *Amer. Birds* 282, *Red-Backed Sandpiper—Pelidna alpina sakhalina.* . . Some twenty-five or more local names, among which are: . . Leadback. . . Crooked-Bill.

  2 also *lead-backed salamander:* The red-backed **salamander** *(Plethodon cinereus).* [From its gray color phase]

  1919 *Copeia* 72.64 **NY,** *Plethodon cinereus.* . . Lead-backed Salamander. **1953** Schmidt *N. Amer. Amphibians* 33, *Plethodon cinereus cinereus.* . . *Common name.*—Red-backed salamander, lead-backed salamander (names for the two color phases). **1958** Conant *Reptiles & Amphibians* 230, *Plethodon cinereus cinereus.* . . Two distinct colorations: (1) *red-backed* . . ; (2) *lead-backed*—uniformly dark gray to almost black. . . Similar species: Ravine Salamander (colored as a leadback) is more slender. **1979** Behler–King *Audubon Field Guide Reptiles* 336, *Red-backed Salamander.* . . Two color phases: "Red-backed". . . "Lead-backed" is light gray to almost black, without stripe.

lead coot n Also *leadhead*

  =**coot** n¹ **1.**

  1802 in 1965 *AmSp* 40.199, Went a gunning with H. Sloven had 12 Lead Coots & Shell Drakes. **1968** *DARE* (Qu. Q9, *The bird that looks like a small, dull-colored duck and is commonly found on ponds and lakes*) Inf **PA**165, Leadhead.

leader n

  1 A tendon, ligament. **Sth, S Midl** [*OED leader* sb.¹ 10 1708 →]

  1899 (1912) Green *VA Folk-Speech* 258, *Leader.* . . A sinew; a tendon. **1902** *DN* 2.238 **sIL,** *Leader.* . . Tendon, exclusive use. **1906** *DN* 3.120 **sIN,** *Leader.* . . A tendon. The only word used. **1907** *DN* 3.223 **nwAR,** *Leader.* . . Tendon, exclusive use. **1912** *DN* 3.581 **wIN,** *Leader.* . . A tendon. "He cut the leader in the lamb's hind leg." **1930** *DN* 6.84 **cSC.** **1938** Stuart *Dark Hills* 200 **eKY,** We went out behind the corn crib to skin the rabbits. . . He cut the flesh through under the leader of the hind leg and hung it over the nail. **1946** *PADS* 6.19 **ceNC** (as of 1900–10), *Leader.* . . A tendon in the neck . . Common. **1950** *PADS* 13.18 **cTX,** *Leader.* . . Any tendon, not just the tendon in the neck. **1954** *Harder Coll.* **cwTN,** *Leader*—ligament. **1956** *DE Folkl. Bulletin* 1.24, He chanced to cut the leaders in two of his fingers. **1969** *DARE* FW Addit **GA**51, Leader—a sinew or tendon, for example, in wrist. **1986** Pederson *LAGS Concordance* **Gulf Region,** 1 inf, That there little leader—ligament in the joint; 1 inf, Bones and leaders—bones and tendons—of humans; 1 inf, The leaders—tendons; 1 inf, Leaders—term for joints [sic], may refer to animals; 1 inf, Leaders—in human back, treated by chiropractor. **1990** Cavender *Folk Med. Lexicon* 26 **sAppalachians,** *Leaders* . . tendons or ligaments, most frequently used in reference to the ligaments in the neck and ankle.

  2 A blood vessel. [Cf *EDD leader* sb. 4 "An artery"]

  1935 Hurston *Mules & Men* 177 **FL,** When Ah was studyin' doctor Ah found out dat you got a leader dat runs from yo' big toe straight to yo' heart. **1990** Cavender *Folk Med. Lexicon* 26 **sAppalachians,** *Leaders.* . . veins in the leg; the phrase "bad leaders" commonly used in reference to varicose veins.

  3 also *leader pipe:* A downspout; also a roof gutter. **chiefly NY, NJ** See Map *somewhat old-fash* Cf **eaves trough, lead trough**

  1868 *Putnam's Mag.* 11.21 **seNY,** Then, without stay or stopping,/ My first and last eaves-dropping,/ By leader-pipe I sped. **1941** *LANE* Map 349 *(Gutter(s))*, Terms for the horizontal trough. . . 1 inf, **nwCT,** Leaders [old-fashioned]. . . [Terms for] the vertical pipe . . 3 infs, **c,seCT,** Leaders. **1950** *WELS (The pipe that takes the water from the eaves to the ground or a cistern)*, 1 Inf, **WI,** Leader. **1965–70** *DARE* (Qu. D29,

The pipe that takes the collected rain-water down to the ground or to a storage tank) 23 Infs, **chiefly NY, NJ,** Leader; **IA**17, **NJ**4, 28, Leader pipe; **NY**206, Leader (pipe); (Qu. D28, *What hangs below the edge of the roof to carry off rain-water?)* Infs **NJ**5, 9, **NY**39, 45, 90, **PA**78, Leader(s). [26 of 30 total Infs old]

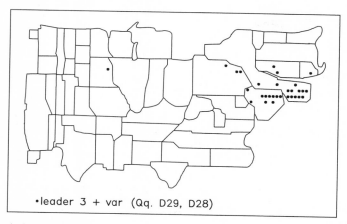

•leader 3 + var (Qq. D29, D28)

4 See **lead horse.**

leader and footer See **head and footer**

leader horse See **lead horse**

leader pipe See **leader 3**

lead flower n [See quot] Cf **lead plant**
    A **mariposa lily** (here: *Calochortus nuttallii*).
    1941 *Jrl. Amer. Folkl.* 54.137 **UT,** The most unusual surface indicator of this nature that I have heard about in Utah is the so-called "lead flower," which is supposed to betray the presence of lead bodies below. . . The flower in question, I think, is the common sego lily.

lead grass n Also *leadweed*
    A **glasswort** (here: *Salicornia virginica*).
    1897 *Jrl. Amer. Folkl.* 10.54 **NY,** *Salicornia ambigua* . . lead grass, lead weed, Southold, L[ong] I[sland]. **1950** Gray-Fernald *Manual of Botany* 599, S[alicornia] *virginica.* . . Leadgrass. . . Sandy sea-strands and borders of salt-marshes, s.N.H. to S.C., perhaps beyond. **1960** Vines *Trees SW* 246, *Woody Glasswort—Salicornia virginica.* . . It is also known under the name of Sea Sapphire, Lead-grass, and Perennial Saltwort.

leadhead See **lead coot**

lead horse n Also *leader (horse), leading horse, lead-side* ~ Cf **follow horse, near** ~, **off** ~ **1**
One of a pair of horses, or of the foremost of several pairs, that are harnessed together, usu the stronger or better trained one; similarly nouns *lead mule,* ~ *ox,* etc. Note: Only instances where the *lead horse* is identified with a *specific* side are included here; *lead horse* in ref to *either* member of the foremost pair is std. Overall, however, the evidence is split about equally as to whether the left-hand or right-hand horse is meant. This variation prob results from a number of factors: different methods of driving, local or individual custom, and imperfect recollection of obsolete terminology. In evaluating the quots, it is important to note that the worksheets of the various projects assoc with the Linguistic Atlas of the United States and Canada, on which quots 1949, 1955, 1966, 1967, 1968, 1972, and 1986 are directly or indirectly based, ask only for terms for the left-hand horse.
    1876 Knight *Amer. Mech. Dict.* 3.2173, *Side-hill Plow.* A plow whose cutting apparatus is reversible, so as to throw its furrow-slice to the right or left. . . This enables the lead horse of the team to return in the furrow just made, the plow throwing the soil down hill while traveling in either direction. **1887** Custer *Tenting* 352 **West,** The number of mules to a wagon varies; sometimes there are four, and again six. The driver rides the near-wheel mule. He holds in his hand a broad piece of leather, an inch and a half in width, which divides over the shoulders of the lead or pilot mule, and fastens to the bit on either side of his mouth. The leaders are widely separated. A small hickory stick, about five feet long,

called the jockey-stick . . is stretched between a pilot and his mate. . . When the driver gives one pull on the heavy strap, the pilot mule veers to the left, and pulls his mate. Two quick, sudden jerks mean to the right, and he responds, and pushes his companion accordingly. **1909** *DN* 3.344 **eAL, wGA,** *Lead-horse.* . . The horse on the right in a team of two, the foremost horse on the right in a team of four or six. **1922** Rollins *Cowboy* 195, Commonly, with animals in a series of spans, the left-hand beast in the front span was the only "lead" animal, and thus alone had the honor of holding the jerk line. [**1923** *DN* 5.211 **swMO,** *In the lead.* . . The position of the left-hand animal in a two-horse team as observed from the rear, or of the foremost animals in a team of two or more pairs.] **1949** Kurath *Word Geog.* 31, The Midland has four different words for the left-hand horse of a team, *lead horse, near-horse, nigh-horse,* and *saddle horse. Lead horse* . . is the regular expression in two large sections: (1) Pennsylvania from the Susquehanna Valley westward, and (2) the Appalachians and the Blue Ridge south of the Kanawha-James River line. . . South-central Pennsylvania is probably the original home of *lead horse.* **1954** *Harder Coll.* **cwTN,** *Lead mule.* . . The mule on the driver's left in a team. **1955** Potter *Dial. NW OH* 81, In these days of mechanized farming many informants are without terms for the left horse of a team. Only thirty-four responses were noted for this item. Sixteen of the informants, scattered through the counties, gave *lead horse (leader). Ibid* 126, *Lead horse,* the term which is gaining, went from 1 in 5 for the old to better than 1 in 2 for the middle-aged, to all but one of the seven youngest informants. **c1960** *Wilson Coll.* **csKY,** In plowing or driving, the lead horse was the one to the driver's left; the other one was the off-horse. **1965–70** *DARE* (Qu. K32a, *With a team of horses,* . . *the horse on the driver's right hand*) 134 Infs, **widespread,** Lead (horse); 11 Infs, **scattered,** Leader; **GA**77, **NY**57, Leading horse; **AL**47, Lead horse—in WWI artillery; **AK**8, Lead horse—on right side, in front of driver sitting on right side of wagon seat; **IL**142, Lead horse—best horse is on the right, he leads; **MI**23, Lead horse—the best horse is always put on the right; **MN**37, Lead horse—the larger one; **OK**27, Lead—could be on either side; **LA**12, Leader horse; **ME**1, Leader—when pulling boat with two horses, the one you rode was the leader; **ND**2, Lead-side horse; (Qu. K32b, *The horse on the left side in plowing or hauling*) 121 Infs, **widespread, but more freq Midl, MS,** Lead (horse); 12 Infs, **scattered,** Lead-side horse; **AZ**2, **GA**14, **MD**20, 24, 29, **PA**75, 137, **VA**10, Leader; **MD**18, Lead horse, under the line—because both horses used to be guided by one line; this one was nearest the line; **PA**23, Lead horse—one on left when a single line was used; **PA**158, Lead horse—on left front for two teams; **WA**20, Lee [sic] horse. **1966** Dakin *Dial. Vocab. Ohio R. Valley* 2.292, Only two terms [for the horse on the left]—*near-horse* and *lead horse* (occasionally *leader horse* and rarely *leading horse*)—are common. *Ibid* 295, North of the Ohio, this usage [=*off-horse* "horse on the left"] is almost always in contrast to *near-horse* = "horse on the right," but in Kentucky it is in contrast to *lead horse* with this meaning. **1967** Faries *Word Geog. MO* 96, To distinguish the left from the right horse in a team, the Missouri informants use a variety of regional expressions, the most prevalent of which are *lead horse* (leader) (291 occurrences [from 700 infs]) and *near horse* (195 occurrences). **1968** *PADS* 49.13 **Upper MW,** There are a few examples of regional farm terms increasing in usage. . . The third regional farm term in this group, the Midland *lead horse* for the left-hand horse in a team, is a riddle. Offered once five times by the [208] field informants . . this term was offered by 25% of the students. It is indeed curious that while the use of teams of horses and the percentage of informants offering any variant are declining, 61% of the students having any term at all have this one. It is worth noting that these students are from all five states, not just Iowa and Nebraska. **1972** *PADS* 58.19 **cwAL,** West Midland and South Midland *lead horse* (11) and *leader* (2) are most frequent [for left-hand horse]; however, one informant used *lead horse* for the right horse. **1986** Pederson *LAGS Concordance* **Gulf Region** (*Horse on the left*), [About 230 infs responded *lead (horse)* (not counting those who, to judge from the comments recorded, were referring to the front horse(s) in a team); many expressed some doubt about their response. Typical comments were: "The best horse, walks in the furrow"; "on the left, in the furrow"; "on right side, walks in furrow"; "walks in furrow, doesn't know which side"; "on right, not always in furrow"; "left or right, depends on plow type"; "on left, leads team into turn"; "one you tell to turn, hauling logs"; "on left, if two; in front, if team." Other responses were *leader* (18 infs), *lead mule* (13 infs), and *lead ox* (2 infs).]

leadman n
An unidentified children's game.
    1901 *DN* 2.143 **csNY,** *Leadman.* . . The name of a game. Oneida Co., N.Y. **1957** *Sat. Eve. Post Letters* **IL** (as of c1895), Lead man. **1991**

DARE File **cIL**, *"Leadman"*: I heard the game mentioned but once (ca. 1960), in a conversation with my best friend (deceased, 1981) who was born and raised in central Illinois. He did not detail what its objective was, or how it was played, but his pronunciation was "Leedman".

lead mule See **lead horse**

lead-off trough See **lead trough**

lead ox See **lead horse**

lead-pencil cactus n Cf **pencil cactus**

A **cactus** n[1] **B1** (here: *Cereus poselgeri*) with slender stems.

1960 Vines *Trees SW* 770, *Wilcoxia poselgeri*. . . is also known under the vernacular names of Sacasil and Lead Pencil Cactus. Rather rare, but also easily overlooked owing to its occurrence among thick chaparral.

lead piece n Also *lead washer* Cf **iron man 1**

A silver dollar.

1950 *WELS* (A silver dollar) 1 Inf, **WI**, Lead washer. **1968** *DARE* (Qu. U27) Inf **MN38**, Lead piece—because so heavy.

lead pipe See **lead trough**

lead plant n Also *leadwort* [See quot 1931]

=**false indigo 1.**

1833 Eaton *Botany* 15, *Amorpha . . canescens* . . lead plant. **1844** Lapham *Geogr. Descr. WI* 78, *Amorpha canescens* . . lead plant. Said to indicate the presence of lead bearing fissures, when found growing in lines across the prairies in the mineral country. **1901** Lounsberry *S. Wild Flowers* 269, An old superstition exists among the country people that wherever Amorpha grows lead is to be found. No doubt at some time this substance was discovered in its vicinity, and so the idea may have originated. Of itself, however, the lead plant [=*A. vigata*] would attract many an eye, for it is very unusual looking, and pretty. **1922** *Amer. Botanist* 28.72, *A[morpha] canescens* is commonly known as "lead plant". . . Other names are "lead-wort" and "wild tea." **1931** U.S. Dept. Ag. *Misc. Pub.* 101.83, There is a local superstition in many places that the presence of this plant indicates the existence of lead ore, but the common name, leadplant, appears to refer rather to a plumbic hue or habitat. **1960** Vines *Trees SW* 518, Lead-plant Amorpha—*A. canescens* . . The name in use refers to the leaden hue of the leaves. *Ibid* 522, Dwarf Indigo-bush Amorpha—*Amorpha nana*. . . It is also known locally as Fragrant Dwarf Indigo and Lead Plant. **1979** Niering–Olmstead *Audubon Guide N. Amer. Wildflowers E. Region* 518, *Leadplant; False Indigo*. . . Indians used the leaves for tobacco and for making a tea. **1991** Heat Moon *PrairyErth* 242 **ceKS**, Homesteaders, seeing the gray hairiness of the leaves, called it lead plant and believed it drew its color from ore deposits beneath it.

lead-side horse See **lead horse**

lead tree n [*OED* 1864 →]

A tree of the genus *Leucaena*, esp *L. lencocephala*. For other names of var spp see **false koa, haole ~, mimosa 2a, popinac, wahoo, wild tamarind**

1908 Britton *N. Amer. Trees* 526, Lead trees—genus *Leucaena. Ibid*, Mexican lead tree—*Leucaena pulverulenta. Ibid* 527, Lead tree—*Leucaena glauca.* **1929** Neal *Honolulu Gardens* 133, False koa, jumpybean, lead-tree. . . *Leucaena glauca.* **1953** Greene–Blomquist *Flowers South* 53, Lead-Tree (*Leucaena glauca*)—A shrub or small tree. . . In hammocks and cleared ground, Fla. to Tex. **1979** Little *Checklist U.S. Trees* 160, *Leucaena*. . . Leadtree. . . *Number of species:* native trees, 2, naturalized trees, 1.

lead trough n Usu |lid trɔf|; for varr see quots Also *lead, lead-off trough, lead pipe* **chiefly S Midl** Cf **leader 3**

A trough or pipe, esp a gutter or downspout, used to convey liquid.

1902 *DN* 2.238 **sIL**, *Lead-pipe* [lid paɪp]. . . Any small pipe for conveying water. Lead never omitted from this or following word. *Lead-trough* [lid trəf [sic]]. . . Any small trough, especially an eavetrough. **1904** *DN* 2.382 [Oil industry language], *Lead-pipe*. . . The pipe which continues the tubing, when that rests on the bottom of the well, to the tank. **1906** *DN* 3.120 **sIN**, *Lead-pipe*. . . Any small pipe used for conveying water. *Lead* never omitted. *Lead-trough*. . . An eaves trough, or one at a well. **1907** *DN* 3.223 **nwAR**. **c1960** *Wilson Coll.* **csKY**, *Lead-troughs* . . gutters. **1966** Dakin *Dial. Vocab. Ohio R. Valley* 2.59, *Lead troughs* or the simplex *leads* [for *gutters*] is fairly common in the eastern Bluegrass and Knobs, in the northern Pennyroyal, in the interior hill country and lower White River–Wabash area of Indiana, and is used in southern Illinois. **1966–69** *DARE* (Qu. D28, *What hangs below the edge of the roof to carry off rain-water?*) Inf **KY28**, Lead-off troft; **KY46**, Lead troft [lid trɔft]; **KY52**, Lead troths; (Qu. D29, *The pipe that takes the collected rain-water down to the ground or to a storage tank*) Inf **OK42**, Lead [lid] pipe—runs to the cistern; **TX2**, Lead [lid] pipe; **KY52**, Lead troths. **1983** *MJLF* 9.1.46 **ceKY**, *Lead trought* . . an "older" term for gutters. **1986** Pederson *LAGS Concordance (Eaves)* 1 inf, **neTX**, Lead troughs—carry water to cistern, made of tin. **1995** *DARE* File **cnKY**, The 'lead trough' . . is indeed so named because it leads into the downspout.

lead washer See **lead piece**

leadweed See **lead grass**

leadwood n [From the density of the wood]

The black ironwood (*Krugiodendron ferreum*).

1946 West–Arnold *Native Trees FL* 138, One of the more common small trees on the lower East Coast [of Florida], leadwood is inconspicuous among the scrub oaks. There are no outstanding gross characters to distinguish it. . . However, the hard, red-brown wood is unique because it is the heaviest wood growing naturally within the boundaries of the United States. **1962** Harrar–Harrar *Guide S. Trees* 495, Leadwood is of no commercial value at the present time. **1979** Little *Checklist U.S. Trees* 158, *Krugiodendron ferreum* . . leadwood. . . S. Fla. incl. Fla. Keys, n. on e. coast to Cape Canaveral.

leadwort See **lead plant**

leaf n[1] Pronc-spp *leabe, leave* Cf Pronc Intro 3.I.15, 17 Cf **leave** n[1] **A**

A Forms.

1922 Gonzales *Black Border* 310 **sSC, GA coasts** [Gullah glossary], *Leabe*—leaf, leaves. **1968** *DARE* Tape **GA30**, You just pull the leave [liv] from them . . and use it. **1981** Pederson *LAGS Basic Materials,* 1 inf, **cnAL**, Leaf [liˑ·v] catchers.

B Senses.

1 =**needle 1**—often in comb *pine-leaf.* Note: The use of *leaf* generically to include both broad and needle-shaped leaves, or in technical botanical contexts, is std and is not illustrated here. [The pointed leaves of conifers appear not to have had a distinct name in general use until the 19th cent, when *needle* (*OED* 1798 →) became the standard term, at least in the US. The earlier terminology is reflected in a number of tree names, esp **longleaf pine** and **shortleaf pine**, both of which were coined in the 18th cent.]

1834 in **1894** Whittier *Complete Poet. Wks.* 496 **MA**, In the pine-leaves fine and small,/ Soft and sweetly musical. **1856** Stowe *Dred* 1.102, No sound was heard but the shivering wind, . . through the long pine-leaves. **1885** NH Forestry Comm. *Report* 83 (as of 1881), Mulching with sphagnum, chaff, sawdust, or pine leaves, will preserve a more uniform degree of humidity. **1908** Rogers *Tree Book* 38, The leaves of *Pinus palustris* yield by distillation an essential oil . . that closely resembles oil of turpentine. The weaving of florists' baskets from the long, shining needles is just beginning. **1966–67** *DARE* (Qu. T6, *The pointed leaves that fall from pine trees*) Inf **LA8**, We don't call 'em nothing but leaves; **SC10**, Pine straw; needles; pine leaf.

2 A grade of tobacco leaves; see quot 1966. **KY** Cf **bright adj 1, flyings 2**

1941 *Sun* (Baltimore MD) 21 Jan 12/7 *(Hench Coll.)* **KY**, Leaf, lugs and flyings were showing unusual strength. **1966** *PADS* 45.2 **KY**, The leaves on a stalk of Burley tobacco were divided into five main grades by the farmer before marketing. . . The standard of quality was set by the "leaf" grade found around the middle of the stalk. Its strength and color at full maturity have the attributes of a leaf with "spit" in it. *Ibid* 3, The Burley tips and leaf . . brought high prices, while the flyings and lugs were hardly marketable. *Ibid* 17, *Leaf.* . . A grade of leaf just under the tip grades. It is medium in body, smooth in texture, and medium in color. **1969–70** *DARE* Tape **KY35**, Years ago . . we'd make flyin's, trash, lugs, and leaf, and damaged. *Ibid* **KY75**, The trash, lugs, and leaf are the grades. . . When you start to stripping a crop you just don't know until you really get into it how many grades you will have. . . The best sellin' grade, is what we call lugs and then leaf is the next grade.

leaf n[2] See **leave** n[1]

leaf v See **leave** v **A1**

leafcup n [See quots 1847, 1931]

A plant of the genus *Polymnia*. For other names of *P. uvedalia* see **bear foot**

1822 Eaton *Botany* 402, *Polymnia . . canadensis . .* white leaf-cup. . . *[P.] uvedalia, . .* yellow leaf-cup. **1847** Wood *Class-Book* 335, *P[olymnia] Canadensis.* Leaf-cup. . . Flowers light-yellow, the rays short, surrounded by the concave leaflets of the double calyx in such a manner as to form a sort of cup, hence called leaf-cup. **1931** Harned *Wild Flowers Alleghanies* 567, *Large-flowered leafcup (Polymnia uvedalia* L.) . . The flower is surrounded by about 5 large, involucral bracts, leaf-like in appearance, forming a sort of cup . . hence the name "Leaf Cup." **1941** Walker *Lookout* 50 **TN,** Wild ginger, . . smooth leafcup, . . and purple gerardia are abundant.

leaf frog n
A tree frog.

1950 *WELS* (Tree frog) 1 Inf, **WI,** Leaf frog. **1966** Dakin *Dial. Vocab. Ohio R. Valley* 2.389 **swIL,** Speakers in southern Illinois regularly call this frog [=tree frog] a *rain frog* and in the American Bottom it is called a *leaf frog.*

leaf jelly See **jelly leaf 2**

leaf mover n Cf **tree mover**
=**trash mover.**

1986 Pederson *LAGS Concordance* (Heavy rain) 1 inf, **cwAR,** Leaf mover.

leaf peeper n Also *leaf peeker* **NEng, esp VT**
A tourist who comes to view autumn foliage.

c1965 *DARE* File **nwVT,** *Leaf peepers*—Tourists who come to Vermont to view the colored leaves. **1978** *UpCountry* Oct 26 **swVT,** "Leaf-peepers are very nice, appreciative people," the Chamber [of Commerce] lady told me. **1980** *Verbatim Letters* **cwVT,** Leaf-peeper refers to tourists who visit Vermont in the autumn to view the foliage. It is in common conversational usage at this time of year, as in "There is a bus load of leaf-peepers" and is also used in newspapers in articles and headlines, often in quotation marks, in stories referring to the tourist business. **1985–90** *DARE* File **VT,** Leaf peepers—what Vermonters call "flatlanders" who visit their state to see the fall foliage; **wMA, Upstate NY,** *Leaf peeper*—very common for tourists looking for fall colors. They come in busloads. However, my husband and I grew up in the 1950s and 1960s saying "leaf peeker." I think "leaf peeper" is a more recent term. **1990** *Yankee* Oct 35 **NEng,** When legions of leaf peepers descend on New England, the best strategy may be to ascend.

leafworm n
1 =**cotton leafworm.**

1918 U.S. Dept. Ag. *Weekly News Letter* 16 Jan 6/1, The boll weevil, . . cotton aphis, . . leaf worm, . . and wireworm are only a section of the category. **1940** Faulkner *Hamlet* 126 **MS,** He would be sitting over the books which he did not love so much as he believed he must read, . . measuring the turned pages against the fleeting seconds of irrevocable time like the implacable inching of a leaf worm. **1967–68** *DARE* (Qu. R27, *. . Kinds of caterpillars or similar worms*) Inf **LA10,** Cotton caterpillar or leafworm; **TX52,** Leafworm.

2 Appar an **earthworm;** see quot.

1982 Sternberg *Fishing* 56, The leaf worm resembles a small nightcrawler. Seldom exceeding 4 inches in length, it has a tail that is somewhat flattened.

league n Usu |lig|; also |lɪg| [Cf *OED league* sb.², Scots forms *lig(g), lyge, lyig* from 15th, 16th cents]
Std senses, var form.

1930s in 1944 *ADD* **n,eWV,** [*League* is pronounced] [lɪg]. . . Usual. **1941** *Ibid* **WV,** Always [lɪg] by many. **1964** *AmSp* 39.157 **Philadelphia PA,** Before [g] the "long e" ([ɪi]) and "long a" ([ɛɪ]) of English are commonly shortened . . and lose the second element of their normal diphthongal pronunciation. . . Thus *league* tends to become [lɪg].

leak v
Std sense, var forms.
Past: usu *leaked;* also *leck(ed).* [Scots, nEngl dial]

1916 *DN* 4.340 **seOH,** Leaked [lɛkt]. **1917** in 1944 *ADD* **sWV,** Leck = leaked.

leak n [Cf *EDD leak* sb. 3] **esp KY**
=**drip** n 2.

1942 Clark *Kentucky* 119, Rub a wart with the skin of a chicken gizzard, and bury the gizzard under a stone at the "leak of the house." **1946** *AmSp* 21.273 **neKY,** Leak. . . The flow from a downspout or gutter (the gutter or spout itself?) '. . . a bucket under the leak of the house.' **1958** Browne *Pop. Beliefs AL* 126, To make hair grow longer, when you cut your hair put the cuttings in the leak of the house (where eaves drain). **1982** Slone *How We Talked* 22 **eKY** (as of c1950), "Under the leak of a house"—Under the edge of the roof, where the rain ran off. Tubs or barrels were set here to catch rain water.

‡leak finder n

1969 *DARE* (Qu. B25, *. . Joking names . . for a very heavy rain. . . "It's a regular _____."*) Inf **WI75,** Leak finder.

leaky adj Pronc-sp *l'aky*
Std sense, var form.

1933 in 1944 *ADD* **Tangier Is. VA,** *Leaky. . .* L'aky [leɪkɪ].

leaky roof n Also *leaky road* esp **MO**
A small, branch railroad; see quots.

1913 in 1983 Truman *Dear Bess* 121 **MO,** He wanted me to go with him to K.C. by the leaky-roof route. . . You know the leaky-roof branch of the Frisco runs to Belton via Olathe. **1942** *Ibid* 485, The crookedest and roughest track I've ridden over since the Leaky Roof quit running from Kansas City to Springfield. **1960** Criswell *Resp. to PADS* 20 **Ozarks,** *Leaky roof*—name for a branch line of a railroad with poor accommodations. Very common years ago. **1967** *DARE* (Qu. N37, *Joking names for a branch railroad that is not very important or gives poor service*) Inf **MO11,** They used to have one here they called the "leaky road." It ran from Clinton to Kansas City.

lean v
A Forms.

Past and past pple: usu *leaned* |lind|; also **esp Sth, S Midl** *leant* |lɛnt|; pronc-sp *lent.*

1893 *DN* 1.277 **nwCT,** *Lean*—leaned (leant pron. [lɛnt]). **1903** *DN* 2.319 **seMO,** *Lent,* pret. and *pp.* Leaned. 'He lent over and spoke to the child.' **1906** *DN* 3.120 **sIN,** *Lent, pt.* and *pp.* of lean. "He lent over an' talked to her." **1907** *DN* 3.232 **nwAR,** *Lent. . .* Leaned. **1909** *DN* 3.345 **eAL, wGA,** *Lent.* **1912** *DN* 3.581 **wIN,** *Lent.* **1942** Hall *Speech* 14 **wNC, eTN,** Middle English open *ē* occurs as [ɛ] in . . *leaned* [lɛnt] (beside [lind]). **1960** Hall *Smoky Mt. Folks* 10, He "lent" (leaned) down to get a mess of fish that he left in the creek when a panther darted out from a thicket and got him by the seat of the "britches." **1962** *Mt. Life* Spring 17 **KY,** The *-d* and *-ed* endings of past forms of verbs are frequently pronounced *-t,* particularly when the ending is preceded by *l, m, n,* or *r.* A few such words are *bound, bount . . leaned, lent.*

B Senses.

1 To depart hurriedly—usu in phr *lean for home. old-fash*

1833 Catlin *Indians* I.98 *(DAE),* He darts forth . . , wraps his robe around him and 'leans' as fast as possible for home. **1840** *Knickerbocker* 15.424 **NEng,** Mr. Bruce . . plunged out of the window . . 'leaning' for home. **1851** (1969) Burke *Polly Peablossom* 109 **MO,** "Lean, Sam," cried Ike, "she's goin' to rip, sartin. . ." Satisfied that they had seen the telegraph in motion, Ike and Sam *leaned.* **1888** Jones *Negro Myths* 21 **GA coast** [Gullah], De ole man dat scade eh . . lean fur home. [=The old man was so scared he . . leaned for home.] **1922** Gonzales *Black Border* 310 **sSC, GA coasts** [Gullah glossary], *Lean fuh*—lean for—set out for with haste and speed.

2 Of the sun: to descend.

1908 *S. Atl. Qrly.* 7.342 **seSC** [Gullah], [In the afternoon] *de sun duh lean, de sun duh lean fuh down.*

3 in phr *lean toward Jones's,* also **NEng** *lean toward Sawyer's,* and varr: To slant, tilt, be out of plumb; also fig.

1905 *DN* 3.86 **nwAR,** *Lean towards Jones's. . .* To slant, be out of plumb. 'That wall leans towards Jones's.' A carpenters' expression. **1957** *Sat. Eve. Post Letters* **IL,** Leaning towards Fisher's (anything out of plumb). **1967–68** *DARE* (Qu. KK20a, *Something that looks as if it might collapse any minute: "That old shed is certainly _____."*) Inf **MA71,** Leaning toward Sawyer's—upcountry northern New Hampshire; **TX1,** Leaning over towards Jones's; (Qu. KK70, *Something that has got out of proper shape: "That house is all _____."*) Inf **IN40,** Leanin' toward Cooper's; **NY22,** Leaning towards Perkins's; **OH61,** It leans toward Fisher's; **PA118,** Leaning toward Schoonover's—a name of a family around here; **WA30,** Leans off toward Jones's. [All Infs old] **1969** *DARE* FW Addit **ceVT,** "That building is leaning towards Sawyers'"—it's out of plumb. **1975** Gould *ME Lingo* 242, Anything in Maine which is . . visibly out of plumb . . is said to "lean toward *Sawyer's.*" . . It comes . . from lumbering. . . When things go as planned, the tree will fall away from them [=the sawyers], but if for any reason it . . tips backward, it is said to lean toward (the) sawyers. **1982** *Smithsonian Letters* **ME,** *Leaning toward Sawyer,* meaning that things have come to a pretty pass. . . [I]t referred to the deplorable situation when two men cut a pine with a cross-cut saw and the pine leans toward the sawyers, and jams the saw, rather than leaning toward the undercut. **1985–86** *WI Alumnus Letters* **WI,** *Leaning toward Jone's* [sic]—In common use in . . Taylor County, except that everything out of plumb leans toward Fischer's. My father used this phrase. . Certainly [I use it] every December as I am trying to straighten the Christmas tree. *Ibid* **WI,** Leaning toward Jones's. . . In 1925 I was a "line foreman" for a power co[mpany] in Platteville. . . This term was in use by "boomer linemen" at that time. I believe it was common in the Midwest when lining up poles. *Ibid* **sePA,** The auctioneer said [of a wardrobe missing a caster] "We'll have to fix this, it's leaning toward Jones's."

4 in phr *lean on one's own breakfast:* To sit up without leaning on another; fig: to rely on oneself. *somewhat old-fash*
    1910 *DN* 3.444 **wNY,** *Lean on your own breakfast.* . . "Sit up; don't lean on me." **1942** Warnick *Garrett Co. MD* 9 **nwMD** (as of 1900–18), *"Lean on your own breakfast,"* . . meaning depend on yourself. **1942** McAtee *Dial. Grant Co. IN* 39 (as of 1890s), *Lean on your own breakfast* . . meaning don't lean on me. **1956** McAtee *Some Dialect NC* 26.

lean n[1] [Abbr for **lean-to**]
An addition to the side or back of a building, with a single-pitched roof abutting the existing wall.
    1928 Chapman *Happy Mt.* 292 **seTN,** Rashe Lowe aims to build him a lean on his house against Waits brings Allardene Howard home. **1941** *LANE* Map 352 *(Ell)* 3 infs, **sNH,** Lean [one of these infs described this term as old-fashioned]. **1968** *DARE* (Qu. D16, . . *Parts added on to the main part of a house)* Inf **CA63,** Lean; **MN12,** Lean—has a slanting roof; (Qu. M9, *The part of a barn where horses are kept)* Inf **CA63,** A lean-to, or shed, or lean put to the barn. **1986** Pederson *LAGS Concordance (Shelter for cows)* 1 inf, **cwFL,** Lean—shelter from rain.

lean n[2], **lean char** See **lean trout**

lean for home See **lean** v B1

‡**lean-off** n
=**lean** n[1].
    1950 *Eaton Coll.* **Washington Is. WI,** We always called it [=a lean-to] a lean-off.

lean on one's own breakfast See **lean** v B4

leant See **lean** v A

leanth See **length**

lean-to n Usu |'lin,tu|; also chiefly **NEng** |'lɪntə(r)| Pronc-spp *leenter, lenter, linter;* for addit pronc and sp varr see quots
Std senses, var forms.
    1704 (1825) Knight *Jrls.* 48, Arriving at my apartment found it to be a little Lento Chamber. **1736** in 1870 NH *Prov. & State Papers* 4.714, The cause was from a spark falling out of a lintan [sic] chimney (which was lower than the house). **1774** in 1915 *New Engl. Hist. & Geneal. Reg.* 69.121 **MA,** I Began to Hew the timber for my Back Linter. . . I Begun to Board my Back Leanture. **1793** *Old Farmer's Almanac for 1794* Sept np, Bind and carry them into your cow linters. **1801** *Spirit Farmers' Museum* 35 **NEng,** She conducted him into a back lintow, where a negro . . usually slept. **1816** Pickering *Vocab.* 122, *Leanto* or *lean-to* . . (commonly pronounced *linter).* **1862** (1882) Stowe *Pearl of Orr's Is.* 5 **ME coast,** A brown house of the kind that the natives call "lean-to" or "linter". **1894** *DN* 1.332 **NJ,** *Lenter:* for "lean-to" = an addition to a house. Pron: ['lɛntr̩], ['lɪntr̩], and ['lɪntr̩]. **1894** *Century Illustr. Mag.* 47.855, In New England and the whole Northern region, the sloping, shed-like addition to a main building, whether house or barn, is in rustic speech called the "linter," or "lenter," and the pronunciation is as old as the settlement of the Northern colonies. I find it in the earliest writings "linter," "lenter," and "leantor," as well as "lenetoe." **1909** *DN* 3.413 **nME,** *Linter.* . . A cow stable. **1914** *DN* 4.76 **ME, nNH,** *Linter.* . . Tie-up, for cattle. **1924** *DN* 5.295 **csNH,** *Linter.* . . Also leenter. **1930** *AmSp* 5.419 **csNH,** Linter. **1939** *LANE* Map 108 *(Cow stable),* [Lean-to/linter is a common response in ME, NH, eMA; proncs of the type [lɪntə] (rarely [lɪntɚ]) are considerably more frequent than those of the type [lintu]. Proncs occurring only once are [lɪntl̩], [lɪntɨʲl], and [liʲtə]. **1941** *Ibid* Map 352 *(Ell),* [Lean-to with proncs of the type [lɪntu] is fairly common throughout **NEng;** 6 scattered infs gave proncs of the type [lɪntə] and one [lɪntɨj].] **1969–70** *DARE* (Qu. D7, *A small space anywhere in a house where you can hide things or get them out of the way)* Inf **RI12,** Linter—a corruption of lean-to—applies to a saltbox house; (Qu. D16, . . *Parts added on to the main part of a house)*

[66 Infs, **scattered,** Lean-to;] **NY209,** Lenter; **NY233,** Linter; (Qu. M10, *The part of the barn where cows are kept)* Inf **MA37,** ['lɪntɚ]—old-fashioned.

lean toward Jones's (or Sawyer's) See **lean** v B3

lean-tree n
=**hornbeam 1.**
    1960 Vines *Trees SW* 144, Vernacular names [of *Carpinus caroliniana*] are Blue-beech, Water-beech, Lean-tree, and Ironwood.

lean trout n Also *lean (char)* Cf **fat lake trout**
=**lake trout 1.**
    1983 Becker *Fishes WI* 323, Lake Trout—*Salvelinus namaycush namaycush.* . . lean trout, lean char, lean. *Ibid* 330, Commercial fishermen and buyers recognize and assign different monetary values to at least four variants: *lean trout* (lake trout), *fat trout* (siscowet), *half-breeds,* and *humpers* (bankers). Two of the variants, the lean and the fat trout, are clearly distinct, at least at larger sizes, and have been accorded subspecific rank as *S. namaycush namaycush* and *S. n. siscowet.*

‡**leany** adj
Thin, scrawny.
    1966 *DARE* (Qu. K44, *A bony or poor-looking horse)* Inf **SC26,** Leany, poor [po].

leap v
Std senses, var forms.
    1 pres exc 3rd pers sg: usu *leap;* rarely *lep.*
    1928 Chapman *Happy Mt.* 54, Leaping mad she was. She just le'p up at me. 'Leave her le'p,' thinks I. **1935** Porter *Flowering Judas* 163, It's enough to make a man lep out of his shoes.
    2 past and past pple: usu *leaped, leapt;* pronc-spp *lep;* rarely *lope.*
    1891 Johnston *Primes & Neighbors* 119 **GA,** People ought to be allays keerful not only to look whar they leap, but whar they lope. **1899** Chesnutt *Conjure Woman* 186 **csNC** [Black], Des ez [=just as] soon ez he got close ter 'im, he le'p' out en ketch' her by de th'oat. **1923** *DN* 5.213 **swMO,** *Lep.* . . Leaped. Seldom used, 'jumped' being employed instead. **1928** [see **1** above]. **1962** *Mt. Life* 38.1.16 **sAppalachians,** Verbs which retain either the strong preterites of Middle English or variant preterites of the English dialects . . *Present*—leap[₍], *Past*—lope[₍] *Past Participle*—lope[₍].

leaper n
    1 The Atlantic **salmon** *(Salmo salar).* [See quot 1889]
    1889 *Century Dict.* 3390, *Leaper.* . . An anglers' name for the salmon, from its leaping over obstructions in streams. **1975** Evanoff *Catch More Fish* 76, The Atlantic salmon *(Salmo salar)* is also called the Kennebec salmon and the leaper. . . Now it's rare in the United States except for small runs in some rivers in Maine.
    2 See **leapfrog.**

leapfrog n Also *leaping frog, (spring) leaper*
A **bullfrog 1** (here: *Rana clamitans)* or similar frog.
    1851 *De Bow's Rev.* 11.53 **LA,** *Rana Musica* or *Clamitans,* croaker, and also leap or spring frog. **1950** WELS *(Small frogs that sing or chirp loudly in spring)* 1 Inf, **WI,** Leapfrog. **1966** Dakin *Dial. Vocab. Ohio R. Valley* 2.388, A bewildering list of names appear to be used for the small frogs whose shrill peeping announces the coming of spring in late March or April. . . Only one Illinois record has any name recorded. [One informant] . . says *spring leapers.* **1967** *DARE* (Qu. P22, *Names or nicknames for a very large frog that makes a deep, loud sound)* Inf **MO21,** Leaping frogs—has longer legs; found near water. **1986** Pederson *LAGS Concordance (Spring frog)* **Gulf Region,** 2 infs, Leapfrogs; 2 infs, Leapfrog—(brown) small; 1 inf, Leapfrog = spring frog, green jumping frog, smaller than bullfrogs, amphibious; 1 inf, Leapfrog—holler all night long; 1 inf, Leaper—small green water frog; *(Bullfrog)* 2 infs, Leapfrog; 1 inf, Leaping frog—small; [1 inf, Mile leaper [*LAGS* scribe queries headword]—they ain't fit for no thing].

leapfrog milk n [Folk-etym for *Liebfraumilch*]
    1975 Newell *If Nothin' Don't Happen* 165 **Chicago IL,** Near the hotel was a fancy German eatin' place . . the lady ordered up a lot of stuff. . . To drink she ordered somethin' called leap-frog milk. . . It didn't look or taste like much of anything, but I was thirsty and she kept fillin' my glass. And I'll guaran-dam-tee that was a well-named drink. I felt like hoppin' all over Chicago. **1989–90** *DARE* File **nWI,** At a small tavern in the North Woods, we ordered some Liebfraumilch with our dinner.

When the check came, the bar tab noted a bottle of Leapfrog Milk; **csWI,** One of my students, who worked as a waitress in northern Wisconsin, said that she had heard *Leapfrog Milk* for *Liebfraumilch.*

leaping frog See **leapfrog**

learn v Usu |lɜ(r)n|; also **esp Sth, S Midl** |lɑ(r)n|; **chiefly NYC, sLA** |lɜɪn| Pronc-spp *larn, loin* Similarly vbl n *larning;* ppl adj *larned,* also sp *larnt* For addit pronc and sp varr see **A** below Cf Pronc Intro 3.I.1.f

A Forms.

   1784 in 1956 Eliason *Tarheel Talk* 313 **seNC,** *Larned.* **1795** Dearborn *Columbian Grammar* 136, *List of Improprieties. . . Larnin* for *Learning.* **1810** (1912) Bell *Journey to OH* 51 **MA,** I could make them believe in ten minutes, that I was a girl of great larnin. **1817** in 1830 Royall *Letters AL* 23 **VA,** This comes o' larnin gals to write! A darter o' mine shouldn't lan [sic] to write, to save her life! **1818** Fessenden *Ladies Monitor* 171 **NEng,** Provincial words . . which ought to be avoided by all who aspire to speak or write the English language correctly. . . *larnt* for learned. **1843** (1916) Hall *New Purchase* 55 **IN,** Maybe Mrs. Callten . . will larn how too. *Ibid* 271 **IN,** Poor, unlarn'd, ignorant men. **1893** Shands *MS Speech* 9, By the illiterate of both colors [ɑ] is substituted for [ɝ] in . . [lɑɑn] for *learn.* **1899** Eggleston *Hoosier Schoolmaster* 119 **IN,** Do you think he'd help a poor, unlarnt Flat Cricker like me? **1913** Kephart *Highlanders* 80 **sAppalachians,** I reckon he'll pick up some larnin' in the next two, three days. **1922** Gonzales *Black Border* 309 **sSC, GA coasts** [Gullah glossary], *Laa'n*—learn, learns, learned, learning. **1927** *AmSp* 3.139 **ME coast,** The older people spoke of "young uns". . . "larnin' " "sartin". **1933** Rawlings *South Moon* 27 **nFL,** Where did you l'arn that figger? **1942** in 1944 *ADD* **NYC,** *Learn. . . |lɔɪn|.* Who can loin him better than you? **1942** *AmSp* 17.151 **seNY,** *Learn . . [ɝ] . . 3* [infs], [ɜ] . . 3 [infs] . . [ɜɪ] . . 6 [infs]. **1943** *LANE* Map 666 *(Taught),* [32 infs, **chiefly ME, NH,** gave proncs of *learned* or *learnt* with the vowels [ɑ, a, æ]; 21 of them described such proncs as older though still in use.] **1950** Hubbell *Pronc. NYC* 5, I have described the well-known homonymy of *curl* and *coil, learn,* and *loin* as uncultivated. *Ibid* 11, A careful sampling of the usage of a large number of speakers would undoubtedly show that the homonymy of *learn* and *loin* was far more frequent in Elmhurst in the Borough of Queens than in the east Sixties between Fifth and Lexington Avenues. But such facts as this can be better explained in social, than in geographic terms. **1950** *PADS* 14.43 **SC,** *Larnin'.* **c1960** Hall Coll. **wNC, eTN,** Pronounced [lɜrn] by those exposed to some education, but [lɑrn] by others. . . I also heard the pronunciation [lɛrn] several times on Cosby Creek. **c1960** Wilson Coll. **csKY,** *Learn. . . Often* [lɑrn] among elderly. **1965–70** *DARE* (Qu. N8, *If somebody gave you lessons in driving a car . . "He _____ me how to drive.")* 56 Infs, **scattered, but less freq West,** [Proncs of the type [lɜ(r)nd]]; 31 Infs, **esp Sth, S Midl,** [Proncs of the type [lɜ(r)nt]]; **GA72, IN13, IA30, MN12,** [Proncs of the type [lɜ·nɪd]]; **IA19,** [You] hear often [lɜ·nɪd]; **LA8, 12,** [lɜɪnt]; **KY34,** [laɝnt]; **VA27,** [lɑrnt]; **TN36,** [lɑrnd]; **SC26,** [lɛrn]; (Qu. OO21a, *To learn: "Even as a child, he _____ fast.";* total Infs questioned, 75) 50 Infs, **scattered,** Learned; 6 Infs, **scattered,** Learnt; **MS69,** Learned; learnt (heard); [lɑrnt] Negro; **OK6,** Learned; learnt—oldsters; (Qu. OO21b, *To learn: "He has always _____ quicker than the others.";* total Infs questioned, 75) 50 Infs, **scattered,** Learned; 6 Infs, **scattered,** Learnt; **FL18,** Learned; [they are] teaching *learnt* in Graceville; **OK6,** Learned; learnt—oldsters; (Qu. Z14b) Inf **KY34,** Don't know no better, never larnt nothing. **1967** *DARE* FW Addit **LA12,** Learned [lɜɪnt]; **TN17,** They'll larn right quick, too. **1989** Pederson *LAGS Tech. Index* 357 **Gulf Region,** *Learn* [is usu pronounced [lɜ·n, lɜn]; 1 inf [lɑrn]; 1 inf [lærn]]. **1990** *DARE* File **New Orleans LA** (as of c1960), In remarking how similar Irish Channel speech was to that of Brooklyn, NY, one word they particularly recalled was *learn,* [lɜɪn] for [lɜrn].

B Senses.

1 To teach. **scattered, but less freq West** See Map *somewhat old-fash; esp freq among speakers with gs educ or less*

   c1769 in 1953 Woodmason *Carolina Backcountry* 158 **SC,** I wish Capt. Canty wou'd'nt let them cheat one another at Cards as they Do—for that learns them to be Sharpers. **1817** [see **A** above]. **1845** Kirkland *Western Clearings* 79 **MI,** I'll larn him who he's got to deal with! **1893** Shands *MS Speech* 43, *Learn.* . . Largely used by all classes for *teach.* **1899** Garland *Boy Life* 241 **nwIA,** Oh, if you weren't Sheriff! I'd learn you to strike me. **1902** *DN* 2.238 **sIL,** Learn me how to do this. **1906** *DN* 3.120 **sIN.** **1907** *DN* 3.223 **nwAR, sIL.** **1909** *DN* 3.343 **eAL, wGA.** **1910** *DN* 3.444 **wNY.** **1923** *DN* 5.213 **swMO.** **1932**

(1974) Caldwell *Tobacco Road* 82 **GA,** I had the hardest time learning him to wear his socks in the bed. **1943** *LANE* Map 666 **NEng,** [Forms of *learned* for *taught* in the context "Who taught you that?" are common **throughout NEng,** often given alongside *taught.*] **1965–70** *DARE* (Qu. N8, *If somebody gave you lessons in driving a car . . "He _____ me how to drive."*) 51 Infs, **scattered, but less freq West,** Learned; **GA74, NY1, TN1, 6, VA50, 54,** Learned—some people (*or* most, they, illiterates, uneducated) say; **NY210,** Learned—out West; **TN11,** Learned—not common; **GA84,** Learned—not proper; **NY164,** Learned—anyone knows this isn't correct; taught; 29 Infs, **esp Sth, S Midl,** Learnt; **LA18, MN13,** Learnt, [corr to] taught; **NY27,** Learnt—that's not right, though; **KY34, VA27,** Larnt; **TN36,** Larned; **SC26,** Learn [Of all Infs responding to the question, 30% were gs educ or less; of those giving these resps, 59% were gs educ or less.]; (Qu. P9, *When you're fishing but not catching any*) Inf **NY233,** [I'm] just learning the worm to swim. **1965–70** *DARE* Tape **FL66,** He learned me to play chess; **IN12,** He . . had been learnt not to do those things; **IL69, KY23, LA27, MI96, 125, SC19, TN15, TX26, 49, 94, VA27, WV8,** Learn [for *teach*]. **1973** Allen *LAUM* 1.398 **Upper MW** (as of c1950), Although nearly one-third of the uneducated use *learn* in the sense of 'teach,' only a handful of Type II [=mid-aged, with approx hs educ] do, and none in Type III [=mid-aged, with coll educ].

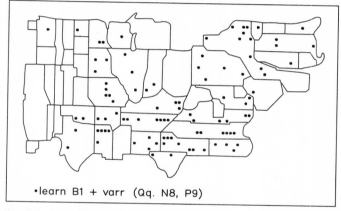

•learn B1 + varr (Qq. N8, P9)

2 with *for:* To study, prepare for.
   1948 Manfred *Chokecherry* 42 **nwIA,** You're the boy that's learnin' for the ministry, ain't you?

3 See quot.
   1939 Hall Coll. **eTN,** *Learn.* . . To become acquainted with. "Ye didn't learn him, did ye?" . . "Where did you learn him?"

learn for See **learn B2**

leary adj [Cf *EDD leary* "half-witted" (at *lear* adj.[1] 1.(3))]
   1911 *DN* 3.545 **NE,** *Leary, adj.* To lack nerve; to be dazed or bewildered. . . To be foolish, half-imbecile, etc: compare, *batty, daffy,* etc.

lease n, v Usu |lis|; for varr see quots Pronc-sp *least* Cf Intro "Language Changes" I.8
   Std sense, var forms.
   1926 Lardner *Love Nest* 89, But durin' the winter Johnnie got a hold of some specialist somewheres that fixed his knee, and he came South with a new least of life. **1965** *DARE* FW Addit **cnOK,** [les]—pronunciation of *lease* (to lease land, etc).

least adj **chiefly S Midl, esp sAppalachians**
1 Smallest in size; also, for those who use the superlative in comparative degree, smaller; rarely, small, tiny. Cf **leastest, less** adj
   1902 *DN* 2.238 **sIL** [Pioneer dialect], *Least.* . . The smaller or smallest. The word small is not used, but *little.* **1904** *DN* 2.419 **nwAR,** *Least.* . . Smallest. 'She's the least child in the class.' [*Ibid, Less.* . . Smaller. 'My brother's less than you.'] **1906** *DN* 3.144 **nwAR,** *Least little.* . . "He's the least little thing." **1909** *DN* 3.344 **eAL, wGA,** *Least little.* . . Tiniest. "She's the least little thing you ever saw." **1928** Chapman *Happy Mt.* 81 **seTN,** The least girl [of the two] 'n' prettiest ran and called her sister. **1931** Hannum *Thursday April* 277 **wNC** (as of 1917), Don't hit make my eyes seem a least mite bluer, Joe? *Ibid* 282, Jest a least pinch of tobacco, Joe. **1939** Hall Coll. **neTN,** Jim, you sleep in the middle. You're the least one of the three. **1958** Randolph *Sticks* 5 **nwAR,** A penny is the least money there is. **1962** Dykeman *Tall*

Woman 39 **NC** (as of c1860), Then she flung out her arms and the least children rushed into her wide embrace while Kate and Lydia followed to kiss her shyly. **1968** *DARE* (Qu. LL6b, *A small, indefinite amount . .* "I'll put in just a _____ of butter.") Inf **GA**30, Least bit.

2 Youngest; also, for those who use the superlative in comparative degree, younger—often in comb *least one.*

1887 *Scribner's Mag.* 2.479 **AR** [Black], How'd ye enj'y hevin' them two least ones tolled off by a gang er cotton-pickers? **1902** *DN* 2.238 **sIL** [Pioneer dialect], The *least un,* the youngest of a family. **1910** *DN* 3.456 **seKY**, Lincoln used to take the least ones on his knee. **1926** Roberts *Time of Man* 325 **KY**, Five youngones [sic] I got, all told, Hen the oldest, and then Nan, she's next, then Joe, then Ellie and then Dick, the least one. **1939** Writers' Program *Guide KY* 239, But it delights most of the mountain people, from the "leastuns" (youngest children) to the grandsires. **1944** *PADS* 2.58 **MO**, Least chap. . . The youngest boy . . in a family. **1958** Randolph *Sticks* 3 **nwAR**, The oldest one was carrying a magic tablecloth. . . The second boy come in leading a magic mule. . . The least boy didn't have nothing but an old knapsack. **c1960** *Wilson Coll.* **csKY**, The *least one* . . the baby, usually in a big family. **1962** Dykeman *Tall Woman* 68 **NC** (as of c1860), I know my mammy, the day before she died, told me she saw the figure of her least 'un that had been buried years before during an awful siege of the bloody flux. **1986** Pederson *LAGS Concordance,* 1 inf, **csGA**, The least child. **1987** Jones-Wheeler *Laughter* 150 **Appalachians**, You can't sleep with them leastl'uns [=least little ones]. You're liable to roll on 'em and clubfoot 'em. **1993** *DARE* File **nwAR**, My neighbor down the road here calls his youngest daughter his least daughter or his least one.

3 =no-account.

1934 Hurston *Jonah's Gourd Vine* 24 **AL** [Black], Humph! Talkin' after po' white trash! If Ah wuz ez least ez dey is, Ah speck Ah'd fret mahself tuh death.

least conj [Arch and Scots dial var of *lest*]

1960 Criswell *Resp. to PADS* 20 **Ozarks**, Least, conj. For *lest.* Common once.

least n See **lease**

leastaways See **leastways**

least bittern n

Std: a small heron *(Ixobrychus exilis)* native chiefly to the eastern half of the US. Also called **cattail hen, citron 3, little green heron 1, mud hen 2c, poke, shitepoke, sungazer, swamp-pumper**

leaster adj Cf **least** adj 1, **leastest, less** adj

Smaller in physical size.

1953 Randolph–Wilson *Down in Holler* 260 **Ozarks**, *Less* and *leaster. . .* Smaller and smaller. When anything is getting *less an' leaster,* it is dwindling away, like a lump of melting ice.

leastest adj [Redund; cf Intro "Language Changes" II.2] Cf **least** adj 1, **less** adj

Least; smallest; hence n *leastest* the least.

1795 Dearborn *Columbian Grammar* 136, *List of Improprieties. . .* Leastest for Least. **1838** Kettell *Yankee Notions* 122, Peggy Downer was here yesterday forenoon . . and she never mentioned the leastest word about it. . . I don't believe Hannah Downer ever gin [=gave] Peet Spinbutton the leastest encouragement in the universal world. **1871** (1882) Stowe *Fireside Stories* 71 **MA**, Jist give 'em the leastest sprig of any thing. **1939** Cheney *Lightwood* **GA** *(ADD),* It 'ud take 3 days at the leastest. **1953** Brewer *Word Brazos* 52 **eTX** [Black], An las', but'n no wise de leastes', Ah wants euh livin' soul heah tonight to keep dis.

least one See **least** adj 2

least sandpiper n

Std: a very small sandpiper *(Calidris minutilla)* found chiefly in Southern Atlantic and Pacific coastal areas of the US. Also called **biddy** n[1] **2, bumblebee peep, green-legged ~, gunwad, hawk's-eye 2, humility 1, jack snipe 6, little peep, marsh peep, meadow oxeye, mud peep, mudsucker 2, oxeye 1a, pea snipe, peckie, peep, peewee, pennywinkle, sand bird, ~ chicken, ~ oxeye, ~ peep, ~ snipe, sea chicken stint, teeter**

least spotted woodpecker See **little spotted woodpecker**

least tern n

Std: a very small tern *(Sterna albifrons).* Also called **jack-knife gull, killing-peter, little striker, mosquito gull, oyt, pond tern, sand peter, sea swallow, striker, tearr**

leastways adv Pronc-spp *leasways, leastaways* [Varr of *leastwise*] esp **Sth, S Midl**

At least; in any case.

1871 Eggleston *Hoosier Schoolmaster* 116 **sIN**, I 'low God don't no ways keer to be remembered by sich as him. Leastways I wouldn't if I was God. **1875** (1886) Woolson *Castle Nowhere* 118 **nMI**, Leastways so Mrs. Malone said. **1887** (1967) Harris *Free Joe* 123 **GA**, He's over on Sweetwater, I reckon. Leastways thar's whar he started to go. **1891** (1967) Freeman *New Engl. Nun* 133, I ain't goin' to, Davy. Leastways not fur more'n two or three minutes. **1905** *DN* 3.57 **eNE**, *Leastways.* **1909** *DN* 3.344 **eAL, wGA**, *Leas(t)ways. . .* Leastwise. The latter is not heard. **1913** Kephart *Highlanders* 380 **sAppalachians**, The Bible says they're human—leastways some says it does. **1936** *AmSp* 11.316 **Ozarks**, *Leastways. . .* At least. Used indiscriminately with *leastwise.* **1938** Caldwell *Southways* 32 **GA**, "I just naturally figured on you helping me out, Mr. Jule," he said. "Leastaways, that's about the only way I know of getting out of this here well." **1946** *PADS* 6.19 **eNC** (as of 1900–10), *Leastaways. . .* Occasional. **1947** *PADS* 8.19 **IA**, *Leastways.* **c1960** *Wilson Coll.* **csKY**, *Leastways.* **1968** Moody *Horse* 23 **nwKS** (as of c1920), It'll take leastways four months to put a two-hundred-pound gain on him [=a steer]. **1976** Lynn–Vecsey *Loretta Lynn* 62 **eKY**, But something that's really important to women, like birth control, they don't want no part of, leastways not on the air.

leather n

1 In var phrr referring to the leather of a saddle, as:

a *pull* (or *claw, go to, hunt, take, touch*) *leather:* To hold on to the saddle while riding a horse; also fig. **West**

1915 *DN* 4.245 **MT**, *Pull leather. . .* To hang on to the saddle. "He rode the outlaw without pulling leather." **1918** Mulford *Man from Bar-20* 17 **West**, I'm gettin' lonesomer and lonesomer all th' time, but I manages to stick on th' job by pullin' leather, because I was drawin' down a foreman's pay. **1922** Rollins *Cowboy* 290 **West**, Less accomplished men . . might be willing to "hunt leather," "take leather," "touch leather," "pull leather," or "go to leather," as a hand hold upon any part of the saddle, its accoutrements or the horse was interchangeably known. **1925** Raine *Troubled Waters* 186, Stick to the saddle, Mac. Don't you pull leather, old scout. **1933** *AmSp* 8.1.28 **TX**, *Pull leather.* To grab the saddle horn—the unforgivable sin. This expression came into interesting figurative use, meaning to begin to feel the insecurity of one's position in an argument, a love affair, or any other precarious undertaking. **1937** *DN* 6.619 **swTX**, The cowboy violates the rules of the game if he catches hold of the pommel or any part of the saddle in order to stay on the pitching horse. . . *pulling leather* and *clawing leather.* **1940** Writers' Program *Guide NV* 75, The contempt of true cowhands for the flat-heeled *peeler* who must *pull leather* (grasp the saddle horn) in order to remain with his mount. **1947** Lomax *Advent. Ballad Hunter* 17 **TX**, Ed . . made a beautiful figure astride a horse. He never pulled leather; "I never was throwed," he claims.

b *pound leather:* To ride (a horse) fast; hence n *leather pounder* a cowboy.

1907 Mulford *Bar-20* 118, But didn't yu see too much of 'em once, or was yu poundin' leather in the other direction? **1936** Adams *Cowboy Lingo* 22, The cowboy was known, too, by such slang names as . . 'saddle-stiff,' 'leather-pounder,' . . or 'waddie.' **1941** Writers' Program *Guide WY* 464, *Pound leather . .* to ride.

2 A rein.

1885 Howells *Rise Lapham* 113, Jerry, suppose you let me have hold of the leathers a minute. **1967** *DARE* Tape **IA**8, [FW:] That's the call for the mules? [Inf:] Yep, pick up your leather and say "ya-hey-up" and away they go.

3 Pureed fruit spread in a thin sheet and dried; see quots. Cf **leather apron**

1849 Howitt *Our Cousins in OH* 158, The fruit, when pared, was cut into slices, and . . if intended for peach-leather, it was first boiled to a fine, smooth pulp, and then spread out to dry. . . When needed for use, it was soaked, and again dissolved by boiling to a pulp, sweetened, and made into pies, which were very delicious in winter. **1866** *Hours at Home* 3.507, Think of apple butter, apple-leather, and apple-jack. **1877** Bartlett *Americanisms* 16 **PA, MD**, *Apple-Leather. .* Apples parboiled and stirred into a paste of considerable consistency; then rolled out and dried in the sun. When dry, it is about as tough as leather, and comes away in sheets of the thickness of tanned cowhide,—whence its name. **1915** *DN* 4.187 **swVA**, *Peach leather.* . . Peaches crushed, spread out, and dried. **1948** *Sun* (Baltimore MD) 29 Sept 14/3 *(Hench Coll.),* I recalled the era in Maryland when most families . . put up all their own preserves. . . Apple leather and peach leather, too—sprinkled with sugar and rolled up in cylinders. **1966–70** *DARE* (Qu. H63, *Kinds of desserts*) Inf **SC4**, Peach leather—dried peaches; (Qu. H80, *Kinds of candy . . made at home*) Inf **VA98**, Peach leather. **1976** *Yankee* Oct 190, Fruit butters and leathers are a traditional and increasingly popular method of preserving fruits. *Ibid* 201, To produce a paper-thin leather, lightly oil a cookie sheet. . . Spread puree ¼ inch thick. . . Place in a 120° to 150° oven. **1979** Woolf *Woolfs VA* 78 **cnVA** (as of c1900), Her popularity among the young was enhanced by her practice of keeping a supply of peach leather in her pocket. **1986** Pederson *LAGS Concordance* (Snits . . *dried pieces of [fruit]*) 1 inf, **cwGA**, Apple leather = dried apples, peach leather; 1 inf, **seLA**, Apricot leather—pounding dried fruit, West Coast.

4 See **leather fern 3.**

leather apron n **NEng, Upstate NY** Cf **frog** n **B9, jack wax 1, leather 3, maple wax, sheepskin**

A sheet formed by pouring hot maple syrup over snow; see quots.

1939 Wolcott *Yankee Cook Book* 346 **VT**, *A Sugar-On-Snow Party.* . . Provide each person or couple with a pan of snow, a small pitcher of hot [maple] syrup and a fork. Pour the syrup on the snow, a little at a time. . . Some people call the syrup "sheepskins"; others refer to it as "leather aprons" or "maple wax." *Ibid* 347, For a real Vermont maple sugar party, doughnuts and pickles are necessary to complete the menu. The tartness of the pickles makes it possible to enjoy and consume more "leather aprons." **1947** Bowles–Towle *New Engl. Cooking* 246, First we have told how to prepare Sugar on Snow, or leather aprons or frogs, if you prefer the country names. **1959** *VT Hist.* 27.146, *Leather aprons.* . . Sugar on snow. **1988** *Yankee* Oct 27 **Upstate NY**, When we were kids in upstate New York our maple syrup was boiled and dribbled over snow, and the result was called "Leather Aprons."

leatherback n

1 also *leatherback(ed) turtle, leather tortoise, ~ turtle:* A very large marine turtle *(Dermochelys coriacea)* of both the Atlantic and the Pacific oceans. [See quot 1972] Also called **trunkback**

1811 *Niles' Weekly Reg.* 1.119, It is a *Testudo Cariaria* or *Leather tortoise*, a native of the East Indies. **1842** DeKay *Zool. NY* 3.5, The Leather Turtle, although a native of tropical American seas, is a great wanderer: it has been seen on the coast of England, and in the Mediterranean. **1935** Pratt *Manual Vertebrate Animals* 242, Leather-turtle. . . Northward as far as Maine. **1947** Pickwell *Amphibians* 62, This family of marine Leather-backed Turtles [=Dermochelidae] has but one genus and one species in our region, *Dermochelys schlegelii*, the Pacific Leather-backed Turtle. **1952** Carr *Turtles* 443, The size attained by the leatherback turtles cannot be determined with accuracy. *Ibid* 446, There is considerable variation in the coloration of mature specimens of the leatherback. **1968** *DARE* (Qu. P24, . . *Kinds of turtles*) Inf **CA80**, Leatherback—the huge sea turtle. **1972** Ernst–Barbour *Turtles* 249, Leatherbacks. . . The carapace lacks horny plates but is covered with a ridged, leathery skin.

2 also *leatherback(ed) turtle, leather(y) turtle:* A **soft-shell turtle** (here: either *Trionyx muticus* or *T. spiniferus*). **esp N Cent**

1879 Smith *Catalogue Reptilia MI* 7, *Amyda mutica.* . . Leathery Turtle. **1883** WI Chief Geologist *Geol. WI* 1.423, *Amyda mutica.* . . Leathery Turtle. All the tributaries of the Mississippi river within the state. **1891** in 1895 IL State Lab. Nat. Hist. Urbana *Bulletin* 3.246, *Aspidonectes spinifer* . . Soft-shelled Turtle, Leather-back. *Ibid* 247, Very similar to *Amyda mutica.* . . Both species appear in the fish markets at Peoria, but are not discriminated, all passing under the name of soft-shells or leatherbacks. **1928** Baylor Univ. Museum *Contrib.* 16.21, *Amyda emoryii* . . In the eastern half of Texas, *Leather Turtle, Soup Turtle,* and *Soft-shelled Terrapin* are names applied to this species. **1950** *WELS (Kinds of turtles found in your neighborhood)* 3 Infs, **WI**, Leatherback. **1965–70** *DARE* (Qu. P24, . . *Kinds of turtles*) Infs **IL29, IA29, MI84, 109, MN21, 42, OH47, 67**, Leatherback; **AR56**, Leatherbacks—soft-shelled turtles; **CO22**, Leatherback—mud turtle (soft-shell); **OH33**, Soft-shell or leatherback—good to eat; **WI6**, Leatherback—brown back,

water; **WI32**, Leatherbacks—same as soft-shell turtle; **MI112**, Leatherback turtle; **NY183, TX5**, Leatherbacked turtle. **1986** Pederson *LAGS Concordance* (Turtle) 1 inf, **neTX**, Leatherback—15–20 pounds; edible; in water.

3 =**ruddy duck.**

1888 Trumbull *Names of Birds* 113, At Charleston, S.C., [the ruddy duck is called] *leather-back.* **1949** Sprunt–Chamberlain *SC Bird Life* 144, *Ruddy Duck: Oxyura jamaicensis rubida.* . . Local Names: Spiketail. . . Leatherback. **1982** Elman *Hunter's Field Guide* 192, *Ruddy Duck.* . . Common & Regional Names: booby . . leatherback.

4 A **redbelly dace** (here: *Phoxinus eos*), the finescale **dace** (*P. neogaeus*), or the pearl **dace** (*Semotilus margarita*).

1943 Eddy–Surber *N. Fishes* 134, *Northern Pearl Dace.* . . Leather Back. . . *Margariscus margarita nachtriebi.* **1983** Becker *Fishes WI* 451, *Finescale Dace—Phoxinus neogaeus.* . . bronze minnow . . leatherback. *Ibid* 459, *Northern Redbelly Dace—Phoxinus eos.* . . redbelly dace . . leatherback.

5 The common carp *(Cyprinus carpio).* Cf **leather carp**

1949 Caine *N. Amer. Sport Fish* 154, German Carp—Leatherback. **1967** *DARE* (Qu. P3, *Freshwater fish that are not good to eat*) Inf **SC40**, German carp—same as leatherback. **1983** Becker *Fishes WI* 419, Mirror carp, leather carp, leatherback.

6 A **lae** (here: *Scomberoides sancti-petri*). [See quot] **HI**

1960 Gosline–Brock *Hawaiian Fishes* 169, *Scomberoides sancti-petri.* . . Leatherback. . . Its leathery, silver skin is frequently used in making trolling lures.

7 The larva of a **crane fly.** Cf **leatherjacket 3**

1949 Palmer *Nat. Hist.* 422, One species [of crane fly] lays about 1,000 eggs in wet soil. These hatch in about 1 week into black worms or "leatherbacks" that develop in a few weeks into pupae.

8 See quot. Cf **buckram, papershell**

1968 *DARE* File **Brooklyn NYC**, Leatherback—a soft-shell crab turning hard.

leatherback(ed) turtle See **leatherback 1, 2**

leatherbark See **leatherwood 1**

leather bat See **leather-winged bat**

leather bird n

=**long-billed curlew.**

1956 *AmSp* 31.182 **NC**, Toughness of flesh has been commemorated in the term *pine knot* for the American bittern and old squaw . . the long-billed curlew has been called *leather bird* for the same reason.

leatherbread n Cf **blanket 3, flannel cake, liver pad**

See quot.

1933 Miller *Lamb in His Bosom* 71 **GA**, Lonzo enjoyed his breakfast the best of any meal—fried bacon . . , grits . . , hoecake, and syrup. Sometimes lately Cean stole a little flour from her barrel and made leatherbread and baked it on a greased spider.

leather breeches n pl

1 also *leather britches (beans), ~ britchy beans:* **green beans** dried and cooked in the pod. [Because when they are hung up to dry they resemble leather pants on a clothesline] **chiefly S Midl, esp sAppalachians** Cf **bean stringing, fodder bean, shelly bean**

1913 Kephart *Highlanders* 292 **sAppalachians**, Beans dried in the pod, then boiled 'hull and all,' are called leather-breeches (this is not slang, but the regular name). Green beans in the pod are called snaps; when shelled they are shuck-beans. **1939** *Hall Coll.* **wNC**, *Leather britches.* . . They'd dry their beans, yes. They'd dry leather britches beans. . . I dry mine in the sun. My grandmother dried hers on a string. Hung 'em up in the porch or around the fireplace and dried 'em. . . I still dry those leather britches beans—that's what they called 'em then. **1940** Brown *Amer. Cooks* 634 **NC**, *Leather Britches*—String full-bodied green string beans, using a darning needle and coarse thread. Hang in an airy place away from sun until thoroughly dry. Store in cloth bags. Soak overnight, and cook with a piece of fat back (salt pork), 3 hours. The flavor is unique. North Carolina shares Leather Britches with Georgia and South Carolina. **1950** *PADS* 14.44 **SC**, *Leather britches beans.* **1953** *PADS* 19.12 **sAppalachians**, *Leather britches.* . . Beans dried and cooked in the shell, also called *shelly beans* and, in Kentucky, *shucky beans.* **1961** *Mt. Life* 37.3.9 **sAppalachians**, She's down thar now a-whackin' off chunks o' hog's jowl as big as yer hand an' a-throwin' 'em in the pot o' leather-britchy beans. **1966–69** *DARE* (Qu. H50, *Dishes made with beans, peas, or corn that everybody around here knows, but people in other places might not*) Inf **GA**70, Leather britches; **NC**31, Leather britches—dried snap beans, soak over night or par boil, then cook with ham hock; **VA**13, Leather britches—these are your green beans which are dry, then later on they are soaked and cooked; (Qu. I12, *The outside covering of dry beans*) Inf **NC**33, Leather britches. **1968** *DARE* FW Addit **KY**40, 44, Leather britches—dried green beans, old-fashioned [FW: Infs used in conv]; **VA**7, Long beans strung up and dried; when they are cooked and eaten they are called leather breeches [bričǝz]. **1969** *DARE* Tape **GA**71, She dries beans, green beans. . . and makes what they call leather britches out of them. **1986** Pederson *LAGS Concordance (Green beans)* 2 infs, **cn,neGA**, Dried green beans (called) leather breeches.

2 =**Dutchman's breeches 1.**

1898 *Jrl. Amer. Folkl.* 11.222 **IL**, *Dicentra Cucullaria* . . leather breeches. [**1970** *DARE* FW Addit **KY**83, Leather britches—a plant, old-fashioned [*DARE* Ed: Plant not identified].]

3 =**ruddy duck.**

1949 Sprunt–Chamberlain *SC Bird Life* 144, *Ruddy Duck: Oxyura jamaicensis rubida.* . . Local Names: Spiketail . . Leather Breeches. **1950** *PADS* 14.44 **s,cSC**, *Leather breeches.* . . The ruddy duck.

4 See quot.

1966 Dakin *Dial. Vocab. Ohio R. Valley* 2.323, A few miscellaneous terms are used: . . *leather britches* (a cruller type doughnut of two long strips of dough twisted together at one end).

leather britches (beans), leather britchy beans See **leather breeches 1**

leather bush n

1 See **leatherwood 1.**

2 =**sweet pepperbush.** [Prob folk-etym for **latherbush**]

1938 Matschat *Suwannee R.* 33 **Okefenokee GA**, Here, too, the swamp folk come to gather the foliage of the leather or lather bush, which makes an excellent substitute for soap when crushed and worked to a lather in water.

leather carp n Cf **leatherback 5, mirror carp**

A variety of the common carp (*Cyprinus carpio*) in which the scales are absent or few.

1883 GA Dept. Ag. *Pub. Circular No. 34* 8.12, Three varieties of carp are cultivated. . . the scale carp. . . the mirror carp. . . the leather carp; which has on the back either only a few scales or none at all, and possesses a thick, soft skin, which feels velvety to the touch. **1905** U.S. Bur. Fisheries *Rept. for 1904* 533, Some authors state that the leather carp should be entirely destitute of scales; others that it may have a row of scales along the back and a row on each side. **1955** Zim–Shoemaker *Fishes* 57, Most Carp are scaled, but . . Leather Carp have no scales at all. **1983** Becker *Fishes WI* 419, The scaled carp with its large, thick cycloid scales, the mirror carp with its occasionally enlarged and scattered scales, and the leather carp in which the scales are absent, are varieties of the same species. . . Mirror and leather carp are quite rare today, constituting less than 2% of all wild carp.

leather-ear n

1 also *leather-eared perch, leather-ear sunfish:* Usu the **redbreast sunfish,** but also rarely the **longear sunfish.** [See quots 1911, 1949]

1911 *Century Dict. Suppl., Leather-ear.* . . One of the sunfishes, *Lepomis megalotis,* having a long dermal opercular flap, found in the fresh waters of the eastern United States. **1935** Caine *Game Fish* 26, *Redbreasted Sunfish—Lepomis auritus.* . . Leatherear—Leather-eared Perch. **1949** Caine *N. Amer. Sport Fish* 43, Leather-ear—Leather-ear Sunfish. . . *Redbreast Sunfish—Lepomis auritus* . . the redbreast sunfish has a long black noticeably narrow gill flap, or "ear." Its range is much the same as the long-ear sunfish.

2 pl: See **leatherhead.**

leather-eared perch, leather-ear sunfish See **leather-ear 1**

leather fern n

1 also *leatherleaf:* A **polypody** (here: *Polypodium scouleri*) native to Pacific coastal regions.

1923 in 1925 Jepson *Manual Plants CA* 29, *P[olypodium] scouleri.* . . *Leather-leaf.* . . On trees or rocks; Redwood belt. **1961** Thomas *Flora Santa Cruz* 57 **cwCA**, *P[olypodium] scouleri.* . . Leather Fern. . . Rock

crevices on exposed hills along the coast. [**1973** Hitchcock–Cronquist *Flora Pacific NW* 52, Leather-l[ea]f p[olypody]. *P[olypodium] scouleri.*]

2 A fern of the genus *Acrostichum* native to southern Florida.

1938 *Small Ferns SE States* 67, *Acrostichum.* . . Leaflets leathery, the blades thick-coriaceous. . . *Leather-ferns.* . . *A. aureum.* . . *Leather-fern.* . . The leather-ferns are quite suggestive of primeval vegetation. *Ibid* 69, *A. danaeaefolium.* . . *Leather-fern.* . . When the coastal regions of southern peninsular Florida were the only well-known parts, it was taken for granted that the leather-fern was confined to the coast and adjacent lowlands. **1975** Natl. Audubon Soc. *Corkscrew* 23, *Leather Fern (Acrostichum danaeaefolium)*—These huge, rankly growing plants. . . attain their greatest growth in the fresh water areas south of Lake Okeechobee. **1976** Bailey–Bailey *Hortus Third* 23, *[Acrostichum] aureum.* . . *Leather fern.* . . *[A.] danaeaefolium.* . . *Leather fern.*

3 also *leather, leatherleaf (fern):* A fern (*Ruhmohra adiantiformis*) commonly used for foliage in the florist trade.

1976 Bailey–Bailey *Hortus Third* 988, *[Rumohra] adiantiformis.* . . *Leather fern, leatherleaf f[ern].* . . *L[ea]v[e]s leathery.* **1986** Pederson *LAGS Concordance,* 1 inf, **neGA**, Leatherleaf (type of flower her husband sells). **1994** *DARE* File **seWI**, My mother's word for the ferns in a florist's bouquet is simply "leather."

leatherfish n [From the leathery skin] Cf **leatherjacket 1**

A **filefish,** usu *Monacanthus ciliatus* or *M. hispidus.*

1896 U.S. Bur. Fisheries *Rept. for 1895* 423, *Monacanthus ciliatus.* . . *Leather-fish.* . . West Indies and Florida; Florida Keys. . . *Monacanthus hispidus.* . . *Leather-fish.* . . South Atlantic Coast and Florida Keys. **1905** NJ State Museum *Annual Rept. for 1904* 358, Genus *Stephanolepis* [=*Monacanthus*]. . . The Leather Fishes. **1933** John G. Shedd Aquarium *Guide* 157, These slow-swimming fishes [=the filefishes] with rough leathery skins are common in all warm seas. . . *Monacanthus ciliatus*—Leatherfish. **1991** Amer. Fisheries Soc. *Common Names Fishes* 145, Leatherfish—see filefishes.

leather flower n [See quot 1953]

=**virgin's bower,** esp *Clematis viorna.*

1822 Eaton *Botany* 241, *[Clematis] viorna* . . leather flower. **1891** Coulter *Botany W. TX* 7, *C[lematis] Drummondii.* . . Leather flowers. . . *C. Pitcheri* . . the most common "leather flower." **1936** Whitehouse *TX Flowers* 29, *Texas Leather Flower.* . . *Clematis texensis.* . . The leaves are thickened. . . The leather flowers have no petals, the showy bells being made up of 4 thickened sepals. . . *Purple Leather Flower (Clematis pitcheri),* together with the marsh leather flower, is often called blue bell. **1953** Greene–Blomquist *Flowers South* 35, Our native species of *Clematis* with relatively large, bell-shaped flowers and thick, leathery sepals are generally called "leather-flowers" but may also have other local names. **1966** *DARE* (Qu. S26a, . . *Wildflowers.* . . *Roadside flowers*) Inf **SC**27, Leather flower (*Clematis viorna*). **1966** *DARE* Wildfl QR Pl.74 Inf **CO**29, Leather flower. **1979** Niering–Olmstead *Audubon Guide N. Amer. Wildflowers E. Region* 732, The vine Leather Flower (*C[lematis] crispa*) has . . extremely fragrant flowers . . [and] occurs . . from southeast Virginia to Florida and west to Texas and southern Missouri.

leatherhead n Also *leather-ears* [*OED* leather-head (at *leather sb.*6) a1700 →] Cf **head** n **C1a**

A stupid person; a fool; hence adj *leather-headed;* n *leather-headedness.*

1873 in 1917 Twain *Letters* 1.203, You leather-head, if I talk in Boston both afternoon and evening March 5, I'll have to go to Boston the 4th. **1879** (1880) Twain *Tramp Abroad* 41, They [=jays] . . got off as many leather-headed opinions about it as an average crowd of humans could have done. *Ibid* 215, His [=the ant's] leather-headedness is the point I make against him. **1903** *DN* 2.299 **Cape Cod MA** (as of a1857), *Leather-ears.* . . A person slow of comprehension. *Ibid, Leather-head.* **1907** *DN* 3.246 **eME**, *Leather-head.* . . Blockhead. "Don't know that, do you, leatherhead?" **1916** *DN* 4.264 **Cape Cod MA**, His son if stupid in "tendin' store" would be reprimanded as "leather-ears." **1919** *DN* 5.61 **NM**, *Leather-head,* a dumb-head. **1941** *LANE* Map 465, Derogatory names applied to a stupid person [44 infs, **NEng**, Leatherhead; 2 infs, Leather-ears]; 2 infs, **wMA**, Leatherhead—used only of men; 1 inf, **cME**, Leatherhead, rare. *Ibid* Map 379 *(Kid, Tot)* 1 inf, **cnRI**, Leatherhead. **1959** *VT Hist.* 27.147, *Leatherhead.* . . A stupid person. . . Occasional. **1960** Criswell *Resp. to PADS 20* **Ozarks**, *(A stupid person)* Lunkhead, leatherhead.

leatherjack See **leatherjacket 2, 3**

leatherjacket n

1 A fish of the family Balistidae, esp a **triggerfish** (here: *Balistes capriscus*). [*OED* 1770 →; see quot 1933] For other names of fishes of this family see **filefish, triggerfish** Cf **leatherfish**

1882 U.S. Natl. Museum *Bulletin* 16.855, *B[alistes] capriscus.* . . *Leather-jacket.* Uniform brownish. . . Common on our Gulf coast. **1884** Goode *Fisheries U.S.* 1.172, The Leather-jacket of Pensacola [FL], *Balistes capriscus,* called "Trigger Fish" in the Carolinas, and at Key West . . known as the "Turbot," occasionally finds its way as far north as Massachusetts. **1889** *Century Dict.* 3392, *Leather-jacket.* . . A balistoid fish, *Balistes Capriscus,* having three dorsal spines. . . It occurs along the Gulf coast of the United States. **1926** Pan-Pacific Research Inst. *Jrl.* 1.1.13, *Monacanthidae* [=Balistidae]. The Leather-Jackets. **1933** John G. Shedd Aquarium *Guide* 156, *Balistes capriscus.* . . The name Leather Jacket applies to the leathery appearance of the skin. *Ibid* 158, *Cantherines verecundus*—Leather Jacket. . . *Cantherines sandwichiensis*—Brown Leather Jacket. **1991** Amer. Fisheries Soc. *Common Names Fishes* 69, Balistidae—leatherjackets.

2 also *leatherjack:* A carangid fish (here: *Oligoplites saurus*). Also called **runner, skipjack, yellow jacket, yellowtail**

1879 U.S. Natl. Museum *Bulletin* 14.43, *Oligoplites occidentalis.* . . Leather Jacket. **1884** Goode *Fisheries U.S.* 1.332, The Leather-jacket—*Oligoplites saurus.* This fish . . has since 1875 been several times observed between Florida and Newport, Rhode Island. **1902** Jordan-Evermann *Amer. Fishes* 297, *Genus Oligoplites.* . . The Leather-Jacks. . . The common leather-jack or zapatero (*Oligoplites saurus*), is found on both coasts of Tropical America, and is common in the West Indies and along the Florida coast, ranging north to New York and Lower California. **1911** U.S. Bur. Census *Fisheries 1908* 316, *Skipjack.* . . A local name applied to the . . leather jacket (*Oligoplites saurus*) on the Atlantic coast. **1944** *Richmond Times–Dispatch* (VA) 20 Oct 15/2 **ceFL,** I got some ladyfish up to three or three and a half pounds and I also got hold of quite a few jack, as well as some small fish called leatherjack. **1991** Amer. Fisheries Soc. *Common Names Fishes* 52, *Oligoplites saurus* . . A[tlantic] . . leatherjack.

3 also *leatherjack:* =**crane fly,** esp in its larval stage. [*OED* 1881 →; see quots 1909, 1980] Cf **leatherback 7**

1905 Kellogg *Amer. Insects* 304, The swarms of dancing midges and the sprawling long-legged crane-flies, or leather-jackets, are not unfamiliar. *Ibid* 321, Tipulidae . . long-legged, narrow-winged members are familiarly known as crane-flies, leather-jackets, and "grandaddy-long-legs." **1909** Smith *Insect Friends* 80, The crane-flies have larvae that live underground and feed on the plant roots. They are sometimes called "wire-worms" because of their long slender form, and "leather-jackets" because of their texture. **1911** *Century Dict. Suppl., Leather-jack.* . . The larva of any one of several species of crane-flies of the family *Tipulidae.* It lives underground in pasture-lands and has an especially tough skin. **1926** Essig *Insects N. Amer.* 530, The larvae [of the acute crane fly (*Tipula acuta*)] are typical leather jackets and feed on the roots of grasses and succulent plants, including the tubers of dahlias, wherever decay occurs. **1980** Milne–Milne *Audubon Field Guide Insects* 634, Tipulidae. . . The larvae, called leatherjackets because of their tough skin, live in shallow water or moist soil and feed mainly on decaying plant matter.

leatherleaf n

1 A low evergreen shrub (*Chamaedaphne calyculata*).

1817 Eaton *Botany* 47, *Andromeda.* . . *calyculata,* (leather-leaf). **1870** *Amer. Naturalist* 4.217, The Leather Leaf (*Cassandra calyculata*), and *Andromeda polifolia,* are both worthy of attention. **1901** Lounsberry *S. Wild Flowers* 394, *Leather-Leaf.* . . is . . one of the very pretty inhabitants of luxuriant swamps and moist, shady places. **1924** *Amer. Botanist* 30.60, "Leatherleaf" (*C[hamaedaphne] calyculata*). . . refers to the small leaves which at the approach of cold weather don the colors of russet leather and remain on the plant until spring like a new sort of evergreen. **1942** Hylander *Plant Life* 420, Leatherleaf (*Chamaedaphne*), a low-growing shrub with narrow evergreen leaves, bears its drooping white urn-shaped flowers all on one side of the tip of the stems, in the axils of the leaves. This bog plant is found from New England to Georgia, westward to Alaska. **1961** Douglas *My Wilderness* 287 **nME,** The low, evergreen-like shrub known as leatherleaf (*Chamaedaphne calyculata*) was showy. **1966–68** *DARE* Wildfl QR Pl.155A Inf **MI57,** Leatherleaf—an andromeda; Pl.157A Infs **MI7, 31, MN14,** Leatherleaf. **1987** *Nature Conserv. News* 37.2.15 **IN,** 24-acre portion of large leatherleaf bog.

2 A shrub of the genus *Maytenus.*

1960 Vines *Trees SW* 664, It [=*Maytenus phyllanthoides*] is known also under the vernacular names of Leatherleaf, Mangle, . . and Aguabola. **1970** Correll *Plants TX* 999, *Maytenus texana* . . Gutta-percha, leatherleaf, mangle duce.

3 =**false nettle.**

1968 *DARE* Wildfl. QR Pl.45 Inf **NY91,** Leatherleaf.

4 See **leather fern 1**

5 See **leather fern 3.**

leatherleaf ash n

=**velvet ash.**

1897 Sudworth *Arborescent Flora* 326, *Fraxinus velutina.* . . Leather-leaf Ash. **1923** Davidson–Moxley *Flora S. CA* 275, *Fraxinus coriacea.* . . Leather-leaf Ash. **1931** U.S. Dept. Ag. *Misc. Pub.* 101.137, *Leatherleaf ash* or desert ash . . is found from Utah to southern California and Arizona in deserts, canyons, along dry watercourses and the like in the creosote bush and sagebrush belt. **1945** Wodehouse *Hayfever Plants* 124, The desert or leatherleaf ash . . [is] distinguished principally by its thicker and leathery leaves and less pubescent branchlets. **1961** Douglas *My Wilderness* 90 **csAZ,** His stone farmhouse, set in a beautiful canyon of leather-leaf ash, western walnut, and Arizona sycamore, now looks like a tiny globe of rocks.

leatherleaf fern See **leather fern 3**

leatherleaf grape n

A **mustang grape** (here: *Vitis mustangensis*).

1920 *Torreya* 20.23, *Vitis coriacea* . . Leatherleaf, Caloosa or Florida grape. **1953** Greene-Blomquist *Flowers South* 72, Mustang-grape (*V. candicans*) of Ark., Okla., and Tex. is represented in Fla. . . by the variety *coriacea* known as leather-leaf or caloosa-grape.

leatherneck n

1 See quot. Cf **leatherhead**

1919 *DN* 5.62 **NM,** *Leather-neck,* an uncouth person. "See that boy, what a leather-neck he is!"

2 See quot.

1966 Barnes–Jensen *Dict. UT Slang* 28, *Leatherneck* . . a real roughened cowboy of many trail accomplishments.

leather oak n

A **scrub oak** (here: *Quercus durata*) native to California.

1910 Jepson *Silva CA* 219, *Quercus durata.* . . Leather Oak. Low spreading shrub with rigid branches . . ; foliage and branchlets closely wooly when young, at least minutely so in age. **1926** Essig *Insects N. Amer.* 803, From a few to many larvae [of the California gallfly] inhabit the galls. The hosts are blue, scrub and leather oaks. **1961** Thomas *Flora Santa Cruz* 137 **cwCA,** *Q[uercus] durata.* . . Leather Oak. **1976** Bailey–Bailey *Hortus Third* 933, *Leather o[ak].* . . L[ea]v[e]s . . dark green above, leathery.

leather plant n

1 See quot. Cf **leather flower, leatherleaf**

1916 *DN* 4.302 **cwFL,** *Leather plant.* . . A tall flower with drooping stem bearing fruit.

2 also *leather stem:* =**sangre de draco.**

1970 Correll *Plants TX* 954, *Jatropha dioica.* . . Leather stem. . . Scarcely woody (though usually described as a shrub or woody plant); . . stems (which are perennial) thick, fleshy. . . In scrub in s. and w. Tex. **1988** Schoenhals *Span.–Engl. Gloss.* 97, "Leather plant" . . A multi-stemmed, semi-succulent bush with astringent, reddish sap.

leather pounder See **leather 1b**

leatherroot n

1 A **scurf pea** (here: *Psoralea macrostachya*). [See quot 1911]

1911 Jepson *Flora CA* 233, *P[soralea] macrostachya.* . . *Leather Root.* . . Along rivers and larger streams in the valleys, following the cañon bottoms in the mountains, and common in the salt marshes, always in the richest soils. The most common and widely distributed species of the genus, occurring both in the Coast Ranges and Sierra Nevada foothills. Roots furnishing to the Pomos and other native tribes a very tough fibre. **1923** Davidson–Moxley *Flora S. CA* 200, *H[oita] macrostachya.* . . Leather-root, the Hoita of the Indian, widely distributed along streams and wet meadows throughout the Transition Zone. **1961** Thomas *Flora Santa Cruz* 211 **cwCA,** *P[soralea] macrostachya.* . . California Hemp, Leather Root.

2 A **burdock 1.**

1968 *DARE* (Qu. S15, . . *Weed seeds that cling to clothing*) Inf **VA**24, Leatherroot = dog tick = beggar lice.

leatherside minnow n Also *leatherside (chub), leather-sided minnow* **esp UT**

A **minnow B1** (here: *Gila copei*).

1882 U.S. Natl. Museum *Bulletin* 16.234 **UT**, *S[qualius] taenia*. . . Leather-sided Minnow. . . Salt Lake Basin; abundant in Provo River. **1889** *Century Dict.* 3393, *Leatherside*. . . A small cyprinoid fish, the leather-sided minnow, *Tigoma tænia*, used in Utah as a bait for catching white-fish, or mountain herring, *Coregonus williamsoni*. **1963** Sigler–Miller *Fishes UT* 74, *Gila copei* . . Common Names: Leatherside chub, leatherside minnow. . . This species is an excellent bait minnow and has been used for this purpose in Wyoming and also in the lower Colorado River. . . It has become established . . , evidently by way of the bait bucket, in Strawberry Reservoir. **1964** Lowe *Vertebrates* 141, Leatherside Chub. . . Now inhabits parts of the upper Colorado basin in Utah. **1991** Amer. Fisheries Soc. *Common Names Fishes* 20, *Gila copei* . . leatherside chub.

leather snake n
=**queen snake.**

1879 Smith *Catalogue Reptilia MI* 6, *Regina leberis*. . . Leather Snake. **1892** IN Dept. Geol. & Nat. Resources *Rept. for 1891* 504, *Leather-snake*. . . The color above varies from olive brown to chestnut brown. **1908** Biol. Soc. DC *Proc.* 21.89 **AR**, Leather snake. **1928** Pope–Dickinson *Amphibians* 61 **WI**, Queen Snake. . . Other common names are Striped Water Snake, Yellow-bellied Snake and Leather Snake." **1958** Conant *Reptiles & Amphibians* 122, The . . "leather snake," as it sometimes is called, likes small stony creeks and rivers, especially those abounding in crayfish, but it is by no means confined to such habitats.

leather stem See **leather plant 2**

leather tortoise See **leatherback 1**

leather turtle See **leatherback 1, 2**

leatherweed n

1 also *leatherweed croton*: A croton (here: *Croton pottsii*). Also called **chaparral tea, encinilla**

1960 Vines *Trees SW* 617, *Leather-weed Croton—Croton corymbulosus*. . . It is reported that the Indians make tea from the foliage. **1970** Correll *Plants TX* 936, *Croton Pottsii*. . . Leather-weed.

2 Prob a **virgin's bower.** Cf **leather flower**

1960 Williams *Walk Egypt* 262 **GA**, The worst thing in the world was watching Wick's field go back to woods, a cluster of blackjack oak creeping in here, a strand of leatherweed there, and everywhere love-entangling vine killing all it twined.

leatherweed croton See **leatherweed 1**

leather-winged bat n Also *leatherwing (bat), leather bat* [Cf *EDD* leather(-winged) bat (at *leather* sb. 1.(2), 1.(22)); in US, appar used to distinguish the true bat (Chiroptera) from a **bat** n[1] or a **bullbat 1** or 2] **chiefly Sth** See Map

A bat of the family Vespertilionidae, esp a pipistrelle (here: *Pipistrellus subflavus*). Also called **mouse bat, pulley bat**

1805 in 1904 Lewis *Orig. Jrls. Lewis & Clark Exped.* 2.200 **VA**, I have not seen the leather winged bat for some time. **1867** Harris *Sut Lovingood Yarns* 79 **TN**, A Yankee pedlar's soul wud hev more room in a turnip-seed tu fly roun in.[sic] than a leather-wing bat hes in a meetin-hous. **1899** Bergen *Animal Lore* 61 **neMD**, Leather-winged bat, for any of the family *Vespertilionidae*. **1899** (1912) Green *VA Folk-Speech* 259, *Leather-wing-bat*. . . The common bat, from its leathery wings. **1909** *DN* 3.344 **eAL, wGA**, *Leather-wing(ed) (bat)*. . . The common mouse bat. **1927** Boston Soc. Nat. Hist. *Proc.* 38.271 **Okefenokee GA**, The residents of the region scarcely distinguish between the various local species of Chiroptera, referring to most of them simply as 'bats,' or 'leather-winged bats.' **1950** *PADS* 14.17 **SC**, *Bullbat:* . . The Florida nighthawk . . ; the common leather-winged bat. **1965–70** *DARE* (Qu. Q3, . . *Birds that come out only after dark*) 10 Infs, **chiefly Sth**, Leatherwing bat; **DE**3, Leather-winged bat; **NJ**67, Leather(wing) bat. [8 of 12 Infs also gave the response *bull bat* to this question.] **1976** Ryland *Richmond Co. VA* 373, *Leatherwing bat*—the common bat. **1986** Pederson *LAGS Concordance*, 1 inf, **cnGA**, Leather-winged bat (same variety as pulley bat).

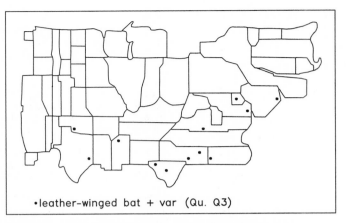

•leather-winged bat + var (Qu. Q3)

leatherwing mosquito hawk See **mosquito hawk 2d**

leatherwood n

1 also *leatherbark, leather bush*: A plant of the genus *Dirca*, usu *D. palustris*. For other names of this sp see **Indian wicopy 1, leaverwood 2, moosewood 2, ropebark, swampwood, thong bark, wicopy**

1743 (1946) Gronovius *Flora Virginica* 155, Thymelæa floribus albis, primo vere erumpentibus: foliis oblongis acuminatis: viminibus & cortice valde tenacibus, unde *Leather-wood* appellatur. [=Thymelæa with white flowers, blooming in early spring; leaves oblong and pointed; the twigs and bark very tough, whence it is called *leatherwood*.] **1787** in 1793 Amer. Acad. Arts & Sci. *Memoirs* 2.1.159, Leather Wood Bushes. Leather Wood bark is an excellent substitute for cord . . : it grows only in low and very rich lands. **1837** Darlington *Flora Cestrica* 243, The pliable branches of this shrub are so strong and tough that they may be used as ligatures;—whence the common name, *Leatherwood*. **1859** (1968) Bartlett *Americanisms* 239, *Leather-Wood. (Dirca palustris.)* A small shrub with flexible branches and a tough, leathery bark, which grows in woods in the Northern States. **1887** Eggleston *Graysons* 157 **cIL**, Bob now went out and down to the brookside, where he cut up and stripped three or four leatherwood bushes. **1900** Lyons *Plant Names* 138, *D. palustris*. . . Leather-wood, Leather-bush. **1940** Clute *Amer. Plant Names* 95, *D[irca] palustris*. Leatherwood. *Ibid* 258, Leatherbark, swamp-wood. **1942** Tehon *Fieldbook IL Shrubs* 206, Dirca [spp] . . The Leatherwoods. **1969** *DARE* FW Addit **KY**39, Leatherwood—bark used as thongs for leather substitute; **KY**41, Leatherwood—stems and inner bark of this shrub used to be used as thongs in place of leather. **1976** Bailey–Bailey *Hortus Third* 391, *Dirca*. . . *Leatherwood*. . . Two spp., one in e. U.S., the other in Calif.

2 also *mountain leatherwood*: A **flannel bush** (here: *Fremontodendron californicum*).

1897 Parsons *Wild Flowers CA* 160, *Fremontia Californica*. . . Among the mountaineers it is generally known as "leatherwood." **1908** Sudworth *Forest Trees Pacific* 382, *Fremontodendron californicum*. . . is also called . . "leatherwood," because of its tough twigs and bark. **1979** Little *Checklist U.S. Trees* 138, *Fremontodendron californicum*. . . California flannelbush, mountain leatherwood.

3 also *southern leatherwood, swamp* ~: =**he-huckleberry 1.**

1897 Sudworth *Arborescent Flora* 277 **AL, FL**, *Cyrilla racemiflora*. . . Leatherwood. **1911** *Century Dict. Suppl., Leatherwood*. . . In the southeastern United States, *Cyrilla racemiflora*, a bush or small, wide-spreading tree. . . More often called *ironwood* and sometimes *he-huckleberry*. . . Sometimes called *Southern leatherwood*. **1976** Bruce *How to Grow Wildflowers* 148, A shrub native to the Coastal Plain from Virginia to Florida which is surprisingly hardy, valuable for late summer bloom, and of surpassing botanical interest is the Swamp Cyrilla or Leatherwood, *Cyrilla racemiflora*. **1979** Little *Checklist U.S. Trees* 122, Leatherwood, swamp leatherwood, southern leatherwood.

‡**leathery ice** n Cf **bendy leather**
=**rubber ice.**

1969 *DARE* (Qu. B35, *Ice that will bend when you step on it, but not break*) Inf **IN**69, Leathery ice.

leathery turtle See **leatherback 2**

leave v
A Forms.

325

1 pres (exc 3rd pers sg): usu *leave;* infreq *leaves;* pronc-spp **chiefly Sth** *esp freq among Black speakers,* leab(e), leaf, lef(f) (cf Pronc Intro 3.I.15, 17); for addit varr see quots.

1823 Cooper *Pioneers* 1.246 **cNY** [Black], Leab it to Massa Jone—leab it to lady. **1853** Simms *Sword & Distaff* 200 **SC** [Black], Leff it to me to hab 'em ready for eat. **1867** Allen *Slave Songs* xxxi **SC,** Very commonly, in verbs which have strong conjugations, the forms of the past tense are used for the present; "What make you leff we." **1883** (1971) Harris *Nights with Remus* 346 **GA** [Black], "You min' dem lil one well, me luf you be." Da ole 'Gator gone 'way; 'e luf da lil boy Bear fer min' 'e chillun. *Ibid* 347, 'E no leaf 'e head, 'e no leaf 'e tail; 'e yent leaf nuttin' 't all. **1884** Lanier *Poems* 178 **Sth** (as of 1875), Den, Lord, please take ole Jim, and lef young Dinah hyar below! **1888** Jones *Negro Myths* 32 **GA coast** [Gullah], Eh cant tek one an leff tarruh [=the other]. *Ibid* 52, Dem all gree fuh leff. Dem did leff. **1899** Chesnutt *Conjure Woman* 45 **csNC** [Black], I got ter go off en [=and] leab you. *Ibid* 208 [Black], Ef you leabe it layin' roun'. **1922** Gonzales *Black Border* 310 **sSC, GA coasts** [Gullah glossary], *Leabe . .* leave, leaves, left, leaving. . . *Lef'*—leave, leaves, left, leaving. **1927** *AmSp* 3.168 **SW** [Cowboy speech], Moving fast is "foggin'," "leffin' here," "sailin' away," "draggin' 'is navel in the sand," or "goin' like the heel flies are after 'im." **1930** Stoney–Shelby *Black Genesis* 132 **seSC,** I'll lef' 'em right here handy. **1956** Eliason *Tarheel Talk* 221 **NC,** In the following spellings [from 1856] a post-vocalic glide seems clear: *lieav* for *leave . .* This pronunciation is still current in North Carolina, but I hear it only occasionally. **1986** Pederson *LAGS Concordance,* 1 inf, **cLA,** You leaves.

2 pres 3rd pers sg: usu *leaves;* also *esp freq among Black speakers,* leave; pronc-sp lebe.

1942 *Sat. Eve. Post* 3 Oct 68 **sSC** [Gullah], Dis train lebe for Glory. **1986** Pederson *LAGS Concordance,* 1 inf, **csTN,** Your husband leave you; 1 inf, **csGA,** She just going over some of the rooms and leave the rest. [Both infs Black]

3 past, past pple: usu *left;* also *leave;* pronc-spp *esp Sth esp freq among Black speakers,* leabe, lef(f).

1838 (1852) Gilman *S. Matron* 127, "Miss Neely, if Maus Lewis tak two piece of cake, he an't lef enough for sarve all." **1867** Harris *Sut Lovingood Yarns* 34 **TN,** I . . felt like my bones were all what lef the shut [=shirt]. **1883** [see **A1** above]. **1888** Jones *Negro Myths* 21 **GA coast** [Gullah], De ole man . . leff eh dog der wood, an eh lean fur home. **1922** [see **A1** above]. **1942** Faulkner *Go Down* 70 **MS** [Black], I lef the next day. **1986** Pederson *LAGS Concordance,* 1 inf, **seLA,** He leave him have it.

B Senses.

1 To let; to allow, permit (someone or something) to—usu foll by bare infin, but sometimes with ellipsis of infin. [Cf quot 1916; some quots are doubtless infl by Ger use] Cf **leave out 2, let** v C

1865 in 1983 *PADS* 70.40 **ce,sePA,** Were ordered to . . proceed on our march, which we did but not without blessing the officers that would not leave us worn out soldiers rest. **1887** Amer. Philol. Assoc. *Trans. for 1886* 17.40 **Sth,** Lef' be, for 'let be,' *or* 'let alone.' **1901** *DN* 2.143 **seIA, ceNY,** Leave . . Let, allow, as in "leave me go," "mother won't leave me." **1916** *DN* 4.325 **KS,** Leave . . To let: used esp. by persons of Pennsylvania German antecedents and in less degree in general by nearly all of German extraction,—a confusion consequent on the German word *lassen,* which means both 'let' and 'leave.'. . "He won't leave me go." "Throw that piece down and leave it lay there." **1927** *AmSp* 2.359 **WV,** Leave that rest a bit . . , let the matter alone for a while. **1931** (1991) Hughes–Hurston *Mule Bone* 132 **cFL** [Black], Leave de man talk! **1935** *AmSp* 10.168 **sePA,** The untutored Pennsylvania German uses the two English words [=*leave* and *let*] but frequently with the meanings reversed. Examples are: From that time I left cats go their way. . . Don't leave that man on [the bus] (keep him off)! . . The man wanted to kiss the girl, but she hadn't left him yet. **1937** *AmSp* 12.205 **sePA,** 'Rutchies' pavement,' and 'spritz,' for example, merit regular newspaper use, as also does, 'he left me do it.' **c1938** in 1970 Hyatt *Hoodoo* 1.63 **seVA** [Black], Leave us go to church. **1950** *WELS* **WI** (*To let something go undecided*) 1 Inf, Leave it ride; 1 Inf, Leave it rest; 1 Inf, Leave it stand that way. **1965–70** *DARE* (Qu. KK47, *Something that is left undecided or unfinished: "Perhaps we'd better just _____."*) 30 Infs, **scattered,** Leave it go (for a while *or* now); 11 Infs, **scattered,** Leave it be (for a while); 5 Infs, Leave it lay; 4 Infs, Leave it (*or* that) hang fire; **MD8, VA21,** Leave it hang; **PA94,** Leave it go at that; **MD19,** Leave it wait; **PA27,** Left it hang fire; (Qu. Y17, *When two people agree to stop fighting and not be enemies any more . .*

"I hear they _____.") Inf **TX31,** Agreed to leave bygones be bygones; (Qu. Y20, *To run fast: "You should have seen him _____!")* Inf **PA241,** Leave go; (Qu. Y51, . . *Ways of saying 'to avoid' things or people . . "He's not your kind—you'd better _____ him."*) Infs **GA44, MO3,** Leave him go; **MD20,** Leave him be; (Qu. GG35a, *To sulk or pout: "It won't do any good to _____."*) Inf **IN68,** Leave it get you down; (Qu. JJ43, *To give away a secret or tell a piece of news too soon: "He wasn't supposed to know. Somebody must have _____."*) Infs **IL61, MD28,** Left the cat out (of) the bag; (Qu. NN22b, *Expressions used to drive away children*) Inf **CA87,** Leave me be. **1966–67** *DARE* Tape **AZ4,** It was that black horse he left that fella take; **MI36,** I picked it [=a bird] up and I brought it down by the house and left it go. **1986** Pederson *LAGS Concordance* **Gulf Region,** 4 infs, Leave it (*or* them) be; 2 infs, Leave it (*or* them) lay; 1 inf, Leave it stay there; he leave [=let] him have it; 1 inf, Leave the ashcake be; 1 inf, I just left it go. **1987** Dillard *Amer. Childhood* 111 **cwPA,** One kind relative brightened our morning by mentioning why she'd brought her son to visit: "He wanted to come with me, so I left him."

2 in phr *leave go of:* To relax one's hold on, let go of.

1912 *DN* 3.568 **cNY,** Leave go of . . let go. "Leave go of me."

3 with *on:* To let on, pretend.

1967 *DARE* (Qu. JJ46, . . *To pretend: "Let's _____ we don't know a thing about it."*) Inf **PA15,** Let on; leave on—sometimes.

leave n[1] Usu |liv|; also **chiefly Sth, S Midl** |lif| Pronc-spp *leaf, lief*

A Forms.

1843 (1916) Hall *New Purchase* 355 **IN,** 'Leftenint! . . gimme leaf to kill that red devil ahind the log . . !' 'My brave fellow. . I daren't give you leave—I mustn't *see* you go.' **1892** *DN* 1.239 **cwMO,** *Lief.* Children on the street (Kansas City) in time of snowballs cry to the passers, "Give me a lief?" = "permission to throw at you." [*DN* Ed: Common in Michigan in similar cases. . . Also in New England.] **1893** Shands *MS Speech* 33, Give me a lief . . *allow me to.* . . generally employed as equivalent to *give me permission.* . . This use of *lief* is . . merely a corruption of *leave.* **1905** *DN* 3.13 **cCT,** *Lief.* . . Permission. 'Give me lief to go.' **1905** *DN* 3.102 **nwAR,** Abnormal consonants . . [lif] (give me leave). **1906** *DN* 3.120 **sIN,** *Leaf.* . . Permission. "Give me leaf to throw." *Ibid* 144 **nwAR,** *Leaf.* . . "Give me (a) leaf?" **1909** *DN* 3.344 **eAL, wGA,** *Leaf, lief.* . . Leave, permission. **1911** *DN* 3.545 **NE,** *Leaf, lief.* . . Permission. **1915–23** in 1944 *ADD* **cNY,** [lif], 'Give us a lief [to throw a snowball at you]?' Usual. Always with *a.* **1937** (1963) Hyatt *Kiverlid* 50 **KY,** I'd never give lief. **1941** in 1944 *ADD* 357 **nWV,** Gi' me a lief! **1945** FWP *Lay My Burden Down* 108 **AR** (as of 1865), "I wants to bless you and hope you always is happy and tell you you got all the right and lief that any white people got," the man say, and then he git on his hoss and ride off. **1946** *PADS* 6.19 **eNC** (as of 1900–10), *Leaf.* . . Permission; reward. **c1960** Wilson *Coll.* **csKY,** *Lief.* . . Permission. **1974** *AmSp* 49.63 **swME** (as of c1900), *Lief.* . . Permission "I'll do it by your lief."

B Sense.

See **leave-over 1.**

leave n[2] See **leaf** n[1]

leave adv See **lief** adv

leave alone conj [Cf **leave** v **A1, B1**]
To say nothing of; not to mention.

1942 Faulkner *Go Down* 139 **MS** [Black], You's de onliest least thing whut ever kep up wid me one day, leff alone fo weeks.

leave between two days v phr
See quot 1916.

1916 *DN* 4.325 **KS,** Leave between two days. . . To leave a community in bad repute;—literally, at night. "Whether he was afraid of prosecution, or in debt, I don't know, but he left between two days." **1927** *AmSp* 2.359 **swWV,** Leave between two days . . to leave unexpectedly, with the implication of disgrace. "Our teacher had to leave between two days." **1929** *AmSp* 5.128 **ME,** He left between two days.

leave go of See **leave** v **B2**

leaven v [*leave,* prob infl by Ger *lassen* to let, leave]
=**leave** v **B1.**

1907 *German Amer. Annals* 9.380 **sePA,** *Leaven.* . . Allow; let. "Leaven me see your book."

leave off v phr

1 To avoid; to refrain from dealing with; to postpone. **chiefly Sth, S Midl** See Map Note: *leave off* + vbl n is std and not treated here.

1845 in 1956 Eliason *Tarheel Talk* 142 **NC**, I wish cousin grissy had lefft her wedden off until we had went home. **1965–70** *DARE* (Qu. Y51, . . *Ways of saying 'to avoid' things or people* . . *"He's not your kind—you'd better _____ him."*) Infs **GA**73, **NJ**69, **NC**62, **SC**7, 24, Leave him off; (Qu. KK47, *Something that is left undecided or unfinished: "Perhaps we'd better just _____."*) Infs **FL**6, **KY**47, **MS**21, **MO**22, **SC**24, **VA**69, Leave it off (for now).

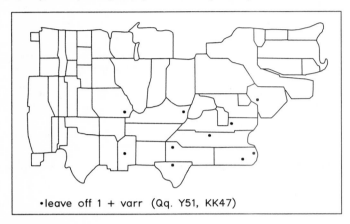

•leave off 1 + varr (Qq. Y51, KK47)

2 =**leave out 1.**
1973 *DARE* File **swPA**, Leave off. . . Depart. . . Area of Pittsburgh PA.

leave on See **leave** v **B3**

leave out v phr

1 also *leave (on) out of*: To depart; to depart from. **Sth, S Midl** Cf **lean** v **B1**
1917 in 1944 *ADD* **sWV**, He left out yesterday. **1938** *AmSp* 13.6 **seAR**, Leave out. . . To go; to leave. 'I'm going to leave out on the bus.' **1939** *Hall Coll.* **eTN**, Leave out. . . To leave, depart. "They left out of here." **1943** Writers' Program NC *Bundle of Troubles* 115, She begged Jim to marry her, and they could leave out, and go sommers else to live. **1944** *AmSp* 19.110, [Among sailors] there are traditional misuses . . you always *leave out*. Ibid 156 **IN**, Leave out, to (to leave). 'The bus leaves out in twenty minutes.' **1944** *PADS* 2.9 **AL, NC, SC, TN, VA**, *Leave out of here.* . . To get out, leave. **1945** FWP *Lay My Burden Down* 114 **LA** (as of c1865) [Black], Next day the whole bunch leave on out of that part. **1955** Ritchie *Singing Family* 73 **seKY**, Then they finally all left out, and Katty flaxed about . . blowing out lights . . to save waste. **1959** Lomax *Rainbow Sign* 26 **AL** [Black], She wouldn't leave out the neighborhood; she'd just be gone from home. **1964** Will *Hist. Okeechobee* 300 **FL**, No longer do the farmers leave out when the storm flags are hoisted now. **1965–70** *DARE* (Qu. Y18, *To leave in a hurry: "Before they find this out, we'd better _____!"*) Infs **KY**84, **MS**63, **NC**37, **TX**5, Leave out; (Qu. Y19, *To begin to go away from a place: "It's about time for me to _____."*) Infs **KY**19, 28, 42, Leave out [FWs: used by Infs in conv]. **1966–69** *DARE* Tape **KY**28, What my grandmother said . . about them wolves when they left out of here; **OK**25, Then when we left out, why the volunteer and regulars would call in on this recorder; **TX**69, We left out early then Monday morning. **1972** Davis *Culture Class & Lang. Variety* 210 **swTN** [Black], Only time I left out was when it was intermission. **1986** Pederson *LAGS Concordance* **Gulf Region**, 2 infs, Leave out—depart; 1 inf, It would leave out; 1 inf, Every so many years they [=eels]'d leave out; 1 inf, Leaving out—moving away; 1 inf, Leaving out—leaving; going out; 1 inf, Left out—went away; 1 inf, Left out—moved away; he just left out—went away suddenly; 1 inf, We left out from there; 1 inf, I left out; 1 inf, The colored came in, and the whites left out. **1990** *DARE* File, [Country music singer introducing a song:] A fallin' out between a boy and a girl . . she says she's leavin' out, and he says, "See if I care."

2 Of school: to let out, be dismissed. [See quot 1949] **chiefly Ger settlement areas, esp PA** Cf **leave** v **B1**
1935 *AmSp* 10.168 **sePA**, The untutored Pennsylvania German uses the two English words [=*leave* and *let*] but frequently with the mean-

ings reversed. . . [For example:] It happened just after school had left out. **1949** Kurath *Word Geog.* 33 **PA**, *School leaves out* . . instead of *lets out*, is the usual expression in common speech from the Delaware to the Allegheny River. The western-most part of the state does not have it, and it is less general west of the Alleghenies than farther east. The expression is not used on Delaware Bay. The confusion in the application of *let* and *leave* to render German *lassen* suggests that *leaves* has a Pennsylvania German background in this expression. The geographic distribution confirms this suspicion. *Ibid* 79, Pennsylvania has the local expression *leaves out*, which is used by the common people, often beside *lets out*, all the way from the Delaware to the Allegheny River, especially in the Pennsylvania German centers. **1967** Faries *Word Geog. MO* 119 **MO**, *School Lets Out.* . . Of the eleven occurrences of *leaves out*, a Pennsylvania term, nine occur in the St. Louis vicinity, a German settlement area. **1977–78** Foster *Lexical Variation* 60 **NJ**, The Closing of School. . . The Pennsylvania *leaves out* is recorded once, from an elderly woman in Essex County. **1985** *AmSp* 60.233 **sePA**, (School) . . *lets out* 47%, *closes* 23%, *leaves out* 17%, *gets out* 10%, other repsonses [sic] *[is out, is done]* 3%. **1986** Pederson *LAGS Concordance* **seLA** (School) 1 inf, Leaves out; 1 inf, It would leave out. **1990** *DARE* File **csPA** (as of c1960), School leaves out at 3:30.

leave out of See **leave out 1**

leave-over n

1 also *leave*: A layover; see quot.
1969 *DARE* (Qu. N38, *On a trip when you have to change trains and wait a while between them* . . *"I have a two-hour _____ in Chicago."*) Inf **NY**156, Leave; **NY**198, Leave-over.

2 A leftover.
1986 Pederson *LAGS Concordance* (*Of food cooked and served a second time*) 1 inf, **cwTN**, We are having leave-overs.

leaverwood n Also *leverwood* [Varr of *leatherwood*]
A **leatherwood 1** (here: *Dirca palustris*).
1876 Hobbs *Bot. Hdbk.* 63, Leaver-wood, Leatherwood, Dirca palustris. **1900** Lyons *Plant Names* 138, D[irca] palustris. . . Leaver-wood, Lever-wood. **1940** Clute *Amer. Plant Names* 95, D[irca] palustris. . . Leatherwood. . . leather-bush, leaver-wood.

leaves See **leave** v **A1**

‡**leavesdrop** v Pronc-sp *leavesdrap* [Folk-etym for *eavesdrop*] Cf **leave trough**
1924 (1946) Greer-Petrie *Angeline Gits an Eyeful* 8 **csKY**, Hit wan't our intinshun to *leavesdrop* the old lady, but we kept on a-hearin' a strange voice in thar.

leave trough n [Prob folk-etym for *eave trough* (at **eaves trough**)]
1968 *DARE* (Qu. D28, *What hangs below the edge of the roof to carry off rain-water?*) Inf **IN**27, Leave troughs; **MO**9, Leave troths.

lebe See **leave** v **A2**

lebem, leben, leb'm, lebun See **eleven**

lebkuchen n [Ger] **esp in Ger settlement areas**
A spicy cookie or cake often made with honey, citrus peel and nuts.
1906 *Country Life* Dec 164, We drank his health in wine, with Lebkuchen. **1909** (1910) *WNID*, Lebkuchen . . pl. -*kuchen*. . . A cake of flour and honey or sirup, variously flavored; also, a kind of gingerbread. **1920** Kander *Settlement Cook Book* 434 **Milwaukee WI**, Lebkuchen . . eggs . . brown sugar . . cinnamon . . citron . . almonds. **1938** Hark *Hex* 187, Then, there are . . *lebkuchen* (spice cakes), and chocolate drops, and nut kisses. **1940** Brown *Amer. Cooks* 521 **NE**, *Gute Lebkuchen* (good German Honey Cakes). *Ibid* 670 **OH**, Lebkuchen should ripen in cakebox at least 1 day before using. **1948** *AmSp* 23.107 **swIL**, German names having to do with foods and cooking are sufficiently numerous in the local vocabulary to give a decided German atmosphere. . . frequently heard . . *lebkuchen*. **1948** *Chi. Tribune* 12 Dec. (Grafic Mag.) 22 (*DA*), These Christmas cookies are: rum balls, lebkuchen, cherry queens, sandbakkels, pecan patty cakes. **1948** Hutchison *PA Du. Cook Book* 166, *Lebkuchen* . . This recipe comes from an old German cookbook. . . Lebkuchen, literally translated, could be "honey cakes." These are traditional Bethlehem Christmas cookies. **1949** (1986) Leonard *Jewish Cookery* 298, Lebkuchen. **1950** Klees *PA Dutch* 420, The *Lebkuchen* is another great favorite. This is a satisfying tasty, chewy cooky to which citron gives a distinctive flavor. **1981** Hachten *Flavor WI* 297, Ione . . remembered that her grandmother stored the *Lebkuchen* in stone crocks with a plate on top.

lechillo n [MexSpan]
=**hornbeam 1.**

1970 Correll *Plants TX* 463, *Carpinus caroliniana.* . . American hornbeam, blue-beech, lechillo. **1979** Little *Checklist U.S. Trees* 71, *Carpinus caroliniana.* . . American hornbeam. . . Other common names—blue beech . . lechillo (Spanish).

lechuguilla n Also *lechugilla, letchugia* [MexSpan *lechuguilla*] **SW, esp TX**

An **agave**, usu *Agave lecheguilla.* For other names of this sp see **amole 1c, dagger grass**

1834 (1847) Lundy *Life & Travels* 96 **TX**, It [=istle] consists of the fibres of a plant, called "*letchugia.*" **1844** Gregg *Commerce* 2.78 **TX**, One of the most useful plants to the people of El Paso is the *lechuguilla*, which abounds on the hills and mountain sides of that vicinity. **1905** Bray *Vegetation* 4, Mr. Vernon Bailey . . estimates that the area covered by lechuguilla in Texas would exceed twenty thousand square miles. **1937** Parks *Plants TX* 16, *Agave heterocantha.* . . One of the common Lechuguillas. **1940** Writers' Program *Guide TX* 24 **cwTX**, Here rare varieties include . . the lechugilla and sotol, which served in prehistoric times as the chief weaving material of the cave dwellers, [and] are still used in making twine and other products. **1971** Green *Village Horse Doctor* 18 **cwTX** (as of 1940s), Lechuguilla. . . is a dagger-like cactus plant that grows in the high rimrock and remote regions of the hills and is seldom eaten by sheep or goats until after cold weather. **1985** Dodge *Flowers SW Deserts* 97, Many species of agave are found in various parts of the desert. . The larger species are called centuryplant or mescal . . , while the small ones are spoken of as lechuguillas (Letch-you-*ghee*-ahs).

leck(ed) See **leak** v

'lection cake See **election cake**

'lection day See **election day**

lectren n [Metath for *lectern;* cf Intro "Language Changes" I.1] Cf **modern**

1968 DARE (Qu. CC6, *The place where the preacher stands to give the sermon*) Inf **PA**134, Lectren ['lɛktrən].

lectric(al), lectricity See **electric**

led See **lid**

ledder See **letter**

ledge hawk n [See quot 1955]
=**duck hawk.**

1927 Forbush *Birds MA* 2.164, *Falco peregrinus anatum.* . . American peregrine falcon; ledge hawk. **1955** MA Audubon Soc. *Bulletin* 39.442, Peregrine falcon. . Ledge Hawk (Mass. From a favorite nesting site, "ledge" being taken to mean cliff.)

lee See **little**

leech n [Transf < *leech* bloodsucking worm (ult < *leech* physician)]

1931–33 LANE *Worksheets*, 1 inf, **nwCT**, Leech—a sponge-like bandage made of four or five chicken feathers. You put a leech into proud flesh and it works from the bottom.

leedamoren See **little more(, a)**

Leeds devil n Also *Leeds's ghost* [Prob after *Leeds Point, NJ;* but see quot 1968 McPhee] **NJ**
=**Jersey devil.**

1939 FWP *Guide NJ* 126 **cs,seNJ**, By default, the title of official State demon has rested for nearly a century with the Leeds Devil, a friendly native of Atlantic County who has traveled extensively throughout southern New Jersey. . . Cloven-hoofed, long-tailed, and white; with the head of a collie dog, the face of a horse, the body of a kangaroo, the wings of a bat, and the disposition of a lamb—that is the Leeds Devil. **1945** Beck *Jersey Genesis* 204 **NJ**, The alias of the Jersey Devil is Leeds's Ghost. **1968** McPhee *Pine Barrens* 76 **NJ**, A woman named Leeds. . had her thirteenth child, and it growed, and one day it flew away. It's haunted the earth ever since. It's took pigs right out of pens. . . The Leeds Devil is a crooked-faced thing, with wings. **1968** DARE (Qu. CC17, *Imaginary animals or monsters that people . . tell tales about*) Inf **NJ**39, Leeds devil—woman was to have unwanted baby she said: "I hope he's so ugly he looks like the devil." He did.

leef See **lief** adv

leek see **lick** v

leek-hook n
See quots.

1930 Shoemaker *1300 Words* 38 **cPA Mts** (as of c1900), *Leek-hook*—An implement worn like a spur to dig up wild leeks in Potter County, Pa. **1983** Glimm *Flatlanders* 151 **cnPA**, Now, those folks in Potter County are born with little spurs on their feet, and these spurs get bigger as they get older. They're leekhooks, you see, for digging leeks out of the ground.

leeks n Cf **houseleek 2**
=**orpine.**

1892 *Jrl. Amer. Folkl.* 5.96, *Sedum Telephium.* . . Leeks. Stowe, Vt.

leeky adj **MI, WI**
=**garlicky.**

1950 WELS (*Milk that has a taste from something the cow ate in the pasture*) 3 Infs, **WI**, Leeky. [2 Infs indicated that the word was common, 1 that it was old-fashioned.] **1966–69** DARE (Qu. K14) Infs **MI**23, 27, 98, **WI**77, Leeky; [**MI**47, Cow has been eating leeks; **MI**94, Tastes like leeks].

leely See **little**

leeman n [Prob var of **lingman**] Cf **feeble man**
The ring finger.

1950 PADS 13.17 **cTX** (as of c1920), The form [for the names of the fingers] in Runnels County was *little-man* ['lɪtlmən], *leeman, longman, lick-pot,* and *thumb-ball.*

leenter See **lean-to**

lee rows to catch meddlers See **layover(s) to catch meddlers**

leery adj

1890 DN 1.62 **swOH**, Leery . . drunk. "Looking leery."

lee set n **NEng**
See quot 1916.

1903 Wasson *Cap'n Simeon's Store* 37 **ME**, Here there's been a lee-set herming up [=clouding up] stiddy since noontime to-day. **1909** DN 3.420 **Cape Cod MA** (as of a1857), *Lea* [sic] *set.* . . A cloud which has blown over to leaward [sic]. **1916** Macy-Hussey *Nantucket Scrap Basket* 138 **seMA**, "*Lee Set*"—A low bank of clouds to leeward—sometimes presaging a storm.

leetle See **little**

lef(f) See **leave** v **A1, 3**

lefse n Usu |'lɛfsə|; for varr see quot 1965–70 Pronc-spp *lefsa, lefsi* [Norw *lefse*] **Norw settlement areas, esp MN, WI**
A thin, unleavened bread made with mashed potatoes.

1902 DN 2.258 **csWI**, In Stoughton . . the words *flat-bread* . . *lefse,* . . and *prim-ost* . . are everywhere used like native English words. Stoughton is a town of about 3500 inhabitants, two-thirds of which are Norwegians. **1934** AmSp 9.152 **ceNE**, In "Little Norway," . . *Lefsi* is . . rolled into thin sheets which are baked on top of the unwashed kitchen range. These are turned again and again until the crust is a spotted brown. **1950** WELS (*Special kinds of bread*) 2 Infs, **WI**, Lefse. **1961** Sackett-Koch *KS Folkl.* 230, Lefse. **1965–70** DARE (Qu. H18, . . *Special kinds of bread*) Inf **MN**13, Lefse—Norwegian bread; **MN**16, Lefse—a flat bread like a thin pancake; **MN**28, Lefse: **WI**53, Lefse ['lɛfsə]; **WI**76, ['lɛfsa]—some people still make it; looks like pancakes and roll up; (Qu. H45) Inf **SD**1, ['lɛfsə]—Scandinavian; (Qu. H65, *Foreign foods favored by people around here*) Infs **MN**28, **WI**71, Lefse; **ID**5, Lefse ['lɛfsə]; **IL**40, ['lɛpsɑ] [sic]; **MN**1, Lefse ['lɛfsə]—Swedish potato pancake type thing; **MN**6, Lefse is a rather leathery, flat sort of unleavened bread made from mashed potatoes; it is fried in a frying pan, comes out a bit like a leathery pancake; it is usually rolled up to eat, sprinkled with sugar, buttered; **MN**39, Lefse—Norwegian. **1966** *Stoughton Courier* (WI) 1 Dec sec 2 [12/2], Also served is lefse, a thin unleavened bread made mostly of mashed potatoes, rather than of flour. A special rolling pin is used to roll small balls of dough into this thin flat bread. These pins are grooved to give the pastry more surface for browning. Old Norwegians carved their own pins from regular rolling pins or brought them from Norway. **1968** *Cook Co. News-Herald* (Grand Marais MN) 9 May 5/5, Sytende [sic] Mai Dag . . Menu . . Parsley Buttered Potatoes—Vegetable and Salad—Lefsa, Bread and Rolls. **1984** MJLF 10.152 **cnWI**, Lefsa. A potato pancake. Norwegian. **1994** *Courier Hub* (Stoughton WI) 12 May Special marketing sec 4/1, The secret of making thin lefse is using a covered rolling pin. The last roll across dough use grooved lefse rolling pin, which marks the dough and makes it thinner. . . Spread with butter to eat. Some people sprinkle brown or white sugar on them. Roll up.

-left suff S Atl Cf **-bit**

In comb *bus-left:* Left behind by (a bus).

1967 *DARE* FW Addit **nwSC**, I got bus-left. [Used mostly by school children.] **1975** *DARE* File **neGA**, I was late to class because I was bus-left. **1995** *NADS Letters* **cGA**, After we got bus-left, the principal had to come pick us up. *Ibid* **nwNC** (as of c1960), You're gonna get bus-left. **1995** *DARE* File **cGA**, Bus-left.

left eye, over the See **left, over the**

left-foot See **left-hander**

left-handed relation n

An in-law rather than a blood relative.

1931–33 *LANE Worksheets,* 1 inf, **csCT**, Left-handed relation . . in-law. He is a left-handed relation to me.

left-handed sugar bowl n Also *left-hand sugar bowl, left-handed thunder mug*

A chamber pot.

1967–68 *DARE* (Qu. F38, *Utensil kept under the bed for use at night*) Infs **NJ3**, **NY70**, Left-hand sugar bowl; **CT2**, Left-handed sugar bowl; **CO47**, Left-handed thunder mug.

left-hander n Also *left-foot, left-legger* Cf **left-winger**

A Protestant.

1950 *WELS* (*Nicknames for different religions*) 1 Inf, **seWI**, Right-handers (Catholics); Left-handers (Lutherans). **1960** Wentworth-Flexner *Slang* 315, *Left-foot.* . . A Protestant. **1964** *PADS* 42.33 **Chicago IL**, Protestant: *lefthander.* **1968** *DARE* FW Addit **NY45**, *Left-leggers*—Catholics used to call Protestants this. **1970** *DARE* (Qu. CC4, . . *Nicknames . . for various religions or religious groups*) Inf **CA213**, Left-handers (non-Catholics).

left-hand sugar bowl See **left-handed sugar bowl**

left-legger See **left-hander**

leftment n Cf **-ment B**

A leftover, remainder.

1928 Chapman *Happy Mt.* 185 **seTN**, It was a tobacco barn, and smelled strong of it, for that the rain had leaked in from the roof upon the leftments. *Ibid* 240, After dinner Sam gave out a job of work to each and they went on with redding the new sawmill out of the heap of trash leftments from the old one.

left, over the adv phr Also *over the left shoulder,* ~ *eye*

Absolutely not; not at all—used to indicate that the speaker means the opposite of, or cancels, what has just been said.

1705 *Rec. Hartford County Court (U.S.)* 4 Sept. in *Newcastle Daily Jrnl.* 28 July 1891 *(OED),* The said Waters, as he departed from the table, he said, 'God bless you over the left shoulder'. **1897** *KS Univ. Qrly.* (ser B) 6.55, *Left,* over the: not serious. It is a children's trick to make an improbable assertion to attract attention, and then to save themselves by adding, 'over the left,' or, 'over the left shoulder.' **1905** *DN* 3.15 **cCT**, *Over the left.* . . An expression used to give to the words it accompanies a meaning directly opposite to that which they would otherwise have [known to 1 inf]. With . . [a second inf] it is *over the left eye.* **1907** *DN* 3.215 **nwAR**, *Over the left.* **1942** McAtee *Dial. Grant Co. IN* 47 (as of 1890s), *Over the left* . . saucy denial; "Yes, you will _____". **1950** *PADS* 14.44 **SC**, *Left.* . . In the phrase, *over the left,* meaning dubious, false, deceitful, said of a promise not meant to be kept, a threat that is futile on its face, a boast incapable of fulfillment. A contemptuous commentary upon anything evidently untrue. **c1960** *Wilson Coll.* **csKY**, *Left.* . . Used in sayings to indicate the exact opposite of what is said: "That's a fact, over the left."

‡left-winger n [Cf *OEDS left-footer* (at *left* a. A.4) "a Roman Catholic"] Cf **left-hander**

A Roman Catholic.

1969 *DARE* (Qu. CC4, . . *Nicknames . . for various religions or religious groups*) Inf **PA228**, Left-wingers (Catholics).

leg n Usu |lɛg|; also **scattered, but more freq Sth, S Midl** |le(ɪ)g|; occas |læg| Pronc-spp *lag, laig* Cf Pronc Intro 3.I.6.a

Std senses, var forms.

1867 Harris *Sut Lovingood Yarns* 172 **TN**, I hes the longes' par ove laigs ever hung tu eny cackus. **1884** *Anglia* 7.261 **Sth, S Midl** [Black], *To cuss a bile* [=curse a boil] *orf* (or *off*) *yo' laig* = to fly into a passion. **1891** *DN* 1.129 **cNY**, [leg]. **1892** *DN* 1.239 **cwMO**, *Leg.* Very often indeed [leg] or [leɪg] in Kansas City [*DN:* and New England. Cf. *egg, keg*]. **1895** *DN* 1.373 **seKY, eTN, wNC**, It takes a heap o' misery to git the bones out of your laig [leg]. **1899** (1912) Green *VA Folk-Speech* 254, *Laig.* . . For *leg.* **1907** White *AZ Nights* 224, The first was these low-set, heavy-weight propositions [=chickens] with feathers on their laigs . . called Cochin Chinys. **1909** *DN* 3.343 **eAL, wGA**, [leg]. *Ibid* 413 **nME**, *Leg.* . . Pronounced with a long vowel. **1917** *DN* 4.414 **IL, IA, KS, KY, NY, wNC, neOH**, *Laig.* Variant of *leg.* **1917** Garland *Son Middle Border* 364 **IA**, I'm just as lame in one laig as I am in t'other. **1923** *DN* 5.213 **swMO**, *Lag* or *laig.* **1931** *PMLA* 46.1315 **sAppalachians**, E, short, becomes highland *a* in *past,* as in "bag," v., "kag," and "lag." **1933** *AmSp* 8.2.44 **neNY**, [eɪ] is usually found in place of [ɛ] in *measure* [meɪʒər], *leg* [leɪg], *egg* [eɪg], *edge* [eɪdʒ]. **1934** *AmSp* 9.211 **Sth**, Some words with standard [ɛ] before [g] or [k] change [ɛ] to [eɪ] or [e]. This pronunciation is decidedly vulgar. . . *Beg, egg, keg . . , leg,* [etc]. **1936** Reese *Worleys* 14 **MD** (as of 1865) [Black], He got his laig shot off in de Wah. **1942** Hall *Smoky Mt. Speech* 20 **wNC, eTN**, [æ] is common . . in *beg, keg, leg* (also *bench-legged, boot-legging*). **1953** Randolph–Wilson *Down in Holler* 13 **Ozarks**, Egg and leg sound pretty much like *aig* and *laig.* **c1960** *Wilson Coll.* **csKY**, *Leg* is often /leg/. **1966–67** *DARE* FW Addit **ceLA**, *Leg* [læg] Occas. probably more often by people in the hilly part of the parish. *Ibid* **cwNC**, *Leg* [læg]. **c1970** Pederson *Dial. Surv. Rural GA,* [In southeast Georgia, *leg* is usually pronounced [leɪg], but [lɛg] also occurs, especially among Whites, and [læg] is occasional.] **1985** *Amer. Jrl. Med.* Feb 183 **eTN**, *Laig.*

leg v[1], hence vbl n *legging,* n *legger* Pronc-sp *lag* [Abbrs for *bootleg(ging), bootlegger*]

To make or distribute illegal whiskey.

1926 *Flynn's Weekly* 16 Jan 640, I sashayed for a legger an' run into a rube hip agent with a bottle and some jake which helped some. **1929** *Variety* 5 June 58, Leggers claim the tonic is as potent as a fifth of gin selling for three times the price. **1950** *WELS* (*A person who sells illegal liquor*) 1 Inf, **WI**, Legger. **1952** Callahan *Smoky Mt.* 176, The 'legger had to move. He went to Union County, where he resumed his occupation of making moonshine. **1972** Hall *Sayings Old Smoky* 92 (as of 1956), *Lag.* Short for bootleg. "I didn't 'lag myself. My business was farmin'." *Ibid* 88, (as of 1936), *Bootleggin', bootlaggin'.* . . Making bootleg (moonshine) liquor. Sometimes shortened to *'leggin',* etc. **1991** Ruff *Call to Assembly* 56 **nwAL**, Bootlegging was the center of Muscle Shoals's social commerce. . . The enormous appeal "leggin" enjoyed in our world, I always suspected, was rooted in the fact that it was so deliciously outside the law and so universally admired.

leg v[2] See **lag** v[1]

leg v[3]

?To remove the stem from.

1925 Dargan *Highland Annals* 209 **cwNC**, An' here's these gooseberries got to be legged 'fore I can git supper.

legger See **leg** v[1]

leggerstreamer See **laggerstreamer**

legging vbl n See **leg** v[1]

legging n Usu |ˌlɛgən, -ɪŋ|; occas |ˈlɛgɚn|

Std sense, var form.

1942 Hall *Smoky Mt. Speech* 95 **wNC, eTN**, Leggings [ˈlɛgɚnz] (reported). **c1960** *Wilson Coll.* **csKY**, Leggings often has an excrescent R.

leggings case n

A situation in which the punishment consists of a lashing with leggings.

1920 Hunter *Trail Drivers TX* 299 (as of 1880), After a meal, if a luckless cowboy happens to put his tin plate and cup on the chuck box lid instead of the "round pan" (a tin tub for dishes), this constitutes a "leggins case;" that is, he is laid over a barrel and treated to a dose of leggins in the hands of the most athletic cowboy.

leghorn n Pronc-spp *laycorn, legon, leg'rn*

Std sense, var forms.

1906 *DN* 3.144 **nwAR**, *Leg'rn.* . . Leghorn fowl. "Leg'rns can sure lay eggs." **1909** *DN* 3.345 **eAL, wGA**, *Legon.* . . A Leghorn fowl:

usually with a qualifying adjective, as *brown, white*. **1941** O'Donnell *Great Big Doorstep* 72 **sLA,** If I owned this piece, you'd see . . all kindsa kitchen food sprouting . . and gangs and gangs of white lay-corn hens.

legislature n Usu |ˈlɛȷɪsˌlɛčə(r)|; occas |-ˌletə(r)| Pronc-spp *leg-islatur, legislater* Cf **creature, nature**
Std sense, var forms.

1843 (1916) Hall *New Purchase* 404 **IN,** And what's more to the pint, Carltin, won't the Major go agin us next legislatur? **1891** *DN* 1.166 **cNY,** [t] is also common in words pronounced with [č] by educated people, when the [t] is older, and probably in these words originally. Examples are . . [krɪtr̩z] < *creatures* . . [lɛȷɪsletr̩] < *legislature*. **1931** *PMLA* 46.1316 **sAppalachians,** *U* (as in mon*u*ment) worries the high-lander. In this word it becomes short *i*. . . We also find: "nater" (na-ture) . . and "legislater" (legislature).

legitimate See **illegitimate**

legless lizard n
A **glass snake,** esp *Ophisaurus ventralis*.
1930 *Copeia* 2.28, *Ophisaurus ventralis*. . . Glass-snake; legless lizard. **1949** *Scientific Mth.* Jan 55, The traditional American glass snake is not, however, a true snake but rather the legless lizard *Ophisaurus ventralis*.

legon, leg'rn See **leghorn**

leh See **let A2a**

lehua See **ohia 2**

lei n |leɪ| [Haw] **chiefly HI, but more widely recognized**
A garland usu of flowers or leaves, worn on the head or around the neck.
1840 in 1934 Frear *Lowell & Abigail* 152 **HI,** Brother Armstrong is doing good in that church and congregation. Not one fourth the leis to be seen here today that there usually has been. **1911** *Mid-Pacific Mag.* 2.425 **HI,** Invariably the . . white is relieved by lei after lei of flowers of gorgeous hues that often hide the wearer. . . These leis are for friends and visitors aboard ship. **1955** Day *HI People* 301, The favorite adornment was the *lei,* a necklace or headband made of many kinds of material, which is still the symbol of love and friendship in the islands. **1967** Reinecke–Tsuzaki *Hawaiian Loanwords* 102, *Lei:* /leɪ/. . . A garland or wreath for the neck or head, generally made of flowers or leaves. Paper and silk imitations of flower wreaths are also worn, and wreaths for hats are often made of feathers. Necklaces of seeds, candy, coins, and the like are also called *leis*. **1991** Saiki *From the Lanai* 99 **HI,** They were one man and two women wearing plumeria leis, obvious tourists. **1995** *DARE* File **swCA** (as of 1978), As I got off the plane in San Diego, I was given a lei, as all passengers were as part of a promotion of tourism.

Lei Day n **HI**
May Day.
1929 in 1985 *King Benny Nawahi Hot Hawaiian Guitar* (Phonodisc), [Song title:] *May Day is Lei Day in Hawaii*. **1949** Clark *All the Best HI* 35 **HI,** *May Day is Lei Day,* in the words of a familiar song. Don Blanding originated this idea in 1928 and it has developed as a popular and beautiful pageant. Practically every individual, from governor to bus boy and from oldest kamaaina to newest malihini, wears a lei on Lei Day. . . Lei queens are chosen. **1967–68** *DARE* (Qu. FF12a, . . *The first day of May*) Inf **CA**65, Lei Day—Don Blanding's term for the Hawaiian celebration he inaugurated [FW: Inf put Mr. Blanding's verse into Braille]; **HI**1, May Day is Lei Day in Hawaii. **1968** *Jrl. Engl. Ling.* 2.82 **HI,** *Lei Day*. . . May Day in Hawaii, celebrated with pageants, *lei* exhibits, and programs of various kinds highlighting Hawaiian culture, old as well as new.

lein See **line tree** n[2]

leingister See **linguister**

l'em See **let A2b**

‡lemine v [Cf *nemine* (at **never A**)]
1909 *DN* 3.345 **eAL, wGA,** Lemine. . . Never mind, don't bother. Used when a speaker asks for something and then changes his mind. "Bring me the ax. Lemine, I don't need it now."

lemita n Also *lameta* **West** Cf **lemonade berry**
A **sumac,** esp **fragrant sumac.**
1904 *NM Ag. Exper. Station Bulletin* 51.27, Lemita. Three-Leaved Sumach. *(Rhus trilobata).* This is a many-stemmed shrub which grows

upon our dry mesas, in the rocky arroyos in the mountains, and on our ditch banks in the valley. **1931** *U.S. Dept. Ag. Misc. Pub.* 101.96, The most valuable of the sumacs from a forage viewpoint are the lemonade sumacs, sweet-sumacs, or lemitas (genus Schmaltzia of some authors), also known as lametas and three-lobed sumacs. . . Lemonade sumac, by far the commonest and most widely distributed species *(Rhus trilo-bata)* . . ranges from Alberta to Missouri, northern Mexico, and southern Oregon. **1947** (1976) Curtin *Healing Herbs* 112 **SW,** Lemita—*Rhus trilobata*. . . The leaves of the *lemita* do not possess the shiny glossiness of the poison oak's, are somewhat smaller, and release a pungent scent when bruised. **1960** Vines *Trees SW* 630, Skunk-bush Sumac—*Rhus aromatica*. . . Other vernacular names are Ill-scented Sumac . . and Lemita. **1976** Elmore *Shrubs & Trees SW* 27, Squawbush. . . lemita.

lemme See **let A2b**

lemon See **lemon-belly**

lemonade n Also *lemonade station* Cf **bum, bum, bum, where are you from; here I come; jolly, jolly butcher boy; New Orleans B; New York B2; pretty girls' station**
A children's game involving pantomime and chasing; see quot 1957.
1952 Brown *NC Folkl.* 1.62 **IN,** *Pretty Girls' Station*. . . In Indiana and, I believe, in neighboring states, the game is known as 'Lemonade.' The questions and responses are as follows: "Here we come!"/ "Where from?"/ "New York!"/ "What's your trade?"/ "Lemonade!"/ "Go to work!" **1957** *Sat. Eve. Post Letters* **MI** (as of 1918–37), New Orleans or Lemonade—As many or want can play; choose sides. One side is first: they choose an action (washing clothes; man digging worms and going fishing) and acted [sic] it out silently for the other side to guess. If the other side guessed it, they chased after the other side. If they caught anyone before they crossed their own goal line, that one had to go over to the other side. The game was played till one side had won all the other players. A little song went along with it. After you had chosen your act you started toward the other side singing: "Here we come!" "Where from?" "New Orleans!" "What's your trade?" "Lemon-ade!" "Show us some, if you're not afraid!" Then the action began. **1965–70** *DARE* (Qu. EE33, . . *Outdoor games . . that children play*) 15 Infs, **scattered,** Lemonade station [*DARE* Ed: Three Infs who said that *lemonade station* referred to selling lemonade have been omitted; some of the remaining Infs were perhaps also referring to running a lemonade stand.]; 11 Infs, **scattered,** Lemonade; **NJ**54, Lemonade—sit in a cool spot and 2 would get up and act something out; others would guess; like charades. **1966** *DARE* File **IN,** Lemonade—a type of children's game. **1988** *DARE* File **sIN** (as of c1912), We used to play "Lemonade." There were two lines of children that would advance toward each other with each line of the rhyme. We'd say, in turn, "Here I come." "Where from?" "New York 'n' Pennsylvania." "What's your trade?" "Lemon-ade." "Go to work!" Then one side would act out some kind of a job and the other side would try to guess what the job was.

lemonade berry n Also *lemonade bush, ~ sumac, ~ and sugar tree* [From its use in preparing a beverage] Cf **Indian lemon-ade, lemita**
A western **sumac,** usu *Rhus integrifolia*.
1896 *Jrl. Amer. Folkl.* 9.185, *Rhus integrifolia* . . and *rhus ovata* . . lemonade and sugar tree. . . San Diego County, Cal. **1897** Parsons *Wild Flowers CA* 204, In the mountains from Santa Barbara to San Diego is found another species—*R[hus] ovata*. . . This has large leathery, pointed leaves, and is known as "lemonade-and-sugar-tree," as the acid berries are coated with a sweet, waxen substance, which the Indians value as sugar. **1931** [see **lemita**]. **1951** Abrams *Flora Pacific States* 3.51, *Rhus integrifolia*. . . Lemonade Bush or Coast Sumac. . . Drupes very viscid and acid. **1960** Vines *Trees SW* 630, Skunk-bush Sumac—*Rhus aro-matica*. . . Other vernacular names are Ill-scented Sumac. . . Lemonade Sumac. **1974** (1977) Coon *Useful Plants* 57, Lemonade berry. . . Take a couple of cups of the berries, bruise and wash them until the juice turns a good pink color. Strain carefully, . . sweeten with sugar and chill before serving. **1980** Little *Audubon Guide N. Amer. Trees W. Region* 519, Lemonade Sumac—"Lemonade-berry" . . *Rhus integrifolia*.

lemonade station See **lemonade**

lemonade sumac See **lemonade berry**

lemon balm n Also *balm lemon* [From the scent of the leaves]
A naturalized plant *(Melissa officinalis)* of the eastern US and parts of California. Also called **balm B1a, beebalm 2, cure-**

all 3, dropsy plant, garden balm, honey plant, lemon lobelia, ~ verbena 2, sweet Mary

    1873 in 1976 Miller *Shaker Herbs* 131, Lemon Balm. . . *Melissa officinalis.* **1876** Hobbs *Bot. Hdbk.* 29, Cureall, Balm lemon, Melissa officinalis. *Ibid* 32, Dropsy plant, Balm lemon. **1894** *Jrl. Amer. Folkl.* 7.96 **NEng,** *Melissa officinalis* . . lemon-balm . . lemon lobelia (pronounced lobely). **1930** Sievers *Amer. Med. Plants* 8, Lemon balm, . . lemon lobelia. . . The plant is lemon scented. **1953** Piercy *Shaker Cook Book* 33 **csNH,** Lemon balm . . was widely cultivated as a garden herb and bee plant. Its leaves give off a lemony, minty aroma. **1972** GA Dept. Ag. *Farmers Market Bulletin* 58.42.8, *What Is Lemon Balm?* A hardy perennial which reaches a height of from one and a half to two feet, lemon balm has broad, dark-green leaves with a faint lemon flavor. **1974** (1977) Coon *Useful Plants* 160, *Melissa officinalis* . . lemon balm.

lemon beebalm See **lemon mint 1**

lemon-belly n Also *lemon (crab)* [From the yellow color of the egg mass attached to the underside of the female blue crab] **Chesapeake Bay** Cf **orange crab**

=**bally** n[1].

    1968 *DARE* FW Addit **MD**43, *Lemon-belly*—mother crab about to spawn. **1970** *DARE* Tape **VA**112, Did you see the lemon crabs . . the ones with the lemon underneath of 'em, real yellow? **1976** Warner *Beautiful Swimmers* 143 **eMD,** In addition to sponges, the egg-heavy females [=of *Callinectes sapidus*] are variously known as "lemon bellies," . . and "punks." **1984** *DARE* File **Chesapeake Bay** [Watermen's vocabulary], Spong [sic] crab, brood crab, cushion crab, lemon, orange crab—all terms for an egg-laden female crab.

lemon butter n Also *lemon cheese*

Lemon curd.

    1853 (1982) Lea *Domestic Cookery* 136 **MD,** *Lemon Butter or French Honey.*—Take half a pound of butter, melt it in an earthen dish and squeeze in the juice of six lemons; beat twelve eggs with two pounds of brown sugar, stir it in with the rind of two lemons grated, mix it all together, and let it boil twenty minutes, when it will be about the consistency of honey; the flavor is agreeable, and it may be eaten on bread, or as a sauce for boiled pudding. **1882** F. Owens *Cook Book* 265 (*DA*), *Lemon Butter.* Use as sauce, filling for tarts, or as jelly for layer cake. **1940** Brown *Amer. Cooks* 98 **DE,** Lemon butter is still in demand in Delaware and once was considered a supper delicacy in many states, especially in New Jersey. In England it was known as "lemon cream." *Ibid* 570 **NJ,** *Lemon Butter*—Put grated lemon, water, sugar, and butter into a saucepan and let come to a boil. Stir beaten eggs into boiling liquid, stir carefully to prevent butter from burning until it thickens, then remove and cool. **1968** *DARE* (Qu. H57, *Tasty or spicy side-dishes served with meats*) Inf **NJ**15, Lemon butter. **1982** Weaver *Quaker Woman's Cookbook* xliii, Among the Quakers, apple butter was acculturated from the Germans at a very early date, but it was generally called cider cheese in local dialect—a cheese being any sort of food thickened or partially dehydrated by slow cooking or pressing, as in the case of cream cheese . . , head cheese, and lemon cheese (also called lemon butter).

lemon crab See **lemon-belly**

lemon-eater See **lemon-pelter**

lemonfish n esp **LA**

=**cobia.**

    1933 LA Dept. of Conserv. *Fishes* 197, The Cobia, *Rachycentron canadus* . . is invariably known in Louisiana as the Ling or Lemon Fish. **1946** LaMonte *N. Amer. Game Fishes* 44, Cobia—*Rachycentron canadus.* . . Lemonfish. **1967** LeCompte *Word Atlas* 213 **seLA,** *Name the different types of edible salt water fish.* . . lemon [4 of 21 infs]. **1968** *DARE* (Qu. P2, . . *Kinds of saltwater fish caught around here . . good to eat*) Inf **LA**37, Lemonfish is cobia. **1968** *DARE* FW Addit **swLA,** *Lemonfish*—South Louisiana term for the fish usually called cobia in books. **1986** Pederson *LAGS Concordance* **Gulf Region,** 3 infs, Lemonfish; 1 inf, Lemonfish—cobia; crabeater; between shark and catfish.

lemon horsemint See **lemon mint 1**

lemon lily n [From the yellow color of the flower]

1 A day lily 1 (here: *Hemerocallis fulva*).

    1897 *Jrl. Amer. Folkl.* 10.145, *Hemerocallis flava* . . lemon lily, Sulphur Grove, Ohio. **1911** *Century Dict. Suppl., Lily.* . . *Lemon-lily,* the day-lily, *Hemerocallis fulva.* **1966** *DARE* Wildfl QR Pl. 12 Inf **OH**14, Lemon lily or day lily. **1968** *DARE* Tape **IN**14, I like the flowers that put out and come up every year. I do have a lemon lily and an orange

lily. **1994** *DARE* File **cOH** (as of c1960), My mother used to grow lemon lilies in the back garden. They were day lilies, bright yellow, with no stripes. *Ibid* **nwMA** (as of 1960s–70s), Yellow day lilies were called lemon lilies.

2 A lily (*Lilium parryi*) native to southern California and Arizona.

    1897 Parsons *Wild Flowers CA* 103, *L[ilium] Parryi* . . is found in the San Bernardino Mountains. This is known as the "lemon lily," and has clear yellow flowers. **1911** Jepson *Flora CA* 95, *L[ilium] parryi.* . . Lemon Lily . . flowers clear lemon yellow. **1915** (1926) Armstrong–Thornber *Western Wild Flowers* 34, *L[ilium] Parryi,* the Lemon Lily, of southern California and Arizona. **1949** Moldenke *Amer. Wild Flowers* 325, In the Southwest, in moist situations on the higher mountains of southern California and Arizona, one meets the lovely *lemon lily, L[ilium] parryi,* with fragrant, clear lemon-yellow flowers, sparingly dotted with minute, purple-black spots. **1976** Bailey–Bailey *Hortus Third* 663, *[Lilium] Parryi.* . . Lemon lily.

lemon lobelia n

=lemon balm.

    1894 [see **lemon balm**]. **1930** [see **lemon balm**]. **1940** Clute *Amer. Plant Names* 264, *Melissa officinalis.* . . lemon lobelia, cure-all.

lemon mint n [From the scent of the leaves]

1 also *lemon beebalm, ~ horsemint:* =**horsemint 1,** esp *Monarda citriodora.* **esp Plains States, SW**

    1930 OK Univ. Biol. Surv. *Pub.* 2.78, *Monarda citriodora.* . . Lemon Mint. **1932** Rydberg *Flora Prairies* 691, *Monarda.* . . Lemon Mint. *Ibid* 692, *M. pectinata.* . . Lemon Mint. Plains, especially in sandy soil. **1937** U.S. Forest Serv. *Range Plant Hdbk.* W132, Beebalms (*Monarda* spp.) . . Other names applied to species of *Monarda* are lemon-mint and wildbergamot, the latter being employed chiefly in the East. **1949** Moldenke *Amer. Wild Flowers* 295, On the dry plains from Nebraska and Colorado to Texas and Arizona, it [=common horsemint] is replaced by the plains lemonmint, *M[onarda] pectinata.* . . The purple lemonmint, *M[onarda] dispersa,* is often found in tremendous colonies on low plains and prairies. **1967** *DARE* Wildfl QR (Wills–Irwin) Pl.43B.1 Inf **TX**44, Lemon horsemint. **1970** Correll *Plants TX* 1372, *Monarda citriodora* . . Lemon beebalm, Lemon-mint. **1972** Brown *Wildflowers LA* 157, Lemon Beebalm—*Monarda citriodora.* . . Widely distributed in Louisiana but not common. Also Texas and Mississippi. **1990** *Plants SW* (Catalog) 30, *Monarda citriodora*—Lemon Mint. . . A wonderful scent of lemons to the foliage.

2 A pennyroyal (here: *Hedeoma* spp); see quots.

    1936 Whitehouse *TX Flowers* 121, Prairie pennyroyal. Lemon Mint. Mexican Tea (*Hedeoma drummondii*) is a low perennial plant characterized by the lemon-like odor of the foliage. **1939** Tharp *Vegetation TX* 67, Lemon mint (*Hedeoma*); all regions.

lemonneck See **limberneck**

lemon nut See **lemon walnut**

lemon-pelter n Also *lemon-eater, ~-sucker*

An English person.

    1968 *DARE* (Qu. HH28, *Names and nicknames . . for people of foreign background*) Inf **NY**66, Limey; Lemon-pelter. **1983** Allen *Lang. Ethnic Conflict* 55, *English.* . . *lime-juicer* [Allen: 1880s. From the lime juice historically served on British ships. Also *lime-juice, lemon-eater, lemon-sucker*].

lemon-scent n esp **Plains States** Cf **fetid marigold 2, headache weed 1**

A chinchweed (here: *Pectis angustifolia*).

    1932 Rydberg *Flora Prairies* 860, Lemon-scent. . . *P[ectis] angustifolia.* **1940** Gates *Flora KS* 239, *Pectis angustifolia.* . . Lemonscent. Sandy soils of plains. **1968** Barkley *Plants KS* 367, *Pectis angustifolia.* . . Lemon-scent. Pectis.

lemon sole n

1 An **English sole** (here: *Pleuronectes vetulus*). Also called **flounder** n B, **sole**

    1953 Roedel *Common Fishes CA* 62, English Sole—*Parophrys vetulus.* . . Unauthorized Names: Common sole, California sole, lemon sole. **1973** Knight *Cook's Fish Guide* 391, Lemon sole—English [sole] or see Flounder, Winter. **1991** Amer. Fisheries Soc. *Common Names Fishes* 174, Sole, . . lemon—see English sole . . winter flounder.

2 A winter flounder (here: *Pleuronectes americanus*).

    1966 *DARE* Tape **ME**17, [FW:] What do they drag for? [Inf:] Haddock, codfish, graysole, lemon sole, black backs, dabs. **1969** *DARE* (Qu. P2, . . *Kinds of saltwater fish caught around here . . good to eat*) Inf **MA**40, Lemon sole; (Qu. P14, . . *Commercial fishing . . what do the fishermen go out after?*) Inf **MA**40, Lemon sole. **1973** [see **1** above]. **1991** [see **1** above].

lemon-sucker See **lemon-pelter**

lemon sumac n [From the scent of the leaves]
=**fragrant sumac**.
 1950 Gray–Fernald *Manual of Botany* 977, R[hus] aromatica. . . Lemon-sumac. **1970** Correll *Plants TX* 991, *Rhus aromatica*. . . Polecat bush . . lemon sumac. **1973** Stephens *Woody Plants* 330, *Rhus aromatica* . . lemon sumac.

lemon verbena n [From the scent of the leaves]
 1 A **frogfruit** or a related cultivated plant *(Aloysia triphylla)*.
 1869 Brace *New West* 37 **cwCA**, Every house [in San Francisco], with bits of yards like ours in New York, makes the most splendid show of flowers; scarlet geraniums, ten feet high, lemon-verbenas which are small trees, fuchsias of immense size. **1889** *Century Dict.* 3406, Lemon-verbena. . . A garden-shrub, *Lippia (Aloysia) citriodora*, related to the verbena. Its leaves have a lemon fragrance. **1942** Hylander *Plant Life* 447, Lemon Verbena [=*Lippia lanceolata*] . . , also known as Mat Grass, ranges from the Atlantic coast to southern California. **1969** *DARE* (Qu. S26e, *Other wildflowers not yet mentioned;* not asked in early QRs) Inf **CA**167, Lemon verbenia [sic]—fragrant. **1976** Bailey–Bailey *Hortus Third* 61, *Aloysia* [spp]. . . The lemon verbena is a popular greenhouse plant.
 2 =**lemon balm**.
 1940 Clute *Amer. Plant Names* 264, *Melissa officinalis*. . . garden balm, lemon verbena. **1968–69** *DARE* (Qu. I35, . . *Kitchen herbs . . grown and used in cooking around here*) Inf **GA**55, Mint, chives, rosemary, lemon verbena; (Qu. S26e, *Other wildflowers not yet mentioned;* not asked in early QRs) Inf **RI**1, Lemon verbena—this is often cultivated.

lemon walnut n Also *lemon nut*
=**butternut 1**.
 1873 in 1976 Miller *Shaker Herbs* 145, Butternut—*Juglans cinerea*. . . Lemon Walnut. **1900** Lyons *Plant Names* 207, *J[uglans] cinerea*. . . Lemon Walnut. **1930** Sievers *Amer. Med. Plants* 18, Butternut . . lemon walnut. **1971** Krochmal *Appalachia Med. Plants* 148, Butternut . . lemonnut. **1974** (1977) Coon *Useful Plants* 154, *Juglans cinerea* . . lemon nut.

lemonweed n [From the scent of the leaves]
 1 Any of var **chinchweeds**; see quots. Cf **lemon-scent**
 1911 *Century Dict. Suppl.*, Lemonweed. . . In the southwestern United States, *Pectis filipes, P. papposa*, and *P. longipes*, small yellow-flowered lemon-scented composites with linear leaves dotted with oil-glands. These plants are used medicinally by the Indians and the white settlers, in the form of a decoction. **1979** Spellenberg *Audubon Guide N. Amer. Wildflowers W. Region* 382, On a hot summer afternoon where these plants [=*Pectis papposa*] are numerous, the air is saturated with a heavy, lemon odor. A look-alike, Lemonweed *(P. angustifolia)*, . . is denser and has only one gland at the tip of each bract.
 2 A **gromwell** (here: *Lithospermum ruderale*).
 1937 St. John *Flora SE WA & ID* 347, *Lithospermum ruderale* . . Cat's Tooth; Lemonweed.

lend v Cf **borrow** v **B1, loan B1**
To borrow.
 1931 *AmSp* 7.20 **swPA**, Lend. Borrow. "May I lend your pencil?"

lend the loan of v phr Also *loan the lend of* [*EDD* lend the loan of (at *loan* sb.[1] 1.(2))]
To lend.
 1911 Pryor *Colonel's Story* 19 **VA**, Ask Miss Prissy to len' me the loan of her sleeve pattern. **1916** *DN* 4.338 **KS**, Loan the lend of. . . To lend.

length n Usu |lɛŋ(k)θ|; also freq |lɛnθ, lɪŋθ|; for addit varr see quots; cf Pronc Intro 3.I.4, 20 Pronc-spp *leanth, len(g)k, lent(h)* Cf **strength**
Std sense, var forms.
 1798 in 1956 Eliason *Tarheel Talk* 313 **cs,seNC**, Lenth. **1835** (1927) Evans *Exped. Rocky Mts.* 14.198 **IN**, At leanth *Iatan* . . was traveling one day alone. **1840** in 1952 Green *Samuel Maverick* 133 **AL**, I have at lenth determined to write you a letter. **1878** *Appletons' Jrl.* 5.413 **PA**,

The Pennsylvanian says *strenth* and *lenth* for *strength* and *length*. **1891** *DN* 1.125 **cNY**, [lenθ] . . 'length.' Ibid 166, [lɛŋks] < *lengths*. **1892** *DN* 1.233 **KY, NEng, MI**, *Len'th* [lɛnθ]. [Also in New England. . . Occasional in Michigan.] **1893** Shands *MS Speech* 15, Negroes do not pronounce the *g* before *th* in such words as *strength, length*. **1899** Chesnutt *Conjure Woman* 42 **csNC** [Black], De same lenk er time. **1902** *DN* 2.238 **sIL**, Length. . . Often pronounced [lenθ]. **1905** *DN* 3.58 **eNE**, Sometimes [n] appears for [ŋ] in *strength, length,* especially among those of Irish descent. **1907** *DN* 3.224 **nwAR**, Length. . . Often pronounced [lɛnθ]. **1922** Gonzales *Black Border* 310 **sSC, GA coasts** [Gullah glossary], Lengk—length, lengths. **1930** *AmSp* 5.205 **Ozarks**, The hillman nearly always substitutes *n* for *ng* in such words as *length* and *strength*. **1936** *AmSp* 11.234 **eTX**, *Lengths* is [lēɪŋks]. **1937** *AmSp* 12.126 **Upstate NY**, *Length* occurs 308 times with [ŋ], 40 times with [ŋk], three times with [n]. **1937** *AmSp* 12.286 **wVA**, Typical pronunciations in the Valley are . . [lɛnθ] for *length*. **1942** *AmSp* 17.156 **seNY**, *Length* has [ŋ] 42, [ŋk] 2, [n] 6. **1950** *WELS Suppl.*, Lent . . for length. "You take a 20-foot lent of pipe. . ." "It comes in 20-foot lents." **1952** Brown *NC Folkl.* 1.559, Lenth [lɛnθ, lɪnθ]. **1959** *VT Hist.* 27.147, Length [lēnth] . . pronc. Occasional. **1991** *DARE* File (as of c1956) **MI**, A close friend of mine from Detroit, Michigan, used always to pronounce *length* "lenth" and *strength* "strenth" to my endless disbelief and dismay. Ibid **KY**, Extend it to its full [lɛnθ]. Ibid **csWI**, I've always said [lɪŋθ].

‡**lennegy** adj [Prob var of *EDD lennucky* (at *lennock* adj.) "1. Limp. . . 2. Pliant. . . 3. . . long, slender."]
 1943 Writers' Program NC *Bundle of Troubles* 132, Dick Wilson's a lean and lennegy feller what always has a twist of hillside navy in his jeans and a good-size hunk of the same in his guzzle.

lent v See **lean** v **A**

lent n[1] [Perh < Span *lento* slow, sluggish]
A greenhorn; hence adj *lenty* inexperienced, green.
 1920 Hunter *Trail Drivers TX* 298, A green cow hand is called a "lent," and his greenness is expressed by the word "lenty."

lent n[2] See **length**

lenter See **lean-to**

lenth See **length**

Lent wind n **LA**
A southerly wind typical of the Lenten season; hence n *Lent weather* weather characterized by such a wind.
 1967 LeCompte *Word Atlas* 94 **seLA**, Summer storms with wind and rain. . . Lent weather [1 of 21 infs]. **1968** *DARE* (Qu. B18, . . *Special kinds of wind*) Inf **LA**20, Lent wind—a south wind that blows all the time in March; **LA**31, Lent wind (vent carême).

lenty See **lent** n[1]

leopard See **leopard dog**

leopard cat n
 1 =**ocelot**.
 1845 Green *Jrl. Texian Exped.* 50, [He] wore a cap made by himself out of a skin which he took from a leopard-cat in a Brasos canebrake. **1898** Canfield *Maid of Frontier* 205 (*DAE*), He knew the track of the leopard cat. **1928** Anthony *N. Amer. Mammals* 162, Ocelot. . . Names. . . Leopard-cat. . . A medium-sized, spotted or marbled Cat, with a fairly long tail. . . Only in southwestern Texas. **1953** *Sun* (Baltimore MD) 18 Sept 10/4 (Hench Coll.), Ocelots . . tame easily, even to pets, despite their wild jungle markings and nicknames of "tiger cat" or "leopard cat."
 2 See quot.
 1966–67 *DARE* (Qu. J5, *A cat with fur of mixed colors*) Infs **AL**14, **OK**43, Leopard cat.

leopard cod n
=**lingcod 1**.
 1953 Roedel *Common Fishes CA* 139, *Ophiodon elongatus*. . . Spots and blotches of brown, green, orange, or yellowish. . . Leopard cod.

leopard dog n Also *(Catahoula) leopard, Texas leopard* esp **LA, TX** Cf **blue leopard**
A spotted **Catahoula hog dog**.
 [**1952** *Argosy* (NY) June 99 **LA**, Characteristics of the Catahoula dog suggest at least three breeds in its lineage . . Dalmatian . . for the dark spotting and blotching of its coat, which in the "blue leopard" strain resembles that of the blue-tick hound. . . Besides the leopard

strain, which comes in blue, brown and tawny, there are brindled Catahoulas.] **1954** *True* June 65 **LA,** The animal Slim Williams talks about is called the Texas leopard, a box-jawed, bell-eared dog weighing from 65 to 75 pounds. . . "You could just about say I was put out to run with leopard dogs when I was a kid the way they put a sheep-dog pup out to run with lambs," he says. . . There is a lot of doubt about the ancestry of the Catahoula dog, although it probably goes back to a "leopard"-dog strain developed in north Georgia and mentioned as far back as 1800. *Ibid* 66, Leopards began working stock—and hogs—further east. **1958** Humphrey *Home from the Hill* 48 **neTX,** One of the fabulous, blue-spotted, glassy-eyed Catahoula hog dogs, sometimes called leopard dogs. **1967** *DARE* Tape **LA2,** Well, I just don't know but that's what they call all leopard dogs, a Catahoula cur. **1986** Pederson *LAGS Concordance (Mongrel)* 1 inf, **cwFL,** Catahoula leopards—curs are called in the west; 1 inf, **ceTX,** Leopards—dogs; "bluish-spotted"; [1 inf, **cnLA,** They're leopardy looking—of Catahoula curs].

leopard flower n [From the spotted perianth]
=blackberry lily.

    1889 *Century Dict.* 3411, *Leopard-flower.* . . A garden-flower from China, *Belamcanda (Pardanthus) Chinensis,* of the iris family . . the fruited receptacle resembles a blackberry, whence the plant is also called *blackberry-lily.* **1910** Graves *Flowering Plants* 128 **CT,** *Belamcanda chinensis.* . . Leopard Flower. **1976** Bailey–Bailey *Hortus Third* 155, *B[elamcanda] chinensis* . . leopard flower.

leopard frog n

Any of several prominently spotted frogs of the genus *Rana* such as the **pickerel frog,** but usu *Rana pipiens* in the northern and western US and *R. sphenocephala* in the southern US. For other names of the latter two see **meadow frog, shad ~, spotted ~, spring ~, Texas bullfrog;** for other names of *R. pipiens* see **bullfrog 1, grass frog a**

    1839 MA Zool. & Bot. Surv. *Fishes Reptiles* 237 **MA,** *R. halecina* [=*R. pipiens*] . . [is] better known in this state as the *leopard frog,* from its ocellated appearance. **1842** DeKay *Zool. NY* 3.63, *Rana palustris.* . . is one of our most beautiful frogs. . . It has a strong and disagreeable odor; and from being used as bait, it is called, in various districts, *Pickerel Frog,* and also *Tiger* and *Leopard Frog. Ibid* 64, In Massachusetts, they [=*Rana halecina*] are better known under the name of *Leopard Frogs.* **1861** Holmes *Venner* 1.66 **NEng,** The green frog . . sat waiting to be victimized . . long after the shy and agile leopard-frog had taken the six-foot spring that plumped him into the middle of the pool. **1892** IN Dept. Geol. & Nat. Resources *Rept. for 1891* 474, The Leopard Frog is our commonest, best known, and most beautiful frog. . . Its voice may be imitated by the syllables chock, chock, chock; but at times is has a cry that sounds like derisive laughter, and again, a sort of low, querulous tone. **1928** Baylor Univ. Museum *Contrib.* 16.6 **TX,** Thousands of Leopard . . Frogs (*Rana sphenocephala* . . and *Rana pipiens* . .) are shipped north from this State and are served in restaurants and on dining cars. **1930** *Copeia* 2.27 **OK,** *Rana sphenocephala.* . . Southern leopard frog. *Ibid* 4.154 **GA,** *Rana sphenocephala.* . . Southern leopard frog. **1966–70** *DARE* (Qu. P22, *Names or nicknames for a very large frog that makes a deep, loud sound*) Inf **IA29,** The leopard frog; **NY97,** Leopard frog—has spots on him; (Qu. P23, *Names for the animal similar to the frog that lives away from water*) Infs **IL119, PA58,** Leopard frog; **OK18,** Toad-frog [mentioned by FW] is what they call a "leopard frog" here—small, striped, live in damp places, but they don't stay in the water. **1973** Allen *LAUM* 1.325 (as of c1950), *Spring frog* . . leopard frog [1 inf, **csMN**]. **1979** Behler–King *Audubon Field Guide Reptiles* 370, Rio Grande Leopard Frog (*Rana berlandieri*). . . Plains Leopard Frog (*Rana blairi*). *Ibid* 376, Relict Leopard Frog (*Rana onca*). . . Northern Leopard Frog (*Rana pipiens*). *Ibid* 379, Southern Leopard Frog (*Rana sphenocephala*). **1981** Vogt *Nat. Hist. WI* 82, Pickerel frogs are often confused with leopard frogs. Pickerel frogs differ by having a blunter snout, more rectangular body, 2 rows of distinct square chocolate-brown spots [etc]. . . The western leopard frog *(Rana blairi)* is possibly found in extreme southwestern Wisconsin. **1985** Clark *From Mailbox* 46 **ME,** The small frogs which go leaping through the grass on the back lawn are young leopard frogs. **1986** Pederson *LAGS Concordance (Bullfrog; spring frogs)* 3 infs, **LA, MS,** Leopard frog(s); 1 inf, **ceTX,** Leopard frog—lighter skin with spots; 1 inf, **csTX,** Leopard frog—used for catfish bait.

leopard lily n [From the spotted perianth]

  1 Either of two **lilies** native to California: usu *Lilium pardalinum,* but also *L. parvum.* Also called **tiger lily.** For other names of *L. pardalinum* see **panther lily, sunset lily**

    1859 in 1863 CA Acad. Sci. *Proc. for 1858–1862* 2.12, *L. pardalinum,* (Kellogg), Leopard Lily. **1897** Parsons *Wild Flowers CA* 182, Leopard-lily. . . *Lilium pardalinum.* **1902** *Out West Mag.* Sept 349 **cCA,** The leopard-lily lights the heather dun. **1920** Rice–Rice Pop. *Studies CA Wild Flowers* 99, The . . small Leopard Lily, *L[ilium] parvum,* . . is far more fragile appearing than its showy relative, *L. pardalinum,* the larger Leopard Lily. . . These plants vary somewhat in appearance in different localities, but. . . the flowers. . . are bright-orange-yellow in color, spotted with purple. **1938** MacFarland et al. *Garden Bulbs* 136, Lilium pardalinum. Sometimes called the Western Tiger Lily, this highly esteemed California native also has the common names of Leopard Lily and Panther Lily. **1979** Spellenberg *Audubon Guide N. Amer. Wildflowers W. Region* 585, The . . Leopard Lily . . (*L. pardalinum*), which grows along forest streams or near springs over most of California, has bright orange-red flowers.

  2 The southern **red lily** (*Lilium catesbaei*).

    1933 Small *Manual SE Flora* 291, *L[ilium] Catesbaei.* . . Leopard-lily. **1949** Moldenke *Amer. Wild. Flowers* 323, A great favorite in the Southeast is the *leopard lily* . . *L[ilium] catesbaei,* found in pinelands and acid swamps on the coastal plain from North Carolina to Florida and Louisiana. **1972** Brown *Wildflowers LA* 17, Leopard Lily. . . Open flower about 5 inches in diameter.

  3 A fritillary: usu *Fritillaria atropurpurea,* but also *F. lanceolata.*

    1932 Rydberg *Flora Prairies* 216, Leopard Lily. . . *F[ritillaria] atropurpurea.* **1963** Craighead *Rocky Mt. Wildflowers* 24, Leopard Lily—*Fritillaria atropurpurea.* . . Only plant likely to be confused with this is another species of leopard lily (*F. lanceolata*). **1970** Kirk *Wild Edible Plants W. U.S.* 165, Our native species of *F[ritillaria] atropurpurea.* . . Leopard Lily . . and *F. purpurea* . . are well known to be edible.

leopard lizard n

A spotted **lizard** of the genus *Gambelia* native to the western US. For other names of *G. wislizenii* see **red-spotted lizard**

    1893 in 1900 U.S. Natl. Museum *Annual Rept. for 1898* 260, The habits of *Crotaphytus wislizenii* are given . . as follows: "The leopard lizard is abundant in most . . of the Lower Sonoran deserts." **1915** *Nature & Sci.* 111 **CA,** The fleet-footed leopard lizards and whip-tails are among the first to attract the attention of a rider across the desert. **1928** Baylor Univ. Museum *Contrib.* 16.11, Leopard Lizard—*Crotaphytus wislizenii.* . . In the Trans-Pecos country. **1946** Smith *Lizards* 158, The Leopard Lizards Genus *Gambelia. Ibid* 163, The leopard lizards. . . ran . . at great speed across the dunes, and disappeared into a low, spreading type of bush. **1979** Behler–King *Audubon Field Guide Reptiles* 507, Blunt-nosed Leopard Lizard (*Gambelia silus*). *Ibid* 508, This lizard usually "freezes" when danger threatens, only to dash for cover if closely approached. . . Leopard Lizard (*Gambelia wislizenii*). . . *Gray or brown with many dark spots on body and tail.*

leopard muskellunge n Also *leopard muskie*

A **muskellunge 1** with prominent spots.

    1943 Eddy–Surber *N. Fishes* 170, Other muskellunge are marked with more or less distinct spots on a light background and are called locally "leopard muskies." **1949** Caine *N. Amer. Sport Fish* 98, Muskellunge. . . Colloquial Names . . Leopard Muskellunge. **1983** Becker *Fishes WI* 405, *Muskellunge.* . . Other common names: . . leopard muskellunge [etc].

leopard oak n

Either of two oaks: a **red oak** (here: *Quercus rubra*) or the **Shumard oak.**

    1903 Small *Flora SE U.S.* 351, *Quercus rubra.* . . The trunk clothed with a rough, close, often mottled bark. . . in woods, Nova Scotia and Ontario to Minnesota and Kansas, Florida and Texas. *Red Oak. Leopard Oak.* **1908** Britton *N. Amer. Trees* 281, *Quercus rubra.* . . is also called Yellow oak, Black oak, Leopard oak, and Spanish oak. **1933** Small *Manual SE Flora* 429, *Q[uercus] shumardii.* . . *Leopard-oak.* . . Woods, bottoms, and river-bluffs, . . Coastal Plain and adj. provinces, N Fla. to Tex. and Ia. **1960** Vines *Trees SW* 186, *Quercus rubra.* . . Leopard Oak. . . The wood is considered to be better than that of other Red Oaks. *Ibid* 192, *Quercus shumardii.* . . Leopard Oak. . . is a beautiful tree with a symmetrical leaf design.

leopard's bane n [*OED* 1822–34]
=arnica B1.

    1830 Rafinesque *Med. Flora* 2.195, Arnica [spp] . . *Leopard's Bane.* . . It is a narcotic, producing burnings, hemorrhage, vertigo and coma in large doses. Vinegar cures these symptoms. **1837** Darlington *Flora Cestrica* 496, *A[rnica] nudicaulis.* . . Leopard's Bane. **1903** Small *Flora SE U.S.* 1300, *Arnica acaulis.* . . Leopard's-bane. **1931** Harned *Wild Flowers Alleghanies* 596, Leopard's-bane (*Arnica acaulis* . .). **1963** Craighead *Rocky Mt. Wildflowers* 193, *Arnica cordifolia.* . . Heart-leaf Arnica, Leopard's Bane.

leopard shark n

1 A cat shark (*Triakis semifasciata*) of California waters. Also called **dog shark**

1896 U.S. Natl. Museum *Bulletin* 47.31 **CA,** Cat Shark; Leopard Shark. . . 3 feet. Cape Mendocino to San Diego, common ; a handsome shark, readily known by its variegated coloration. **1939** Natl. Geogr. Soc. *Fishes* 257, The leopard shark may be distinguished . . by conspicuous black bars across the back and upper sides. Along the lower sides are round black spots mostly opposite and between the ends of the crossbars. It is one of the commonest species in the markets of southern California and is frequently taken on hook and line by anglers. **1953** Roedel *Common Fishes CA* 18, Leopard Shark *Triakis semifasciata.* . . Caught quite frequently by Southern California fishermen. Taken throughout the year in Northern California. . . Commonly marketed for its flesh. The liver contains no vitamins. **1991** Amer. Fisheries Soc. *Common Names Fishes* 13, *Triakis semifasciata* . . P[acific] leopard shark.

2 The tiger shark (*Galeocerdo cuvieri*).

1905 NJ State Museum *Annual Rept. for 1904* 61, *Galeus tigrinus.* . . Spotted Shark. Leopard Shark. Reaching a length of 30 feet, this large shark may be distinguished by its variegated coloration, which has earned for it the above vernaculars. **1946** LaMonte *N. Amer. Game Fishes* 3, Tiger Shark . . Names: Leopard Shark. . . The markings are much plainer in young specimens which are also browner, with distinct large spots. **1960** Amer. Fisheries Soc. *List Fishes* 69, [Shark,] leopard . . see also shark, tiger.

leopard's tongue n

A **hawkweed** (here: *Hieracium venosum*).

1898 *Plant World* 2.14 **sPA,** During a recent visit to the mountains of Southern Pennsylvania, the following local names of plants were noted as in use: . . Leopard's Tongue, for *Hieracium venosum.* . . (The radical leaves with their reddish undersurfaces and oblong outline might remind one of the tongue of that animal.)

lep See **leap** 1, 2

leppy n, also attrib Also sp *leppie* [MexSpan *lepe* an orphan calf] **West**

An orphan calf, lamb, or colt.

1924 James *Cowboys N. & S.* 107, The dry stock was in good condition, outside the few old stuff and cows with calves and "leppies" (orphant calves). **1934** (1940) Weseen *Dict. Amer. Slang* 101 **West,** *Leppy*—An orphan calf. **1936** McCarthy *Lang. Mosshorn* np **West** [Range terms], *Leppy.* . . A name applied to an orphan calf. **1940** Writers' Program *Guide NV* 76, *Leppie* . . motherless lamb, calf, or colt. Also sp *leppy.* **1940** (1966) Writers' Program *Guide AZ* 236 **cAZ,** The celebration ended, they return to their "leppies" (dogies) in Arizona's "back countries." **1942** Whipple *Joshua* 192 **UT,** As soon as Pal told him, he had brought up a leppy-lamb from the herd to raise for a playmate for 'Butch.' **1967** *DARE* (Qu. K83) Inf **CA31,** Leppy calf ['lɛpi]. **1967** *DARE* FW Addit **NV,** *Leppy*—a calf without a mother, a dogie. **1971** Bright *Word Geog. CA & NV* 168 **csCA,** Dogie / motherless calf / . . leppy 9% [of 300 infs]. **1981** KS *Qrly.* 13.2.68, *Leppy* . . an unweaned orphaned calf requiring special care for its survival.

lerp See **larrup** n 2

lerrupy n [Prob *EDD lerrup* sb. 3. "*pl.* Scraps of meat, liver, &c., sold by butchers. Cor[nwall]"] Note: Southwestern Wisconsin had significant numbers of Cornish settlers.

See quots.

1967 *DARE* FW Addit **swWI,** *Lerrupy*—Food prepared or intended for a dog. "You've eaten Purp's lerrupy." **1974** *DARE* File **swWI,** Lerrupy—Mixed stew, as prepared for a dog. "Have you given Rover his lerrupy?"

les See **let** A2c

les'n See **lessen** conj²

lespedeza n Usu |ˌlɛspəˈdizə|; for pronc and sp varr see quot 1965–70 [See quot 1803]

A bush clover of the genus *Lespedeza*, esp *Lespedeza striata*

which is naturalized in the southeastern US. For other names of *L. striata* see **buffalo clover 3, China ~, old-field ~ 2**

[**1803** Michaux *Flora Boreali-Americana* 2.70, *Lespedeza.* . . Lespedez, gubernator Floridae, erga me peregrinatorem officiosissimus. [=*Lespedeza.* . . Lespedez [sic for *Zespedes*] the governor of Florida, [who was] most helpful to me when I was a visitor.] **1881** Phares *Farmer's Book of Grasses* 10, *L[espedeza] repens.* Creeping Lespedeza lies flat on the ground. . . It is utterly worthless. *Ibid* 12, Within a few years the *L. bicolor* has been introduced. . . But this two-colored lespedeza can never become a useful forage plant. **1901** Mohr *Plant Life AL* 576, *Lespedeza striata.* . . Lespedeza. Japanese Clover. . . During the past thirty years extensively and copiously spread over the Southern States from Maryland to the Gulf and southern Arkansas. . . Economic uses: Fodder plant, important for pasture and as spontaneous hay crop. **1929** (1951) Faulkner *Sartoris* 58 **MS,** I expect every spring to find corn or lespedeza coming up in the hyacinth beds. **c1940** Newman–Murphy *Conserv. Notes* 7 **neLA,** The chief products of this section are . . alfalfa, lespedeza, sorghum. **1948** Wolfe *Farm Gloss.* 192, *Lespedeza*—Summer legume very popular in the South for hay following small grain, for pasturing and to furnish seed for wildlife food. **c1960** Wilson Coll. **csKY,** Grass, etc., used for hay . . lespedeza—very recent. **1965–70** *DARE* (Qu. L9b, *Hay from other kinds of plants [not grass]; not asked in early QRs*) 98 Infs, **chiefly Sth, W Midl, Cent,** Lespedeza [=proncs of the types [ˌlɛspəˈdizə], [ˈlɛspəˌdizə]]; **IL**19, [ˌlɛspəˈdeɪzə]; **AR**56, Japanese lespedeza, Kobe lespedeza, sericea lespedeza; **SC**40, Sericea lespedeza; **AR**9, 29, 32, 36, **KY**6, 86, **LA**18, **NC**6, 54, Lespedezer; **AR**21, **MS**9, 28, 53, Lesperdezer; **AR**4, **IN**13, 30, **KY**27, **MO**8, 34, Lespedezy; **NC**85, **SC**69, [ˌlɛspəˈdidə]; **VA**70, [ˈlɛspəˌdidə]; **IL**93, 134, [ˈlɛspədiz]; **GA**77, [ˌlɛˆspəˈdivr]; **MS**87, [ˈlɛspəˌbizə]; **NY**99, [ˈlɛpsudiziə]; **SC**7, [ˈlɛpsɪˌdizə]; (Qu. L9a, . . *Kinds of grass . . grown for hay*) 33 Infs, **chiefly Sth, W Midl, Cent,** Lespedeza; **MS**63, Lespedezer; **AR**4, **KY**49, Lespedezy; (Qu. L8, *Hay that grows naturally in damp places*) Infs **GA**19, **LA**7, **VA**97, Lespedeza; **GA**77, **LA**10, Wild lespedeza; (Qu. L22, *When talking about a crop he intends to plant . . a farmer might say, "This year, I'm going to . ."*) Inf **NC**6, Sow lespedeza. **1966–70** *DARE* Tape **AR**33, We have been quite successful over the years of planting lespedeza in our rice stubble. . . It goes on an' makes either a hay or a seed crop. *Ibid* **TN**53, We raise alfalfa hay, and . . we have what we call jap or lespedeza hay also. **1986** Pederson *LAGS Concordance,* 17 infs, **Gulf Region,** Lespedeza.

less adj [*OED less* a. 1. "*Obs.* with reference to material dimensions (superseded by *smaller*)."] **chiefly S Midl** Cf **least** adj 1, **leaster**

Smaller; shorter.

1859 in 1942 Hafen *Overland Routes* 11.110 **VA,** He had no white neighbors within a less distance than thirty-seven miles. **1886** *S. Bivouac* 4.349 **sAppalachians,** Less (not so tall). **1904** *DN* 2.419 **nwAR,** Less. . . Smaller. 'My brother's less than you.' **1910** *DN* 3.456 **seKY,** Less. . . Smaller. "Give me the less apple." **1953** [see **leaster**]. **1968** Haun *Hawk's Done Gone* 73 **eTN,** A Spirit is not any bigger nor any less than the body it comes from. **1969** *DARE* Tape **GA**51, The little 'un is the she, female cat, it's less in size and a little longer tail than the bobcat . . it's the male and female of the same cat.

less conj **chiefly Sth, S Midl** Cf **lessen** conj¹

Unless.

1871 Eggleston *Hoosier Schoolmaster* 24 **sIN,** Boys won't larn 'less you thrash 'em. **1899** Chesnutt *Conjure Woman* 12 **csNC** [Black], I would n' spec' fer you ter b'lieve me 'less you know all 'bout de fac's. **1906** *DN* 3.144 **nwAR,** 'Less. . . Unless. "I'll not go, 'less something happens." **1909** *DN* 3.345 **eAL, wGA,** Less. . . Unless. **1922** Gonzales *Black Border* 310 **sSC, GA coasts** [Gullah glossary], 'Less—(or onless) unless. **1930** *AmSp* 5.208 **Ozarks,** Ben Jonson . . very often used *'less* instead of *unless,* exactly as the Ozark hillman does today. **1967** *DARE* Tape **TX**8, You don't wanna cut the water off less you have to, 'cause that's more expensive for irrigation. **1970** *AmSp* 45.77 **PA,** Unless. I ain't going 'less you do.

less v See **let** A2c

lessen conj¹ Also sp *less'n, lessun* [Cf *EDD* (at *less* conj.¹ 2), where it is interpreted as *less than,* but perh instead **less** conj + **and** conj B1; cf **iffen, unlessen**] **chiefly Sth, S Midl**

Unless.

1887 (1967) Harris *Free Joe* 105 **GA,** "He's a mighty early bird," said Abe, "less'n he's a-headin' fer the furder side." **1893** Shands *MS Speech* 73, Lessen. . . A word used by negroes and illiterate whites for *unless.* **1896** *DN* 1.420 **swNC,** I'll send, lessen you want to go yourself. **1902**

DN 2.238 **sIL**, *Lessn*. . . Unless. **1903** *DN* 2.319 **seMO**, I won't go lessun you do. **1905** *DN* 3.63 **eNE**, Lessn you change your mind. **1907** *DN* 3.224 **nwAR**, *Lessn*. . . Unless. *Ibid* 232 **nwAR**, *Lessun*. . . Unless. **1909** *DN* 3.345 **eAL, wGA**, He'll go to perdition, lessen the Lord have mercy on him. **1917** *DN* 4.414 **KS, KY, wNC**, Men don't do nothin' fer amusement, lessun they chaw terbacker. **1924** (1946) Greer-Petrie *Angeline Gits an Eyeful* 6 **csKY**, I don't reckon she ever done a day's work in her life, less'n you'd call hit work 'broiderin' 'nishils on handkerchers. **1928** Peterkin *Scarlet Sister Mary* 87 **SC** [Gullah], "How come you got de headache?" "I dunno, lessen so much sun-hot today done it." **1931** (1991) Hughes–Hurston *Mule Bone* 85 **cFL** [Black], Some folks think you ain't workin' lessen you smellin' a mule. **1938** Matschat *Suwannee R.* 65 **neFL, seGA**, But no poachin' on gov'ment land, mind, lessen ye be compelled for food. **1949** Webber *Backwoods Teacher* 11 **Ozarks**, This here dog won't hurt you all less'n I say fer 'im to. **1967** *DARE* Tape **SC35**, Never did know one of them to ever break lessen you cut it a little bit with a knife. **1968** *DARE* FW Addit **LA29**, I don't know, lessen you'd say she was oversize, something like that. **1970** *DARE* (Qu. I3) Inf **SC70**, Rutabagas and turnips are the same thing, lessen you talkin' about the white-bottomed turnip and the rutabaga turnip. **1976** Garber *Mountain-ese* 53 **sAppalachians**, I kain't do the job lessen somebody gives me a hand. **1986** Pederson *LAGS Concordance*, 22 infs, **Gulf Region**, Lessen. **1987** Jones–Wheeler *Laughter* 97 **Appalachians**, Lessen I stub my toe on one of your stills in the middle of the street, I'll not harass you.

lessen conj[2] Pronc-sp *les'n*

Lest, for fear that.

1899 Chesnutt *Conjure Woman* 25 **csNC** [Black], His noo marster begin ter git skeered les'n he gwine ter lose his fifteen-hunder'-dollar nigger.

lessen prep Pronc-sp *lessn* [*EDD* less conj.[1] and prep. 3]

Except.

1905 *DN* 3.63 **eNE**, They are all coming lessn him.

lessen adj [Prob *less* + var of **on** prep **B1**]

Smaller of.

1975 in 1993 Major *Calling the Wind* 374 **KY** [Black], She said I was the lessen two evils.

lesser scaup n

Std: a **scaup** (here: *Aythya affinis*) common esp to inland waters. Also called **blackhead 1, blackjack 1a, blackneck b, bluebill 1, broadbill 1, bullhead 2c, bullneck 1, coldshin, cottontail bluebill, creek broadbill, dogs, dos gris, drift fowl, floating fowl, flock duck, flocking fowl, grayback 1d, greenhead 4a(2), lake duck, March bluebill, marsh ~ 1, polridge, quinder, raft duck, shuffler, troop fowl, widgeon**

lesser yellowlegs See **yellowlegs**

less more adv phr

Let alone, much less.

1954 *PADS* 21.32 **SC**, *Less mo*. . . Much less. "He can't stand up, less mo' walk."

less'n conj See **lessen** conj[1]

lessn prep See **lessen** prep

lessun See **lessen** conj[1]

let v Usu |lɛt|; for varr see **A** below

A Forms.

1 |lɪt|; pronc-sp *lit.*

1821 Cooper *Spy* 2.88 **seNY**, Pooh! man, away wid yee . . march on hurry-skurry; and lit the mare trot. **1859** in 1956 Eliason *Tarheel Talk* 314 **cnNC**, *Lit.* **1932** in 1944 *ADD* **cnVA**, Speaker aged 17. |lɪt|. 'to lit another fam'ly know.' [**1956** Eliason *Tarheel Talk* 222 **NC**, An |ɪ| variant occurs very frequently. From Middle English times an *e/i* alternation has been common . . but the variation persists in folk speech. . . Illustrative spellings include . . *git* . . *kittle* . . *tin* for ten . . *whtstone*, and *yellow*.]

2a pronc-spp *l', le(h), luh.* **chiefly S Atl** *esp freq among Black speakers*

1853 Simms *Sword & Distaff* 446 **SC** [Black], Ef you skear [=scared], nebber le' Miss Ellen see you skear. **1922** Gonzales *Black Border* 310 **sSC, GA coasts** [Gullah glossary], *Leh*—let. . . *Leh we*—let us. *Le'm*—let them. **1927** Adams *Congaree* 9 **cSC** [Black], But dem chillun ain't luh 'im res' while dey Daddy set up dere. *Ibid* 37, But sometimes de law protects 'em an' ain't l'um be try. **1939** Griswold *Sea Is. Lady* 122 **csSC** (as of 1865) [Gullah], "Don' le'm lan'!" [=Don't let them land!] a voice yelled from the rear.

b Spec; in comb *let me:* pronc-spp *le'm, lemme.* Cf **give A1d**

1795 Dearborn *Columbian Grammar* 136, List of Improprieties. . . Lemme for Let me. **1884** *Anglia* 7.270 **Sth, S Midl** [Black], *Lemme 'lone!* = let me alone! **1894** Riley *Armazindy* 49 **IN**, Flick me with a pizenvine / And yell "Yip!" and lem me loose! **1899** Chesnutt *Conjure Woman* 27 **csNC** [Black], So you des lemme know. **1899** Garland *Boy Life* 144 **nwIA** (as of c1870s), Lem me put the kibosh on that puffball. **1906** *DN* 3.120 **sIN**, *Lemme*. . . Let me. "Lemme go." The universal form. **1909** *DN* 3.345 **eAL, wGA**, *Lemme*. . . Let me. Universal. **1922** Gonzales *Black Border* 310 **sSC, GA coasts** [Gullah glossary], *Lem'lone*—let, lets him, her, it, them alone. *Ibid, Lemme*—let me. **1932** *Sat. Eve. Post* 3 Dec 42 **MS** [Black], Weddel jerked the Negro's head up, shaking him. . . The Negro struck out. . . "Le'm be," he said. "Le'm go." **1966** *DARE* (Qu. EE20, *When two boys are fighting, and the one who is losing wants to stop, he calls out, "_____."*) Inf **SC21**, Lemme go.

c Spec; in contr *let's:* pronc-spp *les(s);* less freq *es(s), e.*

1867 Harris *Sut Lovingood Yarns* 28 **TN**, Less all drink! **1884** *Anglia* 7.276 **Sth, S Midl** [Black], *Less des call him* = let's just call him. **1892** *DN* 1.233 **KY**, Less go [lɛs go]: let's go. [*DN* Ed: Also very common in New England and Michigan, where *let's* is hardly used except as a result of education.] **1899** Garland *Boy Life* 264 **nwIA** (as of c1870s), Le's see you get back where we started from. **1899** (1912) Green *VA Folk-Speech* 260, Less go to-morrow. **1908** Fox *Lonesome Pine* 28 **KY**, "Less see you laugh that-a-way agin," said Bub. **1908** *DN* 3.309 **eAL, wGA**, *Es*. . . A contraction of *let us.* "I tell you what es do." Sometimes further contracted to *e*. **1909** *DN* 3.345 **eAL, wGA**, *Less*. . . A common contraction of *let us.* Sometimes further contracted to *es*, and *e*. *Ibid* 399 **nwAR**, Le's go now and do it. **1917** *DN* 4.395 **neOH**, *Les'see* [lɛs'si]. . . Let see; let us see. "Les'see your knife." **1928** *AmSp* 3.405 **Ozarks**, *Let us* or *let's* is always pronounced *less*. **1933** Rawlings *South Moon* 20 **nFL**, "Le's be done when we be done," old man Wilson suggested. **1934** Hurston *Jonah's Gourd Vine* 18 **AL** [Black], When us gather de crops dis yeah less mow. **1942** McAtee *Dial. Grant Co. IN* 39 (as of 1890s), Less go. **1960** Criswell *Resp. to PADS* 20 **Ozarks**, *Let's*. . . [ɛs]. The pron[unciation] *ess* for this contraction has always been extremely common and still is, more common even than *less*. "Ess you and me go down there and steal that watermelon." **1968** *DARE* (Qu. NN6b, *Expressions of joy used mostly by children*) Inf **MO16**, Le's go. **1976** Ryland *Richmond Co. VA* 373, Less go.

B Gram forms.

1 in redund phrr *let's us* (or *we*); See quots. **chiefly Sth** *esp freq among Black speakers*

1914 Dickinson *WI Plays* 36, If we're going to do it, let's us do it. Let's us have ice-cream or nothin. **1927** Adams *Congaree* 22 **cSC** [Black], Less we hear it, Ber Tad. **1927** Kennedy *Gritny* 88 **sLA** [Black], Come on, lessus go. **1931** (1991) Hughes–Hurston *Mule Bone* 147 **cFL** [Black], Less us git married right now. **1934** Hurston *Jonah's Gourd Vine* 47 **AL** [Black], "Less we run in whilst she gone de other way." "Naw, less we lay low 'til she git tired uh huntin' us and give us free base." **1946** McCullers *Member* 4 **AL**, 'Less us have a good time,' John Henry said. 'Us have a good time?' Frankie asked. 'Us?' **1986** Pederson *LAGS Concordance*, 1 inf, **nwTN**, Let's us try [inf White]; 1 inf, **swGA**, Let's we eat; dinner's ready [inf Black].

2 Used with a second person pronoun to reinforce an imperative. [Cf *EDD let* v.[1] II.2] Cf **do** v **C1b**

1941 Ward *Holding Hills* 132 **IA** (as of early 20th cent), "Here," one of the big girls would say, "grab it tight by the ears, one of ye, and sack it up, let ye." *Ibid* 133, An' go home, let ye, all the way around the road, up by Jack's Corner, and not through all them wire-gates.

C Sense.

To leave behind; to allow to remain. [See quot 1934] **chiefly Ger settlement areas, esp sePA**

1907 *German Amer. Annals* 9.380 **sePA**, *Let*. . . "Let your books here when you go." . . fr. Pa. Ger. *Lusă*, Ger. *lassen*, which in both languages is used for *let* and *leave*. **1914** *DN* 4.109 **cKS**, He threw the book on the table and let it there. **1931** *AmSp* 7.20 **swPA**, *Let*. Left. "I let it there." **1931** Jacobson *Milwaukee Dial.* 16 **WI**, Leave and let. . . "Leave us let a piano in your home" for "let us leave a piano in your home." "He persuaded me to let it." **1934** *Language* 10.4 **cPA**, The interchange of *leave* and *let* would seem to be of German origin, as *lassen* has both meanings; only the untutored Dutchman keeps the two words quite distinct, with the meanings reversed: *Leave me go, I left him do it, I'll let my tools here.* **1935** *AmSp* 10.168 **sePA,** One very common sort of error is a confusing of *let* and *leave. . .* The untutored Pennsylvania German uses the two English words but frequently with the meanings reversed. Examples are: . . A parking place is a place where you let the car to have its tail light knocked off. . . Why not let the snow and ice behind and go with us to Florida for two months? **1937** *AmSp* 12.204 **sePA,** The doctor, lawyer, or professor in a Pennsylvania German community . . will not be able to resist the almost unanimous practice of reversing the meanings of *let* and *leave.* **1967** *DARE* (Qu. KK47, *Something that is left undecided or unfinished: "Perhaps we'd better just _____."*) Inf **MO26,** Let it unsettled. **1982** *Barrick Coll.* **csPA,** Let the dishes until tomorra.

let all holts go v phr *Also let all holts loose, ~ loose all holts* Cf **hold** n **A1**

To relax or lose one's grip; to abandon one's position, "let oneself go."

   1894 Riley *Armazindy* 10 **IN,** Inch by inch,/ He let *all* holts go; and so / Took to drinkin'. **1940** *Hall Coll.* **ceTN,** So when the bear got in the right position, I pulled the trigger on it. It just let all holts go and fell over on two limbs there and just laid there, just as dead as it could be. **1943** McAtee *Dial. Grant Co. IN Suppl. 2* 10 (as of 1890s), *Let loose all holts* . . suddenly interrupt or stop what one is doing; "He _____ and vamoosed." **c1960** *Wilson Coll.* **csKY,** *Let all holts loose. . .* Be unhampered.

let alone v phr
To break off, discontinue.

   1884 *Anglia* 7.265 **Sth, S Midl** [Black], *Let 'lone doin sump'n* = to leave off doing.

let-boat n
A rental boat.

   1903 Wasson *Cap'n Simeon's Store* 157 **ME,** Rowin' round and round the Cove into one o' them hotel let-bo'ts.

letchugia See **lechuguilla**

let down v phr

1 also *let down rain:* To rain heavily.

   1972 *DARE* File **csIL,** The rain sure let down last night. **1973** *Ibid* **csIL,** It really let down, but further on it was as dry as a powder horn. **1986** Pederson *LAGS Concordance,* 1 inf, **ceFL,** One time it really opened up and let down rain.

2 Of wind: to abate.

   1973 Allen *LAUM* 1.156 (as of c1950), The wind is *letting up. . .* Letting down [1 inf, **nwMN**]. **1986** Pederson *LAGS Concordance (Wind is letting up)* 2 infs, **cGA, swAL,** Letting down.

3 To cost, "set (one) back."

   1967 *DARE* (Qu. U8a, . . *"It cost me ten dollars."*) Inf **IL15,** Let me down.

4 To dismantle (a portion of a rail fence) to allow passage; by ext, to manipulate any kind of fence to allow passage. Cf **letdown** n

   1843 (1916) Hall *New Purchase* 137 **IN,** Their business was to keep the true course through the woods, clear away brush and let down fences. **1956** Ker *Vocab. W. TX* 94, (To) let down—(to) hold down wire fence for person to drive over.

letdown n [**let down** v phr **4**] Cf **gap** n[1] **2**

   1956 Ker *Vocab. W. TX* 91, Place to let cars or trains pass through a fence. . . let down [2 of 67 infs]. *Ibid,* Let down fence whether of board or wire [1 inf].

let down rain See **let down** v phr **1**

let drive See **drive** v **B5**

let fire v phr Cf **drive** v **B5**
To begin shooting; to open up.

   1953 Randolph–Wilson *Down in Holler* 260 **Ozarks,** *Let fire. . .* To discharge a firearm. "Willy hollered for 'em not to shoot, but Jim he let fire anyhow, an' killed him dead as a doornail." **1954** *Harder Coll.* **cwTN,** *Let fire,* to discharge a firearm.

‡let go adv phr

   1895 *DN* 1.372 **seKY, eTN, wNC,** *Let go* . . say. "The road is back yander, let go abeout [sic] a mile."

let-her-go n

   1901 *DN* 2.143 **ceNY,** *Let 'er go. . .* The name of a boys' street game. Albany, N.Y.

let in v phr

1 To make a start (on something); to begin (to do something). **esp Sth, S Midl**

   1859 Taliaferro *Fisher's R.* 219 **nwNC** (as of 1820s), Long Jimmy let in on a large tray of hog's feet that was set on the table. **1884** *Anglia* 7.262 **Sth, S Midl** [Black], *To let in on* = to begin with. *Ibid* 278, *To let in en'* = to go to work to. **1904** (1972) Harben *Georgians* 143, He let in to cussin' wuss'n I ever heard anybody in my life. **1940** (1968) Haun *Hawk's Done Gone* 97 **eTN,** Then he let in to fussing at me because I let her go over there to spend two weeks with Amy. **1984** Wilder *You All Spoken Here* 191 **Sth,** *Let in:* Began, as in "It let in to rainin' 'bout an hour 'fore day."

2 Of an assembly: to admit people, begin. Cf **leave out 2**

   1904 *DN* 2.398 **NYC,** *Let in. . .* To begin. "The party will let in about nine o'clock." **1986** Pederson *LAGS Concordance (When does school start?)* 1 inf, **csGA,** Lets in.

let it go it phr Cf **it ain't done it**

   1954 *Harder Coll.* **cwTN,** *Let it go it. . .* Leave something alone, let something go undecided: "Don't ye touch that, I say; let it go it."

let loose all holts See **let all holts go**

‡let-loose, have one on the v phr
To be ready to terminate one's employment.

   1934 Hurston *Jonah's Gourd Vine* 246, De Black Herald [=the grapevine] got it dat dey got *you* [=a preacher] on de let-loose and de onliest thing dat keeps some of 'em hangin' on is dey don't b'lieve nobody kin preach lak you, but if dis man dey got here tuhday kin surpass yuh, den dere'll be some changes made.

let off v phr Cf **let down** v phr **2**
Of wind: to abate, let up.

   1986 Pederson *LAGS Concordance,* 2 infs, **LA, TX,** (The wind is) letting off.

let on v phr [Scots dial] **widespread exc NEng** See Map Cf **make like, play like**
To pretend, feign.

   1826 Royall *Sketches* 58 **WV,** When they would say *pretence,* they say *lettinon,* which is a word of very extensive use among them. It signifies a jest, and is used to express disapprobation and disguise; "you are just lettinon to rub them spoons—Polly is not mad, she is only lettinon." **1884** *Anglia* 7.269 **Sth, S Midl** [Black], *To let on* = to pretend. **1902** *DN* 2.238 **sIL,** *Let on. . .* To feign; to pretend; to talk to an ostensible purpose. 'He lets on like he was going to do so and so.' **1906** *DN* 3.120 **sIN,** *Let on. . .* To feign, pretend. "He let on like he was goin' to go." **1907** *DN* 3.224 **nwAR. 1909** *DN* 3.399 **nwAR,** Don't let on like you don't understand. **1921** *DN* 5.116 **KY,** *Let on,* to feign, or pretend. Probably Scottish. **1926** *DN* 5.401 **Ozarks,** *Let on. . .* I jes' let on like I wasn't a-keerin'. **1950** *WELS* (To pretend: "Let's _____ we don't know.") 3 Infs, **WI,** Let on. **1960** Criswell *Resp. to PADS 20* **Ozarks,** He's not as bad off as he lets on. Very common always. **1965–70** *DARE* (Qu. JJ46, . . *To pretend: "Let's _____ we don't know a thing about it."*) 151 Infs, **widespread exc NEng,** Let on; **AR**3, 16, 56, **KY**21, 50, **NY**83, **TX**77, Let on like. **1986** Pederson

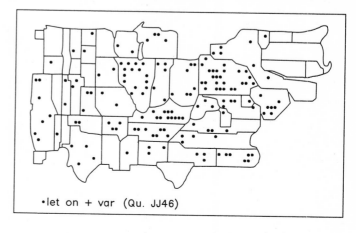

•let on + var (Qu. JJ46)

LAGS Concordance (He didn't know what was going on, but he _____ he knew it all) 6 infs, **AR, TN, TX,** Let on like.

let out v phr Cf **let in 1**
Foll by infin: To start; to prepare.
1858 in 1966 Boller *MO Fur Trader* 162 **MO,** Malnouri, Jeff and I followed after them [=buffaloes] keeping well together, and Malnouri was just on the point of "letting out" to deliver *his* ball [=bullet]. **1955** Ritchie *Singing Family* 64 **seKY,** She let out to give them a piece of her mind then.

let's us, let's we See **let B1**

letter n Pronc-sp *ledder*
1 See quot. [Scots, Engl dial]
1899 (1912) Green *VA Folk-Speech* 260, *Letter.* . . A spark on the wick of a burning candle, foretelling the coming of a letter.
2 in phrr *(there's a) letter in the post office* and varr: Used to indicate that there is a hole in one's trousers or that one's underwear is showing. **chiefly east of Missip R** See Map Cf **Charlie's dead**
1855 Hammett *Wonderful Advent.* 28 **seNY,** That something white, which is fluttering in the breeze from his midships is . . merely a bit of linen which under such circumstances is known to our *gamins* as "a letter in the post office." **1894** *DN* 1.341 **wCT,** *Letter in the post-office:* expression current among boys, denoting that the seat of the trousers is so out of repair that the shirt-tail is visible. **1907** *DN* 3.192 **seNH,** *Letter in the post-office, n. phr.* as *interj.* Shirt-tail visible in a hole in the seat of a boy's breeches. **1912** Green *VA Folk-Speech* 37, One has a letter in the post-office when he has a piece of his shirt-tail sticking through a hole in his trowsers. **1912** *DN* 3.568 **cNY,** *Letter in the post office.* . . Used by a boy to inform another that part of his shirt shows through a hole in his pants. Used also in Connecticut, Illinois, Massachusetts, Missouri, Pennsylvania, and Vermont. **1954** *Harder Coll.* **cwTN,** *Letter in the post office:* . . Warning for a tear in the pants. **1960** Bailey *Resp. to PADS 20* **KS,** *Letter in the post office* . . expression current among boys, denoting that the seat of the trousers is so out of repair that the shirttail is visible. **c1960** *Wilson Coll.* **csKY,** *Letter in the post office*—signal to a person whose clothes are undone. **1965–70** *DARE* (Qu. W24a, . . *Expressions* . . *to warn a woman slyly that her slip is showing*) Infs **CT36, NC36,** You have a letter; **CA101,** Got a letter in the office; **CO20,** You're getting a letter; (Qu. W24b, *Sayings to warn a man that his pants are torn or split*) Infs **AL61, CA101, 157, CT23, 36, NY205, NC87, SC11, VT12, WV13, 18,** There's a letter in the post office; **NY214,** Letter in the post office; (Qu. W24c, . . *To warn a man that his trouser-fly is open*) Inf **WV16,** There's a letter in the post office.

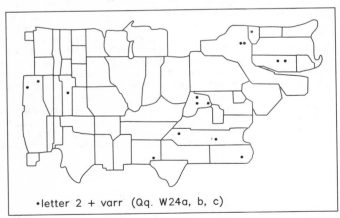

•letter 2 + varr (Qq. W24a, b, c)

3 also *almond letter, butter ~, Dutch ~:* An almond-filled pastry orig made in the shape of a letter of the alphabet. [See quot 1982] **Dutch settlement areas, esp NJ, IA** Cf **banket**
1982 *DARE* File, The original Dutch is *banket letters,* almond filling in puff pastry baked in the shape of your initial for your birthday. . . In New Jersey they are called *almond letters,* even though they are never made in the shape of letters anymore. . . In Pella [IA] they are called *Dutch letters,* or *letters,* again always sold in sticks. I once saw a bakery sign in Pella for *ledders.* When I asked . . he said . . " . . It's a Dutch word for almond pastry!" [*Ibid* **cCA,** I make banket in pieces about 12 inches long and about 2 inches in circumference. It can also be shaped into letters, like if you want to give it as a Christmas gift. Then you

might shape it into the form of someone's initial.] **1984** *Ibid* **neNJ,** Our Dutch relatives here call *banket* "butter letters." **1994** *Ibid,* I bought an almond-flavored pastry called a *Dutch letter* in Pella, Iowa.

letter carrier n Also *letter toter* [See quot 1949] Cf **news bee**
A **hover fly** or similar insect.
[**1949** Webber *Backwoods Teacher* 201 **Ozarks,** When a yellow news bee hovers around you it means you'll get a letter with good news, and . . a black one foretells bad news.] **1968** *DARE* (Qu. R12) Inf **VA15,** News bee—"letter carrier, letter toter"—yellow, looks like a sweat bee, but didn't sting. When they buzzed around your head they were supposed to be giving you good news.

letter-egg See **litter-egg**

letterfly n
See quot 1932.
1932 Farrell *Young Lonigan* 274 **Chicago IL** (as of 1916), They all stood around in a circle. The object was for everyone to say some word with fly at the end of it. When you couldn't think of another word, without hesitating, you had to say letter fly. . . By the time it was Andy's turn, the flies were pretty well exhausted. . . They gave him thirty to think of some fly. He couldn't. He said: Letter fly. Come on guys. Let ur fly! said Kenny. . . They all let ur fly, and Andy got so many pastes in the mush, he was dizzy. **1977** Talman *How Things Began* 201 **seNY** (as of c1910), Boys in a group took names such as Butterfly, Dragonfly, and Horsefly. The new arrival was told his name would be Letterfly. When the roll was called the new kid answered "let 'er fly"—they did, with whatever over-ripe fruit each had hidden behind his back. All but the newcomer and his mother thought it was good, clean fun.

letter from home n
Something or someone that triggers nostalgia.
1939 (1973) FWP *Guide MT* 138, Cornish (Cousin Jack) miners of earlier days contributed the pasty, or meat pie, to Butte cuisine. They called it "a letter from 'ome." **1945** *CA Folkl. Qrly.* 4.322 **CO** [Mining terms], *Letter from home:* Pasty. **1971** Roberts *Third Ear* np [Black], *Letter from home* . . 1. a watermelon. 2. another black person in a foreign country. **1978** *DARE* File **Chicago IL,** A black woman of about 80, born and reared in Pulaski, Tennessee, when she saw a man in Chicago buy a watermelon, said, "Oh, he has a letter from home." She said she first heard the expression when she came to Chicago. **1979** *NYT Article Letters* **West** [Copper mining expressions], The "letter from 'ome" was the Cornish Pasty. **1994** *Ibid* **cwCA,** If you are in a new or strange place and you see, hear, or taste something that reminds you of your upbringing, you might exclaim, "Isn't that a letter from home!"

letter in the post office(, there's a) See **letter 2**

letter-mail n Cf **mail,** Intro "Language Changes" I.4
1944 *PADS* 2.34 **wNC,** *Letter-mail.* . . A letter.

let the cat die See **cat n 7**

let the hammer down v phr [From the action of uncocking a gun; see quot 1966] **SW**
To give a restive horse a preliminary, calming warm-up.
1944 Adams *Western Words* 91, *Let the hammer down*—To take the rough edges off a horse. **1961** Adams *Old-Time Cowhand* 301, The buster's job was to give the hoss his start as a cow hoss. After the first few tries to take the rough edges off, he turned 'im over to the other riders as gentled . . but it'd be a long time before the rider . . could ride 'im on duty without takin' the kinks out of his backbone, which the cowboy speaks of as . . "toppin' off," . . "lettin' the hammer down." **1966** *DARE* Tape **NM13,** Some of those old horses that he rode on a circle would buck if allowed to. And he knew when he got on that horse he'd wanna keep him started, and he'd have a hold of the horn of the saddle with one hand and the reins in the other. And as is common practice, he'd kinda let the hammer down on him. In other words, uncock him by slowly trotting off. But as soon as he had him where he thought he could handle him, why, he broke into a lope.

let the hide go with the tallow See **hide n² 7a**

let the hogs out v phr Also *let the mules out*
1954 *Harder Coll.* **cwTN,** Let the hogs (mules) out . . to make an embarrassing mistake.

let the old cat die See **cat n 7**

let the tail go with the hide See **hide n² 7a**

lettle See **little**

lettuce n

1 =**water lettuce.**

1885 Thompson *By-Ways* 31, The snake-bird, too, that veritable water-dragon of the South, was there, wriggling and squirming in the amber-brown pools amongst the lily-pads and lettuce. **1975** Natl. Audubon Soc. *Corkscrew* 20 **FL**, *Lettuce lakes*—Here and there among the large cypresses there are deeper lakes, most of which are covered with water lettuce . . which floats freely on the surface. . . The lettuce is one of the principal sources of the dead vegetable matter . . deposited as a rich organic peat or muck. . . From a distance the thickly growing lettuce has the appearance of clipped lawn. . . The name of "lettuce" has been conferred on this plant because of its superficial resemblance to leaf lettuce.

2 See **lettuce saxifrage.**

3 A **wintergreen** (here: *Pyrola rotundifolia*).

1958 Jacobs-Burlage *Index Plants NC* 173, *Pyrola americana. . . Lettuce. . .* This species . . is found throughout North Carolina and South Carolina in damp woods.

lettuce bed n

=**hell 1.**

1917 Kephart *Camping & Woodcraft* 2.24 **eTN, wNC**, Those great tracts of rhododendron . . cover mile after mile of steep mountainside where few men have ever been. The natives call such wastes "laurel slicks," "woolly heads," "lettuce beds," "yaller patches," and "hells." **1939** in 1972 Hall *Sayings Old Smoky* 94 **eTN, wNC**, A humorous understatement for rhododendron thicket: "The dogs was in the Devil's Courthouse fightin' the bear. . . We hit in after it, and it wandered through them roughs—we called it 'lettuce beds.'"

lettuce bird n [See quot 1891] **chiefly Midl** See Map

A **goldfinch 1** (here: *Carduelis tristis*).

a1782 (1788) Jefferson *Notes VA* 75, Fringilla tristis . . American goldfinch. Lettuce bird. **1808** Wilson *Amer. Ornith.* 1.21, [Goldfinches] pass by various names expressive of their food, color, &c. such as Thistle-bird, Lettuce-bird, Sallad-bird. **1874** NY Acad. Sci. *Annals Lyceum Nat. Hist.* 10.371 **IL**, *[Chrysomitris] tristis . . .* American Goldfinch; Black-winged Yellow Bird; Lettuce Bird. **1891** *Leighton News* (AL) 1 Oct np, One of our sprightliest and most noticeable birds during summer and the first half of September is the Goldfinch, Yellow-bird, Wild Canary, Thistle-bird, or Lettuce-bird, as it is variously called. The first three names apply to its beautiful plumage . . and the latter two to its habit of feeding upon seeds of the thistle and other plants. **1934** Vines *Green Thicket* 60 **cnAL**, He had a little old trunk nearly full of feathers and down from . . lettucebirds. **1956** MA Audubon Soc. *Bulletin* 40.254, *Goldfinch. . . Lettuce Bird . . Rather general.* **1965–70** DARE (Qu. Q14, . . *Names . . for these birds:* . . *goldfinch*) Infs IL143, IN31, 42, 45, MD30, OH33, 82, TN6, 11, Lettuce bird.

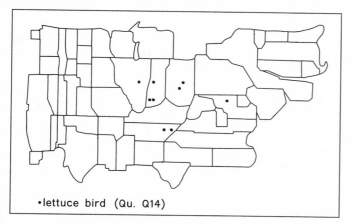

•lettuce bird (Qu. Q14)

lettuce saxifrage n Also *lettuce* **chiefly Appalachians**

A **saxifrage:** usu *Saxifraga micranthidifolia*, but also *S. michauxii*.

1848 Gray *Manual of Botany* 149, *S[axifraga] erosa. . . Lettuce Saxifrage. . .* Penn . . , and throughout the Alleghanies southward. **1903** Porter *Flora PA* 160, *Saxifraga micranthidifolia. . . Lettuce Saxifrage. . .* In cold brooks. **1943** Fernald-Kinsey *Edible Wild Plants E. N. Amer.* 225, *Lettuce-Saxifrage, Saxifraga . . micranthidifolia. . .* According to Asa Gray, "Under the name of Lettuce, the leaves are eaten by the

inhabitants [of the Carolina mountains] as salad." **1959** Gillespie *Compilation Edible Wild Plants WV* 60, Lettuce-Saxifrage (*Saxifraga micranthidifolia*). . . Uses: As a salad ingredient. **1970** Campbell et al. *Gt. Smoky Wildflowers* 56, *Michaux's Saxifrage. . .* Another common name is *lettuce saxifrage.*

leuch See **laugh**

leusifee See **lucivee**

leve See **lief** adv

levee n[1] |ˈlɛvi| Also sp *levy* [Fr *levée*]

1 An embankment, spec:

a One built along a river to control flooding. **chiefly Missip Valley, esp LA** See also **marching around the levee**

[**1719** in Winsor *Narr. & Crit. Hist.* V.39 *(DA)*, Devant la ville [New Orleans] il y a une levée et par derriere un fossé. [=Before the city there is a levee and behind it a ditch.]] **1766** in 1916 Mereness *Travels* 481 **Missip R**, [They] are obliged to have Levée's of Earth to keep off the Floods. **1833** (1847) Lundy *Life & Travels* 34 **New Orleans LA**, The river is up to the levee, and the streets are watered by sluices. **1854** (1932) Bell *Log TX–CA Trail* 36.66 **cCA**, At an expense of two hundred thousand dollars a splendid Levee has been built around the city [=Sacramento], water is plentifully supplied. **1862** (1922) Jackson *Col.'s Diary* 53 **neAR**, A levee some five feet high protected the farms from being overflowed by the Mississippi River. **1903** DN 2.319 **seMO**, *Levy. . .* an embankment for protecting land from the overflow of a river. **1907** DN 3.232 **nwAR**, Levee. **1967** *Catahoula News–Booster* (Jonesville–Harrisonburg LA) 23 Nov 3/5, The $35 million project now underway south of Jonesville which includes the locks and dam, diversion canal, levees and road improvement. **1967–69** DARE (Qu. EE1, . . *Games*) Inf GA58, Up and down the levee; TX12, Marching round the levee; (Qu. EE33, . . *Outdoor games*) Inf KY17, Marching around the levee; (Qu. MM24, . . "*The river is just . . _____ from the house.*") Infs LA8, 11, Across the levee. **1968** *Daily Republican Eagle* (Red Wing MN) 1 May 12/5, Plans for repair of the Levee wall from the lift station to Broad st., and installation of bulkhead along the waterfront . . were okayed. **1969** DARE Tape IL69, It was in 1917 when they started putting the levee [ˈlɛvi] up, and 1918 they got it complete. **1986** Pederson *LAGS Concordance*, c75 infs, **Gulf Region, esp LA**, Levee(s). [DARE Ed: Some of these infs may refer instead to other senses below.] **1994** *WI State Jrl.* (Madison) 10 July sec B 1/3 **swIL**, The hardy residents rebuilt then, just as they did in 1919 when the federal levee was built following another flood [of the Missip R]. . . But the worst jolt came last July 22. The angry floodwaters punched a 700-foot gap in the island's 15-mile levee.

b One that serves as a landing or wharf. **chiefly Missip Valley**

1813 *Cramer's Pittsburgh Almanack for 1814* 52 **New Orleans LA**, This class confine themselves to the levee and levee street principally. **1842** H. Caswall *City of Mormons* 3 *(DA)* **MO**, The landing-place [at St. Louis] (or levee, as it is denominated) was literally swarming with life. **1948** WELS Suppl. **swWI**, Boats landed at the 'levee', not 'wharf'. **1949** *Time* 5 Sept 58 **ceMO**, For eleven weeks, St. Louis playgoers had gone down to the *Goldenrod's* mooring by the cobblestoned levee and paid 75¢ a head to sass the actors in his hokum-logged version of *Hamlet.* **1986** Pederson *LAGS Concordance (Wharf)* 13 infs, **chiefly LA, AR**, Levee.

c One built around a field to confine irrigation water.

1855 *NY Tribune* (NY) 16 June 2/2 **seSC**, We . . found two hundred stalwart men and women . . engaged in repairing a breach of some hundred feet in length of one of the levees or mud dams which surround each division of the field to regulate the flow of water. **1898** U.S. Geol. Surv. *Water-Supply Papers* 18.80 **cwCA**, In alfalfa fields the levees inclosing them are often made so flat and low that farming implements can pass over them. **1941** *Daily Oklahoman* (Oklahoma City OK) 30 Sep. *(DA)*, In addition to crop losses, farmers feared heavy damage from erosion, loss of levees and irrigation canals. **1966–67** DARE Tape AR33, Each levee, each dike, whatever you called it, is one . . elevation from one end to the other. The next one is . . an inch and a half lower than the one above it, and progressively on down. . . The effect of that is to hold your water evenly distributed over your [rice] field. *Ibid* TX8, You build your levees [ˈlɛˑəviˑz̧], and it just depends on how you're gonna plant your rice what you do. If you're gonna plant it in water by airplane, you build your levees up and then you put your water on the soil.

d One that carries a road across low ground; hence, a highway. Cf **fill** n[1] **1**

1903 *DN* 2.319 **seMO**, *Levy*. . . A turnpike road. **1907** *DN* 3.232 **nwAR**, *Levee* ['lɛvi]. . . A turnpike road. **c1960** *Wilson Coll.* **csKY**, *Levee*. . . A fill or embankment; the word meant both a stream levee and a fill across a valley.

2 Used as the nickname for a red-light district, esp one in Chicago. [Transf from **1b** above]

1882 *Chicago Daily Tribune* (IL) 25 Jan 8/2 **neIL**, Maggie Moore, one of the old-time residents of the levee, was arrested last night . . upon charges of abduction and keeping a house of ill-fame. **1901** Dunne *Mr. Dooley's Opinions* 211 **Chicago IL**, If Fate had condemned me to start in business on th' Levee, I'd sarve th' black man that put down th' money as quick as I wud th' white. . . But bein' that I'm up here in this Cowcasyan neighborhood, I spurn th' dark coin. **1903** *Sun* (NY NY) 8 Nov 3/4 **Chicago IL**, *To Segregate Vice Mayor Harrison Favors Fixing Three Places in Chicago for It to Settle.* . . Three levees, one for each of the three leading parts of the city, are to be sanctioned by the city of Chicago. **1948** *Chicago Sun-Times* (IL) 11 Aug 2/5 *(DA)*, [His] beat was the infamous old Chicago Levee District. **1970** *DARE* (Qu. C35, *Nicknames for the different parts of your town or city*) Inf **IL**126, Levee—taverns.

levee n[2] |lə'vi, lɛ-| **chiefly NEng** *old-fash*
A formal or informal social event, often held in someone's honor; a less formal social gathering, often held as a fundraiser.

1766 (1888) Cutler *Life* 1.12 **ceMA**, A second grand levee at Ellis' Inn. **1813** (1927) Gerry *Diary* 179 **OH**, Mrs. Madison also entertained me with an account of her levees &c., &c. of similar things. **1823** in 1894 Stockbridge *Model Pastor* 36 **NH**, Last night attended a levee at Dr. Staughton's, where were the Faculty, some of the trustees, and the young gentlemen who exhibited the day before, entertained in the politest manner. **1870** Smith *20 Yrs. Wall St.* 33 **seNY** (as of c1800), Mrs. Washington's levees were very fashionable. Mrs. Adams wished to introduce at these levees of state the French custom of announcing visitors. **a1890** (1944) Robinson *Hist. Morrill* 64 **ME** (as of 1863), The women were not behind, and levees and sociables were held to raise subscriptions; socks, mittens, and underclothes for the army. Two levees were held in the Sons of Temperance Hall. **1907** *DN* 3.192 **seNH**, *Levee* [lə'vi]. . . A public entertainment at night held to raise funds for some purpose. Contributions of cooked food are made by those interested, and a supper is served in order to increase the financial receipts as much as possible. Londonderry and Salem, N.H. **1930** *AmSp* 6.149 **cME** (as of 1880s), They're a-gettin' up a levee (church fair) an' Mis' Smith is head-cohooter. **1941** *LANE* Map 414 *(Social gathering)* 1 inf, **ceMA**, *Levee* [ləvɪi], old-fashioned; 1 inf, **seNH**, *Levee* [łɛvɪ⁺ˆ], includes supper and perhaps a play at the theater; [łəvij], older pron.; 1 inf, **csME**, *Levee* [ləvij], a church fair. **1969** *DARE* (Qu. FF2, *. . Kinds of parties*) Inf **MA**38, Levee [lɛ'vi]—used to have them in winter—a big turkey dinner—had them over a hundred years—danced, too. **1979** *DARE* File **cnMA** (as of c1915), When I was a small child I used to hear people talk about going to the Petersham levee ['pitəs,hæm lə'vi] in the next town. It must have been a grand affair, for women talked of having new evening gowns for it.

levee walker n [levee n[1] **1c**]
=little blue heron.

1938 Oberholser *Bird Life LA* 60, One of the peculiarities of this bird [=the little blue heron] is its fondness for crawfishes, and on this account it has gained the friendship of the rice growers, who regard it as exceedingly useful in keeping down these crustaceans, which infest the rice field levees. From the habit of seeking its food in this way it has acquired the name 'levee walker.'

level n **chiefly Mid and S Atl** See Map Cf **flat** n[1] **1**
An area of flat ground; a plain, plateau; also used in place names.

1637 *Patents* 1.513 *(AmSp* 15.280) **VA**, Upon a barren Levell which goeth from Martins hundred to Chiskiacke. **1650** (1923) Bland *New Brittaine* 2 **seVA**, We journied . . from the first Towne upon a very rich levell of Land. **1795** in 1907 *OH Archeol. & Hist. Qrly.* 16.380 **swOH**, From this to Hamilton is the most beautiful level that ever my eyes beheld; the soil is rich, free from swampy or marshy ground and the growth mostly hickory. **1797** Imlay *Western Terr.* 28 **cnWV**, You ascend a considerable distance from the shore of the Ohio, and when you would suppose you had arrived at the summit of a mountain, you find yourself upon an extensive level. **1842** in 1959 *IN Mag. Hist.* 55.350 **wPA**, **neKY** (as of 1766–1842), Gosset and myself travelled in company; we

proceeded up the big levels, crossed the Droop mountain, and up the little levels to the Clover-lick. **1905** *DN* 3.87 **nwAR**, *Marching on the level*. . . The name of a children's game. **1959** McAtee *Oddments* 10 **cNC**, *Frog Level*—Now known as Smith Level, near Dogwood Acres. **1965–70** *DARE* (Qu. C29, *A good-sized stretch of level land with practically no trees*) Inf **TN**14, Level; **VA**75, A level; **DE**4, The levels—up here back of Smyrna; **VA**47, Levels; (Qu. C34, *Nicknames for nearby settlements, villages, or districts*) Infs **NC**46, **SC**56, Frog Level; (Qu. C35, *Nicknames for the different parts of your town or city*) Inf **VA**5, Frog Level; (Qu. EE1, *. . Games . . children play . . in which they form a ring, and either sing or recite a rhyme*) Infs **FL**18, **GA**8, 9, Marching (a)round the level. **1986** Pederson *LAGS Concordance* (Swamp) 1 inf, **cAL**, Frog level—where his house is; was wet ground.

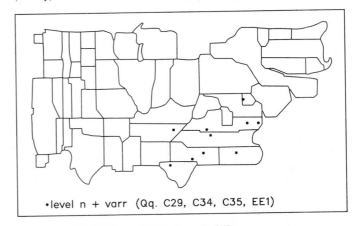

•level n + varr (Qq. C29, C34, C35, EE1)

level v [*OED* 1552 →; "*Obs. exc. dial.*"]
1892 *DN* 1.230 **KY**, *Level*: levy. "To level on one's property."

level adv
1972 Carr *Da Kine Talk* 136 **HI**, *Level* vs. *straight along*—"Den you go level da road, eh?" The Hawaiian woman . . meant 'straight along the road'. This use of *level* may well have come from a loose translation of the Hawaiian word *pololei*. . . The Japanese language has a number of words for 'flat', 'level', and 'straight along'.

level down v phr
To work away.
1928 Peterkin *Scarlet Sister Mary* 311 **SC** [Gullah], "Do looka how Emma [=an infant] duh level down on de milk. E's pure a-starvin, po lil creeter," Seraphine sympathized. And while Emma leveled down, Mary untied the strings of Unex's wet shoes.

level full adj phr **scattered, but esp Sth, Midl** See Map Cf **even full**
Completely full.
1902 *DN* 2.238 **sIL**, *Level full*. . . Even full. **1965–70** *DARE* (Qu. LL28, *. . Entirely full: "The box of apples was _____."*) 32 Infs, **scattered, but esp Sth, Midl**, Level full.

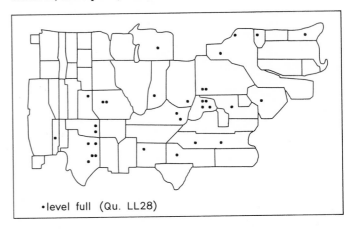

•level full (Qu. LL28)

lever n Also *lever cart*
A handcar.
[**1889** *Century Dict.* 3427, *Lever hand-car*, a hand-car which is driven

by means of levers attached to cranks.] **1895** *DN* 1.372 **seKY, eTN, wNC,** *The lēver* is the common expression at Roan Mountain for hand-car. **1986** Pederson *LAGS Concordance,* 1 inf, **neFL,** Lever carts—on railroad.

leverwood n[1] [See quots 1843, 1938] **esp NEast**
=hop hornbeam 1.
   1755 in 1827 NH Hist. Soc. *Coll.* 2.102, In this meadow, they left a bow, made of lever wood, and several arrows. **1843** Torrey *Flora NY* 2.185, *Ostrya Virginica. . . Hop Hornbeam. . .* The wood of this tree is white, very compact, and of great strength. It is often used for levers, and is hence called *Lever-wood* in some places. **1859** (1880) Darlington *Amer. Weeds* 323, The wood of this small tree is remarkably firm and tough; and although neither very common nor very important, it may be well, perhaps, for the intelligent farmer to know what it is when he meets with it. According to Mr. Emerson, it is known by the name of Lever-wood in New England. **1900** (1927) Keeler *Our Native Trees* 318, When woodmen need a lever they seek at once for a Hop Hornbeam, whence its wild-wood name of Leverwood. **1938** Brown *Trees NE U.S.* 177, *Ostrya virginiana. . .* Hop Hornbeam, Ironwood, Leverwood. . . Wood very heavy, hard, strong, tough, close-grained. . . Used for tool handles, mallets, levers, fence posts and for fuel. **1960** Vines *Trees SW* 145, *Woolly American Hop-hornbeam—Ostrya virginiana. . .* Vernacular names are Ironwood, Leverwood. . . The wood is used for posts, golf clubs, tool handles, mallets, and woodenware.

leverwood n[2] See **leaverwood**

levy n[1] [Abbr for *elevenpence* or *elevenpenny bit;* see quots 1848, 1859] **chiefly C Atl** *old-fash* Cf **escalin, fip**
   Originally a Spanish real; hence, the sum of 12½ cents; also fig.
   1829 in 1944 *AmSp* 19.197, "But them fips and levies," throwing a dirty leather bag, with a dozen small silver coins on the table, "must first go." **1835** (1906) Bradley *Jrl.* 217, I was tempted to try a glass of lemonade. Charge, a levy or ninepence. [*DARE* Ed: Writer is from NH; at the time of this entry he was near Cincinnati OH.] **1838** Neal *Charcoal Sketches* 98, A fip's worth of dinner, or a levy's worth of sleep. **1848** Bartlett *Americanisms* 135, The old system of reckoning by shillings and pence is continued by retail dealers generally; and will continue, as long as the Spanish coins remain in circulation. In consequence of the abovenamed diversity in the colonial currencies, in New England the Spanish real of ⅛ of a dollar or 12½ cents is called *ninepence;* in New York, *one shilling;* in Pennsylvania, *elevenpence* or a *levy;* and in many of the Southern States, a *bit.* **1859** (1968) *Ibid* 142, [In the commercial cities and along the sea-board, Spanish coins of a dollar and fractional parts of a dollar were very common, and passed currently for their original value, until the act of February 21, 1857, which . . caused the foreign coinage to be suddenly withdrawn from the currency.] *Ibid* 242, *Levy.* Elevenpence. In the State of Pennsylvania, Maryland, and Virginia, the Spanish real, or eighth part of a dollar, or twelve and a half cents. Sometimes called an *elevenpenny bit.* **1883** Albany Inst. *Trans.* 10.336 **NY,** The "shilling" of our own State is the "levy" of Pennsylvania, the "bit" of San Francisco, the "ninepence" of old New England, and the "escalan" of New Orleans. **1928** Ruppenthal *Coll.* **KS,** *Levy. . .* 12½ cents, used by immigrants to Kansas from Philadelphia and vicinity. "Calico was a levy a yard." **1940** Writers' Program *Guide MD* 8 **cnMD,** In Baltimore's Lexington Market, the obsolete term 'levy,' meaning approximately 12½¢, is occasionally heard. For instance, the huckster may offer his *Anaranel* (Anne Arundel County) strawberries at 'a levy a quart.' **1982** Barrick *Coll.* **csPA** (as of a1960), *Levy*—twelve-and-a-half cents; a "bit." Auctioneer use. "Fifty cents, three levies, a quarter."

levy n[2] See **levee** n[1]

Lewis's woodpecker n
   Std: a **woodpecker** (here: *Melanerpes lewis*) native to the western US. Also called **apple bird 1, black woodpecker 2, crow ~ 1**

li See **little**

liar n[1] Usu |ˈlaɪə(r)|; also |lɑr| Pronc-sp *lor* See Pronc Intro 3.I.1.g
   1923 *DN* 5.211 **swMO,** In such words as *fire, hire, . . liar, briar,* etc., [i] is sounded as 'ah'. **1923** (1946) Greer-Petrie *Angeline Doin' Society* 20 **csKY,** I'm the biggest lor (liar) in the world. **c1960** Wilson *Coll.* **csKY,** *Liar* is often [lɑr].

liar n[2] See **lawyer**

liar's bench n
   See quots.

1975 Gould *ME Lingo* 162, Liars' bench—A settee before the village store, inside by the stove, or at the post office, where gentlemen exchange veracities. **1977** *DARE* File **csWI,** [Advt for Mt. Horeb Lumber Co.:] Liar's bench. [*DARE* Ed: Illustr shows a wooden bench with curved metal legs, intended for outdoor use.] **1980** in 1983 Beyle *How Talk Cape Cod* 26, Liar's bench—The wooden seat adorning the front porch of the town's general store, post office or bait shop.

liar weed n
   A **plantain;** see quot.
   1978 *DARE* File **WI,** Liar weed = plantain; as you pulled the strands from the leaves, the longer the strand, the bigger the lie you told.

lib v See **live** v

lib adv See **lief** adv

lib'ary See **library**

libel n, v Also sp *libill;* folk-etym sp *lie-bill* Cf **label**
   A Forms.
   1875 in 1955 Lee *Mormon Chron.* 2.373 **UT,** My portrait in Tribune was Burles[q]ue & I ought to Sue them for lie bill. **1909** *DN* 3.345 **eAL, wGA,** Lie bill. . . Libel. Facetious. **1917** *DN* 4.414 **wNC,** Lie-bill. . . Perversion of *libel.* Also Kan. **c1920** in 1993 Farwell–Nicholas *Smoky Mt. Voices* 104 **sAppalachians,** An' him a Baptis' preacher an' my son-in-law! I knocked a hole with him in the Chatooga [sic] River big enough to drown a cow in, an' now he goes a-lyin' and a-lie-billin' me! **1923** [see B below]. **1928** [see B below]. **a1975** [see B below].
   B As noun.
   A formal declaration admitting a previous lie; hence phr *take the libel* to admit formally that one has lied. **esp S Midl**
   1919 *Law Notes* Oct 138 **NC,** In your issue for . . July, 1919 . . , you have an article headed "The Founder of the Ananias Club," quoting an old court record of Cumberland county, North Carolina, . . 1822 one William Jones had an entry made that "I do hereby acknowledge myself a Public Liar, and that I have told unnecessary lies on Jesse Northington, and his family," etc . . a paper of this character is still in use in some rural communities of the South and is known as a 'Lie Bill.' **1923** *DN* 5.213 **swMO,** Lie-bill. . . Libel. "He signed a lie-bill," i.e., made a written retraction and confessed therein that his previous statement was false. **1928** Ruppenthal *Coll.* **KS,** Lie bill . . an acknowledgment of slander or libel—probably lie bill and libel are confused in the minds of many. **1953** Randolph–Wilson *Down in Holler* 261 **cwAR,** An old settler named Rice (*Arcadian Life* [Caddo Gap, Ark.], October, 1936, p. 11) was accused of stealing silver from a deacon; after a "church trial" resulted in acquittal, the deacon gave Rice "a *libel* written on paper cambric." **a1975** Lunsford *It Used to Be* 162 **sAppalachians,** "Libill" is used for the term "libel," a legal term. The expression would be used in this way, "I'll make him take the libill and his word will be no more account in court."

liberry See **library**

liberty n
   A **club moss** (here: *Lycopodium complanatum*).
   1892 *Jrl. Amer. Folkl.* 5.105 **cnMD,** *Lycopodium complanatum . .* liberty. **1898** *Ibid* 11.283 **cnMD,** *Lycopodium* (sp.), liberty.

liberty stripe n Also *liberty strip*
   A red, white, and blue frozen confection.
   1969 *WI State Jrl.* (Madison) 8 June sec 4 1, I want a grape popsicle or some liberty strips and a big sucker. **1992** *DARE* File **seWI** (as of c1955), In summer we often bought "liberty stripes," a sort of "flag"-colored popsicle which was blue at the bottom, white in the middle, and red on top.

liberty tea n
   A **loosestrife 1** (here: *Lysimachia quadrifolia*); also a tea made from this plant.
   1837 NH Hist. Soc. *Coll.* 5.84, Many adopted the use of what was called *Liberty tea,* as a substitute for the Chinese herb. "It was made of four-leaved loosestrife." **1898** *Jrl. Amer. Folkl.* 11.274 **seME,** *Lysimachia quadrifolia . .* liberty tea. [Footnote: Used rather than pay the tax on tea.] **1929** *Torreya* 29.150, Lysimachia quadrifolia, "liberty-tea," (we were always told it was so-named because this plant was used to avoid tea-taxes). **1940** Clute *Amer. Plant Names* 112, *L[ysimachia] quadrifolia.* Whorled Loosestrife . . crosswort . . liberty-tea.

libery See **library**

libill See **libel**

library n Usu |ˈlaɪˌb(r)ɛri|; also esp Atlantic |ˈlaɪbri|; for addit varr see quots Pronc-spp *lib'ary, liber(r)y, libry*

A Forms.

1893 *DN* 1.280, 'Lib(r)ary' (sounded [ˈlaɪbrɪ] or [ˈlaɪbrɪ] [sic]; I have also heard [ˈlaɪbˌɛrɪ], only recently from a professor in Williams College, a native of Williamstown [Massachusetts]. **1893** Shands *MS Speech* 43, *Liberry* [ˈlaɪbɛrɪ]. Negro for *library.* **1907** *DN* 3.246 eME, *Lib'ary.* . . Library. Common pronunciation. **1909** *DN* 3.345 eAL, wGA, *Libery* [ˈlaɪbɛrɪ]. . . An illiterate pronunciation of *library.* **1923** (1946) Greer-Petrie *Angeline Doin' Society* 16 csKY, They had a liberry full of books. **1926** *AmSp* 2.83 ME, I realize that I have by no means exhausted this subject of the Maine speech. . . For example nothing has been said about the omission of the *r* in such words as "libry," . . and "govner." **1931–33** [see B3 below]. **1942** in 1944 *ADD* 356 seNY, *Library.* . . 1st *r* omitted by 6 persons, (both *r*s pron. 37). **c1955** Reed–Person *Ling. Atlas Pacific NW,* 7 infs [of c50], Liberry. **c1960** *Wilson Coll.* csKY, Library is often [ˈlaɪˌbɛrɪ]. **1961** Kurath–McDavid *Pronc. Engl.* 173, Two major types of pronunciation are current in the Eastern States: (1) trisyllabic /ˈlaɪˌbrɛri ~ ˈlaɪˌbɛri/, with half-stress on the second syllable; and (2) /ˈlaɪbrəri ~ ˈlaɪbəri ~ ˈlaɪbri/. Type (1) occurs everywhere, but with greatly varying frequency; type (2) is largely confined to several subareas on the Atlantic seaboard. The disyllabic variant /ˈlaɪbri/ predominates in Eastern New England, in Maryland (along with Philadelphia and vicinity), in northeastern North Carolina, and in the Low Country of South Carolina and Georgia. **1968** Kellner *Aunt Serena* 83 IN, I get 'em at the Public Liberry. **1973** *PADS* 60.57 seNC, *Library.* . . Only one informant used the disyllabic variant . . /ˈlaɪbri/. All the rest used the trisyllabic version /ˈlaɪˌbɛri/. **1975** Gould *ME Lingo* 162, *Liberry*— At least 999 out of 1000 times. **1976** Garber *Mountain-ese* 53 sAppalachians, *Liberry.* **1989** Pederson *LAGS Tech. Index* 306 Gulf Region, [308 infs responded with proncs of the type [ˈlaɪbrɛrɪ]; 207 infs, [ˈlaɪbɛrɪ]; 81 infs [ˈlaɪbrʌrɪ]; 57 infs [ˈlaɪbʌrɪ]; 55 infs [ˈlaɪbrɪ]; 18 infs, [ˈlaɪbrɛ]; 7 infs, [ˈlaɪbrɛrɪ]; 6 infs, [ˈlaɪbrɪrɪ]; 6 infs, [ˈlaɪbrɪ]; 4 infs, [ˈlaɪbrɛrɪ]; 3 infs, [ˈlaɪbrʌrɪ]; 2 infs, [ˈlaɪbæɪ]; 2 infs, [ˈlaɪbræɪ]; 2 infs, [ˈlaɪbɛrɪ]; 2 infs, [ˈlaɪbɪrɪ]; 2 infs, [ˈlaɪbɛrə].]

B Senses.

1 A book borrowed from a library. [Engl dial]

1907 *DN* 3.193 seNH, *Lib'ry.* . . "Did you take the lib'ries back, Herbert?"

2 also *outdoor library, Sears-Roebuck* ~: A toilet or outhouse. [See quot 1949] joc Cf **reading room**

1931–33 *LANE Worksheets* ceRI, Library [ˈlaɪbrɪ]—Outhouse. **1949** *PADS* 11.8 wTX, *Library* . . an outdoor privy. Humorous euphemism arising from the reading material usually present in outdoor privies. **1965–70** *DARE* (Qu. F37, . . *An indoor toilet*) Infs CA94, IL34, 98, PA150, TX28, WI47, Library; (Qu. M21b, *Joking names for an outside toilet building*) Infs AL47, CA36, 145, NE11, PA33, TX43, 45, WA30, Library; AL62, IN8, 11, IA33, OR17, PA29, 127, 193, 232, TN44, WI63, Outdoor library; MI19, Sears-Roebuck library. **1973** Allen *LAUM* 1.181 (as of c1950), *Privy* . . library [2 infs, seMN, cwNE].

lice See **louse A1**

license n

Gram forms.

1 Understood as pl, pronc |ˈlaɪsn̩z|; hence, by back-formation, sg |ˈlaɪsn̩|, pronc-spp *licen, lysun.* chiefly S Midl

1890 *DN* 1.65 KY, *A pair of license* = a license to marry. **1903** *DN* 2.319 seMO, *License.* . . Pronounced licenze. 'He axed me for the licens and I handed them to him.' This is one of the numerous instances in which a plural form is taken as if it had a plural meaning. **1906** *DN* 3.144 nwAR, *License, n. pl.* Licenses. "He couldn't get those license." **1909** [see 2 below]. **1915** *DN* 4.180 swVA, The following words are thought of as plurals: . . license, cheese. **1923** *DN* 5.213 swMO, *License.* . . Used as if plural in form. "Them license aint no good fer they aint signed up." **1923** *DN* 5.236 swWI, *License.* . . A singular used as a plural, as of two or more hunting licenses. "Have ye got them license?" **1940** Harris *Folk Plays* 101 NC, "You have the license of course." "Yes, sure. Here they are." **1941** in 1944 *ADD* 356 eWV, [ˈlaɪsn̩]. **1950** *WELS Suppl.* csWI, License . . used as plural. "They're being married Saturday. Their license were in the paper tonight." **1983** Allin *S. Legislative Dict.* 17 Sth, *Lysuns (always plural):* a permit to operate or act. "When the game warden ast for my lysuns, I couldn't find them."

2 Used with std pl form to indicate a single document.

1909 *DN* 3.345 eAL, wGA, *License.* . . Frequently used as a plural. Sometimes the form *licenses* is used. "Did you get your licenses?" **1968** *DARE* File neAL, *Licenses* . . driver's license—always plural. "He got arrested because he didn't have his licenses on him."

lices See **louse A2**

licey adj

1986 Pederson *LAGS Concordance*, 1 inf, cnAL, Licey—full of lice.

lick v Pronc-sp *Gullah, leek*

A Forms.

1888 Jones *Negro Myths* 98 GA coast [Gullah], Buh Wolf meet Buh Rabbit duh seddown een de big road, dist es content es ef nuttne bin happne, duh leek isself. [=Brother Wolf met Brother Rabbit sitting down in the big road, just as content as if nothing had happened, licking himself.] **1922** Gonzales *Black Border* 310 sSC, GA coasts [Gullah glossary], *Leek*—lick, licks, licked, licking—with the tongue.

B Senses.

1 To strike, beat—often used with advs; hence ppl adj phr *licked up* (pronc-sp *lick up*). Gullah Note: The senses 'to beat (someone) severely (esp as a punishment)' and 'to defeat (someone)' are widespread and not illustrated here. Cf *DJE,* where exx of *lick* 'to hit, strike, beat' occur, like those below, in contexts where most varieties of Amer Engl would not select this verb.

1888 Jones *Negro Myths* 93 GA coast [Gullah], Buh Elephunt . . roll ober an try fuh out de fire een eh yez. Eh tek eh trunk an try fuh lick um out, but befo de fire done out, eh bun de hinge er all two eh yez. [=Brother Elephant . . rolled over and tried to put out the fire in his ears. He took his trunk and tried to beat it out, but before the fire was fully out it had burned the hinges of both his ears.] *Ibid* 120, Buh Rocoon ax Buh Possum wuh mek, wen de dog tackle um, eh double up ehself, . . an wunt fight lucker man an lick de dog off. [=Brother Raccoon asks Brother Possum what's the reason, when the dog attacks him, he doubles himself up, . . and won't fight like a man and beat the dog off.] *Ibid* 126, Buh Wolf all lick up so eh casely kin walk. [=Brother Wolf was all beaten up so he could scarcely walk.] **1966** *DARE* Tape SC15, Then by the lamp or the fire, they cannot run, they cannot move. Then we take that switch and lick them at the neck, kill them. Put 'em in the sack, keep on going. And in that way we call that lick coot; SC16, We used to catch birds and lick coot and shoot duck. We made money on bird, coot, and duck.

2 with *it:* To move fast. Cf **lickety-split**

1850 Garrard *Wah-to-yah* 17, The mad animal . . charged. How they did "lick it" over the ground! **1884** Smith *Bill Arp's Scrap Book* 64 nwGA, He rode seven miles and back as hard as he could lick it. **1901** Harben *Westerfelt* 222 nGA, Toot drove nipitytuck down the street from the Hawkbill as fast as he could lick it. [**1903** *DN* 2.302 Cape Cod MA (as of a1857), Various phrases are used to describe the speed of an animal, as 'he went . . clear lick-it.']

3 with *back:* To turn suddenly, dart back.

1888 Jones *Negro Myths* 2 GA coast [Gullah], Eh run dis way, de fire meet um. Eh lick back an try tarruh [=the other] side. **1922** Gonzales *Black Border* 310 sSC, GA coasts [Gullah glossary], *Lick back*—turn, turns, turned, turning back, while moving rapidly.

4 in phrr *lick one's calf over* and varr: To do something again; to repeat an action inadequately done. Sth, S Midl

1931 *PMLA* 46.1307 sAppalachians, Go back and lick your calf over. (Do the job over.) **1942** Hurston *Dust Tracks* 280 FL [Black], Thus the congregation could judge whether they had really "got religion" or whether they were faking and needed to be sent back to "lick de calf over" again. **1944** *AmSp* 19.156 sIN, *Lick your calf over* (do again some task that was not done well the first time). **1946** *PADS* 6.39 cwVA (as of 1900–10), You'll have to *lick* your calf over. (Parental reproof to a child who has slighted his work and must do it over.) [**1969** *DARE* FW Addit KY21, *Lick one's calves*—To make someone do something he should have but hasn't. "If he doesn't get over here and fix that tire, I'm going to make him lick his calves."] **c1970** Halpert *Coll.* 10 wKY, wTN, Calf—Go back and lick your calf over = advice to one whose job has failed. (Rare). **1972** *Atlanta Letters* cnGA, "You'll have to lick that calf over again." The reference is to a job poorly done which must be done over. **1979** *DARE* File Columbia SC, *Lick (the) calf over* v phr—meaning there's something out of place in your grooming. For example, your slip might be showing or your stocking seam is crooked or your hem is coming down, etc. Refers to a cow grooming her calf by licking her. **1982** *Ibid* **NC,** [From a 30-ish woman, Black, from Winterville, NC. . .] We'll lick this calf again (We'll try to do it again and get it right this time). **1992** *Houston Chron.* (TX) 5 Apr sec G 4, Shera . . explained her cousin's expression "to lick the calf over," a term for starting over. "When calves are born, the mother cow licks the calf until he stands on his spindly legs," she wrote. "If the calf doesn't stand, the mother has to lick that calf over.["]

lick n

1 A sharp blow or stroke, as with the fist, a weapon, or a tool. **chiefly Sth, S Midl, TX, OK** See Map See also **hit a lick**

1851 (1969) Burke *Polly Peablossom* 171 **S Midl,** A wicked sort of dig in my side, which I thought might be inflicted with the naked elbow; this was intended as a kind of interest on the operation, given in "have-the-last-lick" spirit of mind. **1899** (1912) Green *VA Folk-Speech* 260, *Lick.* . . A blow; a stroke. . . *Lick amiss.* . . When a person had received some punishment thought to be deserved, it was said: "He didn't get a lick amiss, unless they hit at him and missed him." **1902** *DN* 2.238 **sIL,** *Lick.* . . A blow or stroke. The latter words are not used. If one strikes another, it is said, 'He hit him.' But 'Hit it a lick,' 'He don't do a lick' (of work), are common expressions. **1907** *DN* 3.224 **nwAR,** *Lick.* . . A blow or stroke. **1909** *DN* 3.345 **eAL, wGA,** *Lick.* . . A stroke or blow. **1922** Gonzales *Black Border* 310 **sSC, GA coasts** [Gullah glossary], *Lick* . . a blow. **1929** Dobie *Vaquero* 261, I was too hot under the collar to pay any attention to them, and whizzed the rock at the loafer and killed him dead as a doorknob with a lick over the eye. **1937–39** *Hall Coll.* **wNC, eTN,** "Let's make it a sure lick [*Hall:* fatal blow] this time." . . "I knocked it [a bear] in the head ever so many licks before I could get it to lay over and hush hollerin'." **1965–70** *DARE* (Qu. Y11, . . *A very hard blow:* "You should have seen Bill go down. Joe really hit him a _____.") 132 Infs, **chiefly Sth, S Midl, TX, OK,** (Hard, heavy, severe, etc) lick; **OK**7, Give him a lick; **IL**140, Lick and a half; [(Qu. U8a, . . "*It cost me ten dollars.*")] Inf **TX**5, Hit me a lick for;] (Qu. X20, . . *A black eye*) Inf **TN**37, Lick on the eye; (Qu. Y12b, *A real fight in which blows are struck*) Inf **GA**1, Passing licks; (Qu. Y14a, *To hit somebody hard with the fist*) Infs **KY**28, **NC**55, **OK**1, **SC**46, Give him a (hard) lick; **AR**51, Hit him a hard lick; (Qu. KK15, *A disagreement or quarrel:* "They had _____ about where the fence was to be.") Inf **VA**25, A squabble, probably went into licks; (Qu. KK53, *When one thing suddenly hits hard against something else:* "He ran _____ into a car.") Inf **GA**7, A hard lick; (Qu. NN21b, *Exclamations caused by sudden pain—a hard blow on the chest*) Inf **AR**47, Man, that's a lick. **1966–69** *DARE* Tape **GA**7, One'll hold the ax level, crossways the tree. . . the other one takes the maul and hits that ax. If he's a good mauler, he can usually complete the job in about three licks. *Ibid* **KY**13, There was a hole in the middle of that you put your handle in and you just hit a very short lick. **1986** Pederson *LAGS Concordance,* **Gulf Region,** 1 inf, One more lick; 1 inf, Lick—blow with buggy switch; 1 inf, A lick; 1 inf, A lick—a blow in a fight; 1 inf, Give him a lick; 1 inf, Lick in the nose—two small boys might say; 1 inf, Never did get a lick—with hand; 1 inf, My last three children—I never hit a lick; 1 inf, A lick or two; 1 inf, Must have didn't get a good lick at him—of a snake; 1 inf, The lick you hit him; 1 inf, Licks; 1 inf, Hit a lick or two—give it a couple of strokes. **1987** *NADS Letters* **csOK,** In Duncan, Oklahoma, my home town, boys when I was growing up would *trade licks*—see how hard a blow each other could take on the arm without flinching.

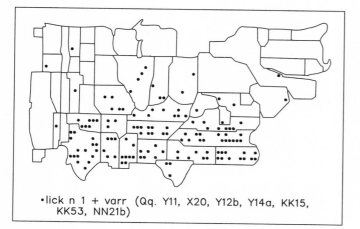

•lick n 1 + varr (Qq. Y11, X20, Y12b, Y14a, KK15, KK53, NN21b)

2 An act of physical or verbal aggression; an opportunity for attack; hence phr *get in one's licks* to get one's chance; to get one's way.

1834 Davis *Letters Downing* 103, We have had the first lick at him [in an election fight], and that, the Gineral says, is the best part of the battle. **1949** *Marshfield* (Wisconsin) *News–Herald* 19 July 4/1 *(OEDS),* The power lobby got in its licks through a subcommittee of the Senate Appropriations Committee passing on the bill for funds for the Department of Interior. **1959** Faulkner *Mansion* 6 **MS,** *They* . . could not harass . . a man forever without some day . . letting him get his own just and equal licks back in return . . they could even just sit back and watch everything go against him right along without missing a lick. . . They were even testing him, to see if he was . . man enough to take a little harassment and worry and so deserve his own licks back when his turn came. **1967** *Chagrin Valley Herald* (Chagrin Falls OH) 21 Sept sec A 1/7, Republican Council members leveled a blast at Mayor Forrest Fram for alleged disregard of Council policy. But Fram wasn't there to get in his licks. **1968** *DARE* (Qu. FF18, *Joking words . . about a noisy or boisterous celebration or party:* "They certainly _____ last night.") Inf **OH**71, Got in their licks.

3 A skill, knack; an effective method. *?obs*

1851 Hooper *Widow Rugby's Husband* 31 **AL,** Trust in Providence— that's the lick! **1884** Smith *Bill Arp's Scrap Book* 66 **nwGA,** The furrows I left behind looked like the track of a crazy snake. I used to could plow, but *it looks like I have lost the lick.*

4a A brief burst of activity; a "go," "turn," "stroke" of work; hence phrr *at a lick* and varr: at once, at a time.

1835 *Vade Mecum* (Phila.) 14 Feb. 3/4 *(DA),* When you come to put in the scientific licks, I squat. **1836** (1838) Haliburton *Clockmaker* (1st ser) 127, That are colt can beat him for a lick of a quarter of a mile. **1884** *Anglia* 7.261 **Sth, S Midl** [Black], *De same lick, de same pop* = at the same time. **1885** in 1917 Twain *Letters* 2.463, He will not desert us now, after putting in four licks to our one on this book all this time. **1894** *Congressional Record* 18 Apr 26.4.3830 **MS,** Most of the money that is made in the section of the country from which I come is made by hard licks under the hottest sun of summer. **1932** Randolph *Ozark Mt. Folks* 106, After each crossing of the shuttle Aunt Elvy reached out her hand and pulled the batten toward her with a sudden jerk, which forced the last thread of the woof tightly up against its predecessors, thus insuring a close, firm cloth. The jerk of the batten is a "lick." **1942** McAtee *Dial. Grant Co.* **IN** 40 (as of 1890s), *Lick* . . action or effort; same as clip, *q.v.* [*Ibid* 19, *Clip.* . single action or effort; "He knocked 'em over two at a clip".] **1959** *VT Hist.* 27.147, *Lick.* . . A brief or brisk stroke of activity. . . Common. **1965–70** *DARE* (Qu. A23, *To do something at the very first try:* "He got the right answer _____.") Inf **CA**210, First lick; (Qu. KK49, *When you don't have the time or ambition to do something thoroughly:* "I'm not going to give the place a real cleaning, I'll just _____.") Inf **IA**5, Give it a few licks. **1967–69** *DARE* Tape **AR**50, They can square these logs up on the main saw . . and then they just cut it all up at one lick, with a gang saw. *Ibid* **KY**5, You pull that thread up and then you'd throw her back through and bring it up and cross your thread and throw her back . . you beat one lick. **1969** *DARE* FW Addit **cKY,** Put him [=a fish] in the boat with one lick; **KY**39, *Lick* . . a try . . "Give it a lick." **1976** Warner *Beautiful Swimmers* 48 **eMD,** The crabs spill out on the deck. If it is a poor lick, as each scrape of the bottom is called, there will be no more than a discouraging two dozen. **1986** Pederson *LAGS Concordance,* 1 inf, **seLA,** At one lick—at one time; 1 inf, **ceTX,** Growed ten thousand at a lick—at once: of chickens; 1 inf, **ceTN,** Give it a lick—when sharpening on one side [of the]. **1993** *NY Times* (NY) 17 Oct sec 1 1/2 **Chesapeake Bay VA,** He groped for the muddy treasure hidden seven feet below the river's surface. Then, when the heft of the tongs was just right, he raised them and, with the muscular grace of a man who has tonged [for oysters] for 37 of his 56 years, swung the dripping mess aboard in a smooth arc, dumping it with a resounding clatter. "Good lick, good lick," he said, a grin of satisfaction creasing his ruddy, weathered face.

b Esp:

(1) in phrr *put in one's (best) licks* and varr: To work hard, do one's best.

1847 (1962) Robb *Squatter Life* 106, He was puttin' in the biggest kind a licks in the way of courtin'. **1851** (1969) Burke *Polly Peablossom* 111, I saw comin' my gray mule, puttin' in her best licks, and a few yards behind her was a grizzly. **1871** Eggleston *Hoosier Schoolmaster* 124 **sIN,** You mean, then, I'm to begin now to put in my best licks for

Jesus Christ, and that he'll help me? **1903** *DN* 2.299 **Cape Cod MA** (as of a1857), *Licks. . .* In expression 'put in the licks,' that is, work hard. **1905** *DN* 3.13 **cCT,** *Licks. . .* Exertions. "He put in big licks." [**1907** *DN* 3.214 **nwAR,** *Licks. . .* Exertions.] **1968** *DARE* (Qu. JJ22, *To express your opinion . . "I went to the meeting, and _____."*) Inf **MN38,** Put in my best licks.

(2) in var neg phrr: The smallest amount of work; a bit of work. Note: This sense shades imperceptibly into sense **5** below; somewhat arbitrarily, all phrr meaning "didn't do any work at all" are collected here, except *hit* (or *strike*) *a lick* and varr, which appear to be more closely related to sense **1** above and are treated at **hit a lick 1** and **strike a lick.**

1902 Harben *Abner Daniel* 94 **nGA,** But all day yesterday an' to-day he hain't worked a lick. **1902** [see **1** above]. **1903** *DN* 2.319 **seMO,** I haven't done a lick of work this spring. **1939** in 1984 Lambert–Franks *Voices* 13 **OK,** It didn't look like I could get a lick of work to do. **1945** *Harder Coll.* **cwTN,** His Dad was rich, didn't have to work a lick. **1960** Criswell *Resp. to PADS 20* **Ozarks,** "He never did a lick of work all day." . . Still very common. **1965–70** *DARE* (Qu. LL18, *To do no work at all, not even make any effort: "She hasn't _____ all day."*) 47 Infs, **scattered,** Done a lick; 18 Infs, **scattered,** Done a lick of work; **MD49,** Done a lick's work; **KY40,** Done one lick; **LA37,** Laid a lick of work on it; **IL11,** Turned a lick; **CA133,** Worked a lick. **1969** *DARE* FW Addit **KY39,** Won't work a lick. **1986** Pederson *LAGS Concordance,* 1 inf, **neTN,** Won't work a lick and living on welfare.

5 A small amount, bit; the smallest amount (of something); hence in quasi-adverbial use, a bit, at all—usu in neg contexts. **chiefly Sth, S Midl** Note: See note at **4b(2)** above.

1853 P.B. St. John *Amy Moss* 50 *(OED)* **Ohio Valley,** Everybody brought 'sunthin'—some a lick of meal, some a punkin'. **1930** (1935) Porter *Flowering Judas* 69 **TX,** They can't say He wasn't dressed every lick as good as Adna. **1954** *Harder Coll.* **cwTN,** At dog wun't bark a lick 'till 'e come to the raght [*sic*] tree. **1956** Gipson *Old Yeller* 55 **TX,** None of that made a lick of difference now. **1960** Criswell *Resp. to PADS 20* **Ozarks,** "Didn't have a lick of sense." Still very common. **1966** Barnes–Jensen *Dict. UT Slang* 28, *Lick of sense, hasn't got a.* **1966–67** *DARE* Tape **SC5,** I couldn't swim a lick but that didn't make a difference. *Ibid* **TN15,** He couldn't, couldn't play a lick and he never couldn't try to. I tuned it back up for him. **1967** *DARE* (Qu. LL18, *To do no work at all, not even make any effort: "She hasn't _____ all day."*) Inf **NY22,** Moved a lick. **1969** *DARE* FW Addit **KY39,** Don't worry a lick. **1976** Garber *Mountain-ese* 53 **sAppalachians,** He don't have a lick uv sense. **1980** *Houston Chron.* (TX) 9 June sec 3, [She] recalls a friend telling her about a book the friend had just finished reading. "But I couldn't understand a lick of it." **1986** Pederson *LAGS Concordance,* 1 inf, **neAL,** Haven't sewed a lick; 1 inf, **seAL,** I can't swim a lick; 1 inf, **ceTX,** Hadn't got a lick of sense; 1 inf, **neTX,** Haven't got a lick of sense. **1991** *DARE* File **NC** (as of c1915), Growing up in North Carolina, I often heard, "He/She hasn't got a lick of sense." I don't believe I've heard this meaning outside the South.

6 Pace, rate of going; hence phr *mend one's licks* to go faster. **esp S Midl** Cf **mend 5**

1864 in 1938 Twain *Washoe Giant* 108, He [=George Washington] kept up his lick for seven long years, and hazed the British from Harrisburg to Halifax. **1869** Twain *Innocents* 48, By George, she [=a watch] *is* good on shore, but somehow she don't keep up her lick here on the water—gets seasick, may be. **1892** *DN* 1.230 **KY,** *Licks.* "To mend one's licks" = to quicken one's steps. "When the dog got after me, I mended my licks." **1899** (1912) Green *VA Folk-Speech* 260, *Lick. . .* The act of doing a thing very fast. "Who was that playing the piano at such a lick." **1905** *DN* 3.86 **nwAR,** *Lick. . .* Gait, rate of progress. 'You'll have to hit a different lick, if you expect to accomplish anything.' Common. **1909** *DN* 3.400 **nwAR,** *Mend one's licks. . .* To quicken one's steps. *Ibid* 345 **eAL, wGA,** *Lick. . .* Rate of speed. "We were makin' a good lick."

7 Syrup, molasses. **chiefly West** Cf **larrup n 2, lickings, longlick**

1893 (1958) Wister *Out West* 198, *Lick, Larrup*—syrup, molasses. **1909** *Sat. Eve. Post* 20 Mar 9 **West,** The range boss, Uncle Henry and Maize [*sic*] trifled with bits of biscuit and "lick" so that he might not be uncomfortable sitting alone. **1915** *DN* 4.227 **wTX,** *Lick. . .* Syrup; molasses. **1927** *Sat. Eve. Post* 23 July 36 **West,** That chuck box also holds lick—sirup—pieces of salt pork, and all the main things to sort of season the grub with. **1940** (1966) Writers' Program *Guide AZ* 63, Lick (syrup) took the place of butter. **1941** Cleaveland *No Life* 163 **NM,** Our stock dessert was bread and 'lick.' Lick is syrup, molasses, or any

viscous sweetening. **1967–68** *DARE* (Qu. H21, . . *The sweet stuff that's poured over these [pan]cakes*) Inf **CA87,** Molasses called lick; **TX3,** Lick—cowboys use for molasses. **1974** Fink *Mountain Speech* 15 **wNC, eTN,** *Lick . .* molasses. "Give him some lick for his dodger."

8 A spring or stream. [See quot 1945] **chiefly Allegheny Mts**

1945 Stewart *Names on Land* 152 **KY,** Not all the springs were good for drinking; some had films of oil upon them, and some were brackish with salt. Near these last the clay was salt to the taste, and the buffalo and deer came there in hundreds to lick it. So these were the best hunting-grounds. They were called *licks* and that name survived upon many streams and towns. **1948** *WELS Suppl.* **PA,** *Lick*—Does Wisconsin have this word which is also frequent in Pennsylvania? It means the same as *run* or *creek*. **1955** Assoc. Amer. Geogr. *Annals* 45.331, The use of *lick* as a full generic term for stream occurs in scattered localities in West Virginia and in the adjoining portions of Virginia, Kentucky, Ohio, and western Maryland—as well as in north-central Pennsylvania. **1961** Field *Guide KY Place Names* 14, *Standard Designator Abbreviations. . .* Lick—Spr[ing]. . . Lick—Str[ea]m.

licka-licka-lacka n Cf **icky-acky-over**

=Antony-over.

1966 *DARE* (Qu. EE22, . . *The game in which they throw a ball over a building . . to a player on the other side*) Inf **DC5,** Licka-licka-lacka; run round and tag—other.

lick back See **lick v B3**

lick block n Cf **lick-log n 1**

A type of salt lick; see quot 1968.

1878 in 1929 Summers *Annals* 1602 **swVA,** A gang of horses had come in from the range to the lick-blocks, about one hundred yards from the house. **1968** Adams *Western Words* 176, *Lick block*—A block of hard salt put out for cattle to lick.

lick-dab n Cf **lick n 7**

1911 *DN* 3.545 **NE,** *Lick-dab. . .* Gravy. "Please send the lick-dab this way."

licked up See **lick v B1**

lickerish See **licorice**

lickerty toot, lickety-brindle See **lickety-split**

lickety-clip v Cf **lick v B2**

1893 *KS Univ. Qrly.* 1.140 **KS,** *Lickety-clip. . .* to go fast, as 'He lickety-clipped it.'

lickety-clip adv, **lickety-cut** adv See **lickety-split**

lickety-cut n

=lapjack.

1917 *DN* 4.395 **neOH,** *Lickety cut. . .* A game or contest in which two bare-legged boys use whips on each other's legs till one gives in. Local. **1948** Hedrick *Land Crooked Tree* 20 **MI** (as of 1870s), 'Lickety-cut' was a favorite game. Two boys with blue-beech gads, five or six feet long, stood foot to foot, each thrashing the other in alternate strokes. The one who first cried or turned tail was defeated.

lickety-split adv Also *lickety-brindle, lickety-cut;* first element also sp *lickity;* for addit varr see quots [Cf *SND lickitie* (in phr *fast as lickitie*) and **lick v B2**]

With great speed or vigor.

1831 *Boston Eve. Transcript* (MA) 4 June 2/2, He ran down the street licketty cut, and is probably at home by this time. **1847** (1962) Robb *Squatter Life* 116, Away they started, "lickety click," and arrived at the winning-post within touching distance of each other. **1848** in 1935 *AmSp* 10.40 **Nantucket MA,** *Lickoty liner. Lickoty split.* **1892** *DN* 1.236 **MO,** *Lickity-split . .* at full speed. Kansas City. [*DN* Ed: *lickity-split* and *lickity-cut* in Michigan . . and New England. . .] **1889** *NY Herald* (NY) 25 Apr 8/4, The New York Central trains can now run thirty miles an hour, or at a rate which small boys call "lickerty smash," through any town or village containing less than fifty thousand inhabitants. **1895** *DN* 1.398 **NYC,** *Lickity-switch.* **1896** *DN* 1.420 **c,w,swNY,** *Lickity blinder, lickity brindle.* **1898** Westcott *Harum* 264 **cNY,** In about a few minutes back she come, lickity-cut, an' pulled up in front of me. **1903** *DN* 2.302 **Cape Cod MA** (as of a1857), Various phrases are used to describe the speed of an animal, as 'he went . . *clear lick-it,*' or *lickety-split,* or *lickety-cut.* **1904** *DN* 2.427 **Cape Cod MA** (as of a1857), *Lickety whittle. . .* Recklessly fast. **1905** *DN* 3.13 **cCT,** He went lickety split down hill. *Ibid* 63 **eNE,** *Lickety-split, -cut, -brindle, -switch. Ibid* 86 nwAR, *Lickity-brin'le—lickity-split(tle)*. . . At a rapid gait. **1907** *DN* 3.193 **seNH,** He was going by lickety larrup. *Ibid* 207 **nwAR,** The old man went down the hill lickety-cut, with the bear about four feet behind him. **1909** *DN* 3.345 **eAL, wGA,** Lickity-split. *Ibid* 413 **nME,** *Lickerty toot.* **1910** *DN* 3.444 **wNY,** *Lickety cut, lickety split.* **1911** *DN* 3.545 **NE,** *Lickety leap, lickety scoot.* **1912** *DN* 3.581 **wIN,** *Lickety-brindle . . lickety-cut.* **1914** *DN* 4.109 **cKS,** *Lickety-clip*. . . Also *lickety-brindle.* **1915** *DN* 4.227 **wTX,** *Lickety-brindle.* **1917** *DN* 4.395 **neOH,** *Lickety cut*. . . At high speed (with trivial or humorous sense); one would not say, "He went for the doctor lickety cut." "He went down the lane lickety cut." General. **1923** *DN* 5.213 **swMO,** *Likkety-whoop*. . . Rapidly and more or less at random. "He went down the road likkety whoop." Also *likkety-hell, likkety-rip, likkety-damn, likkety-scoot,* etc. **1935** Davis *Honey* 140 **OR,** She went through it, jumping logs lickety-bang. **1938** *AmSp* 13.6 **seAR,** He was going lickety-brindle. **1943** Writers' Program NC *Bundle of Troubles* 75, We movin' 'long top speed, lickety bump, down the road. **1947** *PADS* 8.14 **IN, NC, VA,** *Lickety-split. Ibid* 25 **NC, wNY, VA,** *Lickety-split.* **1959** *VT Hist.* 27.147, *Lickety cut* and *lickety split* are used commonly. **1966–70** *DARE* (Qu. A23, *To do something at the very first try: "He got the right answer _____."*) Inf **CA**113, Lickety-split; (Qu. Y20, *To run fast: "You should have seen him _____!"*) Inf **MD**24, He went lickety-split; **OH**98, Lickety-larrup; **PA**7, Run lickety-cut; **MN**28, Run lickety-split; (Qu. EE21b, *When boys were fighting very actively . . "For a while those fellows really _____."*) Inf **GA**18, Went lickety-split; (Qu. KK53, *When one thing suddenly hits hard against something else: "He ran _____ into a car."*) Inf **GA**15, Lickety-split. **1967** *DARE* File **neWI,** They were going lickety-brindle! **1969–70** *DARE* FW Addit **MA**61, Lickety-cut = quickly; **cNY,** Lickity-rip. **c1970** *DARE* File **seNE,** Lickety-larrup, lickety-split. **1983** *DARE* File **ceWI,** Lickety-larrup. **1986** Pederson *LAGS Concordance,* 3 infs, **ce,csTX, swTN,** Lickety-split.

licking good adj phr Also *lickum (good)* **chiefly Nth, esp NEast** See Map Cf **lapping good**

Of food: very good.

1893 *KS Univ. Qrly.* 1.140 **KS,** *Licking good:* very good. **1896** *DN* 1.427 **NY,** *Licking* . . very. Licking good pie, licking good candy. **1914** *DN* 4.75 **ME, nNH,** Them pies was lickin' good. *Ibid* 109 **KS,** *Lickin good*. . . Highly palatable. Also *lickum good.* **1923** *DN*5.213 **swMO,** *Lickum*. . . Very palatable. **1942** in 1944 *ADD* 357, *Licking, lickum*. . . Lickin' good, ain't it? Radio. *Ibid,* A dish that's lickin' good. Radio advt. **1965–70** *DARE* (Qu. LL35, *Words used to make a statement stronger: "This cake tastes _____ good."*) 15 Infs, **chiefly Nth, esp NEast,** Lickin(g).

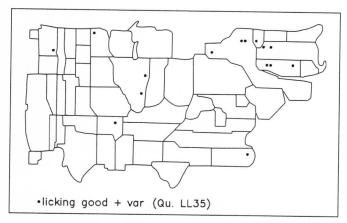

•licking good + var (Qu. LL35)

licking post See **lick-log 2**

lickings n pl Cf **lick** n 7

1973 *News & Courier* (Charleston SC) 25 Nov sec E 4, *Lickings*. . cane syrup that remains in the evaporating pan after the syrup is poured out and which is eaten by the syrup makers . . the syrup pan . . [is] lifted off the fire and . . the syrup is strained into a tub. Workers gather around to sample lickings from the pan.

lick it See **lick** v **B2**

lickity-brindle (or -cut, -split) See **lickety-split**

lick-log n **chiefly S Midl**

1 A notched log or, rarely, a wooden trough, used to hold salt for livestock.

1851 Hooper *Widow Rugby's Husband* 60 **AL,** I knew you'd be about the old lick log 'a fishin' with Betsy. **1852** *Yankee Notions* 1.269 **AR,** Logan went down . . to the bank of the creek, and sat himself down on a "lick log." **1867** Harris *Sut Lovingood Yarns* 79 **TN,** She sorter lean'd tu me . . sorter like a keerful man salts uther pepil's cattil in the mountin, barly enuf tu bring em back to the lick-bog [sic] sum day—that's the way she salted me, an' I 'tended the lick log es reg'lar es the old bell cow. **1889** Roosevelt *Winning the West* 2.212 **KY,** To provide for the latter [=farm stock] a tree was chopped down and the salt placed in notches or small troughs cut in the trunk, making it what was called a lick-log. **1939** *Hall Coll.* **eTN,** Trip with Ranger Kirkland of 20-mile Creek. At Salt Gap made picture of 15-hole "lick-log". This was the center of grazing activities of several families on 20-mile creek and other[s] further down the Tennessee River. **1953** Randolph–Wilson *Down in Holler* 260 **Ozarks,** *Lick-log*. . . A fallen tree with big notches cut in the trunk to hold salt for the cattle. . . Where a trough made of boards is used, I have heard it called a "built lick-log." **c1960** *Wilson Coll.* **csKY,** *Lick-log* . . a fallen tree trunk with a place chopped out for salt for the cattle in the woods. Cf lick-log school on the eastern border of the park. [**1966** *DARE* (Qu. C34, *Nicknames for nearby settlements, villages, or districts*) Inf **NC**15, Lick-log.] **1983** *MJLF* 9.1.46 **ceKY,** *Lick log* . . a fallen tree, with notches cut in it to hold salt for cows.

2 also *licking post;* Fig: a gathering place; a point of contention or decision—often in phrr *stand to one's lick-log, salt or no salt* to stand firm, act decisively; *come to the lick-log* and varr: to face facts, make a difficult decision.

1834 Crockett *Narrative* 89 **TN,** From this place I returned home, leaving the people in a first-rate way; and I was sure I would do a good business among them. At any rate, I was determined to stand up to my lick-log, salt or no salt. **1840** Haliburton *Clockmaker* (3d ser) 175, I like a man to be up to the notch, and stand to his lick-log; salt or no salt, say the word, or it's no offer. **1887** *Congressional Record* 17 Feb 1880 **NC,** It is not necessary to bait him [=a recusant witness] or take him to a lick-log. **1898** Lloyd *Country Life* 15 **AL,** When I got back to the old family lick log I found things powerful changed around. **1942** Perry *Texas* 135, To bring him to taw: to make him "come up to the lick log." **1962** Dykeman *Tall Woman* 290 **NC** (as of c1860), "Why, you only pledged away your selfhood, son," Jesse Moore said, "your narrow little self for a larger manhood. And now you're up to the lick-log: you've been called to keep that pledge." **1962** Faulkner *Reivers* 145 **MS,** "All right, all right," Boon said. . . "That train will be along in four or five hours while we're still debating who's first at the lick dog [sic]." **1966** *DARE* File **WI,** "He'll get right up to the licking-post without ever tasting the salt." Said of a man who stops just short of getting actually involved. **1971** Green *Village Horse Doctor* 267 **cwTX,** He was able to fly and save time. He started to recite to me . . I would have to come to the licklog and progress with the times or I would lose my practice. I said, "You may know what you're talkin' about, but you're overlookin' my distaste for licklogs." **1975** McDonough *Garden Sass* 156 **AR,** The term "lick-log" was sometimes applied to preaching places. **1982** *DARE* File **OK,** Some few years ago my husband heard businessmen in Oklahoma at a time when their company had drilled a well . . to the intended depth and there had been no show of oil or gas, a decision would have to be made as to whether the well should be drilled deeper . . (this can be a very expensive decision). One of the men said, "we are at the lick log" (meaning we must now decide.) **1986** *DARE* File **CO,** She said when she was a little girl her grandmother, who was a full blooded Cherokee, had taken her to the woods to look for herbs. Later on that day the grandmother said she had to go to the lick-log. The little girl thought she meant to go sit down on any log, but the grandmother said she was going there to decide if they needed more herbs or could go home. **1992** *Milwaukee Jrl.* (WI) 2 Aug sec A 8/5, Texas Gov. Ann Richards . . said Democrats were encouraged that Clinton had proved to be a fighter on the campaign trail. "When it really gets down to the licklog, we're going to have somebody in the Democratic Party who's going to get in there and slug it out with them," she said.

lick-'n'-like n Cf **lickstick**

1968 *DARE* (Qu. H81, *Candy on a stick for children to lick*) Inf **NC**55, Lick-'n'-like.

lick one's calf over See **lick** v **B4**

lick one's flint v phr

See quot 1953.

1929 *AmSp* 5.14 **Ozarks,** *Lick th' flint.* **1953** Randolph–Wilson *Down in Holler* 260 **Ozarks,** *Lick your flint*. . . To prepare for a difficult task, to take precautions against disaster. "If you aim to play cards with them Turney boys, you sure better lick your flint." It is said that in the days of the flintlock a rifleman moistened the flint with his tongue, to insure a good fat spark. **1984** Wilder *You All Spoken Here* 23 **Sth,** Lick your flint and try again: Start over. In days of "long rifles," when the flint failed to strike fire and set off the powder charge, the way to insure a fat spark was to dampen the flint with the tongue and pull the trigger again.

lickoty-split See lickety-split

lick out v phr
1978 *NADS Letters* **nwSC,** An expression I have heard used by Blacks is that a person licks out his tongue rather than sticks it out.

lick-over n Cf lick n 4b(2)
A quick once-over.
1966–68 *DARE* (Qu. KK49, *When you don't have the time or ambition to do something thoroughly: "I'm not going to give the place a real cleaning, I'll just _____."*) Inf **NY70,** Give it a lick-over.

lick-pot n [*OED* 1387 →; *EDD* (at *lick* v. 1.[8])] Cf potlicker
The index finger.
1946 *PADS* 6.13 **eNC** (as of 1900–10), *Finger—little, ling, long, lick-pot, and thumb-ball.* . . The little finger, ring finger, long finger, index finger, and thumb. . . Common among children. **1950** *PADS* 13.17 **cTX** (as of c1920), The form in Runnels County was *little-man . . , leeman, longman, lick-pot,* and *thumb-ball.*

lickrish See licorice

lickskillet n

1 A contemptible person; a lickspittle.
1893 Shands *MS Speech* 43, *Lickskillet* ['lɪkskɪlɪt]. Used by illiterate whites to mean a *contemptible or detestable person.* **1958** *Resp. to PADS* 29, Among the Norwegians of my native Wisconsin I had often heard the expression "skrape Gryde" used in expressing contempt for a disagreeable person. One day down here in North Carolina I listened to some one who was speaking disparagingly of another woman. "She's nothing but an old lick skillet," she declared. It struck me immediately that her expression was almost an exact parallel to the epithet, "Skrape Gryde."

2 also *lickskittle:* Used as a place name; see quots. **esp Sth, S Midl** See Map
1961 Field *Guide KY Place Names* 144, [The list includes four entries with *Lickskillet.*] **1965–70** *DARE* (Qu. C34, *Nicknames for nearby settlements, villages, or districts*) Inf **FL15,** Lickskittle; **GA9,** Lickskillet—near Rayle, Georgia; **GA80,** Lickskillet—Adamsville, ten miles from Austell; **IL17,** Lickskillet—Dutch settlement on the Sangamon River; **KY68, TN60,** Lickskillet; **TN37,** Lickskillet in KY, which is about twelve miles away; (Qu. C35, *Nicknames for the different parts of your town or city*) Inf **GA9,** Lickskillet—colored section, named by inhabitants; **TN52,** Lickskillet; (Qu. II25, *Names or nicknames for the part of a town where the poorer people, special groups, or foreign groups live*) Inf **TX104,** Lickskillet, poor town. **1970** Stewart *Amer. Place-Names* 256, *Lickskillet*—A derogatorily humorous appellation for a place so poor or so boorish that people licked their skillets, in early times often applied as a habitation-name, usually by people who did not live there, rarely or never being official, and now largely vanished. **1986** Pederson *LAGS Concordance,* 1 inf, **nwTN,** Lickskillet—[a place in] TN.

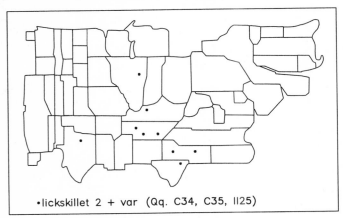

•lickskillet 2 + var (Qq. C34, C35, II25)

licksplit v Cf lickety-split
To go as fast as possible; hence adv *lick-splitting* very rapidly.
1931 Hannum *Thursday April* 11 **wNC,** You licksplit as fast as yore

worthless legs'll tote you up to Penlin Graham's and carry Phoebus Woodley down hyere. *Ibid* 245, The blacksmith shop and mill with the creek squeezing in between, wider and lazier than back up yonder where it went lick-splitting past Christmas Tree. **1946** *AmSp* 21.98 **sIL,** Some other forms from the dialect of Appalachia which are in more or less common use in Southern Illinois are as follows: . . *lick-splittin',* in haste. **1972** Cooper *NC Mt. Folkl.* 94, *Lick-splitting*—walking rapidly.

lickstick n
A lollipop 1a.
1968 *DARE* (Qu. H81, *Candy on a stick for children to lick*) Inf **VA33,** Lickstick.

lick the red off one's candy v phr Also *lick the molasses off one's biscuit*
Fig: to frustrate, anger, torment.
1972 *Atlanta Letters* **cnGA,** "Who licked the red off your candy?"—When someone is in a bad humor. **1978** *AP Letters* **Sth,** I first heard "he licked all the red off my candy" about five years ago from the 62 year old secretary to my then-boss' associate, and I had never heard the expression before, nor have I heard it used since that time. I believe the lady . . was from somewhere in the southern part of the U.S., although she did not have a typically "deep south" accent. *Ibid* (as of c1900), There are some [words] that are still used by old-timers, such as: . . Somebody licked the 'lasses off his biscuit (made him angry).

lick thumbs v phr [From an old Scottish custom of sealing a bargain by licking thumbs and pressing them together; cf *SND lick* v. 1.(16)]
1958 *PADS* 29.12 **cnTN,** *Lick thumbs:* To reach an agreement. "Let's lick thumbs and quit, [used] to settle accounts when the country doctor had an account against a farmer [who had brought] a ham or a load of hay or corn along, and neither had much records."

lickum (good) See licking good

lick up See lick v B1

licorice n Usu |ˈlɪk(ə)rɪš, ˈlɪk(ə)rɪs|; also chiefly S Midl, nNEng (See Map) |ˈlɪkwɪš| Pronc-spp *lick(e)rish, lic(o)rish, liquorish, lickwish* For addit pronc and sp varr see **A** below

A Forms.
1783 Webster *Grammatical Inst.* 77, *Liquorice.* . . Not *lickerish.* **1892** *DN* 1.234 **KY,** *Lickerish. Ibid* 239 **cwMO,** *Licorice.* Generally [lɪkərɪš] in Kansas City. [In Michigan [lɪkrɪš]. . .] **1893** Shands *MS Speech* 43, *Lickerish* [lɪkə·ɪš]. Negro and illiterate white for *licorice.* Used also in New England. **1899** (1912) Green *VA Folk-Speech* 261, *Lickwish. Ibid* 263, *Liquorish.* **1906** *DN* 3.145 **nwAR,** *Liquish.* . . Licorice. A common pronunciation. **1907** *DN* 3.193 **seNH,** *Licorish.* . . Licorice. "Licorish cost a penny a stick." **1909** *DN* 3.345 **eAL, wGA,** *Lic(o)rish.* . . Licorice. **1910** *DN* 3.444 **wNY,** *Licorish* and *licrish.* . . Licorice. **1915** *DN* 4.185 **swVA,** *Liquish.* . . Licorice. **1917** Garland *Son Middle Border* 29 **WI,** A piece of candy or a stick of "lickerish root". **1921** Haswell *Daughter Ozarks* 30 (as of 1880s), Then I wallers them pills around in some powdered lickkerish. **1936** *AmSp* 11.155 **eTX,** *Licorice* is [ˈlɪk-rɪs/š], [ˈlɪkwɪs/š], [ˈlɪkə·ɪs/š]. **1940** *Sat. Eve. Post* 6 Apr 17, He gave him a plug of black candy. Lonnie stared at it and said, "What is it?" "Licorish." **1944** *ADD* **cNY** (as of 1914–23), *Lickrish* [ˈlɪkrɪš]. Usual among children & adults. **1957** *Sat. Eve. Post Letters* **CA, IL, NY,** *Lickerish.* **1959** *VT Hist.* 27.147, *Licorice* [ˈlɪkərɪš] . . pronc. Also [ˈlɪk-rɪš]. Common. **1960** Criswell *Resp. to PADS* 20 **Ozarks,** *Licorice* . . [lɪkwɪš]. **c1960** *Wilson Coll.* **csKY,** *Licorice* is, locally, nearly always

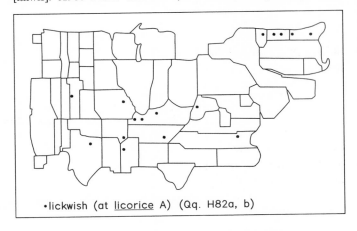

•lickwish (at <u>licorice</u> A) (Qq. H82a, b)

['lɪkwɪš]. **1965–70** *DARE* (Qq. H82a, b) 252 Infs, **widespread**, Lickrish
(sticks *or* whips, etc) [including proncs of the type ['lɪk(ə)rɪš]]; 163 Infs,
widespread, Licorice (sticks *or* whips, etc) [including proncs of the type
['lɪk(ə)rɪš]]; 16 Infs, **chiefly S Midl, nNEng**, Lickwish; **NJ**30, ['likərɪš];
LA40, ['lɪkrɪš]; **PA**9, ['lɪkris]; **NC**10, ['lɪkɚɑɪs] sticks; **WV**6, ['lɪkəɪš];
OH21, Lickish sticks.

B Senses.

1 Std: a plant of the genus *Glycyrrhiza*, either the cultivated
G. glabra widely used as a flavoring, or *G. lepidota* native
chiefly to the western half of the US. Also called **licorice
root 2**. For other names of *G. lepidota* see **Deseret weed, wild
licorice**

2 =**hog peanut 1.**

1922 *Amer. Botanist* 28.74, *Amphicarpa monoica* is "hog peanut",
"wild pea-vine" and "wild peanut" which names refer to the underground pods. . . The name "licorice" sometimes found in books, seems
to be a misnomer for our plant which but slightly resembles the true
licorice. **1940** Clute *Amer. Plant Names* 17, Hog peanut. Wild peanut,
wild peavine, (licorice). **1959** Carleton *Index Herb. Plants* 74, Licorice:
Amphicarpaea monoica.

3 See **licorice fern.**

licorice bush See **licorice vine**

licorice fern n Also *licorice, licorice-root (fern)* [See quot 1970]
A **polypody** (here: *Polypodium glycyrrhiza*) native chiefly to
coastal areas of the Pacific Northwest and Alaska. Also called
rock fern

1898 *Jrl. Amer. Folkl.* 11.283 swWA, *Polypodium falcatum* . . liquorice. . . Root eaten by children. **1923** Abrams *Flora Pacific States* 1.8,
Polypodium glycyrrhiza. . . Licorice Fern. **1937** St. John *Flora SE WA
& ID* 4, *Polypodium vulgare* L., var. *columbianum* . . Licorice-root Fern.
1970 Kirk *Wild Edible Plants W. U.S.* 192, Licorice Fern. . . The stem
of the leaf, when chewed long enough, develops a distinctive licorice
flavor. . . Licorice Fern is found on moist, shaded, rock ledges, old logs,
and mossy trunks of deciduous trees from Alaska southward into California. **1974** Welsh *Anderson's Flora AK* 23, *Polypodium glycyrrhiza* . .
Licorice-root; Licorice Fern—Rhizomes thickish, licorice flavored.

licorice marigold n
A native marigold (*Tagetes micrantha*).

1970 Correll *Plants TX* 1687, *Tagetes micrantha*. . . Licorice-mari-
gold. . . Local in high moist canyons . . ; Ariz., N.M. and Tex.

licorice root n
1 Any of var **sweet vetches.**

1870 Dall *Alaska* 438, [The Indians pick] the roots of *Hedysarum
Mackenzii*, the "liquorice root" of the trappers. **1939** Medsger *Edible
Wild Plants* 199, Licorice Root, Hedysarum Mackenzii, is found in
central Canada west to Alaska. Its long flexible roots are sweet, resembling licorice and are much eaten in spring by the Indians. This is the
wild licorice of the trappers of the Northwest. **1943** Fernald–Kinsey
Edible Wild Plants E. N. Amer. 249, Licorice-root, Hedysarum alpinum,
vars. *americanum* and *grandiflorum*. **1974** (1977) Coon *Useful Plants*
167, *Hedysarum (various species)*—Sweetvetch, sweetbroom, licorice
root. . . There are several species of this sweet vetch which inhabit only
parts of the West, growing as low shrubs in dry ground. The roots are
nourishing and edible, with *H. occidentale* having a mild licorice taste.

2 =**licorice B1.**

1870 U.S. Dept. Ag. *Rept. of Secy. for 1870* 407, *Glycyrrhiza lepi-
dota*. . . This American form of licorice root is eaten by the Indians of
Alaska and the northwestern States. **1876** Hobbs *Bot. Hdbk.* 64, Licorice
root. . Glycyrrhiza glabra and species. **1896** *Jrl. Amer. Folkl.* 9.185 CA,
Glycyrrhiza lepidota . . licorice root. **1973** Hitchcock–Cronquist *Flora
Pacific NW* 261, *Glycyrrhiza* [spp] . . Licorice; Licorice-root.

3 =**lovage.**

1973 Hitchcock–Cronquist *Flora Pacific NW* 326, *Ligusticum* [spp] . .
Lovage; Licorice-root.

4 See **licorice fern.**

licorice-root fern See **licorice fern**

licorice vine n Also *licorice bush* [From the flavor of the leaves]
Cf **Indian licorice**
=**crab's eye.**

1876 Hobbs *Bot. Hdbk.* 64, Licorice bush, Love pea, Abrus precatorius.
1933 Small *Manual SE Flora* 743, *A[brus]* Abrus Crab's-eye, Indian-
licorice, Licorice-vine. . . Woods, thickets and roadsides, pen[insular]

Fla. **1976** Bailey–Bailey *Hortus Third* 3, *[Abrus] precatorius* . . Indian
licorice . . licorice vine.

lic(o)rish See **licorice**

lid n Usu |lɪd|; also **esp Sth, S Midl** |lɛd| Pronc-sp *led*
A Form.

1878 (1879) Harte *Drift* 68 **NEast**, She could sing hymns; he knew
every text between "the leds" of a Bible. **1890** *DN* 1.74 **MA**, Led: for
lid. **1891** *PMLA* 6.165 **WV**, The sounds [ɪ] and [ɛ] are often interchangeable, as [lɛd] for *lid*, [rɛd] for *rid*, [ɛf] for *if*. **1892** *DN* 1.234
KY Led. **1893** Shands *MS Speech* 43, Led [lɛd]. Negro for *lid*. **1899**
(1912) Green *VA Folk-Speech* 259, Led. . . A lid; the lid of a chest; or
of a book. "The led of the kittle." **1902** *DN* 2.238 **sIL**, Led. . . Lid.
1903 *DN* 2.319 **seMO**, My text will be found somewhere betwixt the
leds of the Bible. **1905** *DN* 3.103 **nwAR**, Led (lid). **1907** *DN* 3.232
nwAR, Lid. . . Pronounced led. **1909** *DN* 3.344 **eAL, wGA**, Led. . .
Lid. **1942** Hall *Smoky Mt. Speech* 15 **wNC, eTN**, Laxer and lowered
varieties of [ɪ], often reaching [ɛ], may frequently be heard in *different,
lid, rid*, etc. **c1960** *Wilson Coll.* **csKY**, Lid, as spoken by many older
people, cannot be distinguished from *led*. **1976** Garber *Mountain-ese* 53
sAppalachians, Put the led on the sugar bowl.

B Senses.

1 One of the covers of a book. **chiefly S Midl**

1878 [see **A** above]. **1896** Harris *Sister Jane* 90 **nGA**, You've pored
and pored over them books in yander till you can't make head nor tail
out of anything that ain't to be found betwixt their leds. **1899** [see **A**
above]. **1903** [see **A** above]. **1927** *DN* 5.475 **Ozarks**, "No sir, you caint
find hit nowhar 'twixt th' lids o' th' Book!" The word *Book*, in the
Ozarks, means the King James version of the Bible. **c1960** *Wilson Coll.*
csKY, You can't find that between the lids of the Bible.

2 also *lid door:* See quot.

1966–70 *DARE* (Qu. D20, *Names for a sloping outside cellar door*)
Inf **MD**21, Lid (but not absolutely sure); **NC**88, [Aux Inf:] Lid; **WA**11,
Lid door.

3 =**cap** n[1] **1.**

1968–69 *DARE* (Qu. L31, . . *The top bundle of a shock*) Inf **IL**41,
Lid; **VA**27, Lid: set up ten [bundles] and put two on top—a dozen in a
sheave.

lidard See **lightwood** n[1]

lid door See **lid B2**

lider(d) See **lightwood** n[1]

lie v[1] Note: The use of *lay* as an intransitive in place of *lie* is
very common in US folk and colloq speech; senses and combs
in which *lay* is the only or preponderant form in our evidence
are entered under *lay* or its compounds.

1 also with *down, low;* Of the wind: to abate. [*OED lie* v[1] 9
a1000–1689; "*Obs.*"] **esp Sth** See Map

1806 (1905) Clark *Orig. Jrls. Lewis & Clark Exped.* 5.348 **VA**, I
directed the hunters . . if the wind Should lie that I should proceed on
down to their Camp. **1966–70** *DARE* (Qu. B13, *When the wind begins
to decrease . . it's _____*) Inf **AL**52, Lying [FW: Inf not sure, perh
laying]; **FL**7, **SC**3, **TX**32, Lying; **ID**5, **SC**56, **TX**102, **WI**58, Lying
down; **GA**22, A-lyin'. **1986** Pederson *LAGS Concordance* **esp coastal
Gulf Region** (*The wind is letting up*) 8 infs, (A-)lying; 3 infs, Lie; 1
inf, (A-)lying down; 1 inf, Lying low.

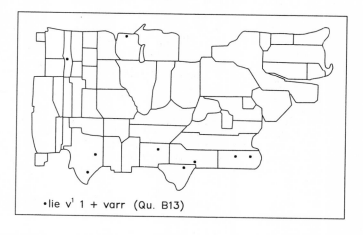

•lie v[1] 1 + varr (Qu. B13)

2 also *lay;* in phrr *lie well* (or *good*); Of land: to have a situation or aspect favorable for cultivation.
1814 (1922) Tatum *Jrl.* 7.41 **NC,** The lands on the left are rich and lie well. **1859** (1968) Bartlett *Americanisms* 238, "The land lays well," for lies well. **1966** *DARE* (Qu. C29, *A good-sized stretch of level land with practically no trees*) Inf **AL23,** Land lies well (for farming). **1976** *DARE* File **nwMO,** The land lays good: it's fairly level, kind of rolling, but not too ditchy or hilly. **c1977** *Ibid* **nwMO,** [Real estate advt:] *Farm land . . 90% tillable, lays good. . . 200 Acre . . land, lays well practically all tillable.*

3 freq *lay;* Of food in the stomach: to make itself felt; to cause discomfort—often in phrr *lay heavy* (or *hard*) *on one's stomach.* **esp NEast, Midl** See Map
1950 *WELS* **WI** (*When food is hard on your stomach, you say that it _____*) 1 Inf, Lays on the stomach; 1 Inf, Lays heavy on my stomach; 1 Inf, Lies heavy on the stomach; 1 Inf, Lies like a rock. **1966–70** *DARE* (Qu. H69) Infs **CA54, IN27, 30, NY37, 80, 240, OH47, OK19, TN11,** Lays heavy (on my stomach); **CT12, KY37, ME19, VT16,** Lays hard (on my stomach); **NJ26, OH42, WI13,** Lays (or laying) on your stomach; **NY94, VT3, WA3,** Lays like a lump of lead (or a piece of lead, a rock); **CT12, KY34, MD8,** Lays on my stomach (or in your stomach, there); **NJ21, NY220, NC41,** Laid in my stomach (or too heavy on your stomach, there); **KY15, NY104, 123,** Lies heavy; **NY72, RI1,** Lays (kinda) heavy on your stomach; **NC14,** Doesn't lie well on my stomach. [12 of 30 Infs mid-aged, 18 old]

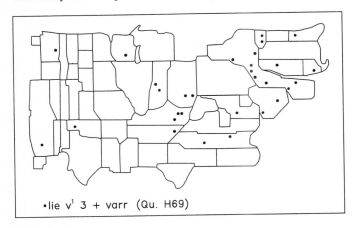

•lie v¹ 3 + varr (Qu. H69)

lie v² See **lie** n 2

lie n

1 A liar. **esp Sth, S Midl**
1894 Riley *Armazindy* 5 **IN,** But she wuz a cunnin', sly,/ Meek and lowly sorto' lie,/ 'At men-folks like me and you / B'lieves jes 'cause we ortn't to. **1909** *DN* 3.345 **eAL, wGA,** *Lie.* . . Liar. "He called me a lie, and I knocked him down for it." Universal. **1922** Gonzales *Black Border* 310 **sSC, GA coasts** [Gullah glossary], *Lie*—liar, liars. **1926** Roberts *Time of Man* 288 **cKY,** He told a tale and made me out a lie. **1934** Carmer *Stars Fell on AL* 215 [Black], "You been crawlin' some other woman while Cena was pregnant," she said in a loud clear voice. . . "You're a damned lie," said the man gruffly. **1937** (1977) Hurston *Their Eyes* 223 **FL** [Black], "You'se uh lie," Sop retorted. "Ah ain't through and Ah ain't ready tuh git up."

2 A story; a tall tale; hence v *lie* to tell such a story.
1934 Hurston *Jonah's Gourd Vine* 314 **AL,** *Lies,* stories, tales. **1935** Hurston *Mules & Men* 23 **FL** [Black], "Ah come to collect some old stories and tales and Ah know y'all know a plenty of 'em. . . " "What you mean, Zora, them big old lies we tell when we're jus' sittin' around here on the store porch doin' nothin'?" *Ibid* 217, "But de very next night after they buried her, she took de shape of uh owl and wuz back dere shivverin' and cryin'. And dats how come us got squinch owls." "Dat sho waz uh true lie, A.D.," Carrie said. *Ibid* 115, We got plenty to do—lyin' on Ole Massa and slavery days. . . Y'all ever hear 'bout dat nigger dat found a gold watch? **1954** *Harder Coll.* **cwTN,** *Lie* . . short, humorous story such as people tell each other. "He's allus a-tellin' old lies, gits people to laugh at 'im." **1987** Jones-Jackson *When Roots Die* 37 **sSC coast** [Gullah], The Sea Island tradition has been to tell tales (called "lies" by the islanders) as a form of entertainment. *Ibid* 38, In the words of one of the islanders, "some people de gift for lie" [=have a gift for telling lies]. The word *lie* . . is also a term associated with any kind of fictional tale told primarily for entertainment.

lie-bill See **libel**

lie detector n Cf **jeep stick**
=gee-haw whimm(e)y-diddle.
1963 *Chr. Sci. Monitor* (Boston MA) 26 Apr 6/6 **OH,** The whimmy-diddle. . . Ohio folks call it a lie detector.

lie down v phr

1 also *lay down;* also refl: To retire for the night, go to bed. [By ext from std sense (Cf *OED* at *lie* v.¹ B.21.a); appar euphem for *go to bed;* see quot 1931] **scattered, but chiefly Sth, S Midl** See Map
1859 (1968) Bartlett *Americanisms* 243, *To lie down.* To go to bed. In Tennessee, when a stranger is asked if he will retire for the night, the question is, "Will you lie down?" **1886** *S. Bivouac* 4.343 **sAppalachians,** Lie down (go to bed). **1887** *Amer. Philol. Assoc. Trans. for 1886* 17.46 **Sth,** List of common Southern expressions—many of them vulgarisms—that have not, so far as I know, either old English or provincial English authority. . . *Lie* down (go to bed). **1903** *DN* 2.319 **seMO,** *Lie down.* . . Go to bed. 'Your room is ready whenever you wish to lie down.' This is considered more polite than to say 'go to bed.' **1909** *DN* 3.345 **eAL, wGA,** *Lie down.* . . To go to bed. *Retire* is rarely used. *Lay down* is by far the common form. **1911** *DN* 3.538 **eKY,** *Lie down.* Specifically, to go to bed. **1923** *DN* 5.213 **swMO,** [*Lay*] *down.* . . To retire for sleep. **1931** Randolph *Ozarks* 81, Sex is very rarely mentioned save in ribaldry, and is therefore excluded from all polite conversation between men and women. . . This taboo is extended to include a great many words which have no real connection with sex. . . Even the word *bed* is seldom used before strangers, and the Ozark women do not *go to bed*—they *lay down.* **c1960** *Wilson Coll.* **csKY,** *Lie down.* . . Go to bed for the night; bed, somehow, suggested something bad. **1965–70** *DARE* (Qu. X40, . . *Ways . . of saying, "I'm going to bed"*) Infs **IN27, KY40, LA8, ME4, MN2, SC29, TN1, TX76,** Lay down; **AR47, GA59, MA25, MO34, NY24, 236, OH76,** Lie down; **GA43, NC49, 55, 79, PA248,** Going to lie down; **CO33, MS63, MO6, NC37,** Go (going to, *or* gotta) lay down; [**SC42,** Lay it down;] **SC21,** Lay me down to sleep; **TN52,** Gone [=going to] lie down; **MS23,** Lie myself down.

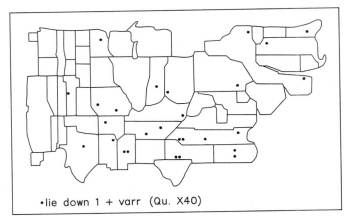

•lie down 1 + varr (Qu. X40)

2 See **lie** v¹ 1.

lief adv Usu |lif|; also freq |liv|; sometimes |lɪv|; also esp **NEng** |livz, lɪvz| Pronc-spp *le(a)ve, leef, lieve(s), live(s), livs;* for addit pronc and sp varr see quots **chiefly NEast, Midl**
Willingly, soon—used in phrr *had* (or *would, should,* or with ellipsis of the verb) *as lief* (or *liefer*) and varr.
1810 (1912) Bell *Journey to OH* 3 **MA,** She did not know but she should as lieve see a wild Indian as to see that scene over again. **1835** Longstreet *GA Scenes* 29, He *jist as live* go agin the house with you. **1843** (1916) Hall *New Purchase* 436 **IN,** I'd just as leef marry. . . down here as not. **1844** Stephens *High Life in NY* xi, *Livs.* As lieve as. *Jest as lives*—just as lieve as. **1858** in 1983 *PADS* 70.40 **ce,sePA,** He as leave have a female doctor as a man. **1863** in 1986 Messer *Civil War Letters* 16 **VT,** I had just as lives chaw him as not if it was not for nastying my mouth. **1864** (1868) Trowbridge *3 Scouts* 75 **TN,** Just as lieves have a kidnapped nigger as any other. **1875** *Atlantic Mth.* 32.417 **ceOH,** He'd just as lief quit work. **1890** Holley *Samantha among Brethren* 107 **NY,** I'll talk to her, mother, I'd jest as leve as not. **1890** *DN* 1.74 **NEng,** *Lives* [lɪvz]: lief. "I'd just as lives do it." **1896** *DN* 1.420 **NY,** *Lief:* sometimes pron. [liv]. . . *Lief:* have as lives [livz] for have as *lief.* "I'd just as lives go as not." **1903** *DN* 2.319 **seMO,** I'd

liefer go than not. **1905** *DN* 3.13 **cCT**, *Liefer* or *liever*. . . Rather. 'I'd liefer read than work.' . . *Liefs* or *lieves*. . . A corruption of *lief* or *lieve*. **1906** *DN* 3.144 **nwAR**, *Lief*. . . Pronounced [liv]. . . Common. Also common in the adv. gen. [livz]. . . *Liefer* [livə]. . . Rather, preferably. "I'd liefer walk than ride." **1907** *DN* 3.193 **seNH**, "I'd as livs do it for him as for anybody." Note the adverbial genitive ending as well as the vowel shortening. Common. **1909** *DN* 3.344 **eAL, wGA**, *Leave* . . lief. *Ibid* 346, *Live*. . . Lief. **1910** *DN* 3.444 **wNY**, *Lief*. . . Commonly pronounced [liv]. *Ibid* 454 **seVT**, I'd just as livs. **1912** *DN* 3.581 **wIN**, I'd just as leave do it as eat. **1913** *DN* 4.1 **cME**, He had just as lifs work as not, and a little lifser. **1915** *DN* 4.184 **swVA**, *Leave*. **1916** *DN* 4.277 **NE**, I would just as liv, or a little liver. **1942** Faulkner *Go Down* 112 **MS**, I reckon I just as lief to if you wants to. **1942** Hall *Smoky Mt. Speech* 13 **wNC, eTN**, The historical variation of |i|/|ɪ|, as in *sleek/slick*, is reflected in *breeches, lief, negro*, which have |ɪ| in the Great Smokies. **1965–68** *DARE* FW Addit **MS**, I'd as lief do this as that; **ceOK**, I'd just as leave—I'd just as soon; **seNY**, I'd just as lief take my car. **1966–70** *DARE* (Qu. JJ32, *If you have to make up your mind between two things*—for example, a dog and a cat . . "*I'd _____ [have a dog].*") Inf **CA97**, As lief have; **MI26, MA5, NY194**, Just as lief [lif]; **CT15**, Lief [lif]; **CA97, PA236, WI5**, Liefer ['lifɚ]; **PA230**, Just leave; **TX51**, Live [lɪəv]. [4 of 9 total Infs said this was old-fash.] **1966** *DARE* Tape **SC7**, I'd just as leave have a peck of dry lima beans. **1974** *AmSp* 49.63 **swME** (as of c1900), I'd lievser do it. **1985** Rattray *Advent. Dimon* 233 **Long Is. NY**, We've got a cash book for that. I'd just as lib they put it on their account, though.

lief adj [Du]
Dear, charming, sweet.

1979 *DARE* File **sHolland IL** [Letter], I talked to Joyce Sat. and she said you had been at their place & Becky is so *lief* (sweet) I will enclose a couple pictures of Becky with her grandparents.

lief n See **leave** n[1]

liefer, liefs See **lief** adv

lie good See **lie** v[1] **2**

lie in v phr Also *lay in* Cf **sleep in**
To stay in bed; esp, to sleep late, oversleep.

1950 *WELS* **WI** (*If you sleep later than usual on purpose:* "*I _____ this morning.*") 1 Inf, Lay in late; 1 Inf, Laid in. **1958** *DE Folkl. Bulletin* 1.32, *Lay in a while* (sleep late). **1966–70** *DARE* (Qu. X43b) Infs **CA2, 36, IL25, 96, KY74, MD33, ME10, PA29, 164**, Laid in (longer); **DC8, MS37, NY59**, Lay in (late); **PA199**, Laying in; (Qu. X43a, *If you sleep later than usual one day by accident . .* "*I _____.*") Infs **CA170, CO15**, Laid in; (Qu. BB41, *Not seriously ill, but sick enough to be in bed:* "*He's been _____ for a week.*") Inf **CA9**, Lying in.

lielock See **lilac**

lie low v phr See **lie** v[1] **1**

lie low(s) to catch meddlers See **layover(s) to catch meddlers**

lie out v phr Also freq *lay out*

1a To spend the night away from home; to sleep outdoors—often used in ref to farm animals. [*OED* (at *lie* v.[1] 26.b) "to sleep out, now *dial.* of cattle. . . *Obs.*"] **chiefly Sth, S Midl**
1852 Stansbury *Expedition* 171 **UT**, They were almost famished for water, and had "laid out," or bivouacked, for four successive nights. **1903** *DN* 2.319 **seMO**, *Lay out* or *lie out*. . . Applied to cows. Not coming home at night. It is customary in many places to turn cows out and keep the calves at home to insure the return of their mothers. 'Our cows laid out last night and we have no milk this morning.' **1905** *DN* 3.86 **nwAR**, The cows laid out all night. **1907** *DN* 3.246 **eME**, *Lay out*. . . Used of farm animals in the sense of *spend the night in the pasture*. Secondarily, of human beings in the sense of *spend the night outside of a house and a bed*. "We slept on a hay-mow that night; when we got home the boys spotted us and said, "We knew you laid out last night."[*] [**] **1909** *DN* 3.344 **eAL, wGA**, *Lay out*. . . Of cows, to stay away from home at night. **1939** Hall *Coll.* **wNC, eTN**, *Lay out*. . . To camp out. . . "Me and a party were on Big Creek a-fishin', layin' out, campin' out in the woods." . . "We was layin' out in the mountains." . . "They had old flint rocks to strike fire out of when they lay out." **1954** *Harder Coll.* **cwTN**, *Lay out*. . . Of a husband or wife, to stay away from home. **1955** Roberts *S. from Hell-fer-Sartin* 111 **seKY**, And he traveled all that day and called to stay all night, and nobody wouldn't let him stay all night. . . He aimed to lay out in that house. **1958** McCulloch *Woods Words* 104 **Pacific NW**, *Lay out*. . . To sleep out in

the open, no blankets or camp. **1970** *DARE* (Qu. Y29b, . . *About a man [who doesn't stay home much]:* "*He's always _____.*") Inf **MO23**, Laying out. **1986** Pederson *LAGS Concordance*, 1 inf, **neAL**, Laying out—sleeping outside; 1 inf, **cnAR**, They'd lay out of a night—sleep outside at night.

b in fig phr *lay out with the dry cattle* and varr: See quots. **esp Gulf States**
1936 *AmSp* 11.368 **nLA**, Lay out with the dry cattle. To remain out late at night; as 'The boys have been laying out with the dry cattle.' **1941** Dobie *Longhorns* 51 **TX**, [He] decided that if he mavericked on his own he could . . have a herd of his own. . . He bought three cow ponies, took a supply of coffee, salt, and meal . . two blankets, a running iron and an extra rope, and went to "laying out with the dry cattle." **1950** *PADS* 14.79 **FL**, *Lyin' out with the dry cattle*. Staying out late at night with the unmarried set. **1984** Wilder *You All Spoken Here* 94 **Sth**, *Layin' out with the dry cattle*: Said of young bucks who carouse most of the night with amiable gal chillun. When cows are dry they don't come in from pasture at night, and some women who are inclined to shirk domestic responsibilities are likewise nonchalant. **1986** Pederson *LAGS Concordance*, 1 inf, **nwAL**, Lay out with the dry cows—stay out too late.

c To hide; see quots.
1958 McCulloch *Woods Words* 104 **Pacific NW**, *Lay out*. . . To hide out with a truck load of logs which is thought to be overweight, until the state highway department scales are shut down for the day. **1974** Fink *Mountain Speech* 15 **wNC, eTN**, *Lay out* . . hide. "They laid out in the woods 'til the law was gone." **1976** Garber *Mountain-ese* 52 **sAppalachians**, *Lay-out*. . . stay hidden—Joel will hafta lay-out in the hills a few days till the heat cools off.

2 To stay away from work, school, or other commitments, usu without permission; to loaf, malinger; also with *of, from*: to stay away from (school, etc). **Sth, S Midl, esp sAppalachians, GA, SC** See Map
1896 *DN* 1.420 **cTX**, *Lay out*: "cut" recitation. "He laid out of Latin." **1905** *DN* 3.86 **nwAR**, *Lay out*. . . To stay away, to absent one's self deliberately. . . 'He laid out of Latin to-day.' General. **1923** *DN* 5.213 **swMO**, [*Lay*] *out*. . . To remain away intentionally, as from a public gathering. **1945** Saxon *Gumbo Ya-Ya* 372 **LA**, *To lay out* is to take a few days off. **1949** Kurath *Word Geog.* 79, *Played truant. . . lay out (of school), laid out (of school)* . . in Western North Carolina and adjoining parts of Virginia and South Carolina, and . . in the contiguous easterly parts of North Carolina and South Carolina lying between the Neuse and the Peedee. Scattering instances of *lay out* and *laid out* have also been noted on the James and the Rappahannock. **1951** *AmSp* 26.75 **csIL**, 'Did you lay out of school?' To *lay out* means either 'playing hooky' for a day or 'skipping' school for a lengthy period. Common. **1960** Criswell *Resp. to PADS 20* **Ozarks**, *Lay out of school*. . . play hooky, miss school. **c1960** Wilson *Coll.* **csKY**, *Lay out*. . . Skip school, play hookey. **1965–70** *DARE* (Qu. JJ6, *To stay away from school without an excuse*) 34 Infs, **chiefly S Midl, S Atl, esp sAppalachians, GA, SC**, Lay out; **AR51, GA73, 86, IL116, KY21, SC39**, Lay out of school; **SC3**, Lie out of school; (Qu. A9, . . *Wasting time by not working on the job*) Inf **LA15**, Laying out; (Qu. A18, . . *A very slow person:* "*What's keeping him? He certainly is _____!*") Inf **KY6**, Laying out [laughter]; (Qu. BB27, *When somebody pretends to be sick . . he's _____*) Inf **GA59**, Laying out, lying out; **GA67**, Laying out [laughter]. **1966** Dakin *Dial. Vocab. Ohio R. Valley* 2.511, *Skip class*. . . lay out of/from school. *Ibid* 512, In all of southern Kentucky, in the Mountains south of the upper Kentucky and Licking Rivers, and among older

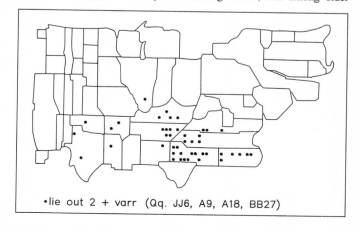

•lie out 2 + varr (Qq. JJ6, A9, A18, BB27)

speakers in the southern Knobs the expression of the Carolinas and western Virginia *lay out (of school)* is usual. **1968** *DARE* Tape **VA**17, And then if they lay out of school she finds out. **1971** Wood *Vocab. Change* 39, In Tennessee and Georgia the next term [after *play hookey*] is to *lay out.* . . *Lie out* may simply be an elegant variation of *lay out;* if so its scattered distribution is an indication of the results from classroom drill in the difference between *lie* and *lay*. **1990** Pederson *LAGS Regional Matrix* 210, [*Lay out* meaning 'to skip class' occurs most frequently in **eTN**, less frequently in **nGA**, and **cTN;** it is found infrequently in other areas of the Gulf Region.]

3 Of land: to lie fallow, remain uncultivated; hence v phr trans *lay out* to leave fallow. **esp S Midl, Sth**

1829 *S. Agriculturist* 2.460 **cSC**, We have adopted . . what may be termed a medium course—that is, to commence the *turning under*, or *listing* a field, having *laid out,* (commonly termed,) during the hot months, about the first of September. **1850** U.S. Patent Office *Annual Rept. for 1849: Ag.* 402 **neNC**, After the corn crop, do not suffer the land to "lie out." **1927** *DN* 5.475 **Ozarks**, *Lay out.* . . To lie idle or unused. A phrase applied to cleared land not under cultivation. "I jes' had t' let th' east forty lay out this year." **1937** Johnson *Ante-Bellum NC* 486 (as of c1850–60), But the land, once having been "burned up" by the turpentine and tar industry, was usually left "lying out" a generation or more until it again grew up in pines. **1945** FWP *Lay My Burden Down* 74 **GA** (as of c1865) [Black], Old Marse and Old Miss, they never had a hand left there on that great big place, and all that ground laying out. **1963** Owens *Look to River* 126 **neTX**, They were following the brushy turnrow of a field left to lie out so long that sassafras and persimmon sprouts grew in patches waist high. **1965** *DARE* FW Addit **swOK**, *Laying out.* Of land: lying idle. **1967** *DARE* Tape **TX**8, [FW:] What do you do with the land, if you don't plant rice on it? Do you put anything else on it? . . [Inf:] I haven't been puttin' anything else on, just lettin' it lay out; **TX**12, They have three tracts that they plant, an' they'll start out at this one this year, an' then they plant the next one next year, and the first one would lay out. . . Then next year they'd plant the next one, an' two of 'em will lay out. . . Each one is laid out two years between times. **1968** *DARE* (Qu. T2a) Inf **NC**49, Land is lyin' out; uncultivated. **1986** Pederson *LAGS Concordance*, 1 inf, **csAL**, Letting his field lie out—if growing in weeds; 1 inf, **seAL**, Laid out—land not in use.

4 To be in recess, take a break.

1976 Gt. Smoky Mt. Nat. Park *Recordings* 114:2 *(Montgomery Coll.)*, [School] lay out . . two weeks to pull fodder, then another two weeks to pick peas.

lie out from (or of) See **lie out 2**

lie up v phr See **lay up** v phr **3, 5**

lieve(r), lieves See **lief** adv

lievo See **relievo**

lievser See **lief** adv

lie well See **lie** v¹ **2**

life bird n
=horned lark.

1917 (1923) *Birds Amer.* 2.212, Horned Lark—*Otocoris alpestris alpestris*. . . Life Bird.

life elastic n [Folk-etym] Cf **live devil aspirin**
=life everlasting 1.

1928 Peterkin *Scarlet Sister Mary* 121 **SC**, She must come in and sit down and have a cup of newly steeped life-elastic tea that he had just finished brewing; it would do her good. Nothing is better in the fall than life-elastic tea.

life everlasting n

1 rarely *live-and-everlasting*: **=cudweed 1.** [Because it keeps its form and color when dry] **chiefly Sth, S Midl** Cf **everlasting n 1, life elastic** Note: Some of these quots may refer instead to senses below.

1629 Parkinson *Paradisi* 374, *Argyrocome sive Gnaphalium Americanum*. Live long or Life everlasting. This silver tuft or Indian Cotton weede, hath many white heads of leafes. **1784** in 1785 Amer. Acad. Arts & Sci. *Memoirs* 1.480, *Life-Everlasting*. Blossoms white. In pastures and fields. September. **1822** Eaton *Botany* 293, *Gnaphalium . . polycephalum* . . sweet-scented life-everlasting . . *decurrens* . . neglected life-everlasting . . *plantagineum* . . early life-everlasting . .

uliginosum . . mud life-everlasting. **1864** *Catalogue of Herbs* **swME**, *Life everlasting*—Gnaphalium polycephalum. **1905** *DN* 3.13 **cCT**, *Life everlasting*. . . An herb. Ibid 86 **nwAR**, *Life everlasting*. **1909** *DN* 3.345 **eAL, wGA**, *Life-everlasting*. . . The plant commonly known as rabbit-tobacco. **1925** Glasgow *Barren Ground* 509 **VA**, She could see the white fire of the life-everlasting. **1937** in 1977 *Amer. Slave Suppl. 1* 1.93 **AL**, Den us used life everlasting tea fur fever. **c1938** in 1970 Hyatt *Hoodoo* 2.934 **ceVA**, This here's the bub [Hyatt: bulb] off of w'a' choo call the *live-an'-everlastin'*. [Hyatt: His *live* pronounced *lyve*.] **1959** Lomax *Rainbow Sign* 151 **LA** [Black], Along-side the road there was an old weed—life-everlastin, we called it—that we used to chew for the cramps. **1966–70** *DARE* (Qu. S6) Inf **NC**41, Life everlasting; (Qu. S20) Infs **VA**2, 43, Life everlasting; (Qu. S26a, . . *Wildflowers . . Roadside flowers*) Inf **VA**26, Life everlasting = tobacco plant = rabbit tobacco; (Qu. S26e, *Other wildflowers not yet mentioned;* not asked in early QRs) Inf **SC**19, Life everlasting—you can smoke the leaves—grows in fallow fields; **SC**27, Life everlasting (Negroes say ['lɑɪfmələstɪn])—same as rabbit tobacco—medicinal—smoked it to cure sinus trouble—made tea from it; (Qu. BB22) Inf **OH**95, Life everlasting: dried and tea made; (Qq. BB50a, b, . . *Remedies*) Inf **SC**10, Life everlasting: make a tea from the flowers—good for fever; will break a cold out; it will drive the phlegm down. **1986** Pederson *LAGS Concordance*, 1 inf, **seGA**, Life everlasting (to cure malaria); 1 inf, **swGA**, Life everlasting (rabbit tobacco; makes tea); 1 inf, **swMS**, Tea made of life everlasting for cold and fever; 1 inf, **cLA**, Life everlasting; 1 inf, **nwFL**, Life everlasting tea (mother made); 1 inf, **nwAR**, Life everlasting (what rabbit tobacco was called); 1 inf, **cnLA**, Life everlasting (used for tea or to smoke); *(Cigars and cigarettes)* 1 inf, **neTN**, Life everlasting; 1 inf, **neTN**, Life everlasting (smoked as a boy); 1 inf, **cTN**, Life everlasting (herb smoked for chest ailments).

2 A **pearly everlasting** (here: *Anaphalis margaritacea*). [Because it keeps its form and color when dry]

1822 Eaton *Botany* 293, [Gnaphalium] margaritaceum . . large-flowered life-everlasting. **1840** MA Zool. & Bot. Surv. *Herb. Plants & Quadrupeds* 125, [Gnaphalium] margaritaceum . . Life Everlasting. A common downy or wooly plant, over fallow fields, about 2 feet high, bearing many very white or pearly flowers. *Ibid* [Gnaphalium] polycephalum. . . Sweet Life Everlasting. **1847** Wood *Class-Book* 351, A[ntennaria] margaritacea . . Common Life-everlasting. **1876** Hobbs *Bot. Hdbk.* 64, Pearl flow[ere]d Life everlasting, Gnaphalium margaritaceum. **1937** U.S. Forest Serv. *Range Plant Hdbk.* W13, Pearl everlasting [=*Anaphalis margaritacea*], a bunched or loosely tufted perennial herb of the aster family, also called pearly everlasting, cudweed, . . and life everlasting. **1969** *DARE* (Qu. S25, . . *The small wild chrysanthemum-like flowers . . that bloom in fields late in the fall*) Inf **MO**15, Life everlasting.

3 An **orpine** (here: *Sedum telephium*). [Perh from its ability to regenerate] Cf **live-forever 2**

1959 Carleton *Index Herb. Plants* 74, *Life everlasting*: Anaphalis margaritacea; Gnaphalium (v); Sedum telephium.

4 A **yarrow** (here: *Achillea millefolium*).

1969 *DARE* FW Addit **KY**5, *Life everlastin'*—common yarrow or Achillea millefolium.

5 also *lifesavers*: Gravy.

1966 *DARE* (Qu. H37, . . *Words . . for gravy. Any joking ones?*) Inf **NC**44, Lifesavers. **1984** Wilder *You All Spoken Here* 87 **Sth**, Life everlasting: Gravy made from country ham grease, milk or water, and flour.

life-of-man n

1 A **spikenard** (here: *Aralia racemosa*). [See quot 1971] Cf **old-man's-root**

1784 in 1785 Amer. Acad. Arts & Sci. *Memoirs* 1.432, Aralia. . . Pettymorrel. Life of Man. . . It is aromatic. The berries give spirits an agreeable flavour. **1795** Winterbotham *Amer. U.S.* 3.397, Among the native and uncultivated plants of New-England . . employed for medicinal purposes . . [is] Pettimorrel, or life of man. **1832** Williamson *Hist. ME* 1.126, *Life-of-man* . . bears clusters of purple berries, large as shot and wholesome; its root is excellent in a poultice. **1891** *Jrl. Amer. Folkl.* 4.148 **ME**, A family visiting us from Maine called it [=*Aralia racemosa*] Life of Man, and I have met the same name elsewhere since then. **1892** *Ibid* 5.97 **NH**, Aralia racemosa, Indian root; life of man; petty morrell. **1894** *Ibid* 7.90 **sME coast**, Aralia racemosa . . life-o'-man. **1930** Sievers *Amer. Med. Plants* 63, The American spikenard (*Aralia racemosa* L.), known also as spignet . . life-of-man, and old-man's root. **1971** Krochmal *Appalachia Med. Plants* 56, Life-of-man, old man's root. . . Roots and rhizomes have been used to treat rheumatism, syphilis, coughs, and shortness of breath. In Appalachia, a tea made of roots is used for backache. **1974** (1977) Coon *Useful Plants* 68, *Aralia racemosa*—Indian-root . . life-of-man . . pigeon weed.

2 Perh **pearly everlasting** (here: *Anaphalis margaritacea*). Cf **life everlasting 2**

1892 *Jrl. Amer. Folkl.* 5.98 seNH, *Anaphalis margaritacea* (?), life-of-man.

3 A **cudweed 1** (here: *Gnaphalium obtusifolium*).

1892 *Jrl. Amer. Folkl.* 5.98 **NH**, *Gnaphalium polycephalum* . . life-of-man. Stratham, N.H.

4 An **orpine**.

1893 *Jrl. Amer. Folkl.* 6.142 cMA coast, *Sedum Telephium*, life of man. **1896** *Ibid* 9.188 cME, *Sedum telephium* . . life-of-man. **1910** Graves *Flowering Plants* 214 CT, Orpine. . . Live-forever. Live-long. . . Life-of-Man. **1931** Clute *Common Plants* 134, That cheerful and persistent plant, the live-for-ever (*Sedum purpureum*) whose other name, life-of-man, makes plain who is to do the living.

5 A **mountain ash 1** (here: *Sorbus americana*).

1897 Sudworth *Arborescent Flora* 211, *Pyrus americana*. . . Life of Man. **1930** Sievers *Amer. Med. Plants* 7, *American Mountain-Ash—Sorbus americana*. . . Other common names.—Roundwood . . life-of-man . . moose-misse. **1971** Krochmal *Appalachia Med. Plants* 238, *Sorbus americana*. . . American mountainash . . dogberry . . life-of-man.

liferoot n

1 also *liferoot plant*: =**golden ragwort**.

1843 Torrey *Flora NY* 1.402, *Senecio aureus*. . . Life-root. **1876** Hobbs *Bot. Hdbk.* 95, Ragwort, Life root plant, Senecio aureus. **1892** (1974) Millspaugh *Amer. Med. Plants* 91–1, *Senecio*. . . Golden Ragwort . . life-root. **1952** Taylor *Plants Colonial Days* 44, Golden ragwort—*Senecio aureus*. . . Common names include groundsel, liferoot, and swamp squawweed. **1971** Krochmal *Appalachia Med. Plants* 234, *Senecio aureus*. . . liferoot. . . The herb is an expectorant and pectoral. . . an emmenagogue and vulnerary. **1974** (1977) Coon *Useful Plants* 115, *Senecio aureus* . . life-root plant, butterweed.

2 =**cocash 2**.

1873 in 1976 Miller *Shaker Herbs* 156, Cocash—*Aster puniceus*— . . Life Root.

liferoot plant See **liferoot 1**

lifesavers See **life everlasting 5**

lifs(er) See **lief** adv

lift n[1] [Scots, nEngl dial]

1952 Brown *NC Folkl.* 1.559 eNC, Lift. . . The sky.

lift v

1a also with *over*: To pick up and carry; to bring or take away. [Scots dial]

1965–70 *DARE* (Qu. Y30b, *To take something heavy up and move it from one place to another—for example, a bushel of apples*) 48 Infs, **scattered, but esp freq OH, wPA,** Lift; MO19, Lift it over; CO15, Lift them over; (Qu. Y30a, *To take something up and move it from one place to another—for example, a paper sack of groceries*) 23 Infs, **scattered, but esp freq OH,** Lift; IA5, Lift and take; PA202, Lift over. **1973** *DARE* File swPA, Will you lift my skirt from the dry cleaner when you go to town? *Ibid* swPA (as of 1920s), To remove (ashes from a stove or fireplace). . . In our home, that was called "lifting the ashes." **1986** Pederson *LAGS Concordance* **Gulf Region** (I lugged) 2 infs, Lift it; 2 infs, Lifted (it); 1 inf, Lift it up the stairs.

b Spec:

(1) To take up (a collection); to collect. [Scots dial]

1881 Pierson *In the Brush* 177 SW, I preached on to the end of my sermon; and, as usual, "lifted a collection" for the Bible Society, which . . amounted to about seven dollars. **1894** *DN* 1.332 **NJ,** Lift the collection: take up the collection. In common use in some localities. **1931** *AmSp* 7.20 swPA, Lift. Collect. "Church ushers lift the collection." **1935** Hurston *Mules & Men* 182 **FL,** The preacher descended from his fiery cloud and lifted the collection in his hat. **1945** Hubbard *Railroad Ave.* 351, Lift transportation—Collect tickets. **1984** Wilder *You All Spoken Here* 183 **Sth,** Lift the collection: Take the collection.

(2) To take up (a dish or meal) and bring it to the table; to serve (a meal); hence ppl adj *lifted* of a meal, prepared; served. **esp Midl** [Scots dial]

1912 *DN* 3.581 wIN, Lift. . . To put on the (dining room) table; to serve. "It is twelve o'clock; we had better lift the dinner." **1916** *DN* 4.277 **NE,** Lifted. . . Ready, prepared. "Dinner is lifted." **1927** *AmSp* 2.359 cwWV, Lifted . . prepared. "Supper is lifted." **1952** Brown *NC Folkl.* 1.560 wNC, Lift. . . To take food from the stove or fireplace to be served on the table. "Janie, lift the beans while I go get some onions." **1953** Randolph–Wilson *Down in Holler* 261 **Ozarks,** Lift. . . To bring forward, especially to serve food and drink. I have heard a backwoods housewife say: "The dinner's all cooked, Paw. Are you-uns ready for me to lift it?" **1959** *DARE* File swPA, You hear the cook of the house say "lift the potatoes" which means take the potatoes out of the cooking well. **1963** in 1982 *Barrick Coll.* csPA, Lift—remove (something cooking) from the stove to serve at the table. "I'm gonna lift the potatoes now." . . "The potatoes is to lift yet." **1966** *DARE* File PA, Lift . . to lift a meal from the stove. **1973** *Ibid* swPA, Lift . . to serve a meal. "I'm just ready to lift the supper."

2 To pay off (a debt). [Cf *SND* lift v. 4.(2) "To take up, accept and pay (a bill of exchange)"] **esp S Midl**

1784 in 1956 Eliason *Tarheel Talk* 281 c,csNC, I Can a sure you if I had Cash I Could by 20 horsis in a week of pepel who want to Lift There plots out of the ofis. **1801** *Ibid* 281 nw,cwNC, Lifted this Deed. . . & gave him a Deed for 311 acres in room of it. **1834** Crockett *Narrative* 19 **TN,** He informed me that he owed a man . . the sum of thirty-six dollars, and that if I would set in and work out the note, so as to lift it for him, he would discharge me from his service. **1868** Beecher *Sermons* (1869) I.190 *(DAE)*, I want to lift a mortgage, and two hundred dollars would lift it. **1903** *DN* 2.319 seMO, Lift (a note or mortgage). . . Pay off indebtedness. 'If my crops do well I will be able to lift my mortgage this fall.' **1907** *DN* 3.232 nwAR, Lift (a note or mortgage). . . To pay off indebtedness. **1909** *DN* 3.345 eAL, wGA, Lift. . . To pay off (a mortgage, a debt).

3 To strike up (a song). [Scots, nEngl dial] Cf **hoist C1i(1)**

1884 *Anglia* 7.278 **Sth, S Midl** [Black], *To lif' de song* = to start the chorus. **1934** Carmer *Stars Fell on AL* 62, "Brother John Muckle, will you begin histin' the rhyme?" A raucous barytone lifted a plaintive questioning: "How long, O Savior, O how long shall this bright hour delay?" Scatteringly the song gathered volume.

4 To haul in (a fishnet or netted fish); to make a haul, fish with nets. **Gt Lakes**

1889 *Century Dict.* 3443, *To lift the crib*, in the Great Lakes fisheries, to gather in the netting of a crib or bowl of a pound-net. **1911** (1913) Johnson *Highways Gt. Lakes* 222 cnMI, He was . . an undesirable citizen, with a habit of lifting other people's nets, and examining their hooks. **1966–68** *DARE* Tape MI21, The only ones that could really make money on it was the smaller outfits that, when they got bait, they'd set all the hooks they had, when they didn't have bait, they'd lift; MI29, He had trap nets, and fish are alive in those—you know, when they catch them they swim around—and he just fished along the shores; he'd go and lift them himself—they were about six feet deep—and, when he'd get in with them, I was always there, and I dressed all those fish; MI54, We wanted to get a lift 'cause after the season we couldn't lift, so I and my partner went out and lifted; WI75, Here about two weeks ago, we lifted the weir out in deep water in the middle of the lake. **1988** Kriehn *Fisherfolk* 32 seWI, The work was very strenuous. Nets had to be lifted by hand and set from an open stern. *Ibid* 35, The warden found the men legally engaged in lifting herring (chubs).

lift n[2] [Cf *SND* lift n.[2] II.3 "The amount of fish, esp. herring, that can be lifted aboard by hand in the net"] **Gt Lakes** Cf **lift v 4**

A haul of fish; the quantity of fish caught at one time.

1966–67 *DARE* Tape MI21, After the fishermen learned how to fish the right way with hooks, a lot of 'em got some very good lifts; MI54, [FW:] Now getting a lift, what is that, what does that mean? [Inf:] Well, that means a lift of fish. [FW:] Pulling the nets. [Inf:] Yeah. . . We had five nets up there that fall; WI75, A lot of these fishermen . . if they hear of you gettin' a lift, they go sit right on top of you. **1988** Kriehn *Fisherfolk* 35 seWI, The harvest for the fishermen was enormous. Two to three thousand pounds per lift were normal. Once the Tesslers had a seven-thousand-pound lift in one night.

lifted See **lift v 1b(2)**

lifter n Cf **wedgie**

1991 *DARE* File **AR**, The act of reaching into another person's belt, and either grabbing the underwear or the belt and lifting the person off the ground. . . Lifter [1 response].

‡**lifting rag** n
  1981 Pederson *LAGS Basic Materials (Dishcloth)* 1 inf, **nwMS**, Lifting rags (in the kitchen for taking up crumbs, etc., from table and sink).

lift, on the adj phr [Cf *SND lift* v. I.1.(8) "To raise a farm animal to its feet . . after it had become weakened . . freq. in phrs. *a-liftin . . at the liftin . .* in a very debilitated state"] **chiefly Sth, S Midl**

1 Too weak to stand unaided, **down** adj D4; ill or exhausted, usu seriously.
  1888 *Harper's New Mth. Mag.* 76.486 **VA** [Black], De ole ox is done took sick, and is on de lift. **1895** *DN* 1.390 **cwIN**, *Lift,* to be on the: to be too weak to rise from bed. **1899** (1912) Green *VA Folk-Speech* 261, *On the lift.* Said of an animal so poor and weak that it has to be lifted up and helped to be able to walk; at the point of death. **1912** *DN* 3.584 **wIN**, *On the lift. . .* Sick; "ailing." "Harry is on the lift this week." **1915** *DN* 4.184 **swVA**, *On the lift,* sick or very weak. **1923** *DN* 5.216 **swMO**, *On the lift. . .* Unable to arise because of illness or weakness. **1933** *AmSp* 8.1.29 **nwTX**, *On the lift.* Sick (applied to a cow). The term comes from the fact that each morning all the sick cows not able to stand were *tailed up* or lifted with a portable block and tackle . . , and encouraged to remain standing for a time. Sometimes applied to persons. **1937** *DN* 6.620 **swTX**, The boys say there are some cows on the lift down on the Rio Grande. I reckon you'll have to ride bog today and tail 'em up. **1941** Cleaveland *No Life* 309 **cwNM**, We tried to save old cows who 'got on the lift,' meaning that they must be helped to their feet when down. **1942** Warnick *Garrett Co. MD* 10 **nwMD** (as of 1900–18), *Lift, on the . .* animals suffering from lack of food and unable to get on their feet were said to be "on the lift." **1952** Brown *NC Folkl.* 1.560, *Lift, on the. . .* Mainly of an animal: to be sick or injured to the point that the animal is unable to stand and must be lifted.—General. *Ibid, Lift, down on the. . .* Same as *on the lift.* **1959** Lahey-Hogan *As I Remember It* 89 **swKS** (as of c1885), A cow "got down" and was what they called "on the lift." They would put belts around her body and her quarters and swing her up to a beam in the stable. Then they would coax her to eat a little. A cow will not eat when it is down. **1966** *DARE* (Qu. BB39, *On a day when you don't feel just right, though not actually sick . . "I'll be all right tomorrow—I'm just feeling _____ today."*) Inf **SC27**, On the lift (old).

2 Convalescent. [Appar infl by *on the mend* and similar phrr]
  1892 *DN* 1.230 **KY**, "On the lift" = convalescent. "He is on the lift." **1903** *DN* 2.319 **seMO**, *Lift (on the). . .* Just able to be up. 'I was sick a week and am on the lift now.' **1907** *DN* 3.232 **nwAR**, *Lift (on the). . .* Just able to be up. **1983** *MJLF* 9.1.49 **ceKY**, *On the lift . .* getting better after an illness.

lift over See **lift** v 1a

lig n Cf **lag line**
  1969 *DARE* FW Addit **cKY**, *Lig*—starting point in the game [of marbles].

liggle adj [Pronc-sp for *legal*] Cf **league**
  c**1930** in **1944** *ADD* 354 **eWV**, *Liggle* ||lɪgl|. Common.

light n See **lights** 1

light v[1], hence vbl n *lighting* Cf **fire-lighting, light-hunting** =**jacklight** v.
  1967–70 *DARE* (Qu. P35b, *Illegal methods of shooting deer;* not asked in early QRs) Infs **IL115, MD34, MI65**, Lighting. **1969** *DARE* Tape **VA52**, You can't light ducks in real windy weather. . . That's when you didn't want no wind at night when you're lightin' ducks . . and . . you get up to 'em better and your light wouldn't flicker. . . There's a lot of people . . you know, lit ducks in them days, a lot of 'em.

light v[2]
1 occas with *down:* To dismount, alight—often used in formulas inviting one to stop and visit or share a meal. **scattered, but chiefly Sth, S Midl** Cf **alight and look at one's saddle**
  1794 (1936) Parry *Jrl.* 34.385 **PA**, Came to a place like a sink-hole—with an entrance into it; which induced me to light & view it. **1889** Edwards *Runaways* 221 **GA**, "Howdy, Cis'ly Toomer, howdy. 'Light," she answered back. Cis'ly Toomer guided her thin plow-horse under a tree and slid to the ground. **1899** (1912) Green *VA Folk-Speech* 261, *Light. . .* To get down off a horse. **1899** Chesnutt *Conjure Woman* 122 **csNC** [Black], W'en he got ter de do', he lit en hitch' de mule. **1903** *DN* 2.319 **seMO**, *Light. . .* Alight. 'Light, Sir, and stay all night.' Addressed to a person on horseback. **1906** *DN* 3.144 **nwAR**, *Light and hitch (your beast). . .* An invitation to stop and gossip. **1907** White *AZ*

Nights 75, The biggest asked me very grudgin' if I wouldn't light and eat, I told them "No," that I was travellin' in the cool of the evenin'. **1909** *DN* 3.345 **eAL, wGA**, *Light. . .* To alight. **1918** *DN* 5.18 **NC**, Won't you light and come in. **1921** Haswell *Daughter Ozarks* 98 (as of 1880s), As soon as he recognized his visitors he hastened to the gate, with the old time Ozark greeting: "Light, boys, Light!" **1929** in **1952** Mathes *Tall Tales* 99 **sAppalachians**, "Howdy, doc! How's all?" . . "'Bout as common, Harrison. Light an' blow yer hosses!" **1932** Randolph *Ozark Mt. Folks* 21, The old man was sitting in his rocking-chair on the "gallery" as I rode up the trail. "Light down an' set a spell," said he, and urged the only chair upon me. **1935** Sandoz *Jules* 211 **wNE** (as of 1880–1930), The Old Man and the boys ain't home, she says, but won't they light and set down to a bit a breakfast? **1939** FWP *ID Lore* 242, *To light and set*—to dismount and talk awhile. **1944** *PADS* 2.27 **Sth**, Light down and take grub. **1966–69** *DARE* (Qu. II15, *When somebody is passing by and you want him or her to stop and talk a while*) Inf **TN12**, Light and come in: to a person on a horse or in a car—country people; **NC30**, Light and rest your saddle; **CT37**, Light and set [laughter]—no one ever says that anymore. **1985** *DARE* File **Appalachians**, Light and come in = In Appalachia, in horseback riding days, this was an invitation to stop for a visit.

2 with *in:* To make a vigorous start on something. **scattered, but esp S Atl, sAppalachians** See Map
  1878 Beadle *Western Wilds* 187, They double-quicked into town and lit in generally. **1909** *DN* 3.346 **eAL, wGA**, *Light in. . .* To begin, enter into operations. "Light in and help yourself to that chicken-pie." **1912** *DN* 3.581 **wIN**, *Light in. . .* To begin operations vigorously. "Light in and help clean up these apple dumplings." **1915** *DN* 4.185 **swVA**, *Light in. . .* To begin work vigorously. "Light in and help me peel these apples." **1942** McAtee *Dial. Grant Co. IN* 40 (as of 1890s), *Light in . .* begin. **1952** Brown *NC Folkl.* 1.560, *Light in. . .* To begin. **1965–70** *DARE* (Qu. A22, *'To start working hard':* "She had only ten minutes to clean the room, but she _____.") 25 Infs, **scattered, but esp S Atl, sAppalachians**, Lit in; **FL35**, Lit in and had it done in no time flat; (Qu. KK29, *To start working very hard:* "He was slow at first but now he's really _____.") Inf **GA31**, He really lights in.

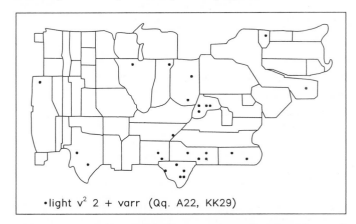

•light v[2] 2 + varr (Qq. A22, KK29)

3 To move quickly. [Cf *light out* to leave in a hurry] **esp S Midl**
  1866 in **1938** Twain *Letters Sandwich Is.* 22, And you want to know what made me light out of bed so sudden last night? Only a "santipede." **1913** Kephart *Highlanders* 101 **sAppalachians**, He [=a bear] riz an' knocked me down with his left paw, an' walked right over me, an' lit up the ridge. **1938** Matschat *Suwannee R.* 53 **neFL, seGA**, Come calm o' day, we-uns'll take our bearin's off the sun an' light for home. **1969** *DARE* (Qu. Y20, *To run fast:* "You should have seen him _____!") Infs **TN31, 33, 34, 36**, Light.

light and shut v phr Cf **open-and-shut**
  1890 *DN* 1.19 **seNH**, *Light and shut:* of the weather. 'It lights and shuts,' that is, the sun peeps out at intervals. The common New England maxim is "Open and shet's a sign of wet." [*DARE* Ed: Author suggests this may be peculiar to Portsmouth NH.]

light a shuck v phr Also *light a rag* [Prob from the use of a corn shuck or rag as a makeshift torch; see quot 1941] **Sth, S Midl** Cf **fire, come to borrow**

To leave in a hurry, run fast; hence v phr *light one's shuck* to cause someone to leave in a hurry.
  1903 *DN* 2.319 **seMO**, *Lit a rag. . .* Humorous for 'started suddenly.'

'He got skeered and lit a rag for home.' **1905** *DN* 3.86 **nwAR**, *Light a shuck*. . . To go in a hurry, to move on, to keep away from danger. **1908** (1966) Thorp *Songs Cowboys* 9, So he saddled up old Chaw one night and "Lit a shuck" this way / Thought he'd try and paddle now his own canoe. **1916** *DN* 4.344 **NC**, *Light a shuck*. . . To leave quickly. **1917** *DN* 4.414 **wNC, SC**, *Light a rag*. . . To decamp. "I lit a rag for home." **1919** *DN* 5.37 **OK**, *Light a shuck, to*. . . To strike out, in a hurry. "You ought to have seen that jack-rabbit light a shuck out across the prairie." In Kentucky, "light a rag." **1920** Hunter *Trail Drivers TX* 213 (as of 1878), Mr. Withers gave him his time [=his wages due] and told him to "light a shuck." **1929** *AmSp* 4.204 **Ozarks**, He geared up his ol' piedy cribber an' lit a shuck fer Gotham Holler. **1930** *DN* 6.85 **cSC**, *Light a rag, to*, to leave in a hurry. **1930** Stoney-Shelby *Black Genesis* 102 **seSC**, Br' Rabbit light a rag back up de pat', an' he is scared for true! **1935** Hurston *Mules & Men* 206 **nFL**, Nobody don't keer, long as she don't put her hand on me. Sho as she do dat Ahm gointer light her shuck for her. **1936** *AmSp* 11.368 **nLA**, When he saw the old man coming, he lit a shuck. **1941** TX Folkl. Soc. *Pub.* 17.10, The departing guest would light the tip of one of the whole corn shucks in the fire and lift it high above his head. The bright blaze would last for a matter of only a minute or two. . . Consequently, when a departing guest lit his shuck, he had to leave instantly or its light would be wasted. So, "He lit a shuck and left." **1952** Giles *40 Acres* 182 **KY**, He was down at Lacey's and Sereny came, so he lit a shuck out the back door and came up here until she left. **1962** Atwood *Vocab. TX* 71, *To leave in a rush.* The most common single expression for hurried departure is *light a shuck.* **1966-69** *DARE* (Qu. Y18, *To leave in a hurry: "Before they find this out, we'd better _____!"*) Infs **IL96, TX23, 29**, Light a shuck; **NC62**, Light a rag; (Qu. Y20, *To run fast*) Inf **AL6**, Light a rag, light a shuck; **LA31**, Really lit a shuck.

light beetle See **light bug 2**

light-bellied brant n
A **brant 1** (here: *Branta bernicla*).
   1910 Eaton *Birds NY* 1.233, *Branta bernicla glaucogastra*. . . Brant; Light-bellied Brant. **1923** U.S. Dept. Ag. *Misc. Circular* 13.37 **Long Is. NY**, Light-bellied brant. **1944** Hausman *Amer. Birds* 507.

light biscuit n Also *light bread biscuit* Cf **beaten biscuit**
A biscuit made with wheat flour and usu leavened with yeast.
   1853 (1982) Lea *Domestic Cookery* 69 **MD**, *Light Biscuit.*—Boil a quart of milk, and when nearly cold, stir it in the middle of your pan of flour, with two spoonsful of yeast, and one of butter and salt; let it lighten for two or three hours; knead the flour in it and let it rise again: a little while before you bake, roll it out, and cut it with the top of your dredging-box. Let them rise a few minutes in the dripping-pan. **1879** (1965) Tyree *Housekeeping in Old VA* 43, *Excellent Light Biscuit.* [*DARE* Ed: Recipe calls for flour, mashed potatoes, lard, milk, and yeast.] *Ibid*, Light Biscuit. [*DARE* Ed: Recipe calls for flour, shortening, salt, soda, and buttermilk.] **1969-70** *DARE* (Qu. H19, *What do you mean by a biscuit? How are they made?*) Inf **OH98**, Light biscuit—bread dough, cut from a roll and made into small pat—flat round bun; **IN65**, Light biscuits—made of light bread dough; **IN70**, Light biscuits—made with yeast: **TX21**, Light bread biscuit.

light bread n [*OED light* a.[1] 9.b "Of bread, pastry, etc.: That has 'risen' properly"; c1460 →] **chiefly Sth, S Midl, OK, TX** See Map Cf **bread n B1, flour bread 1, loaf bread**
Yeast-leavened bread, esp made with wheat flour; hence attrib, made of yeast-leavened wheat dough.
   1821 W. *Carolinian* (Salisbury NC) 27 Mar [1/2], *Crackers* and light *Bread*, will always be found in his shop. **1833** in 1956 Eliason *Tarheel Talk* 281 **neNC**, Supper litebread and butter. **1887** Amer. Philol. Assoc. *Trans. for 1886* 17.46 **Sth**, List of common Southern expressions—many of them vulgarisms—that have not, so far as I know, either old English or provincial English authority. . . *Light-bread* (loaf bread). **1895** *DN* 1.390 **wFL**, *Light bread*: wheat bread, in distinction from "bread," which means corn bread. **1902** *DN* 2.238 **sIL**, *Light-bread* (first part accented). . . Raised or leavened bread. **1903** *DN* 2.319 **seMO**, *Light-bread*. . . Raised bread; common bread. **1904** *DN* 2.419 **nwAR**, *Light bread*. . . Common wheaten loaf-bread as distinguished from biscuit. The generic term *bread* is used of cornbread. **1915** *DN* 4.185 **swVA**, *Light-bread*. . . Ordinary bread made with yeast, distinguished from biscuit. **1916** *DN* 4.325 **KS**, *Light-bread*. . . Bread leavened with yeast. **1940** Hench. Coll. **VA**, Heard in conversation by members of the Univ. of Va. English Department. . . [He] asked the group what their ideas about the meaning of "light bread" were. Some of the group said it was loaf bread, baker's

or home-made. Others vociferously said, "No. It is only home-made loaf bread," All agreed that it was "risen" bread, i.e. bread made with yeast, not with baking powder. **1944** *PADS* 2.9 **Sth**, *Light-bread*. . . Yeast-raised wheat-bread in a loaf. **1949** Kurath *Word Geog.* 39, Wheat bread baked in loaves is apt to be called simply *bread* in the Midland and the North. In the South and the South Midland, however, *light-bread* . . is the usual designation, and this compound word is encountered up to the Pennsylvania line, although the simplex *bread* is common enough in this sense in Delaware, Maryland, and West Virginia. *Ibid* 67, In the South and the South Midland this type of bread is commonly known as *light-bread*, in the coastal area also as *loaf bread*, as distinct from *pone bread* for corn bread. **1965** in 1983 Johnson *I Declare* 52 **nwFL**, You don't have to be from very far out in the country to know that "light bread" is bread made with white flour, like you buy at the store, as distinguished from cornbread or pone. **1965-70** *DARE* (Qu. H15, *Bread made with wheat flour*) 177 Infs, **chiefly Sth, S Midl, SW**, Light bread; **LA19, 28, TN37**, Homemade light bread; (Qu. H13, *Bread that is not made at home*) 141 Infs, **chiefly Sth, S Midl, TX, OK**, Light bread; [**NC76**, Light loaf bread;] (Qu. H18, . . *Special kinds of bread*) 24 Infs, **scattered**, Light bread; **TX37**, Homemade light bread; **KY85, TN31, 61, 64**, Corn light bread; **TN66**, Homemade cornmeal light bread; (Qu. H14, *Bread that's made with cornmeal*) Infs **NC55, SC46**, Corn light bread; (Qu. H17, . . *Kinds [of yeast]*) Inf **IN52**, Light bread east; (Qu. H19, *What do you mean by a biscuit? How are they made?*) Infs **TX21, WA1**, Light bread (biscuit); (Qu. H32, . . *Fancy rolls and pastries*) Inf **AR32**, Light bread; (Qu. H41, . . *Kinds of roll or bun sandwiches*) Inf **VA1**, Light bread buns, light bread rolls. **1966** *DARE* Tape **AL1**, I don't know anything about no light bread. If we didn't have hoecake corn bread, we had biscuits. . . We had corn bread, 'cause my daddy raised a lot of corn, but now flour—we just didn't have it; **FL41**, [FW:] Do you ever make any bread yourself? [Inf:] No, not light bread, you know, not loaf bread. I've never bothered with that, somehow. . . I just use biscuits and corn bread, then I buy loaf bread quite a bit, now. **1967** Fetterman *Stinking Creek* 79 **seKY**, Austria, strangest kind of country. They have the blackest kind of light bread there ever was. **1967** *DARE* FW Addit **LA11**, *Light bread* . . homemade bread. **1973** Allen *LAUM* 1.282 (as of c1950), 1 inf, **seIA**, Light bread doughnut. **1978** Massey *Bittersweet Country* 21 **Ozarks**, Light bread (yeast bread) was reserved for special occasions in most homes. **1989** Pederson *LAGS Tech. Index* 151 **Gulf Region**, [For loaf bread 502 infs used *light bread* alone or in various combs.] *Ibid*, Other flour breads . . light bread rolls (1 [inf]). *Ibid* 152-54, Corn breads . . corn light bread (9 [infs]) . . light bread (1 [inf]). *Ibid* 155, [For store-bought bread 167 infs used *light bread* alone or in various combs.]

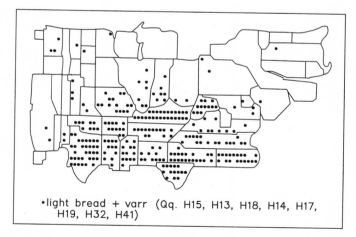

•light bread + varr (Qq. H15, H13, H18, H14, H17, H19, H32, H41)

light bread biscuit See **light biscuit**

light bug n
1 also *firelight bug*: =**firefly 1.** Cf **lightning bug**
   1939 *LANE* Map 238 *(Lightning bug)* 1 inf, **seMA**, Light bug, firelight bugs. **1966-68** *DARE* (Qu. R1, . . *The small insect that flies at night and flashes a light at its tail*) Infs **LA6, PA143, SC9**, Light bug. **1967** LeCompte *Word Atlas* 203 **seLA**, Light bug. [4 of 21 infs]. **1973** Allen *LAUM* 1.329 (as of c1950), 1 inf, **ND**, Light bug. **1986** Pederson *LAGS Concordance* **Gulf Region** *(Firefly)* 16 infs, Light bug(s).
2 also *light beetle*: A beetle, moth, or other insect attracted to light. Cf **electric light bug**
   1969 *DARE* File **Hatteras Is. NC**, *Light beetle*—little brownish beetle which comes to lights. **1986** Pederson *LAGS Concordance* **Gulf Region**

(Moth) 35 infs, Light bug(s); 1 inf, Light bug—small brown bug, like beetle, butterfly; 1 inf, Light bug—clay-colored, black wings, hums; 1 inf, Light bugs—i.e. candle flies; 1 inf, Light bugs—all sorts of little bugs, fly at light; 1 inf, Light bugs—all varieties found around lights; *(Firefly)* 1 inf, Light bug—flies around lights.

light cake n Cf **light bread**

  1930 Shoemaker *1300 Words* 38 **cPA Mts** (as of c1900), *Light cake*—A bun or "roll" made from white flour.

‡light dabber n

  A **miller 1** or similar moth.

  1986 Pederson *LAGS Concordance* (*The insect that flies around a light and tries to fly into it*) 1 inf, **cnTX**, Light dabber.

light dough n

  Yeast dough; yeast dough starter.

  1879 (1965) Tyree *Housekeeping in Old VA* 20, Under no circumstances use soda or saleratus in your light dough. **1959** Lahey–Hogan *As I Remember It* 143 **swKS** (as of c1886–1910), He said . . ma was going to bake bread so I could have a couple of loaves till I could get some light dough started. **1968** *DARE* (Qu. H26) Inf **DE4**, Doughnut—has light dough in it.

light down See **light v² 1**

lighten v Cf **-en suff⁵**, **outen v 1**

  To light (a lamp).

  1968 *DARE* (Qu. Y41a, . . *To tell someone to light a lamp or lantern:* "_____ *the lamp.*") Inf **NY100**, Lighten.

lighten bug See **lighting bug**

lightening n, freq attrib Also sp *lightning*

  Yeast or **emptins 1.**

  1842 Kirkland *Forest Life* 2.105 **MI**, An old man . . came in with a long-handled dipper, and asked if we kept lightning in the house. **1940** Brown *Amer. Cooks* 480 **MO**, The mush mixture, like homemade yeasts, was called variously "rising," "risin'," or "lightnin'," according to local custom. **1949** *AmSp* 24.110 **cnGA**, *Lightning bread*. . . Raised bread, whether of flour or corn meal. **1966–68** *DARE* (Qu. H13, *Bread that is not made at home*) Inf **LA2**, Joking term—lightning bread—because it goes so fast; **NC51**, Lightenin' bread; (Qu. H16, *What do people use to raise the bread before it's baked?*) Inf **NY69**, Lightenin' (old-fashioned?); (Qu. H18, . . *Special kinds of bread*) Inf **NC11**, Sourdough rolls or lightening rolls—a big roll of white bread.

lightening bug See **lightning bug**

lightening wood n Also sp *lightning wood*

  1 also *light wood*: =**fox fire 1a.**

  1818 in 1847 *Knickerbocker* 29.472 **NY**, There's in the rottenness of sin / Something that shines like lightning-wood. **1966** *DARE* (Qu. CC16, *A small light that seems to dance or flicker over a marsh or swamp at night*) Inf **ME4**, Lightening wood (occas) or light wood (doesn't flicker and dance).

  2 also *lightning*: =**lightwood n¹.**

  1968 *DARE* (Qu. T8, *Joints of pine wood that burn easily and make good fuel*) Inf **GA53**, Lightning wood. **1986** Pederson *LAGS Concordance,* 1 inf, **neTN**, Lightning wood = dry, flaky wood; heard at camp; 1 inf, **cnGA**, Rich lightning = lighterd.

light entry n

  In bituminous coal mining: =**air course.**

  1973 *PADS* 59.40 **eKY**, *Light entry* . . air course.

lighter(d), lighterd-wood See **lightwood n¹**

‡lighter fly n

  =**firefly 1.**

  1956 Ker *Vocab. W. TX* 236, Lighter fly. [1 of 67 infs]

lightern, lighter-wood See **lightwood n¹**

light-fingered adj **scattered, but chiefly NEast, N Cent** See Map Cf **long-fingered**

  Thievish; given to stealing.

  1899 (1912) Green *VA Folk-Speech* 261, *Light-fingered*. . . Thievish; addicted to petty thefts. **1915** *DN* 4.218, *Long-fingered,* lightfingered, epithet for a thief. **1960** Criswell *Resp. to PADS 20* **Ozarks,** A few literate people may have said *light-fingered gent*. **1965–70** *DARE* (Qu. V6, . . *Words . . for a thief*) 30 Infs, **chiefly NEast, N Cent**, Light-

fingered; **CT11, MI118**, Light-fingered—refers to shop-lifter(s); **ME21**, He's kind of light-fingered—he takes things unseen; **MI10**, Light-fingered—you hear; **MA5**, Light-fingered—he's despicable; **NH6**, He's light-fingered—picks up things and puts in pocket, etc, slyly; **OH97**, Light-fingered (adj)—small-scale theft out of shop; **ID5, PA131, VT13**, Light-fingered person; **FL27**, Light-fingered gentry; **SC55**, Light-fingered gent; (Qu. V5a, *To take something of small value that doesn't belong to you*) Inf **NY210**, Light-fingered; (Qu. HH37, *An immoral woman*) Inf **NY209**, Light-fingered—if she's a thief; (Qu. OO42a, *About stealing money:* "He admitted that he _____ *[the money].*") Inf **MA30**, Was light-fingered.

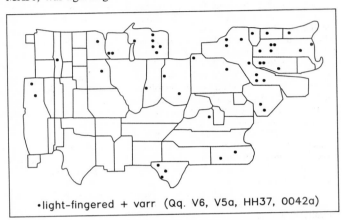

•light-fingered + varr (Qq. V6, V5a, HH37, OO42a)

light-fishing vbl n Also *light-jumping* Cf **fire-fishing**

  1967 *DARE* (Qu. P13, . . *Ways of fishing . . besides the ordinary hook and line*) Inf **SC40**, Light-fishing: lower a light from the bridge or build large fire on the bank to attract fish; **SC45**, Light-fishing: fish at night, dropping a flashlight or sealed beam down in a closed jar to attract fish—drop hook down beside it; **FL7**, Light-jumping—with net and light.

light-houses n

  An **amaranth** (here: *Amaranthus retroflexus*).

  1897 *Jrl. Amer. Folkl.* 10.53 **seNY**, *Amarantus* [sic] *retroflexus* . . light-houses.

light-hunting vbl n Cf **light v¹**

  =**fire-lighting.**

  1966 *DARE* (Qu. P35b, *Illegal methods of shooting deer;* not asked in early QRs) Inf **SC4**, Light-hunting.

light in See **light v² 2**

lighting See **light v¹**

lighting bug n Also *lighten bug* Cf **lightning bug**

  =**firefly 1.**

  1966 *DARE* (Qu. R1, . . *The small insect that flies at night and flashes a light at its tail*) Inf **SC9**, Lightin' bug. [FW: not *lightning*] **1966** Dakin *Dial. Vocab. Ohio R. Valley* 2.406, The variant *lighting bug* is heard from some older speakers in Ohio and is also attested once in Indiana and Illinois. **1970** Tarpley *Blinky* 177 **neTX**, Two informants [of 200], both in the lowest educational bracket, say *lighten bug*. **1973** Allen *LAUM* 1.329 (as of c1950), 2 infs, **MN, NE**, Lighting bug. *Ibid, Lighting bug:* Inf. distinguishes this from 'lightning bug,' the latter naming something with a "hard shell" (perhaps hence = *glowworm*). **1982** Slone *How We Talked* 45 **eKY** (as of c1950), "Lighten' bug"—firefly. We loved to catch them and play with them. Sometimes we would rub the bugs on our finger-nails to make them glow in the dark. **1986** Pederson *LAGS Concordance,* 2 infs, **neFL, csTN**, Lighting bug; 1 inf, **seAR**, Lighten bug.

light-jumping See **light-fishing**

light moon n **Sth, S Midl** Cf **dark moon**

  The part of a month in which the moon gives light, esp the **light of the moon.**

  1920 Hunter *Trail Drivers TX* 255 (as of 1867), This threw him in the region where, on each light moon the Indian left his trail of blood along some mountain side or valley. **1937** in 1976 *Weevils in the Wheat* 247 **VA** [Black], Ain't no use o' nobody killin' no hogs on the dark of de moon, 'cause all de meat'll draw up an' dar won't be nothin' but grease. Kill hogs on de light moon. Ain't nothin' gonna mount to nothin' on de dark moon 'cept i'ish 'taters [=Irish potatoes]. Kin plant dem dark nights in March. Do all plantin' an' killin' hogs on de light moon. **1937** (1963) Hyatt *Kiverlid* 41 **KY,** Can't hardly git grease out'n cracklin's if you kill a hog on the light moon. **1958** Browne *Pop. Beliefs AL* 248, Don't plant corn or anything that makes a crop above the ground in the light moon. . . Plant sorghum seed during the light moon and the crop will grow tall and slim. **1976** Wolfram–Christian *Appalachian Speech* 171 **sWV,** He said if you killed it [=a hog] in light moon that the meat, when you fried it, would turn up around the edges.

light night n Cf mischief night
See quot.

1985 *NADS Letters* **seNY** (as of c1945), *Light night* . . occurred around Halloween. We'd go down to a deserted stretch of Yonkers Avenue near the Saw Mill River Parkway and fling rocks at bare street lights placed under corrugated metal light reflectors.

lightning n[1] Also *lightning liquor;* for addit combs see quots scattered, but esp S Midl, West Cf chain lightning 2, Jersey ~, white ~
Whiskey, cheap liquor.

[**1858** *Calif. Spirit of Times* (San Francisco) 7 Aug. 1/4 *(OEDS),* Having in his possession a few kegs of liquid lightning upon which he was avariciously desirous of reaping a speedy profit.] **1858** in 1941 Hafen *CO Gold Rush* 194, Wine List. Hockheimer; madeira; champagne; . . Taos lightning. **1873** Miller *Modocs* 94 **CA,** In one of the saloons where men were wont to . . drink lightning. **1901** Root–Connelley *Overland Stage* 229 **CO,** The vile whisky, some of which was drank by the overland stage-drivers, was by them given the very appropriate name of "Taos lightning." **1935** *AmSp* 10.18 [Lingo of the good-people], *Lightning.* Rotgut whiskey. **1942** (1960) Robertson *Red Hills* 180 **SC,** Bill fed the mules, cut stovewood, played on a banjo, drank lightning liquor, hunted possums, talked about the world and everything on the broad piazza. **1949** Webber *Backwoods Teacher* 125 **Ozarks,** The enterprising fellow who supposedly was running a "thumper"—a "light-nin' " still—at the fork of Little and Big Piney creeks. **1967–70** *DARE* (Qu. DD21b, *General words . . for bad liquor*) Infs **MD**15, **MA**58, **SC**69, Lightning; **CO**27, Taos lightning; (Qu. DD21c, *Nicknames for whiskey, especially illegally made whiskey*) Infs **NY**36, **WV**7, Lightning; **WV**2, 3, Mule lightning. **1986** Pederson *LAGS Concordance,* 3 infs, **AR, MS,** Lightning.

lightning n[2] See lightening

lightning n[3] See lightening wood 2

lightning brush n Cf matchweed
=snakeweed (here: *Gutierrezia* spp).

1942 *Torreya* 42.165, *Gutierrezia* spp.—Fireweed, lightning-brush, Utah.

lightning bug n Also sp *lightening bug* widespread, but slightly less freq Nth, Pacific See Map and Map Section
=firefly 1.

1778 Carver *Travels N. Amer.* 491, The *Lightning Bug* or *Fire Fly* is about the size of a bee. **1849** Howitt *Our Cousins in OH* 108, The fire-flies, or lightning-bugs, as the people called them, had now made their appearance in the evening. **1867** Harris *Sut Lovingood Yarns* 268 **TN,** The cats' eyes 'zembled a flag ove truce, kivered wif litnin-bugs. **1899** (1912) Green *VA Folk-Speech* 261, *Lightning-bug.* . . A firefly. **1909** *DN* 3.346 eAL, wGA, *Light(e)nin(g)-bug.* *Ibid* 399 **nwAR,** *Lightning-bug.* **1912** *DN* 3.581 **wIN,** *Lightnin(g)-bug.* . . A firefly. In some localities *firefly* is unknown. **1946** *PADS* 5.28 **VA,** *Lightning-bug:* Firefly; common among all classes. *Ibid* 6.45 **cME coast** (as of 1904–21) [Words in common use], Lightning bug. **1947** *PADS* 8.24, **wNY** (as of 1904–28) [Words in common use], Lightning-bug. **1949** Kurath *Word Geog.* 17, *Fire fly* . . is a common rival of *lightning bug* in all of New England except western Vermont. . . In New York State, as in Vermont, *lightning bug,* our national term, has largely eliminated *fire fly.* **c1960** Wilson *Coll.* **csKY,** Lightning bug. . . The firefly; universal. Firefly is decidedly literary. **1962** Atwood *Vocab. TX* 58, *Lightning bug* . . is very heavily favored; the alternate *firefly* . . is distinctly an educated variant. **1963** North *Rascal* 17 **WI** (as of c1918), A phosphorescent stump . . gleamed at night with foxfire, as luminescent as all the lightning bugs in the world. **1965–70** *DARE* (Qu. R1, . . *The small insect that flies at night and flashes a light at its tail*) 795 Infs, **widespread, but slightly less freq Nth, Pacific,** Lightning bug. **1973** Allen *LAUM* 1.328 (as of c1950), U[pper] M[idwest] infs. rather evenly divide their responses between older *firefly* and the Americanism *lightning bug.* . . Literary and New England *firefly* is more favored by Type II [=mid-aged, with approx

hs educ] speakers than by older and less educated Type I, though not by the small sample of college graduates. . . Regional distribution is also uneven. Despite the dominance of *lightning bug* in neighboring Wisconsin (68%) and in New York state, this term is weighted less heavily than *firefly* in the Northern speech area of the UM. It is, however, the most frequently used designation in the Midland speech zone, though without a sharp isoglossic contrast. **1989** Pederson *LAGS Tech. Index* 213 **Gulf Region,** 760 infs, Lightning bug; 149 infs, Firefly.

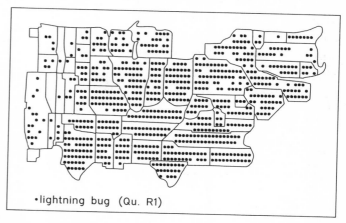

• lightning bug (Qu. R1)

lightning-bug church n
=brush arbor.

1949 Webber *Backwoods Teacher* 113 **Ozarks,** Preachers from the "poke-root" and "lightnin'-bug" churches (brush arbors) . . were "just naturally agin doctors," as one of them said to me.

lightning conch See lightning shell

lightning liquor See lightning n[1]

lightning oil n Also *light oil* Cf lamp oil 1
Kerosene.

1949 *AmSp* 24.110 **seSC,** *Lightning oil.* . . Kerosene. *Ibid* 111 **nw,cwSC,** *Light oil.* . . Kerosene.

lightning shell n Also *lightning conch,* ~ *venus,* ~ *whelk* [From the zigzag markings]
Either a whelk (here: *Busycon contrarium*) or a venus clam (*Pitar fulminata);* see quots.

1951 Teale *North with Spring* 20 **swFL,** We became fascinated in turn with slipper limpets, apple murexes, turkey's wings, and lightning shells. **1954** Abbott *Amer. Seashells* 236, Lightning Whelk. . . South Carolina to Florida and the Gulf States. . . A very common species in west Florida. *Ibid* 414, Lightning Venus. . . North Carolina to Florida and the West Indies. . . Exterior whitish with spots and/or zigzag markings of yellowish brown. . . Moderately common in shallow water. **1969** *DARE* File **eNC,** *Lightning conch*—shell on display in museum at Cape Hatteras, NC. Also called *left-handed conch.* **1981** Rehder *Audubon Field Guide Seashells* 563, Lightning Whelk (*Busycon contrarium*). . . In sand, from near low-tide line to water 10′ (3 m) deep. *Ibid* 797, Lightning Venus (*Pitar fulminata*). . . The species name is derived from the Latin word *fulmen* ("a flash of lightning") and refers to the rays of zigzag markings. **1981** Meinkoth *Audubon Field Guide Seashore* 504, *Lightning Whelk.* . . White or cream-colored, with longitudinal zigzag streaks of brown.

lightning snake n
=fence lizard 1.

1951 Teale *North with Spring* 125 **FL,** Curiously enough, in this land of dangerous reptiles one of the most dreaded creatures is a harmless blue-headed, striped lizard that lives in bushes. Locally it is known as the lightning snake.

lightning-splitter n
1992 *DARE* File **ceRI** (as of c1920), A roof that came to a sharp peak was known as a lightning-splitter.

lightning strike n
1975 Gould *ME Lingo* 162, *Lightning strike*—A forest fire started by lightning, and also the browned-out area that remains an eyesore for years to come. A *lightning strike* will be used as a landmark: "Fish down

the lake to the lightning strike, but you won't likely hook anything beyond that."

lightning tree n

A **mountain ash 1.**

1913 *Torreya* 13.30, There is a superstition among country people that lightning will not strike a house near which grows either a white locust or a mountain ash. In some localities the latter is known as "lightning tree" because of this belief.

lightning venus (or whelk) See **lightning shell**

lightning wood See **lightening wood**

light of the moon n Cf **dark of the moon, light moon**

The period of the waxing moon.

1935 Hyatt *Folkl. Adams Co. IL* 31, If you spread manure over the ground in the light of the moon, it will dry up and blow away. *Ibid* 33, Frost during the light of the moon will not damage plants. **1949** Webber *Backwoods Teacher* 191 **Ozarks**, Lonnie . . assured me it was a well-known fact that meat butchered in the light of the moon would not be of good flavor. **1952** Giles *40 Acres* 96 **KY**, We plant . . things that ripen on the vine above the earth, in the *light* of the moon. And we plant . . things which mature beneath the earth, in the *dark* of the moon. The theory is that in the light of the moon the pull is up, so things that ripen above the earth must be planted in the light of the moon to do well. **1958** Browne *Pop. Beliefs AL* 248, Plant corn in the light of the moon for tall stalks and small ears; plant in the dark of the moon for low stalks and large ears. **1966** *DARE* Tape **MI**21, In the dark of the moon, that's when you get your most whitefish; in the light of the moon they can see the net. **1967–69** *DARE* (Qu. B29, *A frost that does not kill plants*) Infs **IL**15, 19, **MO**32, Light-of-the-moon frost; **MO**18, Frost in the light of the moon; [**KS**5, Frost in the moon]. **1968** *DARE* FW Addit **IA**30, *Light of the moon*—Bad to butcher hogs in, because the bacon of such a hog will always curl. Used occas. **1972** *Foxfire Book* 221 **NC**, Take taters . . on th' light of th' moon they makes more vine and less tater. **1986** Pederson *LAGS Concordance,* 1 inf, **ceTX**, Should plant cotton on the light of the moon.

light oil See **lightning oil**

light one's shuck See **light a shuck**

light out v phr [See quot] Cf **out C3, outen v 1**

To turn off (a light).

1931 Jacobson *Milwaukee Dial.* 16 **WI**, Light out the light. . . commonly used. It is taken from the German verb ausloschen which means to light out.

light roll n chiefly **Sth, S Midl** Cf **light bread**

A bun made from yeast dough.

1847 (1852) Crowen *Amer. Cookery* 283, Light rolls.—Take a piece of risen dough . . from mixed bread . . make it in rolls between your hands, about one inch thick, and the length of the finger . . and bake fifteen minutes in a quick oven. **1943** McAtee *Dial. Grant Co. IN Suppl. 2* 10 (as of 1890s), Light-rolls . . small bread made from the same mix as were large loaves; our only use of the term "roll" for bread. **1944** *PADS* 2.10 **AL**, Light rolls. . . Yeast-raised rolls. **c1960** Wilson Coll. **csKY**, Light-rolls. . . Lightbread made into rolls rather than a loaf. **1965–69** *DARE* (Qu. H15, *Bread made with wheat flour*) Infs **GA**88, **MO**3, **VA**13, Light rolls; (Qu. H18, . . *Special kinds of bread*) Infs **GA**10, **IN**65, **MO**2, Light rolls; (Qu. H32, . . *Fancy rolls and pastries*) Infs **AR**32, **FL**21, 26, Light rolls; [(Qu. H41, . . *Kinds of roll or bun sandwiches*) Inf **VA**1, Light bread roll]. **1986** Pederson *LAGS Concordance* **Gulf Region** (*Wheat bread . . when it is made to rise with yeast*) 6 infs, Light rolls; 1 inf, Light roll (rolls made of light bread dough); (*Boughten bread*) 1 inf, Light rolls.

lights n pl

1 rarely *light:* The lungs, esp of an animal; broadly, the internal organs. **scattered, but chiefly Sth, S Midl**

1848 Lowell *Biglow* 19 **'Upcountry' MA**, Though I myself can 't rightly see it 's any wus achokin' on 'em / Than puttin' bullets thru their lights, or with a bagnet pokin' on 'em. *Ibid* 145, Lights, the bowels. **1848** (1855) Ruxton *Life Far West* 55, From that moment . . "he felt queer," he said, "all over, like a buffalo shot in the lights." **1899** (1912) Green *VA Folk-Speech* 261, Lights. . . The lungs, more especially of brute animals. **1923** *DN* 5.213 **swMO**, Lights. . . The lungs of an animal. **1935** *AmSp* 10.172 [Engl of PA Germans], Other terms more rarely used include the following . . *lights* for the viscera, especially the lungs, of a person or a slaughtered animal. **1937** in 1977 *Amer. Slave Suppl. 1* 1.184 **AL**, Atter cleanin' de hogs, dey w'uld gib us de livers,

and lights. **c1940** Eliason *Word Lists FL* 9 **wFL**, Lights: Lungs. **1950** *PADS* 14.44 **SC**, Lights. . . Lungs of a slaughtered animal. In the expression "to knock one's lights out" the word may refer to the human lungs. **1954** *Harder Coll.* **cwTN**, Lights . . lungs of a slaughtered animal. **c1960** Wilson Coll. **csKY**, Lights. . . Lungs, esp. of animals. Facetious expression—"lights, lungs, and liver." **1965–70** *DARE* (Qu. H43, *Foods made from parts of the head and inner organs of an animal*) Infs **CA**15, **LA**20, **SC**7, 51, Lights; **LA**6, Boiled lights; **MS**85, Hog lights; **IL**30, **SC**34, Liver and lights; **VA**48, Liver and light hash; (Qu. X8, . . *General words . . for the organs inside the body*) Inf **TX**35, Liver and lights; **MA**30, Lights and lungs; **AK**1, Livers and lights. **1972** *Foxfire Book* 205 **nGA**, Lights (more commonly known as lungs)—Nowhere did we run into as much difference of opinion as with this item. One said, "It's very good—*very* good." Another said, "Lots'a folks like th' lights, but I never did." **1986** Pederson *LAGS Concordance* **Gulf Region**, [In response to a question about the internal organs of animals, about 270 infs gave *lights,* often in var combs with *liver;* 4 infs gave the singular form *light.*]

2 Spec:

a in phr *liver and lights* and varr: The living daylights—used in var hyperbolic or exclamatory expressions. **esp Sth, S Midl**

1885 Twain *Huck. Finn* 259, It most scared the livers and lights out of me. **1894** in 1983 Zeigler *Lexicon Middle GA* 104, If two or three of 'em would whirl in on him they could knock his very liver and lights out him. **1935** Sandoz *Jules* 21 **wNE** (as of 1880–1930), You'll find Frenchy scratching the dirt in the Flats until July comes to cook his liver and lights. **1942** McAtee *Dial. Grant Co. IN* 44 (as of 1890s), *My lights and livers* (or sometimes lights, lungs, and livers), interj., facetious exclamation. **1944** Smith *Strange Fruit* 3 **GA**, Now git—before I knock the liver-an-lights out of you. **1977** Miles *Ozark Dict.* 6, Liver-lights—Your "innards." "It don't matter no-how; Verna says her daddy's gonna whup the liver-lights out of Clyde if 'un he sees him." **1986** Pederson *LAGS Concordance*, 1 inf, **nwGA**, Scares the lights out of you—lungs. **1993** *Houston Post* (TX) 24 Feb sec A 17 **csTX**, If you think there is any check on the greed for profits of most big corporations other than the fear of getting the liver and lights sued out of themselves . . , you're a bigger damn fool than I ever took you for.

b in phrr *put (or knock) one's lights out:* To kill one; to knock one out or down; also fig. [Perh infl by *light* 'one's vital spark' (cf *OED* and *OEDS light* sb. 1.i) or by *lights* eyes (*OED light* sb. 4 "now only *slang*")]

1866 in 1966 Twain *Letters HI* 152, The old man caught him, and he had more than two notions to put his lights out. [**1906** *DN* 3.145 **nwAR**, *Light.* . . Eye. "Stand back, or I'll shoot your damn lights out."] **1910** W.M. Raine *Bucky O'Connor* 25 (*OEDS*), Mebbe I'd a-put his lights out for good and all. **1935** Pollock *Underworld Speaks* 92 (*OEDS*), Put his lights out, to kill. **1936** *WV Review* Aug 346, Longer expletives that are heard in West Virginia. . . Well, knock the lights out of me! **1941** Percy *Lanterns* 78 **nwMS**, What consolation is there in trying to knock [a bully's] lights out and having your own dimmed in the effort? **1950** [see **1** above].

lightship basket n Also *lightship handbag* **seMA**

A type of basket orig made esp by Nantucket lightship crews.

1929 Starbuck *My House* 118 **Nantucket MA**, He always carried a shallow rattan basket, the sort known as 'lightship baskets,' but in those days almost any seafaring man could and did make them. **1976** *Yankee* May 110 **seMA**, From the early days of whaling, Lightship crews guarding the shoal waters of Nantucket would while away tedious hours weaving baskets ornamented with delicate whalebone carvings. . . Whitten also makes the popular Lightship handbag as well as a variety of other baskets. . . Though expensive . . a Lightship basket will last a lifetime. **1978** Whipple *Vintage Nantucket* 226 **MA**, There are excellent imitations of the real thing, most of them made in Hong Kong and available for a fraction of the price—and any owner of a Nantucket lightship basket can spot a Hong Kong basket at one hundred paces. **1978** Amer. Heritage Soc. *Americana* 6.64 **seMA**, By virtue of its price alone, a lightship basket from the island of Nantucket . . is no ordinary souvenir: a medium-sized basket used as a woman's handbag sells new for three hundred dollars.

lights out exclam

In the game **statues:** used as a call to tell players to close their eyes.

1975 Ferretti *Gt. Amer. Book Sidewalk Games* 209, Another game . . is Statues, known also in the eastern part of the country as *Freeze.* . . "It" then calls, "Lights out," and all the statues close their eyes.

lightwood n[1], also attrib Pronc-spp *light'ud, lighter(d), litered, lidard, lightern;* also *fat lightwood;* also in redund combs *lighter(d)-wood;* for addit varr see quots [Prob from its use to give light (cf Scots *licht-coal* coal burned to give light), but now often understood as a ref to its use in lighting a fire; this may have infl the development of the form *lighter(-wood)*] **chiefly Sth, esp S Atl** See Map Also called **fatwood** See also **lightwood-knot floater**

Resinous pine wood, esp the heartwood and knots of the **longleaf pine** or the **pitch pine;** a piece of such wood—often in comb *lightwood knot.* Note: The form *lighter* is occas used as a count noun; *lightern* is prob a result of metanalysis of the comb *lighter knot.*

1705 Beverley *Hist. VA* 3.12, [The Indians] generally burn Pine, or Lightwood, (that is, the fat knots of dead Pine). **1743** Catesby *Nat. Hist. Carolina* 2 [app] xxiii, These are first tried with a Chop of an Ax, whether it be Lightwood, which is the Name by which Wood that is fit to make Tar of is called. **1775** (1962) Romans *Nat. Hist. FL* 79, The chapel was destroyed before i came there in 1771, but the cross (being of lightwood [Footnote: The heart of yellow pine]) stood yet. **1801** in 1969 *AmSp* 44.304 **GA,** Lightwood. **1844** Thompson *Major Jones's Courtship* 13 **GA,** Ther was nothin but a lighterd chunk burnin to give light. **1856** Simms *Eutaw* 74 **SC,** She knew where the lightwood lay . . and in a moment . . a rich, cheering blaze, such as . . good *fat* lightwood only could afford. **1893** Shands *MS Speech* 43, *Light'ud* [laɪtud]. **1909** *DN* 3.345 **eAL, wGA,** *Liderd, lighterd.* . . Lightwood, pine rich with resin, fat pine. *Liderd knot.* . . A pine knot or root, rich with resin. *Ibid* 346, *Lightwood.* . . Rich pine. So called because of its use for making torches or lights. Usually pronounced *liderd.* **1910** *DN* 3.458 **FL, GA,** *Lightud.* . . Light wood. **1912** Green *VA Folk-Speech* 262, *Lightwood-knot.* . . The resinous knot of a pine tree. A hard, strong man is said to be made out of a lightwood-knot. **1917** *DN* 4.421 **LA,** *Lighter wood.* . . Same as *light-wood.* **1922** Gonzales *Black Border* 310 **sSC, GA coasts** [Gullah glossary], *Light'ood*—lightwood. **1928** Peterkin *Scarlet Sister Mary* 18 **SC,** He sat on the wood-pile cutting wood and fat lightwood splinters. **1934** Hurston *Jonah's Gourd Vine* 11 **FL,** He seized a lidard knot from beside the fireplace and limped threateningly towards John. **c1938** in 1970 Hyatt *Hoodoo* 1.518 **ceNC,** Take some *lighters.* You get them from offen the north side of a pine, you know, the *lighter pine. Ibid* 153 **DC,** Git yo' three *fat-lighter* splinters. *Ibid* 2.1051 **csNC,** Cut chew . . a *fat-lighter* [Hyatt: piece of *fat-lighter* pine] 'bout dat long. **1938** Rawlings *Yearling* 189 **nFL,** I'd a heap ruther a woman tore me down with a lighter'd knot, than speakin' sharp. **1945** FWP *Lay My Burden Down* 62 **NC** (as of 1850s) [Black], When the boys would start to the quarters from the field, they would get a turn of lider [lightwood] knots. I 'specks you knows 'em as pine knots. **1946** *PADS* 5.28 **VA,** *Lighterd, lightwood:* Kindling; everywhere east of the Blue Ridge. **1950** *PADS* 14.44 **SC,** *Lightered.* . . Lightwood. . . *Lightered knot.* . . A knot or [sic] rich pine used as lightwood. **1965–70** *DARE* (Qu. T8, *Joints of pine wood that burn easily and make good fuel*) 64 Infs, **chiefly VA, S Atl,** Lightwood; **SC11,** Lightwood—old-time name, kindling now; **VA46,** Heartwood that has a lot of lightwood; **VA70,** Lightwood—often found in or by the stump of a pine tree; **AL30, FL17, 20, NC13, 84, SC46, VA79,** Lightwood knots; 17 Infs, **chiefly Sth,** Lighterd; **LA2,** Lighterd—but we usually call it fat pine; 13 Infs, **chiefly S Atl,** Lighterd knots; **GA77,** Lighterd knot—used for back stick in the fireplace; **AL17, FL34,** Lighterd-wood; 20 Infs, **chiefly Sth,** Lighter knots; **AL33, 42, NC33, 67, 72,** Lighter; **NC64, VA47,** Lighter pine; **MS16, NC55,** Pine lighter; **VA38,** (Tar) lighters; **NC52, 60,** Lighter-wood; **AL24, GA25, 38,** ['laɪtəd, -ɪd]; **GA3,** ['laɪtəd]; **GA18,** ['laːtɪd] knots; **GA1, 16,** ['laɪtud]; **GA20, 25,** Lightern; **SC2, 40, 43,** Fat lightwood; **FL26, 35, SC26,** Fat lighterd; **AL25,** Fat lighter-wood; **FL4,** Fat lighter knots; **TX37,** Fat lighter; (Qu. D34, . . *The small pieces of wood and other stuff that are used to start a fire*) 21 Infs, **chiefly S Atl,** Lightwood; 13 Infs, **chiefly S Atl,** Lighterd; **SC3,** Lighterd—the rich pine used to start fires; **SC6, 38, 46, 62,** Fat lightwood (*or* lighterd); **AL25, SC34,** (Fat) lighter-wood; **GA11,** ['laɪdud]; **AL43, MS73,** ['laɪtəd] (splinters); **SC34,** Lighter pine; **VA42,** Lighter—pieces of pine full of rosum; **GA36, SC46,** Lighterd knots; (Qu. D33, *When you build a fire in the fireplace . . the big log that goes behind the others*) Inf **SC38,** Fat lightwood. **c1965** *DARE* FW Addit **AL,** *Lighter knot,* also *lightered.* . . It is a knot of a tree in which the sap has collected (usually pine); also, any small, split kindling made of pine. **1966–69** *DARE* Tape **FL16,** I got out and got me some lighter knots and I lit in on the snake and killed it. *Ibid* **FL41,** When we had the fireplace. . . we used to get the lightwood knots then. *Ibid* **GA22,** Yes sir, lighterd stumps. And they get all the lighterd logs. And ever bit of lighterd-wood they can get. *Ibid*

GA50, Lighterd . . is the old yellow pine. *Ibid* **NC68,** Some calls it lightwood. Some calls it pine. Down east North Carolina they call it lightwood. Through here we call it rich pine. *Ibid* **TX36,** He would always use lighterd, we call it lighterd, you know, it's rich, rich pine. **1967** *Atlanta Constitution* (GA) 6 Mar 5, I know we say light'ard he said but I thought the word was really lightwood. **a1975** Lunsford *It Used to Be* 177 **sAppalachians,** "Litered" is the "light wood" they used to burn as a torch to go 'possum hunting and so on. **1991** Pederson *LAGS Regional Pattern* 199 **Gulf Region,** [Map shows the responses *lightwood* and *lighterd* to be chiefly concentrated in **GA, FL, c,sAL, sMS.**]

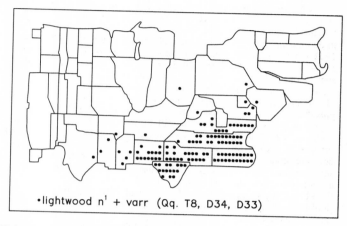

•lightwood n[1] + varr (Qq. T8, D34, D33)

light wood n[2] See **lightening wood 1**

lightwood knot n

1 See **lightwood** n[1].

2 =**ruddy duck.** [See quot 1888]
1888 Trumbull *Names of Birds* 113 **NC,** Another name at Newberne for the Ruddy, and a very popular one, is *Light-wood Knot.* "Lightwood" is a Southern name for very resinous or fatty portions of pine, commonly obtained from trees that have been "scraped" for turpentine. The knot of this "light-wood" is proverbially hard, and the appellation is therefore like "hard-head," "tough-head," "stub-and-twist," etc., and refers to the difficulty sometimes experienced in quieting these creatures. **1944** Hausman *Amer. Birds* 519, Light-wood-knot . . Ruddy Duck.

lightwood-knot floater n **esp S Atl** Cf **chunk-floater**
A heavy rain.
1944 *Clarke Co. Democrat* (Grove Hill AL) 20 July 2/3, Chunk movers and lightwood knot floaters are two names which the Journal omitted. **1950** *PADS* 14.21 **SC,** *Clod buster.* . . Also: *Litered knot floater.* Peedee. **1966–68** *DARE* (Qu. B25, . . *Joking names . . for a very heavy rain.* . . "It's a regular _____.") Infs **FL35, GA7, 36,** Lightwood-knot floater; (Qu. B26, *When it's raining heavily . . "It's raining _____."*) Inf **FL7,** Lightwood-knot floater. **c1970** Pederson *Dial. Surv. Rural GA* (*A very hard rain that doesn't last long*) 3 infs, **seGA,** Lighterd-knot floater.

lightwood-knot grass n
A **dropseed 3** (here: *Sporobolus curtissii*).
1927 Boston Soc. Nat. Hist. *Proc.* 38.213 **Okefenokee GA,** *Sporobolus Curtissii*—'Light'ood-knot grass.'

'ligion n Also *'lijun* [Aphet forms of *religion;* cf Intro "Language Changes" I.7]
1891 *Atlantic Mth.* 68.288, Many of the negroes, during the time for "seekin' 'ligion," tie a cloth about the head, and . . are expected to drop all work and look very woe-begone. **1922** Gonzales *Black Border* 311 **sSC, GA coasts** [Gullah glossary], *'Lijun*—religion. **1945** Saxon *Gumbo Ya-Ya* 242 **LA,** We was all supposed to be Catholics on our place, but lots didn't like that 'ligion.

lignum vitae n Pronc-spp *lingum vite, linkum vit(t)y*
A Forms.
1795 Dearborn *Columbian Grammar* 136, *List of Improprieties.* . . Lingumvite for Lignumvitæ. **1899** Garland *Boy Life* 27 **nwIA** (as of c1870s), This dinner was usually made up of long slices of white bread buttered prodigiously in lumps, and frozen as hard as "linkum vity." **1975** Gould *ME Lingo* 164, Linkumvitty—Maine shipyard pronunciation of *lignum vitae.*

B Sense.

Std: a plant of the genus *Guaiacum*, usu *G. angustifolium* or *G. sanctum*. For other names of the former see **guayacan**, **soapbush**; for the latter see **gumbo-whackum**, **ironwood c(2)**

'lijun See **'ligion**

like v[1], adj, vbl aux, n, adv, prep, conj Pronc-spp **chiefly Sth, S Midl** *la(c)k, lock, loike, luk*

A Pronc varr.

1796 in 1956 Eliason *Tarheel Talk* 314 **ce,seNC,** Loike. **1883** (1971) Harris *Nights with Remus* 133 **GA,** He laks good chilluns. **1899** Chesnutt *Conjure Woman* 43 **csNC** [Black], He lacked de looks er de noo 'oman. *Ibid,* Sandy useter set up all night wid 'er, en den go ter wuk in de mawnin' des lack he had his reg'lar sleep. **1909** [see E2b below]. **1922** Gonzales *Black Border* 311 **sSC, GA coasts** [Gullah glossary], *Luk*—like, alike. **1927** Shewmake *Engl. Pronc. VA* 24, In the [standard] speech of Eastern Virginians . . in such words as *bright, like,* and *price.* . . this diphthong is approximately that of *a* as in *father* plus that of *i* as in *pin*; the dialectal sound is approximately that of *u* as in *hut* plus that of *i* as in *pin.* **1928** McKay *Home to Harlem* 273 **NYC,** I ain't no lonesome wolf lak you is. **a1930** in 1991 Hughes–Hurston *Mule Bone* 30 **cFL** [Black], Fact is, the town aint run lak it might be. **1930** *AmSp* 6.166 **seVA,** [aɪ] tends toward [ɑ] or [a] in *I, mind,* [etc]. . . An opposite tendency often appears in *like,* [etc]. . . The first element is shortened and the second seems to be raised and to have acquired finally a certain consonantal character. . . It may be transcribed, in *like,* as [laɪjk] or [lajk]. Occasionally the first element is raised to [ɛ] or [e], e.g., [leɪjk]. . . A diphthong which approaches [ɔɪ], and which I transcribe [əɪ], is heard occasionally in . . *like,* [etc]. . . This pronunciation is common in Charleston, S.C., and, with a difference, in New York City. It is reported also in Southern Mississippi. **1937** in 1976 *Weevils in the Wheat* 187 **VA** [Black], Dey broke into smoke houses an' dey would throw de bigges' hams, whole meat sides, an' de lak. **1942** Faulkner *Go Down* 139 **MS** [Black], She lacked you too, same as me. **1942** Hall *Smoky Mt. Speech* 43 **wNC, eTN,** The tendency observed elsewhere in Southern speech to reduce [ai] before voiced consonants, but to retain it before voiceless consonants is assuredly not characteristic of Smokies speech. . . The following pronunciations represent the speech of a single individual, but he is typical: . . *like* [lak], [la:k]. (For the last mentioned, cf. the spelling *lock,* which appears in a letter to the writer: 'Mother is just lock she was when you left.') **1958** Humphrey *Home from the Hill* 80 **neTX,** One lak that other un ye got that time. **c1965** *DARE* FW Addit **MS,** *Lack*—this is frequently used to mean "like." **1984** Burns *Cold Sassy* 229 **nGA** (as of 1906) [Black], Mr. Will, yo pa he ack lak he got a dimon ring in his pocket!

B Gram form.

Past: usu *liked;* also *esp freq among Black speakers* pleonastic *lakted, likeded, likted.* Cf **-ed suff 1**

1931 (1991) Hughes–Hurston *Mule Bone* 143 **cFL** [Black], Yeah, you rubbed my head all right, and I lakted that. **1935** Hurston *Mules & Men* 64 **nFL,** Massa had two hawses and he lakted John, so he give John one of his hawses. **1959** Lomax *Rainbow Sign* 36 **AL** [Black], They put me and him together because they knowed we likted each other. **1971** Mitchell *Blow My Blues Away* 156 **nwMS** [Black], She seed I likeded peanut candy and she'd . . get me a block of peanut candy. **1986** Pederson *LAGS Concordance* **swGA,** 1 inf, He just likeded him; 1 inf, I likeded to go to school. [Both infs Black]

C As verb.

1 intr: To be happy with one's location or situation; to feel comfortable in a place. [*EDD like* v.[2] 4 "To take a liking to a place or situation"] **NEng, Sth, S Midl** *somewhat old-fash*

1849 (1982) Schlissel *Women's Diaries* 157 **MA,** I suppose you would like to hear how we like this country. . . I did not like [it] very well but after we had taken our claim and became settled once more I began to like [it] much better and the longer I live here the better I like [it]. [*DARE* Ed: The editor of this collection was appar unfamiliar with this intransitive use of *like.*] **1914** *DN* 4.76 **ME, nNH,** So, you was to Floridy las' winter? How'd ye like? **1918** *DN* 5.20 **NC,** "I liked there very much." I liked that place very much. **1926** *AmSp* 2.78 **ME,** Your foot will hardly be across the first threshold before you are confronted with the question: "How do you like here?" **1926** *DN* 5.388 **ME,** *Like here.* . . To appreciate a locality. "How do you like here?" "How do you like in Boston?" Common. **1926** Roberts *Time of Man* 20 **KY,** You'll like right well once you get broke to the ways of the place. *Ibid* 26, "We moved in." "Do you like?" "We like well enough." *Ibid* 291, We

could go to Phillip's place, and if we don't like there we will go further until we find the land we want. **1934** *Hanley Disks* **sNH,** The postmaster . . takes his dinners and his suppers there . . and he's fussy . . and he likes; **nME,** They was given land in New Brunswick. . . He didn't like over there. **1944** *PADS* 2.10 **AL, GA, NC, VA,** "You go to _____ College? How do you like?" "I like fine." **c1973** *DARE* File **MA** (as of c1920), In Massachusetts in my youth *like* was used as an intransitive verb. You might ask a person about a daughter who'd accepted a teaching job in another town. "How are things going?" Her mother might answer, "Oh, she likes. She likes very much." **1976** Wolfram–Christian *Appalachian Speech* 96 **sWV,** It *liked around people.*

2 foll by adv of place, with ellip of infin: See quots. Cf **want**

1916 *DN* 4.282 **NE,** Would you like in? Would you like out? etc. = "want in," "[s]want out." Frequent. [*DN* Ed: Also N. Car., Kan., Ia.] **1942** in 1944 *ADD* **nWV,** Would you like out? **1982** *Barrick Coll.* **csPA,** "The dog wants out." "The kids like out."

D As adj.

1 foll by infin: Likely (to do something); on the point, in danger (of doing something). [*OED like* a. 9.a, b]

1793 in 1890 MI Hist. Comm. *MI Hist. Coll.* 17.575 **PA,** Short nob hills, sometimes one side, then another, like to overset. **1875** (1876) Twain *Tom Sawyer* 38, He so worked upon his feelings . . that he had to keep swallowing, he was so like to choke. **1884** Jewett *Country Dr.* 7 **ME,** She's like to marry again for all I can see, with her good looks. **1889** Twain *CT Yankee* 143, I was like to get fried in that stove. **1967** *DARE* Tape **TX49,** If you do, he like to get up, come in there, and kill you right dead and go off, and he really ought to. **1986** Pederson *LAGS Concordance,* 1 inf, **ceAR,** Like to come up killed—apt to get killed.

2 in ellip adj phr *something like (it):* Very much as one expects or hopes; highly satisfactory. [*OED like* a. A.2.e 1702 →; cf the modern colloq phr *that's more like it*]

1926 *AmSp* 2.80 **ME,** A piece of work well done brings the complimentary remark, "that's something like." **1928** Weseen *Crowell's Dict. Engl. Gram.* 595, *Something Like.* Not in good use in such elliptical constructions as "That pie was something like," that is, "That pie was good." **1939** Pinkerton *Wilderness Wife* 40, That's something like. . . You've been setting a pace that keeps me humping. **1942** Berrey–Van den Bark *Amer. Slang* 29.4, Something like (it), *as it should be.*

E As vbl aux.

Used in var constrs to indicate that the action referred to nearly occurred:

1 in phr *had like(d) to,* foll by perf infin or past finite verb. [Appar from *was like to,* perh by analogy with *had liked to* = "would have liked to" (*OED like* a. 9.b c1560 →, *like* v.[2] 2.b 1599 →)]

1800 (1907) Thornton *Diary* 10.117 **PA,** Joe. . . said they had liked to have been lost in Pohick run. **1823** Cooper *Pioneers* 2.174 **cNY,** We'd like to have had a bad job of that panther. **1967–68** *DARE* Tape **IA45,** She'd like to killed him. *Ibid* **TX24,** She'd like to 'a' had a fit.

2 in phrr *like(d) to:* See below. **chiefly Sth, S Midl** See Map

a foll by perf (less freq pres) infin. [Appar from **D** or **E1** above, with ellip of *was/were* or *had;* cf *OED like* a. 9.b, *like* v.[2] 2.b.]

1808 (1892) Summer *Tour OH* 1.52 **VA,** Strother was 150 votes behind Roberts & like to have lost his election in consequence of his opposing Madison. **1865** (1922) Jackson *Col.'s Diary* 189 **PA,** I went out among the boys and like to have got intoxicated. **1886** *S. Bivouac* 4.345 **sAppalachians,** Like(d) (for *had like,* or *was like,* as "I like(d) to have fell"). **1893** Shands *MS Speech* 43, *Like to have done it.* Used by educated classes to mean *to have come very near doing it.* Uneducated people say "Like to done it." By these examples I mean to show that some of our best people use the perfect infinitive after *like,* and that the ignorant use the past participle. General. **1905** *DN* 3.87 **nwAR,** "That fellow liked to die." "I liked to 'a' killed myself laughing." **1906** *DN* 3.160 **nwAR,** They like to 'a' taken the roof off. **1909** [see E2b below]. **1915** *DN* 4.185 **swVA,** He liked to a fell into the river. **1916** *DN* 4.277 **NE,** "I liked to have died laughing." Oftener [laɪktuv] or [laɪktə]. **1932** Wasson *Sailing Days* 49 **cME coast,** The Boston steamer . . like to have rolled the sponsons off'n her. **1938** Liebling *Back Where* 31 **NYC,** Then when we got him aboard he liked to kick our brains out. **1946** *PADS* 6.19 **ceNC** (as of 1900–10), We like to have got run over. **1954** *Harder Coll.* **cwTN,** I like to a split a gut laughin'. **c1960** *Wilson Coll.* **csKY,** "We like to have drownded." Sometimes like to only. **1965–70** *DARE* (Qu. LL30, . . *'Nearly' or 'almost':* "He fell off the ladder and _____ [*broke his neck*].") 46 Infs, **chiefly Sth, S Midl,** Like to have; (Qu. BB18, *To vomit a great deal at once*) Inf **OK**18, Like to throw up his insides; (Qu. FF21b, . . *About old jokes people say: "The first time I heard that one _____."*) Inf **IL**126, I liked to die; (Qu. GG31, *To laugh very hard: "I thought I'd _____."*) Inf **KY**45, Like to have died. **1968–69** *DARE* FW Addit **cwNC,** I like to 'a' went through the floor; **GA**44, We like to have ragged him to death; **swNJ,** Like to have froze. **1973** *PADS* 60.79 **seNC,** Among our informants, three said *like to fell down,* two said *like to have fallen down,* and five said *almost fell down.* The remaining two avoided the item. My schoolteachers in Craven County made a firm distinction with regard to this idiom. "like to have fallen" was considered grammatically correct; "like to fell" was ungrammatical and therefore forbidden. **1986** Pederson [see E2b below].

b also pronc-sp *liketa:* foll by past pple or past finite verb. [Cf *EDD* (at *like* adj. 4.(7)(a), v.[1] 18) for exx of *was like to, had liked to* + past pple] Note: The ambiguity of weak forms and the frequent leveling of past and past ppl forms of strong verbs have apparently led to a reanalysis of the idiom as *like to* adv [="nearly"] + past tense verb by some speakers. Contrast the negative forms "I like to not knowed ye" (quot 1986) and "we . . like not to got it" (quot 1990) with "we like to didn't make it" (quot 1965).
1845 Thompson *Pineville* 50 **cGA,** It like to tuck the wind out o' me. **1855** (1929) DeLong *Jrls.* 8.340 **NY,** Like to never got back myself. **1864** in 1983 *PADS* 70.41 **ce,sePA,** But I like to forgot to tell you the purty part. **1892** *DN* 1.236 **cwMO,** *I like to* = I came very near; as in "I like to died laughing." **1893** [see E2a above]. **1905** [see E2a above]. **1909** *DN* 3.343 **eAL, wGA,** *Lack to, like to.* . . Equivalent to 'almost,' and used with preterite forms. . . "I lack to fell." . . Sometimes *have* is inserted . . especially in the reduced form *a.* "He lack to 'a' killed his fool self." The present of the verb is used in questions like the following: "Did you lack to fall?" **1912** *DN* 3.581 **wIN,** He lack to had a fit when I told him. *Ibid* 582, I like to never got ready for church. **1916** [see E2a above]. **1930** *DN* 6.84 **cSC,** *Like to,* adv., almost. **1939** *LANE* Map 173 **cwCT,** I heard a fellow from Maine talk about doubletrees; God! I like to died laughin'. **1942** Warnick *Garrett Co. MD* 10 **nwMD** (as of 1900–18), I like to never got there. **1949** *PADS* 11.23 **CO,** *Like to, liked to.* . . Almost. "I like to fell off the horse." **c1960** *Wilson Coll.* **csKY,** The recess like to never come. **1965** Will *Okeechobee Boats* 34 **FL,** It seemed as how nobody had thought about measurin' the width of the bridge's openin', and we like to didn't make it through. **1965–70** *DARE* (Qu. LL30, . . *'Nearly' or 'almost':* "He fell off the ladder and _____ [*broke his neck*].") 84 Infs, **chiefly Sth, S Midl,** Like to; **IN**80, Liked to; (Qu. K45) Inf **WV**7, Like to pulled my legs off; (Qu. FF21b, . . *About old jokes people say: "The first time I heard that one _____."*) Infs **AR**51, **FL**14, **TX**40, I like to died (or croaked, cracked up); (Qu. GG2, . . *'Confused, mixed up'*) Inf **KY**17, Like to went raving mad; (Qu. GG20) Inf **MS**45, So surprised I like to dropped my teeth; (Qu. KK11, *To make great objections or a big fuss about something: "When we asked him to do that, he _____."*) Inf **LA**32, Like to croaked; (Qu. OO28a, *Talking about running: "John was so scared he _____ [all the way home]."*) Inf **AR**47, Like to flew. **1966–68** *DARE* Tape **IA**45, She like to killed him; **MS**75, He just like to scared us to death; **NC**7, We farmers all like to went broke; **SC**7, She like to died one time, but she got by with harm. She had a stroke. **1968–69** *DARE*

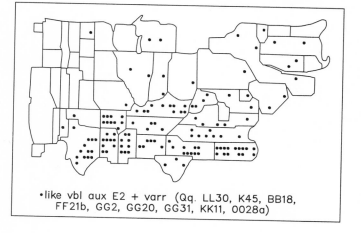

• like vbl aux E2 + varr (Qq. LL30, K45, BB18, FF21b, GG2, GG20, GG31, KK11, OO28a)

FW Addit **ceNC,** I like to died; **ceNC,** I like to fell off; **csNC,** That gal like to got killed. **1973** [see E2a above]. **1976** Wolfram–Christian *Appalachian Speech* 91 **sWV,** We liketa never got waited on. *Ibid* 92, She's liketa threw me, thrown me through a wall before. Matter of fact, she died one time. **1986** *DARE* File **ceKY,** I like to not knowed ye. **1986** Pederson *LAGS Concordance* **Gulf Region,** [Of responses involving *like to* and the verb *fall,* the distribution of constructions was as follows: 105 *like to fell,* 40 *like to have* (or *to've*) *fallen,* 29 *like to have fell,* 8 *like to fall,* 4 *like to fallen,* 1 *like to 've fall.* Similar constructions are recorded for many other verbs.] **1990** Simpson *Gt. Dismal* 8 **nNC, sVA,** Took two days and we still like not to got it. **1992** *NY Times* (NY) 18 Nov sec B 6/3 **NM,** "Papa took a bite and it liked to burn him to death," said his 68-year-old daughter, . . resting her feet in her kitchen after a hard week of processing the last of her green chili pods.

F As noun.
In phr *the like of:* Such an abundance of. [Cf *the like of* "something like," usu in exclam sentences such as *I've never seen the like of it* "I've never seen such a remarkable _____."]
1937 *Hall Coll.* **wNC, eTN,** "I never saw the like of houses," i.e. so many houses. . . "I never saw the like of soldiers in my life." **1968** *Foxfire* Fall/Winter 24 **neGA, cwNC,** Recently a man was talking to us about a huge still he ran across, and he exclaimed, "I never have seen the like of mash boxes since God made me in this world!" **1986** Pederson *LAGS Concordance,* 1 inf, **cnAR,** I never seen the like of potatoes in my life.

G As adv.
Seemingly, so to speak, rather, to some extent—used to qualify a preceding word or phr, as: see below. [Cf *OED like* adv. B.7 "dial. and vulgar"; *SND like* adv. 1.(1) "Gen.Sc."] Cf **-like** suff

a following an adv phr.
1843 (1916) Hall *New Purchase* 79 **sIN,** Turn to the left, but not quite—'cos the path goes to the rite like. **1986** Pederson *LAGS Concordance,* 1 inf, **ceFL,** Behind the door like; 1 inf, **nwFL,** Nobody don't bother with you no more like; 1 inf, **swAR,** Might near like.

b following a noun.
1884 Lanier *Poems* 169 **GA,** A peert little winter branch jest had throw'd / The sand in a kind of a sand-bar like. **1894** Riley *Armazindy* 48 **IN,** Still it peared-like ever'thing—/ Fur away from home as *there*—/ Had more *relish*-like, i jing! **1916** Howells *Leatherwood God* 110 **OH,** And supposin' that . . she felt to need the protection-like of the other one. **1926** Roberts *Time of Man* 79 **cKY,** Some [rocks] have got little worms-like worked on. **1927** *DN* 5.475 **Ozarks,** *Mixtry.* . . A mixture. "This hyar puddin's jes' a kinder mixtry like." **1941** Percy *Lanterns* 302 **nwMS** [Black], He made a motion-like in his bosom before I shot. **1968** *DARE* (Qu. F15, *What you turn to let the vinegar or cider run out of a barrel*) Inf **MO**16, Faucet like.

c following a verb.
1894 Riley *Armazindy* 2 **IN,** Jevver watch a primrose . . / Kindo' loosen-like . . ? *Ibid* 5, 'Stablished-like more confidence. *Ibid* 46, Whilse the old town . . / Dozed-like in the heat o' day. **1927** *DN* 5.474 **Ozarks,** My woman was ailin'-like, but Doc he giv her some powders an' draps. **1931–33** *LANE Worksheets* **cVT,** It was kind of storming like.

-like suff Pronc-sp *-lak* **chiefly Midl, Sth** Cf **like** adv **G**
1 following an adj: Somewhat; seeming; -ish—sometimes used to temper or qualify the adj, but often with little semantic force. [Cf *OED -like* suffix 2.a, *SND -like* suff. 1]
1867 Twain *Jumping Frog* 11, She'd get excited and desperate-like. **1871** Eggleston *Hoosier Schoolmaster* 130 **sIN,** He felt "consid'able shuck up like." **1906** *DN* 3.142 **nwAR,** "He was rather indifferent-like about the matter." "He acted indifferent-like about it." **1911** *DN* 3.538 **eKY,** *Like.* An adjectival suffix (cf. -ish, as in greenish) tempering the idea in the word, e.g., "She is sick-like (=somewhat ill) to-day." **1916** Howells *Leatherwood God* 10 **OH,** He was kind of pale like. *Ibid* 207, It's just your cleverness, and bein' so gentle like. **1926** Roberts *Time of Man* 79 **cKY,** Rocks a-growen now! They don't seem alive. They seem dead-like. **1929** *AmSp* 4.204 **Ozarks,** D'reckly Lee he come a-junin' in all narvish-like an' tetchous. **1934** Carmer *Stars Fell on AL* 59, There's only one nigger in the whole town. . . All the German women couldn't stand havin' 'em round 'cause they was so no-count an' careless like. **1941** Stuart *Men of Mts.* 309 **neKY,** He thought I was actin' lonely-like. **1942** Warnick *Garrett Co. MD* 10 **nwMD** (as of 1900–18), He acted so smart like. **1942** McAtee *Dial. Grant Co. IN* 40 (as of 1890s), *Like* . .

in manner; "He seems so friendly _____". Dial. **c1960** *Wilson Coll.* **csKY,** *-like* . . smooth-like, sad-like, cool-like. **1965–70** *DARE* (Qu. B4, *A day when the air is very still, moist, and warm—it's* _____) Inf **SC43,** Heavy-like; (Qu. B14, *When the wind is blowing unevenly, sometimes strong and sometimes weak,* . . *it's* _____) Inf **IN76,** Sorta ragged-like; (Qu. B35, *Ice that will bend when you step on it, but not break*) Inf **OK1,** Soft, mushy-like; (Qu. I8, *When root vegetables get old and tough and are not good to eat*) Inf **SC43,** Woody-like; (Qu. L5, *When a farmer gets help on a job from his neighbors in return for his help on their farms later on*) Inf **MD26,** Neighborly-like; (Qu. BB7, *A feeling that lasts for a short while, with difficult breathing and heart beating fast*) Inf **IL126,** Faint-like; (Qu. DD1, . . *Forms* . . *[of] chewing tobacco*) Inf **MO16,** Loose-like; (Qu. HH38, *A womanish man*) Infs **CA36, SC11,** Feminine-like. **1986** Pederson *LAGS Concordance* **Gulf Region,** [Examples of adjs formed by adj + -*like* include: awkward-like, black-like, crazy-like, dancing-like (of a party), foggy-like, funky-like, hairy-like, mushroomy-like, queer-like, ritzy-like, sandy-like (soil), scary-like, snappy-like, soft-like, sour-like, speckledy-like, strong-like, swampy-like place, tan-like, watery-like, yellow-like (skin).]

2 following an adj and forming an adv: In a (specified) manner. [Cf *OED* -*like* suffix 2.b, *SND* -*like* suff. 2]
    1870 Harte *Luck Roaring Camp* 63 **CA,** Sez I,—confidential-like, as between man and man,—'What should a man know of his pardner?' **1899** Dunbar *Lyrics Hearthside* 167 [Black], De watah stan's so quiet lak. **1909** *DN* 3.377 **eAL, wGA,** She died sorter suddent-like. **1916** Howells *Leatherwood God* 79 **OH,** Says he, kind o' harsh like. **1921** Haswell *Daughter Ozarks* 44 (as of 1880s), They had seen how easy like we had done our work. **1926** Roberts *Time of Man* 292 **cKY,** Your fingers on my neck and on my throat, they are soft, Ellie, like feathers, and they rub gentle-like up and down. **1938** Matschat *Suwannee R.* 232 **neFL, seGA,** An' all de colored folks an' animals lived right spang under 'em, in de shade, peaceable lak. . . One day Br'er Rabbit stepped crost to de quarters an' he say, perlite lak to a big tree, 'Good mawnin', Sis Coontie.' **1941** Faulkner *Men Working* 17 **MS,** He said, 'Naw,' kind of madlike. **1970** *DARE* (Qu. H11a) Inf **VA56,** Eats fast-like. **1986** Pederson *LAGS Concordance,* 1 inf, **nwFL,** Fast like; 1 inf, **cwAR,** Right quick like.

like v² See **lack** v¹

like a chicken on a June bug See **June bug 4**

like a dog killing snakes See **kill** v **C4d**

like a duck on a June bug See **June bug 4**

like a hen on a hot griddle See **hen** n¹ **B6**

like a hen (or nighthawk) on a June bug See **June bug 4**

like all nature See **nature B3**

likeded See **like** v¹ **B**

liked to See **like** vbl aux **E2**

like for See **for** prep **B3**

like forty See **forty** n **B2**

like fury See **fury**

like hell beating tanbark See **hell 5**

like hell bent for election See **hell-bent for election**

like hell on stilts See **hell 5**

like in See **like** v¹ **C2**

like killing (black) snakes See **kill** v **C4c**

likely adj Pronc-sp *lackly*
    1 Handsome, attractive; good-natured; pleasing. *somewhat old-fash*
        1809 in 1816 Pickering *Vocab.* 126, Throughout the British dominions, and in most parts of the United States, the epithet *likely* conveys an idea of mere personal beauty, unconnected with any moral or intellectual quality. In *New England* a man or woman as deformed as a Hottentot or as an Orang Outang may be *likely,* or *very likely.* **1823** *Natl. Intelligencer* (DC) 1 May (*DN* 4.48) [Yankee dialect], *Likely.* . . Handsome, pretty, intelligent. **1843** (1916) Hall *New Purchase* 258 **sIN,** Them two likely young gals. **1899** (1912) Green *VA Folk-Speech* 262, *Likely.* . . Such as may be liked; pleasing; agreeable; good looking; promising. "A very likely dark, chestnut, sorrel horse." *Examiner,* 1805. **1927** Krapp *Comprehensive Guide* 363, *Likely,* adj., colloquial in the sense . . *good-looking,* as in *a healthy, likely sort of person.* **1946** (1954) Patton *Good Morning* 70 **NC,** Jincey had been a likely child. Not intellectual or

original, but thoroughly nice—cheerful, obliging, and amenable to suggestion. **1955** Leach *Ballad Book* 720, [Ballad:] On Springfield Mountain there did dwell / a likely youth 'twas known full well,/ Left'ts [sic] Merrick's only Son,/ A likely youth near twenty-one. [*DARE* Ed: Other versions of this ballad say "A lovely youth" or "A comely youth."] **1986** Pederson *LAGS Concordance (Good-natured)* 1 inf, **neMS,** Likely. [Inf young]
    2 Sensible, intelligent. **NEng**
        1809 [see **1** above]. **1823** [see **1** above]. **1878** *Appletons' Jrl.* 5.415 **NEng,** In New England a likely person is a sensible, well-educated person. Elsewhere the word refers to physical excellence. . . In New England, as nowhere else, "handsome *is* as handsome *does.*"
    3 Able-bodied, competent.
        1899 Chesnutt *Conjure Woman* 85 **csNC** [Black], A trader . . wuz gittin' up a gang er [=of] lackly niggers fer ter ship off. **1927** *AmSp* 2.359 **cwWV,** *Likely* . . able-bodied. "He is a likely hand." **1975** Gainer *Witches* 13 **sAppalachians,** *Likely* . . capable. "The big feller is the likely one to do the job."

liken v [*OED liken* v. 3 →1838]
To resemble.
    1956 Ker *Vocab. W. TX* 296, For "he resembles his father in appearance and in other traits". . . Informant 39f offers the antiquated verb form likens. . . The birthplace of the parents of 39f is Kentucky and of the informant Wichita Falls; he has been a resident of West Texas for forty-two years.

liken vbl aux [*EDD liken* v. 2] *esp S Atl* Cf **like** vbl aux **E2**
In phrr *liken(ed) to,* foll by pres or perf infin or past finite verb form: Used to indicate that the action referred to nearly occurred.
    1907 *German Amer. Annals* 9.380 **sePA,** *Liken (v.)* or *Like.* . . "I likened to die of cold last week." **1928** Peterkin *Scarlet Sister Mary* 308 **SC** [Gullah], I liken not to a got here. **1966–67** *DARE* (Qu. LL30, . . 'Nearly' or 'almost': *"He fell off the ladder and* _____ *[broke his neck].*") Inf **LA2,** Liken to have ['laɪkṇ ˌtuv]; **SC11,** Likened to. **c1970** Pederson *Dial. Surv. Rural GA* (*I slipped on the ice and I just barely managed to keep my balance; I* _____ *fell down*) 1 inf, **seGA,** Liken to fall. **1975** Newell *If Nothin' Don't Happen* 82 **FL,** It made a mighty splash and throwed water all over me and likened to have scared me to death. **1986** Pederson *LAGS Concordance,* 1 inf, **swGA,** I liken to fell = I liked to have fell.

liken conj Pronc-sp *lacken* [From *like* conj, perh by analogy with **iffen, withouten**]
As if.
    c1937 in 1972 *Amer. Slave* 2.1.214 **SC,** Lacken she think I'd fergit such as dat.

likened to See **liken** vbl aux

likens n
In phr *one's likens:* Someone like one, the likes of one.
    1956 Ker *Vocab. W. TX* 296 **eTX,** As a noun, it [=*likens*] has currency in East Texas. It means "the kind or type of person" in such contemptuous expressions as "your likens will end up in jail."

liken to vbl aux See **liken** vbl aux

liken to, like ontu prep phr See **like unto**

like out See **like** v¹ **C2**

likeso adv
Also in phr *by likeso* (ellip for *by doing likeso*): Likewise.
    1922 Gonzales *Black Border* 311 **sSC, GA coasts** [Gullah glossary], *Likeso*—likewise, also. **1956** *DE Folkl. Bulletin* 1.24, Likeso (something similar—as in "All in favor signify by raising the right hand; all opposed by likeso.")

liketa See **like** vbl aux **E2b**

like that adj phr *esp Sth* Cf **that way,** *DS* AA28
Pregnant.
    1976 Ryland *Richmond Co. VA* 373, *Like that*—starting a family. **1983** Reinecke *Coll.* 7 **LA,** *Like-that*—see "*Comme-ça.*" [Ibid 3, *Comme-ça* . . pregnant. "that way" mainly among Creole Black population.] **1993** *DARE* File **seTX,** I've heard *like that* used to describe a pregnant woman under two circumstances: 1) in front of children (sort of like "She's in the family way") as a euphemism to protect innocent ears from hearing the word *pregnant,* and 2) as a rather catty remark among "respectable" women about a woman they disapprove of. Usually, this

is accompanied by a gesture, an arc made outwards from the belly by the talker's hand. *Ibid* **AL**, I am familiar with people using *like that* for "pregnant"—one of those euphemisms for one of those conditions.

like to See **like** vbl aux **E2**

like unto prep phr Also sp *liken to, like ontu* [*OED like* adj. 1.a "*Const. to, unto* (now arch.)"] **esp Sth**
Similar to; in the manner of.
   1867 Harris *Sut Lovingood Yarns* 32 **TN**, Hit rattled like ontu a sheet ove iron. **1933** Rawlings *South Moon* 132 **nFL**, I been trappin' Ma some wild hogs been actin' jest like unto that. **c1970** Pederson *Dial. Surv. Rural GA*, 1 inf, **seGA**, He's something like unto a muskrat; It belongs to be somethin' like unto a frog; 1 inf, **seGA**, Kind of like unto Boston brown bread. **1986** Pederson *LAGS Concordance*, 1 inf, **cAL**, Hit mostly grows liken to a collard plant or something liken to that; The mushroom is shaped liken to a umbrella; 1 inf, **nwFL**, But it's liken to an oak.

likkety-whoop See **lickety-split**

likted See **like** v¹ **B**

lil See **little**

lilac n, adj Usu |ˈlaɪlək, -ˌlæk, -ˌlɑk|; also *old-fash* |ˈleɪˌlɑk|
Pronc-spp *la(y)lock;* for addit varr see quots
   A Forms.
   1786 (1925) Washington *Diaries* 3.12 **VA**, The buds of the lylack were much swelled and seemed ready to unfold. **1837** *Knickerbocker* 10.167 **NY**, That youg [*sic*] woman, yender, . . with that lay-lock dress on to her. **1860** Holmes *Professor* 38 **MA**, Lalocks flowered late that year, and he got a great bunch off from the bushes in the Hancock front yard. **1871** (1882) Stowe *Fireside Stories* 129 **MA**, She come to meetin' . . her bunnet all tipped off with laylock. **1878** Eggleston *Roxy* 2 **sIN**, Lilacs—lay-locks the people call them. **1884** Jewett *Country Dr.* 27 **ME**, 'T was like setting a laylock bush to grow beside an ellum tree. **1887** Kirkland *Zury* 538 **IL**, Laylock. **1892** Torrey *Foot-Path Way* 58 **Cape Cod MA**, At my elbow stood a bunch of lilac bushes ("laylocks" they were probably called by the man who set them out). **1899** (1912) Green *VA Folk-Speech* 258, Laylock. **1903** *DN* 2.291 **Cape Cod MA** (as of a1857), Short vowels frequently differed in quality from those in normal English: . . [ɑ] for [æ] . . lailock = lilac. **1927** *AmSp* 2.359 **cwWV**, Laylock bush. **1927** Ruppenthal *Coll.* **KS**, Lilac . . lilak, lilock, lilark, laylark. **c1960** Wilson *Coll.* **csKY**, Lilac is always [ˈlaɪˌlæk]. **1965** *DARE* File **csWI**, [laɪlɑk]—most common; [laɪlæk]—occasional in all age groups; [ˈleɪˌlɑk]—still heard from old timers. **1968–69** *DARE* (Qu. S26e) Inf **MD9**, [ˈlaˈlæks]; (Qu. T16) Inf **NY73**, [ˈlaɪˌlɑk]; **RI17**, [ˈlaɪlæk]. **1983** *Greenfield Recorder* (MA) 21 May [Hemenway column], The old folks called them "laylocks" or "lielocks."
   B As noun.
   1 =**ceanothus.** Cf **California lilac, mountain ~, wild ~**
   1872 McClellan *Golden State* 163 **CA**, Throughout the central and northern part of the State may be found . . lilac, cherry, plum, grapevine, vine-maple, and *sequoia*, (mammoth tree.) **1889** *Garden and Forest* 2.279 **cwCA**, The Ceanothus in these mountains are commonly called "Lilacs," or, as I have frequently heard, "Laylocks." **1896** *Jrl. Amer. Folkl.* 9.184 **CA**, *Ceanothus divaricatus* . . lilac, Santa Barbara County, Cal. **1937** U.S. Forest Serv. *Range Plant Hdbk.* B39, Probably the names in most general use [for *Ceanothus* spp] have been bluebush (or bluebrush), buckbrush, lilac, and myrtle.
   2 A purple-flowered cruciferous plant (*Thelypodium torulosum*).
   1957 Barnes *Nat. Hist. Wasatch Spring* 53 **UT**, Over the same field is blooming that thin-stemmed, purple-flowered member of the mustard family, known as the "lilac" (*Thelypodium torulosum*). . . Frail little flower when seen alone, yet in great numbers it hues the field.

lilac lily n
=**chaparral lily.**
   1923 Abrams *Flora Pacific States* 1.417, *Lilium rubéscens*. . . Lilac Lily. **1961** Peck *Manual OR* 219, *L[ilium] rubescens*. . . Lilac Lily. . . Wooded slopes, southern Josephine and Jackson Cos. to Calif. **1979** Spellenberg *Audubon Guide N. Amer. Wildflowers W. Region* 586, Lilac Lily . . has smaller flowers . . that are at first white with purple spots but age to a rich wine color.

lilac sunbonnet n
A **gilia** (here: *Langloisia punctata*).
   1925 Jepson *Manual Plants CA* 808, *L[angloisia] punctata* . . Lilac Sunbonnet. . . Ranges in the desert, 1700 to 4500 ft.: Mohave Desert;

Inyo Co. **1941** Jaeger *Wildflowers* 192 **Desert SW**, Spotted gilia, lilac sunbonnet. *Gilia punctata.* **1979** Spellenberg *Audubon Guide N. Amer. Wildflowers W. Region* 666, Lilac Sunbonnet. . . Pale violet or lilac, purple-dotted flowers peering from among the leaves. . . Southeastern California, southern Nevada, and western Arizona.

lilark See **lilac**

lilian n Also *lillette*
=**dogtooth violet.**
   1933 Small *Manual SE Flora* 292, *Erythronium*. . . About 12 species, all, except one, North American. . . Dog-tooth violets. Adder's-tongues. Lillette. Lilians. Trout-lilies.

lilikoi n [Haw; see quot 1948] **HI**
The passion fruit (*Passiflora edulis*).
   1929 Neal *Honolulu Gardens* 216, Lilikoi. . . While practically confined to gardens on Oahu, . . [it] grows rank and wild in forests on Kauai. [*Ibid* 217, The juicy orange pulp contained in the brittle-shelled, purple fruit is fragrant and edible and affords gratifying refreshment to a thirsty walker.] **1930** Degener *Ferns of HI* 222, As this passion-flower [=*Passiflora edulis*] was unknown to the Hawaiians, they called it *lilikoi*, a name by which it is now known to everyone throughout the Hawaiian Islands. **1948** Neal *In Gardens HI* 523, The liliko'i is named for Lilikoi Gulch, east Maui, where the seeds were first planted. **1967** *DARE* (Qu. H32, . . *Fancy rolls and pastries*) Inf **HI6**, Lilikoi pie, with grahamcracker crust; (Qu. I46, . . *Kinds of fruits that grow wild around here*) Inf **HI1**, Lilikoi [ˈlɪlɪˌkɔɪ]; (Qu. I53, . . *Fruits grown around here . . special varieties*) Inf **HI3**, Lilikoi [ˈlɪlɪˌkɔɪ]—passion fruit (yellow), or small red passion fruit; **HI1**, Lilikoi—passion fruit. **1994** Stone–Pratt *Hawai'i's Plants* 199, Liliko'i leaves are three-parted and similar in shape to those of banana poka, but the smaller flowers are white and purple.

lillette See **lilian**

lilliput n
A **freshwater clam** (here: *Carunculina parva*).
   1982 U.S. Fish & Wildlife Serv. *Fresh-Water Mussels* [Wall chart], Lilliput. . . Sexes often different, female often inflated and . . with caruncle.

lily n
1 Std: a plant of the genus *Lilium*. For other names of these plants see **chaparral lily, field ~, leopard ~ 1, 2, meadow ~ 1, 2, nodding ~, orange ~, Oregon ~, red ~, roan ~, Shasta ~, swamp ~, tiger ~, turk's-cap ~, wild yellow ~, wood ~**
2 Any of var plants resembling those of the genus *Lilium*, as:
a A **dogtooth violet** (here: *Erythronium albidum*).
   1894 *Jrl. Amer. Folkl.* 7.101 **nwIL**, *Erythronium albidum*, lily, Peoria.
b also *iris lily:* =**iris B1.** Cf **blue lily, flag ~**
   1898 *Jrl. Amer. Folkl.* 11.281 **CA**, *Iris* (sp.), lilies. **1949** *WELS Suppl.* **csWI**, Blue flag carried the name of lily. **1966–70** *DARE* (Qu. S24, *A wild flower that grows in swamps and marshes and looks like a small blue iris*) Infs **AL11, IL69, 83, 84, 86, IA43, ME14, MS47, NY150, NC64, OH83, RI4, TX19**, Lily; **TN52**, Lilies; **MO22**, Iris lilies.
c =**fire flag.**
   1933 Small *Manual SE Flora* 362 **FL**, *T[halia] geniculata*. . . Lilies. . . Pools, ponds, marshes, swamps, and river-shores.
d =**trillium.**
   1950 *WELS* (A flower with 3 white petals that blooms in early spring . . , turns pink as the flower gets older) 1 Inf, **cWI**, Trillium, lily. **1966–70** *DARE* (Qu. S2) Infs **ID1, MI92, OH78, OR13, WI78**, Lily; **MI53**, Lily—it's a trillium, actually, but "lily"; **MI116**, Trillium—lily [is the] common name.
e also *lilybush:* A **Rose-of-Sharon** (here: *Hibiscus syriacus*).
   1967–69 *DARE* FW Addit **KY34**, Lilybush = Rose-of-Sharon, a cultivated flowering shrub; has white, blue, or yellow blooms; **seKY**, Lily = Rose-of-Sharon, a cultivated bush.

lily bell n
1 A **mariposa lily** (here: *Calochortus albus, C. amabilis*, or *C. pulchellus*). **CA**
   1897 Parsons *Wild Flowers CA* 54, *Calochortus albus*. . . Wherever they grow, these flowers win instant and enthusiastic admiration; and they have received a variety of common names . . , being known as "snowy lily-bell" [etc]. *Ibid* 144, Golden Lily-bell. *Calochortus pulchel-*

lus. **1911** Jepson *Flora CA* 98, *C[alochortus] amabilis.* . . *Golden Lily Bell.* . . North Coast Ranges. **1915** (1926) Armstrong–Thornber *Western Wild Flowers* 56, *Golden Lily Bell* . . *Calochortus amabilis.* . . These lovely flowers, common in northern California, are peculiarly fresh in color. **1920** Rice–Rice *Pop. Studies CA Wild Flowers* 28, This soft, lemon-colored flower [=*Calochortus pulchellus*] is often confused with the Golden Lily Bell, *C. amabilis.* **1923** in 1925 Jepson *Manual Plants CA* 237, *C[alochortus] pulchellus.* . . Also called Golden Lily Bell and Fairy Lantern.

2 A **fritillary** (here: *Fritillaria pudica*).

1959 Barnes *Nat. Hist. Wasatch Winter* 96 **UT,** Children on the road are carrying bouquets of that pretty yellow member of the lily family known locally as buttercup (*Fritillaria pudica*) though properly as . . lily bell, or orange fritillaria.

lily bonnet n

A **bonnet B1.**

1941 Faherty *Big Old Sun* 36 **FL,** Gator's eyes were every place, like lily bonnets in fresh water.

lily-bulb rice n Cf **Indian rice 3, rice root**

A **fritillary.**

1940 White *Wild Geese* 205 **AK** (as of c1896), "Goose tang," enumerated Sally, depositing aboard a double handful of green, "the stuff Len told us about, lily-bulb rice, wild celery, Hudson Bay tea."

lilybush See **lily e**

‡lily-liquor-leaf n

1968 *DARE* (Qu. BB50c, *Remedies for infections*) Inf **MD**30, Lily-liquor-leaf—a petal of the madonna lily, stored in whiskey, placed over cut to prevent infection; [**PA**14, Lily leaves in whiskey].

lily milkweed n

A **green milkweed** (here: *Asclepias lanuginosa*).

1987 *Nature Conserv. News* 37.2.20 **IL,** The grassland also harbors . . lily milkweed (*Asclepias lanuginosa*).

lily nut n

=**water chinquapin.**

1885 Thompson *By-Ways* 103, From Florida to Michigan one may run the gamut of nuts, beginning with the lily-nuts, or water chinquepins, and running up to the great black-walnut.

lily of the valley n Cf **false lily of the valley, wild ~**

1 Std: a plant of the genus *Convallaria,* usu *C. majalis* naturalized in the eastern US. For other names of *C. majalis* see **barney clapper 2, Jacob's ladder 11, maybell 1, mayflower 11, May lily 1**

2 A **false lily of the valley,** usu *Maianthemum canadense.*

1892 *Jrl. Amer. Folkl.* 5.104 **NH,** *Maianthemum Canadense.* . . Lily-of-the-valley. **1931** Harned *Wild Flowers Alleghanies* 118, *Maianthemum canadense.* . . A familiar little woodland plant having a zigzag stem and two leaves. . . Its flowers are very small and creamy-white. . . arranged in a terminal raceme. . . It is rather unfortunate that this plant should have been given the name Lily-of-the-Valley, for it is in no sense like it. **1959** Carleton *Index Herb. Plants* 75, Lily-of-the-valley: Convallaria majus; Maianthemum canadense; Smilacina stellata. **1967** *DARE* Wildfl QR Pl.19 Inf **OR**12, Lily of the valley.

3 A **false Solomon's seal** (here: *Smilacina stellata*).

1959 [see **2** above]. **1967** *DARE* Wildfl QR (Craighead) Pl.1.9 Infs **CO**15, 29, Lily of the valley. **1976** Bailey–Bailey *Hortus Third* 1050, [*Smilacina*] *stellata.* . . *Star-flowered lily-of-the-valley.* . . Fl[ower]s whitish, in almost sessile racemes to 2 in. long.

lily-of-the-valley tree n [See quot 1980]

=**sourwood.**

1897 Sudworth *Arborescent Flora* 314, *Oxydendrum arboreum.* . . *Common Names.* . . Lily-of-the-Valley-tree. **1908** Britton *N. Amer. Trees* 757, Sourwood. . . is locally known as . . Lily-of-the-Valley tree. . . The numerous white flowers are in nodding, clustered racemes at the ends of branches. **1950** Peattie *Nat. Hist. Trees* 529, Sourwood . . *Other Names.* . . Lily-of-the-valley-tree. **1980** Little *Audubon Guide N. Amer. Trees E. Region* 625, Sourwood . . "Lily-of-the-valley tree". . . Tree with conical or rounded crown of spreading branches, clusters of flowers recalling Lily-of-the-valley, and glossy foliage that turns red in autumn.

lily-of-the-valley vine n

A **Solomon's seal** (here: *Polygonatum biflorum*).

1951 *PADS* 15.29 **TX,** *Polygonatum biflorum.* . . Lily-of-the-valley vine.

lily pad n

1 also *pad:* Usu the floating leaf of a **water lily** (here: family Nymphaeaceae) such as that of **spatterdock,** but also the plant itself. **formerly chiefly NEast, now widespread** Cf **bonnet B1**

1814 Bigelow *Florula Bostoniensis* 132 **MA,** *Nymphaea advena.* . . *Yellow water lily.* . . The floating leaves of this . . are well known to anglers under the name of "lily pads." **1843** *Knickerbocker* 22.1 **SC,** A huge moccasin darting away beneath the dense reeds and lily-pads of the swamp. **1848** Lowell *Biglow* 145 'Upcountry' **MA,** *leaves of the water-lily.* **1857** Hammond *Wild N. Scenes* 145 **NY,** A moose . . was feeding upon the lily pads and flag grass. **1868** in 1911 Lowell *Poet. Wks.* 287, A pike / Lurks balanced 'neath the lily-pads. **1883** *Century Illustr. Mag.* 26.383, The fisher, holding the long rod in front of him . . , allows it to dip or 'bob' at frequent intervals in the water, among the lily-pads, deer-tongue, and other aquatic plants. **1900** Higginson *Outdoor Studies* 90 **MA,** Let us rest our paddles . . while the idle motion sways our light skiff onward, now half embayed among the lily-pads. **1937** *Natl. Geogr. Mag.* Aug 216, Its [=the purple gallinule's] brilliant plumage and bright yellow legs present an attractive picture among the deep-green "bonnets" or lily pads. **1949** Moldenke *Amer. Wild Flowers* 15, Both the flowers [of *Nymphaea odorata*] and the leaf blades (called "lily pads") float upon the water and rise or fall with the level of the water. **1961** Jackson *Mammals WI* 276 **WI** (as of 1918), On June 18, 1918, I saw one [=a porcupine] feeding on pond lily pads (*Nymphaea advena*) along Spring Creek, Vilas County, and the same day saw another, well out in a sphagnum bog near Spring Lake, feeding upon *Nymphaea* pads in a swampy bay. **1965–70** *DARE* (Qu. S22, . . *The bright yellow flowers that bloom in clusters in marshes in early springtime*) Infs **AZ**9, **IA**47, Lily pads; (Qu. S26b, *Wildflowers that grow in water or wet places*) Infs **IL**119, **MI**123, **PA**73, **TX**26, **WI**12, Lily pad(s); **NY**21, Pond lily or lily pads; **WI**50, Lily pad = water lily. **1977** *Parade* 21 Feb ceMA, *Joe Froggers.* . . are large, molasses-flavored cookies. . . Somebody thought they resembled lily pads. **1994** *DARE* File **cOH,** The water lily is the flower; its floating leaves are the lily pads. I've used this term since childhood [=c1960]—in fairy stories frogs are always on lily pads. *Ibid* **NYC,** Lily pads are the whole plant.

2 A **mud-baby** (here: *Echinodorus cordifolius*).

1913 *Torreya* 13.226 **AR,** *Echinodorus radicans.* . . Lily-pads, Lake Wapanoca.

lima bean n Usu |ˈlaɪmə|; also |ˈlaɪmɚ, ˈlaɪmi| Also *lima (butter bean)* Pronc-spp *limar, limer, limey* Cf Intro "Language Changes" IV.1.b **widespread, but less freq Sth, S Midl** See Map Cf **butter bean 1**

A cultivated bean (here: either *Phaseolus limensis* or *P. lunatus*) which produces flattened edible seeds; also the seed itself. Also called **butter bean 1.** For other names of *P. lunatus* see **butter pea, half-and-half c, sieva bean**

1819 Cobbett *Amer. Gardener* 109, The *Lima*-bean, which is never eaten green (that is, the *pod* is never eaten). **1822** *Amer. Jrl. Science* 4.173 **CT,** October 19, the Lima beans and peppers, of the second crop, have come almost to perfection. **1863** Burr *Field & Garden* 495, *Lima Bean. Phaseolus lunatus.* . . The Lima is one of the latest, as well as one of the most tender, of all garden-beans; and seldom, if ever, entirely perfects its crop in the Northern States. **1899** (1912) Green *VA Folk-Speech* 98, *Brunswick Stew.* . . A stew made of squirrel or chicken meat, lima beans and green corn cooked together and seasoned with pepper and salt. **1930s** in 1944 *ADD* eWV, Limar bean. [ˈlaɪmr̩]. Also *Limar.* . . Very common. **1942** Hall *Smoky Mt. Speech* 77 **wNC, eTN,** Lima (beans) [ˈlaɪmɚ]. **1946** *PADS* 5.28 **VA,** Lima beans (see *butterbeans*): Considered a modern term. **1947** *PADS* 8.24 **wNY,** Lima beans: The usual term. **1949** Kurath *Word Geog.* 73, *Butter beans* is a common expression for lima beans in all of the Southern area. Many people in this section differentiate between the large *lima beans* and the smaller *butter beans.* **1961** *AmSp* 36.269 **CO,** Commercial use seems to account for *hotcakes* and *butter beans* as alternative expressions for *pancakes* and *lima beans.* **1965–70** *DARE* (Qu. I16, *The large flat beans that are not eaten in the pod*) 760 Infs **widespread, but less freq Sth, S Midl,** Lima bean(s); **SC**57, Bush lima beans, bush lima butter beans; **CA**63, Green lima beans; 36 Infs, **scattered,** Limas; 10 Infs, **scattered,** (Baby or bush, pole, small) limas; **KY**69, Limey [ˈlaɪmi] beans; (Qu. I20, . . *Kinds of beans*) 28 Infs, **scattered,** Lima beans; **CA**57, 175, Baby lima beans; **NY**36, 43, Pole lima beans; **OH**22, Big and little lima beans; **PA**49, Fordhook lima beans; 16 Infs, **scattered,** (Bunch *or* bush, climbing, Henderson baby, little, pole) limas; **NJ**16, Bush limers, pole limers; **NJ**17, Pole limer. [Further exx throughout *DS;* all exx are mapped.] **1972** *PADS* 58.21 **cwAL,** Lima beans. Southern and South Midland *butter beans* (19) is more common than *lima beans* (8) as a primary response. The informants differ in their use of the terms: eight said that they were the same thing; eight thought that the butter bean was smaller; and two thought that the lima bean was smaller. **1990** *Seed Savers Yearbook* 69, *Henderson* . . old reliable baby lima, . . easy to pick and shell.

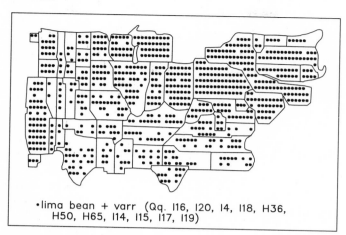

• lima bean + varr (Qq. I16, I20, I4, I18, H36, H50, H65, I14, I15, I17, I19)

limb n See **limb of Satan**

limb v

1 also with *off, out, up;* Esp in logging: to cut the branches from (a tree); rarely, to prune; also fig; hence vbl n *limbing;* n *limber* one who trims the branches from felled trees. **chiefly NEng, West** Cf **knot** v **1**

[**1835** (1927) Evans *Exped. Rocky Mts.* 14.202 **IN**, Weather beaten cotton wood trees limbed and shattered by the storms of the prairies.] **1839** Holmes *Rept. Aroostook R.* 53 **ME**, The best mode undoubtedly is, to fall the trees and *"limb"* them, (that is, cut off the limbs,) in June. **1889** *Harper's New Mth. Mag.* 78.231, It [=a beaver dam] seemed to be built principally of alder poles well limbed off, and placed, roughly speaking, side by side. **1905** U.S. Forest Serv. *Bulletin* 61.41 [Logging terms], *Limb.* . . To remove the limbs from a felled tree. . . (P[acific] C[oast] F[orest].) *Limber.* . . One who cuts the limbs from felled trees. (Gen[eral].) **1907** *DN* 3.246 **eME**, *Limb* (a tree). . . To chop the limbs off a tree, in part, if it remains standing; wholly, if it has been felled. **1914** *DN* 4.75 **ME, nNH**, *Limb out.* . . To cut the limbs from a felled tree. **1950** *Western Folkl.* 9.381 **neCA** [Lumberjack language], *Limber.* A man who cuts the limbs off trees. **1956** Moody *Home Ranch* 68 **CO** (as of 1911), He had a couple of dozen trees felled before I had six limbed out. **1966–68** *DARE* Tape **ME6**, Trimming the tree, cutting the top off—the man that does that we call him the limber ['lɪmɚ], one that does the limbing ['lɪmɪn]. *Ibid* **MA5C**, Sometimes they'd have just one man that wouldn't do anything but limbing ['lɪ‍ᵛmɪn]. *Ibid* **NH14**, [FW:] You call that anything when you cut the branches off the tree, limbs off a tree? [Inf:] Browsin' it would be one [term], for an old one; limbin' ['lɪmɪn] it up. **1968** *DARE* File **SC**, *Limb up.* . . To trim up or prune. The hydrangea in bloom would have been prettier but "'e lim(b) 'em up too late." Uneducated Black male. **1975** Gould *ME Lingo* 163, *Limb out*—To cut the limbs and top from a tree that has been felled. Accordingly, if somebody gets *limbed out,* he's been trimmed down considerably: "The new schoolteacher limbed out that Huxley kid this morning!" **1982** *Smithsonian Letters* **ME**, After I had felled the tree and limbed it, I put a chain around its butt and twitched it out with my tractor.

2 To beat severely.

1949 Arnow *Hunter's Horn* 168 **eKY**, Shut up that trashy talk, young-ens. . . Suse, I'll limb you fer sassen your mom. **1953** Randolph–Wilson *Down in Holler* 261 **Ozarks**, *Limb.* . . To whip, to flog. "I'm a-goin' to limb hell out of that boy!" **1954** *Harder Coll.* **cwTN**.

limber adj, hence adv *limber(ly)* **scattered, but more freq Sth, S Midl**

Limp, weak, exhausted—often in phr *limber as a dishrag* and varr.

1818 Weems *Drunkard's Looking Glass* 35, Then pale and limber as a rag, . . down he sprawls. **1825** Neal *Brother Jonathan* 2.67 **swME**, A minnet afore . . , he was chock full o' fight . . but, now . . if he ain't as limber as a rag. **1866** Smith *Bill Arp* 97 **GA**, In a short space of time she became affected with drowsiness. Her neck became as limber as a greasy rag. **1909** Porter *Roads of Destiny* 186 **West**, A man . . walked

rapidly up the main street of the town. There were other passengers . . , but they either slouched limberly over to the railroad eating-house . . or joined the groups of idlers. **1909** *DN* 3.346 **eAL, wGA**, *Limber as a dishrag.* . . Very limber, exhausted, lacking in nervous energy. **1912** *DN* 3.582 **wIN**, *Limber as a dishrag.* . . Completely exhausted. "When I got through mowing away hay I was as limber as a dishrag." **1927** *AmSp* 2.359 **cwWV**, *Limber as a dishrag* . . without muscular strength. "He lies there limber as a dishrag." **1929** *AmSp* 5.19 **Ozarks**, *Limber sick.* . . Weak, unable to stand or walk because of illness. **1949** Arnow *Hunter's Horn* 129 **eKY**, He jerked the warm shirt from his bosom and went to work on the lamb, a little ewe, limber lifeless, with its ears frozen and its nose frosted. **1951** *Sun* (Baltimore MD) 30 Mar 17/8 *(Hench Coll.),* Vera Connelly came from behind to win the seventh race when the early leaders became "limber" in the last furlong. **1954** *Harder Coll.* **cwTN**, *Limber sick.* . . *Limber as a dishrag.* **1956** McAtee *Some Dialect NC* 27, *Limber as a dishrag:* simile; i.e., limp. **1967–70** *DARE* (Qu. BB6, *A sudden feeling of weakness, when sometimes the person loses consciousness*) Inf **PA70**, Limber; (Qu. GG26, *A feeling of weakness from fear: "When she saw the dog coming at her she got _____."*) Inf **MA100**, Legs got limber; **OH95**, Her knees were limber; **TX35**, Limber-legged. **1972** *GA Dept. Ag. Farmers Market Bulletin* 1 Mar 1/4, "Limber legs" in Jersey calves, a condition in which calves are unable to control their legs, has been found to be inherited. **1986** Pederson *LAGS Concordance,* 1 inf, **csMS**, He was just as limber as he could be = sick; 1 inf, **cnGA**, Of a calf—limber-legged.

limber n See **limb** v **1**

limber as a dishrag See **limber** adj

limber belly (ice) See **limber ice**

limber board See **limber jack 4**

limber ice n Also *limber belly (ice), limber bridge, ~ jack, ~ jim* Cf **limber lead**

=**rubber ice.**

1950 *WELS Suppl.* **csWI**, *Limber bridge*—The layer of ice on which we used to go skating was called limber bridge. It wobbled. **1954** *Ibid* **csWI**, We called the flexible ice "tickle-y bender." . . My husband says it was called "limber belly" in Horicon [WI]. **1965–70** *DARE* (Qu. B35, *Ice that will bend when you step on it, but not break*) Infs **TN36, UT4, WV16**, Limber ice; **MA15**, Limber ice—usu new ice; **AL1**, Limber bridge; **OH38**, Limber jim; **OH47**, Limber—when it starts to melt it's limber jack; [**NY82**, Limber; **NJ28**, Limber—limber lead more common]. **1966** *DARE* File **nWI**, *Limber belly ice*—rubber ice. South side of Lake Superior.

limber jack n

1 also *limber jim:* A whip or other flexible instrument of punishment.

1860 Hundley *Social Relations S. States* 224, Messrs. abolitionists, we warn you to beware of your instructor's ferule, beware of his limber-jack; for he [=the Southern Bully] will cane you and cowskin you. **1940** *Amer. Mercury* 50.209 **eKY**, She wouldn't spare the limber-jim. **1982** Slone *How We Talked* 32 **eKY** (as of c1950), *Limber-jim*—a small switch used to whip children.

2 also *limber jim:* A loose-jointed, flexible person; a contortionist.

1909 *DN* 3.346 **eAL, wGA**, *Limber-jack.* . . A limber person, one who goes through bodily contortions. Common. **1912** [see **3** below]. **c1930** Swann *Lang. Circus Lot* 11, *Limber Jim:* A contortionist.

3 =**jumping jack 5.** **esp Sth, S Midl** Cf **supplejack**

1912 Green *VA Folk-Speech* 262, *Limber-jack.* . . A wooden toy held by the head and the legs and arms made to move in an odd way by pulling a string between the legs. "*Limber-jack*" is a person that moves his arms and legs in a loose way. **1946** *PADS* 6.19 **eNC** (as of 1900), *Limber jack.* . . Jumping jack. . . Rare. **c1960** Wilson Coll. **csKY**, *Limberjack* . . toy, a jumping-jack. [**1975** Thomas *Hear the Lambs* 144 **nwAL**, I thought you couldn't be so pleasant if you knew they had been dancing at the hall most every day, after school. He's been throwing her around and catching her, like he used to do; you know, he used to throw her up like a limber doll.] **1978** *DARE* File **cwOR**, A limber jack is a wooden doll with jointed shoulders, elbows, hips, and knees which, when held so that it just touches a thin piece of wood that is tapped rhythmically, can be made to dance. I learned of this from someone who knew it in Maine about 1925. The dolls were being sold at the Eugene Farmers Market as part of a folk-life revival. **1989** Flynt *Poor But Proud* 226 **ceAL**, Carefully joined wooden creatures called "limber jacks" could buck dance or jig to the finest fiddle tune.

4 also *limber board:* **=joggling board.**

1986 Pederson *LAGS Concordance (Joggling board)* 2 infs, **cnGA, cwMS,** Limber jack; 2 infs, **seAL, seMS,** Limber board.

5 See **limber ice.**

limber jim n

1 See **limber jack 1.**

2 See **limber jack 2.**

3 See **limber ice.**

limber lead n |'lɪmbɚ ˌlɛd| **NJ** Cf **kittly-bender, limber ice**
=**rubber ice;** a game played on such ice.

1965–70 *DARE* (Qu. B35, *Ice that will bend when you step on it, but not break*) Infs **NJ**2, 4, Limber lead [lɛd]; **NJ**1, 28, Limber lead; (Qu. EE27, *Games played on the ice*) Inf **NJ**1, Limber lead—skating over thin ice in a series. **1967** *DARE* FW Addit **NJ,** [lɪmbɚ lɛd]—rubbery ice that will support a light person such as a child. They used to run across to see who would be the first to go through or the last to attempt the feat.

limberly See **limber** adj

limberneck n Pronc-sp *lemonneck* **chiefly Sth, Midl** See Map
An avian botulism that often affects domestic poultry; see quots.

1910 Valentine *How to Keep Hens* 271, The disease called "limberneck," in which the affected bird is unable to control the head, which droops to the ground, is said by many who have had large experience with it to be the result of stomach irritation brought on by eating maggots. **1931** Dickinson–Lewis *Poultry* 216, When flies and maggots infest putrid meat and other spoiled feeds, fowls eating them are likely to show symptoms of limber neck disease. **1948** Wolfe *Farm Gloss.* 195, *Limberneck*—Disease of chickens caused by eating maggots in dead meat. Causes paralysis of the neck muscles and is often fatal. Is a form of botulism. **1965–70** *DARE* (Qu. K78, . . *Diseases . . chickens commonly get*) 98 Infs, **chiefly Sth, Midl,** Limberneck; **AL**14, **KY**80, **MS**60, 81, Lemonneck; [(Qu. BB49, . . *Other kinds of diseases*) Inf **FL**49, Limberneck ['lɪmənɛk]—more children died of that—my boy died of that.] **1967** *Merck Vet. Manual* 1166, The toxin affects the nervous system, causing a flaccid paralysis which is well described by the name "limberneck", given to the disease. In addition, the feathers are loose and come out easily.

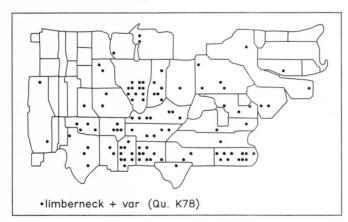

•limberneck + var (Qu. K78)

limber pine n [From the tough and flexible branches]

1 also *limber-twig pine:* A pine *(Pinus flexilis)* native to the Rocky Mts and parts of the Southwest. Also called **bull pine 1b, nut pine e, soft pine, white pine**

1897 Sudworth *Arborescent Flora* 15 *Pinus flexilis.* . . Limber Pine. *Ibid* 16 **CA,** *Common names.* . . Limber-twig Pine. **1908** Rogers *Tree Book* 29, This "limber pine" [=*Pinus flexilis*] is notable because it thrives where other pines fail. . . The best specimens grow in New Mexico and Arizona—sturdy trees, as broad as they are high, with trunks 5 feet through, and limbs of exceeding length, flexibility, and toughness. From these characters the tree takes its specific name and the common name given above. **1913** Wooton *Trees NM* 17, The Western White Pine or Limber Pine *(Pinus flexilis)* and its nearly related congener *Pinus strobiformis,* to which both of the foregoing common names are also applied, occur in the higher mountains. **1917** Eaton *Green Trails* 53 **nwMT,** Over her, dwarfed like a print by Hiroshige, a twisted, limber pine flaunted its pink cone buds. **1961** Douglas *My Wilderness* 14 **CO,**

Limber pine grows high in isolated spots. **1967–70** *DARE* (Qu. T17, . . *Kinds of pine trees;* not asked in early QRs) Inf **CA**208, Limber pine; **CO**9, Limber pine—a species of white; **CO**37, Bull pine or the limber [pine]. **1980** Little *Audubon Guide N. Amer. Trees W. Region* 278, Limber Pine. . . The very tough and flexible twigs . . can sometimes be twisted into a knot.

2 =**Mexican white pine.**

1913 [see **1** above]. **1979** Little *Checklist U.S. Trees* 198, *Pinus strobiformis.* . . *Southwestern white pine.* . . *Other common names . .* border limber pine. [**1980** Little *Audubon Guide N. Amer. Trees W. Region* 291, This species [=*Pinus strobiformis*] of the Mexican border region was formerly considered a southern variety of Limber Pine, which has a broader, more northern distribution, is smaller, and has smooth-edged needles with white lines on all surfaces.]

limber-twig pine See **limber pine 1**

limbery adj Cf Intro "Language Changes" III.1
Limber, flexible.

1930 Stoney–Shelby *Black Genesis* 121 **seSC,** Br' Frog is dat limbery, till he jus' sort o' snap roun' dat t'ing, an' ride it all de res' o' de way to de creek. **1969** *DARE* (Qu. KK25, *Something that bends or yields easily:* "*That willow branch is very _____.*") Infs **IN**80, **KY**5, Limbery.

limb hook See **limb line**

limbing See **limb** v **1.**

limb line n esp **S Midl**
A fishing line attached to a tree limb; hence n *limb hook* a hook attached to such a line.

1967–69 *DARE* (Qu. P13, . . *Ways of fishing . . besides the ordinary hook and line*) Infs **MO**20, 37, Limb lines; **MO**12, Limb line: Limb line is just a piece of a branch off of a tree, stuck into the side at the bank with your line on it, and you put those in in the evening about dusk, then you run 'em during the night or early in the morning; **TN**37, Limb lines—used for catfish—hang line from limb of tree. **1969** *DARE* Tape **KY**21, They catch 'em on . . limb hooks, some in early spring. Top hooked onto a limb and let it go down in the water. **1982** Sternberg *Fishing* 46, *Trotlines* and *limblines* . . are commonly used on large rivers and reservoirs. . . A limbline has only a single hook. It is tied to an overhanging branch so the baitfish dangles in the water. Both types of lines are set one day and picked up the next. **1986** Pederson *LAGS Concordance,* 1 inf, **swMS,** Limb lines—many fishing lines fixed to limbs.

limb off See **limb** v **1**

limb of Satan n Freq abbr *limb* [*OED limb of Satan* →1607; *limb* 1625 →; cf *EDD limb* sb. 2, 8]
A wicked or mischievous person, esp a child.

1851 (1852) Stowe *Uncle Tom's Cabin* 2.36 **KY** [Black], See there. . . [D]on't that show she's a limb? **1887** Kirkland *Zury* 538 **IL,** Limb. . . A limb of Satan. **1899** (1912) Green *VA Folk-Speech* 262, Limb. . . A mischievous or roughish person, especially a young person; an imp; a scamp; a scapegrace. **1927** *AmSp* 2.359 **cwWV,** Limb of Satan . . a mischievous child. "That youngster is surely a limb of Satan." **1929** *AmSp* 5.121 **ME,** Elders would say . . "I will lam you, you imp or limb of Satan," or "I will wear out a stick on you." **a1930** in 1991 Hughes–Hurston *Mule Bone* 35 **cFL** [Black], You impident limb you. **1950** *WELS* (*A small child that is rough or does not behave well*) 1 Inf, **cnWI,** A regular limb; (*Words or expressions for someone who enjoys going out a great deal—men:*) 1 Inf, **csWI,** Gay limb. **1951** Johnson *Resp. to PADS 20* **DE** (*To play jokes on people:* "*He's an awful _____.*") Limb of Satan. **1954** *PADS* 21.32 **SC,** Limb of Satan. . . A wicked, vicious person. **1985** Rattray *Advent. Dimon* 168 **Long Is. NY** (as of c1890), There was maybe five hundred dollars worth of whalebone in that mouth, he said, and those limbs of Satan weren't going to run off with it a shilling at a time. He chased them back up the beach to tend the fire.

limb out (or up) See **limb** v **1**

limby adj
See quot 1953.

1953 Randolph–Wilson *Down in Holler* 261 **Ozarks,** Limby. . . Having many limbs or branches. "Them is the limbiest cedars I ever seen." **1954** *Harder Coll.* **cwTN.**

lime elm n
=**cedar elm.**

1960 Vines *Trees SW* 210, Cedar Elm—*Ulmus crassifolia.* . . Vernacular names are Scrub Elm, Lime Elm, Texas Elm, Basket Elm, Red Elm, and Southern Rock Elm.

limer See **lima bean**

lime tree n[1] [*OED* 1625 →; var of *line* < *lind*] See also **black lime tree**

A **linden,** usu *Tilia americana.*

1785 (1925) Washington *Diaries* 2.343 **VA,** Also four Lime or Linden Trees. **1792** Belknap *Hist. NH* 3.98, Basswood or Lime-tree (tilia americana) is sometimes sawed into boards, which are very white, but soft, and easily warped. **1813** Michaux *Histoire des Arbres* 3.311, *Tilia americana.* . . Elle se trouve dans le Canada, mais elle est encore plus commune dans le Nord des Etats-Unis, où elle est le plus habituellement désignée par le nom de *Baas wood* [sic]; quelquefois aussi on lui donne celui de *Lime tree.* [=*Tilia americana.* . . It is found in Canada, but it is even commoner in the north of the United States, where it is most often called *Baas wood* [sic]; it is also sometimes known as *Lime tree.*] *Ibid* 316, Ils les [=*T. alba* et *T. pubescens*] désignent également par les mêmes noms d'*American lime tree* et de *Baas wood.* [=They call them [=*T. alba* and *T. pubescens*] both by the names *American lime tree* and *Baas wood.*] **1814** [see **line tree** n[2]]. **1860** Curtis *Cat. Plants NC* 78, *Linn* or *lime trees.* . . They are known in the Northern States by the names of *Lime Tree* and *White Wood,* but more generally by that of *Bass Wood.* **1897** Sudworth *Arborescent Flora* 301, *Tilia americana.* . . Limetree (R.I., N.C., S.C., Ala., Miss., La., Ill.). . . Black Limetree (Tenn.). Smooth-leaved Limetree (Tenn.) *Ibid* 303, *Tilia heterophylla.* . . Smooth-fruited White-leaved Limetree (Tenn.). Large-leaved Lime Tree (Tenn.) **1932** Rydberg *Flora Prairies* 537, *Tilia* [spp] . . Linden, Basswood, Lime-tree. **1960** Vines *Trees SW* 733, *Tilia* [americana]. . . has many vernacular names such as Bast-tree, Lin-tree, Lime-tree [etc].

lime tree n[2]
=**Ogeechee lime.**

[**1765** (1942) Bartram *Diary of a Journey* 3 Oct **GA,** A rare tupelo with large red acid fruite called limes.] **1785** Marshall *Arbustrum* 97, *Nyssa Ogeche.* . . The fruit is nearly oval, of a deep red colour, of the size of a Damascene Plumb, and of an agreeable acid taste, from which it is called the Lime-tree. **1830** Rafinesque *Med. Flora* 2.247, *Ogeechee tree, Lime tree* has a red acid fruit, size of a plumb, used like limes in the South. **1898** Sudworth *Forest Trees* 101, *Nyssa ogeche.* . . Names in use. . . Limetree.

limey n[1] [Abbr for *lime-juicer* a British ship or sailor; *OED* 1884 →] **widespread, but less freq Sth, S Midl** See Map
An English person; someone of English ancestry.

1918 Depew *Gunner Depew* 18, So, all over the world, British ships are called "Lime-juicers" and their sailors "Limeys". **1929** *AmSp* 4.342 [Vagabond lingo], *Limey*—An Englishman. **1930** *AmSp* 5.384 [A[mer.] E[xpeditionary] F[orces] English], *Limey.* Any British soldier. **1931** Linklater *Juan in Amer.* 115, 'An Englishman,' he marvelled, 'the first limey I ever saw shot in Chicago.' **1965–70** DARE (Qu. HH28, *Names and nicknames . . for people of foreign background: English*) 159 Infs, **widespread, but less freq Sth, S Midl,** Limey. **1986** Pederson *LAGS Concordance* **Gulf Region** (*Englishman*) 30 infs, Limey(s).

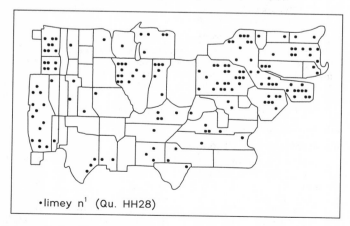

•limey n[1] (Qu. HH28)

limey n[2] See **lima bean**

limit n **MS**

=**furnish;** hence n *limit day* the first day on which credit is advanced against the year's crop.

1950 *AmSp* 25.230 **ceMS,** The following list includes a few of the expressions used currently by tenants and landowners around Stoneville, Mississippi. . . *Limit,* n. 'Furnish.' [*Ibid, Furnish.* . . Groceries provided on credit to the tenant by the plantation owner.] **1954** Smith *Yazoo River* 190 **MS,** The plantation year was built around the cotton crop and the financial arrangements to produce it. March 1 was Limit Day, on which the first allowance was made by the plantation commissary for the rations through the year. There was no obligation of the planter to extend credit before this date.

limpa n Also *limpa (rye) bread* [Sw] **chiefly IL, MN, ND, WI**
A rye bread made with molasses.

1951 Tufford *Scandinavian Recipes* 28, *Swedish Limpa.* . . Mix sugar, shortening, salt, molasses and water and bring to a boil. Add soda to buttermilk, then add hot liquid mixture. Add rye flour. Mix well and add yeast. Add white flour and knead well. **1967–69** DARE (Qu. H18, . . *Special kinds of bread*) Inf IL20, Limpa—Swedish rye; MN42, Limpa—molasses . . rye flour; IL12, Limpa rye bread—Swedish bread; MN14, Swedish limpa—made of rye, a round flat bread; (Qu. H65, *Foreign foods favored by people around here*) Inf IL30, Limpa bread—Swedes. **1973** Allen *LAUM* 1.278 (as of c1950), [Other kinds of bread:] 4 infs, 1 **MN,** 3 **ND,** Limpa. **1979** Flagg *Cape Cod Cooking* 204, *Rye bread—Limpa*—This is somewhat similar to the former recipe, but with perhaps more of the Swedish influence. **1994** *Courier Hub* (Stoughton WI) 12 May Special marketing sec 5/1, [Advt:] *Norwegian Specialties*—Fattigman[,] Stollen[,] Rosettes[,] Julekage . . Lefse . . Limpa. **1994** DARE File **cnWI** (as of 1980s), We always looked forward to stopping at the bakery in Boulder Junction for their special and unusual breads and pastries. The limpa bread was a light rye with pieces of citron in it—no caraway seeds—in a round loaf. *Ibid* **neWI,** Swedish limpa is still sold in Door County.

limping Kate n Also *limping Katie, Kit* [By analogy with **hopping John;** see quot 1952] **SC** Cf **limping Susan**
A dish of rice or **hominy** and **cowpeas;** see quots.

1950 *PADS* 14.45 **SC,** Limpin' Kate, limpin' Kit . . Cowpeas and hominy cooked together. **1952** *PADS* 17.38, As lineal descendants of *hoppin' John* a whole family of halting females has arisen: *limpin' Susan, limpin' Kate, limpin' Kit, limpin' Sal,* and the like, representing dishes of similar composition, mostly with hominy to replace the rice. **1954** *PADS* 21.32 **SC,** Limpin' Katie, limpin' Kate, limpin' Kit, skippin' Jinny: . . Originally, cowpeas and hominy cooked separately and eaten together. Other reports have it that cowpeas and hominy were cooked together. [Footnote, quoting letter:] I was born in 1873. . . My father ran a farm—an eight or ten horse farm—could get labor cheap in those days. . . Sometimes the housewife found her rice out. Her pot of peas was on cooking and no rice. Hands all in the field, no time to stop and beat rice. . . So a pot of grits was the answer. . . So my mother would say to her help: 'Well, Mary, we will have *limping Katie* today.' The hominy had to be limp or soft to get that name. So *limping Katie* is hominy and peas, but not cooked together. **1967** DARE (Qu. H50, *Dishes made with beans, peas, or corn that everybody around here knows, but people in other places might not*) Inf SC43, Limping Kate—grits and peas, beans.

limping Susan n [Cf **limping Kate**] **SC**
A dish of rice and okra cooked together; see quots.

1952 [see **limping Kate**]. **1954** *PADS* 21.32 **Charleston SC,** Limpin' Susan . . Okra pilau, a dish made of chopped bacon, okra, rice, and seasoning.

limpkin n [See quot 1946]

A goose-sized, long-legged marsh bird *(Aramus guarauna)* of southern Georgia and Florida. Also called **carau, clucking hen 2, crying bird, Indian pullet 5, marsh hen 4, nigger boy**

1871 Cambridge Univ. Museum Compar. Zool. *Bulletin* 2.3.362 **eFL,** Its popular name in Florida is "limpkin." **1898** (1910) Willoughby *Across Everglades* 111 **sFL,** A bird which we became intimately acquainted with later on, and which we then saw for the first time, was the limpkin. **1932** Rawlings in *Scribner's Mag.* 91.284 **FL,** "You got you a voice like a limpkin." "A limpkin?" she puzzled. "Thet brownified crane screeches like a wild-cat?" **1946** Hausman *Eastern Birds* 233, Limpkin. . . The bird often bobs or teeters as it stands, and in flight both flaps and sails. When rising from the long grasses and flying only a short distance, it dangles its legs after the manner of a Rail. Its delicate, rather limping gait gives the bird its name. **1966** DARE (Qu. Q8) Inf FL35, Limpkin; (Qu. Q10, . . *Water birds and marsh birds*) Infs FL4, 35, Limpkin(s). **1975** Natl. Audubon Soc. *Corkscrew* 25 **swFL,** A large dark brown bird may walk jerkily along or fly off through the trees with a stiff awkward wingbeat. This is the peculiar limpkin.

limpy adj

Lame; crippled.

1955 Stong *Blizzard* 120 **IA**, "Leg's fine, nurse," said Rut Cameron. "Or will be if he keeps off it for a few more days. I've explained to him what will happen if he doesn't. It will be limpy." **1968** *DARE* (Qu. BB1, *When a person has been injured so that when he walks he steps more heavily on one foot than the other: "He _____."*) Inf **WI62**, He's limpy.

limu n |ˈlimu, ˈlɪmu| [Haw] **HI**

An alga or moss, esp any of var edible seaweeds; also fig.

1928 Pan-Pacific Research Inst. *Jrl.* 3.2.3 **HI**, *Algae. . .* Includes a great variety of seaweeds (limu), spirogyra, pond scum, etc. **1933** Bryan *Hawaiian Nature* 81, The common people lived mainly on fish and poi, augmented by such plant products as seaweed (called limu). *Ibid* 86, Some seventy different kinds of seaweeds which grow about the Hawaiian Islands were eaten. . . About half of these were generally used, the commonest being *limu eleele, limu kohu,* and *limu lipoa. Ibid* 138, Limu is the Hawaiian name for algae, especially the large, marine forms known as seaweeds. Many kinds of limu are relished by the Hawaiians as food. . . and even today no luau is considered complete without limu. **1938** Reinecke *Hawaiian Loanwords* 22, *Limu. . .* Edible sea-moss, of many varieties; an important food in Hawaii, especially among the natives. V[ery] F[requent]. **1954–60** Hance et al. *Hawaiian Sugar* 4, *Limu. . .* Moss, seaweed. **1955** Day *HI People* 297, Relishes were salt, roasted kukui nuts, dried octopus, and a seaweed called limu. **1967** Reinecke–Tsuzaki *Hawaiian Loanwords* 103, *Limu;* [limu]. . . 1. Edible sea-moss, of many varieties; an important food in Hawaii, esp. among the natives. 2. Algae, such as those found in showers and sinks. 3. As a recent slang term applied esp. to music and dancing, it means "It stinks!" [Tsuzaki indicates that this word is widely recognized by all age groups, on the basis of a survey of 26 infs.] **1967** *DARE* (Qu. I35, . . *Kitchen herbs . . grown and used in cooking around here*) Inf **HI3**, Limu [ˈlɪmu]; (Qu. FF21a, *A joke that is so old it doesn't seem funny any more: "His jokes are all _____."*) Inf **HI6**, They all have limu (=seaweed) [laughter]. **1994** Stone–Pratt *Hawaiʻi's Plants* 55, In addition to the coralline algae, sea lettuce . . and other limu (seaweeds) grow firmly attached to the substrate. *Ibid* 73, The green turtle . . feeds largely on pastures of algae, or limu, growing on coral and rocks near the main Hawaiian Islands.

limus cooter n [Prob pronc-sp for *little musk cooter;* cf **little, musk turtle**]

1922 Gonzales *Black Border* 60 **sSC, GA coasts,** He jerked quickly, only to bring swinging over the boat one of the malodorous little black turtles commonly called "limus cootuh" by the low-country negroes.

linch n [Var of *leech*]

1968–69 *DARE* (Qu. R23b, *Blood-sucking creatures—in water*) Inf **NC54**, Linches [ˈlɪnčɪz]—yellowish, brown; **TX59**, Linches [ˈlɪnčɛz].

Lincoln fence See **Abe Lincoln fence**

lind See **linn 1**

linded See **lineded**

linden n

Std: a tree of the genus *Tilia*. Also called **basswood 1, bee tree, boxwood 5, cucumber tree 3, daddynut, honeywood, horse ball tree, lime ~ n¹, linn n, monkey-nut 3, wahoo, whitewood;** for other names of *T. americana* see **bast-tree, black lime tree, line ~ n², spoonwood, whistlewood, wicopy;** for other names of *T. heterophylla* see **white basswood.** For other names of a bract of such a tree see **monkey n¹ 7**

line n¹

1 A driving rein. **widespread, but less freq NEng** See Map Cf **checkline, jack line, jerk ~ 1, rein**

1834 Smith *Letters Jack Downing* 190, Ever since they told the Squire to take the lines, they haint lost a linchpin or broke a strap. **1845** Hooper *Advent. Simon Suggs* 167 **AL,** Uncle Kit reassuming the lines, said—"Well, *now* I'm off sure, 'squire!" **1905** *DN* 3.13 **cCT,** *Lines. . .* Reins for driving. **1907** *DN* 3.214 **nwAR,** *Lines.* **1910** *DN* 3.445 **wNY,** *Lines.* **1939** (1962) Thompson *Body & Britches* 199 **NY,** The old-time Long Islander speaks of *lines,* not reins (but so do many Yorkers inland). **1965–70** *DARE* (Qu. L51, *The leathers or ropes that a driver holds to*

guide a horse) 511 Infs, **widespread, but less freq NEng,** Lines; **AR**51, **KY**29, **MS**81, **TN**58, **VA**40, Plow lines; **MS**81, **WA**18, Guide lines; **DC**5, **PA**6, Lead lines; **GA**84, **TN**58, Wagon lines; **TN**62, Cross lines—for work horse; **NC**60, Driving lines; (Qu. L49, *Leathers or ropes, fastened to the collar, that a horse or mule pulls by*) 18 Infs, **scattered,** Lines; **MI**78, Lines—guide them with; **NC**38, Reins, lines; **CA**16, Guide lines; **GA**17, **NJ**10, 35, **TX**71, Line; [*DARE* Ed: These Infs appear to have confused the reins with the tugs or to have misunderstood the qu.] (Qu. K34, *What do you say to make the horses stop?*) Inf **NM**13, Say "wo" and pull on lines; (Qu. K36a, *What do you say to make a horse go faster?*) Inf **OH**80, Flap the lines; **NM**13, Pop with lines and whistle; **AR**40, **OK**43, Slap (them) with lines; **MD**26, Smack him with the line; **OK**8, Snap lines on back; **VA**10, Tap of the line; **AR**29, Tap with lines; (Qu. K36b, *What do you say to make a horse go backwards?*) Infs **OH**80, **OK**43, **MS**4, Pull (on *or* on the) lines; **AL**29, **GA**84, Just pull (on the) lines; **OK**43, Pull on lines and holler "back." **1966–68** *DARE* Tape **CA100,** We hooked the lines over the whipstock. *Ibid* **MI**10, He hands the lines to Ma. **1972** *NYT Article Letters* **cNY,** Harnesses included hames, belly-bands, cheek straps, spreaders (colored cellulloid rings on the reins, (pardon *me,* the "lines" not the reins)[)]. **1984** *MJLF* 10.152 **nME,** Lines. . . reins.

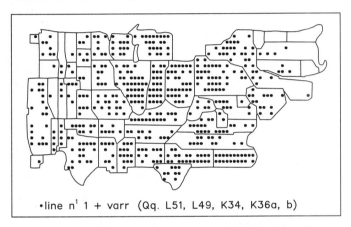

•line n¹ 1 + varr (Qq. L51, L49, K34, K36a, b)

2 A red-light district, skid row; an area of cheap housing.

1927 *DN* 5.454 [Underworld jargon], *Line. . .* The red light district. **1930** Irwin *Amer. Tramp* 121, *Line.*—A tenderloin or restricted district. In smaller cities and towns the disorderly resorts are situated on one or more streets, close together, and usually within one or two blocks. Going "down the line" is applied to the weekly or more frequent visits by the men who visit these resorts in search of "pleasure." **1965** Bancroft *Racy Madams* 5 **CO,** Uniformly throughout Colorado the old-timers speak of "The Row" or "The Line" when they mean the street where the parlor houses, cribs, variety halls, saloons, gambling houses and, in Denver, the opium dens congregated. **1966** *DARE* (Qu. II25, *Names or nicknames for the part of a town where the poorer people, special groups, or foreign groups live*) Inf **SC3**, Negroes: down on the lines—the nigger lines. **1992** Martone *Townships* 54 **cIN,** "Does your father work on the line?" Clark asked. "No," I said, insulted. Anyone knew that only women and hopeless losers worked the lines.

line n² [Pronc var of *loin*] Cf Pronc Intro 3.I.11

1815 Humphreys *Yankey in England* 106, *Lines,* loins. **1899** (1912) Green *VA Folk-Speech* 263, *Lines. . .* Loins. "I got such a pain across my lines that I can hardly stand up." **1931** (1991) Hughes–Hurston *Mule Bone* 50 **cFL** [Black], If she was mine, I'll be hen-fired if I wouldn't break her down in de lines (loins)—good as dat man is to her! **c1960** Wilson *Coll.* **csKY,** *Loin* is rarely [lɑɪn] among the uneducated.

line v See **line out 1**

line-back(ed) adj Cf **lobo stripe**

Of a horse or cow: having a stripe down the back; hence n *line back* an animal so marked.

1841 *New Engl. Farmer & Horticult. Reg.* 13 Jan 222, They say, neighbor B. that you was fool enough to give $50, in November, for that line-backed cow of yours. **1856** Holmes *Lena Rivers* 97 **MA,** Our old line back cow has got a calf. **1893** G.W. Curtis *Horses* 154 *(DA),* Kerry cattle are . . black, but this is only a fashionable point of the last 10 or 15 years; so that black and white—'line backs'—are still found. **1941** Writers' Program *Guide CO* 45, A "line-back" buckskin, it is said, is the toughest of all horses. **1947** Scobee *Old Ft. Davis* 77, Some longhorns, with all sorts of mixtures—red, black, spotted, lineback. **1949** Webber *Backwoods Teacher* 165 **Ozarks,** Aimin' to borry the cash money off 'n him to buy me that there team o' lineback mules o' Rash's. **1952** Dobie *Mustangs* 297, No buck was ever wilder, no buffalo bull fiercer, than the line-backed, mealy-nosed, "mustang" bull descended from the *ganado prieto* (black stock) introduced by Spaniards into California and Texas. *Ibid* 313 **TX** (as of 1939), He had around 250 head of dun and grullo horses, all line-backed. **1994** *DARE* File **seWI** [Heard at Old World Wisconsin Historical Site], [Interpreter:] Here we have pigs, those two red oxen over there, and a lineback cow. [Visitor:] Is it called lineback because it has a stripe down the middle of its back? [Interpreter:] Yes.

line ball n Cf **long ball**

A bat-and-ball game; see quots.

1983 *Wall St. Jrl.* (NY NY) 22 Aug 15/2, I played line ball in Chicago over 40 years ago. It was a popular game in our school yard; played with a 16-inch softball, slow pitch, and two or three-men teams. **1993** *NADS Letters* **Chicago IL** (as of c1950), He identifies line ball as a "Chicago game." It was and is a version of baseball, customized to be played in the streets, without full nine-player teams. It was most often played with 2 to 4 players, either on two teams or cut-throat. The only equipment was a bat and a 16-inch (circumference, not diameter) softball, as opposed to the regulation 12-inch softball that we generally think of. Gloves were not permitted. Lines were agreed upon, signifying hits or outs: Home run, Triple, Double, Single. . . There were no base-on-balls, and one strike made an out. . . With parked cars and apartment windows lining both sides of the playing field, bat control was very important. Only a ball hit straight back up the middle of the street/field could result in a hit.

line boat n Also *hook-and-line boat*

A boat used for fishing with a hook and line.

1911 *Century Dict. Suppl.,* Line-boat. . . A boat used for hand-line fishing in the sea. **1953** (1977) Hubbard *Shantyboat* 285 **Missip-Ohio Valleys,** The man who towed us in was a fisherman from the Yazoo River, and this was his "line boat," meaning that he had another, larger one for net fishing. **1986** Pederson *LAGS Concordance (Kind of boat . . you go fishing in)* 1 inf, **nwFL,** I started fishing with a hook-and-line boat.

line cabin n **AK**

See quot 1965.

1934 *Anchorage Daily Times* 17 Sept 3 (Tabbert *Dict. Alaskan Engl.*), I know of not a single trapper's cabin in our district where our good friend Mr. O'Connor is not more than welcome. At present my upper line cabin is the home of two miners. **1965** Bowen *Alaskan Dict.* 21, *Line cabin*—A small trapper's cabin used for overnight stops on a long trap line. A line cabin is often accompanied by a cache of rations for the trapper and his sled dogs. **1988** *Fairbanks Daily News–Miner* 17 Feb 17 (Tabbert *Dict. Alaskan Engl.*), With this latest addition we now have three line cabins and two tent camps to keep supplied.

line camp n **West** Cf **line house 1**

A cabin and livestock enclosure on the outskirts of a ranch, used esp by a **line rider;** see quots.

1888 *Century Illustr. Mag.* 35.667 **MT,** The men in the line camps lead a hard life. . . The camps are established along some line which it is proposed to make the boundary of the cattle's drift in a given direction. . . The camps are usually for two men each, and some fifteen or twenty miles apart. **1920** Hunter *Trail Drivers TX* 299, In a cattle outfit. . . Before the days of fences, line riding was following an imaginary line between two ranches and turning the cattle back. The "line rider" has charge of a "line camp." **1929** *AmSp* 5.55 **NE** [Cattle country talk], In the "old days" there were "line camps," far-off outpost cabins of cowboys working out from the ranch. These cowboys might be "line riders" . . men who look for "breaks" in fences and repair them. **1933** *AmSp* 8.1.30 **TX,** *Line-camp.* Permanent camp for *line-riders;* later, a camp for *fence-riders.* **1936** McCarthy *Lang. Mosshorn* np **West** [Range terms], *Line Camp.* . . A camp consisting of a cabin, barn and corral with a supply of hay for saddle horses. **1967** *DARE* Tape **TX5,** The saddle horse that the cowboy used was often penned up, and it was very handy to have extra hay at the ranch headquarters or in the line camp. **1981** *KS Qrly.* 13.2.68, *Line camp.* . . a parcel of private property usually surrounded by Federal grazing lands containing a bunkhouse (cabin), horse corral, and fenced area for cattle, usually with a nearby water supply; more properly, "cow camp," "buckaroo camp."

lineded adj Also *linded* Cf Intro "Language Changes" II.5, **-ed** suff **6**

Lined.

1883 (1971) Harris *Nights with Remus* 125 **GA** [Black], De sight er dat nice meat all lineded wid taller is nuff fer ter run a body 'stracted. **1972** *Atlanta Letters* **cGA,** Southernisms. . . Hung wid gold and linded wid diamonds thick as fish scales.

line ditch n Also *line furrow*

See quots.

1950 *PADS* 14.45 **SC,** *Line ditch.* . . A ditch marking a property line. **1994** *DARE* File **cwTN** (as of c1950), A "line ditch" marks a boundary between land properties, that is, not manmade. Sometimes the ditch was a natural boundary, that is, not manmade. Sometimes it was a "ditch" ploughed out to separate fields that had no natural boundaries but which had different owners. Sometimes . . the two owners would plough a "line furrow" to indicate the boundary. The furrow was less permanent than the ditch, lasting during only one growing season.

line fence n Cf **line road**

A fence located on a property line or boundary.

1845 J. Comly *Reader & Bk. Knowl.* 96 (*OEDS*), Always keep good line-fences. **1854** Hammond *Hills* 250 **neNY,** Later still, the old line fence was pulled away. **1859** in 1862 Colt *Went to KS* 256 **NY,** I hinted to you my intention of improving my little home by . . having my line fence made over. **1912** (1914) Sinclair *Flying U Ranch* 93, Andy . . loped along outside the line fence to a point opposite the sheep. **1937** Sandoz *Slogum* 6 **NE,** A tumbleweed, freed in a shift of wind from the line fence. **1939** (1973) FWP *Guide MT* 415, *Line fence*—Dividing fence between range outfits. **c1940** Eliason *Word Lists FL* 3 **nwFL,** *Line fence.* . . Fence between properties. **1966–67** *DARE* (Qu. L61, *Fences made of solid logs, now or in the past*) Inf **NC38,** Line fence; (Qu. L63, *Kinds of fences made with wire*) Inf **NY1,** Line fence—designates line of property; **TN7,** Line fence—between two properties; **MI67,** Line fence; (Qu. L65, . . *Kinds of fences*) Inf **SD5,** Line fence—marks boundary.

line furrow See **line ditch**

line gale See **line storm**

line horse n [**line** n[1] **1**] esp **Sth, S Midl**

=**near horse;** similarly n *line mule.*

1949 Kurath *Word Geog.* 41, In the Virginia Piedmont the near-horse is most commonly known as the *line horse.* **1966** Dakin *Dial. Vocab. Ohio R. Valley* 2.294, *Line horse* . . appears only once. **1967** *DARE* (Qu. K32b, *The horse on the left side in plowing or hauling*) Inf **LA8,** Line horse. **1967** Faries *Word Geog. MO* 96, *Near horse.* . . Other regional expressions . . known to a few of the informants: *line horse. Ibid* 145, 17 [out of 700 infs gave the response *line horse*]. **1971** Wood *Vocab. Change* 45 **Sth,** For the horse on the left side of a team the general word is *lead horse.* . . *Line horse, near horse, nigh horse,* and *saddle horse* are next. **1976** Sublette Co. Artist Guild *More Tales* 159 **cwWY** (as of c1900), The horse on the right in lead was the "Jockey Horse". There was an iron rod from the curb strap in his bridle bit to the hame ring of the line horse. Thereby the line horse would use such a "Jockey Bar" or "Jockey Stick" to jockey or push his teammate wherever he wanted him to go. **1986** Pederson *LAGS Concordance (Horse on left)* 1 inf, **cGA,** Line horse or saddle horse—in furrow; 1 inf, **cLA,** The line mule—one on left.

line house n [*line* boundary]

1 also *line shack:* See quot 1968. Cf **line camp**

1907 Mulford *Bar-20* 266 **TX,** Each ranch had one large ranch-house and numerous line-houses scattered along the boundaries. These latter, while intended as camps for the outriders, had been erected in the days . . when Apaches, Arapahoes, Sioux and even Cheyennes raided southward, and they had been constructed with the idea of defense paramount. **1968** Fulbright *Cow-Country Counselor* 90 **AZ,** A line shack is a small wooden cabin. It is used by a cowman, when riding the range and checking on his cattle, to stop in part of a day or even all night if he is caught in a storm. It contains all the necessary food and fuel to keep him and his cowboys comfortable during their stay.

2 also *line store:* See quots.

1909 *DN* 3.413 **nME,** *Line house.* . . A rum shop. *Line store.* . . A store standing on the boundary line of Maine and New Brunswick engaged in illicit liquor traffic. **1969** *DARE* (Qu. DD30, *Joking names for a place where liquor is [or was] sold and consumed illegally*) Inf **VT16,** Line house.

line mule See **line horse**

linen britches winter n Cf **linsey britches**

A period of cold weather in the spring.

1950 *Courier–Jrl.* (Louisville KY) 11 Dec sec 2 11/2, Linen britches winter comes after dogwood winter and blackberry winter. It also come [sic] after locust winter, magnolia winter, etc. It is a settled fact of barnyard science that we have winter in the spring every time there is a blooming of white blossoms. . . Every spring, when we think all the winters have come and gone, there is one more winter. That is what we call linen britches winter.

line out v phr

1 also *line*, rarely *line off*: =**deacon** v **1**; hence vbl n *lining (out)*. **chiefly Sth, S Midl** Cf **give out** v phr **1b**

1822 *MA Spy* (Worcester MA) 13 Feb [4/4], I was very sorry to observe that our custom of lining out the hymn as sung scarcely exists [on the Atlantic Coast]. **1834** in 1964 Sweet *Relig. Amer. Frontier* 4.393 **MI**, The 3 Resolution appended was That all preachers of this conf be instructed to line their Hymns in all our publick congregations. **1858** Hammett *Piney Woods Tavern* 225 **TX**, He . . concluded with a recitation of his ode, which was sung by the whole company *pleno ore* [=with hearty utterance], being *lined off* by the author. **1859** *Harper's New Mth. Mag.* 19.420, The old style [in Methodist churches] was a "brother" to "lead the singing," while the hymn was *lined* by the minster. **1899** (1912) Green *VA Folk-Speech* 263, *Line out* a hymn; to give out a hymn a line or two at a time to the singers. **1903** *DN* 2.319 seMO, *Line out.* . . To read hymns from the pulpit, one or two lines at a time, the congregation singing them after the preacher. This enables those to sing who have no books or who cannot read. **1906** Casey *Parson's Boys* 31 **sIL** (as of c1860), Following this reading he lined out a hymn. **1907** *DN* 3.232 nwAR, *Line out.* **1909** *DN* 3.346 eAL, wGA, *Line (out).* **1915** *DN* 4.185 swVA, *Line out.* **1920** Hunter *Trail Drivers TX* 77 (as of 1847), He [=the preacher] casts a searching glance over his audience . . and he commences in a sonorous voice to line out the hymn. **1942** (1971) Campbell *Cloud-Walking* 137 seKY, He lined it out, saying off a line to the congregation and then singing it with them when they caught the words. **1967** Jacobs *Rejoicing* 179 cIN (as of a1920s), A "professor" who had actually "lined out" the songs in pioneer schools was the director. **1970** *DARE* Tape OH91, We go to church, and at ten they line out a hymn, and we sing it. . . After the first hymn then another one will get up and line a hymn. **1978** Wolfe *I'm On My Journey Home* 6 **KY**, There are some obvious changes of meter and accent between Grandpa Isom's lining and the congregation's response, and in one case . . the congregation does not sing the same phrase Grandpa Isom lines out.

2 To reprimand, discipline, or punish; hence n *lining out* a scolding.

1927 *AmSp* 2.359 cwWV, *Line one out* . . to punish. "Your father will line you out when he comes home." **1945** Pickard–Buley *Midwest Pioneer* 50 (as of 1800), He regretted that he did not get more severely lined out, for early discipline saved many a man from a bad end. **1966** *DARE* Tape MA6, The third day he called me and he started givin' me a linin' out. **1969** *DARE* (Qu. II27, *If somebody gives you a very sharp scolding* . . *"I certainly got a _____ for that."*) Infs NY190, VT16, Lining out.

3 To arrange in a line; to guide in a particular direction; fig: to straighten out, organize.

1903 (1965) Adams *Log Cowboy* 296 **West**, They would have balked at this second channel . . we lined them out, however, and they breasted the current. **1924** [see **jughead 1**]. **1926** James *Smoky* 116 **West**, Covering territory felt mighty good to the little horse for a change and he wasn't caring much where the cowboy lined him out to. **1938** Stuart *Dark Hills* 284 neKY, My mind was in a muddle. If ever I could get lined out just right, I'd show them I wasn't a fake. **1966** *DARE* (Qu. JJ26, *If somebody has been doing poor work or not enough, the boss might say, "If he wants to keep his job he'd better _____."*) Inf MS6, Get lined out. **1969** *AmSp* 44.19 **Pacific NW** [Painter jargon], *Line out.* . . To size up the job; [to] unload only the equipment and materials needed for the job from the truck.

line rider n **West** Cf **fence rider 1, outrider**

One who patrols the boundary of a ranch to keep cattle from straying or to repair fencing; hence v phr *line ride*, vbl n *line riding*.

1880 (1883) U.S. Census Office *Rept. Ag.* 971 **TX**, The cattle-raisers were obliged to fence or to "line-ride" to keep their cattle from trespass-

ing. *Ibid* 973, The cattle of northwest Texas are in a large measure controlled or held on their ranges by a system of "line-riding." The cowboys engaged in this work are called "line-riders." **1920** Hunter *Trail Drivers TX* 298 (as of a1915), The "fence rider," also called the "line rider," is employed to ride fences and repair them. Before the days of fences, line riding was following an imaginary line between two ranches and turning the cattle back. The "line rider" has charge of a "line camp." **1929** [see **line camp**]. **1933** *AmSp* 8.1.30 **TX**, *Line-rider.* A cowboy who rode the imaginary line between two ranches and kept the cattle pushed back toward the ranch where they belonged. **1935** Sandoz *Jules* 83 wNE (as of 1880–1930), For several years the Newman and Hunter ranches hired line riders to turn the stock back from the hills. **1941** Dobie *Longhorns* 198 **TX** (as of 1884-85), Line riders patrolled the new Texas and Pacific Railroad—its right of way unfenced—to guard against the passing of cattle. **1956** Ker *Vocab. W. TX* 187, The *line rider* (5 [of 67 infs]) patrols the boundary and looks after the welfare of the cattle. The *line rider* leads a more interesting life than a *fence rider* but both are very lonely.

line road n Cf **section road**

A road built along a section line or other boundary.

1881 in 1882 MI Laws *Genl. Statutes* 1.389, Whenever a line road shall have been laid out. **1914** *DN* 4.109 cKS, *Line-road.* . . A road which follows a section line of U.S. government survey. **1948** *Clarke Co. Democrat* (Grove Hill AL) 19 Aug. 4/2 *(DA)*, [She] lives near the intersection of the Line Road and the Grove Hill-Monroeville highway.

line shack See **line house 1**

linesides n Also *lineside (bass)*, *line-sider* [See quots 1946, 1953] **esp Ozarks**

Usu the **largemouth bass** or the **spotted bass**, but also the **smallmouth bass**.

1927 *DN* 5.475 Ozarks, *Line-sider.* . . The large-mouthed black bass. Until recently this was the commonest term in the Ozarks, but now one often hears *bass* and *government-fish*—since many streams have been stocked by the state hatcheries. **1931** Randolph *Ozarks* 253, Whenever'n th' river gits good an' muddy like, them 'ar linesides lays in th' weeds. **1933** Williamson *Woods Colt* 225 Ozarks, A lineside bass that's worth takin'. **1935** Caine *Game Fish* 3, Large-mouthed Black Bass—*Micropterus salmoides.* . . Linesides. *Ibid* 7, Small-mouthed Black Bass—*Micropterus dolomieu.* . . Linesides. *Ibid* 9, Spotted Small-mouthed Black Bass—*Micropterus pseudoplites.* . . Linesides. **1946** Richmond *Times-Dispatch* (VA) 16 June 12B/1 *(Hench Coll.)*, When a largemouth bass grows big enough to be clearly seen, he will have a broad dark band along his sides which is so pronounced that the largemouth is often spoken of as "old linesides." **1953** Randolph–Wilson *Down in Holler* 261 Ozarks, *Line-side.* . . Either the largemouth black bass (*Micropterus salmoides*), or more likely the spotted black bass (*Micropterus punctulatus*), which often has a black stripe along its side.

line store See **line house 2**

line storm n Also *line gale* [*line* equator] **chiefly NEng**

Severe weather associated with the spring and autumn equinoxes; an equinoctial storm.

1836 *Knickerbocker* 7.17 **NEng**, That blamed line gale has kept me in bilboes such a dog's age. **1850** (1914) Kingsley *Diary* 115 **CT**, A fine day with a strong West wind rather think the line storm is over. **1874** VT State Bd. Ag. *Rept. for 1873–74* 2.730, It is well enough to look for a line storm, study the almanac, and watch the thermometer. **1915** (1916) Johnson *Highways New Engl.* 187, Sunday and a Monday it blew a living gale here. That was the line storm. We always get a specially heavy one about the time the sun crosses the equator. **1927** in 1931 McCorrison *Letters Fraternity* 146 **NEng**, Another cold windy day. When we have *no* line gale, it's an old saying, "It will blow all summer." **1942** ME Univ. *Studies* 56.57, The *line storm* or equinoctial gale is a heavy storm expected on the coast about the time of the autumnal equinox. **1950** *WELS* (Storms with thunder and lightning that come in March and September at the beginning of spring and fall) 1 Inf, cWI, Line storms. **1955** Taber *Stillmeadow Daybook* 132 swCT, The line storm, as we call it, usually comes in September. **1966** *DARE* Tape NH19, When you get a string of . . line storms. . . It's a very high tide, very rough, usually accompanied by northeast winds. . . They always last for three days. . . Why are they called a line storm? Because all the way down the coast it hits . . it can be very easily predicted because you can tell in a few hours when you see 'em; it goes right down the line. **1967–70** *DARE* (Qu. B17, *A destructive wind that blows straight*) Infs CT21, 25, RI12, Line storm; (Qu. B18, . . *Special kinds of wind*)

Inf **CT**10, Line storm—his mother called one big storm in the spring and fall each year; **MA**82, Line storm—lasts a week or so, northern wind in September; **MA**100, Line storm—hurricane that never grew up; September at autumnal equinox—equinoctial storm. **1988** Nickerson *Days to Remember* 136 **Cape Cod MA** (as of c1900), *Line storm*—Nowadays, every summer and fall the news media are trumpeting word of "hurricanes." Whatever happened to the old "line storms", which were as certain each year as the sun crossing the equator, north-bound in March and south-bound in September?

line tag n

A children's game: see quot.

1909 (1923) Bancroft *Games* 131, *Maze Tag* (Line Tag; Right Face) 15 to 100 players. . . All but two of the players stand in . . ranks, one behind the other, with ample space between each two players and each two ranks; all the players in each rank clasp hands in a long line. This will leave aisles between the ranks, and through these a runner and chaser make their way. . . One player . . stands aside, giving the command, "Right face!" or "Left face!" at his discretion. When one of these commands is heard, all of the players standing in the ranks drop hands, face in the direction indicated, and . . clasp hands with the players who are then their neighbors. . . This brings about a change of direction in the aisles, and . . necessitates a change of direction in the course of the two who are running.

line tree n¹

A tree serving as a boundary marker or located on a property line.

1743 in 1882 *Documents Colonial & Post-Revol. Hist. NJ* 6.161, Lett the Line Trees be markt with Your Notches on two Sides where the Line cutts them. **1832** *Louisville Directory* 107 *(DAE)*, The practice of blocking out the chops on the corner and line trees of surveys has been universally adopted. **1899** (1912) Green *VA Folk-Speech* 263, *Line-tree*. . . Certain trees standing on the boundaries between tracts of lands are *chopped* every few years, and kept to mark metes and bounds. They are chopped every three years by "possessioners," appointed by the court. **1917** Kephart *Camping & Woodcraft* 2.66, Starting from an established corner, all trees that stand directly on the line of survey have two chops or notches cut on each side of them, without any other marks whatever. These are called "sight trees" or "line trees" (sometimes "fore and aft trees"). **1948** [see **long forty**]. **1958** McCulloch *Woods Words* 107 **Pacific NW**, *Line tree*—A tree smack on a survey line. **1975** Gould *ME Lingo* 164, *Line tree*—A tree growing precisely on the common land line of two owners. When one owner cuts lumber and the other doesn't, the usual practice is to start at one corner and take every second *line tree* as it comes. But regrettable mistakes occur, and many a man has found that his neighbor cut off and left no *line trees* at all. You can go to law about it. **1976** Ryland *Richmond Co. VA* 373, *Line-tree*—boundary tree kept to mark lines between neighboring properties.

line tree n² Also sp *lein* [*OED* (at *lind*) c1510 →] *obs*

A **linden** (here: *Tilia americana*). Cf **lime tree**

1814 Pursh *Flora Americae* 2.362, This tree is known by the name of *Lime-* or *Line-tree; Basswood; Spoonwood*. **1897** Sudworth *Arborescent Flora* 302 **IN**, *Tilia americana*. . . Lein.

‡**line up** v phr Cf *DS* K70

1949 *AmSp* 24.111 **seGA**, *Line up*. . . To castrate.

ling n Cf **scaled ling**

1 A fish of the cod family, spec:

a =**burbot. chiefly Nth**

1857 [see **lawyer B4**]. **1882** U.S. Natl. Museum *Bulletin* 16.802, *L[ota] maculosa* . . Burbot; Lake Lawyer; Ling. **1884** Goode *Fisheries U.S.* 1.236, [The burbot] is known as the "Ling" in Lake Ontario (Professor Baird), lakes of Western New York (Baird and Blackford), and New York Market (Blackford). **1906** NJ State Museum *Annual Rept. for 1905* 417, *Lota maculosa*. . . Mud Blower. Ling. . . The only fresh-water representative of the family. **1943** Eddy–Surber *N. Fishes* 235, *Eastern Burbot* . . Lawyer, Ling. . . a large, dark-olive fish, thickly marbled and reticulated with blackish markings of a decidedly reptilian appearance. **1966–68** *DARE* (Qu. P1, . . *Kinds of freshwater fish . . caught around here . . good to eat*) Infs **MT**3, **ND**1, 9, Ling; (Qu. P3, *Freshwater fish that are not good to eat*) Inf **MN**29, Ling—a lizard or eel; **NY**1, Ling (Lake Champlain, good-sized); recipe for fixing ling: prepare on board, throw away fish and eat the board; **NY**110, Ling—old-fashioned. **1971** *WI Conserv. Bulletin* 36.6.23 **WI**, Burbot is more commonly referred to as eelpout, lawyer, or ling. **1978** *AK Fishing*

Guide 79, *Fresh-water Ling* . . , also called the lawyer, . . or burbot, is found in most Alaskan drainages. *Ibid* 80, The ling . . by any name . . isn't too attractive. **1991** Tabbert *Dict. Alaskan Engl.* 143, In present-day Alaskan usage ling (cod) as a name for the burbot occurs primarily in the Tanana River drainage and perhaps also in Southcentral.

b A **hake 2**, usu either *Urophycis chuss* or *U. tenuis*. **chiefly NEast**

1616 Smith *Descr. New Engl.* 29, [There are] Whales, Grampus, Porkpisces, . . Cole, Cusk, or small Ling, Shark. [*DARE* Ed: This quot may refer instead to the European ling *(Molva molva)*.] **1873** in 1878 Smithsonian Inst. *Misc. Coll.* 14.2.17, *Phycis chuss*. . . Squirrel hake *(Mass.)*; ling; chuss *(formerly at New York)*. **1887** Goode *Amer. Fishes* 360, Owing to their great similarity, *Phycis chuss* and *P. tenuis* are usually known . . by . . "Hake." . . In the Gulf of St. Lawrence and the Bay of Chaleur, and also south of Cape Cod, they are invariably called Ling. **1906** NJ State Museum *Annual Rept. for 1905* 419, The Hakes. . . *Phycis tenuis* . . Hake. Ling. . . *Phycis chuss* . . Ling. **1955** Zim–Shoemaker *Fishes* 74, *Lings and Hakes* are Cod-like fishes. . . The Squirrel or Red Hake (or Ling) is smaller . . averaging 1 to 3 lb., but is otherwise very similar to the White Hake. . . [The] Southern Hake, or Florida Ling [=*U. floridanus*], is still smaller. **1968–70** *DARE* (Qu. P2, . . *Kinds of saltwater fish caught around here . . good to eat*) Infs **NJ**39, **NY**36, 40, Ling; (Qu. P14, . . *Commercial fishing . . what do the fishermen go out after?*) Inf **NJ**67, Ling. **1971** Kieran *Nat. Hist. NYC* 83, If a Coney Island angler hauls in a fish that he calls a "Ling," it may be either the Common Hake *(Urophycis tenuis)* or the Squirrel Hake *(Urophycis chuss)*. . . The hakes or "lings" are cold weather visitors in our waters.

2 An **eelpout 1** (here: *Macrozoarces americanus*). **esp N Atl coast**

1839 MA Zool. & Bot. Surv. *Fishes Reptiles* 67, *Z. anguillaris*. . . The eel-shaped Blenny. . . is incorrectly called by our fishermen *"ling."* **1862** Acad. Nat. Sci. Philadelphia *Proc. for 1861* 45, *Zoarces anguillaris*. . . "Ling," "Conger Eel." **1884** Goode *Fisheries U.S.* 1.247, The Mutton-fish, *Zoarces anguillaris*, called Congo Eel and Ling, and also Lamper Eel, especially by the Maine fishermen, is often seen near the shore north of Cape Cod, and in winter especially is frequently taken with hook and line from the wharves. **1889** *Century Dict.* 1190, *Conger-eel*. . . Along the Atlantic coast of the United States, *Zoarces anguillaris*, a fish of the family *Zoarcidae* or *Lycodidae*. Also called *congo, lamper-eel, ling,* and *mutton-fish*.

3 =**cobia. Gulf States**

1882 U.S. Natl. Museum *Bulletin* 16.909, *Elacate canada* is known in Florida as "Sergeant-fish," from its lateral stripes; also, as "Snooks" and "Ling." **1888** Kingsley *Riverside Nat. Hist.* 3.212, In eastern Florida it [=*Elacate canada*] is called the sergeant-fish, and along the western coast of the peninsula it is known as the ling or snooks. **1933** LA Dept. of Conserv. *Fishes* 197, The Cobia, *Rachycentron canadus* . . , is invariably known in Louisiana as the Ling or Lemon Fish. . . Some of these names are completely misleading. The Cobia is not a Ling. The true Lings are members of the Cod family. **1946** LaMonte *N. Amer. Game Fishes* 44, Cobia. . . Names: . . Lemonfish, Ling. . . Common in summer on the Gulf coast. **1967** *DARE* (Qu. P2, . . *Kinds of saltwater fish caught around here . . good to eat*) Infs **AL**31, **TX**14, Ling; (Qu. P4, *Saltwater fish that are not good to eat*) Inf **TX**17, Ling. **1968** *DARE* FW Addit **sLA**, Ling—South Louisiana term for the same fish usually called *cobia* in books. **1986** Pederson *LAGS Concordance*, 1 inf, **swLA**, Ling; 1 inf, **ceTX**, Ling—fish.

4 =**lingcod 1.**

1882 U.S. Natl. Museum *Bulletin* 16.646, *O[phiodon] elongatus*. . . Cultus Cod; . . Ling. . . Pacific coast, Alaska to Santa Barbara. [**1884** Goode *Fisheries U.S.* 1.267, Cultus Cod *(Ophiodon elongatus* Girard*)*. . . About Puget Sound the English call it "Ling."] **1946** LaMonte *N. Amer. Game Fishes* 90, Pacific Cultus—*Ophiodon elongatus*—Names: Ling, Cultus Cod. **1973** Knight *Cook's Fish Guide* 383, Ling—Lingcod or see Hake or *(f[resh] w[ater])* Burbot.

lingberry See **lingonberry**

lingcod n

1 A large, greenish-fleshed food fish *(Ophiodon elongatus)* of the Pacific coast. Also called **blue cod 1, buffalo ~, codfish n¹, cultus cod, green ~ 2, greenling, leopard cod, ling 4, muttonfish 4, Scotchman, white cod**

1928 Pan-Pacific Research Inst. *Jrl.* 3.3.13, *Ophiodon elongatus*. . . Ling-cod. **1938** *Natl. Geogr. Mag.* Oct 481, The Ling, or Cultus Cod *(Ophiodon elongatus)* . . is confined in its wanderings to the northeastern Pacific Ocean, and bays from the Gulf of Alaska to San Diego, California. . . Probably the name "ling cod" was bestowed by European fishermen, who knew the ling of the North Sea. **1953** Roedel *Common Fishes CA* 139, *Lingcod*. . . A market fish of moderate importance. . . A leading Central California sport fish, it. . . [is] taken by sportsmen from boats or rocky shores with cut sardines or jigs. **1955** U.S. Arctic Info. Center *Gloss.* 50, Ling cod. A large, coarse, marine food fish, *Ophiodon elongatus*, occurring along the Pacific coast. Also called 'ling' and 'buffalo cod.' **1967–69** *DARE* (Qu. P2, . . *Kinds of saltwater fish caught around here . . good to eat*) Infs **CA**25, 65, 105, 109, 187, **OR**1, Lingcod; (Qu. P14, . . *Commercial fishing . . what do the fishermen go out after?*) Inf **CA**109, Lingcod. **1983** *Audubon Field Guide N. Amer. Fishes* 726, Lingcods feed on various large fishes, crustaceans, and mollusks. This . . is one of the most highly esteemed sport fishes, primarily because it makes excellent eating. It is also a valuable commercial species. **1989** Mickelson *Nat. Hist.* 31 **AK**, Rock greenling and lingcod are the dominant fishes of bull kelp beds along the outer coast of P[rince] W[illiam] S[ound].

2 =burbot.

1946 Dufresne *AK's Animals* 280, While the name most often applied to this fish in Alaska is Ling Cod *(Lota maculosa)*, it parades under many local terms such as lush, ling, lawyer, burbot, freshwater cusk and eel-pout. **1956** Harlan–Speaker *IA Fish* 157, Burbot. . . is also known locally as the ling cod, lawyer, and fresh-water cod. **1983** Becker *Fishes WI* 747, Burbot. . . Other common names: lawyer, lake lawyer, ling, ling cod. **1991** Tabbert *Dict. Alaskan Engl.* 143, Still another term for the burbot in Alaska is *ling* or *ling cod,* names which are used also for other, often quite diverse fish.

3 =greenling.

1955 U.S. Arctic Info. Center *Gloss.* 36, Greenling. . . Any of several . . food fishes of the family Hexagrammidae. . . Also called 'ling cod.' *Ibid* 50, Ling cod. . . a misnomer for the 'greenling.'

lingen See **lingin**

lingenberry See **lingonberry**

linger n |ˈlɪŋə(r)| Cf **lunker**

A large or excellent example of its kind.

1893 in 1899 Garland *Prairie Folks* 90, I'd rather have Sim Burns work for me one day than some men three. He's a linger. **1895** [see **lingin**]. **1899** Garland *Boy Life* 188 **nwIA** (as of c1870s), The men were full of admiration of the stack. "She's a linger, and no mistake."

linger v Freq with *on* [By weakening from std *linger* to remain alive although painfully or terminally ill]

To ail; to have a continuing illness.

1859 in 1955 Lee *Mormon Chron.* 1.225 **IL**, Aggathean Still lingering. This Eving I sent M.H. Darrow to Parowan for Dr. Meeks. **1917** *DN* 4.414 **IL, LA, wNC**, Linger on. . . To be ailing. "I 'low Mr. Brooks is takin' the fever. He's been a lingerin' on for two or three days." **1927** *AmSp* 2.359 **cwWV**, Lingerin' . . to be ailing. "I don't know what is the matter with me. I've just been lingerin' on for several days." **1954** Harder *Coll.* **cwTN**, Lingering on—Ailing.

ling finger See **lingman**

lingin adj |ˈlɪŋɪn| Also sp *lingen* Cf **linger** n

Great, remarkable.

1895 *DN* 1.390 **eCT, ME, eMA, VT**, Linger . . lingen, lingin . . pron. [ˈlɪŋə(r), ˈlɪŋɪn]: used to denote unusual size or quality. "Jim caught a lingin big pickerel yesterday." "Was it a big one?" "O yes, 'twas a linger."

lingister See **linguister**

lingman n Also *ling finger* [Varr of **ringman**, *ring finger*, appar influenced by the names of the other fingers] Cf **leeman**

The ring finger.

1946 *PADS* 6.13 **eNC** (as of 1900–10), Finger—little, ling, long, lick-pot, and thumb-ball. . . The little finger, ring finger, long finger, index finger, and thumb. . . Common among children. **1972** Jones–Hawes *Step it Down* 12 **eGA** [Black], John Davis . . told us the finger names he had learned when he was a boy on St. Simons Island: thumb, potlicker, longman, lingman, littleman.

lingonberry n [Sw *lingon*] Also *ling(en)berry* **chiefly AK**

A **mountain cranberry 1** (here: *Vaccinium vitis-idaea*); also the fruit of this plant.

1900 Lyons *Plant Names* 386, *V[accinium] Vitis-Idaea*. . . Ling-berry. . . *Fruit* acid, edible. **1952** Williams *AK Wildfl. Glimpses* 39, Mt.

Cranberry or Lignonberry [sic]. . . In Southeastern Alaska at least, it can often be found on drier hummocks in muskegs. **1959** Anderson *Flora AK* 372, Lingen Berry. Low evergreen subshrub, leaves thick, . . green and shining above. **1966** Heller *Wild Flowers AK* 34, Lingonberry. . . Fruit a small bright red acid-tasting berry. . . In mossy woods and bogs throughout most of Alaska. **1968** Hultén *Flora AK* 731, Lingonberry. . . The berry is edible and makes an excellent jam. A tasty beverage can also be prepared from the berries. **1972** Viereck–Little *AK Trees* 233, Mountain-cranberry. . . Other names: lingenberry, lingberry. . . The berries are abundant and usually picked in the fall after the first frost. . . Although sour, they have a better flavor than the commercial cranberry. **1989** Mickelson *Nat. Hist.* 185 **seAK**, V[accinium] vitis-idaea—lingonberry.

linguister n Pronc-spp *languister, leingister, ling(i)ster, link(i)ster* **chiefly sAppalachians** *old-fash* Cf **languager**

An interpreter; hence v *linkister* to interpret.

1645 (1908) Winthrop *Jrl.* 2.246, He, being linkister, (because he could speak the language . .). **1670** in 1897 SC Hist. Soc. *Coll.* 5.228, Thay left Captain Bayly in the Fryers hands and went away he being a person of verie good worth and a good linguister. **1713** in 1895 Sheldon *Hist. Deerfield* 1.350 **MA**, J Jmployed my Jndian Languister to talk to her. **1789** in 1924 Steele *Papers* 1.52 **NC**, Bennet Belew aplyed to sd. Forman for to assign him as linguister to bring about a liese or purchase of land from the Cherokee Indians. **1795** Dearborn *Columbian Grammar* 136, *List of Improprieties*. . . Linguister for Linguist. **1849** Lanman *Letters Alleghany Mts.* 97, [The preacher] wished to know if he should preach with the *'linguister,'* or interpreter, for the benefit of the young stranger. **1868** Goulding *Marooner's Is.* 65 **GA, FL**, Linkster . . is a word in common use in many parts, being a corruption of *linguister*, . . and means *interpreter*. **1896** *DN* 1.420 **swNC**, Linkister . . interpreter . . to interpret. "He's going to preach to the Injuns to-day, but who's going to linkister for him?" **1913** Kephart *Highlanders* 290 **sAppalachians**, In our county some Indians always appear at each term of court, and an interpreter must be engaged. He never goes by that name, but by the obsolete title linkister or linguister, by some lin-gis-ter. **c1920** in 1993 Farwell–Nicholas *Smoky Mt. Voices* 105 **sAppalachians**, Lingister. . . Also *leingister*. **1924** in 1952 Mathes *Tall Tales* 31 **sAppalachians**, Why, Mister, a linkster's a feller that can read writin' er understand talkin' in a furrin tongue—say like Injun er Dutch er somethin' thataway. **1944** *PADS* 2.46 **NC, VA**, Link(i)ster, lingster. . . An interpreter. **1974** Fink *Mountain Speech* 15 **wNC, eTN**, Linkster (linquister [sic]) . . interpreter.

lingum vite See **lignum vitae**

lining (out) vbl n See **line out 1**

lining out n See **line out 2**

link v [*OED link* v.² "*Sc.* and *north. dial.* . . To move nimbly, pass quickly along"]

1 with *in:* See quot.

1902 *DN* 2.238 **sIL**, Link in, v. phr. i. To devote one's energies to a work; to work as fast as possible.

2 with *down:* See quot.

1935 Davis *Honey* 168 **OR**, Link down offen that horse this minute.

link n Also *link cat* Also sp *lynk* [Back-formation from *lynx* understood as pl]

Usu a **lynx 1**, but also occas a **wildcat** (here: *Felis rufus*) or the **mountain lion**.

[**1873** Howells *Chance Acquaintance* 44 **Quebec Canada**, You say deer for deers, and link for lynx.] **1897** *Outing* 29.380 **MI**, A link is mighty curious an' is forever a-smellin', an' a-pryin' about. **1913** Johnson *Highways St. Lawrence to VA* 57 **seNY**, We have . . once in a while a link or a catamount. **1927** in 1944 *ADD* **WV**, Link-cat. **1930** Shoemaker *1300 Words* 39 **cPA Mts** (as of c1900), Link—The Canada lynx, or "deer wolf." **1965** *DARE* FW Addit **nME**, Link = lynx (occasional). **1966–69** *DARE* (Qu. P31, . . *Names or nicknames . . for the . . wildcat*) Inf **AK**1, Lynx—common term; "a link" the trappers say; **AK**9, Link; [**MN**16, Some people confuse [the bobcat] with the link;] **CA**156, **NM**10, Link cat; (Qu. P31, . . *Panther*) Inf **NV**8, Link—has tufted ears; a gray cat mainly here; **MN**16, Link—a stray once in a while; **MN**15, Link family; **VT**16, A Canadian link is larger than a bobcat but not really a panther. **1966–68** *DARE* Tape **MI**2, There is a link too, but a very odd one; **NC**53, He said he seen a link over there, said that's what they told him it was, a link, and it's a short-legged animal. They ain't none no more, but he said it was real big and long but had real short legs. **1969** *DARE* File **neWI**, Link = a lynx; used by an old man, third generation on Washington Island. **1977** McPhee *Coming Country* 288 **AK,** A "cat" is a lynx. A "lynk" is also a lynx. Nine times out of ten, people who say "lynk" are trying to sound like trappers. **1988** *Fairbanks Daily News–Miner* (AK) 3 Apr sec H 8, Another villager brings five marten and one "link" (Interior Alaska jargon for lynx).

link down See **link** v 2

link in See **link** v 1

link(i)ster See **linguister**

linkum vit(t)y See **lignum vitae**

linn n Also *linnwood* Also sp *lin*

1 also *linn tree;* also sp *lind, lynn:* =**linden.** [*OED linn* sb.² c1475 →; "Now *dial.*" Cf also *OED lind* "Obs."; it seems likely, however, that US examples of *lind* reflect infl (often purely orthographic) of *linden* on *linn* rather than a survival of the earlier *lind.*] **chiefly Midl** See Map
   1787 in 1793 *Amer. Acad. Arts & Sci. Memoirs* 2.158, Lynn, of three feet and a half diameter, a light white wood very proper for finishing the inside of dwelling houses. **1796** Morse *Amer. Universal Geog.* 1.538 **PA,** Elms, and linds are not here so stately as farther north. **1804** (1904) Clark *Orig. Jrls. Lewis & Clark Exped.* 1.54, The 2nd or high bottom of rich furtile Soile of the groth of Cotton, Walnut . . Lynn & Sycamore. **1860** Curtis *Cat. Plants NC* 78, Linn or lime trees. . . They are known in the Northern States by the names of *Lime Tree* and *White Wood,* but more generally by that of *Bass Wood. Ibid* 79, There are but 3 species of Linn in the United States, and all are found in North Carolina. **1872** (1876) Knight *Amer. Mech. Dict.* 1.668, In the West, linn-wood, sawed *through and through* the width of the log, . . is ripped into plastering-lath by the cutting-gage. **1892** *DN* 1.240 **cwMO,** Lin. A popular shortening of *linden* in Kansas City; also called *bass.* **1897** Sudworth *Arborescent Flora* 301, *Tilia americana.* . . Linn (Pa., Va., W. Va., Ala., La., Ill., Ind., Ohio, Mo., Iowa, Kans., Nebr., Wis., S. Dak.) *Ibid* 303, *Tilia heterophylla* . . Lin (Ind.) **1903** *DN* 2.319 **seMO,** Linn. . . Linden; basswood. *Ibid* 352 **swOH,** Lind. . . The linden. *Ibid* **neOH,** Lin-wood. . . The wood of the linden. **1905** *DN* 3.87 **nwAR,** Linn. . . Linden, basswood. . . *Linn-tree.* . . American linden, bass-wood. **1926** *WV Legislative Hdbk.* 508, "He calls yew pine spruce," was the old time criticism of the northerner. And "he calls linn basswood," was another complaint. **1938** Hench *Coll.* **cwVA,** They asked a native farmer what a certain tree was and his reply was "It's a lee-un tree." Lee-un is probably dialectal pronunciation of *lin*—another name for the linden tree. **1965–70** *DARE* (Qu. T13, . . *Names . . for these trees:* . . *linden*) 39 Infs, **chiefly Midl,** Lind; **IN**35, [lɪnt]; **KY**24, **TX**32, [lɪn]; **VA**27, Lind—white lind; **KY**34, **MO**5, **OH**44, **TN**1, 14, 22, Linn; **WV**2, White linn; **AL**38, **AR**51, **IN**32, 44, **OH**85, **PA**198, **WV**3, 7, Lindwood; **TN**1, Linnwood; [**OH**82, Linne [*DARE* Ed: appar a Ger dial form];] (Qu. T15, . . *Kinds of swamp trees*) Inf **AR**28, Lind; (Qu. T16, . . *Kinds of trees* . . *'special'*) Inf **VA**24, Lind; **NC**30, Linnwood. **1968** *DARE* Tape **OH**85, Some call 'em linn trees or linnwood trees, but linden tree is the right name. **1986** Pederson *LAGS Concordance,* 2 infs, **swAR, cwMS,** Linn tree; 1 inf, **cTN,** Linn wood—"lightweight wood"; 1 inf, **cnGA,** Linn wood tree—in swamp; plait chair bottoms.

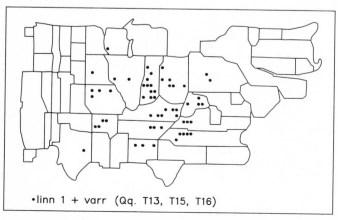

•linn 1 + varr (Qq. T13, T15, T16)

2 also *black linn, yellow linn:* A **magnolia 1** (here: *M. acuminata*). [Perh from the resemblance of the wood to that of **linn 1**]
   [**1843** Torrey *Flora NY* 1.28, *Magnolia acuminata.* . . The grain resembles that of Bass wood (*Tilia*), but it is more compact and takes a

finer polish.] **1893** *Jrl. Amer. Folkl.* 6.136 **WV,** *Magnolia acuminata,* yellow linn. **1897** Sudworth *Arborescent Flora* 196 **WV,** *Magnolia acuminata.* . . Black Lin. **1911** *Century Dict. Suppl.* (at *linn* n.²), Black linn, yellow linn, the cucumber-tree, *Magnolia acuminata.* **1968** *DARE* (Qu. T13, . . *Names . . for these trees:* . . *linden*) Inf **VA**27, Lind—yellow linn. **1986** Pederson *LAGS Concordance (Magnolia)* 1 inf, **seAR,** Linn wood.

3 as *lynn tree:* =**tulip tree.**
   1960 Vines *Trees SW* 280, *Liriodendron* . . *tulipifera.* . . Other vernacular names in use are Yellow-poplar, . . Lynn-tree.

linnet n [Appar from some resemblance to the European linnet (*Carduelis cannabina*) or its song]
1 =**pine siskin.**
   1805 (1904) Lewis *Orig. Jrls. Lewis & Clark Exped.* 2.130, I observed among them the brown thrush, Robbin, turtle dove linnit goaldfinch. **1946** Kopman *Wild Acres* 185 **LA,** A small finch, the pine siskin, or linnet, enters the lowlands and other country near the coast during or following the colder weather.

2 =**purple finch 1. NEng, esp MA**
   1832 Nuttall *Manual Ornith.* 1.531, They [=purple finches] are here [prob = **MA**] exposed in cages for sale at high prices (by the name of Linnets), and sing pretty commonly in confinement. **1862** NH Laws Statutes *Laws* 2609, If any person shall . . take, kill or destroy any of the birds called . . linnets, fly-catchers or warblers; . . he shall forfeit . . the sum of one dollar. **1895** Minot *Land-Birds New Engl.* 180 **MA,** When much startled, the "Linnets" usually fly for some distance at a considerable height. . . The "Linnets" are much more common and generally distributed through this State than formerly. **1925** (1928) Forbush *Birds MA* 3.10, Purple Finch. . . Red Linnet; Linnet. **1956** MA Audubon Soc. *Bulletin* 40.254, Purple Finch. . . Linnet (Mass. This term usually indicates a good songster.); Red Linnet (Mass., Conn., R.I. The fully-plumaged male has much pinkish red to crimson in its coloration.)

3 usu in comb *redpoll linnet;* also *lintie:* A **redpoll,** usu *Carduelis flammea.* **Nth**
   1839 Audubon *Synopsis Birds* 114, Linaria borealis. . . Mealy Redpoll Linnet. . . More common from Maine northward. . . Linaria minor. . . Lesser Redpoll Linnet. . . From Pennsylvania and New Jersey to Maine, in winter; inland, to Kentucky. . . Abundant. Migratory. **1879** in 1936 Roberts *MN Birds* 2.364, An immense flock of Redpoll Linnets was feeding in an old field grown up in weeds and grass. A Marsh Harrier appeared among them and in its attempts to catch one of the Linnets frightened the whole flock from the locality. **1895** Minot *Land-Birds New Engl.* 188, Red-poll Linnet. . . In the winter season only, being in some years very common and in others altogether absent, at least in Massachusetts. **1903** Dawson *Birds OH* 1.46, *Acanthis linaria.* . . Common Red-poll; Linnet; Lintie. . . When they do come they appear to materialize in great numbers out of the leaden sky along with the snowflakes. **1907** Anderson *Birds IA* 311, The Common Redpoll or Redpoll Linnet is a somewhat irregular but abundant winter visitor. **1946** Hausman *Eastern Birds* 581, *Common Redpoll.* . . Other Names . . Redpoll Linnet, Lintie.

4 also *California linnet, house ~:* =**house finch. West, esp CA**
   1883 *Harper's New Mth. Mag.* 67.707 **UT,** The sage-brush abounded in the nests of . . the linnet, pipit, and blackbird kinds. **1902** *Harper's Mth. Mag.* 104.490 **CA,** Linnets and goldfinches . . came to . . [the water] regularly every day. **1904** Wheelock *Birds CA* 481, The House Finch is popularly known throughout California as the Linnet, and is one bird for whom the residents have little praise. **1923** Dawson *Birds CA* 1.213, *California Linnet. Ibid* 214, The linnet is the bread-and-butter of the bird feast which life daily spreads before us. . . For my part, I confess without shame, that I am fond of the linnets. They may litter my porches and they may strip my vines if they like. **1940** Gabrielson *Birds OR* 539, The rollicking warble of the Common House Finch, or California Linnet, is constantly heard about the towns and farmsteads of eastern Oregon and also in the valleys of the Rogue and Umpqua Rivers in the western part of the State. **1964** Phillips *Birds AZ* 185, House Finch; Linnet—*Carpodacus mexicanus.* **1967–70** *DARE* (Qu. Q14) Inf **CA**120, Linnet; **CA**191, House linnet; (Qu. Q20, . . *Kinds of swallows and birds like them*) Inf **CA**6, Linnet; (Qu. Q21, . . *Kinds of sparrows*) Inf **CA**85, Linnets—small like a sparrow—has a little red on her head; **CA**212, Linnet—smaller than a sparrow; eats peaches and apricots; have red heads. **1994** Stone-Pratt *Hawai'i's Plants* 25, House finches or linnets . . are small . . , brown, thick-billed birds that are often seen around houses, farmlots, and open woods.

linn tree See **linn 1**

linnwood See **linn**

linsey britches n [Cf *linsey-woolsey*] Cf **linen britches winter, woollen breeches**

Prob a **waterleaf** such as *Hydrophyllum virginianum*.

1969 *DARE* (Qu. I28b, *Kinds of greens that are cooked*) Inf **KY**28, Linsey [lɪntsɪ] britches. [FW: =whitetop]

lint bells n

A **flax** n; see quots.

1929 Stemen–Myers *Spring Flora OK* 84, *Linum usitatissimum* . . Flax. Lint-bells. **1940** Clute *Amer. Plant Names* 122, *[Linum] usitatissimum*. Common Flax. Lint-bells, linseed, linn, flix [sic], lint. **1959** Carleton *Index Herb. Plants* 75, Lint bells: *Linum perenne*.

lint-catcher n Also *lint-getter, ~-strainer*

See quot.

1967–68 *DARE* (Qu. X34, *. . Names and nicknames for the navel*) Inf **OR**1, Lint-catcher; **PA**76, Lint-getter; **HI**8, Lint-strainer.

linter See **lean-to**

lint-getter See **lint-catcher**

linthead n Sth, S Midl *derog*

A cotton-mill worker; by ext: =**poor White**.

1933 Caldwell *God's Little Acre* 108 **GA**, I'd rather be a God-forsaken lint-head and live in a yellow company house. **1934** Carmer *Stars Fell on AL* xiii, Hill-billies and niggers, poor whites, and planters, Cajans and Lintheads are sometimes aware of the intangible net that encompasses them. **1940** McCullers *Lonely Hunter* 149 **Sth**, I would have just been a preacher or a linthead or a salesman. **1948** *Time* 31 May 18, The "lint-heads" in the Tennessee and Carolina mills . . were showing signs of kicking over the belts and bobbins. **1967** *DARE* (Qu. HH18, *Very insignificant or low-grade people*) Inf **SC**54, Linthead—textile worker, although generalized. **1986** Pederson *LAGS Concordance* (*Caucasian—neutral, jocular, and derogatory terms*) 1 inf, ceAL, Linthead— used years ago for textile workers; *(Poor whites)* 1 inf, seAL, Linthead. **1989** Flynt *Poor But Proud* 106 ceAL (as of 1900–30), But for many workers the larger community never let them forget they were "lint heads," no matter how many new commodes their mill had or what color uniforms they wore.

lintie See **linnet 3**

lint-strainer See **lint-catcher**

lion n *formerly widespread, now chiefly West*

=**mountain lion**.

c1613 in 1910 Smith *Travels & Wks.* 1.cvi **VA**, Ther be in this cuntry Lions, Beares, woulues [etc]. **1635** (1976) *Relation MD* 18, In the upper parts of the Countrey, there are Bufeloes, Elkes, Lions, . . and Deare. **1648** in 1832 MA Hist. Soc. *Coll.* 2d ser 9.120 **VA**, Beasts great and small as followeth; above twenty several kinds. 1. Lions. 2. Bears. 3. Leopard. 4. Elks. But all these four sorts are up in the higher parts of the country, on the hills and mountains, few to be seen in the lower parts. **1681** in 1879 MA Hist. Soc. *Coll.* 5th ser 6.16, Newes is brought of Mr. Deans son . . Killing a Lion with his Axe at Andover. **1840** MA Zool. & Bot. Surv. *Herb. Plants & Quadrupeds* 35, Felis concolor. . . The Puma, or American Lion. **1913** (1979) Barnes *Western Grazing* 330, There are places in the Rocky Mountain region where, due to the inroads of lions, it is almost impossible to raise horses on the open ranges, as the lions kill the young colts as fast as they are born. **1940** (1966) Writers' Program *Guide AZ* 432, He has been called catamount, American lion, cougar, puma, painter, and panther; but in Arizona he is simply lion. There are two varieties here, the Mexican cougar, which ranges throughout the state but avoids the open treeless valleys and mesas, and the Yuma lion. **1957** Barnes *Nat. Hist. Wasatch Summer* 42 **UT**, We are surprised to see a yearling mountain lion run from the creek. . . It is one of the rarest sights in nature—an unhunted lion in daylight and only a few yards away. **1967–70** *DARE* (Qu. P31, *. . Names or nicknames . . for the . . panther*) Infs **AZ**11, **CA**62, 72, 87, 211, **KY**53, **TX**10, Lion. **1968** *DARE* Tape **CA**87, He didn't want the lion to scratch the life out of that hound dog. **1991** *AZ Highways* Aug 23, Today game managers believe that lions and other killers are essential to the health of the deer herd in this place [=the Grand Canyon].

lion-heart See **lion's-heart**

lion-mouth See **lion's-mouth 1**

lion's beard n *chiefly West*

1 A **pasqueflower** (here: *Pulsatilla patens*); also the fruit of this plant. [See quot 1979] Cf **little dish mops**

1931 Clute *Common Plants* 104, *Anemone pulsatilla* is the lion's beard. **1932** Rydberg *Flora Prairies* 333, Pasque-flower, . . Lion's Beard (Fruit). **1976** Bailey–Bailey *Hortus Third* 76, *[Anemone] Nuttalliana*. . . Pasqueflower, . . lion's-beard. . . Alaska s. to Wash., Utah, Nebr. **1979** Spellenberg *Audubon Guide N. Amer. Wildflowers W. Region* 703, Lion's Beard (*Anemone patens*). . . A hairy plant. . . Fruit: seed-like base has a hairy style that in fruit becomes a silky plume.

2 The fruit of a **virgin's bower** such as *Clematis hirsutissima*. [See quot 1979] Cf **grandfather's beard 2**

1932 Rydberg *Flora Prairies* 335, Leather-flower, Old Man's Whiskers or Lion's Beard (Fruit). **1979** Spellenberg *Audubon Guide N. Amer. Wildflowers W. Region* 710, Another common name for this species [=*Clematis hirsutissima*], Lion's Beard, refers to the shaggy fruit head.

lion's foot n

=**rattlesnake root** (here: *Prenanthes* spp), esp *Prenanthes serpentaria*.

1814 Pursh *Flora Americae* 2.499, *Prenanthes*. . . *Serpentaria*. . . is known by the inhabitants [of Virginia and Carolina] under the name of *Lion's-foot*, and is in high esteem as a specific in curing the bite of the rattlesnake. **1830** Rafinesque *Med. Flora* 2.253, *Prenanthes*. . . *Lion's foot*. Many sp. . . Root and milk very bitter, used in dysentery and to cure snake bites in men and cattle in poultice. **1848** in 1850 Cooper *Rural Hours* 283 **NY**, These plants [=*Prenanthes* spp] are sometimes called lion's-foot, rattlesnake-root, &c., but the name of Bird-bell is the most pleasing. **1901** Lounsberry *S. Wild Flowers* 493, Lion's-foot. . . Tall, weedy-looking plants are these, and . . their . . drooping flower heads . . are quite without the charm of colour. **1941** Walker *Lookout 50 TN*, Wild ginger, . . lion's foot, . . and purple gerardia are abundant. **1968** Radford et al. *Manual Flora Carolinas* 1021, *P[renanthes] serpentaria*. . . Lion's foot. . . Leaves palmately 3–5 lobed or dissected or unlobed. **1979** Niering–Olmstead *Audubon Guide N. Amer. Wildflowers E. Region* 398, Lion's Foot (*P[renanthes] serpentaria*) . . has white bristles on its fruit and the stem lacks bloom.

lion's-heart n Also *lion-heart*

Usu =**false dragonhead 1**, but also a **dragonhead 1** (here: *Dracocephalum parviflorum*).

1789 Morse *Amer. Geog.* 415, Lyons hart . . is a sovereign remedy for the bite of a serpent. **1795** Winterbotham *Amer. U.S.* 3.200, [North Carolina] abounds with medicinal plants and roots; among others are . . lion's heart, which is a sovereign remedy for the bite of a serpent. **1847** Wood *Class-Book* 426, *P[hysostegia] Virginiana*. . . Lion's Heart. . . A beautiful plant, native in Penn., S. and W. States! **1900** Lyons *Plant Names* 287, *Physostegia* . . Lion's-heart. . . *P. Virginiana*. . . False Dragon-head, Obedient-plant, Lion's-heart. **1931** Clute *Common Plants* 104, In such a list, the king of beasts naturally comes first, and we find two related species known as lionhearts (*Dracocephalum parviflora* and *Physostegia Virginiana*). **1950** Stevens *ND Plants* 243, *Physostegia parviflora* [=*Dracocephalum p.*] . . is also called false dragonhead and lion's heart. **1961** Wills–Irwin *Flowers TX* 194, Lion-heart [=*Physostegia intermedia*] occurs in damp places from Lamar, Travis, and Gonzales counties east to the pine forests of extreme East Texas. **1968** Barkley *Plants KS* 298, Physostegia virginiana. . . Virginia Lions-heart. **1976** Bailey–Bailey *Hortus Third* 869, *Physostegia* . . False dragonhead, lion's-heart, obedience, obedient plant.

lion's mane n Also *lion's-mane jellyfish* [Prob < Sir Arthur Conan Doyle's "The Adventure of the Lion's Mane," 1926]

A common jellyfish (*Cyanea capillata*).

1979 McPhee *Giving Good Weight* 101, They once caught so many lion's-mane jellyfish they could not haul the net in. **1981** Meinkoth *Audubon Field Guide Seashore* 362, Lion's Mane (*Cyanea capillata*). . . This is the largest jellyfish in the world. **1989** Mickelson *Nat. Hist.* 45 **AK**, Lion's mane jellyfish often reach high densities in mid to late summer in shallow water and channels over sand flats.

lion's-mouth n [From the shape of the flower]

1 also *lion-mouth*: A **snapdragon**, usu the cultivar *Antirrhinum majus*. [*OED* 1706 →]

1773 *Hist. Brit. Dominions N. Amer.* 2.189 **LA**, The flower called lion's-mouth . . forms a sweet nosegay of itself, and is worthy the gardens of kings. **1892** *Jrl. Amer. Folkl.* 5.101 **OH**, *Antirrhinum majus*, lion-mouth. Mansfield. **1923** *Amer. Botanist* 29.61, So like the toad-flax in appearance as to be joint owner of some of the common names in [sic] the "snapdragon" (*Antirrhinum majus*). . . Other names for the plant are . . "lion's-" . . and "dragon's" mouth. **1959** Carleton *Index Herb. Plants* 75, Lion's mouth: Antirrhinum (v). **1973** Hitchcock–Cronquist *Flora Pacific NW* 415, Common snapdragon, lion's-mouth; occ escaped from cult[ivation].

2 =**butter-and-eggs 1.** [*EDD* 1878–86]

   1949 *WELS Suppl.* seWI, "Wild snapdragon" = sometimes called "lion's mouth." **1950** *WELS (Other names for . . wild snapdragon)* 1 Inf, ceWI, Lion's-mouth. **1969** *DARE* (Qu. S11, . . *Wild snapdragon*) Inf CA157, Lion's-mouth, dragon's-mouth; MI93, Lion's-mouth.

3 A **false dragonhead 1** (here: *Physostegia virginiana*).

   1959 Carleton *Index Herb. Plants* 75, *Lion's mouth* . . Linaria vulgaris; Physostegia virginiana.

lion's tongue n Cf **dragon's-tongue**
=**pipsissewa.**

   1942 *Hench Coll.* ceNC, Lion's tongue = pipsissewa. **1970** *Foxfire* Spring-Summer 75 nGA, All turkey hunters we talked to used a call of some sort to attract the bird. . . "Th'real old hunters uses what they call a lion's tongue. Cut's'em in half an' lets'em wilt an' puts'em in their mouth, and they just make a hen ashamed of itself." **1970** *NC Folkl.* 18.10, Leaves and stems of lion's tongue, packed in fruit jar with some water and then some whiskey poured over it, were used as spring tonic, a bitter concoction given three times daily. *Ibid* 28, Lions tongue was good for rheumatism.

lion's-tooth n [*OED* 1562 →]
=**dandelion 1.**

   1889 *Century Dict.* 3471, Lion's-tooth. . . the common dandelion. **1915** (1926) Armstrong–Thornber *Western Wild Flowers* 578, This plant [=dandelion] has many common names, such as Blow-ball, Monk's-head, Lion's-tooth, etc. **1935** (1943) Muenscher *Weeds* 521, *Taraxacum officinale* . . Dandelion, Lions-tooth, Blow-ball, Cankerwort. **1968** *DARE* (Qu. S11, . . *Dandelion*) Inf VT4, Lion's-tooth. [FW: Inf uncertain]

lip v, hence vbl n *lipping*

1 To place (snuff) between the lip and gums; hence n *lipper*. **chiefly Sth, S Midl** Cf **dip v 1**

   1938 Rawlings *Yearling* 59 nFL, Ma Forrester lipped a little snuff. **1940** Harris *Folk Plays* 88 NC, I'm a-goin' to have me a dip o' my snuff. I'm near 'bout perished. . . Where's my bresh? Well, 'tain't no matter, I can lip it. *Ibid* 293, *Lip it*, to place a small quantity of snuff between the lower lip and gums. **1951** Giles *Harbin's Ridge* 15 eKY, She just lipped her snuff and looked wise. **1966–67** *DARE* (Qu. DD3a, . . *A person who uses snuff*) Infs CA7, NC33, TX35, (Snuff) lipper; (Qu. DD3b, *How . . people take snuff*) Inf FL7, Lipping it. **1969** *TenneScene* (Union City TN) 2.11.2/1, If you are an old hand or just a curious youngster, try a pinch of snuff. Carl makes it a curiosity to try in his story about lipping and dipping.

2 also with *off*: To talk, usu volubly, esp in an abusive or argumentative fashion; hence n *lipper-off*.

   1943 Writers' Program NC *Bundle of Troubles* 24, Rabbits is the sassiest critters in the woods. I near bust my sides listenin' to they sassy lippin'. **1966–70** *DARE* (Qu. HH7b, *Someone who talks too much, or too loud: "He's always _____."*) Infs FL52, NY32, Lipping; MI10, OH42, Lipping off; (Qu. II36a, *Somebody who talks back or gives rude answers: "Did you ever see such a _____?"*) Inf NY123, Lipper-off; (Qu. KK13, . . *Arguing: "They stood there for an hour _____."*) Inf NJ70, Lipping. **1972** Claerbaut *Black Jargon* 71, *Lip off* . . to engage in backtalk; to verbally rebel. **1982** *Smithsonian Letters*, For the past five or six years I have secretly recorded some of the unusual phrases that continually pop up in my mother's conversation. She is seventy years old, grew up in Dodderidge County, W. Va. . . *Lip off* = to talk too much.

lip battle n

An argument; hence v phr *lip battle* to argue.

   1969 Emmons *Deep Rivers* 59 eTX [Black], His aunty, who should have been looking after him, stood at the fence "lip-battlin' with that gal next door." **1970** *DARE* (Qu. Y12a, *A fight between two people, mostly with words*) Inf FL48, Lip battle.

lip fern n [See quot 1900]

A small fern of the genus *Cheilanthes*. For other names of var spp see **fairy sword, lace fern**

1822 Eaton *Botany* 234, *Cheilanthes . . vestita* . . Lip fern. **1861** Wood *Class-Book* 819, *Cheilanthes* [spp] . . Lip Fern. **1900** Lyons *Plant Names* 94, *Cheilanthes* . . Lip-Fern. . . From Greek, "lip flower", alluding to the lipped indusium. Small rock-loving ferns. About 65 species; 21 in U.S. **1937** Stemen–Myers *OK Flora* 13, *Cheilanthes alabamensis* . . Alabama Lip-Fern. **1946** Tatnall *Flora DE* 3, Hairy Lip-fern. **1973** Hitchcock–Cronquist *Flora Pacific NW* 49, *Cheilanthes* . . Lip-fern.

lip off See **lip 2**

lipper See **lip 1**

lipper-off See **lip 2**

lippin v [Scots, nEngl dial *lippen*]

   1950 *PADS* 14.45 SC, Lippin. . . To trust, to have faith. "You don't have to understand, just lippin."

lipping See **lip**

lipping full adj phr [*SND* lip v. 3.(2) "To be full to the brim, or overflowing"]

Full to overflowing; brimful; hence n *lipping fulness*.

   1851 (1899) Reid *Scalp Hunters* 142, The first little rivulet that trickled forth from their lipping fulness would be the signal of their destruction. **1953** *Univ. Kansas City Rev.* Summer 286 (*Hench Coll.*) SC, Pa . . pumped water into the tin basin until it was lipping full. **1967–68** *DARE* (Qu. LL28, . . *Entirely full: "The box of apples was _____."*) Inf LA7, Lippin' full; SC59, Lippin' full—of a bucket full of water; over the lip of the bucket; WV1, Lippin' full—of liquids.

lippity-click adv phr Also *lippity-clip*, ~*-cut* [Varr of **lickety-split**]

   1909 *DN* 3.346 eAL, wGA, Lippity-click (clip). . . Rapidly: imitative of the sound. **1912** *DN* 3.582 wIN, Lippity-cut. . . Same as *lickety-cut*.

lippy adj [*lip* impudent talk] **esp Nth** Cf **flippy, lip 2**

Impudent, rude; talkative.

   1893 (1896) Post *Harvard Stories* 195 eMA, Ain't he getting pretty flip? The lippy dude! **1930** Shoemaker *1300 Words* 36 cPA Mts (as of c1900), Lippy—Talkative, pert, disrespectful. **1939** Aurand *Quaint Idioms* 25 [PaGer], Don't get so *lippy* (smart), or I'll *whack* you a swift one over your mouth; and I mean it, too! **1939** *AmSp* 14.91 eTN, Lippy. Extremely talkative. 'I'm tired of her being so lippy.' **1942** Berrey–Van den Bark *Amer. Slang* 189.5, Talkative. . . Lippy. *Ibid* 351.7, Impudent; Audacious. . . Lippy, sassy, saucy. **1965–70** *DARE* (Qu. HH7a, *Someone who talks too much, or too loud: "He's an awful _____."*) Inf MO27, Lippy; (Qu. II36a, *Somebody who talks back or gives rude answers: "Did you ever see such a _____?"*) Inf OH16, Lippy guy; (Qu. II36b, *Of somebody who talks back or gives rude answers . . "She certainly is _____!"*) Infs IA27, MI123, NY209, PA185, 242, RI17, Lippy.

liquidambar n Also *liquidambar tree, liquidamber*
=**sweet gum.**

   1748 in 1970 Kalm *Resejournal* 2.241 NJ, Af förenämda Peter Rambo fick iag veta, hvad namn som de svenska här boende hafva på en hop med träd, som til exempel: sweet gum eller liquidambar kalla de gyllenträd. [=From the aforementioned Peter Rambo I was able to learn what names the Swedes living here have for a lot of trees, for example: sweet gum or liquidambar they call "gyllen-träd."] **1785** Marshall *Arbustrum* 77, *Liquidambar Styraciflua*. Maple-leaved Liquidambar-Tree. . . They have a strong, sweet, glutinous substance, exuding through their pores in warm weather, rendering them clammy to the touch. **1803** Ellicott *Jrl.* 286, Sweet gum, (liquid-amber,) . . in great abundance in some parts of the Mississippi Territory. **1897** Sudworth *Arborescent Flora* 205, Sweet Gum. . . Common Names. . . Liquidamber (R.I., N.Y., Del., N.J., Pa., La., Tex., Ohio, Ill.) **1900** (1927) Keeler *Our Native Trees* 162, The starry five-pointed leaves of the Liquidambar suggest the Sugar Maple, and its fruit balls as they hang upon their long stems resemble those of the Buttonwood. **1939** Medsger *Edible Wild Plants* 227, The Sweet Gum, or Liquidambar, is a large forest tree found in damp woods on the coastal plain from Connecticut to Florida and Texas, north in the Mississippi valley to Missouri and Illinois. **1950** Peattie *Nat. Hist. Trees* 307, Sweet Gum—*Liquidambar Styraciflua* . . Other Names: Red or Star-leaved Gum. Gumtree. Liquidamber. Alligatorwood. **1967–68** *DARE* (Qu. T14, . . *Kinds of maples*) Inf CA20, Liquidambars—has maple-shaped leaf—imported; (Qu. T16, . . *Kinds of trees . . 'special'*) Infs CA53, 79, Liquidambar; CA42, Liquidambar—related to sycamore but goes straight up—only tree in southern California to turn red.

liquid lightning See **lightning** n[1]

liquor head n [**head** n C1c] **chiefly Sth**

A drunkard.

1944 *PADS* 2.35 **NC, SC, TN, VA,** *Liquorhead.* . . A habitual inebriate. . . Common. **1950** *PADS* 14.45 **SC,** *Liquor head.* . . A drunkard. **1952** Brown *NC Folkl.* 1.560, *Liquor-head.* . . A drunkard. **1956** McAtee *Some Dialect NC* 27, *Liquor-head.* . . Drunkard. **1965–70** *DARE* (Qu. DD12, . . *A person who drinks steadily or a great deal*) Infs **AL31, FL35, GA74, NY249, NC72, SC26, 58, 69,** Liquor head. **1986** Pederson *LAGS Concordance,* 1 inf, **ceLA,** Liquor heads.

liquorice, liquorish See **licorice**

lisa See **liza** n[2]

lisen, liss(e)n See **listen**

list n

1 A raised ridge or bed in a field. **chiefly Sth Cf middle**

1768 (1925) Washington *Diaries* 1.267 **VA,** Began to cross gd. at Muddy hole . . , having Run only a single furrow for a list. **1887** Amer. Philol. Assoc. *Trans. for 1886* 17.40 **SC,** List, 'a bed,' . . (of a cotton row). . . is common in South Carolina. **1899** (1912) Green *VA Folk-Speech* 263, *List.* . . A ridge of earth thrown up by a plough, as in cultivating corn. **1948** Wolfe *Farm Gloss.* 197, List—Small ridge formed by throwing two furrows together. **1966** *DARE* Tape **GA1,** Listing, that's making a small list.

2 A stripe, esp one around the body of an animal; hence adj *listed* striped or banded. **chiefly sAppalachians**

1805 (1904) Lewis *Orig. Jrls. Lewis & Clark Exped.* 2.151 **VA,** One other [bear] that we killed . . had a white stripe or list of about eleven inches wide entirely arround his body just behind the shoalders. **1899** (1912) Green *VA Folk-Speech* 263, *List.* . . A stripe of any kind, or streak. *Ibid* 264, *Listed.* . . Encircled by a list. A "listed-sow," a sow with a white list around her black body, or the reverse. **1917** *DN* 4.414 **wNC,** *Listed.* . . Striped. "That's a listed pig." **1941** (1944) Leisenring *Art of Tying* 16, By choosing a hackle with a blue or dun list and yellow tips you imitate both the wings and the legs. **1976** Garber *Mountain-ese* 54 **sAppalachians,** *Listed-hogs* . . hampshires—The listed hogs are the ones with the stripe around the shoulder.

list v

1 also with *up*: To throw (land) into **lists** n **1**; to make **lists** n **1** in a field; with *in*: to plow (weeds) into **lists** n **1**; hence vbl nouns *listing (in), listing up.* **chiefly Sth Cf lister 1**

1768 (1925) Washington *Diaries* 1.267 **VA,** Began plowing at Doeg for Corn—that is to list. **1770** *Ibid* 374, Finished listing Ground for Corn at Muddy hole. **1829** *S. Agriculturist* 2.444 **SE,** We seldom list in this growth [=hog fennel] earlier (for want of time) than January. *Ibid* 460 **cSC,** Two Freeborn . . Ploughs, would thus be able from the 1st September to the 1st November . . to plough *flush,* at least one hundred and eighty acres, or, if you prefer *listing* the vegetable matter *in,* (a furrow run for the purpose,) a much larger proportion of land. **1835** Ingraham *South-West* 2.281 **MS,** Several ploughs . . are kept constantly running . . in "listing up" corn and cotton ground. **1856** Olmsted *Journey Slave States* 432 **S Atl,** Boys and girls, "listing" an old corn-field with hoes. **1861** in 1877 Bartlett *Americanisms* 359 **SC,** The next step [in cotton culture] is the listing, done with the hoe, and making the beds where the alleys were at the previous raising of the crop, and the alleys being made where the beds were before. **1899** (1912) Green *VA Folk-Speech* 264, *Listing.* . . The throwing up of the soil into ridges. **1930** Woofter *Black Yeomanry* 30 **seSC,** At listing and hauling in preparation for planting. **1935** *Sun* (Baltimore MD) 5 Apr 3/1 (Hench Coll.) **KS,** Farmers were reported of the opinion it was impossible to list hard soil at 10 cents an acre—the Federal allowance—but willing to accept the money "as they were going to list their land for corn anyway." **1938** FWP *Guide SD* 85, *Listing:* plowing a field with trench-like furrows to conserve moisture. **1939** Griswold *Sea Is. Lady* 587 **csSC** (as of c1895), The height of the January plowing and February listing. **1966** *DARE* (Qu. L18, *Kinds of plows*) Inf **MS21,** Listing plow. **1966–70** *DARE* Tape **GA1,** [In cotton-growing:] Plow up your land, break it, tear it up good, and lay it off, list it, bed it. . . Listing, that's making a small list and then you get back out further and throw your dirt on up and make what they call a bed. *Ibid* **OK18,** [In wheat-growing:] Most of 'em used listers, at that time would list their ground. . . pull the ridges in and then harrow it. *Ibid* **TX5,** [In cotton-growing:] We list our land and throw it into ridges. *Ibid* **TX10,** The ground is listed and watered [for cotton]. *Ibid* **VA40,** [In tobacco-growing:] They . . lay the row off, and list it

up. **1986** Pederson *LAGS Concordance,* 1 inf, **cwGA,** List—do to soil before breaking up middle; 1 inf, **nwLA,** Listing—first plowing; 1 inf, **neTX,** Listing—with plow.

2 also with *in*: To plant (a crop, esp corn) between **lists** n **1,** esp by using a **lister 2;** hence vbl n *listing* planting in this way; ppl adj *listed* planted in this way. **chiefly Plains States**

1887 [see **lister 1**]. **1888** *Scientific Amer.* 12 May 298, A fender for cultivators has been patented. . . being designed more particularly for use on growing check-rowed and listed corn. **1924** *Amer. Botanist* 30.144, I believe it was somewhere in Nebraska that we first saw the practice of "listing" (planting in furrows), which is the usual one in southern Nebraska and in Kansas. **1929** Bell *Some Contrib. KS Vocab.* 239, *List.* . . To prepare ground for corn by plowing with an implement which turns a furrow both ways, the corn being dropped in the ditch between the furrows. . . This method of preparing and planting a corn field is typical of Kansas, for the deep furrow in which the grain is planted catches and holds the moisture. In Indiana, for instance, where there is more rainfall, it is not necessary to *list* in the corn. **1950** Reeves *Man from SD* 182, We examined the cornfield, where the listed rows waited patiently for a rain to sprout the corn. **1967–68** *DARE* (Qu. L22, *When talking about a crop he intends to plant . . a farmer might say, "This year, I'm going to _____ a crop of oats/corn/cotton, etc."*) Infs **CO12, 19, KS1, 12, 20,** List corn; (Qu. L23, . . *Machinery . . used . . in putting in the seed*) Inf **KS5,** Corn is all listed here.

listed adj See **list** n **2**

listed ppl adj See **list** v **2**

listen v Eye-dial *lisen, liss(e)n*

1 with *at*: To listen to (someone or something). **chiefly Sth, S Midl**

1884 *Anglia* 7.275 **Sth, S Midl** [Black], Lissen at de racket. **1893** *KS Univ. Qrly.* 1.140 **KS,** Listen at: listen to. **1899** (1912) Green *VA Folk-Speech* 264, Listen at the sound of the rain on the roof. **1902** *DN* 2.238 **sIL,** *Lissn at.* . . To listen to. **1904** *DN* 2.419 **nwAR,** I told my wife to listen at the music. **1909** *DN* 3.346 **eAL, wGA,** *Lis(t)en at.* . . "Listen at the mockin-bird." **1930** *DN* 6.84 **cSC,** *Listen at,* listen to. **1932** Randolph *Ozark Mt. Folks* 127, I want ever'body t' listen at me keerful so's thar won't be no mistakes made. **1944** *PADS* 2.46 **nwSC,** *Listen at.* . . To listen to. Common in some sections of the South, even among the educated. One professor of English from S.C. writes: "I use *listen at* regularly. In my dialect . . *listen at* implies less formal attention than *listen to.*" **1946** McCullers *Member* 81 **AL,** Listen at me! **1952** Brown *NC Folkl.* 1.560, *Listen at.* . . Listen *to.* Used in some places by educated as well as by the uneducated. **1962** Fox *Southern Fried* 37 **SC,** And some body would say, "Lord, listen at him." **1965–70** *DARE* FW Addit **seGA,** Listen at—"listen at that bird," "listen at him!"; **seKY,** Listen at—to understand what he says, "you have to listen at him careful"; **MS,** Listen at me—another way of saying "Listen to me." Used primarily by uneducated people; **cwNC,** Listen at—listen to. "Listen at me!"; **VA39,** Listen at someone, TV, radio, etc. Common. **1966–70** *DARE* Tape **MS68,** Oh, now listen at that; **TN16,** They just sat and listened at me. *Ibid* **VA38,** I stood there and listened at it. **1968** *DARE* (Qu. HH7a, *Someone who talks too much, or too loud: "He's an awful _____."*) Inf **GA19,** Listen at that bird run off at the mouth. **1976** Ryland *Richmond Co. VA* 373, Listen at. **1986** Pederson *LAGS Concordance,* 35 infs, **Gulf Region,** Listen at (him, it, me, that music, that rain, etc); 3 infs, **cnAR, cnGA,** Listened at (it, the preaching); 3 infs, **cAL, csLA, cwTN,** Listening at others (*or* that, what she said).

2 with *on*: See quot.

1907 *German Amer. Annals* 9.381 **sePA,** Listen on. Listen to. "Just listen on him!" . . fr. Pa. Ger[.] *ufharā* or *awharā;* Ger. *anhören.*

3 with *out*: To be alert to catch an expected sound; hence n *listen* a state of alertness or watchfulness.

1913 Johnson *Highways St. Lawrence to VA* 338, I must n't forget to kind o' keep a listen out for her team to come in the yard. **1973** *Patrick Coll.* **cAL,** Listen out—Please listen out for the phone.

listen at See **listen 1**

listener n [Cf *EDD* listener an ear]

A pig's ear.

1970 *Thompson Coll.* **AL** (as of 1920s) [Black], Listeners—pig ears—as sold in markets. **1972** *Atlanta Letters* **neGA,** Southern Colloquialisms from Georgia. . . Have you ever bought "listeners and whistlers" (pig ears and tails)?

listen on See **listen 2**

listen out v See **listen 3**

lister n, also attrib

1 also *lister plow:* A double-moldboard plow, a **middlebuster 1. chiefly Sth, S Midl** Cf **list** v **1**

1884 *Prairie Farmer* 16 Aug 521/4 **NE,** The "lister" is becoming more popular every year. **1887** *Scientific Amer.* 1 Jan 6 **KS,** When grain is planted by the so-called "combined lister and drill," the listing forms a ditch or furrow several inches deep, in which the seed is deposited. **1925** *Book of Rural Life* 3.1367, The almost universal practice in the South is to plant cotton on ridges or beds. . . In most cases these ridges are formed by means of an ordinary mold-board plow. . . An improvement on this practice would be the use of a double-mold-board plow, or lister. **1948** Wolfe *Farm Gloss.* 197, *Lister*—Double moldboard plow used for opening a deep furrow and throwing up ridges. **1965–70** *DARE* (Qu. L18, *Kinds of plows*) Inf **AR**4, Lister; **OK**27, Lister—for planting cotton—factory name; **OK**52, Lister—throwed both ways, used for cotton; **NM**13, Lister plow or double-shovel plow; (Qu. L20, *The implement used in a field after it's been plowed to break up the lumps*) Inf **VA**40, Lister—tobacco fields; (Qu. L25, *The implement used to clean out weeds and loosen the earth between rows of corn*) Inf **MO**38, Lister. **1966–70** *DARE* Tape **OK**18, [In wheat-growing:] Most of them used listers, at that time would list their ground. *Ibid* **TX**5, [In cotton-growing:] We list our land and throw it into ridges . . with the top of the lister ridge out of water. *Ibid* **VA**40, [In tobacco-growing:] They got the lister what they hook the tractor to and that put down the gas, put down the fertilizer, lay the row off, and list it up. **1986** Pederson *LAGS Concordance (Plow)* 1 inf, **neAR,** Lister or buster—two wings; 1 inf, **cMS,** A Blount's lister—of brand name and the plow.

2 also *lister drill* (or *planter*): A **lister 1** with a planting attachment. **chiefly Plains States** See Map Cf **list** v **2**

[**1887** see **1** above]. **1909** (1910) *WNID, Lister.* . . A double-moldboard plow which throws a deep furrow, and at the same time plants and covers grain, generally Indian corn, or maize, in the furrow. **1925** *Book of Rural Life* 7.4345, [Caption:] Planting corn with a three-row lister drill. **1950** Reeves *Man from SD* 171, The corn I planted did not come up. I had planted it carefully with a lister, a tool which deposited the kernel in a moisture-conserving ditch. **1965–70** *DARE* (Qu. L23, . . *Machinery . . used . . in putting in the seed*) Infs **IL**18, **KS**1, 12, 15, Lister—(for) corn; **CO**19, Lister—row crop; **CO**22, Lister—corn, planted in furrows; **KS**9, Lister—corn, milo, bean[s]; **KS**20, Lister—corn, feed [*DARE* Ed: =var sorghums]; **NM**10, **OK**33, Lister planter.

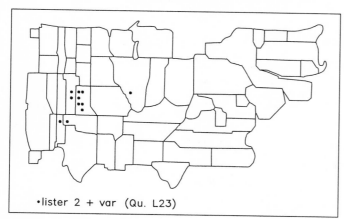

•lister 2 + var (Qu. L23)

lister plow See **lister 1**

list in, listing See **list** v **1, 2**

listing in, list(ing) up See **list** v **1**

Lit n [Abbr for *Lithuanian*] Cf **Lute** n² =**lugen.**

1964 *PADS* 42.40 **Chicago IL,** Of the nine informants with names for Lithuanians, . . one Irishman offer[ed] *Lit.* **1970** *DARE* (Qu. HH28, *Names and nicknames . . for people of foreign background*) Inf **PA**245, Lits—Lithuanians. **1995** *DARE* File **Chicago IL,** *Lit* is a fairly common term for a Lithuanian in the Chicago area. It's neutral when used by people of Lithuanian descent, but mildly derogatory when used by outsiders.

lit v See **let** A1

literary n Also *literary social* **chiefly Cent**
See quot 1916.

1897 in 1984 Gilmore *Ozark Baptizings* 28 **MO,** The young men of this place are trying to elevate themselves to a social political degree by coming out to the literary where they speak in a most distinguished manner. **1904** *DN* 2.419 **nwAR,** *Literary.* . . Literary society. "We organized a literary at the schoolhouse." **1916** *DN* 4.325 **KS, neOH,** *Literary.* . . A kind of literary society or club; a gathering of persons, esp. in rural districts at the schoolhouse, nearly always in winter, and in the evening, where a program is presented, such as reciting or declaiming poetry or prose selections, reading selections, engaging in dialogues (committed to memory); debating propositions, reading original papers, essays, etc. Sometimes contests in spelling are included and even burlesque trials. **1928** *AmSp* 4.130 **cnNE,** In many districts a "literary" is held every Friday night, when the "sandhillers" of the district recite and sing and debate. **1929** *AmSp* 5.72 **NE,** Some of the "ranch hands" may attend the "literary," generally a twice-a-month Friday night event held at the school house. Then they "recite pieces," sing songs, and debate, generally with more or less humor. **1935** Sandoz *Jules* 92 **wNE** (as of 1880–1930), Sometimes there was a dialogue at the literaries, painstakingly prepared and put on without scenery. **1949** Webber *Backwoods Teacher* 47 **Ozarks,** We bought some fancy round-wick lamps so we could have literaries and spellin' matches on Friday night. **1959** Lahey-Hogan *As I Remember It* 134 **swKS** (as of 1903), I had twenty-eight students, all joyful, rollicky youngsters. . . We had a literary on Friday nights and the whole countryside came. **1963** Ottoson *Land Use Policy* 59 **nwNE** (as of c1910), The women, particularly the young ones, brought some gaiety to the homestead regions with . . pie socials, square dances, play parties, literaries at the schools, and shivarees for the newlyweds. **1966–68** *DARE* (Qu. FF1, . . *A kind of group meeting called a 'social' or 'sociable'. . . [What goes on?]*) Inf **MI**4, Literary—there was a clubhouse, of which the men had daily use, for the men of the tannery; the "literary" was a once-a-month gathering for the families of the men as well: theatricals, boxing bouts, all amateur entertainment; **ID**5, Literary social—food, cultural program; [**CA**39, Literary society—got together and had readings; (Qu. FF16, . . *Local contests or celebrations*) Inf **TX**40, Literary program at school—recitations]. **1984** Gilmore *Ozark Baptizings* 51 **MO,** A successful program at one literary was likely to be copied and repeated by other groups.

literary school n [Cf *DAE* literary institution "A school, academy, or college. Often in grandiose use."]

A public school; see quots; hence n *literary teacher* a public school teacher.

1933 *AmSp* 8.1.50 **Ozarks,** *Literary school.* . . The ordinary public school, as distinguished from singin' school or Sunday school. A veteran singin'-teacher once told me: *Th' schools I taught warn't helt jest of a night—they run all day long, jest like a liter'ry school.* **1966** *PADS* 46.27 **cnAR,** *Literary teacher.* . . A public school teacher as distinguished from a singing school teacher or Sunday school teacher.—"Are you studying to be a literary teacher?" **1986** Pederson *LAGS Concordance,* 1 inf, **cwFL,** Literary school—after kindergarten.

literary social See **literary**

literary teacher See **literary school**

litered See **lightwood** n¹

litsy bitsy, littabitty See **little bitty**

litter n

1 Manure, often mixed with straw or other bedding material. [*OED* litter sb. 3.b "Bedding. . . For animals. In mod. use also, the straw and dung together."] **chiefly S Midl** See Map on p. 374 *euphem*

1899 (1912) Green *VA Folk-Speech* 264, *Litter.* . . Manure made by cattle or horses; droppings. *Stable-litter.* Loose straw or anything thrown into a farmyard for cattle to lie on and tread into manure. **c1960** *Wilson Coll.* **csKY,** *Litter.* . . Euphemism for barnyard manure. **1965–70** *DARE* (Qu. L17, . . *Names . . for manure used in the fields: [Also joking names]*) Infs **IN**30, **VA**3, 24, 43, 75, 95, Litter; **TN**7, 10, Litter—polite term; **KY**9, Litter—old-fashioned; **NC**54, Litter—around women sometimes; **KY**16, 68, Barn litter; **AL**2, Chicken litter—from brood houses . . sawdust and shavings, wheat straw, oat straw—where it got its name, "litter"; **TX**33, Chicken litter; **TN**53, Cow litter, horse litter. **1967** Fetterman *Stinking Creek* 50 **seKY,** Bargo . . loaded the sled with "barn litter," and began throwing the rotted manure and straw on his garden plot.

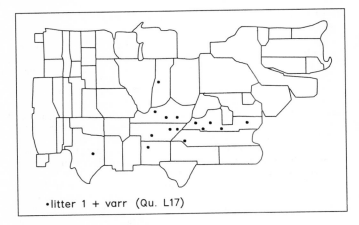

•litter 1 + varr (Qu. L17)

2 pronc-sp *letter:* A clutch (of eggs).
 1892 [see **litter-egg**]. **1903** *DN* 2.299 **Cape Cod MA** (as of a1857), *Litter.* . . In expression 'lay a litter out,' of hens. **1986** Pederson *LAGS Concordance (A setting hen)* 1 inf, **ceTX,** Done laid her litter out; 1 inf, **cAL,** A litter of eggs; 1 inf, **seGA,** Litters—batches of eggs laid by birds.

litter-egg n Pronc-sp *letter-egg* [**litter 2**]
 1892 *DN* 1.210 **NEng,** *Letter-egg:* a small egg, the last of the *letter* (litter).

little adj, n, v Pronc-spp *leetle, lettle, lil;* **sSC, GA coasts** among *Gullah speakers, lee(ly), li(lly)*

A Forms.
 1815 Humphreys *Yankey in England* 106, *Leetle,* little. **1850** in 1969 *AmSp* 44.304 **GA,** *Lettle.* **1861** Holmes *Venner* 2.178 **NEng,** Isn't it a leetle rash to give him the use of his hands? **1867** Allen *Slave Songs* xxxv **coastal SC,** He feel a lee better'n he been, ma'am. **1871** Eggleston *Hoosier Schoolmaster* 195 **sIN,** A leetle too much. **1884** *Anglia* 7.277 **Sth, S Midl** [Black], *Leetle mo'n* = a little more, and. . . **1888** Jones *Negro Myths* 46 **GA coast** [Gullah], A leely Gal bin a gwine home. **1908** Fox *Lonesome Pine* 54 **KY,** Oh, I knowed somethin'd happened an' I wanted to skeer 'em a leetle. **1909** *DN* 3.344 **eAL, wGA,** *Leetle.* . . A pronunciation of *little* with special and prolonged emphasis on the [i] sound to indicate a very small amount, etc.: used in this way by all classes. "Just a leetle (bit) more, please." **1922** Gonzales *Black Border* 310 **sSC, GA coasts** [Gullah glossary], *Leely, Lilly*—little, in size or quantity. **1923** *DN* 5.213 **swMO,** *Leetle.* **1927** Kennedy *Gritny* 15 **sLA** [Black], A cheap li'l thing like a few scat'ring vi'lets. **1931** (1991) Hughes–Hurston *Mule Bone* 49 **cFL** [Black], I don't want yo' lil ole measely turnip greens. **1935** Hurston *Mules & Men* 133 **FL,** It was Ole Man Boll-Weevil whippin' li' Willie Boll-Weevil. **1938** Rawlings *Yearling* 2 **nFL,** You hurted the leetle thing. **1942** Warnick *Garrett Co. MD* 1 **nwMD** (as of 1900-18), *Leetle.* **1960** Criswell *Resp. to PADS 20* **Ozarks,** *Little:* [litl]—pronunciation used years ago, obsolete except humorously. **1967–69** *DARE* (Qu. HH6, *Someone who is out of his mind*) Inf **GA19,** He's a leetle tetched; (Qu. LL1, *Something very small: "I only took a _____ one."*) Inf **CO4,** Leetle [litl]; **GA23, IN75, MA3, TX39, WI6,** Leetle. **1987** Jones-Jackson *When Roots Die* 145 **sSC coast** [Gullah], Know Mama de kill me / Bout the three li pear.

B As adj.
1 Younger, junior.
 1915 *DN* 4.185 **swVA,** *Little.* . . Junior. "I saw little Pat yesterday." Pat weighs 250 pounds, and has six children. His father, under normal size, is called Big Pat. **1939** *New Yorker* 13 May 36 **NC,** When Uncle Dockery was almost sixty, he and Aunt Dolly had a son. Aunt Dolly always referred to her husband as Old Man Dock, and their son came to be known as Little Dock. **1970** *DARE* (Qu. Z6, *Nicknames and affectionate words meaning 'sister'*) Inf **NC88,** Little Mary (Sue, etc), if mother is Mary or Sue. **1994** *DARE* File **neIL,** As long as my eponymous grandfather lived, my grandmother would distinguish between us, in cases of ambiguity, as "big George" and "little George," though as an adult I was several inches taller. *Ibid* **cOH** (as of 1960s), Because my grandmother and I had the same name, she was "big Mary Jo" and I was "little Mary Jo." *Ibid* **AL, GA, MO, MS, NY, TN, TX.**
2 See quot.
 1956 McAtee *Some Dialect NC* 27, *Little* . . slender. "I used to be little, but look at me now." "She has a nice, little figure."

C As noun.
1 in adv phrr *a little the* and varr: Used ironically with a superlative adj or adv; see quots. [*OED a little of the biggest* (at *little* sb. B.4.c) 1654] Cf *a few of the* (at **few, a** adv phr **2**)
 1835 Longstreet *GA Scenes* 21, I'm the boy . . perhaps a *leetle*—jist a *leetle* of the best man, at a horse swap, that ever trod shoe-leather. **1843** (1916) Hall *New Purchase* 116 **sIN,** That would be near about shootin a little bit the closest of any other chap, young or old. **1858** Hammett *Piney Woods Tavern* 131 **TX,** I'd like to know what kinder top-dressin' [=hair tonic] they put on; I'd make a fortin out on't a leetle the quickest. *Ibid* 290, The wool was pulled over their eyes a leetle the slickest, and no mistake. **1903** (1965) Adams *Log Cowboy* 76 **West,** When we returned from looking at the colt, we went into the parlor. Say, fellows, it was a little the nicest thing that ever I went against. **1986** Pederson *LAGS Concordance,* 1 inf, **swMS,** Little the baddest = a little bit worse.
2 in phrr *from little up* (or *on*), *from small on:* From child-hood. [Calque of Ger *von klein auf* (or *an*), PaGer *vun glee uff*] **Ger settlement areas, esp PA, WI**
 1914 *DN* 4.158 **PA,** *Little.* . . Childhood. "From little up," from childhood up. **1935** *AmSp* 10.167 **sePA,** From little up, I learned to avoid girls. **1950** *WELS (Speaking of a person who has always been the same way: "He's been a cheat from _____.")* 2 Infs **cw,csWI,** Little up; 1 Inf, **ceWI,** Little on. **1965–70** *DARE* (Qu. A24, . . *Someone who has always been the same way: "He's been hot-tempered from _____."*) Infs **WI**60, 71, Little on; **KS**18, **OH**91, **PA**5, 141, 146, Little up; **WI**10, Small on. **1966** *DARE* File **cWI,** We called them that from little on. **1968** *Helen Adolf Festschrift* 38 **sePA,** *From little up* (Pennsylvania German *vun glee uff*) for 'from the time that I was small or little'; for example, "From little up I hated that." **1979** *DARE* File **sWI** (as of 1940s), When I was growing up, both adults and children, given a bit of information which seemed obvious to them, scoffed and said, "I've known that from little on!" My own children continue to use the expression.

D As verb.
1 To make small or insignificant; to make narrow. Cf **big v 2**
 1931 *AmSp* 6.267 **KY,** Ole Uncle *littled* his eyes at me quarish. **1949** Guthrie *Way West* 173, This here country puts its mark on a man, and the mark is that he ain't sure who he is, being littled by the size of it.
2 with *along:* To maintain by small additions; see quot.
 1953 (1977) Hubbard *Shantyboat* 173 **Missip-Ohio Valleys,** Against the cold we bought a few bushels of coal since there was not enough wood around the house to burn. . . He spoke of "littling the fire along."

little Abner n [From the comic strip *Li'l Abner* by Al Capp, 1934–79]
1 A blunt or square-toed shoe.
 1947 Berrey–Van den Bark *Amer. Slang Suppl.* 13.7, Li'l Abners, rugged Rogers, *government-issue shoes.* **1968** *DARE* (Qu. W42b, . . *Nicknames for men's square-toed shoes*) Inf **GA59,** Li'l Abners.
‡**2** See quot.
 1950 *WELS (What names or nicknames do you have for large yellow turnips?)* 1 Inf, **csWI,** None except "little Abners."

little along See **little D2**

little barn See **little house**

little-bird orchid n
 =**three-birds orchid.**
 1948 Wherry *Wild Flower Guide* 35, *Little-bird Orchid.* . . Flowers few, suggesting, as the common name implies, tiny birds on the wing. **1979** Niering–Olmstead *Audubon Guide N. Amer. Wildflowers E. Region* 662, Little Bird Orchid (*Triphora trianthophora*). *Ibid* 663, As the common name implies, the flowers resemble a small bird in flight.

little bit, a adv phr
 In neg constrs: At all, whatsoever.
 1909 *DN* 3.400 **nwAR,** *Little bit.* . . At all. "He didn't like it a little bit." **1942** McAtee *Dial. Grant Co. IN* 40 (as of 1890s), *Little bit* . . at all; "I don't care a _____". ([Also in] Tenn.) **1956** McAtee *Some Dialect NC* 27, I don't care a little bit. **1975** Gould *ME Lingo* 164, *Little*—A rather nice variation occurs in Maine usage: "He hit his thumb with the hammer, and he didn't like it a little bit!"

little bitch See **little bitty**

Little Bits n

1970 *DARE* (Qu. Z6, *Nicknames and affectionate words meaning 'sister'*) Inf **NC**88, Little Bits [FW sugg; Inf has heard]; **VA**69, Lots of girls are called "Little Bits" or "Tootsie." [Both Infs and FW Black]

little bitty adj phr Also *littabitty, little bitsy, litsy bitsy;* rarely *little bitch* [Cf Intro "Language Changes" I.4]

Small, tiny.

1905 *DN* 3.87 **nwAR**, *Little bitsy, little bitty.* . . Little, tiny. . . Common. **1909** *DN* 3.346 **eAL, wGA**, *Little bitsy, little bitty.* . . Very small, 'little bit of a.' "She was a little bitsy thing then." **1923** (1946) Greer-Petrie *Angeline Steppin'* 33 **csKY**, A couple of women came along a-totin' two of the prettiest little, bitty dawgs. **1926** *DN* 5.394 **KS**, *Littlebitty, littabitty, littlebitsy,* adjective. The pronunciation is distinctly that of a single word. This nursery term appears incongruously in the serious speech of many adults, even adults of considerable education. "My mother's a littlebitty woman" (a college student). **1930** *VA Orly. Rev.* 6.247 **S Midl**, Backwoods speech abounds in pleonasms . . little bitty. **1940** in 1976 *Weevils in the Wheat* 338 **VA** [Black], She lef' two little bitty children, Shirley an' John. **1945** FWP *Lay My Burden Down* 61 **NC** (as of 1850s) [Black], Every evening at three 'clock Old Mistress would call all us litsy bitsy children in. **1954** *Harder Coll.* **cwTN**, *Little bitch (bitsy) (bitty) piece.* . . A very small, indefinite amount. **1955** Roberts *S. from Hell-fer-Sartin* 192 **seKY**, We children were only very small when this happened, but I can remember every little bitty detail. **1957** Byrd *Little Bitty Pretty One* [song title]. **1965–70** *DARE* (Qu. LL2, . . *Too small to be worth much: "I don't want that little _____ potato."*) 214 Infs, **widespread, but somewhat less freq NEng**, Bitty; **TX**19, Old bitty; (Qu. LL1, *Something very small: "I only took a _____ one."*) 88 Infs, **scattered, but chiefly Sth, S Midl**, Little bitty; **LA**17, **TN**26, Little old bitty; **CO**13, **KY**74, **LA**35, Little bitsy; (Qu. X21c, *If the eyes are very round*) Inf **AR**51, Little bitty small eyes. **1966–69** *DARE* Tape **AL**2, A little bitty fellow taught it that was crippled; **AR**50, They make hardwood floors, you know, little bitty narrow strips; **KY**9, When they hatch out, they're just little bitty; **TX**27, Just for a little bitty while; **TX**33, We lived in a little bitty country town. **1984** Burns *Cold Sassy* 20 **nGA** (as of 1906), When I was little bitty . . Cudn Doodle told me to lick a frozen wagon wheel and my tongue stuck to the ice. **1986** Pederson *LAGS Concordance,* 65 infs, **Gulf Region**, Little-bitty (baby, chickens, boy, bulb, church, fellow, girl, etc); 1 inf, **csTN**, Little-bitsy—very small; 1 inf, **cnLA**, Little-bitsy—of tomatoes; 1 inf, **neMS**, Little-bitsy boy.

little bitty old See **little old**

little black and white duck n

The male **bufflehead 2.**

1747 Edwards *Nat. Hist. Uncommon Birds* 2.100, Little Black and White Duck. **1917** (1923) *Birds Amer.* 1.140, *Buffle-head—Charitonetta albeola* . . *Other Names.*—Buffle-headed Duck . . Little Black and White Duck (male). **1944** Hausman *Amer. Birds* 512, Little Black and White Duck—see Buffle-head.

little black-headed gull n

A Bonaparte's gull *(Larus philadelphia).*

1874 NY Acad. Sci. *Annals Lyceum Nat. Hist.* 10.391, *C[hroicocephalus] Philadelphia* . . Bonaparte's Gull; Little Black-headed Gull.

little blue corporal See **little corporal**

little blue crane n Cf **blue crane**

1 =**little blue heron.** Cf **crane 2**

1913 Bailey *Birds VA* 45, *Florida caerulea.* . . Little Blue Heron. . . Little Blue Crane. **1916** *Times–Picayune* (New Orleans LA) 2 Apr mag sec 5, Little Blue Heron . . Little Blue "Crane." . . The first-year birds are white, with a tinge of blue on the foreheads and the tips of the wings. **1955** MA Audubon Soc. *Bulletin* 39.312, Little Blue Heron. . . Little Blue Crane . . (general).

2 =**sandhill crane** (here: *Grus canadensis*).

1923 U.S. Dept. Ag. *Misc. Circular* 13.39, *Megalornis canadensis.* . . *Vernacular Names.* . . *In local use.* . . Little blue crane (Nebr.) **1932** Bennitt *Check-list* 27 **MO**, *Grus canadensis canadensis.* . . Northern sandhill crane; little blue crane; small crane. . . Mostly in western Missouri.

little blue heron n Also *blue heron*

Std: a small heron *(Egretta caerulea)* native chiefly to the Atlantic and Gulf states. Also called **blue crane 1, crane 2, Indian hen 2c, levee walker, little blue crane 1, little white**

~ **2, powder touch, scoggin, shitepoke, spotted crane, white crane,** ~ **heron,** ~ **poke**

little bluestem n Also *little Indian bluestem* [See quot 1979] Cf **big bluestem**

A **beardgrass** (here: *Schizachyrium scoparium*) common from the Rocky Mountains eastward. Also called **big bluestem, bluejoint 3, bluestem 1, broomgrass, broom sedge, bunchgrass 3, Indian grass 1b, poverty** ~, **wire** ~, **wolf** ~

1911 *Century Dict. Suppl.* (at *blue-stem*), Little blue-stem, *Andropogon scoparius.* **1912** Baker *Book of Grasses* 53, This grass, sometimes known as Indian Grass or Little Blue-stem, is late in starting and the leaves, often tinged with red and bronze, are seldom noticeable until June. **1939** FWP *Guide KS* 11, Bluestem has the greatest forage value, and both species—big and little bluestem, also known as bluejoint turkeyfoot and prairie beardgrass—grow in almost all parts of the state. **1965** *DARE* (Qu. L9a, . . *Kinds of grass . . grown for hay*) Inf **OK**1, Little Injun bluestem—shorter and finer than bluestem. **1966** *Badgerland* (Stoughton WI) 15 Oct 6/2, Prairie grasses (big bluestem, little bluestem, and Indian grass) change color in the fall just as do the shrubs and trees. **1979** Niering–Olmstead *Audubon Guide N. Amer. Wildflowers E. Region* 685, Little Bluestem Grass. . . gets its name from the bluish color of the stem bases in the spring, but most striking is the plant's reddish-tan color in fall, persisting through winter snows. **1989** Frazier *Gt. Plains* 160 **seWY**, This is little bluestem. Cattle don't eat that so much.

little boy's breeches n Also *boy's britches, little boy britches,* ~ *plant* [From the shape of the flower]

=**Dutchman's breeches 1.**

1893 *Jrl. Amer. Folkl.* 6.137 **cIA**, *Dicentra cucullaria,* little boy's breeches. **1910** Graves *Flowering Plants* 198 **CT**, *Dicentra Cucullaria.* . . Little-boy's-Breeches. **1964** Campbell et al. *Gt. Smoky Wildflowers* 20, Dutchman's-Breeches—*Dicentra cucullata.* . . Because of the extended "trouser legs," it is sometimes called Little Boy Plant. **1967** *DARE* (Qu. S2, . . *The flower that comes up in the woods early in spring, with three white petals that turn pink as the flower grows older*) Inf **IL**14, Little boy's britches; (Qu. S3, *A flower like a large violet*) Inf **MO**18, Boy's britches; (Qu. S26c, *Wildflowers that grow in woods*) Inf **IL**14, Little boy britches; (Qu. S26e, *Other wildflowers not yet mentioned;* not asked in early QRs) Inf **IL**83, Boy's britches—look like little pants.

little breeches n Also *little britches*

A child.

1856 Kelly *Humors* 280, We boys didn't like him no how, . . because his pride made it imperiously necessary that some of the "little breeches" should do small chores . . which might otherwise devolve upon himself. **1903** *DN* 2.299 **Cape Cod MA** (as of a1857), *Little breeches.* . . Epithet of a small boy. **1967** *Tyler Co. Booster* (Woodville TX) 10 Aug 1/5, A Little Britches Rodeo, for children 15 years of age and under, will be held at the Tyler County Roping Club Arena Saturday night. **1968** *DARE* (Qu. FF16, . . *Local contests or celebrations*) Inf **KS**13, Little britches rodeo.

little brown crane n

A **sandhill crane,** usu the western subsp *Grus canadensis canadensis.*

1886 Turner *Contribs. AK* 145, The Little Brown Crane is one of the earliest arrivals . . , it being in advance of the Geese and nearly contemporary with the Swan. **1891** Goss *Hist. Birds KS* 133, *Grus canadensis.* . . Little Brown Crane. . . Migratory; not uncommon. **1898** (1900) Davie *Nests N. Amer. Birds* 121, The Little Brown Crane is almost exactly like the next species [=*Grus canadensis tabida*], but smaller. **1926** *Auk* 43.303 **AK**, Little Brown Crane.—On May 7 . . several were heard calling. . . From that time on they were common. **1948** Bailey *Birds Arctic AK* 194, *Grus canadensis canadensis.* The migration of the Little Brown Cranes is one of the first signs of spring. **1961** Ligon *NM Birds* 106, The Little Brown Crane, presumably a subspecies, occurs in far greater numbers than the true Sandhill. The two are so similar that it is difficult for the average observer to tell them apart. **1982** Elman *Hunter's Field Guide* 310, Although game regulations and hunters often refer to the subspecies [=*Grus canadensis canadensis*] by the name "little brown crane," only juveniles are predominately brownish.

little brown duck n Cf **little black and white duck**

The female **bufflehead 2.**

1731 Catesby *Nat. Hist. Carolina* 1.98, The little brown Duck . . the Body and Wings are dark brown. . . This was a Female. The Male was pyed black and white. **1917** (1923) *Birds Amer.* 1.140, Buffle-head—*Charitonetta albeola* . . *Other Names.*—Buffle-headed Duck . . Little Brown Duck (female). **1944** Hausman *Amer. Birds* 512, Little Brown Duck (female)—see Buffle-head.

little brown house See **little house**

little brown jug n Cf **jug** n 1
=**wild ginger;** also its flower.
1964 Campbell et al. *Gt. Smoky Wildflowers* 36, *Little Brown Jug. Asarum arifolium.* . . Its arrow-shaped leaves and fleshy jug-shaped calyx—a flower without petals—give this plant a unique appeal. **1969** *Foxfire* Winter 23 **nGA,** They got th'little heart leaves from th'woods where we find th'little brown jugs in th'spring [ginger].

little brown shack See **little house**

Little Buffalo medicine n
=**wood anemone.**
1958 Jacobs–Burlage *Index Plants NC* 175, *Anemone quinquefolia.* . . Little Buffalo medicine. . . The flowers are said to be . . poisonous to cattle, producing bloody urine and convulsions.

little, by a See **by the littles**

little caille n
=**hermit thrush 1.**
1916 *Times–Picayune* (New Orleans LA) 30 Apr mag sec 5/8, *Hermit thrush.* . . Little Caille; Caille Petite; Half Caille.—This little brown-backed thrush with the spotted breast is a common wintering bird throughout the state.

little cane n
=**maiden cane.**
1942 *Torreya* 42.157 **LA,** *Panicum hemitomon.* . . Little cane, canouche.

little captain n
=**dandelion 1.**
1967 *DARE* (Qu. S11, . . *Dandelion*) Inf **MI**67, Little captain—heard it called that when I was a child.

little chief hare n Also *chief hare* [*W3* "trans. of Chipewyan *bucka-thrae-gga-yaze*"]
=**pika.**
1829 Richardson *Fauna Boreali-Amer.* 1.227 **Rocky Mts,** The Little-Chief Hare resembles the pika (Lagomys alpinus). **1868** *Proc. Calif. Acad. Sci.* IV.6 (DA), Lagomys princeps Richardson—'Little Chief Hare;' Rat-rabbit. **1875** *Amer. Naturalist* 9.150, They stretch clear away to the Rocky Mountains . . ; but a day's march . . from the rocky haunts of the little chief hare (*Lagomys princeps*). **1917** Anthony *Mammals Amer.* 271, *Ochotona princeps.* . . Little Chief Hare. . . A small rodent lacking a tail and having somewhat the appearance of a diminutive rabbit. *Ibid* 272, It [=the pika] is also called Chief Hare [etc]. **1937** U.S. Forest Serv. *Range Plant Hdbk.* W127, This plant [=*Mertensia ciliata*] is a favorite of the rockrabbit, known as . . little chief hare or cony (*Ochotona princeps*). **1946** Dufresne *AK's Animals* 124, The pika, little chief hare, or "squeaker," is commonly found among the rock slides of the Alaska Range. **1949** Palmer *Nat. Hist.* 619, Pika, Cony, Little Chief Hare. . . Allied to rabbits, although they may look like rats.

little Chihuahua See **Chihuahua town**

Little Christmas n
=**Old Christmas.**
1922 (1926) Cady *Rhymes VT* 183, He knows when Little Christmas comes,/ And when it's time for grafting. **1932** *Sun* (Baltimore MD) 2 Jan 4/2 *(Hench Coll.),* Twelfth Night . . throughout many sections of the Delmarva Peninsula . . is known as Old Christmas or Little Christmas. **1969** *DARE* (Qu. FF11, . . *The night of December 31st*) Inf **CT**35, Little Christmas—no, that's the 6th of January, the Epiphany.

little corporal n Also *(little) blue corporal, little corporal hawk* [With reference to Napoleon, the "*Little Corporal,*" prob from its small size and pugnacity]
=**pigeon hawk.**
1832 Nuttall *Manual Ornith.* 1.61, Little Corporal Hawk. (*Falco temerarius* . .). **1874** Coues *Birds NW* 346, I have little to add to the published accounts of this elegant and spirited Hawk [=the pigeon hawk], aptly styled "The Little Corporal." **1914** Eaton *Birds NY* 2.102,

The Pigeon hawk, Bullet hawk, or Little blue corporal is a fairly common migrant through New York State. **1928** Bailey *Birds NM* 192, The "intrepid" little Blue Corporal or Bullet Hawk, as the Pigeon Hawk is locally known, frequents the edges of woods and shores of large bodies of water, where it preys upon birds up to its own size and sometimes larger. **1955** Forbush–May *Birds* 129, Eastern Pigeon Hawk. . . Blue Bullet; American Merlin, Little Corporal.

little crane n
1 =**green heron.**
1913 Bailey *Birds VA* 47, *Butorides virescens.* . . Scow. Fly-Up-the-Creek. Little Crane. Scout.
2 =**black-crowned night heron.**
1955 MA Audubon Soc. *Bulletin* 39.312, Black-Crowned Night Heron . . Little Crane (Maine. Herons are often miscalled cranes; "Little" by contrast to the Great Blue.)

little curlew n
=**Eskimo curlew.**
1844 DeKay *Zool. NY* 2.234, The Small Esquimaux Curlew. *Numenius Borealis.* . . This species, which is known to our sportsmen under the names of *Little Curlew, Futes,* and *Dough-bird,* is much esteemed by epicures. **1880** *Forest & Stream* 15.4, Esquimaux curlew (*Numenius borealis*). . . is called . . in parts of the South the little curlew. **1923** U.S. Dept. Ag. *Misc. Circular* 13.67, Eskimo Curlew. . . little curlew. **1963** Gromme *Birds WI* 214, Curlew, . . Little (Eskimo Curlew).

little dish mops n
The seed head of a **pasqueflower** (here: *Pulsatilla occidentalis*).
1949 Peattie *Cascades* 254 **Pacific NW,** A few people call them [=*Anemone occidentalis*] pasqueflowers and more than a few call the seed heads little dish mops.

little diver n Also *little white diver* Cf **diver**
Either the **horned grebe** or the **pied-billed grebe.**
1899 Howe–Sturtevant *Birds RI* 25, *Columbus auritus* . . Horned Grebe. Hell-diver, Little Diver. **1925** (1928) Forbush *Birds MA* 1.11, *Pied-billed Grebe.* . . didapper; hell-diver; little diver. **1932** Howell *FL Bird Life* 75, Horned Grebe: *Columbus auritus* . . Other Names: Hell Diver; Little White Diver. **1936** Roberts *MN Birds* 1.158, Pied-billed Grebe. . . Thick-billed Grebe or Chicken-billed Grebe, Little Diver.

little dove n
=**ground dove.**
1946 Hausman *Eastern Birds* 344, Eastern Ground Dove—*Columbigallina passerina passerina* . . Other Names . . Moaning Dove . . Little Dove.

Little Easter n Cf **Little Christmas**
1968 *DARE* FW Addit **cwVA,** Little Easter—Whitsunday, old-fashioned.

little egret See **little white egret**

little elephants n Also *little elephant*
An **elephant's head** (here: *Pedicularis groenlandica*).
1934 (1943) *W2,* Little elephant. Elephants'-heads. *Western, U.S.* **1937** U.S. Forest Serv. *Range Plant Hdbk.* W143, Elephanthead, also called . . little . . elephant, is. . . a conspicuous plant in wet meadows and grasslands. **1949** Moldenke *Amer. Wild Flowers* 282, No one who has visited the Yellowstone or Grand Teton National Parks will soon forget the fields of little-elephants there. **1959** Anderson *Flora AK* 425, *Pedicularis groenlandica.* . . The Little Elephants has been reported from Alaska. **1967** *DARE* FW Addit **CO**7, Little elephant grows with rattlesnake plantain.

little end of nothing n For varr see quots
Something very small or insignificant.
1825 Neal *Brother Jonathan* 1.145 **CT,** Not bigger . . than the leetle eend—o' nothin'—sharpened; as the Irishman said. **1853** Simms *Sword & Distaff* 349 **SC,** I'll knock you into the leetle eend of a sarcumstance ef you don't let go. **1865** Crockett *Life* 380, Finally they were whittled down to the little end of nothing in the distance. **1919** *DN* 5.73 **CA,** *Whittled down to a point, little end of nothing,* said of an insignificant person. "That preacher is the little end of nothing whittled down to a point." **1923** *DN* 5.238 **swWI,** Little end of nothing. . . A derogatory intensive. "Why, he don't amount to the little end o' nothin' whittle [sic] off to a point an' the point cut off!" **1953** Randolph–Wilson *Down in Holler* 192 **Ozarks,** As for that man Hoover, . . I think he's *the little end of nothin'.* . . That there *thing* . . is smaller than the little end of

nothin', *whittled down to a p'int.* **1967** *DARE* (Qu. HH20a, *An idle, worthless person:* "*He's a _____.*") Inf **PA**13, Little end of nothing.

little end of the horn, come out (of) the See **horn** n 8b

little few, a See **few, a** adv phr 1

little field lark n [See quot 1877] Cf **field lark**
=**dickcissel.**

1874 Coues *Birds NW* 166 **OH**, *Euspiza Americana* . . Black-throated Bunting. . . It is there known as the "Little Field Lark." **1877** in 1955 Forbush–May *Birds* 489 **IL**, Perhaps the prevalent popular name of this species is "Little Field Lark" or "Little Meadow Lark," a name suggested by his yellow breast and black jugular spot, which recall strongly the similar markings of the *Sturnella.* **1898** (1900) Davie *Nests N. Amer. Birds* 406, Dickcissel. *Spiza americana.* . . Known as the Black-throated Bunting, "Little Field Lark," and "Judas-bird." **1946** Hausman *Eastern Birds* 576.

little garden house See **little house**

little goose n
=**Hutchins's goose.**

1929 Forbush *Birds MA* 1.295, *Branta canadensis hutchinsi* . . Hutchins's Goose. Other names: . . little goose; mud goose. **1943** Musgrove–Musgrove *Waterfowl IA* 10, Hutchins's Goose . . *Branta canadensis hutchinsi* . . Other names: Richardson's goose . . brant, little goose.

little gray coot See **gray coot**

little gray owl See **gray owl** 2

little gray rattlesnake See **gray rattlesnake**

little green heron n
1 =**least bittern.**

1904 (1910) Wheelock *Birds CA* 92, The Least Bittern, or Little Green Heron, as it is sometimes called, is a smaller and much shyer bird than the American bittern.
2 See **green heron.**

little green house See **little house**

little green man n
=**ginseng B1.**

1968 *Foxfire* Mar 73 **nwGA**, Sang [=ginseng] hunters . . would keep their own finds a secret, referring to the plant by the name of a person such as Pete or Long John, or merely as "the little green man."

little guinea woodpecker n Cf **guinea woodpecker**
=**downy woodpecker.**

1917 (1923) *Birds Amer.* 2.141, Downy Woodpecker—*Dryobates pubescens medianus* . . Other Names.—Little Guinea Woodpecker [etc.]. **1930** OK Univ. Biol. Surv. *Pub.* 2.123, *Dryobates pubescens* . . Southern Downy Woodpecker. . . *Local Names:* Little guinea woodpecker [etc.].

little hangbird n Cf **hangbird**
=**red-eyed vireo.**

1792 Belknap *Hist. NH* 3.173, Little Hang-bird, *Parus pendulinus?* **1956** MA Audubon Soc. *Bulletin* 40.129 **NH**, Red-eyed Vireo. Little Hang Bird. [*Ibid,* The nest is suspended in the fork of a twig.]

little hangnest n Cf **hangnest, hangnest bird**
=**red-eyed vireo.**

1917 (1923) *Birds Amer.* 3.102, Red-Eyed Vireo—*Vireosylva olivacea* . . Little Hang-nest. **1946** Hausman *Eastern Birds* 486, Red-Eyed Vireo—*Vireo olivaceus* . . Little Hangnest. **1963** Gromme *Birds WI* 215, Hangnest₍ₛ₎ . . Little (Red-eyed Vireo).

little hawk n
=**broad-wing.**

1946 Goodrich *Birds in KS* 316, Little hawk—broad-winged hawk. **1955** *Oriole* 20.1.5, *Broad-winged Hawk.*—Little Hawk.

little hominy n Also formerly *small hominy* [**hominy** B1] Cf **big hominy**
See quot 1899.

1708 (1865) Cook *Sot-weed Factor* 5 **MD**, Syder-pap is a sort of Food made of Syder and small Homine, like our Oatmeal. **1850** U.S. Patent Office *Annual Rept. for 1849: Ag.* 153 **MS**, When meal is ground for bread, the mill is set rather wide, that the flinty part of the grain may not be cut up too fine, this being sifted out for "small hommony;" the

farinaceous part of the grain is left for bread. **1899** (1912) Green *VA Folk-Speech* 396, Small-hominy. . . Corn ground finer than for big hominy, and boiled in water for food. **1918** *DN* 5.18 **NC**, Big-hominy, lye hominy of whole corn; contrasted with little hominy, or grits. **1986** Pederson *LAGS Concordance,* 1 inf, **ceAL**, Little and big hominy—grits = little, hominy = big.

little horned owl n Cf **horned owl**
Usu =**screech owl,** but also **long-eared owl.**

1895 (1907) Wright *Birdcraft* 211, Screech Owl. . . Little Horned Owl. . . Conspicuous ear tufts. **1898** (1900) Davie *Nests N. Amer. Birds* 239, Screech Owl. . . The nest of the Little Horned . . Owl, as it is often called, is made in a hollow tree or stump, sometimes in the topmost corner inside of an old barn or shed. **1917** (1923) *Birds Amer.* 2.109, *Otus asio asio.* . . Little Horned Owl. **1923** WV State Ornith. *Birds WV* 22, The screech owl is sometimes called . . little horned owl. **1946** Hausman *Eastern Birds* 362, *Long-eared Owl.* . . *Other Names* . . Lesser Horned Owl, Little Horned Owl. . . The ear tufts of this owl are set close together, not far apart as are the tufts of the Great Horned and Screech Owls. **1946** Goodrich *Birds in KS* 317, Owl, little horned—owl, screech.

little house n

1 also *little barn, ~ office;* for addit varr see quots: An outdoor privy. Note: The sense of *little house* in quots 1789, 1804 is not certain. [*OED* 1720–1812 "now *dial.*"; *SND* 1764 →] *euphem*

1789 in 1915 *New Engl. Hist. & Geneal. Reg.* 69.305 **MA**, [June 30] Marshall & I fraimed me a Little house & raised it. . . [July 11] Charles worked on my Little house. **1804** in 1956 Eliason *Tarheel Talk* 282 **cn,cNC**, New Sellin [ceiling] to the Little House. **1899** (1912) Green *VA Folk-Speech* 264, Little-house. . . An out-door privy. **1941** *LANE* Map 354 **scattered NEng**, Privy. . . Back house, out house, . . [6 infs] *little house* . . , the normal terms, originating as euphemisms but no longer felt as such. **1952** Brown *NC Folkl.* 1.560, Little-house. . . A privy.—General. **1954** *PADS* 21.28 **SC**, Garden house. . . A privy. Also called *little house.* **1956** Ker *Vocab. W. TX* 191, Outdoor toilet. . . little house. [1 of 67 infs] **1965** Carmony *Speech Terre Haute* 151 **csIN**, Privy . . little house. [1 of 16 infs] **1965–70** *DARE* (Qu. M21b, *Joking names for an outside toilet building*) 27 Infs, **scattered, but rare NEast, West,** Little house; **MD**42, **OH**45, **PA**56, Little house behind the big (*or* other) house; **CA**195, **NY**72, Little house (*or* shack) out back; **DE**1, **KY**62, Little brown house (*or* shack); **NC**21, **TX**33, Little garden (*or* green) house; **GA**77, Little Mary doll house; **MO**2, Little shed. **1967** Faries *Word Geog. MO* 75, Privy. . . *little house, little office, little barn.* **1973** Allen *LAUM* 1.181 **IA, ceNE** (as of c1950), Privy. . . [4 infs] Little house. **1986** Pederson *LAGS Concordance* (Outhouse) 17 infs, **Gulf Region,** Little house; 1 inf, **cwTN**, Little white house outside—joking term.
2 See quot.

1994 NC Lang. & Life Project *Harkers Is. Vocab.* 7 **eNC**, Little house. . . Shed. *Dad's out back working in the little house.*

little Indian bluestem See **little bluestem**

little indigo n [See quot]
=**indigo bunting.**

1955 *Oriole* 20.1.13 **GA**, Blue Grosbeak.—Big Indigo (that is, indigo bird; "big" in contrast to the smaller Indigo Bunting of the same general coloration). *Indigo Bunting.* . . *Little Indigo.*

little Jack n [Cf *EDD* little Dick]
=**littleman.**

1950 *WELS* (Nicknames for the . . little finger) 1 Inf, **ceWI**, Little Jack.

little jag See **jag** n² **1c**

little Joe n

1 See quot. Cf **little John 1**
1969 *DARE* (Qu. K54, . . *The smallest pig in a litter*) Inf **NY**140, Little Joe.
2 also *little Joe harrow:* See **Joe harrow.**

little John n

1 A calf. Cf **little Joe 1**
1973 Allen *LAUM* 1.408 (as of c1950) 1 inf, **SD**, Little John. A baby calf of either sex.
2 See **little John the conqueror.**

little johnny n

1 The young leaf of a **wintergreen** (here: *Gaultheria procumbens*).

 1894 *Jrl. Amer. Folkl.* 7.93, *Gaultheria procumbens* . . (young leaves) little Johnnies, Calais, Me.

2 A **violet.** Cf **johnny 3**

 1908 Johnson *Highways Pacific Coast* 143 **nCA,** There were multitudes of delicate bluebells, and there were "nigger toes" and "popcorn" and dainty snowdrops and "little Johnnies" and many more.

little John the conqueror n Also *little John* Cf **conquer John, Solomon's seal**

A plant used in **hoodoo 1a**, prob a **false lily of the valley** (here: *Maianthemum canadense*).

 1931 *Jrl. Amer. Folkl.* 44.413 **LA,** Little John the Conquerer [sic]. It is also put in Notre Dame Water or Waterloo in order to win. **1945** Saxon *Gumbo Ya-Ya* 543 **LA,** Some of the roots and herbs (used under various names): Big John the Conqueror; Little John the Conqueror (used to win). **1946** Tallant *Voodoo* 225 **LA,** There is Big John and Little John. . . High John is the same as Big John; that is the strongest.

little laurel n Cf **laurel 2, 3**

1 A **rhododendron** (here: *Rhododendron minus*).

 1901 Lounsberry *S. Wild Flowers* 381, R[hododendron] *punctatum,* little . . laurel, . . is the smallest of our evergreen species. **1932** *Country Life* 62.66 **Appalachians,** The oddest and the smallest of them all is Rhododendron punctatum, called by the natives Little Laurel and Dotted-leaf Rhododendron.

2 =**calico bush 1.**

 1937 *Torreya* 37.99, *Kalmia latifolia.* . . Little laurel, western Maryland.

little loon n Cf **big loon**

=**red-throated loon.**

 1899 Howe–Sturtevant *Birds RI* 26, Red-throated Loon. *Little Loon.*— An uncommon winter resident off the ocean cliffs and beaches, and occasionally seen in Narragansett Bay. **1917** (1923) *Birds Amer.* 1.15, Red-throated Loon—*Gavia stellata* . . Little Loon. **1944** Hausman *Amer. Birds* 519, Little Loon . . Red-throated Loon. **1955** Forbush–May *Birds* 5, Red-Throated Loon—*Gavia stellata* . . Little Loon. **1963** Gromme *Birds WI* 215, Loon, . . Little (Red-throated Loon [=*Gavia stellata*]).

little mackerel n Cf **mackerel 1**

=**Pacific mackerel.**

 1884 Goode *Fisheries U.S.* 1.305 **CA,** [The] 'Little Mackerel'. . . reaches a length of about fourteen inches. It ranges northward to Monterey Bay, appearing in the fall in irregular and often large schools. **1911** U.S. Bur. Census *Fisheries 1908* 309, *Scomber japonicus.* . . is also called . . "little mackerel." . . On account of its small size very little attention is paid to it where the common mackerel is found.

little mamma See **mamma** n[1] **3**

littleman n [*OED* c1290 →; "*Obs.* exc. *dial.*"] Cf **little Jack**
The little finger.

 1972 Jones–Hawes *Step it Down* 12 **eGA** [Black], John Davis . . told us the finger names he had learned when he was a boy on St. Simons Island: thumb, potlicker, longman, lingman, littleman. **1987** *NADS Letters* **cUT,** [From a children's song, "Thumbkin Says":] Little-man says, "I'll dance."

little martin n Cf **martin**

=**tree swallow.**

 1929 Forbush *Birds MA* 3.153, *Tree Swallow.* Other names . . *little martin.* **1956** MA Audubon Soc. *Bulletin* 40.84 **ME,** *Tree Swallow.* . . Little Martin.

little Mary doll house See **little house**

little meadowlark n Cf **meadowlark**

1 =**dickcissel.**

 1877 [see **little field lark**]. **1929** Forbush *Birds MA* 3.121, Dickcissel . . Little Meadowlark. **1946** Goodrich *Birds in KS* 317, *Little meadowlark* . . dickcissel. **1963** Gromme *Birds WI* 216, Meadowlark, . . Little (Dickcissel).

2 =**lark sparrow.**

 1917 (1923) *Birds Amer.* 3.31, *Lark Sparrow.* . . *Other Names.* . . Little Meadowlark. **1946** Hausman *Eastern Birds* 601, *Chondestes*

grammacus grammacus. . . Little Meadowlark. . . Ridgway describes the famous song of this sparrow as " . . one gust of sprightly music."

3 A **redpoll** (here: *Carduelis flammea*). Cf **linnet 3**

 1944 Hausman *Amer. Birds* 519, Meadowlark, Little . . also Redpoll.

little million n

 1914 *DN* 4.76 **nNH, ME,** Little million. . . A great many.

little mite, a adv phr [Cf Intro "Language Changes" I.4] **chiefly Nth, esp NEast**
Somewhat; slightly.

 1913 Wharton *Custom of Country* 12 **NY,** Well—I'll stay a little mite longer if you want. **1927** *AmSp* 3.136 **ME coast,** Intoxication was indicated by such terms as "tight," . . "a little mite *how come ye so?*" **1932** Stong *State Fair* 255 **IA,** Would you mind putting up the truck? I'm feelin' just a little mite sleepy myself. **1938** Rawlings *Yearling* 88 **nFL,** I hoped you'd git up a leetle mite pacified. **1941** *LANE* Map 417 **ME, eMA, NH, VT,** *A little bit.* . . *A little mite* is restricted by two informants to the figurative sense. . . The expression *a little mite* is described as the more common by . . [3 infs]; as less common or rare by . . [5 infs]; and as older though still in use by . . [3 infs]. **1942** McAtee *Dial. Grant Co. IN* 40 (as of 1890s), *Little mite* . . little bit, somewhat; of a price, "That's a leetle mite steep, aint it?" **1959** Martin *Gunbarrel* 169 **WY,** Don't push none at all an' only pull a little mite. It don't take strength to run a crosscut saw. **1966** *DARE* Tape **MA5C,** If your storage tub outside is awful full, there's a little more pressure on your float so that it might come up just a little mite more. **1970** *DARE* FW Addit **eMA,** *Little mite short, a*—as of money to pay for something. Old-fashioned.

little more and(, a) adv phr Pronc-sp *leedamoren* [Cf *DJE* quot 1839 at *little most:* "A lilly mo him die dis morning."] *among Black speakers; old-fash*
Nearly, almost; otherwise, under other conditions.

 1883 (1971) Harris *Nights with Remus* 93 **GA** [Black], Hit's des na'tally a born blessin' dat you struck up wid me w'en you did . . kaze little mo' en bofe un us would 'a' bin bobbycu'd. **1884** *Anglia* 7.268 **Sth, S Midl** [Black], Er little mo'n = almost (a little more, and . .) **1952** Brown *NC Folkl.* 1.558, *Leedamoren.* . . Little more than; almost. "That fall leedamoren killed him."—Granville county. Negroes. Obsolescent.

little muscadine (grape) n

=**bird grape 1.**

 1938 Van Dersal *Native Woody Plants* 289, *Vitis munsoniana* . . Little muscadine grape. *Ibid* 337, Little muscadine (*Vitis munsoniana*).

littleneck n Also *littleneck(ed) clam*

1 A **quahog,** esp when small. [See quot 1883] **chiefly N Atl**

 1883 U.S. Natl. Museum *Bulletin* 27.234, Another name [for a small quahog] is "Little Neck," derived originally from a neck of land on the north shore of Long Island, known as Little Neck, whose clams had a superior flavor; but the demand for a young, small, and tender clam which has sprung up of late years . . has caused dealers generally to apply the term "Little Neck" to all small clams. **1896** (c1973) Farmer *Orig. Cook Book* 164, Little Neck Clams are served raw on the half shell, in the same manner as raw oysters. **1911** *Century Dict.* 3485, *Little-neck.* . . [*Century* Ed: So named from a locality on the north coast of Long Island (*Little Neck*), whence these originally came into favor.] A local epithet, noting young, round, hard clams of a size preferred for eating raw. They are simply ungrown quahaugs. . . The epithet is wrongly but very generally supposed to refer to the absence of the long siphon or "neck" which is conspicuous in the common clam. **1939** Wolcott *Yankee Cook Book* 26 **RI,** At private bakes chowder, clam-cakes and little-necks (young quahogs about the size of a half-dollar) are served for luncheon. **1939** *LANE* Map 235 **NEng,** The *littleneck* or *littleneck clam* (stress on *little*), defined as a small hardshelled clam or as a young quahog, was mentioned incidentally by eighteen informants. **1951** Taylor *Surv. Marine Fisheries NC* 160, The hard clam is known by various names: "little neck," quahaug or quohog, hard-shell clam, round clam, and "cherrystone." *Ibid* 166, Clams are sold chiefly in the shell and are graded according to size. Four grades are generally recognized: Cherrystones, little necks, large, and chowders. **1968–70** *DARE* (Qu. P18, . . *Kinds of shellfish*) Infs **CT42, RI6,** Littlenecks; **DE4,** Littleneck—smaller than cherrystone; **RI17,** Quahogs—some people call them littlenecks. **1968** *DARE* Tape **DE4,** [Inf:] There are the littlenecks, the cherrystones, and the chowder clams. . . these are the regular quahog clams. . . [FW:] How big are they? [Inf:] About as big as a silver dollar, a little larger. **1982** Heat Moon *Blue Highways* 345 **ME,** I bought two pounds of steamed quahogs (also called "littlenecks" and "cherrystones" when small). **1984** *DARE* File **Chesapeake Bay** [Watermen's vocab], Little-necked clams. . . Little necks.

2 An edible clam of the genus *Protothaca,* esp *P. staminea.* [Prob from a resemblance in form or use to **1** above; see quot 1884] **Pacific** For other names of var spp see **carpet shell, hard-shell clam 2, papershell cockle, rock ~, softshell ~, steamer clam**

   1879 U.S. Natl. Museum *Bulletin* 14.256 **wCA,** "Little Neck clams" . . *Chione succincta. . . C. simillima. . . Tapes laciniata. . . T. staminea.* **1884** *Ibid* 27.240, *Tapes staminea. . .* This species, known as the "Carpet-Shell", "Little-Neck Clam," and "Hard-Shelled Clam", is abundant on the whole Californian coast, and is found in all the markets. . . This and other species designated as "Little-Neck Clams" occupy a similar place in San Francisco markets to that of the small-sized *Venus mercenaria,* used so extensively in the Eastern States. *Ibid* 241, *Tapes laciniata . .* is a closely allied species. . . No distinction is made in the markets between them, both being sold as "Little-Neck" or "Hard-Shell" clams. **1920** CA Fish & Game Comm. *Fish Bulletin* 4.5, *Paphia* [=*Protothaca*] *staminea . .* Little-neck. **1949** Palmer *Nat. Hist.* 358, *Littleneck Clam. Protothaca staminea. . .* Edible. Of some commercial importance. **1967** *DARE* (Qu. P18, *. . Kinds of shellfish*) Inf **WA20,** Littleneck or butter clam. **1989** Mickelson *Nat. Hist.* 47 **AK,** Gravel intertidal areas in well protected bays [of Prince William Sound] support butter and littleneck (steamer) clams. Harvestable clams average 5 butters/sq. ft. and 17 littlenecks/sq. ft. *Ibid* 186, Littleneck [clam] *Protothaca staminea.*

3 A venus clam (here: *Chione succincta* or *C. simillima*). **CA** [Prob from a resemblance to **1** above] **CA**

   1879 [see **2** above]. **1884** U.S. Natl. Museum *Bulletin* 27.241 **CA,** *Chione succincta . .* and *Chione simillima . .* are also known in the markets as "Little-Neck" clams, but are not so abundant as *Tapes.*

little office See **little house**

little old adj phr Also *little bitty old, ~ old bitty* **chiefly Sth, S Midl**

Used to express disparagement, familiarity, or affection; see quots.

   1893 in 1958 Wister *Out West* 158, Texas Vocabulary. . . *Little old* applied to anything, e.g., a little old pony; hard to say what it means. **1907** [see **jerk line 1**]. **1910** Schwartz *There's Only One Little Old New York* [song title]. **1913** Kephart *Highlanders* 283 **sAppalachians,** Them bugs—the little old hatefuls! **1928** Aldrich *Lantern* 258 **NE,** I've had a crush on him ever since I first saw him striding along with his little old textbooks across the campus. **1938** Rawlings *Yearling* 3 **nFL,** There'll come a little old drizzly rain before night-fall. **1939** *Hall Coll.* **wNC,** I was borned in Jackson County in a little old log cabin. **1941** Faulkner *Men Working* 13 **MS,** Ain't hardly enough room left in these two little old narrow tracks for a car to git through. **1944** *PADS* 2.10 **Sth,** *Little old* ['lɪt lo, 'lɪl lo]. . . Term of affection, derogation, or diminution—irrespective of age. . . Low popular. **1965–70** *DARE* (Qu. LL2, *. . Too small to be worth much: "I don't want that little _____ potato."*) 7 Infs, **scattered,** Old; **GA68,** Old nothing; **MO35,** Old piece; **TN6,** Old weasy; **TX19,** Old bitty; (Qu. N37, *Joking names for a branch railroad that is not very important or gives poor service*) Inf **MS59,** Little old branch line; (Qu. N40a, *. . Sleighs . . for hauling loads*) Inf **AR47,** Little old sled; (Qu. P32, *. . Other kinds of wild animals*) Inf **LA7,** Little old polar bears; [(Qu. DD27, *. . Nicknames . . for wine*) Inf **IL40,** Stuff the little old winemaker makes]; (Qu. LL1, *Something very small: "I only took a _____ one."*) Inf **SC26,** Little old; **LA17, TN26,** Little old bitty. **1966–68** *DARE* Tape **FL32,** These little old black flies . . they get 'em [=cattle] by the millions and they'll sting 'em day and night; **GA30,** There was a little ol' creek, what we call a gully, that run out from the swamp. **1986** Pederson *LAGS Concordance* **Gulf Region,** 288 infs, Little-old (ball, boat, boy, branch, etc); 11 infs, Little-bitty-old (cow, garage, lights, etc).

little peep n Cf **peep**

Either the **least sandpiper** or the **semipalmated sandpiper.**

   1910 Eaton *Birds NY* 1.313, The Least sandpiper, Little peep, or Oxeye, is a common migrant along our coast and inland waters. It contests with the Semipalmated sandpiper the place for greatest abundance among our shore birds. **1917** (1923) *Birds Amer.* 1.238, *Semipalmated Sandpiper. . . Other Names. . .* Little Peep. **1923** U.S. Dept. Ag. *Misc. Circular* 13.55 **NY,** *Least Sandpiper. . . Vernacular Names. . . In local use. . .* Little peep. **1946** Hausman *Eastern Birds* 281, *Least Sand-*

piper. . . Other Names . . Little Peep. . . The smallest of all our sandpipers. *Ibid* 286, *Semipalmated Sandpiper. . . Other Names . .* Little Peep. . . This is our commonest little beach sandpiper. It closely resembles the Least Sandpiper but is slightly larger.

little pickerel n

A **grass pickerel 1** (here: *Esox americanus vermiculatus*).

   1882 U.S. Natl. Museum *Bulletin* 16.352, *E[sox] salmoneus . .* Little Pickerel. **1902** Jordan–Evermann *Amer. Fishes* 234, Little Pickerel; Grass Pike. . . It rarely exceeds a foot in length which precludes it being more than a boy's fish. **1908** Forbes–Richardson *Fishes of IL* 206, *Esox vermiculatus . .* Little Pickerel. **1939** Natl. Geogr. Soc. *Fishes* 139, Another species, the banded pickerel (*Esox americanus*), is smaller than the eastern pickerel. . . In the Great Lakes region and in the Mississippi and Ohio Valleys it is called the little pickerel. **1983** Becker *Fishes WI* 393, Grass Pickerel—*Esox americanus vermiculatus . .* mud pickerel . . little pickerel.

little pigeon n

=**dovekie.**

   1956 MA Audubon Soc. *Bulletin* 40.80, Dovekie . . Little Pigeon (Maine. Among sea birds known as "pigeons," this is the smallest.)

little pollom n Cf **red pollom, white ~**

=**fringed polygala.**

   1830 Rafinesque *Med. Flora* 2.63, *Polygala paucifolia . .* Vulgar. Little Pollom, Evergreen Snakeroot. **1876** Hobbs *Bot. Hdbk.* 65. **1959** Carleton *Index Herb. Plants* 75, *Little pollum* [sic]: Polygala pauciflora.

little Polly n

A **polypody** (here: *Polypodium polypodioides*).

   1920 *Torreya* 20.91 **GA,** This interesting little plant, known to science as *Polypodium polypodioides,* is closely related to the common polypody (*P. vulgare*) of the North, and one of its local names, "Little Polly," is evidently a popular recognition of the relationship.

little redfish n **NW, AK** Cf **landlocked salmon 2, redfish**

The lake-dwelling **sockeye salmon.**

   1902 Jordan–Evermann *Amer. Fishes* 156, In certain small lakes in central Idaho, northeastern Oregon, Washington and British Columbia are found 2 forms of this salmon [=*Oncorhynchus nerka*], one . . known as the redfish, the other. . . as the little redfish, Kennerly's salmon, or walla. **1946** Dufresne *AK's Animals* 277, This dwarf salmon . . in nearly all instances . . is known to be one of the landlocked forms of the Sockeye Salmon. . . In other parts of the northwest coast it is known as the Kennerly's salmon, . . or little redfish. **1948** Baumann *Old Man Crow's Boy* 55 **ID,** Here also we saw the descendants of sockeye salmon, called little-red-fish, that have lost all their instinct to go downstream to the ocean and live all their lives out in the mountain lakes. **1978** *AK Fishing Guide* 56, Sockeye that become landlocked are commonly found in various lakes from Oregon into Alaska. Called "kokanee" or "little redfish," they follow the same life cycle as their sea-going relatives, except that they grow to maturity in lakes, and they mature at a much smaller size.

little redhead n

A **goldeneye 1** (here: *Bucephala clangula*); see quot.

   1923 U.S. Dept. Ag. *Misc. Circular* 13.22 **MI,** Goldeneye (*Glaucionetta clangula*). . . In local use . . little redhead (for female and young).

little ring n Cf **big ring 1**

A marble game; see quot 1968.

   1950 *WELS Suppl.,* Little ring—in marbles, a small, football-shaped ring is used. The players "lag" and the one getting closest to the ring is allowed first shot. **1957** *Sat. Eve. Post Letters* **MA,** Little ring—corrupt game taken from the "big ring." More often played in a small triangle with marbles. Same rules, but more marbles were used. **1966–68** *DARE* (Qu. EE7, *. . Kinds of marble games*) Infs **MI14, TX9,** Little ring; **PA167,** Little ring—shoot from a line. **1966** *DARE* Tape **MI14,** We played little ring . . an oval ring maybe ten inches the longest way and six inches the short way. . . You stood back and, I forgot, I think you roll your shooter up to this little ring and then you could knock 'em out of the ring. Anything you knock out you kept. **1968** *Ibid* **MD51,** Then we had little ring. This was a ring about twelve inches in diameter and you also stood back about ten foot, behind a line, and you put up about three to four marbles . . into this twelve-inch circle. Now the two men stood back and throwed toward the circle. . . Now he had a chance of knocking out as many marbles as he could. . . He had to go outside the ring every time he hit a marble; . . if it stayed in, he lost his shot and it went on to the next player. This continued until all the marbles were out of the ring.

Little Rock n [*Little Rock,* Arkansas]

A marble game; see quot.

1905 *DN* 3.87 **nwAR,** *Little Rock.* . . The name of a game of marbles. 'First go, Little Rock.' Common.

little roncador n

A food and game fish (*Genyonemus lineatus*) of the southern California coast. Also called **croaker** n[1] **1a(2), herring** n[1] **3b, kingfish 3, roncador, shiner, tomcod, white croaker**

1882 U.S. Natl. Museum *Bulletin* 16.574, *G[enyonemus] lineatus* . . Little Roncador. **1884** Goode *Fisheries U.S.* 1.379, This species [=*Genyonemus lineatus*] is known about San Francisco as the Little Bass. Southward it is called the Little Roncador. **1911** U.S. Bur. Census *Fisheries 1908* 314, Roncador (*Roncador stearnsi*).—A food fish of excellent quality, found from Santa Barbara southward. . . Related species are known as "red roncador," "little roncador," "yellow-finned roncador," etc.

little Sally Ann (or Saucer) See **little Sally Water(s)**

little Sally Walker n Also *Sally Walker;* for addit varr see quots [See quot 1883; *EDD* (at *Sally* sb.[1] 2.(6)) shows *Sally Walker* to be the dominant form in Scotl as well as nEngl.] **scattered, but esp Sth, S Midl** See Map *esp freq among Black speakers* =**little Sally Water(s).**

[**1883** Newell *Games & Songs* 70, *Little Sally Waters.* . . In the north of England the heroine's name is *Sally Walker.*] **1916** Wolford *Play-Party IN* 86 **IN,** *Sally Walker.* . . This like "London Bridge" is definitely and exclusively a children's game. **1950** *WELS* (Games in which the players form a ring and either sing or recite a rhyme) 1 Inf, **cwWI,** Little Sally Walker. **1965–70** *DARE* (Qu. EE1, . . *Games . . children play . . in which they form a ring, and either sing or recite a rhyme*) 30 Infs, **scattered, but esp Sth, S Midl,** Little Sally Walker; **GA**1, Little Sally Walker sitting on the saucer; **SC**5, Sally Walker. [18 of 32 Infs Black] **1991** Pederson *LAGS Social Matrix* 273, Little Sally Walker [and varr]. [*DARE* Ed: The matrix indicates that 17 of 18 infs who offered these terms were Black; 12 of 18 were women. The 1986 *LAGS Concordance* notes that 2 Black women also responded with *Sally Walker.*]

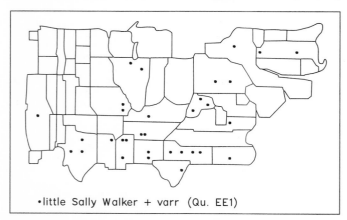

•little Sally Walker + varr (Qu. EE1)

little Sally Water(s) n Also *little Sally Ann,* ~ *Saucer, Sally Water;* for addit varr see quots [*EDD* "*Sally Water(s, Warty,* or *Walker,* children's singing games" (at *sally* sb.[1] 2.(6))] **chiefly east of Missip R, esp PA** See Map Cf **little Sally Walker**

A children's singing game; see quot 1883.

1883 Newell *Games & Songs* 70, *Little Sally Waters.*—A girl in the centre of the ring, seated, and covering her face with her hands. At the word "rise," she chooses and salutes any one whom she pleases.—Little Sally Waters,/ Sitting in the sun,/ Crying and weeping,/ For a young man./ Rise, Sally, rise,/ . . Fly to the one you love best.—In the north of England the heroine's name is *Sally Walker.* **1888** *Amer. Anthropologist* 1.248 **DC,** *Little Sally Waters.* A girl in the center pretends to weep. The others sing: Little Sally Waters, sitting in the sand,/ Weeping, crying, for a young man. **1920** *Jrl. Amer. Folkl.* 33.122 **MI,** *Sally Water.* . . A ring is formed, with a girl seated in the middle of it. The players dance around and sing. When they reach, "Rise, Sally, rise!" the girl in the

middle rises, and goes through the motions of wiping out her eyes. **1950** *WELS* **WI** (Games in which the players form a ring and either sing or recite a rhyme) 2 Infs, Little Sally Water; 1 Inf, Little Sally Walters. **1965–70** *DARE* (Qu. EE1, . . *Games . . children play . . in which they form a ring, and either sing or recite a rhyme*) 28 Infs, **chiefly east of Missip R, esp PA,** Little Sally Water; **GA**58, Little Sally Waters; **MD**2, 8, Little Sally Ann; **GA**58, **IL**83, 100, **NY**28, **PA**163, 167, Little Sally Saucer; **PA**1, Little Sally Walters; **FL**48, Little Sally Ann,/ Sitting in the sand,/ Weeping and a-crying / 'Cause of some young man./ Rise, Sally, rise,/ Wipe your weeping eyes,/ Turn to the east,/ Turn to the one that you love best; **VA**1A, Little Sally Saucer,/ Sitting in a saucer,/ Wipe your weeping eyes; **WV**12, Little Sally Ann sitting in the sand,/ Weeping and crying for someone to come;/ Rise, Sally, rise,/ Point to east,/ Point to west,/ Point to one you like best. **1968** *DARE* Tape MD8, Little Sally Ann, do you know that? . . She would turn around and whoever she would point to would be her partner. **1986** Pederson *LAGS Concordance,* 1 inf, **nwFL,** Little Sally Salter; 1 inf, **cAR,** Little Sally Saucer; 2 infs, **cwMS, seAR,** Sally in the saucer. **1988** *DARE* File **Chicago IL** (as of c1970), I remember playing a game when I was younger called Little Sally Saucer. Both boys and girls played and it didn't matter how many kids there were, but you needed at least four. One person would be Sally and the rest of us would form a circle around her. Before starting, someone would turn "Sally" around a few times. Then we would march around in a circle, singing: "Little Sally Saucer,/ Sitting in the water,/ Cry, Sally, cry,/ Wipe off your eyes./ Now turn to the east,/ And turn to the west,/ And turn to the one that / You love best." Throughout this singing "Sally" had to keep her eyes shut, and as we sang . . she had to turn and point to someone in the circle and then that person was the next "Sally."

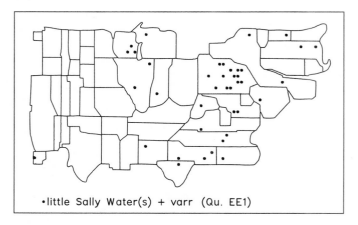

•little Sally Water(s) + varr (Qu. EE1)

littles, by See **by the littles**

little shack, little shed See **little house**

little sister n euphem Cf **friend 2,** *DS* AA27

1948 *Word* 4.183, Female anthropomorphisms [for menstruation] . . are numerous: . . *little sister's here, Aunt Jane, my country cousin.*

little snowball n Also *little snowballs* Cf **snowball**

1 =**buttonbush 1.**

1828 Rafinesque *Med. Flora* 1.100, *Cephalanthus occidentalis* . . English Name—Button-Wood Shrub. . . Vulgar Names—White Ball, Little Snowball . . Globe flower. **1959** [see **2** below]. **1960** Vines *Trees SW* 938, Common Button-bush—*Cephalanthus occidentalis.* . . Vernacular names for the shrub are Spanish Pincushion . . Little-snowball . . and Crouper-brush.

2 =**wild chamomile.**

1959 Carleton *Index Herb. Plants* 75, Little snowballs: Cephalanthus occidentalis; Matricaria inodora fl[ore] pl[eno].

little snowy n Cf **long white**

=**snowy egret.**

1917 (1923) *Birds Amer.* 1.188, *Snowy Egret.* . . To the plume-hunters the bird is known as the "Little Snowy," to distinguish it from the larger species [=*Casmerodius albus*]. **1928** Bailey *Birds NM* 92, The local names, Little Egret, . . Little Snowy, and Bonnet Martyr, give a clue to the sad history of this hunted bird. Its delicate plumes, recurved at the tip, are the "cross aigrettes" of the millinery trade, whose sale . . has been prohibited by law. **1946** Hausman *Eastern Birds* 103, *Snowy Egret*. . . *Other Names*—Little White Egret, . . Little Snowy, . . Little Egret.

little speckled woodpecker n Cf **speckled woodpecker**
=**downy woodpecker.**

1930 OK Univ. Biol. Surv. *Pub.* 2.123, *Dryobates pubescens* . . Southern Downy Woodpecker. . . Local Names: Little guinea woodpecker . . little speckled woodpecker. . . Little spotted woodpecker.

little spikebill n Cf **spikebill**
=**hooded merganser.**

1923 U.S. Dept. Ag. *Misc. Circular* 13.7 **NY**, Hooded Merganser *(Lophodytes cucullatus.)* . . In local use . . little spikebill.

little spotted woodpecker n Also *least spotted woodpecker* Cf **spotted woodpecker**
=**downy woodpecker.**

1791 Bartram *Travels* [289 *bis*], P[icus] pubescens, the least spotted woodpecker. **1930** [see **little speckled woodpecker**].

little squeaking goose n
=**cackling goose.**

1918 Grinnell *Game Birds CA* 234, Cackling Goose—*Branta canadensis minima* . . Other Names—Cackler . . Little Squeaking Goose. **1923** U.S. Dept. Ag. *Misc. Circular* 13.37 **CA,** Cackling Goose *(Branta canadensis minima)*. . . In local use.—Brown brant . . little squeaking goose, yelper. **1953** Jewett *Birds WA* 105, Alaskan Cackling Goose. *Branta hutchinsii minima* . . Other names: Cackling Goose . . Little Squeaking Goose.

little striker n [See quot 1938] Cf **striker**
=**least tern.**

1898 (1900) Davie *Nests N. Amer. Birds* 42, The "Little Striker," as it is called, is found nesting on the Atlantic coast as far north as Massachusetts. **1904** (1910) Wheelock *Birds CA* 45, Sea Swallow and Little Striker are the common names applied to this little tern, although sea swallow is used of all terns. **1932** Howell *FL Bird Life* 266, *Least Tern*. . . Little Striker. [*Ibid* 267, In flight the Least Tern is . . extremely graceful, . . frequently pausing . . to make a swift and sudden plunge.] **1938** Oberholser *Bird Life LA* 297, It [=the least tern] darts downward and readily catches a fish if near the surface, from which habit it has acquired the name of 'little striker.' **1969** Longstreet *Birds FL* 68, *Little Striker*. . . The smallest as well as the most elegant member of the tern family living in the United States.

little sugar pine n [See quot 1948] **CA** Cf **sugar pine**
A **white pine** (here: *Pinus monticola*).

1897 Sudworth *Arborescent Flora* 15 **CA,** *Pinus monticola*. . . Common Names. . . Little Sugar Pine. **1911** Jepson *Flora CA* 18, Silver Pine, or "Little Sugar Pine," is found in the Sierra Nevada at somewhat higher elevations than the Sugar Pine. **1947** Peattie *Sierra Nevada* 157, The sugar pine has a very characteristic effect on the skyline, approached only by . . the western white pine, mountain pine, or little sugar pine, as it is variously called. **1948** *Pacific Discovery* Nov–Dec 20, The silver pine *(Pinus monticola)*. . . Because of its cones the silver pine is sometimes called the "little sugar pine."

little tomato n
A **ground-cherry** (here: *Physalis heterophylla*).

1975 Hamel–Chiltoskey *Cherokee Plants* 37, Ground cherry, little tomato—*Physalis heterophylla*. . . Edible berry.

little tunny n Cf **tunny**
1 also *little tuna:* A **tuna** of the genus *Euthynnus*, esp *E. alletteratus* in Atlantic waters, but also the **kawakawa** in Hawaii.

1873 in 1878 Smithsonian Inst. *Misc. Coll.* 14.2.24, *Orcynus alliteratus* [sic] . . Little tunny; albicore . . (found in large numbers at *Wood's Hole, Massachusetts, August,* 1871). **1882** U.S. Natl. Museum *Bulletin* 16.429, *Euthynnus* [spp] . . Little Tunnies. *Ibid* 430, *E[uthynnus] alliteratus* [sic] . . Little Tunny; Albicore. **1933** Bryan *Hawaiian Nature* 226, The name "tuna" is loosely applied to several species of mackerel-like fishes. In Hawaiian waters these include . . the little tunny or *kawa-kawa.* **1946** LaMonte *N. Amer. Game Fishes* 25, False Albicore—*Euthynnus alletteratus*—Names: Little Tunny, Little Tuna, Bonito. **1951** Taylor *Surv. Marine Fisheries NC* 268, *Euthynnus alletteratus* . . False albacore; little tuna. **1960** Gosline–Brock *Hawaiian Fishes* 258, *Euthynnus yaito* . . Little tuna. . . A small species rarely exceeding 30 inches in length.

1971 Pukui–Elbert *Hawaiian Dict.* 129, *Kawakawa*. . . Bonito, little tunny *(Euthynnus yaito).* Sometimes called *pohopoho.*
2 =**bonito 1.**

1935 Caine *Game Fish* 53, Bonito—*Sarda sarda*. . . Little Tunny. **1946** LaMonte *N. Amer. Game Fishes* 20, Common Bonito—*Sarda sarda*. . . Little Tunny, Bloater. **1947** Caine *Salt Water* 16, For its size, the bonito is one of the most powerful fish that swims and is often referred to as "the torpedo of the sea". It is also known as bone-eater, false albacore, Boston mackerel, bonejack, little tunny and skipjack.

little up v phr
1932 *DN* 6.283 swCT, *Little-up.* To finish many half-completed tasks. You "little-up" to get rid of some of your irons in the fire.

little vinegar plant n
A **dock** n[1] (here: *Rumex acetosa*).

1974 (1977) Coon *Useful Plants* 214, *Rumex acetosa*. . . The mild sour taste has made it "the little vinegar plant" and every nature lover should make use of it as a real "gourmet" item.

little washerwomen n Also *little washerwoman* [Perh from the bonnet-shaped flower] Cf **Quaker ladies**
A **bluet 2** (here: *Houstonia caerulea*).

1896 *Jrl. Amer. Folkl.* 9.190, *Houstonia caerulea* . . little washerwomen, Bethlehem, Pa. **1900** Lyons *Plant Names* 194, *H[oustonia] coerulea* [sic]. . . Bluets . . Little-washerwoman. **1959** Carleton *Index Herb. Plants* 75, *Little washerwoman:* Houstonia caerulea.

little white crane n Also *little white heron* Cf **white crane, ~ heron**
1 =**snowy egret.**

1916 *Times-Picayune* (New Orleans LA) 2 Apr mag sec 5/3, *Snowy egret (Egretta candidissima).* Heron Blanc; Little White "Crane." **1917** (1923) *Birds Amer.* 1.188, Snowy Egret—*Egretta candidissima candidissima* . . Other Names . . Little White Heron. **1940** Trautman *Birds Buckeye Lake* 164 **OH,** It is curious that Little Blue Herons [=*Florida caerulea caerulea*] were not recorded during more than 2 years of the investigation. . . A few old residents stated that "little white cranes" were present during occasional summers before 1900; however, it is not known whether the "little white cranes" were of this species or were Snowy Egrets. **1962** Imhof *AL Birds* 93, Snowy Egret—*Leucophoyx thula* . . Little White Crane. **1963** Gromme *Birds WI* 215, Little White Heron . . Little Blue Heron [=*Florida caerulea*] . . Snowy Egret [=*Leucophoyx thula*].
2 =**little blue heron,** usu the young.

1925 (1928) Forbush *Birds MA* 1.332, *Florida caerulea* . . Little Blue Heron . . Little White Heron. **1932** Bennitt *Check-list* 15 **MO,** *Florida caerulea caerulea* . . Little white crane or heron (white young). **1940** [see **1** above]. **1963** [see **1** above].

little white diver See **little diver**

little white egret n Also *little egret* Cf **white egret**
=**snowy egret.**

1872 Coues *Key to N. Amer. Birds* 267, Little White Egret. Snowy Heron. . . *[Egretta] candidissima.* **1878** U.S. Natl. Museum *Proc.* 1.163, Besides the Ibises, the Great and Little White Egrets, Louisiana and Night Herons . . were breeding there. **1898** (1900) Davie *Nests N. Amer. Birds* 116, Snowy Heron. *Ardea candidissima.* . . It is called Little White Egret, and is doubtless the handsomest bird of this tribe. **1928** [see **little snowy**]. **1940** Gabrielson *Birds OR* 110, The "Little White Egret" . . is found in the same locality [as the Great White Egret]. **1957** Pough *Audubon W. Bird Guide* 293, Egret, . . little. See snowy [egret]. **1963** Gromme *Birds WI* 214, Egret, . . Little (Snowy Egret).

little white heron See **little white crane**

little wild goose n Cf **wild goose**
Usu **Hutchins's goose,** but also a **Canada goose** (here: *Branta canadensis leucopareia*).

1874 NY Acad. Sci. *Annals Lyceum Nat. Hist.* 10.388 **IL,** A[nser] *Canadensis*. . . Little Wild Goose. **1898** Elliot *Wild Fowl* 70, Hutchins' Goose is known to sportsmen and baymen under various names, many of which are bestowed on account of its small size. Some of these are, Lesser Canada Goose, Small Gray Goose, Little Wild Goose, etc. **1932** Bennitt *Check-list* 17 **MO,** *Branta canadensis leucopareia*. . . Little wild goose; brant [etc]. . . *Hutchins's goose*. . . Vernacular names as above.

1953 Jewett *Birds WA* 105, *Branta canadensis leucopareia.* . . Little Wild Goose. . . Occurs commonly along the Columbia River.

little Willie n *euphem* Cf **Horace**

1948 *Word* 4.183, Male personifications [of menstruation] in American are limited: *Little Willie* and *entertaining the general.*

littling n Cf **little D2**

An endearment; a caress.

1963 Edwards *Gravel* 14 **eTN** (as of 1920s), The oldsters went off to bed leaving the newlyweds to retire as soon as they cared to. The young couple stayed up late enjoying the wonderful littlings of love, but finally went to bed.

live v *Pronc-sp* **lib**

A Pronc varr.

1892 (1893) Botume *First Days* 54 **seSC** (as of 1864) [Black], Susie said, "Me an' my ole man lib here, an' we sister lib wid we." **1899** (1967) Chesnutt *Wife of Youth* 11 [Black], I heerd you wuz a big man an' had libbed heah a long time. **1922** Gonzales *Black Border* 310 **sSC, GA coasts** [Gullah glossary], *Lib*—live, lives, lived, living. c**1937** in 1976 *Weevils in the Wheat* 189 **VA** [Black], He kept we alls tergether, and we libed in a little cabin in de yard.

B Gram forms.

1 pres (exc 3rd pers sg): usu *live;* also *lives.*

1921 Haswell *Daughter Ozarks* 107 (as of 1880s), "Wal," drawled the old woman, "Ye see I'm jest old Mis' Brannick, and I lives on the Bryant Fork over in Douglas county." **1945** FWP *Lay My Burden Down* 109 **AR** [Black], Lula married a Thomas, and it's her I lives with. **1986** Pederson *LAGS Concordance,* 22 infs, **Gulf Region,** Lives [3rd pers pl]. [Typical resps are: "Only three of them lives in Hawkins County now"; "There's people that lives down along the riverbank"; "A bunch of Swedes that lives here"; "I got two lives here."]

2 pres 3rd pers sg: usu *lives;* also *live. esp freq among Black speakers*

1892 [see **A** above]. **1899** (1967) Chesnutt *Wife of Youth* 10 [Black], "Is dis yere whar Mistuh Ryduh lib, suh?" she asked, looking around her doubtfully. **1922** [see **A** above]. **1986** Pederson *LAGS Concordance,* 24 infs, **Gulf Region,** Live [3rd pers sing]. [Typical resps are: "A neighbor live across street"; "He live down here"; "My sister live out there"; "Old bachelor live there by hisself."] [14 of 24 infs Black].

3 past: usu *lived;* also *live.*

1922 [see **A** above]. **1937** in 1976 *Weevils in the Wheat* 149 **VA** [Black], It's hard to believe dat dese things did happen, but dey did 'cause I live in dat time. **1986** Pederson *LAGS Concordance,* 1 inf, **nwMS,** I ain't never live nowhere else; 1 inf, **ceTX,** A woman who live to be ninety-two.

live adv[1] See **lief** adv

live adv[2]

Briskly, fast.

1967 Fetterman *Stinking Creek* 42 **seKY,** It's snowing pretty live.

live-and-everlasting See **life everlasting 1**

live-box n Also *live-boat, ~-car*

=**car** n[2].

1933 Rawlings *South Moon* 182 **FL,** He picked them [=young alligators] up with a hand closed over their jaws and dropped them one by one into a live-box, counting as he dropped. **1978** *Pioneer Amer.* June 89 **Missip Valley,** Another type of watercraft is not even a boat, but a vehicle for transporting fish. The *live-car* (also called *live-boat, tow-car, well-car,* and *fish-car*) is a boat-shaped structure made of widely spaced wooden slats. Water can circulate freely through the live-car, thus fish placed in it can be transported alive. A similar device is the *live-box,* a box made of wooden slats or . . of wire stretched over a wooden frame; it is always in the water with the top just above the waterline. *Ibid,* Ice was first used by the fishing industry in the Atchafalaya Swamp in 1899; as a result, live-cars very quickly declined in popularity. **1984** *DARE* File **Chesapeake Bay** [Watermen's vocab], Live box. **1986** Pederson *LAGS Concordance,* 1 inf, **swGA,** Live-box—on fishing boat, container to keep fish.

live devil aspirin n [Folk-etym] Cf **life elastic**

=**life everlasting 1.**

1986 Pederson *LAGS Concordance,* 1 inf, **csTN,** Live devil aspirin = rabbit tobacco.

live fence n Also *live fencing, living fence* Cf **half-live fence**

A hedge.

1804 Roberts *PA Farmer* 84, When the hedge is full grown, then there is a perfect live fence. **1829** *MA Spy & Worcester Co. Advt.* (Worcester MA) 25 Mar [1]/4, Messrs. Grant Thorburn & Son of New York, imported 75,000 hawthorns, for "live fencing." **1833** (1847) Lundy *Life & Travels* 57 **TX,** Among this undergrowth was a species of thorn that would be excellent for live fence. **1860** (1955) Lee *Mormon Chronicle* 1.240 **UT,** Bro. [Walter E.] Dodge has done much to encourage Horticulture & has introduced the living Fense, which is cheap and durable. This is done simply by cutting & setting black willows & cotton wood sticks . . in the Earth about 16 inches deep & some inches apart. **1885** *Century Illustr. Mag.* 29.795, The cuts will be protected from snowdrifts, and long lines of "live fences" be secured. **1968–69** *DARE* (Qu. L65, . . *Kinds of fences*) Inf **MD9,** Living fence—rosebushes or other bushes forming a hedge; can be used for animals or just around the house; **NY109,** Living fence—multiflora rose or hemlock; **NY182,** Live fences—made by growing thickets and brush in rows along the edges of fields.

live-forever n

1 A cudweed **1.** Cf **life everlasting 1, life-of-man 3**

1674 Josselyn *Two Voyages* 77, Live for ever, it is a kind of *Cud-weed,* flourisheth all summer long till cold weather comes in. **1959** Carleton *Index Herb. Plants* 76, *Live-forever:* Gnaphalium (v); Sedum (v); Sempervivum (v). **1968** *DARE* (Qu. BB50c, *Remedies for infections*) Inf **NJ53,** Live-forever and salt—to draw a boil.

2 An **orpine,** usu *Sedum telephium.* [*OED* 1597 →; see quot 1979] Cf **bag plant 1, life everlasting 3, life-of-man 4**

1817 Eaton *Botany* 51, *[Sedum] telephium,* (liveforever, or orpine). **1848** Gray *Manual of Botany* 146, *S[edum] Telephium* . . Garden Orpine, or Live-for-ever. **1853** *Knickerbocker* 42.171, Here and there a straggling red rose-bush and a patch of yellow lilies or 'live-for-ever.' **1880** *Scribner's Mth.* 20.101, Live-forever . . thrives and multiplies under the plow and harrow. **1905** *DN* 3.87 **nwAR,** Live forever. . . Everlasting. Also called 'life everlasting.' **1931** [see **life-of-man 4**]. **1957** *Sat. Eve. Post Letters* **swWI** (as of 1890s), We chewed the bark of the slippery elm, and we blew up the leaves of the live forever plants. **1959** [see **1** above]. **1979** Niering–Olmstead *Audubon Guide N. Amer. Wildflowers E. Region* 480, Live-Forever (*Sedum purpureum*). . . It can regenerate from almost any fragment; hence the common name.

3 =**houseleek 1.** [Calque of the generic *Sempervivum;* see quot 1840] Cf **bag plant 2**

1840 MA Zool. & Bot. Surv. *Herb. Plants & Quadrupeds* 94, *S[empervivum] tectorum.* . . Houseleek, or Live-for-ever. A well-known plant of the gardens, with thick, fleshy, mucilaginous leaves. . . The plant is so succulent, that a twig of it will grow, if the end be only stuck fast under the shingles of a roof; hence its generic, specific, and common name. In popular use as an emollient . . and a vulnerary. **1929** *Torreya* 29.150 **ME,** Sempervivum tectorum, *"Live Forever," "Bag-plant"* (because the children blew up the leaves), and *"Aaron's Rod."* **1959** [see **1** above].

4 A low-growing succulent plant of the genus *Dudleya.* [From its ability to regenerate] **chiefly CA** For other names of var spp see **bluff lettuce, desert savior, hen-and-chickens 1a(2), rock lettuce, sea ~, stonecrop**

1925 Jepson *Manual Plants CA* 452, *Cotyledon* . . Live-for-ever. **1949** Moldenke *Amer. Wild Flowers* 53, On remote sea bluffs and cliffs in California dwell 8 species of live-forever of the genus *Cotyledon.* **1974** Munz *Flora S CA* 383, *Dudleya* [spp] . . Live-Forever. **1987** *Nature Conserv. News* 37.3.10 **CA,** Botanists encountered . . new plant forms: hairy manzanita . . , Fraser Point live-forever (*Dudleya nesiotica*). *Ibid* 12, Live-forever literally seemed to "creep" back over the cliff edges and bask in the open sun.

5 An **onion B** (here: *Allium cepa* Aggregatum Group). Cf **evergreen onion, everlasting ~**

1966 Dakin *Dial. Vocab. Ohio R. Valley* 2.367, Numerous miscellaneous terms [for spring onions] are used by scattered speakers: . . *table onions, garlic onions,* and *live-forevers* all appear once or twice. **1971** Wood *Vocab. Change* 42 **Sth,** Live forevers, potato onions, rare ripes are rarely reported [for early onions].

live in adultery v phr [Cf std colloq *live in sin*] **scattered, but chiefly W Midl, S Atl** See Map

To live together outside of marriage.

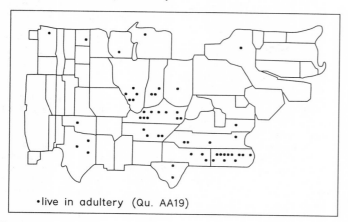

•live in adultery (Qu. AA19)

lively n
Liveliness.

1993 Mason *Feather Crowns* 91 **KY,** "The littlest one ain't stirred none," said Mrs. Willy. "But the other ones have got more lively to 'em."

lively lad n [Trademark] Cf lazy boy 1
1966–69 *DARE* (Qu. L35, *Hand tools used for cutting underbrush and digging out roots*) Inf **FL4,** Lively lad—handle, blade, you swing it; **FL29,** Lively lad; (Qu. L37, *A hand tool used for cutting weeds and grass*) Infs **FL29, TN37,** Lively lad; **FL12,** Lively lad—a swinging sling; **TN26,** Lively lad [FW illustr: handle with a blade shaped like an open triangle].

live neighbor(s) to (or by) See neighbor n B

live oak n

1 Any of var usu evergreen **oaks** native chiefly to the Southeast and Gulf States such as *Quercus minima* or **laurel oak 2,** but usu *Quercus virginiana.* For other names of *Q. virginiana* see **encino;** for other names of *Q. minima* see **oak runner, scrub oak**

1610 in 1844 Force *Tracts* 3.1.22 **VA,** Sarsafrase, liue Oake, greene all the yeare. **1709** (1967) Lawson *New Voyage* 99 **NC, SC,** Live-Oak chiefly grows on dry, sandy Knolls. This is an Evergreen, and the most durable Oak all *America* affords. **1731** Catesby *Nat. Hist. Carolina* 1.17, The usual Height of the Live Oak is about 40 foot; the Grain of the wood course, harder and tougher than any other Oak. . . The Acorns are the sweetest of all others; of which the *Indians* usually lay up store, to thicken their venison-soop. **1812** Michaux *Histoire des Arbres* 2.67, *Quercus virens.* Live oak. Cette espèce de Chêne, qui appartient exclusivement à la partie maritime des Etats méridionaux, des deux Florides, et de la Basse Louisiane, est connue dans tous ces pays, sous le seul nom de *Live-oak*, Chêne vert. [=*Quercus virens.* Live oak. This species of oak, which belongs exclusively to the coastal parts of the southern states, the two Floridas, and lower Louisiana, is known in all these places by the single name of *Live-oak*, green oak.] **1833** (1847) Lundy *Life & Travels* 35 **New Orleans LA,** Timber of various kinds abounds, among which the live oak is very common. **1882** *Bot. Gaz.* 7.48 **cTX,** The sides and part of the top of this great bluff are covered with a thick growth of mountain cedar (*Juniperus occidentalis,* var. *conjungens*), red oak (*Quercus rubra*), live oak (*Q. virens*), and shin oak (*Q. sinuata,* var.?) **1905** Chesnutt *Col.'s Dream* 20 **Sth,** The house possessed . . a solidity of construction that resisted sturdily the disintegrating hand of time. Heart-pine and live-oak, mused the colonel, like other things Southern, live long and die hard. **1938** Rawlings *Yearling* 79 **nFL,** A live oak spread its branches across half the sink-hole. **1945** Wodehouse *Hayfever Plants* 80, Three other species of live oak belong to the southeastern area of the United States. . . the eastern or Texas live oak (*Q. virginiana* . .). . . the dwarf live oak or scrub live oak (*Q. minima* . .) . . and the twin live oak or scrub oak (*Q. geminata*). **1965–70** *DARE* (Qu. T10, . . *Kinds of oak trees*) 134 Infs, **chiefly SE, Gulf States,** Live oak; (Qu. T5, . . *Kinds of evergreens, other than pine*) 43 Infs, **SE, Gulf States,** Live oak; (Qu. T16, . . *Kinds of trees . . 'special'*) 11 Infs, **SE, Gulf States,** Live oak; (Qu. T15, . . *Kinds of swamp trees*) Infs **FL17, 35,** Live oak. **1966–68** *DARE* Tape **FL5,** There are at least two kinds of oaks in our yard—live oak and water oak; **GA18,** I always think of

that story . . when I look at our live oaks . . the one near the coast, it seems that the leaves are just pushed off by the new ones; they are not exactly deciduous; **TX24,** Papa had been here fourteen years before he saw the river higher than where that old live oak stump stands down there now; **TX25,** [FW:] What kind of things make up the brush around here? [Inf:] Mesquite, shin oak, live oak, all kinds of trees; **TX47,** Mustang grapes grew better on live oak than anything else; **TX75,** They met out in a live oak grove; **TX89,** They have oak, various kinds of oak—red oak, post, live oak. **1986** Pederson *LAGS Concordance,* 60 infs, **Gulf Region,** Live oak(s); 4 infs, **swLA, csTX,** Live oak tree(s); 1 inf, **swAL,** Live oak—stays green the year round; 1 inf, **nwLA,** Live oak—lives all year.

2 Any of several usu evergreen **oaks** native to the West such as **canyon oak 1,** but esp such trees as *Quercus agrifolia* or *Q. wislizeni* in California, or *Q. turbinella* in California and the Southwest. Also called **encino.** For other names of *Q. agrifolia* see **evergreen oak b, holly ~ 2, scrub ~;** for other names of *Q. wislizeni* see **highland oak, post ~;** for other names of *Q. turbinella* see **gray oak 3, scrub ~** Cf **California live oak, mountain ~, white ~**

1845 Frémont *Rept. Rocky Mts.* 241, The prevailing tree was the evergreen oak . . which, by way of distinction, we shall call the *live oak.* **1884** Sargent *Forests of N. Amer.* 146, *Quercus chrysolepis.* . . Live oak. Maul oak. Valparaiso oak. . . An evergreen tree of great economic value. **1894** *Jrl. Amer. Folkl.* 7.99 **CA,** *Quercus oblongifolia* . . evergreen white oak, live oak. **1897** Sudworth *Arborescent Flora* 163, *Quercus chrysolepis.* . . Live Oak (Cal., Oreg.) *Ibid* 179, *Quercus densiflora* . . Tanbark Oak. . . Live Oak (Oreg.) **1908** Britton *N. Amer. Trees* 309, California Live Oak—*Quercus agrifolia.* . . It is also called Evergreen oak, Coast live oak, and Live oak. **1910** Jepson *Silva CA* 223, No other Californian oak has so many folk-names in use. Being evergreen it [=*Quercus chrysolepis*] is called Live Oak or Mountain Live Oak, especially in those portions of the mountains where it is the only live oak. *Ibid* 229, Interior Live Oak. [Footnote:] It is almost universally known in the field simply as Live Oak. **1913** Wooton *Trees NM* 54, The Live Oak (*Quercus arizonica, Q. grisea,* and *Q. oblongifolia*) (the last of which is known only from the extreme southwestern corner of the State) are low spreading trees, with comparatively small leaves of extremely variable. . . outline that occur in the mouths of canyons and along arroyos in the foothills of the drier and hotter mountains. **1945** Wodehouse *Hayfever Plants* 80, Regardless of their botanical group, many of the evergreen oaks are called Live Oaks. Usually their leaves are thick and leathery and very stiff and more or less evergreen. Three of these are western. The coast live oak or encina (*Q. agrifolia* . .) . . . The interior or highland live oak (*Q. Wislizenii* . .) . . . The maul oak (*Q. chrysolepis* . .) . . . In common parlance, . . they are the live oaks so characteristic of the landscapes of California. **1965–70** *DARE* (Qu. T10, . . *Kinds of oak trees*) 36 Infs, **chiefly CA,** Live oak; (Qu. T5, . . *Kinds of evergreens, other than pine*) 9 Infs, **CA,** Live oak; **CA136,** Live oak brush; (Qu. T16, . . *Kinds of trees . . 'special'*) Infs **CA20, 22, 80, 161,** Live oak. **1970** *DARE* Tape **CA182,** At this time of year the canyon is especially green. We have a lot of native live oak and sycamore; **CA200,** It [=a fire] was blowing and got into some live oak. Live oak leaves are kind of oily and they burn like nobody's business. **1979** Little *Checklist U.S. Trees* 243, *Quercus tomentella* . . island live oak.

liver n[1] [*OED* 1377 →]
An inhabitant, resident.

1678 *New Castle Ct. Rec.* 195 (DAE), Hee hath forced ye people whoe are Livers wth in the Jurisdiction of this Court to Pay Custome. **1747** in 1851 PA *Prov. Council Minutes* 5.87, One John Powle, a Liver on Sasquehanna River. **1781** (1925) Washington *Diaries* 2.210 **VA,** Mr. John Flood (at present a liver at lower Salem). **1850** Mitchell *Lorgnette* 1.41 **NYC,** My friend . . is an up-town liver. **1954** *PADS* 21.32 **seSC,** Liver. . . An inhabitant, dweller. "He de oldes' liver on dis block." Negro usage, Charleston and Sumter.

liver adv See lief adv

liver n[2] [Appar from the color of its plumage]
=glossy ibis 1.

1917 (1923) *Birds Amer.* 1.177, Liver. . . Adults: Rich purplish-chestnut shading on head, back, wings and tail. **1946** Hausman *Eastern Birds* 115, Eastern Glossy Ibis. . . *Other Names*—Black Curlew, . . Liver. Field Marks—Long curved bill. The dark brown plumage causes the bird to appear a dull black in the distance.

liver and lights See **lights 2a**

liverberry n [See quot 1894]

=**twisted-stalk** (here: *Streptopus* spp).

1894 *Jrl. Amer. Folkl.* 7.102 nME, *Streptopus amplexifolius . . , Streptopus roseus. . . liver-berry. . .* From the supposed medicinal value of the cathartic fruit, which is freely eaten by children wherever the Streptopus grows. **1923** in 1925 Jepson *Manual Plants CA* 248, S[treptopus] *amplexifolius. . . Liver-berry. . .* Margins of cold streamlets in the woods. **1968** *DARE* (Qu. S26a, . . *Wildflowers. . . Roadside flowers*) Inf MN14, Liverberry. **1970** Kirk *Wild Edible Plants W. U.S.* 161, Liverberry. . . The red, juicy berries may be eaten raw or cooked in soups or stews. . . In some localities . . [it] is reported to be somewhat cathartic, but not so in other areas. **1976** Bailey–Bailey *Hortus Third* 1081, [*Streptopus*] *amplexifolius. . .* var. *americanus . . Liverberry*.

liver-bound See **liver-grown**

liver cheese n Cf **headcheese 1, liver mush**

=**liver sausage.**

1965–70 *DARE* (Qu. H43, *Foods made from parts of the head and inner organs of an animal*) Inf FL51, Liver cheese—no cornmeal, grind liver up, add seasonings, hold and let it jell; KY81, Liver cheese—similar to liver pudding; SC62, Liver pudding, liver cheese—mostly liver, a loaf affair, has rice in it; GA4, IN7, MI68, MO1, NY123, Liver cheese. **1973** Allen *LAUM* 1.289 seIA, cwSD (as of c1950), *Liver cheese*. Apparently the expression is equivalent to *liver sausage.* **1986** Pederson *LAGS Concordance* (*What do you call the dish prepared by cooking and grinding up hog liver?*) 37 infs, Gulf Region, Liver cheese; 1 inf, cwGA, Liver cheese—ground liver, made by mother; 1 inf, swGA, Liver cheese—different from hash; 3 infs, ceAR, nwFL, cTX, Liver cheese—(her) mother made; 1 inf, cnFL, Liver cheese—liver, lights, rice, packed in casing; 1 inf, swAL, Liver cheese—not made with cornmeal; 1 inf, nwFL, Liver cheese—ground fine, in square pack with fat; 1 inf, nwTN, Liver cheese—you can buy now; 1 inf, swTN, Liver cheese—made with heart, lights, liver; 1 inf, nwMS, Liver cheese—North Carolina dish, "we ain't never had" here; 1 inf, cnMS, Liver cheese—ground up liver, seasoned; 1 inf, cwMS, Liver cheese—liver and haslet boiled, ground up; 1 inf, cwMS, Liver cheese—has bought, never made; 1 inf, seLA, Liver cheese—not from hog liver; 1 inf, cnAR, Liver cheese—not sure; 1 inf, swAL, Goose-liver cheese—a sausage; [1 inf, nwMS, Cheese].

liverelle n Also sp *liverel*

=**liver sausage.**

1949 *AmSp* 24.111 cnSC, Liverel. . . Liver pudding, a sausage prepared of hog liver. **1967** *DARE* (Qu. H43, *Foods made from parts of the head and inner organs of an animal*) Inf SC29, Liverelle = liver mush—cornmeal and flour, cook liver and grind it, make mush, put them together. **1986** Pederson *LAGS Concordance* (*Haslet*) 1 inf, swTN, Liverelle—from heart, lights, liver; (*What do you call the dish prepared by cooking and grinding up hog liver?*) 1 inf [DARE Ed: same inf as above], Liverelle.

liver-grown adj, also used absol [*OED* 1645 →] Also *liver-bound, ~-growed* chiefly sAppalachians, PA

Having enlargement or adhesion of the liver, or suffering from symptoms supposed to be caused by this condition; hence n *liver growth* enlargement of the liver.

1903 Dunbar *Lyrics of Love* 23 [Black], Den she lif's 'em up head down'ards, so's dey won't git livah-grown,/ But dey snoozes des' ez peaceful ez a liza'd on a stone. **1924** Raine *Land of Saddle-Bags* 207 sAppalachians, I thought maybe hit were liver-growed. You don't know what that is? Well, you take the child by the right hand and left heel, and make them touch behind. Then I tuk the left hand and right heel and they wouldn't touch. So I jest pulled. The child cried mightily, but I knowed hit had to be done. . . [W]ith . . its liver let loose . . hit stands a good chance to get well. **1930** Shoemaker *1300 Words* 38 cPA Mts (as of c1900), *Liver-grown*. **1933** *AmSp* 8.1.50 Ozarks, Liver-grown. . . Subject to a mythical disease of the liver. I have seen sick children picked up by the heels and shaken vigorously, in the belief that the liver has grown fast to the body wall, and that it must needs be *shuck loose.* **1935** Hyatt *Folkl. Adams Co. IL* 131, A baby becomes liver-grown by lying continually in the same position. The character of this disease is such that the child's liver sticks to the back or to some other internal part of the body. **1964** Smith *PA Germans* 135, In the Shenandoah Valley, the German element had a belief that if a child were taken out in the cold, windy, night air and jounced around during a ride in the horse-and-carriage, that it would become liver-grown. . . [I]t was thought that the

liver would attach itself to the ribs causing severe pain and discomfort. Adults could also become liver-grown and suffer sharp shooting pains with each breath. Informants in five counties in Virginia and two in West Virginia reported that greasing for the liver-grown was a widespread practice. One woman said, "I greased my children. The roads were rough in those days, you'd be afraid they'd get shook up and get livergrown. . . If they took a ride in the buggy any distance, we'd grease the children. We used hog lard and camphor." **1982** *Barrick Coll.* csPA, Livergrowed. **1982** Slone *How We Talked* 104 eKY (as of c1950), Little children were said to be "liver grown" if they were listless and not active. Cure: lay them on their stomach on your lap, bring their left foot up over their back and touch their right hand, then do the same with the right foot and left hand. If they meet, then everything is all right. **1983** Glimm *Flatlanders* 155 cnPA, We went down home when Donna was small and she got the liver growth. You know how they used to get that liver growth? Well, when babies are young like that and you bounce 'em around too much, their liver gets bigger. You cause an inflammation of the liver, and that's what they call the liver growth. **1990** Cavender *Folk Med. Lexicon* 26 sAppalachians, Liver grown . . also known as "liver bound". . . [having] a physical disorder . . [in which an infant's] liver becomes attached to the spinal cord due to remaining flat on the back too long in the crib; disorder prevented by using the "liver shakes", a process involving holding the infant by its feet and shaking it up and down.

liver hash n chiefly Sth, S Midl Cf **hash n 1, hog-head hash**

=**liver sausage.**

1965–70 *DARE* (Qu. H43, *Foods made from parts of the head and inner organs of an animal*) Inf FL26, Hog-head cheese, liver hash, chitlins; GA88, Liver hash—without cornmeal; SC38, Hog-liver hash. **1986** Pederson *LAGS Concordance* chiefly GA, TN, AL (*What do you call the dish prepared by cooking and grinding up hog liver?*) 21 infs, Liver hash; 2 infs, Liver hash = liver pudding; 1 inf, Liver hash—onions, cornmeal, same as liver pudding; 1 inf, Liver hash—mother made, had "lights" in it; 1 inf, Liver hash—liver, onion, salt, pepper, potatoes; 1 inf, Liver hash—from liver and lights and heart; 1 inf, I call that liver hash—ground up liver, lights; 1 inf, Liver hash—not liver pudding; 1 inf, Liver hash—boiled, ground, cooked with sage, onions; 1 inf, Liver hash or haslet; (*Chitterlings*) 1 inf, Liver hash.

liverleaf n Also *liverwort* [*OED* 1578 →]

=**hepatica.**

1622 'Mourt' *Relation* 62 (*DAE*), We found heere in Winter . . Brooklime, Liver-wort, Water-cresses. **1784** in 1785 Amer. Acad. Arts & Sci. *Memoirs* 1.458, Anemone. . . *Liverwort.* Blossoms white, tinged with red. In woods and shady places. April. **1817** Eaton *Botany* 63, [*Hepatica*] *triloba,* (liverleaf). **1832** Williamson *Hist. ME* 1.126, Lungwort and *Liverwort* [Footnote: Hepatica], used as preventives, or cures of the consumption. **1873** in 1976 Miller *Shaker Herbs* 12, Concentrated Syrup of Liverwort (*Hepatica triloba*)—A new safe, and valuable medicine for cough spitting of blood and consumption. *Ibid* 198, Liverwort—*Hepatica americana*—Noble liverwort. **1876** Burroughs *Winter Sunshine* 112, In the woods the liverleaf and arbutus had just opened doubtingly. **1916** Keeler *Early Wildflowers* 78, The names Hepatica and Liverwort hark back to the age of the simpler and echo the doctrine of signatures. . . As the leaf of the Hepatica is three-lobed it suggested the liver; thence the plant was considered a specific for diseases of that organ. **1950** Gray–Fernald *Manual of Botany* 660, Hepatica . . Liverleaf . . (Feminine of the Latin *hepaticus,* pertaining to the liver, from the shape of the leaves.) **1967–68** *DARE* (Qu. S21, . . *Weeds . . that are a trouble in gardens and fields*) Inf GA18, Liverwort; (Qu. S23, *Pale blue flowers with downy leaves and cups that come up on open, stony hillsides in March or early April*) Inf PA60, Liverwort. **1968** *DARE* Wildfl QR Pl.51B Inf NY91, Liverwort—known locally as this.

liver moss See **liverweed**

liver mush n NC, SC, GA, TN Cf **mush n[1] 2**

=**liver sausage.**

1918 *DN* 5.18 NC, Liver-mush, liver pudding. **1941** Writers' Program *Guide SC* 429, Nothing is allowed to go to waste—head cheese, liver mush, liver pudding, sausage, and souse meat account for the various odds and ends. **1952** Brown *NC Folkl.* 1.560 wNC, Liver-mush. . . Liver-pudding. **1957** *Hall Coll.* wNC, Liver pudding. . . Also called *liver mush.* **1966–69** *DARE* (Qu. H43, *Foods made from parts of the head and inner organs of an animal*) Infs GA75, NC31, Liver mush—with cornmeal; NC52, Liver mush—head and liver and meal; SC42, Liver mush—has cornmeal, a liver sausage; SC29, Liver mush, liverelle—cornmeal and flour, cook liver and grind it, make mush, put them together; **NC**36, 48, Liver mush. **1972** *Foxfire Book* 205 **nGA**, Most of our contacts used the liver [of a hog] for "liver pudding" or "liver mush." **1981** Howell *Surv. Folklife* 103 **neTN, seKY**, Liver mush is a liver sausage made with meal and sausage seasonings. **1982** Ginns *Snowbird Gravy* 36 **nwNC**, We made livermush from the liver. You know, we buy it in the store now, and it isn't fitten to eat. Always, when I made it, I cooked the onions and everything with it—salt, pepper, and onions. And then we'd make it out in cakes so we could slice it. **1986** Pederson *LAGS Concordance (What do you call the dish prepared by cooking and grinding up hog liver?)* 18 infs, **GA, TN**, Liver mush; 1 inf, **ceTN**, Liver mush—same as liver pudding, made of liver and lights; 1 inf, **ceTN**, Liver mush—cook liver, stir in meal before done; 1 inf, **csTN**, Liver mush—I never did make none; 1 inf, **cnGA**, Liver mush—cornmeal, stirred in hog liver; 1 inf, **cnGA**, Liver mush—ground liver, pepper, sage; 1 inf, **neGA**, Liver mush—can be made with cornmeal; 1 inf, **neGA**, Liver mush—a favorite; *(Chitterlings)* 1 inf, **cnGA**, After cooking, haslet is liver mush; *(Mush)* 1 inf, **neGA**, Liver mush.

liver nip n [Var of **knip**] esp **SC** Cf **liver sausage**
A liver dumpling; see quot 1978.

1954 *PADS* 21.32 **SC**, *Liver nips.* . . A viand prepared with a base of ground or minced beef liver highly seasoned with onions, pepper, and many other ingredients. There are many varying receipts. A favorite dish in the Dutch Fork. **1968** *DARE* Tape **SC**57, We're gonna have liver nips . . liver dumplings for dinner. **1978** Mayer *Beef Club* 7 **cSC** (as of 1840–1940), The customary meal after butchering was a popular dish of German descent, liver dumplings or liver nips. They took all morning to prepare and had to be eaten quickly to avoid the coating of grease which formed in the mouth when they cooled. [Footnote to *liver nips*: Liver nips are a mixture of ground or hacked liver, flour, egg, onion, salt, and pepper. They are dropped by tablespoonfuls into a pot of cooking beef broth and are done when they rise to the top.] *Ibid* 9, *Liver nips (liver dumplings)* . . popular among German settlers in America, including those in the Dutch Fork of South Carolina and in Pennsylvania.

liver pad n [From *liver pad* a pad worn over the region of the liver] *joc* Cf **blanket 3**, *DS* H20b
A pancake.

1942 Berrey–Van den Bark *Amer. Slang* 91.14, *Griddle cakes.* . . Liver pads. **1950** *Western Folkl.* 9.381 **neCA** [Lumberjack language], *Liver pads.* Hotcakes. **1958** McCulloch *Woods Words* 107 **Pacific NW**, *Liver pads*—Flapjacks. **1973** Allen *LAUM* 1.284 (as of c1950), *Griddle cakes* (of wheat). . . Liver pads [2 infs, **cn,swNE**].

liver-pin n Also *liver-string* [Cf *EDD* *liver-pin* "a pin jocularly supposed to secure the liver"] Cf **gizzard string, pop one's; string**
A supposed part of one's liver; see quots.

1899 (1912) Green *VA Folk-Speech* 264, *Liver-pin.* . . A figurative term to express the centre or most important part of the liver. A part not clearly located, but a special and vital part of the anatomy. "Damn his liver-pin." **1910** *DN* 3.458 **Chicago IL** [Expressions heard from Chicago people of New England antecedents], *To burst the liver-strings,* or *to strain the liver-pin.* . . Said of some violent exertion, as "If you laugh so hard you'll burst your liver-strings."

liver pudding n **chiefly S and Mid Atl** See Map Cf **boudin 2, hog-head pudding**
=**liver sausage.**

1879 (1965) Tyree *Housekeeping in Old VA* 223, *Liver pudding.* . . Take two hog's heads, . . two livers, two lights, and . . half a dozen milts; half a dozen sweetbreads; half a dozen kidneys. . . Soak, . . Boil, . . grind it in a sausage mill. . . Season. **1887** *Boston Jrnl.* (Mass.) 31 Dec. 2/4 *(OED)*, A liver-pudding completed this typical Georgia repast. **1937** *Hall Coll.* **wNC**, *Liver-pudding.* . . Hog's liver mixed with corn meal and fried. **1942** (1960) Robertson *Red Hills* 68 **SC**, At my grandfather's house at noontime we had soup and two or three kinds of meat, fried chicken, fried ham, or spareribs or liver pudding. **1951** Johnson *Resp. to PADS 20* **DE**, Meat from the head & inner organs of an animal cut up and pressed into a mold—liver pudding. **1951** *NY Folkl. Qrly.* 7.189 **NY**, In the North Country one frequently finds *blood pudding* for *blood sausage,* less frequently *liver pudding.* **1957** *Hall Coll.* **wNC**, *Liver-pudding.* . . Boil hog's or cow's liver till tender, mash and thicken with corn meal, add salt and pepper, make into a mold and keep in a cool place. Slice and fry if wanted. **1965–70** *DARE* (Qu. H43, *Foods made from parts of the head and inner organs of an animal*) 28 Infs, **chiefly S and Mid Atl**, Liver pudding; **AL**33, Liver pudding—with cornmeal; **FL**6, Liver pudding—from hog livers and one hog head, add

rice, seasonings; **FL**49, Liver pudding—black pepper, salt, sage, make into jelly, chill, slice; **GA**46, Liver pudding—liver, lean meat, onions, stuffed into a casing; **GA**79, Liver pudding—with cornmeal; **GA**81, Liver pudding—with cornmeal, with ears and snoot; **MD**14, Liver pudding—mostly liver, mixed with cornmeal, very like scrapple, except liver predominates; **SC**19, Liver pudding, hog pudding—they don't lose nothing but the squeal of a hog; **SC**46, Liver pudding—used to use lights in it, too; **SC**67, 70, Liver pudding—(with) rice, no cornmeal. **1967–68** *DARE* Tape **SC**46, Back in those days, my grandmother's days, they used lights and liver and a little bit of meat, sometimes it was even maybe the skins off of the sausage meat . . cooked with the lights and liver, and maybe a foot, a hog foot cooked, so that makes it stick together, congeal. When you cook that it will set up and it looks like it's pressed, or you can mold it. . . People mold it now and sell it. . . That's liver pudding. *Ibid* **SC**56, That's what we call. . . liver pudding. You put this meat in the pot, the head, . . the liver and the heart and all the inside of a hog, you might say, and you cook it good and done, and then you take that meat out and grind it up and put pepper and salt and your other flavoring for it . . and stuff it in the entrails. . . You can bake it or fry it, either. **1972** [see **liver mush**]. **1986** Pederson *LAGS Concordance* **chiefly eTN, GA, FL** *(What do you call the dish prepared by cooking and grinding hog liver?)* 134 infs, Liver pudding; 1 inf, Liver pudding—some call liver hash; 1 inf, Liver pudding = liver mush, made of liver and lights; 1 inf, Liver pudding—liver, souse, cornmeal; 1 inf, Liver pudding = liverwurst; 2 infs, Liver pudding = liver hash; 1 inf, Liver pudding = liver cheese, not packed in casing; 1 inf, Liver pudding = blood pudding; 1 inf, You ain't never had no liver pudding, dear?

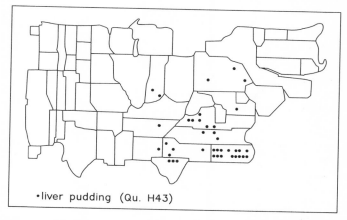

• liver pudding (Qu. H43)

liver sausage n [Calque of Ger *leberwurst*] **chiefly Gt Lakes, Upper Missip Valley** See Map on p. 386 Cf **braunschweiger 1, hog-head sausage**
Liver (usu of a pig) that is cooked, ground, seasoned, and often mixed with cornmeal, meat, and other internal organs, then molded into a loaf or stuffed in casings.

1853 (1982) Lea *Domestic Cookery* 170 **MD**, *Liver Sausage.* Take four livers, with the lights and hearts; have two heads cleaned, and boil them with any scraps, or skinny pieces you have . . ; when they are done, pick out the bones, and chop all together; season with sage, thyme, sweet marjoram, salt and pepper. **1868** in 1920 James *Letters* 1.136, [Letter from Germany:] The sausages (liver sausages, blood sausages, and more). **1950** *WELS* **WI** *(Kinds of sausage most eaten in your neighborhood)* 30 Infs, Liver (sausage); 4 Infs, Smoked liver (sausage); 1 Inf, Smoked and fresh liver sausage. **1951** *NY Folkl. Qrly.* 7.188 **NY**, On the Niagara frontier one finds *blood sausage* and *liver sausage* as products of home butchering (possibly a cultural influence from German settlers). **1965** *Colonial Kitchens* 74 **GA**, *Liver sausage*—Two hog livers and one hoghead. Boil together until thoroughly done. . . Run the meat through sausage grinder, season with salt, pepper and sage. Add about 1 quart of the water the meat was boiled in. . . and add 1 pint of meal and 1 pint of flour to thicken. . . When done pour in pans to mold. To serve cut in slices dip in flour and fry in a very little fat. **1965–70** *DARE* (Qu. H43, *Foods made from parts of the head and inner organs of an animal*) 15 Infs, **chiefly Gt Lakes, Upper Missip Valley**, Liver sausage; **MI**77, Liver sausage—same as liverwurst; **NY**226, Liver sausage—little liver, no cornmeal—wheat flour; **OH**4, Liver sausage—with cornmeal; **NC**72, Pork liver sausage; (Qu. H39, *Kinds of sausage;* total Infs questioned, 75) Inf **FL**19, Liver sausage. **1973** Allen *LAUM* 1.289 **Upper MW** (as of c1950), *Liver sausage.* The expression is widely scattered in the U[pper] M[idwest], without regional weighting. **1986** Pederson *LAGS Concordance* **Gulf Region** (*What do you call the dish prepared by cooking and grinding up hog liver?*) 46 infs, Liver sausage; 1 inf, Liver sausage = liverwurst; 1 inf, Liver sausage—mother made this; 1 inf, Liver sausage—like pate; 1 inf, I guess that's liver sausage; 1 inf, Liver sausage—seasoned with sage, black pepper; 1 inf, Liver sausage—German mother-in-law made; 1 inf, Goose liver sausage—at the store; 1 inf, Liver sausage—made with chicken livers; 1 inf, Liver sausage—ate for breakfast; 1 inf, Liver sausage—mother-in-law made; 1 inf, Liver sausage—tastes like ham and liver; 1 inf, Liver sausage—not haslet.

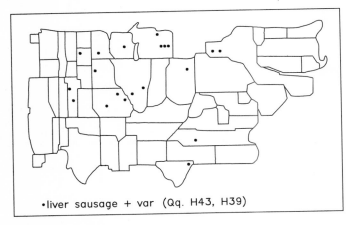

•liver sausage + var (Qq. H43, H39)

liver-string See **liver-pin**

liversworth See **liverworth**

liverweed n Also *liver moss*
A **hepatica** (here: *Hepatica nobilis obtusa*).
1828 Rafinesque *Med. Flora* 1.238, *Hepatica Triloba* . . Common Liverwort . . Vulgar Names—Liverweed, Trefoil, Noble Liverwort. **1876** Hobbs *Bot. Hdbk.* 65, Liver moss . . *Hepatica Americana.* **1892** (1974) Millspaugh *Amer. Med. Plants* 2-1, Hepatica. Liver-leaf . . Liver-weed. **1911** Henkel *Amer. Med. Leaves* 10, *Hepatica hepatica.* . . kidney liver-leaf, liverwort (incorrect), noble liverwort, heart liverwort . . liverweed. **1930** Sievers *Amer. Med. Plants* 40, Liverleaf . . *Hepatica americana* . . liverweed. **1940** Clute *Amer. Plant Names* 3, Hepatica . . *H. triloba* . . liver-moss.

liverwish n [Folk-etym or pronc-sp for **liverwurst**] Cf **liver mush**
1952 Brown *NC Folkl.* 1.561 **wNC**, Liver-wish. . . Liver-pudding. From Ger. *Leberwurst* (?).

liverwort n
1 See **liverleaf.**
2 A **polypody** (here: *Polypodium virginianum*).
1898 *Jrl. Amer. Folkl.* 11.283, *Polypodium vulgare* . . liverwort, Southport, Me. [Footnote to *liverwort:*] Whole plant steeped and used as a tonic.
3 A lichen (here: *Sticta pulmonacea*).
1916 Kephart *Camping & Woodcraft* 1.350, *Lungwort Bread.*—On the bark of maples, and sometimes of beeches and birches, in the northern woods, there grows a green, broad-leaved lichen variously known as lungwort, liverwort, lung-lichen, and lung-moss, which is an excellent substitute for yeast. This is an altogether different growth from the plants commonly called lungwort and liverwort—I believe its scientific name is *Sticta pulmonacea*.
4 also *liverwort lettuce*: A **wintergreen** (here: *Pyrola rotundifolia*).
1900 Lyons *Plant Names* 312, *P[yrola] rotundifolia*. . . Liverwort Lettuce. **1958** Jacobs-Burlage *Index Plants NC* 173, *Pyrola americana*. . . Liverwort. . . This species . . is found throughout North Carolina and South Carolina in damp woods.

liverworth n Also *liversworth* [Folk-etyms] **esp S Midl**
=**liverwurst.**
1965–70 *DARE* (Qu. H43, *Foods made from parts of the head and inner organs of an animal*) Infs **IN34, KY85**, Liverworth; **KY90**, Liverworth—with corn bread; **MO19**, Liverworth—duke's mixture; **OK3**,

My husband's mother used all these things and stuffed them in a piece of intestine; they called that liverworth; **IN16**, Liversworth.

liverwort lettuce See **liverwort 4**

liverwurst n Pronc-sp *liverwursch* [Partial calque of Ger *Leberwurst*] **chiefly Nth, N Midl, West** See Map
=**liver sausage.**
[**1869** *Atlantic Mth.* 24.483 **PA**, Our Dutch neighbors make *liver-wurst* ("woorsht") or meat pudding, omitting the meal, and this compound, stuffed into the large entrails, is very popular in Lancaster market.] **1925** *Book of Rural Life* 8.4908, Cooked sausages include liverwurst, head cheese and blood sausage. **1945** Lewis *Cass Timberlane* 34 **MN**, Coca-Cola, liverwurst, stuffed olives, and chocolate layer cake. **1950** *WELS* (*Kinds of sausage most eaten in your neighborhood*) 1 Inf, **seWI**, Liver "wursch." **1965–70** *DARE* (Qu. H43, *Foods made from parts of the head and inner organs of an animal*) 40 Infs, **chiefly Nth, N Midl, West**, Liverwurst; **CA105**, Liverwurst—mostly German; **MO3**, Liverwurst—that's what the Germans used to call it. **1973** Allen *LAUM* 1.289 **Upper MW** (as of c1950), Liverwurst. This German loanword for liver sausage is fairly common, though better known in German background areas, such as in Nebraska. **1986** Pederson *LAGS Concordance* **Gulf Region** (*What do you call the dish prepared by cooking and grinding up hog liver?*) 67 infs, Liverwurst; 2 infs, Liverwurst = liver sausage; 1 inf, Liverwurst = liver pudding; 1 inf, Liverwurst = bologna; 1 inf, Liverwurst = goose liver, unsure what made of; 1 inf, Liverwurst—sausage in a cloth bag; 1 inf, Liverwurst—mixed liver with lean part of head; 1 inf, Liverwurst—pressed in a vessel; 1 inf, Liverwurst—blacks made this; 1 inf, Liverwurst—in stores; 1 inf, Liverwurst—has bought it, never saw it made; 1 inf, Liverwurst—he has heard, not a natural term.

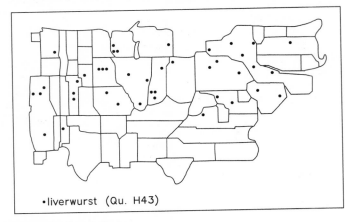

•liverwurst (Qu. H43)

lives adv See **lief** adv
livestock n pl [*OED* 1785 →] *joc*
Vermin, esp lice.
1891 Maitland *Amer. Slang Dict.* 169, Live stock, vermin. **1950** *WELS* **WI** (*Body and head lice*) 1 Inf, Bugs, livestock; 1 Inf, Livestock. **1966–68** *DARE* (Qu. R24, . . Names . . *for a bedbug*) Inf **NM9**, Livestock; (Qu. R25, *Joking names for a head louse, or body louse*) Infs **IL27, IA34, MI47, NY100, PA58, WI58**, Livestock; **MI51**, Livestock—lots of people say that. **1969** Sorden *Lumberjack Lingo* 70 **NEng, Gt Lakes**, Livestock—Body lice, crumbs, blue jackets, gray backs.

live storm n Cf **line storm, living gale**
1975 Gould *ME Lingo* 165, Live storm—A gale with rain or snow, as distinguished from a *dry gale.*

live water n [Cf Lat *aqua vitae* water of life] Cf **aggie forti(e)s**
1940 *AmSp* 15.447 **eTN**, Live water. Liquor. 'The mash will make ten gallons of live water.'

living fence See **live fence**

living gale n
See quots.
1889 *Century Dict.* 3489, Living. . . Furious; fierce: applied by seamen to a gale: as, a *living gale* of wind. **1915** (1916) Johnson *Highways New Engl.* 187, We're havin' fine weather now; but Sunday and a Monday it blew a living gale here. **1942** ME Univ. *Studies* 56.32 **NEng**, It might be *dead calm* or *blowing great guns*, a *living gale*. **1942** Berrey–Van den Bark *Amer. Slang* 790.4, *Wind.* . . Living gale, *a furious gale.*

livs See **lief** adv

li-yer See **lawyer**

Liza n¹ Also *Liza Jane*

A lie; a liar; hence v *lizar* to lie.

1909 *DN* 3.346 eAL, wGA, Liza (Jane). . . Used euphemistically for lie or liar. "He's a Liza." "You told me a Liza Jane." Occasionally as a verb, "He lizared on me."

liza n² Also *lisa* [Span *lisa, liza* mullet]

1 A **mullet** n¹ **1**, usu *Mugil liza* or the **white mullet.**

1882 U.S. Natl. Museum *Bulletin* 16.403, M[ugil] brasiliensis. . . White Mullet: Liza. **1896** U.S. Natl. Museum *Bulletin* 47.810, Mugil brasiliensis. . . Liza. . . Body elongate, more slender than in any other American Mugil. Ibid 813, Mugil curema. . . (White Mullet; . . Liza . .). Cape Cod to Brazil. . . A food-fish of importance, entering the sea more freely than does Mugil cephalus, which is a bay fish. **1902** Jordan–Evermann *Amer. Fishes* 251, Liza. . . Mugil brasiliensis. **1911** *Century Dict. Suppl.*, Lisa. . . The Spanish (and American Spanish) name of several species of mullet. **1911** U.S. Bur. Census *Fisheries 1908* 312, The "white mullet" [=Mugil curema] [is found] from Cape Cod southward. Local names are "bluefish mummichog," . . "liza." **1946** LaMonte *N. Amer. Game Fishes* 15, The White Mullet, Mugil curema (Blue-back Mullet, Liza . .), runs as large as 3'. It is a southern fish but occasionally straggles to Cape Cod, Massachusetts. **1966** *DARE* (Qu. P2, . . Kinds of saltwater fish caught around here . . good to eat) Inf FL27, Mullet or lisa ['lisə]. **1991** Amer. Fisheries Soc. *Common Names Fishes* 57, Mugil liza . . liza.

2 A **ten-pounder** (here: *Elops saurus*).

1902 Jordan–Evermann *Amer. Fishes* 87, The bony-fish [=Elops saurus] rejoices in a multiplicity of vernacular names, among which are . . Liza, . . ten-pounder, and John Mariggle. **1946** LaMonte *N. Amer. Game Fishes* 14, Elops saurus. . . Names . . Lisa . . The name[s] "bonefish" . . and "Ladyfish" for this [fish] . . would be better forgotten, as they are causes of much confusion. . . Feeds in open ocean, coming in in schools with the tide. Coastal in rivers and inlets. Present all year in southern Florida. **1973** Knight *Cook's Fish Guide* 383, Liza—or see Ladyfish or Mullet.

Liza Jane, lizar See **Liza** n¹

lizard n Cf **stinging lizard**

1 Std: a scaled reptile of the order Squamata, suborder Lacertilia. For names of var of these see **alligator lizard 1, 2, blind worm, blue scorpion, dog lizard, fence ~ 1, Gila monster 1, 2, glade devil, glass snake, gray bitch, green lizard, gridiron-tailed ~, horned toad 1, leopard lizard, mountain boomer 3, poison lizard, ring-necked ~, scorpion, skink, swift, worm lizard, zebra-tailed ~**

2 =**salamander** (here: order Caudata), such as the **tiger salamander,** the **hellbender 1,** or the **mud puppy b**; see quots. Cf **spring lizard, water ~**

1867 *Amer. Naturalist* 1.109 MA, The several species of Salamanders (improperly called "Lizards") are also to be found. **1899** Bergen *Animal Lore* 38 nME, Don't kill a lizard (salamander), or you will die within a year. **1905** U.S. Bur. Fisheries *Rept. for 1904* 603, I suspect that by no means the least enemy to these eggs is the common mud puppy (Necturus maculosus—called "lizard" by the fisherman). **1925** *Book of Rural Life* 6.3250, To many people, any long, narrow, four-legged creature which drags its body along on the ground and has a well-developed tail is a lizard. For this reason, many people call salamanders "lizards". **1926** TX Folkl. Soc. *Pub.* 5.63, In the plains region of western Texas, the large tiger salamander [=Ambystoma tigrinum] is a common animal. . . Small specimens are sometimes called "lizards." **1928** Baylor Univ. Museum *Contrib.* 16.8 TX, Poor whites and negroes, who know all lizards as "Scorpions," classify all salamanders as lizards. Ibid, Lizard that leaves a silver streak is a name describing the Slimy Salamander [=Plethodon glutinosus] on account of the viscous matter it exudes from the pores of its body and tail. As a result of this viscous exudation, the animal sometimes leaves a slug-like trail among rotten wood and leaf mould. **1938** *AmSp* 13.43 VT, In my childhood I knew the little sorts [of caudate amphibians] that are found now in clear water and now under big sticks or stones among the fallen leaves of the woods, and my mother (from eastern Vermont) taught me to call them lizards. **1966** Wheeler–Wheeler *Amphibians & Reptiles ND* 31, Tiger Salamander. . . These salamanders are seldom seen but when they are encountered they are usually misnamed "lizards" and are often greatly feared.

3 also sp *lizzard:* A crude sledge made from the fork of a tree; hence v *lizard* to transport with this device. Cf **crotch** n¹ **3**

1870 Nowland *Early Indianapolis* 16, One end was placed on a sled called a "lizard," to which the horse was hitched. **1902** *DN* 2.238 sIL, Lizard. . . A sled or slide framed from the fork of a tree of convenient size. **1906** Johnson *Highways Missip. Valley* 114 AR, The forward end of the log lay on a "lizard," a rude V-shaped sledge about six feet long, upturning at the point, and made out of the fork of some large tree. **1906** in 1931 *AmSp* 6.465 TX, Down in Texas a sledge or jumper is evidently called a lizzard. An effort is now being made to locate a lizzard made by Davy Crockett out of the fork of a bois d'arc tree in 1835, and upon which he hunted and hauled deer. If the lizzard is found it will be placed in the Alamo as a historical relic. **1917** Kephart *Camping & Woodcraft* 2.64, Where logging operations have already begun, then, wherever a stump stands it will not be hard to determine the direction in which the logs were twitched to the nearby "lizard road," where they were loaded on lizards (forks of timber used as sleds), or on wagons, and dragged to the river or saw-mill. **1931** *AmSp* 7.49 Sth, SW [Lumberjack lingo], The timber is sometimes "skidded" on the ground; sometimes it is loaded, one end on a forked sapling, and "lizzarded" to the "stack ground." **1942** Whipple *Joshua* 516 UT (as of c1860), Once a day Ole Oleson came to the back door to collect the swill, which he hauled off in a big barrel on a 'lizard.' **1948** Dick *Dixie Frontier* 106, A type of sled used in Missouri before the era of the wagon was known as a lizard. It was made of a V-shaped forked tree and furnished with a bed of brush to haul a load. **1966** Dakin *Dial. Vocab. Ohio R. Valley* 2.161, Scattered informants in all four of the Valley states mention a lizard—a crude drag vehicle consisting of a bed of planks, etc., constructed on a tree fork which serves as runners. **1966–69** *DARE* (Qu. L57, A low wooden platform used for bringing stones or heavy things out of the fields) Inf DC8, Lizard [lɪzəd]; NC54, Lizard—for hauling tan bark; NJ16, Stone-boat, lizard; OH89, Lizard—this was used to haul logs out of the woods; SC30, Lizard—made from a tree fork with planks over it; SC57, Lizard—made from a tree crotch by nailing boards across it; (Qu. N40c, Other kinds of sleighs) Inf IL66, Lizard—horse pulls it, a kind of forked stick that can haul logs. **1967** Faries *Word Geog. MO* 84, Stone boat. . . The informants list a few occurrences of lizard (6 [of c700 infs]). **1968** *DARE* FW Addit swTN, Lizard—forked log beam for dragging logs. The log was laid in the fork and the chain put across it. A mule was hitched to the other end of the lizard. **1973** Allen *LAUM* 1.219 (as of c1950), Stone boat. . . 2 infs, cIA, cSD, Lizard.

4 See quot. Cf **shotgun house**

1923 *DN* 5.244 LA, Lizard. . . A long, narrow house, with the narrow end facing the street, and rooms opening on an alley along the side.

lizard v See **lizard** n **3**

lizard bird n

=**roadrunner.**

1904 (1910) Wheelock *Birds CA* 181, Road-runner.—Geococcyx californianus. (Common names: Chaparral Cock; Ground Cuckoo; Lizard Bird.) [Ibid 182, A Road-runner killed by Mr. Anthony had just swallowed a large lizard. Undoubtedly its fondness for lizard diet has given it one of its many nicknames.] **1917** *Wilson Bulletin* 29.2.81, Lizard bird, long-tailed pheasant, . . road-runner [etc]. **1950** *WELS* (Road runner) 1 Inf, csWI, Lizard bird. **1955** *AmSp* 30.183 CA, NM, Lizard bird, for the road runner . . , a devourer of lizards. **1958** *AZ Highways* May 2, Its scientific name, Geococcyx californianus, signifies "ground cuckoo," . . Lizard bird, war bird, snake-eater, medicine bird, cock of the desert, and ground cuckoo are names met with in print, though not used to any extent, I think, by people belonging to the land.

lizard's claw n Also *lizard claw*

A **mushroom B1** (here: either *Lysurus gardneri* or *L. mokusin*).

1981 Lincoff *Audubon Field Guide Mushrooms* 832, Lizard's Claw. Lysurus gardneri. . . Several short, pinkish, incurved or spreading arms atop a tall, white stalk; . . odor fetid. Ibid 833, The similar Small Lizard's Claw (L. mokusin) is considered a great delicacy by the Chinese. **1987** McKnight–McKnight *Mushrooms* 344, Lizard Claw. Anthurus gardneri. . . Widespread in N. America. . . Late summer. Edibility: Unknown. Ibid 345, Ribbed Lizard Claw. Lysurus mokusin. . . Reported from Chesapeake Bay area southward. Common in California.

lizard's tail n

1 also *lizard tail:* A plant (*Saururus cernuus*) native chiefly to swampy areas in the eastern half of the US. [*OED* 1753 →; see quot 1931] Also called **breastweed, culver's root 2, swamp dragon, ~ lily, water dragon, ~ lily**

1791 in 1793 *Amer. Philos. Soc. Trans.* 3.168, *Saururus, cernuus.* Lizards-tail. **1817** Eaton *Botany* 43, *Saururus. . . cernuus,* (lizard-tail). **1822** Eaton *Botany* 448, *Saururus. . . cernuus* (Lizard's tail . .). Stem leafy, many-spiked. **1869** Porcher *Resources* 373 **Sth**, *Lizard's tail. . .* The roots can be abundantly and easily obtained in almost every swamp along the seaboard. **1872** *Amer. Naturalist* 6.728, In lower spots [of the lower Wabash Valley] the "lizard-tail" (*Saururus cernuus*) was the predominant plant. **1901** Mohr *Plant Life AL* 125, In the openings the shallow pools are filled with . . *Saururus cernuus* (lizard's tail). **1931** Harned *Wild Flowers Alleghanies* 145, The sharp-pointed tip of the [flower] spike and abrupt curve give the common name, Lizard Tail, to the plant. **1966–68** *DARE* (Qu. S26b, *Wildflowers that grow in water or wet places*) Inf **GA**35, Lizard tail; **SC**27, Lizard's tail—Saururus cernuus. **1972** in 1983 Johnson *I Declare* 145 **nwFL**, There are the buckeyes, lizard tails, . . and deer tongues[s], all descriptively named by American discoverers. **1979** Ajilvsgi *Wild Flowers* 131 **wLA, eTX**, *Lizard's tail. . .* [It forms] large colonies of plants in shallow water or mud.

2 =**yerba mansa**.

1940 Writers' Program *Guide NM* 15, *Oshá* (mountain celery) and *yerba de mansa* (lizard's tail) are among those still gathered in New Mexico mountains as valuable foods and remedies.

lizard tail n

1 See **lizard's tail 1**.

2 A **woolly daisy** (here: *Eriophyllum staechadifolium*). **CA**
1911 Jepson *Flora CA* 437, *E[riophyllum] staechadifolium. . . Lizard Tail. . .* Sandy hills and fields near the ocean. **1954** CA Div. Beaches & Parks *Pt. Lobos Wild Flowers* 9, Lizard-tail . . is probably the most abundant wildflower at Point Lobos. Beginning early in June and lasting throughout summer, Lizard-tail covers entire seaward-facing slopes with its golden hue. **1961** Thomas *Flora Santa Cruz* 366 **cwCA**, Lizard Tail. . . May–November, but individual plants may be found in flower during the remaining months of the year. **1976** Bailey-Bailey *Hortus Third* 442, Lizard-tail. . . Coastal, s. Ore. to s. Calif.

3 A **butterfly weed 2** (here: *Gaura parviflora*).
1961 Wills-Irwin *Flowers TX* 166, Other *Gauras* known from Texas include Lizard-tail, *G. parviflora* . . our tallest, sometimes reaching 8 ft. **1970** Correll *Plants TX* 1124, *Gaura parviflora* . . Lizard-tail.

lizzard See **lizard** n 3

Lizzie See **Lizzy**

Lizzie-run-in-the-hedge n
=**ground ivy 1**.
1940 Clute *Amer. Plant Names* 265, *Nepeta glechoma* . . Lizzie run in the hedge.

Lizzy n Also sp *Lizzie*

1 A saddle horn.
1936 Adams *Cowboy Lingo* 44 **West**, This [saddle] 'tree' was comprised of a longitudinal 'fork' and a transverse 'cantle,' and upon the front end was bolted a metal 'horn,' which went by such slang names as 'nubbin',' 'apple,' 'Lizzie,' 'biscuit,' and many others.

2 See quot.
1969 *DARE* (Qu. M21b, *Joking names for an outside toilet building*) Inf **RI**15, Lizzy, "going to Lizzy's."

Lo See **Lord** n[1]

load v Also with *up*
To deceive, trick, mislead; also n *load* a lie, liar.
1883 Twain *Life on Missip.* (Boston) 266, He went on . . reeling off his tranquil spool of lies. . . and proceeded to load me up in the good old-fashioned way. **1906** *DN* 3.145 **nwAR**, *Load. . .* To deceive or intimidate by a hint, to convey unpleasant information by insinuation. "He just loaded them." **1933** *AmSp* 8.1.31 **nwTX** [Cowboy lingo], *Load.* To deceive by *yarns* or *windies* [=lies]. Also a prevarication, a prevaricator. **1953** Randolph-Wilson *Down in Holler* 262 **Ozarks**, *Load. . .* To deceive with a *windy* or a tall tale. "The boys has been a-loadin' them pore tourists ag'in."

loaded for bear adj phr [See quot 1955]

1 Fully prepared for a situation; esp, ready and eager for a confrontation.
1896 *DN* 1.420 **cwNY**, *Loaded for bear. . .* Said of one who has a big supply of anything. *Ibid* **MA, NY**, *Loaded for bear. . .* Full of indignation which is likely to be vented upon its object. **1909** *DN* 3.400 **nwAR**,

Loaded for bear. . . Full of indignation . . or well supplied with arguments and facts to support an argument, or anything that will enable a person to succeed in what he sets out to do. **1927** *AmSp* 2.359 **cwWV**, We were loaded for bear before we started to the mountains. **1928** Ruppenthal *Coll.* **KS**, *To be loaded for bear*—to be prepared. **1955** Funk *Heavens to Betsy* 206, *Loaded for bear*—To be fully prepared for any contingency; to be well prepared; hence, ready to fly into a rage. Originally this had a hunting significance; the bear, being the largest of dangerous American wild animals and likely to be encountered in any region of wild game, a hunter did not regard himself as prepared unless his gun carried a charge heavy enough to kill a bear. **1966** *DARE* Tape **MI**10, If you [=a lumberjack] left your job, walked off voluntarily. . . and if you were thirsty, which you were apt to be, and loaded for bear, everybody conceded that you were stakebound [=well provided with money]. **1976** Garber *Mountain-ese* 54 **sAppalachians**, *Loaded-for-bear* . . war-minded. **1978** *Capital Times* (Madison WI) 11 Aug [46]/1, Carley has been trying for months to get Schreiber to react directly to his criticisms. . . So Schreiber came out loaded for bear in the Green Bay debate. **1985** *DARE* File **cwIN**, *Loaded for bear*—Meaning preparedness for any situation. Referring to having enough ammunition in a shotgun to shoot a bear if one happened on one. Akin to "rarin' to go." **1986** Pederson *LAGS Concordance* (*Dressed up*) 1 inf, **cwGA**, Loaded for bear.

2 See quots. [Infl by *loaded* drunk]
1896 *DN* 1.420, Loaded for bear. . . Very drunk. **1967** *DARE* (Qu. DD15, *A person who is thoroughly drunk*) Inf **TX**26, Loaded for bear.

loaden v, hence ppl adj *loadened* [*load* v + -*en* suff[5]; *OED* 1568–1889; "*Obs. exc. dial.*"; see also *EDD, SND*] old-fash
Note: The form *loaden* is also an obsolete strong past pple of *load* v.
To load.
1795 Dearborn *Columbian Grammar* 136, *List of Improprieties. . .* Loaden'd for Loaded. **1829** Kirkham *Engl. Grammar* 193, *Provincialisms. . .* Md. Va. Ky. or Miss. . . I seen his boat was loadend too heavy. **1835** in 1930 Meine *Tall Tales* 141 **GA**, Please to observe, gentlemen, that at the word 'fire!' you must fire; that is if any of your guns are loaden'd, you must not shoot in yearnest, but only make pretence like. **1885** Twain *Huck. Finn* 332, He was just loadened down with . . chances . . to make a name for himself. **1899** (1912) Green *VA Folk-Speech* 265, *Loaden. . .* To load. *Ibid*, *Loadened. . .* Loaded. "A loadened gun." **1930** *AmSp* 5.495, To the double past participles . . may be added yet another such formation, *loadened*: "A truck passed loadened with machinery." This sentence was heard on the street, but *loadened* may not be a twentieth century nonce-form.

loadinin See -**ing** B2

load of hay n
See quot.
1922 Rollins *Cowboy* 157, Long hair did not meet with public approval. A man with a "load of hay on his skull" might be an actual "bad man," but usually he was diagnosed as being either weak-minded or a mere "bluffer."

load up See **load**

‡loady adj [Cf *EDD* *loady* "top-heavy, loaded," but cf also **logy 1**]
1969 *DARE* (Qu. BB16b, *If something a person ate didn't agree with him, he might just feel a bit _____*) Inf **TN**37, Loady ['lodɪ].

loaf bread n [Scots, Engl dial] **chiefly Sth, S Midl** See Map Cf **bread** n B1, **light bread**
Yeast-leavened bread, esp made with wheat flour, that is shaped into a loaf (as contrasted with cornbread, biscuits, etc).
1635 in 1850 Dorchester *Antiq. & Hist. Soc. Coll.* 3.12, Many went on shoare. . . and brought. . . loafe bread, fresh fish, &c. **1775** in 1921 *Jrl. Amer. Hist.* [Abilene] 7.366 **VA**, We git some good loaf Bread & good Whiskey. **1879** (1965) Tyree *Housekeeping in Old VA* 29, *Loaf bread. . .* Ingredients . . flour . . salt . . sugar . . water . . yeast. . . When risen work in two pints of flour. . . and set to rise. . . then bake it slowly. **1949** Kurath *Word Geog.* 67, *Wheat bread* (in loaves). . . In the South and the South Midland this type of bread is commonly known as *light-bread*, in the coastal area also as *loaf bread*, as distinct from *pone bread* for corn bread. **1952** Giles *40 Acres* 103 **KY**, Bread is corn bread to ridge folks. Biscuits are biscuits, loaf bread from the store is light bread or boughten bread, but when you say bread, you mean corn bread. **c1960** Wilson *Coll.* **csKY**, *Loaf bread. . .* Yeast, homemade bread rather than biscuits or cornbread; also store-bought loaves. **1965–70**

DARE (Qu. H13, *Bread that is not made at home*) 58 Infs, **chiefly Sth, S Midl**, Loaf bread; **NC**76, Light loaf bread; (Qu. H15, *Bread made with wheat flour*) 17 Infs, **chiefly Sth, S Midl**, Loaf bread; **VA**56, Loaf; (Qu. H16, *What do people use to raise the bread before it's baked?*) Inf **VA**56, East—for loaf bread; (Qu. H18, . . *Special kinds of bread*) Inf **NC**38, Loaf bread; **NY**39, White loaf bread. **1971** Wood *Vocab. Change* 44 **Sth**, Homemade bread (or its commercial equivalent) made of wheat flour and baked in loaves is generally called *light bread. Loaf bread* is next in Georgia and Alabama. **1972** *PADS* 58.20 **cwAL**, *Bought bread.* Southern and South Midland *(store)-bought bread* (11) is most frequent, but *light bread* (6), *loaf bread* (3), *bakery bread* (2), and *baker's bread* (1) occur. *Ibid* 19 **cwAL**, *Wheat bread.* Southern and South Midland *light bread* (12) and Coastal Southern *loaf bread* (7) are most frequent; four informants used both terms, apparently as synonyms. **1990** Pederson *LAGS Regional Matrix* 115 **Gulf Region, esp AL, GA** (*Wheat bread in loaves*) 137 infs, Loaf bread. *Ibid* 119, (*Bought bread*) 94 infs, Loaf bread. **1993** *DARE* File, Among other things, my family says "sweet milk" and "loaf bread" (as opposed to pan-bread or pan-biscuits) because Mom grew up in Silsbee, Texas. We've lived in Eugene, Oregon since 1946. *Ibid* **GA**, How 'bout . . loaf bread.

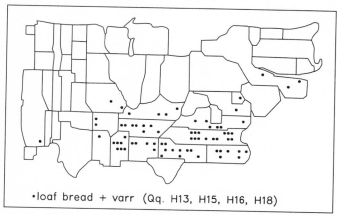

• loaf bread + varr (Qq. H13, H15, H16, H18)

loafer n Also *loafer wolf, lover ~* [Folk-etyms for Span *lobo* wolf] **chiefly SW** Cf **lobo 1**
=**gray wolf 1**.

1877 McDaniel–Taylor *Coming Empire* 314 **cwTX**, The Mexicans call these big wolves "lobos," and the Texans call them "loafers," which is a corruption of the Mexican word. **1893** (1958) Wister *Out West* 159 **TX**, *Loafer* large wolf (Spanish Lobo). **1929** Dobie *Vaquero* 280 **TX**, These lobos—"loafers," most of the old timers call them—are now approaching extinction. They were by far the most predatory animals that the cowmen ever knew. **1940** Writers' Program *Guide AZ* 466, For years George trapped "loafer" (lobo) wolves and hunted mountain lion and bear on the Cross-S range. **1941** Vestal *Short Grass Country* 48 **wOK**, One day John R. (Jack) Abernathy, cowboy and U.S. Marshal, took after a big "loafer" *(lobo)* wolf. When he reached the animal, he found one of his dogs slashed and dying by the loafer's teeth. **1958** Blasingame *Dakota Cowboy* 156 **SD**, A pair of loafers lived for years and raised six or eight pups each season. **1966** *DARE* (Qu. P32, . . *Other kinds of wild animals*) Inf **NM**3, Loafer wolf—similar to a German police dog—big. **1969** *DARE* Tape **TX**70, In the early days they had what they call lobo wolves. That's a big old wolf that would kill calves. We called 'em loafers, but they were lobos, that's the name of 'em. They were as big as these old German shepherd dogs. **1976** Dillard *Amer. Talk* 104, Another such doublet was *lover wolf,* an expression generated not by any sexual connotations but by folk-etymological associations with the Spanish word for wolf, *lobo.*

loafer v, hence ppl adj and vbl n *loafering,* n *loaferer* Also with *about, around* **chiefly sAppalachians** See Map
To loiter, idle, lounge; to gad about.

1837 J.D. Whitney in *Life* (1909) 19 (1933 *OED Suppl.*), There is another thing which is a sad enemy to time, namely 'loafering', i.e. visiting one another's rooms without any ostensible purpose, to pass away time. **1842** (1843) Norman *Rambles Yucatan* 88 **LA**, The Casa-real in this, as in other towns of the province, was the loafering-place of the Indians. **1859** (1968) Bartlett *Americanisms* 248, To loafer. . . To lounge; to idle away one's time. **1860** Hundley *Social Relations S. States* 239, The poor Southern Bully, in nine cases out of ten, is a loafering ex-overseer, whose drunken dissolute habits have lost him his situation.

1913 Kephart *Highlanders* 203 **sAppalachians**, Yea, la! I'm jist loaferin' about. *Ibid* 277, Loaferer, musician. **1931** Hannum *Thursday April* 57 **wNC** (as of 1897), I declar', he's the loaferingest man about. **1949** Hornsby *Lonesome Valley* 282 (Hench Coll.) **eKY**, He's done shaved and cleaned up! Plans to go down and loafer with Crit Marcum! **1953** Randolph–Wilson *Down in Holler* 262 **Ozarks**, That boy just loafers around all day, an' comes home to sleep. **1966–70** *DARE* (Qu. A9, . . *Wasting time by not working on the job*) Inf **MT**37, Loafering; **KY**39, Loafering around; (Qu. Y27, *To go about aimlessly, with nothing to do:* "*He's always _____ around the drugstore.*") Infs **KY**33, 42, **OH**61, **VA**39, Loafering; (Qu. Y28, *A person who loiters about with nothing to do*) Inf **VA**11, Loaferer; (Qu. Y29a, *To 'go out' a great deal, not to stay at home much:* "*She's always _____.*") Inf **NC**55, A-loafering; **VA**2, Loaferin'; (Qu. Y29b, . . *About a man [who doesn't stay home much]:* "*He's always _____.*") Inf **KY**28, Loafering about; **VA**2, Loafering around; (Qu. KK31, *To go about aimlessly looking for distraction:* "*He doesn't have anything to do, so he's just _____ around.*") Infs **KY**40, **NC**55, **TN**30, **VA**11, Loafering. **1971** Wood *Vocab. Change* 369 **Sth**, [A worthless dog]—*loafering dog, mutt, plain dog.* **1984** Wilder *You All Spoken Here* 191 **Sth**, Loafer around: Loaf; engage in aimless endeavors.

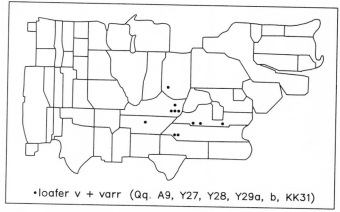

• loafer v + varr (Qq. A9, Y27, Y28, Y29a, b, KK31)

loafer rake n **NEng** Cf **bull rake, lazy man's ~**
A type of hand rake; see quots.

1907 *DN* 3.193 **seNH**, *Loafer rake.* . . Largest kind of hand hay-rake. Usual. **1913** *DN* 4.56 **seMA**, *Loafer-rake.* . . Another name for the "bull-rake," [=a large drag-rake, drawn by hand]. **1942** Cannon *Look to the Mt.* 4 **NH**, Even old David Gillmor was haying, but he couldn't mow or pitch this year; he was pulling a loafer rake. **1967** *Amer. Agric. & Rural New Yorker* 164.6.30 **ME**, [In a list of old words not now commonly known:] Jack or loafer rake—a rake for raking scatterings.

loafer's bread n

1980 *Commercial Appeal* (Memphis TN) 4 July 2/3, Mrs. Sadie Gilbert said light bread was bread you made at home. Storebought bread was "loafers bread," because only loafers didn't bake their own.

loafer wolf See **loafer** n

loafing barn n Also *loafing parlor, ~ shed* **scattered, but chiefly Inland Nth, Midl** See Map on p. 390 Cf **lounging barn**
A building, part of a building, or a shelter that allows free movement for livestock; similarly nouns *loafing area, ~ lot, ~ pen, ~ space, ~ yard* an enclosure that allows such movement.

1950 *Sun* (Baltimore MD) 15 June 40/2 (Hench Coll.) **nwMD**, Bankers touring the farm . . near here saw one of Maryland's few "loafing barns" today. Although widely used further west, the "loafing barn" is still rare in the east. It is an arrangement for wintering dairy cattle so they have floor space, well bedded with straw, to roam around during the long winter months, rather than being kept, as is more usual, at a particular stall with their necks through a stanchion. **1950** *WELS* (Rough or temporary shelter for livestock outside the barn) 1 Inf, **ceWI**, [lofiŋ] pen—just a roof and maybe a couple of sides—mostly for beef cattle. **1962** *Daily Progress* (Charlottesville VA) 30 Jan 3/2–4 (Hench Coll.), Workmen . . start to clear away debris of the large loafing barn that burned after an unexplained explosion Sunday night. . . More than 100 head of Holstein cattle were in the 240 by 40-foot barn. **1962** *Hench Coll.* **cVA**, Loafing barn. . . A barn (or feed lot) in which cattle feed on grain or silage without having to forage or graze in pastures. For fattening cattle. **1965–70** *DARE* (Qu. M1, . . *Kinds of barns . . according to their use or the way they are built*) Infs **MO**33, **PA**207, **SD**2, Loafing barn; **CT**24, Loafing barn—loose housing barn; **GA**84, Loafing barn—for cows; **IL**108, **KS**8, Loafing shed—for cattle; **IA**6, Loafing shed—one side open for beef cattle; **MD**34, Loafing barn—big shed with metal roof where cows can seek shelter from elements; **MN**4, Loafing shed—for livestock shelter, for cold weather or flies; **MN**34, Loafing barn—a barn with a large open area inside and a milking parlor; **NC**63, Loafing barn—a place for cows to rest; open on one side; **ND**1, Loafing barn—cattle roam free, day and night, summer and winter; **PA**141, Pole-loafing barn; **WA**30, Loafing shed—for cows to get out of the weather; **WI**43, Loafing barn—cattle loose, not stanchioned; (Qu. M10, *The part of the barn where cows are kept*) Infs **KY**72, **MO**21, **NC**33, **OH**60, Loafing shed (*or* barn); **GA**84, Loafing shed—cows are outdoors all year; **KY**53, Keep 'em in loafing sheds and milk 'em in parlors; **MI**49, Now the more up-to-date barns have loafing parlors and milking parlors; **MS**4, Loafing shed—a place for cows if there is no barn; **OH**75, Loafing parlor—now; cow stable—old-fashioned; (Qu. M11) Inf **OH**58, Loafing shed; (Qu. M13, *The space near the barn with a fence around it where you keep the livestock*) Infs **IL**41, **OH**48, Loafing pen; **GA**68, Loafing shed—for a dairy herd; **MD**29, Loafing shed—if covered over; **MI**97, Loafing area—covered on one side and the roof; (Qu. M14, *The open area around or next to the barn*) Infs **IL**56, **MD**29, **OH**75, **OR**1, Loafing area; **IL**4, Loafing shed—partially open area where livestock eats; **MD**13, Loafing lot; **MD**26, Loafing yard; **MD**32, Loafing shed—only in modern days, same as loafing parlor; **OH**81, Loafing pen; **OK**43, Many people have a loafing space (fenced in) to keep cattle in overnight for milking the next day; (Qu. M22, . . *Kinds of buildings . . on farms*) Inf **GA**68, Loafing barn—modern term for cow lot; **MD**20, Loafing shed—for heifers, dry cows, to keep them from being knocked around by full-grown cows and those who, because they are milking, have big appetites and prevent others from eating; **MO**19, Loafing shed—shed for cattle where they can find shelter if they wish to; **OR**1, Loafing shed; **VA**10, Loafing shed—where cows go after being milked and fed in the milk barns. **1968** *DARE* Tape **NJ**10, They built a new barn, what they call a loafing barn, and they have a milk parlor. They're all modern. . . He's on Wall Street, and he's got money to spend. **1968** *ID Daily Statesman* (Boise) 25 Feb sec D 6/1, Barn, loafing shed, silo and corrals. **1984** *MJLF* 10.111 **cnWI**, Emery . . built a modest loafing barn. . . To the west of the enclosure was the building, closed on the back and ends, open in the front, with one end used to store straw for bedding. To the east was a roofed-over feeding bunker. . . Such a building allows the farmer to leave his large heifers outside all winter. . . There are also times when a cow . . will benefit from being turned out to move about the loafing yard. *Ibid* 152 **cnWI**, *Loafing barn*. A low, sheet metal and pole structure, open on one side, usually to the south. Used to house heifers, save barn space, and reduce daily chores. **1992** *DARE* File **cwID**, A loafing shed is a rudimentary shelter with a roof and perhaps two walls where livestock can get out of the sun in the summer and out of the wind in the winter. It wouldn't be way out on the range, but probably near the feed lot. I first heard the term about 1960.

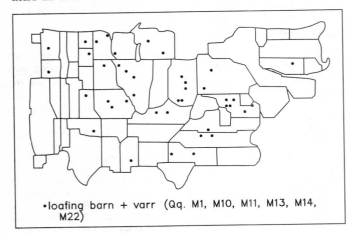

•loafing barn + varr (Qq. M1, M10, M11, M13, M14, M22)

loaker See **locust**

loam n Usu |lom|; also **scattered, but more freq NEast** *esp freq among speakers with little formal educ* |lum|; also **esp nNEng** |lum|; for addit varr see quots Pronc-sp *loom;* hence adj *loomy* [*OED* loam sb., pronc-sp *loom* 18th and 19th cents; see also *EDD* loomy (at loamy adj.¹)] Cf **gum** n¹, v¹

Std sense, var forms.

1801 in 1956 Eliason *Tarheel Talk* 314 **ce,seNC**, *Loom.* **1806** (1970) Webster *Compendious Dict.* 178, *Loam* or *loom. . . a fat earth.* [*DARE* Ed: The form *loom* does not appear in Webster's English model.] **1892** *DN* 1.240 **cwMO, NEng**, *Loam* [lum]. **1907** *DN* 3.193 **seNH**, You want some good loom in this garding. **1959** *VT Hist.* 27.147, *Loam* [lʌm] . . pronc. Occasional. **1961** Kurath–McDavid *Pronc. Engl.* 158, *Loam.* . . Checked /ʊ/ predominates decidedly in northeastern New England and New Brunswick, both in folk speech and in common speech, and is even used by some cultured speakers. It is also regular on the islands of Martha's Vineyard and Nantucket. Scattered instances survive in southern Vermont and on Long Island. . . The free vowel /u/ of *two* is common in this word elsewhere in New England, and only less so in New York State, East Jersey, Pennsylvania (except the southeastern and south-central counties . .), and the Ohio Valley from Pittsburgh to Huntington, W. Va. . . [T]his pronunciation is characteristic of folk speech, but is also more or less widely used by the middle group in rural sections. It is rare in urbanized areas and not current in cultivated speech. **1965–70** *DARE* (Qu. C30, . . *Loose, dark soil*) 462 Infs, **widespread**, Loam (soil); 31 Infs, **scattered**, Black (*or* sandy, dark, clay, etc) loam; 13 Infs, **esp Sth, S Midl**, Loamy (soil, land(s), *or* dirt); **AL**25, Black loamy; [**CA**5, Sloam [sloum]]; 64 Infs, **scattered, but more freq NEast**, Loom; **CA**63, **IL**69, 134, **IA**22, **MI**71, **NC**81, Black (*or* sandy, clay, dark) loam; **GA**28, **NY**195, **NC**20, **OH**89, **PA**70, Loomy (soil); [**MD**8, Loomis] [Of all Infs responding to the question, 31% were gs educ or less; of those giving responses with *loom(y)*, 43% were gs educ or less.]; (Qu. C31, . . *Heavy, sticky soil*) Infs **IA**11, **OK**4, **VA**75, **WI**19, (Heavy) clay loam; **CA**90, **DC**3, **NJ**21, **OH**99, Loam(y); **CT**21, Muddy loam. **1975** Gould *ME Lingo* 169, Mainers spell it *loam* but pronounce it *loom*. "Bring a lo'd a loom to smooth up my lawn when you get to it." **1976** Allen *LAUM* 3.255 (as of c1950), *Loam.* . . No instances of /lum/ appear at all in the U[pper] M[idwest] records, but /lum/ has persisted with some strength. Predictably, it has clear Northern orientation, nearly three-fourths of the occurrences being in Northern speech territory, especially Minnesota and North Dakota. It also remains clearly nonstandard, in that 33 of the 40 users are in type I [old, with little educ], only seven type II [mid-aged, with approx hs educ], and none in type III [mid-aged, with coll educ]. **1989** (1990) Baden *Maryland's E. Shore* 39, The Nassawango ore was six to eight inches thick under a foot of lush, loomy soil. **1989** Pederson *LAGS Tech. Index* **Gulf Region**, 298 infs, [lom]; 43 infs, [ˈlomɨ]; 2 infs, [ˈloəm]; 4 infs, [lon]; 19 infs, [lum]; 3 infs, [ˈlumɨ]; [1 inf, [ˈluməs]]; 3 infs, [laʊm]; 2 infs, [lʌm]; 1 inf, [ˈlʌmɨ]; 7 infs [lɔm].

loan v

A Forms.

1 infin, pres: usu *loan;* also *loand;* pronc-sp *lun.* [Cf Intro "Language Changes" I.8] **esp Lower Missip Valley** Cf **drown 1**

1940 (1941) Bell *Swamp Water* 165 **Okefenokee GA**, "Maybe you could lun me a little," Jeb said, unsmilingly, watching them. "That money's long gone." **1942** Faulkner *Go Down* 68 **MS**, Yo mind might change about loandin us the money. **1942** Rawlings *Cross Creek* 100 **FL**, Mis' Rawlings, do you remember loandin' your truck to Dorsey Townsend last Monday? **1966–67** *DARE* (Qu. U16, *If somebody was caught short of money and went to a friend to get some . . "I need five dollars . . will you _____ it to me?"*) Infs **AR**30, **MS**6, 72, 73, Loand; **AR**15, [ˈlond]; **LA**11, [Loʊnd]. [All Infs old]

2 past: usu *loaned;* pronc-sp *lont.* [Cf Intro "Language Changes" IV.4]

1929 Sale *Tree Named John* 101 **MS**, Ah had on a heavy close-weave coat whut Miss Millie's cook lont me.

B Sense.

To borrow. [Cf PaGer *lehne*, Ger *leihen* to lend, loan, borrow] **chiefly Ger settlement areas** Cf **borrow** v **B1**

1935 *AmSp* 10.171 **sePA** [Engl of PA Germans], *Loan.* To borrow. 'Ask John if you can loan his rake off of him.' **1941** Faherty *Big Old Sun* 35 (*Hench Coll.*), Me, I can always get money. I loaned me a flashlight and a hamper and I went into a pepper field up yonder in the night and picked me a hamper of bell peppers. **1950** *WELS Suppl.* **WI**, I was wondering if I could loan them from you for a day or so. **1967** *DARE* (Qu. V5b, *If you take something that nobody seems to own . . "Before anybody else gets it, I'm going to _____ this."*) Inf **KS**3, Loan [FW: Ger speaking community]. **1968** *Helen Adolf Festschrift* 38 **c,cePA** [Influence of Pennsylvania German Dialect on English], *Loan* (Pennsylvania German *lehne*) for 'borrow'; for example, "Go over to Bohner's and ask if you can loan their shovel." **1986** Pederson

LAGS Concordance, 1 inf, **ceTX,** Loan some—same as borrow; 1 inf, **csTN,** Loan it—borrow [inf of German ancestry]. **1991** *DARE* File **sePA,** The use of *loan* meaning 'borrow' is common around the Lancaster area, though less common today than a generation ago.

loand See **loan A1**

loan the lend of See **lend the loan of**

lob n [*EDD lob* sb.[1] 1 "A lump; a large amount; a wide extent or surface."]
A lump, large quantity.
   1941 Ward *Holding Hills* 115 **IA** (as of early 20th cent), They bought lob after lob of land, and then kept and fed more cattle. **1968** Adams *Western Words* 180, *Lob of gold*—In mining, a small but rich deposit of gold.

lobber v Also *lopper;* hence ppl adjs *lobbered, loppered;* rarely *labbered* (pronc-sp *labber*) [nEngl, Scots dial *lopper, lapper;* cf *OED lopper* v. 1, *SND lapper* v.[1] I.1] **chiefly NEast, Gt Lakes, esp Upstate NY, CT, MI** See Map and Map Section Cf **blink** v 1, **cruddle** v, **curdle** v, **thick milk**
=clabber v 1.
   1856 (1857) *Cincinnatus* 1.521, At the end of twelve hours more, that in the tin was thick *clabber* or *lobbered,* as the Yankees call it, and that in the glass *began* to turn. **1889** *Century Dict.* 3519, *Lopper. . .* To curdle or coagulate, as milk which has become sour. . . Prov. Eng. and U.S., where sometimes *lobber.* **1890** James *Mother James' Cooking* 387, Pour hot water over a pan of "loppered milk" or set the pan on the back of range. **1916** *DN* 4.277 **NE,** *Loppered. . .* Clabbered. "Loppered milk." One contributor. **1917** *DN* 4.395 **neOH,** *Lobber(ed). . .* Of milk; coagulated. I am not familiar with *lopper,* but it is reported from Ashtabula Co. "This milk will lobber before morning." "I don't like lobbered milk." M[edina County]. Geauga Co. **1939** Wolcott *Yankee Cook Book* 215, In Connecticut they call thick sour milk "loppered" milk. In Massachusetts they refer to it as "clabbered" milk. **1948** Davis *Word Atlas Gt. Lakes* 75, *Lobbered milk, loppered milk . .* Fairly common [in **MI, nIL, nIN, nOH**]. **1949** Kurath *Word Geog.* 70, *Clabbered milk . .* seems to have replaced *lobbered milk* in the Western Reserve of Ohio. . . From the Connecticut River westward to the Great Lakes as well as in Rhode Island west of Narragansett Bay, around New London, on Long Island, and in Northern New Jersey (but not in Metropolitan New York), *lobbered milk* or *loppered milk* or both are in general use. The variant *lobbered milk* is regular in Rhode Island and the New London area and in the Rhode Island towns in the northern part of the Berkshires, *loppered milk* in the lower Connecticut Valley and the southern part of the Berkshires, and on Long Island. In the Hudson Valley and in Vermont *lobbered* and *loppered* are equally common, while *loppered* predominates in central New York State and farther west. *Ibid* 71, It is of interest to note that in New England relics of *clobbered, clabbered,* and *labbered* have survived by the side of the usual *lobbered* and *loppered.* **1950** *WELS* **WI** (Milk that becomes thick as it turns sour) 1 Inf, Loppered—common; 1 Inf, Loppered—rare; lobbered—[used by] Grandma Roberts; 1 Inf, Lobbered milk—common. **1951** *NY Folkl. Qrly.* 7.176, Throughout New York State a farmer may . . wonder what to do with the *loppered* (or *lobbered*) milk. **1959** *VT Hist.* 27.148, *Loppered. . .* Sour, as *loppered* milk. Common. Rural areas. **1961** *Folk Word Atlas N. LA* map 1013, Milk that has soured and thickened . . [infreq responses include] lobbered milk. **1963** Adamson *Household Hints* 244 **NEng** (as of late 1800s), Skim the cream as soon as the milk has become *loppord* [sic], which will, in hot weather, be in about thirty

hours. **1965–70** *DARE* (Qu. H59, *Milk that becomes thick as it turns sour*) 40 Infs, **esp Upstate NY, CT, MI,** Loppered (milk); (Qu. H58, *Milk that's just beginning to become sour*) Inf **NY5,** Lobbered. **1966** Dakin *Dial. Vocab. Ohio R. Valley* 2.341, Greater Cincinnati has *sour(ed) milk* regularly, and a single instance of *labber milk* is attested here. **1973** Allen *LAUM* 1.291 **Upper MW** (as of c1950), The variant *lobbered milk . .* survives with 3 scattered infs.—two in Minnesota of Canadian and of New York parentage and one in South Dakota with New York parents.

lobbered See **lobber**

lobby n
1 Among loggers: see quots. [Cf *W3* [1]*lobby* 1.b "*archaic:* a small room or enclosure"] Cf **lobbyhog**
   1930 Shoemaker *1300 Words* 37 **cPA Mts** (as of c1900), *Lobby*—The living room, or smoking room at a lumber camp. **1964** Clarkson *Tumult* 366 **WV,** *Lobby*—Room in a logging camp where the men congregated after meals, before bedtime, on Sundays, etc. **1968** Adams *Western Words* 180, *Lobby*—A logger's name for the place in a logging camp where the men wash and wait for mealtime.
2 =corral 1. [*OED lobby* sb. 2.c "A small enclosure for cattle adjoining the farm-yard."]
   [**1828** Webster *Amer. Dict.* np, *Lobby. . .* In *agriculture,* a confined place for cattle, formed by hedges, trees or other fencing, near the farm-yard. *Cyc.* [*DARE* Ed: =Rees' *Cyclopedia,* a British work]] **1967** *DARE* (Qu. M13, *The space near the barn with a fence around it where you keep the livestock*) Inf **WA27,** Lobby.

lobbyhog n [Cf **lobby 1**]
Among loggers: see quots.
   1930 *DN* 6.88 **cWV,** *Lobbyhog,* the caretaker of the bunkhouse; a roustabout who does everything from building fires to making beds. **1958** McCulloch *Woods Words* 21 **Pacific NW,** *Bull cook. . .* A man who puts in firewood, makes beds, does odd jobs around camp. A roustabout, descended from the "lobby hog" of New England logging camps. **1964** Clarkson *Tumult* 366 **WV** [Logger's terms], *Lobby hog*—Man who carried coal, swept floors, built fires, lit lamps, and did a multitude of other chores. Usually an undesirable job.

lobcock See **logcock**

lobelia n Usu |ˌloˈbiljə|; for addit varr see quots at **A** Cf **lowbelia**
A Forms.
   1942 Hall *Smoky Mt. Speech* 76 **wNC, eTN,** In the speech of most old people, of many middle-aged and young, both *-a* and *-ia . .* appear as [ɪ]. . . The words in which [ɪ] was heard . . [include] Alabama . . lobelia . . Pennsylvania . . pneumonia . . soda. **1967–69** *DARE* (Qu. S24) Inf **CA156,** [loˈbiljə]; **PA70,** Blue [loˈbejə]; (Qu. S26b) Inf **TN22,** [ˌloˈbiljə]; (Qu. BB22) Inf **WI44,** [ˌləˈbiljə]. **1967** *DARE* Tape **TX1A,** That's what he treated—oh them pills I made and lobelia [ˈlobiljɪ] was what the way he treated pneumonia. **1968** *DARE* FW Addit **VA1,** Lobelia—[ˌloˈbilə, ˌloˈbili].
B Senses.
1 Std: a plant of the genus *Lobelia.* For other names of var spp see **blue lobelia, cardinal flower, highbelia, Indian tobacco 1, purple dewdrop, swamp lobelia, water gladiole, ~ lobelia**
2 =death camas, usu *Zigadenus venenosus.* **West**
   1897 Parsons *Wild Flowers CA* 6, The bulb is poisonous, and our Northern Indians call it "death camass," while the farmers in the Sierras call it "Lobelia," not because of any resemblance to that plant, but because its poisonous effects are similar to those of the latter. **1920** Saunders *Useful Wild Plants* 245, On the Pacific slope . . is a plant of the Lily tribe in general appearance resembling Camas but with a bulb that is poisonous. It is realistically known as Death Camas, and also as White Camas and Lobelia. **1922** U.S. Dept. Ag. *Farmers' Bulletin* 1273.4, Quite generally throughout the Pacific States they [=*Zigadenus* spp] are known as "lobelia." *Ibid* 5, *Zygadenus* [sic] *venenosus. . .* is known quite generally in the Pacific States as lobelia. **1937** U.S. Forest Serv. *Range Plant Hdbk.* W209, Deathcamases, sometimes known as poison-segos, poison-camases, poison-soaproots, and erroneously called lobelias, are herbaceous perennials of the bunchflower family.

loblolly n
1a A thick gruel, stew, or gravy; a soft or gelatinous food. [*OED loblolly* sb. 1 "Now *dial.*" 1597–1786] **esp Mid Atl**
   1637 (1972) Morton *New Engl. Canaan* 342, The Colony servant in

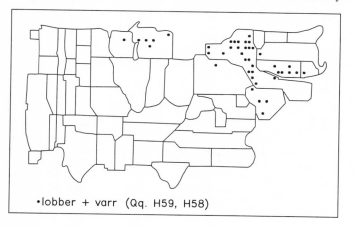

•lobber + varr (Qq. H59, H58)

Virginea. . . called to his wife to set on the loblolly pot. **1785** (1925) Washington *Diaries* 2.421 **ceVA**, The Water is made as thick as Loblolly, or very thick cream. **1899** (1912) Green *VA Folk-Speech* 265, *Loblolly-stick.* . . A stick used for stirring *loblolly* or gruel. **1902** *DN* 2.238 **sIL**, *Loblolly.* . . Jelly; pudding; gravy. **1956** [see **2** below]. **1968** *DARE* (Qu. H37, . . *Words . . for gravy. Any joking ones?*) Inf **OH**87, Loblolly.

b By ext: food in general, esp an unappetizing meal.

1916 *DN* 4.277 **NE**, *Loblolly.* . . Dinner prepared by a dirty cook. "We had to eat their loblolly." **1950** *Western Folkl.* 9.139, *Grub, chuck,* and *loblolly* . . were common words for food in pioneer days.

2 A mudhole, mire; a slushy mess. **scattered, but esp freq Sth, S Midl**

1865 in 1981 Williams *From That Terrible Field* 154, We are in the midst of what appears to be the rainy season; drills and fatigue duty are "easy", streets and crossings a loblolly. **1902** *DN* 2.238 **sIL**, *Loblolly.* . . Ooze, or mud. **1903** (1965) Adams *Log Cowboy* 164 **West**, His ineffectual struggles caused him to sink further to the flanks in the loblolly which the tramping of the cattle has caused. **1906** *DN* 3.120 **sIN**, *Loblolly.* . . A mud hole. **1909** *DN* 3.346 **eAL, wGA**, *Loblolly.* . . Any slushy or sloppy mass, as of mud. "The rains have made a perfect loblolly of the roads." **1909** *DN* 3.400 **nwAR**, Dickson Street in winter is a loblolly. **1912** *DN* 3.582 **wIN**, The hogs have made a perfect loblolly around the watering trough. **1916** *DN* 4.277 **KS, MS, NE, NC**, That road's a regular loblolly. **1941** *AmSp* 16.23 **sIN**, *Loblolly.* A very muddy stretch of road. **1941** *Hench Coll.* **cVA**, Pour in water in the pipe so that down under the ground there is a mushy wet area, a loblolly. **1944** *PADS* 2.58 **nMO, NC, VA**, *Loblolly* ['lab,lalı]. . . A mud-hole. **1948** *Hench Coll.* **cVA**, Describing the condition she feared a pie would be in that had been driven around in a car: "It will be nothing but a loblolly." **1950** *PADS* 13.18 **cTX** (as of 1911–29), *Loblolly.* . . Any very unsightly mess, but usually a liquid one. "He made a loblolly in the kitchen." **1956** McAtee *Some Dialect NC* 28, *Loblolly.* . . various gooey things, among them a mud-puddle. . . also a stew as of okra, tomatoes, and corn. **c1960** *Wilson Coll.* **csKY**, *Loblolly.* . . A mess, like mud. **1964** Jackman–Long *OR Desert* 273, In November it rained for days on end and the road along Crooked Creek north of Lakeview became a loblolly; no surface, just a grade. **1986** Pederson *LAGS Concordance,* 1 inf, **ceLA**, Loblolly—mud and water. **1991** *DARE* File **cMD** (as of c1930), And the flower seeds are in, and soon they are up, and before you can turn around comes a "loblolly rain" and behold, there's a "season." . . No gardener thinks of meals or mending or any such unnecessary things when there is "season."

3 See quot 1970. [Cf *EDD loblolly* sb. 2 "A stout, well-developed child."]

[**1853** *Yankee Notions* Oct 296 (*Mathews Coll.*), There stood Jabez, a great loblolly of a slab-sided, do-less-looking whelp, digging for dear life.] **1970** *DARE* (Qu. X50, *Names or nicknames for a person who is very fat*) Inf **KY**94, Loblolly.

4 See **loblolly bay.**

5 See **loblolly pine 1.**

loblolly bay n Also *loblolly* [loblolly 2]

1 also *lolly bay:* An evergreen tree (*Gordonia lasianthus*) native to swamps and sandhills of the southeastern US. Also called **black laurel 1, holly bay 1, red ~, swamp laurel, tan bay**

1731 Catesby *Nat. Hist. Carolina* 1.44, The Loblolly Bay. This is a tall and very streight Tree, with a regular Piramidal shaped Head. Its Leaves are shap'd like those of the common Bay, but serrated. . . It grows in *Carolina;* but not in any of the more Northern Colonies. **1772** in 1924 Phillips *Notes B. Romans* 121 **FL**, The Middle River has few or no rich Swamps upon it, only in some places there are Boggs Overgrown with that Species of Hypericum, which is here Called the Loblolly Bay. **1822** Eaton *Botany* 311, *Gordonia lasianthus* . . lolly bay. **1853** *Natl. Cyclop.* 1.356 **AL**, The forest trees in . . the south, pine, cypress, and loblolly. **1897** Sudworth *Arborescent Flora* 272, *Gordonia lasianthus* . . Loblolly Bay (N.C., S.C., Ga., Ala., Fla., Miss., La.) **1938** Rawlings *Yearling* 182 **nFL**, The red bay and the loblolly were in full blossom. **1951** Teale *North with Spring* 59 **FL**, All around the curve of the ampitheater-like depression in the earth, it [=dogwood] rose in clouds of white above the dark green of magnolia and loblolly bay. **1966–68** *DARE* (Qu. T5, . . *Kinds of evergreens, other than pine*) Inf **GA**35, Loblolly bay; (Qu. T15, . . *Kinds of swamp trees*) Inf **SC**28, Loblolly bay—rare. **1968** *Patriot-Tribune* (Glenmora–Lecompte LA) 15 Feb 5/4, *Gordonia lasianthus* (Loblolly Bay) native tree or shrub likes moist places to grow well. **1990** Simpson *Gt. Dismal* 145 **nNC, sVA**,

The third species in that family is a plant that doesn't come quite this far north, called *Gordonia*—loblolly bay is a common name for that.

2 also *loblolly magnolia:* =**southern magnolia.**

1913 *Auk* 30.485 **Okefenokee GA**, The tree growth here consists of such species as . . 'loblolly' (*Magnolia grandiflora*), [etc.]. **1927** Boston Soc. Nat. Hist. *Proc.* 38.220 **Okefenokee GA**, *Magnolia foetida*—'Loblolly bay'; 'magnolia.' **1953** Greene–Blomquist *Flowers South* 37, Of the several species of *Magnolia* occurring in the South, the evergreen loblolly- or southern-magnolia (*M. grandiflora*) . . is the best known being planted far beyond its natural range of Fla. to La., s. Ark., and s.e. N.C. **1960** Vines *Trees SW* 281, Vernacular names [of *M. grandiflora*] are Bull-bay, Great Laurel Magnolia, and Loblolly Magnolia.

loblolly pine n [loblolly 2]

1 also *loblolly, lolly pine:* A large, commercially important pine (here: *Pinus taeda*) often found in poorly drained floodplains of the southern US. Also called **bastard pine 1c, black ~ 1a, blackjack ~ 3, bull ~ 1c, cornstalk ~, foxtail ~ 3, frankincense ~, hard ~ 3, Indian ~, longleaf ~ 2, longshat ~, longshucks, longstraw pine 2, meadow ~ 1b, nigger ~ 2, old-field ~, pitch ~, rosemary ~, sap ~, shortleaf ~, slash ~, spruce ~, swamp ~, torch ~, Virginia ~, white ~, yellow ~**

1760 in 1881 GA (Colony) Genl. Assembly *Acts* 219, Squared Timber. . . made of swamp or loblolly pine and Shipped or offered to Sale. **1810** Michaux *Histoire des Arbres* 1.97, Cette espèce de Pin est connue, dans toute la partie basse des Etats méridionaux, sous le nom de *Loblolly pine;* et quelquefois sous celui de *White pine,* aux environs de Richemond et de Petersburgh en Virginie. [=This species of pine is known, in all the lowlands of the southern States, by the name of *Loblolly pine;* and sometimes by that of *White pine* in the neighborhood of Richmond and Petersburg in Virginia.] **1860** Curtis *Cat. Plants NC* 22, Loblolly or Old Field Pine. . . This tree has its northern limit in or near the District of Columbia, gradually becoming more abundant to the southward, until, in this State, it is the most common Pine, next to the Long-leaf, in the lower district. It is there found wherever the soil is dry and sandy, as well as in some of the smaller swamps. **1900** (1927) Keeler *Our Native Trees* 452, Loblolly Pine. . . Inhabits the low lands adjacent to tide-water: rarely makes pure forests. Loves the swamps, but is found in the sandy borders of Pine-barrens. **1934** Carmer *Stars Fell on AL* 91, The little tufted tops of the tall lolly pines beside the singers shivered. **1934** *Daily Progress* (Charlottesville VA) 17 Feb 3/3 (*Hench Coll.*), Pederson said that the largest number of trees distributed from the forest tree nursery last year were loblolly pines, the common species of the Tidewater Section. **1942** Perry *Texas* 163, The noble forests of short leaf, long leaf, and loblolly pine. **1950** Peattie *Nat. Hist. Trees* 25, Down in eastern North Carolina a loblolly is a natural pocket or depression, and in such situations grows the Loblolly Pine. But it is not confined to such areas. **1965** Wolfe *Kandy-Kolored Baby* 224, Any old boy from the loblolly flatlands of Georgia knows how Sunday is supposed to work out in the United States. **1965–70** *DARE* (Qu. T17, . . *Kinds of pine trees;* not asked in early QRs) 87 Infs, **chiefly Sth, S Midl**, Loblolly (pine); (Qu. T16, . . *Kinds of trees . . 'special'*) Inf **OK**20, Loblolly pine. **1966** *DARE* Tape **MS**14, We don't have as much longleaf now because the loblolly and slash will grow faster. **1990** Simpson *Gt. Dismal* 140 **nNC, sVA**, See those pines? These hardwoods, and the loblolly, that means you've got a drier area.

2 A **pond pine** (here: *Pinus serotina*).

1898 Sudworth *Forest Trees* 27, *Pinus serotina*—Pond Pine . . Loblolly Pine (N.C., Fla.) **1908** Britton *N. Amer. Trees* 32, Pond Pine—*Pinus serotina.* . . It is also known as Loblolly pine . . Meadow pine, and Spruce pine.

‡loblopper n Cf clodhopper 4

1969 *DARE* (Qu. X38, *Joking names for unusually big or clumsy feet*) Inf **GA**77, Lobloppers.

lobo n [Span]

1 also *lobo(s) wolf:* =**gray wolf 1. chiefly TX** Cf **loafer n**

1852 in 1853 U.S. Congress *Serial Set* 666 Doc 54 215, Large Lobos wolf. Above Cross-Timbers. **1877** [see **loafer** n]. **1892** *DN* 1.191 **TX**, *Lóbo:* a wolf. In Texas the larger wolf is called *lobo wolf (Canis occidentalis)* to distinguish it from the prairie wolf or *coyote (Canis latrans).* **1920** Hunter *Trail Drivers TX* 72 (as of 1879), The country was full of deer, antelope, elk and lobo wolves. **1945** Thorp *Pardner* 239 **SW**, There, sitting in the trail . . not a hundred and fifty yards from the ranch house, was a big lobo wolf. **1966** Barnes–Jensen *Dict. UT Slang* 29, *Lobo.* . . Spanish name for the wolf. The Utah wolf (*Canis* *youngi*) is sometimes called a lobo, especially in southern Utah. It is now practically extinct; but it once was common all over the state. **1969** [see **loafer** n].

2 =**coyote** n **B1. Cf gray wolf 2**

1967 *DARE* (Qu. P32, . . *Other kinds of wild animals*) Inf **TX**3, Lobos [ˌloˈbouz] = [ˌkɑˈjoʊɾ].

3 also *lobo wolf:* A loner; an outcast.

1907 Porter *Heart of West* 236, I'm not one of them lobo wolves . . who are always blaming on women the calamities of life. **1939** (1973) FWP *Guide MT* 415, Lobo—Wolf that hunts alone. Hence, a solitary person. **1947** Boulware *Jive & Slang* [5] [Black college slang], Lobo— Ugly girl. **1949** in 1960 Wentworth-Flexner *Slang* 322, 'What's a lobo?' 'A lobo's a gun, thug, hoodlum—downstate [California].' . . Movie, *Scene of the Crime.*

lobo stripe n [**lobo 1**] Cf **coyote** n **B4, line-back(ed)**

1941 Dobie *Longhorns* 22 **West,** Solid blacks were not uncommon [among early Spanish-American cattle], but line-backs were very characteristic—a stripe white, yellow or brown in color going down the back to the tail and up the top of the neck. . . This line-back was remarkable on not only Spanish cattle, burros and mules but on Spanish horses of dun shades. Texans called it a "lobo stripe"—a parallel to the *bayo coyote* name for a dun horse with the stripe down its back.

lobos wolf See **lobo 1**

lobo wolf See **lobo 1, 3**

lobscouse n Also sp *lobscouce*

1 Orig a sailor's stew that included **hardtack 1;** now, any similar dish. [*OED* "Naut. and dial." 1706–1894; *EDD*] **chiefly NEng Cf hishy-hash(y), loblolly 1a**

[**1823** Cooper *Pioneers* 1.63, He [=a British sailor] acquired the art of making chowder, lobskous, and one or two other sea-dishes.] **1858** (1929) Taylor *Life on a Whaler* 127 **NEng,** Lobscouce, a dish resembling hash with the exception that sea biscuit softened with water supplied the place of vegetables, had been made for their breakfast and caused no complaint. **1889** *Century Dict.* 3495, Lobscouse. . . A dish made of pilot-biscuit, stewed in water with pieces of salt meat. **1893** Barra *Tale of 2 Oceans* 151, Lobscouse is a sea dish and is made of one onion cut and put into a gallon of water, a dozen potatoes peeled and cut into quarters, four cakes of navy bread soaked and broken up. Boil for half an hour. Cut up salt beef into small square pieces equal to one-third of the whole mass and boil all again half an hour. **1916** Macy–Hussey *Nantucket Scrap Basket* 157, In the old days Lob Scouse was a prominent feature of the menu of a whaleship. It was a stew of soaked hard tack, pork fat, or "top o' the pot" (grease left after boiling "salt horse"— beef), or any sort of "slush" (sailor's term for grease), boiled with molasses and water. **1940** Brown *Amer. Cooks* 695 **OR,** Jack London, whose Slumgullion was made of canned bully beef and bacon, stewed in water and thickened with broken hardtack. Old West Coast sailors call Jack London's stew a "loubscouse [sic]." **1945** Colcord *Sea Language* 120 **ME, Cape Cod, Long Island,** Lobscouse. The sailor's term for a hash of meat, onions and hard bread, pounded up. . . It is applied jokingly alongshore to hash of any kind. "Are you going to have lobscouse for supper?" **1947** Bowles–Towle *New Engl. Cooking* 47 (as of c1850), Cooks on Nantucket whalers and other sea going vessels frequently served lobscouse, a dish made of salt beef—familiarly known as "salt horse"—potatoes, onion, and pepper stewed together.

‡**2** See quot.

1895 *DN* 1.383 **NJ,** Lobscouse: an awkward, hulking fellow.

lobster n Usu |ˈlɑbstə(r)|; also esp **NEng** |ˈlɔbstə| Pronc-sp *lopster;* for addit pronc and sp varr see quots

A Forms. [*OED lopster* "obs."; cf *SND, EDD lapster;* cf also Pronc Intro 3.I.15]

1835 in 1956 Eliason *Tarheel Talk* 314 **ceNC,** Laffsa pot. **1941** *LANE* Map 464 (*Awkward person, lummox*) 1 inf, **Long Island,** [laˆbstə]; 2 infs, neMA, [lɑbstə]; 1 inf, seNH, [lɒbstə]; 1 inf, seNH, [lɒbstə]; 1 inf, **sME,** [lɔ·bstə], one who is 'behind the times' in ways and ideas. **1967–70** *DARE* (Qu. H45) Inf **MA**40, Lobster stew [lɒbstəstu]; (Qu. P14) Inf **MA**55, [ˈlɔbstəz]; (Qu. P18) Infs **MA**3, 4 [lɑbstə]; **MA**2, [lɑbstə·]; **RI**4, [labstə]; **VA**84, [ˈlabstəz]. **1979** *AmSp* 54.93 **sME** (as of 1899–1910), [b] is unvoiced in *lopster*. **1981** Pederson *LAGS Basic Materials* **Gulf Region,** [16 infs responded with proncs of the type [ˈlɑ(ə)bstə]; 11 infs with proncs of the type [ˈlabstə·]; 1 inf, [ˈla·b̥stə·]; 1 inf, [ˈlɛ·bstə].]

B Senses.

1 Std: any of var familiar saltwater crustaceans, but esp

Homerus americanus. For other names of *Palinurus* spp see **crawfish** n **B2, Florida lobster**

2 =**crawfish** n **B1. Cf freshwater lobster**

1817 *Amer. Monthly Mag. & Crit. Rev.* 2.42, *Astacus limosus*. . . Vulgar name mud-lobster. . . *Astacus fossor.* . . Vulgar name, burrowing lobster. . . *Astacus pusillus*. . . In brooks near Saratoga, Lake George, Lake Champlain, Utica, Oswego, &c. length one or two inches; vulgar name, brook prawn, shrimp, or lobster. **1950** *WELS* (What kinds of shell fish are common in your neighborhood) 2 Infs, **cWI,** Lobsters. **1967–69** *DARE* (Qu. P19, . . *Small, freshwater crayfish*) Infs **HI**4, **NH**18, **NY**35, 62, Lobster(s); **RI**4, People call 'em "young lobsters," but they ain't. **1971** Bright *Word Geog. CA & NV* 186, *Crawfish* . . lobster 13% [of 200 infs] P[attern] XIII [=chiefly San Francisco area]. **1986** Pederson *LAGS Concordance* **Gulf Region,** (Crawfish) 10 infs, Lobster(s); 1 inf, Baby lobster; [1 inf, [Crawfish] Look like a miniature lobster].

3 =**red-headed woodpecker.** [See quot]

1956 *AmSp* 31.184, The red-headed woodpecker. . . That the bird has a red head has been considered sufficient excuse in North Carolina for dubbing it *lobster.*

lobster mushroom n [From the bright color resembling that of a cooked **lobster B1**]

A **mushroom B1** (here: *Hypomyces lactifluorum*).

1981 Lincoff *Audubon Field Guide Mushrooms* 373, Lobster Mushroom. . . *Bumpy, bright orange to orange-red mold growing on various white species of* Lactarius *and* Russula *mushrooms*. . . The parasitic Lobster Mushroom transforms its ordinarily unpalatable *Lactarius* and *Russula* hosts into excellent edibles. . . If the host cannot be confirmed, avoid this.

lobster roll n esp **ME, MA Cf crabburger**

A sandwich made with lobster meat in a roll or bun.

1966 *N. Berwick Enterprise* (ME) 29 Apr 1/4, Griffin's Take-Out . . Fried Clams . . Lobster Rolls—etc. **1967–70** *DARE* [(Qu. H41, . . *Kinds of roll or bun sandwiches* . . *in a round bun or roll*) Inf **MA**98, Lobster salad—rolls;] (Qu. H42x, . . *[A sandwich]* . . *in a much larger, longer bun, that's a meal in itself;* not asked in early QRs) Inf **MA**50, Lobster roll. **1977** Anderson *Grass Roots Cookbook* 9 **cME,** And to make Lobster Rolls, she adds, she "piles a slew of lobster salad" into buttered hamburger buns. **1992** *DARE* File **ME coast** (as of 1970s), Lobster rolls are always served cold. The mayonnaise lobster salad in a hot dog roll makes a delicious lunch, and is served all up and down the coast of Maine. **1992** *NYT Mag.* 8 Nov 83/2 **seME,** Pre-lecture chatter was of lobster rolls, continuing-education budget cuts and the goddess Ishtar.

lobster shrimp n [Appar from the orange color resembling that of a cooked **lobster B1**]

A shrimp (here: *Penaeus setiferus*).

1951 Taylor *Surv. Marine Fisheries NC* 200, The spring run of "lobster shrimp" in Louisiana is . . a shoreward migration of individuals that have spent the winter in deeper waters.

local preacher n Also *local minister* **scattered, but chiefly Sth, S Midl, C Atl** See Map on p. 394 Cf **jackleg** adj **1, locus preacher**

A part-time preacher, esp a Methodist layman licensed to preach in a specified region.

1834 Peck *Gaz. IL* 89, The *Methodist Episcopal denomination*. . . The Illinois conference . . has five districts, fifty-six circuit preachers, about twice the number of local preachers, and 13,421 members of the classes. **1840** *Niles' Natl. Reg.* 18 Apr 112, In the United States the Methodist episcopal church has. . . about 5,800 local preachers. **1888** (1889) Lawrence *Life* 237, He was to be seen in the Methodist meeting-house listening to the local preacher, or a negro exhorter. **1956** Ker *Vocab. W. TX* 339, *Local preacher* is reported by two old-timers of Lubbock and Lynn counties. **c1960** Wilson *Coll.* **csKY,** Local preacher. . . A preacher who is ordained but does not have a church regularly. **1961** Folk *Word Atlas N. LA* map 1312, A part-time preacher . . [less freq responses include] local preacher. **1965–70** *DARE* (Qu. CC10, . . *An unprofessional, part-time lay preacher*) 24 Infs, **chiefly Sth, S Midl, C Atl,** Local preacher; **GA**56, Local preacher—Methodists; **MD**32, Local preacher— called associate minister; **SC**24, Local preacher—filled in when they didn't have preaching every Sunday; **TN**37, Licensed to preach—(Methodist) not ordained yet but officially allowed to preach; same as "local preacher"; **MD**24, Local minister. **1970** Tarpley *Blinky* 236 **neTX,** *Local preacher*—part time and not ordained . . local preacher [5 of 200 infs; all 5 were 60 yrs old or older]. *Ibid* 237, The Baptists call such men *local preachers,* but the Methodists call them *licensed preachers.* **1971** Wood *Vocab. Change* 38 **Sth,** A part-time preacher whose professional training may lie only in what he has read from the Bible. . . *Brother-so-and-so* is preferred in all states except Tennessee and Georgia where *jackleg preacher* is the first choice and *local preacher* is second. [215 of 1000 infs in the 8 states investigated by Wood responded with *local preacher.*] **1981** Pederson *Basic Materials* **Gulf Region,** 5 infs, Local preacher; 1 inf, Local preacher—no regular work; 1 inf, Local Methodist preacher—doesn't serve a specific church; 1 inf, Local preachers—in Methodist church. [All infs old]

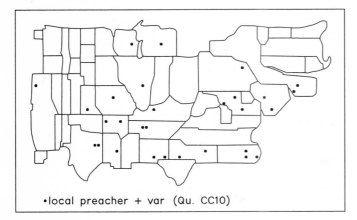

•local preacher + var (Qu. CC10)

locar See **locust**

locate v
See quot 1936.
 1920 Hunter *Trail Drivers TX* 311 **TX** (as of c1882), Each stockman, or ranch, had a line rider, who rode the line or limits of his particular ranch in order to get his cattle "located," or used to their grazing grounds. *Ibid* 385 (as of c1860), Myself and brother, Jack, a third brother older than I, range herded [=herded on a particular range] the cattle to locate them. *Ibid* 386, Then each man wouuld [sic] . . range herd the dry cattle for a few days and locate them. **1936** Adams *Cowboy Lingo* 73, To hold a herd of cattle on a new range until they felt at home was to 'locate' them.

locator n Also *land locator* Also sp *locater* Cf **landlooker**
One who acts as an agent for others in finding public land suitable for farming or lumbering.
 1816 in 1915 *MD Hist. Mag.* 10.364, Where-ever the Corners & lines are lost those present Land Locaters Surveys will hold good until the former can be Established. **1825** in 1924 Austin *Papers* 1.1016 **TX,** The locaters have property that suits you. **1839** U.S. Congress *Congressional Globe* 25th Cong 3d Sess 23 Jan 7 app 266 **TN,** In the legal vocabulary of the day, the land "locator" was as familiarly known by his name as the attorney and clerk of the court by their respective titles. It was the business of this active undertaker . . to scan, with practised eye, all the advantages of water, soil, and situation. . . The information thus acquired became the merchandise of this agrarian broker; and its rapid demand . . by the owners of land warrants, seldom failed to enrich the shrewd and frugal "locator." **1896** *Home Missionary* 69.341 **eCO,** Immigration into that region was greatly stimulated by real estate men, by the locaters of town sites, and by the railroads that were pushing across that vast unoccupied region to reach Denver and the mountains. **1937** Sandoz *Slogum* 166 **NE,** He worked to encourage the drouth-stricken settlers, to bring in the new ones as fast as he could. Times would get better. The rains would come; the cattlemen have to get out. Other locators, all along the free-land region from Indian Territory to Canada, said the same thing to the new wave of homeseekers. **1947** Croy *Corn Country* 42, So widespread did claim jumping become that a low tribe of human beings, known as "locators," sprang up. For a specified sum they would take the newcomer to claims that the locators said had been abandoned. The emigrant would pay the locator and move in. . . Then the rightful owner would show up. **1958** McCulloch *Woods Words* 108 **Pacific NW,** Locator. . . A man who made a business of "locating" timber tracts for distant buyers, in the days when the public domain was still open for purchase. Some locators were honest.

loch(e) See **lush**

locie n Also sp *loci, lokie, lokey;* for addit varr see quots **Nth, esp Pacific NW** Cf **hog B6, loco** n²

In logging: a locomotive.
 1938 (1964) Korson *Minstrels Mine Patch* 316 **nePA, Lokie:** Diminutive for locomotive. **1950** *Western Folkl.* 9.118 **nwOR** [Logger speech], *Loci.* Steam logging locomotive. **1958** McCulloch *Woods Words* 108 **Pacific NW,** Locie (or lokie, or lockie, or loky)—A logging locomotive, known also as a hog. The first models were hardly more than toys, and often were so light that they ran satisfactorily on wooden track. **1961** Labbe–Goe *Railroads* 258 **Pacific NW,** [Glossary:] *Lokey:* Also Locie. Common term used in the woods for locomotive. **1967** *DARE* Tape **WA24,** Big steam lokie ['loki]. Fired 'em with coal for awhile, then they used oil on them afterwards. **1969** Sorden *Lumberjack Lingo* 73 **NEng, Gt Lakes,** Lokey man—A man who worked on a locomotive that hauled logs from the woods to the mill. **1977** Churchill *Don't Call* 49 **nwOR** (as of c1918), "Sam, they got so many goddamn locies [logger term for locomotives] over there a feller don't dare sit on a rail for fear one will come along and nip off a piece of his ass," was how Uncle Marsh described life at Polson Logging Company to Dad.

lock n
1 The corner formed by the intersection of two sections of a rail fence; rarely, a stake or pole used to secure the rails at this intersection. Cf **fence lock, jamb** n
 1851 Pickett *Hist. AL* 2.274, In front of the northern line of picketing was a fence, . . in every lock of which many warriors had placed themselves. **1866** Acad. Nat. Sci. Philadelphia *Proc. for 1866* 329 **TX,** It [=an ant road] is over a hundred yards in length, goes through twenty yards of thick weeds, underruns heavy beds of crop grass 60 yards, and then through the weeds growing in the locks of a heavy rail fence 20 yards more. [**1869** in 1951 *S. Folkl. Qrly.* 16.147, In Kansas, . . a worm fence must be at least four and a half feet high to the top of the rider, or if not ridered, four and a half feet high to top rails, the corners to be locked with strong rails, posts, or stakes.] **1887** Tourgée *Button's Inn* 54 **cwNY,** The drifts had hidden the fences, save . . where the "locks" and "riders" rose above the rounded hillocks that marked their courses. **1899** (1912) Green *VA Folk-Speech* 265, Lock. . . The corner made by joining two pannels [sic] of worm fence. "In the lock of the fence." **1942** Giese *Farm Fence Hdbk.* 8, [Caption:] Rail fence with prop. In some cases, two props were used at each lock. **1986** Pederson *LAGS Concordance,* 1 inf, **nwLA,** A lock—rail extension at corner of rail fence; [1 inf, **ceGA,** Locking the fence—protecting from high winds].
2 A joint of the body; see quots.
 1917 *DN* 4.414 **wNC,** Lock. . . Joint. "The pain's way back in the lock o' my jaw." **1927** *AmSp* 2.360 **cwWV,** Lock . . joint. "He stuck the axe in the lock of his knee." **1954** *Harder Coll.* **cwTN,** Lock. . . joint of knee.
3 Wedlock; see quots. Cf **lock** v **1**
 1969 *DARE* (Qu. AA24, *A man whose wife is dead*) Inf **NY209,** Widdower, out of lock. **1986** Pederson *LAGS Concordance (Bastard)* 1 inf, **swGA,** Out of lock—out of wedlock. [Inf Black]
4 in var phrr indicating something in its entirety; also as adv phr: Completely, wholly. [Varr of *lock, stock, and barrel*]
 1948 Bean *Yankee Auctioneer* 108 **wMA,** The owner followed my advice—and sold everything at once, lock, stock and firing pin. **1966–68** *DARE* (Qu. LL25, . . *Entirely, completely:* "He sold out the whole place, _____.") Infs **NJ11, WI44,** Lock and barrel; **CO4,** Lock, barrel, and stock; **NC14,** Lock, stock; **TX10,** Lock and caboodle.

lock v
1 also with *up, with:* To form a close relationship with; to bind in a relationship; to marry; hence ppl adj *locked up.* [Cf *SND lock* v. I.6 "to bind or engage oneself to (a person)."] Cf **lock** n **3**
 c1938 in 1970 Hyatt *Hoodoo* 2.1736, A man can *lock* a woman, you know, with her sock. He get a sock and hang it up about de house, and if she [has] gone to Halifax, Nova Scotia or California—any place she may go, and he'll do the right thing. He call her three times through de keyhole at sharp nine o'clock at night and burn some of dis *High John de Conker* into his house, and fill it with dis here incense. And I guarantee she'll come back. She can't stay away. **1965** Brown *Manchild* 77 **Harlem NYC** [Black], I knew K.B. about a year before we became ace boon coons. K.B. was the first cat I locked with up at Wiltwyck. We had three fights before we decided we couldn't beat each other, but it was a year before we got tight. **1967–70** *DARE* (Qu. AA4a, . . *A man who is very eager to get married.* . . "He's _____.") Inf **NY241,** Ready to lock up; (Qu. AA15a, . . *Joking ways . . of saying that people got married* . . "They _____.") Inf **TN1,** Got locked; **CT18,** Were locked; (Qu. II3, *Expressions to say that people are very friendly toward*

each other: "They're _____.") Inf **NY**241, Locked up. **1986** Pederson *LAGS Concordance (Married)* 1 inf, **nwAL**, Got locked up—humorous.

2 To cause constipation in (the bowels); to become constipated; hence ppl adj (phr) *locked (up).* Cf **locked bowels 1**

c1938 [see **locked bowels 1**]. **1954** *Harder Coll.* **cwTN**, 'Is bowels locked on 'im; 'e died 'fore 'e git to doctor. **1967–69** *DARE* (Qu. BB21, . . *Being constipated*) Inf **GA**77, His bowels are locked; **SC**44, Locked up.

lock adv See **like** v[1], adj, vbl aux, n, adv, prep, conj

lock bowels See **locked bowels**

lockbox n

A safe-deposit box in a bank.

1949 *Time* 28 March 22 **cIN**, It's still back there in those lock-boxes, at least $8 or $9 million of it. **1969** *DARE* FW Addit **KY**38, *Lockbox*—safety-deposit box at a bank. **1974** *DARE* File **cwOH**, What I [from Westfield, NY] call a bank box is a safe deposit (*never* safety) box or a lock box in Springfield, Ohio. . . An elderly lady . . told me that I should be careful not to say *safety.* She admitted that her use of *lock box* was old fashioned. **1986** Pederson *LAGS Concordance,* 1 inf, **cMS**, Lockbox, in bank—safety-deposit box. [Inf old] **1992** *DARE* File **csWI** (as of c1980), My grandmother always called her safe-deposit box a lockbox. "Mildred," she would say to my mother, "would you go down to the bank and put these insurance papers in my lockbox?" **1995** *Ibid,* I grew up in Kansas where we called it a lockbox. I still call it that, though I also call it a safety-deposit box.

lock closet See **lock room**

locked See **lock** v 2

locked bowels n pl Pronc-sp *lock bowels*

1 rarely sg: Constipation; obstruction of the intestines. **chiefly Sth, S Midl** See Map Cf **lock** v 2

c1938 in 1970 Hyatt *Hoodoo* 2.1432 **SC**, [Inf:] Yo' lock dere bowels shure as yore bo'n. . . [Hyatt:] Well, are you stopping this person's *urinate* [=urine] now or are you stopping his *business* with this thing? . . [Inf:] Stopping his business—yo' know, locked bowels. **1947** (1964) Randolph *Ozark Superstitions* 118, Another case is that of a hillman who had what was called "locked bowels." . . The father of the dead man said sadly: "Too bad we couldn't save Jim. I've saw several fellers with locked bowels cured that-a-way." **1954** *Harder Coll.* **cwTN**, 'Em old locked bowels is hard on ye. Gitchie down or under weather 'fore ye know it. **1965–70** *DARE* (Qu. BB21, . . *Being constipated*) 24 Infs, **chiefly Sth, S Midl**, Locked bowels; **IL**118, A locked bowel; **NC**52, Lock bowels; (Qu. K28, . . *Chief diseases that cows have*) Inf **GA**16, Locked bowels. **1983** *MJLF* 9.1.47 **ceKY** (as of 1956), *Locked bowels* . . prolonged constipation. **1986** Pederson *LAGS Concordance,* 1 inf, **seAR**, Lock bowels—not the same as "appendicitis"; 1 inf, **ceAL**, Locked bowels—didn't relate this to appendicitis. **1990** Cavender *Folk Med. Lexicon* 26 **scAppalachians**, *Locked bowels* . . impaction of the bowels . . intestinal obstruction.

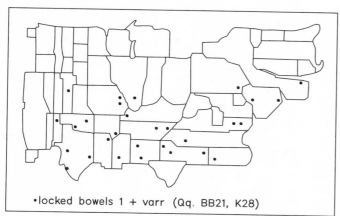

•locked bowels 1 + varr (Qq. BB21, K28)

2 Appendicitis.

1967 *DARE* (Qu. BB49, . . *Other kinds of diseases*) Inf **TN**1, Locked bowels—appendicitis, old-fashioned. **1986** Pederson *LAGS Concordance* **Gulf Region** *(Appendicitis)* 2 infs, Lock(ed) bowels—old term; 2 infs, Lock bowels.

locked up See **lock** v 1, 2

locker n

1 also *food locker:* A cupboard, **safe**; a pantry. **esp Sth**

1899 (1912) Green *VA Folk-Speech* 265, *Locker.* . . A small cupboard. [*DARE* Ed: Specific sense is uncertain.] **1927** (1970) Sears *Catalogue* 561, [Index:] Lockers, Kitchen. **1967–68** *DARE* (Qu. D8, *The small room next to the kitchen [in older houses] where dishes and sometimes foods are kept*) Inf **LA**23, Pantry; in older homes it's called a butler's pantry; food locker—old-fashioned, used occasionally; (Qu. D9, *To prevent bread and cake from drying, you put them in a _____*) Inf **NY**11, Locker. **1986** Pederson *LAGS Concordance (A pantry)* 1 inf, **seLA**, Locker; 1 inf, **seMS**, A big locker—for canned goods; movable; 1 inf, **seGA**, Food locker; 1 inf, **swFL**, Metal locker—for dishware. **1993** *NADS Letters* **LA, OK, TX** (as of early 20th cent), Food lockers were quite common in rural Oklahoma, Louisianna [sic], and Texas in the Twenties and Thirties. My mother-in-law . . of Munday, Texas used one until her death, a few years ago. It was about four by four feet square, some eighteen inches deep. There were shelves on which to store dried and canned food. Two wooden framed doors opened outward. Instead of wood or glass, the doors were made of tin in which had been punched designs. *Ibid,* I have heard *pie locker* for [what] used to be called a *pie safe.*

2 also *clothes locker:* A closet, wardrobe; a small storage area. **chiefly LA** See Map Cf **clothespress**

1961 *PADS* 36.11 **sLA**, We might begin with a small group of words that are positively confined to the informants of southern Louisiana. . . *(clothes) locker* (closet)—18.6 [percent of 70 informants]. **1965–70** *DARE* (Qu. D7, *A small space anywhere in a house where you can hide things or get them out of the way*) Infs **LA**43, **TX**102, Locker; **LA**20, Locker—now they say this; **LA**33, Locker—newfangled, occasional; (Qu. E1, *A piece of furniture that stands against the wall, and you hang clothes in/on it*) Inf **LA**20, Locker; (Qu. E2, *A built-in space in a room for hanging clothes*) Infs **LA**11, 20, Locker; **LA**23, Often referred to as lockers in classified ads; [(Qu. E5, *A piece of furniture with a flat top for keeping tablecloths, dishes, and such*) Inf **WA**11, Locker, linen cabinet, linen closet]. **1967** LeCompte *Word Atlas* 118 **seLA**, *Locker:* Closet, built in. [1 of 21 infs] **1971** *Today Show Letters* **seLA**, A clothes closet in Detroit is a locker in New Orleans. **1975** *Times–Picayune* (New Orleans LA) 9 Jan sec 3 3/1, Closets are lockers. **1984** Stall *Proud New Orleans* 168, *Locker:* Equivalent to a closet. **1986** Pederson *LAGS Concordance* **esp c,seLA; also sMS, wFL** *(Built-in clothes closet)* 8 infs, Locker; 1 inf, Locker—heard in New Orleans; 1 inf, Locker—a closet, common New Orleans term, from boat; 1 inf, I got a locker in each room—clothes closet; 1 inf, Lockers—closets on a boat; 1 inf, Lockers—[has] heard friends use for closets; 2 infs, Walk-in locker(s); 1 inf, Built-in lockers—closets; 1 inf, Clothes locker; *(Movable wardrobe)* 1 inf, Locker; 1 inf, Locker—movable closet, i.e., wardrobe. [*DARE* Ed: Other infs used the term, but the context was unclear.]

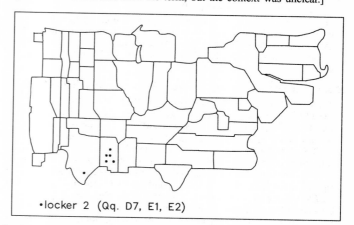

•locker 2 (Qq. D7, E1, E2)

lock-eye n [Cf *EDD lock* v.[1] 5 "To shut. . . Lock up your eyes"]

1895 *DN* 1.398 **cNY**, *Lock-eye:* the game of hide-and-seek.

lockhair fern n

A **maidenhair fern** (here: *Adiantum pedatum*).

1938 Small *Ferns SE States* 116, This maiden-hair fern [=*Adiantum pedatum*] has a wide geographic distribution. . . The plants are sometimes known as *lockhair-fern.*

lock horns v phr **esp S Midl, West**

Fig: to come into conflict, disagree, fight.

1836 Howard *Hist. Virgil A. Stewart* 23, They are enemies, and let them lock horns. **1846** (1973) Porter *Quarter Race* 89, So we locked horns without a word, thar all alone, and I do think we fit an hour. **1901** in 1917 Myers *Hist. Tammany Hall* xi **NYC**, We should hardly feel warranted in locking horns with Tammany Hall. **1912** Green *VA Folk-Speech* 266, *Lock horns. . . To have a contention, or conflict.* "They locked horns about it whenever they met." **1942** Perry *Texas* 97, He was in Round Rock with a view to sticking up the local repository, when he locked horns with the Rangers. **1944** Adams *Western Words* 93, *Lock horns*—To engage in an argument or fight with another. Very commonly male animals of the plains, during fights, get their horns locked together, and, being unable to free themselves, remain in this state until they starve to death. **c1960** *Wilson Coll.* **csKY**, *Lock horns. . .* Engage in argument or a quarrel. **1966** Barnes–Jensen *Dict. UT Slang* 29, *Lock horns with . .* to compete; to combat. "They locked horns with their fists and went at it." **1966–68** *DARE* (Qu. Y12b, *A real fight in which blows are struck*) Inf **MO**38, They locked horns; (Qu. EE21b, *When boys were fighting very actively . . "For a while those fellows really _____."*) Inf **OK**28, Locked horns; (Qu. KK68, *When people don't think alike about something: "We agree on most things, but on politics we're _____."*) Inf **KS**19, Lock horns. **1976** Garber *Mountain-ese* 54 **sAppalachians,** These two have been feudin' fer so long they are abound to lock horns. **1978** *AP Letters* **neGA** (as of c1900), There are some [words] that are still used by old-timers, such as: . . They locked horns (disagreed).

lock open v phr [Calque of PaGer *uffschliesse*, Ger *aufschliessen*] **esp PaGer area** *old-fash*
To unlock.

1907 *German Amer. Annals* 9.381 **sePA**, *Lock open.* Unlock. "Lock the door open. I want to come in." **1935** *AmSp* 10.167 [Engl of PA Germans], Lock open the door. . . accepted currency of daily speech. **1968** *Helen Adolf Festschrift* 38 **c,cePA** [Words borrowed from PaGer], *Lock open . .* for 'unlock'; for example, "You run ahead and lock open the door." [**1987** *Jrl. Engl. Ling.* 20.2.171 **ePA**, *Lock open* 'to unlock', . . 0% (0). *unlock* 92%, other responses (*open* 8%). The item now appears to be extinct.] **1992** *DARE* File **seWI** (as of c1940), In Dodge County where I grew up people said "lock open" to mean unlock. I'm not sure you would hear it as much today though. You might still hear older people use this expression, but probably not so much the younger people. I think I remember hearing it in Ohio too, in the Cincinnati area.

lock room n Also *lock closet* Cf **locker 1, 2**
1966–67 *DARE* (Qu. D7, *A small space anywhere in a house where you can hide things or get them out of the way*) Inf **LA**6, Lock room; **MS**48, Lock room—a cubbyhole; **SC**11, Lock closet; (Qu. D8, *The small room next to the kitchen [in older houses] where dishes and sometimes foods are kept*) Inf **LA**6, Lock room.

lock the barn door v phr [**barn door 2**] Cf **cow barn is open**
Fig: to fasten one's trouser fly.

1968 *DARE* (Qu. W24c, *. . To warn a man that his trouser-fly is open*) Inf **CA**36, Lock the barn door—to men and with men only; **MI**78, **PA**79, (Better) lock the barn door; **WI**64, Lock the barn door before the horse gets away; **NY**109, You better lock the barn door before the horse gets out.

lockup n **scattered, but less freq West** See Map Cf **calaboose**
A jail, esp a small or local one; a detention center.

1839 *Knickerbocker* 14.110, He was seized, and carried to the 'lock-up.' **1928** *Ruppenthal Coll.* **KS**, Lockup. . . A place of detention of persons under arrest. . . especially temporary or for lighter penalties. **1938** *Sun* (Baltimore MD) 2 Sept 6/2 (*Hench Coll.*) **csPA**, State motor policemen from the Gettysburg substation conducted an inspection of jails and borough lockups in Gettysburg and Adams county and returned reports on the lockups in Littlestown and McSherrystown as unfit. **1950** *WELS* (*Joking or nicknames for a county or city jail*) 13 Infs, **WI**, Lockup. **1959** *VT Hist.* 27.147 **cw,swVT**, *Lock up. . .* Jail. Occasional. **1962** Carrell *Autobiog.* [8] **ceMA** (as of 1880s), Some times a tramp [w]ould stay all night at the "Lock up" which was a small brick building on Central St. He had to get permission from some body in authority. **1965–70** *DARE* (Qu. V11) 132 Infs, **scattered, but less freq West,** Lockup; **NY**75, Town lockup. [Of all Infs responding to the question, 66% were old; of those giving these responses, 76% were old.] **1969** *DARE* Tape **NJ**54, This was the county prison. . . The other facilities would be . . what we call local lockups. **1970** Tarpley *Blinky* 270 **neTX**, Lockup [rare]. . . A common distinction made by many informants is that *calaboose, lockup, cooler,* etc. refer to the building where prisoners are detained overnight in a small town before being transferred to the jail at the county court house. **1986** Pederson *LAGS Concordance* **esp**

seLA, 5 infs, (Central) lockup; 1 inf, Central lockup—[for] minor crimes; 1 inf, Lockup—local term, where [they] stay before arraignment.

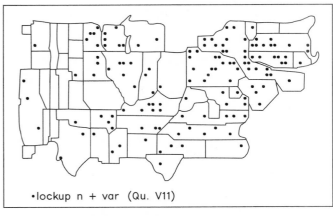

•lockup n + var (Qu. V11)

lock up v, **lock with** See **lock** v 1

loco adj [Span "crazy, insane"] **orig chiefly West, now more widespread** Cf **locoweed**
Crazy, out of one's mind; affected with **loco** n[1] **2a;** obsessed.

1887 *Outing* 10.7 **West,** You won't be able to do nuthin' with 'em, sir; they'll go plumb *loco.* **1918** [see **loco** n[1] **3**]. **1929** *AmSp* 5.68 **NE** [Cowboy talk], "Loco" is commonly used to denote crazy. **1935** Sandoz *Jules* 410 **wNE** (as of 1880–1930), I stayed with him till he went loco. **1942** Perry *Texas* 136, A foolish person we sometimes call "a hollow horn." Or we may say that he is "loco," because a horse that eats the loco weed behaves idiotically. **1947** Williams *Streetcar* 115 **LA**, Regarded as not just different but downright loco—nuts. **1949** Emrich *Wild West Custom* 198, The foolhardy hunter, the man overconfident in the desert, the prospector once too gold-loco to heed warnings of Apaches. **1950** *WELS* (*Words and expressions about someone who is insane*) 5 Infs, **WI**, Loco. **1956** Moody *Home Ranch* 174 **CO** (as of 1911), Reckon I'm loco as a range maverick to let you try it, gal. **c1960** *Wilson Coll.* **csKY**, *Loco. . .* Mentally deranged; obviously a "drift-in" from "out west." **1965–70** *DARE* (Qu. HH6, *Someone who is out of his mind*) 24 Infs, **scattered,** Loco; (Qu. K16, *A cow with a bad temper*) Inf **NM**13, Loco—liable to get mad; has been eating loco, a plant; **CA**161, Loco—very bad; (Qu. K42, *A horse that is rough, wild, or dangerous*) Inf **NM**13, Loco—from eating loco; **OK**27, **OR**4, Loco; (Qu. K47, *Diseases . . horses or mules commonly get*) Inf **CO**7, Go loco; (Qu. DD22) Inf **VA**15, Loco, crazy, off his rocker; (Qu. GG2, *. . 'Confused, mixed up': "So many things were going on at the same time that he got completely _____."*) Inf **DC**1, Loco—from the West; (Qu. GG15, *. . A person who became over-excited and lost control, "At that point he really _____."*) Inf **DC**1, Went loco; (Qu. GG40, *Words or expressions meaning violently angry*) Inf **DC**1, Loco—the nth degree; (Qu. HH4, *Someone who has odd or peculiar ideas or notions*) Inf **MA**73, Loco—on the borderline between a kook and insane; (Qu. HH9, *A very silly or light-headed person*) Inf **DC**1, Sort of loco; (Qu. HH13, *Expressions meaning that a person is not very alert or not aware of things: "He's certainly _____."*) Inf **NM**6, Loco—often used for someone who has an "off-idea." **1967** Green *Horse Tradin'* 69 **TX**, I stood up in my stirrups, looked at that mule, and said: "Mr. Merritt, people are the only things that have got little enough sense to go crazy. She must be loco." **1986** Pederson *LAGS Concordance*, 1 inf, **swMS**, Loco.

loco n[1] [**loco** adj] **chiefly West**
1 See **locoweed.**

2a also *loco disease:* A livestock disease characterized by impaired coordination, erratic behavior, and sometimes lethargy, caused by poisoning, esp by any of var **locoweeds.**

1889 *Century Dict.* 3499, *Loco. . .* A disease of animals resulting from eating loco-weeds. . . *loco-disease. . .* A disease of horses resulting from eating the loco-weed or crazy-weed. Also called *grass-staggers. . .* Western U.S. **1925** *Book of Rural Life* 3255, It has long been known that in the arid and semiarid regions of the West and Southwest there is a disease called *loco* which causes enormous losses of horses, cattle and sheep. **1967–69** *DARE* (Qu. K28, *. . Chief diseases that cows have*) Inf **AZ**2, Loco—from locoweed; (Qu. K47, *. . Diseases . . horses or mules commonly get*) Inf **TX**71, Loco—from eating locoweed; distemper.

b in phr *miner's loco;* Transf: an insatiable lust for gold; gold fever.

1916 *Sunset* Jan 29 **CO,** She shifted for herself until, aged fourteen, she made her way west to Colorado and the "miner's loco" claimed her. . . She has been playing the miner's game ever since. Every cent that she could earn during the winter she would put into the ground during the summer. Despite the many valuable claims which she owns she has barely enough to live on. Yet . . she hopes for gold that her son's education may be of the best.

3 also *loco blossom:* One who is out of his mind or obsessed. *derog*

1852 Alvarez *Alvarez Papers* (Carlisle *Southwestern Dict.*), Jerry Folger your friend has been trying to injure you his best giving out on all sides that you are a *loco.* **1918** Griffin *Ballads Regiment* 23, We are the lads who'll smoke him out./ On the trail of Loco Billy [=Wilhelm II, Emperor of Germany and King of Prussia],/ Billy, the Dutch Loco. **1941** Cleaveland *No Life* 196 **cNM** (as of c1890), 'I ain't had so much fun since Moses was a nigger baby,' announced the man whose name wasn't Red. . . 'Only, it shore grieves me to have to set in a game with two such loco-blossoms. I'll take four cards to keep my ace company. A royal flush, by golly!' **1986** Chapman *New Dict. Amer. Slang* 262, She's acting like a loco.

loco v, hence ppl adj **locoed** [loco n[1]] **chiefly West**
To poison with **locoweed;** by ext, to craze, derange, frenzy.

1884 Aldridge *Ranch Notes* 186 **West,** An animal previously perfectly gentle will frequently, after being locoed, commence 'bucking' as soon as you put the saddle on him. **1887** *Scribner's Mag.* 2.510 **West,** From the substantive [=loco-weed] a verb sprang into use; cattle showing signs of madness are said to be "locoed," and so finally the word extended to human beings. **1889** *Century Dict.* 3499 **West,** Loco. . . To poison with the loco-weed or crazy-weed. **1892** *Chambers's Jrl.* 17 Dec 816 **SW,** In localities where loco is found, . . if people are deficient in intellect, or odd and eccentric, they are designated 'locoed!' **1892** *DN* 1.249 **TX,** Sheriff Cooke brought down from the Quemado, yesterday, two Mexican families,—who all have the appearance of being locoed. **1897** Lewis *Wolfville* 119 **AZ,** Wolfville intelligence is too well founded to let any law loco it or set it to millin'. **1907** Mulford *Bar-20* 70 **West,** "Locoed son-of-a-gun," complained Pete. **1913** *DN* 4.27 **NW,** Locoed. . . Crazed, or crazy mad,—of persons. The poisonous loco weed causes horses or cattle which eat it to go crazy. "He is plumb locoed." Used throughout the cattle-raising country. **1929** *AmSp* 5.68 **NE** [Cowboy talk], "Saged" and "locoed" cattle are those stiffened and crazed by eating sage brush and loco weed. **1933** *AmSp* 8.1.30 **TX** [Ranch terms], A *locoed* animal is characterized by a slow gait, glassy eyes, excitability, delirium, and emaciation, and will wear a circular path in the grass, pacing round a patch of *loco.* Figuratively, a person mentally unbalanced. **1967** *DARE* (Qu. K16, *A cow with a bad temper*) Inf **CO**44, Locoed.

loco n[2] Cf **locie**
A locomotive.

1833 (1877) Breck *Recollections* 274, With the *loco,* when established, he may start from one city in the morning and return again in the evening from a visit to the other. **1937** in 1953 Botkin–Harlow *Treas. Railroad Folkl.* 278, Exact-scale locomotives run by real steam. Vincent Astor . . has a miniature railroad with a live-steam loco at his place. **1942** Berrey–Van den Bark *Amer. Slang* 774.18 [Railroad terms], *Locomotive. . .* loco.

loco blossom See **loco** n[1] **3**

loco disease See **loco** n[1] **2a**

locoed See **loco** v

locoweed n Also *loco (plant),* ~ *grass,* ~ *vetch* **West** See Map Cf **crazyweed**
Any of var, usu leguminous, plants which cause **loco** n[1] **2a,** but esp **milkvetch** or a plant of the genus *Oxytropis,* esp *O. lambertii;* see quots. For other names of *Oxytropis* see **crazyweed, pointvetch;** for other names of var spp of this genus see **frijolillo 2, purple loco, rattleweed, white loco**

1844 *St. Louis Reveille* (MO) 8 Dec 2/4, He was girt about the neck with a leather bridle, and his meat was locos and wild onions. **1882** *Bot. Gaz.* 7.76, *Astragalus mollissimus,* Torr.—A short time ago, my friend . . received from a stock breeder in Western Kansas, a wild plant, know [sic] there by the name of *"loco,"* and said to cause injurious and often fatal effects upon cattle and horses who eat it, causing paralysis and other functional disturbances. **1884** *Amer. Naturalist* 18.1148, Experiments . . prove that *Crotalaria sagittalis,* the Rattle-box, is a "loco-plant." **1887** KS State Bd. Ag. *Biennial Rept. for 1885–1886* part 2 209, Dr. Tipton, of Las Vegas, . . states that the Spanish were not acquainted

with the term loco until Americans became familiar with its virtue, who christened it with this name because of its effects. **1891** Coulter *Botany W. TX* 82, A[stragalus] mollissimus. . . High prairies and mesas in northwestern Texas and west of the Pecos. The most common "loco" plant, and said to be very poisonous to cattle. *Ibid* 84, O[xytropis] Lamberti. . . Extending from the plains into northern and western Texas. Reputed to be a "loco" plant. **1892** *DN* 1.191 **TX,** Loco grass, loco weed. **1896** *Jrl. Amer. Folkl.* 9.185 **CA, NE,** *Astragalus mollissimus,* Torr., rattle-box weed, loco-weed. *Ibid* **NE,** *Crotalaria sagittalis,* L., loco-weed. *Ibid* 186 **NE, IA, MO,** *Oxytropis Lamberti,* Pursh. loco, loco-weed. **1898** *Ibid* 11.225, *Astragalus* (sp.), rattle weed, loco weed, Cal. *Astragalus mollissimus,* Torr., loco, Wyo. *Ibid* **WY,** *Oxytropis Lamberti,* Pursh, and its varieties, loco. **1914** Georgia *Manual Weeds* 239, Woolly Loco-weed—*Astragalus mollissimus.* . . *Other English names:* Crazyweed, Purple Loco, Stemmed Loco, Texas Loco. *Ibid* 241, Stemless loco-weed—*Oxytropis Lamberti,* Pursh. (*Aragallus* [sic] *spicatus,* Rydb.) *Other English names:* Colorado Loco-vetch, White Loco-weed. **1937** U.S. Forest Serv. *Range Plant Hdbk.* W41, The term "Loco", as a definite common plant name, appears to have been first applied to *Astragalus mollissimus* in western Texas. . . Subsequently, a large number of plants, chiefly of the genera *Astragalus* and *Oxytropis* have, at one time or another, been called loco, because of their poisonous effects on domestic animals. **1951** *PADS* 15.35 **TX,** *Astragalus mollissimus* Torrey.—Loco weed. . . *Oxytropis lamberti* Pursh.—Loco weed. **1967–70** *DARE* (Qu. K16) Inf **NM**13, Has been eating loco, a plant; (Qu. K28) Inf **AZ**2, Loco—from locoweed; (Qu. K42) Inf **NM**13, Loco—from eating loco; (Qu. K47) Inf **NM**13, They can eat locoweed; **TX**71, Loco—from eating locoweed; (Qu. S17, . . *Kinds of plants . . that . . cause itching and swelling*) Inf **CA**115, Locoweed—belongs to lupine family; **TX**68, Locoweed—cause sickness; (Qu. S21, . . *Weeds . . that are a trouble in gardens and fields*) Infs **CO**7, **HI**6, **TX**42, 66, Locoweed(s); **CA**189, Loco weed—same as jimson weed; (Qu. S26e, *Other wildflowers not yet mentioned;* not asked in early QRs) Infs **AZ**2, **WY**5, Locoweed. **1970** Correll *Plants TX* 852, *Oxytropis.* . . Crazy-weed. Purple Loco. *Ibid* 853, [*O. lamberti* is] one of the most dangerous of the loco weeds because it is readily eaten by grazing animals.

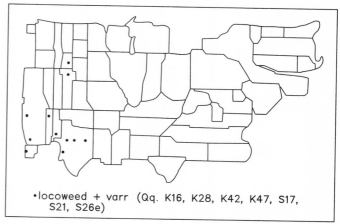

•locoweed + varr (Qq. K16, K28, K42, K47, S17, S21, S26e)

locus See **locust**

locus preacher n Also *locus (pastor)* [Varr of **local preacher,** perh infl by *locus* (var of **locust**)] **SC, GA** *esp Gullah*
1922 Gonzales *Black Border* 224 **sSC, GA coasts** [Gullah], Him is de class-leaduh een my chu'ch, en w'en eeduhso de preachuh on de sukkus [=circuit], elsehow de locus preechuh, onable to filfil de pulpit, den B'Cudjo does hol' saa'bis. *Ibid* 311, *Locus pastuh*—local pastor, or preacher. **1926** Smith *Gullah* 31 **sSC, GA coasts,** *Popular Etymologies*— . . *Locus preechuh* (local preacher). **c1940** *LAMSAS Materials,* 6 infs, **SC,** Locus preacher; 3 infs, **SC,** Locus preacher—heard; 3 infs, **SC,** Locus preacher—heard from Negroes; 1 inf, **SC,** Locus (preacher)—heard; 1 inf, **GA,** Locus preacher; 1 inf, **GA,** Locus. **1950** *PADS* 14.45 **SC,** *Locus.* . . Local. Only in the phrase "*locus* preacher." General Negro usage. Probably Southwide.

locust n Usu |ˈlokɪst, -əst|; also freq |ˈlokɪs|, rarely |ˈlokə(r)| Pl usu |ˈlokɪsts|; also |ˈlokɪsəz, ˈlokəsɪz, ˈlokɪs| Pronc-spp *locus, locar, loaker;* for addit pronc and sp varr see **A** below
A Forms.
1640 Parkinson *Theatrum Botanicum* 1550, The *Virginian* Locus tree. *Ibid* 1552, The second is called Locus by our Nation resident in Virginia. **1805** in 1965 *AmSp* 40.199 **Long Is. NY,** Went up to Flatlands at

Evening came up a Shower I was near a where it struck a Locar Tree. **1807** (1904) Roe *Diary* 55 **NY,** We have been .. makeing crotch & pole fence along by our Locus orched. **1899** (1912) Green *VA Folk-Speech* 266, A fine row of locusses. **1903** *DN* 2.319 seMO, His food was locusses and wild honey. **1906** *DN* 3.145 nwAR, *Locus',* pl., locusses. **1909** *DN* 3.346 eAL, wGA, *Locus.* . . Pl. *locusses.* **1916** [see **B3** below]. **1933** Hanley *Disks* seMA, Locusses. **1957** Battaglia *Resp. to PADS* 20 eMD (*The tree with large heart-shaped leaves, clusters of white blossoms, and long slender seed pods*) Locus. **c1960** Wilson *Coll.* csKY, *Locust*—['lokəs]; *locusts* ['lokəsɪz]. Both common. **1965–70** *DARE* (Qu. R7, *Insects that sit in trees or bushes in hot weather and make a sharp, buzzing sound*) 257 Infs, **widespread,** (Seventeen-year, seven-year, *etc*) locust(s); **CT**11, Locust bug; 106 Infs, **scattered,** (Every-year, seven-year *etc*) Locus [proncs of the type ['lokəs, -ɪs]]; **MD**15, 20, ['lokɪs] (pl); **MD**34, **OH**49, **PA**205, ['lokəs] (pl); **IN**73, **OH**2, ['lokəsəz]; **DE**4, ['loukəsɪz]; **GA**25, ['lokɪsɪz]; **MD**42, ['lɛokɪsɪz]; **MO**13, 20, ['loukɪst], pl: ['loukɪsz]; **LA**44, Loaker ['loukə]; (Qu. R6, . . *Grasshoppers*) 72 Infs, **scattered,** (Seventeen year) locust; 68 Infs, **scattered,** Locus; **OH**2, [lokəsəz]; **WA**6, We don't have any locus, just grasshoppers; **WV**2, Locus are called grasshoppers here; (Qu. R8, . . *Kinds of creatures that make a clicking or shrilling or chirping kind of sound*) 27 Infs, **chiefly Sth, S Midl,** (Seven-year) locust; **KY**9, **SC**32, ['lo(u)kəsɪz]; **GA**35, Tree locus ['lokəs]; (Qu. R5, *A big brown beetle*) 20 Infs, **scattered, but esp N Midl, Cent,** (Singing) locust; **MO**2, **PA**73, **TX**26, Locus [proncs of the type ['lokəs, -ɪs]]; **MO**9, ['loukɪs], pl ['loukɪs:, 'loukɪsz]; **MO**11, [loukɪs:] pl; **MA**26, ['lokəs] have a kind of a croak, too; (Qu. T16, . . *Kinds of trees*) 103 Infs, **widespread,** (Black, honey, *etc*) locust; **CT**11, **MD**13, 42, **PA**134, **TX**75, Locust tree; **CT**42, **MD**15, **NY**211, 213, **RI**10, **TN**24, (Yellow) locus; **CA**24, **MD**20, **NC**52, Locus tree; (Qu. T9, *The common shade tree with . . long thin seed pods*) 17 Infs, **scattered,** (Black, honey, *etc*) locust; 9 Infs, **scattered,** Locust tree; **AR**41, **CT**40, **NE**1, **NY**22, **PA**234, **VT**13, (Black) locus; **GA**65, **NM**2, **NY**20, Locus tree. [Further exx throughout *DS*] **1967** *DARE* Tape **MI**61, In our front yard at home were locus trees. **1967** *DARE* FW Addit **TN**22, Locusts ['lokəsɪz]. **1981** Pederson *LAGS Basic Materials* **Gulf Region,** [4 infs, Proncs of the type ['lo·ukəs] for *locusts;* 3 infs, Proncs of the type ['lo·ukəsɪz] for *locusts.*]

B Senses.

1 also *locust tree:* Usu a tree of the genus *Robinia,* esp *R. pseudoacacia,* but also a **honey locust 1;** also the wood or pod of such a tree. For other names of trees in the genus *Robinia* see **black locust, moss ~, rose acacia, ~ of Sharon** Cf **plume locust, river ~**

c1612 (1849) Strachey *Hist. VA Britannia* 130, A kynd of low tree, which beares a cod like to the peas, but nothing so big: we take yt to be locust. **1640** [see **A** above]. **1739** (1946) Gronovius *Flora Virginica* 82, Pseudoacacia floribus albis racematim congestis pendulis odoratis, foliis pinnatis. [=Pseudoacacia, flowers white, arranged in racemes, pendulous, sweet-smelling; leaves pinnate] Sweet-Smelling Locust. **1792** Belknap *Hist. NH* 3.98, *Locust (robinia pseudo-acacia)* is excellent fewel. Its trunk serves for durable posts set in the ground, and may be split into trunnels for ships, which are equal to any wood for that purpose. **1807** [see **A** above]. **1821** Cobbett *Amer. Gardener* 331 **NY,** The finest flowering trees and shrubs [are]. . . the *Wild Cherry* . . ; the *Locust,* most beautiful of trees and best of timber. **1897** Sudworth *Arborescent Flora* 254, *Gleditsia triacanthos.* . . Locust (Nebr.) Ibid 258, *Robinia pseudoacacia.* . . *Common Names.* Locust (Me., N.H., Vt., Mass., R.I., Conn., N.Y., N.J., Pa., Del., W. Va., N.C., S.C., Ga., Ala., Miss., Tex., Ky., Ark., Ariz., Ill., Wis., Ohio, Ind., Kans., Nebr., Mich., Iowa, Minn.) . . Black Locust. . . Yellow Locust. . . White Locust. . . Red Locust. . . Green Locust. **1937** U.S. Forest Serv. *Range Plant Hdbk.* B134, New Mexican locust, sometimes (though erroneously) called algaroba or, colloquially, agarroba, is a large, thorny shrub or small tree, varying from several feet up to 20 or 25 feet in height. **1950** Peattie *Nat. Hist. Trees* 404, Not unnaturally a sweet-tasting pod on an American tree [*Gleditsia triacanthos*] received the name of Locust. The pods are eagerly eaten by cattle when they can find them on the ground. **1965–70** *DARE* (Qu. T16, . . *Kinds of trees* . . *'special'*) 54 Infs, **scattered,** Locus(t); **CA**24, **CT**11, **MD**20, 42, **NC**52, **PA**134, **TX**75, Locus(t) tree; **KY**49, Locust—fenceposts; **KY**62, Locust—white, pink; **LA**31, Locust—makes long thorns and heavy seed pods; **MD**13, Locust tree—shade tree—finger-size leaf; **NY**75, Locust—makes best posts; **TN**24, Locust—for posts; **VA**70, Locust—used to be used for fence-posts; (Qu. T9, *The common shade tree with large heart-shaped leaves, clusters of white blossoms, and long thin seed pods or 'beans'*) 26 Infs, **scattered,** Locus(t) (tree); (Qu. C28, *A place where underbrush, weeds,*

vines and small trees grow together so that it's nearly impossible to get through*) Inf **KY**60, Locust thicket; (Qu. I46, . . *Kinds of fruits that grow wild around here*) Inf **GA**13, Locusts, persimmons, plums; **VA**69, Wild cherry, simmons, locusts; (Qu. L64, *The kind of wooden fence that's built around a garden or near a house*) Inf **PA**29, Locust posts; (Qu. S13) Inf **WI**32, Locus; (Qu. S26a, . . *Wildflowers.* . . *Roadside flowers*) Inf **ME**7, Locus—a wild tree; **NY**88, Locust—grows on a bush—low to the ground—no beans; (Qu. S26e, *Other wildflowers not yet mentioned;* not asked in early QRs) Inf **CA**208, Locust tree flowers; (Qu. T1, . . *A bunch of trees growing together in open country, especially on a hill*) Inf **LA**8, Locust patch; (Qu. T12) Infs **MA**50, **RI**15, Locust; (Qu. T13) Inf **MA**62, Locust; (Qu. T15. . . *Kinds of swamp trees*) Infs **IL**82, **MD**30, Locust. **1986** Pederson *LAGS Concordance* **Gulf Region** (*Common trees*) 20 infs, Locust.

2 A **rattlebox** (here: *Sesbania punicea*). Cf **red locust**
1960 Vines *Trees SW* 546, *Sesbania punicea.* . . Other names are . . Locust, and Red Siene Bean. A very handsome shrub in flower with good horticultural uses on the Gulf Coast plain area.

3 =cicada. [See quot 1972]
1709 (1967) Lawson *New Voyage* 139 **NC, SC,** The Reptiles, or smaller *Insects,* are too numerous to relate here, this Country affording innumerable Quantities thereof; as the Flying-Stags with Horns, Beetles, Butterflies, Grashoppers, Locust, and several hundreds of uncouth Shapes. **1789** Morse *Amer. Geog.* 62, Of the astonishing variety of *Insects* found in America, we will mention . . Cicada or Locust. **1854** Emmons *Agriculture NY* 5.145, The name *locust* is applied usually in this country to our harvest-fly, which is commonly called *the seventeen-year locust.* **1884** (1885) McCook *Tenants* 313 **PA,** In short, what people call "locusts" in America are called "Cicadas," or "Harvest-flies," in Europe; and what in the Old World are known as "locusts" are called "grasshoppers" in the United States. **1903** *DN* 2.319 seMO, Locust. . . Pronounced locus; cicada. **1916** *DN* 4.346 LA, Loaker ['lokə·']. = a cicada. **1950** *WELS* **WI** (*Insects that sit in trees or bushes and make a sharp buzzing sound in hot weather*) 19 Infs, Locust; 2 Infs, Seventeen-year locust; 1 Inf, Seventeen-year locust [FW sugg]; (*Other creatures that make a clicking, shrilling, or chirring sound*) 6 Infs, **WI,** Locust. **1965–70** *DARE* (Qu. R7, *Insects that sit in trees or bushes in hot weather and make a sharp, buzzing sound*) 318 Infs, **widespread,** Locus(t); 7 Infs, Locust [Infs indicated a seventeen-year locust]; 6 Infs, Locusses; **IA**29, Locus—seven-year locust—a special kind; **KS**1, Locust—that's what most people call the cicada; **KY**60, Locust—seven-year variety; **LA**3, Locust—sheds its shell on trees and comes out with wings; **LA**6, Locust—they shed out of their hull; **LA**14, Locust—same as cicada; cicada = learned word; **LA**37, Locust—cigalle; **MI**120, Locus—chirper; **MN**38, Locust—a different one from the grasshopper; **MO**5, Locus, we call 'em—some of 'em call 'em jarflies; **MO**13, Locust—that's not what they are, but that's what they're usually called; **NC**81, Locust—one-inch body, two-inch wing; **NY**44, Locust—they're hollerin' for heat; **NY**93, Seventeen-year-old locust or harvest bee; **OH**82, Locust—more common name, though they are cicadas; **OK**31, Locus now—July flies when I was a kid; **OK**42, Jarfly or locus (real name); **PA**88, When the locust sings you know it's going to be hot; **SC**4, Locust—continuous sound; **SC**63, Locust—cicada—upper-state name; **TX**59, Locust—jarfly; **VA**75, Locust—hot bug; **LA**44, Loaker—this is a mud diver before it turns into a loaker; before that it's a cuckoo. They sing like a son of a gun; (Qu. R8, . . *Kinds of creatures that make a clicking or shrilling or chirping kind of sound*) 22 Infs, **chiefly Sth, S Midl,** Locust; **KY**9, **SC**32, Locusses; **SC**46, (Seven-year) locusts; (Qu. R5) 20 Infs, **scattered,** Locus(t); **LA**37, Cigalle, locust; **LA**40, Locust, cicada; **MA**26, Locust—have kind of a croak, too—a shrill sound, a buzzing sound; **PA**17, Locust—eggs in trees; (Qu. R6, . . *Names* . . *for grasshoppers*) 11 Infs, Locust(s) [Infs indicated they are different from grasshoppers.]; **AL**2, Locust—something else—big a[s] thumb—makes a high sound; **AL**6, Locust are different here, they scream at night; **AL**10, Locust—big black ones; **DC**8, Locust—dark gray to brown—every seventeen years—holler at night—the ground is like a sieve when they come out; **IA**36, Locus—but they're up in the trees too, I think; **KY**65, Locus—some say cicada locust; **MI**36, Some people call them locusts but the grasshopper is not a locust; the locust I've seen in West Virginia is a fly; **MI**65, Locus—there are seventeen-year locusts; I don't know whether they'd be considered grasshoppers or not; **NY**36, Locusts are different from grasshoppers; usually in trees; **NY**53, Locust—seventeen-year locust—eggs hatch every seventeen years; **OK**31, Some might call them a locus but I think they're different; **WA**6, Locus—we don't have any locus, just grasshoppers; (Qu. P6x, . . *Kinds of worms* . . *used for bait;* not asked in early QRs) Inf **PA**168, Locust; (Qu. R4, *A large winged insect that hatches in summer in great numbers* . . *and is good*

fish bait) Infs **MO**5, 32, Locusts; **MO**3, Locus; (Qu. R9a) Inf **MO**10, Locus; (Qu. R30, . . *Kinds of beetles; not asked in early QRs)* Inf **NJ**8, Locus; **IL**93, Locust—but I don't know whether it's a beetle or not; **NY**105, Locust—sings; **DC**12, Locust, sixteen-year-old locust—but not in a close city. **1967** *PA Game News* Sept 53 **PA,** Some of my elderly friends would no more touch a cicada than bed down with a rattlesnake. They *know* the "locust" has a poisonous sting—book learning to the contrary notwithstanding. **1969** *DARE* FW Addit **Hatteras Is. NC,** *Locust* (pretty sure this is a cicada). One old-timer said that he used to go out and eat their sheddings, which taste like potato chips. **1972** Little *Genl. Entomol.* 147, Cicadas or Harvest Flies. . . are probably better known in the United States as locusts than by any other name. . . The name was given them by early settlers in the eastern states when they observed swarms of the periodical cicada *(Magicicada septendecim)*. . . [which] reminded them of locusts (grasshoppers) of the Old World. **1981** Pederson *LAGS Basic Materials,* 1 inf, **csGA,** Locust; 1 inf, **ceAR,** Seven-year locust; 1 inf, **cwAR,** Jar flies or July flies—local terms for locusts.

4 A **grasshopper 1** of the family Acrididae, esp any of var migratory grasshoppers. [*OED* c1300 →]

1737 (1911) Brickell *Nat. Hist. NC* 166, The Locust, is an Insect or fly with a head like a Horse, six Legs and as many Wings. **1819** in 1823 Faux *Memorable Days* 137 *(DAE),* Grasshoppers, so called, but in fact a species of locust about the length of my little finger, swarm in countless millions. **1905** Kellogg *Amer. Insects* 133, In 1866 and again in 1874 and 1875 the locusts had come; first a thin silvery cloud high overhead—sunlight glancing from millions of thin membranous fluttering wings—and then a swarming, crawling, leaping and ever and always busily eating horde of locusts over all the green things of the land. *Ibid* 149, The general reader of natural history should always keep clearly in mind the sharp distinction made by naturalists between "scientific" and "vernacular" names. The vernacular name locust is applied to insects of the family Acriidiae, but not to any of the members of the family whose scientific name is Locustidae. **1926** Essig *Insects N. Amer.* 84, The Rocky Mountain locust . . is the most famous of all the destructive, migrating locusts of this country. **1950** *WELS* **WI** *(Other names for the grasshopper* . . *Include joking and nicknames)* 15 Infs, Locust; 1 Inf, Locust—short horn grasshopper. **1965–70** *DARE* (Qu. R6, . . *Names* . . *for grasshoppers)* 112 Infs, **widespread,** Locust; **OH**2, Locusses; **MN**38, Locust—the bigger grasshopper; **MN**42, Locust—the big brown flying one; **MA**66, Not too far from here—somewhere in Massachusetts—they went through a place and ate everything green; they were a locus; **NY**40, Locus—different from regular grasshopper—it flies and grasshopper hops and glides; **NY**75, Locus—they look like a grasshopper, only larger; **TX**66, Locust—there is a difference between locusts and grasshoppers; locusts come in droves, eat everything; **WV**2, Locust are called grasshoppers here; (Qu. R7) Inf **FL**48, Locust—another bug; **RI**17, Locusts—flying grasshoppers; (Qu. R8, . . *Kinds of creatures that make a clicking or shrilling or chirping kind of sound)* Inf **KY**40, Locusts—call "Pharoah, pharoah," all the time. **1980** Milne–Milne *Audubon Field Guide Insects* 417, Short-horned grasshoppers (Family Acrididae). . . Many members of this large family attack crop plants. Some are called locusts from the Latin word for grasshopper. **1981** Pederson *LAGS Basic Materials,* 6 infs, **Gulf Region,** Locus(t)(s); 1 inf, **ceAL,** Locuses—like crickets, come in swarms; 1 inf, **ceAR,** Locuses; 1 inf, **cwGA,** Locust—in grasshopper family—some people call it a grasshopper; 1 inf, **csTX,** Grasshopper, locust—nearly the same.

5 =**katydid B1.**

1968 *DARE* (Qu. R8, . . *Kinds of creatures that make a clicking or shrilling or chirping kind of sound)* Inf **GA**25, Locust—same as a katydid; **LA**44, We call katydids locusts. **1981** Pederson *LAGS Basic Materials,* 1 inf, **neTX,** Locust—same as katydid.

locust beer n Also *locust (and) persimmon beer* **chiefly SE** Cf **persimmon beer**

A fermented beverage made with the pods of **locust B1.**

[**1830** Rafinesque *Med. Flora* 2.224, *Honey Locust.* . . The pods have a sweet acid pulp, good to eat, good beer and metheglin made with it.] [**1863** Porcher *Resources* 388 **Sth,** *Persimmon Beer.* . . The addition of a few honey locusts, roasted sweet potatoes, or apple peelings, will make the beer more brisk.] **1949** Barringer *Nat. Bent* 189 **Sth,** Beer was just coming, unless we except "persimmon beer" and "locust beer" made on every plantation and in many village homes. **1952** Brown *NC Folkl.* 1.274, *Locust Beer.*—Take locust, persimmons, and a little corn meal, put it in a barrel, cover with water, and let it remain a few days. To this may be added dried apple peelings and cores. **1966–70** *DARE* (Qu. DD28b, . . *Fermented drinks* . . *made at home)* Inf **AL**4, Locust and

persimmon beer; **NC**47, Locust persimmon beer; **SC**32, Locust beer—very little alcohol, weak; **VA**39, Locust beer. **1980** *Americana* Nov/Dec 44 **cSC** (as of late 1800s) [Black], Among her discoveries was a home-brewed beverage called locust beer, made from locust pods and persimmons. **1981** Pederson *LAGS Basic Materials,* 1 inf, **cnGA,** Locust beer—make it out of a little honey locust. **1984** Burns *Cold Sassy* 20 **nGA** (as of 1906), At the time, Papa made and drank locust beer, and Mama made scuppernong and blackberry wines for church communion.

locustberry n [*DJE* 1727 → for *Byrsonima coriacea*]

A small shrubby tree *(Byrsonima lucida)* native to southern Florida.

1933 Small *Manual SE Flora* 756, *Locust-berry.* . . Hammocks and low pinelands, Everglade Keys, Fla. and Florida Keys. **1938** Baker *FL Wild Flowers* 118, Locust berry. . . Fruit a small drupe. Pinelands and hammocks. All the year. **1953** Greene–Blomquist *Flowers South* 63, *Locust-Berry.* . . is a shrub or tree with opposite, evergreen, lustrous leaves and . . white or pink flowers, fading to yellow. **1971** Craighead *Trees S. FL* 201, Locustberry. **1979** Little *Checklist U.S. Trees* 67, *Byrsonima lucida.* . . *Other common names*—locust-berry.

locust fern n

=**royal fern.**

1938 Small *Ferns SE States* 342, The extensive geographic distribution has . . allowed this fern [=*Osmunda regalis*] to accumulate a rather large number of common names. Besides royal-fern, we find . . locust-fern, and others.

locust persimmon beer See **locust beer**

locust plant n Cf **locust B1**

A **wild senna** (here: *Cassia marilandica*).

1873 in 1976 Miller *Shaker Herbs* 230, *Senna, American.* . . Locust Plant. A mild cathartic. **1911** Henkel *Amer. Med. Leaves* 13, *Cassia marilandica.* . . Locust plant. . . The leaves. . . consist of from 12 to 20 leaflets placed opposite to each other on the stem. **1958** Jacobs–Burlage *Index Plants NC* 123, *Cassia marilandica.* . . Locust plant. . . The leaves are almost identical in action to senna. **1974** (1977) Coon *Useful Plants* 166, *Cassia marilandica* . . locust plant. . . This brightly yellow-colored plant gives us the drug "senna" which is made from the dried leaves.

locust tree See **locust B1**

Lod See **Lord** n[1]

lodde n [Norw]

=**capelin 1.**

1896 U.S. Natl. Museum *Bulletin* 47.520, *Mallotus villosus* . . Capelin; Lodde.

lodestone n Cf **madstone**

=**beazlestone.**

1938 Matschat *Suwannee R.* 89 **neFL, seGA,** *Love Potions and Charms.* . . A lodestone from a deer (a hard substance sometimes found in a deer) and carried in the pocket or around the neck gives the power to produce twins at will.

lodge v, hence ppl adj *lodged,* vbl n *lodging* [*OED* 1593 →; *EDD*] **chiefly Nth**

Of hay, grain, etc: to fall flat, be beaten down or laid flat as by wind or rain; also, esp of wind or rain: to beat down or flatten (crops).

1828 (1970) Webster *Amer. Dict., Lodge.* . . To fall flat, as grain. Wheat and oats on strong land are apt to *lodge.* **1884** *Harper's New Mth. Mag.* 69.247 **seNY,** The growth had been so heavy that . . it had "lodged," or fallen. **1889** *Century Dict.* 3502, *Lodge.* . . To . . beat down; lay flat: said especially of vegetation. . . To be beaten down or laid flat, as grain. **1936** (1972) Ise *Sod & Stubble* 208 **KS** (as of c1880s), The wheat that had been pronounced dead in January became a billowy sea of yellow and gold in early July, so tall that it was feared it might lodge. **1958** *AmSp* 33.271 **eWA** [Ranching terms], *Lodged.* Of hay or grain, not standing erect (usually because of wind or rain). If very badly lodged, the crop may be worthless. **1959** *VT Hist.* 27.148 **cn,neVT,** *Lodge the oats.* . . To flatten oats or other grain, as after a heavy rain. Common. Orleans [County]. **1965** *Bee* (Phillips WI) 19 Aug [9/3], About ¼ of the small grain harvest is complete. . . While showers and high humidity have slowed machinery operation there has been little lodging even among the tall stands on western farms. **1966** *DARE* Tape **AR**33, [Inf:] Quite often we have rice that lodges. [FW:] What do you mean by lodges? [Inf:] Well, that means fall down. The term for it is lodging. **1975** Gould *ME Lingo* 165, Grass or grain which has been trampled or laid down by a storm is said to be *lodged,* and is difficult to mow with a scythe: "Persnickety as lodged oats." **1984** *MJLF* 10.152 nME, cnWI, *Lodged hay.* Hay that has been pressed to the ground by wind and rain, making it hard to mow. **1994** *DARE* File csWI, I walked out into that cornfield the other day and saw that a lot of it is lodging; they are so late in cutting it. *Ibid* cWI, We used to grow oats, and after a heavy rain or wind they would often be lodged.

lodge n See **lodging** n

lodged See **lodge** v

lodgepole pine n Also *lodge pine, lodgepole* [See quot 1924]
A pine tree (*Pinus contorta* and varr) of the western US. Also called **birdeye pine, black ~ 2a, bull ~ 1b, hackmatack 1c, jack pine 2c, pitch ~, prickly ~, red ~, ridgepole ~, sand ~, screw ~, scrub ~, tamarack ~, twisted ~, white ~**

1859 in 1935 *Colorado Mag.* 12.205, Cut the top off a small lodge pole pine. **1884** Sargent *Forests of N. Amer.* 195, *Pinus Murrayana*. . . Tamarack. Black pine. Lodge-pole pine. Spruce pine. **1903** (1965) Adams *Log Cowboy* 330 NM, He . . went back about a mile to a thicket of lodge poles. **1905** *NY Post* (NY) 29 Apr Sat suppl 2/3, The lodgepole pine, . . bears the common name of "lodgepole" from the fact that the Indians used its long slender trunks as supports for their wigwams, or lodges. **1924** Hawkins *Trees & Shrubs* 8, If this region had been named for its most salient botanical feature, the Lodgepole Pine Park would vie with the French and Indian name of Yellowstone. . . In August of each year, the Indians made journeys to these forests to cut and peel the light, strong, slender poles for lodges and travoys. **1962** Sweet *Plants of West* 10, Lodgepole Pine, *P[inus] contorta*. Usually has straight trunk, but scraggly branches. **1965–70** *DARE* (Qu. T17, . . *Kinds of pine trees; not asked in early QRs*) 24 Infs, **West**, Lodgepole pine; CA144, Lodge pine; (Qu. T13, . . *Names . . for . . tamarack*) Inf CA105, Lodgepole pine—because Indians used it for their tents; (Qu. T15, . . *Kinds of swamp trees*) Inf AK1, Lodgepole pine. **1994** *USA Today* (Arlington VA) 4 Feb sec A 6 **MT**, Missoula—An appeals court has OK'd a plan for logging of log lodgepole pine in the Upper Yaak River drainage of the Kootenai National Forest.

lodging n Also *lodge* [Cf *OED lodging* vbl. sb. 3.c "Material to lie or sleep on. *Obs.*"] **chiefly eNC, Delmarva**
A makeshift bed on the floor, a **pallet.**

1814 in 1956 Eliason *Tarheel Talk* 282 NC, Let me advise you to let [the baby] sleep on a lodging made with blankets, in a cradle on feathers is too debilitating this warm weather. **1946** *PADS* 6.19 eNC (as of 1900–10), *Lodging*. . . A sleeping place on the floor. Pamlico [County]. Common. **1949** Kurath *Word Geog.* fig 88 **sDE, eMD, eVA**, Pallet . . lodge [7 infs]. **1966–70** *DARE* (Qu. E18, *A temporary or emergency bed made up on the floor*) Inf NC1, Lodging—old-fashioned; NC25, 82, Lodging (on the floor); VA48, Lodge—old-fashioned; make up a lodge on the floor. **1967** Faries *Word Geog.* MO 87, *Pallet* . . is used almost exclusively by the Missouri informants (685 [of c700] occurrences). A few use the Delamarvian *lodge*. **1970** *DARE* FW Addit Tangier Is. VA, Lodge—an emergency bed made up on the floor. Common. **1971** Wood *Vocab. Change* 298 **Sth**, [Of 1000 infs, 3, in TN and OK, reported *lodge*].

lodging vbl n See **lodge** v

loft n

1 also *hayloft:* The upper part of a barn used esp to store hay. [*OED* 1530 →] **widespread, but less freq Nth, N Midl, Pacific** See Map Cf **mow** n[1] **2, hayrack 3**

1806 (1970) Webster *Compendious Dict.* 140, *Hayloft*. . . a scaffold for hay. [*DARE* Ed: This entry does not appear in Webster's English model.] **1899** (1912) Green *VA Folk-Speech* 266, "Barn-*loft*"; "Hay-*loft*." **1923** *DN* 5.213 swMO, *Loft*. . . The upper story of a . . barn. **1949** Kurath *Word Geog.* 53, The upper part of a barn is called the *loft* in the greater part of the Eastern States: regularly so (1) in the southern area and in the mountains south of Kanawha, and (2) in New England and its offshoots; less commonly in the North Midland. *Loft* is not current in central Pennsylvania and in the adjoining part of West Virginia, and it is infrequent in other parts of Pennsylvania and most of New Jersey. **c1960** *Wilson Coll.* [see **2** below]. **1962** [see **2** below]. **1965** Carmony *Speech Terre Haute* 18 cwIN, For the upper part of a barn where hay may be stored, the usual expression in Terre Haute is *loft* or *hay loft*. [14 of 16 infs] **1965–70** *DARE* (Qu. M3, *The place inside a*

barn for storing hay) 487 Infs, **widespread, but less freq Nth, N Midl, Pacific,** (Hay)loft; 16 Infs, **chiefly S Midl,** Barn loft; FL18, MO16, SC32, Lofts; (Qu. M12, *What do you keep food for the cattle in over winter?*) 32 Infs, **scattered, but esp Sth, S Midl,** (Hay)loft; IL93, TN37, Hay in (the) loft; AL34, FL26, (Fodder) lofts; KY34, Barn loft; MS67, Loft of the barn; (Qu. M5, . . *The hole for throwing hay down below*) Infs AR29, CA156, FL27, 37, SC26, Up in (or out of, hole in) the loft; MO10, OK27, SC26, TN1, Loft hole (or door); LA43, Hayloft; (Qu. L15, *When you are putting hay into a building for storage . . you are* _____) Infs GA60, LA22, NC10, Carrying it up to (or loading it in, putting it in) the loft; MD9, 24, ND3, Filling (or putting it in) the hayloft; NY68, Putting it in a mow; I've heard it called hayloft too; (Qu. L32a, *In early days, how was the grain separated from the straw?*) Inf TN42, Drop from loft onto sheet; (Qu. L32b, *In early days, how was the grain separated from the chaff?*) Inf TN42, Drop from loft onto sheet; (Qu. M1, . . *Kinds of barns . . according to their use or the way they are built*) Infs CA99, ND3, VA10, (Hay)loft barn; AR36, NV8, Barn with (a) loft; AR36, Barn without loft; GA33, Hayloft—over horse lot; (Qu. M6, *The place where grain is kept in a barn*) Infs GA17, LA20, (Hay)loft. **1967** Faries *Word Geog.* MO 75, The general term *loft* (85 percent [of c700] infs), to denote the space for hay in the upper part of a barn, is clearly the widespread expression among the informants. **1971** Bright *Word Geog.* CA & NV 151, Upper part of barn . . *loft* 56% [of 300 infs] . . *hayloft* 51%. **1972** *PADS* 58.14 cwAL, Loft. **1973** Allen *LAUM* 1.183 **Upper MW** (as of c1950), Place for hay in the barn. . . The two common designations for the second story area are *(hay)loft* and *(hay)mow*. Their distribution weight reflects the dominance of *loft* in New England and the dominance of *mow* in the North Midland, although both terms are so common in the U[pper] M[idwest] that only percentages are indicative. **1981** *PADS* 67.22 **Mesabi Iron Range MN,** Loft. **1989** Pederson *LAGS Tech. Index* 55 **Gulf Region** [*Upper part of the barn*] 556 infs, Loft; 191 infs, Hayloft; 37 infs, Barn loft; 3 infs, Fodder loft; 1 inf, Open loft; 1 inf, Stable loft.

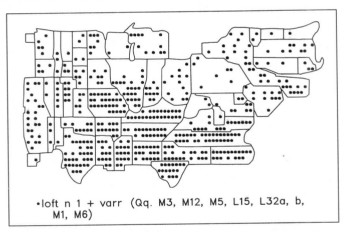

•loft n 1 + varr (Qq. M3, M12, M5, L15, L32a, b, M1, M6)

2 The attic or upstairs of a house. **scattered, but chiefly S Midl, Sth** See Map Cf **cockloft 1**

1852 Bickley *Hist. Tazewell Co. VA* 150 swVA, [Footnote:] Even now the second stories of some of our most costly mansions are termed "lofts," by the older persons. **1899** (1912) Green *VA Folk-Speech* 266, *Loft*. . . A room in the upper part of a house, occupying the whole house. **1915** *DN* 4.185 swVA, *Loft*. . . The second story of a house; upstairs. **1923** *DN* 5.213 swMO, *Loft*. . . The upper story of a house. **1937** *Hall Coll.* eTN, The attic or garret of a house, the space under the roof, sometimes used for sleeping. Called "upstairs" even if no stairs, or "up in the loft." **1941** *LANE* Map 345 (*Attic*) 2 infs, seVT, neME, Loft; 1 infs, neRI, Loft, the usual term; 1 inf, seNH, Loft, an unfinished attic. **1950** *WELS* (*The room up under the roof of a house, used for storing things*) 1 Inf, seWI, Loft—old-fashioned. **1960** Criswell *Resp. to PADS 20* Ozarks, *Loft*. In the older houses here [this] is where the boys and hired men slept. Attic is a much later term for the same thing and is now the common term, though many attics are not used for this purpose at all. **c1960** *Wilson Coll.* csKY, *Loft*—The attic or unfinished top story of a house. Commoner as a term for this area in a barn or stable: *barn loft, hay loft, stable loft.* **1962** Atwood *Vocab. TX* 43, For the part of a house immediately under the roof . . a few informants use *loft* (15 [% of 273 infs]), apparently regardless of whether the structure is a barn or a house. **1965–70** *DARE* (Qu. D4, *The space up under the roof, usually used for storing things*) 54 Infs, **scattered, but chiefly S Midl, Sth,**

Loft; (Qu. D7) Inf **WA2**, Loft. **1967** *DARE* Tape **NC41**, "Well, that'll be in the loft," "It's up in the loft."—That was a common word. **1989** Pederson *LAGS Tech. Index* 39 **Gulf Region** [*Attic*] 215 infs, Loft; 3 infs, Garret loft; 1 inf, Cock loft; 1 inf, Loft overhead; 1 inf, Loft room.

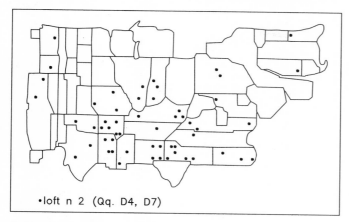

•loft n 2 (Qqs. D4, D7)

3 See quot. Cf **mow** n[1] **3**
1965–70 *DARE* (Qu. D40, *Names and nicknames . . for the upper balcony in a theater*) 10 Infs, **scattered,** Loft.

loft v, hence vbl n *lofting* Cf **mow** v
To store or put up (a crop), esp in a **loft** n **1.**
1785 in 1891 Washington *Writings* 12.229 **eVA**, The remainder of the Crop which was measured and lofted must be accted. for by the Over-seer. **1786** (1925) Washington *Diaries* 3.136 **eVA**, Began to gather Corn in the Neck and at the Ferry for lofting. **1800** (1907) Columbia Hist. Soc. *Records* 10.90 **PA**, Part of the Ton of hay arrived . . as soon as it was lofted—went to see Mrs. T.—Peter. **1968–69** *DARE* (Qu. L15, *When you are putting hay into a building for storage . . you are* _____) Inf **GA80**, Lofting hay—put it in the loft; **NJ31**, Lofting hay. [Both Infs old] **1986** Pederson *LAGS Concordance*, 1 inf, **cwAL**, Have it lofted overhead—[said] of hay in the barn. [Inf old]

loft adj [Var of *loath;* cf *EDD*]
1899 (1912) Green *VA Folk-Speech* 266, *Loft. . .* Unwilling. "He was very loft to do it."

lofting See **loft** v

log v
1 in phr *log it:* See below. **esp NEast**
a To engage in logging; see quots.
1914 *DN* 4.76 **ME, nNH**, *Log it. . .* To work in the lumber-woods. **1917** *DN* 4.395 **neOH, NEng**, *Log it. . .* To cut and haul logs to the saw-mill; especially to do so for a period of time. "I'm logging it while the snow lasts."
b See quot.
1901 *DN* 2.143 **sNY**, *Log. . .* "To log it," draw logs for burning, not for lumber.
2 with *up:* To reduce to logs; to prepare for use as firewood.
1916 Kephart *Camping & Woodcraft* 1.113, With this one tool a good axeman can . . quickly fell and log-up a tree large enough to keep a hot fire before his lean-to throughout the night. **1917** *Ibid* 2.192, *Logging up.*—When the tree is down, trim off the branches for firewood. . . Then log up the trunk. . . Make the outside chip not less in length than the diameter of the log. . . Make two outside nicks, as in felling a tree, split out the block between them, and so go on, making big chips, and cutting at a considerable angle to the grain of the wood instead of across it. . . Having cut one notch half through the trunk, go on to the next ones until the end piece is reached; then turn around and work back until all cuts have been severed. **1949** Graham *Niagara Country* 79, In exchanging his services for those of the oxen, the young settler was able to get the assistance of these patient animals for a day now and then to haul the logs for the cabin and to "log up" the timber he had cut for burning to clear the land. **1969** *DARE* (Qu. LL24, *To keep firewood neat you have to cut it, split it, and* _____ *it up*) Inf **NC61**, Log.
3 Fig: see quots. Cf **cook** v **5**
1930 Williams *Logger-Talk* 27 **Pacific NW**, *Now you're loggin'* or *now you're railroadin':* Words of high praise no matter if one is cleaning a trout or fighting a forest fire. **1958** McCulloch *Woods Words* 123 **Pacific**

NW, *Now you're logging*—a. On the right track. b. Getting the work done in highball fashion. **1975** Gould *ME Lingo* 166, "Now we're loggin'!" means we have everything under control and going well. **1979** *NYT Article Letters* **seWA**, "Now you're loggin(g)" as an expression of commendation, whether or not actually working in lumbering.

log n
1 =**drag** n **1.**
c1960 *Wilson Coll.* **csKY**, *Log. . .* A home-made drag or clod-buster. My own usage as a boy was *log,* but I found *drag* when I went to Hickman County to teach in 1907. *Ibid, Drag. . .* A series of logs or planks fastened together to make a crusher of clods. Sometimes called a *log,* regardless of its make.
2 pl:=**jimmies** n pl[2].
1982 *DARE* File **cnVT**, Here the bits of candy, called jimmies or sprinkles in other places, are called logs. Some of them are shaped, like tiny logs, made of chocolate.
3 See quot.
c1965 *DARE* File, *Log*—used as a measure of time, is the amount of time it takes to split a log (into fence rails). Reported by a graduate student in Boston. He heard the expression used by an army man in 1944, who may have been from Kentucky, and who said it was an old expression. "Well, it's about three logs till noon."

logan n Also sp *login* [Prob abbr for **pokelogan**] **chiefly ME** Cf **bogan**
=**pokelogan.**
[**1881** *Harper's New Mth. Mag.* 63.826 **Canada**, Is it merely a coincidence that the sheet of water the Indian calls *logan* we name *lagoon,* from the Italian *lagune.*] **1903** *Jrl. Amer. Folk.* 16.128 **ME**, *Bogan*—a still creek or bay branching from a stream—exactly the same thing the Indians call a *pokologan. . .* Now, curiously enough, exactly the same thing is generally called in Maine a *logan*—which must be another form of the same word. These words are in good local use, and occur in articles on sporting, etc. **1905** U.S. Forest Serv. *Bulletin* 61.43 **nNEng, nNY, MN, nWI, nMI** [Logging terms], *Pokelogan. . .* A bay or pocket into which logs may float off during a drive. . . Syn[onym]: logan. **1907** *DN* 3.246 **eME**, *Lōgin. . .* A stretch of still water in a river or bay. An Indian word. **1913** *DN* 4.2 **cME**, *Logan. . .* A damp thicket. "We can't get through the logan." **1914** *DN* 4.76 **ME, nNH**, *Logan. . .* A wet, marshy piece of land. **1942** Rich *We Took to Woods* 15 **NEng**, The country is criss-crossed with ridges, dotted with swamps and logans, and covered with dense forest. **1946** Attwood *Length ME* 15 [Geographical terms], *Logan*—A cove formed by the rise of a stream, causing water to back into a tributary. **1971** *DARE* File **sME coast**, In my fishing expeditions to the Maine Lakes I heard *logan* applied to little swampy places which would fit the definition of *bogan.* In some instances it was called a *pokelogan.* **1975** Gould *ME Lingo* 166, *Logan*—A small cove or inlet in fresh water, usually off a pond, and often where a stream comes into a pond. The word suggests sluggish or still water, not too deep, and often a *logan* makes good trout fishing.

loganberry See **logging berry a**

log-and-block fence n
A type of timber fence; see quot.
1983 *High Country News* (Paonia CO) 5 Sept 8, Timber fencing is a dying craft. . . A litany of types: stake-and-rider, buck-and-pole, ripgut, log-and-block, post-and-rail, worm. [Photo caption:] *Log* and *Block* for big timber. [Photo shows a fence of long, notched logs, three-high, supported by short logs perpendicular to them at about ten- or twelve-foot intervals. Because the short logs support the ends of one set of horizontal logs and the beginnings of another, set about a foot apart on the short logs, the parallel sets of rails are offset.]

log berry See **logging berry a**

log boat n Cf **boat 1**
=**stoneboat.**
1968–69 *DARE* (Qu. L57, *A low wooden platform used for bringing stones or heavy things out of the fields*) Inf **NY75**, Log boat; (Qu. N40a, *. . Sleighs . . for hauling loads*) Inf **MA15**, Log boat—about all there is now; double-runner sleighs—in the past.

log buggy n Cf **log cart**
In logging: see quot.
1967 *DARE* (Qu. N41b, *Horse-drawn vehicles to carry heavy loads*) Inf **MI47**, Travois—used in the woods to haul the log from the tree site

to the skidway. The travois was also called a "dray" around here. Old-timers called it "the little log buggy."

log cabin n, also attrib Cf **barn raising 2**

A quilt pattern; see quots 1949, 1979.

1887 *Harper's New Mth. Mag.* 76.36, Reluctantly she slipped her book under the log-cabin quilt and said, "Come in." **1907** Obenchain *Aunt Jane* 57, There seemed to be every pattern that the ingenuity of woman could devise and the industry of woman put together,—"four-patches," "nine-patches," "log-cabins," "wild-goose chases," "rising suns." **1928** Aldrich *Lantern* 57 **NE**, A box of intricate quilt blocks, The Rose of Sharon and The Star of Bethlehem, The Rising Sun or the Log Cabin. **1949** Ickis *Quilt Making* 86, The popular Log Cabin design. . . The pattern of each block is built around a central square with narrower rectangular pieces surrounding this center. These narrow pieces of varying lengths are laid end to end and represent the overlapping logs in cabins of the early settlers. **1967** *DARE* Tape **MA**117, [Inf:] I made hundreds of bed quilts. [FW:] You remember some of the patterns that you used? . . [Aux Inf:] Well, log cabin. You probably made those. [Inf:] Yes, yes. I made log cabin. **1979** *WI Then & Now* 7 July 7, "Log Cabin" patterns of folded narrow strips set in rectangles usually are made of wool and usually have red wool squares in the center of the blocks, some say to represent the red brick chimney of a cabin. **1986** Pederson *LAGS Concordance*, 1 inf, **cnGA**, A log cabin—quilt pattern.

log-cabin raising See **log-raising**

log canoe n Chesapeake Bay Cf **brogan 3, bugeye** n², **maul-head 1**

A usually double-ended boat made of several timbers fastened together and carved to shape, orig designed for sailing but now sometimes used with an inboard motor; also in combs *two-log canoe, three-log ~,* etc.

[**1880** in 1881 Ingersoll *Oyster-Industry* 164 **MD**, The size of the tonging-canoe ranges from 15 or 16 feet to 30 feet or more, the larger ones being called 'bugeyes.'] **1906** *Forest & Stream* 67.898, One cannot travel far on the [Chesapeake] bay waters without discovering places where the heavy log canoes give way to lighter skipjacks. . . Here and there one will find a one-log dugout, here and there a two-log canoe, but new ones are not made, and the old ones are fast passing out of existence. . . Why should not a bugeye, a bugeye with a bustle, a three-log canoe, a five-log one, . . and all the other small boat rigs of Chesapeake Bay be hung as they are rigged for the edification of the near generation which will have forgotten these strange craft? **1935** Chapelle *Hist. Sailing Ships* 257, On the Chesapeake the work [of the oyster-fishery] was done largely by the "bugeyes," a local two-masted, leg-of-mutton rigged and double-ended type of centerboard ketch. The smaller but somewhat similar log-canoes are also employed in the fishery. **1942** Footner *MD Main* 206, Sails are seldom seen now, but many of the infinitely graceful "log-canoes" survive, driven by engines. Since three great logs form the keel of a canoe, they are almost indestructible. **1953** *Sun* (Baltimore MD) 18 Oct mag sec 17/1 *(Hench Coll.)* Chesapeake Bay, It was a crude counterpart of this craft [=log canoe] that the settlers found when they first arrived on these shores. . . The settlers adapted these to their own use and . . improved upon them. Through the years they found it simpler to build a canoe from two or three logs than from a single great log. Eventually sails and centerboards were added to more refined hulls built of even more logs, to bring about the perfection of the type as we know it today. Many log canoes exist today in bay waters as power boats. A few carry on under sail as pleasure craft. **1960** *Hench Coll.,* Moran (who knows a lot about Chesapeake Bay boats) says that originally the log canoe was a sailing boat (work boat) made of logs but that now it is a motorized low-lying, wide boat. **1968** *DARE* (Qu. O9, . . *Kinds of sailboats*) Inf **MD**34, Chesapeake Bay log canoe—a class-boat, built according to the size and style regulations required for the type; **MD**36, Log canoe—built from three pieces of timber, hewed out with an ax, has one to three sails, depending on size; **MD**42, Log canoe—hewn out of a log, no longer made, peculiar to Chesapeake Bay; (Qu. O10, . . *Kinds of boats*) Inf **MD**11, Log canoe—series of logs bolted together, hollowed out with adz; about thirty feet; originated in Chesapeake Bay area; usually sail powered, sometimes has inboard engine; **MD**15, Log canoe—hewn out of several logs; like the bugeye [canoe], but smaller; (Qu. FF16, . . *Local contests or celebrations*) Inf **MD**41, Log canoe race—held at annual regattas. **1984** *DARE* File **Chesapeake Bay** [Watermen's vocab], Log canoe.

log cart n Also *log carrier, logging cart* esp C and S Atl See Map Cf **big wheels, high wheel, logging wheels**

A vehicle for hauling logs, consisting of two large wheels

joined by an axle and having a long tongue that attaches to one or more draft animals.

1913 Bryant *Logging* 180, *Log Carts.*—In all types of carts the logs are swung beneath the wheels with the rear ends dragging on the ground. The height of wheels ranges from 5 to 10 feet with a corresponding variation in gauge. *Ibid* 184, From two to six animals are employed to haul log carts. . . Mules are preferred in the South, and horses in the North and West. **1966–70** *DARE* (Qu. N41b, *Horse-drawn vehicles to carry heavy loads*) Infs **NJ**1, **NC**6, 49, Log cart; **SC**31, Logging cart—two wheels; **SC**57, Log cart—two big wheels (only) with bowed axle, let small end of log drag behind; **VA**78, Log cart—just for logs; **MD**36, Log carrier—two big wheels, log was wound up by rope underneath, hauled beneath wagon. **1986** Pederson *LAGS Concordance*, 1 inf, **csAL**, Log cart—pulled by oxen; 1 inf, **swGA**, Baby-doll log cart—pulled by oxen, [used for] hauling logs. [*LAGS* Ed queries]

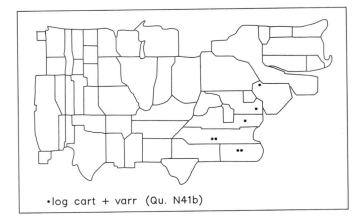

•log cart + varr (Qu. N41b)

log city See **log town**

logcock n Also *lobcock*

1 =**pileated woodpecker.**

1806 (1905) Lewis *Orig. Jrls. Lewis & Clark Exped.* 4.132, The large woodpecker or log cock. **1811** [see **2** below]. **1839** Audubon *Synopsis Birds* 176, Pileated Woodpecker.—Log-cock. . . From Texas to the Columbia River, and along the Atlantic coast, as well as in the interior, to the Fur Countries. **a1883** (1911) Bagby *VA Gentleman* 51, He hears the . . log-cocks drumming, but sees no human being. **1896** Robinson *In New Engl. Fields* 9, You hear the loud cackle of a logcock making the daily round of his preserves, but you are not likely to get more than a glimpse of his black plumage or a gleam of his blood-red crest. **1899** (1912) Green *VA Folk-Speech* 265, *Lobcock.* . . Logcock, a large woodpecker. *Ibid* 488, *Wood-cock.* . . The large, red-crested Woodpecker: Lobcock. **1951** [see **log god 2**]. **1968–70** *DARE* (Qu. Q17, . . *Kinds of woodpeckers*) Inf **VA**75, Logcock—pileated; (Qu. Q18, *Joking names and nicknames for woodpeckers*) Inf **MN**18, Logcock. **1988** *DARE* File **wMA**, The pileated woodpecker is sometimes called the *logcock* in this area.

2 =**ivory-billed woodpecker.**

1811 Wilson *Amer. Ornith.* 4.24, The more intelligent and observing part of the natives . . distinguish them [=ivory-billed and pileated woodpeckers] by the name of the large and lesser *Log-cocks*. **1822** Latham *Genl. Hist. Birds* 3.369, *White-billed woodpecker.* Picus principalis. . . found in Georgia, according to Mr. Abbot, and there called Lobcock by some, by others Woodcock. **1874** NY Acad. Sci. *Annals Lyceum Nat. Hist.* 10.377 **IL**, C[ampephilus] principalis . . Ivory-billed Woodpecker; "Big Log Cock." **1911** Howell *Birds AR* 46, Some persons do not distinguish this species [=Campephilus principalis] from the pileated woodpecker, with which it shares the names of "logcock," "woodcock," "woodchuck," etc. **1917** (1923) *Birds Amer.* 2.138, Ivory-Billed Woodpecker. . . Woodcock; Logcock; Woodchuck. **1953** *AmSp* 28.284, Other woodpeckers share some of these names [with the pileated woodpecker; e.g.:] . . the ivory-billed (*lobcock*, Ga.; *logcock*, Ala., La., Ark., Texas; *big logcock*, Fla., Ill.)

log dirt n

Decayed wood used to enrich garden soil.

1949 Arnow *Hunter's Horn* 55 **KY**, Suse and Lureenie had worked themselves half to death traipsing in the woods hunting log dirt—Lureenie was going to have a flower garden like her mother used to have.

log dog n

=**dog** n[1] **B3.**

1986 Pederson *LAGS Concordance (Andirons)* 1 inf, **neTN,** Log dogs—more of a grate, a modern artifact; 2 infs, **cnGA, neFL,** Log dogs.

logfish n

1 A **rudderfish** (here: *Hyperoglyphe perciformis*). [See quot 1884]

1884 Goode *Fisheries U.S.* 1.334, The Black Rudder-fish—*Lirus perciformis.* This fish is also called by the fishermen "Log-fish" and "barrel fish." . . They are almost always found in the vicinity of floating barrels and spars. . . Sometimes as many as from fifty to seventy-five were observed under a single spar. **1896** U.S. Natl. Museum *Bulletin* 47.964, *Log Fish.* . . Length 1 foot. Atlantic Coast of North America, from Cape Hatteras to Maine; rather common northward, especially about Cape Cod. **1933** John G. Shedd Aquarium *Guide* 81, *Logfish.* . . Found playing around floating logs, boxes, or other wreckage, . . [it] has been recorded far from its natural range, having followed these drifting bits of flotsam.

2 =**green sunfish 1.**

1983 Becker *Fishes WI* 822, Green Sunfish—*Lepomis cyanellus* . . Other common names: green perch, black perch, logfish . . sand bass.

log-floater n Also logroller Cf chunk-floater, cob-floater

1968 *DARE* (Qu. B25, . . *Joking names . . for a very heavy rain.* . . *"It's a regular _____."*) Inf **GA**31, Log-floater. **1985** Ladwig *How to Talk Dirty* 15 **Ozarks,** It was a log-roller and a toad-choker . . heavy rain.

logger See log wagon 1

loggeredy-headed adj [Var of loggerheaded; cf Intro "Language Changes" III.1]

1964 *Mt. Life* Spring 54 **sAppalachians,** A body mightenigh as well whup a gin pole . . , withouten he wants . . to cut the blood outen the poor little stubborndy, loggeredy headed mule.

loggerhead n

1 A stupid, dull-witted, or mulish person. [*OED* 1588 →; *EDD*] Cf **loggerheaded**

1806 (1970) Webster *Compendious Dict.* 179, Loggerhead . . a blockhead, dunce, stupid person. [*DARE* Ed: This entry was carried over from Webster's English model] **1889** *Century Dict.* 3504, Loggerhead. . . A blockhead; a dunce; a dolt; a thickskull. **1928** *AmSp* 3.408, "Blockhead," "dunderhead," . . "loggerhead," . . are terms of unequivocal disparagement. **1941** *LANE* Map 465, Derogatory names applied to a stupid person [include *loggerhead*, offered by 3 infs, in **swMA, nME, seNH**]. **1950** *WELS Suppl.* **seWI,** Loggerhead . . stubborn and a bit dull-witted. **1966** *DARE* (Qu. HH3, *A dull and stupid person*) Inf **ME**13, Loggerhead.

2 A person's head; see quots. [Cf *OED loggerhead* sb. 2 "a large or 'thick' head"; 1598–1816]

1911 *Century Dict. Suppl.,* Loggerhead. . . A large, heavy head, out of proportion to the body. **1967–69** *DARE* (Qu. X28, *Joking words . . for a person's head*) Infs **LA**8, **NC**61, **PA**123, Loggerhead.

3 also *loggershead;* in phr *go to loggerheads* and varr: To come into conflict, argue, come to blows; now usu in adj phr *at loggerheads:* In strong disagreement or conflict, at odds. [*OED* (at *loggerhead* sb. 8) 1680 →] **chiefly Inland Nth, N Midl, C Atl** See Map

1755 in 1968 Laurens *Papers* 1.304 **SC,** Some of them went to Loggerheads & bid so upon each other that some very fine Men sold for £300. **1775** in 1966 U.S. Naval Hist. Div. *Naval Documents Amer. Revol.* 2.576, Here we are at Loggerheads. *Ibid* 899, Lord Dunmore is at Logger heads with the Virginians. **1803** in 1945 Paine *Complete Writings* 2.1101, I send you, Sir, a tale about some Feds,/ Who, in their wisdom got to loggerheads. **1806** in 1904 Jefferson *Writings* 11.126, In order to destroy one member of the administration, the whole were to be set to loggerheads to destroy one another. **1815** Humphreys *Yankey in England* 33, If ever we Yankeys cum to loggerheads, we'll show whose heads are hardest. **1825** Neal *Brother Jonathan* 1.257 **NEng,** He [=the New Englander] never fights; never goes to loggerheads. **1828** Webster *Amer. Dict.* np, Loggerhead. . . *To fall to loggerheads, To go to loggerheads,* to come to blows; to fall to fighting. **1899** (1912) Green *VA Folk-Speech* 266, At *loggerheads,* engaged in bickerings or disputes. **1927** Ruppenthal *Coll.* **KS,** They were at loggerheads over several matters. **1932** *WV Review* June 379, Phrases . . that I have not been able to trace to any great length are . . "at loggersheads," [etc]. **1950**

WELS (She and I are _____ *where that's concerned*) 2 Infs, **WI,** At loggerheads. **1965–70** *DARE* (Qu. KK68, *When people don't think alike about something: "We agree on most things, but on politics we're _____."*) 28 Infs, **chiefly Inland Nth, N Midl, C Atl,** At loggerheads; **OR**1, A [sic] loggerhead; **SD**8, At loggershead; (Qu. II11b, *If two people can't bear each other at all . . "Those two are _____."*) 20 Infs, **esp Inland Nth, C Atl,** (Always) at loggerheads; **NC**1, Really at loggerheads with one another; [**NC**36, Loggerheads;] **PA**15, At loggershead; (Qu. KK13, . . *Arguing: "They stood there for an hour _____."*) Inf **HI**1, At loggerheads; (Qu. KK15, *A disagreement or quarrel: "They had _____ about where the fence was to be."*) Inf **NJ**39, Got to loggerheads—this refers to big snapping turtles, loggerheads, that are stuck head to head in a fight. **1995** *WI State Jrl.* (Madison) 30 June sec A 11, [Headline:] Syrian, Israeli generals at loggerheads on Golan plan.

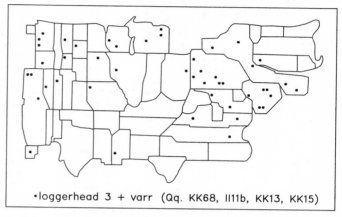

•loggerhead 3 + varr (Qq. KK68, II11b, KK13, KK15)

4 A part of a harness; see quots 1976, 1981.

1939 *Harper's Mag.* 179.92 **MS,** His father . . who was now adjusting the logger-head in the hame. **1976** Brown *Gloss. Faulkner* 122, *Loggerhead . . :* a double-ended, U-shaped hook used (one on each side) to fasten the *traces* to the *hames.* The hames have a series of holes (illogically called a ratchet), and the loggerhead's two hook-ends are fitted into two of these. The choice of holes permits variation of the line of draft and hence of the depth of plowing. (This term seems to be unknown to lexicographers.) **1981** Pederson *LAGS Basic Materials,* 1 inf, **ceAR,** You know what a horse collar is. Well, the hames go right through that little trench around there, and you tie it down with a hame string. . . It's got loggerheads on the hames, right about [in the] middle of his shoulder to hold that trace chain there; 1 inf, **cnGA,** The loggerhead is a keeper that fastens in the hames, and [the] hames is a main part for the draw chain, and the loggerhead hooks in there; 1 inf, **cwGA,** Loggerhead—part of gear on [a] mule.

5 A turtle:

a Std: a large sea turtle *(Caretta caretta)* of warm waters. [*OED* 1657 →]

b also *loggerhead cooter, ~ snapper, ~ turtle, loggerheaded turtle, loghead (terrapin), ~ turtle:* Either of two **snapping turtles:** usu the **alligator turtle 2,** but also the **alligator turtle 1. chiefly S Atl, Gulf States, Lower Missip Valley** See Map on p. 404

1807 (1935) Janson *Stranger in Amer.* 318 **S Atl,** The swamps produce a variety of what may be denominated land turtle. The natives call them loggerheads, tarapins [etc]. **1829** NY Acad. Sci. *Annals Lyceum Nat. Hist.* 3.127, *Chelonura serpentina.* . . Alligator tarapin of the southern states; loggerhead or snapping turtle of the northern. . . Inhabits from New-England to Florida in rivers, and seems to prefer muddy and impure water to that which is clear. **1842** DeKay *Zool. NY* 3.9, The Snapping Turtle. *Chelonura serpentina.* . . This is one of our largest turtles. . . They feed upon frogs and fishes, and snap greedily at ducks in ponds, dragging them under water to be devoured at leisure. It is this propensity to snap at every thing within its reach, which has obtained for it its popular name. In other sections, it is known under the names of *Loggerhead, Alligator Turtle* and *Couta.* **1859** Taliaferro *Fisher's R.* 198 **nwNC** (as of 1820s), They [=brawlers] would . . bite like loggerhead turtles. **1883** WI Chief Geologist *Geol. WI* 1.423, *Macrochelys lacertina* . . Loggerhead Snapper. This ferocious turtle is occasionally found in the Mississippi river as far north as the mouth of the Wisconsin. **1894** U.S. Natl. Museum *Proc.* 17.320, The alligator turtle [=*Chelydra serpentina*] is not very common in south Florida. . . As the head is very large, some ignorant people call it the "loggerhead" which name properly belongs to *Chelonia caretta.* **1928** Baylor Univ. Museum *Contrib.* 16.20, Alligator Snapper *(Macrochelys temminickii)* . . Alligator Turtle and Big Loggerhead are the names by which this species is known in eastern Texas. . . Common Snapper *(Chelydra serpentina)* . . This species is . . known as the Loggerhead and Small Loggerhead. **1938** Burman *Blow for a Landing* 33 **Lower Missip Valley,** The can was leaping wildly now; occasionally beneath it showed the monstrous shell and fierce snapping jaws of a loggerhead turtle. **c1940** Eliason *Word Lists FL* 9 **wFL,** *Loggerhead turtle:* A very large turtle . . having a very large head with a mouth that will slice a fish or another turtle into two or more pieces with all ease. Its massive jaws are as dangerous for human beings as for fish and other turtles. **1965–70** *DARE* (Qu. P24, . . *Kinds of turtles*) 56 Infs, **chiefly S Atl, Gulf States, Lower Missip Valley,** Loggerhead(s); **GA**76, **LA**7, **MS**6, 60, **NC**78, Loggerhead turtle; **KY**43, Loggerhead turtle—very large head; **GA**11, Green loggerhead; **LA**26, Loggerhead—head look like a log!—gets big; **MS**1, Loghead ['tɛr,pɪn]; **MO**24, Loghead turtle; **NJ**39, Loggerhead—big snapper; **TN**24, Loggerhead—grow to be fifty pounds; **TX**35, Loggerheaded turtle. **1966** *DARE* Tape **LA**5, The loggerhead gets a whole lot bigger than the snapper, and he got kinda hacks, like sawteeth . . on the top of his back. **1968** *DARE* FW Addit **csLA,** *Loggerhead*—a turtle that gets as large as 200 pounds. Since the French name of this turtle is *tortue cocodri,* I take it to be the alligator snapper. **1986** Pederson *LAGS Concordance Gulf Region (Turtles)* 47 infs, Loggerhead(s); 3 infs, Loggerhead(s)—[same as] snapping turtle(s); 1 inf, Loggerheads—spurs on back, savage, they'll bite; 1 inf, Loggerhead—will bite, large head; 1 inf, Old loggerhead—most folks eat; 1 inf, Loggerhead—lives in mudholes, damp places; 1 inf, Loggerhead—large, as much as one hundred pounds; 1 inf, Loggerhead—very large; 1 inf, Loggerhead—resembles terrapin, mean scamp; 1 inf, Log-head—hard shell, round; 1 inf, Log-head turtle; 29 infs, Loggerhead turtle(s); 2 infs, Loggerheaded turtle(s); 1 inf, Loggerhead turtle—large head, rough hull; 1 inf, Loggerhead turtle—human-sized head, eighty pounds and up; 1 inf, Loggerhead turtle—looks dreadful, lives in mud; 1 inf, Loggerhead turtles—[same as] snapping, alligator turtles; 1 inf, Loggerhead turtle—large head, snapping; 3 infs, Loggerhead cooter(s).

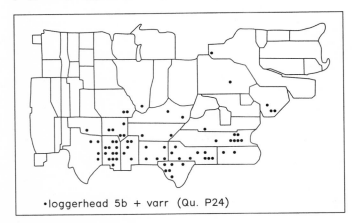

•loggerhead 5b + varr (Qu. P24)

c See **loggerhead musk turtle.**

6 See **loggerhead shrike.**

7 A **sponge:** usu *Spheciospongia vesparia,* but also *Ircinia strobilina.*

  1889 *Century Dict.* 3504, *Loggerhead.* . . A kind of sponge found in Florida. **1898** (1910) Willoughby *Across Everglades* 92 **sFL,** What annoys the sponge-fisherman is, that he sees so many sponges of different kinds before he meets one that is marketable. The largest of the worthless kind is the "Loggerhead." This sponge is on the bottom in enormous quantities. It is the shape of a round life-preserver, and sometimes attains the diameter of five feet. **1981** Meinkoth *Audubon Field Guide Seashore* 329, The loggerhead sponge is the largest sponge known. . . This species [=*Spheciospongia vesparia*] shares its common name with an unrelated sponge, *Ircinia strobilina.*

8 A **channel catfish** (here: *Ictalurus punctatus*).

  1957 Trautman *Fishes* 415, Channel Catfish—*Ictalurus punctatus.* . . Largest adults (colloquially called channel and blue cats [usually males], canal boaters, black warriors and loggerheads) are dark steel-blue with whitish bellies. **1966** *DARE* (Qu. P1, . . *Kinds of freshwater fish . . caught around here . . good to eat*) Inf **NM**3, Blue cat—called "loggerhead."

9 also *loggernut:* See quot.

  1966–68 *DARE* (Qu. I43, *What kinds of nuts grow wild around here?*) Inf **AL**38, ['lɔgərnʌt], loggerhead (a big walnut); **MS**45, Loggerheads.

10 A **woodpecker;** see quots. **esp GA** Cf **logcock**

  c1970 Pederson *Dial. Surv. Rural GA (What do you call a bird that makes a hole in a tree trunk with its bill?)* 1 inf, **seGA,** Loggerhead. **1972** *LAMSAS Materials* **seGA,** Loggerhead—woodpecker. **1981** Pederson *LAGS Basic Materials,* 1 inf, **seGA,** Loggerheads—a bird with a stripe on its head; eats mosquitoes; there used to be a lot of them in the area; 1 inf, **seGA,** Loggerhead—husband calls some kind of bird that pecks on trees; 1 inf, **seGA,** Loggerhead—a large woodpecker; 1 inf, **cnFL,** Loggerhead—large woodpecker.

loggerhead cooter See **loggerhead 5b**

loggerheaded adj [*OED* loggerheaded a. 1 1596–1831] Cf **loggerhead 1, 3, loggeredy-headed, log-headed**

Stupid; pigheaded; stubbornly at odds; also adv *loggerheaded.*

  1806 (1970) Webster *Compendious Dict.* 179, *Loggerheaded* . . dull, stupid. [*DARE* Ed: This entry was carried over from Webster's English model.] **1889** *Century Dict.* 3504, *Loggerheaded.* . . Dull; stupid; doltish. **1968** Haun *Hawk's Done Gone* 8 **TN,** I told Jake I wanted him to have some other woman come too. But he went loggerheaded on and didn't do it. **1969** *DARE* (Qu. II11b, *If two people can't bear each other at all . . "Those two are _____."*) Inf **GA**77, Loggerheaded with each other.

loggerheaded shrike See **loggerhead shrike**

loggerheaded turtle See **loggerhead 5b**

loggerhead musk turtle n Also *loggerhead* [See quot 1979]

A **musk turtle 1** (here: *Sternotherus minor*).

  1952 Carr *Turtles* 77, Loggerhead Musk Turtle—*Sternotherus carinatus minor.* **1955** Carr-Goin *Guide Reptiles* 231, Loggerhead Musk Turtle. . . A small turtle with a big, spotted or mottled head. **1972** Ernst-Barbour *Turtles* 46, The loggerhead musk turtle . . ranges from central Georgia and southwestern Alabama to central Florida. **1979** Behler-King *Audubon Field Guide Reptiles* 444, Loggerheads [=*Sternotherus minor*] are as pugnacious as Stinkpots; the young are capable of expelling musk even before they hatch.

loggerhead shrike n Also *loggerhead, loggerheaded shrike* **chiefly SE**

A bird *(Lanius ludovicianus)* known for impaling its prey on sharp objects. For other names of this bird and var subspp see **catbird 2, cricket hawk, dumb mockingbird, English ~ 4, flathead ~, French ~ 2, grasshopper hawk 2, hedge bird, Indian mockingbird, joree n 2, kite n 1, Mexican mockingbird, migrant shrike, mockingbird 4, ~ hawk, mouse bird, ~ hawk 2, shrike, southern shrike, Spanish mockingbird, summer shrike, white-rumped ~, wire bird**

  1803 Davis *Travels* 81 **SC,** The note of the red-bird is imitated with nice precision by the mocking-bird; but there is a bird called the loggerhead that will not bear passively its taunts. **1811** Wilson *Amer. Ornith.* 3.57, Loggerhead Shrike. *Lanius carolinensis.* . . This species inhabits the rice plantations of Carolina and Georgia. **1872** Coues *Key to N. Amer. Birds* 125, Loggerhead Shrike. . . South Atlantic States. **1903** Dawson *Birds OH* 1.294, The Loggerhead, or Migrant Shrike, has increased somewhat within recent years, except in those localities where it has been subjected to a thoughtless persecution. **1908** *DN* 3.313 **eAL, wGA,** *French mocker* . . The butcher bird. Also called *loggerhead.* **1913** *Auk* 30.499 **Okefenokee GA,** *Lanius ludovicianus ludovicianus.* Loggerhead Shrike. **1938** Oberholser *Bird Life LA* 491, The Loggerhead Shrike, in common with the other American species, has the habit of killing considerably more prey than it can possibly use, and of hanging its booty on thorns, on the barbs of wire fences, or similar places, to which it frequently never returns. **1967** *PA Game News* Aug 6 **PA,** We don't often see shrikes in our valley, but today a loggerhead dropped from an apple tree . . and skimmed to another tree on flickering wings. **1968–69** *DARE* (Qu. Q14, . . *Names . . for . . shrike*) Infs **GA**18, **PA**155, Loggerhead shrike; **GA**25, Loggerhead; **CA**140, Loggerhead shrike. **1977** Bull-Farrand *Audubon Field Guide Birds* 514, The loggerhead preys upon insects more than its northern relative. . . Since it has no talons, it impales its prey—usually a small bird, mouse, or insect—on a thorn or barbed wire fence to facilitate tearing it apart then or at a later time; hence its other name, "Butcher Bird."

loggerhead snapper (or turtle) See **loggerhead 5b**

loggernut See **loggerhead 9**

logger's smallpox n

Among loggers: marks left by the spikes in logging boots.

1938 (1939) Holbrook *Holy Mackinaw* 6 [Logger talk], In any case, he had been in a heap of fights. . . I was impressed by the deep marks of "loggers' smallpox" all over his chest, shoulders, and stomach—the work of many steel-calked boots stamped there by opponents. **1958** McCulloch *Woods Words* 110 **Pacific NW,** *Logger's smallpox*—This is the result of being stomped on by a man wearing calked shoes. **1964** Hargreaves–Foehl *Story of Logging* 59 **MI,** *Loggers' small-pox*—Saw-mill towns' wood plank sidewalks, saloon and dancehall floors—and the faces of victims of barroom brawls always showed signs of "loggers' small-pox." It was a common malady during the brawling days of the logging era—marks left by the riverhogs' corked boots. **1969** Sorden *Lumberjack Lingo* 71 **NEng, Gt Lakes,** *Logger's smallpox.* **1972** *Yesterday* 1.2.27 (as of c1890) [Lumberjack lingo], Most of the fights weren't serious, although "logger's smallpox" was caused when one of the combatants landed on his fallen opponent's chest with his caulked boots.

logger wagon See **log wagon 1**

logging berry n

Esp among loggers:

a also *log berry, loganberry:* A prune.

1928 *Ruppenthal Coll.* **KS** [Army slang], *Loganberries*—prunes. **1941** Writers' Program *Guide WV* 403 **csWV,** Although changed in other respects, the West Virginia logger has retained his jargon. Cooks are still 'stomick robbers'; their helpers are 'cookees'; coffee is 'jerkwater'; prunes, 'log berries'; biscuits, 'cat-heads'; and milk is 'cow.' **1956** Sorden–Ebert *Logger's Words* 22 **Gt Lakes,** Logging-berries, Prunes. **1964** Clarkson *Tumult* 366 **WV** [Logger's words], *Log berries*—Prunes. **1966** *DARE* Tape **MI**10, Prunes, which like dried apples constituted the fruit [in the logging camps], became logging berries. *Ibid* **NC**30, They [=loggers] called a prune a loggin' berry.

b See quot. Cf **strawberry**

1979 McPhee *Giving Good Weight* 168 **ME,** Big red boiled "logging berries"—the lumberjacks' term for beans.

logging cart See **log cart**

logging wagon See **log wagon 1**

logging wheels n pl Cf **big wheels, high wheel, log cart**

See quot 1905.

1905 U.S. Forest Serv. *Bulletin* 61.42 [Logging terms], *Logging wheels.* A pair of wheels, usually about 10 feet in diameter, for transporting logs. . . Syn.: big wheels, katydid, timber wheels. [**1968** *DARE* (Qu. N41b, *Horse-drawn vehicles to carry heavy loads*) Inf **MI**97, Lumber wagon with logging wheels.] **1969** Sorden *Lumberjack Lingo* 72 **NEng, Gt Lakes,** *Logging wheels*—Big wheels, from ten to fourteen feet high, used for transporting logs from the woods. Same as katydid, sulky, timber wheels, big wheels, high wheels.

log god n [Perh blend of **logcock** + **lord god**]

1 =**ivory-billed woodpecker.**

1916 *Times–Picayune* (New Orleans LA) 16 Apr mag sec 9/2, Ivory-Billed Woodpecker. . . Log God; Pique Bois, Poule d'Bois.—This is the largest and rarest of the woodpeckers found in this country. . . It should not be confused with the pileated woodpecker.

2 also *log guard:* =**pileated woodpecker.**

1945 McAtee *Nomina Abitera* 46, The most godified of our birds. . . is none other than the pileated woodpecker, a bird of crow size, noisy both in voice and in its hacking on trees. . . this bird's roll of godly titles [includes] . . log God (Georgia, Louisiana). **1951** *AmSp* 26.93, The most complicated examples of folk etymology provided by North American bird names are in those of the pileated woodpecker. . . lobcock (Va.) logcock (generally) . . log god (Ga.; La.) . . log guard (Ga.) **1955** Lowery *LA Birds* 347, Pileated Woodpecker. . . This is the "log-god," "Indian hen," "woodchuck," or "cock-of-the-woods" that is so familiar to hunters, fishermen, and others who roam our woods and paddle our forest-lined streams. **1981** Pederson *LAGS Basic Materials,* 1 inf, **cnFL,** "Lord-god" or "log-god" is the same as "woodchuck"—large woodpecker, big black or blue one with red head and long bill; [1 inf, **seLA,** Lord god—sound like "log"].

loggy See **logy**

log-haul n

1975 Gould *ME Lingo* 166, *Log-haul*—A wilderness roadway built for hauling logs either to a river or all the way to a mill. After the *Lombard* [=a steam tractor] . . was perfected, log-hauls were engineered for trains of sleds, and were as well graded as railway lines. Since vestiges of such *log-hauls* are frequent in the Maine wilderness, references to them will be heard often. A logging road is not necessarily a *log-haul,* and the *tote-road* should never be confused with either.

loghead See **loggerhead 5b**

log-headed adj [*OED log-headed* "having a head like a log; *Obs.*" (at *log* sb.[1] 9)]

=**loggerheaded.**

1889 *Century Dict.* 3504, *Log-headed.* . . Stupid. **1971** Wood *Vocab. Change* 369 **Sth,** [Footnote 42:] Volunteered [for *obstinate*] . . log headed.

loghead terrapin (or turtle) See **loggerhead 5b**

login See **logan**

loginess See **logy 1**

‡**logings** n Cf **backings, low wine**

1911 *DN* 3.538 **eKY,** *Lōgings.* . . A grade of whiskey intermediate in strength between first-shot . . and singlings.

log iron n Cf **dog iron 1, iron B2**

=**andiron.**

1948 Davis *Word Atlas Gt. Lakes* 176, [Based on mail questionnaires to 59 communities:] *Log irons* fairly common except Ind. **1955** Potter *Dial. NW OH* 60, [Based on 60 mail questionnaires:] *Andirons* . . is the most frequently used term for the metal fireplace equipment, except in Paulding County. There *log irons* was offered in three of the five responses and *hand irons* was given once. In all of the counties *log irons* is in use but . . is a definite minority item everywhere but in Paulding. *Ibid* 99, *Log irons* is fairly common in all [age] groups. . . *log irons* was offered by almost 40% of farmers, 29% of manual workers, but only 19% of skilled workers. The use of *log irons* clearly declines as education increases. In the least educated group *log irons* is the most common term (given by 53% of the informants), but it was offered by only 19% of the high school group and not at all by the college educated. **1966** Dakin *Dial. Vocab. Ohio R. Valley* 2.36, Log irons (1 [of c207 infs]). **1969–70** *DARE* (Qu. D32, *The metal stands in a fireplace that the logs are laid on*) Infs **CA**177, **NY**209, Log irons [Infs query]. **1971** Wood *Vocab. Change* 50 **Sth,** *Log irons* [along with *dog irons*] . . second choice in Oklahoma. *Log irons, dogs, fire irons,* and *hand irons* have small and scattered distributions. [*Log irons* is offered by 29 of 1000 infs.] **1986** Pederson *LAGS Concordance (Andirons)* 1 inf, **cwFL,** Log irons; 1 inf, **cAR,** Log irons—most people probably say.

log it See **log** v **1**

log jumper See **jumper sled**

‡**log leg** n Cf **log iron**

=**andiron.**

1970 *DARE* (Qu. D32, *The metal stands in a fireplace that the logs are laid on*) Inf **TX**80A, Log legs.

log perch n

A **darter 1** of the genus *Percina,* usu *P. caprodes.* For other names of this latter see **hogfish b, hog molly 2, ~ perch, manitou darter, Oklahoma son-of-a-bitch, rockfish, sand perch, zebra fish**

1877 NY Acad. Sci. *Annals Lyceum Nat. Hist.* 10.375, We heard several peculiar vernacular names for fishes on the Rock Castle and Cumberland . . Log Perch . . *Percina caprodes.* **1884** Goode *Fisheries U.S.* 1.417, The Log Perch—*Percina caprodes.* . . This species is known as the "Rock-fish," "Hog-fish," or "Log Perch." It is the largest of a large group of little perch-like fishes known as "Darters." **1908** Forbes–Richardson *Fishes of IL* 281, *Percina* . . Log-perches. . . As compared to the other darters, the skull of *Percina* is much broader. **1929** OK Univ. Biol. Surv. *Pub.* 1.100, *Percina caprodes caprodes* . . Southern log-perch. **1943** Eddy–Surber *N. Fishes* 198, The northern logperch, the largest and one of the most common of the darters, ranges from Minnesota to Vermont and intergrades southward with *Percina caprodes caprodes.* . . The logperch is widely distributed in the lakes and larger streams of Minnesota and Wisconsin. **1991** Amer. Fisheries Soc. *Common Names Fishes* 50, *Percina caprodes* . . logperch. . . *Percina car-*

bonaria . . Texas logperch. . . *Percina jenkinsi* . . Conasauga logperch . . *Percina rex* . . Roanoke logperch.

log-raising n Also *log-cabin raising* old-fash Cf **barn raising 1** =**house-raising.**
 1840 *Daily Picayune* (New Orleans LA) 12 Aug 2/1, The cars were at the time full of people, going to a log-cabin raising in Jersey City. **1864** Gilmore *Down in TN* 43, In April, 1862, he and his band came upon a party of neighbors collected at a log raising in Fentress County. **1896** (1897) Brodhead *Bound in Shallows* 169 **KY,** Law, the log-raisin's and corn-huskin's they used to have! **1908** Fox *Lonesome Pine* 291 **KY,** At corn-cutting in the autumn, or sorghum-making time or at log-raisings or quilting parties. **1923** Adams *Pioneer Hist. Ingham Co.* 320 **csMI** (as of c1850), There were many scenes, incidents and accidents I might recall, and will mention a few: pike pole barn raisings with hair raising incidents and accidents; bull push log raising with many happenings. **1981** Pederson *LAGS Basic Materials,* 1 inf, **neFL,** Log raisings—community house-building parties; put everything up but the roof.

logroller n
1 See **logrolling 3.**
2 In marble play: a large marble; see quots. **esp Sth, S Midl**
 1963 *KY Folkl. Rec.* 9.3.58 **eKY,** Large marbles . . log-roller. **1967–69** *DARE* (Qu. EE6a, . . *Different kinds of marbles—the big one that's used to knock others out of the ring*) Infs **TN**33, 35, **VA**1A, Logroller; (Qu. EE6d, *Special marbles*) Inf **TX**33A, Logrollers. **1986** Pederson *LAGS Concordance,* 2 infs, **sGA,** Logroller—large marble.
3 See **log-floater.**

logrolling vbl n
1 Clearing land, esp by piling and burning the cut trees; moving logs into place for constructing a building; hence n *logrolling* a community or social gathering for such a purpose. **chiefly Sth, S Midl** See Map *old-fash* Cf **corn shucking 1, house-raising**
 [**1781** *View of N. Amer.* 93, Another capital frolic, but of a more laborious nature, and totally performed by men, is, the rolling, or heaping for burning, all the deadned [sic] trees which have fallen down in a field through the course of the winter.] **1813** in 1956 Eliason *Tarheel Talk* 282 **c,csNC,** _____ is good for nothing unless you had a *log rolling or corn shucking* on Capitol Hill. **1832** Paulding *Westward Ho* 1.161 **S Midl,** The good villagers resorted to what, in woodland phrase, is called "log-rolling," which means a combined effort of many to do that which is either difficult or impossible to one. They gathered together and built the colonel a house. **1846** Monette *History* 2.8 **Ohio Valley,** The standard "dinner dish" at log-rollings, house-raisings, and harvest days was a large "pot-pie." **1883** *Harper's New Mth. Mag.* 66.282 **CA,** After hearing his report, the old man replied: "We got to give him a log-rol-lin'." *Ibid* 283, The great festivals of Western life are camp-meetings, barbecues, and log-rollings. **1903** *DN* 2.320 **seMO,** Log-rolling. . . Piling logs for burning in clearing land. **1907** *DN* 3.233 **nwAR,** Log-rolling. . . Piling logs for burning when land is being cleared. **1915** *DN* 4.185 **swVA,** Log-rollin'. . . A gathering of neighbors to roll logs for burning on uncultivated land. **1917** Baldwin *Making of a Township* 119 **ceIN,** A farmer would either burn or cut a large number of logs in lengths that could be handled. Then he would invite his neighbors to a log rolling. They would come early and stay late. You would see them with their favorite handspike in hand ready to roll logs and out lift their neighbor. . . Great numbers of logs would be piled by the men, to be burned at the pleasure of the owner. **1927** *AmSp* 2.360 **cwWV,** There will be a log rolling at Mr. Wiant's next Tuesday. **1935** Hurston *Mules & Men* 128 **FL** [Black], It was almost like a log-rolling or a barbeque. [Footnote to *log-rolling:*] When people used to get out logs to build a house they would get the neighbors to help. Plenty of food and drink served. Very gay time. **1954** *Harder Coll.* **cwTN,** Log-rolling. . . A social gathering to clear land. **1960** Hall *Smoky Mt. Folks* 59, *Log-rollin:* clearing an area of logs for home construction and farming. **1965–70** *DARE* (Qu. L5, *When a farmer gets help on a job from his neighbors in return for his help on their farms later on*) Inf **FL**15, Logrolling—for housebuilding; old-fashioned; (Qu. L36, . . *When you dig up roots and underbrush to make a new field*) Inf **AL**15, Had logrolling; invite neighbors, cut logs, burn brush, dig stumps; don't do it anymore; **SC**57, Logrolling—in clearing land, logs would be piled up and burned so the land could be farmed; old-fashioned [FW: used by Inf in conv]; (Qu. FF1, . . *A kind of group meeting called a 'social' or 'sociable'. . . [What goes on?]*) Inf **LA**11, Logrolling—when they were clearing up land, had jugs, food, etc.; old-fashioned; (Qu. FF2, . . *Kinds of parties*) Infs **AR**18,

NC49, Logrolling (—after clearing land); **KY**19, Logrolling—old-fashioned; **SC**46, Logrolling—clearing land, cutting trees only; **SC**19, Logrollings—to clean up an area; get a bunch of men to come and help pile up the logs to burn, give them a big meal; **TX**98, Logrollings—neighbors help a man clear his land to get it ready for farming; old-fashioned; **TX**37, Logrolling—work party where they helped a man move logs he had chopped to clear land; (Qu. FF4, *Names and joking names for different kinds of dancing parties*) Inf **FL**29, Logrolling—built house in day, danced at night; old-fashioned; (Qu. FF16, . . *Local contests or celebrations*) Inf **TX**35, Logrollings. **1965** *DARE* Tape **VA**114, The neighbors would all go in and help. . . And they'd have the logrollin' . . or a clearing . . they'd clean up a new field. **1971** *Foxfire* 5.103 **nGA** (as of c1925), In log rollin's, you'd go all over th'community and gather up maybe twenty-five men. Then they'd cut logs and clear land and do a whole lot a'work in a day. **1986** Pederson *LAGS Concordance* **Gulf Region, esp LA, MS, AL,** 8 infs, Logrolling(s); 1 inf, A logrolling—a favorite community pastime; 1 inf, This man was going to have a logrolling; 1 inf, Logrolling—men would have while women quilted; 1 inf, Logrolling—preparing logs for neighbor's house; 1 inf, Logrolling—neighbors helped pile logs, clearing; 1 inf, Many a damn logrolling; 1 inf, They'd have logrollings to get land cleared; 1 inf, Logrollings—men cut firewood, stovewood; 1 inf, Logrollings—boys piled logs, girls made quilts; 1 inf, Logrollings—community pastimes in his childhood; 1 inf, Logrolling—men did this, women cooked dinner; 1 inf, Logrollings—community activities; 1 inf, Logrollings—used to have as parties. [*DARE* Ed: In some cases the meaning is not clearly indicated.]

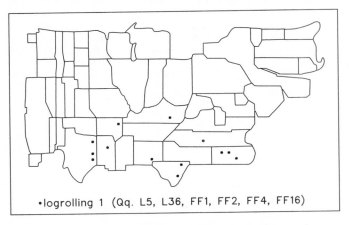

•logrolling 1 (Qq. L5, L36, FF1, FF2, FF4, FF16)

2 Moving cut and trimmed trees from the woods to a river or work site; hence n *logrolling* a cooperative effort for such a purpose.
 1848 Bartlett *Americanisms* 214, Log-rolling. In the lumber regions of Maine it is customary for men of different logging camps to appoint days for helping each other in rolling the logs to the river, after they are felled and trimmed—this rolling being about the hardest work incident to the business. **1848** *Union Mag.* (NY NY) 3.73, Occasionally there was a small opening on the bank, made for the purpose of log-rolling. **1889** *Century Dict.* 3506, Log-rolling. . . A joining of forces. . . In lumbering, for rolling logs into a stream, where they are bound together and floated down to the mills. **1940** Writers' Program *Negro in VA* 202 [Black], We lived in a log cabin at de foot of a hill, out in de field nearby some thick woods. Well, dere was a log-rolling path through dem woods, an' all of a sudden here come de Yankees 'long dat path. **1967** *Warrensburg–Lake George News* (Warrensburg NY) 11 May 4/1, When I was a young girl the men for miles around cut their logs and sold them to companies. The markers came and put their mark on each log[;] then they were drawn to the river bank ready for the log rolling when the right time came. . . When the water was high the river drivers came and drove the logs down the river.

3 Staying upright on a floating log while turning it with the feet; hence n *logrolling* the sport of so doing; n *logroller* one who does so. Cf **birl**
 1893 *Westminster Gaz.* 16 May 5/1 *(DA),* For the special benefit of the distinguished spectators. . . an elaborate display of log-rolling was given. *Ibid (OED),* Canoes, shells, dug-outs, water-cycles, logs and log-rollers, and water-walkers, were present too in large numbers. . . At the start one of the log-rollers managed to drop off his log. **1938** (1939) Holbrook *Holy Mackinaw* 127, About once a year loggers give some serious attention to the only sport that has come out of the woods—the

sport of logrolling. . . Two men get on one log, floating in pond or river, to turn it with their feet to see who can ride it the longer. **1941** *Time* 21 July 57, In birling, two sure-footed log-rollers . . try to spin it so as to roll each other off. **1948** *Hyde Park Herald* (Chi.) 1 Jan. 4/3 *(DA)*, Canadian woodsmen. . . will participate in log rolling, canoe tilting and other water and woods thrillers. **1966** *DARE* (Qu. FF16, . . *Local contests or celebrations*) Inf **WA**3, Logrolling competition—at Lewiston Lumber Mill. **1969** Sorden *Lumberjack Lingo* 73 **NEng, Gt Lakes**, *Log rolling*—An authentic word coming directly from the woods and the drive. A sport where two men vied with each other to stay on a rolling log in the water.

logs, saw (or cut) See **saw wood**

log town n Also *log city,* ~ *village*

A town made up of log buildings; by ext, a small or unimportant town; also used as a place-name.

1790 *Daily Advt.* (NY NY) 19 Feb 2/1, Lines descriptive of a Tavern at *Log-Town,* a small Place in the Pine Barrens of *North-Carolina.* **1817** Brown *Western Gaz.* 106 **KY**, *Vangeville,*—A *log city,* . . has fifteen or twenty old log houses. **1834** (1898) Kemper *Jrl.* 403, We passed one or two log villages, one a country town of Michigan. **1836** Hildreth *Dragoon Campaigns* 70, The remains of a log-town long since evacuated, that had formerly been the settlement of a tribe of the Delawares. **1943** Benét *W. Star* 70, The log-village that hunters can leave behind. **1950** *WELS Suppl.* **csWI**, Log town—An unimportant village. **1967** *DARE* (Qu. C34, *Nicknames for nearby settlements, villages, or districts*) Inf **IL**7, Log City—the original settlement before [it became known as] Galesburg.

log up See **log** v 2

log village See **log town**

log wagon n

1 also *logger (wagon), logging wagon:* In logging: a large, heavy wagon used for hauling logs; see quots. **scattered, but esp lower Missip Valley, Ohio Valley, C Atl** See Map Cf **log cart**

1779 in 1906 *Documents Revol. Hist. NJ* 3.69, To be sold. . . a good log waggon and four horses. **1958** McCulloch *Woods Words* 110 **Pacific NW**, *Log wagon*—A heavy four-wheeled cart used for hauling logs in the pine country, before the days of trucks. **1965–70** *DARE* (Qu. N41b, *Horse-drawn vehicles to carry heavy loads*) 60 Infs, **scattered, but esp lower Missip Valley, Ohio Valley, C Atl**, Log wagon; **CA**114, **PA**104, Logging wagon; **AR**51, Log wagon to haul big loads of logs; **IN**46, Log wagon—about the heaviest; **KY**72, Logger wagon; **KY**84, Log wagon—heavy loads; **LA**2, Log wagon—some had four wheels, some had eight; **LA**3, Logging wagon—pulled by ox teams or horse teams; **LA**20, Log wagon—may be pulled by a tractor, used to be pulled by oxens; **LA**29, Log wagon—had eight wheels with eight-inch tires; drawn by oxen or mules; **PA**131, Logger—wagon for carrying logs; **SC**57, Log wagon—no floor, braces to keep logs on; **TN**24, Log wagon—lower and longer, with bigger wheels than regular wagon. **1968** *DARE* FW Addit **VA**14, Log wagon—special wagon used to haul logs; pulled by oxen. The wagon bed, supported by bolsters, was level with the wheel tops. Cuffs were attached to the bed. They hung over each wheel as a support for planks used as inclined planes. The logs [were] rolled on the wagon with cant hooks. **1969** *DARE* Tape **KY**14, Out in the county here we hauled 'em—a lot a logs—from way out in the country, and

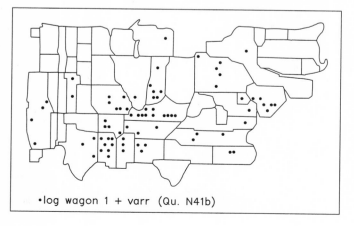

•log wagon 1 + varr (Qu. N41b)

we hauled them on log wagons with mules, four mules and six mules hooked to a log wagon, and we put anywhere from six, seven, or eight hundred logs on these wagons and haul 'em into the mill. **1969** Sorden *Lumberjack Lingo* 73 **NEng, Gt Lakes**, *Log wagon*—Very heavy four-wheeled wagon for hauling logs, usually used in the summer. **1986** Pederson *LAGS Concordance* **esp AR, LA**, 2 infs, (A) log wagon; 1 inf, Log wagon—for hauling logs; 1 inf, Log wagon—heavy; flat bumper across top; six mules; 1 inf, A log-wagon team—four mules; 1 inf, Log wagons—for hauling timber; 1 inf, Log wagons—large; require six horses.

2 See quot. Cf **logroller** 2

1958 *Resp. to PADS 29,* Log-wagon, any large out-size marble. The latter [=log-wagon] may belong in the category of slang rather than strict marbles terminology.

log watch n

In logging: see quots 1905, 1975.

1905 U.S. Forest Serv. *Bulletin* 61.39 [Logging terms], *Head driver.* An expert river driver who, during the drive, is stationed at a point where a jam is feared. Head drivers usually work in pairs. . . Syn[onym]: log watch (N[orthern] F[orest]). **1969** Sorden *Lumberjack Lingo* 73 **NEng, Gt Lakes**, *Log watch*—An expert river driver stationed at a point where a jam was feared during a river drive. **1975** Gould *ME Lingo* 167, *Log watch*—Even though river-driving has waned, the *log watch* will remain for some time as a wilderness bogeyman. It was his job to patrol the river banks and make sure nobody stole marked wood from the drives. Since unmarked wood was up for salvage, there were frequent disputes between him and farmers along the stream who were "catching" firewood. It wasn't any fun to catch five cords of wood and then find the *log watch* had thrown it back in the river. Children very often grew up thinking the *log watch* was something like a wicked ogre; "The *log watch*'ll get you if you don' watch out!"

logwood n [From its use as a dyewood, like the std *logwood* of commerce (*Haematoxylon campechea*)]

=**bluewood.**

1884 Sargent *Forests of N. Amer.* 40, *Condalia obovata.* . . Blue wood. Logwood. Purple haw. **1898** Sudworth *Forest Trees* 297, *Condalia obovata.* . . Common Names . . Logwood (Tex.) **1931** U.S. Dept. Ag. *Misc. Pub.* 101.112, Bluewood, known locally as brasil, capulin, logwood, and purple haw . . is limitedly browsed. **1960** Vines *Trees SW* 697, Bluewood Condalia (*Condalia obovata*). . . Other vernacular names are Brazil, Logwood, Bluewood, . . and Chaparral. The wood yields a blue dye and is sometimes used as fuel.

log wrench n

Esp among loggers: a cant hook or peavey; see quot 1959.

1938 *AmSp* 13.71 [Lingo of railroad linemen], *Log wrench.* Cant hook. **1958** McCulloch *Woods Words* 110 **Pacific NW**, *Log wrench*—A peavey. **1959** *AmSp* 34.78 **nCA** [Logger lingo], *Peavey, log wrench.* . . A stout lever five to seven feet long, fitted with a socket and spike and a curved steel hook that works on a bolt; it is used in handling logs. It was invented by Joseph Peavey in 1858 near Bangor, Maine. **1969** Sorden *Lumberjack Lingo* 73 **NEng, Gt Lakes**, *Log wrench*—A term sometimes used for a cant hook.

logy adj Usu |'lo(ʊ)gi, -ɪ|; also |'lɑgi, -ɪ, 'lɔgi|; for addit varr see quots Also sp *loggy*

1 Heavy, slow, lethargic; dull, stupid; waterlogged; hence n *loginess.* [Cf *EDD louggy, loogy* "Tired, 'fagged'; slow" (Corn dial) and *loggy* adj. 2 "Heavy, slow-moving, dragging" (Hampshire and Isle of Wight)] **scattered, but more freq Nth, N Midl, West** See Map on p. 408

1848 Bartlett *Americanisms* 215, *Logy.* . . He's a logy man, i.e. a slow-moving, heavy man. 'He is a logy preacher,' i.e. dull. **1883** *Harper's New Mth. Mag.* 67.452, Outside ballast . . made boats logy. **1884** *Forest & Stream* 21 Feb 69, How in the world is it that so many pickerel which have been securely hooked manage to get off? I think it is their very calmness and "loginess," as many writers call it, that deceive you; one thinks that they are all exhausted and played out . . when in reality they are only waiting to get an opportunity to bolt. **1895** *DN* 1.390 **eME coast**, *Logy:* slow-moving, "dead and alive." Term used by fishermen. . . (Form *loggy*) Boston, Mass. **1899** (1912) Green *VA Folk-Speech* 266, *Logy.* . . Heavy; slow; stupid. **1902** *DN* 2.238 **sIL**, *Logy* [logɪ]. . . Languid, dull, heavy, in disposition or movement. **1903** (1965) Adams *Log Cowboy* 21, We strung the cattle out, now logy with water. **1905** *DN* 3.13 **cCT**, *Logy.* Ibid 63 **NE**, *Logy.* . . Heavy. "Logy bread." **1907**

DN 3.246 **eME,** *Logy.* . . Sluggish; dull; heavy. **1927** *Ruppenthal Coll.* **KS,** Logy, loggy . . (pron[ounced with] long o)—dull, stupid, stolid, sleepy. He acted loggy to me. He can't work. He would be very slow in his work. He couldn't hustle. **1935** Sandoz *Jules* 197 **wNE** (as of 1880–1930), The crack of the long whips swung by men toiling along beside the logier animals. **1936** *Hench Coll.* **cVA,** Logy. . . This word usually is pronounced [logi], but now and then I hear [lɔgi]. Quite clearly the word is coming to be associated with *log* in the minds of speakers. Dr. Macon said today . . : "One thing I don't like about his condition now-a-days. He's becoming logy [lɔgi]—you know, water-logged." *Ibid* **seVA,** Betty . . down at Virginia Beach, after being in the water longer than she should have been, complained of being [lɔgi]. **1940** Stong *Hawkeyes* 232 **IA,** Where the farmer of my grandfather's time knew that soil was "sour," or else "loggy," they know now that it needs lime, phosphates. **1950** *PADS* 14.45 **SC,** Logy [logɪ]. . . Dull, inert, slow. Used to describe a person's feelings. "After a heavy meal I feel logy." **1950** *WELS,* 2 Infs, **WI,** Logy. **1960** Criswell *Resp. to PADS* 20 **Ozarks,** Logy. . . draggy, mentally and physically below par. **1965–70** *DARE* (Qu. KK30, *Feeling slowed up or without energy: "I certainly feel _____."*) 48 Infs, **chiefly Nth, N Midl, CA,** ['lo(ʊ)gi, -ɪ]; **CA8, OH43, PA74, TX19, 95,** ['lagi, -ɪ]; **PA150, TX81, WI61,** ['lɔgi]; **MD2,** ['lɛogi]; **MI104,** ['lɔki]; (Qu. BB39, *On a day when you don't feel just right, though not actually sick . . "I'll be all right tomorrow—I'm just feeling _____ today."*) 12 Infs, **chiefly Nth, esp NEast,** ['lo(ʊ)gi]; **MA98, NY96, WA9,** Log(g)y; **NY88,** ['lougɪ]; (Qu. B4, *A day when the air is very still, moist, and warm—it's _____*) Inf **ID5,** Loggy; (Qu. H69, *When food is hard on your stomach, you say that it _____*) Inf **GA85,** Feels loggy ['lougiᵛ] on my stomach; (Qu. X47, . . *"I'm very tired, at the end of my strength"*) Inf **NY96,** ['lougɪ]; (Qu. Y21, *To move about slowly and without energy*) Inf **MN12,** ['logi]; **NY96,** Be logy ['lougɪ]; (Qu. BB5, *A general feeling of discomfort or illness that isn't any one place in particular*) Infs **MA98, MI81, NY96,** (I'm feeling) logy; **CA137, NE9, NV8,** ['logi]; **NY196,** ['loʒi]; (Qu. HH13, *Expressions meaning that a person is not very alert or not aware of things: "He's certainly _____."*) Inf **TX5,** ['logi]; (Qu. HH25, *One who never has anything to say: "What's the matter with him?"*) Inf **NH14,** He's logy; (Qu. KK56, *Wood that is heavy from being in water a long time: It's _____*) Infs **CA8, IN76, NE8, NH14, TX79,** Log(g)y; **GA67,** ['logɪ]; **NM12,** ['logi]; **NC38,** ['lagi]. **1979** *DARE* File **MA** (as of c1915), It seems to me that when I was a child, people had a wider variety of words that described their physical and mental condition. I never hear now of anyone's feeling logy, but I ride the bus every morning with many who *are* logy.

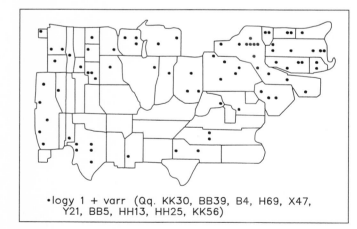

•logy 1 + varr (Qq. KK30, BB39, B4, H69, X47, Y21, BB5, HH13, HH25, KK56)

‡**2** See quot. [Cf **loady**]
1917 *DN* 4.395 **neOH,** Logy [logɪ]. . . I recall the sense "top heavy" in addition to the usual sense. Is this personal only?

Lohd See **Lord** n[1]

loike See **like** v[1], adj, vbl aux, n, adv, prep, conj

loin See **learn** v **A1**

lokey, lokie See **locie**

lolapalooza, lollapaloosa See **lalapalooza 1**

lolligate v [Var of **lollygag**] Cf **lollygag** v **B2**
1940 *Hench Coll.* **cAR** [Black], Lolligating—mixing around and chat-

ting. *Ibid,* Murphy would say to their colored cook: "Are you going . . [out] tonight?" "Yes I'm going lolligating tonight down on 9th street."

lolliper See **lolloper**

lollipop n Also sp *lollypop*
1a A piece of hard candy on a stick. [Cf *OED lollipop* sb. a "dial." a sweetmeat; 1796 → (*OEDS* 1784 →); *OEDS lollipop* sb. a "now a sweet or water-ice on a stick."] **widespread, but esp freq NEast** See Map and Map Section Cf **lickstick, mollycoddle 1, sucker**
[**1939** Wolcott *Yankee Cook Book* 345, *Taffy apples* [Often called Lollipop Apples]. . . Stick a wooden skewer in the stem end of apples, dip . . into the hot syrup.] **1950** *WELS* **WI** *(Candy on a stick for children to lick)* 21 Infs, Lollipop(s); *(Candy sold especially for children in your neighborhood)* 13 Infs, Lollipop(s). **1951** Johnson *Resp. to PADS 20* **DE,** Lollipop. **1960** Bailey *Resp. to PADS 20* **KS,** Lollipop—common. c**1965** Randle *Cookbooks (Ask Neighbor)* 3.70, Arrange skewers on lightly buttered cookie sheets and pour syrup over point of skewer to make a lollipop. **1965–70** *DARE* (Qu. H81) 444 Infs, **widespread, but esp freq NEast,** Lollipop; (Qu. H82a, *Cheap candies sold especially for schoolchildren*) 22 Infs, **scattered,** Lollipops; (Qu. H82b, *Kinds of cheap candy that used to be sold years ago*) Infs **LA19, NY57, RI3, VT3, 16,** Lollipops; (Qu. HH22c, . . *A very mean person . . "He's mean enough to _____."*) Inf **NJ45,** Take a lollipop from a baby.

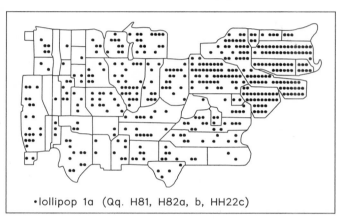

•lollipop 1a (Qq. H81, H82a, b, HH22c)

b A popsicle; see quot. [See **1a** above]
1968 *DARE* (QR, near Qu. H81) Inf **LA28,** Lollipops here are frozen on a stick.
2 A sweetheart—also used as an affectionate nickname.
1913 *NY Eve. Jrl.* (NY) 1 Mar 8 *(Zwilling Coll.),* [In cartoon:] Say Harry I just called up the old lady and told her that I wouldn't be home until quite late and she was nice as pie. Just said allright my lollypop and hung up. **1941** *LANE* Map 379 **ceRI,** Affectionate names. . . used in addressing both boys and girls . . [1 inf] lollipop. **1942** Berrey–Van den Bark *Amer. Slang* 185.2, *Pet names; terms of endearment.* . . lollypop. **1942** Warnick *Garrett Co. MD* 10 **nwMD** (as of 1900–1918), Lollypop. . . sweetheart. **1956** *Sun* (Baltimore MD) 19 Apr 16/1 *(Hench Coll.),* Grace Kelly, who vies with Gina Lollobrigida as the world's reigning lollipop, has now got herself a real title or two. **1956** Roberts–Levy *My Boy Lollipop* np, My Boy Lollipop,/ You made my heart go giddyup—/ You are as sweet as can-dy,/ You're my sug-ar dan-dy. c**1960** *Wilson Coll.* **csKY,** Lollipop. . . Sweetheart; obviously from the candy on a stick.
3 Nonsense, poppycock. Cf *DS* NN13
1950 *WELS (When you think that the thing somebody just said is silly or untrue: "Oh, that's a lot of _____!")* 1 Inf, **csWI,** Lollipop.

lollipop bite n Cf **hickey** n[2] **a**
1968 *DARE* (Qu. X59, . . *The small infected pimples that form usually on the face*) Inf **NY48,** Lollipop bites [FW: used by Inf and friends].

lollop v Also *lallop*
1 To loll, lounge around. [*OED* 1745 →]
1825 Neal *Brother Jonathan* 3.314 **swME,** Poor Walter began to feel a serious disposition to "lollop" and sprawl about. **1867** in 1919 Hale *Letters* 26 **ceMA,** And just lollop on the deck [of a steam-boat] with an awning, and eat delicious things, and stop when we please to go on

shore. **1899** (1912) Green *VA Folk-Speech* 266, *Lollop. . .* To loll or lounge idly.

2 To bound, lurch; to move heavily. [*OED* 1851 →]

1899 (1912) Green *VA Folk-Speech* 266, *Lollop. . .* To . . move heavily or be tossed about. **1941** *Time* 20 Oct 107, He is not the riproaring Mencken of the 1920s, . . when he himself was scorching Fundamentalists at the Scopes trial, sitting up all night with characters like Rudolph Valentino, and lalloping around Manhattan with Ernest Boyd and Jim Huneker. **1944** in 1953 Botkin–Harlow *Treas. Railroad Folkl.* 289, A branch of the New Haven, an inter-urban trolley line (which terrified me the way it went lolloping around curves).

3 also with *around:* To stir or swish (something) around; see quots.

1956 McAtee *Some Dialect NC* 28, I used to like to lollop my sweet tater around in the gravy. **c1960** *Wilson Coll.* **csKY,** *Lollop. . .* To move something around, like food in the mouth.

lolloper n Also *lolliper* Cf **lalapalooza, walloper**
An unusually large, pleasing, or admirable person or thing.

1918 *DN* 5.26 **NW,** *Lolloper. . .* A very bulky object; often a fat person. Variant of wolloper probably. **1927** *DN* 5.475 **Ozarks,** *Lolliper. . .* Something particularly admirable or pleasing. "Look at thet 'ar Paisley gal! Aint she a lolliper, now!" **1933** Williamson *Woods Colt* 227 **Ozarks,** "Oh, that redhorse [=a fish] is a lolliper," she says. "Too bad we ain't got no grease. Bass you can cook any old way, but suckers got to have corn meal an' grease."

lolluhgag See **lollygag**

lolly n [Cf *EDD lolly* sb.³ "Obs. . . Broth, soup, or other food boiled in a pot."] Cf **loblolly** n **1a**

1967 *DARE* (Qu. H37, . . *Words . . for gravy. Any joking ones?*) Inf **CO47,** Lolly—from an Oklahoma friend.

lolly bay See **loblolly bay 1**

lollygag v, n Usu |'lɑlɪ͵gæg|; also |'læli͵gæg| Also sp *lallygag, lalligag;* pronc-sp *lollygog;* for addit pronc and sp varr see **A** below

A Forms.

1862 [see **C1** below]. **1869** [see **B1** below]. **1883** [see **B1** below]. **1906** *DN* 3.120 **sIN,** Lollygog. **1940** [see **B2** below]. **1949** *PADS* 11.24 **CO,** Lolligag. **1950** [see **C1** below]. **1952** Brown *NC Folkl.* 1.556, *Lalligag* ['lɑlɪ͵gæg, lɔ-]. **1953** [see **B2** below]. **1959** [see **B1** below]. **1965–70** *DARE* (Qu. A9) Inf **ME16,** Lallygagging [FW: [æ] in first syll]; **MI100,** Lollygogging; (Qu. A11) Inf **MD24,** ['lɑlɪ͵gægɪn]; (Qu. A18) Inf **ME16,** Lallygagger [FW: [æ] in first syll]; (Qu. Y21) Inf **CT11,** Lollygag ['lɑlɪgæg] around; (Qu. AA8) Inf **AZ11,** ['lɔli͵gægɪn]; **IL54,** [͵lɑli'gagɪn]; **KY84,** Lollygogging ['lɑli͵gagɪn]; **OK6,** ['læli͵gæg]; (Qu. KK31) Infs **MI15, 55,** ['lɑlɪ͵gægɪŋ].

B As verb.

Also with *around;* also vbl n, ppl adj *lollygagging,* n *lollygagger.*

1 To make a public show of affection, neck, flirt, gush; to flirt with. **widespread, but less freq Sth**

1868 *N. Vindicator* (Estherville IA) 30 Dec [3]/2, The lacivious lollygagging lumps of licentiousness who disgrace the common deacencies of life by their love-sick fawnings at our public dances. **1869** *Tidal Wave* (Silver City ID) 15 Jan 3/2, They are too pious to encourage dancing, and *the* feature of their entertainments may be what the boys call "lally-gagging." [*DARE* Ed: This quot may belong instead to sense **B2.**] **1883** Victor *Bad Boy Abroad* 11, Pa likes to lalligag the gals, wen Ma ain't round. **1890** *Jrl. Amer. Folkl.* 3.311 **ME,** *Lallygag.*—To 'spoon,' make love. **1906** *DN* 3.120 **sIN,** *Lollygog. . .* Used with disgust for expression of affection in a too public way, especially of kissing. "They lollygog around before people like two fools." **1907** *DN* 3.246 **eME,** *Lalligag. . .* It's getting down to business when a couple begin to lalligag. **1909** *DN* 3.413 **nME,** *Lallygag. . .* To spoon. **1911** *DN* 3.545 **NE,** *Lollygag. . .* To be effusive in the expression of affection. "Oh, please stop lollygagging." There is also a noun, *lollygagger,* "She's a regular lollygagger." **1912** *DN* 3.582 **wIN,** *Lollygag. . .* At the fair the other day George and Sue were lollygagging around like two sick kittens. **1922** *DN* 5.148 **sePA** [College slang], *Lollygagger*—a young man addicted to attempts at hallway spooning. **1927** in 1947 Runyon *Trials* 112 **NY,** When your correspondent was a "necker" of no mean standing back in the dim and misty past, they called it "lally-gagging". **1931** Randolph *Ozarks* 52, A self-respecting mountain man would never permit his daughter to go "traipsin' round" the country roads at night

with any young man, nor tolerate the indiscriminate "lallygaggin' " which he sees so often among the tourists. **1933** Williamson *Woods Colt* 145 **Ozarks,** She warn't doin' nothin' except lallygaggin' aroun' with the fellers. **1939** FWP *ID Lore* 242, To lallygag—to flirt. **1941** *AmSp* 16.23 **sIN,** *Lollygagging.* Kissing, 'necking.' **1942** McAtee *Dial. Grant Co. IN* 39 (as of 1890s), *Lallygag . .* indulge in mawkish display of affection. **1949** *PADS* 11.24 **CO,** *Lolligag. . .* To be overly effusive, overly flattering. **1959** *VT Hist.* 27.146, *Lallergag. . .* To court; to pay attention to the opposite sex. . . To loiter. Common. **c1960** *Wilson Coll.* **csKY,** *Lally-gagging. . .* courting, being coquettish. *Ibid, Lollygagging. . .* Making love in public. **1965–70** *DARE* (Qu. AA8, *When people make too much of a show of affection in a public place . . "There they were at the church supper _____."*) 58 Infs **scattered, but less freq Sth,** Lollygagging; **NY223, PA234,** Lollygagging around; **KY84,** Lollygogging. **1983** *MJLF* 9.1.47 **ceKY** (as of 1956), *Lollygagging . .* courting in public.

2 rarely with *off:* To loiter, lounge, fool around; to chatter idly; to gad about; also fig.

1870 *N. Vindicator* (Estherville IA) 19 Feb [3]/1, The weather once more is 'salubrious' and balmy, and indicates that winter will not lollygag in the lap of spring. **1893** Owen *Voodoo Tales* 160 **MO,** He bin kip 'wake o' nights a-lissenin' at de gigglin' an' lallygaggin' (humbugging, chaff). **1898** Smith *Caleb West* 322 **NEast,** The major . . was about to compliment Bowles on the wonderful progress of the work so largely due to his efforts, when the man at the hoisting-engine interrupted with, "Don't stand there now lallygaggin', Lonny. Where ye been this half hour? Hurry up with that monkey-wrench. Do you want this drum to come off?" **1910** *Sat. Eve. Post* 30 July 19, Frank lally-gagged through his first term and came back for the second. **1940** (1942) Clark *Ox-Bow* 88 **NV** (as of 1885), Half an hour since I seen how they was lally-laggin' around and started timin' them. **1944** Duncan *Mentor Graham* 127, The children begged for cracklins and ate them while they lallygagged around under the table. **1949** *PADS* 11.24 **CO,** *Lolligag. . .* To dawdle, recline, sprawl. "Don't lolligag at the table." . . To fool along, loiter, "Don't lolligag on the way home from school." **1950** *PADS* 14.43 **SC,** *Lallygag, lollygag. . .* To chatter, talk idly. **1950** *WELS* (*To move about slowly*) 1 Inf, **ceWI,** Lallygag. **1952** Brown *NC Folkl.* 1.556, *Lalligag* ['lɑlɪ͵gæg, lɔ-]. . . To talk in an idle manner. **1953** Brewer *Word Brazos* 16 **eTX** [Black], He allus lolluhgag in de ol' long ez he kin. **1956** McAtee *Some Dialect NC* 26, *Lallygag . .* indulge in idle talk. **1959** [see **B1** above]. **1959** *Wall St. Jrl.* (NY NY) 6 Apr 1/6 (Hench Coll.) **cwCA,** A 250-acre camp site in the Santa Cruz mountains "just for our citizens . . to lollygag around in," says a city official. **1960** Criswell *Resp. to PADS* 20 **Ozarks,** Lollygag. . . To act the fool, loiter around. **1965–70** *DARE* (Qu. A9, *Wasting time by not working on the job*) Inf **ME16,** Lallygagging; **MI100,** Lollygogging; (Qu. A10, . . *Doing little unimportant things: . . "What are you doing?" . . "Nothing in particular—I'm just _____."*) Inf **NY230,** Lollygagging around; (Qu. A11, *When somebody takes too long about coming to a decision . . "I wish he'd quit _____."*) Inf **MD24,** Lollygagging; (Qu. A18, . . *A very slow person*) Inf **ME16,** Lallygagger; (Qu. X43a, *If you sleep later than usual one day by accident . . "I _____."*) Inf **NY205,** Lollygagged; (Qu. Y21, *To move about slowly and without energy*) Infs **MA58, VA54,** Lollygag; **CT11,** Lollygag around; **MA74,** Lollygag—to Inf this means to move slowly, take your time.; **VT12,** Lollygagging; (Qu. Y27, *To go about aimlessly, with nothing to do: "He's always _____ around the drugstore."*) Infs **MN42, NY92, 114, SC70, VA5,** Lollygagging; **OH28,** Lallygagging; (Qu. Y29a, *To 'go out' a great deal, not to stay at home much: "She's always _____."*) Inf **VA5,** Lollygagging; (Qu. Y29b, . . *About a man [who doesn't stay home much]: "He's always _____."*) Inf **RI17,** Lollygagging; (Qu. AA8) Inf **CA106,** Lollygagging—not doing too much of anything; **NY223,** Lollygagging around—could also mean just fooling around; (Qu. KK31, *To go about aimlessly looking for distraction: "He doesn't have anything to do, so he's just _____ around."*) Infs **AK5, CA66, MI15, 55, NY114, 230,** Lollygagging; (Qu. KK60, *Having nothing in particular to do: "I'd just as soon go with you this afternoon—I'm _____ anyway."*) Inf **NY163,** Lollygagging around. **1970** *DARE* Tape **CA183,** They oughta just get it over with instead of just lollygagging around, playing politics. **1973** *Springfield Union* (MA) 25 Sept 14/1 (*OEDS* at *lallygag*), The Dow Jones average of 30 industrials, which lollygagged most of the day, gained strongly in afternoon trading. **1978** Massey *Bittersweet Country* 207 **Ozarks,** *Lolly-gagging* (loafing): She was just lolly-gagging around. **1986** Pederson *LAGS Concordance,* 1 inf, **seMS,** Time to lallygag around—mess around, goof off; 1 inf, **cMS,** Lallygag off—try to avoid work.

C As noun.

1 Foolishness, nonsense; idle talk. [Cf **B2** above]

1862 *Harper's New Mth. Mag.* 25.324 **NY,** The gentleman inside addressed him: " . . Try er lobstaw, bossy?" "Ain't got no money," said Mr. Biggs, still fingering the morsels. "Oh, come now, none o' that ere lallygag," responded the gentleman. **1880** Wheeler *Boss Bob* 9, I kin get lots o' jobs, if I'd take my pay in friendship an' all sech lollygag. **1950** *PADS* 14.43 **SC,** *Lallygag.* . . Chatter, idle talk.

2 pl: See quot. [**lollygag B1**]

1914 *DN* 4.76 **ME, nNH,** *Lollygags.* . . Airs, affectations, love-making.

3 Used as a term of disparagement; see quot.

1940 in 1944 *ADD,* You think I'd let my girl marry a lollygag who squints at peepstones?

lollygag around, lollygagger, lollygagging See **lollygag** v **B**

lollygag off See **lollygag** v **B2**

lollygog See **lollygag**

lollypaloozer See **lalapalooza**

lolly pine See **loblolly pine 1**

lollypop See **lollipop**

lolo adj, n [Haw *lōlō* paralyzed, numb; feeble-minded] **HI**
Crazy; foolish, stupid; a crazy or stupid person.

1938 Reinecke *Hawaiian Loanwords* 22, *Lolo* ['lo:'lo:]. . . Crazy or foolish (not so strong a word as *pupule*). . . A crazy or very silly person. . . A "dumb" person in the sense of being slow witted. V[ery] F[requent]. **1954–60** Hance et al. *Hawaiian Sugar* 4, *Lolo* . . ['lo'lo]—Crazy, insane. **1967** *DARE* (Qu. HH3, *A dull and stupid person*) Inf **HI4,** ['lolo]—literally: paralyzed; figuratively: stupid; **HI13,** You [lo:lo:]! **1972** Carr *Da Kine Talk* 87 **HI,** *Hawaiian Words Commonly Heard In Hawaii's English.* . . *Lōlō.* Stupid. **1981** *Pidgin To Da Max* np **HI,** *Lolo* . . Someone who would be glad to give you the time of day—if he knew how to read a clock.

loma n Also dimin *lomita* [Span] esp **SW**
A hill, mound, or ridge—often used in place-names.

1857 in 1941 *AmSp* 16.265 **CA,** *Spanish Words Frequently Used in English Conversation* . . Loma, Hill. **1859** (1968) Bartlett *Americanisms* 255, *Loma.* (Spanish.) A hill or ridge of hills with a flat summit. A term in general use on the Mexican frontier. The diminutive *Lomita* is also sometimes employed. **1863** U.S. Congress *Serial Set* 1174 Doc 1.20 **SW,** The new road is to follow the bottom at the edge of the *lomas.* **1892** *DN* 1.191 **TX,** *Spanish and Mexican Words used in Texas.* . . *Lóma:* a hill, an eminence. Often found in proper names of places. **1923** Saunders *S. Sierras* 75 **swCA,** All about are rounded hills, or lomas, rising in baldness. **1931** (1960) Dobie *Open Range* 307 **West,** *Names* . . *Peculiar To The Open Range Country.* . . *Loma de Harina.* . . Hill of Flour; Flour Hill. *Ibid* 308, *Loma Escondida.* . . Hidden Hill. **1941** *Harper's Mag.* 183.498 **csCA,** Stand on the "knoll" at Yucca Loma, drink in the desert, and then look down at your feet. **1967** *DARE* (Qu. C17, . . *A small, rounded hill*) Inf **CA4,** Loma—Spanish origin, used in English.

lombard n [Trademark *Lombard,* orig for a steam tractor used in logging]

1975 Gould *ME Lingo* 167, Mainers often use *lombard* for something huge and spectacular, as if it were a synonym for *rauncher, baister, lunker.* A person who is big, strong, and able may be called a "reg'lar *lombard* of a man." The Lombard family made lumbering equipment in Waterville, and around the turn of the century came up with a steam tractor that greatly changed the harvesting of Maine timberlands. . . The *Lombard* moved west as lumbering did, and was the prototype of the British army tank used in World War I. In the 1920s the steam drive was changed to an internal combustion engine. In Maine usage, *Lombard* is pronounced [sic] *lum-b'd.*

lomi v Also redup *lomilomi* [Haw] **HI**

1 To mash fine, crush; hence (ppl) adj *lomi(ed)* mashed fine. Cf **lomi salmon**

1938 Reinecke *Hawaiian Loanwords* 22, *Lomi* ['lo:mi] . . v., adj., n . . To massage. . . To mash fine, as salmon ("*lomi* salmon") to be eaten with *poi.* . . Mashed fine. The word *lomied* is also used. . . Massage. . . V[ery] F[requent]. *Lomilomi* ['lo:mi'lo:mi], [Reduplicated form of *lomi.*] The same as *lomi,* in all senses. V[ery] F[requent]. **1940** [see **lomi salmon**].

2 To massage, rub, squeeze; hence nouns *lomi(lomi)* a massage.

1850 (1852) Colton *Deck & Port* 347 **HI,** I was bruised and fatigued, and determined to try . . the bath and the "lomi-lomi." The latter is a kind of shampooing much resorted to here to relieve fatigue. A kanacka who understood it was at hand, and . . commenced his kneading process. He used me much as a baker would a lump of dough. . . I sank to sleep softly. **1873** in 1966 Bishop *Sandwich Is.* 66 **HI,** I suffered . . from pain and stiffness, and was induced to try a true Hawaiian remedy, which is not only regarded as a cure for all physical ills, but as the greatest of physical luxuries; *i.e. lomi-lomi.* This is a compound of pinching, pounding, and squeezing. **1938** [see **1** above]. **1954–60** Hance et al. *Hawaiian Sugar* 4, *Lomilomi* . . ['lomi'lomi]—Rub, massage. **1955** Day *HI People* 298, Sometimes eating would be interrupted while the diners enjoyed a relaxing massage or lomi-lomi. **1972** Carr *Da Kine Talk* 87 **HI,** *Hawaiian Words Commonly Heard In Hawaii's English.* . . *Lomilomi.* Massage. *Ibid* 115, The verb *lomi* means 'to rub, press, squeeze'. **1984** Sunset *HI Guide* 85, *Lomi* (or *lomilomi*)—rub, press, massage.

lomi n See **lomi salmon**

lomi(ed) ppl adj See **lomi** v **1**

lomilomi v See **lomi** v

lomilomi n
1 See **lomi salmon.**
2 See **lomi** v **2.**

lomi salmon n Also redup *lomilomi (salmon);* abbr *lomi* [**lomi** v **1**] **HI**
A dish consisting of fish, traditionally mashed with the fingers, seasoned with onions and spices.

1938 [see **lomi** v **1**]. **1940** Bazore *Hawaiian Foods* 150, *Lomi Salmon (Kamano Lomi).* . . [S]hred the fish into small pieces. . . Chop the onions fine. Combine the tomatoes and salmon; mash them with a fork. . . The Hawaiians. . . lomi (crush) the green onions . . using the fingers or a wooden potato masher. **1951** *AmSp* 26.21 **HI,** At a 'luau,' or Hawaiian feast, one may hear many native words. . . 'lomi' salmon ('mashed fine'). **1967** *DARE* (Qu. H45, *Dishes made with meat, fish, or poultry that everybody around here would know, but that people in other places might not*) Inf **HI6,** Lomilomi salmon (salted, from Alaska); literally: softened in the fingers. **1968** *Jrl. Engl. Ling.* 2.82 **HI,** *Common Hawaiian Words and Phrases Used in English.* . . Lomilomi salmon. . . Salmon mashed with the fingers and mixed with onions and spices. Also called *lomi, lomi* salmon, and *lomilomi.* **1972** Carr *Da Kine Talk* 115 **HI,** *Lomi salmon* (Hawaiian + English). Salmon or other fish, usually raw and salted, worked with the fingers and mixed with green onions, tomatoes, and seasonings. The verb *lomi* means 'to rub, press, squeeze'. *Lomilomi salmon,* the reduplicated form, is very frequently used. **1991** Saiki *From the Lanai* 3 **HI,** [Mr. Finch] goes in for island food, things like lomi salmon, saimin and raw fish.

lomita See **loma**

lommix See **lummox**

lomo adv Also sp *lowmow*

1970 *Thompson Coll.* **AL, FL** (as of 1930–1960s), He lomo gitten it = he is really going fast, taking a walloping, dancing in a remarkable way, etc. Asseverative: really. Negro men, B[irming]ham AL 1930's; two white Alabamans in Europe 1944. Heard from both blacks & whites Miami 1960's. *Ibid* **FL** [Black], "He lowmow gittin it" would be said of a guy in a car making a fast getaway. Very fast. "All over Florida", "colored talk", "backwoods expression used by older generation: running scared, as of a rabbit being hunted or chased," "Lowmow means fast; heard older folks use the expression."

lompus adj [Cf *EDD lompus* (at *lumpus*) heavily, headlong, in a lump; a heavy fall] Cf *DS* MM13, 15, KK70
=**catawampus** adj

1991 *DARE* File, My husband was putting a casserole on a warmer and it was in danger of sliding off the trivet—it was *lompus* or crooked. I hollered out—"Watch out, it's going to *tump* over!" [Inf grew up in the Panama Canal Zone, and now lives in Baltimore.]

London loo n Cf **hill dill**
=**pom-pom-pullaway.**

1957 *Sat. Eve. Post Letters* **cwPA** (as of c1895–1910), *London Loo—* This game we played in a yard where we could have limits, or frequently we played it on the street, as there were very few cars in those days. . .

One player was "It," and stood in the center of the street. The others would line up on one side of the street and would say "London Loo catch one or two" and would run across and "It" would try and catch them. Of course he could only catch one at a time and that one would join him to catch the others and the game would go on from one side of the street to the other until all were caught, each one caught helping to catch the others. We used telegraph poles or trees as limits and if one went beyond that he would be considered caught.

London pride n

1 =Maltese cross. [*OED* 1688 →] **NEng**

1891 *Jrl. Amer. Folkl.* 4.148 **NEng**, Lychnis Chalcedonica . . was *London pride*. **1902** Earle *Old Time Gardens* 443, A great favorite in the old garden was the splendid scarlet Lychnis, to which in New England is given the name of London Pride. **1938** Damon *Grandma* 81 **CT** (as of late 1800s), The plants were mostly perennials. . . There were sweet rocket, purple and white, London pride, very stiff and very scarlet. **1950** Gray–Fernald *Manual of Botany* 630 **NEast**, London-pride. . . Spreading from cult. to thickets, open woods and roadsides. **1959** Carleton *Index Herb. Plants* 76, London pride. . . Lychnis chalcedonica; Saponaria officinalis. **1976** Bailey–Bailey *Hortus Third* 688, L[ychnis] *chalcedonica* . . Maltese-cross . . London-pride.

2 =bouncing Bet 1.

1892 *Jrl. Amer. Folkl.* 5.92 **MA**, Saponaria officinalis, old maid's pink; London pride. **1900** Lyons *Plant Names* 334, S[aponaria] officinalis . . London-pride. **1958** Jacobs–Burlage *Index Plants NC* 35, Londonpride. . . is common from New York to Georgia and west to Indiana and in all parts of North Carolina. **1959** [see **1** above].

lone n [Scots, Engl dial; *OED lone* a. 6.b, 1375 →; *EDD lone* sb.[2] 5; *SND lane* adj. 2] Cf **lonesome B1**

In phr *by one's lone* and varr: Alone, by oneself.

[1884 *Anglia* 7.273 **Sth, S Midl** [Black], All by it lone se'f = entirely alone.] **1890** Farmer–Henley *Slang* 1.36, All of my lone. . . (American).—A negro vulgarism for 'alone.' **1910** Raine *Bucky O'Connor* 24 **West**, But whyfor do they let a sick man like you travel all by his lone? **1917** in 1944 *ADD* **sWV**, I was here all my lone. **1935** Porter *Flowering Judas* 198, "It's not half she deserves," he answered sternly, "leaving me here by my lone, and for what?"

lone man See **lone woman**

lonesome n, v, adj, adv Pronc-sp *lontsome* Cf Intro "Language Changes" I.8, Pronc Intro 3.1.23

A Form.

1898 in 1919 Hale *Letters* 332 **ceMA**, When I get tired and "lontsome" I shall just git up and git, back to excellent old Boston.

B As noun.

1 in phr *one's lonesome*: Oneself, one's own. [See *SND one's lanesome* (at *lane* adj. 1.(6))] Cf **lone**

1897 *KS Univ. Qrly.* (ser B) 6.89 **neKS**, Lonesome: as "All by my lonesome." **1905** *DN* 3.60 **eNE**, All by my lonesome. . . Alone. **1928** *Ruppenthal Coll.* **KS**, By his lonesome, all by his lonesome—entirely alone (playfully) or to children. He went up to bed all by his lonesome. **1940** *Sun* (Baltimore MD) 16 Jan 10/8 (*Hench Coll.*), She must go with the gang or else be shelved and left by her lonesome. **1963** Owens *Look to River* 107 **TX**, Sing it agin on your lonesome. **1986** Chapman *New Dict. Amer. Slang* 3, All by one's lonesome. . . Alone; solo: *She did it all by her lonesome.*

2 Loneliness.

1942 (1971) Campbell *Cloud-Walking* 232 **seKY**, Ways to pleasure Sary and make her forget her lonesome.

3 in phr *shake a lonesome*: To get going, be on one's way. Cf **high lonesome** n **2**

1966 *DARE* (Qu. Y19, *To begin to go away from a place: "It's about time for me to _____."*) Inf **SC26**, Shake a lonesome (and haul ass) [laughter].

C As adj.

Plaintive, melancholy, gloomy; hence adv *lonesome*. **chiefly S Midl** *esp freq among Black speakers*

1883 (1971) Harris *Nights with Remus* 79 **GA** [Black], Nobody dunner [=don't know] whar de quills cum fum, . . yit ev'ybody want um on account er der playin' sech a lonesome chune. [Footnote:] This word "lonesome," as used by the negroes, is the equivalent of "thrilling," "romantic," etc., and in that sense is very expressive. **1884** *Anglia* 7.264

Sth, S Midl [Black], To look lonesome = to be depressed. **1887** (1967) Harris *Free Joe* 89 **GA** [Black], He'd set out on de peazzer en sing by hese'f, en it make me feel so lonesome dat I bleeze ter cry. **1931** *AmSp* 7.93 **eKY**, Hit were a lonesome-like tune the lad wuz a singin' that evenin' as he went acrost Duty's Knob. **1939** *FWP Guide TN* 209, The Negroes' old "lonesome songs" inspired the "blues" of W.C. Handy. **1941** Stuart *Men of Mts.* 195 **neKY**, The wind kindly blowed lonesome over the place [=a graveyard]. **1947** Lomax *Advent. Ballad Hunter* 58 **TX** (as of c1868), The tune is typically of the western ballad breed, drawling, whiney, creepy, saturated with gloom. Negroes classed it among their lonesome tunes. **c1950** *Hall Coll.* **wNC, eTN**, Lonesome. . . Sad. "That was the lonesomest picture I ever saw." (The picture referred to was the moving picture "The Shepherd of the Hills.") . . This use heard a number of times; also the expression "a lonesome song" for a *sad* song. **1970** *DARE* (Qu. B2, *If the weather is very unpleasant . . it's a _____ day*) Inf **VA69**, Lonesome, bad. [Inf Black] **1982** Powers *Cataloochee* 363 **cwNC**, Os Deaver, a master fiddler before the Civil War, improvised a hauntingly lonely tune. . . A woman, half-drowsing on a cot, sat up to cry, 'Oh, play that lonesome thing again!' His tune was called Lonesome Laurel thereafter. **1986** Pederson *LAGS Concordance (A gloomy day)* 1 inf, **seTN**, Cloudy, lonesome day.

D As verb.

To suffer from loneliness, pine away.

1902 in 1984 Gilmore *Ozark Baptizings* 71 **MO**, The young people are about to lonesome to death. **1942** (1971) Campbell *Cloud-Walking* 44 **seKY**, She looked to Nelt like she was nigh about to lonesome to death for her kin.

E As adv.

See **C** above.

lonesome bird n

=hermit thrush 1.

1956 MA Audubon Soc. *Bulletin* 40.128 **ME**, Hermit Thrush . . Lonesome Bird. . . In reference to its seclusive habits.

lonesome water(s) n esp **KY**

Water from a source near one's childhood home which, when drunk, causes one to stay or return home.

1930 Helton *Lonesome Water* 1 **KY**, Drank lonesome water:/ Weren't but a tad then / Up in a laurel thick / Digging for sang. *Ibid* 5, But I never been way from here,/ Never got going:/ I've drunk lonesome water./ I'm bound to the hills. **1931** in 1959 *KY Folkl. Rec.* 5.70, I drunk th' lonesome water / An left the hills, by gum / But let me tell ye, mister,/ Back I wuz boun' to cum. **1938** Stuart *Dark Hills* 222 **eKY**, I knowed you'd come back to drink of lonesome water. Once you get a drink of lonesome water you always come home. . . lonesome water is good. I drunk of it when I was a little shaver and I never left the hills. . . that boy's not goin' to leave these hills. . . He's drinking lonesome waters. . . I never could forget the lonesome waters. . . The gravels clean it and the willer shade flavors it. . . I want to drink of lonesome water before I die. I couldn't forget the old Kentucky lonesome waters. [1947 (1964) Randolph *Ozark Superstitions* 332, It is said that a man who takes three drinks in three minutes from any Ozark spring is bound to return for another drink before he dies. In one form or another, that story is heard all over the Ozark country. But whether it is really old-time stuff, or was cooked up by the Chamber of Commerce propagandists, I have been unable to find out.] **1950** Stuart *Hie Hunters* 247 **eKY**, "Once you git the taste of the fragrant light burley, ye'll always have the taste, so they say. It's the same as drinkin' lonesome water! I know," she added, "when you once git the smoke from light burley, it's too pleasant ever to fergit." **1960** Williams *Walk Egypt* 11 **nGA**, She warned him not to drink water that ran under hollow stones. "It's lonesome water. You do, and you'll never get going again." He drank it. It tasted of heart leaf, and a month later they were married. He never left Plum Gap, nor wanted to. **1963** *KY Folkl. Rec.* 9.3.76 **eKY**, An ambivalent love-hate for his environment is implicit in the highlander's expression that *if once you take a drink of lonesome waters, you'll come back some day*, implying that nostalgia will draw the wanderer home to die. **1965** *S. Folkl. Qrly.* 29.155 **eKY**, Lonesome Waters. . . The usual implication is that nostalgia for one's native hills and streams will draw him homeward to die. Field informants.

lone star tick n [See quot 1935] Cf **Texas fever tick**

A tick (*Amblyomma americanum*).

1935 Pratt *Manual Invertebrate Animals* 522, *Amblyomma americanum* . . Lone star tick . . the hinder end of which has a conspicuous yellowish spot, which gives the animal its popular name: often common on cattle, also on man. **1938** Brimley *Insects NC* 488, *A[mblyomma] americanum* Linn. *Lone-star tick.* Raleigh, Chapel Hill, Kinston, May, July, August; Onslow and Craven counties, January, October.

lone woman n [*EDD* lone woman (at *lone* adj. 3.(2)); see also *OED* lone a. 2 1548–1859]

A woman who is not living with a man; similarly n *lone man.*

1899 (1912) Green *VA Folk-Speech* 266, *Lone-woman.* . . A widow; left alone. **1903** *DN* 2.320 seMO, *Lone woman.* . . A widow or 'grass widow.' 'I am a lone woman with four little children.' **1942** Berrey–Van den Bark *Amer. Slang* 447.1, *Lone man or woman, an unmarried or widowed man or woman.*

loney v [Cf *EDD* loney "A cry made to a child to encourage it in its first attempts to walk alone"; see also *SND* lane adj. 2.(2)]

1909 *DN* 3.346 eAL, wGA, *Loney.* . . To stand alone: said to a baby.

long adj, n, prep, adv[1] Usu |lɔŋ|; also |lɑŋ|; for addit varr see **A** below See Pronc Intro 3.I.6.c, 3.III.4

A Forms.

1890 *DN* 1.39 csME, *Long* . . [lɔŋ] rather than [lɑŋ]. *Ibid* 68 **KY**, *Long.* Pronounced [lɔŋ]. **1893** Shands *MS Speech* 11, One of the most characteristic marks of the Southern pronunciation is the substitution of [ɔ] for short *o* . . as . . [lɔŋ] for *long.* **1927** Shewmake *Engl. Pronc. VA* 30, *Long.* . . the vowel sound of *hot* is still so generally heard that it may still be regarded as the typical pronunciation of educated Virginians. **1931** *AmSp* 6.164 seVA, There is a tendency to unround [ɔ] to [ɑ], particularly in *foggy, log* and *long.* (In the records *long* is always [lɑŋ].) **1939** *AmSp* 14.126 ne,ceTN, [ə lɔŋ kɔrɪdr]. **1950** Hubbell *Pronc. NYC* 84, Before the nasal . . [ɔə] . . occurs in . . *long.* **1961** Kurath–McDavid *Pronc. Engl.* 164, The North, the North Midland, large sections of the South Midland, and the Lower South have the /ɔ ~ ɒ/ of *law* in *long, strong* almost universally. On the other hand, Virginia east of the Blue Ridge and all of North Carolina have in these words the /ɑ/ of *lot* with similar regularity. Outside this large section of the South, more or less scattered instances of /ɑ/ appear in southern West Virginia, eastern Pennsylvania, northeastern New Jersey, Brooklyn, and western New England. **1965** Carmony *Speech Terre Haute* 113 cwIN, /ɔ/, phonetically [ɔᵛ] or [ɒ], is the usual vowel of . . *long* . . in Terre Haute speech. **1973** *PADS* 60.53 seNC, *Long.* . . The Carteret speakers. . . All said /ɔ/ but one lone /ɑ/ user. **1976** Allen *LAUM* 3.265 **Upper MW** (as of c1950), The common Northern and North Midland /ɔ-ɒ/ vowel range in *long* and *strong* is paralleled by its universality in the U[pper] M[idwest]. . . Although fully rounded /ɔ/ occurs generally throughout the five states, weakly rounded /ɒ/ is less common. . . /ɒ/ in *long* has a rather obvious Midland orientation, with greatest frequency in Iowa and Nebraska. Of the 12 infs. with /ɒ/ in both words, 10 are in Midland speech territory. Unrounded /ɑ/ . . survives in *long* and *along* with only two U[pper] M[idwest] infs., and not at all in *strong.* But unrounded /ɑ/, not recognized in eastern field practice as distinct from /ɑ/, appears in the speech of nine widely scattered infs., few of whom have family ties with eastern /ɑ/ areas.

B As adj.

1 Tall. [*OED* long a.[1] A.1.b c900 →; "Now *rare* exc. in jocular use."; *SND* lang adj. 2 "Gen. Sc[ots]"] Cf **low** adj

1889 *Century Dict.* 3509, *Long.* . . Tall: as, *long* Tom Coffin. . . Now only colloq. or humorous. **1907** *DN* 3.193 seNH, *Long, lean and lank.* . . Often said of a tall, thin person, "He's long, lean, and lank, and can run like a greyhound." **1912** Green *VA Folk-Speech* 266, Long. . . In the sense of tall. "He was a long brother." **1923** *DN* 5.239 swWI, He's a long, ganglin' feller. **1927** *AmSp* 3.168 **SW** [Cowboy speech], The description of a tall man . . may be "he's so long he has to shorten his stirrups to keep from wearin' out his boot soles." **1986** Pederson *LAGS Concordance* (He's so _____) 1 inf, **nwLA**, Long and skinny.

2 in comb *longhead:* An intelligent, farseeing mind. [*OED* (at *long* a.[1] A.1.c) 1809, 1889] Cf **longheaded 1**

1799 *Aurora Genl. Advt.* (Philadelphia PA) 11 June [2]/4, Men so remarkably gifted with *long heads* would never have credited it. **1889** *Century Dict.* 3510, *A long head,* a mind characterized by sagacity, foresight, and shrewdness with caution.

3a Of a price or offer: high; undiscounted. [*OED* long price (at *long* a.[1] A.5.b) 1840; see also *EDD* (at *long* adj. 5), *SND* (at *lang* adj. I.3)]

1887 *Amer. Field* 27.134, Mr. Frank Van Ness is reported as saying

that Mr. J.H. Temple, the owner of Harry Wilkes [=a race horse], having received a "long" offer for this celebrated trotter from a New York man, has concluded to dispose of him. **1899** (1912) Green *VA Folk-Speech* 267, *Long.* . . Great. "A hundred dollars is a long price for that horse." **1911** *Century Dict. Suppl.,* Long price, the full retail price, without deduction, discount or rebate. **1928** Weseen *Crowell's Dict. Engl. Gram.* 380, *Long Price.* Colloquial in the general sense of a high price, as "We paid a long price for that house." Commercial cant in the sense of the full price, without any discount. **1942** Berrey–Van den Bark *Amer. Slang* 551.3, *High price.* . . Juicy figure, long price, neat *or* tidy sum. **1964** (1965) Gould *You Should Start* 18 **ME**, I pointed out that this didn't warrant the long price on a new saw (they cost more than they should, anyway).

b Of money: possessed in large amounts; abundant. [Prob infl by *long green* cash, paper money] *esp freq among Black speakers*

1947 *AmSp* 22.168 [Argot of the three-shell game], *Long dough.* A considerable amount of money, usually in the possession of a mark. **1965** in 1993 Major *Calling the Wind* 242 **NYC** [Black], He was happy at the thought that while Wade and a lot of suckers were risking their lives . . he would be making that long money putting in hours and hours of overtime. **1970** *DARE* (Qu. U37, . . *Somebody who has plenty of money)* Inf **DC**11, Long bread; long funny money. [Inf Black] **1970** Major *Dict. Afro-Amer. Slang* 78, *Long bread:* (1940's) a great deal of money. **1971** Roberts *Third Ear* np [Black], *Long green* . . a lot of money. Ant[onym] chump change. **1980** Folb *Runnin' Down* 84 **Los Angeles CA** [Black], I wanna Jag—Jag 70 XKE, Benz 70. They cost some dough. My money ain' long enough—maybe sometime. *Ibid* 85, It was magnificent. Few of the cars I saw were so elaborately decked out ("long money" or a hustler's resourcefulness are required to get such elaborate accessories together). *Ibid* 112, The ultimate name of the game in American society is money. You can get away with imitation clothes, but *long green* or *long bread* speaks loudly and for itself.

4 In comb with a noun specifying an animal's age: fully that age; approaching the next year of age—esp in phr *long yearling;* also transf. **chiefly West** Cf **out** B8, **short**

1907 Love *Deadwood Dick* 52 **West,** Short yearlings were those over one year old and short of two years, long yearlings those two years and short of three years. [*DARE* Ed questions this explanation.] **1923** *DN* 5.225 swMO, A 'long' or a 'short' yearlin' is one more or less than a year old, respectively. **1927** *Ruppenthal Coll.* **KS**, Long—used of ages of cattle, etc. . . Several in this bunch are long yearlings (that is, somewhat more than a year old the preceding spring), and a few long twos (that is, two year olds who were two years old somewhat more than two years before the spring of the year preceding the time of the statement). Similarly with "lon[g]" threes, etc. **1929** Dobie *Vaquero* 278 **West,** Some of my neighbors and myself contracted with a man from Colorado City to deliver 700 long yearlings—yearlings that would be two's in early spring—to a point in Dawson County. **1936** Adams *Cowboy Lingo* 67, A 'long yearling' was an animal eighteen months old or older. **1939** (1973) FWP *Guide MT* 415, *Long yearling*—Colt or calf between one and two years old. **1944** *PADS* 2.58 neMO, *Long-year-ling.* . . A beef between one and two years old. **1944** Wellman *Bowl* 55 **KS**, "Two year olds?" Til asked. "Long twos. I been figgerin' on having them broke." *Ibid* 170, The animals—which were what was known as "long tens," that is, going on eleven years. **1948** Baumann *Old Man Crow's Boy* 245 **ID**, So Bert and I went to buy the five thoroughbred long-yearlings from Stanfield. **1949** Guthrie *Way West* 29 **MO**, "How old's he [=a boy]?" Summers asked. "Long seventeen." **1959** Martin *Gunbarrel* 274 **WY**, It's not uncommon to see a bull and cow moose with a long yearling and a new calf together.

5 Of a horse: having great endurance.

1897 Hough *Story Cowboy* 81 **West,** He had to hold up his horse with a good stiff rein, keep it from running its wind out the first mile, and so growing weak and apt to stumble on the rough ground over which the run was made. It needed the best and "longest" of his own stock for this work. **1922** Rollins *Cowboy* 275, A horse that could travel notably far, particularly when at high speed, was termed a "long horse." Consequently, the best stayer in one's band would be called one's "longest horse." There was no such phrase as "long pony," though any given animal might coincidently be both a "cow-pony" and a "long horse." **1936** Adams *Cowboy Lingo* 85, An easy-gaited saddle horse was called a 'saddler,' and one that could travel great distances at high speed was a 'long horse.'

6 Of speech: slow; hence adv *long* slow.

1912 Paine *Mark Twain* 1.52 **KY,** Perhaps it was just a commonplace remark that his peculiar drawl made amusing. . . His mother always referred to his slow fashion of speaking as "Sammy's long talk". Her own speech was still more deliberate, but she seemed not to notice it. **1966** *PADS* 46.27 **cnAR** (as of 1952), *Long-talking*. . . Slow rate of speed in speech.—"He was a long-talking old boy."

7 in phrr *have* (or *be on*) *long ears:* To have a tendency to eavesdrop.

1935 Sandoz *Jules* 264 **wNE** (as of 1880–1930), He talks everything out and she has long ears. **1942** Berrey–Van den Bark *Amer. Slang* 139.5, *Eavesdrop*. Be on the . . *long ear*. . . *have* . . *long* . . *ears, to be given to eavesdropping.*

C As noun.

Pl: **=longies.**

1969 *DARE* (Qu. W14, *Names for underwear*) Infs **NY**130, 201, Longs—men's long.

D As adv.

1 in phr *think long:* To long, yearn; see quot. [*OED long* a.[1] A.9.b "Chiefly Sc[ots]"; [c1200]–1788; see also *SND lang* adj. 7.(7) "Gen. Sc[ots]"]

1872 Schele de Vere *Americanisms* 502, *Long,* as an adverb . . is used in some parts of America, especially in the Cumberland Valley, merging into the meaning of the kindred word *"to long."* "Don't you think *long* to be at home?" "A relic doubtless of English in the Middle Ages, for to *think long* is still common in the Cumbrian districts of England, supplying the missing link between the adjective *long* and the verb *long.* We *long* for a thing, when we think it is *long* before we attain it." (Henry Reeves).

2 See **B6** above.

E As prep.

=along of 2.

1888 Jones *Negro Myths* 3 **GA coast** [Gullah], Ef me ebber ketch you close dis ribber, me guine larne you how ter come fool long me. *Ibid* 34, De man wuh bin mek sich pooty music fuh dem fuh dance long.

long v

A Gram forms.

Past: usu *longed;* also *esp freq among Black speakers, longs(t).*

1937 [see **B1** below]. c**1937** [see **B1** below].

B Senses.

1 To belong; to be the property of. [*OED long* v.[2] 2 "*Obs.*"; *EDD long* v.[2]] **esp VA** *relic* Cf **belong A**

1899 (1912) Green *VA Folk-Speech* 266, *Long.* . . To belong. "It longs to me." **1937** in 1976 *Weevils in the Wheat* 218 **VA** [Black], De first 'oman I longsta was Mistress Martha Leonard; she was mighty nice to me. c**1937** *Ibid* 124 **VA** [Black], Yes mam, dese old folks whats livin' will tell you dey's seen hit, yes, right on de place whar I longst. *Ibid* 163 **VA** [Black], Say you is writin' hist'ry? Lord, Lord, po' nigger ain't got much fer you to git 'cause in dem times he longst to de white man. *Ibid* 266 **VA** [Black], I was . . jes' a spare little gal, wid t'other slaves dat 'longst to Parker Jurden. **1952** Brown *NC Folkl.* 1.561, *Long.* . . To belong to.

2 =belong B.

1952 Brown *NC Folkl.* 1.561, *Long.* . . He longs to work till five o'clock.

'long adv[2] See **along**

long already adv phr [PaGer *schun lang,* Ger *schon lange*] **Ger settlement areas**

Since long ago, for a long time.

1935 *AmSp* 10.167 **PA** [Engl of PA Germans], He has lost his respect for her long already. **1950** Klees *PA Dutch* 281, [Pennsylvania] Dutch words . . adopted into the English of southeastern Pennsylvania. . . Especially conspicuous are the attempts at English by the country Dutch that give birth to sentences overly rich in adverbs. "I've known her long already." **1987** *Jrl. Engl. Ling.* 20.170 **ePA,** *Long already*—'for a long time'. . . 6% (7), ages 19–67. . . Though attested in a variety of age and educational groups, the item is used by a small number of speakers. **1994** *DARE* File **seWI, swOH,** I remember the expression *long already* meaning 'for a long time' from my childhood. This expression was quite common in the Dodge County, Wisconsin area in the 1930s, 40s, and 50s, and in southwestern Ohio as well, esp in the Cincinnati area. You

still hear it today, especially in the rural communities. "We belong to that church long already." "We've had Holstein cows long already."

long-ass butterfly n *joc*

=dragonfly.

1968 *DARE* (Qu. R2, . . *The dragonfly*) Inf **OH**79, Long-ass butterfly [laughter].

long ball n Also *long base*

A bat-and-ball game; see esp quots 1937, 1940 Harbin. Cf **cat n 3c, line ball, one old cat 1, town ball**

1932 (1953) Smith *Games* 120, *Long ball.* . . This is an indoor adaptation of One Old Cat. . . Boundary lines are unnecessary, since every hit is a fair ball. For that reason the fielders must scatter over the entire playing area. *Ibid* 121, As long as one player is at home to bat, the others may remain on the long base. . . Even if a player bats what in baseball is called a "foul tip," he must run for the long base. **1937** (1947) Bancroft *Games* 569, *Long-ball.* . . At a distance of sixty-five feet from the home plate . . a field base is outlined. . . The batter continues to bat until he touches the ball. Any touch of the ball with the bat entitles the batter to run to the field base, but only on a fair strike may he return to home plate and score a run. . . Any number of runners may be waiting in the long base (field base) for a chance to run home. . . Each player who gets safely to the field base and back to home base scores one point for his team. **1940** Harbin *Fun Encycl.* 437, *Tip-tap-bat* (Long ball—one-old-cat).— Only two bases are used in this game, home plate and a base back of the pitcher's position. . . Any ball touched by the bat is fair. The batter must then run to the designated base and back. He may be put out by the catcher holding the ball on home base before he can return. Or a player may put him out by throwing the ball across his path. . . Where two batters are available. . . players may run to first base, and then to second as in regular baseball. . . With four batters the runners complete the circuit to home base. **1940** Kennedy–Harlow *Schoolmaster* 229 **IN** (as of c1880), And there was Long Ball or Long Base, in which the bases were two long pieces of plank perhaps a hundred feet apart, and sometimes nearly all of a ten- or twelve-man team might be perched on one of them at once. **1957** *Sat. Eve. Post Letters* **CA, WA** (as of 1910–1944), The following activities . . were popular. . . Long ball. **1968–70** *DARE* (Qu. EE11, *Bat-and-ball games for just a few players [when there aren't enough for a regular game]*) Inf **OH**80, Long ball—just hit it long; (Qu. EE33, . . *Outdoor games . . that children play*) Inf **NC**88, Long base—a kind of practice game for baseball. Use two bases. Pitcher throws ball to person at bat, . . [who] tries to run to the base and get back home.

long-barrel underwear n Cf **long john 1**

1969 *DARE* (Qu. W14, *Names for underwear . . Men's—long*) Inf **KY**44, Long-barrel underwear.

long base n

1 See **long ball.**

2 The base to which the batter runs in **long ball.**

1932 [see **long ball**]. **1937** [see **long ball**].

longbill n

1 also *long-billed plover:* **=dowitcher,** esp *Limnodromus scolopaceus.*

1923 U.S. Dept. Ag. *Misc. Circular* 13.52, *Dowitcher* . . Vernacular Names . . In local use. . . longbill (Idaho); long-billed plover (Wash.) **1929** Forbush *Birds MA* 1.399, *Limnodromus griseus scolopaceus* . . Long-billed Dowitcher . . The Long-bill feeds on the same food as the Dowitcher. **1977** Udvardy *Audubon Field Guide Birds* 413, In fall and winter, this species [=the short-billed dowitcher] is found mainly on coastal mud flats, whereas the Long-bill prefers freshwater ponds.

2 Any of several other birds with markedly long bills; see quots.

1923 U.S. Dept. Ag. *Misc. Circular* 13.50 **WI,** *Wilson Snipe.* . . Long-bill. **1953** Jewett *Birds WA* 256, Bowles found a pair of nesting long-bills [=*Numenius americanus*] at Kiona in 1904. **1956** MA Audubon Soc. *Bulletin* 40.19, *Red-backed Sandpiper.* . . Long-bill (Mass. That is, compared to other "peeps.") **1977** Bull–Farrand *Audubon Field Guide Birds* 622, Many nests have been found, but details of the Long-bill's [=*Toxostoma longirostre*] habits remain relatively unknown.

long-billed beach robin n Cf **beach robin, robin snipe**

A **dowitcher.**

1955 *AmSp* 30.181 **NC,** The dowitcher is a *robin snipe* rather generally and is the *long-billed beach robin* in North Carolina.

long-billed curlew n
Std: a **curlew 1** (here: *Numenius americanus*). Also called **buzzard curlew, daddy longlegs 6, fish duck 2, hen curlew, leather bird, longbill 2, maybird 5, old hen curlew, sabre-bill, screecher, sicklebill, smoker, Spanish curlew**

long-billed dowitcher See **dowitcher**

long-billed plover See **longbill 1**

long-billed rail n
=**Virginia rail.**
　　1888 Trumbull *Names of Birds* 129, *Rallus virginianus*. . . In the vicinity of Salem, Mass., it is distinguished from the common rail, as Long-billed Rail . . by gunners and marketmen. **1925** (1928) Forbush *Birds MA* 1.355, *Rallus virginianus* . . Virginia Rail . . small mudhen; long-billed rail. **1955** MA Audubon Soc. *Bulletin* 39.443, *Virginia Rail.* . . Long-billed (Mass.)

long bit n [*bit* a unit of value equal to 12½ cents] **West** *hist*
The sum of 12½¢ or 15¢ (as opposed to the **short bit** or 10¢).
　　1852 *Yankee Notions* 1.295, How many liquors can I get for two long bits? **1857** *S.F. Call* (CA) 8 Jan. 1/1 (*DA* at *bit* n. 2.c.(2)), *Dissolved,* Dat from and after dis date. . . we will receive nuffin but long bits for brackin of boots. **1877** Wright *Big Bonanza* 354, The smallest coin in use is the bit, ten-cent piece—sometimes spoken of as a "short bit," as not being twelve and one-half cents, the "long bit." **1879** in 1944 *ADD* 59 **Pacific,** *Short bit* . . *long bit.* **1889** *Century Dict.* 567, *A long bit,* fifteen cents. . . Western U.S. . . *A short bit,* ten cents. . . Western U.S. **1907** *N&Q* 10th ser 8.63, South of the Potomac and in the West the real was a "bit." . . The American dime was called a "short bit" to distinguish it from the other, the "long bit." **1944** *ADD* 59, In the West, when small coins . . were scarce, a dime was accepted in payment for anything priced at one bit. A *long bit* was the equiv. of 15¢, being the price paid when a dime was returned as change from a quarter tendered for a purchase priced at one bit. **1957** *Seattle Daily Times* (WA) 25 July 11, When dimes finally came in, they were called short bits, and eight of them passed for a dollar. When one bought something for a bit and tendered a 25-cent piece, he received a dime in change, and paid a long bit.

long blackberry n Also *black longberry* Cf **fingerberry, sow-tit**
A blackberry such as *Rubus alleghaniensis.*
　　1896 *DN* 1.412 **cNY,** *Black long-berries:* blackberries (to distinguish them from black raspberries). *Ibid* **nNY,** *Long blackberries* is heard. **1968–69** *DARE* (Qu. I44, *What kinds of berries grow wild around here?*) Inf **NY**224, Long blackberries; **PA**102, Black longberries.

long-boned rockfish n
=**black grouper 1.**
　　1933 John G. Shedd Aquarium *Guide* 100, *Trisotropis bonaci*—Black Grouper; Black Rockfish; Long-boned Rockfish . . a valuable fish in the markets at Key West [FL], where it is abundant. **1935** Caine *Game Fish* 71, Black Grouper—*Mycteroperca bonaci*. . . Long-boned Rockfish.

long boy n
1 =**submarine sandwich.** Cf **poor boy**
　　1965–70 *DARE* (Qu. H42, . . [*A sandwich*] . . *in a much larger, longer bun, that's a meal in itself*) Inf **CA**54, Long boy—advertised as; **WA**30, Long boy. **1986** Pederson *LAGS Concordance* (Hero sandwich) 1 inf, **swTN,** Long boy.

‡2 A type of doughnut; see quot. Cf **long john 2**
　　1967 *DARE* (Qu. H30, *An oblong cake, cooked in deep fat*) Inf **MO**2, Long boys.

long bread n Also *long cake*
　　1941 *Sun* (Baltimore MD) 3 Nov 6/7 (*Hench Coll.*) **eMD,** This corn-meal Johnnycake of which these fellows have been talking was nothing compared with the long cake of the Eastern Shore—consisting of a great cake the size of a griddle and baked flat out on the griddle, made from bread dough, yeast raised, and when brought on the table quickly opened with a fork and spread deep inside with butter, and then eaten, with the melted butter running down your chin. Good-by Johnnycake when I have long bread!

long butt n esp **Pacific NW** Cf **jump butt**
The lower end of a tree trunk discarded by loggers because of a defect; hence v phr *long butt* to cut off such a section.
　　1905 U.S. Forest Serv. *Bulletin* 61.32 [Logging terms], *Butt off, to.* . . To cut a piece from the end of a log on account of a defect. . . Syn[onym]: long butt, to. **1950** *Western Folkl.* 9.381 **neCA** [Lumberjack language], *Long butt.* A short log that is usually spoiled and cut from the butt end of a tree. **1958** McCulloch *Woods Words* 112 **Pacific NW,** *Long butt.* . . A cull chunk cut off the bottom log of a tree because of rot or other defect. . . To cut off a long butt. **1959** *AmSp* 34.78 **nwCA** [Logger lingo], *Long butt.* . . To cut a piece from the end of a log because of a defect. **1967** *DARE* Tape **WA**20, In the old days when they felled that tree [=one with its trunk growing parallel to the ground before turning upward], they would move up past the crook and cut it off and leave it [=the stump] in the woods and they'd call that a long butt. **1967** *DARE* FW Addit **cwWA,** The long butt—"stump rot" section (rotted stump) of tree which is left in the woods because it will only sink in the water. **1969** Sorden *Lumberjack Lingo* 73 **NEng, Gt Lakes,** *Long butt*—The first log of a tree when culled for rot or other defects. Generally discarded in the woods as it had no value.

long-butted adj [Cf **long butt**]
Having very short legs.
　　1958 McCulloch *Woods Words* 112 **Pacific NW,** *Long-butted*—A short man (suggesting that part of his legs had been cut off, leaving him kind of stumpy).

long cake See **long bread**

long cat n Cf **long ball**
A children's game, perh **cat** n **3a** or **3c.**
　　1964 *Mt. Life* Summer 41 **sAppalachians** (as of c1900), In the winter we skated on the ice behind the school house and in the summer we played roundtown, or long cat or short cat, or drop-the-hat or hot pepper.

long chair n [Cf *SND lang chair* (at *lang* adj. I.6.(10)) "a long bench used as a settee in farm kitchens"; cf also *OEDS long chair* (at *long* a.[1] 18) a chaise longue < Fr, literally "long chair"]
A type of couch, daybed, or lounge.
　　c1938 in 1970 Hyatt *Hoodoo* 1.399 **seNC** [Black], An' he tells 'uh [=her] to lay down. He had a *long chair* in de room an' he tell 'uh to lay down in de chair. An' she . . laid down in de chair. **1968** *DARE* (Qu. E7, *The piece of upholstered furniture that you can stretch out on to rest*) Inf **NC**50, Long chair; (Qu. E9, *A piece of upholstered furniture that seats three people*) Inf **NC**50, Long chair [FW: Inf showed me this and it was a davenport]. [FW: Inf talked of Scots origin of community.] **1986** Pederson *LAGS Concordance (Sofa)* 1 inf, **seAL,** Long chair—lounge; 1 inf, **swAL,** Long chair. [Both infs Black]

long chalk n [From *chalk* chalk mark used to record a debt or score; cf *OED chalk* sb. 4, 5, 6.b]
1 also *long chalks:* A great deal, large amount, long way.
　　1836 (1838) Haliburton *Clockmaker* (1st ser) 18 **NEng,** But if it is behind us in that respect, it is a long chalk ahead on us in others. *Ibid* 108, It whips English weather by a long chalk. **1848** Lowell *Biglow* 131 **'Upcountry' MA,** 'T will take more emptins, a long chalk, than this noo party 's gut. **1872** Schele de Vere *Americanisms* 318, To beat by *long chalks* . . is also not unfrequently heard here.

2 in phr *not by a long chalk* and varr: By no means, not at all.
　　1848 Bartlett *Americanisms* 71, *Not by a long chalk.* When a person attempts to effect a particular object, in which he fails, we say, "He can't do it by a long chalk." **1848** (1855) Ruxton *Life Far West* 14 **Cent,** 'Twas about 'calf-time,' maybe a little later, and not a hundred years ago, by a long chalk, that the biggest kind of rendezvous was held 'to' Independence. **1872** Schele de Vere *Americanisms* 318, Even the *tavern-keeper's* . . chalk must lend itself to such figurative language. "You can't do that by a long chalk," is a common expression for a man's inability to accomplish his purpose, derived from the chalk-marks of credit on the owner's door or shutter. **1899** (1912) Green *VA Folk-Speech* 109, *Chalk.* . . Not by a long *chalk;* not on any account; not by any means; not at all. **1905** *DN* 3.5 **cCT,** *Chalk.* . . Distance, in the expression 'not by a long chalk,' not by a great deal. **1929** *AmSp* 5.126 **ME,** "Not by a jug full," "not by a long chalk," . . were common expressions. **1932** Stribling *Store* 5 **AL,** Do you get it at five cents a pound? Not by a long chalk! **1961** Cole *Idioms New Engl.* 39 (as of c1900–10), Not by a *long* chalk.

long chalks See **long chalk 1**

long clam n

1 also *long-neck (clam)*, *long-necked clam*: **=soft-shell clam.** **chiefly NEast** Cf **littleneck 1**

1843 DeKay *Zool. NY* 5.240, *Mya Arenaria.* . . is known under the various appellations of *Long Clam* and *Piss Clam*, to distinguish it from the common *Round Clam*. **1882** *Amer. Naturalist* 16.882, In New England the clam is *Mya arenaria*, in New York it is *Venus mercenaria*. In the former region the Venus is known as the "hard" or "round" clam; in the latter the Mya is called "soft shell" or "longneck" clam. **1884** Goode *Fisheries U.S.* 1.707, Next upon the list comes the 'Soft Clam,' 'Long Clam,' or 'Nanninose' *(Mya arenaria)*, dear to New Englanders. **1911** U.S. Bur. Census *Fisheries 1908* 308, "Long clam". . . Dredges, rakes, tongs, hoes, forks, and baskets are used in gathering them. **1939** *LANE* Map 235, Several names for the soft clam were incidentally recorded: *long clam* [23 infs, **chiefly CT**]. **1975** Gould *ME Lingo* 168, *Long neck*—The true Maine clam, also called the soft shell. **1981** Meinkoth *Audubon Field Guide Seashore* 572, *Soft-shelled Clam.* . . This delicious clam is also known as the Long Neck Clam. . . A spurt of water shooting out of a hole in the sand betrays the presence of a clam contracting its neck when disturbed. **1984** *DARE* File **Chesapeake Bay** [Watermen's vocab], Long-necked clams.

2 also *long-shell clam*: A **razor clam** of the family Solenidae.

1792 Belknap *Hist. NH* 3.183, Razor shell clam, *Solen ensis*. Long shell clam, *Solen radiatus*. **1881** Ingersoll *Oyster-Industry* 245, Long Clam.—See *Razor-fish*. (Massachusetts bay.) **1887** Goode *Fisheries U.S.* 5.2.614, Under the name of "long clam," "knife-handle," and "razor clam," they are occasionally seen in New York market.

long-come-short n

1 See quot.

1884 *Anglia* 7.271 **Sth, S Midl** [Black], *Dis long-come-short* = this long time.

2 pl: See quot.

1984 Wilder *You All Spoken Here* 89 **Sth**, *Eating short:* On short rations; in a tight; up against it. *Short commons:* Same as above. *Long come shorts:* Ditto.

long corn n

See quot 1899.

1786 (1925) Washington *Diaries* 3.143 **VA**, Measured at the latter 19 Barrls. of long Corn and 6 of Short. **1899** (1912) Green *VA Folk-Speech* 267, *Long-corn.* . . The longest and best ears of corn, used for bread corn. "You are eating your long-corn now."

long corner n Cf **gore** n[1] **1, long forty, odd corner**

In logging: see quot.

1958 McCulloch *Woods Words* 112 **Pacific NW**, *Long corner*—An odd piece of timber, often costly to reach from a donkey setting. Usually it is a somewhat pie-shaped chunk of timber left at the back end where the yarding of two neighboring settings does not fully overlap. Also left because of rock bluff or other hindrance to logging. Such timber is often left to satisfy seed source requirements of state forest conservation laws.

long-coupled adj [By ext from *long-coupled* of a horse: having a relatively long back] Cf **long-geared**

1933 Rawlings *South Moon* 258 **nFL**, You done a good job for me when you was a knob-jointed, long-coupled young scaper, and I don't want you to miss no fun now you're a growed man.

long cut adj phr used absol [Abbr for *long-cut tobacco*] Cf **fine cut**

A type of loose or shredded tobacco; see quots.

1950 *WELS* **ce,seWI** *(Tobacco used for chewing)* 2 Infs, Long cut; 1 Inf, Long cut—in loose pieces, shredded; 1 Inf, Long cut—in loose pieces. **1960** Heimann *Tobacco* 164, Long cut, or ribbon cut, was shredded strip leaf. More often than not it was dipped Burley or a Burley blend, and could be made in a variety of strand widths. Cigarette tobacco is a variety of long cut. **1967–69** *DARE* (Qu. DD1, . . Forms . . *[of]* chewing tobacco) Infs **IA**14, **MI**103, **NJ**1, **NY**59, 219, Long cut; **NJ**28, Long cut—shredded; **NY**68, Long cut—loose type. [All Infs old]

long day n [Cf *OED long* a.[1] 12] Cf **longest day one (ever) lives**

A time far distant in the past or future.

1889 *Century Dict.* 3510, *A long day*, a far-off time; extended postponement. **1931–33** *LANE Worksheets* **nwCT**, Long day . . long time.

It's a long day since I heard that. **1986** Pederson *LAGS Concordance*, 1 inf, **cLA**, I've [sic] been a-many long day since I've had one.

long drawers n pl Also *long draws*, *long-leg drawers* **scattered, but chiefly SE, C Atl, seNY** See Map

=long john 1.

1965–70 *DARE* (Qu. W14, *Names for underwear*) 44 Infs, **scattered, but chiefly SE, C Atl, seNY**, Long drawers; **FL**33, **MS**88, **NY**48, **SC**40, Long draws; **FL**48, Long-leg drawers [FW: used by Inf's grandmother]. **1986** Pederson *LAGS Concordance*, 2 infs, **cnAL, nwTN**, [Them] long drawers; 1 inf, **cwMS**, Long drawers—winter underwear.

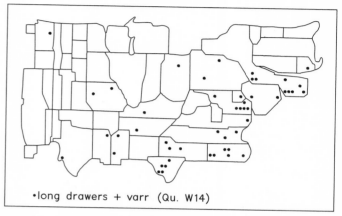

•long drawers + varr (Qu. W14)

long drink of water n Also *long-legged drink of water* [*SND lang drink (o water)* (at *lang* adj. I.6.(14)) "a tall, lanky person. . . Gen.Sc."] **chiefly Nth**

A tall, thin person; see quots.

1942 Berrey–Van den Bark *Amer. Slang* 429.5, *Tall, lanky person.* . . long drink of water. **1950** *WELS* (*Expressions about a person who is very thin*) 1 Inf, **ceWI**, Long drink of water. **1960** Wentworth–Flexner *Slang* 324, *Long drink of water*—A tall, thin man, esp., but not necessarily, if dull or boring. **1968–69** *DARE* (Qu. X49) Infs **GA**75, **IL**47, **PA**162, **WI**57, (A) long drink of water; **MA**25A, A long drink of water [FW: Inf heard this expression in Maine]. **1975** Gould *ME Lingo* 168, *Long drink*—Of water. Used to describe a tall person, and usually a female: "Migod, but she's a long drink of water!" *Ibid*, The girl compared to a *long drink* of water may be amended to a *long-legged drink* of water. **1991** Isaacs *Magic Hour* 43 **Long Is. NY**, One of them, a gangly kid my grandmother would have called a long drink of water, came into the tent on the far side of the pool. **1995** *DARE* File **NYC** (as of late 1950s), Growing up, I was tall and skinny and my relations, especially my uncles, used to speak of me as "a langer loksh" (a long noodle) and "a long drink of water."

long Dutch n Cf **Dutch ball, long ball**

A bat-and-ball game; see quot.

1950 *WELS* (*Bat-and-ball games for a few players [when you don't have enough for a regular game]*) 1 Inf, **ceWI**, Long Dutch—old game; used first and home, 3 and 4. When hit, run to first; must steal home while pitcher and catcher play catch.

longe n[1] See **lunge** n[1]

longe n[2] See **lunge** n[2]

longear n

1 usu *longears*: A mule or donkey; also adj *long-eared*, in var combs referring to a mule or donkey; see quots. **chiefly N Cent, West** See Map on p. 416

1889 *Century Dict.* 3511, *Long-ears.* . . A humorous name for a donkey. **1942** Berrey–Van den Bark *Amer. Slang* 120.21, *Donkey; burro.* . . longear. *Ibid* 120.68, *Mule.* . . longear. *Ibid* 916.21 [Western terms], *Mule; donkey.* . . long-eared chum. **1944** Adams *Western Words* 93, *Long-eared chuck wagon*—A humorous name for the mules which pack the provisions when these animals have to be used instead of wagons in rough country. **1949** *PADS* 11.24 **CO**, *Long-ear.* . . A mule. **1950** *WELS* **WI** (*Joking names for mules*) 3 Infs, Longears; 1 Inf, Long-eared jack; 1 Inf, Long-eared s.b.—[heard in] army; used occasionally. **1962** Wyld *Low Bridge* 23 **cnNY** (as of 1800s), Mules, in Erie parlance, said one informant, were "long-eared robins." Steam packet men later called them "hayburners." **1965–70** *DARE* (Qu. K50) 10 Infs, **chiefly**

N Cent, West, (Old) longears; IN30, 67, KY9, 16, MI8, Long-eared bastard (*or* critter, mule, son of a bitch, son of so-and-so's).

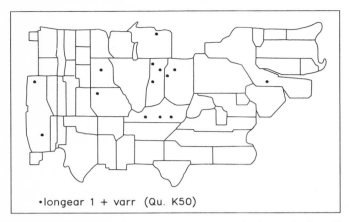

•longear 1 + varr (Qu. K50)

2 A steer or calf not branded or earmarked; similarly adj *long-eared.* **West** Cf **orejana**

1885 Siringo *TX Cowboy* 85, The way I would go about it would be to rope and tie down one of the long-eared fellows and . . "run" my brand on his hips or ribs. **1913** (1919) *WNID, Longear.* . . An unbranded calf. *Local, Western U.S.* **1941** Dobie *Longhorns* 51 **TX,** Huffmeyer decided that if he mavericked on his own hook he could average at least six long-ears a day and in the course of a few months have a herd of his own. *Ibid* 288, Here open range conditions existed, and despite the fact that men were roping and branding "longears" the year round, there were at times hundreds of mavericks on the range. **1941** [see **long rope**].

3 A type of dog; see quot. Cf **Catahoula hog dog, leopard dog**

1967 *DARE* Tape **LA2,** Some of those black and tans are big dogs, but she was a small dog. . . Them old longears was slow, but she didn't have no extra-long ears.

4 See **longear sunfish.**

long-eared See **longear 1, 2**

long-eared owl n

A widely distributed owl (*Asio otus*) distinguished by prominent ear tufts. Also called **cat owl, graveyard ~ 1, horned ~, little horned ~, long-horned ~, swamp ~**

1812 Wilson *Amer. Ornith.* 6.73, Long-Eared Owl. *Strix Otus.* . . is much more numerous in Pennsylvania than the White, or Barn Owl. **1832** Nuttall *Manual Ornith.* 1.130, Long-Eared Owl. . . ear-tufts, long, of about 6 feathers. **1842** DeKay *Zool. NY* 2.27, The *Long-eared Owl* is found chiefly in the Eastern and Middle States, where it breeds. . . It is peculiar to America, and represents here the *Otus vulgaris* of Europe. **1874** Coues *Birds NW* 304, *Otus vulgaris* var. wilsonianus . . American Long-eared Owl. **1923** Dawson *Birds CA* 3.1087, The Long-eared Owl enjoys a high reputation as a mouser, and has been passed with honor by the examining board of governmental experts. **1950** *WELS* **WI** (*Kinds of owls*) 1 Inf, Long-eared owl; 1 Inf, Long-eared owl—long ear tufts. **1967-69** *DARE* (Qu. Q2, . . *Kinds of owls*) Infs CT5, IA3, PA155, 162, Long-eared owl; CA78, NY155, American long-eared owl. **1977** Bull–Farrand *Audubon Field Guide Birds* 676, *Long-eared Owl.* . . Only by peering intently upward can one detect the round face and telltale long ear tufts.

long-eared sunfish See **longear sunfish**

longears n

1 See **longear 1.**

2 See **longear sunfish.**

long ears, have (or be on) See **long** adj **B7**

longear sunfish n Also *longear(s), long-eared sunfish* [See quot 1955]

A **sunfish:** usu *Lepomis megalotis*, but also the **redbreast sunfish.** For other names of *L. megalotis* see **blackears, blacktail sunfish, bream B3, green sunfish 2, leather-ear 1, long-scale sunfish, perch, pumpkinseed, redbelly, ~ bream, redeye, ~ sunfish, sun perch, tobacco box**

1877 NY Acad. Sci. *Annals Lyceum Nat. Hist.* 11.361, The com-

mon long-eared Sunfish of the North-east . . is probably identical with *Lepiopomus auritus.* **1882** U.S. Natl. Museum *Bulletin* 16.477, *L[epomis] auritus* . . Long-eared Sun-fish. *Ibid, L[epomis] megalotis* . . Long-eared Sun-fish. **1903** NY State Museum & Sci. Serv. *Bulletin* 60.478, *Lepomis auritus.* . . Long-eared Sunfish. . . The opercular flap is long, narrow and pointed, its length equal to that of the snout and about twice its width. **1933** LA Dept. of Conserv. *Fishes* 349, The Longear has now many common names . . Long-eared Sunfish, Big-eared Sunfish, . . Long-scaled Sunfish [etc]. *Ibid* 350, The Longears is too small to be of commercial importance. **1955** Zim–Shoemaker *Fishes* 100, *Longear Sunfish* is so named because of the long flaps or lobes that are extensions of its gill covers. **1983** Becker *Fishes WI* 834, Longear Sunfish—*Lepomis megalotis.* . . Other common names . . longear, blue and orange sunfish, pumpkinseed.

long east and a short west n [Cf *EDD longer east, shorter west* (at *long* adj. 3.(8)) "a deficiency in one part is compensated by abundance in another"]

1955 *DE Folkl. Bulletin* 1.20, Let's make it a long east and a short west (i.e., work until about 1:00 p.m. and then for a shorter time in the afternoon).

longest day one (ever) lives n Cf **long day**

The end of one's life; hence adv phr *the longest day one has to live* always; for the rest of one's life.

1774 in 1866 MA Hist. Soc. *Proc. for 1864–65* 340 **ceMA,** I shall never get the idea out of my mind the longest day I have to live. **1911** Harrison *Queed* 321, You'd be a marked man to the longest day you lived. **1946** *PADS* 6.36 **ceNC** (as of 1900–10), The longest day you (he, etc.) live. (Always. "You'll remember that the longest day you live.") Pamlico. Occasional. **1951** *PADS* 15.57 **neIN** (as of 1890s), You'll remember that the longest day you ever live. **1956** McAtee *Some Dialect NC* 28, Longest day: . . in the saying: "You'll remember that the longest day you ever live," that is, always. **c1960** Wilson *Coll.* **csKY,** You'll regret this the longest day you live.

longest, for the (last) adv phr [Cf *OED with the longest* (at *long* a.[1] B.1.h) "for a very long time. *Obs.*"; see also *DBE*] esp freq among Black speakers

For a very long time.

1926 *DN* 5.401 **Ozarks,** *Longest.* . . A long time. "I haint ben over thar fer th' longest!" **1933** Hurston in *Story* Aug 69 **FL** [Black], "You ain't got no business choppin' wood, and you know it." "How come? Ah been choppin' it for de last longest." **1937** (1977) Hurston *Their Eyes* 128 **FL** [Black], He seen he wuz sick—everybody been knowin' dat for de last longest. **1945** Saxon *Gumbo Ya-Ya* 499 **LA** [Black], Fo' the longest I believed that. **1945** FWP *Lay My Burden Down* 72 **GA** (as of c1865) [Black], When the war start to break out, Marse Sam 'listed in the troops and was sent to Virginny. There he stay for the longest.

long eye n [Cf *DBE long-eye* "covetous"; 1918; cf also *SND* (at *ee* n. I.2.(1)) 1944] Cf **big eye**

1987 Jones-Jackson *When Roots Die* 140 **sSC coast** [Gullah], Idioms . . still very much apparent in daily communication . . long eye: envy.

‡**long-eyed** adj

Walleyed.

1969 *DARE* (Qu. X26b, *If a person's eyes look in different directions, looking outward, he's _____*) Inf **IL60,** Long-eyed [laughter].

long-faced adj

Bald; balding.

1936 *AmSp* 11.275 **c,ceTN,** Long faced. Bald headed. 'He is a long faced old man.' [**1986** *Amer. Tongues* (Video recording) **TX,** [To a man whose hairline has receded:] You know your face is gettin' longer?] **1995** *NADS Letters* seMI, My father (a life-long Michigan resident born in 1919). . . also recognized *long-faced* 'balding.' He says that it was in use when he was young but that he has not heard it lately. **1995** *DARE* File **eTN,** Long-faced—"bald." [Recollected by 2 infs]

long feed See **long food**

Longfellow n [In joc ref to Amer poet Henry Wadsworth *Longfellow* (1807–82)]

Pl: Large feet; long legs.

1967-68 *DARE* (Qu. X38, *Joking names for unusually big or clumsy feet*) Infs **NY123, TX41,** Longfellows; **CO20,** Longfellows—you're a

Shakespeare, all but your feet and they're Longfellows. **1981** Pederson *LAGS Basic Materials*, 1 inf, **csTX**, If I'd had the training, I'd been a poet; my feet show it; they [are] both long fellows. **1994** *DARE* File **cwCA** (as of 1950s), When I was a child, if someone unintentionally said something that rhymed, someone else might say, "You're a poet and don't know it." The expected response was, "But I know it, because my legs are Longfellows." *Ibid* KS (as of 1950s), You're a poet and don't know it. Your feet show it; they're Longfellows.

long finger n

1 The middle finger. [*OED* (at *long* a.¹ A.18); *EDD* (at *long* adj. 1.(50))] Cf **lick-pot, longman**

1946 *PADS* 6.13 **eNC** (as of 1900–10), *Finger—little, ling, long, lick-pot, and thumb-ball.*. . The little finger, ring finger, long finger, index finger, and thumb. . . Common among children. **1968** *DARE* Tape **WI60**, I caught it with my left long finger—middle finger.

2 in phr *have long fingers:* To be thievish; to filch. [Cf Ger *lange Finger machen* (or *haben*), Du *lange vingers hebben* to steal, be thievish] Cf **long-fingered**

1950 *WELS* (A thief) 1 Inf, **seWI**, We say: "He has long fingers." **1967–69** *DARE* (Qu. V5a, *To take something of small value that doesn't belong to you—for example, a child taking cookies*) Inf **IN66**, He has long fingers; [(Qu. X32, *Joking or uncomplimentary words for the hands* . . *"Those are mine. You keep your _____ [out of them]."*) Inf **IN66**, Long fingers;] (Qu. JJ19, *If somebody has dishonest intentions, or is up to no good* . . *"I think he's got _____."*) Inf **MN6**, Long fingers—for stealing; **WI51**, Long or sticky fingers.

long-fingered adj [*EDD* (at *long* adj. 1.(51)) 1842; Ger *langfingerig* thievish] **chiefly Gt Lakes, PA** See Map Cf **long finger 2**

=light-fingered.

1915 *DN* 4.218, *Long-fingered*, lightfingered, epithet for a thief. "Johnnie is long-fingered." Colloquial. **1936** in a1972 *Hench Coll.*, [Glossary of prison language:] Long-fingered louse—an inmate who steals from other inmates. **1950** *WELS* (A thief) 7 Infs, **WI**, Long-fingered. **1965–70** *DARE* (Qu. V6, . . *Words* . . *for a thief*) Infs **MI35, PA107, WI12, 49, 76,** (He's) long-fingered; **IL2, PA205,** Long-fingered gent; **MI24,** He's long-fingered [FW sugg]; **MN16,** Long-fingered—especially with things rather than money; **MN42,** Long-fingered—takes things indiscriminately; old-fashioned; **NJ33,** Long-fingered—works anytime—[in] stores, homes, workshop, boats, etc; **NY36,** Long-fingered gent—[a] pickpocket; **PA126,** Long-fingered gent—old term [FW sugg]; **PA177,** Long-fingered gent [FW sugg].

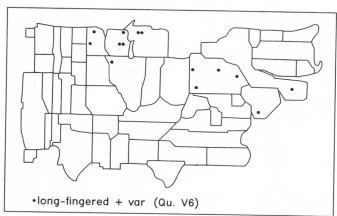

•long-fingered + var (Qu. V6)

long fingers, have See **long finger 2**

long fire n

See quot a1975.

a1975 Lunsford *It Used to Be* 168 **sAppalachians**, "Long fire" is used in speaking about a gun firing, and the time it takes from the time the hammer comes down on the little cap that's put just over the tube in the old squirrel rifle that carries the fire down to the powder till the gun is fired. When the powder is damp the gun will take "long fire." The cap will fire and the powder will be a long time burning enough to explode the entire amount of powder so that we say it "took long fire." **1986** Pederson *LAGS Concordance*, 1 inf, **cwTN**, A long fire—in muzzle-loading rifle, delayed.

long food n Also *long fodder, ~ feed, ~ forage* [Cf *OED long forage* (at *long* a.¹ A.1.f)] "straw and green fodder, as distinguished from hay, oats, etc."]

Hay, fodder.

1823 in 1910 Commons *Doc. Hist. Amer. Industrial Soc.* 1.256, As much corn or oats and hay and fodder as our horses can destroy (usually half a bushel of grain and a rackful of long food). **1917** in 1944 *ADD* **cWV**, *Long fodder.* **1939** Montgomery *Days of Old* 60 **eNC** (as of 1861–65), The animals were entirely without long food. **1942** *Hench Coll.* **cVA**, [They] were talking about all sorts of things, mostly farm things. One was "long feed." Long feed is hay and other fodder; it is not grain. **1986** Pederson *LAGS Concordance*, 1 inf, **seGA**, Long forage—what we call hay down here. [Inf old]

long forty n Cf **forty** n **B1, gore** n¹ **1, long corner**

See quot 1994.

1948 Polleys *Stories* 49 **cwWI**, Some parties feigned ignorance of survey lines, which could be obliterated by cutting the line trees and witness trees, thereby procuring what was called a "long forty", cutting much timber that did not belong to them and acquiring valuable stumpage that cost them nothing. **1994** *DARE* File **csWI**, A long forty is a forty-acre piece of land that actually is larger than the usual 1,320 feet on a side due to boundaryline adjustments made in township plat books to compensate for the curvature of the earth. *Ibid* **cnWI**, A long forty is what you get where the survey lines don't come out exactly due to the curvature of the earth.

longful adj [*OED* "dial."; see also *EDD*]

Long.

1927 *AmSp* 3.139 **eME** [Vanishing expressions], A longful while . . common.

long-geared adj [Cf **gear** n **2,** *gear* the axles, coupling pole, and associated parts of a wagon] Cf **long-coupled**

Long-bodied.

1891 *Harper's New Mth. Mag.* 83.208 **SW,** One of the most successful bronco riders . . was a long-geared, lank Texas lad. **1958** Blasingame *Dakota Cowboy* 83 **SD,** A close-built, short-backed horse was usually as active as a cat and handled himself better than a long-geared horse although that is a flexible statement.

long gravy n esp **LA** Cf **loose 2**

A thin gravy, esp one diluted to increase the quantity.

1952 Henderson *Home Is Upriver* 97 **Lower Missip Valley,** Come eat with us; we're still eatin'—but not what we like. Ain't got nothin' but a *little* fish—but we'll make a l-o-n-g gravy. **1968** *DARE* (Qu. H37, . . *Words* . . *for gravy*) Inf **LA24,** Gravy in stew is called long gravy; **LA28,** Long gravy—meat drippings and water; it is called this because the water makes it go a long ways. [Both Infs old]

long gray n Cf **gray duck c**

=pintail (here: *Anas acuta*).

1955 *Oriole* 20.1.3 **GA,** *Pintail* . . *Long Gray* (the neck and pointed tail make it appear long and pointed).

long green (tobacco) n **chiefly S Midl** Cf **hillside, homespun**

Tobacco that is dried but not processed.

[**1788** Schöpf *Reise Staaten* 2.115 **VA,** Long-green Tobacco hat grosse, fette und lange Blätter, und liebt festen Boden. [=Long green tobacco has large, glossy and long leaves, and loves loamy soil.]] **1897** *Outing* 30.380 **Allegheny Mts,** It seems that they were out of tobacco, and had been able to get only the "long green" that the mountaineers used. **1906** *DN* 3.145 **nwAR,** *Long green.* . . Chewing tobacco. "A typical hayseed was sitting on the other side masticating long green." **1923** *DN* 5.213 **swMO,** *Long green.* . . Home grown tobacco. **1933** Williamson *Woods Colt* 50 **Ozarks,** Well, she's chawin' terbaccer, an' somethin' else besides, by the way her jaws grind together. Long green ain't as tough as all that. **1941** Ward *Holding Hills* 99 **IA** (as of early 20th cent), It was a poor place, wooded on the side toward the road, and said to be roughly cleared back of the house where in an earlier day they had raised a handful of wheat, a pipeful or two of longgreen and a few nubbins of corn. **1942** McAtee *Dial. Grant Co. IN* 41 (as of 1890s), *Long green* . . tobacco leaves used for chewing with no other preparation than drying; for sale in the stores these were twisted into figure-eights and known as Virginia twist or simply twist. **1944** Howard *Walkin' Preacher* 120 **Ozarks,** Hill-fashion, the men squatted on the ground or upon logs after dinner and filled their corncob pipes with long green tobacco. **1944**

PADS 2.67 **S Midl,** *Long-green.* . . A poor quality of tobacco. . . Freshly cured tobacco being used directly for chewing or smoking before it has aged properly. **1947** Steed *KY Tobacco Patch* 98, In order to control mosaic, the men who are working the plant beds should not smoke, chew or handle unprocessed tobacco ("Long Green"). **1950** *WELS* (*Home-grown and home-cured tobacco*) 2 Infs, **swWI,** Long green. Common. **c1960** *Wilson Coll.* **csKY,** Long green. . . Tobacco from the barn, not twisted, not "manufac." **1966** *PADS* 45.16 **cnKY,** *Homespun.* . . = *long green.* *Ibid* 17, *Long green.* . . Cured, but unprocessed tobacco. Farm workers often chew leaves taken directly from the barn. Contact with long green, or with spittle from users, may cause mosaic in tobacco plants. . . "We don't let workers chew long green around the beds." **1966–70** *DARE* (Qu. DD1, . . *Forms* . . [*of*] *chewing tobacco*) Inf **IL135,** Long green; **KY60,** Long green—home-cured; **AR39,** Long green in a twist. **1967** *Key Tobacco Vocab.* 146 **TN,** *Long green*—home-made, not manufactured tobacco. *Ibid* **MO,** *Long green*—home spun.

longhair n
An American Indian who observes traditional ways; a White person who has adopted Indian ways.
1937 La Farge *Enemy Gods* 137 **SW,** The long-hair turned his mount aside and swung to earth under the partial shelter of a thick tree. **1957** *Sat. Eve. Post* 16 Mar 25 **TX** (as of 1874), Some awful old long-hair [=a White man]—he's been watching us. Sitting the dreadfulest old horse, out on the burn. **1969** Stegner *Sound of Mt. Water* 95 **West,** The day before the shindig [=a rodeo] you can watch them [=Navajos] coming . . groups of young men riding and leading prized running or roping horses; longhairs in tall hats; lean adolescents in Levis and dark glasses. **1980** *NYT Mag.* 13 July 32, When Neil Brafford tried to share what he had learned with his fellow citizens, he found himself dismissed as a troublemaking "longhair," as traditional Indians are known in South Dakota. **1988** Erdrich *Tracks* 208 **ND,** She [=an American Indian who works for the federal government] stared at me without shame, and said, "Get out you old longhair."

long-handle(d) drawers See **long handles**

long-handled squash See **long-neck squash**

long handles n pl Also *long-handle(d) drawers,* ~ *underwear;* for addit varr see quots **chiefly Sth, S Midl, West** See Map and Map Section Cf **gourd handles, handlebars**
=**long john 1.**
[**1882** in 1948 *MO Hist. Rev.* 43.95, Found—A pair of long-handled hose, [or] Grandmother socks.] **1943** *Yank* 18 June 6, One piece of shrapnel swung out the seat of his GI long-handles. **1945** *Time* 24 Dec 41, [Advt:] From friends and relatives in America have come tons of food, plus sweaters, bobby-sox, coats and longhandle underwear to fill Norway's needs. **1950** Moore *Candlemas Bay* 112 **ME,** There they hung, stiff as shingles . . the children's little pants and Pa's long-handled underwear caught in a frozen dance. **1950** *WELS* **WI** (*Names for underwear*) 4 Infs, Long handles; 2 Infs, Long-handled [underwear]. **1954** *Harder Coll.* **cwTN,** Long handles. . . Men's long underwear. **1958** McCulloch *Woods Words* 112 **Pacific NW,** *Long handle underwear*—Heavy wool underwear, long sleeves and legs. A loggers' favorite was black to begin with; this saved washing. **1960** Criswell *Resp. to PADS* 20 **Ozarks,** Long-handled underwear. . . Underwear for winter with legs to the ankles. Common. . . Sometimes called long-handles. **c1960** *Wilson Coll.* **csKY,** Long-handled underwear. **1964** Wallace *Frontier Life* 88 **OK** (as of 1893–1906), In winter, I wore "long-handles," knitted

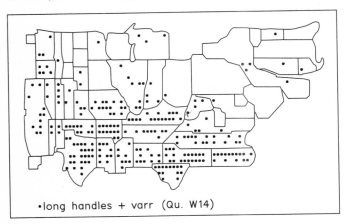

•long handles + varr (Qu. W14)

union-suits, which reached to the tops of my shoes. **1965–70** *DARE* (Qu. W14, *Names for underwear*) 244 Infs, **chiefly Sth, S Midl, West,** Long handles; **CA106, GA6, 13, KS10, KY24, MO13, NH14, RI12,** Long-handled underwear (*or* drawers); **CA208, CT27, MO34, NC30, OH76, OK47,** Long-handle (drawers, johns, *or* underwear); **KY24,** Long-handleds. **1969** Sorden *Lumberjack Lingo* 73 **NEng, Gt Lakes,** *Long-handled underwear*—Heavy wool underwear with long sleeves and legs. Very often they were red in color. **1976** Sublette Co. Artist Guild *More Tales* 351 **WY** (as of c1900), Does Rex wear long handles all year? **1986** Pederson *LAGS Concordance* **Gulf Region,** 5 infs, Long handles—(long *or* men's) underwear; 2 infs, Long-handle(d) underwear; 1 inf, Them long-handle drawers.

longhead n
1 See **long** adj **B2.**
2 See quot. Cf **jughead 1, longear 1**
1950 *WELS* (*Joking names for mules*) 1 Inf, **cwWI,** Longhead.
3 Transf: used as a derog epithet; see quots. Cf **longheaded 2**
1968 *DARE* (Qu. BB53b, . . *A doctor who is not very capable or doesn't have a very good reputation*) Inf **MO34,** Longhead. **1986** Pederson *LAGS Concordance,* 1 inf, **ceTX,** A long head—obstinate, mule-headed.

longheaded adj
1 Discerning, shrewd, foresighted; hence n *longheadedness.* [*OED* a1700 →; cf also *EDD* (at *long* adj. 1.(64)), *SND* (at *lang* adj. I.6.(22))] Cf **long** adj **B2**
1806 (1970) Webster *Compendious Dict.* 179, *Longheaded.* . . having great extent of thought. [*DARE* Ed: This entry does not appear in Webster's English model.] **1864** in 1888 Lowell *Political Essays* 173 **MA,** Mr. Lincoln is a long-headed and long-purposed man. **1866** in 1871 Lowell *Study Windows* 216 **MA,** Ulysses was the type of long-headedness. **1899** (1912) Green *VA Folk-Speech* 267, *Long-headed.* . . Shrewd; far seeing; discerning; as, a *long-headed* man. **1920** Hunter *Trail Drivers TX* 188, For nearly a hundred years, some in Texas, men have been solving problems that required . . the peculiar quality called longheadedness, which is the ability to foresee the effect of untried experiment. **c1960** [see **2** below]. **1986** Pederson *LAGS Concordance,* 1 inf, **ceAL,** Longheaded—having forward-looking ideas.
2 Stubborn, obstinate, pigheaded. **Sth, S Midl** Cf **longhead 2, 3**
1883 (1971) Harris *Nights with Remus* 254 **GA** [Black], Dish yer youngster gittin' too long-headed fer me; dat he is. **1939** *Hall Coll.* **wNC,** "I was long-headed—wasn't afraid of nothin'." (The speaker was a woman of 70, formerly a 'granny woman' or midwife.) **1940** *AmSp* 15.447 **eTN,** *Long headed.* Stubborn. **1954** *Harder Coll.* **cwTN,** *Long-headed.* . . of one who is detested: "He's a long-headed old fool, votin' lak 'at." **c1960** *Wilson Coll.* **csKY,** *Long-headed.* . . Obstinate; usually foresighted. **1966** *DARE* (Qu. GG18, . . '*Obstinate*': "*Why does he have to be so* _____.") Inf **MS45,** Longheaded. **1986** Pederson *LAGS Concordance,* 1 inf, **seGA,** Longheaded—obstinate children.

longheadedness See **longheaded 1**

long-heel n [See quot 1865] Cf **longneck 2**
A Black person; hence adj *long-heeled* (pronc-sp *long-heel*).
[**1865** Bowen *Treatise* 236, *Black* is a part of *negro* in the sense of being only one of his attributes, since he has many others, such as being *long-heeled, prognathous,* &c.] **1955** Warren *Angels* 261 **LA** (as of c1905) [Black], She a colored lady—yeah, she doan look lak it in a pore light, Gin'l, but she long-heel, Gin'l. . . You, ain't you long-heel, Honey? **1960** Wentworth-Flexner *Slang* 324, *Long-heel.* . . A Negro. *Southern white use; archaic.* **1983** Allen *Lang. Ethnic Conflict* 47, *Afro-Americans*—Allusions to Other Physical Differences. . . *long-heels.*

long hog n Cf **side meat**
See quots.
1964 Clarkson *Tumult* 366 [Loggers' words], *Long-hog*—Pork but not in referring to hams or shoulders. Syn[onyms] side meat, sow belly. **1967** *DARE* (Qu. H38, . . *Words for bacon*) Inf **CO5,** Long hog. **1988** *Atlanta Constitution* (GA) 4 Apr 16/3, Long hog was that part of the hog butchered between the shoulder and ham, and part of the tenderloin.

long home n [*OED long home* (at *home* sb.[1] 4) 1303–1722; *EDD* (at *long* adj. 1.(66))] *old-fash* Cf **home E**
The grave, death—usu in phr *go to one's long home* to die.
c1657 in 1965 Wigglesworth *Diary* 115 **MA,** God would come . . and

send them packing to their long home. **c1725** (1942) Byrd *Another Secret Diary* 456, The poor soule is not far from his long home. **1825** Neal *Brother Jonathan* 2.404 **CT**, "Let us go home, Harry," said our hero; after a good hour's walk.—"We are going home."—"To our long home, possibly; but, where now?" **1840** in 1934 Frear *Lowell & Abigail* 154 **MA**, On perusing the Heralds and newspapers and periodicals we find that a large number of our friends and acquaintances are dying off and going to their long home. **1863** in 1962 Truxall *Respects To All* 88 **PA**, I am very sorry to hear of so many of my old acquaintances that had enlisted in the Army that have gone to their long homes. **1863** in 1943 Wiley *Life Johnny Reb* 140 **TX**, If a man treats me well I will stick up to Him till I die and then see that my spirit helps him when I am gone to my long Home. **1912** Green *VA Folk-Speech* 267, *Long-home*. . . When a man dies he goes to his *long-home*. A House not made with hands eternal in the Heavens. **1936** *AmSp* 11.198, [Euphemisms for dying:] Gone to his long home. **1970** *DARE* (QR, near Qu. BB61b) Inf **NJ67**, He's gone to his long home. [Inf old]

longhorn n

1 also attrib; also *Texas longhorn*: A type of long-horned cattle once common in the western states, esp Texas. **chiefly West** Cf **broadhorn 2**

1856 in 1857 IL State Ag. Soc. *Trans.* 2.425, The "long horns" appeal both to our feelings and our pockets, for timely and ample preparations for food and shelter. **1898** Post *10 Yrs. Cowboy* 48 **TX**, Maxwell had in this drive a good round five thousand longhorns, or Texas steers. **1936** McCarthy *Lang. Mosshorn* np **West** [Range terms], *Longhorn*. . . The term was originally applied to a type of cattle brought from Texas. **1946** *Natl. Geogr. Mag.* Jan 17 **NV**, Cattle then were the rangy Texas longhorns—more head, horns, and tail than thick, juicy steaks. **1967–68** *DARE* Tape **CA90**, Then Dad decided to get some milk cows. . . And so he got some cows . . these wild Texas longhorn steers. . . **TX13**, Many herd of longhorn cattle from south Texas cross Oxcart Road near here en route to market. **1972** *Sat. Review* 6 May 20 **TX**, Those are white-faced Herefords and black Angus. . . Don't see many longhorns anymore. **1984** Smith *SW Vocab.* 107, *Long horn:* The breed of cattle raised by ranchers throughout the Southwest in pioneer times. The breed is so named because of the enormous spread of the horns. They were introduced into the Southwest from Mexico, having originated in the high plains of Central Spain. **1986** Pederson *LAGS Concordance*, 2 infs, **AR**, Texas longhorn; 1 inf, **csTX**, Longhorn—draft animal; 1 inf, **cTX**, Longhorn steer; 1 inf, **seFL**, Longhorn.

2 Transf: a Texan or other Southwesterner, esp a savvy, tough old-timer. **chiefly West** Cf **mosshorn**

1896 in 1980 Turner *Earps Talk* 137 (as of 1877), In the vernacular of the feud the . . [Texans] were "longhorns," and the Northerners "shorthorns." **1897** Lewis *Wolfville* 109 **AZ**, Speakin' wide flung an' onrestrained, Cherokee . . is the modestest, decentest longhorn as ever shakes his antlers in Arizona. **1903** (1965) Adams *Log Cowboy* 356, Some of those old long-horns didn't think any more of a twenty-dollar gold piece than I do of a white chip. **1905** *N.Y. Times* 28 May (1939 Thornton *Amer. Gloss.*), There was a big chief on the range, an old longhorn called Abraham, and his lil' ole squaw. **1911** *Century Dict. Suppl.*, *Longhorn*. . . An old inhabitant, shrewd and knowing. [*Century* Ed: Slang, western U.S.] **1929** *AmSp* 4.342 [Vagabond lingo], *Longhorn*—A Texan. **1930** Irwin *Amer. Tramp* 123, *Longhorn*.—A Texan, or any man from the South-West. Taken from the "longhorn" cattle which once ranged the Western ranches. By and large, any wild and rather "hard" individual, one like a "longhorn" in action or habit. **1945** in 1983 McGuire *Taps* 163 **GA** [Black], We often laughed at how the longhorn used to pray when they heard they were going overseas.

3 pl; also *long-horned underwear*: =**long john 1.**

1950 Hemingway *Across the River* 11, I don't have to get up before first light and wear long-horned underwear. **1966** *DARE* (Qu. W14, *Names for underwear. . . Men's—long*) Inf **MS45**, Longhorns.

long-horned owl n Cf **horned owl**
=**long-eared owl.**

1968 *DARE* (Qu. Q2, . . *Kinds of owls*) Inf **NH14**, Long-horned owl.

long-horned underwear See **longhorn 3**

longhorn pepper n Cf **cowhorn 1**
A long hot pepper (*Capsicum* spp).

1966–67 *DARE* (Qu. I22a, . . *Peppers—small hot*) Inf **TX4**, Longhorn [peppers]; (Qu. I22b, . . *Peppers—large hot*) Inf **GA3**, Longhorn peppers.

longhouse n

1 A long, narrow structure used as a communal dwelling or a ceremonial or council building by some American Indian peoples, esp the Iroquois.

1643 Williams *Key into Language* 146, Toward Harvest, when they set up a long house . . sometimes an hundred sometimes two hundred foot long . . where many thousands, men and Women meet, where he that goes in danceth in the sight of all the rest. **1753** (1925) Washington *Diaries* 1.50, We met in Council at the *Long-House*. **1826** Cooper *Last of Mohicans* 1.vi, One branch of this numerous people was seated on a beautiful river . . where the "long house," or Great Council Fire, of the nation was universally admitted to be established. **1906** Ruttenbar *Footprints* 137 **NY**, The Indian Long House was from fifty to six hundred and fifty feet in length by twenty feet in width, the length depending upon the number of persons or families to be accommodated, each family having its own fire. They were formed by saplings set in the ground, the tops bent together and the whole covered with bark. The Five Nations compared their confederacy to a long house reaching, figuratively, from Hudson's River to Lake Erie. **1984** Lesley *Winterkill* 5 **cnOR**, The old village with its salmon-drying shacks and Wy-Am longhouse was gone now. . . Yellow corrugated plastic sealed the east end of the new cedar-shake longhouse. **1994** *DARE* File **csWA** (as of c1940), I don't remember in detail what I saw in the longhouse at Wishram (the town is now under water). . . The part I saw was a dance with a chanter and drums for the music. The men and women were in traditional Indian costume. . . Outside of the longhouse (which was a long, narrow building), were suitcases and Stetson hats, reminding us that they were a part of two worlds.

2 also attrib: Used in ref to traditional American Indian religion; see quots. Cf **longhair**

1949 Graham *Niagara Country* 256, It might be added that the Indians on the Tuscarora Reservation are regarded as Christian rather than "longhouse" Indians. **1967** *DARE* (Qu. CC2, . . *Predominant religious denominations*) Inf **NY18**, Longhouse—Indian religion.

3 A brothel; see quot 1935. Cf **jook n 2**

1933 Hurston in *Story* Aug 68 **FL** [Black], He had come home to buy from her as if she were any woman in the long house. Fifty cents for her love. **1935** Hurston *Mules & Men* 93 **FL**, What does he say when he gets to the jook and the long-house? *Ibid* 307, *Long House*. Another name for jook. Sometimes means a mere bawdy house. A long low building cut into rooms that all open on a common porch. A woman lives in each of the rooms.

longie See **long john 2**

longies n pl **widespread, but chiefly Nth, N Midl** See Map and Map Section
=**long john 1.**

1950 *WELS* (Underwear: long) 21 Infs, **WI**, Longies. **1951** Johnson *Resp. to PADS 20* **DE**, Longies. **1953** in 1960 Wentworth–Flexner *Slang* 324, "The lace-covered pantelettes [sic] which were that day's version of today's 'longies'" C. Lawry. **1957** Battaglia *Resp. to PADS 20* **eMD**, Longies. **1965–70** *DARE* (Qu. W14, *Names for underwear*) 156 Infs, **widespread, but chiefly Nth, N Midl**, Longies; **NJ8**, Men's longies.

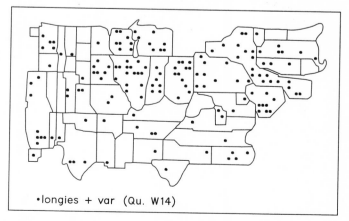

•longies + var (Qu. W14)

longjaw n Also *longjaw chub*, *~ cisco* **Gt Lakes**
A *cisco*: esp *Coregonus alpenae*, but also *C. hoyi* or *C. zenithicus*.
1896 U.S. Natl. Museum *Bulletin* 47.471, *Argyrosomus prognathus* . .

Long Jaw. **1908** Forbes–Richardson *Fishes of IL* 55, *A[rgyrosomus] prognathus*, the longjaw . . [is] more or less commonly taken in Lake Michigan. **1941** Writers' Program *Guide WI* 453 **nwWI,** In 1938, 18 fishing boats, from 26-foot cabin cruisers to 60-foot tugs, all equipped with gasoline engines, operated from this base. They range as far as Isle Royale for trout, whitefish, and longjaw. **1947** Hubbs–Lagler *Fishes Gt. Lakes* 42, Longjaw chub—*Leucichthys alpenae* . . Lakes Michigan and Huron at various depths. **1983** Becker *Fishes WI* 350, *Coregonus zenithicus* . . longjaw. *Ibid* 353, Longjaw Cisco—*Coregonus alpenae* . . Other common names: the longjaw, longjaw chub.

long-jawed adj
Long-drawn-out, long-winded; tiresome.
    1911 *Century Dict. Suppl., Long-jawed.* . . Extended; long-drawn: said of a long-winded person or a great talker. **1975** Gould *ME Lingo* 168, A tiresome speech is *long-jawed,* and it's a *long-jawed* walk to round up a stray cow.

long jeans n pl Also *jeans* **scattered, but esp C Atl, NEast**
See Map
=**long john 1.**
    [**1889** *Century Dict.* 3223, *Jean.* . . A twilled cotton cloth, used both for underwear and for outer clothing: commonly, of garments, in the plural.] **1965–70** DARE (Qu. W14, *Names for underwear, including joking names*) 16 Infs, **scattered, but esp C Atl, NEast,** Long jeans; **NJ**53, **NY**165, (Red) jeans; **WA**9, Jeans, [corr to] long johns.

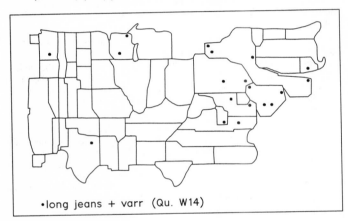

•long jeans + varr (Qu. W14)

long john n
1 pl; also *johns, long johnnies:* Long underwear. **widespread, but somewhat less freq Sth, S Midl** See Map Cf **long** n C, **long drawers, ~ handles, longhorn 3, longies, long jeans, ~ leg 2**
    1943 St. George *c/o Postmaster* 12, Some odd garments affectionately known as "longjohns." **1950** *WELS,* 12 Infs, **WI,** Long johns. **1957** Battaglia *Resp. to PADS* 20 **eMD,** Long johns. **1957** *Daily Progress* (Charlottesville VA) 13 Nov 16/4 *(Hench Coll.),* Now long johns come in the quilted down suit, therma knit . . and other styles and fabrics. . . Long live the long johns! **1958** McCulloch *Woods Words* 112 **Pacific NW,** Long Johns—Same as long handle underwear. **c1960** Wilson Coll. **csKY,** *Long johns.* . . Men's long underwear. **1965–70** DARE (Qu.

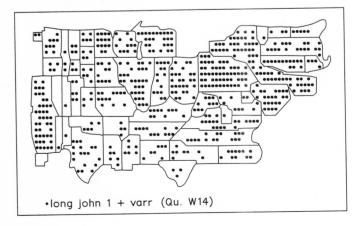

•long john 1 + varr (Qu. W14)

W14, *Names for underwear, including joking names*) 579 Infs, **widespread, but somewhat less freq Sth, S Midl,** Long johns; **KS**18, **PA**26, 29, **VT**3, Johns; **LA**33, **PA**139, Long johnnies. **1976** Garber *Mountainese* 55 **sAppalachians,** Be shore to wear yore long-johns when you go deer huntin'. **1977** *Yankee* Nov 57 **ME,** Once the lights were out, he would step out into the night air in his longjohns to sniff the air and consult the sky. **1986** Pederson *LAGS Concordance* **Gulf Region,** 3 infs, Long johns—(winter *or* long) underwear; 1 inf, Long johns—underwear, facetious; 1 inf, Long johns—what I wear in the wintertime; [1 inf, Long john is underwear—not [a] doughnut]. **1991** Still *Wolfpen Notebooks* 162 **sAppalachians,** *Long-johns:* long underwear.

2 also *longie:* An oblong pastry, usu with a cream or jelly filling and often frosted or glazed. **scattered, but chiefly Upper Missip Valley, Upper MW, Plains States, MI** See Map Cf **bismarck 1, Chicago B2, long boy 2, maple bar**
    1945 *Hench Coll.* **cVA,** Talking about the awful food that the children are offered at . . [s]chool. The thing she thinks is the worst is a *long john,* a long round hollow cake with something like whipped cream inside. **1948** [see **lunch roll**]. **1949** in 1986 DARE File **seMI,** Long John, offered on the breakfast menu at the drug store next to Slater's, is described as a long rectangular piece of pastry, a breakfast roll with cocoanut and nuts and a cream filling. **1950** Bissell *Stretch on River* 53, We carried the damnedest assortment of food aboard that old tugboat—. . long johns. **1950** *WELS* **WI** (*Names for different shapes or sizes of [doughnuts]*) 13 Infs, Long john(s); (*A long cake cooked the same way*) 30 Infs, Long john. **1965–70** DARE (Qu. H30, *An oblong cake, cooked in deep fat*) 161 Infs, **scattered, but chiefly Upper Missip Valley, Upper MW, Plains States, MI,** Long john; **IL**49, Longie; (Qu. H28, *Different shapes or types of doughnuts*) 17 Infs, **chiefly IL, IN, MI, WI,** Long john; (Qu. H29) Inf **IL**134, Long john; (Qu. H32, . . *Fancy rolls and pastries*) Inf **OR**5, Long johns—[with] whipped cream. **1966** DARE Tape **NM**7, [Inf:] We had sweet rolls of any description you wanted: cream puffs, eclairs, long johns, doughnuts. [FW:] What's a long john? [Inf:] It's a doughnut that's [a] long, cut strip. **1967** *Galena Gaz. & Advt.* (IL) 29 June 2/7, Cream Filled Long Johns Reg. 90¢ Dozen 75¢. **1967** DARE FW Addit **WA,** Long john—a maple bar cake, cut, with rum-flavored whipped cream and dusted with powdered sugar. **1973** Allen *LAUM* 1.281 (as of c1950), *Doughnut* (made with sweetened, unleavened dough). . . long John [1 inf, **seIA**]. *Ibid* 282, *Doughnut* (made with slightly sweetened and leavened dough). . . long John: Long and sugar coated [1 inf, **seND**]. **1986** Pederson *LAGS Concordance* **Gulf Region** (*Kinds of things . . you buy at a bakery*) 5 infs, Long john; 1 inf, Long john—something like an eclair; 1 inf, Long john—straight, not twisted; 1 inf, Long john—rectangular, [with] icing; 1 inf, Long john—long sweet bread, like wiener bun; 1 inf, Long john is [a] piece of sweet bread what has, it's a doughnut really, but it's long, and it's got lemon filling inside; 1 inf, Long johns—long, thin, frosted; 1 inf, Long johns—oblong jelly doughnuts; (*Doughnut*) 1 inf, Long john—bar-shaped, has jelly inside; 1 inf, Long johns—seen in bakeries, glaze, filling.

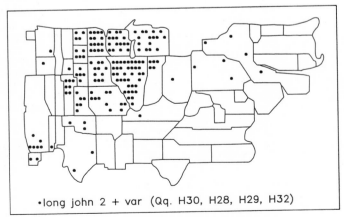

•long john 2 + var (Qq. H30, H28, H29, H32)

3 See quot. Cf **long boy 1, submarine sandwich**
    1966–69 DARE (Qu. H40, *A small sausage that is put into a long roll or bun to make a sandwich*) Inf **IL**99, Long john; (Qu. H42x, . . *[A sandwich] . . in a much larger, longer bun, that's a meal in itself;* not asked in early QRs) Infs **IN**70, **NC**11, Long john; **MN**37, Long john—piled long [FW queries]; **TX**43, Long john [FW: Inf uncertain].

4 pl: =**tom walkers.** Cf **johnny walkers**

1968 *DARE* (Qu. EE35, *Long wooden poles with a footpiece that children walk around on to make them tall*) Inf **NC**53, Long johns.

5 A type of sleigh; see quot.

1968 *DARE* (Qu. N40a, . . *Sleighs . . for hauling loads*) Inf **OH**56, Long john—for parties.

6 A **ginseng B1** (here: *Panax quinquefolium*).

1968 *Foxfire* Mar 73, Sang hunters would try to find out where their competitors had success, and in turn would keep their own finds a secret, referring to the plant by the name of a person such as Pete or Long John, or merely as "the little green man."

7 An **earthworm** or similar worm. Cf **john-jumper 1**

1986 Pederson *LAGS Concordance* (Earthworm) 1 inf, **neGA**, Long johns; 1 inf, **swGA**, Long johns— a foot long or so; 1 inf, **ceAL**, Long john—pink worm.

long johnnies See **long john 1**

long jumper See **jumper 6**

longleaf pine n [Cf **leaf** n¹ **B1**]

1 also *longleaf, long-leafed pine, long-leaved ~:* A large **pine** (*Pinus palustris*) native chiefly to the southern US which has conspicuously long needles. Also called **broom pine, brown ~, fat ~ 1, Florida ~, Georgia ~, hard ~ 1, heart ~, hill ~, long-needle ~, longstraw ~ 1, pitch ~, red ~, rosemary ~, rosin ~, southern ~, swamp ~, turpentine ~, Virginia ~, yellow ~**

1765 (1942) Bartram *Diary of a Journey* 14 **SC**, Trees which naturaly grows there is . . very fine long-leaved pine[,] pitch pine[,] yapon[,] fartle berry[,] chinkapin. **1792** Pope *Tour U.S.* 46 **FL**, Notwithstanding the natural Sterility of Soil . . the Long-leaf'd *Pine, Hickory, . .* and *Walnut* Trees grow to their usual Height. **1832** Browne *Sylva* 229, This invaluable tree [=*Pinus australis*] is known both in the countries which produce it, and in those to which it is imported, by different names: in the first it is called *Long-leaved Pine, Yellow Pine, Pitch Pine* and *Broom Pine.* . . We have preferred the first denomination, because this species has longer leaves than any other eastward of the Mississippi. **1896** Mohr–Roth *Timber Pines* 28, Local or Common Names. . . Longleaved Pine (Del., N.C., S.C., Ga., Ala., Fla., Miss., La., Tex.) . . Georgia Longleaved Pine (Atlantic region) . . Florida Longleaved Pine (Atlantic region) . . Texas Longleaved Pine (Atlantic region). **1904** (1905) Watson *Bethany* 8 **GA**, Ours was just a plain house . . built . . of timbers torn from the heart of the long-leaf Georgia pine. **1933** Rawlings *South Moon* 119 **nFL**, Towards Riverside men had boxed the long-leaf yellow pine; had sent out rosin and turpentine, leaving the great trees to rot before their time. **1965–70** *DARE* (Qu. T17, . . *Kinds of pine trees;* not asked in early QRs) 137 Infs, **chiefly Sth, Midl**, Longleaf pine; **TN**22, Georgia longleaf pine; (Qu. T5, . . *Kinds of evergreens, other than pine*) Infs **FL**18, 34, **NC**18, Longleaf pine; **DC**8, Longleaf; (Qu. T16, . . *Kinds of trees . . 'special'*) Infs **FL**16, 18, 22, **NJ**56, **NC**3, **TX**35, Longleaf pine. [*DARE* Ed: Some of these Infs may refer instead to **2** below.] **1966** *DARE* Tape **MS**14, This part was known as the longleaf pine area. **1976** Bruce *How to Grow Wildflowers* 26, These [=needles] are quite long in the Loblolly Pine, and enormously long in its close relative, the Longleaf Pine of farther south—so long in the latter species that one common name, "Broom Pine," alludes to the practice of making brooms from bundles of the dried needles. **1986** Pederson *LAGS Concordance* **Gulf Region** (*Common trees*) 26 infs, Longleaf pine(s); 7 infs, Longleaf; 1 inf, Longleaf pine.

2 also *long-leaved pine:* Any of var other **pines** with long needles such as Apache pine (*Pinus engelmannii*), **loblolly pine 1**, ponderosa ~, or a **pitch** ~ (here: *Pinus rigida*); see quots.

1897 Sudworth *Arborescent Flora* 20, *Pinus ponderosa.* . . Longleaved Pine (Utah, Nev.) *Ibid, Pinus ponderosa scopulorum.* . . Longleaved Pine (Colo.) *Ibid* 26, *Pinus rigida.* . . Long-leaved Pine (Del.) **1908** Britton *N. Amer. Trees* 25, It [=*Pinus ponderosa*] is also called Yellow pine, Big pine, Longleaf pine [etc]. *Ibid* 31, It [=*Pinus rigida*] is known by many names, such as Hard Pine, Long-leaved pine [etc]. **1950** Moore *Trees AR* 17, Loblolly Pine (*Pinus taeda* L.)—Local names . . Longleaf Pine. (Not to be confused with *Pinus palustris*, the longleaf pine of the Gulf region). **1960** Vines *Trees SW* 16, It [=*Pinus engelmannii*] is also known under the vernacular name of Arizona Longleaf Pine. **1980** Little *Audubon Guide N. Amer. Trees W. Region* 277, "Arizona Longleaf Pine"—*Pinus engelmannii. Ibid* 278, The seedlings pass

through a grasslike stage with a short stem and very long needles to 15″ (38 cm) as does Longleaf Pine (*Pinus palustris . .*) in the Southeast.

longleaf slash pine See **slash pine**

long-leaved pine See **longleaf pine 1, 2**

long leg n

1 The drumstick of a chicken.

1960 Criswell *Resp. to PADS 20* **Ozarks**, Long leg. . . drumstick of a chicken; thigh piece is the short leg. **1986** Pederson *LAGS Concordance*, 1 inf, **seFL**, The long leg of a chicken.

2 pl: =**long john 1**.

1969 *DARE* (Qu. W14, *Names for underwear . . women's—long*) Inf **WI**76, Long legs.

long-leg crane See **longlegs 3**

long-leg drawers See **long drawers**

long-legged adj

Of a ship: see quots.

1905 Wasson *Green Shay* 274 **NEng**, She's an extry long-legged [Footnote: Deep] built vessel, and her stern is going to be hove out all high and dry. **1911** *Century Dict. Suppl., Long-legged.* . . Having a great draft of water; said of a vessel of great length, or long in comparison with its beam. **1975** Gould *ME Lingo* 168, *Long-legged*—A vessel with a deep bottom disproportionate to beam.

long-legged crane See **longlegs 3**

long-legged drink of water See **long drink of water**

long-legged duck n Also *long-legged tree duck* =**tree duck** (here: *Dendrocygna* spp).

1858 Baird *Birds* 770 **TX**, Long-legged Duck. . . Valley of Rio Grande. **1898** (1900) Davie *Nests N. Amer. Birds* 103, The Autumnal Tree-duck is a species of variegated plumage and long legs. . . It is commonly called "Long-legged Tree-duck." **1898** Elliot *Wild Fowl* 95 **LA**, *Fulvous Tree Duck.* . . Called . . the Yellow-bellied Fiddler Duck, and Long-legged Duck. **1911** *Forest & Stream* 77.173 **LA**, *Dendrocygna bicolor.* . . Long-legged Duck. **1918** Grinnell *Game Birds CA* 251, *Dendrocygna autumnalis* . . Long-legged Duck. **1923** U.S. Dept. Ag. *Misc. Circular* 13.51, *Dendrocygna autumnalis.* . . Cornfield duck, long-legged duck, summer duck. The last three are said to be vernacular use in Texas. [**1977** Bull–Farrand *Audubon Field Guide Birds* 422, *Dendrocygna bicolor.* . . These long-legged ducks do most of their feeding on land, eating green grass, seeds, and acorns.]

long-legged Mother Carey's chicken See **Mother Carey's chicken 1**

long-legged mouse n

A **jumping mouse 1** (here: *Zapus hudsonicus*).

1961 Jackson *Mammals WI* 262, *Zapus zapus hudsonicus.* . . In Wisconsin usually called jumping mouse or jumping jack. Other names include . . long-legged mouse.

long-legged sandpiper n

=**stilt sandpiper**.

1828 NY Acad. Sci. *Annals Lyceum Nat. Hist.* 2.316, *Long-legged Sandpiper.* . . Inhabits the middle states in summer and autumn. **1844** Giraud *Birds Long Is.* 232 **NY**, *Tringa himantopus.* . . On Long Island, the Long-legged Sandpiper is not abundant. **1898** (1900) Davie *Nests N. Amer. Birds* 136, The Long-legged Sandpiper, of slender form and very long legs, breeds north of the United States. **1944** Hausman *Amer. Birds* 285, Stilt Sandpiper—*Micropalamus himantopus* . . Other Names—Frost Snipe . . Long-legged Sandpiper, Mongrel. **1963** Gromme *Birds WI* 217, Sandpiper, . . Long-legged (Stilt Sandpiper).

long-legged spider n Also *longleg spider* [*OED* (at *long-legged*) 1848] Cf **longlegs 1**

Prob =**daddy longlegs 1**.

1967–70 *DARE* (Qu. R28, . . *Kinds of spiders*) Inf **MO**21, Long-legged spider; **NJ**67, Longleg spider.

long-legged tree duck See **long-legged duck**

longlegger n Cf **codhead**

1924 *DN* 5.286 **Cape Cod MA**, The hip-length gum boot is called 'longlegger', a name which is quite appropriate.

longlegs n

1 Prob =**daddy longlegs 1**. Cf **long-legged spider**

1911 *Century Dict.* 3512, *Long-legs.* . . An insect having long legs, such as . . the spiders of the family *Phalangiidae.* See *daddy-long-legs.* **1968** *DARE* (Qu. R28, . . *Kinds of spiders*) Inf **IN**34, Longlegs. **1986** Pederson *LAGS Concordance,* 1 inf, **cAL**, Long legs—[a] spider.

2 =**black-necked stilt**. [*OED* 1713 →] Cf **daddy longlegs 5, longshanks 2**

1929 Forbush *Birds MA* 1.384, The Black-necked Stilt is known in parts of its range as . . "Long-legs" and "Daddy-long-legs" in some localities. Despite its apparently unnecessarily long legs, it is a graceful and handsome bird. **1946** Hausman *Eastern Birds* 294, Black-necked Stilt—*Himantopus mexicanus.* . . Stilt, . . Longlegs. **1967** *DARE* (Qu. Q8) Inf **NJ**1, Longlegs.

3 also *long-leg(ged) crane:* =**great blue heron**. Cf **long Tom 5**

1966–69 *DARE* (Qu. Q10, . . *Water birds and marsh birds*) Inf **IA**3, Longlegs; **MS**16, Long-leg crane; **MO**32, Long-legged crane.

longleg spider See **long-legged spider**

longlick n esp **MA** Cf **lick** n 7, **long sugar, ~ sweetening**
Molasses.

1897 (1909) Bullen *Cruise Cachalot* 6, A pot of something sweetened with "longlick" (molasses), made an apology for a meal. **1924** *DN* 5.286 **Cape Cod MA**, Few grocers outside of Cape Cod would know what to produce when someone asked for a gallon of 'Porty Reek long lick'. But a real Cape Codder would know that a gallon of Porto [*sic*] Rico molasses was desired. **1937** FWP *Guide MA* 331, Molasses was 'Porty Reek long-lick,' or 'long-tailed sugar.' **1941** Cleaveland *No Life* 163 **NM**, Lick is syrup, molasses, or any viscous sweetening. There was a distinction between 'short lick,' sugar, and 'long lick.'

long-lifed adj [Var of *long-lived;* cf *OED* long-lif't (at *long-lived*) 17th cent]

1909 *DN* 3.346 **eAL, wGA**, *Long-lifed.* . . Long-lived. **1949** *Sun* (Baltimore MD) 12 Apr 4/1 (*Hench Coll.*), [Headline:] Editor Starts Debate Over Long-Lifed Cats.

long line n Cf **skinner**
=**jerk line 1**—used in comb *long-line skinner* a driver of a large team of draft animals.

1927 *DN* 5.454 [Underworld jargon], *Long line skinner.* . . A driver of a mule team of more than one pair. **1927** *AmSp* 2.392 [Vagabond argot], A teamster, on construction jobs and on western ranches, is a *skinner,* because he skins up the animals with the reins. He is facetiously known as a *long-line skinner.* **1964** Jackman–Long *OR Desert* 276, The "long line skinner," driver of the jerk-line teams . . was hundreds of times more useful than the short-lived pony express . . . [H]e kept entire communities supplied with goods. **1969** *DARE* FW Addit **nCA** [Teamster talk], *Long-line skinner*—a jerk line driver.

long loop See **long rope**

longman n [*OED* (at *long* a.[1] A.18) "Obs."; *EDD* (at *long* adj. 1.(105))] Cf **littleman, long finger 1, middleman 2, tallman**
The middle finger.

1950 *PADS* 13.17 **cTX** (as of 1911–50), The form in Runnels County was *little-man* ['lɪtlmən], *leeman, longman, lick-pot,* and *thumb-ball.* **1972** Jones–Hawes *Step it Down* 12 **eGA** [Black], John Davis . . told us the finger names he had learned when he was a boy on St. Simons [*sic*] Island: thumb, potlicker, longman, lingman, littleman.

long milk n

1973 Allen *LAUM* 1.291 (as of c1950), For milk that has become so sour as to form curds. . . *long milk* and *tet milk* proffered by a Swedish inf. in northern Minnesota.

long minnow n
A **minnow B1** (here: *Macrhybopsis aestivalis*).

1943 Eddy–Surber *N. Fishes* 132, Speckled Dace (Long Minnow). . . reaches a length of 2½ inches [and] . . ranges from southern Minnesota and Ohio to Alabama. **1983** Becker *Fishes WI* 495, Speckled Chub. . . Other common names: long minnow; northern longnose chub.

long moss n
=**Spanish moss** (here: *Tillandsia* spp).
[**1744** in 1840 GA Hist. Soc. *Coll.* 1.105, I observed here a kind of long moss I had never seen before.] **a1782** (1788) Jefferson *Notes VA* 39, Long moss. *Tillandsia Usneoides.* **1827** *Western Mth. Rev.* 1.315

seLA, Palmetto, or latanier, peet, and long moss, add an aspect of novelty to the view in the eye of strangers. **1851** (1969) Burke *Polly Peablossom* 128 **MS**, From their branches grow in profusion the Spanish long moss. **1903** Murrie *White Castle LA* 40, The whole fence was festooned with black moss, which had been hung to dry by the occupant, whose business was making horse-collars of the long moss gathered in the adjacent woods. **1941** Writers' Program *Guide LA* 24, Spanish moss, or "long moss" (*Tillandsia usneoides*), grows profusely in southern Louisiana and more rarely in the northernmost part of the State. **1974** Morton *Folk Remedies* 153 **SC**, Spanish Moss . . Florida Moss; Long-Moss. . . Coastal plain of South Carolina and North Carolina, north to Virginia, south to southern Florida and west to Texas.

long mouth n Cf *DJE* long out one's mouth (at *long out*)

1922 Gonzales *Black Border* 311 **sSC, GA coasts** [Gullah glossary], *Longmout'*—long mouth—descriptive of the surly or contemptuous pushing out of the lips of an angry or discontented Negro.

longneck n

1 also *longnecker:* A liquor or beer bottle, esp one with an elongated neck; such a bottle with its contents. Cf **fruit jar**

1907 *DN* 3.246 **eME**, *Long-necker.* . . Round quart whiskey-bottle. **1914** *DN* 4.76 **nNH, ME**, *Long-necker.* . . A bottle of hard liquor. **1969** Sorden *Lumberjack Lingo* 74 **NEng, Gt Lakes**, Long neck—A bottle of whisky. **1981** Jenkins *Baja OK* 216 **nTX**, Juanita sang: *He wore a longneck in his hand and he hardly ever grinned.* **1986** Pederson *LAGS Concordance,* 1 inf, **csTX**, Longnecks—glass beer bottles; 1 inf, **csTX**, Long live longnecks—bumper sticker for beer. **1988** [see **icehouse 2b**]. **1990** *Village Voice* (NY NY) 24 July 158, In the clubhouse the pitchers sit in silence before their lockers, numbly sipping from long-necks; the hitters exit quickly, choosing to say Kaddish over their dead bats in the privacy of the bridge traffic. **1995** *DARE* File **cTX**, Longnecks—beer bottles, of course, and not the disposable ones or cans. . . "Grab some longnecks and I'll meet you by the river." (It's easier to carry a handful of beer bottles if they are longnecks!)

2 A White person. Cf **long-heel, red-neck**

1986 Pederson *LAGS Concordance* (A Caucasian) 1 inf, **seMS**, Long-neck—inf never used [this term] himself; (*The poor whites, white man's terms*) 1 inf, **seMS**, Longneck—poor whites use [this term]; (*The poor whites, black man's terms*) 1 inf, **seMS**, Longnecks—unsure of meaning. [All infs Black]

3 also *long-necked duck:* =**pintail** (here: *Anas acuta*).

1888 Trumbull *Names of Birds* 39 **NJ**, At Pleasantville and Atlantic City we hear Long-neck for the pintail duck. **1946** Hausman *Eastern Birds* 143, American Pintail. . . Other Names . . Long-necked Duck. . . Field Marks—Long, graceful neck. **1955** MA Audubon Soc. *Bulletin* 39.314, Pintail. . . Long-neck (Mass. Also a British provincial name.) **1982** Elman *Hunter's Field Guide* 156, Pintail. . . longneck. [*Ibid* 157, The back of the neck, almost as long as that of a small goose, is black or dark brown, shading into the gray of the back.]

4 See **long-neck squash**.

5 See **long clam 1**.

long-neck(ed) clam See **long clam 1**

long-necked duck See **longneck 3**

long-necked goose n Cf **short-necked goose**
=**Canada goose**.

1925 (1928) Forbush *Birds MA* 1.292, *Branta canadensis canadensis.* . . Other names: wild goose; honker; long-necked goose. **1955** MA Audubon Soc. *Bulletin* 39.313, Canada Goose. . . Long-necked Goose (Mass. For the larger Canada subspecies.) **1982** Elman *Hunter's Field Guide* 269, Canada Goose (*Branta canadensis*)—Common and Regional Names . . wild goose, long-necked goose.

long-necked squash See **long-neck squash**

longnecker See **longneck 1**

long-neck squash n Also *long-handled squash, longneck, long-necked squash* Cf **gooseneck squash**
A summer squash (here: *Cucurbita pepo* var).

1835 *Vade Mecum* (Phila.) 10 Jan. 3/4 (*DA*), The editor of the National Eagle. . . offered a couple of long necked squashes, a huge pumpkin, and flour enough to make them into pies, for the best New Year's Address. **1868** (1870) Gray *Field Botany* 160, *Long-neck* . . *Squash.* . . Fruit mostly hard-fleshed at maturity. **1889** *Century Dict.* 1388, *Cucurbita.* . . *C. Pepo* and its varieties yield the pumpkin, the warty, long-neck, and crookneck squashes and vegetable marrow. **1965–70** *DARE* (Qu.

I23, . . *Kinds of squash*) 14 Infs, **scattered,** Long-neck squash; **IN**76, **MI**44, **MO**6, **PA**206, **TX**11, Long-necked squash; **MO**1, Long-necks; **GA**1, Long-handled squash. **1986** Pederson *LAGS Concordance (Squash)* 2 infs, **seMS, cnLA,** Longneck (squash).

long-needle pine n Also *long needle, long-needled pine* Cf **shortleaf pine**

A **longleaf pine 1** or any **pine** with notably long needles.

    1965–70 *DARE* (Qu. T17, . . *Kinds of pine trees; not asked in early QRs*) 19 Infs, **chiefly Nth, N Midl,** Long needle; **AL**8, **MO**7, 21, **NJ**2, 58, **UT**10, **WV**5, Long-needle(d) pine; (Qu. T5, . . *Kinds of evergreens, other than pine*) Infs **MI**67, **NM**6, Long-needle pine; **DC**8, Long needle.

longnose n

    1 A busybody or meddler. [Cf *EDD* **longneb** "a prominent nose . . *fig.* of an impertinent intrusion; . . **long-nebbit** . . prying" (at *long* adj. 1.(110),(111))]

    1938 in **1942** *AmSp* 17.104 [Truck driver lingo], *Long nose.* Snooper or spotter. **1968–69** *DARE* (Qu. GG36a, *The kind of person who is always poking into other people's affairs:* "She's an awful _____.") Infs **IN**75, **WI**20, Longnose.

    2 See **longnose gar.**

    3 See **longnose sucker.**

longnose dace n Also *long-nosed dace*

A **dace** (here: *Rhinichthys cataractae*). Also called **gudgeon 1, minnow B1, rock minnow, stream shooter**

    1882 U.S. Natl. Museum *Bulletin* 16.207, *R[hinichthys] cataractae* . . Long-nosed Dace. . . Head long, the muzzle flattened, narrowed, and extremely prominent. **1906** NJ State Museum *Annual Rept. for 1905* 150, Long Nosed Dace. Dace. . . This little dace—for it never exceeds more than 5 inches—differs from the common species in the long prominent snout, which projects well beyond the mouth. **1943** Eddy–Surber *N. Fishes* 132, Great Lakes Longnose Dace (Black Minnow). **1963** Sigler–Miller *Fishes UT* 85, The longnose dace occurs chiefly in cool to cold creeks and rivers. **1983** Becker *Fishes WI* 472, Longnose Dace. . . Other common names: longnosed dace, Great Lakes longnose dace.

long-nosed gar(pike) See **longnose gar**

long-nosed sucker See **longnose sucker**

long-nosed wind splitter See **wind splitter**

longnose gar n Also *longnose, long-nosed gar(pike)* [*OED* 1836 →]

A **gar** n **1** (here: *Lepisosteus osseus*). Also called **billfish 2, bony pike, garpike, great gar, swordfish** Cf **shortnose gar**

    1882 U.S. Natl. Museum *Bulletin* 16.91, *L[epidosteus] osseus.* . . Long-nosed Gar. . . Snout a little more than twice the length of the rest of the head. **1889** *Century Dict.* 2453, *Long-nosed gar, Lepidosteus osseus,* the common garpike or bill-fish, attaining a length of 5 feet, of which the head is about one third, found in North America from the great lakes to Carolina and Mexico. **1933** LA Dept. of Conserv. *Fishes* 404, [Caption:] Most widely distributed of all the Gars, the Long-nosed Gar-pike or Billfish occurs from the Great Lakes to the Gulf Coast, and, like its relatives, carries on, steadily and stealthily, its sinister work of destruction. **1943** Eddy–Surber *N. Fishes* 65, The snout is narrower than that of the shortnose but is not as narrow as that of the longnose. *Ibid,* Northern Longnose Gar. . *Lepisosteus osseus oxyurus.* . . The longnose gar. **1983** Becker *Fishes WI* 244, Longnose Gar. . . Other common names: northern longnose gar, gar, garpike [etc].

longnose sucker n Also *longnose, long-nosed sucker*

A **sucker** (here: *Catostomus catostomus*). Also called **black sucker, mullet n¹ 2, red sucker, sturgeon ~**

    1878 U.S. Natl. Museum *Bulletin* 12.175, Long-nosed Sucker. . . New England to Nebraska and north to Alaska and the Arctic Sea. **1886** Mather *Memoranda* 33 **NY,** Long-nosed sucker, generally [so called]. . . This species is common in most Adirondack waters and is readily distinguished by its long nose. **1908** Forbes–Richardson *Fishes of IL* 84, *Long-nosed Sucker.* . . Found in lower Lake Michigan at Miller, Indiana, and doubtless occurring in the lake within the limits of Illinois. **1950** Everhart *Fishes ME* 33, The young of the longnose, as the other suckers, are of value as forage fish. **1971** Brown *Fishes MT* 122, The longnose sucker . . is generally disliked by fishermen who find it a nuisance and suspect it of damage to the game fish population. . . The flesh of the longnose sucker is white and tasty but the profusion of bones

discourages its use. **1991** Amer. Fisheries Soc. *Common Names Fishes* 24, *Catostomus catostomus* . . longnose sucker.

long oat n [See *EDD* **to give a horse long corn** (or *oats*) to whip it (at *long* adj. 1.(113))] Cf **oatburner**

    [**1896** Farmer–Henley *Slang* 4.228, Long-oats . . (military).—A broom or fork-handle used to belabour a horse.] **1969** Sorden *Lumberjack Lingo* 74 **NEng, Gt Lakes,** Long oat—The horse whip used by teamsters on tote roads and long haul roads.

'long of See **along of**

'long-of-the-path adj phr Cf **of B1h**

    1950 *PADS* 14.45 **SC,** Long-o'-de-paat chillun [ˌlɔŋ-ə-də-ˈpæːt]. . Illegitimate children. Children begotten *along the path.* Negro usage.

long out v phr [Cf *OED* **long** v.¹ I.1. "To grow longer; to lengthen. *Obs.*"] Cf **long** adj **B1**

To grow tall.

    1987 Kytle *Voices* 163 **NC** [Black], He favored his mother, and when he was little he was real pretty. Like a big fat doll. Older, when he longed out and shaped up, he was trim-built but well set up and noways poor.

long pasture n [*EDD* (at *long* adj. 1.(117)) "the pasture on the roadside"]

    1984 Weaver *TX Crude* 117, Long pasture. Right of way along roadsides, where cattle are sometimes staked out to graze.

long potato n

=**sweet potato.**

    1808 Ashe *Travels America* 58, [*Popular Name:*] Long Potatoes.—[*Linnean Name:*] Convolvulas [sic] Batatas. **1899** (**1912**) Green *VA Folk-Speech* 267, Long-potatoes. . . Sweet potatoes.

long red n esp **S Midl** Cf **long green (tobacco)**

A high-quality grade of tobacco leaf; see quots 1944, 1970.

    1944 *PADS* 2.67 **S Midl** [Tobacco words], *Long-red.* . . The (small) upper leaves of high marketable quality. **1949** Arnow *Hunter's Horn* 69 **KY,** LeeRoy sat a long time . . not far from the schoolhouse and took a chew of long red. **1960** Williams *Walk Egypt* 204 **GA,** He had taken to raising Burley and had two acres. . . At the last sale the "long red" had fetched fifteen cents a pound. **1967** Key *Tobacco Vocab.* 135 **TN, MO,** Long red. **1970** *DARE* Tape **KY**72, When the tobacco is stripped, it is put in anyway from two to six grades. . . mostly it's trash or flyings, and lugs, and leaf, and red—long red, short red—and tips, and then . . oftentimes you have your green grade that you have to pick out of this tobacco and . . sell separately.

long rider n **West**

An outlaw.

    1936 Adams *Cowboy Lingo* 161, Members of the lawless fraternity of the West were 'outlaws,' 'long riders,' . . and 'road-agents.' **1941** Writers' Program *Guide WY* 129, 'Long riders' robbed mines and pay-roll trains and spent their money freely over hand carved bars. **1963** Burroughs *Head-First* 178 **CO** (as of 1900–20), The Steamboat Springs youngster who did not aspire to be either a cavalryman, a bronco buster, or possibly, a long rider . . was indeed a queer fish.

long rooter See **rooter**

long rope n Also *long loop* **West**

Used in var combs and phrr in ref to a cattle thief; hence n *long roper.*

    1924 James *Cowboys N. & S.* 95, If Bob would of had better luck the first time . . , most likely by now he'd been just a prosperous cowman and kept his "long ropes" to home. **1931** James *Big-Enough* 155 **West,** [He'd been anxious to have a good size herd quick, and he begin to using his rope and a running iron, and claiming cattle that wasn't his.] *Ibid* 165, They just had a failing for using the "long rope," got a lot of pleasure in the dangerous work of changing a brand, and pride in how they'd get away with it. . . The big stockmen . . also went to hiring "Long rope artists." Them riders stole from inside of the territory. **1936** McCarthy *Lang. Mosshorn* np **West** [Range terms], *Packin' a Long Rope.* A cowboy suspected of or known to be rustling cattle. **1936** Adams *Cowboy Lingo* 158, He [=the rustler] was also spoken of by such names as 'brand-burner,' . . 'long rope,' or 'rope and ring man.' **1941** Cleaveland *No Life* 97 **cwNM,** The more successful of our business competitors were those who 'swung a long loop' and got more than their proportional share of the 'longears,' calves as yet unbranded but old enough to wean. **1965** *DARE* File **West,** But it's the cattle thief that really catches it. He's a rustler, a brand-burner, a brand-artist₍₃₎ a long-roper and an outlaw. **1979** *NYT Article Letters* **ceAL** [Cowboy lingo],

A 'long rope' was used by a rustler reaching into someone else's territory.

long-runner n Cf **double-runner, long sled**
    1966 *DARE* (Qu. N40a, . . *Sleighs . . for hauling loads*) Inf **NH**5, Long-runner—up to half a ton.

longs See **long** v

long sauce n *obs* Cf **garden sauce, green ~, short ~, sauce**
Root vegetables, esp those with elongated roots; a prepared dish of such vegetables.
    1809 Irving *Hist. NY* 1.176, To this end he takes unto himself for a wife, some dashing country heiress . . deeply skilled in the mystery of making apple sweetmeats, long sauce and pumpkin pie. **1815** Humphreys *Yankey in England* 41, Long sairse and short sairse; consisting of a variety of leetle notions too tedious to mention, among which were inions, parsnips, butter, candles, soap, and ile. **1853** *S. Lit. Messenger* 19.666, Cabbages, beets, turnips, and "long sarce" abound. **1859** (1968) Bartlett *Americanisms* 255, *Long Sauce*. Beets, carrots, and parsnips are *long sauce*. Potatoes, turnips, onions, pumpkins, etc. are *short sauce*. **1872** Schele de Vere *Americanisms* 397, The *Sass* of New England is scientifically spoken of as *Long Sauce*, when beets, carrots, parsnips, and the like are referred to, and as *Short Sauce*, if onions are meant, and other bulbs. **1911** *Century Dict. Suppl.* (at *sauce*), *Long sauce*, beets, carrots, parsnips, etc.: opposed to *short sauce*, the vegetables that are shorter in shape and size and grow above the ground, as peas, beans, tomatoes, etc. **1942** Berrey–Van den Bark *Amer. Slang* 91.72, Long sauce *or* sass, *root vegetables served with meat.* **1947** Bowles–Towle *New Engl. Cooking* 104, Garden sauce and green sauce were old English terms. . . Corrupted in New England to garden sass, it included all the vegetables raised in the garden. At one time some of the vegetables were classified as short sauce, others as long sauce, but these finer distinctions have been lost, and in northern New Hampshire and Maine, even today, garden sass is the accepted phrase for all green vegetables.

longscale sunfish n Also *long-scaled sunfish*
A **longear sunfish** (here: *Lepomis megalotis*).
    1933 [see **longear sunfish**]. **1949** Caine *N. Amer. Sport Fish* 43, Long-ear Sunfish—Long-scale sunfish.

longschat pine See **longshat pine**

longshanks n
    1 also pl: A tall or long-legged person. [Cf *OED* longshanks 1 "A nickname given to Edward I of England on account of his long legs"; → a1661] Cf **gander-shanked, long-sparred**
    1889 *Century Dict.* 3512, *Longshanks*. . . A long-legged person. **1909** White *Certain Rich Man* 110 **KS**, It's funny, ain't it—the way we all pick big ones—we sawed-offs? . . Yes—by hen, and you long-shanks always pick little dominickers. **1915** *DN* 4.206, There comes long-shanks across the fields. Making good time too.
    2 =**black-necked stilt.** Cf **longlegs 2**
    1813 (1824) Wilson *Amer. Ornith.* 7.54, *American Stilt. Himantopus Mexicanus*. . . arrives on the seacoast of New Jersey about the twenty-fifth of April. . . The names by which this bird is known on the seacoast are the Stilt, Tilt, and Long-shanks. **1844** [see **lawyer 2**]. **1859** (1968) Bartlett *Americanisms* 238, (*Himantopus nigricollis*.) The black-necked Stilt; a small bird which lives on our shores, known also by the names of Stilt and Longshanks. **1955** [see **lawyer 2**].

longshat pine n Also sp *longschat pine* [shat] **C Atl** Cf **longshucks, longstraw pine, longtag ~, shortshat ~**
Either a **pitch pine** (here: *Pinus rigida*) or **loblolly pine 1.**
    1896 Mohr–Roth *Timber Pines* 106, *Pinus taeda*. . . *Local or common names*. . . Long Schat Pine (Del.) **1897** Sudworth *Arborescent Flora* 26, *Pinus taeda*. . . Longschat Pine (Del.) *Ibid* 27, *Pinus rigida*. . . Longschat Pine (Del.) **1908** Britton *N. Amer. Trees* 31, Leaves . . bright green, . . 6 to 12 cm. long. . . It [=*Pinus rigida*] is known by many names, such as . . Longschat pine. **1968** *DARE* (Qu. T17, . . *Kinds of pine trees;* not asked in early QRs) Inf **DE**1, Longshat pine.

long-shell clam See **long clam 2**

longshucks n Also *longshucks pine* Cf **longshat pine, longstraw ~, longtag ~, shortshucks**
=**loblolly pine 1.**
    1896 Mohr–Roth *Timber Pines* 106, *Pinus taeda*. . . *Local or common names*. . . Long Shucks (Md., Va.) **1960** Vines *Trees SW* 22, [*Pinus taeda*. . . *Leaves*. . . 5–10 in. long.] *Ibid* 23, Vernacular names are Frankincense Pine, . . Long-shucks Pine, . . Shortleaf Pine.

long sight See **sight**

long sled n Also *long sleigh* esp **NEast** Cf **long-runner**
A type of sled; see quots.
    1966–68 *DARE* (Qu. N40a, . . *Sleighs . . for hauling loads*) Inf **CT**14, Long sleds—runners all in one piece; **ME**9, Long sled—one bottom, two runners; **NY**75, Long sleigh; **VT**7, Long sled—long, flat platform. **1973** Allen *LAUM* 1.219 (as of c1950), Terms for a vehicle for traveling over snow. . . long sled [1 inf, **cwMN**].

longsome adj [Prob calque of Ger *langsam* slow, perh infl by arch or Brit dial *longsome* long, tedious] Cf **-some**
See quots.
    1911 *DN* 3.545 **NE**, *Longsome*. . . Used for *long*, especially in German settlements. **1916** *DN* 4.277 **swMO**, *Longsome*. . . Long. Reported from a German community in Polk Co.

long-sparred adj [From the nautical sense]
Having long arms or legs.
    1916 *DN* 4.335 **Nantucket MA**, *Long-sparred*. . . Having long limbs: of people. **1945** Colcord *Sea Language* 174 **ME, Cape Cod, Long Island**, Alongshore, long-sparred and short-sparred were terms to describe people and animals with long or short limbs.

longspur n
Often with modifier: A bird of the genus *Calcarius*. [See quot 1895] For other names of var spp see **butterfly bird 2, painted bunting, ~ longspur**
    1832 Nuttall *Manual Ornith.* 1.463, Lapland Longspur. (*Emberiza lapponica*). *Ibid* 464, The Longspur, like the Lark, sings only as it rises in the air. **1874** Coues *Birds NW* 122, *Plectrophanes Ornatus* . . Chestnut-collared Bunting; Black-bellied Longspur. **1895** Minot *Land-Birds New Engl.* 195, The "longspurs," as their name indicates, have remarkably long hind claws, such as also belong to the Snow Buntings. **1898** (1900) Davie *Nests N. Amer. Birds* 367, Chestnut-collared Longspur. . . This bird is called the Black-shouldered or White-tailed Longspur. It is one of the most abundant birds of the Western plains. *Ibid* 368, The Black-breasted or Bay-winged Longspur breeds in abundance throughout the prairies of Colorado, Wyoming, and Montana. **1917** (1923) *Birds Amer.* 3.22, The Lapland Longspur and its varieties, the Alaska and Siberian Longspurs (*Calcarius lapponicus alascensis* and *Calcarius lapponicus coloratus*), inhabit a broad subarctic belt around the world during the breeding season. **1977** Bull–Farrand *Audubon Field Guide Birds* 533, Lapland Longspur. . . *The only longspur in most of the East.*

longst See **long** v

longstraw pine n [straw] Cf **longshat pine, longshucks, longtag pine, shortstraw ~**
    1 =**longleaf pine 1.**
    1859 Perry *Turpentine Farming* 26, Among the various qualities of pines, we may distinguish four in particular, viz., common short-straw pine; rosemary, or what some call spruce pine; pitch, or long-straw pine, and the white pine of Mississippi. **1896** Mohr–Roth *Timber Pines* 28, *Pinus palustris*. . . *Local or common names.* . . Long-straw Pine (Atlantic region). **1933** Small *Manual SE Flora* 4, Long-straw Pine. . . The giant of our pines, as well as the one with the longest leaves and the largest cones. **1947** Collingwood–Brush *Knowing Trees* 54, *Pinus palustris*. . . is commonly known as "longstraw" pine. **1967–70** *DARE* (Qu. T17, . . *Kinds of pine trees;* not asked in early QRs) Inf **LA**2, Long-straw; **NC**87, Longstraw—choice timber; **TN**24, Longleaf or longstraw pine; **TX**35, Longstraw. **1979** Little *Checklist U.S. Trees* 195, *Longleaf pine*. . . *Other common names*. . . longstraw pine.
    2 =**loblolly pine 1.**
    1896 Mohr–Roth *Timber Pines* 106, *Pinus taeda*. . . *Local or common names*. . . Long-straw Pine (Va., N.C.) in part. **1911** *Century Dict. Suppl.*, Long-straw pine, the long-leafed pine, and sometimes the loblolly-pine, which also has the needles rather long. **1950** Peattie *Nat. Hist. Trees* 24, *Pinus taeda*. . Longstraw Pine. [*Ibid* 25, *Needles*. . 6 to 9 inches long.] **1960** Vines *Trees SW* 22, [*Pinus taeda*. . . *Leaves*. . . 5–10 in. long.] *Ibid* 23, Vernacular names are Frankincense Pine, . . Long-straw Pine, . . Shortleaf Pine.

long sugar n Cf **longlick, long sweetening, long-tailed sugar**
Molasses.
    c1738 (1929) Byrd *Histories* 92, Their molasses comes from the same country, and has the name of "Long Sugar" in Carolina, I suppose from the Ropiness of it, and Serves all the purposes of Sugar, both in their Eating and Drinking. **1889** (1971) Farmer *Americanisms* 351, *Long*

sugar.—A North Carolina term for molasses; in New England, the same product was formerly named *long sweetening*. **1940** Fletcher *Raleigh's Eden* 79 **NC** (as of late 18th cent), Ebon came into the room carrying a large Sheffield tray with coffee cups and put them on a table in front of one of the little love seats which flanked the fireplace. Mary looked to see if there were plenty of long sugar in the silver box and if the cream jug were filled. **1942** Berrey–Van den Bark *Amer. Slang* 91.65, Long sugar *or* sweetening, *molasses used to sweeten coffee &c.*

long sweetening n Also sp *long sweetning* [Cf *OED long* a.[1] A.4 "Of liquors: Ropy. ? *Obs*."; a1648 →] **chiefly Sth, S Midl** *somewhat old-fash* Cf **lick** n 7, **long sugar, short sweetening**
Liquid sweetening such as molasses, syrup, honey, as contrasted to sugar; see also quot 1960.
1714 in 1886 NC *Colonial Rec.* 2.132, Let who will go unpaid, Rum long sweet'n alias Mollasses . . must be had. **1848** Lowell *Biglow* 145 'Upcountry' **MA**, Long-sweetening, *molasses.* **1859** (1968) Bartlett *Americanisms* 256, *Long Sweetening.* Molasses, so called formerly in New England. **1884** *Anglia* 7.272 **Sth, S Midl** [Black], *Long-sweetnin'* = molasses. **1887** Amer. Philol. Assoc. *Trans. for 1886* 17.34 **Sth**, A gentleman from Ohio . . has attempted to indicate for me the words that were imported during or after the war from the South into Southern Ohio. . . *Long sweetening* (molasses), he says, came to them from Virginia, and is still used in remote districts. **1893** Shands *MS Speech* 43, *Long-sweetening.* . . still used by the illiterate whites of Mississippi. . . To this day that class of people in this State ask their guest whether he will have *long-sweetening* or *short-sweetening* in his coffee; i.e. will he take molasses or sugar. **1895** *DN* 1.372 **seKY, eTN, wNC,** Will you have some long sweetening from this jug? **1903** *DN* 2.332 **seMO,** I like long sweetnin on my hoe-cakes. **1909** *DN* 3.378 **eAL, wGA,** *Long sweetnin.* **1911** *DN* 3.538 **eKY,** *Long-sweetening.* . . Sorghum molasses used in coffee for sugar. **1931** Randolph *Ozarks* 33, The juice is taken off into large kettles and boiled down to the consistency and sweetness of ordinary commercial molasses. This is the standard "long-sweetenin' " of the mountain table, and is used in all sorts of cooking. **1938** Matschat *Suwannee R.* 220 **neFL, seGA,** "Why do the Negroes and crackers along the river call syrup and molasses long sweetnin'—the same name the swamp folk give to wild honey?" she asked. "Can't rightly say, ma'am," Ben replied. "Jest a custom." **1939** *AmSp* 14.91 **eTN.** **1944** Adams *Western Words* 93, *Long sweetenin'*—Slang name for molasses. **1945** *Richmond Times–Dispatch* (VA) 13 Mar 8/5 *(Hench Coll.)* **TN,** Going into a Memphis drug store after a cup of coffee one cold and . . rainy day recently, we found the establishment all out of sugar. . . As for us, we went right back to our country raising and persuaded the waitress to add a small dash of syrup to the coffee. Time was when a guest at dinner in a great many rural homes in these and adjacent parts of the South would be asked whether he wanted "short sweetening" or "long sweetening" in his coffee. Sugar was "short" and syrup, sorghum and such like "long" sweetening. **1950** *PADS* 14.45 **SC.** **1952** Brown *NC Folkl.* 1.561. **1960** Criswell *Resp. to PADS 20* **Ozarks,** *Long sweetening.* . . Syrup or molasses or heavy "Orleans" sugar, latter much heavier than pressed brown sugar. *Short sweetening,* sugar of our time. Old terms, now *obs.* **c1960** Wilson Coll. **csKY.** **1966–67** *DARE* (Qu. H21, . . *The sweet stuff that's poured over these [pan]cakes*) Inf **MO**11, Long sweetening—more prevalent in southern part of the state, but used here occasionally; **NC**34, Long sweetening—older [term]; **SC**46, Long sweetening—a syrup [FW sugg]. **1968** Allen *It Happened* 212 **sIL** (as of c1900), Long sweet'nin' was honey, maple sirup, or sorghum, regularly called molasses. **1969** Sorden *Lumberjack Lingo* 74 **NEng, Gt Lakes,** *Long sweet'nin*—Black molasses to sweeten coffee. **1976** Garber *Mountain-ese* 55 **sAppalachians,** We hain't got no boughten sugar but we've got plenty uv long-sweetenin'. **1981** Pederson *LAGS Basic Materials* **Gulf Region,** 5 infs, Long sweetening—molasses; 3 infs, Long sweetening—syrup; 1 inf, Long sweetening—is honey, term used by relatives; 1 inf, Take your coffee with long sweetening—sorghum; 1 inf, Long sweetening—[inf has] heard of; thinks it may mean molasses; 1 inf, Long sweetening—[inf] has heard—not sure what it is; 1 inf, Long sweetening—says he's heard of it.

longtag pine n Cf **longshat pine, longshucks, longstraw pine, shorttag ~**
A **shortleaf pine** (here: *Pinus echinata*) or similar **pine.**
1950 Gray–Fernald *Manual of Botany* 57, *P[inus] echinata.* . . *Long-tag* or *Short-leaf P[ine]*—Leaves . . 7–13 cm. long. **1970** *DARE* (Qu. T17, . . *Kinds of pine trees;* not asked in early QRs) Inf **VA**46, Longtag pine same as Virginia pine. **1976** Bailey–Bailey *Hortus Third* 875, *[Pinus] echinata.* . . *Long-tag p[ine].* To 100 ft. or more.

longtail See **long-tailed duck**

long-tail blackbird See **long-tailed blackbird**

long-tailed adj
See quot.
1941 Ward *Holding Hills* 14 **IA** (as of early 20th cent), The family might have been unlucky and what is called a long-tailed family, for there were seven daughters in it, but it also had three or four sons.

long-tailed blackbird n Also *long-tail blackbird*
=**purple grackle.**
1945 Eifert *Birds* 180, These are the . . long-tailed blackbirds with a brilliant gloss of purple and green on heads and backs, and rather startling, cynical white eyes. **1956** MA Audubon Soc. *Bulletin* 40.130 **ME,** *Purple Grackle.* . . Long-tailed Blackbird. **1967–69** *DARE* (Qu. Q11, . . *Kinds of blackbirds*) Inf **KY**24, Long-tail blackbird—grackle; **NY**209, Long-tailed blackbird—not its right name; **PA**29, Long-tail blackbird.

long-tailed chippy n
=**brown towhee.**
1904 (1910) Wheelock *Birds CA* 248, The Californian Towhee is the brown chippie, or long-tailed chippie, of common parlance throughout most of California west of the Sierra Nevada.

long-tailed dove n
=**mourning dove 1.**
1899 Howe–Sturtevant *Birds RI* 56, Mourning Dove. *Long-tailed Dove. Carolina Dove*—A not uncommon summer resident in the northern and western portions of the State.

long-tailed duck n Also *longtail* [*OED* 1766]
=**old-squaw.**
1814 Wilson *Amer. Ornith.* 8.93, Long-Tailed Duck. *Anas glacialis.* . . This Duck is very generally known along the shores of the Chesapeake Bay by the name of *South Southerly*. **1839** MA Zool. & Bot. Surv. *Fishes Reptiles* 394, The *Long-tailed Duck, Fuligula glacialis,* is . . seen regularly and abundantly on the shores of Massachusetts. **1858** Baird *Birds* 800, *Long-tail.* . . *Female.* Lacks the long points to the tail and scapulars. **1876** *Forest & Stream* 7.245 **eMA,** The . . long-tailed duck . . is also called the "old squaw." *Ibid* 276 **NY,** *Harelda glacialis.* Old squaw; . . long tail. **1884** Roe *Nature's Serial Story* 184 **seNY,** Well, there is the old squaw, or long-tailed duck. **1909** Field Museum Nat. Hist. *Zool. Ser.* 9.339, *Harelda hyemalis.* . . *Local names:* Old Wife. Long-tailed Duck. . . Abundant on Lake Michigan in the late fall and winter and occurs occasionally on inland waters in both Illinois and Wisconsin. **1955** MA Audubon Soc. *Bulletin* 39.375, *Old-squaw.* . . Long-tail (Mass. The middle tail feathers of the male are elongated.); Long-tailed Duck (Mass., Conn., R.I.) **1982** Elman *Hunter's Field Guide* 232, *Clangula hyemalis* . . *Common & regional names:* longtail.

‡**long-tailed fox** n Cf **fox and hounds 1**
1968 *DARE* (Qu. EE33, . . *Outdoor games . . that children play*) Inf **IA**29, Long-tailed fox—dogs were one group—had a master—one guy was long-tailed fox who dipped his tail, a broom, into an outhouse; the lead dog was a "nice" guy who grabbed . . [the] fox's tail.

long-tailed jaeger n
Std: a **jaeger** n[1] (here: *Stercorarius longicaudus*). Also called **gull hunter, marlinspike 1, sea hen, whiptail**

long-tailed sugar n Also *long-tail sugar old-fash* Cf **long sugar, ~ sweetening**
Molasses.
1858 (1929) Taylor *Life on a Whaler* 142, Empty bottles . . they slyly fill from the vinegar cask or "long-tailed sugar" (molasses) hogshead. **1868** Whymper *Travel AK* 175, Molasses (known by us as "long-tailed sugar"), and coffee, pleased our Russian friends well. **1937** [see **longlick**]. **1959** Tallman *Dict. Amer. Folkl.* 180, *Long-tail sugar*—This was an early Cape Cod expression for molasses used for fishing. . . [T]he account goes that one put the molasses on the fishhook, threw it into the air and thus attracted bees, which as they hovered over the surface of the water appeared like flies to the fish. . . [T]he bees then stung the fish to death, thus affording the fisherman success with his long-tail sugar.

long taw n Also *long tawl* [*EDD long tawl* (at *long* adj. 1.(157)]] Cf **taw**
A marble game; see quots 1922, 1958.
1892 *DN* 1.220 **MO,** A *taw* is the playing marble, especially in the game of simple rolling; as, "Long Taw." **1916** in 1944 *ADD* **sAp-**

palachians, Long taw(l), in marbles. **1922** *DN* 5.187, *Long-taw.* . . A game like the Berkshire game. Two play, each taking a shot at the other with his taw, a "marble" being paid in forfeit to the one making a hit. Also *long-tawl, tracks.* **1958** *PADS* 29.36 **WI,** *Long tawl.* . . A marble game in which the objective marbles are set at the end of a "lane" as in bowling, and shot at from a starting line.

long time n
=fast time 2.
  1931 *AmSp* 6.467 **cnNE,** Central time is spoken of as "fast time," and mountain time as "slow time." . . One frequently finds synonyms of these different times. Fast time is sometimes "long time" and, less frequently, "high time." Slow time is called by some "short time" or "low time."

long tom n
1 often cap: Any of var long-barreled guns, esp one with a large bore. **chiefly Sth, S Midl** See Map
  1849 *Daily Picayune* (New Orleans LA) 13 May 2/1, How to begin to describe our gun, puzzles us. There is no use in calling it a "long tom," for that would convey no idea at all. **1920** Hunter *Trail Drivers TX* 308 (as of 1876), It will not be amiss to state what our artillery consisted of at that time. We used the long and trusty cap and ball rifle, familiarly known as "Long Tom." *Ibid* 309, After a bit the boys came up and finished the animal with their "Long Tom" rifle. **1927** (1970) Sears *Catalogue* 503, *Long Tom—Long Range Single Barrel Gun With Automatic Ejector—*Long range 36-inch barrel gun, used for geese, turkeys, jack rabbits, etc. Strongly built for heavy loads. *Barrel—*Blued steel, fitted with a heavy lug. . . *Frame—*Solid steel . . made extra heavy and reinforced. . . 12-gauge. . . [or] 16-gauge. **1939** *AmSp* 14.91 **eTN,** *Long Tom.* A shot gun. 'He took his long tom to the woods.' **1940** Writers' Program *Guide MD* 119 **cn,neMD,** The name of Susquehanna Flats is synonymous with good duck hunting. To old-timers it brings to mind sink boats, sneakboxes, swivel guns, 'long tom' and pump guns. **1956** in 1972 Hall *Sayings Old Smoky* 97 **neTN,** He had an old Long Tom hog rifle, called it 'Rattlesnake.' **1958** Humphrey *Home from the Hill* 126 **neTX,** You orter seen that shotgun. . . The stock looked like it'd been hacked out of a stump with a hatchet by a blind man on a drunk. An old single-barrel Long Tom. **c1960** Wilson *Coll.* **csKY,** *Long Tom.* . . nickname for rifle. **1965–70** *DARE* (Qu. P37b, *Nicknames for a shotgun*) 12 Infs, **chiefly Sth, S Midl,** (Old) long tom; **GA19, 34,** Long tom—single-barrel; **KY28,** Long tom—a name of a gun; **KY84,** Long tom—old 36-inch barrel; **LA2,** Long tom—any shotgun with a long barrel, usually a single barrel; **MI10,** Long tom—high-powered duck gun, with a big bore; **OK25,** Long tom—10- or 12-gauge with 36-inch to 40-inch barrel; **SC40,** Long tom—old-time single-barrel; **SC57,** Long tom—a very long-barreled one, 38 to 40 inches; [**TX67,** Long-tong;] (Qu. P37a, *Nicknames for a rifle*) Infs **FL7, IA8, KY24, MS32, NJ21, VA8, WI58,** (Old) long tom; **IL89,** Long toms—muzzle-loaders; **MD34,** Long toms—for a very long one. **1967** *DARE* FW Addit **AR55,** *Long tom*—a shotgun with a 32″ to 36″ barrel, becoming old-fashioned. **1968** *WI Conserv. Bulletin* 33.5.17 **WI,** The gun. . . should have an open choke because in thick brushy woods the Long Tom with a full choke is a definite handicap. **1984** Smith *SW Vocab.* 108, *Long Tom:* The long-barreled rifle of the American frontier. It originated in Pennsylvania in the middle 1700's, and was the work of expert German gunsmiths. In the beginning the calibre was large, ranging from .45 to .60, and the gun-stock was straight, and thick in the butt. Refinement of the weapon reduced the calibre to an average of .40 to .45.

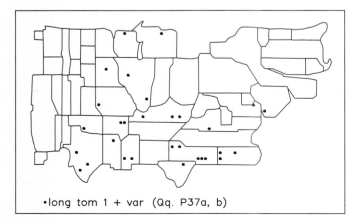
•long tom 1 + var (Qq. P37a, b)

2 In mining: a trough used for gold washing; see esp quot 1859. **chiefly West** *old-fash* Cf **tom**
  1839 *Amer. Railroad Jrl.* 8.98, The Long Tom . . consists merely of a trough. **1855** Marryat *Mountains & Molehills* 236, They [=miners] return to their *camps* and *long-toms* [Footnote: Gold-washers]. **1859** (1968) Bartlett *Americanisms* 256, *Long Tom.* An apparatus used by the Californians for washing gold from the earth or gravel in which it is found. It consists of a wooden trough from twelve to twenty-five feet long and about a foot wide. At its lower end it widens and its floor there is of sheet-iron pierced with holes half an inch in diameter, under which is placed a flat box a couple of inches deep. The long tom is set at a slight inclination over the place which is to be worked, and a stream of water is kept running through it by means of a hose; and while some of the party shovel the dirt into the *tom,* one man stands at the lower end stirring up the earth as it is washed down, and separating the stones, while the earth and small gravel fall through the sieve into another box, where it undergoes another process of sifting. **1925** Stuart *40 Yrs.* 1.69 **CA** (as of c1852–57), The west branch of Feather river rose fifty feet; sweeping away nearly all the miners' cabins . . and all of their tools, such as long toms, rockers [etc]. **1940** Writers' Program *Guide GA* 383 **cnGA** (as of c1830s), Placer mining, known here as deposit mining, utilized crude apparatus and was an inefficient process; as two men worked together, one would shovel gravel into the "long tom" or trough. **1941** Writers' Program *Guide CO* 276 **cCO** (as of c1860), During the peak of the gold rush . . men worked feverishly stripping sand bars, building dams and sluices, and shoveling "pay dirt." Some used the regulation shallow pan; . . still others used a log hollowed into a trough—known as a "Long Tom"—rolled from side to side with a stick handle. **1957** *Seattle Daily Times* (WA) 15 Sept 22, A midget long-tom rocker is exactly like those which miners use to wash gold from gold-bearing earth. **1967** *DARE* Tape **OR2,** [Inf:] A long tom is just a long riffle . . shake the loose stuff out of the riffles and let the gold accumulate. . . [FW:] So it's like a longer sluice box. [Inf:] That's right. It's a combination between a rocker and a sluice box. *Ibid* **OR3,** One they called a long tom. It was very much the same as this rocker. . . The only benefit there would be that it had more chance to save the gold than the shorter one. [Both Infs old] **1969** *DARE* FW Addit **CA114,** *Long Tom*—long sluice box used to separate gold from stream water and dirt. Gold mining term. [Inf old]

3 A type of corn bread; see quot.
  1966 Dakin *Dial. Vocab. Ohio R. Valley* 2.315 **KY,** Miscellaneous terms recorded once or twice [for corn bread baked in large cakes include] . . *long Tom* . . a sweet corn pone.

4 A **bullgrass 1** (here: *Paspalum lividum*).
  1950 Hitchcock–Chase *Manual Grasses* 605, *Paspalum lividum.* . . *Long-tom.* . . Low ground, wet savannas, and swamps, and along streams and ditches. **1970** Correll *Plants TX* 162, *Longtom.* . . Often basally decumbent and freely rooting for up to 1 m., then ascending at the floriferous ends. . . Moist tight clay loam in ditches, tanks, resacas and shallow lakes, s.e. Tex. and coastal parts of Rio Grande Plains, . . n. to Ala., La. and Tex.

5 **=great blue heron.**
  1962 Imhof *AL Birds* 81, Great Blue Heron—*Ardea herodias* . . Other Names: Blue Crane, Big Blue Crane, Long Tom.

long tongue n
1 A gossip, loudmouth; loquacity, a tendency to gossip or prate; hence adj *long-tongued* loquacious, given to gossip. [*OED;* cf also *EDD* (at *long* adj. 1.(164)(a),(165))]
  1899 (1912) Green *VA Folk-Speech* 267, *Long-tongue.* . . A tale-bearer; a gossip. *Long-tongued.* . . Prating; babbling; loquacious. **1930** Shoemaker *1300 Words* 38 **cPA Mts** (as of c1900), *Long-tongued—*Gossiping or vindictive. **1960** *VT Hist.* 28.223, To be born with a long tongue. (To be a great talker.) **1965–70** *DARE* (Qu. GG23b, *If you speak sharply to somebody to make him be patient* . . *"Hold _____!"*) Inf **UT4,** Your long tongue; (Qu. GG36a, *The kind of person who is always poking into other people's affairs: "She's an awful _____."*) Inf **IN60,** Has a long tongue; (Qu. HH7a, *Someone who talks too much, or too loud: "He's an awful _____."*) Infs **NY43, TX40,** Long tongue; **KY40,** Got an awful long tongue; **MS1,** Long-tongued; [**MS56,** His tongue is too long;] **SC10,** Got a long tongue.

2 See quot. [*EDD* (at *long* adj. 1.(164)(b))]
  1983 *MJLF* 9.1.47 **ceKY,** *Long tongue* . . the spleen of a hog.

‡3 A type of doughnut; see quot. Cf **long john 2**
  1970 *DARE* (Qu. H30, *An oblong cake, cooked in deep fat*) Inf **IL117,** Long tongue.

long-tongued See **long tongue 1**

long town (ball) See **town ball**

long-way-around adj phr

Of a relative: distant, remote.

1991 Still *Wolfpen Notebooks* 55 **sAppalachians,** We're long-way-round kinfolks. Not enough to do much bragging.

long ways, by a adv phr Cf **long chalk**

1 also *a long ways:* By far; far and away. Cf **heap n 3**

1952 Brown *NC Folkl.* 1.561, *Longway(s), a. . .* A great deal, very much. "I'd a longways rather work than be hungry."—Central and east. **c1960** *Wilson Coll.* **csKY,** By a long ways (or *long ways* alone). . . By all odds. "He's a long ways the best fiddler in this part of the country." **2** in neg phrr *not by a long way(s):* Not at all; by no means.

1956 McAtee *Some Dialect NC* 28, *Longways. . .* A great deal. "Not by a longways." **1966–68** *DARE* (Qu. KK55a, *To deny something very firmly: "No, not by a _____.")* Infs **CO**7, **GA**7, **IN**49, **MD**19, Long way(s).

long white n [From the long white plumes borne on the back during the mating and nesting season] **esp FL** Cf **little snowy**

The American **egret** (*Casmerodus albus*).

1917 (1923) *Birds Amer.* 1.186, Egret—*Herodias egretta* . . Great White Egret; Great White Heron; Long White. *Ibid* 188, To the plume-hunters the bird [=the snowy egret] is known as the "Little Snowy," to distinguish it from the larger species called by them the "Long White." **1954** Sprunt *FL Bird Life* 29, Even exceeding its larger relative in popularity during the plume-trade days, because of its beautifully re-curved *aigrettes,* it [=the snowy egret] suffered the curse of beauty to a greater extent than the "Long-whites." **1964** Will *Hist. Okeechobee* 94 **FL,** After 1910 the scalp of a "long white" or American egret brought $5. **1969** Longstreet *Birds FL* 23, American Egret—Other Names: White Crane; Long-white; Big Plume Bird.

long yearling See **long adj B4**

lont See **loan A2**

lontsome See **lonesome**

loo v, n¹ [Var of **low** v, n] **chiefly NEast, N Midl**
=**low** v, n.

1903 *DN* 2.306, *Bawl. . .* Bellow (of cattle), to low. The northern provincialism is 'loo.' **1914** *DN* 4.76 **ME, nNH,** *Loo. . .* To low (of a cow). **1948** Davis *Word Atlas Gt. Lakes* app qu 62a (*Name for gentle sound made by cow at feeding time*) 3 (of 233) infs, Loo; qu 62b (*Name for loud sound made by cow when calf is taken away*) 8 infs, **OH,** Loo. **1949** Kurath *Word Geog.* 62, *Loo,* a variant of it [=*low*], is fairly common in rural New England and has survived to some extent in northern Pennsylvania and central New York State. **1965–70** *DARE* (Qu. K19, *Noise made by a calf that's taken away from its mother*) Inf **TN**53, Looing; (Qu. K21, *The noise a cow makes, calling for her calf*) Inf **AL**34, Loo [lu]; **NY**233, She loos [luz]; **TN**53, Loo. **1966** [see **low** v, n]. **1967** Faries *Word Geog. MO* 134, Loo *(Moo)* 5 [of c700 infs]. **1973** Allen *LAUM* 1.252 (as of c1950), *Low. . .* Loo, a minor form in Northern New England and New York state, remains in the speech of an eastern South Dakota Type I [=old, with little educ] inf., three of whose grandparents came from New York.

loo n² [Abbr for *hullabaloo*]

1952 Brown *NC Folkl.* 1.561, *'Loo* [lu]. . . Hullabaloo.—Central and east.

looby n, adj Pronc-sp *loobry* [*OED* 1377 →]

A dull, clumsy person; awkward, doltish.

1806 (1970) Webster *Compendious Dict.* 179, *Looby. . .* an awkward heavy person, clown, lubber. [*DARE* Ed: This entry was carried over from Webster's English model.] **1899** Woerner *Rebel's Daughter* 246 **Ozarks,** Was it quite the thing, Leslie, for me to make a spectacle of myself, for the amusement and gratification of vulgar loobies? **1953** Randolph–Wilson *Down in Holler* 262 **Ozarks,** Looby. . . Clumsy, awkard [sic], perhaps stupid. In Galena, Mo., I heard of a "great big fat *looby* boy that would step on himself an' fall down." Some hillmen put an *r* sound in this word, so that it sounds like *loobry.*

looby-loo n Also *loop-de-loo(p);* for addit varr see quots

A children's singing game; see quot 1909.

[**1894** Gomme *Traditional Games* 1.352, *Lubin. Ibid* 355, II. [Chorus:] Now we dance looby, looby, looby, Now we dance looby, looby, light;/

Shake your right hand a little,/ And turn you round about. *Ibid* III. [Chorus:] Fal de ral la, fal de ral la,/ Hinkumbooby round about./ Right hands in and left hands out,/ Hinkumbooby round about. *Ibid* 357, V. [Chorus:] How do you luby lue . . O'er the Saturday night? *Ibid* 359, A ring is formed and the children dance round.] **1909** (1923) Bancroft *Games* 280, *Looby Loo. . .* Here we dance, looby, looby, looby./ Here we dance, looby, looby, light./ Here we dance, looby, looby, looby, loo,/ Every Saturday night./ Put your right hand in / Put your right hand out / Give your right hand a shake, shake, shake,/ Hinkumbooby round-about. [*Ibid* 282, The players stand in a ring. . . On the last two lines . . the circle gallops halfway around . . and reverses the action. . . For the alternate verses which describe action the movements are suited to the words.] **1940** *Handy Play Party Book* 135 [Children's Games], *Looby Loo. . .* Chorus[:] Here we come, Looby Loo, Here we come, Looby Light; Here we come, Looby Loo, All on a Saturday night. [Verse:] Put your right foot in, Put your right foot out; Give your foot a shake, shake, shake, And turn yourself about,—Oh. At the beginning . . all join hands in a circle and skip around, singing. **1965–70** *DARE* (Qu. EE1, . . *Games . . children play . . in which they form a ring, and either sing or recite a rhyme*) Inf **CA**133, Here we go loop-de-lu; **NY**67, Here we go loopedy-loop; **LA**3, Here we go loopity lie, Here we go loopity loop, All on a Saturday night; **NJ**30, Looby-loo ['lubɪ,lu]; **KS**13, Looby-loo [lubɪ'lu]; **CO**35, Looby-loo—I put my right hand in, I put my right hand out; I give my right hand a shake-shake-shake and turn myself about—Here we go looby-loo, here we go Looby light, all on a Saturday night; **NY**235, **OH**93, Loop-de-loo; **SC**44, Loop-the-loop; **DC**11, **GA**72, Loopy-de-loop; **RI**15, Loopy-loo; **ND**9, Sloopedy-loo ['slupədɪ,lu]—Norwegian? **PA**126, Lu-by-lu—now called hokey-pokey; (Qu. EE33, . . *Outdoor games . . that children play*) Inf **MA**57, New game [lupilu]—Saturday night we lupilu, all on a Saturday night; played to music; **NC**72, Loop-de-loop.

loocervia, loocivee See **lucivee**

Loogin See **Lugen**

look v

A Forms.

Imper: usu *look;* also:

1 *lookee, lookie, look(e)y;* foll by *here, there,* etc, also *look a,* and, perh by hypercorrection, *look at.* [Reduced forms of *look you, look ye;* cf *OED* look v. 4.a]

1744 in 1967 *AmSp* 42.217, Why lookee Gentlemen . . suppose a great stone lies in the street and you want to move it, unless there be some moving cause, how the devil shall it move? **1844** Stephens *High Life in NY* 1.173, Look a here, cousin John, why don't you ask if he ever plays all fours. **1871** Eggleston *Hoosier Schoolmaster* 63 **sIN,** Looky here, marm. **1871** (1892) Johnston *Dukesborough Tales* 59 **cGA,** Look a-here, Sebe! . . fun's fun, but too much is too much. *Ibid* 74, Lookee here, squire, I didn't take it, did I? **1887** Freeman *Humble Romance* 256 **NEng,** Look-a here, I want to know ef Alferd drove you out of the house 'cause you give him gentian? **1894** Riley *Armazindy* 143 **IN,** Looky there! **1899** (1912) Green *VA Folk-Speech* 268, Look a-here, don't forget to call at the store. **1908** *DN* 3.285 **eAL, wGA,** "Look ahere, what I found." This intrusive *a* is probably a survival of the pronoun *ye* or *you,* 'look ye here.' It occurs frequently in such expressions as 'look ayonder,' 'look athere,' etc. **1911** Wharton *Ethan Frome* 46 **wMA,** But look at here, ain't it lucky I got the . . cutter . . waiting for us? **1912** *DN* 3.570 **wIN,** Look ahere at this, will you? **1915** *DN* 4.180 **swVA,** Look a here. *Ibid* 227 **wTX,** Lookey. . . Look! **1917** *DN* 4.395 **neOH,** Look-a-here [lʊkəˈhɪɚ], *looky* ['lʊkɪ]—is the native form. *Looky* I first heard from boys in Cleveland. It may also be native. There is possibly confusion in *look-a-here* with *look-a-that,* in which *a* is *at* or *on.* . . [*DN* Ed: *look-ahere* is general.] **1929** *Ruppenthal Coll.* **KS,** Lookee, look a here. . . A call to direct attention to the speaker or what he wishes to show. "Now look a here. We can't make it this way." **1930s** in 1944 *ADD* **eWV,** ['lʊkɪ]. Looky yonder. **1935** Hurston *Mules & Men* 233 **LA,** But looka here, Zora. **1960** Criswell *Resp. to PADS 20* **Ozarks,** Lookee here what I got. **1966** *DARE* (Qu. NN6b, *Expressions of joy used mostly by children*) Inf **GA**9, Look-a here. **1968** *DARE* Tape **AK**8, Look-a here, I said you're not going back on the farm. **1982** Barrick Coll. **csPA,** Lookie—diminutive of command *look* "Lookie here." **1986** Pederson *LAGS Concordance Gulf Region,* 55 infs, Look-a-here; 16 infs, Look-a-there; 3 infs, Look-a-yonder; 8 infs, Lookee yonder; 1 inf, Lookee—to show you something, serious or not; 1 inf, Oh, lookee; 1 inf, Well, lookee—quoting others; 1 inf, Lookee, look-a-there; 1 inf, Lookee here—semi-jokingly; 1 inf, Lookee there at that snake. **1993** Delany–Delany *Having Our Say* 17 cNC [Black], Hey, nurse, come on over here and looky-here at this old woman, she's in such good shape.

2 *look at,* pronc-sp *lookit.* Note: *lookit* as pronc-sp for *look at* in std constrs is not illustrated here.

1917 *DN* 4.396 **neOH**, Look-at ['lʊkət]. . . used among school children for *look!* Apparently recent. Portage Co. General. Cf. *look-it* in Mass., Mich. **1919** *DN* 5.76 **wMA**, Look-at. With the pronunciation *look-it,* familiar to me all my life. **1928** in 1944 *ADD* **WV**, Look it! **1939** Barry *Philadelphia Story* 6, Lookit, Tracy: don't you think you've done enough notes for one day? **1940** Lewis *Bethel Merriday* 224, Lookit, kids. I'll be in and buy you a drink, soon as you get settled in your hotel. *Ibid* 265, Iris chilled her elegant little nose against the shop window. "Lookit! They call it the 'Demoiselle's D-e-l-i-t-e'—'delight,' I guess that must be." **1967** *DARE* File **csMA** (as of c1947), *Lookit* for "See here." **1968** *DARE* (Qu. NN6b, *Expressions of joy used mostly by children*) Inf **MN26**, Lookit. **1970** *DARE* Tape **CA**185, You'd like to stop and talk to them and say "Lookit kids, life isn't a bowl of cherries and straighten up and fly right." **1978** *DARE* File **cnMA**, Children never said "hey look" but "hey lookit" or just "lookit," to indicate something of interest. It's not a warning. "Hey lookit, here comes that crazy old lady that keeps stopping to shake the spirits off her skirt."

B Senses.

1 To examine, look over; spec:

a To evaluate, appraise (land) for its suitability for a specific purpose. Cf **landlooker, landlooking**

1805 (1904) White *Jrl.* 31 **MA**, Towards night there came four men to look land. **1856** in 1862 Colt *Went to KS* 86 **NY**, Father and my husband have been off east upon Big Creek, looking claims. **1910** Cox *Fearsome Creatures* 33 **eTN**, According to woodsmen who have been "looking" timber in eastern Tennessee, the whimpus . . has a gorilla-shaped head and body.

b To inspect with the purpose of removing what is undesirable; to pick over. [*OED look* v. 6.a 13 . . →; "Now *dial.*"]

1912 Green *VA Folk-Speech* 268, Look. . . To *look* one's head for lice there. **1942** in 1944 *ADD* **IN**, Look. . . 'Mary will you help your mother look this spinach?; **sIL**, To look the berries = stem the berries, not just to pick out poor or crushed fruit. Reported by 15 persons. **1982** Slone *How We Talked* 62 **eKY** (as of c1950), Some of the greens we used were not cooked, but eaten raw. They were "looked" (checked for bugs and rotting spots), washed, sprinkled with salt and wilted or "killed" by pouring real hot pork grease over them. **1984** Wilder *You All Spoken Here* 85 **Sth**, Look: Examine; before cooking greens or beans, they should be washed and looked thoroughly to remove bugs, pebbles, trash.

2 with *out:* To search for and discover; to view and select. [*OED* (at *look* v. 40.h) 1535 →] *arch*

1658 in 1855 New Plymouth Colony *Records* 3.141 **MA**, Liberty is graunted vnto Mr. Josias Winslow, . . to looke out a place to supply him with twenty fiue acres of land. **1768** E. Cleaveland in B.P. Smith *Hist. Dartmouth Coll.* (1878) 36 *(OED)* **NH**, The Deputy Surveyor, . . offered his assistance to look out the township and survey it. **1835** (1930) Sewall *Diary* 167 **IL**, Went over the river and looked me out another timber lot. **1840** in 1940 VT Hist. Soc. *Proc.* new ser 8.148 **VT**, Mr. Mansfield came and looked out some boards—I sent them over by Monroe. **1873** in 1955 Lee *Mormon Chron.* 2.229 **UT**, To day I looked out a waggon Road or rather a rout. **1898** in 1953 Botkin–Harlow *Treas. Railroad Folkl.* 195, We came up to this country to look out a place to take [=rob] a train. **1903** (1965) Adams *Log Cowboy* 197 **West**, Before leaving, we rode over and looked out the trail after it left Duck [Creek], for it was quite possible that we might return during the night. *Ibid* 351 **West**, He set out to look out the country. . . We scouted out some five or six miles.

3 To search for. [*OED look* v. 6.d "To seek, search for; = *look for*"; *OEDS* "*rare,* now *dial.*"]

1991 *DARE* File **seNY**, Look eggs = gather the eggs.

4 rarely with *out;* foll by full or partial infin: To expect, intend (to do something). **chiefly Sth, S Midl**

1851 (1852) Stowe *Uncle Tom's Cabin* 87, I'm glad Mas'r didn't go off this morning, as he looked to. **1891** *PMLA* 6.170 **WV**, Another (Bible) construction is retained in this: *they looked for to see him die every day. For to* instead of *to* is now obsolete. **1902** *DN* 2.238 **sIL**, I look for him to do it. **1934** Carmer *Stars Fell on AL* 44, Monkey kin play that fiddle o' his'n in any conceivable position o' the body. I look to see him try. **1938** Rawlings *Yearling* 394 **nFL**, I more'n half looked for him to do it. **1939** *Hall Coll.* **eTN**, "He's lookin' for to quit." (Expecting to give up his job.) *Ibid* **cwNC**, We had to help [our parents]

at home, and we didn't look out to ever need any much education. **1943** *LANE* Map 704 *(I intend to go)* 1 inf, **seNH**, Looking. **1944** *PADS* 2.30 **eKY**, We are a-goin' to set up with Aint Hanner. She is a-looking to die. **1946** Stuart *Tales Plum Grove* 224 **seKY**, They're not looking for Roy to live until midnight tonight. **1957** *Hall Coll.* **eTN**, Look to. . . Expect. "The man was in the hospital lookin' to die." **1969** *DARE* FW Addit **NC**, I'm not looking for anyone to come—expecting. **1986** *WI Alumnus Letters* **Ozarks**, I look to be there come Friday. **1986** Pederson *LAGS Concordance* **Gulf Region**, 1 inf, I don't look for it to (of his community changing); 1 inf, They look for you to give them something now; 2 infs, (I was) looking for it to happen; 1 inf, I'm looking for her to come in soon; 1 inf, They look to go to the store for everything; 1 inf, Just about look to have a flat tire; 1 inf, I look to have company; 1 inf, Looking to be confined; 1 inf, I ain't looking to die soon; 1 inf, Looking to go back to work; 1 inf, Looking to go to the hospital.

5 with *for:* To expect, anticipate (someone or something).

1963 in 1982 *Barrick Coll.* **csPA**, Look for—expect. "I look for them this evening." **1966** *DARE* Tape **ME**26, My sister was lookin' fer a baby, first one. **1986** Pederson *LAGS Concordance* **Gulf Region**, 1 inf, I will look for her; 2 infs, (I'll) look for you; 1 inf, I'm going look for you; 2 infs, I'll be looking for you; 2 infs, We be looking for you; 1 inf, I was looking for him, i.e., expecting him; 1 inf, I'm looking for company—expecting; 1 inf, Looking for a calf; *(She is pregnant)* 4 infs, Looking for a baby; 1 inf, Looking for offspring.

6 with *for;* Of weather: to promise, portend. [Calque of PaGer; see quot 1968]

1968 *Helen Adolf Festschrift* 38 **ePA**, It looks for rain (Pennsylvania German *Es guckt fer Regge*) for 'It looks as though it were going to rain.' **1987** *Jrl. Engl. Ling.* 20.171 **ePA**, It looks for rain 'it looks as though it is going to rain'. . . [2 infs], ages 83–84. . . The two informants who marked this expression are over 80; it thus seems to be strongly recessive.

‡7 with *at:* To speak to (someone) on a telephone.

1967 *DARE* FW Addit **ceCO**, "Let me look at him"—on the telephone, "let me speak to." Common.

look n Cf **sight** n

The distance or the extent of land that can be seen from one's observation point; a view.

1852 *Knickerbocker* 40.548, A resident in Florida . . informed me that a neighbor . . had *honey-fackled* him in the matter of a *heap* of logs, which they had been getting out on a *quarter* about a *look* from a *branch* near the *old-field. Ibid* 549, A 'look' is a mile. **1941** Writers' Program *Guide WI* 389 **csWI** (as of 1830s), Thibault sold to Caleb Blodgett of Vermont as much of his claim as could be encompassed by "three looks," a standard Indian unit of measurement. **1953** Randolph–Wilson *Down in Holler* 262 **Ozarks**, Look. . . A view, usually from a slight eminence. Asked how far off a certain cabin is, the hillman may reply, "Three looks an' a couple of jumps." He means that the trail traverses three hills, and that the house in question is only a few yards beyond the crest of the third ridge. **1954** *Harder Coll.* **cwTN**, Look. . . A view. **1983** Allin S. *Legislative Dict.* 17 **Sth**, Look and a holler: a moderate distance. Two looks and a holler: A long walk.

look-a-here See **look** v **A1**

look a little out v phr [Infl by Ger *pass ein bisschen auf* watch out, be a little careful]

To be on guard; to be careful.

1928 *Ruppenthal Coll.* **KS**, To look a leedle (or leetle, or little) out. . . To beware; to take care; to be careful. "You better look a leedle out, or you may get hurt." **1950** *WELS* (*If somebody has been doing poor work or none at all:* "If he wants to keep his job, he'll have to _____.") 1 Inf, **cWI**, Knuckle down, get going, look a little out.

look at See **look** v **A1, A2, B7**

look-a-there See **look** v **A1**

lookdown n [From the shape of the head, which has the appearance of looking down]

A **moonfish 2** (here: *Selene vomer*). Also called **dollarfish 3, hogfish e, horsehead 1a**

1882 U.S. Natl. Museum *Bulletin* 16.439, S[elene] vomer . . Moonfish; Look Down; Horse-head. Bluish above, sides and below silvery with golden reflections. **1884** Goode *Fisheries U.S.* 1.323, The Silver Moon-fish—Selene Argentea. . . In the Chesapeake this fish is often called by the names "Horse-head" and "Look-down." **1933** LA Dept. of Conserv. *Fishes* 41, [Caption:] The Lookdown. . . Brilliantly silver and extremely compressed so that it has become thin through its body, this beautiful species, common in our Louisiana salt waters, appears much like a decoration from a Japanese screen. **1955** Zim–Shoemaker *Fishes* 93, The Lookdown is similar to the Moonfish but has elongated dorsal and anal fins and an even blunter head. **1991** Amer. Fisheries Soc. *Common Names Fishes* 52, *Selene vomer* . . lookdown.

look down one's nose v phr
To look embarrassed or unhappy; to submit (to someone).

1914 DN 4.109 **cKS**, *Look down one's nose.* . . To look chagrined, baffled, or ashamed. "I guess he didn't succeed, for he was looking down his nose." **1923** DN 5.213 **swMO**, *Look down one's nose.* . . To look sorrowful, discouraged or ashamed. **1927** AmSp 2.360 **cwWV**, *Look down the nose* . . to become discouraged. "Mother looked down her nose when the clothes line broke." **1946** AmSp 21.273 **KY**, *Look down one's nose.* In addition to the usual senses (to scorn or despise, and to sulk or pout), one speaker was heard to use it in the sense of to listen perforce, to agree under cumpulsion: 'They really made old Buck look down his nose to them.'

lookee See **look** v A1

lookers n pl
1 Eyes. [Cf *EDD* looker sb. 1 "An eye."] Cf DS X21a–c
1913 DN 4.4 **ME**, *Lookers.* . . Eyes. **1950** WELS (*Names or nicknames for a person's eyes*) 5 Infs, **WI**, Lookers.
2 Eyeglasses.
c1935 Smiley *Gloss. New Paltz* **seNY**, In speaking of my glasses Joe Evans used the expression "So you have to use 'lookers' also". I have no idea how general its use may be. **1966–70** DARE (Qu. X23, . . *Joking words . . for eyeglasses*) Inf **FL**33, Lookers; **NC**86, Lookers—don't hear it used often, though; **SC**58, Lookers [laughter].

lookey See **look** v A1

look for See **look** v B5, 6

lookie See **look** v A1

lookingest adj Pronc-sp lookinest
Most extraordinary in appearance.
1932 Wasson *Sailing Days* 47 **cME coast**, The *Burmah* was one of the lookinest objects you ever see in the shape of a vessel still goin'. **1975** Gould *ME Lingo* 169, *Lookinest*—The superlative of looking, coined by Mainers for oddest, most peculiar, most amusing, and usually the most utterly ridiculous spectacle. The tourist in vacation garb doesn't realize that a lobsterman's reaction is often, "That's the lookinest thing we've seen all season!"

looking glass n [Prob rhyming slang]
1966–68 DARE (Qu. X35, *Joking words for the part of the body that you sit on* . . "*He slipped and came down hard on his _____.*") Inf **MD**19, Ass, behind, looking glass; **ND**3, Ass shiner, looking glass; **VA**2, Butt, bottom, looking glass [laughter].

lookit See **look** v A2

look on v phr [OED a1548 →; "Now dial."]
To regard, esteem.
1899 (1912) Green *VA Folk-Speech* 268, *Looked on.* . . Respected. "He is very much looked on." **1984** Wilder *You All Spoken Here* 103 **Sth**, Looked on: Regarded, as in "Glen Rounds is looked on right well in some parts."

look, on the adv phr
See quots.
1952 Brown *NC Folkl.* 1.561, *Look, to be on the:* . . To be courting. "I hear Henry's on the look again."—West. **1969** DARE (Qu. AA4a, . . *A man who is very eager to get married.* . . "*He's _____.*") Inf **KS**16, On the look, on the prowl.

look out v See **look** v B2, 4

lookout n [OED lookout 3 1779 → (in metaphorical sense c1825 →); but perh reversed compound; cf Intro "Language Changes" I.1]
1899 (1912) Green *VA Folk-Speech* 268, *Lookout.* . . A prospect or view; an outlook. Future prospect.

look over v phr [OED (at look v. 19.b) 1666 →, but perh reversed compound; cf Intro "Language Changes" I.1] chiefly **Sth, S Midl**
To disregard, forgive, overlook.
1887 Amer. Philol. Assoc. *Trans. for 1886* 17.46 **Sth**, List of common Southern expressions—many of them vulgarisms—that have not, so far as I know, either old English or provincial English authority. . . *Look over* (overlook). **1899** (1912) Green *VA Folk-Speech* 268, *Look over.* . . To forgive. "I don't see how he can look over that." **1903** DN 2.320 **seMO**, *Look over.* . . Overlook. 'O Lord, forgive our trespasses and look over our faults!' A common form of prayer. **1907** DN 3.233 **nwAR**, *Look over.* . . To overlook. **1909** DN 3.347 **eAL, wGA**, *Look over.* . . To overlook. Rare. **1938** Stuart *Dark Hills* 398 **eKY**, We'll look over all these lies he makes up. **c1960** Wilson Coll. **csKY**, *Look over.* . . Forgive, overlook.

look-see v [look-see a general survey, inspection]
To investigate; to determine, ascertain.
1939 (1966) Chandler *Big Sleep* 42, I'm dropping down to look see. **1940** Faulkner *Hamlet* 340 **MS**, I reckon I'll go on a day or two and look-see them Northern towns. Washington and New York and Baltimore. **1966** DARE Tape **SC**9, Then they go around there and look-see if he'd sprout. You can look right through the water and see the sprout. *Ibid* **SC**25, Have to go look-see if I can't find it.

lookup n [See quot 1844]
A **bittern** (here: *Botaurus lentiginosus*).
1844 Giraud *Birds Long Is.* 286, This species [=*Ardea lentiginosa*] . . is known to many persons by the name of "Indian Hen" or "Pullet," though more familiarly by the appellation of "Look-up," so called from its habit, when standing on the marshes, of elevating its head, which position, though probably adopted as a precautionary measure, frequently leads to its destruction. **1932** Bennitt *Check-list* 15, *American bittern* . . Indian pullet; look-up.

looky (here or there) See **look** v A1

looloo n
=lalapalooza 3.
1896 Lillard *Poker Stories* 87, He threw down four aces and reached for the money. "Hold on! . . I've got a looloo." . . The stranger was dazed. . . "Well, what is a looloo, anyway?" "Three clubs and two diamonds," coolly replied the miner, raking in the stakes. . . The game proceeded, but it was plainly evident that the unsophisticated young tiger hunter had something on his mind. . . [he] threw down his cards with an exultant whoop. . . [and] reached for the money. "There's a looloo for you—three clubs and two diamonds." "Tut, tut!" exclaimed the miner. "Really this is too bad. You evidently don't understand our rules at all. . . Why, look at that rule over there." . . The Chicagoan read his doom in the handwriting on the wall. . . *The looloo can be played but once a night.* **1938** Asbury *Sucker's Progress* 30, The most famous of all eccentric hands, the Looloo, is said to have been invented in a saloon in Butte, Montana, during the 1870's in a game between a stranger and a Butte miner.

loom See **loam**

loom end n
A mill end.
1906 DN 3.145 **nwAR**, *Loom-end.* . . Remnant. "They're having a loom-end sale."

loomy See **loam**

loon n
1 Std: a diving bird of the genus *Gavia*. Also called **diver**; for other names of the common loon (*G. immer*) see **big loon, call-up-a-storm, devil-diver 3, dipsy doodle 3, fencediver, German goose, great northern diver, greenhead 4c, guinea duck, hell-diver 3, pond loon, ring-necked ~, sheep ~, walloon**; for other names of other birds of this genus see **red-throated loon**
2 A grebe. [OED 1678 →] Cf **dipper 3a, peggy loon, sheldrake ~, shitepoke, tinker loon**
1968–69 DARE (Qu. Q10, . . *Water birds and marsh birds*) Inf **NY**207, Loon—dipper duck; **PA**168, Shypoke, also shitepoke, are loons.
3 also *black loon*: =double-crested cormorant. Cf **nigger-goose, nigger loon**

1936 Roberts *MN Birds* 1.166, Double-crested Cormorant . . *Other names* . . Black Loon. 1963 Gromme *Birds WI* 215, Loon, Black (Double-breasted Cormorant). 1966 *DARE* (Qu. Q10, . . *Water birds and marsh birds*) Inf **SC**21, Loon—a nigger goose—food for the Negro.

‡loons n pl
A great amount.
1969 *DARE* (Qu. U38a, . . *A great deal of money:* "*He's got _____ [of money].*") Inf **KY**28, Lots, loons [lunz].

loop-de-loo(p) See **looby-loo**

looper n
Often with modifier: The larva of any moth of the family Geometridae. [See quot 1842; *OED* 1731 →] Also called **inchworm, measuring worm, spanworm, tape measure, yardstick**
1842 Harris *Treatise Insects* 330 **NEng**, The caterpillars of the *Geometrae* of Linnaeus, earth-measurers, as the term implies, or geometers, span-worms, and loopers, have received these several names from their peculiar manner of moving. . . in creeping, they arch up the back while they bring forward the hinder part of the body, and then, resting on their hind-legs, stretch out to their full length, in a straight line, before taking another step with their hind-legs. 1884 (1885) McCook *Tenants* 104 **PA**, The Geometers, or span-worms . . are so called from the mode of walking peculiar to the larvae. . . This mode of progression is popularly called 'looping,' and the caterpillars are called 'loopers.' 1905 [see **inchworm**]. 1926 Essig *Insects N. Amer.* 698, Geometridae. Loopers, Measuring Worms, Cankerworms. . . They move in the characteristic looping manner and also drop from the trees on a silken thread. 1941 Writers' Program *Guide IN* 302 **cnIN**, Until 1926, Indiana peppermint was free from pests, but in that year the flea-beetle . . made its first appearance. . . The mint looper also feeds on the growing plants. 1958 McCulloch *Woods Words* 113 **Pacific NW**, *Looper*—The hemlock looper, a small moth whose larval stage, a small green worm, is a serious killer of coast timber. 1966–67 *DARE* (Qu. R6) Inf **FL**16, Looper; (Qu. R27, . . *Kinds of caterpillars or similar worms*) Infs **AR**41, **GA**84, **KY**75, Cabbage looper; **HI**14, Inchworm—looper; **SC**63, Looper—a green vegetable worm—feeds on leafy vegetables. 1970 *DARE* File **neNY**, Looper—a measuring worm. 1989 Entomol. Soc. Amer. *Common Names Insects* 165, *Nepytia phantasmaria* . . phantom hemlock looper.

loophole n
1967 *DARE* (Qu. HH44, *Joking or uncomplimentary names for lawyers*) Inf **TX**13, Loophole, liar, shyster; **TX**43, Old loophole, shyster.

looping bird n [Perh from the somewhat erratic flight pattern] =**flicker** n² 1.
1911 *Forest & Stream* 77.174 **NC**, *Colaptes auratus*. . . Looping Bird, Church's Island, N.C.

loop-legged adj Also *loop-legged drunk, loopy-legged* [*looped* drunk]
Thoroughly inebriated.
1944 Wellman *Bowl* 43 **KS**, Them Welshmen drinkin' theirselves looplegged every night. 1960 Wentworth–Flexner *Slang* 325, *Loop-legged.* . . Drunk. *Not common.* 1966–70 *DARE* (Qu. DD15, *A person who is thoroughly drunk*) Infs **AR**56, **OK**42, **TX**18, 20, Loop-legged; **AR**3, Loop-legged drunk; **NM**11, Loopy-legged.

loose adj
1 In bulk; unpackaged.
1939 Hall Coll. **wNC**, Loose. . . In bulk. "The loose calomel that you buy at the drug store." 1943 *LANE* Map 555 (*In bulk*) **scattered NEng, but more freq eNEng, esp ME**, Loose. *Loose* is described as the usual or more common expression by . . [4 infs] . . and as less common by . . [4 infs]. . . 1 inf, **ceRI**, Loose, not of sugar; 1 inf, **seMA**, Loose, of prunes, taken from a box in the store; 1 inf, **neMA**, Loose, of raisins and the like; 1 inf, **neMA**, [ɬuˑwz]. c1970 Pederson *Dial. Surv. Rural GA* **seGA** (*Unpackaged material is material that is bought in _____* [or:] *Now we buy peanut butter in a jar, but years ago when the grocer dipped it out of a barrel, we bought it _____*) 1 inf, Loose. 1980 *DARE* File **Brooklyn NY** (as of c1920), "Loose milk" is milk you take a container to the store to buy. No one outside of Brooklyn ever seems to have heard of it. 1981 *AmSp* 56.63 **eTN**, He says, "Hey, Lucy," says, "you got this milk in a vessel or just poured out here loose on the table?" 1986 Pederson *LAGS Concordance*, 178 infs, **Gulf Region**, Loose (sugar); 1 inf, **ceGA**, Loose lard—dipped from a pail; 1 inf, **cnMS**, Loose lard; 1 inf, **neGA**, Loose peanut butter; 1 inf, **ceAR**, Loose salt; 1 inf, **cGA**, It's sold loose—of sugar and crackers; 1 inf, **seAL**, Loose flour; 1 inf, **swAL**, Loose juice/beer; 1 inf, **ceMS**, You could buy it loose—flour or sugar; 1 inf, **cwMS**, Loose—referring to feed, bought loose; 1 inf, **cMS**, Loose—speaking of buying apples; 1 inf, **seMS**, Chicken feed or mash sometimes sold loose; 1 inf, **cLA**, Loose—speaking of rice; 1 inf, **cLA**, Loose—referring to flour; 1 inf, **ceAR**, Flour would come loose; 1 inf, **swAR**, Crackers were sold loose; 1 inf, **cTX**, Loose—speaking of crackers; 1 inf, **cAR**, Bulk is loose; 1 inf, **ceTN**, Loose coffee—bulk coffee; 1 inf, **cnAL**, Loose feed.
2 Of gravy or grits: thin, watery. Cf **long gravy**, *DS* H37
1967 *DARE* FW Addit **SC**, Loose grits—thin grits, watery. Stiff grits—very thick grits. 1970 *Thompson Coll.* **cnAL** (as of 1920s), *Loose gravy* . . unthickened gravy.

loose-herd v, hence vbl n *loose-herding* **West** Cf **close-herd**
To allow animals to range widely; also fig.
1882 Chase *Editor's Run* 109 **NM**, Loose herding prevailed; that is, everybody, after putting their mark upon their animals, turned them loose upon the prairie, to run where they would. 1892 U.S. Congress *Serial Set* 3124 Doc 105 985 **eOR, eWA**, His [=the herder's] best skill is brought into play to let his flock feed over fresh ground every day in the most leisurely manner consistent with preventing any from getting permanently separated from the main flock and so lost. This is called "loose herding," and more often consists of restraining the active and strong than in driving the weak. 1925 Mulford *Cottonwood Gulch* 148 (*DA*), We've got to round-up, loose herd durin' the day, an' close herd nights. 1939 (1973) FWP *Guide MT* 415, *Loose herdin'*—Dancing with decorous space between partners. 1968 Adams *Western Words* 186, *Loose-herd*—To let cattle scatter somewhat while herding them.

loose-meat sandwich n esp **IA** Cf **sloppy joe**, *DS* H41
A sandwich of ground or shredded beef served on a bun.
1986 *DARE* File **seSD**, Reported orally from a Milwaukee, Wisconsin resident: "In Yankton, SD, a sloppy Joe is called a loose-meat sandwich." [1986 *Cook's* 7.2.24 (*W3* File), The kick of so much of America's vernacular cookery is its take-no-prisoners nomenclature: . . snoots (fried pig snouts) in St. Louis, loosemeats in Sioux City, Iowa, and garbage plates (round-the-world wieners) in upstate New York.] 1994 *NYT Mag.* 30 Oct 18/2, Murray pines for his lily-white town in Iowa. But Iowa? Corn shows and loose-meat sandwiches? Give me a break. 1995 *NADS Letters*, On one of the "Roseanne" [television show] segments, Roseanne's sister returns from a trip to Iowa . . and raves about a place that makes loose meat sandwiches, something unheard of in Roseanne's Illinois town. And on a later segment . . [they] go to the Iowa diner to try to figure out the recipe. *Ibid,* In northwest Iowa (around Sioux City), loose meat sandwiches were common; but . . they were also known as "taverns." *Ibid* **ID**, *Loose-meat sandwich:* also used in Idaho. *Ibid,* First mentioned in a 1991 episode [of "Roseanne"], "loose meat" was described as "sloppy joe without the slop." 1996 *DARE* File **IA** (as of c1980), College friends of mine who had grown up in Iowa used to talk about loose-meat sandwiches. When I asked what loose meat was, I got a variety of answers. One person told me it was seasoned pork roast that had been cooked until it was tender enough to fall apart. Another said it was shredded pork or beef in a gravy or sauce. Someone else claimed it was ground beef that had been browned without being formed into a patty. The only thing everyone seemed to agree on was that a loose-meat sandwich was always served on a bun.

looservee See **lucivee**

loosestrife n
1 Std: a plant of the genus *Lysimachia*. [*OED* 1548 →] For other names of var spp see **five sisters, liberty tea, moneywort 1, swamp candle, wild tea, yellow loosestrife**
2 Std: a plant of the genus *Lythrum*. [*OED* 1548 →] For other names of var spp see **milkweed 6, milk willow herb, purple loosestrife**

lop v¹
1 usu with *about* or *(a)round:* To move slowly or aimlessly; to loll; to idle. [*OED* 1587 →]
1851 (1852) Stowe *Uncle Tom's Cabin* 101, She . . cried about it, she did, and lopped round, as if she'd lost every friend she had. 1882 *Century Illustr. Mag.* 23.652, The señora . . could only lop about in her saddle. 1914 *DN* 4.154 **NH**, Lop. . . To lean, as if drunk. 1965–70 *DARE* (Qu. A9, . . *Wasting time by not working on the job*) Inf **MO**36, Lopping around; (Qu. Y27, *To go about aimlessly, with nothing to do:*

"He's always _____ around the drugstore.") Infs **GA**77, **MA**6, Lopping; (Qu. KK31, *To go about aimlessly looking for distraction: "He doesn't have anything to do, so he's just _____ around."*) Infs **GA**77, **IL**11, **KS**2, **NY**43, 169, Lopping.

2 usu with *down:* To flop down; to lie down and rest; to sit or set (oneself) down. **esp NEast**

1822 [see **lopseed**]. **1839** Kirkland *New Home* 17, Jist come in, and take off your things, and lop down, if you're a mind to. **1862** (1882) Stowe *Pearl of Orr's Is.* 78 **ME**, Ruey said she thought she'd jist lop down a few minutes on the old sofa. **1892** F.P. Humphrey *New Eng. Cactus* 34 (*OEDS*), You'd best lop down on the lounge and get a nap. **1901** *DN* 2.143 **NY, OH**, *Lop.* . . "To lop oneself down," i.e., to recline comfortably. **1929** *AmSp* 5.122 **ME**, Frequent expressions were, "All I want to do is lop." **1968–69** *DARE* (Qu. OO19a, *Talking about stretching out to rest: "He felt tired, so he went to the couch . . and _____ [down for a while]."*) Inf **NY**75, Lopped down; (Qu. OO19b, *Talking about stretching out to rest: "He'll feel better after he has _____ [down a while]."*) Inf **NY**75, Lopped down; (Qu. OO44b, *About somebody in a chair: "All day long he has just _____ [in that chair]."*) Inf **IL**43, Lopped—Inf's mother used to say. **1987** [see **lop n**].

3 See quot.

1969 *DARE* (Qu. Y25, *To walk heavily, making a lot of noise: "He came _____ into the house."*) Inf **GA**72, Lopping.

lop v² [Cf *EDD lap* v.³ 1 "To flog, beat"] Cf *DS* Y14a

1939 *Hall Coll.* **wNC**, *Lop.* . . To strike with the fist. "He lopped him one in the jaw."

‡**lop** n [Prob < **lop** v¹ 2]

A sofa.

1967 *DARE* (Qu. E7, *The piece of upholstered furniture that you can stretch out on to rest*) Inf **NY**31, Lop [lɑp]. **1987** *DARE* File **NY**, *Lop*—a couch or sofa on which one can lop.

lop about See **lop** v¹ 1

lopann n

=**great blue heron.**

1927 Audubon Soc. NH *Bulletin* 7.14, "Lopann"—the name which I first heard given to the great blue heron—was probably only local; I have not heard it now for many years, and fear that it has fallen entirely out of use, but lopann so perfectly describes the flight and manner of this particular species, that its passing can only be contemplated with regret.

lop around See **lop** v¹ 1

lop down v phr¹ [*lop* to cut off branches from]

1959 *VT Hist.* 27.148 **cs,seVT**, *Lop down.* . . To mow, as hay or grass. Common. Windham.

lop down v phr² See **lop** v¹ 2

lope v¹ [Scots, Engl dial var of Scots *loup, lowp* to leap]

1902 *DN* 2.238 **sIL**, *Lope.* . . 2. To mount. 3. To leap upon. 4. To assail. 5. To importune.

lope v² See **leap** 2

lope n [Abbr for *cantalope*] Cf *mater* (at **tomato**)

1969 *DARE* (Qu. I26, . . *Kinds of melons*) Inf **NJ**58, Lopes [lops]—nickname for cantalope. **1994** *DARE* File **ID**, I've heard farmers call cantalopes both "cants" and "lopes."

loper n [Prob **lope** v¹]

1895 *DN* 1.383 **NJ**, *Loper:* a worthless, intrusive fellow.

lop-jawed adj [*lop* to droop]

=**flop-jawed.**

1966–70 *DARE* (Qu. X6, *If a person's lower jaw sticks out prominently . . he's _____*) Inf **IL**140, Lop-jawed [lɑp jɔd]; **MO**17, Lop-jawed.

loplolly adj [Cf *EDD lop-lolly* (at *loblolly* sb. 1) "A lazy, clumsy, hulking fellow; . . also used attrib."; cf also Pronc Intro 3.I.15] Cf **loblolly**

See quots.

1895 *DN* 1.398 **cNY**, *Lop-lolly* [lɑplɑlɪ]: careless, slouchy; used of one's gait and dress. "Mrs. W. is a lop-lolly creature." **1981** Pederson *LAGS Basic Materials* (Kitty-cornered) 1 inf, **csMS**, Loplolly, catty-cornered—furniture at an angle.

lop onto v phr

=**glom** v¹ 2.

1934 Stribling *Unfinished Cathedral* 6 **AL**, Cheap prices fuh evahbody wid de brains to lop onto 'em!

lopper(ed) See **lobber**

lopper-jawed adj Cf **whopper-jawed**

Out of alignment, crooked; also adv *lopper-jawed* askew.

1916 *DN* 4.277 **NE, NC**, *Lopper-jawed.* . . Askew. "That picture hangs lopper-jawed." **1927** *AmSp* 2.360 **cwWV**, *Lopper-jawed* . . crooked. "That picture hangs lopper-jawed." **1940** in 1944 *ADD* 708 **nwVA**, I can't get this window up, it's lopperjawed. **1966** *DARE* (Qu. KK70, *Something that has got out of proper shape: "That house is all _____."*) Inf **FL**31, Lopper-jawed [laughter].

lopping See **lap** v²

loppus n [Cf *EDD loppus* a lazy fellow (at *lop* v² 1.(3))]

See quots.

1914 *DN* 4.109 **cKS**, *Loppus.* . . A large, clumsy creature. "A great, overgrown loppus." **1930** Shoemaker *1300 Words* 37 **cPA Mts** (as of c1900), *Loppus*—A big, fat, ungraceful person.

lop round See **lop** v¹ 1

lopseed n [See quot 1961]

A perennial plant (*Phryma leptostachys*) of the eastern half of the US. Also called **jump plant, tickseed**

1822 Eaton *Botany* 389, Lopseed. . . As the fruit begins to form, it lops down against the rachis. **1840** MA Zool. & Bot. Surv. *Herb. Plants & Quadrupeds* 173, Lopseed. The reflexed seed-vessel is a very distinct character. . . This is an American genus of only one species. **1910** Graves *Flowering Plants* 360 **CT**. **1936** Winter *Plants NE* 121, Lopseed. Eastern U.S. in woods and thickets. Found throughout the state, particularly in the eastern portion. **1961** House *Wild Flowers* 264, Lopseed—*Phryma leptostachya.* . . Flowers erect at first, soon becoming at right angles to the stem when in full bloom and later as the fruit matures becoming abruptly deflexed against the axis of the stem, whence the name "lopseed." **1979** Niering-Olmstead *Audubon Guide N. Amer. Wildflowers E. Region* 678, Lopseed (*Phryma leptostachya*). . . The downward-hanging fruit, which accounts for the common name, makes the plant easily recognizable.

lopster See **lobster**

‡**lopsy lows** n Cf **lop** v¹ 2

1968 *DARE* (Qu. BB28, *Joking names . . for imaginary diseases: "He must have the _____."*) Inf **NJ**18, Lopsy lows [loz].

lopsy-wise adv

Askew.

1900 Day *Up in ME* 46, Maria's [=a hen's] comb hung lopsy-wise / And flapped athwart her filmy eyes. **1914** *DN* 4.76 **nNH, ME**, *Lopsy-wise.* . . In a lopsided manner.

Lor n¹ See **Lord** n¹

lor n² See **law** n¹

lorchel n Also *lorel* [Ger *Lorchel*]

=**false morel.**

1964 Kingsbury *Poisonous Plants U.S.* 97, *Gyromitra esculenta* . . is a fleshy ascomycetous fungus closely related to, and in appearance much like, the highly prized morel. . . The false morel or lorchel, as it is commonly called, bears a brownish or orange irregularly convoluted fleshy mass on a thick, somewhat fluted stem. **1981** Lincoff *Audubon Field Guide Mushrooms* 337, Common names include "Brain Mushroom," "Beefsteak Morel," "Lorchel," and "Edible False Morel." Scientists have discovered that the Conifer False Morel develops a compound similar to one used in the manufacture of rocket fuel. It causes acute illness. **1985** Ammirati et al. *Poisonous Mushrooms* 122, Lorel (lorchel), edible gyromitra, elephant ears.

Lord n¹ Pronc-spp *Lard, Lawd, Lo(h)d, Lo(r), Lud* Cf **law** n², intj

A Pronc varr.

1823 Cooper *Pioneers* 2.182 **cNY** [Black], Nebber tink he die! Oh, Lor-a-gor! **1872** [see **B**1 below]. **1873** [see **B**1 below]. **1884** *Anglia* 7.254 **Sth, S Midl** [Black], Yea, Lawd . . Lawd, jes' so . . to be sure. **1885** in 1976 Rose *Doc. Hist. Slavery* 398 **SC**, As he clasped me in his arms, he said "bres de Lo, my son, wat is de matter? **1893** Shands *MS Speech* 43, Lawd [lɔd]. Negro and illiterate white for lord. **1902** (1904)

Rowe *Maid of Bar Harbor* 166 **ME**, Lor, gran'daddy, don't ye know? **1906** *DN* 3.145 **nwAR**, *Lo'* [lɔ] *bless us.* . . Lord bless us! A woman's ejaculation. **1924** *DN* 5.260 [Exclams], *Substitutes for "Lord".* . . Lo(h)d-a-massa. . . oh lud. **1928** Peterkin *Scarlet Sister Mary* 274 **SC** [Gullah], Do yunnah hurry, fo Lawd's sake. **1958** Humphrey *Home from the Hill* 210 **neTX**, "Oh, Lard, yessum!" she said, both scandalized and amused. **1959** McAtee *Oddments* 5 **cNC**, Dear Lawd! **1963** Owens *Look to River* 100 **TX**, Oh, Lawdy, oh, Lawd. **1967–70** *DARE* (Qu. NN7) Inf **LA**7, Lawd have mercy [ˌlɔdəˈmɛsɪ, ˌlɔdˌhævˈmɛsɪ]; (Qu. NN27a, *Weakened substitutes for 'god': "My _____!"*) Infs **RI**6, **SC**69, Lawd; (Qu. NN28a, *Exclamations beginning with 'good': "Good _____!"*) Inf **SC**54, Lawd. **1993** *DARE* File **UT**, My Utah students say . . "Lard" when they warship.

B Senses.

1 in phr *Lord have mercy*, also minced phrr *Lawk 'a' mercy*, *Lawsy mercy*, *Lordy mercy* and varr: Used to express surprise, dismay, etc. **chiefly Sth, S Midl** See Map *esp freq among Black speakers* Cf **lawks, lawsy, mercy**

1851 Hooper *Widow Rugby's Husband* 85 **AL**, Lord-a-massey, 'Squire, how you talk! **1872** Schele de Vere *Americanisms* 616, *Lord a mussy* or *Luddy Mussy*, for Lord have mercy! are ejaculations heard with almost equal frequency in New England and in the South, where they are much affected by the negroes. "Lud a mussy, Mas Bob, is dat you? whar on arth is you gwine to?" **1873** Giles *Slang* 15, *La, Law*, and *Lawk* are vicious pronunciations of *Lord*. "Lauk a mercy on me" is "Lord have mercy on me." **1883** Harris *Nights with Remus* 240 **GA** [Black], Lawdy mussy, Brer Rabbit! Whar my vittles? **1884** Baldwin *Yankee School-Teacher* 9 **VA** [Black], I kin hoof it as easy as ter grub up a sassafras root; but laws-a-mussy! you can't tote yerself ha'f dat dist'nce, Missy! **1896** Harris *Sister Jane* 87 **GA** [Black], Well, the lawsy Massy! . . What'll folks do next? **1906** *DN* 3.144 **nwAR**, Lawsy mercy. . . A woman's exclamation. **1909** *DN* 3.344 **eAL, wGA**, Lawsy mussy (pon my soul). . . Lord have mercy upon my soul: a feminine ejaculation. Sometimes among negroes *lawsee massy* is heard. *Ibid* 347, Lordy, Lordy mussy (pon my soul). **1913** Kephart *Highlanders* 229 **sAppalachians**, As a woman described it, "Dew pizen comes like a risin', and laws-a-marcy how it does hurt!" **1917** *DN* 4.395 **neOH**, Land-a-massy! Lord-a-massy! Lordy-massy! Lordy! . . [*DN* Ed: Also Mass. [lɔksamæsɪ]]. **1924** *DN* 5.260 [Exclams], *Substitutes for "Lord".* . . Lawsamassa, lawse-a-massy, lo(h)d-a-massa (*or* -massy) (*for* Lord have mercy). **1937** NE *Univ. Univ. Studies* 37.110 [Terms from play-party songs], *Lord a massy, Laws a massy, Lawsie Massa*, int. See "Old Dan Tucker." **1944** *PADS* 2.58 **swMO, VA, NC, SC**, Lawsy mercy [ˈlɔzɪ ˈmɝsɪ]. **1946** *PADS* 6.39 **VA** (as of 1900–10), Lack o'mercy on me, this is none of I. (Used when something pleasant and unexpected happens to the speaker.) Bridgewater, Va., region. Fairly common. **1947** *PADS* 8.36 **csVA**, Lack o'mercy me, this is none of I. (In the Mother Goose story about the old woman whose petticoats were cut off by the pedlar, *lawk* is used: "Lawk 'a' mercy me [Lord have mercy on me], this is none of I.") **1954** *Harder Coll.* **cwTN**, Lawsy mercy. **1959** McAtee *Oddments* 5 **cNC**, Law mercy. **1959** *VT Hist.* 27.147, Laws of Mercy! . . Rare. **1962** Atwood *Vocab. TX* 70, *Exclamations of disgust.* . . lordy mercy. **1965–70** *DARE* (Qu. NN4, . . *Ways of answering 'no': "Would you lend him ten dollars?"* "_____.") Inf **VA**15, Lordy mercy, no; (Qu. NN7, *Exclamations of surprise*) Infs **KY**30, **TN**46, Lord have mercy; **LA**7, [ˌlɔdəˈmɛsɪ] or [ˌlɔdˌhævˈmɛsɪ]—also used as an exclamation of intensification: "We had fun back then. Lawd have mercy!";

GA84, Laws-a-mercy [ˌlɔːsəˈmɛsi]; (Qu. NN8a, *Exclamations of annoyance or disgust: "Oh _____. I've lost my glasses again."*) Inf **KY**47, Lord have mercy; (Qu. NN9a, *Exclamations showing great annoyance*) Inf **KY**42, Lord have mercy; (Qq. NN20a, b, 21a, c, *Exclamations caused by sudden pain*) Infs **FL**2, **MS**16, 43, Lord have mercy; **SC**26, Lord have mercy—fits anywhere pain is concerned; **VA**15, Lordy mercy; (Qu. NN28a, *Exclamations beginning with 'good': "Good _____!"*) Inf **MD**30, Lord have mercy on us—in conversation; (Qu. NN29b) Inf **GA**89, Lord o'mercy; (Qu. NN32) Inf **FL**48, Lord ha' mercy. [6 of 14 total Infs Black] **1970** Tarpley *Blinky* 300 **neTX**, Mild expression of disgust. . . Lordy mercy. **1989** Pederson *LAGS Tech. Index* 342 **Gulf Region** *(Land's sakes)* 58 infs, (My) Lord, have mercy; 6 infs, Lordy mercy; 1 inf, Oh, Lordy, have mercy. [22 of 64 total infs Black]

2 also lower case; also *lord bird*: =**harlequin duck**, esp the male; hence n *cock lord* the male; n *lady lord* the female. Cf **lord and lady 1**

1844 Giraud *Birds Long Is.* 337, The Harlequin Duck is an inhabitant of both continents. . . Its singular and handsome markings render it very conspicuous, and it is known to the gunners by the high-sounding appellation of the "lord." **1888** Trumbull *Names of Birds* 91, *Harlequin duck.* . . Known also as *Squealer* at Machias Port, Me., and as *Lord* simply, at Jonesport, same state. **1955** MA Audubon Soc. *Bulletin* 39.376, *Harlequin Duck*. Cock Lord (Maine. The male . .); Lady Lord (Maine. This name is both logical in designating the female of a species often called simply "lord," and illogical in implying that "lord" can be feminine.); Lord (New England); Lord and Lady (Maine, N.H., Mass. In allusion to its handsome plumage; while these terms refer basically to the sexes, they are customarily used together to indicate the species and usually in the plural, "Lords and Ladies"); Lord and Lady Duck (Maine, Mass.); Lord Bird (Maine).

lord n²,v See **lard** n¹, v

lord-a-mighty See **lord god 1**

lord and lady n

1 also *lord and lady duck*: =**harlequin duck**—usu used in pl in ref to groups containing both sexes. [See quot 1929] **chiefly NEng** Cf **Lord n¹ B2**

[**1770** in **1792** Cartwright *Jrl. Labrador* 1.20, I shot four eider ducks, and seven lords and ladies.] **1792** Belknap *Hist. NH* 3.168, Lord and Lady, or Sea Pigeon,—*Anas histrionica?* **1832** Williamson *Hist. ME* 1.142, The *Lord and Lady*, or *Noddy* is as large as a pigeon, good for food. . . Its perpetual whiffles with the wings when flying, give it name. **1888** Trumbull *Names of Birds* 91, *Harlequin duck.* . . Along the coast from New Brunswick to Salem, Mass., *Lord and lady*; farther south than this the species is rare. **1927** in **1931** McCorrison *Letters Fraternity* 135 **NEng**, But I once shot four ducks, two cocks and two hens, called "Lords and Ladies." **1929** Forbush *Birds MA* 1.261, Harlequin! Rightly named, fantastically decorated. . . The bird is so elegant that the people of the north coasts have well named its little companies the "Lords and Ladies" of the sea. **1953** Jewett *Birds WA* 144, Painted Duck, Lord and Lady; Rock Duck [etc]. **1955** [see **Lord n¹ B2**]. **1977** Bull–Farrand *Audubon Field Guide Birds* 355, In the Northeast these [=harlequin] ducks are known locally as "Lords and Ladies."

2 A pair of **old-squaws**.

1903 Dawson *Birds OH* 2.612, Old-squaw. . . Synonyms.—Long-tailed Duck . . Lord and Lady (male and female). *Ibid* 613, A pair of them seated upon the water are handsome enough to merit the name applied to them by the hunters of the Pacific Coast, "Lord and Lady."

lord and lady duck See **lord and lady 1**

lord bird See **Lord n¹ B2**

Lord Chesterfield See **chesterfield 2**

lord god n

1 also *lawd gawd, lord god almighty*, ~ *bird*, ~ *peckerwood*, ~ *woodpecker, lord-a-mighty, lord cock*, ~ *guard*, ~*-to-god*, *lordy god*: =**pileated woodpecker**. [Prob folk-etym varr of **logcock**] **chiefly SE, esp Gulf States** See Map Cf **do lord n, good god 1, great god**

1909 *DN* 3.347 **eAL, wGA**, Lord-god. . . A red-headed woodpecker. **1913** *Auk* 30.496 **Okefenokee GA**, Pileated Woodpecker . . Lord-God Woodpecker. **1942** Faulkner *Go Down* 202 **MS**, A bird, the big woodpecker called Lord-to-God by negroes. **1945** McAtee *Nomina Abitera* 47, Lord God would follow naturally from Good God but even so it seems more probably a corruption of the very appropriate vernacular,

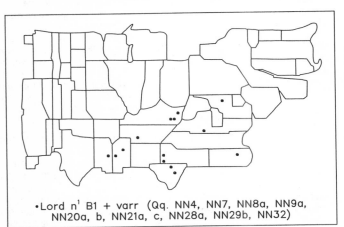

•Lord n¹ B1 + varr (Qq. NN4, NN7, NN8a, NN9a, NN20a, b, NN21a, c, NN28a, NN29b, NN32)

logcock. Lord guard doubtless is of the same derivation. The matter evidently is one of sounds for other combinations of the basic syllables are used as good guard and log guard. **1947** (1964) Randolph *Ozark Superstitions* 248, The great pileated woodpecker, rare in most sections of the country, is still fairly common in the Ozarks. Most Ozarkers call it a woodhen, but it is also known as "God Almighty" or "Lord God Peckerwood," doubtless because of its large size; it looks as big as a teal duck, or a crow. **1950** *PADS* 14.43 **SC**, *Lawd-Gawd . . Lord God.* The pileated woodpecker. "So called in Negro dialect because of his impressive look." This derivation is suggested by Mr. C.M. McKinnon. Another name for this bird is *logcock,* of which our entry may be a corruption. However, the fact that this bird is also known among the Negroes of the *Pee-Dee* as *Doctor Jesus,* lends support to Mr. McKinnon's theory. **1951** *AmSp* 26.93, It is evident that *logcock* is the basic word. . . More extravagant terms, both in form and range [include] . . *lord god almighty* (Fla.); and *oh my god* (Miss.) **1955** *Oriole* 20.1.9 **GA**, Pileated Woodpecker. . . *Logcock* (general); *Log God, Log Guard, Lord Cock, Lord Guard* (corruptions of the preceding term). **1965–70** *DARE* (Qu. Q18, *Joking names and nicknames for woodpeckers*) Infs **AR**48, **LA**7, **MS**53, Lord god; **MS**60, Lord god [lɔːəd gɑɪd]; **AL**22, **GA**35, Lord god bird; **FL**4, Lord-a-mighties; **TN**22, Lord god almighty; **MS**16, Lordy god; (Qu. Q14) Inf **AR**48, Pileated woodpeckers—lord gods—negroes call them that; (Qu. Q17, . . *Kinds of woodpeckers*) Inf **MS**53, Lord gods. c**1970** Pederson *Dial. Surv. Rural GA* (*What do you call a bird that makes a hole in a tree trunk with its bill?*) 1 inf, **seGA**, Lord gods. **1975** Newell *If Nothin' Don't Happen* 65 **nwFL**, Once in a while a big old "Lord God" would light on a dead light'd snag out by the hog pen and hammer that iron-hard wood till it would ring. This here woodpecker is two or three times as big as the ordinary kind and is sort of speckledy-black with a red top-knot. **1981** Pederson *LAGS Basic Materials,* 1 inf, **ceAR**, My stepdaughter, there, told me the other day, there was one of them old big ones down there in her yard the other day on that old rotten stump. And he's called a *lord-god.* He's a big old bird; he's a redhead; looks just like a peckerwood, but he's just about five times, six times as big. He fly lazy, you know. He go down to the woods, "Lord, God; Lord, God; Lord, God," just as hard as he could go. That's what it sounds like . . he's saying; [1 inf, **csMS**, Lord God [FW: expletive; speculating on how lord god woodpecker was named]]. **1986** Pederson *LAGS Concordance,* 25 infs, **Gulf Region,** Lord god(s); 1 inf, **ceAL**, Lord god—biggest one; 1 inf, **seAR**, Lord god—big old redheaded peckerwood; 1 inf, **nwLA**, Lord god—great big old bird—woodpecker; 1 inf, **nwLA**, Lord god—great big redheads with loud call; 1 inf, **seLA**, Lord God bird. [*DARE* Ed: Of 22 infs who provided information other than the headword, 17 mentioned the large size of the bird.]

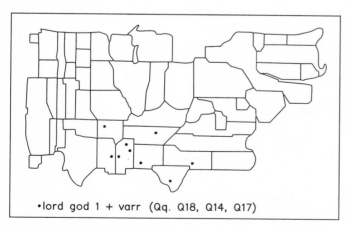

•lord god 1 + varr (Qq. Q18, Q14, Q17)

2 =**ivory-billed woodpecker.**
1951 *AmSp* 26.94, The larger, but now very rare, relative of the pileated, that is, the ivory-billed, woodpecker, shares several of the names cited. These include . . *good god, lord god* (Texas), and *log god* (La., Texas).

3 Perh a **sandhill crane.**
1981 Pederson *LAGS Basic Materials,* 1 inf, **swMS**, Lord god—a crane, not a woodpecker—brown color—water fowl.

lord god almighty (or bird, peckerwood, woodpecker), lord guard See **lord god 1**

Lordie See **Lordy**

Lord's breadwagon n Cf **breadwagon 2, corn wagon, mud ~ 2, potato ~**
Thunder.
1913 *DN* 4.58 **TN**, *Lord's bread-wagon.* . . Thunder: noted at Montvale Springs.

Lord's candlestick, Lord's candle yucca See **Our Lord's candle(stick)**

Lord's fertilizer n *joc*
=**poor man's fertilizer.**
1985 *DARE* File **neOH, cVT**, "The Lord's fertilizer"—Spring snow.

lord-to-god See **lord god 1**

Lordy intj Also sp *Lordie;* pronc-spp *Lawdy, Luddy* esp **Sth, S Midl** See Map Cf *Lordy mercy* (at **Lord** n[1] **B1**)
Used as an expression of surprise, dismay, annoyance, etc.
1853 *S. Lit. Messenger* 19.602 **Gulf States,** On the sofa . . you sank down and bounded up and said Lordy! **1897** Stuart *Simpkinsville* 155 **AR**, Lordy, but it all but takes my breath away. **1903** *DN* 2.299 **Cape Cod MA** (as of a1857), *Lordy,* interj. Exclamation of surprise. **1906** *DN* 3.145 **nwAR**, *Luddy.* . . A woman's exclamation. **1923** in 1983 Taft *Blues Lyric Poetry* 66, [Title:] Ida Cox's Lawdy, Lawdy Blues. [Lyrics:] Lord Lord : Lordy Lordy Lord / Oh the man I love : treats me like a dog. **1924** *DN* 5.260 [Exclams], *Substitutes for "Lord".* . . Lawdy. . . Lordie. **1925** *DN* 5.359 **seGA** [Black], But Lawdy Jedus [lɔːdɪ jidəs]. **1928** *Sat. Eve. Post* 12 May 20 **NY**, But seven hundred dollars and his pocket piece back again! Phew! Lordy! **1950** *WELS* (*Exclamations of surprise*), 1 Inf, **swWI**, Lawdy. **1965–70** *DARE* (Qu. NN4, . . *Ways of answering 'no': "Would you lend him ten dollars?" "_____."*) Inf **VA**2, Oh Lordy, no; (Qu. NN6a, *Exclamations of joy*) Inf **SC**40, Do-Lordy Mamma! (Qu. NN8a, *Exclamations of annoyance or disgust: "Oh _____. I've lost my glasses again."*) Infs **KY**84, **VA**2, Lordy; (Qu. NN9a, *Exclamations showing great annoyance: "_____. The electric power is off again."*) Inf **TN**23, Oh Lordy; (Qu. NN20b, *Exclamations caused by sudden pain—a slight burn*) Inf **KY**6, Oh Lordy; (Qu. NN21a, *Exclamations caused by sudden pain—a pinched finger*) Infs **KY**21, **NJ**50, (Oh) Lordy; (Qu. NN27a, *Weakened substitutes for 'god': "My _____!"*) Infs **NM**11, **VA**21, (Oh) Lordy; (Qu. NN28a, *Exclamations beginning with 'good': "Good _____!"*) Inf **GA**13, Lordy. **1966** Barnes–Jensen *Dict. UT Slang* 29, *Lordy!* . . an exclamation of surprise or astonishment. **1986** Pederson *LAGS Concordance* **Gulf Region,** 11 infs, Oh, Lordy; 6 infs, My (or good, hey, hoo, well, why) Lordy; 2 infs, Lordy; 1 inf, Lordy, no; 1 inf, Oh, Lordy, have mercy.

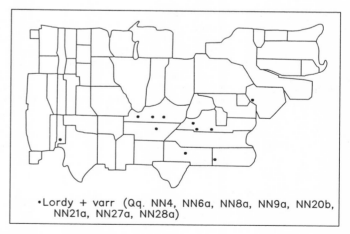

•Lordy + varr (Qq. NN4, NN6a, NN8a, NN9a, NN20b, NN21a, NN27a, NN28a)

lordy god See **lord god 1**

Lordy mercy See **Lord** n[1] **B1**

lorel See **lorchel**

lose v
A Gram forms.
1 pres: usu *lose;* also *loss, lost.* [Scots, Ir, nEngl dial *loss,* swEngl dial *lost*] Cf *DNE* (at *lose* v)
1837 Sherwood *Gaz. GA* 70, *Loss,* for lose; he *loss* it, for loses it or lost it. **1847** Hurd *Grammatical Corrector* 50, *Loss,* for *lose;* as, "Where did you loss it?" "You will loss more than you will gain by the

enterprise." *Principally Irish—very gross.* **1884** *Anglia* 7.273 **Sth, S Midl** [Black], To los' his politeness. **1907** *German Amer. Annals* 9.381 **sePA,** *Loss. . . Lose.* "Be careful of that or you'll loss it." **1922** Gonzales *Black Border* 311 **sSC, GA coasts** [Gullah glossary], *Loss*—lose, loses, lost, losing. **1940** (1941) Bell *Swamp Water* 16 **Okefenokee GA,** "I ain't aiming to go in that swamp and lost myself," Bud said. *Ibid* 70, Ben, you'll lost yourself in that swamp, and I won't never see you again. **1982** *Barrick Coll.* **csPA,** *Loss . . lose.*

2 past, past pple, ppl adj: usu *lost;* also *lose(d), loss, losted, losten.*

1829 Kirkham *Engl. Grammar* 192, *Vulgarisms. . .* Irish. . . Loss it—lost it. **1837** [see **1** above]. **1884** *Anglia* 7.252 **Sth, S Midl** [Black], To the regular forms of the Irregular verbs as used by the whites, the Negro adds the following forms of his own. . . *Pres.* lose (loss)—*Past.* losed, loss—*Pass. Part.*—[=same forms as for past]. **1933** Rawlings *South Moon* 131 **nFL,** Don't you fellers git losted in the scrub? **c1938** in 1970 Hyatt *Hoodoo* 2.1122 **wTN,** Yo' mostly have an idea which way whatevah yo' had losted went. **1942** (1971) Campbell *Cloud-Walking* 156 **seKY,** 'Charming Beauty Bright' ain't got but three verses now the ways folks sings it. Tothers are losted. **1953** Brewer *Word Brazos* 4 **eTX** [Black], Dey say dat de why he comed an' jined de chu'ch dat Sunday was 'caze he losed all his money in a dice game down to Falls on de Brazos, and de Lawd meck hit come to 'im to git shed of his sinful ways an' live a good life. **1966** *DARE* (Qu. K48, *When a horse is short of breath*) Inf **SC9,** He losten he wind—can't work anymore after that. **1970** *Thompson Coll.* **TN, seMI, swCA, seLA, MO,** I've heard lose for the past tenses since the 1930's. . . Two of the men (a Tennesseean and a Missourian) with whom I played poker, 1945, said e.g. "hell, I lose forty bucks last night.["] [Also heard Detroit 1946–60, Los Angeles 1960's, New Orleans 1961, etc] One of my friends, a disgusted millionaire . . recently said, "I drilled seven wells up there las-cheer, an I lose my ass on ever one of em." **1986** Pederson *LAGS Concordance,* 1 inf, **neFL,** He lose his temper; 1 inf, **cLA,** Losed on it = lost on it.

B Sense.

To bleed. [Prob ellip for *lose blood*]

1913 *DN* 4.4 **ME,** *Lose. . .* To menstruate. "She was losing all the time she was carrying her baby."

lose an eye v phr Cf **blink** v **1, blinky** adj **1**
Of milk: to turn sour.

1967 *DARE* (Qu. H58, *Milk that's just beginning to become sour*) Inf **NE7,** Lost an eye.

losed See **lose** A2

lose flesh See **flesh** n B

losel n, also attrib [*OED* 1362 →]
A worthless person; hence n *loselry* the character or behavior of such a person.

1806 (1970) Webster *Compendious Dict.* 180, *Losel. . .* a scoundrel, worthless fellow, cheat. *ob.* [*DARE* Ed: This entry was taken over from Webster's English model, exc that Webster added *"ob."*] **1849** (1857) Irving *Hist. NY* 283, Though descended from a family which suffered much injury from the losel Yankees of those times, . . yet I should have passed over all these wrongs with forgiveness and oblivion. **1928** Chapman *Happy Mt.* 73 **eTN,** I recall he said the boy had on a suit of washed-away overalls and a broken hat and he wondered efn such a losel could be trusted with so much goods. **1970** *DARE* File **nwTN,** *Losel* ['lɑsəl] = a worthless person; *loselry* ['lɑsəlrɪ] = "no-accountness."

lose off v phr
1 To drop or come off.

1874 VT State Bd. Ag. *Rept. for 1873–74* 717, I think that tin buckets are preferable for catching sap to wooden ones, as they . . have no hoops to lose off. **1906** *DN* 3.145 **nwAR,** *Lose off. . .* To come off, be lost. "A wheel lost off as they were driving to town."

2 also *lose out:* To miss from one's possession; to lose.

1966 *DARE* Tape **ME26,** He was comin' . . with a load of beans. There was a little quick place there they had to come through; the road was just grubbed out. . . When he come up over this, he lost off a bag of beans. **1986** Pederson *LAGS Concordance,* 1 inf, **ceGA,** You lose them out—they fall out of your pockets. **1994** *DARE* File **NEng** (as of 1960s–present), "Are you missing a button on your coat?" "Oh, I must have lost it off somewhere."

lose one's cookies See **cookie** n¹ **3**

lose one's okra See **okra** C2

lose out See **lose off 2**

lose time v phr esp **Sth, S Midl**
To waste time; to fool around; hence n *time-loser* one who wastes time.

1967–70 *DARE* (Qu. A9, . . *Wasting time by not working on the job*) Infs **GA30, NC49, 78, SC43, TX36,** Losing time; **MO21,** Lost his time; **NJ51,** Lost time; (Qu. Y28, *A person who loiters about with nothing to do*) Inf **IL48,** Time-loser; (Qu. KK31, *To go about aimlessly looking for distraction:* "He doesn't have anything to do, so he's just _____ around.") Inf **VA39,** Loafing, losing time. **1970** Hyatt *Hoodoo* 1.549 (as of c1935) **neFL,** Now it was [=there was] a man there she had been knockin' aroun' wit, an' another woman come and commence to *lose time* with him.

losh See **lush**

loss See **lose** A1, 2

lossage n
Waste.

1986 Pederson *LAGS Concordance,* 1 inf, **seAL,** Lossage; 1 inf, **ceTN,** No lossage of meat in the country, used all of it.

lossenger See **lozenger**

losset n [Obs Ir, nEngl dial < Ir *losad* kneading-trough] Cf **keeler**
1939 Wolcott *Yankee Cook Book* 367, [In answer to a quiz about old-fashioned kitchen utensils:] *Losset:* wooden container for holding milk.

lossyme See **lawsy**

lost n [Var of *loss; OED* →1671; but cf Intro "Language Changes" I.8] Cf **acrost,** *clift* (at **cliff**)
[**1925** *DN* 5.335 **Nfld,** *Lost. . .* Loss. "De lost o' her'm dear son."] **1970** *DARE* (Qu. KK68, *When people don't think alike about something:* "We agree on most things, but on politics we're _____.") Inf **PA247,** At a lost. **1986** Pederson *LAGS Concordance* (*He had to sell it at a loss*) 1 inf, **neTX,** At a lost on it.

lost v See **lose** A1

lost-and-found n
Any of var children's hiding games; see quot.

1968–70 *DARE* (Qu. EE3, *Games in which you hide an object and then look for it*) Inf **FL48,** Lost-and-found; (Qu. EE13a, *Games in which every player hides except one, and that one must try to find the others*) Inf **MO35,** Hide-and-seek, lost-and-found.

lost bread n [Calque of Fr *pain perdu*] **LA**
French toast.

1967 LeCompte *Word Atlas* 285 **seLA,** Bread slices dipped in a mixture of beaten eggs, sugar and milk and then fried. . . lost bread [1 of 21 infs]. **1980** (1987) Syatt *Like We Say* 213 **New Orleans LA,** *Lost bread*—French toast sprinkled with powdered sugar. **1983** Reinecke *Coll.* 7 **LA,** *Lost bread* ['lɔs‚brɛːd]—French Toast, also in English "pain perdu." **1986** Pederson *LAGS Concordance,* 1 inf, **csLA,** Lost bread; 1 inf, **seLA,** Lost bread—blacks say, most people unaware of it; 1 inf, **cnLA,** Lost bread—French toast, cinnamon, sugar.

losted, losten See **lose** A2

lost John n Cf **john constant, johnnycake,** *DS* H14
1986 Pederson *LAGS Concordance,* 1 inf, **seFL,** Lost John—another expression for corn bread.

lost-my-handkerchief n Cf **handkerchief** B
The game of drop-the-handkerchief.

1970 *DARE* (Qu. EE1, . . *Games . . children play . . in which they form a ring, and either sing or recite a rhyme*) Inf **FL48,** Lost-my-handkerchief—same as drop-the-handkerchief.

lost salmon n [See quot 1887]
=humpback salmon.

1881 *Amer. Naturalist* 15.178, Hump-back . . [vernacular names include] holia, lost salmon, Puget Sound salmon. **1887** Goode *Amer. Fishes* 481, *Oncorhynchus gorbuscha. . .* The English-speaking people call it generally the "Hump-back Salmon". . . In the Sacramento and Columbia it is only an estray, on the latter river being sometimes called "Lost Salmon". **1902** Jordan–Evermann *Amer. Fishes* 150, In the Sacramento River it [=*Oncorhynchus gorbuscha*] occurs each year but in very limited numbers and is there known as the lost salmon. **1911** U.S.

Bur. Census *Fisheries 1908* 315, The humpbacked salmon, or lost salmon *(O[ncorhynchus] gorbuscha),* ranges from the Sacramento River to Alaska.

lost sheep n
   1968 *DARE* (Qu. EE28, *Games played in the water*) Inf **NJ39,** Water tag, lost sheep—dive and hide (in meadows), hide and seek in water.

lot n
   1a A small enclosure or pen for domestic animals, often near a barn; a **barnyard 1.** Note: For use in compounds see **1b** below. **scattered, but chiefly Sth, S Midl, TX** See Map Cf **chipyard, corral 1**
   1831 Peck *Guide for Emigrants* 166 **IL,** In autumn they [=oxen] were shut up in a lot, fed with corn in the ear, . . with water. **1886** *Harper's New Mth. Mag.* 74.48 **VA,** He heard some of his young mules galloping around the yard, and he made a sleepy resolve to sell them all, or to dismiss his overseer for letting them get out of the lot. **1893** Shands *MS Speech* 44, If one is told that anything is in the *lot,* he is to understand that it is in the same enclosure as the stables. **1909** *DN* 3.347 **eAL, wGA,** *Lot.* . . Barn-yard. The latter word is never used. **1923** *DN* 5.213 **swMO,** *Lot.* . . A small enclosure. . . "Put your mule in the lot." **1930** *DN* 6.82 **cSC,** *Lot.* . . A stable yard. Never used in compounds. Universal. **1942** Faulkner *Go Down* 83 **MS,** He . . waited beside the lot fence while the rapid beat of the mare's feet died away in the dusk and then returned. **1949** Kurath *Word Geog.* 55, The yard adjoining or surrounding the barn is regularly called *barn yard* north of the Potomac, *lot* (or *stable lot, barn lot, farm lot*) to the south of it. **1950** *AmSp* 25.230 **ceMS** [Southern plantation terms], *Lot.* Barnyard. **1963** Owens *Look to River* 56 **TX,** Times past, he would have waited for Basil and held the lot gate for him. **1965–70** *DARE* (Qu. M13, *The space near the barn with a fence around it where you keep the livestock*) 156 Infs, **chiefly Sth, S Midl, TX,** Lot(s); (Qu. M14, *The open area around or next to the barn*) 93 Infs, **chiefly Sth, S Midl, TX,** Lot; **MO27,** Lot in front of the barn; **FL26,** Lot yard; (Qu. M15, *The place outdoors where pigs are kept*) Infs **FL12, LA8, NC24, PA132,** Lot; (Qu. L17, *. . Manure*) Infs **GA17, MS81,** Lot fertilize; **MS81,** Lot raking. **1966** [see **1b(2)** below]. **1967** *PADS* 47.27 **MS,** *Lot.* . . 'An enclosure for domestic live stock, usually situated near a dwelling.' . . The lot is really a small pasture almost always near a barn. In it the animals can be 'kept up' rather than 'let out to pasture.' **1973** Allen *LAUM* 1.189 **Upper MW** (as of c1950), For the area near or around the barn where stock may be kept or fed. . . The Southern and South Midland *lot,* with such combinations as *cow lot, feed lot, feeding lot,* and *cattle lot* occur chiefly in the southeastern quadrant of the U[pper] M[idwest], with the basic *barnlot* almost limited to the South Midland speech area of southern Iowa. **1978** Mayer *Beef Club* 4 **SC** (as of 1840–1940), He would select a choice young steer . . from his herd and would pen it up in the lot. *Ibid* 9, *Lot*—a pen for livestock, usually smaller and nearer the house than a pasture. **1989** Pederson *LAGS Tech. Index* 58 **Gulf Region,** 398 infs, Lot.

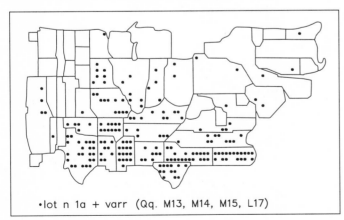

•lot n 1a + varr (Qq. M13, M14, M15, L17)

b In var combs:
   (1) *barn lot:* See **barn lot.**
   (2) *hog lot, pig ~, cow ~, farm ~, stable ~,* etc. **widespread, but less freq N Atl, West** See Map Cf **cow lot, hog ~, horse ~ 1**
   1835 (1841) Cooper *Monikins* 2.145, They would fence it up at each end, and turn it into a hog-lot. **1850** U.S. Patent Office *Annual Rept. for 1849: Ag.* 144 **GA,** The man . . has . . no time to make manure, or

to haul out and spread the little that is dropped in his horse-lot. **1896** (1909) White *Real Issue* 156 **OH,** Colonel Hucks went for a prowl down in the cow lot. **1939** *Hall Coll.* **ceTN,** They was to go to the mule lot. **1949** [see **1a** above]. **1965–70** *DARE* (Qu. M15, *The place outdoors where pigs are kept*) 140 Infs, **widespread, but less freq N Atl, West,** Hog (*or* pig) lot; (Qu. M13, *The space near the barn with a fence around it where you keep the livestock*) 38 Infs, **chiefly SE, Lower Missip Valley, OK, TX,** Cow lot; 24 Infs, **chiefly S Atl, Inland Sth, OK, TX,** Horse lot; 18 Infs, **scattered,** Calf (*or* cattle, chicken, dry, exercise, hog, stable, etc) lot; (Qu. M14, *The open area around or next to the barn*) 38 Infs, **scattered,** Cow (*or* barnyard, farm, horse, stock, etc) lot; (Qu. L65) Inf **KY43,** Hog-lot fence. **1966** Dakin *Dial. Vocab. Ohio R. Valley* 2.88, The simplex *the lot* or more specific varieties *horse lot, cow ~, mule ~, calf ~, stock ~,* and *chicken ~* are used frequently in addition to or instead of *barn lot.* In the areas where *lot* competes with *barn yard,* the full *barn lot* is more common. **1967** *PADS* 47.27 **MS,** Terms like *mule lot* or *calf lot* are often used to designate the type of animal to be kept in the small pasture. **1973** [see **1a** above]. **1989** Pederson *LAGS Tech. Index* 58 **Gulf Region,** 53 infs, Cow lot; 48 infs, Horse lot; 18 infs, Calf (*or* cattle, hog, mule) lot; 17 infs, Back (*or* barnyard, catch, farm, front, grassy, milk, open, pasture, puncheon, stomp) lot; [73 infs, Barn lot; 18 infs, Feedlot].

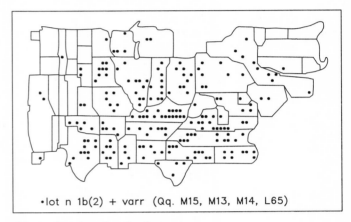

•lot n 1b(2) + varr (Qq. M15, M13, M14, L65)

(3) *feeding lot:* See **feedlot.**
   2 often in combs: A field or pasture. **formerly chiefly NEast; now more widespread** Cf **woodlot**
   1840 (1940) Arnold *Diaries* 147 **VT,** 3 cows of Mr. Stoddard began to go in my mowing lot. **1845** Judd *Margaret* 325 **NEng,** I kept him [=a colt] here in the mow-lot. **1894** *DN* 1.341 **wCT,** *Lot:* field. In all compounds; pasture-lot, corn-lot, meadow-lot, etc. *Ibid* 342 **wCT,** *Lot-rows:* when several men are hoeing in a "lot" where the rows are of unequal length, the farm etiquette requires the outside man to take the next row to his own in returning, and the others to follow in order, so that each shall do the same amount of work in the "bout." **1912** *DN* 3.584 **wIN,** *Pasture-lot.* . . A small pasture. **1939** *LANE* Map 114 *(Pasture),* The terms *lot* and *field,* denoting a fenced-in pasture adjoining the barn or the barnyard, . . are entered in the commentary. . . 11 infs, **CT, seMA,** Lot = pasture (*or* small pasture); 1 inf, **swCT,** Lot, 'where cows are turned out to grass'; 1 inf, **cCT,** Sheep lot = sheep pasture; 1 inf, **seCT,** Lot, any fenced-in piece of land; 1 inf, **cCT,** Pasture, 'nice and clean'; lot, 'not so clean'; 1 inf, **cCT,** Lot, used for grazing; 1 inf, **Long Is. NY,** Pasture lot; 1 inf, **seMA,** Pasture, 400–500 acres; lot, smaller; 1 inf, **seMA,** Lot, for mowing; 1 inf, **seMA,** Lot, pasture lot; 1 inf, **neMA,** Lot = pasture or woodland. [*DARE* Ed: Some of these infs may refer instead to **1** above.] *Ibid* Map 120 *(Field),* The map shows the terms *field, ground, lot, plot,* . . designating a piece of cultivated land where potatoes, corn, or other crops are grown. . . 33 infs, 29 **CT, MA,** Lot (*or* potato lot, cabbage lot, tobacco lot, rye lot, etc). **1946** *PADS* 5.29 **VA,** *Lot.* . . A field (of tobacco, etc.); not common. **1951** *NY Folkl. Qrly.* 7.180, Three terms characteristic of the Virginia Piedmont are found frequently in the Genesee Valley and the Finger Lakes, occasionally elsewhere: *waistcoat* or *weskut* . . , *potato lot* . . , and *nicker.* . . However, one must be cautious about attributing the presence of these terms to Virginia influence: *potato lot* is fairly common in Connecticut. **1965–70** *DARE* (Qu. L6a, *. . A piece of land under cultivation—less than an acre*) 40 Infs, **scattered,** Lot; [**CT6,** Building lot;] (Qu. L6b, *A piece of land under cultivation—if it's several acres*) 19 Infs, **chiefly NEast, nAppalachians,** Lot; **MA31,** Back lot, meadow lot; (Qu. I1, *. . The garden where you grow carrots, beans, and such things, to eat at*

home) Inf **PA**159, Lot; (Qu. L7, *A piece of land with a hay crop planted on it*) Infs **CT**13, 36, **MA**15, **NY**53, 127, **VA**49, Hay lot; **CT**29, **RI**12, Mowing lot; (Qu. L22, *When talking about a crop he intends to plant . . a farmer might say*) Inf **CT**36, I'm going to put that lot in corn or oats.

3 in phr *a lots:* A large number or amount; a great deal. [Blend of *a lot (of)* + *lots (of)*] **chiefly Sth**

1913 *DN* 4.49, *A lots.* "How much? Why, a whole lots." "A whole lots of people." **1967** *DARE* FW Addit **LA**12, A lots of times = often. Common in Inf's speech, occasional in rest of community. **1968** *DARE* Tape **GA**50, That's another thing we'd eat a lots of out there, we'd eat a lot of ducks and fish. **1972** *DARE* File **cwGA**, Lots = lot. "All them other cats out there's a whole lots the same like you." **1975** Newell *If Nothin' Don't Happen* 83 **nwFL**, There was a whole lots of commercial fishermen too who didn't like them big seines. **1975** *Thompson Coll.* **AL**, It's gonna take a whole lotsa money to ever finish this bridge. *Ibid* **cwGA**, I shore done a lotsa surveying with that old mule. *Ibid* **cnGA**, I need a lots of them. **1986** Pederson *LAGS Concordance* **Gulf Region**, [The Concordance has 49 exx of the phrr *a (whole) lots of,* in various contexts, concentrated esp in **AL, GA, FL**.]

lot v[1] [*OED* 1642 →] **chiefly NEng** Cf **allot**

With *on, upon;* rarely with *to:* To count on; to intend to; to look forward to.

1829 *VA Lit. Museum* 1.459, To *lot* or allot, (with upon) "to court [sic] upon"—as, "I lot upon going thither." *New England.* **1838** Gilman *S. Matron* 51 **MA**, I have taken to farming, and lot upon seeing the Carolina seeds come up that you gave me. **1884** Baldwin *Yankee School-Teacher* 216 **NY**, I didn't mean it should spile my visit, I tell ye, when I've been a-lottin' on seein' you all this mortal winter past. **1891** Cooke *Huckleberries* 283 **NEng**, I do 'lot on seein' our folks in t'other world. **1893** Frederic *Copperhead* 27 **nNY**, You know Dad lots a good deal on names. **1902** (1904) Rowe *Maid of Bar Harbor* 11 **ME**, But I'd lotted so on them four boys, a farmer, a doctor, a lawyer an' a sea cap'n. That's the plan I'd staked out. **1905** *DN* 3.2 **cCT**, *Allot,* v.i. Usually lot in the phrase *to lot upon,* to intend, as *I lotted upon going.* **1943** *LANE* Map 704 **scattered NEng**, The map shows verbs of intention or purpose, recorded in the context *I intend to go. . . I'm lotting on going, . . lot (on, to). . .* Several informants say that *lotting on* differs from other expressions in connoting pleasant anticipation as well as or instead of intention. **1959** *VT Hist.* 27.148 **cwVT**, *Lot on. . .* To look forward to. Rare. **1975** *DARE* File **cnMA** (as of c1915), She was dreadfully disappointed when it rained. She'd lotted on the picnic all week.

lot v[2] Also with *up*

To put (animals) in a **lot** n **1a**.

1874 McCoy *Cattle Trade* 171, In Central Illinois many of the most successful dealers in Southern cattle, feed them upon the blue grass pastures, and never lot them up. **1923** *DN* 5.213 **swMO**, Lot the cows to-night. **1962** *Hall Coll.* **wNC**, He keeps them [=cattle] lotted all the time. He caint let them out.

lotebush n Also *lotebush condalia, lotewood ~, lotibush* [*OED* 1846 →] Cf **jujube**

A plant of the genus *Ziziphus*, native to the US. Also called **abrojo, crucillo 1.** For other names of *Z. obtusifolia* see **chapparal B1, gray thorn, gumdrop tree, Texas buckthorn, whitethorn;** for other names of *Z. parryi* see **wild plum** Note: These two spp were formerly included in the genus *Condalia*.

1886 Havard *Flora W. & S. TX for 1885* 508, Lote-bush; Texas Buckthorn. . . Next to Mezquit, the most widespread and abundant shrub in Western and Southern Texas. . . The large, round, black berries are eaten by Mexicans although nearly tasteless. **1903** Small *Flora SE U.S.* 749, *Ziziphus obtusifolia.* . . Lotibush. Texas Buckthorn. **1930** OK Univ. Biol. Surv. *Pub.* 1.71, *Condalia obtusifolia* . . Chapparal. Lote-bush. **1939** Tharp *Vegetation TX* 61, Lotibush (*Zizyphus*). **1960** Vines *Trees SW* 694, Lotebush Condalia—*Condalia obtusifolia.* **1979** Little *Checklist U.S. Trees* 300, *Ziziphus obtusifolia.* . . lotewood condalia, gumdrop-tree. **1981** Benson-Darrow *Trees SW Deserts* 146, *Ziziphus* [spp]—Jujube, Lotebush. *Ibid* 148, *Ziziphus Parryi* . . California Lotebush.

lot fertilize(r) See **lot manure**

lotibush See **lotebush**

lotman n [**lot** n **1**]

See quot 1930.

1930 *DN* 6.82 **cSC**, *Lotman.* . . The farm hand . . whose especial duty

it is to have charge of the lot. General. **1942** Faulkner *Go Down* 83 **MS**, The lotmen . . brought the drove in from pasture that evening.

lot manure n Also *lot fertilize(r)*

Manure collected from a **lot** n **1a**.

1848 in 1927 Jones *FL Plantation Rec.* 57, I dont think I will get done hawling out the lot manure under 3 weeks yet. **1967** *DARE* Tape **SC**46, Everybody used pine straw in the lots, horse lots and cow lots. And it was used in the springtime, put in the fields, fertilizer. You had rich fields so long as you had lot—they called it lot manure, that was the word they used here. See, the animals trampled it underfoot during the winter and . . by springtime it was pulverized. . . My father didn't think he could plant wheat unless he had some fertilizer, some lot fertilizer, you know, to mix with the other. **1967–70** *DARE* (Qu. L17, . . *Names . . for manure used in the fields: [Also joking names]*) Infs **GA**17, **MS**81, Lot fertilize.

lot on See **lot** v[1]

lottest adj Cf **-est 6**

1896 *DN* 1.420 **cwNY**, *Lottest:* "The lottest of people," a large number. Ithaca.

lot to See **lot** v[1]

lot up See **lot** v[2]

lot upon See **lot** v[1]

lotus tree n [*OED* 1548 for *Celtis australis*]

A **hackberry** (here: *Celtis occidentalis*).

[**1763** Catesby *Hortus* 41, The Lote, or Nettle-tree of America. These trees are natives of Carolina and most of the northern colonies in America. . . They grow to a large size, of a regular pyramidal form, the wood close-grained, and fit for many mechanical uses.] **1952** Taylor *Plants Colonial Days* 46, Hackberry—*Celtis occidentalis.* . . Other common names are nettle tree . . and lotus tree.

lotwaer(r)ick See **lattwaerrick**

loud adj Usu |laud|; also |læud, lɑud|; for addit varr see **A** below Cf Pronc Intro 3.II.14

A Forms.

1927 Shewmake *Engl. Pronc. VA* 24 **eVA**, Diphthongal ou or ow is given the dialectal sound represented by (uh-oo). . . Examples . . are: . . growl, loud, mountain. **1936** *AmSp* 11.34 **eTX**, If a norm may be said to exist for this diphthong in East Texas, it is [æu], but variations in the first element produce also [au] and [æʸu]—all of these with various degrees of lengthening and nasalization. Examples: . . cloud, . . crowd, . . loud [etc]. **1941** *AmSp* 16.7 **eTX** [Black], [au]. . . This diphthong is not often flattened to [æu] as in 'hill type' speech, but retains its standard form, with lengthening of the first element. . . *About, allow, . . loud.* . . [ba:ut], [la:u] [etc]. **1942** *AmSp* 17.150 **seNY**, Loud . . [æu] 5 [infs] . . [au] 5 [infs] . . [ɑu] 8 [infs]. **1958** Francis *Structure of Amer. Engl.* 523 **eVA**, [əu, ʌu] . . before voiceless consonants (*house, out*) against [æu] . . before voiced (*down, loud*). . . (Also Charleston [SC] area and Canada).

B Sense.

Of a smell: strong, offensive. [*OED* 1651 →; "Now chiefly *U.S.*"] **chiefly Sth, S Midl**

1842 Dickens *Amer. Notes* 71 **OH**, Pretty loud smell of varnish, sir? **1887** Goode *Fisheries U.S.* 5.2.473, The natives [of the Aleutian Islands] . . prefer to have the meat tainted rather than fresh, declaring that it is most tender and toothsome when decidedly "loud." **1899** (1912) Green *VA Folk-Speech* 269, *Loud.* . . Strong in smell; of evil odour. **1940** Stuart *Trees of Heaven* 26 **eKY**, They are damp with sweat and loud with smell. *Ibid* 31, I love that loud sweet smell. **c1960** *Wilson Coll.* **csKY**, *Loud.* . . Having a very bad or offensive odor. **1967** *Key Tobacco Vocab.* **TN**, The tobacco smells loud when the stem gets rotten. **1968** *Foxfire* Fall–Winter 25, If something has. . . a strong scent, some say, "It has a good, loud scent." **1986** Pederson *LAGS Concordance,* 1 inf, **neAR**, Begin to smell loud—smell bad, of hog lard; 1 inf, **cnTN**, It smells too loud; 1 inf, **nwFL**, Loud smell; 1 inf, **seAL**, A loud smell—strong; 1 inf, **cwAL**, Smells loud—referring to rancid butter. **1994** *DARE* File **cwCA** (as of c1960), A skunk sprayed in the neighborhood last night, and boy, was the smell loud!

loud school n *hist*

A school in which students practice their lessons by saying them out loud; a blab school.

1907 Cockrum *Pioneer IN* 463, They were all what was termed 'loud schools,' the scholars studying their lessons out loud, making a singing sound all over the house. **1914** Whitson *Centennial Hist. Grant Co. IN* 1.157, Back of this period of reform and progress was the "Loud School" where you could hear the uproarious noise on your approach a good fraction of a mile away.

loud-talk v Cf hootenkack

To bully, impress, or convince (someone) by using assertive speech or double-talk.

1930 Williams *Logger-Talk* 26 **Pacific NW**, *Loud-talk:* Argue in coarse strident tones, as *loud-talk* a man out of a smoke. **1934** Hurston *Jonah's Gourd Vine* 315 **AL**, *Loud talk me,* making your side appear right by making more noise than the others. **1935** Hurston *Mules & Men* 192 **FL**, "Look at her puttin' out her brags." Big Sweet nudged me. "Loud-talkin' de place." *Ibid* 206, She always tryin' tuh loud talk somebody. **1958** McCulloch *Woods Words* 113 **Pacific NW**, *Loud talk him*—To argue a man out of something. **1974** Foster *Ribbin'* 258 **NYC**, Loud talk the teacher. Murphy and psych him out with double talk.

Louisiana n Usu esp Nth, N Midl |luˌ(w)ɪzɪ'ænə, lə-|; also esp Sth, S Midl |ˌluzi'ænə(r)|; for addit varr see quots Pronc-spp *Loueesiana, Louisianer, Louizzyan, Lousiana, Lousy Anna*

Std senses, var forms.

1891 Garland *Main-Travelled Roads* 192 **WI**, This knocks the swamps of Loueesiana into kingdom come. **1927** *AmSp* 2.387 [Vagabond argot], *Lousy Anna* is an affectionate title for an important part of Jefferson's purchase. **1941** *AmSp* 16.15 **eTX** [Black], [ˌluzi'ænə]. **1943** *New Yorker* 12 June 10, Miss Eppinette comes from Winnsboro, a hamlet in Lou'siana. **1965–70** DARE (Qu. H57, *Tasty or spicy side-dishes served with meats*) Inf **PA**248, Louisiana [lwizijanə] red hot sauce; (Qu. H74a, . . *Coffee . . very strong*) Inf **TX**33, Louisiana [ˌluzi'ænə]; (Qu. P5, . . *The common worm used as bait*) Inf **GA**54, Louisiana ['luzi,jænə] pink worm; (Qu. Q10, . . *Water birds and marsh birds*) Inf **GA**20, Louisiana [ˌluzi'ænə] heron; (Qu. R15b) Inf **TX**59, Louisianer mosquitoes; (Qu. S24, *A wild flower that grows in swamps and marshes and looks like a small blue iris*) Inf **LA**4, Louisiana [ˌluzi'ænə] iris; (Qu. FF22b, . . *Clubs and societies . . for men*) Inf **LA**23, Louisiana [luˌwizi'ænə] Club. **1977** *MS Folkl. Reg.* 11.79, The data for the present study were derived from the *Linguistic Atlas of the Middle and South Atlantic States*. . . *Louisiana* has perhaps as many patterns of pronunciation as any other state name. . . The five-syllable pronunciation, normally with a secondary stress on the /i/ of the second syllable and primary stress on the penultimate syllable, is heavily predominant in the North, and in the Midland with the exception of the Carolina-Georgia mountains. . . Four-syllable forms . . appear in all regions but are least common in Pennsylvania and southern New Jersey. In the South they predominate below Baltimore. *Ibid* 80, Three-syllable pronunciations, nowhere dominant, are scattered throughout the South. . . A pronunciation with breaking of /lu'i-/ to /le'wi-/ [sic for /lə'wi-/] is fairly common in upstate New York, along the corridor from metropolitan New York to Washington, and in the South Carolina-Georgia Lowcountry [sic]. . . Though nowhere the dominant form, it is common in cultivated speech. . . A falling diphthong . . is dominant in three- and four-syllable pronunciations in eastern Virginia and western North Carolina, and is common in the rest of the coastal South and in southern New York. . . Forms with /u/ as in *two* in the initial syllable predominate in eastern North Carolina, South Carolina, and Georgia, and are common elsewhere except in northern Pennsylvania. Alternatives of /zi/ nowhere predominate. Those with /zj/, in various phonetic shapes, are generally confined to North Carolina. . . Forms with /z/ are scattered from the Northern Neck of Virginia to the Pee Dee Valley. . . The /ž/ forms, resulting from assimilation, cluster in northern New Jersey and southern Maryland. Those with /s/ . . cluster in the German area of eastern Pennsylvania, but there are scatterings elsewhere. *Ibid* 81, A constricted vowel, making *Louisiana* rhyme with *tanner*, is most common in eastern North Carolina. . . Final /i/, a form that rhymes with *Annie*, is most common in West Virginia and eastern Ohio. **1989** Pederson *LAGS Tech. Index* 320, [Most proncs for *Louisiana* throughout the **Gulf Region** are of the type [luzi'ænə(r)]; also common are proncs of the type [luˌ(w)ɪzɪ'ænə]; somewhat less common are [ləˌ(w)ɪzɪ'ænə, luˌ(w)ɪz-]]. **1994** *Houston Post* (TX) 4 Sept sec F 4 **seLA**, Dar's no place, I gar-run-tee, like dis place . . Lou-izzy-an.

Louisiana grass n

=carpet grass 1, usu *Axonopus compressum.*

1889 U.S. Dept. Ag. *Rept. of Secy. for 1889* 389, *Paspalum platycaule* [=*Axonopus compressus*], called lawn grass or Louisiana grass, usually grows on low rich land, but is perfectly at home in poor pine land. As a pasture grass it can not be excelled, and is also an excellent lawn grass. **1898** FL Ag. Exper. Sta. Gainesville *Bulletin* 8.14, Some recent experiments with the Paspalum platycaule (Louisiana grass) indicates [sic] that in it there is a fair prospect for the needed pasture grass for Florida. It is . . a native grass, and is as nutritious as the best pasture grasses of the North. **1922** U.S. Dept. Ag. *Farmers' Bulletin* 1254.15, Carpet grass (*Axonopus compressus* . .) is also known as Louisiana grass and by the Creoles of Louisiana as petit gazon. It is a perennial creeping grass, forming a dense, close turf. . . It was introduced into the United States prior to 1832 and is now abundantly established on the Coastal Plain soils from southern Virginia to Texas.

Louisiana heron n

Std: a slender gray-blue heron (*Egretta tricolor*) of the Atlantic and Gulf coasts. Also called **blue crane 2, crane 2, demoiselle 2, gray scoggin, lady of the waters, poor joe, shitepoke**

Louisiana kite n

=**Mississippi kite.**

1946 Hausman *Eastern Birds* 181, *Mississippi Kite. . . Other Names*—Louisiana Kite, Blue Kite, Mosquito Hawk. **1955** Forbush–May *Birds* 98, Louisiana Kite. . . General bluish tone, almost white head, darker wings and black fan-shaped tail.

Louisiana lobelia n

A **cardinal flower** (here: *Lobelia siphilitica*).

1970 Correll *Plants TX* 1522, *Lobelia siphilitica* . . Big blue lobelia . . Louisiana lobelia.

Louisiana pink worm n Also Louisiana pink chiefly GA Cf red worm

An **earthworm.**

1966–68 DARE (Qu. P5, . . *The common worm used as bait*) Infs **GA**54, **TX**33, Louisiana pink worm; (Qu. P6, . . *Kinds of worms . . used for bait*) Infs **GA**7, **SC**40, Louisiana pink. **c1970** Pederson *Dial. Surv. Rural GA* se**GA** (*Large worms used for bait*) 1 inf, Louisiana pinks. **1986** Pederson *LAGS Concordance* **GA**, 3 infs, Louisiana pink(s); 1 inf, Louisiana pink—great big-old worm; 1 inf, Louisiana pink—large red worm; 1 inf, Louisiana pink—reddish; 1 inf, Louisiana pinks—worms sold in bait store; 1 inf, Louisiana pinks—sold locally; 1 inf, Louisiana pinks—variety [of worm].

Louisianer, Louizzyan See Louisiana

louk n Also lout [Du luik trapdoor; cf also EDD lout v.² 1 "To stoop"] eNY Cf klop door

An outside cellar door.

1968–69 DARE (Qu. D20, *Names for a sloping outside cellar door*) Infs **NY**70, 220, (Cellar) louk [laʊk]. **1988** DARE File ce**NY**, Cellar Lout—The low doorway to a cellar approached by outside steps. Albany.

loulu n Also loulu palm

A palm of the genus *Pritchardia* native to Hawaii.

1929 Neal *Honolulu Gardens* 41, Loulu palm. . . Most are from Hawaii, where they grow wild in the mountains. **1948** Neal *In Gardens HI* 97, Pritchardias, Loulu. *Pritchardia.* . . is the only genus of palms native to Hawaii. **1967** *Malamalama* 9.1.6 **HI**, The three small loulu palms (*Pritchardia hillebrandii*) will get to be about 21 feet tall. . . Hawaiians used the loulu leaves for thatching, but Europeans found they made better fans and hats. **1970** Carlquist *Hawaii* 303, A loulu palm, *Pritchardia macdanielsii*, emerges from low, wet forest on the windward crest of the Koolau Mountains. . . Although many species of loulus have been recognized, many represent minor differences. **1994** Stone–Pratt *Hawai'i's Plants* 177, Loulu leaves are bright green, large, and fan-shaped, usually more than 3 ft broad. . . As the leaves die and turn brown, they . . are retained for a while at the base of live leaves where they form a sort of "hula skirt" at the top of the trunk.

lounce out v phr Pronc-sp lounch out (cf Pronc Intro 3.I.18) [Prob varr of allowance out; cf EDD lowance v. "To put on an allowance. . . Also with off"]

To dole out.

1934 Hurston *Jonah's Gourd Vine* 229 **AL** [Black], ["Ah needs uh pair uh shoes." . . "Ain't yuh got no money?" "You ain't gimme none, is yuh?"] *Ibid* 230, "Here, take dis two bits and do anything you wanta wid it." She threw it back viciously. "Don't come lounchin' me out no two bits when Ah ast you fuh shoes." **1937** in 1976 *Weevils in the Wheat* 245 **VA** [Black], De rashon de white fo'ks lounce out fo' de week done give out. [**1946** *PADS* 6.20 **eNC** (as of 1900–10), '*Lowance* [laʊns]: *vb. Allowance.* Pamlico. Occasional.]

lounging barn n Cf **loafing barn**
   1968 *DARE* (Qu. M1, . . *Kinds of barns . . according to their use or the way they are built*) Inf **NC**54, Lounging barn.

loup-garou n [Fr] *chiefly* ME, LA
   A werewolf.
   1847 Longfellow *Evangeline* 38, He told them tales of the Loup-garou in the forest. **1939** (1962) Thompson *Body & Britches* 115 **NY**, By all odds the most interesting of the French Canadian tales concern the *loup-garou*, the man-wolf so feared by the Continental French in the seventeenth century. Why a man should be transformed into a beast's shape, or should run about in man's shape acting like a beast, is variously explained; one common theory is that this is a punishment for the neglect of Easter duty during seven consecutive years. **1945** Saxon *Gumbo Ya-Ya* 191 **LA**, Cajun children are constantly warned, 'The *loup-garous* will get you, yes! You better be good.' . . '*Loup-garous* is them people what wants to do bad work, and changes themselves into wolves.' **1958** Grau *Hard Blue Sky* 436 **sLA**, The shutter rattled. And he wondered if a loup-garou were banging away out there. **1959** Tallman *Dict. Amer. Folk.* 181, *Loup-garou*—This French word for werewolf was used in parts of Maine where the French-Canadians had introduced some of their beliefs. **1967** LeCompte *Word Atlas* 396 **seLA**, *A tormented soul in the body of an animal. . .* loup-garou [2 of 21 infs]. [**1967** *DARE* (Qu. CC17, *Imaginary animals or monsters that people . . tell tales about— especially to tease greenhorns*) Inf **MA**5, Loup-garou [lup gə'ru]— French-Canadian term for pantherlike animal.] **1982** *Smithsonian Letters* **ME**, Regional names for the two-footed, hairy, human-like "monster" known as bigfoot . . and probable equivalents . . the loupe [sic] garou (werewolf) of Maine/French Canada.

loury See **lower** v[1]

louse n
   A Gram forms.
   1 sg: usu *louse;* also *lice.*
   1909 *DN* 3.345 **eAL, wGA**, *Lice, n. sing.* Louse. "I found a lice on me." Not common, but the plural *lices* is fairly common among the illiterate. **1937** (1977) Hurston *Their Eyes* 101 **FL** [Black], Ah'm go-intuh run dis conversation from uh gnat heel to uh lice. **1966** *DARE* Tape **DC**5, Something like a chicken lice.
   2 pl: usu *lice;* also *lices, louses.*
   1908 *DN* 3.284 **eAL, wGA**, Louses, mouses, mices. **1909** [see **A1** above]. **1986** Pederson *LAGS Concordance*, 1 inf, **seAL**, Lices—plural of "louse"; 1 inf, **swMS**, Them lices.
   B Senses.
   1 Std: a parasitic, chewing or sucking insect of the order Mallophaga or Anoplura. For other names of those which infest the human body, *Pediculus humanus* and *Pthirus pubis,* see **Arkansas lizard, blue jacket 1, boo boo** n[1], **booger** n[1] **2, boogie 4, bug** n[1] **1, bugaboo 4, chemmy lizard, chinch 3, cooter** n **6, cootie** n[1], **crab** n **2, crawler** n[1] **2, creeper 3, crotch pheasant, crumb** n, **Cuban itch, diaper dragon, galloping dandruff, grayback 2a, graybow, livestock, oule, pants rabbit, poor folks' plague, rice, seam squirrel, shirt rabbit, ~ rat, ~ squirrel, string of pearls, striped tiger, tenant, traveler, visitor**
   2 The bedbug (*Cimex lectularius*). Cf **bed louse**
   1965–70 *DARE* (Qu. R24, . . *Names . . for a bedbug*) 16 Infs, **scattered**, Louse; **IL**97, **IN**62, **MA**7, **MS**6, Lice.
   3 A **beggar ticks 1.** Cf **beggar's lice 3**
   1970 *DARE* (Qu. S14, . . *Prickly seeds, small and flat, with two prongs at one end, that cling to clothing*) Inf **OK**54, Lice.

louse around v phr Also *louse* Pronc-sp *louze around* [Cf Scots, nEngl dial *lowse* to stop working] *esp S Midl*
   To waste time; to loaf or idle about.
   1917 *DN* 4.414 **wNC**, . . To play the parasite. **c1920** in 1993 Farwell–Nicholas *Smoky Mt. Voices* 107 **sAppalachians**, I don't see no use in jist louzin' around. **1923** *DN* 5.214 **swMO**, *Louse around. . .* To loiter about aimlessly. **1932** *AmSp* 7.334 [Johns Hopkins jargon], *Louse around*—to loiter; to "kill time." **1966–70** *DARE* (Qu. A9, . . *Wasting time by not working on the job*) Inf **OK**42, Lousing ['laʊsɪn]; (Qu. BB41, *Not seriously ill, but sick enough to be in bed:* "*He's been _____ for a week.*") Inf **MO**35, Lousin' around [lɑ^ʊzɪn];

(Qu. KK31, *To go about aimlessly looking for distraction:* "*He doesn't have anything to do, so he's just _____ around.*") Inf **GA**28, Lousin' around ['læuzɪn].

louse burr n
   A **cockleburr 1** (here: *Xanthium strumarium*).
   1900 Lyons *Plant Names* 398, *X[anthium] strumarium* . . Louse-bur.

louses See **louse A2**

louseweed n [See quot]
   A **St. John's wort** (here: *Hypericum gentianoides*).
   1883 *Bot. Gaz.* 8.296, I have long been interested in local names of plants. Here are some Rhode Island names. . . *Hypericum Sarothra* is called "Louseweed," because the seed-pods crack between the fingers in a rather suggestive manner.

lousewort n
   1 Std: a plant of the genus *Pedicularis.* Also called **fernleaf**; for other names of var spp see **beefsteak plant 2, butterfly tongue, chicken head 1, duckbill 1, elephant flower, elephant's head, ~ snout, ~ trunk 2, greaseweed 2, head betony, high heal-all, Indian warrior, little elephants, mountain figwort, parrot's head, pink elephants, red rattle, sickletop, snaffles, wood betony**
   2 A **false foxglove** (here: *Aureolaria pedicularia*).
   1876 Hobbs *Bot. Hdbk.* 65, Louse wort, . . Gerardia pedicularia. **1900** Lyons *Plant Names* 131, *D[asystoma] Pedicularia. . .* Fern-leaved False Foxglove . . Lousewort. **1910** Graves *Flowering Plants* 355 **CT**, *Gerardia pedicularia. . .* Lousewort. **1959** Carleton *Index Herb. Plants* 3, *American lousewort:* Gerardia pedicularia (Aureolaria).

lousey See **lousy** adj

Lousiana See **Louisiana**

lousy adj Also sp *lousey*
   1 Excessively supplied (with money or other valuables); rich.
   1843 *Spirit of Times* 4 Mar 7/3 (*OEDS*), He was lousy with money. **1856** *Porter's Spirit of Times* 22 Nov 194/2 **CA**, The bed of the river is perfectly "lousy" with gold. **1906** Canfield *Diary Forty-Niner* 10 (as of 1850), Wednesday I struck a crevice in the bed-rock on the rim of the creek and it was lousy with gold. **1927** (1943) Hammett *$106000* 14, Everybody in on it will come home lousy with cash. **1929** *AmSp* 4.357, If you wish to boast of having a great deal of money, you may speak . . of being *filthy* or *lousy* with money. **1951** Salinger *Catcher* 81 **NYC**, I'm not kidding, that hotel was lousy with perverts. **1965–70** *DARE* (Qu. U37, . . *Somebody who has plenty of money*) 36 Infs, **scattered**, Lousy with money (*or* it, dough, etc); **NC**31, 38, **VA**70, Lousy; (Qu. U19a, . . *Money in general:* "*He's certainly got the _____.*") Inf **MI**105, Lousy with money; (Qu. U31, . . *A person who spends money very freely:* "*He's certainly _____*"; total Infs questioned, 75) Inf **FL**37, Lousy with money; (Qu. U38a, . . *A great deal of money:* "*He's got _____ [of money].*") Inf **MD**33, Lousy with money; (Qu. LL9b, . . *All you need or more . .* "*She's got clothes _____.*") Inf **OH**16, Lousy with clothes. [33 of 43 Infs old] **1967** *DARE* FW Addit **LA**8, Lousy with money.
   2a Bad, poor, contemptible. [*OED* c1386 →] **widespread, but less freq Sth, S Midl** See Map
   1839 in 1898 Griswold *Corresp.* 24, I never will stand tamely by, and see the True Friends of Freedom assailed with lousy lies from any quarter. **1899** (1912) Green *VA Folk-Speech* 266, *Lousey.* . . Degraded; mean; contemptible. **1928** *AmSp* 3.345, 'Lousy.' How long will the vogue of this unpleasant adjective continue? It is applied indiscriminately and means nothing in particular except that it is always a term of disparagement. **1932** *AmSp* 7.334 [Johns Hopkins jargon], *Lousy*—a term used to describe anything or anyone causing an unfavorable impression. **1944** Woodward *Way Our People Lived* 316 (as of 1849), I wish I could never hear the word *lousy* again. I am willing to bet that Tommy Plunkett uses it fifty times a day, but he is no worse than the others. It is "lousy" this and "lousy" that. The rain is lousy, the trail is lousy, the bacon is lousy, . . and Gus Thorpe, losing in the card game, has just said that he has had a lousy deal. **1965–70** *DARE* (Qu. KK6, *Something low-grade or of poor quality—for example, a piece of merchandise:* "*I wouldn't buy that, it's _____.*") 17 Infs, **scattered, but esp Nth, N Midl**, Lousy (material); (Qu. N12, . . *Somebody who drives carelessly or not well*) 12 Infs, **scattered exc Sth, S Midl**, Lousy driver; (Qu. FF19, . . *A very dull or unenjoyable time:* "*The party was _____.*") 11 Infs, **scattered**, Lousy; (Qu. P9, *When you're fishing but not catching any*) Infs **CA**3, **IL**104, **MN**16, (Having) lousy luck; **MN**22,

PA185, Lousy (today); **CA**147, Fishing is lousy; **CA**153, Lousy fishing; **PA**240, Lousy spot; (Qu. FF21a, *A joke that is so old it doesn't seem funny any more: "His jokes are all _____."*) Infs **CA**32, **DE**7, **FL**48, **GA**13, **MS**84, **PA**94, Lousy; (Qu. LL13, *Not full or sufficient: "She gave us a _____ meal."*) Infs **CA**133, **CT**27, **NY**70, **PA**245, **UT**14, Lousy. [Further exx throughout DS; all exx are mapped.] [35 of 75 total Infs old]

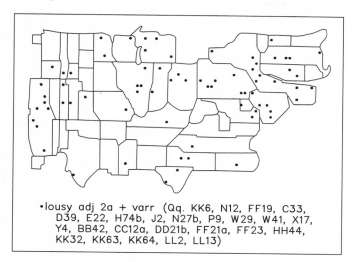

•lousy adj 2a + varr (Qq. KK6, N12, FF19, C33, D39, E22, H74b, J2, N27b, P9, W29, W41, X17, Y4, BB42, CC12a, DD21b, FF21a, FF23, HH44, KK32, KK63, KK64, LL2, LL13)

b Used broadly as a derog intensive.

1965–70 *DARE* (Qu. H71, . . *The last piece of food left on a plate*) Inf **MN**42, One lousy bite; (Qu. X9, *Joking or uncomplimentary words for a person's mouth . . "I wish he'd shut his _____."*) Inf **MO**19, Lousy mouth; (Qu. LL14, *None at all, not even one: "This pond used to be full of fish but now there's _____ left."*) Infs **MA**58, **WI**77, Not a lousy one left; (Qu. LL36, *To make a statement much stronger: "Poor fellow. I think it's a _____ shame."*) Infs **CA**107, **GA**72, **ID**1, **IL**44, **OH**43, Lousy; (Qu. NN17, *Something that keeps on annoying you—for example, a fly that keeps buzzing around you: "That _____ fly won't go away."*) Infs **CA**107, **IL**51, **IA**4, **NY**42, **UT**4, Lousy.

c Spec; in ref to weather: unpleasant, threatening. **widespread, but less freq Sth, S Midl** See Map

1944 [see 2a above]. **1965–70** *DARE* (Qu. B2, *If the weather is very unpleasant . . it's a _____ day*) 92 Infs, **scattered, but less freq Sth, S Midl**, Lousy; **NY**72, Lousy weather; (Qu. B5, *When the weather looks as if it will become bad . . it's _____*) Inf **CA**107, Going to be a lousy day; **MA**7, Lousy; **NY**118, Turning lousy; (Qu. B6, *When clouds begin to increase . . it's _____*) Inf **PA**88, Lousy; (Qu. B8, *When clouds come and go all day . . it's _____*) Inf **MA**7, Another lousy day. [53 of 94 total Infs old]

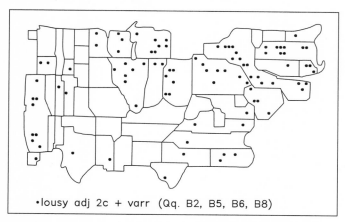

•lousy adj 2c + varr (Qq. B2, B5, B6, B8)

d Spec; in ref to one's health or spirits: unwell, tired, depressed. **widespread, but somewhat less freq Sth** See Map

1933 'N. West' *Miss Lonelyhearts* (1949) 46 (*OEDS*) **CA**, I felt swell before you came, and now I feel lousy. **1934** Cain *Postman* 17, "How are you . . ?" "Lousy." **1950** Ransome *Deadly Miss Ashley* 176, She felt too lousy to come to work. A foul cold, she said. **1961** Salinger *Franny* 19 **NYC**, I'm feeling absolutely lousy. **1965–70** *DARE* (Qu.

BB39, *On a day when you don't feel just right, though not actually sick . . "I'll be all right tomorrow—I'm just feeling _____ today."*) 65 Infs, **widespread, but less freq Sth**, Lousy; **CT**23, Kind of lousy; (Qu. BB5, *A general feeling of discomfort or illness that isn't any one place in particular*) 51 Infs, **scattered, but less freq Sth, West**, (Feel or feeling) lousy (all over); **LA**11, 15, **MI**33, **NY**167, I (just) feel lousy; **FL**15, **NY**92, Just feel(ing) lousy; **OH**47, Feels lousy; (Qu. KK30, *Feeling slowed up or without energy: "I certainly feel _____."*) 33 Infs, **scattered**, Lousy; (Qu. GG34b, *To feel depressed or in a gloomy mood: "She's feeling _____ today."*) 12 Infs, **scattered exc West**, Lousy; (Qu. X52, . . *A person . . who had been sick was looking _____*) Infs **MA**7, **MN**6, **NY**81, 119, Lousy; (Qu. BB38, *When a person doesn't look healthy, or looks as if he hadn't been well for some time . . "He looks _____."*) Infs **CA**176, **MA**7, Lousy; (Qu. BB41, *Not seriously ill, but sick enough to be in bed: "He's been _____ for a week."*) Inf **VA**105, Feeling lousy; (Qu. GG34a, *To feel depressed or in a gloomy mood: "He has the _____ today."*) Inf **MA**7, He feels lousy. [77 of 139 total Infs old]

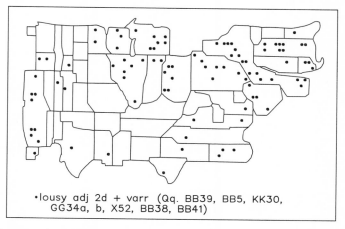

•lousy adj 2d + varr (Qq. BB39, BB5, KK30, GG34a, b, X52, BB38, BB41)

lousy adv Cf **filthy** adv
Very, extremely.

1932 *AmSp* 7.436 **CA** [Stanford University expressions], A man drunk is . . "lousy drunk." **1942** Berrey–Van den Bark *Amer. Slang* 377.7, *Wealthy*. . . lousy-rich. **1965–70** *DARE* (Qu. U37, . . *Somebody who has plenty of money*) Infs **AR**56, **IN**73, **MI**82, **MN**2, **MO**39, **NJ**3, 55, **PA**27, Lousy rich; (Qu. DD15, *A person who is thoroughly drunk*) Infs **NC**1, 22, **UT**5, Lousy drunk.

Lousy Anna See **Louisiana**

lout See **louk**

louze around See **louse around**

lovage n
Std: a plant of the genus *Ligusticum*. Also called **love root**. For other names of var spp see **angelica 2, chuchupate 1, coughroot 2, licorice root 3, mountain celery, nondo, osha, petrushki, sea parsley, wild celery, ~ parsley, ~ parsnip**

love n, v Usu |lʌv|; also |lʌb|; in comb *love to*, |lʌf| Pronc-spp *lub, luf*

A Pronc varr.

1853 Simms *Sword & Distaff* 349 **SC** [Black], I lub you better dan all de worl'. **1899** Chesnutt *Conjure Woman* 13 **csNC** [Black], Ef dey's an'thing a nigger lub, nex' ter 'possum. **1922** Gonzales *Black Border* 311 **sSC, GA coasts** [Gullah glossary], *Lub*—(n. and v.) love, loves, loved, loving; like, likes, liked, liking. **1937** Crane *Let Me Show You VT* 29, There are some of us who "lufto" (love to) tie our words together. **1959** *VT Hist.* 27.148, *Love to* [lʌftu]. . . Common. **1967** [see **D1** below]. **1967–68** *DARE* FW Addit **MO**, "I would [lʌf] to do that." Unvoicing of [v] in this word occurs commonly before infinitive around here. Cf "I have [hæf] to get going," also common. *Ibid* **DE**, Love [lʌf] . . "I'd love to have one."

B Gram forms (of verb).

1 pres (exc 3rd pers sg): usu *love*; also *loves*.

1986 Pederson *LAGS Concordance*, 1 inf, **ceTX**, I loves everybody; 1 inf, **swGA**, I loves fishing; 1 inf, **cFL**, Spanish people really loves gopher; 2 infs, **swMS**, I (really) loves it; 2 infs, **csGA, neLA**, Some (people just) loves it; 1 inf, **nwFL**, People loves it that way; 1

inf, **nwFL**, I loves that too; 1 inf, **cnGA**, I loves to eat; 1 inf, **csGA**, All three of us loves to fish; 1 inf, **csGA**, I loves to scrub with them; 1 inf, **swAL**, I loves to work; 1 inf, **nwFL**, It's good to know that people loves you. [7 of 14 infs Black]

2 pres 3rd pers sg: usu *loves;* also *love. esp freq among Black speakers*

1914 [see **D2** below]. **1922** [see **A** above]. **1986** Pederson *LAGS Concordance* **Gulf Region,** 1 inf, God love = loves; 1 inf, Love her; 1 inf, He love to read; 1 inf, He love to sheik down; 1 inf, He love to talk; 1 inf, That child love to wash dishes. [All infs Black]

3 past: usu *loved;* also *love, loveded.*

1922 [see **A** above]. **1937** in 1976 *Weevils in the Wheat* 149 **VA** [Black], Pa love dogs an' kep' one wid him all de time. **1968** *DARE* Tape **GA**30, We had ivory-billed woodpeckers in this swamp. It was full of 'em. You could hear 'em hollerin'. I loveded to hear 'em holler. **1986** Pederson *LAGS Concordance,* 1 inf, **ceAL,** Really love [*LAGS* Ed: preterit tense verb]. [Inf Black]

C As noun.

In phr *make one's love come down* and varr: To cause one to feel loving or amorous; to arouse one sexually; also fig. *esp freq among Black speakers*

1928 in 1983 Taft *Blues Lyric Poetry* 104, Let's get our gauge up papa : let our love come down. **1938** *Ibid* 312, Now you got fruit on your tree : lemons on your shelf / But you know loving mama : that you can't squeeze them all yourself /. . . Now if you let me be your lemon-squeezer : Lord until my love comes down / Now it makes no difference baby : what your mama don't allow. **1942** Hurston *Dust Tracks* 243, So I sensed early, that the Negro race was not one band of heavenly love. . . Being black was not enough. It took more than a community of skin color to make your love come down on you. **1946** (1972) Mezzrow-Wolfe *Really Blues* 336, Make your love come down: *arouse your passion, put you in a romantic mood.* **1969** Beck *Mama Black Widow* 127 [Black], Ah ain't drunk, Sedalia. Mah luv jes come down fer yu, sugah. . . Ah'm yu man. **1982** Walker *Color Purple* 187 **GA** [Black], Reefer, say Harpo. What kind of a thing is that? Something make you feel good, I say. Something make you see visions. Something make your love come down.

D As verb.

1 in weakened sense: To like, prefer, favor; see quot 1939. **chiefly Sth, S Midl**

1859 (1968) Bartlett *Americanisms* 257, To Love, for to like. "Do you love pumpkin pie?" "I'd love to have that bonnet!" **1895** *DN* 1.372 **seKY, eTN, wNC,** Love: like. "I love it splendid." "Would you love to buy some eggs?" **1903** *DN* 2.320 **seMO,** Love. . . Like. 'I'll do it, but I don't love to!' **1905** *DN* 3.13 **cCT,** Love. . . To like. 'I love pumpkin pie.' **1907** *DN* 3.214 **nwAR,** Love. . . To like. *Ibid* 233 **seMO, nwAR,** Love. . . To like. "I love sweet potatoes." **1913** Kephart *Highlanders* 293 **sAppalachians,** Your hostess, proffering apple sauce, will ask, "Do you love sass?" . . The word love is commonly used here in the sense of like or relish. **1917** *DN* 4.414 **wNC, IA, KS, KY, OH,** Love. . . To like: applies to taste in food. "Do you love pickle-beans?" **1939** *Hall Coll.* **wNC, eTN,** Love . . to like (used without the emotional tone commonly associated with the word elsewhere. . .) "I'd love to see him." "Won't you love the fan?" (=wouldn't you like to have the fan?—said by a young woman to her husband. . . The day was very hot.) **c1960** *Wilson Coll.* **csKY,** Love. . . Standard in the area for like. **1967** *DARE* FW Addit **ceLA,** I coulda shot and maybe crippled it, but I don't love to [ˈlʌftə] do that; **cnLA,** Oh, yes, I love to [ˈlʌftə] do that. . . I'm about carrots the way I am about turnips. I don't love 'em; **TN,** Can't eat nothin' but soup. I don't love soup. . . I'd rather sit out here. I don't love [lʌf] to sit in the house. **1983** *MJLF* 9.1.47 **ceKY,** Love . . to like (food). **1986** Pederson *LAGS Concordance,* 1 inf, **nwMS,** I don't love it too good = I don't much like it; (You agree with a friend when he says, "I'm not going to do that," or, "I'm not going to vote for that guy." You say, "_____!") 1 inf, **swAL,** Well, I didn't love neither one; 1 inf, **cwGA,** I don't never love to be behind in nothing.

2 also with *on, up;* also ppl adj *loved up:* To hug, caress, fondle; to kiss, neck.

1876 Habberton *Helen's Babies* 35, I was only a-lovin' you, cos you was good, and brought us candy. **1889** *Harper's New Mth. Mag.* 79.271 **seGA,** Putting his arms round her neck, [he] "loved" her with his cheek against hers. **1914** *DN* 4.159 **cVA,** Love. . . To hug. "Baby love Sis hahd." **1923** *DN* 5.214 **swMO,** Love. . . To fondle or caress. "Jim's a-lovin' his ol' 'oman." **1931** Randolph *Ozarks* 84, Even *love* is considered more or less indecent, and the mountain people very seldom use

the term in its ordinary sense, but nearly always with some degrading or jocular connotation. If a hillman does admit that he *loved* a woman he means only that he caressed and embraced her—and he usually says that he *loved her up.* **1965–70** *DARE* (Qu. AA8, *When people make too much of a show of affection in a public place . . "There they were at the church supper _____ [with each other]."*) 12 Infs, **scattered,** Loving; 9 Infs, **scattered,** Loving each other up; 8 Infs, **scattered,** Loving it up; 6 Infs, **scattered,** Loving each other (*or* one another); **IN**3, **ME**2, **PA**163, **SC**11, **VA**69, Loving up; **CT**43, Loving and kissing; **TX**87, Loving it; **KY**59, **TN**15, All loved up. **1986** Pederson *LAGS Concordance* **Gulf Region** (*Kissing, bussing, smooching*) 11 infs, Loving; 1 inf, Loving—hugging, kissing; 1 inf, Loving—old-fashioned term; 1 inf, They'd be a-loving; 1 inf, Keen loving, by God; 1 inf, They've been loving each other; 1 inf, Kissing and a-loving; he's been loving the girl [laughing]; 1 inf, He's been loving the girls; 2 infs, (Been) loving up. **1993** Mason *Feather Crowns* 161 **KY,** "Little Bunch always causes trouble," said Dulcie, exasperated. . . "She just wants to love on the babies," said Lena, defending her sister.

love-and-tangle See **love-entangle 2**

love apple n

1 also *love's apple, lover's ~:* A **soda-apple** or similar **nightshade 1.** Cf **apple of Sodom, kiss apple**

1953 Greene-Blomquist *Flowers South* 106, Love-apple (*Solanum aculeatissimum*). . . bears relatively large, orange to red, papery berries . . often seen in florists' shops in the fall. . . Sandy fields, thickets, and roadside, Coastal Plain, Fla. to Tex. n. to s.e. N.C. **1965–70** *DARE* (Qu. S21, *. . Weeds . . that are a trouble in gardens and fields*) Inf **HI**2, Love's apple, lover's apple—deadly poison, Solanum. **1976** Bailey-Bailey *Hortus Third* 1054, [*Solanum*] *aculeatissimum.* . . *Love apple.* . . Widespread in s. US.

2 also *lover's apple:* **=mayapple 1.**

1954 *Harder Coll.* **cwTN,** Love apple—a May apple. **1968–70** *DARE* (Qu. S4, *. . Mayapple: [Woodside plant, not a tree, with two large spreading leaves; they grow in patches and have a small yellow fruit late in summer]*) Infs **IN**48, **KY**83, **VA**28A, Love apple; **MO**10, Lover's apple.

love baby See **love child**

love bite n Also *love mark* Cf **hickey** n² c, **monkey bite 1**
A "passion mark."

1965–70 *DARE* (Qu. X39, *A mark on the skin where somebody has sucked it hard and brought the blood to the surface*) Infs **CA**93, **IL**99, **PA**72, 165, 243, Love bite; **CT**7, Love bite—a woman will do it to a man sometimes when they're having intercourse; **MO**32, Love mark; **FL**51, Love mark—if it comes from a boy sucking a girl's neck.

love bone n *among Black speakers* Cf **marriage bone**
=pully bone.

c1960 *McDavid Coll.* **GA,** Love bone—wishbone. [Inf Black] **1965** *DARE* (Qu. K74, *A bone from the breast of a chicken, shaped like a horseshoe*) Inf **OK**14, When we were little, we called it the "love bone"—the one that got the short piece would get married first. [Inf Black] **c1970** Pederson *Dial. Surv. Rural GA,* 1 inf, **seGA,** Love bone; wishbone. [Inf Black] **1986** Pederson *LAGS Concordance* (*Wishbone*) 3 infs, **nw,swGA,** (The) love bone. [All infs Black]

love-box See **love-pat**

love bubble See **love bump 2**

love bug n [Because it is found in copulating pairs] **Gulf States** Cf **March fly**

A fly (*Plecia nearctica*). Also called **fuck bug, honeymoon fly, telephone bug**

1968 *DARE* FW Addit **cnFL,** Love bugs—black-and-orange insects which mate in late August through September. They are seen coupled in thick swarms for as long as three weeks. *Ibid* **seLA,** Love bug—a little black-and-orange insect about three-eighths of an inch long. They mate at certain times of the year, smearing windshields and covering pedestrians. You never see one separately; they are always coupled. **1968** *DARE* File **seMS,** Love bug—a dark black bug shaped like an enormous mosquito. It flies in huge clouds along the roads near the Gulf around Mississippi and New Orleans. These bugs darken the windshield and must be cleaned off frequently, especially during the day. **1972** *Milwaukee Jrl.* (WI) 24 Sept 27/1, Thousands of visitors to Disney World and other central Florida attractions are being introduced this month to a comparatively new Florida phenomenon, the love bug. Millions of the three-quarter inch insect tandems—male and female fly linked together, hence the name—are swarming over the area's highways. **1986** Pederson *LAGS Concordance* **coastal Gulf Region,** 3 infs, Love bug(s); 1 inf, Love bug—bred to eat mosquitoes—now a problem; 1 inf, Love bugs—travel in pairs; 1 inf, Love bugs—get on windshield; 1 inf, Love bugs—stick to car windshields. **1992** FL Div. Plant Industry *Entomol. Circular No. 350* Jan–Feb [1], *Plecia nearctica* . . is the lovebug that motorists frequently encounter as a serious nuisance when traveling in southern states. *Ibid* [2], Lovebugs are attracted to irradiated automobile exhaust fumes (diesel and gasoline) when the ultraviolet light incident over the highway ranges from 0.3 to 0.4 microns . . between 10 AM and 4 PM, with a temperature above 28° C. Hot engines and the vibrations of automobiles apparently contribute to the attraction of lovebugs to the highways. *Ibid,* Large numbers of lovebugs can cause overheating of liquid cooled engines, reduce visibility, and etch automobile paint.

love bump n

1 =**jack bump. esp Sth, S Midl**

1954 *Harder Coll.* **cwTN,** Love bump—small, infected pimple, usually on the face. **1966–68** *DARE* (Qu. X59, . . *The small infected pimples that form usually on the face*) Infs **AR**18, **TX**28, Love bumps; **FL**19, Love bumps—old-fashioned; **GA**28, Love bumps—they have them when they's havin' change of life; **SC**7, Love bumps—on single people.

2 also *love bubble, ~ point:* See quot.

1966–69 *DARE* (Qu. X31, . . *A woman's breasts*) Inf **GA**13, Love bubbles; **IN**75, Love bumps; **WA**11, Love points.

love child n Also *love baby* [OED *love child* 1805 →] **scattered, but more freq NEast, N Cent, Mid Atl** See Map Cf **outside child**

An illegitimate child.

1942 Berrey–Van den Bark *Amer. Slang* 383.8, Illegitimate child . . love child. **1954** *Harder Coll.* **cwTN,** Love baby. . . Illegitimate child. "Love babies are always best babies there are." c**1955** Reed–Person *Ling. Atlas Pacific NW,* 2 [of 52] infs, Love child. **1956** Ker *Vocab. W. TX* 318, Love child [1 of 67 infs]. **1962** Atwood *Vocab. TX* 66, Uncommon . . terms, occurring from one to six times each, include *brat, bush child, fatherless child, foundling, love child* [etc]. **1965–70** *DARE* (Qu. Z11b, . . *[A child whose parents were not married]*) 78 Infs, **scattered, but more freq NEast, N Cent, Mid Atl,** Love child; [**PA**126, Child of love]. **1967** *DARE* File **csMA** (as of c1945), Love child—illegitimate child. **1970** Tarpley *Blinky* 220 **neTX,** Child of an unwed mother. . . [Infreq responses include:] love baby[,] love child. **1973** Allen *LAUM* 1.344 **Upper MW** (as of c1950), Other unusual equivalents are *chance child, . . illegal child, . . love child* [1 inf, **IA**], and *outlaw baby.* **1986** Pederson *LAGS Concordance* **Gulf Region,** 10 infs, Love child; 2 infs, Love child—old(er) term; 1 inf, Love child—has heard; 1 inf, Love baby.

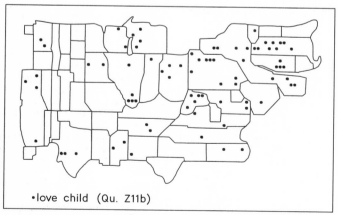

•love child (Qu. Z11b)

loveded See love B3

loved up See love D2

love-entangle n

1 also *love-entangling vine, love(-in-a-)tangle:* =**dodder.** Cf **love-in-a-mist 2, love vine 1**

a**1936** in 1943 *Colorado Mag.* 20.194 **West** (as of 1860), I gathered flowers to place on the grave and found it grown over with that flower of the prairie called "love-entangle," a pale yellow vine set thickly with

pink blossom. **1960** Williams *Walk Egypt* 262 **GA,** The worst thing in the world was watching Wick's field go back to woods . . and everywhere love-entangling vine killing all it twined. **1973** Hitchcock–Cronquist *Flora Pacific NW* 365, *Cuscuta* [spp] . . Dodder; Love-tangle; Coral-vine. **1975** Hamel–Chiltoskey *Cherokee Plants* 32, Love-in-a-tangle . . *Cuscuta gronovii*—Poultice for bruises.

2 also *love-and-tangle, love-entangled:* A **wall pepper** (here: *Sedum acre*).

1892 *Jrl. Amer. Folkl.* 5.96 **nOH,** Sedum acre, love entangled. **1900** Lyons *Plant Names* 340, Sedum acre . . Love-entangle. **1950** Gray–Fernald *Manual of Botany* 733, S[edum] acre . . Mossy S[edum], Wallpepper, Love-entangle. **1959** Carleton *Index Herb. Plants* 76, *Love-and-tangle:* Sedum acre.

love-entangling vine See love-entangle 1

love flower n

=**matilija poppy.**

1902 Smith *Golden Poppy* 228, It was the custom . . for gallant lovers to seek diligently for the first love-flower (Matilija poppy) that opened in the spring. . . If a fatal accident befell the seeker the nearest love-flower would, it is said, bloom pink the coming spring.

love gentian n

A **gentian.**

1975 Zwinger *Run River* 30 **UT,** The big fringed gentians and the more delicate lavender love gentians are beginning to close.

love grass n

Std: a grass of the genus *Eragrostis.* Also called **meadow grass 2c.** For other names of var spp see **candy grass, lace ~, petticoat climber, skunk grass, snake-~, spear ~, stink ~, tickle ~, tumble ~**

love-hole n Cf kiss-me-quick 3

1926 *DN* 5.401 **Ozarks,** Love-hole. . . A gully or ditch across the road.

love-in-a-huddle n

=**cypress spurge.**

1898 *Jrl. Amer. Folkl.* 11.278 **CT,** *Euphorbia Cyparissias* . . love-in-a-huddle. **1959** Carleton *Index Herb. Plants* 76, *Love-in-a-huddle:* Euphorbia cyparissias.

love-in-a-mist n

1 also *love-in-the-mist:* =**fennel-flower.** [See quot 1966; *OED* 1824 →] Cf **maid-in-a-mist, love-in-the-puzzle**

1891 *Jrl. Amer. Folkl.* 4.148, We knew Nigella damascena only as *Lady in the Green;* afterwards Love in a Mist and Devil in the Bush. **1909** Doubleday *Amer. Flower Garden* 250, Love-in-a-mist (*Nigella Damascena*). . . Flowers 1 inch across nestling in finely cut fennel-like foliage. **1940** Gates *Flora KS* 142, Nigella damascena L.—love-in-a-mist. **1966** *DARE* FW Addit **WA**15, Love-in-a-mist . . blue flower like thistle flower, with fuzzy, misty stuff all around flower. **1969–70** *DARE* (Qu. S11) Inf **NY**233, Love-in-the-mist—looks like cornflower, but a bit lacier; (Qu. S26e, *Other wildflowers not yet mentioned;* not asked in early QRs) Inf **KY**60, Love-in-a-mist—fringy pink flower. **1976** Bailey–Bailey *Hortus Third* 767, [*Nigella*] *damascena* . . Love-in-a-mist, wild fennel.

2 =**dodder.**

1956 McAtee *Some Dialect NC* 56, *Love-in-a-mist* . . dodder (*Cuscuta*). Marshall, and Mitchell County.

love-in-a-puff n Cf puffball

=**balloon vine.**

1839 *S. Lit. Messenger* 5.751 **GA,** A particular spot in his garden was appropriated to the culture of old maids, . . and lady slippers, . . and even love in a puff. **1965** Teale *Wandering Through Winter* 150 **TX,** All across Texas, a host of . . names have been bestowed on the wild plants. . . They run from angel's trumpet, . . love-in-a-puff, . . to shame vine.

love-in-a-puzzle n Also *puzzle-love* [OED 1824] Cf love-in-a-mist 1, love-in-a-tangle 2

=**fennel-flower.**

1889 *Century Dict.* 3528, Love-in-a-puzzle. . . Same as *love-in-a-mist.* **1900** Lyons *Plant Names* 224, N[igella] Damascena . . Love-in-a-puzzle. **1959** Carleton *Index Herb. Plants* 76, *Love-in-a-puzzle:* Nigella damascena. *Ibid* 96, *Puzzle-love.*

love-in-a-tangle n

1 See **love-entangle 1.**

2 =**fennel-flower.** Cf **love-in-a-mist 1, love-in-a-puzzle**

1959 Carleton *Index Herb. Plants* 76, *Love-in-a-tangle:* Nigella damascena.

love-in-the-mist n

1 See **love-in-a-mist 1.**

2 A **virgin's bower** (here: *Clematis drummondii*).

1936 Whitehouse *TX Flowers* 28, The vine is covered with iridescent masses of silky, feathery plumes, 2–4 in. long, which grow out from the seed cover. These plumes are elongated, persistent styles and are responsible for many common names given to the vine, including grandfather's beard, gray beard, goat's beard, and love-in-the-mist. **1960** Vines *Trees SW* 265, Drummond Clematis—*Clematis drummondii.* . . Vernacular names for the plant are Texas Virgins-bower . . Love-in-the-mist.

love-in-winter n

A **pipsissewa** (here: *Chimaphila umbellata*).

1892 *Jrl. Amer. Folkl.* 5.100 **ME,** *Chimaphila umbellata.* . . Love-in-winter. **1911** Henkel *Amer. Med. Leaves* 16, Love-in-winter. . . has shining evergreen leaves of a somewhat leathery texture. **1930** Sievers *Amer. Med. Plants* 45, Love-in-winter. . . Dry, shady woods, especially in pine forests. **1971** Krochmal *Appalachia Med. Plants* 90, Love-in-winter. . . The dried leaves are reportedly used as a diuretic, astringent, tonic, and antirheumatic.

love knot n Also *lover's knot*

A pastry in the shape of a knot.

1906 *Pocumtuc Housewife* 34 **nwMA,** Crullers, Matrimony or Love Knots. **1946** Harris *Cooking* 99, Swedish Klannter or English Lovers' knots or Norwegian Fattigmandes Bakkles. **1967** *DARE* (Qu. H28, *Different shapes or types of doughnuts*) Inf **MI**69, Lover's knot—long piece of dough tied in the middle.

love leaves n

A **burdock 1** (here: *Arctium lappa*).

1959 Carleton *Index Herb. Plants* 77, *Love-Leaves:* Arctium lappa.

love-lick See **love-pat**

love-lies-a-bleeding See **love-lies-bleeding 1, 2**

love-lies-bleeding n

1 also *love-lies-a-bleeding, lady bleeding, lovely bleeding:* An **amaranth,** esp *Amaranthus caudatus.* [From the drooping spikes of red flowers; *OED* c1610 →]

1784 in 1785 *Amer. Acad. Arts & Sci. Memoirs* 1.490, *Amaranthus.* . . *Bloody Amaranthus. Love-lies-a-bleeding. Princes Feather.* Amongst rubbish. August. **1822** Eaton *Botany* 169, *[Amaranthus] melancholicus* (love-lies-bleeding). **1830** Rafinesque *Med. Flora* 2.190, The *A[maranthus] sanguineus,* L. called *Lovely bleeding,* is a powerful styptic, the decoction is in popular use to stop the flow of menses, when other remedies have failed. **1868** (1870) Gray *Field Botany* 286, *A[maranthus] melancholicus,* love-lies-bleeding. **1909** Doubleday *Amer. Flower Garden* 246, Amaranthus, Love-Lies-Bleeding (*Amaranthus caudatus*). Scarlet to yellow. . . too gaudy for dainty gardens. **1947** (1976) Curtin *Healing Herbs* 24, Alegría . . *Amaranthus paniculatus* . . Lady bleeding. **1952** Taylor *Plants Colonial Days* 57, Love-lies-bleeding—*Amaranthus caudatus*—This annual herb with a fanciful common name grows up to 3 feet in height. . . Introduced into England from the East Indies in 1596, love-lies-bleeding was grown in Gerard's garden the same year. . . [It] was advertised for sale in Boston in 1760. **1964** De Vries *Reuben* 259, He found himself remembering the story of the amaranth flower. He was not thinking of the real life plant—of which he had often picked a variant called love-lies-bleeding—but the mythical bloom of the poets, which according to legend never fades. **1974** (1977) Coon *Useful Plants* 53, *Amaranthus hybridus*—Smooth pigweed . . love-lies-bleeding. . . Just as with so many common names, quite similar species can be noted as *A. melancholicus, A. caudatus, A. tricolor, A. paniculatus,* and *A. hypochondriacus.*

2 also *love-lies-a-bleeding:* A **bleeding heart 1** (here: *Dicentra spectabilis*). [*EDD* 1882]

1896 *Jrl. Amer. Folkl.* 9.181 **nOH,** *Dicentra spectabilis* . . love-lies-bleeding, bleeding hearts. **1984** Wilder *You All Spoken Here* 177 **Sth,** *Love lies a-bleedin':* Bleeding heart; luxuriant.

3 A **prince's-feather** (here: *Polygonum orientale*).

1940 Clute *Amer. Plant Names* 139, *P[olygonum] orientale.* Prince's Feather. Ragged sailor, gentleman's cane, love-lies-bleeding.

lovely bleeding See **love-lies-bleeding 1**

loveman n [From the strong attachment of the seeds to clothing]

A **cleavers,** usu *Galium aparine.*

1889 *Century Dict.* 3529, *Loveman.* . . The common goosegrass or cleavers, Galium Aparine. **1931** Harned *Wild Flowers Alleghanies* 465, Owing to the number of sharp prickles the plant (*Galium aparine*) has been given numerous names, among which are, Sweethearts, Loreman [sic], Stick-a-back . . all quite suggestive. **1940** Clute *Amer. Plant Names* 52, *G[alium] aparine* . . love-man. *Ibid* 259, *Galium asprellum.* Kidney vine, . . love-man.

love mark See **love bite**

love-me n

1 A **forget-me-not 1a** (here: *Myosotis scorpioides*). [*EDD* 1876]

1900 Lyons *Plant Names* 255, *M[yosotis] palustris* . . Forget-me-not, . . Love-me. **1959** [see **2** below].

2 also *love-me-not:* =**oxeye daisy 1.**

1959 Carleton *Index Herb. Plants* 77, *Love me:* Chrysanthemum leucanthemum; Myosotis scorpioides. *Ibid, Love-me-not:* Chrysanthemum leucanthemum.

love on See **love D2**

love-pain n [Engl dial; cf *EDD*]

1899 (1912) Green *VA Folk-Speech* 270, *Love-pain.* . . Toothache.

love-pat n Also *love-box, ~-lick, ~-tap*

An affectionate blow or caress.

1879 (1880) Twain *Tramp Abroad* 333, She gave Neddy a love-box on the arm with her fan. **1889** Twain *CT Yankee* 426, When I make up my mind to hit a man, I don't plan out a love-tap. **1943** McAtee *Dial. Grant Co. IN Suppl. 2* 10 (as of 1890s), *Love-tap* . . caress, possibly not gentle. **1951** *PADS* 15.67 **cwNH** (as of 1920s), *Love-pat.* . . Caress. **1953** *PADS* 19.12 **sAppalachians,** *Love lick.* . . Rough caress. **1954** *Harder Coll.* **cwTN,** *Love-lick.* . . A rough caress. **c1960** *Wilson Coll.* **csKY,** *Love-lick.* . . A rough caress; also love-tap.

love pea n

=**crab's eye;** also the seed of this plant.

1830 Rafinesque *Med. Flora* 183, Abrus precatorius . . *Liquorice bush, Red bean, Love pea.* A small ornamental and medical shrub, found from Florida to Brazil. . . Well known by its beautiful scarlet seeds with a black spot. **1876** Hobbs *Bot. Hdbk.* 139, Abrus precatorius . . Love pea, Wild liquorice. **1900** Lyons *Plant Names* 8, *A[brus] precatorius* . . Seeds . . Crab's-eyes . . Love-peas. **1976** Bailey–Bailey *Hortus Third* 3, *A[brus] precatorius* . . Rosary pea, love p[ea] . . Prayer-beads.

love point See **love bump 2**

love root n

=**lovage.**

1937 U.S. Forest Serv. *Range Plant Hdbk.* W106, Loveroots—*Ligusticum* spp.—The loveroots, known commonly as wildcelery, lovage, . . and ligusticum, are smooth perennial herbs of the carrot, or parsnip, family (Umbelliferae). . . With perhaps two or three exceptions, all the North American species are confined to the western part of the continent and about 18 species occur on the mountain ranges of the West. **c1938** in 1970 Hyatt *Hoodoo* 2.1391 **VA,** You places in the black bottle what they call a *King Solomon*—the root of *King Solomon root,* then you put the *love root,* then you put the devil's-shoestring root in there and that *Conker* what they call the *Conkerin' John.* **1940** (1968) Haun *Hawk's Done Gone* 289 **eTN,** I . . broke mullein leaves and all else that I had heard tell of, even asking Gertie Cocke's ma if she knowed love root when she seed it. **1963** Craighead *Rocky Mt. Wildflowers* 125, Poison-hemlock (*Conium maculatum*) can quite easily be confused with Water-hemlock and with Loveroot (*Ligusticum filicinum*). . . Loveroot . . has leaves finely divided into linear segments, the basal leaves large and long-stemmed; fruit narrowly winged.

lover's apple See **love apple 1, 2**

lover's chain See **love's chain(s)**

lover's knot See **love knot**

lover's pride n

A **lady's thumb** (here: *Polygonum persicaria*).

1900 Lyons *Plant Names* 300, *P[olygonum] Persicaria.* . . Heart's-ear, Lover's-pride. **1935** (1943) Muenscher *Weeds* 197, Ladys-thumb . . Lovers-pride. **1940** Clute *Amer. Plant Names* 139, Lover's pride, black-heart, willow-weed.

lover wolf See **loafer** n

loves See **love B1**

love's apple See **love apple 1**

love's chain(s) n Also *chain of love, lover's chain*
=**coral vine 3.**

1929 Neal *Honolulu Gardens* 105, Chain of love (*Antigonon leptopus*). . . Much of the year it brightens many parts of Honolulu with its masses of beautiful rose-pink flowers (rarely white). . . The seed cases . . are also attractive, but not conspicuous among the wavy-edged, heart-shaped leaves. **1955** *S. Folkl. Qrly.* 19.232 **FL**, Lover's Chain, or Love's Chain (*Antigonon leptopus*), also a vine, produces festoons of pink and rose colored flowers in masses from six to eight feet wide. **1959** Carleton *Index Herb. Plants* 25, Chain of love: Antigonon leptopus. *Ibid* 77, Love's chains: Antigonon leptopus. **1982** Perry–Hay *Field Guide Plants* 80, Chain of love. . . A pretty, tuberous-rooted, deciduous creeper ascending by means of tendrils.

‡loveship n Cf **love D1**
Fondness, liking.

1955 *DE Folkl. Bulletin* 1.17, [A] man told me of a hunter who, as he said it, "had too much loveship" for whiskey.

love's lost n

1989 Kingsolver *Homeland* 149, It's divided, the way a house can be split down the middle when a landlord sees how he could get twice the rent for the same piece of pie, and makes it a duplex. *There's doors that go right through between my bedroom and his living room, but they're nailed shut and painted over,* she writes Aunt Reima. *Mr. McClure's side must have got the real kitchen because mine's a closet with a hot plate. But it went vice versa on the bathrooms.* And Aunt Reima writes back that yes she's heard those called "love's losts" or some people say "bereaved apartments," because, she supposes, each one is missing something it once had.

love spoons n

A pair of spoons chained together and given as an engagement or wedding gift; see quots.

1941 Writers' Program *Guide WI* 539 **csWI**, There are hand-turned articles, ranging from iron hinges and silverware to "lovespoons," chained together and carved from a single stick of wood. **1995** *DARE* File **csWI** (as of c1960), "Love spoons" were sometimes given as a wedding or shower gift when I was quite small. A set of love spoons consisted of two rather ornate silver spoons fastened together by a ring or rings that went through the top of each handle. Sometimes the spoons were engraved, usually with the names of the bride and groom. They were meant to be purely decorative, but sometimes at the wedding reception, the bride and groom would be made to attempt to eat a few bites of their food with the love spoons. This was jokingly said to be a test of how well they would "pull together" in their new life. I haven't seen (or heard of) love spoons in recent years.

love's test n

A **pussytoes** (here: *Antennaria plantaginifolia*).

1896 *Jrl. Amer. Folkl.* 9.191 **IN**, Antennaria plantaginifolia, . . love's test, Ind. . . The test is in this wise: A leaf is taken by the ends, a person of the opposite sex is thought of, and the ends pulled apart. If the tomentum beneath is drawn out long, the affection is supposed to be proportionate. Sometimes this is varied by naming both ends, when the relative length of the tomentum determines the stronger love. **1959** Carleton *Index Herb. Plants* 77, Love's test: Antennaria plantaginifolia.

love-swindle n

=**barn owl 1.**

1954 McAtee *Suppl. to Nomina Abitera* [8] **SC**, Barn Owl (*Tyto alba*)—Wm. W. Neeley of Chester, S.C., submitted a name heard in that vicinity which he could not explain, which was "love-swindle." Departing for [sic] the prevailing policy of Nomina Abitera, I offer a hypothesis. The barn owl has been credited with a cry like . . the last agonized shriek of a despairing soul. May we not speculate that this hair-raising scream has startled lovers out of near consummation often enough to fasten on the bird the name of "love-swindle."

love-tangle See **love-entangle 1**

love-tap See **love-pat**

love up See **love D2**

love vine n

1 =**dodder.** [See quot 1909] esp **Sth, S Midl**

1833 Eaton *Botany* 116, Cuscuta americana, dodder, love-vine. . . A bright yellow leafless vine, twining around other weeds in damp places. **1876** Hobbs *Bot. Hdbk.* 66, Love vine . . Dodder . . Cuscuta Americana. **1892** *Jrl. Amer. Folkl.* 5.101 **cTX**, Cuscuta, sp., love-vine, Fort Worth. **1894** *Ibid* 7.95 **nwNC**, Cuscuta compacta, . . love-vine, Banner Elk, N.C. . . Probably because used in love-divinations. **1897** *Ibid* 10.51 **swMO**, Cuscuta, sp., love vines. . . From a popular custom among young people of throwing a portion of this plant backward over the head of another plant, and naming it for someone. If it lives, that one loves them. **1899** (1912) Green *VA Folk-Speech* 270, Love-vine. . . Gold-thread. **1909** *DN* 3.347 **eAL, wGA**, Love-vine. . . A yellowish, thread-like, twining parasitic plant; the dodder. So called because of the custom among young people of plucking a section of the vine and, after naming it and circling it over the head three times, throwing it on another bush. If it grows, the person after whom it is named loves the one who throws it. **1951** *PADS* 15.38 **TX**, Cuscutaceae . . Love vine; strangle-weed [etc]. **1967** *DARE* Wildfl QR (Wills–Irwin) Pl.34A Inf **TX**44, Plant is called strangleweed and love vine; grows on *cadillo* and purple nightshade. **1969–70** *DARE* (Qu. S5) Inf **CA**87, Love vine—a little different; waxy orange, grows like a wire and tangles itself in the bushes; (Qu. S21, . . Weeds . . that are a trouble in gardens and fields) Infs **CA**185, **VA**77, Love vine; **GA**84, Dodder—another name of love vine; **MO**19, Love vine—a little yellow vine that gets started in the garden or field or anyplace—you can't get rid of the darn stuff; (Qu. S26b, *Wildflowers that grow in water or wet places*) Inf **KY**40, Love vine—yellow vine, no flower (dodder); (Qu. S26e, *Other wildflowers not yet mentioned;* not asked in early QRs) Inf **SC**43, Love vine—delicate yellow flower. **1970** (1971) Walls *Chickenbone Special* 49 **NC**, The tobacco shoots sometimes are born with a tiny vine clinging to them. . . the search for them is a diligent one. For every youngster . . knows the little parasite as a "love vine" said to possess magical powers over matters of the heart.

2 A **virgin's bower** (here: *Clematis virginiana*).

1900 Lyons *Plant Names* 107, C[lematis] Virginiana . . Canada to Georgia and Kansas. . . Devil's-darning-needle, Devil's-hair, Love-vine. **1910** Graves *Flowering Plants* 190 **CT**, Devil's Hair. Traveler's Joy. Love Vine. **1942** Tehon *Fieldbook IL Shrubs* 75, Virginia Virgin's-Bower . . Love Vine. . . A climbing vine with more or less woody stems as much as 18 or 20 feet long.

3 A parasitic vine (*Cassytha filiformis*) native to Florida and Texas which resembles **dodder.** Also called **woevine** [Cf **love vine 1**]

1933 Small *Manual SE Flora* 925, C[assytha] filiformis. . . Love-vine. . . The plants thrive on both herbaceous and woody hosts. **1969** Lyons *My Florida* 19, My Florida. . . is scrub-oaks covered with orange love-vines and a saucy towhee scratching. **1970** Correll *Plants TX* 661, Cassytha filiformis. . . Love-vine. Parasitic vine superficially resembling Cuscuta, with yellowish or pale-green wiry entwined stems and branches with a spicy fragrance.

4 =**coral vine 3.** Cf **love's chain(s)**

1976 Bailey–Bailey *Hortus Third* 86, [Antigonon] leptopus. . . Love vine. . . Fl[ower]s bright pink. . . Tubers are edible. **1982** Perry–Hay *Field Guide Plants* 80, Antigonon leptopus . . Coral creeper; love vine. . . A pretty, tuberous-rooted, deciduous creeper ascending by means of tendrils up to 12 m (40 ft), or, in the absence of supports, scrambling across the ground.

loving paper n

1930 Shoemaker *1300 Words* 38 **cPA Mts** (as of c1900), Lovin' paper—A marriage certificate, or license.

low v, n, hence vbl n, n *lowing* |lo(ʊ)| [*OED* c1000 →] **chiefly Sth** See Map on p. 444 Cf **bellow, loo** v, n[1]
To make the usu resonant, sustained sound of a cow, esp when it is not disturbed; this sound.

1806 (1970) Webster *Compendious Dict.* 180, Low . . to . . bellow, make a noise. . . Lowing . . the noise made by oxen, &c. a bellowing. [*DARE* Ed: This entry was carried over from Webster's English model.] **1899** (1912) Green *VA Folk-Speech* 270, Low. . . To utter the soft bellow peculiar to animals of the cow-kind; moo. **1939** *LANE* Map 194 *(Moo)* 43 infs, **chiefly sNEng**, Low(ing). **1948** Davis *Word Atlas Gt. Lakes* app qu 62a *(Name for gentle sound made by cow at feeding time)* 19 (of 233) infs, **MI, IL, IN, OH,** Low; qu 62b *(Name for loud sound made by cow when calf is taken away)* 3 infs, **MI, IL,** Low. **1949** Kurath *Word Geog.* 62, Moo. . . This expression is used also by some of the younger generation in the South, but the usual expression from Baltimore southward is *low* (riming with *so*). . . *Low* occurs also in southern New England. **1965–70** *DARE* (Qu. K21, *The noise a cow makes, calling for her calf*) 122 Infs, **chiefly Sth,** Low [lo(ʊ)]; 18 Infs, **chiefly Sth,** Lowing; (Qu. K19, *Noise made by a calf that's taken away from its mother*) 9 Infs, **chiefly Sth,** Low(ing). **1966** Dakin *Dial. Vocab. Ohio R. Valley* 2.251, The usual Southern term, *low* (very rarely *loo* in the Ohio Valley), is in general use in southern Kentucky, where it is the most common expression, and is also quite common in the Bluegrass portion of the lower Kentucky River valley. North of the Ohio it is less common and frequently is mentioned in addition to *moo* or as an expression the informants hear others use. **1966** *DARE* Tape MS72, We'd go out and give two or three hollers, and the cows would bunch up, and them little calves a-runnin' . . and the cows a-lowin', and the little calves would run with their little curl in the tail. **1967** Faries *Word Geog.* MO 145, Low *(Noise made by cows)* 71 [of c700 infs]. **1972** *PADS* 58.17 **cwAL,** Moo. Usage for the sound a cow makes at feeding time is equally divided between Southern *low* (8) and Northern and Midland *moo* (8, educated usage). . . Besides representing educated usage, the *moo* responses are from informants by residence or occupation tend to be urban. On the other hand, the *low* responses come from informants who have engaged in farming or who live in rural communities. **1973** Allen *LAUM* 1.252 (as of c1950), *Low,* surviving either as a relic carried west from the South Atlantic coast, a relic of British usage, or a literary term, occurs three times in Iowa, twice in Nebraska, and twice in Minnesota. **1989** Pederson *LAGS Tech. Index* 136 **Gulf Region,** *(Bawl [of calf])* 43 infs, Low; *(Low [of cow])* 277 infs, Low.

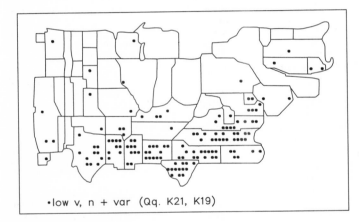

•low v, n + var (Qq. K21, K19)

low adj **chiefly Sth, S Midl** Cf **long** adj **B1**
Of a person: short.
    1885 *Daily Amer.* (Nashville TN) 4 Mar 2/2, Mr. Cleveland . . would no more reform it [=the tariff] by a horizontal reduction than he would cut off the heads of tall and low men to equalize their stature. **1886** *S. Bivouac* 4.343 **Sth,** Low (short). **1899** (1912) Green *VA Folk-Speech* 270, *Low.* . . Short in height. "Mighty low man." **1902** *DN* 2.239 **sIL,** *Low.* . . Short in stature, as 'a low man,' 'a low woman.' **1909** *DN* 3.347 **eAL, wGA,** *Low.* . . Short. The latter word is rarely or never used of a person. "Look at that little low man." **1923** *DN* 5.214 **swMO,** *Low.* . . Short of stature. "He's a low, fat feller." **1939** Hall *Coll.* **eTN,** The Foxes are low, not tall. **1959** Lomax *Rainbow Sign* 76 **AL** [Black], He was a kinda low, brown-skin man with a few freckles across his face. **1971** *Today Show Letters* **cnAL** (as of a1940), Being referred to as a . . "low" person had no reference to one's character, but was referring to height.

low adv Cf **high** adv **2**
In ref to the seasoning of food: lightly.
    1966 *DARE* Tape **SC15,** We . . salt it [=crab meat] just like you want it salted, high or low.

'low See **allow**

low-backs n pl Cf **high back 2**
    1954 Harder *Coll.* **cwTN,** *Low-backs.* . . A type of overalls: galluses button in back. "Em low-backs shore cause twisted galluses."

lowbarkahighrum n Cf **highbarkalorum**
    1967 *DARE* Tape **TX1,** They had this old doctor. . . and they asked him, "You make two kinds o' medicine outta pecan bark. . What do yer call it?" "Highbarkalorum 'n' lowbarkahighrum [ˌlobɑɚˈkə ˈhaɪrəm]. . . Cut the bark down at the bottom of a tree . . strip it up. That's lowbarkahighrum."

low beam n Also *lower beam* **chiefly Nth, N Midl, C Atl, West** See Map Cf **high beam 2**
The short-range, right-directed light of an automobile headlight.
    1939 *Daily Progress* (Charlottesville VA) 19 Aug 4 *(Hench Coll.),* An important step in reducing traffic accidents at night is reported from Cleveland. . . A 'sealed beam,' . . at once provides greatly increased range and breadth of light with stronger intensity through its high, or 'country,' beam and reduction of glare with increased illumination of the right side of the road with its low or 'traffic' beam. **1965–70** *DARE* (Qu. N10, . . *Words . . for the bright and dim lights on a car*) 164 Infs, **chiefly Nth, N Midl, C Atl, West,** Low beam(s); **IN**80, **MA**55, **MI**97, **NY**170, **OH**87, **SC**40, Lower beam(s).

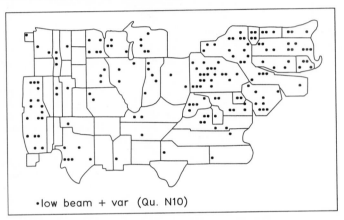

•low beam + var (Qu. N10)

lowbelia n [Folk-etym; see quot 1841] Cf **highbelia**
=Indian tobacco 1.
    1841 in 1843 Torrey *Flora NY* 1.424, In the application of one of the common names to this plant, is a curious instance of committing a pun without committing a sin. Being much taller and more robust than the *L. inflata,* which is frequently used in domestic practice under the name of *Low belia,* it was supposed as a matter of course by those better acquainted with its near affinity to the latter, than with its etymology, that it must be *High belia!* **1859** (1968) Bartlett *Americanisms* 257, The quacks who use the *Lobelia inflata,* or "Indian tobacco," suppose the name to be *Lowbelia,* and it is so written in the description of a patent. **1894** *Jrl. Amer. Folkl.* 7.93, *Lobelia inflata.* . . low belia. **1904** Henkel *Weeds Used in Med.* 11, Lobelia—*Lobelia inflata* . . low belia. **1930** Sievers *Amer. Med. Plants* 40, Lobelia—*Lobelia inflata* . . low belia.

low blood n **chiefly Sth, S Midl** Cf **high blood**
Low blood pressure, anemia, or another disorder associated with the blood.
    1965 Weller *Yesterday's People* 119 **sAppalachians,** Other common complaints are a "beeled head," "low blood," and "nerves." **1966–70** *DARE* (Qu. BB48, *When a person has too much sugar in his blood and may have to take insulin for it . . he has* _____) Inf **FL**39, Diabetes—Negroes call it low blood; (Qu. DD24, . . *Diseases that come from continual drinking*) Inf **TN**53, High or low blood. **1982** Mason *Shiloh* 132 **wKY,** You've been looking peaked lately. I believe you've got low blood. **1982** Slone *How We Talked* 113 **eKY** (as of c1950), *Low blood*— Cure: Yellow Dock; also, drink Sassafrass tea (This was a good tasting tea and was often used just for the taste.) **1984** Wilder *You All Spoken Here* 203 **Sth,** He's down sick with the low blood. **1984** *Annals Internal Med.* 100.6.900 **cwAL,** *Low blood* is a common folk diagnosis for a vague admixture of low blood pressure, anemia, and lack of energy. **1986** Pederson *LAGS Concordance,* 1 inf, **cnFL,** Low blood—low blood pressure. **1987** *DARE* File **seWI,** My Black patients at Mt. Sinai Hospital in Milwaukee use *high blood* to mean 'high blood pressure' and *low blood* to mean 'anemia.' **1990** Cavender *Folk Med. Lexicon* 26 **sAppalachians,** Low blood—a. low blood pressure. b. an anemic condition. c. an abnormally low quantity of blood. d. low blood count. **1993** Mason *Feather Crowns* 276 **KY,** "You're thinning out," Alma said

to her. "You don't want to lose that weight too fast, or you'll have low blood."

low blueberry n

A **blueberry 1**: usu *Vaccinium vacillans*, but also *V. angusti-folium* or *V. tenellum*. For other names of *V. vacillans* see **blue huckleberry 1, half-high blueberry, huckleberry 2, lowbush ~, sugar ~, sweet blueberry**

1824 Bigelow *Florula Bostoniensis* 150, Vaccinium tenellum. *Low Blueberry.* . . A low early flowering shrub upon hills and pastures. **1836** (1840) Phelps *Lectures on Botany* app 148, Vaccinium. . . *pennsylvanica,* low blue-berry. **1847** Wood *Class-Book* 369, V[accinium] Pennsylvani-cum . . Common Low Blueberry. **1889** *Century Dict.* 599, The swamp or tall blueberry is the *Vaccinium corymbosum;* the low blueberry, *V. vacillans;* and the dwarf blueberry, *V. Pennsylvanicum.* **1903** Porter *Flora PA* 242, Vaccinium vacillans . . Low Blueberry. **1946** Tatnall *Flora DE* 201, V[accinium] vacillans . . Low Blueberry . . rare south of the Maryland-Virginia line. **1976** Bailey–Bailey *Hortus Third* 1143, [Vaccinium] vacillans . . low blueberry, low sweet blueberry. . . A source of edible wild blueberries.

low-bred adj, n [Folk-etym, by analogy with **high-bred**] Non-hybrid; non-hybrid corn.

1940–41 Cassidy *WI Atlas* **Prairie du Chien WI**, Last year I tried the high-bred corn and it done so good that I ain't planting the low-bred no more. [**c1980** *DARE* File **csWI**, [Sign:] Welcome to Highbred Corn Association Meeting.]

low bridge exclam

See quot 1916.

1898 Westcott *Harum* 250 **cNY**, I'd like to bet you . . that if all them fellers we seen this afternoon, that air over fifty, c'd be got together, an' some one was suddinly to holler *"Low bridge!"* that nineteen out o' twenty 'd *duck their heads.* **1913** Allen *Low Bridge Everybody Down* [title]. **1916** *DN* 4.326 **KS**, *Low bridge!* A cry of warning on approach-ing an obstruction overhead; originally used on canal boats. General. **1926** *Sat. Review* 13 Nov 295 **NEng**, "Low bridge," cries Jeff, as we turn into the home lane, apple-bordered with trees bending to the walls, propped in their magnificent fruition by dozens of crooked birch poles. **1940** *San Francisco Examiner* (CA) 17 Nov pictorial rev 2, It was one of these new squatty stream-lined cabs and when Ethel was getting in she bumped her head and the driver ses low bridge there lady. **1995** *NADS Letters* **seMI**, Both my father and I are familiar with *low bridge* as a warning. . . The item is not very common, but occasionally heard.

low-built adj Also *low-set* Cf **low** adj

Of a person: short.

1906 *DN* 3.145 **nwAR**, *Low-built and heavy-set.* . . Stocky. "He's low-built and heavy-set." **1930** Shoemaker *1300 Words* 38 **cPA Mts** (as of c1900), *Low-built*—Short legged, a term often applied to plump, medium-sized girls. **1984** Wilder *You All Spoken Here* 54 **Sth**, *Low set and on the heavy side:* Stocky; built from the ground up.

lowbush blueberry n

A **blueberry 1**: usu *Vaccinium angustifolium*, but also *V. pallidum* or *V. vacillans*. For other names of *V. angustifolium* see **blue huckleberry 1, crackerberry 2, dewberry 2, huck-leberry 2, low blueberry, sugar blueberry, ~ huckleberry, sweet blueberry, ~ hurts, ~ juniper, whortleberry**

1900 Lyons *Plant Names* 386, V[accinium] Pennsylvanicum. . . Dwarf, Low-bush or Sugar Blueberry. **1939** Medsger *Edible Wild Plants* 72, *Low-bush blueberry* . . *Vaccinium angustifolium*—This is the early-mar-ket blueberry, ripening in June and July or, farther north, in August. The bushes rarely grow more than twenty inches high and often not half that. **1973** Wharton–Barbour *Trees KY* 263, Vaccinium vacillans . . Lowbush Blueberry—Stems 8–20 inches tall. *Ibid* 264, Vaccinium pallidum . . Lowbush Blueberry—Stems 1–3 feet tall.

lowbush blue huckleberry See **lowbush huckleberry**

lowbush cranberry n [*DCan* 1833 →] chiefly **AK** Cf **high-bush cranberry**

A **mountain cranberry 1** (here: *Vaccinium vitis-idaea*).

1900 *Explor. AK 1898* 85, Blueberries are especially large and plenti-ful in their season, while the high and low bush cranberry grows in favorable places, with the salmonberry and others. **1938** (1958) Sharples *AK Wild Flowers* 149, V[accinium] Vitis-Idaea. "Lowbush Cranberry." A bog species; dwarf, matted growth. . . Fruit red. **1939** Medsger *Edible*

Wild Plants 70, Low-Bush Cranberry—*Vaccinium Vitis-Idaea* . . Like the cranberry, the fruit is not good raw but when properly sweetened is excellent for sauce and jelly. **1955** U.S. Arctic Info. Center *Gloss.* 53, *Mountain cranberry.* A low creeping shrub. . . Also called . . 'low-bush cranberry.' **1966** Heller *Wild Flowers AK* 34, Mountain or low-brush [sic] cranberry, lingonberry—*Vaccinium vitis idaea*. . . A creeping evergreen subshrub 2 to 6 inches high. **1967–69** *DARE* (Qu. I44, *What kinds of berries grow wild around here?*) Inf **AK**3, Lowbush cranber-ries—around Juneau; **MI**53, Cranberries—highbush and lowbush; **NH**14, Lowbush and highbush cranberries. **1972** Viereck–Little *AK Trees* 233, Lowbush cranberry. . . The berries are abundant and usually picked in the fall after the first frost. . . They are commonly used for jams, jellies, relishes, and beverages. Although sour, they have a better flavor than the commercial cranberry. **1977** *New Yorker* 9 May 94 **AK**, The trails would go along, well cut and stamped out through moss campion, . . low-bush cranberries, lichens, Labrador tea; then, abruptly, the trails would disappear.

lowbush huckleberry n Also *lowbush blue huckleberry, low huckleberry* Cf **highbush huckleberry**

A **blueberry 1**: usu *Vaccinium vacillans*, but also *V. tenellum*.

1859 Perry *Turpentine Farming* 9 **NC**, After this, the land needs no cultivation, but every kind of turf should be turned over, such as low bush huckleberry, gallberry, percosan bush, . . and broom-sage grass. **1926** (1949) McQueen–Mizell *Hist. Okefenokee* 124 **seGA**, The low-bush blue huckleberry is a very large berry—larger than a pea—and grows only on high land, where the water never overflows. **1940** Stey-ermark *Flora MO* 406, Low-bush Huckleberry . . *Vaccinium virgatum* Ait. var. *tenellum*. . . Low plant, usually 8–12". *Ibid*, Low-bush Huck-leberry, Low-bush Blueberry (*Vaccinium vacillans* Kalm). *Ibid*, Low-bush Huckleberry, Low-bush Blueberry (*Vaccinium vacillans* var. *crini-tum*). **1960** Vines *Trees SW* 822, Blueridge Blueberry—*Vaccinium vacillans*. . . It is locally known under the vernacular names of Low Huckleberry . . Low Blueberry, Early Sweet Blueberry. *Ibid* 825, *Vac-cinium . . tenellum*. . . Also known under the vernacular name of Low Huckleberry. **1966–68** *DARE* (Qu. I44, *What kinds of berries grow wild around here?*) Infs **CT**17, **SC**1, 7, Lowbush huckleberries. **1973** Stephens *Woody Plants* 436, *Vaccinium vacillans* . . lowbush huckle-berry.

lowbush lightning n Cf **lightning** n[1], *DS* DD21c

1946 *PADS* 6.20 **ceNC** (as of 1900–10), *Low-bush lightning.* . . Whisky hidden by "blind tiger" in bushes. . . Common for a while after 1908, the year of the beginning of prohibition in N.C.

lowbush merkle n Cf **myrtle** n[1] A, B9

A **groundsel tree** (here: *Baccharis halimifolia*).

1974 Morton *Folk Remedies* 35 **SC**, Lowbush Merkle . . Groundsel Bush . . Silver Sage. *Baccharis halimifolia*. . . *Shrub*, very bushy, with short, woody trunk. . . Root decoction taken for colds and for pain in stomach.

low cornel n

=**bunchberry 1.**

1822 Eaton *Botany* 251, Cornus canadensis . . low cornel. **1848** in 1850 Cooper *Rural Hours* 85 **NY**, The low-cornel is opening: its cups are greenish now, but they will soon bleach to a pure white. **1869** Fuller *Uncle John* 72 **NY**, The *Canadensis* is an interesting species. It is usually called *Low Cornel*. It is a little herb, . . not more than four or six inches high. **1910** Graves *Flowering Plants* 304 **CT**, Cornus canadensis . . Low Cornel. **1940** Clute *Amer. Plant Names* 97, C[ornus] Canadensis. Bunch-berry. . . low cornel, . . crackerberry, (bear-berry).

low cotton n chiefly **Sth, S Midl** Cf **high cotton 1**

In phrr *be* (or *feel*) *in low cotton*: To feel ill; to be in a state of malaise or depression; hence adj *low cotton* unwell, listless.

1941 Percy *Lanterns* 291 **nwMS**, I was in what Ford would call "low cotton." **1946** *PADS* 6.20 **seNC** (as of 1900–10), *Low cotton.* . . Puny. "I'm feeling sort o' low cotton today." Craven Co., N.C., 1941–42. **1971** Dwyer *Dict. for Yankees* 29 **Sth, S Midl**, *Low cotton*—State of depres-sion, i.e., "She's always in low cotton." **1965–68** *DARE* (Qu. BB5, *A general feeling of discomfort or illness that isn't any one place in particular*) Inf **NC**11, Low cotton; (Qu. GG33b, *To feel very sad and upset about something: "I never saw a woman _____ so."*; total Infs questioned, 75) Inf **OK**6, Really in low cotton; (Qu. GG34b, *To feel depressed or in a gloomy mood: "She's feeling _____ today."*) Infs **OK**6, **TX**37, 54, In low cotton. **1984** Wilder *You All Spoken Here* 206 **Sth**, *In low cotton:* In depression; morbid; in the dismals; low in spirit.

1986 Pederson *LAGS Concordance* (Peaked . . as a result of ill health) 1 inf, **cnLA,** In low cotton.

low-down adj

1 Mean, contemptible; hence adv *low-down.* **formerly chiefly Sth, S Midl; now more widespread**

1868 [see **lowdowner**]. **1884** *Anglia* 7.270 **Sth, S Midl** [Black], *De lowdonest cuss* = the lowest creature. **1885** Twain *Huck. Finn* 30 **ceMO,** I was so ignorant and so kind of low-down and ornery. **1899** (1912) Green *VA Folk-Speech* 270, *Low-down.* . . Far down in the scale of existence; a very rude or mean person. **1903** *DN* 2.320 **seMO,** *Low-down.* . . Very mean. 'He is a low-down fellow.' **1906** *DN* 3.121 **sIN,** *Low-down.* . . Very mean. *Ibid* 145 **nwAR,** *Low-down.* . . Despicably. "He's low-down mean." **1907** *DN* 3.233 **seMO, nwAR,** *Low-down.* . . Low, vile, mean. **1909** *DN* 3.400 **nwAR,** *Low-down.* . . Despicably; contemptibly. "They're low-down stingy. They won't even give away buttermilk." *Ibid* 347 **eAL, wGA,** *Low-down.* . . Mean, low, vulgar. "He's a low-down scoundrel." *Ibid* 400 **nwAR,** *Low-down.* . . Very mean. "Polly Ann is low-down, and I won't play with her." **1937** (1963) Hyatt *Kiverlid* 50 **KY,** Atter all she's only a blatherskite and not a low-down woman. **1938** Rawlings *Yearling* 73 **nFL,** They ain't low-down, Ma. **1942** (1960) Robertson *Red Hills* 188 **SC,** "Brer Rabbit," said Bill, "had trouble with his low-down, sorry, trifling tramp of a wife." **1952** *DE Folkl. Bulletin* 1.11, Lowdownest trick he ever hearn of. **1954** *Harder Coll.* **cwTN,** *Lowdown(er): Adj.* . . [Used of a] deceiving person. " 'E's plumb lowdown." " 'At set's lowdowner'n a bunch o' maddogs." "He is just it for lowdown meanness." **1965–70** *DARE* (Qu. HH18, *Very insignificant or low-grade people*) 30 Infs, **scattered,** Low-down; (Qu. U17, *Names or nicknames for a person who doesn't pay his bills*) Inf **IL28,** Low-down skunk; (Qu. V2a, . . *A deceiving person, or somebody that you can't trust*) Inf **NC50,** Dirty and low-down; **TX41,** Low-down snake; (Qu. V6, . . *Words* . . *for a thief*) Inf **CT23,** Low-down skunk; **KY5,** Low-down thief; (Qu. AA7b, . . *A woman who is very fond of men and is always trying to know more—if she's not respectable about it*) Inf **MO38,** Low-down; (Qu. GG18, . . *'Obstinate': "Why does he have to be so* _____ *."*) Inf **MS88,** Low-down; (Qu. GG38, *Somebody who is usually mean and bad tempered: "He's an awful* _____ *."*) Inf **NY217,** Low-down; (Qu. HH20a, *An idle, worthless person: "He's a* _____ *."*) Inf **PA247,** Low-down; (Qu. HH22b, . . *A very mean person* . . *"He's meaner than* _____ *."*) Inf **CA66,** Low-down snake; (Qu. HH34y, *Disrespectful words around here for a woman*) Inf **OK31,** Low-down; (Qu. HH37, *An immoral woman*) Inf **IN14,** Low-down; (Qu. II21, *When somebody behaves unpleasantly or without manners: "The way he behaves, you'd think he was* _____ *."*) Inf **OH13,** Just plain low-down; (Qu. KK37, *Words to describe a very sly person: "He's* _____ *."*) Inf **MS61,** Low-down person; (Qu. LL36, *To make a statement much stronger: "Poor fellow. I think it's a* _____ *shame."*) Infs **HI13, KY85, TN52, VA15,** Low-down; (Qu. NN9b, *Exclamations showing great annoyance: "He's run off with my hammer again,* _____ *!"*) Inf **MS16,** Low-down dirty dog. **1968** Haun *Hawk's Done Gone* 266 **eTN,** Of course they done me low-down. But Ad brung Elzie up to be that way. And poor Froney don't know any better. **1989** Flynt *Poor But Proud* 210 **ceAL,** We ain't got nothin' but a shirt tail an' a prayer, but we ain't low-down.

2 Lacking energy; under the weather; low in spirits. **esp Sth, S Midl** See Map

1965–70 *DARE* (Qu. X47, . . *"I'm very tired, at the end of my strength"*) Inf **TX42,** Low-down; (Qu. BB39, *On a day when you don't feel just right, though not actually sick* . . *"I'll be all right tomorrow—I'm just feeling* _____ *today."*) Infs **KY94, NJ4, PA66, VA74,** Low-

down; (Qu. GG34b, *To feel depressed or in a gloomy mood: "She's feeling* _____ *today."*) Infs **DC12, GA1, 11, IN32, LA17, NY88, VA31,** Low-down; (Qu. KK30, *Feeling slowed up or without energy: "I certainly feel* _____ *."*) Infs **GA11, KY65, NC7, VA29, 31,** Low-down. **1986** Pederson *LAGS Concordance,* 1 inf, **csGA,** It seems to me that he's real low-down = ill.

low-down adv See **low-down** adj **1**

low-down n

1 pl; with *the:* Depression, malaise.

1967–70 *DARE* (Qu. GG34a, *To feel depressed or in a gloomy mood: "He has the* _____ *today."*) Infs **MN2, OH80, WV16,** Low-downs.

2 A critical or uncomplimentary remark, a "put-down."

1969 *DARE* (Qu. Y4, . . *A very uncomplimentary remark*) Inf **MO15,** Low-downs.

lowdowner n

=poor White.

1868 *Putnam's Mag.* new ser 1.704 **wSC,** [I was occasionally obliged to deal with . . that wretched caste commonly spoken of as the "mean whites" or the . . "low-down people."] *Ibid* 706, When . . candidates refreshed their adherents by the barrelfull, the low-downer enjoyed his periodical benders without expense. **1872** Schele de Vere *Americanisms* 45, *A corn cracker* . . appears as *Conch* or *Low Downer* in North Carolina, and as *Sandhiller* or *Poor White Trash* in South Carolina and Georgia. **1883** Stevenson *Silverado Squatters* 131 **cwCA,** They are at least known by a generic byword, as Poor Whites or Low-downers.

lower v[1] Usu |ˈlaʊə(r)|; also, prob a sp-pronc, |ˈloʊə(r)|; for addit varr see quots **chiefly NEng, Upstate NY** See Map

Of the weather or sky: to be or become dark or threatening; hence ppl adj *lowering,* adj *lowery,* also sp *loury* dark, threatening.

1775 (1971) Calk *Jrl.* 36 **VA,** This a very loury morning and like for Rain. **1806** (1970) Webster *Compendious Dict.* 180, *Lower* . . to be cloudy. [*DARE* Ed: This entry was carried over from Webster's English model.] **1863** in 1878 Longfellow *Poems* 225, Between the dark and the daylight,/ When the night is beginning to lower,/ Comes a pause in the day's occupations,/ That is known as the Children's Hour. **1873** in 1955 Lee *Mormon Chron.* 2.242 **IL,** To day warm & lowery. Strong indications of Rain. **1899** (1912) Green *VA Folk-Speech* 270, *Low-ery.* . . Threatening, said of the weather. **1907** *DN* 3.193 **seNH,** *Lowery* [ˈlaʊərɪ]. . . Overcast with clouds, gloomy. "It's a lowery day." Universal. **1926** in 1931 McCorrison *Letters Fraternity* 84 **NEng,** Another warm lowery day—fine for pickerel fishing. **1939** *LANE* Map 88 **NEng,** *A cloudy day.* . . The most variable of the terms is *lowery.* This is very often (usually?) used merely as an emphatic or colloquial synonym of *cloudy* . . but occasionally has a more complex or a different meaning. Six informants define *lowery* as 'foggy, misty' . . , while another says that a lowery day is damper than a dull day. . . Ten informants use *lowery* of a day 'when it looks like rain' . . ; twelve use it as a synonym of *rainy, showery* or *drizzly.* . . Four informants call a day lowery only if a storm is brewing . . or actually in process. **1949** Kurath *Word Geog.* 19, *Lowery,* riming with *flowery,* for 'gloomy,' is not an unusual weather term in New England, except for Cape Cod and the Merrimack Valley, but it does not seem to have survived west of the Hudson. **1951** *PADS* 15.67 **cwNH** (as of 1920s), *Lowery weather.* . . Threatening a storm. **1959** *VT Hist.* 27.148, *Lowery* [ˈlaʊrɪ]. . . Cloudy with intermittent showers. **1965–70** *DARE* (Qu. B5, *When the weather looks as if it will become bad* . . *it's* _____) Infs **MA72, NY23, 93, 95, 220,**

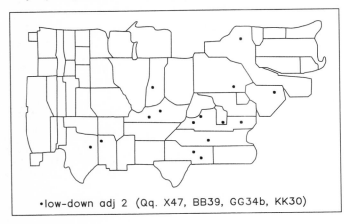

•low-down adj 2 (Qq. X47, BB39, GG34b, KK30)

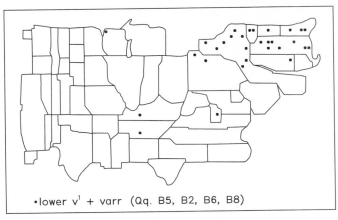

•lower v[1] + varr (Qq. B5, B2, B6, B8)

230, 233, **PA**233, ['la(ʊ)ɚi, -ɪ]; **ME**9, **MA**6, **PA**115, ['lɑʊri]; **ME**16, ['loɚi]; **NY**19, ['lɔəri]; **MA**5, 100, **WI**64, ['la(ʊ)wɚɪŋ]; **KY**83, ['laɚ‧ɪn]; **NY**218, ['laʊɚ‧i]; **VT**12, ['lɑərɪŋ]; **TN**52, ['lowɪn] [FW sugg]; **NY**155, Lowering; (Qu. B2, *If the weather is very unpleasant . . it's a _____ day*) Infs **ME**1, **NH**10, ['lauɚi]; **MA**30, ['lauwɚi]; **VT**16, Lowery; (Qu. B6, *When clouds begin to increase . . it's _____*) Inf **MA**4, ['lɑuwɚri]; **MA**23, ['lauwɚiʃ]; **MA**55, ['lowɚ‧i, 'lauwɚi]; **DC**3, ['lowɚɪŋ]; (Qu. B8, *When clouds come and go all day . . it's _____*) Inf **CT**29, ['lauɚ‧i]—old-fashioned. **1981** Pederson *LAGS Basic Materials*, 1 inf, **ceTX**, Lowering ['loˢʊɚ‧ɪŋ] day—has heard this; clouds coming down before rain.

lower adj

1 In combs with terms for var types of **earmark** n: Made in the lower edge of the ear. Cf **over** C, **under**, **upper**
   1906 *DN* 3.157 **nwAR**, A lower (*right* or *left*) *slope* [is taken] from the lower part [of the ear]. **1967** *DARE* (Qu. K18, *. . Kind of mark . . to identify a cow*) Inf **LA**2, Lower figure seven, lower half-crop.

2 Used in var combs referring to the states of the US other than Alaska, esp the contiguous, continental states: see below. **chiefly AK** Addit exx in Tabbert *Dict. Alaskan Engl*. Cf **down below 1b, outside** n **1**, adv

a *lower forty-eight.*
   1959 *Anchorage Daily News* 29 Aug 1 (Tabbert *Dict. Alaskan Engl.*), Albert B. Cross of Sacramento was uninjured in the crash of his Culver plane, which was flying from the lower 48 to Unalakleet. **1962** *AK Sportsman* Oct 30, Our life, complete with TV, was much the same as it had been in the "lower 48," with only the spectacular setting to change it. **1968** *DARE* FW Addit **AK**8, The lower forty-eight. **c1970** *DARE* File **AK**, We haven't had a shipment from the lower 48. **1977** *New Yorker* 20 June 49, Some, of course, are interested only in a year or two's work, then to return with saved high wages to the Lower-Forty-eight. **1980** *Fairbanks Daily News–Miner* 23 Sept 4 (Tabbert *Dict. Alaskan Engl.*), One guest speaker from Outside told an audience, "I had never heard the term 'Lower 48' before. I shall now refer to Alaska as the 'Upper 1.'" **1987** *AK Mag.* Oct 20, Alaskans will be a little closer to the Lower 48 this fall, when Alascom Inc. hooks up access to toll-free telephone numbers nationwide.

b *lower states.*
   1960 *AK Sportsman* Dec 30, Game biologists in the lower states are accustomed to complaints from the public that deer are eating ornamental shrubbery. **1988** *Fairbanks Daily News–Miner* 28 Sept 13 (Tabbert *Dict. Alaskan Engl.*), Although the school was modern the administrators still depended largely on teachers from the lower states.

c *lower forty-nine (states).*
   1972 Attla *Everything I Know About Training and Racing Sled Dogs* 26 (Tabbert *Dict. Alaskan Engl.*), The first big race of the year which attracts mushers from all over Alaska and the Lower 49 is usually the State Championship race at Kenai–Soldotna. **1987** *AK Mag.* Oct 20, No longer will Alaskans have to feel left out of offers which include toll-free telephone numbers in the Lower 49 states.

lower n, v², hence vbl n *lowering* |'louɚ| [See quot 1949]
=low v, n.
   1949 Kurath *Word Geog.* 62, In the lower James River Valley *low* is sometimes changed to *lower*. This is an overcorrection on the model of *four,* which has a folk pronunciation riming with *so* beside the cultivated pronunciation. **1967** Faries *Word Geog. MO* 145, Lower (*Noise made by cows*) 1 [of c700 infs]. **1969** *DARE* (Qu. K21, *The noise a cow makes, calling for her calf*) Inf **MA**55, Lowering ['lowrɚɪn] [sic], ['laʊrɚɪn] [sic]. **1981** Pederson *LAGS Basic Materials* (*Low–of cow or calf at feeding time*) 1 inf, **csLA**, Bellering ['bɛ‧ɫɟ̣ɚ‧ɪnd], lowering ['loˆʊɚnd̩] (part[iciple]).

lower beam See **low beam**

lower forty-eight See **lower** adj **2a**

lower forty-nine (states) See **lower** adj **2c**

lowering ppl adj See **lower** v¹

lowering vbl n See **lower** n, v²

lower states See **lower** adj **2b**

lowery See **lower** v¹

low fence n Cf **high fence**
   1935 Hurston *Mules & Men* 270 **LA**, He told me, "That a low fence." He meant a difficulty that was easily overcome.

low-gear n Also *low-gear corn* [Folk-etym, by analogy with **high-gear**]
A low-growing **sorghum**; see quot.
   1970 *DARE* File **TX**, Low-gear (corn) . . used alongside *high-gear (corn)* in Texas panhandle. The low-gear grows only about 3 ft. high, but produces two crops per year.

low ground(s) n **chiefly Mid Atl** See Map Cf **bottom** n **1a**
Alluvial land, esp low-lying land near a stream.
   1608 Smith *True Relation* [2] **VA**, The south side is plaine low ground, and the north side high mountaines. **1659** *R.I. Col. Rec.* I.464 *(DAE),* In all meadowes, Swamps and low ground. **1750** in 1898 Filson Club *Pub.* 13.36 **VA**, This night we lodged in Adam Beard's low grounds. **1841** *S. Lit. Messenger* 7.452 **VA**, The level land, called in Virginia low grounds, extends in many places for more than a mile. **1888** Johnston *Mr. Absalom Billingslea* 165 **GA**, Everybody had to complain of the ravages made by crows and blackbirds on the newly planted low-ground corn. **1899** (1912) Green *VA Folk-Speech* 270, *Low-grounds. . .* Meadow or bottom land. **1946** *PADS* 5.29 **VA**, *Low-grounds. . .* Low; common south of the Rappahannock in the Piedmont and Tidewater. **1949** Kurath *Word Geog.* 61, Low-lying flat meadow lands and fields along large and small watercourses. . . *Low-lands* is characteristic of Maryland, Delaware, and southeastern Pennsylvania but occurs sporadically also on the southern coast and in New England. . . Other regional expressions are . . *low-grounds* in the Virginia Piedmont and the greater part of Eastern North Carolina. **1950** *PADS* 14.45 **SC**, Lowgrounds. . . Bottoms, bottom land. **1965–70** *DARE* (Qu. C7, *. . Land that usually has some standing water with trees or bushes growing in it*) Infs **NC**62, **VA**42, Low ground(s); (Qu. C19, *. . Low land running between hills [With and without water]*) Infs **NC**15, 62, **VA**42, 82, 96, Low ground(s); (Qu. C29, *A good-sized stretch of level land with practically no trees*) Inf **NC**15, Low ground; (Qu. R28, *. . Kinds of spiders*) Inf **VA**38, Low-ground spider; (Qu. S9, *. . Kinds of grass that are hard to get rid of*) Inf **NC**80, Low-ground wire grass. **1986** Pederson *LAGS Concordance (Bottomland)* 3 infs, **nwAL, cs,seGA**, Low ground; 1 inf, **cwTN**, Low ground—slough/swamp; 1 inf, **ceGA**, Piece of low ground in a river valley.

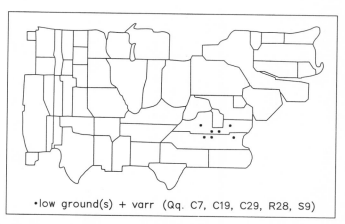

•low ground(s) + varr (Qq. C7, C19, C29, R28, S9)

low huckleberry See **lowbush huckleberry**

lowins See **low wine**

lowland fir n Also *lowland white fir*
=grand fir.
   1898 Sudworth *Forest Trees* 26, *Abies grandis . .* Lowland Fir. . . from Vancouver Island to California . . and from Washington and Oregon to northern Idaho and Montana. **1910** Jepson *Silva CA* 120, *Abies grandis . .* Lowland Fir. **1967** Gilkey–Dennis *Hdbk. NW Plants* 33, *Abies grandis . .* Grand fir. Lowland white fir. **1979** Little *Checklist U.S. Trees* 35, *Abies grandis . .* grand fir . . Other common names—lowland white fir, lowland fir, . . giant fir.

lowland grass n
A **cordgrass** (here: *Spartina pectinata*).
   1920 *Torreya* 20.18 **MO**, *Spartina michauxiana . .* Prairie grass, ramrod grass . . lowland grass, sawgrass, rip-gut.

lowland plover n Cf **highland plover**
=golden plover.
   1916 in 1917 *DN* 4.427 **LA**, *Lowland plover.*=*gros yeux.* **1923** U.S.

Dept. Ag. *Misc. Circular* 13.69 **LA**, Golden Plover (*Pluvialis domin-ica*). . . Lowland plover.

lowland spruce n Cf **highland spruce**
=**black spruce 1.**
    1968 *DARE* (Qu. T5, . . *Kinds of evergreens, other than pine*) Inf **MN**29, White spruce or highland spruce; black spruce or lowland spruce.

lowland white fir See **lowland fir**

low laurel n Cf **high laurel**
    A **sheep laurel** (here: *Kalmia angustifolia*).
    1824 Bigelow *Florula Bostoniensis* 170, A low shrub with rose col-oured flowers, very common in low grounds, and known by the names sheep poison, lambkill, low laurel, &c. **1941** *LANE* Map 249 (*Mountain laurel*) 1 inf, **seMA**, Low laurel = kill kid = lamb kill.

lowly adj [Prob hypercorrection; cf Intro "Language Changes" II.12]
    1968 *DARE* (Qu. GG34b, *To feel depressed or in a gloomy mood: "She's feeling _____ today."*) Inf **NY**92, Lowly.

low maple n
=**mountain maple.**
    1813 Muhlenberg *Catalogus Plantarum* 95, [*Acer*] montanum—Mountain m[aple]. low m[aple]. **1832** Browne *Sylva* 102, It [=*Acer montanum*] is sometimes called Low Maple, from the dwarfish stature of the tree. **1901** Lounsberry *S. Wild Flowers* 323, A[*cer*] spicatum, mountain maple, sometimes known as the low maple, is found through our range mostly in the mountains and usually as a shrub of from six to ten feet high. **1950** Peattie *Nat. Hist. Trees* 470, Mountain Ma-ple . . Other Names: Moose, Low, or Water Maple. **1971** Krochmal *Appalachia Med. Plants* 28, Acer spicatum. . . Common Names: Moun-tain maple, goosefoot maple, low maple.

lowmow See **lomo**

low noon n [By analogy with *high noon* 12:00 o'clock noon]
    1966 *DARE* FW Addit **OK**18, Low noon—About 11:30 a.m. Expres-sion used when time was told by sun and shadows—clocks were scarce.

low order See **order** n 1

low-posted adj Cf **high-posted**
    Of a room: having a low ceiling.
    1965 *DARE* File **MA** (as of 1953), High-posted, low-posted: of a room, having a high or low ceiling. Used by one Mass. native . . and verified by another.

low-quarter(ed) shoe n Also *low-quarter* chiefly **Sth** See Map
    A low-cut shoe, esp an oxford.
    1879 (1880) Twain *Tramp Abroad* 275, He wore . . very low-quarter patent leather shoes. **a1883** (1911) Bagby *VA Gentleman* 73, Give me a straw hat, an oznaburg shirt, no waistcoat, . . and a pair of low-quarter shoes, moderately thick-soled. **1909** *DN* 3.347 **eAL, wGA**, Low-quar-tered. . . Used of oxfords. "He wore low-quartered shoes." **1916** *DN* 4.269 **New Orleans LA, NC**, Low-quarters. . . Oxford shoes. "He wears low quarters all the year round." **c1960** Wilson Coll. **csKY**, Low-quarters, low quarter shoes—Oxfords, slippers. **1965–70** *DARE* (Qu. W11, *Men's low, rough work shoes*) 21 Infs, chiefly **Sth**, Low-quarters; **TX**106, Low-quarters—them's Sunday shoes; **VA**74, Low-quarters—good shoes as well as work shoes; most work shoes were high-top; **FL**36, **GA**1, Low-quartered shoes; **FL**15, Southeastern cracker

low-quarter shoes. **1971** Green *Village Horse Doctor* 119 **cwTX** (as of 1940s), Anybody wearin' low quarters or a white shirt and was bare-headed was bound to be a stranger. **1986** Pederson *LAGS Concordance*, 1 inf, **swTN**, Low quarters—men's oxfords; 2 infs, **csTX**, Low quar-ters—men's shoes.

low-rate v chiefly **Sth** See Map
    To belittle or disparage.
    1906 *DN* 3.145 **nwAR**, Lowrate. . . To depreciate, set a low estimate on. "That's lowrating him some." **1930** *DN* 6.85 **cSC**, Lowrate, to, to denounce. **1931** (1991) Hughes–Hurston *Mule Bone* 143 **cFL** [Black], Whut you come here low-ratin' me for, Dave Carter? **1939** *Hall Coll.* **wNC**, I don't like it [=Kephart's book] because he low-rates the moun-tain people too much. **1942** Hurston *Dust Tracks* 195 **FL**, Play the dozens, which . . is a way of saying low-rate your enemy's ancestors and him. **1950** *PADS* 14.45 **SC**, Low-rate. . . To deprecate; to set a low estimate on. Usually of persons. **1953** Randolph–Wilson *Down in Hol-ler* 262 **Ozarks**, That feller better quit low-ratin' my kinfolks! **1965–70** *DARE* (Qu. Y3, *To say uncomplimentary things about somebody*) 11 Infs, chiefly **Sth**, Low-rate; **NC**49, Low-rating him or his name. **1975** Newell *If Nothin' Don't Happen* 15 **nwFL**, You fellers have my permis-sion to climb onto anybody who low-rates the memory of your dad. **1984** Burns *Cold Sassy* 211 **nGA** (as of 1906), She was just too busy low-rating Miss Love to fool with me.

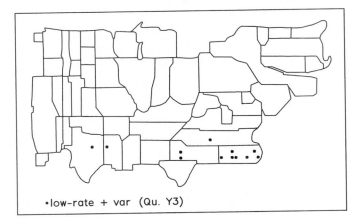
•low-rate + var (Qu. Y3)

low-set See **low-built**

low sick adj phr **Sth, S Midl, esp Gulf States** See Map
    Seriously ill.
    1937 in 1958 Brewer *Dog Ghosts* 93 **TX** [Black], She tuck low sick wid de pneumonia an' died in less'n a week. **1941** Percy *Lanterns* 304 **nwMS**, The sister of a friend of his was low sick. **1948** *AmSp* 23.305 **Ozarks**, Are you *low sick* or jist porely? **1959** *New Yorker* 25 Apr 40 **cAL**, Lilly Belle had asked the neighbor friend to write Bessie, warning her that Mama was low sick. **1965–70** *DARE* (Qu. BB42, *If a person is very sick . . he's _____*) Infs **AL**43, **AR**55, **KY**94, **LA**2, 8, **MO**29, Low sick; **OK**58, Pretty low sick; **AL**43, Real low sick; (Qu. BB54, *When a sick person is past hope of recovery . . he's [a] _____*) Inf **LA**6, Low, low sick. **1986** Pederson *LAGS Concordance*, 1 inf, **cnAL**, My wife got so low sick. **1990** Cavender *Folk Med. Lexicon* 27 **sAp-palachians**, Low sick—feeling very ill and near death.

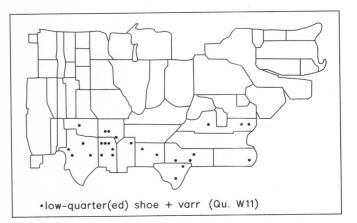
•low-quarter(ed) shoe + varr (Qu. W11)

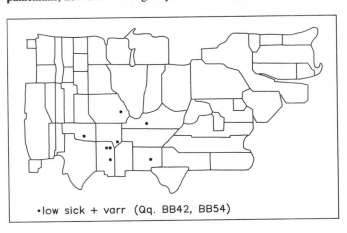
•low sick + varr (Qq. BB42, BB54)

low-test adj, used absol **chiefly NEast, Mid Atl, N Cent** See Map Cf **high-test**

Regular, low-octane gasoline.

1965–70 *DARE* (Qu. N15a, . . *Gasoline* . . *cheaper kind*) 52 Infs, **chiefly NEast, Mid Atl, N Cent**, Low-test.

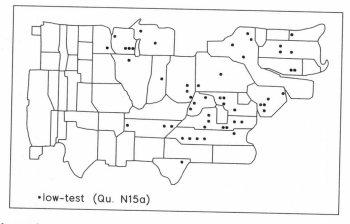

•low-test (Qu. N15a)

low wine n Also *low wines, lowins* [*OED low wines* 1641 →; Scots *lowins*] **chiefly Sth, S Midl**

Low-proof liquor, esp from the first distillation or from the end of a run.

1794 in 1855 U.S. Congress *Debates & Proc.* 3d Cong 1460, Every rectifier of low wines, or other distilled spirits, . . shall enter at some office of inspection, all or any such low wines. **1872** (1876) Knight *Amer. Mech. Dict.* 2.1360, *Low Wine.* The product of the first distillation of *wash.* Its specific gravity at 60° is about 0.978, containing 20 per cent of alcohol. **1933** Rawlings *South Moon* 234 **nFL**, He had two demijohns of whiskey and one of low-wine. **1952** Brown *NC Folkl.* 1.561, *Lowins.* . . Low-proof whisky. **1962** Fox *Southern Fried* 153 **SC**, The doubler re-distills before you hit your condenser box. This eliminates "low-wine". Low wine is when it finishes off too low in proof and has to be re-run. **1968** *DARE* (Qu. DD21c, *Nicknames for whiskey, especially illegally made whiskey*) Inf **MD13**, Low wine—last, weak solution in batch of homemade whiskey, low alcoholic content. **1969** *DARE* Tape **GA72**, When it breaks at the worm, it don't stop runnin'—but in different sections of the countries it's called different names. Here the most popular name for it is backins. Up in Virginia and West Virginia and quite often in East Tennessee it's called low wines. **1972** *Foxfire Book* 316 **nGA**, *Backings*—also *singlings* and *low-wines*—What results after beer is run through a thumperless operation once. They have a good percentage of alcohol, but they won't hold a bead. **1974** Maurer–Pearl *KY Moonshine* 41, Some moonshiners . . use only a beer still and a flakestand to produce what a legitimate distiller would call low wines. They then run the low wines through a so-called liquor or whiskey still. **1986** Pederson *LAGS Concordance* (*Terms for cheap whiskey and for home-brewed beer or whiskey*) 1 inf, **csGA**, Low wine = rotgut; 1 inf, **csAL**, Low wine—from turpentine, cures ground itch; 1 inf, **nwFL**, Low wine—last part of the cooking; 1 inf, **cnLA**, Low wine—legal; 1 inf, **swAL**, The low wine—the last of the run, not so strong.

lozenger n Also *lossenger* [Scots, Engl dial varr of *lozenge*] **scattered, but chiefly NEast**

1861 Holmes *Venner* 1.90 **NEng**, Boxes containing "lozengers," as they were commonly called. **1890** *DN* 1.74 **NEng**, *Lozenger* ['lɔznʤə]: a lozenge. Common in New England. **1892** *DN* 1.234 **KY**, *Lozenger.* **1899** (1912) Green *VA Folk-Speech* 270, Lozenger. **1903** *DN* 2.299 **Cape Cod MA** (as of a1857), *Lozenger.* **1905** *DN* 3.63 **eNE**, He took a lozenger. **1906** Kildare *My Old Bailiwick* 85 **NYC**, A penny represents a great deal to a child of the slums. For it "sticky apples," "all-day" candy, "lossengers," and other sweet "dainties" may be purchased. **1907** *DN* 3.193 **seNH**, *Lossenger.* . . Lozenge, a round dry confection. **1909** *DN* 3.347 **eAL, wGA**, Lozenger. **1910** *DN* 3.445 **wNY**, *Lozenger.* . . Lozenge, a small dry confection; as "peppermint lozengers." **1916** Lincoln *Mary-'Gusta* 75 **MA**, How about sassafras lozengers? Like them? **1941** *LANE* Map 257, 1 inf, **cwVT**, [frɛntʃ lasŋʤɝrz], jocular name for onions. **1968–69** *DARE* (Qu. H82b, *Kinds of cheap candy that used to be sold years ago*) Inf **CT18**, ['lasənʤərz]; **MD39**, Peppermint ['lasŋʤərz]; **PA115**, Peppermint lozengers; **PA210**, ['lozɛnʤɚ·]. **1982** Barrick *Coll.* **csPA**, Smith Brothers cough lozengers. **1993** *DARE* File **csOH** (as of 1940s), The treat my mother gave [at Halloween] was

usually a piece or two of unwrapped candy such as peppermint lozengers—sometimes cookies, and once when she ran out, Ritz crackers.

lua n [Haw *lua* hole, pit] **HI**

A toilet.

1938 Reinecke *Hawaiian Loanwords* 22, *Lua.* . . A privy. **1967** *DARE* (Qu. F37, . . *An indoor toilet*) Inf **HI6**, Lua (=hole), slang; (Qu. M21a, *An outside toilet building*) Inf **HI3**, Lua liilii—small house, movable toilet was used anciently. **1981** *Pidgin To Da Max* np **HI**, *Lua* . . Hawaiian benjo [=toilet]. "Mits went lua. Too much beers." **1984** Sunset *HI Guide* 85, *Lua*—toilet.

luau n [Haw *lūʻau* young taro tops] **HI**

1 The edible leaves of the taro; a dish prepared with these.

1843 in 1934 Frear *Lowell & Abigail* 168 **HI**, The table on the ground spread with leaves was . . loaded with an immense quantity of food—pigs, turkies, flowls [sic], ducks, bread, potatoes, taro, luau, etc. **1873** in 1966 Bishop *Sandwich Is.* 191 **HI**, The food was cooked in Polynesian style, by being wrapped up in greens called *luau,* and baked underground. **1930** Degener *Ferns of HI* 84, The young leaf blades of the taro are gathered while yet tightly rolled together and enclosed in the groove of the old leaf stalk. Before cooking, the lower epidermis of their midrib is stripped off and discarded. This dish, known as *luau,* which name is also applied to a native feast, is eaten like spinach. **1938** Reinecke *Hawaiian Loanwords* 22, *Luau.* . . Young taro leaves cooked for food. **1967** *DARE* (Qu. H45, *Dishes made with meat, fish, or poultry that everybody around here would know, but that people in other places might not*) Inf **HI9**, Chicken luau—with spinach or squid. **1972** Carr *Da Kine Talk* 113 **HI**, *Chicken lūʻau* (English + Hawaiian). Chicken cooked with young taro tops (*lūʻau*), one of the dishes served at a Hawaiian feast (the feast is also called a *lūʻau*).

2 A Hawaiian-style feast. **chiefly HI, but widely recognized**

1853 *Putnam's Mag.* 2.18 **HI**, It was on a Saturday afternoon in the year 1852, that a merry party of us started forth to attend a *luau* or native feast, given by a chief who lived some miles from Honolulu. **1940** Bazore *Hawaiian Foods* 38, Chicken or other fowl is stewed and combined with coconut milk or with cooked taro leaves and coconut milk. (This last combination is a favorite dish for a luau.) **1954** *Ellery Queen's Mystery Mag.* 4.41 **HI**, We're invited to a *luau* tomorrow. **1965** Krauss–Alexander *Grove Farm* xv **HI**, Luau—Hawaiian feast. **1967** *DARE* (Qu. H45, *Dishes made with meat, fish, or poultry that everybody around here would know, but that people in other places might not*) Inf **HI1**, Luau ['lu,aʊ] food—pig cooked in an ['imu] or underground oven; (Qu. AA18, . . *A noisy neighborhood celebration after a wedding, where the married couple is expected to give a treat*) Inf **HI1**, A luau—often at a certain level—Hawaiians and people closer to the earth; **HI6**, Luau—sometimes parents of the bride and groom. **1972** Carr *Da Kine Talk* 115 **HI**, *Lūʻau torch* (Hawaiian + English). A form of outdoor or garden lighting used in Hawaii. The original fuel was the *kukui* nut; now kerosene or gas is used. **1994** *DARE* File **nwMA** (as of c1970), My mother was always wanting to go to a restaurant in the next town called The Luau, where they served Chinese and Polynesian food.

luau foot n [luau 2] **HI**

A big foot.

1967 *DARE* (Qu. X38, *Joking names for unusually big or clumsy feet*) Inf **HI8**, Luau feet; **HI9**, Luau feet—a *luau* is a *big* feast. **1972** Carr *Da Kine Talk* 115 **HI**, *Lūʻau feet* (Hawaiian + English). The large bare Hawaiian feet seen at a *lūʻau* 'Hawaiian feast'. **1981** *Pidgin To Da Max* np **HI**, *Luau feet.* . . Big feet. . . [Cartoon text:] You people have Hawaiian words for everything! Why *do* you call this the Luau Feet Special?

lub See **love**

lubber n [*OED* 1362 →] **chiefly Nth, esp NEng** Cf **lubber grasshopper**

A clumsy, stupid person; a lout; hence adjs *lubber(l)y* clumsy, loutish.

1806 (1970) Webster *Compendious Dict.* 180, *Lubber* . . a lazy sturdy fellow, a clown. *Ibid, Lubberly* . . lazy and bulky, clumsy, awkward. [*DARE* Ed: These entries were taken over from Webster's English model.] **1848** Bartlett *Americanisms* 217, *Lubber.* . . A sturdy drone; an idle, fat, bulky fellow. **1916** Lincoln *Mary-'Gusta* 102 **MA**, The cheeky lubber! **1919** *DN* 5.68 **NM** [Among hs students], *Lubber,* an overgrown boy. A big, awkward person. "He is such a lubber for one so young." **1922** McNeal *When KS Was Young* 69, Haskell insisted that the fish in Kansas were too big and lubberly to climb [fish] ladders over dams. **1930** Shoemaker *1300 Words* 37 **cPA Mts** (as of c1900), *Lubber*—A big, fat ungainly person. **1941** *LANE* Map 465 (*Fool*) 3 infs, **NEng**, Lubber. **1950** *WELS* (*Uncomplimentary words with no definite meaning—just used when you want to say something unfavorable about a person*) 1 Inf, **ceWI**, Lubber. **1968–70** *DARE* (Qu. X50, *Names or nicknames for a person who is very fat*) Inf **OH**70, Lubberly; fatso; (Qu. HH1, *Names and nicknames for a rustic or countrified person*) Inf **MA**89, Non-sea-oriented greenhorn, lubber. **1985** Clark *From Mailbox* 18 **ME**, Yet in this lubbery, musky, musty condition, what does this rough-furred creature [=a woodchuck] do as soon as he crawls out of his winter bed?

lubber grasshopper n [**lubber**] Cf **luger**
Any of several large **grasshoppers 1** of the sub-family Cyrtacanthacridinae. For other names of *Dracotettix monstrosus* see **gray dragon**; for other names of *Romalea microptera* see **Georgia thumper, graveyard hopper**

  1877 *Field & Forest* 2.160, The "Lubber" Grasshopper. . . [is the] large grasshopper *Romalia microptera*. **1888** Kingsley *Riverside Nat. Hist.* 2.194, The "Lubber Grasshopper," or the Clumsy Locust, of the plains, *Brachystola magna*, . . [is] confined to the central portion of North America. **1889** *Century Dict.* 3533, *Lubber-grasshopper*. . . 1. The clumsy locust, *Brachystola magna*, a very large lubberly insect common on the great plains of the western United States. . . 2. The large short-winged insect *Romalea microptera*, which abounds in the Gulf States and feeds on all succulent plants. . . It is from 2.75 to 3.15 inches long, very thick-bodied, and clumsy in its movements. **1928** Metcalf–Flint *Destructive & Useful Insects* 410, Large and small, lubberly grasshoppers often invade cotton from near-by waste lands and defoliate the plants. *Lubber grasshoppers, differential grasshoppers.* **1941** Writers' Program *Guide CO* 19, The greatest scourge of the prairie land is the grasshopper. . . they range from the bulky "lubber," occasionally two inches long, to the small "Carolina locust." **1980** Milne–Milne *Audubon Field Guide Insects* 418, Lubber Grasshopper (*Brachystola magna*). . . The Lubber Grasshopper eats and sometimes destroys the scanty vegetation of its habitat. *Ibid* 420, Dragon Lubber Grasshopper—"Gray Dragon." *Ibid* 424, Southeastern Lubber Grasshopper (*Romalea microptera*). . . This slow-moving grasshopper cannot fly. *Ibid* 427, Horse Lubber Grasshopper (*Taeniopoda eques*).

lubber(l)y See **lubber**

lucerne n Also *lucern, lucifer, luzerne* [*OED* 1626 →] **formerly more widespread, now esp UT, ID**
Alfalfa (*Medicago sativa*).
  1739 (1850) Pinckney *Jrl. Eliza Lucas* 5, Wrote my father . . on the pains I had taken to bring the Indigo, . . Lucern and Casada to perfection. **a1782** (1788) Jefferson *Notes VA* 40, Our grasses are lucerne, . . greenswerd, blue grass, and crab grass. **1817** Bradbury *Travels* 326, The emigrant . . should take with him. . . a small quantity of lucerne, saintfoin, and vetches. **1859** (1880) Darlington *Amer. Weeds* 99, *M[edicago] sativa* . . Lucerne. Spanish Trefoil. French Luzerne. **1868** in 1955 Lee *Mormon Chron.* 2.100 **UT**, I have also sown about 2 acres of Lucerne. **1883** GA Dept. Ag. *Pub. Circular No. 34* 8.44, They [=cows] will leave nice, well-cured lucern or crab-grass hay for the ensilage. **1883** *Harper's New Mth. Mag.* 67.705, Utah would have found it as difficult to struggle into permanent existence without lucern as the early Briton without . . acorns. **1900** Lyons *Plant Names* 242, *M[edicago] sativa* . . Lucerne . . Lucifer. **1925** *Book of Rural Life* 6.3286, *Lucern*, . . a name for *alfalfa* commonly used in eastern United States and in Utah. **1957** *Sat. Eve. Post Letters*, [My grandmother had] been a school teacher many years in Southern Utah during pioneering times. . . Rhubarb was pie plant, and alfalfa was lucerne—and still is in our family, though my husband, from Kansas and Colorado, thinks the latter is a funny name for alfalfa. **1967** *DARE* Tape **ID**6, [FW:] And that's what they [=Mormons] called alfalfa? [Inf:] Yeah, lucerne ['lusən]. At one time I think it was in the dictionary, but I don't believe it's pronounced quite that way; it's something like ['lu,fɚn]. **1968** *DARE* (Qu. L7, *A piece of land with a hay crop planted on it*) Inf **UT**9, Lucerne field. **1982** Brooks *Quicksand* 42 **swUT** (as of c1904), It was that [honey] gathered . . before the clover and lucerne and fruit trees in town came in bloom. **1994** *DARE* File **sID** (as of c1930), People used to say that you could be sure a man was a Mormon if he said "By Hell!" and called alfalfa "lucerne."

lucifee See **lucivee**

lucifer n
1 See **lucifer match 1**.
2 See **lucerne**.
3 See **lucivee**.

lucifer match n
1 also *lucifer*: A friction match; also fig. *old-fash*
  [**1836** (1838) Haliburton *Clockmaker* (1st ser) 214, Having lighted it [=a cigar] by a lucifer, and ascertained that it was 'true in draft,' he resumed his reins.] **1843** *Amer. Pioneer* 2.251 **OH**, They had not the advantage of modern lucifer matches. **1859** (1968) Bartlett *Americanisms* 257, *Lucifer match*. Matches which ignite by friction, also called Locofoco matches. Both these expressions, however, are now being supplanted by the more appropriate term, *Friction-match*. **1859** Taliaferro *Fisher's R.* 212 **nwNC**, There were no lucifer matches then. **1869** Browne *Adventures* 453, Here's Richmond—this crushed box of lucifers; and here's Jeff Davis—a smashed oyster! **1940** Writers' Program *Guide OH* 580, In 1840 Willard Ballard arrived here from Connecticut, bringing with him his wife and children, $1.25 in cash, and a chemical formula. . . He chipped little sticks off a pine slab, tipped them with his malodorous mixture, and sold them in packages as lucifer matches. **1942** Whipple *Joshua* 458 **UT** (as of c1860), Be glad for Lucifer matches. **1962** Carrell *Autobiog.* [45] **ceMA** (as of 1880s), In those days, matches came by the card and you broke of [sic] each one as you used it. Some called them brimstone matches and some called them Lucifer. **1967–69** *DARE* (Qu. F46, . . *Matches you can strike anywhere;* not asked in early QRs) Infs **CA**54, **CT**37, **KS**8, **MA**72, **NJ**2, **NY**66, Lucifers. [5 of 6 Infs old] **1973** Allen *LAUM* 1.160 (as of c1950), *Kitchen matches* (that will strike anywhere). . . Lucifer matches [1 inf, **csMN**]; Lucifers [1 inf, **cwSD**].

2 pl: A **hedge mustard 1** (here: *Sisymbrium officinale*).
  1900 Lyons *Plant Names* 347, *S[isymbrium] officinale* . . Hedge Mustard . . Lucifer matches.

lucivee n Also *loocivee, looservee, lucifee, lucifer;* for addit varr see quots [Pronc-spp for Fr *loup-cervier;* cf *DCan loup-cervier* 1744 →; *lucivee* 1774 →] **esp ME**
Usu **=lynx 1**, but occ a **wildcat** (here: *Felis rufus*).
  1791 *Mass. Laws 1780–1800* (1801) I.509 (*DAE*), No person . . shall hereafter, in either of the months of June, July, August or September . . kill any Otter . . Fisher or Black-Cat, Leusifee [etc]. **1817** *Amer. Monthly Mag. & Crit. Rev.* 2.46, *Lynx*. . . Their vulgar names are Catamount . . Wild-cat, Loocervia. **1860** *Harper's New Mth. Mag.* 20.302 **ME**, "Keep still, Cap'n," says I, "he's after that lucive." **1872** Schele de Vere *Americanisms* 370, The *Lucyver* of Maine, a wildcat or lynx. **1903** *NY Tribune* (NY) 18 Oct (*DAE*), The lynx has almost entirely disappeared. In the Maine woods it is called lucervee. **1904** Day *Kin o' Ktaadn* 138 **ME**, The looservee, the coon an' fox, the deer an' gruntin' bear. **1909** *DN* 3.413 **nME**, *Lúcifee*. . . The *loup cervier*. **1914** *DN* 4.76 **nNH**, **ME**, *Lucivee*. . . The loup-cervier, or "Injun devil," apparently a half-mythical "specie" of wild-cat. **1930** Shoemaker *1300 Words* 39 **cPA Mts** (as of c1900), *Lucivee*—The Canada lynx, or "Lucifer." **1966** *AmSp* 41.24, *Looservee*. . . A Canada lynx. . . The Maine dial. form alone seems to preserve the *r* of the second element of the French compound, so that in Maine today Day's form, the folk etymology of it—*Lucifer* . . —and the French word itself can be heard. . . Mrs. Ethelind Palmer, a librarian from Islesboro, Maine, informs me that in the Penobscot region the name for the lynx is either *looservee* or *Lucifer*. **1966** *DARE* (Qu. P31, . . *Names or nicknames . . for the . . panther*) Inf **ME**8, Lucifees [lusɪfiz]—years ago, not a panther but a Canada lynx, from *loup cervier*. **1966** *DARE* Tape **ME**8, That was the lucifee, so called; I guess they call it the mountain lion or panther in other places. . . They've been reported several times in the wintertime up in the deep woods. . . It's a Canada lynx. *Ibid* **ME**26, Bobcat and the lucivee is the same animal. **1975** Gould *ME Lingo* 169, *Loocivee*—Mainer's approximation of the *loup cervier* of the French-Canadian woodsmen; the Canada lynx. Through mis-identification and in error, *loocivee* is sometimes applied to the bobcat.

luck bag See **lucky bag**

luck bean n
=Kentucky coffee tree.
  1933 Small *Manual SE Flora* 665, *G[ymnocladus] dioica*. . . Kentucky coffee-tree. Luck-bean. **1960** Vines *Trees SW* 531, *Gymnocladus*. . . *dioica*. . . Also known under the vernacular names of Chicot, Luck-bean, Coffee-nut [etc].

luck bone See **lucky bone 1**

lucker See **lukkuh**

luck off See **luck up 2**

luck up v phr

1 with *on;* also *luck upon:* To come upon by chance.

1946 (1972) Mezzrow-Wolfe *Really Blues* 335, Luck up on: get by luck, come into possession of unexpectedly. **1952** Foote *Shiloh* 140 (as of 1862), No one knew where Beauregard's headquarters was, until we lucked up on Colonel Jordan, his chief of staff. **1954** Armstrong *Satchmo* 26 **seLA,** Before I lucked up on store trousers I used to wear my "stepfathers'" trousers, rolling them up from the bottom so that they looked like plus fours or knickers. **1970** *DARE* (Qu. A23, *To do something at the very first try:* "He got the right answer _____.") Inf **NY248,** He lucked up on it. **1973** *Black Panther* (Oakland CA) 29 Sept 2/3, Riggs happened to luck up on a good hustle. **1986** Pederson *LAGS Concordance,* 1 inf, **cLA,** I lucked up on getting work here; 1 inf, **neMS,** I lucked up on it; *(I ran across him)* 1 inf, **cnLA,** Just happened to luck upon.

2 also *luck off:* To have good luck, "luck out."

1952 Brown *NC Folkl.* 1.561, Luck up. . . To have good luck in some venture. "I sure lucked up getting a good car."—Guilford and Iredell counties. Rare. **1968** *DARE* (Qu. CC11, *When somebody has had a lot of good luck . . he* _____) Inf **GA54,** Has lucked up. **1984** *Lutz Coll.* **LA,** I was just hoping that maybe I'd luck off and get the correct book.

luck up on, luck upon See **luck up 1**

lucky See **lucky stone**

lucky bag n Also *luck bag* Cf **mojo** n **1**

A small bag containing various items thought to bring good fortune.

c1938 in 1970 Hyatt *Hoodoo* 1.552 **wTN,** Yo' kin use shammy [=chamois] skin an' yo' make yo' a little luck bag. Yo' put . . a little silver dime in de're. An' yo' put . . about three pieces of that lump incense. *Ibid* 605 **seLA,** Some of these little bags they call *lucky bags.* Yo'll string that an' put it aroun' yore neck. **1946** Tallant *Voodoo* 229 **New Orleans LA,** One Voodoo merchant lists the following as being necessary to "the work": Love Powder, White & Pink[?] Drawing Powder. . . The list also includes candles, lucky bags and certain books.

lucky bone n

1 also *luck bone:* **=pully bone.** Cf **good-luck bone**

1837 Walker in 1940 Drury *Pioneers Spokanes* 58 **ME,** I pulled two luck bones with sister P. . . I got the larger half both times. **1903** *DN* 2.299 **Cape Cod MA** (as of a1857), *Lucky bone.* . . Wishbone. **c1938** in 1970 Hyatt *Hoodoo* 1.536 **Richmond VA,** It's a little [chicken] bone right on the backbone-like—join on together, whut people call a *luck bone.* Some people say if two people be right together an' break it, the one who had the longest bone has good luck. **1946** *PADS* 5.29 **VA,** *Lucky-bone . . :* Wishbone; east of the Blue Ridge, scattered. **1949** Kurath *Word Geog.* 63, Wishbone. . . The V-shaped clavicles of a fowl. . . *Lucky-bone* is the usual folk word between the Kennebeck and the Merrimack in northern New England and has some currency also in eastern Virginia. **1965–70** *DARE* (Qu. K74, *A bone from the breast of a chicken, shaped like a horseshoe*) Infs **CA116, FL18, NY211, NC33, SC19, 26, WA27,** Lucky bone; **DC5, NJ67,** Luck bone. **1966** Dakin *Dial. Vocab. Ohio R. Valley* 1.260, *Lucky-bone* [for *wishbone*] is rare, but appears in the Virginia Military District, the western Bluegrass, and just west of the Little Wabash in Illinois. **1967** Faries *Word Geog. MO* 91, Wishbone. . . There are a few occurrences of . . lucky bone. **c1970** Pederson *Dial. Surv. Rural GA* **seGA,** 1 inf, Wishbone, lucky bone, pulley bone. **1986** Pederson *LAGS Concordance,* 1 inf, **cnFL,** Lucky bone—old people said long piece was good luck; 1 inf, **nwTN,** Lucky bone—shortest piece marries first [laughs]; 1 inf, **csLA,** Lucky bone—biggest part is good luck.

2 The gastrolith of a **crawfish** n **B1.** Cf **eyestone 2, lucky stone**

1931 Randolph *Ozarks* 99, The two circular "lucky bones" found in their [="crawpappies'"] bodies, which are carried in the pocket to ward off syphilis. The bigger the bones the better, it is said, and really large lucky-bones are hard to find.

lucky bug n Cf **dollar bug**

=whirligig beetle.

1899 Bergen *Animal Lore* 12 **eMA,** *Gyrinidae* are called "lucky bugs." . . In some places it is believed that the capture of a "lucky bug" brings good fortune; if you catch a "lucky bug," bury him, and make a wish; you will get your wish. **1962** Carrell *Autobiog.* [18] **ceMA,** If you never laid on your belly, on the nice warm moist sand next to the water, you have missed a good deal—Pollywogs, minnows[?], lucky bugs all came close if you kept very still—and the dragon flies.

lucky hand See **hand** n **B4**

lucky stone n Also *lucky* Cf **eyestone 2, jewelhead, lucky bone 2**

The otolith of the **freshwater drum.**

1887 Goode *Amer. Fishes* 143, The ear bones or otoliths [sic] of the Lake Drum are large and have a texture like ivory. They are often carried as amulets by the negroes of the South, and are also prized by boys in Wisconsin and elsewhere in the West, who call them "lucky stones," perhaps in allusion to the fact that they are marked by a figure which resembles the letter L. **1897** *Outing* 30.435, In the head of this fish [=freshwater drum] are two enamel-like substances, roughly circular in shape, and about the size of a nickel in larger specimens. These were termed "lucky stones." . . No boy . . would dream of casting away the dead fish without first "gettin' his luckies." **1899** Bergen *Animal Lore* 11 **TX,** Two little bones found in the head of a certain fish are called lucky stones; but the good luck comes only after they are lost. *Fort Worth, Tex.* **1903** NY State Museum & Sci. Serv. *Bulletin* 60.591, The name jewel head probably refers to the otoliths or ear-bones, frequently called lucky stones, which are found in the skull of this species [=*Aplodinotus grunniens*]. **1943** Eddy-Surber *N. Fishes* 226, *Aplodinotus grunniens.* . . The ear bone furnishes the famous lucky stone so prized by many youthful fishermen. The ear bones are so hard that they often remain intact long after the rest of the skeleton has disintegrated. **1949** Caine *N. Amer. Sport Fish* 136, The ear bones of the fresh water drum are the prized "lucky stones" of our boyhood days. These two "stones," located in each side of the head, are about the size of a little finger nail. *Ibid* 138, "Lucky stones" are round and flat and each bears a rough letter "L" on it for "luck," They were fancied by Indians as well as successive generations of American youths. Perhaps every angler ought to have one in his tackle box!

Lucy Bowles n Also *Lucy (Bowels)* **scattered, but esp PA, NJ, seNY** See Map *joc, euphem*

Diarrhea; loose bowels.

1965–70 *DARE* (Qu. BB19, *Joking names for looseness of the bowels*) 12 Infs, **scattered, but esp PA, NJ, seNY,** Lucy Bowles; **TX51,** Lucy; **PA175,** Lucy Bowels [sic] by Carrie Paper.

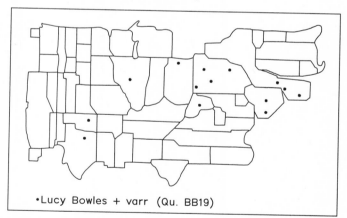

•Lucy Bowles + varr (Qu. BB19)

lucyver See **lucivee**

Lud See **Lord** n[1]

luddle n

The penis of a horse.

1978 Wiersma *Purpaleanie* 86 **nwIA,** What made Frank's [=a horse's] luddle suddenly hang quite low? . . Frank drew his luddle up as promptly into his pouch as if you had hit it head on. *Ibid* 87, Even then I understood one principle so I can never forget it: Horseflesh does not expose its luddle while in harness.

Luddy See **Lordy**

ludefisk See **lutefisk**

luf See **love**

lug n[1] [*lug* to carry with effort]

1 also *lug box, lugger:* A container for fruit or vegetables; see quot 1934. **chiefly Upper Missip Valley, West** See Map on p. 452 Cf **hamper 1a**

1934 (1943) *W2, Lug* . . a box, basket, or other container suitable for handling or shipping such a load, esp. of fruit or vegetables; specif., as orig. in California a box having an inside width of 13½ inches, an out-side length of 17½ inches, and a depth of from 4¼ to 7¾ inches. **1939** *Sun* (Baltimore MD) 29 Sept 24/6 *(Hench Coll.)*, Grapes—Cal[ifornia]. Display Lugs. **1944** *Ibid* 15 Feb 7/7 *(Hench Coll.)*, [Advt:] *Tomato Lugs* One Million Wanted . . Florida Type Tomato Lugs with or without tops . . Hector Supply Company Miami, Florida. **1949** *L.A. Times* 2 July 5/4 *(DA)*, It takes an hour for a lug of grapes to pass through the [precooling] tunnel, which handles 768 lugs an hour. **1965–70** *DARE* (Qu. F17, *What peaches come in—different kinds*) 80 Infs, **chiefly Upper Missip Valley, West,** Lug; 9 Infs, **CA,** Lug box; **CA**59, Field lug; **OR**13, Lugger; (Qu. F16, *The container apples come in;* total Infs questioned, 75) Inf **NM**12, Lug; (Qu. F18, *The container grapes come in;* total Infs questioned, 75) Infs **NM**12, **OK**42, **UT**3, Lug. **1966** *DARE* Tape **WA**13, [Inf:] The lugs are brought in from the orchard. . . [FW:] What are the lugs? [Inf:] That's the big, picking lugs that holds these several . . bushels of fruit. They pick the fruit from the tree and dump right into that lug in the orchard. **1968** *Chicago Daily News* (IL) 24 Sept 18/6 *(Mathews Coll.)*, Grape pickers receive a base wage of $1.50 an hour, plus 25 cents for each 36-pound "lug" they fill.

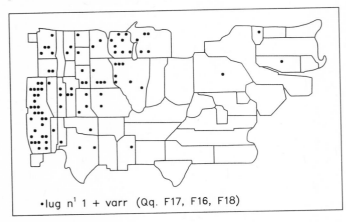

•lug n¹ 1 + varr (Qq. F17, F16, F18)

2 pl: Elegant or showy clothing; by ext: affectations, airs—usu in phr *put on lugs* and varr.

1889 Munroe *Golden Days* 188 **CA**, If you notice me . . piling on any lugs . . you just bump me down hard. **1903** *DN* 2.352, *Lugs.* . . Clothes, in expression 'sling on lugs,' put on style. **1905** *DN* 3.13 **cCT**, *Lugs.* . . Proud manners. **1920** Lewis *Main Street* 326 **MN**, Oh, the lugs he puts on—belted coat, and piqué collar. **1932** *WV Review* June 378, Numerous other Americanisms have changed. "Put on lugs" for putting on style, although sometimes heard, seemed to have evolved pretty generally into "putting on dog." **1941** *LANE* Map 358 **cCT**, She's putting on lugs (i.e. giving herself airs). **1968** *DARE* (Qu. W40, . . *A woman who overdresses or . . spends too much on clothes*) Inf **CT**15, Put on the lugs.

lug n² [*lug* an ear; a projecting part]

1 usu pl, but sg in attrib use: A poor grade of tobacco, usu the bottom leaves of the plant. **chiefly KY, VA** Cf **flyings 2**

1827 (1935) Bolling *Diary* 43.245 **VA**, Engaged in cutting and hauling wood for a plantpatch, and in sorting, tying and prizing my lug tobo. **c1830** Martin *VA & DC* 175, An eminent tobacco manufacturer of Richmond has offered the inhabitants of this district to take all of their tobacco, (lugs included,) at $10 a hundred. **1859** (1968) Bartlett *Americanisms* 258, *Lugs.* Ground leaves of tobacco when prepared for market. **1890** *DN* 1.65 **KY,** Lugs [lʌgz]. "Give me some lugs" is *Give me a chew of tobacco.* **1895** (1896) Bruce *Economic Hist. VA* 1.442, The lowest grade was known as lugs as early as 1686. **1940** *AmSp* 15.134 [Tobacco market language], *Lugs.* The leaves just above the flyings on a tobacco plant. **1944** *PADS* 2.67 **sVA,** *Lugs.* . . The lower leaves . . not the best quality of tobacco. **1965–70** *DARE* Tape **KY**9, Another one is called a lug; **KY**21, Three to four grades. . . I call them trash, lugs, red, and tips; **KY**23, We make three grades out of our tobacco: You take off the trash, then the lugs, and then the tips; **KY**53, Flyings would be the first leaves comes [sic] off, off of the bottom. Then we'll have . . trash. Then we have a lug; **KY**64, Going from the bottom of the stalk to the top of the stalk the grades are flyings or trash, which are the most ragged leaves, then coming on up the stalk, the lug grade, then the leaf and then the tip; **NC**8, The lugses . . are so very dirty, and sometimes they will bring a good price, but, as a rule, they don't bring the money that the second, third, and fourth pullings will bring; **SC**17, [FW:] How

about lugs? [Inf:] That's bottom tobacco; **VA**38, We'd usually have what we'd call a scrap and then . . a lug; **VA**40, Next would be your lugs. **1966** *PADS* 45.17 **cnKY,** Lugs. . . A grade of leaf found just above the flyings on the stalk. They are heavier in body and darker in color than the flyings. . . "The lugs are the longest leaves on the plant."

2 See quot.

1966–67 *DARE* (Qu. X31, . . *A woman's breasts*) Inf **MA**5, Lugs, dugs—both very old; **SD**2, Lugs.

Lugan See **Lugen**

lug box See **lug** n¹ **1**

Lugen n |'lugən| Also *Loogin, Lugan, Lugie* [Perh transf from slang *loogan* a fool, dope, lout] **chiefly Chicago IL** Cf **Lit**

A Lithuanian or person of Lithuanian descent.

1947 Motley *Knock on Any Door* 103 **Chicago IL,** Inside a bunch of the neighborhood men, polacks and lugans and a big Russian with an accordion, got together week ends. **1957** in 1995 *W3* File, Lugan = a Lithuanian. Used by a Chicagoan in my hearing. **1964** *PADS* 42.40 **Chicago IL,** Pejoratives for the Lithuanian. All . . instances of *lugen* /'lugən/ . . are in the speech of Chicagoans with social or business contacts in the Lithuanian communities of the South Side. . . Eight of the nine informants with names for Lithuanians . . had *lugen,* with one Irishman offering *Lit.* **1969** *DARE* (Qu. HH28, *Names and nick-names . . for people of foreign background*) Inf **IL**96, Lithuanians—Lugies ['lugiz]. **1980** in 1984 Royko *Like I Was Sayin'* 105 **Chicago IL,** Do you have any feelings about Lithuanians? "Yeah. They're almost as dumb as the Polacks, and they're twice as mean. The day we let the first Loogin in this country, the average IQ in America dropped by ten points." **1995** *DARE* File **Chicago IL,** *Lugen* seems to be a distinctively Chicago term (specifically, southwest Chicago, near Marquette Park) for a Lithuanian. My Lithuanian friends in other parts of the country don't know it. It's used by non-Lithuanians, and can be neutral or derogatory. *Ibid* **Chicago IL,** Although I've not heard the term *Lugen* for around ten years, I used to hear it frequently in the conversation of assembly-line workers to refer to people of Lithuanian descent. One worker might say of another "He's a Lugen"—much the same as you might say "He's a Jew," or a Polack, or something else. It was used by men referring to men only and was semi-derogatory—it wasn't really bad, but it wasn't really good—it could imply, for example, laziness. *Ibid* (as of 1930s), I heard the term [=*Lugen*] all through my childhood and early years on the south side of Chicago. *Ibid,* Ten years ago, several of my under-graduates reported *Lugen* as a 'common' term in South Chicago for a person of Lithuanian extraction.

luger n [Prob var of *lubber;* cf **lubber grasshopper**]

A **grasshopper 1;** see quot.

1966 *DARE* (Qu. R6, . . *Names . . for grasshoppers*) Inf **FL**27, Lugers [ˌlugɚz]—the big ones.

lugger n¹ [*lug* < *lugsail;* but quot 1817 prob infl by Du *logger* in same sense] **now chiefly sLA**

A small boat with lugsails; hence n *luggerman* one who sails such a boat.

1806 (1970) Webster *Compendious Dict.* 181, Lugger . . a vessel with three masts, a running bowsprit and lug-sails. [*DARE* Ed: This entry does not appear in Webster's English model.] **1817** in 1869 Irving *Life & Letters* 1.289 **seNY,** He . . is as slow getting under way, as a Dutch lugger. **1885** Cable *Dr. Sevier* 130 **LA,** Made friends with Sicilian luggerman. Slept in his lugger. **1927** Kennedy *Gritny* 231 **sLA** [Black], Quick as I could git yonder to de boat landin' on de Basin, an' make 'rangements wid de man on de charcoal lugger to take Chester 'long wid 'im to do de cookin' on de trip over. [**1938** FWP *Guide MS* 169 **seMS,** Growing directly out of the fishing and seafood industry is the trade of shipbuilding. The Biloxi lugger (a power-propelled boat from 30 to 46 feet in length) represents the experience of generations in building boats suitable for coastal waters. Nearly all the shrimp and oyster boats operating out of Biloxi, as well as many of the luggers used in Louisiana, are Biloxi-built.] **1967** *Good Old Days* 4.2.15 **seLA,** Also plying back and forth to New Orleans were over-sized boats of the skiff variety. These were known as "luggers." They had very large sails and travelled fast when the wind was favorable. Their business was supplying people along the way with fruits, ice and sometimes meat. **1968** *DARE* (Qu. O9, . . *Kinds of sailboats*) Inf **LA**45, Luggers—a working sailboat not used any more. **1986** Pederson *LAGS Concordance* **seLA** (*What kind of boat would you go fishing in on a small lake?*) 1 inf, Luggers—big skiffs; 1 inf, Luggers—can stay out a while.

lugger n² See **lug** n¹ **1**

luggerman See **lugger** n¹

luggish adj [Cf *EDD* luggish "Dull, heavy, stupid"] Cf **logy 1**
   1933 *AmSp* 8.1.50 **Ozarks,** Luggish. . . Slow, heavy, sluggish. *Seems like th' turkeys was kinder luggish that day, an' th' boys kilt seven of 'em.*

luggy adj [Prob var of **logy 1**]
   c1938 in 1970 Hyatt *Hoodoo* 1.26 **NYC,** As long as they [=spirits] are around everything is heavy and luggy and you think something is going to happen every minute.

Lugie See **Lugen**

luh See **let** v A2a

luk See **like** v¹, adj, vbl aux, n, adv, prep, conj

luke fisk See **lutefisk**

lukkuh prep, conj Also *lucker* [Pronc-spp for *like* + *-a*; cf *DJE* A⁸ "intrusive transition sound, dial; freq after *like, must*, etc., prob due to phonetic analogy with W. African languages" and *laka*] *Gullah*
   Like; as.
   1888 Jones *Negro Myths* 83 **GA coast,** Eh hab on new beber hat, wuh shine lucker glass. **1922** Gonzales *Black Border* 189 **sSC, GA coasts,** You nebbuh see none dem t'ing trabble lukkuh me trabble w'en uh staa't fuh run!

lull v Also with *away, down, off* **chiefly Mid and S Atl, nNEng** Of the wind: to diminish in force.
   1804 (1904) Clark *Orig. Jrls. Lewis & Clark Exped.* 1.86 **VA,** At 7 oClock the wind luled and it Commns'd raining. **1849** (1914) Kingsley *Diary* 27 **CT,** Wind lulled a little this morning but freshed again at noon. **1939** *LANE* Map 92 *(The wind is going down)* 11 infs, **chiefly ME, NH,** Lulling down; 8 infs, **chiefly ME, NH,** Lulling; 2 infs, **ME, NH,** Lulling away; 1 inf, **ceRI,** Lulling away, sailors' term; 1 inf, **wME,** Lulling off, older term; 1 inf, **neNH,** Lulling, when the wind begins to come in puffs instead of blowing steadily; 1 inf, **eME,** Lulling down, to a dead calm; 1 inf, **eME,** Lulling, especially of the pause between squalls. **1965–70** *DARE* (Qu. B13, *When the wind begins to decrease . . it's _____)* 10 Infs, **chiefly Mid and S Atl,** Lulling; **NJ67,** Lulling away; **NJ67, SC26,** Lulling down; **GA27,** It lulls; **VA74,** Lulled. **1966** Dakin *Dial. Vocab. Ohio R. Valley* 2.28, It's . . *letting up. . .* [1 inf] *lulling.* **1973** Allen *LAUM* 1.155 (as of c1950), *Lulling down,* recorded in Maine by New England Atlas fieldworkers, survives in the speech of a Brookings, South Dakota informant of New England ancestry. **1986** Pederson *LAGS Concordance (If . . the wind has been strong and is getting weaker and weaker, you say it's doing what?)* 2 infs, **cwLA,** Lull down; 1 inf, **swTN,** The wind has lulled; 3 infs, **seGA, nwFL,** (The wind is) lulling; 1 inf, **swGA,** The wind's going [=going to] lull.

lumber n¹

1 Disused or discarded articles that are kept around; junk, stuff. [*OED* 1552 →] **esp VA** Cf **lumber** v² **1, lumber room, ~ sleigh, ~ wagon**
   1642 in 1916 **MA** (Colony) Probate Court (Essex Co.) *Records* 1.22, Barrells & butte[r] Cherne & other lumb., 18s. **1774** (1900) Fithian *Jrl.* 257 **VA,** Fanny & Harriot by stuffing rags & other Lumber under their Gowns just below their Apron-Strings, were prodigiously charmed at their resemblance to Pregnant Women. **1804** (1904) Lewis *Orig. Jrls. Lewis & Clark Exped.* 1.31 **VA,** The Sergt. at the helm, shall . . see that no cooking utensels or loos lumber of any kind is left on the deck. **1899** (1912) Green *VA Folk-Speech* 271, Lumber. . . Things more or less bulky and cumbersome, thrown aside as of no present use or value. **1935** [see **lumber** v² **1**]. **1946** *PADS* 5.29 **VA,** Lumber. . . Junk; common everywhere. **1986** Pederson *LAGS Concordance (Junk, old worthless furniture and implements)* 1 inf, **neMS,** Lumber; 1 inf, **cTX,** Junk lumber.

2 also *lumber sauce:* A toothpick. *joc* See also **dining-room lumber**
   1936 *AmSp* 11.44 [Soda jerker jargon], Lumber. Toothpick. **1942** Berrey–Van den Bark *Amer. Slang* 815.1, Lumber, dining-room lumber, saw-logs, toothpicks. **1950** *WELS* (Names and nicknames for a toothpick) 1 Inf, **seWI,** A piece of lumber. **1967–69** *DARE* (Qu. G11, *Other names or nicknames for a toothpick)* Infs **HI9, NY215,** Lumber; **CA80,** Lumber sauce.

lumber v¹ [*OED* a1529 →] **chiefly S Midl**
   To make a loud thumping or rumbling sound; hence nouns *lumber(ing), lumberment, lumbrage* a loud rumbling noise.
   1855 Cooke *Ellie* 207 **VA,** Keeping the footman lumberin' at the knockers on both sides o' the streets. **1890** *DN* 1.65 **KY,** Lumber [lʌmbə]. "Listen how he lumbers," said of a deep-mouthed dog's barking when he has treed a 'coon or 'possum. **1899** (1912) Green *VA Folk-Speech* 271, Lumber. . . To make a heavy rumbling noise; rumble. . . To make a loud noise, as, a person or animal. "He lumbered when he fell." *Ibid,* Lumbering. . . A dull, heavy, prolonged sound. The sound of distant thunder. "It kept lumbering in the west all day yesterday." **1902** *DN* 2.239 **sIL,** Lumber. . . To make a noise, as by moving things about. The sound of an earthquake or of thunder is called *lumbering.* **1907** *DN* 3.224 **nwAR,** Lumber. . . To make a noise, as by moving things about. **1909** *DN* 3.347 **cAL, wGA,** Lumber. . . To go with great noise. **1915** *DN* 4.185 **swVA,** Lumber. . . Loud noise. Also *lumberment.* **1953** Randolph–Wilson *Down in Holler* 262 **Ozarks,** Lumbrage ['lʌmbreʤ]. . . A loud rumbling or crashing noise. A woman told reporters: "I jumped out of bed when I heerd the lumbrage," meaning the noise made by a drunken man as he fell down a flight of rickety stairs.

lumber v²

1 also ppl adj *lumbered up:* See quots. [**lumber** n¹ **1;** *OED* 1678 →]
   1899 (1912) Green *VA Folk-Speech* 271, Lumber. . . To heap together in disorder. To fill with lumber; to encumber with anything useless. *Ibid,* Lumbered up. . . A room or yard is said to be *"lumbered up"* when it is overcrowded with furniture or implements. **1935** *AmSp* 10.160 **PA,** 'The room is *lumbered up,*' meaning 'cluttered up,' an expression reported from Pennsylvania, recalls the British and older meaning of *lumber,* i.e., disused articles, as in *lumber-room.*

2 To cut down, or clear land of, timber; to mill timber; also with *off:* to cut trees from; to cut (timber).
   1809 Kendall *Travels* 3.73 **ME,** The verb *to lumber . .* has also the . . sense, *to procure,* or even *to manufacture lumber.* **1850** (1851) Johnston *Notes N. Amer.* 1.52, We clean up two or three acres every year of the lumbered land (land from which the timber has been cut). **1901** *DN* 2.143 **sePA,** Lumber. . . To clear land. In Webster, but not in this sense. **1902** in 1904 *DN* 2.399 **NY,** A lumberman . . decides to lumber some certain tract. **1905** U.S. Forest Serv. *Bulletin* 61.42 [Logging terms], Lumber. . . To log, or to manufacture logs into lumber, or both. (Gen.) **1967** *DARE* FW Addit **AR**47, Lumber—cut trees; **cnNY,** Lumbered off—the forests were cleared of lumber, they were lumbered off. **1968–70** *DARE* Tape **MI**96, They would lumber their own farms but they didn't make the woods their occupation; **MI**121, The owners of these hardwood tracts, they commenced to lumber off their hardwoods. **1969** Sorden *Lumberjack Lingo* 74 **NEng, Gt Lakes,** Lumber a tract—To cut the trees on a certain specified area. **1986** Pederson *LAGS Concordance,* 1 inf, **seLA,** Lumbered—cutting wood off land.

lumber n² See **lumber** v¹

lumber box n

1 See **lumber sleigh.**

2 See **lumber wagon.**

lumber-box wagon See **lumber wagon**

lumbered up See **lumber** v² **1**

lumber fence n Cf **pale fence, plank fence**
   A wooden fence.
   1967 *DARE* (Qu. L64, *The kind of wooden fence that's built around a garden or near a house)* Inf **TX**31, Lumber fence. **1986** Pederson *LAGS Concordance* (Picket fence) 4 infs, **swGA, nwFL, seAR, ceTX,** Lumber fence(s); 1 inf, **csMS,** Lumber fence.

lumber-heels n Cf **lubber**
   1895 *DN* 1.398 **NY,** Lumber-heels; a lout, a lazy, ungainly fellow.

lumbering See **lumber** v¹

lumberjack n Also *lumberjack bird* [See quot 1959] **Gt Lakes** Cf **jack** n¹ **23d**
   =**Canada jay.**
   1950 *WELS* (Birds that stay all winter in your neighborhood) 2 Infs, **cWI,** Lumberjacks. **1956** Sorden–Ebert *Logger's Words* 22 **Gt Lakes,** Lumber-jack-bird, See camp robber. **1959** *Names* 7.115, A number of

names of the gray or Canada jay have been given because these birds
are fancied to be the embodied spirits of dead lumbermen. Such are
cruiser's spirit (Wash.), lumberjack (Mich., Wis., Minn., Alta.), and old
logger and woodman's ghost (N.Y.) **1966–68** *DARE* (Qu. Q14) Inf
MN5, Lumberjack—a winter bird around lumber camps—small bird,
not teeny; (Qu. Q16, . . *Kinds of jays*) Inf **MI**10, Canada jay—also
called the fool bird or the lumberjack; **MN**16, Lumberjacks or camp
robber—a gray jay; **MN**29, Lumberjack—a jay in the heavy-timbered
area; a gray one.

lumberjack coffee n
   1970 *DARE* File **nWI**, Lumberjack coffee = Norwegian coffee. Coffee
made with an egg in it (not merely eggshells).

lumberjack match n Cf **cowboy match, farmer ~**
   A wooden match that can be struck on any rough surface.
   1968 *DARE* (Qu. F46, . . *Matches you can strike anywhere;* not asked
in early QRs) Inf **WI**52, Lumberjack matches—people around here
say this.

lumber lot n
   =**timber lot.**
   1966–68 *DARE* (Qu. T2a, . . *A piece of land covered with trees . .
only a few acres*) Inf **VT**4, Woodlot for firewood or pulp, lumber lot
for lumber; (Qu. T2b, . . *A piece of land covered with trees . . a large
acreage*) Inf **ME**14, Lumber lot.

lumberment See **lumber** v[1]

lumber off See **lumber** v[2] 2

lumber room n [**lumber** n[1] 1] **scattered, but chiefly Sth, S
Midl**
   A storage room, esp for unused or discarded items.
   1773 in 1898 Bristol Parish VA *Vestry Book & Reg.* 238, A Dairy
Sixteen by Ten to be built and one end to [be] fitted up Close for a
Lumber Room. **1935** [see **lumber** v[2] 1]. **1941** *LANE* Map 345 *(Attic)*,
1 inf, **neMA**, 'The garret is usually a lumber room', i.e. a store room.
It was unfinished and unplastered. **1949** Kurath *Word Geog.* 52, *Store
room.* . . Many houses have a room in the attic or the cellar for storing
old furniture and utensils. . . *Lumber room* is the Virginia Piedmont and
Tidewater term. **1950** *WELS (Any small space in a house where you
can hide things or get them out of the way)* 1 Inf, **cnWI**, Lumber room,
storeroom. **1955** Stong *Blizzard* 16 **IA**, They went up unenclosed steps
to the lumber room. **1956** Ker *Vocab. W. TX* 101, Unfinished space at
top of house. . . lumber room. [1 of 67 infs] **1966** *DARE* (Qu. D4, *The
space up under the roof, usually used for storing things*) Inf **SC**4,
Lumber room—a spare room for storage in the main house; (Qu. D7,
*A small space anywhere in a house where you can hide things or get
them out of the way*) Inf **AR**7, Lumber room. **1982** Powers *Cataloochee*
316 **cwNC**, Out in the 'lumber' room, a general storage place, was a
loom. **1986** Pederson *LAGS Concordance (Junk room)* 3 infs, **cGA**,
nwAL, cnMS, Lumber room; 1 inf, **swMS**, Lumber room—for storing
junk; 1 inf, **swAR**, Lumber room—old term, heating stove here; [1 inf,
ceTX, Lumber room—for lumber, building materials]. **1986** Wear *Sugarlands* 80 **ceTN**, As I would survey things in the storage room, I
wondered why that my father called it the lumber room; I could see no
lumber.

lumber sauce See **lumber** n[1] 2

lumber sleigh n Also *lumber box, ~ sled* [Cf **lumber** n[1] 1] Cf
lumber wagon
   A box sleigh for general hauling.
   1823 Cooper *Pioneers* 1.44 **cNY**, A large lumber-sleigh, drawn by four
horses, was soon seen dashing through the leafless bushes. **1827** in 1927
Mag. Hist. Extra Nos. 33.4.34 **NEng**, Set off to buy a second-hand
lumber sleigh. [**1829** Mactaggart *3 Yrs. in Canada* 1.252, For some
years, the Americans coming from the States with their *notions* to the
Montreal great mart, were in the habit of running the Canadians off the
road, their lumber-sleighs being much heavier.] **1834** Smith *Letters Jack
Downing* 26 **ME**, Here I am, about half way to Portland, with one shu of
the old lumber box broke down, and tother one putty rickety. **1862** U.S.
Congress *Congressional Globe* 37th Cong 2d Sess 31 Mar 32.2.1463/2,
Mr. *White*, of Indiana. I move to amend by adding, "pleasure sleighs
valued at fifty dollars or over, one per cent. *ad valorem.*" . . Mr. *Stevens*
[of Pennsylvania]. I think the gentleman from Indiana had better with-
draw his amendment, or insert "pungs and lumber boxes, at ten cents
each," for they are the same kind of vehicles. **1901** *Rhodora* 3.153 **ME**,
Our camp equipage was transferred to a "jumper," or rough lumber sled.

1966–70 *DARE* (Qu. N40a, . . *Sleighs . . for hauling loads*) Infs **NY**32,
219, Lumber sleigh; **WI**48, Lumber sled; (Qu. N40c, *Other kinds of
sleighs*) Infs **MI**118, **SD**1, Lumber sleigh.

lumber stretcher See **stretcher**

lumber wagon n Also *lumber-box (wagon)* [Cf **lumber** n[1] 1]
chiefly Nth, Cent See Map Cf **lumber sleigh**
   A box wagon for general hauling, esp on a farm.
   1831 in 1927 *MI Hist.* 11.472, Breakfast swallowed we stepped into
our next rig, which was a lumber wagon drawn by two very good horses.
1848 Bartlett *Americanisms* 217, *Lumber-waggon.* A waggon with a
plain box upon it, used by farmers for carrying their produce to market.
It is sometimes so arranged that a spring seat may be put in it, when
it is very comfortable for riding in. **1903** *DN* 2.299 **Cape Cod MA**
(as of a1857), *Lumber wagon.* . . A lighter four-wheeled cart. **1910**
DN 3.445 **wNY**, *Lumber-wagon.* . . Second word strongly accented.
1917 *DN* 4.396 **neOH, IL, VT, KS, NE, KY**, *Lumber wagon* [lʌmbɹ̩
'wægən]. . . A two horse farm wagon with box, for general hauling.
Strongly strest [sic] on the second word. Strest on the first element, it
would indicate a wagon specifically for hauling lumber. **1965–70** *DARE*
(Qu. N41b, *Horse-drawn vehicles to carry heavy loads*) 71 Infs, **chiefly
Nth, Cent**, Lumber wagon; **CT**14, You carted grain or wood on a lumber
wagon; **CT**29, Lumber wagon—never used for hauling lumber, more
produce like hay, apples, coal, wood; **MI**2, Lumber wagon—a) high-
wheel, b) low-wheel, used more on a farm; **MI**47, Lumber wagon—52
inches wide, two or four horses; **MA**5, Lumber wagon—all-purpose
hauling; **MA**47, Lumber wagon—for very heavy loads; **NY**88, Lumber
wagon—the common one used on a farm; **PA**44, Lumber wagon—
no springs; **PA**223, Lumber wagon—for deep mud; [**MD**10, Lumber
wagon—for hauling lumber around lumberyard; open, no sides, just a
long platform;] **MI**97, Lumber wagon with logging wheels; **NY**70, 82,
Lumber-box wagon; **NY**209, Lumber box; **NY**52, Lumber box—had a
box body; (Qu. L13, *The kind of wagon used for carrying hay*) Infs
CT26, **MI**2, **NY**99, 164, 200, **RI**15, Lumber wagon; **CT**14, You put a
"hay rigging" or "hayrack" on your "farm wagon" or "lumber wagon";
MN23, Hayrack put on lumber wagon; **MN**33, Hayrack—the special
frame put on the lumber wagon; **NY**69, They put a hayrack on top of
an ordinary lumber wagon; **NY**72, Lumber wagon—same kind used
around the farm all the time; **NY**88, Lumber wagon with racks, but they
always call it the lumber wagon; **OK**10, Big old lumber wagon or farm
wagon with a hayrack on it; **WI**6, Lumber wagon, and put a rack on
it; **NY**224, Lumber wagon with hayrack; (Qu. N41a, . . *Horse-drawn
vehicles . . to carry people*) Infs **KS**20, **WI**26, Lumber wagons; (Qu.
N41c, *Horse-drawn vehicles to carry light loads*) Infs **IL**7, 27, **MI**108,
Lumber wagon; **NY**75, Lumber wagon—the ordinary wagon used on a
farm; **NY**69, 72, Light lumber wagon; **NY**69, One-horse lumber wagon.
1965–66 *DARE* Tape **CA**2, These people that I was boarding with took
me over in the lumber wagon to Calico for the day. . . A box wagon
that they used to use on farms; **OK**6, [FW:] What kind of wagons did
they use around here? [Inf:] Mostly lumber wagons. . . [FW:] What
were the lumber wagons built like? [Inf:] Just an old wooden wheel
wagon. **1967** Schilla *Prairies* 71 **ND**, Jasper Jesperson spoke of going
with his father to Dickinson in a lumber wagon.

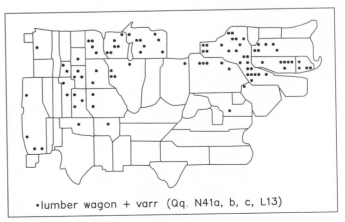

•lumber wagon + varr (Qq. N41a, b, c, L13)

lumbrage See **lumber** v[1]

luminaria n [Span]
   1 A small bonfire lit as part of a Christmas Eve custom; see
quots. **chiefly NM**

1940 Writers' Program *Guide NM* 115, *Luminarias*— . . Small bonfires. **1951** Fergusson *New Mexico* 211, Before the people had paper sacks, they built tiny fires on the roofs or in front of the houses, as the Indians still do in Taos, to light the Christ Child on his way. These were the *luminarias*. Purists prefer to call the lighted sacks *faroles* (lanterns). But so many people have learned to say *luminarias* that the word has become part of our common speech. **1973** [see **2** below]. **1989** *Gourmet* Dec 216 **Santa Fe NM,** All the houses here and on adjoining streets are decorated with *farolitos*, and *luminarias* burn for warmth along the way, in a procession that is beautifully reminiscent of what we're told old Santa Fe was like. **1991** *Sunset* Dec 20 **NM,** In Santa Fe, Christmas Eve brings the lighting of farolitos along Canyon Road, and bonfires known as luminarias (not to be confused with farolitos) burn all over town.

2 By ext: a votive candle set in sand in a paper bag, used with others to line a sidewalk, driveway, etc, esp on Christmas Eve. **orig NM, now more widespread**

1949 Dickey *NM Village Arts* 23, Instead of the juniper vigil fires of former days, the natives [=Hispanic Americans] make *farolitos*, little lanterns of burning candles set in sand inside paper bags. . . The custom has appealed to Anglo-American residents, and they too announce Christmas Eve with candles in grocer's bags, calling them *luminarias*. **1951** [see **1** above]. **1973** *Holiday* Nov–Dec 70, New Mexico's famous "Little Lights of Christmas" are lanterns made of sand-set candles in paper bags called *luminarias*—(*farolitos* among the natives of northern New Mexico, where *luminarias* are small bonfires). **1977** Amer. Automobile Assoc. *TourBook AZ NM* 45 **Albuquerque NM,** On Christmas Eve, the Luminaria (little bonfire) Tour takes place when millions of candles placed in small paper bags and inserted in sand, outline streets, sidewalks, windows and rooftops providing an interesting display of light. **1988** *Pittsburgh Press* (PA) 10 Aug (*W3* File), Whether they were dancing in the street, spelling messages in luminaria, or playing "black watch trivia," Pittsburgh residents made it clear that they're determined to keep neighborhoods free of crime. **1994** *DARE* File **cwCA** (as of c1958), At our Christmas Eve church service, the walkways were lined with luminarias—small paper bags holding a few inches of sand, into which a candle was inserted, and then lighted. Nowadays, luminarias in colorful bags, often with decorative cutouts, are sold in gift and specialty shops all around the country.

lummox n [Engl dial] Also sp *lommix, lummix, lummucks, lummux* **chiefly Nth, N Midl, West** See Map

An awkward or ungainly person; an oaf.

1841 *Spirit of Times* 23 Oct 408/3 **MA,** Not he, the darn'd lummucks—no, the critter has choose this way to get out of the country. **1854** Paige *Dow's Sermons* IV.149 *(DAE)*, Man in his original state is little more than a big lummux of a baby. **1889** Twain *CT Yankee* 382, As a rule, a knight is a lummux, and sometimes even a labrick. **1890** *DN* 1.62 **NEng, sePA,** Lummox. In use in and around Philadelphia to designate an uncouth fellow, awkward in body or in mind. **1899** (1912) Green *VA Folk-Speech* 271, Lummox. . . An unwieldy, clumsy, stupid fellow. **1903** *DN* 2.299 **Cape Cod MA** (as of a1857), Lummux. . . An awkward booby. **1905** *DN* 3.63 **eNE,** Lummux. **1906** Casey *Parson's Boys* 218 **sIL** (as of c1860), I ain't afeard of no lummix like you. **1907** *DN* 3.214 **nwAR,** Lummox. . . A stupid, awkward fellow. **1909** *DN* 3.413 **nME,** Lummox. . . A large awkward person. **1912** *DN* 3.582 **wIN,** Lommix or lummix. . . "Watch the big lommix fall; he can't skate." **1917** *DN* 4.396 **neOH,** Lummox ['lʌməks]. **1919** *DN* 5.69 **NM,** Lum-

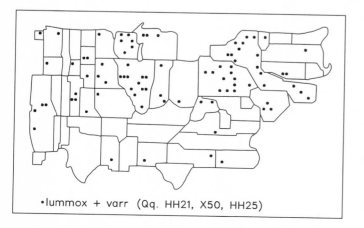

•lummox + varr (Qq. HH21, X50, HH25)

mox, an awkward, overgrown boy or girl. "That Fox girl is the biggest lummox in town." **1927** *AmSp* 3.135 **eME,** An awkward or clumsy man was . . "a great gorming lummox." **1938** Farrell *No Star* 50 **IL,** What do I find but a big lummox on top of him, pounding the daylights out of him. **1947** Ballowe *The Lawd* 186 **LA,** Git outer heah, you big lummox. **1965–70** *DARE* (Qu. HH21, *A very awkward, clumsy person*) 82 Infs, **chiefly Nth, N Midl, West,** Lummox; **CA**74, **NY**219, **SD**3, Big (*or crazy, lazy*) lummox; (Qu. X50, *Names or nicknames for a person who is very fat*) Inf **CA**73, Fat lummox; (Qu. HH25, *One who never has anything to say: "What's the matter with him? _____?"*) Inf **LA**40, Lummox; [(Qu. LL5, *Something impressively big: "That cabbage is really a _____."*) Inf **SD**3, Lummox]. **1977** *Yankee* Jan 113 **Isleboro ME,** If it happens that you're so conked out that you trip on your way out the door, you might feel like a lummox—which is a clumsy oaf. **1982** *Barrick Coll.* **csPA,** *Lummox*—Usu. *big lummox*. Heavy, ungainly person.

lumped jaw See **lump jaw**

lumper n [Etym uncert; cf quot 1915] **esp NEng**

An unskilled laborer; a freight handler.

1833 Hamilton *Men & Manners* 99 **eMA,** There is, however, a class of men, consisting of ten or twelve, called *runners* and *lumpers*, whose duty consists in moving about the [prison] yard. **1887** *Battle Creek Moon* 17 Dec. *(DAE)*, Converse prison number is 4,234, and the position he occupies is known as a 'lumper.' His duties are to assist the forman [sic] of the shop in sorting and packing and putting goods in shape for shipment. **1895** *DN* 1.390 **Boston MA,** Lumper: common unskilled laborer. **1915** (1916) Johnson *Highways New Engl.* 165, They are what is known as "lumpers"—that is, they are shore workers who discharge cargoes and do other jobs about the vessels and wharves for a lump sum. **1916** *DN* 4.356 [Railroad terms], Lumper. . . A freight shed laborer. **1975** Gould *ME Lingo* 171, Lumper—Originally used to designate a laborer who helped load or unload vessels, it now generally refers to a man engaged in any unskilled work. "We could do with a lumper to clean up the mess around this place." **1980** Banks *First-Person America* 106 **VT** (as of c1939), I was a lumper for a while [in a marble quarry]. You have to chain the blocks so they can be moved.

lumphead n
=lunkhead.

1969 *DARE* (Qu. HH3, *A dull and stupid person*) Inf **NJ**6, Lumphead.

lump in v phr

To contribute money toward a collective goal; to chip in.

1965–70 *DARE* (Qu. II9, *If several people have to contribute in order to pay for something . . "Let's all _____."*) Infs **MS**45, 60, **VA**46, Lump in.

lumping adj [*EDD* lumping ppl. adj. 1 "Large and clumsy; heavy"] Cf **lumpus** n

1899 (1912) Green *VA Folk-Speech* 271, Lumping. . . Bulky; chunky; heavy.

lump jaw n Also *lumped jaw, lumpy ~* [So called from the suppurating swellings which occur esp on the jaw] Also called **holdfast, wooden tongue** Cf **wolf**

Actinomycosis; an animal suffering from this disease; hence adj phr *lumpy-jawed* suffering from this disease.

1884 *Prairie Farmer* 5 Apr 224/3 *(Mathews Coll.)*, Diseased cattle of all kinds, especially those having lump-jaws, cancers, and running sores, are condemned and killed by health officers. *Ibid* 9 Aug 500/3 *(Mathews Coll.)*, People have often been assured in positive terms . . that eating the flesh of cattle affected with 'lumpy jaw' or actinomycosis will not injure human beings. **1890** OH Ag. Exper. Sta. *Bulletin* 3.107, Actinomycosis, commonly called lump jaw, or lumped jaw, is not a new disease. **1890** *Congressional Record* 29 May 21.6.5428/2, "Lumpy-jawed cattle" means cancerous cattle, cattle with cancer. The "lumpy-jaw" is simply a cancer. **1913** (1979) Barnes *Western Grazing* 286, Big jaw, also called lumpy jaw and wooden tongue, is an infectious disease found generally all over the West. **1925** *Book of Rural Life* 6.3286, *Lump jaw*, or *actinomycosis* . . , is a common disease of cattle characterized by a large swelling or tumor on the jaws. . . Lump-jaw cattle are slaughtered under veterinary inspection at the stockyards, and the meat is allowed on the market if found fit. **1935** Sandoz *Jules* 88 **wNE** (as of 1880–1930), Nor were they trail-gaunted longhorns, or grotesque lump-jaws, such as beef contractors sold the government for them [=Amer Indians]. **1940** (1948) Seton *Trail of Artist* 307, When seeking some beef for wolf bait, we usually sought out a "lumpy jaw." **1965–70**

DARE (Qu. K28, . . *Chief diseases that cows have*) Infs **IL**5, **IN**17, **IA**8, **KY**6, **NH**5, **NM**6, **OR**1, **WV**8, Lump jaw; (Qu. K47, . . *Diseases . . horses or mules commonly get*) Inf **KY**80, Lump jaw. **1971** Green *Village Horse Doctor* 151 **TX**, Lump jaw is caused by an iodine deficiency. **1976** Sublette Co. Artist Guild *More Tales* 306 **cwWY** (as of c1900), I had trailed a bunch of bulls and lump-jaws down. **1992** Attebery *Sheep* 16 **ID**, Lumpjaw is an ailment caused by such a seed [=that of cheatgrass] working its way into the soft tissue of the mouth or throat of a grazing animal.

lump-jawed adj Also *lumpy-jawed* [**lump jaw**]
Having a swollen face or jaw; having a prominent jaw.
  1967–70 *DARE* (Qu. X6, *If a person's lower jaw sticks out prominently . . he's* _____) Inf **TN**65, Lump-jawed; (Qu. BB32, *If somebody had a swelling—for example, in his whole face . . "Last week his face was all* _____.") Inf **CA**36, Lump-jawed; **NV**2, Lumpy-jawed—like the cattle have.

lump off v phr
To divide (something) by rough estimate; to guess at the measure or value of (something).
  1916 *DN* 4.326 **KS, NY, neOH**, Lump off. . . To guess; to make an approximation as to quantity, size, value, etc. "We didn't measure the field but just lumped it off." **1927** *AmSp* 2.360 **cwWV**, *Lump off* . . to guess at or estimate. "I will lump off the flour to you at fifty pounds." **1949** *PADS* 11.24 **CO**, *Lump off.* . . To separate in a mass without counting. "They lumped off a group of horses from the others." **1954** *Harder Coll.* **cwTN**, Lump off—to guess or estimate [a size or quantity]. **1958** McCulloch *Woods Words* 114 **Pacific NW**, *Lump it off*—To make a guess as to the amount of timber on a given piece of ground.

lumpous See **lumpus** adv

lumpus n [Cf *EDD* lumpus "A heavily-built, rough, clumsy person"] Cf **lumping**
  1903 *DN* 2.299 **Cape Cod MA** (as of a1857), *Lumpus.* . . A clumsy fellow.

lumpus adv Also sp *lumpous* [Engl dial; cf *EDD*]
  1899 (1912) Green *VA Folk-Speech* 271, *Lumpous.* . . Lumpus. All of a heap. "She came down lumpous." All of a lump; of a heavy fall.

lumpy jaw See **lump jaw**

lumpy-jawed adj
  1 See **lump jaw.**
  2 See **lump-jawed**

lun See **loan A1**

luna n [Haw] **HI**
A foreman, supervisor.
  1873 in 1966 Bishop *Sandwich Is.* 76 **HI**, The native *lunas*, or overseers, are not always reasonable. **1951** *AmSp* 26.23 **HI**, *Luna* (boss, foreman). **1965** Krauss–Alexander *Grove Farm* 67 **HI**, They were divided into gangs under supervisors, usually Hawaiians, called lunas. **1967** *DARE* (Qu. HH17, *A person who tries to appear important, or who tries to lay down the law in his community: "He'd like to be the* _____ *around here."*) Inf **HI**13, Luna; (Qu. HH43a, *The top person in charge of a group of workmen*) Infs **HI**1, 6, 13, Luna. **1967** *DARE* Tape **HI**2, In the field, the man who is in charge of a work gang is called a luna. **1972** Carr *Da Kine Talk* 116 **HI**, *Number-one-luna* (pidgin English + Hawaiian). The head boss in charge of a gang of laborers on a plantation. *Luna* means 'foreman', 'supervisor'. **1980** Bushnell *Water of Kane* 119 **HI**, You will be the luna of this gang.

lunch n
  1 also *luncheon:* A light meal or snack taken at any time. Cf **piece** n
  1861 in 1865 IL Dept. Ag. *Trans.* 5.197, Mrs. A., at ten and again at four o'clock, sends out a lunch to the harvesters. **1899** *Scribner's Mag.* 25.106, I should like to inquire if you have any authority for your use of the word 'lunch'? As employed by the appropriating and the arrogant it has long meant a meal or a bite between breakfast and dinner; but, as used by democracy, it seems to apply to afternoon tea or late supper equally well. **1957** *Sat. Eve. Post Letters* **ceMO**, Lunch rather than snack, tea, etc., at any time from 10 a.m. to 2 a.m. Ex. "I won't have dinner, I'll just have a lunch"—a distinction recognized in restaurants. . . I had never heard the word *snack* used outside of English novels until the rise of TV. **c1960** *Wilson Coll.* **csKY**, Lunch. . . Food eaten between meals. **1965–70** *DARE* (Qu. H5, . . *A small amount of food eaten*

between regular meals) 174 Infs, **widespread**, Lunch; **NY**130, **PA**71, Light lunch; **ME**19, **MS**72, (Have a) little lunch; **CA**22, **ME**19, Luncheon [Of all Infs responding to the question, 68% were comm type 4 or 5, 70% old, 28% gs educ or less; of those giving these responses, 81% were comm type 4 or 5, 81% old, 40% gs educ or less.]; [**NY**20, **OH**48, Lunching]. **1968** *PADS* 49.16 **Upper MW**, Vocabularies sometimes change because a word from one dialect appears to have more prestige than that of another dialect. . . *Snack*, originally Southern and South Midland but now virtually international, is replacing the Northern *lunch* as the word for food eaten between meals. **1968** *DARE* FW Addit **MD**34, A little lunch—light meal, regardless of time of day. **1969–70** *DARE* Tape **IL**77, [FW:] What time would they eat lunch? [Inf:] Oh, around nine o'clock in the morning, and noon if sometimes they brought their meals out in the field; **MI**120, [Inf:] A corn-husking bee . . would be at night, and a whole bunch of us kids get together, and get in the barn, and husk corn. Shuck it. [Aux Inf:] We'd sing and then he'd serve us lunch. **1981** Bly *Letters* 9 **swMN**, We were outside all day, from six in the morning to eight at night—coming in only for noon dinner. We ate our lunches on a messy truck flatbed. (For city people who don't know it: *lunch* isn't a noon meal; it is what you eat out of a black lunch pail at 9 A.M. and 3 P.M.) **1981** *KS Qrly.* 13.2.68, *Lunch* . . a light, cold snack. **1987** Mohr *How Minnesotan* 17 **MN**, Lunch can also occur at other odd times of the day. It is then called "a little lunch."
  2 See **lunch roll.**

lunch bucket n See **bucket 2e**

lunch bucket is open, your phr Cf **barn door 2c**, *DS* W24c
Used as a warning to a man that his trouser fly is open.
  1980 *DARE* File **cwIN** (as of 1950s), Kids used to tease boys by saying "Your lunch bucket's open," meaning that the fly was open. When a boy looked down to check, the taunt would be, "That's a funny place to keep your lunch."

lunch bun See **lunch roll**

lunch counter See **lunch pail**

luncheon See **lunch 1**

lunchery n Cf **beanery 1**
See quot 1925.
  1921 *DN* 5.112 **CA**, Lunchery. . . A lunch room; a restaurant. **1925** *AmSp* 1.38 **CA**, *Lunchery*, a place where lunches are sold.

lunch grabber See **grabber 1**

lunchground(s) n
An outdoor area where meals can be taken; a picnic area.
  1956 Sorden–Ebert *Logger's Words* 23 **Gt Lakes**, *Lunch-grounds*, Where a meal will be served out of doors usually with a bonfire. **1975** Gould *ME Lingo* 171, *Lunchground*—A wilderness picnic area designated by a forestry warden where fires may be made without permit. Some have been in use a long time and have special names: Canoe Pool Lunchground, Fontinales Lunchground, etc. Mainers would not use *lunchground* for a highway rest area or just any picnic spot.

lunch hook n *joc* Cf **biscuit hooks**, *lunch grabber* (at **grabber 1**)
A hand or finger.
  1896 (1898) Ade *Artie* 101, It was right in the dead serious part, just when Florence and Tommy put their lunch-hooks together. **1945** Hubbard *Railroad Ave.* 351, *Lunch hooks*—Your two hands. **1950** *WELS* (*Joking or uncomplimentary names for the hands*) 2 Infs, **WI**, Lunch hooks. **1956** Sorden–Ebert *Logger's Words* 23 **Gt Lakes**, *Lunch-hook*, The hand of the lumber-jack. **1966–68** *DARE* (Qu. X32, *Joking or uncomplimentary words for the hands . . "Those are mine. You keep your* _____ *[out of them]."*) Infs **CA**93, **ME**21, **MT**2, **OH**47, **SD**8, Lunch hooks. **1985** De Vries *Prick of Noon* 76 **AR**, Jack has big rather lumpy lunch hooks, with heavy knuckles.

lunch kit n Cf **kit** n **1**
A usu metal container for a noon meal.
  1961 Folk *Word Atlas N. LA* map 410, Metal container for carrying dinner or lunch . . lunch kit. **1962** Atwood *Vocab. TX* 46, Words for the container in which a man carries his noon meal are . . [8% of 273 infs] *lunch kit.* **1967–68** *DARE* (Qu. F22b, *A smaller paper container for carrying a lunch: "He had his lunch in a* _____.") Infs **CA**36, **OH**54, **TX**27, Lunch kit; **MI**43, The men use lunch kits in the mine. **1967** LeCompte *Word Atlas* 136 **seLA**, *Metal container for carrying dinner or lunch.* . . lunch kit [4 of 21 infs]. **1995** *DARE* File **cTX**, If memory

serves me correctly, I used the term "lunch kit" as a child in San Antonio in the late 50s and early 60s. I must have learned it from my mother, who grew up in Wiemar, TX. . . The term referred to the flat rectangular metal box that came with a thermos bottle.

lunch-mouth n

A gluttonous person.

1964 *AmSp* 39.235 **KS,** Lunchmouth. . . A heavy eater. **1967** *DARE* (Qu. H9, *If somebody always eats a considerable amount of food, you say he's a _____*) Inf **OR**1, Lunch-mouth. **1994** *DARE* File **ID** (as of c1965), When I was in college we called people who seemed to be eating all the time either *lunch-mouths* or *munch-mouths.*

lunch pail n Also *lunch counter* Cf *dinner bucket* (at **dinners**)

1965–69 *DARE* (Qu. X31, . . *A woman's breasts*) Inf **PA**209, Lunch counter; **OK**7, Lunch pails.

lunch roll n Also *lunch (bun),* ~ *stick* chiefly **MI** Cf **long john 2**

A kind of **friedcake 1.**

1948 *WELS Suppl.* **seMI,** Two other nouns common to Wisconsin which were totally unfamiliar to me before I came here [from Detroit MI] are *bismark . .* and *long John.* We always referred to these . . as *jelly doughnuts* and *lunch buns* respectively. **1965–70** *DARE* (Qu. H28, *Different shapes or types of doughnuts*) Inf **MI**94, Lunch roll—oblong with icing; **MI**95, Lunch roll—long, twisted; (Qu. H29, *A round cake, cooked in deep fat, with jelly inside*) Inf **OH**70, Lunch roll; (Qu. H30, *An oblong cake, cooked in deep fat*) Inf **MI**122, Filled lunch; **MI**94, **OH**70, Lunch roll; **MI**69, Lunch stick—sometimes filled, sometimes not; **NY**199, Lunch stick.

lunge n[1] Also *longe* esp **VT**

=**lake trout 1.**

1838 *Spirit of Times* 13 Oct 272/1 *(Mathews Coll.)* **VT,** The Lunge, from the lakes in the upper part of this and Essex county, Vermont, is taken, weighing from six to 35 pounds. **1866** *Vt. Acts & Resolves* 71 *(DAE),* No person shall be permitted to take any trout or longe in this State. **1882** U.S. Natl. Museum *Bulletin* 16.317, *S[alvelinus] namaycush . .* Great Lake Trout; Longe (Vermont). **1902** Jordan–Evermann *Amer. Fishes* 204, In Vermont it [=*Salvelinus namaycush*] is called "longe," in Maine it is the "togue," while among the Canadian Indians it is the "namaycush" or "masmacush." **1911** U.S. Bur. Census *Fisheries 1908* 311, Lake trout *(Cristivomer namaycush).*—The trout found in the Great Lakes and in the smaller lakes of the Northern states. In different localities the individuals . . are known by the local names "salmon trout," . . "reef trout," "longe," etc. **1946** LaMonte *N. Amer. Game Fishes* 115, Namaycush, Longue, Togue, Forktail Trout, Lunge, Laker.

lunge n[2] Also *longe* [Abbr for **muskellunge**]

=**muskellunge 1.**

1894 *Outing* 24.368, It's a 'lunge. . . he'll weigh at least fifteen pounds. **1902** *Jrl. Amer. Folkl.* 15.246, *Longe* or *lunge.* A common abbreviation of *muskelunge (maskalonge)* among English-speaking people in the region about the Great Lakes, especially the north shore of Lake Ontario. **1933** John G. Shedd Aquarium *Guide* 58, The "Lunge" is the largest of the American pikes, reaching a length of six feet and a weight of over seventy-five pounds. **1949** Caine *N. Amer. Sport Fish* 98, Muskellunge. *Colloquial Names* . . Lunge . . Longe. **1983** Becker *Fishes WI* 404, Muskellunge. . . Other common names . . muskie (musky), lunge.

lunger n chiefly **West** Cf **lung fever**

A person or animal suffering from a chronic lung disease, esp tuberculosis.

1893 Sanborn *Truthful Woman* 14 **sCA,** The rainy season is . . hard . . for "lungers" and . . nervous invalids. **1913** Johnson *Highways St. Lawrence to VA* 15 **NY,** The air is fine for consumptives. Saranac Lake is a great resort for lungers. **1935** *AmSp* 10.77 **sAZ,** On reaching the arid southwest the [tuberculosis] patient . . is referred to as a *lunger.* **1937** *AmSp* 12.104 **eNE,** An aged sheep. . . A *lunger* is one that has lost a lung. **1941** Cleaveland *No Life* 290 **NM,** There was a 'lunger' who insisted he was equal to any man in the crew and *almost* proved it. **1948** *AmSp* 23.318 [Stockyard terms], *Lungers.* Cattle with any lung disease. **1949** *PADS* 11.24 **CO,** *Lunger.* . . Someone who comes West because of tuberculosis. **1956** Algren *Walk on the Wild Side* 12 **TX,** The townsfolk knew . . that Byron smoked too much potiguaya bush for a lunger. **1961** *AmSp* 36.147, *Lunger.* . . A patient with chronic lung disease, such as tuberculosis or, more commonly, emphysema. **1965–70** *DARE* (Qu. BB10, . . *Names or nicknames . . for tuberculosis*) Inf **CA**7,

He was a lungers [sic]; **CA**87, A lunger—the human with T.B.; **MS**1, T.B., consumption, lunger; [**KS**13, **NY**24, **WA**13, Lunger's; **MO**11, Lunger's—heard that this term was used farther west [*DARE* Ed: prob for *lunger's disease*]]. **1967** *DARE* Tape **CA**15, After working for about five years in the bank, I contracted tuberculosis one winter. This was a dreaded disease in the nineteen-twenties. It was called the "con," a clipped form of the word consumption. And a person was said to be a lunger because it was thought that one was coughing up one's lungs. **1967** *Merck Vet. Manual* 951, Progressive pneumonia is a slowly developing, chronic disease of the lungs. . . Sheep affected with this disease are commonly known as "lungers" in the Northwestern States. **1969** O'Connor *Horse & Buggy West* 185 **AZ,** It was generally believed that he was a lunger, as people with tuberculosis were called.

lung fever n chiefly **Nth, N Midl** See Map

Pneumonia; tuberculosis.

1823 (1922) Anthony *New Bedford* 19 **MA,** Capt. Silas Parker died about 11 o'clock of a lung fevre. **1838** Martineau *Retrospect W. Travel* 3.171 **NEng,** Breathing the frosty air of a winter's night, after dancing, may be easily conceived to be the cause of much of the "lung fever" of which the stranger hears. **1879** U.S. Dept. Ag. *Special Rept.* 12.195 **KS,** *Mitchell* [County]. Murrain, black-leg, and lung-fever have prevailed to some extent among cattle. **1888** *Walla Walla Union* (WA) 24 Nov 3/6, Frank Ingalls is very sick with lung fever. **1925** *Book of Rural Life* 6.3287, *Lung fever,* the name given to the infectious disease of animals more commonly called *pneumonia.* **1943** *LANE* Map 510 *(Tuberculosis)* 5 infs, chiefly **CT,** Lung fever; 2 infs, **sVT,** Lung fever—old-fashioned term; 1 inf, **cCT,** Lung fever = pneumonia; 1 inf, **csMA,** Lung fever— 'that used to be the old name for pneumonia'; 1 inf, **nwMA,** Lung fever—'the older term for pneumonia'. **1945** Pickard–Buley *Midwest Pioneer* 22, Pneumonia, or "lung fever," attacked many people in winter. **1965–70** *DARE* (Qu. BB10, . . *Names or nicknames . . for tuberculosis*) 25 Infs, chiefly **Nth, N Midl,** Lung fever; (Qu. K47, . . *Diseases . . horses or mules commonly get*) Infs **CA**131, **KS**11, **PA**23, 198, Lung fever; (Qu. BB49, . . *Other kinds of diseases*) Inf **MN**23, Lung fever or pneumonia; **OH**82, Lung fever—for pneumonia. [29 of 31 Infs old] **1966** *DARE* Tape **MI**32, They keep saying that . . the deer are starving to death. . . None of them get T.B. or . . heart trouble or lung fever.

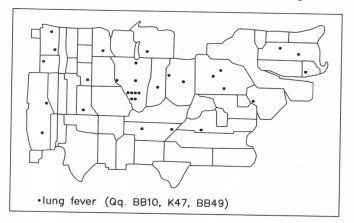

•lung fever (Qq. BB10, K47, BB49)

lung-tied adj

1967 *DARE* (Qu. K48, *When a horse is short of breath*) Inf **NV**1, Lung-tied.

lungwort n

1 A bluebell **1g,** esp **Virginia bluebells.**

1791 in 1793 *Amer. Philos. Soc. Trans.* 3.163, Pulmonaria, virginica. Lungwort. **1837** Darlington *Flora Cestrica* 117, Virginian Pulmonaria . . Virginian Cowslip, Lungwort. **1857** Gray *Manual of Botany* 323, *M[ertensia] Virginica* . . Virginian Cowslip or Lungwort. . . Alluvial banks, W. New York to Wisconsin, Virginia, Kentucky, and southward. **1901** Mohr *Plant Life AL* 690, Virginia Lungwort. **1937** U.S. Forest Serv. *Range Plant Hdbk.* W126, Bluebells [=*Mertensia* spp], sometimes called lungworts and languid-ladies, are well-known perennial herbs of the borage family. **1975** Hamel–Chiltoskey *Cherokee Plants* 26, Lungwort . . *Mertensia virginica.* . . For whooping cough; consumption.

2 A **mullein** (here: *Verbascum thapsus*). [*OED* 1538 →] Cf **hungwort**

1889 *Century Dict.* 3543, *Bullock's* or *cow's lungwort,* the mullen, *Verbascum Thapsus,* formerly used as a remedy for lung-disease in cattle, because its leaf resembles a dewlap. **1904** Henkel *Weeds Used in Med.* 24, Mullein. . . Other common names . . bullock's lungwort, cow's or clown's lungwort. **1940** Clute *Amer. Plant Names* 32, Common Mullein. . . cow's lungwort, bullock's lungwort. *Ibid* 274, *Verbascum thapsus*. . . clown's lungwort. **1974** (1977) Coon *Useful Plants* 246, Mullen, verbascum, flannel plant, candlewick, lungwort, as well as some 25 other common names. . . Among the Navajos it is also smoked for the alleviation of "mild mental disturbances."

lunker n
A large specimen of its kind, esp a large fish.

1911 Shute *Plupy* 14 **NH**, Pewt knew where there were some bully perch, old lunkers. **1912** *DN* 3.582 **wIN**, Lunker. . . A large specimen. "Isn't that calf a lunker?" **1920** *Outing* 76.197, I said that I caught trout in a tin pan, and here's the proof. This old lunker of a rainbow gave me a bath. **1945** *Eaton Coll.* **seWI** (as of 1930s), Them's lunkers, ain't they!—Said of logs. **1964** Jackman–Long *OR Desert* 394 [App.], Lunker—big, heavy-boned. **1966–69** *DARE* (Qu. LL5, *Something impressively big: "That cabbage is really a _____"*) Infs **CT**29, **KS**16, **ME**6, **NY**96, **OK**18, **VT**6, **WI**61, Lunker; (Qu. P22, *Names or nicknames for a very large frog that makes a deep, loud sound*) Inf **NY**2, Lunker. **1975** Gould *ME Lingo* 171, Lunker—A big deer will be termed a *rauncher*, but a big game fish is a *lunker*. *Baister* means about the same. **1987** Childress *Out of the Ozarks* 124, The minute he [=a fish] slacked off, I wound the line around my winch, started my truck, and got ready to haul that lunker out. **1988** Kingsolver *Bean Trees* 2 **KY**, The way Mama would carry on you would think I'd caught the famous big lunker in Shep's Lake that old men were always chewing their tobacco and thinking about.

lunkhead n Cf head n C1a, lumphead
A dull-witted person.

1885 Twain *Huck. Finn* 194 **MO**, So the duke said these Arkansaw lunkheads couldn't come up to Shakspeare. **1889** *Advance* (Chicago IL) 19 Dec 936/4, You dear, old lunkhead, I congratulate you! **1904** *DN* 2.426 **Cape Cod MA** (as of a1857), Lunkhead. . . A numbskull. **1909** *DN* 3.413 **nME**, Lunkhead. . . A stupid person. **1912** *DN* 3.582 **wIN**, Lunk-head. . . A dull, stupid person. **1919** Kyne *Capt. Scraggs* 149 **CA**, "I mean, you lunkhead," said Mr. Gibney, "that luck is found where brains grow. No brains, no luck." **1919** *DN* 5.61 **NM**, Lunk-head, a slow, dull fellow. "I can't have such lunk-heads in my class." **1929** *AmSp* 5.119 **ME**, A stupid individual was a "mutton head," "punkin head," "lunk head," or "dumber than a stump." **1965–70** *DARE* (Qu. HH3, *A dull and stupid person*) 60 Infs, **scattered**, Lunkhead; (Qu. GG41, *To lose patience easily: "You never did see such a _____ person."*) Inf **MI**17, Lunkhead; (Qu. HH1, *Names and nicknames for a rustic or countrified person*) Inf **MA**11, Lunkhead; (Qu. HH2, *Names and nicknames for a citified person*) Inf **MI**13, Lunkhead; [(Qu. X28, *Joking words . . for a person's head*) Infs **NY**96, 197, **UT**7, Lunkhead].

lupine n
Std: a plant of the genus *Lupinus*. Also called **bluebonnet 1, buffalo pea 3, Quaker bonnet, sundial.** For other names of var spp see **buffalo clover 2, chinook licorice, deer cabbage 2, grandma's cap, Indian bean 4, lady lupine, lavender 3, monkeyface 4, old-maid's-bonnet, peavine, seven-year weed, sheep poison, silver lupine, Texas bluebonnet, wild alfalfa, ~ bean, ~ lupine, ~ pea, wolfbean**

lurgy n [*EDD lurgy*, also *lurgy-fever, the fever of lurgy* "Idleness, laziness"] Cf fever and lurk(s)
1968–69 *DARE* (Qu. BB28, *Joking names . . for imaginary diseases: "He must have the _____."*) Infs **CA**107, **OH**47, Lurgy ['lɜˑgi].

lurky n [*EDD lerky* "A noisy game, played with any old tin"] Cf nurky
=kick the can 1.
1968 *DARE* (Qu. EE13a, *Games in which every player hides except one, and that one must try to find the others*) Inf **VA**33, Lurky—base is a moveable object such as a tin can; if one of the players could kick the base, the "it" player had to get the base before finding the rest of the players.

lush n Also loch(e), losh, lush fish [CanFr *loche* < Fr *loche* loach] chiefly AK Cf *DCan*
=burbot.
[**1808** (1890) Keith *Letters* 81 [*DCan*], The active squirrel commanded

his attention, a pike, a loche and a mouse [moose].] [**1842** DeKay *Zool. NY* 4.285, *[Lota maculosa]* is known under the various local names of *La Loche, Methy, Dog-fish* and *Eel-pout*. [*DARE* Ed: This may refer to Canadian usage; see quot 1884 below.]] **1862** in 1942 James *First Scientific Explor.* 127 **AK**, "Loch." (*Lota?*) Decidely [sic] a "queer fish." . . It resembles our catfish somewhat in shape, and has no scales. It is a river fish, and it [sic] never found in the small lakes. . . In the Yukon they are smaller and much less numerous than east of the mountains. **1870** Dall *Alaska* 180, The first fish which are caught in early winter on the Yukon, are the *"losh"* (*Lota maculata*) of the Hudson Bay men. [**1884** Goode *Fisheries U.S.* 1.236, In Canada, [the burbot is known] as *"la Loche."*] **1886** Turner *Contribs. AK* 92, *Lota Maculosa*. . . This species is the *"Losh"* of the Hudson Bay men; and the name has been introduced into Alaska also, as the Russians, in speaking of this fish, always use the word *"Losh."* **1889** *Century Dict.* 3523, *Losh*. . . The burbot, *Lota maculosa*: so called in parts of British America and in Alaska. *Ibid* 3546, *Lush*. . . The burbot: same as *losh*. **1899** in 1968 *AK Sportsman* Oct 12, On the Yukon they set traps and nets under the ice and catch whitefish and lush (burbot). **1915** Stuck *10000 Miles* 368 **AK**, The rivers still teem with salmon and grayling and the lakes with whitefish, ling, and lush. **1946** Dufresne *AK's Animals* 280, Throughout interior Alaska rivers and lakes is found the only freshwater member of the cod family. While the name most often applied to this fish in Alaska is Ling Cod (*Lota maculosa*), it parades under many local terms such as lush [etc]. **1955** U.S. Arctic Info. Center *Gloss.* 50, *Loche*. . . The burbot. **1966–68** *DARE* (Qu. P1, . . *Kinds of freshwater fish . . caught around here . . good to eat*) Inf **MI**2, Losh [laš]—long, slim fish; long fin most of the way down back; no scales—skin; whiskers or feelers like a bullhead; (Qu. P4) Inf **AK**1, Burbot and lush [lʌš] are names for freshwater ling on Yukon River. **1987** *Theata* 95 **AK** (Tabbert *Dict. Alaskan Engl.*), During the winter we fish for lush and pike. *Ibid* 112, In the spring we have swans, geese, ducks, lush fish, black fish, ptarmigans and a variety of fresh vegetables from the shore.

lusty adj
1 Of a person: large, fat; big with child. [Scots, Engl dial] **chiefly Sth**
1708 *Boston News–Letter* (MA) 15 Nov 4/2, [Advt:] A Lusty Carolina Indian Woman fit for any Dairy Service, to be Sold on Reasonable Terms. [*DARE* Ed: This may instead mean "robust, vigorous."] **1798** in 1956 Eliason *Tarheel Talk* 282 **NC**, I very lusty with my second child. **1839** (1863) Kemble *Jrl. Georgian* 143 **GA**, I came upon a gang of lusty women, as the phrase is here for women in the family-way. **1899** (1912) Green *VA Folk-Speech* 272, *Lusty*. . . Full-bodied; or stout from pregnancy. **1973** *DARE* File swPA, Lusty. . . Large, fat . . Ligonier Valley PA, 1973 and before. **1975** Dwyer *Thangs* 22 **Sth, S Midl**, When the wife became pregnant, she was said to be "lusty." **1984** Wilder *You All Spoken Here* 98 **Sth**, Pregnant; in a family way. . . Lusty.

2 See quot. [*OED* a1240 →; "*Obs.*"]
1930 Shoemaker *1300 Words* 36 **cPA Mts** (as of c1900), Lusty—Beautiful, cheerful, agreeable.

lute n¹, v [Appar by ext from *lute* a tool used to level off brick molds, freshly poured concrete, or asphalt] Cf fresno 2
1975 Gould *ME Lingo* 171, Lute. . . A scoop used with a horse for excavating. It has two handles like a wheelbarrow, and when the handles are held down it digs. It then rides with the dirt flat on the ground, and dumps itself when the handles are lifted. Seems to be a word unique to Maine. It is also a verb: *to lute* a cellar hole. When similar tools became available for attaching to farm tractors, the manufacturers offered them as *scoops*, but Maine farmers continued to call them *lutes*.

Lute n² [Abbr for *Lutheran*, infl by Ger and Scan pronc] Cf cat-licker, DS CC4
1959 Lahey–Hogan *As I Remember It* 131 **swKS** (as of early 20th cent), The Boslers were Lutherans and supposed to be very religious. The Barnes were Catholic and that was a very great bone of contention. On the school ground they would yell, "Catlickers" and the other side would call, "Lutes who follow a crazy Catholic monk who never did know anything."

lutefisk n Also *ludefisk, lukefisk, lutefish, lutfisk* [Norw *lutefisk*; Sw *lutfisk*; Dan *ludfisk*] **chiefly Upper MW, WI, nwIL** See Map
Dried fish (usu cod) that is soaked in lye water in preparation for cooking.

1936 (1947) Mencken *Amer. Lang.* 215, In Minnesota and the adjacent

States many Swedish terms are in common use, *e.g.*, *lutfisk* (a fish delicacy). **1940** Brown *Amer. Cooks* 896 **WI**, Lutfisk Feasts—Lutfisk, or lutefisk, is the Norwegian and Swedish term for "lyed fish" or stockfish . . dried in the open air without being salted, and then soaked in lye water for several days to prepare it for cooking. . . Lutfisk suppers are generally church feasts, a popular form of entertainment among Lutheran communities throughout the state. . . The fish is only part of the feast and after being properly soaked is merely boiled and eaten with oodles of melted butter sluiced over it. **1950** *WELS* (*What other holidays or festivals do you have?* [*Include church suppers, fairs, bazaars, etc.*]) 1 Inf, **swWI**, Lutefisk suppers; 1 Inf, **cwWI**, Fall church lutefisk supper with lefse; 1 Inf, **cwWI**, Lutefisk and lefse dinner; (*Dishes made with fish*) 4 Infs, **WI**, Lutefisk. **1961** Sackett–Koch *KS Folkl.* 196, Swedish Christmas Customs. . . Christmas Day foods were *lutfisk*, lingon berries, rice cooked in milk, fruit soup (made from dried apricots, prunes, and raisins), Rye Krisp. **1965–70** *DARE* (Qu. H45, *Dishes made with meat, fish, or poultry that everybody around here would know, but that people in other places might not*) 23 Infs, **chiefly Upper MW, WI, nwIL**, Lutefisk ['lutəfɪsk, 'ludə-, 'lut-]; **MN**17, 28, Lutefish ['lutəfɪʃ]; **IL**12, 20, ['luk‚fɪsk]; **WI**5, ['lukfɪš]; **WI**60, ['ludəfɪš]; **SD**3, ['lɪutəfɪsk]; (Qu. H65, *Foreign foods favored by people around here*) Infs **IL**40, **MN**28, **ID**5, **IL**30, **NE**3, **WI**72, Lutefisk; **WI**5, 49, ['lutəfɪsk]; **OR**4, Lutefish—dried cod soaked in lye and then cooked; **MA**50, ['lytfɪsk]; **IL**12, Lukefisk—Norwegian fish, chopped and made into balls. **1966** *Stoughton Courier* (WI) 1 Dec sec 2 [12/2], Lutefisk, a dried codfish treated in lye brine and boiled in salted water, is served in great hunks with a melted butter sauce. **1967** *Arlington Times* (WA) 5 Jan 3/8, On Christmas Mr. and Mrs. Oscar Sundberg . . had lutefish dinner at the Agnes Danielson home. **1968** *Hungry Horse News* (Columbia Falls MT) 20 Dec 9/1, A complete selection, will (can) be found at B&B of Ducks, Geese, . . Self Basting Turkeys, . . Cornish Game Hens, Ludefisk, Pickled Fish. **1981** Bly *Letters* 140 **swMN**, The publicity committee had drawings of a thirty-six- to forty-foot-long lutefisk (lye-drenched codfish—a Norwegian *Vestlandets specialitet*), to be about six feet high of aluminum tubing and green-gold cloth stretched about. Five guys, the chairman explained, would walk along inside the lutefisk at parades in Madison and neighboring towns. (This would show the flag a little: Madison, Minnesota, consumes more lutefisk per capita than any city in the world except Bergen.) **1993** *DARE* File **neIL**, My . . grandfather is a Norwegian immigrant; both his parents . . spoke with strong accents. Naturally, *lutefisk* and *lefse* are familiar to us.

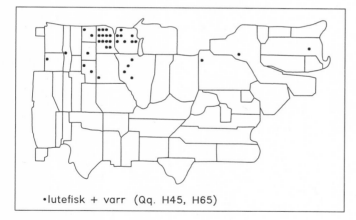

•lutefisk + varr (Qq. H45, H65)

luzerne See **lucerne**

lye corn n Also *lyed corn*
    =**lye hominy.**
    1804 (1904) Lewis *Orig. Jrls. Lewis & Clark Exped.* 1.33 **VA**, The day after tomorrow lyed corn and grece will be issued to the party. **1819** in 1991 Heat Moon *PrairyErth* 563 **ceKS**, Another very acceptable dish was called leyed [Heat Moon: lyed] corn; this is a maize of the preceding season shelled from the cob, and first boiled for a short time in a ley of wood ashes until the hard skin . . is separated from them; the whole is then poured into a basket, which is repeatedly dipped into clean water until the ley and skins are removed; the remainder is then boiled in water until so soft as to be edible. **1826** Biggs *Narrative* 21 **IL** (as of 1788), I had a plenty to eat while I remained with the baker—good light bread, bacon and sandy-hill crains, boiled in leyed corn, which made a very good soup. **1899** Catherwood *Mackinac Stories* 21 **Gt Lakes**, One pint

of lyed corn with from two to four ounces of tallow was the daily allowance of a voyageur. **1986** Pederson *LAGS Concordance* **Gulf Region** (*Coarsely ground corn*) 5 infs, Lye corn; 2 infs, Lye corn—hominy, big hominy; 2 infs, Lye corn—(same as) hominy; 1 inf, Lye corn—fed to hogs and chickens, not for people; 1 inf, Lye corn—whole grain.

lyed hominy See **lye hominy**

lye-gum n [Cf **gum** n[2] 3]
    1923 *DN* 5.233 **swWI**, Ash-gum. . . A piece of a tree, generally of the trunk, hollowed out used to collect ashes for soap. A barrel thus employed is often so called. When water is poured upon the ashes, the receptacle becomes a *lye-gum*.

lye hominy n Also *lyed hominy, lye homily* **chiefly Sth, S Midl** Cf **big hominy, hominy B1, lye corn**
    Whole kernels of corn soaked in lye to remove the hulls before being prepared as food.
    1821 in 1858 Dewees *Letters TX* 20, Our subsistence was principally upon . . a kind of lye hominy seasoned with hickory nut kernels. **1905** *DN* 3.87 **nwAR**, Lye hominy. . . Maize hulled by being boiled in lye. Common. **1909** *DN* 3.347 **eAL, wGA**, Lye-hominy. . . Hulled corn: made by soaking the grains in lye. Also called *big hominy*. **1919** Dunn *Indiana* 2.1170, A woman situated like Mrs. McCoy, in her Indian boarding school, with no food but lye hominy in the house for weeks at a time, "degraded her soul" by cooking lye hominy. **1939** FWP *Guide NC* 298, *Roanoke Island*. . . Roanoke hominy, commonly called big or lye hominy, is still prepared in some rural sections as the Indians made it. **1945** FWP *Lay My Burden Down* 189 **Sth** (as of 1850s) [Black], They know he likes good eats, so they 'ranges for a quilting and gives chitlins and lye hominy. **1950** *PADS* 14.45 **SC**, Lye hominy. . . Hulled corn. Also called *big hominy*. In the trade called *hominy*. **1966** *DARE* (Qu. H25, . . *Names or nicknames . . for fried cornmeal*) Inf **NC**44, Lye hominy—don't fry it, rinse twice, put pinto beans under, put one cup black walnuts, boiling. **1966** *DARE* Tape **NC**36, Call 'em hominy grits. They also have big lye hominy, which is a large . . pearl hominy. **1968** *DARE* FW Addit **GA**33, "Lyed hominy" or "hominy grits"—big grain hominy, made with potash lye (breakfast cereal variety is just called "grits"). **1986** Pederson *LAGS Concordance* **Gulf Region** (*Coarsely ground corn*) 18 infs, Lye hominy; 6 infs, Lye homily [Pederson: =hominy].

lye water n Cf **chamber lye**
    Urine.
    c1938 in 1970 Hyatt *Hoodoo* 1.470 **New Orleans LA**, You take your *lye water*—you see, water that you *urinate* out. . . Take that water and you pour it on your step, rinse your step down—wash it, scrub it off with that and let it drip. . . and that [Hyatt: hoodoo] won't *hurt* you.

lynk See **link** n

lynn See **linn** 1

lynn tree See **linn** 3

lynx n
    1 Std: a large North American cat (*Felis lynx*) distinguished from the common **wildcat** (here: *Felis rufus*) by its usu larger size and black ear tufts. Also called **bar cat** n[2], **Canada lynx, carcajou 2, catamount 1, link** n, **lucivee, mountain cat 1, wildcat**
    2 also *lynx cat*: A **wildcat** (here: *Felis rufus*). Cf **bay lynx**
    1791 Bartram *Travels* 110 **FL**, This cunning fellow hunter, was a large fat wild cat (lynx) he saw me, and at times seemed to watch my motions, as if determined to seize the delicious prey before me. **1817** *Amer. Monthly Mag. & Crit. Rev.* 2.46, *Lynx floridanus* . . Ears beardless, fur greyish, sides varied with yellowish brown spots and black waved streaks. . . lives in Florida, Georgia, and Louisiana. This is the Lynx or Wild cat of Bartram. **1829** Richardson *Fauna Boreali-Amer.* 1.104, Banded Lynx. . . The ears are black on the outer side, covered with fine, short hair, except at the upper point, which is furnished with a pencil of hair, fine, straight, and black, three-fourths of an inch in length. **1937** Grinnell et al. *Fur-Bearing Mammals CA* 605, Pallid Wildcat—*Lynx rufus pallescens* . . Other Names . . Washington Lynx; Pallid Lynx. . . [M]any individuals of the pallid wildcat have been reported as Canada lynx, which is a very distinct species not known to have occurred in California. **1950** *WELS* (*Names for . . wild animals found in your part of the country*) 3 Infs, **WI**, Lynx. **1961** Jackson *Mammals WI* 401, *Lynx rufus superiorensis*. . . Vernacular names . . bay lynx, catamount, lynx

cat . . and red lynx. **1966–70** *DARE* (Qu. P31, . . *Names or nick-names . . for the . . wildcat*) Infs **CA**31, **CT**9, **IA**5, **MA**26, **TX**9, Lynx; **CA**136, 211, **TX**5, 72, Lynx cat; **CA**23, Lynx—large ones; **CA**80, Lynx—has tufted ears; **CA**87, Lynx cat—tufted ears, broader chest, bigger; **CA**120, Lynx cat—a little bigger than a bobcat; **CA**160, Lynx cat—if large; (Qu. P32, . . *Other kinds of wild animals*) Inf **NM**13, Lynx; **NC**30, Bobcat, lynx cat. [*DARE* Ed: Some of these Infs may refer instead to **1** above.] **1982** Elman *Hunter's Field Guide* 333, Bobcat *(Lynx rufus)*—Common & regional names: wildcat, bay lynx, red lynx, pallid lynx, desert lynx.

lyreman n
=cicada.

1889 *Century Dict.* 3555, *Lyreman.* . . A cicada or harvest-fly; a homopterous insect of the family *Cicadidæ,* such as *Cicada tibicen.* **1901** Howard *Insect Book* 232, This is a group of insects [=Cicadidae] commonly known by the popular name of "harvest flies" or cicadas, and frequently in this country by the erroneous term "locust." . . The commonest form in the more Northern States is the so-called "dog-day harvest fly" or "lyreman"—the insect which every summer, toward the end of July or early in August, begins its doleful but resounding buzzing hum in the tree tops. **1905** Kellogg *Amer. Insects* 167, But few species of cicadas, dog-day locusts, harvest-flies, or lyremen, as they are variously called, occur in this country.

lysun See **license 1**

-'m n See **ma'am** n[1]

-m- infix See **-ma-** infix

ma n [*OED* 1823 →]

A Forms. Cf **pa A**

1 |mɑ, ma|; pronc-sp *mah*. Note: The "std" sp *ma* is also included here; in cases where the pronc is neither given nor implied by contrast with the sp *maw,* it is possible that some other pronc was intended. **widespread, but more freq Nth, N Midl** See Map

1852 in 1983 *PADS* 70.41 **ce,sePA,** Pa and Ma went to Charles Thomon on business. **1893** Shands *MS Speech* 44, *Ma* [mɑ] and *maw* [mɔ] are also frequently used for *mother;* the first generally by educated, the second by uneducated, people. **1894** *Century Illustr. Mag.* 48.872, I remember how surprised I was when a boy, visiting in Virginia, to find that "mama" in a letter was pronounced "ma." **1897** (1952) McGill *Narrative* 12 **SC,** He hitches his horse in the . . chimney corner, and feeds him before going into the house to his mah for a cold corn biscuit and a cup of butter milk. **1903** [see **A2** below]. **1961** Kurath–McDavid *Pronc. Engl.* 164, The final syllable in *grandma* has a great variety of vowels. . . /ɑ∼ɑ∼a/ . . is used (1) throughout the North, including Metropolitan New York, and (2) in large parts of the South. . . /ɔ∼ɒ/ . . (1) predominates in the Midland from the Susquehanna Valley westward to Ohio and from there southward to the Carolinas and northern Georgia. . . (2) /ɔ/ occurs also, besides /ɑ/, from Albemarle Sound northward to lower Chesapeake Bay. . . /æ/ . . predominates (1) in the Low Country of South Carolina, (2) on the Eastern Shore of Maryland and in southern New Jersey, and occurs (3) as a minority variant in western Pennsylvania. . . In . . *ma,* the regional dissemination of the variants is nearly the same. . . However, *ma* . . often has the /ʌ/ of *hut* or the /ɜ/ of *her* in the folk speech of the Neuse Valley in North Carolina . . , and scattered instances have been noted elsewhere. **1965–70** *DARE* (Qu. Z2, . . '*Mother*') 138 Infs, **widespread, but more freq Nth, N Midl,** Ma [no transcriptions recorded]; **GA**13, **MI**5, 9, 13, **MA**27, **SC**24, 26, 46, [mɑ]; **LA**37, **ME**5, **NY**69, 75, 83, 88, [mɑ]; **SC**34, 55, 58, [mɑ̃]; (Qu. M21b) Inf **MI**36, Ma and pa; (Qu. Z4) Infs **AL**6, **NY**96, Ma; (Qu. AA20) Inf **MN**15, Tough luck, ma; (Qu. HH22c) Inf **SC**69, Kill his ma; (Qu. KK62) Inf **MD**47, Ma; (Qu. NN12a) Infs **SC**69, **WI**30, Go ask

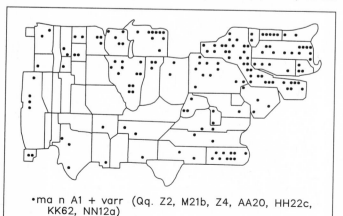

•ma n A1 + varr (Qq. Z2, M21b, Z4, AA20, HH22c, KK62, NN12a)

your ma. **1973** Allen *LAUM* 1.339 **Upper MW** (as of c1950), *Ma* and *maw* are also widespread but less frequent forms [than *mother* and *mama*]. . . *Maw* . . is more favored in Iowa, with a 20% frequency in contrast with only 9% in Minnesota. Both *ma* and *maw* seem now to be old-fashioned, since they are used by 20% and 22% of the Type I speakers [=old, with little educ] respectively, but by only 10% of the Type II speakers [=mid-aged, with approx hs educ]. . . The frequency of *mom* is twice as great on the checklists [as in the field records], and *maw* is much less common.

2 |mɔ, mɒ|; pronc-sp *maw.* **widespread, but less freq NEast** See Map

1857 in 1983 *PADS* 70.41 **ce,sePA,** I got a letter from Maw after school. **1890** *DN* 1.68 **KY,** *Ma* [mɑ], often [mɔ] = mother. **1892** *DN* 1.240 **MO,** *Ma.* The native pronunciation in Kansas City for *ma* (=mother) is [mɔ]. . . [*DN* Ed: So in southern Indiana.] **1893** [see **A1** above]. **1902** *DN* 2.239 **sIL,** *Mommy.* . . grown children . . generally use ma [mɔ]. **1903** *DN* 2.324 **seMO,** *Paw, maw.* . . (In the North *pa; ma.*) **1905** [see **A3** below]. **1906** *DN* 3.121 **sIN,** *Maw.* . . Mother. Latter never used. **1909** *DN* 3.348 **eAL, wGA,** *Maw.* **1942** McAtee *Dial. Grant Co. IN* 42 (as of 1890s), *Maw,* and *grandmaw* . . only pronunciation known. **1961** [see **A1** above]. **1965–70** *DARE* (Qu. Z2) 136 Infs, **widespread, but less freq NEast,** Maw [no transcriptions recorded]; **AL**22, **FL**26, **GA**1, 6, **LA**14, 37, **MS**30, 36, [mɔ]; **MO**5, [mɒ]; **SC**3, [mɑw]; **SC**29, [mɔ̃] [Of all Infs responding to the question, 65% were old; of those giving these responses, 76% were old.]; (Qu. F37) Inf **AR**47, Maw's room; (Qu. N37) Inf **MD**31, Maw and paw; **TX**51, Paw and maw; (Qu. Z4) 8 Infs, **Sth, S Midl,** Maw; (Qu. HH22c) Inf **MS**35, Kill his maw; (Qu. NN12a) Inf **MI**112, Go talk to your maw. **1973** [see **A1** above].

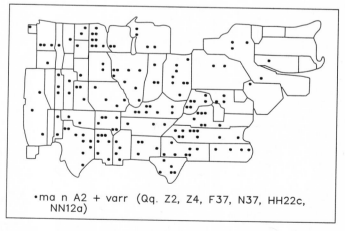

•ma n A2 + varr (Qq. Z2, Z4, F37, N37, HH22c, NN12a)

3 |mæ|. **esp SC, C Atl** See Map on p. 462

1888 *Amer. Jrl. Philol.* 9.205 **Charleston SC,** *Pa, ma,* are pronounced [pæ, mæ]. **1890** *DN* 1.8 **MD,** He also mentioned some Baltimore peculiarities, such as [pæ], [mæ] for *pa, ma.* **1894** *DN* 1.332 **NJ,** [mæ]. **1905** *DN* 3.103 **nwAR,** [pæ, mæ, pɔ, mɔ]. **1930** *DN* 6.82 **cSC,** *Ma* and *pa* [mæ, pæ]. . . Fairly common; once universal. **1955** *PADS* 23.46 **e,cSC, eNC, seGA,** /æ/ in *pa, ma.* **1961** [see **A1** above]. **1965–70** *DARE* (Qu. Z2) 13 Infs, 10 **SC,** [mæ]; **SC**44, [mæǣ].

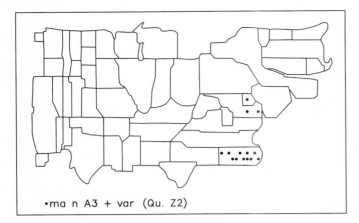

•ma n A3 + var (Qu. Z2)

4 |mʌ, mɜ|; pronc-spp *mu(h)*. **esp NC** Cf **mother dear**
1927 in 1939 Green *Out of South* 280 **NC,** Muh run out and said Pa was gone. **1961** [see **A1** above]. **1967–70** *DARE* (Qu. Z2) Infs **NC**40, 88, **PA**94, [mʌ]; (Qu. Z4) Inf **NC**40, Old |mʌ|. **1992** in 1993 Adero *Up South* 172 **GA** [Black], Sister put the food basket Mu'd prepared snugly under her seat. *Ibid* 173, Just as Mu reached the front door Sister was stepping onto the porch. Feeling like a little girl, she threw her arms round her Mama's neck.

5 pronc-sp *mar*. Cf *marm* (at **ma'am** n[1])
1873 Harte *Mrs. Skaggs* 66 **CA,** Mar sez that everywhere else but yer everybody gives things to everybody Chrismiss.

B Senses.

1 A grandmother. **esp Sth, S Midl** Cf **old mamma**
1965–70 *DARE* (Qu. Z4) Infs **GA**37, 89, **KY**10, 74, **SC**7, **TN**15, **TX**90, **VA**13, Maw; **AL**6, **NY**96, Ma; **NC**40, Old ma. **1989** Pederson *LAGS Tech. Index* 227 **Gulf Region** (*Grandmother*) 22 infs, Ma [*DARE* Ed: as quasi-personal name].

2 Used as a title for a matronly woman or woman of authority; also fig.
1926 *AmSp* 1.659, He [=a lineman] must beware of all "Maw Bell" (telephone) wires. **1926** *NY Times* (NY) 18 July sec 8 10/1 **TX,** [Headline:] "Ma" Ferguson to test her record at polls. **1935** *Ibid* 17 Jan 1/6, Federal agents trailed "Ma" Barker and her son, Fred . . to their Florida hiding place. **1942** Berrey–Van den Bark *Amer. Slang* 184.14, *Nicknames of prominent persons.* . . Ma Ferguson, Miriam A. Ferguson. *Ibid* 808.1, *Telephone.* . . Maw Bell. **1963** Mencken–McDavid *Amer. Lang.* 332, The Hon. Frances Perkins, who became Secretary of Labor in 1933, was often called *Ma* in her early days, but after a while it became a custom in Washington to speak of her, and even to address her, as *Madam.* **1966** *DARE* Tape **MI**10, His devoted wife, Ellen, . . came to be known to a small army of lumberjacks as Ma Culhane. **1976** Horn *World Encycl. Comics* 291, He [=Harold Gray] added a long-lived Sunday gag strip *Maw Green* on January 1, 1933. **1978** *Capital Times* (Madison WI) 14 July 3/1, So many people have complained, in fact, that Ma Bell has decided to scrap its method of handling PhoneCenter customer complaints in favor of a streamlined process, the phone company spokesman said. **1983** Von Auw *Heritage & Destiny* 360, Where and when the term "Ma Bell" arose is obscure. Some people say the term arose in the 1930s when in the depths of the Depression AT&T kept on paying its famous $9 dividend. Others say Ma Bell reflects the character of the old-time chief operator who always took care of "her girls."

-ma- infix Also *-m-, -me(r)-, -mie-, -muh-,* and, appar by folk-etym, *-my-* [Cf *SND* *ma-* "An intermediate syllable appearing freq. in Sc. compound words, usu. of obscure, imit., or ludicrous origin. It is apparently for rhythmic effect only."]
Used for rhythmic effect to expand existing words or phrr, or as an element in "nonsense" words, often with jocular, ironic, or derisive force.
1856 in 1962 Nathan *Dan Emmett* 68, In *O Hush!* he becomes "Sambo Johnson," a "consumquelcial darkey" who has made money in the lottery and therefore, so he figures, has acquired "edgemcation". **1871** (1892) Johnston *Dukesborough Tales* 188 **GA,** "Philadelphia, Henry!" said Mely . . ; "not Philamadelphy." **1898** Lloyd *Country Life* 104 **AL,** They ain't runnin off after any newfangled notions or third party Jack-o-mer-lanterns. *Ibid* 139, It so happened by some hook or mercrook. [**1922**

(1926) Cady *Rhymes VT* 152, The supremetendent, Dr. Small,/ Slipped in each term and that was all.] **1923** Parsons *Folk-lore Sea Islands* 76 **csSC** [Black], De mawsah [=master] go to Philamadelphia. **1931** (1991) Hughes–Hurston *Mule Bone* 139 **cFL** [Black], [Song lyrics:] You may leave an' go to Halimuhfacks, but my slow drag will bring you back. **1931** *AmSp* 6.258, Doomiejig, doomawadja, doomiewadjie . . fumadiddle . . rigamajig . . thingumajig . . thingumajigger [etc]. **1940** *AmSp* 15.221 **wTX,** He is pretty obviously 'snoozemarooed' (drunk). **1941** *AmSp* 16.307, *Kissamaroo* ('the old Ohio kissamaroo,' MGM film 'Third Finger Left Hand'). **1942** Berrey–Van den Bark *Amer. Slang* 75.4, Domajigger . . flumadiddly, fumadiddle . . gigamaree . . hootmalalie . . jigamaree . . jigmarig . . rigamajig . . thingmajigger . . thingumabob . . thingamadad . . thingamaree . . thingumagadget. **1950** *WELS,* 1 Inf, **cnWI,** Cigamagar, cigamarute. **1960** Wentworth–Flexner *Slang* 641, *Infixes.* . . Elomacution, flipmagilder—a "chiseler," hickeymadoodle—a thingamajig, ouchimagoocha . . , photomagenic, psycholomagee, razzamatazz, razzmatazz, snoozemarooed . . , stratemagee, thingamadoger, thingamadudgeon, thingamajig, thingamananny, thingumabob, thingumadoodle. **1966–69** *DARE* (Qu. NN12b) 147 Infs, **widespread,** Thingamajig; **IA**11, Fiddle-ma-dab; **MA**37, Jack-ma-diddly-fidmy-yol, Jack-ma-jiggly-figmy-yol; **NY**69, Thingamawhatses; **PA**227, Whoseamajigger; **CA**105, Fillamajig; (Qu. R1) Inf **AR**5, Jack-o-my-lantern; (Qu. W38) Inf **PA**93, Dressed up like a Philamadelphia lawyer; (Qu. CC16) Inf **GA**5, Jack-a-ma-lantern; **MS**1, Jack-o-my-lantern; (Qu. JJ12) Inf **IN**8, Whirlimacues. **1967** Williams *Greenbones* 52 **GA** (as of c1910), My jacky-my-lanterns lived in swamps.

ma'am n[1] Usu |mæm, mam|; also |mɑrm, mʌm|; in comb with *yes, no* |-(ə)m| Pronc-spp *ma(r)m, mom, mum, -'m, -'n, -um;* for addit pronc and sp varr see **A** below [Pronc-spp for *madam; OED* 1668 →]

A Forms.
1836 [see **B2** below]. **1838** [see **B1** below]. **1845** Judd *Margaret* 52 **NEng,** No, Marm, they drink pupelo and rum. **1885** [see **B1** below]. **1887** [see **B1** below]. **1887** (1967) Harris *Free Joe* 184 **ceGA,** " 'Twuz a gal." "A gal!" exclaimed Mrs. Stucky. "Yes'n, a gal." **1891** *DN* 1.122 **cNY,** [mæ·m] ([mæm]) < *madame.* **1893** Shands *MS Speech* 44, Marm [mɑrm]. Illiterate white for *madam;* as, "Yes, marm, I think so, marm." **1899** (1912) Green *VA Folk-Speech* 275, *Marm.* . . A form of *ma'am, madam;* "yes'm;" "no'm." In answer to a call: as, "John!" "Marm." **1904** *DN* 2.419 **nwAR,** Ma'am [mæm]. . . Madam. 'Yes, ma'am, I am a graduate of the university.' **1913** *DN* 4.1 **cME,** Yessum. . . Yes, ma'am. **1934** Hurston *Jonah's Gourd Vine* 10 **AL** [Black], From way down in the cotton patch, "Yassum! Us comin'!" **1936** *AmSp* 11.166 **eTX,** For *yes ma'am, well ma'am* ['jæsəm], ['wɛləm] are common among almost all speakers. **1940** in 1944 *ADD* 373 **WV,** |mam|. 'Yes, mom' = ma'am. Repeatedly on phone. **1941** *LANE* Map 444 (*School teacher*), [*Schoolma'am* is offered by most infs; the vast majority of them offer proncs of the type [-mam, -mæm]. 19 infs, **scattered,** offered proncs of the type [-mæm]; 8 infs, **wNEng,** proncs of the type [-mɑrm] or rarely [-mærm, -mɜrm]; 2 infs, **Nantucket MA,** proncs of the type [-mʌm]; and 2 infs, proncs of the type [-mɒm].] **1943** *LANE* Map 588, [In the context *yes ma'am,* proncs of the type [mæm] are somewhat more common than those of the type [mɑm, mam]; there are two instances of the type [mʌm]. Abbreviated forms of the type [-m] are also common.] **1960** (1966) Percy *Moviegoer* 53 **New Orleans LA,** "What is it you want out of life, son?" she asks with a sweetness that makes me uneasy. "I don't know'm." **1965–70** *DARE* (Qu. JJ1a, . . *A schoolteacher—a woman*) 474 Infs, **widespread,** Schoolmarm; 220 Infs, **widespread,** Schoolmam; 18 Infs, **scattered,** Schoolmom; 6 Infs, Schoolmum; 5 Infs, Schoolma'am [Of the 84 proncs recorded, 54 were of the type [-mam], 15 [-mæm], 10 [-mɑrm], 4 [-mʌm], and 1 [-mɛrm]; judging from this sporadic sample, the sp varr usu represents [-mam] or [-mɑrm], and *-mam* represents [-mɑm] or, less freq, [-mæm].]; (Qu. N30, . . *A sudden short dip in a road*) 99 Infs, **chiefly NEast,** Thank-you-ma'am; 18 Infs, **chiefly NEast exc NYC, NJ,** Thank-you-mom(s); **CT**13, **MA**30, **NY**1, **TN**11, Thank-you-marm(s); **IL**32, **NY**75, 205, 214, Thank-you-mum(s). **1995** *DARE* File **csWI,** My father, who grew up in southeastern Iowa, invariably refers to a petite family friend who teaches at a local elementary school as "the little schoolmom."

B Senses. Cf **mom** n[1] 1

1 Used as a term of address for a woman. Note: While this use was formerly common throughout the US, it now appears to occur more often and in a wider range of contexts in the **Sth and S Midl.**
1838 (1852) Gilman *S. Matron* 51 **CT,** I am well, as also are, sir and

mar'm, my sister Nancy, and all the rest of our folks. **1843** (1916) Hall *New Purchase* 54 **IN,** Most time, mam, you'll have to work your own ash-hopper. **1873** *Atlantic Mth.* 32.416 **ceOH,** Thankee, marm. It's so long since I've had on anything but that old bag. **1885** Twain *Huck. Finn* 280 **MO,** Don't say yes'm—say Aunt Sally. *Ibid* 288, I'm surprised at you, m'am. **1887** (1956) Kirkland *Zury* 143 **cIL,** Ye must excuse her₍₅₎ mom: she ain't got no manners. **1899** [see **A** above]. **1903** Murrie *White Castle LA* 166 (as of c1865) [Black], I'd rutheh go to school to you, please marm. **1938** Daniels *Southerner* 335, One of the best indices of the Southern region . . [is] a line on one side of which all nice children say, "No, ma'am" and "Yes, ma'am," to the teacher and on the other side of which they get laughed at for saying it by all including teacher. Such a line, I understand, no longer exists. **1940** [see **A** above]. **1943** *LANE* Map 588, The phrases *yes sir* and *yes ma'am* are widely felt as old-fashioned. Many of our informants never use them under any circumstances . . ; others offer one phrase or the other, or both, but characterize them as rare. . . Several state that they used these phrases commonly in their younger days, but now use them only rarely . . or only in jest . . or not at all. . . Many were taught as children to say *yes sir* or *yes ma'am* or both in addressing their elders, but now use only *yes.* . . Some report that these phrases are nowadays used only by children. . . On the other hand, most of our informants still use *yes sir* and *yes ma'am* as polite forms, to show respect for the person addressed or in somewhat formal conversation. **c1960** *Wilson Coll.* **csKY,** Ma'am? is also used as a question, asking over. **1965–70** *DARE* (Qu. X18, . . *When one person doesn't quite hear what another person said, what does he say?*) Infs **AL24, GA59, MD19, 21, 49,** Ma'am; **VA35,** Repeat that please, ma'am; (Qu. II39, . . *'Thank you'*) Inf **MO32,** Thank you, ma'am; (Qu. KK55c, . . *Expressions of strong denial*) Inf **NC23,** No, ma'am; (Qu. NN1, . . *Words like 'yes': "Are you coming along too?"*) Infs **KY40, 85,** Yes, ma'am; **LA15,** Yes'm; yes, ma'am; (Qu. NN2, *Exclamations of very strong agreement*) Inf **TN39,** Yes, ma'am; (Qu. NN4, . . *Ways of answering 'no'*) Infs **FL28, MN28, NY83, NC79,** No, ma'am; (Qu. NN10b, *Greetings used when you meet somebody you do not know well*) Inf **SC45,** How are you, ma'am? **MA58,** How do you do, ma'am? **1968** *DARE* FW Addit **MD,** *Ma'am* is a general term of address for women; it is entirely polite and does not carry the connotations of excessive politeness and/or impatience that it does further north (i.e., New York). **1976** Garber *Mountain-ese* 56 **sAppalachians,** You allers say yes ma'am to yer teacher, Junior.

2 Used as a title of respect or deference.

1836 (1838) Haliburton *Clockmaker* (1st ser) 69 **NEng,** Marm Pugwash is as onsartin in her temper as a mornin in April. **1887** Freeman *Humble Romance* 107 **NEng,** Marm Lawson was not a duchess; but she was Marm Lawson. The "Marm" itself was a title. In a more ambitious and cultured town than this it would have been Madam; but the Marm proved just as well her simple neighbors' recognition of her latent dignity of character. **1899** Garland *Prairie Folks* 100 **IA,** "Why, they ain't a harder-workin' woman in the hull State of Ioway than she is—" "Except Marm Councill." **1903** Wasson *Cap'n Simeon's Store* 208 **eME,** Ole marm Grommet she tended out on Joe Ez for a consid'ble spell.

3 A woman schoolteacher, "schoolmarm"; in phr *ma'am school* a dame school.

1857 Goodrich *Recollections* 1.39 **CT,** I found a girl . . keeping a ma'am school for about twenty scholars. **1889** (1971) Farmer *Americanisms* 354, *Marm school.*—Formerly, what in England and also in Connecticut, was known as a "dame school." **1940** Mencken *Happy Days* 14, I encountered a ma'm in horn-rimmed spectacles teaching a gang of little girls ring-around-a-rosy. . . In the days of my own youth no bossy female on the public payroll was needed to teach games to little girls. **1942** *Time* 12 Jan 37, Matthay-trained teachers are still a distinct minority among the 100,000 piano-marms of the U.S. *Ibid,* [Photo caption:] Many a marm might be alarmed. **1942** Berrey–Van den Bark *Amer. Slang* 826.1, Ma'am . . *a woman teacher.* **1965–70** *DARE* (Qu. JJ1a, . . *A schoolteacher—a woman*) 12 Infs, **scattered,** Marm; **AR52,** [maəm]—more formal, more common in [Inf's] speech; [ma:rm] occasionally; **CA105,** [mæmz]; schoolmam—townspeople; schoolmarm—woods people. **1986** Pederson *LAGS Concordance (Woman teacher)* [1 inf, **cnAL,** Used to call her ma'am;] 1 inf, **neTX,** A ma'am—old term.

ma'am n² See **mom** n¹

ma'ar See **marrow**

maash See **marsh**

mab See **marb** n

macadam n Also *MacAddam, McAdam* [*OED* 1826 →; from J.L. *McAdam* (1756–1836), Scottish engineer]
1 Orig a road pavement made of layers of packed crushed rock, sometimes strengthened by applying a bituminous binder; now usu blacktop or a similar paving material; also fig. **widespread, but chiefly NEast, Mid Atl, N Cent** See Map

1837 Jenkins *OH Gaz.* 117, Cincinnati, Newport and Covington having attained their present population, commerce and manufactures, without the aid of any internal improvement, but that of the Miami canal, and two Macadam turnpikes. **1838** Kettell *Yankee Notions* 152, For I shall grippe you faste untille / You reach that house near Bunker's Hille,/ Where you shall pound MacAddam. **1839** IN House of Repr. *Jrl.* 216, Mr. Dumont offered the following amendment: "And that the State Board of Internal Improvement be instructed to re-locate that portion of the said road . . *Provided,* in their opinion, a good McAdam can be made on said route." **1879** Taylor *Summer-Savory* 160 **cNY,** The streams . . run along their rough McAdams. **1897** *Outing* 30.135, The width of the macadam is eighteen feet, while the crushed rock is ten inches deep. **1961** Hall *String Too Short* 9 **sNH,** We jumped across a ditch at the wood's edge onto the macadam. **1965–70** *DARE* (Qu. N21, *Roads that are surfaced with smooth black pavement*) 173 Infs, **widespread, but chiefly NEast, Mid Atl, N Cent,** Macadam; **NY68,** Macadam road; **MD36,** Macadam top; **CT17,** Water-bound macadam; **CA147,** Asphalt macadam; (Qu. N23, *Other kinds of paved roads*) 43 Infs, **esp Nth, eN Midl,** Macadam; **MA5,** Macadam road; **RI17,** Water-bound macadam; (Qu. N27a, *Names . . for different kinds of unpaved roads*) Infs **CO7, IN17, IA19, MO12, NC36, OH58, OR13, PA82,** Macadam road. **1971** *Today Show Letters* **cNY,** The black covering on roads in the east is called macadam. **1986** Pederson *LAGS Concordance (Designations of roads)* 22 infs, **Gulf Region,** Macadam(s); 3 infs, Macadam road(s).

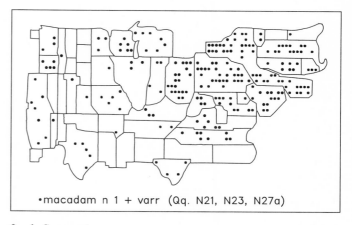

•macadam n 1 + varr (Qq. N21, N23, N27a)

2 pl: See quot.
1906 *DN* 3.145 **nwAR,** Macadams. . . Small, broken stones used to form a smooth, hard, convex surface on a road. "Resolved, that the Commercial League recommend to the City Council that they furnish crushed rock or macadams free of charge, etc."—Fayetteville Daily.

macadam v, hence ppl adj *macadamed*
=**macadamize.**
1906 *DN* 3.145 **nwAR,** Macadam. . . To macadamize. "The property owners are going to macadam Washington Avenue." **1967** *DARE* (Qu. N27a, *Names . . for different kinds of unpaved roads*) Inf **CA15,** Macadamed road.

macadamize v, hence vbl n *macadamizing,* ppl adj *macadamized* (pronc-sp *macadamize,* aphet forms *acadami(z)ed, cadamized*) Also sp *macadamise, McAdamize*
To surface (a road) with **macadam** n **1.**
1825 *Boston Auditor* 10 (DAE), Stones for McAdamizing. **1830** *Western Mth. Rev.* 3.481, What we now achieve, in the way of road making, is well done, and McAdamized, the only kind of road, that will stand in our deep loamy soils. **1854** (1932) Bell *Log TX-CA Trail* 35.220, A heap of stones . . seemed to have been broken for macadamising purposes. **1890** Jefferson *Autobiog.* 24, These smooth hair trunks . . would have made slippery seats even on a macadamized road. **1965–70** *DARE* (Qu. N21, *Roads that are surfaced with smooth black pavement*) 11 Infs, **Nth, CA,** Macadamized; **NY45,** Cadamized; **TX26,** Acadamied

[ə'kædɪ,maɪd]; (Qu. N23, *Other kinds of paved roads*) Infs **IL104,** **PA104, SC31, SD1, VA33,** Macadamized; **IL46,** Macadamized road; **MA76,** Acadamized [ə'kædə,maɪzd]—not paved; (Qu. N27a, *Names . . for different kinds of unpaved roads*) Inf **OR3,** Macadamized road. **1967** *DARE* Tape **IL7,** Before we started using the cement slab and the [ə'kædəmaɪzd] road. **1986** Pederson *LAGS Concordance (Designations of roads)* 10 infs, **Gulf Region,** Macadamized (road); 2 infs, Macadam-ize road.

macadamy n Also aphet *cadamy* Cf **macadamize**
=macadam n 1.
 1968 *DARE* (Qu. N21, *Roads that are surfaced with smooth black pavement*) Inf **NY70,** Macadamy; **MD43,** Cadamy.

MacAddam See **macadam** n

macaltha worm n [Var of **catalpa**]
=catalpa B2.
 1966 *Wilson Coll.* **csKY,** Macaltha [mə'kælθə] worm.

macardy See **mecate**

macaroni n [From the shape]
1 Among loggers: see quot 1958.
 1938 (1939) Holbrook *Holy Mackinaw* 262, Macaroni. Sawdust. **1942** *AmSp* 17.223 **Nth,** Macaroni. Sawdust. **1956** Sorden–Ebert *Logger's Words* 23 **Gt Lakes. 1958** McCulloch *Woods Words* 115 **Pacific NW,** *Macaroni*—Long curls of sawdust cut by a well-filed crosscut saw.
2 Among fishermen: see quot.
 1930 *AmSp* 5.391 [Language of N Atl fishermen], *Macaroni.* . . Clay bottom which collects in the nets in peculiar tube-like formations.

macaroni seed n
A nonexistent item used as the basis of a practical joke.
 1966 *DARE* (Qu. HH14, *Ways of teasing a beginner or inexperienced person—for example, by sending him for a 'left-handed monkey wrench':* "Go get me _____.") Inf **GA12,** Macaroni seed.

macaroni-smacker n *derog* Cf **mackerel-snapper**
 1969 *DARE* (Qu. HH28, *Names and nicknames . . for people of foreign background: Italian*) Inf **PA227,** Macaroni-smacker.

macarte See **mecate**

macaw plant n
A **rattlebox** (here: *Sesbania punicea*).
 1955 *S. Folkl. Qrly.* 19.235 **FL,** The blossom . . of the *Macaw Plant* (*Daubentonia punicea*) is colored like the macaw—orange, scarlet, rose, and crimson against a dark green foliage.

macheer n Also sp *machere, mecheer* [Var of **mochila**] **West** *old-fash*
 1847 *Calif. Star* (S.F.) 21 Aug. 2/3 *(DA),* [A] man declares his *macheres* (saddle cover) was stolen from under him, although seated upon his horse and his horse in motion. **1853** in 1930 Brewerton *Overland* 49 **SW,** Our saddles were of the true Mexican pattern, wooden trees covered with leathers called *macheers.* **1857** in 1941 *AmSp* 16.262 **CA,** The *mochilas* (vulgarly called 'mecheers') are a pair of leather flaps, each about two feet wide by three feet long, which are tied together and used as a cover for the saddle-tree in riding. **1873** Miller *Modocs* 50 **nCA,** The Prince unfastened his cloak from the macheers behind my saddle. **1927** (1944) Russell *Trails Plowed Under* 166 **MT,** I've seen bronc riders use an old macheer saddle with a Texas tree.

machete n [Appar from the body shape]
1 A cutlass fish (here: *Trichiurus lepturus*).
 1902 Jordan–Evermann *Amer. Fishes* 290, *Trichiurus lepturus,* known as the cutlass-fish, . . silver-fish, machete, . . a long, slender, ribbon-like fish[₂] . . is taken occasionally in the lower Chesapeake and along the South Atlantic coast. . . Though not abundant enough to be of commer-cial importance, it is nevertheless an excellent food fish. **1933** LA Dept. of Conserv. *Fishes* 162, (*Trichiurus lepturus*) also called . . Machete, is, at least in some localities, the principal food of the Tarpon.
2 A **ten-pounder** (here: *Elops affinis*).
 1960 Amer. Fisheries Soc. *List Fishes* 10, Machete . . *Elops affinis.* **1973** Knight *Cook's Fish Guide* 384, Machete . . p[oor]. **1983** *Audubon Field Guide N. Amer. Fishes* 372, *Machete.* . . These smaller relatives of the Tarpon are excellent fighters but are not considered edible because of their oily flesh.

machilla See **mochila**

machine shed n Also *machinery shed;* for addit varr see quots **widespread, but esp freq Plains States, Upper Missip Valley** See Map Cf **wagon shed**
An outbuilding where farm equipment is stored.
 1925 *Book of Rural Life* 9.5032, Machine sheds are often fitted with large sliding doors on each side so that any piece of machinery can be easily removed. **1965–70** *DARE* (Qu. M22, . . *Kinds of buildings . . on farms*) 151 Infs, **widespread, but esp freq Plains States, Upper Missip Valley,** Machine shed; 27 Infs, **scattered Inland Nth, N Midl,** Machin-ery shed; **NY105, NC47,** Machine shelter; **MN28, OH41, TX8,** Ma-chinery barn; **NC85, OH61,** Machinery house; (Qu. M1, . . *Kinds of barns . . according to their use or the way they are built*) Infs **CO38, DE5, IL77, IN42, MD38, NJ10, TN36,** Machine shed; **CA16, IL83,** 85, **IA39, KS7, MD38,** Machine barn; **FL27, MI56, NY123,** Machinery barn; **FL12, TX8,** Machinery shed. **1991** *DARE* File (as of c1960), My cousins in southern Idaho kept their tractors and other farm machinery in what they called the machine shed.

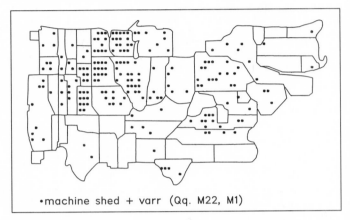
•machine shed + varr (Qq. M22, M1)

macht nichts phr For varr see quots [Ger] **chiefly Nth**
It doesn't make any difference to me; I don't care.
 1934 Stone *Studien* 83, I have not seen *es macht nichts aus* in any book on Americanisms, but I have heard it quite as often as the others here mentioned. **1956** *AmSp* 31.142, Mox nix (an Americanization of *'s macht nichts*) means 'I don't care' or 'it doesn't matter.' The expression's terse form and end alliteration make it an active tool in the hands of the GI, who has produced numerous variations of the phrase, including *mox f—g nix, mox nix stick* (a signaling device on cars), *Tom Mix,* and *mox nix to old ich* ('makes no difference to me,' showing *ich*—pronounced *ik*—used as an object by the poetic, if grammatically unresponsive Americans). **1966–69** *DARE* (Qu. KK26, *Something that makes no difference at all to you:* "He can think what he likes, it _____ me.") Inf **CT37,** [mɑks nɑt]—old-fashioned; my mother used to live in Ger-mantown, PA; **DC3,** [mɑks nɪš aus]—sometimes, German expression; **IL35, MI68,** Es macht (mir) nicht aus; **NY194,** Es machts mir nichts aus; **OR3,** [mɑks nɪks aus tə'mi]; **OR15,** [mɑks nɪks aus]; **PA46,** Machs nix—makes nothing; **WI34,** It's [mɑks nɪks].

mack See **make** v[1]

mackerel n
1 Std: any of var fishes of the family Scombridae, but esp of the genus *Scomber,* and in particular the common *S. scombrus.* Cf **bonito 1, tuna** For other names of var spp of *Scomber* see **chub mackerel, Pacific ~;** for other names of *S. scombrus* see **blink** n[2], **Boston mackerel 1, spike, spring mackerel, tinker ~** Note: For other fish names with *mackerel* as an element, see **fall mackerel, frigate ~, horse ~, jack ~, king ~, Monterey Spanish ~, painted ~, ship ~, skip ~, snap-ping ~, snake ~, Spanish ~, thimble-eye ~, yellow ~**
2 A **greenling** (here: *Pleurogrammus monopterygius*). **AK**
 1886 Turner *Contribs. AK* 96, *Pleurogrammus monopterygius.* . . When I arrived at Unalaska in 1878 I heard much talk about the "Mackerel." During the summer of that year I had an opportunity of conversing with those who frequented the western islands of the Chain where these fish were said to abound. Several persons referred to these fish as . . "Horse Mackerel" and "Alaskan Mackerel." **1939** *AK Sports-man* July 22 (Tabbert *Dict. Alaskan Engl.*), And last, but by no means least, is the possibility of developing a use for the millions upon millions

of Attu mackerel and codfish that are so plentiful throughout western island waters in the summers. The locally-named mackerel are a somewhat different-looking fish than the North Atlantic species.

3 =**bluefish 1.**

1903 NY State Museum & Sci. Serv. *Bulletin* 60.446, Some of the many names applied to this widely distributed fish are the following: mackerel (New Jersey) [etc]. . . Bluefish is the name most extensively used on the coast and in the Gulf of Mexico. **1905** NJ State Museum *Annual Rept. for 1904* 265, *Pomatomus saltatrix*. . . Blue Fish. Mackerel. . . A large fish, reaching 3 feet in length, and extremely destructive to other fishes.

4 =**walleye pollack.**

1946 Dufresne *AK's Animals* 284, Alaska Pollack *(Theragra chalcogrammus)*. . . Its lack of sporting qualities are not at all improved by calling it a "mackerel" as is sometimes the habit around Juneau.

5 See **mackerel sky.**

mackerel bird See **mackerel goose**

mackerel cloud See **mackerel sky**

mackerel-eater, mackerel-gobbler See **mackerel-snapper**

mackerel goose n Also *mackerel bird* [See quot 1951]

A **phalarope**: either *Phalaropus fulicarius* or *P. lobatus*.

1917 (1923) *Birds Amer.* 1.218, *Northern Phalarope. . . Other Names. . . Mackerel Goose.* **1923** U.S. Dept. Ag. *Misc. Circular* 13.47 **NEng,** The red phalarope and the northern phalarope. . . share a number of names. . . *Vernacular names. . .* Mackerel-geese. **1951** Pough *Audubon Water Bird* 255, Fishermen call phalaropes "whale" or "mackerel" birds and watch to see where flocks settle, believing that they depend upon feeding schools of crustacea-eating whales, mackerel, or other fish to help them locate abundant supplies of the small reddish copepods, commonly known as brit, that are one of the phalarope's chief foods at sea. **1955** Forbush–May *Birds* 210, *Red Phalarope. . . Other Names* . . Mackerel-goose.

mackerel gull n

1 =**laughing gull.** [See quot 1956]

1792 Belknap *Hist. NH* 3.169, Mackerel Gull, *Larus ridibundus.* **1832** Williamson *Hist. ME* 1.145, The *mackerel*, or *fishing Gull* [Footnote: Larus Ridibundus] . . is nearly as large as a goose. **1956** MA Audubon Soc. *Bulletin* 40.22 **ME, MA,** Laughing Gull. . . Mackerel Gull (. . From being seen at the time of the mackerel fishery.)

2 =**tern.** [See quot 1955] **chiefly NEng**

1844 DeKay *Zool. NY* 2.299, *Sterna hirundo*. . . In Massachusetts it is called Mackerel Gull, from its simultaneous appearance with that fish. **1852** in 1876 *Forest & Stream* 7.212 **eMA,** *Sterna.* All varieties. Mackerel gulls. **1917** *Wilson Bulletin* 29.2.75 **seMA,** All terns. . . Mackerel gulls. *Ibid* 29.2.76 **ME,** *Sterna hirundo.* . . Mackerel or medric gull. **1955** Forbush–May *Birds* 229, *Sterna hirundo hirundo.* . . Mackerel Gull. . . When mackerel or bluefish, coming in great hordes, find a school of 'bait,' the larger fish chase the little ones until the latter, in their efforts to escape, break water in all directions. . . The sharp-eyed terns . . flock from afar to feast on the luckless 'fishlings.' . . The birds had given the signal to the fishermen to come out from shore. **1956** MA Audubon Soc. *Bulletin* 40.22 **MA, RI,** Roseate Tern. . . Mackerel Gull. *Ibid* 40.22 **ME, MA, NH, RI,** Common Tern. . . Mackerel Gull. . . From association with schools of mackerel. *Ibid* 40.22 **ME, MA,** Arctic Tern. . . Mackerel Gull. **1966** DARE (Qu. Q7, *Names and nicknames for . . game birds*) Inf **ME**22, Mackerel gull.

3 =The black-legged **kittiwake** *(Rissa tridactyla).*

1956 MA Audubon Soc. *Bulletin* 40.22 **MA,** Common Kittiwake. . . Mackerel Gull.

mackerel hawk n Cf **mackerel gull 2**

Appar a **tern.**

1947 Coffin *Yankee Coast* 298 **ME,** The mackerel . . come in August with the mackerel-hawks, marked with the same markings and moulded into the same projectile-like bodies, crying and screaming over the fish.

mackerel scad n

A fish of the genus *Decapterus.* For other names of var spp see **opelu, round robin**

1873 in 1878 Smithsonian Inst. *Misc. Coll.* 14.2.25, *Decapterus macarellus.* . . Mackerel scad. Cape Cod to Florida. **1882** U.S. Natl. Museum *Bulletin* 16.432, *Decapterus.* . . Mackerel Scads. **1897** NY Forest Fish & Game Comm. *Annual Rept. for 1896* 238, Decapterus macarelius

[sic], . . Mackerel Scad, . . was found common at Southampton, Long Island. **1902** Jordan–Evermann *Amer. Fishes* 302, The genus *Decapterus* contains the mackerel scads. . . The common mackerel scad, *D. macarellus*, . . is found in the warmer parts of the Atlantic. It strays northward on our coast to Cape Cod. **1960** Amer. Fisheries Soc. *List Fishes* 29, Mackerel scad . . *Decapterus macarellus.*

mackerel scale See **mackerel sky**

mackerel shark n

1 A shark of the family Lamnidae, usu of the genera *Isurus* or *Lamna.* [See quot 1839] For other names of *Lamna* spp see **salmon shark**

1819 *Plough Boy* 1.135 **eMA,** The revenue cutter brought in two very strange fish, found eating a dead horse, supposed to be *mackerel sharks.* **1839** MA Zool. & Bot. Surv. *Fishes Reptiles* 185, *L[amna] punctata.* . . As this species is generally seen following shoals of mackerel upon which it feeds, it is commonly known among the fishermen as the *Mackerel Shark.* **1884** Goode *Fisheries U.S.* 1.670, The Mackerel Shark—*Lamna cornubica.* . . They are very abundant on the coast of Massachusetts in the mackerel season, and are a great annoyance to the fishermen who use nets. **1903** NY State Museum & Sci. Serv. *Bulletin* 60.38, The mackerel shark reaches the length of 10 feet. It occurs from Cape Cod to the West Indies; but is rarely captured in most localities. **1953** Roedel *Common Fishes CA* 109, *Lamna ditropis.* . . Coastal north Pacific from Alaska south to Southern California. . . Mackerel shark. **1969** DARE (Qu. P4, *Saltwater fish that are not good to eat*) Inf **MA**55, Mackerel shark. **1975** Evanoff *Catch More Fish* 213, *Isurus oxyrhynchus* . . [and] *Isurus glaucus* . . are also called mackerel sharks.

2 The blacktip shark *(Carcharhinus limbatus).*

1939 Natl. Geogr. Soc. *Fishes* 163 **sFL,** The black-tip shark *(Carcharhinus limbatus)* is a small species of ground shark. . . They are frequently hooked by tarpon fishermen, who erroneously call them "mackerel shark," and put up a spirited fight.

mackerel sky n [*OED* 1669 →; from its resemblance to the mottled markings of the **mackerel 1**] **scattered, but chiefly NEast** See Map Cf **fish scale**

A sky filled with rows of high-altitude clouds (esp cirrocumulus clouds); hence nouns *mackerel (cloud), mackerel scale* one of these clouds.

1903 *DN* 2.294 **Cape Cod MA** (as of a1857), *Mackerel sky.* . . A sky covered with fleecy cirrus clouds. 'Mackerel sky and mares' tails / Make lofty ships carry low sails.' **1909** *DN* 3.347 **eAL, wGA,** *Mackerel sky.* . . A sky characterized by numerous small white cumulous [sic] cloud formations somewhat resembling mackerel. **1933** Cannell *Signs* 11 **NE,** Mackerel sky, mackerel sky,/ Never leaves the ground dry. *Ibid,* Mackerel sky, mackerel sky,/ Never long wet, never long dry. **1933** Cheley *Camping Out* 184 *(DA),* 'Mackerel scales,' which are *cirro-stratus clouds,* also indicate rain. **1945** Colcord *Sea Language* 124 **ME, Cape Cod, Long Island,** *Mackerel sky.* Mottled cirrus clouds foretelling a change of weather. **1958** *DE Folkl. Bulletin* 1.32, Mackerel sky, two days wet and one day dry. **1965–70** DARE (Qu. B11, . . *Other kinds of clouds that come often)* 108 Infs, **chiefly NEast,** Mackerel sky; **FL**15, **MA**58, **NY**194, 218, 230, **OH**36, Mackerel (clouds); **NY**95, Mackerels [Of all Infs responding to the question, 72% were old; of those giving these responses, 82% were old.]; (Qu. B10, . . *Long trailing clouds high in the sky)* 10 Infs, **chiefly NEast,** Mackerel sky; **NE**9, **NY**218, Mackerel clouds; **MO**39, **NC**81, Mackerel scales; (Qu. B8, *When clouds come*

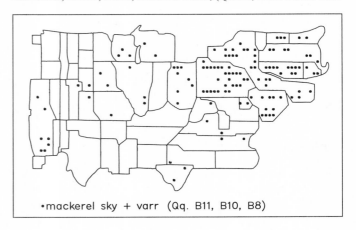

•mackerel sky + varr (Qq. B11, B10, B8)

*and go all day . . it's _____) Inf **CO**2, Mackerel sky. **1975** Gould *ME Lingo* 173, *Mackerel sky. . .* The mottled pattern . . suggests the back markings of a mackerel. . . "Mares'-tails and mackerel sky, never twenty-four hours dry." **1991** *DARE* File **seNY,** Mackerel sky = cloud formation peculiar to the area: lines of small cumulus clouds resembling the rows of bumpy backs in a school of mackerel. Sign of good weather coming.

mackerel-snapper n Also *mackerel-eater, ~-gobbler, ~-smacker, ~-snatcher* [From the Roman Catholic practice of eating fish on Friday] **esp Inland Nth, N Midl, West** See Map *usu derog* Cf **fish-eater, minnie nibbler**

A Roman Catholic.

   1960 Wentworth–Flexner *Slang* 330, *Mackerel-snapper. . .* A Roman Catholic. *Not common.* **1965–70** *DARE* (Qu. CC4, *. . Nicknames . . for various religions or religious groups*) 28 Infs, **esp Inland Nth, N Midl, West,** Mackerel-snappers; **FL**15, **PA**202, **WI**68, Mackerel-eaters; **NY**48, **PA**197, 228, Mackerel-smackers; **CT**9, **NY**42, 131, **PA**223, **RI**13, Mackerel-snatchers; **CA**59, Mackerel-gobblers; (Qu. HH28, *Names and nicknames . . for people of foreign background: Irish*) Inf **MI**26, Mick, mackerel-snappers, Romans. [22 of 41 Infs young or mid-aged, 19 coll educ] **1968** Bradford *Red Sky* 11 **AL,** Every spare dime she gets she gives it to the mackerel-snappers. I should have married a nice Methodist girl when I had the chance. **1977** in 1982 *Barrick Coll.* **csPA,** Mackerel snapper—Catholic. . . Not common. **1985** *DARE* File **IA,** Mackerel-snappers: What Iowans once called nuns because they ate fish on Fridays. **1986** Pederson *LAGS Concordance (Roman Catholics)* 4 infs, **Gulf Region,** Mackerel snappers. **1989** *NY Times* (NY) 13 Dec 31/1 **cnMD** (as of 1930s–40s), It wasn't until I met a youth from suburban Catonsville, three miles to the west and much snootier than our inner-city neighborhood, that I heard the term "mackerel snappers." **1993** *DARE* File **Detroit MI area** (as of 1950s), Reference to Catholics as "fish eaters" reminded me that the term I grew up hearing was "mackerel snapper."

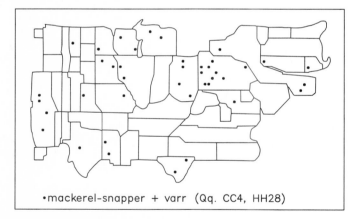

•mackerel-snapper + varr (Qq. CC4, HH28)

Mackina(c) boat See **Mackinaw boat**

Mackinac trout See **Mackinaw trout**

Mackinaw n

1 See **Mackinaw trout.**

2 See **Mackinaw boat.**

3 in phrr *holy (old) Mackinaw:* Used as an exclam or mild oath. **esp NEng**

   1907 Mulford *Bar-20* 350 **TX,** Th' Lord help Billy! Holy Mackinaw! **1924** *DN* 5.273 **ME** [Exclams], Holy Mackinaw (surp[rise] . .) **1938** (1939) Holbrook *Holy Old Mackinaw: A Natural History of the American Lumberjack* [title]. [*Ibid* 7 **ME,** He never used . . vulgar and shopworn phrases like "blue-eyed, bandy-legged, jumped-up ol' whistlin' Jesus H. Mackinaw Christ."] **1959** *VT Hist.* 27.148, *Holy Mackinaw! . .* Rare. **1975** Gould *ME Lingo* 173, "Holy Old Mackinaw!" became . . a favorite mild, Maine-woods expletive.

Mackinaw boat n Also *Mackinaw (sailboat), ~ skiff* Also sp *Mackina(c) boat* [*Mackinaw* City, MI] **now esp MI** *old-fash*

A flat-bottomed boat with oars, sails, or both, formerly common, esp on the Upper Great Lakes and in the Mississippi Valley.

   1812 (1920) Luttig *Jrl.* 54 **NE,** The Mackina Boat took 5 hunters to

the Island. **1817** (1890) Long *Jrl.* 80 **MN,** In the spring of the year deep floods usually prevail in the river, which render it navigable for mackinaw boats. **1880** *Scribner's Mth.* 20.125 **cnMT,** All available space in the overladen mackinaws needed to be reserved for the indispensable whisky. **1882** *Harper's New Mth. Mag.* 64.554 **cnMI,** The surface of the lake is flecked with the . . overgrown, and stanch double-enders known as Mackinac boats. **1948** Hedrick *Land Crooked Tree* 38 **nMI** (as of c1875), One day in mid-November, father and son made a trip up the coast in a Mackinaw boat to see what the sea might be dispensing. They were caught in a sudden gale; and, though the two masted, double-pointed Mackinaw is as safe as any craft afloat, they were wrecked. **1950** *WELS (Kinds of boats common in your locality)* 1 Inf, **neWI,** Mackinaw. **1966** *DARE* (Qu. O9, *. . Kinds of sailboats*) Inf **MI**10, Mackinaw sailboat—fishermen called it Mackinaw skiff. **1969** *DARE* Tape **MI**109, [FW:] Is that a schooner—the Mackinaw? [Inf:] No, no, no, she's just a little Mackinaw boat . . a single mast on 'er, triangular sail. . . We finally put a one-lung gasoline engine on it.

Mackinaw lake trout See **Mackinaw trout**

Mackinaw sailboat, Mackinaw skiff See **Mackinaw boat**

Mackinaw trout n Also *Mackinac trout, Mackinaw (lake trout)* [*Mackinaw* City, MI] **chiefly Gt Lakes, Rocky Mts** =**lake trout 1.**

   1838 Geol. Surv. OH *Second Annual Rept.* 195, S[*alvelinus*] *manycash* [sic]. This name was applied to the Mackinaw trout. . . A few stragglers are occasionally taken in Lake Erie. **1840** *S. Lit. Messenger* 6.604 **MI,** The celebrated Mackinaw trout, so called after the town, near which they are only found, is generally caught by the hook. **1887** Goode *Amer. Fishes* 463, The Namaycush reaches its greatest perfection in the northern parts of Lakes Huron, Michigan and Superior, where it is quite generally known as the "Mackinaw Trout." **1902** *Jrl. Amer. Folkl.* 15.246, *Mackinaw. . .* A species of lake trout, also called "*Mackinac* trout." **1905** U.S. Bur. Fisheries *Rept. for 1904* 102 **AK,** Mackinaw trout (*Cristovomer namaycush*). **1908** Forbes–Richardson *Fishes of IL* 56, In our Illinois markets it is known almost wholly by the name of lake trout, but farther north the names of Mackinaw trout, salmon-trout, and namaycush are sometimes used. **1966** *Flathead Courier Vacation Guide* (Polson MT) 16 June sec B 2/5, [Caption:] Mackinaw trout go over 40 pounds in Flathead Lake. *Ibid* 7/4, [Caption:] These are mackinaw lake trout caught in winter here. **1966–69** *DARE* (Qu. P1, *. . Kinds of freshwater fish . . caught around here . . good to eat*) Infs **CO**9, **MI**105, **MT**4, **NV**8, Mackinaw trout; **WY**1, Mackinaw—lake trout. **1968** *Green River Star* (WY) 25 Jan 7/6, The Mackinaw is an important fish in Wyoming, chiefly because of its size; it is the largest of all trouts and chars and may reach a weight of 60 pounds.

mackly adj [From *macle* spot, stain; cf *EDD mackled* "spotted"]
   1975 Gainer *Witches* 13 **sAppalachians,** *Mackly* (adj.), spotted or soiled. "Jenny got her dress all mackly."

macoola See **makoola**

MacTavish See **McTavish**

mad adj

1 Used in var compar phrr meaning "very angry": see below. Note: Many phrr of this type occur; only those that are well attested and demonstrably regional are treated here.

a *mad as a wet hen* and varr. **widespread, but more freq Sth, S Midl** See Map

   1821 in 1823 Doddridge *Logan* 42, A weddin made a great rumpuss in a neighborhood every body that was not ax'd was mad as a wet hen. **1901** *DN* 2.143 **cNY,** Madder'n a hen. . . Madder'n a hatter. **1902** Harben *Abner Daniel* 54 **nGA,** The Colonel is as mad as a wet hen about the whole thing. **1907** *DN* 3.214 **nwAR,** Mad as a wet hen. **1909** *DN* 3.347 **eAL, wGA,** Mad as a wet hen. . . Also *madder 'n a wet hen. Ibid* 413 **nME,** Mad as a wet hen. **1910** *DN* 3.445 **wNY,** Mad as a wet hen. **1912** *DN* 3.582 **wIN,** Madder (tha)n a wet hen. **1913** in 1983 Truman *Dear Bess* 112 **MO,** He'd be as mad as a wet hen if he knew I thought that. **1929** *AmSp* 5.123 **ME,** The frequent expressions "mad as a hornet," "madder than a wet hen," "mad enough to bite off a board nail," "slower than cold molasses," "has got the wrong pig by the ear," "I am not afraid of him nor a dozen like him," "she pulled the wool over his eyes," "got him where the wool is short" . . need no explanation. **1965–70** *DARE* (Qu. GG40, *Words or expressions meaning violently angry*) 163 Infs, **widespread, but esp freq Sth, S Midl,** Mad as a wet hen; 18 Infs, **scattered,** Mad as a(n) old wet hen; **FL**6, Mad as a wet hen with her tail pulled out; **OH**68, Mad as a hen; **NJ**68, Mad as a red hen; **AK**8, **DC**1, **ME**19, **NY**88, Madder than a wet hen; (Qu. GG4, *Stirred up, angry: "When he saw them coming he got _____."*) Infs **AR**51, **IL**116, **MT**5, Mad as a wet hen; **AK**8, **CO**21, **MA**58, **NY**42, Madder than a wet hen; (Qu. GG7, *. . Annoyed or upset: "Though we were only ten minutes late, she was all _____."*) Infs **GA**67, **NJ**23, **VA**31, Mad as a wet hen. **1987** *DARE* File c**eNY** (as of 1932), If the victim retaliates, he may "rear up on his hind legs" and get "as mad as a wet hen."

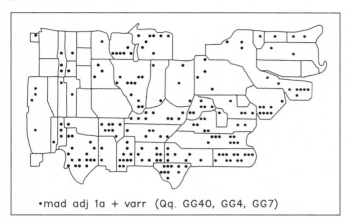

•mad adj 1a + varr (Qq. GG40, GG4, GG7)

b *mad as a (wet) setting hen* and var. **chiefly Sth** See Map
1965–70 *DARE* (Qu. GG40) 17 Infs, **chiefly Sth,** Mad as a (wet) setting hen; **NY**88, Madder than a setting hen. **1984** Wilder *You All Spoken Here* 45 **Sth,** *Mad as a settin' hen:* Angry and puffed up.

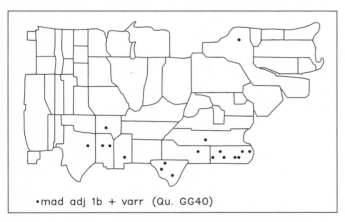

•mad adj 1b + varr (Qu. GG40)

c *mad as a hatter* and varr. **chiefly Nth** See Map Note: Instances of these phrr in the sense "very crazy" are not treated here.
1836 (1838) Haliburton *Clockmaker* (1st ser) 58 **NEng,** He . . never said another word, lookin' as mad as a hatter the whole blessed time. **1878** Shillaber *Ike Partington* 163 **NEng,** Draper went off as mad as a hatter, because the fickle crowd had left his sled to patronize the "barge." **1901** [see **1a** above]. **1922** *DN* 5.170 **NH,** *Mad as a hatter.* **1965–70**

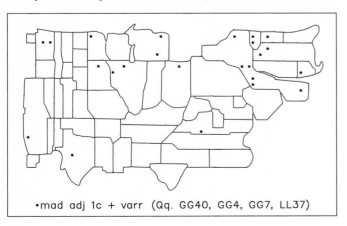

•mad adj 1c + varr (Qq. GG40, GG4, GG7, LL37)

DARE (Qu. GG40) 15 Infs, **chiefly Nth,** Mad as a hatter; **MI**51, 55, **MN**6, Madder than a hatter; (Qu. GG4) Infs **IL**28, **OH**68, **VA**11, Mad as a hatter; **MA**58, **VT**12, Madder than a hatter; (Qu. GG7) Inf **RI**13, Mad as a mad hatteras; (Qu. LL37) Inf **NH**5, Mad as a hatter.

2 See quot.
1953 Randolph–Wilson *Down in Holler* 263 **Ozarks,** *Mad sow. . .* A sow in heat. Butchered at this time, the meat has a strong odor. A man smelling some bacon in a store remarked, "It's either a old boar or a mad sow."

mad v
To anger, make angry.
1815 Humphreys *Yankey in England* 106, *Mad* (not in the usual sense, insane), to make angry. **1864** Weiss *Life Parker* 1.191 ce**MA** (as of 1843), You have madded Parker and in this way he shows his spite. **1873** (1891) Holley *My Opinions* 249 **NEng,** At the same time it madded some of the Republicans. **1893** (1904) French *Stories W. Town* 85, "I didn't mean to mad you," Tim grunted. **1913** *DN* 4.1 c**ME,** He will mad a person. **1916** *DN* 4.285 s**Appalachians,** Adjectives become verbs, and are used without the infinitive ending, *-en,* as to *glad* and to *mad* for to *gladden* and to *madden.* **1922** Brown *Old Crow* 271 **NH,** The old man down the road . . forbade secular talk in the household during a thunder shower. It "madded" the Almighty. You might be struck. **1968** *DARE* (Qu. GG4, *Stirred up, angry: "When he saw them coming he got _____."*) Inf **MO**35, Madded.

mad n
Anger, irritation; a fit of anger; hence phrr *in the mad(s)* angry; *have* (or *get*) *a mad on, get one's mad up* to be or become angry or resentful.
1834 in 1925 Bassett *Southern Overseer* 65 nw**AL,** I will be damde if I can do anythinge with them and they all ways in the mads. **1867** Harris *Sut Lovingood Yarns* 188 **TN,** He stood a-top ove the meal barril, . . his har a-swayin about wif pure mad, . . an' his eyes wer es roun an' es red as a bull's. **1897** *Outing* 30.487, Let the pony get his mad up. **1909** Porter *Girl Limberlost* 59 **IN,** Kate, . . you needn't take out your mad over our little racket on Maggie. **1926** Roberts *Time of Man* 366 **KY,** Her mouth gives up its mad and smiles again. **1941** *Sat. Eve. Post* 13 Sept 56 **SC,** I don't aim to get my mad up again. . . I'm too honed down to fire up a mad. **1941** Stuart *Men of Mts.* 294 ne**KY,** Oh, I was in the mad enough to a bit . . nails in two. **1958** Latham *Meskin Hound* 35 c**TX,** Jim had walked his mad off; and suddenly he burst out laughing. **1967–70** *DARE* (Qu. GG35b, *[To sulk or pout:] "Because she couldn't go, she's been _____ all day."*) Infs **CA**201, **WA**22, Had a mad on. **1973** Gordon *Informant* 128 s**CA,** Well, thanks a lot! I go through hell for you and you take your mad out on me. **1976** Garber *Mountain-ese* 33 s**Appalachians,** Ever time Jeb goes to town Maud gits a mad on.

madam n Also sp *madame* Usu with *the* **chiefly Sth** See Map
The mistress of a household; one's wife.
1863 *Rio Abajo Weekly Press* (Albuquerque NM) 28 July 1/1, W.F.M. Arny will . . make a visit to Washington, for the purpose of advising Mr. Lincoln . . and for the purpose of paying his respects to "The Madame" in the shape of a Navajo blanket. **1879** (1880) Tourgée *Fool's Errand* 78 **Sth,** I've brought back the books I borrowed of the madam the other day. **1902** *Harper's Mth. Mag.* 104.603 **CA,** I only just dropped over to ask about the little madam, and when is she coming home. **1941** *LANE* Map 375 *(My wife)* 1 inf, ne**MA,** Madam, also used.

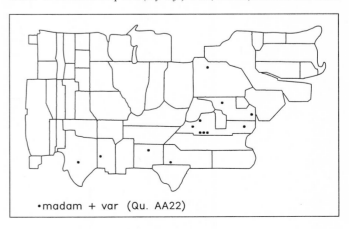

•madam + var (Qu. AA22)

1956 Ker *Vocab. W. TX* 313, *My wife. . .* The madam [4 of 67 infs]. **c1960** *Wilson Coll.* **csKY,** *The madam. . .* Deliberately humorous reference to one's wife, esp. to mean she is the head of the household. **1965–70** *DARE* (Qu. AA22, *Joking names that a man may use to refer to his wife: "I have to go down and pick up my _____."*) Infs **AL39, GA44, MD28, PA221, TX13, VA5, 11, 27,** The madam; **LA28, MD39, VA13, 46,** Madam; **VA31,** The madam—also used as a serious term. **1986** Pederson *LAGS Concordance,* 12 infs, **Gulf Region,** The madam.

Madam's off-ox n Also *Madam's housecat* [By metanalysis of *from Adam's;* see quot] Cf **Adam's housecat**
=**Adam's off-ox 1.**
1966 *DARE* (Qu. II26, *Joking ways of saying that you would not know who somebody is: "I wouldn't know him from _____."*) Inf **MS73,** Madam's housecat, Madam's off-ox.

mad as a dog See **dog** n **B17g**

mad as a hatter See **mad** adj **1c**

mad as a hoe See **hoe** n[1] **3**

mad as a setting hen See **mad** adj **1b**

mad as a wet hen See **mad** adj **1a**

mad as a wet setting hen See **mad** adj **1b**

mad ax n [Folk-etym for **mattocks**] Cf **ad ax**
=**mattock;** the ax blade of a **mattock.**
1948 Hench *Coll.* **cVA,** *Mad-ax,* the ax-end of a grubbing hoe. "Turn the hoe around and use the mad-ax if you want to get that tree out." **1948** Mencken *Amer. Lang. Suppl. 2* 239, Newcomers have brought [to Alaska] terms from far-distant American dialects, e.g., . . *mad-ax* for *mattock* from Appalachia. **1950** *WELS (Hand tools for cutting underbrush)* 1 Inf, **seWI,** Mattock—often called "mad ax." **1965–70** *DARE* (Qu. L35, *Hand tools used for cutting underbrush and digging out roots)* 16 Infs, **scattered,** Mad ax. [13 Infs old, 3 mid-aged] **1986** Pederson *LAGS Concordance,* 1 inf, **sGA,** A madax [=**mattock**].

madder n Also *madders* Cf **wild madder**
=**dog fennel 1.**
1900 Lyons *Plant Names* 37, *A[nthemis] Cotula. . .* Madder. **1940** Clute *Amer. Plant Names* 251, Madder. **1959** Carleton *Index Herb. Plants* 77, *Madders:* Anthemis cotula.

maddick See **mattock**

mad-dog skullcap n Also *mad-dog (weed), madweed* [See quot 1822]
A **skullcap 1** (here: *Scutellaria lateriflora*).
1818 *Amer. Jrl. Science* 1.371 **nwMA,** Mad dog weed *(Scutellaria lateriflora)* and purple vervain *(Verbena hastata)* in blossom. **1822** Eaton *Botany* 455, *[Scutellaria] lateriflora* (mad-dog scull-cap . .). Much has been said and published on the wonderful virtues of this plant. It is said to be an antidote to the hydrophobia, to the poison of serpents, &c. W. Coleman, Esq. editor of the New-York Ev. Post, has certainly merited public gratitude for his diligence in collecting and publishing so many well-attested facts in relation to this subject; even if it should finally appear, that the plant does not possess those virtues. **1830** Rafinesque *Med. Flora* 2.81, *Scutellaria lateriflora. . .* Madweed. [*Ibid* 2.82, The *S. lateriflora* is lately become famous as a cure and prophylactic against hydrophobia. This property was discovered by Dr. Vandesveer, towards 1772, who . . is said to have . . prevented 400 persons and 1000 cattle from becoming hydrophobous, after being bitten by mad dogs.] **1885** *Outing* 7.180 **MA,** A delicate little herb with dainty, blue flowers is called mad-dog skull-cap, from its imputed power of curing hydrophobia. **1894** *Jrl. Amer. Folkl.* 7.96 **WV,** *Scutellaria lateriflora, . .* mad-dog skull-cap. **1971** Krochmal *Appalachia Med. Plants* 232, *Scutellaria lateriflora. . . Common Names* . . mad-dog, mad-dog skullcap, mad-dog weed, madweed. . . This plant has been used for treating hydrophobia, but without much success. **1974** (1977) Coon *Useful Plants* 163, *Mad-dog weed. . .* A widely-grown plant in wet places, it was once an "official" drug recommended for use for the nerves, sedative, etc.

mad-dog stone See **madstone**

mad-dog weed n
1 See **mad-dog skullcap.**
2 A water plantain: usu *Alisma plantago-aquatica,* but also *A. subcordatum.*
[**1830** Rafinesque *Med. Flora* 2.187, *Alisma plantago. . . Water Plantain.* Had once much celebrity in Russia, as a cure for hydrophobia; time

has not confirmed this valuable property.] **1832** *MA Hist. Soc. Coll.* 2d ser 9.146 **cwVT,** Alisma plantago . . Water plantain, mad-dog-weed. **1854** King *Amer. Eclectic Dispensatory* 192, *Alisma plantago. . .* This is a perennial, caulescent herb, sometimes called *Mad-dog weed.* [*Ibid* 193, At one time the root was in great repute as a cure for hydrophobia, but subsequent experiments have proved it inefficacious. The leaves are the parts used.] **1936** Winter *Plants NE* 6, *A[lisma] subcordatum. . .* Called also . . Mad-dog Weed. **1976** Bailey–Bailey *Hortus Third* 47, *[Alisma] Plantago-aquatica. . . Mad-dog weed. . .* Widespread, mainly in temp. zones.

made See **make** v[1] **C8**

made-down (bed) See **make down** v phr **1**

Madeira n Also *Madeira redwood* [*OED* 1663 →; var of Span *madera* wood, infl by *Madeira*] **FL**
A **mahogany 1** (here: *Swietenia mahagoni*).
[**1743** Catesby *Nat. Hist. Carolina* 2.42 **Bahamas,** This is an excellent Wood, and next to what is here called *Madera* (which is the *Mahogony of Jamaica*), is the best Wood these Islands afford.] **1884** Sargent *Forests of N. Amer.* 34, *Mahogany. Madeira. . .* Wood . . rich reddish-brown, turning darker with age, the thin sapwood yellow. **1897** Sudworth *Arborescent Flora* 270 **FL,** *Swietenia mahagoni. . . Common Names. . .* Madeira. **1908** Britton *N. Amer. Trees* 594, This important tropical tree [=*Swietenia mahagoni*] enters our area in peninsular Florida and the Keys, where it was formerly more abundant than now, as the large trees have been cut down for their valuable timber. . . It is sometimes called Madeira and Madeira redwood. **1967** Will *Dredgeman* 67 **FL,** On high ground there was the madeira or Florida mahogany, whose wood when freshly cut is white, but which turns red after being exposed to sunlight. **1971** Craighead *Trees S. FL* 96, Once mahogany was abundant, as evidenced by the term "Madeira Hammocks" and numerous madeira stumps still remaining. **1976** Bailey–Bailey *Hortus Third* 1086, *Madeira redwood. . .* The original mahogany of commerce, now largely replaced as a source of timber by *S[wietenia] macrophylla.*

Madeira nut n
The English **walnut** *(Juglans regia).*
1821 Cobbett *Amer. Gardener* 325 **NY;** *Walnut. . .* The English and French Walnut, called here the *Madeira Nut,* is too sensible of the frost to thrive much in this climite [sic]. . . It is *possible,* that the Madeira Nut grafted upon the black walnut . . might thrive in this climate. **1822** Eaton *Botany* 321, *[Juglans] regia* (madeira nut . .). It is said that this variety is indigenous to North America. **1856** U.S. Patent Office *Annual Rept. for 1855: Ag.* xiv, *The Persian Walnut,* or *Madeira Nut,* . . appears to be well adapted to the climate of the middle and southern latitudes of the United States. **1892** (1974) Millspaugh *Amer. Med. Plants* 156–1, The following fruits or nuts . . are esteemed on account of their rich oily "meats": The black walnut . . , the butternut . . , the Madeira nut or English walnut. **1976** Bailey–Bailey *Hortus Third* 614, *Madeira nut. . .* Nut somewhat wrinkled, thick- or thin-shelled. . . Much planted as a nut tree in the warmer parts of the country, particularly in Calif.

Madeira redwood See **Madeira**

Madeira vine n
A vine of the genus *Anredera.* Also called **mignonette vine.** For other names of *A. cordifolia* see **door potato**
1854 *S. Lit. Messenger* 20.622, Behind so impervious a screen as honeysuckle and Madeira vine, 'tis needless to say I cannot discern you. **1876** Hobbs *Bot. Hdbk.* 66, Madeira vine, Boussingaultia baselloides. **1899** Bergen *Animal Lore* 106, It is bad luck to have a Madeira vine growing around the house. *Chestertown, Md.* **1907** *St. Nicholas* May 651, In this bed . . were planted the bulbs of Maderia [sic] vines and seeds of moon-flowers and morning-glories. **1933** Small *Manual SE Flora* 470, *Madeira-vine. . .* Widely cultivated for its bright-green foliage and very fragrant flowers. **1960** Carpenter *Tales Manchaca* 163 **cTX,** If a pimple progressed to the boil or carbuncle stage, Ma applied one of several poultices "to draw the fever out." One was made by crushing the thick Madeira vine leaves. **1976** Bailey–Bailey *Hortus Third* 81, *[Anredera] cordifolia. . . Madeira vine. . .* Rapidly growing twiner, to 20 ft. or more.

mademoiselle n
A small food-fish *(Bairdiella chrysura)* of the Atlantic and Gulf coasts. Also called **corvina a, croaker** n[1] **1a(1), Lafayette 3, sand perch, silver ~, white ~, yellowtail**
1882 U.S. Natl. Museum *Bulletin* 16.570, *Mademoiselle.* Greenish above, silvery below, each scale with a series of dark punctuations through the centre. **1884** Goode *Fisheries U.S.* 1.375 **FL,** *Bairdiella*

chrysura. . . At Pensacola they are known by the name "Mademoiselle." . . They are regarded as excellent pan-fish. **1902** Jordan–Evermann *Amer. Fishes* 461, The . . mademoiselle . . is a well-known fish, very common from New England to Texas on sandy shores. **1942** Chesapeake Biol. Lab. *Pub.* 53.17 **MD,** The . . mademoiselle, *Bairdiella chrysura,* was a frequent captive [of the pots]. **1973** Knight *Cook's Fish Guide* 384, Mademoiselle—Perch, Silver.

maden See **make** v¹ **B**

made over ppl adj phr **esp Sth, S Midl**

In phr *be (someone) made over:* To resemble (someone) strongly.

1956 Ker *Vocab. W. TX* 296, He resembles his father in appearance; in other traits. . . Made over [1 of 67 infs]. **1966–69** DARE (Qu. Z10, *If a child looks very much like his father . . "He _____ his father.")* Infs **KY**66, **MS**6, Is his daddy made over; **TN**15, Just his father made over. [All Infs old] **c1970** Pederson *Dial. Surv. Rural GA (If the boy's behavior is similar to his father's, you would say that the boy _____ his father.)* 1 inf, **seGA,** Is his father made over. **1986** Pederson *LAGS Concordance (The boy resembles his father)* 5 infs, **Gulf Region,** His father (*or* daddy) made over.

maderone See **madrone**

made up See **make up 1**

mad fence n Cf **devil's lane**

See quots.

1946 PADS 6.20 **cVA** (as of c1890), *Mad fence.* . . A boundary fence between adjoining farms. **1992** NADS Letters **nwTX,** My father in the early 70s erected a chain link fence to separate his front yard from the neighbors' in Lubbock. Both my parents referred to the fence as a *mad fence.* . . The back yards, by the way, were already completely enclosed by fences, so the chain link fences running along the property lines were clearly designed to mark boundaries and to impede neighborhood children from running through my parents' front yard.

madick See **mattock**

mad itch n [Cf *mad itch* pseudorabies, a disease of animals]

A severe itching rash.

1966–68 DARE (Qu. BB24, . . *A rash that comes out suddenly—from hives or something else: "He's got some kind of _____ all over his chest."*) Inf **GA**33, Mad itch; (Qu. BB25, . . *Common skin diseases around here*) Inf **GA**3, Mad itch—same as seven-year itch only worse. **1980** NYT Article Letters **NC,** The "mad-itch" is when you are so upset and angry your body rebels and begins to itch. When we were in North Carolina last year we met a wonderful woman, whose language fascinated us. When her daughter was having a bout with hives or some similar itching problem, Reba told us her daughter had the "mad-itch."

Madonna candle n Cf **desert candle 1, God's candle, Our Lord's candle(stick)**

The flower stalk of a **yucca.**

1941 Writers' Program *Guide CO* 295, The yucca, better known as Spanish bayonet or soapweed, bristles with dagger-like leaves and bears tall spikes of ivory white blossoms, often referred to as Madonna candles.

madreselva n [Span "honeysuckle"]

A **honeysuckle 2** (here: *Lonicera albiflora*).

1951 PADS 15.41 **TX,** *Loniceca* [sic] *albiflora.* . . madreselva. It is gratifying to see that in western Texas . . all the madreselvas are carefully saved. . . The berries are relished by birds.

madrick See **medrick**

madrone n Also *maderone, madrona, madroña, madrono* [Span *madroño*] **chiefly CA**

A plant of the genus *Arbutus,* native to the Southwest. Also called **manzanita 2, mountain mahogany 3.** For other names of var spp see **lady legs, laurel 5, naked Indian, paperbark tree**

[**1769** Crespi *Diary* 5 Nov. *(DA)* **CA,** En estas dos jornadas ultimas, se han encontrado muchos madroños, aunque la fruta es mas chica que la de España pero si de la misme especie. [=In the last two days' travel, we have met with many madroños; although the fruit is smaller than that of the Spanish variety, it is certainly the same species.]] **1841** (1937) Bidwell *Journey to CA* 32, Madrone—Grows as abundant as the oak, it is one of the most beautiful trees I have ever seen—is an evergreen . . but that which renders it so pleasing, is the coler [sic] of the bark of all

its branches, it is smooth like the Sicamore, and of a lively scarlet color, is a most excellent fire wood, and I have been informed by creditable gentlemen, that it is an ellegant substitute for Mahogany. **1850** (1968) Taylor *Eldorado* 130 **CA,** Clumps of the madrono—a native evergreen, with large, glossy leaves, and trunk and branches of bright purple—filled the ravines. **1857** in 1941 *AmSp* 16.261 **CA,** *Maderone,* a kind of tree. **1902** U.S. Natl. Museum *Contrib. Herbarium* 7.374 **nwCA,** In February and March the madroña is thickly covered with white, globular, wax-like flowers, which furnish an abundance of wild honey. **1908** Britton *N. Amer. Trees* 758, Madroña. . . A large evergreen tree extending from British Columbia to southern California. . . It is also called Madroña tree, Madrove [sic], Manzanita, Laurelwood, and Laurel. **1965–70** DARE (Qu. T5, . . *Kinds of evergreens, other than pine*) Infs CA20, 105, 150, Madrone; CA31, ['mædron]; (Qu. T16, . . *Kinds of trees . . 'special'*) Infs CA97, 130, 144, 150, Madrone(s); CA20, 24, ['mʌdron]; CA107, Madrona. **1968** DARE Tape CA97, The kind of wood we used around here for the fireplace, it would be a mixture of fir . . mixed up with manzanita and madrone [mə'dron], which are very hot and made a very hot fire. **1968–75** DARE File CA, Madrones ['mædrənz]—small bush with red berries and red bark; cwCA, Madrone [mə'dron] trees have smooth, shiny wood under the peeling bark. **1970** Stewart *Amer. Place-Names* 272, Madrone, Madrona—From the tree, a common name in the Coast Ranges of CA, and northward, e.g. Madrona Peninsula WA.

madstone n Also *mad-dog stone* **chiefly Sth, S Midl** Cf **beazlestone, moonstone 1**

A stone or stonelike object, often a calculus found in a deer's stomach, which is supposed to draw the dangerous material from the bite of a rabid or venomous animal.

1816 in 1824 Knight *Letters* 70 **VA,** Besides, near Loretto, they have a reputed remedy against canine rabiosity; two *mad-dog stones,* of long-extolled efficacy. . . The stones are about an inch and an half cube; resemble a piece of hone, or hard soap; and are powerful astringents and absorbents. **1834** *S. Lit. Messenger* 1.182 **VA,** He should be able to form a concrete mass, by means of beef gall and alkali, which would resemble and equal in virtue the mad stone. **1889** Amer. Philos. Soc. *Proc.* 26.336, Among the various individuals in Pennsylvania who profess ability in exorcism and charms, we occasionally find one who is reputed to possess a mad-stone. . . A specimen, which had a high reputation in the State from which it had been brought, was described by the present writer as consisting of a worn piece of white feldspar. **1906** DN 3.146 **nwAR,** *Madstone.* . . A stone supposed to cure hydrophobia. **1944** Wellman *Bowl* 190 **KS,** I'm snake-bit. . . If we only had a madstone. **1947** (1964) Randolph *Ozark Superstitions* 141, Many old people allege that the madstone in a deer is always found in the stomach, while others place it in the intestines or the bladder, or in the udder of a doe, or even "betwixt the windpipe and the lights." Uncle Lum Booth . . said that so long as the deer was *white* it made no difference in what part of the body the stone appeared. **1949** Webber *Backwoods Teacher* 273 **Ozarks,** Uncle Johnny used to have a madstone which he got out of a deer. . . Folks came . . when they were mad-dog-bitten. **1963** Watkins–Watkins *Yesterday Hills* 134 **cnGA,** His madstone. . . looked like a worn creek rock about the size of a partridge egg with a chip broken off one end. **1966** *S. Folkl. Qrly.* 30.198 **csKY,** Cover the [snake]bite with a madstone, a stone-like accretion found in the stomach of a deer or cow; the madstone will adhere until it has drawn all the poison out or until it is saturated with it; soak the stone in sweet milk and keep on applying as long as it will stick. **1966** DARE Tape OK51, Treatment of a person bitten by [a] rabid or mad dog was by the use of . . a madstone which was supposed to have been taken out of the heart of a white albino deer. **1970** Anderson *TX Folk Med.* 58 **ceTX,** Rabies—Apply a madstone, which can be obtained from a creek bed. **1986** Pederson *LAGS Concordance,* 1 inf, **cwTN,** Madstone—for dog bites; 1 inf, **csTN,** Madstone—supposedly cures hydrophobia; 1 inf, **swTN,** Madstone—kept it soaking in sweet milk; 1 inf, **cwAR,** Madstones—every white deer has one in paunch.

mad-tail weed n

Perh a **skullcap 1.** Cf **mad-dog skullcap**

1970 DARE (Qu. S26e, *Other wildflowers not yet mentioned*) Inf **VA**46, Mad-tail weed.

madtom n

=**stonecat.**

1896 U.S. Natl. Museum *Bulletin* 47.144, *Mad Toms.* . . Very small catfishes of the fresh waters of the Eastern United States. *Ibid* 147, *Schilbeodes insignis.* . . Mad Tom. . . One of the largest species, reaching the length of nearly a foot. Pennsylvania to South Carolina; very common in streams east of the Alleghanies. **1933** John G. Shedd Aquarium *Guide* 54, The Stone Cats or Mad-toms. . . have a poison gland at the base of the pectoral spines and are capable of inflicting a painful sting. **1968** *DARE* (Qu. P3, *Freshwater fish that are not good to eat*) Inf **VA**8, Madtoms—same as mud catfish; used for bait when cut up; (Qu. P7, *Small fish used as bait for bigger fish*) Inf **VA**33, Madtom—if you don't handle them right, they sting; look like a miniature catfish. **1983** Becker *Fishes WI* 721, When hooked through the lips, madtoms survive for a long time, and several walleyes can be taken on a single madtom. In the late 1970s, madtoms sold for bait cost the fisherman about $1.50 per dozen.

mad violet n

A **shooting star,** usu *Dodecatheon meadia.*

1897 Parsons *Wild Flowers CA* 205, *Mad Violets. Dodecatheon Meadia. Ibid* 206, Among the children the various forms are known by a number of names, such as "mad violets," . . and "roosters'-heads." **1898** *Jrl. Amer. Folkl.* 11.274 **CA,** *Dodecatheon . .* cyclamen, mad violets. . . Near Naples, Italy, the peasants call the true cyclamens mad violets. **1920** Rice–Rice *Pop. Studies CA Wild Flowers* 86, The most common of these [names] are Shooting Stars, Mad Violets [etc]. *Ibid* 87, One can easily catch the meaning of the name "Mad Violets," for the flower is somewhat like a violet that has laid its petals back in anger. **1931** Clute *Common Plants* 60, The name of mad violets given to the plants usually called shooting stars (*Dodecatheon meadia),* has all the ear-marks of being a made name, though it is suggestive, for the reflexed petals make the flowers appear as if they were laying back their ears as some animals do when angry. The plant is not a violet, however, nor is its relative, the cyclamen.

madweed See **mad-dog skullcap**

madz n [Var of *adz*] Cf **ad ax, mad ax**

1893 *DN* 1.278 **wCT,** In my boyhood . . I learned to know a common carpenter's tool as a "madz," and I think most of the fellow-workmen of my father, who was a carpenter, used that name. The explanation of the prefixed *m* is to my mind undoubtedly this: The word on account of its form was looked on as a plural, and always took a plural verb, as I remember the usage. The form with a demonstrative pronoun would then always be, in the dialect of the region, *them adz,* and the *m* was transferred to the noun.

ma'ed See **marry**

magdad coffee n Also *mogdad coffee*

A **senna** (here: *Cassia occidentalis*).

1890 *Century Dict.* 1088, *Negro coffee,* or *Mogdad coffee,* the seeds of *Cassia occidentalis,* which are roasted and used in the tropics as a substitute for coffee, though they contain no caffein [sic]. **1901** Lounsberry *S. Wild Flowers* 261, *C[assia] occidentalis,* coffee senna, [is] a native of Virginia and the states southward. . . In the slightly curved and linear pods there are found numerous seeds. These the negroes make into what they call Magdad coffee. **1922** *Amer. Botanist* 28.30, *Cassia occidentalis* is called . . "magdad-coffee". We are unable to explain the last mentioned term. **1949** Moldenke *Amer. Wild Flowers* 127, A cheap grade of coffee, called negro or magdad coffee, used occasionally by the southern Negroes, is made from the seeds of the *coffee senna.*

maggie n [Var of **aggie,** perh infl by name *Maggie*]

In marble play: see quots.

1968 *DARE* (Qu. EE6b, *Small marbles or marbles in general*) Inf **PA**94, Maggies. **c1970** Wiersma *Marbles Terms* **IA** (as of 1960), *Maggie*—same as boulder, large marble.

Maggie and Jiggs n [From the characters in the comic strip "Bringing Up Father," by George McManus] *joc*

An outdoor toilet building.

1950 *WELS* (An outside toilet building) 1 Inf, **swWI,** Maggie and Jiggs. **1968** *DARE* (Qu. M21b) Inf **PA**71, Maggie and Jiggs.

maggot-eater n [See quot 1970] **NC, VA**

Any of var birds of the family Scolopacidae; see quots.

1890 *Century Dict.* 3571, *Maggot-eater.* . . A book-name for birds of the genus *Scolecophagus.* **1911** *Forest & Stream* 77.453 **neNC,** Turnstone. . . Maggot Eater, Cape Lookout. **1917** *Wilson Bulletin* 29.2.80 **NC,** *Actitis macularia.* . . This and other small sandpipers are known as gray-backs, maggot-eaters and sea-chickens at Beaufort, N.C. **1923** U.S. Dept. Ag. *Misc. Circular* 13.47 **NC,** Shorebirds. . . maggot eaters. *Ibid* 71 **NC, VA,** Common Turnstone (*Arenaria interpres).* . . maggot eater. **1970** *DARE* FW Addit **VA**52, Maggot-eater (turnstone)—they go around

shell-piles, piles of discarded oyster and clam shells, where they find and eat blowfly maggots.

maggot-fish n [Appar folk-etym for **margate fish**] =**margaret grunt.**

1890 *Century Dict.* 3628, *Margate-fish.* . . Also called *market-fish, maggot-fish, margaret-grunt.*

maggot fly n

Usu a **blowing fly,** but also any of var other flies; see quots.

1851 *De Bow's Rev.* 11.56 **LA,** Maggot Fly—Three kinds; *large green, large gray,* and *small gray;* about the size of a house fly. . . They infested animals, depositing their *larvæ* (not eggs) in the least sore or filthy place, and in the sulci and sheaths of mares and horses. **1905** Kellogg *Amer. Insects* 345, The cabbage maggot-fly lays its eggs also on the stem just above or even below the ground, and the larvae burrow into the roots. **1965–70** *DARE* (Qu. R12, . . *Other kinds of flies* . . *for example, those that fly around animals*) Inf **NM**13, Maggot fly (also called blowfly); (Qu. R13, *Flies that come to meat or fruit*) Infs **GA**9, **IN**17, **TX**35, Maggot fly; **CA**78, Bluebottle—the maggot fly; **NY**75, Maggot fly—gets on meat; **WI**77, Apple maggot fly; **CA**155, Onion maggot fly. **1980** Milne–Milne *Audubon Field Guide Insects* 675, Apple Maggot Fly *(Rhagoletis pomonella).*

maggot snipe n Cf **maggot-eater** =**ruddy turnstone.**

1888 Trumbull *Names of Birds* 186 **NY,** *[Arenaria interpres:]* At Moriches, *maggot-snipe.* **1923** U.S. Dept. Ag. *Misc. Circular* 13.72 **NC,** Maggot snipe.

magical music See **magic music**

magic lantern n

See quots.

1906 *DN* 3.146 **nwAR,** *Magic lantern.* . . Japanese lantern; an oriental paper lantern used for decorative illumination. "Magic lanterns were strung all around the lake." **1909** *DN* 3.347 **eAL, wGA,** *Magic lantern.* . . Japanese lantern.

magic music n Also *magical music*

A children's game, usu played to music or singing; see quots 1899, 1937.

1842 in 1956 Eliason *Tarheel Talk* 263 **seNC,** Yesterday being Grandma's birthday, we had a great deal of company to the candy boiling, and Col Childs' family was invited to tea, after which Couzin Eliza Dickinson sung and played, and then we pulled the candy, and played magical music and redeemed pawns, and then the company went home. **1899** Champlin–Bostwick *Young Folks' Games* 410, *Magical Music,* a kind of Hide the Handkerchief, in which the seeker is told by music, generally that of a piano-forte, whether he is near or far from the object. **1937** (1947) Bancroft *Games* 288, Hide the thimble (Magic Music). . . When the object is hidden, the absent player is recalled, and proceeds to hunt for the hidden object. While he is doing this, the others sing or clap their hands, the sound being very soft and low when the hunter is far away from the object, and growing louder as he approaches it. The piano music is desirable.

maginitis See **-itis**

magnolia n

1 Std: a tree of the genus *Magnolia.* Also called **beaverwood 1, cucumber tree 1, elkwood 2, laurel 1, umbrella tree.** For other names of var spp see **beaver tree, broadleaf tree, buffalo tree 2, elephant-leaf tree, elk bark, Indian bitter 2, Indian physic 2, linn 2, mayball tree, mountain magnolia, silverleaf, southern magnolia, sweet bay, water lily tree, wahoo**

2 =**tulip tree.**

1893 *Jrl. Amer. Folkl.* 6.136, *Liriodendron tulipifera.* . . Magnolia. White Haven, Pa.

magnolia bay n

A **sweet bay** (here: *Magnolia virginiana*).

1964 Batson *Wild Flowers SC* 49, *Magnolia Bay . . Magnolia virginiana.* . . Usually a shrub with semi-evergreen elliptic leaves which are about 4 in. long, whitened beneath and fragrant.

magnolia bird n [See quots] =**red-eyed vireo.**

1949 Sprunt–Chamberlain *SC Bird Life* 431, *Red-eyed Vireo. . . Local Names:* Magnolia Bird. . . Wayne noted that the Red-eyed particularly likes seeds of the magnolia. . . The oil in these bright red seeds makes the birds very fat. Wayne added that he had seen as many as fifty in a single magnolia, feeding on the seeds. **1955** *Oriole* 20.1.12 **GA,** *Red-eyed Vireo. Magnolia Bird* (from its feeding on magnolia seeds).

magnolia snake n

The yellow **rat snake** *(Elaphe obsoleta quadrivittata).*

1952 Ditmars *N. Amer. Snakes* 97, *Magnolia Snake. . . Habits:* Typical of the other species of *Elaphe* with exception of partially arboreal habits in climbing into old magnolia and live-oak trees, where it hides in disintegrated knotholes.

magnolia vine n

=**bay star vine.**

1960 Vines *Trees SW* 287, *Carolina Magnolia-vine. Schizandra coccinea. . . Range.* In rich woods; Texas, Louisiana, and Arkansas; eastward to Florida and north to South Carolina.

magnolia warbler n [See quot 1977]

A black and yellow warbler *(Dendroica magnolia).*

1872 Coues *Key to N. Amer. Birds* 102, *Black and Yellow Warbler. Magnolia Warbler. . .* Eastern United States; a dainty little species, abundant in woodland. **1895** Minot *Land-Birds New Engl.* 128, *"Magnolia Warbler." . .* The nest is usually built in a low spruce, . . and is finished in the first week of June. **1902** White *Blazed Trail* 296 **MI,** Myrtle and Magnolia warblers, oven birds, peewits . . passed silently or noisily. **1919** Pearson et al. *Birds NC* 288, The Magnolia Warbler . . [has] been observed in spring at Raleigh only four times. . . In fall it is more often seen. **1977** Bull–Farrand *Audubon Field Guide Birds* 687, *Magnolia Warbler. . .* This pretty warbler got its name from the first specimen obtained by the famous ornithologist Alexander Wilson among some magnolia trees in Mississippi in the early 1800s. It actually breeds in conifer trees in the North, but the name has remained.

magnolia water lily n

A **water lily** (here: *Nymphaea tuberosa).*

1948 Stevens *KS Wild Flowers* 78, *Nymphaea tuberosa. Magnolia Waterlily. . .* The plants of this species are notably efficient in the formation of extensive dense colonies. **1951** Martin *Amer. Wildlife & Plants* 451, Two of these attractive aquatics . . more common than all the others. . . are American waterlily . . , common in acid waters near the seaboard, and magnolia waterlily . . which occurs in limey areas farther inland. **1976** Bailey–Bailey *Hortus Third* 773, *Magnolia w[ater] l[ily]. . .* Fl[ower]s pure white, 4–9 in. across, with little or no fragrance, open until shortly after noon.

magofer n Also *magooffer, megopher, mungofa* [Etym unknown; perh of Afr or AmInd origin; cf **gopher** n¹ **1a**] esp **GA** *obs*

=**gopher** n¹ **1a.**

1789 *Augusta Chron. & Gaz. of the State* (GA) 11 July 4/2, [The dog] at last expired by the mouth of a megopher's hole, where she had lain twenty days keeping the owner from his habitation. **1795** *Gaz. U.S.* (Philadelphia PA) 16 Mar [3/2] **GA,** To make Mr. Watkins feel he must be used like a magoffer by putting fire on his back. **1829** in 1836 NY Acad. Sci. *Annals Lyceum Nat. Hist.* 3.97, *Testudo Polyphemus,* Dandin. . . Mungôfa, vulg. [Footnote to *mungôfa:* The letter ô in this word has the sound of the French ou, or the English oo.] **1840** *S. Lit. Messenger* 6.509 **GA,** I'd have taken a magofer's grip upon him, and not let go. **1879** *Encycl. Brit.* (9th ed) 10.780, The flesh of the gopher, or mungofa, as it is also called, is considered excellent eating.

magpie n

1 also *black-billed magpie, yellow-billed* ~; Either of two similar black-and-white birds: the black-billed *Pica pica* native to much of the western US and Alaska, or the yellow-billed *Pica nuttalli* native to California.

1805 (1965) Lewis–Clark *Hist. Lewis-Clark Exped.* 1.272, Many geese were feeding in the prairies, and a number of magpies. **1806** in 1810 Pike *Expeditions* 170 **CO,** Our horses . . were attacked by the magpies, who attracted by the scent of their sore backs, alighted on them, and in defiance of their wincing and kicking, picked many places quite raw. **1869** *Amer. Naturalist* 3.80, Black-billed Magpie *(Pica Hudsonica)* . . continued common throughout the route westward [from the Bad Lands to Vancouver]. **1898** (1900) Davie *Nests N. Amer. Birds* 320, The Black-billed Magpie. . . A common species on the plains, mountains

and hills of Colorado. . . The Yellow-billed Magpie is confined exclusively to California. **1955** Forbush–May *Birds* 341 **CO,** The Magpie is impossible to confuse with any other North American bird. Conspicuously marked with iridescent black and gleaming white . . its long kite-shaped tail trailing behind, and seeming to constitute more than half of the bird's total length, it is striking and unmistakable. **1963** Murie *Birds Mt. McKinley* 66 **AK,** Back in the hills I have met extremely tame magpies. . . On one occasion a young of the year walked into the Igloo cabin and hopped up on the bed while I was preparing a meal. **1965–70** *DARE* (Qu. Q4) Inf **WA24,** Magpie; (Qu. Q11) Inf **CO3,** Magpie—white-tipped wings, mean bird; **TN46,** Magpies; **WY4,** Magpie; (Qu. Q14) Infs **MT2, SD8, WA8,** Magpie. **1967** *DARE* FW Addit **WA7,** Local birds. . . Magpie.

2 See quot. [From the black-and-white coloring]

1941 Writers' Program *Guide WY* 395, Scattered among the red and white range animals are lean, angular Holstein steers, locally called 'magpies,' which have little physical beauty or commercial value.

maguay See **maguey 2**

maguey n [AmSpan]

1 =**agave. Gulf States, SW**

[**1830** Rafinesque *Med. Flora* 2.187, *Agave americana. . . Maguey* of Mexico. . . From Carolina and Florida to Mexico. . . The central stem grows in a few months 18 to 20 feet high, bearing a beautiful pyramid of yellow blossoms. It is a false notion to suppose that it blossoms only once in 100 years; this happens once in 15 to 25 years, and afterwards the plant dies.] **1831** (1973) Pattie *Personal Narr.* 63, It was a vegetable, called by the Spanish, mascal, (probably maguey.) **1837** (1962) Williams *Territory FL* 34, The eastern side. . . is covered with luxuriant grass and herbs, among which the maguy [sic] . . raises her pendulous white flowers. **1859** (1968) Bartlett *Americanisms* 260, *Maguey: (Agave americana.)* A genus of American tropical plants commonly called Aloes or Century plants. They are found in Texas, New Mexico, and California. The different species furnish pulque, sisal hemp, aguardiente, bagging, etc. **1892** *DN* 1.191 **TX,** *Maguéy:* a succulent plant *(Agave Americana).* Often applied indiscriminately to any species of *Agave.* **1894** *Jrl. Amer. Folkl.* 7.101 **NM,** *Agave* sp., Indian maguey. **1932** Bentley *Spanish Terms* 160, *Maguey* . . [ma'ge:]. . . The term *maguey* is not used with discrimination by Americans, nor by Mexicans, but is applied to the Agave of whatever species. The word is used alone, or in conjunction with "plant," as in the "maguey plant." **1967** *DARE* (Qu. S26a, . . *Roadside flowers)* Inf **TX11,** Maguey. **1967** *DARE* Tape **TX29,** [FW:] What are the native brushes? [Inf:] Chaparral, . . catclaw, . . maguey [mə'geˇ:ɪ].

2 also *maguay;* pronc-sp *McGay:* A rope, esp a **lasso,** made from the fibers of a **maguey 1. West**

1899 in 1921 Thorp *Songs Cowboys* 169 **NM,** And Bill he landed his old maguey / Around old blackie's horns. **1936** McCarthy *Lang. Mosshorn* np **West** [Range terms], *Maguey. . .* An expression seldom used meaning a rope. **1936** Adams *Cowboy Lingo* 55, The Mexican 'maguey'—pronounced 'McGay'—was made from the fiber of the century plant. It was a splendid rope, but owing to its extreme stiffness many ropers did not care for it. **1940** Writers' Program *Guide NV* 77, A rope is sometimes *seagrass, twine, string, Tom Horn,* or *maguey.* **1940** *Cattleman* May 19, We now come to the Mexican *maguey* rope, a four-strand rope of a scant ⅜″ diameter, which is made from the fibers of the *maguey* plant by the natives of Old Mexico. . . The *maguey* is an extra hard rope, holds a big wide loop, and throws very fast. It is the rope which trick ropers use in making their fancy catches. **1946** *NYT Mag.* 20 Oct 35 [Rodeo lingo], *Maguay:* rope, originally made in Mexico, from fiber of cactus plant; smaller than most lariat ropes and used in precision roping (pron. muh-GAY). **1980** *AZ Highways* Feb 7, American cowboys used a shorter grass rope like a *maguey,* made from the fibers of the century plant.

mah See **ma** n **A1**

mahala n [Yokuts *mokel* women] **chiefly CA**

1 also *mahaly, majella, mohale:* An Indian woman or wife.

1850 *Calif. Courier* (S.F.) 31 Aug. 2/1 *(DA),* All this is the work of the squaws—or, as they call them—'Mo-hales.' **1864** in 1942 *CA Folkl. Qrly.* 1.278 **CA,** The mahalies sat each astride a rock / Beating grasshoppers and acorns into smock. **1901** James *Indian Basketry* 227 **CA,** The majella is forced to weave salable baskets in order to support her family. **1903** (1950) Austin *Land of Little Rain* 41 **neCA,** It was Dimmick's squaw from Aurora way. If Dimmick had been anything except New Englander he would have called her a mahala. **1907** Hodge *Hdbk.*

Amer. Indians 1.786, *Mahala,* more often *mohale,* is often used as synonymous with "squaw" in California by the whites. If not from Spanish *mujer,* 'woman,' it is from Yokuts *muk'ela,* having the same meaning. **1969–70** *DARE* Tape **CA**163, The mahalies [mə'heliz] and squaws, they play that game a lot, too; **CA**208, Here come this big fat mahaly in the house. She knocked at the door, you know, and came in, and the father was there, too, and the mother. **1971** Metcalf *Riverside Engl.* 12 **CA,** *Mahala* is now as rarely heard as *squaw.*

2 See **mahala mats.**

mahala mats n Also *mahala (mat)*

A **ceanothus** (here: *Ceanothus prostratus*). Also called **snow-brush, squaw's carpet**
   1896 *Jrl. Amer. Folkl.* 9.184 **CA,** *Ceanothus prostratus,* . . mahala-mats. **1897** Parsons *Wild Flowers CA* 328, The children of our mountain districts know it as . . "mahala mats." Among the Digger Indians the word "Mahala" is applied as a title of respect to all the women of the tribe indiscriminately, and they always refer to one another as "Mahala Sally," "Mahala Nancy," etc. **1898** *Jrl. Amer. Folkl.* 11.225 **CA,** *Ceanothus prostratus* . . *mahala, mahala* mats. **1926** Essig *Insects N. Amer.* 633 **West,** The caterpillars [of *Papilio eurymedon*] feed on coffee berry, and on mahala mats and other species of *Ceanothus.* **1937** U.S. Forest Serv. *Range Plant Hdbk.* B45, Mahala-mats. . . is probably most abundant in the northern Sierras and southern Cascades. **1940** Writers' Program OR *Mt. Hood* 17, Mahala mat, or squaw mat, is a dwarf creeper bearing dainty balls of lavender that blooms in May and June. **1959** Munz–Keck *CA Flora* 984, *Mahala Mats.* Prostrate, the branches rooting and forming mats 1–2.5 m. across.

mahalo exclam |mɑ'hɑlo| [Haw *mahalo* to thank] **HI**
Thank you, thanks; hence phr *mahalo nui (loa)* thank you very much, many thanks.
   1938 Reinecke *Hawaiian Loanwords* 23, *Mahalo.* . . Thanks; thank you. V[ery] F[requent] This word is used in several phrases: *mahalo nui; mahalo nui loa.* Many thanks; thanks very much indeed. F[requent]. **1954–60** Hance et al. *Hawaiian Sugar* 4, *Mahalo.* . . Thanks, thank you. *Mahalo nui.* . . Thank you very much. **1967** *DARE* (Qu. II39, . . *'Thank you'*) Infs **HI**6, 13, Mahalo [mɑ'hɑlo]. **1972** Carr *Da Kine Talk* 87 **HI,** *Hawaiian Words Commonly Heard In Hawaii's English.* . . *Mahalo.* Thank you, thanks. **1981** *Pidgin To Da Max* np **HI,** *Mahalo.* . . Tourist-ese for "T'anks eh?" Used mostly by entertainers, aunties, and inter-island flight attendants.

mahaly See **mahala**

mahape See **mahope**

mahied See **marry**

mahimahi n Also *mahihi* [Haw] **esp HI**
=**dolphin 1.**
   1926 Pan-Pacific Research Inst. *Jrl.* 1.1.8 **HI,** Coryphaena hippurus. . . Mahihi. Mahimahi. **1947** Caine *Salt Water* 18, Often called the "off-spring of the rainbow," the dolphin certainly is one of the most beautiful fish that swims, and a speedy scrapper as well. It is also known as dorado, dourade and, in Hawaii, as mahimahi. **1951** *AmSp* 26.20 **HI,** Many terms for varieties of fish have been borrowed [from Polynesia]; among these are *aku* (bonito), *mahimahi* (dolphin fish). **1960** Gosline–Brock *Hawaiian Fishes* 181, The mahimahi will follow a flying fish by swimming swiftly below it, ready to seize it when it drops back into the sea. **1967** *DARE* (Qu. P2, . . *Kinds of saltwater fish caught around here . . good to eat*) Infs **HI**2, 4, 14, Mahimahi; (Qu. P14, . . *Commercial fishing . . what do the fishermen go out after?*) Inf **HI**2, Mahimahi. **1967** *DARE* Tape **HI**9, Mahimahi, the white, flat fish . . used to catch it on the Kona side. . . a good size, about two feet to two and a half feet, I guess. . . [caught] out in the [deep] water. **1972** Carr *Da Kine Talk* 87 **HI,** *Hawaiian Words Commonly Heard In Hawaii's English.* . . *Mahimahi.* Dolphin, a game fish popular for food. **1994** *DARE* File swCA, Mahimahi is often on restaurant menus in San Diego. *Ibid,* Twenty years ago mahimahi could be found in California restaurants; now it's even in the Midwest.

mahkoolah See **makoola**

mahn See **man** n A

mahogany n Cf **desert mahogany, Florida mahogany, mountain mahogany, white mahogany**
   1 Std: a tree of the genus *Swietenia.* For other names of *S. mahagoni* see **Madeira**

2 Any of var trees or shrubs with wood resembling that of **mahogany 1,** as:

a also *Kentucky mahogany:* =**Kentucky coffee tree.**
   1780 in 1916 Mereness *Travels* 633 **KY,** I met with a tall tree 60 or 70 feet in the body and two feet or three in diameter, . . the bark something like a Cheery tree the wood when cut a crimson red and cald by some Mahogany the grains of the wood resemble the Mahogany some thing but vastly coarser, when dry the red colour vanishes and it appears a glistening white, the leaf I do not know but am informed it bears a pod a foot long containing beans of a flat round form in a sweet acrimonious visid Juice. **1785** Marshall *Arbustrum* 56, I have lately received several seeds from Kentucky, supposed to be of this tree, where it is said to grow plenty, and is called the Coffee or Mahogany tree. **1876** Hobbs *Bot. Hdbk.* 61, Kentucky mahogany, American coffee bean, Gymnocladus Canadensis. **1942** Hylander *Plant Life* 289, The Kentucky Coffee Tree, also known as Mahogany . . , is a fairly large tree of rich bottom lands from New York south to Oklahoma and west to Minnesota. **1953** Strausbaugh–Core *Flora WV* 537, *Kentucky Mahogany.* **1960** Vines *Trees SW* 531, *Gymnocladus dioica* [sic]. . . Also known under the vernacular names of . . Kentucky-mahogany [etc].

b =**mountain mahogany 2** (here: *Cercocarpus* spp). **West**
   1889 Union Pacific RR *Wealth & Resources* 21 **Pacific NW,** There are plenty of good timber lands, on which abound pine, fir, cedar, juniper and mahogany, in the mountains. **1908** Sudworth *Forest Trees Pacific* 338, Curl-leaf Mahogany. . . Cercocarpus ledifolius. . . Freshly cut wood is a distinct mahogany red, browning with exposure. *Ibid* 340, Birch-leaf Mahogany. . . Cercocarpus parvifolius. . . Wood . . rarely used except locally for firewood. **1940** *Jrl. Mammalogy* 21.154 **UT,** One adult doe mule deer . . was seen in the . . mahogany brush. **1949** *Pacific Discovery* Jan-Feb 7, Under present conditions it would be virtually impossible for the mahogany to reproduce, since seedlings would be eaten as fast as they appeared. **1959** Robertson *Ram* 154 **UT** (as of c1875), Father went to "the mahoganies" to get part of our winter's supply of fuel. . . This was a new kind of timber to Father; it was short, scrubby, brittle and hard as iron. The sharpest ax would make no more than a dent, but even the largest tree could be broken off by a good pulling horse. **1967–69** *DARE* (Qu. T5, . . *Evergreens*) Infs **CA**136, **OR**13, Mahogany; (Qu. T16, . . *Kinds of trees . . 'special'*) Infs **CA**156, 163, Mahogany. **1970** Kirk *Wild Edible Plants W. U.S.* 92, *Cercocarpus ledifolius* and related species. . . Mahogany sometimes covers many acres in almost pure stands.

c also *mahogany sumac:* A **sumac** (here: *Rhus integrifolia*). **CA**
   1897 Parsons *Wild Flowers CA* 203, Lemonade-berry. Mahogany. Rhus integrifolia. . . The wood of these shrubs is of a dark-red color, which is responsible for the common name, "mahogany." **1898** *Jrl. Amer. Folkl.* 11.225 **CA,** *Rhus integrifolia,* . . mahogany. **1908** Sudworth *Forest Trees Pacific* 385, Mahogany Sumach. Rhus integrifolia. . . The field name of mahogany sumach is simply "mahogany," and refers to the brilliant red color of its wood. To avoid confusion with the true mahogany . . , the name "mahogany sumach" is suggested. **1938** Van Dersal *Native Woody Plants* 229, *Mahogany sumac.* . . A small to large evergreen shrub; forms remarkably dense thickets. **1942** Hylander *Plant Life* 366, In southern California there are the Laurel Sumac, . . the Lemonade Berry or Mahogany, . . and the Sugar Bush. **1979** Little *Checklist U.S. Trees* 251, *Rhus integrifolia.* . . Lemonade sumac. . . *Other common names*—mahogany sumac.

d See **mahogany birch.**

mahogany birch n Also *mahogany* [See quot 1950] Cf **hogany**
=**sweet birch.**
   1813 Muhlenberg *Catalogus Plantarum* 88, [*Betula*] *lenta* . . soft. . . Black b[irch]—sweet b[irch]—mahagony b[irch]. Pens.-Georg. **1847** Wood *Class-Book* 498, *B[etula] lenta.* . . Mahogany Birch. . . In spring the cambium affords the boys a delicious morsel. **1884** Sargent *Forests of N. Amer.* 162, *Betula lenta.* . . Mahogany birch. . . Wood heavy, very strong and hard, close-grained, compact, satiny, susceptible of a beautiful polish. . . "Birch beer" is obtained by fermenting the saccharine sap of this and perhaps some other species of the genus. **1950** Peattie *Nat. Hist. Trees* 172, *Betula lenta.* . . Mahogany Birch. . . Two characteristics in combination easily identify this lovely tree. The first is the strong wintergreen aroma of the bark and the leaves . . the second is the close, lustrous mahogany-red bark. **1951** *PADS* 15.10, *Betula lenta.* . . Mahogany, hogany, Mitchell County, N.C. **1966–67** *DARE* (Qu. T16, . . *Kinds of trees . . 'special'*) Inf **NC**30, Mahogany birch; **PA**17, Laurel, white birch, mahogany.

mahogany bracket n

Prob a **conk** n[2] **1** such as *Ganoderma applanatum.*

1969 *DARE* (Qu. S19, *Mushrooms that grow out like brackets from the sides of trees*) Inf **NY**134, Mahogany brackets—kids write things on them.

mahogany clam n [Appar from the color]

=**quahog 2.**

1954 Abbott *Amer. Seashells* 382, *Arctica islandica.* . . A common, commercially dredged species found in sandy mud. . . Also called the Black Clam and Mahogany Clam. **1981** Rehder *Audubon Field Guide Seashells* 792, *Ocean Quahog.* . . Also known as Black Clam and Mahogany Clam, this is a highly esteemed food source and the basis of an extensive commercial fishery from Rhode Island south to Virginia.

mahogany flat n [Prob from the color, or association with furniture, and shape]

A bedbug *(Cimex lectularius).*

1896 U.S. Dept. Ag. Div. Entomol. *Bulletin* 4.33, Almost everywhere there are local names for this parasite, as, for illustration, around Boston they are called "chintzes" . . and from Baltimore comes the name "mahogany flat." **1911** *Century Dict. Suppl.* (at *flat* n.[1] II) **Sth**, *Mahogany flat*, the bedbug, *Cimex lectularius.* **1950** Herms *Med. Entomology* 96, Among the local names applied to bedbugs are "chinches," . . "mahogany flats."

mahogany snapper n [From the color]

A **snapper** (here: *Lutjanus mahogoni*).

1898 U.S. Natl. Museum *Bulletin* 47.1272, Mahogany Snapper. . . Color in life deep brown, silvery below, everywhere shaded with red, especially on head. **1902** Jordan–Evermann *Amer. Fishes* 415, *Mahogany Snapper.* . . A small snapper. **1960** Amer. Fisheries Soc. *List Fishes* 26, Mahogany snapper . . *Lutjanus mahogoni.* **1965** McClane *McClane's Std. Fishing Encycl.* 502, *Mahogany Snapper.* . . Taken around southern Florida. . . General coloration reddish-brown with bronze streaks.

mahogany sumac See **mahogany 2c**

mahope adv Usu |mɑˈhope|; for varr see quot 1938 Pronc-sp *mahape* [Haw; see quot 1938] **HI**

Afterwards; later; by and by.

1938 Reinecke *Hawaiian Loanwords* 23, Mahope [ˈmɑːˈhoːpe] [mɑˈhɑːpe, mɑˈhɑːpı..], adv. . . Behind; after; afterward. . . Later in time; late; hindermost. . . By and by; *manana.* This is the most common usage, especially in the expression, "See you mahape." F[req]. **1951** *AmSp* 26.21, Common localisms in Hawaii, used for convenience or more colorful expression, are . . *mahope* (by-and-by; equivalent to the Mexican *mañana*). **1954–60** Hance et al. *Hawaiian Sugar* 4, Mahope [mɑˈhope]. . . Later, behind, late, afterwards.

mahself See **myself**

mahster See **master** n

mahtterr See **matter** n[1], v

mahu adj, n [Haw] **HI**

Of a man; effeminate, homosexual; an effeminate or homosexual man; see quot 1938.

1938 Reinecke *Hawaiian Loanwords* 5, Mahu . . at one extreme means a pervert, at the other a chaser after women—obviously also an unmanly thing to be, in the eyes of some. *Ibid* 23, Mahu . . adj., n. 1. Sissified. 2. An effeminate or sissified man. 3. A male sex pervert, especially a sodomite. 4. "Girl crazy." **1967** *DARE* (Qu. HH39, *A homosexual man*) Inf **HI**1, Mahu [ˈmɑhu]—used all over the islands, euphemistic; **HI**6, Mahu; **HI**13, Mahu [ˌmɑˈhu]. **1972** McCormick *Vocab.* HI 74, *Mahu* n—Homosexual. **1981** *Pidgin To Da Max* np **HI**, *Mahu.* . . Guys who like fool around with guys. . . Drag queen. "No mess aroun' wit dose mahus down Hotel Shtreet, brah! Dose buggahs radical!"

mahukona violet n [*Mahukona* city on north end of Island of Hawaii] **HI**

=**nohu 1.**

1900 Lyons *Plant Names* 375, *T[ribulus] cistoides.* . . Mahukona Violet (Hawaii, with allusion to the fragrance). **1924** *Amer. Botanist* 30.112 **HI**, Here and there the sand near the shore may be carpeted with Nohu *(Zygophyllum tribulum),* and surely nothing could be more gay than the gold of its delicately fragrant blossoms—Mahukona violets they are called locally.

mahvil See **marvel** n[1]

maid bride See **maid's bride**

maiden n Chesapeake Bay Cf **fair maid**

=**scup** (here: *Stenotomus chrysops*).

1903 NY State Museum & Sci. Serv. *Bulletin* 60.559, In Norfolk Va. Mr Bean heard the name maiden for the young of the common scup. **1939** Natl. Geogr. Soc. *Fishes* 69, The *Scup* of New England . . is . . the maiden . . in Chesapeake Bay. **1984** *DARE* File **Chesapeake Bay** [Watermen's vocab], Scup, porgy, maiden, fair maid.

maidenbush n

A small, usu straggling, shrub *(Andrachne phyllanthoides).*

1960 Vines *Trees SW* 609, *Missouri Maiden-bush.* . . Dry rocky soil of ledges, arroyos, and barrens. **1970** Correll *Plants TX* 925, *Andrachne phyllanthoides.* . . Maidenbush. . . Mo., Ark., Okla. and Tex.; reportedly also in Ala.

maiden cane n [See quot 1925] **S Atl, Gulf States**

A **panic grass** (here: *Panicum hemitomon*). Also called **little cane, paille fine**

1806 (1905) Lewis *Orig. Jrls. Lewis & Clark Exped.* 5.107, Among the grasses of this country [=MT] I observe a large speceis which . . has much the appearance of the maden cain as it is called in . . Ge[o]rgia. **1901** *Torreya* 1.115 **swGA**, *Panicum digitarioides.* . . Maiden cane. **1925** *Book of Rural Life* 6.3300, Maiden cane . . (*Panicum hemitomum*), the most nutritious native grass that occurs in the Southern swamps. . . Maiden cane blooms but rarely, and then under exceptional conditions. Its lack of blossoms probably gave rise to its common name. **1927** Boston Soc. Nat. Hist. *Proc.* 38.245 **Okefenokee GA**, There are acres of water lilies, . . thick green beds of 'maiden cane' *(Panicum),* . . and a host of other plants. *Ibid* 247, *Panicum hemitomon*—'Maiden cane'. **1938** Matschat *Suwannee R.* 72 **neFL, seFL**, The big bulls [=alligators], who trumpet their love songs from half-submerged logs along the winding Suwannee, or from the shelter of the maiden cane that covers the prairies. **1947** *Jrl. Wildlife Management* 2.55 **seLA**, Cattails, bulrushes . . , and wapato . . are the principal food plants, but maidencane . . eventually is the dominant plant. **1966** *DARE* (Qu. S9, . . *Kinds of grass that are hard to get rid of*) Inf **FL**7, Maiden cane; (Qu. S21) Inf **FL**35, Wild maiden cane. **1969** Lyons *My Florida* 174, I got the yen to grow Kentucky Wonder pole beans, went out on the bank of St. Lucie Canal and cut a couple of hundred maiden-cane poles. **1969** *DARE* File **seGA**, Maiden cane choke up a water-run.

maidenhair n

1 See **maidenhair fern**.

2 Either of two related plants: a **water avens** (here: *Geum rivale*) or **prairie smoke**.

1893 *Jrl. Amer. Folkl.* 6.141, *Geum rivale.* . . Maiden hair. Brodhead, Wis. **1950** Stevens *ND Plants* 171, *Geum canadense.* . . This is an attractive and popular wild flower. Also called Maidenhair.

3 A **meadow rue** (here: *Thalictrum pubescens*).

1911 Waters *Ferns* 88, Another common error is to call the common meadow-rue maidenhair, probably because of the resemblance in shape of its leaflets and those of the maidenhair-ferns common in greenhouses. One glance at the pale stems will show that the plant is not the fern in question. They are not only green, instead of polished, dark brown, but they branch in an entirely different manner.

maidenhair-berry n

A **wintergreen** (here: *Gaultheria hispidula*).

1924 *Amer. Botanist* 30.56, *Chiogenes hispidula.* . . "Maidenhair-berry" is probably another popular misnomer. **1943** Fernald–Kinsey *Edible Wild Plants E. N. Amer.* 311, *Maidenhair-berry.* . . Rarely fruits in abundance in the southern part of its range. . . Eaten fresh the berries are pleasantly acid, . . but when eaten with cream and sugar they are one of the greatest delicacies of the northern woods. **1959** Carleton *Index Herb. Plants* 77, *Maidenhair-berry:* Chiogenes hispidula.

maidenhair fern n Also *maidenhair, maiden's hair*

Std: a fern of the genus *Adiantum.* Also called **lady fern 2.** For other names of var spp see **dudder-grass, five-finger fern, hair fern, lockhair fern, mattress fern, rock fern, sweet fern**

maidenhair moss n

A **pondweed** (here: *Potamogeton foliosus*).

1913 *Torreya* 13.226, *Potamogeton foliosus.* . . Maiden-hair moss, Menasha, Ark.

maiden's blushes n [See quot 1901]

=**fever tree.**

1901 *Torreya* 1.117 **GA,** *Pinckneya pubens.* . . Maiden's blushes. . . Doubtless so called on account of the color of its enlarged calyx-segments. **1926** *Ibid* 26.84 **FL,** Pinckneya pubens (maiden's blushes).

maiden's hair See **maidenhair fern**

maiden's tears n

=**bladder campion.**

1911 *Century Dict. Suppl.,* Maiden's-tears. . . The bladder-campion, *Silene vulgaris.* **1950** Gray–Fernald *Manual of Botany* 632, *S[ilene] Cucubalus.* . . *Maiden's-tears.* . . Roadsides, borders of fields, gravelly shores, etc. **1976** Bailey–Bailey *Hortus Third* 1045, *[Silene] vulgaris.* . . Bladder campion, maiden's-tears.

maiden's tit n

A **thimbleberry** (here: *Rubus parviflorus*).

1945 McAtee *Nomina Abitera* 13 **NW,** Salmonberry *(Rubus parviflorus)*—Maiden's tit.

maiden's tresses n

Prob a **ladies' tresses.**

1969 *DARE* (Qu. S26c, *Wildflowers that grow in woods*) Inf **CT37,** Maiden's tresses.

maid-in-the-mist n

=**fennel-flower.**

1896 *Jrl. Amer. Folkl.* 9.180, *Nigella Damascena.* . . Maid-in-the-mist, Acton, Mass.

maid marian n

=**meadow beauty 1.**

1933 Small *Manual SE Flora* 925, *Rhexia.* . . Maid-marian. Meadow-beauties. **1949** Moldenke *Amer. Wild Flowers* 105, The only herbaceous genus [of the family Melastomaceae] in our area [=the eastern US] is *Rhexia,* the meadowbeauties or maidmarians.

maid-of-the-mist n

1 =**meadow rue.**

1903 Small *Flora SE U.S.* 445, *Thalictrum.* . . Meadow Rue. Maid-of-the-Mist. **1952** Taylor *Plants Colonial Days* 58, Meadow rue— *Thalictrum minus adiantifolium* . . or maid-of-the-mist, blooms in June. The loose, filmy clusters of yellow-green flowers . . give the plant a delicate, lacy appearance.

2 See **mist maiden.**

maid's bride n Also *maid bride* [Reversed compound; cf *bridesmaid* and Intro "Language Changes" I.1]

1965 *McDavid Coll.* **cGA,** Maid's bride—bride's maid. **1986** Pederson *LAGS Concordance,* 1 inf, **sMS,** Maid bride [=bridesmaid].

maied See **marry**

maikai adj, adv [Haw] **HI** Cf **mahalo**

See quots.

1873 in 1966 Bishop *Sandwich Is.* 71 **HI,** There is no word for "thank you." *Maikai* "good," is often useful in its place, and smiles supply the rest. **1938** Reinecke *Hawaiian Loanwords* 23, *Maika'i* ['mɑːɪkɑʔɪ, 'mɑɪ'kɑɪ]. . . Good; beautiful; in a good state. . . F[req]. **1972** Carr *Da Kine Talk* 87 **HI,** *Maika'i.* Good, well; good-looking. **1984** Sunset *HI Guide* 85, *Maika'i*—good, fine.

mail n Cf Intro "Language Changes" II.7, **letter-mail**

A piece of mail.

1972 Carr *Da Kine Talk* 137 **HI,** "Five of the outgoing mails need to have stamps on them." "Helen, what do you know! You have a mail in the box!" These examples are from the Type IV speech [=near-standard Hawaiian English]. . . In both, there are humorous overtones.

mail carrier n

A **wildcat** (here: *Felis rufus*) that appears to make regular rounds from place to place.

1970 *Foxfire* Spring–Summer 11 **nGA,** Sometimes they'd be one old big'un [=a wildcat]. He'd come an' kill a bunch a'pigs, an' then he'd

go back t'another section a'th'country. That's th'ones they always called th' mail carriers, and they'd all lay fer'em.

maile n [Haw] **HI** Note: Haw has only one liquid consonant, which early writers often represented with *r* rather than *l.*

A twining shrub *(Alyxia olivaeformis).*

1825 Ellis *Jrl. HI* 42, Six women . . crowned with garlands of flowers, having also wreaths of flowers on their necks, and branches of the fragrant *maire,* (a native plant,) bound round their ancles, now made their way by couples through the crowd. **1929** Neal *Honolulu Gardens* 252, The *maile* is a favorite plant of the Hawaiians, the fragrant bark of its stems and the fragrant, elliptical, and highly polished leaves being indispensable decorations at festive times for houses as well as for people. **1930** Degener *Ferns of HI* 249, The *maile* is a straggling or weakly twining shrub emitting . . milky juice when wounded. **1965** Krauss–Alexander *Grove Farm* 288 **HI,** Daisy and Ralph were married under a bower of daisy chains and maile. **1968** *Jrl. Engl. Ling.* 2.82 **HI,** Maile. . . A vine in the periwinkle family *(Alyxia olivaeformis),* the fragrant leaves and bark of which are used for decoration and *leis.* **1980** Bushnell *Water of Kane* 371 **HI,** The men of Japan . . were sent into the woods to gather ferns, ti leaves, strands of maile, and other greenery for decorating the tables. **1994** *WI State Jrl.* (Madison) 6 Nov sec H 3 **HI,** Maile. . . The Maile Lei—made from the vinelike shrub that grows in the mountains and valleys of the [Hawaiian] islands—is usually reserved for special occasions.

maile haole n [Haw < **maile** + **haole;** see quots] **HI**

1 =**myrtle** n[1] **B1.**

1948 Neal *In Gardens HI* 555, Myrtle, maile haole. Myrtus communis. . . A favorite garden plant of Hawaiians, who strung the leaves into leis as they did maile leaves. . . Today, it sometimes serves for bridal wreaths.

2 A **star jasmine** (here: *Trachelospermum jasminoides*).

1965 Neal *Gardens HI* 694, *Trachelospermum jasminoides.* . . Due to the similarity of this vine to maile and due to its similar use for leis, locally it is sometimes called maile-haole.

maile pilau n [Haw < **maile** + *pilau* putrid] **HI**

A woody vine *(Paederia foetida)* with a strong odor. Also called **stink vine**

1929 Pope *Plants HI* 223, *Paederia foetida.* . . Maile Pilau is the common name for this plant in Hawaii. It is not a difficult plant to control in cultivated fields and gardens. **1929** Neal *Honolulu Gardens* 312, *Maile pilau.* . . The leaves look like those of the true *maile* but unlike them have a strong unpleasant odor. **1965** Neal *Gardens HI* 794, Maile pilau. . . *Paederia foetida.*

Mailey See **Maley**

mail-order adj Cf **catalog woman**

Of a woman: located through a matrimonial or advertising agent.

1935 Sandoz *Jules* 162 **wNE** (as of 1890s), Hans . . had answered a matrimonial advertisement and got a mail-order wife. **1937** Sandoz *Slogum* 54 **NE** (as of 1900–20), Mostly they were just gut-starved hoe men . . come west to get away from some woman or another. But before long they were looking for cooks, somebody to sleep with—mail-order women. **1958** McCulloch *Woods Words* 115 **Pacific NW,** *Mail order woman*—A wife secured through a matrimonial bureau. **1995** *DARE* File **csWI** (as of c1930), A mail-order bride might be found through a lonely hearts column.

mail-order cowboy n Also *Monkey Ward cowboy* Cf **Monkey Ward**

A would-be cowboy.

1926 Branch *Cowboy* 17, The range came to expect and recognize the "mail-order cowboy," who arrived already fitted in cowboy-wear as he knew it from his reading and the assurances of some Middle Western store-keeper. **1936** McCarthy *Lang. Mosshorn* np **West** [Rodeo terms], *Mail Order Cowboy.* A westerner who wears a cheap outfit. **1942** *AmSp* 17.75 **NE,** Nearly every community boasts a *Monkey Ward cowboy,* a waddie who sports loud shirts, fancy trousers, fancy boots and a big Stetson.

main n[1] [*OED* 1555 →; "*arch.*"] chiefly **Atlantic**

The mainland.

1608 Smith *True Relation* [6] **VA,** The Towne adjoyning to the maine by a neck of Land of sixtie yardes. **1766** (1942) Bartram *Diary of a*

Journey 47 **S Atl,** A large point of land projects out from the main. **1774** in 1940 *AmSp* 15.282 **VA,** A very valuable Tract of Land . . , being on the Main opposite gwyn's Island. **1785** in 1847 *Olden Time* 2.493 **Ohio Valley,** Here are fine cane-brakes, both on the island and the main on the south side. **1842** (1927) Rodman *Diary* 237 **MA,** She [=a steamboat] makes a trip from and to the island daily which . . is almost like taking Nantucket from her ocean bed and uniting her to the main. **1903** Wasson *Cap'n Simeon's Store* 171 **eME,** I was borned . . across the Gut from Wrack Islant, on the main. **1945** Colcord *Sea Language* 124 **ME, Cape Cod, Long Island,** *Main, the.* An islander's term for the mainland. "I'm going over to the main for the week end." **1951** *DE Folkl. Bulletin* 1.7, *Main* (the mainland). **1970** *DARE* FW Addit **VA**51, *Main*—used by islanders to refer to the mainland of the eastern shore. **1975** Gould *ME Lingo* 174, The mainland is still called *the main* by people on Vinalhaven, Matinicus, Criehaven, and Monhegan, who say, "I'm going to the main tomorrow."

main *adj* chiefly **S Midl**
Great, excellent; notable.

1887 *Scribner's Mag.* 2.484 **AR,** Ain't it a main mussy [=mercy] the critter died. **1924** Raine *Land of Saddle-Bags* 103 **sAppalachians,** He's a *main* worker; he has *breskit.* **1937** *Hall Coll.* **eTN, wNC,** He took after it and had a main race down there till the turkey flopped up agin a big log, and there they caught it; **ceTN,** He was a main hunter. [Both infs old] **1937** (1963) Hyatt *Kiverlid* 31 **KY,** You air a main hand to try to have somethin'. **1942** (1971) Campbell *Cloud-Walking* 139 **seKY,** He was a right main preacher but he had a heap of bother keeping his store teeth from falling plumb outen his mouth. **1945** FWP *Lay My Burden Down* 201 **AL** [Black], I seed most the mainest generals in the Union army and some in the Rebel army. **1968** *DARE* FW Addit **LA**18, *Mainest*—main, chief. "The big one is the mainest one you see." **1991** Still *Wolfpen Notebooks* 85 **sAppalachians,** Goose grease is the main-est thing for waterproofing shoes.

main *adv* chiefly **sAppalachians**
Very, exceedingly—often in comb *main big.*

1853 Simms *Sword & Distaff* 582 **SC,** He's gone off now, I'm main sartin, to pop the question to the widow. **1892** *KS Univ. Qrly.* 1.97 **cMA,** *Main:* very, as, It's main strange. **1895** *DN* 1.372 **seKY, wNC, eTN,** "I seen a main big rabbit to-day." "Hit's the main biggest rabbit ever I see." **1937–39** *Hall Coll.* **ceTN,** It was a main old big one; **wNC,** I looked back and I seed no panter [=panther]. I don't know where he went, but he was a main big 'un! **wNC,** It's a main big old house. [All infs old] **1955** Ritchie *Singing Family* 198 **seKY,** That's the main best eating in the world! **1974** Fink *Mountain Speech* 16 **wNC, eTN,** A main high mountain.

main *n*[2] [*OED* 1760 →]
1 A series of cockfighting matches. Cf **hack** *n*[1] **5**

1937 in 1972 *Amer. Slave* 2.232 **SC,** I 'tend Marse Ed to a chicken main once. **1939** FWP *Guide FL* 455, Known as 'mains,' 'hacks,' or 'meetings,' the [cock]fights are not advertised by press or radio. **1941** Koenigsberg *King News* 176 **El Paso TX** (as of 1896), Why should the abysmal brutality of pugilism bring to mind the gaiety that would fade from a Mexican fiesta without bullfights and cock mains? **1945** *Grit & Steel* Dec 55, He fought a main against Styles with his own chickens and again won; and a main against Tony DeLess. **1945** *Feathered Warrior* Dec 9, Back 25 or more years ago John Madigan and Hanky Dean made a main with Seneca Falls, N.Y., cockers. . . The main was to be fought at another location in the same locality.

2 By ext: the collection of cocks assembled for a series of cockfighting matches.

1945 *Feathered Warrior* Dec 9, They stoped [sic] for a drink at a local hotel, and someone stole the entire main of cocks.

main big See **main** *adv*

Maine(i)ac See **Mainiac**

main girl, main guy See **main man**

main house *n* Cf **big house 2, house B1**
A living room or parlor.

1942 (1971) Campbell *Cloud-Walking* 193 **seKY,** The other women set back in the cook room and talked, there not being room for all the folks in the main house. **1948** *McDavid Coll.* **SC,** *Main house*—living room. **1949** *AmSp* 24.111 **neSC,** *Main-house.* . . Living room.

Mainiac *n* Also sp *Maine(i)ac* [Blend of *Maine* + *maniac*] esp **NEng** *joc*

A resident of Maine.

1837 (1932) Hawthorne *Amer. Notebooks* 10 **MA,** The British have lately imprisoned a man who was sent to take the census; and the Mainiacs are much excited on the subject. **1852** *Lantern* (N.Y.) I.145/2 *(DA),* On the 15th of April there is to be a great *Fast* throughout the State of Maine. The Mainiacs are to be *Fastmen,* which is a clear confession they are *loose* at present. **1856** *Santa Barbara Gaz.* (CA) 10 Jan [4/2], Listen to the ravings of a Maine-ac. **1939** *AmSp* 14.234, Names for natives of American places . . Mainiac. **1966** *Ellsworth Amer.* (ME) 29 June 6/6, I'm what you call a real Mainiac. . . You're never going to get me out of Maine from now on. **1968** *DARE* (Qu. HH28) Inf **NH**14, Mainiac—someone from Maine. **1975** Gould *ME Lingo* 175, *Maineiac*—The homonymic implications of this word do not offend Maine people, and they do not take umbrage when it is applied to them. *Maineiac* is more used by out-of-staters than by bona fide residents of the Pine Tree Precinct, but the latter are capable of tossing it off to describe themselves when it suits, and with more than a little pride. **1992** *DARE* File **cME** (as of 1970s), Both *Mainiac* and *Mainer* were used in general conversation for someone from Maine. Though the homonym *maniac* was not lost on people, I've never had the impression that *Mainiac* was derived from it.

main iron *n* Also *main steel* Cf **high iron a**
A principal railroad line.

1931 *Writer's Digest* 11.42 [Railroad terms], *Main Iron*—Main track. **1932** *RR Mag.* Oct 369. **1938** Beebe *High Iron* 222 [Railroad terms], *Main iron:* Main track, high iron. **1977** Adams *Lang. Railroader* 97, *Main steel:* A main track.

main line *n*

1 In logging: the chief cable used to haul logs. **Pacific NW**

1925 *AmSp* 1.136 **Pacific NW** [Logger talk], The cable that hauled the logs was called "the main line." **1950** *Western Folkl.* 9.118 **nwOR** [Logger speech], *Main line.* Heavy wire cable, 1¾ inches to 2 inches in diameter, used to skid logs. **1956** *AmSp* 31.151 **nCA,** *Main line.* . . The hauling line on a cable logging operation. **1961** Labbe–Goe *Railroads* 258 **Pacific NW,** *Mainline:* The main line on a donkey, which is used for the heavy pull.

2 A fashionable residential district. [Orig in ref to wealthy suburbs of Philadelphia, through which the main line of the Pennsylvania Railroad runs] Cf **gold coast, Nob Hill**

[**1939** Barry *Philadelphia Story* 34, There are a very few old ones [=houses] on the Main Line. *Ibid* 54, There'll be time to run you out to some other places on the Main Line.] [**1951** Longstreet *Pedlocks* 15 **Philadelphia PA,** She liked to have Peter there, so young and handsome and so popular with the Main Line families.] [**1968** *DARE* (Qu. II24, *Names or nicknames for the part of a town where the well-off people live*) Inf **PA**172, The Main Line. [*DARE* Ed: Inf is from Philadelphia.]] **1982** *This Remarkable Continent* 96, One result of these processes of choosing a place to live is the creation of neighborhoods and communities that are easily stereotyped and labeled. For example, we can all think of "high-class" and "low-class" neighborhoods, ghettos, . . suburbs, . . "the mainline," as geographically defined places that contain . . relatively homogeneous groups of people.

main man *n* Also *main guy,* *~ nigger* chiefly among Black speakers

A favorite male friend; a male sweetheart or lover; similarly nouns *main girl,* *~ whore* a female sweetheart or lover.

1967 Baraka *Tales* 19 **NYC,** "Hey, man, I saw that ol' fagit Bobby Hutchens down in the lobby with a real D.C. queer." . . "Hey, man you cats better cool it . . you talkin' about Ray's main man." **1970** Abrahams *Deep Down* 266 [Black], *Main who'*—Best girlfriend. **1970** *DARE* (Qu. AA3, *Nicknames or affectionate names for a sweetheart*) Inf **TN**46, My main man; (Qu. II1, . . *A close friend*) Inf **NY**238, Main man. [Both Infs Black] **1971** Roberts *Third Ear* np [Black], *Main man* . . 1[.] a woman's boyfriend. 2. a man's closest friend. **1979** *Capital Times* (Madison WI) 12 Feb 16, ["Doonesbury" comic strip:] "Minorities, poor Blacks in particular, see him as a valuable ally in an otherwise reactionary world." "Ally, *nothin'!* He's our *main man!*" **1986** Pederson *LAGS Concordance* (Best friend—nonromantic relationship with member of same sex) 1 inf, **cwTN,** Main man, used to call a black best friend; 1 inf, **swAL,** Main man, not necessarily best friend; 2 infs, **swAL, cTX,** My main man; (Her boyfriend) 1 inf, **cwTN,** Main man; 1 inf, **cnGA,** My main man; 1 inf, **swAL,** My main nigger; 1 inf, **cnGA,** My main guy; (Pimp) 1 inf, **neTN,** Their main man = pimp to prostitutes; (His girl friend) 1 inf, **swAL,** Main girl—formerly used; 1 inf, **cLA,** Main girl. [8 of 9 total infs Black] **1988** Lincoln *Avenue* 194 **wNC** (as of c1940) [Black], Well, I do believe it's my main man. . . What you gon' say, country boy!

main pin n
Among railroad workers: a company official.

1931 *Writer's Digest* 11.42 [Railroad terms], *Main Pin*—An official. **1932** *RR Mag.* Oct 369.

main squeeze n Cf squeeze
1 also *big squeeze, head ~:* A boss or foreman; an important person.

1896 (1898) Ade *Artie* 63, I went in and asked the main squeeze o' the works how much the sacque meant to him. **1926** Finerty *Criminalese* 39, *Main squeeze*—A head fellow. **1927** (1943) Hammett *$106000* 13, Vance seems to be the main squeeze. **1935** *AmSp* 10.18 (as of c1900), *Main squeeze.* . . The chief or leader of a gang. . . The head of any organization. **1938** *AmSp* 13.71 [Railroad lingo], *Main squeeze.* Foreman. **1958** McCulloch *Woods Words* 115 **Pacific NW**, *Main squeeze*— The boss. **1966** Barnes–Jensen *Dict. UT Slang* 29, *Main squeeze* . . chief operator. **1966–67** *DARE* (Qu. HH17, *A person who tries to appear important, or who tries to lay down the law in his community:* "*He'd like to be the _____ around here.*") Infs **OR**1, **WI**127, Big squeeze; **MO**5, Head squeeze; (Qu. HH43a, *The top person in charge of a group of workmen*) Inf **MT**3, Main squeeze.

2 A close friend, sweetheart, or favorite sexual partner. *esp freq among Black speakers* Cf **main man**

1970 *DARE* (Qu. AA3, *Nicknames or affectionate names for a sweetheart*) Inf **TN**46, Main squeeze. [Inf Black, female] **1971** Roberts *Third Ear* np [Black], *Main squeeze* . . a man's closest woman friend. **1980** Folb *Runnin' Down* 133 **Los Angeles CA** [Black], Like dude tell you, 'You my main squeeze, my one-an'-only.' *Ibid* 246, *Main squeeze.* . . Male's favorite or most frequent sexual partner. . . Male's mate, lover, girlfriend. **1983** De Vries *Slouching* 66 **ND**, I use to snitch them [=birth control pills] for my main squeeze, so she's got practically a year's supply without going to the family doctor. **1986** Pederson *LAGS Concordance (Her boyfriend)* 1 inf, **swTN**, Main squeeze; *(His girlfriend)* 1 inf, **swAL**, Main squeeze. [Both infs Black, male]

main steel See main iron

main strength and awkwardness n Also *main strength of ignorance;* for addit varr see quots *esp Sth, S Midl*
Brute force, simple persistence.

1928 in 1952 Mathes *Tall Tales* 78 **sAppalachians**, The five noncombatants improvised a rude stretcher from poles and blankets, and by main strength and prodigious awkwardness bore the unconscious victor down the rough ridge. **1928** Ruppenthal Coll. **KS**, You have to learn these principles by main strength and pure awkwardness. **1942** Smiley *Gloss. New Paltz* **NY**, He did it by main strength of ignorance. **1943** McAtee *Dial. Grant Co. IN Suppl. 2* 10 (as of 1890s), *Main strength and awkwardness* . . used in such expressions as, "I'll get there by _____," or "We'll make it by _____," conveying such senses as "muddling through" and "slow but sure." **c1960** Wilson Coll. **csKY**, *By main strength and awkwardness* . . with difficulty, often clumsily. **1962** Dykeman *Tall Woman* 86 **NC** (as of 1860s), He had strained and lifted and pushed and mauled their cabin together—"by main strength and awkwardness," as Aunt Tildy said. **1968** *DARE* Tape **LA**29, We didn't have no way . . of gettin' the stumps out, only just main strength and awkwardness [laughter]. **1986** Pederson *LAGS Concordance,* 1 inf, **cwAR**, Main strength and awkwardness.

maintainance n [Var of *maintenance,* infl by pronc of *maintain; OED* 16th–18th cents]
1950 *WELS Suppl.* **WI**, We're called "Building Maintainance [ˌmeɪnˈtenənts] Helpers." **c1980** *DARE* File **csWI**, If the pipes give you any more trouble, call the maintainance men. **1992** *Ibid,* In Georgia during the early 1970s, I heard *maintenance* pronounced *maintainance* [ˌmeɪnˈtenənts] on numerous occasions.

maintainer n Also *road maintainer* chiefly Upper Missip Valley, esp IA, MO See Map
One who keeps roads in good repair.

1965–70 *DARE* (Qu. N33, *A man whose job is to take care of roads in a certain locality*) 29 Infs, **chiefly Upper Missip Valley, esp IA, MO**, (Road) maintainer. **1995** *DARE* File **nwKS**, I hired a maintainer about three years ago for this road. Look at how it's washed out since then.

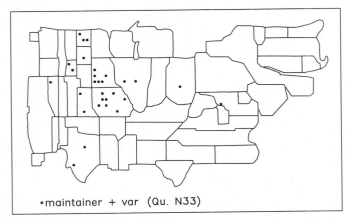

•maintainer + var (Qu. N33)

main whore See main man

mais conj [Fr "but"] LA
See quot 1992.

1968 *DARE* FW Addit **LA**33, Mais no [ˌmeˈno]—*no* not nasalized. "Mais no, she was supposed to be here an hour ago." **1983** Reinecke Coll. 7 **LA**, *Mais.* [me]—Introduces sentence with senses "contrariwise," or merely "indeed". **1992** Scott *Cajun Vernacular Engl.* 48 **sLA**, *Mais* is a French conjunction used as an interjection roughly synonymous with "well" or "but." It usually precedes a sentence and often serves to emphasize the meaning of the speaker's statement as in "Mais, why you gotta do what he says? If he tells you jump in the bayou, you gonna jump?" The phrases *Mais yeah, Mais non,* and *Mais cher* are common.

maize See milo maize

maize bird n [See quot 1890] obs Cf maize thief
=redwing blackbird.

1837 Richardson *Fauna Boreali–Amer.* 2.280, Red-winged Maize-bird. *Ibid* 286, Later in the season it [=the rusty blackbird] joins the flocks of the Maize-birds, Boat-tails, and Cuckoo-bunts in committing depredations in the corn fields. **1890** *Century Dict.* 3584, *Maize-bird.* . . An American blackbird of the family *Icteridæ* and subfamily *Agelæinæ;* one of the troopials or marsh-blackbirds: so called from its fondness for Indian corn.

maize thief n obs Cf maize bird
Either the **redwing blackbird** or the **purple grackle**.

1772 Kalm *Travels N. Amer.* (transl. Forster) 1.372, The laws of Pensylvania [sic] . . have settled a premium of three-pence a dozen for dead maize-thieves. **1811** Wilson *Amer. Ornith.* 4.37, [Red-winged starlings] are known by various names . . such as the *Swamp Blackbird,* . . *Corn* or *Maize Thief,* Starling, &c. **1887** Coues *Key to N. Amer. Birds* 404, The blackbird [=*Agelaius phoeniceus*] collects in August and September in immense flocks, . . visiting and doing much damage to grain-fields. . . At other seasons the "maize-thief" is innocuous, if not positively beneficial, as it destroys its share of insects. **1914** Eaton *Birds NY* 2.232, In the early days of the country the Redwing was called the maize thief from his depredations upon the cornfield, but now when the cornfields are so numerous and the marshes of such comparatively slight extent and, consequently, the redwings are so few in number, the damage they do is so small as scarcely to be noticeable except in a few instances. **1917** (1923) *Birds Amer.* 2.267, *Purple Grackle.* . . *Other names.* . . Maize Thief. [*Ibid* 2.270, The Purple Grackle . . needs watching, for the grain he eats amounts to 45 per cent. of his food.]

majella See mahala

majig n Also *majigger, majiggie* Cf *domajig(ger)* (at doojig-ger), -ma- infix
=thingumajig.

1867 in 1919 Hale *Letters* 26, Mr. Tarvil sent me . . a long box containing an amber necklace with gold majigs hanging from it. **1928** *DN* 6.3, *Majig.* . . Short for *thingamajig.* **1931** *AmSp* 6.258 [Indefinite names], Majig, majiggie. **1942** Berrey–Van den Bark *Amer. Slang* 75.4, *Contrivance; indefinite object;* "gadget." . . Majig, majigger, majiggie.

major n
1 Used as an unofficial title of respect, sometimes applied joc or ironically. **esp Sth, S Midl** Cf **captain B2, colonel B1, Georgia major, Kentucky colonel**

1746 *London Mag.* June 324, Wherever you travel in *Maryland* (as also in *Virginia* and *Carolina*) your Ears are constantly astonished at the Number of *Colonels, Majors,* and *Captains,* that you hear mentioned. 1852 *S. Lit. Messenger* 18.680, Every man that ever comes from Georgia *is* a major,—repaying the honor of . . the title by undeviating fidelity to the democratic ticket. 1873 Twain–Warner *Gilded Age* 515, When we first came here, I was *Mr.* Sellers, and *Major* Sellers, and *Captain* Sellers, . . but the minute our bill went through the House, I was *Colonel* Sellers every time. 1908 (1915) Calhoun *Miss Minerva* 42 **cwTN,** He kilt 'bout a million Injuns and Yankees and he's name' Major 'cause he's a Confed'rit vetrun. 1942 Berrey–Van den Bark *Amer. Slang* 459.1, Superintendent; manager. . . Boss . . the Major. 1968 *DARE* (Qu. HH17, *A person who tries to appear important . . "He'd like to be the _____ around here."*) Inf **VA25,** Major.

2 =**great blue heron.** [See quot 1955]

1955 *Oriole* 20.1.2 **GA,** Great Blue Heron. . . Major (in recognition of its imposing appearance). 1966 *DARE* (Qu. Q10, . . *Water birds and marsh birds*) Inf **GA3,** Blue crane—major. 1969 Longstreet *Birds FL* 21, Great Blue Heron. Other names: *Blue Crane; The "Major".* These majestic birds . . [have] attributes associated with royalty: gorgeous clothing, stately bearing, grace of movement, a slow dignified walk.

majordomo n Also *mayordomo* [AmSpan *mayordomo*] **SW**

1 The overseer of a ranch or mission; a person in charge of a group or project.

1834 in 1929 *CA Hist. Soc. Qrly.* 8.228, Four ranchos [near San Luis Rey], each one made up of an Indian village, a house for the *mayordomo* directing it, storehouses suitable for the harvests, and a very fine chapel. 1848 Bryant *What I Saw in CA* 352, We inquired for the *major domo,* or overseer. 1856 in 1948 *Western Folkl.* 7.13 **CA,** [A man named Castillo] told the mayor-domo that Don Ramon ordered him to let Castillo have a horse, which he obtained. 1892 *DN* 1.249 **TX,** *Mayordómo:* the manager on a ranch or *hacienda.* 1899 Thomas *Arizona* 94, Pa . . says you're the best Major Domo the ranch ever had. 1910 J. Hart *Vigilante Girl* xiv.195 (*OEDS*) **CA,** Arthur's chair was taken to the *portal,* where they found the major-domo and a group of *vaqueros* waiting. 1967 *DARE* (Qu. HH43b, *The assistant to the top person in charge of a group of workmen*) Inf **TX5,** Mayordomo ['maɪə,domo].

2 A manager or official in charge of irrigation. **esp NM** Cf **ditch rider**

1885 *Harper's New Mth. Mag.* 70.692 **NM,** The *acequias* [=canals] are public works, and in each place are under the control of the highly important local official called the *mayor domo.* 1902 Newell *Irrigation* 107, He is usually known as the "watermaster" or "ditch-rider"; or, in Spanish-speaking communities, as majordomo or zanjero. *Ibid* 349 **NM,** The ditches, as a rule, are owned in common by the farmers of each community, and one of the irrigators is annually elected superintendent, or majordomo. 1940 Fergusson *Our Southwest* 251, Every man owed so many days' ditch work under the elected *mayordomo,* ditch boss, who also doled out the water so the man living up the stream did not rob his down-stream neighbor. 1966 *DARE* Tape **NM6,** There's usually three members of the ditch commission and one member is usually called the mayordomo ['mɛrə,domo] or overseer. 1988 Crawford *Mayordomo* xii **nNM,** The *mayordomo* is the ditch manager and is usually paid a monthly salary during the irrigation season.

mak See **make** v[1]

makahiki n [Haw] **HI**

See quots.

1938 Reinecke *Hawaiian Loanwords* 23, Makahiki ['maka'hi:ki]. . . [Reinecke: Originally, a New Year festival at which athletic sports were held.] The annual meet of the Boy Scouts. F[requent]. 1954–60 Hance et al. *Hawaiian Sugar* 4, Makahiki [ma'kɑhiki]—Celebration. 1972 Carr *Da Kine Talk* 87 **HI,** *Hawaiian Words Commonly Heard In Hawaii's English. . . Makahiki.*

makai adv, adj [Haw; see quot 1938] **HI** Cf **kai** n, adv, **mauka**

Toward the sea; seaward.

1873 in 1966 Bishop *Sandwich Is.* 71 **HI,** I hear on all sides . . two words, *makai,* signifying "on the sea-side," and *mauka,* "on the mountain side." These terms are perfectly intelligible out of doors, but it is puzzling when one is asked to sit on "the *mauka* side of the table." 1938 Reinecke *Hawaiian Loanwords* 23, Makai . . , adv. [*Ma,* at, and *kai,* sea.] Toward or at the sea, as opposed to *mauka,* inland. This is a legal as well as a popular direction. . . V[ery] F[requent]. 1951 *AmSp* 26.22, More common than the usual compass directions in Hawaii are *mauka* (toward the mountains) and *makai* (toward the sea). In Honolulu these

are combined with the names of towns along the shore, *Ewa* and *Waikiki.* The newspaper may report an auto accident at the 'waikiki-makai' corner of an intersection. 1969 *DARE* FW Addit **HI,** [Newspaper item:] Mayor Frank F. Fasi already has agreed to purchase the land makai of Diamond Head Road, but is opposed to acquiring the mauka land. 1980 *AmSp* 55.209 **Honolulu HI,** The following are used to give directions: . . *makai* (literally, 'toward the sea') 'south'. 1991 *Chicago Tribune* (IL) 21 July sec 12 4/3, *Memorize a few basic Hawaiian words.* Even just to be able to understand the local weather report—"Mauka showers drifting Makai," for instance. . . Rain from the mountains will blow out to sea.

make v[1] Usu |me(ɪ)k|; also **chiefly Sth, S Midl** |mɛk| Pronc-spp *ma(c)k, me(c)k*

A Pronc varr. [The proncs [mɑk, mɛk] are common in nEngl, Scots dial.]

1813 in 1956 Eliason *Tarheel Talk* 314 **NC,** Mack. 1838 [see **B** below]. 1888 Jones *Negro Myths* 3 **GA coast** [Gullah], Buh Alligatur yent hab time fuh mek answer. [=Brother Alligator didn't have time to answer.] 1893 *Harper's New Mth. Mag.* 86.976 **Sth** [Black], Sometimes die gits in de skin an' mecks 'em kick up an' run. 1894 in 1941 Warfel–Orians *Local-Color Stories* 741 **sAR** [Black], De way a cockroach run fur 'is life meck me draw back my brogan an' let 'im go. *Ibid* 742, I gwine meck de movement. 1897 [see **B** below]. 1899 (1912) Green *VA Folk-Speech* 279, Mek. 1906 Casey *Parson's Boys* 138 **sIL** (as of c1860), Here they come; Ringwell, Tingwell, Towser, the old slut and nine pups, screamin' an' yellin', jist a-meckin' things hark! 1922 Gonzales *Black Border* 143 **sSC, GA coasts** [Gullah], Ef de Lawd haffuh tek'um, uh glad 'E yent tek'um 'tell de crap done mek. [=If the Lord had to take him, I'm glad He didn't take him till the crop was made.] 1941 *AmSp* 16.4 **eTX** [Black], Make, take, frequently [mɛk], [tɛk]. 1942 Hall *Smoky Mt. Speech* 18 **eTN, wNC,** He was making ['mɛkən] for the creek. 1969 *DARE* (Qu. A20) Inf **AL52,** Make haste [mɛk 'ɛst].

B Gram forms.

Past pple, ppl adj: usu *made;* rarely *maden, make(d).*

1838 (1852) Gilman *S. Matron* 125 **SC,** "Kate," said papa, "what have you put in the coffee?" "Me an't put nottin 'tall in 'em, sir. He mak like he always been mak." 1897 (1952) McGill *Narrative* 4, They made repeated inquiries of him, as "who made them pretty shoes," when he said with some pride . . , "They ain't meck, they buy." 1950 *WELS Suppl.* **csWI,** Kids said of such things as maybaskets and valentines: "Was it boughten or maden?" 1967 Key *Tobacco Vocab.* 47 **TN,** These new kind of tobacco setters clicks every time they plant . . but ours is a home-maden one. 1969 *DARE* (Qu. W36, *What . . people say . . about a woman who uses a lot of cosmetics*) Inf **IN66,** All maked up [laughter].

C Senses.

1 To raise or yield (a crop); to produce a crop of. **chiefly Sth, S Midl**

1714 *Boston News-Letter* 9–16 Aug. 2/2 (*DA*), We have had an extraordinary drought . . which makes us apprehensive of a Scarcity of Corn, and little or no Tobacco like to be made. 1818 *Wkly. Recorder* (Chillicothe, O.) 4 Dec. 135/1 (*DA*), There are great crops of corn made in this country. 1844 in 1956 Eliason *Tarheel Talk* 282 **c,csNC,** Cotton is so low that those that Make Cotton Cant Pay. 1883 GA Dept. Ag. *Pub. Circular No. 34* 8.27, Owing to the short corn crop and the small supply of pork made last year, farmers have bought some bacon and some corn. 1884 Smith *Bill Arp's Scrap Book* 72 **GA,** I continue to like farmin . . exsep that the wheat is sumwhat doubtful about making a crap. 1902 *DN* 2.239 **sIL.** 1903 *DN* 2.320 **seMO,** 'I expect to make a thousand bushels of corn this year.' 'He hasn't made a crop for three years.' 1906 *DN* 3.146 **nwAR,** "Dr. Jacobs of Hunt will make a corn crop on his farm this year." "Since that time Lou has decided not to make any crop; says he can make more money doing nothing than he can in making a crop." 1909 *DN* 3.347 **eAL, wGA,** Make a crop. . . To raise a crop. Universal. "My school will be out in time for me to make a crop." 1917 *DN* 4.414 **IL, KY, wNC,** I can't make a crap (crop) on such land. 1932 *Scribner's Mag.* 91.285 **FL,** They made beans as fine as old man Tainter. 1956 Hall Coll. **wNC,** She made some of the finest corn that was ever made in there [i.e. The Bend of the River]. 1965–70 *DARE* (Qu. L22, *When talking about a crop he intends to plant . . a farmer might say, "This year, I'm going to _____ a crop of oats/corn/cotton, etc."*) Infs **AR47, FL15, KS17, MS28, NC87, OK53, VA70,** Make (corn, cotton, oats). [All Infs old] 1966–70 *DARE* Tape **AL1,** Folks made crops then; **GA30,** Of course they'd make little vegetables and stuff; **GA**71, We make all of our vegetables. We don't buy anything; **KY**85, It [=cotton] is just a hard crop to make; **LA**10, We generally made about a hundred bales [of cotton] every year; **NC**54, They made their crop that summer. **1972** *Foxfire Book* 279 **nGA**, I'd bought a little old coon-footed mule that I's tryin' t'make a crop with.

2 Of crops, fruits, etc: to grow, mature; to produce grain or fruit.

1763 (1925) Washington *Diaries* 1.187 **VA**, Observed that my y[oun]g Corn was just beginning to show. . . Quere, has it time to make or Ripen? **1899** (1912) Green *VA Folk-Speech* 272, *Make.* . . The ripening of grain or fruit. "The grain didn't make well this year." **1906** *DN* 3.146 **nwAR**, Cotton will make on this place every year. **1923** *DN* 5.214 **swMO**, *Make.* . . To mature, to produce grain or fruit. "Hit's too dry fer corn t' make." **1930** Faulkner *As I Lay Dying* 28 **MS**, Clouds like that dont lie, and the cotton making every day the Lord sends. **1943** Writers' Program NC *Bundle of Troubles* 186, You could never get peppers to make. Peppers has got to be planted by somebody with a high temper. **1956** McAtee *Some Dialect NC* 29, *Make* . . develop. "The leaves were just makin'." **1959** *VT Hist.* 27.148 **nVT**, *Make.* . . To ripen and dry. Said of hay during the summer, particularly during the sultry season. Common. **1966–70** *DARE* Tape **SC**17, You know tobacco is a quick thing. When it do come, it makes right now; **TX**107, You don't have to fool with it [=cotton] no more. It's large enough to make for itself. **1970** GA Dept. Ag. *Farmers Market Bulletin* 5 Aug, Blue Java peas will make until middle of Aug. **1976** Ryland *Richmond Co. VA* 373, *Make*—mature, "the corn didn't make."

3 Of ice: to form.

1774 in 1906 Litchfield *Diary* 318 **MA**, I worked till after Sunset and the Ice made very fast on my fleshing knife. **1784** in 1912 Ford *Notes N. Webster* 1.88, Cold; ice makes in the river. **1890** *NY Tribune* (NY) 12 Dec 3/3, Several good native guides . . will assist him in an attempt to reach Kadiak [sic] Island by crossing Alaska Peninsula before the ice makes. **1967** *DARE* FW Addit **MI**55, When the ice would make in the fall.

4 occas with *up;* Of food or drink: to undergo a process that prepares it for consumption.

1915 *DN* 4.239 **MA** [Colonial cookery terms], Wait until the pye shall make up, then you may eat. **1967–70** *DARE* (Qu. H72, *. . Preparing tea:* "Pour on the water and let it _____.") Infs **OK**56, **SC**42, Make. **1967** *DARE* Tape **TX**32, You use 5 cups of juice and 7 cups of sugar and a box of Sure-Jell, and it doesn't take but just a few minutes for it to make. **1975** Newell *If Nothin' Don't Happen* 236 **FL**, Kelly Runnels were first man up and when he got a fire goin' and some coffee makin' he went up on the porch and hollered, "Rise and shine, all you so-called deer hunters."

5 See quot.

1949 *PADS* 11.24 **CO**, *Make: v.i.* To take place. "The dance is going to make here in this hall."

6 To prepare (something) for use, as:

a To preserve (fish or meat). [*OED make* v.[1] 39 (in ref to fish) 1555–1809; "*Obs.*"]

1623 in 1912 Bradford *Hist. Plymouth* 353, [Footnote:] A good fishing place . . and well stoed [sic] with fish neer at hand, and convenient places to make it. **1769** in 1904 Colonial Soc. MA *Pub.* 6.29, Thare was not one House that he knew off . . except one on Damariscove an Island to make Fish on. **1846** Sage *Scenes Rocky Mts.* 53, We commenced the process of "making meat," . . cutting into thin slices the boneless parts of buffalo, or other meat, and drying them in the wind or sun. **1855** in 1940 MT Hist. Soc. *Contrib.* 10.128, Found some Grosvonts [=Gros Ventres] camp'd making meat. **1859** (1968) Bartlett *Americanisms* 261, *To make fish.* To cure and prepare fish for commerce. A New England phrase. **1930** *AmSp* 5.391 [Language of N Atl fishermen], *Make fish.* . . To preserve fish, usually by splitting and pickling or drying them. **1971** Morison *European Discovery* 491, In our times "making fish," as the Maine people call curing cod, haddock, and pollock in the sun, is simple enough. . . You simply soak the gutted, split, and washed fish in brine for two or three days, slack-salt them, and spread them on home-made flakes to be cured in the sun.

b To cook (something). Note: When the direct object can be interpreted as the result of preparation, as in "make a cake," *make* is std.

1905 *DN* 3.63 **eNE**, Make the potatoes for supper. **1907** *German Amer. Annals* 9.381 **sePA**, She made a beefsteak for breakfast. **1930** *AmSp* 5.391 [Language of N Atl fishermen], *Make fish.* . . Also used of preparing fish for the table. **1939** Aurand *Quaint Idioms* 25 [PaGer],

Make an egg for my supper. **1949** in 1986 *DARE* File **sePA**, Shall I make the potatoes for you? **1954** *WELS Suppl.* **csWI**, [My mother] would have made a cake, but she never would have used the expression "make an egg" or "make me some potatoes" such as I have heard here. **1995** *DARE* File **csWI**, I made steak and potatoes and corn, and we had a real sit-down dinner.

c To cut and work up (wood) for burning.

1958 McCulloch *Woods Words* 116 **Pacific NW**, *Make wood*—To work as a wood splitter on a donkey or locie. **1984** *MJLF* 10.152 **cnWI**, *Making wood.* Cutting the winter's supply of firewood. **1987** *DARE* File **cWI**, There's so much relief on that land, I sure wouldn't want to try to make wood on that piece. **1992** *Ibid* **cME** (as of 1970s), Making wood is a year-round affair. You are always making wood, not for the coming winter but for the next one; by that time the firewood will be good and dry. Making wood includes the whole process from cutting down the standing timber through the hauling, splitting, and stacking. Sometimes the cutting to stove length and splitting part is called fitting up wood.

7 To prepare (a meal). **widespread, but more freq Nth, N Midl** See Map Cf **fix** v **B1e**, **get** v **C2**, **make** v[1] **C6b**

1905 *DN* 3.63 **eNE**, Make supper. **1935** *AmSp* 10.168 **PA** [Engl of PA Germans], It is customary *to make supper.* **1943** *Time* 11 Jan 38, Veronika lit her improvised lamp . . and made breakfast. **1948** *AmSp* 23.109 **swIL**, She will make dinner now. (Prepare, cook.) **1965–70** *DARE* (Qu. H7, *When a housewife is about to prepare a meal . . "I have to go and _____ supper."*) 100 Infs, **widespread, but more freq Nth, N Midl**, Make.

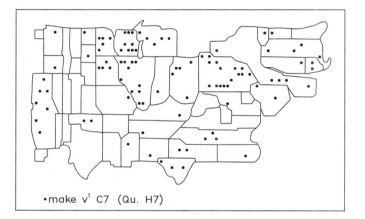

•make v[1] C7 (Qu. H7)

8 To straighten or curl (hair) artificially; hence ppl adj *made*. Cf **conk** v[2]

1942 *Amer. Mercury* 55.223.95 **Harlem NYC** [Black], *Made hair*—hair that has been straightened. **1950** *WELS Suppl.,* "I'm going to have my hair made soon," to get a permanent. **1970** Major *Dict. Afro-Amer. Slang* 79, *Made:* had one's hair straightened (female). **1978** *DARE* File **SC** [Black], I've had my hair made—how do you like it?

9 To distill liquor illegally. **chiefly S Midl**

1942 Thomas *Blue Ridge Country* 105 **sAppalachians**, I've been makin' all my life right here in these Dug Down Mountains alongside this clift. **1953** *Hall Coll.* **eTN**, We found that we'd made about sixteen months [when] we found that the revenuers [were coming]. . . They knocked the flake stand down. Next day we went back and made for sixteen months longer. **1956** *Ibid* **wNC**, He had his still right close to the house. So he'd been makin' there for some years—several years. *Ibid* **eTN**, Jake used to make up at the Spence Place. Him and George Cooper used to make up there. **1963** Carson *Social Hist. Bourbon* 113 **KY**, "Is your father around, sonny?" "Nope. Pap's up thar makin'." "Makin'?" "You know—'shine."

10 also with var advs; Of geographical features or phenomena: to extend, reach, flow.

1785 in 1971 Denny *Military Jrl.* 58, Opposite the most prominent parts of the bottoms, the hill makes in and forms what is called narrows. **1787** in 1853 Jefferson *Writings* 2.136, Spurs, or ramifications of high mountains, making down from the Alps. **1803** (1965) Ordway *Jrls.* 68, [We] passed a Small Creek on the Larbd Side near the point of a ridge [of] high Land makeing to the river. **1807** (1919) Bedford *Tour to New Orleans* 121 **VA**, The Bayou Manchac . . makes from the Mississippi to Lake Pontchartrain. **1853** Kennedy *Blackwater Chron.* 5 **VA**, The

Blackwater is a stream that makes down from the north into the Cheat river. **1885** Jewett *Marsh Is.* 94 **NEng,** Right over beyond the crossroads . . where the crick makes in. **1903** *DN* 2.352 **eMA,** *Make up.* . . To enter and occupy, as a river makes up into the land. **1914** *DN* 4.152 **csME,** *Make in.* . . To form a bay or indentation in the coast. "It isn't right out on the shore, it makes in there." **1915** (1916) Johnson *Highways New Engl.* 209, The tide runs very strong here, and when it makes out it generally clears some places so the steamer . . can work her way in and out. **1929** Starbuck *My House* 176 **Nantucket MA,** What causes a protracted freeze-up is a season of bitter cold, when the ice makes out from our shores; and the northwest wind brings down from the coast of Maine and farther north great floes of heavy ice, and fills in the chord of the bay . . the great cakes meet the shore ice until the harbor is completely sealed. **1945** Colcord *Sea Language* 125 **ME, Cape Cod, Long Island,** A point of land makes out from the coast; a bay makes in. **1968–69** *DARE* Tape **GA**30, St. Mary's River don't make out of the swamp; **MA**40, He'd have to probably go 'round the Taunton River, and all those rivers that make down into the ocean.

11 Usu of the tide, wind, sea, etc: to increase; to get rougher. Cf **make up 2**

1903 Wasson *Cap'n Simeon's Store* 155 **eME,** Ef the sea keeps on a-makin' same's she has sence noontime. **1930** Faulkner *As I Lay Dying* 63 **MS,** It had been a misdoubtful night, with the storm making. **1936** (1951) Faulkner *Absalom* 356 **MS,** There will be a little time yet for them to sit side by side upon the log in the making light of dawn. **1939** FWP *ID Lore* 243, The sky looks like it's making big for a storm. **1945** Colcord *Sea Language* 125 **ME, Cape Cod, Long Island,** The tide makes—i.e., comes in. **1949** WELS *Suppl.* **Washington Is. WI,** *"Making"* for "increasing," of rough weather for fishing tugs, as of the rising ocean tide. "She's a good boat . . when a sea is making." **1967** *DARE* (Qu. B5, *When the weather looks as if it will become bad . . it's* _____) Inf **TN**11, Making; (Qu. B12, *When the wind begins to increase . . it's* _____) Inf **AK**2, Making; **TN**11, Making—sea expression, not local.

12a To grow into, turn into. Note: This sense is to be distinguished from the std sense "to have the essential qualities of, serve as."

1940 Hall *Coll.* **cwNC,** Their drinking and wild-hogging would come to an end./ Perhaps they would make better women and men. **1959** Pearsall *Little Smoky Ridge* 102 **eTN,** He now begins to "make a man," which means he forsakes the world of women to follow his father and older brothers everywhere they go. **1968** *DARE* FW Addit **GA**28, He'll make a big dog [referring to a puppy]. . . A tadpole makes a frog; **GA**46, The sparkleberry doesn't make a big tree.

b Spec: to study or be in training to become (a member of a particular profession. **esp Sth, S Midl**

1941 Writers' Program *Guide WY* 463, *Makin' a hand*—Learning to become a full-fledged cowpuncher. **1966–68** *DARE* FW Addit **nAL,** He's making a preacher, doctor, etc = he is studying to be a preacher, doctor, etc; **MS,** When a person is studying to become a member of a professional group, he is said to be "making a doctor, lawyer, etc." **1968** *DARE* File **neAL,** He went off to the city and made a dentist. **1975** Gainer *Witches* 13 **sAppalachians,** He went to the normal school to make a teacher. **1982** Mason *Shiloh* 22 **wKY,** Judy's in college—first one to go. We're proud. She says she's going to make a doctor. **1986** Pederson *LAGS Concordance* **Gulf Region,** [16 infs gave resps "he made a Baptist preacher," "his brothers made doctors"; one said "one of the boys made farmer."]

13 To stay in place or stay a course for (a season).

1916 *DN* 4.326 **KS,** *Make season.* . . To pursue a course for a season. **1967** Green *Horse Tradin'* 189 **swTX** (as of 1920–30), He wanted to settle down some good place to make the winter, and running that good café sounded like an awful easy thing to him.

14 To light (a lamp). Cf **D8** below, **make on 3**

1967–70 *DARE* (Qu. Y41a, . . *To tell someone to light a lamp or lantern:* "_____ *the lamp.*") Infs **IA**4, **MS**23, **SC**66, Make; **WI**13, Make the light.

15 See quot. [Perh abbr for *make over*]

1969 *DARE* FW Addit **KY**17, "He'll probably make his money to her"—he'll probably will his money to her.

16 To matter. Cf **macht nichts**

1933 Smiley *Gloss. New Paltz* **seNY,** "It doesn't make" (any difference left out). **1983** Lutz *Coll.* **seNY, neNJ,** "It don't make!" meaning "It doesn't make any difference." That is, "Don't bother about it. I don't care. It's O.K."

17 in var senses infl by Ger idiom: See below. **chiefly PaGer area**

a foll by adj: To be, get, become. Cf **make nice**

c1902 Clapin *New Dict. Amer.* 267, In parts of Pennsylvania inhabited by Germans . . *make* is used in many senses. . . "We were talking politics, and it made hot." **1908** *German Amer. Annals* 10.32 **sePA,** I want to make done by sundown. *Ibid* 33, It's dinner time; I must go and make ready. *Ibid,* It might make ugly yet before the war is over. **1939** Aurand *Quaint Idioms* 25 [PaGer], (He makes so funny (he is so comical). **1948** *AmSp* 23.237 **cPA** [Engl of PA Germans], *Make,* as a verb of general utility in Pennsylvania German as in High German. 'It makes wet: P.G. *Es macht nass.*' **1950** WELS *Suppl.* **ceWI,** "That makes a lot of fun" = is a lot of fun. Common. **1966** *DARE* FW Addit **cePA,** He makes loud. Used to refer to a hunting dog's baying when he was on the trail.

b To do.

1907 *German Amer. Annals* 9.381 **sePA,** What did you make, that you tore your coat so? **1935** *AmSp* 10.168 [Engl of PA Germans], 'When your Pop wouldn't be here, what would we make?' meaning, 'If your father hadn't been here, what would we have done?' **1948** *AmSp* 23.109 **swIL** [German language influences], What does the father make? (Do).

c in var other senses and collocations: See quots.

1916 *DN* 4.338 **PA,** *Make.* . . "When it makes a little red house, it's all," i.e., when the caboose passes, the train has gone by. **1931** Jacobson *Milwaukee Dial.* 16 **WI,** *Make fun.* . . Go on, we'll make some fun. The German is *spass machen. Machen* is make and hence the expression. *Ibid, Making her hairs.* . . "she is making her hairs" for she is fixing her hair. **1935** *AmSp* 10.168 **sePA** [Engl of PA Germans], A Lebanon [County] dentist is alleged to have put a sign on his door reading: 'The bell don't make. Bump.' . . To 'make the tree over' means to cut the tree down. **1937** *AmSp* 12.203 [PaGer], He tried to make the corner around. **1940** Yoder *Rosanna* 28 **PA** [Amish], To avoid imposing on neighbors to help haul their household goods so far, they made sale, keeping only the essentials of housekeeping. *Ibid* 250, On the following Sunday a vote of the [Amish] church was taken on "making a preacher" and the vote was unanimous in the affirmative. "Then," said the Bishop, "at the Communion service in two weeks we will cast lots for preacher and may the Lord's will be done." **1948** *AmSp* 23.109 **swIL** [German language influences], Did you make your Christmas tree yet? (Trim, decorate.) . . I made my lesson. (Prepared, studied.) **1956** *DE Folkl. Bulletin* 1.24, *Make* (trim, or clean up—as in "Mister, can I make your yard?") **1978** *DARE* File **sePA,** Wait until I make my dirt away.

d See **make down** v phr **3.**

18 in var senses infl by Fr idiom: See below. [Calque of Fr *faire*]

a To have, do; see quots. **chiefly LA**

1933 Hurston in *Story* Aug 69 **FL,** On Saturday he went to Orlando to make his market. . . Meat and lard, meal and flour, soap and starch. . . All the staples. **1938** FWP *New Orleans Guide* 409, *Make ménage:* To clean house. A typical local translation of French *faire le ménage,* to clean house. **1947** Ballowe *The Lawd* 167 **LA,** Men from the settlements from along the river come to make the grinding [of sugarcane], as they call it. **1975** [see **D10** below]. **1983** Reinecke *Coll.* 7 **LA,** Make . . menage [me'naʒ] = household cleaning. . . "I made my menage [or made menage] early.["] Obsolescent. **1983** [see **C18b** below]. **1986** Pederson *LAGS Concordance,* 1 inf, **seLA,** Make the market. [Inf is a French speaker.] **1992** Scott *Cajun Vernacular Engl.* 40, *Make*— This verb is translated from *faire,* a general verb meaning "to do, make, create, or form." Some examples of C[ajun] V[ernacular] E[nglish] usage follow: I'm going to make a Novena for you and your *pauvre Grandmère.* We're going make groceries at Simon's. Y'all need some milk or bread? Alphonse is making a *boucherie* this weekend. Y'all wanna pass by?

b in phr *make (the) groceries:* To buy food, do one's food shopping. **chiefly Gulf States, esp LA**

1966–70 *DARE* (Qu. U1b, . . *Buying groceries*) Infs **TX**86, **VA**70, To make groceries; **MS**6, Make groceries—heard by Inf. [2 of 3 Infs Black] **1970** *DARE* File **sLA,** Among Blacks the most common term for grocery shopping is "make groceries." **1982** *Anthro. Ling.* 24.316 **csLA,** In Vacherie, one can use expressions such as. . . to make groceries. **1983** Reinecke *Coll.* 7 **sLA,** Make groceries or make market = do shopping. . . "Make the groceries" is more common. **1984** Stall *Proud New Orleans* 168, *Making groceries:* Shopping at a supermarket for food items. **1984** *Yeah You Rite* (Video recording) **New Orleans LA,** We forget that some of the words we use every day might not make sense to somebody from out of town: words like . . *make groceries.* **1986** Pederson *LAGS Concordance (Shopping)* 1 inf, **swMS,** Make groceries = buy groceries; 1 inf, **csMS,** I'm going to make groceries—blacks say; 1 inf, **seLA,** Make the groceries. **1989** *DARE* File **New Orleans LA,** Around here, people are more likely to "make groceries" than to "go to the grocery store" or "buy groceries." That expression is so common that the slogan of the biggest local supermarket is "Make Groceries at Schwegmann's." **1992** [see **C18a** above].

D Phrases. (See also following phrasal headwords.)

1 *make (a) bag;* Of a cow: to show enlargement of the udder as a sign of advanced pregnancy. [*bag* udder]

1950 *WELS Suppl.* **WI,** *Making bag.* Said of a cow whose udder is developing before freshening. "I dried old Boss off last month, and now she is making bag." **1968** *DARE* (Qu. K10, *Words used about a cow that is going to have a calf*) Inf **WV2,** She's making a bag; (QR, near Qu. K11) Inf **NJ10,** When she [=a cow] starts to make bag, she's a springer. **1984** *MJLF* 10.152 **cnWI, nME,** *Making bag.* The filling out of a cow's udders as she approaches the delivery of a calf. With heifers a sure sign that they are with calf.

2 *make a beginning:* To say grace before a meal. Cf **brag the potatoes**

1893 Shands *MS Speech* 18, The methods used by illiterate whites in requesting one to ask the blessing, or say grace, are numerous and interesting. I give some specimens: . . "Make a beginnin'." **1895** *DN* 1.372 **seKY, eTN, wNC,** *Make a beginning:* ask the blessing. "Brother Morin, will you make a beginning?" **1942** *AmSp* 17.130 **IN,** *Make a beginning* (to ask a blessing at table).

3 *make a branch:* To urinate. [*branch 1*] **chiefly Sth, S Midl**

1948 *Hench Coll.* **seGA,** From a letter of a former graduate student: Some [regionalisms] around Savannah: . . make a branch (urinate). **1952** Brown *NC Folkl.* 1.522, *Branch, to make a.* . . To urinate.—General. **1954** *Harder Coll.* **cwTN,** Make a branch—to urinate. **c1960** *Wilson Coll.* **csKY,** *Make a branch.* . . A small child's word.

4 *make a chat:* To have conversation. Cf **D34** below

1975 Gould *ME Lingo* 88, One does not bring socks to darn when making a chat with a neighbor over tea.

5 *make a damn* and varr: To make a difference, be a concern—used in neg constrs.

1966–68 *DARE* (Qu. GG21a, *If you don't care what a person does . . "You can go ahead and do it_____."*) Infs **AR51, GA11, TX33,** (It) don't make a damn (to me); (Qu. KK26, *Something that makes no difference at all to you*) Infs **AL40, MO3,** Don't make a darn to; **GA13,** Don't make a tinker's damn.

6 *make a die of it:* To die. [*OED make a die (of it)* (at *die* sb.²) 1611 →]

1825 Neal *Brother Jonathan* 1.398 **CT** (as of 1775), I wonder . . [the dog] didn't go mad; or make a die of it. **1853** Bird *Nick of Woods* 371 **KY** (as of 1780s), Why, Tom, my boy, you don't mean to make a die of it? **1867** Harris *Sut Lovingood Yarns* 204 **TN,** Ole feller, yu're gwine tu make a die ove hit. **1883** *Century Illustr. Mag.* 26.238, "I believe . . you're *trying* to make a die of it," said the doctor. **1930** Shoemaker *1300 Words* 40 **cPA Mts** (as of c1900), *Make a die of it*—To die, or pass away. **1930** Williams *Logger-Talk* 26 **Pacific NW,** *Make a die of it:* Die. **1968** Kellner *Aunt Serena* 146 **sIN** (as of c1910), It's no use, Doc. This time I'm going to make a die of it. **1968** *DARE* (Qu. BB56, *Joking expressions for dying*) Inf **AR47,** Make a die of it.

7 *make a hand:* To work; to lend a hand. Cf **hand's turn 1, 2**

[**1902** *DN* 2.239 **sIL,** *Make a hand.* . . To do as much, in a stated time [sic], as 'make a hand's work.'] **1927** Adams *Ranch on Beaver* 105 **West,** Twenty-one years ago last fall he was making a hand with a beef herd . . when the Comanches attacked them. **1968** *DARE* FW Addit **neOH** [Amish], "I make a hand at threshing" = I plan to thresh today. **1995** *DARE* File **csWI** (as of c1968), My grandmother, whose first language was German, said "make a hand" rather than "lend a hand." For example, if I came home from school and found her folding laundry, she might say, "Don't just stand there—make a hand."

8 *make a light:* To light a lamp. Cf **C14** above

1950 *WELS* (*Expressions used to tell somebody to . . turn on the light: "_____ the light."*) 2 Infs, **WI,** Make a light. **1965–70** *DARE* (Qu. Y41a, . . *To tell someone to light a lamp or lantern: "_____ the lamp."*) 12 Infs, **chiefly Sth, S Midl,** Make a light.

9 *make a long arm* (or *long arms*): To reach across a table, esp to help oneself to food.

1914 *DN* 4.76 **ME, nNH,** *Long arms, make.* . . To help one's self at

table. "Make long arms, everybody." **1916** *DN* 4.326 **KS,** *Make a long arm.* . . To reach far, esp. at table when trying to help oneself to food. **1939** *AmSp* 14.267 **IN,** If he [=a farmer] is working for another and is having dinner with the latter's family, he will be urged by Sam's 'woman' to 'make a long arm and reach.' **1986** Pederson *LAGS Concordance,* 1 inf, **cwAL,** Make a long arm and reach what you want.

10 *make a party* (or *bee*): To plan or give a party; to have a **bee** n².

1801 in 1889 MA Hist. Soc. *Proc.* 2d ser 4.130 **MA,** In the evening Mr. William Hammatt and Mr. Josiah Barker . . called and invited us to a party they had made for us to the East end of the Island. **1816** in 1924 Kittredge *Old Farmer* 169 **NEng,** Husking is now a business for us all. If you make what some call a *Bee,* it will be necessary to keep an eye on the boys, or you may have to husk over again the whole heap. **1834** (1898) Kemper *Jrl.* 443 **WI,** When he wants to have the garden of one of the farms hoed, after waiting a week there doing nothing, made a bee & treated the Indians to whiskey while they hoed the garden on a sunday. **1836** in 1934 Frear *Lowell & Abigail* 108 **MA,** The residents are making many parties these days. **1975** *Times–Picayune* (New Orleans LA) 9 Jan sec 3 3/1, Sidewalks are called banquettes in Newer Leans and people make parties rather than give them and even make laundry rather than doing it. **1983** *Lutz Coll.* **neNJ,** I noticed that friends in the largely Polish community of West Mahwah, N.J., would say, "We're going to make a party for Mary's birthday," when I would have said "to have a party." Then I found a note among Katharine Garrison's papers: "Granny made a party." Her family was old Jersey-Dutch on both sides.

11 *make a picture* (or *photograph*): To take a photograph. **esp GA, NC**

1905 *DN* 3.87 **nwAR,** *Make a picture.* . . To take a photograph. 'Have your picture made at Grabill's.' Common. [**1906** *DN* 3.146 **nwAR,** *Make faces.* . . Facetious for "take photographs," "be a photographer."] **1910** Univ. NC *Mag.* 40.3.6 **Hatteras Is. NC,** On one of my earliest visits to Hatteras a young man asked: 'Won't you make a picture of my may and me?' **1967** *DARE* FW Addit **NC,** To make a picture = to take photographs. "Let's go out and make us some pictures today." **1978** *DARE* File **Atlanta GA** (as of 1960s), Someone had brought a camera, so we all had our pictures made in front of Stone Mountain. **1990** *Natl. Geogr. World* Dec 21, Maiya's parents lived in Nepal years ago. Photographs they made there gave Maiya ideas for her poster. **1993** *DARE* File **NC** (as of 1988), When I moved to North Carolina to go to college, . . I asked . . if everyone was going to have their pictures taken. Everyone stopped and stared at me and then laughed. . . Later, my roommate . . said "Here in High Point, NC, we don't have our pictures 'taken,' we have them 'made'!" *Ibid* **nwGA,** We all say that we're fixin' to have a picture made, if we can find someone to carry us over to the photographer's. *Ibid* **nGA,** I don't think I would say "I made a lot of pictures of my son in the back yard." In that case it would be "took," but when [a professional photographer is] . . doing the taking . . ,"made" is probably even more common than "taken," although both are possible. . . [We would also say] "They made a Polaroid picture of Thomas with Santa Claus at the mall." *Ibid* **cVA,** [She] had come in all spiffied up and people asked what was going on. Betty . . said she was going [to the studio] to get her picture made.

12 *make a spoon or spoil a horn* and varr: Either to succeed or to fail decisively. [In ref to the former practice of making spoons from the horns of cattle; cf *SND spune, EDD spoon*] *old-fash*

1833 in 1834 Davis *Letters Downing* 83, Zekel is one of them 'ere folks . . who would spile a horn, or make a spoon. **1906** *DN* 3.146 **nwAR,** *Make a horn or spoil a spoon.* . . To succeed or fail. **1912** Green *VA Folk-Speech* 35, Make a spoon or spoil a horn. **1924** *DN* 5.291, *Make a spoon or spoil a horn.* This is the correct order of the phrase. **1929** *AmSp* 4.464, Make the spoon or spoil the horn. **1949** *Western Folkl.* 8.114 **CA,** To make a spoon and spoil a horn.

13 *make a talk:* To give a talk, make a presentation.

1966–68 *DARE* (Qu. JJ22, *To express your opinion . . "I went to the meeting, and_____."*) Infs **LA8, NC79, OK51, TX36,** Made a talk. **1967** *DARE* Tape **CO22,** The guards that take you through [Carlsbad Caverns]. . . They take you on and make talks about this and that, what caused it. **1986** Pederson *LAGS Concordance,* 1 inf, **seGA,** He can make a better talk than I can.

14 *make belly:* To be pregnant.

1969 *DARE* (Qu. AA28, . . *Joking or sly expressions . . women use to say that another is going to have a baby . . "She['s]_____."*) Inf **VT16,** Making belly.

15 *make buckle and tongue meet:* To live within one's means; to make ends meet. **esp Sth**

[**1773** (1965) Carter *Diary* 2.763 **VA,** The Pernicious company generally he Keeps, Gamesters and Spendthrifts; who by taking no care, are reducing themselves, whilst I am keeping as well as I can, my buckle and thong together.] **1859** Taliaferro *Fisher's R.* 249 **AL** (as of 1845), All they cared for was "to make buckle and tongue meet" by raising stock, a few bales of cotton, and a little corn for bread. **1888** *Harper's New Mth. Mag.* 76.703 **GA,** Beginning without money, he had as much as he could do to make "buckle and tongue meet," as the phrase goes. **1899** (1912) Green *VA Folk-Speech* 35, Make both ends meet. Make buckle and tongue meet. **1952** Brown *NC Folkl.* 1.376, Make buckle and tongue meet. **1958** Babcock *I Don't Want* 131 **eSC,** If I can sell old Blue's calf and get two-three days boat paddling on the river this fall, and if those old hens will start laying again, we can make buckle and tongue meet. We'll just take it a thing at a time and see how it works out. **1960** Williams *Walk Egypt* 220 **GA,** You just about making buckle and tongue meet, and the gov'ment says, 'Take a tuck in your belly.'

16 *make bullet patches:* See quot 1953.

1933 Randolph in *AmSp* 8.1.50 **Ozarks,** Make bullet patches. . . I have heard this expression many times. **1953** Randolph–Wilson *Down in Holler* 263 **Ozarks,** A man whose trousers fit very tightly over the seat is said to be *makin' bullet patches.* In loading an old-fashioned rifle, the hunter stretched his *patching* tightly across the muzzle before inserting the bullet, after which the surplus cloth was trimmed off with a knife.

17 *make feet for shoes:* To be pregnant; to have a baby.

[**1785** Grose *Classical Dict.* sig B1[r] **Engl,** *Basket making.* . . The good old trade of basket-making, copulation, or making feet for children's stockings.] **1933** Hurston in *Story* Aug 65 **FL** [Black], They had been married more than a year now. They had money put away. They ought to be making little feet for shoes. A little boy child would be about right. *Ibid* 69, He found Missie May chopping wood. . . "You ain't got no business choppin' wood, and you know it. . . Ah ain't blind. You makin' feet for shoes." "Won't you be glad to have a lil baby chile, Joe?" [**1970** *DARE* (Qu. AA28, . . *Joking or sly expressions* . . *women use to say that another is going to have a baby* . . *"She['s]* _____.")* Inf **SC68,** Making boots for two.]

18 *make fight at:* To attack.

1956 Gipson *Old Yeller* 15 **TX,** It was such a surprise move, Little Arliss making fight at me that way, that I just stood there . . and let him clout me a good one.

19 *make friends:* To settle a fight or argument amicably; to make up. **scattered, but esp Sth, S Midl** See Map

1884 *Anglia* 7.267 **Sth, S Midl** [Black], *To make friends* = to become reconciled. **1965–70** *DARE* (Qu. Y17, *When two people agree to stop fighting and not be enemies any more* . . *"I hear they* _____.")* 66 Infs, **scattered, but esp Sth, S Midl,** Made friends; **OK**18, **VA**11, Shook hands and made friends. [Of all Infs responding to the question, 29% were comm type 5, 27% gs educ or less; of those giving these responses, 43% were comm type 5, 53% gs educ or less.]

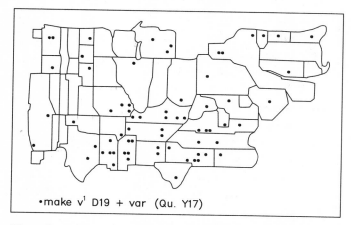

•make v[1] D19 + var (Qu. Y17)

20 *make game:* To mock; to make fun (of), jeer (at); hence n *make-game* one who makes fun of another. [*OED game* sb. 2.b c1460 →] **esp Sth** Cf **game v 1**

1899 (1912) Green *VA Folk-Speech* 191, *Game, v.* To make game of. *Ibid* 273, *Make-game.* . . One who makes a laughing-stock of another;

one who makes fun of another. **1927** Adams *Congaree* 7 **cSC** [Black], He cuss, an' steal, an' make game at God's work. *Ibid* 93, It ain't no fun, and it ain't no joke, and it ain't nothin' fuh make game. **1927** Kennedy *Gritny* 104 **sLA** [Black], Don' laugh an' make game dat way. **1984** Wilder *You All Spoken Here* 190 **Sth,** *Make game of:* Make fun of.

21 *make haste;* pronc-spp *make ase, mek'ace, mek hase:* To hurry—often used in imper. [*OED haste* sb. 5 1535 →] **formerly widespread, now esp Sth, S Midl** See Map *esp freq among Black speakers* Cf *DJE mikies*

1871 (1882) Stowe *Fireside Stories* 266 **NEng,** I must make haste home. **1888** Jones *Negro Myths* 84 **GA coast** [Gullah], Den eh mek hase an heng de key way eh bin fine um. [=Then I hurried and hung the key where I had found it.] **1898** Westcott *Harum* 163 **cNY,** I made 's much haste 's I could. **1908** *DN* 3.287 **eAL, wGA,** Make ase, and let's get this job done. **1922** Gonzales *Black Border* 260 **sSC, GA coasts** [Gullah], Mek'ace, gal, en' come'yuh [=come here]. **1929** *AmSp* 5.121 **ME,** Children were told to . . "make haste." **1948** Hurston *Seraph* 29 **wFL** [Black], "Make haste!" Maria screamed. "Git that spoon in her mouth before she bites her tongue!" **1965–70** *DARE* (Qu. A19, *Other ways of saying "I'll have to hurry": "I'm late, I'll have to* _____.")* 23 Infs, **chiefly Sth, S Midl,** Make haste; **TX**89, Make haste while the sun shines; **NC**83, Make some haste; (Qu. A20, *Joking ways of telling somebody to hurry*) Infs **AL**52, **NY**213, **NC**15, Make haste; **TX**86, Make haste, man; **MO**22, Make haste, ole snail; (Qu. A22, . . *'To start working hard': "She had only ten minutes to clean the room, but she* _____.")* Inf **OH**4, Made haste; (Qu. Y18, *To leave in a hurry: "Before they find this out, we'd better* _____!")* Infs **MI**75, **SC**26, Make haste. [13 of 31 Infs Black] **1972** *Atlanta Letters* **GA,** Not long ago . . an old lady . . when we left . . followed us out on to the porch, calling after us, "Now, y'all make haste and come back."

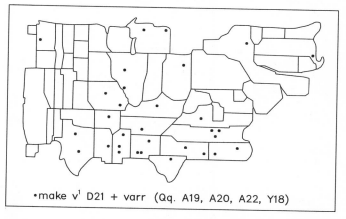

•make v[1] D21 + varr (Qq. A19, A20, A22, Y18)

22 *make hole;* Among oil drillers: to make progress in drilling.

1903 *DN* 2.342 [Oil well language], *Make hole.* . . To make headway in drilling the well. **1939** in 1984 Lambert–Franks *Voices* 14 **OK,** We just had three hours to get rigged up and start makin' hole. **1941** Writers' Program *Guide OK* 40, In cable-tool drilling there is no weight on the tools; the cable by which they are raised and dropped becomes less manageable as the hole deepens, and at a depth below four thousand feet it is an expert driller, indeed, who can give the bit the necessary motion to "make hole." **1959** *Wall St. Jrl.* (NY NY) 20 July 14/5 **cwTX,** "Making hole faster"—oil crew parlance for drilling wells at increasing speeds—is the prime aim. *Ibid* 1/1 **cwTX,** "We're making only 50 feet of hole today," complained brawny Mr. Davidson.

23 *make old bones:* To grow old; to survive to adulthood or old age—usu in neg phrr.

1833 in 1941 Pintard *Letters Daughter* 4.139 **NYC,** It was often predicted . . that I shd never live to make old bones. **1912** Green *VA Folk-Speech* 304, "He will not make old bones." Said of a person not expected to live to old age. **1941** Smiley *Gloss. New Paltz* **seNY,** He never would have made old bones. **1947** Ballowe *The Lawd* 142 **LA,** Poor fellow, he knew that he wasn't going to make old bones, and was living the short time allotted to him quietly and pleasantly. **1952** Brown *NC Folkl.* 1.373, He'll never make old bones. **1980** *DARE* File **wNC,** *Make old bones*—I know the phrase with the meaning "live to adulthood," applied to a child. **1983** *Lutz Coll.* **nNJ,** "He'll never make old bones." Said of someone not expected to live to great age, such as a sickly young person.

24 *make (one) awake:* To waken (someone). [Calque of PaGer *wacker mache*]

c1902 Clapin *New Dict. Amer.* 267, In parts of Pennsylvania inhabited by Germans. . . *Make awake,* to waken. "Make me awake at five." **1916** *DN* 4.338 **PA,** *Make awake,* to awaken.

25 *make one hard to find:* See quot 1951.

1951 *PADS* 15.55 **neIN** (as of 1890s), *Hard to find, make.* . . A threat of condign punishment. "I'll make him hard to find." **1954** *Harder Coll.* **cwTN.**

26 *make (one's) brags:* To boast, claim. [**brag** n 1]

1865 Byrn *Advent. Fudge Fumble* 170, I heard of a certain young lady who . . had made her brags that no man could win her affections. **1898** Lloyd *Country Life* 128 **AL,** But I ain't makin no brags about that. **1903** Wasson *Cap'n Simeon's Store* 95 **eME,** Sairy . . made her brags everywheres round how one o' these days she'd git a come-uppance 'long of Skip' Nate in a way he nor nobody else ever once dremp' on. **1914** *DN* 4.76 **ME, nNH,** *Make brags.* . . To brag, boast. "You've allus made yer brags you'd go." **1924** (1946) Greer-Petrie *Angeline Gits an Eyeful* 12 **csKY,** I heer'd her *makin' her brags* bekase she'd . . lost ten pounds the past month. **1953** Goodwin *It's Good* 103 **sIL** [Black], They made their brags that anybody Buddy was for they would work against.

27 *make oneself home:* To go home. [Calque of PaGer; see quot 1908]

c1902 Clapin *New Dict. Amer.* 267, In parts of Pennsylvania inhabited by Germans . . *make* is used in many senses. . . *Make one's self,* to go. "Make yourself home at once." **1908** *German Amer. Annals* 10.32 **sePA,** "I must make myself home now." . . fr. Pa. Ger. *sich ham mŏchă.* **1935** *AmSp* 10.168 [Engl of PA Germans], A dog or child may be told *to make himself home.*

28 *make one's haslet curl:* See quot. [**haslet**]

1914 *DN* 4.76 **ME, nNH,** *Make one's haslet curl.* . . To surprise or injure one.

29 *make one stand around:* See quots.

1942 Warnick *Garrett Co. MD* 10 **nwMD** (as of 1900–18), *Make 'em stand around* . . to make behave. **c1960** Wilson *Coll.* **csKY,** *Make 'em stand around.* . . Be domineering, bossy.

30 *make pretend;* pronc-sp *make tend:* To make believe.

1968–70 *DARE* (Qu. BB27, *When somebody pretends to be sick* . . *he's* _____) Inf **DE**2, Making tend; (Qu. JJ46, . . *To pretend: "Let's* _____ *we don't know a thing about it."*) Infs **DE**1, **VA**80, Make pretend.

31 *make quick:* To hurry.

1972 Carr *Da Kine Talk* 138 **HI,** "Mo' bettah you make quick an' close da light!" 'Hurry up and put out the light!'

32 *make shut* (or *make to*): To shut (a door, window, etc); to fasten. [Calques of Ger *zumachen,* as in "Mach die Tür zu!"] **Ger settlement areas**

c1902 Clapin *New Dict. Amer.* 267, In parts of Pennsylvania inhabited by Germans . . *make* is used in many senses. . . "Make the door shut." . . "Make the window to." **1908** *German Amer. Annals* 10.33 **sePA,** "Make the door shut"—i.e., close the door, not implying any difficulty. *Ibid,* *Make to.* (Rare.) "Make the door to." **1931** Jacobson *Milwaukee Dial.* 16 **WI,** *Make shut.* . . "make my apron shut" for tie my apron. **1935** *AmSp* 10.168 [Engl of PA Germans], It is customary . . *to make the door shut.* **1951** *Milwaukee Jrl.* (WI) 26 Aug sec 5 2/3, Johnny! Make that window shut. **1978** *DARE* File **sePA,** Go make the door shut.

33 *make small of:* To belittle, ridicule. [Cf *make light of, make much of*]

1899 (1977) Norris *McTeague* 167 **San Francisco CA,** "You can't make small of me *always.*" "Well, never mind that. You know I'm not trying to make small of you." **1949** Guthrie *Way West* 190, Or the married ones like Mack that he felt thankful to for being nice to her family that the rest made small of? **1968** *DARE* [(Qu. Y3, *To say uncomplimentary things about somebody*) Inf **MN**42, Make small;] (Qu. GG16, . . *Finding fault* . . : *"You just can't please him—he's always* _____.") Inf **DC**12, Criticizing, picking to pieces, making small of.

34 *make talk:* To confer, converse. Cf **D4** above

1940 *Sat. Eve. Post* 20 July 55 **GA** [Black], Could I make private talk with you fo' just a minute? **1942** (1971) Campbell *Cloud-Walking* 5 **seKY,** Squire . . and Fess . . sat in the back door and made talk while Squire washed off his feet.

35 *make up a hat:* To pass the hat, take up a collection.

1931 *AmSp* 7.48 **Sth, SW** [Lumberjack lingo], A true "rosin-belly" detests the "swamp angels" and the cotton pickers who come to his camp. . . Yet, he will "make up a hat" for them and buy them, on occasion, food and clothing. **1934** (1940) Weseen *Dict. Amer. Slang* 82 [Loggers' and miners' slang], *Make up a hat*—Take up a collection. **1969** Sorden *Lumberjack Lingo* 76 **NEng, Gt Lakes,** *Make up a hat*—Take up a collection for some worthy cause.

make adj, v², n |'make, 'mʌkɪ| Pronc-sp *mucky* [Haw] **HI** Dead; to die; death; also fig.

1934 *AmSp* 9.58 **HI,** *Make,* the Hawaiian loan word for 'dead,' is often heard *mucky.* **1938** Reinecke *Hawaiian Loanwords* 24, *Make* ['mɑ,ke]. . . 1. Dead. 2. To die. 3. Physically exhausted. 4. Spent, as a spinning top. V[ery] F[requent]. **1951** *AmSp* 26.21 **HI,** Some localisms are handy euphemisms: . . *make* (dead). **1954–60** Hance et al. *Hawaiian Sugar* 4, *Make* ['make]—Death, to die. **1966** Morimoto *Hawaiian Dial. Engl.* 98, Eventually mainland Nisei troops adopted many Hawaiian words or pidgin English words. . . I believe I continued to use some of these words long after my separation from the 442[nd Regimental Combat Team] at the end of the war. Examples: . . *make* [dead]. **1967** *DARE* (Qu. N2, *The car used to carry a dead body for burial*) Inf **HI**13, Make ['mɑ,ke] man car. **1969** *DARE* FW Addit **HI,** "Ma-ke" means dead. **1972** Carr *Da Kine Talk* 87 **HI,** *Make.* To die, dead; to faint. *Ibid* 115, *Make,* pronounced ['make] or often nowadays ['mʌkɪ].

make a bag See **make** v¹ **D1**

make a bee See **make** v¹ **D10**

make a beginning See **make** v¹ **D2**

make a branch See **make** v¹ **D3**

make a chat See **make** v¹ **D4**

make a damn See **make** v¹ **D5**

make a die of it See **make** v¹ **D6**

make a Dutchman See **Dutchman 4**

make against v phr
See quots.
1926 *DN* 5.401 **Ozarks,** *Make agin.* . . To injure. "I done quit a-chawin' terbacker—I seed hit was a-makin' agin' me." **c1960** Wilson *Coll.* **csKY,** *Make against (agin).* . . Injure, work against.

make a hand See **make** v¹ **D7**

make a high-hat See **high-hat** n 2

make a holler See **holler** n¹ **C4**

make a light See **make** v¹ **D8**

make along v phr
To make one's way, come along on one's own.
1936 Morehouse *Rain on Just* 125 **NC,** You be toting Matthew Mark, he's least, and I'll take Luke John. Hector and Lector can make along.

make a long arm See **make** v¹ **D9**

make a mess See **mess** n 5

make a mock of See **mock** n

make a party See **make** v¹ **D10**

make a photograph (or picture) See **make** v¹ **D11**

make a poor out See **out** **F1**

make a raise See **raise** n

make ase See **make** v¹ **D21**

make a sorry out See **out** **F1**

make a spoon or spoil a horn See **make** v¹ **D12**

make a talk See **make** v¹ **D13**

make awake See **make** v¹ **D24**

make bag See **make** v¹ **D1**

make belly See **make** v¹ **D14**

make brags See **make** v¹ **D26**

make buckle and tongue meet See **make** v¹ **D15**

make bullet patches See **make** v¹ **D16**

make by v phr
To make ends meet, get by.

1930 Faulkner *As I Lay Dying* 125 **MS,** You know how tight it is for us to make by, yet you bought a horse for me to feed.

maked See **make** v[1] **B**

make down v phr

1 To arrange (a temporary sleeping place) on the floor; hence ppl adj *made-down,* rarely adj *make-down.* **chiefly Sth, S Midl** Cf **down bed, pallet, Baptist ~, Methodist ~**

1903 *DN* 2.323 **seMO,** I haven't got a spare bed, but I can make down a pallet for you. **1941** Smith *Going to God's Country* 182 **MO** (as of 1899), It was too late to get any bedsteads so we just unpacked our boxes of beding [sic], made down beds on the floor and put the youngsters to bed. **c1960** *Wilson Coll.* **csKY,** Make a bed down. . . Arrange a temporary bed on the floor when the company is too great for the regular beds. **1964** Wallace *Frontier Life* 7 **OK** (as of c1900), We awoke late the next morning to find ourselves on a "made-down" bed in a strange new home. **1966** Dakin *Dial. Vocab. Ohio R. Valley* 2.198 **KY, sIN,** This term [=*shake-down*] . . is quite possibly related to *a made-down bed* [2 infs] and *a bed-down*—expressions which are used in eastern Kentucky. . . A Mountain speaker also uses the verbal expression *(to) make down a bed;* an Estill County, Kentucky, speaker uses a similar *(to) make a pallet down;* and Hancock County, Kentucky, and Jackson County, Indiana, speakers say *(to) make a bed down.* **1966–70** *DARE* (Qu. E18, *A temporary or emergency bed made up on the floor*) Infs **GA72, KY5, TN27, TX32, 94,** Made-down bed; **AR14,** Making down a bed pallet. **1970** Tarpley *Blinky* 104 **neTX,** Bedding spread on the floor when you have too much company. . . Made-down bed [8 of 200 infs] . . make-down-bed [fewer than 3 infs]. *Ibid* 105, *Made-down bed* and *mattress* are non-city expressions of old-timers. **1986** Pederson *LAGS Concordance* **Gulf Region** *(Pallet)* 3 infs, Made-down bed; 1 inf, Make down; 1 inf, They'd make down beds; 1 inf, Make down pallets.

2 To put or pull down.

1935 *AmSp* 10.168 [Engl of PA Germans], 'It's time to make the hay down' means it's time to put the hay down the hay-chute for the horses. **1968** *DARE* (Qu. E13, . . *To pull the shades . . down:* "When the sun is too bright, you go to the window and _____.") Inf **PA162,** Make the shade down.

3 also *make:* To rain, snow, etc; to drop (rain). [Calque of PaGer; see quot 1948] **chiefly PA**

1935 *AmSp* 10.168 [Engl of PA Germans], The local weather prophet looks at the clouds and thinks it's going *to make down,* and later the comment is, 'It's making rain down.' **1939** Aurand *Quaint Idioms* 25 [PaGer], Do you think it will *make,* or *give,* rain? *Ibid* 29, During a shower the girl was heard to say: "My goodness its [sic] making down hard." **1946** *PADS* 6.20 **swVA** (as of 1900–10), *Making down. . .* Snowing hard. (Cf. *putting down.*) Salem. Reported, 1940. **1947** *PADS* 8.19 **ceIA,** *Making down:* Also raining or hailing hard. **1948** *AmSp* 23.237 **cPA,** 'It makes down, i.e., is raining: P[a] G[er] *Es macht runner* [=*herunter*]. . . It's getting ready to make, i.e., to rain. **1969** *DARE* FW Addit **csPA,** "It's really making down outside" = it's raining very hard.

make-down adj See **make down** v phr **1**

make ducks and drakes of See **ducks and drakes 2**

make feet for shoes See **make** v[1] **D17**

make fight at See **make** v[1] **D18**

make flesh See **flesh** n **B**

make friends See **make** v[1] **D19**

make game v phr See **make** v[1] **D20**

make-game n See **make** v[1] **D20**

make groceries See **make** v[1] **C18b**

make haste See **make** v[1] **D21**

make hole See **make** v[1] **D22**

make it out See **make out** v phr **1**

make it up See **make up 1**

make jack See **jack** n[1] **14**

make like v phr Pronc-sp *may like* [For std *make as if, make as though*] **widespread, but esp freq Sth** See Map Cf **make on 4, make out** v phr **2, play like**
To pretend.

1870 in 1884 Lanier *Poems* 171 **GA,** Then he . . made like he neither had seen nor heerd. **1884** *Anglia* 7.270 **Sth, S Midl** [Black], *To make*

like = to pretend. **1912** Green *VA Folk-Speech* 273, *Make like. . .* To act in a certain way: "I made like I didn't see him." (2) To pretend to do a thing. **c1960** *Wilson Coll.* **csKY,** *Make-like:* . . Pretend, play-like. **1962** Faulkner *Reivers* 182 **MS,** Make like this is it, so when he sees that real track tomorrow, he'll already know beforehand what to expect and to do. **1965–70** *DARE* (Qu. JJ46, . . *To pretend:* "Let's _____ we don't know a thing about it.") 67 Infs, **widespread, but esp freq Sth,** Make like [Of all Infs responding to the question, 63% were old; of those giving this response, 49% were old.]; (Qu. II6, *If you meet somebody who used to be a friend, and he pretends not to know you:* "When I met him on the street he _____.") Inf **PA94,** Made like he didn't see me. **1977** Smitherman *Talkin* 259, *May like,* to pretend, to "make like" something is true when it isn't, as in "She may like she was sick." **1986** Pederson *LAGS Concordance* **Gulf Region** *(He acted as if he knew it all)* 16 infs, Made like; 5 infs, Make like; 1 inf, He's just making like; 1 inf, They made like they walk = pretended like; 1 inf, They know it all and they don't make like they know it all.

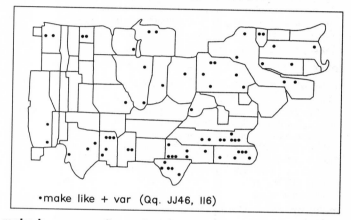

•make like + var (Qq. JJ46, II6)

make long arms See **make** v[1] **D9**

make market See **make** v[1] **C18a**

make medicine See **medicine**

make menage See **make** v[1] **C18a**

make miration See **miration**

make mock of See **mock** n

make nice v phr Cf **make** v[1] **C17a**

1 To be friendly, considerate; to behave oneself; to behave affectionately—often used as an admonition.

1957 *Eaton Coll.* **Washington Is. WI,** Make nice on the kitty—pet gently. **1993** *DARE* File [**MT** (as of 1954), Haven't heard the term for years, but remember as a child, one of our neighborhood mothers [a German speaker] would break up scuffles, arguments, etc. with the admonition, "Okay, you kids, make nice now!" I don't think it was an ethnic thing, though, more of a useful substitute for "be nice" or "make up" in the lexicon of a woman struggling to learn English.] *Ibid,* It was Molly Goldberg on TV circa 1952 who said "Make nice." *Ibid* **IN** (as of 1964), I was staying with my grandparents in Michigan City . . and the girls who lived next door had a few bad habits regarding cheating at jacks. . . Many times that summer my grandmother ran from the house yelling, "Make nice, now, you kids!" *Ibid* **RI,** As far as *making nice*—this is something Rhode Islanders (Road Dielandahs) tell their babies to do: "Make nice with Uncle Mario, little Louie!" Making nice seems to be what you tell a kid to do when the kid is tearing off someone's glasses or doing something else unacceptable. *Ibid* **MN,** I remember hearing it [=*making nice*] among certain Yiddish speakers in my family, WWII generation, as a directive to those who were arguing, fighting, disagreeing. . . Another meaning [of *make nice*] has to do with literally patting or stroking another, as in "making nice." This can be between a parent and child, but might be between two lovers.

2 To act (not necessarily sincerely) in a friendly or accommodating way; to curry favor.

1991 Isaacs *Magic Hour* 272 **Long Is. NY,** He'd planned on taking the ten-fifteen morning flight, but instead he decided to go over to the set, to make nice to everybody because he knew morale wasn't all that high. **1993** *DARE* File **RI,** Here in RI . . lots of shady deals go on. *Make nice* is definitely akin to schmooze but schmoozers are more likely to be more of a social networking nature—i.e. schmoozing with the boys at certain Italian restaurants in Providence enables you to make calls for favors later. But making nice seems like more of foreplay to being able to officially schmooze. *Ibid* **NYC,** I hear *make nice* all the time. I thought it was a New Yorkerism. On the subject of investors, etc., having an independent [theatre production] company carries with it the advantage . . of not having to make nice to *anybody*. *Ibid* **Upstate NY,** I remember *make nice* from my Jewish friends. Is the derivation Yiddish? *Ibid* **NYC** (as of 1980s), My husband and his partner, both theatre producers, often spoke of having to make nice to potential investors. They talked about how much time is spent in L.A. finding out who to make nice to.

3 To smooth things over; to gloss over or suppress something unpleasant.

1993 Norris *Dakota* 81 **SD,** A more immediate consequence of the local history mentality is the tendency to "make nice," If we can make the past harmonious, why not the present? Why risk discussion that might cause unpleasantness? **1993** *DARE* File **Upstate NY,** *Make nice* . . smooth over something that wasn't. [*Ibid* **sOntario** (as of 1950s), As a kid in southern Ontario . . [I knew] *make nice,* at least in . . [the sense of] to prettify or smooth over or make better something that wasn't such.]

make no mind See **mind B4**

make no nevermind See **nevermind 3**

make of v phr [Scots, nEngl dial] **chiefly NEast** Cf **make over**
To pet, fuss over, flatter.

1913 *DN* 4.5 **ME,** *Make of.* . . To pet. "She was stroking the cat and making of it when it scratched her." **1914** *DN* 4.110 **cKS,** *Make over.* . . To treat with demonstrations of affection or esteem. . . [*DN* Ed: *Make of* in Mass.] **1938** Damon *Grandma* 110 **CT** (as of late 1800s), They say he never makes of her, never shows her no attention, 't all. **1959** *VT Hist.* 27.148 **cn,neVT,** *Make of.* . . To make over: to fondle. Occasional. **1970** *DARE* FW Addit **csNY,** Making of him—fussin' over him [occasional usage].

make off See **make up 1**

make old bones See **make v¹ D23**

make on v phr
1 To build or light (a fire). [*OED* (at *make* v.¹ 90.a) 1634 →; "dial."]
1851 in 1956 Eliason *Tarheel Talk* 283 **cnNC,** I did not wake before John had made on . . a fire. **1885** Howells *Rise Lapham* 49 **VT,** I'll be the death of that darkey *yet* . . if he don't stop making on such a fire. **1903** *DN* 2.320 **seMO,** *Make on a fire.* . . To make or build a fire.

2 To proceed, get on. [*OED* (at *make* v.¹ 90.b) 1608 →]
1931 (1991) Hughes–Hurston *Mule Bone* 100 **cFL** [Black], Hit's makin' on to three now. **1955** *DE Folkl. Bulletin* 1.17, If the Nanticoke is a guest in your house, when the time comes to leave he may say, "I guess I'll be makin' on home."

3 To turn on (a light), light (a lamp). [Prob infl by Ger *anmachen* to light (a fire), turn on (a light, etc)] **esp in Ger settlement areas** Cf **make v¹ C14**
1950 *WELS* **WI** (*Expressions used to tell somebody to. . . turn on the light:* "_____ the light.") 3 Infs, Make on the lamp (*or* light); 2 Infs, Make the lamp (*or* light) on. [All Infs of Ger background] **1966–69** *DARE* (Qu. Y41a, . . *To tell someone to light a lamp or lantern:* "_____ the lamp.") Infs GA77, SD2, Make on; (Qu. Y41b, . . *To light an electric light:* "_____ the light.") Infs ME21, PA152, SD2, WI12, Make on. [4 of 6 Infs in Ger settlement comms] **1987** *Jrl. Engl. Ling.* 20.2.172 **ePA,** *Make on* 'to turn on'.

4 usu with infin or *as if, like,* etc: To pretend. Cf **make like, make out** v phr **2**
1843 (1916) Hall *New Purchase* 225 **IN,** Let's you and me make on to be Injins. **1914** *DN* 4.110 **cKS,** *Make on.* . . To feign; pretend. "She makes on as tho she thought much of him." **1928** *Ruppenthal Coll.* **KS,** She makes on a good deal in the matter. **1939** Aurand *Quaint Idioms* 31 [PaGer], Well, you can *make on* as *if* you knew something. **1967–68** *DARE* (Qu. JJ46, . . *To pretend:* "Let's _____ we don't know a thing about it.") Infs TX53, VA26, Make on; LA11, Make on like. **1986** Pederson *LAGS Concordance* (He acted as if he knew it all) 1 inf, **cAR,** Made on like.

make one awake See **make v¹ D24**

make one hard to find See **make v¹ D25**

make one no mind See **mind B4**

make one no nevermind See **nevermind 3**

make one's brags See **make v¹ D26**

make oneself home See **make v¹ D27**

make one's haslet curl See **make v¹ D28**

make one's head save one's heels See **head n D2**

make one's jack See **jack n¹ 16**

make one's love come down See **love C**

make one's manners See **manner n 1**

make one's market See **make v¹ C18a**

make one's rise See **rise**

make one stand around See **make v¹ D29**

make on like See **make on 4**

make on over See **make over**

make out v phr
1 also *make it out:* To manage (to do something). [Cf *make out* to fare, get along]
1776 in 1875 J. & A. Adams *Familiar Letters* 231 **MA,** Amidst these interruptions, how shall I make it out to write a letter? **1839** Walker in 1940 Drury *Pioneers Spokanes* 257 **ME,** Mrs. Whitman . . refused to let me have a bottle to feed him [=a baby] with cow milk but I made out to find one & so fed him. **1845** (1968) Simms *Wigwam & Cabin* (1st ser) 68 **NC,** But I made out to skin and to cut up the b'ar, and a noble mountain of fat she made. **1847** Hurd *Grammatical Corrector* 51, "I made out to find him," instead of "succeeded in finding him." . . This very common but erroneous phrase has no particular locality. **1860** Holmes *Professor* 60 **MA,** What with foreboding looks and dreary death-bed stories, it was a wonder the child made out to live through it. **1864** in 1983 *PADS* 70.41 **ce,sePA,** I made out to damage . . a loaf of bread and three cups of coffee. **1876** in 1969 *PADS* 52.53 **seIL,** It just made out to freeze a little last night. **1885** Jewett *Marsh Is.* 36, I guess he may make out to come back if he don't like. **1887** (1967) Harris *Free Joe* 224 **cGA** [Black], My young marster year [=heard] dat Yankee man holler fer water; en he des [=just] make out fer ter crawl whar he is. **1914** *DN* 4.76 **nNH, ME,** *Make out to.* . . To succeed, accomplish, or come to do (something). **1923** *DN* 5.214 **swMO,** I fin'ly made out t' git hyar. **1943** Peattie *Great Smokies* 100, He made out to get the lantern lit—and then like to died.

2 with *like, as though:* To act as if; to pretend; to pretend to be. [Varr of std *make out;* cf **make like, make on 4**] **chiefly Sth, S Midl** See Map
1891 Johnston *Primes & Neighbors* 103 **GA,** He ain't the old man he make out like, not nigh. **1902** *DN* 2.239 **sIL,** He made out like it mighty nigh killed him. **1906** *DN* 3.121 **sIN,** He's makin' out like they want to go. **1909** *DN* 3.348 **eAL, wGA,** He made out like he was drunk. **1944** *PADS* 2.10 **Sth,** Don't make out like you don't know me. **1946** *PADS* 6.20 **eNC** (as of 1900–10), *Make out like.* **1947** *PADS* 8.14 **sIN** (as of early 1900s), Make out like. **1949** *PADS* 11.24 **CO,** He made out like he was going to town. **1951** *PADS* 15.57 **neIN** (as of 1890s), Make out like you don't know him. **1959** Lomax *Rainbow Sign* 103 **AL** [Black], Nora make out like she don't do this and that and the other, but don't you know she do! **c1960** Wilson Coll. **csKY,** Make out like. **1965–70** *DARE* (Qu. JJ46, . . *To pretend:* "Let's _____ we don't know

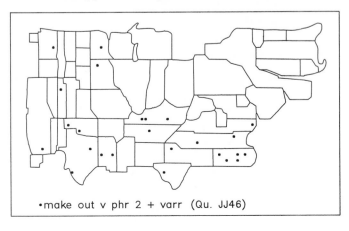

•make out v phr 2 + varr (Qu. JJ46)

485

a thing about it.") 24 Infs, **chiefly Sth, S Midl,** Make out like; **WA**3, Make out as though. **1967** *DARE* FW Addit **AR**55, We'll just make out like we're looking at something in the back yard. **1986** Pederson *LAGS Concordance Gulf Region (He acted as if he knew it all)* 63 infs, Made out like; 3 infs, Made out like—heard, but wouldn't use; 14 infs, Make out like; 1 inf, Making out like something when he ain't; 1 inf, Making out like = pretending.

3 To put out (a light or fire). [Calque of Ger *ausmachen;* but cf also *EDD make* v.[1] II.(15)(a)] **chiefly Ger settlement areas** Cf **make on 1, 3**

c1902 Clapin *New Dict. Amer.* 267, In parts of Pennsylvania inhabited by Germans . . *make* is used in many senses. . . "Make the light out and go to bed." **1908** *German Amer. Annals* 10.33 **sePA,** Make the light out. I do not need it. **1931** Jacobson *Milwaukee Dial.* 16 **seWI,** *Make out the light.* . . uneducated Milwaukeeans have adopted "make out" from the German ausmachen. **1935** *AmSp* 10.168 [Engl of PA Germans], It is customary . . *to make the fire out.* **1948** *AmSp* 23.109 **swIL,** Make the light out. **1948** *WELS Suppl.* **seWI** (as of 1930), Our neighbors made the light out. **1950** *WELS* **WI** (. . *To put out the light:* "_____ the light.") 1 Inf, Make out; 1 Inf, Make the lamp out. [Both Infs of Ger background] **1950** *WELS Suppl.* **seWI,** "Make out the lights" is very commonly used in Milwaukee. **1966–69** *DARE* (Qu. Y42, *Expressions for putting out a lamp or light*) Infs **IA**27, **PA**161, 199, Make out; **WI**48, Make out the light; [**NY**89, Make out with the light;] (Qu. Y43b, . . *To put out a fire*) Infs **PA**57, **WA**6, Make out; **WI**48, Make it out.

4 To put into final form; to shape.

1856 in 1862 Colt *Went to KS* 66 **NY,** She was frying cakes in buffalo grease. . . and she was making them out round on the bottom of an iron dish, cutting them across grid-iron fashion. **1914** *DN* 4.76 **ME, nNH,** *Make out.* . . To make, as "to make out the butter." **1966–67** *DARE* Tape **NC**4, Grease your hands when you make it [=bread dough] out; **TX**32, They're better if they're made up and let rise at least one day before you make 'em out to bake; **TX**40, She'd thicken it with flour or something and make it out in little cakes. . . And then make it out in loaves and let it rise again.

5 To eat.

1954 *Harder Coll.* **cwTN,** Make out. . . To eat. "Make outchie [=out your] dinner." **1954** *PADS* 21.33 **SC,** *Make out one's meal.* . . To eat heartily, as when a guest is urged to make out his meal. Dutch Fork.

6 To plan. [Calque of Ger *ausmachen*]

1935 *AmSp* 10.167 [Engl of PA Germans], We made out to go at five (we had planned to go at five). **1968** Helen Adolf *Festschrift* 38 **sePA,** *Make out* . . for 'plan'; for example, "We made that out long already." **1968–70** *DARE* (Qu. JJ36, *To work out a plan, especially a secret plan:* "*Mary knows more about that, you and she can* _____ *together.*") Infs **PA**130, 242, **SC**26, Make it out. **1987** *Jrl. Engl. Ling.* 20.172 **ePA,** *Make out* 'to plan.' . . All informants [=3 of 100] are Mennonites over age 65.

7 See quot. [*OED* (at *make* v.[1] 91.m) 1558 →; "?Now only dial."]

1952 Brown *NC Folkl.* 1.563, *Make (right) out.* . . To hurry, to escape.—Central and east.

make-out n

A substitute; a pretense; a pretender.

1899 (1912) Green *VA Folk-Speech* 273, *Make-outs.* . . Things with which one can manage to get along in place of something else. Also, people who pretend to be something that they are not: as, "They are great make-outs." **1922** Gonzales *Black Border* 312 **sSC, GA coasts** [Gullah glossary], *Mek out* . . a makeshift. **1946** *AmSp* 21.190 **eKY,** *Make-out* . . a pretense. 'That ain't nothin' but a make-out.' **1953** Randolph–Wilson *Down in Holler* 263 **Ozarks,** Sometimes one hears *make-out* used as a noun, meaning makeshift. An old gentleman said of his new dentures, "I can make out with these here teeth, I reckon. But it's a damn' poor make-out."

make out as though, make out like See **make out** v phr **2**

make over v phr Also rarely *make on over* **chiefly S Midl; also West** See Map Cf **make of**

To pet, fuss over, flatter.

1914 *DN* 4.110 **cKS,** *Make over.* . . To treat with demonstrations of affection or esteem. "She was miffed because they didn't make over her." **1923** *DN* 5.214 **swMO,** They shore did make over me when I driv up. **1942** McAtee *Dial. Grant Co. IN* 42 (as of 1890s), *Make over.* **1942**

Warnick *Garrett Co. MD* 10 **nwMD** (as of 1900–18), *Make over* . . give excessive or preferential attention. **1944** *PADS* 2.58 **MO,** *Make over.* . . To show affection for. "Her grandmother made over her too much." . . General. [*PADS* Ed: Rather common in a number of Southern states] **1954** *Harder Coll.* **cwTN,** Make over. **1956** McAtee *Some Dialect NC* 29, Fathers are inclined to make over their girl children. **1956** Gipson *Old Yeller* 41 **TX,** I petted him and made over him till he was wiggling all over to show how happy he was. c1960 *Wilson Coll.* **csKY,** *Make over.* . . Spoil, pet, pay a lot of attention to. **1966–70** *DARE* (Qu. Z14a, *To give a child its own way or pay too much attention to it:* "*Everyone* _____ *that child.*") Inf **GA**72, Make over; **AR**37, **CA**87, **KY**42, **NE**1, **WV**2, Makes over; **TN**41, Makes on over; (Qu. AA8, *When people make too much of a show of affection in a public place* . . "*There they were at the church supper* _____.") Infs **IL**131, **TX**29, Making over; **TN**2, **TX**32, **WA**13, Making over each other. **1981** Mebane *Mary* 130 **cnNC,** Joyce and Teddy . . soon would be in this or that aunt's kitchen, introducing me as their cousin from down south. Everybody made over me, they were so glad we'd come.

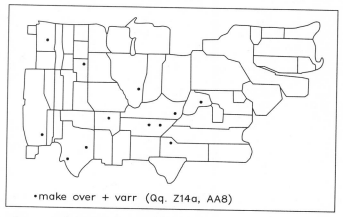

•make over + varr (Qq. Z14a, AA8)

make pretend See **make** v[1] **D30**

make quick See **make** v[1] **D31**

maker n [Prob because it is used to *make* someone obedient]

1953 *PADS* 19.12 **cnNC,** *Maker.* . . Switch. "Johnny, run and get a maker off the apple tree."

make shut See **make** v[1] **D32**

make small of See **make** v[1] **D33**

make strange See **strange**

make talk See **make** v[1] **D34**

make tend See **make** v[1] **D30**

make the fence See **build the fence**

make the groceries See **make** v[1] **C18b**

make the high-hat See **high-hat** n **2**

make the market See **make** v[1] **C18a**

make the riffle See **riffle**

make to See **make** v[1] **D32**

make up v phr

1 also *make off:* To plan, arrange (something); hence v phr *make it up* to plan, decide (to do something); hence ppl adj *made up* planned, contrived. [*OED* (at *make* v.[1] 96.l.(a)) "To arrange, settle (a marriage, etc.); to conclude (a treaty)"; 1562 →] **scattered, but esp Sth, S Midl**

1892 *DN* 1.230 **KY,** Make up. Referring to something planned, it is asked, "When did you all make that up?" **1893** Shands *MS Speech* 73, "That was a made-up job"; i.e. something that had been thought about and planned before. **1905** *DN* 3.87 **nwAR,** Make up. . . To plan. 'When did you make up this party?' **1909** *DN* 3.400 **nwAR,** Make it up. . . To plan. "They made it up to get married Thanksgivin'." **1941** Faulkner *Men Working* 124 **MS,** They was a bunch of us had made it up to go grabbling yestiddy. **1941** Hall Coll. **wNC,** We made it up not to work tomorrow. **1943** Chase *Jack Tales* 156 **wNC,** Jack and I made it up to go out together the next mornin'. **1950** *WELS Suppl.,* To arrange. "You'll have to make that off with Renee yourself." **1955** Ritchie *Singing*

Family 67 **seKY,** Granny knew by the way they acted that they were up to something, so she strained her ears and she heard them a-making it up to "git Balis out and fix him up proper." **c1960** *Wilson Coll.* **csKY,** *Make it up. . .* Plan something to be done. **1966–70** *DARE* (Qu. JJ36, *To work out a plan, especially a secret plan: "Mary knows more about that, you and she can _____ together."*) Infs **AK**8, **CT**39, **GA**1, **IA**7, **MA**55, **NY**22, 209, **SC**10, **TX**102, Make it up; **TN**31, 34, Make it off.
2 Of storm clouds, the sea, etc: to become increasingly threatening; of the weather: to grow stormy; to threaten (a storm, to snow, etc); to be preparing (for a storm, etc); of the wind: to cause (the sea) to become rough. **chiefly Atlantic** See Map Cf **make** v¹ C11

1902 *DN* 2.239 **sIL,** *Make up. . .* To approach. Used particularly of a storm-cloud. **1939** *LANE* Map 90 *(Clouding up)* 33 infs, 24 **ME,** Making up for a storm. **1945** Colcord *Sea Language* 125 **ME, Cape Cod, Long Island,** A storm cloud, or the sea, makes up—i.e., gets rougher or more threatening. **1956** Rayford *Whistlin' Woman* 170 **AL,** We took our party out in the Gulf o' Mexico, and we saw a squall making up. **1957** Beck *Folkl.* ME 137, As the seas made up, the vessel would bore through them, taking solid water her whole length and flinging spray almost masthead high. **1965–70** *DARE* (Qu. B6, *When clouds begin to increase . . it's _____*) Infs **MA**6, 30, **NC**17, **OK**13, **SC**66, **TN**52, **TX**4, Making up; **GA**11, **LA**7, Clouds making up; **MA**6, Making up for a shower; **NC**11, Making up in the northward; (Qu. B5, *When the weather looks as if it will become bad . . it's _____*) Infs **NY**106, **SC**69, Making up; **MA**58, **NY**52, Making up a storm; **FL**29, Making up for a squall; **FL**1, Making up for bad weather; **NC**25, Storm making up; (Qu. B12, *When the wind begins to increase . . it's _____*) Infs **ME**16, **MA**55, 58, **SC**69, Making up. **1975** Newell *If Nothin' Don't Happen* 105 **FL,** I was wonderin' whether I'd make it before the rain—a real frog-strangler makin' up to the southeast. **1975** Gould *ME Lingo* 175, *Make*—Weather *makes* up in various Maine expressions: "Looks like it's making up to snow." A stiff sou-westerly may make up such seas that lobstermen will stay ashore. **1976** Warner *Beautiful Swimmers* 135 **Chesapeake Bay,** "In a slick ca'm, carry eighty or one hundred pots," the watermen will say. "Seas making up, can't take half that number safely." **1986** Pederson *LAGS Concordance* **coastal Gulf Region,** 3 infs, A storm is (or [the] weather's) making up; 3 infs, Making up for a rain (or a storm, a weather); 3 infs, Making up (a) cloud (or the rain); 1 inf, It could be a tornado making up; 1 inf, Making up—of clouds; 1 inf, The weather is making up the rain.

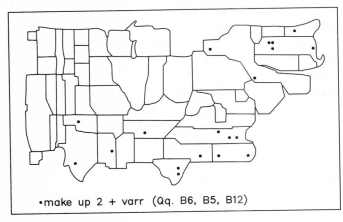

•make up 2 + varr (Qq. B6, B5, B12)

3 See **make** v¹ C4.
4 in phr *make up a hat:* See **make** v¹ D35.

makiawa n Also *mikiawa* [Haw] **HI**
A **round herring** (here: *Etrumeus micropus*).
  1926 Pan-Pacific Research Inst. *Jrl.* 1.1.5 **HI,** *Etrumeus micropus. . . Maki-awa.* **1960** Gosline–Brock *Hawaiian Fishes* 95, *Etrumeus micropus (Makiawa)*—This species occurs around Honolulu from time to time in some numbers. It reaches a length of at least 10 inches. **1967** *Honolulu Star–Bulletin* (HI) 31 May sec F 1/4, *Mikiawa . .* Hawaiian sardine.

makings n **chiefly West**
Loose tobacco and paper for hand-rolled cigarettes.
  1905 *Everybody's Mag.* Dec 817 **TX,** He took out his "makings," and rolled a cigarette. **1907** White *AZ Nights* 161, "Well," agreed Rogers, "pass over the 'makings' and I will." **1912** *DN* 3.583 **wIN,** *Makin(g)s. . .* The tobacco for a cigarette or pipe. **1913** *DN* 4.27 **NW,** *Makin's. . .*

Tobacco for a cigarette. "Got the makin's?" **1916** Sinclair *Phantom Herd* 116 **MT,** Luck . . trailed over to a table and gleaned "the makings" from among the litter of papers . . and rolled himself a much-needed smoke. **1930** Irwin *Amer. Tramp* 126, *Makins*—Cigarette tobacco and papers, the makings of a smoke. Before the days of cheap "tailor made" cigarettes most vagrants carried their "makins" and rolled their own cigarettes as wanted. **1940** *AmSp* 15.335 **NE.** **1941** Writers' Program *Guide WY* 463. **1948** Manfred *Chokecherry* 227 **nwIA,** "You smoke cigarettes?" "When I got the makin's." **1949** Emrich *Wild West Custom* 167 **West,** After eating, the cowboy relaxed with the *makings,* rolling a smoke with cigarette papers from his *prayerbook* and tobacco from his Bull Durham *sack.* **1949** *Sat. Eve. Post* 9 Apr 136 **SW,** I got out his makin's and rolled him one. **1965** *DARE* FW Addit **neNM.**

making up bread n
A children's rope-jumping maneuver.
  1946 TN Folk Lore Soc. *Bulletin* 12.1.18, Rope jumping . . offered a chance for the exhibition of individual skill in endurance, speed, and special stunts through "Rocking the Cradle," "Making up Bread," . . and such things.

makoola n Also sp *macoola, mahkoolah* [See quot 1991] **AK**
Home-brewed liquor; see quots.
  1882 Elliott *Seal Islands* 174 **AK,** *Kvass* or *Quass* (Russian).—Native home-brewed beer; . . also called "mahkoolah", after a Russian brewer. **1945** *AK Sportsman* Feb 35 (Tabbert *Dict. Alaskan Engl.*), Some of the village boys made an alcoholic drink called *macoola. . .* Anything that would add flavor was put into the macoola barrel. . . The best macoola I ever tasted used only graham flour for flavoring. **1965** Bowen *Alaskan Dict.* 21, *Makoola* (muh-cool-a)—Native booze on the order of raisin jack or worse and produced as moonshine. Leave it alone. **1991** Tabbert *Dict. Alaskan Engl.* 88, *Makoola*—Another name used for homebrew in the Aleutian and Alaska Peninsula areas. It is probably from Russian. Dean Worth suggests that it may be from Russian *muka* 'flour.' . . The word is probably now obsolete.

maktak See **muktuk**

makule adj, n [Haw] **HI**
See quots.
  1938 Reinecke *Hawaiian Loanwords* 24, *Makule. . .* 1. Old (of things); aged (of persons). . . 2. An old person. 3. "The old man," used familiarly of one's father. V[ery] F[req]. **1954–60** Hance et al. *Hawaiian Sugar* 4, *Makule . .* [mɑ'kule]—Old.

malafee See **malawu**

malahack v Pronc-spp *mallyhack, mollyhack, mollyhawk* [*EDD malahack*] **scattered, but esp NEng** Cf **ballyhack** v
1 To cut or chop rudely or roughly; to injure, beat, maltreat.
  1867 Lowell *Biglow* lviii **'Upcountry' MA,** *Malahack:* to cut up hastily or awkwardly. **1901** *Nation* 22 Aug 148 **cwME,** He don't know how to cut up a critter, and he's jes' malahacked it all to pieces. *Ibid* 205 **seNH** (as of 1854), She did not wish to have him *malahacked* by his teacher. The boy had been feruled unjustly, and she was indignant. *Ibid* 245 **cwNH** (as of c1850), The word *Malahack* was used less in the sense of "to cut awkwardly" than in that of "to cut injuriously," *e.g.* to disfigure or maim—a tree, a piece of furniture, or an animal. *Ibid* 264 (as of 1872–85), The word *malahack* was in common use there [=Roane Co. WV], in the sense of deface or injure; *e.g.* "Who mollyhacked your hair?" "If you dare do it, I will mollyhack you." **1913** *DN* 4.5 **ME,** *Mollyhawk. . .* To tease, to abuse. "The child was mollyhawking the cat all over the floor." **1953** Randolph–Wilson *Down in Holler* 263 **Ozarks,** *Mallyhack. . .* To cut up, or to beat severely. "I'll mallyhack that feller within a inch of his life!" I have heard a man with many knife wounds and bruises described as *mallyhacked.* The word seems to be used only when the injuries are severe. **1954** *PADS* 21.33 **SC,** *Malahack. . .* Ballyhack or ballywack.
2 To act boisterously, to roughhouse.
  1901 *Nation* 12 Sept 205 **neCT,** He will say . . either in a jesting tone or in a tone of reproof, "Don't go malahacking around here," or "Don't malahack all around."

malapai(s) See **malpais**

malaria n Usu |mə'lɛriə, -'lær-, -'ler-|; also |mə'lɛrɪ, mə'lerɪ, mə'lerə| Pronc-sp *malary* Cf **idea**
Std sense, var forms.
  1891 *DN* 1.157 **cNY,** [mə'lerɪ] < *malaria.* **1928** *AmSp* 3.402 **Ozarks,** *Ida* is turned into *Idy. . .* Something of the same sort occurs in words like *pneumonia* and *malaria,* which are nearly always pronounced neu-

mony and *malary.* **c1938** in 1970 Hyatt *Hoodoo* 1.458 **seGA**, It wus *malary* fever. **1966–68** *DARE* Tape **FL19**, They used to have what they called chills and fever—that's malaria [mə'lerɪ], you know; **IN3**, That was for the chills, I know that—like malaria chills [mə,lɛrɪ 'čiəlz]; **MS77**, They get . . malaria [mə'lerɪrə]. **1981** Pederson *LAGS Basic Materials,* 1 inf, **cMS**, [mə'le·ʳ·ɾɪ]; 1 inf, **csMS**, [mə'le·ʳɔ·ɬ^]; 1 inf, **cTN**, [mɬ'e·ɔ·ɬ^ ˌfiˡvə].

malashagany n [See quot]
=freshwater drum.

   1896 Gerard in *N.Y. Sun* 30 July *(DA),* Malashagany, a name of the sheepshead of Lake Huron, the 'bass' of the English of Canada, and the 'gros bossu' (from its rounded back) of the French of the same country. The name is, through French Canadian, 'malachegane,' from Nipissing 'manashigan,' 'the ill-formed bass.'

malassada n Pronc-sp *mully sobber* [Port "an omelet or pan-cake made with eggs"] **HI, seNEng** Cf **Berliner**
A round cake cooked in deep fat and coated with sugar.

   1967 *DARE* (Qu. H26) Inf **HI6**, [ˌmɑlɑ'sɑdɑ]—a sugared doughnut with no hole, like a ball; (Qu. H29, *A round cake, cooked in deep fat, with jelly inside)* Inf **HI9**, [ˌmɑlɑ'sɑdɑs]—dough not sweetened; sugar outside. **1968** *DARE* File **seMA, seRI**, Mully sobbers [mʌlɪ 'sabəz]— Fried bread dough eaten at breakfast. This came from Portugal, and was learned from the Portuguese workmen on the farms in Middletown, R.I., and from women working in the kitchens. This is even available in S. Dartmouth, Massachusetts in the Portuguese section. The Middletown nickname for this was foopers ['fu:pəz], which the informant thought was very funny. **1972** Carr *Da Kine Talk* 96 **HI**, Hawaii's Portuguese heritage, gastronomically speaking, comes to mind in connection with the popular . . *malassada,* a kind of doughnut raised with yeast. **1981** *Pidgin To Da Max* np **HI**, *Malasada. . .* Portuguese donut. No hole. **1981** Pap *Port.–Americans* 216, In Hawaii, . . Portuguese sweetbreads *(pão doce)* and doughnuts *(malassadas),* too, are quite popular. **1982** Chaika *Speaking RI* [7], *Malasadezh* [sic] = Pawtuguese dough boys, but with a slight lemon taste. **1991** Kirlin–Kirlin *Smithsonian Folklife Cookbook* 277 **HI**, Malassadas (Portuguese Doughnuts).

malawu n Also *malafee* [See quot 1949] *Gullah* Cf *DJE*
Whiskey.

   1923 Parsons *Folk-lore Sea Islands* xxi **csSC**, Maria Middleton told me that she had heard that *malafee* was African for "whiskey." **1949** Turner *Africanisms* 198 **sSC, GA coasts** [Gullah], [Words used in conversation:] [mɑ'lɑwu] 'whiskey'; 'any alcoholic beverage'. *Ibid* 306, None of my Gullah informants were familiar with *malafee,* but most of them knew *maʹlawu,* i.e. [mɑ'lɑßu] ([mɑ'lɑθu]). The word *malavu* 'wine' is found in the Kongo language, spoken in Angola and the Belgian Congo, the very areas from which thousands of slaves were being brought direct to South Carolina throughout the eighteenth century and the first half of the nineteenth.

Malay apple n
Std: a tree *(Syzygium malaccensis)* which produces an edible, red-skinned fruit. Also called **mountain apple, ohia** n[1] 1

mal de ojos n [MexSpan; see quot]
=globe mallow 1.

   1951 *PADS* 15.17 **AZ**, *Sphaeralcea coccinea. . .* Mal de ojos, the thread-like attachments of the carpels causing sore eyes.

mal de raquette n [CanFr, literally "snowshoe sickness"; *DCan* 1821]
   1992 *DARE* File **ME**, Mal de raquette [ˌmæl də 'rækət] is a painful affliction of the muscles and joints of the legs caused by the unnatural gait required when using snowshoes.

male adj, often used absol **widespread, but chiefly Sth, Midl** See Map *euphem* Cf **beast B2, brute, bull** n 1, **gentleman** n **B2**
Used to refer to a male farm animal, usu an uncastrated one kept for breeding purposes—freq in combs *male cow,* ~ *hog.*

   1859 (1968) Bartlett *Americanisms* xxvi, Among some of the Western people there are strange ideas regarding the use of certain words, which has led the mock-modest to reject them and substitute others. . . The essentially English word *bull* is refined beyond the [Appalachian] mountains, and perhaps elsewhere, into . . *male-cow. . . Male sheep, male hog,* etc., are of a piece with the preceding. **1903** *DN* 2.320 **seMO**, *Male-brute. . .* Bull. *Male-hog. . .* Boar. **1906** *DN* 3.121 **sIN**, *Male-hog. . .* Not used playfully. **1907** *DN* 3.233 **nwAR**, *Male-hog.* **1909** *DN* 3.400 **nwAR**, *Male-hog. . .* Not used playfully. **1909** *DN* 3.348 **eAL**,

wGA, *Male-cow. . .* A squeamish term for bull, used occasionally by women. **1915** *DN* 4.185 **swVA**, *Male. . .* Bull. *Male-hog.* **1917** *DN* 4.414 **KS, KY, wNC**, *Male. . .* Used attributively, in affectation of sexual propriety, in combinations; as, *male-brute,* bull; *male-hog,* boar. **1923** *DN* 5.214 **swMO**, *Male. . .* Any male animal kept for breding [sic] purposes. Bull, boar, stallion and jack are not used in mixed company. **1927** *AmSp* 2.360 **WV**, *Male. . .* used in combinations for affected propriety. . . *Male-hog. . . Male-cow. . . Male-brute.* **1933** Rawlings *South Moon* 134 **FL**, "Hit's that male hog," she said fervently. "He's like to drove me crazy." **1946** *PADS* 5.29 **VA**, *Male. . .* Bull; used everywhere, mostly in the presence of women. . . *Male, male hog. . .* Boar, used in the presence of women, not common. . . *Male horse* . . : Stallion; used mostly in the presence of women, fairly common. **1949** *AmSp* 24.111 **nwSC**, *Male ox. . .* Bull. **1949** Kurath *Word Geog.* 62, New England expressions for the bull are: . . *animal* or *male animal. . .* Southernisms are equally varied: *male* and *male cow* in Virginia, adjoining parts of North Carolina, and on Delamarvia (occasionally also in New England); . . *male brute* in westernmost North Carolina. . . In the Southern area such expressions as the *male,* the *beast,* and the *brute* are common. **1958** *PADS* 29.13 **cnTN**, *Male brute* . . used for either bull or stallion. **c1960** Wilson *Coll.* **csKY**, *Male-brute, male-calf, male-horse, male-sheep. . .* Euphemism[s] for [boar or bull, bullock, stallion, ram respectively]. **1965–70** *DARE* (Qu. K22, *Words used for a bull)* 112 Infs, **widespread, but chiefly Sth, Midl**, Male; 64 Infs, **chiefly Sth, Midl**, Male cow; **IL18, 19, KS1, OK10, OR7, VA68**, Male animal; **GA3, NC49**, Male beast; **MO3**, Male calf; **FL15**, Male thing; (Qu. K23, *Words used by women or in mixed company for a bull)* 88 Infs, **chiefly Sth, Midl**, Male; 84 Infs, **chiefly Sth, Midl**, Male cow; **IL5, 9, KS6, 18, NM6, OR7, PA207**, Male animal; **NC31, VA57**, Male ox; **GA3, NC10**, Male beast; **KY29**, Male brute; **TN53**, Male calf; (Qu. K52, *A male pig kept for breeding)* 67 Infs, **chiefly Sth, Midl**, Male hog; 23 Infs, **chiefly Sth, Midl**, Male; **MD18, 38, MN12, SC43, VA38**, Male pig; **MO10**, Brood male; **LA8**, Stock male; **MS81**, Stud male. **1983** *MJLF* 9.1.47 **ceKY**, *Male* . . a euphemism for bull . . for boar . . for ram. . . *Male animal* . . a euphemism for boar. . . *Male hog.*

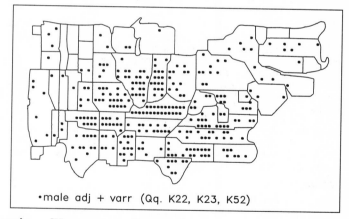

• *male adj + varr* (Qq. K22, K23, K52)

male v [Haw pronc-sp for *marry*]
   1938 Reinecke *Hawaiian Loanwords* 24, *Male* ['mɑle]. . . To marry. F[requently used].

Male n See Maley

maleberry n Also *male blueberry, male-huckleberry* [Cf *OED male* a. A.2.b]
A **staggerbush**: usu *Lyonia ligustrina,* rarely *L. mariana.* For other names of *L. ligustrina* see **buckberry 1, he-huckleberry 3, pepperbush, white alder, white bush, whitewood**

   1797 Smith *Nat. Hist.* **GA** 2.161, Its food is the *Andromeda mariana,* vulgarly called the Male Huckleberry, which grows round ponds and on the margins of running streams. **1897** *Jrl. Amer. Folkl.* 10.49 **sME coast**, *Andromeda ligustrina* . . maleberry. **1910** Graves *Flowering Plants* 310 **CT**, *Lyonia ligustrina. . .* Male Berry. Frequent or common. . . Like the preceding species [=*Lyonia mariana*], [it] is poisonous to stock, especially to sheep. **1942** *Torreya* 42.163 **VA**, *Xolisma ligustrina. . .* Male berry, staggerbush. **1950** Gray–Fernald *Manual of Botany* 1123, *Maleberry* or *Male Blueberry. . .* A polymorphous wide-ranging species. **1966** Grimm *Recognizing Native Shrubs* 228, *Maleberry. . . Range.* Central Maine to central New York and Kentucky; south to Florida, Louisiana, and Oklahoma. . . Also known as . . Male-huckleberry. **1973** Wharton–Barbour *Trees* **KY** 84, *Male-berry* . . is scattered from eastern and southeastern to southwestern Kentucky. **1976** Bailey–Bailey *Hortus Third* 690, *Male berry, . . male blueberry.* Deciduous shrub, to 12 ft., but often less.

male cow See **male** adj

male fern n Cf **female fern**
Std: a shield fern *(Dryopteris filix-mas).* Also called **bear's-paw root, wood fern**

male hog See **male** adj

male-huckleberry See **maleberry**

male paloverde n
A paloverde (here: *Parkinsonia microphylla).*
1925 Jepson *Manual Plants CA* 513, *P[arkinsonia] microphylla. . . Male Palo Verde.* Shrub . . or a small tree up to 25 ft. high, with light green bark. **1938** Van Dersal *Native Woody Plants* 343, Male . . paloverde *(Parkinsonia microphylla).*

Maley n Also sp *Mailey, Male* Cf **melungeon**
=**Guinea** n[1] **2.**
1946 *Social Forces* 24.442 **WV, MD,** Word "Guinea" said to be an epithet applied to anything of foreign or unknown origin. Other names applied locally are "West Hill" Indians, Maileys. **1947** *AmSp* 22.83 **C Atl,** A rather hesitant effort by a mixed-blood group to find a name at once more distinctive and more inclusive than a generalized family name which might also be found among Negroes and whites is reflected in the terms *Our People* (which the *Guineas* use of themselves, together with the name *Maleys).* **1963** Berry *Almost White* 20 **cnWV,** The most frequent [surname] in occurrence is Male (or Mayle, Mail, Mahle). So common, in fact, is that family name that in some localities the Guineas are called Males, and some even say they are an off-shoot of the Malay race.

malice See **mallow**

malihini n, also attrib [Haw] **HI** Cf **kamaaina**
A stranger, newcomer; a neophyte; hence adj *malihini* strange, uncharacteristic.
1914 *Outing* 64.26 **HI,** A couple of canoes are launching . . where the neophytes, the "malihini," learn their first lessons in riding the rollers. **1938** Reinecke *Hawaiian Loanwords* 24, *Malihini. . .* A newcomer; one not established socially and psychologically in the community. . Foreign to Hawaii; characteristic of outsiders. V[ery] F[req]. **1954** *Ellery Queen's Mystery Mag.* 4.31 **HI,** Seeing our guests in more formal clothes didn't faze him; he said, *"Malihinis?"* and added, with his brilliant smile, *"Aloha nui loa!"* **1967** DARE (Qu. HH31, *Somebody who is not from your community, and doesn't belong)* Infs **HI**1, 4, 13, Malihini. **1969** DARE FW Addit **HI,** Malihini [ˌmɑləˈhini]—a new-comer. Common. **1972** Carr *Da Kine Talk* 87 **HI,** *Hawaiian Words Commonly Heard In Hawaii's English. . . Malihini.* Visitor, tourist, newcomer. **1984** Sunset *HI Guide* 85.

malipi See **malpais**

mall n Cf **boulevard**
1 A highway median strip. **chiefly Upstate NY** See Map
1947 *Engineering News-Rec.* 138.131 **NY,** The center mall, never less than 20 ft., will keep opposing lanes of traffic far enough apart as to make head-on collisions virtually impossible. **1965–70** DARE (Qu. N17, . . *The separating area in the middle [of a four-lane road])* 34 Infs, **chiefly Upstate NY,** Mall.

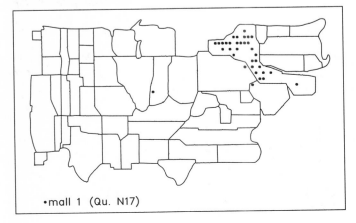
•mall 1 (Qu. N17)

2 See quot.
1967–70 DARE (Qu. N44, *In a town, the strip of grass and trees between the sidewalk and the curb)* Infs **MA**122, **NE**11, **NY**32, 63, 123, **OH**87, Mall.

mallapy See **malpais**

mallard n
1 Std: a common and widely distributed duck *(Anas platyrhynchos).* Also called **black duck 1, drake** n[2] **1, duck-inmallard, English duck 1, French duck 1, frosty-beak, grass mallard, gray duck d, ~ mallard, greenhead 4a(1), icebreaker, ice duck 1, ~ mallard, Irish mallard, northern ~, prairie ~, redlegs, snow mallard, yellowlegs, ringneck, twister, weed duck, wild ~** Cf **Florida duck, gadwall, white-winged scoter**
2 A **black duck 1** (here: *Anas rubripes).*
1923 U.S. Dept. Ag. *Misc. Circular* 13.9 **VA,** *Black Duck (Anas rubripes). . . Vernacular Names. . . In local use. . .* Mallard. **1955** *Oriole* 20.1.3 **GA,** Black Duck. . . Mallard.

mallard weed n
=**duckweed 1.**
1951 *PADS* 15.27 **TX,** *Lemnaceae.* Duckweeds, mallard weeds; several species eaten by river ducks.

maller See **mallow**

malley See **malpais 2**

mallow n Also *maller, malice, mallis*
A Forms.
1873 in 1976 Miller *Shaker Herbs* 200, *Malva rotundifolia.* Cheeses. Cheese Plant. Maller. **1893** *Jrl. Amer. Folkl.* 6.139 **cwVT,** *Malva rotundifolia,* malice. **1894** *DN* 1.342 **wCT,** *Mallis:* probably for *mallows;* a plant whose seed-vessels resemble cheeses in shape, and are called *mallis-cheeses* by children. **1924** *Amer. Botanist* 30.105, In some sections the word mallow has been corrupted into "malice." **1959** Carleton *Index Herb. Plants* 76, *Malice: Malva (v).* **1968–70** DARE (Qu. S9, . . *Kinds of grass that are hard to get rid of)* Inf **CA**212, Marsh malice; (Qu. S21, . . *Weeds . . that are a trouble in gardens and fields)* Inf **NY**107, Malice.
B Sense.
Std: a plant of the family Malvaceae. For other names of var malvaceous plants see **buttonweed 4, cheese B1, desert fivespot, dollar weed 2, false mallow, felt-plant, flower-of-an-hour, glade mallow, globe ~, ground ivy 2e, gumbo 1, hibiscus, hollyhock, ilima, Indian mallow 1, mangrove mallow, marshmallow 1, milo** n[2]**, pancake plant, parcheese, poppy mallow, ribbonwood, rockrose, shirt-button plant, snow cup, teaweed, velvetleaf, Virginia mallow, waxmallow, whiteweed, wild hollyhock, ~ ilima, ~ okra**

mallow bug See **mellow bug**

mallow rose n [OED 1840 →] Cf **rose mallow**
A **hibiscus** (here: *Hibiscus moscheutos).*
1843 Torrey *Flora NY* 1.115, *Hibiscus Moscheutos. Mallow Rose. . .* Flowers about as large as in the common *Hollyhock. . .* A showy plant, sometimes cultivated in gardens. **1893** *Jrl. Amer. Folkl.* 6.139 **NY,** *Hibiscus moscheutos,* mallow rose. **1903** Porter *Flora PA* 210, *Hibiscus Moscheutos. . . Mallow Rose. . .* In brackish marshes, Mass. to Fla. and La., and on lake shores and in saline situations locally in the interior to W. Ont. **1950** Gray-Fernald *Manual of Botany* 1006, *H[ibiscus] Moscheutos. . . Mallow-Rose. . .* Marshes. . July–Sept. **1966** DARE Wildfl QR Pl.129 Inf **AR**44, Mallow rose. **1968** DARE (Qu. S26a, . . *Roadside flowers)* Inf **GA**18, Mallow rose; (Qu. S26e, *Other wildflowers . . ;* not asked in early QRs) Inf **MN**13, Mallow rose. **1976** Bailey-Bailey *Hortus Third* 562, *Mallow rose. . .* Petals 3–4¼ in. long, white, pink, or rose, usually with crimson base.

mallyhack See **malahack**

malma n Also *malma trout*
=**Dolly Varden 1.**
1882 U.S. Natl. Museum *Bulletin* 16.319, *S[alvelinus] malma. . . Dolly Varden Trout; . . Malma. . .* Head large, snout broad, flattened above. **1904** *Salmon & Trout* 286, The Dolly Varden trout; Oregon charr; bull trout; malma; golet. *Ibid* 295, The Dolly Varden trout . . malma trout. **1933** John G. Shedd Aquarium *Guide* 37, *Dolly Varden Trout;*

Malma Trout. . . This fish is very abundant in Alaska, where thousands are destroyed annually because they feed largely on Salmon eggs and fry. **1949** Caine *N. Amer. Sport Fish* 88, Dolly Varden trout. . . *Colloquial Names* . . Malma Trout.

malo n [Haw] **HI** Note: Haw has only one liquid consonant, which early writers often represented with *r* rather than *l.* Cf **holoku, muumuu**

A loincloth.

1825 Ellis *Jrl. HI* 103, Their only clothing was their *maro,* a narrow girdle worn round their loins, one end of which passes between the legs and fastens in front. **1873** in 1966 Bishop *Sandwich Is.* 47 **HI,** His only clothing was the *malo,* a narrow strip of cloth wound round the loins, and passed between the legs. **1938** Reinecke *Hawaiian Loanwords* 24, *Malo.* . . Loincloth. F[req]. **1940** Von Tempski *Paradise* 235 **HI** (as of 1900–25), A tall Hawaiian, naked except for a scarlet *malo,* waited. **1967** *DARE* (Qu. FF16) Inf **HI9,** Malo. **1972** Carr *Da Kine Talk* 87 **HI,** *Hawaiian Words Commonly Heard In Hawaii's English.* . . *Malo.* Loincloth.

malolly n Also *malollypop, molly* Cf **-ma-** infix
Nonsense, bunk.

1966–69 *DARE* (Qu. NN13, *When you think that the thing somebody has just said is silly or untrue: "Oh, that's a lot of _____."*) Inf **GA5,** Malollypop [məˈlɑlɪpɑp]; **IN83,** Malolly; **GA45,** Molly [laughter].

malolo n [Haw] **HI**
=**flying fish 1.**

1926 Pan-Pacific Research Inst. *Jrl.* 1.1.6 **HI,** *Exocoetidae.* Flying-Fishes. Malolo. **1960** Gosline-Brock *Hawaiian Fishes* 6, Aside from the malolo (flying fish), which attaches its eggs to floating objects such as seabird feathers, the other pelagic species of fish . . lay and fertilize numerous small eggs in the sea itself.

malpais n Pronc-spp *malapai(s), malipi, mallapy, malpiar* [Span *mal* bad + *pais* country] **SW** Cf **aa, pahoehoe**
1 Rugged terrain, esp of heavily eroded basaltic lava.

1844 (1846) Kendall *Santa Fé Exped.* 2.384, We had crossed the *mal pais,* or bad country, as it is called. **1892** *DN* 1.249 **TX,** *Malpais:* bad lands, lava country. **1907** White *AZ Nights* 96, Sometimes we skipped . . over little gullies, barrancas, and other sorts of malpais. **1932** *DN* 6.231, *Malpais* or *Malapais.* Somewhat used in the Southwest, in much the same sense as badlands. As a place name I have met with it only in New Mexico, but it is apparently heard now and then in Western Texas, New Mexico, Arizona, and Southern California. **1942** Kearney *Flowering Plants* 17 **AZ,** Some of these are limestone areas, whereas others are volcanic, locally known as "mallapy" *(mal pais).* **1948** Peattie *Inverted Mts.* 61 **nAZ,** The lava is so rough and jagged and so black that it appears to have flowed forth just yesterday. This is the type of lava referred to as "malpais," meaning badlands, by the natives of the southwest. **1951** Fergusson *New Mexico* 407, *Malpais*—country underlain by dark lava, especially basalt. **1956** Ker *Vocab. W. TX* 90, Term for wastelands. . . For the Spanish word *malpais,* which means "bad country," eight scattered responses suggest the Spanish influence upon the speech of the Southern Plains. **1970** Hillerman *Blessing Way* 164 **NM,** To get there you had to go through the Oscura Range and Jicarilla Apache Reservation or over the malpais—across seven miles of broken lava country. You can't even get a horse over that.
2 also abbr *malley:* Basaltic lava; a piece of lava.

1881 U.S. Bur. Indian Affairs *Report* 7 **AZ,** The hills are covered with large stones or malipi rock. [**1885** *Harper's New Mth. Mag.* 70.692, These *mesas* are here of *mal país* (bad lands), as the Mexicans call the ancient lava formations which are blotted in inky blackness over the Rio Grande landscape.] **1919** Chase *CA Desert* 193, The spur ran out at last in a tongue of yellowish rock of the *malpais* kind. **1949** *Chicago Tribune* (IL) 9 Jan sec 6 3/3 **AZ,** They made manos and metates from malpai, in which they ground their meal. **1956** Ker *Vocab. W. TX* 95, Wagon load with the sideboards on chuck full of them malpiar rock. **1967** *DARE* (Qu. C26, . . *Special kinds of stone or rock*) Infs **AZ**1, 7, [mæləpi]; **AZ**10, Malapai rock; **TX**5, Malpai [mælpɑɪ]; **NM**11, Malley—a rough piece of lava of any size.

malt corn n **chiefly S Midl** Cf **corn malt**
Sprouted corn used in making liquor.

1949 *AmSp* 24.10, *Malt corn.* . . Sprouted corn or corn malt. Barley malt is generally used in large operations, but corn malt is universally used in the eastern Kentucky mountains. **1959** Hall *Coll.* **eTN,** *Malt corn grinder* . . used in grinding sprouted corn (malt corn) for fermenting still mash. **1959** Roberts *Up Cutshin* 62 **eKY,** We'd sprout what was

called malt corn. Take and put corn in a coffee sack in water until it sprouted good. **1967** *DARE* Tape **KY**34A, Then we put malt corn, that's sprouted corn.

maltee n, adj [Back-formation from *Maltese,* understood as a pl; cf **Chinee**]
1896 *DN* 1.420 **wCT,** c,n**NY,** *Maltese:* often pron[ounced] [mɑlˈti]. **1897** Stuart *Simpkinsville* 5 **AR,** Maltee is a good enough color for a cat. **1907** *DN* 3.193 se**NH,** *Maltee.* . . Maltese cat. **1911** *DN* 3.549 **NE,** Folk-etymological singulars are . . *Maltee, Chinee, Portugee.* **1918** Lincoln *Shavings* 45 **MA,** Nate Rogers' old maltee never shed all that alone. **1950** *WELS* (A cat with fur of mixed colors) 2 Infs, **WI,** Maltee. **1966–68** *DARE* (Qu. J5) Infs **DE**1, 4, **MI**47, **MO**1, **MA**32, **NY**72, **OK**18, Maltee; **TN**26, Maltee cats.

Maltese cross n [See quot 1979]
The scarlet lychnis (*Lychnis chalcedonica*). Also called **London pride 1, scarlet lightning, sweet William**
1868 (1870) Gray *Field Botany* 65, *L[ychnis] Chalcedonica,* Maltese-Cross or Scarlet *L[ychnis].* Very common in country-gardens. . . The bright scarlet or brick-red petals deeply 2-lobed. **1909** Doubleday *Amer. Flower Garden* 62, Maltese Cross. . . Scarlet flowers, the four petals with squared ends like a Maltese cross. **1910** Graves *Flowering Plants* 178 **CT,** Maltese . . Cross. . . Roadsides and about old houses. **1949** Moldenke *Amer. Wild Flowers* 65, Even more vivid are the . . scarlet flowers of the *maltesecross,* . . occasionally seen along roadsides and around dwellings from Massachusetts west to Minnesota and south to New Jersey. **1979** Niering-Olmstead *Audubon Guide N. Amer. Wildflowers E. Region* 457, Maltese Cross. . . The common name reflects the similarity of the petal arrangement to the shape of the cross adopted by the Knights of Malta. **1993** Comstock Ferre *1993 Seed Catalog* 44, Maltese Cross (*Lychnis*).

malungeon See **melungeon**

mam n |mæm|
1 A mother; a grandmother—often used as a quasi-personal name. [*OED* 1573 →] Cf **mammy** n[1], **mom** n[1], **mum** n[1]
1845 Kirkland *Western Clearings* 8 **MI,** Mam says supper's ready. **1867** Harris *Sut Lovingood Yarns* 23 **TN,** He allers wer a mos' complikated durned ole fool, an' mam sed so when he warnt about. **1890** *DN* 1.68 **KY,** Mam, mama [mæm, mæmɪ]: for mother. **1894** *DN* 1.332 **NJ,** Mam, mom . . for mamma or mother. **1894** in 1983 Zeigler *Lexicon Middle GA* 107, You tell your mam, my son, that there's no danger of such as that. *Ibid,* Pap, I'm ready to go back home, if you are. Mam said we mustn't stay too long. **1923** *DN* 5.214 sw**MO,** Mam. . . Used in speaking to or of mother. **1930** Shoemaker *1300 Words* 39 c**PA Mts** (as of c1900), *Mam*—Mother. **1953** Randolph-Wilson *Down in Holler* 264 **Ozarks,** Maw. . . Mother. Mam, mammy, and mommy are also common. **1966–70** *DARE* (Qu. Z2, . . *'Mother'*) Infs **FL**8, **KY**86, **NY**1, [mæm]; **VA**11, [mæm]—old-fashioned; (Qu. Z4, . . *'Grandmother'*) Infs **KY**10, **MO**9, **RI**6, Mam. **1973** Allen *LAUM* 1.339 (as of c1950), 2 infs [of 203], cs**MN,** Mam. **1981** Pederson *LAGS Basic Materials (Mother)* 2 infs, cs**AR,** ne**TN,** [mæᶜm]; *(Grandmother)* 1 inf, c**TX,** Mam—she is called by her grandchildren.
2 See **mammy** n[1] **2.**

mama n[1] See **mamma** n[1]

ma-ma n[2] See **mam-maw**

mamani n Also sp *mamane* [Haw]
A yellow-flowered tree (*Sophora chrysophylla*) native to Hawaii.
1892 in 1903 Bernice P. Bishop Museum *Special Pub.* 6.436 **HI,** The food of the Palila is to a very large extent derived from the Mamani trees, on the seeds of which it chiefly feeds. **1915** Bryan *Nat. Hist. HI* 245, The . . oo. . . sipped the nectar from the blossoms of . . the yellow *mamani,* and also ate a few insects. **1930** Degener *Ferns of HI* 179, The tree known by the Hawaiian name of *mamani.* . . at present . . is found on all the larger islands excepting Molokai. **1944** Munro *Birds HI* 125, The palila. . . feeds to a great extent on the seeds of the mamane (*Sophora*), holding the pod down with its foot and tearing it open with its hooked bill. **1972** Berger *Hawaiian Birdlife* 121, The birds sometimes foraged in the understory, . . feeding on lobelias, . . the ieie vine, and, occasionally, mamani. **1994** Stone-Pratt *Hawai'i's Plants* 247, Māmane, like ʻaliʻi and koa, is one of the few native Hawaiian plants that often survives fires. . . While resistant to fires, māmane trees are vulnerable to the impacts of browsing by feral goats and sheep.

mama-san n [**mamma** n[1] **1** + Japanese *san* worthy] **HI**
See quot 1972.

1934 *AmSp* 9.57 **HI**, *Mama-san* and *papa-san* [are] hybrid words applied to the old peasant type of Japanese. **1967** *DARE* (Qu. Z2, . . *'Mother'*) Inf **HI**1, Mama-san, among Japanese. **1972** Carr *Da Kine Talk* 115 **HI**, *Mama-san* (English + Japanese). 'Good mother' or 'worthy mother', a term often used in Hawaii by non-Japanese speakers in addressing or speaking of an older Japanese woman. It implies friendship and affection. . . *San* is the well-known honorific term in Japanese.

ma-maw See **mam-maw**

mamère See **mémère**

mamma n[1] Usu |ˈmamə, ˈmɔmə|; also |məˈma|; esp SC |ˈmæmə, məˈmæ|; for addit proncs see quots Also sp *mama, mauma, maumer, maumuh, momma, mommer*

1 A mother—often used as a quasi-personal name, esp by a woman's children or husband. [*OED* 1579 →] **widespread, but less freq Nth, N Midl** See Map Cf **mom** n[1], **mum** n[1]

　　1776 in 1859 Moore *Diary Amer. Revol.* 1.204, A set of great lounging infants tied to mamma's apron at two-and-twenty . . would put a Sybarite to the blush. **1789** *Amer. Museum* 5.204, But lest mama should chide her stay,/ She enters soon the gliding sleigh. **1808** *Balance* (Hudson NY) 15 Mar 44, His little son, a lad of merit,/ Who oft had view'd him steep'd in spirit,/ In great surprise, cri'd, "Mamma, see / A miracle, a prodigy." **1907** [see **mum** n[1]]. **1925** *DN* 5.349 **SC**, Charleston, (S.C.) has kept the [æ] in *palm,* and *calm,* and (with stress on the ultima) . . in papa and mamma. [pəˈpæ, məmæ]. **1929** (1954) Faulkner *Sound & Fury* 19 **MS**, [Black speaker addressing White child:] Your mommer going to whip you for getting your dress wet. **1941** *LANE* Map 372 (*Mother, ma*), *Mama* regularly has initial stress, except in the speech of four informants who offer variant pronunciations with initial and final stress . . , and of eleven who offer only the form with final stress. . . Note that most of these informants are well educated. . . Two cases of *mama* with initial stress are exceptional in having the same vowel in both syllables: ˈmaˣmaˣ . . and ˈmaᶜˑᵊmaᶜˑᵊ. [*DARE* Ed: The map shows *mama* (usu with stressed [ɑ, ɑˣ, aᶜ, or aˣ] in the first syllable) as virtually the only reduplicated form used in wNEng; it is also common in **RI** and **eMA**, where, however, *mumma* is somewhat more common.] **1942** [see **mammy** n[1] 1a]. **1942** Berrey–Van den Bark *Amer. Slang* 446.15, *Wife.* . . mamma. **1945** Mencken *Amer. Lang. Suppl.* 1 519, In England *Mamma* usually had the accent on the last syllable, but in the United States it more often fell upon the first. The first *a,* in this country, gradually became indistinguishable from *o.* **1949** Dos Passos *Grand Design* 20, It was like talking to Dan'l Boone's mommer. **1965–70** *DARE* (Qu. Z2, . . *'Mother'*) 386 Infs, **widespread, but less freq Nth, N Midl**, Mamma (*or* momma) [no transcriptions recorded]; 27 Infs, **scattered**, [ˈmamə]; 25 Infs, **scattered**, [ˈmɔmə]; **SC**42, **TX**12, 15, [ˈmamə]; **NC**49, **SC**64, [ˈmɒmə]; **PA**131, [ˈmɑmə]; **WI**76, My kids said [ˈmɑmə]; **CT**16, [məˈma]; **NM**5, [məˈma]; **GA**12, [ˈmɑmə]; **LA**14, [ˌmæˈmæ]—old-fashioned; **SC**11, [məˈmæɪ]; in Charleston they say [ˈmæmə]; **SC**40, [ˈma,mæ]; **SC**44, [ˈmæmə]—old-fashioned; **SC**46, [ˈmæmə]; **TX**74, [ˈmæmə] [FW: in conv]; (Qu. AA21) Inf **CA**117, Momma wears the pants; (Qu. AA22, *Joking names that a man may use to refer to his wife: "I have to go down and pick up my _____."*) Infs **FL**28, **MS**73, **TX**74, Mamma (*or* momma); **MO**17, Old lady [FW: Inf addressed his wife as "Mamma"—not joking, however]; (Qu. AA28) Inf **IL**131, Become a mamma. [Further exx through-

out *DS;* all exx are mapped.] **1973** *Black World* Apr 57 **Philadelphia PA**, My momma always set more places than there was folks to eat. **1973** Allen *LAUM* 1.339 **Upper MW** (as of c1950), *Mother* and *mama* are the two almost equally widespread designations, . . the latter usually informal and sometimes described as used mostly during childhood. *Ibid* 337, A wife with children is by some referred to familiarly with *Ma, Mama* [1 inf, **nwMN**], *Mom,* or *Mother* as proper names. **1988** *Atlanta Constitution* (GA) 30 Dec sec D 1/1, They reminded me . . of the standard question in bereaved country households where everybody whispered, "How is Mommer a-holding up?"

2 rarely *maumey:* An older Black woman, esp a child's nurse—often used as a title (also abbr *maum*) or term of address. **GA, SC** *obs* Cf **mammy** n[1] 2

　　1803 Davis *Travels* 86 **csSC**, The children of the most distinguished families in *Carolina,* are suckled by negro-women. Each child has its *Momma.* **1810** Lambert *Travels* 2.414 **SC**, An old negro woman is called *momma,* which is a broad pronunciation of *mama.* **1835** Longstreet *GA Scenes* 110, [Footnote:] ["]*"Aunt"* and *"mauma,"* or *"maum,"* its abbreviation, are terms of respect, commonly used by children, to aged negroes. The first generally prevails in the up country, and the second on the sea-board. **1838** (1852) Gilman *S. Matron* 33 **eSC** [Black], Bro' Jim ride more better dan Maus John. [Footnote to *Bro':*] Brother. The terms daddy, maumer, uncle, aunty, broder and titter . . , are not confined to connexions among the blacks, they seem rather to spring from age. *Ibid* 49, Maum Phillis entered with her usual drawl, "Little maussa want for nurse, marm." *Ibid* 161, Little Patsey [=a White child], carried by her *maumer* [=a Black woman], dipped her dimpled feet into the shallow wave. **c1885** in 1981 Woodward *Mary Chesnut's Civil War* 40 **SC** (as of 1861), At church today, saw one of the peculiar local traits—old Negro maumeys going up to the communion in their white turbans. **1922** Gonzales *Black Border* 209 **sSC, GA coasts**, [White man addressing old Black woman:] Mauma, have you seen anything of a deer or dogs? *Ibid* 312 [Gullah glossary], *Maum*—same as "maumuh," when used with the name of the person spoken to or of, as "Maum Kate." *Maumuh*—mauma, the equivalent of the up-country "mammy." **1928** Peterkin *Scarlet Sister Mary* 14 **seSC** [Gullah], Maum Hannah and Budda Ben were the only parents she knew. **1950** *PADS* 14.46 **SC**, Mauma [ˈmɔːmə]. . . Name by which elderly Negro women were called by the children of the family with which they were connected. When the name followed the title, the final *a* was elided: "Maum' Dinah." In the upcountry this title of respect was *aunty* and *aunt*.

3 also *little mamma, mamma-two:* A grandmother—also used as a title or term of address. **chiefly Sth, S Midl** Cf **big mamma, mam-maw**

　　1965–70 *DARE* (Qu. Z4, . . *'Grandmother'*) 9 Infs, **chiefly Sth, S Midl**, Mamma (*or* momma); **LA**20, [məˈmɒ]; **LA**15, Mamma Myrtle [FW: Inf's grandchildren say this.]; **TN**65, Mamma plus given name, as Mamma Ruby; **GA**57A, Little mamma; **VA**41, Mamma-two. **1986** Pederson *LAGS Concordance* **Gulf Region** (*Grandmother*) 76 infs, Mamma; 17 infs, Mamma [plus first or last name]; 2 infs, Little mamma; 1 inf, Mamma Honey—she called her French grandmother; 1 inf, Honey mamma—her mother is called by her children; [1 inf, Little mamma—of a grandmother of short stature]. **1992** Hunter-Gault *In My Place* 59 **GA** [Black], My Grandmother Hunter, whom we called Momma, was a saint in her own right. **1993** *DARE* File **Montgomery AL** (as of 1950s), I'm not your Mamma [=grandmother], I'm your Mom [=mother].

4 also *mammy* and in var phrr: Used as an exclamation of surprise or pleasure.

　　1895 *Harper's New Mth. Mag.* 91.841 **West**, Do you think you'd catch anybody reading a contract wrong to old Meakum? Oh, momma! Why, he's king round here. **1909** *NY Eve. Jrl.* (NY) 29 Apr (*Zwilling Coll.*) [Cartoon:] Oh mommer!! There's a bearcat. **1924** *DN* 5.273 [Exclams], Oh mamma (surp[rise]), sweet mamma (joy: Penn.) **1942** Berrey–Van den Bark *Amer. Slang* 277.7, *Interj. of pleasure.* . . Mamma! Mammy! . . Oh mama! Oh mammy. **1967** *DARE* (Qu. NN6a, *Exclamations of joy . . when somebody gets a pleasant surprise, he might shout "_____."*) Inf **SC**40, Do lordy-mamma; (Qu. NN30, *Exclamations beginning with the sound of 'j'*) Inf **TX**35, Gee mammy.

5 A woman, esp an attractive one; a wife or girl friend—also used as a term of address. *esp freq among Black speakers*

　　1920 in 1965 Bradford *Born with the Blues* 81 **Sth** [Black], 'Twill even drive your "itty bitty" Mama mad. **1926** Van Vechten *Nigger Heaven* 286 [Black], *Mama:* mistress or wife. **1942** Berrey–Van den Bark *Amer. Slang* 382.2, A female, esp. a girl or young woman. . . Mamma. **1967–70** *DARE* (Qu. HH34, *General words . . for a woman,*

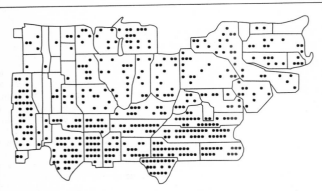

•mamma n[1] 1 + varr (Qq. Z2, D14, Y24, Z9, Z14b, AA21, AA22, AA28, EE20, EE33, FF21b, HH10, HH12, HH16, HH22c, HH28, HH38, JJ3b, KK62, NN6b, NN12a, b, NN22b, NN32)

not necessarily uncomplimentary) Infs **ID**5, **MD**41, **NY**239, 249, **OR**1, Mamma; **IA**15, Momma; (Qu. AA7a, . . *A woman who is very fond of men and is always trying to know more—if she's nice about it*) Inf **TN**46, Cool mamma. **1970** *Major Dict. Afro–Amer. Slang* 80, *Mama: a pretty black girl.* **1972** Claerbaut *Black Jargon* 72, *Momma* . . a very attractive female; beautiful girl. **1977** Smitherman *Talkin* 255, *Momma,* both males and females use this term to address black women; generally limited to younger or stomp-down shonuff-into-a-Black-Thang women.

6 =**mother** n¹ **Ba.**
   1941 Writers' Program *Guide CO* 198 **neCO,** Sugar companies raise their own seed beets, termed "mamas," and sell the seed to growers.

7 Prob =**mother** n¹ **Bb.**
   1950 *PADS* 14.46 **SC,** *Mauma* ['mɔːmə]. . . An overgrown, two-year-old potato.

8 See quot.
   1966 *DARE* FW Addit **SC,** Momma—the knot or head of a boil.

9 =**mammy** n¹ **5.**
   1970 *DARE* (Qu. LL9b, . . *All you need or more* . . *"She's got clothes* ————.") Infs **MS**88, **TN**46, Mamma [*DARE* Ed: i.e., clothes' mamma]. [Both Infs Black] **1988** Naylor *Mama Day* 226 **GA, SC coast** [Black], It could be I'm getting beyond old, she thinks, stirring cinnamon, vanilla, and sugar into her peaches. Could be I'm getting to be Old's mama.

mam-ma n² See **mam-maw**

mam-mam See **mom-mom**

mamma, may I See **mother, may I**

mamma-peg See **mumblety-peg 4**

mamma's bedroom See **mamma's room**

mamma's bread is burning, your phr For var see quot 1970 A children's game.
   1970 *DARE* (Qu. EE33, . . *Outdoor games* . . *that children play*) Inf **GA**90, My mamma's bed [sic] is burning. **1986** Pederson *LAGS Concordance* (*What kind of games did you play as a child?*) 1 inf, **cnTN,** Your mama's bread is burning—circle [game].

mamma's room n Also *mamma's bedroom, mom's room* See quots.
   c1960 *Wilson Coll.* **csKY,** Mom's room. . . The family or living room. **1966** *DARE* (Qu. D14, *The room where members of the family spend most of their time together when they are at home;* total Infs questioned, 75) Inf **MS**22, Mamma's room; **MS**48, Mamma's bedroom (as a girl), family room (today). **1986** Pederson *LAGS Concordance,* 1 inf, **ceTN,** Mamma's bedroom = den in most houses.

mamma-two See **mamma** n¹ **3**

mam-maw n Also *ma-ma(w), mam-ma, maw-maw;* for addit varr see quots [Prob hypocoristic varr of **grandma**] chiefly **Sth, S Midl** See Map Note: It is the secondary stress on the second syllable that differentiates these resps from those at **mamma** n¹. Cf **mamma** n¹ **3, mee-maw** n, **mee-mee, mom-mom**

A grandmother or great grandmother; rarely, a mother or stepmother.
   1942 Hall *Smoky Mt. Speech* 77 **wNC, eTN,** A curious form is ['mæˌmɔː], which I heard a middle-aged man employ in addressing his grandmother. **c1960** *Wilson Coll.* **csKY,** Ma-maw. . . Becoming common as a small child's name for grandmother. **1962** Dykeman *Tall Woman* 135 **NC** (as of c1860), "What happened to Mamaw Moore?" Martha asked, as Lydia braided her hair. **1965–70** *DARE* (Qu. Z4, . . 'Grandmother') 28 Infs, **chiefly Sth, S Midl,** Mam-maw ['mæˌmɔ]; 11 Infs, **chiefly Sth, S Midl,** Maw-maw ['mɔˌmɔ]; **OH**46, 61, 78, **TX**104, Mam-ma ['mæmɑ]; **SC**40, 44, Mam-ma ['mæˌmæ]; **GA**89, **MO**32, **VA**35, **WV**14, Ma-maw ['mɑˌmɔ]; **GA**9, **PA**247, Ma-ma; **GA**77, May-maw. **1967** LeCompte *Word Atlas* 263 **seLA,** *Grand-mother / usual term of affection.* . . [2 of 21 infs] Maw-maw. **1991** Still *Wolfpen Notebooks* 162 **sAppalachians,** Maw-maw: grandmother. **1992** *NADS Letters* **cIN,** *Mamaw & papaw.* . . Our local Monroe County people use these two words, often in death and thank-you notes in paper . . and many seem to use it as an affectionate term for a grandparent or even parent. *But my local life-long resident cleaning lady insists that its real true and correct meaning is: Step-father and Step-Mother. Ibid* **nwTX,** Growing up in Lubbock, Texas in the 40s and 50s, I heard the term *meemaw* but

never encountered *meepop*. In my family, the terms used were *mamaw* [mɑmɔ] or *mawmaw* [mɔmɔ] and *papaw* [pɑpɔ] or *pawpaw* [pɔpɔ]. **1993** *New Yorker* 1 Nov 56 **KY,** She asked her mother, and she said, 'That's how your grandmother taught me,' The grandmother said, 'I don't know, that's how my mother taught me.' The mamaw was alive, and they said, 'Mamaw, why did you do this?'

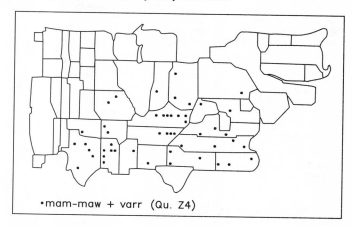

•mam-maw + varr (Qu. Z4)

mammere See **mémère**

mammock n Also sp *mommick, mommock, mommuck, mommix, momox* [*OED* a1529 →; "*arch.* and *dial.*"; see also *EDD*]
1 A fragment, scrap.
   [**1828** Webster *Amer. Dict.* np, *Mammoc*. . . A shapeless piece. [*Not used.*] Herbert.] **1899** (1912) Green *VA Folk-Speech* 274, *Mammock*. . . A shapeless piece; a fragment. **1935** Davis *Honey* 24 **OR,** Each man singed a mammock of mutton on a stick and ate it in the empty tent.
2 A mess; a botch; by ext, someone who makes a mess. chiefly **S Midl**
   1867 Harris *Sut Lovingood Yarns* 92 **TN,** The nex tail fus' experdishun wer made against the cati-corner'd cupboard, outen which he made a perfeck momox. **1913** Kephart *Highlanders* 294 **sAppalachians,** If the house be in disorder it is said to be all gormed or gaumed up, or things are just in a mommick. **1952** Brown *NC Folkl.* 1.566, Mommick. . . A foul, torn-up mess. **1953** Randolph–Wilson *Down in Holler* 265 **Ozarks,** Mommix. . . A mess, a task badly done. "That there barber sure did make a mommix out of Pappy's whiskers." **c1960** *Wilson Coll.* **csKY,** Mommock (or *mommick*). . . A mess. **1968** *DARE* File **TN,** Mommick ['mɑmɪk]. Someone who makes a mess. **1982** *Smithsonian Letters,* My mother's family was from Warrenton, Virginia. . . They were of English and some Scottish stock and the first of the family had come to America in the 18th century. Two household words I never heard anywhere else were "mommock" and "gorm." "Mommock" could be either a verb (meaning to make a mess of) or a noun. ("I mommocked it"—usually referred to some kind of handwork—sewing, for example. Or, "I made a mommock of it.") **1994** NC Lang. & Life Project *Dial. Dict. Lumbee Engl.* 8 **seNC,** I told him, "Don't make a mommuck of it," but he still mommucked up his homework.
3 Something strange and distasteful; see quot.
   1923 (1946) Greer-Petrie *Angeline Doin' Society* 11 **csKY,** Hit looked like a great big red crawfeesh, and I hope to my die, if the thing didn't have laigs with *claws* on 'em, but . . he gulped hit down like hit was nick nacks. . . That mommix Bob Bowles et had turned my stummick.
4 See quot.
   1953 Randolph–Wilson *Down in Holler* 265 **Ozarks,** Sometimes the noun [=*mommix*] seems to mean merely a state of excitement or confusion, as in the sentence, "No use to get yourself into a mommix about it."

mammock v Also *mammox, mommick, mommix, mommuck, mummick, mummox;* for addit varr see quots [*OED* 1607 →; "Now chiefly *dial.*"; see also *EDD*] chiefly **Sth, S Midl** Cf **bollix** v
1 also with *up:* To tear into pieces, mangle; to beat severely, maul; hence vbl n *mommicking* a beating.
   [**1828** Webster *Amer. Dict.* np, *Mammoc*. . . To tear in pieces. [*Not used.*] Milton.] **1867** Harris *Sut Lovingood Yarns* 206 **TN,** I'll bet yu my shut [=shirt] agin that ar momoxed up roas'in har [=a partly-eaten ear of corn]. **1870** *Nation* 28 July 56 **sePA,** A bad carver was said to

"mammock" the joint. **1872** Schele de Vere *Americanisms* 616, *Mammoxed* means, in Southern and Western slang, to be seriously injured. **1886** S. *Bivouac* 4.349 sAppalachians, *Momox or mommocks*—(cut any thing awkwardly). **1899** (1912) Green *VA Folk-Speech* 274, *Mammock*. . . To tear in pieces; mangle. **1942** *AmSp* 17.171 sIL, To mommock. . . "to break or cut in pieces; to crumble, tear, or mangle." . . When asked to give an example of the use of this verb, my informant said that when her husband failed to kill a chicken at the first blow of the axe, she said, "You've mommocked it all up!" **1952** [see **2** below]. **1959** Lomax *Rainbow Sign* 67 AL [Black], If you have to do anything like fightin, don't just touch your man, don't just shove him around. *Mommick* him up good, because you've got to go to jail anyhow. **1968–69** *DARE* (Qu. Y16, *A thorough beating:* "He gave the bully an awful _____.") Inf **NC76**, Mommicking; (Qu. EE21b, *When boys were fighting very actively* . . "For a while those fellows really _____.") Inf **NC82**, Giving each other a mommicking. **1969** *DARE* FW Addit neNC, Mommickin'—meaning "beating." "He gave me a mommickin'."

2 also with *up:* To botch, mess up, mix up, confuse; hence vbl n *momoxing.*

1867 Harris *Sut Lovingood Yarns* 298 **TN**, Mout a-lookt fur a gineral durn'd momoxin ove things tho', when dad tuck the job wif Squire Haney tu help. **1895** *DN* 1.391 ceKY, *Mommixed:* mixed up, in confusion. **1895** *DN* 1.398 PA, *Mummick* . . to soil, as one's clothing. **1899** (1912) Green *VA Folk-Speech* 291, *Mummick*. . . To cut awkwardly; mess or make a mess of: as, he mummicks his food. *Mommick. Mommuck.* **1903** *DN* 2.321 seMO, *Mommick*. . . To mix up; to make a mess of. **1906** *DN* 3.147 nwAR, *Mommix*. . . To mix, confuse. "He got it all mommixed up." **1909** *DN* 3.350 eAL, wGA, *Mommux* (up). . . To botch, spoil in the making. "He mommuxed up that house." . . To mix badly, confuse utterly. "He got all mommuxed up on that job." **1917** *DN* 4.415 wNC, *Mommick*. . . To ruin by bungling. "That was a waste of timber, Uncle Bill; they jist mommicked it up." **1920** *DN* 5.86, *Mommix, mommix* also has the meaning 'to mess, to spoil.' **1942** McAtee *Dial. Grant Co. IN* 44 (as of 1890s), *Mummox* . . mishandle, botch, mess up. **1950** *PADS* 14.48 SC, *Mummock, mommock, mommick*. . . To make a mess of, to spoil, to confuse. . . "You certainly have got this job mommocked up to a fare-you-well!" **1952** Brown *NC Folkl.* 1.566, *Mommick*. . . To tear up, mess up, befoul. **1953** Randolph-Wilson *Down in Holler* 265 Ozarks, Them fellers is a-mommixin' everything. **1962** *Mt. Life* 38.1.18 sAppalachians, The farmer scolds the child for taking out more "grub" than he can eat and "a-smoulin' around over it and a-mommickin' it up till nobody else can stommick it." **1966** *DARE* FW Addit, Mommick—used by a woman from Ralph, Alabama, to indicate mixing non-homogeneous items. One might serve leftovers by mommicking them up and heating. **1968–69** *DARE* (Qu. GG2, . . '*Confused, mixed up*': "So many things were going on at the same time that he got completely _____.") Inf **NC72**, ['maməkt]; (Qu. KK63, *To do a clumsy or hurried job of repairing something:* "It will never last—he just _____.") Inf **MD39**, Mommocked ['mɑmək't] the job [FW: Inf learned from father, has heard local people say]. **1982** [see **mammock n 2**]. **1994** [see **mammock n 2**].

3 To harass, tease, impose on. esp NC

1918 *DN* 5.19 NC, *Mommick*, to take advantage of. **1946** *PADS* 6.21 seNC (as of 1900–10), *Mommock* ['mɑmək]. . . To tease, annoy, torment, "impose on." A large boy mommocks a small boy. A cat mommocks a mouse before killing it. . . Common. **1950** *PADS* 14.48 SC, *Mummock, mommock, mommick*. . . To browbeat, to harass. **1966** *DARE* FW Addit Ocracoke NC, *Mummick*—to beat down, harass badly. "She's always trying to mummick him." **1979** *DARE* File Ocracoke NC, *Mommick*—to tease or beat on someone. **1994** NC Lang. & Life Project *Harkers Is. Vocab.* 8 eNC, *Mommock*. . . To harass or bother.

mammock up See **mammock v 1, 2**

mammoth adj, n chiefly Nth See Map

Large, enormous; something that is very large.

1802 *Balance* (Hudson NY) 19 Oct 331 ceNY, No more to do with the subject, than the man in the moon has to do with the mammoth cheese. **1824** *MA Spy & Worcester Advt.* (Worcester MA) 14 Jan [3/3], The last load, as we Yankees say, was a "*Mammoth*": . . producing an aggregate of nearly twelve cords! **1842** Buckingham *Slave States* 2.326 **VA**, It being the custom of this country to call every thing very large by the epithet of "mammoth;" so that one hears of a mammoth cake, a mammoth pie, a mammoth oyster. **1965–70** *DARE* (Qu. LL5, *Something impressively big:* "That cabbage is really a _____.") 22 Infs, chiefly Nth, Mammoth; **MI15**, Mammoth head; **CA170**, Mammoth one; (Qu. LL4, *Very large:* "He took a _____ helping of potatoes.") 12 Infs,

esp Nth, Mammoth. **1986** Pederson *LAGS Concordance*, 1 inf, neTN, Mammoth—many large varieties of watermelons.

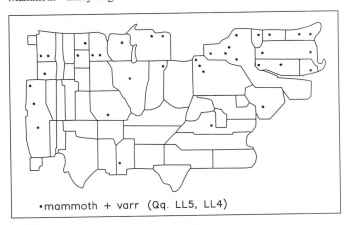

•mammoth + varr (Qq. LL5, LL4)

mammoth clover n Also *mammoth red clover*

Usu zigzag clover, but also red clover.

1895 Gray-Bailey *Field Botany* 126, T[rifolium] medium. . . Zigzag C[lover], Mammoth C[lover]. **1911** CA Ag. Exper. Sta. Berkeley *Bulletin* 217.1001, Trifolium pratense. . . Red Clover. . . Mammoth. **1911** *Century Dict. Suppl.*, Clover. . . Mammoth or mammoth red clover, a robust red clover referred by recent American authors to *Trifolium medium*, the zigzag clover. It resembles common red clover, with which it is often confused, but it may be distinguished, particularly by the long stalks of the heads. **1949** Moldenke *Amer. Wild Flowers* 143, The mammoth clover, T[rifolium] medium, has large heads of bright purple flowers. **1966–70** *DARE* (Qu. L9b, *Hay from other kinds of plants [not grass];* not asked in early QRs) Infs **MI8**, **OH10**, 95, Mammoth clover; **MI2**, Red mammoth clover.

mammoth tree n

The giant sequoia (*Sequoiadendron giganteum*).

1854 in 1856 U.S. Congress *Serial Set* 795 Doc 91 257 CA, Mammoth Trees. August 7. We left Murphy's in the afternoon for the grove of "Big Trees." [*Ibid* 258 CA, The largest tree now standing, called the *Mammoth*, is about the same size [=25 feet in diameter], but imperfect on one side, a portion having been burned out by a fire at the roots. *Ibid* 259 CA, From the Mammoth Grove we passed by a horse-trail . . over the hills for about eighteen miles.] **1857** *Bulletin* (San Francisco CA) 19 May 2/2 CA, This is a most agreeable season of the year to visit the Grove of Mammoth Trees. **1858** *Harper's New Mth. Mag.* 16.259 CA, Another grove of mammoth trees has been discovered in Mariposa County. The trees are said to average three hundred feet in height, and to measure from ten to thirty feet in diameter. **1872** [see lilac B1]. **1897** Sudworth *Arborescent Flora* 62 CA, Sequoia washingtoniana. . . Common Names. . . Mammoth-tree. **1908** Britton *N. Amer. Trees* 87, This enormous tree [=Sequoiadendron giganteum] is also called Sequoia, Giant sequoia, and Mammoth tree, and is noteworthy for its size, massive trunk, and great age. **1968** *DARE* Tape CA104, These great big mammoth trees . . they're a thousand years old or more.

mammox See **mammock v**

mammy n[1]

1a also *maamy:* A mother—sometimes used as a quasi-personal name by a woman's children or husband. [*OED* 1523 →] chiefly Sth, S Midl See Map Cf **mam 1, mamma** n[1] **1**

1835 Longstreet *GA Scenes* 22, I am perhaps a *leetle* . . of the best man at a horse swap, that ever stole *cracklins* out of his mammy's fat gourd. **1887** (1967) Harris *Free Joe* 103 GA, An' ef you don't want me chunk me chunk your mammy fer ole acquaintance sake. **1890** *DN* 1.68 KY, Mam, mama [mæm, mæmɪ]: for mother. **1890** (1895) Riley *Rhymes of Childhood* 85 IN, His Mammy heered him holler, an' his Daddy heered him bawl. **1893** Shands *MS Speech* 44, Mammy [mæmɪ]. A word used by negro children for *mother*. **1901** *DN* 2.182 neKY [Black], Mammy. **1903** Murrie *White Castle LA* 165 (as of c1865), Sancho . . never spoke of his "maw" and "paw" like so many of the other negroes; it was "mammy" and "pappy." **1906** *DN* 3.121 sIN, Mommy. . . Used with mammy exclusively for mama. **1907** *DN* 3.224 nwAR, Mammy. . . Mama. Used by children. **1909** *DN* 3.348 eAL, wGA. **1922** Gonzales *Black Border* 311 sSC, GA coasts [Gullah glossary], Maamy—mother, mothers. **1923** *DN* 5.214 swMO, Mammy. . . Mother. Applicable also to the lower animals. **1928** Peterkin *Scarlet Sister Mary* 111 seSC

[Gullah], My lil blue hen stole a nest . . and hatched dese beedies, all blue like dey mammy. **1929** (1954) Faulkner *Sound & Fury* 3 **MS** [Black], Mammy say keep him out the kitchen today. **1937** *Hall Coll.* **neTN**, My kinfolks on mammy's side settled in Greene County. **1941** *LANE* Map 372 (*Mother, ma*) 5 infs, **NEng**, Mammy. **1942** Hall *Smoky Mt. Speech* 29 **wNC, eTN**, For *mamma*, usually now ['mɑmɪ], ['mɑmə], the old-fashioned ['mæmɪ] may sometimes be heard, though mostly from elderly people. **1946** *Sewanee Rev.* 54.402 **TN**, She thought of how hard they had worked this week and with what unaccustomed deference they had treated her, calling her "Mama" sometimes instead of Mother, sometimes even being so playful as to call her "Mammy." **1965–70** *DARE* (Qu. Z2, . . '*Mother*') 38 Infs, **chiefly Sth, S Midl**, Mammy; (Qu. Y24, . . *To walk, to go on foot: "I can't get a ride, so I'll just have to _____."*) Inf **TX40**, Go on mammy's colts; (Qu. EE12) Inf **PA247**, [Game rhyme:] Old mammy witch, may we go out to play? We won't go near the riverside to chase the ducks away. **1983** *MJLF* 9.1.47 **ceKY**, Mammy cow brute . . a cow. **1989** Pederson *LAGS Tech. Index* 226 **Gulf Region**, *Mother*. . . Mammy (28 [infs]). . . mammy (7). *Ibid* 224, *Wife*. . . Mammy (1).

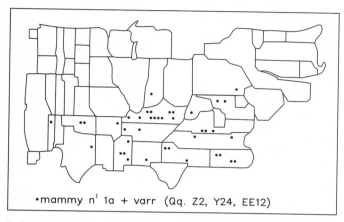

•mammy n¹ 1a + varr (Qq. Z2, Y24, EE12)

b in phr *mammy-made*: Homemade; similarly *mammy-washed*. *among Black speakers*

1905 *DN* 3.87 **nwAR**, Mammy-washed shirt. . . A shirt washed at home by the mater familias. Negroism. **1953** Brewer *Word Brazos* ix **eTX** [Black], David's "mammy-made pants" didn't have a pocket. **1970** *DARE* (Qu. U2, . . *A piece of clothing not made at home—one that you buy*) Inf **FL48**, Store-boughten as opposed to mammy-made [laughter]; (Qu. W29, . . *Expressions . . for things that are sewn carelessly . . "They're _____."*) Infs **FL51, TN53**, Mammy-made. [All Infs Black] **1992** Morrison *Jazz* 109 **NYC** (as of c1926) [Black], Had she braved mammymade poisons and mammy's urgent fists, she could have had the best-dressed hair in the City.

2 An older Black woman, esp a child's nurse—often used as a title or (also abbr *mam*) term of address. **chiefly Sth, S Midl** *old-fash* Cf **hand-mammy, mamma** n¹ **2, mammy cloth**

1837 *S. Lit. Messenger* 3.744, [Aged Negro domestics] were greeted always by the kind appellatives of "daddy and mammy." **1838** (1852) Gilman *S. Matron* 50 **SC** [Black], Mammy Phillis send missis some egg for buy, ma'am. **1893** Shands *MS Speech* 44, Mammy is also used by white children when speaking of their old black nurses. **1898** Page *Red Rock* 23 **VA**, An old mammy in a white apron, with a tall bandanna turban around her head, suddenly appeared. **1899** (1912) Green *VA Folk-Speech* 274, Mammy. . . Also applied to the old black nurses. **1903** *DN* 2.320 **seMO**, Mammy. . . A negress nurse. 'Next to my mother I love my old mammy.' **1909** *DN* 3.348 **eAL, wGA**, Mammy. . . Also a negro nurse, especially one who cares for a very young baby. **1936** Reese *Worleys* 4 **MD** (as of 1865), Run on down to Mam Rachel and ask her to give you a cake or something. **1960** (1966) Percy *Moviegoer* 90 **LA**, "This sure beats typing. Mhm—M!"—as singsongy and shut off to herself as her mammy in Eufala. Southern girls learn a lot from their nurses. **1966–68** *DARE* (Qu. Z2, . . '*Mother*') Inf **MS59**, Mammy—usually this is what the Negro woman who looks after a child is called; **SC21**, Mammy—a Negro who raised the kids; (Qu. AA30, *An older woman who comes in . . to help when a baby is going to be born*) Infs **PA79, SC2**, Mammy; **WV10**, Mammy—old-fashioned; mammies were all Negro—they helped when babies were born and became nurses to the babies. **1993** Delany-Delany *Having Our Say* 76 **cNC** [Black], You know, white people were always looking for good colored maids and mammies.

3 A grandmother—also used as a term of address. Cf **grandma** n **A10**

1966–70 *DARE* (Qu. Z4, . . '*Grandmother*') Infs **AL39, FL26, LA12, MS1, NJ35, PA142, 184, 243, TN27, TX51**, Mammy. [Of these Infs, only **TN27** offered *mammy* at Qu. Z2, where she labeled it old-fashioned.] **1989** Pederson *LAGS Tech. Index* 227 **Gulf Region**, *Grandmother*. . . Mammy (9 [infs]). **1992** *DARE* File, My sister-in-law called her grandmother, who was from South Carolina, "Mammy." **1993** Mason *Feather Crowns* 161 **KY**, "Look who's here, Mammy," said Dulcie. The old woman squinted in the lantern light.

4 See **mother** n².

5 in phr (*something's*) *mammy*: A great deal of, the epitome of (something). *among Black speakers* Cf **mamma** n¹ **9**

1942 *Amer. Mercury* 55.92 **Harlem NYC** [Black], What I want to steal her old pocketbook with all the money I got? . . I got money's mammy and Grandma change. **1970** *DARE* (Qu. LL9b, . . *All you need or more . . "She's got clothes _____."*) Inf **TN52**, Mammy [DARE Ed: i.e., clothes' mammy]. **1971** Roberts *Third Ear* np [Black], *Mammy* . . the ultimate; the most; e.g. A wealthy person is said to have money's *mammy*. There is confusion's *mammy* in that room. **1993** Mason *Feather Crowns* 186 **KY** [Black], You got so much milk, you got milk's *mammy*.

6 See **mamma** n¹ **4.**

mammy v [**mammy** n¹ **1**]

1 See quot.

1954 *Harder Coll.* **cwTN**, Mammy. . . To mother a child or animals.

2 See quot. Cf **daddy** v **3, pappy** v

1953 Randolph-Wilson *Down in Holler* 263 **Ozarks**, Mammy. . . To transmit the mother's likeness to offspring. My neighbor, looking at a cat and kittens, said, "Well, she didn't mammy 'em," meaning that the kittens did not resemble the mother cat.

3 with *up*: See quot. Cf **mother up**

1942 *Sat. Eve. Post* 5 Sept 55 **csFL**, Mammying-up . . is a cow term for matching up every cow mother with her own calf at calving time. . . With hundreds of cows and calves to mammy-up, how can you always tell which calf belongs to which cow?

mammy n²

A **stone roller** (here: *Campostoma anomalum*).

1896 U.S. Natl. Museum *Bulletin* 47.205, *Campostoma anomalum*. . . *Stone-roller*: . . Mammy; *Dough-belly*. . . Color brownish, with a brassy luster above, the scales more or less mottled with dark. **1983** Becker *Fishes WI* 476, *Central Stoneroller*. . . Other common names . . dough-belly, mammy.

mammybush n

An **inkberry 1** (here: *Ilex glabra*).

1974 Morton *Folk Remedies* 77 **SC**, "Mammybush" . . *Ilex glabra*. . . The bush is used as a yard broom in the Low Country.

mammy cloth n Cf **granny rag 3**

1970 *DARE* (Qu. W3, *A piece of cloth that a woman folds over her head and ties under her chin*) Inf **SC68**, Mammy cloth—tied behind the neck [Inf Black].

mammy coot n

1 =**purple gallinule.**

1923 U.S. Dept. Ag. *Misc. Circular* 13.44 **SC**, Purple Gallinule. . . *Vernacular Names*. . . *In local use*. . . Mammy-coot. **1956** *AmSp* 30.183, A peculiarly Southern way of indicating superiority in size is exemplified in the title *mammy coot* for the Virginia rail and purple gallinule (S.C.), as being larger than the sora, there known as *coot*.

2 =**Virginia rail.**

1956 [see **1** above].

mammy-dodging adj *euphem*

Damnable—used as a derog intensifier; hence n *mammy-dodger* a despicable person.

1970 *Thompson Coll.* **AL** (as of 1920s), Why that mammy-dodging potlicker didn't even know what shoes was till he was twenty-nine. **1980** Banks *First-Person America* 256 **NYC** (as of 1939) [Black], I said: "Hell yes, mammydodger, I stink! . . You'll never catch me carrying a bunch of you poor sonsabitches up there."

mammy duck n Also *old mammy* [See quot 1955] Cf **mommy** n **4**

=**old-squaw.**

1917 *Wilson Bulletin* 29.2.77, *Harelda hyemalis.*—Old mammy, Bay Shore, Long Island, mammy duck, Wallops I[slan]d, Va. **1955** MA Audubon Soc. *Bulletin* 39.375 **CT**, *Old-squaw.* . . Old Mammy. . . From its "garrulity."

mammy greens n pl

A type of **cress.**

1968 *DARE* (Qu. I28b, *Kinds of greens that are cooked*) Inf **VA9**, Cress = mammy greens.

mammy-made See mammy n¹ 1b

mammy up See mammy v 3

mammy-washed See mammy n¹ 1b

ma-mom See mom-mom

mamoose n Also *mamouche, moose*

A **sturgeon** (here: *Acipenser oxyrhynchus* or *A. brevirostrum*); see quots.

1905 NJ State Museum *Annual Rept. for 1904* 85, *Acipenser sturio.* . . Sturgeon. Mamoose. Mamouche. Moose. *Ibid* 86, Usually in the Delaware and fairly abundant. . . The river fishermen still call the young "mamoose" or "mamouche." **1907** NJ State Museum *Annual Rept. for 1906* 136, Dr. Kendall writes, "we had a number of this species [=*Acipenser brevirostrum*] from the Delaware (Gloucester, N.J.) under the name of 'mamoose.' . . They were not recognized by the fishermen, and even some ichthyologists were puzzled, but they were undoubtedly *brevirostrum*."

mamou n [See quot 1931] LA

A **coral tree** (here: *Erythrina herbacea*).

1931 Read *LA French* 48, *Mamou.* . . Coral Tree; a shrub known to botanists as *Erythrina herbacea* . . ; found at Mamou, Evangeline Parish, and in the vicinity of that village. Mamou tea—*thé de Mamou*—is made of the leaves, the roots, or the seeds of this shrub and is given to persons ill of pneumonia. The seeds, which are coral-red, are worn as necklaces by little girls. . . (Information given by Miss Ann Spotswood Buchanan). *Mamou* is a corruption of St[andard] Fr[ench] *Mammouth,* "Mammoth." Bones of the mammoth have been discovered in Lower Louisiana. **1945** Saxon *Gumbo Ya-Ya* 527 **LA**, Medicine [for colds, croup]: Mamou tea made with the beans or the roots. Also crapeau [sic] (toadgrass) tea. **1972** Brown *Wildflowers LA* 79, *Mamou, Coral Bean. Erythrina herbacea.* . . The fruit is a typical bean pod which splits open at maturity to expose bright red seeds. **1977** *Mais Jamais* 17 **LA**, The herbs and roots they had to collect were mamou roots, Bull Sickle roots, Prickly Ash bark, Sea Merkle roots, Blue Brier roots, and Cotton Marais roots [to make a cough syrup].

mamouche See mamoose

man n

A Pronc varr.

Sg: usu *man;* pronc-sp *mahn;* also (esp in sense **C2** below) **chiefly Sth** *chiefly among Black speakers* pronc-spp *mon, mun.*

1861 Holmes *Venner* 1.43 **NEng**, Major Bush was what the natives of the town called a "hahnsome mahn." **1883** [see **C2** below]. **1891** Amer. Hist. Assoc. *Papers* 5.475 **NC**, They [=the Croatans] begin their salutations with "mon-n-n," *i.e.,* man. . . "Mon, my fayther told me." **1899** [see **C2** below]. **1926** Smith *Gullah* 27 **sSC, GA coasts**, The narrow or flat sound of *a* as in "fat", "hat", "rat", etc., is broadened to *o* or *ah,* giving . . *ba(h)k, cra(h)k, fa(h)c'* and *ma(h)n* for back, crack, fact, and man. By this reversal of *a* sounds, curious results follow. **1929** (1954) Faulkner *Sound & Fury* 371 **MS** [Black], He sho a preacher, mon! **1930** Woofter *Black Yeomanry* 49 **seSC**, The Sea Islander pronounces words like *man* . . with a broad *a.* **1962** [see **C2** below].

B Gram forms.

1 sg: usu *man;* also *mans.*

1883 Harris *Nights with Remus* 199 **GA** [Black], Bumbye 'e see one ole Affiky mans. **1945** Saxon *Gumbo Ya-Ya* 77 **New Orleans LA** [Black], If he is a white mans I really doesn't think so much of him. . . He's a real mans, and not no ghost.

2 pl: usu *men;* occas *mans;* also **chiefly Sth, S Midl** *esp freq among Black speakers* double pl *mens;* rarely triple pl *menses.*

1867 Allen *Slave Songs* xxxiii **SC** [Gullah], De morest part ob de mens dey git heaps o' clo' [=clothes]. **1893** Shands *MS Speech* 45, *Menses.* . . Sometimes used by illiterate whites for *men.* An uneducated old white woman once invited a party of my friends to dinner by saying: "Menses, take a seat and have some of the fry." **1894** Riley *Armazindy* 162 **IN**, He mocks the mens 'at rides 'em [=horses], too. **1922** Gonzales *Black*

Border 70 **sSC, GA coasts** [Gullah], Cap'n, all dese'yuh mans blonx to quality! **1923** Parsons *Folk-lore Sea Islands* 45 **csSC** [Gullah], De girl was cou'tin' [=courting] de diffun' mans. **1927** Adams *Congaree* 6 **cSC** [Black], I see a heap of mens come out de big swamps. **1928** Peterkin *Scarlet Sister Mary* 240 **SC** [Gullah], Mens is different from womens. **1938** Matschat *Suwannee R.* 111 **neFL, seGA** [White speaker], Howdy, mens. Come an' et. **1945** FWP *Lay My Burden Down* 85 **AL** (as of c1860) [Black], They whupped the women and they whupped the mens. **1945** Saxon *Gumbo Ya-Ya* 75 **New Orleans LA** [Black], Them Needle Mens is everywhere. **1953** Randolph–Wilson *Down in Holler* 50 **Ozarks**, Many Ozarkers who . . would never say gentlemens, do use *fishermens* as the plural of fisherman. **1966–70** *DARE* Tape **GA50A**, Lots o' fishermans; **FL50**, The mens wasn't smoking it enough; **IL69**, That's a-gonna make 'em have less mens [mɛnz] over there; **LA8**, One man can do the work with one tractor that made with six mens and twelve mules; **ME26**, All the mens slept in that one big room; **SC17**, At that time we didn't buy seed; the warehousemans ['wɛəhausmənz] give us seed; **VA52**, There's three mens [mɪnz] sitting out there; **VA55**, Some mens [were] in Sandler's Neck; **WV2**, That put the icemans outa business. **1967** *DARE* (Qu. II24, *Names or nicknames for the part of a town where the well-off people live*) Inf **LA8**, Where the money mens live at. **1968** *DARE* FW Addit **IA31**, "Of all the foremans"—common usage. **1986** Pederson *LAGS Concordance* Gulf Region, 16 infs, Mens [14 of 16 infs Black]; 1 inf, Colored mans; 1 inf, Italy mans; 1 inf, Single mans. **1992** Kincaid *Crossing Blood* 227 **nwFL** [Black], Them two mens living next door to each other is like two rocks rubbing.

C Senses.

1 One's husband. [*OED man* sb.¹ 8 a1300 →; "Now only *Sc.* and *dial.,* exc. in phr. *man and wife*"; in US prob reinforced by the parallel use of the cognates in other Germanic languages.]

1875 (1886) Woolson *Castle Nowhere* 242 **ceOH**, "A stupid beast! He's none of mine; belongs to my man." "Your husband?" "Yes, my man. He works in the coal-mine over the hill." **1902** *DN* 2.239 **sIL**, *Man.* . . Husband, a word which is not used. **1903** *DN* 2.320 **seMO**, *Man.* . . Husband. Latter seldom used. **1906** *DN* 3.121 **sIN**, *Man.* . . Husband. The latter word never used. "He's Liz Cole's man." *Ibid* 146 **nwAR**, *Man.* . . Husband. "Your man said he wanted roun' steak." Common among the uneducated. **1908** *DN* 3.348 **eAL, wGA**, *Man.* . . Husband. Not usual except in the form *old man.* **1930** Shoemaker *1300 Words* 40 **cPA Mts** (as of c1900), "My man", name always used for husband. **1933** *AmSp* 8.1.51 **Ozarks**, *Man.* . . Husband. When used with the possessive "my" or "her" the word is always taken in this sense. I recall a widow from the North who shocked her neighbors by referring to a hired farmhand as *my man.* **1935** *AmSp* 10.167 [Engl of PA Germans], My man had a wonderful night last night. Ach! he was very sick. **1940** *AmSp* 15.82 **MI**, A woman refers to her husband as 'my man.' With these people, undoubtedly a translation of the Dutch phrase *mij man.* **1941** *LANE* Map 374 (*My husband*), The expression *my man* or *the man* is described as common by . . [3 infs]; as rare by . . [6 infs]; and as older but still in use by . . [9 infs]. [*DARE* Ed: *My man* occurs throughout NEng, but rarely as a first response.] **1950** *WELS Suppl.* **csWI**, When I was a young child I often heard a woman's husband called her "man" and the wife his "woman." I never hear that anymore. **1965–70** *DARE* (Qu. AA23, *Joking names that a woman may use to refer to her husband: "It's time to go and get supper for my _____."*) 47 Infs, **scattered**, Man; [579 Infs, **widespread**, [The] old man]. **1973** Allen *LAUM* 1.336 **Upper MW** (as of c1950), [5 of 203 infs offered *my man* in the context "I must ask (my husband)"; 3 of these indicated that they had heard this but did not use it themselves.] **1986** Pederson *LAGS Concordance* Gulf Region (*Husband*) 15 infs, My man; 6 infs, Her man; 4 infs, (The) man. **1991** *DARE* File **neMO**, In Kirksville, a woman might say "My man gets off at 5" if her husband finishes work then.

2 Used as a term of address to a man (rarely to a woman or child). [This usage is common in Scots and Engl dial, often with phonetically reduced forms represented by spp *min, mon,* or *mun;* it is also characteristic of West Indian Creoles; cf *DJE.*] Note: Such emphatic uses of *man* as in "Man, it's hot!" or "Man, oh man!" are not illustrated here; however, *man* in final position (see esp *DARE* resps) demonstrates the shift in use from a term of direct address to one of emphasis; cf *sir(ee)* as in "No *sir(ee)*." **chiefly Sth, S Midl** See Map *esp freq among Black speakers*

1883 (1971) Harris *Nights with Remus* 15 **GA** [Black], In dem days Brer Rabbit wuz a singer, mon. *Ibid* 127, En he is take keer un it, mon—dat he is. **1891** [see **A** above]. **1899** (1912) Green *VA Folk-Speech* 292, Mun. . . A familiar term of address applied to persons of either sex and of any age. Usually at the end of a sentence and practically expletive: as, "Mind what I'm telling you, mun." "Yes, mun;" used to give emphasis to an assertion. **1922** Gonzales *Black Border* 160 **sSC, GA coasts** [Gullah], Go 'way, man, snake ent gwine bite you. **1923** Parsons *Folk-lore Sea Islands* xvii **csSC** [Gullah], "Man" as a form of address . . [is] alike Carolinian and Bahaman. *Ibid* 16, "Man," he say, "I ain't grow so big."—"Oh, yes, man! Le' me measure you by dis stick!" **1929** [see **A** above]. **1942** *Amer. Mercury* 55.87 **Harlem NYC** [Black], Aw, man, can't you take a joke? *Ibid* 89, Man, I don't deal in no coal. **1959** *AmSp* 34.305, In the colloquial speech of Negro men, *man* is extremely common in direct address and as an exclamation; it does not seem to have this function in the speech of women, except the déclassée. **1962** Faulkner *Reivers* 71 **MS** [Black], And hot under there too, mon. **1965–70** *DARE* (Qu. II10b, *Asking directions of somebody on the street when you don't know his name—what you'd say to a man: "Say, _____, how far is it to the next town?"*) 10 Infs, **chiefly Sth, S Midl**, Man; (Qu. II10a, *Asking directions of somebody on the street when you don't know his name—what you'd say to a boy: "Say, _____, where's the post office?"*) Infs **FL48, IL138, 139, MS88, PA94, 236, VT16, WV21,** Man; (Qu. A20) Inf **TX86,** Make haste, man; (Qu. A21, *When someone is in too much of a hurry . . "Now just slow down! Don't _____."*) Inf **DC12,** Rush me, man; (Qu. W24b, *Sayings to warn a man that his pants are torn or split*) Inf **TN50,** Man, your ass is out; (Qu. W24c, *. . To warn a man that his trouser-fly is open*) Inf **MO4,** Button your britches, man; (Qu. X18) Inf **TX73,** Speak up, man; (Qu. Y52, *To move over—for example on a long bench: ". . . Can you _____ [a little]?"*) Inf **NY249,** Man, move; (Qu. EE20) Inf **NY250,** I quit, man; (Qu. II15, *When somebody is passing by and you want him or her to stop and talk a while*) Inf **FL48,** Say, man, whatcha doing? **NY238,** Why don't you lay for a while, man? (Qu. KK55c, *. . Expressions of strong denial*) Inf **LA37,** No, man; (Qu. NN2, *Exclamations of very strong agreement: Somebody says, "I think Smith is absolutely right," and you reply, "_____."*) Infs **FL16, MD37,** Yeah, man; **TX88,** Sure, man; (Qu. NN4, *. . Ways of answering 'no': "Would you lend him ten dollars?" "_____."*) Inf **SC26,** No, man; (Qu. NN6a) Inf **LA45,** Hell yeah, man, let's go again; (Qu. NN10a, *Expressions [such as 'hello'] used when you meet somebody you know quite well*) Inf **DC13,** Hi, man; **FL52,** Hey, man; **TN54,** What's going on, man? **VA71,** What you say, man? [11 of 32 Infs young, 21 Black, 18 male] **1971** *Black World* June 54, Hey, only the squares, man, only the squares have it to keep.

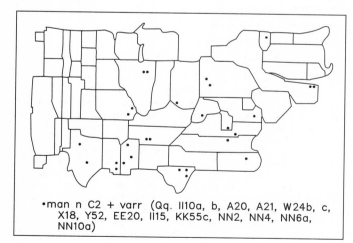

•man n C2 + varr (Qq. II10a, b, A20, A21, W24b, c, X18, Y52, EE20, II15, KK55c, NN2, NN4, NN6a, NN10a)

3 A male friend, esp a close and trusted one. *esp freq among male Black speakers* Cf **main man**

1970 *DARE* (Qu. II1, *. . A close friend . . "He's my _____."*) Infs **NY241, PA236, 247,** Man. [All Infs Black, two male] **1980** Folb *Runnin' Down* 75 **Los Angeles CA** [Black], Then, his boys got me—he had all his boys wid 'em. I was tellin' my man to help me. Guess he split. *Ibid* 246, Man, my. . . (form of address between black males that connotes positive feelings between the two.)

4 A playing marble. [By ext from *man* a piece used in var board games] **esp S Midl**

1890 *DN* 1.24 **KY,** "Dubs" means "doubles" or two "men" (marbles). . . To "take everys" . . is to move around so as to get *every* "man" in range. **1965–70** *DARE* (Qu. EE6a, *. . Different kinds of marbles—the big one that's used to knock others out of the ring*) Infs **DE3, 7, GA1,**

MO9, PA148, Man; (Qu. EE6b, *Small marbles or marbles in general*) Infs **GA75, MO39,** Men; (Qu. EE6c, *Cheap marbles*) Inf **NC33,** Men. **1966** *DARE* Tape **AL3,** We'd make a ring . . it'd be a square—and put . . a man on each corner. **1986** Pederson *LAGS Concordance*, 1 inf, **swGA,** Middle man—marble in the ring.

5 with *the*:

a A man who is in a position of power, esp over the speaker; the boss. [*SND man* n. 6 c1895 →]

1918 in 1920 Battey *70000 Miles* 302, Anybody in authority is "the man." **1930** *AmSp* 6.133, *Man, the. . .* Warden. **1933** *AmSp* 8.3.29 [Prison terms], *Man (the).* Executive Officer; as when a guard yells, *Unuther goddam word out o' you-all, an' Ah'll send ev'ry goddam one of ye up t' the Man.* **1934** *AmSp* 9.288 [Black], *Man.* Anyone in authority. *When I rode* (q.v.) *in that exam I took the Man out!* means 'When I cheated in that exam I put one over on the professor!' **1942** Kennedy *Palmetto Country* 265 **FL,** The supreme authority in the [turpentine] camp is the foreman. To the niggers he is the law, judge, jury, and executioner. . . In speaking to him they call him Capm, but among themselves they call him The Man. **1942** [see **C4c** below]. **1950** *WELS Suppl.* **Upstate NY,** The man in charge of the whole job is referred to as "The Man." **1953** Burroughs *Junkie* 87, When I first hit New Orleans, the main pusher—or "the Man," as they say there—was a character called Yellow. **1962** Baldwin *Another Country* 251, One of the musicians came to the doorway, and said, "Ida, honey, the man [=band leader] says come on with it if you coming." **1964** *PADS* 42.45 **Chicago IL,** *The Man* and *Miss Ann* refer more specifically to the boss and the fair, young white lady of the plantation. . . Both, of course, are used ironically, and . . are not intended to designate all Caucasians. **1969–70** *DARE* (Qu. HH17, *A person who tries to appear important, or who tries to lay down the law in his community: "He'd like to be the _____ around here."*) Inf **MA73,** Man; (Qu. HH43a, *The top person in charge of a group of workmen*) Infs **FL52, IL138,** Man; (Qu. II20b, *A person who tries too hard to gain somebody else's favor: "He's always trying to _____ the boss."*) Inf **TN50,** Kiss the man's ass—around fellows. [3 of 4 Infs Black] **1970** *DARE* Tape **NY242,** "Meet the man" of course is pretty much still a Black expression which we use which means going to see the boss or going to work. **1986** Pederson *LAGS Concordance (Master)* 5 infs, **AL, MS,** The Man; *(Pimp)* 1 inf, **cwGA,** The Man; *(Drug seller)* 1 inf, **nwLA,** The Man—controls supply, sells to dealer.

b By ext: the White man in general; White society. *among Black speakers*

1931 (1991) Hughes–Hurston *Mule Bone* 142 **cFL** [Black], Dis railroad belongs to de *man*—I kin walk it good as you, cain't I? **1963** *NY Times* (NY) 18 May 12/2 [Black], A well-educated Negro said today: "The demonstrations, I think, suggested to 'The Man' that tokenism won't make it and that he has to come to grips with the problem right now." "The Man," in Negro parlance, is the white man. **1970** Updike *Bech* 122, Here [in the South], in an economic and social way, they've had integration all along, though of course entirely on the Man's terms. **1970** *Time* 6 Apr 71 **Brooklyn NYC,** The Man systematically killed your language, killed your culture, tried to kill your soul, tried to blot you out. **1986** Pederson *LAGS Concordance (Caucasian)* 3 infs, **Gulf Region,** The Man.

c Spec: a law-enforcement officer.

1942 *Amer. Mercury* 55.96 **Harlem NYC** [Black], *The man*—the law, or powerful boss. **1952** Callahan *Smoky Mt.* 110, Some bootleggers figure probable nabbings by "the men," as they call the Federal Alcohol Tax Unit personnel, in their tentative budgets, allowing a certain estimated loss for future fines. **1957** *Sat. Eve. Post* 30 Mar 102, The drug trade's slang for a law enforcer was, indicatively, "The Man." **1962** *AmSp* 37.270 **sCA,** *Man. . .* A policeman. A word used by teen-age drivers. 'When I heard the siren, I knew it was the Man.' **1965–70** *DARE* (Qu. V9, *. . Nicknames . . for a policeman*) Infs **DC11, FL48, IL137, IN75, PA66, TX88,** The man; **NC38,** The man—used by Negroes; (Qu. V10a, *. . Joking names . . for a sheriff*) Infs **FL48, GA9, TX26, 37, VA70,** The man. [6 of 11 Infs Black] **1966** *AmSp* 41.72, **Philadelphia PA** [Teen-gang talk], *Man. . .* A policeman in uniform. **1968** *Intermountain Observer* (Boise ID) 27 Jan 7/1, I drove into Salt Lake City one jump ahead of The Man with a warrant charging parole violation. **1969** Keiser *Vice Lords* 42 **Chicago IL** [Black], No man, don't do that. The Man liable to come in your house, and if he find the radio he'll bust . . you. **1986** Pederson *LAGS Concordance (Policeman; this question was asked chiefly in urban areas)* 12 infs, **Gulf Region,** The Man.

6 usu attrib: =**male** adj. *euphem* Cf **gentleman** n B2

1939 *LANE* Map 190 *(Bull)* 1 inf, **sRI,** Man cow. **1949** *AmSp* 24.111 **seSC,** *Man dog. . .* Male dog. **1954** *Harder Coll.* **cwTN,** Man cow. . .

Bull; used by women in mixed company. Not frequent. **c1960** *Wilson Coll.* **csKY,** *Man-cow.* . . Euphemism for bull. *Ibid, Man-hog.* . . Euphemism for boar. **1967–69** *DARE* (Qu. K22, *Words used for a bull*) Infs **GA**84, **MO**14, Man cow; (Qu. K23, *Words used by women or in mixed company for a bull*) Infs **OH**4, **PA**174, Man cow. **1986** Pederson *LAGS Concordance* **Gulf Region,** 4 infs, Man cow; 2 infs, Man hog; 1 inf, Man horse; 1 inf, The man [=bull].

7 in phr *on one's man:* See quot.
> **1950** *PADS* 14.45 **SC,** *Man.* . . Physical strength; superior powers, physical or otherwise. "How did you get the piano here?" "I did it on my man." "He stopped that mob by himself on his man."

‡8 See quot.
> **1952** Brown *NC Folkl.* 1.563, *Man.* . . A cake.—West.

9 A pint of whiskey. Cf **half man 1**
> **1988** Lincoln *Avenue* 64 **wNC** (as of c1940) [Black], If you want a man . . then pay your $3. *Ibid* 75, "Let me have a man." Coley fumbled quickly under the bed and withdrew a pint of corn whiskey. "With all the stuff you got," he told Jipson, "you don't need a man, you need a jug to burn your mouth out."

man v [*OED man* v. 9 c1330 →; "*Obs. exc. dial.*"]
To manage, subdue.
> **1917** *DN* 4.414 **wNC,** *Man.* . . To master. "You can't hardly man that [tough steak], can you?" Also Ky. **1952** Brown *NC Folkl.* 1.563 **c,eNC,** *Man.* . . To apply manpower. "He was cutting up so much that we had to man him."

manada n Pronc-sp *manather* [Span "herd"] **chiefly SW**
A herd of horses, esp a wild herd consisting of a stallion and a number of mares and young horses.
> **1826** in 1924 Austin *Papers* 1.1482, He replied, that but one obstacle presented itself to prevent my taking in 12. *Manadas:,* or 300 head. **1842** in 1940 *CA Hist. Soc. Qrly.* 19.209, I was much interested in the lively scene of a *remonta,* when at a designated place, the *remudadero,* a *manada* of thirty to forty horses . . is driven into a *corral.* **1846** (1848) Bryant *What I Saw in CA* 377, We crossed in the course of the day a wide flat plain, upon which were grazing large herds of broodmares *(manadas)* and cattle. **1857** in 1941 *AmSp* 16.263 **CA,** The *manada* (vulgarly called 'manather') is a herd of mares and colts, led by a garañon or stallion. **1892** *DN* 1.191, *Manáda:* a flock, a herd. In Spain it usually means a flock of sheep. In Texas it is applied specifically to a small drove of horses, about a score. *Ibid* 249, *Manáda.* . . Add: The word is more specifically applied to mares. **1931** (1960) Dobie *Open Range* 91 **SW,** One summer I located . . a *manada* of mustangs that I decided to capture. **1945** Thorp *Pardner* 73 **SW,** It was a colorful and exciting spectacle, because at these times the stallions heading the *manadas* would fight for supremacy, the victors stealing the mares of the vanquished.

managing ppl adj Cf **faculized**
Skillful in management; capable.
> **1914** Furman *Sight* 38 **KY,** She were the smartest, most managing woman in these parts.

mananosay, mananose See **maninose**

manapua n [See quot 1972] **HI**
A steamed bun filled with meat or vegetables.
> **1938** Reinecke *Hawaiian Loanwords* 24, *Manapua* ['mɑːnɑ'puːɑ]. . . [Reinecke: Said to be a corruption of *meanapua.*] A Chinese cake made of rice flour, stuffed with pork, shrimp, etc. [**1967** *DARE* (Qu. H18, . . *Special kinds of bread*) Inf **HI**6, [ˌmeaono'puɑ]—pork-filled bun (encased and cooked), steamed.] **1972** Carr *Da Kine Talk* 87 **HI,** *Hawaiian Words Commonly Heard In Hawaii's English.* . . *Manapua* (a telescoped word from *mea* 'thing' + *ono* 'delicious' + *pua'a* 'pig'). Originally any of several Chinese delicacies, but now usually referring to only one—a large steamed bun enclosing a small amount of meat or vegetable stuffing.

manatee grass n
A submerged plant *(Cymodocea filiformis)* with grasslike leaves found in warm saltwater shallows.
> **1933** Small *Manual SE Flora* 18, *Manatee-grass.* . . Coastal creeks and bays, Fla. to La. **1970** Correll *Plants TX* 94, *Cymodocea filiformis.* . . *Manatee-grass.* . . In shallow salt water of bays along the Gulf Coast . ., frequent in sea drift. **1971** Craighead *Trees S. FL* 85, The principal flowering plants of this community [=mud flats of Florida Bay] are turtle grass, horned pondweed, sea grass, and manatee grass.

manather See **manada**

man-at-the-pot n, exclam **West**
See quots.
> **1939** Rollins *Gone Haywire* 66 **MT** (as of 1886), Conversation ended when eating began. The nearest approach was an occasional cry of "Man at the pot!" If in any cow camp a man rose to refill his coffee cup and that cry was given, it was his duty to go around with the pot and replenish all the cups held out to him. **1940** Writers' Program *Guide NV* 76, *Man-at-the-pot* is the first buckaroo to pick up the coffee pot when out with the chuck wagons. It becomes his duty to pour the coffee for the outfit.

manavel v [*OED manarvel* 1867]
> **1899** (1912) Green *VA Folk-Speech* 274, *Manavel.* . . To pilfer eatables or articles of small value.

manavelins n pl Also sp *manavellings* [*OED manavilins* 1865 →] Cf **manavel**
1 Odds and ends of food; delicacies. **esp eNEng**
> **1887** Goode *Fisheries U.S.* 5.2.228, To the above-mentioned fare should be added, . . the "manarolins" [sic] of the whalemen—that is, fresh meat, vegetables, milk, butter, eggs, and fruits. **1894** *Jrl. Amer. Folk.* 7.150 **Salem MA,** *Manavellings*—This word . . is in this town applied to remnants of a meal, the "leavings." **1895** *DN* 1.390 **seNY,** *Manavelins:* small scraps of choice portions of meat accidentally detached in carving; and hence, more generally, toothsome bits of any dish at table. Staten Island. **1899** (1912) Green *VA Folk-Speech* 274, *Manavellings.* . . Odds and ends of food; scraps, "leavings;" remnant of a meal. "Dog's leavings." Small perquisites. **1945** Colcord *Sea Language* 126 **ME, Cape Cod, Long Island,** *Manavelins.* Small stores on board ship; the sailors' contemptuous term for fancy, fixed-up victuals, and used in the same sense alongshore. **1980** *Yankee* Jan 166, Whalemen . . dined on giant sea turtles, seal liver, bananas, coconut, caribou, porpoise, and foods of the natives in all lands they touched, from the Arctic to the tropics. Of course these manavelins were perishable and lasted only a short time.

2 sg; also *monobilie;* Spec: =**hush puppy 1.**
> **1949** *Jrl. Amer. Folk.* 62.63 **FL,** There are many explanations of the origin of the Southern dish known by the alternate names of hush puppy or monobilie. **1968** *DARE* (Qq. H14, 25) Inf **GA**36, Manavelins [ˈmænəvəlɪnz]—same as hush puppies; (Qu. H32) Inf **GA**36, Danish pastry—flaky, lighter than manavelins.

manawahi See **manuahi**

manaze See **mayonnaise**

man-body See **man-person**

man cage (or car) See **man trip b**

man catcher n Also *man getter, ~ grabber, ~ hunter, ~ shark*
A recruiter of laborers; an employment agency.
> **1926** *AmSp* 1.652 [Hobo lingo], *Man catcher*—employment agency. **1927** *AmSp* 2.391 [Vagabond argot], A *mancatcher* is . . a shark looking for men. **1927** *DN* 5.454 [Underworld jargon], *Man catcher.* . . A runner or agent for a hobo employment agency. Also *man hunter.* **1930** Irwin *Amer. Tramp* 127, *Man catcher.* . . An employment agency or labour exchange. **1942** Berrey–Van den Bark *Amer. Slang* 511.1 [Logging terms], *Man catcher* or *grabber* . . an employment agent. *Ibid* 527.5 [Labor union slang], Employment agent . . *man catcher* or *grabber.* **1956** Sorden–Ebert *Logger's Words* 23 **Gt Lakes,** *Man-catcher,* A man employed by a lumber company to recruit lumberjacks. No charge was made and often the company paid their fares to the camp. **1958** McCulloch *Woods Words* 116 **Pacific NW,** *Man catcher*—a. An employment agent, hangs around pool halls trying to round up a crew. b. A foreman or other company man trying to hire a crew. . . *Man getter*—Same as man catcher. *Man grabber*—Same as man catcher. *Man shark*—An employment agent, particularly the one who played a logger dirt by taking his money and sending him to a camp where there was no job.

man critter n Cf **cow critter, critter B3**
A human being.
> **1940** *AmSp* 15.51 **sAppalachians,** A characteristic of mountain dialect is its abundance of noun compounds in which an initial noun is used attributively: . . man-critter. **1952** Brown *NC Folkl.* 1.563, *Man-critter.* . . A human being.—General. Illiterate.

mandarin n Cf **rose mandarin, white mandarin**
A **fairy bell 2;** esp in combs *nodding mandarin (Disporum lanuginosum), yellow mandarin (D. maculatum).*

1933 Small *Manual SE Flora* 299, *[Disporum maculatum:]* Nodding-mandarin. . . *D. lanuginosum.* . . Yellow-mandarin. **1942** Hylander *Plant Life* 560, The eastern representative of this genus [=*Disporum*] is Yellow Mandarin, . . found from Minnesota eastward; it has white, green, or yellow nodding flowers, borne singly or in pairs. **1949** Moldenke *Amer. Wild Flowers* 335, In the *noddingmandarin,* . . the yellowish tepals are black-dotted. In the *yellowmandarin,* . . the tepals are greenish and not dotted. **1963** Craighead *Rocky Mt. Wildflowers* 22, *Fairybells. Disporum trachycarpum.* . . *Other names:* Mandarin. **1968** Radford et al. *Manual Flora Carolinas* 294, *Disporum.* . . *Mandarin.* . . Berry red or orange, ellipsoid. **1976** Bailey–Bailey *Hortus Third* 392, *[Disporum] lanuginosum.* . . Yellow mandarin. . . *[D.] maculatum.* . . Nodding mandarin.

mandarin apple n
=mayapple 1.

   1968 *DARE* (Qu. S4, . . *Mayapple: [Woodside plant, not a tree, with two large spreading leaves; they grow in patches and have a small yellow fruit late in summer]*) Inf **NY**123, Mandrake, mandarin apple.

mandrake n Also *mandrake apple,* ~ *pear, wild mandrake* **chiefly NEast, N Cent** See Map
=mayapple 1; also its fruit.

   1778 Carver *Travels N. Amer.* 118, In the country belonging to these people [=Pawnee Indians] it is said, that Mandrakes are frequently found, a species of root resembling human beings of both sexes. **1807** in 1810 Schultz *Travels* 1.144 **seOH**, The only fruits I have met with, with which you are unacquainted, are the mandrake and the papaw. **1817** Eaton *Botany* 60, *Podophyllum.* . . *peltatum,* (wild mandrake) leaves peltate, pedate. **1854** King *Amer. Eclectic Dispensatory* 746, *Podophyllum peltatum.* . . Wild mandrake. . . Mandrake is found in abundance in almost all parts of the United States, in damp and shady woods, and sometimes in dry and exposed situations. **1893** *Jrl. Amer. Folkl.* 6.136 **NJ**, *Podophyllum peltatum,* mandrake pear. **1916** Keeler *Early Wildflowers* 85, *Wild Mandrake.* . . *Flowers.* Saucer-shaped, cream-white, nodding, borne in the fork between the two leaves, one and a half to two inches across. **1950** *WELS* **WI** (*Other names in your locality for the mayapple*) 23 Infs, Mandrake; 1 Inf, Wild mandrake. **1953** *Chicago Daily Tribune* (IL) 29 Oct 16/1, And by the time the bushes had leafed out, violets and mandrake and Solomon's seal were blooming in their speckled shade. **1965–70** *DARE* (Qu. S4, . . *Mayapple: [Woodside plant, not a tree, with two large spreading leaves; they grow in patches and have a small yellow fruit late in summer]*) 87 Infs, **chiefly NEast, N Cent**, Mandrake; (Qu. I37, *Small plants shaped like an umbrella that grow in woods and fields—which are safe to eat*) Infs **IL**31, **NY**233, **PA**70, Mandrake; **NY**227, Mandrake apples, mandrakes; (Qu. I38) Inf **PA**234, Mandrakes; (Qu. I46) Inf **NY**123, Mandrake; (Qu. S26b) Inf **NY**75, Mandrake; (Qu. S26c) Inf **MI**82, Mandrakes; (Qu. BB22) Inf **NY**234, Mandrake root. **1966** *DARE* Wildfl QR Pl.76 Infs **MI**57, **NH**4, **SC**41, Mandrake; **NY**91, Mandrake or mandrake apple. **1979** Ajilvsgi *Wild Flowers* 144, *Mandrake.* . . Berry . . lemon-shaped, to 2 in. long.

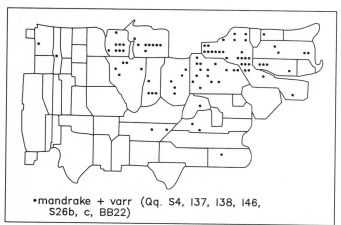

•mandrake + varr (Qq. S4, I37, I38, I46, S26b, c, BB22)

man-eater n

1 also *man-eating shark:* Any of several sharks reputed to eat humans, as:

a also *man-eater shark:* The great white shark (*Carcharodon carcharias*).

   1832 Williamson *Hist. ME* 1.161, The *Shark,* among fishermen, is

called the "maneater," the "shovel-nose," and the "swingle-tail;" these being varieties of the species. **1851** (1857) Hawthorne *Twice-Told* 2.259, To ascertain that the maneater [=a shark] had already met his own death. **1882** U.S. Natl. Museum *Bulletin* 16.30, *Man-eater Shark; Atwood's Shark.* . . American specimens have been named *C[archarodon] atwoodi.* **1884** Goode *Fisheries U.S.* 1.671, The enormous fossil Sharks' teeth which are found in the phosphate beds of South Carolina belong to a Shark closely related to our Man-eater. *Ibid* 1.676 **CA**, *Carcharodon carcharias.* . . Man-eater Shark. Monterey Bay and southward. **1903** NY State Museum & Sci. Serv. *Bulletin* 60.40, *Carcharodon carcharias* . . *Great White Shark; Man-eater.* . . The ferocity of the man-eater shark may be inferred from the following account. **1923** *NY Times* (NY) 13 Sept 23/7 **seNY**, [Headline:] Shark-Hunters Hook Man-Eater, Then Cut Line to Escape Him. **1933** LA Dept. of Conserv. *Fishes* 221, The Man-eater or Great White Shark . . is a species clearly dangerous to man. . . The Man-eater can be distinguished . . by the fact that it possesses large triangular saw-edged teeth. . . Formidable as is the Man-eating Shark, more terrifying still must have been its extinct ancestors. **1953** Roedel *Common Fishes CA* 15, A man-eater was probably responsible for the only fatal attack recorded from California. **1972** Sparano *Outdoors Encycl.* 370, *White shark. Common names:* White shark, great white shark, man-eater.

b The dusky shark (*Carcharhinus obscurus*).

   1903 NY State Museum & Sci. Serv. *Bulletin* 60.26, The dusky shark. . . Abundant in Great Egg bay where it is called the "man-eating shark." **1906** NJ State Museum *Annual Rept. for 1905* 61, *Carcharhinus obscurus.* . . Dusky Shark. . . Man Eater. Man Eating Shark. **1908** NJ State Museum *Annual Rept. for 1907* 127, About Cape May the large sharks usually reported as "man eaters" may probably be this species [=*Carcharhinus obscurus*].

2 A **salamander** such as the **hellbender 1** or a **water dog**.

   1859 (1968) Bartlett *Americanisms* 502, *Water-dogs.* The Western name for various species of salamanders, or lizard-shaped animals, with smooth, shiny, naked skins; sometimes called Water-puppies and Ground-puppies. In Pennsylvania and the Eastern States they are called Spring-keepers and Man-eaters.

3 **=hellgrammite 1.**

   1890 *Century Dict.* 3607, *Man-eater.* . . The dobson or hellgrammite. [*Century* Ed: Local, U.S.]

man-eater shark See **man-eater 1a**

man-eating shark See **man-eater 1**

man-faced owl n [See quot]
=barn owl 1.

   1955 *AmSp* 30.180, Barn owl. . . Likeness to man has not escaped attention, witness the name *man-faced owl,* heard in California.

man-faced spider n
Prob **=Jerusalem cricket.**

   [**1947** Dodge *Poisonous Dwellers* 40, The Jerusalem cricket . . is shy and nocturnal in its habits. Its striking appearance is due to its head which is round, bald, and with markings on top that form, with the use of a little imagination, a simple, smiling face. . . The Navajo Indians call it woh-seh-tsinni meaning Old Man Baldhead.] **1967** *DARE* (Qu. R28, . . *Kinds of spiders*) Inf **AZ**2, Man-faced spider.

manful adv [Cf Intro "Language Changes" II.8]
Vigorously, energetically.

   1895 *DN* 1.372 **seKY, eTN, wNC**, *Manful:* vigorous(ly). "The engineer'd whistle manful ef he'd see us on the track." **1929** Sale *Tree Named John* 140 **MS**, My daddy say de sho prayed manful.

mang n Also sp *mung* [Ult from OE *gemang* mixture, crowd; cf *EDD mang* "A mixture, confused mass," *mung* sb. 3 "A crowd of people; a rabble."]
1 See quots.
   1884 Amer. Philol. Assoc. *Trans. for 1883* 14.51 **WV**, *Mang* means in West Virginia the 'slush about a pig-sty.' **1994** *DARE* File, [mʌŋ], usually spelled *mung,* but not often used in writing, was a synonym for *crud, guck,* for a messy substance of infinite repulsiveness but little specificity, by University of Massachusetts students in the 1970s.
2 See quot.
   1884 Amer. Philol. Assoc. *Trans. for 1883* 14.51 **wTN**, A student of Vanderbilt University (from West Tennessee) was heard to say recently: "Well, if I fail on my examination, I'll have the consolation that I'm in the mang [i.e. 'the crowd'], as the old people in my country say."

mangana n [Span "lasso"] **SW** Cf **forefoot**
A throw with the **lasso** intended to catch an animal by its forefeet.

1929 Dobie *Vaquero* 8 **TX,** I picked up my rope . . and, as she came down the side fence, threw a *mangana* on her fore-feet and at the same time tossed a half hitch over a post. *Ibid* 262, One of the neatest throws in common use is the *mangana,* which means catching an animal by the forefeet, "forefooting." . . The *mangana* is seldom used outside the pen, but can be cast from the saddle as well as from the ground. **1939** Wellman *Trampling Herd* 240 **SW,** The deadliest throw was called "forefooting." The noose caught the animal by the forefoot and spilled it. In the Southwest this was known as the *mangana.* **1940** *Cattleman* May 22, *Mangana.* . . This is undoubtedly one of the best throws to forefoot a horse and when used for that purpose it is held closer to the ground, releasing the loop but continuing to hold the rope. . . This is a loop which needs perfect timing to be a success as it will cause an animal to stop rather than hit it if it is stood up too far ahead of him.

mange n [Var of *manes, mane* being understood as a count noun; cf **hair** n **B1**] *among Black speakers*
1888 Jones *Negro Myths* 112 **GA coast** [Gullah], So eh drap de bridle an heng on ter eh mange fuh keep from fall off. **1922** Gonzales *Black Border* 312 **sSC, GA coasts** [Gullah glossary], *Mange*—mane. **1986** Pederson *LAGS Concordance,* 1 inf, **nwFL,** Mange [=mane]—as on a horse. [Inf Black]

mange grass n [Perh folk-etym for **Means grass**]
=**Johnson grass 1.**
1967–68 *DARE* (Qu. S8, *A common kind of wild grass that grows in fields: it spreads by sending out long underground roots, and it's hard to get rid of*) Inf **SC31,** Mange grass, if it grows tall and otherwise fits the description; (Qu. S9, . . *Kinds of grass that are hard to get rid of*) Inf **SC57,** Mange grass, same as Johnson grass.

mangel-wurzel n Also *mangel, mangle(wurzel);* for addit varr see quots [*OED* 1787 →]
A beet (*Beta vulgaris* Crassa Group) usu grown for fodder.
1788 (1925) Washington *Diaries* 3.427 **neVA,** I sowed 19 Rows of the Yellow bearded Wheat between the Rows of the Mangel Wurzel and those of the Carrots. **1792** in 1801 Society Useful Arts *Trans.* 1.29 **NY,** The mangel-wurtzel, or root of scarcity, seems not to have succeeded among us in a degree equal to the character given of it by the French and English writers. **1844** Stephens *High Life in NY* 2.173 **CT,** Mr. Tyler, between you and I and the post, I don't like that hair of your'n, it makes you look tu much like a manglewozzle-beet a running to seed. **1869** Porcher *Resources* 412 **Sth,** *Beet; Mangel-wurzel.* . . The juice of one bushel of beet . . will make from five to six gallons of vinegar, equal to the best made of elder wine. *Ibid* 714, Mangel-wirzel. **1872** Ellet *New Cyclop.* 78, The chicory itself . . is adulterated with roasted corn, parsnips, manglewurzel [etc]. **1882** (1971) Gibbons *PA Dutch* 352, He had four men hoeing . . "mangles" (mangel-wurzels?), and kohl-rabi. **1883** *Harper's New Mth. Mag.* 66.652, Mangel-wurzel is the principal root crop raised on the farm, and is fed to the cows in winter. A cow gets daily one bushel of sliced mangel. **1925** *Book of Rural Life* 3324, *Mangel-wurzel* . . is one of the most important root crops grown for stock feeding. . . Most of the mangels produced in the United States are grown in New York, Maine, Michigan, Wisconsin, Minnesota, Oregon and Washington. *Ibid* 3325, The mangel-wurzel beet . . yields enormously and keeps well in storage. **1950** *WELS* **WI** (*Other names in your neighborhood for . . beets*) 1 Inf, Mangel-wurzel—in seed catalog . . abbreviated to mangel [mæŋgl] here; 1 Inf, Mangel. **1966–69** *DARE* (Qu. I3, . . *The large yellowish root vegetable, similar to a turnip, with a strong taste*) Inf **MA68,** Mangel; (Qu. I4, . . *Vegetables . . less commonly grown around here*) Inf **MI23,** Mangels. **1976** Bailey–Bailey *Hortus Third* 160, *Beet.* . . The Crassa Group includes the kinds grown chiefly for their roots, used as a vegetable, forage, or source of sugar, and known as *garden beet,* . . *mangel, mangel-worzel* [etc].

man getter See **man catcher**

mangeur maringouin n [LaFr "mosquito-eater"]
=**chuck-will's-widow.**
1916 *Times–Picayune* (New Orleans LA) 16 Apr mag sec 9, *Chuck-will's widow.* . . Mangeur Maringouin. . . It feeds on flying insects (so earned its local Creole name, which means "mosquito eater." [**1931** Read *LA French* 95, *Mangeur maringouins,* "mosquito eater," is one of the names of the Nighthawk or Bull Bat (*Chordeiles virginianus virginianus* Gmel.) and the Florida Nighthawk (*Chordeiles virginianus*

chapmani Coues). The Chuck-Will's-Widow (*Antrosfomus carolinensis* Gmel.) is also called *Mangeur Maringouins.*]

mangeur poulette n [LaFr "chicken-eater"]
A **sparrow hawk** (here: *Falco sparverius*).
[**1831** Audubon *Ornith. Biog.* 1.84, The French and Spaniards of Louisiana have designated all the species of the genus Falco by the name of *"Mangeur de Poulets."*] **1916** *Times–Picayune* (New Orleans LA) 9 Apr mag sec 2, *Sparrow Hawk* . . Mangeur poulette. . . The food consists mostly of grasshoppers, small mice and, rarely, small birds. [**1931** Read *LA French* 37, Other names of the sparrow hawk are *cli-clique* (echoic), *émerillon,* and *mangeur poulets.*]

mangla n
A **sumac;** see quots.
[**1920** Saunders *Useful Wild Plants* 156, *R[hus] integrifolia.* . . The Spanish people call it *mangla,* a name they give to some other sumacs as well.] **1938** Van Dersal *Native Woody Plants* 343, Mangla (*Rhus laurina*).

mangle n[1] [Span < Taino]
1 Std: =**mangrove 1.**
2 Any of var plants appar thought to resemble **1** above in some way, as:
a =**black mangrove.**
1833 Eaton *Botany* 48, *Avicennia . . tomentosa.* . . Mangle. . . Flowers in sub-sessile clusters. **1876** Hobbs *Bot. Hdbk.* 67, Mangle, Avicennia tomentosa. **1946** [see **mangrove 2d**]. **1961** *W3, Mangle.* . . Any of several trees or shrubs (as *Avicennia nitida* and *Laguncularia racemosa*).
b An **indigo bush 2** (here: *Psorothamnus spinosus*).
1931 U.S. Dept. Ag. *Misc. Pub.* 101.85, *Tree-pea . . ,* the familiar, spiny-twigged plant of the Colorado Desert region and Sonora, frequently becomes a small tree. . . Other names for this species include indigobush, mangle [etc].
c A **groundsel tree** (here: *Baccharis halimifolia*).
1940 Clute *Amer. Plant Names* 219, *Baccharis halimifolia.* Mangle, white mangle.
d A **marsh elder 1** (here: *Iva frutescens*).
1940 Clute *Amer. Plant Names* 225, *Iva oraria.* Green mangle, mangle, poverty-weed.
e A **white mangrove** (here: *Laguncularia racemosa*).
1961 [see **2a** above].

mangle n[2] See **mangel-wurzel**

mangle n[3] See **mango 2**

manglewurzel See **mangel-wurzel**

manglier n [Fr "mangrove"] Also *mung*
A **groundsel tree** (here: *Baccharis halimifolia*).
1942 *Torreya* 42.165 **LA,** *Baccharis halimifolia.* . . Manglier; mung.

mangly See **mingledy**

mango n
1 Any of var fruits or vegetables (as a **muskmelon,** peach, pepper, or cucumber) filled with a usu highly spiced stuffing and pickled. [*OED mango* sb.[1] 4 1699 →; the East Indian mango (*Mangifera indica*) was at first known only as a pickle; the "mangoes" illustr here were made in imitation of that imported delicacy.]
1806 (1970) Webster *Compendious Dict.* 184, Mango, . . a fruit from the E. Indies pickled, a green musmelon [sic] pickled. [*DARE* Ed: The second part of this definition does not appear in Webster's English model.] **1830** Child *Frugal Housewife* 89, Musk-melons should be picked for mangoes, when they are green and hard. **1847** (1852) Crowen *Amer. Cookery* 390, *Melon Mangoes.*—Get the large, small, smooth, green melon. [*DARE* Ed: The melons are stuffed with horseradish, cucumbers, green beans, nasturtiums, onions, mustard seed, peppercorns, cloves, and allspice, and then pickled.] **1890** James *Mother James' Cooking* 391, *Pickled Mangoes.* Select green or half-grown muskmelons. . . *Peach Mangoes.* . . *Green Pepper Mangoes.* *Ibid* 392, Cucumber Mangoes. . . Take fresh vinegar, a gallon to one and one-half pounds of brown sugar, boil for fifteen or twenty minutes and pour over mangoes. **1903** *DN* 2.320 **seMO,** *Mango.* . . A kind of pickle made of small green melons stuffed with tomatoes, etc. **1940** Brown *Amer. Cooks* 395 **MA,** *Stuffed Mangoes.* . . Either green peppers or small muskmelons may be used

for mangoes. Mix all well together and fill each mango. **1953** Piercy *Shaker Cook Book* 187, *Pickled Bell Peppers. . .* The North Union (OH) Sisters made literally hundreds of crocks of these pickled peppers, or pickled mangoes. **1982** Weaver *Quaker Woman's Cookbook* lxvi, In Pennsylvania and western Maryland, mangoes were generally made with green bell peppers. In Tidewater Maryland . . muskmelons provided the most popular form of local mango.

2 also *mango pepper;* pronc-sp *mangle:* A pepper, esp a **green pepper 1. chiefly W Midl** See Map

   1948 *WELS Suppl.* VA, I was surprised while living in Virginia to see green peppers advertised and sold as "mangoes." **1950** *WELS (Large sweet peppers)* 2 Infs, WI, Mangoes. c**1960** *Wilson Coll.* **csKY,** Mango. . . Sweet pepper, bell-pepper. **1964** *Gourmet* May 2, [Letter:] The use of the term mango for bell pepper . . is not limited to Indiana. I have heard it used in Louisiana and Georgia. We once had an old English gardener up in Vermont many years ago, and he always called the green pepper a mango. Bird and chili peppers are also referred to as mangoes. **1965–70** *DARE* (Qu. I22d, . . *Peppers—large sweet*) 113 Infs, **chiefly W Midl, esp sIL, sIN, sOH,** Mangoes; **IN**41, 48, Sweet mangoes; **MO**39, Mango peppers; **MO**5, **MO**27, Mangles; **MO**4, Tomato peppers—also called the little mangle peppers; (Qu. I22c, . . *Peppers—small sweet*) 15 Infs, **chiefly N Midl,** Mangoes; **IL**85, Small mangoes; **OK**3, Mango peppers; (Qu. I22b, . . *Peppers—large hot*) Infs **IN**76, **KS**1, **PA**150, Mangoes; **MO**6, Mangoes—not so hot nor so small; **KS**6, **KY**52, **VA**28, Mango peppers; **IN**41, 48, Hot mangoes; (Qu. I22a, . . *Peppers—small hot*) Infs **IL**7, **MO**18, Mango peppers; **NJ**2, Mangoes. **1970** *DARE* File **KY, sOH,** Mango—bell pepper. **1972** *NYT Article Letters* **cnIN,** In my home area, *green (bell) peppers* are called *mangos.*

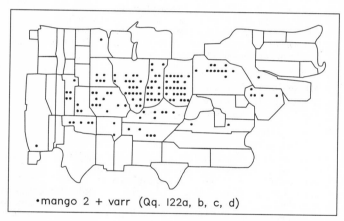

•mango 2 + varr (Qq. I22a, b, c, d)

3 also *mango melon:* A melon (*Cucumis melo* Chito Group). [See quot 1988] Also called **vegetable peach**

   1934 (1943) *W2,* Mango melon. . . A muskmelon (*Cucumis melo chito*) bearing orangelike fruit used as pickles and preserves. **1970** *DARE* (Qu. I26, . . *Kinds of melons*) Inf **VA**108, Mangoes—small cantaloupes, not an actual mango. **1976** Bailey–Bailey *Hortus Third* 342, [*Cucumis*] *Melo.* . . Chito Group. . . *Mango m[elon], orange m., garden lemon, melon apple, vegetable orange, vine peach.* . . Fr[uit] yellow or orange, the size and shape of a lemon or orange, flesh white and firm, not fragrant. Used to make preserves and pickles. **1986** Pederson *LAGS Concordance (Muskmelon)* 1 inf, **cnGA,** Mango. **1988** Whealy *Garden Seed Inventory* (2d ed) 229, *Vine Peach* (Mango Melon, Vegetable Peach) . . native American annual, peach size and color, flavor & texture much like mango, easy to grow, . . best when cooked for canning & preserves & pies & pickling whole (for pickling pick while still green).

mango croaker n

A **grunt 1** (here: *Conodon nobilis*).

   1931 *Copeia* 2.48 **TX,** *Conodon nobilis.* . . The "mango croaker" was common in a fisherman's haul from the Gulf surf near Corpus Christi Pass on July 21.

mango melon See **mango 3**

mango pepper See **mango 2**

man grabber See **man catcher**

mangrove n Cf **mangle** n[1]

1 Std: a plant of the family Rhizophoraceae, usu a tree (*Rhi-*

zophora mangle) known for its stilt-like roots. Also called **mangle** n[1] **1, red mangrove, mangrow**

2 Any of var plants appar thought to resemble **mangrove 1** in some way, as:

a =**sea grape.**
   1900 Lyons *Plant Names* 109, *C[occoloba] uvifera.* . . Mangrove. *Fruit* edible.

b also *mangrove brush;* pronc-sp *mongo tree:* =**marsh elder 1.**
   1913 *Torreya* 13.234, *Iva frutescens.* . . Mangrove, Cameron, La.; mangrove brush, Vermilion Bay, La.; mongo tree, Chef Menteur, La. **1941** *Ibid* 41.52 **swLA,** *Iva* spp.—Mangrove.

c A **groundsel tree** (here: *Baccharis halimifolia*).
   1941 *Torreya* 41.53 **swLA,** *Baccharis halimifolia.* . . Mangrove.

d =**black mangrove.**
   1946 Kopman *Wild Acres* 22 **LA,** The seaside sparrow nests principally in bushes of honey-mangrove, or Avicennia, known locally as "mangle," sometimes as "mangrove."

e =**white mangrove** (here: *Laguncularia racemosa*).
   1946 West–Arnold *Native Trees FL* 153, *Laguncularia racemosa* . . is the least efficient of the erosion-resisting mangroves.

f =**buttonwood 3.**
   1976 Fleming *Wild Flowers FL* 39, *Buttonwood* . . is often called a mangrove. It attains a tree height of 60 feet but remains a shrub in many areas.

mangrove brush See **mangrove 2b**

mangrove clapper rail See **mangrove hen**

mangrove crab n

A brightly-colored crab (*Goniopsis cruentata*) native to Florida.
   1933 John G. Shedd Aquarium *Guide* 202, From Florida comes the . . *Mangrove . . Crab.* . . The *Mangrove Crab* rivals the colors of the tropical fishes with its bright scarlet and yellow legs and jet black carapace dotted and lined with white. **1937** *Natl. Geogr. Mag.* Feb 209 **FL,** Brightly colored mangrove crabs (*Goniopsis cruentata*), their square carapaces aglow with scarlet marked with brilliant yellow and blue, scamper over the oyster beds.

mangrove cuckoo n

A cuckoo (*Coccyzus minor*) native to southern Florida. Also called **rainbird, rain crow**
   [**1782** Latham *Genl. Synopsis Birds* 1.2.537, *Mangrove C[uckow]*]. **1832** Nuttall *Manual Ornith.* 1.558, *Mangrove Cuckoo.* . . It lives upon insects, and is particularly fond of the large caterpillars which prey upon the leaves of the Mangrove, and in the dense forests of which it consequently takes up its principal residence. **1898** (1900) Davie *Nests N. Amer. Birds* 254, The Mangrove Cuckoo is very much like the yellow-billed species, . . with the lower parts of the plumage more deeply colored. **1917** *DN* 4.427 **LA,** *Mangrove cuckoo* (Coccyzus minor). A bird much like the Yellow-billed Cuckoo. **1946** Hausman *Eastern Birds* 347, Mangrove Cuckoo. . . *Notes.* . . A sort of clucking note, low and guttural, repeated slowly, and suggesting the notes of a squirrel rather than those of a bird. **1977** Bull–Farrand *Audubon Field Guide Birds* 487, *Mangrove Cuckoo.* . . Found only in the Florida Keys and on the adjacent Gulf Coast as far as Tampa Bay.

mangrove hen n Also *mangrove (clapper) rail* =**clapper rail.**
   1897 *Auk* 14.287 **LA,** *Rallus crepitans saturatus. Louisiana Clapper Rail.* A common species wherever found; its range, however, is restricted to the mangrove islands along the southeast coast. . . Locally known as Mangrove Hen. Resident. Breeds. **1923** U.S. Dept. Ag. *Misc. Circular* 13.41 **FL,** *Clapper Rail (Rallus crepitans).* . . *Vernacular Names.* . . *In local use.* . . Mangrove rail. **1932** Howell *FL Bird Life* 205, *Mangrove Clapper Rail: Rallus longirostris insularum.* . . Little is known about the habits of this subspecies except that it dwells in the mangrove swamps. **1953** *AmSp* 28.281 **FL,** Mangrove hen. Clapper rail. **1955** Forbush–May *Birds* 161, *Mangrove Clapper Rail.* . . It probably differs somewhat from the other races of Clapper Rails in feeding habits on account of its quite different environment, the ecological factors in the mangrove swamps being very unlike those of the salt marshes of the Atlantic coast.

mangrove mallow n

A **mallow B** (here: *Pavonia racemosa*).
   1971 Craighead *Trees S. FL* 111, The mangrove mallow and Christ-

masberry are found sparingly [under the shade of the mangrove forests]. *Ibid* 201, Mangrove mallow, *Pavonia racemosa.*

mangrove rail See **mangrove hen**

mangrove snapper n FL

1 =**gray snapper.** [See quots 1898, 1933]

1734 Royal Soc. London *Philos. Trans.* 38.316, The *Mangrove Snapper* . . is esteemed pretty good food. **1743** Catesby *Nat. Hist. Carolina* 2.9, The *mangrove Snapper.* . . The Colour of it was that of Umber, dark on the Back, and light on the Belly: The Sides of the Mouth were red. **1882** U.S. Natl. Museum *Proc.* 5.275 **FL,** *Lutjanus stearnsi.* . . *Mangrove Snapper.* . . Not uncommon on the "Snapper Banks" at Pensacola. **1898** U.S. Natl. Museum *Bulletin* 47.1256, In Florida and the Bahamas, where the coasts are lined by mangrove bushes among which the young of this species abound, the name mangrove snapper comes into use. **1933** John G. Shedd Aquarium *Guide* 104, *Lutianus* [sic] *griseus.* . . It gets the name Mangrove Snapper from its habit of lying in very shallow water among the mangrove roots. **1955** Carr–Goin *Guide Reptiles* 102, *Lutjanus griseus* . . Mangrove Snapper. . . *General Distribution.*—Massachusetts to the West Indies. *Florida Range.*—Both coasts. **1973** Knight *Cook's Fish Guide* 391, Snapper[,] . . mangrove—Gray.

2 A **snapper** (here: *Rhomboplites aurorubens*).

1879 U.S. Natl. Museum *Bulletin* 14.48, *Rhomboplites aurorubeus* [sic]. . . Mangrove Snapper. **1882** U.S. Natl. Museum *Bulletin* 16.549, *Mangrove Snapper.* . . Vermilion-red above, rosy below. **1884** Goode *Fisheries U.S.* 1.396, Two other brilliant red species occur . . in the Gulf of Mexico—the Pensacola Snapper, *L[utjanus] Stearnsii,* and the Mangrove Snapper, *Rhomboplites aurorubens.*

mangrove terrapin n

A subsp of the **diamondback terrapin** *(Malaclemys terrapin rhizophorarum)* native to the Florida Keys.

1952 Carr *Turtles* 178, I have seen the mangrove terrapin only in mangrove swamps and mangrove-bordered creeks and around the shores of the hundreds of little keys in Florida Bay. **1958** Conant *Reptiles & Amphibians* 48, *Mangrove Terrapin.* . . Dark spots on neck fused together, producing boldly streaked appearance; . . has striped "pants." The Florida Keys, chiefly among mangroves. **1972** Ernst–Barbour *Turtles* 104, *M. t. rhizophorarum* . . , the mangrove terrapin, is restricted to the Florida Keys. **1979** Behler–King *Audubon Field Guide Reptiles* 467, Mangrove [terrapin].

mangrow n [Prob folk-etym for **mangle** n¹; cf *OED mangrove* sb.¹ 1 quot 1613, *DJE mangrow*]

=**mangrove 1.**

1966 *DARE* (Qu. C7, . . *Land that usually has some standing water with trees or bushes growing in it*) Inf **FL**24, ['mæŋgrə swɔmp]; (Qu. T15, . . *Kinds of swamp trees*) Inf **FL**39, Mangrow ['mæŋgrouw]—more than a bush.

man-grown adj Also *man-growed* [*OED man* sb. 19.f 1587 →] Having reached manhood, grown-up; similarly n *man grown* an adult man.

1907 London *Road* 173 **West,** A gay-cat is a newcomer on The Road who is man-grown, or, at least, youth-grown. **1930** Faulkner *As I Lay Dying* 34 **MS,** I aint no call to expect no more of him than of his man-growed brothers. **1939** *Hall Coll.* wNC, eTN, "Just a man grown," of one who has just reached manhood . . : "I could tell you what the weather used to be back when I was a boy like or just a man grown." *Ibid,* There's one man living there yet . . that was a man grown when I was just a little boy; he told me the other day that he was ninety-four years old. **1953** *Ibid* wNC, Well, he was a young man grown, and his wife was raised right there on Hazel Creek [Hall: i.e., he became a grown young man there, etc].

manhad(d)en, manhayden See **menhaden 1**

man hunter See **man catcher**

manienie n [Haw] **HI**

1 also *manienie haole:* Bermuda grass (here: *Cynodon dactylon*).

1929 Neal *Honolulu Gardens* 31, Bermuda grass, manienie haole *(Cynodon dactylon* . .). . . spreads rapidly over the ground, rooting at the joints of creeping stems. **1954–60** Hance et al. *Hawaiian Sugar* 5, Manienie ['mɑnieniɛ]—Bermuda grass, Cynodon dactylon. **1967** *DARE* (Qu. L9a, . . *Kinds of grass . . grown for hay*) Inf **HI**2, Manienie [,mɑnjə'niɛ]—Bermuda grass; (Qu. S9, . . *Kinds of grass that are hard*

to get rid of) Inf **HI**2, Bermuda grass, called manienie here—grows rapidly; **HI**4, Manienie [,mɑnji'niɛ]—common lawn grass; **HI**11, Manienie [,mɑnjə'niɛ]—same as Bermuda grass. [**1971** Pukui–Elbert *Hawaiian Dict.* 219, *Mānienie. 1.* Bermuda grass *(Cynodon dactylon),* a fine-leafed, cosmopolitan grass, much used for lawns in Hawaii. *Ibid* 220, *Mānienie-haole.* Bermuda grass *(Cynodon dactylon),* said to have been introduced by Dr. G.P. Judd about 1835; called *mānienie* because it creeps like buffalo grass (see *mānienie-maoli*), which the Hawaiians originally called *mānienie.*]

2 also with modifiers: =**St. Augustine grass.**

1929 Pope *Plants HI* 28, *Stenotaphrum secundatum.* . . The old time Hawaiians called this grass . . "Manienie mahikihiki". . . This grass was found in Hawaii by the early plant collectors and it was the original "manienie" (creeping grass) of the old time Hawaiian, being used for medicinal purposes. **1929** Neal *Honolulu Gardens* 29, Buffalo grass, . . *manienie maoli [Stenotaphrum secundatum* . .]. A valuable lawn grass for warm countries. It is also used for fodder. [**1971** Pukui–Elbert *Hawaiian Dict.* 219, *Mānienie.* . . Short for *mānienie-'aki'aki. Ibid, Mānienie—'aki'aki.* . . Buffalo grass *(Stenotaphrum secundatum),* a coarse-leafed grass from the southern United States, used for lawns in Hawaii. Sometimes qualified by *haole* and also called *mānienie-māhikihiki.*]

manienie haole See **manienie 1**

manifac n, adj Also sp *manufac, manyfac(k)* [Abbrs for *manufactured*] *old-fash*

See quots.

1909 *DN* 3.348 **eAL, wGA,** *Manyfac.* . . Manufactured tobacco in contradistinction to home-raised, or natural leaf tobacco. **1942** Berrey–Van den Bark *Amer. Slang* 111.6, Manyfack, tailor-mades, *factory-made cigarettes.* **1950** *PADS* 14.45 **SC,** *Manifac* ['mænɪfæk]. . . *Manufactured,* as contrasted with home-made. "Manifac smoking tobacco," etc. **c1960** *Wilson Coll.* **csKY,** *Manifac* (or *manufac*). . . Plug tobacco rather than hillside, or home-made twist.

man-in-a-boat n Also *two-men-in-a-boat, three-men-in-a-boat* =**Moses-in-the-bulrushes 1.**

1976 Bailey–Bailey *Hortus Third* 966, *[Rhoeo] spathacea.* . . Man-in-a-boat, Two-men-in-a-boat, Three-men-in-a-boat.

manini n [Haw] **HI**

1 A **surgeonfish** (here: *Acanthurus sandvicensis*).

1926 Pan-Pacific Research Inst. *Jrl.* 1.1.11 **HI,** Acanthurus sandvicensis. . . Manini. **1960** Gosline–Brock *Hawaiian Fishes* 246, The manini is the most abundant of Hawaiian surgeonfishes and occurs in nearly all habitats occupied by reef fishes. . . Like other surgeonfishes it grazes on algae. **1967** *DARE* (Qu. P2, . . *Kinds of saltwater fish caught around here* . . *good to eat*) Inf **HI**4, Manini—striped. **1972** Carr *Da Kine Talk* 115 **HI,** The *manini* is a common reef fish.

2 A banana; see quots.

1948 Neal *In Gardens HI* 212, An excellent cooking banana, or plantain *(M[usa] paradisiaca* ssp. *normalis* . .) is a tree to about 25 feet high. . . Probably a form of this plantain, in Hawaii called . . manini, with green and white striped leaves and fruits, is generally eaten cooked. [**1971** Pukui–Elbert *Hawaiian Dict.* 220, *Manini.* . . A kind of banana generally eaten cooked; leaves and fruits green and white striped.]

manini adj [Haw; see quot 1967 Reinecke–Tsuzaki] **HI**

Small, inferior; stingy.

1966 Morimoto *Hawaiian Dial. Engl.* 98, Eventually mainland Nisei troops adopted many Hawaiian words or pidgin English words. . . I believe I continued to use some of these words long after my separation from the 442[nd Regimental Combat Team] at the end of the war. Examples: . . *manini* [Morimoto: stingy]. **1967** Reinecke–Tsuzaki *Hawaiian Loanwords* 105, *Manini.* . . [Reinecke–Tsuzaki: Fr. *manini,* coral reef surgeonfish *(Acanthurus sandvicensis).*] Small; mean; stingy. V[ery] F[req]. **1967** *DARE* (Qu. LL2, . . *Too small to be worth much:* "*I don't want that little* _____ *potato.*") Inf **HI**13, Manini [mə'nini]. **1972** Carr *Da Kine Talk* 115 **HI,** *Manini-looking* (Hawaiian + English). 'Skimpy looking' or 'inadequate.' The *manini* is a common reef fish. *Manini* also means 'stingy.' **1981** *Pidgin To Da Max* np **HI,** *Manini.* . . Stingy. . . Undersized.

maninose n Also *mananosay, man(n)anose, manninose, mannoe(s), man(n)ose, man(n)ynose, man-of-nose, mano(s), nan(n)y-*

nose; for addit varr see quots [Of Algonquian origin; see quot 1907] **chiefly Delmarva, NC**
=soft-shell clam.

1677 in 1896 *Archives of MD* 15.146, He was an Indian belonging to the King of Checonesseck . . last summer he came among them to trade, and brought with him some Mannanoses wch he sold for Peake. **1709** (1967) Lawson *New Voyage* 165 **NC, SC,** Man of Noses are a Shell-Fish commonly found amongst us. They are valued for increasing Vigour in Men, and making barren Women fruitful. **1843** DeKay *Zool. NY* 5.240, It [=*Mya arenaria*] is known under the various appellations of *Long Clam* and *Piss Clam* to distinguish it from the common *Round Clam.* . . In some districts it still retains its ancient aboriginal appellation of *Maninose.* **1859** (1968) Bartlett *Americanisms* 84, The Soft Clam, or Mananosay *(Mya arenaria),* obtained from the shores of tidal rivers. . . has a long, extensible, cartilaginous snout, or proboscis, through which it ejects water; whence it is also called Stem-clam and Piss-clam. **1884** U.S. Natl. Museum *Bulletin* 27.229, *Mya arenaria* . . is the "Mananose" of the Southern States. **1890** *Century Dict.* 3612 **MD, VA,** *Maninose.* . . Also *manninose, mannynose, manynose, nannynose,* etc. . . The soft clam, *Mya arenaria.* **1899** (1912) Green *VA Folk-Speech* 274, *Maninose.* . . Mannose. The soft clam. **1907** Hodge *Hdbk. Amer. Indians* 1.800, *Maninose.* A name used in Maryland for the soft-shell clam *(Mya arenaria),* called *mananosay* in more northerly parts of the Atlantic coast. . . [T]he local name at Lewes, Del., is *mullinose.* The word appears also as *mannynose.* The word is derived from one of the southern Algonquian dialects, Virginian or Delaware; probably the latter. The derivation seems to be from the radical *man-,* 'to gather.' **1911** U.S. Bur. Census *Fisheries 1908* 309, *Clam.* . . Various species . . are known by the names of . . "mananose," "nanninose," "squirt clam" [etc]. **1933** Hanley *Disks* **ceVA,** Little manos from down in the earth. Did you ever see a clam? Clam is kinda round, like a horsefoot, and manos is long. We call them manos. *Ibid* **VA,** Mano is a little longer than a clam. A mano's more like a mussel. It has a snout or a nose on it. **1943** Weslager *DE Forgotten Folk* 201, Today the word Mannose, or Manose is still used by both the Moors and Nanticokes. It is their name for the soft-shelled clam. **1951** Taylor *Surv. Marine Fisheries NC* 178, The soft-shelled clam is commonly known as the "mananose" ("maninose," "nanynose") in North Carolina. **1958** *DE Folkl. Bulletin* 1.32, Mannose (soft-shelled clam, maninose). **1967–70** *DARE* (Qu. P18, . . *Kinds of shellfish*) Inf **DE4,** ['mænə,nouz], same as "piss clam"—they squirt water; **MD13,** Mannose—kidney-shaped clam; **MD36, 42, VA79,** Mannoe; **VA47, 55,** Mannoes; (Qu. H45, *Dishes made with meat, fish, or poultry that everybody around here would know, but that people in other places might not)* Inf **MD39,** Mannoe fritters, mannoe soup; (Qu. O10, . . *Kinds of boats*) Inf **VA79,** Mannoe dredge. **1970** *DARE* Tape **VA55,** [Inf:] They ain't but two kinds . . a clam, and a butterfish we dig out the bottom. . . [FW:] And then the mannoes. [Inf:] Some call them mannoes, . . but . . soft shellfish is what it's called. Some calls 'em mannoes, but what they're generally called is soft shell. *Ibid* **VA112,** [FW:] A mannoe, that's a kind of a clam. [Inf:] That's them big, long ones. . . But the mannoe'll have a snout hole that'll run right up so he can breathe, like a . . periscope. **1981** Rehder *Audubon Field Guide Seashells* 812, Northeastern American Indians called it [=*Mya arenaria*] the Manninose. It has long been important as a food source.

man-in-the-ground n

1 also *man-under-the-ground:* **=man-of-the-earth 1.**

1828 Rafinesque *Med. Flora* 1.123, *Convolvulus panduratus.* . . *Vulgar Names* . . Man in the ground. . . Root perennial, very large, cylindric or fusiform, from two to four feet long, as thick as the arm. **1854** King *Amer. Eclectic Dispensatory* 391, *Convolvulus pandurata.* . . This plant, likewise known as . . *Man in the Ground,* . . *Man of the Earth,* etc., has a . . very large . . *root.* . . It is asserted that the Indians can handle rattlesnakes with impunity, after wetting their hands with the milky juice of this root. **1876** Hobbs *Bot. Hdbk.* 67, Man-in-the-ground, Wild potato, *Convolvulus pandurata.* **1969** *DARE* (Qu. S5, . . *Wild morning glory)* Inf **NJ58,** Man-under-the-ground—from flower book.

2 A **bigroot 1** (here: *Marah fabaceus* or *M. oreganus*). [See quots]

1893 *Jrl. Amer. Folkl.* 6.142, *Megarrhiza Californica,* man-in-the-ground. S[anta] Barbara Co., Cal. . . So named from the enormous roots. **1897** Parsons *Wild Flowers CA* 26, Seeing its rather delicate ivy-like habit above ground, one would never dream that it came from a root as large as a man's body. . . From this root, it has received two of its common names, "big-root" and "man-in-the-ground". **1915** (1926)

Armstrong–Thornber *Western Wild Flowers* 518, *Chilicothe.* . . A graceful, decorative vine, . . springing from an enormous bitter root as large as a man's body, . . this is also called . . Man-in-the-ground. **1934** Haskin *Wild Flowers Pacific Coast* 355, The roots of this plant attain a great size, and from them the plant is sometimes given the name of . . "man-in-the-ground."

maniportia n Usu |ˌmænɨˈpo(r)čə|; for addit proncs see quot 1965–70 [Var of Lat *mania a potu* literally "madness from drinking"] **chiefly MD** See Map
Delirium tremens.

[**1837** *S. Lit. Jrl.* new ser 1.6.515 **seSC,** "Mania a potu," as physicians say [in ref to a drunkard's hallucinations].] [**1850** Garrard *Wah-to-yah* 265 **SW,** So ended Hatcher's tale of Wah-to-yah, or what the mountaineer saw when he had the *mania potu.*] [**1872** (1973) Thompson *Major Jones's Courtship* 75 **GA,** And old Miss Stallins seems like she'd have the hidrafoby or manupotu about it.] **1965–70** *DARE* (Qu. DD22, . . *Delirium tremens)* Infs **MD20, 48,** [ˌmænɨˈpočə]; **MD29, 31,** [ˌmænɨˈporčə]; **DC8,** [ˌmænəˈpočə]; **MD11,** [ˌmænəˈporčə]; **MD15,** [ˌmænɨˈpeočə]; **MD36, 42,** [ˌmænɨˈpročə]; **LA14,** [ˈmɔnəˈpoučə]; **MD26,** [ˌmænɨˈporči]; **MD34,** [ˌmænɨˈporšə]; (Qu. DD24, . . *Diseases that come from continual drinking)* Inf **MD20,** [ˌmænɨˈpočə]. **1983** *NADS Letters* **sMD,** Used by the older native population, "maniportia" denotes madness from overindulgence in alcohol. It carries the implication of near violent behavior. . . The following is an excerpt from a local doctor. . . "When the word Maniportia is used it obviously has the same meaning as 'Delerium [sic] Tremens' . . the symptoms seen in alcohol withdrawal."

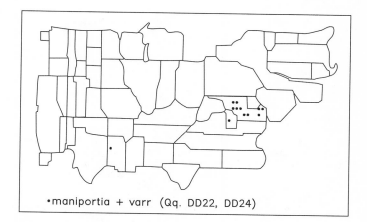

•maniportia + varr (Qq. DD22, DD24)

Manitoba maple n Cf *DCan*
=box elder.

1950 *WELS (Trees that are found in your neighborhood and . . other names used for them . . Box elder)* 1 Inf, **ceWI,** Manitoba maple. **1950** Peattie *Nat. Hist. Trees* 472, *Box Elder.* . . *Other Names* . . Manitoba Maple. **1960** Vines *Trees SW* 677, *Acer negundo.* . . Vernacular names are Maple-ash . . and Manitoba Maple. **1967–68** *DARE* (Qu. T13) Infs **MN29, NY22,** Manitoba maple. **1979** Little *Checklist U.S. Trees* 41, *Acer negundo.* . . *Other common names* . . boxelder maple, Manitoba maple.

manitou darter n
A **log perch** (here: *Percina caprodes*).

1903 NY State Museum & Sci. Serv. *Bulletin* 60.506, *Manitou Darter.* . . Lakes of northern Indiana, Michigan, Wisconsin and northward to Lake Superior; the common form in the Great lakes. . . Evermann and Bean obtained the Manitou darter in the Racket river [NY], . . and in the St. Lawrence. **1943** Eddy–Surber *N. Fishes* 198, *Northern Logperch* (Zebra Fish, Manitou Darter). . . When fried . . [a] desirable . . food fish. **1983** Becker *Fishes WI* 907, *Logperch.* . . Other common names . . Manitou darter.

manitowoc n [*Manitowoc* WI]
In marble play: see quot.

1950 *WELS (Different kinds of marble games)* 1 Inf, **ceWI,** Manitowoc—also called big ring. Marbles are placed in the center of a ring; players try to knock them out. If alley stayed in, you had to pay to get it out.

man jack n [*OED jack* sb.[1] 2.c 1840 →] Cf **jack** n[1] **1**

An individual man—usu in phr *every man jack.*

1935 Sandoz *Jules* 159 **wNE** (as of 1880–1930), If anybody ever gets the drop on him there'll be one man jack deader'n a doughnut. **1940** (1942) Clark *Ox-Bow* 124 **NV** (as of 1885), You'll pay for it, you and every damned man-jack of your gang. **1949** Guthrie *Way West* 112, Tadlock had appointed other riders, until nearly every last manjack was gone. **1962** Fox *Southern Fried* 41 **SC**, Every man jack one of us is guilty—and I mean we know it.

manker See **calamanco**

man-killer n

An implement that is exhausting to use; see quots.

1876 VT *State Bd. Ag. Rept. for 1875–76* 3.614, Improvements in farm machinery are no more conspicuous than in *the horse rake*. Any man who ever held the old Kimball Rake, usually called the "man killer," or "scratch rake," will admit the truth of the foregoing remark. **1967** *DARE* FW Addit **CO3**, Man-killer, meaning a scythe. "Let me borrow your man-killer."

manna grass n

Std: a grass of the genus *Glyceria*. Also called **meadow grass 2d, sugar grass.** For other names of var spp see **floating meadow-grass, fowl manna grass, fowl meadow grass, rattlesnake grass, reed manna grass, reed meadow grass, sweet grass**

mannanose See **maninose**

manner n

1 in phr *make one's manners:* To perform conventional rituals of courtesy or respect. **formerly widespread, now chiefly Sth**

1824 Cooper *Pilot* 239, The ship is to be so cluttered with she-cattle [=women], that a man will be obligated to spend half his time in making his manners! **1849** *Knickerbocker* 34.276 **MA**, He never noticed us, except to reprove us when we failed to 'make our manners to him.' **1857** Goodrich *Recollections* 1.127 **CT**, All children were regularly taught at school to "make their manners" to strangers; the boys to bow and the girls to courtesy. **1859** (1968) Bartlett *Americanisms* 261, *To make one's manners.* To make a bow or salute, on meeting a friend or stranger. The term is applied only to children. Formerly, in New England, the custom was universal among juveniles. **1922** Gonzales *Black Border* 209 **sSC, GA coasts** [Gullah], Git up, gal, ent you hab sense 'nuf fuh mek yo' mannus. **1929** *AmSp* 5.121 **ME**, Elders would say: . . "Keep a civil tongue in your head," "mind (or make) your manners." **1939** Griswold *Sea Is. Lady* 131 **csSC** (as of 1865) [Gullah], You blin', 'oman?—make you' mannuh! **1942** (1971) Campbell *Cloud-Walking* 45 **seKY**, He just give the blackberries to them and made his manners and went off down the mountain towards his homeplace. **1962** Faulkner *Reivers* 77 **MS**, Then Ned went off with Ephum and I made my manners to Miss Ballenbaugh. **1968** *DARE* File **SC**, Make your manners [means] to perform the necessary courtesies. It is an old expression used by a mother or grandmother to admonish a child. **1991** King *Needful Things* 416 **ME**, Ole Harry Samuels said you ast if I'd stop by this mornin if I had a chance. . . I'm just makin my manners to you, sir.

2 in phrr *in a manner* (or rarely *in the manner of*): Nearly, almost; to some extent. [*OED manner* sb.[1] 10 c1420 →] **chiefly S Midl**

1822 (1972) Deane *New Engl. Farmer* 134, But let farmers beware of building their log fences of bass wood . . ; for as they will be soon rotten, the labour of building them is in a manner lost. **1834** Smith *Letters Jack Downing* 151 **ME**, The President's got in a manner cooled down again. **1894** in 1941 Warfel–Orians *Local-Color Stories* 738 **sAR**, I don't see it . . less'n me a puttin' 'im out'n de house in a manner aggervated 'im ter it. **1913** Kephart *Highlanders* 225 **sAppalachians**, Ike Morgan Pringle's a-been horse-throwed down the clift, and he's in a manner stone dead. **1952** Brown *NC Folkl.* 1.563, *Manner, in a.* . . Almost, after a fashion, not quite satisfactorily. **1953** Randolph–Wilson *Down in Holler* 170 **Ozarks**, The phrase *in a manner.* . . seems to mean nearly, virtually, or almost. "Them biscuit is in a manner done," a housewife said, "an' we'll have 'em on the table in a minute." **c1960** *Wilson Coll.* **csKY**, *In a manner.* . . Nearly, almost. "I'm in a manner through stripping tobacco." **1974** Fink *Mountain Speech* 13 **wNC, eTN**, *In a manner* . . nearly. "He's in a manner blind." **1982** *Barrick Coll.* **csPA**, *Manner*—to an extent or degree. "This table is in the manner of new."

3 In ref to the custom of leaving a small amount of food at meals as a gesture of politeness:

a pl; also *manners piece;* for addit varr see quot 1965–70: Such a piece of food. [*EDD to leave some manners in the dish, manners-bit* (at *manner* sb.[1] 1.(6), 2)] **chiefly S Midl, Gulf States, TX** See Map Cf **old maid 4**

1950 *WELS (Words for the last piece of something on a plate)* 2 Infs, **WI**, Manners piece. **1965–70** *DARE* (Qu. H71, . . *The last piece of food left on a plate*) 31 Infs, **chiefly Sth, S Midl**, Manners piece; 23 Infs, **chiefly S Midl, Gulf States, TX**, Manners; **CA101, MI95**, Manners and all (is gone); **GA24, 46**, Don't eat (the) manners; **KY62**, You took manners; **LA40**, I'll take manners; **MS1**, When you leave it, you are saving manners; **MS72**, Manners is left; **SC7**, Manner piece; **AL34**, They ate ill manners; **DC7**, Good manners; **GA79**, Table manners. **1980** *Hand Coll.* **LA**, You "take the manners" if you take the last food from a dish.

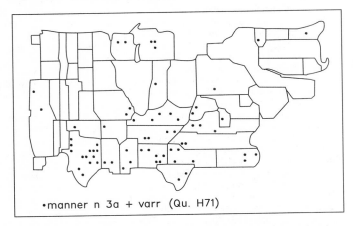

•*manner* n 3a + varr (Qu. H71)

b personified, in phrr *leave something for Miss* (or *Mr.*) *Manners* and varr: To leave such a piece of food.

[**1859** Elwyn *Glossary* 73 **NEng**, "Leave some for manners," was always enjoined on us, as school-boys, and was always practiced by all, old and young.] **1968** *DARE* (Qu. H71, . . *The last piece of food left on a plate*) Inf **CT8**, You "leave something for Miss Manners"; **CT16**, Left for Mr. Manners; **NY48**, Leave it for Mr. Manners; **WI62**, Leave a piece for Little Miss Manners; [**CA136**, One left for Manners, and I'm him; **IL103, KY15, NY237**, (That's *or* piece) left for manners; **KY41, MS8**, Leave that (*or* something on your plate) for manners].

manner v

To teach (someone) manners.

1968 *DARE* FW Addit **ID**, The only thing I don't like about working is I don't have time to manner the kids like I should.

mannerable adj [*OED* c1460 →; "*Obs.* exc. *dial.*"] **Sth, S Midl** Cf **mannersable, mannersly, mannersome**

Polite, well-mannered.

1937 in 1972 *Amer. Slave* 2.1.214 **SC**, I likes mannerable white fokes, mysef, and den, I likes mannerable niggers fer as dat goes. **1943** *Sat. Eve. Post* 16 Oct 10 **sMS**, Course, she's too mannerable to go around bragging about it. *Ibid* 101, It wouldn't have been mannerable to grin at a colonel. **1953** [see **mannersome**]. **1968** Haun *Hawk's Done Gone* 15 **eTN**, He was always mannerable toward Tiny. **1971** Dwyer *Dict. for Yankees* 29 **Sth, S Midl**, I like him 'cause he's so mannerable.

mannersable adj Pronc-spp *mannusubble, manussable* **esp SC** Cf *DJE*

=**mannerable.**

1922 Gonzales *Black Border* 261 **sSC, GA coasts** [Gullah], De hen aig' is too mannusubble fuh hatch'out befo' de odduh'res' aig' [=the rest of the eggs]. **1928** Peterkin *Scarlet Sister Mary* 166 **SC** [Gullah], An' whilst we are a-stayin we may as well try to act mannersable. *Ibid* 244, Seraphine is a good manners-able gal. **1950** *PADS* 14.45 **ceSC**, *Manussable* ['mænəsəbl]. . . Courteous, polite, having good manners.

manners dish n Cf **manner** n **3**

1896 Bergen *Current Superstitions* 144 **nOH**, "Manners dish" is the dish put on for show, and not expected to be eaten.

mannersly adj Cf **mannersable**, *DJE*
=**mannerable.**

    1929 Sale *Tree Named John* 28 **MS** [Black], He *is a* mighty good chile. . . Ah nevuh *is* seed a mo' *mannersly* chile in m'life.

mannersome adj [*OED* 1876 →; "*dial.*"] Cf **-some**
=**mannerable.**

    1895 *Outing* 26.65 **nMI**, Canady's a slick-spoken feller 'bout huntin', 'an a mannersome feller, too. **1953** Randolph–Wilson *Down in Holler* 264 **Ozarks**, *Mannerable*. . . Polite, having good manners. "He's a mannerable old feller, anyhow." *Mannersome* is sometimes used with the same meaning.

manners piece See **manner** n 3a

manninose See **maninose**

mannish adj **chiefly Sth, S Midl** *esp freq among Black speakers* Cf *DJE*
Bold, forward, "uppity"—said of both sexes and of children.

    1930 Stoney–Shelby *Black Genesis* 133 **seSC**, Out dere in de warm sunshine, 'sputin' wid Br' Rabbit, he been mighty mannish, but in dese cool woods all to heself, he aint near so sure o' t'ings. **1934** Hurston *Jonah's Gourd Vine* 81 **AL** [Black], He [=the speaker's adolescent stepson] must smell hisself—done got so mannish. Some fast 'omanish gal is grinin' in his face and he tries tuh git sides hisself. **1939** Harris *Purslane* 71 **cNC**, She made Mr. Smith a good wife, yes. And now already he's gettin' frisky and real mannish at church Sundays. **1969–70** *DARE* (Qu. GG19a, *When you can see from the way a person acts that he's feeling important or independent: "He surely is _____ these days."*) Inf **GA**84, Acting mannish; (Qu. II36b, *Of somebody who talks back or gives rude answers . . "She certainly is _____!"*) Inf **NC**88, Mannish; (Qu. NN12a, *Things that people say to put a child off when he asks too many questions: "What's that for?"*) Inf **TN**54, You're being too mannish, son. [2 of 3 Infs Black] **1970** Bullins *Electronic* 162 [Black], Don't you talk to me like that, frownin' up your face an' rollin' yo' eyes. You gittin' too mannish 'round here. **1972** Claerbaut *Black Jargon* 72, *Mannish* . . a black child's way of acting which is deemed rebellious and disrespectful by his mother: *Stop acting mannish!*

mannoe(s), mannose See **maninose**

mannusubble See **mannersable**

mannynose, mano See **maninose**

man o' day intj
    1969 *DARE* FW Addit **csPA**, Man o' [ə] day—a very common exclamation.

man-of-earth See **man-of-the-earth** 1

man-of-nose See **maninose**

man-of-the-earth n [From the large root]
    1 also *man-of-earth, wild man-of-the-earth*: A **morning glory** 1 (here: *Ipomaea pandurata*). Also called **bigroot** 3, **bindweed** 5, **hog potato** 2, **Indian potato** 1, **Indian purge**, **man-in-the-ground** 1, **manroot** 2, **man-vine**, **mechameck**, **peavine**, **scammony**, **sinkfield**, **trumpet vine**, **wild jalap**, **wild morning glory**, **wild potato**, **wild potato vine**, **wild sweet potato**, **wild rhubarb**

    1833 Eaton *Botany* 105, [*Ipomaea*] *panduratus* [sic] . . man of the earth. . . A mild cathartic, and resembles rhubarb in its effects. **1891** *AN&Q* 7.118, Singular Plant-names.—I should like to gather a few of these, and beg leave to open the list with the following: Man of the Earth, Good King Henry; Life of Man; Lad's Love; Seven years' Love; Robin-run-the-edge. **1924** *Torreya* 24.39 **NJ**, I wonder how many botanists have . . tried to dig out a plant of the Man-of-the-Earth or Wild Potato Vine, *Ipomoea pandurata*. *Ibid* 40, Like the Sweet Potato, the roots of the Man-of-the-Earth are brittle and slightly milky when fresh. **1951** Voss–Eifert *IL Wild Flowers* 208, The flowers of man-of-the-earth vine are luminous white trumpets with a purple throat which open broadly in the summer sunshine. **1964** Batson *Wild Flowers SC* 96, *Wild Man-of-the-Earth*. . . Large, deep, tuber-like root. . . Connecticut to Florida. **1972** Brown *Wildflowers LA* 147, *Man of Earth*. . . A host for the sweet potato weevil. **1976** Bruce *How to Grow Wildflowers* 288, Man-of-the-Earth . . is a true morning glory, related closely to those of our gardens and to the sweet potato of commerce, another species with

a tuberous root. Botanically *Ipomoea pandurata*, the species is a trailing plant.

    2 =**bush morning glory. West**
    1871 U.S. Dept. Ag. *Rept. of Secy. for 1870* 407, *Wild potato vine, (Ipomoea leptophylla.)* This showy plant of the dry deserts of the West is commonly called man root, or man of the earth. . . The Cheyennes, Arapahoes and Kiowas roast it for food when pressed by hunger. **1897** *Jrl. Amer. Folkl.* 10.51 **CA**, *Ipomaea leptophylla*, . . man of the earth. **1940** Clute *Amer. Plant Names* 92, *I[pomaea] pandurata*. Man-of-the-Earth. *Ibid* 261, *Ipomoea leptophylla*. Man-of-the-earth. **1970** Kirk *Wild Edible Plants W. U.S.* 288, *Ipomaea leptophylla*. . Man-of-the-Earth. . . The flavor of the edible root of this plant apparently varies widely according to locality, growing conditions, and age. . . The plant is a perennial with deeply buried (and consequently hard to dig), huge roots, sometimes weighing 25 pounds or more.

man-of-war See **man-o'-war**

man-on-a-horse n Also *man-on-horseback*
A **mushroom** (here: *Tricholoma flavovirens*).

    1980 Smith–Weber *Mushroom Hunter* 155, Tricholoma flavovirens (Man-on-a-Horse). . . a common and widely distributed species in the conifer forests of North America. **1985** Weber–Smith *Field Guide S. Mushrooms* 189, *Tricholoma flavovirens* . . (Man-on-a-Horse). . . Another name formerly used for the species is *T. equestre*. That specific epithet means belonging to a horseman; by extension it was interpreted to mean of distinguished appearance and is the apparent source of the common name. **1987** McKnight–McKnight *Mushrooms* 186, Cavalier (Man-on-horseback)—*Tricholoma flavovirens*.

manos(e) See **maninose**

man-o'-war n Also *man-of-war* [See quot 1898]
=**parasitic jaeger.**

    1898 (1900) Davie *Nests N. Amer. Birds* 26, The Parasitic Jaeger, like the others of this family, is eminently rapacious, and it is known as the "Man-of-War", from its habits of pursuing and robbing the terns and smaller gulls. **1917** (1923) *Birds Amer.* 1.35, Parasitic Jaeger. . . *Other Names*. . . Man-o'-war. **1946** Hausman *Eastern Birds* 301, *Stercorarius parasiticus*. . . Man-of-war. . . This species seems to victimize the Kittiwake Gull on the fishing banks more often than the others. It is the commonest jaeger off our coast.

man-o'-war bird n Also *man-o'-war*
Std: a frigate bird (here: *Fregata magnificens*). Also called **frigate hawk**, **~ pelican, hurricane bird, pirate ~, poison ~, Spanish man-of-war, storm bird**

man-person n Also *man-body* [Redund; cf Intro "Language Changes" I.4] **chiefly S Midl** Cf **man critter**
A male human being; a man.

    1867 Harris *Sut Lovingood Yarns* 87 **TN**, I'll jis' gin yu leave tu go tu the devil ha'f hamon, ef I didn't make fewer tracks tu the mile . . than wer ever made by eny human man body. **1887** *Scribner's Mag.* 2.476 **AR**, Ye got good sense fur a man person, Jeff. **1916** *DN* 4.294 **sAppalachians**, Among the noun-compounds are: . . man-person. **1917** *DN* 4.414 **wNC**. **1924** Raine *Land of Saddle-Bags* 105 **sAppalachians**, [The] desire for exactness has given such expressions as . . ham-meat . . cow-brute, man-person. **1930** *VA Qrly. Rev.* 6.248 **S Midl**, There are the analogous compounds (. . usually overplayed by fiction writers): . . man-person, [etc]. **1937** (1963) Hyatt *Kiverlid* 22 **KY**, Law, they's a-plenty a man-person can allus find to do. **1937** Hall Coll. **wNC, eTN**, Man-person—a man. **1942** (1971) Campbell *Cloud-Walking* 37 **seKY**, Hatty giggled a heap to have a man person plaiting up their hair. **1952** Brown *NC Folkl.* 1.563, *Man-person*. . . A human being; a man. "Yes, these are right good shoes; maybe some man-person could fix them up like new."—General. Illiterate. **1953** Randolph–Wilson *Down in Holler* 54 **Ozarks**, "An' it ain't right nohow," he added, "for a man-person to be thar when a woman's a-havin' a baby." **1986** Pederson *LAGS Concordance*, 1 inf, **nwFL**, The next man person.

man-power v esp **sAppalachians**
To move (something) by human effort.

    1913 Kephart *Highlanders* 32 **sAppalachians**, Often it meant to chop a fallen tree out of the road, and then, with handspikes, "man-power the log outen the way." **1952** Brown *NC Folkl.* 1.563 **wNC**, *Man-power*. . . To employ the force of man. "I don't know whether I can man-power this boat against that current or not." **1976** Garber *Mountain-ese* 56 **sAppalachians,** We'll have to manpower the train back onto the tracks.

manroot n

1 =**bush morning-glory.** [See quot 1949] **West**
1848 Emory *Notes Reconnoissance* 13 **cKS,** The principal growth is the buffalo grass, . . and very rarely that wonderful plant, the Ipomea [sic] leptophylla, called by the hunter man root. **1900** Lyons *Plant Names* 203, *I[pomaea] leptophylla.* . . Nebraska to New Mexico and Texas. . . Man-root. **1949** Moldenke *Amer. Wild Flowers* 268, *Bush morning-glory* . . grows from an enormous, deep-seated, fleshy root. . . Because of this root the plant is often called . . *manroot.*

2 =**man-of-the-earth 1.**
1876 Hobbs *Bot. Hdbk.* 68, Man root, Convolvulus panduratus. **1895** U.S. Dept. Ag. *Farmers' Bulletin* 28.26, Manroot . . Ipomaea pandurata. Delaware to Missouri. **1951** Voss–Eifert *IL Wild Flowers* 208, Man-root. . . The root is huge and deeply hidden in the earth, but there is so much food in it that the effort in digging it out is worthwhile. **1968** Radford et al. *Manual Flora Carolinas* 868, *Man-root.* . . Often dry, open roadsides, fence rows, old fields and waste places. **1974** Morton *Folk Remedies* 83 **SC,** *Man-root.* . . *South Carolina* (Current use): Infusion of the vine taken for chills and fever.

3 =**bigroot 1.** [See quots 1901, 1902]
1901 Jepson *Flora CA* 320, Roots, sometimes as large as and not unlike the shape of a man's body. . . *E[chinocystis] fabacea* . . Common Man Root. . . *E[chinocystis] Marah* . . Hill Man Root. **1902** U.S. Natl. Museum *Contrib. Herbarium* 7.390, *Micrampelis marah.* . . On account of its [=the root's] resemblance in size and shape to a man's head, it is not infrequently called "man root." **1966** *DARE* FW Addit **WA**10, A Washington variety of wild cucumber is manroot, with root three feet long and perhaps four inches in diameter. **1973** Hitchcock–Cronquist *Flora Pacific NW* 457, *Marah.* . . Bigroot, Manroot. . . much enlarged, woody root.

4 A coral tree (here: *Erythrina herbacea*). [See quot]
1926 *Torreya* 26.5, *Erythrina herbacea.* . . Sapelo I[slan]d, Ga. At this locality the root of the plant has a reputation as a tonic, and is called man-root, or woman-root, according to the sex of the person seeking it.

mans See **man** n B1, 2

man's breeches n
=**Dutchman's breeches 1.**
1969 *DARE* (Qu. S26c, *Wildflowers that grow in woods*) Inf **TN**33, Man's breeches.

man shark See **man catcher**

man's side n Cf **near horse,** DS K32b
1949 *AmSp* 24.111 **cnFL,** Man's side. . . The near side of a horse or wagon.

mansworn adj [Ult < OE *mánswerian; OED* a1300 →; "Obs. exc. Sc. and north. dial."]
Perjured.
1944 *PADS* 2.46 **wNC,** Man-sworn: adj. Breaking one's oath, swearing falsely.

manta n [Span "blanket, cloak"]
1 also *manto:* See quots.
1887 *Outing* 10.5 **AZ,** We had some scrambling and sliding, which cost me 200 pounds of flour, . . and one manta, or pack cover. **1929** (1978) Watt *Mule Train* 42 **eWA** (as of 1860s), Packs were protected from the weather by "mantos;" large 9 by 12 pieces of canvas which were laid over the packs in camp, or folded over the loads on the trail in heavy rains or snow storms. **1945** Atwood *Rocky Mts.* 62, A top pack, usually a tent, may be added, and then a large piece of canvas, called a manta, is used to cover and protect the entire load. **1984** Smith *SW Vocab.* 64, *Manta.* . . A piece of canvas or heavy cloth about six feet on a side used in Spanish and Mexican pack-trains for wrapping a load before placing it upon the aparejo, or pack-saddle.

2 also *manta ray:* =**devilfish 1,** usu *Manta birostris.*
[**1760** *Juan & Ulloa's Voy.* (ed. 3) I.130 *(OED),* The mantas or quilts. . . The name manta has not been improperly given to this fish . . ; for being broad and long like a quilt, it wraps its fins round a man, or any other animal, . . and immediately squeezes it to death.] **1794** Morse *Amer. Geog.* 576, The fish common to both oceans are, whales, dolphins, . . manitis, mantas, porpoises [etc.]. **1882** U.S. Natl. Museum *Bulletin* 16.52, *M[anta] birostris.* . . Sea Devil; Devil Fish; Manta. . .

North to North Carolina and San Diego. **1905** Jordan *Guide to Fishes* 1.448, The devil rays or mantas of the tropical seas, *Manta* and *Mobula* being the most specialized genera. **1933** LA Dept. of Conserv. *Fishes* 242, The Manta . . appears to be ordinarily quite harmless. It is a common thing along the Louisiana Gulf Coast to observe these great fishes slowly swimming along the sea surface. A smaller species of Manta, . . *Mobula olfersi* . . also occurs. **1955** Zim–Shoemaker *Fishes* 25, Devil rays . . are common in the Gulf Stream. The flesh is good eating and is sometimes used as food. The harmless Manta is considered a sports fish in southern waters [of the US]. **1967** *DARE* (Qu. P4, *Saltwater fish that are not good to eat*) Inf **HI**14, Manta ray.

mantel n Also *mantelpiece, mantelshelf* esp **NEast, N Cent** See Map
A wall shelf.
1941 *LANE* Map 328 *(Mantel shelf)* 1 inf, **cnCT,** *Chimney shelf,* over the fireplace; *mantel shelf,* elsewhere; 1 inf, **seMA,** *Mantel piece,* may also refer to a separate shelf bracketed to the wall, not connected with the fireplace; 1 inf, **neMA,** *Mantel piece,* a wall shelf not over the fireplace; 1 inf, **neMA,** *Mantel,* a shelf not over the fireplace; 1 inf, **seNH,** *Shelf,* over the fireplace; cf. *mantel,* at the side of the room. **1965–70** *DARE* (Qu. E6, *A small shelf hanging on the wall with small decorative articles on it*) Infs **IL**70, **IN**54, **MO**36, **MA**9, 27, **NJ**64, **OH**48, Mantel; **MA**72, Mantel—not restricted to the fireplace area; **OH**51, Mantel, [corr to] whatnot; **ME**5, Mantelpiece—not necessarily over fireplace; **ME**16, Mantelpiece; **NY**11, Mantelshelf; **IN**19, Clock mantel.

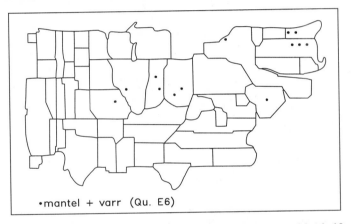

•mantel + varr (Qu. E6)

mantelboard n [Cf *OED* mantel-board 1885–87; "A wide shelf of wood . . fixed upon the mantelshelf"] esp **TX, Lower Missip Valley** See Map Cf **fireboard 1**
=**mantelshelf 1.**
1948 Davis *Word Atlas Gt. Lakes* 177 **IN,** Shelf over fireplace. . . [2 of 63 infs] mantel board. **1962** Atwood *Vocab. TX* 43 **TX, OK, AR, LA,** Shelf over the fireplace. Mantel is the most frequent word, in all areas and groups; *mantelpiece* is somewhat less common. *Mantelboard* also occurs. *Ibid* map 73, [Map shows 50 instances of *mantelboard* out of 468 total infs.] **1965–70** *DARE* (Qu. D36, . . *The shelf over the fireplace*) 16 Infs, **esp TX, Lower Missip Valley,** Mantelboard. **1966** Dakin *Dial. Vocab. Ohio R. Valley* 2.38 **sKY, sOH,** Mantel board . .

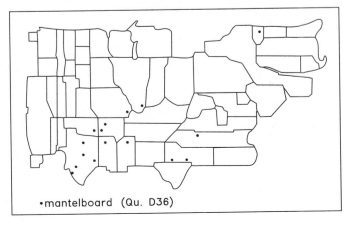

•mantelboard (Qu. D36)

appears a few times in southern Kentucky and once in Lawrence County, Ohio. **1972** *PADS* 58.13 **cwAL**, Two informants [of 27] gave South Midland *fire/mantel board* as their primary responses. **1986** Pederson *LAGS Concordance (Mantel)* 59 infs, **Gulf Region, esp Lower Missip Valley, sAL**, Mantel board(s).

mantelpiece n Also sp *mantlepiece* [*OED* 1686 →]

1 The ornamental facing surrounding a fireplace, esp the shelf over a fireplace. **chiefly Sth, S Midl, Atlantic** See Map Note: *Mantel* in this sense is used throughout the US.

1744 in 1887 Franklin *Complete Wks.* 1.504, The mantel-piece or breast of the chimney. **1807** Irving *Salmagundi* 255 **NY**, He would . . contemplate the little shepherdesses on the mantel-piece for a few minutes. **1829** in 1956 Eliason *Tarheel Talk* 283 **NC**, [Two] figures. . . sit on the mantelpiece. **1833** *Knickerbocker* 1.179, Take your feet from the mantle-piece and let me get nearer the fire; you deserve Fitz. to be laid on the shelf entirely for that vile trolloping habit. **1859** Elwyn *Glossary* 73, *Mantel-piece,* the *chimney-piece.* (Hallamshire Glossary.) This, which formerly meant the whole of the work about a chimney, seldom is applied to more than the piece of wood or marble that crosses its top. **1899** (1912) Green *VA Folk-Speech* 274, *Mantelpiece.* . . The work or wainscotting around a fireplace, including usually one shelf or more. **1949** Kurath *Word Geog.* 51, The shelf over the opening of the fireplace is known as the *mantel* or *mantel piece* in most parts of the Eastern States. **1958** *PADS* 29.13 **TN**, *Mantel.* . . The wood facing of a fireplace and the shelf above it. "We heard mantel piece but were taught it was redundant." **1961** *PADS* 36.14 **sLA**, Since informants for this survey were almost equally divided among three age groups (under 40, 40–60, and over 60), we might very briefly examine what evidence there is for the obsolescence of certain terms. . . It might be well . . to observe a list [of words] which shows at least twice as great a frequency in the oldest group as in the youngest: . . *mantelpiece.* **1965–70** *DARE* (Qu. D36, . . *The shelf over the fireplace*) 167 Infs, **chiefly Sth, S Midl, Atlantic,** Mantelpiece. **1967** LeCompte *Word Atlas* 126 **seLA**, Shelf over fireplace. . . mantelpiece [8 of 21 infs]. . . mantle [4 infs]. **1971** Bright *Word Geog. CA & NV* 143, *Mantel* 88% [of 300 infs]. . . *Mantelpiece* 15%. **1972** *PADS* 58.13 **cwAL**, *Mantel.* The terms *mantel* (20 [of 27 infs]) and *mantel piece* (5) predominate. **1973** Allen *LAUM* 1.162 **Upper MW** (as of c1950), *Mantel shelf.* . . Mailed replies provide an even distribution of a 61% return for *mantel* and of a 28% distribution for *mantelpiece.*

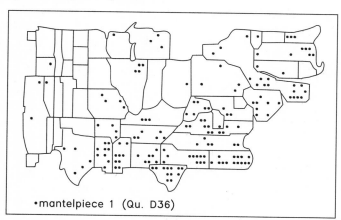

•mantelpiece 1 (Qu. D36)

2 See **mantel.**

mantelplace n Also sp *mantleplace*
=**mantelshelf 1.**

1845 (1968) Simms *Wigwam & Cabin* (1st ser) 91 **SC**, You have a very singular ornament for your mantle-place. **1872** Schele de Vere *Americanisms* 504, *Mantle-place* is the curious form which the English *mantle-piece* has assumed in some parts of the South. **1966** Dakin *Dial. Vocab. Ohio R. Valley* 2.38, The wooden or stone shelf or ledge above a fireplace. . . *Mantel place* and simple *board* are each attested once. **1986** Pederson *LAGS Concordance (Mantel)* 2 infs, **sAL**, Mantel place. [Both infs young]

mantelshelf n Also sp *mantleshelf*

1 The shelf over a fireplace.

1828 Webster *Amer. Dict.* np, *Mantle-piece, Mantle-shelf.* . . The work over a fire-place, in front of the chimney. **1880** Cable *Grandissimes* 84 **LA**, They stood beneath their lofty mantel-shelf, each with a foot on a

brazen fire-dog. **1891** (1967) Freeman *New Engl. Nun* 91, I had gilt vases as tall as that on my parlor mantel-shelf. [*DARE* Ed: This may instead belong at **2** below.] **1911** Harrison *Queed* 152 **NY**, The balled-up veil and gloves [were] on the mantel-shelf. [*DARE* Ed: This may instead belong at **2** below.] **1924** Raine *Land of Saddle-Bags* 76 **sAppalachians**, He putt the pins in the bottle and set it on the fire board (mantel-shelf). **1945** Saxon *Gumbo Ya-Ya* 294 **LA**, A new tenant discovered a yellowed love letter between the mantel-shelf and the chimney. **1965–70** *DARE* (Qu. D36, . . *The shelf over the fireplace*) 13 Infs, **chiefly Sth, S Midl,** Mantelshelf. **1986** Pederson *LAGS Concordance (Mantel)* 44 infs, **Gulf Region,** Mantelshelf.

2 See **mantel.**

mantel stone n Also sp *mantle stone*
1946 McDavid *Coll.* **neGA**, Mantle stone = mantelpiece.

manteltree n Also *manteltree piece* Also sp *mantletree, manteltry* [*OED* 1482 →] **esp NEng** *old-fash*
The beam or shelf over a fireplace.

1688 (1892) Hammond *Diary* 148 **MA**, Ye Lightning came downe ye Chimney, brake out som bricks just above ye manteltree. **1704** (1825) Knight *Jrls.* 53 **MA**, [In New York City] The fire places have no Jambs (as ours have) But the Backs run flush with the walls, and the Hearth is of Tyles . . , and the peice over where the mantle tree should be is made as ours with Joyners work. **1806** (1970) Webster *Compendious Dict.* 184, Mantle or Mantletree . . the part of a chimney in front lying on the jambs. [*DARE* Ed: The word *mantletree* does not appear in Webster's English model.] **1833** in 1834 Davis *Letters Downing* 153 **NY**, We cock'd our feet on the mantle-tree, and in less than five minutes you couldn't see no more on us than our toes. **a1861** (1880) Eastman *Poems* 3 **VT**, And the old brass clock on the mantletree / Had plodded along to almost three. **1887** (1895) Robinson *Uncle Lisha* 84 **wVT**, Set it [=a gun] in the corner, er heng it up on the hooks over the mantel-tree there. **1890** Holley *Samantha among Brethren* vii **NY**, Josiah . . see me walk up and take my ink stand off of the manteltry piece. **1916** Macy-Hussey *Nantucket Scrap Basket* 97 **seMA**, He would sit with his feet on the mantel-tree (mantelpiece) and spit, and spit, and spit. Oh! He was so sociable. **1941** *LANE* Map 328 (*Mantel shelf*) 2 infs, **seCT, sVT,** Manteltree [one inf indicated that the term was old-fashioned]; 2 infs, **RI, seMA,** Manteltree piece [one inf indicated that the term was old-fashioned]. **1949** *AmSp* 24.111 **nwSC**, *Mantel tree.* . . Mantel. **1986** Pederson *LAGS Concordance (Mantel)* 1 inf, **cnGA**, Manteltree—heard this. [Inf old]

mantis shrimp n [See quot 1890]

1 A crustacean of the family *Squillidae,* esp *Squilla empusa,* which is also called **sea mantis, shrimp snapper.** [*OED* 1871 →]

1884 U.S. Natl. Museum *Bulletin* 27.121, There are three common species of Mantis Shrimp (*Squilla empusa* and *dubia,* and *Coronis glabriusculus*) living upon the eastern coast of the United States, one or more of which are occasionally used as bait in the Southern States. **1884** Goode *Fisheries U.S.* 1.823, The Mantis Shrimps—Squillidae. The Mantis Shrimp . . Squilla empusa . . is often thrown on the beach by the waves, and probably it usually burrows in the mud below low-water mark. **1890** *Century Dict.* 3618, *Mantis-shrimp.* . . *1.* A stomatopodous crustacean of the family *Squillidae,* . . so called from the resemblance to the insect called *mantis.* . . *2.* A laemodipodous crustacean of the family *Caprellidae,* . . so called for the same reason as above. **1965** McClane *McClane's Std. Fishing Encycl.* 512, Mantis shrimp. . . can be caught with a baited wire snare by poking it into the burrow. **1981** Meinkoth *Audubon Field Guide Seashore* 598, *Gonodactylus oerstedii.* . . This small mantis shrimp is the only American species whose claw is not armed with a row of sharp spines. *Ibid* 600, *Common Mantis Shrimp (Squilla empusa).* . . Range: Cape Cod to Florida and Texas.

2 =**skeleton shrimp.**
1890 [see **1** above].

mantlepiece See **mantelpiece**

mantleplace See **mantelplace**

mantleshelf See **mantelshelf**

mantle stone See **mantel stone**

mantletree See **manteltree**

manto See **manta 1**

man train See **man trip b**

man trip n

In mining:

a A trip made by a mine train or elevator car to carry workers to or from the work area.

1929 *AmSp* 4.372 swPA, *Man-trip*—A trip on which the men themselves are hauled near to work in the morning and away in the afternoon. **1947** Natl. Coal Assoc. *Gloss.* 14, *Man trip*—A trip made by mine cars and locomotives to take men rather than coal, to and from the working places. **1968** Adams *Western Words* 190, *Man trip*—In mining, a trip of the lift up the shaft with a load of men. **1973** *PADS* 59.42, *Man trip* . . a complete circuit of the [coal] *mine* made by a locomotive and cars specifically designated to carry men to and from the working *places* in the *mine*, usually at the beginning and end of a shift.

b also *man train*, ~ *cage*, ~ *car*: The train or car itself.

1890 *Century Dict.* 3604, *Man-car.* . . A kind of car used for transporting miners up and down the steeply inclined shafts of some mines on Lake Superior. **1941** *Sun* (Baltimore MD) 30 Oct 7/4 *(Hench Coll.)*, Grundy, Va., . . Approximately 1,100 miners at the three mines . . failed to report to work today after a dispute over a "mantrip." . . Miners . . were hauled into the operations on "man trips," which are strings of empty coal cars. **1960** Climax Molybdenum Co. *Manual* 48 [Mine terms], *Man-train, mantrip, man-cars*—Specially built cars to carry men to and from mine workings. **1967–69** *DARE* Tape **CA**128, [FW:] Why do you call 'em a hauling shaft? . . [Inf:] Well, that's where your skips [=ore buckets] go up and down, your haulage. You lower the men down, see, the men ride with the skips too. . . [FW:] Do they have little wire cages? [Inf:] Well, some of 'em do, yeah, a little cage put around it. . . Course there's places that have regular man cages . . and there's bigger [gold] mines that have one side that's all they use is for men, see, and maybe timber; **WY**4, It blew the man trip clear out over 'bout a quarter of a mile outside the [coal] *mine*, over in a field—this string of cars, a man trip, you know. **1968** Adams *Western Words* 189, *Man cage*—A miner's name for a cage used to raise and lower men in a mine shaft. **1973** *PADS* 59.42 [Bituminous coal mining vocab], *Man trip* . . a locomotive and cars specifically designated to carry workers to and from the working *places* in the *mine*.

manuahi n, adj Also *manawahi, manuwahi* [Haw; see quot 1938 at **1** below] **HI**

1 See quot 1938.

1938 Reinecke *Hawaiian Loanwords* 24, *Manuahi* . . sometimes corrupted to *manawáhi*. . . [Reinecke: Said to be derived from the name of a clerk, Manuahi, who used to give extra measure.] . . A gift; a lagniappe. . . Free; gratis. **1954–60** Hance et al. *Hawaiian Sugar* 5, *Manuahi*. . . Free, gratis. **1967** *DARE* (Qu. U15, *When you're buying something, if the seller puts in a little extra to make you feel that you're getting a good bargain*) Inf **HI**1, Manuahi [ˌmɑnuˈɑhi]—Hawaiian word I grew up with; **HI**4, [ˌmɑnuˈwɑhi]—widely used. **1972** Carr *Da Kine Talk* 115 **HI**, *Manuahi* (or *manuwahi*) means 'gratis, free of charge'. **1984** Sunset *HI Guide* 85, *Manuahi*—free, gratis.

2 By ext: see quots.

1938 Reinecke *Hawaiian Loanwords* 24, *Manuahi*. . . A concubine. (Also *wahine manuahi*; applied also to common law wife; prostitute; loose woman.) F[requent]. **1967** Reinecke-Tsuzaki *Hawaiian Loanwords* 105, *Manuahi, manuwahi*. . . Illegitimate child. **1972** Carr *Da Kine Talk* 115 **HI**, *Manuahi* (or *manuwahi*) means . . also 'adulterous'.

manufac See **manifac**

man-under-the-ground See **man-in-the-ground 1**

manure n Usu |məˈn(j)ʊə(r)|; for varr see quots Pronc-sp *manyo* Std sense, var forms.

1899 Chesnutt *Conjure Woman* 29 csNC [Black], Fix up a mixtry er lime en ashes en manyo, en po' it 'roun' de roots er de grapevimes. **1966–68** *DARE* (Qu. L17) Inf **DC**8, [məˈnjə]; **GA**68, [məˈnjɔwə]; **SC**26, Black [məˈnjo]. **1981** Pederson *LAGS Basic Materials*, 1 inf, ceMS, [məˈnjɚ]; 1 inf, seLA, [mĩˈnjɔ̝]; 1 inf, csLA, [ˈmĩ̢ˈnjə]; [10 infs gave proncs of the type [məˈn(j)ʊə(r)]].

manure beetle n

A **dung beetle**.

1967 *DARE* (Qu. R30, . . *Kinds of beetles;* not asked in early QRs) Inf **ID**5, Manure beetle.

manure fly n

1 A gnat *(Sciara coprophila)*.

1911 *Century Dict. Suppl., Mushroom gnat.* . . *Sciara coprophila* has

also been reported as injurious to mushrooms. It lives chiefly in manure, whence it is also called *manure-fly*.

2 Perh a dung fly *(Scatophaga stercoraria)*.

1966–68 *DARE* (Qu. R12, . . *Other kinds of flies*) Infs **ME**12, **NY**109, Manure fly.

manure worm n

An **earthworm** such as a **red worm** or a **red wiggler**.

1941 *Nature Mag.* 34.137, Redworm . . may be a common, easily-recognized species known also as manure worm. I have personal acquaintance with the use of both of these appellations for this smelly species in Indiana. **1968–69** *DARE* (Qu. P5, . . *The common worm used as bait*) Infs **IL**81, **NY**151, **WI**50, Manure worm; **PA**168, Manure worm—striped, 2 to 3 inches; (Qu. P6, . . *Kinds of worms . . used for bait*) Infs **IN**69, **NY**142, **PA**168, Manure worm. **1982** Sternberg *Fishing* 56, The manure worm is red with whitish bands along its 3- to 4-inch body. It is raised by bait suppliers in the South and sold as the *red worm*. Another commercially grown type is the *red wiggler*, which grows to about 2 inches in length. **1991** *DARE* File csWI (as of c1920), Manure worms are those little bright red ones we found around and in manure piles—they wiggled like the dickens. Some people used them for bait, but we didn't—the perch didn't like 'em. *Ibid* csWI, Manure worms are red with whitish stripes around them. You find them in the dirt after the manure has aged for a while, and use them for fishing bait.

manussable See **mannersable**

manuwahi See **manuahi**

man-vine n

=**man-of-the-earth 1**.

1976 Bruce *How to Grow Wildflowers* 288, Man-of-the-Earth, Man-vine, or Wild-potato Vine is a true morning glory, related closely to those of our gardens and to the sweet potato of commerce, another species with a tuberous root. Botanically *Ipomoea pandurata,* the species is a trailing plant.

manway n Cf **man trip**

In mining: see quots.

1929 *AmSp* 4.372 swPA, *Manway*—Men's entrance to the mine, except when they go on the man-trip which goes along the dilly road. **1938** (1964) Korson *Minstrels Mine Patch* 316 nePA, *Manway:* A passage in or into a mine used as a footpath for workers. **1939** (1973) FWP *Guide MT* 146, The miner goes down a gallery to the main drift (lateral tunnel) on the vein, and then to his stope (work chamber), which usually has two or more floors 10 feet apart, reached by ladders up a manway. **1950** *Western Folkl.* 9.39, [Footnote:] A "manway" is a passageway, usually by ladder, up into a raise. **1960** Climax Molybdenum Co. *Manual* 48 **CO**, *Manway*—Any opening for the express purpose of allowing men to pass to and from any area. **1966–69** *DARE* Tape **CA**128, They have what they call a manway with a ladder . . so's they can get up and down and bring their timber up; **SD**4A, The majority of 'em were used for manways.

manyberry n Cf **minny-berry**

A **hackberry** (here: *Celtis occidentalis*).

1859 (1880) Darlington *Amer. Weeds* 294, *Western Celtis.* Nettle-tree. Sugar-berry. Hack-berry. Many-berry. . . *Drupe* edible, the pulpy coat thin, sweetish. **1911** *Century Dict.* 3622, *Manyberry.* . . Same as *hackberry*.

manyfac(k) See **manifac**

manynose See **maninose**

manzana apple n [Redund; Span *manzana* apple] **FL**

The manchineel *(Hippomane mancinella)*.

1967 Will *Dredgeman* 70 **Everglades FL**, This area also has its poisonous trees, one of which is the manchineel, called by the natives here manzana apple. . . This tree struck me as resembling a rubber tree, but with drooping branches. Its fruit is the size of a crab apple and it has an apple odor.

manzanilla n [Span dimin of *manzana* apple]

1 =**pineapple weed.**

1915 (1926) Armstrong-Thornber *Western Wild Flowers* 562, *Matricaria matricarioides* is another little weed, common along roadsides, . . which has a strong pleasant fruity smell when crushed, giving it the name [sic] of Pineapple-weed and Manzanilla.

2 A waxmallow (here: *Malvaviscus arboreus* var *drummondii*).

1931 U.S. Dept. Ag. *Misc. Pub.* 101.114 **wTX,** In the same region occurs Drummond waxmallow *(Malvaviscus drummondii),* sometimes known as . . manzanilla, a good-sized bush having edible fruits, which is probably browsed to some extent by sheep and goats. **1960** Vines *Trees SW* 742, *Drummond Wax-mallow. . .* Vernacular names are Texas Mallow, . . Manzanilla, and Wild Turk's Cap.

manzanilla coyote n
=**chinchweed.**

1896 *Jrl. Amer. Folkl.* 9.192, *Pectis papposa,* . . manzanilla coyote, Cal. Desert. [Footnote: So called by the Mexicans.]

manzanillo n
=**dog fennel 1.**

1906 (1918) Parsons *Wild Flowers CA* 16, *Anthemis Cotula. . .* The Spanish-Californians know it as "manzanillo," and use it, dried and powdered, as a remedy for colic.

manzanita n [Span dimin of *manzana* apple] **West**

1 also *manzanito:* =**bearberry 2** or its fruit. Note: Many of the numerous spp of *Arctostaphylos* are confined to California. For other names of var spp see **Indian manzanita, pinemat ~**

1846 (1848) Bryant *What I Saw in CA* 236, We have met . . with a reddish berry called by the Californians, *manzanita,* (little apple.) The berry is produced by small trees which stand in clumps, about ten or twelve feet in height, shedding their bark annually, leaving a smooth red surface. The flavor of the fruit is an agreeable acid, something like that of our apple. **1872** *Overland Mth.* 9.333 **CA,** She had reached a clump of *manzanita*-bushes, growing on the edge of a ravine. **1887** (1888) Harte *Phyllis* 202 **CA,** A bent manzanito-bush . . flew back against his breast. **1903** (1950) Austin *Land of Little Rain* 68 **CA,** Here begins the manzanita, adjusting its tortuous stiff stems to the sharp waste of boulders, its pale olive leaves twisting edgewise to the sleek, ruddy, chestnut stems. **1910** Hart *Vigilante Girl* 141 **nCA,** With these he would, ever and anon, take a pot-shot at a chipmunk, a squirrel, or a jack-rabbit, scared out of the roadside manzanita. **1918** Mulford *Man from Bar-20* 220, He pushed through matted thickets of oak brush and manzanito. **1932** Bentley *Spanish Terms* 162, *Manzanita. . .* A shrub *(Arctostaphylos,* various species . .) common to the mountains of the border region and California. . . In popular parlance the smaller species are called *manzanita* bushes and the larger species *manzanita* trees. The fruits are known as *manzanita* berries and are edible. **1967–70** *DARE* (Qu. I44, *What kinds of berries grow wild around here?)* Infs **CA**77, 136, Manzanita berry; (Qu. S26a, . . *Wildflowers. . . Roadside flowers)* Inf **CA**4, Manzanita; (Qu. S26d, *Wildflowers that grow in meadows;* not asked in early QRs) Inf **CA**144, Manzanita; (Qu. S26e, *Other wildflowers not yet mentioned;* not asked in early QRs) Inf **CA**117, Manzanita; **CA**87, Pink manzanita; **CA**140, White-leaved manzanita; (Qu. T5, . . *Kinds of evergreens, other than pine)* Infs **CA**20, 161, 204, 208, Manzanita; **CA**136, Manzanita bush; (Qu. T16, . . *Kinds of trees . . 'special')* Infs **CA**20, 24, 87, 97, Manzanita. **1968–70** *DARE* Tape **CA**97, The kind of wood we used around here for the fireplace—it would be a mixture of fir . . with manzanita and madrone, which are very hot and made a very hot fire; **CA**200, Most of the country here comes to manzanita after a fire. You know, brush. And I mean brush. You can't get through it. **1976** Elmore *Shrubs & Trees SW* 124, "Manzanitas" [little apples], shaped like flattened marbles are yellowish brown to creamy white and follow the flowers. **1987** Bowers *100 Roadside Wildflowers* 21 **SW,** Manzanita is a major component of chaparral in California, where more than forty species challenge even the expert botanist.

2 =**madrone** or its fruit.

1897 Sudworth *Arborescent Flora* 312 **OR,** *Arbutus menziesii. . . Common Names. . .* Manzanita. *Ibid* 313, *Arbutus xalapensis. . . Common Names. . .* Manzanita. **1908** Britton *N. Amer. Trees* 758, *Arbutus Menziesii. . .* A large evergreen tree extending from British Columbia to southern California. . . It is also called . . Manzanita, Laurelwood, and Laurel. *Ibid* 759, *Arbutus texana. . .* A small evergreen tree or shrub, . . southwestern Texas, . . quite abundant. . . It is also called . . Manzanita, and Laurel. . . The fruit ripens in late summer, . . the flesh thin, stone thick. **1960** Vines *Trees SW* 805, *Arbutus texana. . .* Also known under the vernacular names of Texas Arbutus, . . Manzanita. . . The fruit is sweetish and is eaten by a number of species of birds. It is also browsed lightly by cattle and heavily by goats.

3 A nakedwood 1 (here: *Columbrina greggii*).

1970 Correll *Plants TX* 1009, *Columbrina greggii. . .* Manzanita. Shrub or small tree.

4 A Barbados cherry *(Malpighia glabra).*

1970 Correll *Plants TX* 913, *Malpighia glabra. . . Barbados cherry,* . . *manzanita. . .* Fruit red, broadly ovoid, . . edible. In thickets, brushlands and palm groves in s. Tex.

manzanito See **manzanita 1**

maomao n [Haw] **HI**
A **demoiselle 1** (here: *Abudefduf abdominalis*).

1926 Pan-Pacific Research Inst. *Jrl.* 1.1.11 **HI,** Abudefduf abdominalis. . . Maomao. **1933** John G. Shedd Aquarium *Guide* 138, *Abudefduf abdominalis—Banded Damselfish; Maomao.* A demoiselle from the Hawaiian Islands. **1960** Gosline–Brock *Hawaiian Fishes* 208, *Abudefduf abdominalis. . .* The maomao is certainly not the most abundant of our pomacentrids. However, it is much the best known. This arises from the fact that it occurs in the same areas as the shore fisherman.

map See **map turtle**

maple n Cf **flowering maple, ground ~**
Std: a tree of the genus *Acer.* For other names of var spp see **big-leaf maple, black ~, box elder, branch maple, chalk ~, dwarf ~, fern-leaf ~, flame ~, Florida ~, frosted-trunk tree, hard maple, hardwood ~, highland ~, honey ~, mountain ~, purple ~, purpleleaf ~, red ~, she-~, silver ~, slick ~, split-leaf ~, striped ~, sugar ~, sycamore ~, vine ~** Cf **key n 2**

maple ash See **ash maple**

maple bar n Also *maple stick;* for addit varr see quots **West** See Map Cf **bar** n[1] **3, long john 2**
A pastry, usu oblong in shape, with maple-flavored frosting.

1965–70 *DARE* (Qu. H30, *An oblong cake, cooked in deep fat)* 17 Infs, **West,** Maple bar; **CA**2, 113, **MT**1, 5, **ND**10, **OR**3, Maple stick; **NV**1, Maple nut bar; **OR**10, Maple roll; **WY**3, Maple square; (Qu. H28, *Different shapes or types of doughnuts)* Infs **CA**146, **OR**4, **WA**1, 6, 13, 19, Maple bar; **AZ**8, **CA**59, **OR**3, Maple stick; [**NY**186, Maple-covered doughnut;] (Qu. H32, . . *Fancy rolls and pastries)* Inf **WA**13, Maple bars. **1980** *DARE* File **nwKS,** Maple sticks are long rectangular pastries with maple-flavored frosting, called long johns in other parts of the country. **1981** *Ibid* **wOR,** Maple bars—rectangular doughnuts with maple frosting; **cwCA** (as of c1960), Maple bars are like raised doughnuts (not cake doughnuts), only they are oblong and have a maple glaze.

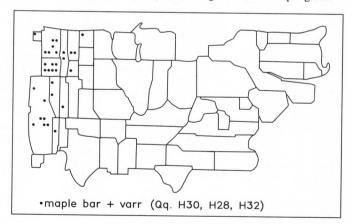

•maple bar + varr (Qq. H30, H28, H32)

maple borer n Also *sugar-maple borer, maple tree borer*
An insect larva, usu of a beetle such as *Glycobius speciosus,* which bores into maple trees.

1881 U.S. Entomol. Comm. *Bulletin* 7.103, The sugar-maple borer. *Glycobius speciosus. . .* bores for several inches into the trunks of healthy trees. **1890** *Century Dict.* 3623, *Maple-borer. . .* One of the different insects which bore the wood of maples. . . Such are *Ægeria* (or *Sesia*) *acerni* in its larval state, *Tremex columba,* and *Plagionotus speciosus.* **1905** Kellogg *Amer. Insects* 284, The sugar-maple borer, *Plagionotus speciosus . . .* is a serious pest of sugar-maples in New York and elsewhere in the East. The beetle, 1 inch long, is black, brilliantly marked with yellow. *Ibid,* Maple-tree borer, *Elaphidion villosum.* **1932** Felt–Rankin *Insects & Diseases Trees* 323, The sugar maple borer *(Glycobius speciosus)* is one of the most dangerous and insidious enemies of this maple. . . It is unusual to find a group of sugar maples in the northeastern United States uninfested by this insect. **1966** *DARE* (Qu. R30, . . *Kinds of beetles; not asked in early QRs*) Inf **NH5**, Maple borer (drills into maple tree). **1972** Swan–Papp *Insects* 448, Sugar-maple borer: *Glycobius speciosus*. . . The larvae mine under the bark of hard maples, work into the heartwood; they are very destructive to open stands.

maple bug n [From its feeding on **maple**]
A **box-elder bug** (here: *Leptocoris rubrolineatus*).
1967 *DARE* FW Addit **swOR**, Maple bug—only starlings eat them; a shieldlike pattern in thin red lines on the back.

maple bush n [bush n¹ B1a] esp **NEast** Cf *DCan*
=**sugar bush.**
1844 *Chambers's Jrl.* 1.264 **nNY**, Mr. Jones had also a maple bush, or a small wood containing sugar maple trees. **1881** *Harper's New Mth. Mag.* 62.646 **VT**, Many farmers would no more part with their maple bush or orchard than with any precious heirloom. **1929** *AmSp* 5.157 **eNY**, The word [=bush] is hardly used now except in *sugar bush* or *maple bush*. **1940–41** Cassidy *WI Atlas* **seWI**, Maple bush. [**1941** *LANE* Map 247 (*Sugar maple grove*) 1 inf, **cwMA**, ?Maple bush, first response, an error.] **1968** *DARE* (Qu. T4, *The place where . . trees grow together and sap is gathered*) Inf **CT4**, Maple bush.

maple butter See **maple cream**

maple camp n Also *maple sugar camp*, ~ *syrup camp* [camp 2] esp **NEast, Gt Lakes** Cf *DCan*
=**sugar camp.**
1884 Roe *Nature's Serial Story* 169 **NY**, We'll improvise a maple-sugar camp of the New England style a hundred years ago. **1931–33** *LANE Worksheets* **csRI**, Maple camp—had shacks for living. **1965–70** *DARE* (Qu. T4, *The place where . . trees grow together and sap is gathered*) Infs **MD22, OH33, PA176**, Maple camp; **IA29, MN33**, Maple sugar camp; **IN73**, Maple syrup camp. **1973** Allen *LAUM* 1.335 (as of c1950), North Midland *sugar camp* appears once in Iowa, as does a new hybrid, *maple camp*.

maple cream n Also *maple butter* esp **NEast, Gt Lakes**
Maple syrup concentrated by boiling and stirred while cooling to a creamy consistency.
1907 Bailey *Cyclop. Amer. Ag.* 2.434 **OH**, Perhaps one-tenth of the crop is made into "maple cream," a delicious, almost white, soft, creamy candy. . . It is made by boiling best-grade syrup a little less than it is boiled to make the hard, coarse-grained cake sugar. While hot it is rapidly stirred till it comes to a thick, whitish, creamy condition and is poured into molds when as thick as it will pour. **1923** U.S. Dept. Ag. *Farmers' Bulletin* 1366.31, Maple cream is produced by boiling the sirup to a density slightly heavier than that for soft sugar and suddenly cooling the product, stirring all the time with a large spoon. . . This product, called maple butter in some sections, is frequently prepared by farmers. **1966–68** *DARE* (Qu. H21, . . *The sweet stuff that's poured over these [pan]cakes*) Inf **VT8**, Maple cream—more concentrated [than maple syrup], cooked down considerable; (Qu. H80, *Kinds of candy . . made at home*) Inf **MI1**, Maple cream; **OH1**, Maple cream—boil down maple syrup, put in real cream. **1982** Heat Moon *Blue Highways* 339 **NH**, Maple cream too. If there's something better to eat, I never ate it. Twice-boiled syrup almost to crystallization it is. **1993** *DARE* File **neVT**, [From a mail-order catalog:] The favorite Maple product of many, Maple Cream—called Maple Butter by some—is a wonderfully rich, creamy spread made from 100% Pure Maple Syrup whipped into a thick, spreadable consistency.

maple-head n
1953 Randolph–Wilson *Down in Holler* 264 **Ozarks**, Maple-head. . Any man with a noticeably small head. This term is very common in Stone and Lawrence counties, Mo. The old-timers say that it began with a pioneer family named Maples. "The Maples boys all got funny little heads," said an old man at Hurley, Mo. "You can tell a Maples as far as you can see him."

maple honey n esp **NEast**
Maple syrup, esp when boiled to the consistency of honey.
1850 *Bentley's Misc.* 27.159, The uncrystalizable sugar which remains is called "maple honey," and with the addition of a small portion of alcohol, will keep for months without turning sour. This is esteemed as a great delicacy, and is much used in the consumption of buckwheat pancakes. **1923** U.S. Dept. Ag. *Farmers' Bulletin* 1366.31, Maple honey is the name often given to a light-colored maple sirup which has been

boiled to a density slightly greater than that of sap sirup, or similar to that of strained honey. **1941** *LANE* Map 307 (*Maple syrup*), [19 infs, **nNEng**, gave the resp *maple honey*. 6 indicated that this was an older or old-fashioned term; 1 said that it was thicker than maple syrup, another that it was "pure syrup," as opposed to *maple syrup*, "an adulterated commercial product."] **1953** Van Wagenen *Golden Age* 174 **NY**, Syrup cooked down to the point where it cools to sugar . . when stirred with a spoon . . will become "maple honey," which even now remains the most delicious of confections.

mapleleaf n **Upper Missip Valley**
A **freshwater clam** (here: *Quadrula quadrula*).
1908 Kunz–Stevenson *Book of the Pearl* 73 **Missip Valley**, Other well-known species are . . the maple-leaf (*Quadrula wardi*), and the hackle-back (*Symphynota complanata*). **1938** FWP *Guide IA* 327, The fisherman's haul usually contained a wide assortment of shells: the niggerhead . . commanded the highest price; others, all salable, were the warty black [sic], yellow back, mucket, washboard, pocketbook, pig toe, maple leaf. **1941** *AmSp* 16.155, The following list gives the common names [of freshwater clams] as applied by the cutter and fisher of shells. . . Maple Leaf [etc]. **1966** *WI Conserv. Bulletin* May–June 27, Other less important species [of mussel] are the wartyback, mapleleaf and pigtoe. **1979** *WI Week-End* 6 Apr 6, Such clams as the maple leaf, washboard, and three-ridged varieties were harvested [from the Mississippi River] for the overseas market. **1982** U.S. Fish & Wildlife Serv. *Fresh-Water Mussels* [Wall chart], Mapleleaf . . *Quadrula quadrula*. . Shell color highly variable.

maple-leafed viburnum See **maple-leaved viburnum**

mapleleaf mallow See **maple-leaved mallow**

maple-leaf viburnum See **maple-leaved viburnum**

maple-leaved mallow n Also *mapleleaf mallow, maple ~* [See quot 1949] **West**
A **globe mallow 2** (here: *Iliamna rivularis*).
1932 Rydberg *Flora Prairies* 541, Maple-leaved Mallow. . . Along streams. **1949** Moldenke *Amer. Wild Flowers* 113, Mapleleaf mallow . . is a tall leafy perennial attaining a height of almost 7 feet, with . . strikingly maplelike leaves about 6 inches long and wide. **1952** Davis *Flora ID* 468, I[liamna] rivularis. . . Maple Mallow. . . Stream banks, mountain slopes and meadows. **1963** Craighead *Rocky Mt. Wildflowers* 114, Maplemallow . . grows from lower foothills to almost 9000 ft., and is distributed from Alberta to B.C., south to Nevada and Colorado.

maple-leaved viburnum n Also *maple-leaf(ed) viburnum, maple ~* [See quot 1847]
=**dockmackie.**
1824 Bigelow *Florula Bostoniensis* 116, *Viburnum acerifolium*. . . Maple Viburnum. . . Dry woods, Roxbury. June, July. **1847** Wood *Class-Book* 302, V[iburnum] acerifolium. Maple-leaved Viburnum. . . Leaves broad, rounded and sometimes cordate at base, . . a form not very unlike that of the maple leaf. **1911** NJ State Museum *Annual Rept. for 1910* 708, Maple-leaved Viburnum. . . Common in the woods of the northern counties. **1924** Deam *Shrubs IN* 305, Mapleleaf Viburnum. . . Most frequently associated with beech and white oak. **1937** Thornburgh *Gt. Smoky Mts.* 24, The maple-leafed viburnum and the withe-rod viburnum are also found. **1960** Vines *Trees SW* 963, Maple-leaf Viburnum. . . Shrub attaining a height of 2–6 ft, sometimes forming thickets. **1976** Bruce *How to Grow Wildflowers* 132, Very different from the foregoing (and belonging to a different section of the genus) is Dockmackie or Maple-leaved Viburnum, *V. acerifolium*.

maple mallow See **maple-leaved mallow**

maple molasses n [molasses C1] esp **NEast** Cf *DCan*
Maple syrup.
1788 *Amer. Museum* 4.350 **sePA**, Maple melasses . . may be made in three ways. **1843** (1916) Hall *New Purchase* 156 **cIN**, Maple molasses . . is indeed as superior to all far east and down east molasses and syrups as cheese is to chalk. **1857** *Knickerbocker* 49.38 **ceMA**, My more ordinary dissipation did n't generally go beyond buying two or three pennies' worth of . . maple-molasses candy. **1887** Freeman *Humble Romance* 252 **NEng**, Then you don't want to hev one [=a griddle cake], with some maple merlasses on it? **1930** *AmSp* 5.419 **sNH**, Maple-molasses: maple syrup. "We ate maple molasses on our griddle cakes." **1941** *LANE* Map 307 (*Maple syrup*) 2 infs, **wCT**, Maple molasses. **1968** *DARE* Tape **IN30**, Of course we didn't have very many treats then because it would have to be taffy or maple molasses or

parched corn or popcorn balls or something like that would be just about all. **1982** *Greenfield Recorder* (MA) 20 Mar sec A 4/2, Grandma used to speak of "maple molasses" referring I think to the rather dark, thick syrup.

maple orchard n Also *sugar maple orchard* Cf **sugar orchard**
A grove of maple trees, esp one planted for systematic production of maple syrup.

  1867 Beecher *Norwood* 399 **NEng,** The woods and maple orchards were filled with sounds of industry. **1881** *Harper's New Mth. Mag.* 62.642, The maple orchards [of Shrewsbury VT] are famous. **1931–33** *LANE Worksheets* **csRI,** Maple orchard—trees set out as apple trees are in New York and Pennsylvania. **1941** *LANE* Map 247, Terms for a grove or plantation of sugar maples, where sap is drawn from the trees for the manufacture of sugar and syrup: *(sugar) maple grove, ~ orchard, (maple) sugar grove, ~ orchard.* **1947** *PADS* 8.7 **VT,** *Maple orchard. . .* A grove of maple trees which produce sap. **1949** Kurath *Word Geog.* 76 **C Atl,** Only scattered instances of *. . maple orchard, sugar grove,* and *sugar camp* have been noted here. **1950** *WELS Suppl.* **NH,** *Maple orchard*—Grove of trees from which maple sugar is taken. More frequently called *sap yard.* **1965–70** *DARE* (Qu. T4, *The place where . . trees grow together and sap is gathered*) 16 Infs, **chiefly Nth, Midl,** Maple orchard; **IL**78, Sugar maple orchard. **1992** Phelps *Famous Last Words* 12 **NEng** (as of 1920s), We also had *. .* quite a large maple orchard which kept us busy in the spring.

maple snow See **maple wax**

maple stick See **maple bar**

maple sugar camp See **maple camp**

maple sugar orchard See **sugar orchard**

maple syrup camp See **maple camp**

maple tree borer See **maple borer**

maple tree worm See **maple worm 1**

maple viburnum See **maple-leaved viburnum**

maple wax n Also *maple snow* esp **NEast, Gt Lakes** Cf **cackany, larbo, leather apron**
=**jack wax 1.**

  1883 Shields *Hunting* 257 **nWI,** Oh, what a delicious *bon bon* is a dish of warm maple wax, pure and fresh from the woods! **1939** Wolcott *Yankee Cook Book* 346 **NEng,** Provide each person *. .* with a pan of snow, a small pitcher of hot syrup and a fork. Pour the syrup on the snow, a little at a time. *. .* Some people call the syrup "sheepskins"; others refer to it as "leather aprons" or "maple wax." **1940** Brown *Amer. Cooks* 819 **VT,** Maple snow has a number of other descriptive names—maple wax, sugar-on-snow, sheepskins, and leather aprons. **1947** *AmSp* 22.152 **NEast,** *Maple wax.* Sirup boiled to a density equal to that of hard sugar, but without stirring, and then poured over snow or ice to secure immediate cooling. [Not common in wPA.] **1967** *DARE* Tape **MI**42, He used to make maple syrup and maple sugar, and what he called maple wax. *. .* It was pulled like the old-fashioned taffy.

maplewing n
  1950 *WELS Suppl.* **ceWI,** Maplewings—maple seedpods.

maple worm n
1 also *maple tree worm:* The larva of the rosy maple moth *(Dryocampa rubicunda).*
  1873 *Winfield* (Kans.) *Courier* 24 July 1/5 (*DA*), I find the maple worm is a peculiarly Kansas institution. *. .* Its body is constructed like a joint snake. **1892** Kellogg *Common Insects KS* 4, The crawling, biting, sluggish, green Maple-worm. *Ibid* 101, *Green-striped maple-worm . . Anisota rubicunda. . .* a naked caterpillar, about 1½ inches long, pale yellowish-green, longitudinally striped with lighter and darker green lines, two small, black horns on body behind the head. **1932** Felt–Rankin *Insects & Diseases Trees* 301, The green-striped maple worm *(Anisota rubicunda) . .* appears to be a more serious pest in the western states. **1966–70** *DARE* (Qu. R27, *. . Kinds of caterpillars or similar worms*) Infs **NY**93, 191, Maple tree worm(s); **KY**75, Maple worm—green. **1981** Pederson *LAGS Basic Materials,* 1 inf, **nwFL,** Maple worms.

2 The green fruitworm *(Lithophane antennata).*
  1932 Felt–Rankin *Insects & Diseases Trees* 302, The green maple worm *(Xylina antennata)* occasionally defoliates soft maples.

map turtle n Also *map* [See quot 1890]
A turtle of the genus *Graptemys.* Also called **sawback.** For other names of var spp see **grayback 3d, moss turtle, mud ~ 2c(3), ringed ~, slider**
  1879 Smith *Catalogue Reptilia MI* vii, *Graptemys geographica. . .* Map Turtle. **1890** *Century Dict.* 3623, *Map-turtle. . .* A common pond-turtle of the United States, *Malaclemmys geographicus:* so called from the markings of the shell. **1891** in **1895** IL State Lab. Nat. Hist. Urbana *Bulletin* 3.234, *Malacoclemmys lesueuri. . .* Map Turtle. *. .* Throughout the State, but less common north. *. .* This species resembles *M. geographica* in a general way, but is very different in the size of its head and the width and character of the grinding surface of its jaws. *Ibid* 3.235, *Malacoclemmys geographicus. . .* Map Turtle. **1908** Biol. Soc. DC *Proc.* 21.79 **cnTX,** *Graptemys geographica. . .* Map Turtle. *. .* I captured two specimens in the North Bosque River. **1928** Pope–Dickinson *Amphibians* 79 **WI,** Map Turtle. *. .* The carapace of this turtle is dull olive-brown with fine, yellow lines, more or less distinct. **1967** *DARE* (Qu. P24, *. . Kinds of turtles*) Inf **LA**14, Map turtle. **1972** Ernst–Barbour *Turtles* 112, The flesh of map turtles is palatable, but the difficulty of capturing them in numbers precludes commercial use. **1979** Behler–King *Audubon Field Guide Reptiles* 461, Shy like other map turtles, they [=*Graptemys geographica*] quickly slide into the water when disturbed. **1981** Vogt *Nat. Hist. WI* 110, On October 1, 1976, I caught 56 Ouachita map turtles, 25 false maps, and 4 common maps behind one rock pile in the Mississippi River. Behind the same rock pile in 1977 I caught 131 maps of all three species.

maque chou(x) n |ˈmɑkšu| [LaFr; perh of AmInd origin] **LA**
A dish whose principal ingredient is sweet corn; see quots.
  [**1931** Read *LA French* 143, *Maquechou. . .* A dish made of young corn cut from the cob and smothered with onions. Such is the meaning assigned to *maquechou* by most of my informants. Some of my friends, however, insist that *maquechou* is a thick soup in which corn is the principal ingredient. Finally some Acadians make *maquechou* of cabbage and give the name as *moque-chou,* "mock cabbage."] **1983** *Reinecke Coll.* 12 **LA,** *Maquechou. . .* [ˈmɑkšu]—a dish of young corn smothered with onions. La. Fr. (from Indian?) Fairly common among Cajuns. **1985** *NYT Mag.* 1 Sept 37/2, Around New Orleans, every Cajun family quarrels over the best way to make the creamed corn they call "maque choux." **1986** Pederson *LAGS Concordance,* 1 inf, **cLA,** Maque choux—boiled corn, bell peppers, seasoning; (*Sweet corn*) 1 inf, **cLA,** Maque choux—cooked corn, cut from cob and fried; 1 inf, **cwLA,** Maque choux.

mar n[1] See **mare**

mar n[2] See **ma** n A5

mar n[3] See **marrow**

maracle See **miracle**

marais n [Fr] **chiefly LA, eTX**
A swamp—often used in place names.
  1839 *Maysville* (Ky.) *Eagle* 18 Dec. 1/3 (*DA*), Among these is one appropriatly [sic] named 'Clear Lake,' or the *Grand Marais.* **1853** Hammett *Stray Yankee in TX* 56 **eTX,** Three miles below us was a *"marais"* or slough. **1896** Clendenin *Prelim. Rept.* 177 **eLA,** The bayous, "marais" and "coulees" *. .* meander through or extend across this "bluff" area. **1961** *PADS* 36.12 **sLA,** Marais for a swamp. **1968** *DARE* (Qu. C7, *. . Land that usually has some standing water with trees or bushes growing in it*) Inf **LA**20, A little marais [ˌmɑˈreʲ]. [**1970** Detro *Generic Terms* 216 **LA,** The first recorded use of *"marais"* as a toponymic generic was on the D'Anville (1732) map along the lower Red River. The term signified a swamp area.] **1992** *DARE* File, Both Minnesota and Michigan have towns called *Grand Marais,* but I wonder how many know that *marais* means 'swamp'?

marb v [Prob var of *OED mob* v.[2] 4 "To abuse, scold, rail at. *dial.* Also *absol.*"]
  1936 *AmSp* 11.191 **swWY,** *To Marb.* To growl or grumble, complain, condemn unceasingly. 'The father sure did marb because the baby got hurt. He thought the women should take better care of it.'

marb n Pronc-sp *mab* [Abbrs for *marble*]
  1942 Berrey–Van den Bark *Amer. Slang* 665.2, *Marble. . .* Marb. **1957** *Sat. Eve. Post Letters* **ceWI** (as of c1890), We called marbles "mibbs" or "marbs." **1969** *DARE* (Qu. EE6b, *Small marbles or marbles in general*) Inf **CT**23, Mabs [mæbz]. [FW: Inf unsure]

marble n See **marble tomato**

marble v See **marvel** v

marblebelly n Also *marbled-breast*
=**white-fronted goose.**
> **1923** U.S. Dept. Ag. *Misc. Circular* 13.34 **CA,** *White-fronted Goose. . . Vernacular Names. . . In local use. . .* Marbled-breast. **1936** Roberts *MN Birds* 1.212, *White-fronted Goose . . Other names . . Marblebelly. . .* Underparts whitish blotched with black.

marbleberry n [Prob by folk-etym]
=**marlberry.**
> **1946** West-Arnold *Native Trees FL* 170, *Marbleberry, Marlberry. . . Fruits*—maturing all year, smooth, shining, black globose, about ¼ inch in diameter. . . The marbleberry, one of the common and well-known small trees of the coastal hammocks, occurs inland to some extent in . . the southern part of the peninsula. **1979** Little *Checklist U.S. Trees* 57, *Ardisia escallonioides. . . Other common name*—marbleberry.

marble board n Also *marble bridge*
In marble play: a board set on edge, with arches or openings cut into that edge, through which marbles are rolled; the game played with such a board.
> [**1894** (1964) Gomme *Traditional Games* 1.45, *Bridgeboard*—A game at marbles. The boys have a board a foot long . . ; any number of holes at the ground edge, numbered irregularly. The board is placed firmly on the ground, and each player bowls at it.] **1950** *WELS,* 1 Inf, **cwWI,** Marble board—with openings cut into it and it is placed with slits to the floor and you roll marbles from a given distance to try to roll through the openings. **1985** Runyan *Knuckles Down* 17, *Golden Arches, Marble Bridge* or *Bridgeboard*—Object: Score the most points by rolling marbles under arches.

marble cat n
1 also *marble(d) bullhead, marbled cat(fish):* =**brown bullhead 1.** [See quot 1903]
> **1877** U.S. Natl. Museum *Bulletin* 10.89, *Amiurus marmoratus. . . Marbled Catfish. . .* This beautiful and singular species seems to have been overlooked. **1903** NY State Museum & Sci. Serv. *Bulletin* 60.89, *Ameiurus nebulosus marmoratus . . Marbled cat. . .* Body much mottled with brown, greenish and whitish. Lowland streams and swamps from New York to southern Indiana and Florida. The type of the marmoratus of Holbrook was from South Carolina. **1932** OH Bur. Scientific Research *Bulletin* 23.2, *Brown or Marble Bullhead. . .* is the big "Yellow-belly" or "Marble Cat" of the four largest state-owned reservoirs. **1949** Caine *N. Amer. Sport Fish* 140, Channel catfish. . . *Colloquial Names . .* Marble Cat. *Ibid* 149, Brown bullhead. . *Colloquial Names . .* Marbled Cat. **1983** Becker *Fishes WI* 702, *Ictalurus nebulosus. . .* Other common names . . marbled bullhead, marble cat.

2 A **channel catfish** (here: *Ictalurus punctatus*).
> **1949** [see **1** above].

marble city See **marble orchard**

marbled-breast See **marblebelly**

marbled bullhead, marbled cat(fish) See **marble cat 1**

marbled godwit n Also *marble godwit*
A godwit (here: *Limosa fedoa*). Also called **badger bird, brant-bird 3,brownback 3, brown snipe 2, bull ~, doughbird 2, horsefoot marlin 2, humility 1, marlin** n[1] **1a, redbird, red curlew, ~ marlin, sea snipe, spike-billed curlew, straight-billed ~**
> [**1787** Pennant *Arctic Zool. Suppl.* 68, *Marbled godwit . . Inhabits* Hudson's Bay.] **1834** Nuttall *Manual Ornith.* 2.174, The Marbled Godwit, in large flocks, appears in the salt marshes of Massachusetts, about the middle of August, particularly towards the eastern extremity of the Bay, around Chatham and the Vineyard. **1849** Herbert *Frank Forester's Field Sports* 2.23, The Great Marbled Godwit, or 'Marlin,' as our gunners term it, arrives on the shores of Long Island in the month of May. **1881** *Forest & Stream* 17.225, The marlin of the West is the marble godwit of the East. **1916** *Times–Picayune* (New Orleans LA) 2 Apr mag sec 11/1, *Marbled Godwit* (Limosa fedoa). . . A large bird with a long bill that curves upward to a slight degree. **1944** Hausman *Amer. Birds* 105, The Marbled Godwits are birds of the seashore, where they follow the retreating surf, feeding as they go. **1967** *DARE* (Qu. Q10, . . *Water birds and marsh birds*) Inf **CO7,** Marbled godwit. **1977** Bull–Farrand *Audubon Field Guide Birds* 396, *Marbled Godwit. . .* One of

our largest shorebirds, it breeds on the vast grassy plains of the West but less abundantly than in former days.

marbled murrelet n
A small murrelet (*Brachyramphus marmoratus*) native to the Pacific coast from Alaska to California. Also called **fog bird**
> **1886** Turner *Contribs. AK* 185, *Brachyramphus marmoratus. . .* Marbled Murrelet. **1898** (1900) Davie *Nests N. Amer. Birds* 16, *Marbled Murrelet. . .* This is another of the diminutive Murres. **1904** Wheelock *Birds CA* 10, *Marbled Murrelet. . .* In California they are common near the coast all winter as far south as San Diego. **1940** Gabrielson *Birds OR* 314, Marbled Murrelets are rather shy and difficult to approach. . . Ordinarily this little diver is found in the mouths of bays and in the ocean just offshore. **1953** Jewett *Birds WA* 323, Marbled murrelets were found quite constantly near canneries, though not known to eat refuse. **1977** Udvardy *Audubon Field Guide Birds* 365, Most alcids use burrows or ledges on coastal cliffs, but Marbled Murrelets, burdened with fish, take off from the sea at twilight and disappear inland.

marbled sculpin n
A **cabezon** (here: *Scorpaenichthys marmoratus*).
> **1939** Natl. Geogr. Soc. *Fishes* 241, *Marbled Sculpin. . .* Its color is highly variable, usually mottled with rich dark brown or reddish brown. . . The marbled sculpin in the Puget Sound region has been found to spawn during the spring. **1946** LaMonte *N. Amer. Game Fishes* 87, *Cabezone. . . Names:* Marbled Sculpin. . . These fishes run from San Diego, California, north. **1953** Roedel *Common Fishes CA* 141, *Cabezon. . .* An important game fish in the Monterey and Santa Barbara areas. . . *Unauthorized Names . .* marbled sculpin, bull cod.

marble eye n
1 A large, round eye; hence adj *marble-eyed* round-eyed. **scattered, but esp Sth, S Midl, Missip Valley** See Map
> **1930** Faulkner *As I Lay Dying* 181 **MS,** Jewel had come back now, standing there, looking at Anse with them marble eyes of hisn. **1965–70** *DARE* (Qu. X21c, *If the eyes are very round*) 33 Infs, **scattered, but esp Sth, S Midl, Missip Valley,** Marble-eyed; **FL15, SC26, VA34,** Marble eye(s).

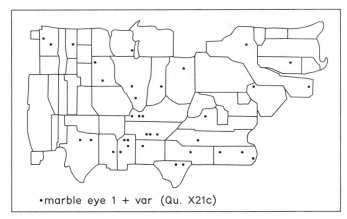

•marble eye 1 + var (Qu. X21c)

2 A **walleye** (here: *Stizostedion vitreum vitreum*). Cf **glasseye** n[2]
> **1949** Caine *N. Amer. Sport Fish* 115, The walleye is blessed . . with an abundance of aliases. . . The most common are: Blue Pike . . Marble-eye [etc]. . . The walleye has large whitish glassy eyes and strong canine teeth.

marble-eyed See **marble eye 1**

marble godwit See **marbled godwit**

marble golf n Cf **bunny-in-the-hole**
A marble game; see quots.
> **1950** *WELS* **ceWI,** Marble golf—dig a hole in ground. Try to shoot marble in hole. **1953** Brewster *Amer. Nonsinging Games* 135 **ID,** *Marble golf. . .* A number of holes (usually six) are dug in a smooth bit of ground. . . The object of the game is to shoot a marble into each of the holes in rotation. **1958** *PADS* 29.36 **WI,** *Marble golf. . .* A marble game in which the players try to shoot their marbles into a hole dug in the ground. **1985** Runyan *Knuckles Down* 17, *Marble golf. . .* Object: To complete the "golf course" with the lowest number of shots. . . The courses are marked off with fairways being 12–25 inches wide and small

mounds of packed dirt become the tees. Holes may be anywhere from 10–80 feet.

marblehead n

1 See **marbleheader**.

2 A cultivated **winter squash** (*Cucurbita maxima* var). **WA**
   1967 *DARE* (Qu. I23, . . *Kinds of squash*) Inf **WA**25, Marblehead—big, green-and-white mottled. **1985** *Seed Savers Exchange* (Harvest ed) 206, *Cucurbita maxima.* . . The following varieties all belong to the species "maxima" . . Marblehead, Marblehead (Umatilla), Marblehead (Yakima). **1988** Whealy *Garden Seed Inventory* (2d ed) 322, *Marblehead*—Large storage type, nearly round grey-green fruits, late-maturing, good keeper. . . *Marblehead, Yakima*—Late-maturing, round, gray-green, a variant of Umatilla Marblehead. **1990** *Seed Savers Yearbook* 200, *Marblehead, Umatilla.* . . Oval-shaped greyish-green squash weighing 8–25 lbs. with . . very good flavor, good keeping quality. *Ibid* 201, *Marblehead, Yakima.* . . Round to oval shape, grayish-green color, . . some stringiness, 10–40 lb.

3 See quot.
   1950 *WELS* (*Names for other kinds of stones of particular size, shape, color, etc*) 1 Inf, **cwWI**, Marbleheads—large, fairly smooth, hard rocks found when plowing.

marbleheader n Also *marblehead* [See quot 1955] NEng
=**fulmar**.
   1884 U.S. Bur. Fisheries *Rept. for 1882* 320, (*Fulmarus glacialis*). This species, known by a variety of names to the New England fishermen, such as . . "marbleheader," . . is found on the fishing banks north of Cape Cod in winter. *Ibid* 321, The marbleheader is quite as greedy as the hagdon. **1890** *Century Dict.* 3625, *Marblehead.* . . The fulmar petrel. . . *Marbleheader.* . . Same as *marblehead.* **1917** *Wilson Bulletin* 29.2.76, *Fulmarus glacialis.* . . Marble-header . . Northeastern Banks. **1925** (1928) Forbush *Birds MA* 1.135, *Fulmar.* . . Other names . . marbleheader. **1955** MA Audubon Soc. *Bulletin* 39.310, *Fulmar.* . . Marbleheader (as being frequently seen off Marblehead, Mass.)

Marblehead turkey n
=**Cape Cod turkey**.
   1859 (1968) Bartlett *Americanisms* 264, *Marblehead Turkeys.* Codfish. So called in Massachusetts.

marble hill See hill n 6

marble orchard n Also *marble city;* for addit varr see quots
scattered, but rare Sth, S Midl *joc* or *euphem* Cf **bone orchard**
A cemetery.
   1925 *WI News* (Milwaukee) 5 June 18 (*Zwilling Coll.*), [Cartoon:] Listening to one of those ancestor pests as you stroll through an old marble orchard. **1936** *AmSp* 11.201 [Euphemisms for the cemetery], The marble orchard. . . The Marble City. **1940** *AmSp* 15.447 **eTN**, *Marble orchard.* Cemetery. 'I don't like to pass through that marble orchard of a dark night.' **1941** *AmSp* 16.23 **sIN**, *Marble orchard.* Cemetery. **1941** in 1946 Cain *3 Novels* 3.158 **swCA**, You'll get your names in this marble orchard soon enough. **1950** *WELS WI* (*Other names . . for a cemetery*) 6 Infs, Marble orchard; 1 Inf, Marble forest. **1965–70** *DARE* (Qu. BB61b, . . *Joking names for a cemetery*) 32 Infs, **scattered, but rare Sth, S Midl**, Marble orchard; **CT**37, Marble city (of the dead); **CA**140, Marble hill; **MI**108, Marble park; (Qu. BB61a) Inf **MO**35, Marble yard. **1970** Major *Dict. Afro-Amer. Slang* 80, *Marble town:* (1940's) a cemetery. **1978** Doig *This House* 59 **MT**, *Just waitin' for the marble farm,* Pete McCabe said of them with sorrow, for he enjoyed the old gaffers and set them up a free beer now and then.

marbleseed n
=**false gromwell**.
   1948 Stevens *KS Wild Flowers* 164, *Onosmodium. Marbleseed (False Gromwell).* . . The parts of the ovary becoming mostly shining white, sometimes brownish, nutlets, but usually only 1 or 2 maturing. **1950** Gray–Fernald *Manual of Botany* 1200, *Onosmodium.* . . Marble-seed. **1970** Correll *Plants TX* 1309, *Marble-seed.* . . Mericarps 4 mm. long or less, usually but one or two maturing, globular to ovoid, smooth or sometimes sparingly pitted.

marble tomato n Also *marble* [From the size]
A small-fruited cultivar of the tomato (*Lycopersicon lycopersicum*); a cherry tomato.
   1966 *DARE* (Qu. I21, *Names or nicknames for tomatoes; total Infs*

questioned, 75) Inf **FL**15, Marble tomatoes. **1981** Pederson *LAGS Basic Materials* (*Tomatoes*) 4 infs, **cnAR, cwLA, cwMS, swMS,** Marble tomatoes; 1 inf, **cwMS,** Marble. **1990** *Seed Savers Yearbook* 250, *Yellow Marble.* . . Bright golden, large marble-sized fruit, excel[lent] flavor, very productive.

march See marsh

March bird n Cf marsh bird
A **spring peeper** (here: *Hyla crucifer*).
   1930 Shoemaker *1300 Words* 41 **cPA Mts** (as of c1900), *March-bird*—Pickering's frog, the "peeper," the popular harbinger of spring in Pennsylvania mountains; usually beginning their choruses early in March.

March bluebill n
=**lesser scaup**.
   1951 *AmSp* 26.271 **IL**, A few names particularize individual months, as *March bluebill* for the lesser scaup duck.

March clematis See marsh clematis

March fleabane See marsh fleabane 3

March flower n

1 A daffodil (*Narcissus* spp). Cf **Easter flower 2**
   1937 (1963) Hyatt *Kiverlid* 12 **KY**, Bed of March flowers, all solid yeller 'fore they faded down. **1944** *PADS* 2.35 **wNC**, *March flower.* . . The Daffodil. **c1960** *Wilson Coll.* **csKY**, March flowers. . . Daffodils.

2 Appar an anemone (*Anemone* spp). Cf **Easter flower 1**
   1966 *DARE* (Qu. S23, *Pale blue flowers with downy leaves and cups that come up on open, stony hillsides in March or early April*) Inf **NC**35, March flowers.

March fly n [See quot 1895] Cf love bug
A fly of the family Bibionidae.
   1895 Comstock–Comstock *Manual Insects* 450, They [=Bibionidae] are most common in early spring; which has suggested the name March-flies; but some occur later in the season. **1926** Essig *Insects N. Amer.* 550, *Bibionidae.* March Flies. . . They often appear in great numbers on blossoming fruit trees and other plants in the spring of the year and attract a good deal of attention. **1966** *DARE* (Qu. R10, *Very small flies that don't sting, often seen hovering in large groups or bunches outdoors in summer*) Inf **GA**11, March fly. **1972** Swan–Papp *Insects* 603, *March Fly: Bibio albipennis.* . . March flies appear in large numbers early in the spring. They are small to moderate in size, usually quite hairy and dark in color. **1980** Milne–Milne *Audubon Field Guide Insects* 649, March flies are clumsy fliers, often bumping into plants and even people. **1992** FL Div. Plant Industry *Entomol. Circular No. 350* [1], Another bibionid, *Dilophus sayi* . . is a March fly (Bibionidae) in which the behavior of the adults is somewhat similar to that of *P[lecia] nearctica,* but the adults do not congregate noticeably on highways.

March hill n Also *May hill* Cf fool's hill
Fig: March (or May) regarded as a barrier to be overcome.
   1832 in 1941 Pintard *Letters Daughter* 4.17 **NYC**, If I live to climb March Hill, I trust to be relieved by milder weather. **1904** Day *Kin o' Ktaadn* 8 **ME**, Content went scraping along on poor sleddin' when we came to "March Hill." The big rafters in the barn had lost their thatching; . . the cellar bins were hollowly empty in the gloom: all the fresh aroma of the harvest days had succumbed to the damp chill of winter. Climbing March Hill! It is always a hard pull for many a rural household. **1929** *AmSp* 5.122 **ME**, Of a sick person it might be remarked "he is a goner", "he won't climb May hill" (also March hill).

marching around the levee n Also *marching around the level, up and down the levee;* for addit varr see quots [From the first of the verses recited in playing the game. The commonest Brit version begins "Round and round the village," but an Ir version begins "Marching round the ladies" (1898 Gomme *Traditional Games* 2.122–43).] **chiefly Sth, S Midl** Cf **in-and-out-the-window 1**
A children's game; see quot 1964.
   [**1883** Newell *Games & Songs* 128 **NYC**, *Go Round and Round the Valley.* . . Go round and round the valley,/ As we are all so gay. . . Go in and out of the windows. . . Go back, and face your lover. . . Such love have I to show you.] **1903** (1963) Newell *Games & Songs* 229, *Walking on the Levy.* . . I'm walking on the levy,/ For you have gained the day./ Go in and out the windows. . . Stand up and face your lover. . . I measure my love to show you. . . . I kneel because I love you. . . . It

breaks my heart to leave you. **1905** *DN* 3.87 **nwAR**, *Marching on the levee, marching round the levee, marching on the level*. . . The name of a children's game. **1946** *TN Folk Lore Soc. Bulletin* 12.1.18, Marching Around the Levee. **1964** Wallace *Frontier Life* 47 **OK** (as of c1900), "Marching around the Levee." What a thrill . . to have nice-looking boy [sic] choose me as his "lover[,]" take me by the hand inside the ring of boys and girls, marching merrily around hand-in-hand, singing hilariously the phrases that told him how to proceed in the game. . . Lastly, as the boys and girls (usually girls) sang "Goodbye, I hate to leave you," the boy shook my hand and stepped back into the ring again, and I was left to "March forth and choose my lover," and proceed as my partner had done. **1965–69** *DARE* (Qu. EE1, . . *Games . . children play . . in which they form a ring, and either sing or recite a rhyme*) Infs **GA**8, 9, Marching around the level; **TX**12, Marching round the levee; **FL**18, Marching round the level; **GA**58, Up and down the levee; (Qu. EE33, . . *Outdoor games . . that children play*) Inf **KY**17, Marching around the levee—form a ring, march around boy in the middle, others squat, last or first to squat gets to kiss the boy in the middle. **1966–67** *DARE* Tape **AL**3, [Aux Inf:] I think that the prettiest game that boys and girls used to play in my day was "marching round the levee." . . They get in a great circle and there's a boy or a girl, one, in there that chooses their lover. The circle marches and sings, "We're marching round the levee, we're marching round the levee, we're marching round the levee, for we all came today. Go in and out the windows, go in and out the windows, go in and out the windows, for we all came today"; **TX**40, There's one we called marching round the levee. **1986** Pederson *LAGS Concordance* (*Child's game; ring game*) 1 inf, **swLA**, Marching around the levee.

marching through Georgia n
=**musical chairs.**
   1950 *WELS* (*Games with an extra player: at a signal the other players change places, and the extra tries to get a place*) 1 Inf, **ceWI**, Marching through Georgia.

marching to Jerusalem See **Jerusalem, going to 1**

March lily n
1 A **dogtooth violet** (here: *Erythronium albidum*).
   1897 *KS Univ. Qrly.* (ser B) 6.52 **KS**, *Easter-bells* . . March lilies. . . Erythronium albidum.
2 An **Easter lily 4.**
   1968 *DARE* (Qu. S26d, *Wildflowers that grow in meadows;* not asked in early QRs) Inf **MD**43, March lily—yellow, comes up around Easter, also called Easter lily; grows near fences of people's yards, not in marsh. [FW: Inf corrects FW that it should be *March lily*, not *marsh lily*, because it grows in that month.]

March meeting n Also *March town meeting* **NEng** *old-fash*
An annual **town meeting** held in March.
   1728 in 1883 Boston Registry Dept. *Records* 8.222, If the Money apropriated . . at the last march meeting be Insofficient. . . Henry Gibbon will advance and pay what falls Short. **1766** in 1850 Adams *Works* 2.188 **MA**, Major Miller and James Bracket, Jr. were heard, since March meeting, raving against Deacon Palmer. **1867** Lowell *Biglow* 221 **'Up-country' MA**, Mr. Hosea Biglow's Speech in March Meeting. **1907** *DN* 3.193 **seNH**, Bad weather for March meeting this year. **1939** Wolcott *Yankee Cook Book* 252, In the old days of long drawn out March Town meetings, nearby taverns were heavily patronized during the noon hour. **1944** Holton *Yankees* 35 *(DA)*, Town meeting was a big event in our community when I was growing up. We called it March Meeting then, and would have continued to do so if some busybody hadn't succeeded in shifting the date back to February.

March meeting cake n [**March meeting**] Cf **election cake**
See quot 1907.
   1907 *DN* 3.193 **seNH**, *March meetin' cake*. . . Simple thin cake sold at town meetings. **1939** Wolcott *Yankee Cook Book* 252 **NEng**, March Meetin' or 'Lection Cakes were sold in the village stores all day [on March town meeting day] at four pence a baker's dozen.

March peeper n **NEng** Cf **marsh peeper, spring peeper**
A **tree frog.**
   1939 *LANE* Map 231 *(Frog)*, Names of the small shrill-voiced frog, *hyla, peeper, peeping frog*, . . March peeper. . . Seven informants mention that peepers appear in early spring . . , three specify the time of their appearance as March. **1965** *PADS* 43.26 **seMA**, 4 [infs] March peepers. **1969** *DARE* (Qu. P21, *Small frogs that sing or chirp loudly in spring*) Infs **RI**8, 15, March peepers; **MA**40, March peepers.

March town meeting See **March meeting**

Marco Polo n
A tag game played in the water; see quots.
   1965–70 *DARE* (Qu. EE4, *Games in which one player's eyes are bandaged and he has to catch the others and guess who they are*) Inf **TX**68, Marco Polo—close your eyes and say "Marco," another answers "Polo" and you try to catch them, guided by sound of voice; (Qu. EE28, *Games played in the water*) Infs **AL**37, **CA**182, **PA**126, **TX**81, **VA**83, Marco Polo; **LA**23, Marco Polo—in the water, everybody scatters around the leader; he yells "Marco" and they yell "Polo"; he, with eyes closed, tries to find them and guess who they are; **VA**65, Marco Polo—water tag; **VA**93, Marco Polo—water tag with "it" blindfolded; **VA**109, Marco Polo—blindfolded water tag. **1968** *DARE* FW Addit **VA**, Marco Polo—water form of blindman's bluff.

marc'ry, marcury See **mercury 1**

Mardi Gras n [Fr, literally "fat Tuesday"] Cf **Fat Tuesday**
1 A festival held on the last day (or several days) preceding Lent, characterized by elaborate costumes, parades, music, and feasting. **chiefly LA (esp New Orleans), but widely recognized elsewhere**
   1839 *Daily Picayune* (New Orleans LA) 13 Feb [2]/1, Thus has passed "Mardi Gras," and may we all live to see fifty more just like it. **1883** Twain *Life on Missip.* (Boston) 465, The largest annual event in New Orleans is . . the Mardi-Gras festivities. **1945** Saxon *Gumbo Ya-Ya* 24 **New Orleans LA**, This is the Mecca of all Negroes on Mardi Gras Night, for here the Zulu Ball, the grand climax of the day, takes place. *Ibid* 166, The Mardi Gras gradually became the most important event in the year, as it is today. Street masking and balls were popular in the earliest years of the nineteenth century. Young Creole blades would march on foot through the Vieux Carré in costume on Fat Tuesday, while young ladies on the galleries would shower them with flowers, all in imitation of the centuries-old festival in Europe. *Ibid* 198, Peculiarly Cajun is the Mardi Gras custom of begging for small coins and for chicken to make gumbo on that day. **1965–68** *DARE* (Qu. FF16, . . *Local contests or celebrations*) Infs **LA**6, 16, 23, 25, 32, 46, Mardi Gras; **FL**17, Mardi Gras in New Orleans. **1983** [see **3** below].
2 A local festival or celebration similar to **Mardi Gras 1. scattered, but esp Gulf States, NYC**
   1904 *NY Post* (NY) 17 Sept 3/4, At a special meeting of the Coney Island business men. . . $25,000 was subscribed to pay the expenses of the semi-centennial celebration and mardi gras on September 21, 22, 23. **1930** Dixon (Ill.) *Ev. Tribune* 24 Sep. 1 *(heading) (DA)*, Mardi Gras, Fireworks End Centennial Tonight. **1941** *Sat. Eve. Post* 15 Mar 14, Mardi Gras at Coney. **1965–70** *DARE* (Qu. FF16, . . *Local contests or celebrations*) Infs **IA**38, **MS**73, **NY**45, Mardi Gras; **AL**19, 25, 30, Mardi Gras—in Mobile; **IL**98, Mardi Gras—gone now; **NY**40, Mardi Gras—used to have at Coney Island during Labor Day week, with parades, floats; different churches participated; twenty years ago; **NY**48, Mardi Gras—day at Coney Island; parade in costumes, pranksters poured confetti on you; **NY**57, Mardi Gras at Coney Island; **NY**249, Calypso Mardi Gras. **1966** *DARE* Tape **FL**17, [FW:] What is this Mardi Gras that you mentioned? [Inf:] Mardi Gras is like fiestas of different places.
3 pronc-sp *mardygraw;* Transf: a costumed participant in **Mardi Gras 1;** the costume of such a participant; also fig.
   1916 *DN* 4.269 **New Orleans LA**, *Mardi-gras* ([grɒ]; plural [grɒz]). . . A street masker. "See the cute mardi-gras." **1917** *DN* 4.420 **New Orleans LA**, *Mardi gras*. . . A participant in the street masquing on Mardi Gras. **1951** *AmSp* 26.111 **New Orleans LA**, *Mardygraw:* A costume worn on Mardi Gras; a masker (used mainly by children). **1983** Reinecke Coll. 7 **LA**, *Mardi Gras* . . Shrove Tuesday, also a "masker," one who is costumed on Mardi Gras—"You gonna be a mardigras this year?" By extension one outlandishly, over-colorfully dressed. "She's a real mardi gras in that getup."

mardling n [*EDD* (at *mardle* sb.²)]
A **duckweed 1** (here: *Lemna* spp).
   1900 Lyons *Plant Names* 218, *Lemna*. . . Duckweed. . . Synonyms, Duck's-meat, . . Mardling. **1911** *Century Dict. Suppl.*, *Mardling*. . . Duckweed; especially, the lesser duckweed, *Lemna minor*.

mardygraw See **Mardi Gras 3**

mare n Usu |mɛr, mɛə, mær, mæə|; for addit proncs see quots
Pronc-spp **chiefly Sth, S Midl** *mar(r), myah* Cf **bare, bear n¹ A, hair,** Pronc Intro 3.I.1.b
Std sense, var forms.

1817 in 1830 Royall *Letters AL* 22 **TN**, *For* they sound like *faw* or *fow*. . . Also . . stars for stairs—mar for mare, &c. **1823** *Natl. Intelligencer* (DC) 1 May (*DN* 4.47), *Western Dialect*. . . *Marr.* . . A female horse. **1871** (1892) Johnston *Dukesborough Tales* 62 **GA,** I have ast you not to ride this mar. **1891** Page *Elsket* 124 **VA** [Black], What's in de myah will come out in de colt. **1893** Shands *MS Speech* 44, *Mar* [mɑ]—Negro and illiterate white for *mare*. **1939** *LANE* Map 196, [Of 47 infs whose proncs of *mare* were recorded, 21 gave proncs of the type [mæə, mær], 25 of the type [mɛə, mɛr], and 1 [maˀə].] **1976** Garber *Mountain-ese* 56 s**Appalachians,** Mar. **1989** Pederson *LAGS Tech. Index* 129 **Gulf Region,** [Of 683 infs giving the resps *mare(s)*, 520 used the vowel [æ], 118 [ɛ], 29 [e], 6 [ɪɛ] or [jɛ], 5 [ɑ], 4 [ʌ], and 1 [ɪ].]

mare's egg n
A puffball.
1973 Allen *LAUM* 1.408 (as of c1950) 1 inf, **cwSD,** Mare's egg. A puff ball.

mare's nest n Cf **hurrah's nest 1, 3**
An untidy jumble, mess; spec, a tangle of debris in a stream.
1948 *New Yorker* 21 Feb 23 **NYC,** Two ladies who were lodged (so they bitterly reminded one another) in an outrageous and expensive mare's-nest at a hotel on Madison. **1951** Gibson *Basic Seamanship* 367, *Mare's nest:* term applied to a stowage space where gear is piled up in hit-or-miss fashion. Also called a *hurrah's* . . *nest.* **1952** *Nation* 6 Dec 521 **NJ,** The settings of the stage in Balzac, the antiquarian preliminaries of Scott, are often mare's-nests of this littered non-functional style. **1967–68** *DARE* (Qu. E22, *If a house is untidy and everything is upset* . . *"It's a _____!" or "It looks like _____."*) Infs **DC**1, **KS**18, **LA**14, **OH**38, **WI**29, Mare's nest. **1975** Gould *ME Lingo* 176, *Mare's-nest.* . . Any wild jumble of unrelated things; a mess of *culch.* A *mare's-nest,* actually, is a bunching up of debris in a stream where a fallen log catches what comes down. Sticks and leaves and stuff.

mare's shanks See **shank's mare**

mare's tail n
1 also *mare tail:* A long, thin cirrus cloud. Cf **cow's tail 4, lamb's tail 2, mackerel sky**
1854 Kane *Grinnell Exped.* 246 **PA,** It resembled the mackerel fleeces and mare's tails of our summer skies at home. **1899** (1912) Green *VA Folk-Speech* 275, *Mare's-tails.* . . Long, straight fibres of grey cirrus cloud, an indication of the approach of stormy weather. **1931** *PMLA* 46.1304 s**Appalachians,** Jedging from them mare's-tails (small streaks of white clouds), hit looks like warm weather. **1933** Cannell *Signs* 11 **NE,** Mare-tail clouds signify rain within three days. **1965–70** *DARE* (Qu. B10, . . *Long trailing clouds high in the sky*) 157 Infs, **widespread,** Mare's tail(s); **OH**67, Old mare's tails; 18 Infs, **scattered,** Mare tails; **GA**71, Mare-tail clouds; (Qu. B11, . . *Other kinds of clouds that come often*) Infs **CA**87, **NY**53, 69, **OR**1, **PA**242, Mare's tail(s); **OR**10, Mare tails.
2 A plant of the genus *Hippurus*. [*OED* 1762 →] Also called **bottlebrush 3, cattail 2c**
1817 Eaton *Botany* 7, *Hippurus.* . . *Vulgaris,* (marestail). **1868** (1870) Gray *Field Botany* 141, *Hippurus,* Marestail. . . The linear acute leaves in whorls of 8–12. **1876** [see **3** below]. **1911** Jepson *Flora CA* 284, *Mare's Tail.* . . Shallow margins of ponds and about springs. **1950** Gray–Fernald *Manual of Botany* 1076, *Mare's-tail.* Flaccid or fleshy plants of cool reg[ions] of N. and S. Hemisph[ere]. **1976** Bailey–Bailey *Hortus Third* 565, *Mare's-tail.* . . In deep or running water, st[em]s may be several ft. long, remaining submersed and sterile.
3 =**horsetail 1.** [*OED* 1868 →]
1876 Hobbs *Bot. Hdbk.* 172, Marestail, Hippurus vulgaris. Marestail . . Equisetum hyemale. **1916** *Torreya* 16.236, *Equisetum arvense.* . . Mare's-tail, Matinicus Id., Me. **1974** (1977) Coon *Useful Plants* 131, *Equisetum hyemale* . . mare's-tail. **1985** Clark *From Mailbox* 109 **ME,** Horse-tail, also called mare's tail, moves into poorly drained soil, which is not a problem on my hilltop.
4 A **horseweed 1** (here: *Conyza canadensis*).
1900 Lyons *Plant Names* 221, *L[eptilon] Canadense.* . . Mare's-tail. **1911** Henkel *Amer. Med. Leaves* 38, *Canada Fleabane.* . . *Other common names* . . mare's-tail [etc]. . . The erect stem is bristly hairy or sometimes smooth, and in the larger plants usually branched near the top. . . This weed . . produces from June to November numerous heads of small, inconspicuous white flowers. **1931** Harned *Wild Flowers Alleghanies* 562, *E[rigeron] canadensis.* . . A very coarse, unattractive weed familiarly known to the farmer under the names . . Mare's tail, Butterweed and Hogweed. . . It contains a resinous, bitter juice that is

quite irritating to the skin. **1935** (1943) Muenscher *Weeds* 483, Marestail. . . Common throughout North America. Native; also introduced in some localities.
5 An aster (here: *Aster ericoides*).
1900 Lyons *Plant Names* 52, *A[ster] ericoides.* . . Mare's-tail. **1940** Clute *Amer. Plant Names* 76, *A[ster] ericoides.* . . Mare's tail.

mare tail See **mare's tail 1**

margaret See **margaret grunt**

margaretfish n
1 See **margaret grunt.**
2 A **sailor's choice** (here: *Haemulon parrai*).
1935 Caine *Game Fish* 79, Bastard Margaret Grunt—*Haemulon parra* [sic]. . . *Synonyms* . . Margaretfish.

margaret grunt n Also *margaret(fish), margarite* [Appar folk-etym for *margate fish; DJE* 1892 →]
A **grunt 1** (here: *Haemulon album*). Also called **maggot-fish, margate fish a, marketfish, pompon, porgy, sailor's choice**
1898 U.S. Natl. Museum *Bulletin* 47.1295, *Haemulon album.* . . *Margaret Grunt.* . . Reaches a length of 2 feet or more, and is an important food-fish at Key West, . . and Jamaica. **1902** [see **margate fish a**]. **1935** Caine *Game Fish* 85, The margaretfish or margaret grunt is one of the largest members of the grunt family, and is found from Florida south to Brazil. **1946** LaMonte *N. Amer. Game Fishes* 64, *Haemulon album* . . Margaret Grunt. . . Averages 1 to 2 pounds; runs up to 10 pounds and a length of over 2′. **1973** Knight *Cook's Fish Guide* 382, Grunt₍₅₎ . . margaret see Margate.

margat See **margate fish a**

margate See **margate fish a, c**

margate fish n
Any of several **grunts 1,** as:
a also *margat, margate (grunt), margotfish:* =**margaret grunt.** [See quot 1902; *OED* 1734 →]
1734 Royal Soc. London *Philos. Trans.* 38.315, *Perca marina Gibbosa cinerea.* The *Margate-Fish.* This is esteem'd very good Meat. **1775** (1962) Romans *Nat. Hist. FL* app xix, A little to the north . . is a small reef . . , where vast quantites [sic] of groopers, snappers, amber-fish, porgys, margate-fish, rock-fish, yellow-tails, Jew-fish, &c. may be taken. *Ibid* app lii, These most commonly caught are such as seamen know by the following names, viz. *King-fish,* . . *margate-fish,* . . and an immense variety of others. **1876** U.S. Natl. Museum *Bulletin* 5.53, The Margate-fish of the fishermen is probably this species [=*Haemulon album*]. . . The fishermen recognize several others. **1902** Jordan–Evermann *Amer. Fishes* 422, The name margate-fish appears to have been derived from Margate, a well-known seaport and watering-place in England, from which some of the "conchs" . . originally came. In the Bahamas and at Key West the name is now variously corrupted into margat, market, margaret, and margarite. **1946** LaMonte *N. Amer. Game Fishes* 64, *Margate Fish.* . . *Names* . . Margate, Margate Grunt, Margot-fish. The fish may turn greenish if disturbed. **1973** Knight *Cook's Fish Guide* 384, Margate (. . g[oo]d).
b A **redmouth** (here: *Bathystoma aurolineatum*).
1884 U.S. Natl. Museum *Bulletin* 27.443, *Diabasis chrysopterus.* . . *Margate-fish.* . . Atlantic coast of the southern United States.
c also *margate (grunt), margotfish:* A **pompon** (here: *Anisotremus surinamensis*).
1933 John G. Shedd Aquarium *Guide* 109, *Anisotremus surinamensis*—Black Margate; Pompon. . . A large fish, reaching a length of two or three feet. It is fairly common on the south Atlantic coast. **1935** Caine *Game Fish* 114, Pompon. . . Synonyms: Black Margatefish. . . Margatefish. Margate Grunt. Margotfish. **1946** LaMonte *N. Amer. Game Fishes* 67, Pompon. . . *Names* . . Black Margate, Margate Fish, Margate Grunt. . . Usually gray, with dark fins and a broad dark band encircling the body just under the pectoral fin. **1960** Amer. Fisheries Soc. *List Fishes* 30, Black margate . . *Anisotremus surinamensis.*

margate grunt See **margate fish a, c**

margil n esp **TX**
=**moonseed 2.**
1936 Whitehouse *TX Flowers* 31, *Moonseed Vine.* . . is also called . . margil [etc]. **1951** *PADS* 15.31 **TX,** *Epibaterium carolinum.* . . Margil. **1960** Vines *Trees SW* 275, Vernacular names [for *Cocculus carolinus*] are . . Moonseed, Carolina Moonseed, . . Margil.

margotfish See **margate fish a, c**

margus, margut See **marrow gut**

maria n [*DCan* 1909 →]
=**burbot.**

1960 *Amer. Fisheries Soc. List Fishes* 62, Maria—see burbot. **1973** Knight *Cook's Fish Guide* 384, Maria—Burbot. [**1983** Becker *Fishes WI* 747, Burbot. . . Other common names . . maria (Saskatchewan, Manitoba, northern Ontario).]

marigold n
A **gaillardia** (here: *Gaillardia pulchella*).

1920 Pellett *Amer. Honey Plants* 154, Marigold (*Gaillardia pulchella*). . . This particular species. . . is the source of large quantities of yellow honey in Texas, where it is highly regarded as a honey plant.

marigut See **marrow gut**

maringouin n Also *marronguin* [Fr < Tupi–Guarani *marigoui* mosquito] **chiefly LA** Cf *DJE* **merrywing**
A **mosquito** n[1] **B1**, esp a large one.

[**1679** in 1876 Margry *Découvertes* 1.465 **cwIL**, On n'y est presque point incommodé de maringouins ny d'autres animaux nuisibles. [=One is hardly troubled at all there by maringouins or other harmful creatures.]] **1917** *DN* 4.420 **New Orleans LA**, Marronguin [mærɔən'guɛə]. . . A large mosquito. [*DN* Ed: Nasal *n* in second syl.] [**1931** Read *LA French* 95, Maringouin, "wiggletail"; *moustique*, "mosquito." *Place* St. Francisville. *Parish* West Feliciana.] [**1939** *AmSp* 14.112 **seMO** [Creole dial], Maringouin was used as early as 1632. . . The word recurs regularly from that time on in the letters and narratives of explorers and missionaries. . . It is only natural that one should hear it today in Canada, Missouri and Louisiana.] **1941** Writers' Program *Guide LA* 690, Maringouin. . . A mosquito. **1968** *DARE* (Qu. R15a, . . *Names or nicknames . . for mosquitoes*) Inf **LA**37, [,mar,æ'gwæ]; (Qu. R15b, . . *An extra-big mosquito*) Inf **LA**26, [,mare'gɔ̃].

mariola n [MexSpan] **chiefly SW**
A **guayule** (here: *Parthenium incanum*).

1913 Wooton *Trees NM* 145, Mariola is a Spanish name for *Parthenium incanum*, a low shrub 2 to 3 feet high, with gray-green leaves and inconspicuous white flowers. **1931** U.S. Dept. Ag. *Misc. Pub.* 101.165, Mariola (*Parthenium incanum*) . . is a shrubby plant, growing scatteringly but commonly . . from extreme western Texas to southern Arizona and south into Mexico. **1938** Van Dersal *Native Woody Plants* 179, Mariola. . . New shoots and flower heads sometimes nibbled by livestock. **1970** Correll *Plants TX* 1626, Mariola. . . Shrub . . intricately branched from the base. . . Very frequent in Trans-Pecos deserts. **1981** Benson–Darrow *Trees SW Deserts* 298, Mariola is of interest as a relative of the Mexican rubber plant . . (*Parthenium argentatum* . .).

marionette n esp **LA, AL**
=**bufflehead 2.**

1838 Audubon *Ornith. Biog.* 4.217, Buffel-headed Duck . . being known to these different districts by the names of . . Marrionette [sic], Dipper, and Die-dipper. **1888** Trumbull *Names of Birds* 82, The Bufflehead is . . Marionette . . [in] the state of Louisiana. **1921** LA Dept. of Conserv. *Bulletin* 10.61, Rarer in more recent years and more beautifully marked than the golden-eye is the buffle-head or "marionette". **1923** U.S. Dept. Ag. *Misc. Circular* 13.23 **AL, LA**, Bufflehead. . . *Vernacular Names. . . In local use.* . . Marionette. **1962** Imhof *AL Birds* 154, Bufflehead. . . *Other names:* Marionette, Butterball. This diminutive duck looks like a teal-sized goldeneye with different head markings. **1982** Elman *Hunter's Field Guide* 211, Bufflehead . . *Common and regional names:* butterball, . . dipper duck, marionette.

mariposa n [Span "butterfly"]
1 See **mariposa lily.**
2 =**opah.**

1896 U.S. Natl. Museum *Bulletin* 47.954, *Lampris luna*. . . Mariposa; Opah; Moonfish. . . Color a rich brocade of silver and lilac, rosy on the belly; everywhere with round silvery spots; head, opercles, and back with ultramarine tints; jaws and fins vermilion. **1902** Jordan–Evermann *Amer. Fishes* 326, The single known species is the opah, mariposa, or moonfish. . . This interesting fish is found in the open waters of the Atlantic and Pacific. . . It has also been taken at Monterey and other places on the California coast.

mariposa lily n Also *mariposa (tulip)* [See quot 1868] esp **CA**
A plant of the genus *Calochortus* native to the western US. Also called **butterfly weed 3, cat's-ear 1, fairy bell 3, fairy**

lantern 1, globe tulip, Indian potato d, mountain tulip, pretty grass, sego lily, star tulip, wild tulip. For other names of var spp see **air castle flower, beavertail grass, dew-bell, globe lily, golden bowl mariposa, golden lantern, hairbell 2, Indian bells, lead flower, lily bell 1, mouse-ear 6, prairie lily, pussy's ear, sand lily, satin bell, snowdrop**

1868 Acad. Nat. Sci. Philadelphia *Proc.* [20].169, This splendid flower [=*Calochortus venustus*] . . has long been known to the native Californians by the name of *Mariposa* (Spanish for butterfly). **1869** (1911) Muir *First Summer* 43 **ceCA**, The grasses and flowers in glorious array, . . monardella, Mariposa tulips, lupines. **1888** Lindley–Widney *CA of South* 330, Mariposa is the Indian [sic] word for butterfly, and butterfly-like, these flowers are poised upon their delicate stems, each cup a chalice, and every petal irised at its heart. **1894** *Jrl. Amer. Folkl.* 7.101, *Calochortus* (several species), Mariposa lilies, Santa Barbara Co., Cal. *Calochortus Nuttallii*, . . Mariposa lily, Deer Lodge, Mont. **1899** in 1919 Hale *Letters* 345 **cwCA**, Mariposa lilies, painter's-brush, poppies, and dozens of others. **1920** Rice–Rice *Pop. Studies CA Wild Flowers* 27, It would probably be more correct to say Mariposa Tulip than Mariposa Lily, for botanists place them in the tulip family. **1934** White *Folded Hills* 198 **cwCA**, Here also were . . yuccas; chollas; mariposas; cascara and artemisia bushes from the mountains. **1947** *Natl. Geogr. Mag.* July 60 **West,** And the Mariposas . . mostly spurn permanent sanctuary with humans. **1966** *DARE* FW Addit **WA**12, Sand lily (or mariposa)—grows on tall, slender stalk; bloom is like flock of butterflies. **1973** Hitchcock–Cronquist *Flora Pacific NW* 686, *Calochortus* . . Butterfly, Mariposa, or Star Tulip; Mariposa or Sego Lily; Mariposa; Cats-ear.

mark n Cf **earmark** n
An identifying mark put on a domestic animal, esp one made by cutting or notching the ear.

1636 in 1836 New Plymouth Colony *Compact* 43, That every man's marke of his cattle be brought to the towne booke where he lives & that no man give the same but shall alter any other bought by him & put his owne upon them. **1660** in 1865 MA Hist. Soc. *Coll.* 4th ser 7.244, Bring in all your horses & mares, & brand them with this mark . . in the sholder. **1746** in 1886 Braintree MA *Records* 145, One White Ram Lamb, ye artificial Mark is a swallows tail cut out of rear (vizt.) ye left Ear & a slit in ye Right Ear. **1885** U.S. Bur. Indian Affairs *Report* 126 **MT**, They [=American Indians] use their own brands and marks. **1899** (1912) Green *VA Folk-Speech* 275, Mark. . . Made on the ears of animals by various cuts with a knife to distinguish the ownership. **1915** *DN* 4.185 **swVA**, Mark. . . A cutting of the ear (of hogs, sheep, cattle) for identification. **1929** *AmSp* 5.70 **NE,** Cattle are frequently given . . a "mark," often called a "jaw lap," if the skin on the jaw is cut, or an "ear mark" . . if the ear is notched or the tip of it cut. **1936** Adams *Cowboy Lingo* 130, Like brands, each mark had a name. **1956** *Hall Coll.* **eTN**, Sometimes they'd split the end of the ear [of livestock]. They [=the owners] all had different marks. **1965–70** *DARE* (Qu. K18, . . *Kind of mark . . to identify a cow*) Infs **NC**13, 81, Mark in the ear; **FL**27, **NY**58, Mark(s); **CT**14, The time was when cows were either branded or had marks in their ears; **FL**6, Stock mark—on ears, cut; use clips now; **ME**12, Used to paint a mark on sheep, on shoulder; **ME**19, Mark on their ears—with a metal tag; **MS**60, Mark—cut them on the ear; **NM**13, Mark (earmark)—not used much now. **1967–68** *DARE* Tape **NJ**73, [FW:] How'd you tell whose pig it was when you went out to get 'em? . . [Inf:] Every man had a mark. . . Maybe your mark would be a slit in the left ear; **NC**41, If I seen your mark, I'd say, well, that's Miss Williamson's cow. **1975** Gould *ME Lingo* 176, Creature *marks* were notches cut in the ears of cattle to identify ownership; precursors of branding *marks;* all Maine farmers had their *marks.*

mark v[1]
1 To put an identifying mark on (a domestic animal), esp by cutting or notching the ear; to make such a mark on (the ear or other part of an animal); hence vbl n *marking.*

1657 in 1913 *MD Hist. Mag.* 8.33, Complaint of many [was made against someone] . . for common frequenting the wild gang, killing cattle, and marking calves, all of which he pretended to be his own. **1672** in 1887 Huntington NY *Town Rec.* 1.196, These farmers shall from time to time Duly mark [the ears of] all their calves, Lambs and Piggs within . . 20 Days after they be fallen. **1814** *Niles' Natl. Reg.* 6.393, Westward of the *Mississippi* it is said not to be uncommon for one man to mark from *one* to *three thousand* calves in a season. **1941** Dobie *Longhorns* 66, When a bull is castrated on the range, he is invariably earmarked and branded or . . at least marked. **1956** *Hall Coll.* **eTN,**

They marked the ears [of the stock]. Sometimes they'd split the end of the ear. **1965–68** *DARE* (Qu. K18, . . *Kind of mark . . to identify a cow*) Infs **CA23, GA28, LA3, 18, MO37, OK20,** Mark the (*or* their) ears; **FL17,** You mark ears and brand shoulder; **FL29,** Mark or cut ear; **NC79,** Mark them on the ear; **SC26,** Mark the hoof. **1970** [see **2** below]. **1992** [see **2** below].

2 By ext: used broadly to include other operations, as docking and castration, usually performed at the same time as earmarking; hence, euphemistically, to castrate; rarely, to spay; hence vbl n *marking*; ppl adj *marked*. [Cf *AND* 1883 →; also *OEDS mark* v. 2.f "*Austral.* and *N.Z.*"] **chiefly Sth, S Midl** See Map
  1912 *DN* 3.583 **wIN,** Mark. . . To castrate. "Did you mark your colt yesterday?" **1934** Vines *Green Thicket* 69 **cnAL,** Greenberry . . threw the hog. . . And Lat cut out his stones . . and laid them on a chestnut log. And time and again Greenberry brought out little boars, threw them and held them while Lat worked on some of them and marked the ears of those unmarked with a split in the left and a half undercrop in the right. . . By this procedure Lat marked all the shoaty pigs and spayed some of the sows about grown. **1935** Hyatt *Folkl. Adams Co. IL* 97, You will kill a pig, if you "mark" it in the sign of the "private parts." **1952** Brown *NC Folkl.* 1.563, *Mark.* . . To castrate; probably a euphemism.— General. Obsolescent. **1954** Jordan *Hell's Canyon* 117 **ID,** "Marking" is the final indication of the year's program of breeding, herding and lambing. . . All lambs' tails are cut off, and their ears are notched to show age and ownership. In addition, the wether (male) lambs are castrated. **c1960** *Wilson Coll.* **csKY,** Mark. . . Castrate. **1965–70** *DARE* (Qu. K70, *Words used . . for castrating an animal*) 44 Infs, **chiefly Sth, S Midl,** Mark; (Qu. J3a, *To make a female dog so that she can't breed, she must be* _____) Inf **WV17,** Marked; (Qu. J3b, . . *A female cat*) Inf **WV17,** Marked; (Qu. K58, *A castrated pig*) Infs **CA193, LA12, OK43, TN33, 35, VA7,** Marked pig. **1970** *DARE* Tape **AR56,** She just had these pigs. . . Dad marked them things, casterated the males, marked their ball of their ears; **KY93,** We have a very small little knife called a casterating knife. . . We mark 'em [=pigs] with that. **1992** Attebery *Sheep* 40 **swID, eOR,** There are four distinct processes subsumed under the term "marking"; the branding or marking itself, earmarking, docking, and castrating, all done as steps in the single operation.

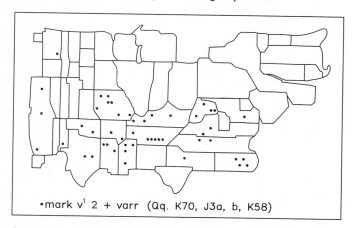

• mark v¹ 2 + varr (Qq. K70, J3a, b, K58)

3 To cause (an unborn child) to have some physical or mental peculiarity, supposed to be a direct consequence of an experience of the mother's; hence n *marking* such a peculiarity; ppl adj *marked*. **chiefly Sth, S Midl** Cf **birthscald**
  c1738 (1929) Byrd *Histories* 54 **VA,** Milk is so Scarce . . that were a Big-belly'd Woman to long for it, She would lose her Longing. And, in truth, I believe this is . . a very good reason why so many People in this Province are markt with a Custard Complexion. **1928** Chapman *Happy Mt.* 223 **seTN,** I got a terrible dread o' beasts . . owing to my mother marking me afore I was born. **1928** Peterkin *Scarlet Sister Mary* 270 **SC,** Mary was almost afraid to look at them for fear she might mark her child. **1930** Shoemaker *1300 Words* 41 **cPA Mts** (as of c1900), *Marked*—A child mentally or physically disfigured as a result of a pre-natal experience of the mother. **1933** Rawlings *South Moon* 202 **FL,** "I said to him, 'Willy, I've took the biggest notion for some white sugar. Fetch me back a half a pound.' . . He comes back and he hands me the sack and he says, 'Here's your white sugar, Py-tee.' I opens the sack. Kezzy, the sugar were brown. I says, 'Willy, the sugar's brown.' When I said it, I could feel the young un turn over inside me. You see I marked him. Willy felt awful bad about it." "You marked him for white sugar,

a'right." **1949** Webber *Backwoods Teacher* 194 **Ozarks,** If ary lady was to come along that was in the family way, hit might mark the baby if she was to be give a turn by the sight of the blood. **1954** Harder *Coll.* **cwTN,** Mark. . . To cause a spot on an unborn baby by the mother's being frightened. **1965** Hyatt *Folkl. Adams Co. IL* 113, Children are marked during the last three months of pregnancy. **1990** Cavender *Folk Med. Lexicon* 27 **sAppalachians,** *Marking*—a birthmark, physical characteristic or behavior trait caused during pregnancy by the mother having a frightening/unfortunate experience or violating a taboo.

mark v² See **mock** v

markary See **mercury 1**

marked See **mark** v¹ **2, 3**

markel See **merkel** n²

marker n

1 A distinctively marked or colored animal (esp a black sheep), used in making an estimate of the size of the herd. **West**
  1913 (1979) Barnes *Western Grazing* 382, *Markers.*—The black sheep in a herd. Every herder knows exactly how many of such he has and by running over them occasionally he feels fairly sure that if they are all there he has lost no sheep. **1931** *AmSp* 6.357 **West,** He checks [the number of his sheep] every few days by . . counting his "markers," the black and spotted members of his flock. A "bell" is also a marker, as are other sheep with sufficient individuality to make them memorable. . . Markers are thus numerous enough so that no considerable number of the band could ordinarily get lost without taking one of them along; if all markers are present there is good reason to believe that the herd is intact. **1936** Adams *Cowboy Lingo* 72, 'Markers' were animals with certain coloration or other marks easily distinguished and remembered by the owner and his riders. Such animals have frequently been the downfall of rustlers when used as proof of theft. **1938** FWP *Guide SD* 87, *Marker:* usually a black sheep, but may be any unusual one used in checking up on possible lost sheep. **1992** Attebery *Sheep* 68 **ID,** He [=a sheepherder] will probably count his markers—one black sheep for every 200 ewes—at least once a day.

2 A license plate.
  1921 CT Laws *Public Acts* 3452, Abandoned markers of motor vehicles. . . Any person who shall have found any . . number plates of any motor vehicle of the current year not issued to him shall immediately deliver them to the commissioner or to any officer. **1981** *DARE* File, The usual term for license plate in northern New England is number plate. This summer I heard a cousin of mine—originally from Massachusetts but a resident of Connecticut for 35 years or so—refer to one as a marker.

markery See **mercury 1**

marketfish n Also *market* [Folk-etym for **margate fish**]
A **grunt 1:** either **margaret grunt** or a **pompon** (here: *Anisotremus surinamensis*).
  1884 Goode *Fisheries U.S.* 1.394 **FL,** The Margate-fish. . . At Key West it is brought to market in well-boats, and sells readily. . . The large ones [are called] "Margate-fish" and "Market-fish." **1902** [see **margate fish a**]. **1911** U.S. Bur. Census *Fisheries 1908* 312, *Margate-fish* (*Haemulon album*). A grunt found in southern Florida; known also as . . "market-fish," etc. **1935** Caine *Game Fish* 85, *Margaret Grunt.* . . Synonyms . . Marketfish. *Ibid* 114, *Pompon.* . . Synonyms . . Marketfish. **1946** LaMonte *N. Amer. Game Fishes* 64, *Haemulon album.* . . Names . . Marketfish. *Ibid* 67, *Anisotremus surinamensis.* . . Names . . Marketfish. **1973** Knight *Cook's Fish Guide* 384, Marketfish—Margate.

marketing n

1 Shopping, esp for groceries. **scattered, but esp east of Missip R** See Map on p. 516 Cf **storing**
  1943 *LANE* Map 554, The terms *shopping,* . . *marketing* and *purchasing,* usually recorded in the context *I must go to town* (or *downtown*) *to do some shopping.* . . *Marketing* differs from the other terms in that it usually refers specifically to the purchasing of food. **1965–70** *DARE* (Qu. U1b, . . *Buying groceries*) 88 Infs, **scattered, but esp east of Missip R,** Marketing; (Qu. U1a, *When you are going to a store or several stores to buy things* . . *"I'm going* _____.") Infs **CT1, KS3, NE10, NY126, OH48, 73, PA186, 245,** Marketing. **1992** *DARE* File **cwCA** (as of c1950), A friend of my mother's used to talk about doing the "marketing" rather than doing the grocery shopping. I always thought it was because she had lived in New York for a while.

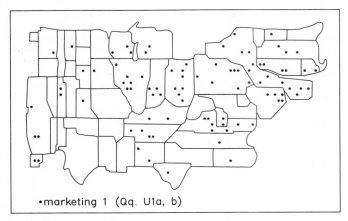

•marketing 1 (Qq. U1a, b)

2 By ext: see quot.

1899 (1912) Green *VA Folk-Speech* 275, *Marketing*. . . Groceries or other articles bought by people when they go to market.

market road n
=farm-to-market road.

1967–70 *DARE* (Qu. N27a, *Names . . for different kinds of unpaved roads*) Inf **TN53**, Market road; (Qu. N28, *A road that connects a big highway with stores and business places set back from it*) Inf **OR3**, Market road; (Qu. N29, *. . Names . . for a less important road running back from a main road*) Inf **OR1**, Market road.

market-wagon n esp **NEast** *old-fash* Cf **farm-to-market wagon**

A horse-drawn wagon used to carry produce or other loads, often serving as a stand from which to sell goods.

1802 in 1851 U.S. Congress *Debates & Proc.* 18 Mar 1027, In the State of New Jersey five hundred and forty two [of the carriages taxed] are . . principally market-wagons, and not designed for pleasurable purposes. **1882** (1971) Gibbons *PA Dutch* 405, The Halloween visitors limited themselves . . to propping up one end of the market-wagon on the fence. **1890** Howells *Boy's Town* 3 **OH**, I must not forget the market-house, with its public market twice a week, and its long rows of market-wagons. **1895** Warner *Golden House* 9, Here and there [was] a lumbering market-wagon from Jersey. **1948** Rittenhouse *Amer. Horse-Drawn Vehicles* 84, *Market or express wagon*. (Period: 1870. . .) These rather top-heavy wagons were used in cities after the Civil War. Body was 86 by 45 inches, with lower side panels 12 inches high. Wheels 39 and 51½ inches. Top, which was removable, was 60 inches above the floor. Canvas sides. **1967** *DARE* Tape **PA29**, [Inf:] Yeah, that's what we call a market-wagon. . . [FW:] It's all closed in with glass. [Inf:] All closed in. **1968–69** *DARE* (Qu. N41a, *. . Horse-drawn vehicles . . to carry people*) Inf **NJ16**, Market-wagon; (Qu. N41b, *Horse-drawn vehicles to carry heavy loads*) Inf **NY62**, Market-wagon; (Qu. N41c, *Horse-drawn vehicles to carry light loads*) Inf **MA19**, Market-wagon—same as spring wagon; **NY205**, **OH56**, **RI6**, Market-wagon. **1983** *PADS* 70.41 *ce,sePA*, *Market wagon*. . . A covered wagon used to haul farm products to the city markets.

marking vbl n See **mark** v[1] **1, 2**

marking n See **mark** v[1] **3**

markingbird See **mockingbird**

markry See **mercury 1**

mark (something) in the chimney corner v phr

To take note of (something).

1968 *DARE* FW Addit **PA169**, Mark that in the chimney corner—don't forget. [**1992** *DARE* File *sePA*, My table companions, all thoroughly Dutch, agreed with me that the P[ennsylvania] G[erman] expression "in der Schannschtee schreiwe," "to write it in the chimney," meaning to make note of an unusual event, is widely known in the Dutch country.]

markweed n [Prob folk-etym for **mercury**]

A **poison ivy** (here: *Toxicodendron radicans*).

1892 *Jrl. Amer. Folk.* 5.94, *Rhus toxicodendron*. . . Mark-weed. Kennebec Co., Me. **1914** Georgia *Manual Weeds* 274, *Poison Ivy*. . . *Other English names* . . Markweed. . . A very poisonous plant, far too common everywhere, for to many persons the touch of it brings disaster,

blotching the skin with burning "water-blisters". **1940** Clute *Amer. Plant Names* 126, *R. toxicodendron. Poison Ivy.* . . Mark-weed. **1964** Kingsbury *Poisonous Plants U.S.* 209, Markweed. . . Vigorous woody vine, shrub, or subshrub with trifoliate, alternate leaves.

marlberry n [Perh *marl* Brit var of *marble*, but perh *marl* calcareous soil; cf quots 1946, 1971]

A small tree *(Ardisia escallionoides)* native to southern Florida. Also called **marbleberry**

1884 Sargent *Forests of N. Amer.* 100, *Marlberry.* . . Wood heavy, hard, very close-grained, compact, susceptible of a beautiful polish. **1897** Sudworth *Arborescent Flora* 316 **FL**, *Icacore paniculata.* . . *Common Names.* Marlberry. **1919** Smithsonian Inst. *Annual Rept. for 1917* 384 **sFL**, In addition to these are the paradise tree, or bitterwood; soapberry tree; . . marlberry [etc]. **1946** [see **marbleberry**]. **1971** Craighead *Trees S. FL* 175, [The shallow marl soil . . is often only 4 to 10 inches deep with little humus. *Ibid* 176, Where the rocky outcrops break off to meet the marl glades . . there is a well-formed gully with a distinct change in vegetation.] *Ibid* 177, On the rim hammocks [of this gully] the important trees include live oak, marlberry, . . two species of wild coffee [etc]. **1979** Little *Checklist U.S. Trees* 57, *Marlberry.* . . *Range*— S. Fla. incl. Fla. Keys, n. on e. coast to Volusia and Flagler Co[untie]s and on w. coast to Pinellas Co.

Marlboro blue n [See quots 1945, 1947] Cf **brass ankle**

A member of a group of racially mixed people in eastern South Carolina.

1945 *Amer. Jrl. Sociol.* 51.34 **SC**, In Chesterfield they [=persons of mixed racial background] are known as "Marlboro Blues," a slur on the adjoining county, whence they came. **1946** *Social Forces* 24.439 **SC**, These peoples are located mainly on the coastal plain area of the State. They are called by a variety of names, depending on the county. . . They are termed Brass Ankles . . in Dorchester . . and Charleston counties; . . Marlboro Blues in Chesterfield. **1947** *AmSp* 22.84, The names *Blue-Eyed Negroes* and *Marlboro Blues,* . . probably both call attention to the blue eye-color found in some members of mixed-blood groups but rarely among pure Indians or Negroes. **1963** Berry *Almost White* 16, The derogatory terms usually employed by both whites and Negroes in the localities where these marginal Indians live—terms such as "red niggers," "half-niggers," "marlboro blues," "yellow hammers," "free jacks." **1966** *DARE* (Qu. HH29a, *. . People of mixed blood—part Indian*) Inf **SC2**, In Marlboro county, Marlboro blues—part Negro, White, and Indian.

Marlborough pie n Also *Marlborough tart,* ~ *pudding pie* Also sp *Marlboro pie* esp **NEng**

A pie with a custard-like filling usu consisting of crushed apples and flavored with lemon.

1869 Stowe *Oldtown Folks* 340 **NEng**, Pumpkin pies, . . apple pies, Marlborough-pudding pies . . attested the boundless fertility of the feminine mind. **1893** (1900) Hale *New Engl. Boyhood* 115 **MA**, In any old and well-regulated family in New England, you will find there is a traditional method of making the Marlborough pie, which is a sort of lemon pie. **1906** *Pocumtuc Housewife* 24 *nwMA*, *Marlborough Pies.* Steam until tender six large tart apples and strain. . . One spoonful of butter. When cool add two eggs, the rind and juice of a lemon, and one cup of sugar beaten together. **1947** Phillips *Salem* 347 **MA** (as of c1800), And then, of course, a few pies of various sorts from squash through apple, cranberry, and gooseberry, according to seasons, to Marlborough, named for the great Duke. **1949** Brown *Amer. Cooks* 546, I wonder how many people know Marlborough pie, which I attribute to New Hampshire origin. Certain am I that the pie is well-nigh unknown outside a few communities. **1964** Amer. Heritage *Cookbook* 582, *Marlborough Tart.* **1970** *DARE* File, *Marlborough pie*—I never knew this in New England, but a friend in Cleveland used to make it—and spoke of it as a Yankee kind of pie. **1979** *Cuisine* Sept 74, Countless versions of the Marlborough, or Marlboro, pie, beginning with Marlborough puddings and thence similar formulas baked in pie shells were published in America. One popular form was made with grated apples.

Marley Bright See **Molly Bright**

marlin n[1]

1 A godwit:

a also *big marlin, brown* ~, *common* ~, *marlin curlew:*
=marbled godwit. [See quots 1888, 1956]

1844 Giraud *Birds Long Is.* 260, The Great Marbled Godwit, or

"Marlin," as our gunners term it, arrives on the shores of Long Island in the month of May. . . The flesh of the Marlin is tender and juicy, and is prized as game. **1880** *Forest & Stream* 15.4, Great marbled godwit. . . Known along the seaboard, from Maine to Maryland, as the marlin. **1881** *Ibid* 17.225, The marlin of the West is the marble godwit . . of the East. **1886** *Ibid* 27.25, Mr. R.B. Roosevelt . . says, "Saw the marlins go past as many as thirty in a flock." My acquaintance with the birds of Long Island . . leads me to class both the godwits, commonly known as the brown and ring-tailed marlin, as rare. Will Mr. Roosevelt kindly state which of the marlins he refers to, if either. I apprehend he saw flocks of Hudsonian curlew *(Numenius hudsonicus)* which is sometimes called crooked-bill marlin. **1888** Trumbull *Names of Birds* 206, Marbled Godwit. . . At Newport, R.I., *Common Marlin*. . . On Long Island . . and . . in New Jersey . . and at Eastville, Va., *Marlin*. . . The name Marlin comes from a resemblance in the bird's bill to the old-fashioned marline-spike, which was more or less curved in shape. **1917** *Wilson Bulletin* 29.2.80, *Limosa fedoa*. Marlin curlew. Wallops Id., Va. **1925** (1928) Forbush *Birds MA* 1.427, Marbled Godwit. Other names . . marlin; brown marlin; big marlin. **1956** MA Audubon Soc. *Bulletin* 40.20, Marbled Godwit. Big Marlin (R.I. . .). Brown Marlin (Maine, Mass. General color pale cinnamon marked with dusky brownish.); Common Marlin (R.I. . .). Marlin (Maine, Mass. The long pointed bill suggests a marlinspike, traditional tool of a boatswain.)

b *also blacktail marlin*: **=Hudsonian godwit.**

1886 [see **1a** above]. **1923** U.S. Dept. Ag. *Misc. Circular* 13.59 **VA,** *Hudsonian Godwit*. . . *Vernacular Names*. . . *In local use*. . . Marlin. **1956** MA Audubon Soc. *Bulletin* 40.20 **MA,** Hudsonian Godwit. . . Black-tail Marlin. . . The tail, chiefly black, is white at tip and base.

2 *also crooked-bill(ed) marlin*: **=Hudsonian curlew.**

1886 [see **1a** above]. **1888** Trumbull *Names of Birds* 200, *Hudsonian Curlew*. . . In New Jersey . . at Pleasantville and Cape May C[ourt] H[ouse], *Marlin* . . ; again, at Pleasantville and at Somers Point, *Crooked-billed Marlin*. **1895** Elliot *N. Amer. Shore Birds* 156, This species [=*Numenius phaeopus*] bears many names among the gunners in various parts of our country, among which I may cite . . Crooked-bill Marlin. **1923** U.S. Dept. Ag. *Misc. Circular* 13.66, Hudsonian Curlew. . . *Vernacular Names*. . . *In local use*. . . Crooked-billed marlin (N.J.) . . marlin (N.J.) **1946** Hausman *Eastern Birds* 268, Hudsonian Curlew. . . *Other Names* . . Crooked-billed Marlin. . . The Hudsonian Curlew migrates in our area along the Atlantic coast; rarely through the interior of the country.

marlin n² See **merlin**

marlin curlew See **marlin** n¹ **1a**

marlinspike n Also sp *marlinespike, marlingspike*

1 *also marlin(g)spike bird*: **=jaeger** n¹. [See quots 1884, 1956] **chiefly NEng**

1884 U.S. Bur. Fisheries *Rept. for 1882* 324 **NEng,** There are several varieties of jaegers . . which are known to the fishermen by the names of "Marlingspikes," "Whiptails," etc . . , both appellations having a special reference to the two long central tail feathers which is [sic] a distinguishing feature of birds of this species. *Ibid* 327, However predacious the marlinspike may be, so far as the gull is concerned, it never presumes to intimidate the hagdon. **1910** Eaton *Birds NY* 1.116, The Parasitic jaeger is . . fairly common . . on the coast of this State. . . Other names for it are . . Boatswain, Marling-spike. **1917** (1923) *Birds Amer.* 1.35, Parasitic Jaeger. . . *Other Names*. . . Marline-spike. **1951** Pough *Audubon Water Bird* 336, Marling-spike. See Long-tailed jaeger. **1953** Jewett *Birds WA* 289, Parasitic Jaeger. . . Other names . . Marlin-spike. **1956** MA Audubon Soc. *Bulletin* 40.21, Pomarine Jaeger. . . Marlinspike Bird (Maine. In allusion to the projecting middle tail feathers which are compared to the boatswain's familiar tool.). *Parasitic Jaeger*. . . Marlinspike (Maine, Mass.); Marlingspike Bird (Maine). . . *Long-tailed Jaeger*. . . Marlingspike Bird (Maine). **1978** Gromme *Birds WI* 215, Marlinspike (Parasitic Jaeger).

2 A **rattail** (here: *Nezumia bairdi*).

1960 Amer. Fisheries Soc. *List Fishes* 22, Marlin-spike . . *Nezumia bairdi.*

marlinspike bird See **marlinspike 1**

marlow bright See **Molly Bright**

marm n¹ See **ma'am** n¹

marm n² See **mom** n¹

marmot n

Any of var burrowing rodents, spec:

a A rodent of the genus *Marmota*. [*OED* 1607 →] **now chiefly West** Also called **chuck** n², **gopher** n¹ **2b(3), groundhog 1, picket pin, whistlepig, woodchuck.** For other names of *M. monax* see **woodchuck;** for other names of var western spp see **rockchuck, whistler**

1747 Edwards *Nat. Hist. Uncommon Birds* 2.104, The Monax, or Marmotte, of America. **1781** Pennant *Hist. Quadrupeds* 2.398, Marmot. . . *Maryland* M[armot]. . . Inhabits *Virginia* and *Pensylvania:* during winter sleeps under the hollow roots of trees. . . Hoary M[armot]. . . Inhabits the northern parts of *North America*. **1825** in 1974 *Fauna Americana* 158, *Maryland Marmot*. **1840** MA Zool. & Bot. Surv. *Herb. Plants & Quadrupeds* 64, Arctomys monax. . . The Marmot. The Woodchuck. . . This interesting animal is one of the most common in New England. **1917** Anthony *Mammals Amer.* 202, In color the western members range from the grizzled gray of the Hoary Marmot . . to the Yellow-bellied Marmot of the Southwest, . . which can be readily distinguished by the golden hue of its underfur. **1947** Cahalane *Mammals* 337, The marmot does not limit itself to whistles, but when excited may burst forth with a variety of barks, yips and yells. If angry and frightened, it grinds its teeth. **1961** Jackson *Mammals WI* 122, *Marmota monax monax*. . . Vernacular names. . . Marmot [etc]. **1965–70** *DARE* (Qu. P31, . . *Names or nicknames . . for the groundhog*) Inf **CA**130, Often a marmot is called a groundhog; **CA**145, Woodchuck, marmot; **CO**9, Groundhog, marmot; **IL**38, Groundhog, woodchuck, marmot the proper term; **MN**38, Groundhog, marmot the true name; **NM**6, Groundhog—in mountains is marmot; **OR**1, **WA**8, Marmot; (Qu. P32, . . *Other kinds of wild animals*) Infs **GA**7, **WA**11, Marmot. **1980** Whitaker *Audubon Field Guide Mammals* 371, Larger still [than prairie dogs] are the solitary Woodchuck and the marmots *(Marmota)*. *Ibid* 384, Woodchuck—"Groundhog" "Marmot" *(Marmota monax)*. *Ibid* 388, This marmot [=*Marmota caligata*] feeds almost entirely on grasses and many other kinds of green plants and may chase others from feeding grounds it considers its own.

b **=prairie dog.**

1820 in 1823 James *Acct. of Exped.* 1.451 **ceNE,** The high and barren parts of this tract are occupied by numerous communities of the Prairie dog or Louisiana marmot. **1861** Berkeley *Engl. Sportsman* 259 **West,** Has the prairie dog or "marmot," of which class he certainly is, a power of resistance to snake-poison? **1875** *Amer. Naturalist* 9.148, 'Marmot' is sometimes used [*DARE* Ed: for *prairie dog*], the present species being the tawny marmot of some writers, but this is the name of the woodchucks *(Arctomys)*. **1949** Palmer *Nat. Hist.* 611, Hoary Marmot. . . Found in Rocky Mountain areas from Idaho, Washington, and northern Montana. . . See prairie dog for "marmots" farther south.

c *also marmot-squirrel*: A **ground squirrel b** such as *Spermophilus parryi*.

1879 U.S. Natl. Museum *Bulletin* 14.15, Spermophilus Parryi. . . Parry's Marmot. Northern parts of the Continent. **1890** *Century Dict.* 3636, Besides the foregoing [=*Marmota* spp], some of the larger species of the related genera *Cynomys* and *Spermophilus*, which include the prairie-dogs and marmot-squirrels, are sometimes called *marmots*. . . *Marmot-squirrel*. . . Any animal of the genus *Spermophilus*. **1966** *DARE* (Qu. P27, . . *Kinds of squirrels*) Inf **WA**6, Marmot.

d **=mountain beaver.**

1967 *DARE* (Qu. P29, . . *'Gophers' . . other name . . or what other animal are they most like*) Inf **WA**20, Mountain beaver, marmot, varmit [sic]—all same.

marmot-squirrel See **marmot c**

maro See **malo**

marooshka, marowska See **moroshka**

marr n¹ See **mare**

marr n² See **marrow**

marracle See **miracle**

marrell See **morral**

marriageable adj

1916 Macy–Hussey *Nantucket Scrap Basket* 138, A woman speaks of some article of wearing apparel, furniture, or household decoration as her "marriageable," meaning that the dress was a part of her trousseau, or that the table or picture was a wedding present. Examples: "Jane has kept her marriageable dress all these years, and her daughter will be married in it;" or "that bureau was a marriageable present from my aunt."

marriage bone n [nScots dial; the "contest" of breaking a wishbone is sometimes supposed to predict which of two people will marry first.] Cf **love bone, merrythought**
=**pully bone.**
   1949 *AmSp* 24.111 cnSC, Marriage bone. . . Wishbone. [**1977** Mather–Speitel *Ling. Atlas Scotl.* 2.26, [The map shows the term *marriage bone* to occur chiefly in the vicinity of the Moray Firth.]]

marri'd See **marry**

married-in n
   1982 *Smithsonian Letters* KY, Are you familiar with the Kentucky name for in-laws—*married-in* (as "she's a married-in")? This comes from Harlan, Kentucky.

married-man match n Cf **farmer match**
A kitchen match.
   1967 *DARE* (Qu. F46, . . *Matches you can strike anywhere;* not asked in early QRs) Inf IA13, Married-man matches; WI64, Married-man matches—men said this years ago. **1993** *DARE* File MI, Married-man matches. I have heard this phrase many times in Michigan. Referred to large kitchen matches, frequently mounted in holder on wall in kitchen. . . Assumption was that bachelors would not have easy access to kitchens and matches therin. . . A bachelor would be more likely to use book matches.

marrit See **marry**

marronguin See **maringouin**

marrow n Usu |ˈmæro, ˈmɛro, -rə|; also |ˈmɑro, -rə|, **chiefly Sth, S Midl** |mɑr| Pronc-spp *ma'ar, mar(r);* for addit pronc and sp varr see quots at **A** below Cf **bar** n[4], **farrow** adj, **harrow**
A Forms.
   1913 Kephart *Highlanders* 228 sAppalachians, "I've burnt my holler teeth out with a red-hot wire." . . "Kill the nerve?" "No; but it'd sear the mar so it wouldn't be so sensitive." **1914** *DN* 4.103 cKS, The sound [ɑ] occurs similarly in *farrow, harrow, marrow, narrow,* etc. **1925** [see **marrowbone**]. **1942** Hall *Smoky Mt. Speech* 25 wNC, eTN, Arrow, harrow, marrow, narrow, sparrow, wheelbarrow. Usage of [ɑ] and [æ] appears to be about evenly divided in these words. [Footnote:] Local informants say, however, that [ɑ] is much more frequent than [æ]. **1953** Randolph–Wilson *Down in Holler* 17 Ozarks, The nouns marrow, harrow, and sparrow are usually *marr', harr',* and *sparr',* although a gentle *er* ending is sometimes heard even here. **1956** Ker *Vocab. W. TX* 295, Mar . . (bone marrow). c**1960** *Wilson Coll.* csKY, Marrow, as in Marrowbone, is still often [mɑrə] or [mɑr·]. **1964** [see **marrowgut**]. **1965–70** *DARE* (Qu. H43) Inf CA205, Marrowgut; KY34, [ˈmɑrə]; (Qu. H50) Inf PA131, Marrowfat [ˈmɑɪrə,fæt] beans; (Qu. I16) Inf MI23, [ˈmæro] beans; OH75, Marrowfat beans; (Qu. I18) Inf NY109, [ˈmɑrə] beans; NY162, [ˈmɑro] bean; PA181, [mairo] bean; NJ4, OH87, Marrowfat; PA9, 41, 100, [ˈmærə,fæt]; NY83, OH98, [ˈmɛrə,fæt]; (Qu. I20) Inf NY109, [ˈmɑrə] beans; MA6, [,mɛrəˈfæt]; NJ2, [ˈmɛɜ·ɪˈfæts]; NY94, [ˈmɛr,fæt]; (Qu. I23) Inf VA28, [ˈmæərə]; FL9, Boston [ˈmɑrə]; NJ17, Boston [ˈmæro]; CA63, [ˈmærəfæts]. **1969** [see **marrowbone**]. **1974** Fink *Mountain Speech* 16 wNC, eTN, Ma'ar . . marrow. "A ma'ar bone."

B Senses.
1 See **marrowbone.**
2 See **marrowfat (bean).**
3 See **marrowfat (pea).**
4 See **marrow squash.**

marrow bean See **marrowfat (bean)**

marrowbone n Also *marrow* [*OED marrowbone* sb. 3 1532 →]
The knee.
   1806 (1970) Webster *Compendious Dict.* 185, Marrowbone, . . the knee. [*DARE* Ed: This entry was carried over from Webster's English model.] **1854** Stephens *High Life in NY* 79 CT, The gal must be something more than common flesh and blood that would bring Jonathan Slick on his marrow bones. **1865** in 1872 Locke *Struggles Nasby* 220 AL, South Carliny. . . wuz the first to git down on her marrow bones, and beg for peace like a dorg. **1899** (1912) Green *VA Folk-Speech* 275, *Marrow-bones.* . . The bones of the knees; the knees. Used both literally

and figuratively. **1925** Dargan *Highland Annals* 153 cwNC, All she done wuz to git down on her marr's an' pray fer my soul. **1950** *WELS* (Joking names for the knees) 1 Inf, neWI, Marrows [ˈmæroz]. [**1969** *DARE* FW Addit MA30, [ˈmɑrəbonz]—legs.]

marrowfat n
1 See **marrowfat (bean).**
2 See **marrowfat (pea).**
3 See **marrow squash.**

marrowfat (bean) n Also *marrow (bean), white marrow(fat)* **chiefly nNJ, NY, PA** See Map
A cultivated white bean (*Phaseolus vulgaris* var) freq used for baking or in soups.
   1863 Burr *Field & Garden* 479 MA, White Marrow. White Marrowfat. . . As a string-bean, the White Marrow is of average quality: but, for shelling in the green state, it is surpassed by few, if any, of the garden varieties. **1931–33** *LANE Worksheets* swMA, Them ain't no butter bean, them are marrowfat. **1952** Tracy *Coast Cookery* 160 NY, *New York-Style Beans* . . 1 pint navy or marrow beans. **1965–70** *DARE* (Qu. I18, *The smaller beans that are white when they are dry*) Infs NY49, 61, 90, 109, PA181, Marrow bean(s); NJ5, Marrow beans—very small, a kind of bush bean; NY162, Marrow bean—like the navy only large; NJ4, Marrowfat—used for baked beans; NY83, Marrowfats; PA9, 100, Marrowfat; OH87, Marrowfat beans; NJ9, Marrowfat—a little bigger [than pea beans]; OH98, Marrowfat—large; PA41, Soup beans—used to call them marrowfat; PA60, Marrowfat—larger; (Qu. I20, . . *Kinds of beans*) Infs NY109, 113, 115, Marrow beans; NY139, Marrow beans—large pea beans; NY230, Marrow beans—larger than pea beans; KY24, Marrowfat—wide and flat; MA6, Horticultural beans—marrowfat (not used); NY94, Marrowfat—plain white bean like a pea bean only larger; NJ56, PA159, 221, Marrow beans; NJ2, Marrowfats; NY107, White marrow; (Qu. H50) Inf PA79, Marrow beans—white, small; PA131, All sorts of baked beans: marrowfat beans; (Qu. I16, *The large flat beans that are not eaten in the pod*) Inf MI23, Some call 'em marrow beans—I think that's the old English name for lima beans; MI68, Marrowfat beans—slightly smaller than limas; not common, as limas are; OH75, Marrowfat beans; (Qu. I17) Inf NJ64, Marrow beans. **1978** *Wanigan Catalog* 21, *White marrow*—Syn[onym]s: Marrowfat, Mountain, White Cranberry, White Egg. . . Has many names. I carry it under this name as first received. White, plump . . 5″ pods. . . Good baker. **1981** Pederson *LAGS Basic Materials,* 1 inf, cwAR, Butterbeans, baby limas, lima bean, marrowfat.

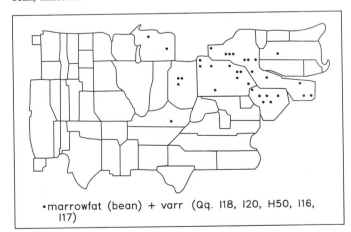

•marrowfat (bean) + varr (Qq. I18, I20, H50, I16, I17)

marrowfat (pea) n Also *marrow (pea)* [*OED* 1733 →]
A cultivated pea (*Pisum sativum* var *sativum* cv).
   1773 (1944) *Jefferson Garden Book* 39, Mar. 12. sowed a patch of Early peas, & another of Marrow fats. **1821** Cobbett *Amer. Gardener* 241, *Pea.* . . The earliest of all is the little white pea . . and . . then come the . . *Dwarf* and *Tall Marrowfats.* . . Sow the May Pea, . . some Marrowfats, and some Knight Pea [sic], all at the same time, and they will come one after another, so as to give you green peas till nearly August. **1829** *Free Press* (Halifax NC) 20 Feb 1/1, Peas. . . Garden, Marrowfat, Early six week, Green Bunch. **1847** (1852) Crowen *Amer. Cookery* 181, *Marrow-fat Peas*—Are the late sort, and as their name indicates, are much richer in taste. The shell of these is more of a yellowish green, and has a roughness, which the earlier peas have not. **1863** Burr *Field & Garden* 533, *Dwarf Marrow.* Dwarf White Marrow.

Dwarf Marrowfat. Early Dwarf Marrowfat. *Ibid* 542, *Matchless Marrow*. . . This is a good marrow-pea. *Ibid* 543, *Missouri Marrow*. Missouri Marrowfat. . . Pods . . wrinkled on the surface as they ripen. . . When ripe, the pea is similar to the Dwarf Marrow in form, but is . . more wrinkled. . . It is of American origin, very productive, of good quality. *Ibid* 551, *Woodford's Marrow*. . . Plants of strong and robust habits of growth, like a vigorous-growing Marrow. **1869** Browne *Adventures* 72, [He] presented me with . . a piece of pure silver about the size of a marrowfat pea. **1925** *Book of Rural Life* 4190, *Pea*. . . Among the better-known varieties are . . Marrowfat, Blackeye Marrowfat. **1990** *Seed Savers Yearbook* 158, *Marrowfat* . . English soup pea.

marrow gut n Pronc-spp *mar(i)gut, margus* **chiefly West**
Any of several inner parts of the cow or bison used as food; now esp the small intestine of a calf.

1846 (1848) Bryant *What I Saw in CA* 96 **wNE**, The choice pieces of a fat [buffalo] cow, are . . the hump-rib; and an intestinal vessel or organ, commonly called by hunters the "marrow-gut," which, anatomically speaking, is the chylo-poetic duct. **1894** *Harper's New Mth. Mag.* 88.351 **csWY**, Inside of the cabin was William . . glowing with heat and pride over his corn cakes and "marrow-gut." **1949** Brown *Amer. Cooks* 530 **NV**, Marrow gut consists of the intestines of nursing veal that still have the curd of mother's milk in them. **1956** Ker *Vocab. W. TX* 295, *Margus*—calf intestine. **1964** Jackman–Long *OR Desert* 102, The cook would come with sharp knives and a big pan to hold the heart, sweetbreads, liver, brains, and, in case it was a young calf, the mar gut. **1968** O'Hare *E. MT Engl. Vocab.* 109, 1 inf, **neMT** ['maɚəgət] all internal organs. **1970** *DARE* (Qu. H43, *Foods made from parts of the head and inner organs of an animal*) Inf **CA205**, Marigut—milk gland of a young cow, fry it. **1986** Pederson *LAGS Concordance*, 1 inf, **seTX**, Marrow guts—small intestines of calf, as food; 1 inf, **csTX**, Marrow guts—of cow or calf, in "cowboy stew"; 1 inf, **csTX**, Marrow guts—small intestines, chitterlings.

marrow pea See **marrowfat (pea)**

marrow squash n Also *marrow(fat)* [See quot 1864] Cf **vegetable marrow**
Often with qualifier: A cultivated **squash:** usu *Cucurbita maxima* var, but also *C. pepo* var.

1843 (1844) Johnson *Farmer's Encycl.* 1009 **MA**, Autumnal marrow squash (*Cucurbita succado*), introduced to notice by John M. Ives, Esq., of Salem. **1858** in 1863 Burr *Field & Garden* 213 **neMA**, [Letter from John M. Ives:] In the spring of 1831, a friend of mine from Northampton, in this State, brought to my grounds a specimen . . which he called "Vegetable Marrow." . . It bore no resemblance to the true Vegetable Marrow, either in its form or color. . . Finding it a superior vegetable, with a skin as thin as the inner envelope of an egg, and the flesh of fine texture, and also that it was in eating early in the fall, I ventured to call it "Autumnal Marrow Squash." **1864** (1873) Webster *Amer. Dict.* 814, *Marrow-squash*, A variety of squash having a soft texture and fine grain, resembling marrow. **1876** Burroughs *Winter Sunshine* 25, [The] small boy . . was as frank and simple as if he had lived on . . marrow-squashes all his days. **1891** *Century Dict.* 5878, Other winter squashes are . . egg-shaped and pointed at the ends, as in the (Boston) marrow, long a standard in America. **1965–70** *DARE* (Qu. I4, . . *Vegetables . . less commonly grown around here*) Inf **CA80**, Marrow—like a rutabaga; (Qu. I23, . . *Kinds of squash*) Inf **MA6**, Marrow—resembles Hubbard, juicier, orange; **RI**12, Marrow—no longer grown, big, round, thick, flat on top; **VA**28, Marrow ['mæɚə]; **FL**9, Boston marrow ['mɑrə]—big, round, like pumpkin; **NJ**17, Boston marrow [mæro]—like pumpkin; **CA**63, Marrowfats ['mærəfæts]—sells to canners, a red and yellow blend. **1976** Bailey–Bailey *Hortus Third* 343, [*Cucurbita*] *maxima*. . . *Autumn* and *Winter squash* and *pumpkin*. . . Among many cvs. are . . 'Boston Marrow', fr[uit] orange, obovoid, to 14 in. long and 11 in. in diam., flesh orange-yellow, moderately moist. *Ibid*, [*Cucurbita*] *Pepo*. . . *Summer* and *Autumn pumpkin* and *squash, gourd, marrow*. **1986** *Seed Savers Exchange* 304, *Cucurbita maxima*. . . The following varieties all belong to the species "maxima" . . *All of the "Marrows"* (Autumnal, Boston, Orange, Prolific, Warted). **1988** Whealy *Garden Seed Inventory* (2d ed) 347, *Squash (Pepo)*. . . Black Italian Marrow.

marry v Usu **chiefly Nth** |'mɛrɪ, -i|, **chiefly Atlantic, Sth** |'mærɪ, -i|; for addit varr see quots Cf Pronc Intro 3.I.2.a Pronc-sp *merry* Similarly ppl adjs *ma'ed, ma(h)ied, marri'd, marrit, merried, morried*
Std sense, var forms.

1860 Holmes *Professor* 86 **MA**, And he as good as married. **1887**
Scribner's Mag. 2.483 **AR**, You uns'll be gittin' married. **1891** Cooke *Huckleberries* 11 **CT**, Fust I know they'll up 'nd git married. **1905** Chesnutt *Col.'s Dream* 211 **GA**, He didn't live hyuh, suh; I used ter live hyuh, an' I ma'ied him down ter Madison, where I wuz wukkin'. **1920s** in 1944 *ADD* **cNY**, ['mærɪd], ['merɪd], not -[ɪd]. **1922** Gonzales *Black Border* 312 **sSC, GA coasts** [Gullah glossary], *Marri'd—married*. **1929** (1951) Faulkner *Sartoris* 290 **MS** [Black], De fust two mont' we wuz ma'ied. **1929** *WV Review* Oct 30, *A* has been given the sound of *o*, as in *married* for married. **1935** *AmSp* 10.295 **cNY**, *Married* . . 55 [infs used] [ɛ] 197 [æ]. *Ibid* 296, *Married* once . . with [a]. **1936** Reese *Worleys* 54 **MD** (as of 1865) [Black], How come I git mahied to dat ole no-count fiel'-han' niggah? **1940** in 1976 *Weevils in the Wheat* 336 **VA** [Black], I b'longed to Mistis. . . When my mistis was ma'ed she drawed fo' slaves. **1941** *LANE* Map 408 (*Married*), [Proncs of the type ['mærɪd] are most frequent, occurring **throughout NEng**; those of the type ['merɪd] are fairly common, occurring most frequently in **wCT, nVT, nNH, seNH, Nantucket, and Martha's Vineyard**; 1 inf, **ceVT**, [maˑˀɚˑɹɪvt], "old local Scotch pron."; 1 inf, **nVT**, [mæ-ɪd], "the most common pron." [of 5 given by the inf.] **1941** *AmSp* 16.15 **eTX** [Black], ['mæˑɪˑvd] . . [mæːᴿɪd]. **1944** Kenyon–Knott *Pronc. Dict.* xxxix, In words like . . *marry* ['mærɪ] . . having historical "short a" [æ] before *r* plus a vowel, a widespread pronunciation with [ɛ] . . ['merɪ] . . is heard in the North . . especially from the younger generations. Many of these speakers pronounce *marry, merry,* and *Mary* all alike—['merɪ]. This variant appears to be rare in the South. **1952** *AmSp* 27.188 **WA**, The words *Mary, marry, merry,* are all pronounced [meɚɪj]. **c1960** Wilson *Coll.* **csKY**, *Marry* ['merɪ]. **1961** Kurath–McDavid *Pronc. Engl.* 125, *Married* has the /æ/ phoneme in all parts of the Eastern States, but /ɛ/ competes with it in several areas, and /ɑ~ɒ/ is rather common in the folk speech of Western Pennsylvania. The vowel /ɛ/ predominates in northern West Virginia (where *marry* is often homophonous with *merry* and *Mary*); it is rather common in southwestern New England and in western New York State . . , and has some currency also in coastal New Hampshire, on Martha's Vineyard and Nantucket, in northeastern Pennsylvania, and on the lower Cape Fear River in North Carolina. The vowel /ɒ/ is a characteristic feature of the folk speech of Western Pennsylvania. Elsewhere only scattered instances of /ɑ/ survive in *married*. **1968** *DARE* FW Addit **MD**13, *Marry* . . always pronounced with [ɑ] instead of the [æ] standard for this area. **c1970** Pederson *Dial. Surv. Rural GA* (*If a man and a woman want to live together, they go to a preacher and get _____*) **seGA**, [Of 64 infs, 52 used proncs of the type ['mæ·rɪˑd, 'mæˑɚ·ɪˑd]; 15 of the type ['mɛ·rɪˑd, 'mɛ·ɚ·ɪˑd]; three infs used both types.] **1976** Allen *LAUM* 3.35 **Upper MW** (as of c1950), *Married* is most successful in keeping historic [æ]. Widespread in the East, this vowel, lower than the [ɛ] of *cherry* is favored by 62% of the [203] U[pper] M[idwest] infs. . . The converse [percentage] would indicate the distribution of the [ɛ] vowel, since no other variant occurs. **1984** Burns *Cold Sassy* 349 **nGA** (as of 1906), "Will, I'm a-go'n git marrit." The sky wobbled. "Get married?"

marry off See **marry up**

marry out of meeting See **meeting 2**

marry up v phr Also *marry off* **esp S Midl, Sth**
To get married.

1955 Roberts *S. from Hell-fer-Sartin* 171 **seKY**, It looked as though they would marry up too, in spite of all the father could do. **1965–69** *DARE* (Qu. AA15a, . . *Joking ways . . of saying that people got married . . "They _____."*) Infs **FL39, MS29**, Married up; (Qu. AA15b, . . *Joking ways . . of saying that a man is getting married. . . "He _____."*) Inf **MA58**, Married up. **1976** Garber *Mountain-ese* 56 **sAppalachians**, I reckon Jed is gonna marry-up with that young McCoy girl. **1986** Pederson *LAGS Concordance*, 1 inf, **neTN**, Before I married off; 1 inf, **csAL**, Some of them had done married off.

mars(e) See **master** n

marsh n[1] Pronc-spp *old-fash, ma(a)sh, march* Similarly adj *mashy* [OED marsh sb., "dial. march, . . mash"]
Std sense, var forms.

1671 in 1897 *SC Hist. Soc. Coll.* 5.336, About ye riuers mouth & vp the riuer beyond ye mashes. **1787** in 1929 *FL State Hist. Soc. Pub.* 9.2.239 **FL**, 1500 Acres one half at least good high land—high swamp rich feeding marches with large natural reserves of water. **1808** in 1956 Eliason *Tarheel Talk* 314 **NC**, *Mash.* **1823** in 1834 *U.S. Congress Amer. State Papers* (Public Lands) Doc 412 3.758 **FL**, The river St. Sebastian . . forms, by its diurnal floods, an extensive march or swamp. **1843** (1916) Hall *New Purchase* 49 **IN**, They had been sufficiently fortunate . . to learn the nature of "mash land." **1875** Twain *Sketches New & Old* (Hartford) 203 **MD** [Black], I wa'nt bawn in the mash to be fool' by trash! **1876** (1882–83) Whitman *Specimen Days* 94 **Long Is. NY**, The sedgy perfume . . reminded me of "the mash" and south bay of my native island. **1888** Jones *Negro Myths* 2 **GA coast** [Gullah], Buh Alligatur . . drag isself trugh de mash. **1899** (1912) Green *VA Folk-Speech* 276, *Mash*. . . A form of *marsh*. **1903** *DN* 2.290 **Cape Cod MA** (as of a1857), *Mash* for *marsh*. **1907** *DN* 3.193 **seNH**, *Ma'sh*. . . Salt marsh on the coast. There are swamps and meadows, but no marshes in Hampstead. **1922** Gonzales *Black Border* 214 **sSC, GA coasts** [Gullah], De nex' week, I bin comin' out de maa'sh on Mr. Rab'nel' place. **1929** *AmSp* 5.160 **Long Is. NY**, *Drain*, a channel in the salt marshes. **1933** *AmSp* 8.2.78 **Cape Cod MA**, Marsh is [mæš] [in everyday speech]. **1939** *LANE* Map 31, *Salt marsh*. . . Pronunciations of the type of [mæš] are still natural to some of the older and less highly educated informants in eastern New England [5 infs] . . and others remember having used or heard it in their childhood. Some use this pronunciation side by side with the type of [mɑ(r)š] [19 infs]. **1941** O'Donnell *Great Big Doorstep* 23 **sLA**, The doctor came in, wearing hip boots and carrying a pirogue paddle. He had been on a confinement case out in the marches. **1961** Kurath–McDavid *Pronc. Engl.* 142, /ɑ∼ɒ∼a/, as in *car*, are the usual vowels in *marsh*, but along the coast the /æ/ of *ashes* . . survives to some extent in folk speech (owing to early loss of /r/ before /š/). **1967–70** *DARE* (Qu. C6, . . *A piece of land that's often wet, and has grass and weeds growing on it*) Inf **NY1**, Mash—they mean a marsh but old guys call it a mash; **PA235**, [mæš] or [mæši] ground; (Qu. C7, . . *Land that usually has some standing water with trees or bushes growing in it*) Inf **NY206**, March, swale; (Qu. C19, . . *Low land running between hills [With and without water]*) Inf **NC87**, [mæš]. **1986** Pederson *LAGS Concordance* (Bottomland) 1 inf, **neMS**, Mashy; (Swamp) 1 inf, **swMS**, Mashy land, mashy place; 1 inf, **seAL**, Mashy place; 1 inf, **neMS**, Too mashy.

marsh n[2] See **mesh** n[1], v

marshal n

An unidentified woodpecker.

    1904 Fountain *Gt. North-West* 224, A bird known locally [in Ohio] as "the marshal", and sometimes "the soldier". . . It is a very gaudy woodpecker with a great deal of scarlet in the colour of its plumage.

marshbanker See mossbunker

marsh barrow n [*barrow* a castrated male hog]

The alligator (*Alligator mississippiensis*).

    1966 *DARE* FW Addit **seGA**, Marsh barrow ['bɑrə]—alligator; used on fishing boats to refer to this reptile. It is considered bad luck to call it an alligator or gator on a fishing boat. Used by shrimp fishermen in Valona, Georgia.

marsh bass n

A **black bass 1**, esp a **largemouth bass**.

    1887 Goode *Amer. Fishes* 56, "Marsh Bass," "River Bass," "Rock Bass," . . are other names applied to one or both species [=largemouth and smallmouth bass]. **1902** Jordan–Evermann *Amer. Fishes* 358, This fish [=*Micropterus salmoides*] has received many vernacular names, among which may be mentioned . . marsh bass. **1933** LA Dept. of Conserv. *Fishes* 313, Large-mouthed Black Bass. . . Lake Bass; Marsh Bass. **1946** LaMonte *N. Amer. Game Fishes* 135, *Large-mouth Black Bass*. . . Marsh Bass. **1978** *Outdoor Life* Sept 56, Scientists call the large-mouth bass Micropterus salmoides. . . But there are many lesser-known names too. Some of them are . . marsh bass, moss bass [etc].

marsh birch n

A **swamp birch** (here: *Betula pumila*).

    1973 Stephens *Woody Plants* 96, *Betula pumila* L. var. *glandulifera* . . Dwarf birch, swamp birch, marsh birch. A freely branched shrub to 2 m high, usually in small colonies.

marsh bird n [*EDD* 1830 →] Cf **March bird**

A frog such as a **spring peeper**; see quot.

    1908 Fox *Lonesome Pine* 103 **KY**, He heard it in the piping of frogs—"Marsh-birds," as he always called them.

marsh blackbird n

=**redwing blackbird**.

    1811 Wilson *Amer. Ornith.* 4.37, [Starlings] are known by various names in the different states of the union; such as the *Swamp Blackbird, Marsh Blackbird, Red-winged Blackbird*. **1831** Audubon *Ornith. Biog.* 1.348, The Marsh Blackbird is . . well known as being a bird of the most nefarious propensities. **1899** (1912) Green *VA Folk-Speech* 275,

Marsh-black-bird. . . A species of blackbird with red feathers on his shoulders living in marshes. **1923** Dawson *Birds CA* 1.114, Red-winged Blackbird. . . *Agelaius phoeniceus neutralis* . . Marsh Blackbird. **1955** Forbush–May *Birds* 465, The Eastern Red-wing is a typical marsh blackbird. It loves the marsh and waterside and seldom nests far from water. **1968** *DARE* (Qu. Q11, . . *Kinds of blackbirds*) Inf **DE3**, Marsh blackbird.

marsh bluebill n [**bluebill 1, 4**]

1 =**lesser scaup**.

    1879 Rathbun *Revised List Birds* 38 **cNY**, "Marsh Blue-bill." (Local.) Lesser Scaup Duck. **1923** U.S. Dept. Ag. *Misc. Circular* 13.20 **NY**, *Lesser Scaup Duck*. . . marsh bluebill. **1951** Pough *Audubon Water Bird* 336, *Marsh bluebill*. . . Lesser scaup duck.

2 =**ring-necked duck**.

    1888 Trumbull *Names of Birds* 60 **seMI**, Ring-necked Duck. . . In the vicinity of Lake St. Clair *Marsh Blue-bill*. **1910** Eaton *Birds NY* 1.208, This species [=*Aythya collaris*], called also Ring-bill, Marsh bluebill, and Bastard broadbill, is a rare migrant in eastern New York. **1940** Trautman *Birds Buckeye Lake* 191 **ceOH**, Market hunters and sportsmen . . stated that the Ring-necked Duck or "marsh bluebill" was very numerous between 1860 and 1890. **1963** Gromme *Birds WI* 213, Bluebill, . . Marsh (. . Ring-necked Duck).

marsh blue violet n Also *blue marsh violet* Cf **marsh violet**

A **violet** (here: *Viola cucullata*).

    1910 Graves *Flowering Plants* 284 **CT**, *Viola cucullata*. . . Marsh Blue Violet. . . Wet meadows, swamps and banks of streams. **1933** Small *Manual SE Flora* 889, *V[iola] cucullata*. . . Blue marsh-violet. **1949** Moldenke *Amer. Wild Flowers* 46, In wet places from Quebec and Ontario south to the mountains of northern Georgia one may usually find the lovely marsh blue violet, *V[iola] cucullata*, noteworthy for its profusion of violet-blue flowers, darker-colored in the throat, borne on long peduncles that usually far surpass the light green leaves. **1968** Barkley *Plants KS* 242, Viola cucullata. . . Blue Marsh-Violet. **1976** Bailey–Bailey *Hortus Third* 1158, *[Viola] cucullata*. . . Marsh blue violet.

marsh buggy n

See quots.

    1939 FWP *Guide FL* 409 **swFL**, Prospecting for oil is carried on in the vicinity with the help of a specialized machine called the 'marsh-buggy,' a motor-driven vehicle with wheels 8 and 10 feet high, which carries prospectors far back into the swamp to make preliminary borings for oil. **1944** Kane *Deep Delta Country* 255 **seLA**, Strange sights appeared at the water edges: drillings in the bays . . catwalks zig-zagging over the waters, and then the grotesque "marsh buggies." The latter are combinations of boat and automobile. **1979** Hallowell *People Bayou* 7 **sLA**, In the 1920s, marsh buggies came along—treaded monsters with bargelike bodies that hauled great plows behind them and heaved the muck to one side.

marsh chicken See **marsh hen 1a**

marsh clematis n Also *March clematis*

A **virgin's bower** (here: *Clematis crispa*).

    1900 Lyons *Plant Names* 106, *C[lematis] crispa*. . . Southeastern U.S. Marsh Clematis, Curl-flowered Clematis. **1901** Lounsberry *S. Wild Flowers* 180, *C[lematis] crispa*, marsh clematis, one of the most beautiful of the genus is a climber which also bears solitary and nodding flowers. They are fragrant, with a silvery sheen and look something as though they had been enameled with blue. **1933** Small *Manual SE Flora* 527, *V[iorna] crispa*. . . Marsh-clematis. Curly-clematis. **1953** Greene–Blomquist *Flowers South* 35, Of the woody vines, one of the most attractive is curly- or marsh-clematis (*C[lematis] crispa*). The calyx tips are pale-blue and crisped on the margins. **1960** Vines *Trees SW* 261, The species name, *crispa*, is for the crinkled margin of the sepals. Also known under the vernacular names of Curl flower, March Clematis.

marsh cotton n

A **cotton grass 1** (here: *Eriophorum callithrix*).

    1966 *DARE* Wildfl QR Pl.2A Inf **MI31**, Marsh cotton.

marsh duck n

=**black duck 1**.

    1923 U.S. Dept. Ag. *Misc. Circular* 13.9 **MD**, Black Duck (*Anas rubripes*) . . marsh duck. **1982** Elman *Hunter's Field Guide* 143, Black Duck (*Anas rubripes*). . . *marsh duck*.

marsh elder n

1 A plant of the genus *Iva*. Also called **high-water shrub, mangrove 2b, povertyweed, sumpweed, salt sage, saltwater myrtle.** For other names of var spp see **careless weed 2, copperweed, deathweed, deep-root, devil's-weed 2d, false ragweed 1, false sunflower 3, half-breed weed, horsebrush 2, horseweed 7, jacko, Jesuit's bark, lavender 2, mangle n¹ 2d, poverty grass, prairie-dog weed, prairie ragweed, Red River weed, saltbush, spearweed**

1848 Gray *Manual of Botany* 220, *Iva* [spp] . . Marsh Elder. **1892** Coulter *Botany W. TX* 208, *Iva* . . Marsh elder. **1930** OK Univ. Biol. Surv. Pub. 2.85, *Iva angustifolia* . . Marsh Elder. . . *Iva ciliata* . . Marsh Elder. . . *Iva xanthifolia* . . Marsh Elder. **1973** Hitchcock–Cronquist *Flora Pacific NW* 532, *Iva* . . Poverty-weed; Marsh-elder.

2 =**groundsel tree.**

1937 *Torreya* 37.101, There is an excusable tendency to confuse *Baccharis* and *Iva* in the application of local names and the terms, marsh elder and hightide bush . . are so confused on the New York coast.

marsh feather(s) n

Among loggers: hay used as a mattress or cushion.

1959 *MI Hist.* 43.405 (as of 1880s) [Among loggers], Cedar or hemlock boughs were laid over the strips with a topping of "marsh feather" or hay, and a grain sack, stuffed with the same kind of "feathers," was used for a pillow. **1969** Sorden *Lumberjack Lingo* 77 **NEng, Gt Lakes,** *Marsh feathers*—Marsh hay used to cushion the sleeping bunk in the logging camp.

marsh felwort n chiefly AK

A plant (*Lomatogonium rotatum*) of the gentian family. Also called **star gentian**

1932 Rydberg *Flora Prairies* 636, Marsh Felwort. . . *P[leurogyne] rotata.* **1938** (1958) Sharples *AK Wild Flowers* 105, "Marsh Felwort." . . Dwarf plant, with much the appearance of a Gentian. **1974** Welsh *Anderson's Flora AK* 244, *Marsh Felwort.* . . Stream banks, lake shores, marshes, and bogs; in much of Alaska. **1987** Hughes–Blackwell *Wildflowers SE AK* 65, Marsh Felwort. . . Up to 16″; flower is star shaped.

marsh fern n Also marsh shield fern

A fern (*Thelypteris thelypteroides*). Also called **meadow fern 3, quill ~, snuffbox ~**

1900 Lyons *Plant Names* 141, *D[ryopteris] Thelypteris.* . . Marsh Shield-fern. . . Marsh, Meadow or Swamp Fern. **1937** Stemen–Myers *OK Flora* 7, *Dryopteris Thelypteris.* . . Marsh Shield-fern. **1938** Small *Ferns SE States* 225, *T. Thelypteris* . . Marsh-Fern. . . Marshes, swamps, bogs, damp woods, and ditches, various provinces, Fla. to Tex. **1950** Stevens *ND Plants* 42, *Dryopteris thelypteris.* . . Marsh Fern. **1968** McPhee *Pine Barrens* 131 **NJ,** Wherry pointed out . . bluish-gray marsh ferns. **1970** Correll *Plants TX* 68, *Thelypteris palustris.* . . Southern marsh fern.

marsh fire See marsh light

marsh fleabane n

1 A plant of the genus *Pluchea*. Also called **stinkweed.** For other names of var spp see **camphor weed 3, pinktop smartweed, plowman's wort, salt-marsh fleabane, stinking ~**

1822 Eaton *Botany* 249, *Conyza* . . *camphorata* . . marsh fleabane. . . About a foot high, near rivers, &c. Odour resembling camphour. **1848** Gray *Manual of Botany* 216, *Pluchea* . . Marsh Fleabane. Heads many-flowered. **1892** Coulter *Botany W. TX* 201, *Pluchea* . . *Marsh-fleabane.* . . Clustered heads of purplish flowers. **1910** Shreve *MD Plant Life* 493, *Pluchea foetida* . . Marsh Fleabane. . . Common in the southern Eastern Shore. **1940** Gates *Flora KS* 240, Pluchea camphorata. . . Marsh Fleabane. Salt marshes. **1964** Batson *Wild Flowers SC* 118, Marsh-Fleabane, Camphorweed. . . *Pluchea camphorata.* . . Wet margins, ditches and shores. Summer. Delaware to Florida. **1970** Correll *Plants TX* 1618, *Marsh-fleabane.* . . Aromatic annual or perennial herbs.

2 also *marsh fleawort:* A **ragwort** (here: *Senecio congestus*).

1900 Lyons *Plant Names* 342, *S[enecio] palustris* . . (northern U.S.), is Marsh Fleawort. **1940** Clute *Amer. Plant Names* 87, *S[enecio] palustris.* Marsh Fleawort. **1950** Gray–Fernald *Manual of Botany* 1532, *S[enecio] congestus.* . . Marsh-Fleabane.

3 also *March fleabane:* =**arrowweed 1.** Note: Now designated *Tessaria sericea,* this plant was formerly included in the genus *Pluchea.*

1960 Vines *Trees SW* 999, It [=*Tessaria sericea*] is also known under the vernacular names of Arrow-weed, March Fleabane. . . The flowers are considered to be a good bee food. **1985** Dodge *Flowers SW Deserts* 121, Marsh-Fleabane. . . *Tessaria sericea.* . . Arizona, California and Texas deserts.

marsh fleawort See marsh fleabane 2

marsh fly n

1 An insect of the family Sciomyzidae.

1954 Borror–DeLong *Intro. Insects* 628, The Sciomyzidae, or marsh flies, are small to medium-sized flies which are usually yellowish or brownish in color. . . Most marsh flies are about the size of a house fly. **1980** Milne–Milne *Audubon Field Guide Insects* 676, *Marsh Flies.* Slender, yellowish or brownish flies . . common along the edges of ponds and marshes.

2 A **midge 1.**

1966 *DARE* (Qu. R10, *Very small flies that don't sting, often seen hovering in large groups or bunches outdoors in summer*) Inf **GA11,** Marsh fly.

marsh frog n

1 =**pickerel frog.**

1745 *London Mag.* Nov 551 **seGA,** The Bull-Frogs, Lizards, Grasshoppers, Marsh Frogs [imitate city noises]. **1842** DeKay *Zool. NY* 3.62, The Marsh Frog. Rana palustris. . . This is one of our most beautiful frogs, and is remarkably active. It has a strong and disagreeable odor; and from being used as bait, it is called, in various districts, *Pickerel Frog.* **1867** *Amer. Naturalist* 1.109 **MA,** Marsh Frog, or Pickerel Frog (*Rana palustris*). **1891** in 1895 IL State Lab. Nat. Hist. Urbana *Bulletin* 3.325, *Rana palustris* . . Marsh Frog. **1928** Pope–Dickinson *Amphibians* 39 **WI,** Pickerel Frog. . . Other common names are Marsh Frog, Tiger Frog, Yellow Legs and Grass Frog. **1939** *LANE* Map 231 *(Frog)* 1 inf, **seRI,** Marsh frog, smaller than a bullfrog, 'the size of a toad,' green and brown.

2 A **tree frog:** usu *Hyla* spp, but also *Pseudacris* spp. Cf **marsh peeper**

1899 Bergen *Animal Lore* 61, Marsh frogs, smaller frogs, *Chorophilus triseriatus. Pike Co., Ill.* **1939** *LANE* Map 231 *(Frog)* **NEng,** Names of the small shrill-voiced frog, *hyla, peeping frog . . , marsh peeper, marsh frog.* **1950** *WELS (Small frogs that sing or chirp loudly in the spring)* 1 Inf, **seWI,** Marsh frog.

marsh gentian n [*OED* 1722 →]

Any of var **gentians,** but usu **soapwort gentian** or **striped gentian.**

1824 Bigelow *Florula Bostoniensis* 105 **MA,** *Gentiana pneumonanthe* . . Marsh Gentian. **1833** Eaton *Botany* 154, *[Gentiana] ochroleuca.* . . marsh gentian. **1854** King *Amer. Eclectic Dispensatory* 494, *Gentiana ochroleuca.* . . This plant is likewise known by the names of *Marsh Gentian, . . Sampson Snakeroot,* etc. . . Also used for bites of snakes, and in typhus fevers, pneumonia, etc. **1900** Lyons *Plant Names* 171, *G[entiana] Saponaria.* . . Marsh or Rough Gentian. *Ibid, G[entiana] villosa.* . . Straw Colored or Marsh Gentian. **1940** Clute *Amer. Plant Names* 57, *Soapwort Gentian.* . . marsh gentian. *Ibid, Striped Gentian.* . . marsh gentian. **1953** Nelson *Plants Rocky Mt. Park* 125, *Blue marsh gentian . . Gentiana affinis.* . . Found on wet ground in the montane zone. . . *Marsh gentian, Gentiana strictiflora.* . . This is abundant in marshes of the montane zone. **1971** Krochmal *Appalachia Med. Plants* 132, *Gentiana villosa.* . . marsh gentian.

marsh goose n

=**Hutchins's goose.**

1888 Trumbull *Names of Birds* 4, *Anser hutchinsii.* . . In the neighborhood of Morehead, North Carolina, *Marsh Goose.*

marsh grass n

Any of var grasses that grow in marshy land, but esp those used for hay, as **cordgrass, canary grass** (here: *Phalaris arundinacea*), **bluejoint 1,** and **salt grass;** see quots. Cf **marsh hay, meadow grass, salt-marsh ~, salt-meadow ~**

1785 in 1925 *MD Hist. Mag.* 20.44 **cnMD,** The Island . . had flaggs or marsh grass growing on it. **1837** *S. Lit. Messenger* 3.738 *(DAE),* The driver told us his horses were fed on . . hay—and this too made of the marsh grass. **1843** Torrey *Flora NY* 2.447, *Spartina.* . . Marsh-grass. **1849** U.S. Congress *Serial Set* 571 Doc 5.2.844 **nwMI,** Many of the drained beaver-ponds have become meadows, from which several tons of bluejoint or marsh grass may be annually cut. **1903** Small *Flora SE U.S.* 132, *Spartina.* . . Often tall grasses, with flat or convolute leaf-blades. . . Marsh Grass. **1913** London *Valley of Moon* 259 **cwCA,** She had even roofed the hole in rough fashion by means of drift wood and marsh grass. **1925** *Book of Rural Life* 3391, *Marsh Grasses.* . . The salt marshes of the Atlantic coast. . grew various grasses, but particularly *black grass* [=*Juncus gerardii*] . . , several kinds of *cord grass* . . and *salt grass.* [*Ibid* 3392, Farther westward, *bluejoint* . . was abundant in marshes. . . Even at the present time great areas are cut annually, especially in Wisconsin and Minnesota. In the interior a slough grass, one of the cord grasses, is found . . , much of which is cut for hay. . . In the alkaline marshes of the West, *salt grass* . . furnishes valuable pasturage. . . In the marshes of the southern coasts important grasses are *roseau cane, cord grass* and *maiden cane.*] **1931–33** *LANE Worksheets* **MA,** Marsh grass—type of hay. **1950** *WELS* **WI** (*Hay that grows naturally in damp places*) 5 Infs, Marsh grass; 1 Inf, Marsh grass—bluejoint; (*What kinds of grass are grown for hay in your neighborhood?*) 2 Infs, Marsh grass. **1965–70** *DARE* (Qu. L8, *Hay that grows naturally in damp places*) 15 Infs, **scattered,** Marsh grass; (Qu. L9a, . . *Kinds of grass . . grown for hay*) Inf **IL31,** Marsh grass. **1981** Pederson *LAGS Basic Materials,* 10 infs, **AR, FL, GA, MS,** Marsh grass. **1992** *DARE* File **cWI,** Marsh grass is canary grass. It's tall, grows right down to the edge of the ponds. We have a lot of lowland, and my uncle cuts marsh grass for hay. Marsh hay's low protein, so it's good for dry cows or for cows that have calved so that they don't get milk fever.

marsh guinea n Cf **pond guinea, swamp guinea, water guinea**
Any of three related birds: the **Florida gallinule, purple gallinule,** or a **coot** n[1] **1** (here: *Fulica americana*).

    1923 U.S. Dept. Ag. *Misc. Circular* 13.44 **LA,** *Purple Gallinule.* . . *Vernacular Names.* . . *In local use.* . . Marsh-guinea. **1953** *AmSp* 28.276, Marsh guinea. Purple gallinule. La., Texas. Common gallinule. Texas. American coot. Texas.

marsh hare n [*DCan* 1930] Cf **marsh rabbit 2**
=**muskrat 1.**

    1947 Cahalane *Mammals* 537 **LA,** By act of the state legislature in July, 1944, the official name [of the muskrat] in Louisiana is "marsh hare." The dark red meat is fine-grained and tender and tastes like wild duck or terrapin. **1968** *DARE* (Qu. P31, . . *Names or nicknames . . for the . . muskrat*) Inf **MD15,** Some people say marsh hare; **NY84,** Marsh hare.

marsh harrier n [*OED* 1802 →]
=**marsh hawk 1.**

    1844 DeKay *Zool. NY* 2.20, Marsh Harrier. *Circus uliginosus.* **1874** Coues *Birds NW* 331, The Marsh Harrier belongs among the "ignoble" birds of the falconers, but is neither a weakling nor a coward, as one may easily satisfy himself by handling a winged bird. **1903** Dawson *Birds OH* 2.394, *Circus hudsonius.* . . Marsh Harrier. **1917** (1923) *Birds Amer.* 2.64, *Marsh Hawk.* . . Harrier; Marsh Harrier. [*Ibid* 65, Slowly and steadily with a gliding flight the Harrier quarters back and forth across the fields with the care and precision of a well-trained dog.] **1955** Lowery *LA Birds* 206, The Marsh Hawk, or "marsh harrier," is a member of a distinct group of hawks that have slim bodies, long legs, and unusually long tails. **1969** Longstreet *Birds FL* 44, *Marsh Harrier.* . . The downy fledglings stay in the nest for about five weeks.

marsh hawk n

1 A hawk (*Circus cyaneus*) of marshes and open grasslands. [*DCan* 1772 →] Also called **blue hawk 1, bog ~, bog-trotter 1, bullet hawk, chicken ~ 1, chock-a-la-taw, frog hawk 1, Georgia boy 1, goshawk 2, harrier, heath hawk, hen harrier, marsh ~, meadow hawk, mole ~, mouse ~ 1a, rabbit ~, rat ~, snake ~, swamp ~, white-rumped ~**

    1791 Bartram *Travels* 290 **Atlantic,** F[alco] ranivorus, the marsh hawk. **1812** Wilson *Amer. Ornith.* 6.67, Marsh Hawk: *Falco uliginosus;* . . is most numerous where there are extensive meadows and salt marshes. **1844** Giraud *Birds Long Is.* 21, Among us the Marsh Hawk or Harrier is a constant resident. It is commonly seen sailing over the salt marshes and meadows in quest of mice. **1898** (1900) Davie *Nests N. Amer. Birds* 201, The Marsh Hawk, Blue Hawk, or Harrier, is distributed throughout the whole of North America. **1944** Nute *Lake Superior* 294 **MI, MN, WI,** A marsh hawk could also be seen now and again enjoying the effortless rides that the air currents afforded over the edge of the land. **1950** *WELS* (*Kinds of hawks in your neighborhood*) 13 Infs, **WI,** Marsh hawk. **1965–70** *DARE* (Qu. Q4, . . *Kinds of hawks*) 30 Infs, **scattered, but chiefly Nth,** Marsh hawk; (Qu. Q3, . . *Birds that come out only after dark*) Inf **NJ21,** Marsh hawk; (Qu. Q10, . . *Water birds and marsh birds*) Inf **MI73,** Marsh hawk. **1977** Bull–Farrand *Audubon Field Guide Birds* 437, Marsh Hawk (*Circus cyaneus*) . . the only North American

member of a group of hawks known as harriers. All hunt by flying close to the ground, taking small animals by surprise.

2 =**everglade kite.**

    [**1954** Sprunt *FL Bird Life* 100, Although somewhat resembling the Marsh Hawk in flight, the kite has a different method of feeding.] **1955** Forbush–May *Birds* 98, *Everglade Kite* (*Rostrhamus socialis plumbeus*). . . *Other names* . . Sociable Marsh Hawk. . . Wings much broader than in other kites, resembling those of Buteos.

marsh hay n Also *marshy hay* [*OEDS* 1742 →] **chiefly Gt Lakes, Atlantic** See Map Cf **salt hay, wild ~**
Hay made from **marsh grass,** esp from **cordgrass,** but also from a **canary grass** (here: *Phalaris arundinacea*), **bluejoint 1,** or **salt grass** (here: *Distichlis spicata*); see quots.

    1839 in 1840 *Cultivator* 7.33 **IA,** The common marsh hay is no better than the "bog meadow hay" of the east. **1852** MI State Ag. Soc. *Trans. for 1851* 3.132 **csMI,** They feed well at the straw stack and thrive on marsh hay. **1862** U.S. Patent Office *Annual Rept. for 1861: Ag.* 344 **seCT,** This hay. . . intelligent farmers value . . for bedding, and the price of straw regulates the price of marsh hay. **1885** Jewett *Marsh Is.* 28 **NEng,** We're a-cuttin' the ma'sh hay. **1948** Pearson *Sea Flavor* 119 **NH,** There are still places up and down the coast where farmers harvest the marsh hay, and one can see the stacks, like pointed tents, dotting the wind-swept areas. *Ibid* 149, The surging tides roll up over the level stretches where the fox, sea spear, and spike grasses [=*Spartina patens, Puccinellia maritima,* and *Distichlis spicata*], which combine to make marsh hay, grow. **1950** Hitchcock–Chase *Manual Grasses* 313, [Bluejoint, *C. canadensis,* is a source of much of the wild hay of Wisconsin and Minnesota.] *Ibid* 509, The marsh hay of the Atlantic coast, much used for packing and formerly for bedding, often consists largely of *S[partina] patens.* [*Ibid* 556, *Reed canary grass.* . . An important constituent of lowland hay from Montana to Wisconsin.] **1950** *WELS* (*Hay that grows naturally in damp places*) 29 Infs, **WI,** Marsh hay; 1 Inf, Not as much marsh hay used since we raise so much tame hay; (*What kinds of grass are grown for hay in your neighborhood?*) 1 Inf, **cWI,** Where there is lowland—marsh grass or hay. **1965–70** *DARE* (Qu. L8, *Hay that grows naturally in damp places*) 55 Infs, **chiefly Gt Lakes, Atlantic,** Marsh hay; **GA8,** Marsh hay—not much here; **NY45,** Marsh hay—this grew in the meadows; **MS2,** Marshy hay; (Qu. L9b, *Hay from other kinds of plants [not grass];* not asked in early QRs) Inf **WI42,** Marsh hay. **1992** [see **marsh grass**]. **1992** *DARE* File **WI,** The grass most commonly used for marsh hay in Wisconsin is reed canary grass. Bluejoint is also used. **1994** *WI State Jrl.* (Madison) 22 Oct sec D 2, Marsh Hay, 2nd cutting, 400 bales @ $1.50 each.

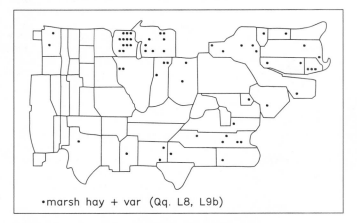

•marsh hay + var (Qq. L8, L9b)

marsh hen n Cf **meadow hen, mud hen**
1 Any of var birds of the family Rallidae; see below. **chiefly Sth** See Map Cf **freshwater marsh hen, saltwater ~**
a also *marsh chicken:* Any of var rails, but esp the **king rail 1** or the **clapper rail.**

    1709 (1967) Lawson *New Voyage* 154 **NC,** Marsh-Hen, much the same as in *Europe,* only she makes another sort of Noise, and much shriller. **1843** in 1898 Poe *Tales* 8 **seSC,** Jupiter . . bustled about to prepare some marsh-hens for supper. **1888** Trumbull *Names of Birds* 125, *King rail.* . . Very generally known throughout the South as *Marsh-hen,* sharing this name, however, indiscriminately with the more common *Salt-*water Marsh-hen. *Ibid* 127, *Clapper rail.* . . At Pleasantville [NJ] . . , at Pocomoke City, Md., on Cobb's Island, Va., and very generally to the southward, *Marsh-hen.* **1896** Robinson *In New Engl. Fields* 121, The absence of the rail's cackle was noticeable. . . We never got sight of the "ma'sh chickens" as they skulked among the sedges. **1923** U.S. Dept. Ag. *Misc. Circular* 13.40, *King Rail. . . Vernacular Names. In general use.* Marsh-hen. *Ibid* 41, *Clapper Rail. . . Vernacular Names. In general use.* Marsh-hen. *Ibid* 42 **MD,** *Virginia Rail. . . Vernacular Names. . . In local use. . .* Marsh-hen. **1953** *AmSp* 28.279, Marsh chicken—King rail [in] N.C. Sora [in] N.Y. *Ibid* 281, Marsh hen. . . Clapper rail—[distribution] General[-] King rail—[distribution] General[-] Slender-billed rail [in] Md., Fla., Minn., La. Sora [in] Del. . . (big [marsh hen])—Clapper rail [in] N.C. . . (little [marsh hen])—Slender-billed rail [in] N.C., Ill. **1965–70** *DARE* (Qu. Q10, . . *Water birds and marsh birds*) 22 Infs, **chiefly Sth,** Marsh hen; **GA**20, Marsh hen—I believe it's a king rail; **LA**29, Marsh hen—about ten or twelve inches high, has a sharp bill; **MD**36, Marsh hen—good to eat, looks like young brown chicken, makes clicking noise; **VA**52, Marsh hen—clapper rail; **VA**84, Marsh hen, sage hen; (Qu. Q7, *Names and nicknames for . . game birds*) Inf **FL**48, Marsh hen—plantation raised; **GA**91, Marsh hen; **LA**26, Marsh hen = rail; **LA**31, Marsh hens—these are rails; **SC**21, Marsh hen = clapper rail; **SC**67, Marsh hen—clamper rail is proper name. [*DARE* Ed: Some of these Infs may refer instead to other senses below.] **1966–70** *DARE* Tape **GA**11, We have what we call marsh hen huntin'. . . It's a bird that lives in the marsh and it's a great sport. . . It's a little kind of a little spindly-legged little gray bird. Oh, they good eatin'! *Ibid* **VA**112, The marsh hens, what you call marsh hens, and these other kind with them long bills, scouts, they call 'em, that place is full of 'em. **1981** Pederson *LAGS Basic Materials,* 1 inf, **seMS,** 2 infs, **seLA,** Marsh hen. **1982** Elman *Hunter's Field Guide* 321, Whatever species of rail is prevalent on the marsh, he [=a hunter] may speak of it as a marsh hen.

b =**coot** n[1] **1.**
 1888 Trumbull *Names of Birds* 117, *Coot. . .* From Bangor to Cape Cod Bay, *Marsh-hen . . ,* and Mr. Everett Smith speaks of hearing it called the *Blue Marsh-hen* in Maine. **1923** U.S. Dept. Ag. *Misc. Circular* 13.46 **MA, ME, RI,** *American Coot. . . Vernacular Names. . . In local use. . .* Marsh-hen. **1967** *DARE* (Qu. Q9, *The bird that looks like a small, dull-colored duck and is commonly found on ponds and lakes*) Inf **AL**22, Mud hen, marsh hen—same as pouldeaux [=**pull-doo**]. **1982** Elman *Hunter's Field Guide* 314, *American Coot. . .* Common & regional names . . marsh hen.

c also *marsh chicken:* Either the **Florida gallinule** or the **purple gallinule.**
 1888 Trumbull *Names of Birds* 122, *Common Gallinule. . .* At Detroit and other points near Lake St. Clair . . *Marsh-hen. Ibid* 123, Some distinguish the Gallinule. . . At Sanford, Fla. . . another darky broke into the conversation with "Naw, dat no coot, coot got a white bill, dat a marsh-hen." **1923** U.S. Dept. Ag. *Misc. Circular* 13.44, *Purple Gallinule. . . Vernacular Names. . . In local use. . .* Marsh-hen (S.C., Ala.) . . *Florida Gallinule. . . Vernacular Names. . . In local use. . .* Marsh-hen (Que., Mich., Md., Fla.) **1949** Sprunt–Chamberlain *SC Bird Life* 203, *Purple Gallinule. . .* Bluepeter; Pond chicken; Marsh Hen. **1953** *AmSp* 28.279, Marsh chicken. . . Common gallinule. N.Y. *Ibid* 281, Marsh hen. . . Purple gallinule. S.C., Fla., Ala., Texas. Common Gallinule. Md., Fla., Texas. **1967** *DARE* (Qu. Q7, *Names and nicknames for . . game birds*) Inf **DE**4, Indian hen or marsh hen—this is black.

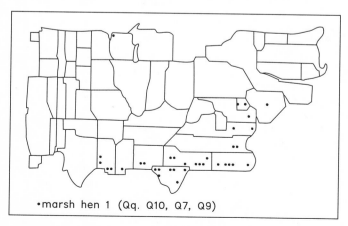

•marsh hen 1 (Qq. Q10, Q7, Q9)

2 A **bittern** (here: *Botaurus lentiginosus*).
 1904 Wheelock *Birds CA* 90, *American Bittern.—Botaurus lentiginosus.* Common names: Marsh Hen [etc]. **1917** (1923) *Birds Amer.* 1.181, *American Bittern . .* Marsh Hen. **1953** *AmSp* 28.281, Marsh hen. American bittern. Rather general [distribution]. . . [Marsh hen] (spotted).

American bittern. Ala. **1967–70** *DARE* (Qu. Q8, *A water bird that makes a booming sound before rain and often stands with its beak pointed almost straight up*) Infs **MD**45, **TX**33, **VA**110, Marsh hen.

3 =**black-crowned night heron.**
 1953 *AmSp* 28.281 **MA, MD, VA,** Marsh hen. Black-crowned night heron. **1968** *DARE* (Qu. Q3, . . *Birds that come out only after dark*) Inf **GA**28, Marsh hen.

4 =**limpkin.**
 1953 *AmSp* 28.281 **GA,** Marsh hen. Limpkin.

marsh-hen tide n [Prob **marsh hen 1a**]
 1969 *Reader's Digest* Apr 115, Down on the Georgia coast where I live, these high tides in the fall of the year are known as marsh-hen tides, because only then can those wary shorebirds be flushed from their hiding places.

marsh lark n
The eastern **meadowlark 1.**
 1792 Belknap *Hist. NH* 3.172, Marsh Lark, *Alauda magna.* **1956** MA Audubon Soc. *Bulletin* 40.130, *Meadowlark. . .* Marsh Lark (Maine, N.H., Mass. It is, however, no lark.)

marsh laurel n
A **groundsel tree** (here: *Baccharis halimifolia*).
 1951 *PADS* 15.42 **TX,** *Baccharis halimifolia . .* marsh laurel.

marsh light n Also *marsh fire*
=**will-o'-the-wisp.**
 1928 Ritchie *Forty-Niners* 246 **CA** (as of c1849), Perhaps the modern psychologist would diagnose this universal attribute as an "escape" from the enormous preoccupation of chasing Fortune's marsh light. **1965–70** *DARE* (Qu. CC16, *A small light that seems to dance or flicker over a marsh or swamp at night*) 18 Infs, **scattered,** Marsh light; **IN**22, **NY**30, 35, Marsh fire; [**RI**13, Marsh air]. **1988** *DARE* File **csWI** (as of late 1920s), It was called a marsh light when it appeared in the vicinity of Buckeye Station in the late 1920s. A St. Elmo's, my Atlantic seagoing friends say, is seen only over the . . ocean.

marshmallow n Cf **salt marshmallow**
1 Std: a common malvaceous plant *(Althea officinalis)*. [*OED* c1000 →] Also called **mallow B, mortification root, sweatweed, sweetweed**
2 A **hibiscus:** usu *Hibiscus moscheutos*, but also *H. militaris.*
 1817 Eaton *Botany* 78, *Hibiscus . . moscheutos,* (. . marsh-mallow). **1869** Porcher *Resources* 102 **Sth,** *Marsh mallow, (Hibiscus Moscheutos . .).* This also is possessed of demulcent properties. **1932** Rydberg *Flora Prairies* 543, *Hibiscus* L. *Rose Mallow. Marsh Mallow.* Herbs, shrubs, or trees. **1940** Gates *Flora KS* 145, Hibiscus militaris. . . Marshmallow. Along river banks. **1952** Taylor *Plants Colonial Days* 72, Rose mallow—*Hibiscus moscheutos. . .* Other common names include . . marshmallow (better applied to the related true marshmallow, *Althaea officinalis*). **1961** Smith *MI Wildflowers* 227, *Marsh Mallow. Hibiscus palustris. . .* In salty, fresh, or brackish marshes. Found in Michigan only in the southern part of the state. **1976** Bailey–Bailey *Hortus Third* 562, [*Hibiscus*] *moscheutos. . .* Subsp. *palustris. . .* Marsh m[allow]. . . Petals white, pink, or rose.

marsh marigold n [*OED* 1578 →] **chiefly Nth, N Midl** See Map on p. 524
A plant of the genus *Caltha,* esp *C. palustris.* Also called **cowslip 1.** For other names of *C. palustris* see **bulldog** n **5, bull flower, bull's-eye 7, butter daisy 2, butterflower 1, butter gold, caper, coltsfoot 4, cow lily 2, cowslop, crazy bet, crowfoot 1c, drunkard 3, English cowslip, false marigold, ground ivy 2c, kingcup 3, maybell 2, mayflower 16, meadow buttercup, swamp robin, water dragon, yellow marigold;** for other names of var spp see **elkslip, mountain marigold 1, white marsh ~**
 1814 Bigelow *Florula Bostoniensis* 134, Marsh Marigold. Meadow cowslip. . . In the spring . . its bright yellow blossoms are very common and conspicuous in meadows and wet situations. **1848** in 1850 Cooper *Rural Hours* 51 **ceNY,** A bunch of the golden flowers of the marsh marigold . . enticed us off the road into a low, boggy spot. . . a handsome flower, this—the country people call it cowslip, though differing entirely from the true plant of that name. **1859** (1880) Darlington *Amer. Weeds* 30, Marsh Marigold . . much used as a pot herb or "greens" in early spring. **1896** Robinson *In New Engl. Fields* 53, Marsh marigolds lengthen their golden chain, link by link, along the ditches. **1943** Fer-

nald–Kinsey *Edible Wild Plants E. N. Amer.* 205, Do not eat Marsh-Marigold raw. The fresh plant contains the poisonous glucoside *helleborin,* which is expelled in boiling. **1965–70** *DARE* (Qu. S22, . . *The bright yellow flowers that bloom in clusters in marshes in early springtime*) 90 Infs, **chiefly Nth, N Midl,** Marsh marigold(s); **RI**4, Wild marsh marigold; **MI**17, The books call it marsh marigold but I think that's nuts; many people know that name too; **MI**31, Marsh marigold is the name of them, but here we call them cowslips; **MI**53, Some people call 'em marsh marigold, but locally it was always cowslip; **NY**223, Marsh marigold—very fancy; **WA**12, Marsh marigold; maybe marsh buttercups; (Qu. S26b, *Wildflowers that grow in water or wet places*) Infs **CT**8, **GA**38, **PA**234, **WI**64, Marsh marigold(s); (Qu. I28b, *Kinds of greens that are cooked*) Inf **NY**30, Marsh marigolds; **MA**58, Wild marsh marigolds. **1989** Mosher *Stranger* 63 **nVT** (as of 1952), We traipsed along past blooming golden cowslips—marsh marigolds, my city-born mother called them, to Dad's amusement.

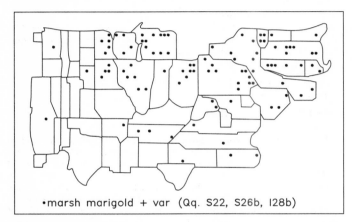

•marsh marigold + var (Qq. S22, S26b, I28b)

marsh milkweed n Also *Indian marsh milkweed*

A **boneset 1** (here: *Eupatorium purpureum*).

1892 *Jrl. Amer. Folkl.* 5.98 **MA,** *Eupatorium purpureum.* . . marsh milkweed. **1940** Clute *Amer. Plant Names* 82, E[upatorium] purpureum. Joe-Pye-weed. . . marsh-milkweed. *Ibid* 259, Indian marsh milk-weed. **1971** Krochmal *Appalachia Med. Plants* 120, *Eupatorium purpureum.* . . marsh milkweed.

marsh muhly n West

A **muhly (grass)** (here: *Muhlenbergia racemosa*).

[**1912** Baker *Book of Grasses* 106, Marsh Muhlenbergia (*Muhlenbergia racemosa*) grows in wet places and has much stouter and more compact flowering-heads, which sometimes resemble spikes of Timothy.] **1940** Gates *Flora KS* 131, Muhlenbergia racemosa. . . Marsh Muhly. **1950** Stevens *ND Plants* 74, *Muhlenbergia racemosa.* . . Marsh Muhly. **1952** Davis *Flora ID* 114, M[uhlenbergia] racemosa. . . Marsh muhly. **1953** Nelson *Plants Rocky Mt. Park* 41, Marsh muhly or green muhly. **1973** Hitchcock–Cronquist *Flora Pacific NW* 651, Marsh muhly.

marsh oats n

An **oat grass b** (here: *Trisetum pennsylvanicum*).

1912 Baker *Book of Grasses* 134, One of the early summer grasses . . is the Marsh Oats, which, although allied to other Oat-grasses, unlike them is found in the low grounds of wet meadows and by brooksides.

marsh owl n

=**short-eared owl.**

1890 Warren *Birds PA* 148, *Asio Accipitrinus.* . . The vulgar name of Marsh Owl is quite appropriate, as this species frequents mostly . . marshy districts and grass fields. **1904** Wheelock *Birds CA* 170, The habits of the Short-eared Owl differ so greatly from those of the rest of its family that it is sometimes called the Marsh Owl. It is rarely seen in a tree, and never in the dense woods. On bright days it sits concealed in the long grass of a marsh. **1914** Eaton *Birds NY* 2.114, This is our Marsh owl par excellence. . . I have often seen it sitting on trees and fence posts in broad daylight watching for its favorite prey. **1944** Hausman *Amer. Birds* 235, Its predilection for fenlands is reflected in the names Marsh Owl or Bog Owl, by which it is known in some sections of the country. **1950** *WELS* (Kinds of owls) 1 Inf, **csWI,** Marsh owl. **1968–70** *DARE* (Qu. Q2, . . *Kinds of owls*) Inf **VA**47, Marsh owl; (Qu. Q3) Inf **NJ**21, Marsh owl. **1981** Pederson *LAGS Basic Materials,* 1 inf, **swGA,** Marsh owl.

marsh pea n

A **vetchling** (here: *Lathyrus palustris*). Also called **Canada pea 2, peavine, sweet pea, wild ~**

1833 Eaton *Botany* 198 **NY,** *Lathyrus. . . palustris,* (marsh pea . .). Peekskill. **1910** Graves *Flowering Plants* 257 **CT,** Marsh Pea. Local. Borders of salt marshes in Groton, Waterford and Old Lyme . . , Old Saybrook. **1940** Steyermark *Flora MO* 312, *Marsh Pea.* . . Flowers . . purple or tinged with rose. Open woods and moist places. **1961** Smith *MI Wildflowers* 207, *Marsh Pea, Vetchling.* . . The shelled peas were cooked and eaten by the Indians.

marsh peep n

=**least sandpiper.**

1881 *Forest & Stream* 17.226, The above species [=*Tringa pusilla*] is designated as a "marsh peep," has olive or yellow bill and feet, and feeds around little pools on the marshes. **1923** U.S. Dept. Ag. *Misc. Circular* 13.55 **ME,** *Least Sandpiper.* . . *Vernacular names.* . . *In local use.* . . Marsh peep. **1932** Howell *FL Bird Life* 240, Least Sandpiper . . Marsh-peep. **1956** MA Audubon Soc. *Bulletin* 40.19 **MA, ME,** *Least Sandpiper.* . . Marsh Peep.

marsh peeper n Cf **March peeper**

A **tree frog.**

1892 Gibson *Sharp Eyes* 9 **NEng,** Pickering's frog. . . [and] the cricket frog . . *Acris crepitans.* . . are the two rival marsh peepers, and it is a "toss up" which you shall chance to hear first in your late winter rambles. **1939** *LANE* Map 231 *(Frog)* 1 inf, **seRI,** Frog; ?March peeper; ?marsh peeper. **1969** *DARE* (Qu. P21, *Small frogs that sing or chirp loudly in spring*) Inf **RI**1, Marsh peepers.

marsh pennywort n

Std: a plant of the genus *Hydrocotyle*. Also called **fairy table 2, pennywort.** For other names of var spp see **dollar grass, nickels and dimes, parasol 1, penny post, sombrerillo, water parsley**

marshpepper smartweed n Also *marsh pepper*

A **water pepper** (here: *Polygonum hydropiper*).

1942 Amer. Joint Comm. Horticult. Nomenclature *Std. Plant Names* 495, [Polygonum] hydropiper . . Marshpepper Smartweed. **1968** Barkley *Plants KS* 124, Polygonum hydropiper . . Marshpepper Smartweed. Wet woods and prairies. **1972** Courtenay–Zimmerman *Wild Flowers* 63, Marsh pepper, *Polygonum hydropiper.* . . Marshes, streambanks, shores / Flowers green, minutely dotted. **1973** Hitchcock–Cronquist *Flora Pacific NW* 86, Smartweed, marshpepper s[martweed]. . . P. hydropiper.

marsh Peter n

=**Florida gallinule.**

1923 U.S. Dept. Ag. *Misc. Circular* 13.45 **NC,** *Florida Gallinule.* . . marsh-Peter.

marsh pine n

A **pond pine** (here: *Pinus serotina*).

1908 Rogers *Tree Book* 36, The Pond, or Marsh Pine . . is the water-loving, round-headed pine, with yellow-green leaves. . . In the flat, peaty and sandy swamps from North Carolina down the coast to the St. John's River in Florida, the traveller finds this pine with the longleaf. **1933** Small *Manual SE Flora* 5, Black-pine, Pond-pine, Marsh-pine. . . Sandy swamps and shallow ponds, frequently acid, Coastal Plain, Fla. and Ala. to S N.J. **1979** Little *Checklist U.S. Trees* 198, *Pinus serotina* . . marsh pine, pocosin pine.

marsh pinegrass n

=**bluejoint 1.**

1937 U.S. Forest Serv. *Range Plant Hdbk.* G41, Bluejoint, also known in some localities as . . marsh pinegrass.

marsh pink n

1 A plant of the genus *Sabatia*. Also called **rose gentian.** For other names of var spp see **eyebright 6, meadow beauty 3, ~ gentian, ~ pink 4, pink bloom, ~ star, Plymouth gentian, prairie gentian, ~ pink, ~ starblossom, quinine flower, rose of Plymouth, rose pink, sea ~, sea star, Texas pink, ~ star**

1900 Lyons *Plant Names* 328, *Sabbatia.* . . Marsh Pink. **1901** Lounsberry *S. Wild Flowers* 427, S[abatia] dodecandra, large marsh pink, flourishes near the coast and from July until September unfolds its most beautiful flowers. **1942** Hylander *Plant Life* 431, The Marsh Pinks (*Sabbatia*) are slender plants with linear or oval leaves, found in wet pinelands and brackish marshes of our eastern states. **1976** Fleming *Wild Flowers FL* 27, White marsh pink (*Sabatia brevifolia*), gentian family, is a much-branched, slender-stemmed herb 1 to 2 feet tall, with small whitish flowers at the ends of the branches. **1982** *Miami Herald* (FL) 24 Oct sec H 10, We are six months away from finding the wild orchids that can color the prairie pink, but we're in time to catch a few marsh pinks in flower.

2 A **sea lavender** (here: *Limonium carolinianum*).

1940 Clute *Amer. Plant Names* 263, *Limonium Caroliniana* [sic]. . . Marsh pink.

marsh plover n
=pectoral sandpiper.

1852 in 1876 *Forest & Stream* 7.212 **eMA**, T[ringa] maculata. Marsh plover. **1923** U.S. Dept. Ag. *Misc. Circular* 13.54 **MA**, Marsh plover. **1936** Roberts *MN Birds* 1.502 **MN**, Pectoral Sandpiper . . Marsh Plover. [*Ibid* 503, From a distance of half a mile they [=Pectorals] were mistaken at first for a flock of Golden Plovers as they rose occasionally and circled about, now low, now high up, in truly ploverine fashion.]

marsh poke n Cf pokeweed
A **water hemp** (here: *Amaranthus cannabinus*).

1937 *Torreya* 37.96 **DE**, *Acnida cannabina*. . . Marsh poke.

marsh pullet n Cf marsh hen 1c
=Florida gallinule.

1888 Trumbull *Names of Birds* 122, At Washington, D.C. [the Florida gallinule is called] *king-ortolan,* and less commonly, *marsh-pullet.* **1913** Bailey *Birds VA* 63, *Florida Gallinule* . . Marsh Pullet.

marsh purslane n
=false loosestrife, esp *Ludwigia palustris.*

1900 Lyons *Plant Names* 204, *Isnardia.* . . Marsh Purslane. . . Succulent herbs. About 4 species, N. America; 3 in U.S. **1931** Harned *Wild Flowers Alleghanies* 333, Marsh purslane. . . a common, low, aquatic species, lying flat in the mud in swamps or ditches. Generally floating, or sometimes partially erect, branching. **1961** Thomas *Flora Santa Cruz* 251 **cwCA**, *Ludwigia.* . . Marsh Purslane. . . *L. palustris.* . . Pacific Marsh Purslane. Occasional along the edges of ponds and puddles. **1970** Correll *Plants TX* 1135, *Ludwigia palustris.* . . Marsh purslane.

marsh quail n [See quots 1914, 1927] NEng
The eastern **meadowlark 1.**

1750 (1916) Birket *Cursory Remarks* 32 **swRI**, Killd . . some very pretty birds called Marsh quails Something bigger then a field fare and fine Eatg. **1821** *Amer. Jrl. Science* 3.273 **cwMA**, April 14. . . The song of the marsh quail has been heard for a few days past. **1850** *Conn. Public Acts* 5 (*DAE*), It shall not be lawful . . for any person to shoot . . [the] meadow-lark or marsh quail. **1895** Minot *Land-Birds New Engl.* 251, They [=meadowlarks] are sometimes pursued by gunners from whom, I suppose, they have received the name of "Marsh Quail," which is not altogether inappropriate, since "they are generally considered, for size and delicacy, but little inferior to the quail." **1914** Eaton *Birds NY* 2.234, The Meadowlark's flight is strong and well-sustained. . . He rises with a buzzing of the wings which reminds one somewhat of a Quail's flight and has given him in many localities the name of "Marsh quail." **1927** Forbush *Birds MA* 2.436, Along the seaboard it [=meadowlark] frequents meadows and salt marshes and there it is known as the Marsh Quail. **1956** MA Audubon Soc. *Bulletin* 40.130 **MA, ME,** Meadowlark. . . Marsh Quail . . (The bird was formerly hunted in much the same way as quail now are.)

marsh rabbit n
1 A dark brown rabbit (here: *Sylvilagus palustris*) native to the southern US. Also called **black hare, pontoon, swamp rabbit**

1869 *Amer. Naturalist* 3.343, It is clear that a Marsh Rabbit has passed this way, planting his fore-feet straight downward, and drawing his hinder ones leisurely after, half squatting at each step, as he loped out of his home in the bushes to nip the beach grass for a change of diet. **1917** Anthony *Mammals Amer.* 291, The *Marsh Rabbit* makes its home in the lowlands along rivers and the coast of the Southeastern States from Dismal Swamp, Virginia, south to Florida, and west to Mobile Bay, Alabama. **1938** Matschat *Suwannee R.* 32 **neFL, seGA**, Marsh rabbits, that swim like ducks and have heavier fur than other species, are thick along the runs and in the sphagnum bogs. **1947** Cahalane *Mammals*

624, The marsh rabbits . . are clothed in dark fur that is short and thin. **1966–70** *DARE* (Qu. P30, . . *Wild rabbits*) Infs **FL**29, 35, **GA**11, **SC**66, Marsh rabbit; **LA**26, Marsh rabbits . . same size [as swamp rabbits] but slightly different color to match surroundings; **LA**44, Marsh rabbit—in the cane; **TX**14, Swamp rabbit—some say marsh. **1982** Elman *Hunter's Field Guide* 370, The small, dark marsh rabbit (S[ylvilagus] palustris) and closely related . . swamp rabbit, or cane-cutter . . both range from Virginia to Florida and across the Gulf states into Texas.

2 also *mush rabbit, musk rabbit:* **=muskrat 1,** esp when regarded as food. **chiefly C Atl, Gt Lakes** See Map Cf **marsh hare, marsh rat 2**

1932 Stieff *Eat in MD* 72, [Recipe title:] *Marsh rabbit (muskrat).* **1943** in 1944 *ADD*, [Clarence Birdseye] claims that muskrats have been avidly eaten in Baltimore for generations, under the more euphonious name of 'marsh rabbit.' Newspaper. **1947** Cahalane *Mammals* 537, Muskrat carcasses are sold as "marsh rabbits" in Washington, Baltimore, Philadelphia, St. Louis, and numerous other places. **1950** *WELS* (*Muskrat*) 2 Infs, **csWI**, Marsh rabbit. **1951** Johnson *Resp. to PADS* 20 **DE**, Muskrat. . . marsh rabbit. **1965–70** *DARE* (Qu. P31, . . *Names or nicknames . . for . . muskrat*) 23 Infs, **chiefly C Atl, Gt Lakes**, Marsh rabbit; **DE**3, Marsh rabbit—they used to sell them three for a quarter; **IL**9, Marsh rabbit—fancy name used in restaurants; **MI**49, Down around Wyandotte they call 'em marsh rabbit; **VA**110, Marsh rabbit—only when it's served as food! **TX**12, Mush rabbit; **NC**6, Musk rabbits. **1975** Jones *Amer. Food* 91, "Marsh rabbit" is an Eastern Shore euphemism for muskrat, a fine flavored meat which, after marinating overnight, is coated with flour and fried. **1982** *Wall St. Jrl.* (NY NY) 17 Mar 1/4 **eMD**, The muskrat stew—which the restaurant diplomatically calls "marsh rabbit"—has a tangy taste, lots of small bones and the consistency of stringy beef.

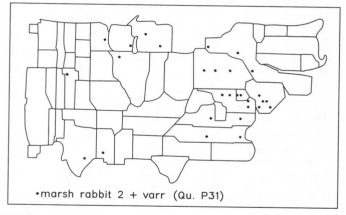

•marsh rabbit 2 + varr (Qu. P31)

marsh rat n
1 A **cotton rat** (here: *Sigmodon hispidus*).

1917 Anthony *Mammals Amer.* 228, *Sigmodon hispidus* . . Marsh Rat. **1968** *DARE* (Qu. P32, . . *Other kinds of wild animals*) Inf **MD**36, Marsh rat—something like house rat—not the same as marsh rabbit.

2 **=muskrat 1.** [*DCan* c1902] Cf **marsh rabbit 2**

1967–69 *DARE* (Qu. P31, . . *Names or nicknames . . for the . . muskrat*) Infs **NH**18, **NY**2, 207, **WI**68, Marsh rat(s); **MD**45, Marsh rat—joking name for muskrat.

marsh rattler n
Prob a **canebrake rattler.**

1966 *DARE* (Qu. P25, . . *Kinds of snakes*) Inf **GA**11, Marsh rattler.

marsh robin n [See quot 1890]
=rufous-sided towhee.

1872 Coues *Key to N. Amer. Birds* 151, Towhee Bunting. Marsh Robin. Chewink. **1890** *Century Dict.* 3640, Marsh-robin, . . the chewink or towhee-bunting, . . so called from its haunts, and the reddish color on the sides of the breast. **1917** *Wilson Bulletin* 29.2.83 **KY**, *Pipilo erythrophthalmus* . . ground or marsh robin. **1946** Goodrich *Birds in KS* 318, Marsh robin. . . red-eyed towhee. **1956** MA Audubon Soc. *Bulletin* 40.254 **ME**, Towhee. . . Ground Robin (General. Its black and cinnamon coloration suggests that of the Robin.) . . Marsh Robin.

marsh rosemary n
=sea lavender.

1784 in 1785 Amer. Acad. Arts & Sci. *Memoirs* 1.432, *Marsh Rose-*

mary. The roots are powerfully astringent. **1824** Bigelow *Florula Bostoniensis* 124, *Statice Caroliniana*. Marsh Rosemary. . . A purple flowering plant of the salt marshes, very conspicuous about midsummer. . . The root is strongly astringent, and with us is an officinal article of considerable consumption. **1854** King *Amer. Eclectic Dispensatory* 908, *Statice caroliniana*. Marsh Rosemary. *Ibid* 909, Marsh Rosemary is found along the seacoast in marshy situations from Maine to Florida. **1862** (1882) Stowe *Pearl of Orr's Is.* 98 **ME**, 'Ma'sh rosemary is the gargle that I always use,' said Miss Roxy; 'it cleans out your throat so.' **1892** Coulter *Botany W. TX* 254, Marsh-rosemary . . Seaside or salt-marsh perennials, with thick and stalked radical leaves, naked flowering stems. **1923** Davidson–Moxley *Flora S. CA* 272, *Limonium*. Marsh Rosemary. . . *L[imonium] californicum* . . Frequent in salt marshes along the coast. **1948** Pearson *Sea Flavor* 119 **NH**, Most conspicuous of all is the marsh rosemary. This is a perennial with a group of long, rather heavy leaves growing from the crown. From June to mid-September the stems hold erect bouquets of interlaced sprays. **1976** Bailey–Bailey *Hortus Third* 664, *Limonium*. . . *Marsh Rosemary*. . . Often grown in rock gardens, in greenhouses, or for cut flowers, some are useful in dry bouquets.

marsh rot n
Thrush of a horse's hoof.
1967 *DARE* (Qu. K47, *Diseases . . horses or mules commonly get*) Inf **MI49**, Marsh rot—the flesh just behind the hoof stinks and falls away.

marsh shield fern See **marsh fern**

marsh shrew n Also *salt marsh shrew*
=**water shrew.**
1829 Richardson *Fauna Boreali–Amer.* 1.5, *Sorex Palustris, American Marsh-Shrew.* **1917** Anthony *Mammals Amer.* 312, *Neosorex palustris*. . . Marsh Shrew. . . The Marsh Shrew ranges from central Minnesota to the east base of the Rocky Mountains. **1928** Anthony *N. Amer. Mammals* 28, Salt Marsh Shrew . . *Sorex halicaetes*. . . Found in salt marshes of Santa Clara County, California. *Ibid* 35, *Neosorex palustris* . . Marsh Shrew. **1935** Pratt *Manual Vertebrate Animals* 254, Marsh shrew. . . Eastern North America from the Pennsylvania mountains to Labrador . . in swamps and wet fields and woods. **1957** Blair et al. *Vertebrates U.S.* 636, *Sorex bendirei* [sic] . . Marsh shrew. **1961** Jackson *Mammals WI* 36, *Sorex palustris hydrobadistes*. . . Names include . . marsh shrew.

marsh snipe n
=**Wilson's snipe.**
1888 Trumbull *Names of Birds* 156 **seMD**, Wilson's Snipe. . . Marsh Snipe. **1895** Elliot *N. Amer. Shore Birds* 47, Wilson's Snipe. . . is called in different sections Jack Snipe, Bog and Marsh Snipe. **1969** *DARE* (Qu. Q10, . . *Water birds and marsh birds*) Inf **NC78**, Marsh snipe.

marsh sparrow n
1 =**song sparrow. chiefly NJ**
1917 (1923) *Birds Amer.* 3.50, Song Sparrow. . . Marsh Sparrow. **1946** Hausman *Eastern Birds* 615, Eastern Song Sparrow *Melospiza melodia melodia*. . . Marsh Sparrow, Swamp Finch. **1968** *DARE* (Qu. Q21, . . *Kinds of sparrows*) Infs **NJ**15, 17, 21, 22, 39, Marsh sparrow.
2 =**Savannah sparrow. CA**
1904 Wheelock *Birds CA* 216, Among the thick rushes of the San Francisco Bay marshes the Bryant Marsh Sparrow makes its home. *Ibid* 218, The Belding Marsh Sparrow is abundant on the salt marshes near the coast of Southern California from Santa Barbara south to Lower California. **1968** *DARE* (Qu. Q21, . . *Kinds of sparrows*) Inf **CA**78, Belding marsh sparrow—in estuaries—local form of Savannah sparrow.

marsh spike-grass n
A **salt grass** (here: *Distichlis spicata*).
1901 Mohr *Plant Life AL* 383, *Distichlis spicata*. . . Marsh Spike Grass. . . Coast of New York to Florida, west to Texas. On the Pacific slope, Vancouver Island to California. **1911** NJ State Museum *Annual Rept. for 1910* 239, Marsh Spike Grass. . . Salt meadows along the coast; common. **1912** Baker *Book of Grasses* 187, Marsh Spike-grass . . is one of the sand-binding grasses, spreading by strong rootstocks. **1913** *Torreya* 13.250 **eNY**, Considerable hay was made from the marsh grasses, composed largely of the marsh spike-grass, *Distichlis spicata*. **1933** Small *Manual SE Flora* 128, *Marsh spike-grass*.

marsh sweater n
=**clapper rail.**

1923 U.S. Dept. Ag. *Misc. Circular* 13.42 **VA**, [Clapper Rail] *Vernacular Names*. . . In local use. . . Marsh-sweater.

marsh tacky n Also *marsh tackey*, ~ *taggy* [**tacky**] **chiefly S Atl, esp SC**
A small horse or pony of southern marshes.
1825 *U.S. Lit. Gaz.* 3.105 **SC**, "Marsh tackies" . . a small but hardy animal. **1838** (1852) Gilman *S. Matron* 131 **seSC**, An accident happening to my horse, I was obliged to hire one of the little animals called 'marsh tackies' to carry me over a creek. They are usually very strong and sure. **1853** Simms *Sword & Distaff* 61 **SC**, A little 'marsh-tacky,' or poney, of Spanish breed, such as are to be found very commonly about the parishes of South-Carolina to this day—a light, hardy, lively creature, very small, but of great endurance. **1890** McAllister *Society* 91 **ceGA**, We all pressed through the crowd to the . . two marsh tackeys, with their manes and tails . . full of burrs. **1936** Smith–Sass *Carolina Rice* 80 **eSC**, Bob rode a marsh-tackey named Jim, who was for his size a fine jumper and a fast pony for a quarter of a mile. **1939** FWP *Guide FL* 302 **neFL**, Herds of wild horses, called marshtackies, roamed this region as late as 1918. These horses, perhaps descended from the animals brought over by the first Spanish settlers, could traverse almost inaccessible swamps and lowlands. **1950** *PADS* 14.45 **SC**, Marsh tacky. . . A small pony raised in the low country. A term of derision. **1966–67** *DARE* (Qu. K39, . . *Names . . for horses according to their colors*) Inf **GA**11, Marsh tackies ['tækɪz]; (Qu. K44, *A bony or poor-looking horse*) Inf **SC**38, Marsh taggy—a wild horse in lower part of the state near the coast. **1984** Wilder *You All Spoken Here* 59 **Sth**, Marsh tacky: Small horses of the sea islands of Virginia, North Carolina, South Carolina, and Georgia.

marsh tea n
1 also *mash tea*: A **Labrador tea** (here: *Ledum palustre*).
1822 Eaton *Botany* 332, *Ledum . . palustre* . . marsh-tea. **1830** Rafinesque *Med. Flora* 2.236, Ledum. . . *Marsh tea* . . very near to Chinese tea, but stronger, owing to a fragrant resin. **1872** Schele de Vere *Americanisms* 396, In the Northwest they have a tea called *Mash*-tea, and another called *Labrador*-tea, made from two plants (Ledum palustre and Ledum latifolium), the leaves of which possess moderate narcotic qualities, and are said to furnish a pleasant infusion. **1892** (1974) Millspaugh *Amer. Med. Plants* 100–2, Marsh Tea (*Ledum latifolium* . .), used in dysentery, diarrhoea, tertian ague, and in some places to render beer heady, though it is said to bring on delirium. **1900** Lyons *Plant Names* 218, *L[edum] palustre*. . . Marsh Tea.
2 A **glasswort** (here: *Salicornia europaea*).
1900 Lyons *Plant Names* 329, *S[alicornia] herbacea*. . . Marsh Tea.

marsh tern n
1 =**gull-billed tern.**
1814 Wilson *Amer. Ornith.* 8.143 **seNJ**, Marsh Tern: *Sterna aranea* . . first met with on the shores of Cape May . . darting down after a kind of large black spider. **1898** (1900) Davie *Nests N. Amer. Birds* 38, In North America the Marsh Tern, as it is commonly called, breeds from New Jersey southward. **1925** (1928) Forbush *Birds MA* 1.96, The earlier writers knew this species [=*Gelochelidon nilotica aranea*] as the Marsh Tern for it once frequented salt marshes of the Atlantic and Gulf States and bred there. **1977** Udvardy *Audubon Field Guide Birds* 409, This marsh tern [=*Gelochelidon nilotica*] often forages for insects in fields around lagoons where it nests, or hawks for them in the air as they swarm over the marsh.
2 =**black tern.** [*OED* 1852]
1909 Field Museum Nat. Hist. *Zool. Ser.* 9.304 **IL, WI**, Black Tern. Marsh Tern. **1932** Bennitt *Check-list* 34 **MO**, *Black tern*. . . Marsh tern.

marsh tiger lily See **tiger lily**

marsh treader n
An insect of the family *Hydrometridae*.
1895 Comstock–Comstock *Manual Insects* 136, The Marsh-treader, *Limnobates lineata* . . crawls about on the surface of the water or mud, or climbs upon water-plants and sticks projecting from the water; it seems to prefer stagnant ponds or marshes. **1905** Kellogg *Amer. Insects* 198, Slender insects, about ½ inch long, with thin long legs and hair-like antennae and long cylindrical head, are to be found on top of the water. But they creep slowly about on the surface or on the soft mud of the shore, and are found mostly where plants are growing in quiet water. These are marsh-treaders, *Limnobates lineata*. **1954** Borror–DeLong *Intro. Insects* 239, Family *Hydrometridae*—Water Measurers or Marsh Treaders. These bugs are small . . , usually grayish in color and very

slender; they resemble tiny walking sticks. **1972** Swan–Papp *Insects* 115, Marsh Treader: *Hydrometra martini.*

marsh trefoil n [*OED* 1597 →]
=**buckbean 1.**

1830 Rafinesque *Med. Flora* 2.33, *Menyanthes verna* . . *Vulgar.* Marsh Trefoil, Water Shamrock, Bitter Root. **1854** King *Amer. Eclectic Dispensatory* 633, *Menyanthes trifoliata.* Buckbean. . . This plant is also known by the names of *Bog-bean, Marsh-trefoil, Water-shamrock,* etc. **1873** in 1976 Miller *Shaker Herbs* 142, Wind Shamrock. Bitterworm. Marsh Trefoil. **1897** *Jrl. Amer. Folkl.* 10.50, *Menyanthes trifoliata* . . marsh trefoil. **1949** Moldenke *Amer. Wild Flowers* 230, The *buckbean* or *marshtrefoil, menyanthes trifoliata,* is a smooth marsh herb with thick, scaly, creeping stems, often a foot long, and long-stalked, 3-parted leaves. **1974** (1977) Coon *Useful Plants* 144, Buckbean, marsh trefoil.

marsh turnip n
A **jack-in-the-pulpit 1** (here: *Arisaema triphyllum*).

1873 in 1976 Miller *Shaker Herbs* 188, *Arum triphyllum.* . . Marsh Turnip. Recommended internally in croup, low typhoid, and externally in scrofulous tumors, and scald head. **1930** Sievers *Amer. Med. Plants* 37, *Jack-in-the-pulpit.* . . *Other common names.* . . Marsh turnip, . . meadow turnip. [*Ibid* 38, The underground portion . . is shaped like a turnip.]

marsh violet n Cf **marsh blue violet**
A **violet**: usu *Viola palustris* or *V. epipsila.*

1784 in 1785 *Amer. Acad. Arts & Sci. Memoirs* 1.485 **neMA**, *Viola.* . . Marsh violet. Blossoms pale blue. In moist meadows. April. **1813** Muhlenberg *Catalogus Plantarum* 26 **PA**, [Viola] asarifolia (uliginosa) . . marsh [violet]. **1848** Gray *Manual of Botany* 44 **cNH**, *V[iola] palustris.* . . Marsh Violet. **1949** Moldenke *Amer. Wild Flowers* 47, *V[iola] palustris,* the marsh violet . . is at home in moist or wet soil from Labrador throughout all of Canada to Alaska, south to Washington and northern California, in the high mountains of New England, and in the Rockies to Colorado. **1966** Heller *Wild Flowers AK* 77, Northern marsh violet—*Viola epipsela.* **1968** *DARE* (Qu. S11) Inf **PA**176, Marsh violet; (Qu. S26b, *Wildflowers that grow in water or wet places*) Inf **PA**99, Marsh violet. **1987** Hughes–Blackwell *Wildflowers SE AK* 106, Marsh Violet (*Viola epipsila*).

marsh widgeon n
=**European widgeon.**

1955 *Oriole* 20.1.4 **GA**, European Widgeon . . *marsh widgeon.*

marsh wren n
Either of two similar birds: the long-billed marsh wren (*Cistothorus palustris*) or the short-billed marsh wren (*C. platensis*). For other names of the former see **prairie marsh wren, reed ~, saltwater marsh ~, swamp ~, tomtit, tule wren**; for other names of the latter see **freshwater marsh wren, grass ~, meadow ~, sedge ~**

1791 Bartram *Travels* 291 **Atlantic**, M[otacilla] palustris, . . the marsh wren. **1823** Latham *Genl. Hist. Birds* 7.202, *Sylvia Platensis.* . . "Inhabits Georgia, frequenting briars and thickets in the marshes, and rice fields, but far from common; and called the Marsh Wren." **1844** DeKay *Zool. NY* 2.56, Marsh wren. . . This little wren, as its name implies, is chiefly found in marshes, where it constructs a curious pensile nest. **1917** (1923) *Birds Amer.* 3.198, Marsh Wrens, like other Wrens, are irrepressible songsters. . . Sometimes when the full moon lights up the marshes the singing of the Wrens becomes almost a continuous performance, ringing over the meadows. **1923** *Frontier & Midland* Mar 12 **MT**, Shall I ever again . . hear the liquid call of the marsh wren? **1950** *WELS* (*Water and marsh birds*), 2 Infs, **WI**, Marsh wren. **1968** *DARE* (Qu. Q10) Inf **CA**78, Marsh wrens; (Qu. Q11) Inf **CT**5, Marsh wren—around water a lot. **1977** Bull–Farrand *Audubon Field Guide Birds* 437, Short-billed Marsh Wren (*Cistothorus platensis*). *Ibid* 438, Long-billed Marsh Wren (*Cistothorus palustris*).

marshy hay See **marsh hay**

marshy milk n Cf **bitterweed milk, blinky 2**
See quots.

1890 *DN* 1.59, "Marshy milk" in Charleston, S.C., is the milk of a cow feeding on the marsh grass, which gives the milk a peculiar marshy taste. **1966** *DARE* (Qu. K14, *Milk that has a taste from something the cow ate in the pasture*) Inf **NC**1, Marshy milk—from cows in marsh.

marster n See **master** n

marster adj See **master** adj

marster adv See **master** adv

marter n[1], v See **matter**

Martha Washington's candle n
=**blazing star 3.**

1951 *PADS* 15.42 **TX**, *Laciniaria* spp.—Martha Washington's candle.

marthy See **methy**

martin n Also *martin bird, martin dove* Cf **bank martin, barn ~, bee ~, billy ~, buddy bee ~, field ~, gully ~, king ~, little ~, mud ~, sand ~, sea ~, white-bellied ~**
A **swallow** (here: Hirundinidae): usu **purple martin,** but at times also any of several related birds such as **tree swallow.** Note: This term is often used in combs for **chimney swift** and **kingbird 1;** hence some Infs may refer to either of these birds.

1709 (1967) Lawson *New Voyage* 149 **NC**, Martins are here of two sorts. The first is the same as in *England;* the other as big as a Black-Bird. They have white Throats and Breasts, with black Backs. The Planters put Gourds on standing Poles, on purpose for these Fowl to build in. **1812** Wilson *Amer. Ornith.* 5.58, I never knew an instance of Martins eating *peas.* **1831** Audubon *Ornith. Biog.* 1.115, At the Falls of the Ohio, I have seen Martins as early as the 15th of March. **1832** Nuttall *Manual Ornith.* 1.599, The food of the Martin is usually the larger winged insects; as wasps, bees, large beetles, such as the common *Cetonias* or goldsmiths, which are swallowed whole. **1844** Giraud *Birds Long Is.* 35, The flight of the Martin is easy and graceful. It is frequently seen it [sic] sailing in the air with so little apparent effort, that feather-like it seems to be floating along. **1891** *Leighton News* (AL) 19 Nov np, About the middle of August the Martins collect in large flocks preparatory to migrating. **1923** *WV State Ornith. Birds WV* 61, No hawk can successfully prey upon a flock of chickens where a colony of martins live. **1956** MA Audubon Soc. *Bulletin* 40.84, *Purple martin* . . Martin bird (Me.). . . *Tree swallow* . . Martin (Maine, Mass.) **1965–70** *DARE* (Qu. Q3, . . *Birds that come out only after dark*) Infs **IA**20, **OK**25, Martins; **IA**22, Martin—feeds at night; (Qu. Q11, . . *Kinds of blackbirds*) Infs **FL**22, **NC**44, **OH**84, **TX**33, Martin(s); **GA**72, Martin—black; **GA**77, Martin—is a blackbird, lives in a barn; (Qu. Q14, . . *Names . . for these birds: . . martin*) 373 Infs, **widespread exc West,** Martin; **MD**20, **MS**63, Martin bird; **FL**1, Martin dove; **LA**14, Martin, sometimes called king martin; (Qu. Q14, . . *Kingbird*) Inf **TN**30, Martin; (Qu. Q15) Inf **IL**69, Martins; (Qu. Q20, . . *Kinds of swallows and birds like them*) 39 Infs, **scattered,** Martin; **LA**8, Martin bird. **1981** Pederson *LAGS Basic Materials* **Gulf Region,** 3 infs, Martin; 6 infs, Martins; 1 inf, Martin bird.

‡**martin-house swallow** n Cf **house martin**
A **martin.**

1966 *DARE* (Qu. Q20, . . *Kinds of swallows and birds like them*) Inf **ME**22, Martin-house swallow.

martin storm n Also *martin winter* Cf **blackbird storm**
See quots.

1953 Randolph–Wilson *Down in Holler* 264 **Ozarks**, Martin storm. . . A late blizzard, at the time the martins return in the spring. **1995** Montgomery Coll. **wNC, eTN**, *Martin winter* n. A frost or freezing spell in early May at the time that martins arrive from the south.

martis See **tomato**

marvel n[1] Also sp *marvell, marvle* Pronc-sp *mahvil* [Engl, Scots dial] **chiefly S Midl**
A playing marble.

1795 Dearborn *Columbian Grammar* 137, *List of Improprieties.* . . Marvels for Marbles. **1846** in 1952 Green *Samuel Maverick* 318 **SC**, If you should go into the marvell trade you must be sure . . never to play marvells for winning, as that is gambling, and that will never do. **1859** (1968) Bartlett *Americanisms* 265, Marvel. A mispronunciation of *marble,* common in the mouths of illiterate people. **1872** Schele de Vere *Americanisms* 504, Marvel has . . usurped, first in pronunciation and afterward even in writing, the place of *marble,* especially in the play with "marbles," so popular in the South. . . A Kentucky divine is reported to have once preached against this "frivolous and childish sport" from the text, "Marvel not, brethren!" (1 John iii.13). **1875** (1876) Twain *Tom Sawyer* 27 **MO**, Jim, I'll give you a marvel. I'll give you a white alley! **1899** (1912) Green *VA Folk-Speech* 272, We'll play a game of mahvils. *Ibid* 275, Marvel. **1909** *DN* 3.348 **eAL, wGA**, Marvel. . .

Marble. *Marvels.* . . The game of marbles. **1915** *DN* 4.185 **swVA**, *Marvel.* **1916** *DN* 4.285 **sAppalachians,** Games at "marvles" (marbles) furnish many [Elizabethan words and phrases]. **1925** *AmSp* 5.19 **Ozarks,** *Marvels.* **1967** *DARE* (Qu. EE6c, *Cheap marbles*) Inf **AR**47, Glass marvels [mɑrvəlz]. **1968** *DARE* FW Addit **neAL,** Little boys play marvels.

marvel v Also *marble, marvil* [Orig unknown]
To depart quickly, move off in a hurry.
  1847 Hurd *Grammatical Corrector.* 52 **PA,** *Marble,* for *move off;* as, "If you do that again you must marble," i.e., move quickly, be off immediately. **1858** Hammett *Piney Woods Tavern* 21 **TX,** I tell *you* we must marvel; so good-bye. *Ibid* 43, We . . marvelled off with our tails atween our legs. **1867** Harris *Sut Lovingood Yarns* 174 **TN,** Yu'd better gird up yer coteails an marvil furder, an' marvil faster, fur his boot hes a powful strong swing. **1894** *Century Illustr. Mag.* 48.870, I cannot suggest any explanation of an Indiana mother's injunction by which she seeks to quicken the pace of the boy "creeping like snail unwillingly to school." She says, "Marvel, now!" **1927** *AmSp* 3.139 **eME,** If [in] a hurry he must "cut along" or "marvel."

marvel n[2]
=horehound 1.
  1900 Lyons *Plant Names* 240, M[*arrubium*] *vulgare.* . . Marvel. **1911** Henkel *Amer. Med. Leaves* 51, Marvel, same as horehound. **1930** Sievers *Amer. Med. Plants* 35, Marvel, marrube. **1974** (1977) Coon *Useful Plants* 158, *Marrubium vulgare*—Horehound, houndsbane, marvel, marrub.

marvelle n Cf **love knot, matrimony 2**
  1950 *PADS* 14.45 **SC,** *Marvelle* [mɑ'vɛl]. . . Rectangular cake of sweet dough slit several times lengthwise and fried. The slit sections are usually twisted, probably to allow the frying fat to penetrate more easily. Also called *lady fingers.*

marvellous adv
Exceedingly, terribly.
  1953 Randolph–Wilson *Down in Holler* 161 **Ozarks,** Nancy Clemens, Springfield, Missouri, quoted a farmer who had been hurt in a motor accident: "No bones broke," said he, "but I sure was scratched up *marvellous.*"

marvel-of-Peru n [*OED* 1597 →]
A **four-o'clock 1** (here: *Mirabilis jalapa*).
  1847 Wood *Class-Book* 472, M[*irabilis*] *jalapa.* . . Marvel-of-Peru. **1876** Hobbs *Bot. Hdbk.* 69, Marvel of Peru. . . Mirabilis Jalapa. **1929** Pope *Plants HI* 63, Four-o'clock or Marvel of Peru. **1949** Moldenke *Amer. Wild Flowers* 96, Of wide geographic distribution, but chiefly American, are the . . four-o'clock family. . . Best known and handsomest is the common four-o'clock or marvel-of-Peru. **1976** Bailey–Bailey *Hortus Third* 735, [*Mirabilis*] *Jalapa.* . . Four-o'clock, Marvel-of-Peru.

marvil See **marvel** v

Marvin See **Melvin**

marvle See **marvel** n[1]

Mary n Usu |'mɛri|; also *esp* Sth, NEng |'me(ɪ)ri|; for addit varr see quots Pronc-sp *Meery*
Std sense, var forms.
  1891 *DN* 1.127 **cNY,** [mɛrɪ] < Mary. **1941** in 1944 *ADD*, Mary. . . ?*Md. Balt.* or gen. vulg. Pron. Meery. *Eve. Sun* Feb. **1950** Hubbell *Pronc. NYC* 75, The partial disappearance of the /ɪ/ [*DARE* Ed: =/ɪ/] -/iɔ/ [*DARE* Ed: =/ɪɔ/] opposition before /r/ is not paralleled in the case of /e/ [*DARE* Ed: =/ɛ/] and /ɛɔ/: *ferry-fairy, merry-Mary, very-vary* are always distinguished. . . Metropolitan usage . . is extremely variable, differing considerably from one social group to another and differing from person to person within what is roughly the same group. And the practice of a single speaker will often show a great deal of variation in successive utterances of the same word. **1961** Kurath–McDavid *Pronc. Engl.* 124, Broadly speaking, *Mary* rimes with *merry* /mɛri/ in the Midland. . . [and] has the vowel /e/ of *eight* in . . the South and New England. . . A third type of pronunciation is in regular use in Metropolitan New York and vicinity, and occurs with varying frequency in Upstate New York, in New England, on upper Chesapeake Bay (Maryland), and in Wilmington, N.C. Here *Mary* contrasts with *merry* as /meəri/ vs. /mɛri/. **c1970** Pederson *Dial. Surv. Rural GA (Jesus's parents were Joseph and _____) seGA,* [Of 62 infs, 29 had proncs of the type ['meˑᵛɪrɪ^, 'meəˑɪ^, 'meˑərɪ^]; 29 of the type ['mɛːrɪ^, 'mɛˑᵊˑɪ^, 'mɛᵊrɪ^]; 2 ['mæ^ᵊˑ(r)ɪ^]; 2 ['mɪːˑrˑ, 'mɪᵛ·ᵊrɪ^].] **1976** Allen *LAUM* 3.34 **Upper MW** (as of c1950), The distinction created by a higher vowel,

[e, eᵛ, ɛ^], in *Mary* than in *merry* has been preserved in the first settled parts of the U[pper] M[idwest] by some speakers directly related to the eastern areas where it occurs, but generally the distinction appears to be headed for obsolescence as more and more younger speakers adopt the [ɛ] vowel in *Mary.* **1991** Pederson *LAGS Regional Pattern* 62, 202, 310, [Of approx 914 primary infs, 449 infs had proncs with [ɛ], 322 with [eɪ], and 208 with [eɪ~eᵛ] in *Mary.*]

Mary Ann(e) adj
See quot 1916.
  1872 Twain *Roughing It* 455, [In Honolulu] I saw cats—Tomcats, Mary Ann cats, long-tailed cats, bob-tailed cats. **1916** *DN* 4.342 **seOH,** *Mary Ann.* Vile; low; mean; e.g. "That is a Mary Anne saloon." [*DN* Ed: "A Queen Anne front and Mary Ann back." N. Eng. . . Also N. Car. . .] [*Ibid, Queen Anne.* Beautiful: opposite of *Mary Anne, q.v.*]

Mary-cut-a-finger n Cf **Mary's-thumbweed**
An unidentified plant.
  1966 *DARE* (Qu. S21, . . *Weeds . . that are a trouble in gardens and fields*) Inf **NC**24, Mary-cut-a-finger.

Mary Jane n
1 A woman's shirt-like garment. *esp freq among Black speakers; old-fash*
  1928 White *Amer. Negro Folk-Songs* 317, Well a white lady wears a hobble skirt,/ A yaller gal tries to do de same,/ But a poor black gal wears a Mary Jane,/ But she's hobbling just de same. **1966** *DARE* (Qu. W15, *A shirt-length undergarment worn by women*) Inf **SC**24, Mary Jane [FW sugg] = chemise (older [term]). **1966** *DARE* Tape **SC**14 (as of c1910), Mary Jane was a coat that fitted like a corset. . . Get your coatsuit and your Mary Jane. **1969** *DARE* FW Addit **SC** [Black], Mary Jane—A wide shirt using 3 to 4 yards of cloth. Old-fashioned.
2 See quot. *euphem*
  1970 *DARE* (Qu. AA27, . . *A woman's menstruation*) Inf **PA**247, Mary Jane.
3 Appar an anemone (here: *Anemone patens*).
  1967 *DARE* (Qu. S23, *Pale blue flowers with downy leaves and cups that come up on open, stony hillsides in March or early April*) Inf **CO**37, Mary Janes.

Maryland beaten biscuit n Also *Maryland (beat) biscuit* chiefly **MD**
=beaten biscuit.
  1853 (1982) Lea *Domestic Cookery* 69 **MD,** *Maryland Biscuit.* Rub half a pound of lard into three pounds of flour; put in a spoonful of salt, a tea-cup of cream, and water sufficient to make it into a stiff dough; divide it into two parts, and work each well till it will break off short, and is smooth; (some pound it with an iron hammer, or axe;) cut it up into small pieces, and work them into little round cakes. **1872** in 1909 Roe *Army Letters* 35, There was no April fool about the delicate Maryland biscuits. **1895** (1900) Arnold *Century Cook Book* 247, *Distinctively Southern Dishes.* . . Maryland Beaten Biscuit. **1896** (c1903) Farmer *Orig. Cook Book* 77, *Maryland Biscuit*—1 pint flour[₍], 1 teaspoon salt[₍], ⅓ cup lard[₍], milk and water in equal quantities. . . Mix flour and salt; work in lard. . . Beat with rolling-pin thirty minutes. **1931** *Sun* (Baltimore MD) 1 May 12/7 (Hench Coll.), Oh, I bought eight of those heavenly biscuits—the last they had!/ Maryland biscuits?/ I *object* to that description. *Beaten* biscuits. They make them *just* as good in Virginia! **1933** *Ibid* 21 June 10/7, I have noticed some degree of controversy recently . . as to the exact nature of the Maryland beat biscuit. . . I have beaten enough Maryland biscuit to know what I am talking about when I say that the whole secret is in the beating. **1968** *DARE* (Qu. H19, *What do you mean by a biscuit? How are they made?*) Inf **CA**97, Maryland biscuits—beaten biscuit made with no yeast; **MD**30, Maryland beat biscuits—dough beaten on wooden block before baking; biscuits came out hard, kept fresh a long time; **MD**33, 35, 37, Maryland biscuits; **MD**41, Maryland beaten biscuit—dough pounded with mallet until light—require no baking powder, beating makes them rise. [5 of 6 Infs old]

Maryland end n Also *Maryland side*
See quots.
  1859 (1968) Bartlett *Americanisms* 265, *Maryland end.* Said of the hock of the ham. The other is the Virginia end. Maryland and Virginia. **1899** (1912) Green *VA Folk-Speech* 276, *Maryland side.* . . The hock of the ham. The other is the Virginia side.

Maryland yellowthroat See **yellowthroat**

Mary's-thumbweed n
Perh a **lady's thumb.**
  1968 *DARE* (Qu. S21, . . *Weeds . . that are a trouble in gardens and fields*) Inf **NC49,** Mary's thumbweed.

Marzetti See **Johnny Marzetti**

masacree See **massacre**

masamacush See **namaycush**

mascal See **mescal**

mascallunge, mascalonge See **muskellunge**

mash v[1]

1 also with *down, in, up:* To apply an injurious blow or pressure to; to crush, smash, squash; to suffer crushing of (some part of the body); to be smashed (esp on something); hence ppl adj *mashed.* **widespread, but chiefly Sth, Midl; also West** See Map Cf **jam** v **1**
  1832 *Political Examiner* (Shelbyville KY) 8 Dec 4/1, I reckon I squashed her into a mashed hat in a little less than no time. **1838** (1852) Gilman *S. Matron* 40 seSC, "He says," answered I, "that John has *mashed* his hand on the *dray.*" . . "You should say, Master Richard, that John has *jammed* his hand on the *truck.*" **1867** Allen *Slave Songs* xxviii eSC [Gullah], *Mash* in the sense of crush; "mammy mash 'em," when the goat had killed one of her kids by lying on it. **1899** (1912) Green *VA Folk-Speech* 276, *Mash.* . . To crush by weight; to break. **1906** *DN* 3.121 sIN, *Mash.* . . To crowd down, push down, crush. "I mashed my finger with the hatchet." **1909** *DN* 3.348 eAL, wGA, *Mash.* . . to crush, press upon. "Get off, you are mashing me." **1909** *S. Atl. Qrly.* 8.41 sSC coast, *Lest he dash his foot against a stone* in Gullah idiom is *Les' 'e fut mash on a rock!* **1928** Peterkin *Scarlet Sister Mary* 45 SC [Gullah], You gwine mash Si May-e's dress. **1932** (1974) Caldwell *Tobacco Road* 123 **GA,** The wagon turned over on him and mashed him. **1950** *WELS* **WI** (*When something hollow is crushed by a heavy weight or by a fall:* "The kids ran the wagon over the coffee pot and _____.") 4 Infs, Mashed it; (*To squeeze or squash:* "I _____ my finger in the door.") 12 Infs, Mashed. **c1960** *Wilson Coll.* csKY, *Mashed.* . . Squeezed, crushed, bruised. **1963** Watkins–Watkins *Yesterday Hills* 48 cnGA, Nobody ever got cold for lack of cover, but it's a wonder why no child ever got mashed to death sleeping under eight or ten quilts. **1965–70** *DARE* (Qu. Y33, . . *Squeezing or crushing something* . . "I _____ my finger in the door.") 459 Infs, **widespread, but chiefly Sth, Midl, West,** Mash(ed); (Qu. KK21, *When something hollow is crushed by a heavy weight, or by a fall:* "They ran the wagon over the coffee pot and _____.") 167 Infs, **widespread, but chiefly Sth, Midl; also West,** Mashed it; 47 Infs, **chiefly Sth, Midl,** Mash(ed) it flat (*or* flat as a flitter, flatter than a pancake, all to flinders); **GA72, KY33, MI44, MS45, 61, SC19, 26,** Mash(ed) it up; **LA20, MS49, SC3, TN66, TX39,** Mashed it in; **NM4,** It was mashed; **OK13,** Just mashed it; (Qu. Y35, *To spoil something so that it can't be used* . . "My new coffee pot—it's completely _____.") Infs **NJ9, OK12, 18, 54,** Mashed; **TX103,** Mashed down. **1986** Pederson *LAGS Concordance,* 1 inf, cMS, You can catch one and mash him, and he might would sting; 1 inf, neFL, Can't mash them—of bugs; 1 inf, cTN, Mash those nails—flatten them; 1 inf, neAR, It would mash—be flattened.

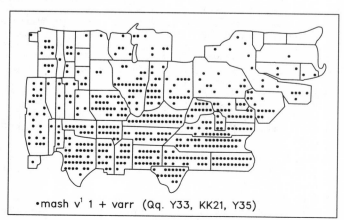

•mash v[1] 1 + varr (Qq. Y33, KK21, Y35)

2 also with *down, in:* To squeeze, press, put one's weight on; to apply pressure; to press (on something). **chiefly Sth, S Midl**

  1845 Hooper *Advent. Simon Suggs* 126 **AL,** When I lay down thar it got wuss and wuss, and 'peared like somethin' was a-mashin' down on my back. **1896** *DN* 1.420 cTX, *Mash:* iron slightly. "Why don't you mash the clothes?" **1903** *DN* 2.320 seMO, *Mash.* . . To push down; not necessarily to crush. 'Mash down on the trunk lid so I can lock it.' **1909** *S. Atl. Qrly.* 8.42 [Gullah], Jane reported that her brother's sprained ankle was so much better "dat him kin mash on it a little now ma'am." [Footnote: The stable-boy reported, of the terrier which had produced a litter of twelve, "He mash on um; two daid."] "Mash down! Mash down!" exclaimed the negro boatman, "Mash down yo' side! dis gunnel awash!" **1936** in 1983 Taft *Blues Lyric Poetry* 147, And when I mash down on your little starter : then your spark plug will give me fire. **1939** *Hall Coll.* wNC, Old man Tom went back, had about a two-year old bear [in the bear trap]. And he said he had him mashed down flat so he couldn't get up on his feet to raise the lid up. **1941** *AmSp* 16.167 [Army slang], *Mash in.* To push in the clutch pedal. **1954** *Harder Coll.* cwTN, *Mash.* . . To press down. . . "Mash down them brakes and she'll stop." **1965–69** *DARE* (Qu. I32, *How do you know when corn is ready to eat?*; total Infs questioned, 75) Inf **MS1,** Mash with finger; **MS23,** Mash grains to see if it has milk in it; (Qu. KK38, . . *"I wish he wouldn't _____ his hair down so!"*) Inf **MO15,** Mash; **CO4,** Mash down. **1966** *DARE* Tape GA7, You have a small . . plastic bottle. . . You get ready to spray that acid, all you have to do is mash that bottle right quick. **1970** *DARE* File SC, Mash the brakes. **1971** *Today Show Letters* **AL,** In the north, we press a button or push it down; in Alabama people commonly call this 'mashing' the button down (as on the telephone). **1972** *Atlanta Letters* **GA,** On an elevator: "mash the button." **1978** *NADS Letters* cnMS, "Mash that button". . . I hear it often, though I think the "preferred" form is "Push that button" or "Press that button." **1986** Pederson *LAGS Concordance,* 1 inf, nwLA, Mash it down—of one's hair; 1 inf, ceAL, Mash your foot—press you[r] foot down on a pedal.

3 also with *up:* To strike or beat (someone).
  1884 Lewis *Sawed-Off Sketches* 78, If you'll step out-doors I'll mash you! **1935** *AmSp* 10.18 [Criminal argot], *To mash.* . . To beat up someone severely. **1954** *Harder Coll.* cwTN, *Mash up.* . . Beat. "He shore got mashed up in that air fight." **1966–69** *DARE* (Qu. Y15, *To beat somebody thoroughly:* "John really _____ that fellow!") Infs **CT23, MA30, NY199,** Mashed; **FL30,** Mashed him to a pulp. **1986** Pederson *LAGS Concordance,* 1 inf, seFL, Mash—hit.

mash n[1] See **marsh**

mash n[2], v[2] See **mesh** n[1], v

mash n[3] See **mast** n[1]

mash back v phr Cf **double** v **4b**
  1974 Maurer–Pearl *KY Moonshine* 117, *Double* or *double back.* . . To remash at the same place, in the same vats, using the slops from the preceding distillation as a part of the mash. . . Also "to mash back."

mash down See **mash** v[1] **1, 2**

mashed See **mash** v[1] **1**

‡**mash frogs** v phr *joc*
  1970 *DARE* (Qu. X55b, *Words for breaking wind from the bowels*) Inf **FL48,** Mashing frogs [laughter].

mash in See **mash** v[1] **1, 2**

mashing See **mesh** v **B2**

mashoo See **mashu**

mash tea See **marsh tea**

mashu n Also *mashoo, masu(e), masru, musho(o)* [See quot 1991] **AK** Cf **Eskimo potato**
A **sweet vetch** (here: *Hedysarum alpinum*).
  [**1890** Wells–Kelly *Engl.–Eskimo Vocab.* 56 nwAK, Musho—Wild parsnip.] **1899** U.S. Naval Inst. *Proc.* 25.815 **AK,** At camp that night [on the Colville River] the natives dug roots called mashoo, they were very succulent and tender, and later on formed my principal food. **1948** in 1957 Meyers *Eskimo Village* 87, We found the root of the mushoo plant that the natives gather in the spring and fall. The root is tender and sweet when eaten raw and tastes like the sweet potato when cooked. **1955** U.S. Arctic Info. Center *Gloss.* 50, *Hedysarum alpinum.* . . Also called 'masu.' **1966** Wilimovsky *Environment Cape Thompson* 1006 **AK,** Only one root is collected extensively. This is the Eskimo potato, *Hedysarum alpinum,* which is called "masue." **1966** Heller *Wild Flowers AK* 33, Eskimo or Indian Potato, "Mashu" (Eskimo), Bear root. **1981** *AK Geographic* 8.3.124, *Masru* or Eskimo potato (*Hedysarum alpinum*)

is the main root harvested to eat. **1991** Tabbert *Dict. Alaskan Engl.* 179, In Athabaskan areas the root [=*Hedysarum alpinum*] is often called *Indian potato* and in Eskimo areas, *Eskimo potato* in English contexts. And because the root has been an important subsistence staple in northwest Alaska, the Inupiaq word for it has regularly been used in English contexts: *masu,* and in the Kobuk River area, *masru*.

mash up See **mash** v[1] **1, 3**

mashy See **marsh**

mask See **mast** n[1]

maskalonge See **muskellunge**

masked (bedbug) hunter See **bedbug hunter**

masketo See **mesquite**

maskinanga, maskinonge, maskinonje, maskinunga See **muskellunge**

mason See **mason wasp**

masonic weed n [See quot 1880]
A **false indigo 1** (here: *Amorpha canescens*).
1856 WI State Hist. Soc. *Coll.* 2.485, The *amorpha canescens,* or "masonic weed," peculiar to the whole country, when found in a cluster of rank growth, also attracted the attention of the Indian as well as the more experienced miner, as it was supposed to indicate great depth of clay or the existence of crevices in the rock beneath. **1880** Gillespie *Recoll. Early IL* 43, I have found the roots of what was called the "Masonic-weed" thirty feet deep. . . This weed, which is called in other localities the "Devil's shoe-string," grows luxuriantly over crevices . . lead ore was found in these crevices. . . This sign was at first known to but a few, and was tried by them to be kept as a secret, and hence the *growth* got the name of the "*Masonic*-weed."

mason swallow n [See quot 1890] Cf **mud dauber 2**
Either the **barn swallow 1** or the **cliff swallow**.
1887 Eggleston *Graysons* 183 **IL**, The mason-swallows whose young were sheltered in adobe houses attached to the rafters. **1890** *Century Dict.* 3647, *Mason-swallow.* . . A swallow which builds a nest of mud, as the barn-swallow or eaves-swallow.

mason wasp n Also *(mud) mason, mud mason wasp* [*OED* 1792 →] chiefly **Mid Atl, sAppalachians** See Map Cf **potter wasp**
Any of var wasps of the families Sphecidae, Vespidae, and Pompilidae, but esp a **mud dauber 1** of the genera *Eumenes* and *Sceliphron;* see quots. Also called **black mason**.
1851 *De Bow's Rev.* 11.56 **LA**, Mason Wasp or clay dauber. **1852** Harris *Treatise Insects* 406 **NEng**, The clay cells of the mud-wasp, plastered against the walls of our houses, each one containing a single egg, together with a large number of living spiders, caught and imprisoned therein solely for the use of the little mason's young. **1890** *Century Dict.* 3647, *Mason-wasp.* . . An aculeate hymenopterous insect of the genus *Odynerus,* family *Vespidae;* a kind of solitary wasp. . . *O. murarius* is an example. **1899** (1912) Green *VA Folk-Speech* 276, *Mason.* . . A wasp that makes its nest with grains of sand mixed with saliva, and fixes it on the sides of walls, and other places. **1905** Kellogg *Amer. Insects* 498, Of mason- or potter-wasps, that is, solitary wasps that make a nest of clay or mud worked up with saliva, there are numerous species belonging to several different families. *Ibid* 499, In this family [=Eumenidae] are found diggers, and miners in the earth, carpenters making their nests in twigs or boards, as well as masons or clay-handlers. *Ibid* 501, Pompilidae. . . is a large family including . . a few mud-daubers or mason-wasps (Agenia). **1928** Hudson *Specimens MS Folkl.* 153 **MS**, Wrap the sprained joint with a mixture of clay and vinegar. A dirt dauber's (mud mason wasp's) nest is better than road clay. **1946** *PADS* 5.29 **VA**, *Masons.* **1950** *WELS (Wasps that build their nests of mud)* 1 Inf, **cwWI**, Mud wasp. Also mason wasp, mud dauber. [Wasp is] long, slender, black, super active. [Nest is] case or cocoon of mud, 1½–3 inches long. Under eaves, inside sheds, granaries etc. **1965–70** *DARE* (Qu. R20, *Wasps that build their nests of mud*) Inf **KY**42, Mud dauber = mason, long tube-like nests; **MD**34, Mason—black or purplish, same size as stinging wasp, nest irregularly shaped, size of apple; **MD**42, Mason, mud dauber same thing—thinner than wasp, black; nest round, holes in it; **NC**41, Mason—black, long tunnels; **SC**57, Dirt dauber = mason; **TN**22, Mason wasp = mud dauber; **DE**4, Masons—they are brown and build a little mud mound an inch thick; **DE**3, Mud mason—a blue-black wasp; makes three or four long finger-like things to lay eggs

in; **MD**32, Mud mason—insect like wasp, but slightly larger; nest is flat, usually built up against board, opening in bottom; **MI**109, Mud mason; **NJ**39, Mud mason—light gray tubes, 2″ long, cemented together, or single tubes; **OH**40, Mud masons—black and thin—smaller than wasps; **VA**30, Mud masons; **VA**79, Mud mason—tubes of mud—bluish-black or brown wasp; **WV**2, Mud masons—looks like wasp—metallic blue—no stinger. **1986** Pederson *LAGS Concordance,* 1 inf, **cLA**, Mason—makes a dirt-dauber's nest; 1 inf, **neTX**, Mud dauber or mud mason.

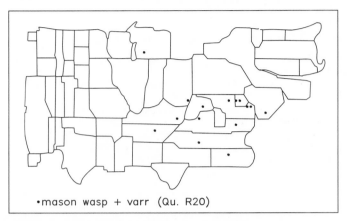

•mason wasp + varr (Qu. R20)

masquenonge, masquinongy See **muskellunge**

ma's room n *joc*
A women's indoor toilet.
1967 *DARE* (Qu. F37, . . *An indoor toilet*) Inf **AR**47, Ma's room.

masru See **mashu**

mass n[1] See **mast** n[1]

mass n[2] See **master** n

mass adv [Perh < **master** adv]
=**master** adv **1.**
1927 *DN* 5.475 **Ozarks**, *Mass dark.* . . Absolutely dark. "Hit's jes' plum mass dark in them 'ar caves—darker'n whut hit ever does git top o' th' ground."

massa See **master** n

Massachusetts n Usu |ˌmæsəˈčusəts|; also chiefly **Sth** |ˌmæsəˈt(j)usə(t)s|; for addit varr see quots Pronc-sp *Massatusits* Std sense, var forms.
1795 Dearborn *Columbian Grammar* 137, *List of Improprieties.* . . Massatusits for Massachusetts. **1961** Kurath–McDavid *Pronc. Engl.* 175, *Massachusetts.* . . The syllable next to the last, which bears the main stress, is pronounced as /ču/, /ju/, /tju/, or /tu/. . . /ču/ . . is in regular use in the North Midland, and with few exceptions also in the North outside of New England. In the South this pronunciation is uncommon, except in cultivated speech. /ju/ . . is fairly common in the folk speech of New England, less so in the speech of the middle group, rare in cultivated speech. . . In the South, /tju/ . . is the usual pronunciation. . . In the transition belt between North Midland /ču/ and Southern /tju/, especially in Delmarva and West Virginia, some speakers say /tu/. **1966** *Wilson Coll.* **csKY**, Massachusetts is often [ˌmæsəˈtjusɪts], occasionally [ˌmæsəˈtjutəsɪts] in southern Kentucky. **1973** *DARE* File **TX**, [ˌmæsəˈtusɛts]. **1989** Pederson *LAGS Tech. Index* 322 **Gulf Region,** [Among the 612 infs who gave proncs of *Massachusetts,* the widest variation was in the third syllable; the major variants were [ču] (205 infs), [čju] (53), [tju] (200) and [tu] (150). The vowel of the second syllable, usu [ɪ] or [ə], was elided by 72 infs. The consonant beginning the last syllable was usu [s], but 31 infs used [š] instead. The final consonant cluster [ts] was reduced to [s] by 199 infs and entirely elided by 48.]

massacre n, v Usu |ˈmæsəkə(r)|; also |ˈmæsəkri|; for addit varr see quots Pronc-spp chiefly **Sth, S Midl** old-fash, *mas(s)acree, massurkree, massycree*
Std senses, var forms.
[**1727** C. Colden *Hist. Five Ind. Nations* 83 *(OED)* **Canada,** Your Warriors . . have Massacreed Men, Women and Children.] **1836** (1928) Underwood *Jrl.* 32.144 **MA**, After they had laid down their arms . . [the enemy] attempted to masacree the whole. **1843** (1916) Hall *New Pur-*

chase 147 **IN**, There's bad Ingins that will steal and maybe *massurkree.* **1876** in 1969 *PADS* 52.53 **seIL**, There is great excitement over a great massacree of Gen. Custer and his intire troupe. **1891** Harris *Balaam* 117 **nGA,** He 'low dat ef dey don't keep mighty close watch on Ananias dey'd all be massycreed in deir beds. **1899** (1912) Green *VA Folk-Speech* 276, If you do that he will massacree you. **1903** Wasson *Cap'n Simeon's Store* 31 **eME**, Somebody was like to be massacreed. **1909** *DN* 3.348 **eAL, wGA,** *Massacr·ee,* v. and n. [*DARE* Ed: =[mæsəˈkri].] **1911** *DN* 3.549 **NE,** Some words showing divergence from the standard accentuation are: *massa·cree.* [*DARE* Ed: =[mæsəˈkri].] **1933** Williamson *Woods Colt* 81 **Ozarks,** I'd of massacreed him plenty, if that gun would of went off. **1942** Hall *Smoky Mt. Speech* 79 **wNC, eTN,** *Massacre* and *sabre* . . in single occurrences were [ˈmæsəkrɪ] and [ˈseɪbrɪ]. **c1960** *Wilson Coll.* **csKY,** Massacre—[ˈmæsə‚kri] among many oldsters. **1967** *DARE* Tape **TX13**, Henry Karnes was at the Alamo, and he was a scout . . and he was carrying a message to Houston when . . the massacree occurred.

massasauga n Also *(massa)sauger, (mis)sauga;* for addit varr see quots [Varr of *Mississauga* (literally "big river mouth"), name of an Amer Ind tribe of southern Ontario and (with var spp) of var places associated with it, as the *Mississagi R., Mississauga,* and *Fort Massassauga*] **chiefly Gt Lakes**
A small **rattlesnake** (here: *Sistrurus catenatus*). Also called **black rattlesnake, ~ snapper 3, gray rattlesnake, ground ~ 2, meadow ~, prairie ~, swamp ~**

    1835 (1906) Bradley *Jrl.* 257 **seMI,** I learned that my conquered enemy was the massassagua, the Michigan rattlesnake. **1839** Kirkland *New Home* 29 **MI,** It's a rattlesnake; the Indians call them Massisangas [sic] an *so folks* call 'em so too. **1899** Garland *Boy Life* 81 **nwIA** (as of c1870s), It was a "Massasauga" or meadow rattlesnake. *Ibid* 317, They overtook a big "Sauga" crossing the road. **1928** Pope–Dickinson *Amphibians* 70 **WI,** Massasauga . . *Sistrurus catenatus catenatus.* **1948** *WELS Suppl.* **csWI,** Jim Goldsmith called rattlesnakes *saugers,* or perhaps *saugas.* I think I found that it was a short thick variety named massauga or was it massatsauga? **1952** Ditmars *N. Amer. Snakes* 67, The Massasauga frequents swampy places and damp meadows. . . It is particularly common in Ohio and Michigan, where it is rated as a reptile of swampy places. **1967–70** *DARE* (Qu. P25, . . *Kinds of snakes*) Inf **MI65,** Rattlesnake—but it's called something else. . . "Massasauga," that's it; **MI76,** Massasauga; **MI84,** Massasauger; **MI115,** Missauga. **1974** Shaw–Campbell *Snakes West* 27, In the East the massasauga *(Sistrurus catenatus)* is called the swamp rattlesnake or sometimes the little gray rattlesnake. The more commonly used name "massasauga" is derived from two Chippewa words which literally mean "great river mouth." The term probably was used because these small snakes are frequently found in the vicinity of streams, ponds, or swamps. **1981** Vogt *Nat. Hist.* **WI** 167, Hundreds of massasaugas were reported killed in a marsh that existed at the foot of Mason Street in Milwaukee in the late 1830s. **1991** *WI State Jrl.* (Madison) 20 Jan sec C 1, The massasauga feeds on frogs and other snakes, but prefers mice, moles, shrews and an occasional blackbird.

Massasip See **Mississippi**

Massatusits See **Massachusetts**

masse-misse See **moosemisse**

Massena quail n Also *Massena, ~ partridge*
=**harlequin quail.**

    1852 Acad. Nat. Sci. Philadelphia *Proc. for 1850–51* 5.221, Massena Quail, or Partridge. . . was not seen before crossing the San Pedro. **1857** U.S. Congress *Serial Set* 834 Doc 108.2.2 23 **TX,** On being shot [the bird] proved to be a male massena. **1898** (1900) Davie *Nests N. Amer. Birds* 167 **wTX, NM, AZ,** Massena partridge. **1917** (1923) *Birds Amer.* 2.10, Mearns's quail . . Messena [sic] Partridge. **1982** Elman *Hunter's Field Guide* 102, The harlequin, or Mearns, quail . . also called Montezuma quail, Massena quail, crazy quail.

Mississippi See **Mississippi**

massurkree, massycree See **massacre**

mast n[1] Pronc-spp *mash, mask, mass* [*OED* 825 →; both *mask* and *mass* are attested in Engl dial] **chiefly Sth, S Midl**
The nuts, seeds, or fruits of wild trees and vines, usu when considered as food for animals (esp hogs); rarely used as a count noun.

    1670 (1937) Denton *Brief Descr.* 4 **NY,** [Long] Island is very full of

Timber, as Oaks white and red, Walnut-trees, Chestnut-trees, which yield store of Mast for swine. **1752** in 1847 Updike *Hist. Episc. Church* 3.12 **NC,** They export *Indian* Corn, and Pork, fatted in the Woods, with what, by a general Name, is called *Mast;* that is, Acorns, Walnuts, Chestnuts, other Nuts and wild Fruits. **1850** Chamberlain *IN Gaz.* 38, Such [hogs] as have become fat on the nuts or *mast* in the fall of the year. **1890** Howells *Boy's Town* 3 **sOH,** There were squirrels in the woods, where there was abundant mast for the pigs that ran wild in them. **1899** (1912) Green *VA Folk-Speech* 276, Mast. . . The fruit of the oak and beech or other forest trees, acorns or nuts collectively, serving as food for animals. **1930** Shoemaker *1300 Words* 41 **cPA Mts** (as of c1900), Mast—Fruit of the beech trees; favorite food of wild pigeons and bears. **1936** *AmSp* 11.316 **Ozarks,** Mass. . . Acorns. The word should be *mast,* but is generally pronounced *mass,* and so spelled in the country newspapers. **1949** Webber *Backwoods Teacher* 106 **Ozarks,** A man might have . . droves of swine chomping acorns in the woods or, when "the mash" (mast) fails, eating corn and protein supplement. **1953** *Hall Coll.* **wNC,** Mast means all kinds of things [for animals] to eat in the woods, such as acorns and chestnuts, and berries and grapes, and all sorts of things. Choicest food for the bear was to get beech nuts. **1954** *Harder Coll.* **cwTN,** Mash . . beech mast, the nuts from beech trees. "Be lots 'a squirrels this year; them trees jes' full o' mash." **1963** *Clarke Co. Democrat* (Grove Hill AL) 25 Apr. 4/1 *(Mathews Coll.),* Not only does there promise to be a bumper crop of beech mast but also of acorns . . , dogwood and magnolia berries and mast of every other type. **1966** *DARE* Tape **FL42,** They know when to gather them [=pine cones] to get the mass when it's in proper condition, and they plant that mass in a field and every year they sell seedlings of pines by the thousand; **NC24,** Woods coveys . . eat mass, pine mass, and even acorns, oak acorns. **1967–68** *DARE* (Qu. I43, *What kinds of nuts grow wild around here?*) Inf **AL38,** Beech masks [ˈbič ‚mæsks]; **AR52,** Beech nuts or mast; **TX37,** Beech mass. **1975** *Foxfire 3* 112 **nwGA,** Hogs roamed the mountains, where there's all kinds of mast-chestnuts. The hogs'd get just as fat on them as they could be. . . And you could bring'em in an' kill'em right off the mast. **1986** Pederson *LAGS Concordance* **Gulf Region,** 6 infs, Mast [=acorns or acorns and other nuts]; 1 inf, Mast; 1 inf, Wild hogs lived on mast, acorns, and chestnuts; 1 inf, Wild hogs ate mast and acorns; 1 inf, Mast—provided by longleaf timber; 2 infs, Beech mast; 1 inf, Beech masts; 1 inf, Bitter mast—acorns, etc., sometimes fed to hogs; 2 infs, (Beech) mash. **1989** [see **mast** n[2]].

mast n[2] [Pronc-sp for *mask*] Cf **ask A1b,** Pronc Intro 3.I.14
    1926 Lardner *Love Nest* 83, Been on this bench since catchers started wearin' a mast, or anyway it seems that long. **1930** Faulkner *As I Lay Dying* 68 **MS,** Cora says his face looked like one of these here Christmas masts that had done been buried a while and then dug up. **1989** Nicholson *Field Guide S. Speech* 10, Mast: something people wear on their faces and trees wear on their limbs. "Leroy says he can hunt better with a camouflaged mast, so I made me one out of acorns and pine cones."

master n Usu |ˈmæstə(r)|; also **chiefly NEng, Sth** |ˈmɑstə(r)| Pronc-spp *mahster, marster;* also **chiefly Sth** *among Black speakers, obs, mars(e), mass(a);* also **chiefly S Atl coast** *among Black speakers, obs, maus(sa), mossa;* for addit pronc and sp varr see quots Note: The monosyllabic forms occur chiefly in conjunction with a proper name; see B1 below.

A Forms. For addit exx see **B1** below
    1803 [see **B1** below]. **1829** Tenney *Female Quixotism* 1.120 **Philadelphia PA** [Black], But what debil put him in your head, Betty, to dress in masser croase? **1838** (1852) Gilman *S. Matron* 15 **eSC** [Black], 'Twas altogedder onnatural to see my poor maussa wid de ragiments [=ragged clothes] on. **1838** [see **B1** below]. **1893** Shands *MS Speech* 44, Mars [mɑs]. Negro form for *master.* Marster [mɑstə] is also used with the same meaning. **1896** Harris *Sister Jane* 133 **GA** [Black], My mars'er ain't set back [=doesn't sit back] an hire his niggers out to Tom, Dick, an' Harry. **1899** Chesnutt *Conjure Woman* 51 **csNC** [Black], Young mars wuz in a tarrible hurry. **1903** *DN* 2.320 **seMO,** Marse or mahster. . . Master. Formerly used by slaves. The flat 'massa' or 'massy' would not be recognised by Southern negroes, because never used by them. **1909** *S. Atl. Qrly.* 8.48, In Tide-Water Virginia, in the language of the dialect-speaking negro, *Master* becomes *Mahsteh,* which the Virginian, perhaps, writes *Marster,* though he does not so pronounce it: this pronunciation is almost entirely confined to the Virginian. In Mississippi and Arkansas the pronunciation, *Massa,* is distinctly heard. But in the coastal plain of Carolina, Georgia and Florida, *Maussa* obtains . . : used disjunctively the form is universally *Mossa* or *Maussa;* but in conjunction with Christian or surname, form and pronunciation change

to *Mass'*. . . The form *Maussa* is used almost entirely by the older negroes . . ; the new negro . . prefers *Misto.*' **1922** Gonzales *Black Border* 50 **sSC, GA coasts** [Gullah], Een slabery time nigguh baig 'e maussuh' paa'd'n. [= . . [He] begged his master's pardon.] *Ibid* 312 [Gullah glossary], While the Gullah can pronounce "mastuh," he reserves this for God, even saying "Maussuh Jedus"—Master Jesus. **1923** Parsons *Folk-lore Sea Islands* 76 **csSC** [Black], Ol'-time story, Rebel time. Ev'y winter dat de mawsah go to Philamadelphia, always go to New York. **1929** (1951) Faulkner *Sartoris* 367 **MS** [Black], De little marster done arrive. **1941** *LANE* Map 444 *(School teacher)* 2 infs, **seMA, RI**, School [mastə]; 1 inf, **seNH**, School [mɑˑˈstə]. [6 infs gave proncs (school) [mæstə(r)].] **1945** Saxon *Gumbo Ya-Ya* 224 **LA**, Cecile White, . . nearly a century old in 1941, remembered being sold. . . "My Marse died, and me and my ma. . . was sold right at the French Market in New Orleans." **1950** *PADS* 14.46 **SC**, *Maussa* ['mɔːsə]. . . Master, in slavery days. **1970** *DARE* (Qu. JJ1b) Inf **MA79**, [mɑrstə]—obsolete.

B Senses.

1 Formerly used by Blacks in the South as a respectful title, deferential term of address, or quasi-proper name for their (male) owners or other White men. *obs* Cf **mistress B1**

    1766 in 1952 *AmSp* 27.283 **SC**, Brought to the Work-House. . . A young slim new negro lad, . . who calls himself Ben, but cannot tell his master's name, only says Masa Johny. **1803** Davis *Travels* 92, When Mossa curse, he break no bone. *Ibid* 211, You call, Mossa *Ryland*? **1823** Cooper *Pioneers* 1.246 **cNY** [Black], Leab it to Massa Jone. **1829** [see **A** above]. **1837** *S. Lit. Messenger* 3.174 **wVA** [Black], Mass Phil been very uneasy about you. **1837** (1976) Simms *Martin Faber* 2.95 **SC**, "Want a hack, mossa?" cried the obsequious negro. **1838** (1852) Gilman *S. Matron* 33 **eSC** [Black], Bro' Jim ride more better dan Maus John. **1858** Hammett *Piney Woods Tavern* 140 **TX** [Black], "I done, done it, mossa," ses he. **1872** Powers *Afoot* 101 **MS** [Black], Jest a quarter, massa, fur a mighty little'll do me. **1881** (1967) Tourgée *Royal Gentleman* 301 **NC** [Black], He gave Toinette to young Marse Geoffrey. **1885** Twain *Huck. Finn* 324 **MO** [Black], Why, Mars Tom, I hain't got no coat o' arms. **1899** (1912) Green *VA Folk-Speech* 275, Marse Bob. **1899** [see **A** above]. **1909** *DN* 3.348 **eAL, wGA**, *Marse, marster*. . . Master: still politely applied by elderly negroes to any prominent or well-to-do white man. **1909** [see **A** above]. **1922** Gonzales *Black Border* 312 **sSC, GA coasts** [Gullah glossary], *Mass, Mas'*—master when used with a name; as, "Mass Clinch," "Mas' Rafe." **1929** (1951) Faulkner *Sartoris* 114 **MS** [Black], You jes' got ter lay down de law ter 'um, Marse John. **1935** Hurston *Mules & Men* 25 **FL** [Black], He always tried to do everything Ole Massa told him to do.

2 A schoolmaster, male schoolteacher.

    1710 in 1882 Boston Registry Dept. *Records* 8.65, We are of opinion the worke of that School do's necessarily require the Attendance of a master and an Usher. **1841** *Knickerbocker* 18.65 **NEng**, Bill Jones . . swore he would whip the master before the week was out. **1888** Sheridan *Personal Memoirs* 1.3 **csOH**, The village school . . was taught by an old-time Irish "master"—one of those itinerant dominies of the early frontier. **1941** *LANE* Map 444 *(School teacher)* 1 inf, **csMA**, [mæstə] (in a high school). [8 infs gave schoolmaster.] **1950** *WELS* (Names or nicknames for schoolteachers: . . a man) 2 Infs, **WI**, Master. **1965–70** *DARE* (Qu. JJ1b, . . A schoolteacher—a man) 18 Infs, **esp NEast**, Master. [*DARE* Ed: 2 Infs said this was old-fashioned or obsolete.]

3 also attrib: See quots. Cf **male** adj, *DS* K22–23

    1842 Kirkland *Forest Life* 1.142 **MI**, In vain is the far-sounding bell strapped round the neck of the master ox or cow, (for we say *master*-cow by catachresis I suppose.) **1939** *LANE* Map 190 **ceVT**, Euphemisms used when a direct reference to the bull is avoided on grounds of delicacy . . *the male, the masculine, . . the master.*

master adj, sometimes used as superl Pronc-sp *marster* [*EDD* *master* adj. 16] **chiefly S Midl, also ME** See also **master hand**
Great, outstanding, large; greatest.

    1834 Smith *Letters Jack Downing* 53 **ME**, The Kennebeckers are master fellers to hold on. **1859** Taliaferro *Fisher's R.* 60 **nwNC** (as of 1820s), I seen a monstrous big [blackberry] brier full uv great big 'uns, big as hen's eggs. . . and, says I to myself, "I'll soon hev my basket full uv these master fellers." **1880** in 1956 Eliason *Tarheel Talk* 283 **cnNC**, In the mountain a hunter says "It was a 'Master' bear, a 'Master' fight, a 'Master' tree, meaning largest or best or greatest." **1896** *DN* 1.420 **swNC**, *Masterest*: most powerful. "He was makin' the masterest noise ever I hearn." **1902** (1904) Rowe *Maid of Bar Harbor* 57 **ME**, That back pastur' o' his is a master place for that kind o' stun. **1903** *DN* 2.320 **seMO**, It's the master apple that ever I saw. **1913** *DN* 4.58 **TN**, *Masterest*. . . Biggest: noted at Brabson's Ferry. "That man has the

masterest orchard!" **1915** *DN* 4.185 **swVA**, *Masterest*. . . Greatest; 'awfulest.' **1917** *DN* 4.414 **wNC**, *Master*. . . Big, powerful. "He was the masterest bear-fighter I ever did see." **1923** *DN* 5.214 **swMO**, "He's the masterest worker in the settlement." "Hit shore was a master storm." **1928** *AmSp* 4.116 **Ozarks**, Well, sir, black actu'lly an' candidly, thet 'ar's th' masterest catfish I ever seed! **1929** *AmSp* 5.129 **eME**, "Ma(r)ster" . . was said of something that tasted especially good. **1933** Miller *Lamb in His Bosom* 84 **GA**, Lias thought I was the master fool. **1953** *PADS* 19.12 **sAppalachians**, I cut a master pile of wood for this winter. **1963** Edwards *Gravel* 139 **eTN** (as of 1920s), All at onct that float started bobbin up and down an this way an that . . —the master lot of splashin ye ever heerd tell of in your life. **1975** Gould *ME Lingo* 177, This is a master dining room!

master adv [*EDD* *master* adv. 17] Pronc-sp *marster* **chiefly ME, sAppalachians** Cf **master** adj

1 Very.

    1834 Smith *Letters Jack Downing* 65 **ME**, It almost made me blush to see what a master substantial ginuin republican he made me. **1877** Jewett *Deephaven* 96 **ME**, He told Kate once that he "felt master old in winter to what he did in summer." **1903** Wasson *Cap'n Simeon's Store* 71 **eME**, He 'lowed how he see the Olive Branch (a ship) hove down by a master-great holler sea. **1929** *AmSp* 5.129 **eME**, "Ma(r)ster, marster good" was said of something that tasted especially good. **1933** *AmSp* 8.1.25 **sAppalachians**, *Master* is used as an adverb to mean *very. He is master strong* means *he is very strong.* **1939** Hall Coll. **wNC**, "He had a master big track;" said of a fox. **1942** (1971) Campbell *Cloud-Walking* 101 **seKY**, A pig . . making a master big mess. **1955** Ritchie *Singing Family* 121 **seKY**, They said Long John played "Killy Kranky" on the jew's-harp, master well too. **1975** Gould *ME Lingo* 177, Joe caught a master big horsefish.

2 Exceedingly, a great deal.

    1913 Kephart *Highlanders* 285 **sAppalachians**, An adjective can serve as an adverb: "He laughed master." **1928** Chapman *Happy Mt.* 52 **seTN**, He sat down upon a big rock and shook master. *Ibid* 56, While he set the coffee to boil, . . he fussed master.

masterful adv
=**master** adv **1.**

    1933 *AmSp* 8.1.25, In West Virginia, particularly in the northern part, and in adjoining Virginia, the word is generally *masterful* [rather than *master*]. In these regions anything is *masterful good* or *masterful bad*.

master hand n [**master** adj + **hand** n B2; perh reanalysis of *master hand* the hand of a master (*OED* at *master* sb. 29 1709 →)] **chiefly NEng, S Midl**
A person who is skillful at something; an expert.

    1806 (1970) Webster *Compendious Dict.* 186, Masterhand . . a person very skillful in any art. [*DARE* Ed: This entry was carried over from Webster's English model.] **1871** (1882) Stowe *Fireside Stories* 144 **NEng**, She was a master hand at cookin'. **1914** *DN* 4.76 **ME, nNH**, *Master*. . . Big, great, superior. "A master hand to fish." **1926** Roberts *Time of Man* 168 **cKY**, My grandpap was a master hand for honey bees. **1927** *AmSp* 3.136 **eME**, A competent person was "a marster hand" to do this or that. **1938** Matschat *Suwannee R.* 119 **neFL, seGA**, Manthy was a master hand for smartin' up. **1944** *PADS* 2.46 **wNC**, He was a master hand at making chairs. **1945** *PADS* 3.11 **CT**, *Master (hand)*. . . Also applied to women: "She's a master hand at making pies." **c1960** Wilson Coll. **csKY**, He's a master hand at log-rolling. **1965–70** *DARE* (Qu. KK5, *A very skilled or expert person—for example, at woodworking: "He's a _____."*) Infs **AR52, CA99, IA34, LA2, NY22, OR6, TN52, VA69, WV3, 4, 5, 7, 14**, Master hand. **1983** *MJLF* 9.1.47 **ceKY** (as of 1956), *Master hand* . . an expert.

master of the woods See **king of the woods**

masterous adj, adv Also sp *mastrous* [**master** adj, adv] Cf **monstrous B, C**
Very large; extremely.

    1904 *DN* 2.419 **nwAR**, *Mastrous*. . . Very, extremely. "You've got a mastrous large school for this district." **c1905** Dunckel *Mollyjoggers* 38 **swMO**, Boy-ees, this yere is a masterous good night to go a coon huntin. **1925** Dargan *Highland Annals* 174 **cwNC**, Granpap pocketed five dollars for the hog, the buyer considering six a "masterous price."

masterwort n

1 A cow parsnip **1** (here: *Heracleum lanatum*).

    1830 Rafinesque *Med. Flora* 2.227, *Heracleum lanatum*. . . Cow parsnep, Masterwort. . . Useful in cardialgy, dyspepsia and epilepsy.

1854 King *Amer. Eclectic Dispensatory* 532, *Heracleum lanatum.* Masterwort. . . This plant, sometimes called *Cow-parsnep,* has a large, spindle-shaped, perennial *root.* **1963** Craighead *Rocky Mt. Wildflowers* 126, Cow-cabbage, Masterwort, Hercules-parsnip. **1974** (1977) Coon *Useful Plants* 259, *Heracleum lanatum* . . masterwort. . . This is one of the largest-growing perennial herbs.

2 =**angelica 1a.**

1793 Morse *Amer. Universal Geog.* 1.171, Angelica, or American Masterwort (Angelica lucida). **1830** Rafinesque *Med. Flora* 2.192, *Angelica atropurpurea.* . . *Masterwort.* The root has a strong smell, when fresh it is a poison, the juice is acrid and blisters the lips. **1873** in 1976 Miller *Shaker Herbs* 127, Purple Angelica. Masterwort. **1971** Krochmal *Appalachia Med. Plants* 46, *Angelica atropurpurea* . . masterwort. . . *Harvest:* Root in fall. **1974** (1977) Coon *Useful Plants* 258, *Angelica atropurpurea* . . masterwort. . . Looks like a huge five foot plant of celery.

mast-fed adj [Transf from *mast-fed* raised on **mast** n[1], appar because it is typically the food of semi-wild hogs that forage for themselves]

1912 *DN* 3.583 **wIN,** *Mast-fed.* . . Irregularly educated. "He's just a mast-fed lawyer; he never went to law school."

mastiff bat n

A bat of the genus *Eumops.*

1906 Stephens *CA Mammals* 275, California Mastiff Bats. . . are known only from southern California. They have been found over a door, behind a signboard, hanging from a window ledge and in a tunnel. **1947** Cahalane *Mammals* 133, The mastiff bat *(Eumops)* is the largest bat found in this country. . . It is sooty brown and has such long ears that they droop over the face. **1964** Lowe *Vertebrates* 251 **AZ,** *Eumops perotis.* . . Western Mastiff Bat. . . In small colonies in rock crevices. . . *Eumops underwoodi.* . . Underwood's Mastiff Bat. . . Known only from the region of Sasabe, Pima County. **1965** Teale *Wandering Through Winter* 18 **CA,** It was not far from here . . that two friends . . had come upon the sooty-brown body of a dead mastiff bat. **1980** Whitaker *Audubon Field Guide Mammals* 334, *Western Mastiff Bat* . . *(Eumops perotis).* . . *Largest bat in North America.* . . Southern California, . . s Nevada, s Arizona, . . sw New Mexico, Big Bend area of Texas. *Ibid* 335, *Underwood's Mastiff Bat (Eumops underwoodi).* . . *Large,* free-tailed bat. . . Pima County, Arizona. *Ibid* 336, *Wagner's Mastiff Bat (Eumops glaucinus).* . . *Large.* . . Extreme se Florida near Miami and Ft. Lauderdale.

masting pine See **mast pine**

mast maple n [**mast** n[1] + **maple**]

A **red maple** (here: *Acer rubrum*).

1969 *DARE* FW Addit **GA51,** Mast maple. [FW: The red maple *(Acer rubrum).* The name may refer to the seeds it drops before leafing out. "Mast" is used by Okefenokee people about the dropped fruit of oak and other trees.]

mastodon flower n

A **ragwort** (here: *Senecio congestus*).

1952 Williams *AK Wildfl. Glimpses* 22, The *mastodon flower* . . is found in the gold dredging creek sands and I was told this romantic story—that its seeds were buried in this gold-bearing muck along with those of the mastodon millions of years ago. When man started moving these gold-bearing sands he uncovered not only gold and mastodon bones, but these seeds which had been buried so many years ago! A very thrilling story but unfortunately this flower can also be found in many other places that have no resemblance to the gold-bearing creeks. **1966** Heller *Wild Flowers AK* 17, Mastodon flower—*Senecio congestus.* . . Common in moist, overturned soil, along roadsides, in mining areas on mainland Alaska from Cook Inlet north to Arctic Coast.

mast pine n Also *masting pine* **nNEng** Cf **king's pine**

A **white pine** (here: *Pinus strobus*), esp one that is old and straight.

1751 (1972) Douglass *Summary* 2.52 **NH,** The Pines may be subdivided into the *Masting,* or white Pine [etc]. **1792** Belknap *Hist. NH* 3.73, Another thing . . is the mast pine. This tree often grows to a height of one hundred and fifty, and sometimes two hundred feet. It is straight as an arrow, and has no branches but very near the top. *Ibid* 102, The *White Pine (pinus strobus)* is undoubtedly the prince of the American forest in size, age and majesty of appearance. More of this species have been produced in New-Hampshire, and the eastern counties of Massachusetts than in all America besides. These trees have a very thin sap, and are distinguished by the name of mast-pine from the succeeding

growth of the same species, which are called saplings. [*Ibid* 106, The best white pine trees are sold for masts, bowsprits and yards, for large ships.] **1832** Williamson *Hist. ME* 1.110, So literally is this erect and lofty *masting-pine* the greatest ornament of our forests, that it was adopted as one of the emblems in the shield of our State coat of arms. *Ibid* 111, The Hemlock in stature almost vies with the mast-pine. **1975** Gould *ME Lingo* 178, *Mast pine*—A richly historical Maine term. It means a native eastern white pine suitable for a ship's mast, and also one that will yield smaller spars and timbers. . . *Mast pine* is still used in Maine for a fine, straight, tall white pine, but seldom is one found that measures up to the admiralty requirements when George III was king. **1992** *DARE* File **ME** (as of late 1970s), Mast pine, also called the king's pine, were the tallest, straightest white pines, reserved, by decree, for masts for the king's ships. I don't think any are left now.

mastrous See **masterous**

masu(e) See **mashu**

mat See **oil mat (road)**

matate See **metate**

matax See **mattock**

matchbrush See **matchweed**

‡**matchmaker** n

1969 *DARE* (Qu. W1c, . . *Joking names . . for an umbrella*) Inf **CT6,** Matchmaker—when a man visited a girl he would leave his umbrella behind as an excuse to return, thus, the matchmaker.

match-me-if-you-can n [See quot 1965] Cf **Jacob's coat**

A **copperleaf** (here: *Acalypha wilkesiana*).

1965 Neal *Gardens HI* 508, *Acalypha wilkesiana.* . . Wide variations of leaf patterns have won for the plant the name "match-me-if-you-can." **1976** Bailey–Bailey *Hortus Third* 8, Match-me-if-you-can. . . The many color strains of this plant are much planted in s. Fla. . . less in s. Calif. **1982** Perry–Hay *Field Guide Plants* 42, Match me if you can. . . No two leaves are exactly alike.

matchweed n Also *matchbrush* [See quot 1924] **chiefly SW** =**snakeweed** (here: *Gutierrezia* spp).

1924 *Amer. Botanist* 30.33, The common name all over the west for *[Gutierrezia]* . . is "torchweed" or "matchweed," not as one might suppose from the abundance of bright yellow flowers but from the readiness with which the dry stems and resinous buds burn in the spring. **1963** Craighead *Rocky Mt. Wildflowers* 213, Matchbrush—*Gutierrezia sarothrae.* **1965** *DARE* (Qu. S26a, . . *Wildflowers . . Roadside flowers*) Inf **UT3,** Matchweed. **1973** Hitchcock–Cronquist *Flora Pacific NW* 524, *Gutierrezia.* . . Matchbrush; Matchweed; Snakeweed. **1987** Bowers *100 Roadside Wildflowers* 45 **SW,** Snakeweed is also known as matchweed.

mater See **tomato**

‡**mater bump** n [Perh blend of **matter** n[1] **B1** + **nature bump**]

1966 *DARE* (Qu. X59, . . *The small infected pimples that form usually on the face*) Inf **GA6,** Mater bumps [metə bʌmps].

material n, adj Usu |məˈtɪriəl, -ˈti-|; also |məˈtɪrəl, -ˈti-| Pronc-sp *mater'al* Similarly adv *mater'lly* Cf **curious, dubious A2, natural**

Std senses, var forms.

1861 Holmes *Venner* 1.165 **wMA,** But I don't propose mater'lly alterin' Miss Darley's dooties. **1867** Lowell *Biglow* xxxii 'Upcountry' **MA,** The "Coventry Mysteries" have . . *naterale, material (material),* and *meracles,* all excellent Yankeeisms. **1906** *DN* 3.146 **nwAR,** *Mater'al* [mɛtɪrəl]. . . Material. "Does it make any mater'al difference when you get this?" Common. **1930s** in 1944 *ADD* **eWV,** Mater'al. **1941** *Ibid* **NC,** [məˈtɪrəl]. **1967** *DARE* FW Addit **AR,** Materials [məˈtɪrəlz]. **1969** *DARE* Tape **GA77,** They produced different materials [məˈtɪɚəlz].

matet(e) See **metate**

mat grama n

A **grama grass 1** (here: *Bouteloua simplex*).

1950 Hitchcock–Chase *Manual Grasses* 537, *Bouteloua simplex.* . . Mat grama. . . Annual, tufted, prostrate or ascending, foliage scant. **1970** Correll *Plants TX* 246, Mat grama. Tufted annual; culms numerous.

matgrass n

1 Any of var grasses, as:

a A **beach grass** (here: *Ammophila arenaria*). [*OED* 1818]

1847 Wood *Class-Book* 601, *P[samma] arenaria. . . Mat Grass. . .* On sandy sea-coasts, Can. to N.J. At Dorchester, Mass., this grass is extensively manufactured into paper. **1881** Phares *Farmer's Book of Grasses* 39, *C[alamagrostis] arenaria . . mat grass. . .* Its roots . . bind the sands and hold them against the action of winds and waves. . . Much property has been saved by a judicious planting of this grass, in the eastern States.

b =**cordgrass.**

1923 Davidson–Moxley *Flora S. CA* 53, *Spartina.* Mat-grass. . . *S. foliosa.* . . Marshes along the coast from Long Beach to San Diego.

c A **dropseed 3** (here: *Sporobolus domingensis*).

1971 Craighead *Trees S. FL* 201, Mat grass (coral dropseed), *Sporobolus domingensis.*

2 =**frogfruit,** usu *Phyla nodiflora.*

1911 Jepson *Flora CA* 352, *L[ippia] nodiflora. . . Mat-grass. . .* Esteemed as a plant covering on levees for the purpose of resisting erosion. **1942** Hylander *Plant Life* 447, Lemon Verbena [=*Lippia lanceolata*]. ., also known as Mat Grass, ranges from the Atlantic coast to southern California. **1970** Correll *Plants TX* 1333, *Phyla nodiflora* . . Mat-grass. **1976** Bailey–Bailey *Hortus Third* 865, [*Phyla*] *nodiflora. . .* Matgrass. . . Creeping and spreading, rooting at the nodes.

3 A **knotgrass 1** (here: *Polygonum aviculare*).

1914 Georgia *Manual Weeds* 97, *Polygonum aviculare. . .* Matgrass. . . A social, almost domesticated, weed, seeming to thrive best where most trampled and abused, growing in thick mats along hard-beaten farmyard paths. **1935** (1943) Muenscher *Weeds* 190, *Polygonum aviculare. . .* Mat-grass. . . Stems slender, . . much branched, mostly forming prostrate mats from thin tap-roots.

mathig(a)lum, mathiglin See **metheglin**

matilija poppy n [See quot 1897]

A plant of the genus *Romneya*, native to California. For other names of *R. coulteri* see **love flower, tree poppy**

1893 *Jrl. Amer. Folkl.* 6.137 **swCA,** *Romneya Coulteri,* Matilija poppy. **1897** Parsons *Wild Flowers CA* 64 **swCA,** The Matilija poppy . . must be conceded the queen of all our flowers. . . Its common name was given it because it grows in particular abundance in the Matilija Cañon. **1915** *Nature & Sci.* 149 **swCA,** The rare Matilija poppy, well known for its magnificent white flowers, is best seen in the Ojai Valley, Ventura County, and in Santiago Cañon, Orange County. **1949** *Los Angeles Times* (CA) 13 Mar (Home Mag) 33, Matilija poppy . . draws attention mostly because of the unusualness of a shrub bearing poppies, especially such huge, glistening, fragrant ones. **1968–70** *DARE* (Qu. S26a, . . *Wildflowers . . Roadside flowers*) Inf **CA**65, Matilija poppies—a large white hill poppy; (Qu. S26e, *Other wildflowers not yet mentioned;* not asked in early QRs) Inf **CA**185, Matilija poppy.

matis See **tomato**

mat muhly n [See quot 1937] **West**

A **muhly (grass)** (here: *Muhlenbergia richardsonis*).

1937 U.S. Forest Serv. *Range Plant Hdbk.* G83, Mat muhly is usually a low, dull-green, perennial grass growing in scattered, dense carpetlike or matlike patches. **1952** Davis *Flora ID* 114, *Mat Muhly.* . . Often found in saline soil. . . This is a fair forage grass. **1953** Nelson *Plants Rocky Mt. Park* 42, *Muhlenbergia richardsonis* . . Mat muhly. **1973** Hitchcock–Cronquist *Flora Pacific NW* 650, Prairies, meadows, and rocky slopes. . . Mat m[uhly].

mato See **tomato**

mat onto v phr

To latch onto.

1914 *DN* 4.76 **nNH, ME,** *Mat onto. . .* To take hold of. "Bill, he matted right onto Zeb, an' took him down." **1927** *AmSp* 3.139 **eME,** "Effet" for eft, "a bare mite," for a little, "much of a muchness" for a similarity, "to mat on to" when an undesired person could not be shaken off, were all common.

matrimony n

1 See **matrimony vine 1, 2.**

2 A type of **cruller;** see quots.

1906 *Pocumtuc Housewife* 34 **nwMA,** Crullers, Matrimony or Love Knots. Three eggs . . sugar . . butter . . soda, nutmeg, flour to make very stiff. Roll thin, cut in strips and tie in knots, or braid three strips together. Fry delicately and sprinkle sugar over while hot. **1941** *LANE* Map 284

(Doughnut) 1 inf, **ceRI,** Matrimony, two slit crullers fastened together with another piece of dough.

matrimony plant See **matrimony vine 2**

matrimony vine n

1 also *matrimony:* =**wolfberry** (here: *Lycium* spp), esp *L. halimifolium.* For other names of this latter sp see **Jackson vine 1, jasmine 2b, privy, tether-devil**

1822 Eaton *Botany* 343, *Lycium . . barbarum* (matrimony vine). **1861** Wood *Class-Book* 581, *Lycium* [spp] . . Matrimony vine. **1895** Gray–Bailey *Field Botany* 315, *L[ycium] vulgare.* . . *Matrimony Vine.* . . Planted, and sparingly running wild in some places. . . Pale greenish-purple 5-cleft corolla. *Ibid* 316, *L[ycium] Chinense.* . . *Chinese M[atrimony Vine].* Less commonly cult. than the last, but more desirable on account of the large . . bright scarlet acute fruit which ripens in August and hangs until early winter. **1915** (1926) Armstrong–Thornber *Western Wild Flowers* 464, Desert Matrimony—*Lycium cooperi.* . . An odd-looking desert shrub, everything about it so closely crowded as to give a queer bunchy and clumsy effect. . . The familiar Matrimony Vine of old-fashioned gardens belongs to this genus. **1939** FWP *Guide NJ* 19, In August, roadside fences and waste places are covered with matrimony-vine and its purple blossoms. **1964** Jackman–Long *OR Desert* 44, Homesteaders' wives needed something green in the middle of the gray desert. Nearly all of them planted a matrimony vine. . . It furnished shade for the kitchen and was kept growing by dishwater and scrub water. **1972** Brown *Wildflowers LA* 164, Salt Matrimony Vine—*Lycium carolinianum.* . . Flowers wheel-shaped to bell-shaped lavender to purple about 1 inch in diameter. Fruit a fleshy, red berry about ½ inch in diameter. **1981** Benson–Darrow *Trees SW Deserts* 195, One species, *Lycium halimifolium,* is the rather frequently cultivated matrimony vine, an excellent plant for training over fences and lattice work.

2 also *matrimony,* ~ *plant:* An **honesty** (here: *Lunaria annua*).

1896 *Jrl. Amer. Folkl.* 9.182 **cME,** *Lunaria biennis* . . matrimony vine. **1923** *Amer. Botanist* 29.156, The name of "matrimony plant" applied to this species [=*Lunaria annua*] is a puzzle unless it too alludes to the round seed-pods—matrimony ever being greatly dependent upon money. It is likely, however, that "matrimony plant" is a corruption of "money-plant." **1940** Clute *Amer. Plant Names* 37, *L[unaria] annua.* . . Matrimony-plant. **1959** Carleton *Index Herb. Plants* 79, *Matrimony:* Lunaria annua (L. biennis).

3 A **bittersweet** (here: *Solanum dulcamara*).

1963 Zimmerman–Olson *Forest* 162, *Bittersweet Nightshade.* . . Flowers all summer. Some call it matrimony vine. **1966** *DARE* Wildfl QR Pl.194A Inf **OR**12, Nightshade or matrimony vine; **WI**34, Matrimony vine.

mat road See **oil mat (road)**

matt n [Abbr for *matter*]

1983 *DARE* File **NC,** (*The stuff in the corner of your eyes when you wake up in the morning*) Matt.

mattawocca See **mattowacca**

mattax See **mattock**

matter n[1], v Usu |ˈmætə(r)|; also **chiefly NEng, Sth** *old-fash* |ˈmɑtə(r)| Pronc-spp *mahtterr, marter, motter*|

A Forms.

1840 in 1938 *AmSp* 13.46 **NEng,** 'The short sound of *a* in father' [is the sound] which the people of New England formerly gave and the vulgar still give to such words as *fathom, ladder, matter.* **1861** Holmes *Venner* 1.52 **NEng,** I'll ye what's the mahtterr. **1884** *Anglia* 7.268 **Sth, S Midl** [Black], To sorter straighten out marters. **1891** Page *Elsket* 145 **VA** [Black], I rehearse de motter wid him f'om de time he had ax me 'bout de tunament spang tell he come to see me hang. **1899** *PMLA* 14.215, One may still hear from elderly New England rustics . . [mɑtə] . . for . . matter. **1943** *LANE* Map 513 (*Pus*), [15 infs, **chiefly nNEng,** gave resps of the type [ˈmɑtə, ˈmɑtə]; 6 of these indicated that the pronc is older or obsolete.]

B As noun.

1 Pus; hence adj *mattered* full of pus. [*OED matter* sb.[1] 4 c1420 →; *mattered* adj. 2 1590] *somewhat old-fash* Cf **mater bump**

1899 (1912) Green *VA Folk-Speech* 276, *Matter.* . . Pus. **1929** *AmSp* 5.122 **ME,** Pus was "matter" or "corruption." **1965–70** *DARE* (Qu. BB35, *The yellowish stuff that comes out of a boil when the head breaks*) 216 Infs, **widespread,** Matter [Of all Infs responding to the question,

10% were young, 66% old; of those giving this response, 2% were young, 81% old.]; (Qu. X59, . . *The small infected pimples that form usually on the face*) Inf **MO**21, Matter pimples; (Qu. BB29) Inf **IN**76, Matter; (Qu. BB36) Infs **IL**143, **WA**3, Mattered; **CA**112, Matter; **NY**70, Got matter in it; (Qu. BB37) Inf **NY**96, Matter running out of his ear. **1967** *DARE* FW Addit **NY**, To get matter out of a boil—chew piece of bread, put mother's milk on it and then put it over boil and it will draw. **1985** *Amer. Jrl. Med.* Feb 183 **eTN**, *Matter* . . purulent running.

2 in phrr *such a matter (as); Usu in ref to an extent of time: thereabouts; in the neighborhood of.* **chiefly Sth, S Midl**

1909 *DN* 3.377 **eAL, wGA**, *Such a matter.* . . Approximately, about that. "A week ago or such a matter, he was here." **1915** *DN* 4.191 **swVA**, Bill was here an hour ago, or such a matter. **1929** Sale *Tree Named John* 12 **MS** [Black], There were three hours "er sich a matter 'fo' time t' start supper." **1931** *PMLA* 46.1305 **sAppalachians**, It wuz about a week ago, er sich a matter. **1946** *PADS* 6.29 **NC** (as of 1900–10), *Such a matter.* . . Approximately (usually of time). "I been here a week or sich a matter." Pamlico. Old persons. **1952** Brown *NC Folkl.* 506, "He was here such a matter as two hours ago."—Central and east.

C As verb.

To form or discharge pus, suppurate; hence ppl adj *mattered* full of pus. [*OED matter* v. 1 1530 →] Cf **matterate**

1806 (1970) Webster *Compendious Dict.* 187, *Matter,* v. to produce matter, signify, regard. [*DARE* Ed: The def "to produce matter" is carried over from Webster's English model.] **1899** (1912) Green *VA Folk-Speech* 276, *Matter.* . . To form pus; . . also, to discharge pus. **1950** *WELS* **WI** (*When pus or yellowish stuff comes out of an open sore, you say the sore is* _____) 6 Infs, Mattering. **1954** *Harder Coll.* **cwTN**, 'At sore place's a-matterin' up some now. **c1960** *Wilson Coll.* **csKY**, *Mattering.* . . Running, suppurating. **1965–70** *DARE* (Qu. BB36) 48 Infs, **scattered exc West**, Mattering; **IL**143, **WA**3, Mattered.

matter n² See **tomato**

matter a difference v phr Cf *DS* KK26

To be of no importance or consequence.

1934 Hurston *Jonah's Gourd Vine* 260 **FL** [Black], "You don't care, then, if Hattie has her freedom?" "Naw suh, Ah sho don't. Matters uh difference tuh me whut she do, uh where she go." **1948** Hurston *Seraph* 23 **wFL**, So far as making up your mind is concerned, that matters a difference. Women folks don't have no mind to make up nohow. *Ibid* 35, "You was borned back there in middle Georgia." "Matters a difference about where I was borned, Maria. I'm talking about what I learned when I was visiting over there in the backwoods of Arkansas."

matterate v, hence ppl adj *matterated* [Var of *maturate* to cause suppuration, to suppurate, infl by **matter** n¹, v **B1, C**] **chiefly NEng, Upstate NY** See Map
=**matter** v **C**.

1917 *DN* 4.396 **neOH**, *Matterate.* . . Maturate. Perhaps by analogy of *matter*, "pus". . . It may, however, be a normal phonetic development from *maturate.* . . "The wound is beginning to matterate." General. **1929** *AmSp* 5.122 **ME**, If a wound were infected, it *"matterated."* **1932** *DN* 6.283 **swCT**, *Matterating.* An inflamed wound or a boil which has matter coming out of it. **1943** *LANE* Map 513, The verb *matterate* 'suppurate' [10 infs] and the adjectives *matterated* [3 infs], *mattery* [1 inf] 'suppurating' were incidentally offered by several informants (including three who do not use the noun *matter*). **1950** *WELS* (*When pus or yellowish stuff comes out of an open sore, you say the sore is*

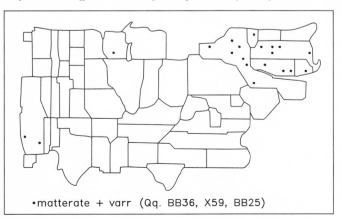
•matterate + varr (Qq. BB36, X59, BB25)

_____) 3 Infs, **WI**, Matterating; 1 Inf, **cWI**, Matterated. **1965–70** *DARE* (Qu. BB36) 18 Infs, **chiefly NEng, Upstate NY**, Matterating; **CT**39, Matterated; (Qu. X59, . . *The small infected pimples that form usually on the face*) Inf **MA**25, Matterated; (Qu. BB25, . . *Common skin diseases around here*) Inf **RI**1, Erysipelas—skin breaks out and matterates. **1995** *DARE* File **csWI** (as of c1945), *Matterate* was known, but considered slightly old-fashioned in the mid-forties.

mattered adj See **matter** n¹ **B1**

mattered ppl adj See **matter** v **C**

mattery adj [*OED* 1398 →]

Containing pus.

1899 (1912) Green *VA Folk-Speech* 277, *Mattery.* . . Purulent; generating pus. **1943** *LANE* Map 513 (*Pus*) 1 inf, **RI**, All mattery. **1955** Denlinger *Complete Boston* 2.152, Small mattery spots on the inside of the thighs . . are often the first indication that a dog is suffering from distemper. **1968** *DARE* (Qu. BB36, *When there's an open sore and this yellowish stuff is coming out of it . . it's* _____) Inf **MN**42, Mattery.

mattock n Also *mattock ax* Pronc-spp *mad(d)ick, mat(t)ax, mattick, mattox* **widespread, but more freq Appalachians** See Map Cf **mad ax**

An agricultural hand tool with a pick- or ax-like steel head used for digging and chopping.

1636 in 1894 Watertown MA *Records* 1.1.3, Ordered . . every man that is Souldier or watchman to come . . with a wheelbarrow, mattock [etc]. **1837** in 1956 Eliason *Tarheel Talk* 314 **c,csNC**, Madick. **1915** *DN* 4.185 **swVA**, Maddick. **1936** *AmSp* 11.316 **Ozarks**, Mattick. **c1938** in 1970 Hyatt *Hoodoo* 2.940 **ceVA**, I took dey own matax . . , goes up on the hill an' git me some bitter apple. . . Dig me up some bitter apple. **1947** Lomax *Advent. Ballad Hunter* 4 **TX** (as of c1880), We went down into the soil around the trees with mattox and grubbing hoe, and cut the taproots, sometimes two feet below the surface. **1950** (1965) Richter *Town* 180 **OH**, She put a mattox, shovel and old axe in the chariot. **1965–70** *DARE* (Qu. L35, *Hand tools used for cutting underbrush and digging out roots*) 221 Infs, **widespread, but esp Appalachians**, Mattock; **GA**52, Grub mattock; **SC**3, **WA**11, Mattock ax; **CT**26, **MI**83, Pick-mattock. **1976** *PA Folklife* Spring 31, Similarly *mattock* has become *mattax* (*mattock* + *ax*).

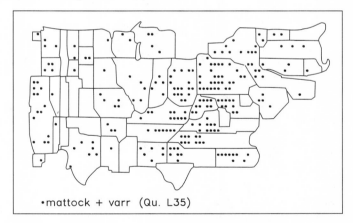
•mattock + varr (Qu. L35)

mattowacca n Also *mattawocca* [See quot 1842]

A **hickory shad:** usu *Alosa mediocris,* rarely *Dorosoma cepedianum.*

[**1842** DeKay *Zool. NY* 4.261, The trivial [=species] name [=*mattowacca*] given by Mitchill [in 1814 to *Alosa mediocris*], was derived from the aboriginal name of the island [=Long Island] *Mattowaka* or *Matowax*.] **1879** U.S. Natl. Museum *Bulletin* 14.60, *Pomolobus mediocris* . . Mattawocca. **1896** U.S. Bur. Fisheries *Rept. for 1895* 281, *Pomolobus mediocris.* . . Mattowacca. Atlantic Coast of United States from Maine to Florida. **1911** U.S. Bur. Census *Fisheries 1908* 312, Mattowacca (*Dorosoma cepedianum*).—A poor food fish found on the Atlantic coast from Cape Cod to Florida, ascending rivers. It is called "hickory shad" and "hicks," particularly in the South.

mattox See **mattock**

mattress n Usu |'mætrəs|; for varr see quots
Std sense, var forms.

1901 *DN* 2.143 **LA**, *Mattress* . . [mə'træs]. . . This pron. is occasionally used in Seneca Co., N.Y. **1903** Dunbar *Lyrics of Love* 80, I kin hyeah dat mattuss squeak. **c1940** Eliason *Word Lists FL* 4 **nwFL**, *Mattress* [mætləs]: Very rare now; though formerly common. [*DARE* Ed: Cf Fr *matelas*] **1993** *NADS Letters*, Texans far and wide say /'mætrɪs/. *Ibid* **ceMS**, /'mætrɪs/.

mattress fern n

A **maidenhair fern** (here: *Adiantum capillus-veneris*).

1951 *PADS* 15.26 **TX**, *Adiantum capillus-veneris* . . Mattress fern (formerly used for stuffing mattresses and pillows).

mattuss See mattress

matweed n Cf pink matweed

An **amaranth** (here: *Amaranthus blitoides*).

1898 *Jrl. Amer. Folkl.* 11.277 **KS**, *Amaranthus blitoides* . . matweed.

mauck See mock n

Maud n [Cf quot 1976] esp Sth, S Midl Cf jenny 1, joe n² 1

Used as a name for a female mule or donkey, rarely for a cow; hence n *Maud mule* a mare mule.

1935 (1944) Rawlings *Golden Apples* 332 **NC**, Is it a Maud mule or a Jo-mule? **1942** Berrey–Van den Bark *Amer. Slang* 120.21, *Donkey; Burro*. . . Maud. *Ibid* 68, *Mule*. . . Maud. **1967–68** *DARE* (Qu. K50, *Joking nicknames for mules*) Inf **LA**15, Maud, Kate—these are common given names for mare mules; **MA**15, Maud. **1976** Horn *World Encycl. Comics* 80, Fred Opper's classic kicking mule strip, *And Her Name Was Maud* (a play on "and her name was mud") technically began publication under that title . . on May 23, 1926. . . Actually, however, Maud the mule was a feature character in many of Opper's Sunday page episodes going well back into the early 1900's. **1986** Pederson *LAGS Concordance*, 1 inf, **nwTN**, Saw, Maud, be still—to Maud, her cow.

mauey-mouthed See mowy-mouthed

mauger adj [Perh of multiple origin; cf *SND maugre* "Appar. an irreg. variant of Eng. *meagre, maigre,* lean, starved-looking"; Dan, Du, Ger, Norw, Sw *mager;* Ital, Port, Span *magro*] NEast old-fash

1 Lean, peaked, sickly.

1890 Holley *Samantha among Brethren* 199 **NY**, And though Jenette wuzn't the one to say anything, she began to look kinder pale and mauger. **1901** *DN* 2.143 **e,cNY**, *Mauger* [mɔgɚ]. . . Sickly, weak in appearance. **1903** *DN* 2.352 **csNY**, *Mauger* [mɑgɚ]. . . Lean, thin. . . Common. **1932** *DN* 6.283 **swCT**, *Mauger.* Poor, thin, peaked. The grown-up word for *puling.* **1941** *LANE* Map 459 *(Emaciated, peaked)* 5 infs, **sNEng**, Mauger [mɔgə, mɔgr, mɒgə]. [3 infs indicated that this word was old-fashioned or obsolete.] **1943** *Ibid* Map 493 *(Feeling bad)* 2 infs, **seMA, RI**, Mauger. [a1949] (1964) Storms *Jersey Du. Vocab.* np **neNJ**, *Maugher*—Skinny; Lean.] **1972** *NYT Article Letters* **cNY**, If grandmother . . [was] ailing only a bit, she was "wumble-cropped." She also sometimes felt "a little mauger." **1983** *Lutz Coll.* **neNJ**, [An elderly man] described someone as being "mauger as a spook."

2 By ext: lazy.

1941 *LANE* Map 459, 1 inf, **wCT**, Mauger [mɒgr] = 'lazy.'

mauka adv, adj [Haw; see quot 1938] HI Cf makai

Inland; toward the mountains.

1873 [see **makai**]. **1938** Reinecke *Hawaiian Loanwords* 24, *Mauka* . . adv. [*Ma,* at, and *uka,* inland.] Mountainward, one of the two standard directions. . . V[ery] F[req]. **1951** [see **makai**]. **1965** Krauss–Alexander *Grove Farm* 284 **HI**, "I suppose you're going to finish furrowing out mauka today?" he asked, one planter to another. **1969** [see **makai**]. **1980** *AmSp* 55.209 **Honolulu HI**, The following are used to give directions: *mauka* (literally, 'toward the mountains') 'north.' **1991** Saiki *From the Lanai* 89 **HI**, Her parents raise sweet potatoes . . on the *mauka,* mountain side of the island.

maul n [From the shape]

c1960 *Wilson Coll.* **csKY**, *Maul.* . . Comic name for chicken leg; more often drumstick.

maul drag v phr

To beat or manhandle (someone).

1917 *DN* 4.421 **New Orleans LA**, *Maul drag.* . . To beat and drag about (a person). **1941** O'Donnell *Great Big Doorstep* 203 **sLA**, I'll mauldrag him!

maulhead n

1 A type of **log canoe. Chesapeake Bay**

1906 *Forest & Stream* 67.898, Why should not a bugeye, a bugeye with a bustle, a three-log canoe, a five-log one, a Pocosin, a maulhead, a jigger rig, a spanker rig, and all the other small boat rigs of Chesapeake Bay be hung as they are rigged for the edification of the near generation which will have forgotten these strange craft? **1907** *Ibid* 68.212 **Chesapeake Bay**, Our canoe was a maulhead—wide at the bow and tapering aft like a tadpole. **1909** *Rudder* 21.353 **Chesapeake Bay**, The next canoe to take her place in the line of development was the three-piece centerboard craft, called the maulhead.

2 Prob a **flathead catfish 1**.

1966 *DARE* (Qu. P1, . . *Kinds of freshwater fish . . caught around here . . good to eat*) Inf **MS**1, Maulhead. **1986** Pederson *LAGS Concordance*, 1 inf, **csMS**, Maulhead = fish.

mauling rails See maul rails 1

maul oak n [See quot 1910] esp CA

=canyon oak 1.

1884 Sargent *Forests of N. Amer.* 146, Live Oak. Maul Oak. Valparaiso Oak. **1897** Sudworth *Arborescent Flora* 163 **CA**, Cañon Live Oak. . . Maul Oak. **1910** Jepson *Silva CA* 223, The wood of Maul Oak is remarkable for its strength, toughness, and close grain; for these reasons and because of its freedom from checks in seasoning it is more valuable than that of any other California oak. . . By reason of the hardness and solidity of the wood it is everywhere used for the heads of mauls and is most widely known as Maul Oak. **1947** Peattie *Sierra Nevada* 145, Golden-cup oak—known by many other names as well, such as maul oak, canyon oak, mountain live oak, etc.—is a tree of the talus slopes. **1961** Thomas *Flora Santa Cruz* 137 **cwCA**, Maul . . Oak. Open woods, . . or growing as a shrub or a small tree in chaparral. **1976** Bailey–Bailey *Hortus Third* 933, [*Quercus*] *chrysolepis* . . Canyon o[ak], Maul o[ak].

maul rails v phr chiefly Sth, S Midl

1 To split logs for fence rails; hence vbl n *mauling rails.* old-fash

1677 in 1894 *VA Mag. Hist. & Biog.* 2.168, Armed men . . were . . commanded to goe to work, fall trees and mawl and toat railes. **1843** (1916) Hall *New Purchase* 321 **IN**, Teachers . . ought . . at least be content with "a dollar a day, which was more nor double what a feller got for mauling rails!" **1880** (1881) Harris *Uncle Remus Songs* 45 **GA**, Brer Fox, he lammed away at dat holler tree, he did, like a man maulin' rails. **1899** (1912) Green *VA Folk-Speech* 277, *Maul.* . . To split with wedges and a maul. "I have mauled two hundred rails to-day." **1903** *DN* 2.320 **seMO**, *Maul* (rails). . . Split out rails. **1906** *DN* 3.146 **nwAR**, *Maul rails.* . . To split rails from logs by means of a wedge and a maul. "It's harder than mauling rails to cut and sell meat all day." **1914** Furman *Sight* 70 **KY**, I laid my plans for to set the farm on its feet ag'in, and clear new ground, and maul rails for the fence. **1949** Webber *Backwoods Teacher* 166 **Ozarks**, He putt Johnny in the timber, maulin' fence rails out of white oak an' walnut. **1982** Slone *How We Talked* 10 **eKY** (as of c1950), "I feel like I been mauling rails"—meaning I am real tired. [**1986** Pederson *LAGS Concordance*, 1 inf, **csAL**, Maul—used to split rails; 1 inf, **cnLA**, Maul—for splitting rails.]

2 Fig: see quot.

1884 *Anglia* 7.270 **Sth, S Midl** [Black], *To maul rails* = to make oneself ridiculous.

mauma See mamma n¹

maumey See mamma n¹ 2

maumuh See mamma n¹

maus(sa) See master n

maverick n Also *mauvric, mav(o)rick* [From Samuel A. *Maverick* (1803–70), a prominent Texan who owned, from 1847–56, a herd of cattle that was allowed to run wild] chiefly West

1 A cow, bull, or calf (rarely a horse) without a brand or other indication of ownership. Note: Properly a calf could only be considered unclaimed if it was not with a branded cow, but any unbranded calf could easily be stolen and passed off as a true maverick. Cf orejana

1867 in 1940 McCoy *Cattle Trade* 83 **San Antonio TX**, The term maverick which was formerly applied to unbranded yearlings is now applied to every calf which can be separated from the mother cow—the consequence is, the fastest branders are accumulating the largest stocks. **1874** McCoy *Cattle Trade* 9, Unbranded animals over a year old are, in ranchmen's parlance, called "Mauvrics," which name they got from a certain old Frenchman of that name, who began stock raising with a very few head, and in a very brief space of time had a remarkably large herd of cattle. . . Of course he captured the unbranded yearlings. **1881** Romspert *W. Echo* 179, A calf that is following no cow, and is unbranded, is called a *maverick;* and though by law these now belong to the state in some places, they used to belong to the man who first put his brand there. **1885** Siringo *TX Cowboy* 71, There being plenty of "Mavricks" close at hand . . I used to try and get the old man to let me butcher one now and then. **1887** Francis *Saddle & Mocassin* 172 **West,** Nowadays you don't dare to clap a brand on a maverick [Footnote: An unbranded motherless calf] even. **1907** White *AZ Nights* 76, "Well," says I to the carcass, "no one's goin' to be able to swear whether you're a maverick or not, but I bet you know the feel of a brandin' iron all right." **1912** (1990) Babb *In the Bosom* 76 **TX** (as of 1871), We gathered about five hundred "mavericks", and drove them to the ranch in Wise County, where we marked and branded them. **1915** *DN* 4.227 **wTX,** *Maverick.* . . An unbranded calf. (Named from a Texas ranchman who did not brand his calves. Accordingly, many of them were stolen and branded by other ranchmen. Hence, *Maverick* may also mean a stolen calf.) **1929** *AmSp* 5.67 **NE,** A "marvick" [sic] is a calf, sometimes a "beef," that is not "ear marked" or "branded." **1933** *AmSp* 8.1.30 **nwTX,** Maverick. **1936** McCarthy *Lang. Mosshorn* np **West,** *Maverick.* An unbranded yearling, either a horse or cow, belonging to the man with the longest loop and the fastest horse. **1940** Writers' Program *Guide NV* 77, A *maverick* or *slick-ear* is an unbranded, unclaimed calf. **1956** Ker *Vocab. W. TX* 223, The Texas term *maverick.* . . shows significant currency, being used by both younger and older informants. **1962** Atwood *Vocab. TX* 57, *Maverick* . . occurs in all parts of Texas except the Northeast and the Trans-Pecos. It does not occur in states to the east. . . No less than thirty-one informants specify that a *maverick* is an unbranded animal; a few others state or intimate that it is a stray. **1967** *DARE* Tape **TX**24, They took out worlds of big mavericks the first time. **1986** Pederson *LAGS Concordance,* 1 inf, **ceTX,** Maverick—calf, not branded; 1 inf, **csTX,** A maverick—unbranded animal.

2 By ext: a rough, untamed, or feral animal.

1965–70 *DARE* (Qu. K42, *A horse that is rough, wild, or dangerous*) 11 Infs, **scattered,** Maverick; **CA**16, Maverick—lacking ownership; **NY**41, Maverick [FW: Inf says she has read it.]; (Qu. K43, *A horse that was not intentionally bred, or bred by accident*) 11 Infs, **scattered,** Maverick; **IN**82, Maverick [FW: Inf later said she thought this was some sort of calf.]; **NJ**6, Maverick [FW: Inf doubtful]; (Qu. K16, *A cow with a bad temper*) Infs **CT**9, **WI**72, Maverick.

3 Fig: see below. Note: The fig sense "an independent-minded person" appears to have been rapidly popularized in the US before 1900 and is now used throughout the country.
a Anything which may be, or has been, appropriated by the finder; something obtained dishonestly.

1890 *Century Dict.* 3666, *Maverick.* . . Anything dishonestly obtained, as a saddle, mine, or piece of land. [*Century* Ed: Western U.S.] **1893** *KS Univ. Qrly.* 1.140, *Maverick:* a waif, any unclaimed article. . . A boy in Wyoming calls a book without the owner's name a maverick.
b An orphan child; an illegitimate child.

1922 *DN* 5.181 **WY, NW,** *Maverick.* . . An orphan (human). Wyoming and the Northwest generally. **1968–69** *DARE* (Qu. Z11b, . . *[A child whose parents were not married]*) Infs **CA**114, **KS**7, Maverick.

maverick v Also sp *mavrick*

1 To lay claim, usu by branding, to (a **maverick** n **1**); to search out and brand mavericks; hence vbl n *mavericking;* n *mavericker.* **West** *hist*

1880 (1883) U.S. Census Office *Rept. Ag.* 965, The Indians stole them, the Mexicans raided them and drove them across the Rio Grande, and the Texans "mavericked" the unbranded. **1889** *Glenrock* (Wyo.) *Graphic* 13 Sep. 1/3 *(DA),* Numerous cases are reported of cows having their throats cut so that the mavericking of the calf would be made easy. **1891** (1958) Wister *Out West* 117, Smith is at present stealing cattle or, more likely, mavericking. **1893** James *Cow-Boy Life in TX* 73, I believe it just possible that some cattle men who made their start after the first great tidal wave of wholesale mavricking (or stealing I should have said) were strictly honest. **1929** Dobie *Vaquero* 293, The story of the cow thieves was the old story of young men beginning their career as maverickers and ending as outright takers of other people's property. **1936** McCarthy *Lang. Mosshorn* np **West,** The term mavericking' is used when an outfit rounds up unbranded stock and applies its own brand. **1945** Thorp *Pardner* 261 **SW,** Some maverickers lost many of their catch by necking two wild ones together. *Ibid* 262, Some of the riders on these mavericking roundups . . took a lot more chances than any other riders going.

1956 Ker *Vocab. W. TX* 223, There was no law against taking a *maverick* and putting one's own brand on it until the cowboy decided to maverick on his own.

2 To appropriate (abandoned or unprotected property).

1890 *Century Dict.* 3666 **West,** *Maverick.* . . To seize or brand (an animal) as a maverick; hence, to take possession of without any legal claim; appropriate dishonestly or illegally: as, to *maverick* a piece of land. [*Century* Ed: Western U.S.] **1897** Lewis *Wolfville* 176 **AZ,** I never tracks up on no sech outrage in my life as this disgraceful Colonel openin' a hurdy-gurdy ag'in Hamilton's, an' mavericking' his music that a-way. **1935** Davis *Honey* 163 **OR,** Hops picked and left in the field overnight were liable to be mavericked and turned in at daylight by the first early riser who found them.

mavis n [Transf from *mavis* a European thrush (*OED* a1366 →)] =**brown thrasher.**

1865 *Atlantic Mth.* 15.523, The Mavis, or Red Thrush, sneaks and skulks like a culprit. **1895** Minot *Land-Birds New Engl.* 45, "Mavis." A common summer resident in southern New England. **1895** (1907) Wright *Birdcraft* 80, Song Thrush, Red Thrush, Brown Mockingbird, Mavis, are four of the local names for this most exultant and . . dashing of our song-birds. **1917** (1923) *Birds Amer.* 3.179, Brown Thrasher—*Toxostoma rufum.* . . Mavis. **1949** (1958) Stuart *Thread* 70 **KY,** A mavis flew from the nest through a broken windowpane in her escape to freedom.

mavorick, mavrick n See **maverick** n

mavrick v See **maverick** v

maw n[1]

1 The stomach or occas other internal organs; also fig, appetite. [*OED maw* sb.[1] 1 c725 →] **chiefly Gulf States, Mid and S Atl** See also **hog maw**

1887 (1967) Harris *Free Joe* 216 **cGA** [Black], I ain't fin' out den w'at war wuz—I ain't know w'at a great big maw she got. **1899** (1912) Green *VA Folk-Speech* 277, *Maw.* . . The stomach of animals, and also of human beings. **1948** Hutchison *PA Du. Cook Book* 50, Stuffed pig's maw. **1967** *DARE* Tape **SC**46, That was just the plain maw. . . Just the plain stomach. And it is thick, and when you cut it open . . you can cut it up in pieces and batter it and fry it, but you got to cook it before you can fry it. **1968** *DARE* (Qu. X8, . . *General words . . for the organs inside the body*) Inf **NC**49, Stomach, intestines, maw [mɔu]. [Inf old] **1986** Pederson *LAGS Concordance* **Gulf Region,** 14 infs, Maw(s); 9 infs, Maw(s) [=stomach or tripe]; 1 inf, The maw—of a hog, when served; 1 inf, His maw—intestines of hog; 1 inf, That haslet is a maw, we call it; 1 inf, Maw—of a deer; 1 inf, Maw—of cow; 1 inf, Chitterlings and maw are edible insides of hog; 1 inf, Maw—of calf, hog—organs inside. [23 of 30 infs old]

2 The gullet, jaws, mouth. [*OED maw* sb.[1] 3 1530 →]

1851 (1976) Melville *Moby-Dick* 41, I saw the open maw of hell. **1938** Rawlings *Yearling* 93 **FL,** He looked down, unbelieving, at the stout form and the great maw [of a bass]. **c1938** in 1970 Hyatt *Hoodoo* 2.1483 **seGA** [Black], Yo'll gag his [=a catfish's] mouth open an' yo'll pop dat little small package right down in his—be sure it's down in his maw. . . He'll stay right dere until dat—until dat stuff in his maw—until he deliver dat out. **1967** *DARE* (Qu. X9, *Joking or uncomplimentary words for a person's mouth . . "I wish he'd shut his _____."*) Inf **IL**5, Maw.

maw n[2] See **ma** n A2

mawk See **mock** v

mawking bird See **mockingbird**

maw-maw See **mam-maw**

mawmouth n Also *mawmouth perch, moremouth (bream), mormouth* **chiefly SC**

A **warmouth** (here: *Lepomis gulosus*).

1839 (1840) Simms *Border Beagles* 1.213 **MS,** Here . . I find you, like a cursed maw-mouth that grows blind when he sees a worm wriggle. **1853** in 1956 Eliason *Tarheel Talk* 152 **cwNC,** Went fishing in the lake [and] caught twenty four more mouths. **1856** Simms *Eutaw* 365 **SC,** He felt sure that we could not withstand the bait, any more than a hungry mawmouth perch in midsummer. **1890** *Century Dict.* 3666, *Mawmouth.* . . The calico-, grass-, or strawberry-bass, *Pomoxys sparoides,* a centrarchoid fish. [*Century* Ed: Local, U.S.] **1922** *Outlook* 130.261 **SC,** In the waters themselves fish abound—black bass, mudfish, . . mormouth [sic]. **1933** LA Dept. of Conserv. *Bulletin* 33.342, Warmouth. . .

Moremouth Bream. **1966–67** *DARE* (Qu. P1, . . *Kinds of freshwater fish . . caught around here . . good to eat*) Infs **SC**9, 19, 26, 43, Mawmouth.

may v

A Gram forms.

Past: usu *might;* also:

a *mought, mout, mowt, mote;* usu |maut|. [*OED may* v. A.4.B "Now *dial.*"] **chiefly Sth, S Midl** *old-fash* Cf **moughty**

1789 Webster *Dissertations Engl. Lang.* 111, *Mought* for *might* is heard in most of the states, but not frequently except in a few towns. **1818** in 1824 Knight *Letters* 107 **KY,** Some words are . . , by the lower classes in society, universally most uncouthly, as . . mought. **1827** (1939) Sherwood *Gaz. GA* 139, *Mout,* for might. **1843** (1916) Hall *New Purchase* 363 **IN,** It moughtn't be that deep. **1843** Thompson *Major Jones' Courtship* 7 **GA,** I mought as well take advantage of the "flood." **1859** (1968) Bartlett *Americanisms* 281, *Mought.* This obsolete preterite of *may* is still heard among old people in the interior parts of New England. **1866** Smith *Bill Arp* 135 **nwGA,** So mote it be. **1883** (1971) Harris *Nights with Remus* 21 **GA,** Dish yer pig-grabber *mought* be dead, en den ag'in he moughtent. **1888** in 1971 Farmer *Americanisms* 375, That beefin' bee mowt ha' happened an' it mowtn't ha', for all I know. **1890** *DN* 1.71 **LA,** *Mought* [maut]: might. . . Common where settlers of English descent have long been isolated. [*DN* Ed: *mought* (pronounced [maut]) is also reported from Kentucky.] **1893** Shands *MS Speech* 46, *Mought* [maut]. Negro for *might* (verb). **1894** *DN* 1.332 **NJ,** *Mought* [maut]. **1895** *DN* 1.370 **seKY, eTN, wNC,** You mout (might) have got a bussy. **1899** Chesnutt *Conjure Woman* 20 **csNC** [Black], She mought be able fer ter take de goopher off'n him. **1899** (1912) Green *VA Folk-Speech* 289, *Mought.* **1903** *DN* 2.321 **seMO,** *Mought.* **1905** *DN* 3.14 **cCT,** *Mought.* . . Still in use among old people. **1906** *DN* 3.147 **nwAR,** *Mout* [maut]. **1908** Fox *Lonesome Pine* 63 **KY,** I'm afeered somethin' mought happen to 'em. **1909** *DN* 3.350 **eAL, wGA,** *Mought.* **1911** *DN* 3.539 **eKY,** *Mout.* **1913** Kephart *Highlanders* 284 **sAppalachians,** Mought (mowt) for might. **1914** *DN* 4.159 **cVA,** That caow mought hawn yo. **1923** *DN* 5.215 **swMO,** *Mought.* **1927** Kennedy *Gritny* 59 **sLA** [Black], Gussie bin able to see de change w'at moughta took place. **1930** Shoemaker *1300 Words* 40 **cPA Mts** (as of c1900), *Mote*—Might, must. **1936** *AmSp* 11.348 **eTX,** *Mought* [maut] . . is used now only by older people among the more ignorant speakers. **1942** Hall *Smoky Mt. Speech* 45 **wNC, eTN,** The following words almost always have [æu] rather than [au]: . . mought (rare obsolescent variant of *might*). **1952** Brown *NC Folkl.* 1.567, Mought [maut]. . . General. Illiterate. **1953** Randolph–Wilson *Down in Holler* 74 **Ozarks,** The equivalent form of might is very often pronounced to rhyme with *out,* at least by the older generation of Ozarkers. **1953** Atwood *Survey of Verb Forms* 18, *Might.* . . The archaic *mought* /maut/ occurs in the S[outh] A[tlantic] S[tates] in a distribution very similar to that of *holp.* . . It extends into the Shenandoah Valley at three points, however, and there are occurrences in the eastern portion of W. Va. and even in w. Md. It is recorded in three scattered communities in c. and n. N.J. . . *Mought* is primarily a rustic form, being used by more than half the Type I informants in Va. and N.C. but by less than one sixth the Type II informants. **1967** *DARE* FW Addit **seLA,** *Mought* [maut]. **1981** Pederson *LAGS Basic Materials,* 1 inf, **cwMS,** [maut ə bɪ·ᵊn] [=might have been]; 1 inf, **cnAR,** [mæ·ᵛ·oᵗ əv bɪᵊ·ᵊn]; 1 inf, **swMS,** [ma⸃oᵗ ə hɪ⸃ᵊd ɪt] [=might have heard it].

b *mighnt.*

1890 *DN* 1.22 **ME,** I mighnt and then again I mightn't. *Ibid* 59 **wNY,** *Might,* pronounced *mighnt,* is quite general among the working people of Western New York. **1905** *DN* 3.58 **eNE,** Intrusive *n,* the "nasal infix," occurs in . . *migh(n)t.*

B Syntax.

Used as the first member of a multiple modal or a non-std multiple auxiliary: see below. [Cf *SND can* v.¹ III.2; *EDD can* v. II.1] **chiefly Sth, S Midl** Cf **must 2, used to** Note: The exx shown below are the most common but not the only attested combinations. For further data including negative and interrogative forms see Mishoe and Montgomery in 1994 *AmSp* 69.3–29.

1 *may can, ~ could, might can, ~ ('a') could:* Probably can or could; may or might be able to; might have been able to.

1859 in 1956 Eliason *Tarheel Talk* 245 **NC,** *I know I* might could *& should enjoy myself.* [*DARE* Ed: It is possible that this should instead be interpreted as "might, could, and should."] **1905** *DN* 3.87 **nwAR,**

Might could. . . Might be able. 'We might could rent the hall over Whittmore's store, if we fail to get this other one.' Rare. **1909** *DN* 3.349 **eAL, wGA,** *Might can, might could.* . . Might be able. "Go to see Mr. Smith. He might can tell you." **1914** *DN* 4.159 **cVA,** *Might-'a could.* . . Might have been able to. "Ah might a could found aout." **1919** *DN* 5.34 **KY,** I might could do it. **1923** *DN* 5.215 **swMO,** I mought 'a' could if I'd 'a' wanted to. **1934** *AmSp* 9.79 **LA,** To the question, Can you do this? even students who habitually used good English slipped naturally into the answer, *I might could,* or *I might could do that,* and infrequently, *I may could.* **1938** *AmSp* 13.4 **seAR,** 'May can' and 'might could' are almost universal. **1941** in 1983 Taft *Blues Lyric Poetry* 286, Now listen here brother : you may can understand / I might would pimp a woman : but I will never pimp a man. **1953** Atwood *Survey of Verb Forms* 35, The phrase *might could,* in the context "I (might could) do it" (future), is recorded wherever it occurred in the M[iddle] A[tlantic] S[tates] and the S[outhern] A[tlantic] S[tates]. The isogloss of this form is peculiar in that it not only indicates a typical South and South Midland form, but shows the form to be current in the German area of Pa. as well. . . [Within this isogloss] Type I informants [=those with little education] offer this form with hardly any exceptions, and it is also used by from two thirds (Va.) to practically all (N.C.) of Type II informants [=those with moderate education] as well. Cultured informants as a rule avoid the construction: there are very few instances of it in this type. **1956** Gipson *Old Yeller* 88 **TX,** Jumper's liable to throw a fit with that hide rattling along behind him, and you might not can hold him by yourself. **1967** *DARE* Tape **SC**46, I might could look it up in my notes; **TX**49, They might could tell you where you got the whiskey. **1984** Burns *Cold Sassy* 100 **nGA** (as of 1906), There was a pause, his face working like he might not could go on, but he did. **1985** *AmSp* 60.233 **sePA,** Apparently *might could* is now a distinctly recessive feature in the Pennsylvania German area. **1989** *AmSp* 64.197 **TX,** Actually Occurring Double Modals . . may could₍₎ may can₍₎ may will₍₎ may should₍₎ may supposed to₍₎ . . might could₍₎ might oughta₍₎ might can₍₎ might should₍₎ might would₍₎ might better₍₎ might had better₍₎ . . may used to₍₎ might supposed to₍₎ might've used to₍₎ may need to₍₎ . . might woulda had oughta. **1994** *AmSp* 69.13 **SC,** Could you might possibly use a teller machine? . . I wonder if we might could get a copy of last year's test?

2 *might better:* Probably should; perhaps should. [*better* vbl auxiliary < *had better*]

1968 *DARE* Tape **NJ**28, When you don't know it you might better keep out. [*DARE* Ed: This may be *might* + *better* adv.] **1970** *DARE* FW Addit **csNY,** I might better—might as well. **1979** Feagin *Variation AL Engl.* 338, And I thought I might better tell you. . . You might better shake it up. **1986** Pederson *LAGS Concordance,* 1 inf, **cGA,** You might better take it off; 1 inf, **cTN,** You might better do it. **1989** [see **B1** above]. **1990** *DARE* File **SC,** You might better try on some of your clothes.

3 *may did, might did:* Probably did; perhaps did.

1986 Pederson *LAGS Concordance,* 1 inf, **ceLA,** He might did; 1 inf, **cnAR,** Well, I might did. **1994** *AmSp* 69.12 **SC,** There weren't no way to be sure; could be he may didn't want to come. . . You might did already do that. . . We waited as long as we could cause we thought he may did want to go with us.

4 *may ought to, might ought to:* Probably should; perhaps should.

1938 *AmSp* 13.4 **AR,** You might ought to go. **1967** Green *Horse Tradin'* 248 **swTX,** I really got to thinking that I might ought to hear the good Reverend preach. **1986** Pederson *LAGS Concordance,* 1 inf, **swGA,** I figured I might ought not to; 1 inf, **cnGA,** You might ought to go see about that; 1 inf, **csTN,** Might ought to—uses form frequently; 1 inf, **neMS,** I might ought to spot-fight them; 1 inf, **seAL,** Might ought to be able; 1 inf, **neMS,** I may not ought to say it. **1989** [see **B1** above]. **1994** *AmSp* 69.17 **SC,** You might ought to have the oil changed.

5 *may should, might should:* Probably should; perhaps should.

1986 Pederson *LAGS Concordance,* 1 inf, **neGA,** We might should. **1989** [see **B1** above]. **1994** *AmSp* 69.13 **SC,** You may should go to the dentist if it's really bothering you a lot. *Ibid* 17, We might shouldn't have done it last night.

6 *may will, ~ shall, ~ would, might will, ~ would:* Probably will (or would); might.

1928 Peterkin *Scarlet Sister Mary* 138 **SC,** I'm 'faid e might would catch cold. **1940** *AmSp* 15.214 **TX,** The most commonly heard examples [of double auxiliaries]: *I might can, . . it might would.* **1941** [see **B1** above]. **1966** *DARE* FW Addit **OK,** "He might would"—used for "maybe he would." **1986** Pederson *LAGS Concordance,* 1 inf, **cAL,**

Sometimes they maybe may would; 1 inf, **neLA,** Some people might would call it a hill, but I wouldn't; 1 inf, **neAR,** Some people might would call them tow sacks; 1 inf, **ceAL,** Yeah, I might would use that term; 2 infs, **cwLA, cwMS,** I might will. **1989** [see **B1** above]. **1994** *AmSp* 69.9 **SC,** They're saying we may shall get some rain. *Ibid* 13, You might would run smack into it. . . I think I may will have me a piece of cake. . . I feel like I might will do all right. *Ibid* 17, I thought y'all may would have had some more of them in by now.

may n [*OED may* sb.¹ *"poet. (arch.)"*]

A young woman; a man's sweetheart.

1910 *Univ. NC Mag.* 40.3.6 **Hatteras Is. NC,** On one of my early visits to Hatteras a young man asked: "Wont you make a picture of my may and me?" **1952** Brown *NC Folkl.* 1.564, *May. . .* A maid, a girl.

mayapple n

1 A plant *(Podophyllum peltatum)* with a globular yellow fruit and spreading leaves that is widely distributed in the eastern two-thirds of the US; also its root or edible fruit. **widespread exc West; less freq NEast, Sth** See Map Also called **billy apple, bitter ~, citron 1, cunnywobble, devil's apple 2, duck's foot 1, ground lemon, hog apple 1, Indian apple 1, ~ physic 5, June apple 3, love apple 2, mandarin ~, mandrake, mayflower 7, maypop 2, mayroot, parasols, raccoon berry, umbrella leaf, ~ plant, vegetable calomel, ~ mercury, wild jalap, ~ lemon, yellowberry, yellowroot**

1730 in 1731 *Royal Soc. London Philos. Trans. for 1729–1730* 36.428 **NC,** *Anapodophyllon Canadense Morini . .* May-Apple. **1795** Winterbotham *Amer. U.S.* 3.517, Podophyllum *peltatum,* foliis peltatis palmatis, May apple, is lately coming into practice as a laxative by an extract of the root that removes its emetic quality. **1849** Howitt *Our Cousins in OH* 82, They brought home the May-apple in full bloom. It is a handsome plant, . . with its large, white blossom, . . and . . large umbrella-like leaves. **1877** Still *Early Recoll.* 207 **cwNJ,** I have found the May-apple root, used as a purgative, to answer every purpose for which calomel is given, in acting on the liver. **1886** *Harper's New Mth. Mag.* 73.58 **seKY,** A local store-keeper told the people . . to go out and gather all the mandrake or 'May-apple' root they could find. **1890** (1895) Riley *Rhymes of Childhood* 32 **cIN,** And will any poet sing / Of a lusher, richer thing / Than a ripe Mayapple, rolled / Like a pulpy lump of gold / Under thumb and finger-tips,/ And poured molten through the lips. **1903** *DN* 2.320 **seMO,** *May-apple. . .* Mandrake. **1950** *WELS* **WI** (*Other names in your locality for the mayapple*) 5 Infs, Mayapple; (*Small plants, shaped like an umbrella, that grow in woods and fields*) 3 Infs, Mayapple(s). **1954** *Harder Coll.* **cwTN,** Mayapple. . . Plant and fruit. If a person eats Mayapple, can't make another crop, bad luck. **1965–70** *DARE* (*Qu. S4, . . Mayapple: [Woodside plant, not a tree, with two large spreading leaves; they grow in patches and have a small yellow fruit late in summer]*) 115 Infs, **widespread exc West; less freq NEast, Sth,** Mayapple(s); **KY21,** Mayapple root—used to be dug for two cents a pound to be sold for medicine; (*Qu. I46, . . Kinds of fruits that grow wild around here*) 17 Infs, **chiefly Midl,** Mayapple(s); **KY74,** Mayapple—kind of a sour whang; (*Qu. I37, Small plants shaped like an umbrella that grow in woods and fields—which are safe to eat*) Infs **IL31, 37, 124, 134, MS59, MO8, PA70, 128, TN26,** Mayapple(s); (*Qu. I38, Small plants shaped like an umbrella that grow in woods and fields—which are not safe to eat*) Inf **IL124,** Mayapples; (*Qu. S2*) Infs

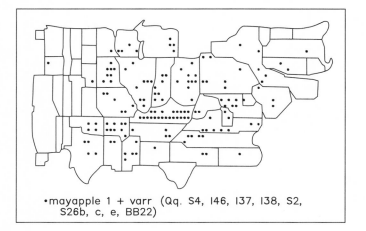

•mayapple 1 + varr (Qq. S4, I46, I37, I38, S2, S26b, c, e, BB22)

IL67, 83, IN83, MI93, MO17, NE9, OK1, PA77, Mayapple; (*Qu. S26b*) Infs **NY75, TX32,** Mayapple; (*Qu. S26c, Wildflowers that grow in woods*) Infs **IA8, IL67, IN54, 76, KY11, 21, 35, 40,** Mayapple(s); (*Qu. S26e, Other wildflowers not yet mentioned;* not asked in early QRs) Infs **KY21, SC31,** Mayapple; (*Qu. BB22, . . Home remedies . . for constipation*) Infs **VA42,** Mayapple root; **GA9,** Mayapple tea; **MD17,** Mayapple-root tea. **1966–68** *DARE* FW Addit **NY15,** Mayapple—mandrake; **VA1,** Mayapple—roots medicinal; **VA15,** Mayapple—woods, common. **1976** Lynn–Vecsey *Loretta Lynn* 18 **eKY** (as of 1930s), One time she made a tea from the mayapple root, but instead of using the female mayapple she used the male. It gave one of the kids a stomachache for days. **1986** Pederson *LAGS Concordance,* 14 infs, **Lower Missip Valley,** Mayapple(s); 8 infs, 7 **TN,** Mayapple root(s).

2 =**maypop 1;** also its fruit. **esp S Atl, Inland Sth**

1775 (1962) Romans *Nat. Hist. FL* 94, They [=Creek Indians] also prepare a cake of the pulp of the species of the *passi flora,* vulgarly called may apple. **1830** Rafinesque *Med. Flora* 2.250, *P[assiflora] incarnata* called May apple, fruit yellow as large as an egg, pulp like jelly. **1869** Porcher *Resources* 21 **Sth,** *Podophyllum. . .* should be distinguished from the "may-apple," or may-pop of our corn fields. (See *Passiflora*). *Ibid* 82, *May* apples; may pops; passion flowers, (Passiflora *lutea* and *incarnata . .*). The fruit of these beautiful climbing plants . . , sometimes called may apple . . , contains a sweetish, acid pulp, and is eatable. **1937** in 1972 *Amer. Slave* 2.96 **SC,** Molasses was made from watermelons in time of de war. Dey was also made from May-apples or may-pops as some call dem. **1954** *Harder Coll.* **cwTN,** Mayapple. . . Fruit of the *Passiflora incarnata.* **1986** Pederson *LAGS Concordance,* 1 inf, **cwTN,** Mayapple—can be eaten off the vine; 1 inf, **neMS,** Mayapple—vine, sweet things on it.

3 =**swamp apple** (here: *Exobasidium* spp). Cf **mock mayapple, cedar apple, huckleberry ~, oak ~**

1872 Schele de Vere *Americanisms* 400, The same term of *May-Apple* is not unfrequently applied to a large, globular excrescence produced by the sting of a wasp on the miniature flowers of the swamp honeysuckle (Azalea mediflora), and, on account of its frequent occurrence, occasionally for the shrub itself. **1892** Gibson *Sharp Eyes* 58, Few New England boys need to be told what the May-apple is—the *real* May-apple of the swamp-pinks . . , not the yellow tomato-like affair known as the May-apple in the States farther south and west, and which the doctors and botanists call *Podophyllum. . .* The May-apple which hangs among the clusters of the wild, fragrant pink swamp-azaleas has no mission in the world but to melt in the mouth of the eager, thirsty small boy. **1897** *Jrl. Amer. Folkl.* 10.148 **NJ,** *Exobasidium,* sp., May apple. **1901** Lounsberry *S. Wild Flowers* 379, There grows we remember on the azaleas a fleshy ball called the May, or swamp apple. **1939** Medsger *Edible Wild Plants* 154, On the leaves or twigs of the Azalea [=*Rhododendron nudiflorum*] there often appears an irregular growth an inch or two across. . . These May apples, as they are sometimes called, are excellent for pickling with spiced vinegar and have been used for that purpose since Pilgrim days. . . They are usually at their best near the end of May. **1965–70** *DARE* (*Qu. S4, Other names around here for the mayapple: [Woodside plant, not a tree, with two large spreading leaves; they grow in patches and have a small yellow fruit late in summer]*) Infs **CT26, MA40, NY205, RI15, 17, VT10,** Swamp apple. [*DARE* Ed: This resp to Qu. S4 probably refers to *Exobasidium* spp and hence implies familiarity with the term *mayapple* in the same sense.]]

4 A rhododendron, esp *Rhododendron nudiflorum.*

1872 [see **3** above]. **1881** Vanderbilt *Social Flatbush* 293 **NY,** Mayapple, or "Pinkster bloomitje," as the Dutch people called it, was abundant early in the season. **1910** Graves *Flowering Plants* 308 **CT,** *Rhododendron nudiflorum. . .* Pinxter Flower. May Apple. **1965–70** *DARE* (*Qu. S26d, Wildflowers that grow in meadows;* not asked in early QRs) Inf **NJ29,** Pinsters [*sic*]—they're mayapples; [[(*Qu. S4, Other names around here for the mayapple: [Woodside plant, not a tree, with two large spreading leaves; they grow in patches and have a small yellow fruit late in summer]*) Inf **CT2,** Azalea; **MA39,** Wild azalea; **NJ29,** Pinkster, wild azalea; **SC7,** Lowbush wild azalea; **MA14,** May pink; **MA39, VT10,** Swamp pink [*DARE* Ed: These responses to Qu. S4 probably refer to *Rhododendron* spp and hence imply familiarity with the term *mayapple* in the same sense.]]

5 A waxmallow (here: *Malvaviscus arboreus* var *drummondii*). **TX**

1891 Coulter *Botany W. TX* 43, *M[alvaviscus] Drummondii. . .* A very handsome plant, known as "may-apple." The scarlet fruit, produced in late summer, is eaten both raw and cooked. **1946** Reeves–Bain *Flora TX* 69, May Apple, Texas Mallow. . . Fruits thicker than long, depressed at both ends, showy red, mostly 1–2 cm. thick, resembling miniature apples. **1960** Vines *Trees SW* 742, *Malvaviscus drummondii.* . . Vernacular names are Texas Mallow, . . May Apple. . . The small, apple-like fruit is edible, either raw or cooked, and has a mealy taste.

6 A vanilla leaf (here: *Achlys triphylla*).
1896 *Jrl. Amer. Folkl.* 9.180 **CA, WA,** *Achlys triphylla,* . . May apple.

7 =calico bush 1.
1941 *LANE* Map 249, 1 inf, **swCT,** We tried to call the laurel [=*Kalmia latifolia*] our state flower, but I don't know as it is. Right or wrong, we used to speak of it as the mayapple. **1986** Pederson *LAGS Concordance,* 1 inf, **swTN,** Mayapple—plant, same as mountain laurel.

8 A hawthorn. Cf apple haw, mayhaw 1
1965–70 *DARE* (Qu. I46, . . *Kinds of fruits that grow wild around here*) Inf **NJ1,** Mayapple—eastern in bush form, several flowers per plant, apples turn yellow in summer; **NY52,** Mayapples—grow on a thorn bush but we don't eat them; (Qu. S4, *Other names around here for the mayapple: [Woodside plant, not a tree, with two large spreading leaves; they grow in patches and have a small yellow fruit late in summer]*) Inf **AR2,** Mayapple—bush; [**IA41, MI9,** Hawthorn (apple); **FL7, 20, GA11, 12, 28, MS6, OK20,** Mayhaw(s); **MI15,** Thornapple [*DARE* Ed: These responses to Qu. S4 probably refer to *Crataegus* spp and hence imply familiarity with the term *mayapple* in the same sense.]]

may-ball tree n
A **magnolia 1.**
1968 *DARE* (Qu. T15, . . *Kinds of swamp trees*) Inf **LA22,** May-ball tree—magnolia.

May basket n Also *May Day basket* **scattered, but esp Nth, N Midl, Plains States** See Map
A small gift basket, usu filled with flowers or candy and left at a friend's door on May Day.
1842 (1927) Rodman *Diary* 235 **MA,** The little girls for the last two days have had the pleasant excitement attending the giving and receiving may baskets of flowers, attended with the usual mystery to heighten the zest. **1869** Fuller *Uncle John* 43 **NEng,** We found the contents of the May-baskets carefully preserved in vases on the library table. **1899** Champlin–Bostwick *Young Folks' Games* 487, [These customs] are not observed to-day as they were fifty years ago, but in New England the hanging of May-baskets is still common. **1948** Coatsworth *South Shore* 64 **MA,** In the early morning one may see May baskets filled with flowers or candy, hung to door knockers. **1950** *WELS* **WI** (*What do you call the night of May first?*) 8 Infs, May-basket night; 1 Inf, May-basket eve; 2 Infs, Night for hanging May baskets. **1965–70** *DARE* (Qu. FF12b, . . *The night of May first*) 42 Infs, **chiefly Nth, N Midl,** May-basket night; 37 Infs, **chiefly Nth, N Midl,** May basket(s); **CA209, CO43, ME11,** (Children) give May baskets; **PA32,** May baskets of flowers; **CT16,** May baskets—rarely; **MN6,** May baskets, maypole; **IA13,** May-basket day; **IL5, KS15,** May-basket evening; **IA38,** May-basket time; **WA1,** May Day baskets hung on doorknob; (Qu. FF12a, . . *The first day of May*) Infs **CT23, IA41, IL60, ME15, MO10, 15, MA29, NC9,** May-basket day. **1966** York Co. *Coast Star* (Kennebunk ME) 28 Apr 8/1, Maybaskets are now on sale. **1969** *DARE* Tape **MA29,** [Inf:] [Children would] go around, just dusk and. . . put the May basket at the door and then run. . . [FW:] What did they put in them? [Inf:] Candy or nuts, animal crackers or something like that. **1978** *UpCountry* May 46 **ME** (as of c1910), The month [=May] was special because of Maybarskets, skun knees, romance, and discovering clothes lines. **1994**

DARE File, In the small town where I grew up in SW. Iowa we "hung" May baskets on May 1. A small container, maybe a nut cup, was filled with a few flowers (violets were best) and a little candy. These were delivered after ringing the doorbell. If the donor was caught she or he got kissed. When we moved to Ames—about 80 miles away I helped my 3 yr. old make May baskets. No one there had ever heard of the idea.

maybe adv Usu |ˈmebi|; also |ˈmɛbi| *Pronc-spp* mebbe, mebby
Std senses, var forms.
1815 Humphreys *Yankey in England* 106, *Meb-be,* may be. **1861** Holmes *Venner* 2.188 **wMA,** When he comes back, mebbe he'll tell ye whar he's gone tew! **1899** Garland *Boy Life* 140 **nwIA** (as of c1870s), The town boy doubled his fists, "Mebbe you want to fight me." **1901** Harben *Westerfelt* 13 **nGA,** Mebby it 'll give you courage. **1935** Sandoz *Jules* 31 **wNE** (as of 1880–1930), Mebby, but they's talk of the railroad coming through, an' the womenfolks wants to live clost to town. **1938** Rawlings *Yearling* 12 **nFL,** I'd . . mebbe have time to set. **1959** *VT Hist.* 27.148, Maybe [ˈmɛbɪ]. . . Common. **1969** *DARE* FW Addits **MA14, 40,** Maybe [ˈmɛbi]. **1982** Barrick Coll. **csPA,** Mebbe.

May bee n
=June bug 1.
1899 Bergen *Animal Lore* 63 **nwMA,** May-bees, . . June-bugs, *Lachnosterna.*

May beetle n [*OED* 1720 →; see quot 1852] **chiefly Nth Cf May bug 1**
=June bug 1.
1838 MA Zool. & Bot. Surv. *Repts. Zool.* 65, The Melolonthae are known in England by the names of *dorrs* or *chaffers* [sic], and in this country, by those of *dorr-bugs,* and *may-beetles.* **1852** Harris *Treatise Insects* 25 **NEng,** During the month of May they come forth from the ground, whence they have received the name of May-bugs, or May-beetles. **1871** IL Dept. Ag. *Trans. for 1869–1870* 8.172, The manure is . . instrumental in breeding the white-grub (May-beetle) which often ruins our meadows and strawberry beds. **c1930** Brown *Amer. Folkl. Insect Lore* 4 **WI,** June-bugs, or May beetles, were disliked and feared, especially by girls and women, because of the delight which they were suppos'd [sic] to take in getting entangled in their hair. **1950** *WELS* (*Big brown beetle that comes out* . . *between spring and summer and flies with a buzzing sound*) 4 Infs, **WI,** May beetle. **1966–68** *DARE* (Qu. R5) Infs **IA6, NH5, OH82,** May beetle; **WI20,** May beetle—turns into a grub; (Qu. R30) Infs **NY22, TX5,** May beetle. **1986** Pederson *LAGS Concordance,* 1 inf, **ceAR,** May beetles is the worst.

maybell n
1 A lily of the valley 1 (here: *Convallaria majalis*). **esp WI**
1950 *WELS* (*Other names in your locality for the lily of the valley*) 2 Infs, **seWI,** Maybells; 1 Inf, **ceWI,** Maybell. **1959** Carleton *Index Herb. Plants* 79, May bells: *Convallaria majus.* **1992** *DARE* File **seWI** (as of c1956), My mother, who grew up in Milwaukee, always referred to lilies of the valley as maybells. It was the only word I had for them.
2 A marsh marigold (here: *Caltha palustris*).
1967 *DARE* (Qu. S22, . . *The bright yellow flowers that bloom in clusters in marshes in early springtime*) Inf **MI69,** Maybells.
3 A harebell 1.
1969 *DARE* (Qu. S26a, . . *Wildflowers.* . . *Roadside flowers*) Inf **CA126,** Maybell—same as harebell.

mayberry n
1 A berry such as a blueberry 1 or a dewberry 1; see quots. esp TX
1960 Vines *Trees SW* 826, A vernacular name [for *Vaccinium elliottii*] is Mayberry. **1967** *DARE* (Qu. I44, *What kinds of berries grow wild around you?*) Inf **LA3,** Mayberries—a lot like dewberries but come in between them and blackberries; **TX99,** Mayberries. **1986** Pederson *LAGS Concordance,* 8 infs, 6 **TX,** Mayberry (or mayberries).
2 A serviceberry (here: *Amelanchier canadensis*). Cf **May cherry**
1898 *Plant World* 2.14, Mayberry (as well as Juneberry), for *Amelanchier Canadensis.*

maybeso adv Cf **may so**
Perhaps.
1919 *DN* 5.38 **OK** [Engl of Cherokee Indians], Maybe-so me go work, too. **1921** Haswell *Daughter Ozarks* 44 (as of 1880s), Maybeso some on 'em had old scores and gredges of their own. **1956** Almirall *From*

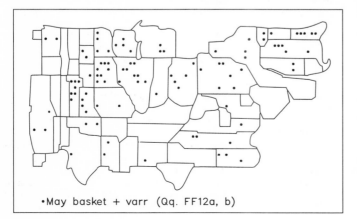
•May basket + varr (Qq. FF12a, b)

College 293 **CO,** Maybeso I oughter phone Rooster to ride up on the road, hunh?

maybird n

1 =dickcissel. *obs*

1791 Bartram *Travels* 291 **Atlantic,** Calandra pratensis [=*Spiza americana*], the May bird. **1951** [see **5** below].

2 =bobolink B. [See quot 1941] **chiefly S Atl, esp SC**

1823 in 1945 Easterby *SC Rice Plantation* 61, The field on the main next to Coachmans was ruined by the may-birds; there is scarcely any rice in it. **1859** (1968) Bartlett *Americanisms* 41, Popular names by which it [=the bobolink] is known in different parts of the country are Rice-bird, . . May-bird [etc]. **1903** in 1961 Pringle *Woman Rice Planter* 12 **GA,** Rice planted between these seasons falls a prey to birds,—Maybirds in the spring and rice-birds in August. **1937** Heyward *Madagascar* 32 **sSC,** The May birds would not remain in the rice fields longer than two weeks. . . By the tenth of September these same little birds would be back again. They had changed their plumage and were known as rice birds. [Footnote:] In Maryland and Delaware these birds are called reed birds, and in New England they are known as bobolinks. **1941** Writers' Program *Guide SC* 389, Rice birds, . . locally called May-birds, because of the time of their arrival, . . settled in chattering multitudes on the growing rice. **1951** [see **5** below]. **1962** Imhof *AL Birds* 497, Bobolink. . . Maybird.

3 A **knot** n[2] (here: *Calidris canutus*).

1838 Audubon *Ornith. Biog.* 4.132, In that country [=SC] it is called the "May Bird," which, however, is a name also given to the Rice Bird. **1844** DeKay *Zool. NY* 2.244, In its spring dress it [=*Tringa canutus*] is called *May-bird.* **1895** Elliot *N. Amer. Shore Birds* 63, The Knot. . . is known by many names . . , a few of which are: Red Sandpiper, . . May Bird, Robin Snipe [etc]. **1951** [see **5** below].

4 =redwing blackbird.

1968 *DARE* (Qu. Q11, . . *Kinds of blackbirds*) Inf **GA**28, Maybird—same as ricebird (black with red on wings).

5 Any of several other birds; see quot.

1951 *AmSp* 26.271, May, by all odds the most popular of these prefixes, is used to indicate the period in which the species is most often seen or heard. Thus *May bird* denotes the turnstone in Delaware and South Carolina, the knot or robin snipe in the latter state, the long-billed curlew in Nebraska, the great crested flycatcher (S.C.), bobolink (S.C., Ga., Fla.), goldfinch (S.C.), and dickcissel (Pa., formerly).

May breakfast n NEng

A social breakfast held on or near May Day.

1968–70 *DARE* (Qu. FF12b, . . *The night of May first*) Inf **MA**82, May breakfast; (Qu. FF16, . . *Local contests or celebrations*) Inf **CT**12, May breakfast—first Saturday in May, mostly for lodges. **1989** *Providence Jrl.* (RI) 1 Jan sec C 1, May breakfasts are Rhode Island, but power lunches aren't. **1989** *DARE* File **RI** (as of 1950), May breakfast: the johnny-cake breakfasts churches sponsor the first day of May.

May bug n

1 =June bug 1. [*OED* 1698 →] **esp N Cent** See Map Cf **May beetle**

1835 *Harvardiana* 1.314, The multiplicity of May-bugs . . rendered writing by candle-light highly inconvenient. **1852** [see **May beetle**]. **1861** in 1865 IL State Ag. Soc. *Trans.* 5.411, The *L[achnosterna] quercina,* or "May-bug," prevails in Northern Illinois. **1882** (1903) Treat

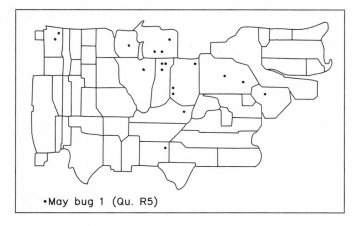

•May bug 1 (Qu. R5)

Injurious Insects 73, The frequent White Grub and the familiar May-bug, or June-bug, or Dor-bug, are different forms of the same insect. **1931–33** *LANE Worksheets,* 1 inf, **swRI,** Maybug = Junebug. **1965–70** *DARE* (Qu. R5, *A big brown beetle that comes out in large numbers in spring and early summer, and flies with a buzzing sound*) 18 Infs, **esp N Cent,** May bug.

2 =mayfly 1.

1950 *WELS* (*A large winged insect that hatches in summer in great numbers around lakes or rivers, crowds around lights, lives only a day or so, and is good fish bait*) 1 Inf, **seWI,** May bugs. **1966–68** *DARE* (Qu. R4) Infs **MO**21, **PA**77, May bug(s); **MA**6, May bug—white, come out suddenly on Northampton bridge.

3 =firefly 1.

1939 *LANE* Map 238 (*Lightning bug*) 1 inf, **seMA,** May bug.

may can See **may** v **B1**

May cherry n Cf mayberry 2

A **serviceberry,** usu *Amelanchier canadensis.*

1884 Sargent *Forests of N. Amer.* 84, *Amelanchier Canadensis.* . . June Berry. Shad Bush. Service Tree. May Cherry. **1901** Lounsberry *S. Wild Flowers* 249, *A[melanchier] Canadensis.* . . May-cherry. . . Those that find it eat it as eagerly as they would cherries. It is even made into pies. **1933** Small *Manual SE Flora* 635, *Amelanchier* [spp]. . . Juneberries. Service-berries. May-cherries. **1952** Taylor *Plants Colonial Days* 75, Common names are Juneberry, shadblow, and May cherry.

maycock n [See quot 1951]

=black-bellied plover.

1888 Trumbull *Names of Birds* 192, [The black-bellied plover is] known also at West Barnstable, Mass., as *May cock.* **1917** (1923) *Birds Amer.* 1.256, Black-bellied plover. . . May Cock. **1951** *AmSp* 26.271, May, by all odds the most popular of these prefixes, is used to indicate the period in which the species is most often seen or heard. . . Of similar time significance [is] . . *May cock* (black-bellied plover, Mass.)

may could See **may** v **B1**

May Day basket See **May basket**

may did See **may** v **B3**

mayfish n

A **killifish 1** (here: *Fundulus majalis*).

1787 Gesellschaft Naturforschender Freunde *Schriften* 8.173 **NY,** *Mayfish.* . . Diese Fische. . . wurden im Ost-River bey Neuyork . . gefangen. [=*Mayfish.* . . These fish. . . were caught in the East River at New York.] **1879** U.S. Natl. Museum *Bulletin* 14.56, *Hydrargyra majalis.* . . *May-fish.* Brackish waters; Cape Ann to Cape Hatteras. **1896** *Ibid* 47.639, *Fundulus majalis.* . . Killifish; *Mayfish.* . . Abundant in shallow bays. . . (*majalis,* pertaining to May, translation of Mayfish). **1905** NJ State Museum *Annual Rept. for 1904* 185, *Fundulus majalis.* . . May Fish. [*Ibid* 188, About Cape May they were abundant, . . though not many were taken in the surf.] **1911** U.S. Bur. Census *Fisheries 1908* 312, Along the eastern coast they are known as "mayfish," "killifish," and "fundulus." **1991** Amer. Fisheries Soc. *Common Names Fishes* 149, Mayfish—see striped killifish.

mayflower n [Usu from the time of blossoming]

1 =arbutus. chiefly NEast

1778 Carver *Travels N. Amer.* 520, May Flowers, Jessamine, Honeysuckles, Rock Honeysuckles. . . I shall not enter into a minute description of the flowers above-recited. **1840** *S. Lit. Messenger* 6.518 **ME,** The little May-flower, earliest and sweetest of our forest-flowers, has passed away. **1854** King *Amer. Eclectic Dispensatory* 447, *Epigea repens.* Trailing Arbutus. . . This plant has several names as *Winter-pink, Gravel-weed, Mountain-pink, Ground Laurel, May-flower,* etc. **1885** Howells *Rise Lapham* 71 **ceMA,** The tints of her cheeks and temples were such as suggested May-flowers and apple-blossoms. **1903** *DN* 2.299 **Cape Cod MA** (as of a1857), *Mayflower.* . . Arbutus. **1926** *DN* 5.388 **ME,** *Mayflowers.* . . Trailing arbutus *only.* Common. **1944** Holton *Yankees Were Like This* 145 **Cape Cod MA** (as of c1890), The mayflower season was always too short, but there was the compensation of knowing the number of days to the end of school was growing beautifully less. **1965–70** *DARE* (Qu. S26c, *Wildflowers that grow in woods*) 13 Infs, **esp NEast,** Mayflower; **MI**120, Mayflower—a small white flower, 5-petaled; **MA**78, Trailing arbutus, mayflower—same; (Qu. S2) Inf **MI**65, Trillium . . looks like a lily. . . and . . is different from what is called the mayflower here; **NJ**8, Mayflowers—windflower, . . arbutus; (Qu. S4) Inf **MA**25, Mayflower—trailing arbutus;

PA89, Mayflower also refers to arbutus; PA234, Mayflower—5-petal blossoms yellow and pink and white; (Qu. S26a, . . *Wildflowers. . . Roadside flowers*) Inf **MN**12, Mayflower—pink flower, very common here—blossoms in May; **MA**5, Mayflower = arbutus; (Qu. S26b, *Wildflowers that grow in water or wet places*) Infs **MI**34, **MA**6, Mayflower = arbutus; (Qu. S26e, *Other wildflowers not yet mentioned;* not asked in early QRs) Infs **NY**106, **PA**225, Mayflower(s); **MA**100, Mayflower = trailing arbutus; **MI**31, Arbutus . . some people here call them mayflowers. **1966–68** *DARE* Wildfl QR Pl.153B Inf **MI**31, Mayflower around here; **NY**91, Called mayflower in Massachusetts along the coast; **OH**14, Mayflower. **1979** *Greenfield Recorder* (MA) 22 Sept sec A 4/2, So many of those old graveyards have weeds, short sparse grass, maybe some checkerberries and dew berries and mayflower leaves that snakes seem to like as a place to sun themselves.

2 =pinkster flower. esp NY, NJ

1838 Loudon *Arboretum Britannicum* 2.1140, *Rhododendron nudiflorum*. . . the American Honeysuckle; May Flowers. **1894** *Jrl. Amer. Folkl.* 7.93 NJ, *Rhododendron nudiflorum*. . . Mayflower. **1924** *Amer. Botanist* 30.59, Chief of these is the "Mayflower" or "wild honeysuckle" (*Azalea nudiflora*). **1968–69** *DARE* (Qu. S26b, *Wildflowers that grow in water or wet places*) Inf **NY**75, Swamp apple or mayflower—not same as mandrake or mayapple; (Qu. S26e, *Other wildflowers not yet mentioned;* not asked in early QRs) Inf **NY**223, Pinksters—wild azalea, also called mayflower. **1968** *DARE* Wildfl QR Pl.154 **NY**91, Mayflower—common name here. **1969** *DARE* Tape **NY**223, Pinksters. . . Really, it's wild azalea, and some of the family, the older ones in the family, called those mayflowers.

3 Any of var plants of the family Ranunculaceae, as:

a An anemone, usu *Anemone caroliniana* or *A. quinquefolia.*

1892 *Jrl. Amer. Folkl.* 5.91 MA, *Anemone nemorosa*. . . Mayflower. Boston. **1893** *Ibid* 6.136 eMA, *Anemone nemorosa,* Mayflower. **1896** *Ibid* 9.179 SD, *Anemone Caroliniana,* . . mayflower, Burnside, S. Dak. **1910** Graves *Flowering Plants* 190 CT, *Anemone quinquefolia*. . . Wood or Spring Anemone. Mayflower. . . An acrid poison with medicinal properties. **1920** Packard *Old Plymouth* 19 seMA, In localities where the arbutus is not common the name mayflower is here most commonly given to the pink and white Anemone nemorosa, the wind flower of the meadow margins and low woods, and to the rock saxifrage, Saxifraga virginiensis, both of which are among the earliest blossoms of the month. **1949** *WELS Suppl.* neIL, We also found "Wind flowers." . . They were delicate, small blossoms—pale pink, white, or sometimes, a faint lavender pink—and grew on the most slender, threadlike stems, with frail, serrate little leaves. There was absolutely no fuzziness on stems or leaves. . . I believe we sometimes called them "Mayflowers," too. *Ibid* cWI, Wood anemone was called Mayflower. Rue anemone, less abundant, was also a Mayflower. **1950** *Ibid* csWI, Mayflower—wood anemone. **1968–69** *DARE* (Qu. S2) Inf **MI**82, Anemone, mayflowers; **NJ**8, Mayflowers—windflower, . . arbutus; (Qu. S26c, *Wildflowers that grow in woods*) Inf **RI**12, Anemones—used to be called mayflower; (Qu. S26d, *Wildflowers that grow in meadows;* not asked in early QRs) Inf **NY**211, Mayflower—small, April, white and pink.

b =pasqueflower. chiefly Upper MW

1892 (1974) Millspaugh *Amer. Med. Plants* 1-1, *Pulsatilla patens*. . . Com[mon] Names. Pasque flower, . . may flower [etc]. [*Ibid* 1-2, The American pasque flower is found in abundance upon the prairies from Wisconsin northward, and westward to the Rocky Mountains, flowering from March to April.] **1906** Rydberg *Flora CO* 440, May-flower *(Pulsatilla)*. **1937** U.S. Forest Serv. *Range Plant Hdbk.* W159, Although pasqueflower is the common name most widely used, such other appellations as . . Mayflower . . have variously designated this species. **1949** *WELS Suppl.,* In northern Minnesota it [=pasqueflower] is called the May flower, because it blooms there in May. **1966–68** *DARE* (Qu. S3) Inf **ND**9, Crocus or mayflower—also called pasqueflower; **SD**2, Mayflower; (Qu. S23) Inf **SD**2, Pale blue flowers with downy leaves and cups that come up on open, stony hillsides in March or early April) Infs **MN**30, 42, Crocus, mayflower; **MN**38, Pasqueflowers, *Anemone patens,* mayflower; **ND**9, **SD**3, Pasqueflowers, crocus, mayflower(s); **SD**2, Mayflowers; (Qu. S26a, . . *Other wildflowers*) Inf **IA**22, Mayflower—white or violet-colored—5 petals; (Qu. S26d, *Wildflowers that grow in meadows;* not asked in early QRs) Inf **MN**34, Mayflower—a small . . flower, blooms in early spring.

c =rue anemone.

1893 *Jrl. Amer. Folkl.* 6.136 eMA, *Anemonella thalictroides,* Mayflower. **1940** Clute *Amer. Plant Names* 1, *A[nemonella] thalictroides.* Rue Anemone. Mayflower. **1949** [see **3a** above]. **1959** Carleton *Index Herb.* Plants 80, *May-flower:* Anemonella thalictroides; Anemone

pulsatilla (Pulsatilla vulgaris); Cardamine pratensis; Convallaria majus; Epigaea repens; Hepatica triloba; Maianthemum bifolium; Saxifraga virginica[.] Although the above species are those most commonly identified as May-flowers, practically any species flowering in that month can [be] and is identified by that.

d =hepatica. chiefly NEast Cf blue mayflower

[**1892** *Jrl. Amer. Folkl.* 5.91, *Hepatica triloba*. . . Mayflower. Hemmingford, P[rovince] Q[uebec].] **1897** *Ibid* 10.49 cME, The hepatica is called mayflower in Norridgewock, Me. **1913** *DN* 4.54 sNY, *Mayflower*. . . The liverwort (*Hepatica triloba*). **1929** Burgess *Wild Flowers* 6, One of the brave little flowers of the early spring is the Hepatica, which in some places is called the Mayflower. **1948** Peattie *Berkshires* 44 wMA, Here in Berkshire hepatica is sometimes called Mayflower, a name reserved in other regions for the arbutus. **1965–70** *DARE* (Qu. S3) Infs **ME**14, **MD**42, **PA**216, Mayflowers; **NY**88, Mayflower—they're bluish-white; **NY**92, Mayflower has leaves like ace of clubs; the flowers come up in the middle—cup-shaped blossoms; **NY**142, Mayflower, capatica [sic]; (Qu. S4) Inf **NY**126, Mayflower, nepatica [sic]; (Qu. S23) Infs **NJ**1, **NY**84, Mayflowers; **MI**102, **PA**176, Mayflower(s), hepatica(s); (Qu. S26c, *Wildflowers that grow in woods*) Infs **VT**16, **WI**68, Mayflower; **WI**50, Hepatica or mayflower; **WI**58, Hepaticas—commonly called mayflower; (Qu. S26e, *Other wildflowers not yet mentioned;* not asked in early QRs) Inf **WI**78, Mayflower—white, pink, blue; many (12) in a bunch—nicest here; this is the Washington Island name for liverwort (hepatica).

4 =spring beauty (here: *Claytonia* spp).

[**1892** *Jrl. Amer. Folkl.* 5.93, *Claytonia Virginica*. . . Mayflower. Hemmingford, P[rovince] Q[uebec].] **1900** Lyons *Plant Names* 106, *C[laytonia] Caroliniana* . . and . . *C. Virginica* . ., of the eastern U.S. are called . . May-flower. **1910** Graves *Flowering Plants* 182 CT, *Claytonia virginica*. . . Spring Beauty. Mayflower. Rich moist woods and more open places. . . April–May. **1966–68** *DARE* (Qu. S2) Inf **PA**176, Mayflower, spring beauties; (Qu. S26c, *Wildflowers that grow in woods*) Inf **MI**67, Spring beauty or mayflower. **1967** *DARE* Wildfl QR Pl.51A Inf **NY**15, Mayflower.

5 A saxifrage (here: *Saxifraga virginiensis*). **esp MA**

1892 *Jrl. Amer. Folkl.* 5.96, *Saxifraga Virginiensis,* Mayflower, Allston, Mass. **1898** *Ibid* 11.226, *Saxifraga Virginiensis,* . . Mayflower, Auburndale, Mass. **1913** *DN* 4.54, *May-flower.* . . In Connecticut, at least at Ivoryton, Deep River, and Middletown, the early saxifrage (*Saxifraga Virginiensis*) is so called. **1920** [see **3a** above]. **1959** [see **3c** above].

6 A phlox (here: *Phlox caespitosa*).

1898 *Jrl. Amer. Folkl.* 11.275 WY, *Phlox caespitosa,* . . May flowers.

7 =mayapple 1. chiefly Nth, Midl

1905 *DN* 3.87 nwAR, *Mayflower*. . . Flower of the May apple (mandrake). Common. **1928** Aldrich *Lantern* 35 NE, She went into the timber to look for anemones and Dutchmen's breeches, for dog-toothed violets and the first signs of Mayflower buds. **1940** Clute *Amer. Plant Names* 117, *P[odophyllum] peltatum*. . . Mayflower. **1965–70** *DARE* (Qu. S4, . . *Mayapple: [Woodside plant, not a tree, with two large spreading leaves; they grow in patches and have a small yellow fruit late in summer]* 49 Infs, **chiefly Nth, Midl,** Mayflower; **CT**17, Mandrake, mayflower; **CT**40, Mayflower—locally used; **IA**34, Umbrella plant, mayflower; **KY**85, Mayflower—roots were boiled to make a syrup for a poultice to put on a mule's shoulder when he got some disease in them; **MI**116, Mandrake, mayflower, umbrella plant; **NJ**4, Mayflower—fruit is light green, edible; **NY**12, Mandrake, mayflower; **NY**219, Mandrake, mayflower; **PA**191, Umbrella plant, mayflower; **VA**26, Mandrake, mayflower; **VA**34, Mayapple, mayflower; (Qu. S2) Inf **MO**17, Mayapple or mayflower; **PA**77, Mayflower, mayapple; (Qu. S26c) Infs **IL**30, **MI**104, Mayflower.

8 =bluet 2.

1910 Graves *Flowering Plants* 364 CT, *Houstonia caerulea*. . . Bluets. Innocence. Mayflower. . . April–June. **1967–69** *DARE* (Qu. S4) Inf **MI**49, The "mayflower" here is a faint purple flower, has four leaves; (Qu. S11, . . *Bluets*) Infs **NJ**6, **NY**21, 97, **PA**181, Mayflowers.

9 A penstemon such as *Penstemon acuminatus.*

1932 Rydberg *Flora Prairies* 712, *Pentstemon* [sic]. . . Beardtongue. Mayflower. **1940** Clute *Amer. Plant Names* 266, *Pentstemon* [sic] *acuminatus.* Baby-blue-eyes, Mayflower.

10 =false lily of the valley, usu *Maianthemum canadense.* Cf Canada mayflower

1931 Harned *Wild Flowers Alleghanies* 118, *False Lily-of-the-Valley (Maianthemum canadense* . .). They are sometimes called May Flowers, but this name is one to which they are not justly entitled. **1959** [see

3c above]. **1976** Bailey–Bailey *Hortus Third* 1264, Mayflower: *Cardamine pratensis, Epigaea repens, Maianthemum.*

11 A **lily of the valley 1** (here: *Convallaria majalis*). Cf **maybell 1, May lily 1**

 1940 Clute *Amer. Plant Names* 12, *C[onvallaria] majalis. Lily-of-the-valley.* Mayflower. **1959** [see **3c** above].

12 A **storksbill** (here: *Erodium cicutarium*).

 1959 Barnes *Nat. Hist. Wasatch Winter* 39 **UT**, A stiff south wind today has rapidly melted the snow . . , revealing a pleasing carpet of alfilaria. . . Locally it is called "clocks," . . or "May flower".

13 =**trillium.**

 1965–70 *DARE* (Qu. S2, . . *The flower that comes up in the woods early in spring, with three white petals that turn pink as the flower grows older*) 23 Infs, **chiefly NEast, Gt Lakes**, Mayflower; **CT**6, Mayflower (on one stalk—three petals—changes color); (Qu. S26c, *Wildflowers that grow in woods*) Inf **IL**30, Mayflower. **1967** *DARE* Wildfl QR Pl.24A Inf **NY**15, Mayflower.

14 A **pipsissewa** (here: *Chimaphila umbellata*).

 1966 *DARE* Wildfl QR Pl.152A Inf **WA**15, Mayflower.

15 =**bunchberry 1.**

 1967 *DARE* Wildfl QR Pl.150 Inf **WA**30, Mayflower.

16 A **marsh marigold** (here: *Caltha palustris*). [*EDD* 1877 →]

 1969 *DARE* (Qu. S22, . . *The bright yellow flowers that bloom in clusters in marshes in early springtime*) Inf **PA**216, Mayflowers.

17 Any of var other, sometimes unidentified, flowers; see quots.

 1959 [see **3c** above]. **1966** *Anderson Valley Advt.* (Boonville CA) 23 Mar 8/2, The early Mayflowers (possibly a more scientific name should apply) and the Wood violets, . . Cream Cups, Lady Slippers. **1968–69** *DARE* (Qu. S26a, . . *Wildflowers. . . Roadside flowers*) Inf **NV**8, Mayflower—a tiny white one close to the ground; (Qu. S26c, *Wildflowers that grow in woods*) Inf **CA**87, Mayflower—a pink, fragrant small flower; **MA**68, Mayflower—fringed.

‡**May flower day** n [Cf **May basket, mayflower**]
May Day.

 1967 *DARE* (Qu. FF12a, . . *The first day of May*) Inf **CO**35, May flower day; [(Qu. FF12b) Inf **CO**35, April 30th (night of)—hung flower baskets on the old people's door].

mayfly n

1 Std: an insect of the order Ephemeroptera. [*OED* 1651–53 →] Also called **bay fly, Canadian soldier 1, cisco fly, drake ~, dun** n, **eel fly, fish ~ 2, flying clipper, Green Bay fly, green fly 2, July fly 3, June bug 3, ~ fly 1, lake fly 1, May bug 2, Mormon fly, periwinkle, river bug, salmonfly, sand fly, shad ~, scobolotch, soldier, spindle, spinner, stickbait, taddle fly, trout ~, twenty-four-hour bug, willow fly 2** =**June bug 1.**

 1899 Bergen *Animal Lore* 63 **nwMA**, Horn-bugs, May-bees, May-flies, June-bugs, *Lachnosterna.* **1968** *DARE* (Qu. R5, *A big brown beetle that comes out in large numbers in spring and early summer, and flies with a buzzing sound*) Inf **PA**163, Mayfly.

3 Perh a **horsefly 1** or similar fly.

 1899 (1912) Green *VA Folk-Speech* 277, May-fly. . . An insect troublesome to horses in spring and summer. **1969** *DARE* (Qu. R4) Inf **GA**76, Mayfly—woolly fly is the same. **1986** Pederson *LAGS Concordance (Stinging insect)* 1 inf, **ceGA**, Mayflies.

maygrass n

A **canary grass** (here: *Phalaris caroliniana*).

 1950 Gray–Fernald *Manual of Botany* 185, *P[halaris] caroliniana.* . . Maygrass.

mayhall See **mayhaw 1**

mayhap adv Pronc-sp *mayhep* old-fash
Perhaps, maybe.

 1843 (1916) Hall *New Purchase* 148 **IN**, I kept creeping slowly along till I'd got from home, mayhap, a matter of two miles. **1872** Burnham *Memoirs U.S. Secret Service* 80 **NYC**, Come to the 'break o' day drum' . . and mayhap I'll p'int him out to yer. **1903** *DN* 2.352 **neOH**, Mayhap. . . Pronounced mayhep. **1938** Matschat *Suwanee R.* 64 **neFL, seGA**, Mayhap ye might git a gator.

mayhaw n

1 also *mayhall, mayhull, mayhour, May hawthorn;* A **hawthorn** native to the southern US: usu *Crataegus aestivalis*, but also *C. opaca.* For other names of the former see **apple haw, summer haw**

 1868 *Amer. Naturalist* 2.468 **TX**, They [=deer] visit the ponds in which the May-haw grows, the fruit of which is juicy with the flavor of the apple. **1884** Sargent *Forests of N. Amer.* 82, May Haw. Apple haw. . . The large, globular, fragrant, red fruit, of agreeable subacid flavor, used as a preserve, in jellies, etc.; ripening in May. **1901** Lounsberry *S. Wild Flowers* 250, *C[rataegus] aestivalis*, May haw, is a tree sometimes twenty or thirty feet tall. . . During May the markets of many southern towns dispose of large quantities of the fruit. **1908** Britton *N. Amer. Trees* 473, The May haw occurs in shallow ponds in the pinelands, and on low banks of streams from South Carolina to northern Florida and west to southern Arkansas and the Sabine River, Texas. **1938** Rawlings *Yearling* 118 **nFL**, He concentrated on light bread and mayhaw jelly. **1960** Vines *Trees SW* 338, May Hawthorn. . . This [=*Crataegus opaca*] is the famous May Haw of the South, from which preserves are made. **1965–70** *DARE* (Qu. I46, . . *Kinds of fruits that grow wild around here*) 10 Infs, **chiefly Gulf States**, Mayhaw(s); **AL**15, Mayhaw—tree fruit—[as big as] end of thumb—[grows] on bottomy place; **MS**13, Mayhall—like a berry—grows in a damp place; **GA**3, Red mayhulls—a berry on a tree; (Qu. I44, *What kinds of berries grow wild around here?*) Infs **FL**6, **LA**18, 28, 32, **MS**72, **TX**33, Mayhaws; (Qu. S4) Infs **FL**7, 20, **GA**12, 28, **MS**6, **OK**20, Mayhaw; **GA**11, Mayhour; (Qu. T15, . . *Kinds of swamp trees*) Infs **LA**14, **TX**9, 35, Mayhaw. **1980** Little *Audubon Guide N. Amer. Trees E. Region* 462, The name May Hawthorn is misleading, because the flowers are borne earlier and the fruits ripen later.

2 A **muscadine** (grape).

 1967 *DARE* File **sAL**, Mayhaw ['meɪˌhɔ]—a wild sweet grape in southern Alabama; in northern Alabama it is called scuppernong.

May hawthorn See **mayhaw 1**

mayhep See **mayhap**

may hide n [From the rhyme used in the game; see quot 1967]
=**hide-and-seek A.**

 1967 *DARE* (Qu. EE13a, *Games in which every player hides except one, and that one must try to find the others*) Inf **KY**34, May hide—"Who may hide hoopie-hide / Who ain't hid mayn't hide over." **1976** Lynn–Vecsey *Loretta Lynn* 29 **eKY**, We were playing "may-hide" out behind the school. (Most people call it "hide-and-seek" but we called it "may-hide.")

mayhop See **maypop 1**

mayhour, mayhull See **mayhaw 1**

may I n Also called **mother, may I** Cf **giant steps**
A children's game in which the other players must ask permission from "it" before performing some action, usu advancing a certain number of specified steps; see quots.

 1948 *Hoosier Folkl. Bulletin* 7.88, May I? One person is "it." The others stand in a straight line. "It" tells players they may take so many steps; they are not ordinary steps but are called scissors, elephant, baby, pin, giant, side steps, etc. If players remember to say, "May I?" they take the steps. If they forget, they go back to starting line. Sneaking steps are allowed, if "it" does not see the sneaker. If he is caught, he goes back to starting line. The one who reaches the goal first is winner, and he is "it" for the next game. **1950** *WELS Suppl.* **csWI**, May I?—Children's game: players' progress is governed by "it," who assigns various steps (giant, baby, pin, pie, elephant, scissor, camel, etc.) in certain numbers. Players *must* turn around and say "may I?" to "it" after the assignment or go back to the starting line. Both "may I?" and "red light" are followed by hiding—from then on, they are like hide-and-go-seek. **1954** *Harder Coll.* **cwTN**, May I. . . A hiding game. . . A requesting game used by teachers to teach children to say "may I" instead of "can I." **1965–70** *DARE* (Qu. EE16, *Hiding games that start with a special, elaborate method of sending the players out to hide*) 24 Infs, **scattered**, May I; **AR**18, 37, **IN**61, **MS**65, May I—not a hiding game; **PA**4, 126, May I—same as giant steps; (Qu. EE33, . . *Outdoor games . . that children play*) 11 Infs, **scattered**, May I; **AL**54, May I—one who is "it" gives directions which players follow; if one forgets to say "may I" before he moves, he must go back; **FL**28, May I—take 2 giant steps; you must say "may I" or go back; **LA**32, May I—"it" gives commands and the others have to say "may I" before proceeding; **MD**39, May I—leader directs players to take certain kinds of steps (giant, scissors, etc) toward goal; if they forget to say "may I" they must go back to the beginning point; **MI**114, May I—permission must be asked of leader to move from line; if they forget to ask, places are exchanged; **NC**63, Red light or may I—where permission is granted to go a certain distance; **OH**98, May I—with giant steps, small steps only by permission; **TX**4, May I—leader gives instruction "take 2 giant steps," etc; others must say "may I" before proceeding or return to start. **1975** Ferretti *Gt. Amer. Book Sidewalk Games* 204 **IL**, Giant Steps as it is known almost everywhere is also called . . *May I?* in Chicago. **1986** Pederson *LAGS Concordance* **Gulf Region**, 3 infs, May I? 1 inf, May I?—giant steps; 1 inf, May I?—old hiding game.

may like See **make like**

May lily n

1 A **lily of the valley 1** (here: *Convallaria majalis*). [See quot 1901; *OED* 1548, 1597 (at *lily* sb. 2)]
1832 Williamson *Hist. ME* 1.126, [We have] May-lily, or "lily of the valley;" and nodding-lily. **1876** Hobbs *Bot. Hdbk.* 69, May lily, Lily of the valley, Convallaria majalis. **1901** Lounsberry *S. Wild Flowers* 60, It is only in the higher Alleghanies that the lily-of-the-valley is found growing wild. . . By the mountaineers it is known mostly as the "May lily," in which month it begins to bloom. **1952** Taylor *Plants Colonial Days* 54, Lily of the valley is prized for the fragrance of the small, white, bell-shaped flowers. . . Blooming in April or May it is also known as May lily. **1959** Carleton *Index Herb. Plants* 80, *May-lily:* Convallaria majalis.

2 A **false lily of the valley** (here: *Maianthemum dilatatum*).
1973 Hitchcock–Cronquist *Flora Pacific NW* 692, *M[aianthemum] dilatatum.* . . May-lily, false lily-of-the-valley. . . Attractive in the wild but apt to prove a nasty pest in the native garden.

mayonnaise n Usu |ˈmeə,nez|; for addit proncs see quots Pronc-spp *manaze, my-nez* Note: The proncs |ˈmeəne, ˈmaɪneɪ| are prob back-formations from |ˈmeənez| understood as pl. Std sense, var proncs.
1966–69 *DARE* FW Addit **nwLA**, Mayonnaise [ˈmaɪ,neɪz]; **LA**40, [ˈmaɪə,neɪz, ˈmaɪ,neɪz]; **csLA**, Mayonnaise—[ˈmaɪ,nɛz] old-fashioned, [ˈmeə,neɪz] recent, [ˈme,nez] occasional; **New Orleans LA**, [ˈmaɪ,nɛz] newer pronunciation, more common now, [ˈmeɪə,nɛz] uptown local pronunciation; **wNC**, Mayonnaise [ˈmɛrə,niz]; **cnIL**, Mayonnaise [ˈmeə,ne] [*DARE* Ed: perh back-formation from [ˈmeə,nez] understood as pl]. **1981** Pederson *LAGS Basic Materials*, 1 inf, **swGA**, [ˌmaʌˈɪˈneʳɪ]; 1 inf, **cwFL**, [ˈmæˆ·ənɪs]; 1 inf, **swLA**, [ˈmãˑ·ə^n,ne^·ə^z]. **1983** Allin *S. Legislative Dict.* 17 **Sth**, *Manaze:* a salad and sandwich dressing. **1992** *DARE* File **cwCA** (as of 1950s), I remember hearing people say [ˈmæ·n,nez], but I was instructed to say [ˈmeɪ,nez]; a friend from northern California says [ˈmeɪə,nez]. **1993** Safire *Quoth the Maven* 24, A primer published in the New Orleans *Times–Picayune* defined . . *dressed* as "How you order your po-boy [sandwich]. It means with lettuce, tomato, and mayonnaise, pronounced my-nez."

mayordomo See **majordomo**

May ought to See **may** v **B4**

May pea n Also *early May* now esp NC Cf **June pea**

A **garden pea** (*Pisum sativum* var *sativum* cv).
1821 Cobbett *Amer. Gardener* 241, The earliest of all is the little white pea, called, in Long Island, the *May-Pea*, and, in England, the *early frame-pea*. **1863** Burr *Field & Garden* 544, *Early May.* . . Pea, when fully ripe, round, cream-colored, approaching to white about the eye. . . Sown May 1, the plants blossomed June 15, and pods were plucked for use July 6. . . As now found in the garden, the variety is not distinguishable from some forms of the Early Frame. **1966–70** *DARE* (Qu. I14, *Kinds of beans that you eat in the pod before they're dry*) Inf **NC**12, June peas, May peas; (Qu. I20, . . *Kinds of beans*) Inf **KY**5, May peas—small green sweet pea; **NC**8, 18, May peas; (Qu. L34, . . *Most important crops grown around here*) Inf **NC**85, Used to raise May peas. **1988** Whealy *Garden Seed Inventory* (2d ed) 265, *Peas.* . . *Early May* . . yellow round-seeded type, can also be used as yellow dry peas.

May pear n Cf **mayberry 2, May cherry**

A **serviceberry** (here: *Amelanchier canadensis*).
1900 Lyons *Plant Names* 28, *A[melanchier] Canadensis.* . . May Pear, Juice Pear, Indian Pear. **1910** Graves *Flowering Plants* 224 **CT**, *Amelanchier canadensis.* . . Sugar, Indian or May Pear.

May pink n

1 =**arbutus**. esp **NJ**

1899 *Plant World* 2.199 **NJ**, Maypink for *Epigaea repens* . . , the pink flower that blooms in May. **1968–69** *DARE* (Qu. S26a, . . *Wildflowers. . . Roadside flowers*) Inf **NJ**55, May pink; (Qu. S26c, *Wildflowers that grow in woods*) Inf **NJ**31, Trailing arbutus—May pink.

2 A **rhododendron**, such as *Rhododendron canadense* or *R. nudiflorum*. Cf **mayapple 4**

1940 Clute *Amer. Plant Names* 229, Rhodora Canadensis. Lamb-kill, May pink. **1969** *DARE* (Qu. S4, . . *Mayapple: [Woodside plant, not a tree, with two large spreading leaves; they grow in patches and have a small yellow fruit late in summer]*) Inf **MA**14, May pinks.

3 =**spring beauty** (here: *Claytonia* spp). Cf **mayflower 4**

1969 *DARE* (Qu. S26c, *Wildflowers that grow in woods*) Inf **VT**13, May pink = spring beauty; tiny, striped (white, pink stripes).

4 =**fringed polygala**. Cf **Indian pink 5, mayflower 17**

1970 *DARE* (Qu. S26e, *Other wildflowers not yet mentioned;* not asked in early QRs) Inf **MI**116, May pinks—same as Indian pinks.

May plover n

=**pectoral sandpiper**.

1923 U.S. Dept. Ag. *Misc. Circular* 13.54 **IL**, Pectoral Sandpiper. . . May-plover.

May plum n

A **wild plum** (here: *Prunus texana*).

1938 Van Dersal *Native Woody Plants* 343, Mayplum (*Prunus texana*).

maypop n

1 also *mayhop*: A plant of the genus *Passiflora*, esp *P. incarnata;* also the fruit of such a plant. [See quot 1902] **chiefly SE, Lower Missip Valley** Also called **apricot B, ground ivy 2d, Holy Trinity flower, mayapple 2, molly-pop, passionflower, pop apple**

1851 *De Bow's Rev.* 11.49 **LA**, May Pop, Passion Flower, is also abundant here. **1869** Porcher *Resources* 82 **Sth**, *May apples; may pops; passion flowers, (Passiflora lutea and incarnata . .).* The fruit of these beautiful climbing plants . . , contains a sweetish, acid pulp, and is eatable. **1887** (1967) Harris *Free Joe* 184 **cGA**, I fotch you some May-pops, too . . I never eat a one, nuther. **1902** *Jrl. Amer. Folkl.* 15.247, According to Dr. J.H. Trumbull *may-pop* is a corruption of *maracaw* or *maracock*,—rendered "apple" by some of the early writers,—the name of a fruit known to the Algonkian Indians of the Maryland–Virginia region. **1909** *DN* 3.348 **eAL, wGA**, *May-pop.* . . The passion-flower, the fruit of this plant. Universal. **1913** Morley *Carolina Mts.* 68, If you look over those fields where, in spite of the efforts of the farmer, the great blue passion-flowers bloomed all summer, you will see leathery-skinned fruits as large as a goose egg lying about by the basketful. These are maypops. **1926** *DN* 5.401 **Ozarks**, *May-pop.* . . The edible fruit of the passion-vine; sometimes called apricot. **1929** Sale *Tree Named John* 76 **MS**, Aunt Emily had covered the "co'pse" with a nice, white piece of tablecloth . . and had laid a May-pop bloom and a rosebud on it. **1953** Randolph–Wilson *Down in Holler* 264 **Ozarks**, *May-hop.* . . The passionflower vine (*Passiflora incarnata*). The term *may-pop* is reserved for the edible fruit of this vine. **1965–70** *DARE* (Qu. S4) 63 Infs, **Sth, SE**, Maypop; **AR**2, Maypop (vine); **AR**35, Maypop, passionflower—same; **FL**16, **GA**38, **NC**10, 16, 21, 24, Maypop, passionflower; **GA**70, Maypop—it pops open and you eat it; **LA**12, Maypop is the local name for passion fruit [sic]; **MS**1, Maypop—this is a vine, passionflower; **MS**70, Maypop is different: this grows on a vine; **NC**80, Maypop—you can eat 'em; **SC**67, Maypop—grown on a vine . . soft when ripe, kids eat; (Qu. S26a, . . *Wildflowers. . . Roadside flowers*) Inf **AR**52, Maypop = passionflower; (Qu. S26e, *Other wildflowers not yet mentioned;* not asked in early QRs) Infs **KY**83, **LA**33, 40, Maypop; (Qu. T16) Inf **GA**84, Maypop. [*DARE* Ed: Some of these Infs may refer instead to **2** below.] **1967** *DARE* Wildfl QR (Wills–Irwin) Pl.27A Inf **TX**34, Passionflower, wild maypop. **1970** *NC Folkl.* 18.16, Calamus root and maypops were an ideal sedative for babies with colic.

2 also *May pop-up:* =**mayapple 1**.

1946 *PADS* 6.20 **eNC** (as of 1900–10), *May pop.* . . The May apple. (*Podophyllum peltatum.*) . . Occasional among farmers about 1900. **1966–69** *DARE* (Qu. S4, . . *Mayapple: [Woodside plant, not a tree, with two large spreading leaves; they grow in patches and have a small yellow fruit late in summer]*) Infs **IL**85, **NJ**21, **PA**18, **WI**64, Maypop; **NC**6, Maypops, hog apples; **IN**1, May pop-ups; **TN**11, Maypop, mandrake; **TN**24, Maypop occasionally, but mayapple is more common. [*DARE* Ed: Some of these Infs may refer instead to **1** above.]

‡3 A fringed gentian.

1968 *DARE* (Qu. S4) Inf **AL42**, Maypop is a name for fringed gentian.

May pop-up See **maypop 2**

May queen moss n

A **haircap moss** (here: *Polytrichum juniperinum*).

1876 Hobbs *Bot. Hdbk.* 69, May queen moss, Hair-cap moss, Polytrichum Juniperum. **1900** Lyons *Plant Names* 301, P[olytrichum] juniperinum. . . May-queen moss.

mayroot n

The root of **mayapple 1**.

1966 *DARE* (Qu. BB50d, *Favorite spring tonics*) Inf **MS45**, Tea made from mayroot.

may shall See **may** v B6

may should See **may** v B5

may so adv [Perh abbr for **maybeso**]

Perhaps, probably.

1969 *DARE* (Qu. NN1, . . *Words like 'yes': "Are you coming along too?"*) Inf **KY47**, I guess, may so, sure. **1992** *NADS Letters*, May so: meaning "perhaps." One student [in Indiana] said she had heard this in Tennessee, where her mother is from.

May star n

A **chickweed wintergreen** (here: *Trientalis borealis*).

1848 in 1850 Cooper *Rural Hours* 85 **ceNY**, The May-star is remarkable for its elegance, a delicate star-like blossom of the purest white. . . Some persons call this chick wintergreen. *Ibid* 86, Discriminating people, when they find its elegant silvery flower growing in the woods beside the violet, call it May-star, and so should everybody who sees it. **1894** *Bot. Gaz.* 19.434 **NY**, *Trientalis Americana*. . . May-star. **1948** Wherry *Wild Flower Guide* 98, Maystar. . . Flowers few, on long stalks from the leaf star, about ½ in. across; petals about 7, white pointed. Spring.

May storm n Cf **blackberry storm**

1957 *Chr. Sci. Monitor* (Boston MA) 12 Oct 8/2, In Nebraska the phrase for such a belated jab by winter in spring is Indian Winter; . . in New England it is the May storm. I was surprised not to find this last phrase in the dictionaries.

May sucker n

1 =**harelip sucker**. [See quot 1957]

1878 U.S. Natl. Museum *Bulletin* 12.68, We have lately received a fine specimen taken in the Scioto River, Ohio, by Mr. J.H. Klippart, where it [=*Quassilabia lacera*] is well known to the fishermen under the name of "May Sucker." **1887** Goode *Amer. Fishes* 439, The "Rabbit-mouth Sucker," *Quassilabia lacera*, "Hare-lip," "Split-mouth" or "May-sucker" is found in abundance in many rivers of Tennessee and in some streams of Ohio. **1896** Jordan–Evermann *Check List Fishes* 243, *Lagochila lacera*. . . May Sucker. **1957** Trautman *Fishes* 263 **OH** (as of 1878), Klippart informed Jordan that this species was well known to Columbus fishermen who called it "May Sucker" because it spawned in May.

2 A **chubsucker 1** (here: *Erimyzon sucetta*).

1878 U.S. Natl. Museum *Bulletin* 12.54, This species [=*Erimyzon sucetta*], known locally as the May Sucker, is abundant in the water-basin of the Alabama.

May tree n Cf **mayhaw 1**

Prob a **hawthorn**.

1966 *DARE* (Qu. T15, . . *Kinds of swamp trees*) Inf **SC3**, May tree.

May water n Also *May dew* [EDD May-dew, May-water (at *May* sb.[1] 1.(12), (36)); cf *OED May-dew* c1430 →, "Dew gathered in the month of May, supposed to have medicinal and cosmetic properties"]

Rainwater or dew collected in May, supposed to have curative and other favorable properties.

1912 Green *VA Folk-Speech* 277, May-dew. . . Dew gathered on a May morning is used for washing the face as a beautifier. **1933** Rawlings *South Moon* 297 **FL**, Sand gnats swarmed in clouds and passed the sore-eyes from one baby to another. Women who had saved May-water from the rains in May doled it out to cure the affliction. **c1938** in 1970 Hyatt *Hoodoo* 1.460 **swTN**, Take May-watah, . . whut it rains lak when it first rains . . an' use it in a bottle. . . Yo' kin use fo' eyes, . . fo' sore places, use it fo' any kinda 'fected part of disease. [**1958** Browne *Pop.*

Beliefs AL 127, To make hair grow long wash it in May rain water.]

1970 *DARE* Tape **TN52**, I don't try to keep rain water. I do try to catch May water and water the flowers. . . that's good. [FW:] You mean when it rains in May? [Inf:] Yes, ma'am.

mayweed n

1 =**dog fennel 1**. [*OED* 1551 →]

1672 Josselyn *New-Englands Rarities* 86, May weed, excellent for the Mother; some of our *English* Houswives call it *Iron-Wort*. **1778** Carver *Travels N. Amer.* 515, Water Cresses, Yarrow, May Weed, [etc]. **1814** Bigelow *Florula Bostoniensis* 202, May weed. . . The road sides are full of the white blossoms of this common, annual weed. **1854** King *Amer. Eclectic Dispensatory* 624, *Maruta cotula*. . . Mayweed. *Ibid* 625, Mayweed is a native of Europe, and is extensively cultivated in this country, where it is known by several other names, as *Wild Chamomile, Dog-fennel*, etc. **1878** (1887) Jackson *Bits of Travel* 186 **NEng**, Rabbits' foot, May-weed, shepherd's purse. **1887** (1895) Robinson *Uncle Lisha* 186 **wVT**, China-asters, sweet-williams, and pansies struggling in a matted tangle of May-weed, posy beans and morning glories. **1901** Mohr *Plant Life AL* 55, In its northward spread this plant [=*Helenium tenuifolium*] has largely taken the place of the mayweed (*Anthemis cotula*). **1936** IL Nat. Hist. Surv. *Wildflowers* 377, Mayweed. . . The flowers of this weed . . are very conspicuous, and as the foliage is also pretty the plant might be used for ornamental purposes but for its disagreeable odor. **1967–70** *DARE* (Qu. S21, . . *Weeds . . that are a trouble in gardens and fields*) Infs **IA13, VA38**, Mayweed; (Qu. S26e, *Other wildflowers not yet mentioned;* not asked in early QRs) Inf **RI15**, Mayweed. **1979** Niering–Olmstead *Audubon Guide N. Amer. Wildflowers E. Region* 357, Mayweed. . . Daisy-like plant with white ray flowers surrounding a dome-shaped yellow disk.

2 =**wild chamomile** (here: *Matricaria* spp).

1900 Lyons *Plant Names* 241, M[atricaria] Chamomilla. . . Mayweed. **1954** Harrington *Manual Plants CO* 580, *Matricaria* L. False Camomile; Mayweed. **1966** Heller *Wild Flowers AK* 67, Mayweed. *Matricaria ambigua*. **1974** (1977) Coon *Useful Plants* 113, *Matricaria chamomilla* . . Mayweed. . . is another escaped weed, and one which is quite similar . . to *Anthemis nobilis*.

May whitewing n Also *great May whitewing* esp **NEng** =**white-winged scoter**.

1888 Trumbull *Names of Birds* 98, In Massachusetts at New Bedford and Fairhaven, and southward along the shore to Newport, R.I., the name *May White-wing* or *Great May White-wing* is applied to certain full-feathered birds, locally regarded as a distinct and larger variety, to be met with only between the 10th and 20th of May "flying west nor'west." **1899** Howe–Sturtevant *Birds RI* 11, The flight consists of "apparently all old birds," and in such fine adult plumage and of such large size that the local gunners believe them to be of a different species from the other less mature White-winged Scoters seen throughout the winter, and have named them May White-wings or Great May White-wings for this reason. **1917** (1923) *Birds Amer.* 1.150, White-winged Scoter. . . May White-wing. **1951** *AmSp* 26.271, *May whitewing* (white-winged scoter, Mass., Conn., R.I.) **1955** Forbush–May *Birds* 85, White-winged Scoter. . . May White-wing.

may will See **may** v B6

maywings n Also *maywing* esp **NEast** =**fringed polygala**.

1848 in 1850 Cooper *Rural Hours* 86 **NY**, As for the May-wings, or "gay-wings," they are in truth one of the gayest little blossoms we have. **1893** *Jrl. Amer. Folkl.* 6.140 **CT, NY**, *Polygala paucifolia*, May wings. **1896** *Ibid* 9.182 **ME**, *Polygala paucifolia*. . . Purple May wing. **1916** Keeler *Early Wildflowers* 141, The common names given to the plant, Gay-Wings, May-Wings, Bird-on-the-Wing, are each and every one . . recognition of the airy-winged suggestion of the blossom. **1959** Carleton *Index Herb. Plants* 80, May wings: Polygala paucifolia.

may would See **may** v B6

maze n [*OED maze* sb. 3 "A state of bewilderment. *Obs. exc. dial.*"; *amaze* sb. 2 "Bewilderment, mental confusion. *Obs.*"]

Amazement, surprise; a state of bewilderment.

1899 (1912) Green *VA Folk-Speech* 277, Maze. . . Bewilderment; perplexity. To be in a maze. **1950** *PADS* 14.46 **SC**, Maze. . . Amazement. "Mek maze," to show delighted surprise. Coastal Negro usage.

'mazin' See **amazing**

mazuka n [Var of *mazuma*]
   1967–68 DARE (Qu. U19a, . . *Money in general:* "*He's certainly got the* _____.") Infs **NJ**25, **OH**11, Mazuka.

McAdam See **macadam** n

McAdamize See **macadamize**

McCart(h)y See **mecate**

McCormack n Also *McCormick*
  =cormorant.
   1951 AmSp 26.90, A variation of the *cormorant* in New Jersey gives the forms *McCormack* and *McCormick*.

McGay See **maguey 2**

McKinley bug n Cf **democrat bug**
  =box-elder bug.
   1980 Des Moines Register (IA) 26 Oct 1 **swIA**, You'll occasionally hear a Democrat call the box elders "McKinley bugs." This is a form of retaliation that got started when Democrats were mocking the infamous Republican president, William McKinley, about 1900.

McKinley spider n
  A garden spider (*Argiope* spp).
   1967 DARE (Qu. R28, . . *Kinds of spiders*) Inf **IA**8, McKinley spider—out in the woods, build a large web; a large spider; gold design on back.

McTavish n, adj Also sp *MacTavish*
  A person of Scottish background; Scottish.
   1967–68 DARE (Qu. HH28, *Names and nicknames . . for people of foreign background: Scotch*) Infs **KS**16, **MI**67, **PA**19, McTavish; (Qu. HH30, *Things that are nicknamed for different nationalities—for example, a 'Dutch treat'*) Inf **WA**20, McTavish whiskey—scotch. **1990** Allen Unkind Words 32, Scotsmen were also nicknamed *MacTavish* and *Saunders*.

me pron
  1 Used with transitive verbs to indicate that the speaker's interests are affected; see quots. [Cf *OED me* pers. pron. 1.c "The so-called ethical dative. . . *arch.*"] Note: There is no sharp line between this and the std indirect object construction. Cf **3** below
   1688 (1892) Hammond Diary 148 **MA**, It [=lightning] killd me a Cow, & in ye stable one Lamb. **1908** German Amer. Annals 10.34 **sePA**, Ethical dative, with put. "Put me some gravy on my bread." **1986** Pederson LAGS Concordance, 1 inf, **swTN**, Mama done put me down a pallet; 1 inf, **cnGA**, He hauled me ten loads.
  2 Used as a subject:
  a As part of a compound subject. [*OED me* pers. pron. 6 "In uneducated speech commonly used where the pron. forms with another pron. or a sb. the subject of a plural verb."]
   1843 (1916) Hall New Purchase 147 **IN**, Me and Mary had a secret conscience that the white deserved his fate. **1866** in 1983 PADS 70.41 **ce,sePA**, Rach & me rested awhile then we all went for a walk. **1903** DN 2.320 **seMO**, Me and you. . . Almost universal for 'you and I.' **1906** DN 3.146 **nwAR**, Me and you both. . . "I agree with you." **1907** DN 3.233 **nwAR**, Me and you. . . You and I. Common. **1924** (1946) Greer-Petrie Angeline Gits an Eyeful 5 **csKY**, Me and him could a-tuck hit turn about a-w'arin' 'em [=could have taken turns wearing them], and been right in the style. **1942** McAtee Dial. Grant Co. IN 42 (as of 1890s), Me . . frequently used for I; "Me'n you". **1955** PADS 23.44 **SC**, Me and you . . can do it. Me and him . . are going. **1976** Lynn–Vecsey Loretta Lynn xi **eKY**, When we started on this book, me and Doolittle talked it over.
  b As a non-compound subject. *chiefly Gullah*
   1838 (1852) Gilman S. Matron 28 **SC** [Black], Me an't got no membrance, if me an't member maussa. **1883** (1971) Harris Nights with Remus 331 **GA** [Black], Me hab plenty reason, B'er Lion. **1888** Jones Negro Myths 3 **GA coast** [Gullah], Me know who mek all dis trouble fur me. **1892** (1969) Christensen Afro-Amer. Folk Lore 42, It are so hot me don't want for go roun' by de big road, so me gwine hire Br'er Alligator for tuk me 'cross. **1908** S. Atl. Qrly. 7.341 **sSC coast** [Gullah], "You hailed them then?" "Me duh holleh [=I did holler]." **1922** Gonzales Black Border 48 **sSC, GA coasts** [Gullah], Me yent hab no maussah! Ibid 217, Me lub um berry well. . . Me cyan' ketch de dog. **1928** Peterkin Scarlet Sister Mary 265 **csSC** [Gullah], Me most ready

though. **1949** Turner Africanisms 260 **seSC** [Gullah], [mi ē gwɒɪn dɛ]. **1986** Pederson LAGS Concordance, 1 inf, **cTX**, That's how come me to know so much about the things; 1 inf, **swLA**, That how me to know [sic] = how I came to know [inf a French speaker]; 1 inf, **swGA**, A lady called me last night and ask me where was me. [2 of 3 infs White]
  3 Used reflexively:
  a As an indirect object or in place of std *for myself.* **scattered, but esp Sth, S Midl** Note: Some of the examples included here verge toward the redundant use treated at **3b** below; it is impossible to draw a sharp line between them. Cf **1** above
   1821 (1930) Sewall Diary 75 **MD**, Purchased me some linens. **1858** in 1983 PADS 70.41 **ce,sePA**, I went over to Mary Bennets to get me some stuff to cure my *lump*. **1863** in 1968 DARE File **csNY**, I bought me a big cup. **1954** Roberts I Bought Dog [1] **KY**, Once upon a time I bought me a dog. **1956** McAtee Some Dialect NC 29, I'm going to kill me a rabbit. **1962** Fox Southern Fried 137 **SC**, I believe I got me an answer. **1976** Wolfram–Christian Appalachian Speech 123, I finally did buy me a coffee pot. . . I shot me a pheasant. **1986** Pederson LAGS Concordance, [Instances of *me* for std *myself* (indirect object) or *for myself* are fairly common throughout the **Gulf Region**; some typical examples are:] 1 inf, **cnGA**, I put me in a furnace; 1 inf, **ceAL**, I just built me a house; 1 inf, **cwAL**, I moved me a bed up in the side room; 1 inf, **swTN**, I bought me a chuck roast; 1 inf, **nwMS**, [I] hired me a man; 1 inf, **csAR**, I bought me a tent; 1 inf, **cwLA**, I found me a hobby; 1 inf, **ceTX**, I bought me a place.
  b Redundantly (with transitive verbs) to emphasize that the speaker's advantage (or disadvantage), well-being, pleasure, or the like is ultimately concerned. **chiefly Sth, S Midl**
   1935 in 1983 Taft Blues Lyric Poetry 304, Going to catch me a Greyhound : going to leave here tonight. **c1938** in 1970 Hyatt Hoodoo 1.68 **cwMS**, Well, I got up and went and got me some of this fish brine. . . I put me some saltpeter in it and I put me some salt in it and heated it. **1963** Owens Look to River 10 **TX**, I'll need me a few clothes. **1969–70** DARE (Qu. X40, . . *Ways . . of saying, "I'm going to bed"*) Inf **MO**29, Catch me a nod; (Qu. X41) Inf **GA**77, I'll take me a catnap, I'll take me a snooze. **1976** Wolfram–Christian Appalachian Speech 124, I'm gonna write me a letter to the President. . . I need to find me a place to live for my family. **1986** Pederson LAGS Concordance, [There are about 30 examples of redundant *me* throughout the **Gulf Region**; some typical examples are:] 1 inf, **nwGA**, I want me a bowlful of it for supper; 1 inf, **ceFL**, [I] had me a couple of heart attacks; 1 inf, **cTN**, I been meaning to open me up a pool hall; 1 inf, **csTN**, I drank me a glass of water; 1 inf, **cwAL**, [I] don't own me a home out here; 1 inf, **seAL**, I use me a dishrag; If I want me some corn bread, I put me a pone in the stove; 1 inf, **nwFL**, I got [=have] me a washing machine; 1 inf, **nwAR**, I caught me a bus.
  4 Used as direct object with normally intransitive verbs referring to physical sensations; see quots.
   1912 Green VA Folk-Speech 277, Me. . . "My head hurts me." **1942** McAtee Dial. Grant Co. IN 42 (as of 1890s), My head hurts me. **1984** Head Brogans 116 **eKY, eTN**, Mom still says "my head aches me" when she has a headache. **1986** Pederson LAGS Concordance, 1 inf, **ceTX**, It itched me so.
  5 Used to reinforce a preceding first person pronoun. [Calque of Fr constr] Note: The use of sentence-initial *me*, as in "Me, I don't care," appears to be widespread.
   1923 DN 5.244 **LA**, Me. . . Used intensively as French moi. "I am not going to-day, me."

me adj
  Used as a possessive adj in distinct regions and with separate origins in Amer Engl: see below. Note: Phonetic reduction of [maɪ] to [mi, mɪ, mə] has prob infl the sense development in both **a** and **b** below.
  a My. [Cf DBE, DJE] **sSC, GA coasts** *Gullah*
   1888 Jones Negro Myths 133 **GA coast** [Gullah], Tunder an lightnin done sen [=sent] meat een me house. **1892** (1969) Christensen Afro-Amer. Folk Lore 59, "Come me son, le' we [=let us] go." So all t'ree chilluns come too wid um. **1908** S. Atl. Qrly. 7.334 **sSC coast** [Gullah], Hoonah yunt yudde me wud! [=You haven't heard my words!] **1922** Gonzales Black Border 32 **sSC, GA coasts** [Gullah], W'en uh yeddy dat wu'd, me h'aa't hebby 'tell 'e ready fuh drap out me t'roat 'pun de du't. [=When I heard that word, my heart was heavy till [=so heavy that] it was ready to drop out of my throat upon the ground.]

b My. [Cf quot 1936 and *OED my* poss. adj. "in [19th-century] representations of Irish speech . . *me*."] **esp NJ, ePA**

1894 *DN* 1.332 **NJ**, *My:* pron. [mi]. **1899** Woerner *Rebel's Daughter* 110 **Ozarks**, D'ye mean me to defend me words agin this—Hessian? **1936** (1947) Mencken *Amer. Lang.* 457, [Footnote:] The archaic misuse of *me* for *my*, as in "I lit *me* pipe," is almost unknown in American, either standard or vulgar, though a correspondent in Philadelphia tells me that it is a localism in that city, and is sometimes used by elderly persons of Irish birth. **1967–70** *DARE* (Qu. H69, *When food is hard on your stomach, you say that it* _____) Infs **PA**41, 60, Upsets me stomach; (Qu. V2b, *About a deceiving person, or somebody that you can't trust . . "I wouldn't trust him* _____."; not asked in early QRs) Inf **NJ**18, Behind me back; (Qu. X47, . . *"I'm very tired, at the end of my strength"*) Inf **NJ**56, End of me string; (Qu. Z5, *Nicknames and affectionate words meaning 'brother'*) Inf **NJ**63, Me bruth. [All Infs old] **1968** *DARE* Tape **NJ**52, Listened me heart, he did.

-me- infix See **-ma-** infix

meach See **meech**

meaching See **meeching**

meadow n Usu **chiefly Nth, N Midl, West** |'mɛdo|; also **chiefly Sth, S Midl, NEng** |'mɛdə|; **chiefly sAppalachians, Ozarks, occas NEng** |'mɛdɚ| Pronc-spp *meader, medah, medder*
A Forms.

1871 (1882) Stowe *Fireside Stories* 57 **MA**, She hed the . . medders mowed in summer. **1875** *Atlantic Mth.* 32.424 **ceOH**, He kep' a going out to that meader. **1904** Day *Kin o' Ktaadn* 77 **ME**, Up on the knoll in the medder land. **1907** *DN* 3.194 **seNH**, *Medder*. **1915** (1916) Johnson *Highways New Engl.* 279, "Well," the older man resumed, "he tells of being at work on the medder one day when the ground shook so strong that it brought the cattle down on their knees." **1923** *DN* 5.214 **swMO**, *Medder*. . . Meadow. **1926** *AmSp* 2.80 **ME**, Swamp lands are called "medders" (meadows). **1933** *AmSp* 8.2.78 **Cape Cod MA**, [mɛdʌ]. **1939** *LANE* Map 29 *(Meadow; swale)*, [Proncs of the type ['mɛdo(ʊ)] are most freq; those of the type ['mɛdə] are also very common; those of the type ['mɛdu] occur occasionally; ['mɛdər] is rare.] **1942** Hall *Smoky Mt. Speech* 80 **wNC, eTN**, A considerable degree of education or subjection to modernizing influences is required before speakers regularly avoid [ɚ] for general American [o]. Examples: Banjo, . . piano, . . meadow, . . yellow. **1959** *VT Hist.* 27.148, *Meadow* ['mɛdɚ]. . . Common. Rural areas. **c1960** *Wilson Coll.* **csKY**, *Meadow*. . . usually /'mɛdə/. **1961** Kurath-McDavid *Pronc. Engl.* 170, *Widow, meadow, yellow*. . . These words end in /o/, /ə/, or /ɜ/. In cultivated speech, the /o/ of *ago* predominates in the North and the North Midland, the final /ə/ of *Martha* in the South Midland and the Lower South; in Virginia the two vowels are rather evenly matched. . . [The] /ɜ/ . . pronunciation is common in the mountains of the South . . , in eastern North Carolina, and on the Delmarva Peninsula, being most frequent among the folk. Relics of /ɜ/ survive in the folk speech of the North. Cultured speakers avoid it altogether. **1968** *DARE* Tape **NY**43, We had an east [mɛdə] and a west [mɛdɚ]. Well, where the west [mɛdɚ] is . . is the . . field today where the airplanes go out. **1976** Garber *Mountain-ese* 57 **sAppalachians**, The cows got out uv the barn lot and are grazin' in the medder. **1976** Allen *LAUM* 3.294 **Upper MW** (as of c1950), With *meadow* the /o/ dominance is greater than with *yellow* and the frequency of /ə/ is less, although still with some indication of Midland orientation. . . But the third variant /u/ is somewhat more frequent than it is in *yellow*, . . though still with Northern orientation. **1982** *Barrick Coll.* **csPA**, *Meadow*—pron. me-dah.

B Senses.

1 often with qualifier; also *meadow marsh:* An open marshy area; a fresh or salt marsh; a cultivated river bottom. **chiefly NEast** Cf **beaver meadow, bog ~**

1670 (1937) Denton *Brief Descr.* 13 **seNY**, [The] River puts into the main Land on the West-side. . . There is very great Marshes or Medows on both sides of it, excellent good Land. **1816** Pickering *Vocab.* 130, *Meadow.* In New England this word means exclusively *grass land, which is moist or subject to being overflowed;* and land, which is not so, is called *upland.* **1894** *DN* 1.332 **sNJ**, *Meadow:* salt marshy tract used for grazing and "shingling." [Ibid 337, *Shingling:* the process of taking cedar logs from the meadows or swamps and converting them into shingles.] **1905** *DN* 3.13 **cCT**, *Meadow*. . . Wet mowing lands. **1926** [see **A** above]. **1939** *LANE* Map 29, The map shows the terms *meadow(s), meadow land, meadow ground, fresh meadow, salt ~, grass ~, river ~, brook ~, bog ~, swamp ~, valley ~* and *upland ~*. . . These

terms denote, in general, low-lying grass land; but their exact meaning varies considerably with the character of the country. Thus the simplex *meadow* is generally applied to a salt meadow along the sea-shore, but to a fresh meadow farther inland. A meadow is usually in grass, but in the uplands of southern New England . . the term is often used of a fertile cultivated river bottom. **1945** Beck *Jersey Genesis* 108 **NJ**, But all the barges have gone now, all except mine, and most of the hay business has gone with them as far as the medders down here are concerned. **1948** Pearson *Sea Flavor* 95 **NH**, On the edge of a marsh meadow on a calm moonlit evening in July one can hear the nighthawks playing their bass horns. *Ibid* 118, Above the thatch-grass area is the zone of the marsh hay, or more properly, the salt grass. This section is called the meadow marsh by farmers who live close to the ocean. Only occasionally, perhaps once a month, do the tides flood this expanse. The surface of the meadow marshes is fairly firm. . . Here . . one can find three grasses—fox grass, spear grass, and spike grass. **1955** Richardson *House on Nauset Marsh* 198 **ceMA**, Many times, while tramping swampy, fresh-water meadows, I have jumped rails, usually soras or Virginians. **1965–70** *DARE* (Qu. C6, . . *A piece of land that's often wet, and has grass and weeds growing on it*) 20 Infs, **scattered, but esp NEast**, Meadow; **CT**14, If it could be mowed it becomes a meadow; **NC**62, Boggy land or a meadow; **NJ**15, In South Jersey the meadows are salt marshes along the coast. Salt hay was harvested here. Muskrats, etc, live in them; **NJ**21, 31, Meadow—these are the salt marshes; **NJ**67, Marsh—nothin' growin' over it, just mud; meadow—that's got grass, etc; **NC**23, Boggy meadow; **PA**22, 41, Meadowland; (Qu. C7, . . *Land that usually has some standing water with trees or bushes growing in it*) Inf **PA**146, Meadow; (Qu. C19, . . *Low land running between hills [With . . water]*) Inf **MA**15, Wet or marshy meadow—with water; **CT**7, Meadows—always water; **NH**16, Meadow—water in and flat; **NJ**8, A meadow here is used for pasture; meadow is a little damp—too damp to plow; (Qu. L8) Inf **NY**45, Marsh hay—this grew in the meadows. **1988** Nickerson *Days to Remember* 136 **Cape Cod MA** (as of c1900), *Meadow Bank*—On the "backside" (ocean side) of beaches, . . where the sand slopes down from the high tide mark to the low, there often appear chunks of peat protruding from the sand. These are the remnants of a marsh which was once on the inside or bay side of the beach. . . This continuing process of rollover of dunes onto marsh and later erosion result in the exposure to the ocean of the old "meadow bank". **1994** *Nature Conserv. WI Chapter* Winter 1, Sedge meadows. . . These wetlands are dominated by grass-like plants of the genus *Carex*, a type of sedge. They do not typically have standing water year round, but the soil is saturated with water.

2 See **meadow hay.**

meadow beauty n

1 A plant of the genus *Rhexia*. Also called **deer flower, deer grass 1, maid marian.** For other names of var spp see **deer hominy, deerweed 2, handsome Harry**

1822 Eaton *Botany* 426, *Rhexia* . . *virginica* (meadow beauty, deer grass). **1840** MA Zool. & Bot. Surv. *Herb. Plants & Quadrupeds* 51, *R[hexia] Virginica*. . . Deer Grass, Meadow Beauty. . . Has no important properties, but great beauty, and is well deserving cultivation. **1863** U.S. Dept. Ag. *Rept. of Secy. for 1862* 159, The *Rhexias*, or, as our people [=Americans] call them, "Meadow Beauties," comprise the only native genus. **1887** *Century Illustr. Mag.* 34.327, Parts of New England have already a midsummer flower. . . in meadow beauty, or rhexia. **1938** FWP *Guide DE* 12, Other plants noted on this brief visit were three kinds of meadow beauties. **1939** Writers' Program *Guide KY* 18, Tall purple composites, the ironweed and meadow beauty (deer grass), grace the open woodlands or low meadows. **1964** Batson *Wild Flowers SC* 78, *Meadow beauty: Rhexia alifanus*. . . Petals four, pinkish-purple and falling usually by noon. **1968–69** *DARE* (Qu. S26c, *Wildflowers that grow in woods*) Inf **GA**35, Meadow beauty—several species; (Qu. S26d, *Wildflowers that grow in meadows;* not asked in early QRs) Inf **IL**37, Meadow beauty.

2 =**poppy mallow.**

1941 *Torreya* 41.49 **nwTX**, *Callirhoë* spp.—Meadow-beauty, wild hollyhock, winecup.

3 A **marsh pink 1** (here: *Sabatia angularis*).

1964 Campbell et al. *Gt. Smoky Wildflowers* 46, *Rose-pink*. . . Another common name for this flower, appropriately, is *meadow beauty*. It flowers in August and September.

meadow bird n

1 =**bobolink B.** [See quot 1890]

1844 DeKay *Zool. NY* 2.144, The *Boblink*, or *Bob-o'link* . . is known in others [=states] by the various names of *Reed-bird, May-bird, Meadow-bird.* **1857** U.S. Patent Office *Annual Rept. for 1856: Ag.* 127, The "Meadow Bird," in Louisiana, the "Reed Bird," in Pennsylvania, the "Rice Bunting," in the Carolinas, and the "Bob-o-link," in New York. **1890** *Century Dict.* 3671, *Meadow-bird.* . . The bobolink, *Dolichonyx oryzivorus:* so called from its usual breeding-place. **1956** MA Audubon Soc. *Bulletin* 40.130 **MA**, Bobolink. . . Meadow Bird. **1963** Gromme *Birds WI* 216, Meadow Bird (Bobolink).

2 The eastern **meadowlark 1.**

1966 *DARE* (Qu. Q15, . . *Kinds of larks*) Inf **MS**47, Meadow bird— same as field lark.

meadow bugle n Cf bog bugle

A **jack-in-the-pulpit 1** (here: *Arisaema triphyllum*).

1966 *DARE* Wildfl QR Pl.3 Inf **NC**28, Meadow bugles—old or obsolete term.

meadow buttercup n

A **marsh marigold** (here: *Caltha palustris*).

1893 *Jrl. Amer. Folkl.* 6.136 **NEng**, *Caltha palustris.* . . Meadow buttercup. **1959** Carleton *Index Herb. Plants* 80, *Meadow-buttercup:* Caltha palustris.

meadow cabbage n

A **skunk cabbage** (here: *Symplocarpus foetidus*).

1854 King *Amer. Eclectic Dispensatory* 922, The whole plant [=*Symplocarpus foetidus*], especially when bruised, emits a very disagreeable alliaceous odor, which has given rise to the several names, *Skunk-weed, Skunk-cabbage, Polecat-weed,* and *Meadow-cabbage.* **1876** Hobbs *Bot. Hdbk.* 69, Meadow cabbage. . . Skunk cabbage. **1900** Lyons *Plant Names* 353, Skunk Cabbage, Skunk-weed, Polecat-weed, Meadow Cabbage, Swamp Cabbage. **1940** Clute *Amer. Plant Names* 152, Meadow cabbage.

meadow chicken n Also meadow chick Cf meadow hen 1

Usu a **sora** (here: *Porzana carolina*), but see quot 1899.

1888 Trumbull *Names of Birds* 132, At East Haddam, Conn., it [=*Porzana carolina*] is the *Meadow Chicken* (or Meadow Chick). **1899** Newton *Dict. Birds* 539, *Meadow-chicken* and *Meadow-hen,* names given in North America to more than one species of Rail or Coot. **1925** (1928) Forbush *Birds MA* 1.357, *Sora.* . . Chicken-bill; Meadow-chicken. **1938** Oberholser *Bird Life LA* 203, The well known Sora, or as it is sometimes called, 'Carolina Rail', or 'meadow chicken', is a rather small bird, easily distinguished from its relatives by its black throat, whitish and pale grayish under parts, and black-streaked olive brown upper surface.

meadow chippy n [meadow n B1] Cf chippy (at chipping sparrow), field chippy, ground ~, winter ~

=**seaside sparrow.**

[**1914** Eaton *Birds NY* 2.299, *Seaside Sparrow.* . . Its call note is a squeaky *"cheep,"* and it has a chippering song of no great melody, uttered from the top of some reed or tall stalk just above the marsh.] **1917** (1923) *Birds Amer.* 3.30, *Seaside Sparrow.* . . *Other Names.* Meadow Chippy. **1946** Hausman *Eastern Birds* 597, *Northern Seaside Sparrow.* . . *Other Names*—Meadow Chippy. . . It does not flush easily, preferring to run mouselike through the grass.

meadow clover n

=**red clover.**

a**1862** (1864) Thoreau *ME Woods* 28, He was at this time engaged in cutting the native grass,—rush-grass and meadow-clover, as he called it,—on the meadows and small, low islands of this stream. **1890** *Century Dict.* 1060, The red, purple, or meadow clover, *T[rifolium] pratense,* is extensively cultivated for fodder and as a fertilizer. **1910** Graves *Flowering Plants* 248 **CT**, Meadow or Pea-vine Clover. **1936** Winter *Plants NE* 97, Red or Meadow Clover. **1971** Krochmal *Appalachia Med. Plants* 252, *Trifolium pratense.* . . meadow clover.

meadow coneflower n

=**black-eyed Susan 2.**

1897 IN Dept. Geol. & Nat. Resources *Rept. for 1896* 694, *R[udbeckia] hirta.* . . Yellow Daisy. Black-eyed Susan. Meadow Cone-flower.

meadow cup n

1 A **pitcher plant** (here: *Sarracenia purpurea*).

1818 in 1826 MA Hist. Soc. *Coll.* 2d ser 8.171 **nwMA**, The purple sarracenia. . . is here called, meadow cups and forefathers' pitcher. **1832** Williamson *Hist. ME* 1.126, *Meadow-cup,* called forefathers' pitcher, or Whippoorwill's shoes. **1940** Clute *Amer. Plant Names* 145, Meadow-

cup, fever-cup, St. Jacob's dipper. **1959** Carleton *Index Herb. Plants* 80, *Meadow cup.* . . Sarracenia purpurea.

2 A **buttercup 1** (here: *Ranunculus acris*).

1959 Carleton *Index Herb. Plants* 80, *Meadow cup:* Ranunculus acris.

meadow daisy n

A **black-eyed Susan 2** or similar flower.

1967 *DARE* (Qu. S7, *A kind of daisy, bright yellow with a dark center, that grows along roadsides in late summer*) Inf **MO**11, Meadow daisy; (Qu. S26d, *Wildflowers that grow in meadows;* not asked in early QRs) Infs **IL**6, 25, **MO**5, 11, Meadow daisy (or daisies).

meadow death n Also meadow death camas

A **death camas** (here: *Zigadenus venenosus*).

1937 U.S. Forest Serv. *Range Plant Hdbk.* W213, *Meadow Death-camas.* Zygadenus [sic] *venenosus.* . . Meadow deathcamas is one of the most toxic range species, being responsible for the loss of thousands of sheep. **1940** Clute *Amer. Plant Names* 275, Zygadenus venosus [sic]. . . meadow death, soap plant, alkali-grass.

meadow fern n

1 =**sweet gale.**

1876 Hobbs *Bot. Hdbk.* 73, Meadow fern,—*Myrica gale.* **1894** *Jrl. Amer. Folkl.* 7.98, *Myrica Gale,* . . meadow-fern, Dover, Me. **1950** Gray–Fernald *Manual of Botany* 524, *M[yrica] Gale.* . . Sweet Gale, "Meadow-Fern." **1974** (1977) Coon *Useful Plants* 190, *Myrica gale.* . . meadow-fern. A widely spread plant in North America, it is a low shrub growing on moist peaty soils.

2 A **sweet fern** (here: *Comptonia peregrina*).

1900 Lyons *Plant Names* 113, *C[omptonia] peregrina.* . . Fern-gale, Fern bush, Meadow Fern. **1930** Sievers *Amer. Med. Plants* 55, Sweetfern. . . fern bush, meadow fern. **1971** Krochmal *Appalachia Med. Plants* 102, *Comptonia peregrina.* . . meadow fern.

3 also **meadow shield fern: =marsh fern.**

1824 Bigelow *Florula Bostoniensis* 390, Aspidium Thelypteris. . . Meadow Shield Fern. . . Common in low, moist grounds, about the edges of meadows and swamps. **1843** Torrey *Flora NY* 2.496, Meadow Shield-fern, Lady-fern. **1900** Lyons *Plant Names* 141, *D[ryopteris] Thelypteris.* . . Marsh, Meadow or Swamp Fern. **1950** Gray–Fernald *Manual of Botany* 33, *D[ryopteris] Thelypteris* . . var. *pubescens* . . Meadow-Fern.

meadow foam n chiefly CA

A plant of the genus *Limnanthes.* For other names of *L. douglasii* see **valley foam.**

1897 Parsons *Wild Flowers CA* 126, When the spring is well advanced, our wet meadows are all a-cream with the meadow-foam, whose dense masses blend exquisitely with the rich red of the common sorrel. **1915** (1926) Armstrong–Thornber *Western Wild Flowers* 278 **CA, OR**, Meadow Foam—*Floerkea Douglasii.* . . A charming plant, often covering the meadows with drifts of creamy bloom. **1949** Moldenke *Amer. Wild Flowers* 81, Californians are well acquainted with the *meadow-foam, Limnanthes douglasii,* 6 to 14 inches tall, with smooth, succulent, yellowish-green foliage and white (occasionally pinkish) flowers, usually yellow at the center. **1968** *DARE* (Qu. S26e) Inf **CA**97, Meadow foam—related to Nemophilia [sic]. **1974** Munz *Flora S. CA* 547, *Limnanthes.* . . Meadow-Foam.

meadow foxtail grass See meadow grass 2b

meadow frog n [See quot 1958]

A **leopard frog:** usu *Rana pipiens,* but also *R. sphenocephala.*

1928 Pope–Dickinson *Amphibians* 38 **WI**, Leopard Frog. . . Other common names are Grass Frog, Common Frog, Meadow Frog and Spring Frog. **1932** Wright *Life-Hist. Frogs* 344 **Okefenokee GA**, The meadow frogs (*R. pipiens* and *R. sphenocephala*). Ibid 419, *Rana sphenocephala.* . . Common Names—Southern Leopard Frog. Southern Meadow Frog. **1958** Conant *Reptiles & Amphibians* 300, Northern Leopard Frog. . . This is the "meadow frog," at least in summertime, a name earned by its wanderings well away from water. **1966** Dakin *Dial. Vocab. Ohio R. Valley* 2.388, Indiana has [the names] night peepers and meadow frog. **1982** Sternberg *Fishing* 112, Leopard frogs are the most common type of frog and the most popular among fishermen. Sometimes called *meadow frogs,* they often wander into grassy fields. **1985** Clark *From Mailbox* 46 **ME**, The small frogs which go leaping through the grass on the back lawn are young leopard frogs. . . Often called the "meadow" frog, this bright and beautiful amphibian has a habit of wandering far from the ponds and marshes.

meadow gentian n

A **marsh pink 1** (here: *Sabatia campestris*).

1948 Stevens *KS Wild Flowers* 174, *Sabbatia* [sic] *campestris*—Meadow Gentian. . . We may say of these flowers that they are among the loveliest of the sweet-scented and long-lasting native flowers.

meadow gold n

Prob a **gold fields.**

1968 *DARE* (Qu. S26a, . . *Wildflowers* . . *Roadside flowers*) Inf **CA**87, Meadow gold—a tiny flower, yellow-green leaf—an early spring flower.

meadow grass n Cf **marsh grass, meadow B1, meadow hay, salt-marsh grass, salt-meadow ~**

1 Any of var grasses which grow in meadow land, but esp those used for hay or pasturage. Note: These quots may refer spec to senses below.

1848 in 1850 Cooper *Rural Hours* 124 **ceNY**, The timothy is also an imported grass; so is the meadow-grass considered as the best of all for pasture. **1884** Shepherd *Prairie Exper.* 216 **West**, If the sage-bush is cleaned off and the land irrigated, good crops of wheat, barley, and meadow grass are gathered. **1905** Valentine *Hecla Sandwith* 255 **PA**, The gale whipped the meadow-grass into leaping silver lines. **1950** Hitchcock–Chase *Manual Grasses* 305, *Arrhenatherum elatius*. . . Cultivated in the northern humid regions as a meadow grass. **1965–70** *DARE* (Qu. L8, *Hay that grows naturally in damp places*) 23 Infs, 18 **Atlantic**, 5 **Pacific NW**, Meadow grass; (Qu. L9a, . . *Kinds of grass . . grown for hay*) Inf **WA**1, Meadow grass; (Qu. L9b, *Hay from other kinds of plants [not grass]*; not asked in early QRs) Inf **OR**13, Meadow grass; (Qu. L34, . . *Most important crops grown around here*) Inf **OR**13, Meadow grass; (Qu. S9, . . *Kinds of grass that are hard to get rid of*) Infs **PA**136, **SC**31, Meadow grass.

2 Spec:

a =**Kentucky bluegrass.** [*OED* c1275 →]

1817 Eaton *Botany* 15, *Poa.* . . *pratensis*, (meadow-grass). **1840** *MA Zool. & Bot. Surv. Herb. Plants & Quadrupeds* 245 **MA**, *Poa.* . . Meadow-Grass. . . One of the most important grasses for the support of cattle. More than 30 species are native or cultivated in England, and 24 are credited to the Northern States, and 18 species to this State. **1891** Jesup *Plants Hanover NH* 54, *Poa.* . . Meadow-Grass. Spear-Grass. . . Wet meadows, and valuable. **1945** Wodehouse *Hayfever Plants* 41, One of the commonest species is . . meadow grass . . *P[oa] annua*. . . in open ground, lawns, pastures. **1976** Bailey–Bailey *Hortus Third* 889, *Poa.* . . Bluegrass, meadow grass, spear g[rass]. . . Palatable and nutritious forage plants, hence important in pastures and ranges.

b also *meadow foxtail grass*: A **foxtail 1** (here: *Alopecurus pratensis*).

1802 Drayton *View of SC* 61, Remarkable Plants. . . indigenous to the state. . . Meadow fox-tail grass. (*Alopecurus* pratensis.) **1822** Eaton *Botany* 168, *Alopecurus.* . . *pratensis* (meadow-grass . .) culm erect: glume villose; corol[la] beardless. **1869** Porcher *Resources* 645 **Sth**, *Alopecurus pratensis*. . . meadow or tall grass, which is found in the Southern States, is . . much relished by horses and cattle. **1935** (1943) Muenscher *Weeds* 139, *Alopecurus pratensis*. . . Meadow foxtail-grass. . . Meadows and pastures in the eastern states. **1968** Barkley *Plants KS* 34, *Alopecurus pratensis*. . . Meadow Foxtail Grass. Meadows and waste places.

c =**love grass.**

1843 Torrey *Flora NY* 2.459, *Poa Eragrostis* [=*Eragrostis minor*]. . . Strong-scented Meadow-grass. . . When fresh, it emits a peculiar and rather disagreeable odor. **1881** Phares *Farmer's Book of Grasses* 58, *E[ragrostis] reptans*, Creeping Meadow Grass, is a beatiful [sic] annual . . found in low, sandy places, gravelly banks of streams, fence corners and open pastures. It is relished by cattle, but not of much value in agriculture. *Ibid* 59, *E. pilosa*, Slender Meadow Grass. . . *E. capillaris*, Hair-panicled Meadow Grass. **1911** Jepson *Flora CA* 61, *Creeping Meadow-grass.* . . Wet places, San Joaquin and Coast Range valleys. **1933** Small *Manual SE Flora* 122, *Eragrostis*. . . Annuals or perennials of various habit. . . *Meadow-grasses.* **1935** (1943) Muenscher *Weeds* 155, *Eragrostis cilianensis*. . . Meadow-grass. . . Cultivated fields, roadsides and waste places. Eastern United States; especially in the South.

d =**manna grass. Cf floating meadow grass, fowl ~, reed ~**

1869 Porcher *Resources* 681 **Sth**, *Floating sweet meadow-grass* . . *Glyceria fluitans*. . . Its seeds form a common and enriching food for fresh water fish, for aquatic fowl, and when gathered and dried they constitute the manna-croup of the shops. **1889** Vasey *Ag. Grasses* 70,

Glyceria nervata (Nerved Meadow Grass). This is similar in appearance to the tall meadow grass, but is smaller, with a lighter panicle and smaller flowers. . . It usually grows along the wet margins of streams and swamps. . . It is especially abundant in the Rocky Mountains. **1933** Small *Manual SE Flora* 131, *Glyceria.* . . Manna-grasses. Meadow-grasses. **1937** U.S. Forest Serv. *Range Plant Hdbk.* G67, Fowl manna-grass, also locally known as . . tall meadowgrass, is a moderately tall, often tufted perennial grass. . . Although it sometimes grows pure in small patches, this grass ordinarily is intermixed scatteringly with other meadow grasses. **1943** Fernald–Kinsey *Edible Wild Plants E. N. Amer.* 93, *Floating Manna-grass, Floating Meadow-grass, Glyceria* (or *Panicularia*), several species.

e =**alkali grass 2.**

1876 Hobbs *Bot. Hdbk.* 47, Grass, sea meadow, *Glyceria maritima* [=*Puccinellia maritima*]. **1906** Rydberg *Flora CO* 48, *Puccinellia.* . . *Meadow-grass.* . . In wet meadows, especially in alkaline soil. **1911** NJ State Museum *Annual Rept. for 1910* 243 **sNJ**, *Puccinellia fasciculata.* . . *Spreading Meadow Grass.* . . Borders of salt marshes on the coast. **1936** Winter *Plants NE* 29, *Puccinellia.* . . Meadow-grass. . . In alkaline soil in western Nebr.

f A **cordgrass** (here: *Spartina cynosuroides*).

1916 *Torreya* 16.237, *Spartina cynosuroides.* . . Meadow grass, Revels Id., Va.

meadow hawk n

=**marsh hawk 1.**

1917 *Wilson Bulletin* 29.2.81 **KY, VA**, *Circus hudsonius.*—Meadow-hawk. **1955** MA Audubon Soc. *Bulletin* 39.442 **MA**, *Marsh Hawk.* . . Meadow Hawk. **1968** *DARE* (Qu. Q4, . . *Kinds of hawks*) Inf **NJ**21, Meadow hawk; **MN**15, Meadow hawk—gets mice in the meadow, a small hawk.

meadow hay n Also *meadow* [*OEDS* 1733 →] Cf **marsh hay, salt ~, slough ~, swale ~, wild ~**

Hay made from **meadow grass,** such as that from **bluejoint 1, bentgrass 1,** or **cordgrass;** see quots.

1851 (1856) Springer *Forest Life* 54 **ME**, Among other preliminaries which anticipate the winter operations of lumbermen is the "putting up" of large quantities of meadow hay. **1859** (1968) Bartlett *Americanisms* 266, *Meadow.* In the United States often applied to mowing lands which are marshy or too wet to be ploughed and producing a coarse kind of hay, which is called "*meadow* hay," in distinction from that which grows on uplands. **1879** Webster *Amer. Dict.* 1566, *Meadow-hay,* . . a coarse grass, or true sedge, growing on uncultivated swamp or river meadow;—used as fodder for cattle, packing for ice, and the like. **1907** *DN* 3.194 **seNH**, *Medder hay.* . . A coarse hay cut on cleared swamps, used for bedding and sometimes as feed for cows and horses. **1940** Writers' Program *Guide NY* 631 **ceNY**, The rich bottom lands grow heavy with meadow, wheat, and corn, potatoes, carrots, celery, onions, lettuce, cabbage, and tomatoes. **1950** *WELS* (*Hay that grows naturally in damp places*) 2 Infs, **nWI**, Meadow hay. **1965–70** *DARE* (Qu. L8) 27 Infs, **scattered, but esp NEast**, Meadow hay; **ME**12, 19, **MA**74, Meadow hay, bluejoint; **TX**63, Meadow hay; cane-reed grass grows tall in damp places; (Qu. L9a, . . *Kinds of grass . . grown for hay*) Inf **TN**62, Herge [sic] grass . . also called redtop and meadow hay.

meadow hen n

1 Any of var birds of the family *Rallidae*: esp the **king rail 1** or **clapper rail,** but also a **sora** (here: *Porzana carolina*) or **Virginia rail. chiefly NEast** Cf **marsh hen 1, meadow chicken**

1842 Hawes *Sporting Scenes* 1.18 **Long Is. NY**, The principal inhabitants are gulls, and meadow-hens. **1844** DeKay *Zool. NY* 2.259, The Saltwater Meadow-Hen. . . *Rallus crepitans*. *Ibid*, The Clapper Rail, Mud-hen, or Meadow-hen, appears along the shores of this State about the latter end of April, and . . departs for the South in October. *Ibid* 260, The Freshwater Meadow-Hen. . . *Rallus elegans*. **1863** Dodge *Gala-Days* 97 **MA**, You know you didn't scare a little meadow-hen. **1888** Trumbull *Names of Birds* 117, *Coot.* . . To some at Salem, Mass., and more commonly at Newport, R.I., *meadow-hen*. *Ibid* 127, *Clapper rail: Meadow clapper: Salt-water meadow-hen.* . . In Connecticut at Stony Creek and Stratford, on Long Island at Bellport, Seaford, and Freeport, and to some on Cobb's Island, Va., *meadow-hen*. **1923** U.S. Dept. Ag. Misc. Circular 40, King Rail (*Rallus elegans*). . . Meadow hen (Conn.) *Ibid* 42, Clapper Rail (*Rallus crepitans*). . . Meadow-hen (Conn., Long Id., N.Y.) *Ibid* 43, Sora (*Porzana carolina*). . . Meadow-hen. *Ibid* 44, Florida Gallinule (*Gallinula chloropus cachinnans*). . . Meadow-hen

(Conn.) *Ibid* 46, American Coot *(Fulica americana)*. . . Meadow-hen (Mass., R.I., Long Id., N.Y.) **1955** *MA Audubon Soc. Bulletin* 39.443, *Virginia Rail.* . . Meadow Hen, Mud Hen (Maine, Mass.) . . *Sora.* . . Meadow Hen (Maine, Mass.) . . *Florida Gallinule.* . . Meadow Hen (Mass., Conn.) **1968** *DARE* (Qu. Q7, *Names and nicknames for . . game birds*) Inf **NY**89, Meadow hen.

2 A **bittern** (here: *Botaurus lentiginosus*). [*DCan* 1896] Cf **marsh hen 2**

1946 Hausman *Eastern Birds* 110, American Bittern. . . Other Names . . Indian Hen, Meadow Hen. **1953** *AmSp* 28.281 **ME, MA, NY**, Meadow hen. . . American bittern. **1966** *DARE* (Qu. Q8, *A water bird that makes a booming sound before rain and often stands with its beak pointed almost straight up*) Inf **ME**8, American bittern or meadow hen.

3 =**black-crowned night heron.** Cf **marsh hen 3**

1953 *AmSp* 28.281 **MA, NY**, Meadow hen—Black-crowned night heron.

meadow holly n

A **holly** n[1] **1** (here: *Ilex decidua*).

1900 Lyons *Plant Names* 199, *I[lex] decidua*. . . Swamp or Meadow Holly. **1901** Lounsberry *S. Wild Flowers* 315, *I[lex] decidua,* swamp or meadow holly, chooses for its home such haunts as swamps and shaded ravines. . . Sometimes it becomes tree-like, about thirty feet high. **1937** Stemen–Myers *OK Flora* 300, *Ilex decidua*. . . Meadow or Deciduous Holly. **1960** Vines *Trees SW* 655, Local names [for possum-haw holly] are Deciduous Holly, Meadow Holly [etc].

meadow hyacinth n

A **camas 1** (here: *Camassia scilloides*).

1933 Small *Manual SE Flora* 292, *Q[uamasia] hyacinthina*. . . Wild-hyacinth. Indigo-squill. Meadow-hyacinth. **1949** Moldenke *Amer. Wild Flowers* 326, Only our eastern species, *C[amassia] hyacinthina,* is called *wildhyacinth, meadowhyacinth,* or *indiansquill.* It may be looked for in thickets and meadows from Georgia and Texas north to Pennsylvania and Minnesota. **1976** Bailey–Bailey *Hortus Third* 208, *[Camassia] scilloides*. . . Meadow hyacinth, Indigo squill.

meadowlark n

1 Either of two similar birds: the eastern meadowlark *(Sturnella magna)* or the western meadowlark *(S. neglecta).* **widespread, but less freq Sth, S Midl** See Map Cf **field lark** For other names of both birds see **fee lark, field ~, lark** n[1] **1, medlark, mud lark** n **2, old-field ~**; for other names of *S. magna* see **marsh lark, marsh quail, meadow bird 2, ~ quail, ~ starling, nigger quail, quail, sail bird**

1775 (1962) Romans *Nat. Hist. FL* 114, Meadow larks, fieldfares, rice birds, &c. &c. are very frequently had. **1811** Wilson *Amer. Ornith.* 3.22, Their general name is the *Meadow Lark;* among the Virginians they are usually called the *Old field Lark.* **1844** Giraud *Birds Long Is.* 148 **NY**, The Meadow Lark is distributed throughout the United States, and it is said to range over the whole of the continent. **1898** (1900) Davie *Nests N. Amer. Birds* 343, In almost any stretch of pastureland may be found a pair or colony of Meadowlarks, and the sweet sound of their wild, ringing, and rather melancholy notes fill [sic] the air at short intervals from sunrise till the gloaming. **1917** (1923) *Birds Amer.* 2.252, *Sturnella neglecta*. . . The Meadowlark has . . a just claim on the respect and affections of the people. **1923** Dawson *Birds CA* 1.130, In passing westward across the prairies of Iowa or Kansas one notices an instant change in the voices of the Meadowlarks. The song of the western bird

is sweeter, clearer, louder, longer and more varied. **1940** Stuart *Trees of Heaven* 248 **eKY**, They 'peared to be happy as two medder larks. **1965–70** *DARE* (Qu. Q15, . . *Kinds of larks*) 699 Infs, **widespread, but less freq Sth, S Midl**, Meadowlark; **CA**78, **CO**7, **IA**20, **WI**58, Western meadowlark; **IA**20, **WI**58, Eastern meadowlark; (Qu. Q7, *Names and nicknames for . . game birds*) Inf **OK**52, Some hunt the meadowlarks and eat them—they used to, but not now; (Qu. Q10, . . *Water birds and marsh birds*) Infs **PA**89, 128, Meadowlark. **1977** Bull–Farrand *Audubon Field Guide Birds* 512, Meadowlarks are often polygamous; more than one female may be found nesting in the territory of a single male.

2 =**bobolink B.** Cf **meadow bird 1, meadowwink**

1950 *WELS* (Other names . . for . . bobolink) 1 Inf, **swWI**, Meadow-lark. **1965–70** *DARE* (Qu. Q14, . . *Names . . for these birds: bobolink*) 16 Infs, **scattered, but more freq N Cent, Cent, IA**, Meadowlark.

3 =**brown thrasher.**

1969–70 *DARE* (Qu. Q14, . . *Names . . for these birds: . . brown thrasher*) Inf **IN**69, We sometimes call it a meadowlark, knowing that it isn't; **TN**65, Meadowlark; (Qu. Q14, . . *Names . . for these birds: . . thrush*) Inf **NY**211, Meadowlark.

meadow lily n

1 The Canada **lily** *(Lilium canadense).*

1832 Williamson *Hist. ME* 1.126, [We have] two varieties of meadow-lilies, the upright has a flower of a red colour, freckled with black, in the other, the pensile is yellow freckled. **1832** *MA Hist. Soc. Coll.* 2d ser 9.152 **cwVT**, Lilium canadense . . Meadow lily. **1894** *Jrl. Amer. Folkl.* 7.102 **NY**, Lilium Canadense. . . meadow lily, nodding lily. **1901** Lounsberry *S. Wild Flowers* 51, *Lilium Canadense,* wild yellow lily, or meadow lily, extends southward as far as Georgia, Alabama and Missouri. **1931** Harned *Wild Flowers Alleghanies* 112, Meadow lily. . . It is said the Indians used the bulbs of the lily [=*Lilium canadense*] for thickening meat soups. **1967** *DARE* (Qu. S26d, *Wildflowers that grow in meadows;* not asked in early QRs) Inf **MN**6, Yellow meadow lily. **1979** Niering–Olmstead *Audubon Guide N. Amer. Wildflowers E. Region* 600, Canada Lily; Meadow Lily; Wild Yellow Lily.

2 A **wood lily** (here: *Lilium philadelphicum*).

1832 Williamson [see **1** above]. **1966–68** *DARE* (Qu. S26d, *Wildflowers that grow in meadows;* not asked in early QRs) Inf **PA**1, Meadow lily; **VA**28A, Meadow lily—dark red with black spots. **1966** *DARE* Wildfl QR Pl.13 Inf **NC**28, Meadow lily.

3 A **zephyr lily** (here: *Zephyranthes atamasco*).

1956 McAtee *Some Dialect NC* 56, *Meadow lily* . . the zephyr-lily *(Zephyranthes atomosco* [sic]). Chapel Hill.

meadow marsh See **meadow B1**

meadow mole n

1 A **mole** n[1] **1** (here: *Scalopus aquaticus*). **esp NEast** Cf **gopher** n[1] **3**

1931–33 *LANE Worksheets,* 1 inf, **swCT**, Meadow moles. **1967–69** *DARE* (Qu. P29, . . *'Gophers' . . other name . . or what other animal are they most like*) Inf **MA**42, Nearest is meadow mole; **NY**27, Meadow moles, [in the] rat family, work under snow in winter; **NY**196, Meadow moles are the same animal [as gopher].

2 A **shrew** (here: *Blarina brevicauda*).

1961 Jackson *Mammals WI* 43, In Wisconsin usually called mole shrew. . . Other names include . . meadow mole.

meadow mouse n [*OED* 1801 →]

A vole of the genus *Microtus,* esp *M. pennsylvanicus.* Also called **field gopher 2, ~ mouse, gopher** n[1] **2c, ground mouse, mole** n[1] **2.** For other names of var spp see **pine mouse, prairie ~**

1812 Wilson *Amer. Ornith.* 6.59, The *meadow mouse* is . . eagerly sought after by . . great numbers of Hawks. **1817** *Amer. Monthly Mag. & Crit. Rev.* 2.46, [The] Meadow-mouse. . . lives near Philadelphia, &c. in meadows and even in salt marshes, where it burrows in all direc-tions . . it has the appearance of the *Ondatra zibethicus,* or Musk-rat; but is only five inches long altogether. **1857** *U.S. Patent Office Annual Rept. for 1856: Ag.* 84, Of Meadow-mice, we have many species. . . [T]hey are commonly considered by farmers as one animal, known under various names, as "Short-tailed Field Rats or Mice," "Bear Mice," "Bull-headed Mice," "Ground Mice," "Bog Mice," &c. **1908** NJ State Museum *Annual Rept. for 1907* 69, The meadow mice are active all the year and on a warm day in winter we may see them passing along their more exposed surface runways with wonderful rapidity. **1946** Dufresne *AK's Animals* 144, The meadow mouse or Vole is the most abundant and widely distributed of all mice in Alaska. **1961** Jackson *Mammals*

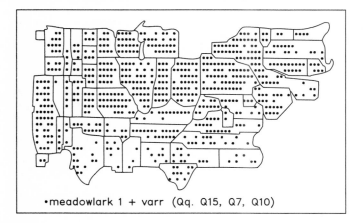

•meadowlark 1 + varr (Qq. Q15, Q7, Q10)

WI 230, *Microtus pennsylvanicus*. . . Most frequently called meadow mouse in Wisconsin. **1963** North *Rascal* 69 **WI** (as of 1918), The rustling of small creatures in the grass, meadow mice perhaps.

meadow muffin n Cf **alley apple 2, nigger pancake**

A lump of manure.

1976 *Business Week* 12 July 45, [The company] is involved in a huge array of international energy deals . . even a modest plan to turn cow manure . . into natural gas. Some people . . refer to this last venture as "the meadow muffin project." **1977** *U.S. News & World Rept.* 25 Apr 64 **CT**, I intend to fight tooth and nail to block passage of this political meadow muffin. **1995** *DARE* File **cMA**, A meadow muffin is a cow pie. *Ibid* **nwMA**, I've known meadow muffin for 'cow manure' since about 1965. *Ibid* **cwCA** (as of 1950s), When I was a child we used the term *meadow muffins* for lumps of manure in a field or on a trail. *Ibid* **MA**, Meadow muffin—a horse apple or road apple. Heard from young people, 1968 to the present. *Ibid* **csWI** (as of c1977), Every time our school band marched in a parade, our director would warn us, "Mind the meadow muffins—we're behind the horses again!"

meadow mushroom n [*OED* 1884]

A **field mushroom**, usu *Agaricus campestris*.

1908 Hard *Mushroom Edible* 5, The common meadow mushroom is found from September to frost. It is known by its pink gills and meaty cap. **1943** Fernald–Kinsey *Edible Wild Plants E. N. Amer.* 381, Meadow or Pasture Mushroom, *Agaricus arvensis* and *campestris*. **1968** *PA Game News* July 54 **PA**, Meadow mushrooms—which every mushroom hunter knows—are going to waste at a shameful rate despite wholesale picking. **1980** Marteka *Mushrooms* 105, Toward the end of summer when rains become more frequent, a short, stocky, white mushroom with pink to chocolate-brown gills appears on lawns, pastures, fields, and golf courses. This is *(Agaricus campestris)*, the meadow mushroom. **1985** Weber–Smith *Field Guide S. Mushrooms* 237, Another common name for this species [=*Agaricus campestris*] is meadow mushroom.

meadow musk n Cf **salt hay**

See quot.

1945 Beck *Jersey Genesis* 161 **seNJ**, The Pleasant Mills plant . . turned out manila paper made from salt hay. Mrs. Albor said she remembered rolls of the stuff, finished paper, big tanks of boiling meadow musk, and the four-mule teams that hauled to Sailor Boy.

meadow mussel n [**meadow B1**]

The Atlantic ribbed **mussel 1** *(Geukensia demissa)*.

1881 Ingersoll *Oyster-Industry* 245 **NY**, Meadow Mussel.—In Great South bay, Long Island, the *Mytilus plicatula* which grows on the tide-flats. **1890** *Century Dict.* 3672 **NY**, Meadow-mussel. . . A kind of mussel found on tide-flats or salt meadows, *Modiola plicatula*. [**1981** Rehder *Audubon Field Guide Seashells* 688, This mussel [=*Geukensia demissa*] is abundant in the salt marshes . . where it occurs in clumps buried in mud among the roots of the marsh cordgrass *Spartina*.]

meadow oat grass n Also *meadow oat(s)*

=**oat grass a.**

1815 *Lit. & Philos. Soc. NY Trans.* 1.71, The avena elatior, or tall meadow oats . . is recommended as the best grass for green fodder and hay. **1822** (1972) Deane *New Engl. Farmer* 171, *Tall Meadow Oat*. . . has been cultivated in Massachusetts, as well as in the State of New-York, and the southern States. **1889** Vasey *Ag. Grasses* 52, *Arrhenatherum avenaceum* . . Meadow Oat Grass. . . When growing with other grasses, cattle and sheep eat it very well, but do not like to be confined to it exclusively. **1937** U.S. Forest Serv. *Range Plant Hdbk.* G22, It [=*Arrhenatherum elatius*] was more or less well established in New England and the Tennessee and Ohio Valleys as early as 1884. At that time it was known as . . meadow oatgrass. **1956** St. John *Flora SE WA* 32, Tall Meadow Oatgrass. . . Sparingly escaped from cultivation.

meadow owl n Cf **marsh owl**

Prob =**short-eared owl**.

1939 *LANE* Map 230, 1 inf, **seNY**, Meadow owl, large.

meadow oxeye n [See quots 1904, 1956]

=**least sandpiper**.

1904 Wheelock *Birds CA* 65, Least sandpiper, or meadow oxeye. *Ibid* 66, Their frequenting the meadows in the vicinity of water and hiding in the long grass has given them the name of "Meadow Oxeye." **1923** U.S. Dept. Ag. *Misc. Circular* 13.55 **NY**, Least Sandpiper . . meadow oxeye. **1932** Howell *FL Bird Life* 240, Least Sandpiper. . . Meadow Oxeye. **1956** MA Audubon Soc. *Bulletin* 40.19 **ME, MA**, Least Sandpiper . . Meadow Oxeye. . . Latter term from the full, round eye.

meadow parsnip n

1 A plant of the genus *Thaspium*. For other names of *T. trifoliatum* see **purple alexanders**

1822 Eaton *Botany* 484, *Thaspium. . . aureum* (meadow parsnip). . . Grows in dry meadows and pastures. **1848** Gray *Manual of Botany* 161, *Thaspium. . .* Meadow Parsnip. **1901** Mohr *Plant Life AL* 642, *Thaspium pinnatifidum.* . . Mountain Meadow Parsnip. **1942** Hylander *Plant Life* 412, Golden Parsnip *(Zizia)* produces yellow flowers. . . Meadow Parsnip *(Thaspium)* has similar leaves but purple flowers; it ranges from the Atlantic coast into the central states. **1968** *DARE* (Qu. S26c, *Wildflowers that grow in woods*) Inf **PA99**, Purple meadow parsnip. **1979** Niering–Olmstead *Audubon Guide N. Amer. Wildflowers E. Region* 334, A common southern Meadow Parsnip of a different genus *(Thaspium trifoliatum)*, sometimes called Golden Alexanders as well, has only 3 lanceolate, toothed leaflets.

2 =**golden alexanders 1.**

1833 Eaton *Botany* 401, *[Zizia] aurea* . . meadow parsnip, alexanders. **1843** Torrey *Flora NY* 1.271, *Zizia aurea*. . . Golden Meadow Parsnep. **1901** Lounsberry *S. Wild Flowers* 370, Golden meadow parsnip. **1916** Keeler *Early Wildflowers* 171, The golden-yellow clusters of the Early Meadow-Parsnip often get into the race in April and are especially noticeable because of the pure brilliant yellow of the massed florets. **1968** Barkley *Plants KS* 264, Golden Alexanders. Meadow Parsnip. Golden Zizia.

meadow phlox n

A **phlox**: usu *Phlox maculata*, rarely *P. glaberrima*.

1933 Small *Manual SE Flora* 1105, *P[hlox] maculata.* . . Meadow Phlox. . . Damp thickets, meadows, and moist open woods. **1940** Clute *Amer. Plant Names* 266, *Phlox glaberrima*. Prairie phlox, meadow-phlox. **1949** Moldenke *Amer. Wild Flowers* 149, The meadow phlox, *P. maculata*, . . [has] smaller, narrower leaves and often strikingly purple-streaked stems. **1965** *Native Plants PA* 54, Phlox maculata pyramidalis—Late Meadow Phlox.

meadow pine n

1 Any of var **pines** native chiefly to the southern US, as:

a A **slash pine** (here: *Pinus elliotii*).

1884 Sargent *Forests of N. Amer.* 202, *Pinus cubensis*. . . Slash Pine. . . Meadow Pine. . . Light sandy soil along the dunes and marshes of the coast, or wet clay borders of ponds, abandoned fields, etc. **1896** Mohr–Roth *Timber Pines* 77, In Florida, where best known, it [=*Pinus heterophylla*] is distinguished as the Slash Pine; and in the flat woods along the seashore in Alabama and Mississippi as Meadow Pine. **1897** Sudworth *Arborescent Flora* 31 **CA, FL, eMS**, *Pinus heterophylla*. . . Cuban Pine. . . Meadow Pine. **1908** Britton *N. Amer. Trees* 37, It [=*Pinus heterophylla*] is also called Swamp pine, Bastard pine, Meadow pine [etc].

b =**loblolly pine 1.** [See quot 1908]

1896 Mohr–Roth *Timber Pines* 106 **FL**, Loblolly Pine. . . Meadow Pine. **1897** Sudworth *Arborescent Flora* 26 **FL**, Loblolly Pine. . . Meadow Pine. **1908** Rogers *Tree Book* 35, "Old-field" and "meadow pine" refer to its habit of invading land abandoned by farmers.

c A **pond pine** (here: *Pinus serotina*).

1908 Britton *N. Amer. Trees* 32, It [=*Pinus serotina*] is also known as . . Meadow pine, and Spruce pine. **1950** Peattie *Nat. Hist. Trees* 24, Pocosin pine. . . Other Names: Pond, Marsh, or Meadow Pine.

2 =**horsetail 1** (here: *Equisetum arvense*).

1914 Georgia *Manual Weeds* 20, *Equisetum arvense*. . . Meadow Pine. **1935** (1943) Muenscher *Weeds* 129, Field horsetail . . Meadow-pine. **1968** Schmutz et al. *Livestock-Poisoning Plants AZ* 84, Meadowpine *(Equisetum arvense)*.

meadow pinegrass n

=**bluejoint 1.**

1937 U.S. Forest Serv. *Range Plant Hdbk.* G41, Bluejoint [=*Calamagrostis canadensis*], also known in some locations as . . meadow pinegrass . . is the most common and widespread species of *Calamagrostis* in North America.

meadow pink n

1 A **swamp azalea** (here: *Rhododendron viscosum*). Cf **honeysuckle 3**

1827 *Western Mth. Rev.* 1.323, Meadow pink, or honey suckle,—a shrub which fringes brooks and creeks, in the pine woods. **1900** Lyons *Plant Names* 56, *A[zalea] viscosa*. . . Swamp Pink, Meadow Pink,

Swamp Honeysuckle. **1940** Clute *Amer. Plant Names* 219, *Azalea visosa* [sic]. Cinnamon honeysuckle. Meadow pink.

2 A fringed orchid (here: *Platanthera grandiflora*).
1892 *Jrl. Amer. Folkl.* 5.103 **MA**, *Habenaria fimbriata,* meadow pink. **1959** Carleton *Index Herb. Plants* 80, *Meadow-pink* . . Habenaria fimbriata.

3 A swamp pink (here: *Arethusa bulbosa*).
1897 *Jrl. Amer. Folkl.* 10.144 **MA**, *Arethusa bulbosa* . . swamp pink, meadow pink.

4 A marsh pink 1 (here: *Sabatia campestris*). **TX**
1936 Whitehouse *TX Flowers* 98, *Prairie Sabbatia (Sabbatia campestris)* is also known as meadow pink. **1961** Wills–Irwin *Flowers TX* 171, Meadow-pink is found in the eastern half of Texas. **1979** Ajilvsgi *Wild Flowers* 226 **TX**, Meadow-pink.

meadow plover n
1 =**killdeer 1.**
1923 U.S. Dept. Ag. *Misc. Circular* 13.69 **PA**, Kildeer. . . meadow plover. **1946** Hausman *Eastern Birds* 256, Meadow Plover. **1955** MA Audubon Soc. *Bulletin* 39.444 **MA**, Kildeer. . . Meadow Plover. **1969** Longstreet *Birds FL* 59, Meadow Plover.

2 =**upland plover** (here: *Bartramia longicauda*).
1903 Dawson *Birds OH* 2.529, Probably the bird [=*Bartramia longicauda*] is better known throughout the state as the Upland Plover, or Meadow Plover.

meadowpride n
=**columbo.**
1873 in 1976 Miller *Shaker Herbs* 159, Colombo, American. . . Indian Lettuce, Pyramid Flower, Meadow Pride, Yellow Gentian. **1900** Lyons *Plant Names* 164, *F[rasera] Carolinensis.* . . Meadow-pride.

meadow quail n Cf **marsh quail, nigger quail**
The eastern **meadowlark 1.**
1956 MA Audubon Soc. *Bulletin* 40.130 **MA**, *Meadowlark.* . . Meadow Quail.

meadow queen See **queen of the meadow**

meadow rattlesnake n
=**massasauga.**
1899 Garland *Boy Life* 81 **nwIA** (as of c1870s), It was a "Massasauga" or meadow rattlesnake. The scythe had clipped his head and about four inches of neck from his body, and he lay sullenly quiet, with his little black, forked tongue playing in and out of his mouth. As Mr. Stewart presented a piece of popple bark, the head opened its mouth wide and flat and struck its fine, curving fangs into it.

meadow rose n
A **wild rose:** usu *Rosa blanda,* rarely *R. carolina.*
1900 Lyons *Plant Names* 324, *R[osa] blanda.* . . Pale, Smooth or Meadow Rose. **1910** Graves *Flowering Plants* 242 **CT**, *Rosa blanda.* . . Meadow, Thornless or Early Wild Rose. **1942** Tehon *Fieldbook IL Shrubs* 124, The Meadow Rose ranges from Newfoundland west to Saskatchewan and south to Pennsylvania and Illinois. **1952** Blackburn *Trees* 252, *R[osa] blanda.* . . meadow rose. **1952** Taylor *Plants Colonial Days* 81, The swamp rose [=*Rosa palustris*], which grows wild throughout the eastern United States, . . is often confused with the meadow rose [=*R. carolina*].

meadow rue n [*OED* 1668 →]
A plant of the genus *Thalictrum.* **chiefly Nth** Also called **maid-of-the-mist 1.** For other names of var spp see **king-of-the-meadow 1, lady rue, maidenhair 3, muskrat weed 2, queen of the meadow, quicksilver weed, rattlesnake bite, rue, rue anemone, shining grass, silverweed, skunk meadowrue, sweet grass**
1817 Eaton *Botany* 62, *Thalictrum.* . . *dioicum,* (meadow rue). **1843** Torrey *Flora NY* 1.23, Common Meadow Rue. . . A common tall plant in wet meadows, varying in its foliage according to the degree of exposure and shade. **1884** Roe *Nature's Serial Story* 311 **seNY**, She never came to the house without bringing . . bunches of meadow-rue from her rambles. **1901** Mohr *Plant Life AL* 515, *Thalictrum.* . . *Meadow Rue.* . . Temperate regions Northern Hemisphere. **1931** Fassett *Spring Flora* 62 **WI**, *Meadow Rue.* . . Staminate and pistillate flowers on different plants. **1960** Teale *Journey into Summer* 11 **ME**, Many of the openings were strewn with spikenard and meadow rue and star flowers in bloom. **1965–70** DARE Wildfl QR Pl.71 Infs **CA**24, **MI**7,

31, 57, **NY**91, **OR**8, **WA**10, 12, Meadow rue; **SC**41, Meador [sic] rue; Pl.72 Infs **NY**91, **WI**79, Meadow rue. **1967–69** DARE (Qu. S26a, . . *Wildflowers. . . Roadside flowers*) Infs **CT**8, 23, **MA**67, Meadow rue; (Qu. S26b, *Wildflowers that grow in water or wet places*) Infs **CT**23, **MA**67, Meadow rue; (Qu. S26d, *Wildflowers that grow in meadows; not asked in early QRs*) Infs **CT**30, **MA**67, **NE**9, **RI**15, Meadow rue. **1979** Niering–Olmstead *Audubon Guide N. Amer. Wildflowers E. Region* 729, The leaves of Rue Anemone [=*Anemonella thalictroides*] are similar to those of the Meadow Rues (*Thalictrum* spp.)

meadow sandpiper n
=**upland plover** (here: *Bartramia longicauda*).
1903 Dawson *Birds OH* 2.529, Probably the bird is better known throughout the state as the Upland Plover, or Meadow . . Sandpiper. . . While it is a true sandpiper in structure, its habits resemble the plover group.

meadow scabish n
=**cocash 2.**
1854 King *Amer. Eclectic Dispensatory* 265, *Aster puniceus.* Red-stalked Aster. . . This plant is variously known by the names of *Cocash, Meadow Scabish, Squaw-weed,* etc. **1900** Lyons *Plant Names* 52, *A[ster] puniceus.* . . Meadow Scabish. **1914** Georgia *Manual Weeds* 435, *Purple-stemmed aster.* . . Meadow scabish, Cocash. **1940** Clute *Amer. Plant Names* 76, *A[ster] puniceus.* . . rough-stemmed aster, swamp-weed,—meadow-scabish, cocash. **1959** Carleton *Index Herb. Plants* 80, *Meadow scabish:* Aster puniceus.

meadow shield fern See **meadow fern 3**

meadow shoe n [**meadow** n B1]
1968 DARE FW Addit **NJ**, Meadow shoes—wide shoes for horses worn over the regular shoe to provide a better footing on wetland or meadows. Some were wooden or leather; others were double loops of iron.

meadow snipe n
1 =**Wilson's snipe.**
1791 Bartram *Travels* 294, S[colopax] minor arvensis, the meadow snipe. **1890** *Century Dict.* 3672, *Meadow-snipe.* . . The common American or Wilson's snipe, *Gallinago wilsoni* or *delicatula.* **1923** U.S. Ag. *Misc. Circular* 13.50 **PA**, Common snipe (*Gallinago gallinago*). . . gray snipe, little woodcock, meadow snipe. **1953** Jewett *Birds WA* 253, *Wilson Common Snipe* . . Meadow Snipe; Marsh Snipe.

2 =**pectoral sandpiper.**
1844 DeKay *Zool. NY* 2.242, It [=the pectoral sandpiper] passes under the various names of *Meadow Snipe, Jack Snipe, Short-neck,* and according to Mr. Giraud it is called *Fat-bird* on the coast of New-Jersey. **1876** *Forest & Stream* 7.68, *Tringa pectoralis.* Creaker; meadow-snipe. **1923** U.S. Dept. Ag. *Misc. Circular* 13.54 **NY, NJ, MI**, Meadow snipe. **1932** Howell *FL Bird Life* 237, Pectoral Sandpiper . . Grass Snipe . . Meadow Snipe. **1955** Forbush–May *Birds* 195, Marsh-plover . . Meadow Snipe.

meadow sparrow n
=**Savannah sparrow.**
1953 Jewett *Birds WA* 629, *Passerculus sandwichensis crassus.* . . Savannah Sparrow, Meadow Sparrow, Grass Sparrow. **1966–67** DARE (Qu. Q21, . . *Kinds of sparrows*) Inf **OH**4, Meadow sparrow; **NC**24, Field sparrow or meadow sparrow.

meadow star n
=**cinquefoil.**
1933 Small *Manual SE Flora* 610, *Cinquefoils. Five-fingers. Meadow-stars.*—Our species all have yellow flowers. **1949** Moldenke *Amer. Wild Flowers* 120, *P[otentilla] simplex,* the meadowstar, [is common] in shaded grassy situations and open woods from Nova Scotia to Minnesota and south to Georgia and Texas.

meadow starling n [See quot 1927]
The eastern **meadowlark 1.**
1839 Audubon *Synopsis Birds* 148, Sturnella. . . Meadow-Starling. **1844** Giraud *Birds Long Is.* 147 **NY**, Starlings. Genus *Sturnella.* Meadow Starling. **1917** *Wilson Bulletin* 29.2.83 **swKY**, *Sturnella magna.*—Meadow starling, marsh quail. **1927** Forbush *Birds MA* 2.436, The Meadowlark is not a lark; it is a meadow starling. . . One can see at a glance that the bird bears a close superficial resemblance in form to a Starling, and its flight is similar to that of the latter. Our Meadow Starling in New England is rather a shy bird and keeps to the open lands.

meadow swallow n
=barn swallow 1.

1946 Hausman *Eastern Birds* 415, Barn swallow. . . Meadow Swallow. . . Very common about farms, or sweeping over fields and meadows.

meadowsweet n [*OED* 1530 →]

1 also *meadowsweet spirea:* **=spirea.**

1814 Bigelow *Florula Bostoniensis* 120, *Spiraea alba.* . . White Spiraea. Meadow sweet. . . A slender shrub three or four feet high, bearing large, terminal bunches of white flowers. **1822** Eaton *Botany* 478, *[Spiraea] tomentosa* (steeple-bush, purple hard-hack, meadow-sweet.) **1854** King *Amer. Eclectic Dispensatory* 902, *Spiraea tomentosa.* Hardhack. . . This plant, known also by the names of *Meadow-sweet, White-leaf,* and *Steeple-bush,* is a small shrub, from two to four feet in hight [sic]. **1860** Curtis *Cat. Plants NC* 103, *S[piraea] salicifolia* . . sometimes called *Meadow Sweet.* **1887** Freeman *Humble Romance* 135 **NEng,** The meadow-sweet and hardhack bushes were powdered thickly with dust, and had gray leaves instead of green. **1935** (1943) Muenscher *Weeds* 298, *Spiraea tomentosa* . . Woolly meadowsweet. **1966** *DARE* Wildfl QR Pl.93A Infs **MI**7, **SC**41, Meadowsweet; **OH**14, Meadowsweet spirea; **NY**91, Spirea, called meadowsweet; Pl.94A Infs **OH**14, **SC**41, Meadowsweet. **1967–70** *DARE* (Qu. S26a, . . *Wildflowers. . . Roadside flowers*) Inf **MA**78, Meadowsweet; **MA**67, Meadowsweet—has sweet, creamy-white flowers—comes out after meadow rue; (Qu. T16) Inf **MA**5, Meadowsweet. **1979** Niering-Olmstead *Audubon Guide N. Amer. Wildflowers E. Region* 760, Meadowsweet *(Spiraea latifolia).*

2 A plant of the genus *Filipendula.* For names of var spp see **bridal wreath 1, honeysweet 1, kiss-me-quick 1, pride of the meadow, queen of the forest, ~ meadow, ~ prairie, sweet bay, ~ William** Note: This genus was formerly included in *Spiraea.*

1815 Lit. & Philos. Soc. NY *Trans.* 1.72, The meadowsweet wastes away the cow, but it is beneficial to the goat. . . Spiraea Ulmaria [=*Filipendula ulmaria*]. **1876** Hobbs *Bot. Hdbk.* 69, Meadow sweet—Spiraea ulmaria. *Ibid* 215, Spiraea palmata . . American meadow sweet. **1910** Graves *Flowering Plants* 235 **CT,** *Filipendula Ulmaria.* . . Meadow-sweet. Honey-sweet. **1933** Small *Manual SE Flora* 610, *F[ilipendula] rubra.* . . Prairie meadow-sweet. **1942** Hylander *Plant Life* 296, Prairie Meadowsweet or Queen of the Prairie *(Filipendula)* has palmately lobed leaves and pink or purple flowers with broad petals. **1976** Bailey-Bailey *Hortus Third* 480, *Filipendula* . . Meadowsweet.

3 An **ocean spray** (here: *Holodiscus discolor).* **CA** Cf **false meadowsweet**

1897 Parsons *Wild Flowers CA* 85, Meadow-sweet. Spiræa [here: =*Holodiscus*] *discolor.* . . Not until midsummer is upon us does the common meadow-sweet make itself noticeable by its large feathery clusters of minute white flowers, which have a pleasant odor, reminiscent of slippery-elm. **1911** Jepson *Flora CA* 204, *H[olodiscus] discolor.* . . California Meadow Sweet. . . Cañons and low hills of the Coast Ranges from the coast to the inner ranges.

meadowsweet spirea See **meadowsweet 1**

meadow turnip n

A **jack-in-the-pulpit 1** (here: *Arisaema triphyllum).*

1900 Lyons *Plant Names* 45, *A[risaema] triphyllum.* . . Indian Turnip, . . Meadow- or Pepper-turnip. **1930** Sievers *Amer. Med. Plants* 37, *Jack-in-the-pulpit.* . . Other common names. . . Marsh turnip, . . meadow turnip. **1971** Krochmal *Appalachia Med. Plants* 62, *Arisaema triphyllum.* . . Meadow turnip.

meadow violet n

Any of several **violets,** but usu *Viola papilionacea;* see quots.

1883 *Century Illustr. Mag.* 26.727, The crane's-bill and the meadow-violet expend their surplus revenue in adding to their [own] attractiveness. **1933** Small *Manual SE Flora* 889, *V[iola] cucullata.* . . Meadow-violet. **1936** Winter *Plants NE* 93, *Viola papilionacea.* . . Meadow or Hooded Blue Violet. **1940** Steyermark *Flora MO* 366, *Meadow* . . *Violet (Viola papilionacea).* . . Frequently a waif in cultivated and waste places. **1949** Moldenke *Amer. Wild Flowers* 45, Almost equally well loved is *V. papilionacea,* the *meadow violet,* so abundant in moist fields, meadows, and groves, frequently around dwellings. . . The corolla is deep violet, white or greenish yellow at the center. **1950** *WELS,* 1 Inf, **cWI,** Meadow violet. **1953** Nelson *Plants Rocky Mt. Park* 106, The meadow violet or wanderer violet, *Viola nephrophylla* . . occur[s] in the montane zone. **1966** *DARE* Wildfl QR Plates 142A, B Inf **NC**28, Meadow violets. **1967–68** *DARE* (Qu. S11, . . *Blue violet*) Inf **IA**3, Meadow violets;

NJ29, Meadow violet—these can also be yellow or white; (Qu. S26e) Inf MD30, Meadow violets—purple or blue, stem about six inches long. **1968** Barkley *Plants KS* 242, *Viola papilionacea.* . . Meadow Violet. Woods, prairies, and flood plains.

meadow willow n

A **willow** (here: *Salix petiolaris).*

1960 Vines *Trees SW* 110, *S[alix] petiolaris.* . . Also known under the vernacular name of Meadow Willow. **1973** Stephens *Woody Plants* 50, *Salix petiolaris.* . . Meadow willow. . . *Habitat:* Stream banks and wet meadows, often associated closely with other species of willow. **1979** Little *Checklist U.S. Trees* 265, *Salix petiolaris.* . . Meadow willow.

meadowwink n [See quots 1890, 1956]

=bobolink B.

1884 Coues *Key to N. Amer. Birds* 400, *D[olichonyx] oryzivorus.* . . Bobolink. Meadow-wink. Skunk Blackbird. **1890** Warren *Birds PA* 206, Bobolinks are known by a variety of common names. The terms "Bobolink" and "Meadow Wink" are applied in imitation of its voice. **1898** (1900) Davie *Nests N. Amer. Birds* 338, In the South he is known as the Rice-bird, in the Middle States as Reed-bird and Meadow-wink, and in the North as Skunk Blackbird. **1923** Dawson *Birds CA* 1.137, Bobolink. . . Rice-bird. Meadow-wink. **1956** MA Audubon Soc. *Bulletin* 40.130 **MA, CT,** Meadow-wink. . . The second element of this name is sonic.

meadow wren n

A **marsh wren** (here: *Cistothorus platensis).*

1895 Minot *Land-Birds New Engl.* 77, The Meadow Wrens have a harsh unpleasant chatter, but also a simple and yet very pleasant song. **1946** Hausman *Eastern Birds* 449, Short-Billed Marsh Wren. . . Other Names—Meadow Wren, Fresh-Water Marsh Wren, Grass Wren. **1963** Gromme *Birds WI* 219, Wren, . . Meadow.

meal v esp **NEng**

To provide food for, feed; to eat a meal, take regular meals (as at a boarding house).

1630 Winthrop *Let. in New Eng.* (1825) I.378 *(OED),* Some more cows would be bought, especially two new milch, which must be well mealed and milked by the way. **1891** Bunner *Zadoc Pine* 201 **NY,** A lodging-house for those who "mealed" at the hotel. **1896** *DN* 1.420 **Nantucket MA,** *Mealing:* in "They're all gone a-mealing," = gone to dinner. **1914** *DN* 4.76 **ME, nNH,** *Meal.* . . To board. "They're mealin' to Drusilly's." **1928** *AmSp* 3.434, The reference to "roomed" . . reminds me of a sign that I saw while in Florida, at Sarasota I think it was: "Tourists Roomed and Mealed."

meal bag See **meal sack**

meal beer n Also *meal mammy* Cf *mammy* (at **mother** n[2]), **corn beer, still beer**

=beer 1.

1985 Wilkinson *Moonshine* 21 **neNC,** Initially, the mash tastes sweet and is sticky; fermented, it is tangy and sour. While turning, it has a two- or three-inch snowy collar, and when ready it is clear on top and the color of dark beer. It is called still beer, or meal beer, or meal mammy. "They call it meal mammy," says Garland, "because after it's processed it's so strong it'll make you fight your mammy."

mealberry n Also *mealyberry* [See quot 1924]

A **bearberry 2** (here: *Arctostaphylos uva-ursi).*

1890 *Century Dict.* 3673, Mealberry. . . The bearberry, *Arctostaphylos Uva-ursi.* **1920** *Torreya* 20.24, *Arctostaphylos uva-ursi* . . Mealyberry, Nantucket, Mass. . . This name is also used in Pine-barren region of New Jersey. **1924** *Amer. Botanist* 30.13, The rather large bright red and attractive fruits are devoid of juice which accounts for "meal-berry" and "meal plum." **1968** Hultén *Flora AK* 729, Kinnikinnick, Mealberry. **1976** Bailey-Bailey *Hortus Third* 101, Mealberry, hog cranberry.

mealer n [**meal**] esp **NEng** *old-fash* Cf **table board**

One who pays to take meals in one place while living elsewhere; hence n *mealery* a place that provides meals to those living elsewhere.

1880 *Harper's New Mth. Mag.* 61.619 **eNEng,** The term "mealer" is applied to those boarders living outside in the cottages, for whom, in wet weather, . . the buckboard . . is sent by the hotel-keepers. **1892** *KS Univ. Qrly.* 1.97 **KS,** *Mealer:* one who takes only meals at a boarding-house. **1896** *DN* 1.420 **Boston MA,** *Mealer* for *table boarder,* like *roomer* for *lodger,* is familiar to the boarding-house language in Boston. So *mealery* in Boston for a cheap boarding-house where meals are provided at a fixed price, generally with a reduction on a ticket for a week's meals. **1912** Woodrow *Sally Salt* 104, Besides the farm, I make something taking in mealers. **1914** *DN* 4.76 **ME, nNH,** *Mealer*. . . A boarder. **1928** *AmSp* 3.434, I remember hearing "roomers and mealers" even in Boston.

meal gravy See **meal soup**

meal of victuals n Also *meal's victuals;* for addit varr see quots [*EDD* *meal's victuals* (at *meal* sb.[1] 1.(4))]
A meal; food enough for a meal.

   1862 in 1967 *DARE* File **AL,** [Letter from Confederate soldier:] A meals vituals. **1878** *Appletons' Jrl.* 5.416 **Sth,** Instead of dining with a friend or taking tea, they eat "a meal's vittles" with him. **1895** Brown *Meadow-Grass* 117 **NH,** You 'ain't acted as if you'd relished a meal o' victuals for nigh onto ten days. **1899** (1912) Green *VA Folk-Speech* 277, *A meal of victuals,* food enough for one meal. **1903** *DN* 2.320 **seMO,** *Meals,* pl. for *sg.* n. Meal of victuals. 'I haven't cooked a meals [sic] of victuals for a year.[*]' **1914** *DN* 4.76 **ME, nNH,** *Meal 'o* [sic] *victuals.* . . Common for "meal." **1929** *AmSp* 5.127 **ME,** Someone in need did not "know where the next meal of victuals was coming from." **1942** (1971) Campbell *Cloud-Walking* 5 **seKY,** I better get a meal's victuals set out against the time Nelt and them two other younguns get back home. **1944** *PADS* 2.19 **sAppalachians,** *Meal's victuals.* . . A meal, repast. Also *meal o'victuals.*

meal plum (vine) See **mealy-plum (vine)**

meal room n [*meal* ground grain]
A pantry.

   [**1842** Kirkland *Forest Life* 1.239 **MI,** A meal-room near at hand [to the kitchen] contains several varieties of flour, and a buttery and milk-house supply other rustic dainties in profusion.] **1967** Faries *Word Geog. MO* 73, The general term *pantry* . . seems to be almost the exclusive name in Missouri for a room in which to keep provisions. . . *Meal room,* a write-in, appears once. **1968** *DARE* (Qu. D8, *The small room next to the kitchen [in older houses] where dishes and sometimes foods are kept*) Inf **VA**13, Meal room. **1986** Pederson *LAGS Concordance (Pantry)* 7 infs, **eTN,** Meal room.

meal sack n Also *meal bag* Cf **bran sack**
A coarse cloth sack.

   1644 *Essex Prob. Rec.* I.46 *(DAE)* **eMA,** Too meal baggs. **1738** in 1914 NH *Prov. & State Papers* 32.622, He knows of no Meal Bag that his son had but what he borrowed of him. **1865** Kellogg *Life & Death* 119 **CT,** The dirt was pushed back . . in a *meal sack,* which we stole from the ration wagon. **1896** Freeman *Madelon* 98 **eMA,** He heaved the meal-sack from his shoulder to the floor. **1899** (1912) Green *VA Folk-Speech* 278, *Meal-bag.* . . Made of a salt-sack, held three bushels of corn or meal, and used for sending "toll" to mill every week. **1902** White *Blazed Trail* 131 **eMI,** They were . . carrying each a bulging meal sack looped by a cord across the shoulders and chest. **1950** Stuart *Hie Hunters* 23 **eKY,** Sparkie pulled a meal-sack towel down from the nail, and he dried on one end while Did dried on the other. **c1960** Wilson *Coll.* **csKY,** *Mealsack.* . . A heavy cotton bag, holding two bushels of corn or ground meal. These sacks were often made into strong, wearever towels for farm families. **1965** *DARE* Tape **KY**3, We had what they call a meal sack that you bought. It was a very coarse knit sack. . . It was very special; it wouldn't let even the dust of the meal go through, and it was long, something around four feet almost, and you could take two bushel of corn in this one sack by balancing it across the saddle on a mule. **1966** Dakin *Dial. Vocab. Ohio R. Valley* 2.140 **Ohio Valley,** Several miscellaneous names are used for the coarse sack. . . *corn sack, bran ~, meal ~.* **1966–70** *DARE* (Qu. F19, *A cloth container for grain*) Infs **FL**49, **IN**19, **MI**68, **OK**21, Meal sack; **ME**5, **OH**98, Meal bag; (Qu. F20, *A cloth container for feed*) Infs **MA**6, **MI**68, Meal bag; (Qu. F21, *A cloth or paper container that you buy flour in*) Inf **VA**53, Meal bag. **1986** Pederson *LAGS Concordance (Sack, made of cloth)* 32 infs, **Gulf Region,** Meal sack.

meal soup n Also *meal gravy*
A soup or gravy made from broth or meat drippings thickened with meal.

   1967 *DARE* FW Addit **KY**34, Meal soup—after cooking a chicken in boiling water, meal was added to the broth to make a thick soup. **1969** *DARE* (Qu. H37, . . *Words . . for gravy*) Inf **TN**37, Meal gravy. **1986** Pederson *LAGS Concordance,* 1 inf, **cwAL,** Meal gravy, meal soup—used to make gravy with meal after frying fatback.

meal's victuals See **meal of victuals**

meal ticket n

1 One who provides for another—usu used of a spouse. Cf **biscuit getter**

   1902 Ade *Girl Proposition* 93, Tessie never came back for she had found her Meal-Ticket. **1925** *Scribner's Mag.* 78.411, Frequently . . a woman will marry a man so worthless . . as to regard him simply in the light of what he calls his "meal ticket." **1929** Wolfe *Look Homeward* 384 **cwNC,** She can't bear to give him [=her son] up. . . He's her meal-ticket. **1950** *WELS* (*Joking names that a woman may use to refer to her husband:* "I wonder if my _____ is home yet?") 8 Infs, **WI,** Meal ticket. **1965–70** *DARE* (Qu. AA15c, . . *Joking ways . . of saying that a woman is getting married. . .* "She _____.") 72 Infs, **scattered,** Got (her *or* herself) a meal ticket; **NE**11, Found a meal ticket; **NJ**28, Married a meal ticket; **IN**32, Took a meal ticket; (Qu. AA23, *Joking names that a woman may use to refer to her husband:* "It's time to go and get supper for my _____.") 15 Infs, **scattered,** Meal ticket; (Qu. AA4b, . . *A woman who is very eager to get married. . .* "She's _____.") Infs **FL**39, **IL**43, **MN**15, **NJ**35, 41, **WI**47, Looking for a meal ticket; **MD**21, Wants a meal ticket; (Qu. AA5, *If a woman seems to be going after one certain man that she wants to marry:* "She's _____ him.") Inf **OH**47, Hunting a meal ticket; (Qu. AA15b, . . *Joking ways . . of saying that a man is getting married. . .* "He _____.") Infs **FL**51, **TX**6, Got a meal ticket.

2 One who gives a handout; see quots.

   1900 Willard *Tramping* 395, [Glossary:] *Meal-Ticket:* a person "good" for a meal. **1927** *DN* 5.455 [Underworld jargon], *Meal ticket.* . . A charitable person who can be inveigled into giving a tramp a meal. **1966** Barnes–Jensen *Dict. UT Slang* 30, *Meal ticket* . . a source of gratuitous money.

3 A livelihood, means of support.

   1969 *DARE* Tape **CA**158, We sold range cattle and dairied for twelve years, and that was our meal ticket. We'd have been starved if it hadn't been for butterfat.

mealy adj [*OED* 1675 →]
Of an animal, esp a horse, cow, or mule: light-colored; flecked with light colors, esp around the nose and mouth.

   1806 (1905) Clark *Orig. Jrls. Lewis & Clark Exped.* 4.139, A species [of gull] somewhat larger of a light brown colour, with a mealy coloured back. [**1872** Powers *Afoot* 279 **West,** Suddenly we saw an enormous "meal-nose" [=a grizzly bear], sitting erect on his haunches, nearly eight feet high.] **1899** (1912) Green *VA Folk-Speech* 278, *Mealy-mouthed.* . . White-mouthed, as if dippped [sic] in meal. "Item. one Mealy-mouthed bull." *Mealy-mouthed.* . . A bay or brown horse having a light-coloured muzzle. **1902** in 1991 Biggers *Buffalo Guns* 35 **wTX,** There were two distinct breeds of buffalo; the 'mealy noses' and the 'black noses,' the noses of the former being yellow, or a smutty brown. **1925** *Book of Rural Life* 6.3712, In earlier times the color [of mule] most sought was black with white (mealy colored) muzzles and flanks. **1928** Ruppenthal *Coll.* **KS,** The mule was brown with light mealy points. **1941** Dobie *Longhorns* 66 **TX,** One such heifer—black, mealy-nosed and line-backed—jabbed her dagger-pointed horn. **1967** Green *Horse Tradin'* 78 **TX,** There was a big, black, mealy-nosed mule tied to its wheel. **1967** *DARE* Tape **TX**24, Those Missoura jacks, they had a white nose, you know—these Spanish burros, they haven't got that mealy nose.

mealyberry See **mealberry**

mealybush n
=**honeycup 2.**

   [**1821** Elliott *Sketch* 1.493 **SC,** [*Andromeda] pulverulenta;* with leaves more round, crenate, and coated, as well as the young branches, with a white dust.] **1830** Rafinesque *Med. Flora* 2.192, The powder on the leaves and buds of *A[ndromeda] pulverulenta* or *Mealybush,* and other kinds is a powerful errhine; even the powdered leaves are such. **1876** Hobbs *Bot. Hdbk.* 70, Mealy bush, Andromeda pulverulenta.

mealy-cup sage n Also *mealy sage* [See quot 1949] **TX**
A *sage* (here: *Salvia farinacea*).

   1946 Reeves–Bain *Flora TX* 161, *S[alvia] farinacea.* . . Mealy Sage. **1949** Moldenke *Amer. Wild Flowers* 297, A handsome Texan species is *S[alvia] farinacea,* the mealycup sage, so called because the violet-blue corollas issue from white-mealy cuplike calyxes in 8-inch-long clusters. **1961** Wills–Irwin *Flowers TX* 197, Probably the most widely distributed [species of sage in Texas] is Blue Sage or Mealy Sage, with bluish-purple flowers from April to July. **1976** Bailey–Bailey *Hortus Third* 999, Mealy-cup s[age].

mealymouth v

To avoid frank speech.

1934 Hurston *Jonah's Gourd Vine* 18 **AL** [Black], You mealy-moufin' round cause you skeered tuh talk back tuh Rush Beasley.

mealy-plum (vine) n Also *meal plum (vine)* [See quot 1924] =**bearberry 2.**

1882 Godfrey *Is. Nantucket* 36 **seMA**, The mealplum vine . . gives a true richness to the commons of Nantucket. **1920** Packard *Old Plymouth* 77 **seMA**, The mealy-plum itself shows faint coral edging of pink young buds. *Ibid*, Mossy mats of mealy-plum. **1924** [see **mealberry**]. **1974** (1977) Coon *Useful Plants* 133, Bearberry, kinnikinnick, mealy-plum vine.

mealy sage See **mealy-cup sage**

mealy tree n

A **viburnum** (here: *Viburnum dentatum*).

1830 Rafinesque *Med. Flora* 2.274, *V[iburnum] dentatum* (Mealy tree, Arrow wood and *Tity* of Indians). Bark used by Indians and Shakers as a diuretic and detergent, bitterish, contains a peculiar fragrant oil. **1854** King *Amer. Eclectic Dispensary* 958, *Viburnum Dentatum,* Arrow-wood, or Mealy-tree, called by the former name on account of its long, straight, slender branches or young shoots, is a somewhat smooth shrub . . growing in low grounds, damp woods, and thickets. **1910** Graves *Flowering Plants* 368 **CT**, *Viburnum dentatum*. . . Arrow-wood. Mealy Tree. Frequent. Swamps and on banks of streams. **1960** Vines *Trees SW* 964, *Viburnum dentatum*. . . is also known under the vernacular names of Southern Arrowwood, Mealy-tree. . . Indians were known to have made arrows from the straight stems.

mean adj

1 Of liquor: inciting combativeness; harmful in effect; poor in quality. **chiefly Sth, S Midl**

1847 in 1930 Meine *Tall Tales* 6 **GA**, That liquor of Sterritt's is mean enough to make a man do anything dirty. **1867** [see **mountaineer**]. **1871** Eggleston *Hoosier Schoolmaster* 195 **sIN**, How Welch's whisky was all-fired mean, and how it allers went straight to his head. **1896** Harris *Sister Jane* 259 **GA**, They had knives, pistols, bad tempers, and a good deal of mean whiskey along. **1904** *Charlotte Observer* 27 Aug. 4 *(DAE)*, There was the usual tough contingent that filled up on mean whiskey. **c1960** *Wilson Coll.* **csKY**, *Mean whiskey*. . . Poor quality, cheap, not made right, harmful. **1966–69** DARE (Qu. DD21b, *General words . . for bad liquor*) Infs **KY**16, **NC**30, **TN**14, 37, Mean (liquor).

2 Of weather: very unpleasant, disagreeable.

1897 Barrère–Leland *Slang* 2.47, The night was dark and stormy, about as mean a night as was ever experienced in Washington. **1936** in 1973 Ade *Letters* 192 **nwIN**, We . . almost immediately ran into mean weather including one snow fall which completely covered the ground. **1939** LANE Map 88 **NEng**, In the context *It's a cloudy day*. . . [26 infs said] *Mean*. **c1960** *Wilson Coll.* **csKY**, *Mean-looking*. . . Likely to become bad, as weather. **1965–70** DARE (Qu. B2, *If the weather is very unpleasant . . it's a _____ day*) Infs **MA**50, 100, **NH**14, **NJ**31, **OH**57, **OK**31, **TN**37, Mean; (Qu. B5, *When the weather looks as if it will become bad . . it's _____*) Infs **AL**6, 11, 14, **NJ**15, **NY**198, **TN**52, **VT**16, Mean-looking; **IA**32, Starting to get mean. **1986** Pederson *LAGS Concordance*, 1 inf, **cwMS**, Going be mean out there today; 1 inf, **ceTX**, A southeast wind is a mean wind—it's cold.

3 Unwell, "under the weather." **esp NEast**

1911 Wilson *Land Claimers* 21, "Feel pretty mean?" the packer asked him kindly. "I'm not just fit," was the brief answer. **1911** Harrison *Queed* 90 **Sth**, Mebbe you could do better writing and harder writing if only you did n't feel so mean. **1931–33** LANE Worksheets **cMA**, I feel kinda mean. **1943** LANE Map 493 **NEng**, Beside or instead of *bad(ly)* [in the context *He is feeling bad(ly)*] many informants offered. . . *Mean*. **1959** *VT Hist.* 27.148, *Mean*. . . Ill; indisposed. . . Common. **1967–69** DARE (Qu. BB5, *A general feeling of discomfort or illness that isn't any one place in particular*) Infs **CA**17, **RI**10, Feel mean; **VT**16, Mean all over; **IN**30, Mean feeling; (Qu. BB39, *On a day when you don't feel just right, though not actually sick . . "I'll be all right tomorrow—I'm just feeling _____ today."*) Inf **NY**35, Mean. **1975** DARE File **cnMA** (as of c1915), I've felt kind of mean ever since I got up this morning. **1976** in 1982 Barrick Coll. **csPA**, *Mean*—not well, ill. "He jist felt mean, ya know."

4 in phrr *mean white (person)*: =**poor White. Sth**

1837 (1966) Martineau *Soc. in America* 2.146 **GA**, He told me that there was great excitement among the negroes in Augusta [about a lynching]; and that many had been saying that "a mean white person"

(a white labourer) would not have been hanged. **1845** *Knickerbocker* 26.336, Half of the songs published as theirs [=Negroes'] are . . the productions of 'mean whites.' **1868** *Putnam's Mag.* 11.704 **wSC**, That wretched caste commonly spoken of as the "mean whites." **1872** Schele de Vere *Americanisms* 617, *Mean Whites* were, in the days of slavery, the white citizens of the South who had no slaves to work for them, and yet deemed themselves too good to work themselves. **1891** Dixon *Dict. Idiom. Phrases* 211, *A mean white*—a name used in the Southern States of America . . to signify "a white man without landed property." **1986** Pederson *LAGS Concordance (The poor whites—[black man's terms])* 1 inf, **ceAR**, A mean white person.

mean adv

Very, exceedingly—used before an unfavorable adj to intensify its meaning.

1940 (1978) Still *River of Earth* 139 **KY**, He puckered his lips; he looked as mean-mad as he could. **1954** *Harder Coll.* **cwTN**, *Mean spoilt:* Said of a child that misbehaves. **1966** Maddux *Spring Rain* 66 **WV**, That Boy, he's been mean bad since he was fifteen years old. . . Why, even his own mother don't like him. **1968** DARE (Qu. HH22b, . . *A very mean person . . "He's meaner than _____."*) Inf **LA**35, He's mean mean.

mean n[1]

Meanness.

1922 Gonzales *Black Border* 312 **sSC, GA coasts** [Gullah glossary], *Mean*—mean, meanness. **1971** *Foxfire* Spring–Summer 84 **GA**, He was full'a mean. He had that born and bred in th'bone.

mean n[2] See **meanie**

mean as one's hide would hold one See **hide** n[2] **3**

meander v Pronc-spp *mi-ander, muander* **scattered, but less freq Sth, S Midl** See Map

Of a person or animal: to wander about with no specific purpose or destination.

1875 Twain *Sketches New & Old* (Hartford) 248, If you'll just give me a lift we'll skeet him into the hearse and meander along. **1890** Johnston *Widow Guthrie* 219 **GA** (as of 1830s), That animal of a colt he'll muander everywhere, all over the lot, and what he can't manage to jump over, he'll jump intoo. **1894** Riley *Armazindy* 9 **IN**, Season done,/ He'd be off mi-anderun. **1911** *San Francisco Examiner* (CA) 2 July 43 *(Zwilling Coll.)*, [Cartoon:] Do you promise to take this thing for a wife as long as you continue to meander on the map? Sure!! I'll try anything once. **1950** WELS (*To move about slowly*) 4 Infs, **WI**, Meander. **1958** *Sat. Eve. Post Letters*, Meander around—(wander aimlessly). **1965–70** DARE (Qu. KK31, *To go about aimlessly looking for distraction: "He doesn't have anything to do, so he's just _____ around."*) 25 Infs, **scattered, but less freq Sth, S Midl**, Meandering; (Qu. Y27, *To go about aimlessly, with nothing to do: "He's always _____ around the drugstore."*) 13 Infs, **scattered, but less freq Sth, S Midl**, Meandering; (Qu. Y21, *To move about slowly and without energy*) 9 Infs, **esp Nth**, Meander (about *or* along); **NJ**56, Meandering; (Qu. Y19, *To begin to go away from a place: "It's about time for me to _____."*) Infs **IL**96, **WA**18, Meander (home).

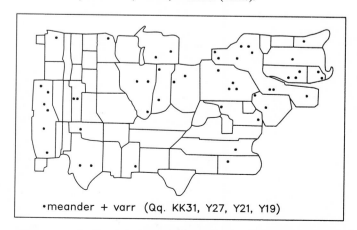

•meander + varr (Qq. KK31, Y27, Y21, Y19)

mean enough to kill his grandmother (or grandma) See **grandmother 3**

meaner than a (mad) dog See **dog** n **B17d**

meanery n

Meanness.

1845 Thompson *Pineville* 47 **cGA,** This town's got a monstrous bad name for meanery . . of all sorts. **1872** (1973) Thompson *Major Jones's Courtship* 138 **GA,** Can any man look over our country, and see the pride, the meanery, the rascality, the corruption . . that characterizes the people of our day? **1909** *DN* 3.348 **eAL, wGA,** *Meanery.* . . Meanness. "The meanery of some folks is past reason."

meanie n Also *mean* [Prob varr of **minnie** n²]

In marble play: see quot.

1967–68 *DARE* (Qu. EE6b, *Small marbles or marbles in general*) Inf **AK5,** Meanies; **NE3,** Means.

‡mean maybe adv phr [Prob abbr for *and I don't mean maybe*]

1954 *Harder Coll.* **cwTN,** *Mean maybe:* Seriously, really, actually. "I went to Knoxville payday nite to a dance hall. I sure had a time mean maybe."

mean-mouth v Cf **badmouth** v

To malign; to give a tongue-lashing to (someone).

c1960 *Wilson Coll.* **csKY,** *Mean-mouth.* . . To bemean, scold. **1969** *DARE* (Qu. Y3, *To say uncomplimentary things about somebody*) Inf **KY24,** Mean-mouth. **1970** *DARE* FW Addit **TN,** Mean-mouth = to insult. "Let's mean-mouth this guy!"

Means grass n [See quot 1914]

=Johnson grass 1.

1858 *S. Cultivator* 16.57, We advise all our readers who are troubled with . . "Means Grass," . . to give this plan a fair trial. **1887** Beal *Grasses N. Amer.* 1.171, *Means' Grass.* . . From several sources I learn that in 1835 Gov. Means obtained the seed from Turkey. **1889** Vasey *Ag. Grasses* 51, *Sorghum halepense.* (Cuba grass, Johnson grass, Means grass, False Guinea grass, Evergreen millet, Arabian millet.) **1914** Georgia *Manual Weeds* 22, Means-grass. [*Ibid* 23, About 1830 there came to Governor Means of South Carolina, a message from the Sultan of Turkey, requesting that an instructor in the art of raising cotton be sent to the Ottoman Empire. . . When the instructor returned, he brought with him the seeds of a number of plants . . , and among them was this grass.] **1948** Wolfe *Farm Gloss.* 179, *Johnson Grass*—Also known as Means Grass. . . Found in many fields, meadows and waste places. **1976** Bailey-Bailey *Hortus Third* 1061, *Means-grass.* . . Cult[ivated] for forage and naturalized in many parts of the U.S.; often a troublesome weed.

mean white (person) See **mean** adj **4**

meany adj

Mean; irritable.

1941 *Sat. Eve. Post* 10 May 113 **KY,** Fern roused, meany for being awakened with a start. **1984** Burns *Cold Sassy* 103 **nGA** (as of 1906), She'd get mad and hit me if I crossed her or sassed her, and I'd do meany things to her, like tripping her up or putting sugar in her salt cellar.

measle v

1917 *DN* 4.414 **wNC,** *Measle.* . . To catch measles. "The old cow measled, and she died last spring."

measure n, v Usu |ˈmɛžə(r)|; also |ˈmežə(r)|; *among Black speakers* |ˈmɛjə(r)|; *for addit varr see quot 1981* Pronc-spp *medjer, medjuh, me(d)jure*

Std senses, var forms.

1838 (1852) Gilman *S. Matron* 49 **SC** [Black], Will mistress please to *medjure* out some calomel? **1884** *Anglia* 7.262 **Sth, S Midl** [Black], *To come out short medjer* = to get less than one expects. **1892** (1969) Christensen *Afro-Amer. Folk Lore* 40, I kin tie you to de tree, an' den I kin medjure an' see whether you head bigger dan de tree or not. **1893** Shands *MS Speech* 44, *Mejure* [ˈmɛjə]. Negro for *measure.* **1922** Gonzales *Black Border* 154 **sSC, GA coasts** [Gullah], Mek 'um fuh po'rum 'tell de muhlassis stop run out de medjuh. [=Make him pour them till the molasses stop running out of the measure.] *Ibid* 312 [Gullah glossary], *Medjuh*—(n. and v.) measure, measures, measured, measuring. **1953** Brewer *Word Brazos* 86 **eTX** [Black], 'Cides dat you mought th'ow in for good medjuh ten thousan' dolluhs in de bank. **1981** Pederson *LAGS Basic Materials* **Gulf Region,** [Of 73 transcriptions of *measure* noun or verb, or *measurement,* 45 were of the type [ˈmɛžə(r)]; 16 were of the type [ˈmeɹžə(r)] or [ˈmeə-]; 3 were of the type [ˈmɛjə(r)], for which all infs were Black; 3 were of the type [ˈmæˆɛžə]; 2 were of the type [ˈmɛžuˠ]; 2 were of the type [ˈmɛ(ə)žɪ]; 1 [ˈmɛjjə]; 1 [mɪˠˈžɚ].]

measuring caterpillar See **measuring worm**

measuring stick n [Perh from the resemblance of the segmented abdomen to a *measuring stick*]

A **dragonfly.**

1968 *DARE* (Qu. R2, . . *The dragonfly*) Inf **NJ5A,** Measuring sticks.

measuring woman n

See quot.

1968 Kellner *Aunt Serena* 148 **cIN** (as of c1920), Once she got him back to Aunt Vidy (the measuring woman) he would pick up. Aunt Vidy measured a young-one with a cord-string and said a secret saying over him, and after that he growed like a Jimpson weed.

measuring worm n Also *measuring caterpillar* [See quot 1899; cf *EDD measuring bug* "A caterpillar"] **widespread exc NEng, West** See Map Cf **inchworm**

=looper.

1844 DeKay *Zool. NY* 6.41, It [=*Caprella geometrica*] walks after the manner of some caterpillars called *Measuring worms.* **1869** U.S. Dept. Ag. *Rept. of Secy. for 1868* 314, The larvae [of moths of the family Geometridae] are known as span-worms, measuring worms, [etc]. **1884** (1885) McCook *Tenants* 109 **PA,** It was a sign we were goin' to git a new coat when one of them caterpillars was seen steppin' off distance on our arms or back. We call them 'measurin' worms' on that account. **1896** (1897) Hughes *30 Yrs. a Slave* 29 **MS** (as of 1844), The newly hatched boll worm walks like a geometrical larva or looper, a measuring worm as it was called. **1899** (1912) Green *VA Folk-Speech* 278, *Measuring-worm.* . . So called from its mode of progression, moving its head, afterwards drawing its tail along making a loop, then moving its head forward again. **1942** Warnick *Garrett Co. MD* 10 **nwMD** (as of 1900–18), *Measuring-worm* . . looper caterpillar. When seen on someone, we said, "It is measuring you for a new dress." **1942** McAtee *Dial. Grant Co. IN* 42 (as of 1890s), *Measuring-worm* . . looper caterpillar. "Knock him off, he's measurin' you for your coffin". **c1960** *Wilson Coll.* **csKY,** *Measuring worm.* . . A small larva that "humps itself." **1965–70** *DARE* (Qu. R27x, . . *Kinds of caterpillars or similar worms;* not asked in early QRs) 139 Infs, **widespread exc NEng, West,** Measuring worm; **IA34,** Measuring worm—if one of these lands or crawls on your dress, you'll get a new dress; **IN1,** Measuring worm—[this name] taught in school; **KY75,** Measuring worm—same as cabbage looper; **OH98,** If a measuring worm gets on your dress, you get a new one; it is measuring your dress; **MO20,** Measuring caterpillar; **CA65,** Measuring caterpillar—measures you for a new suit. **1982** *Barrick Coll.* **csPA,** *Measuring-worm*—larva of geometid [sic] moth.

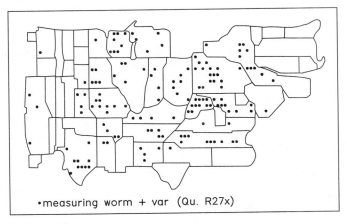

•measuring worm + var (Qu. R27x)

meat n

1 The edible part of a nut or, rarely, of a fruit seed—often used in comb *nutmeat;* sometimes used as a mass noun. [*OED* "?Now only *U.S.*"] **widespread, but less freq S Midl** See Map and Map Section Cf **goody 1, kernel 3**

1775 (1925) Washington *Diaries* 2.179 **VA,** Nuts . . like the Pignut—but longer . . and fuller of meat. **1838** (1932) Hawthorne *Amer. Notebooks* 46 **MA,** An old man selling the meats of butter-nuts under the stoop. **1896** (c1973) Farmer *Orig. Cook Book* 449, To Chocolate Caramels add the meat from one pound English walnuts. **1900** *Boston Even. Transcr.* 29 Mar. 7/3 (*OED*), Force through a meat chopper with one-half pound nut-meats. **1913** Emerson *Ruth Fielding at Snow Camp* 102, The three boys stuck to their work . . until there was a great bowl of nutmeats. **1941** *LANE* Map 268 (*Peach pit*) 1 inf, **RI,** Kernel = peach *meat,* inside the stone. **1965–70** *DARE* (Qu. I41, *The part of the nut that you eat*) 590 Infs, **widespread, but less freq S Midl,** Meat; 34 Infs, **scattered exc Sth, S Midl, NEng,** Nutmeat. **1974** *Aiken (S. Carolina) Standard* 22 Apr. 8-A/5 (*OEDS* at nut sb.[1] 21), Torten are sometimes made with finely ground nut-meats without the inclusion of any flour. **1986** Pederson *LAGS Concordance (Walnut shell)* 1 inf, **ceTN,** Meat—edible; 1 inf, **cwAL,** Meat—inside the kernel; 1 inf, **csMS,** Meat—of the nut.

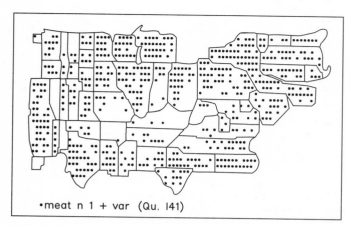

•meat n 1 + var (Qu. I41)

2 Pork; bacon. **chiefly Sth, S Midl** Cf **fresh n 4, meat rind, side meat**

[**1832** Paulding *Westward Ho* 1.124 **wKY,** What a wild goose of a feller, not to know that nothing is called meat in these parts but salt pork and beef.] **1845** Kirkland *Western Clearings* 93, Venison is not "meat," to be sure, in our parlance; for we reserve that term for pork. **1847** Paulding–Paulding *Amer. Comedies* 196, The term *meat* in the West is understood to apply solely to *salt pork.* **1902** *DN* 2.239 **sIL,** Meat. . . Bacon always understood. **1903** *DN* 2.320 **seMO,** Meat. . . Pork. **1906** *DN* 3.121 **sIN,** Meat. . . Pork. **1909** *DN* 3.400 **nwAR,** Meat. . . Pork. **1917** *DN* 4.414 **wNC,** Meat. . . Usually understood to mean 'pork.' **1924** Raine *Land of Saddle-Bags* 211 **sAppalachians,** "Bread" and "meat" are the staples of diet. This means corn and pork. **1939** FWP *Guide NC* 101, "Meat" still means pork to many people in the State. **1942** Rawlings *Cross Creek* 213 **nFL,** "Meat" in Florida is one thing—white bacon. . . [I]t is, simply, salt pork. **1954** *Harder Coll.* **cwTN,** Meat. . . Bacon. **1956** Ker *Vocab. W. TX* 270, Meat. . . is reported in the present survey as a common term for pork, usually with such qualifying adjectives as *[middling, fat, jowl].* **1970** *DARE* (Qu. H38, . . *Words for bacon [including joking ones]*) Inf **NC88,** Meat. **1986** Pederson *LAGS Concordance (Salt pork)* 2 infs, **cnGA, cnLA,** Meat.

3 Beef; salt beef. [Cf *EDD meat* sb. 4 "Beef, as distinct from mutton, &c."]

[**1832** see **2** above.] **1916** Macy–Hussey *Nantucket Scrap Basket* 158, To the whaleman, salt beef was always "meat," while pork was pork. As some preferred one and some the other, a sailor would frequently offer to swap his "meat" for his mess-mate's pork, or vice versa. **1972** Carr *Da Kine Talk* 138 **HI,** "No meat today, only pork." 'No beef today.' This phrase was seen, within the last decade, on a sign in a small restaurant in Honolulu. Several decades ago, *meat* was the general term in Hawaii for 'beef.'

meat v

1 To feed or supply with meat. **esp S Midl**

1913 Kephart *Highlanders* 282 **sAppalachians,** That bear'll meat me a month. **1919** *DN* 5.32 **seKY,** Uncle Roger's got corn enough to bread 'im, and hogs enough to meat 'im fer two year. **1933** Williamson *Woods Colt* 215 **Ozarks,** By golly . . we got to take out after that feller [=a wild or stray hog]. He'll meat us for a hell of a while. **1951** Randolph *We Always Lie* 127 **Ozarks,** Godamighty, boys, that coon was four foot long, an' must have weighed a hundred pounds! He'll meat the whole family a month easy. **1974** Fink *Mountain Speech* 16 **wNC, eTN,** Meat . . supply with meat. "One hog will meat us all winter."

2 To impregnate; hence ppl adj **meated.** [Cf *meat* penis]

1954 *Harder Coll.* **cwTN,** Meat. . . To get a woman pregnant. "He's done went 'n meated her." "He's got her meated."

meat auger n

An imaginary object used as the basis of a practical joke.

1921 *DN* 5.94 **OH,** Meat auger. Butcher's joke, Woodsfield. **c1960** *Wilson Coll.* **csKY,** Meat auger. . . One of the numerous yokel-traps.

"Go to Mr. Jones and tell him to send by you my meat auger." **1965–70** *DARE* (Qu. HH14, *Ways of teasing a beginner or inexperienced person—for example, by sending him for a 'left-handed monkey wrench': "Go get me _____."*) 9 Infs, **scattered,** Meat auger.

meatbird n

1 also *meat hawk:* =**Canada jay. chiefly NEng**

1857 Hammond *Wild N. Scenes* 53 **NY,** Small birds, of the size and general appearance of the cuckoo, save in their hooked beaks, attracted by the scent of our cold meats, came hopping tamely about on the lower limbs of the forest trees around us. They were called by our boatmen 'meat hawks.' **a1862** (1864) Thoreau *ME Woods* 220, Three large slate-colored birds of the jay genus *(Garrulus canadensis),* the Canada-jay, moose-bird, meat-bird, or what not, came flitting silently and by degrees toward me. **1895** Minot *Land-Birds New Engl.* 279, [Footnote:] "Meat Hawk" is also a name in very general use in Maine. **1917** *Wilson Bulletin* 29.2.82 **AK,** *Perisoreus canadensis.*—Meat-bird. **1927** Forbush *Birds MA* 2.384, Canada Jay. . . grease-bird; meat-bird; camp robber; meat hawk. **1941** Writers' Program *Guide WY* 35, Unpopular for his insolence and thievery, the Canada jay, known also as Whiskey Jack, moose bird, meat hawk, and grease bird, is a native of the evergreen forests, where his whistlings, chucks, squalls, and screams are a familiar nuisance to still-hunters. **1956** MA Audubon Soc. *Bulletin* 40.84 **ME, NH,** Canada Jay. . . Meat Bird, . . Meat Hawk. **1961** *Jrl. Amer. Folkl.* 74.1 **ME,** The Canada Jay . . is more commonly called gorbey, moose-bird, meat-bird [etc].

2 Clark's **nutcracker a** *(Nucifraga columbiana).* [See quot]

1917 (1923) *Birds Amer.* 2.234, The Clarke Crow is very fond of meat, and for this reason he has often been called "meat bird."

meat candy n

1968 *DARE* (Qu. H82b, *Kinds of cheap candy that used to be sold years ago*) Inf **NC55,** Meat candy—not very sweet.

meat cart, meat crate See **meat wagon 1**

meated See **meat v 2**

meat fisherman n

1 One who fishes with live bait rather than artificial flies or lures.

1949 Peattie *Cascades* 318 **OR,** [This is the habitat of the famous McKenzie river "redside," a . . rainbow . . marvelous to eat.] *Ibid,* The McKenzie guides will not take "meat fishermen"—the users of salmon eggs and other bait—and have such a low opinion of hardware fishermen that they will consent to the use of spinners with the greatest reluctance. . . This is a splendid river for the dry fly, and the guides hope to keep it that way. **1994** [see **2** below]. **1995** *NADS Letters* **cwCA,** A 'meat fisherman' is one who uses bait like a minnow, worm, or larvae—something like these—on his hook. He is opposed to a fly fisherman, and much scorned by the latter.

2 One who fishes for food rather than purely for sport. Cf **meat hunter**

1993 *NYT Mag.* 5 Sept 20, It is a curious book, revealing [Herbert] Hoover to be both a fly-fishing elitist and a meat fisherman so dedicated that he made fish killing a political virtue. **1994** *DARE* File **NEng** (as of 1960s–70s), A meat fisherman or meat hunter is not out for trophies; they are interested in getting food on the table. *Ibid* **wWA,** [A meat fisherman] is someone who fishes out of a desire to catch a lot of fish—to eat, sure, but also to brag about. . . He is not interested in the sport, but only in "sacking them up." He looks upon flyfishermen who catch and release fish as some kind of deviant species. . . Flyfisherpersons . . might consider a fisherman who uses bait a "meat fisherman."

meat-getter n Pronc-spp *meat-gitter,* ~-*gutter*

1 =**meat-gun.**

1968–70 *DARE* (Qu. P37a, *Nicknames for a rifle*) Inf **PA147,** Meat-getter; **NY233,** Meat-gitter; (Qu. P37b, *Nicknames for a shotgun*) Inf **CA36,** Meat-gutter.

2 also *meat-pusher:* A toothpick.

1968 *DARE* (Qu. G11, *Other names or nicknames for a toothpick*) Inf **GA23,** Meat-gitter; **TX51,** Meat-pusher.

meat-gun n Cf **meat-in-the-pot**

A rifle or shotgun.

1960 Williams *Walk Egypt* 91 **GA,** A meat-gun for sure. Point it at a squirrel and tell the old woman to get the frying pan ready. **1967** *DARE* (Qu. P37b, *Nicknames for a shotgun*) Inf **TX37,** Meat-gun [laughter].

meat-gutter See **meat-getter**

meat hawk See **meatbird 1**

meat hog n **chiefly Sth**

A pig raised for meat.

1856 in 1927 Jones *FL Plantation Rec.* 169, I doe not see but Verry few of the shoats that I turned out for meat hogs this year. **1949** *AmSp* 24.111 seGA, *Meat hog.* . . A hog fattened for butchering. **1965–70** *DARE* (Qu. K58, *A castrated pig*) Infs **FL**7, **IL**104, **LA**40, **SC**26, **TX**35, Meat hog. **1967** *Goliad Advance–Guard* (TX) 13 Apr 7/2, Meat hogs wanted. **1986** Pederson *LAGS Concordance,* 9 infs, **Gulf Region,** Meat hog.

meat hound n

Used as a derog or joc epithet for a dog.

1967–70 *DARE* (Qu. J1, . . *A dog of mixed breed*) Inf **TN**47, Meat hound; (Qu. J2, . . *Joking or uncomplimentary words . . for dogs*) Infs **KY**49, **OR**1, **PA**132, Meat hound. [**1984** Wilder *You All Spoken Here* 58 **Sth,** *Meat dog:* Barks only when he has treed the coon.] **1986** Pederson *LAGS Concordance (Mongrel)* 1 inf, **cnTN,** Meat hound—I refer to them all—not much on dogs. **1995** *NADS Letters* seMI, *Meat hound* is another term that my father recognized from bygone days. He says that it is a dog who 'eats like a horse.'

meat house n

1 A small building where meat is smoked or cured and often stored. **chiefly S Midl** See Map

1805 (1905) Clark *Orig. Jrls. Lewis & Clark Exped.* 3.284, Had the Meet house coverd and the Meat all hung up. **1831** Peck *Guide for Emigrants* 126 **IL,** Around it [=a cabin] are put a meat or smoke house. **1899** (1912) Green *VA Folk-Speech* 278, *Meat-house.* . . The house where the supply of meat is smoked and kept for use. **1906** *DN* 3.146 nwAR, *Meat-house.* . . Smoke-house; a wooden shed in which smoked and preserved meats are kept. **1938** FWP *Guide DE* 417, At the rear of the house is an old shingled "meat house" with batten shutters and a mossy roof. **1950** *WELS* (*Small building where meat or fish are smoked and cured*) 1 Inf, **seWI,** Meat house. **1954** *Harder Coll.* cwTN, *Meat-house.* . . Smokehouse. **1965–70** *DARE* (Qu. M20) 35 Infs, **chiefly S Midl,** Meat house. **1976** Ryland *Richmond Co. VA* 373, *Meat-house.* **1986** Pederson *LAGS Concordance,* 6 infs, **AR, GA, MS,** Meat house.

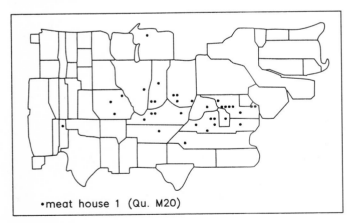

•meat house 1 (Qu. M20)

2 also *meat shanty:* See quots. Cf **bone wagon, cobhouse** n **1** quot 1923

1953 Randolph–Wilson *Down in Holler* 264 **Ozarks,** *Meat-house.* . . Used figuratively to mean hopes or expectations. An old farmer, having agreed to finance his son's education at the village high school, issued this solemn warning: "But if you ever lie to me about them grades, down goes your meat-house!" **1995** *DARE* File csWI (as of 1930s), "You do, and down comes your meat shanty!" A childhood response to a threat such as "I'm going to eat that piece of cake before you get to it."

meat hunter n [Cf earlier *pothunter* in the same sense (*OED* 1781 →)] Cf **meat fisherman 2**

One who hunts primarily to obtain meat; similarly n *meat hunt,* vbl n *meat hunting.*

1889 *Harper's New Mth. Mag.* 78.878 **West,** The meat-hunters are still devoting their attention to the killing of larger game. **1907** Cook *Border & Buffalo* 54 **SW,** In those days it was the custom of the Mexicans to go each fall to border New Mexico and Texas on "meat hunts." *Ibid* 55, Here we overtook another meat-hunting party from Galisteo. *Ibid*

128, He thought the parties that had stolen the hides were meat-hunters from the edge of the settlement on the Clear fork of the Brazos. **1965** Bowen *Alaskan Dict.* 21, *Meat hunter*—A person who takes a moose or other game to provide meat for his table. **1969** *DARE* Tape CA169, They're the last of the meat hunters . . that need the meat. **1994** [see **meat fisherman 2**]. **1995** *NADS Letters,* I've known *meat hunter* for a long time. A meat hunter hunts for food, not sport. The connotations are bad sportsmanship, indifference to game laws, and poverty. *Ibid,* "Meat hunter" is someone who hunts for the purpose of obtaining the meat (of deer, quail, rabbit, squirrel) either for eating or for sale, but *not* for the sport of hunting. . . Occasionally, a game law enforcement official will refer to a poacher as a meat hunter, particularly someone who hunts for meat to sell. I first heard the term in 1961 or 1962, in northern Delaware, from a classmate who criticized meat hunters because they were solely interested in obtaining the meat of game, and not in the joy and sport of hunting, as such.

meat-in-the-pot n **esp West**

Used as a nickname for a firearm; also transf.

1869 *Overland Mth.* 3.126 **TX,** Among names of revolvers I remember the following: Meat in the Pot, Blue Lightning, Peacemaker. **1907** White *AZ Nights* 11, I grabbed old Meat-in-the-pot and made a climb for the tall country. **1967–69** *DARE* (Qu. P37a, *Nicknames for a rifle*) Infs **CA**136, 153, **TX**5, **WY**1, (Old) meat-in-the-pot; (Qu. J2, . . *Joking or uncomplimentary words . . for dogs*) Inf **CA**105, Meat-in-the-pot [FW: Inf's family dog, because he always found a deer for the family to eat].

meat man n

A butcher or retailer of meat.

1907 *DN* 3.194 **NH,** *Meat-man.* . . Butcher. "The meat-man's come." **1910** *DN* 3.445 wNY, *Meat-man.* . . Butcher, or driver of a butcher's wagon. "The meat-man comes around twice a week." **1920** *DN* 5.83 **NW,** *Meat man,* for butcher. The Olympia meat man has again resumed the regular route. *Mason County Journal,* Shelton, Washington. **1943** *LANE* Map 553 (*Butcher*), The terms [*meat man, market man, meat cutter,* and (*meat*) *peddler*] . . denote a man who sells meat at retail. . . 18 infs, **NEng,** Meat man. **1986** Pederson *LAGS Concordance,* 11 infs, **Gulf Region,** Meatman; 1 inf, **TN,** Meatman—used more than "butcher."

meat pie n **NEng** *obs* Cf **mince pie**

A pie consisting primarily of minced meat, along with minced fruits, sugar, spices, and often suet.

1861 Holmes *Venner* 1.126 **NEng,** Mixed conversation chopped very small, like the contents of a mince-pie,—or meat pie, as it is more forcibly called in the deep-rutted villages lying along the unsalted streams. **a1870** Chipman *Notes on Bartlett* 266 (*DA*), *Meat-pie.* A mince pie. Occasionally, in this reference, heard in—N[ew] E[ngland]. **1890** *Century Dict.* 3678, *Meat-pie.* . . 1. A pie made of meat or flesh.—2. A mince-pie [*Century* Ed: Local, New Eng.] **1894** *Harper's New Mth. Mag.* 89.609 **MA,** I dun'no' when I've eat a decent meat pie. . . I 'ain't had a mince pie I could eat since my last wife died.

meat platter n [Cf Intro "Language Changes" I.4] **chiefly N Cent, N Midl, C Atl** See Map

A platter used for serving meat.

1863 Dodge *Gala-Days* 75 **NY,** I decided upon a meat-platter. **1898** *Star* (Kansas City MO) 18 Dec 11/2, Semi-porcelain Meat Platters, nicely embossed. **1965–70** *DARE* (Qu. G6, . . *Dishes that you might*

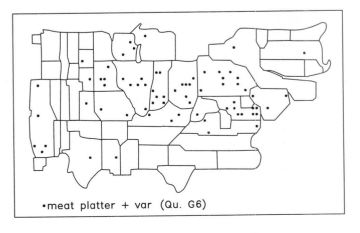

•meat platter + var (Qu. G6)

have on the table for a big dinner or special occasion—for example, Thanksgiving) 69 Infs, **chiefly N Cent, N Midl, C Atl**, Meat platter(s); **WI**20, Cold-meat platter. **1995** *DARE* File **csWI**, I bought a meat platter and two vegetable bowls to match my everyday dishes.

meat pudding See **pudding**

meat-pusher See **meat-getter 2**

meat rind n Also *meat skin* [**meat** n 2]
Pork rind; a piece of cured pork skin.

1867 Harris *Sut Lovingood Yarns* 189 **TN,** The nigger what hed been watchin up at hit all this time, wis'ful like, es a dorg watches a meat-skin when yu holds hit too high fur him tu grab, cotch his fiddil in bof hans. **1917** *DN* 4.399 **neOH,** *Meat-rine,* the tough skin of pork. General. **1943** McAtee *Dial. Grant Co. IN Suppl. 2* 11 (as of 1890s), *Meat-rind . .* skin of cured meat, used for a variety of purposes, two very different being: (1) for a teething baby to chew on, and (2) to lubricate a saw to make it cut with less effort. Used for greasing various things: guns, harness, shoes. **c1960** *Wilson Coll.* **csKY,** Meat rind. . . The skin on cured hog meat especially middlings. "He fishes with strips of bacon rind" or meat rind or pork rind. **1967** *DARE* (Qu. BB50c, *Remedies for infections)* Inf **MO**38, Old-timers used to use meat rinds on 'em [=boils].

meat shanty See **meat house 2**

meat skin See **meat rind**

meat victuals n pl Cf Intro "Language Changes" I.4
See quots.

1894 *DN* 1.342 **wCT,** *Meat-victuals:* the meat course at dinner. "If you're through with meat-victuals, they's some pie comin'." **1914** *DN* 4.76 **ME, nNH,** *Meat-victuals. . .* Meat.

meat wagon n Cf **dead wagon, gutwagon 2a, b**
1 also *(cold) meat cart, meat crate:* A vehicle used to carry dead bodies; a hearse.

[**1820** in 1891 Farmer–Henley *Slang* 151, *Cold-meat cart. . .* A hearse.] **1936** *AmSp* 11.201, The hearse is the 'cold meat cart.' **1942** Berrey–Van den Bark *Amer. Slang* 81, *Hearse. . .* meat cart,—crate *or* wagon. **1943** (1944) Chandler *Lady in Lake* 96 **Los Angeles CA,** Murder-a-day Marlowe, they call him. They have the meat wagon following him around to follow up on the business he finds. **1956** Longstreet *Real Jazz* 7, The band would march out behind the meat-wagon, black plumes on the hearse horses. **1965–70** *DARE* (Qu. N2, *The car used to carry a dead body for burial)* 18 Infs, **scattered,** Meat wagon; [(Qu. BB58, *The person who prepares a dead body for burial;* total Infs questioned, 75) Inf **OK**42, Meat man]. **1986** Pederson *LAGS Concordance (Hearse)* 1 inf, **cMS,** Meat wagon—facetious; 1 inf, **cAR,** Meat wagon—police vehicle for murder victims; 1 inf, **csTN,** Meat wagons.

2 also *live meat wagon:* An ambulance.

1925 Taber *Story of 168th Infantry* 1.189, By this time all of the old members of the regiment . . cheerfully referred to the ambulance as the "meat wagon." **1937** in 1972 *AmSp* 47.77, *Meat wagon. . .* He rode triumphantly back on the seat of the meat wagon which had been hastily despatched to pick up his mangled remains. **1939** *Forum* July 42, He must have pulled his rip cord because he woke up in the meatwagon. **1941** *AmSp* 16.167 [Army slang], *Meat wagon.* Ambulance. **1948** *AmSp* 23.77, We referred to recruits as 'raw meat.' Compare this with the Air Force's use of 'meat-wagon' for ambulance. **1950** *WELS (The kind of car that takes an injured person to the hospital in a hurry)* 6 Infs, **WI,** Meat wagon. **1969** *DARE* (Qu. N1, *. . Names for an ambulance)* Inf **GA**77, Live meat wagon. **1971** Hunter *Hail Hail* 15, We'll need a couple of meat wagons. The minister and two other people were killed, and . . there're a lot of injured. **1986** Pederson *LAGS Concordance (Emergency truck—if someone has a heart attack)* 1 inf, **neMS,** Meat wagon; *(Hearse)* 1 inf, **nwLA,** Meat wagon—ambulance, not hearse.

3 A paddy wagon.

1968–69 *DARE* (Qu. N3, *The car or wagon that takes arrested people to the police station or to jail)* Infs **GA**77, **PA**94, Meat wagon.

meb See **mib**

mebbe, mebby See **maybe**

mecate n Pronc-spp *macarte, macardy, mecarte,* and by folk-etym, *McCart(h)y* [MexSpan] **chiefly West**
A rope usu made of horsehair and used for leading, guiding, or tying horses.

1849 Revere *Tour Duty CA* 260, Picketing our horses by the 'mecate,'

we began telling stories, and . . some of the party fell asleep. **1857** in 1941 *AmSp* 16.263 **CA** [Span words used in English], The *mecate* is a hair rope used in tethering horses on the plains; any other kind of a rope, particularly if it have a particle of grease upon it, being liable to be eaten through by the coyotes. **1877** Bartlett *Americanisms* 387, *Mecate.* (Mexican.) A rope of hair or of the fibre of the maguey, the American *agave.* A term in use in the States bordering on Mexico. **1892** *DN* 1.191 **TX,** *Mecáte:* a rope or cord. This word is often used by cattlemen. From Mexican *mecatl.* **1904** Steedman *Bucking Sagebrush* 48 **OR,** Everything was there, six-shooter and belt, McCarty (or hair rope), sombrero. **1916** Benedict–Lomax *Book of TX* 180, Equally elaborate and beautiful were the mecates, or hair ropes, made of hair from the tails of mares, usually called 'broom tails' in the West. **1919** Chase *CA Desert* 182, Before I left I bought of him a *mecate* or rope of plaited horse-hair, of his own making. **1927** (1944) Russell *Trails Plowed Under* 166 **MT,** They all rode an' broke broncs with a hackamore. . . Looped to this was about fifteen or twenty foot of hair rope called a 'McCarthy.' **1932** Bentley *Spanish Terms* 165, *Mecate. . .* A horsehair headstall with lead rope; a horsehair rope. . . The longest rope possible is obtained. By the aid of a twisting apparatus it is made into strands or *cuerdas* about the size of heavy wrapping cord. These in turn are twisted into a hard rope or *mecate.* **1936** McCarthy *Lang. Mosshorn* np **West** [Range terms], *Mecarte . .* (pronounced McCarty). **1939** Rollins *Gone Haywire* 126 **MT** (as of 1886), At the bottom of the heap lay chaparejos, a bridle, saddle, quirt, mecate, and pair of spurs. **1940** Writers' Program *Guide NV* 75, A *hackamore, . .* a type of halter . . is sometimes known as a *McCarty.* Ibid 76, A *Macarte* or *McCarty* is [a rope] of twisted horse-hair (mane or tail). **1946** Mora *Trail Dust* 68 **West,** The reins for a hackamore are made up from a horse-hair rope called a mecáte (meh-cáh-teh). **1964** Jackman–Long *OR Desert* 84, I found it a good scheme to tuck the McCarty into my belt. Then if a horse fell down, or bucked me off, he wouldn't run off, leaving me to walk. **1981** *KS Qrly.* 13.2.68, *Macardy . .* a long rope of twisted horse tail hair used in ranch work, known elsewhere as *mecate.*

mechameck n [Prob of Algonquian origin; cf Shawnee *mak-,* Menominee *mɛ·c* big (in reference to the large root)]
=man-of-the-earth 1.

1828 Rafinesque *Med. Flora* 1.123, *Convolvulus panduratus.* English Name—Mechameck bindweed. . . Vulgar Names—Mechameck. *Ibid* 125, The native name of Mechameck ought to be given to it as a distinctive appellation. **1854** King *Amer. Eclectic Dispensatory* 391, *Convolvulus pandurata. . .* This plant, likewise known as . . *Mechameck, . .* has a perennial, very large, cylindrical or fusiform *root. . .* It is asserted that the Indians can handle rattlesnakes with impunity, after wetting their hands with the milky juice of this root. **1914** Georgia *Manual Weeds* 320, Wild Sweet Potato Vine. . . Mecha-Meck. **1939** Medsger *Edible Wild Plants* 193, The Indians named this plant the Mecha-meck, and without doubt it was a favorite food among them. **1974** (1977) Coon *Useful Plants* 119, *Ipomoea pandurata. . .* mecha-meck. . . Possible to use as food, but . . it has a reputation as a strong purgative, and is not recommended.

mechanical and artistic purposes See **artistic purposes**

mechanics' avenue n Also *mechanics' alley, mechanic street*
A poor or run-down part of a town or city.

1968–70 *DARE* (Qu. C35, *Nicknames for the different parts of your town or city)* Inf **PA**126, Mechanic street, literally a place where mechanics used to work; (Qu. II21, *When somebody behaves unpleasantly or without manners: "The way he behaves, you'd think he was _____.")* Inf **PA**126, Raised on mechanic street; (Qu. II25, *Names or nicknames for the part of a town where the poorer people, special groups, or foreign groups live)* Inf **NY**102, Mechanics' avenue; **PA**126, Mechanic street—older term, now fashionable; **PA**242, Mechanics' alley. [All Infs old]

mechanized dandruff See **galloping dandruff**

mecheer See **macheer**

meck See **make** v[1]

medaddy-bush n Cf **midaddy**
A **fly honeysuckle** (here: *Lonicera canadensis*).

1896 *Jrl. Amer. Folkl.* 9.189 **cwME,** *Lonicera ciliata. . .* Medaddy-bush. **1940** Clute *Amer. Plant Names* 54, Vernal honeysuckle, medaddy-bush.

medah, medder See **meadow**

meddle v

1 tr: To disturb, annoy, or interfere with (someone or something). Note: Only transitive uses are illustrated here. [Scots, nEngl dial; cf *EDD meddle* v. 3, *SND middle* v. 1] **chiefly Sth chiefly among Black speakers**

1892 (1969) Christensen *Afro–Amer. Folk Lore* 38, Rattlesnake shich a cross ting you know, nobawdy mus'n meddle um. *Ibid* 67, I ain't gwine meddle you 'gen sho' [=again surely]. **1927** Kennedy *Gritny* 68 **sLA** [Black], Dark-skin mens w'at meddled you an' pulled off yo' close. *Ibid* 162, I ain' come hyuh to meddle you. **1928** Peterkin *Scarlet Sister Mary* 200 **SC** [Gullah], Budda never meddled the pesky black devils. He never meddled anybody. **1946** Tallant *Voodoo* 42 **New Orleans LA** [Black], He used to always pass her house and she would meddle him; you know what I mean—she would laugh at him and make fun. **1967–70** *DARE* (Qu. Y7, *When one person never misses a chance to be mean to another or to annoy another: "I don't know why she keeps _____ me all the time!"*) Infs **MS**80, **TX**9, Meddling; (Qu. GG3, *To tease: "See those big boys trying to _____ [that little one]."*) Inf **MS**80, Meddle. [1 Inf Black] **1972** Culbertson *May I Speak* 148 **LA** [Black], Some of their expressions, such as "He meddlin' me," . . I had heard "meddlin' " all my life, but the Negroes on our cotton plantations said "meddlin' with me." Anyway, I knew that meddlin' meant "bothering." **1972** Davis *Culture Class & Lang. Variety* 204 **swTN** [Black], You know she jus*t* be walkin. A*n*d she made up funny. And ney was meddlin he*r*. A*n*d he*r* sister wear glasses. And ney were meddlin he*r* too. **1975** *AmSp* 50.62 **AR** [Black], *Meddle*. . . Bother, irritate, or annoy. **1986** Pederson *LAGS Concordance,* 1 inf, **nwFL**, Meddle us (=bother us). [Inf Black] **1995** *DARE* File **Chicago IL** (as of 1948), When I was teaching 6th grade in an all-black school . . a common complaint I heard, but at first did not understand, was "Teacher, Henry (or some other name) meddlin' me." . . I soon learned that "meddlin' " referred to any physical activity—hitting, pinching, hair-pulling, or the like.

2 also with *at:* To fight; to fight with. [Prob by ext from *meddle with* interfere with, but cf *OED meddle* v. 6 "To mingle in fight; to engage in conflict"; →1601]

1937 *AmSp* 12.232 **NJ**, Negroes use *meddle* in the obsolete sense of 'to fight' (with), 'engage in conflict': 'Him and Turk meddled last night outside the O.K. Bar.' **1986** Pederson *LAGS Concordance (Fight)* 1 inf, **cnAL**, Meddling at one (a)nother. [Inf Black]

3 also with *at:* To make sexual advances; see quots. [Prob by ext from *meddle with* interfere with, "mess with," but cf *OED meddle* v. 5 "To have sexual intercourse *(with)*"; →1655]

1971 Mitchell *Blow My Blues Away* 116 **nwMS** [Black], I thought he was a preacher. I thought the preacher was meddling, you know. *Ibid,* I said to myself after he left, "Now, what that old preacher keep on meddling at me for?" **1975** *AmSp* 50.62 **AR** (as of c1970) [Black], *Meddle*. . . Have sexual intercourse with (one). . . Be intimate with (someone) but not necessarily through sexual intercourse (black use).

4 with *around:* See quots.

1968–70 *DARE* (Qu. KK31, *To go about aimlessly looking for distraction: "He doesn't have anything to do, so he's just _____ around."*) Infs **MD**36, **MO**30, Meddling. [1 Inf Black] **1995** *DARE* File **swCA** (as of c1970), I seem to recall the use of *meddle around* in the sense of "fool around, canoodle, make out" from my teen days in northeast Ohio, Colorado, Los Angeles.

meddle at See meddle 2, 3

meddle(some) box n [box n 5a]
=meddlesome Mattie.

1968–70 *DARE* (Qu. GG36a, *The kind of person who is always poking into other people's affairs: "She's an awful _____."*) Inf **NC**82, Meddle box; **VA**46, Meddlesome box.

meddlesome Mattie n Also *meddlesome Matildy* [From the 1804 poem *Meddlesome Matty* by Ann Taylor]

An interfering nosy person; a busybody.

1946 *Western Folkl.* 5.241 **wOR**, Don't be a Meddlesome Mattie. **1949** *AmSp* 24.24, Now and then one hears remarks about 'Meddlesome Matties.' A friend may say, 'Beware of some Meddlesome Mattie if you try that.' **1965–70** *DARE* (Qu. GG36a, *The kind of person who is always poking into other people's affairs: "She's an awful _____."*) Infs **AR**56, **IN**19, **MS**8, 49, **TX**51, **WV**1, 4, 7, 13, 16, **WI**29, Meddlesome Mattie; **FL**10, Meddlesome Matildy. **1983** *MJLF* 9.1.47 **ceKY**, *Meddlesome Mattie* . . someone who is always in mischief; from a character in a McGuffey reader.

medial (strip) See median (strip) 1b

medialuna n [Span "half moon"] CA

The half-moon (*Medialuna californiensis*).

1884 Goode *Fisheries U.S.* 1.395 **swCA**, The 'Half-moon,' more commonly known by its Spanish name, 'Medialuna,' *Scorpis californiensis,* . . forms the greater part of the catch at San Pedro. **1933** John G. Shedd Aquarium *Guide* 120, The Medialuna is an excellent food fish, abundant on the rocky shores of southern California. It reaches a length of one foot.

median (strip) n

1 The divider that separates opposing lanes of traffic on a four-lane (or larger) road; see below. Cf **boulevard 2**

a as *median (strip)* and varr. **widespread exc Pacific, Rocky Mts, LA, MS** See Map Cf **neutral ground**

1954 Ingraham *Mod. Traffic Control* 31, Choice of the type of median strip—solid concrete, grass and curbing, or grass alone. **1965–70** *DARE* (Qu. N17) 280 Infs, **widespread exc Pacific, Rocky Mts, LA, MS,** Median; 63 Infs, **scattered, but esp Nth, Midl,** Median strip; **NH**5, **TN**37, **WI**65, Median line; **PA**165, Divided median; **CT**22, Median divider. **1967** *Boston Sunday Herald* 7 May 1/1 *(OEDS),* A fence erected on the median strip to discourage the road-crossings. **1995** *WI State Jrl.* (Madison) 18 June sec B 1/2, Civil engineers . . flocked to see the autobahn's state-of-the-art dual-lane highways, separated by 16-foot grassy medians. . . New York's Bronx River Parkway in 1923, [was] the first to use medians.

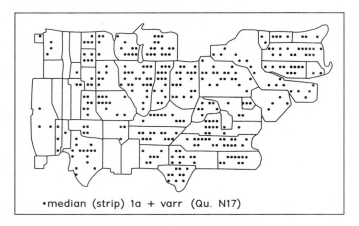

•median (strip) 1a + varr (Qu. N17)

b as *medial (strip).* **chiefly PA, sNJ; also HI** See Map

1965–70 *DARE* (Qu. N17, . . *The separating area in the middle [of a four-lane road]*) 35 Infs, **chiefly PA, sNJ,** Medial (strip). **1972** McCormick *Vocab. HI* 71, Medial strip—Grass strip in center of divided road.

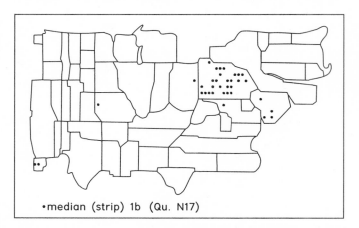

•median (strip) 1b (Qu. N17)

c as *medium (strip).* [Perh by folk-etym] **chiefly Midl** See Map

1965–70 *DARE* (Qu. N17, . . *The separating area in the middle [of a four-lane road]*) 37 Infs, **chiefly Midl,** Medium (strip). **1986** Pederson *LAGS Concordance,* 13 infs, **Gulf Region,** Medium (strip)—concrete or grass strip between road lanes.

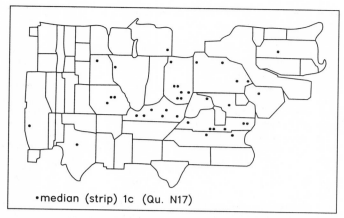

•median (strip) 1c (Qu. N17)

d as *media (strip).* [Perh var of *medial (strip)* by vocalization of [l] (cf Pronc Intro 3.II.27), but perh infl by *media* in other senses]

1966–70 *DARE* (Qu. N17, . . *The separating area in the middle [of a four-lane road]*) Infs **ME**10, **MI**112, **OH**80, **PA**3, 34, 72, **VA**50, Media (strip).

e as *meridian (strip);* pronc-sp *meridan.* **scattered, but rare Sth, West** See Map

1965–70 *DARE* (Qu. N17, . . *The separating area in the middle [of a four-lane road]*) 22 Infs, **scattered, but rare Sth, West,** Meridian (strip); **RI**4, Meridan [mɛrɪdɛn].

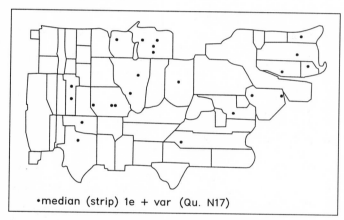

•median (strip) 1e + var (Qu. N17)

f as *medrin.* [Cf Intro "Language Changes" I.8]

1968–69 *DARE* (Qu. N17, . . *The separating area in the middle [of a four-lane road]*) Inf **KY**53, ['midrən]; **MI**97, Medrin ['midrɪn].

2 also *medium:* The grassy strip that separates the street from the sidewalk. Cf **boulevard 1, parking strip**

1968–70 *DARE* (Qu. N44, *In a town, the strip of grass and trees between the sidewalk and the curb*) Infs **DE**4, **SC**66, Median; **MO**2, **VA**20, Medium. 1984 *DARE* File **nCA, CO,** In a town, the strip of grass and trees between the sidewalk and the curb: Median (strip). 1986 Pederson *LAGS Concordance* (*Strip of green grass between the sidewalk and the street*) 4 infs, **nTN, neAL,** Medium.

media (strip) See **median (strip) 1d**

medicine n

1 in phr *make medicine:* To have a discussion and come to agreement.

1903 (1965) Adams *Log Cowboy* 237 **NM,** They will sit and powwow and make medicine for an hour or two. 1929 Dobie *Vaquero* ix **West,** I learned that he was dreaming of writing a book . . about . . his own life. . . [He told me:] "I'll need somebody to go over the writing and put it into shape." We made medicine, and John Young began firing in certain episodes out of his career. 1968 Adams *Western Words* 188, *Make medicine*—To hold a conference; to plan some action; an expression taken from the Indian custom [*DARE* Ed: = Amer. Indian custom of holding ceremonies to gain favor with supernatural powers].

2 Knowledge, information.

1927 *AmSp* 3.169 **SW** [Cowboy speech], When he [=a cowboy] is

without information upon a subject, he tells you: "I ain't got any medicine." 1929 *AmSp* 5.75 **NE** [Cattle country talk], One who has no information on the topic of conversation might say, "I ain't got any medicine."

medicine bird n Cf **war bird**

=**roadrunner.**

1917 *Wilson Bulletin* 29.2.81, Long-tailed pheasant, medicine bird, . . road-runner [etc].

medicine wolf n

=**coyote** n B1.

1837 Irving *Rocky Mts.* 2.147, This little, whining, feast-smelling animal, is . . called among Indians the "medicine wolf." 1848 (1855) Ruxton *Life Far West* 77 **Rocky Mts,** Besides the buffalo wolf, there are four distinct varieties common to the plains, and all more or less attendant upon the buffalo. These are, the black, the gray, the brown, and last and least, the *coyote,* or *cayeute* of the mountaineers, the "*wach-unkamǎnet,*" or "medicine wolf" of the Indians, who hold the latter animal in reverential awe. 1860 in 1938 *Colorado Mag.* 15.30, Went up town and saw a young grizzly bear, a young swift or medicine wolf, much resembling a fox. 1982 Elman *Hunter's Field Guide* 344, Coyote. . . barking wolf, cased wolf, medicine wolf.

medinary adj [Prob blend of *medium + ordinary*] Mediocre.

1944 *PADS* 2.10 **cAL,** *Medinary* ['midɪˌnɛrɪ, 'midn̩ˌɛrɪ]. . . Of indifferent qualities; said of a horse or mule or crop, etc. . . Rural. Rare.

medio n [Transf from *medio* an obsolete Mexican coin worth half a real]

[1844 (1846) Kendall *Santa Fé Exped.* 2.239, One of the lads . . [handed] each of the unfortunate prisoners a *medio.*] 1909 *DN* 3.400 **OK,** *Medio* . . Five-cent-piece.

medium (strip) See **median (strip) 1c, 2**

medjer, medjuh, medjure See **measure**

medlar n[1] See **medlar bush**

medlar n[2] See **medlark**

medlar bush n Also *(snowy) medlar* [See quot 1860] A **serviceberry** (here: *Amelanchier canadensis*).

1785 Marshall *Arbustrum* 90, *Early ripe, Esculent fruited Medlar, or wild Service.* . . The fruit is ripe in June, pretty large and of an agreeable taste. 1837 Darlington *Flora Cestrica* 294 **sePA,** *A[melanchier] Botryapium.* . . *Vulgo*—Wild Service-berry. June berry. Snowy Medlar. Shad-flower. *Ibid* 295, *A[melanchier] ovalis?.* . . *Vulgo*—Medlar-bush. 1860 Curtis *Cat. Plants NC* 69, The fruit [of *Amelanchier canadensis*] is here much sweeter, more juicy and palatable, like the *Medlar* [=*Mespilus germanica*], than in other parts of the State, and trees are sometimes recklessly cut down to obtain it. . . This shrub or tree, when displaying its profusion of clustered white blossoms in early Spring, is not without beauty, and is found enumerated in the catalogues of some northern Nurseries as *The Snowy Medlar.* 1869 Fuller *Uncle John* 31, Another species of the Aronia, or Amelanchier, is known as the "Medlar Bush." It has a small, black berry; and another still has red berries. 1893 *Jrl. Amer. Folkl.* 6.141 **NY,** *Amelanchier Canadensis,* snowy medlar.

medlark n Also *medlar*

=**meadowlark 1.**

1859 *Harper's New Mth. Mag.* 18.603, He had angled for sunfish and bull-pouts, and hunted gophers and med'-larks in Connecticut. 1903 Dawson *Birds OH* 1.22, Meadowlark. . . *Sturnella magna* . . medlark . . medlar (poetical). 1926 *DN* 5.401 **Ozarks,** *Medlar.* . . The meadow lark.

medrick n Also *madrick, medrake, medric (gull)* **ME, MA** Either the common **tern** (*Sterna hirundo*) or the Arctic **tern** (*S. paradisaea*).

1832 Williamson *Hist. ME* 1.145, We suppose there are with us four [species of gulls] . . 4. the *swallow-tail Gull,* or *Medrake.* 1855 in 1911 Lowell *Poet. Wks.* 303, A medrick that makes you look overhead / With short, sharp scream, as he sights his prey. 1890 *Century Dict.* 3687, *Medrick, madrick.* . . The tern or sea-swallow. 1917 *Wilson Bulletin* 29.2.76 **csME,** *Sterna hirundo* . . medric gull and medric, Matinicus I[slan]d. 1925 (1928) Forbush *Birds MA* 1.105, *Common Tern.* . . sea swallow; medrick. *Ibid* 1.115, *Arctic Tern.* . . medrick. 1956 **MA** Audubon Soc. *Bulletin* 40.22, Common Tern. . . Medric Gull (Maine);

Medrick (Maine, Mass. Perhaps sonic). *Ibid*, Arctic Tern . . Medric (Maine, Mass.) **1982** *DARE* File **ME coast,** Medricks.

medrin See **median (strip) 1f**

meech v Also *mi(t)ch* Also sp *meach*
1 To slink, skulk; to cringe. [*OED miche* v. 2.a 1558 →] **chiefly NEng** *somewhat old-fash*
1833 Smith *Life Jack Downing* 176 ME, The old man hauled in his horns and meeched off looking shamed enough. **1857** Paige *Dow's Patent Sermons* 203, When you fall short of the object for which you jump, you go meeching off, like a cat that has missed her mouse. **1890** *DN* 1.19 NEng, *Meech:* cringe, look ashamed. *Ibid* 78, In the phrase *to go meeching about*, to go in a mean or underhand way, it is reported as in familiar use in New Haven, Conn. **1900** Day *Up in ME* 78, She always kept him meechin'; calls him down with sour tone,/ Till the critter hasn't gumption for to say his soul's his own. **1902** Wilson *Spenders* 366 NYC, I'd hate to have you come meachin' around after that stock has kited. **1903** *DN* 2.299 **Cape Cod MA** (as of a1857), *Meech.* . . To slink, of a dog or cat. **1914** *DN* 4.76 ME, nNH, *Meach.* . . To cringe, crawl. **1944** *PADS* 2.46, *Meech, meach* [mitʃ]. . . To get around stealthily; to slink; to appear dishonest, shifty. "I seed a fellow meechin' round up the cove like he might 'a' been a revenuer." . . W[estern]. N.C., but sometimes heard elsewhere in the South.
2 To play truant; hence vbl n *miching,* n *micher*. [*OED miche* v. 2.b 1580 →]
1870 *Nation* 28 July 56 sePA, Genuine English of Shakespeare's time . . is the participle applied to the boy who played truant, and good Scotch, we suppose, is the "scutching" that he received for his "miching." . . Recess, as we say now, the young "micher" of fifty years ago called "little noon." **1958** *KY Folkl. Rec.* 4.100, Two school boys . . were seining for crawfish at a ford; and when I asked for Mr. W_____, the local teacher, they laughed and said: "When you find him, don't tell him we are mitching." . . It was obviously the equivalent of snap, cut, or play hooky.
3 See quot. [*OED miche* v. 3 →1611]
1952 Brown *NC Folkl.* 1.565, *Mich, meech* [mitʃ]. . . To whimper, to grumble.

meeching ppl adj Also *meaching, miching* [**meech 1**] **chiefly NEng** *somewhat old-fash*
Skulking, cringing; self-deprecating, obsequious; contemptible.
1792 *Thomas' MA Spy or Worcester Gaz.* (MA) 22 Mar 1/1, There is a kind of meaching souls in the world. **1818** Fessenden *Ladies Monitor* 172 VT, Provincial words . . to be avoided. . . *Meaching* for mean. **1836** (1838) Haliburton *Clockmaker* (1st ser) 126 NEng, Father goes up to him, looking as soft as dough, and as meaching as you please. **1859** (1968) Bartlett *Americanisms* 267, *Meeching* or *Miching*. Skulking. This old Shaksperian word is still occasionally heard in New York and New England. **1867** Lowell *Biglow* 13 'Upcountry' MA, But I ain't o' the meechin' kind, thet sets an' thinks fer weeks / The bottom's out o' th' univarse coz their own gillpot leaks. **1881** Holley *Wayward Pardner* 25 NY, "She hain't!" says he . . with that dretful meachin' and sheepish look to him. **1892** *DN* 1.217, *Meech.* . . "Common in Boston in my youth, especially *meeching* as an adjective." . . *Michin* ['mitʃin] is reported from Plymouth, Mass. and is in use in various parts of New England. **1895** *DN* 1.391 cNY, *Meecking* [sic]: guilty appearance of one caught pilfering. **1914** *DN* 4.76 ME, nNH, *Meachin'.* . . Cringing. **1916** Macy–Hussey *Nantucket Scrap Basket* 162, "*Meeching*"—Is another word often noted. The dictionary gives "skulking, sneaking, mean," which is just the sense we give it in Nantucket. **1926** *DN* 5.388 ME, *Meeching.* . . "He was so meechin' that butter wouldn't melt in his mouth." Common. **1927** *AmSp* 3.141 eME, "*Meaching*" is provincial English or archaic. . . As generally used in Maine it implied a Uriah Heep [sic] humbleness. **1936** Morehouse *Rain on Just* 177 NC, Young Emmet with his meeching ways. **1942** McAtee *Dial. Grant Co.* IN 42 (as of 1890s), *Meechin'*. . . sneaking. **1945** *PADS* 3.11 NEng, *Meech* . . : I know this expression in "Don't look so meechin'" in the sense of needless humility, without the suggestion of dishonesty. **1951** West *Witch Diggers* 192 sIN, She could act meechin enough, put on a false Irish humility. **1959** *VT Hist.* 27.148, *Meaching.* . . Useless; good-for-nothing. Occasional. **1967** *DARE* FW Addit MA5, Meaching.

meechy adj
1968 *DARE* (Qu. U36b, . . *A person who saves in a mean way or is greedy in money matters: "She certainly is _____."*) Inf **OH**61, Meechy—I don't know what it derives from.

mee-maw n Also *mima;* for addit varr see quots **chiefly Sth, S Midl** Cf **mam-maw, mee-mee, mee-pop**
A grandmother.
1966–70 *DARE* (Qu. Z4, . . 'Grandmother') Infs **AL**10, **KY**84, **TX**61, Mee-maw; **KY**19, Mee-maw ['mimə]; **TX**35, Mee-mo; **GA**11 Mimaw ['mimɔ]; **AL**6, Mee-mamma; **GA**57, Mimo. **1981** *DARE* File, My cousin's child, who grew up in Atlanta, Georgia, called his grandparents mee-maw and pa-paw. The rest of the family, who were all northerners, attributed this to the fact that the child's mother was from Kentucky. **1986** Pederson *LAGS Concordance (Grandmother)* 13 infs, **Gulf Region,** Mima. **1992** *NADS Letters* neSC, I have a late 30s-aged friend . . who always talks of *meemaw* and *peepaw* when referring to little old people who look like grandparents. *Ibid,* My wife's term even today for her grandmother is *meemaw* or *little meemaw*. My wife was born in Texas, (Houston) . . , but moved back to Equality, Illinois when she was two. *Ibid* IN, *Meepop* did not sound very common, but many students were familiar with the term *meemaw* [=grandmother]. *Ibid* Our granddaughter refers to me as Meemaw and has from the first. . . It was a new term both to me (from Pa.) and my husband (from Ohio). However, my Southern friends know it, and, as one told me, "It is very country; you must get her to change it." *Ibid,* Mee ma (with the accent on the "mee") is the very expression used by my siblings and I to address our Acadian Louisiana maternal grandmother. *Ibid,* A friend of mine, born and reared in Massachusetts, is called Meemaw by the children of her three daughters, all of whom were reared in West Virginia. The term was chosen because of *her* suggestion. **1993** *Ibid* TX, Meemaw is quite common in Sweeny, Texas.

meemaw exclam
1992 *NADS Letters* WI, My mother says she heard and used the term *meemaw* in Wisconsin during her childhood (she's 71). . . It meant "Me first" in childhood squabbles.

mee-mee n Also *mimi, mimmy* Cf **mam-maw, mee-maw** n
A grandmother; rarely a mother.
1966–70 *DARE* (Qu. Z4, . . 'Grandmother') Infs **IL**141, **MO**12, **NJ**59, **OK**28, **PA**152, **RI**6, **WA**17, Mee-mee [mimi]. **1970** Tarpley *Blinky* 208 nwTX, Term of affection for grandmother. . . mimi [rare]. *Ibid* 212, Term of affection for mother . . mimi [rare]. **1986** Pederson *LAGS Concordance (Grandmother)* 9 infs, **Gulf Region,** Mimi; 1 inf, **nwFL,** Minny—means "Mimmy"—grandchild calls his wife.

mee-pop n Cf **mee-maw** n
A grandfather.
1969 *DARE* (Qu. Z3, . . 'Grandfather') Inf **TX**61, Mee-pop. **1992** *NADS Letters* AL, TN, I am a Birmingham native who has lived in Nashville for five years now, and I hear these terms for grandparents [=meemaw and meepop] constantly from natives of both cities.

meet v
1 To find; to meet with. [*OED* "Now only *dial.*"] **sSC coast Gullah**
1867 Allen *Slave Songs* xxviii eSC, Meet is used in the sense of *find*. "I meet him here an' he remain wid me," was the cook's explanation when a missing chair was found in the kitchen. **1930** Woofter *Black Yeomanry* 54 seSC, Meet: to find, to observe, to experience. "Did oona [=you] meet a good time?" The fisherman is asked, "Did oona meet plenty feesh?" **1949** Turner *Africanisms* 267 seSC [Gullah], You go there and meet some man broken. [=You go there and come upon a man who has been destroyed.] **1950** *PADS* 14.46 SC, *Meet*. . . To find. "I meet um gone," "I found them gone, they were gone when I arrived." "I meet um here when I come," "I found them here when I came." Negro usage, chiefly coastal area.
2 also in phr *meet up with:* To be the equal of or match for (someone). Cf **meet** n 2
1968–70 *DARE* (Qu. LL32, *Expressions meaning that one man's ability is not nearly as great as another man's: "John can't [or doesn't, or isn't] _____ Bill."*) Inf **SC**69, Can't (*or* doesn't) meet up with; **VA**5, John can't meet Bill.
3 To introduce.
1991 *DARE* File nwAR, If you wanted to introduce a friend to someone you might say "I want to meet you to so-and-so." You'd hear that.

meet n
1 A place where two or more trains come together, esp from opposite directions; see quots. Cf **cornfield meet**

1916 *DN* 4.356, *Meet.* . . Assigned meeting place of trains. **1940** *RR Mag.* Apr 48, *Meet order*—Train order specifying a definite location where two or more trains will meet on a single track, one on a siding, the others on the *high iron.* **1969** *AmSp* 44.258 [Railroad terms], *Meet.* . . Encounter with such a train [=a train going in the opposite direction].

2 An equal or match. Cf **meet** v 2

1969 *DARE* (Qu. LL32, *Expressions meaning that one man's ability is not nearly as great as another man's: "John can't [or doesn't, or isn't] _____ Bill."*) Inf MI93, Isn't a meet for.

3 =**camp meeting**. [Abbr for *meeting*]

1967 Williams *Greenbones* 8 **GA** (as of c1910), Nin . . began capering. "A meet! A meet!" He loved them as much as his mother did, and Doesticks would travel twenty long Georgia miles to a camp meeting or a revival.

meet court v phr
To go to a court of law.

1970 Hyatt *Hoodoo* 1.312 (as of c1935) **MS**, The next day I had a notice in my door to meet court. My husband was putting in for divorce. I had a notice in my door to meet court.

meetiner See **meetinger**

meeting n

1a A religious service; an assembly for worship. **chiefly NEast, S Midl** *somewhat old-fash* (exc in phr **Sunday-go-to-meeting**) Note: Orig used to distinguish the services of dissenters from those of the established church—see *AmSp* 34.5-10. Cf **meetinghouse 1**

1687 in 1861 MA *Hist. Soc. Coll.* 4th ser 5.155, Many are forced to keep three or four horses for the necessary use of their families to ride to meeting. **1772** (1894) Winslow *Diary* 57 **MA**, Yesterday I walk'd to meeting all day, the ground very dry. **1827** (1940) Arnold *Diaries* 110 **VT**, He . . sometimes attended meeting with his wife & children. **1830** (1930) Sewall *Diary* 131 **IL**, Sunday. . . Attended meeting at the Courthouse. Rev. Mr. Herrick . . preached. **1852** in 1983 *PADS* 70.41 ce,sePA, Till and me went to meeting in the forenoon. **1859** Taliaferro *Fisher's R.* 113 **nwNC** (as of 1820s), Most of the people walked to "meetin'." **1890** *DN* 1.65 **KY**, *Meetin':* for church, preaching [as in New England]. "I am going to meetin'." **1902** *DN* 2.239 **sIL**, *Meetin.* . . An assembly for worship. **1905** *DN* 3.14 **cCT**, *Meeting.* . . A religious assembly. **1907** *DN* 3.194 **seNH**, *Meeting.* . . Religious service. **1907** *DN* 3.215 **nwAR**, *Meeting.* . . A religious assembly. **1941** *AmSp* 16.23 **sIN**, Meetin' ain't over till the benediction's said. **1959** *AmSp* 34.9, Around the turn of the nineteenth century . . [the] phrase *going to meeting* transformed itself into *going to church.* **1959** *VT Hist.* 27.148 **nw,cnVT**, *Meeting.* . . Mass. Rare. **1969** *DARE* (Qu. W39, *Joking ways of referring to a person's best clothes*) Inf GA75, Sunday best; my meetin' clothes. **1971** *Down East* Nov 26, When a Mainer "goes to meeting," it's to church, of course; otherwise he'll specify another kind of assembly; town meeting, grange meeting. **1982** Slone *How We Talked* 71 **eKY** (as of c1950), A meetin'—the church service, made up of singing, praying and preaching.

b A series of religious services usu extending over several days. Cf **all-day meeting, big ~, camp ~, protracted ~**

1804 in 1857 Dow *Hist. Cosmopolite* 218 **MS**, We held a quarterly meeting on Clarke's creek. Some supposed I would get no campers, but. . . [a]n old backslider . . came forward and fell upon his knees, and several followed his example. **1909** *DN* 3.348 **eAL, wGA**, *Meetin(g).* . . Divine services; specifically, protracted services. "When are you goin to have your meetin'?" **1938** FWP *Guide MS* 20, Our religion . . possesses . . an emotional background brought forward at yearly "meetings." In other places these meetings are called "revivals," but we are more realistic. If we are Methodist, we refer to our meeting as the "camp-meeting," . . If we are Baptist, we say "protracted meeting." In either case, we mean what the name implies, a series of religious services for a number of days.

2 A local congregation of Quakers; hence v phr *marry out of meeting* to marry one who is not a Quaker; *turn (one) out of meeting* to put (one) out of the Society of Friends.

[**1706** in 1851 Prot. Episc. Hist. Soc. *Coll.* 44 [Scots writer], They had scarce any Notion of Religion but Quakerism: The Quakers had formerly a meeting there [=Oysterbay, Long Is.], but many of them . . became followers of *Thomas Chase.*] **1713** in 1886 NC *Colonial Rec.* 2.37, Friends appoint John Morris & Henry White to represent the state of this meeting to the Quarterly meeting. **1850** Chamberlain *IN Gaz.* 72,

They have nine Quarterly meetings, about 27 Monthly meetings, and about 80 Congregations, or meetings for worship in the State. **1856** MacLeod *Biog. F. Wood* 34 **cwNJ**, He went on fighting for his native land, and was turned out of meeting by his brethren. **1874** in 1983 *PADS* 70.53 ce,sePA, The strangers expect to visit all the meetings composing this quarterly meeting. **1898** Harper *Life Anthony* 1.10, A Quaker was not permitted to "marry out of meeting." **1933** *AmSp* 8.1.13 **Philadelphia PA**, *The meeting.* The church; the local unit of Quakers. . . *The clerk* (of the meeting). The man, or woman, who presides over the Meetings for Business. **1940** Weygandt *Down Jersey* 96, The meeting was split by the troubles between "The Friends" and "The Other Friends" of 1826–1827. **1967** *DARE* Tape PA31, We have about, in this [Quaker] meeting, one hundred and seventy-five members. **1968** *DARE* FW Addit **VA33**, When a Quaker married a non-Quaker, he was said to have married out of meeting and was expelled from the church. **1988** *Isthmus* (Madison WI) 25 Nov 9/3, Madison Friends work locally as well. In past years, the meeting (the term refers to the group as well as the gatherings) operated storefront offices for the "Ban the Bomb" movement and a draft-counseling center.

3 An organizational unit of congregations of Quakers, the size and duties of which are determined by the intervals at which the group meets; see quot 1983.

1713 [see 2 above]. **1831** in 1896 Weeks *S. Quakers & Slavery* 300, There is not a school in the limits of the [North Carolina] Yearly Meeting that is under the care of a committee of either monthly or preparative meeting. **1850** [see 2 above]. **1874** [see 2 above]. **1983** *PADS* 70.42 ce,sePA, *Monthly Meeting.* . . Religious Society of Friends: the basic or local group of Friends having its own meetings for worship each First Day and a meeting for business once a month. *Ibid 46, Quarterly Meeting.* . . Religious Society of Friends: a meeting of representatives of constituent Monthly Meetings. A level of organization between the Monthly and Yearly Meetings. *Ibid 58, Yearly Meeting.* . . Religious Society of Friends: the largest organizational unit of constituent Monthly and Quarterly Meetings in the Society.

meetinger n Pronc-sp *meetiner* [**meeting 1a, b**]
One who takes part in a religious service.

1858 Hammett *Piney Woods Tavern* 49 **TX**, Now, Uncle Billy, I kinder guess if you was at a meetin', and the preacher should stop to take a drink of water . . you'd up and give the preacher and the meetiners ginerally your ideas and views on the subject. *Ibid 68*, So our meetiners wanted to know how the captin *dard* to foller in the same track. **1953** Randolph–Wilson *Down in Holler* 54 **Ozarks**, People going to or from a religious meeting are often called *meetin'ers.* "It must have been about eleven o'clock," said a witness in a murder trial, "because I heard the *meetin'ers* go by just about that time."

meeting-going adj [**meeting 1a**]
Of clothes: =**Sunday-go-to-meeting**.

1954 *Harder Coll.* **cwTN**, *Meetin'-goin' clothes*—Best clothes. " 'Em's my meetin'-goin' clothes."

meetinghouse n

1 A church building. *somewhat old-fash* Note: Orig this term was used to distinguish the buildings of dissenting congregations from those of the established church; it remains the preferred term among Quakers.

1632 in 1901 Cambridge MA *Records* 24 Dec 4, Euery persson . . shall [be] . . wthin [the] meetinghouse In the Afternoone. **1791** Bartram *Travels* 10 **seGA**, It is about nine miles from Sunbury [GA] to Medway meeting-house. **1801** in 1889 MA *Hist. Soc. Proc.* 2d ser 4.134 **MA**, The meeting-house is small but new, very simple and neat in decoration. **1809** Kendall *Travels* 1.132 **CT**, Two meeting-houses, one belonging to quakers, and the other to *baptists.* **1816** Pickering *Vocab.* 60, *Church.* This word . . is generally used in *New-England,* to denote the places of worship of the *Episcopalians.* . . The places of worship of the other denominations of Christians are called *Meeting-houses.* In the *Southern* States, I believe, the word *Church* is used by Christians of all denominations. **1859** Taliaferro *Fisher's R.* 114 **nwNC** (as of 1820s), Boys and "gals" . . would . . walk "side-by-side," the gals . . with their shoes in their "rediculate" till they got in sight of the "meetin'-house." **1891** (1967) Freeman *New Engl. Nun* 26, Folks are gettin' as high-steppin' an' fussy in a meetin'-house as they are in a tavern, nowadays. **1905** *DN* 3.14 **cCT**, *Meeting house.* . . Church. **1906** *DN* 3.121 **sIN**, *Meetin house.* . . Church house. The latter the common term, so that the former seems dialectal. **1907** *DN* 3.215. **1909** *DN* 3.348 **eAL, wGA**. **1910** *DN* 3.445 **wNY**, *Meeting house.* . . Church. Older generation. **1933** *AmSp*

8.1.13 **Philadelphia PA,** *The meeting house.* The building in which the [Friends'] Meeting is held. **1940** Weygandt *Down Jersey* 254, It is not only the Friends, though, whose meeting houses are steepleless. The Cohansey Baptist Church, out from Roadstown, is a true meeting house. **1959** *AmSp* 34.9, Around the turn of the nineteenth century, Baptists, Congregationalists, Presbyterians, and others began dropping the term *meetinghouse* and replacing it with *church.* **1967** *DARE* (Qu. X50, *Names or nicknames for a person who is very fat*) Inf **AL**30, Big as the side of a meetinghouse. **1967** *DARE* FW Addit **TN**16, Meeting-house—old-fashioned term for "church." **1992** *DARE* File **csWI,** The First Unitarian Society's building in Madison is still known as the Meeting House.

2 pl: A **wild columbine** (here: *Aquilegia canadensis*). [Perh from the "steepled" shape of the blossoms]
1892 *Jrl. Amer. Folkl.* 5.91 **NEng,** *Aquilegia Canadensis.* . . meeting-houses. **1910** Graves *Flowering Plants* 192 **CT,** Wild or Red Columbine. Honeysuckle. Meeting-houses. **1961** Smith *MI Wildflowers* 139, Wild Columbine, Rock-bells, Meetinghouses. **1976** Bailey–Bailey *Hortus Third* 93, [*Aquilegia*] *canadensis* . . meeting-houses.

meeting seed n [meeting 1a] **chiefly NEng**
Any of var edible, aromatic seeds; see quots.
1851 *Knickerbocker* 38.372 **nwMA,** Some people call it 'caraway' and 'anise seed,' but we call it 'meetin'-seed,' 'cause we cal'late it keeps us awake in meetin'. **1889** Cooke *Steadfast* 414 **CT,** Mothers of young families distributed fragrant bunches of dried "meetin' seed" among their flocks. **1891** Cooke *Huckleberries* 330 **CT,** She sat down on the bare seat of a corner pew, and choked with the dead odors of "meetin'-seed." **1902** Earle *Old Time Gardens* 341 **NEng,** In the herb garden grew three free-growing plants, all three called indifferently in country tongue, "meetin' seed." They were Fennel, Dill, and Caraway, and similar in growth and seed. . . Their name was given because, in summer days of years gone by, nearly every woman and child carried to "meeting" on Sundays, bunches of the ripe seeds of one or all of these three plants to nibble throughout the long prayers and sermon. It is fancied that these herbs were anti-soporific, but I find no record of such power. **1905** Valentine *H. Sandwith* 25 *(DAE)* **PA,** [He] sat contentedly munching 'meeting seed' which Molly Tucker, the family seamstress, had given him as entertainment on the drive. **1959** Carleton *Index Herb. Plants* 80, *Meeting-seed:* Anethum graveolens; Carum carvi; Eryngium (v); Ferula communis.

meet-me-early n
A **spiderwort** (here: *Tradescantia virginiana*).
1966 *DARE* Wildfl QR Pl.7 Inf **NC**28, Meet-me-early.

meet-up n [Prob folk-etym for **netop**]
A friend.
1903 *DN* 2.299 **Cape Cod MA** (as of a1857), *Meet-ups* . . Chums. 'They were great meet-ups.' Ibid 427, *Meet-up* . . Crony. Cf. Bartlett, *netop,* of which it may be a corruption. [*DN* Ed: See rather the verb.]

meet up with See **meet** v 2

Mef(o)dis See **Methodist**

meg n
1 also *meggie:* A playing marble, esp a small, inexpensive one usu made of clay; pl: a game of marbles. [Cf *EDD* meg, meggy (at *mag* sb.²) "a stone thrown at a mark or other stone"] **chiefly Nth Cf mig**
1949 *PADS* 11.24 **CO,** Meg, mig. . . A marble; a non-agate marble. **1950** *WELS* (Names and nicknames for different kinds of marbles: small ones) 5 Infs, **WI,** Megs. **1957** *Sat. Eve. Post Letters* **cMI,** The game was called "megs." **1966–68** *DARE* (Qu. EE6a, . . *Different kinds of marbles—the big one that's used to knock others out of the ring*) Inf **NY**59, Meg; (Qu. EE6b, *Small marbles or marbles in general*) Infs **MI**61, **NY**66, **WI**20, Megs; **CT**9, Meggies. **c1970** Wiersma *Marbles Terms* **swMI,** Meggies or megs. . . Lower class marble, made of clay and painted various colors. **1971** Bright *Word Geog. CA & NV* 117, Marbles: [1 inf] megs. **1976** *WI Acad. Rev.* June 20 (as of 1920s), We called the painted clay globes "miggies," and the dimpled crockery ones "meggies," not "coffees," and as we grew older disdained both of them—only babies used them.

2 Fig: in phr *have one's megs set to go:* To be ready to go.
1944 *PADS* 2.46 **VA,** *Megs set to go* [mɛgz]. . . "He has his megs set to go"—that is, he is prepared to go.

meggie See **meg** 1

megopher See **magofer**

megrim n Also sp *megrum* [*OED* c1420 →]
See quot 1933.
1933 *AmSp* 8.1.51 **Ozarks,** *Megrum.* . . A severe one-sided headache, migraine. **1953** Randolph–Wilson *Down in Holler* 152 **Ozarks,** An illiterate farmer in Kansas or Illinois would not be likely to say *megrim* when he meant headache, but this word is quite common in the Ozarks.

mejure See **measure**

mek See **make** v¹

mek'ace, mek hase See **make** v¹ **D21**

mele n, v [Haw] **HI**
See quots.
1938 Reinecke *Hawaiian Loanwords* 24, *Mele* ['me:le]. . . A chant for the *hula.* Oli is a non-dance chant. F[req]. **1972** Carr *Da Kine Talk* 88 **HI,** *Mele.* Song or chant; to sing. **1984** Sunset *HI Guide* 85, *Mele*—song.

Mele Kalikimaka exclam [Haw pronc-sp for *Merry Christmas*] **HI**
1950 Anderson *Mele Kalikimaka* [song title]. **1967** *DARE* (Qu. FF10, *What . . people . . say to greet each other on Christmas morning*) Inf **HI**1, [ˈmɛlɪ kɑˌlikiˌmɑkɑ]; **HI**4, [ˈmeli kɑˌlikiˈmɑkɑ]; **HI**9, [ˈmele ˌkɑlikiˈmɑkɑ]. [All Infs old] **1984** Sunset *HI Guide* 85, *Mele Kalikimaka*—Merry Christmas.

melic grass n
Std: a grass of the genus *Melica.* Also called **honey grass, oniongrass 1**

melk See **milk**

‡**mell along** v phr
To mill about.
1966 *DARE* (Qu. KK31, *To go about aimlessly looking for distraction: "He doesn't have anything to do, so he's just _____ around."*) Inf **MS**6, Melling along, ambling.

meller See **mellow**

meller bug See **mellow bug**

mellion See **melon**

mellosses See **molasses**

mellow v Also with *up* Pronc-spp *meller, miller* [Prob *EDD* mell v.¹ "To hammer . . to beat severely" + -*er* frequentative; hypercorrect form *mellow*] **esp S Midl**
Fig: to beat, hit, strike (someone).
1895 Brown *Meadow-Grass* 137 **NH,** I guess you mellered him some, but he's more scairt than hurt. **1923** *DN* 5.236 **swWI,** *Meller.* . . To beat; to pound. "I'll meller him." **1927** *DN* 5.475 **Ozarks,** *Miller.* . . To beat, to pummel. "My boy he ketched thet feller an' jes' millered him up t' a fare-you-well." **1953** Randolph–Wilson *Down in Holler* 264 **Ozarks,** *Mellow.* . . To beat, to pummel, to smash. "I'll just take a stick of wood an' meller that boy's head." **1954** Harder Coll. **cwTN,** *Mellow.* **c1960** Wilson Coll. **csKY,** *Mellow.* . . To beat, smash, whether an apple or a head. **1976** Garber *Mountain-ese* 57 **sAppalachians,** Iffen you cross that boy he'll meller your nose fer you.

mellow bug n Pronc-spp *mallow bug, meller bug* [See quot 1909] **esp GA, AL**
=**whirligig beetle.**
1894 (1922) Harris *Little Thimblefinger* 140 **GA,** Why, I expect it is a mellow bug. . . I used to catch them when I was a girl and put them in my handkerchief. They smell just like a ripe apple. **1909** *DN* 3.348 **eAL, wGA,** *Mellow-bug.* . . A small water-beetle, *Gyranus natator,* the whirligig: so called from its mellow, apple-like odor. **1915** *DN* 4.185 **swVA,** *Meller-bug.* **1941** *Nature Mag.* 34.138 **AL,** Among other characteristics of the whirligig beetles is that of emitting, when, handled, an odor. . . Those finding it agreeable have been the most vocal, for they have called the insects . . mellow bugs. **1951** Teale *North with Spring* 128, Whirligig beetles, the "mellow bugs" of the Okefenokee, spun like pinwheels on the brown water. **1969** *DARE* (Qu. R30, . . *Kinds of beetles;* not asked in early QRs) Inf **GA**89, Mellow bug—sweetish smell. **1972** Swan-Papp *Insects* 352, Gyrinids exude a milky secretion . . for which they have been given such names as "apple smellers"

and "mallow bugs." **1981** Pederson *LAGS Basic Materials,* 1 inf, **csMS,** Mellow bugs; 1 inf, **ceMS,** Mellow bug—stays on top of water.

mellow up See **mellow**

melon n Usu |'mɛlən|; also **chiefly Sth, S Midl** |'mɪljən|; also |'mɪlən| Pronc-spp *mellion, million, millyum, milyun, milon* [Both var types go back at least to the 16th cent; cf such spp as *millian, milion, milon,* and *myllon* in *OED* (at *melon* sb.¹).]
A Forms.

1652 in 1865 MA Hist. Soc. *Coll.* 4th ser 7.63, I have sent you a rariti of seeds which came from the Mouhaks, which is a kinde of milions. **c1770** in 1833 Boucher *Glossary* **MD,** Sweet the day / Ere long, when *water-millions* come in play. **1795** Dearborn *Columbian Grammar* 139, *List of Improprieties* . . Watermilyun for Watermellon. **1818** Fessenden *Ladies Monitor* 172 **VT,** Provincial words . . to be avoided. . . *Million* for melon. **1845** in 1952 Green *Samuel Maverick* 291 **SC,** I am yet taking . . horse redish root Parsley root tea, slippery Elm Tea & water mellion seed Tea for the cholick. **1887** Eggleston *Graysons* 134 **sIL,** Onions and watermelons—"ing-uns and watermillions," in Broad Run phrase. **1893** Shands *MS Speech* 45, Million. . . Negro for *melon.* **1899** (1912) Green *VA Folk-Speech* 282, Million. **1899** Chesnutt *Conjure Woman* 31 **csNC** [Black], Dat Yankee had done bus' de watermillyum. **1903** DN 2.336 **seMO,** Watermillion. **1907** DN 3.238 **nwAR,** *Watermil-lion.* **1909** DN 3.349 **eAL, wGA,** Million. . . Melon. A negroism origi-nally used facetiously, but now often unconsciously. *Milon* is frequently heard among all classes. **1915** DN 4.185 **swVA,** Million. **1915** DN 4.229 **wTX,** Watermillions. . . Often heard for *watermelons.* Commonly used by negroes. **1942** Hall *Smoky Mt. Speech* 19 **eTN, wNC,** The raising of [ɛ] to [ɪ] was observed also in . . melon. **1952** Brown *NC Folkl.* 1.565, Million: . . Melon. **1976** Ryland *Richmond Co. VA* 373, 'Million—(watermillion).

B Sense.
An oil- and blubber-filled bulge on the forehead of certain cetaceans of the family Delphinidae, esp the pilot whale.

1877 U.S. Natl. Museum *Bulletin* 14.225, "Melon" blubber of black-fish *(Globicephalus melas). Ibid* **MA,** "Melon" blubber of grampus *(Grampus griseus).* Cape Cod. **1887** Goode *Fisheries U.S.* 5.2.299, About 30 gallons of oil . . [are] obtained from each fish [=*Globicephala melaena*], besides about 6 quarts of extra oil from the melon. The melons are taken from the top of the head, reaching from the spout-hole to the end of the nose and from the top of the head down to the upper jaw, and when taken off in one piece they represent a half water-melon, weighing about 25 pounds, and when the knife is put into the center of this melon the oil runs more freely than the water does from a very nice water-melon; hence the name melon oil. . . The head oil or melon oil . . is refined in small quantities for the use of watch and instrument makers. **1926** Ashley *Yankee Whaler* 124, Blackfish: A small cetacean. The forehead or "melon" makes the finest lubricant known. Used exclusively for watch oil. **1938** Tripp *Flukes* 188 **New Bedford MA,** In the head of a blackfish is a cavity called the "melon," which contains oil in a liquid state. . . Blackfish oil is used by jewelers to oil clocks and watches. **1983** *Audubon Field Guide N. Amer. Fishes* 798, [The long-finned whale's] large bulbous melon, or bump on the forehead, looks much like an inverted cook pot. *Ibid* 803, False Killer Whale *(Pseudorca crassidens).* . . Rounded bump on forehead, or melon, somewhat over-hangs long lower jaw.

melon loco n [See quots 1886, 1979] **chiefly TX**
A cucurbitaceous plant *(Apodanthera undulata)* native from southern Arizona to western Texas.

1886 Havard *Flora W. & S. TX for 1885* 522, Apodanthera undulata. . . Melon Loco. . . As the name indicates, the fruit is considered poisonous by the Mexicans. **1891** Coulter *Botany W. TX* 124, In rocky valleys, from Eagle Pass to the mountains west of the Pecos. Known as "melon loco." **1892** DN 1.191 **TX,** The plant called *melon loco* is a gourd about the size of an orange *(Apodanthera undulata).* **1939** Tharp *Vegetation TX* 70, Melon Loco *(Apodanthera).* **1979** Spellenberg *Audubon Guide N. Amer. Wildflowers W. Region* 472, Melon loco. . . A bad-smelling, grayish, hairy plant. . . Plants with the name "loco" are usually poison-ous to some degree; several have toxins that produce madness.

melt n [Var of *milt;* Cf *OED melt* "obs. and dial. variant"]
1 The spleen of an animal, esp when prepared as food. **chiefly Sth, S Midl**

1887 *Scribner's Mag.* 2.479 **AR,** I seen ye, myseff, feedin' up that innercent chile on gouber peas an' hogs' melts! **1887** (1895) Robinson

Uncle Lisha 143 **wVT,** A man can tell if it's goin' tu be a hard or open winter by lookin' 't a hawg's melt. **1893** Shands *MS Speech* 44, Melt [mɛlt]. The *milt* of hogs is always thus pronounced by all classes. **1899** (1912) Green *VA Folk-Speech* 279, Melt. . . The spleen. **1913** Kephart *Highlanders* 106 **sAppalachians,** John slapped a bear's "melt" (spleen) upon the table. **1926** DN 5.401 **Ozarks,** Melt. . . The spleen. In com-mon use in connection with the butchering of cattle and hogs. **1939** *LANE* Map 209 *(Pluck, haslet)* 1 inf, **cVT,** 'A hog's melt denotes the winter. . . If it's thick at the front end and thin at the back end, the winter will be severe during the early months and mild later on,' and conversely. **c1940** Eliason *Word Lists FL* 10 **wFL,** Melt: The spleen. **1946** *PADS* 6.20 **NC** (as of 1900–10), Melt. . . Milt (of a hog). . . Common among farmers. (Common in many sections of the South. A butcher in Guilford Co., N.C., once told the Editor that beating a stuttering child with a melt would cure him of stuttering.) **1950** Faulkner *Stories* 372 **MS,** Then there was the tongue, paws and melt of a bear. **1968–70** DARE (Qu. H43, *Foods made from parts of the head and inner organs of an animal)* Inf **WV8,** Melt—part of hog hooked to heart, used with other inner organs to make puddin; **VA42,** Kidneys, lights, melts, heart . . and sweetbread. **1970** Green *Ely* 55, I loved to be around hog-killing. I liked to broil the melts over the blaze and eat them. **1991** Still *Wolfpen Notebooks* 77 **sAppalachians,** At hog killing time what I like best to eat is the melt. I could eat it [even] if I was tolerably sick.

2 See quot 1953. Cf **pluck**
1867 Harris *Sut Lovingood Yarns* 248 **TN,** The idear ove Derringers, an' the melt tu use em, bein mix't up wif es much durned finekey fool es he show'd, never struck me at all. **1953** Randolph–Wilson *Down in Holler* 85 **Ozarks,** The word melt means courage, too, or rather reck-lessness. An old man in our neighborhood was talking about his son's quarrel with some village boys, who were always "layin' for him" after school. "They better let Tommy alone," said the father darkly. "Tommy's a-packin' a big knife, an' he's got the *melt* to use it, too."

melting time n [Cf *OED melt* v.¹ 3.b "to become softened by compassion, or love"; c1200 →]
See quot.

1993 Mason *Feather Crowns* 69 **KY,** "Wasn't that a fine melting time at this morning's service? . . " "We didn't get here that early," Christie said. Melting time, when all the true believers came together to rededi-cate their souls, always made her feel as though she would smother.

melt one's butter v phr
To please one.

1986 DARE File **cnAR,** Whatever melts your butter means whatever pleases you, whatever makes you happy.

Melungeon n Also sp *Melungen, Malungeon* [Perh based on Fr *mélange* mixture, crossing of races] **sAppalachians, esp eTN** Cf **brass ankle, Maley**
A member of a racially mixed group of people centered in northeastern Tennessee and southwestern Virginia.

1840 *Whig* (Jonesborough TN) 7 Oct [3]/5, An effort was made, to get an impudent *Malungeon* from Washington City, a scoundrel who is half *Negro* and half *Indian,* and who has actually been speaking in Sullivan [Co], in reply to Combs! **1849** *Littell's Living Age* 20.618 **neTN,** This gorge and the tops and sides of the adjoining mountains are inhabited by a singular species of the human animal called *Melungens.* The legend of their history, which they carefully preserve, is this. A great many years ago, these mountains were settled by a society of Portuguese adventurers. . . These intermixed with the Indians, and subsequently their descendants . . with the negroes and the whites, thus forming the present race of Melungens. **1889** *Amer. Anthropologist* 2.347 **eTN** (as of 1850s), No one seemed to know positively that they or their ancestors had ever been in slavery, and they did not themselves claim to belong to any tribe of Indians in that part of the country. They resented the appellation Melungeon, given to them by common consent by the whites, and proudly called themselves Portuguese. **1914** Wilson *S. Mountain-eers* 12 **eTN,** Occasionally the student of ethnology may stumble upon a community that is a puzzle, as, for example, that one occupied by the "Malungeons" of upper East Tennessee. **1915** DN 4.185, *Malungeon.* . . One of a race of people in southwestern Virginia and eastern Kentucky and Tennessee said to have partly Indian blood. **1952** Callahan *Smoky Mt.* 162, The first records of them date back to 1784, when . . a colony of strange people with dark complexions of a reddish-brown hue was found in the upper Smokies. . . They called themselves Melungeons. **1963** Berry *Almost White* 17, In the mountains of eastern Tennessee, in the county of Hancock . . a remote spot called Newman's Ridge . . has long been the home of an enigmatic people known as Melungeons. **1968** Haun *Hawk's Done Gone* 124 **eTN**, Drusilla had just enough of Burt's Melungeon blood in her to make her pretty—big black eyes and long black hair. **1968** *DARE* FW Addit **VA**4A, Melungeons [ˌməˈlʌŋɪ̆nz]— dark skinned people who live up in the mountains, supposedly descendents of Moors shipwrecked off Kitty Hawk and escaped to the mountains.

Melvin n Also *Marvin, Uncle Melvin* Cf **wedgie**

1989–91 *DARE* File **AZ, AR, CA, FL, ID, KS, NV, OR, UT, WA**, The act of reaching into another person's belt, and either grabbing the underwear or the belt and lifting the person off the ground. . . Melvin. *Ibid* **OK**, Uncle Melvin. *Ibid* **AK, WY**, Marvin.

memaloose adj, n [Chinook Jargon *memaloost* < Chinook *memalust* to die, dead] **Pacific NW** Cf *DCan* (at *mamaloos*)

See quot 1938—also used in place names.

1938 (1939) Holbrook *Holy Mackinaw* 265 **NW**, In the camps of the Pacific Northwest loggers use a number of Chinook words. . . *Memaloose.* Dead, or death. **1970** Stewart *Amer. Place-Names* 289, *Memaloose*—Chinook jargon, 'death, dead,' usually applied to a place of Indian burial, e.g. the islands in OR and WA. **1989** Lesley *River Song* 67 **cnOR**, Danny stopped the pickup at the Wish-Ham Cemetery. . . Jack walked over to the locked gate. . . "Hey, I know about this place. One of the kids at school told me they moved all the bones here from a burial island in the river." "Two islands," Danny said. "Grave and Memaloose. They were flooded by the dam's backwaters, so the Army Corps of Engineers moved all the bones here."

‡memaloose v [Perh **memaloose** adj, n, infl by **vamoose**]

1967 *DARE* (Qu. Y18, *To leave in a hurry: "Before they find this out, we'd better _____!"*) Inf **OR**3, Memaloose [ˌmɛməˈlus]; (Qu. NN22b, *Expressions used to drive away children*) Inf **OR**3, Memaloos.

member n *among Black speakers*

1 A devout church member. [Cf *OED* member sb. 2 "fig. with reference to a metaphorical 'body'; chiefly in *member of Christ, of Satan*" 13..–1711]

1867 Allen *Slave Songs* 4, Praise, member, praise God. *Ibid* 15, O call all de member to de graveyard. **1891** *Atlantic Mth.* 68.288 [Black], He's tuck a seat wid de member-men. **1959** Lomax *Rainbow Sign* 51 **AL** [Black], This Reverend Gillum. . . [would] go to town and tell the white people, "These members of mine don't have any food and no way to get none and I want to try to get um some." **1977** Dillard *Lexicon* 52, *Member* has a special function in the Black English vernacular. . . It does not indicate someone who is merely carried on the church rolls but rather one who really "belongs"—one who is totally and enthusiastically a part of the church.

2 A fellow Black person. Cf **blood** n **1**

1963 *Freedomways* 3.53 **NYC** [Black], Three more, one of 'em a member, . . sailed over. **1971** Roberts *Third Ear* np [Black], *Member.* . . a fellow black person. *Syn. see* blood. **1972** Kochman *Rappin'* 149, *Club member* or *Member.* Also connotes the kinship or "all-in-it-together" aspect of being black in white America. The label is complimentary. **1977** Smitherman *Talkin* 251, *Member,* club member, positive term, stressing racial bond and togetherness. **1977** Dillard *Lexicon* 52, *Member* was adopted by the Black militant groups, becoming virtually synonymous with in-group participation terms like *blood.* **1980** Folb *Runnin' Down* 246 **cwCA** [Black], *Member*—Another black person.

membranous croup n Also *membrane(ous) croup* [*OED* 1876]

Usu diphtheria; occas a related or similar disease.

1889 *Century Dict.* 1367, *True* or *membranous croup* is inflammation of the larynx (laryngitis) with fibrinous exudation forming a false membrane. Many if not all cases of true croup are diphtheritic in nature. **1925** *Book of Rural Life* 1450, What used to be commonly called *membranous croup* is, as a matter of fact, *diphtheria.* **1937** Thornburgh *Gt. Smoky Mts.* 30, Now take lobelia. . . Its [*sic*] mighty common, and it's mighty good for membraneous croup, too. **1967** *DARE* (Qu. BB49, . . *Other kinds of diseases*) Inf **MI**65, Diphtheria, and they would get membranous croup along with it. **1986** Pederson *LAGS Concordance* (Diphtheria) 1 inf, **nwLA**, Membrane croup; 3 infs, **cAL, cwGA**, Membranous croup.

mémère n Also *(ma)mère, mammere* [Fr] **Fr** settlement areas, esp **sLA**

A grandmother.

1961 *PADS* 36.11 **sLA**, Memere (Grandmother)—18.6[% of 70 infs]. **1967** LeCompte *Word Atlas* 263, **seLA**, Grand-mother, usual term of

affection. . . *me-mère* [7 of 21 infs]. **1968** *DARE* (Qu. Z4, . . *'Grandmother'*) Inf **LA**23, Mère [mɛr]. **1969** Cagnon *Franco–Amer. Terms* 224 **RI**, Mémère . . [mɛmeˡr]; [mœmeˡr]—Grandma. "That's my mémère." "Is mémère coming with us?" "Go see your mémère." **1983** Reinecke *Coll.* 12 **LA**, Mémère, Mère . . [meˈmɜə] . . grandmother. Still quite common in families of F[rench] descent. **1986** Pederson *LAGS Concordance* (Grandmother) 1 inf, **seLA**, Memere = granny; 2 infs, **seLA**, Mere; [(Midwife) 1 inf, **seLA**, Memere—neighbors called midwife; her mother]. **1994** *DARE* File **wMA**, [ˈmɛmɛ] is used for 'grandmother' in western Massachusetts by people of French (Canuck) background. Sometimes it's [ˈmɛmɛ] and [ˈpɛpɛ], and sometimes [məˈmɛɚ] and [pəˈpɛɚ], even among Anglophone kids. *Ibid*, The form of the name which my nieces (and sister) use to call my mother is "mamère" with a schwa in the first syllable. . . My Aunt Merci, who has lived almost all her life in New Orleans, . . uses the pronunciation . . "mémère". . . Obviously, the French pronunciation is still kept in N.O. . . but those of us living away have anglicized it. . . My cousin Louise . . pronounces the name /mæˈmejr/ and she spells it "mammere". It was the name by which her older sisters called their grandmother (. . who died in 1911). . . It is hard to know how the French influence would have been felt in rural Md., except perhaps that the relevant families are all Catholic and convent education for girls tended to stress French then.

Memorial Day flower n Cf **Decoration Day plant**

A peony (*Paeonia* spp).

1969 *DARE* (Qu. S11, . . *Peony*) Inf **IL**30, Memorial Day flower.

memorial times n [Prob < *time immemorial*]

Days long past.

1933 Hurston in *Story* Aug 64 **FL** [Black], You don't know whut been lost 'round heah. Maybe somebody way back in memorial times lost they gold money and went on off and it ain't never been found.

memorize v Usu |ˈmɛməˌraɪz|; infreq |ˈmɛmbəˌraɪz|

A Form. [Cf Intro "Language Changes" I.8; perh infl by *remember;* cf **B** below]

1981 Pederson *LAGS Basic Materials,* 1 inf, **cnAR**, [ˈmɛˀmbɚˀaˀɪzd̟]; 1 inf, **neTX**, [ˈmɛ̃mbə̣ˡˌaˀɪz].

B Sense.

To remember, bring to mind. **esp S Midl**

1924 Raine *Land of Saddle-Bags* 103 **sAppalachians**, I hain't seen my sister in twenty years; I cain't hardly *memorize* her. **1930** *VA Qrly. Rev.* 6.249 **S Midl**, The gentleman of the backwoods . . may say memorize for remember. **1940** (1968) Haun *Hawk's Done Gone* 27 **eTN**, It had been so long since I had heard Tiny say anything that I didn't quite memorize how her voice sounded. **1986** Pederson *LAGS Concordance,* 1 inf, **swMS**, I don't memorize it—= remember it.

memory See **memory root**

memory gem n

A brief text, as a verse, proverb, or portion of Scripture, committed to memory.

1897 in 1984 Gilmore *Ozark Baptizings* 56 **swMO**, 'Memory Gems,' . . culled from the ablest authors and sages of the past. **1942** Whipple *Joshua* 572 **UT** (as of c1860), Looking at their innocent faces like upturned flower-faces, Clory thought they might be reciting a memory-gem in Sunday School. **1968** *DARE* Tape **DE**3, [FW:] Did they have you learn any more verses in school? . . [Inf:] Little memory gems, little four-line verses. **1985** *NC Folkl. Jrl.* 33.45 **wNC** (as of c1920), He . . had a few students recite a Bible verse or what he called a "memory gem"—a proverb such as those from *Poor Richard's Almanac*.

memory root n Also *memory* [See quot 1892]

A **jack-in-the-pulpit 1** (here: *Arisaema triphyllum*).

1892 (1974) Millspaugh *Amer. Med. Plants* 167–2, The corms, when fresh, especially, and all parts of the plant, have a severely acrid juice, imparting an almost caustic sensation to the mucous membranes, and swelling of the parts when chewed. This action upon the mouths of school-boys, who often play the trick of inviting bites of the corm upon each other, gave rise to the common name, "memory-root," as they never forget its effects. **1897** *Jrl. Amer. Folk.* 10.146 **cMA**, Memory root. **1950** *WELS,* 1 Inf, **cwWI**, Indian turnip—also called "memory" because "if you ever bite into one you will remember it!" [FW: said by Inf's old teacher] **1971** Krochmal *Appalachia Med. Plants* 62, *Arisaema triphyllum.* . . memory root, pepper turnip. **1975** *Mt. Eagle* (Whitesburg KY) 26 June sec B3, A third name for the plant [=jack-in-the-pulpit] is "memory Root" [*sic*] because, once tasted raw, it cannot ever be forgotten.

memory string n

1965 Hyatt *Folkl. Adams Co. IL* 440, About sixty-five years ago the girls would ask every man they see for one button off of their clothes and would put the button on a string—it was called a *memory string*—and the hundredth button you got was to be your future husband. I remember I had a memory string when I was a girl and I asked a fellow for a button and he said, 'I hope this is the hundred.' It happen to be. And in about three months after that I was engaged to that fellow, but I didn't marry him—we had trouble and broke up.

mend v

1 To improve in health; to recover from illness. [*OED mend* v. 6.b 1500–20 →] **chiefly Sth, S Midl** See Map See also **mending hand, on the**

1909 *DN* 3.348 **eAL, wGA,** *Mend. . .* To improve in health. **1965–70** *DARE* (Qu. BB46, *. . Someone who has been very sick but now is getting better: "He's _____."*) 27 Infs, **chiefly Sth, S Midl,** Mending; **TX**37, Going to mend; **SC**46, Mending; starting to mend; **NY**8, Starting to mend along. **1974** Fink *Mountain Speech* 16 **wNC, eTN,** *Mend . .* improve physically. "He's mending slowly." **1976** Garber *Mountain-ese* 57 **sAppalachians,** *Mend . .* improve in health—He's been real puny but he's beginnin' to mend uv late. **1986** Pederson *LAGS Concordance,* 1 inf, **csTN,** *A-mending* = recovering from illness.

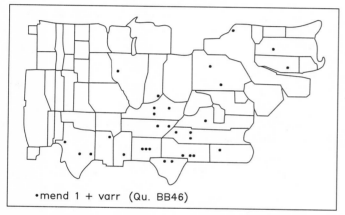

•mend 1 + varr (Qu. BB46)

2 also with *up:* To thrive; to gain weight. [Cf *EDD mend* v. 8 "To grow stout."] **chiefly S Midl**

1903 *DN* 2.320 **seMO,** *Mend. . .* To improve. 'My pigs are mending mighty fast,' that is growing thriftily. **1907** *DN* 3.233 **nwAR,** *Mend. . .* To improve, to grow thriftily. **1953** Randolph–Wilson *Down in Holler* 264 **Ozarks,** *Mend. . .* To gain weight. "That feller's a-mendin' mighty fast" does not mean that his health is improving, but merely that he's putting on weight. **1954** *Harder Coll.* **cwTN,** *Mend up. . .* Gain weight. **c1960** *Wilson Coll.* **csKY,** *Mend. . .* To gain weight or strength.

3 To make well, restore to health.

1967 *DARE* FW Addit **TN,** "If you don't 'noculate, you cain't mend it" [means] if you don't inoculate a sick animal you can't cure it.

4 To tend or add fuel to (a fire). [*OED mend* v. 5.b c1480 →] **chiefly Sth, S Midl**

1884 *Anglia* 7.275 **Sth, S Midl** [Black], *To men' de fier* = to see after the fire. **1899** (1912) Green *VA Folk-Speech* 279, To mend the fire is to add fresh fuel to it. **1953** Stuart *Beatinest Boy* 103 **KY,** I'll mend the fire so we'll have fire all night. **1953** Randolph–Wilson *Down in Holler* 83 **Ozarks,** *Mend the fire* means to keep adding fuel, as "Bill he had to set up an' mend the fire all night." **c1960** *Wilson Coll.* **csKY,** *Mend the fire. . .* Add fuel to it, chunk it up. **1977** Miles *Ozark Dict.* 6, *Mend. . .* Tend to. "Mend the far, it's a gittin' chilly in hyar."

5 in phr *mend one's licks* and varr: To move or travel faster. **esp S Midl** Cf **lick n 6**

1892 *DN* 1.230 **KY,** "To mend one's licks" = to quicken one's steps. "When the dog got after me, I mended my licks." **1899** (1912) Green *VA Folk-Speech* 279, *Mend his gait. . .* To go faster. **1909** *DN* 3.400 **nwAR,** *Mend one's licks. . .* To quicken one's steps. **1922** Gonzales *Black Border* 313 **sSC, GA coasts** [Gullah glossary], *Men' e' pace*—mend his, her, its, their pace; hurry, hurry up, etc.

mending hand, on the adj phr [*OED* (at *hand* sb. 4.b) 1598 →; cf **mend 1**] esp NEng Note: *on the mend* is not regional.

Recovering from sickness or injury; convalescent.

1675 in 1826 Morton *New Engl. Mem.* 435, Our wounded men, some die still, and some on the mending hand. **1890** *DN* 1.19, *On the mending hand:* convalescent. A common New England phrase. *Ibid* 78 **LA,** *On the mending hand* is sometimes heard in Louisiana, but *on the mend* is commoner. **1892** *DN* 1.217 **ceMA,** *On the mending hand. . .* "Common in Boston in my youth." **1899** (1912) Green *VA Folk-Speech* 279, He's been sick but is now on the mending-hand. **1942** *AmSp* 17.130 **IN,** *On the mending hand* (convalescent). **1979** *AmSp* 54.98 **ME** (as of c1905), *Mending hand. . .* (Recuperation from illness)—"He's on the mending hand."

mend one's gait (or licks) See mend 5

mend one's own shoes v phr

1967 *DARE* (Qu. II22, *Expressions to tell somebody to keep to himself and mind his own business*) Inf **ID**5, Mend your own shoes.

mend one's pace See mend 5

mend up See mend 2

menehune n [Haw] HI

See quots.

1938 Reinecke *Hawaiian Loanwords* 25, *Menehune* ['me:ne'hu:ne]. . . "A race of midgets in Hawaiian legends, who are credited with the building of many temples, fishponds and roads which still exist. They worked only in the night and if the work was not completed in that one night it remained unfinished." . . Some people still credit them with existence, invisible to ordinary eyes. V[ery] F[req]. **1967** *DARE* (Qu. CC17, *Imaginary animals or monsters that people . . tell tales about—especially to tease greenhorns*) Inf **HI**4, Menehune—good people; two feet to three feet tall; made fish ponds, tunnels in one night; **HI**9, Menehune—small, grotesque-looking fellow. **1972** Carr *Da Kine Talk* 88 **HI,** *Menehune.* Legendary race of small people who worked at night and were noted for good deeds. **1984** *Sunset HI Guide* 85, *Menehune*—dwarf, legendary race of dwarfs.

menfolk(s) n pl chiefly Sth, S Midl Cf folk C1a, 2b, womenfolk(s)

Men; the men of a family or community.

1843 (1916) Hall *New Purchase* 55 **IN,** We men-folks, my dear Miss, went out to see what sort of weather we were likely to have. **1899** (1912) Green *VA Folk-Speech* 279, *Men-folks. . .* The men of a household or community collectively. **1908** Fox *Lonesome Pine* 80 **KY,** You menfolks don't think less—you jes' talk less. **1913** Kephart *Highlanders* 120 **sAppalachians,** They know thar's a president, because the men folks 's voted for him, and the women folks 's seed his pictur. **1926** Vollmer *Sun-Up* 62 **wNC,** Ain't ye fitten to use yo' law agin' nothin' but wimen, and men folks whut's without guns? **1934** Carmer *Stars Fell on AL* 9, Every day some menfolks would ride in with their guns. **1938** Damon *Grandma* 74 **CT,** Menfolks had said nothing could be grown in such "dirt" as that. **1938** Rawlings *Yearling* 11 **FL,** Men-folks has got to stick together in the name o' peace. **1941** Percy *Lanterns* 6 **nwMS,** If the ladies loved going to New Orleans, the men-folks were never at a loss for reasons to take the same trip. **1967–68** *DARE* FW Addit **wMD,** Menfolks—general term for men; **ceTN,** Menfolks (for *men*)—heard often in conversation with country people. **1967–69** *DARE* Tape **CA**164, When I was four I used to go with the menfolks and ride; **CA**172A, She saw these menfolks hewing logs; **TX**31, Menfolks. **1986** Pederson *LAGS Concordance,* 12 infs, **Gulf Region,** Menfolks; 2 infs, **seMS, cnAL,** (Bunch of) menfolk.

menhaden n Usu |ˌmɛnˈhedn̩, ˌmən-|; for varr see quots 1939, 1965–70

1 also sp *manhad(d)en, manhayden, menhadden:* A fish of the genus *Brevoortia,* esp *B. tyrannus* of the Atlantic coast or *B. patronus* of the Gulf coast. [See quot 1907] Also called **alewife, bugfish, oldwife 1a, pogy, sardine, shad;** for other names of *B. tyrannus* see **bonefish 2, bonyfish 1, bunker n[1], fatback 2b, greentail 1, hardhead 2a, minnie n[4], mossbunker, mossyback 2, mud shad 2, ocean trout, panhagen, pilchard, poghagen, Sam Day, shadine, shiner, skippaug, whitefish, whiting, yellowtail**

[**1643** Williams *Key into Language* 114, Aumsûog, & Munnawhatteaûg. *A Fish somewhat like a Herring.*] **1792** Toulmin *Descr. KY* 42, [In 1787 were exported from Philadelphia PA] Barrels of manhadden 236. **1814** in 1815 *Lit. & Philos. Soc. NY Trans.* 1.453, They are eatable; but as they are too abundant for consumption as food, and as there are multitudes of preferable fish, menhaden are often left to putrify on the shore, or are removed to the fields for manure. . . The aborigines called him [sic] menhaden. **1836** *Farmers' Reg.* 4.306 **RI**, One of their principal manures is the "Manhayden" fish. **1838** MA *Zool. & Bot. Surv. Repts. Zool.* 43, It is computed that a single menhaden of ordinary size is equal in richness to a shovel-full of barn-yard manure. It is getting likewise to be thought worthy of preservation as an article of food. **1843** (1844) Johnson *Farmer's Encycl.* 769, *Manhaden.* . . A species of herring frequenting the waters of New England States and Long Island. **1867** *Amer. Naturalist* 1.224, The Finbacks feed on menhaden, and other small fishes. **1884** U.S. Natl. Museum *Bulletin* 27.1041, An extract of fish made from the juices of the flesh of menhaden was patented several years ago, but has not become popular. The menhaden abounds from Maine to North Carolina. **1907** Hodge *Hdbk. Amer. Indians* 1.841, *Menhaden.* . . The name is derived from the Narraganset dialect of Algonquian. Roger Williams (1643) calls *munnawhatteaug* a "fish like a herring," the word being really plural and signifying, according to Trumbull (Natick Dict., 69, 1903), 'they manure.' The reference is to the Indian custom of using these fish as manure for cornfields, which practice the aborigines of New England transmitted to the European colonists. *Menhaden* is thus a corruption of the Narraganset term for this fish, *munnawhat,* 'the fertilizer.' **1921** LA Dept. of Conserv. *Bulletin* 10.143, The pelican in Louisiana . . feeds largely on the menhadden . . with a slight addition of mullet. **1939** *LANE* Map 233, Brevoortia tyrannus. . . This fish is called . . *menhaden* from Cape Cod westward. . . *Menhaden* . . is now replacing all other terms along the southern shore of New England. [Most common proncs are [mən'he(ɪ)dn̩, mɛn-]; 3 infs, **CT, Long Is. NY,** [mən'hædn̩, mɛn-].] **1945** Beck *Jersey Genesis* 147 **NJ,** "The fish they caught was mossbunkers, and the stuff they made was mostly oil and fertilizer." . . "Most people know mossbunkers as menhaden," Jack said. **1965–70** *DARE* (Qu. P2, . . *Kinds of saltwater fish caught around here . . good to eat*) Infs **AL22, NC1, VA55,** Menhaden; **MA55, 80, NJ39,** [ˌmɛn'hɛdn̩]; **LA44,** ['mɪn,heɪdn̩]; **NC27,** [mæn'hɛdən]; (Qu. P4, *Saltwater fish that are not good to eat*) Infs **DE3, RI**8, [ˌmæn'he(ɪ)dn̩]; **DE4,** ['mæn,heɪdn̩]; **LA31,** [ˌmɪn'heɪdn̩]; **LA44,** ['mɪn,heɪdn̩]; **MA40,** [ˌmɛn'hɛdn̩]; **NJ16,** Menhaden; (Qu. P7, *Small fish used as bait for bigger fish*) Inf **VA47,** Cut ['mɪn,hɛdn̩]; **NJ60,** ['mæn,hɛdənz]; (Qu. P14, . . *Commercial fishing . . what do the fishermen go out after?*) Infs **LA**31, 44, **NC**12, **VA**55, Menhaden; **MS**73, [mæn,hɛdn̩]; (Qu. O10, . . *Kinds of boats*) Inf **SC**63, Menhaden boats. **1976** Warner *Beautiful Swimmers* 127 **Delmarva,** Chesapeake watermen simply say menhaden or bunker. **1983** *Audubon Field Guide N. Amer. Fishes* 382, Menhadens. . . support a large industry on the Atlantic and Gulf coasts. Although all parts of the fish have value, its oil is the principal product. **1986** Pederson *LAGS Concordance (Saltwater fish)* 6 infs, **coastal Gulf Region,** Menhaden.

2 A thread herring (here: *Opisthonema oglinum*).
1873 in 1878 Smithsonian Inst. *Misc. Coll.* 14.2.33, *Brevoortia menhaden.* . . Menhaden *(Vineyard Sound* [MA]). . . *Opisthonema thrissa.* . . Menhaden *(Portland* [ME]). **1890** *Century Dict.* 3707, The name *menhaden* . . is locally misapplied to the thread-herring, *Opisthonema thrissa.*

menominee n Also *menominee whitefish* [Through assoc with *Menominee* an Amer Ind people of northeastern Wisconsin and the Upper Peninsula of Michigan] **chiefly MI, MN, WI** **=round whitefish.**
1882 U.S. Natl. Museum *Bulletin* 16.298, *C[oregonus] quadrilateralis.* . . Menomonee [sic] *White-fish.* . . Abundant in cold, deep waters. **1896** U.S. Bur. Fisheries *Rept. for 1895* 288, *Menominee Whitefish.* . . Upper Great Lakes, northwestward to Alaska, as far south as Yukon River. **1908** Forbes–Richardson *Fishes of IL* 53, The round or Menominee whitefish . . is taken in Lake Michigan, though much more rarely than the common whitefish. **1944** Nute *Lake Superior* 186 **MI, MN, WI,** Menominees, a kind of whitefish, are listed at 14,940 pounds, all caught in American waters. **1966–68** *DARE* (Qu. P1, . . *Kinds of freshwater fish . . caught around here . . good to eat*) Infs **MI**2, 32, 54, **MN**15, Menominee; (Qu. P14, . . *Commercial fishing . . what do the fishermen go out after?*) Inf **MI**54, Menominee. **1969** *DARE* Tape **WI**75, Along comes the lawyer and the sucker and the menominee. . . He's a menominee whitefish. He isn't as fat as a whitefish—he's a different species again. **1974** WI Univ. *Fish Lake MI* 31, *Prosopium cylindraceum.* . . menominee, . . menominee whitefish. . . Those that patrol the coastal waters around the islands and shores of northern Lakes Michigan and Huron are known locally as "menominees." **1983** Becker *Fishes WI* 372, *Round Whitefish.* . . Other common names . . Menominee, Menominee whitefish.

menow See **minnow** A1

mens, menses See **man** n B2

menstruate v Pronc-sp *ministrate* Cf **menstruation**
Std sense, var form.
c1938 in 1970 Hyatt *Hoodoo* 1.305 **cnVA,** She *ministrated* every day for about five years. **c1938** in 1973 *Ibid* 3.2519 **SC,** Dey take de dishrag when dey *ministrate* or have dere monthlies on. **1946** McCullers *Member* 70 **AL,** I'm not so old as some peoples would try and make out. I can still ministrate. **1967** *DARE* (Qu. AA27, . . *A woman's menstruation*) Inf **LA**14, She's ministrating ['mɪnəˌstreɪtɪŋ].

menstruation n Pronc-spp *menustration, ministration* Cf **ministress, menstruate**
A Forms.
c1938 [see **B** below]. **1967** *DARE* (Qu. AA27, . . *A woman's menstruation*) Inf **LA**8, [mɪnɪ'streɪ̌ʃən]. **1992** Hunter-Gault *In My Place* 65 **GA** [Black], My cousin Shirley, who used to come and visit from nearby Oxford—would try to describe menstruation, which everybody called "menustration."
B Sense.
Menstrual discharge; hence adj *ministrational* of or relating to menstrual discharge.
c1938 in 1970 Hyatt *Hoodoo* 1.342 **seGA,** It was some of her ministration. *Ibid* 359 **swTN,** When the moon is on the wane, a person can take a woman's *ministrational cloth* and wash 'em and take that water and put 'em in a tree. *Ibid* 708 **csNC,** If yo's a woman, put some ministration in dere.

-ment suff Pronc-sp *-mint*
A Forms.
With primary or secondary stress; see quots. **chiefly Sth, S Midl**
1893 Shands *MS Speech* 28, *-ent.* . . It is characteristic of the illiterate white inhabitants of the pine district of Mississippi to give special emphasis to the pronunciation of this syllable when final; as, . . commandmént, contentmént. **1909** *DN* 3.349 **eAL, wGA,** *-ment.* . . Commonly with strongly accented pronunciation in . . *settlement, compliment,* etc. **1913** Kephart *Highlanders* 224 **sAppalachians,** In mountain dialect such words as settlement, government, studyment (reverie) are accented on the last syllable, or drawled with equal stress throughout. **1936** *AmSp* 11.162 **eTX,** Words ending in *-ment.* . . *Argument, government, improvement, predicament, president, punishment, statement, temperament,* . . usually carry secondary stress on the final syllable, which is pronounced with nasalized [ī]: ['argjəˌmĩnt]. . . ['prɛzəˌdĩnt], etc. **1940** Stuart *Trees of Heaven* 291 **neKY,** Let's git our heads togither here and come to some settle-ment. **1941** *AmSp* 16.10 **eTX** [Black], *Argument* and *president* have secondary stress on the final syllable, ['agəˌmĩnt], ['prɛzəˌdĩnt]. **1974** Fink *Mountain Speech* 16 **wNC, eTN,** *-ment* (suffix): accented last syllable in such words as settlement', government', treatment', etc. **1984** Burns *Cold Sassy* 285 **nGA** (as of 1906), About then old Mr. Billy Whisnant shuffled in and asked for a jar of lini-ment.
B Sense.
Noun-forming suff—freq redund, occas replacing std suffixes *-ance, -ing, -ion,* etc. **chiefly Sth, S Midl** See also **botherment, conflutement, fixment, foolishment, gabblement**
1844 Thompson *Major Jones's Courtship* 49 **GA,** They got out of ther tanglement. It was a mighty sight of botherment. **1883** (1971) Harris *Nights with Remus* 197 **GA** [Black], Den de Guinnies, dey tuck'n huddle up, . . en hol' er confab. . . Bimeby one . . step out fum de huddlement en make a bow. **1884** *Anglia* 7.269 **Sth, S Midl** [Black], To set up er monst'ous gigglement = to giggle immoderately. **1887** (1967) Harris *Free Joe* 105 **GA,** I'll . . make some inquirements about his famerly. **1891** Page *Elsket* 125 **VA** [Black], P'laske got de notionment . . to ride in a tunament. *Ibid* 131, I tell her I just come to git de reasonment o' de matter. **1898** Lloyd *Country Life* 15 **AL,** That was the general appearment to me. **1912** *DN* 3.588 **wIN,** Scatterment. . . A scattering. **1913** [see **A** above]. **1916** *DN* 4.294 **sAppalachians,** We find the suffix *-ment* attached to words. . . revilement, revengement. **1917** *DN* 4.418 **wNC,** Studyment. . . "He sot thar all in a studyment." **1927** *DN* 5.478 **Ozarks,** Tanglement. . . A thicket. "I shore cain't run th'ough no sich a tanglement as thet 'ar." **1927** Adams *Congaree* 26 **cSC** [Black], Dat old ooman done every kind of devilment. **1927** [see **nurse** n 2]. **1930** *AmSp* 5.427 **Ozarks,** Spenser also used the word *needments,* which still means necessities in the Ozark country. **1932** Peterkin *Bright Skin* 274 **SC,**

Anybody would think I had mistreated you instead savin you from disgracement. **1936** *AmSp* 11.316 **Ozarks,** *Playment. . .* A toy, a plaything. **1942** Thomas *Blue Ridge Country* 51 **sAppalachians,** The chickens made a scattermint before him. **1950** *WELS (General words . . meaning "food")* 1 Inf, **WI,** Eatments. **1970** *DARE* FW Addit **VA38,** *Confusement*—confusion.

menudo n Also *menuda* [Span *menudo* entrails] **chiefly SW**
Tripe soup or stew.

1967–70 *DARE* (Qu. H36, *Kinds of soup*) Inf **TX**11, Menuda [mə'nudə]—tripe and spice soup; (Qu. H43, *Foods made from parts of the head and inner organs of an animal*) Inf **AZ**12, Menudo [mə'nudo]—a soup of tripe; **TX**26, Menuda [ˌmɛ'nudə]; (Qu. H45, *Dishes made with meat, fish, or poultry that everybody around here would know, but that people in other places might not*) Inf **TX**4, Menuda; **TX**28, 29, Menudo. **1983** Santiago *Famous All Over Town* 98 **Los Angeles CA,** Then he spooned out a bowl of menudo, which is every drinker's Sunday breakfast. **1985** Ehrlich *Solace* 120 **WY,** [At an Amer Ind fair:] Between the menudo and the caramel apples were two gambling tents—one for bingo, the other for poker. **1986** Pederson *LAGS Concordance,* 1 inf, **csTX,** Tripe used to make menudo; good for a hangover; 1 inf, **csTX,** Menudo, Spanish dish made from tripe; 1 inf, **csTX,** Menudo—tripe soup, Mexican dish.

menustration See **menstruation**

meow n Cf **cat's ass 1**
Among loggers: see quot 1958.

1958 McCulloch *Woods Words* 117 **Pacific NW,** *Meow*—A bend or snarl in a line, a crook in a road, or anything else out of line. **1977** *WI State Jrl.* (Madison) 16 Jan sec 5 5/1, *Meow*—A kind of bad twist in steel rope.

meow bird n Also *mew bird*
=**catbird 1.**

1966–68 *DARE* (Qu. Q14, . . *Names . . for these birds: Catbird*) Infs **GA**13, **MN**18, Meow bird; **KS**5, Mew bird.

-mer- See **-ma-** infix

meracle See **miracle**

mercury n Cf **three-seeded mercury, vegetable mercury**
1 also *marc'ry, marcury, markary, mark(e)ry, mercury vine:* A **poison ivy,** usu *Toxicodendron radicans.* **NEast, esp ME**

1792 Belknap *Hist. NH* 3.127, Other poisonous plants, are the ivy *(hedera helix)* the creeping ivy or, as it is called by some, mercury *(rhus radicans)* the juice of which stains linen a deep and indelible black. **1843** Torrey *Flora NY* 1.130, *Rhus Toxicodendron. . .* Poison Oak. Poison Vine. Mercury. **1892** *Jrl. Amer. Folkl.* 5.94, *Rhus toxicodendron,* black mercury. Harmony, Me. Mercury or markry. NH. **1896** *Ibid* 9.185, *Rhus toxicodendron. . .* Mercury (marc'ry) . . Hartford, Me. **1907** *DN* 3.246 **eME,** *Marc'ries. . .* Poison ivy plants; "mercuries." "Look out for the marc'ries." Heard near Auburn, western Maine. **1909** *DN* 3.413 **nME,** *Markary. . .* The poison ivy. A corruption of mercury. **1910** Graves *Flowering Plants* 269 **CT,** *Rhus Toxicodendron. . .* Mercury. Marcury. . . A pernicious shrub or vine that is far too plentiful. **1916** *Torreya* 16.238, *Rhus vernix. . .* Mercury, Matinicus Id, Me. **1929** *AmSp* 5.120 **ME,** Poison ivy was "markery" or mercury perhaps because its poison runs as swiftly as the Messenger of the Gods. **1938** FWP *Guide CT* 13, The three-leaved poison ivy, often called mercury, should be avoided. **1941** *LANE* Map 251 **NEng,** 9 infs, [mɚ·krɪ, mɚ·krɪ, mɛ·krɪ]; 1 inf, [mɑ·kjʊrɪ]—grandmother's term; 1 inf, [mɜʳ^kɚɪ^ᵛ]. [*DARE* Ed: Synonyms for poison ivy were not collected systematically.] **1966** Dakin *Dial. Vocab. Ohio R. Valley* 2.411, Another old name, *mercury vine,* is used once in the Ohio Company area (Meigs County). **1966–68** *DARE* (Qu. S16, *A three-leaved plant that grows in woods and countryside and makes people's skin itch and swell*) Infs **ME**7, 20, **NJ**29, Mercury; (Qu. S17, . . *Kinds of plants . . that . . cause itching and swelling*) Infs **NJ**31, 39, Mercury. **1982** *DARE* File **coastal ME,** Mercury: poison ivy.

2 See **mercury weed.**

mercury vine See **mercury 1**

mercury weed n Also *(wild) mercury*
A **three-seeded mercury** (here: *Acalypha virginica*).

1830 Rafinesque *Med. Flora* 2.184, *Acalypha virginica . .* Mercury weed. Common from Canada to Florida. **1900** Lyons *Plant Names* 10, *A[calypha] Virginica. . .* Mercury-weed. . . *Plant* reputed expectorant and diuretic. **1935** (1943) Muenscher *Weeds* 319, *Acalypha vir-*

ginica. . . Mercury-weed. . . Meadows, pastures, abandoned fields and waste places. **1936** Winter *Plants NE* 186, *Acalypha. . .* Mercury. **1975** Hamel–Chiltoskey *Cherokee Plants* 61, Wild mercury. . . *Acalypha virginica. . .* Root for dropsy; gravel; pox.

mercy n Usu ['mɝ(r)sɨ]; also, esp in exclam phrr *Lord have mercy* and varr, ['mæsɨ]; for addit varr see quots Pronc-spp *marci, marcy, marsy, mass(a), mass(e)y, mussy* Similarly adj *marcyful, massiful, mussiful* For further exx see **Lord B1**
Std senses, var forms.

1815 Humphreys *Yankey in England* 106, *Marcy,* mercy. . . *Massiful,* merciful. **1817** in 1830 Royall *Letters AL* 22, Massy upon me. **1827** (1939) Sherwood *Gaz. GA* 139, *Marci,* for Mercy. **1843** (1916) Hall *New Purchase* 277 **IN,** I beseech thee to have marsy on all them there poor sinners. **1851** Hooper *Widow Rugby's Husband* 85 **AL,** Lord-a-massey, 'Squire, how you talk! **1852** *Yankee Notions* 1.354, "Massy alive! Eb's home agin!" says cousin Sally, running into the kitchen. **1867** Harris *Sut Lovingood Yarns* 35 **TN,** Marcyful payrint! thar's been murderin dun yere. **1875** in 1884 Lanier *Poems* 177 [Black], De Lord have mussy. **1891** (1967) Freeman *New Engl. Nun* 162, Do speak to me for massy sake! **1893** Shands *MS Speech* 47, *Mussy* ['mʌsɪ]. Negro for *mercy. Lawdy-mussy* is a favorite exclamation among the negroes, and even to some extent among the whites. **1899** (1912) Green *VA Folk-Speech* 292, Lord a *mussy.* **1903** *DN* 2.290 **Cape Cod MA,** About the years 1835–1850 the common pronunciation lost many of its features, *perfectly* became *perfectly,* and my grandfather's *Aint Massy* became my father's *Aunt Mercy.* **1905** *DN* 3.17 **cCT,** *Sakes! la sakes! massy sakes! sakes alive!* . . All feminine exclamations. *Ibid* 56 **eNE,** Before *r,* especially among those of Irish descent, it [=[ɛ]] sometimes becomes [ɑ]:—*marcy, sarpint, etarnal,* etc. **1909** *DN* 3.421 **Cape Cod MA** (as of a1857), *Mass a body. . .* Mercy on my body. Used with the interjection *Oh.* **1911** *DN* 3.539 **eKY,** *Mercy.* Pronounced ['mɑrsɪ] and ['mæsɪ]. **1922** Gonzales *Black Border* 314 **sSC, GA coasts** [Gullah glossary], *Mussiful*—merciful. *Mussy*—mercy, mercies. **1924** *DN* 5.260 [Exclams], Lawse-a-massy, lo(h)d-a-massa (*or* -massy). **1928** Peterkin *Scarlet Sister Mary* 160 **SC** [Gullah], Jedus axed Gawd to have mussy on em. **1931** *PMLA* 46.1315 **sAppalachians,** *E* (with the sound of *e* in *certain*) often [is pronounced] broad, as in: "consarn," (concern), . . "marchant," "marcy." . . "Massy" is also heard for *mercy.* **1942** Hall *Smoky Mt. Speech* 89 **wNC, eTN,** The pronunciations [hɔs] *horse,* ['mæsɪ] *mercy* (only in the expressions ['lɔɔ·ɚ ə 'mæsɪ], ['lɔz ə 'mæsɪ], now generally replaced by ['lɔɔ·d hæv 'mɝsɪ]) . . seem to belong, on the whole, to the older generations. **1943** *LANE* Map 601–602 (*For goodness sake*), [In the exclam phrr *mercy, mercy on me, mercy sakes,* proncs of the type ['mɚ·sɪ, 'mɜsɪ] are almost universal; only two infs use proncs of the type ['mæsɪ], and one of these offers it only as an older var of the std pronc. In *Lord (a) mercy, Lordy mercy,* however, proncs of the type ['mæsɪ] are by far the commonest; there are a few scattered instances of ['masɪ] and ['mɛsɪ], and only one of ['mɔsɪ].] **1969** *DARE* (Qu. NN7) Inf **GA**84, Laws-a-mercy [ˌlɔːsə'mɛsi].

mercy dinner n
See quot.

1994 *DARE* File **MA,** They'll be coming to the mercy dinner after the funeral.

mercy seat n *esp freq among Black speakers*
=**mourners' bench.**

1942 (1965) Parrish *Slave Songs* 152 **GA coast,** "Gettin' religion" is a soul-stirring matter with the Negro. . . [H]e responds to the appeal of the minister to come forward to the "Mou'ners' Bench"—also called the "Anxious" or "Mercy Seat." There, at the bench directly in front of the pulpit, he kneels while the congregation sings an appropriate song. **1970** *DARE* (Qu. CC5, *Names for seats in a church, especially near the front*) Inf **TN**53, Mercy seat. [Inf Black] **1974** Baldwin *If Beale St. Could Talk* 23 **NYC** [Black], Mrs. Hunt, . . from the moment we walked through the church doors, became filled with a stern love for her two little heathens and marched us before her to the mercy seat. *Ibid* 24, The mercy seat: she led us to the front row and sat us down before it. **1977** Dillard *Lexicon* 56 [Black], When she was twelve, she got on the *mercy seat.* . . She was baptized soon after.

mère See **mémère**

merganser n
Std: any of three diving, fish-eating ducks: the common merganser *(Mergus merganser),* the **hooded merganser,** or the **red-headed merganser.** Also called **bec-scie, Chicago mal-**

lard, diver, fish duck 1, fisherman 1, ganser, garbill, Irish canvasback, pheasant duck, sawbill, sheldrake, shelduck, water witch. For other names of *Mergus merganser* see **bracket, breakhorn, dun diver 2, French drake, gooney 3, ice duck 1, morocco head, orange-breast, pond sheldrake, sawbuck, spike, stud, swamp sheldrake, Swede mallard, tweezer, velvetbreast, water pheasant, winter sheldrake, weaser, wood duck**

mergens, mergins See **murgens**

mericale See **miracle**

meridan, meridian (strip) See **median (strip) 1e**

merit-fish n

A **silversides** (here: *Menidia menidia*).

    1884 Goode *Fisheries U.S.* 1.456 **RI,** The most important species . . is the Green Smelt of the Connecticut coast, *Menidia notata,* also called . . about Watch Hill the "Merit-fish." **1911** U.S. Bur. Census *Fisheries 1908* 316, *Silversides.* . . Different species are known as . . "green smelt," . . "merit-fish." . . They range from 7 to 18 inches in length and are caught in seines.

merkel n¹ See **myrtle** n¹

merkel n² Pronc-spp *markel, merkle, myrtle* [Prob < Ger *morchel* (PaGer *marrichel*), in which case *myrtle* is a hypercorrection (cf **myrtle** n¹ **A**)]

A **morel** n² (here: *Morchella* spp).

    1956 *Hench Coll.* **cnVA,** Merkel [for *morel*]. **1973** *Foxfire 2* 53, Morel (*Morchella esculenta, M. crassipes, M. angusticeps*) (sponge mushroom, markel, merkel). *Ibid* 54, Merkel pie: cut in small pieces. Cover bottom of pie dish with thin bits of bacon. Add layer of merkels, salt and pepper; then layer of mashed potatoes. Put in layers of merkels and potatoes, finishing with potatoes on top. Bake one-half hour. **1980** Marteka *Mushrooms* 68, *Morchella esculenta.* . . Common morel, merkle, myrtles.

merkle n¹ See **myrtle** n¹

merkle n² See **merkel** n¹

merlasse(r)s See **molasses**

merlin n Also *marlin* [From its resemblance to the European *merlin* (*Falco aesulon*)]

=**pigeon hawk 1.**

    1637 (1972) Morton *New Engl. Canaan* 72, There are very many Marlins. **1709** (1967) Lawson *New Voyage* 143 **NC, SC,** The Merlin is a small Bird in *Europe,* but much smaller here; yet he very nimbly kills the smaller sorts of Birds, and sometimes the Partridge; if caught alive, he would be a great Rarity, because of his Beauty and Smalness. **1874** NY Acad. Sci. *Annals Lyceum Nat. Hist.* 10.379, *F[alco] columbarius.* . . American Merlin. **1895** Minot *Land-Birds New Engl.* 366, [*Falco*] *columbarius.* Pigeon Hawk. American Merlin. Not very common in Massachusetts, though known to have bred here. **1917** (1923) *Birds Amer.* 2.90, A darker colored form of the Pigeon Hawk is the Black Pigeon Hawk or Black Merlin. **1968** *DARE* (Qu. Q4) Inf **NJ22,** Merlin—bird hawk or pigeon hawk. **1977** Bull–Farrand *Audubon Field Guide Birds* 682, Merlin—"Pigeon Hawk"—(*Falco columbarius*).

merliton See **mirliton**

merluccio n

=**hake** n **1b.**

    1882 U.S. Natl. Museum *Bulletin* 16.809, *M[erlucius] productus* . . Merluccio. . . Pacific coast, from Santa Barbara northward. **1911** U.S. Bur. Census *Fisheries 1908* 312, Merluccio. . . also called "hake," "horse-mackerel," etc.

mermaid's hair n Also *mermaid's tresses*

Any of var seaweeds; see quots.

    1901 Arnold *Sea-Beach* 50, *L[yngbya] majuscula, mermaid's-hair.* **1942** Hylander *Plant Life* 34, *Cladophora* is a small tufted plant averaging less than six inches in length, made up of densely branching filaments. It is often called Mermaids Tresses. *Ibid* 38, *Ectocarpus,* one of the simplest of the Phaeophyta. . . cover[s] objects in the inter-tidal zone with "Mermaid's Tresses" that resemble a Cladophora except for color.

mermaid's pouch n [Var of *mermaid's purse* (*OED* 1836 →)] Cf **sailor's purse**

The egg case of a skate.

    1978 Whipple *Vintage Nantucket* 237 **MA,** Just above the tide line was the usual litter of skates' egg cases, black rectangles with tiny protuberances at all four corners. Sometimes called "mermaid's pouches" or "sailor's purses," these hollow parchments serve to protect the skate's eggs, and attach themselves to rocks or floating weed. When the eggs hatch the empty cases release their grip and float to shore.

mermaid's shaving brush See **merman's shaving brush**

mermaid's tresses See **mermaid's hair**

mermaid weed n

1 An aquatic plant of the genus *Proserpinaca*.

    1822 Eaton *Botany* 410, *Proserpinaca . . palustris* (mermaid weed). **1840** MA Zool. & Bot. Surv. *Herb. Plants & Quadrupeds* 49, *Proserpinaca* [spp]. . . Mermaid Weed. **1843** Torrey *Flora NY* 1.241, *Proserpinaca palustris.* . . Common Mermaid-weed. . . Shallow ponds, ditches and swamps. *Ibid, P. pectinacea.* . . Cut-leaved Mermaid-weed. **1891** Coulter *Botany W. TX* 111, *Proserpinaca* [spp]. . . Mermaid weed. **1901** Mohr *Plant Life AL* 639, *Proserpinaca palustris.* . . Swamp Mermaid-weed. *Ibid, Proserpinaca pectinata.* . . Comb Mermaid-weed. **1937** Stemen–Myers *OK Flora* 359. **1971** Craighead *Trees S. FL* 54, A great variety of plant communities occupies these solution holes. . . Some holes are occupied with one species exclusively; these may be liverworts, swamp ferns, . . mermaid weed [etc].

2 A similar aquatic plant (*Floerkea proserpinacoides*).

    1940 Clute *Amer. Plant Names* 125, *F[loerkea] proserpinacoides.* False Mermaid. Mermaid-weed. **1959** Carleton *Index Herb. Plants* 81, *Mermaid-weed:* Floerkea proserpinacoides.

merman's shaving brush n Also *mermaid's shaving brush* [See quot 1942]

A seaweed of the genus *Chamaedorus* or *Penicillus*.

    1866 Lindley–Moore *Treas. Botany* 2.737, *Merman's shaving brushes.* A name given in North America to different species of *Chamaedoris* and *Penicillus.* **1884** U.S. Natl. Museum *Bulletin* 27.619 **FL,** *Penicillus capitatus.* . . Mermaid's shaving-brush. **1901** Arnold *Sea-Beach* 58, Genus *Penicillus*—The merman's shaving-brush, characteristic of coral reefs. [**1942** Hylander *Plant Life* 35, *Penicillus* is the Latin word for a small brush, certainly an appropriate name for this seaweed which has a stout whitish-green stalk terminated by tufts of stiff filaments, giving it the appearance of a shaving brush. It is common in Bermuda, the West Indies and Florida.]

merracle See **miracle**

married See **marry**

merry adj Usu |'mɛrɪ|; for addit var see quots Cf **marry, Mary** Std sense, var forms.

    1950 Hubbell *Pronc. NYC* 75, *Ferry-fairy, merry-Mary, very-vary* are always distinguished. **1952** *AmSp* 27.188 **WA,** The words *Mary, marry, merry,* are all pronounced [mɛᵊɪ]. **1961** Kurath–McDavid *Pronc. Engl.* 124, Broadly speaking, *Mary* rimes with *merry* /mɛri/ in the Midland. **c1970** Pederson *Dial. Surv. Rural GA* (A greeting on December 25th is _____ *Christmas.*) **seGA,** 36 infs, ['mɛᵊɪ, -ɪ]; 17 infs, ['mɛrɪ, -ɪ]; 4 infs, ['mɛɑrɪ̈]; 3 infs, [mɛ⁺]; 2 infs, ['mɛɑᵊɑ^]; 1 inf, [mɛ·ᵊ·]. **1989** Pederson *LAGS Tech. Index* 344, [Out of 941 total infs, 552 pronounced *Merry* in Merry Christmas with [ɛ] as initial vowel, 72 with [ʌ], 18 with [e], and 11 with [ɪ].]

merrybells n Rarely *merrybell*

=**bellwort.**

    1933 Small *Manual SE Flora* 299, *Oakesiella.* . . Bellworts. Hay-bells. Merry-bells. Cow-bells. **1948** Wherry *Wild Flower Guide* 18, Sessile Merrybells (*Uvularia sessilifolia*). *Ibid* 19, Great Merrybells (*Uvularia grandiflora*). *Ibid,* Smooth Merrybells (*U. perfoliata*) . . is found chiefly in the Northeastern and Southern states. **1951** Voss–Eifert *IL Wild Flowers* 19, Greater Bellwort (Wood Merrybells). . . a light and airy spring flower with its gold bells twinkling through the woods when April once again is on the land. **1966** *DARE* Wildfl QR Plates 20A, B Inf **OH**14, Merrybell; **WI**80, Merrybells. **1967** Braun *Monocotyledoneae* 346 **OH,** *Uvularia sessilifolia.* . . Merry-bells. **1972** GA Dept. Ag. *Farmers Market Bulletin* 10 May 8/1, Merrybells, Wild Oats, or Bellwort are all common names for this lovely member of the Lilicaceae family.

merryhearts n

A **death camas** (here: *Zigadenus nuttallii*).

    1933 Small *Manual SE Flora* 279, *T[oxicoscordion] Nuttalli.* . . Merryhearts. **1976** Bailey–Bailey *Hortus Third* 1183, *Zigadenus.* . . *Nuttallii.* . . merryhearts.

merrythought n [*OED* 1607 →] Cf **marriage bone,** *DS* K74 =**pully bone;** see also quot 1949.

    1872 Coues *Key to N. Amer. Birds* 14, The lower belly of the curve fits in the space between the legs of the merry-thought *(furcula).* **1899** (1912) Green *VA Folk-Speech* 279, *Merrythought.* . . The wishbone of a fowl's breast; so called from the sport of breaking it between two persons each of them pulls at one of the two ends, to determine which is to be married first. **1905** *New Engl. Cook Book* 274, You will dislodge the V-shaped bone, corresponding to the "merrythought" or "pull-bone" of chickens. **1939** *LANE* Map 215 *(Wishbone)* 1 inf, **nwCT,** Wishbone, merrythought. **1949** *AmSp* 24.111 **csSC,** *Merry-thought.* (1) Wishbone; (2) side-bones of chicken.

merry widow n

1 also *merry widow spider:* The black widow spider *(Latrodectus mactans).*

    1965–70 *DARE* (Qu. R28, . . *Kinds of spiders*) 10 Infs, **scattered,** Merry widow(s); **CT**23, **ID**1, **IL**6, **IN**3, **NY**83, **SC**43, Merry widow spider; **OK**46, Merry widder spider. [16 of 17 Infs old]

2 A **blue-eyed grass 1.** Cf **grass widow 3**

    1966 *DARE* (Qu. S26a, . . *Wildflowers* . . *Roadside flowers*) Inf **WA**6, Merry widows, grass widows.

3 An unidentified fish.

    1956 Rayford *Whistlin' Woman* 149 **AL,** I asked Bert and Ed to name all the fish they knew in Mobile Bay. Here are the fish they named: croakers, . . pilot fish, merry widow, dolphin . . dog shark.

merry-widow cactus n

A **hedgehog cactus 3** (here: *Echinocereus reichenbachii*).

    1959 Carleton *Index Herb. Plants* 81, *Merry-widow-cactus: Echinocereus reichenbachi* [sic].

merry widow spider See **merry widow 1**

merrywing n [From the sound of its wings; see quot 1917] esp CT

A **goldeneye 1** (here: *Bucephala clangula*).

    1888 Trumbull *Names of Birds* 78, Another and very pretty name, heard at Lyme, Conn., but almost exclusively among the old people, is *merry-wing.* **1917** (1923) *Birds Amer.* 1.138, Whistle-wing . . Merry-wing. [*Ibid,* The Golden-eye is commonly known as the Whistler because of the peculiar penetrating whistle made by its wings in flight. There are times when these cutting strokes can be heard even before the bird itself can be clearly made out.] **1923** U.S. Dept. Ag. *Misc. Circular* 13.22, Merrywing (Conn., western end of Lake Erie). **1944** Hausman *Amer. Birds* 519, Merry-wing.

merse'f See **myself**

mesa n |ˈmesə| [Span "table"]

1 A flat-topped hill or mountain; an elevated plateau with steep sides. **chiefly West, esp SW, CO** See Map Cf **bench B, butte**

    1840 (1941) Gregg *Diary* 1.53 **nwTX,** Came today about 20 miles . . over this very level *mesa* almost as firm and more smooth than a turn-pike. **1875** in 1877 Phillips *Letters CA* 34, The city [=Los Angeles] is built at the base of the mesa lands of the mountains. **1887** *Scribner's Mag.* 2.505 **CO,** For over a hundred miles, the eye traverses an enormous extent of plain, mesa, and mountain. **1892** *DN* 1.191 **TX,** *Mésa:* a table; more specifically a flat plateau or mountain top, so common in the geological formation of Texas and other states to the west, as well as of Mexico. **1927** Cather *Death Comes* 90 **NM,** Behind their camp, not far away, lay a group of great mesas. **1949** *Natl. Geogr. Mag.* Sept 392 **UT,** Covered with thick forage, the mesa top makes a fine fenceless cattle range. **1949** Emrich *Wild West Custom* 168 **SW,** The Southwesterner can scarcely pass a day without the casual use of . . *mesa.* **1967–68** *DARE* (Qu. C17, . . *A small, rounded hill*) Inf **AZ**1, Mesa—as long as it's flat on top; **CO**26, Mesa—mountain-size but flat-topped; **TX**43, Mesa—flat top; **TX**54, Mesa—maybe forty feet across; (Qu. C19, . . *Low land running between hills [With and without water]*) Inf **TX**31, Mesa; (Qu. C29, *A good-sized stretch of level land with practically no trees*) Infs **CA**79, **CO**2, **TX**5, **WA**31, Mesa; **CO**28, Mesa, if higher than surrounding ground; (Qu. I124) Inf **CA**1, Desert Mesa—in Victorville; **CO**38, Mortgage Mesa. **1967–70** *DARE* Tape **CA**181, There is a large company that is building a big country club just on the mesa [ˈmesə] up here; **TX**5, The gramma grass on these rolling hills—locally called the mesa—was great enough so that in the fall . . the men could establish a hay camp and mow the grass that grew wild. **1973** Allen *LAUM* 1.237 (as of c1950), The term *butte* is . . identified . . twice in

Nebraska with the southwestern Spanish equivalent *mesa,* a form more common in neighboring Colorado.

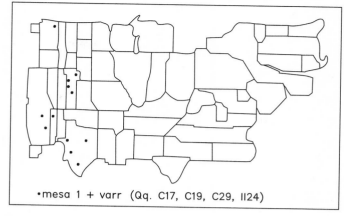

•mesa 1 + varr (Qq. C17, C19, C29, I124)

2 See quot.

    1927 *AmSp* 3.23, In the Nebraska sandhill region mesas are steep gullies along rivers, like the Niobrara or Snake rivers.

mesa oak n **CA**

Engelmann **oak** *(Quercus engelmannii).*

    1910 Jepson *Silva CA* 217, The Mesa Oak inhabits the low hills of San Diego County. . . It ranges south into northern Lower California and apparently ranges north into the San Carlos Mountains and Mt. Hamilton Range. **1923** Davidson–Moxley *Flora S. CA* 98, *Q[uercus] Engelmannii.* . . Mesa Oak. Ranges on the mesas south from Santa Anita through San Diego Co. **1945** Wodehouse *Hayfever Plants* 79, Also of the Pacific coast is the evergreen, mesa or Engelmann's oak. . . It is confined to the mountains of southern California. **1980** Little *Audubon Guide N. Amer. Trees W. Region* 397, *Engelmann Oak*—"Evergreen White Oak" "Mesa Oak."

mescal n Also *mascal, mescale, mezcal, muscal(e)* [MexSpan *mezcal* (in senses **1** and **2** below) < Nahuatl *mexcalli* (in sense **2** below)] **SW**

1 =**agave;** also the root or the head (the young bud stalk) of an agave prepared as food.

    [**1759** Venegas *Hist. CA* 1.44, The mountains and forests yield the mezcal, . . the roots of which boiled is a principal ingredient in the mexcalli.] **1831** (1973) Pattie *Personal Narr.* 63 **NM,** I afterwards ascertained, that it was a vegetable, called by the Spanish, mascal. **1846** in 1848 Emory *Notes Reconnoissance* 59, This afternoon I found the famous mezcal, (an agave,) about three feet in diameter, broad leaves, armed with teeth like a shark. **1854** (1932) Bell *Log TX-CA Trail* 35.226, Took the Muscal plant out of the pit this morning. . . I have eat nothing like it. It is the root of the plant . . and is filled with a fibrous gelatinous matter. The whole tube will weight [sic] from 6 to 9 pounds. **1885** *Outing* 7.24 **AZ,** The old and young squaws . . had brought down from the hillsides donkey-loads of mescal heads, which were piled in ovens of hot stones covered with wet grass and clay. The process of roasting, or rather steaming, mescal takes from three to four days, and resembles somewhat the mode of baking clams in New England. **1890** Bandelier *Final Rept.* 185, Vegetable food was limited mostly to wild fruits, . . to the stalks of the Maguey baked into a sweet conserve called Mezcal [etc]. **1895** *Jrl. Amer. Folkl.* 8.95, The laxative quality [when eaten] is accounted for readily, the Mescal, like its big brother, the Maguey, being a member of the Aloe family. **1914** Saunders *With Flowers in CA* 139, The mescal buds are capable of making by distillation one of the fieriest intoxicants known. **1949** Curtin *By the Prophet* 49 **AZ,** The leaves were removed from the head of the mescal, which is baked for twenty-four hours in a pit with hot stones. **1951** Corle *Gila* 348, The agave. . . is also known as mescal, amole, maguey, and lechuguilla. . . From the agave are made pulque, mescal, and tequila, all three intoxicating beverages. **1962** Balls *Early Uses CA Plants* 17, Within the boundaries of California only two species of Mescal are at all frequent. . Both *Agave deserti* and *Agave utahensis* var *nevadensis* were referred to as Mescal. *Ibid* 58, The fiber . . was . . obtained from the Spanish Bayonet and Mescal plants. **1966–67** *DARE* (Qu. S26a, . . *Wildflowers* . . *Roadside flowers*) Inf **CA**32, Mescal; (Qu. S26e, *Other wildflowers not yet mentioned;* not asked in early QRs) Inf **NM**13, Mescal. **1985** Dodge *Flowers SW Deserts* 97, Many species of agave are found in various parts of the desert. . . The larger species are called . . mescal (mess-KAHL). . . If the young stalk is cut off, the sweet sap may be collected and fermented to form highly intoxicating beverages, some of which are distilled commercially. Among these are mescal, pulque . . , and tequila.

2 also *mescal liquor:* An alcoholic drink made by distilling the fermented juice or pulp of **mescal 1;** any alcoholic drink.

[**1824** Poinsett *Notes on Mexico* 96, *Vino mezcal,* the brandy of the Maguey.] **1833** (1847) Lundy *Life & Travels* 61 **CA,** They have a kind of whiskey here, called muscal, which is distilled from a plant called Maguey. **1854** (1932) Bell *Log TX-CA Trail* 35.235, About one dozen men came over, bringing . . Muscal liquor. . . This Liquor has a tast [sic] between whiskey and brandy, and considerable intoxicating power. **1857** in 1948 *Western Folkl.* 7.11 **CA,** The head . . was then placed in a jar of mescal for preservation. **1892** *DN* 1.192 **TX,** *Mezcál:* spiritous liquor distilled from *pulque. Ibid* 250, Capt. F.H. Hardie, U.S.A., writes me: "*mezcal* is not distilled from *pulque,* but from the bulb of the *maguey* after it has been baked underground." **1907** Mulford *Bar-20* 116 **West,** Some of his brother's old companions were at that moment drinking mescal in a saloon down the street. **1910** Hart *Vigilante Girl* 203 **nCA,** Or in mescal, . . that gives it more of a Mexican flavor. **1910** [see **3** below]. **1936** McCarthy *Lang. Mosshorn* np **West** [Range terms], *Mescal.* . . Primarily a Mexican drink but applied by cowboys to any type of alcoholic beverage. **1946** Waters *Colorado* 316, Dreary mud-floored drinking dens selling mezcal and green tequila began to fill. **1951** [see **1** above]. **1985** [see **1** above]. **1986** Pederson *LAGS Concordance,* 1 inf, **csTX,** Mescal—kept in demijohn—from maguey plant.

3 =peyote.

1887 [see **mescal button**]. **1889** in 1955 *Amer. Anthropologist* 57.217, I desire to call to your special attention to [sic] the report of my predecessor . . on woqui, or mescal. . . The use of this fruit as a stimulant is alarmingly on the increase among the Indians. **1895** *Therapeutic Gaz.* 19.579, In connection with the physiological action of the mescal, its use by the Indians is of great interest. The Kiowa Indians formerly for generations occupied the valley of the Rio Grande, and became addicted to the use of the mescal buttons, which . . are native in that region, and they adopted its use as a regular part of their religious ceremonies. **1896** *Ibid* 20.8, The exercises open with a prayer by the leader, who then hands each man four mescals, which he takes and eats. **1899** *Jrl. Physiology* 25.83, "Mescal" never gives rise to merriment, but rather to a condition of ideal content, and produces wakefulness. **1900** Lyons *Plant Names* 229, *Lophophora.* . . Mescale. . . *L. Williamsii.* . . Source of Mescale buttons, which have remarkable narcotic and intoxicating properties. **1910** Hodge *Hdbk. Amer. Indians* 2.237, By the whites it [=*Lophophora williamsii*] is commonly known as "mescal," from a confusion with the maguey cactus of the S[outh] W[est] from which the fiery intoxicant mescal is prepared. **1920** *Scientific Amer.* 14 Feb 157, The peyote, often popularly miscalled "mescal," through confusion with the maguey cactus from which a fiery intoxicant is prepared, is a species of small cactus widely used for both medicinal and ceremonial purposes by the Indian tribes of the southwestern U.S. **1937** Borg *Cacti* 209, The dried tops of the plant made into bunches or wreaths used to be sold as mescal. **1951** Fergusson *New Mexico* 407, [Glossary:] *Mescal*—a small cactus.

mescal bean n [**mescal 2, 3**]

1 =frijolillo 1.

1856 Derby *Phoenixiana* 46, A solitary antelope, picking up mescal beans. **1931** U.S. Dept. Ag. *Misc. Pub.* 101.87, *Mescalbean* . . is a handsome evergreen shrub or small tree. **1960** Vines *Trees SW* 569, The narcotic properties of the red seeds of Mescal-bean Sophora were well known to the Indians. A powder from them, in very small amounts, was mixed with the beverage mescal to produce intoxication, delirium, excitement, and finally a long sleep. The seeds are poisonous to both humans and livestock. **1980** Little *Audubon Guide N. Amer. Trees W. Region* 505, Mescalbean. . . "Frijolillo." **1988** Schoenhals *Span.-Engl. Gloss.* 189, Mescalbean *(Sophora secundiflora)*—frijolillo.

2 The dried top of **peyote.** Cf **mescal button**

1888 in 1955 *Amer. Anthropologist* 57.216, Its common name here among the whites is mescal bean. In size it is about one-fourth of an inch thick and 1½ inches in diameter. When dry it is hard and about the color of bright tobacco. . . The center of the upper side is covered with a coat of gray fuzz. Its effect on the Indians is believed by medical men to be somewhat like that of bangue [*DARE* Ed: =*bhang*]. **1890** *Ibid* 217, We find that this tribe [=the Tonkawa] is addicted to the use of the mescal bean and we are doing our best to discourage and prevent its use among them. **1946** Foreman *Last Trek* 258 **OK,** Two societies of mescal-bean eaters were organized.

mescal button n [**mescal 3**]

The dried top of **peyote;** by ext, the cactus itself.

1887 *Med. Reg.* 1.276 **SW,** "*Muscale Buttons*"—Physiological Effects—Personal Experience. **1895** *N.Y. Dramatic News* 7 Dec. 3/2 *(DA),* For introducing brilliant coloring into dreams it is as efficacious as the nerve stimulant known as the mescal button, contributed to science by the Kiowa Indians. **1911** *Century Dict. Suppl., Mescal-buttons.* . . The dried tops of a succulent, spineless, turnip-shaped cactus growing in the arid regions of Texas and northern Mexico, known botanically as *Lophophora Williamsii,* and called by the natives in various localities *peyote.* **1920** Saunders *Useful Wild Plants* 252, The cult of another dangerous vegetable poison of the Southwest is still active. This is the . . Mescal-button, . . Peyote, . . names given in common speech to a small cactus. *Ibid* 253, [The cactus. . . top is flat and round, two to three inches across, and wrinkled with radiating ribs.] **1930** Ferber *Cimarron* 295 **OK,** She held out her hand, shaking a little, the mescal button crushed in her palm. **1936** Shiner Cactus Nursery *Illustr. Catalog* 22 **TX,** *Lophophora williamsii.* . . Dried and known as "mescal buttons" this sp[ecies] has been used by N[orth] A[merican] Indians in religious ceremonies for hundreds of years. **1948** *Holland's Mag.* June 18/2 *(DA),* Mescal button cactus . . contains an alkaloid that causes the person who eats it to see gorgeous dreams in riotous colors. **1974** (1977) Coon *Useful Plants* 84, Mescal button. . . is a highly dangerous alkaloid, and its non-liturgic use should be avoided. **1976** Bailey–Bailey *Hortus Third* 682, *Mescal-button.* . . The buttonlike crowns of the plants yield the hallucinogenic alkaloid peyote, long used by Indians in the area where *Lophophora* is native.

mescale See **mescal**

mescal liquor See **mescal 2**

Mescan See **Mexican**

mescat acacia n Also *mescat* [Perh var of **mesquite** + *acacia*] **SW** Cf **mescrew 2**

A **whitethorn** (here: *Acacia constricta*).

1931 U.S. Dept. Ag. *Misc. Pub.* 101.71, Mescat acacia, often known as mescat . . , a common spiny southwestern bush . . , is considered inferior to almost worthless forage, except that the pods are often taken. **1938** Van Dersal *Native Woody Plants* 37, *Mescat acacia.* . . Often with sticky foliage, . . often found in sand. . . A source of honey. **1960** Vines *Trees SW* 494, The seeds of Mescat Acacia serve as food for various species of birds. . . The Indians of Arizona made a coarse meal known as "pinole" out of the legumes. **1971** Dodge *100 Desert Wildflowers* 28, *Mescat-acacia.* . . Cattle and horses eat the bean-like fruits. **1975** Lamb *Woody Plants SW* 68, Mescat acacia or whitethorn is. . . a shrub, usually 6 to 8 feet tall, that may reach heights of up to 18 feet.

mescrew n [Perh blend of **mesquite** + **screw bean**] **SW**

1 =screw bean. esp **NV**

1897 Sudworth *Arborescent Flora* 251 **NV,** *Prosopis odorata.* . . Common Names. Screw Bean. . . Mescrew. **1933** Harrington *Gypsum Cave NV* 194, Wild plant used as food . . *Prosopis pubescens.* . . Screwbean, mescrew (pods and seeds). *Ibid* 197, *Prosopis pubescens.* . . Screwbean mesquite, mescrew. **1982** Brooks *Quicksand* 100 **NV,** A beautiful little mescrew—not a mesquite with heavy dark thorns—but a young, perfect mescrew, just the right size for us to handle. . . The mescrew . . often grew in a thicket of thorns. Its branches were delicate, the thorns smaller and snow-white. The tiny cluster of blooms hardened into a screwed-up little pod so tight and with such tiny seeds inside that the small rodents who depended on them for food ate the whole little pod.

2 A **cat's-claw** (here: prob *Acacia* spp).

1942 Whipple *Joshua* 58 **UT** (as of c1860), The black talons of the grotesque mescrew or cat's-claw . . rubbed at Apostle Snow's trousers.

mesee n

See quot.

1927 *AmSp* 3.141 **ME coast,** "No bigger than a mesee" we always thought referred to the midges or "no see 'ems" of the Indians.

meself See **myself**

mesh n[1], v Usu |meš|; also chiefly **NEng, Sth, S Midl** |mæš|; chiefly **Mid Atl** |marš| and var Pronc-spp *ma(r)sh* [For the earlier hist of these varr see *OED*]

A Forms.

1850 U.S. Congress *Serial Set* 574 Doc 20 155, What I claim as new . . is . . the Shaft H, with the pinions i, mashing into racks II. **1859** (1968) Bartlett *Americanisms* 265, In machinery, one wheel is said to *mash* into or with another, i.e. to "engage" with it. **1899** (1912) Green *VA Folk-Speech* 276, *Mash, n.* A form of *mesh.* **1905** [see **B1** below]. **1923** *DN* 5.214 **swMO,** *Mash,* n. or v. Mesh. **1953** Randolph–Wilson *Down in Holler* 13 **Ozarks,** Mesh is often pronounced *mash.* **1955** *DE Folkl. Bulletin* 1.18, He . . showed us a net he was making with the aid of a hickory netting needle which he had fashioned, and explained the different sizes of "marsh," i.e., mesh. **1966** *DARE* Tape **NC1,** Same type o' net only it was a bigger marsh [mɒrš]. **1968–70** *DARE* (Qu. F19, *A cloth container for grain*) Inf **VA69,** Mash bag for large grains like corn; made of coarser weave—small grain would spill through; (Qu. L63, *Kinds of fences made with wire*) Inf **AK8,** [mæš] wire; **GA28,** Mash wire fence. **1969** *DARE* FW Addit **ceNC,** Marsh [mɑrš]—the spaces between the lines in the net. **1975** Gould *ME Lingo* 177, *Mash*—Mesh. The word is pronounced thus by highlanders who mean a screen or sieve for sifting gravel or some screen wire for a window, and by coastal people who refer to the opening in a net and derivatives therefrom: the finished net, bait bags, trap heads, etc. **1976** Warner *Beautiful Swimmers* 132 **VA,** He is typical of an older generation of civil and extremely courteous Virginians and, in addition to selling pot mesh or "marsh," as it is always spoken of in the tidewater, he raises chickens. **1981** Harper–Presley *Okefinokee* 74 (as of 1929), They check a rope through it, like making up a gill net, with about an eight-inch mash.

B As verb.

1 Of a fish: to become caught in a net. [*OED mesh* v. 3 1589 →]

1905 Wasson *Green Shay* 161 **NEng,** Mack'rel struck off here consid'ble plenty jest then, and commenced to 'mash' [Footnote: to enter the nets] in good shape, so's Abram Spurling he only give the new work a light priming coat to keep the water out like, for the time bein'.

2 To make (a net); to net; hence vbl n *mashing* the act of making a net; n *mashing* the spacing, substance, or material of a net. [*OED meshing* vbl. sb. 1615 →]

1975 Gould *ME Lingo* 177, *Mashin'* is the inclusive term for fishermen's netting; the making of it, the size of the apertures, the twine used . . , and all related thereto. . . The set-up for *mashin'* is a cup-hook screwed into a windowsill to hold the work, and the person *mashin'* sits in a rocker in hopes something like a dog fight may occur outside to give him something to watch.

mesh n[2] [Pronc var of *mash*]

1899 (1912) Green *VA Folk-Speech* 279, *Mesh.* . . "Wheat to the mesh." *Mash,* a mixture of ground grain malted, and water for brewing. (?) **1976** Garber *Mountain-ese* 57 **sAppalachians,** The revenoors poured out ten barrels uv my good sour mesh.

meskeet, mesket(is) See **mesquite**

Meskin See **Mexican**

meskit, mesqui(e)t See **mesquite**

mesquital n [Span *mezquital*] **chiefly SW**

An area where **mesquite B1** is the dominant plant form; a thicket of **mesquite.**

1929 Dobie *Vaquero* x **SW,** The story of the brush and the brush hand has never been written, though the cattle industry of America began in the *mesquitals* along the Rio Bravo. **1938** *AmSp* 13.113 **SW,** In recent years (1929-) the derivative *mesquital,* signifying 'a tract or district covered with mesquite,' has obtained some currency. **1962** Atwood *Vocab. TX* 41, For a brushy, tangled growth of mesquite. . . There are six Texas occurrences of *mesquital* [among 273 infs].

mesquite n Also *mesquit(o), mezquit(e);* abbr *skeet;* for addit varr see quots [MexSpan *mezquite* < Nahuatl *mizquitl*] **chiefly SW, esp TX**

A Forms.

1805 in 1852 U.S. Congress *Debates & Proc.* 9th Cong 2d sess 1083, A bean that grows in great plenty on a small tree resembling a willow, called masketo; the women cook their buffalo beef in a manner that would be grateful to an English squire. *Ibid* 1103, Some small, cultivated fields, fenced round with small cedar and moschete brush. **1817** Darby *Geogr. Descr. LA* 198, There are in the Parish of Nachitoches, two very distinct species of the robinia; one a tree of considerable size, the other a shrub, the latter is known by the name of musquito wood. **1821** [see **B1** below]. **1827** in 1858 Dewees *Letters TX* 63, The country is mostly a prairie country, the prairies being mostly covered with shrubs, musquit trees, and prickly pear. **1831** (1973) Pattie *Personal Narr.* 83 **SW,** We had reached the point where the [Gila] river runs between mountains, and. . . there is here little timber, beside musqueto-wood,

which stands thick. **1834** Pike *Prose Sketches* 56 **SW,** The valley was here wider, and was full of small hills interspersed with mesquito bushes. . . We bought some meat and mesquito meal, made by grinding the beans between two stones. *Ibid* 63, We emerged from the broken hills into the mesquito. **1844** Gregg *Commerce* 2.78 **SW,** The valleys are timbered with cottonwood, and occasionally with *mezquite.* **1845** Green *Jrl. Texian Exped.* 32, Dawson selected his position in a musquet thicket favourable for his rifle-shooting. **1846** [see **mesquite bean**]. **1854** (1932) Bell *Log TX-CA Trail* 35.215, No grass, small mesquit except near the river. **1854** Bartlett *Personal Narr.* 2.563 **Desert SW,** Then come the mezquit or acacia, the tornilla, the fouquiera . . all armed with the most terrific spikes or thorns. **1857** [see **mesquite grass 2a**]. **1858** *TX Almanac for 1859* 185, Along the river banks there is some good timber, but the most common wood is scrubby musquite, which . . is unfit for building purposes. **1870** U.S. Dept. Ag. *Rept. of Secy. for 1870* 410, Mesquite, (*Algarobia glandulosa* . .)—Frequently called mosqueit. **1881** [see **mesquite grass 2a**]. **1881** [see **mesquite grass 2c**]. **1883** *Rep't upon the Statistic of Agriculture* 960 (Mathews Coll.), The term *mesquite* (called also *muskit*) and *grama* are confined to the southern tier. **1886** Havard *Flora W. & S. TX for 1885* 497, *Prosopis juliflora.* . . Mezquit. . . The correct spelling of this Mexican name is Mezquite, with the accent on the penultimate. North of the Rio Grande the final e is generally omitted, but the accent should remain the same and the word be pronounced as if written 'Mezkeet.' **1887** Francis *Saddle & Mocassin* 73, Wave after wave of rolling country, sparsely covered with *mesketis*-bush. **1894** [see **mesquite grass 2e**]. **1920** Saunders *Useful Wild Plants* 63, There is before me . . a jar of coarse mesquit meal, and it is as cloyingly fragrant as so much molasses. **1948** *Western Folkl.* 7.13 **sCA,** *Mesquit, mesquiet, musquit.* A shrub or tree related to the acacia. **1956** Ker *Vocab. W. TX* 79, Meskeet. . . Skeet grove. **1986** Pederson *LAGS Concordance,* 1 inf, **csTX,** Mosquito [=mesquite] tree.

B Senses.

1 also attrib: A shrub or tree of the genus *Prosopis;* also the thicket formed of such plants. For other names of var spp see **algaroba, honey locust 3, honey mesquite, honeypod 1, ironwood d(2), screw bean, tornillo, velvet mesquite** Cf **mesquital, mesquite bean**

1805 [see **A** above]. **1821** (1904) Austin *Jrl. TX* 296, No timber, muskete bushes & grass. **1834** (1847) Lundy *Life & Travels* 119 **TX,** As we approach the Trinity [River], the mesquite and prickly pear first begin to appear. **1844** Kendall *Santa Fé Exped.* 2.108, We encamped . . in a little mesquit valley. **1873** (1876) Cozzens *Marvellous Country* 144 **AZ, NM,** The plains around us were covered with an abundance of cactus . . and mesquit chaparral. **1903** (1965) Adams *Log Cowboy* 45 **csTX,** Suddenly in the dark we encountered a mesquite thicket. **1929** Dobie *Vaquero* 201 **TX,** Perhaps no widely dispersed tree growth responds more apparently to climate, altitude, and latitude than the mesquite. In the southern part of Live Oak County, where it seems generally to reach its maximum growth, it develops into great trees. **1942** Whipple *Joshua* 24 **UT** (as of c1860), Supper fires were being lighted with dry cottonwood limbs or greasewood or mesquite bush. **1945** *New Yorker* 25 Aug 26 **NM,** A railroad bull came walking along the tops of the cars and kicked me into the mesquite. **1962** Atwood *Vocab. TX* 41, *Mesquite thicket* . . is used along with a few other terms such as *mesquite flat(s)* . . and *brush (land or country)* . . , the latter of which is confined to Southwest and West Texas. **1965–70** *DARE* (Qu. T16, . . *Kinds of trees . . 'special'*) 19 Infs, **chiefly TX,** Mesquite tree; **CA2, TX71, 78,** Mesquite; (Qu. I46, . . *Kinds of fruits that grow wild around here*) Inf **TX85,** Mesquite; (Qu. S10, *A shrub that gets covered with bright yellow, spicy-smelling flowers early in spring;* total Infs questioned, 75) Inf **NM2,** Mesquite; (Qu. S15, . . *Weed seeds that cling to clothing*) Inf **CA15,** Mesquite seed; (Qu. T9, *The common shade tree with large heart-shaped leaves, clusters of white blossoms, and long thin seed pods or 'beans'*) Infs **CA12, TX26,** Mesquite; (Qu. T15) Inf **TX31,** Mesquite. **1967–69** *DARE* Tape **TX13,** Grass all over these prairies out here . . it come up to the stirrups on a horse . . then havin' mesquite [məs'kit] trees; **TX24,** Grass was about all 'er was; there was none of that big mesquite [məs'kit] there; **TX25,** [FW:] Just what'll he need protection from? [Inf:] Well, from limbs, mesquite [mɪs'kit] limbs; **TX68,** She came after me, chased me up a mesquite tree, and there's just thorns all over mesquite [mɪs'kit] trees. **1986** Pederson *LAGS Concordance,* 29 infs, **chiefly c,cs,ceTX,** Mesquite(s); 12 infs, **chiefly c,csTX,** Mesquite tree(s); 7 infs, **csTX,** Mesquite wood (*or* leaves, limbs, post).

2 A **horsemint 1** (here: *Monarda citriodora*).

1898 *Jrl. Amer. Folkl.* 11.277, *Monarda citriodora,* . . mesquite, Waco, Tex.

3 A **huisache** (here: *Acacia farnesiana*).

1913 *Torreya* 13.231, *Vachellia farnesiana* [=*Acacia farnesiana*]. . . Mesquite, Cameron, La.

4 See **mesquite grass.**

mesquite bean n chiefly SW

The seed or seedpod of a **mesquite B1.** Also called **Mexican bean 3**

1846 in 1942 *CA Hist. Soc. Qrly.* 21.217, My riding mule was the most refractory of all. I however succeeded at last in making him drink, by covering the water with the musquite bean. **1883** *Harper's New Mth. Mag.* 66.493 **AZ,** The crop of mesquit beans was so large one year as to be beyond their own unaided capacity of consumption. **1886** Havard *Flora W. & S. TX for 1885* 498, The Mezquit "bean" is one of the staple foods of Mexicans and Indians. They grind it on the "matate" and, after removing shell and seeds, boil the flour in water. The infusion of this flour can easily be made to undergo alcoholic fermentation whereby a weak beer is obtained, formerly much used by Comanche and Apache Indians. **1900** Harris *Reminiscences* 94 **TX** (as of 1834), At sunrise, he stopped to rest. He couldn't find water, but ate mesquite beans. **1913** (1979) Barnes *Western Grazing* 38, Mesquite beans (Prosopis) furnish feed of a high nutritive value, and it is a strange sight to see the cattle and horses eating the long yellow pods, often getting down on their knees to reach the beans lying all over the ground under the low-hanging boughs of the trees. **1929** Dobie *Vaquero* 3, Mesquite beans keep horses fat the year round and as strong as corn would make them. **1949** Curtin *By the Prophet* 95 **AZ,** For a good sweet drink, . . mesquite beans . . are pounded in a stone mortar, cold water is mixed with the powder, then the product is strained. **1969** *DARE* Tape **TX71,** They use this small rock, then, to grind the—I guess—corn and mesquite beans.

mesquite grass n Also *mesquite* **chiefly West** Cf **curly mesquite, vine ~**

1 Any of var grasses which often grow in association with **mesquite B1** and are freq used for hay or pasturage. Note: These quots may refer specifically to senses at **2** below.

1823 in 1858 Dewees *Letters TX* 35, The musquit grass grows very thick and about three feet high, and looks very much like a blue grass pasture. **1834** Strubble *Visit to TX* 25, The musquito grass which overspreads the ground is green all the year. **1847** *Western TX* 7, In grasses the glory of the State is the *musquit,* found only in Western Texas. **1889** Vasey *Ag. Grasses* 6 **West,** Many of the grasses of this extensive region . . are popularly known as "mesquite" and "grama grass." These consist of many species of different genera, some of them more or less local and . . others having a wide range. **1899** M. Going *Flowers* 153 (*DAE*), The running mesquit of Arizona and the alkali-grass of the plains help to hold in place the shifting soils of the great thirst-lands. **1916** Thoburn *Std. Hist. OK* 1.5, In the western part of the state . . [are] buffalo grass, mesquite grass and the several species of grama grasses. **1967** *DARE* (Qu. L8, *Hay that grows naturally in damp places*) Inf **TX40,** Mesquite grass; (Qu. L9a, . . *Kinds of grass . . grown for hay*) Infs **TX4, 29,** Mesquite (grass).

2 Spec:

a =**grama grass 1.**

1857 Gray *Manual of Botany* 552, *Bouteloua.* . . Muskit-Grass. **1881** Phares *Farmer's Book of Grasses* 51, The true *Mesket grass* is *Bouteloua hirsuta,* growing also in the Western Prairies. *Ibid,* *Bouteloua.* Mesquit Grass. Three species of this grass grow in the west, and are known . . as . . mesquit, with the many ways of spelling, etc. . . But this name has been applied to a number of other grasses and caused no little confusion. **1889** Vasey *Ag. Grasses* 7, There is a large number of grasses of low growth and of more spreading habit, which are known in the southwest and east of the Rocky Mountains under the names of "mesquite" and "buffalo" grasses. The former belong mostly to the genus *Bouteloua,* the most important species being *B. racemosa,* or tall mesquite, and *B. oligostachya,* or low mesquite. **1894** Coulter *Botany W. TX* 533, *B[outeloua] texana.* . . *Mesquit.* . . Dry hills throughout Texas and northward to Arkansas. **1920** Saunders *Useful Wild Plants* 231, Among the Tewa of New Mexico and Arizona, the plant used for this double purpose [i.e. as a whiskbroom or a hairbrush] is the Mesquitegrass (*Bouteloua curtipendula* . .). **1936** Winter *Plants NE* 25, *Bouteloua.* . . Mesquite-grass. . . In short-grass prairie throughout the state. **1945** Wodehouse *Hayfever Plants* 53, Blue grama . . , also called mesquite . . grass, . . is found in the Great Plains from Manitoba to Mexico. . . Along with buffalo grass it constitutes most of what is known in the Middle West as "Short Grass." **1976** Bailey-Bailey *Hortus Third* 174, *Bouteloua.* . . Mesquite g[rass].

b A **velvet grass** (here: *Holcus lanatus*).

1861 *S. Field & Fireside* 1 Jun 14 **Sth,** *Texas Mesquit Grass.* . . We did not think so favourably of mesquit for grazing purposes last year as we do this. **1869** Porcher *Resources* 682 **Sth,** Consult Dr. Lee's editorials in Southern Field and Fireside, 1861, for much information on the grasses best to be used as fertilizers and for food and manure. He recommends . . the Texas Mesquit grass (*Holcus lanatus*). **1881** Phares *Farmer's Book of Grasses* 51, Many specimens of so called mesquit grass have been sent to me from Texas and from several other states, (the seeds having been first obtained from Texas) and in every instance it has proved to be *Holcus lanatus.* . . And it is this velvet grass, naturalized in Texas, that is generally cultivated in the southern States under the name mesquit. **1911** Jepson *Flora CA* 52, *H[olcus] lanatus.* . . *Mesquit-grass.* . . A conspicuous softly-woolly pale-colored grass of moist bottom lands. **1935** (1943) Muenscher *Weeds* 156, *Holcus lanatus.* . . Mesquite-grass. . . Very troublesome in the Pacific Northwest. **1956** St. John *Flora SE WA* 46, *Holcus lanatus.* . . Velvet Grass or Mesquite.

c =**buffalo grass a.** [See quot 1881] **esp TX**

1881 Phares *Farmer's Book of Grasses* 50 **TX,** *B[uchloe] dactyloides.* . . mostly abounds on the prairies among the mesquit trees, scattered over a large portion of our State, whence it is commonly called mesquit grass in Texas. This name, however, is given to two or three other species of grass which are often associated with it. *Ibid* 51, I saw it in 1869 in Texas, growing abundantly a few miles from Corpus Christi, and in the prairies near Indianola; and it was there called *Meskit grass.* **1886** Havard *Flora W. & S. TX for 1885* 529, Equal or superior to the Gramas in quality . . is the famed Buffalo- or Mezquit-Grass (*Buchloe dactyloides*). This invaluable grass, densely tufted and spreading by stolons into broad mats, is the best constituent of sheep pastures. It extends from Northeastern Texas, San Antonio and Laredo westward to the branches of the Concho. Although hardy and fast spreading, it does not thrive on the dry, sandy plains of the far Southwest, and is rare beyond the Pecos. **1941** *Torreya* 41.46, *Buchloe dactyloides.* . . Mesquite grass, . . Texas Panhandle.

d A **needlegrass 1** (here: *Stipa viridula*).

1892 *DN* 1.192 **wTX,** *Mesquite.* . . Mesquite grass (*Stipa spata* [sic]), which is a fine, short grass found in the same region.

e A **needlegrass 2** (here: *Aristida purpurea*).

1894 *Jrl. Amer. Folkl.* 7.104 **TX,** *Aristida purpurea,* . . muskit grass.

f A **galleta:** either **curly mesquite 1** or *Hilaria jamesii.*

1903 Small *Flora SE U.S.* 68, *Hilaria Texana.* . . On hills and plains, central Texas to Arizona. Spring and summer. Creeping Mesquite. **1906** Rydberg *Flora CO* 20, *Hilaria.* . . Mesquite. **1912** Wooton-Standley *Grasses NM* 34, The other species of the genus [=*Hilaria jamesii*] is . . the Texas Mesquite Grass, so much prized by stockmen. **1913** (1979) Barnes *Western Grazing* 47, Creeping Mesquite (Hilaria cenchroides).

g A **muhly (grass)** (here: *Muhlenbergia porteri*). [See quot 1912]

1912 Wooton-Standley *Grasses NM* 68, One species [=*Muhlenbergia porteri*] is known as Mesquite Grass probably because of its habit of seeming to hide under the spiny protection of the mesquite bushes, but this name . . is never applied to any of the other species. *Ibid* 70, Mesquite Grass (*Muhlenbergia porteri* . .) is a common grass in the southern part of the State where it is commonly to be found on the mesas growing in the protection of the mesquite bushes or other thorny shrubs. **1923** in 1925 Jepson *Manual Plants CA* 122, *M[uhlenbergia] porteri.* . . Mesquite Grass. . . Rocky places, Colorado Desert; e. to Tex., s. to Mex. **1950** Hitchcock-Chase *Manual Grasses* 402, [*Muhlenbergia porteri* is] [k]nown also as mesquite grass and black grama.

mesquite weed n

=**rush-pea.**

1942 *Torreya* 42.161, *Hoffmannseggia* sp. . . Mesquite weed, Hansford County, Texas.

mesquitilla n Cf **false mesquite**

=**fairy duster.**

1985 Dodge *Flowers SW Deserts* 45, False-Mesquite Calliandra—Fairyduster, Calliandra, Mesquitilla.

mesquito See **mesquite**

mess n

1a A prepared dish (of a spec food); a meal; a quantity (of food) sufficient for a dish or a meal. **chiefly NEast, Sth, S Midl**

1697 (1878) *MA Hist. Soc. Coll.* 5th ser 1.455 **MA,** Betty gets her Mother a Mess of English Beans; which she makes a shift to eat. These are our First Fruits. **1766** (1942) Bartram *Diary of a Journey* 44 **S Atl,** Here we cooked a fine mess of palm-cabbage. **1775** (1962) Romans *Nat. Hist.* **FL** 12, He [=a man who is fishing] told me; that his mother had an inclination to eat fish, and he was come to get her a mess. **1817** in 1918 IN Hist. Soc. *Pub.* 6.298 **NY,** We had a fine mess of mussels for breakfast. **1861** in 1903 Norton *Army Letters* 26 **VA,** H. and I got enough [potatoes] for a mess, and some parsnips. **1891** Johnston *Primes & Neighbors* 45 **GA,** She told Billy one day that she wanted a mess of stewed cat-fish. **1899** (1912) Green *VA Folk-Speech* 279, *Mess. . .* A quantity of food sufficient for one or more persons for a single meal. **1916** Macy-Hussey *Nantucket Scrap Basket* 139 **seMA,** "*Mess*"— Enough for a meal—As a mess of clams, or a mess of birds. When such commodities are scarce they say, "it's hard to get enough for a mess." The word is also used to describe certain dishes for the table, as "I'll fix up a mess for dinner," that is, make a chowder or a stew. **1926** *DN* 5.388 **ME,** *Mess. . .* A portion sufficient for a meal. "A mess of peas." Universal. **1929** *AmSp* 5.127 **ME,** The peas, beans, greens were carefully watched and it was announced that a "good mess" of peas or greens, etc., could be had. **1937** *Hall Coll.* **wNC, eTN,** The bear killed lots of stock, sheep, and hogs. He wouldn't eat but two messes out of a big 'un and then kill him another'n. **1939** *Ibid,* There they had him [=a bear] dressed up when we got there. We all, nine of us, just had a mess, around of that bear. **1942** *Esquire* Sept 173 **KY,** Not many invited him to dinner—a little skinny man but he could eat three chickens at a mess besides the other grub he put away. **1944** *PADS* 2.58, *Mess. . .* A portion of, enough to make a meal: "a mess of greens (or turnips)." Mo. Ozarks. . . (Also Va., N.C., S.C., Tenn.) **1946** Stuart *Tales Plum Grove* 41 **KY,** I've et many a good mess of coon there. **1967–68** *DARE* Tape **IN51,** We never even thought about buying a mess of bologna if we'd go to town; **SC38,** A mess of greens, that's what you call it. **1982** *Barrick Coll.* **csPA,** *Mess*—serving quantity. ". . enough squirrels to make a mess."

b The amount of milk given by a cow or herd at one milking. [*OED* a1533] **esp NEng**

a1824 (1937) Guild *Jrl.* 263 **VT,** She said that my fortune has ben just like a Cow giving a good mess of milk and up with her foot and kick it all over. **1842** *Knickerbocker* 19.557 **ceMA,** Sally could n't hardly bring in the pail, she [=a cow] gave such a mess. **1872** VT State Bd. Ag. *Rept. for 1871* 1.197, I tested their milk by weighing every mess for a month. **1874** *Ibid* 2.185, After putting her on to this hay, she gradually increased her mess to two quarts per day. **1877** *Ibid* 4.54, We took off what cream arose on the night's mess, and churned it. **1929** *AmSp* 5.118 **ME,** Of a good hearted person with a high temper who spoiled all the effects of good deeds by violent outbreaks of temper they said that he or she was "like a cow that gives a good mess of milk, then kicks the pail over." **1967** *DARE* Tape **MA32,** She gives a big mess of milk.

c The number or quantity of fish caught at one time. [*OED* "U.S."]

1854 (1969) Thoreau *Walden* 338, I got a rare mess of golden and silver and bright cupreous fishes. **1899** (1912) Green *VA Folk-Speech* 279, *Mess. . .* In *fishing,* the amount or number of fish taken. A *mess of fish.* **1950** *WELS Suppl.* **csWI,** *Mess*—a sizeable catch of fish. **1956** *Hall Coll.* **eTN,** I caught a mess of trouts. **1968** *DARE* Tape **IN36,** I always just catch a good mess [of bass] and come in, you know? **1993** *DARE* File **sID** (as of 1950s), When I was a kid we would go on a fishing trip every summer. My Dad and Grandpa would get up early and catch a mess of trout for breakfast, and then another one for dinner.

2a An indefinite amount or number, usu a large one; a crowd.

1833 in 1834 Davis *Letters Downing* 40, With that, he out with his wallet, and unrolled a mess on 'em [=bank notes]. **1853** *Knickerbocker* 41.502, There was wolves in the Holler—an unaccountable mess of 'em. **1931–33** *LANE Worksheets* **Boston MA,** *Mess. . .* Crowd. "A mess of folks." **1938** Rawlings *Yearling* 103 **nFL,** There was sich a mess of us. **1941** *LANE* Map 415 *(The whole crowd)* 1 inf, **ceMA,** A mess of folks = a crowd, not necessarily derogatory; 3 infs, **wMA, seNH,** A whole mess of 'em. **1954** *Harder Coll.* **cwTN,** *Mess. . .* A large quantity. **1956** (1973) Holiday-Dufty *Lady Sings* 154 **cnMD,** Just before I was set to go on for the second set a big mess of gardenias arrived backstage. **1956** Moody *Home Ranch* 18 **CO** (as of 1911), Wouldn't no self-respectin' cowhand hire out to wrangle a mess of ornery milk cows. **1958** Humphrey *Home from the Hill* 13 **neTX,** He would often return with as many as forty or fifty quail or ducks (which he would have his man Chauncey distribute with his compliments to all the pretty young housewives in town, a mess or a brace to each impartially). **1959** *VT Hist.* 27.148 **c,ceVT,** *Mess. . .* A large amount or quantity of. A *mess* of water. Common. Windsor. **c1960** *Wilson Coll.* **csKY,** *Mess. . .* A large quan-

tity, often too large. . . The gang or crowd, maybe an echo of the messes of Civil War time. **1965–70** *DARE* (Qu. LL8b, *. . A large number . . "She has a whole _____ of cousins.")* 54 Infs, **scattered,** Mess; (Qu. LL10, *A whole group of people: "They made too much noise, so he sent the whole _____ home.")* 25 Infs, **scattered,** Mess (of them); (Qu. U38b, *. . A great deal of money: "He made a _____ [of money]."*) Infs **MD6, PA131,** Mess.

b A mutually understood amount or number that varies according to context; see quots.

1872 VT State Bd. Ag. *Rept. for 1871* 1.634, They will dress a mess of ore to any required per cent. **1975** King *S. Ladies & Gentlemen* 14 **MS,** How could anyone not know what a "mess" was? *Everybody* knew that it meant a dozen or a pound, unless, of course, it meant a bushel or a peck, or, in the country, a truckload. My maturing Southern mind conceived a clear, concise picture of a "mess." It was a neatly arranged and properly weighed collection of anything edible. If it was more than the usual unspecified amount, it was a "nice mess."

3 A witty, clever, or mischievous person; an objectionable or foolish person. **chiefly S Midl**

1936 Mitchell *Gone* 122 **GA,** To have that mealy-mouthed little mess take up for me. **1952** Brown *NC Folkl.* 1.564, *Mess. . .* A person regarded as more witty, lively, entertaining, etc., than most people; a "show." "Now ain't Mr. Jim a mess!"—General. **1954** *Harder Coll.* **cwTN,** *Mess. . .* A person who is jocular. In letter: "He is one mess." **1956** McAtee *Some Dialect NC* 29, *Mess. . .* "One who is the 'life of the party'." . . an unruly or incorrigible person. **c1960** *Wilson Coll.* **csKY,** *Mess. . .* A mischievous or joking person. **1972** *DARE* File **Atlanta GA,** Mrs. Wright had her feelings bruised when someone said that she was a mess. . . The person meant she was fun to be with, not sloppy. **1973** *Patrick Coll.* **cAL,** *Mess*—Usually affectionate or approving: mischievous, a jokester, etc. That chile's a mess. **1982** *Barrick Coll.* **csPA,** *Mess*—mischievous person. "Aint he a mess?" **1986** *WI Alumnus Letters* **Ozarks,** "She's a mess" (affection, admiration, especially for a child or infant). **1986** Pederson *LAGS Concordance,* 1 inf, **cAR,** [Senator Dale] Bumpers was a mess for running.

4 Trash, junk; hence fig: stuff, nonsense; abuse.

1937 in 1976 *Weevils in the Wheat* 4 **VA** [Black], One day he beat me very bad an' de ole man called me an' tol' me, "Don't you let 'im beat you dat way anymo'. You fight 'im back. . . You don' have ter take dat mess offen him." **1956** McAtee *Some Dialect NC* 30, *Mess . .* trash. "The dog is bringing more mess for the front yard." **1965** Bradford *Born with the Blues* 121 **Sth** [Black], I began spreading this "mess:" "Well, . . Mamie Smith has been booked for a vaudeville tour. . . She opens . . next week." **1986** Pederson *LAGS Concordance,* 1 inf, **ceTX,** Mess— husband's term [for junk]; 1 inf, **nwMS,** All such mess as that = all such things as that; 1 inf, **nwMS,** Lots of people believes that mess; 1 inf, **ceAL,** This psychedelic mess [="funky" music].

5 Excrement; hence v *mess,* v phr *make a mess* to defecate. [Cf *EDD mess* sb.² 4 "Ordure, the quantity of dung excreted at one time."]

c1938 in 1970 Hyatt *Hoodoo* 1.436 **New Orleans LA,** I have seen people use the *mess* from a white dog to cure . . lockjaw. **1972** *New Yorker* 30 Sept 44, Happy [=a dog]. . had helped them unpack by . . pulling one of Mrs. Webster's dresses from a hanger and then making a mess on it. **1992** *DARE* File **cwCA,** The mother apologized for being late, explaining that her child had made a mess in his pants just as they were leaving the house. *Ibid* **csWI** (as of 1960s), "Mess" as a euphemism was used in my family—"Don't step in the dog mess." **1993** Mason *Feather Crowns* 293 **KY,** Shoo that hen out of the garden, Nannie. We don't want chicken mess on the turnip greens. *Ibid* 294, "Shoo, shoo," Nannie said. "Don't mess on the turnip greens." **1995** *DARE* File **csWI,** With my luck, as soon as I put the baby in his christening outfit, he'll mess his pants.

mess v

1 To dawdle or putter; to fool around; to kid around. **esp Sth, S Midl**

1966–69 *DARE* (Qu. A10, *. . Doing little unimportant things: . . "What are you doing?" . . "Nothing in particular—I'm just _____."*) Infs **NC20, TN34,** Messing; **IA29,** Messing; **SC42,** Messing [FW sugg]. **1979** *NYT Article Letters* **Ocracoke Is. NC,** Messing—Teasing or kidding. *Ibid,* Oh go on—Means You're just messing. **1984** Wilder *You All Spoken Here* 191 **Sth,** *Messin' and mullin':* Not involved in any worthwhile enterprise. **1986** Pederson *LAGS Concordance (Kissing)* 1 inf, **neTN,** You been messing.

2 See **mess** n 5.

mess-ahead adj [**mess** n 1]

1936 *AmSp* 11.316 **Ozarks**, *Mess-ahead.* . . Shiftless. Used of a man who is perfectly happy as long as he has food enough for one meal in the house.

Messakin See **Mexican**

mess box n **chiefly West**

A chest or box in which cooking and eating utensils and food are carried.

1859–60 Mrs. Witter *Letters* (MS.) 3 *(DAE)*, We had what we call a mess box which contained all our cooking utensils. **1884** Shepherd *Prairie Exper.* 138 **West**, A mess-box was fixed into the hind-end of the waggon. **1890** D'Oyle *Notches* 26 *(DAE at chuck wagon)*, The sun blistered the paint upon the 'mess-box' behind the 'chuck-waggon.' **1894** *Harper's New Mth. Mag.* 89.515, He now returned to Captain Glynn and shared his mess-box. **1910** in 1914 Stewart *Letters* 106 **WY**, Early one morning we started with a wagon and a bulging mess-box for Zebbie's home. **1913** (1979) Barnes *Western Grazing* 116 **SW**, One can still find the old-time 'chuck wagon' and the great mess box with its hospitable lid and cranky cook. **1921** Thorp *Songs Cowboys* 24 **CO**, The way we gathered round that mess-box, scramblin' for tools,/ Showed the disregard for ethics that is taught in other schools.

messed up See **mess up 3**

mess house n Also *mess shack* **chiefly West**

A building in which communal meals are eaten, as by soldiers, cowboys, loggers, etc.

1865 *Atlantic Mth.* 15.66 **SC**, A wooden cook-house to every company, with sometimes a palmetto mess-house beside. **1885** U.S. Bur. Indian Affairs *Report* 179 **UT**, Other head men were taking dinner at the mess house. **1912** (1914) Sinclair *Flying U Ranch* 47, Old Patsy came out of the mess-house, and went, with flapping flour-sack apron, to the wood-pile. **1915** *DN* 4.244 **MT**, Mess house. . . Eating house. "I am going down to the mess house to get something to eat." **1929** Heyliger *Builder of Dam* 209, A great log fire was roaring in the fireplace at the head of the mess-shack. **1929** *AmSp* 5.54 **NE**, If there is a separate eating place of the employees [of a ranch], it is the "mess house" or "grub house." **1936** McCarthy *Lang. Mosshorn* np **West** [Range terms], *Messhouse.* . . A building in which meals are served the cowboys. **1941** Writers' Program *Guide WY* 463, *Mess house*—Place where cowhands eat. **1958** McCulloch *Woods Words* 117 **Pacific NW**, *Mess house*—A cookshack.

mess over v phr *chiefly among Black speakers*

To meddle with, make a mess of, cause pain or trouble for.

1968–70 *DARE* (Qu. V5a, *To take something of small value that doesn't belong to you—for example, a child taking cookies: "Who's been _____ the cookies?"*) Inf **NY**249, Messing over; (Qu. Y37, *To make a place untidy or disorderly: "I wish they wouldn't _____ the room so."*) Inf **NC**49, Mess over that room; (Qu. AA11, *If a man asks a girl to marry him and she refuses, . . she _____*) Inf **TN**46, Let him go, gave him up, messed over—most generally used; (Qu. KK63, *To do a clumsy or hurried job of repairing something: "It will never last—he just _____."*) Infs **FL**48, **SC**69, **TN**46, Messed over it. [4 of 5 total Infs Black, 1 Amer Ind] **1971** Roberts *Third Ear* np [Black], *Mess over* . . to interfere with the freedom or activity of another. **1988** Lincoln *Avenue* 163 **wNC** (as of c1940) [Black], [Chapter heading:] When God messed over Vernon. *Ibid* 182, Suddenly he heard himself saying, "God had been mighty good to them, *but God sho' messed over Vernon!*"

mess shack See **mess house**

mess up v phr

1 intr: To make a muddle of a situation, get into trouble; to fail, flop. **chiefly Sth, Midl** See Map

1933 Rawlings *South Moon* 323 **FL**, He better not mess up around me no more, but if he'll mind his business and leave me mind mine, I got nary call to harm him. **1933** *AmSp* 8.3.29 [Prison slang], Boy, I ain't a-goin' t' mess up no more from now on. I on'y got eighty-one more days 'n' a get-up. **1956** (1973) Holiday-Dufty *Lady Sings* 33 [Black], When the time came to take those bills off the table, I was always messing up. **1965–70** *DARE* (Qu. JJ42, *To make an error in judgment and get something quite wrong: "He usually handles things well, but this time he certainly _____."*) 34 Infs, **chiefly Sth, S Midl**, Messed up; **AL**25, Mess up; (Qu. AA15b, . . *Joking ways . . of saying that a man is getting married. . . "He _____."*) Inf **PA**76, Messed up [laughter]; (Qu. GG15, . . *A person who became over-excited and lost*

control, *"At that point he really _____."*) Inf **SC**26, Messed up; (Qu. KK9, *When someone undertakes something too big for him to handle: "This time you've _____."*) Inf **MO**22, Messed up; (Qu. KK10, . . *Words for something failing* . . *"He didn't work it out carefully enough, and his plan _____."*) Inf **IN**75, Sunk, messed up, flopped; (Qu. KK19, *If a machine or appliance is temporarily out of order: "My sewing machine _____."*) Inf **PA**242, Messed up; (Qu. KK63, *To do a clumsy or hurried job of repairing something: "It will never last—he just _____."*) Inf **TN**52, Messed up. **1972** Kochman *Rappin'* 110 [Black], He wanted to learn badly, they told me, and was messing up by memorizing the signs in the neighborhood and thinking that's all there was to reading.

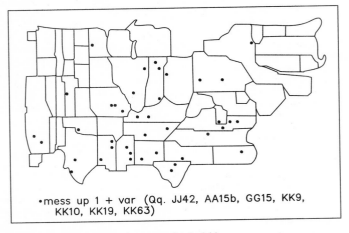

•mess up 1 + var (Qq. JJ42, AA15b, GG15, KK9, KK10, KK19, KK63)

2 To meddle (with), have to do (with).

1933 Rawlings *South Moon* 69 **FL**, "I be dogged," he said, "if I aim to mess up with no school no longer'n I have to." *Ibid* 223, Lant said, "Well, I don't mess up with nobody no-ways. I figger ain't nobody'll mess up with me."

3 ppl adj *messed up*: Pregnant, "in trouble."

1954 *Harder Coll.* **cwTN**, Pregnant. "She's messed up now, been sick for a week." **1986** Pederson *LAGS Concordance*, 1 inf, **cLA**, Messed up—pregnant, not married. [Inf Black]

mestizo n [Span "mixed, hybrid"] **chiefly SW**

A person of mixed blood, esp of Spanish and American Indian ancestry.

1712 in 1840 SC Laws *Statutes at Large* 7.352, All negroes, mulatoes, mustizoes or Indians, which at any time heretofore have been sold . . for slaves, are hereby declared slaves. **1796** in 1855 U.S. Congress *Debates & Proc.* 4th Cong 2d sess 14 Dec 2694 **SC**, Free negroes, mulattoes, and mestizoes, [are taxed] at nine shillings and four pence per head. [**1847** (1848) Bryant *What I Saw in CA* 425, Arriving at the rancho of Don Joaquin Gomez, we found no one but a *mestiza* servant at home.] **1899** *Atlantic Mth.* 83.759 **NM**, Perhaps you have heard or read of beautiful mestizo maidens? **1946** Waters *Colorado* 117, The impassable breach between the mestizo and the Indian. **1950** *WELS* (People of mixed blood . . part Indian) 1 Inf, **seWI**, Mestizo. **1965–70** *DARE* (Qu. HH29a) Infs **CA**4, 56, 66, **NM**12, **TX**28, 31, 43, Mestizo; (Qu. HH29b) Inf **SC**21, Mestizo.

metal sponge n

1965–70 *DARE* (Qu. G14, *The rough metal pad that's used to scour pots and pans*) Infs **IL**11, **MD**35, **MI**28, 66, **MO**38, **NY**220, **PA**9, 41, **TN**57, Metal sponge.

metate n Usu |mə'tate, mɛ'tatɛ|; also |mə'tæt, mə'tæti| Also *matate, matet(e)* [MexSpan < Nahuatl *metatl*] **chiefly SW**

A rectangular stone with a concave surface on which corn and other grains are ground.

1834 in 1942 *SW Hist. Qrly.* 45.330 **Houston TX**, Mrs. Roark had a Mexican utensil for grinding corn, called a *metate*. It was a large rock which had a place scooped out of the center that would hold a peck of corn. It had a stone roller. **1886** Havard *Flora W. & S. TX for 1885* 498, They grind it on the "matate." **1889** Ripley *Flag to Flag* 112 **swTX**, A few frowsy women with stone *matets* were laboriously grinding corn for tortillas. **1892** *DN* 1.192 **TX**, *Metáte*: a hollowed stone on which corn is ground. . . The instrument or pestle with which the grinding is done is called *metlapil* in Mexico. In Texas the first word generally implies both parts. **1903** (1950) Austin *Land of Little Rain* 101 **sCA,** You can hear the *plump, plump* of the *metate* from the alcoves of the vines where comfortable old dames . . are pounding out corn for *tamales.* **1932** Bentley *Spanish Terms* 166, *Metate*—English modifications *matete, matet* (*Spanish* [me:'tɑ:te:]; *English* [mə'tæti:]). . . The word *metate* is as nearly naturalized as such specialized name words become. The spelling of the word often shows metathesis when it occurs in English writings. **1967** *DARE* (Qu. C25, . . *Kinds of stone . . about . . [. . size of a person's head], smooth and hard*) Inf **CA30,** Metate—the Indians used it. **1967–69** *DARE* Tape **TX31,** This is regular corn that is ground on what we call a metate [me'tɑte], and it's gotten together in a ball-like and taken from there and then patted in the hands and spread out. . . A metate is a stone-like ring made from volcanic stones. It's rather porous, rough-like. . . It varies in size but I would usually say about a foot square. . . It's rounded at the edges. . . It's two pieces because it has a stand to be placed on so it is at an angle; **TX71,** We never have found a whole piece of pottery. I found lots of pieces of their metates [mə'tæts] they ground their food with. . . They were just a long sand rock, different lengths, maybe a foot long or a foot and a half. We've found 'em nearly two feet long. Then they have a smaller rock to use in the big one. . . They use this small rock then to grind corn and mesquite beans.

Metdis See **Methodist**

meteor light n [*OED* (at *meteor* sb. 6) 1804; < *OED meteor* sb. 2.b. "Applied to . . the ignis fatuus, etc."] Cf **mineral light**

1968 *DARE* Tape **NC53,** The meteor lights are mineral lights of some kind. . . They're just usually a ball of fire, it looks like, or a big light that goes up into the sky or floats around over the ground. It's a reflection of some kind of mineral in the ground—gold, silver, or it's something like that—it could cause these. . . It could be the Indian pottery.

meter hymn n

A repetitive chant; see quot.

1958 Hughes–Bontemps *Negro Folkl.* 269, Most of the chants were in a minor key and used the same three or four notes over and over again. The Negroes call them "meter-hymns."

Methdis See **Methodist**

metheglin n Also *methelin wine, methiglum;* for addit varr see quots [Welsh *meddyg* medicinal + *llyn* liquor; *OED* 1533 →] **chiefly Nth, Midl** *old-fash*

A beverage usu made from fermented honey.

1633 in 1867 NH *Prov. & State Papers* 1.71, For 6 gallons of mathiglin, beaver 2 lb. **1704** (1825) Knight *Jrls.* 55 **NYC,** A Gentlewoman . . gave us . . choice Beer and metheglin. **1839** Townsend *Narr. Rocky Mts.* 84 **seID,** Among the rest, was some *methiglen* or diluted alcohol sweetened with honey. **1895** *DN* 1.391 **CT, NY,** *Metheglin* . . drink made from honey. **1899** *Harper's New Mth. Mag.* 99.504 **VA** (as of c1800), Many a glass of palate-tickling "methigler" made this easy way to the shining negroes. **1930** Shoemaker *1300 Words* 40 **cPA Mts** (as of c1900), *Methiglum.* **1937** Gardner *Folkl. Schoharie* 3 **ceNY,** I succeeded in allaying suspicions to the extent that I was . . treated to . . "methiglum," a liquor made chiefly from fermented "wild honey." **1939** Writers' Program *Guide KY* 259 (as of 1820s), Meals were 25¢ with whiskey thrown in, or metheglin, a drink made of honey and vinegar, for the temperate. **c1940** Eliason *Word Lists FL* 13 **wFL,** Mathiglum [mə'tɪglʌm]. Metheglin. **1947** Bowles–Towle *New Engl. Cooking* 273 (as of 18th and 19th cents), In addition to fruit wines, metheglin or mead was made in large quantities. **1953** Randolph–Wilson *Down in Holler* 264 **Ozarks,** *Methiglum.* . . Metheglin or mead. . . Many Americans never even heard of metheglin, but the old folks in the Ozarks know all about it. **1963** *Julian Apple Day* 3 **csCA,** When they were extractin honey, the uncapping knives were kept in hot water so they could cut the wax. . . When your knife cooled so it wouldn't cut anymore, you put it back in the pot of hot water. . . Well, there was quite a little honey in the used water and rather than throw it away, Eb put it in gallon jugs and set it along by the honey house. Pretty soon, after the sun shone on it, you got some mighty potent medicine. He called that Mathigalum. **1968** *DARE* (Qu. DD28b, . . *Fermented drinks . . made at home*) Inf **CT16,** [mə'θeglɪn]—from honey; **NY111,** [mə'θɪgləm]—made with honey; **PA118,** Methiglin—raisins and hard cider. [All Infs old] **1970** *NC Folkl.* 18.10, Methelin wine, made from fermented honey, yeast, and water, was good tonic, especially after fermenting a few months. **1986** Pederson *LAGS Concordance,* 1 inf **cnGA,** Metheglin—drink made from honeycomb and water; locust beer was something like metheglin; 1 inf, **swGA,** Fig [me]theglin—made with figs—potent.

methinks v impers, hence past *methought relic*

It seems to me; I think.

1944 *PADS* 2.19 **sAppalachians,** *Methought.* . . I thought. This old form is rare, but is still heard here and there. *Methinks* is not heard. **1953** Randolph–Wilson *Down in Holler* 153 **Ozarks,** Mary Elizabeth Mahnkey reported *methinks* used by her neighbors near Kirbyville, Missouri. I have heard it myself, in both Missouri and Arkansas, but not often.

Methodist n Also rarely *Methodie* Pronc-spp **Sth, S Midl** *Mef(o)dis, Metdis, Meth(o)dis;* hence pl *Methodisis* Cf Pronc Intro 3.I.17, 22

A Forms.

1823 Cooper *Pioneers* 1.189 **nNY,** Nather a Methodie, nor a Papish. **1843** (1916) Hall *New Purchase* 147 **sIN,** And, I dad, if she didn't read clean through all our church histories, . . Baptisis and Methodisis. **1903** *DN* 2.320 **seMO,** *Methodist.* . . Pronounced Methodis. **1907** *DN* 3.233 **nwAR,** *Methodis'.* . . Methodist. **1909** *DN* 3.349 **eAL, wGA,** *Methodist.* . . Almost universally pronounced *Methodis,* and occasionally *Mefodis.* **1922** Gonzales *Black Border* 313 **sSC, GA coasts** [Gullah glossary], Met'dis'—Methodist, Methodists. **a1930** in 1991 Hughes–Hurston *Mule Bone* 32 **cFL** [Black], See whut you Meth'dis' niggahs will do? **1953** Brewer *Word Brazos* 11 **eTX** [Black], De chu'ch hab a haa'd time gittin' on foot, 'caze dey don' be many Mefdis's in dat paa't of de Bottoms.

B Sense.

A **cooter** n 1 (here: *Chrysemys concinna*). Cf **Baptist B, hard-shell** adj 2

1952 Carr *Turtles* 248, In west Florida, where turtles are commonly speared in deep, clear springs, it [=*Chrysemys scripta*] is regularly recognized and is called "Baptist," with reference to the thick, hard shell which is more resistant to gig points than that of the "Methodist," or softer-shelled Mobile turtle.

Methodist ax n [Cf *EDD methody-hammer* "a hammer made with a smooth face on each end."]

A double-bladed ax.

1966 *DARE* (Qu. V2a, . . *A deceiving person, or somebody that you can't trust*) Inf **ME21,** As two-faced as a Methodist ax—a Methodist ax has two blades; (Qu. V7, *A person who sets out to cheat others while pretending to be honest*) Inf **ME21,** As two-faced as a Methodist ax.

Methodist feet n *joc*

Fig: religious objections to dancing.

1935 Sandoz *Jules* 91 **wNE** (as of 1880–1930), The communities split into the dancers and those with Methodist feet, as Elmer Sturgeon called them. **1939** FWP *Guide NE* 109, Those who had "Methodist feet," or religious objections to dancing, skipped, instead, at play-parties or bounce-arounds, to the vigorously rhythmic words and tunes such as "Skip to My Lou." **1942** McAtee *Dial. Grant Co. IN* 43 (as of 1890s), *Methodist feet.* . . "I've got _____" means, "I can't (or don't) dance."

Methodist handshake n Cf **handshaker**

1977 *WI State Jrl.* (Madison) 6 Feb 4/4, *Dear Ann Landers:* . . You advised her, "Give him a nice Methodist handshake and send him on his way." . . How does it differ from other handshakes? . . [Ann Landers:] A Methodist handshake is firm and sincere (a trait of Methodists) with an added air of finality. I first heard the expression when I attended a Methodist college, Morningside, in Sioux City, Iowa. I tried to trace the origin of the term back to 1936, but was unsuccessful.

Methodist howler See **howling Methodist**

Methodist measure n

1 Full measure. [Prob in ref to Luke 6:38] Cf **gospel measure**

1958 *DE Folkl. Bulletin* 132, *Gospel measure* (full to overflowing)—also Methodist measure. **1968–69** *DARE* (Qu. U15, *When you're buying something, if the seller puts in a little extra to make you feel that you're getting a good bargain*) Infs **IN3, KY37, 70, MO15,** Methodist measure; (Qu. LL28, . . *Entirely full: "The box of apples was _____."*) Inf **VA21,** Methodist measure—heaped up and running over.

2 Short measure. [Perh in ref to Methodists' opposition to alcoholic beverages]

1949 *PADS* 11.8 **wTX,** *Methodist measure.* . . Short measure. Often used about a glass filled only two-thirds full of liquid—apparently an allusion to the Methodists' sprinkling rather than immersing for baptism. [**1986** Pederson *LAGS Concordance,* 1 inf, **seFL,** Myself, I was a

Drinking Methodist.] [**1992** *NADS Letters*, As for *methodist measure*, I've never heard this term used, but as a former Methodist I can solve the mystery of its meaning. Methodists are commonly teetotallers, so a "methodist measure" of liquor would be stingy, hence, less than a full measure. It has nothing to do either with baptism or with old and new wineskins, I suspect.]

Methodist pallet n [From the practice of setting up makeshift **pallets** at Methodist **camp meetings**] *esp AR, TX* Cf **Baptist pallet, make down 1**
A temporary bed made on the floor.
   1967–68 *DARE* (Qu. E18, *A temporary or emergency bed made up on the floor*) Inf **AR**47, Methodist pallet; **TX**40, Methodist pallet—at camp meetings. **1970** Tarpley *Blinky* 105 neTX, Informants who recall the use of *pallets* for the children at summertime evangelistic services (usually held outdoors) still refer to the home variety as *Baptist* or *Methodist pallets*. **1986** Pederson *LAGS Concordance*, 1 inf, ceAR, Methodist pallet—clothes piled up on floor; 1 inf, swAR, Methodist pallet—depended on church membership; 1 inf, swAR, Methodist pallets—a lot of them in same place.

methought See **methinks**

methy n Also *marthy* [Of Algonquian origin; *DCan* 1743 →]
=**burbot**.
   [**1743** (1949) Isham *Observations* 169, Mer'thy (as the Natives styles itt,) are a fish Resembles an Eal in taste, they are muddy fish and skin's—the Same as an Eal, but of a Different shape, these are plenty, they are fine Eating in a pye with pork &c.] **1842** DeKay *Zool. NY* 4.285, It [=burbot] is known under the various local names of *La Loche, Methy, Dog-fish* and *Eel-pout.* According to Richardson, it is common in every river and lake from the great lakes to the frozen ocean. **1903** NY State Museum & Sci. Serv. *Bulletin* 60.702, The American burbot. . has received a great many names, including . . marthy, methy [etc].

metiche n [MexSpan]
A busybody, meddler.
   1967 *DARE* (Qu. GG36a, *The kind of person who is always poking into other people's affairs: "She's an awful _____."*) Inf **TX**31, Metiche [mɛˈtičɛ]. **1983** Santiago *Famous All Over Town* 101 **Los Angeles CA**, "Jesus Christ! Shit! Who are you, the FBI?" Lena yelled. "I just happen to be your brother," I informed her. "You're a snot-nose metiche. Get out of my life!" **1991** *DARE* File csWI [Speaker from **TX**], A metiche [mɛˈtičɛ] is someone who has to have his foot in every door. If I catch my daughters listening in on my phone conversations I call them "my little metiches."

metis n [Fr *métis* mongrel, half-breed; cf **mestizo**] Cf *DCan*
A person of mixed blood, esp of French and American Indian ancestry.
   1839 *Penny Cyclo.* XV. 158/2 (DA), The mixed race [in Mexico] is mostly composed of the descendants of the Europeans and the aboriginal tribes: these are called *Metis* or *Mestizos.* **1885** *Boston Herald* (MA) 29 Nov (DA), The paternal ancestors of the Metis were the former employes of the Hudson Bay and Northwest Fur Companies, and their maternal ancestors were indian women of various tribes. **1966** *DARE* (Qu. HH29a, *. . People of mixed blood—part Indian*) Inf **ND**3, Metis. **1977** Dunlop *Wheels West* 44, Jolly Joe Rolette was a métis, or a *bois brûlé*, so called because they were said to be the color of burned wood. . The *métis* lived on both sides of the Canadian border [in the West].

me-too n
A person who imitates or adopts the behavior of another; a copycat; a tagalong.
   [**1942** Berrey–Van den Bark *Amer. Slang* 16.13, *Metooistic*, imitative.] **1950** *WELS (Someone who always imitates other people)* 2 Infs, **WI**, A me-too. **1966** *DARE* (Qu. Y9, *Somebody who always follows along behind others: "His little brother is an awful _____."*) Inf **FL**5, Me-too. **1993** *DARE* File, I know *Me-too* as a character in a comic that was printed on waxed paper and used as a bubble gum wrapper in the early fifties. The brand was Bazooka because Me-too was the kid brother who tagged along with his big brother Bazooka Joe. Me-too only uttered those two words, which he did when he wanted to be included in whatever hi-jinks his brother was planning.

metsel soup See **metzel soup**

mettwurst n Also *metworst* [Ger *mettwurst*, Du *metworst*; *OEDS* 1895 →]
A spiced pork and beef sausage.

1911 *Cosmopolitan* Feb 314, See that I have blutwurst, brattwurst, and mettwurst every morning for breakfast. **1934** Stone *Studien* 78, [ˈmɛtwoˑʳst]. . . Portland, Oregon . . 1932. . . I asked the name of this sausage, and was told that it was *mettwurst*. I protested that this was a German word, and asked if the English name were not *summer sausage.* "Well, yes, sometimes it's called that; but the usual name is *mettwurst*", was the answer I received. **1950** *WELS (Kinds of sausage most eaten in your neighborhood)* 3 Infs, **WI**, Mettwurst. **1967–70** *DARE* (Qu. H65, *Foreign foods favored by people around here*) Inf **MI**122, Metworst; **MA**50, Mettwurst—same as thuringer. **1969** *Cardunal Free Press* (Carpentersville IL) 19 Feb [6], Koeneman's homade mettwurst 89¢ lb. **1970** *DARE* Tape **MI**122, The Polish have a kind of sausage that they call kielbasa, and we [=the Dutch] have a sausage that we call metworst [ˈmɛtwɚst], and it's sausage with different spices in it. They don't taste alike, but it's the same base, which is the sausage, but with different spices in it. **1995** *DARE* File c**WI** (as of 1956), Mettwurst is a spicy, very dry pork sausage. My grandmother used to cut it up and fry it, then pour in eggs and scramble it all together.

metzel soup n Also *metsel soup, metzel soop,* ~ *sup* [sGer *Metzelsuppe* sausage soup] *chiefly* sePA Cf **pudding**
A gift of sausage, etc, given to friends and neighbors by one who has butchered an animal.
   1872 Haldeman *PA Dutch* 57 [Engl infl by German], *Metzel-soup*, originally pudding broth, the butcher's perquisite, but subsequently applied to a gratuity from the animals he has slaughtered. **1872** Schele de Vere *Americanisms* 143, When the "killing season" arrived it was . . a common practice among farmers to send their friends and near neighbors as much of the puddings and sausages they made as was necessary for one meal. . . This gift was called the Metzel-soup. **1882** (1971) Gibbons *PA Dutch* 40, The friends who have assisted [in the butchering] receive a portion of the sausage, etc., which portion is called the "metzel-sup" (or soop). The metzel-sup is very often sent to poor widows and others. **1935** *AmSp* 10.170 se**PA**, Other German words used in English are *metzel,* 'They always give a metzel soup along.'

mew bird See **meow bird**

mewl v [Transf < *mewl* to whimper]
   1939 Hall *Coll.* e**TN**, Mewl. . . To complain. "Many of 'em have been mewling about it (the take over of land by the state for the creation of the National Park)."

Mex See **Mexican town**

Mexican adj, n Pronc-spp *chiefly* **SW**, *esp* **TX** *Mescan, Meskin, Messakin*
A Forms.
   1953 Brewer *Word Brazos* 81 wTX [Black], Dem's yo' white folks; dese heah's yo' Meskins; dere's yo' Germans. **1958** Latham *Meskin Hound* **TX**. **1962** Atwood *Vocab.* **TX** 73, The word *Mexican* [is] often shortened to *Mescan.* **1966** *DARE* Tape **NM**3, There was a one-armed [ˈmɛskɪn] . . with a little burro. **1967** *DARE* (Qu. HH28, *Names and nicknames . . for people of foreign background . . Mexican*) Infs **TX**1, 42, 45, Mescan; **TX**39, [ˈmɛskən]; (Qu. L37) Inf **TX**26, [mɛskɪn] lawnmower; (Qu. N6) Inf **TX**68, [mɛskən] rig. [All Infs old] **1969** O'Connor *Horse & Buggy West* 32 **AZ**, Meskin Town. **1991** *Contemp. S. Short Fiction* 81 **TX**, "Let him sleep," Curly said. "Mescans won't care. I know I sure don't." *Ibid* 86, All I know is that I wake up with a headache the size of Dallas, 'bout a hundred Mescan kids lookin' at me in the back of Curly's pickup, an' when I get out, I'm in Mexico. **1994** *Capital Times* (Madison WI) 5 Oct sec A 11/2, The one thing we [=Texans] never did when we were down was blame the "Messakins." (To Bubba, all people of the Hispanic persuasion are Messakins.)
B As adj.
1 Cheap, inferior; makeshift, substitute; bogus, illegal. *chiefly* **West**, *esp* **SW** *derog* Cf **Irish banjo,** ~ **buggy, nigger** n[1] **B4**
   1912 *NY Eve. Jrl.* (NY) 5 Mar 14 (*Zwilling Coll.*), [Cartoon:] I'm tired of being the boob around town. I'm going to be a mexican athlete. Throw the bull about being a fighter and get away with it. **1935** *AmSp* 10.79 [Sailor slang], *Mexican seabag.* A newspaper or paper bag in which the poor sailor carries his belongings. **1941** Dobie *Longhorns* 225 **TX**, Before barbed wire arrived, according to another saying, Texas was "bound together with rawhide." . . Some people called the binding "Mexican iron." **1955** *AmSp* 30.94 [Truck drivers' language], *Mexican overdrive.* . . A term used for coasting down hill with gears disengaged. **1960** Wentworth–Flexner *Slang* 337, *Mexican* [derog.]. . . Cheap, inferior. *Not common.* Some southwest dial[ect] use. **1960** *AmSp* 35.270

cwCA, Phrases . . I have heard in actual usage in San Francisco building construction and waterfront employment are: . . *Mexican drag line.* **1961** *PADS* 36.29 **West,** *Mexican dragline.* . . A humorous term for a hand shovel. **1962** *Western Folkl.* 21.28, A "Mexican credit card," (a hose and siphon used for pilfering gasoline at night) is known in the Southwest. **1966–69** *DARE* (Qu. K50, *Joking nicknames for mules*) Inf **TX5,** Mexican quarter horse; (Qu. L37, *A hand tool used for cutting weeds and grass*) Inf **TX26,** Mexican lawnmower [laughter]; **TX37,** Mexican lawnmower; (Qu. L41, *A device for moving dirt and other loads, with one wheel in front and handles to lift and push it behind*) Infs **ID3, WY1,** Mexican dragline; (Qu. N6, *An old car that has been fixed up to make it go fast or make a lot of noise*) Inf **TX68,** Mexican rig—for noise; (Qu. HH30, *Things that are nicknamed for different nationalities—for example, a 'Dutch treat'*) Inf **CA169,** Mexican dragline—a shovel; **TX68,** Mexican rig—anything poorly constructed. **1986** Pederson *LAGS Concordance,* 1 inf, **seMS,** Mexican hydraulic lift—wheelbarrow; facetious. **1986** *Barrick Coll.* [Sports announcer at an auto race:] They're working down there with what we call a Mexican speed wrench; that's a sledge hammer. **1993** *NADS Letters,* I have heard . . *Mexican athlete* . . used to describe someone who "throws the bull," that is to say lies or exaggerates. **1993** *DARE* File **GA** (as of 1938–39), *Mexican handcuffs*—a figure-eight slipknot formed in the bight of a length of rope. . . The knot is a ready substitute for metal handcuffs.

2 Of time or events: late; slow; unreliable. Cf **Indian time**

1968 *DARE* (Qu. HH30, *Things that are nicknamed for different nationalities—for example, a 'Dutch treat'*) Inf **CA66,** Mexican time—no time sense; Mexican happening—it never comes about.

3 Of foods: spicy; containing hot peppers. **esp TX, Gulf States**

[**1854** (1932) Bell *Log TX-CA Trail* 35.236, We have the food cooked up in mexican style, that is onions and peper mixed with everything.] **1952** Tracy *Coast Cookery* 236 **TX,** *Mexican Rice* [Recipe includes rice, onion, green pepper, tomatoes, salt, water, and chili powder]. **1967** *DARE* (Qu. H50, *Dishes made with beans, peas, or corn that everybody around here knows, but people in other places might not*) Inf **AR52,** Mexican corn—corn and peppers cooked together. **1968** *Favorite Recipes Univ. Women* 118 **FL,** *Mexican Meat and Beans* [Recipe includes ground beef, onion, garlic, butter beans, tomatoes, chili powder, salt, cheese]. **1986** Pederson *LAGS Concordance,* 1 inf, **neTX,** Mexican cornmeal—with peppers in it; 1 inf, **cTX,** Mexican corn bread which have [sic] all this pimento; 1 inf, **csTX,** Mexican corn bread—peppers, corn kernels, pimento; 1 inf, **ceTX,** Mexican corn bread—green peppers, chili peppers; 1 inf, **seMS,** Mexican corn bread—it's hot; 1 inf, **nwMS,** Mexican corn bread—includes hot pepper, garlic; 1 inf, **cTN,** Mexican corn bread—spices, corn.

4 in var combs referring to diarrhea: See quots. *joc* or *derog* Cf **Aztec two-step**

1962 *Western Folkl.* 21.28 **swCA,** The North American in Mexico has coined a number of names for the inevitable dysentary [sic] and diarrhea: "Mexican two-step," "Mexican fox-trot," "Mexican toothache," and . . "Montezuma's revenge," . . and the "Aztec hop." **1967–69** *DARE* (Qu. BB19, *Joking names for looseness of the bowels*) Inf **IL46,** Mexican disease; **CA4,** Mexican sickness; **CA7,** Mexican two-step.

C As noun.

See **Mexican bean 1.**

Mexican apple n [See quot 1965] esp TX

A **waxmallow** (here: *Malvaviscus arboreus* var *drummondii*).

1936 Whitehouse *TX Flowers* 71, Mexican Apple. Turk's Cap (*Malvaviscus drumondii*) is also called red mallow. . . The red apple-like fruits are nearly an inch broad and half as high. They have a delicious flavor and may be eaten raw or cooked. **1961** Wills–Irwin *Flowers TX* 154, Turk's-cap, also called Red Mallow and Mexican-apple, commonly forms clumps in the shade of East Texas woods. . . The flowers, which never open fully, are followed by edible fruit. **1965** Teale *Wandering Through Winter* 156 **TX,** Mexican mallows. . . are . . known as . . Mexican apples. The . . name comes from the fact that Mexicans eat the small red, apple-shaped fruit.

Mexican ash n esp TX

Berlandier ash (*Fraxinus berlandierana*). Also called **fresno 1**

1938 Van Dersal *Native Woody Plants* 130, *Fraxinus berlandieriana* [sic]. . . *Mexican ash.* . . A large deciduous tree. **1960** Vines *Trees SW* 862, Local names for the tree [=Berlandier ash] are Plumero, Fresno, and Mexican ash. . . The tree is widely planted as an ornamental in western and southwestern Texas. **1980** Little *Audubon Guide N. Amer.*

Trees E. Region 648, *Berlandier Ash* "Mexican Ash". *Ibid* 649, Range: Central and S. Texas and NE. Mexico.

Mexican balsamea n
=hummingbird's trumpet.

1925 Jepson *Manual Plants CA* 667, *Z[auschneria] californica.* . . Mexican balsamea. **1949** Moldenke *Amer. Wild Flowers* 92, The Mexican balsamea, *Zauschneria californica,* has blossoms 1 to 1½ inches long and flourishes best on dry benches, rocky hillsides, and cliffs in the Coast Ranges of southern California.

Mexican banana n
=banana yucca.

1884 Sargent *Forests of N. Amer.* 219, *Yucca baccata.* . . Spanish bayonet. Mexican banana. . . The large juicy fruit edible and an important article of food to Mexicans and Indians. **1900** Lyons *Plant Names* 401, *Y[ucca] baccata.* . . Mexican Banana, Soap-plant.

Mexican bean n

1 also *Mexican:* A kidney or pinto bean (*Phaseolus vulgaris* cv). **chiefly West** See Map Cf **frijole**

1901 *Amer. Mth. Rev.* 24.313, The list includes Mexican beans, oatmeal . . and canned tomatoes and corn. **a1936** in **1943** *Colorado Mag.* 20.183 **NM** (as of 1850s), Massive Indian jars stood there, filled to the brim with pinto or Mexican beans. **1950** *WELS* (Flat beans that are striped or speckled with red) 1 Inf, **cWI,** Mexican beans. **c1955** Reed-Person *Ling. Atlas Pacific NW,* 2 infs, Mexican beans [=pinto beans]. **1956** Ker *Vocab. W. TX* 249, The Mexican brown bean is commonly called *pinto, red bean,* and *frijole.* . . *Mexican bean* is the response of three old-timers of Hartley, Lamb and Lubbock counties. **1965–70** *DARE* (Qu. I17, *Beans . . that are dark red when they are dry*) Infs **CA57, 144, 196, CO45, KS14, MI68, MN36, NC81, OR4, 10, TX53, WA8, 15, 27,** Mexican bean(s); **CA62,** California beans or Mexican beans; **CA126,** Red beans [FW: Inf thinks these may also be called Mexican beans.]; **OH35,** Mexican; [**CO3,** Mexican chili beans; **NH14,** Mexican pinto beans;] (Qu. H50, *Dishes made with beans, peas, or corn that everybody around here knows, but people in other places might not*) Inf **CA59,** California pink beans or Mexican beans; **CA91,** Red beans or Spanish beans or Mexican beans; (Qu. I20, . . *Kinds of beans*) Infs **KS14, MT4,** Mexican beans; **ID1,** Mexican bean—red; **CO20,** Mexican bean—a little larger than a navy, brown; **CO30,** Pintos—Mexican beans; **NM8,** Mexican bean, [same as] pinto beans. **1968** *DARE* Tape **CA87,** Roasting ear, and potato salad, and brown beans; Mexican beans, and a roasting ear, and potato salad. **1978** *Wanigan Catalog* 14, Mexican pinto. *Ibid,* Mexican red—Syns. California Red. Mexican. . . A solid dark red . . fat oval seed.

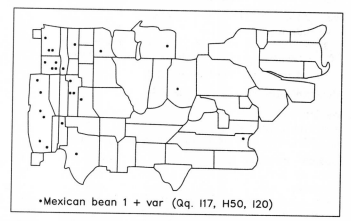

•Mexican bean 1 + var (Qq. I17, H50, I20)

2 A white bean such as a **navy bean;** see quot.

1965–70 *DARE* (Qu. I18, *The smaller beans that are white when they are dry*) Inf **HI11,** Mexican beans, white, with spots or stripes; (Qu. I19, *Small white beans with a black spot where they were joined to the pod*) Inf **OH72,** Mexican beans.

3 =**mesquite bean.**

1921 *DN* 5.113 **CA,** *Mexican bean.* . . Mesquite bean. [**1969** *DARE* (Qu. I17) Inf **CA107,** Mexican beans [are] not a food.]

Mexican bean beetle n Also Mexican beetle

A plant-eating **ladybug** (*Epilachna varivestis*) or other beetle; see quot 1965–70.

1922 Bentley *Mex. Bean Beetle* 3, Chief among the insect pests in Tennessee at present is the Mexican bean beetle (*Epilachna corrupta*).

[*Ibid* 8, It is supposed to be a native of Mexico and Central America and has been known for some 50 years.] **1925** *Book of Rural Life* 6.3512, *Mexican bean beetle,* or what has commonly been known as the *bean ladybird,* migrated into the United States from Mexico, and for some time has been a serious pest of beans in Colorado, New Mexico, Arizona and western Kansas. **1926** Essig *Insects N. Amer.* 426, The Mexican bean beetle or the bean ladybird, *Epilachna corrupta* . . is the most destructive member of the family [=Coccinellidae] in the west and it is proving to be a serious pest wherever found. **1949** Swain *Insect Guide* 135, The Mexican bean beetle (*Epilachna varivestis*). . . has now spread over most of the country and into southern Canada. Adults and larvae skeletonize the foliage and also feed on the flowers and pods of lima and snap beans. **1965–70** DARE (Qu. R30, . . *Kinds of beetles;* not asked in early QRs) 19 Infs, esp Sth, S Midl, Mexican bean beetle; **OH**79, **TX**62, **VA**8, 38, **WV**3, Mexican beetle; **MA**15, Mexican beetle—starlings cleaned them out; **NC**49, Mexican beetle—eat up plants' leaves; (Qu. R5, *A big brown beetle that comes out in large numbers in spring and early summer, and flies with a buzzing sound*) Inf **NC**81, Mexican bean beetle; **NC**80, Mexican beetle; **DC**8, Mexican beetle—big, brown; since Second World War; eat bean crops up. **1989** Entomol. Soc. Amer. *Common Names Insects* 89, *Epilachna varivestis*—Mexican bean beetle.

Mexican bedbug n Cf **bedbug hunter**
A **conenose** (here: *Triatoma sanguisuga*).
1972 Swan–Papp *Insects* 121, *Bloodsucking Conenose.* . . Also called the big bed bug or Mexican bed bug. *Range:* New Jersey to Florida, west to Illinois and Texas; considered a common insect in parts of Kansas. **1980** Milne–Milne *Audubon Field Guide Insects* 474, *Eastern Blood-sucking Conenose*—"Big Bed Bug"—"Mexican Bed Bug" (*Triatoma sanguisuga*). . . If hungry, the adult may fly, but after a full meal it is unable to get off the ground. Bites cause severe allergic reactions in some people.

Mexican beetle See **Mexican bean beetle**

Mexican black hawk n Also *Mexican hawk, ~ buzzard*
A hawk (*Buteogallus anthracinus*) native to the southwestern US. Also called **black hawk 2, crab ~, Mexican eagle 3**
1898 (1900) Davie *Nests N. Amer. Birds* 213, Mexican black hawk. *Urubitinga anthracina.* . . A beautiful Hawk, known as the Mexican or Anthracite Buzzard. . . The general color of the adult bird is coal-black. **1944** Hausman *Amer. Birds* 147, Mexican Black Hawk. **1961** Ligon *NM Birds* 71, Black (Mexican) hawk—*Buteogallus anthracinus.* **1964** Phillips *Birds AZ* 24, The Mexican Black Hawk is a characteristic hawk of running water, but will often soar high above the creeks and rivers.

Mexican blanket n Cf **Indian blanket 2**
An **Indian paintbrush 1.**
1898 *Jrl. Amer. Folkl.* 11.276 **TX**, *Castilleia* (sp.) . . Mexican blanket, Austin Co., Tex. . . From the appearance of a prairie covered with it.

Mexican blue See **Mexican quail 2**

Mexican blue oak See **blue oak 3**

Mexican brant n
=**white-fronted goose.**
1957 AmSp 32.183 **TX**, Mexican brant—White-fronted goose.

Mexican buckeye n Also *New Mexican buckeye, New Mexico ~* [See quot 1980]
A small tree or shrub (*Ungnadia speciosa*) native to Texas and New Mexico. Also called **monilla, Spanish buckeye, Texas ~**
1886 Havard *Flora W. & S. TX for 1885* 507, *Ungnadia speciosa* . . Mexican Buckeye. **1891** Coulter *Botany W. TX* 66, *U[ngnadia] speciosa* . . (Mexican buckeye.)—A shrub or very small tree common . . from the valley of the Trinity through western Texas to New Mexico. **1913** Wooton *Trees NM* 110, *New Mexico Buckeye.* . . The pod . . [contains] 3 spherical smooth dark brown seeds about ½ inch in diameter and resembling the buckeye. *Ibid* 111, *New Mexican Buckeye.* Bushy branched shrubs 6 feet high or less. **1931** U.S. Dept. Ag. *Misc. Pub.* 101.104, Mexican-buckeye . . known also as monillo, Spanish buckeye, and New Mexican buckeye. **1980** Little *Audubon Guide N. Amer. Trees W. Region* 543, Mexican buckeye. . *Ungnadia speciosa.* . . Although not a true buckeye, it is so called because of the similar large capsules and seeds.

Mexican burr See **Mexican sandburr**

Mexican buzzard n
1 =**caracara.**
1854 (1932) Bell *Log TX-CA Trail* 35.223, The Crow is scarce here, the Raven and Mexican Buzzard fill up the compliment [sic], of the feathered tribe. **1898** (1900) Davie *Nests N. Amer. Birds* 230, Audubon's caracara. . . Common to the Southern border of the United States, and known as the Mexican Eagle or Buzzard—intermediate between the Eagles and Buzzards, and resembling both in its habits. **1957** AmSp 32.184 **FL, TX**, Mexican buzzard—common caracara. **1961** [see **Mexican eagle 1**]. **1966** DARE (Qu. Q13, *Names . . for the vulture*) Inf **FL**35, Mexican buzzard. **1967** Will *Dredgeman* 84 **Everglades FL**, You might sight a snowy sea gull, or maybe a heavy bodied "Mexican buzzard," the black vulture, who alternately flaps his wings three times, then soars awhile.
2 See **Mexican black hawk.**

Mexican canary n
1 A **painted bunting** (here: *Passerina ciris*).
1946 Hausman *Eastern Birds* 575, Painted bunting. . . Mexican Canary. **1957** AmSp 32.183 **TX**, Mexican canary. . . Painted bunting. **1970** DARE (Qu. Q23) Inf **TX**84, Mexican canary—a kind of bunting. [**1977** Udvardy *Audubon Field Guide Birds* 674, Though the Painted Bunting's song is not particularly musical, males used to be favorite cagebirds because of their beautiful coloration; they are still sold in Mexico.]
2 Any of several yellow or mostly yellow birds; see quots. Cf **wild canary**
1957 AmSp 32.183 **TX**, Mexican canary—Orchard oriole. *Ibid* **NM**, Mexican canary. . . Yellow warbler [=Dendroica petechia]. *Ibid* 184 **TX**, Mexican canary—Hooded oriole. **1967** DARE (Qu. Q14, . . *Names . . for these birds: . . goldfinch*) Inf **TX**3, Mexican canary.

Mexican cardinal n
=**pyrrhuloxia.**
1957 AmSp 32.185 **TX**, Mexican cardinal—Gray grosbeak.

Mexican clover n [See quot 1889]
A plant (*Richardia scabra*) naturalized in the southeastern US, esp along the Gulf coast, that is sometimes used as forage. Also called **Alabama clover, Florida ~, Florida purslane, John's weed, pigeonweed, poor joe, ~ toes, purslane, Spanish clover, water pusley**
1881 Phares *Farmer's Book of Grasses* 14, Mexican Clover. . . has become naturalized in Florida and the southern parts of other southern States. **1889** Vasey *Ag. Grasses* 103, Mexican Clover. . . is . . not a true clover, that name having perhaps been given from the general appearance of the plant and the fact that the flowers are mostly borne in terminal heads. *Ibid* 104, Dr. Charles Mohr, Mobile, Ala. . . in 1874 . . said. . . "the plant is known here by the name of 'Mexican clover.'" *Ibid* 105, Mr. Matt Coleman, Leesburgh, Sumter County, Fla., in 1878 wrote . . "The tradition is that when the Spanish evacuated Pensacola, this plant was discovered there by the cavalry horses feeding upon it eagerly." **1944** AL Geol. Surv. *Bulletin* 53.209, "Mexican clover". . . A common fall weed in sandy fields in the coastal plain. . . It may have come into Alabama since the Civil War, for it was unknown to Chapman in 1860, but was reported by him from Alabama, Georgia and Florida. . . in 1883 and 1897. **1970** U.S. Ag. Research Serv. *Selected Weeds* 356, *Mexican clover.* . . Mainly along the South Atlantic and Gulf Coast States, from North Carolina to Florida and west to southern Texas. **1975** Duncan–Foote *Wildflowers SE* 188, *Mexican-clover.* . . Weedy annual. . . Common. Open places, fields, roadsides, waste places.

Mexican cormorant n
A **cormorant**: usu *Phalacrocorax olivaceus*, rarely also **double-crested cormorant.** For other names of the former see **niggergoose 1**
1858 Baird *Birds* 879, *Graculus mexicanus* . . Mexican Cormorant. . . Of this species, new to our fauna, there are seven specimens. . . all from the Rio Grande. **1872** Coues *Key to N. Amer. Birds* 303, *Mexican Cormorant.* . . Texas; up the Mississippi to Illinois. **1898** (1900) Davie *Nests N. Amer. Birds* 68, The Mexican Cormorant is. . . a common summer resident in Southwestern Texas, in the vicinity of Fort Brown. **1916** *Times–Picayune* (New Orleans LA) 26 Mar mag sec 1/7, Mexican cormorant (*Phalacrocorax vigua mexicanus*). This . . has a white packet of feathers on each side of the head during the breeding season, known as nuptial plumes. **1938** Oberholser *Bird Life LA* 40, The Mexican Cormorant is a fairly common permanent resident in the Gulf Coast

region of southwestern Louisiana. **1961** Ligon *NM Birds* 28, The Double-crested, also formerly known as the Mexican Cormorant, is the only species of this group which occurs in the state. **1968** *DARE* (Qu. Q13, *Names . . for the vulture*) Inf **WI**32, Mexican cormorant [FW: found on the Mississippi River; they fly in formation same as a goose].

Mexican creeper n

=**coral vine 3.**

1929 Neal *Honolulu Gardens* 105, The Mexican creeper is a sunloving vine with slender, smooth stems and tuberous roots. It has been picturesquely called "hearts-on-a-string." **1976** Bailey–Bailey *Hortus Third* 86, [*Antigonon*] *leptopus* . . Mexican creeper.

Mexican curlew n Cf black curlew, bronze ~

=**white-faced ibis.**

1957 *AmSp* 32.183 **CA,** Mexican curlew—White-faced ibis. [**1977** Udvardy *Audubon Field Guide Birds* 423, *White-faced Ibis*. . In flight to and from the roost they present an unforgettable view as long, wavering lines of large, dark, curlew-like birds speed toward the horizon.]

Mexican devil-weed n

An aster (here: *Aster spinosus*).

1925 Jepson *Manual Plants CA* 1049, *A*[*ster*] *spinosus* . . Mexican Devil-weed. **1941** Jaeger *Wildflowers* 270, Mexican devil-weed. . . Its large size (3–9 ft. high), spiny nature, and easy propagation make it a pest wherever it grows. The almost leafless stems and scraggly flowers which soon turn brown do not commend it as a thing of beauty. **1970** Correll *Plants TX* 1599, *Aster spinosus*. . . Mexican devil-weed.

Mexican disease See Mexican B4

Mexican dove n SW, esp TX

1 also *Mexican ground dove:* =**ground dove.**

1898 (1900) Davie *Nests N. Amer. Birds* 189, Mexican ground dove. *Columbigallina passerina pallescens*. **1917** (1923) *Birds Amer.* 2.51, The Mexican Ground Dove. . . is found in the desert regions of the southwest. **1929** Dobie *Vaquero* 202 **West,** Here are *mogotes* (thick patches) of the evergreen, stubborn, beautiful *coma* with dirk-like thorns, and, in season, with blue berries which the Mexican dove likes so much that it constantly coos—if we are to believe the Mexican folk— *"comer comas, comer comas,"* saying that it wants to eat *coma* berries. **1957** *AmSp* 32.185 **TX,** Mexican dove—Ground dove. **1970** *DARE* (Qu. Q7, *Names and nicknames for . . game birds*) Inf **TX**101, Mexican dove—little bitty fellows.

2 =**Inca dove.**

1957 *AmSp* 32.185 **TX,** Mexican dove—Inca dove.

Mexican duck n

1 also *Mexican wood duck:* A **tree duck** (here: *Dendrocygna bicolor*).

1918 Grinnell *Game Birds CA* 246, *Fulvous Tree-duck*. . . *Other names*—Mexican Duck. **1953** Jewett *Birds WA* 112, Mexican Duck. . . Neck and legs very long for a duck. **1957** *AmSp* 32.185 **CA, TX,** Mexican duck—Fulvous tree duck. *Ibid* **CA,** Mexican wood duck—Fulvous tree duck.

2 also *New Mexican duck:* A small, dark duck native to the southwestern US which resembles the **mallard 1;** see quots.

1977 Udvardy *Audubon Field Guide Birds* 439, Mexican Duck (*Anas diazi*). . . This smaller, darker version of the Mallard is a nonmigratory form. Some ornithologists are undecided about its status as a full species. **1982** Elman *Hunter's Field Guide* 128, The Mexican duck (sometimes called New Mexican), and the mottled duck of the Gulf Coast . . are localized, sedentary races of the mallard in which the male resembles the female and does not acquire the nuptial plumage of typical mallard drakes.

Mexican eagle n

1 =**caracara.**

1835 in 1925 *SW Hist. Qrly.* 28.190 **TX,** The most common birds and fowls found [in Texas] are the Mexican eagle, the hawk. **1858** Baird *Birds* 45, The Caracara Eagle; The Mexican Eagle. . . It is of frequent occurrence also in Mexico and Texas, and is found also in Florida. **1898** [see **Mexican buzzard 1**]. **1928** Bailey *Birds NM* 186, The Mexican Eagle . . is the national emblem of Mexico and figures on the flag with a rattlesnake in its bill. **1957** *AmSp* 32.185 **FL, TX,** Mexican eagle—Common caracara. **1961** Ligon *NM Birds* 77, The Caracara, known both as Mexican Buzzard and Mexican Eagle, is a long-legged, dark bird.

1967–70 *DARE* (Qu. Q4, *. . Kinds of hawks*) Infs **TX**5, 31, Mexican eagle; (Qu. Q13, *Names . . for the vulture*) Inf **TX**84, Mexican eagle; (QR p119) Inf **TX**84, Mexican eagle. **1977** Udvardy *Audubon Field Guide Birds* 508, This bird [=*Caracara cheriway*], magnificent in flight, is the "Mexican eagle" of the flag of Mexico. The Mexican peso coin shows the Caracara hacking a wriggling rattlesnake to death with its beak.

2 =**golden eagle.**

1957 *AmSp* 32.183 **OK, TX, CO,** Mexican eagle—Golden eagle.

3 =**Mexican black hawk.**

1957 *AmSp* 32.185 **TX, AZ,** Mexican eagle—Black hawk.

4 Harris's hawk (*Parabuteo unicinctus harrisi*).

1957 *AmSp* 32.185 **TX,** Mexican eagle—Harris's hawk.

Mexican eagle-hawk n

=**peregrine falcon.**

1957 *AmSp* 32.183 **TX,** Mexican eagle-hawk—peregrine falcon.

Mexican fireball n

A **barrel cactus** (here: *Ferocactus acanthodes* var *lecontei*).

1936 Shiner Cactus Nursery *Illustr. Catalog* 24, Ferocactus lecontei— S. California, W. Arizona. Small plants globular, most colorful, larger ones tall, stout, cylindric. Sometimes called "Mexican fire-ball."

Mexican fire bush See fire bush 2

Mexican fire plant n

1 See **Mexican fireweed.**

2 =**fire-on-the-mountain.**

1911 *Century Dict. Suppl.,* Fire-on-the-mountain. . . Also called *Mexican fire-plant.* **1940** Clute *Amer. Plant Names* 223, *Euphorbia heterophylla.* Hypocrite-plant, Mexican fire-plant. **1976** Bailey–Bailey *Hortus Third* 463, [*Euphorbia*] *heterophylla*. . . Mexican fire plant.

Mexican fireweed n Also Mexican fire plant Cf fireweed

A **summer cypress** (here: *Kochia scoparia*).

1910 Graves *Flowering Plants* 165, Kochia Scoparia. . . Mexican Fire Plant. . . Cultivated for its brilliant autumnal foliage. **1914** Georgia *Manual Weeds* 107, Kochia scoparia. . . Its name of "Mexican fireweed" is a misnomer, for it is an immigrant from Europe. . . In autumn the dense foliage turns fiery red. **1935** (1943) Muenscher *Weeds* 213, Kochia scoparia. . . Burning-bush, Fireball, Mexican fireweed. **1967** *DARE* (Qu. S21, *. . Weeds . . that are a trouble in gardens and fields*) Inf **CA**7, Mexican fireweed. **1968** Barkley *Plants KS* 133, Summer Cypress. Mexican Fireweed.

Mexican flameleaf n

=**poinsettia.**

1976 Bailey–Bailey *Hortus Third* 464, [*Euphorbia*] *pulcherrima*. . . lobster plant, Mexican flameleaf. **1982** Perry–Hay *Field Guide Plants* 58, Euphorbia pulcherrima (*Poinsettia pulcherrima*) . . Christmas star; Mexican flameleaf.

Mexican flats See Mexican town

Mexican fox-trot See Mexican B4

Mexican French duck n LA

=**Florida duck.**

1911 *Forest & Stream* 77.172 **Missip Delta LA,** Mexican French Duck.

Mexican gamecock n

=**chachalaca 1.**

1953 *AmSp* 28.283 **TX,** Mexican gamecock—Chachalaca.

Mexican goldfinch n

A **goldfinch 1** (here: *Carduelis psaltria mexicanus*).

1858 Baird *Birds* 423, Chrysomitris mexicana . . Black Goldfinch; Mexican Goldfinch. **1898** (1900) Davie *Nests N. Amer. Birds* 362, Mexican Goldfinch. Spinus psaltria mexicanus. **1970** *DARE* (Qu. Q14) Inf **TX**84, Mexican goldfinch; Arkansas goldfinch.

Mexican goose n

1 Any of var geese, as:

a A **snow goose** (here: *Chen caerulescens*).

1888 Trumbull *Names of Birds* 9 **RI,** I have heard it [=*Chen caerulescens*] called *Mexican goose.* **1917** (1923) *Birds Amer.* 1.155, Snow Goose. . . Other Names . . Mexican Goose. **1957** *AmSp* 32.183 **IL,** Mexican goose. . . Blue goose. *Ibid* **MA, RI, IL,** Mexican goose. . .

Snow goose. [*DARE* Ed: The blue color phase of the snow goose was formerly considered a separate species and designated "blue goose."] **1982** Elman *Hunter's Field Guide* 287, Lesser Snow Goose. . . Alaska goose, arctic goose, Mexican goose.

b =**Canada goose. esp CA**

1918 Grinnell *Game Birds CA* 222, Canada Goose. . . Mexican Goose, Big Mexican Goose. **1923** U.S. Dept. Ag. *Misc. Circular* 13.35 **CA,** Mexican goose—Canada goose. **1982** Elman *Hunter's Field Guide* 269, Canada Goose. . . Mexican goose, Eskimo goose.

c =**white-fronted goose. Cf Mexican brant**

1957 *AmSp* 32.183 **IL,** Mexican goose. . . White-fronted goose.

2 =**double-crested cormorant. Cf Mexican cormorant**

1957 *AmSp* 32.183 **AZ,** Mexican goose—Double-crested cormorant.

3 =**anhinga.**

1957 *AmSp* 32.183 **TX,** Mexican goose—Anhinga.

Mexican goshawk n [See quot 1898]

A gray hawk (*Buteo nitidus*) native to Arizona.

1874 NY Acad. Sci. *Annals Lyceum Nat. Hist.* 10.381, B[uteo] nitida . . var. plagiata. . . Mexican Goshawk. **1898** (1900) Davie *Nests N. Amer. Birds* 214, Mexican Goshawk. . . is not an uncommon summer resident of the southern portions of Arizona. . . [T]heir flight [is] exceedingly graceful and swift, resembling in many respects that of the American Goshawk. **1928** Bailey *Birds NM* 175, Mexican Goshawks . . [are] readily recognized by their light color. **1964** Phillips *Birds AZ* 23, Gray Hawk; Mexican Goshawk. *Buteo nitidus.*

Mexican gourd n

=**calabacilla.**

1951 *PADS* 15.41, *Curcurbita* [sic] *foetidissima.* . . Spanish or Mexican gourd; calabacilla; chilicoyote.

Mexican ground dove See **Mexican dove 1**

Mexican hat n [See quot c1979] **esp TX**

A **prairie coneflower,** esp *Ratibida columnifera.*

1936 Whitehouse *TX Flowers* 173, *Ratibida columnaris* . . is also called Mexican hat. **1961** Wills–Irwin *Flowers TX* 58, Mexican-hat—*Ratibida columnaris.* **1967** *DARE* Wildfl QR (Wills–Irwin) Pl.58B Infs **TX**34, 44, Mexican hat. **1970** Correll *Plants TX* 1643, *Ratibida* [spp]. . . Mexican Hat. **1972** Brown *Wildflowers LA* 213, Cone-flower, Mexican Hat. **1979** Ajilvsgi *Wild Flowers* 308 **wLA, eTX,** *Mexican-hat.* . . Flowers numerous, of ray and disk types, in head. **c1979** TX Dept. Highways *Flowers* np, *Mexican Hat* is an appropriate name for the flower that resembles the traditional high-crowned, broad-brimmed Mexican sombrero. Common throughout most of Texas from May to July, and later with favorable weather.

Mexican hawk n

1 =**caracara.**

1967–69 *DARE* (Qu. Q4, . . *Kinds of hawks*) Infs **TX**26, 68, Mexican hawk.

2 See **Mexican black hawk.**

Mexican heliotrope n **TX**

1 A **frogfruit** (here: *Phyla cuneifolia*).

1897 *Jrl. Amer. Folkl.* 10.52 **TX,** *Lippia* [=*Phyla*] *cuneifolia.* . . Mexican heliotrope.

2 A **bee brush** (here: *Aloysia gratissima*).

1898 *Jrl. Amer. Folkl.* 11.277, *Lippia lycioides* [=*Aloysia gratissima*] . . Mexican heliotrope, Waco, Tex.

Mexican hog n

1 =**jabalina.**

1819 (1821) Nuttall *Jrl.* 155 **AR,** The *Sus tajassu* or Mexican hog, is not uncommon some distance higher up Red river. **1836** (1935) Holley *Texas* 95, The Pecari or Mexican hog is even yet occasionally met with, on the frontiers, in considerable gangs. **1901** *Amer. Mth. Rev.* 24.309 **TX,** An otherwise magnificent grazing country . . is frequented by wild Mexican hogs, panthers [etc].

2 Prob a **razorback hog.**

1981 Pederson *LAGS Basic Materials,* 1 inf, **neTN,** Mexican hogs—a variety which ran wild.

Mexican jay n

=**scrub jay.**

1957 *AmSp* 32.185 **TX,** Mexican jay—Scrub jay.

Mexican lark n

=**lark sparrow.**

1957 *AmSp* 32.183 **CA,** Mexican lark—Lark sparrow.

Mexican lion n **TX**

=**mountain lion.**

1903 *Everybody's Mag.* 9.599 **TX,** It is well to be reasonably watchful when a Mexican lion sings soprano along the arroyos. **1932** Barry *TX Ranger* 52, He [=a large panther] . . was what some are pleased to call a Mexican lion. **1967–70** *DARE* (Qu. P31, . . *Names or nicknames . . for the . . panther*) Inf **TX**27, Mexican lion; **TX**54, Mexican lion, puma; (Qu. P32) Inf **TX**101, Mexican lions—panthers, like, but not exactly. **1981** Pederson *LAGS Basic Materials,* 1 inf, **csTX,** Mexican lion.

Mexican mallard n **esp LA**

=**Florida duck.**

1911 *Forest & Stream* 77.172 **Missip Delta LA,** Mexican Mallard. **1916** *Times–Picayune* (New Orleans LA) 26 Mar mag sec 2/3, Summer French Duck . . Mexican Mallard. **1921** LA Dept. of Conserv. *Bulletin* 10.53 **LA,** A variety of French and English names are applied to the summer mallard, among which are . . "Mexican mallard," "canard d'ete."

Mexican mockingbird n

Any of three birds: the **scissor-tailed flycatcher,** the **loggerhead shrike,** or the curve-billed **thrasher** (*Toxostoma curvirostre*).

1957 *AmSp* 32.183 **TX,** Mexican mockingbird—Scissor-tailed flycatcher . . Southern shrike. *Ibid* 185 **AZ,** Mexican mockingbird—Curve-billed thrasher.

Mexican mudhen n [Perh from its resemblance to *Fulica americana;* cf **mud hen 1b**]

The least grebe (*Podiceps dominicus*).

1957 *AmSp* 32.185 **TX,** Mexican mudhen—White-winged grebe.

Mexican mulberry n

1 =**Texas mulberry. SW**

1884 Sargent *Forests of N. Amer.* 128, Mexican mulberry. . . most common and reaching its greatest development in the mountain cañons of southern New Mexico. **1938** Van Dersal *Native Woody Plants* 343, Mexican . . mulberry (*Morus microphylla*). **1951** *PADS* 15.30 **TX,** *Morus microphylla* . . Mexican mulberry. **1960** Vines *Trees SW* 219, *Texas Mulberry.* . . Vernacular names are Mexican Mulberry [etc].

2 =**French mulberry.**

1951 *PADS* 15.40, *Callicarpa americana.* . . French mulberry in eastern Texas; . . Mexican mulberry in central and southern parts of the state.

Mexican myrtle n [Appar from its resemblance to **crape myrtle**]

A Barbados cherry (*Malpighia glabra*).

1970 Correll *Plants TX* 913, *Malpighia glabra.* . . Barbados cherry, *Mexican myrtle.* . . Leaves opposite, . . bright-green. . . In thickets, brushlands and palm groves in s. Tex.

Mexican nightshade n

A **nightshade 1** (here: *Solanum eleagnifolium*).

1951 *PADS* 15.39 **TX,** *Solanum eleagnifolium* . . Purple, prickly, or Mexican, nightshade.

Mexican orange n Also *Mexican orange-flower* [See quots 1934, 1945]

A shrub of the genus *Choisya.* Also called **starleaf, zorillo**

1890 *Century Dict.* 4137, *Mexican orange-flower,* a handsome white-flowered shrub, *Choisya ternata.* **1923** Amer. Joint Comm. Horticult. Nomenclature *Std. Plant Names* 79, *Choisya* [spp]—Mexican-orange. **1934** NM Ag. Exper. Station *Bulletin* 714.2, The . . Mexican orange. . . belongs to the citrus fruit family . . and the white flowers resemble orange blossoms very closely, but . . the fruits are small and inconspicuous. [**1945** Benson–Darrow *Manual SW Trees* 213, *Choisya dumosa.* . . When . . crushed, the . . fragrance [of the leaves] resembles that of the foliage of the related citrus fruits.] **1981** Benson–Darrow *Trees SW Deserts* 131, [Caption:] Mexican orange, *Choisya dumosa* var. *dumosa.*

Mexican paisano See **paisano**

Mexican peafowl n Cf **Arizona peacock, California ~**

=**roadrunner.**

1897 *Oölogist* 14.79 **TX,** In Texas this bird [=the roadrunner] is almost universally known as the Chaparal Bird or Mexican Peafowl. **1917**

Wilson Bulletin 29.2.81, *Geoccoccyx* [sic] *californianus.* . . Mexican peafowl.

Mexican persimmon n
=black persimmon.

1846 [see **mustang persimmon**]. **1884** Sargent *Forests of N. Amer.* 105, Black persimmon. Mexican persimmon. Chapote. **1886** Havard *Flora W. & S. TX for 1885* 523, Mexican Persimmon; the Chapote of the Mexicans. . . The black, globose fruit. . . [s]tains black everything it touches, and Mexicans use it to dye sheep skins. **1908** Britton *N. Amer. Trees* 787, Black persimmon. . . is also called Mexican persimmon. **1936** Whitehouse *TX Flowers* 94, Mexican Persimmon *(Diosporos texana)* is also called . . "chapote," and black persimmon. **1970** Correll *Plants TX* 1189, Texas or Mexican persimmon, black persimmon, chapote.

Mexican pheasant n Also *Mexican tree pheasant*
=chachalaca 1.

1923 U.S. Dept. Ag. *Farmers' Bulletin* 1375.36 **TX**, *Open seasons:* . . chachalaca or Mexican pheasant. . . Dec. 1–Jan. 31. **1940** Writers' Program *Guide TX* 28, The chachalaca, often called the Mexican pheasant, found in no other part of the United States, lives in the chaparral thickets along the Rio Grande. **1957** *AmSp* 32.185 **TX**, Mexican pheasant—Chachalaca. . . Mexican tree pheasant—Chachalaca.

Mexican piñon n Also *Mexican pinyon (pine)*
A **piñon** (here: *Pinus cembroides*).

1908 Britton *N. Amer. Trees* 14, *Pinus cembroides.* . . A low bushy tree of Arizona and adjacent Mexico, . . [it] is variously known as Mexican piñon or pinyon [etc]. **1938** Van Dersal *Native Woody Plants* 188, *Mexican piñon.* . . Wood used for fuel. **1951** *PADS* 15.27 **TX**, *Pinus cembroides.* . . Mexican piñon. **1975** Lamb *Woody Plants SW* 112, Mexican pinon. . . The needles are shorter [than those of *Pinus edulis*] and more often occur in bundles of three. **1976** Elmore *Shrubs & Trees SW* 19, *Mexican Pinyon.* . . Its seeds. . . are the largest of the pinyon nuts, reaching ½ to ¾ inch in size. **1979** Little *Checklist U.S. Trees* 190, *Mexican pinyon.* . . *Other common names* . . "Mexican pinyon pine."

Mexican plover n
An **upland plover** (here: *Bartramia longicauda*).

1957 *AmSp* 32.184 **LA**, Mexican plover—Upland plover.

Mexican poppy n Also *Mexican prickly poppy, ~ thorn poppy* chiefly SW, esp TX
A **prickly poppy** (here: *Argemone mexicana*).

1846 in 1962 U.S. Army Corps Topog. Engineers *Abert's NM Rept.* 35, The Mexican poppy was abundant. **1848** Emory *Notes Reconnoissance* 13 **seCO, swKS**, We find in the bottoms . . Mexican poppy. **1868** (1870) Gray *Field Botany* 49, *Mexican P[oppy].* . . Flowers yellow or yellowish, pretty large, in summer. **1900** Lyons *Plant Names* 44, *A[rgemone] mexicana.* . . Mexican Prickly-poppy, Mexican Poppy. **1936** Whitehouse *TX Flowers* 34, *Mexican Poppy* . . is a common weed . . in s. Southwest Texas. . . It is also called . . Mexican thorn poppy. . . The seeds of the Mexican poppy are valued for the painter's oil obtained from them. **1967** *DARE* Wildfl QR (Wills–Irwin) Pl.12B Inf **TX44**, Mexican prickly poppy. **1970** Correll *Plants TX* 664, *Mexican poppy.* Annual with bright yellow latex. **c1979** TX Dept. Highways *Flowers* 36, A yellow variety [of prickly poppy] is called the Mexican Poppy, and other colors range from lavender to rose. **1995** *Smithsonian* Jan 80 **Desert SW**, A few desert basins have been freckled with . . hot oranges of Mexican poppies.

Mexican primrose n
An **evening primrose a** (here: *Oenothera speciosa*).

1959 Munz–Keck *CA Flora* 948, *Oe[nothera] speciosa.* . . Cult. as "Mexican Primrose" and escaping; native of s. Tex. and . . along the Gulf. **1972** Brown *Wildflowers LA* 121, *Mexican Primrose.* . . is widely known in Louisiana as a buttercup in spite of its pink and white flowers. . . Widely distributed, forming conspicuous colonies along roadsides, ditch banks, and idle fields.

Mexican quail n SW
1 A **quail** such as the **bob-white**.

1923 Cook *50 Yrs.* 27, There were wild turkeys by the thousand; also Mexican quail.

2 also *Mexican blue:* =scaled quail.

1929 Dobie *Vaquero* 203 **SW**, *Tasajillo* (rat-tail cactus) . . in winter is bizarre and beautiful with a studding of red berries that are fancied by blue topknot Mexican quail and wild turkeys. **1957** *AmSp* 32.185 **CO**,

TX, Mexican quail—Scaled quail. **1967** *DARE* (Qu. Q7, *Names and nicknames for . . game birds*) Inf **TX5**, Mexican blues or scale quail.

3 =Gambel's quail.

1957 *AmSp* 32.185 **TX**, Mexican quail—Gamble's [sic] quail.

Mexican rail n
=Florida gallinule.

1957 *AmSp* 32.184 **LA**, Mexican rail—Common gallinule.

Mexican ring n
A children's game; see quot.

1968 *DARE* (Qu. EE16, *Hiding games that start with a special, elaborate method of sending the players out to hide*) Inf **CA94**, Mexican ring—a hiding game played by Mohave children in the village; all hide and then on signal run to the base while "it" tries to tag them.

Mexican sandburr n Also *Mexican burr* chiefly KS, OK
=puncture vine.

1930 OK Univ. Biol. Surv. *Pub.* 2.69, *Tribulus terrestris* . . Caltropbur. Mexican Sand-bur. **1966–70** *DARE* (Qu. S14, . . *Prickly seeds, small and flat, with two prongs at one end, that cling to clothing*) Inf **KS1**, Mexican sandburrs—other people here call them [=bullheads] that; **KS15**, Mexican sandburr—used to say "the thorns"; **OK18**, Mexican sandburrs or goatheads—look just like a goat's head; will even puncture tires; (Qu. S15, . . *Weed seeds that cling to clothing*) Inf **CA181**, Mexican sandburrs; **KS6**, Goatheads—they got three prongs on them. They're also called Mexican burrs; **KS12**, Mexican sandburrs—little things with three prongs that really stick.

Mexican sickness See Mexican B4

Mexican squealer n [See quot 1955] Cf squealer
A **tree duck** (here: *Dendrocygna bicolor*).

1923 U.S. Dept. Ag. *Misc. Circular* 13.38 **TX**, *Dendrocygna bicolor.* . . *Vernacular Names.* . . *In local use.* . . Mexican squealer. **1955** Lowery *LA Birds* 158, *Dendrocygna bicolor.* . . The common name is "Mexican squealer," which is appropriate on two counts: the call is a long, squealing whistle; and, by the first week of November, practically the entire Louisiana population has moved southward to southern Texas or Mexico. **1960** Peterson *Field Guide Birds TX* 30, Fulvous Tree Duck—*Dendrocygna bicolor* . . "Mexican Squealer".

Mexican standoff n
1 An impasse, deadlock; an impasse resolved by the backing down of one or both parties; a contest without a clear-cut victory for either side.

1891 *NY Sporting Times* (NY) 19 Sept 4/3, "Monk" Cline, who got a Mexican stand-off from Dave Rowe has signed with Louisville. **1904** *McClure's Mag.* Mar 557 **TX**, Boys, as fur as the coin goes, we're out an' injured; we jest made a 'Mexican stand-off'—lost our money, but saved our lives—and mighty lucky at that. **1944** Adams *Western Words* 99, *Mexican standoff*—Getting away alive from any serious difficulty. The Mexican has never had the reputation, among the cowboys, for being a sticker in a fight. They claim that, if he does not win quickly in a gun battle or if he finds much opposition, he leaves in a hurry. **1967** *DARE* (Qu. HH30, *Things that are nicknamed for different nationalities—for example, a 'Dutch treat'*) Inf **IL11**, Mexican standoff—when two people can't agree; **MI69**, Mexican standoff—when neither side is going to win; **TX33**, Mexican standoff—stalemate argument. **1969** *NY Rev. Books* 6 Nov 24, The attorneys . . have announced that they will not seek review. One can only guess the reasons that have motivated both sides to settle for a "Mexican standoff." Whatever they may be, they are surely linked to the unsatisfactory (to both sides) decision of the US Court of Appeals. **1973** *DARE* File **SW**, Mexican standoff. . . A confrontation that does not lead to an actual fight. **1990** *Springfield (MA) Union–News* 26 July 1 (*W3* File), Real estate brokers warn that the decline [in housing prices] may be a slight one because of a "Mexican standoff" between buyers waiting for prices to come down further and sellers reluctant to discount their properties.

2 By ext: see quot.

1969 *AmSp* 44.249, When two trains traveling in opposite directions on the same track are unable to stop before they collide, the collision is referred to as a . . *Mexican standoff.*

Mexican strawberry n
1 See **strawberry cactus**.

2 See **strawberry**.

Mexican sweat n
1 A card game; see quot 1987.

1969 *DARE* (Qu. DD35, . . *Card games*) Inf **TX**68, Mexican sweat—same as "red dog"; [**LA**37, Seven-card sweat]. **1986** *DARE* File **csTX,** A laborer about 30 yrs old says Mexican sweat is a card game very similar to poker. "It's real cut-throat." **1987** *Ibid* **OK,** Now . . I have actually seen the card game of Mexican sweat played by a father and his two small sons. The game is also known as "Don't peek." Each player gets seven cards face down on the table. The first player to be dealt turns one of his cards face up and bets that no one else can top that card. Then the next player turns up his cards until he has equalled or topped the first player. Then if he chooses, he can turn up one of his cards and bet that the player following him can't top that card, and so on until everybody has all seven cards face up. **1993** *NADS Letters* **csTX** (as of 1960s), *Mexican sweat* (more properly *Meskin sweat*) is a poker game, a variant of 7-card stud. . . The sweating part comes in as the player starts turning over cards until he has a card or a combination of cards that can beat the face up card on the deck. . . The game is very exciting because of the mystery involved in the players' not knowing what cards they have. There is no room for bluffing.

2 See quot 1986.

[**1966–67** *DARE* (Qu. DD37, . . *Table games played a lot by adults*) Infs **OK**25, **TX**27, Mexican dominoes.] **1986** *DARE* File **OK,** *Mexican sweat*—a domino game.

Mexican tea n

1 A **Jerusalem oak 1** (here: *Chenopodium ambrosioides*). Cf **Jesuit tea**

1830 Rafinesque *Med. Flora* 2.208, The *Ch[enopodium] ambrosioides* or Mexican tea, used in Europe for hemoptysis, and to help parturition. **1843** Torrey *Flora NY* 2.135, *Ambrina ambrosioides*. . . Mexican Tea. . . Common near New-York and along the Hudson. **1894** Coulter *Botany W. TX* 368, *C[henopodium] ambrosioides* . . Mexican tea. **1925** *Book of Rural Life* 6.3513, Mexican tea, a name for the common weed, *American wormseed*, whose leaves are sometimes used for making tea. **1944** AL Geol. Surv. *Bulletin* 53.96, Mexican tea . . prefers rich soil near houses and barns. . . Some people assert that sprigs of it laid on top of growing cabbages will keep worms off. **1971** Krochmal *Appalachia Med. Plants* 86, Mexican tea. . . In New Mexico, Spanish speaking people use a tea made of the leaves to encourage milk flow and to relieve post-delivery pains.

2 =**Mormon tea 1.** [See quots 1937, 1945]

1923 in 1925 Jepson *Manual Plants CA* 60, *Ephedra* . . Mexican Tea. Joint Pine. **1937** U.S. Forest Serv. *Range Plant Hdbk.* B73, Other local names [for the joint fir] include Brigham-tea, Mexican-tea [etc]. . . American Indians and Mexicans have long used decoctions of the stems as an alleged specific for certain ailments of the genito-urinary tract, and also as a cooling beverage. **1945** McAtee *Nomina Abitera* 7, Decoctions of these plants [=*Ephedra* spp] are used in the treatment of venereal diseases, a point recognized in the scientific name of one of them—*antisyphilitica*. Such medication and popular opinion of those in need of it are indicated in the vernacular names [including] Mexican tea. **1962** Balls *Early Uses CA Plants* 39, Of the seven species of Mexican Tea which are to be found in California, only one grows west of the Sierra Nevada. **1967** Harrington *Edible Plants Rocky Mts.* 356, Desert Tea, Mexican Tea. . . This plant has been extensively used by both the Indians and white people for making a tea. Sometimes it was taken as a tonic for its reputed medicinal effects, but many persons used it rather regularly by preference as a beverage. **1981** Benson–Darrow *Trees SW Deserts* 379, *Ephedra trifurca*. . . Mexican Tea.

3 A **pennyroyal** (here: *Hedeoma drummondii*).

1936 Whitehouse *TX Flowers* 121, *Mexican Tea (Hedeoma drummondii)*. . . A tea made from the foliage, either fresh or dried, is considered of value for its soothing effect.

4 A **croton** (here: *Croton monanthogynus*). Cf **prairie tea**

1951 *PADS* 15.35 **TX,** *Croton monanthogynus*. . . Mexican tea.

Mexican thistle n

1 =**buffalo burr.**

1914 Georgia *Manual Weeds* 368, *Buffalo Bur*. . . Mexican Thistle. . . The plant frequently becomes a tumbleweed, distributing its burs as it rolls before the winds.

2 A **button snakeroot 2** (here: *Eryngium heterophyllum*).

1970 Correll *Plants TX* 1166, *Eryngium heterophyllum* . . Mexican-thistle.

Mexican thorn poppy See **Mexican poppy**

Mexican toothache See **Mexican B4**

Mexican town n Also *Mexican flats, Mex* **chiefly TX, CO**

The section of a town or city inhabited predominantly by Mexicans or Mexican-Americans.

1930 *AmSp* 6.12 **West** [Sugar beet language], Townsmen and farmers refer to the foreign settlements, usually located near the *sugar towns,* as *The Mex,* and do not associate very much with these alien neighbors. **1956** Algren *Walk on the Wild Side* 18 **TX,** These three shanties . . made a kind of slum Alamo right in the middle of Mexican-town. **1967–70** *DARE* (Qu. C35, *Nicknames for the different parts of your town or city*) Infs **TX**29, 68, Mexican town; **CO**11, Mexican flats; (Qu. II25, *Names or nicknames for the part of a town where the poorer people, special groups, or foreign groups live*) Infs **CO**29, **TX**1, 3, 27, 68, 81, Mexican town; **CO**15, Mexican flats. **1969** O'Connor *Horse & Buggy West* 38 **AZ,** We were a lonely enclave thrust into what was called "Meskin Town"—Mexican Town—and separated from it by a high board fence.

Mexican tree pheasant See **Mexican pheasant**

‡Mexican twala-twala n Cf **filliloo bird**

See quot.

1966 *DARE* (Qu. CC17, *Imaginary animals or monsters that people . . tell tales about—especially to tease greenhorns*) Inf **WA**11, Mexican twala-twala—flies backwards to see only where it's been.

Mexican two-step See **Mexican B4**

Mexican white pine n

A **white pine** (here: *Pinus strobiformis*) native to Arizona, New Mexico, and Texas. Also called **limber pine 2, western white ~**

1908 Britton *N. Amer. Trees* 11, *Mexican White Pine*. . . This tree inhabits cañons and mountain sides. . . Its branches are slender and somewhat drooping. **1938** Van Dersal *Native Woody Plants* 193, *Mexican white pine*. . . Seeds completely shed by the middle of October. **1975** Lamb *Woody Plants SW* 110, Many of the Mexican white pines are of good enough form to be utilized in lumber manufacture. **1980** Little *Audubon Guide N. Amer. Trees W. Region* 290, "Mexican White Pine". . . The large seeds are consumed by wildlife and were eaten by southwestern Indians.

Mexican wild chicken n

=**chachalaca 1.**

1953 *AmSp* 28.279 **TX,** Mexican wild chicken—Chachalaca.

Mexican wood duck See **Mexican duck 1**

Mexican woodpecker n

1 The red-shafted **flicker** n^2 **1.**

1872 Coues *Key to N. Amer. Birds* 198, *Red-shafted* or *Mexican Woodpecker*. Wings and tail showing orange-red underneath, and the shafts of this color. **1880** *News & Press* (Cimarron NM) 23 Dec 1/4, The last member of this family is the red shafted or Mexican woodpecker . . the underparts lilac-brown with numerous circular black spots. **1957** *AmSp* 32.184 **NM,** Mexican woodpecker—Red-shafted flicker.

2 =**ladder-backed woodpecker 1.**

1957 Pough *Audubon W. Bird Guide* 167, *Ladder-backed Woodpecker*. . . (Mexican Woodpecker). **1960** Peterson *Field Guide Birds TX* 150, Ladder-Backed Woodpecker—*Dendrocopos scalaris*. . "Mexican Woodpecker." **1965** Herlan *NV Highway Bird Watcher* 35, *Ladder-backed Woodpecker*. . . Called . . "Mexican" Woodpecker. . . He presents quite a jaunty appearance with his bright sport cap.

Mexico n **OK** Cf **Old Mexico**

New Mexico.

1945 FWP *Lay My Burden Down* 115 (as of c1865) [Black], We come to a little place called Clayton, Mexico, where we camped a while and then went north. That place is in New Mexico now, but Old Master just called it Mexico. **1966** *DARE* FW Addit **OK**25, Generally, New Mexico is called "Mexico," and the country is called "Old Mexico." **1986** *DARE* File **OK,** *Mexico*—New Mexico. This is a very common usage in Oklahoma. **1993** *NADS Letters* **TX,** My friends at that time [=the 1960s] from Oklahoma were always confused when the rest of us referred to *Mexico*. They always wanted to know if we were saying *New Mexico* or *Old Mexico*. Mexico was Mexico, of course, to us, but obviously never to the Okies.

mezcal See **mescal**

mezquit(e) See **mesquite**

M.I.A. See **mutual**

Miami mist n

A **scorpionweed** (here: *Phacelia purshii*).

1847 Wood *Class-Book* 437, C[*osmanthus*] *Purshii*. . . Miami mist. **1935** (1943) Muenscher *Weeds* 377, *Phacelia Purshii*. . . Miami mist, Scorpion weed, a native annual, is locally common in gardens, grain fields, clover fields and waste places in the north central states. **1940** Steyermark *Flora MO* 442, *Miami mist*. . . Flowers numerous, blue or purplish or nearly white, widely open-faced. **1965** *Native Plants PA* 53, Phacelia purshii. Miami-mist.

mi-ander See **meander**

mib n Also *meb, mibbie, mibble, mibsie, mimb* scattered, but chiefly N Cent, NEast See Map Cf **mig, nib** n[2]

A playing marble, esp a small one; pl: any of var marble games.

1883 Newell *Games & Songs* 186, The lads whom we quote never used the word marbles, but *mibs.* "Let's play mibs." **1895** *DN* 1.398 seMI, cNY, *Mib:* a marble; the game is called "playing mibs," or more often simply *mibs;* no other term is used in Ithaca. **1949** *PADS* 11.24 CO, *Mib,* pl. *mibbies.* . . A marble. **1950** *WELS* WI (*Marbles . . small ones*) 9 Infs, Mibs; 1 Inf, Mimbs; (*Marbles . . cheap ones*) 2 Infs, (Clay) mibs; 1 Inf, Clay mebs; (*Marbles . . others*) 2 Infs, Mibs. **1951** *PADS* 15.67 cwNH (as of 1920s), *Mib.* . . Medium-sized clay marble. **1958** *PADS* 29.37 CT, IL, MA, WI, *Mibs.* **1965–70** *DARE* (Qu. EE6b, *Small marbles or marbles in general*) 58 Infs, chiefly Nth, N Midl, Mibs; IL51, Mibbies; CA15, Mibbles; (Qu. EE6c, *Cheap marbles*) Infs MI75, WI56, 77, Mibs. **1966–70** *DARE* Tape MI24, We would get to a level surface and make a hole about the width of our shoes. It would be shaped like the bottom of a rocking chair. There were different types of marbles used. We call the game mibs. . . The shooters would be used to shoot the marbles out of this so-called hole; MI115, We called 'em mibs instead of marbles. **1973** Ferretti *Marble Book* 48, *Mibs.* Object or target marbles. Also Mibbies, Mibsies, Miggs, and Miggles. **1973** Allen *LAUM* 1.404 Upper MW (as of c1950), *Mibs,* with variants *mibbles* and possibly *nibs,* may have a Northern orientation. **1976** *WI Acad. Rev.* Mar 8 seWI (as of 1920s), The most common marble, however, was produced by firing (heating) clay spheres about one-fourth inch in diameter formed in revolving drums. The dull gray globes were then painted with bright colors. These were the most numerous marbles, or "mibs," used in Milwaukee. *Ibid* 9, The most common game [of marbles] was simply called *Mibs.* To have a game of Mibs meant having a flat dirt surface on which was drawn with stick or finger a circle about eight to ten inches in diameter.

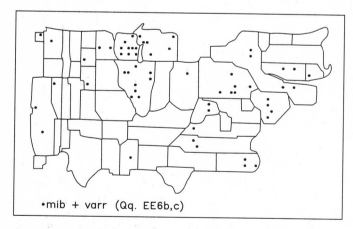

•mib + varr (Qq. EE6b,c)

mica cap n [See quot 1985]

An **inky cap** (here: *Coprinus micaceus*).

1975 Smith *Field Guide W. Mushrooms* 229, *Mica Cap.* . . The tawny to pale crust brown cap when young appearing as if sprinkled with fine sugar. **1981** Lincoff *Audubon Field Guide Mushrooms* 600, *Mica Cap.* . . Also known as the "Common Inky Cap." **1985** Weber–Smith *Field Guide S. Mushrooms* 231, *Mica Cap.* . . The veil, which appears to be composed of tiny particles of mica (and for which the species is named), is seldom obvious on caps large enough to harvest.

mice See **mouse** n A1

mice hawk See **mouse hawk 1a**

mice nut See **mouse nut**

mice pink n

=**garden catchfly.**

1896 *Jrl. Amer. Folkl.* 9.182 cnIL, *Silene armeria* . . mice pink. **1959** Carleton *Index Herb. Plants* 81, Mice-pink: *Silene armeria.*

micer n Pronc-sp *miser*

A mouser.

1892 *DN* 1.210 seMA, *Miser* [mɑɪzə]: mouser. "Her [a kitten's] mother was a dreadful good miser." **1968–70** *DARE* (Qu. J6, *A cat that catches lots of rats and mice . . "She's a good _____."*) Infs NY88, PA248, TN37, TX59, Micer.

mices See **mouse** n A2

mich See **meech**

Michaelmas daisy n [*Michaelmas* church festival celebrated Sept 29; so called from the period of bloom; *OED* 1785 →] chiefly Nth

An aster (*Aster* spp).

1848 in 1850 Cooper *Rural Hours* 105 NY, Violets . . grow there, with . . Michaelmas-daisies of several kinds, perhaps the coptis, or gold-thread, and three or four ferns. **1894** *Jrl. Amer. Folkl.* 7.91 NY, *Asters* of any kind, Michaelmas daisies. **1896** *Ibid* 9.191, *Aster Novae-Angliae,* . . Michaelmas daisy, . . Sulphur Grove, Ohio. **1914** Georgia *Manual Weeds* 434, *Aster Tradescanti.* . . Michaelmas Daisy. . . *Time of bloom:* August to October. **1938** Madison *Wild Flowers OH* 150, *Aster ericoides.* . . Michaelmas Daisy. **1950** *WELS,* 1 Inf, WI, Michaelmas daisies . . a kind of aster. **1963** Craighead *Rocky Mt. Wildflowers* 195, *Aster conspicuus.* . . Michaelmas Daisy. . . Asters and daisies (*Erigeron*) are difficult to distinguish. Usually the asters are later-blooming, larger, and have several series of green bracts surrounding the head. *Ibid* 196, Because they are late-blooming, asters have been called Michaelmas Daisies and Christmas Daisies. **1966–70** *DARE* (Qu. S25, . . *The small wild chrysanthemum-like flowers . . that bloom in fields late in the fall*) Infs IA25, IN38, OR4, RI10, SC36, WA6, 28, Michaelmas daisy (*or* daisies); MI45, OH95, ['mɑɪkəl,məs] daisy; LA17, [,mɑɪkəlməs 'deɪzɪ]; WA3, [mikəlmæs] daisy; (Qu. S26e, *Other wildflowers not yet mentioned;* not asked in early QRs) Inf OR10, Michaelmas daisies. **1966–67** *DARE* Wildfl QR Pl.241 Inf AR45, Wild mickelson [sic] daisy; Pl.245 Inf WA12, Michaelmas daisy; Pl.246B Inf WA12, White Michaelmas daisy; Pl.242A Inf WA30, Michaelmas daisy. **1973** Hitchcock–Cronquist *Flora Pacific NW* 488, *Aster;* Michaelmas-daisy. . . Fl[owers] mostly mid- or late summer and fall.

michael tea n [Cf *mickle* (at **myrtle** n[1])] Cf **mickleberry**

Prob an infusion made from a **wax myrtle** (here: *Myrica cerifera*).

1937 in 1977 *Amer. Slave Suppl. 1* 1.41 AL, Dyed wid copperas mixed wid odder ingre'ents, sich as michael tea. [**1974** Morton *Folk Remedies* 99 SC, *Myrica cerifera.* . . (*Current use:*) Leaves often steeped for "tea," drunk as a beverage; also taken as a remedy.]

micher See **meech 2**

Michigan n Usu |'mɪʃəgən|; for varr see **A** below

A Forms.

1822 Worcester in 1938 *AmSp* 13.263, Michigan—Mish-e-gan'. **1829** in 1938 *AmSp* 13.264, [Letter of Edward Everett in resp to Worcester:] Michigan is accented on the first syllable with a half accent on the last. . . Mitch-e-gan is sometimes heard. **1845** in 1944 *ADD* MI, Michigan. **1942** *Ibid* WV, Michigan. . . |'mɪ|-. **1968** *DARE* Tape TN26, Michigan ['mɪtʃəgən]. **1968** *DARE* FW Addit KY, Michigan ['mɪtʃ-]. **1995** *DARE* File ce,seIA, My father and his brothers pronounce "Michigan" as ['mɪʃəkən].

B Sense.

See **Michigan hot (dog).**

Michigan basement n Also *Michigan cellar*

See quots.

1969 *DARE* (Qu. D18, *The part of the house below the ground floor*) Inf MI100, A dirt floor cellar was called "Michigan cellar." **1977** *WI State Jrl.* (Madison) 2 Oct sec 5 3/3 MI, The deep "Michigan basement" is designed for five-foot snows. **1995** *NADS Letters* seMI, *Michigan basement.* . . My father (a life-long Michigan resident born in 1919) explains that it is a partial basement, just large enough for a furnace room. He says that these basements were usually added to already existing houses and were generally dug out by hand. To gain access to the basement from inside the house, people installed small service stairways or trap door and ladder arrangements.

Michigan grayling n

A **grayling** (here: *Thymallus arcticus tricolor*).
  1879 U.S. Natl. Museum *Bulletin* 14.58, *Thymallus tricolor. . . Michigan Grayling.* Northern portion southern peninsula of Michigan. **1887** (1888) Jordan *Sci. Sketches* 44, In several streams in northern Michigan and in Montana occurs a dwarfish variety of this species, known to anglers as the Michigan Grayling (*Thymallus signifer ontariensis*). **1902** Jordan–Evermann *Amer. Fishes* 222, The Michigan grayling is known from various streams in the southern peninsula of Michigan and from Otter Creek, near Keweenaw, in the northern peninsula. **1935** Pratt *Manual Vertebrate Animals* 49, Michigan grayling. . . Dorsal fin spotted and with rose colored and dark stripes. **1946** Dufresne *AK's Animals* 215, In the Michigan and Montana graylings (*Thymallus tricolor* and *montanus*) . . , the spawning season is in April or May. **1947** Hubbs–Lagler *Fishes Gt. Lakes* 44, *Thymallus signifer tricolor.* . . Originally in the Otter River of the Lake Superior drainage in northern Michigan (where extant until a few years ago). . . Now extinct in the Great Lakes basin. . . "Michigan grayling".

Michigan holly n

A **winterberry** (here: *Ilex verticillata*).
  1938 Van Dersal *Native Woody Plants* 344, Michigan holly (*Ilex verticillata*). **1945** MI Ag. Exper. Sta. *Technical Bulletin* 201.35, The following are not to be cut or removed without the consent of the owner: trailing arbutus, . . Michigan holly. . . The vending of wild plants has become an item of considerable importance in some of the larger cities. . . Offered for sale . . in the fall [is] . . the winterberry (so-called "Michigan holly"). **1952** Taylor *Plants Colonial Days* 96, Winterberry—*Ilex verticillata.* . . Other common names include . . Michigan holly.

Michigan hot (dog) n Also *Michigan*

  c1965 Randle *Cookbooks* (Ask Neighbor) 1.38 **OH**, *Michigan hot dogs.* . . Simmer [sauce containing ground beef, chili sauce, etc] for 1 hr., Place on hot dog in a bun and add a little raw chopped onion. **1967** *DARE* FW Addit **nNY**, Michigan hots—hot dog and chili sauce. Sometimes "Michigans" or "hots."

Michigan pine n Also *Michigan white pine*

A **white pine** (here: *Pinus strobus*).
  1873 Walling *Atlas MI* 20, Michigan pine . . is what is known as white pine, and of this there are several varieties. **1968–69** *DARE* (Qu. T17, . . *Kinds of pine trees;* not asked in early QRs) Inf **MI**79, Michigan pine; **MI**110, Michigan white pine.

miching vbl n See **meech 2**

miching ppl adj See **meeching**

Mick n Also *Mick(e)y* [Abbrs for *Michael;* perh also in ref to the *Mc* of many Irish surnames]

1 An Irishman; a man of Irish descent. **chiefly Nth, N Midl, esp NEast** See Map Cf **paddy**
  1856 *Butte Rec.* (Oroville, Calif.) 20 Sep. 3/3 *(DA),* One of the 'bucks' jerked something from his belt . . and made for a Mick. **1894** (1899) Ford *Peter Stirling* 369 **NYC**, Fortunately it's a Mick regiment, so we needn't worry over who was killed. **1896** *DN* 1.421 **cNY**, Mick: an Irishman. **1897** Barrère–Leland *Slang* 2.49, *Mickey* (American), a com-

mon word for an Irishman, the same as Paddy. **1918** Griffin *Ballads Regiment* 34, But he always loved a soldier be he "Chummy", "Krout" or "Mick". **1929** Ellis *Ordinary Woman* 202 **CO** (as of early 1900s), But soon George starts to complain that it was run by a bunch of 'red necks,' 'chaws,' 'flannel mouths,' 'Micks'—all names for Irishmen. **1940** [see **kike**]. **1941** [see **Mike 1**]. **1942** [see **Mike 1**]. **1946** *Sat. Eve. Post* 3 Aug 48, The people of Pittsburgh . . in earlier days were somewhat ungenerously thought of as Polaks, Hunkies, Wops, and Micks. **1962** Atwood *Vocab. TX* 73, Irishman. . . Very scattered: *Mick* . . and *Mike.* **1965–70** *DARE* (Qu. HH28, *Names and nicknames . . for people of foreign background: Irish*) 138 Infs, **chiefly Nth, N Midl, West**, Mick; **CO**23, **NY**60, **PA**126, Mickey; (Qu. LL26b, . . *'Entirely'—for example, "He's Irish _____."*) Inf **ME**19, Full-blooded Mick; [**NM**9, As Mickey's mother].

2 A Roman Catholic. **scattered, but esp PA** See Map
  1924 Marks *Plastic Age* 201 **NEng**, I suppose you refer to . . my one mick friend, although he isn't Irish. **1965–70** *DARE* (Qu. CC4, . . *Nicknames . . for various religions or religious groups*) 15 Infs, **scattered, but esp PA**, Micks; **PA**110, 197, Mickeys. **1968** *DARE* FW Addit **NY**45, Protestants used to call Catholics "micks."

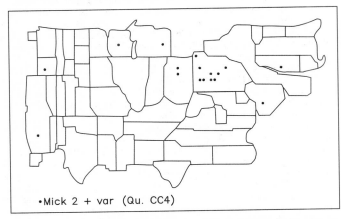

•Mick 2 + var (Qu. CC4)

3 usu as *mickey:* =**white potato. NY, esp NYC** Cf **Irish potato**
  1943 Mitchell *McSorley* 18 **NYC**, Sometimes they roast mickies in the gutter fires. **1957** *Sat. Eve. Post Letters* **Manhattan NYC** (as of c1918), *Mickies:* potatoes cooked in an open fire and eaten with relish, black, burned skin and all. **1967–69** *DARE* (Qu. I9, . . *Names [including nicknames] for potatoes*) Infs **NY**34, 36, 37, 79, 90, 92, Mickey(s); **NY**176, Micks. **1977** *NY Times* (NY) 8 Mar sec C 23 **Long Is. NY**, Once a year at the Wheeler Avenue School, . . the students honor the noble tradition of vacant lots, hot coals, and potatoes roasting to charred perfection. The celebration is called "Mickey Day," a mickey being the hot potato. *Ibid* **NYC** (as of 1920s), "I grew up in the Inwood section of Manhattan. We had some outcroppings of rocks where we'd hide . . and roast potatoes or chestnuts or sweet potatoes." "I grew up in Greenwich Village and we never had roast mickeys," said one mother.

Mickey n[1]

1 See **Mick**.

2 A sparrow.
  1921 *DN* 5.109 **CA**, *Mickey.* . . A sparrow.

mickey n[2] [Var of *miggey* (at **mig**)]

A playing marble.
  1957 *Sat. Eve. Post Letters* **neKS**, Just as boys would appear some spring day, each equipped with a bag of mickeys and aggies, so would each girl have her rubber ball, or ball and jacks. **1965** *DARE* Tape **NY**245, They used to call marbles "mickeys." **1967** *DARE* (Qu. EE6b, *Small marbles or marbles in general*) Inf **OR**6, Mickeys. **1973** Allen *LAUM* 1.404 (as of c1950), *Marbles.* . . mickies [1 inf, **ND**].

mickey n[3]

A children's bat-and-ball game; see quot.
  1977 *NY Times* (NY) 6 July 29/5 **NYC**, It [=a spaldeen or rubber ball] is used for all the old games and for the new ones, too, such a[s] "Mickey,"[*] which, as explained by the gang at P.S. 172 . . is an intricate form of stickball-baseball. In "Mickey," the pitcher stands behind the batter. Both face a wall, preferably brick. The pitcher throws the ball at the wall and as it bounces back, the batter swings. If he misses, it's an

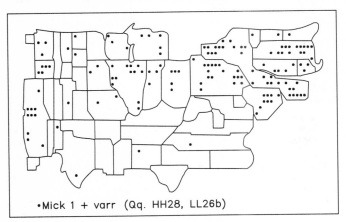

•Mick 1 + varr (Qq. HH28, LL26b)

out. If he tips it, it's an out. Two outs and the next batter comes up. Why is it called "Mickey?" Well nobody seems to know for sure.

mickle See **myrtle** n[1]

mickleberry n [*mickle* (at **myrtle** n[1])]
A **wax myrtle** (here: *Myrica cerifera*).
 1974 Morton *Folk Remedies* 99 **SC**, "Mickleberry". . . *Myrica cerifera.* [*Ibid* 100, Leaves and fruits used for flavoring soups and have been used as a substitute for hops. . . The fresh fruits are boiled in water to release the greenish wax.]

Micky See **Mick**

Micmac potato n Cf **Indian potato a**
=**groundnut B1.**
 1931 Clute *Common Plants* 30, A more famous potato is the mic-mac potato (*Apios tuberosa*) whose tubers were undoubtedly the first potatoes to be sent to Europe from our country. The Indians called this plant *Sagabon* and from this Sag Harbor, on long [*sic*] Island, is said to have derived its name. **1959** Carleton *Index Herb. Plants* 81, Mic-mac-potato: *Apios tuberosa.*

midaddy n Cf **granddaddy 5, medaddy-bush**
A **bullfrog 1** or similar frog.
 1966 *DARE* (Qu. P22, *Names or nicknames for a very large frog that makes a deep, loud sound*) Inf **FL**7, Midaddies [mɪˈdædiz].

Midas tree n
=**golden shower.**
 1929 Neal *Honolulu Gardens* 142, Golden shower, Indian laburnum (*Cassia fistula* . .). . . One of the most beautiful flowering trees in Honolulu is the golden shower or "Midas tree."

middle n **chiefly Sth, S Midl** Cf **middlebuster 1**
The ridge or strip of ground between rows of a crop.
 1825 in **1829** *S. Agriculturist* 2.258 **SC**, The balks, or "middles," are then to be flushed up, either with shovel, skimmer, or double iron mould-board ploughs, according to the state of the weather. **1829** in **1910** Commons *Doc. Hist. Amer. Industrial Soc.* 1.238 **swMS**, Two Ploughs breaking middles in Popular [*sic*] tree cut. **1847** in **1927** Jones *FL Plantation Rec.* 242, 13 [slaves] plowing out middles in brickyard [field]. **1902** *DN* 2.239 **sIL**, Middles. . . The balks between rows in *barring off* a crop. Hence to *bust out* or *split* the middles is to plow the balks, throwing the earth back to the row. **1903** *DN* 2.320 **seMO**, Middles. . . In expression bust out the middles. **1906** *DN* 3.121 **sIN**, Middles. . . Corn row ridges. "He's bustin out middles to plant corn." **1907** *DN* 3.224 **nwAR, sIL**, Middles. **1931** Randolph *Ozarks* 68, I seed him an' his least chaps a-bustin' out middles down in ol' man Price's bottom t'other ev'nin'. **1946** *PADS* 6.20 **eNC** (as of 1900–10), Middle. . . The ridge of earth made between two rows of corn, cotton, etc., by throwing a furrow from each of the adjoining rows. Pamlico. Common. **1959** Faulkner *Mansion* 49 **MS**, Nor did he even count off the years. . . He simply trod them behind him into oblivion beneath the heavy brogan shoes in the cotton middles behind the mule which drew the plow. **c1960** *Wilson Coll.* **csKY**, Middle. . . The area left between corn rows when furrows have been turned to the rows on each side in laying by corn; called the *balk* in western North Carolina. **1967** Key *Tobacco Vocab.* 38 **TN**, The tobacco grows on each side . . and you just bust that middle out; **MO**, The middles of that crop should be busted; **GA, NC**, Bust(ing) the middle. **1986** Pederson *LAGS Concordance* **Gulf Region**, 11 infs, (The) middle; 1 inf, The middle = furrow; 2 infs, Bust the middle (up); 1 inf, Bust the middle out; 4 infs, (The) middles—between the rows; 3 infs, Middles; 1 inf, Bust middles—of plowing; 1 inf, Run the middles—in plowing; 1 inf, Running middles—plowing between cotton rows; 1 inf, Sweep out the middles—of cotton and corn; 1 inf, Grass grows up in the middles; 1 inf, There [*sic*] several different plows you could bust out the middles with; 1 inf, Middles = furrows; 1 inf, Middles—rows in cotton cultivation.

middlebuster n
1 also *middlebreaker, middleburster, middle plow, middlesplitter, middler:* A double-moldboard plow that throws earth to both sides; hence, by back-formation, v *middlebust* to use such a plow. **chiefly Sth, TX** See Map Cf **bust** v **1, buster 4**
 1887 in **1893** Mansur & Tebbetts *Genl. Cat.* D 86 **MS**, The Sunset Middlebreaker is a number one Plow for center furrowing. **1889** *Ibid* **AR**, I tried the No. 10 Deere Mansur "middle splitter" as soon as I got it home. . . One man and two mules can do as much with middle buster

as two men and four mules with turning plow. **1907** (**1910**) Hunt *Forage Crops* 352, By means of a middle 'buster,' which is a double mold board plow. **1944** Clark *Pills* 283 **Sth**, In the warerooms or crowded along the aisles in the stores themselves were the assembled implements such as middle busters, turning plows [etc]. **1950** Faulkner *Stories* 17 **MS**, They were running a middle buster now, his brother holding the plow straight while he handled the reins. **1952** *Clarke Co. Democrat* (Grove Hill AL) 7 Aug 8/6 (Mathews Coll.), For Sale. . . one 2-horse middle burster. **1965–70** *DARE* (Qu. L18, *Kinds of plows*) 79 Infs, **chiefly Sth, TX**, Middlebuster; **NC**68, Middle plow; **NC**6, Middlesplitter; **FL**17, Middler; **LA**8, Walking middlebuster plow; (Qu. L25, *The implement used to clean out weeds and loosen the earth between rows of corn*) Infs **MS**66, **MO**9, **NC**12, **TX**38, 57, Middlebuster. **1967** *DARE* Tape **TX**49, Laying off ground just use one [animal]; breaking, flat breaking, use two; middlebuster, two. **1969** *SC Market Bulletin* 24 July 3, No. 10 John Deere middle buster-plow, $5. *Ibid* 11 Sept 3, Garden tractor . . with turn plow cultivator and middle buster $150. **1972** GA Dept. Ag. *Farmers Market Bulletin* 25 Oct 1/4, Cotton stalks should not just be mowed and harrowed, but uprooted with a middlebuster, subsoiler, peanut plow or bottom plow. **1986** Pederson *LAGS Concordance* **Gulf Region**, 168 infs, **esp Missip Delta**, Middlebuster(s); 3 infs, **c,ceLA, swMS**, Middlesplitter; 2 infs, **nwMS, cTX**, Middlebreaker(s); 1 inf, **seLA**, Middlebreaker—attachment for Georgia stock; 2 infs, **nwGA, cTX**, Middlebust [*LAGS* Ed: infinitive]; 1 inf, **csTX**, To middlebust up the land; 1 inf, **nwLA**, Middlebusted.

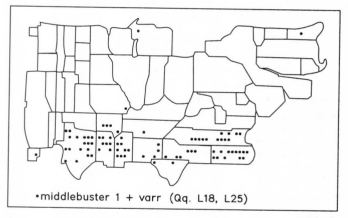

•middlebuster 1 + varr (Qq. L18, L25)

2 Transf: a person's nose.
 1968 *DARE* (Qu. X14, *Joking words for the nose*) Inf **GA**17, If it's big, it's a middlebuster.

middleday n *esp freq among Black speakers* Cf **middlenight**
Noon.
 1922 Gonzales *Black Border* 78 **sSC, GA coasts** [Gullah], W'en middleday come, me en' all dem todduh man . . gone to de Jew fuh buy bittle [=vittles]. *Ibid* 313 [Gullah glossary], *Middleday*—midday, noon. **1928** Peterkin *Scarlet Sister Mary* 246 **SC** [Gullah], De day is young, Si May-e. It ain' middle-day yet. **1981** Pederson *LAGS Basic Materials*, 1 inf, **nwGA**, Middle day; other people call middle day "noon." [Inf Black]

middleman n
1 In marble play: a large marble placed at the center of a ring or of a square whose corners are formed using four marbles; a game in which players try to knock this center marble out of the ring. **Sth, S Midl** See Map on p. 588 Cf **middler 1**
 1909 *DN* 3.349 **eAL, wGA**, The marble in the center of the ring. . . Called middle-man. **1915** *DN* 4.185 **swVA**, Middle-man. . . The marble in the center of the ring. **c1960** *Wilson Coll.* **csKY**, Middle man. . . The big marble in the center in some marble games. **1965–70** *DARE* (Qu. EE6a, . . *Different kinds of marbles—the big one that's used to knock others out of the ring*) Inf **AR**47, Middleman or king marble—the one in the center; **AR**51, The big one's the middleman in the center of the ring; **GA**9, Extra big one in the middle is the middleman; **GA**44, 72, **NC**35, **TN**16, **TX**35, Middleman; (Qu. EE6d, *Special marbles*) Inf **KY**40, Middleman; **LA**12, The middleman—it sits in the middle of the ring; **TN**14, Middleman—large marble in center of ring; (Qu. EE7, . . *Kinds of marble games*) Infs **AR**47, 51, **LA**12, Middleman; **VA**13, In middleman, you played for points. **1967–69** *DARE* Tape **KY**41, If you shot back here from your taw line . . and shot this middle marble out,

there was one on each corner and one in center, and we call that the middleman; **TX**49, [Inf:] You'd have a square about that big . . [with a] marble here, marble here, marble here. [FW:] In each corner. [Inf:] The middleman . . you knock that middleman, there's one game. **1970** Hyatt *Hoodoo* 1.261 **cwFL** (as of c1935) [Black], He picks up de [diamond] ring an' goes in de kitchen an' mix up some wheat dough right quick an' he *bobbled* it up in dere somepin de size of a *marble of a middle-man*—dey used to have middlemen fo' marbles. **1983** *MJLF* 9.1.47 **ceKY**, *Middle man* . . object marble placed in the middle of the square. **1986** Pederson *LAGS Concordance,* 1 inf, **swGA**, Middle man—marble in the ring.

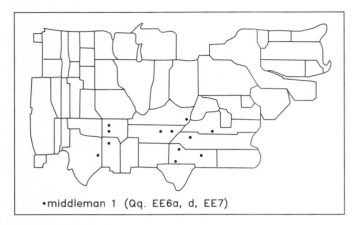

•middleman 1 (Qq. EE6a, d, EE7)

2 The middle finger. Cf **longman**

1987 *NADS Letters* **cUT**, [From a children's song, "Thumbkin Says":] Middle-man says, "I'll dance."

middlenight n Cf **middleday**
Midnight.

1922 Gonzales *Black Border* 313 **sSC, GA coasts** [Gullah glossary], *Middlenight*—midnight. **1937** Heyward *Madagascar* 169 **sSC coast** [Black], At "fus daa'k," "middle night," and "day clean" Cudjo would emerge from the watchman's house and fire his musket.

middle plow See **middlebuster 1**

middler n

1 In marble play: =**middleman 1**. chiefly **Sth, S Midl**

1890 *DN* 1.24 **KY**, Words used in playing at marbles: One may "knock," . . or "plump" the "middler" (middle marble) from "taw." **1909** *DN* 3.349 **eAL, wGA**, *Middler*. . . The marble in the center of the ring. **1916** *DN* 4.345 **TN**, *Middler*. . . The large marble in the middle of the ring. **1955** *PADS* 23.25 **cwTN**, *Middler (middleman)*. . . The center marble, usually larger than the others, of a five-marble square. **1965–70** *DARE* (Qu. EE6a, . . *Different kinds of marbles—the big one that's used to knock others out of the ring*) Infs **AL**3, 29, **AR**28, **IL**126, **IN**32, **MS**30, **PA**11, Middler; (Qu. EE6d, *Special marbles*) Inf **AR**39, Middler—the marble in the center, a big marble; (Qu. EE7, . . *Kinds of marble games*) Inf **KY**36, Middler—make a square ring, one to one and a half feet square, with a smaller marble in each corner and a big one, the middler, in the center; players stand ten feet back and knock out the middler by pitching or tossing the toy. **1966** *DARE* Tape **AL**3, And then this middler, always a big marble. If you knocked the middler from taw, why, you got the game. **1978** Massey *Bittersweet Country* 139 **Ozarks**, He'd get anybody to play marbles with him, a game that had five marbles, one in each corner and one in the middle. If you knocked the middle one out, you won. . . And he just loved to be the first one to have done it. He'd say, "I got a middler."

2 See **middlebuster 1**.

middlesex adj [Prob orig in allusion to *Middlesex* Co. in Connecticut or Massachusetts]
See quot 1975.

1908 Wasson *Home from Sea* 229 **ME**, The plain, common, middle-sex, every-day run of folks ain't always . . going to stand bein' spit on and stomped on. **1975** Gould *ME Lingo* 180, *Middlesex*—Average, ordinary. A *middlesex* kind of dog is half conjecture and half something else. A *middlesex* day is seasonable, but nothing to cheer about. A *middlesex* person is acceptable, but not the *finest kind*.

middlesplitter n

1 See **middlebuster 1**.

2 A heavy fall of rain.

1991 Still *Wolfpen Notebooks* 92 **sAppalachians**, The rain went around to the north, then to the south. Then it come one of these middle-splitters.

middling adj Also sp *midling* Cf **fair to middling**
Of one's health: fair, tolerable, so-so.

1859 (1968) Bartlett *Americanisms* 269, "How are you, to-day?" "Wall, I'm pretty middlin', jest so as to be knockin' around." **1872** in 1983 *PADS* 70.42 **cePA**, The afternoon we stopped at Aaron Burgess' found them all middling. **1893** Shands *MS Speech* 45, *Middling*. . . In moderately good health, used mostly by negroes and illiterate whites. *Tollible* has about the same meaning and is a corruption of *tolerable*. **1899** (1912) Green *VA Folk-Speech* 280, *Middling*. . . Not in good health, yet not very unwell. **1906** *DN* 3.146 **nwAR**, *Middlin'*. . . Pretty well. "How are you?" "I'm just middlin', thank you." **1927** *DN* 5.475 **Ozarks**, *Middling*. . . Tolerable. "How's th' ol' woman, Gabe?" "Oh, she's middlin'—jes' fair t' middlin'." **1927** Adams *Congaree* 94 **cSC** [Black], Is you well? . . Middlin', is you hear de news? **1939** *AmSp* 14.264 **IN**, Ill health or just 'puniness' is indicated by such expressions as 'jest tol'able only,' 'middlin',' 'fair to middlin'.' **1943** *LANE* Map 497 (*Pretty well*) **scattered NEng**, In answer to the casual greeting, 'How are you?' or 'How are you feeling?' . . *middling, kind of [middling]*. **1946** *PADS* 5.30 **VA**, *Middling*. . . Fair, in answer to "how are you?"; common everywhere. **1950** *PADS* 13.18 **cTX**, *Middling*. . . Often fair to middling. Both expressions are felt to be derived from the grading of cotton into middling, fair to middling, etc. **1967** *DARE* (Qu. X52, . . *A person . . who had been sick was looking* _____) Inf **MI**49, Fairly middlin'. **1990** Cavender *Folk Med. Lexicon* 27 **sAppalachians**, *Midlin*—not feeling well, but feeling very sick.

middling adv
Moderately, fairly.

1765 (1942) Bartram *Diary of a Journey* 31 **S Atl**, Travailed over many swamps & bridg[es] & some midling high ground. *Ibid* 32, Ye land . . is hilly & midling good. **1848** Lowell *Biglow* 27 '**Upcountry**' **MA**, Mister Sawin, sir, you're middlin' well now, be ye? **1872** Schele de Vere *Americanisms* 505, The Scotch-Irish in the valley of the Alleghanies . . speak of a man as *middling smart*. **1874** (1895) Eggleston *Circuit Rider* 91 **IN** (as of early 19th cent), He felt in his own mind "middlin' certain," . . he would be saved. **1899** (1912) Green *VA Folk-Speech* 280, *Middling*. . . Tolerably; moderately. **1903** Wasson *Cap'n Simeon's Store* 190 **eME**, Some days I'd r'ally commence to feel kind o' middling smart. **1929** Sale *Tree Named John* 125 **MS**, "Is you feelin' well t'day, Sis Betsey?" "Middlin' well, Sis Em'ly, middlin'." **1930** *AmSp* 6.98 **cNY** [Erie Canal expressions], *Middling-old:* Middle-aged. "It ain't as if I was even middling-old." **1943** *LANE* Map 497, 1 inf, **cnCT**, 'Twas middling still this morning. **1952** Brown *NC Folkl.* 565, Middling peart. . . Fairly well. . . Illiterate. **1974** *AmSp* 49.63 **seME** (as of c1900), He was middling smart.

middling n Also sp *midling*

1 The middle part of a side of meat, esp of salt pork or bacon. chiefly **Sth, S Midl**

1777 in 1875 VA *Calendar State Papers* 1.288, 9338 lbs Bakin [=bacon] in hams, midlings, shoulders, &c. **1804** in 1956 Eliason *Tarheel Talk* 284 **cnNC**, One Midlin of bacon. **1844** Thompson *Major Jones's Courtship* 58 **GA**, Some big-foot fellers lay sprawl'd out on the benches, quiet as a midlin of meat. **1899** (1912) Green *VA Folk-Speech* 280, *Middling*. . . That part of a hog that lies between the ham and the shoulder; a side of bacon. **1903** *DN* 2.320 **seMO**, *Middlings*. . . Sides of bacon. **1907** *DN* 3.233 **seMO, nwAR**, *Middlings*. . . Sides of bacon. **1909** *DN* 3.400 **nwAR**, *Middling of meat*. . . Pork middlings. **1923** *DN* 5.214 **swMO**, *Middlin'*. . . A side of meat, bacon. **1939** *Hall Coll.* **eTN**, We cleaned it [=a bear] and cut it up and cut the middlin's out of it just the same as we was a-cuttin' up a hog. **1953** *Ibid* **wNC**, We hung middlin's of bear up in the house for seasoning. **1966** *DARE* Tape **AL**1, We had some big ol' pieces [of sowbelly]; we used to call them middlings. **1976** Ryland *Richmond Co. VA* 373, *Middling*—part of the hog between ham and shoulder.

2 also pl; also *middling meat,* ~ *bacon*, and varr: Salt pork, bacon. chiefly **Sth, S Midl** See Map Cf **side meat**

c1770 in 1833 Boucher *Glossary* 1 **MD**, But neither *clabber,* with *molasses* sweet,/ . . / Nor *middling,* garnish'd all with dainties nice;/ . . / My palate can regale. **1837** in 1972 Hilliard *Hog Meat* 39 **GA**, Fryed middlin, cornbread, and coffee. **1840** *S. Lit. Messenger* 6.385 **Sth,** This anniversary she is in the habit of celebrating by a dinner of fried middling and ash-cake. **1845** in 1952 Green *Samuel Maverick* 303 **TX,** Do you think it best to get midlins bacon, or Pork here? **1906** *DN* 3.146 **nwAR,** *Middlin'*. . . Pork. "I'll take two bits' worth of that middlin'." **1909** *DN* 3.349 **eAL, wGA,** *Middlin(g)*. . . Side-meat, side of bacon. Universal. Sometimes *middlin(g)-meat* is used. **1927** *AmSp* 2.360 **cwWV,** *Middlings* . . side meat from a hog; used only in the plural. "Have you any middlings for sale?" **1935** Glasgow *Vein of Iron* 58 **wVA,** She must remember before she went to bed to bait a trap with middling rind. **1941** *LANE* Map 301 *(Salt pork)* 4 infs, **sNH,** Middlings. **1946** *PADS* 5.29 **VA,** *Middlin, middlin meat* . . .: Salt pork; common everywhere. **1949** Kurath *Word Geog.* 39, *Middlin(s)* and *middlin meat* are the regular designations for salt pork throughout the South and the South Midland. These terms have gained currency as far north as the Pennsylvania line. **1962** Atwood *Vocab. TX* 62, For the sides of pork preserved in salt, usually at home. . . *Middlin(s)* (17 oc[currences out of c270 infs]). **1965–70** *DARE* (Qu. H38, . . *Words for bacon [including joking ones]*) 16 Infs, **chiefly S Midl,** Middling (meat); **KY**74, **WV**8, 12, 13, Middlin(s); **SC**46, Middling bacon; **KY**85, Middlings. **1969** *DARE* FW Addit **cKY,** Middling meat—meat from sides of a hog, salted but not smoked. **1994** NC Lang. & Life Project *Dial. Dict. Lumbee Engl.* 8 **seNC,** *Middlin' meat*. . . Homemade bacon.

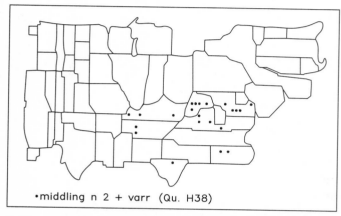

•middling n 2 + varr (Qu. H38)

3 Fig: someone or something of only average quality. [Prob transf from *middlings* medium-sized particles of grain, or *middling* the std grade of cotton against which other grades are measured]
1916 *DN* 4.277 **NE,** *Middlin'*. . . Used in the expression, "How are you?" "O, among the middlin's." **1940** Harris *Folk Plays* 6 **NC,** Tryin' to get in with respectable folks this late day, the old rusty middlin'. *Ibid* 293, Middlin', a cheap person; from "middling" or mediocre cotton.

middling bacon, middling meat See **middling** n 2

midge n

1 Std: any of numerous non-biting dipterous insects of var families, but esp of the family Chironomidae. For other names of the latter see **blind mosquito, bloodworm 2, chizzywink, corn fly, cow ~ 2, crazy ~, green ~ 3, lake ~ 2, marsh ~ 2, midget 2, minge, moth fly 2, nit** n **1, no-see-um 2, punkie, sand fly, trout ~, water mosquito**
2 also *midgie*: A biting dipterous insect: either a **black fly** or a **punkie** (here: family Ceratopogonidae). **chiefly NEast** Cf **midget 1, minge, nit** n 1
1842 [see **no-see-um 1**]. **1852** Harris *Treatise Insects* 483 **NEng,** They [=black flies] are followed, however, by swarms of midges, or sand-flies . . , called no-see-'em by the Indians of Maine, on account of their minuteness. **1909** Smith *Insect Friends* 167, The small black flies, usually called "midges," are not content to attack only the exposed parts of the body. **1950** *WELS (A very tiny fly that you can hardly see but that stings sharply)* 3 Infs, **WI,** Midges. **1954** Borror–DeLong *Intro. Insects* 592, Biting Midges. . . are very small, but because of their blood-sucking habits are often serious pests. **1965–70** *DARE* (Qu. R11, *A very tiny fly that you can hardly see, but that stings*) 11 Infs, **esp NEast,** Midge; **MA**45, Little black midgies; **ME**6, Midgies; (Qu. R10) Inf **MA**5, Midge—they do sting like fury. **1982** Heat Moon *Blue Highways* 339 **NH,** As we walked up the road, air began whiffling down off Bald Peak and pushing invisible biting midges . . downwind.

midget n

1 Usu a **punkie** (here: family Ceratopogonidae), but also a **black fly**; see quots. **NEast, esp NEng** Cf **midge 2, minge**
1851 (1856) Springer *Forest Life* 56 **ME,** One species of fly commonly called the midget . . is so small as to be almost imperceptible. . . The black fly and the musquito can only reach the exposed parts of the body, but to the midget every portion is accessible. **1872** Schele de Vere *Americanisms* 392, The *Midget* of Canada and some of the Northern States, is the *Sand-fly* of Europe. **1915** (1916) Johnson *Highways New Engl.* 51 **cwNH,** Then there's the midgets. They're so small you can hardly see 'em. You don't notice 'em much till they bite. They're worse than the black fly. **1933** Cheley *Camping Out* 203 **NY,** The . . 'midgets' can outstrip them [=mosquitoes] for ferocity and the painful character of the wounds which they inflict. . . The midget is a minute little creature. . . They fly in swarms of thousands, attacking face, hands, and neck. . . Their bites produce great redness and swelling, and the itching is most intolerable. **1966–70** *DARE* (Qu. R11, *A very tiny fly that you can hardly see, but that stings*) Infs **MA**42, **NH**5, **NY**22, 103, **VT**13, Midget; **PA**246, Oat midget—black, ⅛ inch long, bites.
2 =**midge 1.**
1965–70 *DARE* (Qu. R10, *Very small flies that don't sting, often seen hovering in large groups or bunches outdoors in summer*) Infs **NH**4, **NY**22, **VT**13, Midgets; **PA**1, Oats midget.
3 also *midgie*: A small playing marble. Cf *DS* EE6b
1958 *PADS* 29.37 **WI,** Midgies. . . Marbles. **c1970** Wiersma *Marbles Terms,* Midgets: . . A small marble.

midget faded rattlesnake See **faded midget**

midget rattler n
=**faded midget.**
1968 Abbey *Desert Solitaire* 18 **seUT,** If there are midget rattlers in the area there may be diamondbacks too.

midgie n
1 See **midge 2.**
2 See **midget 3.**

‡**midging** adj
1954 *PADS* 21.33 **seSC,** *Midgin'*. . . Middlin', especially in greetings. "How do you feel today?" "Just midgin'." Summerville.

midlady n Also *midwoman* **chiefly Sth** Cf **midnight wife**
A midwife.
1967–69 *DARE* (Qu. AA30, *An older woman who comes in . . to help when a baby is going to be born*) Infs **NY**200, **SC**32, Midlady. **c1970** Pederson *Dial. Surv. Rural GA (A woman who helps at childbirth who isn't a nurse)* 1 inf, **seGA,** Midlady. [Inf Black] **1986** Pederson *LAGS Concordance* **Gulf Region** *(Midwife)* 9 infs, Mid woman; 2 infs, Mid women; 3 infs, Mid lady.

midling adj See **middling** adj

midling n See **middling** n

midmother n **esp Sth, S Midl** Cf **midlady**
A midwife.
c1960 Wilson Coll. **csKY,** Mid-mother. . . A mid-wife or granny. **1970** *DARE* (Qu. AA30, *An older woman who comes in . . to help when a baby is going to be born*) Infs **NY**250, **VA**41, Midmother. [Both Infs Black] **c1970** Pederson *Dial. Surv. Rural GA (A woman who helps at childbirth who isn't a nurse)* 1 inf, **seGA,** Midmother. [Inf Black] **1970** Tarpley *Blinky* 223 **neTX,** *Midwife* is the standard name . . but some of the informants over 60 continue to call them . . *midmother* [5 of 200 infs].

midnight n
A children's chasing game; see quot 1909.
1909 (1923) Bancroft *Games* 133, Midnight. . . One player is the fox and the others sheep. . . The sheep . . scatter around, approaching as close to the fox as they dare. . . When he says "Midnight!" they must run for the sheepfold as fast as possible, the fox chasing them. Any sheep caught changes places with the fox, and the game is repeated. **1950** *WELS (Outdoor games)* 2 Infs, **WI,** Midnight.

midnight fuzz n
1968 *DARE* (Qu. E20, *Soft rolls of dust that collect on the floor under beds or other furniture*) Inf **LA**16, Midnight fuzz.

midnight wife n Also *midnight nurse* [Perh by folk-etym from *midwife*] Cf **midmother**

A midwife.

1940–41 Cassidy *WI Atlas* cwWI, Midnight nurse. . . Midwife. **c1955** Reed–Person *Ling. Atlas Pacific NW*, 1 inf, Midnight wife. **1967–68** DARE (Qu. AA30, *An older woman who comes in . . to help when a baby is going to be born*) Infs **MO**38, **VA**27, Midnight wife.

midshipman n [From the rows of photophores on the underside; see quot 1939] **chiefly Pacific coast**

A fish of the genus *Porichthys*, esp *P. notatus* which is also called **singing fish, toadfish.**

1882 U.S. Natl. Museum *Bulletin* 16.751, P[orichthys] porosissimus. . . Midshipman. [*Ibid* 752, The so-called "shining pores" on the sides are not pores, but bright round pieces of shiny membrane, showing through a translucent skin.] **1896** U.S. Bur. Fisheries *Rept. for 1895* 466, Porichthys. . . Midshipmen. **1928** Pan-Pacific Research Inst. *Jrl.* 3.3.15 **OR, WA**, Porichthys notatus. . . Midshipman. **1939** Natl. Geogr. Soc. *Fishes* 220, Many . . fish . . have luminiferous organs along their sides and on their heads that give off light like a firefly at night. These many luminiferous organs on the . . midshipmen look like the pearl buttons of a uniform when the fish is taken from the water. Hence the name "midshipmen." **1953** Roedel *Common Fishes CA* 144, Slim Midshipman. Porichthys myriaster. . . It is possible, though difficult, to induce an individual to "light up"; when one does it is very spectacular. . . Northern Midshipmen [sic]. Porichthys notatus. **1991** Amer. Fisheries Soc. *Common Names Fishes* 32, Porichthys myriaster . . P[acific:] specklefin midshipman. Porichthys notatus . . P[acific:] plainfin midshipman. Porichthys plectrodon . . A[tlantic:] Atlantic midshipman.

midway n

1 =alley n[1] **7.**

1969 Sorden *Lumberjack Lingo* 78 **NEng, Gt Lakes**, Midway—The roofed-over space between the bunkhouse and the cook shack where barreled beef, pork, venison, lard, and other supplies were stored.

‡2 =median (strip) **1.**

1968 DARE (Qu. N17, . . *The separating area in the middle [of a four-lane road]*) Inf **CT**7, Midway.

midways prep [*midway* + -s; cf Pronc Intro 3.I.23] Cf **anyways**

Between.

1970 DARE (Qu. MM7, *If there's a house on each side of the school . . "The school is _____ the houses."*) Inf **VA**99, Midways.

midwoman See **midlady**

-mie- See **-ma-** infix

miff v Also with *up* [Perh var of *muff* to bungle, botch]

To blunder, make a mistake; to botch (something).

1967 DARE (Qu. JJ42, *To make an error in judgment and get something quite wrong: "He usually handles things well, but this time he certainly _____."*) Inf **NY**32, Miffed; **OH**8, **PA**59, Miffed (it) up.

mig n Also *migalo, migget, miggey, miggie, miggle, miglet* **chiefly Nth, West** See Map Cf **mib, meg**

A playing marble, esp a small or inexpensive one; pl: any of var marble games.

1890 DN 1.76 **NYC, neNJ**, "Miggles" is the generic name for marbles, also meaning the commonest clay marbles. **1895** DN 1.398, Migs: marbles. King's Co., N.Y. **1906** Amer. Mag. 61.562 **NYC**, Boys garner birds' eggs, door knobs, chalk, and miggles. **1924** DN 5.286 **Cape Cod MA**, When Isaiah has lost all of his marbles he has been 'screened of his miglets'. **1926** AmSp 2.66 **Denver CO** [Playground argot], Hear the chatter that comes out of a marble-shooting ring. . . [T]he "migs," "agates," "glassies," "pureys," "commies" and "pottries" they talk about! **1935** AmSp 10.159 **seNE**, Miggles. . . A general term for marbles, of which *migs* is probably a shortened form. **1940** Recreation (NY) 34.110, A list of the many games of marbles played throughout the country follows: . . miggles, mibs. **1949** PADS 11.24 **CO**, Mig. . . Miggle. . . Migget. . . A marble. **c1955** Reed–Person *Ling. Atlas Pacific NW*, 7 infs, Migs. **1958** PADS 29.37 **MA, WA, WI**, Mig. Ibid **MA, WI**, Miggey (miggie). Ibid **CT, MA, NJ**, Miggle. Ibid, Migs. . . A marble game; same as *knuckles* (Cal.). "One player puts marbles up to be shot at; the next player does the same; marbles hit are won by the one who hits them" (Wis.) **1963** Burroughs *Head-First* 99 **CO**, Like as not in an altercation over a game of migs, . . Pinky would call you a dirty name.

1965–70 DARE (Qu. EE6b, *Small marbles or marbles in general*) 69 Infs, **chiefly Nth, West**, Migs; 10 Infs, **esp Nth, West**, Miggles; **CA**181, **NY**213, 223, Miggies; (Qu. EE6c, *Cheap marbles*) Infs **CA**174, **CT**6, **NY**44, 52, 59, 60, Migs; **NY**37, Migalos; **NY**223, Miggies; **KS**16, **NY**80, Miggles; (Qu. EE6a, . . *Different kinds of marbles*) Infs **CT**8, **WA**19, Mig; **NY**59, Miggle; (Qu. EE7, . . *Kinds of marble games*) Infs **MI**101, 103, **MN**2, **NY**99, **WA**30, Migs; **CO**28, **MI**103, Miggles. **1969** DARE Tape **MI**103, The plain ones [=marbles] are the ones that you try to hit the set-up with. You roll it down the sidewalk. . . If you hit the set-up, then it was your turn to sit down. Then the other guys would try to hit that set-up with the common marbles. But meanwhile all the common marbles you took in were yours, and that was miggles. **c1970** Wiersma *Marbles Terms* **neNJ**, Miggle—a hard clay marble, fired by a kiln. **1976** WI Acad. Rev. June 20 (as of 1920s), We called the painted clay globes "miggies," and the dimpled crockery ones "meggies," not "coffees," and as we grew older disdained both of them—only babies used them. **1993** DARE File **cWA** (as of c1943), We played "migs," I think a generic name for "marbles."

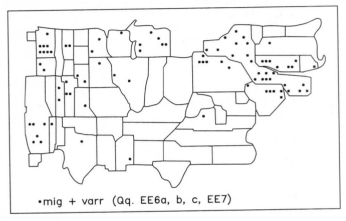

•mig + varr (Qq. EE6a, b, c, EE7)

mighnt See **may** v **Ab**

might v See **may** v **B**

might n [EDD *might* sb. 1] Cf **mort, power**

A considerable amount or quantity.

1834 Caruthers *Kentuckian* 1.28, I'm 'bliged to do a might of business in Baltimore afore I can go on. **1878** Beadle *Western Wilds* 29 **sTN**, It took a might of time. . . At last I got into a more open country. *Ibid* 43, It was a might o' comfort, though, to see 'em 'fore they died. **1911** DN 3.539 **eKY**, Might. . . A large quantity; e.g., "He is selling a might of timber lately."

might adv See **mighty** adv

might 'a' could See **may** v **B1**

might better See **may** v **B2**

might can, might could See **may** v **B1**

might did See **may** v **B3**

mightily adv Also *mightly* [OED *mightily* adv. 3 "Now somewhat *rare*; very common in 17–18 c."]

Greatly, very much.

1744 in 1851 PA Prov. Council *Minutes* 4.707 **sePA**, Finding what great friendship subsisted between us and the Dutch, he approved it mightily. **1876** Twain in *Atlantic Mth.* 35.722 **MS**, They were mightily looked up to. **1884** Murfree *TN Mts.* 254, Caleb war mightily worked up 'bout this hyar finin' business. *Ibid* 260, Tony air mightily outdone. **1899** (1912) Green *VA Folk-Speech* 280, Mightily. . . Greatly; in or to a great degree; very much. "I heard the new preacher and liked him mightily." **1901** DN 2.182 **neKY** [Black], Mightily—might'ly. **c1940** Eliason *Word Lists FL* 3 **nwFL**, Mightily. . . Very much. "Seems like they've spun your graduation out mightily on you." **1970** DARE (Qu. LL35, *Words used to make a statement stronger: "This cake tastes _____ good."*) Inf **KY**84, Mightly. **1984** Wilder *You All Spoken Here* 17 **Sth**, Mightily beliked: Popular.

might near, might nigh See **mighty** adv

might ought to See **may** v **B4**

might should See **may** v **B5**

might will, might would See **may** v B6

mighty adj **widespread, but more freq Sth, S Midl, NEast**
Note: The sense illustrated has undergone depreciation from the std senses, no longer having any necessary implication of power or might.

Big, large, great; extreme.

1774 (1957) Fithian *Jrl. & Letters* 149 **eVA,** I piddled at my Exegessis [sic], but (as they say here in Virginia) I did a mighty little. **1851** Hooper *Widow Rugby's Husband* 93 **AL,** She has a mighty notion of courtin', and ef you sidle up to her, it'll please her. **1871** Eggleston *Hoosier Schoolmaster* 145 **sIN,** A mighty sight of hoss sense fer his age. **1902** (1904) Rowe *Maid of Bar Harbor* 249 **ME,** It makes a mighty sight o' difference where the land is. **1932** (1974) Caldwell *Tobacco Road* 23 **GA,** They got up there and all of them has a mighty pain inside for the land, but they can't come back. **1948** Dick *Dixie Frontier* 313, When a man wished to compliment another on his crop, he said: "You've a mighty heap this year." **1952** Brown *NC Folkl.* 1.565, *Mighty heap more.* . . A great deal more.—Central and east. **1986** Pederson *LAGS Concordance* **Gulf Region,** 1 inf, So-and-so is a mighty blabbermouth; 3 infs, A mighty heap (of it); 1 inf, A mighty heap of land; 1 inf, A mighty heap of water; 1 inf, I studied a mighty lot; 1 inf, We saw a mighty lots [sic] in Miami; 1 inf, He had a mighty need for it; [1 inf, Courting her mighty lot; 1 inf, He hated it mighty lot].

mighty adv Also (esp when followed by *near, nigh*) *might* [*OED* a1300 →] **esp Sth, S Midl** See Map and Map Section
Note: *DARE* QR evidence shows that while the comb *mighty good* is widespread, *mighty* in other combs is regional.
Very, extremely, quite.

1816 Pickering *Vocab.* 133 **VA,** An intelligent friend, who has travelled in *Virginia,* informs me, that he "found the adverb *mighty* in common use, in the conversation of all classes of people in that State, as precisely synonymous with *very. Ex. gr. Mighty* cold—*mighty* near ten o'clock—a *mighty* fine man, &c." **1827** (1939) Sherwood *Gaz.* **GA** 139, *Mighty,* for very, as mighty well, &c. **1843** (1916) Hall *New Purchase* 69 **sIN,** The children were mighty spry. **1879** (1880) Twain *Tramp Abroad* 225 **MO,** You hain't got me so mighty much, nuther. **1884** *Anglia* 7.264 **Sth, S Midl** [Black], *To be mighty right* = to be quite right. **1887** (1967) Harris *Free Joe* 12 **GA** [Black], I ain't seen Lucindy in now gwine on mighty nigh a mont'. **1903** *DN* 2.321 **seMO,** 'We are all mighty glad to see you.' . . 'Did you win your case?' 'You're mighty right I did!' **1905** *DN* 3.14 **cCT,** *Mighty.* . . Very. 'I'm mighty glad to see you.' . . R[are]. **1906** *DN* 3.121 **sIN,** "Mighty right," "mighty powerful." **1907** *DN* 3.215 **nwAR,** *Mighty.* . . Very. **1909** *DN* 3.349 **eAL, wGA,** *Mighty.* . . Quite: in the phrase 'mighty right.' . . Very: extremely common before adjectives. **1910** *DN* 3.445 **wNY,** *Mighty.* . . Very. **1923** *DN* 5.214 **swMO,** A mighty sick baby. . . I'm mighty near thar. **1924** (1946) Greer-Petrie *Angeline Gits an Eyeful* 5 **csKY,** She . . looks might nigh as big as a kiver'd wagon, from the reer. **1939** Hall Coll. **wNC,** I could might' nigh put my foot where hit killed the sheep. **1943** *LANE* Map 716 **NEng,** The map shows the intensive adverbs recorded in the sentence *It's awful(ly) cold* or in a similar context. . . The recorded terms are here listed in the order of their frequency: *awful(ly), terrible, -ly, mighty* [etc]. **1944** *PADS* 2.10 **AL,** *Might nigh.* . . Very nearly, almost. . . Negro. Low popular. **1952** Brown *NC Folkl.* 1.565, *Might nigh.* . . Illiterate. . . *Mighty long:* . . "He didn't live here so mighty long." . . *Mighty much:* . . "I never thought so mighty much of him." **1963** Edwards *Gravel* 123 **eTN** (as of 1920s), Might nigh ever hoss in that company was limpin. **1965–70** *DARE* (Qu. LL35, *Words used to make a statement stronger: "This cake tastes _____ good."*) 116 Infs, **widespread,** Mighty; **NC82, SC54,** Might; (Qu. II3, *Expressions to say that people are very friendly toward each other: "They're _____."*) 18 Infs, **chiefly Sth, S Midl,** Mighty close (*or* thick); **TX43,** Mighty near in love; **TX72,** Mighty simpatico; (Qu. LL30, *'Nearly' or 'almost': "He fell off the ladder and _____ [broke his neck]."*) Infs **AR55, KY25, LA8, MS88, NC82, TN26, TX98, VT6,** Mighty nigh (*or* near); **IL130, KY84, LA17, MS7, NC55, TN65, TX11,** (Come) might near; (Qu. KK27, *A very lively, active old person: "For his age, he's _____."*) 10 Infs, **chiefly Sth,** Mighty spry (*or* frisky, lively); (Qu. GG34b, *To feel depressed or in a gloomy mood: "She's feeling _____ today."*) Infs **AZ3, GA84, MO11, NJ39, NY44, PA214,** Mighty low; **CA22, NJ54,** Mighty blue; (Qu. KK1a, . . *Very good—for example, food: "That pie was _____."*) Infs **AR6, 22, 36, GA9, LA17, VA39,** Mighty good (*or* fine, etc); (Qu. KK41, *Something that is very difficult to do: "I managed to get through with it, but it was _____."*) Infs **DC8, KY47, LA3, MS88, OH41, WV3,** Mighty hard.

[Further exx throughout DS; all exx are mapped.] **1966–70** *DARE* Tape **AL11,** We raised might near everything else; **CA196,** It comes in mighty handy to know how now; **GA9,** They keep a continual bark mighty near all the time; **IL86,** There were automobiles, but mighty few; **TX25,** It's might near the same as our steer wrestling. **1971** *Foxfire* Winter 261 **nGA,** I was might'near froze t'death when I got there. **1987** Jones-Wheeler *Laughter* 127 **Appalachians,** Best crop you might nigh ever seen.

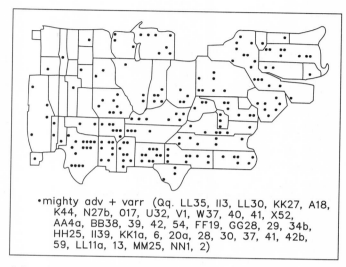

•mighty adv + varr (Qq. LL35, II3, LL30, KK27, A18, K44, N27b, O17, U32, V1, W37, 40, 41, X52, AA4a, BB38, 39, 42, 54, FF19, GG28, 29, 34b, HH25, II39, KK1a, 6, 20a, 28, 30, 37, 41, 42b, 59, LL11a, 13, MM25, NN1, 2)

mighty come a-tooting adj Also *mighty come a-shouting, ~ come a-right, ~ shouting, ~ whistling*
Quite right—usu in phr *you're mighty come a-tooting* and varr.

1905 *DN* 3.88 **nwAR,** *Mighty (come a-)shoutin', mighty whistlin'.* . . Right. 'You're mighty (come a-)shoutin'.' 'You're mighty whistlin'.' **1907** *DN* 3.233 **nwAR,** *Mighty right.* . . Quite right. Also "you're mighty come a-shouting." **1941** Street *In Father's House* 171 **seMS,** "Did you see any good trucks?" "You mighty come a'right. I picked out one and made a down payment." **1970** *Thompson Coll.* **cnAL** (as of 1920s), *Mighty come a-tooting.* . . Enthusiastic affirmative. "You ready?" "You mighty come a-tootin'."

miglet See **mig**

mignonette (madeira-vine) See **mignonette vine 2**

mignonette vine n

1 =**tarweed** (here: *Madia* spp).
1890 *Century Dict.* 3758, *Mignonette-vine,* a plant, *Madia elegans,* from Pacific North America. **1896** Sanders *Encycl. Gardening* 221, *Madaria* (Mignonette Vine).—Ord. Compositæ. Hardy annual. *Nat.* California. . . *Flowers,* yellow. **1900** Lyons *Plant Names* 236, *Madaria.* . . Mignonette-vine. . . Syn[onyms] Anisocarpus, Madia. . . *M. elegans.* . . California. Mignonette-vine.

2 also *mignonette (madeira-vine):* =**Madeira vine.**
1953 Randolph-Wilson *Down in Holler* 240 **Ozarks,** *Door 'tater.* . . The so-called Madeira vine *(Boussingaultia gracilis),* which has buds or fruit like tiny potatoes. This plant is grown in dooryards for shade and ornament, and is sometimes called *mignonette.* **1960** Vines *Trees SW* 256, Mignonette Madeira-vine—*Boussingaultia baselloides.* **1976** Bailey-Bailey *Hortus Third* 81, *Andredera . . cordifolia.* . . Madeira vine, mignonette vine. Rapidly growing twiner, to 20 ft. or more.

migrant shrike n Also *migrant*
A **loggerhead shrike** (here: *Lanius ludovicianus migrans*).
1903 Dawson *Birds OH* 1.294, The Loggerhead, or Migrant Shrike, has increased somewhat in recent years, except in those localities where it has been subjected to a thoughtless persecution. **1914** Eaton *Birds NY* 2.362, The Migrant shrike breeds in eastern America from northern Minnesota, Michigan, southern Quebec, Maine and New Brunswick, southward to eastern Kansas, southern Illinois and western Virginia; winters from the Middle States to Mississippi and Texas. **1917** (1923) *Birds Amer.* 3.101, The Migrant, or Northern Loggerhead, Shrike (*Lanius ludovicianus migrans*) is practically identical with the Loggerhead in coloration. **1936** Roberts *MN Birds* 2.166, The Migrant Shrike [=*Lanius ludovicianus migrans*], or Northern Loggerhead, is an abundant summer resident in southern Minnesota including the prairies of the southwest.

Ibid 167, Any Shrike found nesting in Minnesota is certainly the Migrant. . . Several young Migrants, kept in an indoor aviary by the writer, greedily ate raw meat cut up in small pieces. **1955** Forbush–May *Birds* 398, My chief recollections of the Migrant Shrike picture a gray bird sitting on a telephone wire where he could scan the scenery and from which he occasionally descended swiftly to pick up an unlucky grasshopper.

Mike n

1 =**Mick 1.**

1941 *LANE* Map 454, The map shows the nicknames, jocular or derogatory, applied to an Irishman: . . *Mick* [is very common], *Mickey* [is occasional], . . *Mike* [is rare]. **1942** Berrey–Van den Bark *Amer. Slang* 385.11, *Irishman.* . . Michael, Mick, Mickey, Micky, Mike. **1962** Atwood *Vocab. TX* 73, *Irishman.* . . Very scattered: *Mick* . . and *Mike.* **1968** *DARE* (Qu. HH28, *Names and nicknames . . for people of foreign background: Irish*) Inf **WI**44, Mike.

2 Among miners: a hammer.

1966 *DARE* Tape **SD**4A, They do have a sixteen-pound mike, or hammer. They always called 'em mikes in the mine. **1968** Adams *Western Words* 195, *Mike*—A miner's name for a heavy hammer.

mikiawa See **makiawa**

milch cow n Pronc-sp *milks cow* [*OED milch cow* 1424 →] **scattered, but chiefly NEast, Gt Lakes** See Map *old-fash* Cf **new-milch**
=**milk cow.**

1637 in 1892 Dedham MA *Early Rec.* 3.27, Yt medowe . . shall become a somer pasture for milch Cowes. **1708** *Boston News–Letter* (MA) 25 Oct 4/2, Strayed . . out of a Pasture in North-Boston, a black Milch Cow between 3 and 4 year old. **c1783** in 1941 Woodward *Ploughs & Politicks* 407 **NJ,** 7 Milch Cows. **1899** (1912) Green *VA Folk-Speech* 281, Milch cow. **1933** Rawlings *South Moon* 1 **nFL,** The grey mule was hobbled and the scrub milch cow tethered. **1941** Writers' Program *Guide IN* 400 **swIN,** In the autumn of 1818 the settlers were beset by a fever called 'milk sick' because it attacked cattle and particularly milch cows. **1965–70** *DARE* (Qu. K1, *A cow that is giving milk is a* _____) 76 Infs, Milch cow; 35 Infs, **esp NEng,** Milch cow; 8 Infs, **esp NEast, Gt Lakes,** Milks cow. [Of all Infs responding to the question, 73% were old; of those giving these responses, 85% were old.] **1966–70** *DARE* Tape **NM**13, Some of them even had milch [mɪəlč:] cows; **MI**116, Milch [mɪlč] cows. **1968** Moody *Horse* 31 **nwKS** (as of c1920), You'll be left with . . a couple of milch cows. [**1981** Pederson *LAGS Basic Materials,* 1 inf, **cGA,** Milch [mɪl^tʃ] = milk cow.] **1988** Palmer *Lang. W. Cent. MA* 31, [mɪlč kɑu]—That would be a normal cow that is bred to calf. As soon as they give milk, they were called milch cows.

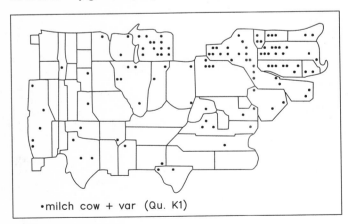

• milch cow + var (Qu. K1)

mild v Also with *down*

Of a wind or storm: to diminish or decrease.

1956 Ker *Vocab. W. TX* 65, [For the phrase:] The wind is not blowing so hard. . . The unusual form, *the wind is milding* . . is reported by one informant. **1970** *DARE* (Qu. B13, *When the wind begins to decrease . . it's* _____) Inf **VA**55, Milding down.

mile n Pronc-spp **chiefly Sth, S Midl, NEng** *mild* (cf Intro "Language Changes" I.8); also *moll*

A Pronc varr.

1795 Dearborn *Columbian Grammar* 137, *List of Improprieties.* . . *Mild* for Mile. **1887** Kirkland *Zury* 63 **IL,** It tuk a mild o' fence t' dew the forty, that makes four mild altogether. **1891** Cooke *Huckleberries* 326 **CT,** He lives three mild back beyond Pond Hill. **1892** *DN* 1.210 **MA,** *Mild:* a mile. **1901** *DN* 2.143 **cNY,** *Mild* [mɑɪld]. . . A form of *mile* with excrescent d. **1902** *DN* 2.239 **sIL,** *Mild.* . . Common pronunciation of mile, both singular and plural. **1903** *DN* 2.321 **seMO,** *Mile.* . . Always mild [mɑɪld]. 'I haven't . . walked a mild in a year.' **1906** Johnson *Highways Missip. Valley* 178 **MO,** Hit [=a cyclone] was only a mild away, and how hit rattled. **1907** *DN* 3.224 **nwAR,** *Mild.* . . Common pronunciation of mile, both singular and plural. **1914** *DN* 4.110 **cKS,** *Mild.* **1923** *DN* 5.214 **swMO,** *Mild.* **1927** [see **B** below]. **1940** *AmSp* 15.48 **sAppalachians, Ozarks,** When [l] is followed by a consonant, a stop [d] or [t] may be made before the next consonant: milds (miles). **1969** Kantor *MO Bittersweet* 46, Folks called the concrete pavement slab. "Yeh, you might have a moll or two of mud, but then you'll hit the slab."

B Gram forms.

Pl: usu *miles;* also **chiefly Sth, Midl** *mile* (cf Intro "Language Changes" II.7); rarely *mileses.* Cf **foot** n **B2b(1), month B**

1837 Sherwood *Gaz. GA* 72, *Two mile,* for two miles. **1840** (1847) Longstreet *GA Scenes* 27, Start 'em together for a hundred and fifty mile. **1843** (1916) Hall *New Purchase* 147 **sIN,** The nearest white settlement warnt nearer nor four mile. **1885** Twain *Huck. Finn* 24 **MO,** We . . pulled down the river two mile and a half. **1891** [see **A** above]. **1899** Chesnutt *Conjure Woman* 44 **csNC** [Black], [It] wuz mo' d'n forty mile off. **1902** [see **A** above]. **1907** [see **A** above]. **1909** *DN* 3.349 **eAL, wGA,** *Mile.* . . For the plural *miles.* **1910** *DN* 3.456 **seKY,** My house is ten mile from here. **1916** Howells *Leatherwood God* 7 **swOH,** Folks there from twenty mile round. **1921** Haswell *Daughter Ozarks* 47 (as of 1880s), He carried me seventy-five mile in nine hours. **1927** *AmSp* 3.10 **Ozarks,** On the state highway north of Neosho, Missouri, there is a large sign which reads "Joplin, Seven Mile From Here." Most natives use *mile* for both singular and plural, but some of the old-timers use the plural form *mild.* **1966** *DARE* (QR p93) Inf **IN**2, About seventeen mile up there. **1968–69** *DARE* Tape **GA**77, A few mile out from Rome; **IN**30, It is located about fifty mile straight west of Indianapolis; **MO**1, [FW:] And you were born here? . . Close to Lancaster? [Inf:] Yes, eight mile Lancaster [sic]. **1982** Barrick *Coll.* **csPA,** Fifty mile an hour. **1986** Pederson *LAGS Concordance,* 1 inf, **seAL,** (A)bout eight mileses. **1989** Pederson *LAGS Tech. Index* 331, Mile [as pl] (173) [infs].

mile-a-minute n [In ref to the rapid growth of these plants; cf **foot-a-night, yard-a-night**]

1 also *mile-a-minute vine:* =**kudzu.**

1956 McAtee *Some Dialect NC* 56, Mile-a-minute . . the kudzu vine (*Pueraria thunbergiana*) . . in allusion to its rapid growth. Chapel Hill. **1984** Wilder *You All Spoken Here* 176 **Sth,** Mile-a-minute: Kudzu. **1985** *Atlanta Constitution* (GA) 30 June sec H 1/4, Called the "mile-a-minute" vine, kudzu is ideal for retarding soil erosion but quickly outgrows its welcome. **1993** *NADS Letters* **GA,** Mile-a-minute vine. . . A neighbor . . said that she remembered the vine, and the "mile-a-minute" label, from when she lived in Atlanta, GA, more than a decade ago.

2 also *mile-a-minute plant, ~ weed:* An introduced **tearthumb** (here: *Polygonum perfoliatum*).

1991 *Wall St. Jrl.* (NY NY) 5 Sept sec B 1/1, Mile-a-minute weed is a new threat to young trees in the middle Atlantic states. . . The weed, a vine with triangular leaves and an iridescent blue berry, . . was first seen by weed scientist Nathan L. Hartwig of Pennsylvania State University in 1972, when a specimen was brought to him. . . He believes the weed came originally from Japan, possibly aboard some rhododendrons imported . . around 1930. **1994** *Houston Chron.* (TX) 8 July sec A 5, They call it the Mile-a-Minute plant, and it's threatening forests and farmland in Maryland and other mid-Atlantic states. . . It can grow 6 inches a day. **1995** *DARE* File, Mile-a-minute (*Polygonum perfoliatum*) is not kudzu but is sometimes referred to as annual kudzu because it is a vine that grows to 25 ft. in one growing season. . . [T]he common name 'mile-a-minute' was probably first used in the 80's. . . It is presently found in 16 counties in southeastern Pennsylvania, eastern Maryland, several counties in northern Virginia, one or two counties in New Jersey . ., two counties in West Virginia, one county of Ohio . ., and very likely in all three counties of Delaware.

mile-jumper n Also *mile-leaper*

Perh a **bullfrog 1** (here: *Rana clamitans*).

[1851 *De Bow's Rev.* 11.53, *Rana . . clamitans*, croaker, and also leap . . frog.] **1986** Pederson *LAGS Concordance (Bullfrog)* 1 inf, **swMS**, Mile jumper—smaller than a bullfrog; not edible; 1 inf, **swMS**, Mile leaper—they ain't fit for no thing.

milermore bird n Cf **clew bird**

1951 Randolph *We Always Lie* 68 **Ozarks**, The fishermen in Taney County, Missouri, still tell tourists about the clew-bird, that sticks its bill into a gravel bar and whistles loudly through its rectum. . . My friend . . , who used to direct float trips on the James and White rivers, says that his guides called this creature the milermore bird, because its whistle can be heard for a mile or more.

mileses See **mile B**

miliquant toast See **milquetoast**

military wedding n Also *military ceremony*
A shotgun wedding.

1916 *DN* 4.326 **KS**, *Military wedding.* . . A marriage where the groom is forced because he has ruined the bride. **1936** *Our Army* Feb 41, Mabel Clank: "Will we have a military wedding, dearie?" Corporal Cluck: "That all depends." . . "Depends on what, dearie?" . . "On whether or not your pa has a shotgun around the house." **1965–70** *DARE* (Qu. AA20, *A marriage that takes place because a baby is on the way*) Infs **IL11, MI104, MO25, NY167, SC11, TX38, VA42, 102**, Military wedding; **TX9**, Military ceremony.

milk n, v Usu |mɪlk|; also freq |mɪə(l)k, mjɪlk, mɛlk|; for addit varr see quots Pronc-sp *melk*
A Forms.

1936 *AmSp* 11.12 **eTX**, *Milk* . . is pronounced [mjɪlk], [mjɪək]. **1937** *AmSp* 12.288 **wVA**, A survey of the speech of a group of young women college students in the Valley elicited the following pronunciations: [mɛlk] for *milk*. **1940** *AmSp* 15.259, In the South the *l* is frequently lost before *-k* when it is preceded by any vowel, especially [ɪ]. Thus *milk, silk* . . are often pronounced [mɪək], [sɪək]. . . *Milk, hill* . . are often pronounced [mɪək], [hɪəl]. **1941** *AmSp* 16.4 **eTX** [Black], *Milk* is [mjɪlk], [mjɪək], and [mjɛək]. **1941** *LANE* Map 297, [Variants of the type [mɪlk, mɪɫk] are common throughout **NEng**; those of the type [mɪəlk] occur occas, esp in **nNEng**; those of the type [mɛlk] are scattered, but esp in **s and wNEng**; those of the type [mɪʊk, mɪuk] occur infreq, but esp in **wMA, wCT**.] **1944** *PADS* 2.30 **nwNC, eKY**, *Milk* [mjɪək, mɛlk]. . . Common. **1952** *AmSp* 27.188 **WA**, The nuclear [il] [=[ɪl]] of *milk* (and similar words) is strongly velarized, so that a number of speakers substitute [e] [=[ɛ]] . . and say 'melk.' **1954** *Harder Coll.* **cwTN**, *Milk* pronounced [mɛək]. **1973** Allen *LAUM* 3.270 (as of c1950), *Milk* with /ɛ/ rather than /ɪ/. . . Although in the U[pper] M[id]west no cultivated speakers have this form, it persists in the speech of [eight infs with high school education or less]. **1975** Gould *ME Lingo* 179, *Melk*—Milk. "When I make my biscuits, I use a whole cup of melk." The transition from *i* to *e* is progressive from west to east, until in far-down Washington County milk rhymes with elk. **1982** Barrick *Coll.* **csPA**, *Milk*—pron. melk. **1989** Pederson *LAGS Tech. Index* 163 **Gulf Region**, [275 infs, [mɪlk]; 129 infs, [mɪuk]; 12 infs [mɪuuk]; 6 infs, [mɪlk]; 5 infs, [mɛlk]; 3 infs, [mjɪlk]; 2 infs each, [mɛuk, mɪl, mɪlʔ]; 1 inf each, [mɪg, mɪu, mɪuug, mjɪuuk].]

B As noun.

1 Buttermilk. Cf **bread** n B1

1924 Raine *Land of Saddle-Bags* 212 **sAppalachians**, The term "milk" usually means buttermilk.

2 in var combs referring to a woman's breast: See quots.

1942 Berrey–Van den Bark *Amer. Slang* 121.16, *Breasts.* . . Milk bottles. **1965–70** *DARE* (Qu. X31, . . *A woman's breasts*) Infs **MI24, OK28, OR1**, Milk cans; **CA165, CO22**, Milk bags; **GA1, IL45, MO29**, Milk bottles; **IN61**, Milk buckets; **WA30**, Milk condensery; **NY197, PA76**, Milk factories; **MN15**, Milk factory; **GA77**, Milk jugs; **PA130**, Milk pails; **ME21, NJ1, NY10, 84**, Milk route; **CA59**, Milk works; **CO47, IN60, NY45, 65**, Milker(s); **MD36, NC72**, Milkshakes; **PA237**, Her milky ways. **1969** *DARE* FW Addit **NC**, Milking jugs—a woman's breasts.

‡**3** See quot. Cf *DS* AA3

1968 *DARE* FW Addit **PA66**, Milk. . . A boy or girl friend.

C As verb.

Vbl n *milking*: Attracting fish with crushed fish eggs; see quot. [Cf *milt*]

1968 *DARE* (Qu. P16, *When fishermen throw bits of bait in the water to attract fish*) Inf **AK9**, Milking [mɛlkɪŋ]—makes the water milky. Take fish eggs in small cloth bag, crush them, tie bag to boot and walk in the water—"milk" washes out and attracts fish.

milk adder See **milk snake 1**

milk and water adj phr
Weak, wishy-washy, insipid.

1783 (1922) U.S. Continental Congress *Jrls.* 24.297 **seNY**, Change the milk-and-water style of your last memorial; assume a bolder tone. **1854** (1883) Cooke *VA Comedians* 1.179 **seVA**, A mere milk-and-water family visitor. **1899** (1912) Green *VA Folk-Speech* 281, *Milk-and-water.* . . Insipid, like milk diluted with water; hence, weak; characterless; wishy-washy. **1915** *DN* 4.220, *Milk and water*, wishy-washy. "Having brought on such a character, can you become milk and water in the treatment?" **1931** Hannum *Thursday April* 55 **wNC**, "He treats his women scandulous mean." "Hit's the Gawd's truth. Why, Thursday April, I've seed Poppy myself hitched to a plow and him a-drivin' her! She was milk and water to stand for hit!" *Ibid* 115, Squinting upward at a black cloud that was crawling across the sky on its stomach to warily swallow a milk-and-water sun. **1951** Morgan *Skid Road* 171 **WA**, In 1906 Judge William Hickman Moore, a milk-and-water reformer, was the Fusion candidate for mayor. **1984** Santmyer *And Ladies* 230, Sally had only a mild liking for one who seemed to her a milk-and-water youth.

milk-and-wine lily n Also *milk-and-wine* [From the colors of the flower]
A cultivated crinum lily (*Crinum* spp).

1923 Amer. Joint Comm. Horticult. Nomenclature *Std. Plant Names* 103, *[Crinum] fimbriatulum*. Milk-and-wine. **1959** Carleton *Index Herb. Plants* 81, *Milk-and-wine-lily:* Crinum fimbriatulum. **1960** Williams *Walk Egypt* 151 **GA**, Milk and wine lilies bloomed by the fence. **1968** *DARE* FW Addit **LA21**, Milk-and-wine—a white lily shaped like a day lily. The name comes from bright red streaks in the white petals. **1982** Perry–Hay *Field Guide Plants* 116, *Crinum latifolium* var *zeylanicum.* . . Milk and wine lily. . . *Flowers* . . white with purplish red markings.

milk bag See **milk B2**

milkball tree n [From the white juice exuded by the fruit]
=Osage orange.

1970 *DARE* (Qu. T13, . . *Names . . for these trees: . . osage orange*) Inf **KY94**, Milkball tree.

milkbark n [From the color of the bark]
A Guiana plum (here: *Drypetes diversifolia*) native to the Florida Keys. Also called **whitewood**

[**1922** Sargent *Manual Trees* 651, *Bark* of the trunk [of *Drypetes diversifolia*] about ½' [sic] thick, smooth, milky white and often marked by large irregular gray or pale brown patches.] **1962** Harrar–Harrar *Guide S. Trees* 416, *Milkbark. Drypetes diversifolia.* . . A small tree or shrub, sometimes 30′ to 40′ in height. **1971** Craighead *Trees S. FL* 82, The principal tree species in the upper keys are . . milkbark, Guiana plum, . . and poisonwood. *Ibid* 201, Milkbark, *Drypetes diversifolia.* **1979** Little *Checklist U.S. Trees* 125, *Drypetes diversifolia.* . . *Milkbark.* . . *Range*—Through Fla. Keys but absent from s. Fla. mainland.

milkberry n
A **snowberry** (here: *Chiococca alba*).

1960 Vines *Trees SW* 938, *Chiococca alba.* . . Vernacular names used within the range of this plant are Snowberry, Milkberry. . . The plant is an attractive shrub. **1970** Correll *Plants TX* 1492, *Chiococca alba.* . . *David's milkberry.* . . In palm groves and brushlands in Cameron and Hidalgo co[untie]s, flowering throughout the year; also, Fla.

milk boat n [**boat** 1]

1968 *DARE* Tape **WI11**, And when we were on the farm . . we didn't take no wagon or anything to haul, we had something that was similar to it. We always called it a milk boat—similar to a stoneboat, but they made runners for that like they did on a sled. And . . then they put irons on the bottom of those runners and that's what we used to take.

milk bonnet n
A **dunce cap** (here: *Conocybe lactea*).

1987 McKnight–McKnight *Mushrooms* 308, *Milk Bonnet. Conocybe lactea.* . . Delicate whitish, conic to bell-shaped cap on a spindly stalk. Common in lawns on summer mornings.

milk bottle See **milk B2**

milk box n Also *milk chest* esp Sth, S Midl

A box, often kept in a well, stream, or spring, for keeping milk and other food cool.

1966–67 *DARE* (Qu. D9, *To prevent bread and cake from drying, you put them in a* _____) Inf **CA**34, Milk chest; (Qu. D10a, *The place to keep food cool, usually with ice, so that it won't spoil*) Inf **AR**17, Milk box; (Qu. M18, *The separate building where milk is kept cool*) Inf **SC**3, Milk box—set in the spring or stream with a weight to keep it steady and upright. **1986** Pederson *LAGS Concordance (Place for milk and butter)* 1 inf, **neTN**, Milk box—placed in the spring; 1 inf, **nwTN**, Milk box—in spring for storing butter; 1 inf, **nwAR**, Milk box—kept in well or below spring; 1 inf, **ceFL**, Milk box—4′ x 6′, with shelves, in the shade; 1 inf, **nwFL**, Milk box—to keep milk cool, outside under trees; 2 infs, **neGA, neMS**, Milk box.

milk brother n Also *milk sister*, ~ *cousin* Cf **kettle cousin**

A person (not a sibling) related to another by the fact of their being nursed by the same woman.

1968 *Territorial Enterprise & VA City News* (VA City NV) 15 Mar 14/4, The baby, named Robert, was nursed by Mrs. Warren. Here an interesting phrase was entered. Robert became a "milk cousin" of the Warren baby. **1990** *DARE* File NC, *Milk brother,* a new one to me. From a man born in rural North Carolina about 1915. He hoped to visit his milk brother this summer. Seems he was quite premature and his mother had no milk, so a neighbor nursed him and her own offspring. This makes the two males milk brothers. He had never heard the word "milk sister." **1991** *NADS Letters,* Yes, I do use the terms "milk brother" or "milk sister." My childhood was spent in Pennsylvania's mountains. . . My friend broke her leg sixteen years ago. I nursed her daughter, along with mine. We call the two girls "milk sisters."

milk bucket See **milk B2**

milk calf n

=**bob calf.**

1967–69 *DARE* (Qu. K20, *A calf that is sold for meat*) Inf **NJ**58, Milk calf; [**AZ**2, Milk-fed calf].

milk can See **milk B2**

milk can dinner n

1995 *DARE* File swWY, *Milk can dinner*—You put all the ingredients for a stew in a regular big milk can and set it outside on a special burner to cook. It is a common way to feed an outdoor gathering.

milk cap See **milky cap**

milk cheese n Cf *DS* H60, **cream cheese 1, sour-milk cheese**

Cottage cheese.

1949 *AmSp* 24.111 neGA, *Milk cheese.* . . Cottage cheese. **1961** *Folk Word Atlas N. LA* map 1011, Homemade cheese made out of milk curd . . milk cheese. **1986** Pederson *LAGS Concordance (Cottage cheese)* 3 infs, **neTN, swMS, cnTX**, Milk cheese.

milk chest See **milk box**

milk condensery See **milk B2**

milk cooler room See **milk room**

‡**milk corn** n [Cf **milk, in the**]

1967 *DARE* (Qu. I33, *. . Ears of corn that are just right for eating*) Inf **NE**7, Milk corn.

milk cousin See **milk brother**

milk cow n Also rarely *milk critter* [*OED* 1535 →; "Now dial."] **widespread, but less freq NEast, Gt Lakes** See Map Cf **critter B2a, milch cow, milking** ~

A cow in milk or kept for milking.

1909 *DN* 3.349 eAL, wGA, *Milk-cow.* . . A milch-cow. *Milch* is not used so far as I know. **1915** *DN* 4.185 swVA, *Milk-cow.* . . Milch cow. **1949** Webber *Backwoods Teacher* 31 Ozarks, Caldwell has got about as good a set of milk critters as you'll find around here. **c1960** *Wilson Coll.* csKY, *Milk cow,* not *milch.* **1965–70** *DARE* (Qu. K1, *A cow that is giving milk is a* _____) 533 Infs, **widespread, but less freq NEast, Gt Lakes**, Milk cow. **1965–70** *DARE* Tapes CA90, 163, IN42, 45, MN11, TX24, Milk cow.

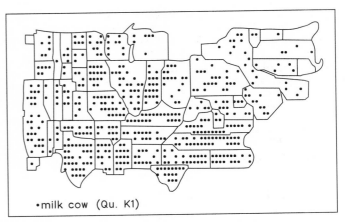

•milk cow (Qu. K1)

milk dairy n [Cf Intro "Language Changes" I.4]

=**dairy 1.**

1966–70 *DARE* (Qu. M18, *The separate building where milk is kept cool*) Infs **NJ**67, **SC**26, Milk dairy. **1986** Pederson *LAGS Concordance (Place for milk and butter)* 29 infs, **Gulf Region**, Milk dairy.

milker See **milk B2**

milk eye n

See quots.

1950 *WELS (Words used to describe people according to their eyes)* 1 Inf, cwWI, Walleyed—slightly bulging and with white around; some call that a milk eye. **1966** *DARE* (Qu. X21c, *If the eyes are very round*) Inf **NM**8, Milk eyes—like a baby, big, round, soft, gentle.

milk factory See **milk B2**

milkfish n [Prob from the color] **HI**

A herring-like fish (*Chanos chanos*). Also called **awa** n[2]

1890 *Century Dict.* 3762, *Milk-fish.* . . A clupeoid fish, *Chanos salmoneus.* **1905** Jordan *Guide to Fishes* 2.45, The single living species is the *Awa,* or milkfish, *Chanos chanos,* largely used as food in Hawaii. **1926** Pan-Pacific Research Inst. *Jrl.* 1.1.5 HI, The Milk-fishes. . . *Chanos cyprinella.* **1933** Bryan *Hawaiian Nature* 101, The principal fish in salt water ponds were the *amaama* or mullet, and the *awa* or milkfish. **1960** Gosline–Brock *Hawaiian Fishes* 97, *Chanos chanos (Awa, Milkfish).* . . Occurs frequently in the markets. . . Attains a length of at least 3 feet—the largest of any Hawaiian herring-like fish. **1967** *Honolulu Star–Bulletin* (HI) 31 May sec F 1/4, Awa—Milk fish. Good for baking. Steam. And for making fishcakes. **1991** Amer. Fisheries Soc. *Common Names Fishes* 19, *Chanos chanos* . . P[acific] . . Milkfish.

milk flatscher n Also *milk flitche* [Cf Ger *Flatsche* a mushy, paste-like substance, a formless mass; cf also swGer dial *Flatsche* a flat cake, patty]

=**milk pie.**

1948 Hutchison *PA Du. Cook Book* 123, *Milk Flitche*—1½ tablespoons flour (sifted)[,] ¾ cup milk[,] 1½ tablespoons sugar[,] 1½ tablespoons butter[,] Cinnamon. . . Pour into the crust. . . Makes one 7-inch pie. . . *Flitche* is considered untranslatable, but may possibly mean something put together with a flick of the wrist, casually. **1967–68** *DARE* (Qu. H63, *Kinds of desserts*) Inf **PA**41, Milk flatscher [flɑčɚ]; **PA**159, Milk flatscher. [Both Infs old] [**1982** Beam *PA Ger. Dict.* 75, *Milk-pie* . . der Millichflitscher.]

milk gap n Also *milking gap* [Cf **gap** n[1] **2, 3**] **chiefly sAppalachians** Cf **milk lot**

An opening in a fence where cows and calves are let in at milking time; the pen where cows are milked, esp a small one in a pasture.

1913 Morley *Carolina Mts.* 172, In some places the people still go to the "milking gap" to milk the cows. **1937** *Hall Coll.* eTN, *Milk gap.* . . A place where cows are penned for milking. **1938** Stuart *Dark Hills* 58, I told her my plans at the milk gap every evening after spring came on and the cows were turned out on the grass. **1946** *PADS* 5.30 VA, *Milk gap.* . .: Pen for cows; in the southern part of the Blue Ridge. **1949** Kurath *Word Geog.* 36, One of the striking South Midland innovations is the term *milk gap, milking gap* . . for a rail enclosure where the cows are milked. We find it in Western North Carolina and Virginia (south of the James), and in all of West Virginia except the upper reaches of the Potomac and the counties bordering on the Ohio north of the mouth of the Kanawha. Not a single instance of this expression has been recorded outside this area. **1952** Brown *NC Folkl.* 1.565, *Milk-gap.* . . The gap through which cows and calves pass at milking time.—West. **1966** Dakin *Dial. Vocab. Ohio R. Valley* 2.90, *Milk lot* appears along the Ohio below the Muskingum and in the southern Mountains, but is greatly outnumbered in these same regions by the distinctive South Midland *milk(ing) gap.* This latter term is almost invariably *milk gap* in the [Ohio R.] Valley. . . *Milk gap* . . is used by almost every informant in the eastern Knobs and Mountains [of KY] from the upper reaches of the Licking River to the Tennessee-Virginia boundaries. *Ibid* 91, The *milk gap* is typically a small enclosure constructed of rails and frequently described as "out in the pasture," "in the corner of a field," etc., although it can also be near the barn. . . Some unquestionably use this term not as a name for the entire enclosure but only for the gate or the place where the rails let down—that is, where cows enter the *cow lot* . . to be milked. **1967** Faries *Word Geog. MO* 77, The Appalachian and the Blue Ridge expressions *milk gap* and *milking gap* muster only thirty-four and five occurrences respectively [out of 700 infs], these occurring mostly in the Ozark Highland area. **1968** *DARE* FW Addit **VA**14, Milking gap—the place in the pasture or barn lot where the women found it most convenient to milk the cows. **a1975** Lunsford *It Used to Be* 165 **sAppalachians**, "Milkgap" is the place where the milkmaid goes to let down the fence. She lets down the bars of whatever gap it might be to let the little calves in to the cows so they can get their part of the milk first before she milks. She lets them go in and stay until they get what milk they're allowed to have, which would be half in each case. Then they are turned back, the gap is closed up, and the milkmaid milks the cows. **1982** Ginns *Snowbird Gravy* 171 **nwNC**, You know, there aren't many people that know what a milk gap is. It's a kind of a fenced in little place. Maybe the cows are all in the pasture, and you call 'em in to milk 'em. And you get 'em in this little corral and feed them and milk them, you know. **1983** *MJLF* 9.1.47 **ceKY**, *Milk gap* . . a rail enclosure alongside a fence, where cows are milked. **1986** Pederson *LAGS Concordance (Place where cows are staked or penned for milking)* 15 infs, **esp eTN**, Milk gap [4 infs say they have only heard this term.]; 1 inf, **neTN**, Milk gap—a barred corner of the field; 1 inf, **ceTN**, Milk gap—down at the slip bars; 1 inf, **cnAL**, Milk gap—has heard; not a pen; crossing at a ditch; 1 inf, **cwMS**, Milk gap—a sort of gate between pen and pasture; 1 inf, **neTN**, Milking gap.

milk gland n
=marrow gut.
   1970 *DARE* (Qu. H43, *Foods made from parts of the head and inner organs of an animal*) Inf **CA**205, Marigut—milk gland of a young cow, fry it.

milk house n **widespread, but less freq Sth, Atlantic** See Map Cf **dairy 1, milk room, spring house**
A small building in which milk and other food can be kept cool.
   1666 in 1887 East Hampton NY *Records* 1.248, Eight boards over the milke house. **1842** Kirkland *Forest Life* 1.239 **MI**, A buttery and milk-house supply other rustic dainties in profusion. **1883** *Wheelman* 1.245 **NEng**, A milk-house, with running-water troughs to convey the refuse milk to the piggery. **1908** Fox *Lonesome Pine* 18 **KY**, Geese and ducks were hunting crawfish in the little creek that ran from a milkhouse of logs. **1913** (1980) Hardy *OH Schoolmistress* 18, In the left hand corner of the yard was the well with its wooden pump and the milk house nearby shaded by young sycamore trees. **1942** Whipple *Joshua* 200 **UT** (as of c1860), The 'milk-house'—around the well Abijah had built a little board house with a hinged lid they could raise. The well was rocked up high, and underneath the lid, just above the surface of the water, were shelves—shelves stocked with wooden bowls of milk, eggs, butter. **1965–70** *DARE* (Qu. M18, *The separate building where milk is kept cool*) 480 Infs, **widespread, but less freq Sth, Atlantic, CA**, Milk house; (Qu. D9, *To prevent bread and cake from drying, you put them in a _____*) Inf **NC**20, Milk house; (Qu. D10a, *The place to keep food cool, usually with ice, so that it won't spoil*) Infs **NM**12, **NC**14, **VA**47, Milk house; (Qu. M22, . . *Kinds of buildings* . . *on farms*) Infs **CA**9, **KS**4, **MO**17, 25, Milk house. **1966–70** *DARE* Tape **CA**156, The milk house was where milk was kept and was built on a spring; **KY**77, I had a milk house, then the spring an' the water run through an' you had a trough built in a little corner of it, and the water run through it all the time an' that's where I kept butter; **OK**32, We had a real good

milk house. . . In those days . . there wasn't such a thing as a refrigerator. . . We kept our milk and eggs and things cool in that with the water running through in a trough. **1982** *Barrick Coll.* **csPA**, *Milk house*—small ancillary building near barn, with trough for cooling milk cans. **1989** Mosher *Stranger* 72 **nVT** (as of 1952), As he was wheeling two forty-quart milkcans down a short ramp to the milkhouse, he tripped and lost the entire load.

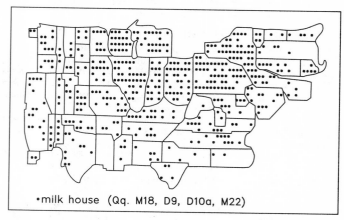
•milk house (Qq. M18, D9, D10a, M22)

milking See **milk C**

milking cow n **scattered, but esp NEast** See Map
=milk cow.
   1965–70 *DARE* (Qu. K1, *A cow that is giving milk is a _____*) 19 Infs, **scattered, but esp NEast**, Milking cow; [**MD**34, **MA**16, She's milking]. **1986** Pederson *LAGS Concordance (Cow: the kind you keep for milk)* 3 infs, **seAL, cwGA, cLA**, Milking cow(s).

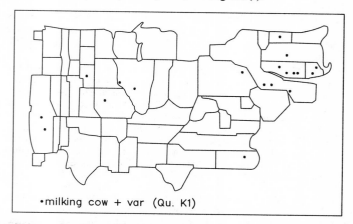
•milking cow + var (Qu. K1)

milking gap See **milk gap**
milking jug See **milk B2**
milking lot See **milk lot**
milking pen See **milk pen**
milking stars n pl
   1936 *AmSp* 11.316 **Ozarks**, *Milking stars.* . . The constellation of Orion. It is said that these stars often rise at milking time.

milk, in the adj phr Also *in milk* Cf **dough, in (the); green corn 2, milk corn**
Of grain, now esp corn: at the stage preceding full maturity, in which the grains exude a milky fluid when pierced.
   1772 in 1904 GA Hist. Soc. *Coll.* 6.213, The Rice came up rather unequal, so that a good deal of those Fields were in Milk. **1778** Carver *Travels N. Amer.* 25 **ceWI**, Whilst their corn is in the milk, as they term it, that is, just before it begins to ripen, they [=Amer Indians] slice off the kernels from the cob. **1835** (1955) *Crockett Almanacks* 14 **wTN**, And in the West, while the ear of Indian corn is still young, soft and tender, or "in the milk," it is very sweet. **1838** MA Ag. Surv. *Rept. for 1837* 98, Late sown wheat is not likely to pass beyond that season before it gets into a condition to be injured, which is while it is in the milk.

1941 *LANE* Map 261, 1 inf, **cCT**, The corn is in the milk. **c1960** *Wilson Coll.* **csKY**, *Corn in the milk:* . . Corn ready to be eaten as roasting-ears. *Ibid,* In the milk. . . Corn or wheat in that immature stage. **1965–70** *DARE* (Qu. I32, *How do you know when corn is ready to eat?*; total Infs questioned, 75) Inf **AR27**, It's in the milk; [**MS34**, Milk comes out when you stick your nail in it; **OK27**, Milk comes out of the kernels when you stick your finger in them;] (Qu. I33, . . *Ears of corn that are just right for eating*) Infs **IL29, IN69, MI23, WI30**, In the milk; **CA196**, Right in the milk; [**NJ56**, Soft and milky].

milk ipecac n Cf **wild ipecac**

1 also *American ipecac:* **=spreading dogbane.**

1874 *Shaker Med. Preparations* 137, Bitterroot—*Apocynum androsaemifolium.* . . Milk Ipecac. **1892** (1974) Millspaugh *Amer. Med. Plants* 132-1, *Apocynum androsaemifolium.* . . American ipecac. [*Ibid* 132-3, *Apocynum A.* is an emetic without causing nausea.] **1935** (1943) Muenscher *Weeds* 360, *Apocynum androsaemifolium.* . . Milk ipecac. . . Widespread throughout the northern states and southern Canada. **1971** Krochmal *Appalachia Med. Plants* 50, *Apocynum androsaemifolium.* . . Common names . . American ipecac, . . milk ipecac. . . This plant . . has been used also as a tonic, diuretic, and purgative. **1974** (1977) Coon *Useful Plants* 61, *Apocynum androsaemifolium* . . milk ipecac.

2 A **spurge:** usu **flowering spurge,** but also *Euphorbia ipecacuanhae.*

1876 Hobbs *Bot. Hdbk.* 70, Milk ipecac, Blooming spurge, Euphorbia corollata. **1900** Lyons *Plant Names* 156, *E[uphorbia] corollata.* . . Milk Ipecac. . . *E. Ipecacuanha* [sic]. . . Milk Ipecac. **1940** Clute *Amer. Plant Names* 98, *E[uphorbia] corollata.* . . Flowering spurge . . milk ipecac.

3 A **boneset 1** (here: *Eupatorium rugosum*).

1959 Carleton *Index Herb. Plants* 81, *Milk Ipecac:* Eupatorium urticaefolium.

milk jug See **milk B2**

milk leg n

1 A painful swelling of the leg, esp of the veins, that occurs esp following childbirth (see quot 1890); transf: varicose veins; a leg with varicose veins; weakness of the leg. Cf **milk vein**

1890 *Century Dict.* 4447, *Phlegmasia dolens* . . puerperal tumid leg: an affection presenting thrombosis of the large veins of the part, with swelling, hardness, whiteness of the skin, and much pain, usually affecting the leg, most frequently after childbirth. Also called . . *milk-leg* and *white-leg.* **1930** (1935) Porter *Flowering Judas* 122 **TX**, Where were you forty years ago when I pulled through milk-leg and double pneumonia? **1950** *WELS Suppl., Milk leg*—Apparently congenital condition of a leg which tends to be weak throughout life; may lead to a decided limp, or even complete paralysis. **1960** Williams *Walk Egypt* 205 **GA**, I had milk leg the worst. **1965–70** *DARE* (Qu. AA29, . . *The blue, swollen veins that a woman often gets on her legs while expecting a baby*) 21 Infs, **scattered**, Milk leg; **NY211, PA139, 152**, Milk legs; **CT27**, Milk leg—legs swell up; **FL18**, Milk leg—swelling of the leg; **GA81**, Milk leg—a leg with varicose veins; **IL135**, Milk leg—a disease; **RI10**, Milk leg—when legs and veins swell; **SC7**, Milk leg—old-time name; **SC24**, Milk veins—generally comes after the baby's born and they call it "milk leg"; **VA31**, Milk leg—following the child's birth; **WY3**, Milk leg—water in tissues; **NY250**, Milk legs—develops sometimes after pregnancy. **1983** *DARE* File **csWI** (as of 1930), They called it a milk leg because it came when a woman was breast-feeding a baby. **1990** Cavender *Folk Med. Lexicon* 27 **sAppalachians**, *Milk leg*—a. phlebitis acquired by women shortly after birth. *b.* an infection in the veins of the legs. *c.* weakening of the arms and legs.

2 Chronic swelling of a horse's leg following an attack of lymphangitis. Cf **big leg**

1966 *DARE* (Qu. K47, . . *Diseases . . horses or mules commonly get*) Inf **ID1**, Milk leg.

3 A disease of lactating cows; perh **milk fever.**

1945 *Richmond Times-Dispatch* (VA) 26 June 6/7 (Hench Coll.), The plagues that ravage the farmers' flocks and herds are as much the children of nature as the herds and flocks they ravage. Nature is the mother of the milk-leg and the anthrax. **1966–69** *DARE* (Qu. K7, *What sickness can a cow get in her udder—for example, if she's left unmilked too long?*) Inf **CA116**, Milk leg—an inflammation; **CA157**, Milk leg; **TX32**, Milk leg—I think this is from giving birth; (Qu. K28, . . *Chief diseases that cows have*) Infs **OK27, SC1**, Milk leg; **CA157**, Milk fever (milk leg).

milk line See **milk train**

milk lot n Also *milking lot* [**lot** n **1a**] **chiefly Sth, S Midl** Cf **milk gap**

An enclosure where cows are milked.

1949 Kurath *Word Geog.* 55, In addition to these terms [=*cow pen, milk gap,* etc], *cow lot* and *milk lot* turn up in scattered fashion in different parts of the South and the South Midland. **1966** Dakin *Dial. Vocab. Ohio R. Valley* 2.90, *Milk lot* appears along the Ohio [River] below the Muskingum and in the southern Mountains, but is greatly outnumbered in these same regions by the distinctive South Midland *milk(ing) gap.* **1967** Faries *Word Geog. MO* 76, *Cow lot* and *milk lot* . . appear to be the prevailing terms in Missouri for an enclosure adjoining a cow barn or shed . . , the latter being least common in the southeastern one-fourth of the state. **1970** Tarpley *Blinky* 128 **neTX**, Small enclosure outside where cows are kept. . . Milk lot [rare]. **1986** Pederson *LAGS Concordance* (Place where cows are staked or penned for milking) 15 infs, **Gulf Region**, Milk(ing) lot.

milkmaids n [In England applied to *Cardamine pratensis* as well as other plants; see *OED, EDD*]

A **toothwort** (here: *Cardamine californica* or *C. integrifolia*). Note: Some authorities place these plants in the genus *Dentaria* instead.

1897 Parsons *Wild Flowers CA* 4, *Dentaria Californica.* . . Various . . names have been applied to these flowers, such as . . "milkmaids." **1911** Jepson *Flora CA* 188, *D[entaria] integrifolia.* . . Milk-maids. . . Abundant in the valleys and on the plains, often whitening the fields in Feb. and Mar. **1932** Rydberg *Flora Prairies* 377, *Dentaria.* . . Toothwort, Milkmaids. **1954** CA Div. Beaches & Parks *Pt. Lobos Wild Flowers* 29, *Milk-maids* (*Dentaria californica*). . . Nearly all of the Milk-maids . . are by the roadside at the Big Mound Meadow. . . The four-petaled, dime-sized flowers are white, tinged with pink, and they close at night. **1961** Thomas *Flora Santa Cruz* 182 **cwCA**, *D. californica* Nutt. var. *integrifolia.* . . Milkmaids. . . In general, plants do not flower in any great number until February. **1973** Hitchcock–Cronquist *Flora Pacific NW* 158, Milk maids. . . *C[ardamine] integrifolia.*

milkmaid's path n [*EDD* (at *milk* sb. 1.(25)) "the milky way"] Cf **milky way 1**

The Milky Way; transf: a band of clouds.

1912 Green *VA Folk-Speech* 281, *Milkmaid's path.* . . The Milky-way. **1943** Weslager *DE Forgotten Folk* 174, Wherever the narrow end of the Milkmaid's Path is, the wind will blow from that direction the next day. [Weslager: Apparently refers to Milky Way.] **1968** *DARE* (Qu. B11, . . *Other kinds of clouds that come often*) Inf **OH39**, Milkmaid's path—sort of a streak of clouds across the sky in the evening, wider than a jet trail.

milk mushroom See **milky cap**

milk pail See **milk B2**

milk parsley See **milk purslane 1**

milk pea n

A plant of the genus *Galactia.*

1843 Torrey *Flora NY* 1.162, *Galactia.* . . Milk Pea. . . Flowers purplish. **1891** Coulter *Botany W. TX* 88, *Galactia.* . . Milk-pea. . . Texas . . to the lower Rio Grande. **1910** Shreve *MD Plant Life* 449, *Galactia regularis.* . . Milk Pea. **1946** Tatnall *Flora DE* 160, *Milk Pea.* . . Frequent in dry, sandy pinelands. **1953** Greene–Blomquist *Flowers South* 60, Elliott's milk-pea . . is a unique species of *Galactia* in having 7–9 evergreen leaflets and white flowers. **1976** Fleming *Wild Flowers FL* 64, *Milk pea* . . is a much-branched perennial vine that may either lie on the ground or climb. . . The pod is flat; the halves twist spirally when mature, which releases the seeds. **1979** Ajilvsgi *Wild Flowers* 176 **wLA, eTX**, *MaCree's milkpea.* . . flowers solitary or in twos or threes.

milk peanut n

=hog peanut 1.

1939 Tharp *Vegetation TX* 59, Milk Peanut (*Falcata*).

milk pen n Also *milking pen* **esp Gulf States, TX**

=milk lot.

1906 in 1921 Thorp *Songs Cowboys* 144 **NM**, But Mollie hed gone to the milk-pen as she heard the milk cows bawl. **1956** Ker *Vocab. W. TX* 165, For a yard or enclosure about the barn . . *pen* has only limited currency with three entries for *cow pen* and one for *milk pen.* **1967** *DARE* Tape **TX24**, I can remember on one occasion they [=wolves] came here and killed a milk pen calf of mine. **1967** Faries *Word Geog.*

MO 77, For an enclosure adjoining a cow barn or shed. . . A few informants list the expressions *barn lot, holding lot,* and *milking pen.* **1986** Pederson *LAGS Concordance (Place where cows are staked or penned for milking)* 15 infs, **Gulf Region,** Milk(ing) pen.

milk pie n **PaGer area** Cf **milk flatscher**
A custard-like pie.

1950 Klees *PA Dutch* 416, I do not mean to imply that . . all Pennsylvania Dutch pies are good. . . Milk pie I consider a pale makeshift of a pie. [**1953** *Reading Times* 8 July 7/2 *(Mathews Coll.)* **PA,** He ate generous quantities of . . millich pie.] **1967** *DARE* (Qu. H63, *Kinds of desserts*) Inf **PA40,** Poor man's pie, same as milk pie. **1982** Beam *PA Ger. Dict.* 75, Milk-pie.

milk pig n
1969 *DARE* (Qu. K51, *. . Pigs, a very young one*) Inf **IL59,** Milk pig.

milk pink n
A **skeletonweed** (here: *Lygodesmia juncea*).

1953 Nelson *Plants Rocky Mt. Park* 179, In addition the following species grow in the park: . . *milkpink* or *skeleton weed, Lygodesmia juncea* . . and *golden curlyhead, Pyrrocoma crocea.*

milk purslane n
1 also *milk parsley, milky pussley;* for addit varr see quots: A **spurge** such as **flowering spurge** or *Euphorbia ipecacuanhae,* but usu *E. maculata.* [From its milky juice]

1828 Rafinesque *Med. Flora* 1.181, *Euphorbia corollata.* . . *Vulgar Names* . . Milk-purslain. **1843** Torrey *Flora NY* 2.176, *Euphorbia maculata.* . . Milk Purselane. . . Fields, cultivated grounds and roadsides, usually in dry soils. **1854** King *Amer. Eclectic Dispensatory* 461, *Euphorbia hypericifolia.* . . This plant, also known by the names of . . *Milk-pursely, Eye-bright,* etc., is an annual plant. **1873** in 1976 Miller *Shaker Herbs* 170, *Euphorbia ipecacuanha* [sic]. . . Milk Purslane. . . Valuable in bilious colic, dropsical affections, . . and sluggishness of the liver. **1876** Hobbs *Bot. Hdbk.* 70, Milk pursely, Blooming spurge, Euphorbia corollata. *Ibid* 94, Purslain, Milk, Blooming spurge, Euphorbia corollata. . . Pursely, Milk, Large spotted spurge, Euphorbia maculata. **1892** (1974) Millspaugh *Amer. Med. Plants* 147-1, *Euphorbia hypericifolia.* . . Com[mon] names. . . Milk parsley or purslane. . . *Euphorbia.* This genus consists of herbs or shrubs with a milky juice. **1901** Lounsberry *S. Wild Flowers* 301, *E. maculata,* . . milk purslane. . . Its leaves are very small, . . and besides being blotched turn to brilliant shades of red and purple. **1931** Harned *Wild Flowers Alleghanies* 273, *Milk Purslane.* . . When cut or bruised the stem and leaves emit a sticky milk. **1950** Gray–Fernald *Manual of Botany* 970, *E. supina.* . . *Milk-purslane.* . . Generally common. **1968** *DARE* (Qu. BB22) Inf **NY68,** Old Frank used to take milky pussley and dry it and take that for when he had diarrhea.

2 as *milk pussley:* A **purslane** (here: *Portulaca oleracea*).
1943 Weslager *DE Forgotten Folk* 161, The following record of Cheswold herbs represents an ethnobotanical study of hitherto unformulated cures and applies only to the Cheswold Moors. . . Milk Pussley—*Portulaca oleracea*—Tea for dysentery.

milk room n Also *milk cooler room* **scattered, but chiefly NEng, Sth, S Midl** See Map Cf **milk house**
A room or small building where food, esp milk, is kept cool.

1836 *Knickerbocker* 8.706 **cNY,** In the rear, is quite a city of additions, in the shape of bed-rooms, bath-rooms, milk-rooms, buttery. **1871** (1882) Stowe *Fireside Stories* 157 **MA,** He was laid out in the back

chamber, you see, over the milk-room and kitchen. **1941** *LANE* Map 344 *(Pantry)* 8 infs, 7 **CT,** Milk room. **1965–70** *DARE* (Qu. M18, *The separate building where milk is kept cool*) 54 Infs, **scattered, but chiefly NEng, Sth, S Midl,** Milk room; **KY27,** Milk cooler room; (Qu. M22, *. . Kinds of buildings . . on farms*) Inf **NC36,** Milk room. **1986** Pederson *LAGS Concordance (Place for milk and butter)* 5 infs, **Gulf Region,** Milk room.

milk route n
1 See **milk train.**
2 See **milk B2.**

milk run See **milk train**

milks cow See **milch cow**

milk shake n
1 A drink made with milk and flavoring vigorously mixed together, but without ice cream. **esp MA, RI** Cf **cabinet, frappe**

1890 *Century Dict.* 3763, *Milk-shake.* . . A beverage composed of milk and carbonated water with the addition of a flavoring, mixed by being vigorously shaken up and down by hand or by a small machine. [*Century* Ed: Recent, U.S.] **1895** (1900) Arnold *Century Cook Book* 557, *Milk Shake*—Fill a glass two thirds full of milk; sweeten it to taste with any fruit syrup, or with a syrup made of boiled sugar flavored with vanilla, orange-flower water, or any liqueur; strained preserve of any kind or liquefied jelly may be used. Fill up the glass with cracked ice and shake together until well mixed. **1965–89** *DARE* File **csMA,** A *frappe* is . . an ice cream milk shake; **cVA,** A [plain] milk shake is made without ice cream; **nCA,** Boston must be infamous for its milk shakes. Before visiting there in 1963 I was warned that if I wanted a *real* milk shake, one with ice cream, I had to order a frappe; **wMA,** A frappe . . a milk shake with ice cream; **Providence RI, Fall River MA,** Cabinet—an ice-cream milk shake. **1971** *Today Show Letters,* In Rhode Island a milkshake is milk and flavoring. If you want ice cream in it, you ask for a "cabinet." **1980** Safire *On Language* 65 **ceMA,** Just south of Boston, ordering a milkshake would get you milk mixed with flavored syrup; no ice cream was included. **1982** Chaika *Speaking RI* [7], *Milk shake* = just what the name says: milk and syrup shook up. *No ice cream.*

2 See **milk B2.**

milksick n [Cf Intro "Language Changes" III.4, 5] **chiefly S Midl**
Milk sickness.

1818 *MO Gaz. & Pub. Advt.* (St. Louis) 14 Aug 3/3, *Milk-sick.* A disease called by the above name prevail [sic] along the marshes of the American Bottom, in Illinois territory, and in certain spots on the Missouri. . . We have no doubt but this disease in cattle is occasioned by . . Water Hemlock. **1885** Murfree *Prophet of Smoky Mts.* 47 **TN,** She [=a cow] lay down an' died o' the milk-sick. **1913** Kephart *Highlanders* 229 **sAppalachians,** A more mysterious disease is "milk-sick," which prevails in certain restricted districts, chiefly where cattle graze in rich and deeply shaded coves. **1913** Morley *Carolina Mts.* 281, And do they still have to guard against the "milk-sick" over there in Pizen Cove? It was in this region that one first saw a "milk-sick pen," and heard of the curious sickness which, attacking cattle that eat grass or leaves in certain well-defined spots, through the milk poisons the people, sometimes fatally. **1941** Writers' Program *Guide IN* 400 **swIN,** In the autumn of 1818 the settlers were beset by a fever called 'milk sick' because it attacked cattle and particularly milch cows, as readily as men and women. There was no cure and the victims usually died quickly. **1960** Williams *Walk Egypt* 255 **nGA,** She said aloud, "Fool cow. . . Now if you went and broke into the milk-sick pen. . . " Good riddance. . . Grass and berries were fine and green, but let a cow crop there, a possum pull the berries, and they would surely die. There was something evil in the earth, and there was nothing you could do about it, soda or lime, nothing but fence it off and put up a sign: "Beware. Milk-sick." **1966–68** *DARE* (Qu. K28, *. . Chief diseases that cows have*) Inf **NC36,** Milksick; (Qu. BB49, *. . Other kinds of diseases*) Inf **IN38,** Milksick. **1971** *Foxfire* Winter 248 **nGA,** Sometimes . . even a doctor can't save a lady. If they take childbed fever or milksick or somethin' like that. **a1975** Lunsford *It Used to Be* 159 **sAppalachians,** "Milksick" is said to be a sort of mold that is found high up in the coves on the mountain and that the cattle eat in the spring of the year. It will make people sick to use the milk, and they say that is "milksick," and they call the mold or the disease "milksick."

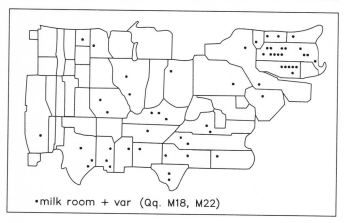
•milk room + var (Qq. M18, M22)

milksick plant n Also *milksick*
A **boneset 1** (here: *Eupatorium rugosum*).
1931 Clute *Common Plants* 125, The milk-sick plant (*Eupatorium ageratoides*) is an abundant wild species . . on the farm it frequently causes a disease in cattle known as "trembles" and produces in human beings who use the milk from such cattle, an affection known as milk-sickness which is often fatal. **1959** Carleton *Index Herb. Plants* 81, Milk Sick: *Eupatorium urticaefolium*.

milk sister See **milk brother**

milk snake n [From the folk belief that it sucks milk from cows]
1 also *milk adder*, *~ sucker*: A **king snake 1**: usu *Lampropeltis triangulum*. **chiefly NEast, N Cent** See Map For other names of *L. triangulum* see **adder, candycane snake, checkered adder, chicken snake 2, coral ~ 2a, cow ~ 2, cowsucker 2, house snake 1, red adder, scarlet king snake, scarlet ~, spotted adder, thunder snake** Cf **barn snake, cane ~**
1800 (1826) Maude *Niagara* 41 **cNY**, Kane killed two Garter and one Black Snake; saw Milk Snake dead on the road. **1807** MA Hist. Soc. *Coll.* 2d ser 3.54, The only snakes found on the island are the black snake . . [and] the milk or house snake, speckled like a rattlesnake; all harmless. **1825** Neal *Brother Jonathan* 1.143 **CT**, Ever seed a snarl o' black sneks thawin' out—in sugar time—under a pooty smart rock heap? Winkin' away . . jess like so many milk adders, at a frog pond. **1842** DeKay *Zool. NY* 3.38, The Milk Snake. *Coluber eximius*. . . In this State, its most usual popular name is *Milk Snake*, although it has various other appellations. **1885** Holder *Marvels Animal Life* 120 **NY**, Many farmers . . believe that the milk-snake . . deprives cows . . of their supply of milk. **1900** U.S. Natl. Museum *Annual Rept. for 1898* 886, *Osceola doliata triangula.* . . This subspecies, the common "milk snake," is abundant in the Middle States. **1911** (1913) Johnson *Highways Gt. Lakes* 86, There used to be quite a few milk-snakes here. I know a fellow who noticed he wa'n't getting the milk he ought to get from one of his cows. So he watched her, and while she was lying down out in the pasture he saw one of those short, thick, light-colored milk-snakes come and suck her. **1925** TX Folkl. Soc. *Pub.* 4.45, The milk snake . . is supposed to visit cow lots and clandestinely to relieve cows of their milk. In some states, the name is applied to a variety of king snake; in Indiana, to *Lampropeltis triangulum* . . , and in southeastern Missouri, to its scarlet cousin, *Lampropeltis triangulum amaura*. **1928** Pope–Dickinson *Amphibians* 57 **WI**, Milk Snake. . . Other local names for this snake are Checkered Adder, Spotted Adder and Milk Sucker. **1950** WELS (*Kinds of snakes*) 2 Infs, **csWI**, Milk snake. **1954** Harder Coll. **cwTN**, *Milk snake.* **1965–70** DARE (Qu. P25, . . *Kinds of snakes*) 76 Infs, **chiefly NEast, N Cent**, Milk snake; **MA**1, Milk snake—said to milk cows; **MA**6, Milk snake—will suck milk from cow's tit; **ME**6, 20, **MA**97, Milk adder. **1974** Shaw–Campbell *Snakes West* 123, The story, told as fact by many dairy farmers, has it that the milk snake obtains a substantial part of its diet by milking cows. . . The method described is quite simple: the snake climbs a leg, coils around it, stretches out its neck, seizes a teat, and sucks away. **1981** Vogt *Nat. Hist. WI* 144, The name milk snake stems from an Old World folk tale about a snake that supposedly sucked the milk of nursing mothers. Similarly to its European counterpart, this species supposedly sucks the milk of cows and causes them to go dry.

2 A **racer** such as the **blue racer 1**. Cf **blacksnake 1, cowsucker 1**
1925 TX Folkl. Soc. *Pub.* 4.45, The milk snake . . is supposed to visit cow lots and clandestinely to relieve cows of their milk. . . In Louisiana . . , the name has been shifted to the southern phase of the blue racer, *Bascanion constrictor*. **1968** DARE (Qu. P25, . . *Kinds of snakes*) Inf **PA**168, Blacksnake—sometimes called a milk snake, but it isn't.
3 A **garter snake 1**.
1967 DARE (Qu. P25, . . *Kinds of snakes*) Inf **NJ**2, Milk snake = garter [snake]—equated by some.

milk-sourer n [See quot]
Either the **black-billed cuckoo** or the **yellow-billed cuckoo**.
1956 MA Audubon Soc. *Bulletin* 40.80 **ME**, Yellow-billed Cuckoo. . . Milk-sourer (Maine. Warm, humid weather, preceding rain, hastens the souring of milk; under those weather conditions, the cuckoo is most clamorous; hence it is superstitiously believed to have some connection with the souring.) . . Black-billed cuckoo. . . Milk-sourer.

milk stop See **milk train**

milk sucker See **milk snake 1**

milksweet n [From its use in making cheese]
A **cleavers** (here: *Galium aparine*).
1971 Krochmal *Appalachia Med. Plants* 126, Galium Aparine . . milksweet.

milk tea n Cf **kettle tea**
=**cambric tea**.
1949 AmSp 24.111 **cSC**, Milk tea. . . Milk diluted with hot water and sweetened.

milk thistle n
1 =**prickly lettuce**. [See quot 1912]
1912 Blatchley *IN Weed Book* 146, Lactuca scariola. . . Prickly Lettuce. Milk Thistle. [Ibid 147, The numerous prickles and bitter milky juice prevent all animals but sheep from feeding upon it.] **1936** IL Nat. Hist. Surv. *Wildflowers* 389, *Milk Thistle.* . . Sheep eat the young leaves quite greedily and cattle seem to like them also. Generally, however, it is considered a noxious weed because its hard stems dull reaping knives and its copious juice is a major annoyance in threshing machinery. **1974** (1977) Coon *Useful Plants* 113, Milk . . thistle. . . can provide a salad basis when the plant is young and tender.
2 A **prickly poppy** (here: *Argemone hispida*).
1915 (1926) Armstrong–Thornber *Western Wild Flowers* 162, *Milk Thistle. Argemone hispida.* . . The prickly, bluish-green foliage of this . . handsome plant is thistle-like both in form and color. The leafy, branching stems . . are covered with dense, white or yellowish prickles and bear several lovely flowers.

milk train n Also *milk line*, *~ route*, *~ run*, *~ stop*; for addit varr see quot 1965–70 **chiefly Nth, N Midl, West** See Map
Orig a slow train that made freq stops to pick up cans of milk; by ext, any slow train.
1965–70 DARE (Qu. N37, *Joking names for a branch railroad that is not very important or gives poor service*) 85 Infs, **chiefly Nth, N Midl, West**, Milk train; 13 Infs, **esp Nth, N Midl, West**, Milk run; **IL**97, **ME**22, **MN**19, Milk route; **OR**1, Milk line; **IL**119, Milk stop; **WI**77,

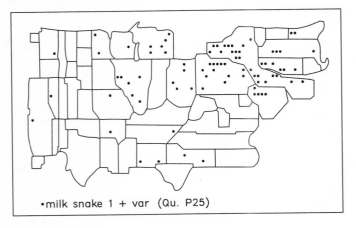
•milk snake 1 + var (Qu. P25)

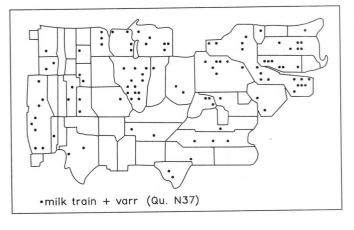
•milk train + varr (Qu. N37)

Milk-wagon express; **WA**28, Morning milk run. **1968** *AmSp* 43.288 [Railroad vocab], *Milk train.* A slow-moving local passenger train that makes frequent stops.

milk vein n Cf milk leg 1

A varicose vein.

1965–70 *DARE* (Qu. AA29, . . *The blue, swollen veins that a woman often gets on her legs while expecting a baby*) 25 Infs, **scattered,** Milk veins.

milk vetch n

Std: a plant of the genus *Astragalus.* Also called **buffalo bean, buffalo pea 1, cow weed, crazyweed, ground plum 1, locoweed, poison vetch, rattlepod, rattleweed.** For other names of var spp see **balloon plant, bird-egg pea, dapplepod, fitsroot, garbancillo, ladyfinger 5, lady's slipper 8, painted pod, pink ladyfingers, prairie apple, purple loco, rattlebox, rattle vetch, red-stemmed peavine, sheep loco, sheep-pod, speedpod, Texas loco, turkey pea, woolly loco**

milkweed n [From the milky juice of these plants]

1 also attrib: A plant of the family Asclepiadaceae, usu of the genus *Asclepias.* **widespread, but less freq Sth** For other names of this genus see **cushion weed, Indian hemp 3, silkweed, speckled John, swallowwort;** for other names of var spp of this genus see **bedstraw milkweed, bee weed 2b, butterfly ~ 1, cotton milkweed, cottonweed 2, green milkweed, horsetail ~, orange ~, poison ~, purple ~, rabbit's ~, redhead, red milkweed, sand ~, sandhill ~, spider ~, sunset flower, swamp milkweed, wax ~, white ~, white-flowered ~, whorled ~, wild cotton**

[**1761** in 1922 Fries *Rec. Moravians* 1.237 **NC,** Careful survey was made of the native herbs, with an eye to their medicinal value, and several useful ones were found . . "Squasweed" for rheumatism, "Milkweed" for pleurisy.] **1814** Bigelow *Florula Bostoniensis* 62, *Asclepias Syriaca.* . . Common Silk weed or Milk weed. . . is used as a substitute for feathers, fur, cotton, &c. **1854** King *Amer. Eclectic Dispensatory* 256, Asclepias Syriaca. . . known as *Milkweed* in many parts of the country, has a large, stout, simple, somewhat branched *stem.* **1871** (1882) Stowe *Fireside Stories* 43 **MA,** Wal, that was the reason why Jeff Sullivan couldn't come it round Ruth tho' he was silkier than a milkweed-pod. **1891** *Jrl. Amer. Folkl.* 4.148, Mrs. Hayward, who came from Middleborough, Mass., when I spoke of *Milkweed,* always understood Asclepias. **1941** Jaeger *Wildflowers* 185 **Desert SW,** *Purple Climbing Milkweed. Funastrum heterophyllum.* . . A climbing perennial, with rank, milky juice. . . *Rambling Milkweed. Funastrum hirtellum.* . . Much like the purple climbing milkweed but with smaller flowers and more hairy herbage. **1953** Greene–Blomquist *Flowers South* 102, *Milkweed-Vine (Funastrum clausum)* A vine with . . white fragrant flowers blooming all year. . . Hammocks of coastal and lake regions of peninsular Fla. and the Keys. **1965–70** *DARE* (Qu. S21, . . *Weeds . . that are a trouble in gardens and fields*) 51 Infs, **scattered, but somewhat less freq Sth,** Milkweed(s); (Qu. S15, . . *Weed seeds that cling to clothing*) 12 Infs, **chiefly Nth, N Midl,** Milkweed; **CT**15, 42, **GA**80, **IA**22, **MD**9, **NY**41, 205, **PA**181, Milkweed pod(s) (*or* seed(s), sticks); (Qu. S26a, . . *Wildflowers . . Roadside flowers*) 15 Infs, **chiefly Nth, N Midl,** Milkweed(s); (Qu. I28b, *Kinds of greens that are cooked*) 10 Infs, **NEast,** Milkweed(s); **NY**106, Milkweed tips; **NY**123, Milkweed greens; **NY**75, Small milkweed; (Qu. S26d, *Wildflowers that grow in meadows; not asked in early QRs*) 11 Infs, **scattered,** Milkweed; (Qu. S26e, *Other wildflowers not yet mentioned; not asked in early QRs*) 11 Infs, **scattered,** Milkweed; (Qu. I28a, . . *Kinds of things . . you call 'greens' . . [Those that are eaten raw]*) Inf **NY**146, Milkweed; **NY**1, Milkweed greens; (Qu. S6) Inf **SD**1, Milkweed; (Qu. S9) Infs **MD**36, **WA**28, Milkweed; (Qu. S11) Inf **NC**6, Milkweed; (Qu. S13) Inf **OH**45, Milkweed; (Qu. S14) Infs **MI**82, **MO**1, **NY**20, Milkweed; **CO**22, **IL**63, Milkweed seed(s); (Qu. S17) Infs **NC**52, **TX**68, Milkweed; (Qu. S20) Infs **CA**9, **MI**2, **NY**79, **OH**80, Milkweed; (Qu. S25) Inf **CA**7, Milkweed; (Qu. S26b, *Wildflowers that grow in water or wet places*) Inf **WI**20, Milkweed; (Qu. BB50c, *Remedies for infections*) Inf **NY**183, Milkweed poultice. [*DARE* Ed: Some of these Infs may refer instead to other senses below.] **1965–70** *DARE* Wildfl QR Plates 171–75, 21 Infs, chiefly **Nth,** Milkweed. **1985** Dodge *Flowers SW Deserts* 11, Readily recognizable because of their milky sap and the pods filled with silky-winged seeds, the milkweeds are generally considered poisonous to livestock, although rarely eaten.

2 A **spurge,** esp **flowering spurge.** [*OEDS* 1598 (for *Euphorbia helioscopia*)]

1828 Rafinesque *Med. Flora* 1.181, *Euphorbia corollata.* . . *Vulgar Names*—Milkweed [etc]. [*Ibid* 187, The milk of all the species of this genus [will] destroy Warts and cure Herpes.] **1854** King *Amer. Eclectic Dispensatory* 460, *Euphorbia corollata.* . . This plant has many common names, as . . *Milk-weed.* **1892** *Jrl. Amer. Folkl.* 5.102 **nOH,** *Euphorbia maculata,* milkweed. **1897** *Ibid* 10.143, *Euphorbia corollata,* . . milkweed, Madison, Wis. *Euphorbia Cyparissias,* . . milkweed, Vermont. . . *Euphorbia marginata,* . . milkweed, . . Waco, Tex. **1950** *WELS (Special cures for corns or warts)* 6 Infs, **WI,** Milkweed, milk from milkweed—for warts. **1959** [see **5** below]. **1965–70** *DARE* (Qu. BB51a, . . *Cures for corns or warts*) 28 Infs, **esp Nth, N Midl,** Milkweed milk; 10 Infs, **esp Nth, Midl,** Milkweed; **NY**68, Milkweed greens; **NY**196, Milkweed juice; **MO**11, Rub milkweed juice on warts; **CA**87, Wild milkweed juice. **1967** *DARE* FW Addit **AR**44, Fire-on-the-mountain—a kind of milkweed. **1972** Brown *Wildflowers LA* 102, *Milkweed . . Euphorbia heterophylla.* . . Annual herbs with milky sap up to 3 feet tall, much-branched.

3 Either of two related plants: usu **spreading dogbane,** but also **Indian hemp 1.**

1828 Rafinesque *Med. Flora* 1.49, *Apocynum androsemifolium* [sic]. . . *Vulgar Names*—Milk-weed, Bitter-root, Honey-bloom [etc]. [*Ibid* 51, All have a bitter milky juice, and yet the flowers smell of honey, and produce that sweet substance.] **1854** King *Amer. Eclectic Dispensatory* 226, *Apocynum androsaemifolium.* Bitter-root. . . This plant, likewise called *Dogsbane, Milk-weed,* etc., is found in nearly all parts of the United States. **1898** *Jrl. Amer. Folkl.* 11.275, *Apocynum androsaemifolium,* . . milkweed, Franklin Co., Me. **1900** Lyons *Plant Names* 40, *A[pocynum] androsaemifolium.* . . Milkweed. . . *A . . cannabinum.* . . Milkweed. **1930** Sievers *Amer. Med. Plants* 34, *Apocynum cannabinum.* . . *Other common names.* . . Milkweed. . . The plant contains a milky juice. . . *Apocynum androsaemifolium.* . . also contains a milky juice. **1968** *DARE* Wildfl QR Pl.170A Inf **WA**30, Wild milkweed. **1971** Krochmal *Appalachia Med. Plants* 52, *Apocynum cannabinum.* . . *Common Names.* . . milkweed. . . This plant is a cardiotonic drug that is extremely poisonous.

4 =**wild lettuce** (here: *Lactuca* spp). Cf **trumpet milkweed**

1891 *Jrl. Amer. Folkl.* 4.148 **swNH,** Lactuca [was] *Milkweed.* **1895** U.S. Dept. Ag. *Farmers' Bulletin* 28.27, Milkweed, wild lettuce. Lactuca scariola. **1896** *Jrl. Amer. Folkl.* 9.192, *Lactuca leucophaea,* . . milk weed, Paris, Me. **1898** *Ibid* 11.230 **ME,** Lactuca (sp.), milkweed. **1935** (1943) Muenscher *Weeds* 506, *Lactuca pulchella.* . . Milkweed. . . Meadows, pastures, grain fields and waste places. . . Juice milky. **1950** Gray–Fernald *Manual of Botany* 1554, *Lactuca.* . . Lettuce. "Milkweed."

5 A **rattlesnake root** (here: either *Prenanthes alba* or *P. altissima*).

1940 Clute *Amer. Plant Names* 71, *P[renanthes] alba.* . . Milkweed. . . *P. altissimus* [sic]. . . Milkweed. **1959** Carleton *Index Herb. Plants* 81, *Milkweed:* Apocynum androsaemifolium; Asclepias (v); Euphorbia (v); Lactuca (v); Lythrum alatum; Prenanthes alba.

6 A **loosestrife 2** (here: *Lythrum alatum*).

1959 [see **5** above].

7 =**Seneca snakeroot.**

1975 Hamel–Chiltoskey *Cherokee Plants* 55, Milk-weed . . *Polygala senega.* . . root tea or powder is expectorant and cathartic in large doses.

milkweed beetle n Cf red milkweed beetle

Often in combs: Any of several leaf beetles of the family Chrysomelidae which feed on **milkweed 1.**

1842 Harris *Treatise Insects* 455, Milk-weed beetle, 106. [*Ibid* 106, The largest species [of chrysomelid] in New England inhabits the common milk-weed, or silk-weed (Asclepias Syriaca), upon which it may be found. . . Its head, thorax, body beneath, antennae, and legs are deep blue, and its wing-covers orange, with three large black spots upon them, namely, one upon the shoulder, and another on the tip of each, and the third across the base of both wing-covers. . . It is nearly three eighths of an inch long, and almost hemispherical.] **1926** Essig *Insects N. Amer.* 469, *The blue milkweed beetle, Chrysochus cobaltinus,* . . is very common on milkweed throughout parts of New Mexico, Arizona, California, Oregon, Washington, and British Columbia. **1980** Milne–Milne *Audubon Field Guide Insects* 604, *Milkweed Tortoise Beetle . . (Chelymorpha cassidea).* . . Range: throughout North America. Food: Foliage of wild morning glory and related plants; sometimes milkweed. *Ibid*

605, *Milkweed Leaf Beetle (Chrysochus cobaltinus).* . . Food: Adult eats foliage of milkweed. *Ibid* 609, *Swamp Milkweed Leaf Beetle (Labidomera clavicollis).* . . Habitat: Marsh and stream edges where swamp milkweed grows. Range: most of North America. Food: Foliage and sometimes flowers of milkweed.

milkweed bug n

A lygaeid bug which feeds on **milkweed 1:** usu either *Lygaeus kalmii* or *Oncopeltus fasciatus.*

1905 Kellogg *Amer. Insects* 211, The milkweed-bug, *Oncopeltus fasciatus,* . . is a common showy bug on various species of milkweed. **1926** Essig *Insects N. Amer.* 346, *The spotted milkweed bug, Oncopeltus fasciatus.* . . feeds and breeds on various species of milkweed *(Asclepias)* and often becomes very abundant. . . It . . is reported in the west only in California and Arizona. *Ibid* 347, *The common milkweed bug, Lygaeus reclivatus,* is smaller than the preceding. . . Like the former, this bug feeds on various species of milkweed. . . It . . is common throughout the Western States. **1954** Borror–DeLong *Intro. Insects* 233, The small milkweed bug, *Lygaeus kalmii* . . , has a red X-shaped area on the hemelytra and a broad red band across the base of the pronotum; the large milkweed bug, *Oncopeltus fasciatus* . . , is broadly banded with red and black. **1980** Milne–Milne *Audubon Field Guide Insects* 478, *Small Eastern Milkweed Bug (Lygaeus kalmii).* . . This insect is immune to toxic chemicals in milkweed but is itself toxic to other insect predators. *Ibid* 479, *Large Milkweed Bug (Oncopeltus fasciatus).* . . The Large Milkweed Bug sometimes sips nectar from flowers of other plants in gardens and crop fields but seems to do no significant damage.

milkweed butterfly n [See quot 1902]

A butterfly of the family Danaidae, usu the monarch *(Danaus plexippus).*

1880 Burgess *Contributions* 10, In the milk-weed butterfly the colon is somewhat pyriform in the female . . , but is longer and more cylindrical in the male. **1892** IN Dept. Geol. & Nat. Resources *Rept. for 1891* 376, *Danais* [sic] *archippus.* . . The Milkweed Butterfly. The Monarch. . . One of the largest and most common butterflies throughout the State. **1902** Holland *Butterfly Book* 80, Euploeinae [=Danaidae] (The Milkweed Butterflies). *Ibid* 82, The larvae of the genus *Anosia* [=*Danaus*] feed for the most part upon the varieties of milkweed *(Asclepias),* and they are therefore called "milkweed butterflies." **1926** Essig *Insects N. Amer.* 639, Milkweed Butterflies. . . The chrysalis is jade green, . . highly ornamented with spots of burnished gold, and is a most beautiful object. **1940** Teale *Insects* 59, Two butterflies you will soon learn to recognize are the Monarch, or Milkweed butterfly, and its "look alike," the Viceroy. **1972** Harris *Butterflies GA* 284, Monarch; Milkweed Butterfly. *Danaus plexippus plexippus.* **1981** Pyle *Audubon Field Guide Butterflies* 711, Milkweed butterfly eggs are raised and blimplike. . . Milkweed butterflies are known for their strong soaring flight, which finds its greatest expression in the Monarch's remarkable migrations. *Ibid* 715, *Tropical Milkweed Butterfly (Lycorea cleobata).* . . Range: S. Texas and S. Florida south to Bolivia. **1986** Scott *Butterflies N. Amer.* 228, *Milkweed Butterflies.* . . A hair pencil on the male's abdomen wafts a scent to seduce the female.

milk willow herb n Also *milk willow*

A **loosestrife 2:** either *Lythrum alatum* or *L. salicaria.*

1822 Eaton *Botany* 346 NEng, *Lythrum* . . *salicaria* . . milk-willowherb. **1900** Lyons *Plant Names* 235, *L[ythrum] Salicaria.* . . Milk Willowherb. . . *L. alatum* . . , Wing-angled Loosestrife, is called also Milk Willow. **1940** Clute *Amer. Plant Names* 94, *Lythrum.* . . *L. alatum.* Winged Loosestrife. Milk willow-herb. . . *L. salicaria.* Purple Loosestrife . . milk willow-herb.

milk works See milk B2

milk worm n

A **ground worm 2** or similar larva; see quots.

1968–70 DARE (Qu. P5, . . *The common worm used as bait*) Inf **IA**29, Milk worm—a large ground worm—a substance in it that glows fluorescent—in very rich soil; (Qu. P6, . . *Kinds of worms . . used for bait*) Inf **AL**53, Milk worm—milkish color, big ones 6 or 8 inches long; **AR**56, Milk worm.

milkwort n [*OED* 1578 →]

Std: a plant of the genus *Polygala.* Also called **candyroot, candyweed 1.** For other names of var spp see **drumheads, fringed polygala, golden button 2, ground centaury 1, October flower 2, orange milkwort, pine-barren ~, pink ~,**

procession flower, purple milkwort, rogation flower, Seneca snakeroot, snakeweed, thimbles, white bachelor's button, white milkwort, wort, yellow bachelor's button, yellow milkwort

milky adj Cf **mulky**

Of the weather: see quots.

1967 Key *Tobacco Vocab.* 188 **PA**, "Milky weather." . . Moist, foggy weather. **1990** DARE File **nOH** (as of c1920), When there's light fog about, it's milky.

milky n

An opaque, whitish playing marble.

1950 WELS (Names and nicknames for different kinds of marbles. . . *Cheap ones*) 1 Inf, ceWI, Milkies. **1967–69** DARE (Qu. EE6d, *Special marbles*) Inf **GA**86, Milkies—opaque ones; **MO**21, **NY**37, Milkies. **c1970** Wiersma *Marbles Terms* swMI, Milkies—white marbles. *Ibid* **NJ, MI** (as of c1958), Milkies—solid white marbles. **1990** *WI State Jrl.* (Madison) 13 June "Neighbors" sec 2, American children know their marbles as kabolas, steelies, jumbos, milkies and peewees in descending order of size.

milky cap n Also *milk cap, milk(y) mushroom, milky* [See quots 1943, 1987]

A fungus of the family Russulaceae, usu of the genus *Lactarius.* For other names of var spp see **shaggy bear**

1939 Medsger *Edible Wild Plants* 233, The following species I have found to be excellent in quality and flavor. . . Delicious Milky Mushroom. *Lactarius deliciosus.* **1943** Fernald–Kinsey *Edible Wild Plants E. N. Amer.* 389, *Orange-milk mushroom, Lactarius deliciosus.* . . The bruised plant [exudes] a thick, milky, pleasantly aromatic, orange or saffron-red juice, which an exposure to the air gradually turns greenish. **1949** Palmer *Nat. Hist.* 65, *Delicious Milky Cap.* . . Some consider this species a favored mushroom but others disagree. **1972** Miller *Mushrooms* 46, *Russulaceae.* The Milk Mushrooms. . . The genus *Lactarius* contains a latex which can be seen by cutting the gills or upper stipe. . . *Russula* has no latex, but various color changes result when the tissue of some of them is cut or bruised. **1981** Lincoff *Audubon Field Guide Mushrooms* 686, *Indigo Milky. Lactarius indigo.* . . Indigo is an unusual color for mushrooms, and so this milky is quite easy to identify. *Ibid* 694, *Pink-fringed Milky. Lactarius torminosus.* . . Although generally considered poisonous in North America, this species is sold commercially in Finland. **1985** Ammirati et al. *Poisonous Mushrooms* 269, *Lactarius rufus.* . . Common names. Red milky cap. . . Fruit bodies often growing in well-drained pine woods. **1987** McKnight–McKnight *Mushrooms* 326, *Milkcaps:* Genus *Lactarius.* . . All parts exude latex when cut or broken; latex clear to white or colored.

milky pussley See **milk purslane 1**

milky-toast See **milquetoast**

milky way n

1 A long band of clouds resembling the Milky Way. Cf **milkmaid's path**

1968–70 DARE (Qu. B10, . . *Long trailing clouds high in the sky*) Inf **CA**147, Milky way—a long, stringy cloud, visible at night, a reflection of the stars on the cloud; **NJ**17, Milky way; **NJ**31, Milky way—clouds building up in a long line, means wind from that direction; (Qu. B11, . . *Other kinds of clouds that come often*) Inf **IL**117, Milky ways—same as skimmery clouds.

2 See **milk B2.**

mill n[1]

1 The circular movement of a herd of cattle, sometimes deliberately created to stop a stampede. **West** Cf **mill v**

1874 McCoy *Cattle Trade* 97, To break the mill and induce the leaders to launch out for the shore—the drover swims his cow pony into the center of the mill and, if possible, frightens the mass of struggling, whirling cattle, into separation. **1897** Hough *Story Cowboy* 146 **West,** Sometimes in the water . . a sudden panic would seize the herd, and they would fall to "milling", . . swimming round and round helplessly. . . [T]he cowboy . . by shouts and blows did all he could to break the "mill" and get the cattle headed properly. **1903** (1965) Adams *Log Cowboy* 47, They [=lead cattle] reentered the rear guard of our string, and we soon had a mill going which kept them busy and rested our horses. Once we had them milling, our trouble, as far as running was concerned, was over, for all two of us could hope to do was to let them exhaust themselves in this endless circle. **1941** Dobie *Longhorns* 82 **TX,** A herd that attempted the same crossing the next day lost eight hundred head in a mill that could not be broken. *Ibid* 92, The object was to swing the leaders around into the tail end of the herd, thus turning it into a mill. **1942** Dale *Cow Country* 55 **West,** Those behind them would follow and a "mill" would be established in which the animals would swim around and around in a circle until they drowned unless it were quickly broken up and the leaders again headed for the opposite shore. **1958** Blasingame *Dakota Cowboy* 105 **SD,** They [=cattle] ran for two hours before they could be turned into a "mill"—or run in a circle and stopped.

2 Among railroad workers and loggers: see quots. Cf **coffee-pot 1**

1926 *AmSp* 1.250 **PA** [Railroading terms], Locomotives are "mills" or "kettles." **1932** *RR Mag.* Oct 369, *Mill*—Steam locomotive. **1958** McCulloch *Woods Words* 117 **Pacific NW,** *Mill. . .* A term for a beat-up old locie, wheels flat, wedges down, steam leaking at every joint, but still running.

3 also *mills, the mill:* The game of **morris;** one of the configurations in the game. [Cf *EDD mill* sb.¹ 5; cf also Ger *Mühle* mill] **esp Gt Lakes** Also called **figmill**

1937 Chicago Park District *Games* 20, The game of mill, sometimes called merelles or nine-men's morris, is played on a board having three concentric squares with straight lines connecting the center points of the corresponding sides. *Ibid* 21, The object of each player is to prevent his opponent from placing three pieces so as to form a row. As soon as either player gets three men in a line, he has formed a "mill." **1938** (1941) Natl. Recreation Assoc. *Games* 26, *Mill. . .* The object is to get a "mill," that is, three men in a row. A mill must run horizontally or vertically on a line. **1951** *Jrl. Amer. Folkl.* 64.305 **wNY,** The . . lay-out. . . makes it easy to form what we called "double mills" (arrangements of five men so that one of them can be shifted back and forth to close a line of three at every move; called "open mills" by Stephens . .). **1968–69** *DARE* (Qu. DD37, . . *Table games played a lot by adults*) Inf **MN**12, The mill, a variation of tick-tack-toe—tried to get three in a row; if you did then you got to take one from your opponent—a German game; **WI**12, Mill—a German game; **MO**30, Mills; (Qu. EE39, . . *Games played on paper by two people*) Inf **MI**93, Mill—draw three rectangles, connect the corners, then slide the buttons in. [All Infs of Ger background or in Ger settlement area] **1988** *DARE* File **WI,** Mill was what my Waukesha cousins called this game [=**figmill**] in the late 1930s. The "board" was carved on the top of a picnic table and the counters were pop-bottle caps. **1992** *Ibid,* [Instructions to game of *Mill:*] A clever player soon learns to take away one peg from his own mill or row, and then move it back on a later turn to form a new mill, thus removing one of his opponent's pegs from play.

4 in phr *go through the mill* and varr: See quots.

1977–78 Foster *Lexical Variation* 85 **NJ,** The most widespread penalty for the losers of children's team games is to receive slaps on the buttocks while crawling between the victors' legs. This custom is known by two classes of names. *Go through the mill* (42 responses [of 166 infs]) has the variants *go under the mill* (4), *go through the tunnel* (2), *goin' under* (1), and *run the mill* (1). **1992** *DARE* File **cwCA** (as of 1950s), When I was a child, at birthday parties the birthday boy or birthday girl would often have to "go through the mill." That meant that he or she would crawl between the outstretched legs of all the other children, who were standing in a line, and submit to their paddling. *Most* kids paddled gently, but there were always a few who wouldn't.

mill v, hence vbl n *milling* **West** Cf **mill** n¹ **1**

Of cattle: to move in a circle; also, to cause (cattle) to move in a circle in order to stop a stampede.

1874 McCoy *Cattle Trade* 101 **TX, OK, KS,** Drovers consider that the cattle do themselves great injury by running round in a circle, which is termed in cow-boy parlance, "milling." **1888** *Century Illustr. Mag.* 35.862 **West,** The cattle may begin to run, and get "milling"—that is, all crowd together into a mass like a ball, wherein they move round and round. **1897** [see **mill** n¹ **1** above]. **1903** [see **mill** n¹ **1**]. **1920** Hunter *Trail Drivers TX* 142, I was the only one on horseback, and one of the men yelled to me to "turn the leaders toward the bluff and mill them." **1929** *AmSp* 5.72 **NE** [Cattle country talk], If there are a hundred or more cattle in the herd, some might become frightened or confused and the "herders" will "get the cows milling," keep them going in a circle, merry-go-round fashion, in order to prevent their "stampeding," and to quiet them down. **1933** *AmSp* 8.1.30 **nwTX,** *Mill.* To cause to drift in a circle. Milling cattle is the best method of checking a stampede. **1941**

Dobie *Longhorns* 77 **TX,** About the time we got the herd milling, here came a posse of citizens with a deputy. **1968** Adams *Western Words* 195, *Milling*—The marching of cattle in a compact circle. This formation is resorted to in stopping stampedes. As the cattle mill in a circle, they wind themselves up into a narrowing mass which becomes tighter and tighter until finally it is so tight they can no longer move. The term is reserved strictly for cattle. When the same action is carried out with horses, it is called *rounding up.*

mill n² [Pronc-sp for *meal;* cf Pronc Intro 3.I.3.c]

1982 McCool *Sam McCool's Pittsburghese* 25 **PA,** Mill: food, a meal—"That was a good mill, Mom."

millard See **miller** n **1**

mill days n pl

1946 *PADS* 6.20 **eNC** (as of 1900–10), *Mill days. . .* Days of moodiness, gloominess, and grouchiness.

miller n Also *moth miller* [So called from the powdery scales on the wings; *OED* 1681 →] Cf **river miller**

1 also freq *miller moth;* occas *miller bug, miller('s) fly;* pronc-spp *millard, millow (moth):* Any of numerous moths often attracted to lights, but esp those of the families Arctiidae and Noctuidae; occas also the larva of such a moth. Also called **dusty miller 5, light dabber**

1783 in 1888 Cutler *Life* 1.94 **neMA,** Tarred apple-trees to keep the millers from going up. **1792** Belknap *Hist. NH* 3.182, *Moth,* or *Miller, Phalœna.*—Numerous species. **1842** Harris *Treatise Insects* 237, The third great section of the Lepidoptera, which Linnaeus named *Phalaena,* includes a vast number of insects, sometimes called millers, or night-butterflies, but more frequently moths. **1871** MO State Entomol. *Annual Rept.* 68, The common yellow bear—*Spilosoma virginica. . .* The moth . . which is very generally dubbed "the Miller," frequently flies into our rooms at night. **1885** Jewett *Marsh Is.* 162 **ME,** Don't flitter about so, mother; you make me think of a singed moth-miller. **1890** *Century Dict.* 3765, *Miller. . .* A moth whose wings appear as if dusted over with flour or meal, like a miller's clothes; hence, almost any small moth, such as fly about lights at night. Common millers in the United States are *Spilosoma virginica,* a moth whose larva is one of the woolly-bear caterpillars, and *Hyphantria cunea,* the web-worm moth. The little yellowish moths of the genera *Crambus* and *Botis* are also commonly called millers. **1898** Lugger *Butterflies* 133 **MN,** The moth [=*Spilosoma virginica*], which is very generally called "The Miller," frequently flies into our rooms at night. It is easily recognized by its pure white color, by having the abdomen orange-colored above, with three rows of black spots. **1899** Bergen *Animal Lore* 41 **NEng,** A white "miller" coming into the house is a sign of bad news. **1905** Kellogg *Amer. Insects* 412, The yellow bears, common caterpillars . . distinguished by their dense but uneven coat of long creamy-yellow, light or even dark brown hairs, are the larvae of the beautiful snowy-white miller-moth, *Spilosoma virginica.* **1926** Essig *Insects N. Amer.* 678, *Noctuidae. . .* This is a large family of very injurious species. . . They are night fliers, many being attracted to lights and commonly known as millers. **1930** Shoemaker *1300 Words* 40 **cPA Mts** (as of c1900), *Miller*—A moth; "Moth-Miller." **1944** *PADS* 2.67, *Miller, tobacco miller. . .* A moth (sometimes as large as a humming bird) which feeds on the nectar in the "Jimson" weed and deposits on the green tobacco its eggs, which hatch into tobacco worms. **c1960** *Wilson Coll.* **csKY,** Miller. . . A night-flying moth. **1964** O'Hare *Ling. Geog. E. MT* 131, The adult form of the cutworm. . . Miller [8 of 10 infs] . . moth miller [2 of 10 infs]. **1965–70** *DARE* (Qu. R4) 9 Infs, **scattered,** Miller(s); **CT**15, Miller = moth; large; **IA**1, Millers—a form of moth; **ME**20, Miller—a small white moth; **NY**219, The miller—gray, different colors . . a little moth; **VT**13, Millers—little, like fuzzy white butterfly; bigger, they're moths; **NE**4, Miller moths; **PA**218, Miller's flies; **MI**112, Millards, moths; **CA**72, Millow moth; **MA**122, Millows; (Qu. P6, . . *Kinds of worms . . used for bait*) Inf **CA**87, Caterpillars . . miller; miller moth; (Qu. R27, . . *Kinds of caterpillars or similar worms*) Inf **TX**71, Miller bug; **NJ**8, Millers. **1986** Pederson *LAGS Concordance,* 46 infs, **Gulf Region,** Miller(s); 7 infs, **AR, GA, TX,** Miller bug(s); 6 infs, **AL, GA, TN,** Miller fly (*or* flies); 1 inf, **ceTN,** Miller moth; 1 inf, **neTN,** Moth miller. **1987** *NADS Letters* **PA** (as of 1950s), My husband and his whole family called these moths *millers.* He says that he stopped using the word at college, when he realized it was not universally understood.

2 A clothes moth of the family Tineidae.

1846 *Penny Mag.* 19 Dec. 728/2 *(Mathews Coll.),* We have before given a minute account of the moth-miller, which lays the eggs, and the destructive little worm which is hatched from them and does all the mischief. **1865** *Harper's Weekly* 25 Nov 747 **NY,** If there is *one* little hole in your linen or paper, some adventurous moth-miller is pretty sure to discover it. **c1930** Brown *Amer. Folkl. Insect Lore* 3 **WI,** All small moths were "millers" and were dreaded because of the injury that all were supposed to cause to clothing and fabrics. A moth singeing its wings in a candle flame or lamp chimney foretold sickness or a dire calamity. A white moth hovering about at night was believed by some persons to be the spirit of a dead relative or friend. **1949** Swain *Insect Guide* 86, Clothes Moths and Allies. . . The better-known species are the "millers," which when seen flying about inside a house are always headed away from the light toward a darkened corner or closet. **1971** Bright *Word Geog. CA & NV* 187, Moths . . in clothes . . millers [8% of 300 infs]. **1986** *DARE* File **swWI,** *Millers*—large, wool-eating moths, from the fact that the moths lay their eggs in sweaters which the larvae then eat. **1987** *NADS Letters* **eME coast** (as of c1900), My mother always called a clothes moth flying around the house a *moth miller* or simply *miller.*

miller v See **mellow**

miller boy n Also *happy is the miller, jolly ~;* for addit varr see quot 1952

A children's singing game; see quots 1883, 1919.

  1883 Newell *Games & Songs* 102 **wNY, OH,** *Happy is the Miller.* An odd number of players, of whom the one not paired stands in the centre of the ring. The others march in couples . . till the sudden end of the song, when each boy grasps the girl in front of him. . . Happy is the miller that lives in the mill;/ While the mill goes round, he works with a will;/ One hand in the hopper, and one in the bag,/ The mill goes around, and he cries out, Grab! **1905** *DN* 3.88 **nwAR,** *Miller-boy.* . . The name of a game. **1916** Wolford *Play-Party IN* 67 **seIN,** *Miller Boy.* . . The person who is without a partner stands in the center. . . The movement is regular and rather quick to imitate the turning of a wheel. At [stanza] 2, each boy drops his partner's arm and tries to get the arm of the girl behind him and at his right. While the change is being made, the one in the center (the Miller) tries to get a partner. **1919** Elsom–Trilling *Social Games* 219 **WI,** *Jolly is the miller.* . . Children join hands with partners. . . As the words in the last line are sung, the outer circle steps backward, the inner circle forward, and each child takes a new partner. As the change is made, the child in the center tries to get a partner. **1937** NE Univ. *Univ. Studies* 37.247 **OK,** *Miller Boy.* **1952** Brown *NC Folkl.* 1.110, *Happy Is The Miller Boy.* . . [Variant titles:] 'The Jolly Miller.' *Ibid* 111, 'Johnny Miller.' *Ibid* 112, 'The Jolly Old Miller.' . . 'There Was A Little Miller.' . . 'Miller Boy.' **1965–70** *DARE* (Qu. EE1, . . *Games . . children play . . in which they form a ring, and either sing or recite a rhyme*) Inf **ID**5, Miller boy; **KS**5, Miller boy—the girl steps back, the boy steps ahead, then they form hands [sic] and march around; (Qu. EE2, *Games that have one extra player—when a signal is given, the players change places, and the extra one tries to get a place*) Inf **OK**48, Miller boy: "Happy is the miller boy who lived by the mill,/ The wheel turns around with a free good will,/ A hand in the hopper and the other in the sack,/ The ladies step forward and the gents fall back"; (Qu. EE33, . . *Outdoor games . . that children play*) Inf **IL**143, Miller boy—singing. **1967** *DARE* Tape **OH**6, They'd play kitchen games. . . One was . . happy is the miller.

miller bug, miller moth, miller('s) fly See **miller** n 1

miller's maid n

A **colicroot 2** (here: *Aletris farinosa*).

  1949 Moldenke *Amer. Wild Flowers* 318, The last, *A[letris] farinosa,* is perhaps the best known of the group because of its wide distribution. It is often called *millers-maid* . . and *bittergrass.*

miller's rule n Also *miller's turn*

See quots.

  1899 (1912) Green *VA Folk-Speech* 282, *Miller's turn.* . . Where every one takes his turn as he comes, as at the mill the "first come first served." **1954** *PADS* 21.33 **SC,** *Miller's rule.* . . The miller's rule is that everyone comes in his turn, and each one must await his turn.

miller's thumb n

1 A **sculpin** of the genus *Cottus,* usu the **mottled sculpin** or *C. cognatus.* [*OED* c1440 →; see quots 1890, 1956]

  1709 (1967) Lawson *New Voyage* 163, Barbouts and Millers-Thumbs, are the very same here, in all respects, as they are in *England.* **1884** Goode *Fisheries U.S.* 1.259, In the lakes and streams of the Northern States are numerous species of *Uranidea* and allied genera, known in

some localities by the English name of "Miller's Thumb." **1890** *Century Dict.* 3765, *Miller's-thumb.* . . The name is due to the fancied resemblance of the head to the form a miller's thumb is popularly supposed to assume from the frequent sampling of meal with the hand. **1899** (1912) Green *VA Folk-Speech* 282, *Miller's thumb.* . . The name of a fish. **1956** Harlan–Speaker *IA Fish* 160, It [=*Cottus cognatus*] is also called the miller's thumb because its broad, flat head resembles the flattened thumb of the unfortunate miller who had . . his thumb crushed between the millstones. **1983** Becker *Fishes WI* 974, Slimy Sculpin. . . northern miller's thumb.

2 =**brown bullhead 1.**

  1906 NJ State Museum *Annual Rept. for 1905* 169, *Ameiurus nebulosus.* . . Miller's Thumb.

miller's turn See **miller's rule**

millet n Cf **duck millet, evergreen ~, Indian ~, Polish ~, Texas ~, wild ~**

Std: a cereal grass *(Panicum miliaceum).* Also called **guinea corn 2, hog millet**

milleton See **mirliton**

mill, go through the See **mill** n[1] 5

millinder n [Pronc var of *milliner;* cf Intro "Language Changes" I.8]

  1924 (1946) Greer–Petrie *Angeline Gits an Eyeful* 19 **csKY,** They must a-patternized [=have patronized] awful pore millinders.

millineer See **millionaire**

milling See **mill** v

million See **melon**

millionaire n Also *millineer, millionairee, millionist, milyinist* Std sense, var forms.

  1893 Shands *MS Speech* 45, *Millineer* [mɪlɪniə]. Illiterate white pronunciation of *millionnaire* [sic]. **1903** Wasson *Cap'n Simeon's Store* 30 **eME,** I never realized ever we had no sich millionist stoppin' up into that section. **1979** *AmSp* 54.98 **swME** (as of 1899–1910), *Millionairee.* . . Millionaire. *Milyinist.* . . Millionaire.

million-dollar-man n Also *million-dollar-husband piece* Cf **handsome husband, old maid 4**

=**manner** n 3a.

  1950 *WELS* **WI** (*Words for the last piece of something on a plate*) 1 Inf, Million-dollar-man; 1 Inf, Million-dollar-husband piece.

million-dollar weed n [See quot 1921] **FL**

=**water hyacinth.**

  1921 *Discovery* Feb 48, The water hyacinth. . . is a beautiful aquatic plant . . but its spread in St. John's River and the enormous sums spent in attempting its suppression have earned it the name of the "million-dollar weed." **1949** Moldenke *Amer. Wild Flowers* 343, In Florida the plant [=water hyacinth] is often called the *million-dollar-weed* because its unbelievably luxuriant growth in the St. Johns and other rivers is a menace to navigation and millions of dollars are spent to keep these waterways open. **1955** *S. Folkl. Qrly.* 19.235 **FL,** The Water Hyacinth, much admired by nature lovers and much hated by those who must keep our rivers navigable, has been called by the latter group the *Million-Dollar Weed* (Eichhornia crassipes).

millionist See **millionaire**

mill kettle See **kettle B3**

millo maize See **milo maize**

millow (moth) See **miller** n 1

millpond roach See **mill roach**

mill post n [*OED* a1704 →]

A fat or thick leg.

  1950 *WELS* (*Words and phrases to describe people's legs . . very thick*) 2 Infs, **WI,** Mill posts. **1954** Harder Coll. **cwTN,** Mill posties. . . People's legs when very thick. [*DARE* Ed: Cf **-es** suff[1] **1a**] **1966** *DARE* (Qu. X37) Inf **AL**6, Mill posts.

mill roach n Also *millpond roach*

=**golden shiner.**

  1966–68 *DARE* (Qu. P1, . . *Kinds of freshwater fish . . caught around here . . good to eat*) Infs **DE**4, **NJ**21, Mill roach; (Qu. P3, *Freshwater* *fish that are not good to eat*) Inf **DE**3, Mill roach; (Qu. P7, *Small fish used as bait for bigger fish*) Inf **NC**15, Millpond roaches. **1968** *DARE* Tape **DE**3, Any little old fish, mill roach, sunfish. **1976** Bruce *How to Grow Wildflowers* 275, The common Mill Roach, for example, with its gleaming silvery body and orange-red fins is a beautiful fish.

millrock n Sth, S Midl Cf grind rock

A millstone; also fig.

1901 Harben *Westerfelt* 283 **nGA,** You've been my mill-rock long enough, an' now I'm goin' to take a new an' a firmer stand in my treatment uv you. **1940** *Hench Coll.* **NC,** Mr. P. Johnson. . . grew up in Pitt County, N.C., the son of a miller. He tells me that their name for mill-stones was "mill-rocks." **1947** *McDavid Coll.* **GA,** Millrock = millstone. **1954** *Ibid* **KY,** Millrock. [**1986** Pederson *LAGS Concordance (Grindstone)* 1 inf, **cwLA,** A mill rock.]

mills See mill n[1] 3

millstone, not by a adv phr

Not by any means; not by a long shot.

1970 *DARE* (Qu. KK55a, *To deny something very firmly: "No, not by a _____."*) Inf **CA**209, Millstone.

milltails of hell, like the adv phr Also *like the milltail of thunder*

In a fast and violent manner.

1914 *DN* 4.76 **ME, nNH,** *Mill tail o' thunder, like the,* . . See "Hell-bent an' crooked." [*Ibid* 74, *Hell-bent an' crooked.* . . In a swift, disorderly, excited manner.] **1923** *DN* 5.214 **swMO,** *Mill tails o' hell.* . . Swiftly, violently. "The creek's a-runnin' like the mill tails o' hell." **1935** Davis *Honey* 62 **OR,** On a grade like this you could drag the wheels and still be goin' like the milltails of hell. **1953** Randolph–Wilson *Down in Holler* 181 **Ozarks,** They was runnin' like the *mill-tails of hell.*

mill town n Also *mill village* Cf sawmill hollow

A section of a city, often the poorest, where there is or was a factory.

1966–70 *DARE* (Qu. C35, *Nicknames for the different parts of your town or city*) Infs **MN**19, **OR**1, **SC**51, Mill town; **NC**17, Mill village; (Qu. II25, *Names or nicknames for the part of a town where the poorer people, special groups, or foreign groups live*) Inf **MA**98, Mill village; **CT**21, **MS**69, Mill town (area). **1969** *DARE* FW Addit **ceCT,** Mill village—area built up by mill for use by its employees.

millyum See melon

milo n[1] See milo maize

milo n[2] [Haw] HI

The portia tree (*Thespesia populnea*).

1929 Neal *Honolulu Gardens* 202 **HI,** Milo. . . The bark is thick and corrugated, . . the bell-shaped flowers . . blossom most of the year. **1930** Degener *Ferns of HI* 209, The *milo* of the Hawaiians, *Thespesia populnea* . . , from whose trunk beautiful bowls were formerly made, is . . found . . near the ocean. **1994** Stone-Pratt *Hawai'i's Plants* 63, During the winter, salt spray from high surf may partially defoliate the canopy of milo trees, but they survive and regain their foliage in the spring or summer.

milo maize n Also sp *milo maizo, millo maize* Also freq abbr *maize, milo* [Sotho *maili*] chiefly Plains States, SW See Map

A naturalized **sorghum** (here: *Sorghum bicolor* Subglabrescens Group).

1883 GA Dept. Ag. *Pub. Circular No. 34* 8.35, My attention was some time since called to the claims of "Ivory wheat" and "Millo Maize" to a place in our long list of profitable food crops. *Ibid* 36, I planted the maize . . on the 20th of April, and it . . made a heavier stalk and much higher (some of it being 12 feet) but it never matured and was quite green when the first heavy frost came. I cut it down and fed away to the cattle. **1884** *N.Y. Wkly. Tribune* 17 Sep. 10/1 (*DA*), The very old and well-known Sorghum halepense [sic] . . has frequently been distributed of late years under many different common names, among the most familiar being Green Valley grass, Johnson grass, Nisan's grass, evergreen millet and Milo maize. **1887** *Florida Dispatch* 10 Jan. 34/3 (*OEDS*), The head of yellow millo maize is formed in sections of smaller heads, lying very close and compact. *Ibid* 14 Feb. 165/3 (*OEDS*), Mr. Jones recommends the substitution of Kaffir corn, Milo Maizo, etc., for a part of the corn crop. **1901** Mohr *Plant Life AL* 135, Cowpeas, millets, various kinds of sorghum, known as . . millo maize [etc] . . furnish green forage and hay crops throughout the summer. **1920** U.S. Dept. Ag. *Farmers' Bulletin* 1147.3, Milo has long since passed the experi-

mental stage as a farm crop in the southwestern United States. . . Milo made its first appearance in the country soon after 1880. **1933** *Small Manual SE Flora* 47, This grass [=sorghum] has been cultivated from prehistoric times in many varieties for food and forage—*Sorgo, Kafir, Milo* . . —and for its sweet juice which is made into sirup. **1945** [see **kafir corn**]. **1949** *Sat. Eve. Post* 24 Sept 125, By August there were foot-deep cracks in the low corners of milo maize and kaffir corn. **1951** Martin *Amer. Wildlife & Plants* 463, *Milo.* . . is closely related to corn and is like it nutritionally. **1965–70** *DARE* (Qu. L34, . . *Most important crops grown around here*) 15 Infs, **esp KS, NE, TX,** Milo; 10 Infs, 7 **OK, TX,** Maize; **OK**3, Combine maize; **TX**26, 31, Milo maize; (Qu. L21, . . *Kinds of grain grown around here;* total Infs questioned, 75) Infs **NM**3, **OK**1, 8, 18, 27, 33, 52, Maize; **MS**1, **NM**6, **OK**27, 33, Milo; **NM**6, **OK**14, Milo maize; **NM**3, Dwarf maize; (Qu. L22, *When talking about a crop* . . *a farmer might say, "This year, I'm going to _____ a crop of oats . . etc."*) Infs **KS**9, 15, **OK**33, Plant milo; **KS**18, **OK**33, Sow milo; **MO**32, Drill milo; **TX**22, Put in milo; **OK**33, Plant maize; **OK**33, Sow maize; **TX**11, Drill maize; (Qu. L9a, . . *Kinds of grass* . . *grown for hay*) Inf **TN**24, Maize; (Qu. L9b, *Hay from other kinds of plants [not grass];* not asked in early QRs) Infs **NC**52, **TX**102, 105, Milo; **TX**4, 82, Maize; **LA**29, Milo maize. **1967–68** *DARE* Tape **TX**23, [FW:] Do they grow a lot of cotton? [Inf:] Yes, and maize, grain; **CA**90 (as of c1902), The man from Davis came down and. . . he said . . , "If you get maize . . , get the giant maize and then plant it." . . Then we got the seed . . which was millet seed, alfalfa seed, and this giant maize. **1973** *Houston Chron.* (TX) 21 Oct 26/6, Cotton, wheat, milo, corn and soybean production can be increased tremendously. **1976** Bailey–Bailey *Hortus Third* 1061, [Sorghum] Subglabrescens Group. . . Milo. . . An important grain sorghum of s. Great Plains.

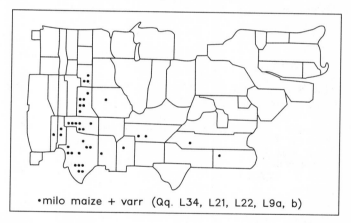

•milo maize + varr (Qq. L34, L21, L22, L9a, b)

milon See melon

milpa n Also sp *milpah* [MexSpan *milpa*] SW

See quot 1938.

[**1844** (1954) Gregg *Commerce* 107 **NM,** The *labores* and *milpas* (cultivated fields) are often . . without any enclosure.] **1856** (1928) Jaeger *Diary Fort Yuma* 122 **PA,** Some [soldiers] hid in the milpa & some ran off. **1860** in 1948 *Western Folkl.* 7.13 **sCA,** As to sowings and milpahs there has been a great falling off in the country. **1894** *DN* 1.325 **TX,** Milpá: a land measure of 177 acres. **1934** White *Folded Hills* 4 **CA,** The cattle throve: the *milpas* and the grain fields flourished. **1938** *AmSp* 13.121, In Texas, the term *milpa* signifies a land-measure of 177 acres, but the expression also occasionally (and in Mexico usually) denotes a cultivated patch.

milquetoast n Also freq *Caspar Milquetoast, Mr. Milquetoast,* rarely *miliquant toast, milky-toast* [From *Caspar Milquetoast* in H.T. Webster's comic strip "The Timid Soul," which first appeared in May 1924] chiefly Nth, N Midl, CA See Map on p. 604

A meek, easily intimidated person; hence adj *milquetoasty* meek, timid.

1938 M. Fishback *Safe Conduct* vi.70 (*OEDS*), Don't be a Milquetoast either, and be afraid to add it [=the bill] up. **1947** *Sun* (Baltimore MD) 20 Dec 6/2 (*Hench Coll.*), Representative Monroney . . called the GOP measure "a 'Casper [sic] Milquetoast' sent out to fight inflation." **1965–70** *DARE* (Qu. HH10, *A very timid or cowardly person: "He's _____."*) 32 Infs, **chiefly Nth, N Midl,** (Mr.) Milquetoast; 7 Infs, Caspar Milquetoast; **MN**18, Miliquant [mɪləkwənt] toast; **CT**3, Milky-toast; **VA**101, Milquetoasty; (Qu. AA21, . . *Joking expressions . . about*

a wife who gives the orders and a husband who takes them from her)
11 Infs, **esp Nth, N Midl,** He's a (Mr.) Milquetoast; 10 Infs, **esp Nth,
N Midl,** (He's) Mr. Milquetoast; **IL**11, **NE**9, **OH**2, **PA**196, 225, **WI**63,
He's (a) Caspar Milquetoast; **CA**82, Good old Caspar Milquetoast;
MI92, **OH**17, **PA**118, (He's) milquetoast; (Qu. HH5, *Someone who is
queer but harmless)* Inf **CA**8, Mr. Milquetoast; (Qu. HH38, *A womanish
man)* Infs **CT**10, **IN**32, **MO**5, **MA**58, **WA**3, Milquetoast. **1978** *Up-
Country* Nov 5 **wMA,** His salute to educated women . . was reaffirmed
for this Milquetost [*sic*] as the audience dispersed in the late golden
afternoon.

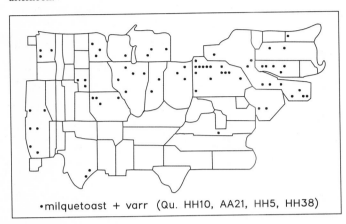

•milquetoast + varr (Qu. HH10, AA21, HH5, HH38)

Milwaukee cider n Also *Milwaukee special,* ~ *water* [*Milwau-
kee,* Wisconsin, in ref to its once-numerous breweries] *joc*
Beer.
  1950 *WELS* **csWI** *(Nicknames for beer)* 1 Inf, Milwaukee water; 1
Inf, Milwaukee cider. **1967–68** *DARE* (Qu. DD25) Infs **OH**82, **WI**26,
Milwaukee cider; **MI**67, Milwaukee special.

Milwaukee goiter n Also *Milwaukee front* Cf **German goiter**
An oversized stomach, esp from drinking beer or liquor.
  1942 Berrey–Van den Bark *Amer. Slang* 121.7, *Drunkard's paunch. . .*
German *or* Milwaukee goitre. **1950** *WELS* **WI** *(An oversize stomach. . .
If it comes from drinking)* 10 Infs, Milwaukee front; 1 Inf, Milwaukee
goiter. **1962** *Western Folkl.* 21.33 **sCA,** Milwaukee goiter—a large mid-
section as the result of drinking too much beer over a period of time.
1967–70 *DARE* (Qu. X53b, *An oversize stomach that results from
drinking)* Infs **IL**9, 114, Milwaukee front; **IL**63, Milwaukee goiter.

Milwaukee shiner n
The emerald **shiner** *(Notropis atherinoides).*
  1968 *DARE* (Qu. P7, *Small fish used as bait for bigger fish)* Inf **WI**38,
Milwaukee shiners. **1983** Becker *Fishes WI* 505, *Emerald Shiner. . .*
Other common names: . . Milwaukee shiner, lake emerald shiner. *Ibid*
508, In Wisconsin it is sold as the "Milwaukee shiner," because large
numbers of them were once taken from southern Lake Michigan. *Ibid*
509, [Until about 1960 it was so abundant that it was regarded as a
nuisance when it congregated in harbors in spring and fall.] *Ibid* 586,
Brassy minnows made up . . 5–20% of the minnows sold as Milwaukee
(lake emerald) shiners.

Milwaukee special, Milwaukee water See **Milwaukee cider**

milyinist See **millionaire**

milyun See **melon**

mima See **mee-maw** n

mimb See **mib**

mimbre n Also *mimbres* [Span *mimbre* osier, willow] **TX**
=**desert willow.**
  1872 Powers *Afoot* 149 **TX,** There are little mimbres, swaying their
long green hair, and bright dwarf walnuts, and vast cottonwoods. **1904**
NM Ag. Exper. Station *Bulletin* 51.26, The Desert Willow or Mimbres
(Chilopsis linearis) has already been brought into cultivation. **1936**
Whitehouse *TX Flowers* 138, Desert Willow *(Chilopsis linearis),* also
called flowering willow, willow-leaved catalpa, and "mimbre," is a common shrub along water courses from West Texas to Southern California
and Northern Mexico. **1951** *PADS* 15.41 **TX,** *Chilopsis linearis. . .*
Flowering willow . . catalpa; mimbre. **1970** Correll *Plants TX* 1444,
Chilopsis. . . Desert Willow, Mimbre.

mimi See **mee-mee**

mimic v
To resemble.
  1913 Kephart *Highlanders* 296 **sAppalachians,** Many common English words are used in peculiar senses by the mountain folk, as . . mimic
or mock for resemble. **1944** *PADS* 2.19 **sAppalachians,** *Mimic. . .* To
resemble in appearance. "He mimics his cousin a sight." **1986** Pederson
LAGS Concordance (The boy [resembles] his father) 1 inf, **ceAL,**
Mimics.

mimic n
  1917 *DN* 4.415 **wNC,** *Mimic. . .* Likeness. "That [photograph]'s a fair
mimic of him."

mimmy See **mee-mee**

mimosa n Cf **mimosa-bush, Texas mimosa**
  1 Std: a plant of the genus *Mimosa.* Also called **cat's claw,
sensitive plant, uña de gato.** For other names of var spp see
**be-shame bush, pink mimosa, powder puff, raspilla, shame
plant, wait-a-minute bush, zarza**
  2 Any of several plants related to **1** above, as:
  a A lead tree, usu *Leucaena pulverulenta.*
    1897 Sudworth *Arborescent Flora* 250, *Leucaena pulverulenta. . .
Common Name.* Mimosa. **1900** Lyons *Plant Names* 222, *Leucaena. . .*
Mimosa. . . Shrubs or trees with white flowers in globular heads. **1908**
Rogers *Tree Book* 345, The . . Mimosa *(Leucaena pulverulenta . .)*
grows as a handsome, round-headed tree near the mouth of the Rio
Grande River in Texas. **1922** Sargent *Manual Trees* 598, *Leucaena
pulverulenta. . . Mimosa. . . Flowers* sessile, fragrant, in heads. **1960**
Vines *Trees SW* 505, *Leucaena retusa. . .* Mostly . . in central Texas and
the Trans-Pecos area. . . It is apparently not abundant enough to warrant
the application of other vernacular names except that of Mimosa and
Wahoo-tree. Much browsed by cattle.
  b See **mimosa tree.**
  c See **prairie mimosa.**

mimosa-bush n
=**huajillo 1.**
  1960 Vines *Trees SW* 515, Apes-earring—*Pithecellobium pallens. . .*
Vernacular names are Huajillo . . and Mimosa-bush.

mimosa tree n Also *mimosa* [See quot 1945]
A **silk tree** (here: *Albizia julibrissin*), naturalized chiefly in
the southern US.
  1938 Van Dersal *Native Woody Plants* 344, Mimosa *(Albizzia* [*sic*]
julubrissin [*sic*], *Leucaena pulverulenta).* **1944** AL Geol. Surv. *Bulletin*
53.123, *A[lbizia] Julibrissin. . .* Commonly called "Mimosa," which is
the technical name of a larger genus in the same family. . . A small or
medium-sized tree . . commonly cultivated in the southeastern states for
shade and ornament. . . This does not seem to have been known as a
wild plant in the United States until a little more than a century ago.
1945 Wodehouse *Hayfever Plants* 114, The mimosa tree. . . bears large
clusters of pink or whitish flowers during spring and most of the summer.
It is . . naturalized in the South from Virginia to Florida and Louisiana. . . Its common name of mimosa is a survival from a time when it
and the acacias were included in the genus *Mimosa.* **1952** Taylor *Plants
Colonial Days* 59, The white-streaked greenish twigs and the doubly
compound leaves . . are characteristic of the mimosa or silk tree. . . Its
introduction into South Carolina at the end of the eighteenth century is
attributed to André Michaux. **1953** Greene–Blomquist *Flowers South*
128, One of the South's outstanding ornamental flowering trees . . is the
picturesque, flat-topped, low-spreading (20″–40″) mimosa tree. **1965–70**
DARE (Qu. T16, . . *Kinds of trees . . 'special')* 24 Infs, **chiefly Sth, S
Midl,** Mimosa (tree); (Qu. T9) Infs **AR**5, 24, 41, **MS**21, 63, Mimosa
(tree). **1968** Radford et al. *Manual Flora Carolinas* 574, *A[lbizia] julibrissin. . . Mimosa. . .* Naturalized along roadsides and woodland borders. . . Va., Ga., Fla., Ala., Miss., Tenn., Ky. **1980** Little *Audubon
Guide N. Amer. Trees E. Region* 517, "Mimosa-tree" . . *Albizia julibrissin. Ibid* 518, Often called "Mimosa-tree" because the flowers are similar to those of the related herbaceous sensitive-plants (genus *Mimosa).*
1986 Pederson *LAGS Concordance* **Gulf Region,** 49 infs, Mimosa(s);
16 infs, Mimosa tree(s).

min See **mind**

minah See **minor**

mince v **widespread, but more freq Sth, Midl** See Map Cf **mincy, timid**

To eat daintily, sparingly, or without appetite; to eat (something) in such a way; hence n *mincer*.

1909 *DN* 3.349 **eAL, wGA,** Mince. . . To eat sparingly. "She minced along through the dinner." **1912** *DN* 3.583 **wIN,** Mince. . . To eat without appetite. "He just minces through all his meals." **1915** *DN* 4.185 **swVA,** Mince. . . To eat slowly and daintily. **1950** *PADS* 14.46 **SC,** Mince. . . To eat without appetite, in a gingerly way; to eat fastidiously. "He's only mincing his food." **c1960** *Wilson Coll.* **csKY,** Mince. . . To eat daintily, too daintily. **1965–70** *DARE* (Qu. H12, *If somebody eating a meal takes little bits of food and leaves most of it on his plate, you say he* _____) 86 Infs, **chiefly Sth, Midl,** Minces; **KS**11, **NC**60, **OH**31, **VT**16, Minces around (*or* along); **CA**174, **OK**44, Minces at it (*or* his food); **MI**51, 66, **MO**6, **NY**21, **TX**1, Minces his food (*or* meals); **CA**87, Mincing it; **NY**69, Minced his food; **MA**50, **MS**13, **MO**1, **NJ**56, **PA**119, Mincer; (Qu. H5) Inf **TX**58, Mincing; (Qu. H10, *If somebody never eats very much food . . he's a* _____; total Infs questioned, 75) Infs **AR**32, **GA**13, **MS**2, Mincer. **1981** *PADS* 67.34 **neMN,** Snack. . . Bite, *Mincing,* and *Picking* occur once each on the Mesabi. **1983** *MJLF* 9.1.47 **ceKY,** Mincer . . a person lacking an appetite.

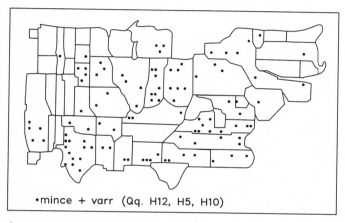

•mince + varr (Qq. H12, H5, H10)

minced pie See **mince pie**

mincemeat n **chiefly Midl** See Map

=**headcheese 1** or a similar food made with head meat or inner organs.

1956 Ker *Vocab. W. TX* 275, Pressed meat loaf made of hogs' jowls. . . mince meat [1 of 67 infs]. **1965–70** *DARE* (Qu. H43, *Foods made from parts of the head and inner organs of an animal*) 20 Infs, **chiefly Midl,** Mincemeat; **NC**30, Souse meat, mincemeat pie. [*DARE* Ed: Some of these Infs describe a mixture of head meat, fruits, and spices.] **1966** Dakin *Dial. Vocab. Ohio R. Valley* 2.339, The edible portions of the head and hocks of a hog when minced, seasoned, cooked, and allowed to cool form a jellied loaf commonly called *head cheese.* . . A number of miscellaneous terms . . appear scattered throughout the Valley. Among them are: *head sausage,* . . and *mince meat.* **1967** Faries *Word Geog. MO* 124, A pressed loaf consisting of a mixture of pork scraps, especially hog jowls. . . A list of terms . . occurring only occasionally follows: *head souse,* . . *mince meat.* **1986** Pederson *LAGS Concordance (Souse)*

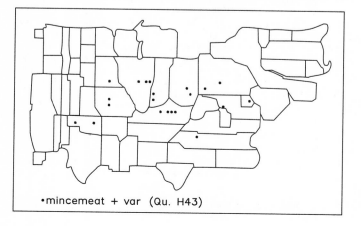

•mincemeat + var (Qu. H43)

2 infs, **nw,cwAR,** Mincemeat; 1 inf, **neTN,** Mincemeat—probably same as souse; seasoned meat; 1 inf, **cwAR,** Mincemeat—also made from hog's head; 1 inf, **cwAR,** Mincemeat—used the head for.

mince pie n Also *minced pie* **esp NEast** See Map Note: The term *mincemeat pie* is not regional.

A pie made with chopped raisins, apples, spices, and sometimes with meat and suet.

1694 (1878) S. Sewall *Diary* 1.394 **MA,** Women din'd with rost Beef and minc'd Pyes, good Cheese and Tarts. **1783** in 1974 Winslow *Amer. Broadside* 193 **MA,** Chesecakes, cold hams, plumb-puddings, and mince-pies! **1821** Willich *Domestic Encycl.* 3.127 **PA,** Mince pie—Of scraped beef . . suet . . currants . . apples. **1872** Schele de Vere *Americanisms* 506, *Minced*–pies represent in America the English Christmaspies. They continue to be popular in the South. **1923** Watts *Luther Nichols* 146 **OH,** They wound up with mince-pie opulently garnished à la mode. **1952** Tracy *Coast Cookery* 247 **VT,** Many Vermont cooks look forward to the November deer-hunting season—and the makings for those holiday mince pies. **1965–70** *DARE* (Qu. H63, *Kinds of desserts*) 12 Infs, **esp NEast,** Mince pie(s).

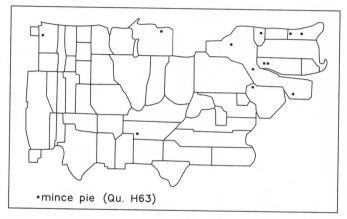

•mince pie (Qu. H63)

mincer See **mince**

mincy adj **esp S Midl** Cf **mince**

Finicky or overly fastidious, usu about eating.

1913 Kephart *Highlanders* 289 **sAppalachians,** A remarkable word, common in the Smokies, is *dauncy,* defined for me as "mincy about eating," which is to say fastidious, over-nice. **1927** *AmSp* 2.360 **WV,** Mincy . . particular in eating. "She is too mincy to suit me." **1952** Brown *NC Folkl.* 1.565 **wNC,** Mincy. . . Over particular, over exact, finicky. "You're mighty mincy about your breakfast today. Are you sick?" **1960** Williams *Walk Egypt* 224 **nGA,** Her voice was mincy, a child playing a woman. **c1960** *Wilson Coll.* **csKY,** Mincy. . . Dainty, said of an eater. **1967–70** *DARE* (Qu. H12, *If somebody eating a meal takes little bits of food and leaves most of it on his plate, you say he* _____) Infs **IN**3, **OH**41, Mincy; **TX**40, **VA**35, Mincy eater. **1972** Cooper *NC Mt. Folkl.* 94, Mincy—finicky. **1984** Wilder *You All Spoken Here* 12 **Sth,** Mincy: Fastidious; finicky; picky; she's so persnickety she wouldn't be happy in a pie factory.

mind n, v Pronc-spp *min(e)* Cf Pronc Intro 3.I.22
A Forms.

1848 Lowell *Biglow* 145 'Upcountry' **MA,** Min', mind. **1884** *Anglia* 7.271 **Sth, S Midl** [Black], *To tu'n de mine over* = to deliberate. **1890** *DN* 1.74, *Mind.* Note the New England phrase, "if he was a mind to" (pronounced [wəz ə maın tu]). **1899** Chesnutt *Conjure Woman* 14 **csNC** [Black], A nigger did n' mine goin' fi' er ten mile in a night. **1901** *DN* 2.182 **neKY** [Black], *Mind*—min'. **1903** *DN* 2.299 **Cape Cod MA,** Mind. . . In expression 'be all mind to,' to be much disposed. 'I'm all min' to hit ye.' **1909** *DN* 3.349 **eAL, wGA,** Mine. . . To mind.
B As noun.

1 An inclination, desire (to do something)—used in phr *have a mind to* and varr. [*OED mind* sb.¹ 13 a1400 →] Cf **a mind**
[**1705** Beverley *Hist. VA* 1.52, Oppechancanough . . was not able to walk alone; but was carried about by his Men where-ever he had a Mind to move.] **1762** *Boston Eve.–Post* (MA) 4 Oct np, Any Person that has a Mind to treat at private Sale may Enquire of the Auctioneer. **1814** in 1947 *AmSp* 22.274 **NEng,** I had a great mind to. **1909** *DN* 3.420 **Cape Cod MA** (as of a1857), *Great good mind* . . a strong inclination. **1910**

DN 3.443 **wNY,** *Have a great mind. . .* To have a strong desire or inclination. "I've a great mind to go to the city and do some trading to-morrow." **1912** DN 3.577 **wIN,** *Have a great mind. . .* To have a pronounced inclination. "I have a great mind to go to town to-day." **1914** DN 4.76 **nNH, ME,** *Mind to, have a great. . .* To be much inclined to. **1946** PADS 6.20 **ceNC,** *Mind. . .* Inclination, desire. "I could do that if I had a mind to." . . Common. **1952** Brown NC Folkl. 1.565, *Mind, to have a great (good). . .* To be inclined to, to have a strong desire. **1955** Ritchie Singing Family 155 **seKY,** The stock . . could have got out through the same hole, if they had a mind to. **1965–70** DARE (Qu. JJ35a, *When you have just about reached the point of telling somebody what you think of him: "By gosh, I have a _____ [to tell him what I think of him]."*) 295 Infs, **widespread, but somewhat more freq NEng, Sth, S Midl,** Good mind; 285 Infs, **widespread,** Mind; 18 Infs, **esp Sth, S Midl,** Great mind; 17 Infs, **scattered,** Half a mind; **MA98, NY92,** 241, Damn (or great) good mind. **1967** DARE Tape TX39, A man can avoid a lot of that trouble whenever . . he has a mind to. **1986** Pederson LAGS Concordance, 1 inf, **cnGA,** If I has a mind to = If I want to; 1 inf, **csGA,** If they'd a mind to; 1 inf, **cGA,** If you've a mind to.

2 rarely pl: Attention, heed—usu in neg phrr. **chiefly Sth, S Midl**
1916 DN 4.269 **seLA,** *Mind. . .* Attention. "I pay no mind to that." **1923** DN 5.214 **swMO,** *Mind. . .* Attention. "He wouldn't give no mind to me." **1932** (1974) Caldwell Tobacco Road 27 **GA,** But he ain't paying no mind to it now, is he? **1933** Rawlings South Moon 74 **nFL,** He someway wa'n't payin' no mind when the tree were throwed. **1939** in 1944 ADD **seAL,** You'd better pay mind to him. **1941** Time 13 Oct 15, But retail merchants paid him little mind. **1941** Stuart Men of Mts. 108 **neKY,** Pa didn't pay us no minds. **1944** PADS 2.10 **AL, NC, SC, TN, VA,** *Mind, to pay* (me) *some (any). . .* To give attention to (me). "I talked with enthusiasm, but he didn't pay me any mind." **1946** PADS 6.20 **eNC** (as of 1900–10), "He paid me no mind." . . Mainly among negroes. **1950** PADS 14.46 **SC,** *Mind. . .* Attention. "He don't pay me no mind." **c1960** Wilson Coll. **csKY,** *Mind. . .* Attention. "Pay him no mind." **1968–70** DARE (Qu. GG27b, *To get somebody out of an unhappy mood . . "Don't _____."*) Inf **MO34,** Pay any mind; (Qu. KK26, *Something that makes no difference at all to you: "He can think what he likes, it _____ me."*) Inf **SC66,** I pay it no mind; **VA25,** Pay him no mind. **1986** Pederson LAGS Concordance **Gulf Region,** 4 infs, (I) didn't pay him (or them, it, her) no mind; 3 infs, (I) never paid it (or that, them) no mind; 1 inf, Don't pay it no mind; 1 inf, I never paid no mind; 1 inf, They don't pay no mind; 1 inf, Pay any mind to it; 1 inf, Don't pay no mind to what he's a-doing.

3 An idea, notion; see quots.
1966–70 DARE (Qu. GG12, *To have an inner feeling that something is about to happen: "There she comes now, I _____ she would."*) Infs **SC26, 69,** Had a (good) mind. [Both Infs Black] **1971** Mitchell Blow My Blues Away 147 **nwMS** [Black], That first mind that come to me told me, don't you go anywhere tonight, you go home and go to bed. . . But instead of me following my first mind, I let this fellow out-talk me to bring him to Boyle that night.

4 in phr *make (one) no mind:* To be of no importance or consequence (to one). [Cf **nevermind 3**]
1966–68 DARE (Qu. KK26, *Something that makes no difference at all to you: "He can think what he likes, it _____ me."*) Infs **NM9, TX1, VA31,** Makes me no mind. **1980** Banks First-Person America 68 **Chicago IL** (as of c1938) [Black], But that don't make no mind; they all friends in the union.

C As verb.

1 To remind; hence ppl adj *minded.* [OED 1340 →, "Now rare"; W3 "chiefly dial"] **chiefly Sth, S Midl**
1858 Hammett Piney Woods Tavern 116, It sorter minded me of bein' made a most a grand fool of . . when I was a boy. **1881** Twain Prince & Pauper 194 **MO,** Here is the stump . . to keep me minded of it. **1899** Chesnutt Conjure Woman 40 **csNC** [Black], Dat saw . . 'min's me er po' Sandy. **1899** (1912) Green VA Folk-Speech 282, *Mind. . .* To remind. . . "He minded me of my purpose." **1909** DN 3.349 **eAL, wGA,** *Mind. . .* To remind. **1923** DN 5.214 **swMO,** *Mind. . .* To remind. "Be shore 'n' mind me o' what I said." **1937** Sandoz Slogum 72 **NE,** You mind me of a girl I had once. **1942** Hall Smoky Mt. Speech 53 **wNC, eTN,** Remind. . . 'He 'minds me o' you.' **1955** Taber Stillmeadow Daybook 139 **swCT,** As I hang them on the line, I am minded of my Uncle Walter. **1968** DARE (Qu. JJ28, *If you are afraid you may forget something, you may tell another person, "Before I leave tonight, be sure and _____ [me to do it]."*) Inf **VA15,** Mind.

2 also with *about, of;* also refl: To remember. [OED mind v. 2 1382 →; "Now arch. and dial."] **esp Sth, Midl**
1769 in 1953 Woodmason Carolina Backcountry 154 **SC,** If any of You should fall out about Your Calves and Your Kine, You be sure mind and think upon Abraham. **1865** Crockett Life 206 **TN,** I saw so many folks, and so many new things, that it's no wander [sic] I should not mind everything. **1873** Harte Mrs. Skaggs 166 **CA,** Do ye mind that morning? **1903** in 1976 AmSp 49.63 **seME,** *Mind. . .* Remember. "D'ye mind the old days?" **1903** DN 2.321 **seMO,** You may have told me, but I don't mind it now. **1907** (1970) Martin Betrothal 105 **sePA,** "Do you mind of him, pop?" . . "Ach, yes, I mind of *him.*" **1907** DN 3.233 **nwAR,** *Mind. . .* To remember. **1907** White AZ Nights 219, I mind when they catched the great-granddaddy of all the bullsnakes. **1909** DN 3.349 **eAL, wGA,** I mind me of a story I heard once. **1918** DN 5.20 **NC,** *Mind about,* remember. **1923** DN 5.214 **swMO,** I mind 'im when he was jist a sprout of a boy. **1933** Rawlings South Moon 6 **nFL,** I mind me o' him tellin' all that. **1935** AmSp 10.172 **sePA,** *Mind* in the sense of 'remember' is frequently heard: 'I mind me that he wanted it last week.' **1936** (1951) Faulkner Absalom 283 **MS,** I hope you minded to thank them. **1954** DE Folkl. Bulletin 1.16, I seemed to mind such a yarn from way back. **1959** VT Hist. 27.149, "I mind the time." . . Old Fashioned. Rare. **c1960** Wilson Coll. **csKY,** *Mind. . .* Remember. "I mind that her daddy lived to be eighty." **1982** Barrick Coll. **csPA,** *Mind*—remember. . . "Yeah, I mind a him."

3 To notice, be aware of. Cf **mind out**
1834 Crockett Narrative 39 **TN,** I reported to Col. Coffee the news. He didn't seem to mind my report a bit, and this raised my dander higher than ever. **1867** Allen Slave Songs 74, O sister, you must mind how you step on the cross,/ Your foot might slip, and your soul get lost. **1899** Garland Boy Life 83 **nwIA** (as of c1870s), You jest want to mind where you step, and where you put your bare hand; that's all. **1963** Owens Look to River 163 **TX,** It'll take a heap more time'n just talking to you about it. You minding the time? **1964** Faulkner As I Lay Dying 203 **MS,** "I never noticed it getting hot," Cash said. "I ought to minded it."

4 To desire, be inclined; to intend. [OED mind v. 6.b "Obs. exc. dial."]
1906 DN 3.147 **nwAR,** *Mind. . .* To like. "I shouldn't mind to." **1926** Roberts Time of Man 328 **KY,** Said a horse could go in by itself if it minded to. **1931** Randolph Ozarks 74, Shakespeare . . also used *mind* in the sense of intend, exactly as the hillman employs the term today.

5 To care for, like. [OED mind v. 7.b →1748]
1895 DN 1.391 **wNC,** Near Asheville, N.C., I heard a mountaineer say, 'I didn't mind it a bit,' meaning he was terrified at looking over a precipice. The same phrase in Ohio would mean that he was wholly indifferent to it.

6 freq with *off:* To scare or drive away (birds, flies, etc). **chiefly Sth, S Midl**
1865 Byrn Advent. Fudge Fumble 152 **TN,** A little boy went out to mind off the dogs. **1892** KS Univ. Qrly. 1.97 **KS,** *Mind off:* to ward off (flies, etc.) **1930** DN 6.82 **cSC,** *Mind the flies. . .* "Shoo the flies." . . "Mind the flies off the food." **c1937** in 1972 Amer. Slave 2.247 **SC,** When I was a boy, I mind de crows out de field. **1942** (1971) Campbell Cloud-Walking 73 **seKY,** Ishmael was left to mind off the flies because Fess had gone off to Viny's. **1942** McAtee Dial. Grant Co. IN 43 (as of 1890s), *Mind flies . .* keep flies away from the table with a fly brush. This is the same use of the word as in the term bird-minding which has been widely used in the Southeast, particularly with reference to efforts to keep destructive birds out of rice fields. **1963** Owens Look to River 14 **TX,** Then came March and the blackbirds. In a week of minding them, Jed hated them more than anything he had ever known. **1966** DARE Tape **FL36A,** We grew rice and we'd mind the birds out of it; **SC15,** Used to min' the bird with the musket. **1968** DARE (Qu. NN22a, *Expressions used to drive away people or animals—for example, flies*) Inf **GA28,** Fan 'em away, mind 'em away. **1975** McDonough Garden Sass 150 **AR,** Now we'd have to keep them [=cats] minded off-a that corpse. **1986** Pederson LAGS Concordance, 1 inf, **neTN,** Always, one of the women, a mother or one of the girls, would have to mind them—flies, during meal.

mindable adj
Well-mannered.
1970 DARE FW Addit **VA35,** Talking about area Negroes, the Inf said some were "mindable"—they have good manners, treat you well and kindly, and are not biggity.

mind about See **mind C2**

minded See **mind C1**

minder n

In combs: One who tends free-ranging animals.

1936 Smith–Sass *Carolina Rice* 68 **SC coast** (as of c1850), The cow-minder resided at the "hog crawl," which lay just outside of the fence that surrounded the cornfields or provision-land. **1937** Heyward *Madagascar* 103 **sSC coast**, Stepney, the hog-minder, who years later worked for me, followed them closely and several times each year penned and counted them.

mindful adj [*mind* to obey]

1952 Brown *NC Folkl.* 1.565 **c,eNC**, Mindful. . . Obedient.

mind of See **mind C2**

mind off See **mind C6**

mind oneself of See **mind C2**

mind out v phr **chiefly Sth, S Midl** Cf **mind C3**

To be careful, to watch out—freq used in imper.

1890 *DN* 1.65 **KY**, Mind out: to take care, to look out. "Mind out what you are doing." **1905** *DN* 3.88 **nwAR**, Mind out. . . Have a care. **1918** *DN* 5.20 **NC**, Mind out. **1938** Stuart *Dark Hills* 66 **eKY**, I tell you John's got a bad boy. He'll go to the pen if he don't mind out. **1959** McAtee *Oddments* 5 **cNC**, Mind out . . watch out. . . "Children playing in the street will get run over if they don't mind out." **c1960** *Wilson Coll.* **csKY**, Mind out. . . Be on the lookout, be particular. **1969** Emmons *Deep Rivers* 81 **eTX** [Black], Honey, ever' time you see a dark Christmas, you just mind out. There's gonna be a lot of colored folks die that year. **1986** Pederson *LAGS Concordance*, 1 inf, **cwMS**, Y'all mind out now = Y'all watch out now.

mine See **mind**

mineral See **minnow A6**

mineral light n Cf **money light**

=**jack-o'-lantern 1.**

1968 *DARE* (Qu. CC16, *A small light that seems to dance or flicker over a marsh or swamp at night*) Inf **NC54**, Mineral [mɪnɚl] lights. **1968** [see **meteor light**].

mineral rod n Cf *DS* CC13a

A divining rod, used esp for locating mineral deposits.

1809 Kendall *Travels* 3.101 **ME**, The mysteries of the mineral-rods are many. **1849** Lanman *Letters Alleghany Mts.* 187 **wNC**, Travelling about the country under the guidance of *mineral rods* or dreams in search of mines. **1903** McFaul *Ike Glidden* 184 **ME**, They've sent for Squire Blunt to come up here in the morning, with a mineral rod, to assist them. **1930** Dobie *Coronado* 107 **swTX**, They possessed a "gold monkey"—a mineral rod—and this instrument they took to the fort; it oscillated towards the west and made two locations. **1939** (1962) Thompson *Body & Britches* 22 **NY**, A good word is to be said for the Mineral-Rod. This valuable apparatus is a fork of witch-hazel, such as our *dowsers* upstate use in finding water-wells; into its straight part is inserted a pure white goose-quill filled with quicksilver and covered tightly with kid.

miner's asthma See **miner's consumption**

miner's bread n [From the old-time miners' practice of making sourdough] Cf **sheepherder's bread**

1968 *DARE* (Qu. H18, . . *Special kinds of bread*) Inf **CA64**, Miner's bread—about the same as sourdough made in a loaf.

miner's candle n Cf **candlewick 1**

A **mullein** (here: *Verbascum thapsus*).

1941 Writers' Program *Guide WY* 23, Tucked into crevices and sun-warmed pockets on the high slopes, or bent by the wind on the drying prairie, are saxifrage, five-fingers, . . miner's candle, beardtongue, arnica. **1990** *Plants SW* (Catalog) 95, *Verbascum thapsus* . . Miner's candle.

miner's cat n [See quot 1980]

=**ringtail cat.**

[**1917** Anthony *Mammals Amer.* 109, Ring-tailed cat. . . They . . are made household pets by California miners and Texas ranchmen. The latter say they make better mousers than domestic cats, and if given free run of the premises, will lose no time in clearing a cabin of rats and mice.] **1937** Grinnell et al. *Fur-Bearing Mammals CA* 172, "Ring-tail". . . The name "miner's cat" was applied because in early days miners and prospectors kept these animals as pets to rid their cabins of

mice and pack rats. **1980** Whitaker *Audubon Field Guide Mammals* 562, Ringtails were placed in frontier mines to control rodents, thus earning the name "Miner's Cat."

miner's consumption n Also *miner's asthma*, ~ *con*, ~ *lung*, ~ *puff, the miner's* **chiefly West, esp CA, NV, CO** See Map Cf **con** n[1]

Any of several lung diseases caused by inhalation of mineral particles or coal dust.

1945 *CA Folkl. Qrly.* 4.322 **CO** [Mining terms], The miners: Silicosis. **1949** Emrich *Wild West Custom* 165 **West**, A miner with silicosis had *rock on the chest, rock on the box, the miner's con* or, succinctly, *the miner's.* **1960** Korson *Black Rock* 351 **PA**, Industrial ballads were sung solo and often without pause between stanzas; exceptions were in the cases of individual singers suffering from anthracosis, or "miner's asthma." **1967–70** *DARE* (Qu. BB10, . . *Names or nicknames . . for tuberculosis*) Infs **CO33, 35, 39, 47, NV2, 8**, Miner's consumption; **CA59, 123, CO14, 33, 47, NV2, 8**, Miner's con; **CO47**, Miner's puff; (Qu. BB49, . . *Other kinds of diseases*) Infs **AK1, NV2**, Miner's consumption; **PA245**, Miner's asthma. **1968** Thrush *Dict. of Mining* 840, Pneumoconiosis. . . Also called miner's asthma; miner's consumption; miner's lung. **1969** Kantor *MO Bittersweet* 287, What are the lungs like, inside that maltreated chest? (Oldtimers in Missouri mining regions used to talk about "miners' con," a form of silicosis which in its later stages ran into tuberculosis.)

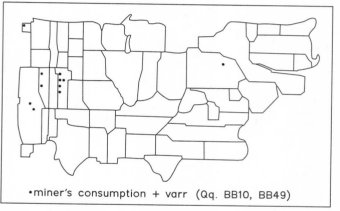

•miner's consumption + varr (Qq. BB10, BB49)

miner's dogwood n

A **dogwood 1** (here: *Cornus sessilis*).

1938 Van Dersal *Native Woody Plants* 110, *Cornus sessilis*. . . Miners dogwood. . . A large shrub to small tree; flowers in April; thicket forming. **1979** Little *Checklist U.S. Trees* 99, *Cornus sessilis* . . black-fruit dogwood. . . Other common name—miners dogwood.

miner's lettuce n [See quot 1967]

Any of var western plants of the closely related genera *Montia* and *Claytonia*, but esp *C. perfoliata.* Also called **Indian lettuce 3, spring beauty.** For other names of var spp see **candyflower, Spanish lettuce, squaw cabbage, toad lily, water chickweed, wild lettuce**

1897 Parsons *Wild Flowers CA* 16, Miner's Lettuce. . . *Montia perfoliata*. . . These little plants are said to be excellent when boiled and well seasoned. **1915** (1926) Armstrong–Thornber *Western Wild Flowers* 120, There are several kinds of Montia, closely related to Claytonia, . . rather succulent plants, very smooth and often with a "bloom." . . *Miner's Lettuce*. . . The tender, bright-green leaves look as if they would taste very nice. **1940** Writers' Program *Oregon* 23, Miners' lettuce took the place of the cultivated vegetable. **1947** *Atlantic Mth.* 180.110 **CA**, Your Farewell to Spring, Cream Cups, Baby Blue Eyes, and Miner's Lettuce have given up their whimsical little ghosts. **1954** Sharpe *101 Wildflowers* 13 **WA**, As are most springbeautys [sic], it [=*Claytonia sibirica*] is also known as miner's lettuce. **1966** *DARE* FW Addit **WA10**, *Claytonia perfoliata*—miner's lettuce; **WA12**, Miner's lettuce—flesh[y] leaf, white blossom. **1967** Harrington *Edible Plants Rocky Mts.* 138, It [=*Claytonia perfoliata*] was very popular during the gold rush to California, hence the name "miner's lettuce." It was one of the fresh native plants that could be used to cure and avert scurvy. **1967–70** *DARE* (Qu. I28a, . . *Kinds of things . . you call 'greens' . . Those that are eaten raw*) Inf **CA196**, Miner's lettuce; (Qu. I28b, *Kinds of greens that are cooked*) Inf **CA87**, Miner's lettuce—a papery cup with a flower in the center, also called Indian lettuce; (Qu. S21, . . *Weeds . . that are a trouble in gardens and fields*) Inf **CA**20, Miner's lettuce—a heart-shaped leaf with a short-stemmed white flower, edible. **1970** Kirk *Wild Edible Plants W. U.S.* 49, An excellent salad can be made of canned tuna mixed with Miners Lettuce leaves, and seasoned with a dressing of olive oil, salt, pepper, vinegar, and spices to suit. **1977** Churchill *Don't Call* 140 **nwOR** (as of c1918), Miner's lettuce was more difficult to find but it was a good substitute for real lettuce, which didn't appear on the market until summer. **1979** Spellenberg *Audubon Guide N. Amer. Wildflowers W. Region* 684, *Miner's Lettuce, Indian Lettuce. . .* As the common names indicate, the leaves are edible.

miner's loco See **loco** n¹ **2b**

miner's puff See **miner's consumption**

miner's strawberry See **strawberry**

mines pron [Perh by analogy with *hers, its, yours, theirs*] *esp freq among Black speakers*

Mine.

    1934 Hurston *Jonah's Gourd Vine* 127 **AL** [Black], Youse a lie [=liar], madam. Eve'y chicken on dis place is mines. **1956** *AmSp* 31.36, *Fin dibs* . . means 'No divisions on what is mine!' or, as Chuck Albert, from Providence, Rhode Island, says, 'All mines, fellas, all mines!' **1959** Lomax *Rainbow Sign* 35 **AL** [Black], If I don't mind, he's gonna have some of mines, too. **1968** *PADS* 50.34 **swTN** [Black], [One inf] has the form /maɪnz/ for *mine*. **1986** Pederson *LAGS Concordance,* 1 inf, **nwFL**, Mines = mine; 1 inf, **neAR**, Mines had to walk—i.e., my children. [Both Infs Black]

minge n Also *mingie* *esp* **ME, NH**

A **midge**, esp a **punkie** (here: family Ceratopogonidae).

    1895 *DN* 1.391 **ME**, *Minges:* for *midges*. **1914** *DN* 4.76 **ME, nNH**, *Mingie*. . . A gnat. **1966** *DARE* (Qu. R11, *A very tiny fly that you can hardly see, but that stings*) Infs **ME**8, 24, Minges ['mɪnjɪz]; **ME**20, Mingies. **1979** [see **no-see-um 1**]. **1982** Heat Moon *Blue Highways* 339 **NH**, As we walked up the road, air began whiffling down off Bald Peak and pushing invisible biting midges ("mingies" Hunter called them) downwind.

mingledy adj Also *mangly, mingly* *esp* **Sth, S Midl** Cf Intro "Language Changes" III.1, **fadedy**, *muckledy-dun* (at **muckledun 1**)

Of mixed colors, variegated.

    1933 Miller *Lamb in His Bosom* 13 **GA**, One dress that she had brought with her from her mother's was brown mingled-y. **1938** Rawlings *Yearling* 309 **nFL**, Blue and white. . . All mingledy . . like a joint snake. **1941** Smith *Going to God's Country* 39 **MO** (as of 1890), The cloth would be mingly. But if we dyed the chain brown the cloth would be solid brown. **1957** *Sat. Eve. Post Letters* **AR** (as of c1930), Some of the Ozark words I liked to hear were . . *mangly* . . —used of dress material which was of multi-colored pattern, such as a flower pattern of different colors. [**1967–68** *DARE* (Qu. J5, *A cat with fur of mixed colors*) Inf **TX**45, Mingled; **NC**52, Mingle; (Qu. K38, *A horse of a dirty white color*) Inf **VA**1, Mingled.] **1986** Pederson *LAGS Concordance,* 1 inf, **csMS**, Striped, colored, mingledy. **1993** Mason *Feather Crowns* 381 **KY**, The mingledy-spotted cats sat on another chair washing each other's faces.

ming-mang n [Cf *EDD* ming-mang "disorder," *ming* "mixture"] Cf **mang**

See quot.

    1936 *AmSp* 11.316 **Ozarks**, *Ming-mang.* . . A mixture of butter and molasses, or butter and gravy.

minichuck n

Prob a **mummichog.**

    1931–33 *LANE Worksheets* **CT**, A minichuck is not very good for bait, but used for it.

minim See **minnow A5**

‡mini-mini in free exclam

In the game of **hide-and-seek**: = **all (in) free.**

    1968 *DARE* (Qu. EE15, *When he has caught the first of those that were hiding what does the player who is 'it' call out to the others?*) Inf **MD**2, Mini-mini in free.

minini n Cf **manini 1**

A butterfly fish of the family Chaetodontidae.

    1967 *Honolulu Star–Bulletin* (HI) 31 May sec F 1/4, Minini . . Angelfish, Coralfish, or Butterflyfish.

minister n

1 =**brown bullhead 1.** [See quots 1872, 1911]

    1839 *MA Zool. & Bot. Surv. Fishes Reptiles* 102, The Horned Pout. . . is known in the interior of the State by the vulgar names of "*Horn Pout*", and "*Minister*." **1842** DeKay *Zool. NY* 4.183, The *Common Catfish, Horn Pout* or *Minister*, has a wide geographic range. It occurs in the great lakes, and along the Atlantic States from New-Hampshire to Florida. **1872** Schele de Vere *Americanisms* 382, A species [of catfish] is known also as *Mudpout,* . . and irreverently, from its black color perhaps, as *Minister*. **1911** *Century Dict.* 3776, *Minister*. . . The catfish, *Amiurus nebulosus:* apparently so called from the silvery white throat, contrasting with the dark back, and likened to a clergyman's white necktie. [*Century* Ed: Local, U.S.] **1949** Caine *N. Amer. Sport Fish* 148, Brown bullhead. . . Minister.

2 Usu the **great black-backed gull**, but also the **glaucous gull**. [See quot 1956] Cf **black minister, white ~**

    1929 Forbush *Birds MA* 1.69, Great Black-backed Gull . . minister. **1946** Hausman *Eastern Birds* 311, *Great Black-backed Gull.* . . *Other Names* . . Minister. . . Distinguishable by its broad, very dark gray mantle (almost black at a distance) contrasting markedly with its white head, neck, underparts, and tail. **1956** *MA Audubon Soc. Bulletin* 40.22 **MA**, *Glaucous Gull.* . . Minister. *Ibid* **MA**, *Great Black-backed Gull.* . . Minister . . From its black mantle and white vest.

minister cat, finding the n

    1969 *DARE* (Qu. EE16, *Hiding games that start with a special, elaborate method of sending the players out to hide*) Inf **KY**5, Finding the minister cat.

minister-of-the-woods n Cf **preacher Jack**

A **jack-in-the-pulpit 1.**

    1950 *WELS (Other names for the jack-in-the-pulpit)* 1 Inf, **ceWI**, Minister-of-the-woods.

minister's face n Cf **parson's nose, preacher's ~**

1 also *minister's head, ~ snout, parson's face:* A boiled or roasted hog's head with eyes and jowls removed. **esp NEng, S Atl**

    1899 (1912) Green *VA Folk-Speech* 283, *Minister's face.* . . The upper part of the head of a hog, from which the ears, nose, and jowl have been cut. Usually boiled, when salt, with beans. **1926** *AmSp* 1.652 [Hobo lingo], *Minister's face*—pigs [sic] head served in cheap restaurant. **1927** *DN* 5.455 [Underworld jargon], *Minister's snout.* . . Boiled pig's head. Also *minister's face.* **1930** Irwin *Amer. Tramp* 129, *Minister's Head.*—Boiled pig's head. Just why this term is used is hard to say unless it is a term of derision for two things but rarely admired by the tramp: the clergy and this particular article of food. **1932** *DN* 6.283 **swCT**, *Minister's face.* The upper part of a pig's face; the eyes are taken out, the head is scored and then is baked. **1934** *Hanley Disks* **csMA**, The head—we usually cut the cheeks off and skinned them and sliced that up for sausage meat, and the rest of the head, the face—well, the old people used to call it the minister's face; **cNH**, They would meet in the evening there . . the old folks . . and have what they called the minister's face baked. [*DARE* Ed: Inf goes on to describe hanging it up in the fireplace, light coming through the holes as the face turned from side to side on a string.] **1941** *LANE* Map 305, A hog's head with jowls and eyes removed, roasted, is sometimes called *minister's face* or *parson's face.* According to one informant . . it was formerly customary after butchering to give the hog's head to the minister. . . 8 infs, 6 **CT**, Minister's face; 1 inf, **CT**, Parson's face. **1952** Brown *NC Folkl.* 1.565, *Minister's-face.* . . A hog's head.—Granville county.

2 Transf: **headcheese 1; souse.** Cf *DS* H43

    1931–33 *LANE Worksheets* **swCT**, They used to call it (souse) minister's face; **nwCT**, Minister's face . . . Headcheese.

ministrate See **menstruate**

ministration See **menstruation**

ministrational See **menstruation B**

mink n Cf **fox n 1**

See quots.

    1899 (1912) Green *VA Folk-Speech* 283, Mink. . . Minx; a pert girl; a huzzy. **1971** Roberts *Third Ear* np [Black], *Mink* . . an attractive lady. **1972** Claerbaut *Black Jargon* 72, *Mink* . . a girl friend; female social companion.

‡mink v
   1969 *DARE* (Qu. X55b, *Words for breaking wind from the bowels*) Inf NY219, He minked [laughter].

mink eye n, hence adj *mink-eyed*
   An eye with a sharp or piercing look; having such an eye.
   1967–69 *DARE* (Qu. X21b, *If the eyes are very sharp or piercing*) Inf VA2, Mink eyes; GA72, KY33, Mink-eyed.

mink feed n Also *mink meat* Cf **dog feed, fox farm, ready for the**
   An old or worn out horse fit only as meat for mink.
   1968–69 *DARE* (Qu. K44, *A bony or poor-looking horse*) Inf VT16, Mink feed; NY99, Mink meat.

mink frog n [See quot 1958]
   A **bullfrog 1** (here: *Rana septentrionalis*). Also called **Hoosier frog 1**
   1883 *Amer. Naturalist* 17.945, The mink or Hoosier frog. . . *Rana septentrionalis*. . . If taken in the hand it emits . . the disagreeable scent of the mink. **1928** Pope–Dickinson *Amphibians* 40 **WI**, In general appearance the Mink Frog *(Rana septentrionalis)* resembles both the Green Frog . . and the Bullfrog. **1958** Conant *Reptiles & Amphibians* 299, Mink Frog—*Rana septentrionalis*. . . The skin produces an odor like the scent of a mink (or rotten onions) when the frog is rubbed or handled roughly. **1981** Vogt *Nat. Hist. WI* 85, Raccoons and great blue herons regularly feed on mink frogs.

minkle See **minnow A6**

mink meat See **mink feed**

minna See **minnow A2**

Minnehaha cake n [*Minnehaha* the Indian maiden in Longfellow's *Hiawatha*]
   A frosted dessert cake; see quots.
   1906 Gregory *Woman's Cookbook* 236, Minnehaha cake. . . Sugar, . . butter, . . milk, . . flour, . . baking powder, the whites of six eggs beaten thoroughly. For filling use . . raisins, . . hickory nut meats, . . sugar. . . Boil down until thick enough to spread on cake. **1968** *DARE* (Qu. H63, *Kinds of desserts*) Inf PA110, Minnehaha cake—white cake, iced. **1969** *DARE* FW Addit ceNY, Minnehaha cake—a layer cake.

minner See **minnow A2**

Minnesota gopher n
   A **ground squirrel b** (here: *Spermophilus tridecemlineatus*).
   1970 *Western Folkl.* 29.171, There is not just one ground squirrel in the upper Midwest; there are three. The most common of the three is the so-called Minnesota gopher or the thirteen-lined ground squirrel.

Minnesota maple n
   =**box elder.**
   1967 *DARE* (Qu. T13, . . *Names* . . *for these trees: box elder*) Inf MI71, Minnesota maple.

Minnesota mutton n Cf **government beef**
   Venison.
   1968 *DARE* (Qu. P35a) Inf WI45, Minnesota mutton. [FW: Inf mentioned this as being on a menu in South Dakota for venison.]

Minnesota thirteen n
   1966–67 *DARE* (Qu. DD21c, *Nicknames for whiskey, especially illegally made whiskey*) Inf MN6, Minnesota thirteen—an illegal corn whiskey made in prohibition days, supposedly named after the brand of corn used; ND3, Minnesota thirteen.

minnew See **minnow A4**

minnie n[1] See **minnow A3**

minnie n[2] [Prob abbr for *miniature*]
   A playing marble.
   1967–69 *DARE* (Qu. EE6b, *Small marbles or marbles in general*) Infs IL47, OH37, Minnies; (Qu. EE6c, *Cheap marbles*) Infs IL47, OH50, Minnies.

minnie n[3] Also *minnie-cat* [Fr *minet* kitten] **chiefly LA** Cf **minou**
   A cat—often used as a call to a cat.
   1916 *DN* 4.346 **New Orleans LA**, *Minnie*. . . Pet name for a cat: now used as a common noun, with children. "The minnie" refers to the cat. **1941** O'Donnell *Great Big Doorstep* 97 **sLA**, 'I bring my minnie-cat

and make her be bad on your chair!' one of the girls yelled. **1968** *DARE* (Qu. J10, *To call a cat to make it come*) Infs LA15, 24, Minnie, minnie; LA44, Here, minnie; MO25, Minnie; (Qu. NN22d, . . *Expressions used to drive away people or animals*) Inf MO25, Get out, minnie. **1983** *Reinecke Coll.* 7 **LA**, Minnie—[mɪnɪ] the way to call a cat. Also, "a minnie", child's word for cat. Minou [mɪ'nu] is also sometimes heard.

minnie n[4]
   A **menhaden 1** (here: *Brevoortia tyrannus*).
   1945 Beck *Jersey Genesis* 147 **NJ**, "Most people know mossbunkers as menhaden," Jack said. "Minnies to you, maybe."

minnie n[5] *euphem* Cf *DS* AA27
   1978 *MJLF* 4.1.38 **cTX**, Euphemisms for menstruation—"Mother Nature" and "Minnie."

minnie-berry See **minny-berry**

minniebush n [See quot 1931]
   A **mock azalea** (here: *Menziesia pilosa*). Also called **false heather 3, mountain heath 2**
   1900 Lyons *Plant Names* 245, M[enziesia] pilosa . . is called Minniebush. **1931** U.S. Dept. Ag. *Misc. Pub.* 101.131, Of the American species [of *Menziesia*] one is confined to the Allegheny Mountains. . . Sometimes called minniebush (a corruption of the Latin name). **1943** Peattie *Great Smokies* 197 **wNC, eTN**, Most of the associated shrubs like mountain laurel, blueberry, and minniebush are of the heath family. **1954** *Sat. Review* 13 Nov 55 **NC**, Up on top of the mountain [=Mount Mitchell] you will find minnie bush (sometimes called he-honeysuckle), balsam trees (sometimes called she-balsams), mountain lettuce, St. John's wort, and the grave of the Rev. Elisha Mitchell, D.D. **1961** Douglas *My Wilderness* 164 **wNC, eTN**, Some slopes [of the Smoky Mts] that are covered with rhododendron, laurel, blueberry, and minniebush . . are called . . "slicks" by the mountain people. **1965** *Native Plants PA* 57, [Native shrubs:] Menziesia pilosa. Minniebush. **1968** Radford et al. *Manual Flora Carolinas* 801, *Minnie-bush*. . . Bogs, thinly wooded slopes and balds. **1976** Bailey–Bailey *Hortus Third* 729, *Minniebush*. . . Late spring. Penn. to Ga. and Ala.

minnie-cat See **minnie** n[3]

‡minnie minnie motion n
   1950 *WELS* (Outdoor games . . *played during your childhood*) 1 Inf, **csWI**, Minnie minnie motion—now called "Tennessee" or "trades."

minnie nibbler n [*minnie* (at **minnow A3**)] Cf *DS* CC4 =**mackerel-snapper.**
   1965 *DARE* FW Addit **IA**, Minnie nibbler ['mini nɪblɚ]—a Catholic. "That's right—you're a minnie nibbler. You'll have to order fish tonight."

minnin See **minnow A5**

minnow n For varr see **A** below
A Forms.

1 *min(n)ow, minno;* rarely *menow.* **widespread, but less freq Sth, S Midl** See Map on p. 610
   1792 Belknap *Hist. NH* 3.180, Menow, An cyprinus? **1796** Morse *Amer. Universal Geog.* 1.222, Bony Fish [found in the U.S. include the] . . Minow / Week [sic] fish / King fish. **1814** in 1815 *Lit. & Philos. Soc. NY Trans.* 1.460, *Brook Minnow. (Cyprinus atronasus.)* With a dark stripe extending round his nose and lengthwise to the end of the tail. . . Lives in the fresh-water brooks, inhabited by trout. **1840** *S. Lit. Messenger* 6.386, Ellen used to fish there for minnoes with a pin-hook. **1877** *NY Acad. Sci. Annals Lyceum Nat. Hist.* 11.363, *Episema callisema.* . . One of the handsomest of our Minnows, both in form and coloration. **1906** *NJ State Museum Annual Rept. for 1905* 140, *Notropis procne.* . . Minnow. Minnie. Swallow Minnow. **1939** *LANE* Map 234, [Proncs of the types ['mɪnoz] and ['mɪnɪz, -ɪz] are common **throughout NEng.** Other widely scattered types are ['mɪnuz] (21 infs), ['mɪnjuz] (14), ['mɪnuz] (22), ['mɪnjuz] (5), and ['mɪnəz] (10). 14 infs, **chiefly eMA**, gave proncs of the type ['mɪnəmz] and 1 inf [mɪnɪnz]. 3 infs gave the compound *minnow-fish* [mɪnfɪʃ, minɪ-].] **1950** *WELS* (Small fish used as bait for bigger fish) 50 Infs, **WI**, Minnow(s). **1965** Carmony *Speech Terre Haute* 100 **IN**, /ɪ/ is the usual vowel of such words as . . *rinse, minnow*, . . and *dish.* . . /ɛ/ occurs in . . *minnows* in [1 inf's] record. **1965–70** *DARE* (Qu. P7) 442 Infs, **widespread, but less freq Sth, S Midl**, (Chub, crappie, *or* golden, etc) minnow; (Qu. P3) 10 Infs, **chiefly Nth**, (Common, rock, *or* shiner) minnow(s); (Qu. P1) Infs MN15, NC44, (Chub) minnows; (Qu. P4) Inf LA37, Minnows. **1966** *DARE* Tapes MI13, 21, ['mɪnoz]. **1971** Bright *Word Geog. CA & NV* 187, **widespread throughout CA, NV**, Minnows—76% [of 300 infs]. **1976** Allen

LAUM 3.295 **Upper MW** (as of c1950), [Of the 219 proncs of *minnow* recorded, the second vowel was /o/ in 147, /i/ in 41, /u/ in 21, /ə/ in 8, and /ɚ/ in 2. The /u/ pronc shows little social bias, but is more than twice as frequent in **ND** than in any other state surveyed. The /i/ pronc shows some bias toward the midland region, and a strong bias toward older and less educated infs.]

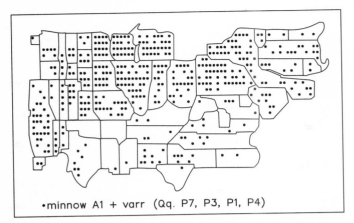

•minnow A1 + varr (Qq. P7, P3, P1, P4)

2 *minna, minner;* rarely *minter.* **chiefly Sth, S Midl** See Map
Cf Pronc Intro 3.I.12.d

1867 Harris *Sut Lovingood Yarns* 27 **TN,** He turn'd durn fool, . . an's in the swimin hole a divin arter minners. **1905** *DN* 3.103 **nwAR,** Final [o] unstressed is invariably [ə]. Cf . . [mɪnə]. **1915** *DN* 4.178 **swVA,** [o] in unaccented syllables at the end of words . . becomes regularly -*er*, in which the r is always heard, even if it is indistinct: . . minner. **1935** (1944) Rawlings *Golden Apples* 139 **nFL,** You kin mess with them painted minners all you o' mind to. **1939** [see **A1** above]. **1941** *Esquire* May 63 **KY,** Little minners playing in the middle of the road took to hiding places under the edges of the banks. **1942** Thomas *Blue Ridge Country* 309 **sAppalachians,** Playful as minner fish. **1954** *Harder Coll.* **cwTN,** Minners. **1965–70** *DARE* (Qu. P7) 224 Infs, **chiefly Sth, Midl,** (Blackhead, branch, *or* chub, etc) minna; 82 Infs, **chiefly Sth, Midl,** Minner; **LA22,** Minna-fishes; (Qu. P14) Inf **OK25,** Minners. **1966–68** *DARE* Tape **AR36,** ['mɪnɚ]; **IN36, TX18,** ['mɪnə(z)]. **1970** *DARE* FW Addit **ceVA,** ['mɪntɚz]. **1976** [see **A1** above].

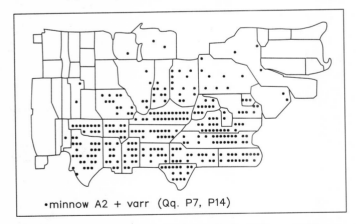

•minnow A2 + varr (Qq. P7, P14)

3 *minnie, minny.* [*OED* (at *minnow* sb. 1) 1558 →; *EDD* min-nie sb.²] **chiefly N Midl, Inland Nth** See Map Note: These forms may be intended as dimins, but might instead be systematic pronc varr; see Pronc Intro 3.I.12.d

1817 *Amer. Monthly Mag. & Crit. Rev.* 2.121 **NY,** *Cyprinus hemiplus.* . . Common in Lake George, Saratoga-lake, &c. vulgar names Shiner or Minny, these names are common to many species. **1842** DeKay *Zool. NY* 4.218, This fish [=*Fundulus heteroclitus*] is known under the names of *Minny* (and more generally of *Big Killie.* **1877** NY Acad. Sci. *Annals Lyceum Nat. Hist.* 11.375 **KY,** We heard several peculiar vernacular names for fishes on the Rock Castle and Cumberland, some of which may be worth recording . . Minny (with contempt), Nototropis micropteryx. **1905** *DN* 3.63 **eNE,** We caught some minnies. **1906** NJ State Museum *Annual Rept. for 1905* 140, *Notropis procne.* . . Minnow. Minnie. *Ibid* 143, *Notropis cornutus.* . .

Red Fin. Shiner. Minny. *Ibid* 145, *Notropis chalybaeus.* . . Minnie. **1910–25** in 1944 *ADD* 390 **cNY,** ['mɪni]. **1936** *AmSp* 11.316 **Ozarks,** *Minny.* **1939** [see **A1** above]. **1940** in 1944 *ADD* 390 **swPA, nWV,** Minny. Old speaker. **1950** *WELS* **WI** (*Small fish used as bait for bigger fish*) 6 Infs, Minnie(s); 1 Inf, Children call them [=minnows] minnies; 1 Inf, Minnies—nickname for minnows. **1950** *WELS Suppl.* **csWI,** I'm fishing with grubs 'cause I haven't got any minnies. **c1955** Reed–Person *Ling. Atlas Pacific NW,* 6 infs, Minnies. **1959** *VT Hist.* 27.149, *Minnows* ['mɪniz] . . pronc. Occasional. **1962** Bailey *Jayhawker* 85 **KS,** I've got my hook baited with minnies. **1965–70** *DARE* (Qu. P7) 61 Infs, **chiefly N Midl, Inland Nth, esp OH, PA, MD, NJ,** Minnie; **WV7,** Sunfish minnie; (Qu. P3) Inf **NY88,** Minnies. **1968** *PADS* 49.14 **Upper MW,** Schools tend to establish literary terms in place of or alongside indigenous folk terms. This influence is also evident in . . the increasing use of *minnows* and the decline of *minnies.* **1976** [see **A1** above].

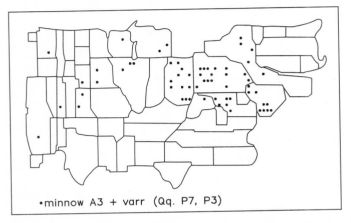

•minnow A3 + varr (Qq. P7, P3)

4 *minnew.* **esp Nth** Note: *OED* shows similar forms from the 16th–18th centuries.

1818 *Amer. Monthly Mag. & Crit. Rev.* 2.204 **NY,** *Notropis Atherinoides.* . . These fishes come on the shores of Lake Erie . . in the spring, in great shoals. . . They are called *Minny* or *Minnew,* together with twenty different other species of fish, and are often considered the young of other fishes. **1820** Rafinesque *Ohio R. Fishes* 46, There are in the United States more than fifty species of small fresh water fishes . . commonly called Minnies, Minnews, Bait-fish, Chubs, and Shiners. **1939** [see **A1** above]. **1966–70** *DARE* (Qu. P7, *Small fish used as bait for bigger fish*) Infs **MI20, 32, 115, ND2, NY24,** ['mɪnu(z)]. **1976** [see **A1** above].

5 *minim, minnin, minnum.* [*OED* mennom 1654 →; *EDD* mennem, mennon; *SND* minnon] **esp eMA, VA**

1828 Webster *Amer. Dict.* np, Minim . . 5. A small fish. **1860** Holmes *Professor* 21 **ceMA,** She has that foolish way of dancing and bobbing like a quill-float with a "minnum" biting the hook below it. **1899** (1912) Green *VA Folk-Speech* 283, Minnum. . . A small fish. **1939** [see **A1** above]. **1970** *DARE* (Qu. P7, *Small fish used as bait for bigger fish*) Inf **VA46,** Minnins ['mɪnɪnz].

6 *mineral, minkle.*

1836 in 1935 Drake *Life & Wks.* 225, Through the transparent waves, the ruddy minkle / Shot up in glimmering sparks his red fin's tiny twinkle. **c1955** Reed–Person *Ling. Atlas Pacific NW,* 1 inf, **WA,** Minerals.

B Senses.

1 Std: a fish of the family Cyprinidae. Also called **baitfish, fryer** n². For other names of var fishes of this family see **Baltimore minnow, bonytail, Boston chub, branch ~, bugle-mouthed bass, bullhead minnow, bull ~, chiselmouth, cocaho, cutlips minnow, dace, fallfish, fathead 1, flathead chub, German carp, Gila trout 1, golden carp, ~ shiner, greaser blackfish, gudgeon 1, hardhead 2f, hardtail 3, hitch** n², **hogfish i, horned dace 2, hornyhead, lake chub, leatherback 5, leather carp, leatherside minnow, long minnow, mirror carp, Missouri minnow, mud chub 2, mudfish h, mud whump, Ozark minnow, peamouth, river chub, roach, roundtail, scale carp, shiner, silver carp, ~ chub, silverjaw minnow, silvery ~, smelt, ~ minnow, speckled chub, splittail, squawfish, stone roller, sturgeon chub, suckermouth**

minnow, tommycod, Utah chub, Verde trout, water hog Cf **ghost minnow, grounder ~, topminnow**

2 Any of var other fishes which resemble **B1** above, as:

a A **darter 1** (here: *Etheostoma* spp).

1820 Rafinesque *Ohio R. Fishes* 37, *Black Hogfish. Etheostoma nigra*. . . Vulgar name Black minny. . . From one to two inches long. **1908** Forbes–Richardson *Fishes of IL* 281, To the fisherman and the ordinary observer these little percoids [=*Etheostoma* spp] are usually either wholly unknown or go by the general name of minnow, or, perhaps, by the more appropriate one of "perch minnow."

b also with modifiers: A fish of the family Cyprinodontidae, usu a **killifish 1.**

1842 DeKay *Zool. NY* 4.218, This fish [=*Fundulus heteroclitus*] is known under the names of *Minny* (minnow), and more generally of *Big Killie*. It abounds in the salt-water creeks and brackish streams in the neighborhood of New-York. *Ibid* 219, *The Transparent Minnow. Hydrargira diaphana*. . . This is described . . from Saratoga lake, where it is used as a bait for other fishes. **1849** (1851) Herbert *Frank Forester's Fish & Fishing* 176, *Minnows. Hydrargyra* [=*Fundulus*]. . . They are generally known as Killy-fish, and are an excellent bait for fish of almost every kind that prey on other fish. **1884** Goode *Fisheries U.S.* 1.466, *Cyprinodontidae*. . . In other localities [than **NEng**], especially in the interior, less correctly known as "Minnow." **1906** NJ State Museum *Annual Rept. for 1905* 185, *Fundulus majalis*. . . Minnow. Killi Fish. *Ibid* 188, *Fundulus heteroclitus macrolepidotus*. . . Minnow. Dog Fish. Killy. *Ibid* 193, *Fundulus diaphanus*. . . Minnow. Killy. **1911** U.S. Bur. Census *Fisheries 1908* 312, *Mummichog*. . . They are known . . in the interior as "minnows." **1943** Eddy–Surber *N. Fishes* 119, *Cyprinidae*. . . The minnows are usually fishes of small size, though. . . several American species reach a weight of several pounds and a length of 18 inches. . . In addition the name "minnow" is often applied locally without discrimination to any small fish, and also there are a number of small fishes called minnows, such as the topminnow [here: =*killifish 1*] and mudminnow, which belong to other families. **1950** Everhart *Fishes ME* 41, *Eastern Banded Killifish*. . . Fishermen frequently refer to this fish as a minnow but the teeth on the jaws serve to distinguish it from the minnow family. **1955** Zim-Shoemaker *Fishes* 66, Killifish and Topminnows are often called minnows, but the term is more correctly used for smaller relatives of the carp. **1983** Becker *Fishes WI* 755, *Banded Killifish*. . . Other common names . . grayback minnow, . . barred minnow.

c Any of var **surfperch**, but esp *Cymatogaster aggregata*. **Pacific coast**

1882 U.S. Natl. Museum *Bulletin* 16.590, *M[icrometrus] aggregatus*. . . "Minnow." . . Pacific coast of the United States, everywhere exceedingly abundant. **1884** Goode *Fisheries U.S.* 1.276, *Embiotocidae*. . . The names "minny," "Sparada," and "Moharra" are also applied to the smaller species [of these fishes] northward [of **OR**]. *Ibid* 278, *Cymatogaster aggregatus*. . . On Puget Sound the Americans call it "Minny," and the Italians "Sparad" or "Sparada." **1911** U.S. Bur. Census *Fisheries 1908* 317, *Surf-fish (Embiotocidae)*. . . Also called . . "minny" . . along their northern range.

d =**mudminnow 1.**

1890 *Century Dict.* 3778, *Minnow*. . . In the United States, one of many different fishes of small size. (*a*) Any cyprinoid. . . This is the correct use of *minnow*. . . (*b*) One of numerous small cyprinodont fishes, otherwise known as *killifishes* and *mummychogs*, and more fully called *top-minnows*. . . (*c*) Any American member of the . . genus *Umbra*, . . more fully called *mud-minnow*. . . (*d*) One of various small . . embiotocoid fishes of California, . . as . . *Cymatogaster aggregatus*. (*e*) One of several small suckers or catostomoid fishes: a loose use. **1933** John G. Shedd Aquarium *Guide* 59, *Umbra pygmaea—Eastern Mud Minnow; Pigmy Minnow*. . . Found only on the Eastern sea board. **1943** [see **B2b** above]. **1950** *WELS* (*Small fish used as bait for bigger fish*) 1 Inf, **WI**, Minnows, minnies—includes chubs, suckers, shiners, silversides, mudminnows.

e also *pin minnow, sucker ~*: A **sucker** (here: family Catostomidae). **esp MN, WI**

1890 [see **B2d** above]. **1943** Eddy–Surber *N. Fishes* 113, *Western Creek Chubsucker (Sweet Sucker, Pin Minnow)*. . . A small sucker rarely exceeding 10 inches in length. **1950** [see **B2d** above]. **1968** *DARE* (Qu. P7, *Small fish used as bait for bigger fish*) Inf **MN**42, Sucker minnow; **MN**15, 35, **WI**68, Sucker minnows. **1983** Becker *Fishes WI* 646, *Lake Chubsucker*. . . Other common names . . pin minnow.

f A **silversides** (here: family Atherinidae). Cf **glass minnow**

1950 [see **B2d** above].

minnow fisher n

=**green heron.**

1944 Hausman *Amer. Birds* 107, Eastern Green Heron—*Butorides virescens virescens*. . . Minnow Fisher. **1951** Pough *Audubon Water Bird* 338, Minnow-fisher. . . Green Heron. **1955** MA Audubon Soc. *Bulletin* 39.312 **CT**, Green Heron. . . Minnow Fisher.

minnow-fole n [Cf *EDD fole* (at *foal* sb.[2]) "A bannock or cake; any soft and thick bread"]

A **duckweed 1** (here: *Spirodela polyrhiza*).

1933 Small *Manual SE Flora* 250, *S[pirodela] polyrhiza*. . . Duckweed, Minnow-fole.

minnow gull n

Prob =**herring gull.**

1968 *DARE* (Qu. Q10, . . *Water birds and marsh birds*) Inf **OH**67, Minnow gull.

minnum See **minnow A5**

minny See **minnow A3**

minny-berry n Also sp *minnie-berry* Cf **manyberry**

A **hackberry** (here: *Celtis occidentalis*).

1883 *Bot. Gaz.* 8.296, *Some Rhode Island Notes.*—I have long been interested in local names of plants. Here are some Rhode Island names. Here, in Warwick [sic], the *Celtis occidentalis* has the name of "Mining berry [corr to *minnie-berry* (*Ibid* 319)]." **1940** Clute *Amer. Plant Names* 164, *C[eltis] occidentalis*. Hack-berry . . minny-berry.

minor exclam Also *minors* Pronc-sp *minah* **HI**

See quot 1972.

1972 Carr *Da Kine Talk* 138 **HI**, A: "Ey, no can go show—wen forget my money." B: "Ah, minah! I get plenty foah two." A popular word with young people, the word means 'of no importance', 'no worry', or 'minor matter'. **1981** *Pidgin To Da Max* np **HI**, Minors. . . No big thing. "But I no mo' money fo' da movies!" "Minors, brah. I get."

minou n esp **LA**

=**minnie** n[3].

[**1931** Read *LA French* 50, *Minou*. . . A cat; a kitten.] **1941** Writers' Program *Guide LA* 690, *Minou*—Fr. *minet*, kitten. Cat. **1968–69** *DARE* (Qu. J10, *To call a cat to make it come*) Inf **LA**20, Come on [ˌmɪˈnu]—minou is just a general word for cat; **LA**33, [ˈmɪnu]; **MA**25, Come [ˈmɪˌnu]; **VT**16, [mɪnu mɪnu]—that's French. **1983** [see **minnie** n[3]].

minow See **minnow A1**

minstress adj [Var of *menstruous*] Cf **menstruation**

Menstrual.

c1938 in **1970** Hyatt *Hoodoo* 2.1501, Fo' instance . . if ah wus a woman an' mah husban' left me an' ah want him back . . ah git me a piece of unbleached sheetin' an' use it as a *minstress* cloth.

-mint suff See **-ment**

mint adj [Reduced from **a mind**; cf Pronc Intro 3.I.15] Cf **mind B1**

1940 Harris *Folk Plays* 91 **NC**, Course sometimes we help shell the peas . . and wash the cabbages if we're mint to. *Ibid* 293, Mint, *willing*.

minter See **minnow A2**

minute pudding n *old-fash* Cf **hasty pudding 1**

See quots.

1847 (1852) Crowen *Amer. Cookery* 211, *Minute Pudding.*—Put a quart of milk in a stew-pan over a clear fire; make a batter of a large teacup of wheat flour and enough cold milk; add a teaspoonful of salt, and when the milk is boiling hot, stir the batter gradually to it; continue to stir it until it thickens, and the flour is cooked. Dip a mould or basin into cold water; pour the pudding in and let it cool sufficiently to keep its form, then turn it out and serve with sugar and butter, or wine-sauce. **1887** Parloa *Miss Parloa's Kitchen Companion* 606, *Minute Pudding*. The materials are: one pint of boiling water, a pint and a half of milk, half a pint of sifted flour, one teaspoonful of salt, and two eggs. **1905** *New Engl. Cook Book* 155, *Minute Pudding.*—Take six eggs, two tablespoonfuls of sugar, one cupful of flour, a lump of butter large as an egg, and half a nutmeg; you may add, if desired, a half pound of raisins; mix well and bake quick. **1932** *DN* 6.283 **swCT**, *Minute pudding*. A handful of wheat flour stirred into boiling milk. It is "lumps and milk."

mippety-nip See **nippity-nip**

miracle n Pronc-spp *mar(r)acle, mericale, mer(r)acle, muracle, murricle, mycle*

A Forms.

1795 Dearborn *Columbian Grammar* 137, *List of Improprieties. . . Marracle* for Miracle. **1837** Sherwood *Gaz. GA* 70, *Maracle* and *muracle*, for miracle. **1853** Simms *Sword & Distaff* 402 **SC**, Tom's a merracle of a cook, and at stew, roast, brile or bake, he ain't got his match. **1890** *DN* 1.71 **LA**, *Maracle* ['mærək], *meracle* ['mɛrək]: miracle. **1893** Shands *MS Speech* 45, *Meracle* ['mɛrk̩]. Negro and illiterate white for *miracle*. This pronunciation is also heard in Louisiana among settlers of English descent. *Maracle* ['meərk̩] is also sometimes used by the lower classes of Mississippi. **1896** Harris *Sister Jane* 277 **GA**, You'd better thank the Lord that the day of meracles ain't gone by. **1912** Green *VA Folk-Speech* 279, *Meracle. . .* For *miracle*. **1916** Howells *Leatherwood God* 124 **OH**, Murricle or no murricle. **1933** *AmSp* 8.2.44 **neNY**, *Miracle . .* ['mɜrək̩]. **1936** *AmSp* 11.155 **eTX**, *Miracle* is also ['mɪrk̩], ['mɜ·k̩]. **1942** Hall *Smoky Mt. Speech* 16 **wNC, eTN**, *Miracle,* ['mɜrɪkə̩] in the older speech, is now usually ['mɜrɪkə̩]. **1947** Lomax *Advent. Ballad Hunter* 216 **swMS** (as of 1940) [Black], The preacher used the not unusual pronunciations "mycles" for "miracles," [etc.]. **1952** Brown *NC Folkl.* 1.564, *Mericale* ['mɛrk̩]. . . Miracle.

B Sense.

In phr *once in a miracle:* See quot.

1980 in 1982 *Barrick Coll.* **csPA**, *Miracle*—[mɪrɪkə̩]. . . "Long time" as in the phrase "Once in a miracle it happens."

miracle baby n

A baby conceived or born out of wedlock, or one whose conception was unexpected.

1966 *DARE* (Qu. Z11b, . . *A child whose parents were not married]*) Inf **FL39**, Illegitimate, miracle babies. **1986** Pederson *LAGS Concordance,* 1 inf, **seLA**, Miracle baby—child born 20 years after another. **1993** *DARE* File **csWI** (as of c1970), As a child, I often heard the term "miracle baby" used sarcastically to refer to a baby born less than nine months after a couple's wedding. (The phrase was particularly appropriate if the new parents were attempting to pass off a nine-pound baby as "premature.")

mirate v [Back-formation from **miration**] **chiefly Sth, S Midl**
To wonder, marvel; to admire (something); to express admiration or wonder, carry on (about or over someone or something).

1893 Shands *MS Speech* 46, *Mirate* [maɪret]. This word is used by negroes to mean *to wonder.* **1903** *DN* 2.321 **seMO**, *Mirate. . .* To wonder at; to admire. **1909** *DN* 3.349 **eAL, wGA**, *Mirate. . .* To make signs of admiration, express wonder. **1934** *AmSp* 9.79 **LA**, *Mirate,* to marvel or express admiration in exaggerated terms. **1939** Griswold *Sea Is. Lady* 509 **csSC** (as of c1893) [Gullah], I yeddy [=heard] you miratin' 'pon 'um, how sweet he stan' an' all. **1941** Daniels *Tar Heels* 78 **NC**, I suspect that Mr. Wiggins died mirating over the powers of evaporation in his climate. **1943** Writers' Program *NC Bundle of Troubles* 3, Seem like, in the dream, ever'body had all a-sudden started miratin' and fussin' 'bout their troubles. **1950** *PADS* 14.46 **SC**, *Mirate. . .* To make a miration over; to express surprise, admiration over a person or thing. **1954** Welty *Ponder Heart* 43 **MS**, Everybody . . had to listen to Uncle Daniel mirate and gyrate over Bonnie Dee. **c1960** *Wilson Coll.* **csKY**, *Mirate. . .* To wonder at, to take on over. **1978** *DARE* File **MS**, I had to go down and mirate his camera. **1983** *Ibid* **nwMS**, Mirate [maɪret]. This word suggests expressing admiration or approval of something or someone. Example: "Mrs. Jones really mirated about the new dress her daughter had bought." . . Mrs. Jones had "carried on" about the dress.

miration n [Aphet form of **admiration**] **chiefly Sth, S Midl** *esp freq among Black speakers*

A display of wonderment, surprise, or admiration; a fuss, clamor—usu in phr *make miration.*

1884 *Anglia* 7.270 **Sth, S Midl** [Black], *To make er great 'miration 'bout* = to wonder at. **1888** Jones *Negro Myths* 102 **seGA** [Gullah], De Cunjur Man mek er great miration ober wuh Buh Rabbit bin done. **1899** (1912) Green *VA Folk-Speech* 283, He made a great miration at it. **1899** Chesnutt *Conjure Woman* 45 **csNC** [Black], He made a great 'miration w'en he hear w'at Tenice say. **1909** *DN* 3.349 **eAL, wGA**, *Miration. . .* An expression of admiration. "He made a great miration over the baby." **1930** Stoney–Shelby *Black Genesis* 7 **seSC**, He jump 'bout an' mek a big 'miration. **1935** Hurston *Mules & Men* 125 **FL** [Black], Aw, man, you done seen Tookie and her walk too much to be makin' all dat miration over it. **1939** *FWP Guide TN* 193, He noticed a crowd in a

roadside field, gathered around a red-faced auctioneer in a beaver hat who was standing on a stump "making a mighty gobbling miration." **1943** *AmSp* 18.237 **neLA** [Black], Folks came to de ole plantation every Sunday and made miration. **1946** *PADS* 6.20 **NC, VA** (as of 1900–10), *Miration. . .* Exaggerated and pretentious wonderment, a carrying-on. "They made a great miration about my killing that squirrel." . . Occasional. **1947** Ballowe *The Lawd* 171 **LA** [Black], They made such a miration over Go-Easy that work on the place almost stopped. **1948** Faulkner *Intruder* 130 **MS**, A whole countryside . . waked and alerted by the sleepless sibilant what Paralee [=a Black man] . . would call 'miration' of the pines. **c1960** *Wilson Coll.* **csKY**, *Miration.* **1982** Walker *Color Purple* 18 **GA** [Black], Your skin. Your hair. Your teefs. Everyday it something else to make miration over.

mire drum n [*OED* 1398 →]

A **bittern** (here: *Botaurus lentiginosus*).

1917 (1923) *Birds Amer.* 1.181, Bittern—*Botaurus lentiginosus. . .* Mire Drum.

mire up v phr Pronc-sp *ma'rr up*

To become mired.

1967 Parris *Mountain Bred* 310 **wNC**, You'd mire up above the hubs and the oxen would have to pull you out. **1972** *Atlanta Letters* **nwGA**, Having lived in Georgia all our lives, my husband and I speak fluent "Southern-isms." Here are a few examples: . . He *mired up* in the mud. (Some say *bogged down*). **1982** Slone *How We Talked* 35 **eKY** (as of c1950), *To ma'rr up*—to sink; "You might ma'rr up in a mud hole."

miring time n

1899 (1912) Green *VA Folk-Speech* 283, Caretakers were used to look after stock in the "miring-time," that is, in the spring when the cattle were thin and weak and apt to get stuck in the soft marshes.

mirliton n Also *merliton* Pronc-spp *milleton, molytone* [LaFr *mirliton, merliton* < Fr *mirliton* kazoo, shako] **LA**
=chayote.

1911 *Century Dict. Suppl.* **LA**, *Mirliton. . .* The chayote, *Chayota edulis.* **1923** *DN* 5.244 **LA**, *Milleton. . .* Vegetable pears. **1941** Writers' Program *Guide LA* 226, Among those [vegetables] usually unfamiliar to visitors are: the *mirliton* (vegetable pear), which is prepared in the same way as squash or egg plant, and frequently stuffed with crabmeat or shrimp. **1958** Grau *Hard Blue Sky* 441 **LA**, There had been fine mirlitons—big and a good light green, their meat soft and tender as a flounder. **1967** LeCompte *Word Atlas* 316 **seLA**, *Green or white pear-shaped vegetables which grow on vines. . .* merliton [16 of 21 infs]. **1968** *DARE* FW Addit **LA**40, ['mɛlə,toun]—a small fruit that tastes like a squash. . . It's raised mostly in New Orleans. The best way to fix them is with shrimp; you stuff them. **1969** *DARE* File **New Orleans LA**, *Merliton. . .* Name seen on the vegetable offered for sale in market, French Quarter. **1979** *NY Times* (NY) 13 Oct 19/1 **sLA**, "They's not a man can beat my molytones," says Alcide Verret over his stove. "I cooks them *nine* different ways." **1981** Pederson *LAGS Basic Materials,* 1 inf, **seLA**, ['mɛlə,ta<ɚ]—pear-shaped; grows on a vine; cooked like squash; 1 inf, **seLA**, ['mɪr˘,lɪt͡ʃ˘ɔz]—like eggplant, grows on vine; 1 inf, **seLA**, [,mɛʌḷi'tn̩]; 1 inf, **csLA**, [ma<'ɛnəto<ʊnz]—like a pear, but a vegetable. **1983** *Reinecke Coll.* 7 **LA**, *Mirliton* ['mɛlɪtən, 'mɪlɪt͡ɔ]. . . Much esteemed in N[ew] O[rleans] cooking.

mirror n Usu |'mɪrə(r)|; also |'mɪr(o), mɪri, mɪr| Pronc-sp *mirry* Std sense, var forms.

1906 *DN* 3.147 **nwAR**, *Mirror. . .* Often pronounced ['mɪro]. **1940** in 1944 *ADD* **AR**, Mirry ['mɪri]. Radio. **1982** *Barrick Coll.* **csPA**, *Mirror*—pron. [mɪr]. **1992** *DARE* File, I have heard *mirror* pronounced [miə·] both in Wisconsin and Chicago. *Ibid* **cwCA** (as of c1950s), I remember hearing people say [mi:ə·] for ['mɪrər].

mirror carp n

A variety of the common carp *(Cyprinus carpio)* with few, large scales.

1879 U.S. Bur. Fisheries *Rept. for 1877* 43, On the 26th of May [1877] Mr. Hessel placed there [=in the ponds] 227 naked and mirror carp and 118 common carp. **1883** GA Dept. Ag. *Pub. Circular No. 34* 8.12, Three varieties of carp are cultivated . . 1 . . the scale carp. . . 2. *Cyprinus carpio specularis,* the mirror carp, thus named on account of the extraordinarily shiny scales, which run along the sides of the body in three or four rows, the rest of the body being bare. 3 . . the leather carp. **1905** NJ State Museum *Annual Rept. for 1904* 430, *Cyprinus carpio. . .* Originally introduced . . as a food fish. . . In domestication it has produced many varieties, principal among these are those with very large scales (mirror carp). **1949** Caine *N. Amer. Sport Fish* 155, The mirror carp . . has a few large scales often the size of a fifty-cent piece. **1957** Trautman *Fishes* 284, On December 8, 1880, the Fish Hatchery Superintendent for the State of Ohio . . received from the Federal Government 750 Mirror Carps, 4.0″-6.0″ long. Distribution of Carps by the state first began in the spring of 1881. **1974** WI Univ. *Fish Lake MI* 29, *Cyprinus carpio.* . . Common names . . German carp, . . mirror carp. . . A large number inhabit shallow stretches all along Lake Michigan's shores, particularly in the southeastern end. **1983** Becker *Fishes WI* 419, Mirror and leather carp are quite rare today, constituting less than 2% of all wild carp.

mirror glass n [Redund; cf Intro "Language Changes" I.4; perh also infl by *looking glass*]
A mirror.

    c1938 in 1970 Hyatt *Hoodoo* 2.1470 **LA**, I'll get me a glass of water and I'll get me a *mirror-glass.* . . And I'll stand right over that glass [Hyatt: mirror] and I'll just talk to that glass.

mirrorweed n
A **Venus's looking-glass** (here: *Triodanis perfoliata*).

    1974 Peden *Speak to Earth* 62 **IN**, In the strawberry patch one year I discovered Venus's looking glass, also called mirrorweed.

mirry See **mirror**

mis n
1 See **mistress.**
2 See **Mrs.**

‡**misagreement** n [Cf *OED misagree* "To disagree. Now *dial.*"]
A disagreement.

    1967 *DARE* (Qu. KK15, *A disagreement or quarrel: "They had _____ about where the fence was to be."*) Inf **KY**33, Misagreement.

‡**misameanness** n [Perh vȧr of *misdemeanor,* infl by *mean*]
Misdeeds, sins.

    1969 Emmons *Deep Rivers* 61 **eTX** [Black], You men all come to meetin' with your slates full of your misameanness. You begin scrapin' 'em off, but before you get all your misameanness scraped off'n your slate, the meetin's over.

misbehave v
See quots.

    1952 Brown *NC Folkl.* 1.565, Misbehave. . . Of children: to urinate or defecate in an improper place or at an improper time. **c1960** *Wilson Coll.* **csKY**, Misbehave. . . Usually said of some small child that defecates or urinates on himself or at somebody's house where he is visiting.

misbobble n Also *miscuebobble, miscobobble, miskubobble* [*mis-* bad + **bobble** n[1] 1] Cf **ker-**
A mistake or error.

    1911 *DN* 3.545 **NE**, Miskubobble. . . Mistake, error. "The printers made a miskubobble in your name." **1912** *DN* 3.566, *Balk.* . . Small strip left unsown or unplowed unintentionally. . . From Missouri *bobble* and *misbobble,* both used in similar senses. **1931** *AmSp* 6.231 **cnNE**, Misbobble. . . A mistake. "I made a misbobble in my crocheting, and I'll have to make it all over again." **1942** Berrey–Van den Bark *Amer. Slang* 170.2, *Error; mistake; blunder.* . . Misbobble, miscue, miscuebobble. **1968** *DARE* (Qu. JJ41, *An embarrassing mistake: "Last night she made an awful _____."*) Inf **IA**27, Miscobobble.

miscall v
1 See quot. [*OED* c1449 →; "Now *dial.*"] Cf **call** v 9
    1899 (1912) Green *VA Folk-Speech* 283, Miscall. . . To give an unworthy name of character to; berate; revile.
2 To mispronounce (a word). [*OED* "*dial.*"]
    1940 *Qrly. Jrl. Speech* 26.265 **VA**, One who *mispronounces* a word "miscalls" it.
3 refl: To speak incorrectly, misspeak.
    1938 Rawlings *Yearling* 354 **nFL**, The sound of hoof beats was unmistakable. . . "Now wouldn't it be fine not to have to go clare to Fort Gates for he'p?" . . The riders were the Forresters. Penny said, "Looks like I mis-called myself."

mischeevous, mischevious See **mischievous**

mischief n Usu |ˈmɪsčəf, ˈmɪš-|; also |ˈmɪsčif, mɪsˈčif, mɪsˈčɪf|
A Forms.

    1891 *PMLA* 6.165 **WV**, *Mischief* is accented on the ultima and pronounced [mɪsˈčɪf]. **1902** *DN* 2.239 **sIL**, Mischief. Pronounced [mɪsˈčɪf] with accent on last syllable. **1907** *DN* 3.224 **nwAR**, Mischief. . . Some-

times pronounced [mɪsˈčif] with the stress on the last syllable. **1967** *DARE* FW Addit **ceTN**, *Mischief* pronounced [ˈmɪsˌčif].
B Sense.
Usu with *the;* often fig: Hell, the devil—freq used euphemistically in exclams.

    1807 Irving *Salmagundi* 147, This unlucky characteristic played the mischief with him in one of his love affairs. **1895** *Century Illustr. Mag.* 50.279, And there's kindnesses and kindnesses, Mr. Ludovic. There's some that cost like the mischief. **1913** Johnson *Highways St. Lawrence to VA* 41, He was bruised up like the mischief. **1924** *DN* 5.273 [Exclams], *Mischief:* the, the mischief you say, what in the mischief. **1941** *LANE* Map 474 (*He ran like a house afire*) 2 infs, **wCT**, Like the mischief. **1966–68** *DARE* (Qu. NN26b, *Weakened substitutes for 'hell': "Go to _____!"*) Inf **MS**16, Mischief, the mischief; (Qu. NN26c, *Weakened substitutes for 'hell': "What the _____!"*) Inf **MO**9, Mischief. **1986** Pederson *LAGS Concordance,* 1 inf, **seGA**, Give them the mischief; 1 inf, **csMS**, Hardheaded as mischief; 1 inf, **seGA**, You've got to work like the mischief; 1 inf, **seGA**, They'll sting the mischief out of you.

mischief night n [In England, *mischief night* was on April 30 in the 19th cent, but is now on Nov 4, the night before Guy Fawkes Day] esp **NJ**, **sePA** Cf **cabbage night, clothesline ~, devil's ~, gate ~, light ~, moving ~**
The night before Halloween; see quots.

    1977–78 Foster *Lexical Variation* 75, Mischief Night—The night before Halloween is a time for minor vandalism in New Jersey and Philadelphia, although not in New York City. On Mischief Night doorbells are rung, gates removed from their hinges, car windows soaped, and houses and walks marked with chalk, egg, or flour. *Ibid* 77, The custom of Mischief Night is so well established that the police advertise the "Mischief Night curfew" in local newspapers. **1988** *WI State Jrl.* (Madison) 23 Oct sec G 14/1, By the last week in October, I'm going to have the largest collection of jack-o'-lanterns in the Northeast. I'm the only woman I know who actually hopes kids will stop by on mischief night and steal her pumpkins. **1993** *DARE* File **sePA** (as of 1930s), The night before Halloween was, as in many places, "mischief night," a night for knocking on doors, then running; soaping automobiles; moving porch furniture; draping toilet paper around yards—all the usual. *Ibid* **sNJ**, If one traveled to South Jersey, the night before Halloween was "mischief night."

mischievous adj Usu |ˈmɪsčivəs|; also |ˌmɪsˈčiv(i)əs|; for addit varr see quot 1965–70 Pronc-spp *mischeevous, mischevious, misch(i)ievious, muscheevous* [*OED* "The stressing on the second syllable was common in literature till about 1700; it is now dialectal and vulgar."] Cf **blasphemious,** Intro "Language Changes" I.8
Std senses, var forms.

    1747 in 1851 *PA Prov. Council Minutes* 5.111, The many mischevious consequences that arose. **1851** Hooper *Widow Rugby's Husband* 72 **AL**, He could shoot enny body's mischeevous steer for jumpin' over it [=a fence]. **1883** (1971) Harris *Nights with Remus* 359 **GA** [Black], Whar you 'speck dat ar muscheevous Brer Rabbit tuck'n kyar' Brer Fox. **1899** (1912) Green *VA Folk-Speech* 283, Mischievous. . . With accent on the *e* in the second syllable. **1902** *DN* 2.239 **sIL**, Mischiievious. Pronounced [mɪsˈčivjəs]. **1909** *DN* 3.349 **eAL, wGA**, Mischee'vous. . . A common pronunciation. Also *mischee'vious.* **1911** *DN* 3.549 **NE**, Some words showing divergence from the standard accentuation are: *massacree'* . . *mischie'v(i)ous.* **1914** *DN* 4.110 **cKS**, Mischievous. . . Mischievous. **1915** *DN* 4.227 **wTX**, *Misch-ievous.* Always pronounced thus or as *misch-ievious.* **1947** Ballowe *The Lawd* 3 **LA**, Hants is cu'ious. They gits mischeevous efn they ain' checked. **1949** in 1986 *DARE* File **seMI**, Mischievious [-vɪjəs]. **1965–70** *DARE* (Qu. Z16) 10 Infs, **scattered,** [mɪsˈčivijəs]; **KY**28, Mischievious; **CT**36, **MD**19, **MS**63, **NC**49, [mɪsˈčivəs]; **SC**10, [mɪsčibəs]; **PA**241, [ˈmɪčiˌvəs]; (Qu. K16) Inf **NJ**67, [ˌmɪsˈčivəs]; (Qu. GG32a) Infs **AZ**10, **MD**15, **MO**2, [mɪsˈčivijəs]; **AL**5, [mɪˈčɪfəs]; **MA**35, [mɪsˈčivəs]; (Qu. GG32b) Infs **FL**14, **NJ**67, [mɪsˈčivəs]; (Qu. HH26) Inf **OK**31, Mischievious. **1969** Emmons *Deep Rivers* 9 **eTX** [Black], Not even the mechanized age with all its devices put a quietus on these "mischeevious", gadabout ghosts.

miscobobble See **misbobble**

‡**miscomput** n Cf **discombobulate, kaput** adj **B**
    c1960 *Wilson Coll.* **csKY**, Miscomput. . . Out of fix or out of order.

misconfuddled See **misfuddled**

miscuebobble See **misbobble**

misdoubt v [*OED* "Now chiefly *dial.* or *arch.*"] **esp Sth, S Midl**

To doubt (that something desirable is true); to fear, suspect, feel sure (that something undesirable is true); to distrust, be suspicious of.

1875 (1886) Woolson *Castle Nowhere* 126 **nMI,** "I misdoubt they'll hang him," said Mrs. Malone. . . "Or worse," said the miner's wife. *Ibid* 256 **ceOH,** The Community ain't got nothing covered to send after you, except the old king's coach, and I misdoubt they won't let that out in such a storm. **1885** *Harper's New Mth. Mag.* 70.830 **NM,** I misdoubt the ladies won't like it. **1903** *DN* 2.321 **seMO,** Misdoubt. . . Suspect. 'I misdoubt his intentions are bad.' **1903** Wasson *Cap'n Simeon's Store* 30 **eME,** That fetched her to her mutton some quick, I don't misdoubt. **1907** *DN* 3.233 **nwAR,** Misdoubt. . . To suspect. **1909** *DN* 3.349 **eAL, wGA,** Misdoubt. . . To suspect, doubt. Rare. **1931** Randolph *Ozarks* 74, The use of the word *misdoubt*, meaning to suspect or distrust, is a typical Ozark barbarism. **1932** Wasson *Sailing Days* 46 **cME coast,** What with doin' for the ailin' folks, and keepin' up the vessel . . , I misdoubted if he didn't go astern [=lose money] the heft o' the time. **1938** Rawlings *Yearling* 287 **nFL,** I mis-doubt could they git their teeth through their old hides. **1942** (1971) Campbell *Cloud-Walking* 10 **seKY,** I don't misdoubt them women will turn out right common and good after they get habited to the pioneering ways of mountain folks. **c1960** *Wilson Coll.* **csKY,** Misdoubt. . . Suspect. **1964** Faulkner *Hamlet* 324, "I misdoubted that damn shell corn all along," the Texan said. **1967** Williams *Greenbones* 4 **GA** (as of c1910), "I'm going." "I m-m-misdoubt Ma'll let you." **1968** *DARE* FW Addit **VA,** While I misdoubt that ye'll misbelieve me . . hit's the gospel truth. **1975** Gould *ME Lingo* 181, To *misdoubt* means to doubt very much. . . "I misdoubt he'll be too happy in that new job."

misdoubtful adj [**misdoubt**]

Dubious, uncertain.

1927 in 1928 Green *In the Valley* 161 **eNC,** Reckon his knees are bended, but I'm mis-doubtful 'bout the prayers. **1964** Faulkner *As I Lay Dying* 65 **MS,** It had been a misdoubtful night, with the storm making.

miser See **micer**

miserable me See **misery me**

misery n Pronc-spp *mizry, mizzery* [Engl dial] **widespread, but more freq Sth, S Midl** *esp freq among Black speakers*

An ache or pain; also, usu with *the*, often pl: a vague internal pain; a general feeling of illness.

1827 (1939) Sherwood *Gaz.* GA 139, *Misery*, for pain, as misery in my head. **1832** Hall *Legends West* 82 **sIN, nKY,** You never *seed sich* a poor afflicted *crittur* as I be, with the misery in my tooth. **1884** Baldwin *Yankee School-Teacher* 102 **VA** [Black], Well, I hed de miz'ry so I couldn't hol' up my hade! **1893** Shands *MS Speech* 46, *Misery* [mɪzrɪ]. Negro for a pain or ache of any kind in any part of the body. Negroes say: "I've got a misery in my head, foot, tooth," etc. When, however, the word *misery* is used not followed by the name of any portion of the body, it refers to *stomach-ache*. When suffering from this ailment, negroes commonly say: "I've got a misery." **1895** *DN* 1.373 **sAppalachians,** Misery: pain. **1902** *DN* 2.239 **sIL,** Misery. . . Pain, as 'I've had a mizzery in my breast all day.' **1903** *DN* 2.321 **seMO,** Misery. . . Pain. Almost universally applied to bodily suffering. **1905** *DN* 3.88 **nwAR,** Misery. . . Pain. . . Rare. **1906** *DN* 3.121 **sIN,** Misery. . . Common word for any pain. **1923** *DN* 5.214 **swMO,** Misery. . . A pain. **1927** Kennedy *Gritny* 121 **sLA** [Black], Sew up a salt-sack full o' hot bran, to lay on Peesah stummick to ease de mizry. **1930** *DN* 6.84 **cSC,** Misery, pain. **1937** Sandoz *Slogum* 342 **NE,** The misery in his middle . . seemed to be pulling him into a knot. **1940** Hall *Coll.* **eTN,** "I'm so full of misery this morning I can't hardly walk." . . "All of them old people around home uses that." **1944** *PADS* 2.10 **Sth,** Misery. . . Pain from rheumatism, arthritis, sciatica, etc. Over much of the South. Negro and older uneducated whites. **1954** *Harder Coll.* **cwTN,** Misery. . . Pain. Some say 'I have misery'—all old people said this. **c1960** *Wilson Coll.* **csKY,** Misery. . . A pain or ache, somewhat indefinite in intensity or location. **1965–70** *DARE* (Qu. BB4, . . *A pain* . . *"He's had a _____ in his arm for a week."*) 74 Infs, **scattered, but less freq West,** Misery [Of all Infs responding to the question, 65% were old, 6% Black; of those giving this response, 80% were old, 18% Black.]; (Qu. BB5, *A general feeling of discomfort or illness that isn't any one place in particular*) 57 Infs, **scattered,** The misery; **ME22,** I get the misery; 16

Infs, **scattered,** (Got) the miseries; 12 Infs, **scattered,** (A) misery; **KS5,** We never used the word "misery" but some do; **GA59,** Misery in my bones; **MT4,** General misery [Of all Infs responding to the question, 6% were Black; of those giving these responses, 13% were Black.]; (Qu. BB8, *When a person's joints and muscles ache and sometimes swell up, especially in damp weather, he may have _____*) Infs **AK1, ME10, NY92, PA199,** The miseries; **OH15, 78,** (A) misery; **AZ2,** The misery—darkies say this here; **GA59,** A misery—Negroes; **MS33,** The misery—Negroes; **LA2,** Misery in the joints; (Qu. AA27, . . *A woman's menstruation*) Inf **KY10,** The miseries; **NJ41,** My miseries; (Qu. BB3a, . . *A pain that strikes you suddenly in the neck*) Inf **AL33,** Misery; (Qu. BB3b, *A sudden pain that strikes you in the back*) Infs **LA14, NY100,** Misery; (Qu. BB3c, *A sudden pain that comes in the side*) Inf **VA30,** Misery; (Qu. BB13, . . *Chills and fever*) Infs **AL43, NY84,** Misery; **NY226,** Miseries; (Qu. BB28, *Joking names . . for imaginary diseases: "He must have the _____."*) Inf **AL48,** Miseries; (Qu. BB49, . . *Other kinds of diseases*) Inf **NC13,** Misery; (Qu. GG34a, *To feel depressed or in a gloomy mood: "He has the _____ today."*) Inf **NY1,** Misery. **1987** Jones-Wheeler *Laughter* 147 **Appalachians,** My woman she's been down with the misery all year, but I got a fair patent medicine for her. **1990** Cavender *Folk Med. Lexicon* 27 **sAppalachians,** (The) miseries—a. menstrual period. b. a tired, aching feeling. *Ibid*, (A) misery—a pain.

misery exclam See **misery me**

misery harp See **misery whip**

misery me exclam Also *miserable me, misery*

Used as an exclam; see quots.

1904 *DN* 2.427 **Cape Cod MA** (as of a1857), *Misery me!* . . Similar to 'Oh dear me!' **1924** *DN* 5.273 [Exclams], Oh misery. **1936** *WV Review* Aug 346, The short expletives that can be shot out for any reason, or for no particular reason, are numerous. . . In this category [is] . . Miserable me.

misery whip n Also *misery harp* [See quot 1984]

Among loggers: a crosscut saw, whipsaw.

1930 Williams *Logger-Talk* 26 **Pacific NW,** Misery-whip: A cross cut saw. **1958** McCulloch *Woods Words* 118 **Pacific NW,** Misery harp—A crosscut saw; those who don't think so have never pulled one. **1977** Jones *OR Folkl.* 14, In the case of loggers, not only do they know what a crosscut saw is (the technical term for a type of hand saw once widely used in the woods), they also know that same item as a *misery whip* or a *Swede's fiddle*. **1982** *Smithsonian Letters*, I was raised in the lower Columbia river logging country . . (Early 1900). . . The fallers used very long saws which were necessary to cut down 8 or 10 feet diameter trees. These saws were known as "misery whips." **1984** Wilder *You All Spoken Here* 153 **Sth,** Misery whip: A crosscut saw. When a crosscut saw buckles while in use, it is said to fold, and when it folds, it whips violently as it regains its shape. **1994** *Jrl.-Patriot* (N. Wilkesboro NC) 25 Aug sec D 5/3 [Logging terms], The seven-foot crosscut saws they used sometimes were called a "misery whip" or a "briar."

misfool v Cf *DS* V1, 2

1953 Randolph-Wilson *Down in Holler* 265 **Ozarks,** Misfool. . . To delude, to deceive. "Them folks didn't mean no harm; they was misfooled by listenin' at a crazy preacher."

misfortune n [*OED* "*dial.* and *colloq.*"] Cf *DS* Z11b

1899 (1912) Green *VA Folk-Speech* 284, *Misfortune.* . . An illegitimate child.

misfuddled adj Also *misconfuddled* Cf **discumfuddled**

Confused, befuddled.

1968–69 *DARE* (Qu. GG2, . . *'Confused, mixed up': "So many things were going on at the same time that he got completely _____."*) Inf **NJ46,** Misconfuddled; **NY219,** Misfuddled.

misht n Also *mitch* [PaGer *mischt* < Ger *Mist* dung, excrement] **sePA**

Manure.

1939 Aurand *Quaint Idioms* 25 [PaGer], You're full of *misht* (manure). **1967–68** *DARE* (Qu. L17, . . *Names . . for manure used in the fields: [Also joking names]*) Inf **PA21,** Mitch [mɪč]; **PA158,** Misht [mɪšt].

miskubobble See **misbobble**

mislick n Also sp *miss-lick* [**lick** n 1] **chiefly Sth, S Midl**

A poorly delivered or badly aimed stroke or blow; by ext, a mistake or error.

1859 (1968) Bartlett *Americanisms* 273, *Miss-lick.* When an axe or knife cuts out of line, it is called in the West a *miss-lick.* **1899** (1912) Green *VA Folk-Speech* 284, *Mislick.* . . When an axe cuts out of line; a false blow. **1903** *DN* 2.321 **seMO,** He made a mislick and cut his foot. **1906** *DN* 3.121 **sIN,** *Mislick.* **1907** *DN* 3.233 **nwAR,** *Mislick.* **1909** *DN* 3.349 **eAL, wGA,** *Mislick.* **1915** *DN* 4.185 **swVA,** *Mislick.* **1917** *DN* 4.415 **wNC,** *Miss-lick.* . . A false blow. Also Ill., N.Y., Kan. **1943** Chase *Jack Tales* 23 **wNC,** When you go to strike me, you make a mis-lick and hit the old woman. **1952** Brown *NC Folkl.* 1.565, I made a mislick and hit my thumb. **1954** *Harder Coll.* **cwTN,** *Mislick.* . . An error. **c1960** *Wilson Coll.* **csKY,** *Mislick* (or *misslick*). . . A false stroke, one that failed to land where it should have. **1975** Newell *If Nothin' Don't Happen* 42 **FL,** Turkeys. . . answer a yelper pretty good. But any time you get an answer, you better not make a mis-lick with your cedar box . . or whatever you're usin', because that old turkey is a-standin' out there really listenin' and so your second call better be right.

mislist v [Perh var of *mislest* to molest] *arch*
To mistreat; to mistrust, suspect.

    1845 Thompson *Pineville* 55 **cGA,** Who is I done any harm to?—what is I done to be mislisted in sich a way? **1950** *PADS* 14.46 **SC,** *Mislist.* . . To mistrust, suspect. Obsolete.

mismean v [*OED mismean* "*Obs*. . . To mean or intend wrongly. . . To misinterpret"] Cf **miscall, misput**
To misspeak, make a mistake.

    1899 (1912) Green *VA Folk-Speech* 284, *Mismeant.* . . Past tense [sic]. To mistake. "It was mismeant on my part."

misorderly adj
Disorderly.

    1938 Stuart *Dark Hills* 257 **KY,** The good wives often take care of the tobacco when the men are put in the Greenup crib for "misorderly conduct."

misput v Also sp *missput*
1 To mislay, misplace; to mislead.

    1923 *DN* 5.215 **swMO,** *Misput.* . . To misplace. "I misput that letter." **1927** *DN* 5.475 **Ozarks,** *Misput.* . . To misplace, to lose, to mislay. **1934** Hurston *Jonah's Gourd Vine* 204 **AL** [Black], Ah done told yuh time and time uhgin dat ignorance is de hawse dat wisdom rides. Don't git miss-put on yo' road. **1993** *DARE* File **AR,** *Misput* meaning "mislay, misplace"—"I misput that letter"—seems familiar from when I lived in Arkansas. *Ibid* **MI,** *Misput*—I heard this as a boy in Michigan, usually by the older folks I was aware of at the time. I often wondered why, but never heard an explanation of why this term was used instead of "misplace."

2 To **discomfit**; also refl: to put oneself out. **esp KY**

    1942 (1971) Campbell *Cloud-Walking* 15 **seKY,** Mostly grannying didn't misput Sary no great sight, but this was one time it set her to mouthing around about being drug out in the night time. *Ibid* 181, Ever last funeral meeting . . or other gathering had its crowd of candidates misputting theirselves to be sociable. **1946** *AmSp* 21.271 **neKY,** *Misput.* . . To inconvenience; to put out. **1951** Giles *Harbin's Ridge* 93 **eKY,** Papa didn't look for Ben to be much account. He misput himself with Ben just to help Faleecy John.

misput adj
1 Annoyed, put out. **esp Sth, S Midl**

    1898 Johnston *Pearce Amerson's Will* 133 **cGA,** Your conduct took me so much by surprise that I got a little mis-put just now. I'm all right again. **1966–67** *DARE* (Qu. GG6, *Talking about a person's feelings being hurt:* "When she said she wouldn't go with him, he was quite _____.") Inf **AR**31, Misput; (Qu. GG7, . . *Annoyed or upset:* "Though we were only ten minutes late, she was all _____.") Inf **TX**40, Misput; (Qu. GG35b, [*To sulk or pout:*] "Because she couldn't go, she's been _____ all day.") Inf **LA**2, Misput. **1984** Wilder *You All Spoken Here* 204 **Sth,** *Misput:* Out of sorts; aggravated; pouty; put out. **1993** *DARE* File **AR,** *Misput* meaning "annoyed, put out"—"He felt quite misput about what I said" seems familiar from when I lived in Arkansas. [*Ibid,* My grandmother, Scotch/Irish/Dutch, who was born in Canada but moved to Connecticut, then Michigan as a young woman, would use this [=*misput* meaning "annoyed"] very occasionally. She rarely got annoyed, but she would say this to my mother about things my mother said to her, "I am misput that you would think that."]

‡**2** Untidy, messy.

    1966 *DARE* (Qu. E22, *If a house is untidy and everything is upset* . .

"It's a _____!" or "It looks like _____.") Inf **OK**26, Misput house, misplaced house, tore-up house.

misremember v *esp S Midl* Cf **disremember**
To forget.

    1909 *DN* 3.349 **eAL, wGA,** *Misremember.* . . To forget. The common form is *disremember.* **1953** Randolph–Wilson *Down in Holler* 265 **Ozarks,** *Misremember.* . . To forget. This is not common, but I have heard a few old-timers use it. **c1960** *Wilson Coll.* **csKY,** *Misremember.* . . Can't remember or else have forgotten.

miss n
1 See **mistress.**
2 See **Mrs.**

miss a figure See **figure B3**

Miss Ann(e) n Also *Miss Annie chiefly among Black speakers; often derog* Cf **Mister Charlie**
A White woman; by ext, a Black woman who puts on airs.

    1926 Van Vechten *Nigger Heaven* 286 [Black], *Miss Annie:* a white girl. **1942** *Amer. Mercury* 55.89 **Harlem NYC** [Black], I had to leave from down south 'cause Miss Anne used to worry me so bad to go with me. *Ibid* 95, *Miss Anne*—a white woman. **1964** *PADS* 42.45 **Chicago IL** [Black], *The Man* and *Miss Ann* refer more specifically to the boss and the fair, young white lady of the plantation. . . Both . . are used ironically. **1970** Major *Dict. Afro-Amer. Slang* 81, *Miss Ann:* a white woman—carry-over from Southern terminology, but now used with a good-natured sneer or with outright maliciousness. **1971** [see **Mister Charlie**]. **1977** Smitherman *Talkin* 68, While *Miss Ann,* also just plain *Ann,* is a derisive reference to the white woman, by extension it is applied to any black woman who puts on airs and tries to act like Miss Ann.

Miss Astor n Also *Mrs. Astor(bilt)* Cf **Astorbilt, Mrs. Astor's (pet) horse**
A woman who dresses ostentatiously or behaves pretentiously; a member of the "best society" of a community.

    1966–70 *DARE* (Qu. W40, . . *A woman who overdresses or* . . *spends too much on clothes*) Inf **IL**17, Looks like Mrs. Astor; **LA**32, Miss Astor; **NY**123, Mrs. Astor; (Qu. HH35, *A woman who puts on a lot of airs:* "She's too _____ for me.") Inf **MO**3, Miss Astor; **LA**2, Thinks she's Mrs. Astor; (Qu. II23, *Joking names for the people who are, or think they are, the best society of a community: The* _____) Infs **TX**19, 61, Miss Astors; **TX**104, She thinks she's Miss Astor; **IA**3, **MS**69, **TX**1, Mrs. Astor; (Qu. NN10a, *Expressions* [*such as* 'hello'] *used when you meet somebody you know quite well*) Inf **SC**39, Hello, Miz Astorbilt.

missauga See **massasauga**

missed-meal colic See **miss-meal colic**

missey-moosey n Also *missy-massy* [Varr of **moosemise**]
A **mountain ash 1** (here: *Sorbus americana*).

    1892 *Jrl. Amer. Folkl.* 5.95 **NH,** *Pyrus Americana.* . . Missey moosey. **1930** Sievers *Amer. Med. Plants* 7, Missey-moosey. . . *Part used.*—The bark with the outer layer removed. **1951** Teale *North with Spring* 218 **NC,** Or he may return with juglans, . . missey-moosey, . . or robin-runaway. **1971** Krochmal *Appalachia Med. Plants* 238, *Sorbus americana.* . . *Common names* . . missy-massy, missey-moosey. **1976** Bailey–Bailey *Hortus Third* 1059, *Missey-moosey.* . . E[astern] N. Amer.

missie See **missy 2**

missionary barrel n
A barrel or box of clothing sent by a church denomination to one of its ministers or missionaries stationed in a remote or poor community in the US.

    1912 (1935) Porter *Pollyanna* 20, I'm not in black. . . But there weren't any black things in the last missionary barrel. **1914** [see **near C1**]. **1952** Giles *40 Acres* 183 **KY,** The next time you pack a missionary barrel remember that I wear a size 14 dress, a 6-½ shoe, and I am badly in need of a lightweight, rainproof coat! [*DARE* Ed: Writer lives in a poor community served by local missionaries from a nationwide denomination.] *Ibid* 187, Their forefathers would not have accepted relief. Their forefathers would have gone hungry before going on the county welfare roll. Their forefathers would have died before taking castoff clothing from the missionary barrel. **1992** *DARE* File, During the Great Depression my grandfather was minister of a small, struggling church in Montana. Sent there as a home missionary by the Congregational

Church, he knew that the local church could not support a minister and would need financial help from the denomination. Part of that help came in the form of the missionary barrel, which was a box of clothing for his family, sent by an eastern congregation that had "adopted" him.

missionary bird n
=**brown thrasher.**
  1956 MA Audubon Soc. *Bulletin* 40.128, Brown Thrasher. . . Missionary Bird (Mass. Hearing in its song the words "Caesar, Caesar, Go to Church, Go to Church, Fishy fisher, Fishy fisher, Devil catch you" persuaded an old negro to stop fishing on Sunday and go to church. Packard, 1921.)

missionary weed n
=**orange hawkweed.**
  1896 *Jrl. Amer. Folkl.* 9.192, *Hieracium aurantiacum,* . . missionary weed, E. Sangerville, Me. **1959** Carleton *Index Herb. Plants* 82, *Missionary-weed:* Hieracium aurantiacum.

mission bells n Also *mission bell* [See quot 1954] **West, esp CA**
A **fritillary:** esp *Fritillaria biflora* or *F. lanceolata,* but also *F. atropurpurea.*
  1897 Parsons *Wild Flowers CA* 264, Mission-bells. Bronze-bells. **1915** (1926) Armstrong–Thornber *Western Wild Flowers* 38, When we found this flower [=Fritillaria atropurpurea] growing in the Grand Canyon, halfway down Bright Angel trail, it seemed entirely suitable to the mysterious spirit of the place. The general effect is bronze-color and the attractive name of Bronze Bells, or Mission Bells, is very appropriate. **1920** *DN* 5.83 **OR,** Mission bells. Fritilaria [sic]. **1923** Davidson–Moxley *Flora S. CA* 89, Mission bells. Brown Lily. Canyon slopes from Santa Barbara to San Diego. **1942** Hylander *Plant Life* 552, Chocolate Lily, also known as Mission Bells *(Fritillaria),* has nodding brownish-purple flowers, borne singly or in small clusters; it grows on grassy slopes in California. **1954** CA Div. Beaches & Parks *Pt. Lobos Wild Flowers* 27, Mission Bells are named for the bell-shaped, mottled green and brownish-purple blossom which produces a clapper-shaped style. **1966** Barnes–Jensen *Dict. UT Slang* 30, *Mission bells* . . a name often given to the Leopard Lily or Spotted Fritillaria *(Fritillaria atropurpurea).* **1967–69** DARE (Qu. S26c, *Wildflowers that grow in woods)* Inf **CA20,** Chocolate lily or mission bells; (Qu. S26d, *Wildflowers that grow in meadows;* not asked in early QRs) Inf **CA144,** Mission bells. **1967** DARE FW Addit **OR,** Mission bells—*Fritillaria lanceolata.* **1970** Kirk *Wild Edible Plants W. U.S.* 166, Our native species of *F[ritillaria] atropurpurea* (Leopard Lily, Mission Bell, Purple Fritillary) . . [is] well known to be edible. **1973** Hitchcock–Cronquist *Flora Pacific NW* 691, Mission bells.

missis See **mistress**

Mississippi n Pronc-spp *Massasip, Massissippi, Missippi*
Std sense, var forms.
  1837 Sherwood *Gaz. GA* 70, *Massissippi,* for Mississippi. **1867** Lowell *Biglow* 122 **'Upcountry' MA,** The banks o' my own Massissippi. **1892** Harris *Uncle Remus & Friends* 123 **GA,** I done hear talk er Massasip long 'fo' you wuz bornded. I done seed um go dar, en I done seed um come back. **1893** Shands *MS Speech* 44, *Massasip.* . . Sometimes used by negroes and illiterate whites for *Mississippi.* **1903** DN 2.320 **seMO,** *Massissippi.* **1929** Sale *Tree Named John* 98 **MS,** Yo' grandaddy, en all de res' uv de folkses come t' Mis'sippi t' live. **1942** Faulkner *Go Down* 12 **MS,** Nothing sweetened a Missippi toddy like the hand of a Missippi lady. **1950** (1965) Richter *Town* 48 **OH,** He'd go . . till safe among his own countrymen on the muddy bayous that flowed slow and brown as molasses into the Massasip. **1968** DARE FW Addit **sKY,** *Mississippi* is often [mɪsˈsɪpi]. **1989** Pederson *LAGS Tech. Index* 321 **Gulf Region,** [The most common pronunciations are [mɪ(s)sɨˈsɪpɨ, mɪ(s)sə-], given by 365 infs, followed by [mɪ(s)ˈsɪpɨ] given by 241.]

Mississippi buck n Cf **sawbuck, spring buck**
=**red-breasted merganser.**
  1923 U.S. Dept. Ag. *Misc. Circular* 13.6 **IL,** *[Red-breasted Merganser:]* Vernacular Names. . . In local use. . . Mississippi buck. **1932** Bennitt *Check-list* 21 **MO,** Mergus serrator. . . Mississippi buck.

Mississippi bullhead n
  1 =**yellow bullhead.**
  1956 Harlan–Speaker *IA Fish* 112, *Yellow Bullhead.* . . Mississippi bullhead. . . Individuals weighing as much as 2 pounds are often taken from the Mississippi River. **1983** Becker *Fishes WI* 708, *Yellow bullhead.* . . Mississippi bullhead, greaser.
  2 =**flathead catfish 1.**

1966 *WI Conserv. Bulletin* July–Aug 14, What is a Mississippi bullhead? First of all it's not a bullhead, nor is it found only in the Mississippi river. . . Many know the fish. . . [as] flathead catfish. **1983** Becker *Fishes WI* 728, *Flathead catfish.* . . Other common names: . . Mississippi bullhead.

Mississippi cat n **Missip-Ohio Valleys**
  1 also *Mississippi catfish:* =**blue catfish 1.**
  1877 U.S. Natl. Museum *Bulletin* 10.84, This species [=Italurus furcatus] is the "Great Fork-tailed Cat" of the Lakes and the "Great Mississippi Cat" of the Mississippi and Ohio Rivers. I have seen . . specimens which I suppose were of this species which weighed nearly a hundred pounds. I have heard of Catfish weighing two or three hundred pounds, but have never seen them, and presume they were "weighed by guess." **1908** Forbes–Richardson *Fishes of IL* 179, "Mississippi cat" is the name given it [=Ictalurus furcatus] by some Illinois River fishermen. **1933** LA Dept. of Conserv. *Fishes* 420, *The Blue Cat.* . . Known also as . . the Mississippi Cat, this is one of . . the Catfishes that make up an important fresh water fishery in the United States. **1957** Trautman *Fishes* 412 **OH,** The readily-identifiable "Mississippi" or "White" catfish was present before 1900 in the Ohio River between the Indiana state line and Belmont County. *Ibid* 414, In Ohio the species is called "Mississippi" or "White Cat," the latter a most appropriate name, for all specimens I have seen were whitish or milk-white. **1967–69** DARE (Qu. P1, . . *Kinds of freshwater fish . . caught around here . . good to eat)* Inf **IN83,** Mississippi cats; **KY6,** Missippi cat; (Qu. H45) Inf **IL3,** Mississippi catfish. **1975** Evanoff *Catch More Fish* 94, The blue catfish. . . is also called the great forktail cat, Mississippi catfish [etc].
  2 =**flathead catfish 1.**
  1956 Harlan–Speaker *IA Fish* 112, *Flathead Catfish.* . . Other Names . . Mississippi cat. **1983** Becker *Fishes WI* 728, *Flathead catfish.* . . Other common names: . . Mississippi cat.

Mississippi catfish See **Mississippi cat 1**

Mississippi kite n
A kite *(Ictinia mississippiensis)* native chiefly to the southern US. Also called **blue kite, grasshopper hawk 4, Louisiana kite, mosquito hawk 1b, pigeon ~, snake-killer ~**
  1811 Wilson *Amer. Ornith.* 3.80 **MS,** [The] Mississippi Kite. *Falco Misisippiensis* [sic]. . . I first observed . . a few miles below Natchez. **1832** Nuttall *Manual Ornith.* 1.92, Mississippi Kite. . . This remarkably long-winged and beautiful Hawk does not appear to extend its migrations far within the United States. **1872** Coues *Key to N. Amer. Birds* 211, Mississippi Kite. . . S. Atlantic and Gulf States, N. to Illinois. **1907** Anderson *Birds IA* 243, The Mississippi Kite has been quoted by nearly all authorities as ranging north "casually to Iowa and Wisconsin." **1921** LA Dept. of Conserv. *Bulletin* 10.92, In the late summer considerable loose flocks of Mississippi kites may be seen hawking over cornfields and other crops on the borders of woodlands, where they capture cicadas, or "locusts", grasshoppers and other insects. **1954** Sprunt *FL Bird Life* 97, Mississippi Kite: *Ictinia misisippiensis* [sic]. . . Breeds from northeastern Kansas, Iowa, Illinois, southern Indiana, and South Carolina south to Texas and Florida. **1977** Bull–Farrand *Audubon Field Guide Birds* 639, Mississippi Kite. . . This graceful, buoyant kite is a marvelous flier and spends hours in the air. **1987** *Nature Conserv. News* 37.3.30 **TN,** This . . area is . . a primary nesting site for the Mississippi kite.

Mississippi mule n [From its powerful kick] Cf **Minnesota thirteen, white mule**
  1967 DARE (Qu. DD21c, *Nicknames for whiskey, especially illegally made whiskey)* Inf **LA14,** Mississippi mule.

Mississippi rosebush n
A **hibiscus.**
  1954 *Harder Coll.* **cwTN,** Mississippi rosebush. . . Hibiscus.

Mississippi skiff n Cf **creole skiff**
  1956 Knipmeyer *Settlement Succession* 168 **eLA,** Intermediate between the lake skiff and the smallest is the "Mississippi skiff." It is generally no shorter than the lake skiff, but has a smaller beam in proportion to the length. The stern board is rectangular and more V-shaped. The lake skiff has a broad, bulging appearance, and the Mississippi skiff is slender.

‡Miss Janet n
=**Mrs. Jones.**
  1969 DARE (Qu. BB20, *Joking names or expressions for overactive kidneys)* Inf **IN76,** Have to go see Miss Janet again.

Miss Jenny Jones n Also *Miss Jennia Jones;* for addit varr see quots [See quot 1883]

A children's group game; see quot 1907.

1883 Newell *Games & Songs* 63, *Miss Jennia Jones*—This childish drama has been familiar in the Middle States since the memory of the oldest inhabitant. The Scotch equivalent shows that the heroine's name was originally *Jenny Jo.* "Jo" is an old English word for sweetheart, probably a corruption of *joy.* . . *Jenny my joy* has thus been modernized into Miss Jennia (commonly understood to be a contraction for Virginia) Jones. The story is originally a love tale. **1907** *DN* 3.246 eME, *Miss Jenny Jones.* . . In this game one player crouches behind a second player, who stands opposite a line. Line advancing: We've come to see Miss Jenny Jones. . . Is she at home to-day? Second player: Miss Jenny Jones is washing. . . And can't be seen to-day. Line advancing: We've come, etc. Second player: Miss Jenny Jones is starching, etc. Line advancing: We've come, etc. Second player: Miss Jenny Jones is ironing, etc. Substitute: mending, —sweeping, —cooking. With refrain; also, Miss Jenny Jones is ill, —dying, —dead. The one crouching falls. Then follows the funeral. **1966** *DARE* FW Addit swIN, Miss Jenny 'n' Jones—a singing type of children's game. **1967** *DARE* (Qu. EE33, . . *Outdoor games* . . *that children play*) Inf CA24, I've come to see Miss Jenima Jones.

Miss Jones('s) See **Mrs. Jones**

miss-lick See **mislick**

Miss Lizzie Tish n Also *(Miss) Tizzie Lish* Cf **catish** =**Miss Astor.**

1994 *DARE* File NY, All dressed up like Miss Lizzie Tish. Ibid NY, Tizzie Lish. **1995** *Ibid* csWI (as of c1968), The mother of one of my childhood friends had a tendency to dress in frilly, fussy outfits and wear a great deal of jewelry and makeup. "Who does she think she is—Tizzie Lish?" my mother would mutter. As I recall, the name was not always used sarcastically. For example, if my grandmother thought I looked nice, she would announce as I came into a room, "Here she is—Miss Tizzie Lish!"

Miss Manners, leave something for See **manner** n 3b

miss-meal colic n Also *missed-meal colic, miss-meal cramp(s)* chiefly Sth

Hunger.

1928 in 1983 Taft *Blues Lyric Poetry* 137, My body feels so weary : because I got the miss-meal cramp / Right now I could eat more : than a whole carload of tramps. **1950** *PADS* 14.46 SC, *Missed-meal colic.* . . Hunger. **1954** *PADS* 21.33 SC, *Miss-meal colic.* . . Hunger. **1965** Bradford *Born with the Blues* 13 **Sth** [Black], My friends was buzzing me with, "Perry, why don't you forget the dream about a colored girl singing on phonograph records. That's causing you to suffer from 'miss-meal-cramps!' " **1966–68** *DARE* (Qu. K47, *Diseases* . . *horses or mules commonly get*) Inf GA63, Miss-meal colic—not getting enough to eat; (Qu. K44, *A bony or poor-looking horse*) Inf MS74, Miss-meal colic—too much to eat gives him the colic and this is where this word came from.

Missouri n Usu |mɪˈzuri, mə-, -ˈzuri, -ˈzurɪ|; also freq |mɪˈzurə| Pronc-spp *Missoura(h), Mizzoura(h);* for addit pronc and sp varr see quots Cf Intro "Language Changes" IV.1.a.

Std sense, var forms.

1822 Worcester in 1938 *AmSp* 13.263, Missouri—Mis-soo′-re. **1829** in 1938 *AmSp* 13.265, [Letter of Edward Everett in resp to Worcester:] Missouri . . My-zoo′-re is heard. **1838** in 1933 *AmSp* 8.4.32, Missoura. **1889** Field *Western Verse* 36 MO, He lives here in Mizzoora. **1893** *Chicago Daily Tribune* (IL) 6 Aug sec B 29/2 MO, Every boy here that respects his parents . . will always say Mizzouraw. **1910** Hart *Vigilante Girl* 133 nCA, One of the first families of Mizzourah. **1911** *DN* 3.500 **Sth, S Midl,** *Missouri*—76 [infs pronounce the final syllable as [ɪ]]—162 [infs pronounce it [ə]]. **1921** Haswell *Daughter Ozarks* 47 (as of 1880s), As rough road as thar is in all Missoury. **1930** *AmSp* 5.421, Announcers and broadcasters in Saint Louis and in Cincinnati are coming right out and saying "Missour-*i*" and "Cincinnat-*i*", instead of "Missour-*a*" and "Cincinnat-*a*," which latter pronunciations quite a number of pretentious people affect. **1933** *AmSp* 8.4.32, The perplexing final vowel was probably originally an [ɪ] if we can go by the French spelling of the Indian word; but the testimony of the old settlers in 1897 tends to show that [ə], as *Mizzoura,* was firmly established by 1840 or 1850. **1936** *AmSp* 11.163 eTX, *Cincinnati* and *Missouri* are [ˌsɪnsəˈnætə], [məˈzurə]. I have never heard [ɪ] as the final vowel of these words in East Texas. **c1960** Wilson *Coll.* csKY, *Missouri* is always /mɪˈzurə/. **1961** Kurath–McDavid *Pronc. Engl.* 169, *Missouri, Cincinnati* . . end

in [ə] or in [ɪ ~ ɪ], the former predominating in Western New England, New Jersey, Pennsylvania, Virginia, and parts of North Carolina, the latter in Eastern New England, Metropolitan New York, Philadelphia, and the Lower South. Elsewhere the two pronunciations are rather evenly matched. There is no marked class cleavage in usage, but urbanites have a preference for [ɪ ~ ɪ]. **1969** *DARE* (Qu. BB17) Inf MO15, [mɪˈzurə]. **1976** Allen *LAUM* 3.351 (as of c1950), The two conspicuous pronunciations of *Missouri,* /mɪˈzuri/ and /mɪˈzurə/ . . reveal clear social and geographical contrast within the region. The variant with final /i/ is somewhat preferred by the more highly educated and by the infs. in Northern speech territory. **1985** *MO Folkl. Soc. Jrl.* 7.1 MO, Both Missour-ee and Missour-uh are in common use to some extent in all parts of the state. **1989** Pederson *LAGS Tech. Index* 321 **Gulf Region,** [410 infs gave proncs ending in [-ɪ] or [-i], chiefly [məˈzurɪ, mɪ-, mɪ-]; 232 proncs ending in [-ə], chiefly [məˈzurə, mɪ-, mɪ-].] **1992** *NYT Mag.* 25 Oct 26/2, In his introduction, he [=Jim Lehrer] said the program originated in St. Louis, "Miz-oor-uh." In his conclusion, he said goodbye from "Miz-oor-ee." . . [Lehrer] confesses: "I did it deliberately. I went to the University of Miz-oor-uh. 'Miz-oor-uh! Tigers!' That was a signal to my friends that I knew that's the way it's pronounced there. But everybody else says 'Miz-oor-ee,' . . so I closed on that." **1992** *DARE* File ceMO, We are a bit archaic in Missouri (pronounced Missourah).

Missouri banana See **banana B1**

‡**Missouri blue** n

See quot.

1968 *DARE* (Qu. S26a, . . *Wildflowers.* . . *Roadside flowers*) Inf IN19, Missouri blues.

Missouri breadroot n Also *Missouri breadnut*

An **Indian breadroot** (here: *Psoralea esculenta*).

1889 *Century Dict.* 4820, *Psoralea.* . . *P. esculenta* . . yields an edible tuberous root, known as . . *Missouri breadroot.* **1900** Lyons *Plant Names* 309, *P[soralea] esculenta.* . . Manitoba to Texas. Indian or Missouri Bread-root. . . Tubers esculent. **1917** Kephart *Camping & Woodcraft* 2.379, Indian or Missouri Breadroot. The *pomme blanche* of the voyageurs. *Psoralea Esculenta.* . . Often sliced and dried by the Indians for winter use. Palatable in any form. **1922** *Amer. Botanist* 28.75, The specific name of *Psoralea esculenta* alludes to its edible properties and among its vernacular names are . . "Indian bread-root", "Missouri bread-nut." **1959** Carleton *Index Herb. Plants* 82, *Missouri-bread-nut:* Psoralea esculenta.

Missouri canary n Also *Missouri hummingbird, ~ mockingbird, ~ songbird* Cf **Arizona nightingale, Colorado mockingbird**

=**mountain canary.**

1937 *Natl. Geogr. Mag.* Aug 150, From all over the South buyers flock to Wichita's busy mule market. "Missouri mockingbirds," they nickname these agile, shapely, but sterile hybrids. **1942** Berrey–Van den Bark *Amer. Slang* 120.21, *Donkey; burro.* . . Missouri hummingbird. **1950** *WELS* (*Joking names for mules*) 1 Inf, csWI, Missouri mockingbirds; 1 Inf, swWI, Missouri canaries or songbirds. **1967** *DARE* (Qu. K50, *Joking nicknames for mules*) Inf AZ2, Missouri canary.

Missouri currant n

A **currant B1:** either *Ribes aureum* or *R. odoratum.*

1837 Darlington *Flora Cestrica* 162, *R[ibes] aureum,* or *Missouri Currant,* is much cultivated, and greatly admired, for the beauty and spicy fragrance of its flowers. **1848** in 1850 Cooper *Rural Hours* 116 cNY, Saw a number of humming-birds. . . They are extremely fond of the Missouri currant. **1891** Jesup *Plants Hanover NH* 14, R[ibes] aureum. . . Missouri Currant. . . Persisting for years about old homesteads. Native of Missouri and the West. **1910** Graves *Flowering Plants* 219 CT, *Ribes odoratum.* . . Missouri . . Currant. . . The fruit is edible. **1915** (1926) Armstrong–Thornber *Western Wild Flowers* 214, *Missouri . . Currant. Ribes aureum.* . . Growing beside brooks and in moist canyons, . . it has at a distance the effect of Forsythia, but purer in color. **1932** Rydberg *Flora Prairies* 401, Missouri . . Currants. . . *Ribes odoratum.* . . *Ribes aureum.* **1963** Craighead *Rocky Mt. Wildflowers* 78, *Ribes aureum.* . . Missouri Currant. . . This shrub could easily be mistaken for other currants . . , but lack of prickles on stems, and long, bright yellow flowers help distinguish it from other *Ribes* in the Rockies. **1973** Stephens *Woody Plants* 202, *Ribes odoratum.* . . Missouri currant. . . The fruit is full of seeds but makes good jam and jellies and is sometimes used in pies. **1976** Bailey–Bailey *Hortus Third* 969, [Ribes] aureum. . . *Missouri c[urrant].* . . Wash. to Mont. s. to Calif. Ibid 970, [Ribes] odoratum. . . *Missouri c[urrant].* . . S. Dak. and Minn. s. to Tex. and Ark. . . Sometimes confused with the related *R. aureum.*

Missouri featherbed n

1961 Adams *Old-Time Cowhand* 101, 'Bout the only mattress the cowhand knowed was the one at the cheap frontier hotel, stuffed with "prairie feathers [=straw]," and knowed as "Missouri featherbeds."

Missouri gooseberry n

A **gooseberry 1:** usu *Ribes missouriense,* but also *R. cynosbati* and *R. setosum.*

1897 IN Dept. Geol. & Nat. Resources *Rept. for 1896* 637, *R[ibes] gracile.* . . Missouri Gooseberry. Dry, upland woods; frequent. **1910** Graves *Flowering Plants* 217 **CT,** *Ribes gracile.* . . Missouri Gooseberry. **1938** Van Dersal *Native Woody Plants* 236, *Ribes missouriense.* . . *Missouri gooseberry.* . . Berries very large. *Ibid* 238, *Ribes setosum.* . . *Missouri gooseberry.* . . A small, spiny shrub; flowers in May. **1953** Strausbaugh–Core *Flora WV* 456, *Missouri gooseberry.* . . Flowers white or greenish, drooping. **1973** Wharton–Barbour *Trees KY* 526, The Missouri gooseberry is found in central and western Kentucky on rocky wooded creek banks and in woodland borders, but is infrequent. **1976** Bailey–Bailey *Hortus Third* 970, *[Ribes] missouriense.* . . *Missouri g[ooseberry].* . . Fr[uit] purplish. . . Tenn., w. to Minn., S. Dak., Kans. *Ibid* 970, *[Ribes] setosum.* . . *Missouri g[ooseberry].* . . Fr[uit] red or black. . . Mich. and Minn. to Sask., s. to Nebr. and Wyo.

Missouri gourd n West

A **calabacilla** (here: *Cucurbita foetidissima*).

1911 *Century Dict. Suppl., Gourd.* . . *Missouri gourd.* Same as *cala-bazilla* [sic]. It extends east to the Missouri river. **1920** Saunders *Useful Wild Plants* 179, Also of the West is a species of gourd. . . in some sections . . known as Missouri Gourd. . . Botanically it is *Cucurbita foetidissima* . . , and the rank, garlicky odor given off by the crushed leaves makes the specific appellation very apropos. **1936** Winter *Plants NE* 135, *Missouri Gourd.* . . Found in southern Nebr., most frequent westward. **1947** Curtin *Healing Herbs* 45 **West,** *Missouri Gourd.* . . is a coarse but decorative creeping vine, adorned with solitary yellow flowers. **1968** Barkley *Plants KS* 329, Missouri Gourd. . . Plains, prairies, waste ground and along roads and railways. **1976** Bailey–Bailey *Hortus Third* 343, *Missouri gourd.* . . Fr[uit] striped green and yellow, of the size and shape of an orange, not edible.

Missouri grape n

=**catbird grape.**

1856 Ferguson *America* 272 **swOH,** Those which are chiefly cultivated are the . . Isabella, and the Missouri grape. **1859** Mackay *Life & Liberty* 1.208 **OH,** He again selected twelve as alone fit for the production of wine. These twelve were the Catawba, . . the Missouri [etc]. **1938** Van Dersal *Native Woody Plants* 337, Grape_[5] . . Missouri *(Vitis palmata).* **1970** Correll *Plants TX* 1019, *Vitis palmata* . . Missouri grape, red grape, catbird grape. . . On margins of ponds or sloughs, or in low woods in e. Tex., n. to Ind., Ill. and Ia.

Missouri hummingbird See **Missouri canary**

Missouri lark See **Missouri skylark**

Missouri minnow n

The goldfish *(Carassius auratus).*

1983 Becker *Fishes WI* 428, Goldfish. . . Other common names: golden carp; . . Missouri minnow.

Missouri mockingbird See **Missouri canary**

Missouri pistol n Cf **coonass pistol, fire C9, Kentucky pill**

1977 Dunlop *Wheels West* 36 (as of c1840), The drivers snapped their "Missouri pistols," long saplings with a lash ending in a buckskin thong.

Missouri primrose n esp TX, OK

An **evening primrose a** (here: *Oenothera macrocarpa*).

1929 Stemen–Myers *Spring Flora OK* 118, *Megapterium missouriensis.* . . *Missouri Primrose.* . . May–July. Frequent. **1936** Whitehouse *TX Flowers* 82, *Missouri Primrose.* . . clings to the side of a gravelly cliff or grows on rocky limestone hillsides from Missouri to Colorado and Texas. **1949** Moldenke *Amer. Wild Flowers* 91, With only a few, but exceedingly showy, yellow flowers . . is the *Missouriprimrose.* **1961** Wills–Irwin *Flowers TX* 164, The Flutter-mill, known also as . . Missouri-primrose, . . is found . . throughout the Panhandle. **1970** Correll *Plants TX* 1129, *Missouri primrose.* . . Flowers opening near sunset.

Missouri rabbit n

Appar a cottontail *(Sylvilagus* spp).

1968 *DARE* (Qu. P30, . . *Wild rabbits*) Inf **OH**47, Missouri rabbit—they're small; **PA**121, Missouri rabbit or cottontail.

Missouri skylark n Also *Missouri lark* [See quots 1898, 1946]

Sprague's **pipit** *(Anthus spragueii).*

1858 Baird *Birds* 234, *Neocorys Spraguei.* . . *Missouri Skylark.* . . This little known species has the general appearance of a titlark. **1874** Coues *Birds NW* 42, At Fort Randall, last year, . . I became perfectly familiar with the Missouri Skylark. It is one of the most abundant and characteristic birds of all the region along the forty-ninth parallel of latitude, from just west of the Pembina Mountains to as far as the survey progressed this year—about four hundred miles. **1898** (1900) Davie *Nests N. Amer. Birds* 461, The Missouri Skylark has the same general habits common to the Titlark, but soaring like the European Skylark when singing, and according to those who have heard it, its vocal powers are not less inferior than those of that celebrated bird. **1910** Wayne *Birds SC* 178, Sprague's Missouri Lark. . . Again, on November 1, 1904, I saw and heard one sing. **1931** OK Univ. Biol. Surv. *Pub.* 3.148, The sweet and silvery-toned flight song of the . . "Missouri Skylark" is given for 20 minutes at a time so high in the air that the singer is almost invisible. **1946** Goodrich *Birds in KS* 264, Sprague's pipit, known also as the . . Missouri skylark because it was first taken in the upper reaches of the Missouri river, is a relatively common migrant through western Kansas. **1955** Forbush–May *Birds* 392, *Anthus spraguei.* . . Missouri Skylark.

Missouri songbird See **Missouri canary**

Missouri sucker n [See quot 1820]

A **sucker** (here: *Cycleptus elongatus*). Also called **black horse, black sucker 2, blue ~, gourdseed ~, muskellunge 3, razorback, sweet sucker, suckerel**

1820 Rafinesque *Ohio R. Fishes* 61, Black Suckrel. *Cycleptus nigres-cens.* . . It is also found in the Missouri, whence it is sometimes called the Missouri Sucker. **1842** DeKay *Zool. NY* 4.203, *C[atostomus] elon-gatus. The Missouri Sucker, Black Horse,* and *Black Buffalo.* **1878** U.S. Natl. Museum *Bulletin* 12.190, From the general use of the name "Missouri Sucker", its abundance in the State of Missouri may be inferred; but, as to the facts in the case, I am not informed. **1884** Goode *Fisheries U.S.* 1.615, The "Black Horse," "Gourd-seed Sucker," "Missouri Sucker," or "Suckerel" is found chiefly in the river channels of the Ohio and Mississippi. It reaches a considerable size, weighing five to twelve pounds, and is said to be a much finer fish in flesh than any other of its family. **1943** Eddy–Surber *N. Fishes* 108, The Missouri sucker ranges from southern Minnesota and Wisconsin southward into Kentucky and Kansas, and possibly farther. **1956** Harlan–Speaker *IA Fish* 71, Blue Sucker. . . Other Names—Missouri sucker. **1983** Becker *Fishes WI* 611, Blue Sucker. . . Other common names: Missouri sucker [etc].

misspend oneself v phr

1953 *PADS* 19.12 **sAppalachians,** *Misspend (oneself).* . . To overreach. "Ben will misspend himself if he hunts on posted land."

missput See **misput** v

miss stays v phr Also, perh by folk-etym, *misstay* [Transf from *miss stays,* of a sailing vessel: to fail to go about]

To fail, make a mistake.

1907 Lincoln *Cape Cod* 68 **MA,** You've missed stays *this* time, for sure. **1916** *DN* 4.335 **Cape Cod MA,** *Misstay.* . . To make a mistake; to fail. [*DN* Ed: N.J. *miss stays,* from failure of a sailboat to go about on another tack.]

miss the figure See **figure B3**

misstis See **mistress**

Miss Tizzie Lish See **Miss Lizzie Tish**

missus n[1] See **mistress**

Missus n[2] See **Mrs.**

miss-woman n

1953 Randolph–Wilson *Down in Holler* 265 **Ozarks,** *Miss-woman.* . . A refined, accomplished young woman, either married or single. "That feller can wash a shirt as good as any miss-woman." Rose O'Neill tells me that she often heard this in Taney County, Mo., in the early nineteen hundreds.

missy n

1 See **mistress.**

2 also cap; also sp *missie:* Used as a title or term of address for a girl or woman. **chiefly Sth**

1810 Lambert *Travels* 2.414 **seSC,** An old negro woman is called *momma,* . . and a girl, *missy.* **1926** Ferber *Show Boat* 30 **Sth,** [Black servant:] "Wha' that you say, missy?" [White employer:] "Don't you missy me!" **1938** Faulkner *Unvanquished* 112 **MS**, Ringo went on to Missy Lena's cabin. *Ibid* 130, "Then who are you going to mind from now on?" . . "You, missy." **1940** Faulkner *Hamlet* 247 **MS** [Black], The negro man had warned her: "He's a horse, missy. But he's a man horse. You keep out of there." **1946** *Sewanee Rev.* 54.404 **TN**, She heard old Mattie's [=a Black woman's] broken voice calling to her, "Miss Harriet! Oh, Missie, Missie!" . . The old fashioned appellative "Missie" told Harriet a great deal. **1986** Pederson *LAGS Concordance* (Mrs. Cooper) 1 inf, **swGA**, Missy—unmarried [inf Black]; (Master) 1 inf, **cnMS**, Missy—blacks' usual term of address, to white; 1 inf, **seMS**, Missy—sometimes used by blacks; as a child.

missy-massy See **missey-moosey**

mist n

1 also *Scotch mist:* A **bedstraw** (here: *Galium mollugo* or *G. sylvaticum*).
1894 *Jrl. Amer. Folkl.* 7.90 **eMA**, *Galium Mollugo* . . (and other sp.), mist, babies' breath. **1898** *Ibid* 11.228 **cME**, *Galium Mollugo* . . Scotch mist. **1961** Smith *MI Wildflowers* 357, The cultivated Scotch-mist or Baby's-breath, *G[alium] sylvaticum*.

2 =**baby's breath 1.**
1896 *Jrl. Amer. Folkl.* 9.182 **eMA**, *Gypsophila paniculata* . . (and other species), mist, babies' breath. **1940** Clute *Amer. Plant Names* 62, Baby's-breath. . . mist. **1959** Carleton *Index Herb. Plants* 82, *Mist* . . *Gypsophila paniculata.*

3 See **mistflower.**

4 A light snowfall. **esp Sth, S Midl** See Map
1965–70 *DARE* (Qu. B39, *A very light fall of snow*) 17 Infs, **esp Sth, S Midl,** Mist (of snow). [10 Infs Black]

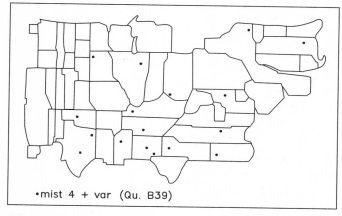
•mist 4 + var (Qu. B39)

mistake v
Gram forms.

1 past: usu *mistook;* also *mistakened.*
1902 [see **2** below]. **1907** *DN* 3.224 **nwAR**, *Mistakened.* . . Mistook and mistaken. **1948** *Hench Coll.* **VA**, [Student quiz response:] The intoxicated guard seeing the moon mistakened it for the sun. **1962** *Mt. Life* 38.1.17 **sAppalachians**, Certain persistent perversities in the use of verbs are also widespread. Strong verbs are often weakened, irregular verbs made regular. The past and past participle of . . mistake [become] mistakened.

2 past pple: usu *mistaken;* also *mistakened, mistook(en).*
1890 Holley *Samantha among Brethren* 8 **NY**, I wouldn't want this told of, for I may be mistook. **1902** *DN* 2.239 **sIL**, *Mistakened.* Preterit and past participle of mistake. 'He was mistakened.' **1907** [see **1** above]. **1927** *AmSp* 3.163 **NE**, Later the gentleman learned he had been mistakened in his information. **1940** (1941) Bell *Swamp Water* 179 **Oke-fenokee GA**, "You'll have to take us to him." Ben laughed with a savage bitterness. "That's where you're plumb mistooken. Go find him." **1942** (1971) Campbell *Cloud-Walking* 148 **seKY**, Right there you are mistook. **1962** [see **1** above]. **1969** *DARE* (Qu. KK59, *To have a mistaken idea, or to be quite wrong about something:* "*If he thinks she'll help him, he's* _____.") Inf **KY5**, Mistakened. **1974** Fink *Mountain Speech* 16 **wNC, eTN**, Mistook . . mistaken or confused. "I've been mistook about that lots of times." **1979** *AmSp* 54.94 **swME** (as of 1899–1910), Nonstandard past participles are likewise numerous: borned, . . mistakened.

3 pres pple: usu *mistaking;* also *mistakening.* Cf **-en** suff[5]
1959 *Hench Coll.* **VA**, [On a student exam paper:] When Troilus is on

the wall mistakening the distant people as his love, the reader is wholly sympathetic with him.

mistakened See **mistake 1, 2**

mistakening See **mistake 3**

mister n

1 usu with *the* or *my:* A husband or head of a household. **scattered, but chiefly N Cent, PA** See Map
1929 Suckow *Cora* 256 **IA**, Mister'll be home today, I suppose? **1931** *AmSp* 7.20 **swPA**, My mister. My husband. **1934** *AmSp* 9.79 **nLA**, The Mister, a wife's term for her husband, appeared occasionally. **1938** Matschat *Suwannee R.* 83 **neFL, seGA**, Afore my mister passed away he found him in the powsture. **1941** *LANE* Map 374 (My husband) 9 infs, **NEng**, The mister. **1943** *Sat. Eve. Post* 17 Apr 24 **ID**, Yes, sir, I wish my mister had 'a' come here. **1950** Klees *PA Dutch* 282, Amusing, too, is the reference to the husband and head of the house as *the mister.* This is the shibboleth of the true country Dutchwoman. **c1955** Reed–Person *Ling. Atlas Pacific NW*, The mister [2 of c50 infs]. **1965–70** *DARE* (Qu. AA23, *Joking names that a woman may use to refer to her husband:* "*It's time to go and get supper for my* _____.") 29 Infs, **scattered, but chiefly N Cent, PA,** Mister; **NY**132, Big mister; **GA**33, The mister. **1986** Pederson *LAGS Concordance* (My husband) 1 inf, **nwMS**, Mister; 1 inf, **swMS**, Mister—has heard; 1 inf, **seMS**, Mister—wife called husband—taught blacks respect; 1 inf, **nwAR**, Mister—older term; 1 inf, **swGA**, My mister.

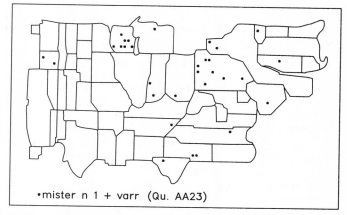
•mister n 1 + varr (Qu. AA23)

2 See quot. Cf **male** adj
1966 *DARE* (Qu. K23, *Words used by women or in mixed company for a bull*) Inf **SD**2, Mister.

mister v [*mist* v + *-er* affix 2]
1970 *DARE* (Qu. B21, *When fine drops of moisture are falling . . it's doing what?*) Infs **VA**39, **TN**52, Mistering (rain). [Both Infs Black]

Mister Charlie n Also sp *Mister Charley, Mr. Charlie among Black speakers; often derog* Cf **Charlie 2, man** n **C5b, Miss Ann(e)**
A White man; the boss; White people.
1928 Fisher *Walls Jericho* 303 **NYC** [Black], *Mr. Charlie*—Non-specific designation of "swell" whites. **1942** *Amer. Mercury* 55.223.95 **Harlem NYC** [Black], *Mister Charlie*—a white man. **1964** Baldwin *Blues for Mister Charlie* [title]. **1965** Brown *Manchild* 274 **Harlem NYC** [Black], She had all the Southern upbringing in her, that business of being scared of Mr. Charlie. Everybody white she saw was Mr. Charlie. **1967** *Manchester Guardian* (England) 12 Jan 2/4, Stokeley Carmichael was there promising "Mr. Charlie's" doomsday. **1971** Clarke *Harlem* 173, He is assured . . his ancestors were happy, shiftless, watermelon-eating darkies who loved Mr. Charlie and Miss Ann. **1971** Roberts *Third Ear* np [Black], *Mister Charley* . . a white man; the boss. **1986** Pederson *LAGS Concordance*, 1 inf, **swGA**, Mister Charley—blacks called her father; 1 inf, **nwTN**, Mister Charley—black servants to her grandfather; 1 inf, **cwFL**, Mister Charley—blacks call police; [same inf:] No, sir, Mister Charley—general name for master; Yes, sir, Mister Charley—general name in slavery.

mistflower n Also *mist* [See quot 1901]
A **boneset 1** (here: *Conoclinium coelestinum*).
1848 Gray *Manual of Botany* 194, *Conoclinium.* . . Mist-flower. **1894** *Jrl. Amer. Folkl.* 7.92 **WV**, *Eupatorium coelestinum* . . mist-flower. **1901** Lounsberry *S. Wild Flowers* 498, *E[upatorium] coelestinum* [is] quaintly

called the "mist-flower," from the soft haze of its violet-blue blossoms growing with bell-shaped involucres in small compact heads. **1936** IL Nat. Hist. Surv. *Wildflowers* 342, The Mist Flower grows in rich soil in partly exposed places from New Jersey to Michigan, Kansas and southwest. **1949** Moldenke *Amer. Wild Flowers* 220, Related to the thoroughworts and bonesets is the *mistflower*, . . so well known to all travelers in the South. **1959** Carleton *Index Herb. Plants* 82, Mist: Eupatorium caelestinum [sic]. **1968** Barkley *Plants KS* 236, Eupatorium coelestinum. . . Mistflower. Wet stream banks in woods. **1979** Ajilvsgi *Wild Flowers* 290, wLA, eTX, Mist-flower. . . Plants usually forming extensive colonies.

mistis(s) See **mistress**

mist maiden n Also *maid of the mist, mist maid(ens)* [See quot 1938]

A plant of the genus *Romanzoffia* native to the Pacific NW and Alaska.

1897 Parsons *Wild Flowers CA* 22, Mist-Maidens. . . In appearance these delicate herbs resemble the saxifrages, and they affect much the same sort of places, decking mossy banks and stream borders with their beautiful scalloped leaves and small white flowers. **1934** Haskin *Wild Flowers Pacific Coast* 290, Mist Maidens. . . love moist rocks . . , where their pure white blossoms nestle among the mosses. **1936** *Nature Mag.* 27.356 AK, The maid of the mist, *Romanzoffia* sitchensis. . . A creamy-colored center breaks the otherwise solid white of these dainty blossoms. **1938** (1958) Sharples *AK Wild Flowers* 124, R[omanzoffia] sitchensis. . . Its nickname, "Mist Maidens," is applied because of its frequent appearance so close to a mountain stream that it is wet by the misty spray. **1949** Peattie *Cascades* 262 Pacific NW, Wherever the rocks are wet we shall see mist-maiden, a succulent plant with slender stems, thin kidney-shaped leaves, and airy sprays of small white blossoms. **1959** Anderson *Flora AK* 401, Mist Maid. . . Kodiak I[sland] east along the coast to Calif. and Alb[ert]a. **1973** Hitchcock–Cronquist *Flora Pacific NW* 384, *Romanzoffia*. . . Mistmaiden. **1987** Hughes-Blackwell *Wildflowers SE AK* 106, Mist-maid. . . *Moist Rocky Places*. . . Stem leaves are alternate (and few).

mistook(en) See **mistake 2**

mist rain v phr chiefly Sth, S Midl See Map Note: The intr form *misting,* pres pple of *mist* v, given as a resp by 544 Infs to Qu. B21, is not regional.

To rain lightly with very small drops; hence n *mist rain* a very light rain.

1909 DN 3.349 eAL, wGA, Mist. . . To drizzle. "It's a mistin' rain now, and it'll be a pourin' befo' you git home." **1965–70** DARE (Qu. B21, *When fine drops of moisture are falling . . it's doing what?*) 46 Infs, chiefly Sth, S Midl, Misting rain. **1968** DARE FW Addit swLA, Misting rain—raining lightly in fine drops. **1986** Pederson *LAGS Concordance,* 1 inf, cGA, It's misting rain; 1 inf, cLA, Misting rain—just starting; 1 inf, neGA, I'd call it a mist rain; 1 inf, cLA, Mist rain—"all day"; 1 inf, cnGA, Little mist rain.

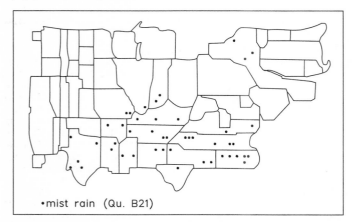

•mist rain (Qu. B21)

mistress n Pronc-spp, *esp freq among Black speakers; old-fash, mis(s), miss(t)is, missus, missy, mistis(s), mistus*

A Std sense, var forms.

1835 [see **B1** below]. **1887** (1967) Harris *Free Joe* 82 GA [Black], My mistiss sot lots by her. **1887** Page *In Ole VA* 454 VA, Didn't none on 'em hol' a candle to his young mistis. **1894** [see **B1** below]. **1899**

[see **B1** below]. **1899** Chesnutt *Conjure Woman* 44 csNC [Black], No marster, ner no mistiss. **1901** DN 2.182 neKY [Black], *Mistress*—Missus. **1909** DN 3.349 eAL, wGA, Mistiss. . . Mistress: still in use by the older negroes. **c1937** in 1976 *Weevils in the Wheat* 142 VA [Black], I was big 'nough to wait on de table den. I stay' in de house with my misstis. **1986** [see **B1** below].

B Senses.

1 Formerly used by Black speakers in the South as a quasi-proper name for their female owners or for other White women. Cf **master** n **B1**

1835 in 1965 *AmSp* 40.130, My old Missus she's mad wid me,/ Kase I wouldn't go wid her into Tennessee / Massa build him barn and put in de fodder / Twas dis ting and dat ting one ting or odder. **1852** Eastman *Aunt Phillis's Cabin* 217 VA, Master George, take it to mistis, and tell her de truth. **1858** Hammett *Piney Woods Tavern* 27 [Black], Why look hea, ole mossa, mistiss done sent Rushey down to the grocery. **1892** (1893) Botume *First Days* 6 seSC [Black], My father and the other boys used to crawl under the house an' lie on the ground to hear massa read the newspaper to missis when they first began to talk about the war. **1893** Shands *MS Speech* 46, Miss. . . Negro for *mistress.* They say "ole Miss" for "old mistress." **1894** in 1941 Warfel–Orians *Local-Color Stories* 737 sAR, Look lak I can't see my way straight dis mornin', mistus. **1899** Chesnutt *Conjure Woman* 204 csNC [Black], Ole mis' tuk her up ter de big house, en l'arnt her ter wait on de w'ite folks, 'tel bimeby she come ter be mis's own maid. **1929** (1951) Faulkner *Sartoris* 367 MS, Like in Mars' John's time, when . . de niggers fum de quawters gathered on de front lawn, wishin' Mistis en de little marster well. **1930** DN 6.79 cSC, Big-Miss, and Little-Miss, vocatives. An older negro speaks to or of a married white woman as Big-Miss and to or of her daughter, regardless of age or weight, as Little-Miss. **1986** Pederson *LAGS Concordance (Master)* 1 inf, swGA, Old miss and old boss—terms used by slaves; 1 inf, neMS, Old Miss, Miss—older blacks still use for "Mistress"; 1 inf, swGA, Old Miss—black man to white woman in story; 1 inf, ceMS, Old Miss—wife of boss; 1 inf, csAR, Old Miss—blacks called informant's wife; 1 inf, nwLA, Old Miss—blacks called her; 2 infs, cAL, cLA, Old Miss; 1 inf, cTN, Master and missy—old terms, used by blacks; 1 inf, swTN, Young Miss—daughter of the house; slaves' term.

2 See **Mrs.**

mistrust v esp NEast

1 To suspect, anticipate, surmise. [OED mistrust v. 3 a1450 →]

1777 *Boston Gaz. & Weekly Republican Jrl.* (MA) 10 Nov 3/3, He said he was taking his own Way to Boston, but is mistrusted to be going to Long or Rhode Island. **1815** (1922) Valpey *Jrl.* 27 MA, The Blacks were near the gates of there Yard Gamboling and not Mistrusting any harm when a dreadful fire from the top of the wall killed several and wounded many. **1840** Hoffman *Greyslaer* 1.109 cNY, I mistrust that your Injun friend there . . didn't help you much . . in finding out old Josie. **1861** Holmes *Venner* 1.124 NEng, I mistrusted he didn't mean to come. **1867** *Harper's New Mth. Mag.* 35.147, They have left the Atlantic coast, given up by physicians as in the last stage of consumption—a fact that would never be mistrusted from their present robust condition. **1909** DN 3.349 eAL, wGA, Mistrust. . . To suspect. "I mistrusted he was at the bottom of it." Not common, *suspicioned* being more frequently used. **1921** in 1969 Frost *Poetry* 209 NEng, But I mistrusted he was none too proud. **1934** *Hanley Disks* csME, I mistrust that a great deal of it [=interest in Paul Bunyan] is prompted by people from the outside. **1942** McAtee *Dial. Grant Co. IN* 43 (as of 1890s), Mistrust . . surmise; "I _____ there'll be trouble". Now rare. **1950** *WELS Suppl.,* When he seen three hogs in the load was dead, he mistrusted something. **c1960** *Wilson Coll.* csKY, Mistrust. . . Surmise. "I mistrusted that he wouldn't come back." **1967** DARE (Qu. GG12, *To have an inner feeling that something is about to happen: "There she comes now, I _____ she would."*) Inf NY1, Mistrusted. **1975** Gould *ME Lingo* 182, Mistrust—The dictionaries say that *mistrust* in the sense of suspect or surmise is rare, but it will be heard every day in Maine speech. "I mistrusted you might come today!" means a premonition is fulfilled. . . Misdoubt and *mistrust* have some interchangeable nuances, but not always. One will misdoubt the future in the negative; i.e., that something will not happen. To *mistrust* the future suggests the likelihood it will happen. **1979** DARE File cnMA (as of c1915), I recall my mother's asking me when I was a small child if I mistrusted that one of our neighbors was going to have a baby.

2 To doubt. Cf **misdoubt**

1935 (1944) Rawlings *Golden Apples* 114 nFL, I most mistrust Mis'

Raynes'd leave one o' her young uns come here. **1938** Rawlings *Yearling* 306 **nFL**, Penny said, "I mistrust kin old Cæsar tote all we got." "I'll walk, Pa. Do the buck weigh more'n me?"

3 See quot.

1975 Gould *ME Lingo* 182, *Mistrust.* . . The word is also used for an error in identification: "He mistrusted I was you."

mist tree n [See quot 1908]

A **smoke tree** (here: *Cotinus obovatus*).

1901 Lounsberry *S. Wild Flowers* 308, *American Smoke-tree. Mist Tree.* . . Only in certain parts of the South does the American smoke-tree grow wild. **1908** Rogers *Tree Book* 359, These panicles [of flowers] show a peculiar feathery development of the bracts. . [and] form in the aggregate a great cloud of rosy haze or smoke, that makes it [=*Cotinus obovatus*] a thing of beauty in late summer. Then it earns its common names, smoke tree and mist tree.

mistus See **mistress**

misty moisty adj phr [Prob from the Mother Goose nursery rhyme "The Wiltshire Wedding"]

Of the weather: misty, foggy; threatening to rain.

1856 in 1894 Lowell *Letters* 1.269 **ceMA**, A misty, moisty morning. **1879** (1888) Brush *Col.'s Opera Cloak* 70, When the day came, it was rather "misty-moisty." **1894** *Forum* 17.731, A misty, moisty island. **1901** *DN* 2.143, *Misty-moisty.* . . Misty, threatening rain. **1909** *DN* 3.400 **nwAR**, *Misty-moisty.* . . Misty, threatening rain. (Facetious.) **1946** *PADS* 6.21 **VA** (as of 1900–10), *Misty moisty, to be.* . . To be threatening rain. Salem. Reported, 1940. **1947** *PADS* 8.19 **IA**, *Misty moisty, to be:* Dewy; foggy. Cf. Mother Goose rhyme beginning, "One misty moisty morning. . . "

mit See **mitt 2**

mitch v See **meech**

mitch n See **misht**

Mitchell Day n [After John *Mitchell* (1870–1919), labor leader and organizer of the anthracite coal miners' strike of 1902]

May first.

1968 *DARE* (Qu. FF12a, . . *The first day of May*) Inf **PA**135, Mitchell Day—miners named it this and they take the day off.

mite n

A small child.

1941 *LANE* Map 379 *(Kid, tot)* 1 inf, **cwMA**, Youngster, tyke, tad, mite. **1963** in 1982 Barrick *Coll.* **csPA**, *Mite*—small child. "Our little mite went to sleep already." **1967** *DARE* (Qu. Z12, *Nicknames and joking words meaning 'a small child': "He's a healthy little _____."*) Inf **PA**29, Mite.

mite v, hence ppl adj *mited* [Ger *meiden* to shun, avoid] *among Amish*

To shun.

1940 Writers' Program *Guide OH* 394, They [=the Amish] censure members who become proud or vain, and place the penalty of 'avoidance' upon all members who have relations with a banned or 'mited' member. **1947** *Time* 8 Dec 12 **PA**, To be "mited" means that a former good member of the Amish Church has gone astray from the Amish interpretation of the Bible, and although he may continue to sleep in Amish homes, he is shunned. Members are advised not to eat with the offender, to refrain from any business dealings or associations with him, and in general to disregard him.

miterwort n Also sp *mitrewort*

1 A plant of the genus *Mitella*, esp *M. diphylla*. [See quot 1979] Also called **bishop's cap, currant-leaf, false sanicle.** For other names of *M. diphylla* see **coolwort 2, fairy cup 1, fringe cup 1**

1848 Gray *Manual of Botany* 150, *Mitella.* . Mitre-wort. Bishop's-cap. . *M[itella] diphylla.* . Common Mitre-wort. **1892** IN Dept. Geol. & Nat. Resources *Rept. for 1891* 142, *Mitella diphylla.* . Mitrewort. Bishop's Cap. **1902** (1909) Mathews *Field Book Amer. Wild Flowers* 184, Mitrewort or Bishop's Cap. . . [T]he tiny white blossom has five petals beautifully fringed, which remind one of a highly ornamental snow crystal. **1937** St. John *Flora SE WA & ID* 184, *Mitella.* . Mitrewort. **1948** Wherry *Wild Flower Guide* 86, *Miterwort.* . . carpels maturing to a miter-shaped capsule, to which the common name refers. **1959** [see **2** below]. **1979** Niering–Olmstead *Audubon Guide N. Amer. Wildflowers*

E. Region 777, Miterwort. . . The common and genus names allude to the fruit, which has the shape of a small cap or bishop's miter.

2 =**false miterwort.**

1822 Eaton *Botany* 487, *Tiarella . . cordifolia* (miter-wort, gem-fruit). . Resembles the Mitella diphylla. **1832** MA Hist. Soc. *Coll.* 2d ser 9.157 **cwVT**, Tiarella cordifolia, Miter-wort. **1840** MA Zool. & Bot. Surv. *Herb. Plants & Quadrupeds* 46, *T[iarella] cordifolia* . . Mitre Wort. . . flowers yellowish-white in a long raceme; grows in woods with *M[itella] diphylla.* **1876** Hobbs *Bot. Hdbk.* 71, Mitre wort, Coolwort, Tiarella (Mitella) cordifolia. **1959** Carleton *Index Herb. Plants* 82, *Mitre-wort:* Mitella diphylla; . . Tiarella cordifolia.

3 A plant of the genus *Cynoctonum* native to the southeastern US.

1857 Gray *Manual of Botany* 174, *Mitreola . .* Mitre-Wort. . . [1 species:] *M. petiolata.* . . Damp soil, from Eastern Virginia southward. **1892** Coulter *Botany W. TX* 272, *Mitreola . .* Mitrewort. **1903** Small *Flora SE U.S.* 923, *Mitreola . .* Mitrewort. **1968** Radford et al. *Manual Flora Carolinas* 833, *Cynoctonum* [spp] . . Miterwort. **1970** Correll *Plants TX* 1202, *Cynoctonum* [spp] . . Miterwort. Hornpod.

mither See **mother** n[1]

mitsy n

A **mosquito** n[1] **B1.**

1968 *DARE* (Qu. R15a, . . *Names or nicknames . . for mosquitoes*) Inf **OH**70, Mitsy.

mitt n

1 See **mitten** n.

2 also *mit:* A hand, fist, or palm. [Abbr for *mitten*] **chiefly Nth, Midl, West** See Map

1896 (1898) Ade *Artie* 116 **IN**, I thought them was gloves you had on. Gee, is them your mits? **1901** Hobart *John Henry* 10 **NYC**, I'm sitting on the sofa with one mitt lying carelessly on the family album and the other bunched around a $1.70 cane. **c1938** in 1970 Hyatt *Hoodoo* 2.1568 **TN** [Black], See, dat's whut dey call *mittmen*, goin' an' tellin' fortunes. . . Dat means he goes in homes an' find people wants dere fortune told. Sometime he tell 'em by lookin' in de palm of dere han' or he tell 'em by card. **1942** Berrey–Van den Bark *Amer. Slang* 121.53, *Hands or fists* . . meat-hooks, mittens, mitts, mudhooks. **1965-70** *DARE* (Qu. X32, *Joking or uncomplimentary words for the hands . . "Those are mine. You keep your _____ [out of them]."*) 205 Infs, **chiefly Nth, Midl, West,** Mitts; **CA**122, **IL**43, **MI**75, **PA**131, **TX**28, **WA**22, 28, Big (*or* clammy, dirty, filthy, grubby) mitts.

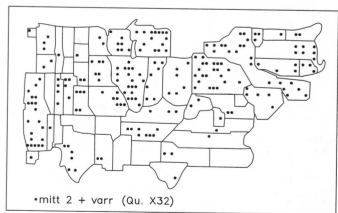

•mitt 2 + varr (Qu. X32)

mitten n Also rarely *mitt* [Prob joc var of *mittimus* a dismissal; cf *OED mittimus* sb. 2 "To get one's *mittimus:* to be dismissed" 1596–1857] **chiefly Nth, N Midl** See Map on p. 622 *somewhat old-fash* Cf **admittance, give one the; buttons, ~; bounce, ~; ditch, ~; dodge, ~; dust-off, ~; glove, ~; door B3; icy mitt**

A rejection or dismissal, usu by a woman of a man's invitation or a proposal of marriage—usu in phrr *give one the mitten, get the mitten.*

1842 Kirkland *Forest Life* 2.217 **MI**, I'm glad enough . . that Candace has given that young scamp the mitten! **1844** (1856) Neal *Peter Ploddy* 14 **ePA**, Young gentlemen that have got the mitten, or young gentlemen who think they are going to get the mitten, always sythe [=sigh]. **1846**

Knickerbocker 27.185, We do not affect the pinings of rejected suitors, in verse or prose. Ink is shed copiously for "mittens" by many of our correspondents. **1871** Eggleston *Hoosier Schoolmaster* 51 **sIN,** Young men were timidly asking girls if "they could see them safe home," which is the approved formula, and were trembling in mortal fear of "the mitten." **1891** Garland *Main-Travelled Roads* 207 **cwWI,** But he's goin' to get the mitten, that red-headed feller is, for I see a feller comin' up behind him. **1894** Freeman *Pembroke* 260 **NEng,** I wouldn't have a daughter of mine chasin' a fellar that had give her the mitten. **1899** (1912) Green *VA Folk-Speech* 284, *To get the mitten,* to receive only the mitten, instead of the hand; be refused as a lover. **1905** *DN* 3.14 **cCT,** 'To get the mitten' is to be jilted. **1907** *DN* 3.215 **nwAR,** "To get the mitten," to be jilted. **1910** *DN* 3.445 **wNY,** "To get the mitten," to have one's suit rejected. **1929** *AmSp* 5.124 **ME,** A young man paying attention to a girl was "shining up to her" and sometimes "got the mitten." **1937** Sandoz *Slogum* 205 **NE,** Tad Green promptly got the mitten from Annette. **1941** *LANE* Map 406 **NEng,** The map shows the expressions *(She) gave him the mitten, ~ the mitt* [1 inf], [etc]. These expressions . . may be used in four distinct senses: (1) 'She refused his proposal of marriage.' . . Even those expressions which are used in other senses . . have this meaning in most cases. (2) 'She jilted him. . . ' This sense is common only for the expression *She gave him the mitten.* . . (3) 'She dismissed him either before or after accepting his proposal of marriage.' This sense is given only for the expression *She gave him the mitten.* (4) 'She refused (on a particular occasion) to go with him to a party or dance.' This sense, often described as 'less serious' than the others, is given only for the expression *She gave him the mitten.* **1946** *PADS* 5.30 **VA,** *(Give someone) the mitten* . . : Jilt (someone); common. **1965–70** *DARE* (Qu. AA11, *If a man asks a girl to marry him and she refuses, . . she* _____) 29 Infs, **chiefly Nth, N Midl,** Gave (*or* give) him the mitten [24 of 29 Infs old]; (Qu. AA12, *If a man loses interest in a girl and stops seeing her . . he* _____) Inf **OH**78, Gave her the mitten; (Qu. II5b, *When you don't want to have anything to do with a certain person because you don't like him . . "I'd certainly like to give him the* _____.") Infs **CT**6, **IL**55, **KS**13, **MI**108, **NY**88, **PA**104, 126, **WA**18, Mitten [7 of 8 Infs old].

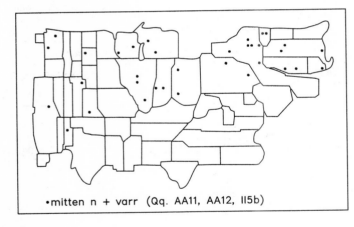

•mitten n + varr (Qq. AA11, AA12, II5b)

mitten v

1 To reject the invitation or marriage proposal of; to give (one) the **mitten** n; hence vbl n *mittening.* **Nth** *old-fash*

1873 (1875) Carleton *Farm Ballads* 19 **MI,** For me she mittened a lawyer, and several other chaps. **1878** (1887) Cooke *Happy Dodd* 289 **NEng,** You a'n't set downright on mittenin' of him then? **1881** (1883) Holmes *Madeline* 114 **NEng,** When she mittened him, it almost took his life. **1941** *LANE* Map 406 *(She gave him the mitten)* 13 infs, **chiefly ME, NH,** Mittened him. **1949** McDavid Coll. **cnNY,** Mitten v. = give the mitten. Male informant 94 years old.

2 with *on to:* To seize, grab.

1899 (1912) Green *VA Folk-Speech* 284, *Mitten on.* . . To sieze [sic] and hold fast. "When you get near enough mitten on to him."

mitten, give one the See **mitten** n

mittening See **mitten** v 1

mitten-kitten n

Prob a kitten having extra toes in the front paws.

1977 in 1982 Barrick Coll. **csPA,** *Mitten-kittens*—kittens born with double paws in front.

mitten money n

1975 Gould *ME Lingo* 182, *Mitten money*—Any kind of a tip, and sometimes a bribe: "I hear he gets more mitten money than salary out of that job." The term comes from an extra charge added to a regular pilot's fee during the winter months, when the added difficulties of navigation and the hardships of the season make it seem only fair.

mitten on to See **mitten** v 2

mitten tree n [From the shape of the leaf]

=sassafras.

1973 Kluger *Wild Flavor* 25 **sIN,** Young sassafras leaves are not all shaped alike . . many are shaped exactly like mittens. Who could pass by a "mitten tree" . . without stopping to search the branches for a matching pair of mitts? [**1984** *Horticulture* Sept 20, *Sassafras albidum* has . . leaves of three different shapes. . . A leaf may . . have a lobe on the left or the right side of the blade that makes it look like a mitten.]

mix bread v phr

To knead bread dough; also fig.

1942 Warnick *Garrett Co. MD* 10 **nwMD** (as of 1900–18), *Mix* . . to knead. . . She was mixing bread (i.e. dough). **1984** *DARE* File **RI** (as of 1930s), To be mixing bread—describing a cat (often purring): to push rhythmically with the front paws and claws against a blanket, clothing or human's body.

mixed bread n Also *half-mix bread* esp SC Cf **awendaw, half bread**

A bread made with a mixture of wheat and cornmeal or hominy.

1954 *PADS* 21.33 **SC,** *Mixed bread.* . . A bread made up of flour, mush or hominy, yeast, and various seasonings according to local tradition. Known and prized in Newberry, Lexington, Fairfield, Richland, and Saluda Counties. Product of the Dutch Fork. **1966–68** *DARE* (Qu. H14, *Bread that's made with cornmeal*) Inf **SC**26, Half-mix bread: lard, sugar, egg, milk, water, half wheat flour; (Qu. H18, . . *Special kinds of bread*) Inf **SC**56, Mixed bread.

mixed-breed n Also *mix-breed* chiefly Sth, S Midl, N Atl See Map Cf **breed** n

A person of mixed racial heritage.

1775 in 1916 *SC Hist. Mag.* 17.99, It was with difficulty I would get away . . after seeing his Indigo fields and Spiral Pumps, and breakfasting with his mixed breed daughters. **1965–70** *DARE* (Qu. HH29a, . . *People of mixed blood—part Indian*) 26 Infs, **chiefly Sth, S Midl, N Atl,** Mixed-breed; **IL**40, **LA**12, **MD**2, Mix-breed [24 of 29 Infs old]; (Qu. HH29b, . . *People of mixed blood—part Negro*) 20 Infs, **chiefly Sth, S Midl, N Atl,** Mixed-breed; **MD**2, **OH**70, Mix-breed [17 of 22 Infs old]; (Qu. HH28, *Names and nicknames . . for people of foreign background*) Inf **WV**21, Mixed-breed. **1986** Pederson *LAGS Concordance* **Gulf Region** *(A child born of a racially-mixed marriage)* 51 infs, (A) mix breed; 4 infs, Mix breeds; 23 infs, (A) mixed breed; 2 infs, Mixed breeds.

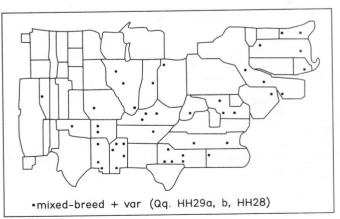

•mixed-breed + var (Qq. HH29a, b, HH28)

‡mixmux n Cf **mux** n[1]

1914 *DN* 4.110 **cKS,** *Mixmux.* . . Confusion; medley.

mixtry n Also sp *mixtery* [Var of *mixture*, prob infl by *-ry* state, condition] chiefly Sth, S Midl

A mixture.

1867 Harris *Sut Lovingood Yarns* 31 **TN,** Betts cooks up sum tarifyin mixtrys ove vittils. **a1883** (1911) Bagby *VA Gentleman* 306, Doubled and twisted, and tied, and turned, and tacked, and tangled into forty-'leven thousand double bow-knots. By jings! it was a mixtery. **1888** Johnston *Mr. Absalom Billingslea* 220 **GA,** Whar's your cousin Sally in all this mixtry an' minglin' up o' men an' childern, women an' boys? **1899** Chesnutt *Conjure Woman* 151 **NC** [Black], I'll gib you some kin' er mixtry fer ter make 'im fergit. **1909** *DN* 3.349 **eAL, wGA,** **1927** *DN* 5.475 **Ozarks,** This hyar puddin's jes' a kinder mixtry like. **1928** Peterkin *Scarlet Sister Mary* 124 **SC** [Gullah], I ain' never seen no man get loose from a 'oman what wears dis mixtry. **1937** *Hall Coll.* cwTN, *Mixtry.* . . A mixture. "A mixtry of purple and white Rhododendron." **1939** *FWP Guide TN* 458, The "mixtry" is eaten with a knife or sopped up with a biscuit. **1942** Hall *Smoky Mt. Speech* 79 **wNC, eTN,** *Mixture,* in several instances ['mɪkstrɪ]. **c1960** *Wilson Coll.* csKY, *Mixture* [mɪk-strɪ], rare. **1962** Faulkner *Reivers* 294 **MS,** Both act like the mixtry of the other just makes it worse. **1986** Pederson *LAGS Concordance,* 1 inf, **cLA,** Mixtry = mixture + mystery—coined by black man.

mixy-maxy adj [Scots, Engl dial; cf *EDD, OED* (at *mixty-maxty*)] Cf **mixmux**

Mixed up, confused.

1960 Williams *Walk Egypt* 123 **GA,** Toy was glad and sorry too—how could a mind be so mixy-maxy?

Miz See **Mrs.**

mize v [Back-formation from *miser*]

To act like a miser; to hoard (money).

1970 *DARE* FW Addit **TN,** Mize—to act like a miser, to hoard one's money. **1991** Still *Wolfpen Notebooks* 154 **sAppalachians,** "How much money have you mized?" he asked.

Mizres See **Mrs.**

mizry See **misery**

mizzel See **mizzle** v[2]

‡**mizzen** n

1901 *DN* 2.144 **csNY,** *Mizzen.* . . A spirit, imp. "It was just as if a sprite or a little mizzen had bobbed up beside me, whistled my tune, and disappeared again into the dark."

mizzery See **misery**

mizzil See **mizzle** v[2]

mizzle v[1] [*OED* 1483 →] **chiefly Sth, S Midl**

To rain in very fine drops; also fig; hence ppl adj *mizzling* drizzly; n *mizzling* =**mizzle** n.

1838 Kettell *Yankee Notions* 106, Who loved to hear roast mutton sizzling,/ And good fat cheer on all sides mizzling. **1843** (1916) Hall *New Purchase* 123 **sIN,** The rain kept mizzling away. **1858** in 1966 Boller *MO Fur Trader* 144, Cloudy and mizzling. **1899** (1912) Green *VA Folk-Speech* 285, *Mizzle.* . . To rain in very fine drops; drizzle. . . *Mizzling.* . . A thick mist of fine rain; a mist. **1952** Brown *NC Folkl.* 1.565, *Mizzle.* . . To rain in fine or foglike drops. **1954** *Harder Coll.* cwTN, *Mizzle.* . . Of rain: fall mistily. **c1960** *Wilson Coll.* csKY, *Mizzle.* **1966** *DARE* (Qu. B21, *When fine drops of moisture are falling . . it's doing what?*) Inf NM11, Mizzlin': too heavy for a mist, not enough for a drizzle—usage not widespread. **1971** *Down East* Nov 68 **ME,** What we had were temperatures in the fifties and a mizzling rain. **1976** Garber *Mountain-ese* 58 **sAppalachians,** It ain't rainin' much, jist a mizzlin' uv fallin' weather. **1986** Pederson *LAGS Concordance* (A steady drizzle) 1 inf, **cwFL,** Mizzling—has heard people say this; 1 inf, **neMS,** Miz-zling—her neighbor used to say, = drizzling.

mizzle n [**mizzle** v[1]; for adj *mizzlety* cf Intro "Language Changes" I.8] **chiefly Sth, S Midl** Cf **dry drizzle**

A very fine or misty rain; hence adjs *mizzly, mizzlety* misty, drizzly.

1899 (1912) Green *VA Folk-Speech* 285, *Mizzle.* . . Fine rain. *Ibid, Mizzly.* . . Misty; drizzly. **1909** *DN* 3.349 **eAL, wGA,** *Mizzlety, adj.* Drizzling. **1923** *DN* 5.215 **swMO,** *Mizzle.* . . Falling mist, a light rain. **1953** Randolph–Wilson *Down in Holler* 265 **Ozarks,** *Mizzle.* . . A very light shower, also called a *dry drizzle* or a *mizzlin'* rain. **1954** *Harder Coll.* cwTN, *Mizzle.* . . A steady, misty rain. **1975** *DARE* File csTX, Mizzle—a cross between a mist and a drizzle. I have never heard it used anywhere except in Texas, and very seldom here. **1984** Wilder *You All Spoken Here* 141 **Sth,** *Mizzly:* Less precipitation per hour than in a sizzle sozzle. **1986** Pederson *LAGS Concordance* (A steady drizzle) 1 inf, **ceGA,** Mizzle.

mizzle v[2] Also sp *mizzel, mizzil* [*OED* mizzle v.[2] 1781 →] *old-fash*

To depart in haste, abscond.

1845 *NY Herald* (NY) 14 May [2/1], The Southern men, say they, will spend their last cent here; whilst the Northern and Eastern men, if they had won, would have buttoned up their pockets and "mizzled." **1848** Bartlett *Americanisms* 227, *To mizzle.* To run away; to abscond. A low word. **1855** Wise *Tales Marines* 15, You don't larn your lessons . . nor go to chapel either, you dam little wharf rats! I've written to the Hon. Soketary of the Navy to send you off to sea; so mizzle. **1867** Harris *Sut Lovingood Yarns* 82 **TN,** All this waked the ole hoss, an' he fotch one rar, one kiek, an' then he went—he jis' mizzel'd, skar'd. *Ibid* 103, The chokin roun' his naik, an' the steel trap sprung ontu his tail, did discum-fort 'im pow'ful. He jis' mizzild. **1899** (1912) Green *VA Folk-Speech* 285, *Mizzle.* . . To disappear suddenly; decamp; run off. **1932** Tooné *Yankee Slang* 26, *Mizzle:* Clear off, vacate, vanish.

mizzle v[3] [*OED* mizzle v.[3] "Obs. exc. dial. rare"; perh infl by *misled*, pronc ['mɪzļd]] *esp Sth*

To confuse, muddle; hence ppl adjs *mizzled, mizzling* confused, muddled.

1938 Matschat *Suwannee R.* 289 **neFL, seGA,** Mizzle [sic]: muddled or confused. **1942** *AmSp* 17.171 **sIL,** *To mizzle.* . . The writer's inform-ant used it in the sense of 'to confuse' or 'to muddle.' **1950** Faulkner *Stories* 28 **MS,** Why He should turn around for the poor, mizzling souls of men that can't even borrow tools in time to replace the shingles on His church, I don't know either. **1984** Wilder *You All Spoken Here* 5 **Sth,** *Mizzled:* Muddled.

mizzlety See **mizzle** n

mizzle-witted adj [Cf **mizzle** v[3]]

Mentally dull, witless, stupid.

1935 Porter *Flowering Judas* 171, A starved-looking woman in a blackish gray dress, and a jaundiced man with red-rimmed eyes, and their mizzle-witted boy.

mizzling ppl adj[1], n See **mizzle** v[1]

mizzling ppl adj[2] See **mizzle** v[3]

mizzly See **mizzle** n

Mizzoura(h) See **Missouri**

mo' See **more**

moan n

1 also *moaning, moon:* The sound a cow or calf makes. Cf **moonie** n[2], **mourn** v 2

1948 Davis *Word Atlas Gt. Lakes* 227, *Name for loud sound made by cow when calf is taken away.* . . 1 inf, **cwOH,** moan, moon. **1965–70** *DARE* (Qu. K19, *Noise made by a calf that's taken away from its mother*) Infs CA193, KY32, Moan; **FL21,** Moaning; (Qu. K21, *The noise a cow makes, calling for her calf*) Inf AR47, Moan. **1966** Dakin *Dial. Vocab. Ohio R. Valley* 2.250 **KY, ceOH,** (Soft noise made by cows) . . moan. **1986** Pederson *LAGS Concordance* (Gentle noise made by a cow during feeding time) 10 infs, **Gulf Region,** Moan(ing).

2 A mournful song, esp a blues song. *among Black speakers* Cf **moan** v 2

1926 in 1983 Taft *Blues Lyric Poetry* 126 **Chicago IL,** [Title:] That Black Snake Moan. **1928** *Ibid* 274 **Memphis TN,** [Title:] Bessie's Moan. **1929** *Ibid* 94 **NYC,** [Title:] Levee Camp Moan. **1939** *FWP Guide TN* 143, There is a large group of regular Negro church songs known as "moans" because they are pitched in the sing-song fashion of prayer or grief.

moan v [By ext of *moan* to lament] **chiefly Sth** *among Black speakers*

1 To hum, usu in chorus, as part of a church service; hence vbl n *moaning*.

1942 in 1959 Lomax *Rainbow Sign* 187 **nMS** [Black], The old women "moan" the hymn into silence. **1942** Jones *Eve's Stepchildren* 106 [Black], The preacher finished his sermon with a shout and a flourish. The congregation moaned and chanted. **1942** (1965) Parrish *Slave Songs* 35 **GA coast,** The "moaning" (as the peculiarly beautiful humming of the Negroes is called) takes on an elemental quality. **1977** Dillard *Lexicon* 54 [Black], Either a deacon or the preacher will deliver prayers, accompanied by a *moaning* backdrop. **1986** Pederson *LAGS Concor-dance,* 1 inf, **nwMS,** Moaning—humming the sermon. [Inf Black]

2 To sing (a blues song); hence n *moaner*. Cf **moan** n **2**

1927 in 1983 Taft *Blues Lyric Poetry* 28 **Chicago IL,** My mind's all churned up : that's why I'm all confused / That's the reason why : I'm moaning these brownskin mama blues. **1927** Sandburg *Amer. Songbag* 232 [Black], It [=*"*Got Dem Blues"] was moaned by resonant moaners in honky tonks of the southwest. *Ibid* 234, This blues was sung in honky tonks of the southwest in years before the appearance of "mean moaners" in cafes where a tuxedo is requisite. **1932** *AmSp* 7.247, Clara Smith evidently deems it a mark of distinction to be known as 'The World's Greatest Moaner.' **1934** in 1983 Taft *Blues Lyric Poetry* 231 **NYC,** [Title:] Moanin' the Blues.

moana n[1] |mo'ɑnɑ| [Haw] **HI** Cf **kai** n, adv

The ocean.

1972 Carr *Da Kine Talk* 88 **HI,** *Hawaiian Words Commonly Heard In Hawaii's English. . . Moana.* Ocean. **1984** Sunset *HI Guide* 85, *Moana*—ocean. **1994** *DARE* File **HI** (as of 1967), In Honolulu directions are generally given as [mo'ɑnɑ] or [mɑ'kai] meaning "toward the ocean," and ['mɑʊkɑ] meaning "toward the mountains."

moana n[2], **moana kea** See **moano**

moan around v phr [Cf *moon around*]

To go about in a depressed or melancholy mood; to mope.

1932 Stong *State Fair* 31 **IA,** I knew I didn't want to marry you all the time, but you moaned around so that I tried to think I loved you. **1969** *DARE* FW Addit **OR,** Moan around—to act depressed.

moaner n[1] See also **moaners' bench**

Prob =**mourner.**

1927 Kennedy *Gritny* 61 **sLA** [Black], The soothing melody of "Po' Moanuh got a Home at Las'." [*Ibid* 118, Dey . . wan' try an' make Aun' Amy git out an' walk to de grave-side, leadin' de moaners.] **1927** Adams *Congaree* 25 **cSC** [Black], Hell was full of moaners and prayer leaders and deacons from all the churches.

moaner n[2] See **moan** v **2**

moaners' bench n [Pronc-sp or folk-etym for **mourners' bench;** cf **moaner** n[1]] **chiefly Sth, S Midl**

1929 (1951) Faulkner *Sartoris* 24 **MS** [Black], Sinner riz fum de moaner's bench. **1954** *Harder Coll.* **cwTN,** *Moaner's bench.* . . *Mourner's bench.* (*Moaner's* common, *mourner's* occasional). **1968** *State* (Raleigh, N.C.) 1 Aug. 11/2 (*Mathews Coll.*), When the sinners finally did get to the moaners bench, they were prayed over long and loud. **1988** *Lincoln Avenue* 25 **wNC** (as of c1940) [Black], When it was all over, those who had tarried faithfully on the moaners' bench until they finally got religion were marched down to the river and baptized.

moaning vbl n See **moan** v **1**

moaning n See **moan** n **1**

moaning bird n [See quot 1972] **HI**

A shearwater.

1944 Munro *Birds HI* 21, *Wedge-tailed Shearwater.* . . *Other names . . Moaning Bird (Midway).* [*Ibid* 22, Its cry is a series of moans, groans, snores and wails, with an intense weird effect when a large number of birds are performing.] **1972** Berger *Hawaiian Birdlife* 45, Beginning shortly after dusk, the adults [of *Puffinus pacificus*] emit a wide variety of moans, groans, and wails, as do many of the other shearwaters. . . Because of these weird calls, which continue throughout most of the night, these species often are referred to as moaning birds. **1977** Udvardy *Audubon Field Guide Birds* 344, Shearwaters. . . are the "Moaning Birds" that sailors on South Sea islands heard after dusk as the birds sat outside their burrows and wailed and yammered in territorial disputes.

moaning dove n

1 =**ground dove.**

1944 Hausman *Amer. Birds* 344, *Eastern Ground Dove. . . Other Names*—Moaning Dove, Mourning Dove. . . *Notes*—Soft, plaintive cooings. **1951** *AmSp* 26.93, Some people call our common dove the *mourning dove.* . . Those deeming the note mournful emphasize that significance in the adjective *moanin'* (N.C.) . . Parallel usage affects names of the ground dove, witness *moanin' dove* (Fla., Ga.) **1955** Forbush–May *Birds* 255, *Eastern Ground Dove.* . . Their soft cooing notes are a characteristic sound in their Florida haunts and have given the bird the local name of 'Mourning Dove' or 'Moaning Dove,' as it is often pronounced, but when seen the bird should never be confused with the real Mourning Dove. **1968** *DARE* (Qu. Q7, *Names and nicknames for . .*

game birds) Inf **GA**35, Moanin' dove ['monɪn] . . called the moanin' dove because he moans.

2 A **mourning dove 1** (here: *Zenaida macroura*).

1949 Sprunt–Chamberlain *SC Bird Life* 288, Eastern Mourning Dove. . . *Zenaidura macroura carolinensis.* . . Local Names: Turtle Dove; Carolina Dove; "Moaning" Dove. **1951** [see **1** above].

moano n Also *moano kea, moana (~)* [Haw *moano* (+ *kea* white)] **HI**

A **goatfish 1,** usu *Parupeneus bifasciatus* or *P. multifasciatus.*

1926 Pan-Pacific Research Inst. *Jrl.* 1.1.10, Upeneus chryseredros . . Moana Kea. . . Upeneus multifasciatus . . Moana. **1933** John G. Shedd Aquarium *Guide* 114, The Moana is one of the most abundant of the Hawaiian fishes and is always found in the markets there. **1960** Gosline–Brock *Hawaiian Fishes* 191, *Parupeneus chryserydros* (Moano kea)—The purplish coloration and bright yellow saddle on the caudal peduncle will immediately distinguish this species. The extremely long snout, small eye, and long barbels are also distinctive. *Ibid* 192, *Parupeneus multifasciatus* (Moano). **1967** *Honolulu Star–Bulletin* (HI) 31 May sec F 1/4, Moana—Goatfish. This one is salmon-colored with black spots. . . Fry.

moashi See **moshey**

‡**moat** n

1969 *DARE* (Qu. N44, *In a town, the strip of grass and trees between the sidewalk and the curb*) Inf **NY**198, Moat.

mobbing sparrow n [From its behavior in groups] =**English sparrow.**

1923 Dawson *Birds CA* 1.223, English Sparrow. . . Gamin. Hoodlum. Mobbing Sparrow. [*Ibid* 227, It discourages and drives out desirable native species by continual annoyance and by the employment of mob tactics.]

mobile v

To run or move fast.

1938 *AmSp* 13.6 **seAR,** *Mobile.* . . To move rapidly. 'The horse mobiled along down the road.' **1970** *DARE* (Qu. Y20, *To run fast: "You should have seen him _____!"*) Inf **CA**205, Mobile away.

mobilized dandruff See **galloping dandruff**

moccasin n Also sp *mocasine, mocassin, moccason, moccos(s)on, mockason*

1 Any of var snakes, as: see below. [Appar from *moccasin* shoe, of AmInd origin, but the connection has not been satisfactorily explained] Cf **water moccasin**

a also *moccasin snake:* Either of two related venomous snakes: **copperhead snake 1** or **cottonmouth.** Cf **black moccasin, dryland ~, highland ~, spreadhead ~, stumptail ~**

1765 (1942) Bartram *Diary of a Journey* 5 Aug **SC,** We killed a Mocasine snake & toward noon it rained & thundred exceedingly. **1784** Smyth *Tour U.S.A.* 1.148, The more silent and dangerous moccossons also abound, especially in and near the swamps. **1784** (1929) Filson *Kentucke* 27, The horned and the mockason snakes. **1788** Schöpf *Reise Staaten* 1.485, Ich habe mich überall nach der Klapperschlange und dem Kupferbauch (Copper belly, auch Moccoson-Snake genannt,) . . erkundiget. [=I gathered information everywhere about the rattlesnake and the copperbelly (Copper belly, also called Moccoson snake).] **1791** Bartram *Travels* 272, The moccasin snake is a large and horrid serpent . . , and there are very terrifying stories related of him by the inhabitants of the Southern states, where they greatly abound, particularly in East Florida: that their bite is always incurable [etc]. *Ibid* 273, There is another snake in Carolina and Florida called the moccasin, very different from this, which is a very beautiful creature, and I believe not of a destructive or vindictive nature. **1832** in 1868 McCall *Letters Frontiers* 259, On reaching the spot, I found a large *moccason* or *cotton-mouth* snake writhing on the ground, with its head crushed . . but there it stood . . disclosing the whole of the interior of his immense dead-white, or, as it is well named, "cotton-mouth." **1894** U.S. Natl. Museum *Proc.* 17.330, In a cypress swamp a few miles south of Kissimmee, Osceola County, I killed a big moccasin (*Agkistrodon piscivorus*), and found in its oesophagus a smaller snake which it had probably just swallowed. **1906** *DN* 3.132 **nwAR,** Cottonmouth. . . A kind of moccasin snake. **1922** Gonzales *Black Border* 313 **sSC, GA coasts** [Gullah glossary], *Moccasin*—water-moccasin, a venomous snake. **1928** Baylor Univ. Museum *Contrib.* 16.6, The venomous Cottonmouth (*Agkistrodon piscivorus* . .) and Copperhead (*Agkistrodon mokasen* . .) snakes are the true Moccasins; but informed [sic] persons always call the harmless water snakes of the genus *Natrix* by the same name and believe them to be poisonous. **1933** Cheley *Camping Out* 206, The moccasins are not so easy. There are two kinds: the water-moccasin, or cotton-mouth, . . and the copperhead, which is the highland, or northern moccasin, or pilot snake. **1958** Harper *Travels William Bartram* 566, [In reference to quot 1791 above:] Moccasin, harmless. . . The name, size, shape, reputation, and to some extent the colors . . fit the Southern Water Snake (*Natrix sipedon fasciata*). . . Moccasin snake, poisonous: Cottonmouth (*Agkistrodon piscivorus* . .) **1961** Douglas *My Wilderness* 85 AZ, Arizona has some poisonous snakes—at least eight species of rattlesnake, the Mexican moccasin snake, and the coral snake. **1965–70** *DARE* (Qu. P25, . . *Kinds of snakes*) 105 Infs, **chiefly Sth, S Midl**, Moccasin(s); **AR55**, Moccasin or blunt-tail; **GA89**, Moccasin—poisonous; **LA10**, All the moccasins are poison except the fish moccasin; **LA15**, [The] copperhead is classed as a moccasin; **LA40**, Moccasin snake—there are different kinds; **MS60**, Moccasins—poison; **VA70**, Moccasin. [*DARE* Ed: Some of these Infs may refer instead to **2** below.] **1970** *DARE* Tape **AR56**, There's still a lot of moccasin snakes on it [=Moccasin Creek]. . . That's where it got its name. **1970** *DARE* FW Addit **VA70**, Moccasins given much respect in these parts. One neighbor of Inf wouldn't put up yard shrubs because she lives close to a creek and moccasins might get in shrubbery and bite children. Some men won't fish in some fishing holes because of moccasins. **1976** Brown *Gloss. Faulkner* 131, The general tendency among people who know snakes in Faulkner's country is to reserve the name *moccasin* (or *water moccasin* . .) for the venomous snake and to call the others water snakes. . . (Such usages are highly localized. In Georgia, for instance, the distinction is usually between moccasins [which are harmless] and cotton-mouth moccasins [which are venomous]. **1981** Pederson *LAGS Basic Materials* **Gulf Region**, 68 infs, Moccasin(s); 1 inf, Moccasins are the poisonous snakes, really; 1 inf, [The] moccasins was thick; 1 inf, He'd stomp them moccasins' heads off.

b also with modifier: **=water snake** (here: *Nerodia* spp). Cf **fish moccasin, gray ~, saltwater ~, striped ~**

1791 [see **1a** above]. **1853** Baird–Girard *N. Amer. Reptiles* 1.166, Mocassin (*N[erodia] sip[edon]* and *N. fasc[iata]*). **1859** Colton *Mt. Scenery* 101 **NC**, The moccasin of the mountains is not considered poisonous; and a gentleman told me he had seen the Indians let them bite their feet, and no bad result ensued. **1882** IN Dept. Geol. & Nat. Resources *Rept. for 1881* 508, Under the impression that it [=*Nerodia sipedon*] is poisonous it is greatly feared by many people, who suppose it to be the same as the poisonous moccasin of the Southern rivers. This is a mistake, and the name moccasin ought not to be applied to our species. **1928** [see **1a** above]. c**1940** Newman–Murphy *Conserv. Notes* 5 **neLA**, There are many and varied reptiles in the parish. Among the . . snakes may be mentioned, the . . yellow-belly moccasin, water snake and small viper. **1949** Dickinson *Lizards & Snakes* WI 48, An extremely vicious species [=*Natrix sipedon*] [is] often given the name "moccasin" though it is harmless. It is found all over the state. The snake reaches over three feet in length. **1958** [see **1a** above]. **1965–70** *DARE* (Qu. P25, . . *Kinds of snakes*) Infs **IL104, MI105, OH65, 72**, Moccasin; **LA10**, All the moccasins are poison except the fish moccasin; **NC21**, Red-bellied moccasin; **OK52**, Spotted moccasin; **PA27**, Moccasin snake—not poisonous; striped black, white, and brown; small; **SC40**, Water snake [same as] copperbelly moccasin—harmless; **TX9**, Three moccasins: copperhead, cottonmouth, water; **TX19**, Speckled moccasin; **VA26**, Water snake = moccasin; **VA41**, Green moccasin. **1976** [see **1a** above]. **1981** Pederson *LAGS Basic Materials* **Gulf Region**, 1 inf, Moccasins (different from cottonmouth); 1 inf, Brown moccasins; 1 inf, Striped moccasin.

c A **black racer 1**. Cf **blacksnake 1**
1966 *DARE* (Qu. P25, . . *Kinds of snakes*) Inf **NH4**, Blacksnake— some call them moccasins, but they aren't real moccasins.

2 A fish, as:

a **=pumpkinseed**.
a**1848** (1954) Foster *Jeffersonian Amer.* 220, The great River Susquehannah, famous for canvass-back ducks, and mocassins, a delicious little round fish caught on the stream. **1859** (1968) Bartlett *Americanisms* 275, Moccason Fish. The sun-fish of Maryland. **1884** U.S. Natl. Museum *Bulletin* 27.463, *Lepomis gibbosus*. . . Pumpkin-seed . . Moccasin. **1902** *Jrl. Amer. Folkl.* 15.248, After the *moccasin* have been named . . the moccasin fish (Maryland sun-fish), [and the] moccasin-snake (the water-*moccasin* . . and the upland *moccasin*. . .)

b Prob **=eel catfish**.
1981 Pederson *LAGS Basic Materials*, 1 inf, **cTX**, Moccasin—fish which resembles snake. **1989** Flynt *Poor But Proud* 33 **ceAL** (as of

c1860), Thar was a moccasin tuk out of it [=the Tallapoosa River] longer than my arm. And nobody wouldn't have it, but Jim. As we was goin' home, Jim a totin' the fish, ses I—Jim, you ain't a gwine to eat that cat [=catfish] surely! Ses he—'pshaw! that moccasin warn't nothing'; I noticed it good, and it warn't rotten a bit.

3 See **moccasin flower**.

moccasin flower n Also *moccasin (plant)* Also sp *moccasine, moccason flower, mockasine ~, molkasin ~* [From the shape of the flower] **chiefly NEast, Gt Lakes** See Map **=lady's slipper 1**.
1680 in 1688 Ray *Historiæ Plantarum* 2.1926, Helleborine flore rotundo luteo, purpureis venis striato. *The Mockasine flower.* **1700** Plukenet *Almagesti* 101, Helleborine *Virginiana*. . . The Molkasin Flower. **1739** (1946) Gronovius *Flora Virginica* 111, *Cypripedium* foliis ovato-lanceolatis. . . *Moccasine.* **1784** in 1785 Amer. Acad. Arts & Sci. *Memoirs* 1.487, Lady's Slipper. . . Catesby says, the flowers of this plant . . were in great esteem with the Indians for decking their hair. They called it the *Moccasin Flower.* **1848** Gray *Manual of Botany* 477, *Cypripedium* [spp] . . Lady's Slipper. . . Also called *Moccason-flower.* **1848** in 1850 Cooper *Rural Hours* 111 **NY**, We found also a little troop of moccasin plants in flower. **1864** *Catalogue of Herbs* **swME**, Moccasin or Valerian—Cypripedium acaule. **1897** IN Dept. Geol. & Nat. Resources *Rept. for 1896* 610, *C[ypripedium] hirsutum*. . . Moccasin Flower. **1902** *Jrl. Amer. Folkl.* 15.248, After the *moccasin* are named the following: Moccasin-flower . . (*Cypripedium*) or moccasin-plant. **1941** Walker *Lookout* 52 **seTN**, Yellow and pink moccasin flowers . . are hiding in cool gulches where few people go. **1950** Correll *Native Orchids* 21, The Pink Moccasin-flower is one of the earliest flowering of our eastern orchids. **1965–70** *DARE* (Qu. S26c) Infs **MN2, 36, 38, MA67, 78, NJ55**, Moccasin flower(s); **ID5**, Moccasin plant; **NC36**, Pink moccasin flower; **WI58**, Indian moccasins; (Qu. S22) Inf **TN36**, Moccasin flower; (Qu. S24) Inf **NY142**, Moccasin; (Qu. S26a) Infs **RI15, VA11**, Moccasin flower; (Qu. S26b) Inf **MI31**, Moccasin flower; **MI53**, Pink moccasin, yellow moccasin; (Qu. S26e) Infs **MN11, MA68**, Moccasin flower. **1965–70** *DARE* Wildfl QR Pl.29 Infs **AR45, MN14, NY91**, Moccasin flower; Pl.30 Infs **MI31, NY91**, Moccasin flower; Pl.31 Infs **MN37, NY91, NC36, WI80**, Moccasin flower; **OH14**, Moccasin; Pl.33 Inf **OH14**, Pink moccasin; **MI57, MN37**, Moccasin flower; **NY91**, Pink moccasin flower. **1968** *PA Game News* May 51 **PA**, Even the most case-hardened outdoorsman will stoop to admire . . stately pink moccasin flowers beneath the hemlocks. . . [and] consider the strangely formed blooms of the . . moccasin flower. **1982** Barrick *Coll.* **csPA**, Moccasin—Lady's slipper. **1987** Case *Orchids* 71, Pink Lady's-slipper, Stemless Lady's-slipper, Moccasin-flower—*Cypripedium acaule.*

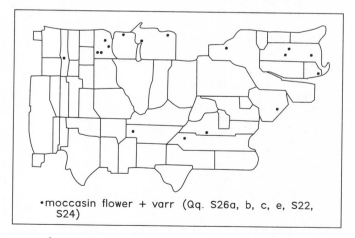

•moccasin flower + varr (Qq. S26a, b, c, e, S22, S24)

moccasin mouth n
Prob a **turtlehead**.
1968 *DARE* (Qu. S26b, *Wildflowers that grow in water or wet places*) Inf **GA35**, Moccasin mouth.

moccasin pie n Cf **flip-over pie, half-moon pie**
1982 Slone *How We Talked* 58 **eKY** (as of c1950), Dried apples. . . were used most for to make fried apple pies, also called "moon pies," "moccasin pies" or "flip overs."

moccasin plant See **moccasin flower**
moccasin snake See **moccasin 1a**

moccasin telegraph n **chiefly NW** Cf **mukluk telegraph,** *DCan*

The informal means by which news is spread in American Indian communities.

1927 *Sat. Eve. Post* 23 July 3 **AK,** That agency known to white men as the Moccasin Telegraph, by which odd bits of news are flashed from one isolated native camp to another. **1931** *Jrl. Amer. Folkl.* 44.3 **nID,** These children are the "moccasin telegraph" by which the coming play party is announced. **1956** Morenus *AK Sourdough* 224, Here it was again, thought Slim, that impossible thing of the Indian, like the dogs, knowing something that had taken place miles away with no apparent means of communication. "Moccasin telegraph," the old-timers called it. **1958** Blasingame *Dakota Cowboy* 183 **SD,** I . . heard all the news that traveled by moccasin telegraph. **1984** Doig *English Creek* 150 **nMT,** Toussaint's words signaled what I had never dreamt of: moccasin telegraph had the story of my sashay with Stanley. **1989** Lesley *River Song* 35 **cnOR,** The man looked at the four empty ladders. "Those wetbacks sure cleared out fast." "The Taco Telegraph," Danny said, and chuckled, because people were always saying Indians got word of things by the Moccasin Telegraph.

moccason See **moccasin**

moccason flower See **moccasin flower**

moccos(s)on See **moccasin**

mochila n, also pl Also sp *machilla, mochiler* [Span] **West old-fash** Cf **macheer**

A saddle cover, often with pockets.

1856 *Harper's New Mth. Mag.* 13.594 **OR,** He rode a heavy black mule with bearskin *machillas.* **1857** in 1941 *AmSp* 16.262 **CA,** The *mochilas* (vulgarly called 'mecheers') are a pair of leather flaps, each about two feet wide by three feet long, which are tied together and used as a cover for the saddle-tree in riding. **1900** Drannan *31 Yrs.* 167 **SW,** A measly redskin shot me through the calf of my leg, pinning me to the mochila of my saddle. The mochila is a large covering for a saddle made of very heavy leather and comes low on the horse's side, thereby affording great protection to horses in cases like this. This shield is of Spanish origin, but they were used by all mountaineers as well as Mexicans. **1913** Bradley *Story of Pony Express* 58 **West** (as of 1860), The *mochila* had four pockets called *cantinas* in each of its corners. **1936** Adams *Cowboy Lingo* 48, A leather covering that fitted over the saddle in one piece . . was a 'macheer,' or 'mochiler.' **1941** Fisher *Illusion* 93 **NV** (as of 1860s), A fresh horse was led out, a mochila stamped Overland Pony Express was thrown on the beast, and the rider was gone. **1982** Heat Moon *Blue Highways* 197 **NV** (as of c1860), The only baggage the boys carried—in addition to the mail mochila—was a kit of flour, cornmeal, and bacon, and a medical pack of turpentine, borax, and cream of tartar.

mock v Usu |mɑk, mɔk|; also |mɑrk| Pronc-spp *mark, mawk, mork*

A Forms.

1899 (1912) Green *VA Folk-Speech* 285, *Mock.* . . Mork, or mawk. To imitate, to mimic. To make sport of by mimicry, ridicule or sarcasm; deride. **1909** *DN* 3.348 **eAL, wGA,** *Mark.* . . To mock. Heard also in marking-bird. **1914** *DN* 4.110 **cKS,** *Mark.* . . To mock. **1934** Hurston *Jonah's Gourd Vine* 173 **AL** [Black], John preached the sermon himself . . and he aped the gestures of the preacher so accurately that the crowd hung half-way between laughter and awe. "You kin mark folks," said Blue. "Dass jes' lak dat preacher fuh de world." **1941** *AmSp* 16.120, In the [Shenandoah] Valley may occasionally be heard such grim pronunciations as . . [mɑɚk] for *mock.*

B Sense.

To mimic, imitate (esp a person's speech or an animal's call); to lure (an animal) by imitating its call. **chiefly Sth, S Midl**

1899 [see **A** above]. **1917** *DN* 4.415 **wNC, IL,** *Mimic.* . . To represent. "That mimics him right smart." . . *Mock.* . =mimic. **1934** [see **A** above]. **1939** Hall *Coll.* **wNC,** He was crippled in a accident and she mocked his way of walkin'. **c1960** Wilson *Coll.* **csKY,** *Mock.* . . To mimic. **1966** *DARE* (Qu. K83, *To call a calf to you at feeding time*) Inf **SC19,** Mock them. **1967** *DARE* Tape **LA3,** I have heard boys that could just mock these different type dogs' voices and almost sound like the race themselves. **1975** McDonough *Garden Sass* 278 **AR,** He got two turkeys, using a leaf to mock them on. *Ibid* 279, We saw a Stone Age Indian tribe in Brazil that hunted fowl by mocking them on leaves, so this must be a very old practice. **1986** Pederson *LAGS Concordance,* 1

inf, **cnFL,** I couldn't mock him [=imitate, of horse noise]; 1 inf, **cMS,** Mock it [i.e., imitate].

mock n Pronc-sp *mauck* [*OED* a1460 →]

An object of ridicule or contempt—usu in phrr *make (a) mock of* to treat with contempt or derision, make a mockery of.

1851 (1857) Hawthorne *Twice-Told* 2.265 **NEng,** My own shadow makes a mock of my fooleries! **1942** Thomas *Blue Ridge Country* 192 **NC,** Becaze he made mauck of Pol Gentry. **1953** *PADS* 19.12 **sAppalachians,** *Mock.* . . Butt of ridicule. "Homer made a mock of me right before the whole school." **1954** *Harder Coll.* **cwTN,** *Mock.* . . Butt of ridicule.

mock apple n

1 A **wild cucumber** (here: *Echinocystis lobata*).

1903 Small *Flora SE U.S.* 1139, *Mock Apple.* . . *Micrampeles* [sic] *lobata.* . . In woods along streams. . . Summer and fall. **1910** Shreve *MD Plant Life* 486, *Micrampelis lobata.* . . Mock Apple. . . Throughout the state; in open situations. **1940** Clute *Amer. Plant Names* 107, *E[chinocystis] lobata.* . . Mock apple. **1959** Carleton *Index Herb. Plants* 82, *Mock-apple:* Echinocystis lobata.

2 See **mock mayapple.**

mockasine flower See **moccasin flower**

mockason See **moccasin**

mock azalea n

Std: a plant of the genus *Menziesia.* For other names of var spp see **fool's huckleberry, minniebush**

mockbird See **mockingbird 1, 2**

mock bishop('s) weed See **bishop's weed 2**

mockboard See **mopboard**

mock cucumber n Also *wild mock cucumber* **chiefly West**

A **wild cucumber** (here: *Echinocystis lobata*).

1948 Stevens *KS Wild Flowers* 323, *Wild Mock Cucumber.* . . The vines . . make a sightly coverage for trellises, arbors, low walls, and wire fences. **1952** Davis *Flora ID* 657, *Mock-Cucumber.* . . Covered with slender spines. Among bushes along streams. **1954** Harrington *Manual Plants CO* 524, *Mock Cucumber.* . . Our records from the eastern half of Colorado at 3500–7500 feet. **1968** Barkley *Plants KS* 329, Wild Mock Cucumber. Alluvial soil. East two-thirds. **1970** Correll *Plants TX* 1512, *Wild Mock-cucumber.* . . In moist soil in thickets of the Trans-Pecos.

mock-eel root n

=**water hemlock.**

1964 Kingsbury *Poisonous Plants U.S.* 373, *Cicuta* spp. Water hemlock. The most useful common name of this genus is water hemlock. In appearance the plant [sic] is not easily distinguished from several other members of the family Umbelliferae. A profusion of common names, locally applied, has resulted. Among such names are cowbane, . . mock-eel root [etc].

mocker See **mockingbird 1, 2, 3**

mockernut hickory n Also *mockernut* [See quots 1917, 1950]

A **hickory B1** (here: *Carya tomentosa*). Also called **bullnut, fragrant hickory, hard-bark ~, hickory nut 1, hognut 1, kingnut, pignut, red hickory, square nut, walnut, white-heart hickory, white ~, white walnut, woodpecker hickory**

1804 Michaux *Voyage à l'Ouest* 17, L'on y observe cependant différentes espèces d'arbres, entr'autres . . le *Juglans tomentosa,* Mockernut. [=One sees there, however, different species of trees, among others . . the *Juglans tomentosa,* Mocker-nut.] **1810** Michaux *Histoire des Arbres* 1.184, *Juglans tomentosa.* . . Dans la partie de l'État de New-Jersey qui avoisine la rivière Hudson, ainsi qu'à New-York et dans les environs de cette ville, cette espèce de Noyer est connue sous le nom de *Mocker nut,* Noyer à noix moqueuse. [=*Juglans tomentosa.* . . In the part of New Jersey bordering the Hudson River, as well as in New York and the surroundings of this city, this species of walnut is known by the name of *mocker nut,* walnut with a teasing nut.] *Ibid* 187, La coquille fort épaisse . . renferme une amande douce, mais petite et difficile à extraire . . ; et c'est probablement pour cela qu'on a donné à cette espèce le nom de Noyer à Noix moqueuse. [=The very thick . . shell encloses a kernel that is sweet, but small and difficult to extract . . ; and that is probably why this species has been given the name walnut with a teasing nut.]] **1814** Pursh *Flora Americae* 2.638, *Juglans tomentosa. . . is* known under the name of *Mocker Nut. . .* the nuts are very hard, with but little kernel in them. **1917** (1923) Rogers *Trees Worth Knowing* 40, The mockernut is a mockery to him who hopes for nuts like those of either shagbark. The husk is often three inches long. Inside is a good-sized nut, angled above the middle, suggesting the shagbark. But what a thick, obstinate shell, when one attempts to "break and enter!" **1938** Brown *Trees NE U.S.* 171, Hicoria alba. . . Mockernut. **1950** Gray–Fernald *Manual of Botany* 529, C[arya] tomentosa. ., Mockernut (in early New York Dutch Moker-noot, heavy-hammer nut). **1960** Vines *Trees SW* 131, Mockernut Hickory. **1967** DARE (Qu. T16) Inf **TN11**, Mockernut hickory. **1980** Little *Audubon Guide N. Amer. Trees E. Region* 355, Mockernut.

mockey See **mocky** n²

mock hawk n
=**northern shrike.**

1956 MA Audubon Soc. *Bulletin* 40.129, *Northern Shrike. . .* Mock Hawk (R.I. From its similarity in predation to a hawk.)

mock heather n
1 A **goldenweed** 1 (here: *Haplopappus ericoides*).

1938 Van Dersal *Native Woody Plants* 54, *Aplopappus ericoides. . .* Mock-heather. **1960** Abrams *Flora Pacific States* 4.286, *Haplopappus ericoides. . .* Mock Heather. **1961** Thomas *Flora Santa Cruz* 347 **cwCA**, *H[aplopappus] ericoides . .* ssp *ericoides.* Mock Heather. Coastal sand dunes.

2 A small shrub *(Frankenia jamesii)* native to the southwestern US.

1976 Elmore *Shrubs & Trees SW* 89, Mockheather. . . *Frankenia jamesii. . .* One of our dwarf shrubs, . . it usually grows no taller than a foot or two. . . They grow in crowded bundles, reminding some of the Old World heathers.

mockie n¹ See **mocky** n¹

mockie n² See **mocky** n²

mocking See **mockingbird** 2

mockingbird n Pronc-spp *markingbird, mawking bird* Cf **brown mockingbird, dumb ~, English ~, flathead ~, French ~, gray ~, Indian ~, Mexican ~, mountain ~, red ~, rusty ~, sandy ~, Spanish ~, yellow ~**

1 also *mockbird, mocker:* A gray-brown bird *(Mimus polyglottos)* known for its ability to imitate the calls of other birds. Also called **English mockingbird 1, imitation bird, mocking thrush, nigger-hater, nightingale a**

1649 in 1838 Force *Tracts* 2.8.15 **VA**, We have . . one Bird we call the Mock-bird; for he will imitate all other Birds notes. **1676** Royal Soc. London *Philos. Trans.* 11.631 **VA**, As to the *Mocking-bird,* besides his own natural notes, which are many and pleasant, he imitateth all the birds in the woods. **1731** Catesby *Nat. Hist. Carolina* 1.27, Hernandez justly calls it the Queen of all singing Birds. The *Indians,* by way of eminence or admiration, call it *Cencontlatolly,* or *four hundred tongues;* and we call it (tho' not by so elevated a name, yet very properly) the *Mock-bird,* from its wonderful mocking and imitating the notes of all Birds, from the Humming Bird to the Eagle. **1773** Royal Soc. London *Philos. Trans.* 63.286, From the attention which the *mocker* pays to any . . sort of disagreeable noises, these capital notes would be always debased. **1791** Bartram *Travels* 11 **S Atl**, Moon-light nights, filled with the melody of the chearful mockbird, warbling nonpareil. **1828** (1938) Bolling *Diary* 46.152 **VA**, Mocking Birds first salute about 4th. **1841** (1952) Cooper *Deerslayer* 450 **cNY**, She's a noble gal . . [with] a voice that's as pleasant as a mocker's. **1887** (1967) Harris *Free Joe* 133 **GA**, Ef a gal puts on a man's hat when she hears a mocker sing at night, she'll git married that year an' do well. **1899** Chesnutt *Conjure Woman* 149 **csNC** [Black], De mawkin'-bird stayed roun' dere 'mos' all day. **1903** Dawson *Birds OH* 1.252, What puzzled me most, however, about his performance was that he always stood silent whenever a bantam rooster, some two blocks or so away, crowed. When his mistress assured me that it was the Mockingbird that crowed, I could scarcely believe my ears. Having always heard the rooster at a distance the Mocker reproduced the sound in exactly the same way. **1909** DN 3.348 **eAL, wGA**, Marking-bird. Ibid 349, Mocker. . . Commonly used for mocking-bird. **1934** Natl. Geogr. Mag. May 618 **sGA**, The mocking bird. . . is . . full of music. . . "Did yer ever hear er mockin' eggs bein' good fer stutterin'?" a man of Okefinokee asked. . . "One time somebody

come ter our house, an' they said mockin' eggs 'd cure me. So nex' time I found one er their nesties I taken some er the eggs an' eat 'em, an' after that I could talk all right." **1950** WELS (Birds that come out only *after dark*) 1 Inf, **seWI**, Mockingbird—day and night. **1965–70** DARE (Qu. Q14) 412 Infs, **chiefly Sth, S Midl, SW**, Mockingbird(s); 12 Infs, **scattered**, Mockbird; 11 Infs, **esp Sth**, Mocker(s); MS63, NC64, Markingbird(s); VA70, Mockingbird mocks all the other birds, has no song of its own; (Qu. Q3, . . *Birds that come out only after dark*) 30 Infs, **scattered**, Mockingbird(s); DC2, Mockingbird sings all night at full moon; DC8, Mockingbird will whistle all night; NJ22, Mockingbird—both day and night, but very busy at dusk; (Qu. Q7) Inf **NC82**, Mockingbird. [DARE Ed: Many Infs responded to Qu. Q14 both at this sense and at **3** below.] **1986** Pederson *LAGS Concordance*, 37 infs, **Gulf Region**, Mockingbird.

2 also *mockbird, mocker, mocking;* also with modifiers: Usu the **brown thrasher,** but also the California **thrasher** *(Toxostoma redivivum).* Cf **mocking thrush**

1688 in 1844 Force *Tracts* 3.12.32 **VA**, The red Mocking is of a duskish red, or rather brown; it sings very well, but has not so soft a Note as the grey mocking Bird. **1709** (1967) Lawson *New Voyage* 147 **S Atl**, The Ground-Mocking-Bird. . . is the same bigness [as the Mocking-Bird], and of a Cinnamon Colour. This Bird sings excellently well, but is not so common amongst us as the former. **1792** Belknap *Hist. NH* 3.172, Thrasher, or Mock-bird,—*Turdus orpheus?* **1832** Williamson *Hist. ME* 1.149, The *Thrasher,* or *Mockbird;* and . . the *Robin,* are species of the *Thrush* family. **1872** Coues *Key to N. Amer. Birds* 75, *Sickle-billed Thrush. Californian Mockingbird.* Dark oily olive-brown. . . Coast region of California. **1883** Nuttall Ornith. Club *Bulletin* 8.75, *Brown Thrasher. . .* Its imitative powers have given it several names, such as . . *American Mockingbird* (Wisconsin); . . *Carolina Mockingbird* and so on. **1895** Minot *Land-Birds New Engl.* 47, Though called "mockers," the "Thrashers" never mimic other creatures. **1936** Roberts *MN Birds* 2.109, This song . . , together with the seeming mimicry of the songs of other birds, has caused the Thrasher to be sometimes called the "Mockingbird of the North." **1950** WELS (Brown thrasher) 1 Inf, **ceWI**, Mockingbird. **1956** MA Audubon Soc. *Bulletin* 40.128 **NH, VT**, This species [=*Toxostoma rufum*] is an occasional, though expert, imitator of the notes of other birds. . . Mockbird. **1966** DARE (Qu. Q14) Infs **CA22, ND1**, Brown thrush—(a) mockingbird.

3 also *mockbird, mocker;* also with modifiers: =**catbird 1.**

1839 Audubon *Synopsis Birds* 88, Black-capped Mocking-Bird.—Cat Bird. . . From Texas to Massachusetts, inland to the Missouri. **1932** Howell *FL Bird Life* 357, Catbird. . . Other Name: *Black Mockingbird.* Ibid 358, The song of the Catbird is not to be compared with that of its near relative, the Mockingbird, but it is nevertheless sweet and varied, and at times contains imitations of other birds' notes. **1946** Hausman *Eastern Birds* 452, Catbird. . . Other Names: Slate-colored Mockingbird, Gray Mockingbird, Black Mockingbird. **1950** WELS (Catbird) 4 Infs, **sWI**, Mockingbird; 1 Inf, **seWI**, Mockingbird—because it mimics other birds; 1 Inf, **csWI**, Mocker. **1956** MA Audubon Soc. *Bulletin* 40.128 **VT**, Mockingbird. . . As a mimic the Catbird falls far short of the Mockingbird, but excels the Thrasher. **1965–70** DARE (Qu. Q14, . . *Names . . for these birds:* . . *catbird*) 153 Infs, **widespread**, Mockingbird; MS63, NC64, Markingbird(s); NY79, Mockbird. [DARE Ed: Many Infs responded to Qu. Q14 both at this sense and at **1** above.] **1969** Longstreet *Birds FL* 116, Catbird—*Other name: Black Mockingbird.*

4 Usu the **loggerhead shrike,** but also the **northern shrike.** Cf **mockingbird hawk**

1822 Latham *Genl. Hist. Birds* 2.7 **GA**, [The cinereous shrike] is found also as far south as Georgia, and known by the name of Big-headed Mocking Bird. **1832** Nuttall *Manual Ornith.* 1.260, Great American Shrike, or Butcher-bird. . . From his attempts to imitate the notes of other small birds, in Canada, and some parts of New England, he is sometimes called a *Mocking-bird.* **1859** (1968) Bartlett *Americanisms* 293, The Northern Butcher-bird. . . in Canada and the Eastern States . . is sometimes called Mocking-bird. **1874** NY Acad. Sci. *Annals Lyceum Nat. Hist.* 10.371 **IL**, "Logger-head;" "Butcher Bird;" "Mocking Bird." **1966–67** DARE (Qu. Q14, . . *Names . . for these birds:* . . *shrike)* Inf **AL22**, Mockingbird—butcher bird. . . catch worms, small snakes and hang them on barbed wire fence for storage; **OH2**, Mockingbird—black and white; [**OK52**, There's a butcher bird that looks the same [as the mockingbird], but he's bigger—he'll stick a grasshopper on a thorn or a barb wire].

5 also *Kentucky mockingbird:* =**yellow-breasted chat. esp KY**

1897 Oölogist 14.69 **KY**, I . . listen to the garrulous notes of the "Kentucky Mockingbird," otherwise known as the Yellow-breasted Chat

(Icteria virens). **1967–69** *DARE* (Qu. Q14) Inf **KY**31, Mockingbird (yellow-breasted chat)—no real mockingbirds here; **KY**47, Mockingbird (yellow-breasted chat); **WV**5, Different mockingbird—yellow.

6 Either the **black-billed cuckoo** or the **yellow-billed cuckoo.**

1968–70 *DARE* (Qu. Q14, . . *Names . . for these birds:* . . *cuckoo*) Inf **MS**87, Mockingbird [same as] rainbird, rain crow; **VA**15, Mockingbird—rain crow: this one eats the tent caterpillars.

mockingbird berry n
A **pokeweed** (here: *Phytolacca americana*).

1951 *PADS* 15.30 **TX**, *Phytolacca americana*. . . Mockingbird berry. It is hard to get out of sight and hearing of a mockingbird in Texas, and where he is, there is almost certainly pokeweed, if it can possibly grow in the soil; the master singer scatters its seeds far and wide.

mockingbird bush n
=**French mulberry.**

1955 *S. Folkl. Qrly.* 19.235 **FL**, Mocking birds, and at least eleven other species of birds, feed upon the berries of the *Mocking Bird Bush* (*Callicarpa Americana*), or *Beauty Bush.*

mockingbird hawk n Cf mockingbird 4
=**loggerhead shrike.**

1955 *AmSp* 30.180, *Mockingbird hawk* (southern shrike, Nev.) derives from the close resemblance in color of the mocking- and butcher-birds.

mockingbird tale n
1950 *PADS* 14.46 **SC**, *Mockingbird tales*. . . Loose tattle of one who receives a bit of scandal in confidence and proceeds to broadcast it as the *mockingbird* does its borrowed songs.

mocking owl n
Perh a **barn owl 1.**

1968 *DARE* (Qu. Q2) Inf **NC**54, Mocking owl.

mocking thrush n Also *mock thrush* Cf mockingbird 2
A bird of the family Mimidae, esp the **brown thrasher.**

1839 Audubon *Ornith. Biog.* 5.336, Townsend's Mocking Thrush. . . [is] cinereous brown above, whitish below, with a long rounded tail. **1847** Emerson *Poems* 230, A mocking thrush,/ A wild-rose, or rock-loving columbine,/ Salve my worst wounds. **1880** *Harper's New Mth. Mag.* 61.74 **NEng**, A "mocking-thrush" he is indeed, for he mimics his own song from morn till night in all the thickets and pasture-lands. **1890** *Century Dict.* 3811, *Mock-thrush*. . . A bird of the subfamily *Miminæ;* especially, one of the genus *Harporhynchus,* as the thrasher, *H. rufus.* **1917** (1923) *Birds Amer.* 3.175, *Mockingbird*. . . *Other Names.* . . Mocking Thrush. **1946** Hausman *Eastern Birds* 451, Eastern Mockingbird. . . *Other Names* . . Mocking Thrush.

mocking wren n [See quot 1832]
=**Carolina wren.**

1832 Nuttall *Manual Ornith.* 1.429, Great Carolina or Mocking Wren. . . This remarkable, mimicking, and musical Wren is a constant resident in the Southern states, from Virginia to Florida, but is rarely seen at any season north of the line of Maryland or Delaware. **1903** Dawson *Birds OH* 1.259, Great Carolina Wren; Mocking Wren. **1917** (1923) *Birds Amer.* 3.189, Carolina Wren. . . Mocking Wren. . . Louisiana Wren. **1955** Forbush–May *Birds* 362, Carolina Wren. . . *Other names:* Great Carolina Wren; Mocking Wren. *Ibid* 363, A great number of phrases are attributed to it, for it is really a very accomplished musician, a ventriloquist also, and something of a mocker. . . On account of its apparent imitative powers, it is known locally as the Mocking Wren. **1969** Longstreet *Birds FL* 113, Carolina Wren. . . *Other name:* Mocking Wren.

mock locust n
A **false indigo 1** (here: *Amorpha californica*).

1925 Jepson *Manual Plants CA* 556, *A[morpha] californica* . . Mock Locust. **1960** Vines *Trees SW* 521, *A[morpha] californica*. . . Also known under the vernacular names of Mock Locust and California Indigo-bush.

mock mayapple n Also *mock apple* [Appar from its resemblance to **mayapple 3**]
A gall found on plants of the genus *Andromeda* and of related genera.

1892 Gibson *Sharp Eyes* 60 **NEng**, There are May-apples and *mock* May-apples, and the small boy may well beware of the latter poisonous variety. These may be seen hanging sometimes in close company with the azalea apples upon the *Andromeda* bushes, and are frequently gathered by mistake. . . These mock-apples turn to black, unsightly pouches when they grow old, and . . the interior of the mock May-apple . . [is] filled with ashen powder and remnants of plant-lice, for this growth is of insect origin.

mock mesquite n
=**fairy duster.**

1959 Munz–Keck *CA Flora* 796, *C[alliandra] eriophylla*. . . Fairy Duster. Mock Mesquite. **1976** Bailey–Bailey *Hortus Third* 200, [*Calliandra] eriophylla* . . Mock mesquite, mesquitilla, fairy-duster.

mock olive n [From the small, black, olive-like fruits]
=**Carolina cherry.**

1908 Britton *N. Amer. Trees* 510, This tree [=*Prunus caroliniana*] is much planted in the South for ornament and for hedges. . . Other common names are . . Carolina cherry, Mock olive.

mock orange n
1 Any of several trees or shrubs:

a =**Carolina cherry.** [See quots 1769, 1895] **Sth**

1769 Stork *Descr. East FL* 2.5, [Footnote:] There is an evergreen sort of this Bird or Cluster-cherry, which grows about 30 feet high in S. Carolina, and from the beauty of its evergreen shining leaves is called the Mock-orange. **1858** *S. Cultivator* 16.56 **Sth**, If an evergreen hedge is needed, we have . . the Wild Olive (*Cerasus Carolinianus*) or "Mock Orange." **1893** *Jrl. Amer. Folkl.* 6.140, *Prunus Caroliniana,* mock-orange. . . Southern States. **1895** Gray–Bailey *Field Botany* 147, *P[runus] Caroliniana*. . . Carolina Laurel Cherry, also called *Mock Orange* at [sic] the South, probably from the coriaceous, smooth, and glossy leaves. **1933** Small *Manual SE Flora* 651, *Mock-orange*. . . Woods, usually in river banks and hammocks. **1953** Greene–Blomquist *Flowers South* 52, Carolina Cherry-Laurel, Mock-Orange. . . An evergreen, small tree. . . native to Coastal Plain from Fla. to Tex. and N.C. **1964** Kingsbury *Poisonous Plants U.S.* 368, Southern mock orange. . . is considered toxic in Louisiana. **1979** Little *Checklist U.S. Trees* 212, Carolina laurel-cherry. . . *Other common names* . . mock-orange.

b A plant of the genus *Philadelphus.* [*OED* 1731; see quot 1915] Also called **syringa.** For other names of var spp see **Indian arrowwood 3, orange-flower tree**

1785 Marshall *Arbustrum* 99, *Philadelphus*. . . Mock-Orange. . . The flowers are pretty large. . . This is impatient of much cold. **1858** Warder *Hedges* 46, The most rapid growth for a tall screen will be furnished by the mock-orange . . which bears a profusion of showy white flowers. **1891** Jesup *Plants Hanover NH* 14, *Philadelphus*. . . Mock Orange. **1915** (1926) Armstrong–Thornber *Western Wild Flowers* 208, They [=*Philadelphus* spp] are often called Mock-Orange, because the flowers often resemble orange blossoms. **1928** Rosendahl–Butters *Trees MN* 135, *Mock Orange*. . . is likely to be found growing spontaneously in Minnesota as it does in some other parts of the United States. **1942** Tehon *Fieldbook IL Shrubs* 89, The mock oranges are branching shrubs. **1954** Harrington *Manual Plants CO* 288, Mockorange. . . Represented in Colorado by . . two . . sub-species, which intergrade rather commonly. **1965–70** *DARE* (Qu. T13) 33 Infs, **scattered, but esp PA, NJ, Mid Atl,** mock orange [*DARE* Ed: These Infs distinguished *Philadelphus* from **1c** below.]; (Qu. S26e) Inf **IL**58, Mock orange—flowering bush. **1967** *DARE* FW Addits **OR**9, **WA**30, (Wild) mock orange. **1973** Wharton–Barbour *Trees KY* 526, Several foreign species of mock-orange . . are used in ornamental planting. Our two native species . . are found on cliffs and in woodland borders in . . Kentucky. **1990** *Plants SW* (Catalog) 70, *Mock Orange*. . . Masses of delightfully fragrant, orange-scented, large, white flowers. . . It is a fine-textured shrub with slender twigs and brown-and-white bark.

c =**Osage orange;** also its fruit.

1814 Brackenridge *Views of LA* 59, There is particularly one very beautiful [tree], *bois jaune,* or yellow wood: by some called the mock orange. **1897** Sudworth *Arborescent Flora* 190 **LA**, Osage Orange. . . Common Names. . . Mock Orange. **1917** *DN* 4.382 **IL, IA, KS, LA, NC, VA**, *Mock orange* = bois d'arc. **1941** Writers' Program *Guide AR* 314 **nwAR**, Small stacks of logs . . may be piles of hard *bois d'arc,* going through a four-year period of seasoning. *Bois d'arc,* known . . as . . mock orange . . , is highly prized by makers of archery equipment. **1944** *AL Geol. Surv. Bulletin* 53.93, *Maclura aurantiaca,* . . known as Osage orange, mock orange, or bois d'arc . . , is supposed to be native near the Red River in Oklahoma and Texas. . . [but] has been widely cultivated in the eastern states. **1965–70** *DARE* (Qu. T13, . . *Names . . for these trees:* . . *osage orange*) 103 Infs, **widespread, but less freq**

NEng, Mock orange; **LA2**, Mock orange—it's not the trees, it's the balls they call that.

d A **snowbell:** either *Styrax americanus* or *S. grandifolius.* [See quot 1860] **chiefly Sth**

1860 Curtis *Cat. Plants NC* 101, *Mock Orange.* (Styrax grandifolia . .). The flowers are from 15 to 20 on loose nodding racemes, white, very fragrant, in size and form very similar to those of the Orange. **1900** Lyons *Plant Names* 360, *S[tyrax] grandifolia.* . . Southeastern U.S. Mock Orange. **1953** Greene–Blomquist *Flowers South* 95, A more common species is *S[tyrax] americana,* often called "Mock-Orange," which occurs along stream banks and in swamps of the Coastal Plain. **1960** Vines *Trees SW* 846, *Styrax grandifolia.* . . Vernacular names are Coast Snow-bell, Storax, and Mock-orange. The fruit is known to be eaten by the wood duck. **1970** Correll *Plants TX* 1191, *Styrax americana.* . . *Mock-orange.* . . In moist woods and along streams in e. Tex. **1979** Ajilvsgi *Wild Flowers* 14 **eTX**, Some of the understory plants of these quiet, watery places are water elm . . , common buttonbush . . , and mock-orange *(Styrax americana).*

e The shaddock *(Citrus maxima).* **obs**

1868 U.S. Dept. Ag. *Rept. of Secy. for 1867* 142, The Shaddock. . . is called . . sometimes in this country Mock-orange, or Forbidden Fruit.

f A **southern buckthorn** (here: *Bumelia lycioides*).

1897 Sudworth *Arborescent Flora* 319 **FL**, *Bumelia lycioides.* . . *Common Names.* . . Mock Orange. **1933** Small *Manual SE Flora* 1034, *B[umelia] lycioides.* . . *Mock-orange.* . . The yellow or light-brown heart-wood is close-grained, heavy, and hard. **1960** Vines *Trees SW* 834, Vernacular names [of *Bumelia lycioides*] are Buckthorn, Mockorange, . . and Gum Elastic. . . Various authors state that the fruit is edible, but the author has found it so bitter as to be unpalatable. **1976** Bailey–Bailey *Hortus Third* 190, *Mock orange.* . . Shrub or small tree, to 30 ft., often thorny.

g A plant of the genus *Murraya,* usu *M. paniculata.* **HI** For other names of *M. paniculata* see **orange jessamine**

1929 Neal *Honolulu Gardens* 167, *Mock orange* . . *(Murraya exotica* . . *).* Because of its rich-looking, shining foliage, . . and its sweet, white flowers, . . the shrub is popular in Honolulu. **1948** Neal *In Gardens* HI 421, *M[urraya] paniculata.* . . The mock orange. . . is ornamental only, its half-inch-long, red, one- to two-seeded berries being inedible. . . In the United States, another plant is known as mock orange (see *Philadelphus*). **1976** Bailey–Bailey *Hortus Third* 744, *Murraya.* . . Mock orange.

h A plant of the genus *Pittosporum.*

1967–69 *DARE* (Qu. T13) Inf **IN58**, Mock orange—a house plant; **LA14**, Mock orange—this word is applied to a real [*sic*] citrus plant with small, knotty, foul-smelling fruit. **1976** Bailey–Bailey *Hortus Third* 881, Pittosporums are useful ornamentals and are cultivated in the Pacific Coast states and southern states because of their good habit, attractive foliage, flowers, and fruits. . . *[Pittosporum] Tobira.* . . *Mock orange, house-blooming m[ock] o[range].* . . Now widely cult. . . *[P.] undulatum.* . . *Victorian box, mock orange.*

2 A plant of the family Cucurbitaceae with fruits that resemble an orange in some way, as:

a A gourd; see quots.

1842 *Lowell Offering* 2.68 **neMA**, There were apples, pears, melons, a mock-orange, a pumpkin, squash, and a crooked cucumber. **1892** *Jrl. Amer. Folkl.* 5.96 **cIL, nOH**, *Lagenaria* sp., mock orange.

b A **calabacilla:** usu *Cucurbita foetidissima,* rarely *C. palmata.* [See quot 1897] **chiefly CA**

1897 Parsons *Wild Flowers CA* 117, *Mock-orange. Gourd.* . . *Cucurbita foetidissima.* . . When the gourds are ripe, these vines look like the dumping-ground for numerous poor, discarded oranges. **1911** Jepson *Flora CA* 271, *C[ucurbita] palmata.* . . Mock Orange. . . Gourd 3 in. in diameter.—Southern California to San Joaquin Co. **1920** Saunders *Useful Wild Plants* 177, It [=*Cucurbita foetidissima*] is known . . in California as Mock Orange. **1936** Whitehouse *TX Flowers* 149, Mock Orange *(Cucurbita foetidissima).* **1947** Curtin *Healing Herbs* 46, The gourds it produces . . resemble spilled oranges—which perhaps accounts for the popular name of "mock orange" given it in California. **1988** Whealy *Garden Seed Inventory* (2d ed) 407, Mock Orange, Calabazilla [*sic*] . . volume round hard-shelled 3 in. fruits, . . grows wild in Southwest and Mexico.

c A **wild cucumber** (here: *Echinocystis lobata*). Cf **mock apple 1, ~ cucumber**

1900 Lyons *Plant Names* 248, *M[icrampelis] lobata.* . . Mock Orange.

1940 Clute *Amer. Plant Names* 107, *E[chinocystis] lobata.* . . Mock orange. **1959** Carleton *Index Herb. Plants* 82, *Mock-orange* . . Echinocystis lobata.

mock oyster n

A vegetable such as eggplant or **vegetable oyster.**

1950 *WELS (Other names in your neighborhood for: Eggplant)* 1 Inf, **ceWI**, Mock oyster. **1965–70** *DARE* (Qu. I4, . . *Vegetables . . less commonly grown around here*) 15 Infs, **scattered,** Mock oyster [11 Infs, FW sugg]; **IL134**, Mock oyster—same as vegetable oyster. **1995** *DARE* File **csWI** (as of 1930s), Salsify was called mock oyster and vegetable oyster.

mock pennyroyal n [See quot 1848]

A **pennyroyal** (here: *Hedeoma* spp).

1848 Gray *Manual of Botany* 317, *Hedeoma.* . . Mock Pennyroyal. . . Low odorous plants with small leaves. [*Ibid* 318, *H. pulegioides.* . . Plant . . with nearly the taste and odor of the true *Pennyroyal* (Mentha Pulegium).] **1933** Small *Manual SE Flora* 1165, *H[edeoma] pulegioides.* . . *Mock-pennyroyal.* . . Dry fields and open woods. **1961** Smith *MI Wildflowers* 327, *Mock Pennyroyal.* . . Flowering July to September. **1970** Correll *Plants TX* 1379, *Mock Pennyroyal.* . . 2 [species occur] in eastern and southern United States. **1976** Bailey–Bailey *Hortus Third* 544, *[Hedeoma] pulegioides.* . . *Mock p[ennyroyal].* . . Nov[a] Sc[otia] to S. Dak., s. to Fla. and Ark.

mock sandburr n

A **crabgrass 1** (here: *Digitaria sanguinalis*).

1898 *Jrl. Amer. Folkl.* 11.283 **KS**, *Panicum sanguinale.* . . Mock sandburr.

mock strawberry n

=**Indian strawberry 1.**

1900 Lyons *Plant Names* 141, Mock Strawberry. . . *D[uchesnea] Indica.* **1910** Graves *Flowering Plants* 232 **CT**, Mock Strawberry. . . Often grown in hanging-baskets for its yellow flowers and handsome but insipid berries. **1933** Small *Manual SE Flora* 612, *Mock-Strawberries.*—The receptacle is red and spongy, but not juicy, at maturity. **1949** Moldenke *Amer. Wild Flowers* 123, In waste places from southern New York and Pennsylvania to Florida and Missouri, as well as in parts of California, one may frequently come across a yellow-flowered, trailing plant. . . This is the *mockstrawberry*. **1961** Thomas *Flora Santa Cruz* 195 **cwCA**, Mock . . Strawberry. Becoming established in lawns and in shaded areas in San Francisco and probably elsewhere. **1976** Bailey–Bailey *Hortus Third* 403, *Mock s[trawberry].* . . Looks like a yellow-fl[owere]d strawberry. . . Naturalized in N. Amer., where often weedy.

mock sweet William n

=**garden catchfly.**

1893 *Jrl. Amer. Folkl.* 6.138 **sIN**, *Silene Armeria.* . . mock sweet William. **1940** Clute *Amer. Plant Names* 63, *S[ilene] armeria.* . . Sweet William Catchfly. . . mock sweet William. **1959** Carleton *Index Herb. Plants* 82, *Mock-sweet William:* Silene Armeria.

mock thrush See mocking thrush

mocky n[1] Also sp *mockie* [Prob Yiddish *makeh* a boil, sore, plague] **chiefly NYC** *usu derog*

A Jew.

1931 *Collier's* 10 Jan 10 **NYC**, I consider this . . disrespectful, like calling Jewish people mockies, or Heebs. **1937** Conwell *Professional Thief* 12 **NYC**, I was over on the East Side and there saw this Jew who was pointed out to me as one of their best mocky cannons. **1942** Berrey–Van den Bark *Amer. Slang* 460.5, *Nationalities and races.* . . Mockie . . *a jew.* **1955** *PADS* 24.90 [Argot of pickpockets], Jewish organizations are referred to as *mocky mobs* or *mocky jew mobs.* "Mocky is not a Jew. It's a Sixth Avenue Jew." **1968** *DARE* (Qu. HH28, *Names and nicknames . . for people of foreign background*) Inf **NY93**, ['mɑkɪz]—Jewish; **NY119**, Mocky—Jewish. **1971** *AmSp* 46.81 **Chicago IL**, Jew: . . *mocky.* **1986** Pederson *LAGS Concordance* **Nashville TN** *(Jews)* 1 inf, Mockies. [Inf Jewish] **1993** *DARE* File **NYC** (as of 1950s), As a Jewish kid growing up in a predominantly Irish neighborhood in the Bronx, I was called a *mocky* on more than just a few occasions, usually when on the way to Hebrew School, and it was almost always the prelude to a fight. However, a contemporary growing up in a Jewish neighborhood in Brooklyn knew it only as a term used by acculturated Jews to refer to more recent arrivals who still retained a great deal of their eastern European ways and were more visibly "Jewish." His parents, for instance, used to refer to the "mockies who run the grocery store." While the tone was derogatory, it wasn't strong enough to be considered contemptuous.

mocky n[2] Also sp *mockey, mockie*

1 A young, usu wild, mare.

1936 Adams *Cowboy Lingo* 81, A wild mare was sometimes called a 'mockey.' **1937** *DN* 6.618 **swTX**, A *mocky* is a young mare, and perhaps the word develops from the fact that she mocks the *bronco-buster* in being frisky and mettlesome. **1942** Berrey–Van den Bark *Amer. Slang* 916.14, Mockie, *a wild range mare.*

2 See quot.

1949 *PADS* 11.8 **wTX**, Mockey ['mɑkɪ]. . . A dun horse with a black mane.

mocky n[3] Cf *DS* H37

1939 *AmSp* 14.91 **TN**, *Mocky.* Gravy. 'My woman makes good mocky.'

modderun See **modern**

mo' dear See **mother dear**

modern adj Usu |'mɑdə(r)n|; also, by metath, |'mɑdrən|; also |'mɑdə·ən|; for addit varr see quots Pronc-spp *modderun, modren, modrun* Cf *Pronc Intro* 3.I.23, **lectren**

Std sense, var forms.

1905 *DN* 3.58 **eNE**, Metathesis, especially of *r*, is very frequent: . . *modren.* **1933** Rawlings *South Moon* 118 **nFL**, Modrun science figgers not havin' no outhouse has got somethin' to do with it. **1936** (1947) Mencken *Amer. Lang.* 353, Consonants are misplaced by metathesis, as in . . *modren.* **1943** in **1944** *ADD* 394 **ePA**, *Modern.* . . 3 syls., modderun. **1950** Faulkner *Stories* 30 **MS**, You don't seem to kept up with these modren ideas about work. **1968** *DARE* Tape **AK6**, They got modren ['mɑdrən] snow-removing equipment. **1968–69** *DARE* FW Addits **NJ, PA**, ['mɑdrɪn]—modern. **1981** Pederson *LAGS Basic Materials Gulf Region*, [10 infs gave proncs of the types ['mɑdṛn, 'mɑd(ə)rṇ]; ['mɑədrɑˀ] and ['mɑədrɔ̃] were each attested once.] **1984** Burns *Cold Sassy* 159 **nGA** (as of 1906), I swanny to God, these modrun women are something else.

modest lily n

A **fritillary** (here: *Fritillaria pudica*).

1959 Carleton *Index Herb. Plants* 82, *Modest-lily:* Fritillaria pudica.

modesty n

1 A **thoroughwax** (here: *Bupleurum rotundifolium*).

1837 Darlington *Flora Cestrica* 191, *Round-leaved Bupleurum.* Vulgo—Modesty. . . Not very common; but is becoming naturalized about gardens, in several neighborhoods. **1843** Torrey *Flora NY* 1.266, *Bupleurum rotundifolium.* . . Thorough-wax. Modesty. . . A weed about gardens and cultivated grounds. . . June-August. **1861** Wood *Class-Book* 382, *Modesty.* . . B[upleurum] *rotundifolium.* . . Fr[uit] crowned with the wax-like, shining base of the styles. **1900** Lyons *Plant Names* 72, B[upleurum] *rotundifolium.* . . Modesty. **1931** Harned *Wild Flowers Alleghanies* 350, *Hare's Ear.* Modesty (Bupleurum rotundifolium . .). Common in cultivated ground and fields. **1959** Carleton *Index Herb. Plants* 82, *Modesty:* Bupleurum rotundifolium.

2 =**flower-of-an-hour.** [See quot 1949]

1896 *Jrl. Amer. Folkl.* 9.183 **swOH**, *Hibiscus Trionum* . . modesty. **1935** (1943) Muenscher *Weeds* 336, *Flower-of-an-hour, Bladder ketmia, Venice mallow, Modesty, Shoo-fly.* **1949** Moldenke *Amer. Wild Flowers* 111, The names *modesty* and *flower-of-an-hour* are applied to this little plant because each of its flowers remains open only for a few hours. **1973** Hitchcock–Cronquist *Flora Pacific NW* 291, *H[ibiscus] trionum* . . modesty.

3 =**yerba de selva.**

1915 (1926) Armstrong–Thornber *Western Wild Flowers* 204, *Modesty. Whipplea modesta.* . . A pretty little under-shrub, with many woody stems, spreading and trailing on the ground, . . bearing clusters of very small flowers with a pleasant honey-like fragrance. **1931** U.S. Dept. Ag. *Misc. Pub.* 101.40, *Whipplea* . . , occasionally called modesty, . . is abundant in places, but its palatability is low and it has at best only slight forage value. **1934** Haskin *Wild Flowers Pacific Coast* 135, *Modesty.* . . Found in open woods from Washington, southward, and very abundant in low mountains. **1961** Thomas *Flora Santa Cruz* 192 **cwCA**, Modesty, Yerba de Selva. Common in the drier parts of redwood-Douglas fir forests.

modren, modrun See **modern**

moe See **more**

moemoe v, n |'mɔɪ'mɔɪ|; for addit varr see quots Also rarely *moe* [Haw; see quot 1938] **HI**

To sleep, lie down; by ext, to be off duty; sleep.

1938 Reinecke *Hawaiian Loanwords* 25, *Moemoe* ['mo-ɛ'mo-ɛ] ['mɔɪ'mɔɪ]. . . [Reinecke: Reduplicated form of *moe*, to lie down to sleep.] 1. To lie down to sleep; to sleep. 2. Sleep. 3. To be off duty. V[ery] F[req]. **1951** *AmSp* 26.23 **HI**, Moe (sleep). **1954–60** Hance et al. *Hawaiian Sugar* 5, *Moemoe* ['mo-ɛ'mo-ɛ]. . . To sleep, lie down; with cane, to lodge. **1967** *DARE* (Qu. X40, . . *Ways* . . *of saying, "I'm going to bed"*) Inf **HI8**, [mɔɪmɔɪ]. **1969** *DARE* FW Addit **HI**, When I was a child my parents always referred to going to sleep as going moemoe ['mɔɪmɔɪ]. **1972** Carr *Da Kine Talk* 88 **HI**, *Hawaiian Words Commonly Heard In Hawaii's English.* . . Moemoe (reduplication of *moe*). Sleep. **1984** Sunset *HI Guide* 85, *Moemoe*—sleep (slang).

mog v Also sp *mogg*

1 freq with *along;* also with *around:* To move, esp slowly or aimlessly; to depart. [*OED mog* v. 3 "To walk *along* slowly but steadily" 1857 →; cf also *OED mog* v. 2 "To move on, depart, decamp. Chiefly with *off* or *on*" 1764 →] **chiefly NEast**

1890 *Jrl. Amer. Folkl.* 3.311 **ME**, *Mogg*—To move slowly. "He mogged along." **1892** [see **mogle**]. **1895** *DN* 1.398 **NY**, *Mog* . . : to walk. "We mogged along slowly." **1927** *AmSp* 3.139 **eME**, A neighbor often said "well, I must be mogging along," mog meaning to move slowly, to depart. **1938** Damon *Grandma* 262 **CT** (as of late 19th cent.), "Giddap." They mogged slowly all the way home in a delicate silence. **1959** *VT Hist.* 27.149 **nw,cnVT**, *Mog along.* . . To move slowly; to jog. Occasional. **1967–69** *DARE* (Qu. Y21, *To move about slowly and without energy*) Inf **MA5**, He mogged [mɔgd] around; (Qu. Y27, *To go about aimlessly, with nothing to do: "He's always _____ around the drugstore."*) Inf **NY145**, Moggin' ['mɑgɪn]. **1983** *DARE* File **ceWI**, *Mog along*—move slowly. **1989** Mosher *Stranger* 16 **nVT**, Val, who all of a sudden I liked better, rolled her eyes toward the ceiling and mogged back out to the kitchen. **1993** *DARE* File **nwMA** (as of 1940s), Sure, I've heard mog, to mog along. 'He's just moggin' along.' But I've never used the term myself. My mother wouldn't have liked that. She brought us up to speak properly.

2 To cause to move quickly.

1867 *Geauga Democrat* (Chardon OH) 24 Apr [1]/2, Thinking the bean-pole a gun, he ran for dear life, and complained of Hutchison for threatening to *"mog"* him. . . Judge Tod . . said, *"Mog* him—what does that mean?"—Hutchison . . says, " . . It means to make a man go where he don't want to, and damned quick, too." **1894** Frederic *Marsena* 200 **nNY**, Well, then, mog your boots out of this as quick as ever you can.

mog along (or around) See **mog** 1

‡**mogate** v Cf **mog**

1938 *AmSp* 13.6 **seAR**, *Mogate.* . . To move rapidly. 'He can sure mogate along.' A negro expression.

mogdad coffee See **magdad coffee**

‡**mogey** v [Perh blend of **mog** + **mosey**]

1968 *DARE* (Qu. Y21, *To move about slowly and without energy*) Inf **CT19**, Mogey ['mogi] along—picked it up from grandparents.

mogg See **mog**

‡**mogle** v [Prob < *mog along* (at **mog** 1)]

1892 *KS Univ. Qrly.* 1.97, *Mog:* to move, as, Mog along with you. *Mogle:* the same.

mogote n [MexSpan < Span *mogote* hillock] **chiefly TX**

A thicket of brush and undergrowth.

1892 *DN* 1.250 **TX**, *Mogóte:* a thicket with heavy undergrowth, the refuge of wild cattle. The divergence of meaning from the Spanish acceptation is striking. In Spain it designates an isolated mountain with a flat top (the American *mesa* . .), or a sand-hill, a down. **1929** Dobie *Vaquero* 201 **TX**, I worked for years in the *mogotes* of huisache and mesquite. *Ibid* 233, The brush here was rather spotted, very thick in some places with open intervals between the *mogotes.* **1932** *DN* 6.231 **wTX**, *Mogote.* A Spanish word for a clump of trees, probably picked up and used now and then in limited territory. I have note of it only in Western Texas. **1932** Bentley *Spanish Terms* 169, *Mogote* (*Spanish*, [mo:'go:te:]; *English*, [mo:'go:ti:]) A hillock; applied also to thick patches of shrubbery. **1941** Dobie *Longhorns* 303 **TX**, They seem to know that riders incline to go merely to the edge of a patch of brush. . .

Tiburcio . . found five outlaws in such a *mogote*. *Ibid* 314, The feller dodged and laid down in a *mogote*.

moh See **more**

mohale See **mahala**

moharra See **mojarra**

Mohave aster n

An aster-like plant (*Xylorhiza tortifolia*).

1933 Jaeger *CA Deserts* 131, When it comes out in force on the gravelly mesas and rocky hills, the Mohave aster . . presents an equally striking spectacle. **1949** *Desert Mag.* Apr 8 **CA,** Golden bush and Mohave aster are in bloom among the rocks. **1957** Jaeger *N. Amer. Deserts* 286, *Mohave aster.* . . Handsome perennial with large lilac-colored flowers. **1981** Bugliosi–Hurwitz *Shadow* 308 **sCA,** He sauntered along the edge of a dry wash. . . As he bent down . . to touch a delicate Mohave aster, his eye strayed from the lilac-colored petals.

Mohave comet n

A **stickleaf** (here: *Mentzelia albicaulis*).

1941 Jaeger *Wildflowers* 154 **Desert SW,** *Mohave comet.* . . *Fl[ower]:* bright yellow.

Mohave diamond rattler (or rattlesnake) See **Mohave rattlesnake**

Mohave flower n Also sp *Mojave flower*

A **desert snapdragon** (here: *Mohavea confertiflora*).

1951 Abrams *Flora Pacific States* 3.788, *Mohavea confertiflòra.* . . Mohave flower. **1979** Spellenberg *Audubon Guide N. Amer. Wildflowers W. Region* 763, *Mojave Flower.* . . Desert washes and rocky slopes. . . Southeastern California to southern Nevada, western Arizona, and northwestern Sonora.

Mohave poppy n As *Mojave poppy*

A **gold poppy** (here: *Eschscholtzia glyptosperma*).

1947 *Desert Mag.* July 27, You can't go far on the Mojave desert without seeing the Mojave Poppy, often in lavish prodigality.

Mohave rattlesnake n Also *Mohave diamond rattler, Mohave diamond rattlesnake, Mojave (rattlesnake)*

A **diamondback rattlesnake** (here: *Crotalus scutulatus*).

1936 *AZ Univ. Genl. Bulletin* 3.104, The Mojave rattlesnake *(C. scutulatus)* occurs in much the same environment as [*Crotalus*] *atrox*. **1947** Pickwell *Amphibians* 59 **sCA,** *Crotalus scutulatus scutulatus,* the Mojave Rattlesnake, has markings consisting of green diamonds on a brown background, and the black tail rings are on the average narrower than the white. In addition there are scale characteristics of the head which separate this Snake from the others of the genus. It occurs in the Mojave Desert of California. **1952** Ditmars *N. Amer. Snakes* 249, Mohave Diamond Rattlesnake, *Crotalus scutellatus.* . . Compared with the powdery-gray Western Diamond-back, . . the Mohave Diamond Rattler is a clearly definable snake. **1974** Shaw–Campbell *Snakes West* 213, Almost as dangerous [as the diamondback rattlesnake] and somewhat similar in appearance is the Mojave rattlesnake, a moderately large, wide-ranging snake with a particularly potent venom that contains elements not unlike those in some of the cobra venoms. *Ibid* 229, On the Mojave's tail are alternating dark and light rings, with the light rings wider than the dark ones. **1981** Vogt *Nat. Hist. WI* 171, Western diamondbacks, prairie rattlesnakes, Mohave rattlesnakes, and sidewinders are easily collected in flat open areas in the desert or on roads at night.

Mohave thorn n

=crucifixion thorn 3.

1931 U.S. Dept. Ag. *Misc. Pub.* 101.116, Canotia (*Canotia holacantha*), also called crucifixion thorn, Mohave-thorn, paloverde, and tree of Christ.

Mohave yucca n Also sp *Mojave yucca*

A **yucca** (here: *Yucca schidigera*).

1897 Sudworth *Arborescent Flora* 107, Mohave Yucca. **1933** Jaeger *CA Deserts* 174, On the high slopes of the New York Mountains and vicinity it consorts with junipers, Mohave yuccas, tree yuccas, and piñons. **1959** Munz–Keck *CA Flora* 1361, *Y[ucca] schidigera.* . . Mohave Yucca. . . Nev., Ariz., L[ower] Calif. . . San Bernardino Co. has plants with blue-green l[ea]v[e]s. **1967** *DARE* (Qu. S26e, *Other wildflowers not yet mentioned;* not asked in early QRs) Inf **CA**4, Mohave yucca. **1981** Benson–Darrow *Trees SW Deserts* 56, *Mohave Yucca.* . . The California Indians made much use of the Mojave yucca as a source

of fiber for ropes and coarsely woven blankets and as a source of soap. The fleshy fruits are eaten raw or roasted as are those of banana yucca.

Mohawk n Also *Mohican* [*Mohawk* an Iroquoian people of the Mohawk River Valley in New York; *Mohican* an Algonquian people of the upper Hudson River Valley in New York] Cf **Apache, Iroquois**

A haircut in which the head is shaved except for a strip of hair running down the center of the scalp.

1950 *WELS (Different kinds of men's haircuts)* 13 Infs, **WI,** Mohawk. **1955** *AmSp* 30.304 **seMI,** *Mohawk.* . . A type of crew haircut. **1965–70** *DARE* (Qu. X5) 64 Infs, **scattered,** Mohawk; **MO**29, **NY**109, 123, **OH**22, **VT**8, Mohican. [Of all Infs responding to the question, 12% were young, 41% hs educ, 47% male; of those giving these responses, 29% were young, 55% hs educ, 36% male.] **1979** *New Yorker* 5 Mar 96 **NY,** Steep, lumpy, rounded hills with stands of forest on top, like Mohawk haircuts. **1986** Pederson *LAGS Concordance (Hairstyles)* 3 infs, **ce,cwFL, cnTN,** Mohawk; 1 inf, **seLA,** Mohican—head shaved except for strip in center.

Mohawk brier n Cf **Indian brier**

Perh a **greenbrier.**

1900 (1901) Munn *Uncle Terry* 157 **coastal ME,** I lost my boat over back here on the shore, and have had a cheerful time among the Mohawk briers.

Mohawk weed n

A **bellwort** (here: *Uvularia perfoliata*).

1876 Hobbs *Bot. Hdbk.* 71, Mohawk weed,—Bellwort,—Uvularia perfoliata. **1900** Lyons *Plant Names* 385, *U[vularia] perfoliata* . . is called Mohawk-weed. **1931** Clute *Common Plants* 29, The Mohawk-weed *(Uvularia perfoliata)* is named for another tribe of central New York. **1959** Carleton *Index Herb. Plants* 82, *Mohawk-weed:* Uvularia perfoliata.

Mohican See **Mohawk**

moi n **HI**

A **threadfin** (here: *Polydactylus sexfilis*).

1926 Pan-Pacific Research Inst. *Jrl.* 1.1.8, Moi. Polynemus sexfilis. . . Reef. **1960** Gosline–Brock *Hawaiian Fishes* 154, The moi is one of the most characteristic and sought-after fish of the sandy shores. **1967** *Honolulu Star–Bulletin* (HI) 31 May sec F 1/4, Moi—threadfish. Bake. Steam. **1984** Sunset *HI Guide* 145, *Moi*—threadfin.

moist n [*OED* a1366–1742]

Moisture.

1966–68 *DARE* (Qu. B4, *A day when the air is very still, moist, and warm—it's* _____) Inf **GA**7, Full o' moist; (Qu. B23, . . *A light rain that doesn't last . . it's just a* _____) Inf **NC**49, Didn't bring the moist up—a lot of people use this. **1981** Pederson *LAGS Basic Materials,* 1 inf, **seGA,** [Land] keeps too much moist on it; 1 inf, **cnGA,** Got more moist = has more moisture.

moist v [*OED* 1382 →, "*obs. exc. dial.*"]

To moisten.

1924 Raine *Land of Saddle-Bags* 79 **sAppalachians,** Then he'd moist it and rub it and grain it through a fine sieve.

moist cake, moist east See **moist yeast**

moisty adj Cf **misty moisty**

Damp; humid.

1966 *DARE* (Qu. B4, *A day when the air is very still, moist, and warm—it's* _____) Inf **GA**7, Moisty. **1966–70** *DARE* Tape **TX**107, If rain come, pretty soon the ground kinda moisty; **SC**17, You want to get a good, moisty place [to plant tobacco].

moist yeast n Also *moist cake* Pronc-sp *moist east* **chiefly Nth, N Midl** See Map on p. 632 Cf **compressed yeast**

Yeast molded and packaged in the form of a small block.

1950 *WELS (What is used to raise bread before baking?)* 6 Infs, **WI,** Moist yeast. **1965–70** *DARE* (Qu. H17, . . *Kinds [of yeast]*) 10 Infs, **esp Nth, N Midl,** Moist (yeast); **MO**12, Moist east; **IA**7, Moist yeast = yeast cakes; **IL**34, Moist yeast—has to be refrigerated; **ME**11, Moist—square cube wrapped in foil; **OH**72, Moist yeast—old-fashioned; **PA**213, Moist yeast—soft; **MI**94, Moist cake; (Qu. H16) Inf **MO**1, Moist east. **1973** Allen *LAUM* 1.285 **MN** (as of c1950), Cake of yeast. . . *moist yeast* [1 inf].

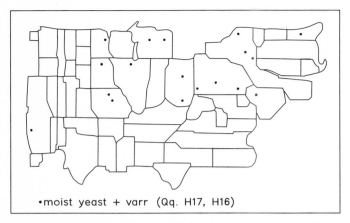

•moist yeast + varr (Qq. H17, H16)

mojarra n Also sp *moharra* [Span *mojarra,* var of *moharra* spearhead]

1 A fish of the family Gerreidae. Also called **silver perch.** For other names of var spp see **Irish pompano, mojarrita, silver jenny**

[**1845** in 1846 *Amer. Acad. Arts & Sci. Memoirs* 6.336, Gerres Brasilianus. . . Called, at Porto Rico, "Moharra."] **1884** Goode *Fisheries U.S.* 1.279, *The Moharra Family—Gerridae* [sic]. . . Represented on our eastern coast by four species, all of which are very small and of little consequence except as food for larger fishes. **1929** Pan-Pacific Research Inst. *Jrl.* 4.4.8 **sCA,** Gerridae [sic]. The Mojarras. **1955** Zim-Shoemaker *Fishes* 118, *Mojarras.* . . are among the commonest Atlantic shore fishes and are also found on the Pacific Coast. More abundant in warmer waters, mojarras are seldom over 6 in. long. **1955** Carr-Goin *Guide Reptiles* 105 **FL,** Mojarra. . . *Florida Range.* Both coasts. *Habitat.* Shallow salt waters and fresh-water streams, especially spring-runs, entering salt water. **1973** Knight *Cook's Fish Guide* 384, Mojarra. . . Can be *f[resh]w[ater]* or *s[alt]w[ater].* **1991** Amer. Fisheries Soc. *Common Names Fishes* 53, Gerreidae—mojarras.

2 Any of var **surfperch.**

1884 Goode *Fisheries U.S.* 1.276, *The Surf-fish Family—Embiotocidae.* . . The names "minny," "Sparada," and "Moharra" are also applied to the smaller species [of these fishes] northward [of Oregon]. *Ibid* 278, *Hypsurus Caryi.* . . This species is known as "moharra" to the Portuguese at Monterey [California]; elsewhere it is a "Perch." **1911** U.S. Bur. Census *Fisheries 1908* 317, *Surf-fish (Embiotocidae).* . . Also called . . "moharra" . . along their northern range.

3 A **demoiselle 1** (here: *Abudefduf saxatilis*).

1882 U.S. Natl. Museum *Bulletin* 16.611, *P[omacentrus] saxatilis.* . . *Cow-pilot; Mojarra.* . . occasional on our South Atlantic coast. **1896** U.S. Bur. Fisheries *Rept. for 1895* 410, *Abudefduf saxatilis.* . . Mojarra Raiado [sic].

mojarrita n

A **mojarra 1** (here: *Eucinostomus* spp).

1896 U.S. Bur. Fisheries *Rept. for 1895* 391, *Eucinostomus.* . . Mojarritas. **1902** Jordan-Evermann *Amer. Fishes* 445, *The Mojarritas.* . . [are] represented in our waters by 5 species. **1911** *Century Dict. Suppl.,* Mojarrita. . . Any fish of the genus *Eucinostomus* and the family *Gerridae* [sic]. These fish are numerous in warm seas.

Mojave See **Mohave rattlesnake**

Mojave flower See **Mohave flower**

Mojave poppy See **Mohave poppy**

Mojave rattlesnake See **Mohave rattlesnake**

Mojave yucca See **Mohave yucca**

mojay, mojh(e)y See **moshey**

mojo n Also sp *mojoe, moojoo;* pronc-sp *monjo* [Of Afr origin; cf Gullah *moco* witchcraft, magic, and Fula *moco'o* medicine man] **chiefly Sth** orig *chiefly among Black speakers* Cf **conjure bag, hand** n **B4, hoodoo** n **1c, jomo,** *DBE*

1 A charm, amulet, or spell; magic.

1926 Puckett *Folk Beliefs S. Negro* 19, The term *mojo* is often used by the Mississippi Negroes to mean "charms, amulets, or tricks," as "to work mojo" on a person or "to carry a mojo." **1928** in 1983 Taft *Blues*

Lyric Poetry 132 **Chicago IL,** My rider's got a mojo : and she won't let me see / Every time I start to loving : she ease that thing on me / She's got to fool her daddy : She's got to keep that mojo hid / But papa's got something : for to find that mojo with. **1934** Couch *Culture South* 585, Fragments of hoodoo and conjuration, whose spells, . . mojos, . . goofer bags are the special province of the Negro "root doctor" or "hoodoo man." **c1938** in 1970 Hyatt *Hoodoo* 1.610 **Memphis TN** [Black], Yo' kin take *High John de Conker* an' git *black lodestone* an' *Adam an' Eve root.* Put them together with violet incense powders, an' sew them in a red flannel. They call that *mojo* an' dat fo' yore luck. *Ibid* **New Orleans LA,** They have some *lucky mojo.* Yo' take an' put it in your house in your room an' that will make—when people come in yer room an' inhale that once, they'll come back again. *Ibid* **MS,** (And she saw this perfume?) Yes. (And it's called?) *Moojoo Lucky Star. (Mojo Lucky Star?)* Yes, sir. (And how do you use that perfume?) You don't use it. The one that you want to come back to you, you put it on them. **1940** Writers' Program *Guide GA* 260, Root doctors and "cunjur" folk ply their trade for a small fee, and at small shops can be purchased . . Lucky Mojoe Drops of Love, or Mojoe Incense to bring love and luck to the buyer and confusion to his enemies. **1946** Tallant *Voodoo* 197 **New Orleans LA** [Black], She gets five dollars for a mojo. You know what a mojo is? It's the leg bone of a black cat that's been killed in a graveyard at midnight. **1958** Hughes-Bontemps *Negro Folkl.* 374, Goin' to Louisiana to git myself a Mojo hand / 'Cause dese backbitin' womens tryin' fo' to steal my man. **1962** *Jrl. Amer. Folkl.* 75.314 **NC,** Local names for amulets are "mojo," "monjo," . . and "jomo." These are all made by the conjurer and may consist of one or more of the following materials or some unknown substance wrapped in a little black, brown, or green cloth bag: roots, rats, lizards, snakes, . . red dirt, steel wool, gray clay, and pumpkin seeds. **1965–70** *DARE* (Qu. CC14, . . *Where one person supposedly casts a spell over another*) Infs **GA**1, 8, 13, **TX**37, Mojo; **GA**3, 9, Put the mojo on (*or* to him); **NY**249, Went into her mojo ['mojo] bag; (Qu. CC13a, . . *A forked stick that's used to show where there's water underground*) Inf **TX**98, Mojo stick—old-fashioned. [7 of 8 Infs White] **1973** Himes *Black on Black* 18 **NYC** [Black], You got the best go and the mojo.

2 By ext; in phr *have the mojo on:* to have the advantage of.

1938 *AmSp* 13.6 **seAR,** Mojo. . . Used as a noun in such instances as 'He has the mojo on me.' That is, he has the upper hand on me.

mojo v

1 To jinx or charm. Cf **conjure** v, **hoodoo** v **1**

1966–70 *DARE* (Qu. CC12b, . . *If a person has a lot of bad luck . . "He's been _____."*) Infs **MS**1, **MO**23, **NC**31, Mojoed; **AR**12, Mojoed—Negroes. **1972** Chapman *New Black Voices* 356, It is overdue time / to mojo the demons . . now it is time for mojo.

2 See quot. Cf **mojo** n **2**

1938 *AmSp* 13.6 **seAR,** Mojo. . . To hoodwink, or to get the best of one. 'I'll mojo you this time.'

mojoe See **mojo** n

moke n Also *black moke* [Etym unknown] usu derog Cf **smoke** A Black person; occas a Filipino or Hawaiian.

1856 White *Oh Hush* 19 **VA** [Black], Rose, don't you interfere, I'll show dis moke a sight. **1875** *Century Illustr. Mag.* 11.142, "See here! my lively moke," said he, "you sling on too much style!" **1882** Peck *Peck's Sunshine* 53 **Milwaukee WI,** They want to hear old fashioned negro melodies, and yet these mokes will tackle Italian opera. **1890** *DN* 1.62 **swOH,** Moke . . a negro. Especially "musical moke," a negro minstrel, who plays on a number of different instruments in succession. **1892** Twain *Amer. Claimant* 87 **DC** [Black], Dat ole moke is losin' his mine. **1896** *DN* 1.421 **cNY,** Moke: a negro. **1927** *AmSp* 3.451 [Naval Academy jargon], Moke alone signifies "dark" or "black," and is the term for a Negro or Filipino. **1933** *AmSp* 8.4.52 **NE** [Pioneer speech], A *moke* (from *smoke*) was a colored servant. **1941** *LANE* Map 452B (Nicknames for a negro) 1 inf, **cCT,** We used to call negroes *mokes;* 1 inf, **sME,** Moke. **1950** *PADS* 14.14 **SC,** *Black Moke.* . . A Negro having the clear, coal-black hue of the African tribe of Mocoes from the valley of the Congo. **1967** *DARE* (Qu. HH28, *Names and nicknames . . for people of foreign background*) Inf **HI**13, Moke [mok]—a Hawaiian. **1981** *Pidgin To Da Max* np **HI,** Moke. . . Local boy whose idea of a good time is to broke [sic] some body's face.

mokihana n Also *mokehana* [Haw] **HI** A tree *(Pelea anisata)* native to Kauai.

1888 Hillebrand *Flora Hawaiian Is.* 64, *P[elea] anisata.* . . Nat[ive] name: 'Mokehana'.—All parts of the tree, but particularly the capsules, when bruised, emit a strong spicy odor of anise. **1915** Bryan *Nat. Hist. HI* 221, The most highly scented of all are the seed pods of the mokihana used in making leis. **1930** Degener *Ferns of HI* 193, *P[elea] anisata. . .* is mentioned because of its high esteem in the eyes of the Hawaiians, who know it as *mokihana.* The plant is peculiar to the Island of Kauai where it grows in the rain forest. **1948** Neal *In Gardens HI* 419, *Mokihana. . .* A slender tree 15 to 20 feet high. . . Fresh fruit sometimes burns the skin. **1954** *Ellery Queen's Mystery Mag.* Oct 45/1 *(OEDS),* She . . hung around her neck a *lei* of mokihana and maile. **1967** *DARE* (Qu. S11) Inf **HI**4, Mokihana—flower of island of Kauai; scented wood; string seeds, dry, will retain smell for years.

moky adj Also sp *mokey* [*EDD moke* sb.³ 1 "A mist, fog. . . Hence . . *moky* . . of weather: dull, hazy"]

Of weather: foggy; hazy.

 1938 Matschat *Suwannee R.* 289 **neFL, seGA,** *Moky:* foggy. **1984** Wilder *You All Spoken Here* 141 **Sth,** *Mokey:* Hazy; foggy.

mola n

Std: a fish of the genus *Mola,* usu *Mola mola.* Also called **headfish 1, ocean sunfish**

‡**molar** n [Perh var of **bowler,** infl by *molar*] Cf *DS* EE6a

 1950 *WELS* (The marble used to knock the others out of the ring) 1 Inf, **ceWI,** Molar.

molar masher n Also *molar jerker,* ~ *tinker* joc

A dentist.

 1950 *WELS* (Joking and nicknames for a dentist) 1 Inf, **csWI,** Molar masher. **1968–70** *DARE* (Qu. BB52) Inf **MD**17, Molar jerker; **PA**245, Molar masher; **NY**79, Molar tinker.

molasses n Usu |məˈlæsɪz, -ɪs|; also |ˌmoˈlæsɪz, -ɪs|; also esp **NEng, Sth** |məˈlɑsɪz, -ˈlasɪz|; freq aphet |ˈlæsɪz, -ɪs| Pronc-spp *merlasse(r)s, molassey, molosses, lass(i)es, lassy;* for addit pronc and sp varr see **A** below

A Pronc varr.

 1730 in 1985 Lederer *Colonial Amer. Engl.* 133, There'll be some a drinking round and some a lapping lasses. **1775** in 1974 Winslow *Amer. Broadside* 141 **NEast,** The 'lasses they eat every day,/ Would keep an house a winter. **1777** in 1956 Eliason *Tarheel Talk* 314 **NC,** Mellosses. **1797** *Ibid,* Moloses. **1807** Irving *Salmagundi* 10.204, This manufacture is called by the bostonians *lasses* candy—by the new-yorkers *cock-a-nee-nee.* **1887** (1967) Harris *Free Joe* 83 **GA** [Black], Dee won' be none lef' fer buy flour en 'lasses fer make mo'. **1893** Shands *MS Speech* 43, Lasses. . . Negro and illiterate white for *molasses.* **1894** *DN* 1.332 **NJ,** *Molasses:* pron[ounced] *merlasses, merlasse, millasses.* **1899** (1912) Green *VA Folk-Speech* 285, A barrel of molosses. **1899** Chesnutt *Conjure Woman* 43 **csNC** [Black], Dey want [=wasn't] no use cryin' ober spilt merlasses. **1909** *DN* 3.344 **eAL, wGA,** Lasses. . . The full form is rarely heard in illiterate speech. **1915** *DN* 4.184 **swVA,** Lasses. **1938** Stuart *Dark Hills* 226 **neKY,** We popped corn. . . We made lassie-popcorn balls. **1940** *Amer. Mercury* 50.213 **KY,** Once a hard winter come. . . Not a lick o' sweetening in the 'lassy barrel. **1941** Stuart [see **C**1 below]. **1941** *LANE* Map 307, 129 infs, **NEng,** [m(ə)ˈlæsɪz, -ɪs]; 28 infs, **chiefly eNEng,** [məˈlasɪz]; 15 infs, **chiefly eNEng,** [məˈlɑsɪz]; 15 infs, **chiefly sNEng,** [moˈlæsɪz, -ɪs]; 10 infs, **neMA, seVT, NH, swME,** [məˈlæəsɪz]; 5 infs, **neMA, NH, swME,** [ˈlæsɪz]; 3 infs, **neMA,** [ˈlɑsɪz]; 3 infs, **neMA, swME,** [ˈlasɪz]; 3 infs, **wCT, swME,** [məˈlæɪsɪz]; 1 inf, **csCT,** [moⁱˈlæsɪz]. **1953** Brewer *Word Brazos* 16 **eTX** [Black], He . . staa't to soppin' his biscuits in his 'lasses an' one-eyed gravy. **1954** Harder Coll. **cwTN,** Molassey candy. *Ibid,* Them folks stick like lasses. **1958** *PADS* 29.13 **TN,** Pronunciation [of *molasses mill*] rep[orted] as *molassy mill* in Lawrence, Perry [counties]. **1965–70** *DARE* (Qq. A18, H21, H80, BB50d) 211 Infs, **widespread,** [məˈlæsɪz, -əz, -ɪz] (and similar proncs); 102 Infs, **scattered,** [məˈlæsɪs, -əs, -ɪs] (and similar proncs); 50 Infs, **scattered,** [ˌmoˈlæsɪz, ˌmoˈlæsɪs, ˈmoˌlæsɪz] (and similar proncs); 22 Infs, **scattered,** [ˈmlæsɪz] (and similar proncs with reduced first syllable); **CA**113, **IL**35, 43, 52, 57, [məˈlæzəz]; **MO**1, [məˈlæːṣzs]; **MA**72, **ME**4, [məˈlasɪs, -ɪz]; **MA**72, [moˈlaːsɪs]; **VA**71, [məˈlɑsɪs]; **NJ**18, [mʌˈlaɪsɪz]; **NJ**22, [moˈlaɪsɪs]; **MD**19, [mlɛɪsɪs]; **MD**24, [məˈlɛɪsɪs]; **NJ**25, [məˈleˀsəz]; **AL**34, [ˌmoˈlæsɪ]; **IL**117, [məˈlæsɪ]; **MS**55, [məˈlesɪ]; **NJ**16, [mʌˈlæsɪ]; **MS**72, [ˈlæsɪz]. **1982** [see **C**1 below]. **1989** Pederson *LAGS Tech. Index* 172 **Gulf Region,** [By far the commonest proncs recorded were [məˈlæ(ɪ)sɪz] (513 infs) and [məˈlæ(ɪ)sz̩, -ɪs] (133). 15 infs gave [məˈlæsɪ], 16 [ˈlæ(ɪ)sɪz, -ɪz, and one [ˈlæsɪ]. For the first syllable, less common varr were [m̩-] (29),

[mɪ-] (26), [m̩-] (14), [mʌ-] (12), [mu-] (7), [mo-] (6); for the middle syllable, [-ˈlɛɪ-] (6), [-ˈlɛ-] (4), [-ˈle-] (3), [-ˈlɑ-] (3), [-ˈlʌ-] (1).]

B Gram form.

Also rarely *molassisis:* Used as pl count noun. **chiefly S Midl** Cf **cabbage A2, cheese A**

 1843 (1916) Hall *New Purchase* 155 **IN,** Also maple molasses, (usually called "them 'ere molassisis,") and preserved apples. **1859** (1968) Bartlett *Americanisms* 275, *Molasses.* Used as a plural in the West; as, "Will you give me some of *those* molasses?" **1895** *DN* 1.373 **seKY, eTN, wNC,** "They's all gone"—the molasses. **1902** *DN* 2.239 **sIL,** *Molasses. . .* Never used as a singular. 'These are good molasses.' **1905** *DN* 3.88 **nwAR,** *Molasses. . .* I like *molasses,* but I can't eat *many* of 'em. **1915** *DN* 4.227 **wTX,** *Molasses. . .* Always used as plural. **1923** *DN* 5.215 **swMO,** *Molasses. . .* Always spoken of as if plural form. "How many molasses did you-all git?" **1927** in 1983 Taft *Blues Lyric Poetry* 3, Oh nigger licked molasses : and the white man licked them too. **1937** *Hall Coll.* **wNC, eTN,** *Molasses. . .* This noun is felt as a plural, e.g., "They are made in a press," where "they" refers to "molasses." **1948** Faulkner *Intruder* 24 **MS,** He thanked him for the molasses and Lucas had answered . . : 'They turned out good this year.' **1950** *PADS* 14.47 **nSC,** *Molasses. . .* "These molasses," "them molasses," etc. c**1960** Wilson Coll. **csKY,** *Molasses* is often (maybe most often) used as a plural. **1974** [see **C**1 below]. **1989** Pederson *LAGS Tech. Index* 172 **Gulf Region,** 238 infs, Molasses is/was; 42 infs, Molasses are/were.

C Senses.

1 Syrup, usu that made by concentrating the sap of various plants, esp sugar cane or sorghum. Note: The std commercial molasses is a by-product of the sugar-manufacturing process and represents only the uncrystallizable fraction of the original juice; it is likely that some of the *DARE* Infs are referring to this sense of *molasses.* **widespread, but less freq Inland Nth, Pacific** See Map See also **maple molasses**

 1777 in 1888 Cutler *Life* 1.63, Boiled some cornstalk juice into molasses. **1864** in 1865 IL Dept. Ag. *Trans.* 5.317 **cwIL,** A near neighbor of mine, . . and his two sons, have a neat molasses house, with an engine to run the crushing mill. **1941** *LANE* Map 307 *(Maple syrup)* 1 inf, **wCT,** Sap molasses; 1 inf, **nwVT,** Molasses, from maple sap. **1941** Stuart *Men of Mts.* 300 **KY,** Cane was getting ripe to make in lassies. **1941** Writers' Program *Guide WV* 415, In autumn, farm families gather . . to reap green cane, which is boiled down into syrupy " 'lasses' and used as sweetening in all home cooking. . . Entire families toil in the making of sorghum. **1950** *WELS* (Names for sweet stuff that you pour over these cakes) 4 Infs, **WI,** Molasses. **1957** *Sat. Eve. Post Letters* **cIN,** In my home I and the family . . always said . . "molasses"—for syrup. **1965–70** *DARE* (Qu. H21) 165 Infs, **widespread, but less freq Inland Nth, Pacific,** Molasses; **AR**47, 55, **IN**54, **MO**3, 38, **OK**1, 21, **TN**52, Sorghum molasses; **AR**32, **MS**72, **TX**1, Lasses; **IN**48, Sugar molasses [Of all Infs responding to the question, 70% were old; of those giving these responses, 79% were old.]; [**AR**52, **DC**7, **GA**36, 79, **NJ**67, **NY**41, **SC**43, Black(strap) molasses; **CT**39, New Orleans molasses]. **1974** Fink *Mountain Speech* 16 **wNC, eTN,** *Molasses* . . sorghum syrup, always plural. "Give me some o' them molasses." **1982** *Barrick Coll.* **csPA,** *Lassy—molasses* or corn syrup.

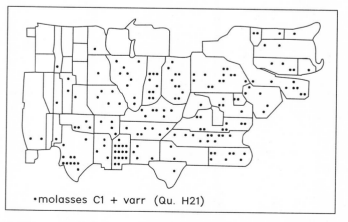

 •molasses C1 + varr (Qu. H21)

2 Nonsense, baloney—sometimes used as an exclam. Cf **molly** n¹ 4

 1924 *DN* 5.273 [Exclams], Oh molasses. **1968** *DARE* (Qu. NN13,

When you think that the thing somebody has just said is silly or untrue:
"Oh, that's a lot of _____.") Inf **WV5**, Molasses.

3 The brown liquid exuded by grasshoppers. Cf **molasses hopper, tobacco juice**

1981 Mebane *Mary* 9 **cnNC**, "Grasshopper, Grasshopper, give me some molasses." If he didn't come across right away, we would talk to him some more and have him to understand that we weren't going to let him go until he deposited some brown liquid in our hands, which he never failed to do.

molasses biscuit n Also *molasses jug*
See quots.
1950 *PADS* 14.47 **SC**, *Molasses biscuit.* . . A biscuit of an earlier period, about the size of an ordinary bakery roll, with a hole thrust into it from the side with the forefinger. The hole is then filled with molasses. . . Probably obsolete. **1954** *PADS* 21.21 **SC**, *Brown jug.* . . A biscuit with a hole punched into it with the forefinger and filled with molasses. Also called *molasses jug.* . . *Molasses biscuit* . . is more generally used. Mainly used by children.

molasses-candy pull(ing) See **molasses pull(ing)**

molasses corn n
A **sorghum**, prob *Sorghum bicolor.*
1904 (1913) Johnson *Highways South* 321 **VA** [Black], The leaves of sorghum, or "molasses corn" as my driver called it, were also saved for cattle feed.

molasses face n
The **dot eye** bean.
1978 *Wanigan Catalog* 22, The yellow eye [sic] which have come to me are of three color combinations. The one I have known since about 1920 is white, with a large, solid yellow eye patch. Look alikes in the collection [of beans] are molasses face and skullcap. **1979** *UpCountry* Jan 21 **ME**, What is called Molasses Face in Maine, for instance, is referred to as Yellow Eye elsewhere. Each year he plants a number of varieties in his own backyard garden and fills nearby areas . . with row on row of different kinds of pole, bush and dwarf runner beans. **1990** *Seed Savers Yearbook* 41 **MN, OH**, *Molasses Face.* . . white seed with yellow around eye, shelling bean . . very productive.

molasses hopper n [**molasses C3**] Cf **tobacco spitter**
=**grasshopper 1.**
1969 *DARE* (Qu. R6, . . *Names . . for grasshoppers*) Inf **CT23**, Molasses hopper.

molasses jug See **molasses biscuit**

molasses making n **sAppalachians** Cf **molasses stew**
A social gathering at which molasses is made and eaten; similarly n *molasses licking* a social event after the making of molasses.
1941 Writers' Program *Guide WV* 416 **cwWV**, Everybody is thinking of the gaiety to come when the last day's work [of making molasses from green cane] is done. The event is celebrated with a ' 'lasses lickin',' attracting neighbors from near and far. The assembled guests are given small wooden paddles to scrape the generous leaving in the boiling pan; games are played; there is group singing; mountain minstrels enliven the gathering. . . [Y]oung folks wander off in couples, for, as everybody knows and expects, 'they's a sight o' courtin' ben did at 'lasses lickin's.' **1966** *Good Old Days* Feb 30 **neKY** (as of c1910), When the neighborhood boys and girls heard about a molasses making going to be at the neighbors [sic] down the way, everybody and his neighbor came to join in the fun of 'lasses soppin! After it was made and poured in new 50-pound lard cans, all the fellows would take their knifes [sic] and whittle a wooden spoon to eat the newly made molasses. **1966** *DARE* (Qu. FF1, . . *A kind of group meeting called a 'social' or 'sociable'.* . . [*What goes on?*]) Inf **NC36**, Molasses making. [**1982** Ginns *Snowbird Gravy* 147 **nwNC** (as of 1930s), We'd have a candy stew . . or we'd have a corn shucking or some event, such as grinding molasses, to get together.] **1991** Still *Wolfpen Notebooks* 19 **sAppalachians**, Getting acquainted didn't take long for I began to attend the community happenings. Depending on the season, bean stringings and corn shuckings and molasses making and hog killings.

molasses pull(ing) n Also *molasses-candy pull(ing)* Cf **taffy pulling**
=**candy pulling.**

1893 *Harper's New Mth. Mag.* 86.441, I invited them all myself late this afternoon; and it is a molasses-candy-pulling. **1939** Coffin *Capt. Abby* 66 **ME** (as of c1860s), He went to molasses candy pulls at his uncles' houses. **1955** Parris *Roaming the Mountains* 151 **cwNC**, An old-timer is one who remembers . . when the social calendar swirled around corn-shuckin's, sewing bees, quiltin' frolics, bean stringin's, apple-butter stirrin's, and molasses pulls. **1975** Dwyer *Thangs* 9 **Sth, S Midl**, In the mountains, candy pullin's, sometimes called "molasses pullin's" started with the molasses-making season and continued through the winter. These "pullin's" provided the excuse for a social gathering at someone's house, particularly for young courting couples.

‡**molasses spit** n Cf *DS* DD4
=**ambeer 2.**
1950 *WELS* (*Saliva colored brown by snuff or chewing tobacco*) 1 Inf, **cnWI**, Molasses spit.

molasses stew n
A social gathering at which molasses candy is made; a **candy stew.**
1872 Schele de Vere *Americanisms* 287, The people of the South had always been fond of *molasses stews*, in which the boiling molasses was pulled or tugged out into long strips. **1943** Writers' Program NC *Bundle of Troubles* 26, They have a big 'lasses stew right here in the sassyfras thicket and ever'body invited to come. . . Atter a while he begins dishin' up the 'lasses, and settin' it 'round in the grass to cool so they can pull it to taffy.

molassey See **molasses**

molassisis See **molasses B**

molboard See **moldboard** n[1]

mold v Also sp *mould* Also with *up* [*OED mould* v.[1] 2 1601 →] Cf **dirt** v 1, **hill** v 1
To heap earth around (a plant).
1746 in 1940 *AmSp* 15.229 **NH**, Moulded my Island corn. **1887** in 1893 Mansur & Tebbetts *Genl. Catalogue D* 86 **MS**, The Sunset Middlebreakers do well to mould up cotton and scrape the middles at the same time. **1945** FWP *Lay My Burden Down* 224 **Sth** (as of c1865) [Black], They were in the field molding corn, going round the corn, hoeing it, and putting a little hill around it. **1967** *DARE* Tape **LA6**, You hoe 'em [=sweet potatoes] off and then you mold 'em back up.

mold n[1] Also *moldboard;* also in combs *shoe mold, toe* ~
A baseboard.
1950 *WELS* (*Strip of wood about 8 inches high along the bottom of a wall inside a room, joining to the floor*) 2 Infs, **WI**, Moldboard. **1966–68** *DARE* (Qu. D37) Inf **GA19**, Mold; **MO2**, Moldboard; **AL27**, **FL9**, **NC81**, Shoe mold; **TN11, 13**, Toe mold.

mold n[2] See **mould**

moldboard n[1] Pronc-spp *molboard, mow(er)board, mulboard* Cf Pronc Intro 3.I.22, 3.II.27
Std sense, var forms.
1917 *DN* 4.396 **neOH**, *Mulboard.* . . Mold-board of a plow. **1965–70** *DARE* (Qu. L18, *Kinds of plows*) 55 Infs, **scattered**, (Double, two-way, or wooden) moldboard (plow); 14 Infs, **scattered**, Molboard plow; 13 Infs, **scattered, but chiefly Nth, Midl**, Mowboard plow; **CT4, 14, IA43, IL90, KS9, PA139**, (Steel) mulboard plow; **IA39**, Lathe and mowboard plow; **IN80**, Mowerboard. **1966** *DARE* Tape **ME5**, [FW:] What are the different parts of a plow? [Inf:] Well, you got the mowboard. . . that throwed the furrow over.

moldboard n[2] See **mold** n

moldosher n [Etym unknown]
1950 *PADS* 14.47 **cnSC**, *Moldoshers.* . . Dumplings made of young spring onions and cooked with a hambone. Newberry County.

mold up See **mold** v

moldwarp n Also sp *mouldwarp;* pronc-spp *molewarp, mortworp* [*OED mouldwarp* (c1325 →; "Now chiefly north. dial.")] a mole; often applied to a person who is literally or figuratively blind] **esp sAppalachians**
A stupid or good-for-nothing person.
1928 Chapman *Happy Mt.* 312 **seTN**, *Moldwarp*—a slack-twisted, worthless man; a downgone wastrel. **1938** Matschat *Suwannee R.* 122

neFL, seGA, Hain't as if Pompano was a mortworp—he's got a fine job in the gov'ment. [*Ibid* 289, Moldwarp: worthless, shiftless—i.e., as a "mole."] **1944** *PADS* 2.46 **wNC,** Molewarp, moldwarp. . . A senseless person. **1952** Brown *NC Folkl.* 1.566, Moldwarp, mouldwarp. . . A stupid person, a dolt. "That fellow's always doing the wrong thing; he's such a moldwarp he hacks me to death."

mole n¹

1 Std: a burrowing animal of the family Talpidae. Also called **gopher** n¹ **3, ground mole.** For other names of var genera and spp see **meadow mole 1, mole shrew 2, shrew mole, star-nosed ~**

2 =**meadow mouse.** *obs* Cf **mole mouse 3**

1839 Buel *Farmer's Companion* 99, Where stones are to be employed, either as a covering to the conduit, or as a drain of themselves, they should be broken to so small a size, that moles or ground-mice cannot penetrate and find a shelter among them. **1857** U.S. Patent Office *Annual Rept. for 1856: Ag.* 84, Meadow-Mice. . . While many persons call them "Moles," . . they are not in the least related to that family.

3 A **shrew;** see quots. Cf **mole mouse 2**

1903 in 1917 Anthony *Mammals Amer.* 308, Considering the abundance of these animals, . . it seems strange that the name 'Shrew' has not come into more general use, especially among persons who live in the country and see them often. When referred to on the farm they are almost invariably designed [sic] 'Mole' or 'Mouse'. **1961** Jackson *Mammals WI* 43, *Blarina brevicauda.* . . *Vernacular names.* . . Baby mole, . . little mole, . . mole (particularly in localities where there are no true moles).

4 See **mole salamander.**

mole n² See **mould**

mole bean n

1 =**bagpod.**

1937 *Torreya* 37.98 **SC,** *Glottidium vesicarium.* . . Mole-bean, Hilton Head [Island].

2 also *mole plant:* The castor bean *(Ricinis communis).* [Because its odor is supposed to repel *moles*] **esp S Midl, S Atl**

1836 *Farmers' Reg.* Sept 288 [sic for 298], There is yet another growth that bids fair to become of great value to the agricultural interest of the Eastern Shore of Maryland, namely, the *palma christi,* or castor bean plant, sometimes known by the name of *mole plant.* **1939** FWP *These are Our Lives* 376 **ceTN,** Nothing left now but that old hanging basket of moss and them mole beans. Castor beans, some calls them. They's supposed to keep a mole from rooting up your ground. **1959** Carleton *Index Herb. Plants* 82, Mole-bean: Ricinus communis. . . Mole-plant: . . Ricinus communis. **1968** *DARE* (Qu. I20, . . *Kinds of beans)* Inf **IN**52, Mole beans. **1969** *DARE* FW Addit **KY**52, Mole beans [FW: prob castor beans]—a tall, bushy, rank-smelling plant put in gardens to ward off moles. This plant is often grown in mountain or old-fashioned gardens. **1969** *SC Market Bulletin* 24 July 4/4, Castor or Mole Bean seed 50c-50. **1972** *GA Dept. Ag. Farmers Market Bulletin* 5 Jan 8/2 **swGA,** [Letter:] The Palma Christi, Castor Bean, or mole bean, are these the same and will they get rid of ground moles? B.C., Albany. [Response:] These are all the same and do, for some reason, cause Mr. Mole to find a new home.

mole crab n

Usu a crab of the genus *Emerita,* but also *Blepharipoda occidentalis.* For other names of *E. talpoida* see **sand bug, sand crab**

[**1884** Goode *Fisheries U.S.* 1.779, *Hippa talpoida.* . . This species burrows like a mole, head first, instead of backward.] **1981** Meinkoth *Audubon Field Guide Seashore* 633, Pacific Mole Crab *(Emerita analoga).* . . These crabs often occur in dense populations on open beaches. . . Atlantic Mole Crab *(Emerita talpoida).* . . This species is commonly used for bait. *Ibid* 634, Spiny Mole Crab *(Blepharipoda occidentalis).* . . The adults are scavengers, feeding mostly on dead mole crabs *(Emerita)* that abound in the same habitat. **1989** (1990) Baden *Maryland's E. Shore* 21, The lower beach is active with the almost invisible life just under the surface. There are mole crabs, who sink into the sand vanishing so fast that you don't know if you really saw them or not.

mole cricket n [See quot 1884; *OED* 1714 →]

An insect of the family Gryllotalpidae. Also called **earth**

crab. For other names of var genera and spp see **changa, go-devil** n **8, gopher** n¹ **6, ground puppy 3**

1792 Belknap *Hist. NH* 3.181, Mole cricket—*grillus gryllotalpa.* **1852** Harris *Treatise Insects* 131, The common mole-cricket. . . The fore legs are admirably adapted for digging, being very short, broad, and strong; and the shanks, which are excessively broad, flat, and three-sided, have the lower side divided by deep notches into four finger-like projections, that give to this part very much the appearance and the power of the hand of a mole. **1884** (1885) McCook *Tenants* 147 **PA,** The mole-cricket is a nocturnal insect, and will not be caught near the door of his den until dusk. *Ibid* 148, "Why is the insect called a mole-cricket?" "From the very fact, in part, that caused you to mistake his burrow for a mole's. The general shape of the insect contributes to this likeness, as well as the strange development of the fore limbs, and the peculiar formation of the first pair of feet, which are not unlike the corresponding members of the mole. . . Like the mole, the mole-cricket passes nearly the whole of its life underground, digging out long passages. . . Like the mole, it is fierce and quarrelsome. . . Like the mole, it is exceedingly voracious." **1926** Essig *Insects N. Amer.* 99 **CA, AZ, NM,** Gryllotalpinae (Subfamily). Mole Crickets. **1967** *DARE* (Qu. R8, . . *Kinds of creatures that make a clicking or shrilling or chirping kind of sound)* Inf **AR**52, Mole cricket. **1967** *DARE* FW Addit **LA**2, Mole cricket—makes a run under the ground like a mole. **1980** Milne–Milne *Audubon Field Guide Insects* 442, Mole Crickets (Family Gryllotalpidae). . . have short antennae and spadelike front legs, which they use for digging. **1993** *Nature Conserv. Mag.* 43.4.21, The male prairie mole cricket may not qualify as one of the world's most eligible bachelors, but its efforts at romance are indisputably handsome.

mole hawk n

=**marsh hawk 1.**

1955 MA Audubon Soc. *Bulletin* 39.442 **CT,** Marsh Hawk. . . Mole Hawk. . . No moles were found in 601 stomachs. **1991** Heat Moon *PrairyErth* 443 **ceKS,** Mole hawk: it will eat a mole if it can find one above the ground.

mole mouse n

1 A **grasshopper mouse** (here: *Onychomys leucogaster).* [See quot 1904]

1904 Hornaday *Amer. Nat. Hist.* 91 **West,** The Grasshopper Mouse, originally described by Audubon and Bachman as the *Missouri Mouse,* and often called the *Mole Mouse.* . . *Its fur is very fine and soft,* and hence it is sometimes called the Mole Mouse. **1917** Anthony *Mammals Amer.* 233, Grasshopper Mouse—*Onychomys leucogaster.* . . Mole Mouse.

2 also *mole rat, mouse mole:* A **shrew** such as *Cryptotis parva* or *Blarina brevicauda.* Cf **ground-mole rat, mole** n¹ **3**

1927 Boston Soc. Nat. Hist. *Proc.* 38.269 **Okefenokee GA,** Shrews in the Okefinokee are generally spoken of as 'Mole-rats' (Billy's Island). **1961** Jackson *Mammals WI* 43, Giant Mole Shrew. . . Vernacular names. . . mole mouse, mole rat, and mouse mole. *Ibid* 56, Indiana Little Short-tailed Shrew. . . mole mouse.

3 also *mole pine mouse:* =**pine mouse.**

1961 Jackson *Mammals WI* 240, Northern Pine Mouse. . . *Vernacular names.* . . Where recognized in Wisconsin commonly called pine mouse or mole mouse. Other names include . . mole pine mouse.

mole plant n

1 also *mole tree, ~ weed:* A **spurge:** usu *Euphorbia lathyrus,* rarely *E. heterophylla.* [See quots 1837, 1892]

1830 Rafinesque *Med. Flora* 2.219, E[uphorbia] lathyrus, Mole plant or Spurge Capers. Milk drastic. **1837** Darlington *Flora Cestrica* 517, *E. lathyrus.* . . Mole-tree. . . This . . has become naturalized about many gardens;—having been introduced under a notion that it protected them from the incursions of *Moles.* **1892** *Jrl. Amer. Folkl.* 5.103 **nOH,** *Euphorbia Lathyrus,* mole-tree. . . Supposed to keep moles out of gardens. **1894** *Jrl. Amer. Folkl.* 7.98 **WV,** *Euphorbia Lathyrus,* . . mole-weed. **1910** Graves *Flowering Plants* 267 **CT,** Mole Plant. . . Well established in Trumbull and Bridgeport. **1940** Clute *Amer. Plant Names* 99, *E. lathyrus.* . . Mole-plant, mole-tree. **1967** Gilkey–Dennis *Hdbk. NW Plants* 246, *Euphorbia lathyrus.* . . Mole plant. . . Not rare in the Willamette Valley [of Oregon]. Children eating the fruits of this species are known to have become severely ill. **1976** Bailey–Bailey *Hortus Third* 463, [Euphorbia] heterophylla. . . Mole plant. . . [E.] lathyrus. . . Mole plant.

2 See **mole bean 2.**

mole rat See **mole mouse 2**

mole salamander n Also *mole*

A burrowing **salamander** of the family Ambystomidae, usu *Ambystoma talpoideum*.

1891 in 1895 *IL State Lab. Nat. Hist.* Urbana *Bulletin* 3.379, *Mole Salamander.* . . Dusky or dark brown, mottled with small gray dots and a few obscure dusky spots. **1892** *IN Dept. Geol. & Nat. Resources Rept. for 1891* 582, *Mole Salamander.* . . It is the smallest, stoutest, and most clumsily constructed of the species of the genus. . . It lives in damp places below logs and stones. **1935** Pratt *Manual Vertebrate Animals* 140, Mole salamander. . . Southern States from North Carolina to Louisiana and up the Mississippi Valley to Illinois. **1958** Conant *Reptiles & Amphibians* 208, *Mole Salamanders.* . . Like moles, these amphibians stay underground most of their lives. **1979** Behler–King *Audubon Field Guide Reptiles* 288, Lack of a nasolabial groove between lip and nostrils distinguishes moles from lungless salamanders. . . Adult mole salamanders are typically terrestrial and confirmed burrowers. **1982** Sternberg *Fishing* 108, *Mole Salamanders.* Named for their habit of burrowing into damp soil, these thick-bodied salamanders seldom come out except on rainy nights. *Ibid* 110, Mole salamanders are abundant and easy to find in spring, especially after the season's first rains.

mole shrew n

1 A **shrew** (here: *Blarina brevicauda*).

1888 Kingsley *Riverside Nat. Hist.* 5.148, The typical species, called the Mole-shrew, *B[larina] brevicauda.* **1891** Jesup *Plants Hanover NH* 79, *B[larina] brevicauda.* . . Mole-Shrew. **1917** Anthony *Mammals Amer.* 310, *Short-tailed Shrew.* . . *Other Name.* Mole Shrew. **1935** Pratt *Manual Vertebrate Animals* 255, *B[larina] brevicauda.* . . Mole shrew. . . Common in woods and fields, bogs and swamps; emits a fetid odor. **1961** Jackson *Mammals WI* 43, *Blarina brevicauda.* . . In Wisconsin usually called mole shrew.

2 A **mole** n[1] **1** (here: *Neurotrichus gibbsi*). Cf **shrew mole**

1890 *Century Dict.* 3823, *Mole-shrew.* . . The name is also applied to *Neurotrichus gibbsi.*

mole skink n

A **skink** (here: *Eumeces egregius*).

1979 Behler–King *Audubon Field Guide Reptiles* 569, Mole Skink (*Eumeces egregius*). [*Ibid* 570, Range: Coastal plain of Georgia, Alabama, and Florida including Keys. . . Adapted for tunneling and digging, as its name implies, this species successfully preys on burrowing or secretive insects, spiders, and small crustaceans.]

mole snake n [See quot 1952]

A **king snake 1** (here: *Lampropeltis calligaster rhombomaculata*).

1952 Ditmars *N. Amer. Snakes* 105, *Lampropeltis rhombomaculata.* . . It sometimes hides in the burrows of small mammals, hence its name, Mole Snake. **1958** Conant *Reptiles & Amphibians* 173, *Mole Snake.* . . A shiny, *smooth*-scaled serpent that may be patterned or not. . . An accomplished burrower often turned up by the plow or during excavation operations. **1979** Behler–King *Audubon Field Guide Reptiles* 618, Mole Snake. . . Spends much of the day in animal burrows or under rocks or several inches of loose soil. Most frequently seen crossing roads after a rainstorm or on warm spring or summer nights.

mole tree See **mole plant 1**

molewarp See **moldwarp**

mole weed See **mole plant 1**

moley, holy See **moly, holy**

molkasin flower See **moccasin flower**

moll n[1]

=**tautog.**

1884 Goode *Fisheries U.S.* 1.269, On the eastern shore of Virginia [the tautog is called] "Moll." **1903** *NY State Museum & Sci. Serv. Bulletin* 60.598, Better known in New York as the blackfish; farther south it is styled . . Moll . . and oyster fish. **1911** *U.S. Bur. Census Fisheries 1908* 317, Moll. **1973** Knight *Cook's Fish Guide* 385, Moll—Tautog.

moll n[2] See **mile**

Molle See **Molly Hogan**

mollie See **molly** n[1]

Mollie Hogan See **Molly Hogan**

molligut n

=**goosefish.**

[**1842** DeKay *Zool. NY* 4.163, Its [=*Lophius piscatorius's*] monstrous form has given rise to many popular names.] **1884** Goode *Fisheries U.S.* 1.173, The Goose Fish or Monk Fish, *Lophius piscatorius.* . . The names of the fish are many; . . in Eastern Connecticut [it is called] "Molligut." **1911** *U.S. Bur. Census Fisheries 1908* 310, Goosefish (*Lophius piscatorius*). . . Local names are . . "bellows-fish," "molligut" [etc].

molly n[1] Also sp *mollie*

1 Used as a nickname for a female horse or mule; hence n *molly (mule)* a mare mule. Cf **jack** n[1] **20, jenny 1**

1944 Wellman *Bowl* 44 **KS** (as of c1900), [Sale advt:] *Livestock*—1– Team Molly Mules smooth mouth. **1966–68** *DARE* (Qu. K50, *Joking nicknames for mules*) Inf **IN**44, Mollies; **OK**18, Mare mule is "Molly"; male mule is "Jack"; mare mule or molly mule. **1986** Pederson *LAGS Concordance*, 1 inf, **cwAR**, Old Molly—their horse; (*Calls to horses*) 1 inf, **swAL**, Come here Molly.

2 A cow; also *molly cow*: a hornless cow. [Var of or folk-etym for **muley** adj, n[2]]

1968–69 *DARE* (Qu. K12, *A cow that has never had horns*) Inf **NJ**29, Molly ['mɑli] cow; (Qu. K16, *A cow with a bad temper*) Inf **CA**131, Mean Molly.

3 in phr *cut up molly*: See quot. Cf **jack** n[1] **14**

1942 Warnick *Garrett Co. MD* 6 (as of 1900–18), *Cutting up molly* . . act[ing] extravagantly or frolicsome; having a high time.

‡**4** Nonsense, baloney. Cf **molasses C2**

1968 *DARE* (Qu. NN13, *When you think that the thing somebody has just said is silly or untrue: "Oh, that's a lot of _____."*) Inf **GA**45, Molly [laughter].

‡**5** pl: Men's long underwear.

1966 *DARE* (Qu. W14, *Names for underwear, including joking names. Men's—long*) Inf **MS**37, Mollies.

6 See **molly cottontail.**

7 Any of several fish, as:

a =**striped mullet.**

1882 *U.S. Natl. Museum Proc.* 5.266, *Mugil albula.* . . Mullet, Molly, Meuille. . . Exceedingly abundant, particularly about Galveston [TX], where they are found even in the gutters along the streets. Held in low esteem as a food-fish, and largely used for bait. **1933** *LA Dept. of Conserv. Fishes* 200, Striped Mullet. . . Other popular names for the species are Callifavor, . . Molly, Common Mullet and Jumping Mullet.

b A fish of the genus *Poecilia*. For other names of *P. latipinna* see **mudfish i**

1933 John G. Shedd Aquarium *Guide* 187, Another cool water livebearer is *Molliensia* [=*Poecilia*] *latipinna*, the *Sail-fin* or *Molly*. **1955** Carr–Goin *Guide Reptiles* 79, Sailfin Molly. . . A pretty little fish with a big dorsal fin. . . *General Distribution.*—The coasts and lowland streams and swamps from the Carolinas to Mexico. **1957** Blair et al. *Vertebrates U.S.* 158, The mollies. Body rather short and deep. Mouth small, the mandible very short. **1971** Brown *Fishes MT* 146, The food of the shortfin molly is rather varied including both plant and animal matter. **1983** *Audubon Field Guide N. Amer. Fishes* 518, Sailfin Molly. . . Saltwater marshes, ponds, and ditches; also freshwater pools, ponds, and ditches. **1991** *Amer. Fisheries Soc. Common Names Fishes* 101, Shortfin molly [is established in] California, Colorado, Idaho, Montana, Nevada, Texas.

c A **pompon** (here: *Anisostremus surinamensis*).

1935 Caine *Game Fish* 114 **Sth**, Pompon. . . Synonyms . . Molly. . . Largest size approximately 20 lbs.

d A **warmouth** (here: *Lepomis gulosus*). Cf **mawmouth**

1941 Writers' Program *Guide SC* 369, Bream and mollies are made into 'pine-bark stew'. **1950** *PADS* 14.47 **SC**, Molly. . . The warmouth.

e Prob =**hogsucker.** Cf **hog molly 1**

1968 *DARE* (Qu. P3, *Freshwater fish that are not good to eat*) Inf **IL**29, Mollies.

8 A **summer cypress** (here: *Kochia americana*). Cf **green molly, red molly**

1936 McDougall–Baggley *Plants of Yellowstone* 53, Molly (*Kochia americana*).

molly n² See **malolly**

Molly Bright n Also *Marley Bright, marlow bright, Molly blight* [Varr of *barley-break* (OED 1557 →); cf **barley bright**] **Mid and S Atl**

A children's outdoor chasing game; see quots; also used as a refrain in the game.

1883 Newell *Games & Songs* 153 **GA**, "Marlow, marlow, marlow bright,/ How many miles to Babylon?" "Threescore and ten." . . This sport, which has been universally familiar in America, is a form of the old English game of "Barley Break," and probably the "marlow bright" of our version is a corruption of that name. **1892** *Jrl. Amer. Folkl.* 5.120, *Marley Bright.* As far as I can bore into the past, this is the oldest of games. **1922** Talley *Negro Folk Rhymes* 74, *Caught by the witch play*— (Human *Call*) "Molly, Molly, Molly-bright!"/ (Witch *Sponse*) "Three scō' an' ten!" [etc]. **1953** Brewster *Amer. Nonsinging Games* 52 **NC**, *Molly Bright*—Players are divided into two groups . . in parallel lines facing each other. . . One player takes his position about midway between the two lines. . . [After the rhyming lines are said] Both groups then start running toward each other, each trying to reach the other's base. A player caught by the "Witch" must take the latter's place. **1968** *DARE* Tape VA9, And we'd play "how far is it to Molly Bright." The other feller'd say, "Well three scores and ten." Well we'd say, "Can we get there by early candlelight"; they'd say, "Yes, if your legs is long and light, but watch out, there's a witch in the middle on the road." And we'd have to shy the witch, but the witch would get the others, but she wouldn't get one for I'd run up and pat the base, and I done had her face. **1968** *DARE* FW Addit VA10, Molly Bright, Molly Bright: players divided into two groups twenty yards or so apart with the witch in between. Rhyme—*Player:* "How far is it to Molly Bright?" *Other group:* "Three score and ten." *Player:* "Can I get there by candlelight?" *Group:* "If your legs is long and light,/ But beware, the witch is out tonight." One player runs to the other group while the witch tries to catch him. Game repeated. **1969** *DARE* (Qu. EE33, . . *Outdoor games . . that children play*) Inf **GA**80, Marley Bright—how many miles to Marley Bright, played with a captain. **1986** Pederson *LAGS Concordance*, 1 inf, **cnGA**, Molly blight [FW: game?].

mollycoddle n

1 =**lollipop 1.**

1957 *Sat. Eve. Post Letters* **neMA**, In Salem, Massachusetts, in my childhood, 1910–1920, we called the candy now termed *lolly-pop, a molly-coddle.* The shape of the candy then was long and slender, unlike that seen today.

2 also pl: An imaginary ailment. [Perh < *mollycoddle* to pamper] Cf **collywobbles, mulligrubs**

1969 *DARE* (Qu. BB28, *Joking names . . for imaginary diseases:* "He must have the _____.") Infs **KY**10, **NY**220, Mollycoddle(s).

molly cottontail n Also *molly, ~ cotton, ~ har(e)* **chiefly Sth, S Midl**

Any of several cottontail rabbits of the genus *Sylvilagus.*

1835 Longstreet *GA Scenes* 188, When I went into the neighborhood . . the common appellation of the rabbit, was "Molly Cotton-tail," as it still is, elsewhere in Georgia. **a1883** (1911) Bagby *VA Gentleman* 48, He must make partridge-traps out of tobacco-sticks; set gums for "Mollie-cotton-tails." **1889** *Jrl. Amer. Folkl.* 2.229 **KY, TN**, *Molly-cotton. . .* rabbit. **1890** *DN* 1.65 **KY**, *Mollie-Cotton-tail:* a hare. **1892** *Outing* 19.362 **KS, OK**, The prairie dog and jack rabbit have firmly established themselves, assisted by the screech owl, rattlesnake and the "Molly cotton tail." **1893** Shands *MS Speech* 46, *Molly har. . .* A hare. **1909** *DN* 3.350 **eAL, wGA**, *Molly-cottontail. . .* The gray rabbit. Also called simply *molly.* "What did ye kill?" "I got a couple of mollies." A familiar negro rime shows the form *molly hare.* "Ole molly hâr,/ What ye doin' dâr." *Ibid* 400, **nwAR**, *Mollie Cotton-tail. . .* A hare. **1915** *DN* 4.227 **wTX**, *Molly. . .* Ordinary term for a *molly-cottontail* (rabbit). **c1960** Wilson *Coll.* **csKY**, *Molly cottontail. . .* The ordinary cotton-tail rabbit known to everybody. **1966–69** *DARE* (Qu. P30, . . *Wild rabbits*) Infs **MS**1, **NY**142, **NC**38, 40, 47, Molly cottontail.

molly cow See **molly** n¹ **2**

‡**molly graw** n

1968 *DARE* (Qu. EE41, *A hobgoblin that is used to threaten children and make them behave*) Inf **LA**40, Molly graw ['mɑlɪ̩grɔ]—Comes from Negro pronunciation of Mardi Gras, from outrageous costumes and masks.

mollygrooms See **mulligrubs**

mollygrub See **mulligrub 2**

mollygrubs See **mulligrubs**

molly gull n [Cf *molly* a fulmar or other large seabird] =**laughing gull.**

1955 Richardson *House on Nauset Marsh* 124 **MA**, Harried laughing gulls, especially the young ones (sometimes called "molly gulls"), are squealing too, and ever making a futile dip just too late.

mollyhack See **malahack**

molly har(e) See **molly cottontail**

mollyhawk See **malahack**

Molly Hogan n Also sp *Mollie Hogan;* abbr *Molle* **NW**

1 In logging: a wire loop used as a temporary link, usu to connect two cables.

1941 *AmSp* 16.233 **NW**, *Mollie Hogan.* A strand of wire from a wire cable which is doubled and twisted together, usually used as a link to hold two pieces of equipment. Incidentally it is the cause of many accidents, and it is forbidden by the safety rules. **1950** *Western Folkl.* 9.119 **nwOR** [Logger speech], *Molly Hogan.* A single strand of wire cable rolled into a loop; it is sometimes used in place of a clevis. *Ibid* 381 **neCA** [Lumberjack language], *Molly Hogan.* Splice put in a cable in the shape of a loop. **1956** *AmSp* 31.151 **nwCA**, *Molly Hogan. . .* An improvised eye on the end of a logging cable. **1958** McCulloch *Woods Words* 118 **Pacific NW**, *Molly Hogan*—Another name for molle. When a straw line is to be taken into the woods it may be carried by the rigging crew in short lengths of 200 feet or so, with an eyesplice at each end. These are tied together with a molle. When no longer needed, the molle, or Molly Hogan, is cut through with an ax. **1977** Churchill *Don't Call* 43 **nwOR** (as of c1918), Molly Hogan wasn't a woman. It was a short length of cable strand that a logger could quickly fashion into a wire loop by wrapping it back on itself. It was used as a temporary link to hook any number of things together, such as the eye ends of two cables. It was often used to replace a lost cotter key or as a guide for a whistle wire.

2 By ext: see quots.

1960 Wentworth-Flexner *Slang* 342, *Molly-hogan. . .* Any complicated or puzzling thing. *Mainly logger use. Dial[ectal].* **1967** *DARE* (Qu. HH14, *Ways of teasing a beginner or inexperienced person—for example, by sending him for a 'left-handed monkey wrench':* "Go get me _____.") Inf **OR**6, Molly Hogan. In the woods they send the boys to look for Molly Hogan. It's a certain knot they tie in the wire.

molly, holy See **moly, holy**

‡**molly-hugging** vbl n [Prob by analogy with *mollycoddle* and similar constr in *EDD: mollicrush, molligrant, molly-prance, mully-puffled*] Cf **lollygag B1**

1944 *PADS* 2.58 **cwMO**, *Molly-huggin'* ['mɑlɪ'hʌgən]. . . Love-making, "petting." Used by a minister's wife whose family came from Ohio. Saline Co. Rare.

mollyjogger n

See quots.

c1905 Dunckel *Mollyjoggers* 10 **swMO**, For those who are not familiar with the different species of the finny tribe found in the James and kindred streams of Southwest Missouri, it will perhaps be interesting to know that there is a minnow inhabiting these waters—a horny-headed, spotted fellow, who is absolutely worthless, not even tempting the versatile appetite of gars and turtles when used as bait, and this fish is called by the natives the "Mollyjogger." **1953** Randolph-Wilson *Down in Holler* 265 **Ozarks**, *Mollyjogger. . .* A kind of minnow, probably the young of the *hogmolly* (Hypentelium nigricans).

molly miller n

A blenny (*Scartella cristata*).

[**1876** U.S. Natl. Museum *Bulletin* 5.28 **Bermuda**, *Molly Miller. . .* Very common under stones in tide-pools and in crevices; their habits closely resembling those of the "Rock-eel" (Muraenoides mucronatus) so familiar to naturalists on the New England coast.] **1933** John G. Shedd Aquarium *Guide* 151, *Blennius cristatus . . Molly Miller.* This little fish is widely distributed throughout the tropical Atlantic and individuals show an equally wide variation in color. **1983** *Audubon Field Guide N. Amer. Fishes* 670, The Molly Miller is the only blenny in

North America with a median row of cirri on top of the head. **1991** Amer. Fisheries Soc. *Common Names Fishes* 63, *Scartella cristata . . molly miller.*

molly moocher n
A **morel** n[2] (here: *Morchella esculenta*).
1980 Marteka *Mushrooms* 68, *Common Morel—Morchella esculenta . . common names . . Molly moocher.*

molly mule See **molly** n[1] **1**

molly-pop n
=**maypop 1.**
1909 DN 3.350 eAL, wGA, *Molly-pop. . . Same as may-pop. Rarely heard.* **1918** DN 5.19 NC, *Molly-pop, a Maypop.*

Molly Putz n [*Molly* a woman, wench + **putz** v; cf also Yiddish *putz* a fool, objectionable person]
See quots.
1950 WELS (*A careless, slovenly woman*) 1 Inf, seWI, Molly Putz. **1970** Bouton *Ball 4* 388, A lot of [baseball] managers say their players look like Molly Putz out there. But never Tom Thumb. **1988** DARE File seWI, [From a radio call-in show:] *Molly Putz*—A woman who is somewhat scatterbrained as to her dress, mannerisms, etc. Reports from Milwaukee, Sheboygan, etc. **1991** Ibid seWI, "She's a real Molly Putz" means 'She's a terrible housekeeper.' Also heard in southeast Pennsylvania.

moloa, moloha See **molowa**

molosses See **molasses**

molowa adj Also *molo(h)a* [Haw] **HI**
Lazy.
1938 Reinecke *Hawaiian Loanwords* 25, *Moloha. . .* [Reinecke: Corruption of *molowa . .* which is occasionally heard also.] Lazy; indifferent. . . F[req]. **1967** DARE (Qu. BB27, *When somebody pretends to be sick . . he's _____*) Inf HI4, Moloa—lazy.

molty adj
Molted; molting.
1949 Guthrie *Way West* 232 (as of 1847), An Indian boy . . standing naked except for a tag of leather, standing dignified with a molty feather in his hair. **1967** DARE (Qu. K72, *When the hen stops laying and begins to sit on the eggs to hatch them, she's*) Inf OR13, Molty [moltɪ]; [7 Infs, **scattered,** Molting (hen); OH66, Molding; IA39, Molter].

moly, holy exclam Also *holy moley, ~ molly, ~ kamoly, ~ tamoly* [Redup var of *Holy Moses;* see quot 1981] *esp freq among young speakers*
Used as an exclam of surprise or astonishment.
1949 in 1981 *Smithsonian Book of Comic-Book Comics* 86, [In the comic "Captain Marvel":] Holy Moley! Sivana has captured Mr. Tawney! Shazam! **1965–70** DARE (Qu. NN29c, *Exclamations beginning with 'holy': "Holy _____!"*) Infs MA1, MI69, 117, OH40, PA94, Moly; UT3, Molly; NY18, Tamoly; TX81, Kamoly. [5 Infs young, 3 mid-aged] **1981** Spears *Slang & Euphem.* 193, *Holy Moly!* a mock oath and an exclamation. The characteristic exclamation of Captain Marvel, a comic-book character [DARE Ed: written by C.C. Beck, 1940-54]. **1993** DARE File cwCA (as of 1950s), When I was growing up, people often said "Holy Moly!" to indicate real astonishment.

molytone See **mirliton**

mom n[1] Also sp *marm, ma'am* [Prob abbr for **mamma** n[1] **1,** but perh infl by **ma'am** n[1] used as a term of address] Note: In most cases the sp *marm* prob represents proncs of the type [mɑm], but may occasionally reflect an intrusive *r* Cf **mam 1, mum** n[1], **mamma** n[1], **mommy**
1 infreq *moms:* A mother—also used as a quasi-personal name by a woman's children or husband. **widespread, but less freq Sth** See Map
1835 (1841) Cooper *Monikins* 1.196 seCT, He could scare one by threatening to tell his *marm* how he behaved. **1838** Cooper *Home as Found* 2.18 NY, Who taught you to call me *marm* . . Say ma', this instant. **1859** *Harper's New Mth. Mag.* 19.573 MA, He knocked down par, and kicked *marm.* **1867** *Atlantic Mth.* 19.21 NEng, Your ma'am don't love no feathers cluttrin' round. **1871** Eggleston *Hoosier Schoolmaster* 73 IN, *Marm* don't like it; but ef Bud and her does . . I don't see as it's *marm's* lookout. **1890** Jewett *Strangers* 9 ME, You've got

real nice features, like your marm's folks. **1894** DN 1.332 NJ, *Mam, mom . .* for mamma or mother. **1902** DN 2.239 sIL, *Mommy. . . Mama.* Used by children. Sometimes abbreviated to mom [mɑm] by grown children, but they generally use ma [mɔ]. **1916** Howells *Leatherwood God* 52 OH, Truly, mom? Oh, Benny, hurrah! She's let me! **1941** Amer. Mercury 52.664 nGA, He went over to Maam's ter git it riddled out. Maam? She's my ma. **1941** LANE Map 372 (*Mother, ma*), [About 70 infs, **esp, NH, ME,** gave proncs of the type [mɑm, mam]; 5 gave proncs of the type [mɔm, mɒm].] *Ibid,* 1 inf, swCT, I call my wife [mɑˑˑm]. *Ibid* Map 375 (*My wife*) 1 inf, swNH, [mɑˑᵊm], very old-fashioned. **c1955** Reed–Person *Ling. Atlas Pacific NW,* 1 inf, Moms [=mother]. **1965–70** DARE (Qu. Z2, . . 'Mother') 631 Infs, **widespread, but less freq Sth,** Mom; AZ11, FL33, NC86, PA162, [mɔm]; CA94, DC1, IN60, MN42, TN12, TX53, Moms; FL2, Marm; (Qu. N37) Inf PA136, Mom and pop; (Qu. W24a) Inf PA110, You think more of your pop than your mom; (Qu. W32) Inf FL51, Sewing moms; (Qu. AA22, *Joking names that a man may use to refer to his wife: "I have to go down and pick up my _____"*) Infs IN13, MN29, Mom; IN73, Disgruntled mom; MO19, [FW: In free conversation he addressed his wife as "mom."]; (Qu. KK1a) Inf WA16, Better than mom's. **1969** DARE Tape CA158, Better put it [=the tape recorder] over this way so it'll get mom [=his wife], huh? **1973** Allen *LAUM* 1.337 **Upper MW** (as of c1950), A wife with children is by some referred to familiarly with *Ma, Mama, Mom* or *Mother* as proper names. *Ibid* 339, Several times characterized as recent or as used by children today, *mom* /mɑm/ is reported in use by only 13% of Type I speakers [=old, with little educ] but by 20% of Type II [=mid-aged, with approx hs educ]. . . The frequency of *mom* is twice as great on the checklists. **1989** Pederson *LAGS Tech. Index* 226 **Gulf Region,** *Mother. . .* Mom [DARE Ed: as quasi-personal name] (124 [infs]). . . mom (29). *Ibid* 224, *Wife . .* Mom (2 [infs]).

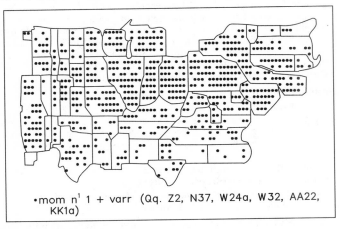

•mom n[1] 1 + varr (Qq. Z2, N37, W24a, W32, AA22, KK1a)

2 A grandmother.
1941 LANE Map 383 (*Grandma*) 1 inf, seNH, Grammy, gram affectionately; [maˑˑᵊm, mʌˑˑm], sometimes in addressing her. **1966–68** DARE (Qu. Z4, . . 'Grandmother') Infs MS10, NJ23, PA74, Mom. **1989** Pederson *LAGS Tech. Index* 227 **Gulf Region,** *Grandmother . .* Mom (5 [infs]).

mom n[2] See **ma'am** n[1]

mom dear See **mother dear**

momma, mommer See **mamma** n[1]

mommick n See **mammock** n

mommick v See **mammock** v

mommicking See **mammock** v **1**

mommix n See **mammock** n

mommix v See **mammock** v

mommock n See **mammock** n

mommock(s) v See **mammock** v

mom-mom n Also *ma-mom, mam-mam* [Cf Sw, Norw *mormor* maternal grandmother] **PA, NJ, DE, MD** See Map Cf **mammaw, mee-maw** n
A grandmother.
1965–70 DARE (Qu. Z4, . . 'Grandmother') Infs NJ48, 54, 59, PA134, Mom-mom; DE2, ['mɑˌmɑm]—recent; DE5, Mom-mom—

nowadays; **MD**33, ['mɑm,mam]; **PA**14, Ma-mom; **PA**66, Mam-mam. **1994** *DARE* File **eDE**, My grandmother (mommom for people who say y'all) would ask me "Ya finished?"

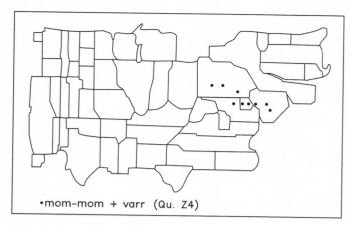

•mom-mom + varr (Qu. Z4)

mommuck n, v See **mammock** n, v

mommux See **mammock** v

mommy n

1 also *marmee, marmy:* A mother—often used as a quasi-personal name by a woman's children or husband.

1858 in 1951 *PA Dutchman* 1 Oct 2, Mei gemuethe freiet sich / Wen die mommy dess krout awricht. . . All my soul is in delight / When mommy fixes crout just right. **1868** (1871) Alcott *Little Women* 1.17 **NEng,** "When will he come home, Marmee?" asked Beth. **1902** *DN* 2.239 **sIL,** *Mommy* [mɑmɪ]. . . Mama. Used by children. Sometimes abbreviated to mom [mɑm] by grown children, but they generally use ma [mɔ]. **1906** *DN* 3.121 **sIN,** *Mommy.* . . Used with mammy exclusively for mama. **1909** *DN* 3.400 **nwAR,** *Mommy.* . . Mama. **1923** *DN* 5.214 **swMO,** *Mammy.* . . Mother. . . Also Mommy. **1942** Hall *Smoky Mt. Speech* 29 **wNC, eTN,** *Mamma* usually now ['mɑmɪ], ['mɑmə]. **1953** Randolph–Wilson *Down in Holler* 264 **Ozarks,** *Mam, mammy,* and *mommy* are also common [beside maw]. **1965–70** *DARE* (Qu. Z2, . . *'Mother'*) 172 Infs, **widespread,** Mommy; **SC**64, [,mɔˈmi]; **CT**5, Marmy [marmɪ]; **PA**162, Marmy [mɔrmɪ] [Of all Infs responding to the question, 29% were comm type 5, 11% young, 65% old; of those giving these responses, 19% were comm type 5, 21% young, 48% old.]; (Qu. NN6b) Infs **IA**2, 3, **MN**15, Oh mommy, look(, look); **NY**73, **SC**67, (Oh daddy,) oh mommy; (QR, near Qu. Z2) Inf **NJ**41, [FW: He calls his wife mommy, which is nickname given her by Ringwood company]. **1970** *DARE* Tape **CA**206, We were all mommies to him [=a nephew]. **1973** Allen *LAUM* 1.339 **Upper MW** (as of c1950), Hypocoristic or childish *mommy* occurs only three times [among 203 infs]. **1989** Pederson *LAGS Tech. Index* 226 **Gulf Region,** Mother. . . Mommy [*DARE* Ed: as quasi-personal name] (25 [infs]). . . mommy (1). *Ibid* 224, Wife. . . Mommy (1).

2 A grandmother.

1968 *DARE* (Qu. Z4, . . *'Grandmother'*) Infs **NY**46, **PA**72, Mommy; [**GA**57, Mamo, mah-mee, marmee]. **1989** Pederson *LAGS Tech. Index* 227 **Gulf Region,** Grandmother. . . Mommy [*DARE* Ed: as quasi-personal name] (2) [infs].

3 See quot. Cf **mamma** n[1] **5**

1970 *DARE* (Qu. AA3, *Nicknames or affectionate names for a sweetheart*) Inf **NY**241, My mommy.

4 =**old-squaw.** Cf **mammy duck**

1888 Trumbull *Names of Birds* 88, Old Squaw. . . In New Jersey . . at Cape May City, *Mommy.* **1923** U.S. Dept. Ag. *Misc. Circular* 13.24 **NJ,** *Old-squaw.* . . *Vernacular Names.* . . *In local use.* . . Mommy.

momona adj, n [Haw] **HI**

Fat; a fat person.

1938 Reinecke *Hawaiian Loanwords* 25, Momona. . . Fat; fleshy; large. . . Applied in the sense of "Fatty" to a fat person. . . V[ery] F[req]. **1967** *DARE* (Qu. X50, *Names or nicknames for a person who is very fat*) Inf **HI**8, Momona—much said. **1981** *Pidgin To Da Max* np **HI,** Momona. . . Fat.

momox See **mammock** n, v

mompsy See **mumsy**

moms See **mom** n[1] **1**

momsey See **mumsy**

mom's room See **mamma's room**

momsy, momzey See **mumsy**

mon See **man** n **A**

monaca nut n

=**water chinquapin.**

1854 Wailes *Rept. on Ag. & Geol. MS* 346, Monoca [sic] nut, Nelumbium speciosum. **1921** LA Dept. of Conserv. *Bulletin* 10.58, The wood ducks. . . find an abundance of food, the most important being duckweeds, . . seeds of grasses, . . and water chinquapin, . . known locally as . . "Monaca nut."

monack See **moonack** 1

monax See **moonack** 1

Monday comes before Sunday phr Also *Saturday is longer than Sunday, Sunday below Monday, Tuesday is longer than Monday;* for addit varr see quot 1968–70

Used to indicate that a woman's slip is showing.

1968–70 *DARE* (Qu. W24a, . . *Expressions . . to warn a woman slyly that her slip is showing*) Inf **NJ**19, Monday comes before Sunday; **MI**108, Monday's longer than Sunday; **MS**88, Sunday below Monday; **GA**81, Tuesday below Monday, your Tuesday is hanging below your Monday; **NJ**30, Tuesday is longer than Monday; **NY**49, Your Tuesday is below Wednesday; **VA**18, Saturday is longer than Sunday; **VA**31, Saturday's longer than Sunday. **1971** Brunvand *Guide Folkl. UT* 38, Monday comes before Sunday. (Swedish saying for "Your slip is showing.")

Monday morning sickness n Also *Monday morning headache, Monday sickness*

An imaginary illness used as an excuse to avoid work or school.

1967–68 *DARE* (Qu. BB27, *When somebody pretends to be sick . . he's _____*) Inf **CT**5, Monday morning sickness—for kids who don't want to hit school; (Qu. BB28, *Joking names . . for imaginary diseases: "He must have the _____."*) Inf **MD**32, Monday sickness; **MO**13, Monday morning sickness; **NY**42, Monday morning headaches.

money n

1 A mass of bubbles floating on a hot drink. [*EDD* money sb. 5 "The scum that rises to the surface of any boiling or fermenting liquor."] Cf **frog-eye gravy**

1899 (1912) Green *VA Folk-Speech* 285, When sugar is put into a cup of coffee and the air-bubbles come to the top and gather in one mass it is called *money,* and if taken into the spoon and drank at once it is a sign you will soon get money. **1935** Hyatt *Folkl. Adams Co. IL* 389, If you can sip the bubbles off your coffee, you are sipping money. . . When pouring coffee into a cup, if the bubbles collect in a circular form and you can drink them before they break, you will be rich. [*Ibid* 428, When I was a boy forty years ago, we were watching it rain and the man with me said, 'O look, we are going to get a lot of money.' I said, 'Why?' He said, 'Just look at all those bubbles; sure sign of money.'] **1966** *DARE* FW Addit **WA,** There's a lot of *money on top* when a white film floats on top of a cup of tea or coffee if it's round like coins. Old-fashioned. **1995** *DARE* File **csWI** (as of 1930s), "Money" was foam on cocoa or Ovaltine, sometimes even root beer. *Ibid* **csWI** (as of c1968), My grandmother and her friends called the bubbles that sometimes floated on a freshly-poured cup of coffee "money." If you had a lot of "money" in your cup, it meant you would soon come into some money.

2 in phr *show one's money:* Of a **green lizard 1** (here: *Anolis carolinensis*): see quot. Cf **pocketbook**

1955 *Clarke Co. Democrat* (Grove Hill AL) 8 Sept 4/5 (Mathews Coll.), This is the lizard which frequently "shows his money," by expanding a red sac under the throat. [Mathews: This was the expression we always used of the action of the little green lizard when he did this.]

moneybags See **money plant** 2

money-called adj Cf **college-called**

Motivated by money rather than by dedication.

1966 *DARE* FW Addit **OK**42, Money-called preacher—a professional preacher who would find some other work if he was not paid well.

money cat n [See quots 1957, 1975] **chiefly NEng, esp ME**
See Map
A calico cat, esp one with at least three colors.

  1957 Beck *Folkl. ME* 66, Among the felines a black cat was considered bad luck, . . a three-colored cat good luck or "a money cat." **1965–70** *DARE* (Qu. J5, *A cat with fur of mixed colors*) Infs **ME**10, 15, 19, **MA**2, 3, 80, Money cat; **ME**9, **PA**102, Calico; money cat; **ME**23, Money cat—three or four colors; **NH**18, Money cat—black, orange, yellow; **NY**79, Money cat, lucky cat. **1966** *DARE* FW Addit **nME**, Money cat—a cat of at least three colors, generally white, black and brown. **1975** Gould *ME Lingo* 182, Money cat—A calico cat whose fur shows at least three or four colors. Mainers have always believed this oddity of color happens only in the female, and that if anybody ever finds it on a tomcat the thing will be "worth money." **1977** *DARE* File **MA**, My nephew says that a money cat is so-called because it is supposedly worth money. He says it is a three-colored male cat, very rare genetically. . . I was told by a biology professor (who raised cats) that all three-colored cats are female.

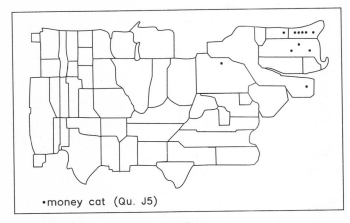

•money cat (Qu. J5)

money-catcher n Cf **fortune-teller**
  1896 *DN* 1.421 **NY**, *Money-catcher:* a dandelion blossom gone to seed.

money child n
A child who is reared by someone for a fee.
  1947 Ballowe *The Lawd* 173 **LA**, " 'Tain' hern. She too ole. . . Hit's a money chile; she paid to raise hit an' keep her mouf shet." . . Gossip finally decided that, in addition to being a money child, it was also a throwback.

money-cleaner n
A nonexistent item used as the basis of a practical joke.
  1969 *DARE* (Qu. HH14, *Ways of teasing a beginner or inexperienced person—for example, by sending him for a 'left-handed monkey wrench':* "Go get me _____.") Inf **CA**113, Money-cleaner, currency stretcher.

money dog See **money hound**

money flower See **money plant 1**

money gold light See **money light**

money grass n [*EDD* 1881]
A **yellow rattle** (here: *Rhinanthus crista-galli*).
  1900 Lyons *Plant Names* 319, *R[hinanthus] Crista-Galli.* . . Money-grass. **c1938** in 1970 Hyatt *Hoodoo* 2.1408, "You are bootlegging and you wanta bring in customers. . . You get some *money grass.*" "What kind of grass?" "*Money grass.*" "Money?" "Money." "Like the money you have in your pocket?" "Yeah, *money grass.*" "Where do you get that?" "At the drug store."

money hound n Also *money dog*
  1970 *DARE* (Qu. U36a, . . *A person who saves in a mean way or is greedy in money matters:* "He's an awful _____.") Inf **SC**68, Money hound; **VA**70, Money dog. [Both Infs Black]

money-in-both-pockets See **money plant 1**

money light n Also *money gold light* Eye-dial sp *munny lite* [Because the light supposedly guides one to hidden treasure] Cf **treasure light**
=**jack-o'-lantern 1.**
  c1938 in 1970 Hyatt *Hoodoo* 1.117 **seMD**, They claim that on certain nights, especially dark nights, people going along this road from

Snowhill to Salisbury see a little light like and this light seems to flicker and it is near this tree. They claim that that's the way you know money is buried there. . . They called it the *money gold light.* **1952** Brown *NC Folkl.* 1.694 [Black], We'd been seein' dem munny lites down neah de ribber, and I knowed dare wuz munny dere. **1966** *DARE* (Qu. CC16, *A small light that seems to dance or flicker over a marsh or swamp at night*) Inf **FL**14, Money lights—they come out most anywhere and are supposed to go where the money is; [**TX**31, There's treasure buried close by].

money miser n [Redund; cf Intro "Language Changes" I.4]
A skinflint, tightwad.
  1968 *DARE* (Qu. U36a, . . *A person who saves in a mean way or is greedy in money matters:* "He's an awful _____.") Inf **LA**25, Money miser. **1986** Pederson *LAGS Concordance* (He's a tightwad) 3 infs, **seTN, swGA, cwLA**, Money miser.

money musk n Also sp *munny muss* [Perh < *Monymusk* a town in Scotland] **chiefly NEng**
A contra dance.
  1844 Stephens *High Life in NY* 1.202 **CT**, A set of folks come from all the four quarters of the globe . . that didn't know how to dance an eight reel or munny-muss as it ought to be done. **1899** Garland *Boy Life* 209 **nwIA**, Sometimes, if there were enough for a set, the young people pushed the table aside and took places for "The Fireman's Dance," or "Money Musk." **1908** Lincoln *Cy Whittaker* 86 **MA**, They were forming sets for "Money Musk"; it was "ladies' choice," and there was a demand for more couples. **1934** *Hanley Disks* **neMA**, In list of dances known to informant: Lancers, Quadrilles, . . Money Musk. **1938** FWP *Guide NH* 118, The morning star, Virginia reel, quadrille, . . and money musk are still danced. Contra-dances have always been more popular in New Hampshire than square dances. . . Two lines of dancers stand opposite each other, whereas in square dances four couples form a square. **1950** WELS (*Names for different steps and figures in dancing*) 1 Inf, **ceWI**, Money musk. [Inf old] **1966–69** *DARE* (Qu. FF5a, . . *Different steps and figures in dancing—in past years*) Inf **MA**6, Money musk—difficult; **MA**29, Money musk; **MA**73, Money musk—a regular hoedown. [All Infs old] **1969** *DARE* Tape **MA**29, Then of course they had the contra dances, money musk, and all those contra dances; **VT**13, We did the contras, and we did Fisher's hornpipe and money musk. **1993** *DARE* File **ME** (as of late 1970s), Lady of the Lake and Money Musk were my favorite contra dances.

money myrtle See **money plant 2**

money plant n

  1 also *money-flower, money-in-both-pockets, money-seed, moneywort:* =**honesty**, usu *Lunaria annua*. [*EDD* 1848 →]
  1900 Lyons *Plant Names* 231, *L[unaria] annua.* . . Money plant. **1902** Earle *Old Time Gardens* 172 **NEng**, As a child this Lunaria was a favorite flower, for it afforded to us juvenile money. Indeed, it was generally known among us as Money-flower or Money-seed, or sometimes as Money-in-both-pockets. The seed valves formed our medium of exchange and trade, passing as silver dollars. *Ibid* 173, Poor Elmer never was able to understand that the money which he and the children saved so carefully each autumn from the money plants was not equal in value to the great copper cents of the village store. **1923** *Amer. Botanist* 29.156, "Honesty" (*Lunaria annua*). . . is also known as "money-plant" and "penny-flower" in allusion to the large flat circular seed-pods. **1940** Clute *Amer. Plant Names* 37, *L[unaria] annua.* . . money-plant, penny-flower. **1950** WELS *Suppl.* **csWI**, Money plant . . another name for silver dollar plant. **1959** Carleton *Index Herb. Plants* 82, *Money-wort:* Lunaria annua (l. biennis). **1976** Bailey–Bailey *Hortus Third* 685, *Lunaria* [spp] . . money plant.

  2 also *moneybags, money myrtle, ~ vine:* =**moneywort 1.**
  1897 *Jrl. Amer. Folkl.* 10.49, *Lysimachia mummularia* [sic] . . money plant, . . Oxford Co., Me. money-bags, Medford, Mass. **1940** Clute *Amer. Plant Names* 112, *L[ysimachia] nummularia.* Moneywort. Money-plant . . money-myrtle. **1959** Carleton *Index Herb. Plants* 82, *Money-plant.* . . *Money-myrtle:* Lysimachia nummularia. **1966** *DARE* (Qu. S21, . . *Weeds . . that are a trouble in gardens and fields*) Inf **GA**11, Money vine . . Dollar weed—same as money vine. **1967** *DARE* Wildfl QR Pl.164A Inf **SC**41, Called money plant by some, though not correctly; loosestrife.

moneys n pl [*OED money* sb. 4 1382 → "pl. . . Now chiefly in legal . . parlance, or as an archaism." Cf also Ger *Gelder* n pl "funds, money"] Cf Intro "Language Changes" II.6, 7
Money.

1949 in 1986 *DARE* File, *Money*. . . In Pennsylvania Dutch section near Reading, Pa., the word "money" is seldom heard in the singular. "Do you have enough moneys to buy a car?" or "Both my mother and father gave me moneys to go shopping."

money-seed See **money plant 1**

money shell n

A **Washington clam** (here: *Saxidomus* spp).

[**1884** Goode *Fisheries U.S.* 1.708, In regard to this latter mollusk (*Saxidomus aratus*) . . its shell was broken into pieces by the Indians of the California coast and worked into flat, circular disks by rubbing upon stone. Eighty of these disks strung upon sinews were in recent use by the Indians of Lake County, California, as a medium of exchange in trade, and were valued at one dollar.] **1920** CA Fish & Game Comm. *Fish Bulletin* 4.35 **cwCA**, Washington Clam—*Saxidomus*. . . The name "money shell" came from the use of *Saxidomus* shells of pearly appearance and unusual thickness as money by the Indians of Bodega and Tomales bays. **1949** Palmer *Nat. Hist.* 358 **CA**, Name money shell refers to use of shells as money by Indians. . . Humboldt Bay to San Diego.

money shower n esp **NEng**

=**greenback shower.**

1967–68 *DARE* (Qu. FF3, . . 'Showers' or 'gift parties') Infs **CA**15, **CT**6, Money showers; **CT**12, Jewish people have money showers; **MA**33, Money, gift [showers].

money-spinner n

A spider; see quots.

1884 (1885) McCook *Tenants* 225 **PA**, Them little bits of spiders . . drop on you from the ceiling or trees by long threads. I've heerd 'em called *money-spinners,* and they'll say they'll bring good luck if you don't kill or hurt 'em. . . When a spider is found upon your clothes, . . we used to say some money is coming toward us. [**1899** Bergen *Animal Lore* 13, If a spider spin down on or near you, pick it up and put it in your pocket, and it will bring you money. *Plymouth, Ohio. Ibid* 39, A spider crawling over a garment means a new garment of the same kind. *Massachusetts*. . . Meeting a white spider signifies finding money; but if you kill the spider, you won't get the money. *Deerfield, Mass.*]

money tree n

1 A small tree or branch decorated with money and given as a gift, esp to mark a wedding anniversary.

1966 Ellsworth *Amer.* (ME) 29 June 5/3, Mr. and Mrs. Almond Reed celebrated their 60th wedding anniversary. . . [They] were presented with a money tree, . . and several beautiful flower arrangements. **1966** *DARE* (Qu. FF3, . . 'Showers' or 'gift parties') Inf **WA**1, Money tree on fiftieth year anniversary. **1979** *Athol Daily News* (MA) 12 Oct 2/1, Thanks also to our neighbors and friends for the money tree. **1993** *DARE* File **NEng**, A money tree is a common way for guests to give gifts at an anniversary celebration. Often it is prepared before the party. A note is added to the invitations stating that there will be a money tree and cash donations should be sent or brought to a certain person. A twiggy branch will be cut from a bush or tree and "planted" in a decorated coffee can or bucket full of sand. Sometimes the branch is spray-painted. The organizer will fold the bills and tie them to the twigs with ribbons. This way, the couple can spend the money however they wish and don't get a bunch of unwanted objects as gifts.

2 An unidentified plant; see quots.

1945 Saxon *Gumbo Ya-Ya* 550 **LA**, When passing a lavender bush, known to the Negroes as the 'money tree,' pluck a sprig of leaves, count the leaves, and repeat the Commandment of the number counted. This brings luck. Nine leaves on a sprig brings money. **1969** *DARE* FW Addit **NC**, *Money tree*—plant common on Hatteras Island, N.C.

money vine See **money plant 2**

moneywort n

1 Std: a **loosestrife 1** (here: *Lysimachia nummularia*). [*OED* 1578] Also called **creeping Charlie 4, creeping Jennie 1, down-hill-of-life, dollar weed 2, infant's breath 1, money plant 2, myrtle** n[1] **B5, tievine, wandering Jenny, yellow myrtle**

2 See **money plant 1.**

mongo tree See **mangrove 2b**

mongrel n Usu |ˈmaŋgrəl|; also |ˈmaŋgrəl, ˈmɔŋgrəl, ˈmɔŋgrəl|; also **widespread, but esp NEast** (See Map) *esp freq among old Infs and those with little formal educ* |ˈmʌŋgrəl|; oc-

cas |ˈmaŋrəl, ˈmʌŋrəl, ˈmʌŋgəl, ˈmaŋgəl| Pronc-spp *mongler, munger, mungrel;* for addit pronc and sp varr see **A** below [See quot 1976]

A Forms.

1939 *LANE* Map 212 (*Mongrel*), [Throughout **NEng** proncs of the type [ˈmʌŋgrəl] predominate by a considerable margin; other types given, in descending order of frequency, are [mɔŋgrəl, mɒn-, mɔn-], [maŋgrəl, man-, maŋ-], [ˈmʌŋgəl], [mɛŋgrəl, mɛŋ-], [mʌŋgrəl]; there are single examples of [mɔˠŋgɪᵛl], [mɛˀŋgrɬ], [mʌŋrɔˠɬ], [mʌᵛŋglə].] **1942** *Sat. Eve. Post* 5 Sept 49, "There ain't no mungers around, but you never can tell." . . Mungers were mongrels. **1952** [see **B1** below]. **1960** *PADS* 34.63 **CO**, Only those [expressions] restricted to older speech—like *shakedown* and the pronunciation [mʌŋgrəl]—may we call relics. **1965–70** *DARE* (Qu. J1, . . *A dog of mixed breed*) 333 Infs, **widespread**, Mongrel ([ˈmaŋgrəl, ˈmaŋgrəl] and varr); 74 Infs, **scattered**, Mongrel ([ˈmɔŋgrəl, ˈmɒŋgrəl, ˈmɔŋgrəl] and varr); 26 Infs, **scattered, but esp Nth, N Midl**, Mongrel ([ˈmaŋrəl, ˈmɔŋ-, ˈmɒŋ-] and varr); 139 Infs, **widespread, but esp NEast**, Mungrel ([ˈmʌŋgrəl, ˈmʌn-] and varr); 14 Infs, **scattered, but esp Nth**, Mungrel ([ˈmʌŋrəl] and varr) [Of all Infs responding to the question, 69% were old, 27% gs educ, 51% male; of those giving the response *mungrel*, 84% were old, 43% gs educ, 71% male.]; **CA**101, **MD**35, **MI**37, **MT**1, **NY**122, **NC**52, 79, Mungel ([ˈmʌŋgəl] and varr); **NY**200, [ˈmʌŋəl]; **MD**21, **MO**12, **NJ**21, Mongel ([ˈmaŋgəl] and varr); **PA**178, [ˈmaŋəl]; **IL**26, **PA**54, **TX**26, Mogrel [ˈmagrəl, -əl]; **CT**29, Mugrel [ˈmʌgrɪl]; **NJ**3, 50, **NY**70, Mungler [ˈmʌŋglə]; **PA**27, Mongler [ˈmaŋglə]; **PA**9, Mongreler [ˈmaŋgrlə]; **PA**1, Monger [ˈmaŋgə]; **ME**1, Munglet [ˈmʌŋlɛt]; **CO**28, [ˈmauŋgrəl]; **PA**211, [ˈmʌŋgrɪl]; **MA**8, [ˈmɒŋgro]; (Qu. J2, . . *Joking or uncomplimentary words . . for dogs*) 16 Infs, **scattered**, Mongrel; **CA**107, **ME**5, 19, **MN**12, **NY**117, **PA**235, **SC**4, Mungrel; **PA**27, Mongler; (Qu. J5) Infs **CA**113, **CO**22, **WA**14, Mongrel; **CT**6, Mungrel; **MO**38, Mungrel color; (Qu. K43) Infs **AK**8, **CA**105, Mongrel; **DC**5, [mʌŋrəl]; (Qu. HH18) Inf **IN**10, [maŋgrɪlz]; (Qu. HH28) Inf **CT**23, Mongrel; (Qu. HH29a) Inf **CT**28, [ˈmaŋgrɪl]; **MD**15, [ˈmʌŋrɪl]; **NC**79, [ˈmʌŋəl]. **1976** Allen *LAUM* 3.336 **Upper MW** (as of c1950), The gradual displacement of a historical pronunciation by an increasingly accepted spelling pronunciation appears clearly in the distribution of two variants of *mongrel,* the older with a mid-central stressed /ʌ/ and the newer with /a/ or, rarely, /ɔ/. In the UM the older original pronunciation occurs most frequently among the oldest and least educated speakers and least frequently within the college group. *Ibid* 337, The data for *mongrel* reveal also the incidence of what is probably another spelling pronunciation, the replacement of /ŋ/ by /n/ . . leaving the form /mʌŋrəl/ or /maŋrəl/. Although only 26 infs. offer this variant . . it is favored by a higher proportion of better educated speakers. . . What may be another spelling pronunciation, /mʌŋrəl/ . . is offered by three infs. . . Three others . . delete the /r/ so as to yield /mʌŋgəl/. Another inf. . . deletes both /g/ and /r/ so as to produce /mʌŋəl/, and the ultimate in deletion is reached by inf. 138 with /mogɪl/.

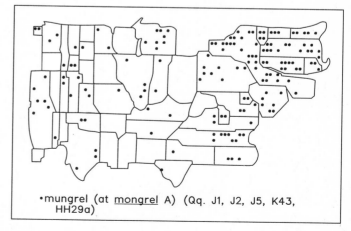

•mungrel (at <u>mongrel</u> A) (Qq. J1, J2, J5, K43, HH29a)

B Senses.

1 A **stilt sandpiper** (here: *Micropalama himantopus*). [See quot 1977]

1899 Howe–Sturtevant *Birds RI* 49, Stilt Sandpiper. *Mongrel. Bastard Yellow-leg.* **1925** (1928) Forbush *Birds MA* 1.400, Stilted sandpiper; mongrel. **1952** *AmSp* 27.294, In Massachusetts and Rhode Island it [=the Bastard Yellowleg] is also termed a *mongrel* and, in New Jersey, a *mongler.* [**1977** Bull–Farrand *Audubon Field Guide Birds* 391, Often associated with dowitchers and yellowlegs, Stilt Sandpipers resemble both species and appear to be intermediate between the two.]

2 also *mongrel drake:* =eider duck. [See quot 1952]

1923 U.S. Dept. Ag. *Misc. Circular* 13.27 **ME,** *King Eider . . Vernacular names . . In local use. . . mongrel drake.* **1952** *AmSp* 27.295, We cite *mongrel* for the common eider (in the mixed plumage of the young male, Mass.) and *mongrel drake* for the king eider (Maine), the 'normal' drake being the common eider or sea drake.

mongrel buffalo (fish) n [From its appearance, which suggests a hybrid between **bigmouth buffalo** and **smallmouth buffalo**]
The black **buffalo fish** *(Ictiobus niger).*

1878 U.S. Natl. Museum *Bulletin* 12.209, *Bubalichthys urus. . . Mongrel Buffalo. . .* This is a very abundant species in the Mississippi and its larger tributaries. **1902** Jordan-Evermann *Amer. Fishes* 40, *Mongrel Buffalo. . .* This species is close to the common buffalo, from which it can be distinguished by its similar, more oblique mouth, and its much darker colour. **1908** Forbes-Richardson *Fishes of IL* 71, The mongrel buffalo appears to vary somewhat more than either *I[ctiobus] cyprinella* or *bubalus,* but we have met with no cases which appear to show intergradation with either. **1933** LA Dept. of Conserv. *Fishes* 434, The Mongrel Buffalo has a mouth . . considerably smaller indeed than has the Common Buffalo. **1943** Eddy–Surber *N. Fishes* 103, The mongrel, or black, buffalofish has an elliptical and robust body. **1956** Harlan–Speaker *IA Fish* 73, Mongrel buffalo. . . This fish rarely takes natural or artificial lures. **1983** Becker *Fishes WI* 621, *Black Buffalo. . .* Other common names: mongrel buffalo [etc]. **1991** Amer. Fisheries Soc. *Common Names Fishes* 120, Buffalo, . . mongrel—see black buffalo.

mongrel bullhead n
A **stonecat** (here: *Noturus flavus*).

1983 Becker *Fishes WI* 725, Stonecat. . . Other common names . . mongrel bullhead.

mongrel drake See **mongrel B2**

mongrel whitefish n [See quot 1903]
A **cisco** (here: *Coregonus artedi*).

1882 U.S. Natl. Museum *Bulletin* 16.301, *C[oregonus] tullibee. . . "Mongrel White Fish". . .* A handsome and well-marked species. **1896** *Ibid* 47.473, *"Mongrel Whitefish". . .* Great Lakes, Lake of the Woods, and northward. **1903** NY State Museum & Sci. Serv. *Bulletin* 60.239, This species is usually called the tullibee, but in Lakes Erie and Michigan it is sometimes styled the mongrel whitefish on the supposition that it is a cross between the common whitefish and the lake herring.

'mongst-em, 'mongst hands of them See **amongst (hands of) them**

mongst-ye See **amongst you**

monilla n Also *monillo* [MexSpan]
=**Mexican buckeye.**

1931 U.S. Dept. Ag. *Misc. Pub.* 101.104, *Mexican-buckeye . . . ,* known also as monillo. . . is usually a bush 4 to 8 feet high. . . It ranges from western Texas, through southern New Mexico, into Mexico. **1960** Vines *Trees SW* 686, *Ungnadia speciosa. . .* Also known under the vernacular names of Monillo [etc]. **1967** *DARE* Tape **TX**29, [FW:] What are the native brushes. . . [Inf:] Chaparral . . guayucan . . mojilla [sic] . . cat claw, coyotillo . . brazil, blackbrush. **1970** Correll *Plants TX* 1006, *Monilla. . .* Flowers . . pink to purplish-pink, fragrant; . . seeds . . dark-brown to blackish, poisonous. **1979** Little *Checklist U.S. Trees* 292, *Mexican-buckeye. . .* Other common names . . monilla.

monjo See **mojo** n

monk v [Abbr for *monkey*] Cf **munk up**

1 See quot. [Prob *monkey* to ape, mimic] Cf **mock** v **B**
1916 *DN* 4.341 **seOH,** *Monk. . .* To make a fool of.

2 also with *around:* =**monkey** v.
c1938 in 1970 Hyatt *Hoodoo* 1.136 **eVA,** She told me one day, "I am going to get even with you." So I told 'er it was all right, that if she was to *monk* [Hyatt: *monkey*] with me I would shoot 'er. **1940** (1941) Bell *Swamp Water* 99 **Okefenokee GA,** They's a few critters, though, that don't aim to run from a body, and them you better not monk with. *Ibid* 134, Well, I hope you don't expect me just to set and sew all the time you're monking around in that swamp. **1941** O'Donnell *Great Big Doorstep* 171 **sLA,** You were seen in the show with him the other night, see? Monking, I'm afraid. Where was your brother?

monk n[1] See **monkfish 2**

monk n[2] See **moonack 1**

monke See **munk**

monkey n[1] Pronc-spp *mawnkey, mongkey*

A Forms. Note: These spp prob represent proncs of the type ['maŋki] or ['mɔŋki]; cf the alternation between ['dʌŋki] and ['daŋki, 'dɔŋki], ['mʌŋgrəl] and ['maŋgrel, 'mɔŋgrəl] (for which see **mongrel**).

1909 [see **B2** below]. **1940** in 1944 *ADD* **LA** [Black], Dey look like a mawnkey and ack like a man.

B Senses.

1 One of any of var kinds of workers, esp one whose job requires clambering around or moving quickly from place to place—usu in combs.

1858 (1929) Taylor *Life on a Whaler* 62 **NEng,** Amid loud cries for the "monkey," a boat-steerer in his stocking feet and stripped to the waist makes his appearance. A rope is fastened around his body and with an axe in his hands . . he is lowered upon the slimy creature's back. **1930** *RR Man's Mag.* June 469, *Air monkey*—Air brake repairman. **1932** *RR Mag.* Oct 369, *Monkey*—Brakeman on hump riding cars. **1941** *AmSp* 16.164 [Army slang], *Deck monkeys.* Deck crew of Army Mine Planter. *Ibid* 166, *Grease monkey.* Air mechanic's assistant. *Ibid* 233 [Lumberjack jargon], *Powder monkey.* The man who lays and shoots the dynamite in logging operations, for example, in shooting stumps. **1945** Hubbard *Railroad Ave.* 340, *Dope. . .* A composition for cooling hot journals. . . *Dope monkey*—Car inspector. **1946** in 1953 Botkin–Harlow *Treas. Railroad Folkl.* 351, As long as railroad books are written and railroad vocabularies are complied, we may expect to hear brakemen called *block-heads . .* bridge workers, *monkeys . .* but in print only. **1965–66** *DARE* (Qu. HH42, *Names and nicknames for a common laborer;* total Infs questioned, 75) Inf **FL**36, Grease monkey = mechanic; **OK**9, Grease monkey—a mechanic or one who greases a car. **1968** Adams *Western Words* 34, *Bridge monkey*—A logger's name for a bridge builder. **1968** *DARE* FW Addit **NY**96, *Monkey*—inferior workman, someone "just on the payroll," or kept on for odds and ends of work. **1980** *DARE* File **WI** (as of c1900), In a steam-driven threshing machine crew, the water monkey was the man who kept the machine supplied with water. He had to get the water wherever he could—from cisterns, wells, streams—anywhere. **1984** *DARE* File **ceCA,** [Letter:] Driving over Donner Summit was exciting. Chains required over most of the mountains. . . I put them on wrong, but found a "chain monkey," as they are called here, to do it right. **1990** *DARE* File **CO** (as of c1915), A water monkey was the man who drove the horses hitched to the water tank on wheels. The tank . . was used to take water to the steam engine out in the harvest field.

2 also *monkey-meat:* See quot.
1909 *S. Atl. Qrly.* 8.40 **seSC,** The *cocoa-nut* is called *mongkey-nut* perhaps from the resemblance of the hairy nut to a brown monkey's head; and hence small cakes of grated cocoanut are cried through the market as *"mongkey"* or *"mongkey-meat!"*

3 also *monkey calf, ~ veal:* A very young veal calf. **sePA, sNJ** See Map
1967–68 *DARE* (Qu. K20, *A calf that is sold for meat*) Inf **NJ**16, Monkey or monkey calf; **NJ**17, Monkey—very young; **NJ**21, Monkey calf—sold immediately—less than a week old; **NJ**31, Monkey veal—two days old—can give dysentery if eaten; **PA**33, One to three days old is called a monkey; **PA**153, They are monkey calves when nine days or so old; **PA**163, Monkey veal if it's very young. [5 of 7 Infs old]

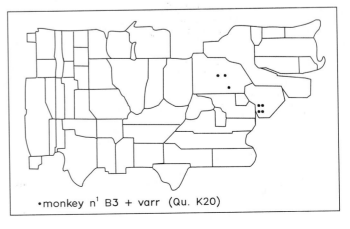

•monkey n[1] B3 + varr (Qu. K20)

4a Fig: a heat wave; heat prostration; hence v phr *see monkeys* to be overcome by heat; adj *monkeyed* exhausted, esp by heat. **SC, NC**

1918 *DN* 5.21 **NC**, *See monkeys,* to be overcome by the heat while working. The heat waves are called "monkeys." When one laborer shows signs of exhaustion, the others say, "Look out, the monkeys are after you." **1930** Stoney-Shelby *Black Genesis* 134 **seSC**, He couldn't run no more. He couldn't eben t'ink. De "Monkey" (exhaustion) most got him. **1952** *PADS* 17.31 **SC**, A similar effect of mirage which makes objects near the ground, such as grass, weeds, bushes, seem to be trembling, dancing in the sunlight, is called *monkeys.* Heat prostration means, therefore, that "the monkeys got you." **1968** *DARE* (Qu. X47, . . *"I'm very tired, at the end of my strength"*) Inf **SC**58, Monkeyed—esp from overwork, heat, fatigue.

b By ext; in railroading: see quot.

1940 Cottrell *Railroader* 132, *Monkey*—If a crew is between terminals when sixteen hours have elapsed since leaving, "the monkey gets them" and they are required by I.C.C. rules to "tie up" until a new crew comes.

5 usu pl: Delirium tremens; also used in var phrr to indicate drunkenness or its aftereffects; see quots. **chiefly S Atl** See Map

1935 Hurston *Mules & Men* 56 **FL**, You drunk, Bennie Lee. You done drunk so much of dis ole coon dick till you full of monkies [sic]. **1950** *PADS* 14.47 **SC**, *Monkeys.* . . Delirium tremens. "To have the monkeys." **1965–70** *DARE* (Qu. DD22, . . *Delirium tremens*) Infs **FL**1, 13, 48, **MS**71, **NC**1, 2, Monkeys; **NC**87, Drunken monkeys; **FL**22, Monkeys and snakes; **FL**39, **NE**11, **SC**69, Monkey on his back; **GA**13, Monkeys after you; **FL**20, **GA**30, Monkeys are (*or* gets) after him; **GA**5, Monkeys on him; **FL**35, **GA**17, 19, 30, **NC**26, Seeing (the) monkeys.

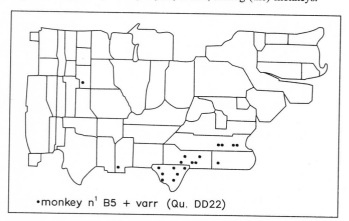

•monkey n[1] B5 + varr (Qu. DD22)

6 also pl; usu in var phrr: Menstruation. [Perh joc var of *monthlies,* or by ext from slang *monkey* female genitals]

1950s in **1982** *Barrick Coll.* **csPA**, Monkies [sic]—menstrual cycle; to have the monkies. **1967–69** *DARE* (Qu. AA27, . . *A woman's menstruation*) Inf **NJ**59, Her monkey's sick; **PA**161, She's got the monkey; **OR**3, Monkey's got a hemorrhage.

7 See quots. Cf **monkeynut 3**

1949 *WELS Suppl.* **ceWI**, Maple seed pods are "monkeys" ([from their] supposed resemblance) to Milwaukee-raised 35 yr.-old. **1970** *DARE* File **NEng, esp MA**, Monkey. . . A bract of linden or the winged seeds of maple or ash.

8 A Black person. *derog* Cf **ape** n **1, monkey in the woodpile**

1968–70 *DARE* (Qu. HH28, *Names and nicknames . . for people of foreign background: Black*) Inf **PA**247, Monkey; **VA**2, Have heard them called monkeys. **1983** Allen *Lang. Ethnic Conflict* 50, *Animal Metaphors* [for Blacks]: ape . . , monkey. **1986** Pederson *LAGS Concordance* (Negro) 1 inf, **cMS**, Monkey—offensive; 1 inf, **nwMS**, A monkey—of a playful black—"full of tricks."

‡9 Nonsense, baloney.

1966 *DARE* (Qu. NN13, *When you think that the thing somebody has just said is silly or untrue: "Oh, that's a lot of _____."*) Inf **SC**26, Monkey.

monkey v, hence vbl n *monkeying* Often with *around;* rarely with *along* **chiefly Nth, N Midl** See Map Cf **monk** v **2, monkeyed up**

To waste time, fool around; to tamper, meddle, or fiddle (with something or someone).

1881 (**1939**) Mayne *Maud* 39 **IL**, What with talking, running back and forth and general monkey-ing Clara slipped and fell. **1885** Siringo *TX Cowboy* 131, You can imagine the boys giving it to me about monkeying with civilized girls. **1887** Kirkland *Zury* 538 **IL**, *Monkey.* To waste time in foolish actions. **1907** *DN* 3.194 **NH**, *Monkey with the buzz-saw.* . . Negatively, don't meddle. **1912** *DN* 3.583 **wIN**, *Monkey with the buzz-saw.* . . To risk injury of any kind. "You'd better quit running around with that fellow. Don't monkey with the buzz-saw." **1916** *DN* 4.277 **IL, IA, KS, MA, NE, NY, NC, PA, TN**, *Monkey around.* . . To waste time, or pass the time aimlessly. "What did you do after supper?" "We just monkeyed around." **1927** *AmSp* 2.360 **cwWV**, *Monkey around . . ,* to pass the time without any aim. "We monkeyed around all afternoon." **1929** *AmSp* 5.119 **ME**, A man who was busy without results was said to be "monkeying around" wasting time. **1930** Shoemaker *1300 Words* 39 **cPA Mts** (as of c1900), *Monkey*—To interfere with or upset anything. **c1960** *Wilson Coll.* **csKY**, *Monkey around.* . . Be idle or meddlesome. **1965–70** *DARE* (Qu. A10, . . *Doing little unimportant things: . . "What are you doing?" . . "Nothing in particular—I'm just _____."*) 13 Infs, **Nth**, Monkeying around; **MI**47, Monkeying; (Qu. A11, *When somebody takes too long about coming to a decision . . "I wish he'd quit _____."*) Inf **NY**93, Monkeying around; (Qu. A12, *When somebody keeps you waiting . . "Hurry up! I don't have all day to _____ you!"*) Infs **OH**4, **WA**24, Monkey around (with); **IN**30, Monkey with; (Qu. A19, *Other ways of saying "I'll have to hurry": "I'm late, I'll have to _____."*) Inf **PA**131, Can't monkey around; (Qu. A20, *Joking ways of telling somebody to hurry*) Inf **FL**11, Quit monkeying around; (Qu. Y27, *To go about aimlessly, with nothing to do: "He's always _____ around the drugstore."*) Infs **PA**234, **WA**22, **WI**66, Monkeying; (Qu. GG32a, *To habitually play tricks or jokes on people: "He's always _____."*) Inf **MD**41, Monkeying around; [**VT**12, Up to some monkey trick; **IL**143, Acting the monkey;] (Qu. JJ26, *If somebody has been doing poor work or not enough, the boss might say, "If he wants to keep his job he'd better _____."*) Infs **MN**10, **TX**27, Quit monkeying around; (Qu. KK31, *To go about aimlessly looking for distraction: "He doesn't have anything to do, so he's just _____ around."*) Infs **CA**202, **IN**61, 73, **NY**109, **PA**234, **WI**65, Monkeying. **1966–69** *DARE* Tape **CA**103, At that time he didn't have any better sense, but, in fact, after he'd monkeyed along, and his folks taught him, . . he owned some timber himself, and that's how he monkeyed around here; **CA**145, They'd start rattlin' and buzzin' and then we'd monkey around and fish him out of there with a stick or wire; **MI**36, I walked in there, monkeyed around with the cars there; **MI**49, Two-thirds of the sailors you wouldn't even want to monkey around with; **MI**96, There were some kids here the other night, that were monkeying around . . with the light out here. **1981** Bly *Letters* 9 **swMN**, You monkey with poultry, unless you're a major egg handler. Or you monkey with ducks or geese. . . The other meaning of monkeying is wrestling with and maintaining machinery. . . Farmers who cornpick the old way . . put up with some monkeying.

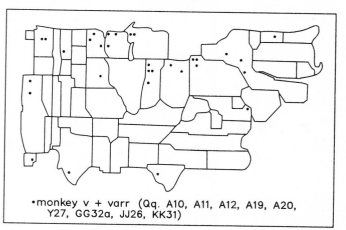

•monkey v + varr (Qq. A10, A11, A12, A19, A20, Y27, GG32a, JJ26, KK31)

monkey n[2] See **munk**

monkey along (or around) See **monkey** v

monkey ball n

1 =Osage orange.

1971 *Today Show Letters* **swPA** (as of c1925), The Osage orange we called "monkey balls." But [when] we used them as weapons in gang warfare, we called them "stink balls."

2 The seed pod of a **sycamore** tree. Cf **buttonball**

1982 Ferguson *All about Trees* 6 **wPA,** Many streets were lined with great sycamores. . . They were dirty trees, shedding leaves, bark, and fuzzy 'monkey balls' in the fall, but they added so much to the quality of that dingy town.

monkey bite n

1 =**hickey** n² **c. chiefly CA, also C and S Atl** See Map Cf **octopus bite, sucker ~**

1942 Berrey–Van den Bark *Amer. Slang* 355.4, Monkey bite, hicky, strawberry kiss, *a red mark caused by sucking or biting.* **1965–70** *DARE* (Qu. X39, *A mark on the skin where somebody has sucked it hard and brought the blood to the surface*) 27 Infs, **chiefly CA, also C and S Atl,** Monkey bite.

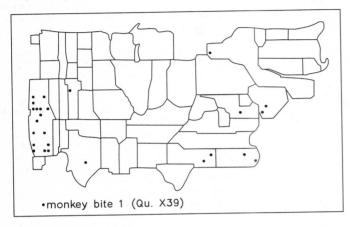

•monkey bite 1 (Qu. X39)

2 See quot.

1967 *DARE* (QR, near Qu. X39) Inf **MA**1, Monkey bite—perfectly innocent—a hand grab, e.g., just above the knee, no bruise.

monkey blanket See blanket 3

monkey blood n Also *monkey's blood* esp TX

An antiseptic solution; see quots.

1986 Pederson *LAGS Concordance,* 8 infs, 6 **LA, TX,** Monkey blood; 2 infs, **cLA, neTX,** Monkey blood = iodine; 1 inf, **ceTX,** Monkey blood—another name for Mercurochrome; 1 inf, **neTX,** Monkey blood—red medicine; 1 inf, **cTX,** Monkey blood—joking term for Merthiolate; 1 inf, **csTX,** Monkey blood—Mercurochrome or iodine; 1 inf, **csTX,** Monkey's blood—Mercurochrome. **1995** *DARE* File **c,seTX** (as of 1940s), Monkey blood. . . I knew that term for Mercurochrome as a child. *Ibid* **nwTX** (as of late 1940s), Let me add the Texas Panhandle (Lubbock) to the "monkey blood" crowd. That was standard usage in my family. *Ibid* **cTX** (as of 1940s–50s), Monkey blood. . . This term was used in my family when I was a child growing up in Fort Worth. *Ibid* **csTX** (as of 1970s), Monkey blood. . . My mother and her parents—all from San Antonio, Texas—used it while I was growing up. *Ibid* **nwIN** (as of 1970s), Monkey blood. . . I heard it in rural NW Indiana as a kid. *Ibid* **csKS,** Monkey blood is alive and well here in Wichita—and has been for as long as anyone can remember. *Ibid* (as of 1940s–50s), Growing up in Los Angeles . . , "monkey blood" was frequently applied to my boyhood wounds. And I think it was an internal family word . . , so that moves its roots back into Arkansas. *Ibid* **swAR,** I grew up knowing that Mercurocrome was monkey blood. . . This was part of our family language that has its origins in southwest Arkansas. *Ibid* **cTX** (as of 1950s–60s), Members of my family referred to Mercurochrome as monkey blood. . . We always begged for monkey blood when we had a cut or scratch—the alternative was Merthiolate, which stung like hell.

monkey bone n

=**funny bone 1.**

1967 *DARE* (Qu. X33, *The place in the elbow that gives you a strange feeling if you hit it against something*) Inf **PA**29, Monkey [mʌki] bone. [FW: Inf has slight nasalization.]

monkey bush n

A **monkey flower 1.**

1968 *DARE* (Qu. S11) Inf **CA**65, Monkey bush—looks like a snap-dragon.

monkey cage See monkey house

monkey calf See monkey n¹ B3

monkey-chaser n esp freq among Black speakers

A dark-skinned native of a tropical country; see quots.

1926 Van Vechten *Nigger Heaven* 286 [Black], *Monkey-chaser:* a Negro from the British West Indies. **1928** McKay *Home to Harlem* 38 [Black], I've seen the monkey-chasers order it when they want to put on style. **1930** Irwin *Amer. Tramp* 130, *Monkey chaser.* . . A West Indian or Central American native; people the average tramp visualizes as spending much of their time in chasing the monkeys and doing but little else. **1942** *Amer. Mercury* 55.223.95 **Harlem NYC** [Black], *Monkey chaser*—a West Indian. **1942** Berrey–Van den Bark *Amer. Slang* 385.26, *South-Sea Islander; Polynesian; Malayan.* . . monkey chaser. **1988** Naylor *Mama Day* 100 **GA, SC coast** [Black], Your eyes got a little misty, and if you still thought of Jamaicans, Trinidadians, or Antiguans as "monkey chasers," you never said it aloud again.

monkey cigar tree n Also *monkey cigar* Cf **cigar tree, Indian cigar**

=**catalpa B1.**

1966–70 *DARE* (Qu. T9, *The common shade tree with large heart-shaped leaves, clusters of white blossoms, and long thin seed pods or 'beans'*) Inf **SC**28, Monkey cigar tree; **VA**64, Monkey cigar.

monkey climb v phr Also *monkey up* Cf **coon v 2**

1965–70 *DARE* (Qu. EE36, *To climb the trunk of a tree by holding on with your legs while you pull yourself up with your hands*) Infs **MO**21, **NC**14, **PA**210, **TN**27, **TX**43, **WA**18, Monkey climb(ing); **NE**11, **GA**23, Monkey(ing) up; [**NY**241, Monkey business; **FL**18, Climbing like a monkey; **FL**48, Skinning the monkey].

monkey cups n

Prob a **pitcher plant.**

1968 *DARE* (Qu. S26b, *Wildflowers that grow in water or wet places*) Inf **MI**96, Monkey cups.

monkeyed See monkey n B4a

monkeyed up ppl adj Cf **monkey v**

Confused, mixed up.

1966 Maddux *Spring Rain* 40 **WV,** "Seem like," Will said, "everything just all monkeyed up." *Ibid* 70, I was workin on a machine . . and it's all monkeyed up.

monkey face n Cf **monkey's face**

1 also *monkey-faced flower:* =**monkey flower 1.** esp Pacific

1921 *DN* 5.113 **CA,** Monkey face. . . Monkey flower. **1966** *DARE* Wildfl QR Pl.191B Inf **OR**8, Monkey face. **1968** *DARE* (Qu. S26a, *. . Wildflowers. . . Roadside flowers*) Inf **CA**80, Monkey-faced flower.

2 =**fringed orchid.**

1938 in 1950 Correll *Native Orchids* 59 **csTN,** Like the other species of Habenaria it [=*H. blephariglottis*] is known locally as 'Monkey-face.' **1950** *Ibid* 59, *Habenaria blephariglottis* . . var *integrilabia*. . . Common name: Monkey-face.

3 A **dayflower** (here: *Commelina communis*). Cf **monkey flower 4**

1969 *DARE* FW Addit **KY**5, Monkey face—dayflower or *Commelina communis.*

4 pl: =**lupine.**

1892 *Jrl. Amer. Folkl.* 5.94 **nOH,** *Lupinus villosus,* monkey faces; sun-dial. **1896** *Ibid,* 9.186 **swOH,** *Lupinus,* sp. sun dial, monkey faces.

5 pl: A **witch hazel** (here: *Hamamelis virginiana*).

1940 Clute *Amer. Plant Names* 147, *H[amamelis] Virginiana.* Witch-hazel. Winter-bloom, monkey-faces.

6 A **freshwater clam** (here: *Quadrula metanevra*).

1941 *AmSp* 16.155, The following list gives the common names [of freshwater clams] as applied by the cutter and fisher of shells. . . Monkey Face [etc]. **1979** *WI Week-End* 6 Apr 6, Such shellfish as the . . monkey face . . go right on living their private lives in the quiet water-ways of the Mississippi. **1982** U.S. Fish & Wildlife Serv. *Fresh-Water Mussels* [Wall chart], Monkeyface. . . Shell yellow or brown, usually with zigzag green lines, especially when young.

7 A malformation in lambs caused by ingestion of **false hellebore 1;** hence n *monkey-faced lamb.*

1968 Schmutz et al. *Livestock-Poisoning Plants AZ* 122, Another disease caused by hellebore is "monkey face" in lambs, a congenital malformation which causes the forehead and lower jaw to protrude and the face to dish in. . . Losses due to monkey-faced lambs may be prevented by delaying breeding until after frost.

8 See **monkey-faced owl.**

9 See **monkey-faced spider.**

10 A type of cookie; see quots.

1947 Bowles–Towle *New Engl. Cooking* 202, No matter how busy grandmother was she always had time to make gingerbread men and monkey faces. *Ibid* 212, *Monkey Faces.* . . Drop [cookie dough] by the spoonful on a buttered baking sheet. Press in two raisins for eyes and one for the mouth. **1957** Showalter *Mennonite Cookbook* 274 **sePA,** *Monkey Faces*—Use preceding recipe [=cookies made with two rounds of dough and a filling of raisins, nuts, sugar, water, and flour]. Before putting top round of dough on cookie, use a thimble to cut eyes and mouth. Do not cut through dough but press deep enough so that shape will remain in baked cookie. **1982** *DARE* File **cnMA,** Monkey faces are cookies baked with three raisins—two for the eyes, one for the mouth. My New Hampshire grandmother made these.

monkey-faced flower See **monkey face 1**

monkey-faced mint See **monkey flower 5**

monkey-faced owl n Also *monkeyface (owl), monkey(-headed) owl*

=barn owl 1.

1893 Fisher *Hawks & Owls U.S.* 138, The peculiar and almost ludicrous expression of the physiognomy of this bird [=barn owl], as it sits upright with half-closed eyes, has suggested to the minds of many a fanciful resemblance to a monkey; hence the origin of the name 'Monkey-faced Owl,' which is a common appellation for the bird in many parts of the country, especially Florida. In this State the credulous have been led to believe that certain birds with monkeys' heads exist in the remote recesses of the Everglades. **1898** (1900) Davie *Nests N. Amer. Birds* 233, A beautiful ochraceous-yellow or amber-colored owl; sometimes called the "Monkey-faced Owl." **1917** *DN* 4.426 **LA,** The American barn owl . . also called *monkey-faced owl.* **1923** *WV State Ornith. Birds* WV 20, Monkey-faced Owl. . . facial disk narrowed and elongated, giving the bird a weird, impish expression, like that of a monkey or and [sic] old thin-faced man. **c1940** *LAMSAS Materials,* (Hoot owl) 1 inf, **PA,** Monkey-face owl—middle-sized. **1955** *AmSp* 30.180, With a facial disk distinctive both in color and shape among our owls, the barn owl is very generally called *monkey-faced owl,* a designation often shortened to *monkey face,* and varied to *monkey owl* (N.J., Md., Fla., Ill., N. Mex.), *monkey-headed owl* (Texas), and *baboon owl* (Kans.) **1961** Ligon *NM Birds* 142, The heartshaped facial disc has given rise to the widely used name "Monkey-face." **1965–70** *DARE* (Qu. Q2, . . *Kinds of owls*) 26 Infs, scattered, Monkey-face(d) owl; **CA78,** Monkey-faced owl—the barn owl; **NJ21,** Monkey-faced owl—this is the barn owl; **WV8,** Monkey-faced owl—very rare; **WI43,** Monkey face—same as brown owl; very rare now; **GA35,** Monkey owl; **CA87,** Monkey-faced owl or monkey owl—a peculiar laugh—sounds like a crazy person laughing. **1973** Allen *LAUM* 1.317 (as of c1950) 4 infs, **NE, SD,** Monkey-faced owl. **1981** Pederson *LAGS Basic Materials,* 1 inf, **neGA,** Monkey-faced owl—a right attractive-looking one; 1 inf, **ceFL,** Screech owl, white owl; monkey-faced owl, some call them; 1 inf, **ceTX,** Screech owls. . . monkey faced owls; 1 inf, **seTX,** Monkey-faced owl—He's got a face just like a monkey; 1 inf, **csTX,** Monkey owl [same as] barn owl.

monkey-faced spider n Also *monkey face, monkey-faced tarantula*

See quot.

1966–68 *DARE* (Qu. R28, . . *Kinds of spiders*) Inf **NM13,** Monkey face—makes a big web; **NE10,** Monkey-faced spiders; **CA62,** Monkey-faced tarantula—the skinny, ugly ones.

monkeyface eel n Also *monkeyface prickleback*

A **prickleback** (here: *Cebidichthys violaceus*).

1953 Roedel *Common Fishes CA* 146, *Monkey-face Eel.* . . It is not an eel though commonly so called. . . Common in the intertidal zone in the northern and central part of the State. **1991** Amer. Fisheries Soc. *Common Names Fishes* 59, *Cebidichthys violaceus* . . P[acific] . . monkeyface prickleback.

monkey fare n

A **potluck** meal.

1939 (1962) Thompson *Body & Britches* 501 **NY,** In old-fashioned apology you may avoid the banal reference to pot-luck by saying, "You'll have to take monkey-fare today—catch as catch can."

‡**monkey fishing** vbl n Cf **telephoning**

Fishing by using an electrical current to stun the fish.

1966 *DARE* (Qu. P13, . . *Ways of fishing . . besides the ordinary hook*

and line) Inf **FL**16, Monkey fishing—give the fish a shock. **1966** *DARE* Tape **FL**16, The next one [=illegal way of fishing] is what they call monkey fishing. That's any—the catfish will—by using a little generator, putting both poles into the ground and turning it, it'll shock the fish and they'll come to.

monkey flower n

1 A plant of the genus *Mimulus.* [See quot 1923] Also called **monkey face 1, wild snapdragon.** For other names of var spp see **eyebright 11, monkey bush, musk plant, purple mouse-ears, wild lettuce, wild tobacco**

1789 Aiton *Hortus Kewensis* 2.361, *Mimulus.* . . *ringens.* . . Oblong-leav'd Monkey-flower. Nat. of Virginia and Canada. **1848** Gray *Manual of Botany* 299, *Mimulus* [spp] . . Monkey-flower. **1892** Coulter *Botany W. TX* 309, *Mimulus* [spp] . . (Monkey-flower.) **1902** (1909) Mathews *Field Book Amer. Wild Flowers* 422, Monkey-flower—*Mimulus ringens.* . . In swamps and beside brooks, generally in meadows, from Me., south to Va. and Tenn., and west to S. Dak., Minn., Neb., and Tex. **1923** *Amer. Botanist* 29.67, *Mimulus ringens* is everywhere known as "monkey-flower" though it requires a great stretch of the imagination to see in the flower any likeness to the face of a monkey. **1949** Moldenke *Amer. Wild Flowers* 280, The monkeyflowers, *Mimulus,* are another strikingly showy group. . . The scarlet or cardinal monkeyflower, *M. cardinalis* . . flaunts flowers 1½ to 2 inches long, and sets fire to streams and ditches in the foothills and middle altitudes almost throughout California and north to Oregon and east to Utah and Arizona. **1967–69** *DARE* (Qu. S11, . . *Wild snapdragon*) Inf **TN22,** Monkey flower (hiking club term; most of the club members are from Knoxville); **CA24,** Monkey flower; **CA150,** Some call [wild snapdragons] monkey flowers, but it's incorrect; (Qu. S26b, *Wildflowers that grow in water or wet places*) Inf **CA20,** Monkey flower—one variety of; (Qu. S26c, *Wildflowers that grow in woods*) Inf **PA176,** Monkey flowers; (Qu. S26d, *Wildflowers that grow in meadows; not asked in early QRs*) Inf **CA87,** Monkey flower; (Qu. S26e, *Other wildflowers not yet mentioned; not asked in early QRs*) Inf **TN22,** Monkey flower. **1967** *DARE* FW Addit **AR44,** Monkey flower—*Mimulus ringens;* **OR12,** Monkey flower—*Mimulus;* **SC41,** Monkey flower—*Mimulus langsdorfi.* **1967–68** *DARE* Wildfl QR Pl.191B Inf **NY91,** Monkey flower; (Craighead) Pl.18.8 Inf **CO29,** Monkey flower. **1987** *Nature Conserv. News* 37.3.12 **CA,** New populations of native buckwheat, monkey flower and bush poppy took hold.

2 A **lady's slipper 1,** usu *Cypripedium calceolus.*

1876 Hobbs *Bot. Hdbk.* 71, Monkey flower—American valerian,—Cypripedium of several species. **1900** Lyons *Plant Names* 130, *C[ypripedium] hirsutum.* . . Monkey-flower. **1930** Sievers *Amer. Med. Plants* 38, Ladyslipper. . . Other common names . . monkeyflower. **1940** Clute *Amer. Plant Names* 221, *Cypripedium parviflorum.* Male nervine, monkey-flower. **1950** Correll *Native Orchids* 24, Yellow Moccasin-flower, American Valerian, Monkey Flower. **1985** Clark *From Mailbox* 188 **ME,** The monkey flower blossom is a delightful orchid when seen through the [magnifying] glass.

3 =**dead nettle 1.**

1933 Small *Manual SE Flora* 1157, *Lamium.* . . Dead-nettles. Monkey-flowers.

4 A **dayflower** (here: *Commelina communis*). Cf **monkey face 3**

1966 *DARE* Wildfl QR Pl.6B Inf **WI80,** Monkey flower.

5 also *monkey-faced mint:* A mint (here: *Mentha canadensis*).

1966–67 *DARE* Wildfl QR Pl.191A Inf **WA30,** Monkey flower; Pl.191B Inf **WA15,** Monkey-faced mint.

monkey food n chiefly Sth

1 Snack food, finger food.

1940 Harris *Folk Plays* 243 **eNC,** It's your Gussie, with some more monkey food. *Ibid* 293, Monkey food, *cakes, sweetmeats.* **1968** *DARE* (Qu. H5, . . *A small amount of food eaten between regular meals*) Inf **GA17,** Snack; monkey food.

2 Spec: **peanuts.** Cf **monkey-nut 1**

1965–70 *DARE* (Qu. I42, . . *Names or nicknames . . for peanuts*) Infs **CA113, GA13, IL98, LA20, NC41, 84, 87, NJ19, SC26, 70,** Monkey food.

monkey-fooler n

A **prickly ash** (here: *Zanthoxylum clava-herculis*).

1951 Teale *North with Spring* 58 **FL,** In the scrub, we came upon a monkey-fooler or toothache tree—our first prickly ash with its silvery bark and thornlike projections.

monkey-fruit See **monkey-nut 1**

monkey grass n

Perh a **bentgrass 1;** see quots.

1968 *DARE* (Qu. S9, . . *Kinds of grass that are hard to get rid of*) Inf **LA**17, Monkey grass—has bulb at bottom, spreads by underground roots. **1979** *DARE* File, *Monkey grass.* . . [One friend] says she's known it all her life in Oklahoma, and [another] . . says he didn't know [it] till he came to Louisiana. *Ibid* **cLA,** [Church newsletter headline:] *Monkey Grass Needed* [Text:] Bob Allen is sending out a plea for monkey grass to help in the church landscaping project. If you have any extra monkey grass just hanging around your yard give Bob a call. He'll even come over and dig it up himself.

monkey-headed owl See **monkey-faced owl**

monkey heater See **monkey stove**

monkey house n Also *monkey cage, ~ hut, ~ wagon*

=**caboose** n¹ 2.

1930 *RR Man's Mag.* June 471, Monkey house—Caboose. **1950** *WELS* (*Names and nicknames for the last car on a freight train, usually used as headquarters for the crew*) 1 Inf, **seWI,** Monkey cage. **1977** Adams *Lang. Railroader* 101, *Monkey cage:* A caboose; also called *monkey house, monkey hut, monkey wagon.*

monkeying See **monkey** v

monkey-in-the-middle n Cf **saluggi**

A three-person game in which two players try to keep a ball or other object away from a third who stands between them.

1993 *DARE* File **csWI,** *Monkey-in-the-middle* is a game like keep-away, except that there are only two people who throw the ball to each other, trying not to let the person in the middle catch it. *Ibid* **nwMA** (as of 1960s), We used to call keep-away *monkey-in-the-middle. Ibid* **csWI,** My children play monkey-in-the-middle, a kind of keep-away with two kids who throw the ball, and one in the middle who tries to catch it. My daughter likes to use a stuffed monkey instead of a ball, but any kind of ball or tossable object will work. *Ibid* **nwMA,** The game Monkey-In-The-Middle. . . I have indeed played the game, and under that particular name, although Keep Away is more common. . . Kids at our middle school still play it, and it's often unpleasant. Two Alpha males usually grab something belonging to someone who's not so aggressive and the poor victim becomes the Monkey-In-The-Middle, hopping around and trying to retrieve whatever was grabbed while the perpetrators amuse themselves tossing it to each other . . just out of the frantic reach of the victim. . . [T]he Monkey-In-The-Middle is almost never a willing participant. . . It's almost exclusively an adolescent male's game. *Ibid* **NYC** (as of c1950), Monkey-in-the-middle. *Ibid* **Bronx NYC,** Salugi is/was a rather malicious "game" . . that *must* have a victim. . . At least for me, monkey-in-the-middle has no such constraints. *Ibid* **eLong Is. NY,** Monkey-in-the-middle [has no malicious intent].

monkey-in-the-ring n

A children's group game; see quot.

1968 *DARE* (Qu. EE2, *Games that have one extra player—when a signal is given, the players change places, and the extra one tries to get a place*) Inf **MD**8, Monkey-in-the-ring.

monkey in the woodpile n [**monkey** n¹ **B6**] Cf **Ethiopian 2**

=**nigger in the woodpile 1a.**

1967 *DARE* (Qu. V1, *When you suspect that somebody is trying to deceive you, or that something is going on behind your back . . "There's _____."*) Inf **SC**63, A monkey in the woodpile; [**VT**13, Monkey work].

monkey jugs n [See quot] Cf **jug** n **1**

=**wild ginger.**

1943 Peattie *Great Smokies* 172 **TN,** Certainly there is no odder flower . . than that of our wild gingers—"monkey-jugs" some mountain folk call them—each with its little jug-shaped calyx half buried in the earth and hidden under its mottled leaf.

monkey-meat See **monkey** n **B2**

monkey-monk See **muck-a-muck 2**

monkey-nut n

1 also *monkey-fruit:* A **peanut.**

1942 Berrey–Van den Bark *Amer. Slang* 91.61, Monkey nuts . . pea-

nuts. **1967–68** *DARE* (Qu. I42, . . *Names or nicknames . . for peanuts*) Inf **GA**23, Pinders; monkey-fruits; **PA**63, Monkey-nuts.

2 A coconut.

1909 [see **monkey** n **2**].

3 also *monkey-nut tree:* A **linden.** Cf **daddynut, monkey** n **B3**

1950 *WELS* (*Other names . . for . . linden*) 1 Inf, **WI,** Basswood, monkey-nut tree. **1969** *DARE* (Qu. T13, . . *Names . . for . . linden*) Inf **IL**30, Monkey-nut.

4 The seed of a **queen palm.**

1948 Neal *In Gardens HI* 106, *Queen palm.* . . The inch-long fruit is ovoid and is covered with a layer of sweet-tasting, orange, pulpy fiber. Within this is a single seed enclosed in a shell with three pores at one end, locally called the "monkey nut" . . and strung for leis and earrings. [**1960** McGeachy *Hdbk. FL Palms* 16, Queen Palm. . . The hard-shelled fruit, or nut, when ripe and peeled from its thin fibrous husk has the familiar monkey-face of the coconut.]

monkey owl n

1 See **monkey-faced owl.**

2 =**burrowing owl.**

1968 *DARE* (Qu. Q2, . . *Kinds of owls*) Inf **CA**62, Monkey owl—little ones that live in the ground.

monkey pile n Cf **dog pile, nigger pile**

=**buck buck 2.**

1984 *DARE* File **csWI** (as of 1930s), Piling people on top of one another was called making a *monkey pile;* it was just something we did for fun. **1994** *Ibid* **KS,** We called it a monkey pile when a bunch of kids piled on top of each other.

monkeypod n

A tree (*Albizia saman*) naturalized in Hawaii. Also called **rain tree**

1888 Hillebrand *Flora Hawaiian Is.* 115, *Pithecolobium Samang,* the Samang or Monkey-pod tree, enjoys great favor as a shade tree. **1934** Frear *Lowell & Abigail* 267 **HI,** The monkey-pod sapling . . lives on to this day and is now the glory of the "Church in the Garden." **1940** Von Tempski *Paradise* 95 **HI,** The curved domes of monkey-pod trees leaning over blossoming oleanders and hibiscus. **1948** Neal *In Gardens HI* 351, A landmark in Kau, Hawaii is a monkeypod planted by Mark Twain. **1965** Neal *Gardens HI* 402, The name, monkeypod, is from the Greek word "pithecellobium," . . referring to the twisted pods of another tree, the opiuma. **1967** *DARE* (Qu. T16, . . *Kinds of trees . . 'special'*) Infs **HI**2, 11, Monkeypod. **1976** Bailey–Bailey *Hortus Third* 1001, *Monkeypod.* . . A fast-growing, ornamental shade tree, suitable for parks or large gardens.

monkey roost n Cf **buzzard roost 2, nigger heaven 1**

A theater balcony.

1970 *DARE* (Qu. D40, *Names and nicknames . . for the upper balcony in a theater*) Inf **SC**69, Monkey roost.

monkey rum n esp S Midl

Raw liquor made from sorghum or cane syrup.

1941 Daniels *Tar Heels* 255 **NC,** Corn liquor and monkey rum (which in North Carolina was the distilled sirup of sorghum cane), were concoctions taken stoically, with retching and running eyes, for the effect beyond the first fusel oil belch. **1975** McDonough *Garden Sass* 165 **AR,** Sometimes the syrup was distilled into a drink called "monkey rum." As H.D. Payne said, molasses was even better if you "Let it set for awhile till it gets fermated." **1985** Wilkinson *Moonshine* 28 **neNC,** In times when the price of sugar has risen high enough to make the use of it unprofitable, bootleggers have substituted molasses. Moonshine made with molasses is called monkey rum.

Monkey's See **Monkey Ward**

monkey's blood See **monkey blood**

monkey's cat n [From the fable of the monkey using the cat's paw to pull hot chestnuts from the fire; cf **cat's-paw 8**]

A dupe, stooge.

1970 *DARE* (Qu. II34, *If you think somebody is trying to use you to his advantage: "I'm not going to be his _____."*) Inf **VA**43, Monkey's cat.

monkey's face n

An **Oswego tea** (here: *Monarda didyma*).

1966 *DARE* Wildfl QR Pl.189 Inf **MN**37, Monkey's face.

monkeyspring n

A handspring, somersault.

1969 DARE (Qu. EE9b, *If children jump forward, land on the hands, and turn over*) Inf **KY**41, Monkeyspring.

monkeys, rain down v phr

To rain heavily.

1967 DARE (Qu. B26, *When it's raining very heavily . . "It's raining ———."*) Inf **LA**7, Down monkeys.

monkey stove n Also *monkey heater* **chiefly Cent**

A small, general-purpose stove; see quots.

1907 in 1996 DARE File nwIN, [Letter:] I . . have the stareway in and 4 hole monkey stove up. **c1920** in 1944 ADD 395 **KS**, Monkey-stove. . . Small auxiliary stove, as for heating water for laundering. **1934** (1970) Wilson *Backwoods Amer.* 124 **AR, MO**, The countryside generally is free to congregate on shady steps . . or to encircle patriarchal monkey-stoves as weather decides. **1943** (1970) Guthrie *Bound for Glory* 176 **cOK**, We didn't have but one or two sticks of furniture in the house. An old monkey heater with room for two small pots, one beans, one coffee. **1946** Driscoll *Country Jake* 55 **KS**, Even when the snow piled high against the shack, all was warm and cozy within, for there was abundance of dry wood to burn in the monkey stove. **1954** *NY Times* (NY) 6 Mar sec C 14/4, This device, designed for the express purpose of heating water for a household, is known by a number of names, some of them unprintable; however it is, in polite circles, called "a bucket-a-day" or a "monkey stove". **1966** *Wichita Eagle* (KS) 9 Apr sec c 7/1, Clearance Sale. . . Brass bed, monkey stove. **1973** Allen *LAUM* 1.408 (as of c1950), 1 inf, **MN**, Monkey stove. A stove, such as was formerly used in railway depots, having a long slender top section and a bulging round base. **1981** DARE File **OK**, Monkey stove—A small stove for room heating. **1994** *NADS Letters* ceMI, Monkey stove . . was my mother's word for laundry stove. Could put the copper boiler on it to heat wash water. It burned everything [DARE Ed: i.e., for fuel]. She was from Akron, Michigan. Born 1890. [DARE Ed: Illustr shows a stove with a flat top and two lids in its surface.]

monkey's wedding n Also *monkey's wedding breakfast*

A state of disorder or disarray.

1884 Jewett *Country Dr.* 276 **ME**, She confessed to having left her own possessions in such confusion . . that Priscilla had called it a monkey's wedding. . . Nan begged to know if anybody had ever heard of a monkey's wedding before, and seemed very much amused. *Ibid* 277, "She called such a disarray in the kitchen one morning the monkey's wedding breakfast," said Miss Prince. . . "Priscilla has always made use of a great many old-fashioned expressions."

monkey tail n [Prob from the appearance of the flower spike]

A **plantain** such as *Plantago major.*

1968 DARE (Qu. S9, . . *Kinds of grass that are hard to get rid of*) Inf **NY**69, Monkey tail. [FW: Inf pointed out a common plantain.]

monkey tree n

1 =**Hercules'-club 1.**

1940 Clute *Amer. Plant Names* 251, *Aralia spinosa.* Monkey-tree, sea ash.

2 The monkey-puzzle tree (*Araucaria araucana*).

1968 DARE (Qu. T16, . . *Kinds of trees . . 'special'*) Inf **CA**53, Monkey tree [has] a sharp leaf, wide, strong, and shiny—they all turn up—monkey could go up and couldn't come down.

3 The China fir (*Cunninghamia lanceolata*).

[**1976** Bailey–Bailey *Hortus Third* 344, China fir. . . Grown as an ornamental in milder parts of the U.S. Propagated by seeds or cuttings.] **1995** *Atlanta Constitution* (GA) 26 Mar sec N 1, One of the trees . . is a type of fir with a nice conical shape and large needles. They are usually large—50 feet or so—and always around older homes. . . I finally found a picture of one . . , and it was called a Chinese fir. I have asked about this tree in a number of nurseries and. . . at Dorsey's. . . Mr. Dorsey . . suggested what I sought was a Cunninghamia or monkey tree. He said it was called that because it is a sticky nasty thing that even a monkey wouldn't climb. . . It has cones of a sort and needles that go around the limb like a spruce but larger so limbs have the appearance of a bottle brush.

monkey up See **monkey climb**

monkey veal See **monkey** n[1] **B3**

monkey wagon See **monkey house**

Monkey Ward n Also *Monkey's, Monkey Ward's* joc

The mail-order house and department store of the Montgomery Ward Company.

1942 [see **mail-order cowboy**]. **1949** Webber *Backwoods Teacher* 248 **Ozarks**, On Thursday, when ever'body got their *Weekly Star* f'm Kansas City, had to lead a mule behind to pack 'em. An' them damn' Monkey Ward catalogues—how I hated them. **1956** Almirall *From College* 106 **CO**, If anything needed was not there, ranchers procured it through either of the two so-called "Ranchmen's Bibles," the catalogues of Montgomery Ward, more familiarly known as "Monkey Ward," and Sears, Roebuck. **1964** Jackman–Long *OR Desert* 334, Of course, everyone had catalogs from Monkey Ward and Sears and Sawbuck. **1975** (1992) Dick *Confessions* 185, Don't stick up anything for her [=a horse] to nip off. They really have strength in those jaws. . . grind the grass, like rotary blades. Bone roto-tillers, and good for a hell of a lot longer than that monkey ward's piece of tin. **1976** Sublette Co. Artist Guild *More Tales* 45 ceWY (as of c1900), To the discomfort of the local merchants much buying was done from Monkeys and Sears. *Ibid* 56, The mail men had brought up . . various Christmas orders from Monkey Wards. **1992** DARE File seWI (as of c1956), I used to say "Monkey Ward" for Montgomery Ward—I heard it from my mother. *Ibid* cwCA (as of 1950s), Our town had Sears, Penney's, and Monkey Ward's stores, all of which also had catalogs through which people could buy what wasn't in the store. *Ibid* nIL (as of c1910–20), Montgomery Ward was known as Monkey Ward.

Monkey Ward cowboy See **mail-order cowboy**

Monkey Ward's See **Monkey Ward**

monkey work n

1 Mischievous or underhanded activity; "monkey business."

1898 *McClure's Mag.* Apr 541 **NY**, Mind you, any monkey work'll get you into more trouble. **1969** DARE (Qu. V1, *When you suspect that somebody is trying to deceive you, or that something is going on behind your back . . "There's ———."*) Inf **VT**13, Monkey work.

2 Trifling or insignificant work.

1933 White *Dog Days* 75 **MI**, If this out-of-season monkey-work with guns has any interest for him [=a dog] at all it is probably only to a not too roseate hope that it may teach us to miss 'em [=targets the dog must retrieve] less often. **1967** DARE (Qu. KK32, . . *The word 'busy-work'. . . What does it mean?*) Inf **CA**33, [FW: described [busywork], got:] Monkey work.

monkfish n

1 =**angel shark.** [See quot 1672; OED 1610 →]

1672 Josselyn *New-Englands Rarities* 96, *Munk Fish,* a flat Fish like scate, having a hood like a Fryers Cowl. **1879** U.S. Natl. Museum *Bulletin* 14.67, *Squatina dumerili* . . Monk-fish; Fiddle-fish.—Cape Cod to Florida. **1903** NY State Museum & Sci. Serv. *Bulletin* 60.45, *Squatina squatina* . . Angel fish; Monkfish. . . Body raylike in shape, flat, depressed. **1933** John G. Shedd Aquarium *Guide* 21, *Squatina Squatina*—Monkfish; Angelfish. **1968** *Cape May Co. Gaz.* (Cape May Court House NJ) 11 July sec D 3/4, Nate High called us up and asked us to stop over and see a picture of what was first called monk fish and later identified as an angel shark.

2 also *monk:* =**goosefish.**

1807 in 1846 MA Hist. Soc. *Coll.* 2d ser 3.55, The sting-ray, the skaite, and the goose fish, or monk, or fishing frog, are common. **1832** Williamson *Hist. ME* 1.157, *Monk-fish* is very plenty about Owl's-head and other bays. **1842** DeKay *Zool. NY* 4.163, Its monstrous form has given rise to many popular names, such as *Sea Devil, Fishing Frog, Bellows-fish, Angler, Goose-fish, Monk-fish,* and various others. **1884** Goode *Fisheries* U.S. 1.173, The names of the fish are many; but that most commonly in use among the Massachusetts fishermen is "Goose Fish." In Maine it is often called "Monk Fish." **1965** *PADS* 43.17 seMA, Fish common in this area . . monkfish or goosefish [1 of 9 infs]. **1973** Knight *Cook's Fish Guide* 385, Monkfish—Goosefish. **1982** Heat Moon *Blue Highways* 352 **ME**, Even more primordial is the monkfish, also called the "goosefish" and "angler fish". . . The death-trap mouth is a cavernous thing, full not so much of spiky teeth as stalagmites and stalactites. But more: around the top half of the body are strange growths of skin resembling sea plants that give a resting monkfish the look of an old weedy stone. Under the mouth, where the pectoral fins should be, are two little finny, clawed hands that it uses to scrape out a depression to hunt from.

monk's cap n

A **prairie clover** (here: *Dalea purpurea*).

1959 Carleton *Index Herb. Plants* 83, Monk's cap . . Petalostemum purpureum.

monkshood n

1 Std: a plant of the genus *Aconitum*. Also called **blue-weed 3.** For other names of var spp see **Adam and Eve 2, Venus's chariot**

2 A **Dutchman's breeches 1.**

1866 Lindley–Moore *Treas. Botany* 2.750, Monkshood. *Aconitum Napellus*; also *Dielytra* [=*Dicentra*] *Cucullaria*. **1900** Lyons *Plant Names* 63, *B[icuculla] cucullaria*. . . Northern U.S. Dutchman's breeches . . Monkshood. **1940** Clute *Amer. Plant Names* 121, *D[icentra] cucullaria*. Dutchman's Breeches. . . monk's-hood.

monk's pepper tree n Also *monk's pepper bush*
=**chaste tree.**

1900 Lyons *Plant Names* 395, *V[itex] agnus-castus*. . . Monk's Pepper-tree. . . *Seeds aromatic.* **1909** Doubleday *Amer. Flower Garden* 177, Chaste Tree, Monk's Pepper Tree *(Vitex Agnus-castus)*. . . Flowers bluish lilac. **1962** Harrar–Harrar *Guide S. Trees* 645, In the South, the monks pepperbush *(Vitex agnus-castus L.)* and certain of the lantanas are prized ornamentals. **1970** Correll *Plants TX* 1340, Vitex Agnus-castus. . . *Monk's-pepper-tree, wild-pepper.* **1979** Little *Checklist U.S. Trees* 294, Vitex agnus-castus. . . monks-peppertree, Indian-spice.

monnie n Cf **moonie** n[1], *DS* EE6a

In marble play: see quots.

c1970 Wiersma *Marbles Terms,* Different names for shooters . . monnies. **1973** Ferretti *Marble Book* 49, Monnies. Another term for shooters.

monobilie See **manavelins 2**

monsous, monstous, monstratious See **monstrous**

‡monstropolous adj [Var of **monstrous**] Cf **obstropolous**

1937 (1977) Hurston *Their Eyes* 239 **FL**, The monstropolous beast had left his bed.

monstrous adj, adv Rarely *monstratious* Pronc-spp *monst(o)us, mons(o)us*

A Forms.

1836 (1955) *Crockett Almanacks* 45 **wTN**, A monstratious great Cat-Fish . . came swimming along close under the bows of my boat. **1851** Burke *Polly Peablossom* 49 **MO**, I've heard of some monsus explites [=exploits] kicked up by the brown bars [=bears]. **1867** Harris *Sut Lovingood Yarns* 31 **TN**, She spied out that his shut [=shirt] wer mons'ous stiff. **1884** *Anglia* 7.270 **Sth, S Midl** [Black], *To feel monst'ous skittish* = to be very timid. **1896** [see **B** below]. **1899** [see **B** below]. **1899** Chesnutt *Conjure Woman* 146 **NC** [Black], Dis yere is a monst'us small pickaninny. **1903** *DN* 2.321 **seMO**, Monstous. **1907** *DN* 3.233 **nwAR**, Monstous.

B As adv.

Exceedingly, very. [*OED* 1590 →] **chiefly Sth, S Midl** Cf **masterous**

1827 (1939) Sherwood *Gaz. GA* 139, Provincialisms. . . *Monstrous,* for very, as monstrous great. **1844** Thompson *Major Jones's Courtship* 80 **GA**, Cousin Pete thought he was monstrous smart. . . it's a monstrous curious feelin when anybody tries to hate somebody that they can't help likin. **1867** [see **A** above]. **1884** *Anglia* 7.264 **Sth, S Midl** [Black], *To be monst'ous full er* = to be very full of. **1885** Twain *Huck. Finn* 122 **MO**, A little ways behind a monstrous long raft. **1896** Harris *Sister Jane* 162 **GA**, I'm monstus glad to see you. **1899** (1912) Green *VA Folk-Speech* 286, Monsus. . . Exceedingly: extremely; wonderfully: as, "That's a monsus hard thing to do." **1903** *DN* 2.321 **seMO**, She's a monstous fine girl. **1905** *DN* 3.14 **cCT**, Monstrous. . . Very. A monstrous pretty city. R[are]. **1907** *DN* 3.233 **nwAR**, Yes'm, I'se monstrous hungry. **1909** *DN* 3.350 **eAL, wGA**, Monst(r)ous. . . Very. **1926** Roberts *Time of Man* 215 **KY**, I'm monstrous tired tonight. **1931** *N. Amer. Rev.* 231.429 **NYC**, You look monstrous well-favored without [a beard]. **c1960** *Wilson Coll.* **csKY**, Monstrous. . . Very.

C As adj.

Used as an intensive. [*OED* 1710-11–1825; "*Obs.*"]

1929 *AmSp* 5.127 **ME**, A person might be . . a "monstrous worker."

mont See **month**

monte n [Span "thicket"] chiefly SW Cf **chaparral B1**

An uncultivated area usu densely covered with shrubs or brush.

1851 (1929) Hayes *Pioneer Notes* 79 **Los Angeles CA**, An American coming from the Monte, whom he presently met, had seen no person on that road. **1854** (1932) Bell *Log TX-CA Trail* 36.63, Came to what is called the *Monte* about noon. This valley is said to be the richest in California. **1855** in 1948 *Western Folkl.* 7.13 **CA**, [Agriculture on the "Plains of Los Angeles" shows promise] in the experimental crops on the "Monte," a few miles east of the city. The Monte lands will yield. . . sixty bushels to the acre. **1856** (1928) Jaeger *Diary Fort Yuma* 107 **sCA**, Pablo got thrown off a horse out in the monte catching cattle. **1892** *DN* 1.250 **TX**, *Mónte*. . . Often used as an equivalent of *chaparral*. **1933** (1955) Rockfellow *Log AZ Trail Blazer* 32 (as of 1870s), This was because of the dense mesquite brush or "monte" through which the road ran. **1941** Dobie *Longhorns* 336 **TX**, Martin told me that one time in the Chapa *monte* he accidentally rode up on some pieces of rope and bones at a mesquite tree. *Ibid* 338, One by one the Chapa Longhorns were roped out of the *monte*. **1967** *DARE* (Qu. C28, *A place where underbrush, weeds, vines and small trees grow together so that it's nearly impossible to get through*) Inf **TX**29, Monte ['mɔnti].

Monterey halibut n [See quot 1884] c,sCA coast

A **flounder** n B (here: *Paralichthys californicus*). Also called **chicken halibut 1, halibut B2, sole**

1882 U.S. Natl. Museum *Bulletin* 16.821, *P[aralichthys] californicus* . . Monterey halibut; Bastard halibut. **1884** Goode *Fisheries U.S.* 1.182, At San Francisco, where the true Halibut is known, this species *[Paralichthys maculosus]* is called the Bastard Halibut, and sometimes the Monterey Halibut, as they are mostly brought from Monterey. **1909** Holder–Jordan *Fish Stories* 323, Our Monterey halibut, or bastard halibut, is a big fish too, but seldom exceeds three feet in length. It . . may be known from true halibut by the form of its tail. . . In the "Monterey halibut" the eyes are normally on the left side, but very often on the right, a piece of carelessness which is very unusual in the making of flounders. **1953** Roedel *Common Fishes CA* 55, California Halibut. . . Unauthorized Names: Chicken halibut, bastard halibut, southern halibut, Monterey halibut.

Monterey mackerel See **Monterey Spanish mackerel**

Monterey pine n

A pine *(Pinus radiata)* native to California. Also called **bull pine 1a**

1874 (1877) Hittell *Resources CA* 358, The Monterey pine *(Pinus insignis)* is extensively cultivated as an ornamental tree. **1884** Sargent *Forests of N. Amer.* 196, *Monterey Pine.* California, Pescadero to Monterey and San Simeon bay. **1910** Jepson *Silva CA* 100, The Monterey Pine is a strictly littoral species, of very limited range, distributed along the coast south of San Francisco Bay, a distance of one hundred and thirty miles. **1961** Thomas *Flora Santa Cruz* 63 **cwCA**, *P[inus] radiata* . . Monterey Pine. **1967–69** *DARE* (Qu. T17, . . *Kinds of pine trees;* not asked in early QRs) Infs **CA**65, 107, 119, Monterey pine; **CA**31, Monterey pine or bull pine; **CA**105, Bishop pine or Monterey [pine] or bull pine. **1979** Little *Checklist U.S. Trees* 197, Monterey pine. . . Rare at 3 localities on coast of c. Calif. (San Mateo, Santa Cruz, Monterey, and San Luis Obispo [counties]).

Monterey Spanish mackerel n Also *Monterey mackerel*

A **Spanish mackerel** (here: *Scomberomorus concolor*).

1884 Goode *Fisheries U.S.* 1.316, The Monterey Mackerel. . . attains a length of about thirty inches and a weight of about five or eight pounds. . . They always bring a very high price in the market . . , the flesh being similar to that of the Spanish Mackerel of the East, which species this fish closely resembles. **1896** U.S. Natl. Museum *Bulletin* 47.873, *Monterey Spanish Mackerel.* . . Monterey Bay, California; appearing about Santa Cruz in moderate numbers every fall; not known elsewhere, and always disappearing in November. **1911** U.S. Bur. Fisheries *Rept. for 1908* 316, In California the Monterey Spanish mackerel *(S. concolor)* is a most excellent food fish. **1953** Roedel *Common Fishes CA* 85, The Monterey Spanish mackerel . . is occasionally caught off Southern California and in years past was known from Monterey Bay. **1973** Knight *Cook's Fish Guide* 384, Mackerel . . Atka . . ; Atlantic . . ; . . Monterey [etc]. **1991** Amer. Fisheries Soc. *Common Names Fishes* 148, Monterey Spanish [mackerel].

Montezuma quail n
=**harlequin quail.**

1917 (1923) *Birds Amer.* 2.10, Mearns's Quail. *Cyrtonyx montezumae* *mearnsi.* . . Other names.—Montezuma Quail; . . Fool Quail; Fool Hen. **1977** Udvardy *Audubon Field Guide Birds* 620, Montezuma Quail—"Harlequin Quail"—*(Cyrtonyx montezumae).* **1982** Elman *Hunter's Field Guide* 102, The harlequin, or Mearns, quail *(Cyrtonyx montezumae),* also called Montezuma quail, Massena quail, crazy quail, black quail, or painted quail.

Montezuma's revenge n [*Montezuma* II (1466–1520), last Aztec emperor of Mexico, killed during the Spanish conquest] Cf **Aztec two-step**

Diarrhea, esp that caused by food or water in Mexico.

1962 *Western Folkl.* 21.28 **CA,** The North American in Mexico has coined a number of names for the inevitable dysentary [sic] and diarrhea: . . "Montezuma's revenge," the "Curse of Montezuma" and the "Aztec hop." **1967–68** *DARE* (Qu. BB19, *Joking names for looseness of the bowels*) Infs **CA**49, 80, **LA**14, **TX**28, 29, Montezuma's revenge. **1978** *Capital Times* (Madison WI) 7 Apr 31/1, A seldom-used antibiotic will soon be routinely prescribed to prevent so-called Montezuma's Revenge, the intestinal misery that afflicts legions of Americans traveling abroad, doctors say. **1979** *NY Times* (NY) 15 Feb sec A 3/1, President Carter . . recalled that on a visit to Mexico while in the Navy, he had suffered what he called "Montezuma's revenge," the tourists' term for diarrhea. The President's remark evoked resentment among the Mexicans present. **1986** Pederson *LAGS Concordance,* 1 inf, **neTX,** Montezuma's revenge—diarrhea from Mexican food.

Montgomery pie n [*Montgomery* Co, Pennsylvania] **sPA** Cf **shoofly pie**

A pie made with a filling (as molasses, lemon custard) and with a layer of cake dough on top.

c1946 Griggs *Sally Cook's Recipe Book* 44 **Philadelphia PA,** Montgomery Pie. **1948** Hutchison *PA Du. Cook Book* 123, *Mrs. Krusen's Montgomery Pie—First Layer* [includes molasses, sugar, water, egg, lemon, flour]. . . *Top layer* [includes sugar, milk, butter, egg, baking powder, flour]. Line 2 pastry tins with pastry. Fill in 2 layers. . . Makes two 8-inch pies. **1955** *Daily Progress* (Charlottesville VA) 1 Feb 7/5, Specialty of Pennsylvania Dutch kitchens—Shoofly Pie. . . [W]e roll out a pastry crust and pour a mixture of molasses, water and baking soda on it. Then we sprinkle a crumbly mixture of flour, sugar, spices, salt and butter or margarine over the liquid. A strange combination to put in the oven and expect to come out an edible pie. But it does—with a flaky bottom crust, then a brown custardy layer and a cake-like top. . . Sometimes it is called Molasses Shoofly Pie. Sometimes it goes under the name of Shoofly Cake or Molasses Crumb Cake. And occasionally it gets its name from a Pennsylvania county and is called Montgomery Pie. **1957** Showalter *Mennonite Cookbook* 375 **csPA,** *Montgomery Pie*—Bottom Part: Molasses . . sugar . . 1 egg. . . Top Part: sugar . . soda . . sour milk . . flour. **1966–69** *DARE* (Qu. H63, *Kinds of desserts*) Inf **PA**1, Montgomery pie—coconut and molasses; **PA**9, Montgomery pies—lemon custard on the bottom with cake dough on top; **PA**18, Montgomery pie—molasses, dough on top, similar to shoofly pie; **PA**203, Montgomery pie. **1969** *DARE* Tape **PA**203, Montgomery pie . . is something on the order of shoofly pie only it's got a liquid in the bottom . . it's got like a cake—you mix up the egg and the sugar, the flour, a little baking powder and put that on top of the syrup that you put in, and bake it.

month n Usu |mʌn(t)θ|; also chiefly **Sth, S Midl** |mʌnt|; also rarely |mɒnθ| Pronc-spp *mont, munt* Note: |mʌn(t)s| for *months* is widespread and is not treated here.

A Pronc varr.

1884 *Anglia* 7.276 **Sth, S Midl** [Black], *Munt' in en munt' out* = for months. **1899** Chesnutt *Conjure Woman* 78 **csNC** [Black], He did n' 'spec' he'd be back fer a mont' er so. **1909** *DN* 3.350 **eAL, wGA,** *Mont.* . . Month. Chiefly among the negroes. **1981** Pederson *LAGS Basic Materials,* 1 inf, **neFL,** [mʌᵊnt]; 1 inf, **swFL,** [mɒnt]; 1 inf, **cAR,** [mɐˆnt]; 1 inf, **ceAL,** [mɒnθs]

B Gram forms.

Pl: usu *months;* also, in ref to an extent of time, *month;* also rarely double pl *mont'sus.* [The use of sg form for pl for this word has been obs in std Engl since the 15th century, but is still common in Scots dial; cf Intro "Language Changes" II.7] Cf **foot** n **B2b(1), mile B**

1915 in 1944 *ADD* 396 **nWV,** The baby was only three month old. **1929** (1951) Faulkner *Sartoris* 290 **MS** [Black], I had to fin' Euphrony fo' new cookin' places de fust we mont' we wuz ma'ied. **1931** *AmSp*

6.171 **seVA** [Black], There are interesting plurals, such as . . [mɔɪl] for *miles,* . . [mʌnt] for *months.* **1931–33** *LANE* Worksheets **Fall River MA,** I was in Middleboro five month. **1934** *Language* 10.3 **cPA,** That baby'll walk till [=by the time that] he's nine month old. [c1938 see **D** below]. **1986** Pederson *LAGS Concordance,* 7 infs, **Gulf Region,** Month [used as pl; 1 Black inf, 1 French-speaking inf, 1 Spanish-speaking inf].

C Syntax.

Used directly after the name of a month. [Scots dial]

1922 Gonzales *Black Border* 284 **sSC, GA coasts** [Gullah], The simple name of the month is seldom sufficient, but must be fortified by the addition of "munt," as: "Uh hab da' gal een June munt'."

D Sense.

Pl: Menstrual discharge. [*OED month* sb. 5 →1694] *relic*

c1938 in 1970 Hyatt *Hoodoo* 2.1563, Well, yo' take her mont'sus [Hyatt: *months*] an' wash it outa her pad.

month hand n Also *monthly hand* [**hand** n **B1**]

A temporary farm worker hired by the month.

1966–67 *DARE* (Qu. L1, *A man who is employed to help with work on a farm*) Inf **NC**6, Month hand; **LA**7, Monthly hand—hired by the month. **1986** Pederson *LAGS Concordance,* 1 inf, **neLA,** A month hand—paid by day/week/month, not by crop.

monthly pink n

=**bouncing Bet 1.**

1896 *Jrl. Amer. Folkl.* 9.182 **swMO,** *Saponaria officinalis,* monthly pink.

mont'sus See **month B**

monument plant n [From its tall form] Cf **pyramid flower**

Either a **green gentian** (here: *Frasera speciosa*) or a **columbo** (here: *F. carolinensis*).

1920 Pellett *Amer. Honey Plants* 162, The monument plant. . . has large, creamy blossoms, . . on tall flower stalks growing to a height of three feet. It is common in the Rocky Mountains and is much sought by bees. **1948** Wherry *Wild Flower Guide* 102, *Midland Monument-plant (Frasera caroliniensis).* . . Range: Midland and adjacent Northeastern states. **1953** Nelson *Plants Rocky Mt. Park* 123, *Monument plant.* . . *Frasera speciosa.* . . A tall stout plant found on open slopes at all altitudes in the park. **1957** Roberts–Nelson *Wildflowers CO* 65, Green Gentian, *Swertia radiata.* . . Sometimes called "monument plant." **1963** Craighead *Rocky Mt. Wildflowers* 144, *Green Gentian.* . . *Other names:* Deertongue, Monument Plant [etc]. **1965** *Native Plants PA* 54, *Swertia carolinensis*—Monument Plant. **1979** Spellenberg *Audubon Guide N. Amer. Wildflowers W. Region* 523, Monument Plant; Deer's Ears *(Frasera speciosa).*

mooch v[1]

1 often with adv: To move slowly or apathetically; to idle about, loaf; hence vbl n *mooching,* n *moocher.*

1927 *AmSp* 2.390 [Vagabond argot], Dinging the stem [=street] is known as *mooching, stemming* and *plinging.* **1933** Hench *Coll.,* My . . student . . uses *mooch.* . . "I mooched around the house all day yesterday, doing little." . . "Bill is a *moocher;* he'll never graduate." **1966–69** *DARE* (Qu. Y21, *To move about slowly and without energy*) Infs **MA**33, **NY**41, **WA**18, Mooch (along); (Qu. KK31, *To go about aimlessly looking for distraction:* "He doesn't have anything to do, so he's just _____ around.") Inf **NY**131, Mooching. **1974** Betts–Walser *NC Folkl.* 13, "One day," said the old fellow, "I was moochin' along a mountain road trail when these here telescope eyes of mine spotted a buck." **1993** *DARE* File **csWI,** Most walked alone, out county roads to Stoughton or De Forest, weaving for miles up the shoulder. The State Patrol regularly picked Henry up mooching along in the grass beside I90.

2 with *over:* To move over, make room. Cf **hitch** v **1, hunch** v **3c**

1967–69 *DARE* (Qu. Y52, *To move over—for example on a long bench:* "*. . . Can you _____ [a little]?*") Infs **IL**110, **NJ**1, **PA**109, 130, Mooch over (a little).

3 See quots.

1984 Doig *English Creek* 9 **nMT,** "Here's how you mooch them, Jick." He eased over to the nearest horse, waited until it put its head down to eat grass, then straddled its neck. When the horse raised its head Alec was lifted, and slid down the neck into place on its back and simultaneously gripped the mane to hang on and steer by. *Ibid* 31, Alec teaching me to mooch my way onto the back of a grazing horse.

4 To troll (for fish); hence vbl n *mooching.*

1965 McClane *McClane's Std. Fishing Encycl.* 984 **WA,** The boats drift-troll (mooch) for salmon 2–15 miles off shore. **1966** *DARE* (Qu. P17, . . *When . . people fish by lowering a line and sinker close to the bottom of the water*) Inf **WA**17, Mooching. **1982** Sternberg *Fishing* 49, Mooching rigs originated on the West Coast where they are still used to catch salmon. Push the rear hook through the tail and the front hook through one gill and out the other. Adjust the front hook to snug up the line.

mooch n, v² [Var of *smooch*]

A kiss; to kiss.

1965–70 *DARE* (Qu. X39, *A mark on the skin where somebody has sucked it hard and brought the blood to the surface*) Inf **IL**12, Mooch spot; (Qu. AA8, *When people make too much of a show of affection in a public place . . "There they were at the church supper _____ [with each other]."*) Infs **CA**53, **IA**7, **KS**16, **MO**12, **NY**235, **OH**50, **TN**1, Mooching; (Qu. AA9, . . *A loud or vigorous kiss*) Infs **NV**9, **MO**34, Mooch(ing). **1986** Pederson *LAGS Concordance* (Kissing) 1 inf, neGA, You've been mooching.

moocher See **mooch** v¹ **1**

mooching See **mooch** v¹ **1, 4**

mooch over See **mooch** v¹ **2**

moochy adj [**mooch** n, v²]

1967 *DARE* (Qu. AA8, *When people make too much of a show of affection in a public place*) Inf **CO**10, Moochy.

moody-colored adj

1950 *PADS* 14.47 **SC,** *Moody-colored.* . . Of a dull or sad color.

moody grass See **muda grass**

moojoo See **mojo** n

mool(e)y See **muley** adj, n²

moon n¹

1 also *mooney:* Illegally made whiskey. [Abbr for *moonshine*] Cf **shine**

1928 *Collier's* 29 Dec 8, Wherever you go in Colorado a bootlegger . . says to you 'Mister, this is good stuff. It's Leadville "moon." ' **1929** *AmSp* 4.385 **KS,** Some of the common names for whiskey—moonshine, moon, mooney. **1934** (1974) Farrell *Young Manhood* 380 **Chicago IL,** They bought another pint of cheap moon and staggered back to Jackson Park. **1950** *Sat. Eve. Post* 27 May 20, I would buy a couple of pints of moon. **1962** Fox *Southern Fried* 35 **SC,** From the rear window we saw them in there drinking "moon" and telling stories. **1965–70** *DARE* (Qu. DD21c, *Nicknames for whiskey, especially illegally made whiskey*) Infs **FL**13, **MI**10, 15, 19, 103, **WV**8, 10, **WI**19, 77, Moon.

2a A crescent-shaped crack in a playing marble; hence v *moon* to crack in this way. Cf **moonie** n¹

1935 *AmSp* 10.159 seNE, Moons. Crescent-shaped nicks which agates receive from hard hits. **1955** *PADS* 23.34 seKY, Moon. . . A marking on an agate caused by its impact against other marbles. If a boy's agate is full of moons, it is indicated that he has been doing some good shooting with it as a taw. **1958** *Resp. to PADS 29,* Here are a few more marble terms. . . Coal Oil Agate. A solid gray agate that was hard to come by and "mooned" very easily giving it a mottled appearance. **1966** *DARE* (Qu. EE6d, *Special marbles*) Inf **NC**14, Moonies—buckeyes which have been hit so much they get cracks or moons.

b See **moonie** n¹.

‡**3** One's navel.

1969 *DARE* (Qu. X34, . . *Names and nicknames for the navel*) Inf **NC**68, Moon.

moon n² See **moan** n **1**

moon v See **moon** n¹ **2a**

moonack n

1 also *monack, mo(o)nax, mooneck, moonox, monk:* A **woodchuck** (here: *Marmota monax*). [See quot 1902] esp **MD, VA**

1666 (1972) Alsop *Character Province MD* 37, The Monack, the Musk-rat, and several others (whom I'le omit for brevity sake) inhabit here in *Mary-land.* **1676** Royal Soc. London *Philos. Trans.* 11.630 **VA,** There are also several sorts of ravenous Beasts, as Wolves, . . Possums, Monacks, Flying Squirrels. **1743** Catesby *Nat. Hist. Carolina* 2 [app] xxviii, *Marmota Americana. The* Monax. This Animal is about the Bigness of a wild Rabbet. . . They are Inhabitants of *Maryland, Pensil-*

vania &c. Their Flesh is esteemed good Meat. **1782** in 1904 Jefferson *Writings* 2.71 **VA,** There remain then the . . wild cat, monax, bison [etc]. **1789** *MD Jrl. & Baltimore Advt.* (MD) 13 Nov [2/3], [Advt:] A Monack or Ground-Hog, presented [to Peale's Museum] by Mr. W.P. Johnston. **1805** (1904) Clark *Orig. Jrls. Lewis & Clark Exped.* 2.377, I have also observed some robes among them of beaver, moonox, and small wolves. **1876** Burroughs *Winter Sunshine* 29, In Virginia, they [=Black women] call woodchucks "moonacks." **1902** *Jrl. Amer. Folkl.* 15.249, *Moonack.* A name applied in the Maryland–Virginia region to the woodchuck or ground-hog (*Arctomys monax*). The origin of the word is seen in the Lenâpé *monachgeu,* "ground-hog," literally "digger," from *mon-han* (=Ojibwa *mona*), "to dig,"—the radical *mona,* "to dig," is widespread among the Algonkian dialects. . . *Moonack* is also the name of a mythic animal much feared by some Southern negroes. **1910** Hodge *Hdbk. Amer. Indians* 2.973, *Woodchuck.* . . Called *moonack* in parts of the S[outh]. **1961** Jackson *Mammals WI* 122, In Wisconsin [*Marmota monax* is] commonly called woodchuck or chuck, sometimes groundhog. Other names include . . monax, monk, moonack. **1967** *PA Game News* Aug, [Inside front cover:] Woodchuck, groundhog, whistle-pig, mooneck—whatever he's called, this heavyset marmot is undoubtedly the favorite target for Pennsylvania's varmint hunters. **1970** *DARE* (Qu. P31, . . *Names or nicknames . . for the groundhog*) Inf **VA**110, Moonax [mʌnæks]. **1982** Elman *Hunter's Field Guide* 408, *Marmot* . . *Common & Regional Names.* . . For eastern or flatland species—woodchuck, groundhog, monax.

2 An appar mythical beast; see quot.

1872 Schele de Vere *Americanisms* 151, It is presumed, though not proven, that the *Moonack,* a mythical animal known to negroes only, is also of African origin. The beast lives, according to their belief, in caves or hollow trees, and the poor negro who meets it in his solitary rambles is doomed. His reason is impaired, till he becomes a madman, or is carried off by some lingering malady. He dare not speak of it, but old, experienced negroes say when they look at him: "He gwine die; he seed the *moonack.*" **1902** [see **1** above].

moon aggie See **moonie** n¹

moon and stars See **moonhouse**

moon ax n¹

An ax used to cut the **box** in a turpentine tree.

1966 *DARE* Tape GA7, Take what you call a moon ax, a broad ax first and smooth the bark down as it goes to the ground, then you'll take what you call a moon ax or cubbing ax.

moonax n² See **moonack 1**

moon-ball n Cf Intro "Language Changes" I.4, **sun-ball**

The moon.

1941 *Sat. Eve. Post* 10 May 36 sAppalachians, Now that hain't asking for the moon ball. **1982** Slone *How We Talked* 29 eKY (as of c1950), *Moonball*—moon.

moonbeam See **moonie** n¹

moon-bill n [Appar from the light-colored mark on the bill] =**ring-necked duck.**

1888 Trumbull *Names of Birds* 61, I am told by two well-informed gunners . . of its [=ring-necked duck's] being known to certain South Carolina duckers as the *Moon-bill.* **1917** (1923) *Birds Amer.* 1.137, *Ring-necked Duck.* . . *Other Names.* . . Moon-bill. **1950** *PADS* 14.47 **SC,** *Moonbill.* . . The ring-necked duck.

mooncalf n

1 A congenitally deformed animal; a monster. [*OED* 1565 →; "Obs."]

1913 Kephart *Highlanders* 287 **sAppalachians,** I had supposed that the words cuckold and moon-calf had none but literary usage in America, but we often hear them in the mountains, . . moon-calf [being employed] in its baldly literal sense that would make Prospero's taunt to Caliban a superlative insult. **1917** Kephart in *DN* 4.415 wNC, Moon-calf. . . In mountaineer's superstition, a shapeless thing, without life, that a steer causes in a cow by worrying her. **1944** *PADS* 2.46 wNC, Moon-calf. . . An imagined misshaped animal, a bastard, a simpleton. . . One college professor reports: "Sometimes used to describe the actions of adolescent love."

2 A fool, simpleton. [*OED* 1620 →]

1896 Harris *Sister Jane* 102 **GA,** Folks useter call him quare, an' some say now he's a half-wit—one o' these here moon-calves. **1932** Tooné *Yankee Slang* 26, Moon-calf: A ninny, simpleton, loon, chump. **1944**

[see **1** above]. **1952** Brown *NC Folkl.* 1.566, *Moon-calf.* . . A fool, an idiot.

3 A bastard.

1944 [see **1** above]. **1952** Brown *NC Folkl.* 1.566, *Moon-calf.* . . A bastard.

moon creeper See **moonflower 1**

moon crumbler See **mooner**

mooncurser n Pronc-sp *mooncusser* [See quot 1937] **NEng old-fash**

One who causes ships to wreck in order to plunder them; one who plunders wrecked ships; also used as an epithet; hence n *mooncussing* taking goods from wrecked ships.

1812 *Old Farmer's Almanac for 1813* Dec np, All the village mooncursers came in for their portion of the wreck. So poor Freeport gave up vessel and cargo to these land pirates. **1937** FWP *Guide MA* 277 **neMA**, This district is Barnegat, long ago named for the town on the New Jersey coast where 'mooncussers' lured vessels to destruction by false lights from shore, with the purpose of plundering their cargoes. (A mooncusser is one who curses the moon for its hindrance to his nefarious designs.) *Ibid* 328, Mooncussing and beachcombing—now synonyms meaning recovery of goods from the beach—were wreckers' work. . . The legend of false lights hung out on moonless nights to lure unwary mariners of those days persists in the Cape's oral traditions. **1945** Colcord *Sea Language* 131 **ME, Cape Cod, Long Island**, *Mooncurser.* A South-of-England name for a wrecker, who enticed vessels ashore by tying a lantern to a horse's bridle and hobbling one leg, so that the animal's stumbling simulated the motion of a vessel. . . This was not, of course, feasible on fair moonlit nights, hence mooncurser. American sailors apply the name chiefly to the inhabitants of the "back shore" of Cape Cod, though they do not accuse these people of jibbering the kibber. **1987** Hamilton *Lights & Legends* 22 **sNEng** (as of c1800), Armed with broomstick handles and lanterns, the "moon cussers" (moonlit nights were bad for business) lured many a ship to destruction on the reefs with false lights and beacons. . . Early rescue stations and lighthouses were not accepted in all communities, because the moon cussers saw them as a threat to their "business." **1988** Nickerson *Days to Remember* 204 **Cape Cod MA** (as of c1900), There were several crews of "wreckers". These were made up of local young men who worked in teams, each team maintaining its own lifeboat for going to rescue wrecks. There are stories that these men were not far removed from being pirates, or "mooncussers".

moondown n [By analogy with *sundown*]

The setting of the moon; the time when the moon sets.

1797 in 1916 Hawkins *Letters* 276 **GA**, Last evening just before moon down, his camp had been fired on by some men supposed to be Georgians. **1861** *N.Y. Tribune* 25 Oct. *(DA),* They landed at Santa Rosa Island, at about a quarter of an hour to moondown, or 11 o'clock p.m. **1899** (1912) Green *VA Folk-Speech* 287, *Moondown.* . . The setting, or time of setting, of the moon. "We'll get there before moon-down." **1908** (1915) Calhoun *Miss Minerva* 147 **Sth**, He got 'way f'om here 'bout moon-down las' night. **1933** Rawlings *South Moon* 100 **nFL**, "Finest kind o' time for the deer." "Moon-down's jest as good," Lant said. **1938** Matschat *Suwannee R.* 68 **neFL, seGA**, Four, five hours till moondown. Hain't no use to hunt gators iffen the moon be up. **1967** Leslie *High Trails West* 170 **AZ**, At moondown coyotes, kit foxes, bobcats, badgers, and ringtail cats began a continuous chorus.

mooneck See **moonack 1**

mooner n Also *moon crumbler* Cf *DS* CC17

An imaginary animal said to live in the woods.

1914 DN 4.76 **ME, nNH**, *Mooner.* . . Mythical creature in logging-woods. **1939** (1962) Thompson *Body & Britches* 299 **NY**, Those numerous creatures of fantasy described by guides, such as . . the barking Moon Crumbler.

mooney See **moon** n[1] **1**

mooneye n

1 A fish of the genus *Hiodon.* [See quot 1967] **esp Upper Missip Valley** Also called **gizzard shad 3, toothed herring.** For other names of var spp see **freshwater herring 4, goldeye, humpie 3, river whitefish, shad, shiner, silver bass, Winnipeg goldeye, wap, white shad, yellow herring**

1842 DeKay *Zool. NY* 4.267, This species [=*Hiodon tergisus*] is common in Lake Erie. At Buffalo and Barcelona it is called *Moon-eye.*

1882 U.S. Natl. Museum *Bulletin* 16.259, *Hyodon* [sic]. . . *Moon Eyes.* **1902** Jordan–Evermann *Amer. Fishes* 90, The *Mooneyes.* . . are all handsome and gamy fishes, of little value as food. **1943** Eddy–Surber *N. Fishes* 69, The mooneyes are silvery fishes with deeply compressed bodies, small heads, feeble mouths, and large eyes. . . The mooneye [=*Hiodon tergisus*]. . . can be distinguished from the goldeye, or northern mooneye, by the keel, or ridge, on the belly. **1950** WELS *(What kinds of fish do commercial fishermen go out for in your section?)* 1 Inf, **WI**, Mooneye—rough fish. **1956** Harlan–Speaker *IA Fish* 61, Moon-eyes are frequently taken by fly-fishermen and anglers using minnows and spinner rigs, but usually incidentally to other fishes, since no special effort is made to catch them. **1967** Cross *Hdbk. Fishes KS* 59, I have seen many goldeyes but no mooneyes [=*Hiodon tergisus*] from the Kansas and Missouri rivers, although the latter name is often used by anglers for *H. alosoides*. . . The "eye shine" of the mooneye (and the related goldeye) is caused by a reflective layer, the tapetum lucidum, in the retina. **1971** *WI State Jrl.* (Madison) 29 Aug sec 4 5/1, Between the four of us we caught one small walleye, three mooneyes [etc]. **1983** Becker *Fishes WI* 284, The mooneye occurs in the Mississippi River and Lake Michigan drainage basins.

2 also *mooneye cisco:* A **cisco:** usu *Coregonus hoyi,* but also **blackfin cisco** or **kiyi.**

1875 *Amer. Naturalist* 9.135, This Indiana *Argyrosomus* appears to be quite distinct from the species found in Lake Michigan; *i.e.,* the shallow-water "herring" . . and the deep-water "moon eye" (*A. Hoyi* Gill). **1896** U.S. Natl. Museum *Bulletin* 47.469, *Moon-eye Cisco.* . . The United States Fish Commission . . find it to be the principal fish caught in the gill nets in the western part of Lake Michigan. **1902** Jordan–Evermann *Amer. Fishes* 136, *Mooneye Cisco—Argyrosomus hoyi.* . . Among other names by which this species is known are mooneye, cisco [etc]. . . It reaches a length of 12 or 13 inches and is one of the smallest and handsomest of our whitefishes. **1908** Forbes–Richardson *Fishes of IL* 55, *A[rgyrosomus] hoyi,* the mooneye cisco . . and *A. tullibee,* the tullibee . . are more or less commonly taken in Lake Michigan. **1983** Becker *Fishes WI* 361, *Kiyi.* . . Other common names . . mooneye. *Ibid* 364, *Blackfin Cisco.* . . Other common names . . mooneye cisco.

moon-eyed adj

1 Partially blind; of a horse: suffering from moon blindness. [*OED moon-eyed* ppl. a. 1 1610 →] **chiefly S Midl**

1889 Murfree *Despot* 105 **eTN**, Do ye know ennything 'bout'n a horse's eyes? I be sort'n 'feard he's moon-eyed, or suthin'. **1899** (1912) Green *VA Folk-Speech* 287, *Moon-eyed.* . . Dim-eyed; purblind. **1905** (1970) Adams *Outlet* 21 **TX**, Tolleston . . took the only blind horse in the entire herd. . . At the time of his purchase, . . no one could see anything in the eyeball which would indicate he was moon-eyed. **1906** *DN* 3.147 **nwAR**, *Moon-eyed.* . . Used of horses suffering from a peculiar ocular affection. "Horse seems partly blind in the right eye during the increase and up to the full of the moon; also has a light or purplish spot on the sight most of the time. The left one does not seem so badly affected." **1912** *DN* 3.583 **wIN**, *Moon-eyed.* . . Half-blind. The term is also applied to a horse that holds its head to one side when it walks. **1941** Writers' Program *Guide WY* 463, *Moon-eyed*—A horse with white, glassy eye or eyes. **1952** Brown *NC Folkl.* 1.566, *Moon-eyed.* . . Of horses: blind during certain phases of the moon. **1960** Bailey *Resp. to PADS* 20 **KS**, All of these I have heard in Kansas . . moon-eyed, bots, heaves. **1972** *Atlanta Letters* **nwGA**, A Blinker—a horse with poor eyesight also called "moon eyed."

2 Able to see better by night than by day. [*OED moon-eyed* ppl. a. 2 1699–1817; "*Obs.*"]

1933 Rawlings *South Moon* 287 **nFL**, "Hit's them cataracks, like." "Must be. I've got to where I'm moon-eyed, Kezzy. I cain't hardly see, day-times, but when the moon's bright I kin see mighty plain." **1940** Writers' Program *Guide GA* 326 **cnGA**, A Cherokee myth about the "moon-eyed folk," a strange white people who could see only at night, is supported in part by the theory of one ethnologist that albinos lived here and built fortifications along the Tennessee River until they were conquered by the Indians.

3 Of a dog: see quots.

1948 *Sat. Eve. Post* 21 Aug 72 **AK**, Many Siberians [=Siberian huskies] are moon-eyed, or watch-eyed, which means they can contract their pupils to a pin point, saving them from easy snow blindness. **1966** *DARE* FW Addit **FL**, Moon-eyed—having one white or very light blue eye and one brown eye. "That old moon-eyed dog ain't good for nothing." Common among country folk.

4 Drunk. Cf *DS* DD15, *pie-eyed*

1737 *PA Gaz.* (Philadelphia) 6–13 Jan 2/1, He sees two Moons, Merry,

Middling, Moon-Ey'd, Muddled. **1940** *AmSp* 15.447 **eTN,** *Moon-eyed.* Intoxicated. 'Sid gits moon-eyed every Saturday night.'

moon-eyed agate See **moonie** n[1]

mooney-mooney wild-dog n
=**doodlebug 1.**

    1963 *DE Folkl. Bulletin* 1.40, A "mooney-mooney wild-dog" is a type of ant eater. The proper name is ant lion. . . If you would like to see one all you have to do is get down close to the hole and call "mooney-mooney wild-dog" over and over again.

moonfish n [From the disc-shaped, laterally compressed body] Cf **sunfish**

1 =**spadefish.**

    1842 DeKay *Zool. NY* 4.99, The Moon-fish. *Ephippus gigas.* **1873** in 1878 Smithsonian Inst. *Misc. Coll.* 14.2.29, *Parephippus faber.* . . Moonfish. . . Cape Cod to Florida. **1884** Goode *Fisheries U.S.* 1.445, The Moon-fish . . has recently come so much into favor in New York that among connoisseurs it is one of the most highly esteemed food-fishes. **1903** NY State Museum & Sci. Serv. *Bulletin* 60.603, The moonfish has occasionally been taken as far north as Cape Cod. **1933** LA Dept. of Conserv. *Fishes* 261, The Spadefish is a familiar fish of the Gulf Coast. . . [It] is often also called Moonfish or Angelfish. **1966** *DARE* (Qu. P2, . . *Kinds of saltwater fish caught around here* . . *good to eat*) Inf **FL24,** Moonfish.

2 A fish of the genus *Selene.* For other names of var spp see **dollarfish 2, horsehead 1b, horsefish 1, humpbacked butterfish, lookdown, pug-nosed shiner, silverfish, sunfish**

    1878 U.S. Natl. Museum *Proc.* 1.376, *Vomer setipinnis.* . . *Moonfish.* . . *Selene argentea.* . . *Moon-fish.* . . Taken on the outer beach in the fall. . . *Argyriosus vomer.* . . *Moon-fish.* **1896** U.S. Natl. Museum *Bulletin* 47.935, *Selene.* . . *Moonfishes.* . . Body very closely compressed and much elevated, the profile very oblique or nearly vertical. . . Coloration silvery. Tropical seas. **1905** NJ State Museum *Annual Rept. for 1904* 259, *Vomer setipinnis.* . . Moon Fish. . . Generally distributed by the Gulf Stream. *Ibid* 260, *Selene.* . . The Moon Fishes. **1939** Natl. Geogr. Soc. *Fishes* 197, With its steep forehead and mother-of-pearl sheen, the *Moonfish* . . seems to seek attention as it preens and scrubs itself on the sandy shallows. **1955** Zim–Shoemaker *Fishes* 93, The Moonfish . . is netted in the south as a food fish. **1970** *DARE* (Qu. P4, *Saltwater fish that are not good to eat*) Inf **CA191,** Moonfish; **MA80,** Moonfish, sunfish—same. **1983** *Audubon Field Guide N. Amer. Fishes* 598, The . . Moonfish is a schooling fish that may be abundant within limited areas during summer months. **1991** Amer. Fisheries Soc. *Common Names Fishes* 52, *Selene peruviana* . . P[acific] . . Pacific moonfish. *Selene setapinnis* [sic] . . A[tlantic] . . Atlantic moonfish.

3 =**opah.**

    1896 U.S. Natl. Museum *Bulletin* 47.954, *Lampris luna.* . . Opah; *Moonfish.* . . One of the choicest of fishes, the flesh rich, firm, and of delicate flavor. **1902** Jordan–Evermann *Amer. Fishes* 326, The . . moonfish. . . is found in the open waters of the Atlantic and Pacific. **1929** Pan-Pacific Research Inst. *Jrl.* 4.4.5, The Opah; Moon-fish. *Lampris regius.* **1939** Natl. Geogr. Soc. *Fishes* 267, I have found the tooth marks of this lamprey in the skin of the opah, or moonfish *(Lampris regius).* **1991** Amer. Fisheries Soc. *Common Names Fishes* 151, Moonfish—see opah.

4 A **harvest fish** (here: *Peprilus alepidotus*).

    1911 *Century Dict. Suppl.* **FL,** *Moonfish.* . . A stromateid fish, *Peprilus paru,* the harvest-fish.

moon-fixer n chiefly Sth, S Midl Cf **hang the moon**
A very tall person.

    c1950 *Halpert Coll.* 43 **wKY, nwTN,** She must be a moon-fixer = girl unusually tall. **1952** Brown *NC Folkl.* 1.566, *Moon-fixer.* . . A very tall person.—Granville county. **1956** McAtee *Some Dialect NC* 30. **c1960** *Wilson Coll.* **csKY,** *Moon-fixer.* . . A nickname for a tall, usually lanky, person; the opposite of shorty. **1978** *AP Letters* neGA (as of c1900), Expressions . . of the pioneers . . from . . mountain and rural areas: . . "So tall he must be a moon fixer." **1979** *NADS Letters* **nMS,** A very tall person, especially a tall girl, was spoken of as a "moonfixer."

moonflower n

1 also *moon creeper, moon vine:* A **morning glory 1,** esp *Ipomoea alba.* [*OEDS* 1857 →]

    1890 FL Ag. Exper. Sta. Gainesville *Bulletin* 8.11, *Aggressive or Troublesome Weeds.* . . Ipomæa Bona nox [=*I. alba*], L.—Moon flower.

1900 Lyons *Plant Names* 202, *I[pomoea] Bona-nox.* . . Moon-flower, Moon Creeper. **1901** NM Ag. Exper. Station *Bulletin* 40.15, Other climbing plants that grow well where a vine is desired are the ordinary hop, . . the moonvine, and the Madeira vine. **1929** Pope *Plants HI* 180, Moonflower—*Ipomoea bona-nox.* . . The flowers open in the late afternoon, and remain open all night, withering the next morning. The effect of the large white flowers is charming, particularly on moonlight nights. The popular name "Moonflower" is no doubt due to its nocturnal habit. In some localities it has the common name "Evening-glory." **1938** FWP *U.S. One* 287 **FL,** Day glories and moonvines are everywhere, and the shoulders of the highway are colored with wild flowers. **1942** (1960) Robertson *Red Hills* 178 **SC,** Our great-aunt loved the fields, . . moon vines, the crimson poke, and the south wind and the fierce Southern sun, shining straight down, a hundred degrees in the shade. **1950** *WELS (Wild morning glory)* 2 Infs, **cWI,** Moonflower. **1961** Douglas *My Wilderness* 135 **Everglades FL,** One morning at Flamingo I rose early to see the sun come up. I was rewarded by moonflowers heavy with dew. They are white and as large as morning-glories. They close by day and open by night. **1966** *DARE* Wildfl QR Pl.164B Inf **TX34,** Moonflower. **1966–69** *DARE* (Qu. S5, . . *Wild morning glory*) Inf **MI17,** Wild moonflower; **PA200,** Wild moonflower; **WA30,** Moon vine; **CA,** Moon vine; (Qu. S26e, *Other wildflowers not yet mentioned;* not asked in early QRs) Inf **AR49,** Moonflower—big white morning glory. **1969** Lyons *My Florida* 21, My Florida is squatty custard apple trees and moon vines. **1993** Comstock Ferre *1993 Seed Catalog* 21, *Moonflower (Ipomoea alba).* . . Heart-shaped leaves on fast-growing vine. Bud opens to large white flower in 2 minutes in evening.

2 =**buckbean 1.**

    1876 Hobbs *Bot. Hdbk.* 71, Moon flower, Buckbean, *Menyanthes trifoliata.* **1900** Lyons *Plant Names* 245, *M[enyanthes] trifoliata.* . . Marsh Clover, Moon-flower. **1911** Henkel *Amer. Med. Leaves* 21, Buck bean. . . *Other common names.* . . marsh clover, moonflower, bitterworm.

3 also *moonlily:* A plant of the genus *Datura* such as **angel's trumpet 1** or **jimson weed.**

    1942 Whipple *Joshua* 142 **UT** (as of c1860), Here was Steadfast Weeks, the doctor, setting a leg with the aid of the foul-smelling Jimson Weed or moonflower beloved of the Indian medicine-man who called it *nea-nump,* or crazy plant. **1968** Abbey *Desert Solitaire* 28 **seUT,** The sacred datura—moonflower, moonlily . . blooms in the night, soft white trumpet-shaped flowers that open only in darkness and close with the coming of the heat. The datura is sacred (to certain cultists) because of its content of atropine, a powerful narcotic of the alkaloid group capable of inducing visionary hallucinations, as the Indians discovered long before the psychedelic craze began. **1968** *DARE* (Qu. S26a, . . *Wildflowers.* . . *Roadside flowers*) Inf **CA41,** Moonflower—a shrub with a white flower—tubular flower. **c1982** *DARE* File **csWI,** Moonflower— another name for angel's trumpet. **1993** *WI State Jrl.* (Madison) 22 Aug sec G 1, Shown here are sunflowers with moonflowers climbing up their stems. Moonflowers, also called angel trumpets, were immortalized by artist Georgia O'Keeffe. The massive white flowers open only at night.

4 A **stickleaf.**

    1963 Craighead *Rocky Mt. Wildflowers* 117, Ten-Petaled Blazingstar— *Mentzelia decapetala.* . . *Other names:* Stickleaf, Eveningstar, Sandlily, Moonflower. . . This flower opens at night and closes during the day. **1967** Dodge *Roadside Wildflowers* 43 **SW,** *Moonflower.* . . Flowers remaining closed and inconspicuous during most of the day opening in late afternoon to create a showy display.

moonfruit pine n [Perh from the crescent-shaped cone-like fruits]
A **club moss** (here: *Lycopodium lucidulum*).

    1822 Eaton *Botany* 345, *[Lycopodium] lucidulum* . . moon-fruit pine . . fruit lunulate. **1832** MA Hist. Soc. *Coll.* 2d ser 9.152 **cwVT,** [Lycopodium] lucidulum, Moon-fruit pine. **1876** Hobbs *Bot. Hdbk.* 188, Lycopodium lucidulum, Moon fruit pine. **1938** Small *Ferns SE States* 405, Besides the common name trailing-evergreen, the plant [=*Lycopodium lucidulum*] is also known as *Shining clubmoss* and *Moonfruit-pine.*

moonglade n esp NEng
The diffused and lengthened reflection of moonlight on water.

    [**1857** (1949) Thoreau *Jrl.* 10.53 **MA,** The Watsons tell me that Uncle Ned uses the expression "a glade" for the sheen of the moon on the water.] **1859** Lowell in *Atlantic Mth.* 4.641 **MA,** Moonglade: a beautiful word for the track of moonlight on the water. **1872** Schele de Vere *Americanisms* 341, Two very beautiful words, used and perhaps invented by our coast-people, are *moonglade* and *grayslick.* The former denotes the soft, silvery track which moonlight traces on the waters, and has come down to sea-faring folk from the days of the pilgrim fathers. **1951** Teale *North with Spring* 38, As we headed for home through the growing chill of the night, the line of moonlight across the water—the 'moonglade' of the New Englanders—moved with us. **1954** Forbes *Rainbow* 194 (as of c1800), We could see the Connecticut River and the strong, straight white moonlight, "the moonglade" country people called it, like a silver sword dividing Vermont and New Hampshire. **1993** *DARE* File **nwWI**, Moonglade, that's the moonlight reflected on the water. I've always called it that.

moon, hang the See **hang the moon**

moon-head n [Cf *loony*] Cf **moon calf 2**, *DS* HH9
See quots.
 1919 *DN* 5.61 **NM**, *Moon-head*, a silly, awkward fellow. "Get out of here you big moon-head." **1942** Berrey–Van den Bark *Amer. Slang* 433.7, *Silly person. . . Spec.* moon-head, . . esp. one who is silly in showing affection. **1969** *DARE* FW Addit **GA**13, Moon-head is a new expression I hear quite often since the moon landing. It means a person has no brains, just a vacuum, because it was discovered there is no oxygen on the moon.

moonhouse n Also *moon and stars* Cf **crescent, half-moon 1**
An outhouse.
 1966–68 *DARE* (Qu. M21b, *Joking names for an outside toilet building*) Inf **MD**9, Moonhouse—because of half-moon design often carved on door; **MI**19, Moon and stars. **1986** Pederson *LAGS Concordance* (Outhouse) 1 inf, **seAL**, The moon house.

moonie n[1] Also *moon (aggie), moonbeam, moon-eyed agate, moon marble* Cf **agate, agate-eye, moon** n[1] **2**
A playing marble, esp a **shooter,** with internal moon-shaped cracks or a moon-shaped streak of color.
 1937 (1947) Bancroft *Games* 161, The term *shooter* is used to denote the offensive marble, variously known as the *taw, moonie, glassie,* etc. **1958** *Sat. Eve. Post Letters* **swMA** (as of 1920s), Moonie—This was the term for an agate, or taw, made of flint. This was derived from moon-like marks inside which developed from contact with other agates. They were desirable because they maintained a smooth outer surface. **1958** *Resp. to PADS 29* **NJ** (as of early 20th cent), In N.J. . . [w]e had moonies, too, very valued. **1960** Bailey *Resp. to PADS 20* **KS** (as of c1900), Others [=marbles]: glassies, aggies, moonies, . . cloudies. **1966–68** *DARE* (Qu. EE6d, *Special marbles*) Inf **NC**14, Moonies—buckeyes which have been hit so much they get cracks or moons in them; **NC**22, 26, Moonies; **NJ**18, Moonies—glass ones that formed moons when hit; **WA**16, Moonie—a glassie with nicks that go clear through; **GA**13, Moon marbles—glass with a moon in the middle; **KS**16, Moon-eyed agates. **1966–68** *DARE* Tape **MD**51, [FW:] Do you know the names of different kinds of marbles? [Inf:] The only three I can remember would be aggie, moonie, boulder; **NC**22, [FW:] How about the other ones . . the glass ones that had the little white streak? [Inf:] We called those moonbeams or moonies. c**1970** Wiersma *Marbles Terms* **swMI** (as of c1960), *Moons* . . or *moonies.* . . Clear untinted glass marbles with a half moon inside. The half moon came in white or yellow. *Ibid,* Moonies—clear marbles with any color in a moon shape. "That's a moonie, not a cat's eye." **1971** Bright *Word Geog. CA & NV* 117, Marbles: . . moonies [1 inf]. **1973** Ferretti *Marble Book* 49, *Moonaggies.* Marbles made of carnelian. So named because when they crack, generally from the inside, moon or crescent shapes form on the surfaces.

moonie n[2] Cf **muley** adj, n[2], *moon* (at **moan** n 1)
See quot.
 1968 *DARE* (Qu. K16, *A cow with a bad temper*) Inf **MD**34, Moonie ['muni].

moon jelly n Also *moon jellyfish*
A common jellyfish (*Aurelia aurita*).
 1981 Meinkoth *Audubon Field Guide Seashore* 363, Moon Jellyfish. . . Saucer-shaped. Whitish, translucent. . . This is the jellyfish most commonly washed up on beaches during high tide or after a storm. **1989** Mickelson *Nat. Hist.* 45 **AK**, Moon jelly and lion's mane jellyfish often reach high densities in mid to late summer in shallow waters and channels over sand flats.

moonlight v
1 To steal, esp at night; to take, latch on to (something).
 1942 Berrey–Van den Bark *Amer. Slang* 490.8, Moonlight . . *to rob at night.* **1969** *DARE* (Qu. V5b, *If you take something that nobody seems*

to own . . "Before anybody else gets it, I'm going to _____ this.") Inf **CA**147, Moonlight it, midnight requisition.
2 To drive or herd cattle at night. Cf **moonshine 5**
 1944 Adams *Western Words* 101, *Moonlight 'em*—To night ride for cattle.
3 To hunt (deer) at night; hence vbl n *moonlighting;* also *moonshining.* Cf **fire-lighting, shine** v
 1965–70 *DARE* (Qu. P35b, *Illegal methods of shooting deer;* not asked in early QRs) Infs **AZ**7, **IL**32, 38, **MI**32, **MN**36, **MO**16, **NY**105, **TX**59, **WA**28, Moonlighting; **NY**69, They moonlight for deer at night; **LA**15, Moonshining; **MI**76, Moonshining, [corr to] shining the deer.
4 vbl n *moonlighting:* Loafing on the job.
 1969 *DARE* (Qu. A9, . . *Wasting time by not working on the job*) Inf **IN**71, Moonlighting. **1993** *DARE* File **swIN** (as of c1950), Moonlighting = slacking on the job.

moonlighting See **moonlight 3, 4**

moonlily See **moonflower 3**

moon marble See **moonie** n[1]

moonox See **moonack 1**

moon pie n [From the shape]
=**half-moon pie.** Note: This is not the trademarked confection of the same name.
 1982 Slone *How We Talked* 58 **eKY** (as of c1950), Dried apples. . . were used most for to make fried apple pies, also called "moon pies," "moccasin pies" or "flip overs."

moonrose n
=**evening primrose a.**
 1936 McDougall–Baggley *Plants of Yellowstone* 91, Moonrose . . *Pachylophus* [spp].

moonseed n
1 also *Canada* (or *Canadian*) *moonseed, moonseed root, ~ vine:* A climbing vine (*Menispermum canadense*). [From the crescent shape of the seed; *OED* 1739 →] Also called **sarsaparilla, Texas ~, vine maple, yellow sarsaparilla**
 1785 Marshall *Arbustrum* 85, *Menispermum.* Moonseed. . . The *Seeds* are solitary, large, and kidney form. **1822** Eaton *Botany* 351, *Menispermum . . canadense* (moonseed). **1876** Hobbs *Bot. Hdbk.* 71, Moonseed root . . yellow parilla . . Menispermum Canadense. **1892** (1974) Millspaugh *Amer. Med. Plants* 14-1, Yellow Parilla, Canadian Moonseed. **1911** (1916) Porter *Harvester* 416 **IN**, She picked up a trailing vine of moonseed. **1920** Saunders *Useful Wild Plants* 242, Noxious berries that sometimes tempt children to their sorrow are those of the Moonseed (Menispermum Canadense, L.), so called because of the curious seeds, which are shaped like a crescent or horseshoe. This is a climbing perennial vine of fence rows and waterside thickets, indigenous from Canada to Arkansas and Georgia. **1951** Voss–Eifert *IL Wild Flowers* 135, When the pulp is cleaned away from the seed, it stands revealed in its almost cryptic shape. It is a perfect crescent moon three-eighths of an inch in diameter, rough and ridged, the seed of the moonseed vine. **1971** Krochmal *Appalachia Med. Plants* 170, Canada moonseed. **1979** Niering–Olmstead *Audubon Guide N. Amer. Wildflowers E. Region* 633, Common Moonseed (*Menispermum canadense*).
2 usu as *Carolina* (or *Carolinian*) *moonseed;* also *red-berried moonseed, red(-berry) ~, moonseed vine:* A related, red-fruited vine (*Cocculus carolinus*). [From the crescent shape of the seed] Also called **coral bead, coralberry 3, margil, sarsaparilla, snail-seed, wild sarsaparilla**
 1785 Marshall *Arbustrum* 86, *Menispermum carolinum.* Carolinian Moonseed. This is much smaller and weaker than the other [=M. canadense], scarcely becoming shrubby. **1900** Lyons *Plant Names* 88, C[ebatha] Carolina. . . Southeastern U.S. Carolina or Red-berried Moonseed. **1936** Whitehouse *TX Flowers* 31, Moonseed Vine (*Cebatha carolina*) is a vine with clusters of small red berries. It is very abundant throughout the state in woods and on fences, ranging north to Kansas and Virginia. It is also called . . red-berried moonseed. **1953** Greene–Blomquist *Flowers South* 36, Red-Moonseed, Carolina Moonseed (*Cocculus carolinus*) . . so named from the crescent-shaped seeds. **1960** Vines *Trees SW* 275, Vernacular names are . . Moonseed, Red-berry Moonseed, Carolina Moonseed, Red Moonseed [etc]. **1976** Bailey–Bailey *Hortus Third* 289, [*Cocculus*] *carolinus* . . Carolina moonseed, red m[oonseed], red-berried m[oonseed].

3 An **honesty** (here: *Lunaria annua*). [Prob from the shape of the silicle]
1959 Carleton *Index Herb. Plants* 83, *Moon-seed:* Lunaria annua (L. biennis).

moonseed root See **moonseed 1**

moonseed vine See **moonseed 1, 2**

moon-set n [Perh from the round, low-set leaves]
A **fringed orchid** (here: *Platanthera orbiculata*).
1950 Correll *Native Orchids* 93, Habenaria orbiculata. . . Common names: Large Round-leaved Orchid, Moon-set, Heal-all. **1976** Bailey-Bailey *Hortus Third* 534, [Habenaria] orbiculata. . . Round-leaved orchid, moon-set, heal-all.

moonshine n Note: *Moonshine* in the sense "illicitly distilled liquor" is now widespread in colloq use.
1 =**pearly everlasting.** [See quot 1848]
1848 in 1850 Cooper *Rural Hours* 310 ceNY, In our walk, this afternoon, observed a broad field upon a hill-side covered with the white silvery heads of the everlastings. The country people sometimes call these plants "moonshine," and really the effect in the evening upon so broad a field reminded one of moonlight. **1900** Lyons *Plant Names* 32, A[naphalis] margaritacea. . . Moonshine, None-so-pretty, Old-sow. **1935** (1943) Muenscher *Weeds* 450, Anaphalis margaritacea. . . Pearly everlasting, Silver leaf, Moonshine. **1959** Carleton *Index Herb. Plants* 83, *Moonshine:* Anaphalis margaritacea; Gnaphalium (v). **1967** *DARE* FW Addit **AR**44, Pearly everlasting—some say "moonshine"—Anaphalis margaritacea.
2 A **cudweed 1** (here: *Gnaphalium polycephalum*).
1894 *Jrl. Amer. Folkl.* 7.92, Gnaphalium polycephalum. . . moonshine, Dorset, Vt. **1900** Lyons *Plant Names* 176, G[naphalium] obtusifolium. . . Fuzzy-guzzy, Indian-posy, Moonshine. **1959** [see **1** above].
3 Any of three water birds: a **bittern** (here: *Botaurus lentiginosus*), a **purple gallinule**, or a **night heron**; see quots. [From their nocturnal habits] SC
1909 *S. Atl. Qrly.* 8.48 sSC coast [Gullah], The bittern, from his nocturnal flitting, is the *Moonshine: him always moonshinin' about.* **1923** U.S. Dept. Ag. *Misc. Circular* 13.44 SC, Purple Gallinule. . . moonshine. **1950** *PADS* 14.47 SC, Moonshine. . . The common night heron. So called on account of its nocturnal habits.
4 =**partridgeberry 1.**
1966 *DARE* Wildfl QR Pl.211B Inf **MI**31, Moonshine.
5 See quot. Cf **moonshining**
1927 in 1941 Dobie *Longhorns* 252 **TX**, One night we made what we called a 'moonshine'—that is, a night ride and a dry camp—with the intention of starting at daybreak on a fifteen- or twenty-mile drive back to the roundup ground.
6 Used as a name for var light-colored or insubstantial foods; see quots.
c1885 in 1981 Woodward *Mary Chesnut's Civil War* 762 **NC** (as of 1865), Moonshine is a sort of paste—light and fairylike, white as snow, twisted and twining, shining, intangible, mystic, wonderful—crumbles under one's fingers when touched—a sort of magical "marvelles," and yet delicious. **1890** James *Mother James' Cooking* 241, Moonshine. Take a glass of tart jelly and beat up until easy to work with. Beat the whites of six eggs to a stiff froth; add . . sugar . . flavor to taste; add the jelly and beat until stiff enough to stand in a pretty erect way on a flat dish. **1933** *AmSp* 8.1.27 cn**TX**, Moonshine. Rice. **1961** McDavid *Coll.* ne**OK**, Moonshine—baker's light bread; derog. **1966** *DARE* FW Addit **NM**13, Moonshine—rice and raisins cooked together (eaten by cowboys).

moonshine grass n
An **oat grass c** (here: *Danthonia spicata*).
1952 Strausbaugh–Core *Flora WV* 120, D[anthonia] spicata. . . Moonshine grass. . . Its presence usually indicates poor land. It is one of the most common pasture grasses in the State.

moonshining vbl n[1] Cf **moonshine 5**
1936 Adams *Cowboy Lingo* 113, 'Moonshinin' ' was working on round-up in a country so rough that packs had to be used in place of chuck-wagons.

moonshining vbl n[2] See **moonlight v 3**

moon-shot adj Cf **moon-eyed 1**
1930 Shoemaker *1300 Words* 41 c**PA** Mts (as of c1900), *Moon-shot*—Affected by phases of the Moon; "Moon blindness."

moon snake n
=**queen snake.**
1930 OK Univ. Biol. Surv. *Pub.* 2.224, Natrix septemvittata. . . Moon Snake. **1935** Pratt *Manual Vertebrate Animals* 214, Moon-snake. . . Color dark brown . . and a bright yellow lateral band; belly yellow, with 2 brown bands. **1953** Schmidt *N. Amer. Amphibians* 158, Natrix septemvittata. . . Common name. . . Moon snake.

moon spider n
An orb weaver (here: prob *Araneus marmoratus*).
1967 *DARE* (Qu. R28, . . Kinds of spiders) Inf **LA**10, Moon spider—builds a big round nest with a crescent thing in the center—a large spider colored black, yellow, and orange.

moonstone n
1 =**madstone.**
1970 Anderson *TX Folk Med.* 64 cs**TX**, Hard, round, bone-like objects called moonstones [Anderson: madstones] are used to neutralize snakebites.
2 In marble play: prob =**moonie** n[1].
1967 *DARE* (Qu. EE6d, *Special marbles*) Inf **IA**11, Moonstone. **c1970** Wiersma *Marbles Terms, Different types of marbles.* . . Moonstone. **1984** *WI State Jrl.* (Madison) 8 Apr sec 9 1/5, Other players have stories about their cat's eyes closing after a hard day of shooting or their "moonstones" changing shapes.

moon-up n [By analogy with *sunup*]
Moonrise.
1907 White *AZ Nights* 90, "Didn't git in till moon-up last night," he growled. **1934** Hurston *Jonah's Gourd Vine* 81 **AL** [Black], Zeke and Zack were in the woods trying out a new coon dog and came in after moon-up. **1938** Stuart *Dark Hills* 303 **KY**, I had stayed from sundown until moon-up. **1941** *Sat. Eve. Post* 1 Mar 84 **MO**, They'd come between first dark and moon-up.

moon vine See **moonflower 1**

Moor n chiefly c**DE**, s**NJ**
A member of a racially mixed people living in central Delaware and southern New Jersey.
1888 Scharf *Hist. DE* 2.1124 cw**DE**, West of the town of Moortown are a class of people who claim that they are original Moors. . . They claim to have settled here about 1710. In 1795 there were several families owning quite large estates. . . They have always lived apart from both white and colored neighbors, and have generally intermarried, and steadily refused to attend the neighboring colored schools. *Ibid* 1271 se**DE**, This race of people are noted as peaceable, law-abiding citizens, good farmers, and are known as Moors, but without any foundation. **1938** FWP *Guide DE* 351, A group of people locally called Moors has lived in the vicinity of Cheswold since Colonial days. Of unknown origin, they have skins varying from nearly white to dark yellow. . . Generally quiet and industrious, they live by themselves, associating little with the whites and considering themselves superior to the Negroes. **1943** Weslager *DE Forgotten Folk* 11, The Indian blood is still perpetuated in forgotten folk who are neither white nor black nor pure Indian. Some of them are called Moors. *Ibid* 17, The term "Moor" is widely used at Cheswold by both the whites and the mixed-bloods. The people do not refer to themselves as Nanticokes or Indians, and their white neighbors do not think of them as Indians. Nevertheless they are no different in appearance from the people in Indian River Hundred who call themselves Indians or Nanticokes. Their skin color ranges from white to brown in all its tones. None has the ebony skin and other characteristic features of the pure Negro. Even the casual traveler comments that the people are strangely different from either whites, Negroes, or mulattoes. **1946** *Social Forces* 24.445, Moors are centered in Cheswold, Kent County, Delaware, and at Bridgeton, Cumberland County in southern New Jersey. Name "Moor" traditionally derived from shipwrecked Moorish sailors. **1963** Berry *Almost White* 23 s**NJ**, In Cumberland county there are two groups—a people of Indian-white-negro ancestry known as "Moors," and who apparently came over from Delaware, and the Gouldtown settlement, whose history traces back to Colonial times. **1968** *DARE* (Qu. HH29b, . . People of mixed blood—part Negro) Inf **DE**1, Moors—there's a bunch near here that call themselves Moors.

moorhead n
=**coot** n[1] **1.**
1917 (1923) *Birds Amer.* 1.214, Coot—*Fulica americana.* . . Moorhead.

moor hen n

1 =**Florida gallinule.** [*OED* c1300 →] esp **MI, Upper Missip Valley**
1888 Trumbull *Names of Birds* 122, *Florida Gallinule: American Gallinule.* . . at Detroit and other points near Lake St. Clair . . Red-billed Mud-hen, Moor-hen. **1923** *U.S. Dept. Ag. Misc. Circular* 13.45 **CA, MI**, *Florida Gallinule.* . . moor-hen. **1932** Bennitt *Check-list* 28 **MO**, Florida gallinule. . . Mud-hen; moor-hen; water-hen. **1951** Pough *Audubon Water Bird* 204, Gallinule. . . Moorhen. **1953** *AmSp* 28.281 **MI, IL, MO,** Moor hen—Common gallinule.

2 =**coot** n[1] **1.**
1888 Trumbull *Names of Birds* 117, *Coot.* . . At Havre de Grace, Md., *Moor-hen*, so termed by all. **1953** *AmSp* 28.281 **MI, WI, ND,** Moor hen—American coot.

moose See **mamoose**

moose antlers n [See quot] Cf **horn mushroom, moose mushroom**
A **mushroom** (here: *Wynnea americana*).
1981 Lincoff *Audubon Field Guide Mushrooms* 345, Moose Antlers—*Wynnea americana.* . . shaped like moose antlers or rabbit ears; outer surface blackish-brown; inner surface pinkish to reddish.

mooseberry n [*DCan* 1789 →] **Nth**, esp **NEng**
Either **highbush cranberry** or **hobblebush**; also the fruit.
1848 Thoreau in *Union Mag.* (NY NY) 3.179, The cornet, or bunchberries, were very abundant, as well as Solomon's seal and moose-berries. **1894** *Jrl. Amer. Folkl.* 7.90 **NH**, *Viburnum lantanoides* . . Mooseberry. **1896** *Jrl. Amer. Folkl.* 9.190 **ME**, *Viburnum lantanoides* . . moose berry. **1940** Brown *Amer. Cooks* 332 **ME**, The mooseberry or heath apple, a berry produced on a single stalk like a mulberry, planted, scientists say, by the migratory birds on the low promontories extending into the Atlantic at Lubec and Jonesport. **1940** Clute *Amer. Plant Names* 56, *V[iburnum] alnifolium* . . moose-wood, moose-bush, mooseberry. **1950** Gray–Fernald *Manual of Botany* 1341, *V[iburnum] edule* . . Squashberry, Mooseberry. **1953** Nelson *Plants Rocky Mt. Park* 149, Arrowwood, high-bush-cranberry, or mooseberry viburnum, (*Viburnum pauciflorum*). **1972** Viereck–Little *AK Trees* 244, High Bushcranberry. . . Other names: squashberry, mooseberry, *Viburnum pauciflorum.* **1974** (1977) Coon *Useful Plants* 91, Squashberry, mooseberry, arrowhead. . . The red or orange fruits are useful for jam.

moosebird n [Etym uncert; see quots 1832, 1956] **Nth**, esp **ME**
=**Canada jay.**
1832 Williamson *Hist. ME* 1.150, The *Moose-bird*, which feeds on the berries of the moose bush. **a1862** [see **meatbird 1**]. **1888** (1971) Hubbard *Woods ME* 153, We heard near by the merry note of the Canada jay, or moose-bird, "What cheer, what cheer, what cheer!" **1925** (1928) Forbush *Birds MA* 2.386, Camp is no more than established when the Moose Birds "rally round" eager to snatch any bit of meat or other edible substance. **1941** Writers' Program *Guide WY* 35, Unpopular for his insolence and thievery, the Canada jay, known also as . . moose bird, . . is a native of the evergreen forests. **1950** *WELS*, 1 Inf, **csWI**, Canada jay—known in the north woods as whiskey jack, moosebird. **1956** *MA Audubon Soc. Bulletin* 40.84 **ME**, *Canada Jay.* . . Moose Bird. . . The Moose permits the bird to alight on it to remove ticks. . . The bird was also believed by Indians to direct hunters to the Moose. **1961** *Jrl. Amer. Folk.* 74.1, Maine woodsmen usually call it [=the Canada jay] either gorbey or moose-bird. **1966–70** *DARE* (Qu. Q16, . . *Kinds of jays*) Inf **ME3**, There is a gorby or moosebird here; **MN14**, Canada jay or whiskey jack; moosebird or camp robber; **NY233**, Whiskey jack, moosebird, venison jay. **1969** Sorden *Lumberjack Lingo* 79 **NEng, Gt Lakes**, *Moose birds*—Canada jays or garbies [sic]. The reincarnated souls of dead lumberjacks. **1975** Gould *ME Lingo* 113, The handsome Canada jay of Audubon, also called moosebird and whiskeyjack.

moosebush See **moosewood**

moose cat n Cf **cat** n **1e**
Among loggers: something or someone extraordinary; see quots.
1926 Rickaby *Ballads Shanty-Boy* 212 **cnMN**, *Moose-cat:* a slang

expression, hard of translation, but applied to anyone possessing great ability, strength, or what not. **1956** Sorden–Ebert *Logger's Words* 23 **Gt Lakes,** *Moose-cat.* . . Anything unusually large or an unusually good lumber-jacket [sic].

moose ear See **moosehead plant**

moose elm n [See quot 1962]
=**slippery elm.**
1810 Michaux *Histoire des Arbres* 1.37, *Slippery elm.* . . Moose elm . . dans le haut de l'Etat de New-York. [=*Slippery elm.* . . Moose elm . . in upper New York State.] **1884** Sargent *Forests of N. Amer.* 122, Red Elm. Slippery Elm. Moose Elm. . . The inner bark [is] mucilaginous, nutritious. **1902** *Jrl. Amer. Folkl.* 15.249, Moose-elm (the slippery elm). **1936** Winter *Plants NE* 178, Moose Elm. Grows in the eastern portion of the state especially along the Missouri and its tributaries. **1962** Harrar–Harrar *Guide S. Trees* 237, Moose are known to browse on the young twigs and foliage of this species [=*Ulmus rubra*], and in certain sections . . the tree is called the *moose elm.*

moose eye n
=**dog eye** n **1.**
1944 *AmSp* 19.106 [Vocab of sailors], The reproachful or supplicatory stare is the *dog-eye* or the *moose-eye.*

moose flower n **NEast**
=**trillium.**
1848 in 1850 Cooper *Rural Hours* 73 **NY**, The moose-flowers are increasing in numbers. **1894** *Jrl. Amer. Folkl.* 7.102 **NY**, *Trillium*, sp., moose-flowers. **1896** Robinson *In New Engl. Fields* 53, The brown forest floor, which is splashed with white moose-flowers. **1940** Clute *Amer. Plant Names* 15, *T[rillium] grandiflorum.* . . Moose-flower.

moose fly n

1 A fly of the family Tabanidae. esp **ME**
1834 Audubon *Ornith. Biog.* 2.437 **ME coast**, The musquitoes and moose flies did their best to render us uncomfortable. **a1862** (1864) Thoreau *ME Woods* 177, While engaged in this search we made our first acquaintance with the moose-fly. **1902** *Jrl. Amer. Folkl.* 15.249, Moosefly (a large brown fly common in Maine). **1934** *Hanley Disks* **ME**, We have what we call the moose fly here. . . They lay right hold and bite. [*DARE* Ed: Inf distinguishes between moose flies and mooseflies.] **1955** U.S. Arctic Info. Center *Gloss.* 53, *Moose fly.* A deer fly. **1966–68** *DARE* (Qu. R12, . . *Other kinds of flies*) Inf **AK9**, Moose fly same as horsefly, bad biters; **ME3**, Moose fly; **ME8**, Deerfly—I've heard these often called moose fly; **NH14**, Moose fly. **1994** *Nature Photographer* 4.5.24 **ME**, Black flies are very active in late May into July [in Baxter State Park], and you may also encounter mosquitoes, moose flies, and midges. **1994** *DARE* File **ME** (as of c1978), Moose flies are bigger than horse flies and deer flies. They are a plain light brown color all over, and have a mean bite.

2 A **punkie** (here: Ceratopogonidae).
1972 Swan–Papp *Insects* 594, The biting midges [=Ceratopogonidae]. . . include some very annoying pests, variously called no-see-ums, punkies, and flies, moose flies, and gnats.

moose grass n
A **squaw grass** (here: *Xerophyllum tenax*).
[**1903** White *Forest* 190 **Canada**, Three times we blundered on little meadows of moose-grass.] **1936** Thompson *High Trails* 86 **nwMT**, The bear grass flower. . . is also listed as pine grass, moose grass, Indian basket grass, and turkey beard.

moosehead plant n Also *moose ear*
=**pickerelweed.**
1866 Lossing *Hudson* 6 **NY**, A winding and narrow river, fringed with rushes, lilies, and moose-head plants. **1901** Eckstorm *Bird Book* 4 **ME**, By the water's edge there are . . clumps of tall *pontederia*, which in Maine we call both "pickerel-weed" and "moose-ear," the latter name being given because its long, pointed leaves look like the ears of the moose.

moose jaw n
A large or protruding jaw; hence adj *moose-jawed.*
1967–69 *DARE* (Qu. X6, *If a person's lower jaw sticks out prominently . . he's _____*) Infs **PA209, 216, WI50,** Moose-jawed; **WY2,** Moose jaw.

moose maple n chiefly NEng Cf **moosewood 1**

Usu either a **mountain maple** (here: *Acer spicatum*) or **striped maple**; rarely, the **box elder**.

1839 Hoffman *Wild Scenes* 1.53 **NY**, We would come to a sort of plateau of swampy land, overgrown with moose-maple. **1897** Sudworth *Arborescent Flora* 282 **VT**, *Acer spicatum.* . . Common Names. . . Moose Maple. **1901** *Plant World* 4.190 **eNH**, Rock or sugar maple . . and the red maple . . were abundant, as well as the moose maple (*Acer pennsylvanicum*). **1950** Peattie *Nat. Hist. Trees* 470, *Acer spicatum.* . . Moose Maple. [*Ibid* 471, There are no commercial uses for the wood of so small a tree, but deer and moose browse the bark.] **1966–70** DARE (Qu. T14, . . *Kinds of maples*) Inf **ME**8, Moose maple—a shrub; **MA**5, Moose maple—has striped bark; **MA**58, Moose [maple]; **MA**78, Moose maples; **NH**5, Moose maple—same as striped maple or box elder; **PA**223, Striped or moose maple; also called whistlewood. **1988** DARE File **cwMA**, Woodsmen call the striped maple "moose maple." **1989** Mosher *Stranger* 254 **nVT** (as of 1952), We . . cut . . down through the summery mixed hard- and softwoods, thick with hobblebush and moose maple.

moosemise n Also sp *moose-misse* [Of Algonquian origin]

1 also *masse-misse*: A **mountain ash 1** (here: *Sorbus americana*). [DCan 1861 →] Cf **Indian mozemize**

1893 *Jrl. Amer. Folkl.* 6.141, *Pyrus americana* . . moose misse. Ferrisburgh, Vt. **1907** Hodge *Hdbk. Amer. Indians* 1.606, Moose misse. The American mountain-ash or dogberry. **1930** Sievers *Amer. Med. Plants* 7, American Mountain-ash. . . Other common names. . . Moose-misse. **1971** Krochmal *Appalachia Med. Plants* 238, *Sorbus americana.* . . Masse-misse.

2 A **wintergreen** (here: *Pyrola rotundifolia americana*).

1902 *Jrl. Amer. Folkl.* 15.249, *Moosemise.* A name current in certain parts of New England (Vermont) for the *Pyrola Americana* or "false wintergreen."

moose mushroom n

Perh =**moose antlers.**

1968 DARE (Qu. S18, *A kind of mushroom that grows like a globe . . sometimes gets as big as a man's head*) Inf **WI**37, Moose mushroom, sponge mushroom.

moose nose n

See quot.

1968 DARE (Qu. H43, *Foods made from parts of the head and inner organs of an animal*) Inf **AK**8, Moose nose—nothing but brisket—pickle it and take for traveling.

moose shank n Cf DCan

A stocking made from the hide of a moose leg; see quot 1887.

1887 *Harper's New Mth. Mag.* 74.458 **nME**, 'Moose shanks' are made by peeling the skin from the hind-legs of the animal. . . The smaller end is then sewn up to form the toe; and thus a moose-hide stocking is formed. **1966** DARE Tape **ME**1, They used to [make] what they call moose shanks out of a moose. You'd take off the hind legs there and they used to skin them and turn the fur in and they was as warm as socks.

moose sled n

1975 Gould *ME Lingo* 183, Moose sled—A wide-runnered hand sled presumably first designed for transporting moose meat into camp. It is a utility sled used in lumber and sporting camps for odd chores, replaced in summer by a wheelbarrow. The *hand shark* is a similar sled.

moose tongue n

A **willow herb** (here: *Epilobium angustifolium*).

1916 *Torreya* 16.239, *Epilobium angustifolium.* . . Moose-tongue, Matinicus I., Me. **1959** Carleton *Index Herb. Plants* 83, *Moose tongue: Epilobium angustifolium.*

moose tree See **moosewood 2**

moosewood n Also *moosebush*

1 also *moosewood maple*: =**striped maple.** [See quot 1792] Cf **moose maple**

1792 Belknap *Hist. NH* 3.163, The *moose* . . is the largest animal of our forest. . . He feeds on the wild grass of the meadows, or on the leaves and bark of a species of the maple, which is called moose-wood. **1822** Eaton *Botany* 154, *[Acer] striatum* . . striped maple, false dogwood, moose wood. **1843** (1844) Johnson *Farmer's Encycl.* 789, Moose wood, or striped maple (*A[cer] striatum*). . . The moose wood maple of the Eastern States was so called by the first settlers, from observing that the moose fed upon its twigs during the latter part of winter and begin-

ning of spring. **1897** Sudworth *Arborescent Flora* 283, *Acer pennsylvanicum.* . . Common Names. . . Moosewood (Me., Vt., N.H., R.I., Mass., N.Y., Pa., N.C., Mich., Minn.) **1931** Harned *Wild Flowers Alleghanies* 284, Striped Maple. . . Known also by the familiar names, Moose Wood, Whistle Wood, and Goose-foot Maple. The tree. . . grows mostly in damp, shady woods. **1961** Douglas *My Wilderness* 173 **wNC**, We saw occasional striped maples, some thirty feet high. This tree . . the mountain folks call moosewood. **1966–67** DARE (Qu. T14, . . *Kinds of maples*) Inf **MI**10, Striped maple—small tree . . synonymous with moosebush; **TN**11, Striped [maple] or moosewood—not a strictly local term; (Qu. T15, . . *Kinds of swamp trees*) Inf **MI**2, Moosewood. **1967** Borland *Hill Country* 160 **nwCT**, We have two small maples here in this area that are commonly called moosewood and elkwood. **1982** DARE File, One of our best local historical architects . . remembers running into a backwoodsy fisherman in Tennessee, once, who was fishing with a "Moosewood" plug. . . It was carved and as heavy as ironwood. . . The architect and a friend . . found a man in Nashville who had done much Forestry and preservation work . . and he told them that there is a variety of "lowland maple"—different from upland maple, that grows along the boggier bottomlands of the Cumberland river and it is called "Moosewood" by the locals.

2 also *moose tree*: A **leatherwood 1** (here: *Dirca palustris*). [See quot 1872]

1778 Carver *Travels N. Amer.* 507, The *Moose Wood* grows about four feet high, and is very full of branches. **1822** Eaton *Botany* 268, *[Dirca] palustris* (leather-wood, moose-wood). **1832** Williamson *Hist. ME* 1.117, *Moose-bush* [Footnote: Or "Moosewood," *Dirca palustris*] is a small tree, or large shrub, not uncommon in the forest. **1854** Greatrex *Whittlings* 119, Jacques caught up a sharp stone, and tried to saw it, but the thong, which was formed out of the tough bark of the moosetree, would not yield. **1872** Schele de Vere *Americanisms* 53, The leatherwood (Dirca palustris), a small shrub with a tough, leathern bark, is a favorite food with these gigantic animals, and hence frequently called *Moose wood*. **1894** Coulter *Botany W. TX* 383, *Dirca* [spp] . . Leatherwood. Moosewood. **1942** Hylander *Plant Life* 402, Leatherwood (*Dirca*), also known as Moosewood; this is a deciduous shrub of damp woods from New England to Louisiana. **1960** Vines *Trees SW* 781, Known by the vernacular names of Wicopy, Wickup, Moose-wood, Rope-bark, Swamp-wood, Leather-bark, Leather-bush, and American Mezereon. **1976** Bailey–Bailey *Hortus Third* 391, *[Dirca] palustris* . . wicopy, ropebark, moosewood.

3 also *moosewood viburnum*: A **viburnum**, usu **hobblebush**. scattered, but esp NEng

1784 (1888) Cutler *Life* 1.102 **NH**, The ground [was] covered with an underwood of moose bush. **1892** *Jrl. Amer. Folkl.* 5.97 **MA**, *Viburnum lantanoides*, Moosewood. **1896** *Ibid* 9.190 **ME**, *Viburnum lantanoides* . . Moose bush. **1910** Graves *Flowering Plants* 368 **CT**, *Viburnum alnifolium.* . . Hobble-bush. Witch Hobble. Moosewood. **1929** *Torreya* 29.6.151 **ME**, *Viburnum dentatum*, "*Withe wood*" *Moose-wood.* **1933** Small *Manual SE Flora* 1271, *V[iburnum] lantanoides* . . Hobblebush. Moosewood. **1973** Hitchcock–Cronquist *Flora Pacific NW* 453, Moosewood v[iburnum], high-bush cranberry, squashberry. . . *V[iburnum] edule.* **1976** Bailey–Bailey *Hortus Third* 1153, *[Viburnum] alnifolium* . . Moosewood, Moose bush.

moosewood maple See **moosewood 1**

moosewood viburnum See **moosewood 3**

moosharoon See **mushroom**

‡**moot** n

A dust ball.

1965 DARE (Qu. E20, *Soft rolls of dust that collect on the floor under beds or other furniture*) Inf **OK**13, Moots.

moozie n [Cf SND *mozie, moz(z)(e)y, mosey, moosie* adjs (at *moze* n. I.1) "(i) decayed, . . fusty, mouldy . . (ii) covered with soft hairs, downy"] Cf **moot, woozie**

1980 *Capital Times* (Madison WI) 26 Aug 13/3 **nIL**, She . . found the . . only other person in the world who called the dustballs under the bed "moozies."

‡**mop** n [Cf *map face, mop* a mass of hair]

1966 DARE (Qu. X29, *Joking or uncomplimentary words for a person's face*) Inf **SC**10, Mop.

mop along v phr [Cf *mope;* see also quot 1939]

To move lethargically.

[**1939** (1962) Thompson *Body & Britches* 497 **NY**, Drag like a mop (a gait).] **1970** *DARE* (Qu. Y21, *To move about slowly and without energy*) Inf **VA47**, Mop along.

mopboard n Rarely *mockboard* **chiefly Nth, West** See Map
Cf **washboard**
A baseboard.

1853 (1880) Fowler *Home for All* 159 **NY**, After mop or base-boards are nailed on, . . fill in between these boards . . with stone or mortar. **1859** (1968) Bartlett *Americanisms* 279, *Mop-board.* The wash-board which extends around the base of the walls in the interior of a house, is so called in New England. **1882** Howells *Modern Instance* 272 **MA**, When he sits on the sofa, and stretches out his legs, his boots touch the mop-board on the other side of the room. **1899** Garland *Boy Life* 51 **nwIA**, Their cowhide boots shrank distressfully . . causing their owners to weep, and kick the mopboard. **1902** Aldrich *Sea Turn* 201 **NYC**, Even the mop-boards were stripped off. **1959** *VT Hist.* 27.149, *Mop-board.* . . The baseboard around the bottom of the walls of a room. . . Common. **c1960** *Wilson Coll.* **csKY**, Mopboard. . . The plank at the bottom of a wall; a baseboard. Widely used. **1965–70** *DARE* (Qu. D37, *The strip of wood about eight inches high along the bottom of the wall [inside a room] joining to the floor*) 168 Infs, **chiefly Nth, West**, Mopboard(s); **NH17**, Mopboard, mockboards. **1967** *San Juan Mission News* (San Juan Bautista CA) 24 Nov 2/5, Frank Bettencourt was repairing the "mop board" in the old cloak room at Community Hall Wednesday morning. **1995** *DARE* File **csWI**, They sure made a mess of my mopboards when they installed the new linoleum in my kitchen.

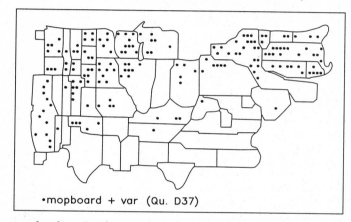

•mopboard + var (Qu. D37)

mop bucket See **bucket 2g**

mopes n pl With *the*
A fit of depression.

1954 *Harder Coll.* **cwTN**, The mopes. . . A fit of being dispirited. **1969** *DARE* (Qu. GG34a, *To feel depressed or in a gloomy mood: "He has the _____ today."*) Inf **IL68**, Mopes.

mophead n
=**hooded merganser.**

1955 *Oriole* 20.1.5, Hooded Merganser. . . Mop-head . . (the head is conspicuously crested).

mop one's hair v phr
1952 Brown *NC Folkl.* 1.566 **wNC**, Mop the hair. . . To wash the hair.

mopround n
=**mopboard.**

1968 *DARE* (Qu. D37, *The strip of wood about eight inches high along the bottom of the wall [inside a room] joining to the floor*) Inf **IA47**, Mopround.

moral law n **nNEng**
In phrr *longer* (or *taller*) *than the moral law* and varr: Very long (or tall).

1914 *DN* 4.76 **nNH, ME**, Longer'n (taller'n) the moral law. . . Very long (tall). **1929** *AmSp* 5.130 **ME**, The following comparisons were common . . "longer than the moral law." **1958** *VT Hist.* 26.277, As long as the moral law.

more adv Pronc-spp *mo', moe, moh*
A Forms.

1884 *Anglia* 7.272 **Sth, S Midl** [Black], En' mo'n dat = and furthermore. **1891** Page *Elsket* 127 **VA** [Black], 'Cuz a full hawg cyarn drink no mo'. **1899** Chesnutt *Conjure Woman* 215 **csNC** [Black], Who wuz

tryin' ter slander Jeff 'ca'se he wuz mo' luckier 'n he wuz. **1899** (1912) Green *VA Folk-Speech* 285, Mo. . . For more. Moe. **1908** *DN* 3.284 **eAL, wGA**, Double comparatives and superlatives are frequent, as in beterer [sic], mo beterer, mo worser, mo puttier. **1915** (1916) Johnson *Highways New Engl.* 214, People wouldn't die so young if they lived mo' plainer and didn't eat such rich food. **1958** Humphrey *Home from the Hill* 129 **neTX**, You don't hear no mo talk bout superstitions. **1976** *DARE* File **cTX**, Many white middle-class r-ful students are familiar with and use [moˈbɛdə] for 'better'. **1991** Saiki *From the Lanai* 96 **HI**, Ever since Dan, things going to pot—moh bettah in old days, I tell you.
B Gram varr.

1 Rarely double compar, pronc-sp *moreder.* Cf Intro "Language Changes" I.8, *nearder* (at **near B**)

1916 *DN* 4.277 **NE**, Moreder. Occasional double comparative of *more.* "I like John moreder than I do his younger brother."

2 Superl: usu *most;* also *morest;* pronc-spp *mo'res', mo'ris'.* Gullah

1867 Allen *Slave Songs* xxxiii **eSC**, De morest part ob de mens dey git heaps o' clo'—more'n 'nuff; 'n I ain't git nuffin. **1922** Gonzales *Black Border* 314 **sSC, GA coasts** [Gullah glossary], Mo'ris', mo'res'—most. **1930** Stoney–Shelby *Black Genesis* 73 **seSC**, Dat back sure is de t'ing in dis worl' dat he needs de more-est. **1937** *S. Folkl. Qrly.* 1.1.100 [Gullah], [Proverb:] A still calf git de mores' milk. **1971** Cunningham *Syntactic Analysis Gullah* 33, The morest time I always be to my niece house.

C Syntax.
See **-er** compar suff **4.**

moreder See **more B1**

more hair n [Folk-etym for *mohair;* cf Intro "Language Changes" I.6, Pronc Intro 3.II.26]
1949 *McDavid Coll.* **nwNY**, More hair 'mohair'.

moreish adj Also *morey* Also sp *morish* [*OED* 1738 →] Cf **taste like more**
Of food: appetizing, tasty.

1905 *DN* 3.63 **eNE**, Morish. . . "That tastes morish." Cf. "that tastes like more." **1961** Sackett–Koch *KS Folkl.* 114, "Has it got a morish taste?" asks a lady offering a second piece of cake. **1968** *DARE* (Qu. LL35, *Words used to make a statement stronger: "This cake tastes _____ good."*) Inf **MN26**, Moreish—Cornish say this. **1975** Gould *ME Lingo* 183, *Morey*—Worth having more of: "That's a real morey cake—don't mind if I do!"

morel n[1] Also sp *morelle, morrel* [*OED* 1265 →, but in Louisiana perh an independent borrowing from Fr *morille*]
A **nightshade 1** (here: either *Solanum dulcamara* or *S. nigrum*).

1900 Lyons *Plant Names* 349, S[olanum] Dulcamara. . . Fever-twig, Morrel, Poison-berry. **1930** Sievers *Amer. Med. Plants* 11, Poisonberry, poisonflower, pushion-berry, morel. **1940** Clute *Amer. Plant Names* 51, Black Nightshade. . . Morelle, morel. **1967** Harrington *Edible Plants Rocky Mts.* 286, A husky, large-fruited form of this species is fairly common in cultivation under the name of "wonderberry, sunberry, garden huckleberry or Morelle." Many people eat these fruits without harm and learn to relish the musky flavor, but even this garden form has been reported to have occasionally caused illness. **1968** *DARE* (Qu. I28b) Inf **LA37**, Morel [ˌmoˈrɛl]—this is French, the common word here; "nightshade" in English.

morel n[2] Usu |məˈrɛl, ˈmorəl, ˈmɔr-|; for addit proncs see quots [*OED* 1672 →] **chiefly N Cent, Upper Missip Valley** See Map on p. 658
A **mushroom** of the family Morchellaceae, usu of the genus *Morchella.* For other names of *Morchella* spp see **dog pecker, dryland fish 1, fat morel, honeycomb mushroom, molly moocher, mountain fish, ~ mushroom, pinecone, sponge mushroom, spring mushroom** Cf **false morel**

1843 (1844) Johnson *Farmer's Encycl.* 832, Morel. . . The *Moschella* [sic] *esculenta* is one of the few edible fungi which may be used as food with safety. It occasionally occurs in woods and orchards, whence it finds its way to the markets. . . It has a hollow stalk an inch or two high, and a yellowish or grayish indented head 2 or 3 inches deep. **1855** U.S. Patent Office *Annual Rept. for 1854: Ag.* 364, Morel. *(Phallus esculentus.)* This vegetable is a native of this country, and closely related to the mushroom, from which it is distinguished by the cap being hollow within. **1885** U.S. Dept. Ag. *Rept. of Secy. for 1885* 105, *Morchella esculenta.* . . The morel is found in April or May in grassy places. **1908**

Hard *Mushroom Edible* 489, Old apple and peach orchards are favorite places for Morels. It makes no difference if the beginner cannot identify the species, as they are all equally good. **1950** *WELS (A large round mushroom, often bright colored)* 3 Infs, **WI**, Morel; *(Small plants, shaped like an umbrella, that grow in woods and fields: Those safe to eat)* 1 Inf, **seWI**, Morels. **1965–70** *DARE* (Qu. I37, *Small plants shaped like an umbrella that grow in woods and fields—which are safe to eat)* Infs **IN**52, **MI**104, **NY**66, **OH**35, Morel(s); **IA**13, ['morəlz]; **IN**7, [mə'rɪlz]; **MI**102, [mə'rɛl]; **MN**36, ['morəlz]; **MA**15, [mə'rɛlz]; **WI**76, [mə'rælz]; **OH**82, Morels—young people call them that; **TN**37, They don't grow here, but they are in Indiana and are called morels [morɛlz]; **IA**22, The northern Illinois morel; *(Qu. S18, A kind of mushroom that grows like a globe . . sometimes gets as big as a man's head)* Inf **WI**43, Morel; **IL**55, ['morəlz]; **MI**17, [mə'rɛl]. **1967–70** *DARE* Tape **MI**65, The morel [mə'ræl] or spring mushroom—it's conical-shaped and looks like a sponge; it's a great delicacy; **MI**120, They pick morels [mə'rɛlz] in the spring of the year now, about the middle of May. . . You find people from all over . . coming up here to pick morel mushrooms. **1987** McKnight–McKnight *Mushrooms* 36, Morels: Family Morchellaceae. . . All species are considered edible after cooking by some people, but bell morels *(Verpa)* do cause poisoning. . . Also, the morels in genus *Morchella* occasionally are responsible for some poisoning, particularly when eaten with alcoholic beverages.

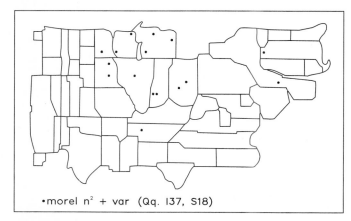

•morel n² + var (Qq. I37, S18)

morelle See **morel** n¹

moremouth (bream) See **mawmouth**

more-rummer n Cf **jugarum**
A **bullfrog 1.**
  1968 *DARE* (Qu. P22, *Names or nicknames for a very large frog that makes a deep, loud sound)* Infs **NJ**16, 21, More-rummer(s).

mo'res', morest See **more** B2

morey See **moreish**

morfadite, morfidite, morfodike See **morphodite**

morgan n Cf **mawmouth**
A **warmouth** (here: *Lepomis gulosus*).
  1950 *PADS* 14.47 **SC,** Morgan. . . The warmouth, a species of fresh water fish.

morgan cat n
=**flathead catfish 1.**
  1908 Forbes–Richardson *Fishes of IL* 193, It is perhaps best known to the fishermen of the Mississippi River as the "Morgan cat." **1946** LaMonte *N. Amer. Game Fishes* 163, *Flathead Catfish.* . . Morgan Cat, Shovelhead Catfish. **1966** *WI Conserv. Bulletin* July–Aug 14, Many know the fish [=*Pylodictis olivaris*] by such local names as yellow cat, mudcat, morgan cat, opelousa or just plain bullhead. **1983** Becker *Fishes WI* 728, *Flathead Catfish.* . . Johnny cat, Morgan cat.

morgue wagon n Cf **meat wagon 1**
A hearse.
  1899 (1977) Norris *McTeague* 7 **CA,** Just say that once more, and . . you'll go back to the city in the Morgue wagon. **1969** *DARE* (Qu. N2, *The car used to carry a dead body for burial)* Inf **NY**156, Morgue wagon.

mo'ris' See **more** B2

morish See **moreish**

mork See **mock** v

Mormon blanket n
  1944 Adams *Western Words* 101, *Mormon blanket*—A quilt made from scraps of faded overalls and jumpers.

Mormon board n Also *Mormon level*
A simple type of road-scraper.
  1926 Bennet *Boss Diamond A* 35 **WY,** Yankem and Doc were driving teams hitched to improvised Mormon levels. **1941** Writers' Program *Guide OK* 122, In general use in the oil-field world are the following expressions: . . Mormon board—A broad board with two handles, used for filling in a ditch. **1957** *Time* 24 June 99, But [in 1917] horses and mules continued to provide most of the motive power for road building, pulling primitive Fresno scrapers and pushing wooden "Mormon Boards."

Mormon brake n Cf **rough lock**
  1873 in 1955 Lee *Mormon Chron.* 2.233, I assistd them to put a Mormon Brake on their waggon. **1944** Adams *Western Words* 101, *Mormon brakes*—A tree tied behind a wagon to retard its speed downhill. This device was first used by Mormon pioneers in crossing the San Bernado [sic for *Bernardino*] Mountains in 1850. **1955** Lee *Mormon Chron.* 2.262, [Footnote:] A Mormon brake consisted of a log placed horizontally in front of the hind wheels of a wagon so it could be drawn up against them on a steep downgrade.

Mormon buckskin n Also *Mormon silk* joc or derog Cf **haywire** adj 1
Baling wire.
  1941 Writers' Program *Guide UT* 507, These are reached by the original ladders—now decrepit with age but reinforced with "Mormon buckskin," which is to say, baling wire. **1966** *DARE* (Qu. L63) Inf **ID**3, Baling wire is called "Mormon buckskin" around here. **1979** Stegner *Recapitulation* 193 **UT,** Gateposts have been bound by windings of baling wire (Mormon silk, says some amused folklorist).

Mormon candy n Also *Mormon currency* Cf **carrot eater**
Carrots.
  1939 FWP *ID Lore* 241, *Mormon candy*—raw carrot. **1942** Berrey–Van den Bark *Amer. Slang* 474, *Mormon currency*, carrots.

Mormon cricket n [See quot 1949] chiefly **Rocky Mts**
A **grasshopper 1** (here: *Anabrus simplex*).
  1896 Smith *Economic Entomol.* 97, At the base of the Rocky Mountains, extending up into the foot-hills. . . the "Mormon cricket," *Anabrus simplex,* occasionally multiplies so greatly that it migrates to the plains below, destroying everything in its path. **1926** Essig *Insects N. Amer.* 92, The Mormon, Western, Great Plains, Idaho or black cricket . . is the most destructive member of this family and one of the most destructive of the order. **1934** *Daily Progress* (Charlottesville VA) 30 Apr 1/6, The devastating "Mormon" crickets, which came into prominence in 1848 when they threatened first colonists in Utah with starvation, have appeared in a half dozen spots of southern Idaho to carry on the destruction they started last year. **1949** Swain *Insect Guide* 13, Mormon Cricket. . . During the critical early days of the Mormon settlement at Salt Lake City, the crops, whose loss would have meant starvation and defeat, were threatened with complete destruction by droves of these insects. Sea gulls . . came to gorge on the pests and were credited, as agents of the Lord, with saving the crops. **1964** Jackman–Long *OR Desert* 213, Mormon crickets are his [=the Oregon grasshopper mouse's] chosen food if there are any around. **1966–67** *DARE* (Qu. R6, . . *Names . . for grasshoppers)* Infs **CO**7, **ID**5, **NV**5, Mormon crickets; *(Qu. R8, . . Kinds of creatures that make a clicking or shrilling or chirping kind of sound)* Inf **MT**4, Mormon cricket; **WY**1, Mormon cricket . . eats crops. **1967** *DARE* Tape **ID**7, But the Mormon cricket. . . that's a great big, about three times bigger than a grasshopper, and they come in plagues. . . Ever since the war, World War II, I haven't heard of cricket plagues. *Ibid* **ID**13, [FW:] Anything besides the weather that caused trouble to the crops? . . [Inf:] There were these crickets, they call 'em Mormon crickets, and I think there were times when those were bad. **1980** Milne–Milne *Audubon Field Guide Insects* 430, Mormon Cricket. . . This common cricket got its common name after thousands suddenly attacked the Mormon pioneers' first crops in Utah in 1848. **1994** *USA Today* (Arlington VA) sec A 12 **seWA,** Franklin County farmers are hoping a federal agency will help fight off an invasion of Mormon crickets.

Mormon currency See **Mormon candy**

Mormon derrick n Also *Mormon stacker* **esp UT, ID, eOR** Cf *DS* L16

A type of **derrick** for stacking hay; see quots.

1927 U.S. Dept. Ag. *Farmers' Bulletin* 1525.11 **CO, ID**, For handling alfalfa with a minimum loss of leaves from shattering and a saving of labor on the stack, the derrick stacker . . excels all other types. All stackers of this type are homemade. . . The Mormon derrick, the style in most general use and perhaps the best, varies slightly in construction in different sections. **1944** U.S. Dept. Ag. Bur. Plant Industry *Info. Ser.* 74.43, Perhaps the stacker most frequently mentioned . . has been the so-called Mormon stacker, or some variation thereof. It has been stated that this stacker has been in use in some sections over fifty years. This is particularly true of Utah—although, there they are more apt to be referred to as hay derricks, swing derricks, or hay stackers. **1951** *Western Folkl.* 10.321 **ID, UT**, Actually the term "Mormon derrick" is a misnomer since it refers not to one particular type but to a group of perhaps fifteen stackers which differ essentially from each other, although all of them have the one point in common that the hay is hoisted by means of pullies [sic] and a cable attached to frames of widely differing structure and function. **1967** *DARE* FW Addit **OR**, *Mormon derrick*—no guy wires; the boom swung across on stirrup from the top of the derrick pole. **c1971** Hall *Snake River Valley, (What do you call a device used as an aid in stacking and storing hay?)* 8 infs, **sID, eOR**, Mormon derrick. **1977** Jones *OR Folkl.* 39 (as of early 1900s), The inventor of the hay derrick is not known. Whether the basic design originated with Mormon settlers in northern Utah and then spread north has never been determined, but this style of derrick is commonly known as a "Mormon derrick." **1985** Atteberry *ID Folklife* 11, [Footnote:] Blueprints of two types of "Mormon stackers" are supplied by the U.S. Department of Agriculture . . [in publications of] 1924, and . . 1925. **1986** Klinkenborg *Making Hay* 94 **MT**, You confront the fundamental problem of haystack building. . . Early solutions to this quandary included the Mormon derrick, nothing more than a huge bipod with a sling attached. The sling lifted the hay and the bipod tilted to drop the load of hay on a stack much taller than a man, but shorter than the derrick. Unc showed me photos of Mormon derricks at work in the Big Hole in the 1890s. They looked like gangly, inefficient hay tools in constant danger of toppling.

Mormon dog n

1968 Adams *Western Words* 200, *Mormon dog*—A tin can filled with pebbles, used in place of dogs in some sections of the Northwest to scare cattle from their hiding places in rough country.

Mormon elder n
=**black-necked stilt.**

1923 U.S. Dept. Ag. *Misc. Circular* 13.48, *Black-necked Stilt. . . Mormon-elder* (Utah); religieuse (nun, its black and white plumage suggesting the garb of a religious order) (La.)

Mormon fly n **Upper Missip Valley**
=**mayfly 1.**

1845 (1946) Moore *Diary* 46 **cwIL**, Our boat and every thing about it is now covered with Mormon flies as they are called, being, I am told, peculiar to this neighborhood. I heard one of the deck hands a little while ago cursing "these damned Nauvoo flies." **1847** Lanman *Summer in Wilderness* 34, I noticed on . . [the upper and lower rapids of the Mississippi River] a certain fly or miller, which is found at the evening hour flying about in immense numbers. They are called the Mormon fly, and I was told were found on these rapids alone. **1950** Bissell *Stretch on River* 29 **eMO**, Out in the street kids were being dragged along by the hand, and the smell of melting tar and squashed Mormon flies filled the air. **1967–68** *DARE* (Qu. R4, *A large winged insect that hatches in summer in great numbers around lakes or rivers, crowds around lights, lives only a day or so, and is good fish bait*) Infs **IL6, 25**, Mormon fly; **WI23**, Mormon fly—more down at Dubuque [IA]. **1983** *Capital Times* (Madison WI) 12 July 2/1 **eIA**, The flies, also known as mayflies and Mormon flies, infest the [Mississippi] river towns annually, as eggs laid a year earlier hatch in the July heat. . . Dead flies were piled a foot deep in spots . . and some steep streets were impassable because of the slippery bodies of the insects.

Mormon iron n Also *Mormon nails* Cf *Mexican iron* (at **Mexican B1**)

1968 Adams *Western Words* 200, *Mormon iron*—Rawhide; perhaps so called because the Mormons used rawhide instead of nails in the construction of their tabernacle as well as other structures. Also called *Mormon nails.*

Mormon level See **Mormon board**

Mormon poison n [So called because beverages containing caffeine are proscribed by the Mormon church] Cf **Mormon tea 2** Coffee.

1984 Lesley *Winterkill* 272 **neOR**, "If there's any leftover coffee in that thermos, bring it here. Got a corpse that needs reviving." "I can't drink that Mormon poison until I've had a shot," Jones said. "You bring any whiskey?"

Mormon rain(storm) n **chiefly ID** Cf **Arizona cloudburst, black blizzard, Idaho rain, Oklahoma rain**

A dust storm.

1939 FWP *ID Lore* 241, *Mormon rain*—a dust storm. **c1971** Hall *Snake River Valley, (A dry storm)* 3 infs, **cs,seID**, Mormon rainstorm. [Hall: None of the infs is a Mormon.] **1973** *DARE* File **swID**, A Mormon rainstorm is a dust storm—it does a farmer no good at all. **1981** *Ibid* **sID**, When a storm brings wind to stir up the dust but doesn't produce the needed rain, it's called a Mormon rainstorm.

Mormon silk See **Mormon buckskin**

Mormon stacker See **Mormon derrick**

Mormon tea n

1 A plant of the genus *Ephedra;* also the drink made from such a plant. [See quot 1985] **chiefly Desert SW** Also called **Brigham tea, canatillo, clapweed, desert tea, joint fir, ~ pine, Mexican tea 2, mountain rush, popotillo, shrubby horsetail, squaw tea, teamster tea, tepopote, whorehouse tea**

1910 AZ Ag. Exp. Sta. *Bulletin* 65.261, The more important are salt-bushes, . . winter fat . . and the green, rush-like twigs of . . Mormon tea. **1933** *Torreya* 3.61, A shrub valued by all desert dwellers is the Mormon Tea (*Ephedra viridis*). Equisetum-like in appearance, the Mormon Tea has slender, jointed stems with leaves reduced to rudimentary scales. . . A tea made from an infusion of the branches is regarded by Indians and Whites alike as a sovereign remedy in the treatment of disease. **1937** AZ Ag. Exp. Sta. *Bulletin* 68.220, Among beverages commonly used and made from other than fresh fruits are the well-known Mormon tea (*Ephedra*) with its sennalike taste. **1945** McAtee *Nomina Abitera* 7, Decoctions of these plants [=*Ephedra* spp] are used in the treatment of venereal diseases, a point recognized in the scientific name of one of them—*antisyphilitica.* **1957** *Plateau* 30.2.33 **AZ, UT**, Shrubby plants dot both the terraces and the higher plateaus. Perhaps the most common are the various species of saltbush or shadscale . . and two species of Mormon-tea. **1965** Teale *Wandering Through Winter* 26 **CA**, One evening . . Riley brewed medicinal-tasting Mormon tea from a desert plant, the naked joint fir. **1967–68** *DARE* (Qu. S26e, *Other wildflowers not yet mentioned;* not asked in early QRs) Inf **CA4**, Mormon tea; (Qu. BB50d, *Favorite spring tonics*) Inf **UT12**, Mormon tea. **1968** Abbey *Desert Solitaire* 28 **seUT**, I can see . . the green ephedra or Mormon tea, from which Indians and pioneers extracted a medicinal drink (contains ephedrine). **1985** Dodge *Flowers SW Deserts* 70, The harsh, stringy stems [of *Ephedra*] are green to yellow-green and, when dried, were used with the flowers in making a palatable brew, particularly by the Utah pioneers; hence the name Mormon-tea. **1990** *Plants SW* (Catalog) 68, *Mormon Tea. . .* Browsed by deer and the seed also attracts quail. . . Not hardy above 7,000 ft.

2 See quot. [So called because beverages containing caffeine are proscribed in the Mormon church] Cf **cambric tea**

1971 Brunvand *Guide Folkl. UT* 31, "Mormon tea" (hot water with cream and sugar added).

Mormon tree n [See quot 1942] **UT**

The Lombardy **poplar** (*Populus nigra* var *italica*).

1942 Stegner *Mormon Country* 21 **UT**, These are the "Mormon trees," Lombardy poplars. Wherever they went the Mormons planted them. They grew boldly and fast, without much tending, and they make the landscape of the long valleys of the Mormon Country something special and distinctive. **1966** Barnes–Jensen *Dict. UT Slang* 31, *Mormon tree. . .* The black or Lombardy Poplar (*Populus dilatata*).

Mormon weed n

A **velvetleaf** (here: *Abutilon theophrasti*).

1872 IL Dept. Ag. *Trans. for 1871* 9.ix, The Indian Mallow . . [is] variously known as . . "velvet leaf," "butter print," "Mormon weed," etc. **1892** *Jrl. Amer. Folkl.* 5.93, *Abutilon Avicenne. . .* Mormon weed; velvet-weed. Quincy, Ill. **1924** *Amer. Botanist* 30.108, *Abutilon Theo-*

phrasti. . . We are at a loss to know the origin of . . "Mormon-weed" also applied to our plant.

morngloam See **gloam**

morning bell n

A **morning glory 1.**

1967 *DARE* (Qu. S5, . . *Wild morning glory*) Inf **MI**69, Morning bells.

morning bloom n Also *morning bloomer*

A **morning glory 1.**

1967 *DARE* (Qu. S5, . . *Wild morning glory*) Inf **KY**34, Morning blooms, morning bloomers.

morning brides n Also *morning bride*

A plant of the western genus *Chaenactis.* Also called **false yarrow, pincushion.** For other names of var spp see **dusty maiden, golden girls**

1915 (1926) Armstrong-Thornber *Western Wild Flowers* 548, Morning Bride—*Chaenactis Fremontii.* . . the flowers are all pure white, or pinkish. **1932** Rydberg *Flora Prairies* 854, *Chaenactis* [spp] . . Morning Brides. Annual, biennial, or perennial herbs. **1963** Craighead *Rocky Mt. Wildflowers* 200, Morning-Brides—*Chaenactis douglasii.* . . This plant is often confused with Yarrow (*Achillea lanulosa*) or Dogfennel (*Anthemis cotula*), but these plants have rayflowers as well as diskflowers; Morning-brides has only diskflowers. **1971** Dodge *100 Desert Wildflowers* 94, Probably because it is one of the attractive white desert flowers, chaenactis is popularly called "morning bride."

morning dove See **mourning dove**

morning glory n

1 A plant of the family Convolvulaceae, usu of the genus *Ipomoea* or a **bindweed 1.** [See quot 1814] For other names of var spp of *Ipomoea* see **beach morning glory 2, bindweed 5, bush morning-glory, climbing glory, creeper 1, cypress vine 1, hat vine, man-of-the-earth 1, moonflower 1, railroad vine, tievine, white star, wild morning glory, wild potato;** for other names of var genera and spp see **alkali weed 1, bindweed 1, creeper 1, hell-vine 2, morning bell, morning bloom, morning vine, ponyfoot** Cf **baby morning-glory, false morning-glory**

1814 Pursh *Flora Americae* 1.146, *Ipomoea Nil.* . . Flowers beautiful pale blue, only open early in the morning, from which it has been called *Morning-glory.* **1848** Gray *Manual of Botany* 348, *Convolvulus.* . . *Bindweed. Morning-Glory.* . . Chiefly twining or trailing plants, often with milky juice. **1871** (1882) Stowe *Fireside Stories* 75 **NEng,** She sat down in the mornin'-glory porch, quite quiet, and didn't sing a word. **1888** (1891) AR State Geologist *Annual Rept.* 249, In cornfields, two species of morning glory (one of them *Ipomoea nil*) and another plant called blue-vine (*Cocculus carolinus*) does [sic] considerable damage. All three are twiners, and choke and bend the cornstalks; frequently so overrunning a field as to seriously impede the progress of a person walking through it. **1939** Tharp *Vegetation TX* 66, Carpet Morning glory (*Dichondra*); all regions. **1949** Moldenke *Amer. Wild Flowers* 267, Yellow flowers are rare in this family [=Convolvulaceae], but *I[pomoea] polyanthes* and *Operculina tuberosa,* both called *yellow morning-glory,* have bright yellow blossoms. They . . reach their northern boundary in our Gulf states. **1964** Munz *Shore Wildflowers* 46, The true Morning-Glory has a number of species near the [Pacific] coast, one of which . . is *Convolvulus Soldanella.* **1965–70** *DARE* (Qu. S5) 91 Infs, **widespread, but chiefly Sth, S Midl,** Morning glory; **OK**52, Blue morning glory; **IL**16, Japanese morning glory; **MN**16, Morning glory vine; **NJ**39, Old morning glory; **VA**75, Tato morning glory; (Qu. S8) Inf **CA**99, Morning glory; **CA**165, Morning glory vines; (Qu. S9) Infs **CA**65, 212, Morning glory; (Qu. S21, . . *Weeds . . that are a trouble in gardens and fields*) 21 Infs, **chiefly Midl,** Morning glory; (Qu. S23) Inf **FL**22, Morning glory; (Qu. S26a, . . *Wildflowers. . . Roadside flowers*) Inf **VA**64, Morning glory; (Qu. S26b) Inf **SC**10, Morning glory; (Qu. S26e, *Other wildflowers not yet mentioned*) Infs **DC**5, **KY**11, **MN**3, **NJ**21, **SC**32, **VT**16, Morning glory; **AR**49, White morning glory. **1967** *DARE* Wildfl QR (Craighead) Pl.17.2 **CA**24, Morning glory. **1976** Fleming *Wild Flowers FL* 65, Morning glory grows over surrounding vegetation, or sometimes trails on the ground; it blooms irregularly all year from central Florida to Louisiana and Texas.

2 =**hooded merganser.**

1923 U.S. Dept. Ag. *Misc. Circular* 13.6 **MI,** Hooded Merganser. . . *Vernacular Names.* . . *In local use.* . . Morning-glory. **1956** *AmSp*

30.185, Morning-glory—Hooded merganser—Mich. Seems to allude to the conspicuous white and black crest.

3 A pancake; a doughnut.

1941 *LANE* Map 284, Terms for various types of cakes fried in deep fat (not always clearly defined) . . *morning glory* [1 inf, **swME**]. **1968** *DARE* (Qu. H20b, . . *Names . . for pancakes*) Inf **MN**14, Morning glories. **1969** Sorden *Lumberjack Lingo* 79 **NEng, Gt Lakes,** *Morning glories*—Pancakes.

‡**4** The navel. Cf **DS** X34

1950 *WELS* (*Nicknames for the navel*) 1 Inf, **cWI,** Morning glory.

morning-glory bush See **bush morning-glory**

morning honeysuckle n

=**butterfly weed 2.**

1933 Small *Manual SE Flora* 952, *G[aura] biennis.* . . Morning-honeysuckle. **1949** Moldenke *Amer. Wild Flowers* 92, Of entirely different aspect are the morninghoneysuckles or butterflyflowers (*Gaura*) with narrow, stalkless leaves and small, white, pink, or red flowers borne in terminal spikes or racemes. Many species abound in the South and the Middle West.

morning, in the adv phr [Cf Scots adv phr *the morn* tomorrow, on the morrow] *arch* Cf **morning soon**

See quots.

1952 Brown *NC Folkl.* 1.566, *Morning, in the.* . . "I'm going to town in the morning about two o'clock [that is, in the afternoon of tomorrow]."—Granville county. Rare now. **1956** McAtee *Some Dialect NC* 30, *Morning, in the.* . . Sometime tomorrow.

morning lark n

See quot.

1967–68 *DARE* (Qu. Q15, . . *Kinds of larks*) Infs **NJ**3, **WI**48, Morning lark.

morning primrose n

An **evening primrose a;** see quots.

1953 Nelson *Plants Rocky Mt. Park* 111, Fragrant morning-primrose, *Oenothera caespitosa.* . . This plant grows in tufts among the rocks and bears large white flowers, 2 to 3 inches across, that turn pink with age. *Ibid,* Common morning-primrose, *Oenothera coronopifolia. Ibid,* Nuttall morning-primrose, *Oenothera nuttallii.* **1963** Craighead *Rocky Mt. Wildflowers* 121, Evening primrose—*Oenothera caespitosa.* . . Other names: Sandlily, Rockrose, Morning Primrose, Gumbo Primrose.

morning's milk n Cf **night's milk**

See quot 1899.

1899 (1912) Green *VA Folk-Speech* 287, *Morning's milk.* . . As the cows are milked twice a day [sic] that gotten in the morning is called *morning's milk.* That in the evening is called night's milk. **1917** *DN* 4.396 **neOH, CA, IL, KS, KY, LA, NEng, NY, SC,** *Morning's milk.* . . Milk that was milkt in the morning of the same day. **1919** *DN* 5.76 **NEng, CA,** *Morning's milk:* so far as I know, the universal use. I know no other; and this expression is common both in New England and California. **1927** *AmSp* 2.360 **cwWV,** *Morning's milk* . . the milk gotten in the morning. "The children like the morning's milk better." **1929** *AmSp* 5.123 **ME,** Morning's milk.

morning's morning n [Scots *morning* a drink of liquor taken before breakfast]

An early-morning drink; transf: an early-morning chew of snuff.

1914 *DN* 4.110 **cKS,** *Mornin's mornin.* . . Morning drink. **1925** *AmSp* 1.139 **Pacific NW,** When he dresses, the logger "rigs up." Usually he feels "haywire" when he wakens and he takes a rear of snoose [=a chew of snuff] for a "morning's morning."

morning soon adv phr Cf **morning, in the; soon**

1939 FWP *Guide NC* 98 **eNC,** The banker [=inhabitant of the outer banks of the NC coast] . . promises to do a task "morning soon," meaning the next day.

morning star n

1 =**hedge bindweed 1.**

1959 Carleton *Index Herb. Plants* 83, *Morning star:* Convolvulus sepium.

2 A **stickleaf** (here: *Mentzelia lindleyi*). Cf **blazing star 4, evening star 1**

1970 *DARE* (Qu. S26e, *Other wildflowers not yet mentioned;* not asked in early QRs) Inf **CA**195, Morning star.

morning sun n

A **goatsbeard 1** (here: *Tragopogon pratensis*).

1914 Georgia *Manual Weeds* 532, Meadow salsify—*Tragopogon pratensis*. . . Morning Sun, Noon-flower, Nap-at-noon. . . Heads solitary, terminal, golden yellow, nearly two inches broad. . . the flowers open at sunrise and are closed again by noon. **1935** (1943) Muenscher *Weeds* 523, *Tragopogon pratensis*. . . Noon-flower, Morning sun.

morning swallow n

See quot.

1969 *DARE* (Qu. Q20, . . *Kinds of swallows and birds like them*) Inf **MA**26, Morning swallow—another bird that lives around cat-of-nine-tails.

morning vine n

A **morning glory 1**.

1967 *DARE* (Qu. S5, . . *Wild morning glory*) Inf **MO**38, Morning vine.

morocco head n [Prob because the head and neck are the typical color of morocco leather]

The common **merganser:**, usu the female.

1888 Trumbull *Names of Birds* 65, [Common merganser:] To some Atlantic City gunners, Morocco-head. **1917** (1923) *Birds Amer.* 1.110, *Mergus americanus*. . . Other Names. . . Morocco-head (female). . . *Adult Female:* Head and neck, reddish-brown. **1928** Bailey *Birds NM* 148, The descriptive names of Buff-breasted Sheldrake for the drake and . . Morocco-head for the duck seem to belong to this species [=*Mergus merganser*]. **1944** Hausman *Amer. Birds* 519, Morocco-head (female)—see Merganser.

morocco jaw n

=**surf scoter.**

1888 Trumbull *Names of Birds* 103 **seNY**, Surf Scoter. . . At Bellport, L[ong] I[sland], Morocco-jaw. **1917** (1923) *Birds Amer.* 1.151, *Surf Scoter*. . . Other Names. . . Morocco-jaw.

Morocco millet n Cf Egyptian grass 2

=**Johnson grass 1.**

1889 Vasey *Ag. Grasses* 36, *Sorghum halepense* [sic] . . Johnson Grass. . . This grass is a native of Northern Africa and the country about the Mediterranean Sea. . . It has been called Egyptian grass . . and Morocco millet. **1914** Georgia *Manual Weeds* 22, *Sorghum halapense*. . . Morocco Millet. **1935** (1943) Muenscher *Weeds* 157, Johnson-grass, . . Morocco millet. . . Widespread throughout the southern states.

moronel n CA

A **honeysuckle 2** (here: *Lonicera subspicata*).

1901 Jepson *Flora CA* 474, [*Lonicera interrupta*] Var. *subspicata* (Gray). Moronel. **1938** Van Dersal *Native Woody Plants* 159, Moronel. . . A climbing or trailing vine or small to large shrub; evergreen. **1970** *DARE* Tape **CA**193, There's another vine that grows all over the scrub oaks . . it's called moronel. We used to make tea out of that.

moroshka n Also *marooshka, marowska, moroshkie* [Russ *moroshka*] AK

A **cloudberry** (here: *Rubus chamaemorus*).

[**1870** Dall *Alaska* 443, All these berries, but especially the salmon berry or *morósky* of the Russians, are excellent anti-scorbutics.] **1882** Elliott *Seal Islands* 174, Moroshka (Russian).—The fruit of *Rubus chamaemorus*. "Little frost berry." **1886** Elliott *Our Arctic Province* 411, The only indigenous fruit which this large population of the Lower Kuskokvim can enjoy is that of the pretty little "moroshkie," or red raspberry [Footnote: *Rubus chamaemorus*], which grows in great abundance on its short, tiny stalks throughout all swales and over rolling tundra. **1901** Brooks et al. *Reconnaissances AK* 166, The salmon berry (*Rubus chamaemorus*), called also cloud berry and marooshka, is probably the most important food plant in the region. The berries are said to be gathered in large quantities by the Eskimo and preserved in seal oil for winter use. **1914** in 1991 Tabbert *Dict. Alaskan Engl.* 177, Associated with the mosses are the "marowskas" and cranberries, both of which are of some importance in that they form a part of the food supply of the people of the island [=Afognak].

morphodite n Also *morfadite, morfidite, morfodike, morphadite, morphidite, morphodike, morphodye, morphydite, mor-*

phydyke [Varr of *hermaphrodite;* cf *OED mophrodite* (also *morphrodite*) 1706 →, *EDD morfreydite*] Cf **muffledice**

A hermaphrodite; a person with characteristics of the other sex; a homosexual person.

1896 *DN* 1.421 **CT, NY,** *Morphodite* . . for *hermaphrodite*. **1909** *DN* 3.400 **nwAR,** *Morphodite*. . . Hermaphrodite. **1921** *DN* 5.118 **KY,** *Morfadite*. . . Hermaphrodite, having the characteristics of both sexes. **1923** *DN* 5.246 **KS,** *Morphodite*. Corruption of hermaphrodite. **c1925** in 1944 *ADD* **cNY,** |mə'rfədaɪk|, -|aɪt|. Usual. **1926** *DN* 5.401 **Ozarks,** *Morphodite*. . . Hermaphrodite. **1930** Shoemaker *1300 Words* 41 **cPA Mts** (as of c1900), *Morfidite*—A person of double sex, a hermaphrodite. **1939** *LANE* Map 212 *(Mongrel)* 1 inf, **sNH,** *Mongrel,* a [mɒθədeɪt] (i.e. hermaphrodite); *cur,* a dog of mixed breed. **1940** Harris *Folk Plays* 139 **NC,** *John Edward*. . . You don't know whether "Babe Ruth" is a girl or boy. *Savannah.* Don't care if she's a morphydite. **1942** McAtee *Dial. Grant Co. IN Suppl. 1* 7 (as of 1890s), *Morfadite, morfodike* . . variants of hermaphrodite. **1943** *New Yorker* 18 Dec 46 **NYC,** Once an older boy whispered that a schoolmate of mine was a 'morphodye,' which was a new one to me. **1944** *PADS* 2.25 **cwOH, cwNC,** *Morfadite* ['mɔrfɪ,daɪt]. . . A hermaphrodite. **1946** McCullers *Member* 17 **AL,** The last booth was always very crowded, for it was the booth of the Half-Man Half-Woman, a morphidite and a miracle of science. **1954** *Harder Coll.* **cwTN,** *Morphodite* [mɔrfidaɪt]. . . Hermaphrodite. **c1960** *Wilson Coll.* **cwKY,** *Morfadite* (or *morphodite* or *-dike*). . . An hermaphrodite. **1965–70** *DARE* (Qu. HH39, *A homosexual man*) 46 Infs, **scattered,** Morphodite; **AR**47, Morphodite—half woman, half man; **AR**55, Morphodite—has parts of both sexes; **IN**73, Morphodite—obsolete; **LA**40, Morphodite—someone who has characteristics of both sexes; **MN**30, Morphodite—a mannish woman; **MA**15, Morphodite—male or female; **NC**84, Morphodite—man's role; **OR**3, Morphodite—a woman can also be a morphodite; **TN**26, Morphodite—has characteristics of both sexes; **VA**69, Morphodite—main word around here—have quite a few like that around here; **IN**10, ['morfədaɪk]; **NJ**53, ['morfidaɪt] [Of all Infs responding to the question, 59% were old, 23% gs educ or less; of those giving these responses, 82% were old, 46% gs educ or less.]; (Qu. HH38, *A womanish man*) 10 Infs, **scattered,** Morphodite; **MA**6, Morphodite—they have both fixtures—called one "the put and take woman"; **OK**28, Morphodite—have both male and female parts; (QR, near Qu. HH38) Inf **IL**143, A mannish woman is a morphodite—did man's work. **1983** *MJLF* 9.1.48 **ceKY** (as of 1956), *Morphadite* . . a hermaphrodite. **1985** Rattray *Advent. Dimon* 169 **Long Is. NY,** "The whale . . suckles his young." "Suckles his young? Is he some kind of morphydyke? Your learning has softened your brain, Doctor."

morral n Usu |mə'ræl, mor'æl| Also sp *marrell, morrall, morrel* [Span *morral*] SW, esp NM, wTX

A coarse cloth sack usu used for carrying provisions or as a nose bag; hence fig phr *put on the morral* to eat.

1915 *DN* 4.227 **wTX,** *Morrall*. . . A nose-bag, from which horses eat grain while in harness. **1920** Hunter *Trail Drivers TX* 176 (as of c1880), The coin, if of considerable amount, was put in saddle bags, morrals, etc., and secreted in remote corners of the house, or up under the roof. **1931** (1960) Dobie *Open Range* 308 **SW,** *Morral*. . . A fibre bag; used both as a nose bag and to carry articles in. **1932** Bentley *Spanish Terms* 169, *Morral* (Spanish, [mo:r'ra:l]; *English*, [mor'æl]) A nose-bag; a feed bag. *Morral* is widely current in the cattle country of the Southwest, particularly in Texas. **1933** *AmSp* 8.1.30 **TX,** *Morral.* A nosebag. *To put on the morral* (applied to a person), to eat. **c1937** in 1970 Yetman *Voices* 39 **TX** [Black], Sometime she take her old morrel—dat a sack make for to carry things in. **1958** Latham *Meskin Hound* 104 **cTX,** Jim saddled Blue, put hammer, pliers, and staples into a morral and hung it over his saddle horn. **1962** Atwood *Vocab. TX* 50, *Bag used to feed a horse*. . . In the old ranch country the Spanish loanword *morral* remains in regular use. . . The *morral,* as some informants point out, was used more often for the carrying of one's belongings than for the feeding of horses. **1966** *DARE* (Qu. F20, *A cloth container for feed*) Inf **NM**12, We called the canvas nose bag a morral [mə'ræl]—made them also from a gunny sack; **TX**43, Morral [mə'ræl]. **1971** Green *Village Horse Doctor* 259 **NM,** He had a cactus-fiber marrell slung over his shoulder . . , and it looked like it was still about half full of grub. **1981** Pederson *LAGS Basic Materials* (Bag or sack potatoes are shipped in) 1 inf, **csTX,** Morral [mə'ræ˞·ə˩]—Mexican term, made of jute or tow sack.

morrel n[1] See morel n[1]

morrel n[2] See morral

married See marry

morris n [Var of *merels; OED* 1590 →] Cf **mill** n¹ **3, nine-men's morris**

A board game in which players place counters at the corners or midpoints of three concentric squares, trying to get three in a row.

1825 Neal *Brother Jonathan* 1.7 **CT,** Peters had beaten him . . first in argument . . ; then, at fox and geese; then, at morris; then, at checkers, or draughts. **1949** *PADS* 11.34 **ME,** Morris. . . A game played with counters, not unlike fox and geese.

mort n [*OED* 1694 →] **chiefly sAppalachians**

A large quantity or number; an abundance.

1899 (1912) Green *VA Folk-Speech* 287, *Mort. . .* A very great number or quantity. **1931** Hannum *Thursday April* 9 **wNC,** They say he got him a heap of doctor l'arnin' down country and can cure a mort of sickness. **1938** Rawlings *Yearling* 196 **FL,** "A heap o' taters, ain't it, son?" "Hit's a mort of 'em." **1939** (1962) Thompson *Body & Britches* 149 **NY,** Heading west toward the Adirondacks, you are bound to hear a mort of tall tales from the guides. **1941** Glasgow *In This Our Life* 317 **VA,** Minerva reminded herself, that she had a mort of things to be thankful for. **1944** *PADS* 2.10 **NC, TN, VA,** *Mort. . .* A quantity. **1952** Brown *NC Folkl.* 1.567, *Mort, a: . .* A great many; very much. **1952** Giles *40 Acres* 217 **csKY,** It took a mort of rocks to build that chimney. **1955** Taber *Stillmeadow Daybook* 96 **swCT,** What a mort of pests we do inherit. **1991** Still *Wolfpen Notebooks* 50 **sAppalachians,** We've had a mort of deaths amongst the old folks the past winter.

mortal adv Pronc-sp *mortial* **esp sAppalachians, NEng**
=**mortally 1.**

1884 Murfree *TN Mts.* 278 **eTN,** He air mortal low with the fever. **1891** (1967) Freeman *New Engl. Nun* 85, It's 'cause . . they're so mortal homely themselves. **1911** (1916) Porter *Harvester* 346 **IN,** You do look mortal tired. **1914** *DN* 4.76 **ME, nNH,** *Mortal, mortial. . .* Very. "She was mortal hum'ly [=homely]." **1937** (1963) Hyatt *Kiverlid* 12 **KY,** She's mortal proud o' her pineys. **1941** *Sat. Eve. Post* 10 May 36 **sAppalachians,** She knelt by the hearth, frying a skillet of hominy, cooking it mortal slow. **1956** McAtee *Some Dialect NC* 30, So mortal hot. **c1960** *Wilson Coll.* **csKY,** He's mortal ugly.

mortally adv

1 Extremely, seriously, intensely.

1930 (1935) Porter *Flowering Judas* 64 **TX,** Oh, I do mortally wish they would keep out of our business. **1942** Perry *Texas* 136, If he leaves in a particular hurry, his neighbors may remark . . "He was mortally toppin' cotton." **1973** *DARE* File **OK,** East Texas hillbilly types [say] Mortally hot, hard, big, etc. **1975** Newell *If Nothin' Don't Happen* 133 **nwFL,** I mortally love to fish—just any kind of fishin'.

2 in neg constrs: At all.

1955 Ritchie *Singing Family* 48 **seKY,** I just couldn't mortally stand to sit still on that log bench and that tune snakin around so.

mortase See **tomato**

mortgage alley See **mortgage hill**

mortgaged property n

A person engaged to be married.

1909 *DN* 3.350 **eAL, wGA,** *Mortgaged property. . .* An engaged person. . . "No use lookin' at her. She's mortgaged property." **1970** *DARE* Tape **TN62,** He was a very fine young man, and several of the girls in the neighborhood would like to have caught him, but he was mortgaged property, so he went back and got his girl.

Mortgage Hill n Also *Mortgage Alley,* ~ *Row;* for addit varr see quot

The well-to-do section of a town or city.

1965–70 *DARE* (Qu. II24, *Names or nicknames for the part of a town where the well-off people live*) 36 Infs, **scattered, but esp Inland Nth, N Midl,** Mortgage Hill; 15 Infs, **esp Inland Nth, N Midl,** Mortgage Row; 13 Infs, **scattered,** Mortgage Alley (or Flat, Heights, Hollow, Knob, Lane, Manor, Mesa, -ville); (Qu. C35, *Nicknames for the different parts of your town or city*) Infs **KS8, KY65, NH10, NC38, PA40, 220, SD2,** Mortgage Hill; **AL30, ID4, IA46, KS5, MI93, MN6, OH12, OR1,** Mortgage Alley (or Row, Heights, Lane, Mountain).

mortial See **mortal**

mortification root n
=**marshmallow 1.**

1876 Hobbs *Bot. Hdbk.* 71, Mortification root, Marsh mallow root,

Althaea officinalis. **1910** Graves *Flowering Plants* 278 **CT,** Mortification Root. . . The root is very mucilaginous and is used in the manufacture of confectionery. **1924** *Amer. Botanist* 30.106, The true marshmallow. . . is an interesting little species. . . Medicinal uses are indicated by such terms as "sweat-weed" and "mortification-root." **1974** (1977) Coon *Useful Plants* 183, *Althaea officinalis. . .* Mortification root. . . The "officinalis" part of the name would indicate its long use in medicine as a demulcent and for conditions of the urinary tract. It has also been used as an ingredient for coughs and bronchitis. Dried and cleaned roots have been recommended for teething babies.

mortworp See **moldwarp**

moscheto See **mesquite**

moschettoe See **mosquito** n¹

Moses n

1 =**Adam 1.**

1967 *DARE* (Qu. II26, *Joking ways of saying that you would not know who somebody is: "I wouldn't know him from _____."*) Inf **IL4,** Moses.

2 See quot.

1968 *DARE* (Qu. F37, *. . An indoor toilet*) Inf **WI52,** Moses.

Moses' firebush n Cf **burning bush 3, fire bush**

Perh a **summer cypress.**

1970 *DARE* (Qu. S26d) Inf **FL48,** Moses' firebush—red leaves at top.

Moses-in-the-bulrushes n

1 also *Moses-in-a-boat, Moses-in-the-bulrush* (or *bullrushes*), *Moses-in-the-cradle, Moses-on-a-raft:* A foliage plant *(Tradescantia spathacea)* often grown in cultivation. **chiefly FL** Also called **man-in-a-boat, oyster plant 3, sailor-in-a-boat**

1916 *DN* 4.302 **FL,** *Moses-in-the-bulrushes. . .* The flower of a kind of spider's-wort *(Tradescontia* [sic] *concolor* [=*Rhoeo spathacea*]). Tiny white flowers are enclosed in red cuplike leaf. **1955** *S. Folkl. Qrly.* 19.233 **FL,** Religious fancy is responsible for the name *Moses in the Bullrushes* (Rhoeo discolor). The plant bears its tiny white flowers in a boat-shaped bract that rises from the axil of pointed, rather stiff green leaves. **1959** Carleton *Index Herb. Plants* 83, *Moses-in-the-bullrushes:* Rhoea [sic] discolor; Scirpus lacustris [=*Scirpus acutus*]. . . *Moses-in-the-cradle:* Rhoea [sic] discolor. **1966** *DARE* (Qu. S1) Inf **FL31,** Moses-in-the-bulrush. **1970** *DARE* Tape **MI112,** I have a lot of things, oddities. . . Moses-in-the-bulrushes, no, no, Moses-in-the-cradle. **1971** Gantz *Naturalist in S. FL* 99, Oyster plant (Moses-in-the-bulrushes): *Rhoeo spathacea. Ibid* 92 **Miami FL,** I have always known it as the oyster plant, but here it has the more colorful name of Moses-in-the-bulrushes. **1976** Bailey–Bailey *Hortus Third* 966, [*Rhoeo*] *spathacea. . .* Moses-on-a-raft, Moses-in-a-boat, Moses-in-the-cradle, Moses-in-the-bulrushes. **1986** Pederson *LAGS Concordance,* 1 inf, **neMS,** Moses in the cradle—plant in her terrarium.

2 also *Moses weed:* A bulrush (here: *Scirpus acutus*).

1942 *Torreya* 8.158 **NM,** *Scirpus acutus. . .* Moses weed. **1959** [see **1** above].

Moses-in-the-cradle, Moses-on-a-raft See **Moses-in-the-bulrushes 1**

Moses weed See **Moses-in-the-bulrushes 2**

mosey See **mossy**

moshey n Also *mosey sugar, sugar mosey* Also sp *moashi, mojay, mojh(e)y, moshie, moszhy, mozey, mozh(e)y* [PaGer *mooschi* taffy] **sePA**

Candy made of boiled sugar syrup or molasses.

1849 W. Duane *Let. to Bartlett* 22 Jan. (MS.) *(DAE),* Sugar Mosey or Mosey Sugar, the name of a cake made of sugar, for children, in Harrisburgh Pa. **1870** *Nation* 28 July 56 **sePA,** "Mosey sugar" was their great delicacy when they grew a little older. . . It was a black molasses candy—not cake, as Bartlett says—scalloped at the edges like our cakes of maple sugar. **1908** *German Amer. Annals* 10.35 **sePA,** *Mozhy (mozhey).* Molasses candy. "We made mozhy at the party." . . fr Pa. Ger. *mozhy; mŏlŏsich,* molasses. **1916** *DN* 4.338 **PA,** *Mozey. . .* Molasses candy; also, nut candy. **1939** Berolzheimer *U.S. Cookbook* 325 [PaGer], *Mojhy apples*—10 apples / 10 wooden lollypop sticks / 1 cup sugar / 1 cup corn sirup / . . Combine sugar and sirup in deep pan. . . Let boil to 300° F. or until a small quantity when dropped in cold water becomes brittle. . . Then dip apples in sirup and wind in circular motion until thoroughly covered. **1950** Klees *PA Dutch* 431 **sePA,** Mojhey is one of the sweets of childhood. . . [I]t is a simple candy and easy to make. . . Boil 1 cup of medium molasses, 1 cup of brown sugar, 1 cup of water, and 1 tablespoonful of vinegar. . . add 2 tablespoonfuls of butter. Pour into small patty pans in the bottom of which peanuts, walnuts, or shellbarks have been placed. **1952** *Reading Times* 8 Sept 1/1, *(Mathews Coll.)* **sePA,** The usual collection of calorie counters, from steak sandwiches to moszhy apples, rang up a good day's business. **1953** *PA Dutchman* May 5/2 *(Mathews Coll.),* And the lad, by custom, was bound to unloose his purse string and buy them some candy, *moashi* perhaps. **1956** *Reading Times* 25 Aug 5/2 *(Mathews Coll.)* **cePA,** There is no better place to be than "on top of the world" via ferris wheel with sweet "moshie" apples. **1968** *DARE* (Qu. H80, *Kinds of candy . . made at home*) Inf **PA**159, Molasses candy; popcorn balls called mojay [moǰe]. [Inf of PaGer background] **1991** *DARE* File **sePA,** He also tells us that real "moshey" contains molasses, whereas the red apples that I thought were "moshey" apples do not contain molasses, but some other substitute for molasses. . . It seems that only us older natives of these parts still know the word "moshey."

moskeet(er) See **mosquito** n[1]

moskeet spider n [**mosquito** n[1]]
A **daddy longlegs 1.**
   1966 *DARE* (Qu. R28, . . *Kinds of spiders*) Inf **AR**5, Moskeet spider, granddaddy—very similar; [moskeet spider] is smaller.

mosqueit See **mesquite**

mosquito n[1] Usu |məˈskito, -tə|; also freq |məˈskitɚ| and aphet |ˈskitɚ| Also sp *moschettoe, moskeet(er), muskeeter, musquito, skeet(er), skitter;* for addit pronc and sp varr see **A** below
A Forms.
   1622 Mourt's Relation *Iournall Plimoth* 46, What with . . fleas within doores, and Muskeetoes without, wee could hardly sleepe. **1682** in 1836 Carroll *Hist. Coll. SC* 2.136, There are few Insects in *Carolina* that can reasonably be complain'd of, except a sort of Gnats, which they call *Muscatoes.* **1765** (1942) Bartram *Diary of a Journey* 21 **Sth,** In Charls town all good livers has what they call muschata curtains. . . We lay down amongst . . muschatoes. *Ibid* 23, A monstrous sised mosketo. . . ye mscketos being as thick as bees in A swarm. *Ibid* 27, Ye muschatos was very troublesom. *Ibid* 32, Lodged . . near A pond & musketoes. *Ibid* 42, Muskatoes. . . The muskitoes [were] troublesome. *Ibid* 50, Musscketoes. **1778** Carver *Travels N. Amer.* 106, All the wilderness between the Mississippi and Lake Superior is called by the Indians the Moschettoe Country. **1785** in 1908 Mathews *A. Ellicott* 41, We are much pestered with Muskeetoes and Knats. **1788** (1821) Asbury *Jrl.* 2.36, The gnats are almost as troublesome here, as the moschetoes in the low-lands of the sea-board. **1806** (1905) Clark *Orig. Jrls. Lewis & Clark Exped.* 5.323, My Musquetor Bear has a number of small holes worn through [which] they pass in. **1817** in 1920 *WI Mag. Hist.* 3.344 **VT,** Moscketoes beat all I ever met with before. **1835** (1927) Evans *Exped. Rocky Mts.* 14.201 **IN,** Muskatoes most intolerably bad. **1838** Kettell *Yankee Notions* 106, You might as well look out for beef / On a moscheto. **1839** *Spirit of Times* 14 Dec 495, I was fas asleep, and dreaming dat a big skeeter was a biten me. **1848** Lowell *Biglow* 23 **'Upcountry' MA,** I felt a thing go thru my leg,—'t wuz nothin' more 'n a skeeter! **1849** Howitt *Our Cousins in OH* 163, It was necessary to put up musquito-curtains to the children's beds. **1872** Twain *Roughing It* 27 **KS,** Here I've sot . . a-bust'n muskeeters. **1873** (1874) Leland *Egyptian Sketch Book* 38, Egypt is inhabited by . . musk-eaters,—as they pronounce the word in New Jersey. **1893** Shands *MS Speech* 57, Skeeter [skitə]. Negro for *mosquito.* **1904** Day *Kin o' Ktaadn* 194 **ME,** Stop that swarm o' moskeeters. **1909** *DN* 3.370 **eAL, wGA,** Skeeter. . . Slang. **1914** *DN* 4.132, Skeet. . . Colloquial. "There were so many skeets on the lake we had to take a smudge along." **1922** Gonzales *Black Border* 314 **sSC, GA coasts** [Gullah glossary], Muskittuh. **1936** *AmSp* 11.149 **eTX,** Words spelled with *o* in initial unstressed open syllables. . . are for the most part regularly pronounced with [ə]. Examples: Bologna, . . mosquito, . . etc. . . The same speakers frequently omit the first syllable of . . *mosquito,* . . [ˈskitə/ɚ]. **1941** *AmSp* 16.9 **eTX** [Black], Spellings with *o.* . . Banjo, mosquito [etc], all end in [ə]. **1942** Hall *Smoky Mt. Speech* 57 **wNC, eTN,** Mosquito. . . [ˈskitə]. **1950** *WELS* **WI** (*Other names or nicknames for a mosquito*) 9 Infs, Skeeter; 2 Infs, Skeet; 1 Inf, [skito]; 1 Inf, Skitter. **1951** Johnson *Resp. to PADS 20* **DE,** Moskeet. **1965–70** *DARE* (Qu. R15a, . . *Names or nicknames . . for mosquitoes*) 360 Infs, **widespread, but less freq NEng,** Skeeter; **OH**45, 66, Skeeta; **NY**142, Skeeto; **MI**96, Skeets; **NC**41, Skaters; 32 Infs, **scattered,** (Black, blind, etc) mosquito(es); **IL**48, **IN**14, **NJ**67, Moskeet; **SC**34, [ˈmʌskitə]; **KY**34, **TX**13, Moskeeter; **SC**32, [ˈmoskitɚz]; **MD**3, [məˈskitə]; **NC**78, [məˈskidɚ]; **NY**34, [ˌməˈskedə]; **CT**26, M'skeete. [Further exx through-

out *DS*] **1966** *DARE* Tape **AL**2, It killed mosquitoes [məsˈkitɚz]. **1968** *DARE* FW Addit **GA**22, [ˈskitɚ]. **1987** Jones–Jackson *When Roots Die* 101 **sSC coast** [Gullah], Don't raise a hand at mosquito. Let skita bite. **1989** Pederson *LAGS Tech. Index* 214 **Gulf Region,** 501 infs gave proncs of the type [məˈskitə], 77 [məˈskitɚ], 61 [məˈskito]. There was considerable variation in the pronc of the first syllable, but only [mɨ-] (in addition to [mə-]) was at all common. There were 8 instances of [ɪ] for [i] in the second syllable. 54 infs gave the aphet forms [ˈskita(r), -to] and 3 [ˈskitə]. 76 infs gave proncs with initial stress, chiefly of the type [ˈmʌskitə]; there was a single instance of the apocopated form [ˈmʌskit].]
B Senses.
1 Std: an insect of the family Culicidae. For names of var genera and spp see **airplane 2, boy dog, brasshead, buzzer 2, cousin 2, day mosquito, dive bomber, drill bug, freshwater mosquito, gallinipper 1a, grandfather graybeard 1, he** n **3, horse mosquito, humpbacked skeeter, jayhawk** n **3, Jersey mosquito 1, katynipper 2, maringouin, mitsy, nighthawk 4, Paul Bunyan mosquito, rain-barrel ~, red-horse ~, salt-marsh ~, saltwater ~, snow ~, spring ~, stinger, summer mosquito, swamp ~, Texas ~, tree-hole ~** Cf **blind mosquito, jack ~, third-shift ~**
2 =**dragonfly.**
   1966–70 *DARE* (Qu. R2, . . *The dragonfly*) Inf **LA**6, He's just a big old mosquito; **MO**8, Big mosquitoes; **PA**246A, Skeeter. **1968** *AmSp* 43.53, Answers written in for 'dragonfly' . . included . . *mosquito* [1 of 1,518 infs].

mosquito n[2] See **mesquite**

mosquito bar See **bar** n[3]

mosquito bill n esp **CA**
=**shooting star.**
   1897 Parsons *Wild Flowers CA* 206, Among the children the various forms [of *Dodecatheon*] are known by a number of names, such as . . "mosquito-bills." **1901** Brooks et al. *Reconnaissances AK* 172, *Dodecatheon frigidum.* . . Mosquito bill. . . Grows in moist grassy places inland. **1920** Rice–Rice *Pop. Studies CA Wild Flowers* 86, The Shooting Star or Dodocatheon [sic] seems to have more popular names than most of the other wild plants. . . The most common of these are Shooting Stars, . . Mosquito Bills, . . and Prairie Pointers. **1949** Moldenke *Amer. Wild Flowers* 235, In . . *D[odecatheon] patulum,* the flowers are white, . . and in the *mosquitobills* . ., *D. hendersonii,* the corolla is purple. . . Both are native of California. **1976** Bailey–Bailey *Hortus Third* 393, [*Dodecatheon*] Hendersonii. . . Mosquito-bills. Rice-grain bulblets present at flowering.

mosquito catcher n
1 also *mosquito chaser:* =**dragonfly.** Cf **mosquito hawk 2a**
   1950 *WELS* (*Other names for the dragonfly*) 1 Inf, **cWI,** Mosquito chaser. **1968–69** *DARE* (Qu. R2, . . *The dragonfly*) Inf **IL**69, Mosquito catchers; **AK**9, Mosquito catchers—on duck flats. **1971** Bright *Word Geog. CA & NV* 114 **cnCA,** Mosquito catchers—1 [inf]—Sierra [County]. **1973** Allen *LAUM* 1.319 (as of c1950), Mosquito catcher [2 infs, **nwMN**]. **1986** Pederson *LAGS Concordance,* 2 infs, **cnAL, seTX,** Mosquito catcher(s).
2 =**nighthawk 1.**
   1967 *DARE* (Qu. Q20, . . *Kinds of swallows and birds like them*) Inf **SC**62, Mosquito catcher.

mosquito chaser See **mosquito catcher 1**

mosquito doctor n [Prob blend of **mosquito hawk 2a** + **snake doctor**]
=**dragonfly.**
   1981 Pederson *LAGS Basic Materials (Dragonfly)* 1 inf, **nwMS,** Skeeter doctor [*LAGS* Ed: inf doubtful]; 1 inf, **cMS,** Mosquito doctors [*LAGS* Ed: long pause between words].

mosquito eater See **mosquito hawk 2b**

mosquito fern n Also *mosquito plant* [See quot 1938]
A fern of the genus *Azolla,* usu *A. caroliniana.* Also called **water fern, water velvet**
   1938 Small *Ferns SE States* 388, *Azolla* floats on the surface of the water and in still bodies of water it propagates rapidly and commonly forms carpets dense enough to conceal the water. It is in fact sometimes called mosquito-fern because it prevents the growth of mosquitoes

in pools. **1952** Davis *Flora ID* 47, *A[zolla] caroliniana* . . *Mosquito Fern* . . very resistant to water, bright green early in season, becoming tinted with red and finally an intense red by autumn. **1968** Radford et al. *Manual Flora Carolinas* 33, *Mosquito Fern.* . . Plants green to dark red, free-floating. **1976** Bailey–Bailey *Hortus Third* 132, *Azolla* [spp] . . Mosquito fern. *Ibid, [Azolla] caroliniana* . . Mosquito plant.

mosquito fish n [See quot 1933]
A small, surface-feeding fish (*Gambusia affinis*). Also called **killifish 2, potgut, topminnow**

1933 LA Dept. of Conserv. *Fishes* 450, The Mosquito Fish has well earned its name. . . Ranging originally in the marshes, ditches and lagoons of the South Atlantic and Gulf States and westward through lowland streams, [it] was found to be an insatiable searcher for mosquito larvae and pupae. *Ibid* 451, Mosquito Fishes have been introduced into many foreign lands including Hawaii, . . and have been of great value in reducing the prevalence of malaria by destroying the mosquitoes. **1947** Hubbs–Lagler *Fishes Gt. Lakes* 78, Mosquitofish were introduced into Michigan during the early 1940's. . . Mosquito larvae . . suspend themselves from the surface film of the water and are ready prey for mosquitofish. **1963** Sigler–Miller *Fishes UT* 120, *Gambusia affinis affinis.* . . serves to some extent as a bait and forage fish. This mosquitofish is native to central United States, from southern Illinois and southern Indiana to Alabama and the mouth of the Rio Grande, Texas. **1967–69** *DARE* (Qu. P3, *Freshwater fish that are not good to eat*) Inf **HI**2, Mosquito fish; (Qu. P7, *Small fish used as bait for bigger fish*) Inf **CA**130, Mosquito fish. **1971** Brown *Fishes MT* 145, The diet of the mosquitofish includes all kinds of tiny aquatic plants and animals. **1991** Amer. Fisheries Soc. *Common Names Fishes* 35, *Gambusia affinis* . . western mosquitofish.

mosquito fly n esp Gulf States, S Atl Cf mosquito hawk 2a
=dragonfly.
1964 O'Hare *Ling. Geog. E. MT* 128, The long insect with two pairs of transparent wings. . . [1 inf] mosquito flies. **1967–68** *DARE* (Qu. R2, . . *The dragonfly*) Infs **GA**17, **SC**63, Mosquito fly. **c1970** Pederson *Dial. Surv. Rural GA*, 1 inf, seGA, Mosquito fly, mosquito hawks, skeeta hawks. **1981** Pederson *LAGS Basic Materials*, 2 infs, **csAL, cnLA,** Mosquito fly; 1 inf, **ceGA,** Mosquito fly—hovers over stagnant water; 1 inf, **cnLA,** Skeeter fly—same as mosquito hawk.

mosquito gull n
Either the **black tern** or the **least tern**.
1956 MA Audubon Soc. *Bulletin* 40.22 **RI,** Least Tern. . . Mosquito Gull . . From its small size. *Ibid* 79 **RI,** Black Tern. Mosquito Gull.

mosquito hawk n
1 Either of two birds:
a =nighthawk 1.
1709 (1967) Lawson *New Voyage* 148 **NC,** *East-India* Bats or Musqueto Hawks, are the Bigness of a Cuckoo, and much of the same Colour. . . They appear only in the Summer, and live on Flies, which they catch in the Air, as Gnats, Musquetos, &c. **1845** Green *Jrl. Texian Exped.* 133 **TX,** In their balldress they look like winged creatures, and the moscheto hawk, in stooping after its tiny prey, does not appear more lightsome. **1873** IL Dept. Ag. *Trans. for 1872* 10.352, No person shall . . kill any . . swallow, martin, mosquito hawk, whip-poor-will [etc]. **1904** (1910) Wheelock *Birds CA* 194, California Nighthawk. . . Common names: Bull Bat; Mosquito Hawk. **1927** Forbush *Birds MA* 2.306, Mosquito hawk. [*Ibid* 309, The late Professor Harvey of the Maine State College found remains of 500 mosquitoes in a Nighthawk's stomach.] **1950** *WELS* **WI,** 1 Inf, Mosquito hawk—a bird similar to a nighthawk, but smaller; (*Other birds that come out only after dark*) 1 Inf, Mosquito hawk. **1956** MA Audubon Soc. *Bulletin* 40.81, Mosquito Hawk. . . It preys to some extent upon mosquitoes. **1966–70** *DARE* (Qu. Q3, . . *Birds that come out only after dark*) Infs **MI**23, **NV**5, **WA**2, Mosquito hawk; **MA**78, Mosquito hawk [same as] nighthawk, nightjar. **1973** Allen *LAUM* 1.319 (as of c1950), 1 inf, ceND, Mosquito hawk . . —a bird, not an insect; = nighthawk. **1981** Pederson *LAGS Basic Materials*, 1 inf, **nwFL,** Mosquito hawk is a bird and an insect; 1 inf, **csLA,** Skeeter hawk is a cuckoo [sic] bird that catches mosquitoes.

b =Mississippi kite.
1924 Howell *Birds AL* 130, In some localities [the Mississippi kite] is known as the "mosquito hawk." **1946** Hausman *Eastern Birds* 181, Louisiana Kite, Blue Kite, Mosquito Hawk. **1955** Forbush–May *Birds* 98, Mississippi Kite. . . Mosquito Hawk.

2 Any of several insects:

a =dragonfly. chiefly Sth, but scattered Missip Valley See Map and Map Section Cf mosquito catcher 1, ~ fly
1737 (1911) Brickell *Nat. Hist. NC* 163, The *Muskeetoe-Hawks*, are Insects, so called, from their continually hunting after *Muskeetoes*, and killing and eating them. **1832** J. Pickering *Inquiries of Emigrant* 59 *(OEDS),* Thousands of long large flies, similar to the English dragon fly, but a little smaller, are flying about the fields; they are called musquito hawks, on account of their killing and living on those insects. **1870** MO State Entomol. *Annual Rept.* 46, "Mosquito Hawks" (*Libellulae*) and bats, doubtless destroy many of the moths. **1903** *DN* 2.321 seMO, *Mosquito-hawk.* . . Dragon-fly or darning-needle. **1907** *DN* 3.233 nwAR, *Mosquito-hawk.* . . Dragon-fly, devil's darning needle. **1909** *DN* 3.350 eAL, wGA, *Mosquito-hawk.* . . The dragon-fly, especially one of the larger varieties. **1946** *PADS* 5.30 **Chesapeake Bay,** Mosquito hawk. *Ibid* 6.21 ceNC (as of 1900–10), *Mosquito hawk.* . . The dragon fly. **1948** Davis *Word Atlas Gt. Lakes* app qu 77, 7 (of 233) infs, **IN, IL, MI,** Mosquito hawk. **1949** Kurath *Word Geog.* 75, *Mosquito hawk* occurs along the coast in a widening belt extending from Delaware Bay to Georgia. It is the usual expression in all of Delmarvia and the Virginia Tidewater, in the southeastern half of North Carolina, and in the greater part of South Carolina. On the periphery of the *mosquito hawk* area some informants say that the *mosquito hawk* is larger than the *snake doctor.* **1950** *WELS (Other names for the dragonfly)* 2 Infs, **WI,** Mosquito hawk. **1955** *PADS* 23.42 e,cSC, eNC, seGA, *Mosquito hawk*— 'dragon fly.' **1955** Potter *Dial. NW OH* 355, Mosquito hawk [4 of 72 infs]. **1960** *PADS* 34.57 **CO,** *Older Folk Speech.* . . Mosquito hawk. **1962** Atwood *Vocab. TX* 58, *Mosquito hawk,* uniformly used in Louisiana, is also solidly established in Southeast Texas. It also extends into Central and Southwest Texas, where it competes with the variant *snake doctor,* which strongly predominates in the western half of the state. **1965–70** *DARE* (Qu. R2, . . *The dragonfly*) 109 Infs, **chiefly Sth,** Mosquito hawk; 32 Infs, **chiefly S Atl, TX,** Skeeter hawk. **1966** Dakin *Dial. Vocab. Ohio R. Valley* 2.405, *Mosquito hawk,* a southern coastal term in the East, appears only in the Jackson Purchase and southern Illinois. It seems quite possible that this may be another case of a term carried into the southwest by the migration from the Carolina plantation country and then northward by the later movement into western Kentucky and across the Ohio. **1967** Faries *Word Geog. MO* 112, The southern *mosquito hawk* seems rather widely used in Missouri (168 [of c700] occurrences). **1970** Tarpley *Blinky* 173 neTX, Mosquito hawk and skiter hawk are found primarily in the age groups above 40 and among the least educated. **1971** Bright *Word Geog. CA & NV* 114, Mosquito hawk—21 [of 300 infs]. [*DARE* Ed: Distribution is chiefly rural.] **1973** Allen *LAUM* 1.318 (as of c1950), In the U[pper] M[idwest] . . *mosquito hawk* . . is found almost exclusively in Minnesota north of the two lower tiers of counties and in eastern North Dakota, that is, in territory having a minimal degree of Midland and no Southern penetration. *Ibid* 319, 16 infs, **chiefly MN,** Mosquito hawk; 2 infs, **nwMN, csMN,** *Mosquito hawk:* Small variety, not the big; 1 inf, **cwMN,** When we were kids, we always called them 'mosquito hawks'; 1 inf, **cnMN,** *Mosquito hawk:* . . Smaller than a darning needle. **1986** Pederson *LAGS Concordance* **coastal Gulf Region,** 362 infs, (Mo)squito hawk(s).

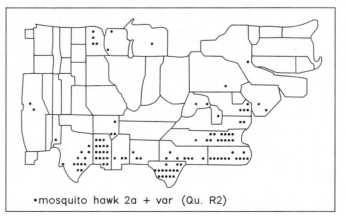

•mosquito hawk 2a + var (Qu. R2)

b also *mosquito eater:* =crane fly.
1938 *Hench Coll.* **VA,** Heard orally. . . Gallinippers . . great big mosquitoes with long trailing legs. . . Others said they knew them as mosquito hawks. **1950** *WELS (Name for an extra big mosquito)* 2 Infs, **nWI,** Mosquito hawk; 1 Inf, **cwWI,** Mosquito hawk—also a Jersey mosquito; 1 Inf, **cwWI,** Mosquito hawk—looks like a huge mosquito—lives on

mosquitoes. **1965–70** *DARE* (Qu. R15b, . . *An extra-big mosquito*) Infs **CA120, MA68, NJ16, 52, NY191, OR1,** Mosquito hawk(s); **AK1,** Mosquito hawk—something like daddy longlegs with wings—don't bite or buzz; **CT29,** Mosquito hawk—they don't bite; **NJ45,** Mosquito hawks—real big, won't bite; **NJ56, RI17,** Skeeter hawk; (Qu. R2) Inf **VA70,** Mosquito hawk—long wings, looks like a huge mosquito. **1968** *AmSp* 43.57, One informant indicated that this insect [=*Tipulidae*] was the referent of *mosquito hawk* for her; another informant indicated that she . . calls crane flies *mosquito eaters*. **1986** Pederson *LAGS Concordance,* 1 inf, **cwMS,** Mosquito hawk—a large mosquito; 1 inf, **ceTX,** Mosquito hawk—large, looked like mosquito; 1 inf, **csTX,** Mosquito hawk—she thought it was a big mosquito; 1 inf, **nwFL,** [Mo]squito hawk—[same as] mosquito-bug; mosquito-like, big; 1 inf, **cMS,** [Mo]squito hawks—2 inches long—one pair of wings. **1987** *DARE* File **cnGA** (as of c1930), In our house in Decatur, Georgia, some sixty-odd years ago, I heard *mosquito hawk* used, not of the dragonfly, which we called *snake doctor,* but of a smaller insect which wasn't considered a biter but was shaped like an out-size mosquito. **1995** *Ibid* **Philadelphia PA** (as of c1950), The mosquito hawk has a small body, with diaphanous wings, supported by long, very thin legs, each with an elbow-like joint. Although it looks like a giant mosquito, I've been told that it kills mosquitoes.

c =praying mantis.

1965 *DARE* (Qu. R4, *A large winged insect*) Inf **FL22,** Mosquito hawks—like a grasshopper, lay eggs in ground, eat mosquitoes. They are a bug. **1968** *AmSp* 43.52 **esp KS,** On 17 [of 1,518] questionnaires, *mosquito hawk* means 'dragonfly'; on 3 others, it means 'praying mantis.'

d also *leatherwing mosquito hawk:* A **robber fly** such as *Promachus fitchii.* Cf **bee catcher 1**

[**1890** (1904) Hyatt–Arms *Insecta* 262, *Asilidae.* . . These insects are rightly named robber-flies, insect-hawks, and Missouri bee-killers, for they have the habit of attacking bees, beetles, dragon-flies, and even other robber-flies, sucking out the soft parts of the body and leaving the chitinous skin.] **1968** *DARE* (Qu. R2) Inf **GA25,** Bee-eater (large moskeeter hawk)—about four times as big as average. Leatherwing moskeeter hawk (brown). **1986** Pederson *LAGS Concordance,* 1 inf, **seGA,** [Mo]squito hawks—catch bees.

mosquito horse n Cf **devil's horse 5**
=dragonfly.

1981 Pederson *LAGS Basic Materials (Dragonfly)* 2 infs, **cwMS, cGA,** Mosquito horse.

mosquito lion n Cf **mosquito hawk 2b**
=crane fly.

1994 *Houston Post* (TX) 21 Mar sec A 14, Some dub them "mosquito lions"—because folk wisdom has it they actually eat mosquitoes for lunch. (No such luck.) Actually, crane fly is the proper name for that huge, mosquitolike creature.

mosquito plant n

1 A **pennyroyal** (here: *Hedeoma pulegioides*). [See quots 1911, 1914]

1911 Henkel *Amer. Med. Leaves* 26, Stinking balm, mosquito plant. [*Ibid,* The odor is very repulsive to insects, and pennyroyal is therefore much used for keeping away mosquitoes and other troublesome insects.] **1914** Georgia *Manual Weeds* 358, American Pennyroyal . . Mosquito Plant. . . The oil distilled from this herb is much used in making the "mosquito dopes" which hunters and fishermen and many other persons are obliged to use in localities where mosquitoes are a plague. **1940** Clute *Amer. Plant Names* 260, *Hedeoma pulegioides.* Mosquito plant, tick-weed, stinking balm.

2 A **giant hyssop** (here: *Agastache cana*).

1942 Amer. Joint Comm. Horticult. Nomenclature *Std. Plant Names* 8, [*Agastache*] *cana* . . Mosquitoplant. **1970** Correll *Plants TX* 1355, *Agastache cana* . . Mosquito plant. . . On rocky slopes and in crevices of ledges in w. Trans-Pecos. **1976** Bailey–Bailey *Hortus Third* 35, *Mosquito plant.* . . New Mex[ico] and w[est] Texas.

3 See **mosquito fern.**

moss n

1 Std: a plant of the class Musci. For the names of various of these see **extinguisher moss, feather ~, haircap ~, plume ~, tree ~, swamp ~, white ~** Cf **club moss, flowering ~, pixie ~**

2 Any of var other plants thought to resemble **moss 1** in some way, as:

a =Spanish moss (here: *Tillandsia* spp). **Sth**

1733 in 1905 *Colonial Rec.* **GA** 3.381, There is no Morse on the Trees, tho' in most Parts of Carolina they are covered with it. **1803** Davis *Travels* 119 **SC,** [Footnote:] This moss. . . is bought [in Charleston] to stuff mattrasses [sic], and chair-bottoms. **1869** Porcher *Resources* 602 **Sth,** It is stated in a journal, 1863, that Messrs. Segur & Bryars, of Union Springs, Ala., are preparing to enter largely on the manufacture of rope from moss. **1901** Mohr *Plant Life* **AL** 429, *Tillandsia usneoides.* . . Moss. Spanish Moss. **1927** Boston Soc. Nat. Hist. *Proc.* 38.348 **Okefenokee GA,** A considerable portion of . . [the nests] were in strands of the 'moss' that were dead and black. **1974** (1977) Coon *Useful Plants* 81, *Tillandsia usneoides*—Spanish or Florida moss, treebeard. This "moss" has been gathered for cushions. **1974** Morton *Folk Remedies* 153 **SC,** *Tillandsia usneoides.* . . When green, the plant is boiled and the "tea" taken for easy delivery. . . The green moss is also put in the shoes as a remedy for high blood pressure. . . Crushed moss is applied to hemorrhoids. **1992** Kincaid *Crossing Blood* 263 **nwFL** (as of 1950s), The screaming insects pulsating through the darkness, the heaviness of the summer air . . , the tree branches where moss hung like unpinned lady's hair—all blended, making the road just as familiar to us this night as our own unmade beds at home.

b A **buttercup 1** (here: *Ranunculus aquatilis*).

1892 *Jrl. Amer. Folkl.* 5.91, *Ranunculus aquatilis,* var *trichophyllus,* moss (gives name to "Moss Creek," Carroll Co., Mo.)

c A lichen (Lichenes) or a liverwort (Hepaticae). Cf **reindeer moss**

1907 Marshall *Mosses* 8, Under the name of moss, in the popular mind, are included all small flowerless plants which grow in cushion-like tufts on stone or wood or bark. The name "moss" is made to do duty for the lichens, the mosses and their near relatives, the Hepatics. **1916** Dunham *How to Know Mosses* 4, The name "moss" is commonly applied to a number of plants that do not belong to the true mosses. . . Lichens are often called mosses by those unfamiliar with the lower forms of plant-life. [*Ibid* 6, The hepatics or liverworts, especially the leafy liverworts, sometimes called "scale mosses" (*Jungermanniales*) somewhat resemble certain mosses.] **1954** Bodenberg *Mosses* 2, I do believe that the name "moss" has been incorrectly applied more often than any other name in the plant world. . . Lichens . . are oftentimes called mosses. . . Festooning trees in the Pacific Northwest are the yellow-green Goat's Beard Moss (Alectoria sarmentosa) and the black Goat's Beard Moss (Alectoria fremontii), but they are both in reality lichens.

d An aquatic plant such as **Irish moss 1** or **muskgrass.** [*OED* "Applied to sea-weed. *rare*"; 1543–1895] Cf **fine moss, sea ~**

1913 *Torreya* 13.225, Submerged aquatic plants in general are known among hunters and others as grass, moss or weeds. **1954** Bodenberg *Mosses* 2, In the spring floating masses of slippery green plants appear in streams and pools of quiet water. Most people refer to these as "moss." In reality, they are composed of green algae. . . It is certain that the so-called Irish Moss which is collected for food along the Atlantic Coast is an alga and not a moss. **1975** Gould *ME Lingo* 142, *Irish moss.* . . Along the Maine coast the *Irish* is usually dropped, and a man who *mosses* is a *mosser,* etc. The plant is pulled or raked at low tide periods, and in warmer weather *mossers* will wade and dive for it.

e See **moss rose 2.**

f See **tree moss.**

3 See quot. [*OED moss* sb.[1] 1 "Chiefly *Sc.* and *north. dial.*"; 975 →]

1930 Shoemaker *1300 Words* 41 **cPA Mts** (as of c1900), *Moss*—A swamp or bog.

4 =house moss.

1959 *VT Hist.* 27.151 **cwVT,** *Noss* [sic]. . . Dust under the bed. Occasional. **1966–70** *DARE* (Qu. E20, *Soft rolls of dust that collect on the floor under beds or other furniture*) Infs **AL52, GA11, MS1, NJ67, TX58,** Moss.

moss v, hence vbl n *mossing*

1 To **chink** v, esp with sphagnum moss.

1905 U.S. Forest Serv. *Bulletin* 61.42 **Nth** [Logging terms], *Moss.* . . To fill with moss the crevices between the logs in a logging camp. **1969** Sorden *Lumberjack Lingo* 79 **NEng, Gt Lakes,** *Moss*—To fill with soft clay, oakum, or mud the crevices between logs. **1975** Gould *ME Lingo*

184, *Moss*. . . In the woods, swamp or sphagnum moss was used to chink log buildings. To *moss* a camp is to chink it between the logs. As soon as enough logs were at hand to start a *camp*, a *mossing* crew would be sent into the swamp to gather chinking.

2 To gather moss or seaweed; hence nouns *mosser, mossie* one who gathers such plants. Cf **moss** n **2d**

1945 Beck *Jersey Genesis* 185 **NJ**, The "mossies" may not know how to spell sphagnum, but they know well enough that it must be valuable to somebody and that it is used by floriculturists all over the country. **1968** *Yankee* Aug 88 **ceMA**, Mossing is still a business requiring long, hard labor. [*Ibid*, Once of little use except to make a tangy blanc mange, the elements of sea moss now find a way into scores of products, including cosmetics, cake frosting, shoe polish, and cardboard.] **1969** *WI Conserv. Bulletin* 34.1.23, The harvest of [sphagnum] moss is still mostly hand labor. Methods have not changed—mossing is much the same today as it was a hundred years ago. What machines are used today result from the efforts of individual "do it yourself" mossers trying to make their work easier. **1969** *New Engl. Galaxy* Winter 63 **seMA**, The mosser in his boat could harvest in the same time between five hundred and two thousand pounds [of sea moss]. **1975** [see **moss** n **2d**]. **1992** *DARE* File **sME coast** (as of 1975), Men wade around at low tide with chest waders on and a small rowboat tethered to them by a rope, to go mossing. They rake and pull the seaweed off the rocks and load it into the boats.

mossa See **master** n

mossback n

1 also *mossyback:* A turtle with an algae- or plant-covered carapace, such as a **snapping turtle** (here: *Chelydra serpentina*) or a **musk turtle 1** (here: *Sternotherus odoratus*); see quots. Cf **moss turtle**

[**1842** DeKay *Zool. NY* 3.23, The color and markings of this species [=*Sternotherus odoratus*] [are] not easily detected in the recently caught animal, as it is usually covered with an agglutination of mud and aquatic plants.] **1943** McAtee *Dial. Grant Co. IN Suppl. 2* 2 (as of 1890s), *Mossback* . . a turtle, usually, if not always, a snapper, with a growth of algae and other water plants on its carapace. [**1966** Wheeler–Wheeler *Amphibians & Reptiles ND* 56, Snapping turtles are often seen pushing slowly about in the shallows with their backs partly out of water. When they are at rest, their algae-covered backs perfectly simulate slimy rocks.] **1968** *DARE* (Qu. P24, . . *Kinds of turtles*) Inf **NY68**, Mossback; **NY71**, Mossback [same as what we used to call] grassyback; **IN42**, Mossyback—same as green turtle; **OH67**, Mossyback.

2 =**black bass 1.** [Appar from the color of the back] Cf **moss bass**

1935 Caine *Game Fish* 3, *Large-mouthed Black Bass*. . . Mossback. *Ibid* 7, *Small-mouthed Black Bass*. . . Mossback. *Ibid* 9, *Spotted* . . *Black Bass*. . . Mossback. **1949** Caine *N. Amer. Sport Fish* 16, Large-mouth. . . *Colloquial Names* . . Mossback. . . The color of the large-mouth will vary in different waters. Those taken in clear . . lakes and streams have green sides shading into white on the belly. Those from mud or moss-bottom lakes or sluggish streams will be almost black on the back and sides.

3 See quot. [Cf *greenback*]

1967 *DARE* (Qu. U26, *Names or nicknames* . . *for a paper dollar*) Inf **MN2**, Mossback.

4 See **mosshorn.**

mossbanker See **mossbunker**

moss bass n

=**black bass 1,** usu **largemouth bass.**

1883 *Century Illustr. Mag.* 26.376, Black bass. . . have received names somewhat descriptive of their habitat, as, lake, . . bayou, moss, grass, and Oswego bass. **1902** Jordan–Evermann *Amer. Fishes* 358, This fish [=largemouth bass] has received many vernacular names, among which may be mentioned . . moss bass. **1935** Caine *Game Fish* 3, *Large-mouthed Black Bass*. . . Moss Bass. *Ibid* 7, *Small-mouthed Black Bass*. . . Moss Bass. *Ibid* 9, *Spotted* . . *Black Bass*. . . Moss Bass. **1946** LaMonte *N. Amer. Game Fishes* 135, *Large-mouth Black Bass*. . . *Names:* Straw Bass, . . Moss Bass. **1978** *Outdoor Life* Sept 56, Scientists call the large-mouth bass Micropterus salmoides. . . But there are many lesser-known names too. Some of them are . . moss bass, and lake bass.

moss beauty n

=**arbutus.**

1892 (1974) Millspaugh *Amer. Med. Plants* 101-1, *Epigaea repens*. . . So closely do the prostrate spreading stems cling to and mingle with the mosses, to which they in their rusty hairiness bear great similitude, that one of its common names in some localities is *Moss Beauty.*

mossberry n

1 A cranberry, usu *Vaccinium oxycoccos.* [*OED* 1732 →]

1784 in 1785 Amer. Acad. Arts & Sci. *Memoirs* 1.439, *Vaccinium*. . . The *Craneberry,* or *Mossberry.* These berries make an agreeable tart. **1830** Rafinesque *Med. Flora* 2.48, *Oxycoca* [sic] *macrocarpa*. . . Vulgar [names]. Common Cranberry, Mossberry. **1900** Lyons *Plant Names* 271, *O[xycoccus] Oxycoccus*. . . Moss-berry. **1940** Clute *Amer. Plant Names* 42, *O[xycoccus] palustris*. Small Cranberry. . . moss-berry. *Ibid* 274, *Vaccinium macrocarpum*. Moss-berry. **1963** Eifert *Journeys* 98 **WI**, They were of many shapes, those choice muskeg fruits—squat, ovoid, oblong, round, with the little speckled moss-berries scattered as accent among them.

2 A crowberry **1** (here: *Empetrum nigrum*). **AK**

1869 U.S. Dept. Ag. *Rept. of Secy. for 1868* 178 **AK**, Among them [=small fruits] may be noted red and black currants . . [and] mossberries. **1870** Dall *Alaska* 442, Among the various kinds may be noted . . mossberries, and roseberries. **1898** Haskell *2 Yrs.* 191 **AK**, Many others [=berries] that are indigenous only to Alaska, such as the roseberries, mossberries, bearberries, and salmonberries. **1951** Winchell *Home Bering Sea* 186 **AK**, Down on hands and knees on the hillside would be another group busily picking and eating the small black moss-berries. **1972** Viereck–Little *AK Trees* 201, Crowberry (*Empetrum nigrum* L.) Other names: mossberry, blackberry, curlewberry. **1982** *AK Geographic* 9.3.101, Food served on these occasions consists of Aleut delicacies such as . . pies filled with mossberries picked during family outings in the fall. **1991** Tabbert *Dict. Alaskan Engl.* 177, In Alaska the name crowberry is widely used. However, two other names are also common, especially in non-urban areas. One is blackberry. . . Still another Alaskan name for *E[mpetrum] nigrum* is *mossberry,* a term recorded in only a few reference works, where it is associated with *Vaccinium oxycoccus,* the European cranberry.

moss bird n

1 A **wood pewee** (here: *Contopus virens*).

1880 Cable *Grandissimes* 237 **LA**, The red-bird, the moss-bird, the night-hawk and the chuckwill's widow. **1909** *DN* 3.350 **eAL, wGA**, *Moss-bird*. . . The wood-pewee: so called because the nest is coated on the outside with lichens and moss.

2 A **gnatcatcher 1** (here: *Polioptila caerulea*).

1917 *Wilson Bulletin* 29.2.85 **swKY**, *Polioptila caerulea.*—Moss-bird. **1956** MA Audubon Soc. *Bulletin* 40.129 **MA**, Blue-gray gnatcatcher. Moss Bird. . . The nest looks as if it were made of moss.

3 =**phoebe.**

1917 *Wilson Bulletin* 29.2.82 **swKY**, *Sayornis phoebe*. . . Bridge, moss, preacher, or spider bird.

mossbunker n Also *marshbanker, mossybank, mossybunker;* for addit varr see quots [Du *marsbanker* the European fish *Caranx trachurus*] esp **NJ, NY** Cf **bunker** n[1]

A **menhaden 1** (here: *Brevoortia tyrannus*).

[**1661** in 1861 Murphy *Jacob Steendam* 38 **NY**, Swart-vis, en Roch, en Haring, en Makreel,/ Schelvis, Masbank, en Voren die (so veel) / Tot walgens toe, die Netten vuld: en heel / Min word ge-eeten. [=The black-and roch-fish, herring, mackerel,/ The haddock, mosbankers and roach which fill / The nets to loathing; are so many, all / Cannot be eaten.]] **1792** Hommedieu in *Amer. Assoc. Proc.* [sic] XXVIII.436n. (*DAE*), The fish called menhaden or mosbanker. **1803** *Med. Repository* 6.176, The fish which Mr. Latrobe describes is the *morsch-banker* of the Dutch settlers about New-York, and the *menhaden* of the Mohegan natives. **1809** Irving *Hist. NY* 2.225, He saw the duyvel, in the shape of a huge Moss-bunker. **1818** Acad. Nat. Sci. Philadelphia *Jrl.* 1.396, It [=*Cymothoa praegustator*] is very commonly found in the mouths of the *Moss-bankers,* (*C[lupea] tyrannus*). **1818** *Amer. Monthly Mag. & Crit. Rev.* 2.206 **NY**, *Clupea neglecta* . . Vulgar names *Fall Herring, Marsbankers,* in common with other species. **1842** DeKay *Zool. NY* 4.260, *Mossbonkers* (or as it is pronounced by our Dutch inhabitants, *Morsebonkers*). **1862** Acad. Nat. Sci. Philadelphia *Proc. for 1861* 34, This genus, established on the well known and very abundant "Morsebunker" or "menhaden" of our eastern coast, is distinguished from almost all of its associates. **1884** Goode *Fisheries U.S.* 1.569, In New York the usage of two centuries is in favor of "Mossbunker." This name is a relic of the Dutch colony of New Amsterdam, having evidently been transferred from the "Scad," or "Horse Mackerel," . . known to the Hollanders as the "Marshbanker." New Jersey uses the New York name with its local variations, such as "Bunker" and "Marshbanker." **1893** *Outing* 22.355 **NJ,** All at once, rushing athwart our wake under our very stern, came a mighty school of moss-bunkers or white-fish. **1894** *DN* 1.332 **NJ,** *Menhaden:* called "moss bunkers," "mossy bunkers." **c1902** Clapin *New Dict. Amer.* 280, *Mossybank*. . . A variation of mossbunker. **1939** *LANE* Map 233, 1 inf, **Block Is. RI,** *Mossbunker,* 'in Connecticut'; 1 inf, **sMaine coast,** Called *mossbunker* 'south of Cape Cod'. **1945** Beck *Jersey Genesis* 147 **NJ,** "Most people know mossbunkers as menhaden," Jack said. "Minnies to you, maybe." **1990** *Yankee* Jan 18 **NJ,** [Letter:] The good ship *Riga* . . was fishing for menhaden, called mossbunkers down here in New Jersey.

moss bush n Also *moss plant* [From its resemblance to moss] Cf **moss heather**

A **mountain heather 3** or the related plant *Harrimanella hypnoides*.

1822 Eaton *Botany* 172, [*Andromeda*] *hypnoides* . . moss bush. . . Small, creeping. **1861** Wood *Class-Book* 486, *Cassiope*. . . Moss-plant. . . Small, alpine, moss-like or heath-like shrubs. **1876** Hobbs *Bot. Hdbk*. 71, Moss bush, Andromeda hypnoides. **1900** Lyons *Plant Names* 84, *Cassiope*. . . Moss-plant, Moss-bush. **1940** Clute *Amer. Plant Names* 39, *C[assiope] hypnoides* [=*Harrimanella hypnoides*]. *Moss-plant*. Moss-bush. **1973** Hitchcock–Cronquist *Flora Pacific NW* 342, *Cassiope*. . . Moss-bush; Cassiope.

moss campion n [*OED* 1791 →]

A **catchfly 1** (here: *Silene acaulis*). Also called **carpet pink, cushion ~, moss ~ 2**

1848 Gray *Manual of Botany* 59 **NH,** *S[ilene] acaulis* . . Moss Campion. . . Alpine summits of the White Mountains. **1900** Lyons *Plant Names* 345, Moss Campion, Moss Pink, Cushion Pink. **1915** (1926) Armstrong–Thornber *Western Wild Flowers* 114, Moss Campion. Cushion Pink. . . It has a long taproot and many spreading stems, crowded with tiny, stiff, pointed, dark-green leaves, forming close tufts . . resembling cushions of marsh moss and spangled all over with pretty little flowers. **1949** Moldenke *Amer. Wild Flowers* 68, Well known to all alpinists is the moss campion, *S. acaulis,* a dwarf, densely tufted perennial, forming mats 1 to 3 inches deep on Cape Breton Island, Gaspé, Labrador, throughout arctic America, and south to the summits of the White Mountains of New Hampshire and the Rocky Mountains, as far south as Arizona. **1966** Heller *Wild Flowers AK* 28, Moss campion, cushion pink. . . A perennial forming low, dense, mossy, cushion-like mounds. . . in alpine situations throughout most of Alaska. **1979** Niering–Olmstead *Audubon Guide N. Amer. Wildflowers E. Region* 459, Moss Campion (*Silene acaulis*). . . This beautiful little mountain-dwelling wildflower forms extensive moss-like carpets in the western mountains, but appears only locally in the East, where Mt. Washington in New Hampshire is its southern limit.

moss cranberry n Cf **mossberry 1**

Perh a **mountain cranberry 1** (here: *Vaccinium vitis-idaea*).

1948 *WELS Suppl.* **cwWI,** Your *calico bean* becomes *cranberry bean* in Taylor, Wis., where there is a small colony of northern York Staters. The moss cranberry is spotted, you know.

mosser See **moss** v 2

moss fern n Cf **fern moss**

A **polypody,** usu *Polypodium polypodioides* or *P. virginianum*.

1900 Lyons *Plant Names* 301, *Polypodium*. . . Moss Fern. **1920** *Torreya* 20.91, *Polypodium polypodioides*. . . Common local names are "fern moss," "moss fern" . . from its epiphytic habit of growing on the trunks of trees. **1938** Small *Ferns SE States* 73, Being such a widespread fern, it [=*Polypodium virginianum*] has received many common names. Some of these are . . *Golden-locks, Moss-fern* [etc].

moss flower n

A male **haircap moss;** see quot.

1954 Bodenberg *Mosses* 63, Polytrichaceae are dioecious and the male plants are easily distinguished from the female by the typical rosettes at their tops. Because of their somewhat flower-like appearance, they are often known as "moss flowers."

moss gentian n

A **gentian:** usu *Gentiana prostrata,* but also *G. fremontii*.

1953 Nelson *Plants Rocky Mt. Park* 124, Moss gentian, *Gentiana prostrata*. . . A diminutive plant of the alpine grassland, also found in moss. **1959** Munz–Keck *CA Flora* 442, *G[entiana] Fremontii*. . . Moss Gentian. **1966** Heller *Wild Flowers AK* 82, Moss gentian. . . Found: on moist, mossy alpine slopes. **1974** Welsh *Anderson's Flora AK* 241, *Gentiana prostrata* . . Moss Gentian. . . Arctic and alpine tundra, heath, or woods and meadows; in much of Alaska . . and most of the Yukon.

mosshead n [From the prominent crest] **esp SC** =**hooded merganser.**

1888 Trumbull *Names of Birds* 74, To the darkies of Charleston, S.C., and its vicinity, [the hooded merganser is known as] *moss-head*. The colored women often use a large bunch of "Florida Moss," *Tillandsia usneoides,* as a cushion for the heavy loads they carry upon their heads, and I am inclined to believe that "Moss-head" was suggested by this practice, rather than by any direct resemblance to moss in the bird's crest. **1917** (1923) *Birds Amer.* 1.112, *Hooded Merganser*. . . *Other Names* . . Hairy-crown; Hairy-head; Moss-head; Tow-head. **1923** U.S. Dept. Ag. *Misc. Circular* 13.8 **SC,** [Names for the Hooded Merganser] Hairy-head, mosshead. **1949** Sprunt–Chamberlain *SC Bird Life* 145, Hooded Merganser. . . Local Names: Hairyhead; . . Mosshead. **1950** *PADS* 14.47 **SC,** *Mosshead*. . . The hooded merganser. **1955** *Oriole* 20.1.5 **GA,** Hooded Merganser. . . Hairy-head, Mop-head, Moss-head.

moss heather n Also *Alaska moss heath* [See quot 1987] **chiefly AK** Cf *DCan*

A low shrubby plant (*Harrimanella stelleriana*).

1968 Hultén *Flora AK* 726, Alaska Moss Heath . . *Harrimanella Stelleriana*. . . Common along the coast. **1972** Viereck–Little *AK Trees* 220, Moss heather, . . Alaska moss heath; *Harrimanella stelleriana*. . . Low spreading, mat-forming . . shrub. **1973** Hitchcock–Cronquist *Flora Pacific NW* 342, Alas[ka] . . m[oss-heather]. (*Harrimanella s[telleriana]*). **1987** Hughes–Blackwell *Wildflowers SE AK* 70, Alaska Moss Heath. . . 2–4″ tall; the mat-forming stems look mossy.

mosshorn n Also *mossback, mossyhead, mossyhorn* [See quot 1929] **West, esp TX**

An old steer; also fig; hence adjs *mossy-headed, mossyhorn* old, wrinkled.

1885 Siringo *TX Cowboy* 75, They were all old mossy horn fellows [=steers], from seven to twenty-seven years old. **1929** Dobie *Vaquero* 12 **TX,** When a Texas steer gets six or eight years old, his horns become wrinkled and scaly; hence the name *mossy horn*. *Ibid* 200, I won my spurs as a vaquero while helping to snare mossy horns out of the thickets. **1936** McCarthy *Lang. Mosshorn* np **West,** *Mosshorn*. . . Old cowboys and old cattle. **1936** Adams *Cowboy Lingo* 68, He [=an old steer] was also called a 'mossback' or 'wrinkle horn.' **1939** FWP *Guide KS* 272, Fearing that the "Texers" and their droves of "mossy horns" would disorganize their community, the citizens rejected his offer. **1941** Dobie *Longhorns* 213, The rough wrinkles probably generated the Texan word *mossy-horn,* not only descriptive of horns but also a name for any old, rough steer. Also, the horns gathered . . the low-hanging Spanish moss from the bottoms, where wild cattle took refuge. **1945** Thorp *Pardner* 196 **SW,** We was ridin' the rimrock, Tom, tryin' to crowd a bunch of mossy-heads down into the canyon. **1967** Green *Horse Tradin'* 81 **TX,** Two old wore-out, mossy-headed, buck-kneed, big-ankled, boghocked, cow horses.

mossie n

1 A playing marble.

1973 Allen *LAUM* 1.404 (as of c1950), *Marbles*. . . [1 inf, **cwIA**] mossies.

2 See **moss** v 2.

mossing See **moss** v

moss locust n Also *mossy locust*

A **locust B1:** usu *Robinia hispida,* rarely *R. kelseyi*.

1889 *Century Dict.* 3501, *Bristly locust,* or *moss-locust, Robinia hispida,* a shrub with pink flowers . . from the Alleghanies. **1901** Lounsberry *S. Wild Flowers* 275, *R[obinia] hispida* . . is really the moss locust, holding among the acacias the same place as the moss rose does among roses. The calyxes of its pink blossoms, petioles, and midribs of the leaves as well as almost every available part of the plant, are covered with bristles purplish, or hazy in colour and which give it an extremely odd and unusual look. **1953** Greene-Blomquist *Flowers South* 58, *Moss-locust.* . . The stems as well as the fruits are densely hispid with reddish bristles. **1976** Bailey-Bailey *Hortus Third* 971, *[Robinia] hispida.* . . *Moss l[ocust]*, . . *mossy l[ocust]*. . . Se. U.S. *Ibid* 972, *[Robinia] kelseyi.* . . *Alleghany moss l[ocust]*. . . Fr[uit] covered with purple glandular hairs. N.C.

moss oak n [From its association with **moss 2a**]
Prob a **live oak 1**.
    1967–70 *DARE* (Qu. T10, . . *Kinds of oak trees*) Infs **AL25, GA93**, Moss oak.

moss phlox n [See quots 1949, 1950]
A **phlox**: either *Phlox hoodii* or *P. muscoides* in the western US and Alaska, or **moss pink 1** in the eastern US.
    1900 Lyons *Plant Names* 285, *P[hlox] bryoides* [=*P. muscoides*] . ., Nebraska to Wyoming, is called Moss Phlox. **1933** Small *Manual SE Flora* 1102, *P[hlox] subulata*. . . Low matted evergreen shrub. . . *Moss-phlox*. **1936** Winter *Plants NE* 116, Moss Phlox. . . *P[hlox] hoodii*. . . Frequent in dry rocky places in western Nebr. and westward. **1949** Moldenke *Amer. Wild Flowers* 248, With needlelike or almost mosslike leaves and a rather woody stem, are the *moss phlox*, *P[hlox] bryoides*, with densely white-woolly leaves, and *P. hoodii*, the *Hood phlox*. **1950** Stevens *ND Plants* 232, *Phlox bryoides*. . . *Moss Phlox*. . . Perennial, forming dense, moss-like mats 1–3 dm. wide on the ground and flowering profusely in May. **1959** Anderson *Flora AK* 399, Moss Phlox. . . Flowers . . at the end of the branches. **1965** *Native Plants PA* 52, Phlox subulata—Moss Phlox. **1973** Hitchcock-Cronquist *Flora Pacific NW* 375, Moss p[hlox]. . . *P[hlox] muscoides*.

moss pink n
1 A **phlox** (here: *Phlox subulata*). [See quots 1901, 1979]
Also called **flowering moss 3, ground phlox, ground pink 1, moss phlox, mountain phlox 1, ~ pink 1, rock pink, sweet William, thrift, wild pink, wild sweet William**
    1847 Wood *Class-Book* 440, *P[hlox] subulata*. . . Moss Pink. Rocky hills and mountains, Penn. to Ga. and Ky., abundant in its localities. **1897** *Jrl. Amer. Folkl.* 10.50 swOH, *Phlox subulata*, L., moss pink, creeping phlox. **1901** Lounsberry *S. Wild Flowers* 442, *Phlox subulata*, ground or moss pink, than which no other phlox is handsomer, spreads over rocky, dry soil a carpet of fine, moss-like foliage. . . Its range extends from Florida to the southern part of New York. **1923** *Amer. Botanist* 29.138, *Phlox subulata* is the moss pink, well known for its predilection for rocks and stony hillsides. **1949** Moldenke *Amer. Wild Flowers* 248, The mosspink . . is widely cultivated in rock gardens for the gorgeous carpets of pink, purple, or white made by its wealth of flowers in early spring, but it is a native American plant. **1979** Niering-Olmstead *Audubon Guide N. Amer. Wildflowers E. Region* 697, Moss Pink. . . This low plant forms *moss-like mats* with pink to lavender (rarely white) flowers in clusters at the ends of the stems, collectively forming a continuous carpet of flowers.
2 =**moss campion**.
    1896 *Jrl. Amer. Folkl.* 9.182 swME, *Silene acaulis* . . moss pink. **1973** Hitchcock-Cronquist *Flora Pacific NW* 118, Moss C[ampion], moss pink, cushion p[ink]. . . *S[ilene] acaulis*.

moss plant See **moss bush**

moss rose n
1 Std: a many-petaled, cultivated rose *(Rosa centifolia)* with "mossy" calyx and pedicels.
2 also *moss, rose moss*: A **purslane**, usu *Portulaca grandiflora*.
    1892 *Jrl. Amer. Folkl.* 5.93 sNE, *Portulaca grandiflora* . . rose-moss. **1893** *Ibid* 6.138 sIN, *Portulaca grandiflora*, moss. **1896** *Ibid* 9.183 swOH, *Portulaca grandiflora* . . rose-moss, Kentucky moss. **1929** Ellis *Ordinary Woman* 16 CO (as of early 20th cent), A pan of moss roses mama had brought from home. **1929** Bell *Some Contrib. KS Vocab.* 183, Moss. . . The common term for *portulaca*, a lowgrowing plant having pink, white, and yellow single flowers, which open only when the sun is obscured by clouds. On the questionnaires, forty-nine [of approximately 100 infs] gave *moss* as their use. . . one offered *moss rose* as her use. **1940** Clute *Amer. Plant Names* 143, Garden Portulaca. Rose-moss. **1959** Carleton *Index Herb. Plants* 83, Moss-rose: Portulaca [spp]. *Ibid* 100, Rose-Moss: Portulaca [spp]. **1961** Wills-Irwin *Flowers TX* 109, Moss-rose—*Portulaca pilosa*. . . In Central, South, and West Texas the Moss-rose grows here and there along roadsides and in sandy fields, producing its pinkish-purple flowers during the brightest hours. In some

places it becomes so abundant as to carpet the ground, blanketing barren waysides with a rosy mantle. **1969** *Richland Observer* (Richland Center WI) 22 May sec 1 9, [Advt:] *Flowers* dozen 69c[s] African Daisy[s] Ageratum[s] . . Phlox[s] Moss Roses[s] Salvia. **1969** *SC Market Bulletin* 24 July 4/4, Moss rose or Rose Moss plants, 10c each. **1993** *DARE* File seWI (as of c1960), When I was growing up, I didn't know there was any such thing as a portulaca. My mother always referred to the flower as a moss rose.
3 also *rose moss*: A **globe mallow 1** (here: *Sphaeralcea coccinea*).
    1896 *Jrl. Amer. Folkl.* 9.183 SD, *Malvastrum coccineum* . . moss rose. **1900** Lyons *Plant Names* 238, *M[alvastrum] coccineum* . . of western prairies is called Red False Mallow, also Moss Rose. **1936** Whitehouse *TX Flowers* 70, Red Star-Mallow. . . The plant is also called prairie mallow, red false mallow, and rose moss. It grows in low clumps, spreading or erect, on prairies from Texas to Southern Canada.

moss turtle n Cf **mossback 1**
A **map turtle** (here: *Graptemys geographica* or *G. pseudogeographica*).
    1883 WI Chief Geologist *Geol. WI* 1.422 **WI**, *Malacoclemmys geographicus*. . . Moss Turtle. Grant county. **1928** Pope-Dickinson *Amphibians* 79 **WI**, Map Turtle. . . Sometimes called the Moss Turtle or Geographic Turtle. The carapace of this turtle is dull olive-brown with fine, yellow lines, more or less distinct.

moss verbena n Sth
A **vervain** (here: *Verbena tenuisecta*).
    1949 Moldenke *Amer. Wild Flowers* 292, The *moss verbena*, *V[erbena] tenuisecta*, . . lays a gaudy blue, purple, or violet carpet along roadsides and in fields and waste places in Georgia, Alabama, Florida, and Texas. Its stems usually are prostrate, with only the gorgeously flowering tips held aloft. **1953** Greene-Blomquist *Flowers South* 108, *Moss-Verbena*. . . resembles a true verbena in its flower characteristics. **1970** Correll *Plants TX* 1324, *Moss verbena*. . . Roadsides, fields, and waste places. **1972** Brown *Wildflowers LA* 156, Moss Verbena. . . Extensive colonies along road shoulders in prairie and pinelands.

moss wood n Cf **moss beauty**
Prob =**arbutus**.
    1928 in 1931 McCorrison *Letters Fraternity* 177 **NEng**, The ground was covered with wild flowers. . . There were two kinds of trilliums . . ladies slipper, . . moss wood, . . and numerous other kinds of a dwarf nature that I can not name.

mossy n Also *mossy mossy man* Also sp *mosey*
A children's game of tag; see quots.
    1896 *DN* 1.421 Brooklyn NYC, *Mosey*: same as *pom-pom-pull-away*. **1901** *DN* 2.138 seNY, *Cross-the-road*. . . A game, the same as mosey . . and mossy. *Ibid* 144 c,wNY, *Mossy*. . . The name of a game; the same as pom-pom-pull-away. **1969** *DARE* (Qu. EE2) Inf **NY219**, Mossy mossy man (catch me if you can)—one player tries to catch others running to goal.

mossyback n
1 See **mossback 1**.
2 A **menhaden 1** (here: *Brevoortia tyrannus*). *obs* Cf **mossbunker**
    1872 Schele de Vere *Americanisms* 67, In the State of New York the same fish appear under the name of *Mossy Back* or *Mossbunkers*.

mossybank, mossybunker See **mossbunker**

mossycup oak n Also *mossycup (white oak), white mossycup, mossy overcup oak* [See quot 1812]
=**burr oak**.
    1812 Michaux *Histoire des Arbres* 2.32 **NY**, *Quercus olivaeformis*—mossy cup oak. . . Les glands, de forme ovale allongée, sont presque entièrement renfermés dans une cupule qui présente à-peu-près la même configuration que les glands, et qui, à sa surface, est garnie d'écailles saillantes dont les pointes se recourbent en arrière, excepté vers le bord supérieur où elles se terminent en filamens déliés et flexibles. C'est à cause de cette disposition particulière, que je lui ai donné le nom de *Mossy cup oak*. [=The acorns, elongate oval in form, are almost entirely covered by a cup which is nearly the same shape as the acorns, and which, on its surface, is protected by projecting scales of which the points curve backward except along the top edge where they end in fine and flexible filaments. It is because of this peculiarity that I have given

it the name of *Mossy cup oak.*] **1890** *Century Dict.* 4050, *Mossy-cup oak.* . . The bur-oak, sometimes distinguished as *white mossy-cup.* **1897** *IN Dept. Geol. & Nat. Resources Rept. for 1896* 616, Over Cup or Mossy Cup Oak. . . Readily known by its thick, rough, shaggy bark . . and large acorn with the cup margined with a moss-like fringe. **1897** Sudworth *Arborescent Flora* 155 **Atlantic, Gulf States, Missip Valley,** Mossycup Oak. *Ibid* **MN,** Mossycup White Oak. **1938** Brown *Trees NE U.S.* 203, Mossy-cup Oak. . . One of the most widely distributed and largest of American oaks. **1950** Moore *Trees AR* 45, Bur Oak. . . Local Names: Mossy Cup, Mossy Cup White Oak. **1968** Pochmann *Triple Ridge* 84 **cWI,** The bur-oak acorn is covered almost entirely by its deep shaggy cup, and because of it the tree is sometimes called the mossy-cup oak. **1979** Little *Checklist U.S. Trees* 236, Mossycup oak, mossy-over-cup oak.

mossyhead, mossy-headed, mossyhorn See **mosshorn**

mossy locust See **moss locust**

mossy mossy man See **mossy**

mossy overcup oak See **mossycup oak**

mossy pink n

An **owl's clover** (here: *Orthocarpus erianthus*).

1898 *Jrl. Amer. Folkl.* 11.176 **CA,** *Orthocarpus versicolor,* . . mossy pinks.

most See **-est 5**

mostest See **-est 3**

mostly adv [Scots, Engl dial] **chiefly Sth, S Midl**

Nearly; almost.

1871 Eggleston *Hoosier Schoolmaster* 40 **sIN,** He got a heap o'money, or, what's the same thing mostly, a heap of good land. **1938** Stuart *Dark Hills* 177 **eKY,** I have done farm work, taught school, cut timber. . . I can do mostly anything. **1941** in 1944 *ADD* 398 **nWV,** I mostly always tell 'em. **1967** *DARE* Tape **AL14,** We mostly always used the dipper to dip the water from that with. **1968–69** *DARE* (Qu. K44, *A bony or poor-looking horse*) Inf **NC79,** Mostly starved; (Qu. LL30, . . *'Nearly'* or *'almost'*: *"He fell off the ladder and _____ [broke his neck]."*) Inf **MO15,** Mostly. **1986** Pederson *LAGS Concordance,* 1 inf, **cwLA,** Mostly always cut it; 1 inf, **nwFL,** We mostly always drinked it up fast as it get ready for drink; 1 inf, **cnGA,** They just set back in the church mostly like usual.

most nearly adv phr Also *most nigh*

Almost, nearly.

c1960 *Wilson Coll.* **csKY,** Most nearly. . . Almost. **1966–70** *DARE* (Qu. LL30, . . *'Nearly'* or *'almost'*: *"He fell off the ladder and _____ [broke his neck]."*) Inf **AR35,** Most nigh; **OK55,** Most nearly.

most time(s) adv phr **esp Sth, Midl** See Map

Usually.

1843 (1916) Hall *New Purchase* 54 **IN,** Most time, mam, you'll have to work your own ash-hopper. **1954** *Harder Coll.* **cwTN,** Most times. . . Usually. "The mail most times comes on at about ten o'clock." **1960** Bailey *Resp. to PADS 20* **KS,** Generally, in generally, most times. **1965–70** *DARE* (Qu. KK40, . . *'Usually'*: *"They come twice a month, _____."*) 27 Infs, **esp Sth, Midl,** Most times; **MS45,** Most time.

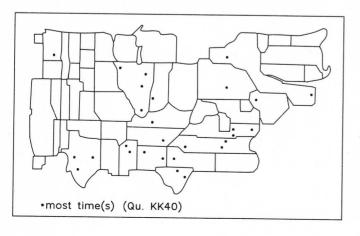

•most time(s) (Qu. KK40)

most-wise adv

Especially, most of all.

1943 Writers' Program NC *Bundle of Troubles* 42, We's all proud of you, most-wise you pappy and mammy.

mot, mote n[1] See **motte**

mote n[2] [Prob var of *moat*]

1890 *DN* 1.74 **NH,** Mote . . a sort of little pond or puddle in an old river bed. Northern and southern New Hampshire.

mote v See **may** v **Aa**

moth n [Cf *OED moth* sb. 1.b "*fig.* Something that eats away, gnaws or wastes gradually and silently. Now *rare.*"]

1927 *AmSp* 3.138 **ME,** A difficult task was "quite a chore" and an extravagance or great expense "an awful moth."

moth dust n

=**house moss.**

1970 *DARE* (Qu. E20, *Soft rolls of dust that collect on the floor under beds or other furniture*) Inf **MS85,** Moth dust.

mother n[1] Usu |'mʌðə(r)|; also |'maðə(r), 'muðə, 'mʌdə(r), 'mʌvə(r)|; for addit varr see quot 1989 Pronc-spp *mither, mothey, mover, mudder, murrah, murruh, muvver* Cf Pronc Intro 3.I.17

A Forms.

1909 *S. Atl. Qrly.* 8.43 **sSC, GA coasts** [Gullah], In *father, mother,* . . the formula is *farrah, murrah.* **1922** Gonzales *Black Border* 314 **sSC, GA coasts** [Gullah glossary], *Murruh*—mother, mothers. *Ibid, Murruh-law*—mother-in-law. **1930** Woofter *Black Yeomanry* 209 **seSC** [Black], It is rather unusual to find the old women living alone. There is usually a 'grand' who can be spared or a 'mudderless' who can be adopted. **1930** Knibbs *Songs Lost Frontier* 9 **West,** He'd sit and blow the foam, And yarn till mither bade me go. **1941** *LANE* Map 372 (*Mother, ma*), The map shows the terms . . *mother, mothey, ma, mama,* [etc]. [Proncs of the type ['mʌðə(r)] are found **throughout NEng;**] 1 inf, **neCT,** ['mʌðɪ]; 1 inf, **cwMA,** ['mʌvr], childish pron. **1954** *PADS* 21.33 **SC,** Mudder. . . Mother. **1966** Dakin *Dial. Vocab. Ohio R. Valley* 2.426, One or two instances of the use of *mummy, mumə, mum* (all from women), and of *muvvə* (the Negro informant in Louisville) and *muvver* (a ninety-six year old Mountain speaker) are recorded. **1973** *PADS* 60.56 **seNC,** *Father, mother.* . . Although coastal North Carolina usually has /ə/ as the final syllable of these words, the speech of coastal Carteret County is marked by strong retroflection. Our informants therefore had [ɚ] only. **1989** Pederson *LAGS Tech. Index* 226 (*Mother*), [393 infs had proncs of the type ['mʌðə(z)]; 371 ['mʌðɚ(z)]; 155 ['maðə, -ɚ]; 8 ['maðə, -ɚ]; 7 ['mʌðə, -ɚ]; 5 ['muðə]; 5 ['mɤðə]; 2 [mʌð]; 2 ['mʌrə, -ɚ]; 1 ['moðɚ]; 1 ['mʌtə]; 1 ['mʌθə]; 1 ['mʌvə]; 1 ['mʌðə]; 1 ['mwʌðə]; 1 [ɓʌðə].] **1993** *Coast Watch* Sept/Oct 13 **Outer Banks NC,** Bankers. . . often use a "v" instead of "th," as in "mover" and "brover" for "mother" and "brother."

B Sense.

Often attrib; a plant used for propagation, as:

a A beet grown for seeds. Also called **mamma** n[1] **6**

1925 *Book of Rural Life* 9.5341, In the production of sugar-beet seed, the first step is the selection of mother beets of high sugar content. . . The progeny of each strain is analysed, . . and the good ones used in producing mother seed, which is increased in sufficient quantity for planting on a large scale. **1930** *AmSp* 6.10, The sugar beet is a *bien-nial* . . the *seed stalks* grow out of the *crown* of the year old *mother* beet. **1941** Writers' Program *Guide WY* 225, 'Mother beets' are raised and tested for shape, size, uniformity, and sugar content. These beets are then planted in greenhouses. . . It requires two years to produce beet seed.

b A sweet potato from which cuttings are taken for planting. Cf **mamma** n[1] **7**

1950 *PADS* 14.47 **SC,** Mother patch. . . Since the smoothest and best keeping sweet potatoes are grown from cuttings, a *mother patch* of plants is set out as early as possible and fertilized for rapid vine growth. From these vines of the *mother patch* cuttings are then secured for general planting. *Ibid,* Mother potatoes. . . The potatoes from which potato slips are grown for planting. **1956** Rayford *Whistlin' Woman* 8 **AL,** He raised sweet potatoes that weighed fifty pounds. . . Those old mother potatoes were enormous. Course, those big 'ns were not good to eat—I mean the old mother potatoes. They were like a sponge. But they never rotted, because there was no frost on Cat Island. I suppose those big old potatoes were fifteen years old. **1976** Bailey–Bailey *Hortus Third* 1086, In areas of long growing seasons, after early plantings are established with transplants, later plantings may be established with vine cuttings obtained by cutting 8–10 inches of tips of growing vines. This involves considerable labor and tends to reduce yields of the "mother" plantings.

mother n² Also *mammy, mother of vinegar* [*OED* mother sb.² 2 1601 →]
A membrane or sediment that forms in fermenting liquids and that can be added to wine or cider to produce vinegar.
    1899 (1912) Green *VA Folk-Speech* 288, *Mother.* . . A st[r]ingy, mucilaginous substance which forms in vinegar during the acetous fermentation. **1930** *DN* 6.82 **cSC,** *Mammy.* . . The sediment (the mother) in vinegar. Common. **1937** *Hall Coll.* **wNC, eTN,** *Mother*—Growth which forms on the top of vinegar after fermentation and which is supposed to be necessary for its preservation. **c1960** *Wilson Coll.* **csKY,** *Mother of vinegar.* . . The bacterial growth often found in vinegar. **1967** *DARE* Tape **TX**1, [FW:] What's that stuff that vinegar gets in it? [Inf:] Mother. Any vinegar has mother in it if you put it up awhile. . . You take some of that mother, if you want to make some vinegar, and get the juice of some fruit and put that piece of mother in there and it will make vinegar right quick. [FW:] What does it look like? [Inf:] Well it looks like a piece of leather. . . It stays on the bottom. [FW:] Oh, how big is it? [Inf:] Different sizes. It, uh, ordinarily I'd say it is six to eight inches square, in pieces. **1969** *DARE* FW Addit **csPA,** *Mother*—the sediment that forms at the bottom of a bottle of vinegar or cider. **1979** *Greenfield Recorder* (MA) 13 Oct sec A 4/2, At least one barrel [of cider] had to have some "mother" added from an old barrel to make the cider "work" and become vinegar. [**1985** Wilkinson *Moonshine* 21 **neNC,** Initially, the mash tastes sweet and is sticky; fermented, it is tangy and sour. While turning, it has a two- or three-inch snowy collar, and when ready it is clear on top and the color of dark beer. It is called still beer, or meal beer, or meal mammy.]

mother bird n Also *father bird*
A children's game; see quot.
    1968 *DARE* (Qu. EE33, . . *Outdoor games . . that children play*) Inf **PA**133, Mother bird or father bird—one or two "it"; two or three hunters. Mother divides the team into names. Mother calls birds to her nest by name. The one named runs; hunters chase.

mother bunch n [Cf *OEDS* (at *mother* sb.¹ 4.b) "*Mother Bunch* . . f. the name of a noted ale-wife of late Elizabethan times"; cf *EDD bunch* sb.¹ 7 "An awkward-looking woman or girl."]
    1899 (1912) Green *VA Folk-Speech* 288, *Mother-bunch.* . . A short, stout girl.

Mother Carey's chicken n
1 also *Carey, Carey chick(en), Kerry chicken, long-legged Mother Carey's ~*: =storm petrel. [*OED* 1767 →] esp **NEast**
    1844 DeKay *Zool. NY* 2.290, This little Petrel, or *Mother Carey's Chicken*, occurs commonly along our coast from Mexico to high northern latitudes. **1858** Hammett *Piney Woods Tavern* 112, You may be sure of it [=foul weather] when you see them pesky little critters, Mother Carey's chickens, a flyin' round the starn. **1899** Howe–Sturtevant *Birds RI* 32, *Oceanodroma leucorhoa.* . . Stormy Petrel. Mother Carey's Chickens. **1925** (1928) Forbush *Birds MA* 1.145, *Oceanodroma leucorhoa leucorhoa.* . . Carey Chicken ("Kerry chicken"). *Ibid* 149, Mother Carey's chicken; long-legged mother Carey's chicken. **1933** *AmSp* 8.3.77 **ME,** *Careys* are stormy petrels, or "Mother Carey's chickens." **1942** ME Univ. *Studies* 56.60, The *stormy petrel*, or *Mother Carey's chicken*, skimming over the water was thought to be an indication of a storm. **1946** Hausman *Eastern Birds* 76, Leach's petrel. . . Mother Carey's Chicken. *Ibid* 77, Storm petrel. . . Mother Carey's Chicken. *Ibid* 78, Wilson's petrel. . . Mother Carey's Chicken. **1953** *AmSp* 28.277, *Carey chick,* for the white-rumped and Wilson's petrels (Northeast), is an abbreviation of *Mother Carey's chicken*. *Ibid* 278, The common petrels are known to sailors and coastwise people as *Mother Carey's chickens*. The complete form, dating at least to Carteret's time (say the mid 1700s), and used on both sides of the Atlantic—in fact, wherever English-speaking sailors go—is applied in the coastal region, on and off shore, from the Middle Atlantic states northward, to the white-rumped, storm, and Wilson's petrels. The shorter form, *Carey's chicken,* also has been recorded from New England. **1968** *DARE* (Qu. Q7) Inf **MD**3, Mother Carey's chickens (stormy petrel); **MD**36, Mother

Carey chicken—comes only before storm, an ocean bird, seems to walk on water.
2 =coot n¹ **1.**
    1917 *Wilson Bulletin* 29.2.79 **swKY,** *Fulica americana.* . . water guinea hen, Mother Carey's chicken.
3 The common crow (*Corvus brachyrhynchos*).
    1956 MA Audubon Soc. *Bulletin* 40.84 **NH,** Common Crow. . . Mother Carey's Chicken. . . Borrowed from the petrels, but apparently facetious, in this instance, for a kind of wild "poultry."

mother dear n Also abbr *mo' dear, muhdear* |məˈdɪə(r), ˈmʌdɪə(r)|; also *mom dear* **chiefly Gulf States, S Atl** See Map *chiefly among Black speakers; chiefly among women*
One's mother.
    1965–70 *DARE* (Qu. Z2, . . 'Mother') Inf **FL**51, Mother dear—the younger generation starting to say this; **IL**68, Mother dear; **NC**88, People are beginning to call grandmothers "mamma" and mothers "mother dear" [ˈmʌðə dɪ]; **MS**47, 60, [məˈdɪr]; **MO**29, **MS**84, [məˈdɪr]; **MS**90, [ˈmʌdɪr]; **AL**24, **TN**46, [məˈdɪə]; **LA**6, [məˈdɪə]—occasionally; **SC**66, Mom dear—new, but becoming more common. [11 of 12 Infs Black, 11 female] **1968** *DARE* FW Addit **nwLA,** Mo' dear [ˌməˈdɪə]—mother. Negro usage. **1972** King *Black Anthol.* 257 [Black], Muhdear [=Mother] monkeyed with my collar again. **1981** Pederson *LAGS Basic Materials* **chiefly coastal Gulf Region,** [6 infs gave the response *mother dear;* 4 of these, and 2 other infs gave *mo' dear* (proncs of the types [ˈmʌdɪə, məˈdɪə]); 2 explicitly said that this was short for *mother dear*.] [8 of 8 total infs Black, 4 female]

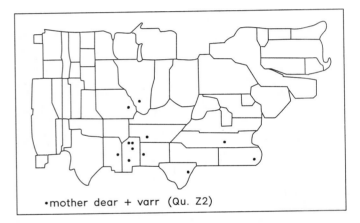

•mother dear + varr (Qu. Z2)

mother eel See **mother of eels 2**

Mother Hubbard loop n Also *Mother Hubbard*
In roping: see quot 1940 *Cattleman;* also fig.
    1940 *Cattleman* May 17 **West,** So here goes a *Mother Hubbard* at the whole subject. *Ibid* 20, A big flat loop is sometimes called a "Mother Hubbard" or a "washer woman," but such loops are not commonly used today. **1940** *Sat. Review* 17 Aug 9/2 **CO,** A number of terms and allusions may be peculiar to one section or another, and the writer, in throwing a "mother hubbard" loop—which in itself may be a limited term—is not always at fault.

Mother Hubbard saddle n Also *Mother Hubbard* [See quot 1955] *old-fash*
See quot 1944.
    1944 Adams *Western Words* 101, *Mother-Hubbard saddle*—An early-day saddle, the first improvement upon the Mexican saddle, which consisted of little more than a tree and stirrup leathers, The Mother-Hubbard had a housing like the mochila, an almost square piece of leather with a hole for the horn and a slit for the cantle, the whole being detachable. Later this was made a permanent part of the saddle, and was designed to give more comfort to both horse and rider. **1955** Harris *Look of Old West* 242, The Anglo-Americans . . soon switched to the Mexican stock saddle. They improved it, first by stitching on the housing or mochila so it wouldn't come off, then by doubling the rigging. The Americans called the result a Mother Hubbard, because of its long skirts. **1967** *DARE* FW Addit **CO,** Side saddle, western saddle and a Mother Hubbard saddle with long skirts—old-fashioned.

Mother Hubbard squash n Also *Mother Hubbard* esp Upper MW
=**hubbard squash.**
   1966–68 *DARE* (Qu. I23, . . *Kinds of squash*) Infs **PA**136, **SD**3, 5, Mother Hubbard; **IA**30, Mother Hubbard—green outside, a hook in it, a gooseneck; **MN**12, Mother Hubbard—dark green, warty; **MO**8, Mother Hubbard squash; **SD**2, Mother Hubbard—hard, green.

mothering adj
   Of weather: pleasant, comforting.
   1966 *DARE* FW Addit **SC,** A mothering day—not too warm, not too cool, just right.

mother-in-law bird n
=**cowbird 1.**
   1968 *DARE* (Qu. Q14, . . *Names . . for . . cowbird*) Inf **NY**123, Mother-in-law bird.

‡**mother-in-law's bite** n Cf **old maid 4**
   1968 *DARE* (Qu. H71, . . *The last piece of food left on a plate*) Inf **PA**131, Mother-in-law's bite.

mother-in-law's button n
   The bachelor's button (*Centaurea cyanus*).
   1968 *DARE* (Qu. S11, . . *Bachelor's button*) Inf **VA**7, Mother-in-law's button.

Mother Jones n [In ref to Mary Harris *"Mother" Jones,* 1830–1930, labor leader who championed, among others, Colorado coal miners]
=**Mrs. Jones.**
   1941 *LANE* Map 354 (*Privy*) 2 infs, **neCT, seMA,** Mother Jones. **1967** *DARE* (Qu. M21b, *Joking names for an outside toilet building*) Infs **CO**7, 19, 44, Mother Jones. **1973** Allen *LAUM* 1.181 (as of c1950), *Privy. . .* Mother Jones [1 inf, **IA**].

mother luck n Cf **mother wit, nigger luck**
   Sheer good luck.
   1985 Wilkinson *Moonshine* 140 **neNC,** Earl said, "If they went in there at five o'clock trying to get the cool of the morning, we're going to be late." "I know," Garland said, "but we might have some mother luck and run up on them carrying the liquor out. I *have* done that."

motherly naked See **mother-naked**

mother mark See **mother's mark**

mother, may I n Also *momma, may I* **chiefly west of Appalachians** See Map Cf **captain may I, freeze n 2**
=**may I.**
   1950 *WELS Suppl.* **csWI,** Simply *may I?* in my childhood. Now the kids say *mother, may I?* **1965–70** *DARE* (Qu. EE16, *Hiding games that start with a special, elaborate method of sending the players out to hide*) 43 Infs, **chiefly west of Appalachians,** Mother, may I; **CA**182, **ID**2, **IL**100, **IN**75, **MS**64, **PA**167, Mother, may I—not a hiding game; **PA**130, Mother, may I—not a hiding game, just a matter of progressing between two points; **PA**133, Mother, may I—actually just an obstacle course sort of thing; not actually a hiding game, more like elaborate tag game; **UT**10, Mother, may I—but you don't hide; you just tell the players how many steps they can take, then they try to sneak forward; they have to say "mother, may I" to move; (Qu. EE33, . . *Outdoor games . . that children play*) Infs **CA**1, **HI**9, **NJ**28, **NY**98, 186, **OH**84, **PA**163, **VA**109, Mother, may I. **1967** *DARE* Tape **IN**1, Mother, may I . . like ol' granny tippy-toes except there's a leader in front. There can be any number of children in the row behind her. The first person in the row would say "Mother, may I take so many baby steps or scissors steps or so many giant steps?" and they try to sneak as they go and catch up to the line where "mother" stands. And if she catches them inching along or taking large steps, then they have to go back to the starting line again. **1977–78** Foster *Lexical Variation* 42 **NJ,** The game known as *Giant Steps, Mother, May I?,* and *May I? . .* is evidently a girl's game. . . While *May I?* responses show fairly even geographical distribution, *Giant Steps* seems to be more common in North Jersey and *Mother, May I?* in the Philadelphia Suburbs and South Jersey. **1986** Pederson *LAGS Concordance* **Gulf Region,** 3 infs, Mother, may I? 1 inf, Mother, may I?—seeks permission, like giant step; 1 inf, Mother, may I?—involves mimicking a leader; 1 inf, Momma, may I?

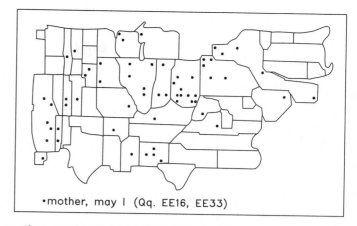

•mother, may I (Qq. EE16, EE33)

mother, mother, the pot boils over n Also *mother, mother, the teakettle is boiling over* Cf **chickamy chickamy craney crow, old witch 1**
   A children's game; see quots 1909, 1957.
   1909 (1923) Bancroft *Games* 135, *Mother, Mother, the Pot Boils Over!* One player represents an old witch, another a mother, another the eldest daughter, another a pot boiling on the hearth, and the balance are children, named for the days of the week. . . [T]he mother says to her . . eldest, "Be sure and not let the old witch take any of your sisters. You can also get the dinner, and be sure not to let the pot boil over." [*Ibid* 136, The old witch comes again, . . until each child in turn has been taken away. *Ibid* 137, When all have been sent home, the mother, joined by the children, chases and catches the witch.] **1953** Brewster *Amer. Nonsinging Games* 71, *Chickamy Chickamy Craney Crow. . .* This familiar game is known by many names . . [including] Mother, Mother, the Pot Boils Over. **1957** *Sat. Eve. Post Letters* **WI,** *Mother, Mother, the teakettle is boiling over*—A group of players called "children" are left in one room. One player is called "mother" and . . [another] "witch." The mother leaves her children . . and tells them . . not [to] let the teakettle boil over. . . [T]he witch . . chases the children[,] catches one and takes it away. The other children cry out "Mother, Mother, the teakettle is boiling over." . . [T]he same thing happens over and over until all the children are gone.

mother-naked adj phr Also *motherly naked* [*OED* c1400 →] **esp Ozarks**
=**bare-naked.**
   1899 (1912) Green *VA Folk-Speech* 288, *Mother-naked. . .* Naked as at birth. Start naked. Quite naked. **1933** *AmSp* 8.1.51 **Ozarks,** *Mother-naked,* adj. Naked. **1959** in 1980 *DARE* File **cAR,** [Newspaper clipping:] Tell any chap, town or country, he main't go swimming, motherly naked, and that's how certain and sure he will go. **1966** *DARE* (Qu. W20, *If somebody has no clothes on at all—for example, "There was Johnny, _____."*) Inf **AR**23, Motherly naked.

Mother Nature n Cf *DS* AA27
   1978 *MJLF* 4.1.38 **cTX,** Euphemisms for menstruation—"Mother Nature" and "Minnie," as a nickname for menstruation, are explainable.

mother of eels n
1 =**eelpout 1.** [See quot 1933]
   1882 U.S. Natl. Museum *Bulletin* 16.784, *Z[oarces] anguillaris. . .* Eelpout; Mutton-fish; Mother of Eels. **1911** U.S. Bur. Census *Fisheries 1908* 313, Mutton-fish (*Zoarces anguillaris*). . . It is also called the "eelpout," "mother-of-eels," [etc.] **1933** John G. Shedd Aquarium *Guide* 153, The species [=*Zoarces anguillaris*] is viviparous, a fact which gives rise to the name "Mother of Eels" which is sometimes applied to it.

2 also *mother eel*: =**burbot.**
   1884 Goode *Fisheries U.S.* 1.236, Professor Jordan gives the names "Aleby-trout" and "Mother of Eels" as in use in the Upper Great Lake region. **1911** U.S. Bur. Census *Fisheries 1908* 308, Burbot. . . In various localities it is called . . "mother of eels," "aleby trout," etc. **1967** Cross *Hdbk. Fishes KS* 229, Burbots that are caught on hook-and-line nowadays attract notice in local newspapers as oddities . . in the lower Missouri River. . . Interestingly, this species is called the "mother eel" by some fishermen in this area.

mother of the church See **church mother**

mother of vinegar See **mother** n²

mothers' bench n Also *mothers' seat* Cf **mourners' bench**

   1970 *DARE* (Qu. CC5, *Names for seats in a church, especially near the front*) Inf **OK**58, Mothers' bench; **MO**29, Mothers' seats.

mother schoolcraft n

A **pennycress** (here: *Thlaspi arvense*).

   1964 *WV Folk.* 14.46 **WV**, Also for cramps, boil the leaves of mother school craft (sometimes called penny grass) and drink.

mother's colt, ride one's v phr Also *ride granny's colt, ~ mamma's colt, ~ one's mother's pony, go on mammy's colts*

esp S Midl Cf **shank's mare**

To go on foot.

   1849 in 1956 Eliason *Tarheel Talk* 159 **NC**, Every horse cart wagon, buggy, carriage and whatever else that was ever made to ride in were filled, besides not a few 'rode their mother's colt.' **1966–69** *DARE* (Qu. Y24, . . *To walk, to go on foot: "I can't get a ride, so I'll just have to _____."*) Inf **AR**40, Ride mamma's colt; **KY**28, Ride granny's colt; **TN**1, Ride my mother's pony; **TX**40, Go on mammy's colts.

mother's heart n [*EDD* 1853 →; see quot 1914]

=**shepherd's purse**.

   1895 U.S. Dept. Ag. *Farmers' Bulletin* 28.28, Shepherd's purse, mother's heart. . . Bursa bursa-pastoris. **1901** Lounsberry *S. Wild Flowers* 198, *Mother's Heart.* . . The popular names which appeal most to us in this country have naturally been bestowed in allusion to the peculiar shape of its pods, they being infinitely better known than its . . flowers. In the early season . . , the whole plant is collected by the people to be used in medicinal preparations. **1910** Graves *Flowering Plants* 201 **CT**, Mother's Heart. . . Common. . . Valued as a pot-herb because of its earliness. **1914** Georgia *Manual Weeds* 180, *Capsella Bursa-pastoris.* . . Mothers' Hearts. . . Flowers white, minute, terminating a . . raceme of triangular, flattened heart-shaped silicles . . ; each "Mother's heart" is partitioned across its narrow thickness and each cell contains about ten reddish brown seeds. **1973** *Foxfire 2* 73 **sAppalachians**, Shepherd's purse . . , mother's heart. . . Flowers are white and followed by flat, heart-shaped seed capsules. The young leaves can be cooked and added to salads; or the seeds used in salads.

mother's mark n Also *mother mark* [*OED mother mark, mother's mark* (at *mother* sb. 16.a)]

A birthmark.

   1899 (1912) Green *VA Folk-Speech* 288, Mothermark. . . Stain on the face or body of a new-born child. **1904** U.S. Dept. Ag. Bur. Animal Industry *Special Rept. Diseases of Cattle* 265, The angiomas are tumors composed mainly of blood vessels or blood spaces and are observed on the skin of man, where they are called "birthmarks" or "mother marks." **1960** Taber *Med. Dict.* M-49, Mother. . . *m.'s mark.* A birthmark.

mothers' seat See **mothers' bench**

mother up v phr **esp West**

Of a cow: to seek out her calf; of a herd: to sort itself out so that each cow has her own calf.

   1940 Writers' Program *Guide NV* 77, When the female stock claim their young they *mother-up*. [**1961** Patterson *Buffalo Head* 134 **wCanada**, At Bull Creek we stopped for a little while to give the calves a chance to "mother-up"; very soon every cow had her calf.] **1981** *KS Qrly.* 13.2.68, *Mother up* (v.)—the action of calves and their mothers locating each other at the end of the day as the herd quiets down for the night on a drive.

mother way, in the adj phr Cf *DS* AA28

=**family way, in a**.

   1990 Cavender *Folk Med. Lexicon* 25 **sAppalachians**, *In the mother way*—pregnant.

mother wit n [*OED* c1440 →] **chiefly Sth, S Midl** *esp freq among Black speakers*

Natural intelligence; common sense; see quot 1973.

   1858 (1929) Taylor *Life on a Whaler* 132 **NEng**, He was naturally good-humored and possessed a great share of that engaging faculty called mother-wit. **1899** (1912) Green *VA Folk-Speech* 288, *Mother wit.* . . Native wit; common sense. Good sense unaided by book-learning. **1926** *DN* 5.401 **Ozarks**, Mother-wit. . . Native intelligence. "Thet 'ar Simpson boy's fine eddicated, but he don't 'pear t' have no mother-wit." **1945** FWP *Lay My Burden Down* 1 **Sth** [Black], Folks claim them

kind of people been bless with plenty good mother wit. **1945** Saxon *Gumbo Ya-Ya* 499 **LA** [Black], I ain't had much schoolin' but I got good mother-wit. **1967–68** *DARE* FW Addit **neLA**, Mother wit = a high degree of common sense; "One of 'em [=Black people] might say, 'That fellow's got a lot of mother wit about him'"; **PA**172, Mother wit—native intelligence [Inf Black]. **1972** Claerbaut *Black Jargon* 73, *Mother-wit* . . common sense; conventional wisdom: *Use the mother-wit, baby.* **1973** Dundes *Mother Wit* xiv, Mother wit is a popular term in black speech referring to common sense. Mother wit is the kind of good sense not necessarily learned from books or in school. Mother wit with its connotation of collective wisdom acquired by the experience of living and from generations past is often expressed in folklore. **1986** Pederson *LAGS Concordance*, 1 inf, **csGA**, She has plenty of mother wit even though she didn't go to school; 1 inf, **csTX**, Good mother wit; 1 inf, **csLA**, Mother wit = common sense. [2 of 3 infs Black] **1988** *Lincoln Avenue* 260 **wNC** (as of c1940) [Black], The coo-koo is not a bird of principle. He ain't got no mother wit. . . He's just a low-down opportunist.

motherwort n

1 Std: a widely distributed, naturalized medicinal plant (*Leonurus cardiaca*).

2 A **boneset 1** (here: *Eupatorium purpureum*).

   1892 *Jrl. Amer. Folkl.* 5.98 **MA**, *Eupatorium purpureum*, motherwort. **1971** Krochmal *Appalachia Med. Plants* 120, Marsh milkweed, motherwort. . . This plant is used for urinary disorders. **1974** (1977) Coon *Useful Plants* 108, Motherwort. . . A plant with as many common names as this is surely one known to people all over the East and South where it grows. . . Among herbalists it is claimed to be of value as a diuretic and tonic.

mothey See **mother** n¹

moth fly n

1 An adult moth (Lepidoptera), as contrasted with its larva (sometimes also called a **moth**). **esp NEast**

   1890 Warren *Birds PA* 310, The House Wren feeds on beetles, spiders, flies, "moth-flies," grasshoppers and larvae. [**1899** Bergen *Animal Lore* 91 **eMA**, Butterflies make moths, therefore they had better be killed.] **1931–33** *LANE Worksheets,* 1 inf, **CT**, Moths come from moth flies. **1939** *LANE* Map 237, 1 inf, **MA**, The moth fly lays eggs from which the moths hatch. **1968** *DARE* (Qu. R4) Infs **DE**3, **PA**112, 138, Moth fly.

2 A **midge 1** of the family Psychodidae. [See quot 1901]

   1901 Howard *Insect Book* 108, *Psychodidae.* . . These are certain very small, weak flies which look like little moths, from which fact they have been termed "moth-flies," which are frequently found upon windows and upon the under surfaces of leaves. **1905** Kellogg *Amer. Insects* 319, "Moth-fly". . . The vernacular name comes from the slight resemblance to minute moths shown by these flies because of the hairy broad wings, which are held over the back when the fly is at rest in the roof-like manner of moths. **1926** Essig *Insects N. Amer.* 532, Moth Flies. . . Very small, hairy, brownish or dark flies resembling brown lacewings or small moths. **1949** Swain *Insect Guide* 187, *Moth Flies.* . . Minute insects, rarely exceeding ⅛ inch in length. **1972** Swan–Papp *Insects* 586, The Psychodidae, or moth flies, have hairy bodies and wings. . . Their flight is short and jerky.

moth miller See **miller** n

motley adj

Of someone's face: dirty, smeared.

   1899 (1912) Green *VA Folk-Speech* 289, Motley. . . Party-coloured; variegated in colour. . . Also dirty. "Where did you get that motley face." **1968–70** *DARE* [(Qu. X29, *Joking or uncomplimentary words for a person's face*) Inf **VA**2, Motley face;] (Qu. Y39, *To get something sticky or smeared up: "The children have been eating candy and they've got their faces all _____."*) Infs **GA**44, **KY**94, Motley.

motorboat n

A children's ring game; see quots.

   1968–70 *DARE* (Qu. EE1, . . *Games . . children play . . in which they form a ring, and either sing or recite a rhyme*) Inf **CA**118, Motorboat, motorboat; **LA**34, **VA**109, Motorboat. **1983** *DARE* File **MI, UT**, (*What games do children play in which they form a ring, and either sing or recite a rhyme?*) Motorboat. [**1995** *DARE* File **csWI** (as of c1968), When I was in grade school, sometimes one kid would start saying the word "motorboat" over and over and others would chime in. The chant would get faster, louder, and less synchronized as more kids joined in; I guess we thought the dull roar we produced sounded like a motorboat.

This wasn't really a game, and we didn't have a name for it; it was just something to do to pass the time while we were waiting in line to go back into the school building after recess or while we were on the school bus.]

motorcycle n Usu |ˈmotə(r)ˌsaɪkəl|; also |-ˌsɪkəl| Pronc-sp *motorsickle*
Std senses, var forms.
    c1960 *Wilson Coll.* **csKY,** Motorcycle [ˈmotəˌsɪkl], common. **1967** *DARE* FW Addit **csPA,** Motorcycle [-sɪkəl]; **neTN,** Motorcycle = "motorsickle" [ˈmotɚˌsɪkl]. **1969** *This is the Arlo Guthrie Book* 83, [Song lyrics:] I don't want a pick-le / Just want to ride on my mo-tor-sick-le. **1976** Garber *Mountain-ese* 59 **sAppalachians,** Motorsickle. **1981** Pederson *LAGS Basic Materials* **Gulf Region,** [Of 20 infs who offered the term *motorcycle,* 7 had proncs of the type [ˈmotɚˌsɪkl].] **1982** *Barrick Coll.* **csPA,** Motorcycle—pron. motor-sickle.

motte n Also sp *mot(e), mott* [Prob ult Fr *motte,* introduced by Irish immigrants to southeast Texas; see quot 1972; cf *EDD moat* sb.] **chiefly TX** See Map Cf **shinnery**
A grove or clump of trees, esp in open prairie.
    1844 (1846) Kendall *Santa Fé Exped.* 1.40 **TX,** We drew up in a body, with a small *mot* of timber close by to which we could easily retreat. [Footnote to *mot:*] In Western Texas a small clump of timber is called a *mot.* **1848** Webber *Old Hicks* 52 **TX,** Our course bearing west of north, over broken prairie, diversified by clumps or motts of scrubby growth. **1858** Hammett *Piney Woods Tavern* 271 **TX,** This prairie is surrounded . . on the west and north by a succession of mots of timber. **1892** Duval *Young Explorers* 142 **swTX,** We've got the wind of them, and by keeping yon little 'mot' bertwixt them and us, we kin git in three or four hundred yards of the drove. **1896** in 1952 Green *Samuel Maverick* 254 **TX** (as of 1842), Immediately in front of the house stood a "mott" of young live oak trees. **1929** Dobie *Vaquero* 203 **TX,** During the past fifty years terrible drouths have decimated noble live oak mottes. **1945** Thorp *Pardner* 31 **SW,** I had camped for the night in a motte of *bois d'arc.* **1962** Atwood *Vocab. TX* 42, *Grove of trees.* A small group of trees together, surrounded by open country. . . *Mott* . . is rather heavily concentrated in South Central and West Texas. **1965–70** *DARE* (Qu. T1, . . *A bunch of trees growing together in open country, especially on a hill)* 11 Infs, **TX,** Motte; **TX3, 4,** [mɑ(ː)t]; **TX13, 22,** [mat]; (Qu. T2a, . . *A piece of land covered with trees . . only a few acres)* Infs **TX22, 101,** Motte. [14 of 16 Infs old] **1972** *S. Folkl. Qrly.* 36.127, There are many reasons why derivation [of *motte*] from Mexican Spanish seems unlikely. First, the most convincing meaning of Mexican Spanish *mata,* "a group of trees in the middle of a prairie", is found only in *southern* Mexico. . . Second, many Spanish words ending in "a" were absorbed into the Anglo-Texan vernacular, . . but never with the loss of pronunciation of the final "a". *Ibid* 129, Of these diverse European minority groups, only the Irish were present in the Coastal Prairie as early as the 1830's, when *motte* entered Texas English. *Ibid* 130, Both of these colonies [of Irish settlement] lay in the zone of present *motte* concentration. . . The leading European source area of the Irish immigrants was County Wexford. . . Significantly, there are many *mottes,* or *motes,* in County Wexford. *Ibid* 132, The use of the word *mote* or *motte* in Ireland can be attributed to the French spoken by these Norman invaders, and it has survived in the vernacular English of the Irish. *Ibid,* *Motte* was used in parts of nineteenth-century Ireland . . to describe mounds that were often, if not usually tree-covered. **1982** *This Remarkable Continent* 136, *Motte* or *mott,* meaning a copse or small stand or

clump of trees on a prairie, is concentrated between the lower Colorado and Nueces rivers in Texas. **1986** Pederson *LAGS Concordance,* 1 inf, **cTX,** Mote—any clump of trees; 1 inf, **csTX,** A motte of trees—orchard; 1 inf, **csTX,** A motte of trees—a cluster; smaller than a grove.

motter See **matter** n[1], v

mottled brant n Also *mottled goose*
=**white-fronted goose.**
    1923 U.S. Dept. Ag. *Misc. Circular* 13.34, *White-fronted Goose.* . . *Vernacular Names.* . . *In local use.* . . Mottled brant (Calif.); mottled goose (Tex.)

mottled cranefly See **cranefly orchid**

mottled duck n
=**Florida duck.**
    1916 *Times–Picayune* (New Orleans LA) 26 Mar mag sec 2/3, Mottled Duck (Anas fulvigula maculosa). Texas Mallard. . . mottled on the breast, instead of streaked. Found in Southern Louisiana near the Texas border. **1921** LA Dept. of Conserv. *Bulletin* 10.53, Two forms of this specie [sic] [=*Anas fulvigula*] are described as occurring on the Gulf coast of the United States, the Florida duck . . and the mottled, or Texas, duck.

mottled goose See **mottled brant**

mottled owl n
A **screech owl** with plumage in the gray color phase.
    1781 Latham *Genl. Synopsis Birds* 1.126, Mottled Owl. . . The length of this species is eight inches and a half. The bill is brown: irides yellow. . . Inhabits *North America.* **1811** Wilson *Amer. Ornith.* 3.17, Mottled Owl. *Strix Naevia.* . . is chiefly a native of the northern regions. **1858** Baird *Birds* 51, *The Mottled Owl.* . . *Adult.*—Upper parts pale ashy brown with longitudinal lines of brownish black, and mottled irregularly with the same, and with cinereous. **1898** (1900) Davie *Nests N. Amer. Birds* 239, The Mottled Owl is resident throughout Eastern United States and Canada; west to the Rocky Mountains. **1923** WV State Ornith. *Birds WV* 22, The screech owl is sometimes called mottled owl. [*Ibid* 23, If you have an owl around your barn or orchard, . . his family will be a mystery to you, for he and his wife may both be gray and their young may be of the red phase. All over the country they have this peculiar trait, part of the family being red, the other gray.] **1953** Jewett *Birds WA* 347, *Otus asio kennicottii.* . . Mottled Owl. **1969** Longstreet *Birds FL* 76, Mottled Owl. . . Two distinct color phases. . . These phases are said to have no connection with sex or season.

mottled sandpiper n
=**stilt sandpiper.**
    1916 *Times–Picayune* (New Orleans LA) 2 Apr mag sec 8, *Stilt Sandpiper.* . . Mottled Sandpiper. **1923** U.S. Dept. Ag. *Misc. Circular* 13.52 **NC, LA,** *Stilt Sandpiper.* . . *Vernacular Names.* . . *In local use.* . . Mottled sandpiper.

mottled sculpin n
Std: a **sculpin** (here: *Cottus bairdi*). Also called **blob** n **1, bullhead 1a, gudgeon 3, lake sculpin, miller's thumb 1, muddler, muffle-jaw, spoonhead, springfish, stargazer**

mottledy adj [Cf Intro "Language Changes" III.1] Cf **fadedy, motley**
Mottled.
    1969 *DARE* (Qu. X29, *Joking or uncomplimentary words for a person's face)* Inf **KY19,** Mottledy [ˈmɑtḷdi] face.

mouf(y) See **mouth**

mougat See **mucket** n[1]

mought See **may** v **Aa**

moughty adj, adv Also sp *mouty;* with *near,* also *mought* [Varr of **mighty,** by analogy with *mought* var of *might* (at **may** v **Aa**)] **Sth, S Midl**
    1893 Shands *MS Speech* 46, Moughty [mauti]. Illiterate white and negro for *mighty,* meaning *very, excessively, exceedingly.* **1913** Kephart *Highlanders* 394 **sAppalachians,** I tell yeou hit teks a moughty reso*lute* gal ter do what that thar gal has done. **1917** in 1944 *ADD* 399 **sWV,** Mouty. **1936** in 1976 *Weevils in the Wheat* 193 **VA** [Black], Mr. Sam Bagos, I member him. He was a little man, but a moughty man. **c1940** in 1995 *Montgomery Coll.* **wNC, eTN,** Hit's gittin raily mought nigh plumb cold. **1942** Thomas *Blue Ridge Country* 288 **nGA,** Johnny's

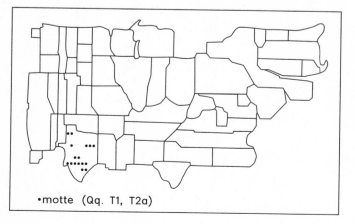
•motte (Qq. T1, T2a)

captain has writ moughty pretty about our boy. **1950** (1965) Richter *Town* 153 **OH,** Moughty few ever heerd gabby birds a talkin'.

mouket See **mucket** n[1]

mould n Also sp *mold;* pronc-sp *mole* [*OED* *mould* sb.[2] c1000 →; *EDD mole* sb.[2]] **Sth**
The top of the head; the fontanel of an infant's head.
   1899 (1912) Green *VA Folk-Speech* 289, *Mould.* . . A soft place on the crown of children's heads where the sutures are not closed, the bones being incomplete. **1912** Green *VA Folk-Speech* 285, *Mole.* . . Space at the top of a child's head before the bones are closed. **1923** Parsons *Folk-lore Sea Islands* 198 **csSC** [Black], Another way for babies is to "blow smoke on mole o' de head [Parsons: fontanella], get um drunk, le' um go to sleep, smoke go right on t'rough." **1927** *Jrl. Amer. Folkl.* 40.150 **LA,** If the mole of a baby's head does not beat, the baby will die. (Negroes make plasters of various kinds to cause it to beat.) **c1938** in 1970 Hyatt *Hoodoo* 1.407 **New Orleans LA** [Black], You cut right in the mole of his head—a strand of hair out of the mole of his head. *Ibid* 2.1475 **seGA** [Black], She cut off . . three strands of hair from de *mole* of head. *Ibid* 1527 **ceSC** [Black], Yo' take yore hair agin from de mole of yore head. **1945** Saxon *Gumbo Ya-Ya* 529 **LA,** For a high fever: Obtain a pigeon which has never flown out of the cage, cut him open and lay him on the 'mole' of the patient's head. **1968** Harris *S. Home Remedies* 82 **NC,** For headache: Pour one tablespoon of salt on the mold of your head and keep it moistened with vinegar. **1981** Pederson *LAGS Basic Materials,* 1 inf, **cwFL,** ['mo<ʊləɨ͈ˌhɛˀ·əd] = center of your head. [Inf Black]

mould v See **mold** v

mouldwarp See **moldwarp**

mounah's bench See **mourners' bench**

mound n See **mow** n[1]

mound v See **mow** v

mound cactus n [See quot 1941]
A **hedgehog cactus 3** (here: *Echinocereus triglochidiatus*).
   1941 Jaeger *Wildflowers* 164, Mohave mound cactus. . . The many small, globose to oblong stems, 6 to 600 in number, are huddled together in cushion-like mounds up to a yard across; and when the plant is in full flower the color effect is most startling. **1959** Munz–Keck *CA Flora* 317, *E[chinocereus] mojavensis* . . Mound Cactus. **1967** Dodge *Roadside Wildflowers* 45, Crimson hedgehog—Mound cactus. Sometimes growing singly but more often in crowded clumps of up to 150 stems, the plants are covered with bright red, trumpet-shaped flowers in May–July. These colorful mounds are visible for considerable distances on open, rocky hillsides.

mound gopher n
A **ground squirrel b** (here: *Spermophilus richardsonii*).
   1970 *Western Folkl.* 29.172 **Upper MW,** *Mound gopher* and *pocket gopher* reveal the informant's confusion, for ground squirrels are not pocket gophers, which belong to the family *Geomyidae.* The true gophers make mounds, but ground squirrels do not. **1973** Allen *LAUM* 1.324 (as of c1950), Flickertail or Richardson's ground squirrel: . . mound squirrel [1 inf, **cwMN**].

mound lily n Also *mound lily yucca*
A **yucca** (here: *Yucca gloriosa*).
   1900 Lyons *Plant Names* 401, *Y[ucca] gloriosa.* . . Mound Lily. **1933** Small *Manual SE Flora* 303, *Y[ucca] gloriosa.* . . Mound-lily yucca. . . Fla. to N.C. **1949** Moldenke *Amer. Wild Flowers* 369, *Moundlily yucca* . . has a stem up to 15 feet tall, sometimes branched. **1952** Blackburn *Trees* 308, Mound-lily . . *Y[ucca] gloriosa.* **1960** Vines *Trees SW* 56, *Moundlily Yucca.* . . Probably only indigenous as a species on the coastal dunes of South Carolina, Georgia, and northeastern Florida. **1979** Little *Checklist U.S. Trees* 297, *Moundlily yucca.* . . Coastal dunes and beaches.

mount n
1 A cowboy's string of horses. **chiefly SW** Cf **string**
   1903 (1965) Adams *Log Cowboy* 14 **csTX,** It was my good fortune that morning to get a good mount of horses,—three sorrels, two grays, two coyotes, a black, a brown, and a *grulla.* **1907** White *AZ Nights* 53, He kept his own mount of horses, took care of them. **1933** *AmSp* 8.1.30 **nwTX,** *Mount.* A string of horses, usually eight or ten, assigned by the boss to one man. **1940** *Sat. Review* 17 Aug 9, If "mount" means, in one range country, a working outfit of several animals, on another range it might be called a "string." When I joined a northwestern Colorado

roundup I was assigned a "string" from the "cavvy." . . I was not assigned a "mount," nor even six "mounts" in the Websterian sense; it was a "string" of six "hosses." **1944** Adams *Western Words* 101, *Mount*—The number of horses assigned to a rider for his personal use during his stay at the ranch. . . The number of horses assigned a rider depends largely upon the size of the ranch and the kind of country to be worked. Seven to ten head is an average mount, and in this number is included one or two broncs which the cowboy rides on circle to get them gradually used to cow work. The word *mount* is usually used in sections which employ the term *remuda* in speaking of the band of saddle horses. In the northern, or *cavvy,* country personal horses are called the *string.* **1966** *DARE* Tape **OK**30, A man's mount generally consisted of about seven horses, or eight. . . Some of them had more, but that was the average.
2 A type of playing marble.
   c1970 Wiersma *Marbles Terms, Mounts*—large marbles midsized between boulder and a perry.

mount v
To furnish with a **mount** n **1.**
   1966 *DARE* Tape **NM**14, There would be one to three wagons usually with the roundups. Each wagon would contain from fifteen to twenty men and every man was mounted with about eight horses.

mountain n Usu |'maʊntən, 'maʊntn̩|; also **chiefly Sth, S Midl** |'maʊntɪŋ|; also |'maʊntɪn, -ɪn|; for addit varr see quots Pronc-sp *mounting* Cf Intro "Language Changes" II.12, Pronc Intro 3.II.14, 19, **-ing B1**
Std senses, var forms.
   1837 Sherwood *Gaz.* **GA** 70, *Provincialisms.* . . *Mounting,* for mountain. **1855** in 1956 Eliason *Tarheel Talk* 314 **nw,cwNC,** Mounting. **1861** [see **-ing B1**]. **1886** *S. Bivouac* 4.349 **wNC,** *Mounting* is heard in [western] North Carolina but not in East Tennessee. **1895** [see **-ing B1**]. **1903** *DN* 2.321 **seMO,** *Mountain.* . . Pronounced mounting. **1906** *DN* 3.147 **nwAR,** *Mounting* ['maʊntɪŋ]. **1933** Rawlings *South Moon* 38 **FL,** They cain't half ketch them fellers makin' moonshine up in them mountings. **1942** Hall *Smoky Mt. Speech* 82 **wNC, eTN,** *Mountain* is occasionally ['mæʊntən] and ['mæʊnɪn], as well as ['mæʊntn̩]. **1955** *PADS* 23.43 **e,cSC, eNC, seGA,** /ɪ/ in unstressed syllables in *funnel, mountain* (also e. Virginia and e. New England). **1959** *VT Hist.* 27.149, *Mountain* . . pronc. ['maʊntɪn]. Common. ['maʊntn̩] is rarely heard. **1961** Kurath–McDavid *Pronc. Engl.* 168, A clear regional pattern appears in the dissemination of the phonemes /ə/ and /ɪ/ in the unstressed syllable of . . *mountain.* . . [T]he incidence of /ɪ/ is largely confined to coastal subareas of the North and South and appears to be more common among older speakers, especially in western and central New England. When *mountain, towel,* etc., do not have /ɪ/, they end in /-ən, -əl/, articulated as [-ən, -əl] or as syllabic [n̩, l̩].

mountain alder n
1 An alder: usu *Alnus crispa* in the eastern US; *A. sinuata* or *A. tenuifolia* in the western US.
   1843 Torrey *Flora NY* 2.203, *Alnus viridis.* . . Mountain Alder. . . Along the mountain streams of Essex county. **1891** Jesup *Plants Hanover NH* 38, A[lnus] viridis. . . Green or Mountain Alder. **1908** Sudworth *Forest Trees Pacific* 266, *Mountain Alder. Alnus tenuifolia.* . . Important as a member of the forest on account of the protection it affords the headwaters and lower courses of mountain streams and springy slopes. **1910** Jepson *Silva CA* 200, *Alnus tenuifolia.* . . The Mountain Alder forms thickets . . at 5000 to 7000 feet altitude in the Sierra Nevada from Donner Pass northward to Mt. Shasta, thence westward to Trinity Summit and the Siskiyous. It has a wide distribution over western America. **1924** Hawkins *Trees & Shrubs* 76 **MT,** *Mountain Alder* (Alnus sinuata) . . is a smaller shrub with greener leaves . . and grows about mountain springs at higher elevations. **1928** Rosendahl–Butters *Trees MN* 102, *Alnus crispa.* . . Mountain alder. A shrub 0.6–3 m. high, bark gray or brownish. **1938** Van Dersal *Native Woody Plants* 322, Alder, . . Mountain *(Alnus crispa, Alnus rhombifolia, Alnus sinuata, Alnus tenuifolia).* **1959** Anderson *Flora AK* 188, Mountain Alder—*A. tenuifolia.* . . A large shrub or small tree. **1976** Elmore *Shrubs & Trees SW* 117, Mountain . . alder . *Alnus tenuifolia.* . . Abundant along mountain streams or in moist meadows. . . Beaver, deer and rabbits eat the bark in spite of its puckery taste (to us anyway). **1980** Little *Audubon Guide N. Amer. Trees W. Region* 380, "Mountain Alder" . . *Alnus sinuata.* . . Along streams and lakes and in valleys. . . In Alaska to alpine zone above timberline; in NW California to 7000'. *Ibid* 381, *Mountain Alder* . . *Alnus tenuifolia.* . . This is the common alder throughout the Rockies.

2 =**striped maple.**

1897 Sudworth *Arborescent Flora* 282 **NC,** *Acer pennsylvanicum.* . . Mountain Alder. **1933** Small *Manual SE Flora* 824, Moosewood. *Mountain-alder.* . . Rocky woods, Blue Ridge and more northern provinces.

mountain anemone n

An anemone (here: *Anemone lancifolia*).

1901 Lounsberry *S. Wild Flowers* 177, Mountain anemone. . . From North Carolina to southern Pennsylvania it occurs, usually in the mountains where its companion often is the sweet lily-of-the-valley. **1931** Harned *Wild Flowers Alleghanies* 177, *Mountain Anemone.* . . Flowers, white, 1 to 1½ in. across. **1953** Strausbaugh–Core *Flora WV* 390, *Mountain anemone.* . . May. Woods, chiefly in the mountain counties.

mountain apple n

The **Malay apple,** naturalized in Hawaii; also its fruit.

1924 *Amer. Botanist* 30.20 **HI,** One of the most common of the forest trees is the ohia or mountain apple (*Eugenia malaccensis*). . . When the fruit is ripe . . the tree is in its glory—great clusters of the deep red, luscious-looking "apples" clinging about its branches and larger limbs everywhere. Juicy and refreshing the fruit is, but rather insipid. **1933** Bryan *Hawaiian Nature* 85, The familiar mountain apple tree . . grows in the valleys and gulches at the lower edge of the rain forest. **1948** Neal *In Gardens HI* 559, *Mountain apple.* . . The trees grow rapidly and begin to bear fruit when seven or eight years old. . . The fruit is eaten both raw and pickled. Some years, it is on sale in the markets from June to early winter. **1967** *DARE* (Qu. I53, . . *Fruits grown around here . . special varieties*) Inf **HI**1, Mountain apple—not a real apple, dark purple-red skin; **HI**11, Mountain apples—bell-shaped. **1980** Bushnell *Water of Kane* 415 **HI,** Crimson mountain apples clung to the branches and trunks of ohia-ai, waiting to be eaten. **1994** Stone–Pratt *Hawai'i's Plants* 329, Large numbers of 'ō'ū once wandered . . downslope . . to exploit fruiting common guava, mountain apple, and other introduced fruits.

mountain ash n

1 A tree of the genus *Sorbus*, esp *S. americanus*. [*OED* 1597 →] **chiefly Nth** See Map Also called **service tree, rowan.** For other names of var spp see **dogberry f, Indian mozemize, life-of-man 5, lightning tree, missey-moosey, moosemise 1, mountain sumac 2, peruve, roundwood, whistlewood, wine tree, witchwood**

1785 Marshall *Arbustrum* 144, Sorbus. The Service tree, Quickbeam, or Mountain ash. [*Ibid* 145, Sorbus americana. . . The flowers are produced at the extremity of the branches in form of an umbel, and are succeeded by roundish berries of a red color when ripe.] **1822** Eaton *Botany* 470 **nwMA,** [*Sorbus*] *americana* . . mountain ash. . . This shrub or tree grows in very great plenty on Saddle mountain near Williams College. **1830** Rafinesque *Med. Flora* 2.265, Sorbus . . *Mountain ash, Service tree.* . . Bark smells and tastes like cherry bark. **1843** Torrey *Flora NY* 1.224, Pyrus Americana . . *Mountain Ash.* . . The handsome red fruit is persistent through the winter. **1873** in 1976 Miller *Shaker Herbs* 124, Ash, mountain. . . The bark is used in bilious diseases to cleanse the blood; the berries for scurvy, and as a vermifuge. **1930** Sievers *Amer. Med. Plants* 7, Sorbus americana. . . The American mountain-ash occurs in swamps, low woods, or moist ground from Newfoundland south along the mountains to North Carolina and to Michigan. It is most abundant in the northern portion of its range. **1952** Blackburn *Trees* 270, S[orbus] *decora.* . . showy mountain-ash. **1965–**

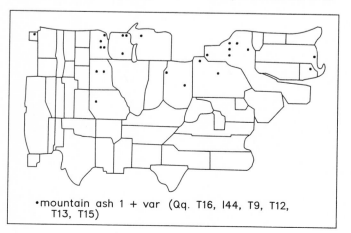

•mountain ash 1 + var (Qq. T16, I44, T9, T12, T13, T15)

70 *DARE* (Qu. T16) 14 Infs, **chiefly Nth,** Mountain ash; **MN**2, Mountain ash—produces red berries; **OH**89, Mountain ash—they're pretty rare; **RI**10, Mountain ash—orange berries; (Qu. I44, *What kinds of berries grow wild around here?*) Inf **MI**34, Mountain ash berries; **NY**97, Mountain ash has berries; **PA**234, Don't eat mountain ash berries; (Qu. T9) Inf **NY**101, Mountain ash; (Qu. T12) Inf **AK**9, Mountain ash; (Qu. T13, . . *Sumac*) Inf **NY**219, Mountain ash; (Qu. T15, . . *Kinds of swamp trees*) Inf **AK**9, Mountain ash; **MN**19, Mountain ash—grows native in swamps here [FW: Inf thinks it's actually a silly name]. **1972** Viereck–Little *AK Trees* 166, Sorbus scopulina. . . western mountain-ash. *Ibid* 168, Sitka mountain-ash . . Sorbus sitchensis. . . Pacific mountain-ash.

2 Any of var ashes (*Fraxinus* spp), esp **Texas ash;** see quots. **West**

1897 Sudworth *Arborescent Flora* 327 **TX,** *Fraxinus texensis.* . . Mountain Ash. **1913** Wooton *Trees NM* 128, Mountain Ash . . (*Fraxinus velutina*). . . The common name is a local one and does not refer to the shrub which ordinarily goes under that name in the eastern and central states (*Sorbus Americana*). **1925** Jepson *Manual Plants CA* 760, F[raxinus] *dipetala* . . Foothill Ash. . . Also called Mountain Ash and Flowering Ash. **1931** U.S. Dept. Ag. *Misc. Pub.* 101.137 **West,** Fragrant ash (F[raxinus] *cuspidata*), locally known as flowering ash and mountain ash, a handsome shrub or low tree with small leaves and showy panicles of white fragrant flowers. **1945** Wodehouse *Hayfever Plants* 124, Mountain ash [=*Fraxinus texana*]. . . is found on the high dry limestone bluffs and ridges in the neighborhood of Dallas and Fort Worth. **1960** Vines *Trees SW* 866, It [=the Texas Ash] is also known as Mountain Ash because of its growth on limestone hills.

mountain balm n

1 An **Oswego tea** (here: *Monarda didyma*).

1830 Rafinesque *Med. Flora* 2.35, Mountain Mint, Oswego tea, Mountain Balm, Horse Mint. [*Ibid* 37, The whole plant has a grateful smell, somewhat similar to Dittany and Balm; much stronger when bruised.] **a1874** in 1976 Miller *Shaker Herbs* 212, Mountain Balm. High Balm. Bee Balm. **1876** Hobbs *Bot. Hdbk.* 72, Mountain balm . . Monarda coccinea. **1971** Krochmal *Appalachia Med. Plants* 178, Mountain balm, mountain mint, Oswego tea.

2 A **yerba santa,** usu *Eriodictyon californicum*. **chiefly CA** Cf **consumptive's weed**

1887 *Overland Mth.* (2d ser) 10.153, The low growth of shrubs . . is made up of . . herba santa, or "mountain balm,"—from which a medicine is prepared for pulmonary affections—and a few others. **1897** Parsons *Wild Flowers CA* 58, Yerba Santa. Mountain Balm. **1902** U.S. Natl. Museum *Contrib. Herbarium* 7.381, The well-known yerba santa (holy herb) of California. . . grows profusely on dry, bushy hillsides throughout Mendocino County, and is known under the names mountain balm, wild balsam, gum leaves, tar weed, and, although incorrectly, "sumac." No plant is more highly valued as a medicine by all the tribes of Mendocino County. It is found in every household either in the dry state or in whisky extract. **1931** U.S. Dept. Ag. *Misc. Pub.* 101.139, Eriodictyon, frequently known as mountain balm, consisting of six or seven species, is a genus confined to the region from southern Oregon to Lower California, Arizona, and southern Utah. **1969** *DARE* Tape **CA**136, Mountain balm—they used to smoke and chew that for cough or cold. . . It's a large bush-like deal, has a kind of a slick, sticky leaf . . sticky when you chew it, has a purple flower on it, . . grows around here, especially after a fire. **1969** *DARE* FW Addit **cnCA,** Mountain balm—cure for coughs and colds. . . It is a plant with ragged leaves and gummy stuff on them. Put leaves in whiskey or brandy; it dissolves the gum. Drink. **1974** (1977) Coon *Useful Plants* 152, *Eriodictyon californicum*—Yerba Santa, mountain balm, consumptive's weed. . . A number of references to this plant indicate its value as an expectorant and again for making an aromatic syrup used as a vehicle for quinine. For those with asthma, recommendations are to dry the foliage, make "cigarettes" and be helped by smoking them. **1981** Benson–Darrow *Trees SW Deserts* 193, *Eriodictyon*—Yerba Santa, California Mountain Balm.

3 A **snowbrush** (here: *Ceanothus velutinus*). **esp Pacific NW**

1924 Hawkins *Trees & Shrubs* 97 **MT,** *Mountain Balm* (Ceanothus velutinus) . . is common throughout the lodgepole pine belt. . . Its fragrance accounts for the common name. **1931** U.S. Dept. Ag. *Misc. Pub.* 101.109, Snowbrush (C[eanothus] *velutinus*) . . for which mountain balm, sticky laurel, and tobacco-brush are variant vernacular names, . . extends from British Columbia to California, Colorado, South Dakota, and Saskatchewan. **1937** U.S. Forest Serv. *Range Plant Hdbk.* B47, Snowbrush refers to the abundant fluffy masses of white flowers; mountain balm to its typically montane habitat and heavy balsamic odor. **1966** *DARE* Wildfl QR Pl.126 Inf **WA**10, Mountain balm—buckbrush if pink;

sticky laurel or mountain balm if white. **1973** Hitchcock–Cronquist *Flora Pacific NW* 290, Mt balm, sticky-laurel, greasewood.

4 A **horse balm** (here: *Collinsonia canadensis*).

1937 *Torreya* 37.100 **VA**, *Collinsonia canadensis* . . Mountain balm.

mountain balsam n

1 =**alpine fir.**

1897 Sudworth *Arborescent Flora* 53, *Abies lasiocarpa*. . . Mountain Balsam (mts. of Utah and Idaho). **1908** Britton *N. Amer. Trees* 77, White Fir. . . This Fir, variously called . . Alpine fir, Downy cone fir, Mountain balsam, . . has probably a greater range than any other American Fir, occurring from Alaska to Washington, Arizona, eastward to Alberta, Montana, Wyoming, Utah, and southern Colorado. **1916** Sudworth *Spruce & Balsam Fir* 327.24, Woodsmen and settlers usually call it [=the alpine fir] "balsam" or "mountain balsam."

2 =**Fraser fir. sAppalachians**

1897 Sudworth *Arborescent Flora* 50 **NC**, *Abies fraseri*. . . Mountain Balsam. **1908** Britton *N. Amer. Trees* 76, Fraser's balsam fir. . . This southern fir, called . . Mountain balsam, . . occurs in the higher mountains of Virginia and West Virginia to North Carolina and Tennessee. **1937** Thornburgh *Gt. Smoky Mts.* 132, "Us mountain people," he explained, "call the spruce 'he-balsam,' and the mountain balsam we call 'she-balsam.' "

3 A **yerba santa** (here: *Eriodictyon californicum*). Cf **mountain balm 2**

1897 *Jrl. Amer. Folkl.* 10.50 **CA**, *Eriodictyon glutinosum*, . . mountain balsam, yerba santa.

4 A **horse balm** (here: *Collinsonia canadensis*). Cf **mountain balm 4**

1940 Clute *Amer. Plant Names* 256, *Collinsonia Canadensis*. . . Mountain balsam.

mountain beaver n [See quot 1980]

A burrowing rodent (*Aplodontia rufa*) native chiefly to the Pacific Northwest. Also called **gopher n[1] 2d, marmot d, mountain boomer 2, whistler, woodchuck**

1884 Kingsley *Std. Nat. Hist.* 5.121, The "Showt'l" or "Sewellel" of the aborigines . . [is] known to more prosaic hunters and trappers as the "Boomer" or "Mountain Beaver." **1906** Stephens *CA Mammals* 95, It would appear that other animals prey on the Mountain Beaver as I caught a weasel and two skunks in traps set for Mountain Beaver. **1928** Anthony *N. Amer. Mammals* 457, The Mountain Beaver is a very hardy animal, and although it fights viciously when first taken from a trap, becomes tame in a remarkably short time. **1941** Writers' Program *Guide WA* 15, Among lesser native mammals. . . Several are of special interest: . . the strange mountain beaver (not a beaver), who burrows in wet hillsides and is found only in the western part of Washington and Oregon. **1947** Cahalane *Mammals* 550, The mountain beaver actually does cut down trees sometimes. Perhaps that is where it got its most common name, but it is a lumberjack in a very small way. **c1965** *DARE* File **WA**, Mountain beaver—a burrowing rodent common in the Seattle area. **1966–69** *DARE* (Qu. P29) Infs **WA**17, 20, 30, Mountain beaver; (Qu. P31) Inf **CA**137, Mountain beaver. **1980** Whitaker *Audubon Field Guide Mammals* 368, The common name "Mountain Beaver" is misleading, as this rodent is neither a beaver nor does it prefer a mountainous habitat: the name may have derived from its beaver-like habit of diverting streams into its tunnels or from its occasional gnawing of bark and cutting of limbs.

mountain beaver baseball n

1980 Whitaker *Audubon Field Guide Mammals* 368, Its [=the mountain beaver's] labyrinthine burrow system is usually shallow, . . and. . . features a nest chamber . . ; dead-end tunnels . . ; and separate chambers for storage of food and "Mountain Beaver baseballs," baseball-size balls of stone or clay encountered in digging, which the animal occasionally gnaws upon to sharpen its teeth and uses to close off nesting or feeding areas when vacated.

mountain berry n

A **wintergreen** (here: *Gaultheria procumbens*).

1971 Krochmal *Appalachia Med. Plants* 128, *Gaultheria procumbens*. . . Common names: . . mountain berry.

mountain birch n

1 A **birch**: usu **western birch,** rarely **sweet birch.**

1908 Sudworth *Forest Trees Pacific* 260, Mountain birch is a slender, graceful tree or tall shrub, long known as *Betula occidentalis* Hooker. . .

The habitat of the tree, in contrast with that of most other birches, is distinctly a mountainous one. **1931** U.S. Dept. Ag. *Misc. Pub.* 101.18, Mountain birch, a common western shrub, is an important browse species on many sheep and goat ranges, its palatability ranging from fair to very good. **1940** Clute *Amer. Plant Names* 253, *Betula lenta*. Mountain birch. **1942** Hylander *Plant Life* 184, West of the Rocky Mountains there is a slender little tree known as the Mountain Birch with shiny reddish-brown bark and small ovate leaves. **1953** Nelson *Plants Rocky Mt. Park* 56, *Mountain birch* or *water birch, Betula occidentalis*. . . In some seasons these birches turn a beautiful clear yellow in the autumn.

2 =**deer brush 1.**

1897 Parsons *Wild Flowers CA* 84, Mountain birch. White tea-tree. Soap-bush. . . The young twigs and leaves have the spicy fragrance of the black birch of the Eastern States. **1898** *Jrl. Amer. Folkl.* 11.225 **CA**, *Ceanothus integerrimus* . . mountain birch.

mountain blackberry n

Any of three blackberries: usu *Rubus alleghaniensis,* but also *R. canadensis* or *R. nivalis.*

1900 Lyons *Plant Names* 326, The Mountain Blackberry of the northeastern U.S. . . is . . *R[ubus] alleghaniensis* [sic]. **1903** Porter *Flora PA* 167, *Rubus Alleghaniensis*. . . Mountain Blackberry. . . In dry soil, Ont. and N.Y. to Pa., perhaps to Va. **1910** Shreve *MD Plant Life* 442, *Rubus alleghaniensis* [sic]. . . Mountain Blackberry. . . In dry forests and open situations; frequent. **1937** Stemen–Myers *OK Flora* 195, *Rubus alleghaniensis*. . . *Mountain Blackberry*. . . Fruit . . thimble-shaped. **1942** *Torreya* 42.161 **OR**, *Rubus nivalis*. . . Small mountain blackberry. **1966** Grimm *Recognizing Native Shrubs* 140, *Mountain Blackberry—Rubus canadensis*. . . Stems unarmed or with only an occasional weak prickle. . . Along the higher Appalachians to northern Georgia.

mountain black cherry See **black cherry**

mountain blacksnake n

=**pilot blacksnake.**

1900 U.S. Natl. Museum *Annual Rept. for 1898* 844, *Coluber obsoletus*. . . is known as the Mountain Black Snake, or Pilot Snake. **1952** Ditmars *N. Amer. Snakes* 40, Mountain Blacksnake. . . In the Atlantic states it ranges as far north as central Massachusetts, thence southward to Florida. Farther inland, however, it ranges much farther north. **1958** Conant *Reptiles & Amphibians* 160, The . . "mountain black snake." Occurs virtually at sea level and to considerable altitudes in parts of the Appalachian mountain chain.

mountain bluebell n

1 A **bluebell 1g** (here: *Mertensia ciliata*). [See quot 1937] **West**

1906 (1918) Parsons *Wild Flowers CA* 340, Mountain Bluebells. . . *Mertensia Siberica* [sic]. . . The handsome blossoms of the mountain bluebell are to be found along water-courses at considerable elevations. These are not true bluebells. **1915** (1926) Armstrong–Thornber *Western Wild Flowers* 430, *Mertensia Sibirica*. . . It is often called Mountain Bluebell, but that name belongs to Campanula and is therefore misleading. **1936** McDougall–Baggley *Plants of Yellowstone* 106, Mountain bluebells *(Mertensia ciliata)*. **1937** U.S. Forest Serv. *Range Plant Hdbk.* W127, Mountain bluebells, one of the large species of its genus, . . is so named because it usually occurs in the mountains and has blue, bell-shaped flowers. **1963** Craighead *Rocky Mt. Wildflowers* 160, Mountain Bluebell covers large grassy meadows or parks among the spruce and fir trees.

2 A **bellflower** (here: either *Campanula divaricata* or *C. rotundifolia*).

1915 [see **1** above]. **1949** Peattie *Cascades* 242 **Pacific NW**, Harebell, the beautiful Campanula rotundifolia. . . They are known to many people by the name of bluebells or mountain bluebells. **1953** Greene–Blomquist *Flowers South* 124, *Mountain-Bluebell (Campanula divaricata)*. . . The most delightful of these [=bellflowers] is the mountain-bluebell with many, drooping, small, blue flowers hanging over ledges and road-cuts in seepages, on edges of mountain streams and waterfalls. Ga. to Ala., Ky., W.Va., and Md.

mountain bluebird n Also *Rocky Mountain bluebird*

A bluebird (*Sialia currucoides*) native to the western US.

1858 Baird *Birds* 224, *Rocky Mountain Bluebird*. . . In this species there is none of the reddish brown of the other two American bluebirds, the color throughout being blue. **1861** U.S. Army Corps Topog. Engineers *Rept. Colorado R.* 5.5 **AZ**, *Sialia arctica*. . . Mountain blue bird.

Fort Defiance, Fort Yuma. **1874** Coues *Birds NW* 14, *Rocky Mountain Bluebird*. . . Eastern foot-hills of the Rocky Mountains to the Pacific, chiefly in mountainous regions. **1904** Wheelock *Birds CA* 506, The exquisite coloring of the Mountain Bluebird renders him easily the most beautiful of all Californian birds. **1961** Ligon *NM Birds* 233, *Sialia currucoides*. . . The Mountain Bluebird prefers a mountainous habitat and is therefore largely confined to western United States. **1977** Udvardy *Audubon Field Guide Birds* 734, *Mountain Bluebird*. . . Open areas where mountain meadows and pastures are interspersed with loose stands or single coniferous trees.

mountain blue grouse See **blue grouse 1**

mountain blue jay See **mountain jay 1**

mountain bog birch See **bog birch 2**

mountain bog gentian See **mountain gentian**

mountain boomer n

1 A **red squirrel** (here: *Tamiasciurus hudsonicus*). **chiefly S Midl**

1855 (1858) Bennett *Chronology of NC* 94, The only inhabitants we saw on these high points were pheasants, cross bills, . . and mountain boomers, a sort of squirrel. **1859** Colton *Mt. Scenery* 100 **NC**, There is upon all the mountains, a little squirrel, in size between the gray and the ground squirrel, called, by the inhabitants, 'mountain boomer.' . . They are a pretty animal, of a light red color, the under portion of the body very white. **1913** Kephart *Highlanders* 87 **sAppalachians,** Out of a tree overhead hopped a mountain "boomer" (red squirrel), and down he came, eyed me, and stopped. **1917** Baldwin *Making of a Township* 437 **ceIN,** A saucy mountain "boomer," perched upon the top rail of a ladder leaning against the rear of the house chattered, daring us to come closer. **1949** *AmSp* 24.106 **nGA,** *Boomer; Mountain boomer*. . . A small gray [sic] squirrel. **1968** *DARE* (Qu. P27, . . *Kinds of squirrels*) Inf **VA**8, Mountain boomer—same as red squirrel. **1981** Pederson *LAGS Basic Materials,* 1 inf, **neTN,** Mountain boomer—not many around here; found in the Smokies and in the knobs; 1 inf, **ceTN,** Red squirrel—mountain boomers.

2 =**mountain beaver.**

1913 *DN* 4.27 **NW,** Mountain boomer. . . A beaver-like animal living at the head of mountain streams in small holes that always lead to water. They make a peculiar noise, whence the name. **1928** Anthony *N. Amer. Mammals* 452, *Mountain beaver.—Aplodontia rufa*. . Mountain Boomer. **1940** Writers' Program OR *Mt. Hood* 21, The sewellel or mountain beaver, sometimes colloquially called "mountain boomer," . . resembles the porcupine and marmot rather than the beaver.

3 The collared **lizard** (*Crotaphytus collaris*). **chiefly Ozarks, SW**

1909 in 1947 Lomax *Advent. Ballad Hunter* 52 **CO,** This is a peculiar country. . . prairie dogs, badgers, rattle snakes, lizards, mountain boomers, owls [sic] and coyotes all live in one hole. **1926** TX Folkl. Soc. *Pub.* 5.65, In Middle and Western Texas, this creature [=the glade devil] is called a "mountain boomer." **1927** *DN* 5.475 **Ozarks,** Mountain boomer. . . A large collared lizard, which the hillmen believe to be very poisonous. **1928** Baylor Univ. Museum *Contrib.* 16.11, In middle Texas it is called *Barking Lizard*, and it is claimed that its bark is as loud as that of a young coyote. In other localities, when it "barks" (?), it is called either *Mountain Boomer* or *Bull Lizard*. **1958** Conant *Reptiles & Amphibians* 77, This reptile has no voice. The name "mountain boomer" may have originated from seeing a Collared Lizard atop a rock while some other animal, possibly a Barking Frog, called from beneath the same rock. **1958** Latham *Meskin Hound* 42 **cTX,** Just an old scaly mountain-boomer lizard skimming across the rocks thrilled him the same way. **1964** Wallace *Frontier Life* 74 **OK** (as of 1893–1906), We found other attractions to interfere with cotton chopping, such as . . a lizard, a small snake, a horned toad, or mountain boomer, all of which required either minute examinations or lengthy discussions. **1966** *DARE* (Qu. P32, . . *Other kinds of wild animals*) Inf **NM**3, Mountain boomer—same as rock lizard; **OK**25, Mountain boomer—a kind of lizard. **1981** Pederson *LAGS Basic Materials,* 1 inf, **cAR,** Has heard of mountain boomer, but not sure what it is. . . it might be "a big old lizard"; 1 inf, **cnAR,** Mountain boomer—heard of, but it's a lizard in Texas; 1 inf, **neTX**; [1 inf, **ceTN,** Mountain boomer—he said it is a 7–8 foot long snake in Arkansas].

4 See quot.

1944 Adams *Western Words* 102, *Mountain boomer*—One of cattle of the hilly country; also a species of large mountain lizard.

5 A rustic, hillbilly. **chiefly sAppalachians** Cf **mountaineer**

1859 Taliaferro *Fisher's R.* 33 **nwNC,** A mountain "boomer," dressed in a linsey hunting-shirt down to his knees. **1913** Kephart *Highlanders* 207 **sAppalachians,** They call themselves mountain people, or citizens; sometimes humorously "mountain boomers," the word boomer being their name for the common red squirrel which is found here only in the upper zones of the mountains. **1915** *DN* 4.185 **swVA,** *Mountain boomer*. . . One from the outlying districts; an uncouth person. **1929** in 1952 Mathes *Tall Tales* 116 **sAppalachians,** I ain't done neither one of ye right, but hit was jist because I'm a ol', ignor'nt, ornery mountain boomer that didn't know no better. **1952** Brown *NC Folkl.* 1.567 **wNC,** *Mountain boomer*. . . A mountaineer. **1967** *DARE* FW Addit **nwAR,** Mountain boomer = "hillbilly." Heard in Clarksville, Arkansas. **1973** Allen *LAUM* 1.351 (as of c1950), Mountain boomer [1 inf, **IA**]. **1986** Pederson *LAGS Concordance* neTN (*A rustic*) 3 infs, Mountain boomer(s); 1 inf, Mountain boomer—only of person; never a squirrel; 1 inf, Down come the mountain boomers; 1 inf, Mountain boomer—I've heard that; (*Poor whites*) 1 inf, Mountain boomer—used "right much" for a hermit.

mountain box n

1 A **bearberry 2** (here: *Arctostaphylos uva-ursi*). [See quot 1924]

1828 Rafinesque *Med. Flora* 1.57, English Name—*Bear-berry*. . . Vulgar Names—Mountain Box, Redberry, Upland Cranberry. **1873** in 1976 Miller *Shaker Herbs* 248, *Arctostaphylos uva-ursi*—Bearberry . . Mountain Box. **1892** (1974) Millspaugh *Amer. Med. Plants* 390-1, Bearberry, mountain box, red berry. **1924** *Amer. Botanist* 30.13, "Box-leaved wintergreen" is descriptive of the plant . . while "barren myrtle," "ground holly" and "mountain-box" embody in different forms the idea that the plant has small, firm evergreen leaves. **1976** Bailey–Bailey *Hortus Third* 101, Sandberry, mountain box, bear's grape.

2 =**Oregon boxwood.**

1973 Hitchcock–Cronquist *Flora Pacific NW* 288, *P[achistima] myrsinites*. . M[ountain]-box.

mountain brome n Also *mountain bromegrass*

A western **bromegrass:** usu *Bromus carinatus*, but also *B. polyanthus* or *B. inermis*.

1923 Abrams *Flora Pacific States* 1.228, *Bromus marginàtus*. . . Large Mountain Brome-grass. **1937** U.S. Forest Serv. *Range Plant Hdbk.* G33, *Big Mountain Bromes* . . *Bromus carinatus, B. marginatus, B. polyanthus*. . . Big mountain bromes are . . considered to include three prominent bromes that are closely related and very similar in appearance, growth habits, and forage value. . . The big mountain bromes have been used to a limited extent in hay meadows and have yielded as high as 2 tons per acre on good soils. [*DARE* Ed: *B. marginatus* is now included in *B. carinatus*.] **1953** Nelson *Plants Rocky Mt. Park* 41, *Bromus pumpellianus* [=*B. inermis pumpellianus*]—Pumpelly brome or mountain brome. **1956** St. John *Flora SE WA* 35, *Bromus marginatus*. . . Mountain Bromegrass. . . Abundant. **1961** Thomas *Flora Santa Cruz* 79 **cwCA,** *B. marginatus*. . . Mountain Brome Grass. Open slopes and coastal bluffs. **1968** Barkley *Plants KS* 40, *Bromus carinatus*. . . Mountain Broma [sic]. **1976** Bailey–Bailey *Hortus Third* 183, [*Bromus*] *marginatus*. . . Mountain brome. . . St[em]s to 4 ft. . . B.C. to S. Dak., s. to New Mex. and Calif.

mountain buckthorn n

A **gum elastic** (here: *Bumela lanuginosa*).

1938 Van Dersal *Native Woody Plants* 77, Mountain buckthorn. . . spiny and straggling.

mountain bunchgrass n

1 A **fescue** (here: *Festuca viridula*). **Pacific NW**

1923 in 1925 Jepson *Manual Plants CA* 83, *F[estuca] viridula*. . . Mountain Bunch Grass. . . Subalpine meadows in the Sierra Nevada. **1937** U.S. Forest Serv. *Range Plant Hdbk.* G65, Green fescue is the mountain bunchgrass of the Blue Mountain country of northeastern Oregon and southeastern Washington. Lambs fed on these ranges are famous for condition and the high market prices they command. **1956** St. John *Flora SE WA* 45, *Mountain Bunch Grass*. Densely tufted, dark green. . . Mountain meadows, Mt. Spokane, and the Blue Mts. **1961** Peck *Manual OR* 91, *Mountain bunchgrass*. . . Mountain meadows at high altitude in the Cascade and Siskiyou Mts. to Wash. and Calif. **1973** Hitchcock–Cronquist *Flora Pacific NW* 642, Slopes and rock slides and meadows to well above timber . . Green f[escue], mt. bunchgrass.

2 A **muhly (grass)** (here: *Muhlenbergia montana*).

1937 U.S. Forest Serv. *Range Plant Hdbk.* G81, Mountain muhly, also known as mountain bunchgrass . . , is a bright green, perennial grass growing in very dense bunches. . . It ranges from Wyoming to California and western Texas.

mountain camellia n

A stewartia (here: *Stewartia ovata*).

[**1901** Lounsberry *S. Wild Flowers* 338, It seems strange that a shrub so bold and striking and fairly enchanting when in blow as the mountain Stuartia [sic] should be so little known. . . Along the southern exposures of the Blue Ridge . . sometimes it is fairly covered with large white flowers looking like single camellias.] **1933** Small *Manual SE Flora* 876, *Mountain camellia.* . . Along streams and rich woods, Blue Ridge to Appalachian Plateau and adj. Piedmont. **1964** Campbell et al. *Gt. Smoky Wildflowers* 52, *Mountain Camellia.* . . The large white flowers of this small tree, when seen from a distance, sometimes cause it to be mistaken for late flowering dogwood. . . The mountain camellia blooms in June, and is found in rich soils at 1,000 to 2,000 feet elevation. **1976** Bruce *How to Grow Wildflowers* 142, The Mountain Stewartia or Mountain-camellia [is] just a little taller [than *Stewartia malacodendron*].

mountain canary n Also *Rocky Mountain canary* **chiefly West**
See Map Cf **Arizona nightingale**

A donkey or mule.

1921 *DN* 5.114 **CA,** *Mountain canary.* . . *Rocky mountain canary.* . . Burro. **1950** *WELS (Joking names for mules)* 2 Infs, **WI,** Mountain canary. **1952** Peattie *Black Hills* 261 **SD,** Occasionally all the other sounds were drowned out, no doubt, by the braying of the burros (mountain canaries) that served as beasts of burden and were as a rule the miner's only family. **1965–70** *DARE* (Qu. K50) 14 Infs, **chiefly West,** Mountain canary; **ID**5, **TX**5, Rocky Mountain canary. **1971** Bright *Word Geog. CA & NV* 113, Mountain canary . . Rocky Mountain canary. **1971** *Today Show Letters* **CO,** "Mountain canary" (miners called their burros & donkeys) (They make such a noise).

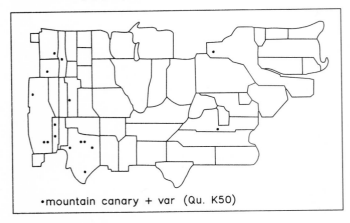

•mountain canary + var (Qu. K50)

mountain cat n

1 A **wildcat** (here: *Felis rufus*) or the **lynx 1.** [*DCan* c1665 → for the lynx] *prob obs*

1709 (1967) Lawson *New Voyage* 123, The Mountain-Cat, so call'd, because he lives in the Mountainous Parts of *America,* . . is a Beast of Prey, as the Panther is. . . His tail does not exceed four inches. . . He is spotted as the Leopard is, tho' some of them are not (which may happen, when their Furs are out of Season). **1817** *Amer. Monthly Mag. & Crit. Rev.* 2.46, Tail thick truncated, not reaching to the knees . . ; long ears often tufted. . . Their vulgar names are Catamount, Mountain-cat, Wild-cat, Loocervia, &c. . . *Lynx canadensis.* . . *Lynx montanus.* . . *Lynx floridanus.* . . *Lynx fasciatus.* **1832** Williamson *Hist. ME* 1.135, The *Wild-Cat,* or mountain cat, is much heavier and fiercer than any of the domestic species. It is of a sallow-ground colour, and its weight about 30 or 40 pounds. **1838** Geol. Surv. OH *Second Annual Rept.* 160, Felix concolor. . . *Mountain Tiger.* Felix montana. . . *Mountain Cat.* Ibid 176, The mountain tiger and the mountain cat. The pioneer hunters blended both these species under the common name of *catamount,* and seemed not to know they were distinct. **1842** DeKay *Zool. NY* 1.51, I suppose the Mountain Cat described . . as having reddish or orange-colored hair, with black streaks, to have been the Bay Lynx.

2 also *mount cat:* =**mountain lion.**

1779 in 1789 Anburey *Travels* 2.433, At that very instant, a ferocious animal . . called the mountain cat, was going to spring upon him. **1956** *DE Folkl. Bulletin* 1.23, And the mount cats sat up in the trees—/ Their

tails were hanging down. **1969** *DARE* (Qu. P31, . . *Names or nicknames* . . *for the* . . *panther*) Inf **GA**80, Mountain cat. **1990** *DARE* File **WI,** There was some excitement a couple of years ago when a mountain cat was rumored to be stalking cattle in northern Wisconsin. More than one person reported having seen the animal.

3 =**ringtail cat. CA**

1872 McClellan *Golden State* 239 **CA,** The wild cat and mountain cat . . are found in the mountains and hill-sides of the State. **1874** (1877) Hittell *Resources CA* 382, The mountain cat, or striped bassaris (*Bassaris astuta*) is abundant along the western base of the Sierra Nevada, between latitudes 36° and 39°. **1890** Langford *Vigilante Days* 1.184, To the agility of a mountain cat he added the quick, sharp eye of an Indian. **1917** Anthony *Mammals Amer.* 109 **CA,** The reader may find other references to it [=*Bassariscus astutus*] as . . "Mountain Cat" and "Ring-tailed Cat." **1937** Grinnell et al. *Fur-Bearing Mammals CA* 166, *California Ring-tailed Cat.* . . *Other Names.* . . Mountain Cat.

mountain cedar n **esp TX**

Any of several **junipers 1,** but esp *Juniperus ashei.* For other names of *J. ashei* see **cedar 1, ~ brake 2, juniper cedar, post ~, rock ~, white ~, yellow ~**

1882 *Bot. Gaz.* 7.48 c**TX,** The sides and part of the top of this great bluff are covered with a thick growth of mountain cedar (*Juniperus occidentalis,* var. *conjungens*), red oak (*Quercus rubra*), live oak (*Q. virens*), and shin oak (*Q. sinuata,* var.?) **1897** Sudworth *Arborescent Flora* 97 **TX,** *Juniperus occidentalis conjungens.* . . Mountain Cedar. *Ibid* 99 **TX,** *Juniperus pachyphloea.* . . Mountain Cedar. **1908** Britton *N. Amer. Trees* 113, *Juniperus pachyphlaea.* . . Oak-barked cedar, Thick-barked cedar, and Mountain cedar. *Ibid* 116, Rock cedar—*Juniperus mexicana* Sprengel [=*J. ashei*]. . . Juniper cedar, Mountain cedar. **1945** Wodehouse *Hayfever Plants* 27, The most important in hayfever is the mountain cedar, Mexican cedar or rock cedar. . . This species is extremely abundant on the limestone hills of Texas. **1960** Vines *Trees SW* 33, Names used [for *J. ashei*] are Mountain Cedar, Cedar Brake, Texas Cedar. **1979** Little *Checklist U.S. Trees* 154, *Juniperus ashei.* . . mountain-cedar . . Mexican juniper.

mountain celery n

A **lovage** (here: *Ligusticum porteri*).

1940 Writers' Program *Guide NM* 15, Oshá (mountain celery) and yerba de mansa (lizard's tail) are among those still gathered in New Mexico mountains as valuable foods and remedies.

mountain cherry n

Any of var plants of the genus *Prunus,* but esp **Chickasaw plum.**

1813 Muhlenberg *Catalogus Plantarum* 48, [*Prunus*] montana . . mountain cherry. **1825** (1933) Sibley *Santa Fe Diary* 142, On my return, I gathered some mountain cherries to preserve for seed. **1837** Darlington *Flora Cestrica* 287, *Chicasaw Plum. Mountain Cherry.* . . The fruit of this is very pleasant. . . It approaches the *Cherry* somewhat, in character. **1871** *Harper's New Mth. Mag.* 43.707 **MD,** We must . . gather mountain cherries (*Prunus cerasus*). **1893** *Jrl. Amer. Folkl.* 6.140 **MD,** *Prunus Chicasa,* mountain cherry. **1898** Bailey *Sketch Native Fruits* 173 **MD, VA,** I suppose that the cherry to which Strachey refers is the Chickasaw plum, which grows abundantly in that region, and which is even now called "mountain cherry" in parts of Maryland and Virginia. **1908** Britton *N. Amer. Trees* 492, Chickasaw plum. . . Also called Mountain cherry, this is a somewhat spiny, small tree or shrub, with spreading branches, often forming dense thickets in dry sandy soils from New Jersey to Florida, westward to the lower Mississippi valley, Arkansas and eastern Texas. **1939** Medsger *Edible Wild Plants* 45, Chickasaw plum, or Mountain cherry. . . The fruit from wild trees is gathered and sold in the markets of the South. **1976** Elmore *Shrubs & Trees SW* 143, Mountain cherry; cerezo. . . *Prunus emarginata.* . . Mostly it tends to be shrubby, forming thickets.

mountain chestnut oak See **mountain oak a**

mountain chickadee n

A **chickadee 1** (here: *Parus gambeli*) native to the western US.

1874 Coues *Birds NW* 22, Mountain chickadee. . . Common in various coniferous mountainous tracts in New Mexico and Arizona. **1917** (1923) *Birds Amer.* 3.212, The Mountain Chickadee of the West is a shade larger, and of slightly different coloration than its well beloved eastern relative, but in habits and disposition the birds are very similar. **1937** Natl. Geogr. Soc. *Book of Birds* 2.138, The calls of the mountain chickadee are closely similar to those of the blackcap species, but are uttered in a slightly slower, drawling tone, so that the notes of the two may be distinguished by a practiced ear. **1977** Udvardy *Audubon Field Guide Birds* 733, *Mountain Chickadee. . . A fearless, constantly active insect-gleaner of the mountain forest, it frequently descends into the lowlands in winter.*

mountain clematis n Cf **Rocky Mountain clematis**

A **virgin's bower** (here: *Clematis verticillaris*).

1910 Graves *Flowering Plants* 190 **CT**, *Clematis verticillaris. . . Purple or Mountain Clematis. . . Occasional about the trap hills of central Connecticut. May.* **1933** Small *Manual SE Flora* 528, *Mountain-clematis. . . Rocky woods, Blue Ridge and more northern provinces.*

mountain clover n

Any of three clovers: *Trifolium cyathiferum, T. virginicum,* or *T. wormskjoldii.*

1902 U.S. Natl. Museum *Contrib. Herbarium* 7.361, *Trifolium cyathiferum. . .* Another tough-stemmed clover which is . . greatly relished by stock. It grows among grass, especially in the mountains, and is therefore known as "mountain clover." **1925** Jepson *Manual Plants* 540, *T. cyathiferum. . . Mountain Clover. . .* Valleys or hillsides, 50 to 6000 ft. **1931** Harned *Wild Flowers Alleghanies* 254, *Prostrate Mountain Clover (T. virginicum . .) . . .* a very small perennial. . . on barren slopes. **1953** Strausbaugh–Core *Flora WV* 546, *T. virginicum . . Mountain clover. . .* Known from 16 counties in four states, . . it occurs in the barest and most sterile situations. **1970** Correll *Plants TX* 808, *Mountain clover. . .* Davis Mts. at about 4,000–6,000 ft. elev., summer; Rocky Mts. and s. in the mts. . . *T. Wormskjoldii.*

mountain coconut n

=**oil nut 2.**

1933 Small *Manual SE Flora* 1250, *P[yrularia] pubera. . . Mountain-coconut. . .* An oil, resembling olive oil, but ill-scented and poisonous, has been pressed from the drupes.

mountain columbia n

Perh =**columbo.**

1983 *MJLF* 9.1.48 **ceKY**, *Mountain columbia . .* a medicinal herb; "for stomach trouble."

mountain cottontail See **Rocky Mountain cottontail**

mountain cottonwood n

A **cottonwood 1** (here: *Populus angustifolia*).

1960 Vines *Trees SW* 88, *Populus angustifolia. . .* Also known under the vernacular names of Black Cottonwood, . . Mountain Cottonwood, and Alamo. . . It is sometimes planted in western cities for ornament. **1966** *DARE* (Qu. T13) Inf **NM**2, Mountain cottonwood. **1980** *Little Audubon Guide N. Amer. Trees W. Region* 340, "Mountain Cottonwood" . . *Populus angustifolia. . .* This is the common cottonwood of the northern Rocky Mountains.

mountain cranberry n

1 Either of two cranberries: *Vaccinium vitis-idaea* in the northern US and Alaska, or *V. erythrocarpum* in the southern US. For other names of the former see **clusterberry, cowberry 1, flowering box, foxberry 5, highland cranberry, lingonberry, lowbush cranberry, partridgeberry, redberry, rock cranberry, squawberry;** for other names of the latter see **dingleberry 1**

1843 Hayward *Gaz. U.S.* 28 **ME**, In autumn, the whole surface of the island [=Cross Island] is red with mountain cranberries. **1848** *Union Mag.* (NY NY) 3.75 **ME**, Mountain cranberries, stewed and sweetened, were the common dessert. **1869** Fuller *Uncle John* 120, A shrub three or four feet high, called the . . *Mountain Cranberry. . .* is a fine ornament for lawn or garden, with its white flowers and bright scarlet fruit, but it loves its own wild haunts best. **1892** Torrey *Foot-Path Way* 72 **Cape Cod MA**, Broad patches of bearberry showing at a little distance like beds of mountain cranberry. **1901** Lounsberry *S. Wild Flowers* 401, *Southern Mountain Cranberry. Oxycoccus erythrocarpus. . .* The bright or dark red berries of this cranberry are knowingly passed by. They in their mountain home are pretty to look at, but most insipid to the taste. **1928** Rosendahl–Butters *Trees MN* 322, *Mountain Cranberry. . .* Locally very abundant in sphagnum swamps in the far northern part of the state, less commonly on granite ledges along Lake Superior. **1933** Small *Manual SE Flora* 1017, *Vaccinium erythrocarpum. . . Mountain-cranberry. . .* The fruit from different mountains is often quite different in flavor. The better kinds make a delicious jelly. **1966** *DARE* (Qu. I44, *What kinds of berries grow wild around here?*) Inf **ME**5, Mountain cranberries. **1972** Viereck–Little *AK Trees* 233, Mountain-cranberry is

common in spruce and birch woods of the boreal forest, in bogs and alpine types in most of Alaska, and in the tundra of the north and western sections. **1987** Hughes–Blackwell *Wildflowers SE AK* 71, Mountain Cranberry. . . Flowers are bell shaped and nodding.

2 =**bearberry 2.**

1876 Hobbs *Bot. Hdbk.* 72, Mountain cranberry, Bearberry, Arctostaphylos Uva Ursi. **1894** *Jrl. Amer. Folkl.* 7.93 **sME**, *Arctostaphylos Uva-ursi. . .* Mountain cranberry. **1924** *Amer. Botanist* 30.13, Such names as "rock-berry," . . and "mountain cranberry" . . mostly indicate a confusion of this [=*Arctostaphylos uva-ursi*] with the true cranberry. **1940** Clute *Amer. Plant Names* 38, *A[rctostaphylos] uva-ursi. . .* Mountain cranberry.

3 =**cascara 1.**

1931 U.S. Dept. Ag. *Misc. Pub.* 101.113, *Cascara buckthorn (R[hamnus] purshiana), . .* locally known as . . mountain cranberry, . . ranges from British Columbia to western Montana and northern California.

mountain cucumber See **cucumber tree 1**

mountain currant n

A **currant B1** (here: *Ribes glandulosum*).

1824 Bigelow *Florula Bostoniensis* 90, *Ribes rigens. . . Mountain Currant. . .* The berries, when bruised, have the odor of Ictodes foetidus [=skunk cabbage]. **1833** Eaton *Botany* 304, Mountain currant . . unarmed: branches straight. **1861** Wood *Class-Book* 361, *Mountain Currant. . .* Fl[ower]s marked with purple. Berries rather large. **1910** Graves *Flowering Plants* 219 **CT**, Mountain Currant. . . Swampy woods. . . May–June. **1933** Small *Manual SE Flora* 602, *R. glandulosum. . . Mountain-currant. . .* Deep woods, Blue Ridge and more N provinces.

mountain daisy n

1 Either of two western **fleabanes:** *Erigeron coulteri* or *E. peregrinus.*

1897 Parsons *Wild Flowers CA* 332, *Lavender Mountain Daisy. Erigeron salsuginosus* [=*E. peregrinus*]. . . Late in the summer it stars the alpine meadows with its charming flowers, or stands in solitude companies on those natural velvet lawns of the mountains. It resembles the feathery, white mountain daisy [=*E. coulteri*], and grows in the same region. **1915** (1926) Armstrong–Thornber *Western Wild Flowers* 534, *E[rigeron] Coulteri,* the large White Mountain Daisy, is a beautiful kind, . . with bright green leaves, . . and the flowers usually single, an inch and a half across, usually with pure white rays. This grows in Yosemite meadows and similar mountain places, in Utah, California, and Colorado. **1934** Haskin *Wild Flowers Pacific Coast* 371, Mountain Daisy. *Erigeron salsuginosus. . .* A beautiful pink flower found at high elevations in the mountains. **1956** St. John *Flora SE WA* 449, *Erigeron salsuginosus. . . Mountain Daisy. . .* Mountain meadows.

2 A composite plant *(Melampodium cinereum)* native chiefly to the southwestern US. Also called **prairie daisy, rock ~**

1936 Whitehouse *TX Flowers* 169, *Mountain Daisy. . .* is very abundant on limestone slopes and in dry soil from Texas to Arkansas, Kansas, and Arizona. **1961** Wills–Irwin *Flowers TX* 231, Mountain Daisy. . . is frequently a handsome plant, the spreading branches covered with heads, strongly resistant to drought and thriving in the most barren situations.

3 A composite plant *(Chrysanthemum integrifolium)* native to Alaska.

1966 Heller *Wild Flowers AK* 66, *Chrysanthemum integrifolium. . . Mountain Daisy. . .* Common in arctic-alpine locations from the arctic slope south to Wiseman; also on Seward Peninsula.

mountain dandelion n Rocky Mts, Pacific

A **false dandelion** (here: *Agoseris* spp).

1954 Harrington *Manual Plants CO* 637, *Agoseris. . .* Mountain-Dandelion. **1962** *Julian Apple Day* [26] **csCA**, [Among items at the annual wildflower show:] The mountain dandelion. **1963** Craighead *Rocky Mt. Wildflowers* 187, *Agoseris glauca. . .* Mountain Dandelion. . . This looks like the common Dandelion, . . but . . in *Agoseris,* seeds [are] reasonably smooth and stems less fleshy. **1973** Hitchcock–Cronquist *Flora Pacific NW* 478, *Agoseris. . .* Mountain-dandelion. . . Fl[ower]s . . yellow or orange, often turning pink or purple in drying.

mountain day n **MA**

A fall day of exceptionally fine weather; transf, a college holiday for the enjoyment of such a day.

1939 *LANE* Map 87 *(A fine day)* 1 inf, **neMA**, Mountain day, a clear, crisp October day. **1995** *DARE* File **MA**, Mountain day. . . Refers to one of those rare days when the sky is blue and the sun is bright and the air is wonderfully clear. . . People would argue about why it was called that: "Some say it's a day that's so bright and clear you can see all the mountains that are covered by the haze in a heat wave; and others say it's a day when the air is so fine it's worth the effort to climb a mountain to get the fine view." *Ibid* **MA** (as of late 1920s), Mountain Day is a spontaneous holiday traditional at Smith College . . and Mt. Holyoke College. . . Everybody knows it is coming . . in October, but nobody knows the exact date. . . Then one golden morning, the president of the college gives the word and . . all the bells ring out and all classes are cancelled for the entire day. *Ibid* **cMA**, I've heard "This looks like a real *mountain day."* Not terribly common because such days are not—but it's always recognized. *Ibid* **cMA** (as of 1977), Mountain Day—An unscheduled holiday from classes at Smith and Mount Holyoke colleges, announced early in the morning by ringing bells and a statement from the college president on a day, usually in October, chosen because the weather promises to give a bright, clear, crisp, perfect fall day.

mountain dew n [*OED* 1816 →] **scattered, but more freq Sth, S Midl** See Map
Whiskey; illegal liquor, moonshine.

1850 Garrard *Wah-to-yah* 191, The first house we passed, was a distillery, where the "mountain dew" of New Mexico—*aguardiente de Taos,* is made. **c1874** in 1929 Summers *Annals* 1617 **swVA** (as of c1840), They repaired to the room soon after nightfall, . . and proceeded with a pack of cards and a bottle of "mountain dew." **1888** *Century Illustr. Mag.* 36.766 **Sth**, Pine tags and even potato peelings went into the impromptu still to come out pure "mountain dew." **1913** Morley *Carolina Mts.* 66, Corn is not only the principal food of the mountaineer, but supplies as well . . "mountain-dew." **1950** *WELS* (Nicknames for . . bad liquor) 1 Inf, **cWI**, Mountain dew; (Illegal liquor) 1 Inf, **neWI**, Mountain dew. **1962** *Mt. Life* 38.4.12 **sAppalachians**, Good "mountain dew," the kind made by expert hands and aged in a charred whiteoak keg, will make "a preacher lay his Bible down." **1965–70** *DARE* (Qu. DD21c, *Nicknames for whiskey, especially illegally made whiskey*) 55 Infs, **scattered, but more freq Sth, S Midl**, Mountain dew; (Qu. BB50d, *Favorite spring tonics*) Inf **NC**35, Mountain dew; (Qu. DD21a, *General words . . for any kind of liquor*) Infs **TN**14, 53, Mountain dew; (Qu. DD21b, *General words . . for bad liquor*) Infs **KY**90, **MD**48, **NY**36, Mountain dew; (Qu. DD31, *Joking names for homemade hard liquor;* total Infs questioned, 75) Inf **OK**52, Mountain dew. **1966** Leisy *Folk Song Abecedary* 251 **Appalachians**, Old Mountain Dew. . . This popular hillbilly song is a tribute to the art—and the product. *Ibid* 252, They call it that old mountain dew,/ And them that refuse it are few./ You may go 'round the bend, but you'll come back again / For that good old mountain dew. **1984** Gilmore *Ozark Baptizings* 174 **MO**, I'd had some of that old mountain dew. . . I went up to the church and I shot that dad-burned pistol until it was red hot. **1986** Pederson *LAGS Concordance,* 14 infs, 8 **GA, FL**, Mountain dew; 1 inf, **seTN**, Mountain dew—general term; 1 inf, **nwGA**, Mountain dew—lower-quality concoction; 1 inf, **cTN**, Mountain dew—laughing; 1 inf, **ceTX**, Mountain dew—in Arkansas.

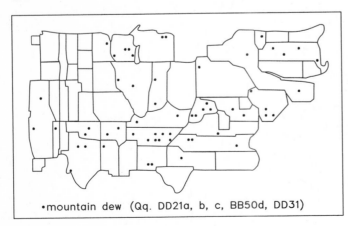

•mountain dew (Qq. DD21a, b, c, BB50d, DD31)

mountain dock n Cf **dock** n[1]
A bistort (here: *Polygonum bistortoides*).
1934 Haskin *Wild Flowers Pacific Coast* 84, *Mountain Dock—Polygonum bistortoides.* . . The stems of the mountain dock are slender and almost grass-like, and the fact that they grow among tall grasses in wet, alpine meadows helps to fix this impression. . . However, . . an examination of the base of the plant will reveal its few, narrow, dock-like leaves. **1956** St. John *Flora SE WA* 121, *Polygonum bistortoides.* . . This

is the beautiful *Mountain Dock* of the alpine meadows of the Cascade Mountains of Washington and Oregon, the Sierras of California, and the Blue Mountains of Washington.

mountain dogwood n
A **dogwood 1** (here: *Cornus nuttallii*).
1938 Van Dersal *Native Woody Plants* 333, Dogwood, . . Mountain (*Cornus nuttallii*). **1952** Davis *Flora ID* 522, *C[ornus] Nuttallii.* . . *Mountain Dogwood.* . . Known from central western portion [of Idaho]. **1959** Munz–Keck *CA Flora* 1035, *Mountain Dogwood.* . . Twigs at first green, later dark red to almost black. . . Mountain woods, below 6000 ft. **1979** Little *Checklist U.S. Trees* 98, *Cornus nuttallii.* . . Mountain dogwood. . . Wash., . . Oreg., . . Calif., . . Idaho.

mountain duck n
=**harlequin duck**.
[**1831** Richardson *Fauna Boreali-Amer.* 2.459, *Clangula histrionica.* (Leach.) *Harlequin Duck.* . . Painted Duck, also Mountain Duck. Hudson's Bay Residents. Lord. Newfoundlanders.] **1917** (1923) *Birds Amer.* 1.142, *Harlequin Duck.* . . *Other Names.* . . Mountain Duck. **1953** Jewett *Birds WA* 144, *Histrionicus histrionicus histrionicus.* . . Mountain Duck. . . In summer north to Skagit River, near the international boundary line, . . and west to the Elwha River, Olympic Mts. **1982** Elman *Hunter's Field Guide* 223, *Harlequin Duck.* . . Common & regional names . . mountain duck.

mountain eagle n
=**golden eagle**.
1856 Simms *Charlemont* 316 **KY**, Her eye [was] no longer uplifted like that of the mountain-eagle. **1874** NY Acad. Sci. *Annals Lyceum Nat. Hist.* 10.381 **IL**, *A[quila] chrysætus.* . . American Golden Eagle; Ring-tailed Eagle; Mountain Eagle. Winter visitant. **1917** (1923) *Birds Amer.* 2.82, Mountain Eagle. . . Now restricted almost entirely to the mountainous regions of the West. **1932** Howell *FL Bird Life* 181, *Golden Eagle.* . . *Mountain Eagle.* . . Mountains of New England (formerly), and in the Alleghenies to North Carolina; casual in winter in the Gulf States. **1955** Forbush–May *Birds* 115, *American Golden Eagle.* . . *Other names:* Mountain Eagle [etc].

mountaineer n Also *mountainite* **scattered, but chiefly Appalachians** See Map Cf **mountain boomer 5, ~ grill**
A person from a remote or isolated area in the mountains; a **hillbilly 1.**
1867 Harris *Sut Lovingood Yarns* 19 **TN**, [He] reined up in front of Pat Nash's grocery, among a crowd of mountaineers full of fun, foolery, and mean whisky. **1913** [see **mountain dew**]. **1934–44** in 1944 *ADD* 399 **nWV**, Mountaineer. . . Popular nickname for a native. **1965–70** *DARE* (Qu. HH1, *Names and nicknames for a rustic or countrified person*) Infs **GA**74, **MD**17, **NJ**36, **NY**92, **PA**93, **SC**32, 45, **TX**26, **VA**5, Mountaineer; **SC**31, Regular old mountaineer. **1967** *IN Engl. Jrl.* Winter 1 **IN**, "What are your expressions for people from the country who look awkward and out of place in town?" Responses offered include . . *mountaineer, mountainite.* **1973** Allen *LAUM* 1.350 (as of c1950), A rustic. . . Mountaineer [1 inf, **IA**]. **1986** Pederson *LAGS Concordance* (A rustic) 43 infs, 31 **GA, TN**, Mountaineer [9 infs state that they live in the mountains, one of those specifying the mountains of nGA, another of TN.]; 1 inf, **ceAL**, Mountaineer something; (Poor Whites) 6 infs, 5 **TN**, Mountaineer(s); 1 inf, **cnAL**, Ignorant mountaineer—from the hills; 1 inf, **cwAR**, Old mountaineer—habitual.

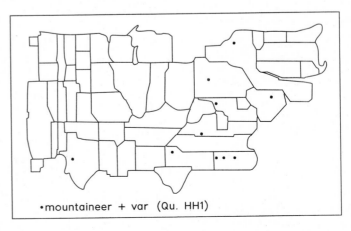

•mountaineer + var (Qu. HH1)

mountain elder n

An elder, such as *Sambucus callicarpa* in the eastern US or *S. cerulea* in the West.

1897 Sudworth *Arborescent Flora* 338, *Sambucus glauca*. . . Mountain Elder (Western States). **1911** *Century Dict. Suppl.*, *Elder*. . . *Mountain elder*. . . The red-berried elder. . . [or] *pale elder* [=*Sambucus cerulea*]. **1938** Van Dersal *Native Woody Plants* 334, Elder, . . Mountain (*Sambucus caerulea*). **1953** Greene-Blomquist *Flowers South* 122, Red-berried or mountain elder (*S[ambucus] pubens*) occurs at higher altitudes as far south as Ga. **1960** Vines *Trees SW* 941, *Sambucus melanocarpa*. . . Rocky, moist stream banks, or canyons in the conifer belt at altitudes of 5,000–10,000 ft. . . Also known as the Black Elderberry and Mountain Elder.

mountain elm n

1 =**winged elm.**

1897 Sudworth *Arborescent Flora* 182 **AR**, *Ulmus alata*. . . Mountain Elm. **1917** (1923) Rogers *Trees Worth Knowing* 215, The Winged Elm. . . is distributed from Virginia to Florida and west to Illinois and Texas. "Mountain elm" and "small-leaved elm" are local names. **1950** Peattie *Nat. Hist. Trees* 248, *Ulmus alata*. . . Mountain . . Elm.

2 =**slippery elm.**

1967 *DARE* (Qu. T11) Inf **PA**44, Mountain elm.

mountaineous See **mountainous**

mountain evergreen cherry See **evergreen cherry 2**

mountain fetterbush See **fetterbush 2**

mountain fever n

Disorientation or confusion suffered by an inexperienced person in mountainous terrain.

1956 Moody *Home Ranch* 82 **CO** (as of 1911), "Are you sure we're going the right way?" "Got the mountain fever a'ready?" he laughed. "By dogies, I seen prairie men get so fuddled up in these here mountains they don't know straight up from Sunday." **1970** Buchanan *Murder of Crows* 10 **KY**, You're not used to being out here in the boondocks. You have what we ridge runners call mountain fever. The first symptom is hallucinating things like exploding crows.

mountain figwort n Cf **figwort**

A **lousewort 1** (here: *Pedicularis racemosa*).

1953 Nelson *Plants Rocky Mt. Park* 144, *Mountain figwort* . . *Pedicularis racemosa*. . . A plant with . . a spike of white or cream-colored flowers. . . This . . is very frequently seen . . in the subalpine zone.

mountain fish n Cf **dryland fish 1**

A **morel** n[2] (here: either *Morchella angusticeps* or *M. esculenta*).

1980 Marteka *Mushrooms* 68, *Morchella esculenta*. . . *Common Names* . . mountain fish. Ibid 69, *Morchella angusticeps*. . . *Common Names*. . Mountain fish. . . Fruits early in the spring when the fiddleheads appear.

mountain flax n

1 A **blue flax** (here: *Linum lewisii*). [*OED* 1718 → for *Linum catharticum*]

1839 (1973) Farnham *Travels Prairies* 2.74 **West**, The mountain flax was very abundant and ripe. The root resembled that of perennial plants, the fibres that of the annual bluebowl of the States, the flower the same. **1959** Carleton *Index Herb. Plants* 84, *Mountain flax*: Linum lewisi; Polygala senega.

2 =**Seneca snakeroot.**

1829 Eaton *Botany* 336, *[Polygala] senega* . . mountain flax. . . Stem erect, simple, leafy. **1842** Kirkland *Forest Life* 1.67 **MI**, Mountain flax, prickly-ash, . . bitter root, Cayenne pepper, laudanum, raw eggs, strong coffee, wormwood, hop tea,—but I might fill a page with the names of nauseous bitters, narcotics and stimulants which we are solicited to try [for the ague]. **1876** Hobbs *Bot. Hdbk.* 72, Mountain flax, Seneca root, Polygala Senega. **1903** Porter *Flora PA* 197, *Mountain Flax*. . . In rocky woods, N.B. to Minn. and the Canadian Rocky Mts., south to N.C. and Mo. **1930** Sievers *Amer. Med. Plants* 50, Mountain flax. . . *Part used.*— The root, collected in autumn. In reasonably constant demand. **1942** Hylander *Plant Life* 339, Seneca Snakeroot or Mountain Flax is a species with greenish-white flowers . . on stems which grow . . from a thickened root. **1959** [see **1** above]. **1974** (1977) Coon *Useful Plants* 211, Mountain flax. . . For a time, it became an accepted "official" drug for uses in chronic catarrh, croup, asthma, and lung disorders.

mountain fly honeysuckle See **fly honeysuckle**

mountain fringe n

1 The climbing fumitory (*Adlumia fungosa*). Also called **Allegheny vine, canary ~, cliff harlequin, colicweed 3, cypress vine 2, fairy creeper, wood fringe**

1847 Wood *Class-Book* 158, *A[dlumia] cirrhosa*. . . *Mountain Fringe*. A delicate climbing vine, native of rocky hills, Can. to N. Car. **1892** *Jrl. Amer. Folkl.* 5.92 **sVT, eMA**, *Adlumia cirrhosa*. . . Mountain fringe. **1896** Ibid 9.181, *Adlumia cirrhosa*, . . mountain fringe, . . Paris, Me. **1896** Robinson *In New Engl. Fields* 124, The cliff towered skyward . . ; its tiny caves were unexplored mysteries, their coral-beaded curtains of Canada yew and delicate netting of mountain-fringe strange foreign growths. **1912** Mathews *Amer. Wild Flowers* 160, *Mountain Fringe*. . . A beautiful and delicate vine climbing and trailing over thickets or shrubbery. **1931** Harned *Wild Flowers Alleghanies* 197, *Mountain Fringe*. . . A . . vine many feet in length. . . Rather common in moist woods and thickets extending into the mountains. **1959** [see **2** below]. **1976** Bailey-Bailey *Hortus Third* 27, *Mountain-fringe*. . . Ont. to Mich., s. to N.C.

2 A **sagebrush** (here: *Artemisia* spp).

1959 Carleton *Index Herb. Plants* 84, *Mountain fringe*: Adlumia fungosa; Artemisia (v).

mountain garland n

A **farewell-to-spring** (here: *Clarkia unguiculata*).

1982 *Plants SW* (Catalog) 22, *Mountain Garland*. . . Flowers in early summer. Native of California coastal ranges.

mountain gentian n Also *mountain bog gentian*

A **gentian** (here: *Gentiana calycosa*).

1961 Peck *Manual OR* 607, *Mountain Bog Gentian*. . . Mountain bogs at high altitude. **1963** Craighead *Rocky Mt. Wildflowers* 146, The Mountain Gentian is well named, for it and its relatives are at home in the Alps, Himalayas, and Andes, as well as the high Rockies. **1967** *DARE* Wildfl QR (Craighead) Pl.16.1 Inf **CO**29, Mountain gentian. **1973** Hitchcock-Cronquist *Flora Pacific NW* 359, Mt. bog g[entian] . . *G[entiana] calycosa.*

mountain geranium n

=**herb Robert.**

1896 *Jrl. Amer. Folkl.* 9.184, *Geranium Robertianum*, . . mountain geranium, Hancock, N.H.

mountain ginger n

Perh **kahili ginger.**

1980 Bushnell *Water of Kane* 414 **HI**, And below those, closer to the ground, grew olona, mountain ginger, and ferns of many kinds.

mountain goat n

Std: a goat antelope (*Oreamnos americanus*) native to the northwestern US and Alaska. Also called **Rocky Mountain goat, white ~**

mountain goose n

=**Hutchins's goose.**

1923 U.S. Dept. Ag. *Misc. Circular* 13.36 **ND**, *Hutchins Goose*. . . *Vernacular Names*. . . *In local use*. . . Mountain goose.

mountain gooseberry n

A **gooseberry 1**: *Ribes montigenum* or *R. rotundifolium*.

1924 Hawkins *Trees & Shrubs* 86 **MT**, Mountain Gooseberry (Ribes montigenum). . . A broadly spreading shrub seldom over two feet high. It grows at higher elevations than *[Ribes parvulum]*. **1933** Small *Manual SE Flora* 603, Ribes rotundifolium. . . Mountain-gooseberry. . . Rocky woods, Piedmont and Blue Ridge. **1938** Van Dersal *Native Woody Plants* 236, Ribes montigenum. . . Mountain gooseberry. . . Of more than average palatability to livestock. **1966** Grimm *Recognizing Native Shrubs* 116, Ribes rotundifolium. . . Massachusetts to New York and Kentucky; south to western North Carolina and eastern Tennessee. Also called Mountain Gooseberry. **1973** Hitchcock-Cronquist *Flora Pacific NW* 200, Mt. g[ooseberry]. . . *R. montigenum.*

mountain grape n

1 also with modifiers: Any of three **grapes**: *Vitis berlandieri, V. monticola,* or *V. rupestris.* **esp TX**

1830 Rafinesque *Med. Flora* 2.130, *V[itis] montana* [=*V. monticola*]. . . Mountain Grape. . . In the Alleghany mountains from New York to Carolina. . . Flowers hardly odorous, fruit hardly good. **1862** U.S. Patent Office *Annual Rept. for 1861: Ag.* 485, *Vitis monticola*. . .

is called the "White or Mountain grape;" differs from *V. rupestris* in its trailing habit and long, slender branches. **1886** Havard *Flora W. & S. TX for 1885* 511, *Vitis rupestris*. . . Mountain Grape. . . Said to grow on the hillsides of the Limpio and other mountains. **1891** Coulter *Botany W. TX* 62, *V. monticola*. . . Mountain grape. . . Peculiar to the hilly limestone region of western Texas. *Ibid* 63, *V. rupestris*. . . In the valley of Devil's River and westward into the mountains west of the Pecos. . . Also called "mountain grape." **1903** Small *Flora SE U.S.* 754, *V. monticola*. . . In sandy or lime soil, Texas. . . *Mountain Grape*. **1938** Van Dersal *Native Woody Plants* 337, Grape. . . Little mountain (*Vitis berlandieri*). . . Mountain (*Berberis aquifolium, Vitis berlandieri, Vitis rupestris*). . . Sweet mountain (*Vitis monticola*). **1960** Vines *Trees SW* 715, *Vitis berlandieri*. . . Also known under the vernacular names of Little-mountain Grape, Fall Grape [etc]. *Ibid* 725, *Sweet Mountain Grape—Vitis monticola*. . . Growing abundantly on top of limestone hills of central-southwest Texas. **1970** Correll *Plants TX* 1020, *Vitis monticola*. . . *Sweet mountain grape*. Rather slender small-leaved climber. **1976** Bailey–Bailey *Hortus Third* 1163, [*Vitis*] *monticola*. . . *Mountain g[rape], sweet m[ountain] g[rape]*. . . Tex. . . [*V.*] *rupestris*. . . *Mountain g[rape]* . . S. Penn. to Mo., s. to Tenn. and Tex.

2 A **barberry,** usu **Oregon grape.**

1925 Jepson *Manual Plants CA* 394, *B[erberis] aquifolium*. . . *Mountain Grape*. . . Berries blue, . . rather large. North Coast Ranges. **1962** Sweet *Plants of West* 17, Mountain Grape, *Berberis* sp . . . Holly-like leaves, fragrant yellow flowers in racemes, . . bluish berries. . . Juice of the fruit fermented with sugar makes an excellent wine. **1974** (1977) Coon *Useful Plants* 75, *Mahonia aquifolium*. . . Mountain grape. . . The berries may be eaten raw or used for jelly. **1976** Bailey–Bailey *Hortus Third* 697, *Berberis aquifolium*. . . *Mountain g[rape]*. . . Nw. N. Amer.

mountain grill n [Cf *OED grill* sb.[2] "*Obs. rare*. . . A quasi-proper name for a person of low tastes or lazy habits."] *derog* Cf **grit** n[1], **mountaineer,** DS HH1

A rustic, hillbilly.

1929 Wolfe *Look Homeward* 29 **PA,** "Mountain Grills!" he roared. "Mountain Grills! The lowest of the low! The vilest of the vile!" *Ibid* 49, Would any one of them give a starving beggar a crust of bread? By God, no! . . 'Twas a bitter day for me when I first came into this accursed country. . . Mountain Grills! Mountain Grills! **1939** Wolfe *Web & Rock* 43 **NC,** Sid Purtle was poor white trash and a mountain grill. . . George Webber's uncle had said that they were nothing but mountain grills no matter if they did live out upon Montgomery Avenue. **1989** *DARE* File **wNC** (as of c1920), A mountain grill was an uncouth, raw, ignorant, often ill-mannered boy or man. (I never heard it applied to girls or women.) I believe it was used only of people known as "poor whites."

mountain grouse n

1 =**dusky grouse.**

1844 in 1925 *CA Hist. Soc. Qrly.* 4.346, No animal Seen no fowl Save a few mountain grouse which can live in any region whare vegitation can grow. **1887** *Century Illustr. Mag.* 33.747 **CA,** There is a bird called the mountain grouse which can be found on Pine Mountain. **1923** U.S. Dept. Ag. *Farmers' Bulletin* 1375.3, Colorado reduced the limit on prairie chickens from 15 to 8 and on mountain and willow grouse from 5 to 3 a day. **1923** Dawson *Birds CA* 4.1591, The "Blue" Grouse, . . or "Mountain" Grouse, . . is found throughout the heavily timbered areas of the West. **1953** Jewett *Birds WA* 196, Mountain Grouse. . . One of the best-known game birds of the state. **1967** *DARE* (Qu. Q7, *Names and nicknames for . . game birds*) Inf **OR**13, Mountain grouse.

2 =**spruce grouse.**

1917 (1923) *Birds Amer.* 2.16, *Franklin's Grouse*. . . *Other Names.* Franklin's Spruce Grouse; . . Mountain Grouse.

3 The white-tailed **ptarmigan** (*Lagopus leucurus*).

1953 Jewett *Birds WA* 208, *Rainier White-tailed Ptarmigan*. . . Other names: Mountain Grouse. . . Permanent resident in the Alpine Arctic Zone of the Cascade Mountains and the mountains of northern Washington.

mountain gum n

A **gum elastic** (here: *Bumelia lanuginosa*).

1960 Vines *Trees SW* 834, Vernacular names used [for *Bumelia lanuginosa*] are Gum-elastic, Chittamwood, Mountain-gum.

mountain hare n [*OED* 1871] **West, AK**

A **jackrabbit 1:** esp *Lepus americanus*, but also *L. townsendii* in the western US, or *L. timidus* in Alaska.

1923 U.S. Dept. Ag. *Farmers' Bulletin* 1375.3, Nevada established

limits of 5 cottontail rabbits, 2 mountain hairs [sic], . . a day. **1959** Barnes *Nat. Hist. Wasatch Winter* 15 **UT,** Suddenly a mountain hare (*Lepus townsendi townsendi*) bounds up a gulch to a ridge. . . This mountain hare or white-tailed jack rabbit, which is almost uniformly dark gray above in the summer, becomes white in the winter, except for the blackish tips of its ears. **1966–70** *DARE* (Qu. P30, . . *Wild rabbits*) Inf **CA**210, Mountain hare; **NV**8, Mountain hare—in between cottontail and jackrabbit in size; **NM**13, Mountain hare—a big rabbit—also called snowshoe rabbit. **1980** Whitaker *Audubon Field Guide Mammals* 358, "Mountain Hare" . . (*Lepus timidus*). . . Western and n Alaska.

mountain heath n

1 =**mountain heather 2. chiefly West, AK**

1900 Lyons *Plant Names* 286, *Phyllodoce*. . . Mountain Heath. **1924** Hawkins *Trees & Shrubs* 100 **MT,** *Mountain Heath* (Phyllodoce empetriformis) . . reminds one of Scotch heather. It is an evergreen shrub growing in dense patches and has the appearance of stunted spruce or fir. **1931** U.S. Dept. Ag. *Misc. Pub.* 101.132, The mountain heaths. . resemble heaths (*Erica* spp.), . . rather than heather (*Calluna vulgaris*). . . All are ordinarily accounted worthless as forage. **1952** Davis *Flora ID* 531, Mountain Heath. Low evergreen shrubs, often growing in mats. **1954** Harrington *Manual Plants CO* 418, Mountain Heath. . . Flowers . . rose-colored (in ours). **1972** Viereck–Little *AK Trees* 217, Aleutian mountain-heath can commonly be found blooming . . in protected depressions and adjacent to snow fields in the mountains . ., both above and below timberline. **1973** Hitchcock–Cronquist *Flora Pacific NW* 346, *Phyllodoce*. . . Mountain-heath; Mountain-heather.

2 =**minniebush.**

1924 *Amer. Botanist* 30.60, Another "mountain heath" is *Menziesia glabella.* **1940** Clute *Amer. Plant Names* 42, *M[enziesia] glabella.* Mountain Heath.

mountain heather n

1 A **sand myrtle** (here: *Leiophyllum buxifolium*).

1901 Lounsberry *S. Wild Flowers* 382 **wNC,** Mountain Heather. . . A prettier, more thrifty form of growth can hardly be imagined than is displayed by this bewitching little shrub as it is seen on the tip top of Roan Mountain. **1932** *Country Life* 62.66 **Appalachians,** In many places close to the Rhododendron . . is found the . . Mountain-heather. . . It is practically an ever-bloomer and is exquisite at all times. **1953** Greene–Blomquist *Flowers South* 88, *Leiophyllum buxifolium* . . ., locally called "mountain heather," with a profusion of white flowers, . . occurs only on certain rocky summits in the s. Appalachian Mountains.

2 A plant of the genus *Phyllodoce*. **chiefly West, AK** Also called **false heather 2, heath 2a, heather 1a, mountain heath 1.** For other names of var spp see **red heather, yellow ~**

1931 U.S. Dept. Ag. *Misc. Pub.* 101.132, *Phyllodoce*. . . A small group of . . northern species, of which about 2 are indigenous to the Alaska region, 3 or 4 others in the Western States, and 1 species in the high mountains of New England and the far North generally. . . These plants are usually called mountain heathers. **1959** Munz–Keck *CA Flora* 402, *Mountain-heather*—Low evergreen shrubs, much-branched, heathlike. **1968** Hultén *Flora AK* 722, Mountain Heather. . . Mountainsides. **1976** Bailey–Bailey *Hortus Third* 866, *Mountain heather*. . . Fl[ower]s greenish, yellow, white, pink, or purple. **1987** Hughes–Blackwell *Wildflowers SE AK* 70, Aleutian Mountain-Heather. . . Flowers, which are urn-shaped, are clustered at the tips of twigs on fuzzy stalks.

3 A plant of the genus *Cassiope*. **AK** Also called **heather 1c, moss bush.** For other names of var spp see **white heather**

1955 U.S. Arctic Info. Center *Gloss.* 53, Mountain heather. Any plant of the genus *Cassiope*. . . Also called 'Cassiope' or 'bell heather.' **1966** Heller *Wild Flowers AK* 62, Mountain heather. . . Flowers . . small, white, bell-shaped. **1972** Viereck–Little *AK Trees* 218, The members of the genus *Cassiope* are often called mountain-heathers, but to distinguish them from the mountain-heaths or mountain-heathers of the genus *Phyllodoce* it is preferable to refer to them as cassiopes. **1987** Hughes–Blackwell *Wildflowers SE AK* 70, Club-Moss Mountain-Heather (*Cassiope lycopodioides*). . . Mertens Mountain-Heather (*Cassiope mertensiana*). . . Mountain Slopes.

mountain hedge n **Rocky Mts** =**Oregon boxwood.**

1952 Davis *Flora ID* 464, *P[achistima] Myrsinites*. . . Mt. Lover, Mt. Hedge. . . Moist slopes of hills and mountains. **1957** Barnes *Nat. Hist. Wasatch Spring* 51 **UT,** Half way up the canyon . . that common evergreen known as mountain hedge or mountain lover is showing its tiny dark red blooms. *Ibid* 58, The mountain hedge now has pin-head buds at the bases of its wedge-shaped evergreen leaves. **1963** Craighead *Rocky Mt. Wildflowers* 111, *Pachistima myrsinites.* . . Mountain-hedge. . . An evergreen shrub with the appearance of a loosely branched boxwood.

mountain hemlock n

A **hemlock 2,** usu *Tsuga mertensiana* of the western US and Alaska.

1884 Sargent *Forests of N. Amer.* 572 **ID,** The timber on these ridges was often small and scattered . . with larch and red fir, balsam, hemlock, and sometimes the mountain hemlock *(Tsuga Pattoniana).* **1892** Apgar *Trees Nth. U.S.* 182, *Tsuga Caroliniana.* . . Mountain-hemlock. . . Wild, but scarce, in the higher Alleghanies, south. **1908** Rogers *Tree Book* 77, *Mountain Hemlock (Tsuga Mertensiana* . .). . . is not likely to be exterminated by lumber companies, for it grows in inaccessible mountain fastnesses, and battles with storms to the very timber line. **1946** Sierra Club *Bulletin* Dec 27 **CA,** Approaching Bond Pass I traversed one of the largest forest associations of mountain hemlock in the Sierra. **1959** Anderson *Flora AK* 28, *T[suga] mertensiana.* . . Mountain Hemlock. . . A small or medium-sized tree . . , but a mere shrub on muskeags and at timberline. **1980** Little *Audubon Guide N. Amer. Trees W. Region* 297, Mountain Hemlock . . *Tsuga mertensiana.* . . is a characteristic species of high mountains.

mountain hen n

=**dusky grouse.**

1953 *AmSp* 28.281 **OR, WA,** Mountain hen—Dusky grouse.

mountain herring n esp UT

A **whitefish** (here: *Prosopium williamsoni*). Cf **herring** n[1] **2**

1877 Hallock *Sportsman's Gaz.* 350, Williamson's Whitefish; Mountain Herring.—*Coregonus williamsoni.* **1884** Goode *Fisheries U.S.* 1.542, *Coregonus Williamsoni.* . . Usually known as the White-fish; in Utah as the "Mountain Herring." **1902** Jordan–Evermann *Amer. Fishes* 134, Like the mountain herring, . . it [=the cisco] will rise to the fly or . . can be taken on the hook. **1949** Caine *N. Amer. Sport Fish* 164, *Colloquial Names* [of *Prosopium williamsoni*] . . Mountain Herring [etc.]. **1966** Barnes–Jensen *Dict. UT Slang* 31, *Mountain herring* . . local name for the native mountain white fish *(Prosopium williamsoni),* which is not very common in Utah rivers, and which is a good game fish. **1973** Knight *Cook's Fish Guide* 382, Herring . . mountain see Whitefish.

mountain hog n Cf *mountain rooter* (at **rooter**)

=**razorback hog.**

1939 FWP *Guide TN* 502, The mountain, or razorback hog, that lives in the woods upon acorns and roots, becomes comparatively fat in the late fall, when it is hunted and shot by the owner. **1986** Pederson *LAGS Concordance* (Wild hog) 2 infs, **cnAL, neGA,** Mountain hogs.

mountain holly n

1 =**Oregon grape.**

1805 (1808) Gass *Jrl.* 185, There is also a small bush . . about 6 inches high, which bears a bunch of small purple berries; some call it mountain holly; the fruit is of an acid taste. **1806** (1905) Lewis *Orig. Jrls. Lewis & Clark Exped.* 4.274, Near the river we find . . two speceis [sic] of mountain holley, & common ash. [**1937** U.S. Forest Serv. *Range Plant Hdbk.* B100, In his journal Lewis referred to Oregon-grape as "mountain holly," probably because of the similarity of its shiny, evergreen, prickly-toothed leaves to those of the common cultivated English holly *(Ilex aquifolium).*] **1963** Craighead *Rocky Mt. Wildflowers* 64, Oregon Grape, . . Mountain Holly . . *Berberis repens.* . . Hollylike leaves . . sometimes turn red in fall.

2 A shrub or small tree of the genus *Nemopanthus,* usu *N. mucronatus,* native to the eastern half of the US. For other names of *N. mucronatus* see **dogberry i, wild holly**

1822 Eaton *Botany* 317, *[Ilex] canadensis* [=*Nemopanthus mucronatus*] . . mountain holly. . . A shrub 3 to 5 feet high. **1832** MA Hist. Soc. *Coll.* 2d ser 9.151 **cwVT,** Illex [sic] canadensis . . Mountain-holly. **1843** Torrey *Flora NY* 2.5, *Nemopanthes* [sic] *canadensis.* . . Mountain Holly. . . Frequent on mountains, but not uncommon in low grounds. Northern and western part of the State, and on the Catskill mountains. **1895** Gray–Bailey *Field Botany* 103, *Mountain Holly.* A much-branched shrub. . . Cold damp woods, Me. to Va. and Ind. **1931** Harned *Wild Flowers Alleghanies* 277, *Mountain Holly.* . . Berries borne on long stalks, a lusterless, light crimson, . . and deeply grooved. **1966** Grimm *Recognizing Native Shrubs* 168, *Mountain-holly.* . . Flowers small, greenish white. . . *Fruits* berry-like. **1979** Little *Checklist U.S. Trees* 176, *Nemopanthus.* . . Mountain-holly. Ibid 177, Nemopanthus col-

linus. . . *Mountain-holly.* . . A shrub or small tree to 13 ft. . . *Nemopanthus mucronatus* . . , mountain-holly. . . Generally a shrub 3–10 ft . . high.

3 A **holly** n[1] **1,** usu *Ilex montana.*

1901 Mohr *Plant Life AL* 71, The fringed stuartia . . [and] mountain holly *(Ilex monticola)* . . extend northerly on the lower of the western Alleghenian ranges to southeastern Kentucky, western Virginia, and Pennsylvania, and reach their southern limit on Sand Mountain. **1903** Small *Flora SE U.S.* 732, *Ilex monticola.* . . In mountain woods, New York to Georgia and Alabama. . . *Mountain Holly.* **1943** Peattie *Great Smokies* 161, A few deciduous trees are frequently found with them [=balsam fir and red spruce]. Such are fire cherry, yellow birch, mountain holly, . . and mountain maple. **1967** *Ozark Visitor* (Point Lookout MO) Feb 6, Pussy-toes, . . mountain holly, wild petunia fringed my path down the hillside. **1968** Radford et al. *Manual Flora Carolinas* 683, *Mountain Holly.* . . Throughout mts. and pied[mont]. . . *I[lex] montana.* **1976** Bailey–Bailey *Hortus Third* 589, *Mountain h[olly].* . . Mass. to Ala. and Ga.

4 =**mountain mahogany 2** (here: *Cercocarpus* spp).

1906 Rydberg *Flora CO* 189, *Cercocarpus.* . . Mountain Holly.

5 =**islay 1.** Cf **hollyleaf cherry**

1976 Bailey–Bailey *Hortus Third* 919 **CA,** *[Prunus] ilicifolia.* . . *Mountain holly.* . . Dense evergreen shrub or small tree . . ; l[ea]v[e]s shining, leathery.

mountain holly fern n Cf **holly fern**

A **sword fern** (here: *Polystichum lonchitis*).

1953 Nelson *Plants Rocky Mt. Park* 34, *Holly fern* or *mountain holly-fern, Polystichum lonchitis.* **1973** Hitchcock–Cronquist *Flora Pacific NW* 53, Mt. h[olly-fern]. *P[olystichum] lonchitis.*

mountain hollyhock n

A **globe mallow 2** (here: *Iliamna rivularis*).

1952 Davis *Flora ID* 468, *I[liamna] rivularis.* . . *Mt. Hollyhock.* . . Stream banks, mountain slopes and meadows. B.C. to Mont., Wyo., and Colo. **1963** Craighead *Rocky Mt. Wildflowers* 114, When you see pinkish-white to rose-purple flowers in dense spikes blooming on a plant that though smaller looks like the garden Hollyhock, you have probably found the Mountain Hollyhock.

mountain honeysuckle n

1 A **rhododendron.** Cf **honeysuckle 3, honeysuckle azalea**

1822 Eaton *Botany* 199, *Azalea.* . . *lapponica* (mountain honeysuckle . .). **1941** Writers' Program *Guide AR* 270 **nwAR,** Sweet-smelling azaleas, known in this region as "mountain honeysuckle," grow in profusion on the rocky soil. The salmon-pink flowers are at their best in May. **1984** Wilder *You All Spoken Here* 176 **Sth,** Kiss-me-over-the-gate; bush honeysuckle, mountain honeysuckle: Azalea.

2 A **honeysuckle 2** (here: *Lonicera dioica*).

1933 Small *Manual SE Flora* 1275, *L[onicera] dioica.* . . *Mountain-honeysuckle.* . . Blue Ridge and more northern provinces. **1938** Van Dersal *Native Woody Plants* 158, *Mountain honeysuckle.* . . A diffuse or twining vine; flowers May–June.

mountain hoof n

A type of horse's hoof suitable for rocky terrain.

1971 Green *Village Horse Doctor* 305 **cwTX** (as of c1940s), The walls of the hooves of horses become thicker and tougher to withstand the wear of pebbly rocks, hard ground, and the rimrock of the canyon regions as well as the rocky surfaces of the mountains. . . [T]he hoof becomes much smaller in width and the sole of the hoof becomes much more concave, which enables the walls to better protect the sole of the hoof, and the receded frog in the hoof is less susceptible to stone bruise and blisters. . . [T]he hoof . . is referred to . . as a rock hoof, or sometimes a mountain hoof.

mountain hoosier See **hoosier B1a**

mountain indigo n Also *mountain indigo bush*

A **false indigo 1** (here: either *Amorpha glabra* or *A. virgata*).

1933 Small *Manual SE Flora* 689, *A[morpha] glabra.* . . *Mountain-indigo.* . . Dry soil and swamp-margins. Ibid 690, *A. virgata.* . . Mountain-indigo. . . Dry woods. **1938** Van Dersal *Native Woody Plants* 51, *Amorpha glabra.* Mountain-indigo. . . A small to large shrub; flowers May–June. Ibid 52, *Amorpha virgata.* Mountain-indigo. **1966** Grimm *Recognizing Native Shrubs* 151, Mountain Indigobush—*Amorpha glabra.* . . North Carolina and Tennessee south to Georgia and Alabama. . . *Mountain Indigobush—Amorpha virgata.* . . Western Florida and Alabama north to Tennessee.

mountainite See **mountaineer**

mountain ivy n Also *mountain ivory* **chiefly sAppalachians, esp VA** Cf **ivory** n², **ivy 4**

A **mountain laurel 1,** usu **calico bush 1.**

1817 Brown *Western Gaz.* 322 neOH, Woodbine, . . mountain ivy, mountain laurel. **1908** Britton *N. Amer. Trees* 755, *Kalmia latifolia.* . . is so well known that it has received a great many common names, such as . . Mountain ivy. **1938** Stuart *Dark Hills* 188 **KY,** But the holly bushes were green, the pines and the mountain ivy were still green. **1941** *LANE* Map 249 *(Mountain laurel)* 1 inf, wCT, In Norfolk [MA] (ca. 35 miles northeast) it's always called *ivy* or *mountain* ~. **1949** Arnow *Hunter's Horn* 356 **KY,** The ewes, fat as they were, wouldn't poison themselves eating mountain ivy bush for a day or two. **1950** Peattie *Nat. Hist. Trees* 523, *Kalmia latifolia.* . . Mountain . . Ivy. **1961** Douglas *My Wilderness* 175 wNC, Mountain people call laurel (whose regional name is ivy) the calico bush or mountain ivy. **1967** *DARE* Wildfl QR Plates 156A, B Inf **SC**41, Mountain ivy. **1968–70** *DARE* (Qu. T16, . . *Kinds of trees* . . *'special')* Inf **VA**2, Mountain ivy—not poisonous to touch, but poisonous if eaten by cattle; **VA**7, Mountain ivy—smaller bloom [than mountain laurel]; **VA**21, Mountain ivy—sheep and cattle eat and die; book word is mountain laurel; **VA**26, Mountain laurel = mountain ivy; (Qu. T5, . . *Kinds of evergreens, other than pine)* Inf **VA**15, Mountain ivy = mountain laurel; (Qu. S26c, *Wildflowers that grow in woods)* Inf **VA**75, Mountain ivory—pink cuplike flowers; **VA**77, Mountain ivory. **1968** *DARE* FW Addit **VA,** The mountain people mistakenly call mountain laurel "mountain ivy."

mountain jack n Cf **mountain boomer 1**

An unidentified squirrel.

1967 *DARE* (Qu. P27) Inf **OH**33, Mountain jack.

mountain jay n Cf **Rocky Mountain jay**

1 also *mountain blue jay:* =**Steller's jay. West, esp CA**

1872 *Amer. Naturalist* 6.398 **UT,** The great-crested, Woodhouse's and the Canada jays were of frequent occurrence in the mountains, the former being familiarly known as the "mountain jay." **1881** (1882) Chase *Editor's Run* 87 **NM,** Magpies, mountain blue jays, and other birds, are plenty about the house. **1917** (1923) *Birds Amer.* 2.219, *Steller's Jay.* . . Mountain Jay; Pine Jay; Conifer Jay. **1923** Dawson *Birds CA* 1.65, *Steller's Jay.* . . Synonyms. Mountain Jay. "Blue Jay." "Jaybird." **1936** Thompson *High Trails* 84 **MT,** Of smaller birds the most showy is the mountain jay. **1968–69** *DARE* (Qu. Q16, . . *Kinds of jays)* Inf **CA**130, Mountain blue jay—bigger than regular jay; **CA**137, Mountain blue jay—bit differently colored; **CA**160, Mountain blue jay; **CA**99, Valley jays and mountain jays are types of jays.

2 =**scrub jay.**

1935 Sandoz *Jules* 215 **wNE** (as of 1880–1930), Then, with his gun across his knees, he sat . . and watched a flock of powdery-blue mountain jays circle about the patch of sweet corn below.

mountain juniper n **chiefly West, AK**

A **juniper 1,** usu *Juniperus communis.*

1897 Sudworth *Arborescent Flora* 97, *Juniperus occidentalis conjugens.* . . Mountain Juniper. **1906** Rydberg *Flora CO* 9, *Juniperus sibirica* [=*J. communis*]. . . *Mountain* . . *Juniper.* Exposed rocky mountains and hills from Labr. to Alaska, Utah and N.Y. **1908** Britton *N. Amer. Trees* 116, *Rock Cedar* [=*Juniperus ashei*]. . . is also called . . Mountain juniper, and Juniper. **1936** McDougall–Baggley *Plants of Yellowstone* 26, *Juniperus sibirica.* . . Also known as *Mountain juniper.* **1968** Hultén *Flora AK* 65, *Juniperus communis.* . . Common Mountain Juniper. **1969** *DARE* (Qu. T16) Inf **CA**130, Mountain juniper. **1973** Hitchcock–Cronquist *Flora Pacific NW* 58, Common or mt. j[uniper]. . . J[uniperus] communis. **1976** Bailey–Bailey *Hortus Third* 616, *[Juniperus communis]* var. *saxatilis.* . . *Mountain j[uniper].* . . Arctic and high mts.

mountain lamb n Also *mountain mutton,* ~ *pork,* ~ *veal* Cf **Adirondack steak, lamb without horns**

Venison from a deer killed out of season.

1887 *Amer. Field* 27.510, Do you know what mountain lamb is? Why, it's venison. **1890** *DN* 1.74 **NH,** *Mountain lamb* or *mountain mutton:* deer killed out of season. **1954** White *Adirondack Country* 118 **neNY,** Hotels served venison in and out of season; out of season, the name

changed to "Adirondack Steak" or "mountain lamb." **1967–68** *DARE* (Qu. P35a, *Names or nicknames for any deer shot illegally)* Inf **IL**27, Mountain veal; **NJ**41, Mountain pork; **NY**6, Mountain lamb.

mountain larch n

A western **tamarack:** either *Larix lyalli* or *L. occidentalis.*

1897 Sudworth *Arborescent Flora* 33, *Larix lyalli.* . . Mountain Larch. **1908** Britton *N. Amer. Trees* 53, *Larix Lyallii.* . . This tree, also called . . Mountain larch, . . and Tamarack, is an alpine species, growing only near the timber-line of mountains between the altitudes of 1350 and 2400 meters. **1979** Little *Checklist U.S. Trees* 159, *Larix occidentalis.* . . Mountain larch.

mountain lark n

=**white-throated sparrow.**

1956 MA Audubon Soc. *Bulletin* 40.255 **MA,** *White-throated Sparrow.* Mountain Lark.

mountain laurel n

1 A plant of the genus *Kalmia,* esp *K. latifolia.* **chiefly Atlantic** Also called **creek ivy, highland myrtle, ivory** n², **ivy 4, laurel 2, mountain ivy, wicky.** For other names of var spp see **calico bush 1, sheep laurel, swamp** ~

1759 Miller *Gardener's Dict.* np, *Kalmia.* . . Ever-green Rose Laurel . . commonly called in *America* Mountain Laurel. **1813** Michaux *Histoire des Arbres* 3.147, *Kalmia latifolia.* . . Cet arbrisseau est assez indifféremment désigné par les noms de *Mountain laurel . . ; Laurel . . ; Ivy . . ,* et de *Calico tree.* [=*Kalmia latifolia.* . . This shrub is rather indifferently designated by the names of *Mountain laurel . . ; Laurel . . ; Ivy . . ,* and of *Calico tree.*] **1892** (1974) Millspaugh *Amer. Med. Plants* 103-1, *Mountain Laurel.* . . In southern Pennsylvania, on the Alleghanies, this shrub often attains the dimensions of a small tree, sometimes reaching as high as 30 feet. **1916** *Torreya* 16.239, *Kalmia angustifolia.* . . Mountain laurel, Matinicus Id., Me. **1941** *LANE* Map 249 **widespread sNEng,** Mountain laurel. **1953** Nelson *Plants Rocky Mt. Park* 116, *Dwarf mountain-laurel* . . *Kalmia polifolia.* . . This little shrub. . . is only a few inches high, but blooms profusely in July with clusters of rose-purple flowers similar in shape to those of the mountain-laurel of the East. **1965–70** *DARE* (Qu. T16, . . *Kinds of trees* . . *'special')* 10 Infs, **Atlantic,** Mountain laurel; **DC**2, Mountain laurel—blossom suddenly opens and throws pollen abroad; **VA**26, Mountain laurel = mountain ivy; (Qu. S17, . . *Kinds of plants . . that . . cause itching and swelling)* Inf **AL**37, Mountain laurel; (Qu. S26a) Infs **PA**60, 68, 181, 231, Mountain laurel; (Qu. S26c, *Wildflowers that grow in woods)* Infs **MD**23, **NH**10, **RI**15, **WV**13, Mountain laurel; **NC**16, Creek ivy or mountain laurel; **VA**75, Mountain ivory—"mountain laurel" book word; **VA**77, Mountain laurel . . [=] mountain ivory; (Qu. S26e, *Other wildflowers not yet mentioned;* not asked in early QRs) Infs **AL**30, **MA**58, **SC**32, 57, Mountain laurel; (Qu. T5, . . *Kinds of evergreens, other than pine)* Infs **GA**80, **KY**68, **NC**45, **PA**104, **WV**3, Mountain laurel; **NC**30, Pink mountain laurel; **VA**15, Mountain ivy—book word "mountain laurel"; (Qu. T15, . . *Kinds of swamp trees)* Infs **CT**21, **WY**1, Mountain laurel. **1980** Little *Audubon Guide N. Amer. Trees E. Region* 624, Mountain-laurel is one of the most beautiful native flowering shrubs. . . The wood has been used for tool handles and turnery, and the burls, or hard knotlike growths, for briar pipes.

2 A **rosebay:** *Rhododendron maximum* in mountainous areas of the eastern US, or *R. macrophyllum* along the Pacific coast.

1785 Marshall *Arbustrum* 127, *Rhododendrum* [sic] *maximum.* Pennsylvanian Mountain Laurel. . . The flowers are pretty large and of a pale rose colour, studded with spots of a deeper red, having their tubes a little bent. **1830** Rafinesque *Med. Flora* 2.256, *Mountain Laurel, Rosebay.* . . Leaves poison cattle. **1837** Darlington *Flora Cestrica* 263 **PA,** *R. maximum.* . . Mountain Laurel. Rose Bay. . . This magnificent ornament of our mountain forests is rare in Chester County. **1908** Britton *N. Amer. Trees* 752, *Rhododendron maximum.* . . is also called . . Mountain laurel. . . It occurs from Nova Scotia and Ontario southward in the mountains to Georgia and Alabama. *Ibid* 754, *Rhododendron californicum* [=*R. macrophyllum*] . . , also called Mountain laurel . . , occurs on rich slopes and in ravines of the Cascade Mountains and along the coast from Mendocino county, California, northward to British Columbia. **1924** *Amer. Botanist* 30.58, *Rhododendron maximum.* . . Other names for [the] plant are . . "mountain laurel" . . and "spoon hutch." **1964** Batson *Wild Flowers SC* 82, *Mountain laurel* . . *Rhododendron maximum.* . . Rich mountain woods, particularly on bluffs along streams where it forms colonies. Late spring. Virginia to Georgia. **1968–70** *DARE* (Qu. S26c,

Wildflowers that grow in woods) Inf **NJ**6, Mountain laurel—rhododendron; **VA**75, Mountain laurel—like a magnolia—"rhododendron" [is] book word; **VA**77, Mountain laurel—rhododendron; (Qu. T16, . . *Kinds of trees . . 'special'*) Inf **VA**7, Mountain laurel—big bloom; mountain ivy—smaller bloom; **VA**21, Mountain laurel—book word is "rhododendron"; (Qu. T5, . . *Kinds of evergreens, other than pine*) Inf **VA**15, Mountain laurel—book word "rhododendron."

3 =**California laurel. chiefly CA**

1884 Sargent *Forests of N. Amer.* 120, *Umbellularia californica. . . Mountain laurel. . .* Used . . in shipbuilding, for jaws, bitts, cleats, cross-trees, etc. **1897** Sudworth *Arborescent Flora* 203, *Umbellularia californica. . . California Laurel. . . Common Names. . .* Mountain Laurel (Cal., Nev.) **1897** Parsons *Wild Flowers CA* 373, This tree [=*Umbellularia californica*] is known in different localities by a variety of names, such as . . "mountain laurel." **1923** Davidson–Moxley *Flora S. CA* 144, *Mountain Laurel. . .* Frequent in canyons of the coast range.

4 A **snowbrush** (here: *Ceanothus velutinus*). **West**

1924 Hawkins *Trees & Shrubs* 97 **MT**, Ceanothus velutinus. . . Mountain laurel, snow bush [etc] . . are other common names. **1932** Rydberg *Flora Prairies* 533, *Mountain Laurel. . . C[eanothus] velutinus. . .* Hillsides: Mont.—S.D.—Colo.—Utah—B.C. **1952** Davis *Flora ID* 467, *C. velutinus. . . Mt. Laurel, Snowbrush. . .* Browsed by game animals. Moist draws of hills. **1963** Craighead *Rocky Mt. Wildflowers* 112, *Snowbrush. . . Other names:* Mountain-laurel. . . Entire plant is pleasantly aromatic. **1966** Barnes–Jensen *Dict. UT Slang* 31, *Mountain Laurel . .* a local name for the Snow Brush or Mountain Lilac (*Ceanothus velutinus*).

5 also *Texas mountain laurel:* =**frijolillo 1. chiefly TX, NM**

1931 U.S. Dept. Ag. *Misc. Pub.* 101.87, Other common names for this plant [=*Sophora secundiflora*] include . . mountain-laurel. **1936** NM Univ. *Biol. Ser.* 4.5.54 **NM**, *Broussonetia secundiflora*, known as "mountain laurel," . . is a beautiful evergreen shrub with glossy dark green leaves, common in the Guadalupe Mountains southwest of Carlsbad. **1939** Tharp *Vegetation TX* 58, *Texas Mountain Laurel (Sophora secundiflora) . .* glossy evergreen foliage. **1951** *PADS* 15.34 **TX**, *Sophora secundiflora. . .* Mountain laurel. . . The fragrance of the wisteria-like purple blossoms is offensive to many. **1970** Correll *Plants TX* 798, *Texas mountain laurel. . .* Tex. and N.M. . . Cultivated for the beautiful evergreen foliage and showy flowers. **c1979** TX Dept. Highways *Flowers* 47, *Mescal bean* is also called Mountain Laurel in Texas. . . This shrub, *Sophora secundiflora,* is not related to the southern mountain laurel (*Kalmia latifolia*) found in other states.

6 =**bearberry 2.**

1941 *LANE* Map 274, 1 inf, **sVT**, *Checkerberries,* grow on a small vine, 'called *mountain laurel* in the White Mountains.'

7 A **sumac** (here: *Rhus ovata*).

1979 Little *Checklist U.S. Trees* 252, *Rhus ovata. . . Sugar sumac. . . Other common names . .* mountain-laurel. . . Mts. of c. Ariz. and s. Calif.

mountain leatherwood See **leatherwood 2**

mountain lettuce n **chiefly Appalachians**

A **saxifrage** (here: *Saxifraga micranthidifolia*).

1903 Small *Flora SE U.S.* 500, *Mountain Lettuce.* **1933** Small *Manual SE Flora* 596, *M[icranthes] micranthidifolia. . . Mountain-lettuce. . .* Brooks, logs, and wet rocks, Blue Ridge and Appalachian provinces, Ga. to Tenn. and Pa. **1939** Medsger *Edible Wild Plants* 153, *Mountain Lettuce. . .* is a perennial plant that grows on the borders of cool mountain streams and in swampy places in the Appalachian Mountains. . . In some of the mountainous sections of southern Pennsylvania, this plant is highly prized by the people. For salads it is probably used more than any other wild plant of the region. **1954** *Sat. Review* 13 Nov 55 **NC**, Up on top of the mountain [=Mount Mitchell] you will find minnie bush (sometimes called he-honeysuckle), balsam trees (sometimes called she-balsams), mountain lettuce, St. John's wort, and the grave of the Rev. Elisha Mitchell, D.D. **1964** Batson *Wild Flowers SC* 131, *S[axifraga] micranthidifolia . .* Mountain Lettuce.

mountain lilac n **West**

Any of several spp of **ceanothus,** such as **buckbrush 3c** or **deer brush 1;** see quots.

1901 Jepson *Flora CA* 254, *Ceanothus* [spp] . . Mountain Lilac. **1911** Chase *Yosemite Trails* 11 **ceCA**, With them arrives the mountain-lilac (*Ceanothus*) in clouds of azure and white that emulate the very sky.

1915 (1926) Armstrong–Thornber *Western Wild Flowers* 282, There are many kinds of Ceanothus, largely western. . . Mountain Lilac is the commonest name, but misleading. Lilacs belong to another family. *Ibid,* Snow Brush, Mountain Lilac—*Ceanothus velutinus . .* West, except Ariz. *Ibid* 284 **CA**, Deer-Brush, Mountain Lilac—*Ceanothus integerrimus.* **1937** U.S. Forest Serv. *Range Plant Hdbk.* B44, Deerbrush, known also as bluebrush, mountain-lilac, and sweetbirch, is a deciduous shrub growing in the mountains from Washington south through California and western Nevada into Arizona. **1960** Vines *Trees SW* 691, *Desert Ceanothus. . .* Also known by the name of Gregg Ceanothus, New Jersey-tea, Indian-tea, Red-root, and Mountain-lilac. **1961** *Julian Apple Day* [37] **csCA**, [At the annual wildflower show in Julian:] Among the unusual flowers are the . . creeping mountain lilac. **1966** [see **mountain laurel 4**].

mountain lily n

1 =**Indian mallow 1.**

1896 *Jrl. Amer. Folkl.* 9.183 **ME**, *Abutilon,* sp., mountain lily.

2 also *Rocky Mountain lily:* A **sand lily** (here: *Leucocrinum montanum*). **West**

1932 Rydberg *Flora Prairies* 215, *Mountain Lily. . . L[eucocrinum] montanum. . .* Hills and plains. **1936** Winter *Plants NE* 11, Mountain Lily. . . Common in the sand-hills of western Nebr. **1954** Harrington *Manual Plants CO* 154, *Mountainlily. . .* scattered over Colorado, none as yet from the extreme western part, at 3500–8000 ft. **1959** Carleton *Index Herb. Plants* 100, *Rocky-Mountain-lily:* Leucocrinum montanum. **1961** Peck *Manual OR* 216, *Mountain Lily. . .* Dry sandy soil east of the Cascades, to the Rocky Mts. and Calif. **1969** *DARE* (Qu. S2) Inf **CA**137, Mountain lily; (Qu. S26e) Inf **CA**165, Mountain lily. **1973** Hitchcock–Cronquist *Flora Pacific NW* 691, Mt. lily. . . Sagebr[ush] des[ert] to open mont[ane] for[ests]. **1979** Spellenberg *Audubon Guide N. Amer. Wildflowers W. Region* 584, *Mountain Lily . . Leucocrinum montanum. . .* With its flowers nestled among the leaves, this distinctive little Lily is unmistakable.

3 A **squaw grass** (here: *Xerophyllum tenax*).

1949 Peattie *Cascades* 248 **Pacific NW**, Squaw-grass . . has the name of Xerophyllum tenax. . . It is so conspicuous and attractive that it has a number of other popular names, some of which are bear-grass, . . and mountain lily.

4 also *Rocky Mountain lily:* A **wood lily** (here: *Lilium philadelphicum*).

1967 *DARE* Wildfl QR Pl.12 Inf **CO**7, Mountain lily. **1979** Spellenberg *Audubon Guide N. Amer. Wildflowers W. Region* 585, *Rocky Mountain Lily . . (Lilium philadelphicum). . .* Once much more common than now. It is too often picked by visitors to the mountains. It also disappears rapidly from intensively grazed meadowland.

5 Prob an **iris B1** such as *Iris missouriensis.* Cf **Rocky Mountain iris**

1967 *DARE* (Qu. S24, *A wild flower that grows in swamps and marshes and looks like a small blue iris*) Inf **OR**16, Mountain lily.

mountain lion n **chiefly West** See Map on p. 686

A large, tawny, unspotted cat *(Felis concolor).* Also called **California lion, catamount 2, cougar, Indian devil 1, ~ panther, lion, Mexican lion, mountain cat 2, panther, puma, tiger, wildcat**

1859 in 1890 Hall *Hist. CO* 2.520, Mountain lion stole all my meat in camp; no supper to-night; d—n him. **1888** Lindley–Widney *CA of South* 123, The mountains are the haunts of the grizzly bear and mountain-lion. **1941** Writers' Program *Guide UT* 336, Mountain lions (they are known as panthers and cougars elsewhere, but not in Utah) will "tree" when too closely pressed. **1961** Douglas *My Wilderness* 97 **AZ**, Then from the mountain at my back came the most fearful sound of the woods—the bloodthirsty screech of the mountain lion. **1965–70** *DARE* (Qu. P31) 112 Infs, **chiefly West,** Mountain lion; **CA**120, California mountain lion; (Qu. P32) Infs **CA**1, **UT**3, Mountain lion. **1966** Barnes–Jensen *Dict. UT Slang* 31, *Mountain lion . .* the puma *(Felis concolor).* Although this large cat is known by almost fifty different names, in Utah it is generally called mountain lion and, less frequently, cougar. **1968** *PA Game News* Mar 5 **PA**, Mountain lions also continued to be numerous in Pennsylvania well into the 19th Century. **1969** *DARE* Tape **CA**145, Their [=wild rams'] natural enemy is the wolf and the wolverine and the bobcat and the mountain lion. **1982** *NY Times* (NY) 3 Jan sec 10 17/6 **AZ**, Once, years before, I had glimpsed a mountain lion in this canyon, following me through the twilight.

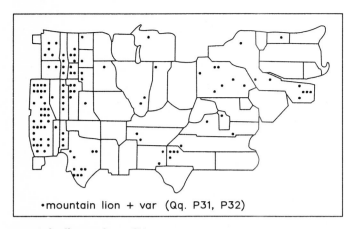

•mountain lion + var (Qq. P31, P32)

mountain live oak n CA
=canyon oak 1.

1908 Rogers *Tree Book* 209, *Mountain Live Oak. . . Quercus chrysolepis. . .* Most valuable timber oak of the Pacific coast. . . The mountain live oak is not a horticultural tree. . . It is a wild thing, untamable as the mountain goat, loving the rocky cañon sides and the high terraces. **1910** Jepson *Silva CA* 223, Being evergreen, it is called . . Mountain Live Oak, especially in those portions of the mountains where it is the only live oak. **1968–70** *DARE* (Qu. T10, . . *Kinds of oak trees*) Infs **CA**97, 200, Mountain live oak.

mountain locust n
A **kidneywood** (here: *Eysenhardtia polystachya*).

1931 U.S. Dept. Ag. *Misc. Pub.* 101.86, It [=*Eysenhardtia polystachya*] is frequently called mountain locust in Arizona, evidently being mistaken for a Robinia.

mountain lover n [Transl of Nuttall's proposed name *Oreophila* for this genus]
Std: a plant of the genus *Paxistima*: *P. canbyi* in Virginia and West Virginia, or **Oregon boxwood** in the western US. For other names of the former see **rat stripper**

mountain magnolia n
A **magnolia 1**: usu *Magnolia acuminata* or *M. fraseri,* but also *M. pyramidata.*

[**1783** in 1788 Schöpf *Reise Staaten* 1.347, Die blaue Magnolie oder Berg-Magnolie (*Magnolia acuminata* . .) war einer der merkwürdigern und dieser Gegend eigenen Bäume. . . Man findet ihn nur in den Gebürgen an trockenen Stellen. [=The blue magnolia or mountain magnolia (*Magnolia acuminata* . .) was one of the more noteworthy and unusual trees of this region. . . One finds it only in the mountains in dry places.]] **1785** Marshall *Arbustrum* 83, Magnolia acuminata. *Long leaved Mountain Magnolia, or Cucumber Tree.* This tree grows sometimes to the height of thirty or forty feet. **1897** Sudworth *Arborescent Flora* 196, *Magnolia acuminata. . . Common Names. . .* Mountain Magnolia (Miss., Ky.) *Ibid* 197, *Magnolia fraseri. . . Common Names. . .* Mountain Magnolia. **1908** Rogers *Tree Book* 254, *Mountain Magnolia (Magnolia Fraseri). Ibid* 255, A peculiarity of the mountain magnolia, umbrella tree and large-leaved cucumber tree is that the foliage of all three falls without any perceptible change of colour. **1938** Van Dersal *Native Woody Plants* 342, Magnolia, . . Mountain *(Magnolia acuminata, Magnolia fraseri, Magnolia pyramidata).* **1950** Grimm *Trees PA* 205, The Cucumber Tree is also known as . . Mountain Magnolia. . . It is often found on rather rocky slopes. **1966** *DARE* (Qu. T16) Inf **NC**36, Mountain magnolia—cucumber tree. **1973** Wharton–Barbour *Trees KY* 357, *Magnolia fraseri. . . Mountain Magnolia.* In Kentucky this lovely tree is restricted to the southeast where it grows as an understory tree. **1980** Little *Audubon Guide N. Amer. Trees E. Region* 439, "Mountain Magnolia" . . *Magnolia fraseri. . .* This species is fairly common in the Great Smoky Mountains National Park. *Ibid* 442, "Mountain Magnolia"—*Magnolia pyramidata. . .* This . . local species of the Coastal Plain is closely related to Fraser Magnolia, a mountain species which has larger leaves and larger flowers with pale yellow petals.

mountain mahogany n
1 **=sweet birch.** [See quots 1860, 1950] Cf **mahogany birch**
1810 Michaux *Histoire des Arbres* 1.26, B[etula] lenta. . . *Mountain*

mahogany . . dans une partie de la Virginie. [=B[etula] lenta. . . *Mountain mahogany* . . in a part of Virginia.] **1830** Rafinesque *Med. Flora* 2.200, *B[etula] lenta. . . Mountain Mahogany.* Wood much used by cabinet makers, takes a fine polish: bark with a sweet spicy smell and taste. **1860** Curtis *Cat. Plants NC* 74, B[etula] lenta. . . In the mountains of Virginia it is called *Mountain Mahogany. . .* Furniture made of it, as chairs, tables, &c., will in time and by careful use, acquire very much the appearance of Mahogany. **1897** Sudworth *Arborescent Flora* 142 **SC,** *Betula lenta. . .* Mountain Mahogany. **1930** Sievers *Amer. Med. Plants* 54, *Sweet Birch. . .* Other common names. . . Mountain mahogany. **1950** Peattie *Nat. Hist. Trees* 173, But it [=*Betula lenta*] has had from the beginning a property which has long tempted the furniture manufacturer, for on exposure to the air the wood slowly deepens in tone, and old furniture of this species, if well cared for, might pass in its color for mahogany. Indeed, it has been sold in the past as "Mountain Mahogany." . . A little doctoring with fillers and stains made the deception nearly perfect. **1976** Bailey–Bailey *Hortus Third* 161, *[Betula] lenta. . . Mountain mahogany. . .* Moist woods, Me. to Ala.

2 A plant of the genus *Cercocarpus*. [See quot 1937] **West** Also called **Apache plume 2, blackbrush 3, buckbrush 3g, deer brush 2, hardtack 6, mahogany 2b, mountain holly 4, quail brush, rabbit ~, sweetbrush, tallow bush.** For other names of var spp see **curl-leaf, desert mahogany, ironwood d(5), plume tree, sweetbrier**

1860 Greeley *Overland Journey* 268, There is a . . small tree which a driver termed a mountain-mahogany and a passenger called a red haw. **1874** (1877) Hittell *Resources CA* 365, The mountain mahogany is an evergreen found on the eastern slopes of the Sierra Nevada, at an elevation of 6,000 feet above the sea. The leaves are bright and glossy, the growth low, the trunk crooked, the wood red, very even in grain, hard, heavy, and susceptible of high polish. **1888** Lindley–Widney *CA of South* 172 **swCA,** The chaparral . . is made up of the grease-wood, mountain-mahogany, buckthorn . . and a few others. *Ibid,* The mountain-mahogany makes good light-colored canes, the sap-wood being nearly white notwithstanding its name. **1897** Sudworth *Arborescent Flora* 207, *Cercocarpus ledifolius. . . Common Name.* Mountain Mahogany (Cal., N. Mex., Utah, Idaho, Mont.) *Ibid* 208, *Cercocarpus parvifolius. . . Common Names.* Mountain Mahogany (Cal., N. Mex., Utah, Idaho, Colo.) **1913** Wooton *Trees NM* 81, *Mountain Mahogany . .* is represented in New Mexico by four species, all of which are more or less valuable for the forage they produce. These plants are also frequently used for firewood. **1935** Davis *Honey* 301 **OR,** The flat below was brushed up with junipers and mountain mahogany and mock orange. **1937** U.S. Forest Serv. *Range Plant Hdbk.* B49, *Cercocarpus spp. . .* The common name, mountain-mahogany, refers to the mountainous habitat characteristic of the genus and to the fact that the wood is very hard and heavy, and often reddish-brown in color, suggesting that of the true mahogany, a well-known tropical . . tree *(Swietenia mahagoni).* **1970** *DARE* (Qu. T5, . . *Kinds of evergreens, other than pine)* Inf **CA**208, Mountain mahogany; (Qu. T16, . . *Kinds of trees* . . *'special'*) Infs **CA**155, **OR**10, Mountain mahogany; **NV**8, Mountain mahogany—a bush 10' high used by early settlers . . to smoke meat in their smokehouses—deer bed down in it. **1981** Benson–Darrow *Trees SW Deserts* 274, The . . name mountain mahogany was applied by the Mormon settlers in Utah.

3 A **madrone.**
1885 *Outing* 7.25, With this pine grew a little mescal and a respectable amount of the "madroña," or mountain mahogany.

4 A western **yew** (here: *Taxus brevifolia*).
1897 Sudworth *Arborescent Flora* 103 **ID,** *Taxus brevifolia. . . Common Names. . .* Mountain mahogany. **1908** Britton *N. Amer. Trees* 123, *Western Yew—Taxus brevifolia. . .* This beautiful evergreen tree or shrub. . . is also known as . . Mountain Mahogany. [*Ibid* 124, The wood is . . bright light red. . . It is very durable, and takes a fine polish and is used for fence posts, fancy cabinet work, bows, canoe paddles, . . and many other useful purposes.]

5 **=sweet gum.**
1940 Clute *Amer. Plant Names* 147, *L[iquidambar] styraciflua. . .* Mountain mahogany.

mountain maple n Cf Rocky Mountain maple
Any of var often shrubby **maples** such as **dwarf maple** in the western US or **vine maple,** but esp *Acer spicatum* of the eastern US. For other names of the latter see **elkwood 1, false**

dogwood 1, goosefoot maple 2, low ~, moose ~, swamp ~, water ~

1785 Marshall *Arbustrum* 2, Acer pennsylvanicum—*Pennsylvanian Dwarf Mountain Maple.* This grows naturally upon the mountains in the back parts of Pennsylvania. **1832** *MA Hist. Soc. Coll.* 2d ser 9.146 **cwVT,** Acer spicatum . . Mountain maple. **1897** Sudworth *Arborescent Flora* 282, *Acer spicatum. . . Common Names.* Mountain Maple (Vt., N.H., R.I., Conn., N.Y., N.J., Pa., N.C., S.C., Mich., Minn.) *Ibid* 283, *Acer circinatum. . . Common Names.* . . Mountain Maple. *Ibid* 284, *Acer glabrum. . . Common Names.* . . Mountain Maple (Colo., Mont.) **1898** *Jrl. Amer. Folkl.* 11.225 **West,** *Acer glabrum.* . . Mountain maple. **1924** Hawkins *Trees & Shrubs* 97 **MT,** Mountain maple has a dashing school-girl color that is always refreshing. In winter, its buds and twigs are a deep red. . . The leaf stems are always pink and the young leaves are covered with bright red galls. **1937** U.S. Forest Serv. *Range Plant Hdbk.* B6, Dwarf maple . . sometimes known as mountain maple. . . is one of the most widespread maples on the western ranges. **1950** Grimm *Trees PA* 275, The Mountain Maple is a large shrub or a small tree which sometimes attains a height of 20 to 30 feet. . . As its name implies, [it] is usually found in the cool, shady, moist, and rocky mountain forests. **1965–70** *DARE* (Qu. T14) Infs **AZ**2, **ME**8, **MN**14, **OH**72, **PA**99, 223, 245, **TN**11, **VA**8, **WA**12, **WV**4, Mountain maple. **1967** Borland *Hill Country* 160 **nwCT,** Elkwood is more generally known as mountain maple. **1973** Stephens *Woody Plants* 346, *Acer glabrum* . . Mountain maple. . . Alaska to California, east to New Mexico, and north to Colorado, western Nebraska, Montana, and Idaho. **1980** Little *Audubon Guide N. Amer. Trees E. Region* 581, Mountain Maple is hardy. . . Rabbits, beavers, deer, and moose browse the bark, and ruffed grouse eat the buds. **1980** Little *Audubon Guide N. Amer. Trees W. Region* 530, "Mountain Maple"—*Acer glabrum.* . . Shrub or small tree with short trunk and slender, upright branches.

mountain marigold n

1 also *mountain marsh-marigold:* **=elkslip. AK**
   1959 Anderson *Flora AK* 238, *C[altha] leptosepala.* . . Mountain Marigold. **1974** Welsh *Anderson's Flora AK* 354, *Mountain Marsh-marigold.* . . Moist heath and alpine meadows, often along streams. **1987** Hughes-Blackwell *Wildflowers SE AK* 56, Mountain Marsh-marigold. . . Usually with just one leaf and one flower.

2 A **ragwort** (here: *Senecio resedifolius*).
   1959 Carleton *Index Herb. Plants* 84, *Mountain-marigold:* Senecio Lyali [sic].

mountain marsh-marigold See **mountain marigold 1**

mountain mint n

1 An **Oswego tea** (here: *Monarda didyma*). Cf **mountain balm 1**
   1817 Eaton *Botany* 9, [Monarda] allophylla . . mountain mint. **1830** Rafinesque *Med. Flora* 2.35, Mountain Mint, Oswego tea, Mountain Balm, Horse Mint. **1876** Hobbs *Bot. Hdbk.* 72, Mountain mint, Monarda didyma. Mountain mint, Pycnanthemum montanum. **1922** [see **2** below]. **1940** Clute *Amer. Plant Names* 26, *M. didyma.* . . Mountain mint. **1971** Krochmal *Appalachia Med. Plants* 178, *Monarda didyma.* . . Common names . . mountain mint.

2 A plant of the genus *Pycnanthemum*. Also called **horsemint 2, wild basil.** For other names of var spp see **pennyroyal**
   1817 Eaton *Botany* 65, [Pycnanthemum] aristatum . . mountain mint. **1837** Darlington *Flora Cestrica* 344 **PA,** Pycnanthemum. . . Mountain Mint. . . Hilly woodlands; Mica-slate hills; frequent. . . This, and all the following species, have a pleasant odor. **1891** Jesup *Plants Hanover NH* 32, Pycnanthemum. . . Mountain Mint. **1922** *Amer. Botanist* 28.122, The name of "mountain mint" applied to *Monarda didyma* suggests a confusion of this plant with *Pycnanthemum Virginianum*. When in leaf, only, the two species are, indeed, very much alike. . . *Monarda* may often be found in elevated places, especially if wet, but the present species is so plentifully distributed in rough country as to be fairly entitled to be considered the true mountain mint. **1931** Harned *Wild Flowers Alleghanies* 432, Basil Mountain Mint (P. clinopodioides . .). Dry soil in the mountains. **1950** Stevens *ND Plants* 244, *Mountain Mint.* . . Branches, leaves and flowers are crowded into a . . dense cluster at top of plant. Fragrant. **1968** McPhee *Pine Barrens* 130 **NJ,** He showed the group mountain mint and cat briar. **1979** Ajilvsgi *Wild Flowers* 258 **wLA, eTX,** *Mountain-mint* . . Pycnanthemum albes-

cens. . . Erect, stout, aromatic perennial to 5 ft. tall. . . Plants with mint fragrance.

mountain misery n

1 A shrub of the genus *Chamaebatia* native to California. [See quot 1915] Also called **bear-clover, bear mat, fernbush 3, Jerusalem oak 2, kittikit, running oak, tarbush, tarweed**
   1897 Parsons *Wild Flowers CA* 92, *Mountain Misery. Chamaebatia foliosa.* . . It is exceedingly abundant, covering considerable areas and filling the air with its balsamic fragrance, strongly suggestive of tansy, though to many not so agreeable as the latter. **1915** (1926) Armstrong-Thornber *Western Wild Flowers* 222, Mountain Misery does not at first seem an appropriate name for so attractive a plant, but when we walk through the low, green thickets we find not only that the tangled branches catch our feet but that the whole plant is covered with a strong-smelling, resinous substance, which comes off on our clothes in a most disagreeable manner. **1925** Jepson *Manual Plants CA* 500, *Mountain Misery.* . . Commonly gregarious and covering extensive tracts. **1937** U.S. Forest Serv. *Range Plant Hdbk.* B52, Bearmat, also known as . . mountain misery, . . is a low, resinous, heavy-scented, evergreen shrub occurring in the ponderosa pine and mixed conifer types on the west slope of the Sierra Nevadas in California. **1959** Munz-Keck *CA Flora* 781, *Mountain Misery.* Shrub . . with many leafy branches. . . Open forests, 2000–7000 ft. **1968** *DARE* (Qu. S16) Inf **CA**60, Mountain misery—looks like a rose leaf, has a tarry substance some people [are] allergic to, a fernlike leaf.

2 **=fern-bush 2.**
   1931 U.S. Dept. Ag. *Misc. Pub.* 101.55, Tansybush (Chamaebatiaria millefolium), frequently called . . mountain misery, is an odorous . . and somewhat woolly shrub . . ranging from northwestern California and eastern Oregon . . to western Wyoming and, through Nevada and Utah, into western and southern Arizona. It is a denizen of steep slopes, dry ridges, rocky canyons, lava beds, . . between about 4,000 and 9,000 feet elevation.

mountain moccasin n Cf **highland moccasin**
Prob a **copperhead snake 1.**
   1986 Pederson *LAGS Concordance*, 1 inf, **nwAL,** Mountain moccasins—snakes.

mountain mockingbird n Also *mountain mocker* [See quot 1953]
=sage thrasher.
   1858 Baird *Birds* 347, *Oroscoptes montanus.* . . Mountain Mocking Bird. . . Rocky mountains. **1874** NY Acad. Sci. *Annals Lyceum Nat. Hist.* 10.2 **UT,** Mountain Mocking Bird. An inhabitant of the valleys and plains. Most abundant in the neighborhood of settlements. **1880** in 1949 Denton *Pages from a Diary* 23 **CA,** I got several nice birds, among them a mountain mocker. **1898** (1900) Davie *Nests N. Amer. Birds* 462, Sage Thrasher. . . Erroneously called Mountain Mocking Bird, for it is exclusively an inhabitant of the sage-brush region of the West, and is partial to the lower portions of the country, though not infrequently met with in the open mountains. **1953** Jewett *Birds WA* 506, *Sage Thrasher.* Other Names . . Mountain mockingbird. [*Ibid* 507, The sage thrasher is famous for its song, which is reminiscent of that of the mockingbird.]

mountain mulberry n
=Texas mulberry.
   1938 Van Dersal *Native Woody Plants* 344, Mountain mulberry (Morus microphylla). **1970** Correll *Plants TX* 497, *Morus microphylla.* . . Mountain mulberry. . . In canyons, limestone and igneous slopes in the w. two thirds of Tex.

mountain mushroom n Cf **mountain fish, sponge mushroom**
A **morel** n[2].
   1967 *DARE* (Qu. I37) Inf **NJ**1, Mountain mushroom—shaped like a sponge.

mountain mutton See **mountain lamb**

mountain myrtle n

1 Prob **=Oregon boxwood.**
   1961 Douglas *My Wilderness* 20 **cCO,** In the lower areas the floor litter is in large part bracken ferns, a tiny blueberry, and mountain myrtle with leathery leaves.

2 A **sand myrtle** (here: *Leiophyllum buxifolium*).

1964 Campbell et al. *Gt. Smoky Wildflowers* 34, *Mountain Myrtle— Leiophyllum lyoni.* . . This small shrub is restricted mainly to the edges of laurel slicks from 4,000 to 6,500 feet elevation in the Smokies. . . The plant, only 15 to 20 inches tall, grows in dense beds. Myrtle Point on Mt. Le Conte was named for this beautiful shrub.

mountain nigger n *derog*
A person of Basque heritage.

1967 *DARE* Tape **OR**18, We [=Basques] used to be called "mountain niggers" out here a lot. **1967** *DARE* FW Addit **seOR,** *Mountain nigger*—a non-Basque expression for Basques.

mountain nightingale n Cf mountain canary
Used as a nickname for the **gray wolf 1.**

1930 Shoemaker *1300 Words* 40 **cPA Mts** (as of c1900), *Mountain nightingale*—A wolf.

mountain oak n
Any of several **oaks,** as:

a also *mountain chestnut oak:* A **chestnut oak** (here: either *Quercus montana* or *Q. prinus*). **east of Missip R** Note: *Quercus montana* is included in *Q. prinus* by some authorities.

1822 Eaton *Botany* 421, [*Quercus*] *montana.* . . Chestnut [sic] oak, mountain oak. **1832** MA Hist. Soc. *Coll.* 2d ser 9.155 **cwVT,** [*Quercus*] *montana,* Mountain oak. **1883** Smith *Rept. for 1881 & 1882* 296 **AL,** On the high lands . . are found . . the mountain or tan-bark oak [etc]. **1908** Britton *N. Amer. Trees* 330, It [=*Quercus prinus*] is also known as Chestnut oak, . . and Mountain oak. **1938** [see **b** below]. **1950** Peattie *Nat. Hist. Trees* 206, *Quercus montana.* . . Mountain Oak. . . is a fine, soldierly sort of Oak, for the column of its trunk may rise 100 feet. **1966–69** *DARE* (Qu. T10, . . *Kinds of oak trees*) Inf **AL**2, Mountain oak—same as chestnut oak; **AL**33, **GA**77, **MA**30, Mountain oak. **1973** Wharton-Barbour *Trees KY* 448, *Quercus montana.* . . *Mountain Chestnut Oak*—Tree up to a height of 70 feet. . . Bark dark and deeply furrowed. **1986** Pederson *LAGS Concordance,* 5 infs, **n,cAL,** Mountain oak.

b Any of three **oaks:** a **black oak** (here: *Quercus kelloggii*), the **blue oak 2,** or the **Gambel oak. West, esp CA**

1897 Sudworth *Arborescent Flora* 153, *Gambel Oak.* . . *Common Names.* . . Mountain Oak (Nev., Oreg.) **1910** Jepson *Silva CA* 216, Blue Oak [=*Quercus douglasii*] has many common names. . . The fuel is most commonly sold under the name of Mountain Oak. **1938** Van Dersal *Native Woody Plants* 346, Oak, . . Mountain (*Quercus kelloggii, Quercus montana*). **1979** Little *Checklist U.S. Trees* 228, *Quercus douglasii.* . . *Blue oak.* . . *Other common names* . . mountain oak. . . N. to s. Calif. mostly in foothills of Coast Ranges and Sierra Nev.

c Either **Lacey oak** or **Texas oak.**

1903 Small *Flora SE U.S.* 353, *Quercus Laceyi.* . . On the summits of Caprina limestone hills, south-central Texas. . . *Mountain Oak.* **1911** *Century Dict. Suppl.,* Oak. . . *Mountain-oak.* (*a*) The chestnut-oak, *Quercus Prinus.* (*b*) Gambel's oak, *Q. Gambelii.* (*c*) The Texan oak, *Q. Texana.* **1960** Vines *Trees SW* 160, *Lacey Oak.* . . Vernacular names are . . Mountain Oak . . and Bastard Oak. The wood is occasionally used for fuel and posts.

d A **red oak** (here: *Quercus rubra*).

1994 *DARE* File **wNC,** *Mountain oak.* . . In this area, a common name for the Northern Red Oak (*Quercus rubra*). "Northern Red Oak (what the old timers call Mountain Oak) . . it sometimes won't float, so they have to get those with some more logs that will float."

mountainous adj Usu |ˈmaʊntənəs|; also |ˌmaʊnˈteniəs| Pronc-spp mounta(i)neous Cf grievous
Std sense, var forms.

1837 Sherwood *Gaz. GA* 70, *Provincialisms.* . . *Mountaneous,* for mountainious [sic]. **1906** *DN* 3.147 **nwAR,** *Mountaneous.* . . Mountainous. **1909** *DN* 3.350 **eAL, wGA,** *Mountain'eous.* . . Mountainous. **1915** *DN* 4.185 **swVA,** *Mountainous* [maʊnteniəs].

mountain owl n
=**whiskered owl.**

1957 Pough *Audubon W. Bird Guide* 301, Mountain owl. *See* Whiskered [owl].

mountain oyster n Also Rocky Mountain oyster chiefly S Midl, West Cf fry n 4, prairie oyster
A testicle of a sheep, bull, or hog, used as food.

1890 *Century Dict.* 4219, *Mountain-oyster,* a lamb's testicle. **1906** *DN*

3.153 **nwAR,** *Rocky Mountain oyster.* . . Lamb-fry. **1929** *AmSp* 5.19 **Ozarks,** *Mountain oysters.* . . The testicles of sheep or hogs. Occasionally used as food, they are supposed to contain a powerful aphrodisiac, and must never be mentioned in polite conversation between the sexes. **1941** *AmSp* 16.236 **ceNE,** Pig testicles are *agates,* sheep testicles *mountain oysters.* **1944** *PADS* 2.19 **sAppalachians, TX,** *Mountain oysters.* . . Testicles of the boar, the bull, [*PADS* Ed: or the sheep], whenever the highland gourmet partakes of these delicacies at the table. **1946** *PADS* 6.21 **swVA** (as of 1900–10), *Mountain oyster.* . . Sheep's testicle. **1947** *PADS* 8.19 **IA,** *Mountain oyster:* Heard in Kansas, 1944. More common term there appears to be *prairie oyster.* **1967–68** *DARE* (Qu. H43, *Foods made from parts of the . . inner organs of an animal*) Inf **NC**51, Mountain oysters—hog testicles; **OH**37, Mountain oysters—testicles of sheep and pigs. **1982** Slone *How We Talked* 119 **eKY** (as of c1950), When hogs were "trimmed," . . crushed tomato leaves or elderberry tree leaves were used to keep flies away and to stop the bleeding. Some people ate this part that was cut from the hog. It was called "mountain oysters" or "hog's nuts." **1982** *DARE* File **seWY,** [Restaurant menu:] Mtn. oysters with french fries. . . $3.75. [When I asked what these were, the waitress explained that they were "the male organs of a bull."] **1983** *MJLF* 9.1.48 **ceKY,** *Mountain oysters* . . hog testicles. **1984** Smith *SW Vocab.* 109, *Mountain oyster:* The testicle of a bull, ram, or steer, considered by mountain men to be a great delicacy. There is a mountain oyster club in Tucson, Arizona, and a mountain oyster bar in the famous old Pioneer Hotel in Tucson.

mountain parrot n
Clark's **nutcracker a** (*Nucifraga columbiana*).

1953 Jewett *Birds WA* 472, Clark Nutcracker. . . Other names: Clark Crow; . . Camp Robber; Mountain Parrot.

mountain partridge n
1 =**mountain quail 1.**

1789 Morse *Amer. Geog.* 60, American Birds [include the] . . Pheasant or mountain Partridge. **1917** (1923) *Birds Amer.* 2.5, *Mountain Quail.* . . *Other Names.* . . Mountain Partridge. **1982** Elman *Hunter's Field Guide* 92, *Common & Regional Names.* . . For mountain quail . . *mountain partridge.*

2 A **woodcock** (here: Philohela minor).

1887 Ridgway *N. Amer. Birds* 191, Pacific coast district, from San Francisco north to Washington Territory. . . *O[reortyx] pictus.* . . Mountain Partridge. **1923** U.S. Dept. Ag. *Misc. Circular* 13.49 **VA,** *American Woodcock.* . . *Vernacular Names.* . . *In local use.* . . Mountain-partridge.

mountain partridgeberry n
A **wintergreen** (here: *Gaultheria hispidula*).

1900 Lyons *Plant Names* 96, *C[hiogenes] hispidula.* . . Mountain Partridge-berry. **1924** *Amer. Botanist* 30.56, It [=*Gaultheria procumbens*] is called "mountain partridge-berry" through a confusion of the plant with the true partridge-berry (*Mitchella*). **1959** Carleton *Index Herb. Plants* 84, *Mountain-partridge-berry:* Chiogenes hispidula.

mountain pay n
In railroading: overtime.

1943 *AmSp* 18.167 [Railroad terms], *Mountain pay.* Overtime. **1945** Hubbard *Railroad Ave.* 352, *Mountain pay*—Overtime.

mountain pheasant n esp Sth, S Midl
=**ruffed grouse.**

1888 Trumbull *Names of Birds* 146, In Virginia and the Carolinas we sometimes hear it [=*Bonasa umbellus*] referred to as the *Mountain Pheasant.* **1917** (1923) *Birds Amer.* 2.17, *Ruffed Grouse.* . . *Other Names.* . . Mountain Pheasant. **1955** *Oriole* 20.1.6 **GA,** *Ruffed Grouse.*—Mountain Pheasant. **1967–69** *DARE* (Qu. Q7, *Names and nicknames for . . game birds*) Infs **GA**76, **TN**11, Mountain pheasant—same as ruff grouse. **1982** Elman *Hunter's Field Guide* 15, *Ruffed Grouse.* . . *Common & Regional Names* . . mountain pheasant, drummer [etc].

mountain phlox n
1 Any of several **phlox:** esp *Phlox ovata* or **moss pink 1** in the eastern US, or *P. austromontana* or *P. diffusa* in the western US.

1901 Lounsberry *S. Wild Flowers* 442, *P[hlox] ovata,* mountain phlox, is another species occurrent through the mountains. In fact on the high peaks of western North Carolina it was . . prolifically in bloom in late August. **1933** Small *Manual SE Flora* 1104, *P. ovata.* . . *Mountain-phlox.* . . Higher Piedmont to Central Lowland and to New England

Upland, Ga. to E. Ind. and E. Pa. **1934** Haskin *Wild Flowers Pacific Coast* 281, Mountain Phlox—*Phlox diffusa*. . . A prickly, moss-like plant, often forming large patches or mats in the mountains above timber line. **1950** Gray–Fernald *Manual of Botany* 1189, *P. subulata*. . . Moss- or Mountain-P[hlox]. *Ibid* 1190, *P. ovata*. . . Mountain-P[hlox]. **1951** Abrams *Flora Pacific States* 3.411, *Phlox austromontàna*. . . Western Mountain Phlox. **1965** *Native Plants PA* 53, Phlox ovata—Mountain Phlox. **1968** *DARE* (Qu. S26c) Inf **PA**99, Mountain phlox. **1976** Bailey–Bailey *Hortus Third* 862, [*Phlox*] *ovata*. . . Mountain p[hlox]. . . Fl[ower]s purple, pink, or rarely white.

2 =wild bouvardia.

   1982 *Plants SW* (Catalog) 25, Mountain Phlox—*Linanthus grandiflorus*—Not a true phlox but a close relative.

mountain pigeon n
=band-tailed pigeon.

   1923 U.S. Dept. Ag. *Misc. Circular* 13.73 **CA,** Band-tailed Pigeon. . . Vernacular Names. . . Mountain pigeon.

mountain pine n
A **pine:** usu **Table Mountain pine** in the eastern US, or a **white pine** (here: *Pinus monticola*) in the western US.

   1814 *Niles' Weekly Reg.* 21 May 194, The mountain pine . . cradles the eagle. **1850** Garrard *Wah-to-yah* 200 **SW,** The hard bread, *biscoche*, is . . a perfect luxury with a cup of coffee by a mountain-pine fire. **1892** Apgar *Trees Nth. U.S.* 173, *Pinus monticola*. . . *Mountain-pine.* . . A large tree, 60 to 80 feet high, resembling the White Pine, . . but the foliage is denser. Pacific coast. **1897** Sudworth *Arborescent Flora* 15 **CA,** *Pinus monticola*. . . *Common Names*. . . Mountain Pine. *Ibid* 28 **TN,** *Pinus pungens*. . . *Common Names*. . . Southern Mountain Pine. **1908** Britton *N. Amer. Trees* 9, *Western White Pine*. . . is also known as . . Mountain pine, . . and Soft pine. *Ibid* 47, *Pinus pungens*. . . A tree of the mountains, . . it is also called Southern mountain pine. **1938** Van Dersal *Native Woody Plants* 192, *Pinus pungens*. . . *Mountain pine*. . . A large evergreen tree; two-needled. **1947** Peattie *Sierra Nevada* 157 **eCA,** The sugar pine has a very characteristic effect on the skyline, approached only by its near relative, the . . mountain pine. **1969** *DARE* (Qu. T17) Infs **GA**80, **KY**21, Mountain pine; **GA**77, Rough-bark mountain pine. **1979** Little *Checklist U.S. Trees* 196, *Pinus pungens*. . . Mountain pine. . . Appalachian Mt. region from Pa. sw. to e. W. Va., Va., nw. S.C., ne. Ga., and e. Tenn. Also local in N.J. and Del.

mountain pink n
1 =moss pink 1.

   1822 Eaton *Botany* 389, [*Phlox*] *subulata* . . mountain pink. **1843** Torrey *Flora NY* 2.94, *Mountain Pink*. . . Rocky banks and hill-sides, particularly along rivers. . . I am not sure that I have found this plant strictly within the limits of the State, but it is abundant on our immediate borders in New-Jersey. **1933** Small *Manual SE Flora* 1102, *P. subulata*. . . Low matted evergreen shrub with numerous . . flowering shoots. . . *Mountain pink*. **1959** Carleton *Index Herb. Plants* 84, *Mountain-pink:* Epigaea repens; Lychnis [*DARE* Ed: =*Silene*] (v) Phlox subulata. **1981** Pederson *LAGS Basic Materials,* 1 inf, **cwTN,** Mountain pinks.

2 =arbutus. Cf May pink 1, winter pink

   1850 (1926) Sawyer *Way Sketches* 12 June 53 **cWY,** We found some grass and some beautiful specimens of what we called mountain pink. It is much smaller than our garden pink, but resembles it somewhat in form, but more in its sweet perfume. **1854** King *Amer. Eclectic Dispensatory* 447, *Epigea repens*. Trailing Arbutus. . . This plant has several names as *Winter-pink, Gravel-weed, Mountain-pink, Ground Laurel, May-flower*, etc. **1876** Hobbs *Bot. Hdbk.* 72, Mountain pink, Mayflower, Epigaea repens. **1911** Henkel *Amer. Med. Leaves* 18, Mountain pink. . . is greatly prized on account of its delicate shell-pink, waxy blossoms with their faint yet spicy fragrance. **1924** *Amer. Botanist* 30.57, *Epigaea repens*. . . "Mountain pink" and "crocus" are . . names transferred from plants better entitled to bear them. **1959** [see **1** above].

3 A centaury such as *Centaurium beyrichii*. **West, esp TX**

   1936 Whitehouse *TX Flowers* 95, *Mountain Pink*. . . (*Erythraea beyrichii*). . . The stems . . often form hemispherical clumps . . which are covered with pink flowers in June. **1961** Wills–Irwin *Flowers TX* 171, The Mountain-pink . . , appearing as pink mounds in June and July on the gravelly roadsides of Central Texas, is another member of the Gentian Family. **1970** Correll *Plants TX* 1207, *Centaurium Beyrichii*. . . *Mountain pink*. . . In seepage on granite boulders. . . Tex. and Ark. **c1979** TX Dept. Highways *Flowers* 16, *Mountain-pink* thrives on gravelly limestone hills of Central Texas, and westward. . . Pioneers used

dried plants to reduce fevers. [**1979** Spellenberg *Audubon Guide N. Amer. Wildflowers W. Region* 522, *Centaurium calycosum*. . . The brilliant pink corolla resembles that of *Phlox*.]

4 A **pinxter flower** (here: *Rhododendron nudiflorum*). Cf **May pink 2, swamp pink**

   1898 *Jrl. Amer. Folkl.* 11.274, *Rhododendron nudiflorum*, . . mountain pink, Bellows Falls, Vt.

5 A low-growing, mat-forming plant (*Douglasia montana*) native chiefly to the northwestern US.

   1926 *Torreya* 26.107 **MT,** The little mountain pink brings a blush of color here and there. **1952** Davis *Flora ID* 537, *Mountain Pink*. . . *Douglasia montana*. . . Dry soil of the mountains. Neb. to Mont., to C. Idaho.

6 A **catchfly 1.** Cf **wild pink**

   1959 [see **1** above]. **1968** *DARE* Wildfl QR Pl.53 Inf **NY**91, Mountain pink.

mountain plover n
A plover (*Charadrius montanus*) native to the western US. Also called **prairie plover, upland ~**

   1858 Baird *Birds* 693, *Mountain Plover*. . . This bird is only known to inhabit the western countries of North America. **1913** *Pacific Coast Avifauna* 9.32 **CA,** The Mountain Plover is a not uncommon winter visitant in suitable places on the west side plains. Its preference, seemingly, is for the open pasture lands. **1932** Howell *FL Bird Life* 220, The Mountain Plover is not well named, for it is found on the dry, grassy plains of the West, rather than in mountainous districts. **1961** Ligon *NM Birds* 113, In size and coloration, the so-called Mountain Plover resembles the Killdeer, though it is slightly smaller. **1977** Udvardy *Audubon Field Guide Birds* 576 **West,** *Mountain Plover*. . . It feeds in small flocks, mostly on insects. **1989** Frazier *Gt. Plains* 163 **eMT,** There were flocks of birds—mountain plovers, mostly. They were olive and taupe-colored above, sooty-white underneath. They always took off in a way that showed the white.

mountain poplar n
=balsam poplar.

   1968 *DARE* (Qu. T12) Inf **VA**8, Mountain poplar; (Qu. T13) Inf **VA**8, Mountain poplar.

mountain pork See mountain lamb

mountain pride n Also *pride-of-the-mountain(s)* chiefly CA
A **beardtongue** (here: *Penstemon newberryi*).

   1897 Parsons *Wild Flowers CA* 250, *Pride of the Mountains. Pentstemon* [sic] *Menziesii, var. Newberryi*. . . One of the most gracious flowers to be found in the Sierras in late summer. **1915** (1926) Armstrong–Thornber *Western Wild Flowers* 480, *Pride-of-the-mountain*. . . A beautiful little shrub, making splendid patches of vivid color on high bare rocks in the mountains. **1925** Jepson *Manual Plants CA* 908, *Mountain Pride*. . . On rocky ledges, 4000 to 10,000 ft. . . North Coast Ranges. **1949** Moldenke *Amer. Wild Flowers* 277, A number of species [of *Penstemon*] cater to hummingbirds. Among these is the *mountain-pride*. . . Its flowers are crimson or bright red, as one would expect. **1979** Spellenberg *Audubon Guide N. Amer. Wildflowers W. Region* 774, *Mountain Pride*. . . Southwestern Oregon to the southern Sierra Nevada of California. . . This handsome species commonly adds bright swatches of color to highway road cuts through the rocky California mountains.

mountain pussycat See pussy

mountain quail n
1 A partridge (*Oreortyx pictus*) distinguished by a long, straight black plume on the head, native chiefly to the far western US. Also called **mountain partridge 1, painted quail, plumed ~, valley ~**

   1858 Baird *Birds* 642, *Oreortyx picta*. . . *Mountain Quail*. . . Mountain ranges of California and Oregon towards the coast. **1888** Lindley–Widney *CA of South* 331, The mountain-quail rears her brood in safety among their guardian bayonets. **1910** Hart *Vigilante Girl* 200 **nCA,** Passed by the ranges covered with *casseroles* containing savory concoctions, and the open roasting fires, before which slowly revolved joints of beef, saddles of lamb, mountain quail, canvas-back. **1923** U.S. Dept. Ag. *Farmers' Bulletin* 1375.4, Nevada established limits of . . 10 valley quail, 5 mountain quail, . . a day. **1944** *Natl. Geogr. Mag.* June 696 **ID,** We did, however, secure some calls of the mountain quail and the chukar partridge. **1965–70** *DARE* (Qu. Q7, *Names and nicknames for . . game birds*) 9 Infs, **CA, OR,** Mountain quail; **CA**130, California mountain quail. **1982** Elman *Hunter's Field Guide* 96, A typical mountain quail weighs more than 8 ounces and is about 10 to 12 inches long—unusually large for a quail. Its plume is also unusual; it is composed of two straight, narrow blackish feathers that stand up when the bird is on the ground, though they sweep back in flight.

2 The white-tailed **ptarmigan** *(Lagopus leucurus).*

1874 *Forest & Stream* 1.390 **CO,** They [=white-tailed ptarmigan] are generally known in Colorado as White and Mountain Quails by the hunters, miners, and ranchmen. **1982** Elman *Hunter's Field Guide* 79, *Common & regional names:* For. . . white-tailed ptarmigan . . *mountain quail.*

mountain ramp See **ramp**

mountain raspberry n Also *high mountain raspberry*

A **cloudberry** or similar raspberry.

1803 (1805) Harris *Jrl. Alleghany Mts.* 65, On these declivities [along the Ohio River] grow the mountain raspberry . . in great plenty. It is a handsome bush; and the flower, which is of a pale pink colour, . . gives it a very ornamental appearance. **1902** (1909) Mathews *Field Book Amer. Wild Flowers* 192, *Cloudberry, or Mountain Raspberry—Rubus Chamaemorus.* . . One of the interesting relatives of the common raspberry which finds its home among the clouds of high mountain-tops. **1940** Clute *Amer. Plant Names* 8, *R. chamaemorus. Cloud-berry.* . . Mountain raspberry. **1966** *DARE* Wildfl QR Pl.101 Inf **NC**36, High mountain raspberry.

mountain rat n **West**

A **wood rat** (here: *Neotoma cinerea*).

1885 *Outing* 7.51 **SW,** If the mountain rats hadn't eaten up my copy of Shakespeare . . , I should have the very best of company. **1897** Hough *Story Cowboy* 41, Small birds twitter and flit about the ranch house, . . and the mountain rats appear from their nests. **1927** (1944) Russell *Trails Plowed Under* 10 **West,** The floor's strewn with pine cones, an' a few scattered bones, showin' it's been the home of mountain-rats an' squirrels. **1929** Ellis *Ordinary Woman* 42 **CO** (as of early 20th cent), The ceiling of our cabin was usually covered with canvas. . . Mountain rats also made their nests just on top of the canvas. *Ibid* 193, We . . find her covered with blood; a mountain rat had bitten her hand through and through. **1967** *DARE* (Qu. P32) Inf **CO**41, Mountain rat.

mountain rattler n Also *mountain rattlesnake*

Either of two **rattlesnakes:** the **timber rattlesnake** in the eastern US, or a **prairie rattlesnake** (here: *Crotalus viridis*) in the West.

1966–70 *DARE* (Qu. P25) Infs **CA**114, **GA**77, **NM**13, **TN**42, Mountain rattler. **1967–68** *WI Acad. Trans.* 56.29 **WI,** The timber rattlesnake, also known as the . . mountain . . rattlesnake, is rarely found far from rock outcrops, and in Wisconsin rock rather than timber would be a more appropriate name.

mountain rice n

A grass of the genus *Oryzopsis,* esp *O. hymenoides.* Also called **ricegrass.** For other names of var spp see **Indian millet 2,** ~ **mountain rice,** ~ **rice 2, sand grass, silk** ~, **smilo** ~, **wild rice, winter grass**

1817 Eaton *Botany* 12, *Oryzopsis.* . . *asperifolia* . . mountain rice. **1843** Torrey *Flora NY* 2.431, *Oryzopsis.* . . *Mountain Rice.* . . Erect perennial grasses. **1894** Coulter *Botany W. TX* 517, *O[ryzopsis] membranacea.* . . *Mountain rice.* . . Mountain regions of western Texas and northward. **1932** Rydberg *Flora Prairies* 85, *Oryzopsis.* . . *Mountain Rice.* . . Grain oblong, free. **1959** Gillespie *Compilation Edible Wild Plants WV* 12, Mountain Rice (*Oryzopsis asperifolia* . .). The dried and ground seeds make an excellent flour, but they are very scarce in West Virginia. **1974** (1977) Coon *Useful Plants* 147, *Oryzopsis hymenoides* . . mountain rice. One of the grasses that grows in the arid parts of the West, the seeds of this and other grasses are best when dried and ground into flour for making breads and cooked mush.

mountain robin n [From its habitat and similarity of appearance to *Turdus migratorius*]

=**varied thrush.**

1923 Dawson *Birds CA* 2.768, *Varied Thrush.* . . *Synonyms:* Mountain Robin. **1953** Jewett *Birds WA* 511, *Ixoreus naevius naevius.* . . Mountain Robin.

mountain rooter See **rooter**

mountain rose n

1 A **bitterroot 2** (here: *Lewisia rediviva*).

1947 *Nature Mag.* 40.444, *Montana's historic bitterroot.* . . Other common names are . . mountain rose [etc].

2 also *rosa de montana, rose-of-the-mountain:* =**coral vine 3.**

1953 Greene-Blomquist *Flowers South* 155, *Coral Vine. Rosa de montana.* . . One of the world's most beautiful climbers, coral vine is at home over the lower South into Calif. **1959** Carleton *Index Herb. Plants* 84, *Mountain-rose:* Antigonon leptopus. *Ibid* 100, *Rose-of-the-mountain:* Antigonon leptopus.

3 See **mountain rosebay.**

mountain rosebay n Also *mountain rose* Cf **rosebay**

The Catawba **rhododendron** *(Rhododendron catawbiense).*

1900 Lyons *Plant Names* 319, *R[hododendron] Catawbiense.* . . Mountain Rose-bay. **1901** Lounsberry *S. Wild Flowers* 379, *Mountain Rose Bay.* . . grows on the highest summits of the mountains throughout its range, following the ridges. **1911** *Century Dict. Suppl., Mountain-rose.* . . The rhododendron. **1941** Walker *Lookout* 48 **TN,** The most beautiful, perhaps, is rhododendron, known as mountain rose bay. **1968** Radford et al. *Manual Flora Carolinas* 798, *Mountain Rosebay.* . . Rocky slopes, ridges and balds, usually over 3000 ft. **1976** Bailey–Bailey *Hortus Third* 953, *Mountain Rosebay.* . . Corolla purple to paler lilac-rose and occasionally white.

mountain rush n

=**Mormon tea 1.**

1911 *Century Dict. Suppl., Mountain-rush.* . . *Ephedra antisyphilitica,* the common joint-fir of the western United States, with somewhat the aspect of a scouring-rush. **1966** Barnes–Jensen *Dict. UT Slang* 31, *Mountain Rush.* . . Another name for Brigham's Tea.

mountain sage n

1 A **sagebrush,** usu *Artemisia frigida* or *A. tridentata.*

1844 Lee-Frost *10 Yrs. OR* 122, Toiling through immense tracts of mountain sage, or, more properly, wormwood. **1900** Lyons *Plant Names* 47, *A[rtemisia] tridentata.* . . Mountain Sage. **1924** *Amer. Botanist* 30.32 **West,** *Artemisia frigida* is . . "mountain sage." **1936** Winter *Plants NE* 162, *A. tridentata.* . . Mountain-Sage. Common sage-brush of the west. **1950** Stevens *ND Plants* 291, *Artemisia frigida.* . . *Mountain Sage.* . . Very common, especially on gravelly hills and prairie. **1953** Nelson *Plants Rocky Mt. Park* 177, *Mountain-sage* or *wormwood, Artemisia.*—A very large genus with many representatives in this region. **1959** Carleton *Index Herb. Plants* 84, *Mountain-sage:* Artemisia frigida.

2 =**desert lavender.**

1931 U.S. Dept. Ag. *Misc. Pub.* 101.141, *Emory bushmint* . . , also known as . . mountain sage is. . . a lavender-scented, scurfy woolly shrub . . growing on rocky gravelly slopes, ravines, desert valleys, alluvial deposits and the like.

3 A **sage** (here: *Salvia regla*).

1970 Correll *Plants TX* 1367, *Salvia regla.* . . Mountain sage. . . On rocky wooded slopes and in canyons of Chisos Mts.

mountain sidewinder n Cf **sidewinder**

A **rattlesnake** (here: *Crotalus pricei*).

1974 Shaw–Campbell *Snakes West* 230, Sometimes called "mountain sidewinder," the twin-spotted rattlesnake *(Crotalus pricei)* is truly a snake of the high mountains, being found most often in habitats between 6,300 and 10,000 feet above sea level.

mountain snow See **snow-on-the-mountain**

mountain sorrel n

1 A **wood sorrel** (here: *Oxalis* spp).

1830 Rafinesque *Med. Flora* 2.46, *Oxalis acetosella. Names.* Common Woodsorrel. . . *Vulgar.* . . Mountain Sorrel. [*Ibid* 47, This plant . . in America seems confined to the boreal and mountain regions.] **1934** Haskin *Wild Flowers Pacific Coast* 203, *Mountain Sorrel—Oxalis oregana.* . . If you are used . . to the small, delicate wood sorrel of the East, you will be amazed when you first enter the deep coastal forests to find acre on acre of the giant mountain sorrel completely covering the forest floor.

2 A perennial alpine plant *(Oxyria digyna)* native chiefly to the western US and Alaska. [*OED* 1843] Also called **scurvy grass**

1847 Wood *Class-Book* 473, *O[xyria] reniformis.* . . *Mountain Sorrel.* . . Found on the summits of the White Mts., in moist ravines, and

N. to the Arc. Sea. The plant is acid to the taste, like *Rumex acetosus*. **1876** Hobbs *Bot. Hdbk.* 109, Sorrel, Mountain, Boreal sour dock, Oxyria reniformis. **1911** Jepson *Flora CA* 134, *Oxyria digyna.* . . Mountain Sorrel. . . Sierra Nevada, 7,000 to 10,000 ft. **1943** Fernald–Kinsey *Edible Wild Plants E. N. Amer.* 168, The *Mountain-Sorrel,* which resembles a miniature rhubarb, with small rounded leaves, has always been highly esteemed in the Arctic regions . . , the new growth up to flowering time being eaten raw. **1954** Harrington *Manual Plants CO* 195, *Mountain Sorrel.* . . Greenland to Alaska, south to New Hampshire and Arizona. . . Our records scattered in the high mountains of Colorado. **1955** U.S. Arctic Info. Center *Gloss.* 53, the mountain sorrel has a circumpolar and alpine range, growing on shaded slopes where snows last late into summer and . . thriving on bird cliffs and Eskimo campsites. **1967** *DARE* FW Addit **OR**12, Buckwheat: one kind is mountain sorrel. **1987** Hughes–Blackwell *Wildflowers SE AK* 51, Mountain Sorrel. . . The oatmeal-shaped flowers are clustered on the upper stem.

mountain spicewood n

A **sweet shrub** (here: *Calycanthus fertilis*).

1901 Mohr *Plant Life AL* 518, *Butneria fertilis.* . . Mountain Spicewood. . . Allegheny Mountains from Pennsylvania and Virginia to Georgia. **1938** Van Dersal *Native Woody Plants* 79, *Calycanthus fertilis.* . . Mountain Spicewood. . . A large shrub. . . considered deleterious to cattle.

mountain spray n chiefly Rocky Mts

=**ocean spray,** usu either *Holodiscus discolor* or *H. dumosus.*

1952 Davis *Flora ID* 394, *Mountain Spray.* Shrubs with simple, toothed or lobed leaves. **1953** Nelson *Plants Rocky Mt. Park* 94, *Mountain spray* . . , *Holodiscus dumosus.* . . A shrub with pyramidal clusters of small white flowers . . , found in rocky canyons. **1954** Sharpe *101 Wildflowers* 16, *Holodiscus discolor.* . . Called mountain spray in the national parks of the Rocky Mountain area. **1974** (1977) Coon *Useful Plants* 226, *Holodiscus discolor* . . mountainspray. . . This plant has white flowers, followed by small one-seeded fruits which were eaten raw or cooked by many western Indians.

mountain sprout n Cf shepherd's sprout

See quot.

1953 (1977) Hubbard *Shantyboat* 59 **Missip-Ohio Valleys,** We learned new kinds of weeds that could be eaten, such as mountain sprout, Indian corn, and sandbar greens.

mountain spruce n

The Engelmann **spruce** (*Picea englemannii*).

1897 Sudworth *Arborescent Flora* 39 **MT,** *Picea engelmanni.* . . Common Names. . . Mountain Spruce. **1908** Britton *N. Amer. Trees* 60, This tree [=*Picea engelmannii*]. . . is also called . . Mountain spruce. **1973** Hitchcock–Cronquist *Flora Pacific NW* 61, Mostly above 3000 ft elev. . . M[oun]t[ain], or silver s[pruce]. . . *P. engelmannii.* **1979** Little *Checklist U.S. Trees* 185, Engelmann spruce. . . Other common names . . mountain spruce. . . Rocky Mt. region.

mountain spurge n

1 The Allegheny spurge (*Pachysandra procumbens*).

1941 Walker *Lookout* 52 **TN,** Pachysandra, or mountain spurge blooms in March and April in the rich soil in Lookout Mountain woods.

2 A **snow-on-the-mountain** (here: *Euphorbia marginata*).

1959 Carleton *Index Herb. Plants* 84, *Mountain spurge:* Euphorbia variegata.

mountain squirrel n

1 A **red squirrel** (here: *Tamiasciurus hudsonicus*). Cf **mountain tacky**

1857 U.S. Patent Office *Annual Rept. for 1856: Ag.* 67, This pretty and active little animal is well known through the Northern States, under the names of "Red-Squirrel," . . and, sometimes, "Mountain Squirrel." **1966–68** *DARE* (Qu. P27, . . *Kinds of squirrels*) Inf **MT**5, Mountain or pine squirrel; **UT**5, Mountain squirrel.

2 A **rock squirrel** (here: *Spermophilus variegatus*).

1986 Pederson *LAGS Concordance* (Gray squirrel) 1 inf, **csTX,** Mountain squirrel = rock squirrel, black squirrel.

mountain sucker n West

A small **sucker,** usu *Catostomus platyrhynchus.*

1896 U.S. Natl. Museum *Bulletin* 47.170, *Pantosteus generosus.* . . Mountain Sucker. . . Great Basin of Utah; very abundant in streams about Great Salt Lake and southwest through the Sevier basin and the

desert. **1902** Jordan–Evermann *Amer. Fishes* 45, *The Mountain Suckers.* . . are all western, chiefly in the Rocky Mountain region and westward, mostly in rocky brooks in the arid districts. . . *P[antosteus] generosus,* known as the mountain sucker, . . reaches 8 or 10 inches in length. **1963** Sigler–Miller *Fishes UT* 100, The mountain sucker [=*Catostomus platyrhynchus*] prefers the clear, cold water of creeks or rivers which have a bottom of gravel, rubble, sand or boulders. *Ibid* 103, *Pantosteus virescens* . . Common Names: Green sucker, mountain sucker. *Ibid* 165, Mountain sucker. This common name was formerly applied . . to all species of *Pantosteus.* [*DARE* Ed: *Pantosteus* is now included in *Catostomus.*] **1971** Brown *Fishes MT* 127, The first mountain sucker [=*Catostomus platyrhynchus*] to be taken in Montana was on July 16, 1805, from the Yellowstone River . . by the Lewis and Clark Expedition, but this species was not described until 87 years later. **1991** Amer. Fisheries Soc. *Common Names Fishes* 24, *Catostomus platyrhynchus* . . F[reshwater] . . Mountain sucker.

mountain sumac n

1 A **sumac** (here: *Rhus* spp), usu **dwarf sumac.**

1813 Muhlenberg *Catalogus Plantarum* 32, *Rhus* . . *copallinum aestivale*—(mountain sumach). **1843** Torrey *Flora NY* 1.129, *Rhus Copallina.* . . Mountain Sumach. . . Rocky and sterile hills. **1854** King *Amer. Eclectic Dispensatory* 808, *R[hus] copallinum,* Mountain or Dwarf Sumach, . . must be carefully distinguished from those [varieties of *Rhus*] which possess poisonous properties. **1901** Lounsberry *S. Wild Flowers* 308, *R. copallina,* Dwarf or mountain sumac . . occurs either as a shrub or a small tree and from Florida northward to Maine. . . This one is collected in large quantities for the sake of its tannin. **1930** Sievers *Amer. Med. Plants* 52, Smooth Sumac—*Rhus glabra.* . . Other common names. Mountain sumac, . . vinegar tree. **1931** Harned *Wild Flowers Alleghanies* 274, *Mountain Sumac* (*Rhus copallina* . .). The leaflets assume a lovely, brilliant scarlet early in the fall. Common in the area. **1950** *WELS (Other names . . for . . sumac)* 1 Inf, **WI,** Mountain sumac. **1974** Morton *Folk Remedies* 127 **SC,** *Mountain sumac. . . Rhus copallina.* . . Woods, old fields and along fences and in dry, hilly regions. . . *(Current use)* Leaf decoction used for bathing painful places.

2 A **mountain ash 1** (here: *Sorbus americana*).

1860 Curtis *Cat. Plants NC* 70, *Mountain Ash.* (P[yrus] Americana . .). It is not very rare on our higher Mountains . . where it is called . . *Mountain Sumach.* The foliage is more like that of a *Sumach* than of any other of our trees. **1897** Sudworth *Arborescent Flora* 210, *Pyrus Americana.* . . Mountain Ash. . . Common Names. . . Mountain Sumach (N.C., S.C.) **1910** Graves *Flowering Plants* 223 **CT,** *Sorbus americana.* . . Mountain Sumac. . . Swamps and about ponds or sometimes on dry ledges or in rocky woods. **1950** Peattie *Nat. Hist. Trees* 331, *Sorbus americana.* . . Mountain Sumac. . . On the mountains. **1971** Krochmal *Appalachia Med. Plants* 238, Mountain sumach. . . The berries have been used to treat scurvy and as a vemifuge [sic].

mountain sunflower n

A **bitterweed** (here: *Hymenoxys acaulis* or *H. brandegei* or *H. grandiflora*).

1963 Craighead *Rocky Mt. Wildflowers* 221, *Hymenoxys grandiflora.* . . Mountain Sunflower. . . *Related species:* There are two mt. sunflowers in Rocky Mt. region: (1) *H. brandegei* . . ; (2) *H. acaulis.*

mountain tacky n Cf mountain squirrel 1, tacky

A **red squirrel** (here: *Tamiasciurus hudsonicus*).

1968 *DARE* (Qu. P27, . . *Kinds of squirrels*) Inf **WV**8, Mountain tacky [tæki]—small, chipmunk-like.

mountain tea n

1 A **wintergreen** (here: *Gaultheria procumbens*); also the beverage made from this plant.

1785 Marshall *Arbustrum* 52, *Gaultheria procumbens.* . . The leaves have been used as a substitute for Bohea Tea, whence the name of Mountain Tea. **1819** *Western Rev.* 1.94, On the Cumberland mountain . . Common Laurel, and . . Mountain tea, grow. **1832** Williamson *Hist. ME* 1.121, This "mountain tea" [from checkerberries] promotes mammillary secretions. **1891** Ryan *Pagan* 65 **Allegheny Mts,** As they reached the level above the cliff, the level carpeted with mountain-tea and rabbit-berries, . . the mountaineer halted. **1892** *Jrl. Amer. Folkl.* 5.100 **eOH,** *Gaultheria procumbens.* . . Mountain tea. **1911** Henkel *Amer. Med. Leaves* 19, Mountain tea. . . This small native perennial frequents . . cool damp woods, occurring especially under evergreen trees in Canada and the northeastern United States. **1950** Stuart *Hie Hunters* 247 **eKY,** I plucked the mountain tea leaves from all the stems that growed on Buzzard Roost mountain. I et the red mountain tea berries.

1964 Campbell et al. *Gt. Smoky Wildflowers* 60, *Gaultheria procumbens*. . . Before the days of synthetics, this plant was a source of wintergreen (or teaberry) flavor. Other common names are *checkerberry,* . . and *mountain tea.* **1968** *DARE* (Qu. I44) Inf **VA**13, Mountain tea berries; (Qu. BB22, . . *Home remedies . . for constipation*) Inf **WI**70, Mountain tea—not common. **1982** Ginns *Snowbird Gravy* 113 **nwNC,** And he stole this here teaberry, which we called mountain tea.

2 usu in comb *blue mountain tea:* A **goldenrod 1,** usu *Solidago odora;* also the beverage made from this plant.

1873 in 1976 Miller *Shaker Herbs* 179, *Solidago odora* . . Blue Mountain Tea. . . As a tea it is diaphoretic when taken warm. It is excellent to use to disguise the taste of medicinal herbs. **1886** *Harper's New Mth. Mag.* 62 **KY,** Another beverage is "mountain tea," which is made from the sweet-scented golden-rod and from winter-green. **1901** Lounsberry *S. Wild Flowers* 509, *Blue Mountain Tea. Solidago odora.* . . Although about the flowers of this golden-rod there is nothing very individual, we find in its leaves, emitting their strong anise scent, an unfailing mark of its identity. **1920** Saunders *Useful Wild Plants* 147, A pleasant and wholesome drink may also be made from the foliage of one of the Goldenrods—*Solidago odora.* . . A common name for it is Mountain Tea, and in some parts of the country the gathering of the leaves to dry and peddle in the winter has formed a minor rural industry, yielding a modest revenue. **1939** Medsger *Edible Wild Plants* 220, This plant [=*Solidago odora*] is sometimes referred to as Blue Mountain Tea. I find it recorded that the dried flowers make a pleasant and wholesome tea substitute. **1940** Clute *Amer. Plant Names* 88, *S[olidago] odorata.* . . Blue Mountain tea. . . *S. rugosa.* . . Blue Mountain tea. **1974** (1977) Coon *Useful Plants* 115, *Solidago odora* . . Blue Mountain tea. . . This particular species rates as a "tea" made from the dried leaves.

3 A **sweet fern** (here: *Comptonia peregrina*).

1898 *Plant World* 2.14 **sPA,** During a recent visit to the mountains of Southern Pennsylvania, the following local names of plants were noted as in use: Mountain Tea, for *Myrica asplenifolia* [=*Comptonia peregrina*] [etc].

mountain tea-tree n Cf **white tea-tree**

A **deer brush 1** (here: *Ceanothus integerrimus*).

1900 *Sunset* July 121 **ceCA,** Those who go to the Yosemite early in the season are often regaled by a wonderful sight upon the journey thither, for then the mountain tea-tree, *Ceanothus integerrimus,* is in full bloom and gives vast mountain slopes the aspect of being covered by a recent snowfall.

mountain thrush n

A **wood thrush** (here: *Hylocichla mustelina*).

1956 MA Audubon Soc. *Bulletin* 40.128 **VT,** Wood Thrush. . . Mountain Thrush.

‡mountain top adj phr

Healthy, well.

1960 Williams *Walk Egypt* 305 **GA,** I been sick some . . but I'm mountain top now.

mountain tree squirrel See **tree squirrel**

mountain trots n pl esp TN Cf **backdoor trot 2**

=**trots.**

1968–69 *DARE* (Qu. BB20, *Joking names or expressions for overactive kidneys*) Infs **TN**31, 34, 36, **WV**3, Mountain trots.

mountain trout n

1 A **trout:** usu **brook trout,** but also **lake trout 1** in the eastern US, and **cutthroat trout, rainbow trout,** or **Dolly Varden 1** in the western US and Alaska. Note: Several of these fishes have been introduced into parts of the US outside of their native ranges.

1805 (1904) Lewis *Orig. Jrls. Lewis & Clark Exped.* 2.151, These trout . . resemble our mountain or speckled trout [=*Salvelinus fontinalis*]. **1820** *Western Rev.* Apr 177, Alleghany Trout. . . It is found in the brooks of the Alleghany mountains falling into the Alleghany and Monongahela. It has the manner of the small Brook-trouts, and is called Mountain-trout, Creek-trout, &c. **1872** Tice *Over Plains* 126 **CO,** She had just finished catching a fine mess of mountain trout. **1884** Goode *Fisheries U.S.* 1.475, The Rainbow Trout. . . is generally known as the "Brook Trout," "Mountain Trout" [etc]. . . *Salmo purpuratus.* . . is known as . . "Mountain Trout," . . "Silver Trout," etc., in the mountains, but when in the ocean, full grown, as "Salmon Trout." **1948** *Trail Riders*

Bul. July 6/1 *(DA),* Nor need they be sparing their optimism as the lake as well as nearby Cerulean and Sunburst are well stocked with scrappy and tasty mountain trout. **1949** Caine *N. Amer. Sport Fish* 84, *Colloquial Names* [for *Salvelinus fontinalis*]. . . derived from appearance and habitat are: Brookie, . . Mountain Trout [etc]. **1965–70** *DARE* (Qu. P1) Infs **CA**137, **CO**12, 33, **NC**41, **SC**39, **UT**9, **VA**1, 8, Mountain trout. [*DARE* Ed: Some of these Infs may refer instead to **2** below.] **1972** Sparano *Outdoors Encycl.* 356, Cutthroat Trout—*Common Names* . . mountain trout. **1974** WI Univ. *Fish Lake MI* 15, Lake Trout—*Salvelinus namaycush.* . . Common names . . mountain trout.

2 A **black bass 1,** usu **smallmouth bass. Sth** Cf **trout**

1884 Goode *Fisheries U.S.* 1.401, The Small-mouth . . in Alabama, according to Professor Jordan, . . is called the "Mountain Trout." **1911** U.S. Bur. Census *Fisheries 1908* 307, The small-mouth bass . . in the Southern states . . is also called . . "mountain trout," etc. **1935** Caine *Game Fish* 3 **Sth,** Large-mouthed Black Bass. . . Synonyms . . Mountain Trout. *Ibid* 7 **Sth,** Small-mouthed Black Bass. . . Synonyms . . Mountain Trout. *Ibid* 10 **Sth,** Southern Small-mouthed Black Bass. . . Synonyms . . Mountain Trout. **1986** Pederson *LAGS Concordance,* 4 infs, **AL, TN,** Mountain Trout.

3 A **redfin pickerel** (here: *Esox americanus americanus*).

1927 Weed *Pike* 42, *Esox americanus.* . . Mountain Trout; Spring Valley Creek, Shannon County, Missouri.

4 Bacon. joc Cf **overland trout, sidehill salmon**

1966 *DARE* (Qu. H38, . . *Words for bacon [including joking ones]*) Inf **GA**1, Mountain trout.

mountain tulip n

=**mariposa lily.**

1949 Peattie *Cascades* 259 **Pacific NW,** One of the fairest of these is the calochortus that adorns many of our mountain meadows. . . It is endowed with a wonderful, delicate beauty, and this winsome charm has given it a number of names, including . . mountain tulip.

mountain veal See **mountain lamb**

mountain watercress n

A bitter cress: usu *Cardamine rotundifolia,* but also *C. douglasii.*

1900 Lyons *Plant Names* 81, *C[ardamine] purpurea.* . . Mountain Water-cress. *C. rotundifolia.* . . Mountain Water-cress. **1923** *Amer. Botanist* 29.107, A species of similar appearance [to *Cardamine bulbosa*] is *C. Douglasii* known as "purple cress" and "mountain water-cress." *Cardamine rotundifolia* is another "mountain water-cress." **1953** Strausbaugh–Core *Flora WV* 436, *C. rotundifolia.* . . Mountain watercress. . . Springs and brooksides, throughout the State. **1979** Niering–Olmstead *Audubon Guide N. Amer. Wildflowers E. Region* 428, Mountain Watercress *(C. rotundifolia),* also white-flowered, has oval leaves with tiny projections on the leafstalk.

mountain whitefish n Cf **mountain herring**

A **whitefish** (here: *Prosopium williamsoni*).

1946 LaMonte *N. Amer. Game Fishes* 124, Among the varieties of this fish [=*Prosopium williamsoni*] well known to anglers are the Oregon Whitefish and the Mountain Whitefish. **1963** Sigler–Miller *Fishes UT* 58, The mountain whitefish is just now becoming important in Utah's fishery. **1966** Barnes–Jensen *Dict. UT Slang* 31, The native mountain whitefish *(Prosopium williamsoni)* . . is not very common in Utah rivers, and . . is a good game fish. **1983** *Audubon Field Guide N. Amer. Fishes* 392, Mountain Whitefish . . has 20–25 gill rakers; inhabits lakes and streams of W. Canada and NW. **1991** Amer. Fisheries Soc. *Common Names Fishes* 28, *Prosopium williamsoni* . . F[reshwater] . . mountain whitefish.

mountain white oak n Cf **mountain oak**

A western oak: esp **blue oak 2,** but also **Oregon oak** or a **gray oak 2** (here: *Quercus grisea*).

1884 Sargent *Forests of N. Amer.* 143, *Quercus Douglasii.* . . Mountain White Oak. Blue Oak. . . South along the western foot-hills of the Sierra Nevada . . and through the Coast ranges to the San Gabriel mountains. **1897** Sudworth *Arborescent Flora* 160 **CA,** *Quercus douglasii.* . . Common Names. Mountain White Oak. **1902** U.S. Natl. Museum *Contrib. Herbarium* 7.343 **CA,** *Quercus garryana.* . . The Pacific post oak, or, as it is more commonly called in this region, mountain white oak. It resembles the valley white oak both in size and appearance of several of its parts, but may be readily distinguished therefrom by . . its habitat, it being confined principally to the lower hills instead of the level valleys. **1908** Britton *N. Amer. Trees* 323, *Quercus douglasii*. . . A tree of dry hills and mountain sides of west central California, . . is also called Mountain white oak. *Ibid* 338, *Quercus Garryana*. . . is the most valuable oak timber on the Pacific slope, where it is used like the White oak of the eastern States. . . It is also called . . Mountain white oak. **1931** U.S. Dept. Ag. *Misc. Pub.* 101.23, *Garry oak* . ., also frequently known as California mountain white oak, is a Pacific tree or shrub, and appears to be the only oak in Washington State. **1938** Van Dersal *Native Woody Plants* 346, Oak, Mountain white *(Quercus douglasii, Quercus grisea).* **1980** Little *Audubon Guide N. Amer. Trees W. Region* 394, "Mountain White Oak" . . *Quercus douglasii.* . . Recognized from a distance by the bluish foliage.

mountain willow n

Any of several, chiefly western, **willows**: esp **Scouler willow,** but also **planeleaf willow, prairie willow,** or *Salix monticola.*

   1848 Gray *Manual of Botany* 428, *S[alix] phylicifolia*. . . *Smooth Mountain Willow.* . . Moist ravines, on the alpine summits of the White Mountains, New Hampshire. **1861** Wood *Class-Book* 653, *S. phylicifolia.* . . *Mountain Willow.* . . White Mts. . . A handsome, low shrub. **1897** Sudworth *Arborescent Flora* 126 **MT,** *Salix nuttallii.* . . *Common Names.* . . Mountain Willow. **1931** U.S. Dept. Ag. *Misc. Pub.* 101.15, *Scouler willow* . ., known also as . . mountain . . willow, is one of the most common, abundant, and widely distributed willows in west North America. **1960** Vines *Trees SW* 98, *Salix scouleriana.* . . Vernacular names are . . Mountain Willow, and Nuttal Willow. It is fair browse for mule deer and livestock. *Ibid* 107, *Mountain Willow—Salix monticola.* . . Along streams, or in boggy meadows at altitudes of 3,500–11,500 ft. New Mexico, Colorado, Utah, and Wyoming. **1975** Hamel–Chiltoskey *Cherokee Plants* 61, Willow . . mountain. . . *S[alix] humilis.* . . Bark for tonic. **1979** Little *Checklist U.S. Trees* 264, *Salix monticola.* . . Mountain willow. . . A shrub only rarely attaining tree size. *Ibid* 266, *Scouler willow.* . . *Other common names* . . mountain willow.

mountain woodchuck n

=**mountain boomer 5.**

   1983 *Lutz Coll.* **seNY** (as of late 19th cent), [A woman] of the Sandyfield–Beaver Pond area of Rockland County said that the folks of the little village there used the term "mountain woodchucks" for a certain family that sometimes came in from the Green Swamp. . . Obviously the folks who lived at the crossroads where there was a store thought themselves better than the woodcutters farther back from the road.

mountain woodpecker n

Nuttall's **woodpecker** *(Picoides nuttallii).*

   1969 *DARE* (Qu. Q17) Inf **CA**130, Mountain woodpecker—a funny, spotted-looking thing—makes a lot of racket.

mountaneous See mountainous

mount cat See mountain cat 2

mounting See mountain

mourn v

1 To moan. [Cf *EDD mourn* v. 1 "To moan; to complain; to be peevish"; however, this may reflect pronc of *mourn* as [mo:n]; cf Pronc Intro 3.I.e, 3.I.21]
   1903 *DN* 2.321 **seMO,** Mourn. . . Moan. 'She was mourning all night with a toothache.' **1912** Green *VA Folk-Speech* 289, Mourn. . . To make a low, mourning noise: "He was mourning and groaning all night long."
2 See quot. [*SND murn* v. 2. "To complain. . . Gen. Sc.; *specif.* of cattle: to low mournfully from hunger or illness"] Cf *DS* K19, 21
   1983 *MJLF* 9.1.48 **ceKY,** Mourn . . to moo.

mourner n chiefly Sth, S Midl See also mourners' bench Cf moaner

One who repents publicly, esp at a revival meeting.
   1807 in 1925 *VA Mag. Hist. & Biog.* 33.284, One shouter, four mourners came to be prayed for. **1883** Sweet–Knox *Mexican Mustang* 110 **ceTX,** Around in front of the preacher's stand was an open space fenced off by a row of reserved seats for the mourners. **1903** *DN* 2.321 **seMO,** Mourner. . . A person 'under conviction,' at revival meetings. **1905** *DN* 3.88 **nwAR,** Mourner. . . A person desirous of religious conversion. 'He was calling for mourners, but when they come up he

didn't even shake hands with them.' Common. **1906** *DN* 3.121 **sIN. 1909** *DN* 3.350 **eAL, wGA. 1921** Haswell *Daughter Ozarks* 37 (as of 1880s), After the sermon there was the usual call for "mourners", to which a score responded and knelt at the bench in front of the pulpit.

mourners' bench n Also *mourner('s) bench, mourners' pew, ~ row, ~ seat* Pronc-sp *mounah's bench* [**mourner**] **chiefly Sth, S Midl** See Map Cf **anxious bench 1, moaners' ~**

A bench, seat, or rail set aside for penitents at the front of a church or revival meeting.
   1834 Lieber *Letters* 312 **sePA,** These tents . . are divided lengthwise by a bench about a foot high, and called the mourners' bench. **1845** Hooper *Advent. Simon Suggs* 126 **AL,** "Bimeby I felt so missuble, I had to go yonder"—pointing to the mourners' seat. **1848** *Ladies' Repository* 8.102, She loves the mourner's bench, for there she found peace and pardon. **1903** *DN* 2.321 **seMO,** Mourner's bench. . . Seat reserved for those seeking religion. **1906** *DN* 3.121 **sIN,** Mourner's bench. **1907** *DN* 3.233 **nwAR,** Mourner's bench. **1909** *DN* 3.350 **eAL, wGA,** Mourner's bench. . . The front bench or seat in a church where the mourners are assembled. **1911** Wright *Barbara Worth* 20 **CO,** When the rush for the mourners' bench come I unlimbered an' headed the stampede pronto. **1912** *DN* 3.583 **wIN,** Mourners' bench. . . The altar-railing (in newer churches) at which penitents kneel. **1915** *DN* 4.186 **swVA,** Mourners' bench. **1916** *DN* 4.326 **KS,** Mourner's bench. . . Seat, bench or rail, etc., near the altar, where in evangelical churches, in 'revivals,' 'protracted meetings,' etc., persons ('mourners,' because of their sadness over their sinful condition) gather, usually kneeling, to 'seek religion', to bewail their sins, etc. Not local. *Ibid* 345 **FL,** Mourner's row. The front row in church. **1953** Brewer *Word Brazos* 14 **eTX** [Black], Hit takes lots of patience to deal wid a sinnuh at de mounah's bench. **1958** Humphrey *Home from the Hill* 282 **neTX,** But what annoyed Fred was having the christening of his son in the very best church in town spoiled by the attendance of any revivalists of the mourners' bench sort. **1965–70** *DARE* (Qu. CC5, *Names for seats in a church, especially near the front*) 100 Infs, **chiefly Sth, S Midl,** Mourners' bench(es); **SC**10, Mourner bench; **MI**92, **MA**68, Mourners' pew(s); **MN**38, Mourners' row; **KS**13, Mourners' seat.

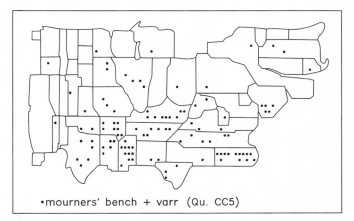

•mourners' bench + varr (Qu. CC5)

mourners to the front exclam

   1895 *DN* 1.398, Mourners to the front: this phrase is used when one who has been defeated in a game of any kind is given the first play or chance in the next game.

mournful widow See mourning bride

mourning aster n

See quot.
   1949 *WELS Suppl.* **seWI,** Until I came to Waterloo . . I always thought gaillardias were "mourning asters" (Ger. "Trauer-Astern.")

mourning bird n MA

=**piping plover.**
   1886 *Forest & Stream* 27.343 **Cape Cod MA,** Along the Cape . . the piping plover [is known] as a "mourning bird." **1917** (1923) *Birds Amer.* 1.264, *Piping Plover.* . . *Other Names.* . . Mourning Bird. . . Its piping calls are plaintive and pretty. **1925** (1928) Forbush *Birds MA* 1.470, *Piping Plover.* . . *Mourning Bird.* [*Ibid* 471, *Voice.*—A plaintive, piping whistle.] **1955** MA Audubon Soc. *Bulletin* 39.444, *Piping Plover.* . . Mourning Bird (Mass. Its notes sound mournful to some ears).

mourning bride n Also *mournful widow, (mourning) widow* [From the colors of the flowers]

A scabious, usu *Scabiosa atropurpurea.* Also called **pincushion**

1847 Wood *Class-Book* 310, S[cabiosa] atropurpurea. *Mourning Bride. . .* A beautiful species, 2–4f[eet] high, with dense heads of dark purple flowers. **1880** Howells *Undiscovered Country* 300 **MA,** Here is bachelor's button, and mourning bride, and marigolds, and touch-me-not. **1896** *Jrl. Amer. Folkl.* 9.190, *Scabiosa atropurpurea, . .* mourning bride, mourning widow, Sulphur Grove, Ohio. **1902** Earle *Old Time Gardens* 339, At the lower end of the long flower border in our garden, grew "Mourning Brides," white, pale lavender, and purple brown in tint. **1943** in 1960 Daly *Elizabeth Daly Omnibus* 2.129, Clara pored lovingly over the sweet williams, marigolds and mourning bride. **1959** Carleton *Index Herb. Plants* 84, *Mournful widow. . . Mourning bride:* Scabiosa (v). *Ibid* 125, *Widow:* Scabiosa (v). **1976** Bailey–Bailey *Hortus Third* 1014, *[Scabiosa] atropurpurea. . . Mourning-bride. . .* Fl[ower]s dark purple, rose, lilac, or white. . . Naturalized in Calif.

mourning dove n Also understood as *morning dove*

1 A long-tailed, buff-colored bird *(Zenaida macroura).* Also called **Carolina dove, long-tailed ~, moaning ~ 2, rain crow, turtledove, wild dove, wood ~**

1838 *Geol. Surv. OH Second Annual Rept.* 164, Columba Carolinensis. . . *Mourning Dove.* **1841** Catlin *Letters Indians* 1.158, The mourning or turtle-dove, . . being, as they call it, a *medicine-bird,* is not to be destroyed or harmed by any one. **1891** *Leighton News* (AL) 15 May np, The Mourning Dove . . is a common and well known resident throughout the year in this locality. . . The cooing or mourning sound made by the male in the spring, and from which it takes its name I used to think was the Dove mourning over the loss of its mate, but it is really expressive of the highest joy and contentment, and is no more meant for mourning than the liveliest song of the Mockingbird. **1923** WV State Ornith. *Birds WV* 13, In the mourning dove we have the most graceful of all our birds, built like a race horse for speed, with his full breast and long, tapering wings and graceful tail. **1951** *AmSp* 26.93, Our common dove the *mourning dove. . .* is also recorded as *morning dove* (Iowa; Kans.). Parallel usage affects names of the ground dove, witness . . *morning dove* (Fla.) **1965–70** *DARE* (Qu. Q7, *Names and nicknames for . . game birds)* 37 Infs, *scattered,* Mourning dove; (Qu. Q14) 9 Infs, *scattered,* Mourning dove; (Qu. Q2) Inf **WA**3, Mourning dove; (Qu. Q3) Inf **NY**100, Mourning dove. [*DARE* Ed: Some of these Infs may refer instead to **2** below.] **1977** Bull–Farrand *Audubon Field Guide Birds* 542, *Mourning Dove. . .* This bird. . . is common in rural areas in all parts of the United States, as well as in city parks and, in winter, [at] suburban feeders.

2 **=ground dove.** chiefly **AL, FL**

1898 (1900) Davie *Nests N. Amer. Birds* 189, *Ground Dove. . .* Mr. Walter Hoxie, of Frogmore, S.C., states that this species is called Mourning Dove by the natives, who used to have a superstition that any one who molested their nest would be "mourned to death" by the grief-stricken owners. **1917** (1923) *Birds Amer.* 2.51, Its [=the ground dove's] soft plaintive note has won for it the name of "Mourning Dove" by many people. **1924** Howell *Birds AL* 125, Ground Dove; "Mourning Dove". . . A local and rather uncommon resident in the southern third of the State. **1951** [see **1** above]. **1954** Sprunt *FL Bird Life* 237, This diminutive dove is a favorite of everyone. . . There is, however, endless confusion regarding it and its larger relative, many insisting that it [=*Columbina passerina*] is the "mourning" dove. **1962** Imhof *AL Birds* 295, *Ground Dove. . .* Its moaning, oft-repeated call has earned it the name of "Mourning Dove" in much of the Alabama Coastal Plain area. **1969** Longstreet *Birds FL* 73, The dove that spends most of its time walking over fields and lawns should always be called by its real name of ground dove. It is incorrectly known as mourning dove, which is the true name of a species that not only has different plumage but is once again as large.

mourning finch See **mourning sparrow**

mourning ragwort n

A **ragwort** (here: *Senecio integerrimus).*

1966 Heller *Wild Flowers AK* 17, Mourning Ragwort. . . Disc and ray flowers yellow . . ; bracts beneath them all black-tipped. . . Scattered throughout interior Alaska.

mourning sparrow n Also *mourning finch* **=Harris's sparrow.**

1929 Forbush *Birds MA* 3.440, *Harris's Sparrow. . . Other names . .*

mourning sparrow. . . A large sparrow with black face and breast or black blotch on breast. **1932** Bennitt *Check-list* 65 **MO,** *Harris's sparrow. . .* Mourning finch. **1936** Roberts *MN Birds* 2.420, *Mourning Finch. . . General Range.*—Central portions of North America. **1946** Hausman *Eastern Birds* 609, Mourning Sparrow. . . Crown, throat, and upper breast more or less black.

mourning warbler n [See quot 1929]

A **warbler** (here: *Oporornis philadelphia).* Also called **ground warbler**

1810 Wilson *Amer. Ornith.* 2.101, [The] Mourning Warbler. *Sylvia Philadelphia. . .* was shot in the early part of June, on the border of a marsh. **1844** DeKay *Zool. NY* 2.81, The *Mourning Warbler* derives its name from its peculiarly melancholy notes, and is a bird of shy and solitary habits. **1911** Howell *Birds AR* 81, The mourning warbler, so named from the black hood it wears, is a regular and not uncommon migrant in the Mississippi Valley, breeding from central Minnesota northward. **1929** Forbush *Birds MA* 3.293, The Mourning Warbler is a striking and beautiful bird, though frontally "veiled in crêpe." This crêpe-like marking about the breast is the only thing about the bird that would suggest mourning, for it seems as happy and active as most birds, and its song is a pæan of joy. **1951** Kumlien–Hollister *Birds WI* 106, *Mourning Warbler. . .* Common summer resident in the northern half of the state and in some localities is the most abundant warbler. **1977** Bull–Farrand *Audubon Field Guide Birds* 651, *Mourning Warbler. . .* This warbler supposedly gets its vernacular name from the black crepe-like patch on the breast of the male.

mourning widow See **mourning bride**

mouse n

A Gram forms.

1 sg: usu *mouse;* also, esp in proverbial phrr, *mice.*

1851 (1969) Burke *Polly Peablossom* 70 **MS,** With that I smelt a mice, and commenced larfin. **1859** in 1966 Boller *MO Fur Trader* 96 **MO,** The men began to "smell a very large sized mice" & all hands burst into tremendous peals of laughter. **1872** Burnham *Memoirs U.S. Secret Service* 182, But he had already smelt an enormous mice, nevertheless! **1903** *DN* 2.299 **Cape Cod MA** (as of a1857), *Mice. . .* In expression 'just like a mice,' that is easily and neatly. **1923** *DN* 5.238 **swWI,** *Mice, like a; slick as a. . .* Easily without trouble. "I'll do that slick's a mice." **1930** Stoney–Shelby *Black Genesis* 4 **seSC,** He mek all de beasts; de goat, an' de horse, an' de cow, de mice an' de rat, de coon an' de possum. **1941** *Sat. Eve. Post* 13 Sept 15 **Sth,** I ain't in the ma'ket for a rabbit, . . a field mice . . or a bullwhip snake.

2 pl: usu *mice;* also *mices, mouses.*

1908 *DN* 3.284 **eAL, wGA,** Mices. **1965–70** [see **B**3 below]. **1986** Pederson *LAGS Concordance,* 1 inf, **cwAL,** Mices = mice; rat and mices; 1 inf, **swMS,** Mices.

B Senses.

1 also *mouser:* A lump or swelling caused by a blow; spec, a black eye.

1860 Holmes *Professor* 245 **MA,** Clap a slice o' raw beefsteak on to that mouse o' yours 'n' 't'll take down the swellin'. (*Mouse* is a technical term for a bluish, oblong, rounded elevation occasioned by running one's forehead or eyebrow against another's knuckles.) **1950** *WELS Suppl.,* Mouse—a black eye. **1965–70** *DARE* (Qu. X20, . . *A black eye)* 61 Infs, *scattered,* Mouse; **FL**27, Mouser; (Qu. X60, . . *A lump that comes up on your head when you get a sharp blow or knock;* not asked in early QRs) Infs **NY**221, **WA**13, Mouse. **1975** (1982) Ludlum *Road to Gandolfo* 55, Sam pressed the sensitive flesh around his eye with his fingers. He hadn't had a mouse in over fifteen years.

2 See quot. Cf **joint mouse**

1959 *VT Hist.* 27.149, *Mouse in your knee. . .* A sharp pain in one's knee. Rare.

3 usu pl; also often *dust mouse;* occas *mousie:* **=dust bunny.** **scattered, but rare Sth** See Map

1941 *AmSp* 16.167 [Army slang], *Mice.* Small balls of lint on floor. **1950** *WELS Suppl.* **WI,** Mouse—roll of dust; *dust mice*—rolls of lint. **1965–70** *DARE* (Qu. E20, *Soft rolls of dust that collect on the floor under beds or other furniture)* Infs **AK**3, **CA**41, 64, **IN**7, **NC**5, **OH**7, **PA**165, **WV**1, **WI**19, 29, Mice; **CA**4, **IA**25, **IN**76, **MA**18, **NJ**3, **PA**88, Dust mice; **NM**5, Dust mouse; **CA**59, Dust mouses; **IA**25, **MA**83, Mouse; **AK**3, Fuzzy mice; **WA**19, Gray mice; **KY**41, **MO**21, **PA**131, White mice; **WI**47, Mousies; [**ID**5, Mouse hair]. **1970** *DARE* File s**NJ,** Dust mice—the rolls of dust that gather under beds, furniture, etc.

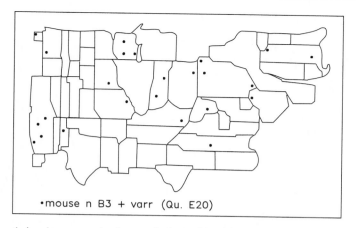

•mouse n B3 + varr (Qu. E20)

4 in phr *mouse in the meal:* Something suspicious, something that needs investigating.

1933 Williamson *Woods Colt* 53 **Ozarks,** What's wrong with her? They never talk very much, but this ain't natural. There's a mouse in the meal, somewhere. **1968** *DARE* (Qu. V1, *When you suspect that somebody is trying to deceive you, or that something is going on behind your back . . "There's _____."*) Inf **MO**10, A mouse in the meal.

5 in phr *to smell a mouse:* To suspect that something is contrary to appearances. [Var of *to smell a rat*]

1851 [see **A1** above]. **1872** [see **A1** above]. **c1905** Dunckel *Molly-joggers* 62 **swMO,** Pa smelled a mouse, and going down to the water's edge, discovered that he had been shooting at a cast iron frog. **1941** Smith *Going to God's Country* 22 **MO** (as of 1890), Then I began to wonder if he had any idea of what I was planing [sic] to do. I wanted to know if he smelt a mouse. **1945** Street *Gauntlet* 226 **MO** (as of 1920s), That's what they say. Maybe she's expecting all right, but I smell a mouse. **1967–68** *DARE* (Qu. V1, *When you suspect that somebody is trying to deceive you, or that something is going on behind your back*) Infs **CA**79, **CO**20, **LA**11, **MN**42, **UT**4, I smell a mouse (someplace).

mouse v

‡1 with *around:* To be indecisive. [Cf *mousy* timid]

1969 *DARE* (Qu. A11, *When somebody takes too long about coming to a decision . . "I wish he'd quit _____."*) Inf **GA**71, Mousing ['mæəsɪn] around.

‡2 To complain or gripe. [Cf *grouse* to complain]

1968 *DARE* (Qu. GG16, *. . Finding fault, or complaining: "You just can't please him—he's always _____."*) Inf **CA**81, Mousing ['maʊzɪŋ].

mouse and rat cat See **mouse cat**

mouse around See **mouse** v 1

mouse bat n

=leather-winged bat.

1909 *DN* 3.344 **eAL, wGA,** Leather-wing(ed) (bat). . . The common mouse bat. **1966** *DARE* (Qu. Q3, *. . Birds that come out only after dark*) Inf **OK**25, Mouse bat.

mouse bird n [See quot 1857] Cf **mouse hawk 2**

A **loggerhead shrike.**

1857 U.S. Patent Office *Annual Rept. for 1856: Ag.* 87, The Southern shrike, *(Lanius ludovicianus,) . .* is also an enemy to be dreaded by the meadow-mice. . . its destruction of arvicolae in summer is well known, and has gained for it the name of "Mouse Bird," in Central Illinois. **1903** Dawson *Birds OH* 1.290, *Lanius ludovicianus excubitorides. . . Mouse Bird.* [*Ibid* 293, The Shrike is a bird of prey, . . [and] searches the ground with his eye until he detects some suspicious movement of insect, mouse, or bird.] **1917** (1923) *Birds Amer.* 3.101, The White-rumped Shrike, or Mouse-bird *(Lanius ludovicianus excubitorides)* is . . found in the arid districts of western North America.

mouse bush n Also *mouse-ear bush* [Cf *OED* mouse-eared a., *DCan* mouse ear, in ref to the catkins of a willow]

A **pussy willow** such as *Salix discolor.*

1833 (1847) Lundy *Life & Travels* 59 **TX,** An endless variety of plants and shrubs are now in blossom: among the rest, my pretty little "mouse-ear" bush is common. **1953** Randolph–Wilson *Down in Holler* 266

Ozarks, *Mouse-bush.* . . The pussy-willow *(Salix discolor).* The catkins do look rather like little gray mice.

mouse cat n Also *mouse and rat cat* **esp Ohio Valley, Gulf States** See Map Cf **rat cat**

1965–70 *DARE* (Qu. J6, *A cat that catches lots of rats and mice . . "She's a good _____."*) 13 Infs, **esp Ohio Valley, Gulf States,** Mouse cat; **IL**93, Mouse and rat cat.

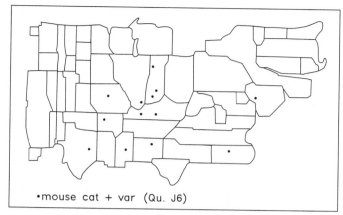

•mouse cat + var (Qu. J6)

mousee See **mousie 1**

mouse-ear n Cf **purple mouse-ears**

1 Any of several often introduced and naturalized plants, as:

a also *mouse-ear chickweed, mouse's ear:* **=chickweed 1b.** [See quot 1895; *OED* 1578 →]

1791 in 1793 *Amer. Philos. Soc. Trans.* 3.169, Cerastium, Mouse-ear. **1829** Phelps *Familiar Lect.* 357, *Cerastium. . . vulgatum,* (mouse-ear, chick weed . .). **1837** Darlington *Flora Cestrica* 277 **PA,** *C[erastium] vulgatum.* . . Mouse-ear Chickweed. Mouse-ear. Plant pale green, very hairy, somewhat viscid when young. **1895** Gray–Bailey *Field Botany* 78, *Cerastium. Mouse-ear Chickweed.* . . Popular name from the shape and soft hairiness of the leaves of the common species [=*C. vulgatum*]. **1910** Graves *Flowering Plants* 177 **CT,** *Cerastium semidecandrum.* . . Spring Mouse-ear. **1936** McDougall–Baggley *Plants of Yellowstone* 55, *Mouse-ear (Cerastium arvense).* . . is a low, hairy plant with white flowers. **1968–69** *DARE* (Qu. I28b, *Kinds of greens that are cooked*) Infs **KY**37, **NC**55, Mouse's ear; (Qu. S21, *. . Weeds . . that are a trouble in gardens and fields*) Inf **WV**3, Mouse-ear. **1979** Niering–Olmstead *Audubon Guide N. Amer. Wildflowers E. Region* 445, Mouse-ear Chickweed *(Cerastium vulgatum).* . . This naturalized European plant takes its common name from the fuzzy leaves. Although a troublesome weed in the garden, its leaves can be boiled and eaten as greens. **1991** Still *Wolfpen Notebooks* 77 **sAppalachians,** What I look forward to in the spring hain't garden sass. Hit's wild greens. . . What you want to look for is plantain, . . mouse's ear, . . and blue thistle.

b **=forget-me-not 1a.** [See quot 1857; *OED* 1597 →]

1814 Bigelow *Florula Bostoniensis* 47, *Myosotis scorpioides.* . . *Mouse ear Scorpion grass.* . . Flowers pointing one way, small, rose coloured. **1857** Gray *Manual of Botany* 323, *Myosotis.* . . In allusion to the aspect of the short and soft leaves in some species: one popular name is *Mouse-ear.* **1900** *Lyons Plant Names* 255, *Myosotis.* . . Mouse-ear. . . *M. palustris.* . . Mouse-ear. **1951** Abrams *Flora Pacific States* 3.542, *Myosotis arvensis.* . . Field Scorpion Grass or Mouse-ear. . . Frequent in western Washington and western Oregon. . . but more widely naturalized in eastern United States. **1972** GA Dept. Ag. *Farmers Market Bulletin* 24 May 8, Myosotis scorpiodes, also known as Forget-me-not, Mouse-ear and Scorpion-grass, is a European flower which has become naturalized throughout the coastal plain states.

c also *mouse-ear cress:* A **cress** (here: *Arabidopsis thaliana*). [See quot 1822; *OED* 1578 →]

1822 Eaton *Botany* 177, *[Arabis] thaliana* . . mousear [sic] cress . . stem erect, rough-haired at the base. **1876** Hobbs *Bot. Hdbk.* 72, Mouse ear cress, Arabis thaliana. **1903** Small *Flora SE U.S.* 475, *Wall Cress. Mouse-ear Cress.* . . In sandy soil and waste places, Ontario to Minnesota, Massachusetts, Georgia and Missouri. Spring. **1910** Shreve *MD Plant Life* 439, Mouse-ear or Thale-cress. **1932** Rydberg *Flora Prairies* 370, *Mouse-ear Cress.* **1944** Abrams *Flora Pacific States* 2.267 **OR, WA,** *Arabidopsis Thaliana.* . . Mouse-ear. . . Waste places, especially in dry ground. **1968** Barkley *Plants KS* 161, Mouse-ear Cress. **1995** Brako et al. *Scientific & Common Names Plants* 188, Mouse-ear cress—*Arabidopsis thaliana*.

d also *mouse-ear hawkweed:* A **hawkweed:** usu *Hieracium pilosella*, but also **orange hawkweed**. [OED c1265 →]

   1890 *Century Dict.* 3880, *Mouse-ear.* . . *Hieracium Pilosella.* . . Also called *mouse-ear hawkweed.* . . *Golden mouse-ear, Hieracium aurantiacum.* **1900** Lyons *Plant Names* 191, *H[ieracium] aurantiacum.* . . Golden Mouse-ear Hawkweed. *Ibid* 192, *H. Pilosella.* . . Mouse-ear Hawkweed. **1910** Graves *Flowering Plants* 414 **CT,** *Hieracium Pilosella.* . . Mouse-ear. **1940** Clute *Amer. Plant Names* 70, *H[ieracium] aurantiacum.* . . Golden mouse-ear hawk-weed. . . *H. pilosella.* Mouse-ear. Mouse-ear hawk-weed. **1950** Gray–Fernald *Manual of Botany* 1564, *H[ieracium] Pilosella.* . . Mouse-ear. . . Very troublesome northw[ard]. **1973** Hitchcock–Cronquist *Flora Pacific NW* 530, Mouse-ear h[awkweed]. . . *H[ieracium] pilosella.* . . Golden mouse-ear h. . . *H. aurantiacum.* **1995** Brako et al. *Scientific & Common Names Plants* 188, Mouse-ear hawkweed—*Hieracium pilosella.*

e A **hedgenettle**. [*OED* 1879 →]

   1933 Small *Manual SE Flora* 1161, *S[tachys] italica.* . . Mouse-ear. . . Fla. to Tenn. and Ont. Nat. of Eur.

2 also *mouse-ear (life) everlasting, mouse-ear plantain, mouse's ear(s):* A **pussytoes** (here: *Antennaria plantaginifolia*).

   1784 in 1785 Amer. Acad. Arts & Sci. *Memoirs* 1.480, *Gnaphalium* [here: =*Antennaria*]. . . *Catsfoot. Woolly Mouse-Ear.* Blossoms yellowish-white. **1824** Bigelow *Florula Bostoniensis* 300, *Gnaphalium plantagineum.* . . Mouse Ear. . . This species flowers early, and is pretty common in pastures and dry hills. **1840** MA Zool. & Bot. Surv. *Herb. Plants & Quadrupeds* 125, Mouse-Ear Everlasting. . . Rises early in the spring from a few inches to a foot in height, and flowers for a long time. **1847** Wood *Class-Book* 351, *Mouse-ear Life-everlasting.* . . Its numerous, scattered leaves [are] clothed with white and cotton-like down. **1887** (1895) Robinson *Uncle Lisha* 25 **wVT,** Half way across the field, Lisha became discernible against the dull whiteness of the mouse ear and everlasting on the sterile hillside. **1896** *Jrl. Amer. Folkl.* 9.191, *Antennaria plantaginifolia.* . . Mouse's ear, Oxford County, Me. . . Mouse-ear, Salem, Mass. **1912** Blatchley *IN Weed Book* 159, Mouse-ear. . . Low woolly herbs. . . common in dry clayey, half-barren soil on the slopes of open upland woods and old fields. **1940** Clute *Amer. Plant Names* 74, *A[ntennaria] plantaginifolia.* . . Pearly mouse-ear everlasting, mouse-ear plantain. **1995** Brako et al. *Scientific & Common Names Plants* 188, Mouse's-ears—*Antennaria plantaginifolia.*

3 also pl: An **aster** (here: *Aster tortifolius* Michx.)

   1869 Porcher *Resources* 455 **SC,** Mouse-ear, (*Aster tortifolius,* Mx.) Vicinity of Charleston; grows in Pine Barrens. . . This plant has some reputation in domestic practice in South Carolina as a diuretic. **1901** Mohr *Plant Life AL* 779, Mouse Ears. . . Common in the pine barrens of the Coast Pine belt.

4 A **cudweed 1**, usu *Filaginella uliginosa*.

   1873 in 1976 Miller *Shaker Herbs* 207, Mouse Ear. . . *Gnaphalium uliginosum* [=*Filaginella uliginosa*]. . . Used in coughs, diarrhea, and obstructions. . . This Mouse Ear is not to be confused with the Hawk-weed which is called Mouse Ear. **1876** Hobbs *Bot. Hdbk.* 72, Mouse ear, *Gnaphalium uliginosum*. **1896** *Jrl. Amer. Folkl.* 9.192, *Gnaphalium uliginosum,* . . mouse-ear, Paris, Me. **1914** Georgia *Manual Weeds* 445, *Gnaphalium uliginosum.* . . Mouse-ear. . . A common weed of flooded ground.

5 pl: A **hepatica** (here: *Hepatica nobilis obtusa*). [Appar from the shape of the leaf]

   1892 *Jrl. Amer. Folkl.* 5.91 **NH,** *Hepatica triloba,* mouse-ears. Mason, N.H. **1910** Graves *Flowering Plants* 189 **CT,** Mouse-ears. . . Rich, usually rocky woods. **1930** Sievers *Amer. Med. Plants* 40, Mouse-ears. . . The thick and leathery evergreen leaves are roundish or kidney-shaped.

6 pl: A **mariposa lily** (here: *Calochortus tolmiei*). [See quot 1920]

   1898 *Jrl. Amer. Folkl.* 11.281, *Calochortus Maweanus,* . . mouse-ears, . . Mendocino Co., Cal. **1920** Rice–Rice *Pop. Studies CA Wild Flowers* 28, *C[alochortus] maweanus,* with tiny, bell-shaped flowers, is white or lilac colored, and barely an inch across. The blossoms are thickly covered with white or purplish hairs. . . This variety, because of its color, is more frequently called "Mouse Ears."

7 A **speedwell** (here: *Veronica officinalis*). [See quot]

   1899 *Plant World* 2.198, Mouse-ear. . for *Veronica officinalis* L., the . . name doubtless suggested by the form of the leaf.

mouse-ear bush See **mouse bush**

mouse-ear chickweed See **mouse-ear 1a**

mouse-ear cress See **mouse-ear 1c**

mouse-ear everlasting See **mouse-ear 2**

mouse-ear hawkweed See **mouse-ear 1d**

mouse-ear life everlasting, mouse-ear plantain See **mouse-ear 2**

mouse-ears See **mouse-ear 3, 5, 6**

mouse-ear violet n

A **violet** (here: perh *Viola pubescens*).

   1967 *DARE* (Qu. S26b, *Wildflowers that grow in water or wet places*) Inf **MI67,** Mouse-ear violet.

mousefish n

The sargassum fish *(Histrio histrio)*.

   1818 *Amer. Monthly Mag. & Crit. Rev.* 2.325, *Mouse-fish.—Lophius gibbus,* . . is a fish scarcely two inches long. . . He was brought on board clinging with his fingered pectorals to some gulf weed that was raised from the surface of the ocean by the boat-hook. **1873** in 1878 Smithsonian Inst. *Misc. Coll.* 14.2.14, *Pterophryne lævigata.* . . Common frog-fish; mouse-fish. . . Accidental on [east] coast. **1898** U.S. Natl. Museum *Bulletin* 47.2716, *Mouse-fish.* . . Abundant on our Gulf coast and occasional northward to Cape Hatteras or beyond, especially in floating masses of *Sargassum.* . . A remarkable fish, excessively variable in coloration. **1933** John G. Shedd Aquarium *Guide* 162, *Mousefish.* This little fish . . is very abundant in the floating beds of Sargassum weed in the . . Atlantic. **1939** Natl. Geogr. Soc. *Fishes* 161, One of the commonest and perhaps the most interesting [of fishes which hide in weed masses] . . , the mouse fish, spends its entire life in the drifting sargassum. **1991** Amer. Fisheries Soc. *Common Names Fishes* 151, Mousefish—see sargassumfish.

mouse food See **mouse nut**

mouse hawk n

1 Any of several hawks:

a also *mice hawk, mouser:* =**marsh hawk 1.**

   1812 Wilson *Amer. Ornith.* 6.67 **eNJ,** Marsh Hawk[s]. . . are usually known by the name of the Mouse Hawk along the sea coast of New Jersey. **1884** *Harper's New Mth. Mag.* 68.620, The marsh-hawk has a bluish or brown plumage. . . In the marshes on the Delaware it is often called the mouse-hawk. **1917** (1923) *Birds Amer.* 2.64, *Marsh Hawk.* . . *Other Names.* . . Mouse Hawk. [*Ibid* 65, The food of the Marsh Hawk varies with the season and with local conditions. In some parts of the country . . it is exclusively small quadrupeds, and of these field mice are the favorites.] **1927** Forbush *Birds MA* 2.99, *Marsh Hawk.* . . Mouse hawk. **1953** Jewett *Birds WA* 178, *Circus cyaneus hudsonius.* . . Mouse Hawk. [*Ibid* 179, It is probably the most active and determined foe of meadow mice and ground squirrels.] **1955** MA Audubon Soc. *Bulletin* 39.442, *Marsh Hawk.* . . Mouse Hawk (General. A well-deserved name; mice were identified in 211 of 601 stomachs.); Mouser (Conn.) **1965–70** *DARE* (Qu. Q4, . . *Kinds of hawks*) Infs **FL7, IL16, KY49, ME3, MO38, 39, MA15, OH87, 97,** Mouse hawk; **NY89,** Mice hawk. [*DARE* Ed: Some of these Infs may refer instead to **1b, c,** or **d** below.] **1969** Longstreet *Birds FL* 44, *Mouse Hawk.* . . Numerous in the winter over marshes and meadows, fields, and prairies, of central and south Florida.

b =**rough-legged hawk.**

   1890 *Century Dict.* 3880, *Mouse-hawk.* . . The rough-legged bustard. . . [*Century* Ed: New Eng.] **1917** (1923) *Birds Amer.* 2.79, *Rough-legged Hawk.* . . *Other Names.* . . Mouse Hawk. . . When mice are abundant, one or two Rough-legs will hunt for weeks in the vicinity. **1944** Hausman *Amer. Birds* 517, Hawk, Mouse—see Hawk, Rough-legged; see also Hawk, Sparrow; also Hawk, Marsh. **1955** Forbush–May *Birds* 113, *Buteo lagopus s[ancti] johannis.* . . Mouse Hawk. [*Ibid* 114, It is now a well-known fact that the food of the American Rough-legged Hawk in the United States consists chiefly of field mice.]

c A **sparrow hawk** (here: *Falco sparverius*).

   1898 (1900) Davie *Nests N. Amer. Birds* 229, It [=*Falco sparverius*] may be seen hovering almost motionless in mid air, when suddenly swooping down to the ground, arises [sic] again with perhaps a field mouse in its talons. From this habit it receives the name of Mouse Hawk. **1904** Wheelock *Birds CA* 162, He [=*Falco sparverius*] is also called "Mouse Hawk" in some sections from his habit of preying on field mice. **1932** Bennitt *Check-list* 25 **MO,** Eastern sparrow hawk. . . Mouse hawk. . . C[ommon] W[inter] R[esident], central and southern Missouri.

1970 *DARE* (Qu. Q4, . . *Kinds of hawks*) Inf **KY**72, Mouse hawk—same as sparrow hawk.

d A **pigeon hawk** (here: *Falco columbarius*).

1946 Goodrich *Birds in KS* 316, Hawk, mouse . . [=] hawk, American, rough-legged . . hawk, eastern, pigeon . . hawk, marsh.

2 A **loggerhead shrike** (here: *Lanius ludovicianus migrans*). Cf **mouse bird**

1956 MA Audubon Soc. *Bulletin* 40.129, *Southern Shrike. . .* Mouse Hawk (Maine. As preying on mice.)

mouse in the meal See **mouse** n B4

mouse mole See **mole mouse 2**

mouse nut n Also *mouse food, mice nut* **AK**

A **cotton grass 1** (here: *Eriophorum angustifolium*) or its tuberous root.

1951 Schwalbe *Dayspring* 47 **AK,** Discarded fish bones were re-boiled with certain grassy roots while the caches of field mice were robbed of the small bulbs known as mice nuts. **1953** (1962) Heller *Wild Plants AK* 62, The underground stem [of the tall cottongrass] . . is collected in the autumn by tundra mice who cache them for winter use. . . The Eskimos call these underground stems "mouse nuts." Mousenuts taste a little sweet. **1975** *River Times* (Fairbanks AK) May 7 (Tabbert *Dict. Alaskan Engl.*), Mouse nuts are the roots of tundra plants. Sometimes the winter root cache of the mouse is found and used. When the people find it, they replace it with dried meat or fat for the mouse had gathered these 'nuts' for the winter. **1980** *Ak'a Tamaani* (Togiak high-school publication) 2 (Tabbert *Dict. Alaskan Engl.*), One other food the Eskimos used to eat as a regular part of their fall diet was mouse food. . . The mouse food is raindrop shaped, tan-colored, and small. It is greenish-yellow after you peel it. It tastes sweet and nutty.

mouse owl n
=**saw-whet owl.**

1946 Hausman *Eastern Birds* 365, Saw-whet Owl. . . *Other Names* . . Mouse Owl. . . Our smallest owl, not more than an inch or so longer than a Bluebird, though its fluffy feathers make it appear larger. **1986** Pederson *LAGS Concordance*, 1 inf, **cwMS,** Mouse owl—smaller than screech owl.

mouser n[1] See **mouse hawk 1a**

mouser n[2] See **mouse** n B1

mouse rail n

The black **rail** (*Laterallus jamaicensis*).

1923 U.S. Dept. Ag. *Misc. Circular* 13.44, *Black Rail.* . . Called also California black rail and mouse rail, the latter name said to be in local use in California.

mouse room n Also *mouse shed* [See quot]

A small attic or storage space.

1968–69 *DARE* (Qu. D4, *The space up under the roof, usually used for storing things*) Inf **WI**5, Mouse room—very old, used when she was a girl; (Qu. D7, *A small space anywhere in a house where you can hide things or get them out of the way*) Inf **IL**53, Mouse shed, my Dutch cousin calls her tiny attic, just a stowaway place; this is a literal translation of the Dutch term "muizehok" ['maɪzə,hɑk].

mouse-root n Cf **mouse nut**

A **wood lily** (here: *Lilium philadelphicum*).

1940 Clute *Amer. Plant Names* 12, *L[ilium] Philadelphicum. . .* Mouse-root.

mouses See **mouse** n A2

mouse's ear See **mouse-ear 1a, 2**

mouse's ears See **mouse-ear 2**

mouse's foot n
=**club moss.**

1928 Pan-Pacific Research Inst. *Jrl.* 3.2.4 **HI,** Lycopodium, ground pine or "mouse's foot," . . extensively used as a Christmas decoration and for wreaths.

mouse shed See **mouse room**

mouse snake n

1 also *spotted mouse snake:* A **rat snake** (here: *Elaphe obsoleta*). **chiefly TX**

1928 Baylor Univ. Museum *Contrib.* 16.16 **TX,** *Elaphe laeta. . .* In

the San Antonio region, small examples are called *Mouse Snake* or *Spotted Mouse Snake.* **1967** *DARE* (Qu. P25, . . *Kinds of snakes*) Infs **TX**19, 42, Mouse snake; **TX**40, Mouse snake—eats mice. **1986** Pederson *LAGS Concordance*, 1 inf, **cTX,** Mouse snake.

2 A **garter snake 1** (here: *Thamnophis marcianus*).

1928 Baylor Univ. Museum *Contrib.* 16.18 **TX,** *Thamnophis marcianus.* . . In half a dozen or more Texas localities, I have heard the name *Mouse Snake* referred to this handsome species.

3 Prob a patch-nosed snake (*Salvadora* spp). Cf **striped mouse snake**

1966 *DARE* (Qu. P25, . . *Kinds of snakes*) Inf **NM**3, Mouse snake—small, black, striped.

mousetail n

A perennial plant *(Ivesia santolinoides)* native to California.

1925 Jepson *Manual Plants CA* 492, *P[otentilla] santolinoides. . . Mouse Tail.* . . Montane, 7200 to 10,000 ft.: Sierra Nevada . . ; San Gabriel Mts.; San Bernardino Mts.

mouse wren n [See quots 1955, 1977]
=**winter wren.**

1917 (1923) *Birds Amer.* 3.194, *Winter Wren. . . Other Names. . .* Mouse Wren. **1946** Hausman *Eastern Birds* 443, Mouse Wren. . . A tiny little wren . . with the shortest tail of all; a dark brown midget, often bobbing up and down as if on springs. **1955** *AmSp* 30.178 **MI,** *Mouse wren* for the winter wren . . refers to the brown color, small size, and elusive movements of this tiny bird. [**1977** Bull–Farrand *Audubon Field Guide Birds* 708, *Troglodytes troglodytes.* . . This wren moves like a mouse, creeping through the low, dense tangle of branches covering the forest floor.]

mousie n

1 also sp *mousee, moussie:* =**rat-tailed maggot. esp WI, MN**

1968 *DARE* (Qu. P6, . . *Kinds of worms . . used for bait*) Inf **MN**21, Mousies—a grayish-white larva . . looks like a mouse—has a tail; **MN**42, Mousie—the larva of a fly. **1969** *DARE* File **cwWI,** *Mousie*—type of fish bait advertised in LaCrosse, Wis. Larva of a syrphid fly, genus *Eristalis,* also called "rat-tailed maggot." **1972** Swan–Papp *Insects* 618, Those [=larvae] that breed in putrid or stagnant water and moist excrement have a long tail-like anal breathing tube with spiracle at the end, and are called "rat-tailed maggots" or "mousies." **1982** Sternberg *Fishing* 88, Mousees, or rat-tailed maggots, live in water, but the pale brown larvae breathe through a tail-like tube so they are considered land insects. **1987** *DARE* File **Madison WI,** Mousies—little grub with a tail on it; also plastic mousies—little jig [*DARE* Ed: from a bait shop]. *Ibid* **Madison WI,** Mousie—soft-bodied grub with a little tail on it, turns into a fly, found in corn silage, used in ice fishing [*DARE* Ed: from a bait shop]. *Ibid* **Madison WI,** Fishermen here all call it "mousie." I've also seen it spelled "moussie." A mousie is the larva of a syrphid fly, *Eristalis* spp, and is also called rattail maggot. It's widely distributed, but only called 'mousie' in ice-fishing areas around here, probably in the Midwest.

2 See **mouse** n B3.

moussie See **mousie 1**

mout v See **may** v Aa

mouth n, v Usu |mauθ|; also **chiefly Sth** chiefly among Black speakers |mauf, maut|; for addit varr see quots c1970, 1989 at **A** below Pronc-spp *mouf* (pl *mouv(e)s*), *mout;* similarly adj *moufy* Cf Pronc Intro 3.I.17
A Forms.

1867 Harris *Sut Lovingood Yarns* 24 **TN,** Thar's a heap ove whisky spilt twixt the counter an' the mouf. **1887** (1967) Harris *Free Joe* 179 **GA,** We'll wipe our mouves. **1893** Shands *MS Speech* 46, *Mouf* [mauf]. Negro for *mouth.* **1905** Chesnutt *Col.'s Dream* 149 **GA,** Den de black cat open his mouf an' showed 'is teef. **1909** *DN* 3.350 **eAL, wGA,** *Mouf.* . . Mouth: a negroism rapidly gaining ground among the whites, especially in the derivatives, as *mouffle* (mouthful). **1922** Gonzales *Black Border* 314 **sSC, GA coasts** [Gullah glossary], *Mout'*—mouth, mouths. **1928** Peterkin *Scarlet Sister Mary* 36 **SC** [Gullah], Shut you mout', gal, befo Gawd strikes you dead. **1929** Sale *Tree Named John* 39 **MS** [Black], Don' stan' dar wid yo' mouf wide op'm, *do* sump'm. *Ibid* 94, Hit's jes lak ole Mis' read out'n de Bible—"out'n de mouvs uv babes en sucklin's comes wisdom." **1937** (1977) Hurston *Their Eyes* 117 **FL** [Black], You gettin' too moufy, Janie. **1940** *Sat. Eve.*

Post 20 July 55 **Sth** [Black], I keep my mouf shut. **1942** *Ibid* 3 Oct 68 **seSC** [Gullah], En' out ob 'he mout' come fiah en' smoke. **1967–68** *DARE* (Qu. X22) Inf **MO**16, Starin' wid his mout wide open [Inf White]; (Qu. HH7a, *Someone who talks too much, or too loud: "He's an awful _____."*) Inf **LA**8, Moufy person; (Qu. HH7b, *Someone who talks too much, or too loud: "He's always _____."*) Inf **LA**8, Moufing [Inf Black]. **c1970** Pederson *Dial. Surv. Rural GA* **seGA** (Mouth), [For *mouth,* from 64 infs (32 Black, 32 White, some of whom had more than one pronc), there were 55 exx of proncs of the type [mauθ], 5 of the type [maut] (4 Black), 4 of the type [mau] (all Black), and 2 of the type [mauf] (both Black).] **1989** Pederson *LAGS Tech. Index* 262 **Gulf Region**, [For *mouth,* there are 776 exx of proncs of the type [mauθ, mauθ, məuθ], 35 of the type [mauf], 15 of the type [maut], 13 of the type [mau], and 4 of the type [maus].]

B As noun.

1 The characteristic voice of an individual hunting dog; in phr *give mouth* to bay. **chiefly S Midl**

1873 Harte *Poetical Wks.* 238, The watch-dog on the distant shore / Gives mouth, and all is still. **1934** (1970) Wilson *Backwoods Amer.* 106 **Ozarks,** The hunters . . do not ride after game. Instead they reckon to perpetuate the venerable sport by sitting about watch fires built high upon hilltops, listening to the yapping and baying of the trailing hounds, identifying the particular "mouth" of each dog. **1952** Brown *NC Folkl.* 1.567, *Mouth.* . . The voice, especially of a hunting dog. "That young dog o' mine's jest naturally got the best mouth I ever heard in a race." **1967** *DARE* Tape **LA**3, All the different mouths. . . Like just different instruments almost in a band. [**1970** *Natl. Geogr. Mag.* Nov 673 **csMO,** "That squawlin' dog's shore pretty, ain't she," declared George. . . "Yeah," agreed Deward. . . "She shore does be a mouth."] **a1975** Lunsford *It Used to Be* 164 **sAppalachians,** His dog has a good mouth. This is speaking of a fox hound. You say, "My dog's got the finest mouth in the whole pack." That means he's got the best voice or he's got an unusual mouth. **1982** Ginns *Snowbird Gravy* 137 **nwNC,** I could tell every one of my dogs. I don't care how many dogs was in that bunch, I could tell my dog's mouth, voice different from any of 'em. **1984** Wilder *You All Spoken Here* 58 **Sth,** *Pretty mouth, sweet mouth:* What a dog in good voice has when he opens, or bays, or begins to mouth on a hunt.

2 in phrr *have one's mouth set for (a particular food)* and varr: To anticipate, have an appetite for (that food).

1859 *Student and Schoolmate* 8.148 *(Mathews Coll.),* We lost the "mackerel steak" for which some of the excursionists had made up their mouths. **1890** *Century Dict.* 3587, *Make. . . To make up one's mouth for,* to expect with desire; have an appetite for: as, his *mouth* was *made up for* a chicken salad. [Colloq.] **1929** *AmSp* 5.129 **ME,** "My mouth was all made up for" whatever one greatly wanted and expected to eat. **1942** Warnick *Garrett Co. MD* 8 **nwMD** (as of 1900–18), *Have your mouth set for* . . pleasurably anticipate some especially palatable food. **1942** McAtee *Dial. Grant Co. IN* 43 (as of 1890s), *Mouth fixed, have one's* . . have an appetite for; "That's fine Sary, I had my _____ fer dumplin's"; often with "all" before *fixed.* **1960** Criswell *Resp. to PADS 20* **Ozarks,** Well, I had my mouth all set for some of that sweet potato pie, and then I couldn't get to the dinner.

3 in phrr *to put (one's) mouth on:* See quots. Cf **bad mouth** n **1**

1950 *PADS* 14.47 **SC,** *Mouth, mouf* [mauθ, mauf]. . . Bad luck; only in the phrase *to put mouf on,* to conjure, and cause to have bad luck. Implied is the pronunciation of some magic formula over a person, or against him. **1952** Brown *NC Folkl.* 1.567, *Mouth, to put (one's) _____ on (a person):* . . To curse one.—Chapel Hill.

C As verb.

1 To examine the teeth of (a horse or mule) to determine its age.

1914 *DN* 4.110 **cKS,** *Mouth.* . . To examine the mouth of (a horse). **1923** *DN* 5.215 **swMO. 1944** Wellman *Bowl* 170 **KS** (as of 1880s), I mouthed 'em [=mules] awhile back. Ten years old, mebbe eleven. **1967** Green *Horse Tradin'* 249 **TX,** I still didn't get a chance to mouth that preacher's mare to see how old she was.

2 also with *off:* To argue or quarrel; with *against, on:* to attack (someone) orally; hence vbl n *mouthing.*

1917 in 1944 *ADD* **sWV,** *Mouth.* . . To quarrel. . . [*ADD* Ed: They] mouthed. **1957** Parris *My Mountains* 174 **cwNC,** It all started over somethin' that had got 'em to mouthin' against each other. **1962** *Mt. Life* 38.4.11 **sAppalachians,** The mildest sort of quarrel, terminating in nothing more serious than one of the antagonists "runnin' out his jaw" at the other because of a "floutin'," is called a "mouthin'." **1967–70**

DARE (Qu. KK13, . . *Arguing:* "They stood there for an hour _____.") Infs **MO**25, **NY**234, Mouthing off; **MO**30, Mouthed on each other; (Qu. Y12a, *A fight between two people, mostly with words*) Infs **HI**9, **OH**82, Mouthing.

3 Of a hunting dog: to bay during the hunt.

1984 [see **B1** above].

mouth against See **mouth C2**

mouth battle n Also *mouth contest,* ~ *fight,* ~ *lashing* Cf **tongue fight**

An argument, verbal fight.

1966–68 *DARE* (Qu. Y12a, *A fight between two people, mostly with words*) Infs **MO**36, **PA**142, 148, 152, Mouth battle; **NE**11, Mouth contest; **MS**6, **MO**25, Mouth fight; **MD**21, Mouth lashing. **1967** *DARE* FW Addit **sePA,** I mostly get into mouth battles.

mouth-bound adj

Tongue-tied.

1966 *DARE* (Qu. HH25, *One who never has anything to say: "What's the matter with him? _____?"*) Inf **MA**6, Mouth-bound.

mouth bow n Also called **Jew's harp B4, music bow, song bow, tune bow**

A simple musical instrument consisting of a string or wire stretched on a wooden bow, which is held near the mouth while the string is plucked and the resulting sound is modified by varying the size of the oral cavity.

1978 Wolfe *I'm On My Journey Home* 3 **Ozarks,** The mouthbow is an ancient instrument that looks something like an Indian bow and works on a principle similar to that of the jew's-harp. One end of the bow is placed against the cheek, and the string is plucked. The player obtains pitches by varying the size and shape of the cavity of the open mouth. Though known to both Anglo- and Afro-American traditions, the mouthbow has been popularized in recent years. . . [Charlie] Everidge recalls that such bows were often played at square dances in the Ozarks in the teens and twenties. **1979** Irwin *Musical Instruments* 59 **eTN,** As a child I remember sitting on the front porch of the home of our next door neighbor . . listening to him play the mouth bow. . . The instrument consisted of a simple bow. . . It was made of red cedar and the "string" was a tiny wire which he unraveled from a piece of door screen. He played it by placing one end of the bow against a firm lower lip and by plucking the string with a rigid finger. The rhythm was acquired by the plucking, and the variation or [sic] the pitch was obtained by increasing or decreasing the mouth cavity in much the same manner as when playing the Jews Harp.

mouth contest, mouth fight See **mouth battle**

mouth glad adj phr

Pretending to be pleased; insincere.

1934 Hurston *Jonah's Gourd Vine* 175 **AL** [Black], "Glad tuh see me, Lucy?" " 'Course, John." "Is you only mouf glad or yuh sho' nuff glad?"

mouth harp n

1 A harmonica. **scattered, but less freq NEast, W Midl** See Map and Map Section Cf **French harp 1, harp 1, mouth organ 1**

1903 Ade *In Babel* 40 **neIL,** I'd walked from Loueyville over to Terry Hut with a nigger that played the mouth-harp. **1913** Johnson *Highways St. Lawrence to VA* 337 **WV,** He produced a guitar and tuned it, put

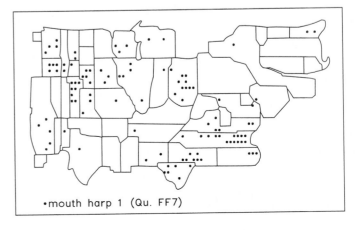

•mouth harp 1 (Qu. FF7)

around his neck a wire so bent as to hold a "mouth-harp" before his face, and then played me various tunes. **1914** *DN* 4.160 **cVA,** *Mouth-harp.* . . Mouth-organ, harmonica. **1926** Roberts *Time of Man* 255 **cKY,** He played tune after tune on the mouth harp, shaking his spittle from it from time to time. **1937** Sandoz *Slogum* 56 **NE,** A slim-hipped young cowpuncher who could play the mouth harp fine. **1962** Fox *Southern Fried* 37 **SC,** He'd play . . songs with . . a lot of sucking noises on the mouth harp. **1965–70** *DARE* (Qu. FF7, *A small musical instrument that you blow on, and move from side to side in your mouth*) 109 Infs, **scattered, but less freq NEast, W Midl,** Mouth harp. **c1970** Pederson *Dial. Surv. Rural GA* **seGA** (*A small musical instrument that you hold up to your mouth and blow on*) 11 [of 64] infs, Mouth harp.

2 A Jew's harp. Cf **harp 2, mouth organ 2**

1965–70 *DARE* (Qu. FF8, . . *Small instrument that you hold between the teeth and pluck on*) 21 Infs, **scattered,** Mouth harp.

3 See quot. [Cf *harp* to repeat an idea with tiresome frequency]

1970 *DARE* (Qu. HH7a, *Someone who talks too much, or too loud: "He's an awful _____."*) Inf **VA46,** Mouth harp [FW: used by Inf in conv].

mouthing See **mouth C2**

mouth lashing See **mouth battle**

mouth off, mouth on See **mouth C2**

mouth organ n

1 A harmonica. **widespread, but chiefly Inland Nth, C Atl; also S Atl, SW** See Map and Map Section Cf **mouth harp 1**

1866 in 1872 Locke *Struggles Nasby* 314 **OH,** He wuz . . playin "Hail to the Chief!" on a mouth organ. **1905** *DN* 3.88 **nwAR. 1912** *DN* 3.568 **cNY. 1916** *DN* 4.347 **neTX, PA. 1938** Rawlings *Yearling* 111 **nFL,** I reckon the mouth organ's wuth more'n a dime. **1946** *Reader's Digest* Mar 142 **cnOK,** A man in a decrepit spring wagon, driving a 17-year-old horse and playing a mouth organ, rode through a line of vigilantes. **1955** *PADS* 23.45 **e,cSC, eNC, seGA,** Mouth organ 'harmonica' (also Northern, North Midland). **1965–70** *DARE* (Qu. FF7, *A small musical instrument that you blow on, and move from side to side in your mouth*) 344 Infs, **chiefly Inland Nth, N Midl, SC, scattered West,** Mouth organ. **c1970** Pederson *Dial. Surv. Rural GA* **seGA** (*A small musical instrument that you hold up to your mouth and blow on*) 21 [of 64] infs, Mouth organ. **1991** Pederson *LAGS Regional Pattern* 320, *Atlantic Coast [Pattern] 3.* . . mouth organ [=harmonica]. [*DARE* Ed: The map shows *mouth organ* to be esp freq in **FL, sGA, seLA.**]

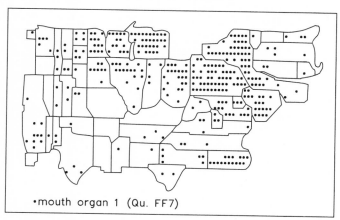

•mouth organ 1 (Qu. FF7)

2 A Jew's harp.

1968–69 *DARE* (Qu. FF8, . . *Small instrument that you hold between the teeth and pluck on*) Inf **CA142,** Mouth organ [Inf queries resp]; **NY55,** Mouth organ. **1986** Pederson *LAGS Concordance (Jew's harp)* 1 inf, **cGA,** Mouth organ; 1 inf, **seFL,** Mouth organ or mouth harp—was mountain term; 1 inf, **csTN,** Mouth organ = juice harp—unsure; 1 inf, **neMS,** Mouth organ [inf queries].

mouthroot n [See quot 1784]

A **goldthread 1** (here: *Coptis trifolia*).

1784 in 1785 Amer. Acad. Arts & Sci. *Memoirs* 1.457, Mouth Root. . . The Roots are astringent, and of a bitterish taste. Chewed in the mouth they cure apthas [sic] and cankerous sores. It is frequently an ingredient in gargles for sore throats. **1854** King *Amer. Eclectic Dispensatory* 399,

Coptis trifolia. Gold Thread. . . This plant, also termed *Mouthroot,* has a small and creeping, perennial root, of a bright-yellow color. [*Ibid* 400, Goldthread. . . is decidedly efficacious, as a wash or gargle, when in decoction, in aphthous and other ulcerations of the mouth.] **1910** Graves *Flowering Plants* 191 **CT,** Mouth-root. . . The roots have been much used as a bitter tonic and in the form of an infusion as an astringent wash. **1930** Sievers *Amer. Med. Plants* 32, Mouth root. . . In reasonably constant demand. **1969** GA Dept. Ag. *Farmers Market Bulletin* 23 Sept 8/1 **GA,** Goldthread or mouthroot . . is a decorative little plant that abundantly carpets the northern bogs and extends southward over the mountains. **1974** (1977) Coon *Useful Plants* 220, Mouthroot. . . A New York State mother has written me that it is very valuable for "baby's sore mouth." A good little plant to know about.

mouthwort n

A **cow parsnip 1** (here: *Heracleum lanatum*).

1974 (1977) Coon *Useful Plants* 259, *Heracleum lanatum* . . mouth-wort. . . The young growth is said to be edible and with an aromatic and sweetish flavor, and is noted as one of the food plants of the Indians.

mouty See **moughty**

mouv(e)s See **mouth**

move night See **moving night**

mover n See **mother** n[1]

move-up n Also *move-up base(ball), ~ piggy, movings up* **esp Ohio Valley, NEast** See Map Cf **piggy move-up, work-up**

Any of var bat-and-ball games; see quots.

1932 Farrell *Young Lonigan* 199 **Chicago IL** (as of 1916), Some young punks . . came around. Joe got the ball and bat from the instructor's office, and they played move-up piggy. **1953** Brewster *Amer. Nonsinging Games* 81 **AL,** Move-Up. . . The usual number of players . . is twelve. To start the game, there must be three batters. The rest of the players are placed in the field just as in baseball. . . There is, however, only one team, which alternates in fielding and batting. . . Each batter continues until he is put out. When one batter has been put out, each player moves up one position. . . The batter who has been put out goes to the bottom, . . from which position he has to work up before he can bat again. **1965–70** *DARE* (Qu. EE11, *Bat-and-ball games for just a few players [when there aren't enough for a regular game]*) Infs **IN49, KY11, MO35, OH87, TX30,** Move-up; **CT16,** Move-up—all but batter in field, rotate through positions; **IL76, NJ13,** Move-up base(ball); **PA1, 49,** Movings up. **1965** *DARE* File **ceMO** (as of c1930), Move-up. . . Elementary baseball game for a few players; the batter runs to first base (the only one) and back to make a run. Fly balls caught or the ball thrown to home base put batter out. No strikes counted. Players "move up" to get turns at bat.

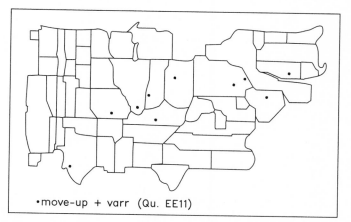

•move-up + varr (Qu. EE11)

moving day n Also *moving time* **esp NY, PA** Cf **flitting 1**

A day on which leases typically expire, causing many people to change residences at the same time.

1828 Paulding *New Mirror* 74 **NYC,** "The first of May, what of the first of May?" " 'Tis moving time." "Moving time! what is that?" "The time when every body moves." **1832** Watson *Hist. Tales NY* 123 **NYC,** "Moving day" was, as now, the first of May, from time immemorial. **1841** *S. Lit. Messenger* 7.661 **NY,** A sudden light bursts upon me! 'tis "moving day"—the dreaded "first of May!" [**1849** (1857) Irving *Hist. NY* 121, This memorable migration [from Communipaw to Manhattan] took place on the first of May, and was long cited in tradition as the *grand moving.* The anniversary of it was piously observed . . by turning their houses topsy-turvy and carrying all the furniture through the streets . . ; and this is the real origin of the universal agitation and "moving" by which this most restless of cities is literally turned out of doors on every May day.] **1855** *Knickerbocker* 45.585, In the southern part of New-Jersey, one who rents or purchases a house or farm usually takes possession . . on the twenty-fifth day of the present month [=March], which is therefore denominated 'moving-day.' [**1859** (1968) Bartlett *Americanisms* 282, *To Move.* . . In the city of New York, it is the custom to hire houses by the year from the first day of May; and as many, especially of the poorer class, remove every year or two, an immense deal of puss-in-the-corner playing takes place on that day.] **1865** Crockett *Life* 188 **NYC,** "Everybody appears to be pitching out their furniture, and packing it off." He laughed, and said this was the general "moving day." Such a sight nobody ever saw unless it was in this same city. It seeemed a kind of frolic, as if they were changing houses just for fun. **1873** in 1983 *PADS* 70.43 **ce,sePA,** Moving time has again returned and by the amount of teams that has passed through Johnsville today it seems as though a great many persons would lodge that night at their new homes. **1910** *Nation* 22 Sept 259, One of the inalienable rights of the free American is the privilege of insuring his domestic tranquility by leaving a domicile before it has become too familiar. An annual moving day fits nicely into our practice of the restless life. *Ibid,* A September Labor Day on which no manual labor is performed is less characteristic of us than our October moving day, . . not without its realistic exhibits and its impressive parade. **1968** *DARE* FW Addit **PA**169, Moving day—April 1. **1983** *PADS* 70.43 **ce,sePA,** *Moving time.* . . April 1 was the day that tenants and farm hands moved to new locations.

moving kitchen furniture See **kitchen furniture**

moving night n Also *move night* esp Baltimore **MD** =**mischief night.**

1935 *Sun* (Baltimore MD) 29 Oct 4/2 (*Hench Coll.*), Tomorrow, they [=schoolchildren] will observe "moving night," to the woes of housekeepers. Everything that is movable—from a back gate to a flower pot—will be in danger of being transported to a neighboring yard. **1941** *Ibid* 31 Oct 8/3 (*Hench Coll.*), [Headline:] *Police Kept Busy For Halloween* [Subhead:] *Gates, Ashcans, Steps Take Flight As "Move Night" Celebrators Call.* . . On "move night" Junior's imagination—and energy—is boundless, it seems. . . [T]he Police Department . . can attest to that. Soaped windows, disappearing back gates and front steps, doorbell ringing, and upset, torn-down or smashed everything(s) kept them on the jump. That was last night. **1992** *DARE* File **Baltimore MD** (as of c1920), The night before Halloween was called *moving night.* Children roamed the neighborhood for an hour or two after supper looking for porch furniture and other portable objects. Those that we found we carried off and deposited on porches or in yards several doors away or even in the next block.

movings up See **move-up**

moving time See **moving day**

mow n[1] Usu |mau|; occas |mo| (see quot 1965–70 at **2** below) Also, by folk-etym, *mound, mown;* freq in comb *haymow*

1 A heap of hay, straw, or unthreshed grain in a field or barn. Note: Only quots in which *mow* refers unambiguously to the heap itself rather than the space enclosing it are included here; see note at **2** below. [*OED mow* sb. 1 c725 →; *haymow* 1483 →]

1695 in 1878 MA Hist. Soc. *Coll.* 5th ser 5.398 **ceMA,** An undermined Mow in the Barn . . fell upon him and kill'd him. **1838** (1932) Hawthorne *Amer. Notebooks* 68, Fields of grass beyond, where stood the hay-mows of last year. **1893** Frederic *Copperhead* 143 **nNY,** I stumbled clumsily once I was inside the barn, and sat down with great abruptness on a milking-stool, leaning my head back against the hay-mow. **1939** [see **2** below]. **1949** Kurath [see **2** below]. **c1960** *Wilson Coll.* **IL,** *Haymound*—A pile of hay, a hayshock or haystack. Heard only once. **1961** *AmSp* 36.267 **CO,** *Hay mow* . . may mean both 'hay loft' and 'hay stack' in Colorado. It even appears twice as *hay mown,* in which its association with *mound* (itself often pronounced [maun]) will perhaps reinforce its reference to a hay stack, the only meaning of the *mown* form. **1965–70** *DARE* (Qu. L14, *A large pile of hay stored outdoors*) 13 Infs, **esp Gt Lakes,** (Hay)mow; **NC**80, Mound of hay; **DE**3, Mow of hay; **FL**22, **NY**36, (Hay)mound; (Qu. L12, . . *The small piles of hay standing in the field*) Infs **IL**73, **MO**25, **NE**11, **NY**216, **PA**246, **WV**5,

(Hay)mounds; **AR**52, **IN**45, **WA**14, (Hay)mows. **1966** Dakin *Dial. Vocab. Ohio R. Valley* 2.74, Several other terms for hay stacks were each used once: *hay mound* (Washington Cty., O.); . . *haymow* (Hickman Cty., Ky.) **1973** Allen *LAUM* 1.185 **Upper MW** (as of c1950), *Haystack.* . . *haymow* [1 inf]. *Ibid* 186, *Haycock.* . . *mound* [3 infs]. . . *hay mound* [2 infs].

2 also in combs *grain mow, straw ~, wheat ~:* An enclosed area for storing hay, etc, usu a bay or loft in a barn. Note: The line between this and the previous sense is not sharp; see especially the comments in quot 1939. [*OED mow* sb. 2 1755 →] chiefly **Nth, N Midl, West** See Map Cf **loft** n 1

1825 Neal *Brother Jonathan* 1.156 **CT,** Feller like you—don't know a pitch-pine hay-mow from a sugar maple-tree. **1847** in 1870 Drake *Pioneer Life* 66 **KY,** We had no barn or mow, and both wheat and hay were stacked out. **1850** Judd *Richard Edney* 113 **MA,** There came . . to his mind, his own barn-yard, and stable, and hay-mow. **1887** Eggleston *Graysons* 182 **cIL,** The people jostled one another closely upon the wide threshing-floor, and the wheat-mow alongside contained . . at least twenty women whose appetite for the horrible had led them to elbow their way early to this commanding situation. The hay-mow at the other end of the floor was full of men and boys. *Ibid* 183, Other curious people had crowded into the horse stables below the wheat-mow. **1937** *AmSp* 12.102 **eNE,** The barn has a *hay mow,* rarely called a hay loft, above, and a stable below. **1939** *LANE* Map 103 (*Mow, bay*) **NEng,** *Mow* usually refers to the section or compartment together with the hay stored in it . . , but it may refer to the hay alone . . or to the compartment alone. [Some typical comments: "*bay,* an empty *mow*"; "The *bay* is the place for the *mow*"; "When the bays get about half full, they call it a *mow*"; "The hay is in the *mow*" but *go up on the mow*"; "*hay mow,* any space filled with hay"; "*grain mow,* of unthrashed grain"; "*mow,* the hay in the barn"; "*mow,* a bent filled with hay."] **1949** Kurath *Word Geog.* 54, In the North Midland, in the Shenandoah Valley, and in West Virginia north of the Kanawha *(hay) mow* is in general use for the upper floor of a hay barn, and this expression is current also in New York State and to some extent in northwestern New England. . . [I]n some sections the term *(hay) mow* is also extensively applied to any stack of hay in the barn, whether it rests on the barn floor or on a raised platform. **1949** *WELS Suppl.* **seWI,** In this area the word "haymow" is used exclusively for the "hayloft" in a barn. **1950** *WELS* WI *(The upper part under the roof of a barn)* 13 Infs, Haymow; 7 Infs, Mow; 1 Inf, Mow—begins from the ground; *(The place for storing hay in a barn)* 31 Infs, Haymow; 18 Infs, Mow; 1 Inf, Haymow—may go clear to ground. **1965–70** *DARE* (Qu. M3, *The place inside a barn for storing hay*) 460 Infs, **chiefly Nth, N Midl, West,** (Hay)mow; **NY**96, Mows; **MD**22, **PA**137, Straw mow; **MO**21, Haymound; **IN**3, Haymow; (Qu. M12, *What do you keep food for the cattle in over winter?*) 52 Infs, **chiefly Nth, N Midl,** (Hay)mow; **IA**1, Mow for hay; **NH**16, **OR**7, **PA**129, Mows; **NY**140, Haymound; (Qu. L15, *When you are putting hay into a building for storage . . you are _____*) Infs **MA**40, **NY**92, 213, **PA**92, **WI**68, **WY**1, Filling the (hay)mow; **CO**47, **MA**55, **NY**75, Putting it in the (hay)mow; **CO**12, Put it in the mow; **VA**24, Putting hay up in mow; **NY**219, Storing hay in the mow; (Qu. M6, *The place where grain is kept in a barn*) Inf **NY**209, Haymow; **ME**12, Mow. [Of 89 Infs for whom proncs were recorded, 78 gave proncs of the type [mau], 14, **chiefly nS Midl,** of the type [mo].] **1973** Allen *LAUM* 1.183 **Upper MW** (as of c1950), The two common designations for the second story area are *(hay)loft* and *(hay)mow.* Their distribution weight reflects the dominance of *loft* in New England and the dominance of *mow* in the

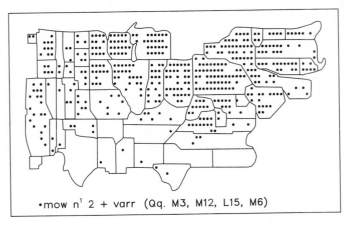

•mow n[1] 2 + varr (Qq. M3, M12, L15, M6)

North Midland, although both terms are so common in the U[pper] M[idwest] that only percentages are indicative. [Percentages show *hay-mow* slightly commoner than *hayloft* in **NE, IA**; slightly less common in **ND, SD, MN**.] *Ibid* 184, [Individual comments:] *Haymow:* Name for loft when full. **1983** *MJLF* 9.1.42 **ceKY** (as of 1956), *Hay mow . . a place for storing hay in a barn.* **1988** *WI State Jrl.* (Madison) 8 Feb sec 3 1/1, *The haymow was a fearsome place. . . I had a vague idea of constructing another hidey-hole for the cats. A cave, sort of, in the hay and chaff laying all over the mow.*

3 See quot. Cf **loft** n 3

 1968 *DARE* (Qu. D40, *Names and nicknames . . for the upper balcony in a theater*) Inf **MN38**, Haymow.

mow v, hence vbl n *mowing* Usu |maʊ|; for varr see quot 1965–70 Also with *back, off, up* Also, by folk-etym, *mound, mown* **chiefly Nth, N Midl** See Map Cf **loft** v

 To stack (hay, etc) into a **mow** n¹ **2**; to store hay.
 1811 (1898) Hunt *Diary* 19 **PA**, Another man was mowed up in Jams Bones's Barn and not found till the smell became offencive. **1849** Howitt *Our Cousins in OH* 208, Besides these apple-butter frolics, there were in that part what were called "husking frolics," and "quilting frolics," and "mowing frolics"—when all the neighbors assembled to help one another, and thus the work went on much more rapidly and pleasantly. **1914** *DN* 4.154 **NH**, Mow. . . To put away hay in the barn from the waggon. **1939** *LANE* Map 103 *(Mow, bay)* 1 inf, **seCT**, The bay is the place where you mow the hay. You mow it off and stomp it down; 1 inf, **RI**, Mowing [maʊɪn] hay; 1 inf, **cMA**, We mowed [maod] the hay. **1965–70** *DARE* (Qu. L15, *When you are putting hay into a building for storage . . you are* _____) 141 Infs, **chiefly Nth, N Midl**, Mowing (hay); **NY226, VA33, WA31**, [ˈmɔɪn] hay; **PA187**, [ˈmɔʊɪn] hay; **PA71**, [ˈmɒɪn] hay; **IL114**, [ˈmoʊwɪn] hay; **WA4**, [ˈmɑrɪn]; 11 Infs, **scattered Nth, N Midl**, Mowing it; **CT26, 32, DC8**, Mow; **IL65**, Mowing the hay; 11 Infs, **chiefly NJ, NY, PA**, Mowing up (hay); **CT7, SD1**, Mowing it back; **MN7**, Mowning [ˈmɔwnɪn] hay; **MO15**, Mounding the hay. [Unless otherwise noted, proncs given were of the type [ˈmaʊ(ɪn)].]

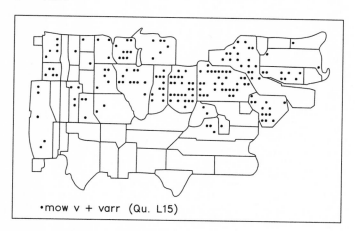

•mow v + varr (Qu. L15)

mow n² See **mowing** n attrib

mow n³ [*OED mow* sb.² 1.a "A grimace; esp., a derisive grimace" c1325 →; 1.b "In phrases . . *mocks and mows, mows and mocks*" 1508–1681] Cf **mowy-mouthed**
 1899 (1912) Green *VA Folk-Speech* 290, Mow. . . An insulting grimace; a mock.

mow away v phr **chiefly NEng, NY, Gt Lakes** See Map =**mow** v.
 1917 *DN* 4.396 **nwOH, NY, NEng, KS**, Mow away [maʊəwe]. . . Stow away hay or grain in the mow. "I pitched off the load and Sam mowed it away." "I've been mowing away all day." *Mow away* is the usual term, not *mow;* moreover, it refers to stowing away, tramping down, not to unloading from the wagon. **1939** *LANE* Map 103 *(Mow, bay)* 1 inf, **ceCT**, Mowing [mɛʊɪn] the hay away up in the ridge. **1965–70** *DARE* (Qu. L15, *When you are putting hay into a building for storage . . you are* _____) 40 Infs, **chiefly NEng, Upstate NY**, Mow(ing) it away; **CT4, MI27, 71, NY209, OH10, RI2, 8, VT12**, Mowing away (hay). **1968** *DARE* FW Addit **cnNY**, Mow [maʊ] the hay away = to store hay in a building.

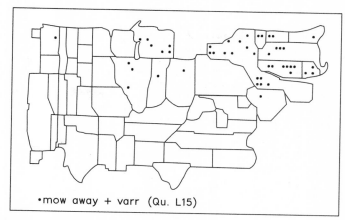

•mow away + varr (Qu. L15)

mow back See **mow** v

mowboard See **moldboard** n¹

mow chute See **mow hole**

mower v [*mower* n]
 To mow, cut (grass).
 1965 *DARE* FW Addit **OK13**, I can't hardly get my lawn mowered.

mower blade See **mowing blade**

mowerboard See **moldboard** n¹

mow hay v phr [Prob *mow* to cut] *joc*
 To snore.
 1970 *DARE* (Qu. X45, . . *Joking expressions . . about snoring*) Inf **CA208**, Mowing hay, sawing wood.

mow hole n Also *mow chute* [**mow** n¹ **2**] **esp Appalachians, PA, NJ** See Map Cf **hay hole 1**
 An opening in the floor of a hayloft for throwing down hay.
 1965–70 *DARE* (Qu. M5, . . *The hole for throwing hay down below*) 13 Infs, **esp Appalachians, PA, NJ**, Mow hole; **NJ50**, Mow chute.

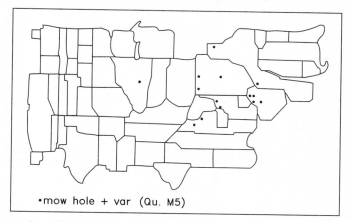

•mow hole + var (Qu. M5)

mowich See **mowitch**

mowing n attrib |ˈmoʊɪn| Also *mow* **chiefly NEng** See Map on p. 702
 Usu of a piece of land: used or suitable for raising a hay crop; hence n *mowing* a hayfield.
 1634 in 1896 Cambridge MA Proprietors *Records* 1 **ceMA**, The Constable . . shall make a surueyinge of the Houses backsids Corne ffeilds Moweing Grounds and other lands. **1663** in 1850 CT (Colony) *Pub. Rec.* 1.402 **cCT**, They are to improue the mowing land as formerly. **1741** in 1915 NH *Prov. & State Papers* 3.71, One Peice [sic] of Woodland . . with about an Acre of mowing. **1800** in 1846 MA Hist. Soc. *Coll.* 1st ser 7.245 **seNH**, [The Isles of Shoals] lie in common, except a few small inclosures for gardens and mowing ground. **1840** (1940) Arnold *Diaries* 147 **VT**, 3 cows of Mr. Stoddards began to go in my mowing lot. **1845** Judd *Margaret* 214 **NEng**, Alders and willows . . yet flourished in their best mow-lands. *Ibid* 325, They let me take the Colt; I kept him here in the mow-lot, made considerable of him, groomed him. **1874** VT State Bd. Ag. *Rept. for 1873–74* 2.206, He thought the American custom of robbing the pasture to enrich the

mowing a ruinous policy. *Ibid* 411, The breeding of wrinkled sheep is like a farmer who ridges up his level mow-land and seeds the ridges with an inferior grass. **1937** Crane *Let Me Show You VT* 33 **VT,** On the west side of our mountains a meadow is a meadow (or a medder), but on the east side a meadow is a mowin'. **1959** *VT Hist.* 27.149, *Mowing* ['mowɪŋ] ['mo·ɪn]. . . A hayfield; a meadow. Common. **1965–70** *DARE* (Qu. L7, *A piece of land with a hay crop planted on it*) Infs **MA**37, 25, 66, Mowing; **CT**24, Mowing field; **NJ**56, Mowing grass; **MA**5, **VA**14, Mowing land; **CT**29, **RI**12, Mowing lot; (Qu. L8, *Hay that grows naturally in damp places*) Inf **CT**26, Natural mowing—land that's seeded by nature and keeps on coming. [All Infs old] **1967** *DARE* Tape **VT**1, [FW:] Did you always call the place where the hay grew a hayfield? [Inf:] Hayfield, yes, a mowing ['mouɪ^n]. **1968** *Yankee* Oct 70 **NEng,** He looked over the mowings, orchards, and homestead, to the hills. **1992** Phelps *Famous Last Words* 4 **NEng,** There was a large brook crossing the farm in the back mowing.

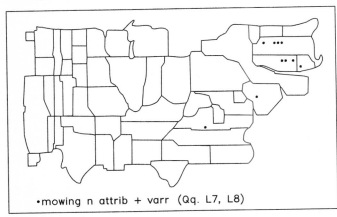

•mowing n attrib + varr (Qq. L7, L8)

mowing vbl n See **mow** v

mowing blade n Also *mower blade, mowing scythe* [**blade 3**] **chiefly S Midl, esp sAppalachians** See Map
   A tool used to cut vegetation (as grass, weeds, grain).
   1779 in 1906 *Documents Revol. Hist. NJ* 3.478 **cnNJ,** For sale, . . a few dozen of mowing scythes. **1902** *DN* 2.239 **sIL,** Mowing-blade. . . A scythe. **1903** *DN* 2.321 **seMO,** Mowing-blade. **1906** *DN* 3.121 **sIN,** *Mowin blade.* **1907** *DN* 3.233 **nwAR,** *Mowing-blade.* **1915** *DN* 4.186 **swVA,** *Mowing-blade.* **1917** *DN* 4.415 **wNC, KY,** *Mowin' blade.* **c1960** *Wilson Coll.* **csKY,** *Mowing-blade.* . . A briar-hook; a long handled scythe used to cut briars and small bushes. **1965–70** *DARE* (Qu. L37, *A hand tool used for cutting weeds and grass*) 12 Infs, **chiefly S Midl, esp eKY,** Mowing blade; 12 Infs, **chiefly S Midl,** Mowing scythe; **MO**25, Mowing sy; **TN**10, Mowing syes; **SC**30, Mower blade; (Qu. L28, *Tools used in the past for cutting grain*) Infs **KY**34, 39, 46, **NC**48, **SC**39, Mowing blade; **IN**35, **OK**18, Mowing scythe; (Qu. L35, *Hand tools used for cutting underbrush and digging out roots*) Infs **KY**29, **NC**48, Mowing blade; **DE**3, Mowing scythe. **1983** *MJLF* 9.1.48 **ceKY,** *Mowing scythe.*

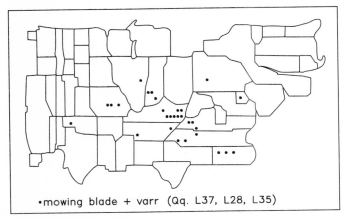

•mowing blade + varr (Qq. L37, L28, L35)

mowitch n Also sp *mowich* [Chinook Jargon]
   1 Venison.
      1958 McCulloch *Woods Words* 119 **Pacific NW,** *Mowich*—Venison.

1968 *DARE* (Qu. P35a, *Names or nicknames for any deer shot illegally*) Inf **AK**1, Side-hill halibut, mowitch ['mauɪč]—Chinook Jargon. [**1970** Thomas *Chinook* 88, *Mow'-itch.* . . A deer, venison.]
   2 A **kittentails** (here: *Synthyris reniformis*).
      1934 Haskin *Wild Flowers Pacific Coast* 323, They [=*Synthyris rotundifolia*] are also called dolly-flowers, and mowich, the latter being an Indian word for deer.

mown n See **mow** n[1]

mown v, **mow off** See **mow** v

mowt See **may** v **Aa**

mow the mustard v phr
   To act self-important or arrogant.
      1967 *DARE* (Qu. GG19a, *When you can see from the way a person acts that he's feeling important or independent: "He surely is _____ these days."*) Inf **CO**21, High and mighty, uppity, mowing the mustard.

mow up See **mow** v

mowy-mouthed adj Also sp *mauey-mouthed* [Prob **mow** n[3]]
   1936 *AmSp* 11.191 **swWY,** *Mauey, mowy* (spelling?). Characterizing speech that is rambling, indefinite, mumbling, evasive. 'You don't know what he says, he's so mauey-mouthed.'

moxa See **moxie 1**

moxey See **moxie 2**

moxie n [Perh < Algonquian base *maski-* (or var) "medicine"; see 1995 *Dictionaries* 16.208–11]
   1 also *moxa, moxie berry, ~ plum, ~ vine:* A **wintergreen** (here: *Gaultheria hispidula*). **ME**
      1894 *Jrl. Amer. Folkl.* 7.93, *Chiogenes serpyllifolia* . . running birch, Vt. [M]oxie berry, Penobscot Co., Me. **1897** *Ibid* 10.49, *Chiogenes serpyllifolia,* . . Moxa or Moxie, Paris and Dixfield, Me. **1907** *DN* 3.247 **eME,** *Moxie.* . . A trailing plant which covers the ground with a thick mat of little leaves. **1916** *Torreya* 16.239, *Chiogenes hispidula.* . . Moxie vine, Matinicus Id., Me. **1924** *Amer. Botanist* 30.56, "Moxie-berry" and "moxie-plum". . . we suspect . . to be of Indian origin. **1943** Fernald–Kinsey *Edible Wild Plants E. N. Amer.* 311, The *Moxie-plum,* as it is called in Maine, . . rarely fruits in abundance in the southern part of its range. . . Eaten fresh the berries are pleasantly acid, with a mild suggestion of checkerberry, but when eaten with cream and sugar they are one of the greatest delicacies of the northern woods.
   2 also sp *moxey:* Energy, initiative; strength, know-how; courage, nerve. [*Moxie* trademark (1924) for a soft drink, modeled after *Moxie* a patent medicine developed c1880 (perh containing **moxie 1**) that was once advertised as a "nerve food"] **chiefly Nth, esp NEast** See Map
      1930 *Collier's* 20 Dec 32 **NYC,** Personally, I always figure Louie a petty-larceny kind of guy, with no more moxie than a canary bird. **1943** Shulman *Barefoot Boy* 158 **MN,** We knew you had the old moxie, the old get out and get. **1955** *PADS* 24.94, If he [=a pickpocket] admits his own limitations, he loses his nerve *(blows his moxie)* and will eventually find it impossible to work. **1957** *Eaton Coll.* **Milwaukee WI,** *Moxie* . . gumption, guts. **1965–70** *DARE* (Qu. HH27b, *Of a very able and energetic person who gets things done . . "He's got lots of _____."*) 13 Infs, **scattered Nth, N Midl,** Moxie; (Qu. GG37, *Somebody who is very brave or courageous: "He's got plenty of _____."*) 9 Infs, **scattered Nth, N Midl,** Moxie; (Qu. GG5, *When someone does something unexpectedly bold or forward . . "Well, she certainly has a lot of _____."*) Infs **CT**42, **MA**71, **NY**64, 78, Moxie; (Qu. KK28, *Feeling ambitious and eager to work*) Inf **PA**46, Got lots of moxie. **1966** *DARE* File **Boston MA,** You've got a lot of moxie [=nerve]. **1971** Roberts *Third Ear* np [Black], *Moxey* . . nerve; daring; e.g. He had the moxey to demand money from the boss. **1971** *Today Show Letters* **seLA,** Here, also, moxie is a word for courage or guts, though one doesn't hear it used much. **1971** *DARE* File **MN,** *Moxie* . . means "sense enough" or "know how". "He hasn't got the moxie to figure that out." (It definitely refers to brain power—not strength or guts or courage.) **1976** *NYT Mag.* 29 Aug 34, So let the doomster take his brood / To Brentwood or Biloxi—/ Our town [=New York] will thrive on pulchritude,/ Mixed with a little moxie. **1979** *UpCountry* Feb 38 **NH,** His biggest tractor wasn't powerful enough ("It don't have the moxie," is how he phrased it) to remove the stumps.

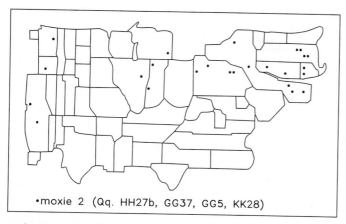

•moxie 2 (Qq. HH27b, GG37, GG5, KK28)

moxie berry, moxie plum, moxie vine See **moxie 1**

mox nix See **macht nichts**

mozey n[1] See **moshey**

mozey n[2] [Cf *SND moshie* (at *mosh* n.[2]) "a hollow scooped in the ground in which the target marble is placed" and *mooshie* (at *mosh* n.[2]) "a game of marbles using three such hollows"]
    1908 *German Amer. Annals* 10.34 sePA, *Mozey.* A marble, any kind except a commy. "I'll trade you a mozey for three commys."

mozh(e)y See **moshey**

Mr. Astorbilt n *joc*
=**Astorbilt 1.**
    1967–68 *DARE* (Qu. U37, . . *Somebody who has plenty of money*) Inf WI48, Mr. Astorbilt; (Qu. GG19b, *When you can see from the way a person acts that he's feeling important or independent: "He seems to think he's _____.")* Inf SC39, Mr. Astorbilt.

Mr. Charlie See **Mister Charlie**

Mr. Dole See **Dole's beard**

Mr. It n *esp Sth* *chiefly among Black speakers*
    A self-important person.
    1965–70 *DARE* (Qu. GG19b, *When you can see from the way a person acts that he's feeling important or independent: "He seems to think he's _____.")* Infs FL52, GA92, IL140, NC88, NY241, SC7, 26, Mr. It; (Qu. HH8, *A person who likes to brag*) Inf MS88, Mr. It; (Qu. HH17, *A person who tries to appear important, or who tries to lay down the law in his community: "He'd like to be the _____ around here.")* Inf FL52, Mr. It; (Qu. HH41, *Someone who has a very high opinion of himself;* total Infs questioned, 75) Inf MS45, Thinks he is Mr. It. [8 of 9 total Infs Black]

Mr. Manners, leave something for See **manner** n 3b

Mr. Milquetoast See **milquetoast**

Mrs. n *chiefly Nth, N Midl, West* |ˈmɪsɪz|; *chiefly Sth, S Midl* |ˈmɪzɪz, mɪz, mɪs|; *also esp Sth, S Midl* |ˈmɪzrɪz, ˈmɪstrɪs| *Pronc-spp Mis(s), Missus, Mistress, Miz(res); for addit pronc and sp varr see quots*
    A Forms.
    1790 *Amer. Mercury* (Hartford CT) 17 Nov 1/2, The use of *Miss* for *Mistress* in this country is a gross impropriety. . . The word *mistress* . . should always be applied to a *married lady,* and *miss* to one who has never been married. 1840 (1847) Longstreet *GA Scenes* 64, I wouldn't have done it if it hadn't o' been on account of *Miss* (Mrs.) Durham. 1848 in 1935 *DN* 6.453 RI, *Miss* is used for married ladies instead of Mrs. 1872 Schele de Vere *Americanisms* 507, *Mistress* is in the South very frequently yet heard pronounced fully, without the usual contraction into "Missess." 1885 Twain *Huck. Finn* 318 MO, "Missus, dey's a sheet gone." . . "*Where's* it gone, Lize?" "Clah to goodness I hain't no notion, Miss Sally." 1886 *S. Bivouac* 4.343 sAppalachians, Mistress (pronounced in full, as in Shakespeare's time, instead of *missess*). 1903 *DN* 2.321 seMO, *Miss.* . . Generally used by negroes and ignorant whites for 'Mrs.' 1904 *DN* 2.419 nwAR, *Mistress.* . . Used for Mrs. on formal occasions, as at the roll-call of a society composed of matrons. Informally, Mrs. Brown is *'Mis' Brown.'* 1909 *DN* 3.349 eAL, wGA, *Miss.* . . Sometimes used by negroes and very illiterate whites for *Mrs.*

The latter is usually pronounced *Miz,* the sonant being very distinct to distinguish it from *Miss.* The forms *mis, mizes, mizres, mistress* are all heard, but *miss* is a recognized negroism. 1910 *DN* 3.445 wNY, *Miss.* . . Used continually, by many people, instead of *Mrs.* 1913 Kephart *Highlanders* 290 sAppalachians, A married woman is not addressed as Missis by the mountaineers, but as Mistress when they speak formally, and as Mis' or Miz' for a contraction. 1927 *DN* 5.475 Ozarks, In ordinary conversation the Ozarker says *Mis'* or *Miz,* but on ceremonious occasions he pronounces *Mistress* very distinctly. 1944 *PADS* 2.15 AL, *Mrs.* [ˈmɪiz, ˈMɪzɪz]. . . [ˈmɪiz] is more common in Ala., even among standard speakers. [*PADS* Ed: In s.Va. and n.N.C.: [mɪz] among old persons, [ˈmɪzɪz] among young persons.] 1950 *AmSp* 25.13, Throughout the Middle Atlantic states and adjoining portions of the South Atlantic states (including all of Delaware and the northern portions of Maryland and West Virginia), the forms with [s] are the only ones in use: there are no instances whatever of the forms [mɪzəz] or [mɪz]. The form [mɪsəz] very strongly predominates throughout this area. . . The area characterized by the occurrence of *z*-forms alone takes in eastern Virginia . . , the adjoining portion of North Carolina, and that part of the Western Shore of Maryland lying between Baltimore and the Potomac. Within this area the only two forms in regular use are [mɪzəz] and [mɪz]. . . To the west, southwest, and south of the *z*-area we find a rather extensive belt of mixed usage, where both *s*- and *z*-forms are current. *Ibid* 16, All the forms with some variety of [r] in the second syllable ([mɪsrz], [mɪzrəs], etc.) are clearly antiquated and are rapidly passing from use. The form *Mistress* [mɪstrəs], [mɪstərs] is also chiefly found in the old-fashioned type, except in southern West Virginia, where it is recorded in the speech of a considerable number of more modern speakers. 1950 *WELS Suppl.* csWI, But the hitch is, Missus [ˈmɪsəs], that they [=berry crates] don't come put together. 1958 Humphrey *Home from the Hill* 9 TX, "Miz Hannah?" cried the waitress. c1960 Wilson *Coll.* csKY, *Mrs.* [mɪz] commonest. [mɪs] sometimes by older people. [ˈmɪzrɪz] fairly common in some groups. 1961 Kurath–McDavid *Pronc. Engl.* 177, *Mrs.* . . The type of /mɪsɪz/ prevails throughout the North and the North Midland, but /mɪsɪs/ is rather common in New England and occurs with some frequency in the northern and the eastern counties of Pennsylvania. In these areas, /mɪsɪz/ and /mɪsɪs/ are reduced to monosyllabic /mɪz/ and /mɪs/, respectively, in rapid speech. In the South, with the exception of parts of North Carolina, the prevalent types are /mɪzɪz/ and its reduced form /mɪz/. Even in North Carolina /mɪsɪs/ is rare, but its reduced variant /mɪs/ . . is rather widely used and not unknown in South Carolina and Georgia. The South Midland presents the same confused situation as North Carolina. 1967–69 *DARE* FW Addit swKY, *Mrs.* [ˈmɪzrəz]—Black usage; LA, *Mrs.* [ˈmɪzrɪz]—this pronunciation is used by the uneducated, especially when speaking formally or distinctly; seAR, *Mrs.* [ˈmɪzrɪz]—careful and/or emphatic; FL, Miz—Mrs. "Have you seen Miz Hill yet?" Common; wTN, Mizres [ˈmɪzrez]—Mrs. Currently used to distinguish between Miss and Mrs. At the doctor's office, I told them my name was Mrs. Miller, and they wrote "Miss" until I spelled out "Mrs." Then they said, "Oh, Mizres Miller." Occasionally Mizres is used for older women in conversation, but generally everyone is Miss So-and-so. 1989 Pederson *LAGS Tech. Index* 241 **Gulf Region,** [In the context *Mrs. Cooper,* 304 infs gave proncs of the type [ˈmɪzɪz], 235 of the type [mɪz], 66 of the type [ˈmɪsɪz], and 63 of the type [mɪs]; 27 gave proncs with *r,* most commonly [ˈmɪzrɪz], and 4 said [ˈmɪstrɪs] or [ˈmɪstrɪz].]
    B Sense.
    Usu with *the:* A wife; one's wife.
    1821 (1930) Sewall *Diary* 81 MD, Arrived at Mrs. Winter's a little before sunset. I found the Mrs. rather indisposed with ague and fever. 1920 *Sat. Eve. Post* 27 Nov 42, I and the Mrs. and Kate was the only ones there in evening clothes. 1925 *AmSp* 1.152 West, "The Missus" is a man's wife. 1931 *AmSp* 7.20 swPA, *My missus.* My wife. 1933 *AmSp* 8.4.78, Apparently *the Missus* is acquiring, or has preserved, the force that is inherent in *the Mistress* and *the Master.* It is occasionally synonymous with 'person in authority' or 'boss'—witness the following instances: "Have you a good cabin for rent?" . . "Yes, the Missus will show them to you," replied the man (not her husband) of whom I inquired. 1937 *AmSp* 12.103 eNE, The farmer will often refer to his wife as *the Mrs.* 1944 *PADS* 2.58 MO, *Mrs., the* [ˈmɪzəz]. . . The wife. 1965–70 *DARE* (Qu. AA22, *Joking names that a man may use to refer to his wife: "I have to go down and pick up my _____.")* 63 Infs, **scattered,** Missus; (Qu. AA21, . . *Joking expressions . . about a wife who gives the orders and a husband who takes them from her*) Inf SC10, She's the Missus *and* the boss; (Qu. HH34x, *General words . . for a woman, not necessarily uncomplimentary;* not asked in early QRs) Infs MN3, NY2, WI44, Missus; IN32, The Missus. 1970 *DARE* File TN,

Mrs. ['mɪzrɪs, 'mɪzərɪs, 'mɪsrɪs]—as title and as noun (preceded by *the* or *a*) = a married woman. "Are you a mizris?" Said to be used by speakers along entire [social] scale. **1976** Garber *Mountain-ese* 58 **sAppalachians**, *Missus* . . the wife—I've gotta take the little missus to the beauty shop.

Mrs. Astor(bilt) See **Miss Astor**

Mrs. Astor's (pet) horse n Also *Mrs. Astor's billy goat, ~ (pet) cow, ~ plush horse;* for addit varr see quots [See quot 1959 at **1** below]

1 =**Astor's pet horse 1.**

1929 in 1947 Runyon *Trials* 211 **NYC**, Bridget . . was certainly all dressed up like Mrs. Astor's horse. **1957** *Sat. Eve. Post Letters* **TX**, All dressed up like Mrs. Astorbilt's plush horse. **1959** Tallman *Dict. Amer. Folkl.* 194, *Mrs. Astor's plush horse*—Mrs. William Astor, widow of the grandson of the first John Jacob Astor, was the dominant figure in New York and Newport society until her death in 1908. Her annual ball at 842 Fifth Avenue was the great affair of the season. Her gilded, over-stuffed magnificence led to the expression that an ostentatiously dressed person looked "like Mrs. Astor's plush horse," or as it sometimes appeared, "Mrs. Astor's pet horse." **1965–70** DARE (Qu. W37, *When a woman puts on her good clothes and tries to look her best . . she's _____*) Infs **KS**12, **NJ**24, 33, **NY**111, **WI**18, 21, 50, Dressed up like Mrs. Astor's horse; **MA**40, **MN**6, **OH**63, Diked out (*or* dressed up) like Mrs. Astor's plush horse; **NY**7, Dressed like Mrs. Astor's pet horse; **MA**79, All dolled up like Mrs. Astor's pet horse on parade; **NY**43, Dressed up like Mrs. Astor's billy goat; **PA**175, Like Mrs. Astor's pet horse; **CA**166, Mrs. Astor's horse; (Qu. W40, . . *A woman who overdresses or . . spends too much on clothes*) Inf **PA**18, Dressed up like Mrs. Astor's horse; **CT**19, Looks like Mrs. Van Astorbilt's horse. **1967** DARE FW Addit **sePA**, You're all dressed out like Mrs. Astor's off-side horse. **1985** DARE File **cwIN**, Someone truly dressed up looked like "Lady Astor's plush horse." **1993** Delany–Delany *Having Our Say* 109 **NYC** [Black], When I put that coat on, honey, I looked sensational. I looked as good as Mrs. Astor's pet mule.

2 =**Astor's pet horse 2.**

1950 WELS (*A woman who puts on a lot of airs: "She certainly is _____."*) 1 Inf, **csWI**, Mrs. Astor's plush horse; 1 Inf, **seWI**, Mrs. Astor's cow. **1968–69** DARE (Qu. GG19b, *When you can see from the way a person acts that he's feeling important or independent: "He seems to think he's _____."*) Infs **LA**23, **PA**175, Mrs. Astor's pet horse (*or* cow); (Qu. II21, *When somebody behaves unpleasantly or without manners: "The way he behaves, you'd think he was _____."*) Infs **CA**119, **MI**110, Mrs. Astor's pet (*or* plush) horse.

Mr. Scratch See **Old Scratch**

Mrs. Jones n Also *Miss Jones('s), Mrs. Jones's house, Jones' place, Widow Jones house;* for addit varr see quots joc Cf **Miss Janet, Mother Jones, Mrs. Murphy, neighbor Jones**

An outhouse or toilet.

[**1855** Halliwell-Phillipps *Dict. Archaic Words* 2.485 **England**, *Johnny*. . . A jakes. . . Also called *Mrs Jones* by country people.] **1899** (1912) Green *VA Folk-Speech* 246, Go to see *Mrs. Jones,* going to the privy. Used in the country. **1941** LANE Map 354 (*Privy*), The old-fashioned privy or 'country toilet', a small structure separate from the main house . . erected over a dry well dug in the ground. . . 41 infs, **scattered**, Miss Jones. . . 4 infs, **eMA, RI**, Mrs. Jones. **1942** Berrey–Van den Bark *Amer. Slang* 84.11, *Toilet.* . . Jones' place . . Mrs. Jones, Mrs. Jones's place. **1950** WELS (*An outside toilet*) 2 Infs, **WI**, Mrs. Jones; 1 Inf, **swWI**, Miss Jones. **1956** Ker *Vocab. W. TX* 191, Outdoor toilet. . . Mrs. Jones [2 infs]. **1960** PADS 34.42 **CO**, Northwestern Colorado—This area is marked by relatively high participation in a set of 14 language features [including]: . . Jones(es [sic] 'outside toilet.' **1965–70** DARE (Qu. M21b, *Joking names for an outside toilet building*) 44 Infs, **scattered**, Mrs. Jones; **VT**12, Calling on Mrs. Jones; **AR**56, **MI**116, Go see Mrs. Jones; **OH**58, Miss Jones; **MO**19, Miss Jones's; **GA**74, **KY**76, Mrs. Jones's house; **NY**224, Widow Jones house; **MI**120, Jones' house; **CA**3, Casey Jones; (Qu. F37, . . *An indoor toilet*) Infs **IL**29, 69, **KS**18, **NY**135, **TN**34, Mrs. Jones; (Qu. M21a, *An outside toilet building*) Infs **IL**31, **RI**2, Mrs. Jones; **IL**31, Jones' house. **1971** *Today Show Letters* **IN**, The modest ladies of back-country Indiana had many interesting names for these buildings such as . . "Miz Jones." **1973** Allen LAUM 1.181 **Upper MW** (as of c1950), *Privy*. . . Mrs. Jones, Mrs. Jones's house . . outdoors Jones. [11 infs, 6 **IA**]

Mr. Slick See **slick-tail**

Mrs. Murphy n
=**Mrs. Jones.**

1968–69 DARE (Qu. F37, . . *An indoor toilet*) Inf **IN**64, Mrs. Murphy; (Qu. M21b, *Joking names for an outside toilet building*) Inf **WI**42, Mrs. Murphy. **1973** Allen *LAUM* 1.181 (as of c1950), *Privy*. . . Mrs. Murphy [1 inf, **ceIA**].

Mrs. Murphy's chowder n [In allusion to the song "Who Threw the Overalls in Mistress Murphy's Chowder," by George L. Geifer (1899), to one of its varr, or to a similar song] See quot 1958.

[**1955** Best–Best *Song Fest* 82, *Mrs. Murphy's Chowder*. . . Won't you bring back, won't you bring back, Mrs. Murphy's chowder /. . . meat balls, fish balls, moth balls, cannon balls,/ come on in, the chowder's fine. *Ibid* 85, *Who Threw the Overalls in Mistress Murphy's Chowder?* . . When Mrs. Murphy dished the chowder out she fainted on the spot;/ She found a pair of overalls at the bottom of the pot.] **1958** McCulloch *Woods Words* 119 **Pacific NW**, *Mrs. Murphy's chowder*—Any unknown stuff found on the table.

Mr. White is out of jail phr Also *Mrs. White is out of jail, White man's* (or *Whitey's*) *out of jail* Cf **Jack White, johnny 5**

Used as a warning that a woman's slip is showing.

1966–70 DARE (Qu. W24a, . . *Expressions . . to warn a woman slyly that her slip is showing*) Infs **MS**72, **RI**8, **TX**51, Mr. White is out of jail (today); **VA**78, **WI**52, Mrs. White is out of jail; **LA**28, White man's out of jail; **LA**23, Whitey's out of jail.

m'se'f See **myself**

mu See **ma** n **A4**

muander See **meander**

mubble-squibble n Cf **Dutch rub, noogie**

1946 PADS 6.21 **ceNC** (as of 1900–10), *Mubble-squibble* ['mʌbḷ 'skwɪbḷ]: *n.* To tease (mommock) a smaller person (male) by running one's knuckles heavily through the victim's hair in order to make the hair "pull" and hurt. Pamlico. Common among school boys.

mubblety-peg See **mumblety-peg 1**

much adj

1 See quots. [OED *much* adj. A.1.a →1573, but perh this is an independent development from **much** n **1**]

[**c1840** in 1930 IL State Hist. Soc. *Jrl.* 23.238 **IL**, The indians, he went to their camps and they said he was a much manitou (meaning an evil spirit).] **1952** Brown *NC Folkl.* 1.567 **c,eNC**, *Much*. . . Strong, great. "He is a much man in his arms."

2 Well, in good health—used in neg constructions. [EDD *much* adj. 2] chiefly **sAppalachians**

1913 Kephart *Highlanders* 224 **sAppalachians**, John's Lize Ann she ain't much; cain't you-uns give her some easin'-powder for that hurtin' in her chist? **1931** (1991) Hughes–Hurston *Mule Bone* 50 **cFL** [Black], "Howdy do, Mrs. Roberts. How's yo' husband?" . . "He aint much and I aint much and my chillun is poly [=poorly]." **1939** Hall Coll. **eTN**, "How are you feeling today, Swede?" "Not much." **1971** Dwyer *Dict. for Yankees* [20] **sAppalachians, SE**, *Ain't much*—Is not very well. . . "She ain't much these days." **1976** Garber *Mountain-ese* 2 **sAppalachians**, How air you feelin'? I ain't much these cold winter days. **1986** Pederson *LAGS Concordance* (In response to "How are you?") 1 inf, **csTN**, I just ain't much.

much adv chiefly **Sth, S Midl**

Modifying an adj: Very—usu in neg or interrog contexts. Note: This sense is std when it modifies past pples or ppl adjs (e.g., *much obliged, much-improved*).

1876 in 1983 PADS 70.43 **ce,sePA**, We did not get much wet as we staid in the buildings most of the time. **1913** Kephart *Highlanders* 297 **sAppalachians**, Your name ain't much common. **1916** DN 4.347 **neTX** (as of 1896), *Much*. . . Very. . . "I don't guess she's much old." **1925** Dargan *Highland Annals* 254 **cwNC**, His wife wuzn't much stout, an' he didn't count on gittin' anything out of her but a little housekeepin'. **1929** (1954) Faulkner *Sound & Fury* 268 **MS**, I . . went up front. "Been much busy?" Earl says. "Not much," I says. **1931** Hannum *Thursday April* 13 **wNC**, "You got purty hands, honey." Thursday April smiled a bit, shook her head modestly. "They hain't purty, much." **1939** Hall Coll. **eTN**, "Is that road much steep?" "He haint up the mountain much fer [=far]." "The old ones couldn't talk much plain." **1955** Ritchie

Singing Family 213 **seKY,** I don't know the road much well. **1986**
Pederson *LAGS Concordance,* 1 inf, **csAL,** Much thankful; 2 infs,
cnGA, csTX, Much grateful; 1 inf, **swMS,** Much appreciative.

much n

1 in phr *much of:* An outstanding example of, esp with regard to strength. Note: In negative, interrogative, or otherwise
qualified contexts (e.g., "That wasn't much of a meal."), this
is std; only exx of unqualified positive use are given here.
chiefly S Midl Cf **considerable n 3**

1903 *DN* 2.321 **seMO,** *Much of a man.* . . A strong, robust man. 'He
was much of a man and ought to have lived to a good old age if he had
taken care of hisself.' **1939** *Hall Coll.* **wNC,** He whupped everybody
he ever tackled; he was much of a man. **1940** Stuart *Trees of Heaven*
254 **neKY,** He can lick three men his size. Anse is a much of a man.
1952 Brown *NC Folkl.* 1.568, *Much of.* . . Strong, great, valuable;
followed by a substantive: "much of a man, car," etc.—Central and east.
1965 Will *Okeechobee Boats* 145 **FL,** Now there was much of a man,
standing six feet two, with shoulders like a cargo hatch. **1986** Pederson
LAGS Concordance (Strong) 5 infs, **AR, LA, MS,** (A) much of a man;
1 inf, **csTN,** Much a man; much of a man; 1 inf, **swGA,** Much of a
man—large, tall, heavy; 1 inf, **ceLA,** Much of a man—of blacksmith;
1 inf, **nwAR,** A much of a worker.

2 An estimable person; a model of excellence.

a1930 in 1991 Hughes–Hurston *Mule Bone* 32 **cFL** [Black], Cose
everybody knows dem Westons is a set uh bullies, but you Baptists aint
such a much. **1993** *DARE* File **Akron OH** (as of 1920s), "He's not such
a much" and "He's not much of a much" were both used by folk
speakers.

3 in phr *not to have much for:* To have little regard or respect for.

1964 in 1986 *Barrick Coll.* **csPA,** "I don't have much for him" [i.e.,
much respect; I don't hold him in very high esteem].

much v Also with *over, up* [Engl dial] **chiefly Sth, S Midl**
To make much of; to pet, stroke.

1848 in 1911 Lowell *Poet. Wks.* 140 **ceMA,** As't were pure cloth of
gold,/ Which, indeed, it all turns to as soon as she's touched it,/ And (to
borrow a phrase from the nursery,) *muched* it. **1887** *Century Illustr. Mag.*
34.119 **AR,** I never cud much her like I cud t'other gells. **1893** Shands
MS Speech 73, *Much up.* This expression is used by illiterate whites to
mean *to pet, to make much of.* . . I have never heard *much* used in this
sense unless followed by *up.* **1896** Harris *Sister Jane* 143 **GA,** Man . .
come 'long take de chil' in he arms an' much 'im, an' den he gi' 'im
sump'n t' eat. **1909** *DN* 3.350 **eAL, wGA,** *Much.* . . To make much of:
usually with *up.* "They muched her up ter(ri)bly." **1917** *DN* 4.415 **wNC,**
Much. **1918** *DN* 5.19 **NC,** *Much,* pet, make much of. **1919** *DN* 5.34
KY, Much him up and see won't he come. **1931** *Sat. Eve. Post* 20 June
9, The old boy would enjoy it. He likes being muched over, though he
pretends that he doesn't. **1933** Rawlings *South Moon* 102 **nFL,** That
Red's a wild un. Cain't nobody but Lant much him. **1939** *Hall Coll.*
wNC, eTN, "So I patted him and muched him." "I muched the dogs a
little and they come up to me." **1944** *PADS* 2.47 **NC,** *Much (up).* . . To
make much of, to show affection for. "I muched the dogs up, and they
got so they'd follow me." Here and there in N.C. Somewhat rare. **1960**
Williams *Walk Egypt* 257 **GA,** The puppy, tail disillusioned, listened
from a safe distance. The children "muched" it. "Aw, you the prettiest
li'l' ole dog. You so pretty and cute." **1986** Pederson *LAGS Concor-*
dance, 1 inf, **neTN,** Muching a dog—making friends; not scolding.

mucher adv Cf **muchly**

1953 Randolph–Wilson *Down in Holler* 266 **Ozarks,** *Mucher.* . .
More, farther. In setting out a row of trees, a man said to his helper: "I
reckon we better set that'n over just a little mucher." The tree he
indicated was a trifle out of line with the others.

much-hunger n
A **trillium.**

1898 *Jrl. Amer. Folkl.* 11.282, *Trillium* (any species), much-hunger,
Farmington, Me. . . Leaves eaten as greens.

muchly adv
Greatly, much.

1862 (1864) Browne *Artemus Ward Book* 195, His gallunt men had
been a little 2 enthoosiastic in confisticatin my show. "Yes," sez I, "they
confisticated me too muchly." **1909** *DN* 3.351 **eAL, wGA,** *Muchly.* . .
Much, greatly. **1967** *DARE* (Qu. Z14b, *If a child expects to have its*

own way or have too much attention . . "That child is _____.") Inf
TX4, Very muchly spoiled. **1986** Pederson *LAGS Concordance,* 1 inf,
neTX, Very muchly; 1 inf, **csTX,** Pinto bean is used very muchly =
frequently.

much o'britches exclam Also *smuch o'britches* [Varr of *much*
obliged] joc

1966–70 *DARE* (Qu. II39, . . *'Thank you'*) Inf **GA44,** Smuch
o'britches; **MS1,** Much o'britches [ɑˈbrɪtʃɪz]; **WV14,** Much o'britches
[laughter].

much of See **much n 1**

much over See **much v**

much-right adj
Of a person: unmarried; see quot 1983.

1934 Hurston *Jonah's Gourd Vine* 97 **AL** [Black], "John, how come
you ain't in de play party? M'haley [is] dancin' wid Bully [=another
young man]." "She's a much-right gal. Much right for Bully ez it
is for me." **1983** *DARE* File, Following are some colloquialisms that
I have heard first-hand. They come from extreme Southern Illinois
and Southeast Missouri, locally known as SwampEast Missouri. . . A
verbal altercation between two men concerning a woman went as follows: "You leave my woman alone," said one man. "You got papers on
this woman?" questions the second man. "No. I ain't got no papers on
her, but she is my woman and you leave her alone," replied man #1.
Man #2 comes back with "If you ain't got papers on her, then she is
just a 'much-right' woman and I'll talk to her all I want". In the language
of the area, a 'much-right woman' is a woman without marital ties, so
one man has as 'much-right' to her as another man.

much up See **much v**

much-what adv [*EDD much* adv. 4.(7)]
Pretty nearly, more than somewhat.

1899 (1912) Green *VA Folk-Speech* 290, *Much-what.* . . Nearly; almost. For the most part.

muck n[1]

1a Dark, moist soil that is high in decomposed organic matter
and very fertile; hence adj *mucky.* **chiefly east of Missip R**
See Map on p. 706

1832 H.L. Barnum *Farmer's Own Bk.* 35 (*OEDS*), On tearing up some
handfuls of the ground, this is well blackened of course, and little is
thought of looking for the sub-soil, as those invariably do, who have
once been deceived by black muck, and these soft beds of leaves. **1839**
Buel *Farmer's Companion* 73 **NEast,** *Peat earth,* or swamp muck, is
vegetable food, in an insoluble state, and requires only such a chemical
change as shall render it soluble, to convert it into an active manure.
1840 Hoffman *Greyslaer* 1.61 **Upstate NY,** He had laid the logs right
down on a piece of deep, mucky soil, made up of old roots, rotten leaves.
1850 Chamberlain *IN Gaz.* 283, The soil being a mixture of clay, marl
and black *muck.* **1889** *Century Illustr. Mag.* 39.217 **seNY,** The soil
proved to be a wet muck overlaying sand with boulders—in fact, a
swamp. **1904** (1977) Porter *Freckles* 52 **cnIN,** The wildly leaping heart
of Freckles burst from his body and fell in the black swamp-muck at
her feet. *Ibid* 63, The thing for you to be thinking of would be to stretch
out in the muck for the feet of her to be walking over. **1965–70** *DARE*
(Qu. C31, . . *Heavy, sticky soil*) 105 Infs, **chiefly east of Missip R,**
Muck; **IL69,** Black muck; **ME5,** Mucky; **NC11,** Mucky dirt; **MO21,**
Mucky ground; **CT14, GA77,** Mucky land; **KY11, NJ69, VT16,** Mucky
soil; **FL35,** Spongy muck; (Qu. C30, . . *Loose, dark soil*) 32 Infs, **esp**
MI, NY, Muck; **MI2, 36, MN15, NJ1, NY24,** Black muck; **GA36,** Dry
muck; **NJ39,** Mucky ground; **FL35,** Soft muck; (Qu. C11, *Soft, wet sand*
in streams or wet places, that draws people and things down into it)
Infs **FL34, GA45, MI56, MA23, MN28, PA182,** Muck; **IN62,** Quick
muck; (Qu. C32) Inf **FL3,** Dried-out muck. **1966** *DARE* Tape **FL39,**
[FW:] What does muck mean around here? [Inf:] It's black and rich-
looking and it's extremely heavy. . . muck is no good for the average
place such as mine—it's too heavy. You'd have to mix it with something
else in your sand 'cause if you just spread it around it'll eventually dry
out and blow away. . . It's way below the surface. **1986** Pederson *LAGS*
Concordance (Loam; bottomland) 25 infs, 21 **FL, GA,** Muck [*DARE*
Ed: 5 infs indicate that it is black soil, 4 that it is rich.]; 1 inf, **seLA,** A
muck-like = gumbo; 1 inf, **seFL,** Rich-looking muck; 1 inf, **seTN,**
Kindly of a blue muck; 25 infs, 15 **FL, GA,** Mucky (land, place, soil);
1 inf, **neFL,** Mucky-type black soil.

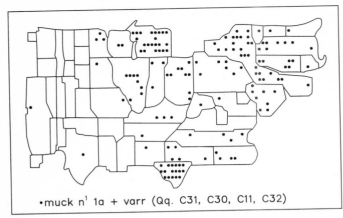

•muck n¹ 1a + varr (Qq. C31, C30, C11, C32)

b Transf: an area having such soil. **esp FL, GA**

1937 (1977) Hurston *Their Eyes* 192 **FL** [Black], "Soon as Ah git over dis lil cuttin scrape, we gointuh do somethin' crazy. . . We goin' on de muck." "Whut's de muck, and where is it at?" "Oh down in de Everglades round Clewiston and Belle Glade where dey raise all dat cane and string-beans and tomatuhs. Folks don't do nothin' down dere but make money and fun and foolishness." **1970** *DARE* (Qu. C7, . . *Land that usually has some standing water with trees or bushes growing in it*) Inf **FL**48, Muck. **1986** Pederson *LAGS Concordance* (Swamp) 1 inf, **cwFL**, Muck—land; 1 inf, **seGA**, A muck; 1 inf, **cwGA**, Muck [inf queries]; (Marshes) 1 inf, **cTN**, Muck; [1 inf, **ceGA**, Muck and mud]. **1991** *DARE* File **cwNY**, There are many muckland farms in western New York—great for growing onions and potatoes, etc. Muck out here means large areas, (probably once a swamp) of decomposed vegetation.

c attrib, esp in phr *muck land*: See quots.

1848 U.S. Patent Office *Annual Rept. for 1847* 358 **cwMA**, They [=potatoes] have been planted the present year, on deep muck lands. **1870** U.S. Dept. Ag. *Rept. of Secy. for 1869* 270 **cGA**, The soil was . . black mud or muck swamp, five feet deep, containing a mixture of sand. **1934** *Hanley Disks* **seNY**, The onions and the muck produce from there, that is, black earth produce. **1942** Kennedy *Palmetto Country* 16 **FL**, After a total expenditure of twenty-two million dollars, thousands of acres of muckland were reclaimed and are now producing truck crops for Northern winter markets. **1967** Will *Dredgeman* 13 **FL**, This . . was Florida's first State Park, established in 1916 . . to preserve the wild royals and the rare flora and fauna of Paradise Key. The beauty of this scene couldn't fail to impress even an old Glades "muck rat" like me. **1967–70** *DARE* (Qu. C31) Inf **VA**44, Muckland; (Qu. C30) Infs **NJ**3, **NY**110, 183, 206, Muckland; (Qu. C11) Inf **OH**81, Muckland; (Qu. I1, . . *The garden where you grow carrots, beans, and such things, to eat at home*) Inf **NY**97, Muck gardens—at Rome [NY], black soil. **1968** *DARE* FW Addit **cWI**, Muck farms—tamarack swamps from which the trees have been taken and vegetable gardening is done, commercially. **1970** *DARE* Tape **MI**116, The Shiawassee River . . goes right down through our farm down back of the barn there, and when that's cleaned out, why then we have several acres of good productive muckland; **MI**122, Like around Kalamazoo . . there's muckland, and that's the same kind of soil. **1986** Pederson *LAGS Concordance* (Loam; bottom-land) 13 infs, 11 **FL**, Muckland(s); 1 inf, **ceAL**, Muckland—12–15' deep in water; in Everglades; 3 infs, **ne,nwFL, seGA**, (Black) muck soil; 1 inf, **nwMS**, Muck-type soil; 1 inf, **nwAL**, Muck loam; 1 inf, **cFL**, Muck farms—real fertile and rich. **1990** Simpson *Gt. Dismal* 28 **nNC, sVA**, The timbermen built a trestle for their train, then went back and filled it in with earth in hopes this muckmire causeway would stay stable. **1991** *NADS Letters* **nwNJ**, The Great Meadows area of Warren County, New Jersey is an old lake bed which has a black, rich soil that is ideal for truck farming. The fields are called black mucklands. *Ibid* **MI**, *Muck farm* and *muckland*: Both are terms that I heard and read about while living in Michigan, from 1970–1978. . . Generally, the term "muck" was used in reference to bog soils left after glaciation. The soil is rich. *Ibid* **cNY**, A muck farmer is someone who does his farming in the muck—that is, in the muddy, sometimes (seasonally?) flooded land by one of the upstate waterways (lakes, rivers, or canals). To the obvious question, "What do they grow on muck farms? Muck?" the answer is: potatoes and perhaps other vegetables.

2 In hardrock mining: excavated rock, soil, or ore; a pile of such rock. [*DCan* 1897 (in placer mining)] **chiefly West** Cf **muck stick**

1918 Peele *Mining Engineers' Hdbk.* 229, Prompt removal of the muck is always essential, for many little things are to be done after the heading is clear. . . On the other hand, if the mucking crew be too large, the men will interfere with one another. **1941** Fisher *Illusion* 10 **NV** (as of 1860s), "Ther's a muck," he said. "Up in the head the gulch ther's a muck." . . She went up to see the thick heavy stuff that was only a nuisance for the gold-seekers. . . Sandy suggested that they might send a chunk of it to California for an assay, but Eilley wanted gold, and there was no gold in these piles of stuff that prospectors were shoveling out of their way. *Ibid* 11, "About that muck, why don't we send some to Californee?" . . Sandy sent a piece of his ore to California for an assay. **1947** Natl. Coal Assoc. *Gloss.* 15, *Muck*—Refuse from a mine; to remove such refuse. **1966–69** *DARE* Tape **CA**120, But you always keep enough muck in the stope so you can work off till you get it through to the next level; SD4, [FW:] What do they call . . the broken-up ore that's been blasted out? [Inf:] Muck pile. That's the muck pile.

3 A state of confusion; a morass; a tangle. [Cf *EDD muck* sb. 6]

1875 (1876) Twain *Tom Sawyer* 183 **MO**, It's a prime comfort to see faces that's friendly when a body's in such a muck of trouble. **1950** *PADS* 14.48 **SC**, *Muck*. . . 1. A snarl, a tangle. "That backlash has my line in a muck." 2. A state of confusion or uncertainty. "He is in a muck over what to do about the boll weevil."

4 in phrr *muck of (a) sweat*: A very sweaty condition or person; fig: =*muck* n¹ 3. [*EDD muck* sb. 7]

1899 (1912) Green *VA Folk-Speech* 290, *Muck of sweat*. . . Excessive perspiration. **1903** *DN* 2.321 **seMO**, I am a muck of sweat and not fitten to come to the table. **1907** *DN* 3.233 **nwAR**, *Muck of sweat*, n. phr. Wet with sweat. **1933** *Sun* (Baltimore MD) 30 Aug 10/7 (Hench Coll.), Already I am in what certain excellent persons on the Eastern Shore call a muck of a sweat. In trying to write this item, I got so mixed up . . that three times I had my informant making the same mistake he said I had made.

muck v, hence vbl n *mucking* [**muck** n¹ 2] **chiefly West** Cf **mucker 1**

To shovel or otherwise remove rock, ore, or debris from a mine.

1918 [see **muck** n¹ 2]. **1932** (1968) Wilson *Amer. Jitters* 218 **NV**, The men, who had been displaced by new mucking machines (mucking is cleaning out the tunnel after the blast), were to be transferred. **1939** FWP *Guide MT* 80, In the deep Butte [copper] mines. . . men . . muck (shovel) the ore into chutes. **1947** [see **muck** n¹ 2]. **1952** Peattie *Black Hills* 297 **SD**, We observe a "mucking" machine shoveling broken rocks into ore cars. **1966** *DARE* (Qu. FF16, . . *Local contests or celebrations*) Inf **MT**1, Mucking contests—years ago. [*DARE* Ed: Inf is a miner.] **1966–69** *DARE* Tape **CA**120, You have to blast it, then you have to muck it [=gold ore], and then we have a gold pan and you pan it; **IA**8, Their extra dirt an' stuff, they'd just muck that back over here; **MT**1, [FW:] Do you start out as a mucker? [Inf:] No. . . I did start muckin' at the Alamo, that's where I contracted first; **NM**15, [FW:] When someone's mucking in a mine, what does he do? [Inf:] That's shovelin'; SD4, [FW:] Do the miners . . call it shoveling or do they say mucking? [Inf:] Most of 'em'll say mucking. . . They have these power shovels or mucking machines.

muck n² See **muck-a-muck 2**

muck-a-muck n [Chinook Jargon]

1 also *muck-muck*: Food. **chiefly NW, AK** Note: This may not be fully naturalized, but cf **high-muck-a-muck 1**.

[**1847** Palmer *Jrl.* 150 **Pacific NW** [Chinook Jargon], *Muck-a-muck*—Provisions, eat.] **1882** Nash *2 Yrs. OR* 84, "Any fish, muck-a-muck?" say you, blandly. Without turning her head . . , the old crone [=an Amer Indian] grunts out, "Halo" (none). **1898** (1983) Conger *In Search of Gold* 122 **AK**, The Indians are few and quite civilized. They live mostly on salmon. They are well pleased to have the white man with them because the white man's muck-muck (food) is better than theirs. **?1939** in 1991 Tabbert *Dict. Alaskan Engl.* 84, On Tanana's banks I'll settle down / As the pioneers did of old,/ A fish wheel furnishing muck-muck,/ I'll let others dig for gold.

2 also *monkey-monk, muck, muck(et)y-muck, muckity-muck*: =**high-muck-a-muck 2**.

1914 *DN* 4.113 **cKS**, *Squeegee*. . . A person of importance; mucka-muck:—used derisively. **1941** O'Donnell *Great Big Doorstep* 61 **sLA**, He said those people, the Governor and the big mucky-mucks from New York with the oil company, was passing close to the levee to let us smell the geese. **1941** Smith *Going to God's Country* 167 **MO** (as of 1901), I knew one man that was a big muck in the bank. . . He was the head of everything. **1954** Armstrong *Satchmo* 213 **LA,** We all thought you had to be . . some kind of a big muckity-muck to play the trumpet. **1955** Warren *Angels* 13, He ain't nuthin—them muck-a-mucks, so high and mighty—ain't nuthin. **1965–70** *DARE* (Qu. HH17, *A person who tries to appear important, or who tries to lay down the law in his community: "He'd like to be the _____ around here."*) Inf **CA**15, Big muck-a-muck; **CT**21, **GA**3, Big muckety-muck; **CA**169, **OK**9, (Big) mucky-muck; **NY**36, Big monkey-monk; (Qu. II23, *Joking names for the people who are, or think they are, the best society of a community: The _____*) Infs **AR**33, **SC**40, **TX**21, Muckety-mucks; **AK**8, **MT**1, **NJ**39, **VA**46, Mucky-mucks; **SC**69, Mucks; (Qu. II24, *Names or nicknames for the part of a town where the well-off people live*) Inf **DC**13, Muckety-mucks. **1995** Lesley *Sky Fisherman* 30 **OR,** Tangent knows all the mucky-mucks on the tribal council. All the big-shot chiefs.

muckeley-dun See **muckle-dun 2**

mucker n[1]

1 One who removes **muck** n[1] **2**; one who works with a shovel; one who excavates. [**muck** v] **chiefly West** Cf **muck stick**

1899 *Harper's Weekly* 20 May 498 **nwID,** [The] Company . . paid $3 for miners and $2 50 for "muckers," or underground laborers [in a lead mine]. **1918** *DN* 5.26 **NW,** *Mucker*. . . A man with a shovel in the mines. **1918** Peele *Mining Engineers' Hdbk.* 260, Empty bucket should always be available at bottom to render muckers independent of irregularities and delays. In large shafts, where more shovelers are employed than can crowd around one bucket or skip, two compartments are sometimes used for hoisting. **1941** Fisher *Illusion* 57, In the California camps they had been common muckers, going from place to place as the winds of rumor shifted, but never getting their hands on more than a toiler's wage. **1945** Hubbard *Railroad Ave.* 353, *Muckers*—Excavators in construction work. **1947** Natl. Coal Assoc. *Gloss.* 15, *Mucker*—One who removes the refuse. **1958** McCulloch *Woods Words* 119 **Pacific NW,** *Mucker*—A man working around a cat or shovel. **1959** Robertson *Ram* 218 **ID** (as of c1875), As one old miner said at a friend's funeral, "Tim was only a mucker, but he was a *good* mucker." I was a good mucker. **1966–69** *DARE* Tape **CA**128, Your miner is the one that does the drilling, see, and a miner can put in a set o' timbers but a mucker all he knows is a shovel; **MT**1, [FW:] What are some of the grades of underground laborers. . [Inf:] Muckers; **NM**15, Muckers . . shovel the ore up an' put it in the cars lots of times when there isn't room enough to work a hoist and a scraper; **SD**4, We had some that was shoveling rock by hand years ago which they have discontinued now. . . We called him a mucker. **1968** Adams *Western Words* 202, *Mucker*—In mining, a workman who removes gravel, hardpan, etc., from a mine; he loads mine cars and in most mines is also a *trammer*, pushing the cars to the mouth of the shaft, tunnel, or adit. **1970** Wilhelm *Last Rig* 303 **West,** Anybody knows that a mucker has the hardest job found around the mines. They had to be young and strong and able to clean up after a blast in time so the miners could lay track, timber or get in another round of holes.

2 One who grows produce on **muck** n[1] **1a.**

1991 *NADS Letters* **seMI,** When he was either delivering or picking up produce. . . it was not unusual for him to point to a farm that we were passing and note that "He's a mucker," proceeding to detail the list of crops grown on the farm.

mucker n[2] See **myrtle** n[1]

mucket n[1] Also *mougat, mouket* [Etym unknown] Cf **fat mucket** A **freshwater clam,** usu *Actinonais carinata.*

1911 *Century Dict. Suppl., Mucket*. . . [Also *mouket, mougat*; origin obscure.] A large dark-brown mussel, *Lampsilis ligamentinus*, found in the Mississippi river and used in the manufacture of pearl buttons. **1935** Pratt *Manual Invertebrate Animals* 657, *A*[*ctinonais*] *ligamentina*. . . Mucket. . . Mississippi and St. Lawrence Valleys; used in button making. **1938** FWP *Guide IA* 327, The fisherman's haul usually contained a wide assortment of shells . . , all salable, . . mucket, . . maple leaf, and elephant's ear. **1940–41** Cassidy *WI Atlas,* 1 inf, **WI,** Clam shells, niggerhead, oyster shell, mucket. **1949** Palmer *Nat. Hist.* 354, *Unionidae*. . . Different species of fresh-water mussels or muckets have different fish species on which they are parasitic in larval stage. **1953** (1977) Hubbard *Shantyboat* 211 **Missip-Ohio Valleys,** Fresh-water pearls are often found in mussel shells, occasionally one of considerable value. The pearls are nearly always found in muckets, especially in shells with a crook at the end. **1982** U.S. Fish & Wildlife Serv. *Fresh-Water Mussels* [Wall chart], *Mucket*. . . *Actinonais carinata*. . . Shell yellow or brown with green

rays. **1982** *WI State Jrl.* (Madison) 22 Aug sec 7 3, Several of the clams that may be found in Wisconsin rivers include . . hickorynut and mucket.

mucket n[2] [Cf Fr *moquette* a decoy bird] A nonexistent item, sometimes used as the basis of a practical joke.

1961 *AmSp* 36.273 **NW, West,** Load of muckets. . . An empty truck. **1967–68** *DARE* (Qu. HH14, *Ways of teasing a beginner or inexperienced person—for example, by sending him for a 'left-handed monkey wrench': "Go get me _____."*) Inf **OR**3, Green-handled mucket (a bird to catch in a sack); (Qu. NN12b, *Things that people say to put off a child when he asks, "What are you making?"*) Inf **NJ**31, A mucket ['mʌkət].

muckety-muck See **muck-a-muck 2**

mucking See **muck** v

muckity-muck See **muck-a-muck 2**

muck land See **muck** n[1] **1c**

muckle adj [Scots *muckle* large, big; mature] Great, much; large.

1838 Kettell *Yankee Notions* 146, [From poem "The Rime of the Ancient Pedler," Canto I:] Thou man of muckle sinne! **1969** *DARE* FW Addit **cCT,** He's a muckle ['mʌkəl] tyke—a healthy, strong, etc.

muckle v

1 To bother, upset.

1916 Macy–Hussey *Nantucket Scrap Basket* 15 **seMA,** 'Twould muckle me dretful to go to bottom in an old tub like this. *Ibid* 139, "Muckle". . . To bother or disturb, as "don't muckle me now."

2 with *up:* To disarrange, jumble. [*EDD* muckle v.[1] 3]

1970 *DARE* (Qu. Y38, *Mixed together, confused: "The things in the drawer are all _____."*) Inf **VA**69, Scrambled up; rumpled; balled up. [FW: When Inf was actually going through such a drawer, she said, "I wish she wouldn't muckle up things so—like scrambled eggs."]

3 also with *away:* To work hard, slog. [Cf *EDD* muck v. 17 (with *about*): "To work hard; to drudge, slave, toil."]

1916 Macy–Hussey *Nantucket Scrap Basket* 139, "Muckle"—To work hard under adverse conditions, as "he muckled away at it till he finally got it right." **1950** *WELS Suppl.* **seWI,** *Muckle through* v phr (of building a road through a marshy place).

4 with *down:* To set to work, buckle down.

1993 *DARE* File **NEng,** There's no use putting it off any longer. I've got to just muckle down and get this job done.

5 with *(in)to:* To set to work on, apply force to.

1944 *PADS* 2.58 **swMO,** *Muckle to it.* . . To work hard. **1968** *DARE* FW Addit, *Muckle* = to use a lot of muscle, as "muckle into it."

6 with *on(to):* To seize firmly, grasp; hence vbl n *muckling (on).*

1977 *Yankee* Jan 73 **csME,** But if you're really upstropolis you might muckle a hold on the scruff of his neck and hist him. **1979** Lewis *How to Talk Yankee* [22] **nNEng,** *Muckle* . . to seize, grasp. "Muckle onto one end of this sofa, will ye? I put my back out yesterday and can't lift nawthin'." **1989** Mosher *Stranger* 17 **nVT** (as of 1952), A common threat of my father when I was growing up [was]. . . that if he were ten years younger he would certainly "muckle onto" someone and throw him into the biggest snowbank south of Labrador. . . I was somewhat unclear in my mind as to exactly what Dad meant by "muckling on." Yet I had no doubt at all that muckling was a most dire form of corporal retribution. *Ibid* 92, I would have loved to see the old man muckle onto Bumper and clean his clock. **1993** *DARE* File **NEng,** Once he muckles onto an idea you'll never convince him otherwise.

7 with *out:* To renege, back out.

1950 *WELS* (When somebody says he will do something and then changes his mind and won't: "At the last minute he _____.") 1 Inf, **seWI,** Muckled out.

muckle n See **myrtle** n[1]

muckle away See **muckle** v **3**

muckle down See **muckle** v **4**

muckle-dun adj [Cf *EDD* muckle sb. 1 "Manure, long straw from the stable"]

1 also *muckledy-dun, muffle-~:* Muddy gray or brown; nondescript in color; hence n *muckle-dun, muckledy-dun(g)* an animal of such a color. **scattered, but esp Missip-Ohio Valleys** Cf **dunkel dun**

1906 *DN* 3.121 **sIN**, *Muckle-dun.* . . Rat colored. "That mule's a muckle-dun." **1916** *DN* 4.278 **NE**, *Muckle-dun*, adj. = *muffle-dun*. Reported as brought from Memphis, Tennessee. [*DN* Ed: Also Kan.] . . *Muffle-dun*, adj. = *dunkel-dun* [="an indefinite gray-brown"]. Term of disparagement. Reported as brought from Indiana. **1942** McAtee *Dial. Grant Co. IN* 44 (as of 1890s), *Muckle-dun* . . a nondescript drab color of a horse or other animal. **1944** *PADS* 2.47 **wNC**, *Muckle-dun.* . . Muddy-brown. **1950** *WELS* (A dark, unattractive brownish color: "They painted the house a _____ color.") 1 Inf, **ceWI**, Muckle-dun. **1966–70** *DARE* (Qu. K37, . . *A horse of mixed colors*) Infs **IA**8, Muckle-dun; (Qu. K38, *A horse of a dirty white color*) Inf **IL**114, **ID**3, Muckledy-dun(g). **1992** *DARE* File **seID**, In describing a cat of mixed, nondescript colors, my mother-in-law said it had a "muckledy-dun" color. She grew up in Idaho after moving there from Missouri as a small child.

2 as *muckeley-dun;* By ext: see quot.

1927 *AmSp* 2.361 **cwWV**, *Muckeley-dun* . . a word of indefinite meaning, which is used to signify contempt, and which has no reference to color. "Look at that old muckeley-dun horse."

muckledy-dun(g) n See **muckle-dun 1**

muckle gall See **gall** n[2] 1

muckle into See **muckle** v 5

muckle mish See **myrtle** n[1] B9

muckle on(to) See **muckle** v 6

muckle out See **muckle** v 7

muckle to See **muckle** v 5

muckle up See **muckle** v 2

muckling (on) See **muckle** v 6

muckluck See **mukluk**

muck-muck See **muck-a-muck 1**

muck of sweat See **muck** n[1] 4

muck stick n [**muck** n[1] 2] **West**

Esp among loggers and miners: a shovel.

1918 *DN* 5.26 **NW**, *Muck-stick.* . . A shovel. **1926** *AmSp* 1.652 [Hobo lingo], *Muck stick*—longhandled shovel. **1930** Williams *Logger-Talk* 26 **Pacific NW**, *Muck-stick*: A shovel. **1940** Writers' Program *Guide NV* 61 [Mining lingo], A *muck-stick* is a shovel. **1958** McCulloch *Woods Words* 119 **Pacific NW**, *Muck stick*—A shovel. **1966** *DARE* Tape **SD**4, It was a small scoop shovel which was plenty large for the weight of this rock. . . Some of them [=miners] called them muck sticks. **1968** *DARE* FW Addit **nwCA**, *Muck stick*—shovel (a mining term).

muck worm n Cf **mudworm**

A worm or insect larva such as that of a **dung beetle** or of a beetle of the genus *Ligyrus*.

1842 Harris *Treatise Insects* 28, There is a grub . . which is frequently found under old manure heaps, and is commonly called muck-worm. It . . is transformed to a dung-beetle called *Scarabæus relictus*. **1882** (1903) Treat *Injurious Insects* 75, A larva of similar size and appearance to the White Grub is often found in manure heaps, and farmers, supposing them to be identical, fear to cause trouble by using the manure. This grub, known as the Muck-worm, is the larva of a different beetle *(Ligyrus)*, and as it feeds only upon decayed vegetable matter, can do no damage to the crops. . . It has a lead-colored appearance, for its whole length, due to the contents of its intestines, which show through the skin; the White Grub shows this dark color only near the tail end. **1939** *LANE* Map 236, 1 inf, **neMA**, Muckworm = mudworm, slimy, caught in the marshes, used as bait; 1 inf, **ceVT**, Muckworm, white, one inch long. **1966–69** *DARE* (Qu. P5, . . *The common worm used as bait*) Inf **NC**32, Muck worm—white worm the size of my finger; **MI**108, Muck worm; (Qu. P6, . . *Kinds of worms . . used for bait*) Inf **MD**20, Muck worm—short, thick.

mucky adj[1] See **muck** n[1] 1a

mucky adj[2] [Prob var of *muggy*, infl by *mucky* sticky] Cf **murky**

Muggy, humid.

1804 Volney *View Soil U.S.A.* 143, [Translator's note:] A mucky breeze from the south *sometimes* discompose him in the sultry mornings

of August. **1950** *WELS* (A day when the air is very still, moist, and warm) 3 Infs, **eWI**, Mucky. **1954** *WELS Suppl.* **nwWI**, A friend from Brule unhesitatingly answered "mucky" to describe hot, moist weather. She never heard of "muggy." *Ibid* **cwWI**, I was amazed to hear that the word "mucky" . . was found in another part of the state. It is a common expression for my next door neighbor, who is Dutch. *Ibid* **seWI**, Mucky rather than muggy. I've heard that too. **1967–70** *DARE* (Qu. B4, *A day when the air is very still, moist, and warm—it's _____*) Infs **CA**129, **IL**13, **KY**39, 52, **NC**78, **OH**45, **VA**39, 47, Mucky; (Qu. B3, *If a day is very hot . . it's [a] _____*) Inf **VA**28, It's mucky; (Qu. B6, *When clouds begin to increase . . it's _____*) Inf **TX**96, Getting mucky. [All Infs comm types 4 or 5] **1993** *DARE* File **csWI**, When the weather is hot and sticky, I always say it's "mucky" outside. My mother, who was born in 1908, also talked about "mucky" weather in this same way.

mucky adj[3] See **make** adj, v[2], n

mucky-muck See **muck-a-muck 2**

mud n[1] See **mud cat 1c**

mud n[2] See **muddy** n

mud exclam

In mining: see quot 1929 *AmSp* 5; hence generally, Stop! Enough!

1929 *AmSp* 4.342 [Vagabond lingo], *Mud*—Enough. **1929** *AmSp* 5.146 **CO** [Mining expressions], *Mud*, the call of a driller to indicate that the water poured into the drill hole has now formed mud and that the hammering on the drill should stop. **1949** *PADS* 11.24 **CO**, *Mud.* . . Stop! That's plenty!

mud v

1 also *muddy;* also with *it:* To stir up mud from the bottom of a lake or stream in order to drive fish to the surface where they can be caught; to stir up sediment in (a lake or stream) for the same purpose; hence vbl n *mudd(y)ing.* **chiefly Sth** See Map

1877 Hallock *Sportsman's Gaz.* 371 (*DAE*), The season for muddying begins. **1938** in 1977 *Amer. Slave Suppl. 1* 1.73 **AL**, I allus like ter go muddin for fish, 'twas easern hook 'n' bait. **1966–70** *DARE* (Qu. P13, . . *Ways of fishing . . besides the ordinary hook and line*) Infs **FL**7, **TN**53, **VA**70, Mudding; **GA**7, Mudding—churn water up with a stick; **MS**47, Mudding—take stick and muddy up hole and dip fish out; **NC**87, Mudding—outlawed, killed young fish; **MS**11, Muddy the creek—makes fish come to the top; **GA**89, **MS**21, 66, Muddying. **1970** *DARE* FW Addit **seNE**, Mudding for fish— . . wading through the water pushing a tree branch so that it stirs the bottom mud and forces the fish to the surface, where they are caught. **1986** Pederson *LAGS Concordance*, 1 inf, **cMS**, Mud it or seine it—methods of fishing.

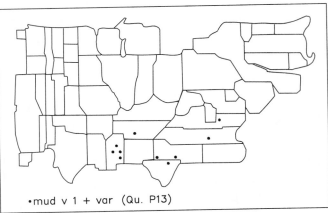

•mud v 1 + var (Qu. P13)

2 with *in:* To plant (a crop) in muddy ground.

1967 *DARE* FW Addit **LA**11, After the flood we repaired fences, "mudded in" cotton, [etc]. **1983** *Champaign-Urbana News-Gaz.* (IL) 29 Apr sec A 3/5, Farmers' annual move into their fields [was] delayed this year by a cold, damp spring. . . 'Last year I would have been mudding the seed in.'

3 with *up;* Of a turtle: to go into hibernation by burrowing in mud.

1937 [see **mud turtle 2a**].

muda grass n Also *moody grass, mudey ~* [Aphet forms of *Bermuda grass*] esp Sth

Bermuda grass (*Cynodon dactylon*).

1933 Rawlings *South Moon* 43 **nFL,** We got a day's work fightin' the 'muda grass. **1949** *AmSp* 24.111 **GA,** *Moody grass. . .* Bermuda grass. 'They calls it that because old man Moody was the first man went around selling the seed.' **1963** Edwards *Gravel* 119 **eTN** (as of 1920s), This 'mudey grass is gettin damp from the dew. **1966** *Wilson Coll.* **csKY,** Bermuda grass is known as "moody grass" in Mammoth Cave and Bowling Green areas. Common. **1968–70** *DARE* (Qu. L8) Inf **GA**52, Muda ['mudə] grass; (Qu. S8) Inf **MS**82, ['mudə] grass; **VA**75, Muda grass. **1971** Dwyer *Dict. for Yankees* 29 **Sth, S Midl,** *Muda grass*—Bermuda grass.

mud-baby n [From the habitat]

A plant of the genus *Echinodorus*. Also called **wampee, water plantain.** For other names of var spp see **lily pad 2**

1933 Small *Manual SE Flora* 21, *Echinodorus. . .* Mud-babies. **1976** Bailey–Bailey *Hortus Third* 414, [*Echinodorus*] *cordifolius. . .* Texas mud-baby. . . Md. to Ill., s. to w. Fla. and s. Tex.

mudbank fiddler crab See **mud fiddler**

mud bass n

1 =**mud sunfish 1.**

1884 Goode *Fisheries U.S.* 1.405, *The Mud Bass—Acantharchus pomotis.* This species is found only in the coastwise streams of the lowlands from New Jersey to North Carolina.

2 =**largemouth bass.**

1909 Webster *Amer. Dict.* 1417/3 (*DAE*), Mud bass, . . the large-mouthed black bass. . . *Indiana.* **1933** LA Dept. of Conserv. *Fishes* 313, *The Large-mouthed Black Bass. . .* Mud Bass. **1935** Caine *Game Fish* 3 **Sth,** *Large-mouthed Black Bass. . . Synonyms . .* Mud Bass.

3 A **warmouth** (here: *Lepomis gulosus*).

1949 Caine *N. Amer. Sport Fish* 47, The warmouth is commonly called "mud bass" because it prefers lakes and streams with mud bottoms. **1956** Harlan–Speaker *IA Fish* 130, *Warmouth. . . Other Names . .* mud bass. . . The warmouth is a . . sunfish strongly resembling the rock bass and often confused with it by many anglers. . . More than any of the other sunfishes, the warmouth has a strong preference for weedy mud-bottom areas and is found largely in the quiet backwater lakes of the Mississippi River. **1957** Trautman *Fishes* 498 **OH,** Although its [=warmouth's] colloquial name was "Mud Bass" it seemed to be less tolerant to turbidity and situation than was the Green Sunfish. **1983** Becker *Fishes WI* 817, *Warmouth. . . Other common names . .* mud bass.

mud bird n

=**wood thrush.**

1955 *Oriole* 20.1.11 **GA,** *Wood Thrush.—Mud Bird* (from using that substance in the construction of its nest).

mud blower n [See quot 1905]

=**burbot.**

1905 NJ State Museum *Annual Rept. for 1904* 417, *Lota maculosa. . .* Mud Blower. Ling. [*Ibid* 418, It [=burbot] was discovered by means of bubbles which were seen to eminate [sic] from certain depressions or holes in which the fish was found buried.] **1946** LaMonte *N. Amer. Game Fishes* 166, *Burbot. . . Names . .* Mud Blower. . . One of the fishes whose value to anglers is dependent on the scarcity of other fishes. **1973** Knight *Cook's Fish Guide* 385, Mud blower—Burbot. **1983** Becker *Fishes WI* 747, *Burbot. . . Other common names . .* mud blower.

mud boat n

1 also *mud skid, ~ sled, ~ wagon:* =**stoneboat.** chiefly **OH, IN, sIL** See Map Cf **boat 1**

1905 U.S. Forest Serv. *Bulletin* 61.43 [Logging terms], *Mudboat. . .* A low sled with wide runners, used for hauling logs in swamps. **1917** *DN* 4.396 **neOH,** *Mud-sled. . .* A long low sled with one pair of broad wooden runners for use in soft snow or mud; a flat-bottom. [*DN* Ed: So *mud-skid,* Cleveland, O.] **1951** *PADS* 15.57 **neIN,** *Mud-boat. . .* A low sled, with or without definite runners, used for farm hauling on dry ground as well as on mud or snow. **1958** McCulloch *Woods Words* 119 **Pacific NW,** *Mud boat*—A flat sled which would skid easily over a mud road. **1965** Carmony *Speech Terre Haute* 22 **cwIN,** The heavy sled-like vehicle used for removing stones from fields . . [1 inf] *mud boat.* **1965–70** *DARE* (Qu. L57, *A low wooden platform used for bringing stones or heavy things out of the fields*) 21 Infs, **chiefly OH, IN, sIL,** Mud boat; **IN**53, Mud wagon; (Qu. N40a, . . *Sleighs . . for hauling*

loads) Inf **IN**58, Mud boat—for hauling stones on snow or mud; poor farmers hauled family in it; **MO**18, Mud boat—homemade, just boards; **NJ**56, Mud boat—like stoneboat but with wider runner; **OH**22, Mud boat—fixed runners; **OH**32, Mud boat—for rocks and stone; **OH**27, 47, Mud boat; **OH**3, Mud sled—carried maple syrup; (Qu. N40b, . . *Sleighs for carrying people*) Inf **MO**18, Mud boat; (Qu. N40c, *Other kinds of sleighs*) Inf **OH**67, Mud boat—put your drag and plow on it; some called it a mud sled; **OH**74, Mud boat—for stones; **OH**88, Mud boat; (Qu. N41b, *Horse-drawn vehicles to carry heavy loads*) Inf **MD**13, Mud boat—platform on runners, pulled by horse or tractor, to haul logs, heavy things, over mud. **1966** Dakin *Dial. Vocab. Ohio R. Valley* 2.160 **sIL, sIN, sOH,** From the Scioto westward the *boat* of *stone boat* continues, but begins to appear as *mud boat* (for its use on wet, muddy ground) and in eastern Indiana this name is common. It is also used, along with *mud sled* (known in southwestern Ohio), in Illinois. **1967** Faries *Word Geog. MO* 84, Stone boat. . . [2 infs] *mud boat.* **1967** Jacobs *Rejoicing* 25 **cIN** (as of c1930), We put harness on Ned. He would pull the mudboat loaded with buckets, axes, hatchets, and other equipment. A mudboat . . was a narrow raft with runners, . . a handy thing in the woods. As the ground started to thaw, it rode lightly on top of the ground. **1967** *DARE* Tape **OH**6, A mud sled, they're similar to a stoneboat . . It's something low that drags right on the ground. . . They still use 'em quite an extent in the woods. **1968** Allen *It Happened* 113 **sIL,** A mudboat. . . was nothing more than the New England stoneboat brought west. . . This boat was made of two heavy crosspieces, often eight by eight inches, and was bottomed by wide two-inch boards or puncheons fastened on by large wooden pegs. **1986** Pederson *LAGS Concordance,* 1 inf, **neAR,** Mud boat—sled for hauling logs on land/water; A mud-boat run—a path dug by mud boat.

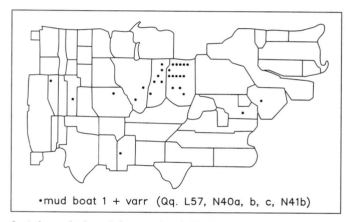

•mud boat 1 + varr (Qq. L57, N40a, b, c, N41b)

2 A boat designed for use in shallow or swampy water.

1968 *DARE* (Qu. O2, *Nicknames . . for an old, clumsy boat*) Inf **MD**20, Old mud boat—type of clumsy boat made of rough boards, square at both ends; (Qu. O10, . . *Kinds of boats*) Inf **IA**36, Mud boats. **1979** Hallowell *People Bayou* 38 **sLA,** We were in Jim's mudboat, an eighteen-foot skiff with an ancient sixteen-horsepower engine planted amidships and a propeller fastened close against the bottom. Most trappers use such boats. . . their inboard motors and propeller arrangement allow them to churn through bayous and channels that are half mud and half water. **1986** Pederson *LAGS Concordance,* 1 inf, **ceTX,** Mud boat—used in local canals; flat bottom; motor; 1 inf, **swLA,** Mud boats—for marshes; flat; propellers; 25–30 mph.

mud boot See **mud shoe**

mud box terrapin See **mud turtle 2b(1)**

mud buffalo n

=**bigmouth buffalo.**

1933 LA Dept. of Conserv. *Fishes* 441, *The Common Buffalo. . .* has come to be known under many popular names. . . [such as] Mud Buffalo and White Buffalo. **1983** Becker *Fishes WI* 615, *Bigmouth Buffalo. . .* Mud buffalo. [*Ibid* 616, It [=bigmouth buffalo] was encountered most frequently in water more than 1.5 m deep over substrates of mud.]

mudbug n Also *bug* chiefly **LA**

=**crawfish** n **B1.**

1955 *Ford Times* Feb 42 **LA,** The commercial crayfishermen use traps in deeper water where the mudbugs are bigger. **1968** *DARE* (Qu. P19, . . *Small, freshwater crayfish*) Inf **LA**22, Mudbug. **1981** *DARE* File **eTX,** The Cajuns eat crawfish where I come from. "Bugs," we'd call them—

that's short for "mudbugs." **1982** Heat Moon *Blue Highways* 116 **sLA,** You know, the Cajun, he sometime call them 'mudbugs.' But I never tell a customer that until he all full inside. But the crawfish, he live smilin' in the mud, he do. **1984** *Unitarian Universalist World* 15 Aug 1/3 **New Orleans LA,** The crawfish, affectionately known as mudbugs, are boiled Cajun-style in a large kettle over an open fire with corn, potatoes, onions, sausage, garlic and secret hot spices. **1993** *DARE* File **sLA,** Down here in Louisiana/Cajun country, mudbug is another name for crawfish. I haven't heard it used too much, but everyone knows what it means, and it is often used on signs, advertisements, and t-shirts. Was at Godfather's Pizza in Lafayette the other day, and there was a sign in the window for mudbug pizza. *Ibid* **LA,** Mudbug is another name for crawfish (not crayfish). **1993** *Gourmet* Apr 83 **LA,** There is no better way to prepare . . crayfish—known in parts of Louisiana variously as crawfish, crawdads, crawdaddies, creekcrabs, or mudbugs—than to boil them.

mud buzzard n
=**gannet 1.**
    1950 *PADS* 14.76 **FL,** *Mud-buzzard. . .* The gannet.

mud carp See **mudfish h**

mud cat n

1 also *mud catfish:* Any of var fishes of the family Ictaluridae; spec:

a A large catfish: usu **flathead catfish 1,** occas **blue catfish 1** or a **channel catfish** (here: *Ictalurus punctatus*). **chiefly Missip-Ohio Valleys, Gulf States**
    1818 *Amer. Monthly Mag. & Crit. Rev.* 3.354, I have pretty nearly explored the ichthyology of the river Ohio, and the following catalogue of its fishes, is complete. . . Silurus punctatus. . . Mud Cat-fish. *Ibid* 447, I have added about 20 species to my former catalogue of the fishes of the Ohio. . . Here follows their scientific and vulgar names. . . Glanis limosus. . . Mud catfish [etc]. **1819** Thomas *Travels W. Country* 211, The mud cat is covered with clouded spots, and is a very homely fish. **c1830** Martin *VA & DC* 347 **VA,** [The New River] is also remarkable for its fine fish, particularly the *mud* and *blue cat.* **1877** U.S. Natl. Museum *Bulletin* 10.95, *Pelodichthys* [sic] *olivaris. . . Mud Catfish. . .* Ohio Valley to Iowa and South. **1883** Twain *Life on Missip.* (Boston) 532, He did n't really catch anything but only just one small useless mud-cat. **1884** Goode *Fisheries U.S.* 1.628, *Ictalurus nigricans. . .* Professor Goode remarks: "I have observed frequently enormous specimens of this species in the Saint John's River [FL], where they are called Mud Cats." *Ibid, Leptops olivaris.* The "Mud Cat" . . is found in all the large rivers of the West and South. . . It is less attractive in its appearance than the other Catfishes, but we are not aware that its flesh is inferior to that of the others. **1908** Forbes–Richardson *Fishes of IL* 194, In the Southern States, fresh hickory-shad is greatly valued as a live bait for the mud-cat. . . The species is found in all suitable waters throughout the Mississippi Valley, and in the Gulf states, from Alabama west and south to Mexico. **c1940** Newman–Murphy *Conserv. Notes* 5 **neLA,** In the varities [sic] of cat-fish might be listed . . mud cat. **1965** Teale *Wandering Through Winter* 173 **OK,** Mud cats sometimes tip the scales at eighty pounds. **1965–70** *DARE* (Qu. P1, . . *Kinds of freshwater fish . . caught around here . . good to eat)* 47 Infs, **chiefly Missip-Ohio Valleys, Gulf States,** Mud cat(s) *or* mud catfish; (Qu. P3, *Freshwater fish that are not good to eat)* Infs DC4, GA77, IL71, IN22, MO20, NC53, TX33, 101, Mud cat(s) *or* mud catfish; KS10, Blue cats and yellow cats are varieties of mud cats; (Qu. P14, . . *Commercial fishing . . what do the fishermen go out after?)* Inf LA15, Mud cat. [*DARE* Ed: Some of these Infs may refer instead to other senses below.] **1966** *WI Conserv. Bulletin* July–Aug 14, Many know the fish [=flathead catfish] by such local names as yellow cat, mudcat, morgan cat, opelousa, or just plain bullhead. **1986** Pederson *LAGS Concordance* **Gulf Region,** 27 infs, Mud cat(s); 1 inf, Mud cat—not much good to eat; 1 inf, Mud cat = yellow cat; 1 inf, Mud cat—yellow; 1 inf, Mud cat = yellow cat, flap-head cat, broad head; 2 infs, Mud catfish.

b A bullhead **1b:** usu either the **brown bullhead 1** or a black **bullhead 1b** (here: *Ameiurus melas*), but also the **flat bullhead.**
    1842 DeKay *Zool. NY* 4.187, *P[imelodus] nebulosus.* The *Mud Catfish,* recognized by the scarified and clouded appearance of its skin. **1870** (1871) *Amer. Naturalist* 4.386 **NJ,** Mud Cat-fish (*Amiurus DeKayi*). **1878** U.S. Natl. Museum *Bulletin* 12.28 **SC,** *Amiurus* [sic] *brunneus. . .* This is the common cat-fish of the Saluda, and is known as the Mud Cat. *Ibid, Amiurus platycephalus. . .* The fishermen confound it with the preceding under the name of Mud Cat. *Ibid* 44 **GA,** *Amiurus*

brunneus. . . This is the most abundant edible fish of the Chattahoochee. . . It is usually known as the Mud Cat. **1897** *Outing* 30.439, The small "mud-cat," or bull-head, also had these weapons [=spikes on the fins] with a complete knowledge of their use. **1906** *DN* 3.147 **nwAR,** *Mud-cat. . .* A small kind of cat-fish. **1940** Stong *Hawkeyes* 246 **IA,** The mudcat is purplish black and very coarse and oily. They will not weigh more than three or four pounds, ordinarily, but the big fellows who come up from the Mississippi in high water may weigh a hundred. **1963** Sigler–Miller *Fishes UT* 111, *Ictalurus melas . .* Common Names: Black bullhead, bullhead, mudcat. [*Ibid* 114, The black bullhead prefers sluggish streams and rivers, especially those with muddy bottoms.] **1967** *DARE* (Qu. P1, . . *Kinds of freshwater fish . . caught around here . . good to eat)* Inf LA12, Mud cat—they get up to several pounds; LA14, Mud cat—name for bullhead. **1967** *DARE* Tape IL9, I personally prefer a catfish about four pounds, and that would have to be a mudcat. I don't want a channel cat . . a mudcat is sweet. **1983** Becker *Fishes WI* 702, *Brown Bullhead. . .* Other common names . . mudcat. [*Ibid* 705, In the late fall, brown bullheads become sluggish and cease feeding, often "mudding up," or burying themselves in soft, leafy ooze along the shore.] **1986** Pederson *LAGS Concordance,* 1 inf, **swGA,** Mud black cat—fish.

c also *mud:* A **stonecat;** see quots.
    1905 NJ State Museum *Annual Rept. for 1904* 171, *Schilbeodes gyrinus. . .* Mud Cat Fish. . . These small cat fish are dangerous to handle, as their small spines are capable of inflicting painful wounds. *Ibid* 173, *Schilbeodes insignis. . .* Mud Cat Fish. . . It is not distinguished from *Schilbeodes gyrinus* by most fishermen, who usually regard all small cat fish as the young of the larger individuals of *Ameiurus.* **1969–70** *DARE* (Qu. P3, *Freshwater fish that are not good to eat)* Inf DC4, Poison mud cat; VA8, Mud catfish = madtoms—used for bait when cut up; (Qu. P7, *Small fish used as bait for bigger fish)* Inf SC66, Muds; TX62, Mud catfish (used when they're small). **1986** Pederson *LAGS Concordance* **Gulf Region,** 1 inf, Mud cat = polliwog, fish.

2 =**muskrat 1.**
    1961 Jackson *Mammals WI* 245, In Wisconsin usually called muskrat. Other names include . . mud cat, mushrat [etc].

3 also *mud rat;* Fig: used as an epithet for a person, esp an inhabitant of Mississippi. *joc* or *derog*
    1872 Schele de Vere *Americanisms* 660, *Mississippi* is occasionally spoken of humorously as the *Mudcat* State, the inhabitants being quite generally known as Mud-cats, a name given to the large catfish abounding in the swamps and the mud of the rivers. **1909** *DN* 3.351 **eAL, wGA,** *Mud-cat. . .* A catfish. Often used as a term of opprobrium. **1945** *Chi. D. News* 16 Aug 10/7 *(DA),* While we are laying down surrender terms for the Japanese, how about a Declaration on Senator 'Dear Dago' Bilbo, the Mississippi mudcat? **1947** Guthrie *Big Sky* 350 **West** (as of 1843), A settler's cabin stood in a clearing, and the settler himself hung to the handles of a plow. . . He whoaed the mules when he saw the pirogue and leaned on the plow to watch. . . His voice boomed out, "Hello, you mud cats." "Hello, grayback." "Grayback maybe I be, but I ain't never seed a mud cat I couldn't handle." "You been foolin' with minners." To Boone Mefford said, "What gits into these damn farmers makes 'em want to mix with river men?" **1948** Mencken *Amer. Lang. Suppl. 2* 630, Schele de Vere . . reported that Mississippi was the *Mudcat State . . ,* but it seems to be obsolescent. The nickname of choice is now *Magnolia State.* **1949** *AmSp* 24.26, Almost every American has heard . . *Mud-cat* for a Mississippian. **1981** Pederson *LAGS Basic Materials,* 1 inf, **ceTX,** Mud rat (from Miss.); cowboy; swamp rat.

mud catfish See **mud cat 1**

mud chicken n Also *mud chick* Cf **mud hen 1b, c**
Either the **coot** n[1] **1** or the **Florida gallinule.**
    1936 Roberts *MN Birds* 1.454, *American Coot. . . Other names:* Mud Hen, Mud Duck, Mud Chicken. **1953** *AmSp* 28.277, We have such terms as . . *mud chick* (American coot, Mont.) *Ibid* 279, Mud chicken. Common gallinule. Texas. American coot. Minn.

mud chub n

1 A **warmouth** (here: *Lepomis gulosus*).
    1933 LA Dept. of Conserv. *Fishes* 342, The Warmouth Bass has come to bear many confusing popular names. These are . . Mud Chub, . . Indianfish. **1935** Caine *Game Fish* 33, *Warmouth. . . Synonyms . .* Mud Chub. [*Ibid* 34, The warmouth prefers . . shallow mud-bottom ponds and lakes.]

2 The creek chub (*Semotilus atromaculatus*).
    1983 Becker *Fishes WI* 437, *Creek Chub. . .* Other common names . .

mud chub. . . Abundant in small- and medium-sized streams and rivers throughout the state.

mud clam n

1 =**soft-shell clam.**

1920 CA Fish & Game Comm. *Fish Bulletin* 4.56, *Mya arenaria. . . Other names*—Soft clam; long clam; mud clam. **1931** Blatchley *My Nature Nook* 178, The smaller mud clam, *Mya arenaria . . ,* so common along the New England coasts, does not occur along the sandy shores of Florida.

2 Prob a **geoduck 1** or similar clam.

1909 U.S. Dept. Commerce Bur. Fisheries *Document* 645.77 **AK,** Large mud clams (probably *Panopea generosa*) have been reported from southeast Alaska. **1967** *DARE* (Qu. P18, . . *Kinds of shellfish*) Infs **OR**5, **WA**20, Mud clams.

3 The bent-nose macoma *(Macoma nasuta).*

1920 CA Fish & Game Comm. *Fish Bulletin* 4.43, *Macoma nasuta. . .* Mud clam. . . The most common and widely distributed species in California. It is typically a form of the sheltered muddy bays.

mud crow n Cf **mud hen 1b, pond crow**

=**coot** n[1] **1.**

1955 MA Audubon Soc. *Bulletin* 39.443 **RI,** American Coot. . . Mud Crow (R.I. In allusion to its dark color and its habit of frequenting mud.)

mud dab n

1 =**winter flounder.**

1873 in 1878 Smithsonian Inst. *Misc. Coll.* 14.2.16 **MA,** *Pseudopleuronectes americanus. . .* Mud dab *(Massachusetts Bay).* **1972** Sparano *Outdoors Encycl.* 384, *Winter Flounder. Common Names . .* mud dab. . . It lies on the bottom, preferring sand or mud.

2 A **flounder** n **B** of the genus *Limanda.*

1898 U.S. Natl. Museum *Bulletin* 47.2644, *Limanda. . .* Mud Dabs. **1905** NJ State Museum *Annual Rept. for 1904* 395, *Limanda. . .* The Mud Dabs.

mud dace n

1 A **mudminnow 1** (here: *Umbra pygmaea*).

1884 U.S. Natl. Museum *Bulletin* 27.470, *Umbra pygmaea. . . Mud Dace; . . Mud Minnow. . .* Eastern United States from New York to South Carolina.

2 A **shiner** (here: *Notropis bifrenatus*).

1891 Jesup *Plants Hanover NH* 59, N[otropis] bifrenatus. . . Muddace. . . Common.

mud darter n chiefly Upper Missip Valley

A **darter 1** (here: *Etheostoma asprigene*).

1943 Eddy–Surber *N. Fishes* 200 **Upper Missip Valley,** The northern mud darter ranges from southern Minnesota and Wisconsin to Arkansas. . . Its preference [is for] the muddy sloughs and river mouths near the Mississippi and its larger tributaries. **1947** Hubbs–Lagler *Fishes Gt. Lakes* 88, Northern Mud Darter. . . Generally over soft bottoms in the sluggish parts of larger rivers. **1956** Harlan–Speaker *IA Fish* 151, The length of the mud darter is about 2½ inches. **1970** WI Acad. *Trans.* 58.289, *Etheostoma asprigene* (Forbes)—Mud darter. **1983** Becker *Fishes WI* 937, In Wisconsin, the mud darter is known only to occur in the Mississippi River drainage basin. **1991** Amer. Fisheries Soc. *Common Names Fishes* 48, *Etheostoma asprigene . .* F[reshwater] . . mud darter.

mud dauber n Also *mud dobber*

1 also *mud-dauber wasp:* Any of var wasps, usu of the families Sphecidae or Vespidae, but also of the family Pompilidae, which build a nest of mud. **chiefly Midl, West** See Map and Map Section Cf **dirt dauber 1, mud wasp** Also called **bricklayer, clay dauber, dauber, daubler, dirt dauber 1, mudder 2;** for other names of var genera and spp see **black hornet, ~ jacket, ~ wasp, blue jacket 2, ~ mud dauber, ~ wasp, clodhopper 5, green wasp, house-builder, jack daubler, mason wasp, mud digger 1, ~ diver, ~ doodler, organ-pipe mud dauber**

1856 *Zoologist* ser 1 14.5030, The species of the genus Pelopaeus are popularly known as mud-daubers in America. **1867** Harris *Sut Lovingood Yarns* 178 **TN,** Mud daubers nestes onder the soundin board. **1884** (1885) McCook *Tenants* 443 **PA,** They [=hornets] . . carry war into the insect world, their weapon not being their sting as with their relations

the Mud-daubers and Digger Wasps, but their formidable jaws. **1899** (1912) Green *VA Folk-Speech* 290, *Mud-dauber. . .* A digger wasp; a mason. **1906** *DN* 3.147 **nwAR,** *Mud-dauber. . .* A harmless black wasp which builds a nest of mud. **1937** Kroll *I Was Share-Cropper* 90, Smoke blowing from the fireplace, and generations of mud-daubers, had made the ceiling an unclean dingy gray. **1946** *PADS* 5.30 **VA,** *Mud daubers. . .* Wasps; not common. **1949** (1958) Stuart *Thread* 70 **KY,** There were wasps' nests, mud-daubers' nests, and birds' nests above the window. **1950** *WELS,* 9 Infs, **WI,** Mud dauber(s). **1951** West *Witch Diggers* 96 **IN,** He had watched a mud-dauber stitching in and out of the opened windows, hunting a spot to lay down its load of clay. **1958** *Hand Coll.* **ID,** Hornets are called "mud dobbers" in Idaho. **1965–70** *DARE* (Qu. R20) 224 Infs, **chiefly Midl, West,** Mud dauber; **MO**5, Mud-dauber wasp; (Qu. R21) Inf **IL**126, Mud dauber. **1974** Dillard *Pilgrim* 214, My life inside the cottage is mostly Tinker Creek and mud dauber wasps. **1986** Pederson *LAGS Concordance,* 67 infs, **Gulf Region,** Mud dauber(s).

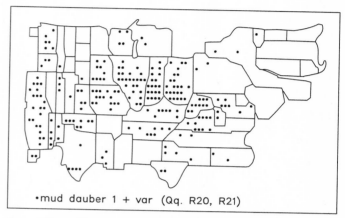

•*mud dauber 1 + var (Qq. R20, R21)*

2 =**cliff swallow. chiefly West** Cf **mud swallow**

1899 Bergen *Animal Lore* 34 **KS,** The building of the mud-daubers, or swallows, on the barn or house is a sign of prosperity to the occupants of the house. The destruction of the nest brings misfortune. **1928** Bailey *Birds NM* 463, At Tres Piedras [NM] where the people call it a "mud dauber," Mr. Gaut found it abundant about the houses. **1945** Pearson *Country Flavor* 49, There was often a phoebe's home to explore and dozens of mud daubers' nests. **1953** Jewett *Birds WA* 449, *Oregon Cliff Swallow. . .* Other names . . Mud Dauber. **1965–70** *DARE* (Qu. Q20, . . *Kinds of swallows and birds like them*) Infs **CA**87, 136, **CO**11, **KS**5, **MT**5, **VA**27, Mud dauber; (Qu. Q14) Inf **KS**6, Mud dauber; (Qu. R20) Inf **OR**13, Mud dauber—that's a swallow.

mud-dauber wasp See **mud dauber 1**

mudder n[1] See **mother** n[1]

mudder n[2]

=**mud dauber 1.**

1967–68 *DARE* (Qu. R20) Infs **MD**40, **MI**65, Mudder.

mud devil n obs

=**hellbender 1.**

1825 in 1826 *Amer. Jrl. Science* 11.278, Menopoma Alleghaniensis. . . Hell-bender. Mud-devil. **1859** (1968) Bartlett *Americanisms* 283, *Mud-devil.* See . . *Salamander* [=*Cryptobranchus alleganiensis*].

muddie n Cf **clayie, dobe** n **5**

In marble play: a baked clay marble.

1942 Berrey–Van den Bark *Amer. Slang* 665.2, Muddie, *a clay marble.* **1955** *PADS* 23.25 **cwTN,** *Muddie. . .* A marble made of clay. **1967** *DARE* (Qu. EE6c, *Cheap marbles*) Inf **PA**19, Muddies. **c1970** Wiersma *Marbles Terms* **cwMI,** Muddie—a clay playing marble.

mud digger n

1 A **mud dauber 1.** Cf **digger wasp**

1968 *DARE* (Qu. R20) Inf **MD**3, Mud digger.

2 See quot.

1970 *DARE* (Qu. HH1, *Names and nicknames for a rustic or countrified person*) Inf **VA**50, Mud digger—he digs clams and oysters.

muddigrubs See **mulligrubs**

mudding See **mud** v

mud dipper n

=**ruddy duck.**

  1888 Trumbull *Names of Birds* 110, *Ruddy Duck*. . . At Eastville, Va., *mud dipper.* **1917** (1923) *Birds Amer.* 1.152, *Ruddy Duck*. . . *Other Names*. . . Mud-dipper. **1944** Hausman *Amer. Birds* 520, Mud-dipper— see Duck, Ruddy.

mud-disk n

=**brass buttons.**

  1959 Anderson *Flora AK* 492, *C[otula] coronopifolia*. . . Mud-Disk. . . Tidal flats, southeast Alaska. **1974** Welsh *Anderson's Flora AK* 139, *Mud-disk*. . . Beaches and tidal flats.

mud diver n Also *mud hornet*

A **mud dauber 1.**

  1969–70 *DARE* (Qu. R20) Inf **CA207**, Mud diver; **CA145**, Mud hornet.

muddle n esp eNC

A stew, usu made with fish; a gathering at which such a stew is featured.

  1833 *Amer. Turf Reg.* 4.404 neNC, To make a Muddle.—Take shad, pike or rock, fresh from the stream. . . Take sundry slices of pork. . . [A]dd red pepper in large quantity . . and as much water as, when done, may leave it doubtful if the muddle be a stew or a soup. . . [P]lunge in the boiling mass slices of corn bread, in the proportion of one-fourth. **1890** *Century Dict.* 4654 neMA, *Pottle*. . . A dish made by Connecticut fishermen by frying pork in the bottom of a kettle, then adding water, and stewing in the water pieces of fresh fish. *Muddle,* made by Cape Ann fishermen, is the same dish with the addition of crackers. **1939** FWP *Guide NC* 105, Fish muddle, a typical Eastern Carolina dish, is made by putting several kinds of fish in a kettle with layers of onions and potatoes, seasoning with fried fat meat, adding water to cover, and cooking to a stew. **1939** Harris *Purslane* 122 **cNC**, They say she used to cook coon muddles by the potful, and she comes here now and then to hunt her some young coons like she use to. **1941** Daniels *Tar Heels* 257 **eNC**, Fish muddle is a name for fish stew, the ingredients of which vary with what you have got. *Ibid* 258, But the barbecues and the fish muddles (both are the names for the gatherings as well as the dishes), in the eastern part of the State, where they are most often held, are occasions for both eating and drinking. **1952** Brown *NC Folkl.* 1.529, *Coon muddle*. . . Brunswick stew—Chapel Hill. **1966** *DARE* (Qu. H45, *Dishes made with meat, fish, or poultry that everybody around here would know, but that people in other places might not*) Inf **NC14**, Rock muddle [rɔk mʌtl]—boil rockfish with potatoes, butter beans, tomatoes, seasoning, carrots, celery; **NC16**, Rock muddle [rɔk mʌtl]—rockfish cooked and seasoned with onion, bacon grease, salt, pepper, parsley; some put potatoes and boiled eggs in it; **NC18**, Rock muddle—rockfish, bacon, onion, potatoes, tomatoes, all stewed together; **NC20**, Fish muddle—rockfish, potatoes, tomatoes, onions, just about everything in it.

muddler n **chiefly Gt Lakes**

A **sculpin** (*Cottus* spp), esp the **mottled sculpin** or *Cottus cognatus.*

  1943 Eddy–Surber *N. Fishes* 230, The northern muddler [=*Cottus bairdii*] commonly rests on the bottom on its enormous, fanlike pectoral fins. It swims short distances with a darting movement that resembles a hop. *Ibid* 231, The slimy muddler [=*C. cognatus*] . . is similar to *Cottus bairdii* in appearance and habits. **1947** Hubbs–Lagler *Fishes Gt. Lakes* 96, The muddlers, as these fishes [=*Cottus* spp] are known in the Great Lakes region, are bottom dwellers. **1950** Everhart *Fishes ME* 50, The freshwater sculpin or slimy muddler is distributed from southern Canada into the Great Lakes drainage and east of the Alleghenies. **1966** *DARE* (Qu. P7, *Small fish used as bait for bigger fish*) Inf **MI**10, Muddler. **1968** *WI Conserv. Bulletin* May–June 15, His knowledge of the slimy sculpin or muddler has been helpful to him. **1983** Becker *Fishes WI* 969, *Mottled Sculpin*. . . Other common names . . northern muddler, muddler. *Ibid* 974, *Slimy Sculpin*. . . Other common names: slimy muddler, common slimy muddler. **1991** Amer. Fisheries Soc. *Common Names Fishes* 152, Muddler—see sculpins.

muddling vbl n [*OED muddle* v. 2 " 'To rout with the bill, as geese and ducks do'. . . To grub in the soil"] Cf **grabble v 2, mud v 1**

  1981 Vogt *Nat. Hist. WI* 93, Muddling is the technique of the serious turtle catcher—feeling rapidly through the muck and weeds along the bottom of ponds with your hands and feet, and grabbing anything that moves.

mud dobber See **mud dauber**

mud doodler n

A **mud dauber 1.**

  1966 *DARE* (Qu. R20) Inf **SC21**, Mud doodler.

mud duck n

1 =**coot** n[1] **1.** chiefly Midl, N Cent   See Map   Cf **mud chicken, mud hen 1b**

  1857 *Porter's Spirit of Times* 26 Sept 54 **IA**, There is duck of every quality, canvas-back, wood, mud, and various other species of ducks. **1923** U.S. Dept. Ag. *Misc. Circular* 13.46 **MN**, *American Coot*. . . *Vernacular Names*. . . *In local use*. . . Mud duck. **1936** Roberts *MN Birds* 1.454, *American coot*. . . Other names: Mud Hen, Mud Duck, Mud Chicken. [*Ibid* 455, The Coot, or Mud-hen, is the most Duck-like member of the Rail family in Minnesota.] **1955** Forbush–May *Birds* 168, *Fulica americana americana*. . . Mud-hen; Mud-duck. **1965–70** *DARE* (Qu. Q9, *The bird that looks like a small, dull-colored duck and is commonly found on ponds and lakes*) 23 Infs, **chiefly Midl, N Cent**, Mud duck; (Qu. Q5, . . *Kinds of wild ducks*) 10 Infs, **scattered**, Mud duck. **1986** Pederson *LAGS Concordance*, 1 inf, **nwLA**, Mud duck = coot, poule d'eau; edible but smells bad.

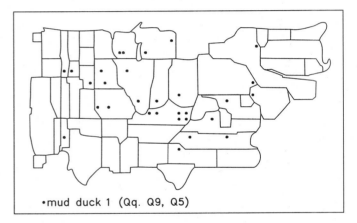

•mud duck 1 (Qq. Q9, Q5)

2 =**shoveler.**

  1923 U.S. Dept. Ag. *Misc. Circular* 13.14 **NE**, *Shoveler*. . . *Vernacular Names*. . . *In local use*. . . Mud duck. **1982** Elman *Hunter's Field Guide* 160, *Shoveler*. . . *Common & regional names* . . mud duck. *Ibid* 161, Shapeless little flocks of shovelers push slowly along, . . behaving like teal in all respects except speed. To shoot a putative teal and collect a mud duck is depressing. [*Ibid* 163, Shovelers. . . slush mud through their bristle-edged bills, taking more bottom food than any other ducks.]

3 =**ring-necked duck.**

  1923 U.S. Dept. Ag. *Misc. Circular* 13.21 **VA**, *Ring-necked duck*. . . *Vernacular Names*. . . *In local use*. . . Mud duck.

muddy n Also abbr *mud* [Cf Ger *Mutti* colloq var of *Mutter* mother] Cf **faddy**

A mother—also used as a quasi-personal name.

  1905 *DN* 3.78 **nwAR**, *Faddy*. . . 'Here's faddy and muddy!' Not uncommon. *Ibid* 88, *Muddy*. . . Mother. Faddy . . , bud(dy), and sis(sy) correspond. **1993** *DARE* File **seWI** (as of c1930s), *Muddy* was a distortion of Mutter, the German for mother, often shortened to *Mud*, . . used regularly by us children.

muddy v See **mud v 1**

muddy-breast n Also *muddy-belly*

=**golden plover.**

  1888 Trumbull *Names of Birds* 196, [Golden Plover] At Newport, R.I. *Muddy-breast.* **1899** Howe–Sturtevant *Birds RI* 54, *Muddy-breast*. . . Becoming scarcer and scarcer each season. **1917** (1923) *Birds Amer.* 1.257, *Golden Plover*. . . *Other Names*. . . Muddy-breast; Muddy-belly. **1955** Forbush–May *Birds* 174, *American Golden Plover*. . . Muddybreast. . . In spring black below, . . in autumn brown below.

muddying See **mud v**

mud eel n

1 Either an amphiuma such as the **congo snake 1,** or the great **siren** (*Siren lacertina*). **chiefly Sth**

1823 in 1929 Weems *Mason Locke Weems* 3.353 **SC,** The British . . fairly chased our militiamen across Broad River, to the huge amazement of the mud eels and cats. **1842** Holbrook *N. Amer. Herpetology* 5.102, Siren lacertina. . . Mud Eel or Siren, *Vulgo.* **1890** *Century Dict.* 3887, *Mud-eel.* . . A long slender salamander which lives in the mud, as *Siren lacertina* or *Murænopsis tridactyla* [=*Amphiuma tridactylum*]. **1892** IN Dept. Geol. & Nat. Resources *Rept. for 1891* 416, *Siren lacertina.* . . *Mud-eel. Siren.* . . Distribution from North Carolina west to Mexico, and up the Mississippi Valley to Alton, Ill., and Lafayette, Ind. **1894** U.S. Natl. Museum *Proc.* 17.337 **FL,** *Amphiuma means.* . . is known under the name of "mud eel." . . People digging in the "muck" find them frequently in such soil, and I have taken them with my net in ponds and small lakes. **1925** *Book of Rural Life* 8.4864, Another group [of salamanders] includes the *mud eel* of the waterways of the southeastern United States. **1926** TX Folkl. Soc. *Pub.* 5.77 **TX,** The "stinging snake" uses this sharp caudal extension as a means of holding the slippery mud eel, or siren, on which he feeds, while he is working it in position to swallow. **1928** Baylor Univ. Museum *Contrib.* 16.9 **Sth,** Mud Eel. The Siren burrows in mud, and this name for it is in almost universal use in some of the Southern States. **1953** Schmidt *N. Amer. Amphibians* 27, *Amphiuma means.* . . *Common name.* . . Congo eel, . . mud eel.

2 A **lamprey** (here: either *Ichthyomyzon unicuspis* or *Petromyzon marinus*).

1903 NY State Museum & Sci. Serv. *Bulletin* 60.15, The silver lamprey or mud eel is found in the Great Lakes region. **1938** Schrenkeisen *Field Book Fishes* 5, The young [of *Petromyzon marinus*] . . are called "mud-eels." [**1947** Hubbs–Lagler *Fishes Gt. Lakes* 26, Lampreys inhabit creeks, rivers and lakes. . . After . . the young appear and drift downstream . . they become lodged in the mud of a bank in some quiet back-water. Here they burrow into the bottom material and spend several years as larvae.]

3 See quot 1890. [See quot 1983]

1840 *Boston Jrl. Nat. Hist.* 3.473, *A[mmocoetes] concolor.* Kirtland. The Mud-Eel. **1890** *Century Dict.* 3887, *Mud-eel.* . . An eel of any kind; especially, in New England, a yellow-bellied sluggish variety of the common eel, found in muddy water. [**1983** Becker *Fishes WI* 260, Eels [=*Anguilla rostrata*] . . usually spend the day . . buried in the mud with only their snouts protruding. . . In winter, in cold regions like New England, the eel burrows in soft mud and hibernates.]

mudey grass See **muda grass**

mud face n

See quots.

1966 Barnes–Jensen *Dict. UT Slang* 31, *Mud face.* . . One whose facial features are always cloudy in expression. **1967** *DARE* (Qu. X29, *Joking or uncomplimentary words for a person's face*) Inf **IA**8, Mug, mud face.

mud-fat adj [Engl dial; of EDD mud-fat (at mud sb.¹ 3) "very fat indeed"; cf also AND (at mud 2)] esp S Midl

Very fat.

[**1912** Green *VA Folk-Speech* 27, Fat as mud.] **1940** *Amer. Mercury* 50.212 **seKY,** Ever see such mud-fat ones [=quail]? [**1940** *S. Folkl. Qrly.* 4.211, Fat as mud.] **1952** Brown *NC Folkl.* 1.568, *Mud-fat.* . . Very fat; generally in reference to an animal.—General. [**1952** TN Folk Lore Soc. *Bulletin* 18.19 **wTN,** Fat as mud. (i.e. "sloppy fat").] **1986** Pederson *LAGS Concordance,* 1 inf, **ceAR,** Get them just mud fat—really fat; for slaughter.

mud fiddler n Also *mudbank fiddler crab*

A **fiddler crab** (here: *Uca pugnax*).

1969 *DARE* FW Addit **Hatteras Is. NC,** Mud fiddler—crab with one claw much bigger than the other; lives in the mud flats. **1976** Warner *Beautiful Swimmers* 98 **MD,** My attention was drawn to great numbers of *Uca pugnax,* or the mudbank fiddler crab, scurrying across the road. **1981** Meinkoth *Audubon Field Guide Seashore* 655, The Mud Fiddler. . . ranges from Cape Cod to northeastern Florida, and from northwestern Florida to Texas. . . This crab prefers a muddy habitat and frequently digs into mud banks along tidal marshes.

mudfish n

Any of var fishes, as:

a =**bowfin. chiefly SE**

1787 Gesellschaft Naturforschender Freunde *Schriften* 8.174, *Amia calva.* . . Mudfish; in Carolina. **1791** Bartram *Travels* 176 **neFL,** The mud fish is large, thick or round, and two feet in length; his meat white and tender, but soft and tastes of mud, and is not much esteemed. **1842** DeKay *Zool. NY* 4.269, *The Western Mud-fish. Amia Occidentalis.* . . This species is found in Lakes Erie and Ontario. **1854** Wailes *Rept. on Ag. & Geol. MS* 333, Amia calva. Mud-fish. **1884** Goode *Fisheries U.S.* 1.659, Though not considered eatable in the North, it [=*Amia calva*] is very highly esteemed by the negroes of the South, who say "there is nothing sweeter than a Mud-fish." **1933** LA Dept. of Conserv. *Bulletin* 33.383, Throughout the rest of its range [=outside Louisiana], the Grindle is known as . . Poisson marais, . . the Mudfish [etc]. **1961** Douglas *My Wilderness* 146 **Everglades FL,** Mary, the Seminole, had smoked fish hanging in the hut where she did the cooking. She and her folks eat bowfin or mudfish and the garfish that most people reject. **1965–70** *DARE* (Qu. P3, *Freshwater fish that are not good to eat*) Infs **FL**4, 9, 32, 35, **GA**3, **SC**63, Mudfish; **FL**7, Mudfish [same as] blacks; **FL**27, Mudfish or dogfish; **SC**40, Jack grindle—usually called mudfish here—scavenger; **SC**43, Mudfish—cottony taste—scavenger; (Qu. P1, . . *Kinds of freshwater fish* . . *caught around here* . . *good to eat*) Infs **GA**16, 41, **KS**3, **SC**19, 26, 66, Mudfish; **GA**19, —same as blackfish; **GA**34, Blackfish—we call 'em mudfish; (Qu. P14, . . *Commercial fishing* . . *what do the fishermen go out after?*) Inf **SC**19, Mudfish. [*DARE* Ed: Some of these Infs may refer instead to **c** or **h** below.] **1974** *DARE* File, In much of the coastal South it [=the bowfin] is called mudfish. **1986** Pederson *LAGS Concordance,* 14 infs, **Gulf Region,** Mudfish; 1 inf, **seAL,** Mudfish = grindle, blackfish; 1 inf, **neFL,** Mudfish—like cat, muddy taste, meat soft; 1 inf, **seLA,** Mudfish = grindle or choupique.

b A **killifish 1:** usu a **mummichog** (here: *Fundulus heteroclitus*), but also *Fundulus majalis.*

1787 Gesellschaft Naturforschender Freunde *Schriften* 8.170, *Cobitis heteroclita* [=*Fundulus heteroclitus*], Mudfish in Carolina. **1882** U.S. Natl. Museum *Proc.* 5.585 **SC,** *Fundulus heteroclitus.* . . *Mud fish.* Many specimens from Charleston enable us to make a more detailed comparison with specimens from the Gulf. **1896** U.S. Natl. Museum *Bulletin* 47.640, *Fundulus heteroclitus.* . . *mudfish.* . . Coast of Maine to the Rio Grande, everywhere very common in brackish waters, often burying itself in the mud in shallow lagoons. **1903** NY State Museum & Sci. Serv. *Bulletin* 60.310, The killifish [=*Fundulus heteroclitus*]. . . is frequently called mummichog or salt-water minnow, and the name mudfish has been applied to it. **1991** Amer. Fisheries Soc. *Common Names Fishes* 152, Mudfish—see bowfin . . mummichog . . sailfin molly . . striped killifish [=*Fundulus majalis*].

c A **chubsucker 1** (here: *Erimyzon oblongus*).

1817 *Amer. Monthly Mag. & Crit. Rev.* 2.121, *Cyprinus vittatus* [=*Erimyzon oblongus*]. . . Found in the Hudson above the falls, vulgar name Mudfish. **1931–33** *LANE Worksheets* **cwCT,** Chub sucker . . a mudfish, same as dace. **1970** *DARE* (Qu. P1, . . *Kinds of freshwater fish* . . *caught around here* . . *good to eat*) Inf **SC**66, Mudfish—same as sucker.

d =**flathead catfish 1. Cf mud cat 1a**

1820 Rafinesque *Ohio R. Fishes* 67, *Pylodictis limosus.* . . is found in the lower parts of the Ohio and in the Mississippi, where it lives on muddy bottoms. . It bears the name of Mudcat, Mudfish, Mudsucker. . . It is good to eat and bites at the hook. **1986** Pederson *LAGS Concordance,* 1 inf, **ceAL,** Mudfish = catfish.

e =**mudminnow 1.**

1855 Smithsonian Inst. *Annual Rept. for 1854* 342, *Mud-Fish. Melanura pygmæa.* . . I have caught them . . on the American shores of all the great lakes except Lake Superior. **1870** (1871) *Amer. Naturalist* 4.99 **NJ,** Other streams, sluggish and thick, . . are paradisiacal to the mud-fish (*Melanura*). **1880** Günther *Intro. Study Fishes* 619, *Umbra limi,* locally distributed in the United States; called . . "Dog-fish" or "Mud-fish" in America. **1905** NJ State Museum *Annual Rept. for 1904* 180, *Umbra pygmæa.* . . Mud Minnow. Mud Fish. [*Ibid* 182, It is . . common . . to take them in shallow pools of clear water that have a deep bottom of soft mud. In such places they remain altogether concealed, but may be easily scooped out with the mud.] **1908** Forbes–Richardson *Fishes of IL* 202, *Umbridae. The Mudfishes.* . . Fishes of small size and carnivorous habit, . . very tenacious of life. *Ibid* 204, Ditches on the plains of Wisconsin, or mere bog-holes containing nothing else beyond tadpoles, may thus be found full of mudfish. **1983** Becker *Fishes WI* 387, *Central Mudminnow.* . . Other common names . . mudfish.

f =**mudsucker 1c.**

1882 U.S. Natl. Museum *Bulletin* 16.636, *G[illichthys] mirabilis. Mud-fish.* . . Pacific coast. [**1898** U.S. Natl. Museum *Bulletin* 47.2250,

Gillichthys mirabilis. . . A most remarkable little fish; very abundant in the mud flats in shallow water along the California coast, burrowing in holes in the mud like a crawfish.]

g =**blackfish 3.**

1893 U.S. Census Office *Rept. Population AK 1890* 120 **AK,** In winter a species of mudfish called blackfish, found in the lakes [of the Yukon delta area], is a great food source.

h also *mud carp, mudhog:* The common carp *(Cyprinus carpio).*

1926 (1949) McQueen–Mizell *Hist. Okefenokee* 53 **seGA,** Fresh water carp (mud fish) up to 14 pounds. **1949** Caine *N. Amer. Sport Fish* 154, Carp fishermen take their sport very seriously. . . *Colloquial Names* . . Mud Carp, Mudhog. **1975** Evanoff *Catch More Fish* 96, [Names for the common carp include] Mud carp, mudhog.

i A **molly** n[1] **7b** (here: *Poecilia latipinna*).

1960 Amer. Fisheries Soc. *List Fishes* 63, Mudfish—see bowfin; mummichog; killifish, striped; molly, sailfin.

mud fishing vbl n

1969 DARE (Qu. P17, . . *When* . . *people fish by lowering a line and sinker close to the bottom of the water*) Inf **NY**198, Bottom fishing, mud fishing.

mudge v Also with *along* [Scots dial]

1950 PADS 14.48 **SC,** Mudge. . . To move along slowly; to work in a leisurely way. Usually with the adv. *along.* . . Aiken County, obsolescent.

mudge n [Perh Scots, Engl dial *mudge* a movement, stir] A state of confusion.

1936 Lutes *Country Kitchen* 186 **sMI** (as of 1880s), I'd ruther go without any dinner. . . than be mixed up in the mudge you'll be in gettin' ready, and the bedlam after they're here.

mudge along See **mudge** v

mud goose n

=**Hutchins's goose.**

1844 Giraud *Birds Long Is.* 292 **seNY,** Hutchins's Goose. . . At Montauk it is known by the name of "Mud Goose." **1898** Elliot *Wild Fowl* 70, Hutchins' Goose is known to sportsmen and baymen under various names . . [such as] Mud Goose. **1917** (1923) *Birds Amer.* 1.160, Hutchins's Goose. . . is generally three or four pounds. . . Variously known also as . . Short-necked Goose, or Mud Goose. **1955** Forbush–May *Birds* 51, *Branta canadensis hutchinsi.* . . Mud Goose.

mud gutter n **NYC, NJ, PA**

A curb or gutter; hence n *mud-gutter band* a street band.

1891 (1893) Campbell *Darkness & Daylight* 237 **NYC,** A "mud-gutter" band in front of one of the dance-halls was making discordant music, while children of all ages . . jostled each other in a rude attempt at dancing. **1966** DARE FW Addit **nNJ,** Mud gutter—a curb. **1968** DARE Tape **NY**36, We used to call 'em mud-gutter bands. They consisted of Germans. They had tubas and trumpets. . . There'd be four or five of 'em. They'd come around every night in warm weather and stop in one spot in the block and play a few old tunes. Then they'd go to the houses with their hands out and expect to pick up a few pennies or a nickel here and there, and that's the way they made their living. **1991** NADS Letters, In deep Southwest Philadelphia . . my grandparents bought a retirement home. . . Along the side of each street there was a gully for runoff of rain and such sewage that didn't empty into cesspools. That gully, usually holding fluids of various derivations, was always encrusted with a green, floating scum. It was a breeding ground for mosquitoes and, I believe, illnesses of all kinds. It was called a "mud gutter." It was not a curb nor was one near it. It was exactly what it says, a place for runoff from the street, mud, horse manure and cowflop, dust and dirt, household fluids and human excrement. . . This was not just a North Jersey term. It had gravitated as far south as Philadelphia in 1922.

mud hake n

A **hake 2** (here: *Urophycis tenuis*).

1933 John G. Shedd Aquarium *Guide* 65, The Mud Hakes are close relatives of the codfishes but look quite different. . . They are soft bodied fishes always found on muddy bottom in comparatively deep water. **1955** Zim–Shoemaker *Fishes* 75, White Hake or Mud Hake . . gets to be 4 ft. long; weight to 40 lbs. . . Its large mouth extends back beyond the eyes. **1967** DARE (Qu. P4, *Saltwater fish that are not good to eat*)

Inf **MA**72, Mud hake. **1991** Amer. Fisheries Soc. *Common Names Fishes* 140, Hake, mud—see white hake.

mudhead n Cf **mud cat 1b**

A **bullhead 1b.**

1967 DARE (Qu. P1, . . *Kinds of freshwater fish* . . *caught around here* . . *good to eat*) Inf **MI**67, Mudhead—also call 'em catfish; has whisker-like things.

mud heaver n Cf **gopher** n[1] **2b(3)**

A **woodchuck** (here: *Marmota monax*).

1968 DARE (Qu. P29) Inf **NH**14, Gopher—also called mud heavers.

mud hen n Cf **marsh hen, meadow hen**

1 Any of var birds of the family Rallidae:

a also with modifier: Any of var rails, but esp the **Virginia rail** and **clapper rail.** esp **Atlantic**

1813 (1824) Wilson *Amer. Ornith.* 7.115, [The Virginian rail] is known to some of the inhabitants along the sea coast of New Jersey, by the name of the Fresh-water *Mud-hen.* **1834** Nuttall *Manual Ornith.* 2.201, The Clapper Rail [=*Rallus longirostris*] is a numerous and well known species in all the Middle and Southern States. . . The arrival of the Mud Hen (another of their common appellations,) is soon announced through all the marshes, by its loud, harsh and incessant cackle. *Ibid* 208, The Small Mud Hen [=*Rallus limicola*] is about 10 inches in length. **1844** Giraud *Birds Long Is.* 208, *Virginian Rail.* . . It is known to gunners and sportsmen by the name of . . "Mud Hen." It inhabits low situations, usually selecting the reedy margins of water courses and rivulets; and I have observed it on the low salt marshes along the sea coast. **1888** Trumbull *Names of Birds* 127, *Clapper Rail.* . . At Freeport [NY], and in New Jersey . . , *Mud-hen.* **1917** (1923) *Birds Amer.* 1.203, *King Rail. Rallus elegans.* . . *Other Names.* . . Mud Hen. *Ibid* 204, *Clapper Rail.* . . Mud Hen. *Ibid* 205, *Virginia Rail.* . . Small Mud Hen. *Ibid* 207, *Sora. Porzana carolina.* . . Mud Hen. **1923** Dawson *Birds CA* 3.1530, *California Clapper Rail.* . . *Synonyms.* . . Mud-hen. . . *Nest:* In salt marsh near tide-gut. **1946** Hausman *Eastern Birds* 242, *Black Rail* [=*Laterallus jamaicensis*]. . . *Other Names.* . . Black Mud Hen. . . Runs about like a little black chicken. **1953** *AmSp* 28.282, Mud hen. . . [Name for] Clapper rail [Distribution of name] Rather general. *Ibid* **NJ, MI, IL, ND, NE,** Mud hen. . . King rail. *Ibid* **ME, MA, NY, CO,** Mud hen. . . Slender-billed rail. *Ibid* **ME, NY, IL,** Mud hen. . . Sora. *Ibid* **NJ, PA, MD,** Mud hen. . . (fresh-water) [for] King rail. *Ibid* **NY, NJ, WI,** Mud hen. . . (fresh-water) [for] Slender-billed rail. *Ibid* **NY, MD,** Mud hen. . . (little) [for] Slender-billed rail. *Ibid* **NJ, MD,** Mud hen. . . (salt-water) [for] Clapper rail. *Ibid* **VT, MA,** Mud hen. . . (small) [for] Slender-billed rail. **1968** DARE (Qu. Q10, . . *Water birds and marsh birds*) Inf **MI**76, Mud hen—spindly legs, looks like a skinny chicken but with a smaller head; **NY**92, Mud hen (rail). **1982** Elman *Hunter's Field Guide* 321, Rails. . . *Common & regional names:* marsh hen, mud hen, meadow hen.

b also *mud-hen duck:* =**coot** n[1] **1. widespread, but more freq Inland Nth, N Midl, West** See Map

1814 Wilson *Amer. Ornith.* 9.62, [The] Common Coot. . . is known in Pennsylvania by the name of the Mud-hen. **1858** Baird *Birds* 751 **West,** *Fulica americana.* . . Mud Hen. . . Head and neck glossy black, with a tinge of ashy. **1898** Grinnell *Birds Pacific Slope* 16 **CA,** *American Coot.* . . These birds are popularly known as "mud-hens," and are killed by hundreds on the duck preserves, as they are considered a nuisance by the hunters. **1907** Anderson *Birds IA* 210, The . . Mud-hen. . . is readily recognized, even at a distance, by its slaty-black plumage and white bill. . . While usually not considered a game bird, the Coot is accounted excellent eating by many sportsmen, equal to the flesh of most ducks. **1916** *Times-Picayune* (New Orleans LA) 2 Apr mag sec 5/6 **LA,** Mud Hen.—This water-loving pond bird is of a dark slate color. **1940** Gabrielson *Birds OR* 235, The *American Coot,* or "Mud-hen," is undoubtedly the most common nesting water bird in the State. **1950** WELS **WI** (*The bird that looks like a small dull-colored duck and is commonly found on ponds and lakes*) 33 Infs, Mud hen(s); (*Kinds of wild ducks in your general neighborhood*) 9 Infs, Mud hen(s); (*Names and nicknames for other kinds of game birds in your section*) 4 Infs, Mud hen(s); (*Other water and marsh birds commonly found in your locality*) 1 Inf, Mud hen. **1964** Phillips *Birds AZ* 32, *Mud hen.* . . Unlike most other Arizona water birds, they are almost never found on open represos or livestock watering holes. **1965–70** DARE (Qu. Q9, *The bird that looks like a small, dull-colored duck and is commonly found on ponds and lakes*) 324 Infs, **widespread, but more freq Inland Nth, N Midl, West,** Mud hen; **KY**53, Mud-hen duck; (Qu. Q5, . . *Kinds of wild* *ducks*) 20 Infs, **West, Upper Missip Valley,** Mud hen; (Qu. Q10, . . *Water birds and marsh birds*) Infs **CA**191, **NJ**31, 39, **NM**6, **NY**177, **PA**168, Mud hen. **1982** Elman *Hunter's Field Guide* 314, (*Fulica americana*) *Common & regional names:* common coot, . . mud hen.

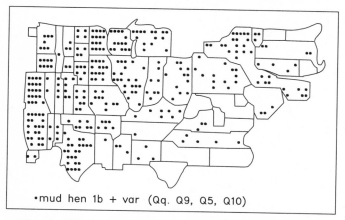

•mud hen 1b + var (Qq. Q9, Q5, Q10)

c Usu the **Florida gallinule,** but also the **purple gallinule.** [*OED* 1611 for *Gallinula chloropus*]

1874 *NY Acad. Sci. Annals Lyceum Nat. Hist.* 10.387 **IL,** Florida Gallinule. Red-billed Mud-Hen. Summer sojourner. **1888** Trumbull *Names of Birds* 122, In the vicinity of Lake St. Clair, about Chicago, and to some at Enterprise, Va., [*Gallinula chloropus* is known as] *Mud-hen,* and a friend writes from latter state as follows . . : "At Indian River I showed it to six men in one day, and each said at once, 'that's a mud-hen.' . . One man said, *'There ain't no other name for that bird but mud-hen.'* " In the western localities mentioned [=Illinois] this species is numerous . . and is commonly recognized as a much superior bird to [the common coot]. Yet many gunners loosely use the term "mud-hen" for each. **1904** Wheelock *Birds CA* 105, *Florida Gallinule, or Red-billed Mud-hen.* . . In form so like a sleek bantam hen, in habits so like a coot, the Florida Gallinule is a most interesting study. . . Feeding on the mud flats, it dips daintily, as it picks its way through the tangled reeds. **1953** *AmSp* 28.282, Mud hen. . . [for] Purple gallinule—Texas. *Ibid,* Mud hen. . . Common gallinule—General [distribution of name]. **1954** Sprunt *FL Bird Life* 150, *Purple Gallinule.* . . *Local Names:* Mud-hen. **1955** *Oriole* 20.1.6 **GA,** *Florida Gallinule.*—Mud Hen. **1962** Imhof *AL Birds* 214, *Gallinula chloropus.* . . Florida Gallinule, Mudhen. **1967** *DARE* (Qu. Q10, . . *Water birds and marsh birds*) Inf **HI**14, Mud hen—alae [*DARE* Ed: =*Gallinula chloropus*].

2 Any of several other birds:

a =**woodcock.** Cf **mud snipe 1**

1888 Trumbull *Names of Birds* 152, Dr. William Jarvis writes of hearing it [=*Philohela minor*] termed . . *mud hen* some ten years ago at Cornish, N.H. **1923** *U.S. Dept. Ag. Misc. Circular* 13.49 **NH,** *American Woodcock.* . . *Vernacular Names.* . . *In local use.* . . Mud-hen. **1953** *AmSp* 28.282 **NH, NJ, LA,** Mud hen. . . [for] American woodcock.

b =**ruddy duck.** Cf **mud dipper**

1943 Musgrove–Musgrove *Waterfowl IA* 71, *Ruddy duck.* . . Other names . . mud hen. **1953** *AmSp* 28.282 **IA,** Mud hen. . . [for] Ruddy duck.

c Either the **bittern** or the **least bittern.**

1953 *AmSp* 28.282 **ME, NY, NJ, PA, MI,** Mud hen. . . [for] American bittern. *Ibid* **NJ,** Mud hen. . . Least bittern. **1966–69** *DARE* (Qu. Q8, *A water bird that makes a booming sound before rain and often stands with its beak pointed almost straight up*) Infs **MO**21, **NY**155, Mud hen; **MI**2, Mud hen—bittern is the right name for them; **NY**92, Stake-driver—about same as a mud hen; **NY**97, The right name is least bittern, but we call 'em mud hens; **OH**4, Mud hen—same as shypoke; (Qu. Q10, . . *Water birds and marsh birds*) Inf **MI**76, Mud hen, shypoke—same.

d A heron such as the **great blue heron, green heron,** or **black-crowned night heron.** Cf **mudpoke**

1953 *AmSp* 28.282 **KS,** Mud hen. . . [for] Great blue heron. *Ibid* **MA, PA,** Mud hen. . . Green heron. *Ibid* **PA,** Mud hen. . . Black-crowned night heron.

e =**pied-billed grebe.**

1953 *AmSp* 28.282 **IN, WI,** Mud hen. . . [for] Pied-billed grebe.

3 A **mud turtle.** Cf **chicken turtle, Suwannee chicken**

1968 *DARE* (Qu. P24, . . *Kinds of turtles*) Inf **IN**13, Mud hen.

‡mud-hen cleaner n *joc*

1968 *DARE* (Qu. B25, . . *Joking names . . for a very heavy rain. . . "It's a regular _____ ."*) Inf **NJ**39, Mud-hen cleaner.

mud-hen duck See **mud hen 1b**

mudhog See **mudfish h**

mud hook n *joc*

1 also *mud hopper,* ~ *masher,* ~ *splasher,* ~ *splitter,* ~ *squasher:* A foot; a heavy shoe or boot. Cf **mud scow 2**

1850 Garrard *Wah-to-yah* 276 **NM,** "This 'mudhook,'[ⁿ] holding out his foot, "has n't a moccasin on for nothin'." **1884** *Century Illustr. Mag.* 29.283 (as of 1862), The boys [=soldiers] called their feet "pontons," "mud-hooks," "soil-excavators," and other names not quite so polite. **1898** Lloyd *Country Life* 239 **AL,** But . . when a farmer goes to foolin with figgers he is puttin his mudhooks on powerful slippery ground. **1915** *DN* 4.244 **MT,** Mud hooks. . . Feet. "Get your big mud hooks out of the way." **1939** *AmSp* 14.91 **eTN,** Mud splitters. . . Heavy shoes. 'My mud splitters are wearing out.' **1948** *AmSp* 23.318 **ceMN** [Stock-yard terms], Mud hooks. Heavy shoes. **1966–70** *DARE* (Qu. X38, *Joking names for unusually big or clumsy feet*) Infs **MT**4, **NC**18, **UT**7, Mud hooks; **ME**5, Mud hoppers; **FL**51, **GA**7, Mud mashers; **TX**36, 42, Mud splashers; **KY**28, **TN**27, Mud splitters; **MA**75, Mud squashers.

2 A hand.

1950 *WELS* (*Joking or uncomplimentary names for the hands*) 4 Infs, **WI,** Mud hooks. **1968** *DARE* (Qu. X32) Inf **MN**42, Mud hooks.

3 A hoe. Cf **mud stick**

1941 Writers' Program *Guide CO* 199 **neCO,** Sugar companies raise their own seed beets, termed "mamas," and sell the seed to growers. . . The initial hoeing is known as the "first chop," hoes are called "mud hooks."

mud hopper See **mud hook 1**

mud hornet See **mud diver**

mud in See **mud v 2**

mud-jack n Cf **jack grindle 2**

=**bowfin.**

1908 Forbes–Richardson *Fishes of IL* 39, The name . . of mud-jack [for *Amia calva* is used] locally in Illinois.

mud lark n

1 A hog; pork. [*OED mudlark* sb. 1 1785; "*slang*"]

1833 Neal *Down-Easters* 1.46 **NEng,** I should like to know . . what upon irth he means by . . mud-larks that's made into Virginny-ham. **1869** *Overland Mth.* 3.129 **Sth,** A hog clandestinely killed outside of camp and smuggled in . . was called a "slow bear." . . "Mud-lark" signified the same thing. **1923** *DN* 5.240 **swWI,** Mud lark. . . Pork. "What d'you have for dinner?" "Boiled potatoes an' mud lark."

2 =**meadowlark 1.** [Prob folk-etym for **medlark**]

1903 Dawson *Birds OH* 1.22, *Meadowlark.* . . *Synonyms.* . . *Mudlark* (corruption). **1917** (1923) *Birds Amer.* 2.251, *Sturnella magna magna.* . . *Other Names.* . . Mudlark.

3 =**shoveler.**

1923 *U.S. Dept. Ag. Misc. Circular* 13.14 **WA,** *Shoveler.* . . *Vernacular Names.* . . *In local use.* . . Mud-lark. **1982** Elman *Hunter's Field Guide* 160, *Shoveler* . . *Common & regional names:* . . mud lark.

4 Either the greater or the lesser **yellowlegs.**

1956 *MA Audubon Soc. Bulletin* 40.18 **MA,** *Greater Yellowlegs.* . . *Lesser Yellowlegs.* . . Mud-lark.

mudlark v, hence vbl n *mudlarking* [*OED* 1840 →; "To carry on the occupation of a mudlark; also, to 'play about' in the mud"] **Chesapeake Bay**

To catch or dig up crabs on mud flats or marshes.

1905 *U.S. Bur. Fisheries Rept. for 1904* 419 **MD,** During the first two or three weeks of May they follow what is known as "mud-larking," that is, scoop-netting in marshes and along the banks of small streams, the crabs being found in the mud at this season of the year. **1969** *DARE* FW Addit **VA**47, Mudlarking—catching crabs by walking over the mud flats exposed by low tide and looking for where the crabs have buried themselves in the mud and digging them up. Common practice in Northampton Co. **1976** Warner *Beautiful Swimmers* 141 **ceVA,** Before the advent of crab pots, mud-larking was practiced rather widely around Poquoson on Virginia's Lower Neck. . . Crabbers used to . . walk out into this marsh, basket in hand, to mud-lark. They snuck up on the resting crabs and snatched them from their bathtubs. **1984** *DARE* File **Chesapeake Bay** [Watermen's vocab], Mudlarking.

mud lily n

A **spatterdock.**

1969 *DARE* (Qu. S26b, *Wildflowers that grow in water or wet places*) Inf **MA42**, Mud lily—big green round leaf, plant is yellow.

mud lump n

A mound of silt or clay characteristic of the Mississippi delta; see quot 1946.

1868 *Putnam's Mag.* May 591, Small islands of bluish clay suddenly emerge from the water. . . These are the famous *mud-lumps* of the Mississippi. **1872** Schele de Vere *Americanisms* 508, *Mud-lumps,* is the technical name of the earliest appearance of soft, spongy land at the mouth of the Mississippi. . . They are at first conical . . and have little craters at the top, from which flows muddy water. . . They have been known to rise to the height of twenty feet, and to become several hundred feet in circumference. **1902** Smithsonian Inst. *Annual Rept. for 1901* 2.71, Within the region lie a number of "mud volcanoes," apparently analogous to the "mud lumps" of the Lower Mississippi. **1941** Writers' Program *Guide LA* 413 **seLA**, "Mud lumps" are masses of river clay and silt that average about an acre in area and rise from three to ten feet above water. Some of these islands, which support no vegetation except cockleburs and other low and weedy growths, are breeding places of the brown pelican. **1944** Kane *Deep Delta Country* 132 **sLA**, The 'mud lumps' of the Mississippi are a phenomenon without counterpart. **1946** Kopman *Wild Acres* 40 **LA**, An average mudlump is less rather than more than an acre in extent and sometimes only a few square rods. It is roughly oval or circular, has a layer-like formation, with edges abrupt or irregularly sloping, and rises seldom more than five or six feet above the level of high tide. . . Nothing grows on these spots except a few cockleburs and other rank weeds.

mud martin n Also *mud packer* esp KY Cf **mud swallow**

=**cliff swallow.**

1969–70 *DARE* (Qu. Q14) Inf **KY11**, Barn martin = mud martin; (Qu. Q20, . . *Kinds of swallows and birds like them*) Inf **KY86**, Mud martin—same as barn swallow; **KY17**, Mud packer.

mud masher See **mud hook 1**

mud mason (wasp) See **mason wasp**

mud-midget n

A **duckweed 1** (here: *Wolffiella floridana*).

1933 Small *Manual SE Flora* 249, *W[olffiella] floridana.* . . Mud-midget. . . Stagnant water. **1976** Bailey–Bailey *Hortus Third* 1173 **FL**, Mud-midget. . . Plant bodies . . forming large mats floating beneath water surface.

mudminnow n

1 also *mudminnie:* A small fish of the family Umbridae. Also called **minnow B2d, mudfish e.** For other names of *Umbra limi* see **dogfish 4;** for other names of *U. pygmaea* see **mud dace 1**

1838 Geol. Surv. OH *Second Annual Rept.* 169, Hydragira [sic] limi. . . *Mud Minnow.* **1882** U.S. Natl. Museum *Bulletin* 16.349, Umbridæ. (The Mud Minnows.) . . Carnivorous fishes living in mud or among weeds at the bottom of clear sluggish streams and ponds. **1896** *Pop. Sci. Mth.* 48.467 **cNJ**, I failed to notice any undue number of the mud minnow (*Umbra limi*). **1908** Forbes–Richardson *Fishes of IL* 203, Mud-minnows are small fishes. . . They rest quietly upon the bottom much of the time, and when disturbed first dart away to a little distance, and then bury themselves, tail downwards, in the mud with one or two quick twists of the body. **1939** Natl. Geogr. Soc. *Fishes* 267, The Washington mud minnow, *Novumbra,* . . is found only in the Chehalis River of western Washington. **1950** *WELS* (Small fish used as bait for bigger fish) 1 Inf, **WI**, Mudminnie. **1968** *DARE* (Qu. P7) Infs **MN**21, 35, **WI**12, 32, Mudminnow. **1982** Sternberg *Fishing* 22, Mudminnows, though not true minnows, live in swamps and sluggish streams in many eastern states. They have a vertical bar near the rounded tail. **1986** Pederson *LAGS Concordance,* 1 inf, **cnFL**, Mudminnow.

2 =**fathead 1.**

1982 Sternberg *Fishing* 20, Fatheads, also called . . *mudminnows,* live in lakes and rivers throughout most of North America. *Ibid* 25, In the South, fatheads may be sold as . . *mudminnows.*

mud packer See **mud martin**

mud peep n

=**least sandpiper.**

1917 (1923) *Birds Amer.* 1.235, Least Sandpiper. . . *Other Names.* . . Mud-peep. **1932** Howell *FL Bird Life* 240, Mud-peep. . . Frequents mud flats and the borders of shallow pools both on salt marshes and in flooded fields on the uplands. **1946** Hausman *Eastern Birds* 281, Mud Peep. . . prefers . . the muddy margins of tidal creeks in the salt marshes and about the mouths of estuaries. **1955** Forbush–May *Birds* 198, Mud-peep. . . Smallest of our sandpipers; sparrow size.

mud pickerel n Cf **mud pike**

A **grass pickerel 1** (here: *Esox americanus vermiculatus*).

1929 OK Univ. Biol. Surv. *Pub.* 1.97, *Esox vermiculatus* . . (Mud or grass pickerel). **1943** Eddy–Surber *N. Fishes* 166, The little mud pickerel, or grass pike, . . is a small pickerel rarely reaching a length of over 12 inches. . . It is distributed in the Ohio Valley and the Lower Mississippi drainage. **1956** Harlan–Speaker *IA Fish* 64, *Esox americanus vermiculatus.* . . Mud pickerel. **1957** Trautman *Fishes* 209 **OH**, Because of its tendency to migrate, occasional specimens were found in such unfavorable conditions as muddy waters flowing over silted bottoms and it was these occasional individuals which have given rise to the general misconception that this pickerel is tolerant to turbid water and clay-silt bottoms, and to its colloquial name of "Mud Pickerel." **1983** Becker *Fishes WI* 393, Grass Pickerel. . . Other common names . . mud pickerel. **1991** Amer. Fisheries Soc. *Common Names Fishes* 157, Pickerel, mud—see grass pickerel.

mud pike n Cf **mud pickerel**

Either a **redfin pickerel** (here: *Esox americanus americanus*) or a **grass pickerel 1** (here: *Esox americanus vermiculatus*).

1870 (1871) *Amer. Naturalist* 4.386, [The] Mud Pike (*Esox porosus*) [is found in the Delaware at Trenton NJ]. **1905** NJ State Museum *Annual Rept. for 1904* 175, *Esox americanus.* . . Mud Pike. . . It reaches a foot in length and is a good pan fish. **1933** John G. Shedd Aquarium *Guide* 56, *Esox americanus*—Red-fin Pickerel; Mud Pike. **1983** Becker *Fishes WI* 393, Grass Pickerel. . . Other common names . . mud pike.

mud plantain n

1 A plant of the genus *Heteranthera.*

1822 Eaton *Botany* 304 **NY**, *Heteranthera. . . reniformis* . . mud-plantain . . in muddy overflowed places. Very abundant in South Bay, below Hudson city. **1894** Coulter *Botany W. TX* 441, Mud Plantain. . . Creeping, floating or submerged low herbs in mud or shallow water. **1933** Small *Manual SE Flora* 266, *Heteranthera.* . . Plants of muddy places. . . *Mud-plantains.* **1976** Bailey–Bailey *Hortus Third* 558, *Heteranthera.* . . *Mud plantain.* . . About 10 spp. of aquatic herbs.

2 =**water plantain.**

1950 Gray–Fernald *Manual of Botany* 84, *Alisma.* . . Water- or Mud-plantain. **1961** Smith *MI Wildflowers* 27, Mud-plantain. *Alisma subcordatum.* . . This plant can be grown in a wet-soil garden, where it gives an attractive lacy effect. **1970** Correll *Plants TX* 96, *Alisma.* . . Mud Plantain. . . Usually in shallow water of marshes, streams and ponds.

mud plover n

=**black-bellied plover.**

1917 (1923) *Birds Amer.* 1.256, *Black-bellied Plover.* . . *Other Names.* . . Mud Plover. [*Ibid* 257, These . . mostly confine themselves to flats and beaches and to pools in the marsh.] **1946** Hausman *Eastern Birds* 258, Mud Plover. . . Very shy birds, running about on the flats in great numbers.

mudpoke n Cf **shitepoke**

Either the **green heron** or the **black-crowned night heron.**

1809 Irving *Hist. NY* 2.86, Squatting himself down on the edge of a pond catching fish for hours together . . [he bore] no little resemblance to that notable bird ycleped the Mud-poke. **1919** Burns *Ornith. Chester Co. PA* 39, *Butorides virescens virescens* . . "mudpoke." *Ibid* 40, *Nycticorax nycticorax nycticorax* . . "mudpoke."

mudpout n

A **bullhead 1b** such as the **brown bullhead 1.**

1804 Fessenden *Poems* 27, Like an otter that paddles the creek,/ In quest of a mud pout, or sucker. **1859** (1968) Bartlett *Americanisms* 72, Catfish. (Genus *Prinelodus* [sic] . .). Also called by the name of . . Mud-pout, . . or simply Cat. **1872** Schele de Vere *Americanisms* 382, A species [=*Ameiurus nebulosus*] is known also as *Mudpout,* from its preference for the mud of rivers and creeks, and, irreverently, from its black color perhaps, as Minister. **1931–33** *LANE Worksheets,* 1 inf,

ceCT, Mudpouts—catfish. **1967–69** *DARE* (Qu. P1, . . *Kinds of fresh-water fish . . caught around here . . good to eat*) Inf CT26, Mudpout (bullhead); NY10, Bullhead [same as] bullpluck [and] mudpout.

mud pullet n Cf **mud chicken, mud hen 1c**
=Florida gallinule.

1888 Trumbull *Names of Birds* 123 **FL,** [The Florida gallinule is known] at Enterprise as *Mud-pullet.* **1953** *AmSp* 28.277 **FL,** *Mud pullet* (the same species [=*Gallinula chloropus*], Fla.)

mud puppy n

Any of var **salamanders** (order Caudata), as:
a =hellbender 1.

1882 *Amer. Naturalist* 16.325, *Vitality of the Mud Puppy.*—The observations on the Menopoma. **1897** *Outing* 30.439, The mud-puppy. . . is a repulsive-looking water-lizard. **1968** *DARE* Tape NC53, [FW:] Is there a kind of big one [=salamander]. . . ? [Inf:] Water dog or mud puppy? Yeah; its real name is hellbinder. **1972** GA Dept. Ag. *Farmers Market Bulletin* 8 Mar 8/2, The reptile you described closely resembles a salamander, known as a hellbender or mudpuppy. They are fairly common in Georgia and Florida. They are not dangerous, however, their bite is painful. **1988** *DARE* File cnOH (as of 1920), We boy scouts caught salamanders in the creeks near Akron and called them hellbenders. Some called them mud puppies.

b A **water dog** (here: *Necturus maculosus*). [See quot 1958] **chiefly Missip Valley** Also called **dogfish 10, ground puppy 1c, lizard 2, puppy, salamander, water lizard**

1879 Smith *Catalogue Reptilia MI* 8, *Menobranchus lateralis.* . . Mud Puppy. **1883** WI Chief Geologist *Geol. WI* 1.426, Found in abundance in most streams and lakes of the state. They are ignorantly supposed to be poisonous and are the subject of many ridiculous newspaper accounts. The Mud Puppies do considerable damage by eating the spawn of various fishes. The Mud Puppy is strictly aquatic, never leaving the water; in fact, many fishes can survive longer when taken from their native element. **1891** in 1895 IL State Lab. Nat. Hist. Urbana *Bulletin* 3.382, *Necturus maculatus.* . . *Mud Puppy.* . . Total length about one and a half feet. [*Ibid* 383, It is often captured on hooks baited for fish, and so dreaded is its bite that the line is frequently cut to let it escape. It is, however, perfectly harmless.] **1899** Bergen *Animal Lore* 62, Mud-puppy, salamander. Lawrence, Kan. **1905** U.S. Bur. Fisheries *Rept. for 1904* 603, I suspect that by no means the least enemy to these eggs is the common mud puppy (*Necturus maculosus*—called "lizard" by the fishermen) which is often taken in numbers in the pound nets. **1925** *Book of Rural Life* 4864, One of these [groups of salamanders] includes the *mud puppy* so well known to fishermen in the Mississippi Valley. It grows about a foot in length. **1930** *Copeia* 3.26 **neOK,** Mudpuppy. . . Commonly found in mud of ponds and ditches. **1958** Conant *Reptiles & Amphibians* 198, *Necturus maculosus.* . . is a Mudpuppy in the North, but Southerners . . refer to it and all its relatives as Waterdogs. Throughout much of Dixieland, Mudpuppy is also used by the country folk, but they reserve that name for adults of . . *Ambystoma.* Both names owe their origin at least in part to the belief that these animals bark. **1968–69** *DARE* (Qu. P1) Inf WI22, Mud puppy; (Qu. P3) Infs MN21, NY87, Mud puppy; (Qu. R23b) Inf OH88, Mud puppy. **1981** Vogt *Nat. Hist. WI* 57, Mudpuppies are found from western New England west through Manitoba and south through the states bordering the shores of the Mississippi River to Louisiana and north of the Fall Line. **1982** Sternberg *Fishing* 108, Mudpuppies . . live in water all of their lives.

c A **salamander** of the genus *Ambystoma.* **chiefly Sth**

1892 IN Dept. Geol. & Nat. Resources *Rept. for 1891* 426, The Ambystomas are familiarly known as "Mud-puppies," and are frequently met with in the operations of plowing, digging ditches and cleaning out cellars. **1925** TX Folkl. Soc. *Pub.* 4.51 **nwLA,** All land salamanders are "mud-puppies." . . I have seen . . negroes jump . . when a small-mouthed salamander, *Ambystoma microstomum* . . , was uncovered at the turning of a log. "When er mud-puppy barks an' yo' heahs it, youse gwine to die." If a mud-puppy crawls across your shadow, unless you kill it, your death will soon follow. A mud-puppy's bite is more dangerous than that of a rattlesnake. **1928** Baylor Univ. Museum *Contrib.* 16.7 **TX,** *Mud-puppy.* . . *Ground-dog.* In Texas, these . . names refer to three species of land salamanders which inhabit the eastern part of the State. . . The three species referred to are . . *Ambystoma maculatum* . . , *A. opacum* . . , and . . *A. texanum.* . . Numerous myths are connected with . . "mud-puppies." **1958** [see **b** above].

d Either the great **siren** (*Siren lacertina*) or an amphiuma such as the **congo snake 1.** Cf **mud eel 1**

1890 *Century Dict.* 3887, *Mud-puppy.* . . See *hellbender,* and *mud-eel,* 1 [=*Siren lacertina* and *Amphiuma tridactylum*]. **1894** U.S. Natl. Museum *Proc.* 17.337 **FL,** *Amphiuma means.* . . is known under the name of . . "mud puppy." . . People digging in the "muck" find them frequently in such soil, and I have taken them with my net in ponds and small lakes. *Ibid* 338, *Siren lacertina.* . . A man living in Oakland, Orange County [FL], told me that he once had taken two specimens of the "*gray mud puppy*" on hook and line in Lake Apopka.

‡mud quacker n
A **tree frog.**

1966 Dakin *Dial. Vocab. Ohio R. Valley* 2.388, Kentucky has . . *mud quackers* [for spring peeper] [1 of 207 infs].

mud rain See **mud-sender**

mud rat n
1 See **mud cat 3.**
2 A **muskrat 1.**

1970 *DARE* (Qu. P31, . . *Names or nicknames . . for the . . muskrat*) Inf CA195, Mud rat.

mud room n

A separate small room or an area near an entry used for storing muddy footwear and other items for outdoor use.

1950 *Architecture & Building Trades Dict.* 212, *Mud room:* In building, a small room or entranceway where members of the family remove their muddy overshoes or rubbers before going into any of the other rooms; found especially in modern farm homes. **1968** *State* (Columbia SC) 4 May sec B 8, Executive home—Kitchen plus; double ovens, dishwasher, and disposal! Breakfast room! Mudroom. **1968** *DARE* (Qu. D16, . . *Parts added on to the main part of a house*) Inf OH70, Mud room—used as a catchall. **1969** *DARE* FW Addit KY36, Mud room—a small room or hall just into the house where muddy boots, rubbers, etc., are removed and stored; neCT, Mud room—extra room in the house for storage; collects junk; the place where you take off your boots (originally). **1972** McDavid Coll. neGA, Mud room—entry way (where one scrapes mud off the feet). **1986** Pederson *LAGS Concordance,* 1 inf, neGA, Mud room—keeps washing machine and dryer here; mud room—entry room of informant's house. **1989** *Yankee* Mar 90 **NEng,** Contrary to its old-fashioned sound, the word mudroom is a relative newcomer in New England. **1992** Martone *Townships* 101 **ceWI,** There was a clumping up the stairs of our mudroom and then there he was, in our kitchen.

mud sail n
=mule n¹ 4.

1953 (1977) Hubbard *Shantyboat* 281 **Missip-Ohio Valleys,** In the next several miles, by rowing and by lowering the mud sail, which at least served as a sea anchor, we managed to hold our position in the flowing water, the wind being across our course now.

mud scow n

1 A flat-bottomed boat used to carry away dredged mud; by ext, an old, broken-down boat.

1766 *Boston News-Letter* (MA) 2 Oct 1/3 **ceMA,** To Be Sold, A new Mud-Scow, 24 Foot long, and can carry 12 or 14 Tons Weight. **1835** (1836) Gilman *Life on the Lakes* 2.259 **Gt Lakes,** Forward she looked exactly like a mud-scow; scarcely any deck, and an open hold exposed to the weather. **1950** *WELS* (An old, clumsy rowboat) 1 Inf, **WI,** Mud scow. **1966–69** *DARE* (Qu. O2, *Nicknames . . for an old, clumsy boat*) Infs CA136, MA30, 35, 62, 68, NH10, Mud scow. **1967** *DARE* Tape NJ2, There was one they called the mud scow. They used to go through every once in a while and cut the weeds.

2 See quots. Cf **barge n 4, canal boat**

1863 *U.S. Army & Navy Jrnl.* I.180/2 *(DA),* Expensive shoes . . are often thrown away unused, for the despised Government 'mudscows.' These 'mudscows' or 'gunboats' . . are low-cut, stitched, very light, and very cheap. . . The sole is very broad, and the heels broad and low. **1909** *DN* 3.413 **nME,** *Mudscows.* . . Large shoes. **1950** *WELS Suppl.* **seWI,** Mud scows—those high, heavy rubbers worn on the farm.

mud season See **mud time**

mud-sender n Also *mud rain* Cf **chunk-floater, dam-buster**

A heavy rain.

1963 *DE Folkl. Bulletin* 1.40, Mud rain (a real downpour). **1968** *DARE* (Qu. B25, . . *Joking names . . for a very heavy rain.* . . "*It's a regular _____.*") Inf CA90, Mud-sender.

mud shad n

1 =**gizzard shad 1.**

1879 U.S. Natl. Museum *Bulletin* 14.60, *Dorysoma* [sic] *Cepedianum. . . Mud Shad. . .* Cape Cod to St. John's River, Fla. **1884** Goode *Fisheries U.S.* 1.610, *Dorosoma cepedianum. . .* In the Chesapeake region it is known as the "Mud-Shad." **1905** NJ State Museum *Annual Rept. for 1904* 107 **NJ,** The vernaculars of this fish, such as mud shad, denote the habit of the fish being found in the mud during winter. **1943** Eddy–Surber *N. Fishes* 72, *Gizzard Shad . . Mud Shad. . .* In quiet, muddy stretches of the Lower Mississippi they are exceedingly abundant and are regarded as a nuisance by fishermen. . . Their stomachs and intestines are often filled with mud. They live on food obtained from the muddy bottoms of very muddy lakes and streams. **1968–70** *DARE* (Qu. P3, *Freshwater fish that are not good to eat*) Inf **DE**3, Mud shad or gizzard fish; **VA**79, Mud shad—full of bones. **1983** Becker *Fishes WI* 273, *Gizzard Shad. . .* Other common names . . mud shad. . . At present the gizzard shad . . functions as a forage fish, and is an interesting part of Wisconsin's fish population.

2 A **menhaden 1** (here: *Brevoortia tyrannus*). **NJ**

1894 *DN* 1.332 **NJ,** *Menhaden:* called . . "mud shad" in Cumberland County. **1945** Beck *Jersey Genesis* 148 **NJ,** "Sometimes," Jack said, "we just called 'em [=*Brevoortia tyrannus*] bony-fish and mud-shad."

mud shark n [See quot 1991] nwAK

=**burbot.**

1936 *AK Sportsman* Aug 17, Then there are such undesirable varieties as mud sharks, dog-fish, devil fish, turbot and a variety of red cod they call "idiots." **1952** Giddings *Arctic Woodland* 3 **nwAK,** Pickerel and lingcod ("mudshark"), as well as the trout-like grayling, furnish an off-season supply of fish to be caught under the ice. **1974** *Fairbanks Daily News–Miner* 10 Dec (Tabbert *Alaskan Engl.*), Howard and his wife, Pearl, are the *mud-shark* champions of Kobuk—they caught 62 the other night in only three hours—now that's real fishing, folks! **1981** *AK Geographic* 8.3.98 **nwAK,** Just after sunset the fishermen may switch to larger lures in order to hook for burbot, which are also on the move as the river freezes over. These unlovely mudsharks are prized not only for their delicate flesh but also for their sweet livers. **1991** Tabbert *Dict. Alaskan Engl.* 143, Although *mudshark* is reported as a common name for various bottom-dwelling true sharks, I find no references to its being used outside Alaska to name the burbot. And in Alaska that usage occurs only in the Kobuk River area. Rather than a transfer of a shark's name, the Kobuk River usage is probably an original formation based on the bottom-dwelling habits (hence *mud*) and a perceived shark-like appearance.

mud sheldrake n

=**hooded merganser.**

1917 (1923) *Birds Amer.* 1.112, *Hooded Merganser. . . Other Names. . . Mud . . Sheldrake.* [*Ibid* 113, The Hooded Merganser. . . frequents clear streams and muddy pools alike.] **1923** U.S. Dept. Ag. *Misc. Circular* 13.6 **MA,** *Hooded Merganser. . . Vernacular Names. . . In local use. . .* Mud sheldrake.

mud shoe n Also mud boot

Any of var types of horseshoes designed for use on soft ground.

1942 ME Univ. *Studies* 57.46 **nwME** [Pulpwood terms], During the summer and early fall horses are shod with a so-called "mud" shoe, which has heavy and blunt toe and heel calks. This shoe is heavy and will stand considerable wear. **1949** Sim *Pages from the Past* 98 **NJ,** When horses were employed on the meadows [to harvest salt hay] their hind feet were enlarged with leather, wood or iron "mud-boots" to keep them from getting mired. . . Heavy straps and buckles held the boot on the foot. **1967** *Amer. Agric. & Rural New Yorker* Mar 76, "Mud shoes" . . were about a foot square, made of hard wood with straps of iron. These could be strapped to a horse's feet and . . [he] could walk on wet soft ground. **1969** Pinto *Treen* 93, Elmwood horse mud shoes, with iron staples, . . were used to give a horse better bearing in the cranberry swamps of Wisconsin. **1994** *DARE* File **WI** (as of c1940), Mud shoes were square wooden devices fastened under the horses' normal shoes to prevent them from sinking in swamp mud.

mud shoveler n Cf mud duck 2, mud lark n 3

=**shoveler.**

1888 Trumbull *Names of Birds* 43, The only time I remember to have heard the name Shoveller in actual usage among gunners . . was at Baltimore. The bird is known however as the *Mud-shoveller* at Sanford,

Fla. **1955** *Oriole* 20.1.4 **GA,** *Shoveler. . .* Mud Shoveler. **1982** Elman *Hunter's Field Guide* 160, *Shoveler. . . Common & regional names . .* mud shoveler.

mud shrimp n

1 The pink shrimp *(Penaeus duorarum)*.

1951 Taylor *Surv. Marine Fisheries NC* 201, Specimens, presumably from the mud, can be collected during the winter months. Examination of these "mud-shrimp" reveals a high percentage of *P. duorarum.*

2 A soft-bodied crab of the genus *Callianassa* or *Upogebia.* Cf **ghost shrimp**

1981 Meinkoth *Audubon Field Guide Seashore* 622, *Flat-browed Mud Shrimp (Upogebia affinis). . .* This crustacean is not a true shrimp, but is more closely related to the hermit crabs. . . The Blue Mud Shrimp *(U. pugettensis)* is larger. *Ibid* 623, The Short-browed Mud Shrimp *(C[allianassa] atlantica)* ranges from Nova Scotia to Florida. It . . burrows in sandy mud. **1982** Sternberg *Fishing* 126, *Mud Shrimp.* This group includes *ghost shrimp* and *blue mud shrimp.* Although called shrimp, they are actually soft-bodied crabs that burrow into sand or mud flats of estuaries. *Ibid* 127, Mud shrimp inhabit tidal flats and beaches along the Pacific and Gulf coasts. *Ibid* 135, Mud shrimp are used in coastal rivers of the Pacific Northwest for steelhead, salmon, sturgeon and smallmouth bass.

mud siren n

A **siren** (here: *Pseudobranchus striatus*).

1953 Schmidt *N. Amer. Amphibians* 15, *Pseudobranchus striatus. . .* South Carolina to Florida. *Common name.*—Mud siren. **1957** Blair et al. *Vertebrates U.S.* 241, *Pseudobranchus striatus. . .* Mud siren. [**1979** Behler–King *Audubon Field Guide Reptiles* 272, During droughts they [=*Pseudobranchus striatus*] encase themselves in mud beneath the pond bottom. When caught, they make faint yelping noises.]

mud skid (or sled) See mud boat 1

mud snake n

Any of three snakes native to the southeastern US: usu **horn snake 1,** but also **rainbow snake** or a **swamp snake** (here: *Liodytes alleni*).

1928 Baylor Univ. Museum *Contrib.* 16.14 **TX,** *Mud Snake . . Farancia abacura. . .* is usually identified with the mythical *Hoop Snake.* **1952** Ditmars *N. Amer. Snakes* 76, *Mud Snake, Liodytes alleni. . .* Georgia and Florida. *Ibid* 122, *Horn Snake, Mud Snake. . .* Mostly the coastal region, or close to river systems, in wet and swampy areas, from southeastern Virginia to western Florida. *Ibid* 124, *Rainbow Snake, Mud Snake. . .* Through the lower, coastal region from southeastern Virginia to Florida, but . . not farther west than Alabama. **1953** Schmidt *N. Amer. Amphibians* 178, *Liodytes alleni. . .* Peninsular Florida and extreme southern Georgia. *Common name.*—Allen's mud snake. **1966–70** *DARE* (Qu. P25) Infs **FL**4, 27, 48, Mud snake. **1979** Behler–King *Audubon Field Guide Reptiles* 609, *Mud Snake (Farancia abacura). . .* Shiny blue-black snake with pink or red belly bars extending upwards on sides. . . Tail short and tipped with a sharp spine.

mud snipe n

1 A **woodcock** (here: *Philohela minor*).

1830 *Cabinet Nat. Hist.* 1.97, This bird is known throughout the United States, under different names, as the snipe, big snipe, red-breasted snipe, and mud snipe, and, in some parts of the country, through ignorance, is not considered fit to eat, although they are generally held in the highest estimation as an article of luxury. **1897** NY Forest Fish & Game Comm. *Annual Rept. for 1896* 322, *Philohela minor. . .* American woodcock. Popular synonyms: Bog-sucker; mud snipe; blind snipe. **1898** (1900) Davie *Nests N. Amer. Birds* 134, Woodcock . . is called Big Mud . . Snipe. [*Ibid* 135, The Woodcock is often called Bog-sucker, from its habits of boring in the mud for worms and animalculæ, of which its food consists.] **1923** U.S. Dept. Ag. *Misc. Circular* 13.49 **NJ, PA,** *American Woodcock. . . Vernacular Names. . . In local use. . .* Mud snipe. **1946** Hausman *Eastern Birds* 265, *Woodcock. . . Other Names . .* Mud Snipe. . . Probes in the mud with its long bill, making many round holes close together.

2 =**Wilson's snipe.**

1955 *Oriole* 20.1.7 **GA,** *Wilson's Snipe. . .* Mud Snipe.

mud splasher (or splitter) See mud hook 1

mud spoon See mud stick

mud squasher See mud hook 1

mud-star n

A starfish (*Ctenodiscus crispatus*).

1950 *Biol. Bulletin* (Lancaster PA) 98.82 **wWA,** Large numbers of the mud-star, *Luidia foliolata* (Grube), were collected by dredging in West Sound on the south side of Orcas Island. **1959** Collins *Complete Field Guide* 629, Mud-star—*Ctenodiscus crispatus*—Of all our starfish this has the shortest arms. **1981** Meinkoth *Audubon Field Guide Seashore* 670, *Mud Star.* . . This sea star not only lives in soft mud, creeping through it on thick, suckerless tube feet, but it eats mud as well, removing from it the digestible organic compounds.

mud stick n Also *mud spoon*

=muck stick.

1939 FWP *ID Lore* 243, Mining jargon in the Pierce City area: . . *Mud stick*—a shovel. **1941** Writers' Program *Guide CO* 199 **neCO,** Beginning in June, fields [of beets] must be irrigated regularly. Those engaged in the undertaking, dubbed "mud pie hands," are equipped with shovels, or "mud spoons."

mudsucker n

1 Any of several fishes, as:

a =**flathead catfish 1.** Cf **mud cat 1a, mudfish d**

1819 *Jrl. de Physique* 88.422, *Pylodictis.* . . Ses noms vulgaires sont: *Mudcat, Mudsucker, Toadcat, Toadfish.* Vers l'embouchure de l'Ohio; . . apparence d'un crapaud. [=*Pylodictis.* . . Its common names are: *Mudcat, Mudsucker, Toadcat, Toadfish.* Towards the mouth of the Ohio; . . appearance of a toad.] **1885** *Outing* 5.336 **LA,** There are . . gaspergoos,—an Indian word meaning "fish," and applied to anything fishy, from the delicate sheep's-head to the nasty mud-suckers of the Mississippi. **1986** Pederson *LAGS Concordance,* 1 inf, **nwLA,** Mudsuckers.

b Any of var **suckers** (family Catostomidae), but esp the **hog sucker;** see quots.

1870 (1871) *Amer. Naturalist* 4.113 **NJ,** The Mud-sucker (*Hylomyzon nigricans*). **1884** Goode *Fisheries U.S.* 1.615, Although called the "Mud Sucker" in the books, it [=*Hypentelium nigricans*] is most characteristically a fish of running streams. **1905** NJ State Museum *Annual Rept. for 1904* 158, *Catostomus nigricans.* . . Mud Sucker. . . This large sucker reaches a length of two feet. **1963** Sigler-Miller *Fishes UT* 98, *Mountain Sucker—Pantosteus platyrhynchus.* . . Common Names . . mud sucker. [*Ibid* 100, Species of this genus of suckers are plant eaters, the stomachs being gorged with algae and slime.] **1967–68** DARE (Qu. P3, *Freshwater fish that are not good to eat*) Infs **NJ**1, 16, **PA**58, Mudsucker. **1969** DARE FW Addit **Hatteras Is. NC,** Mudsucker—type of fish. **1983** Becker *Fishes WI* 682, *White Sucker. Catostomus commersoni.* . . Other common names . . common mud sucker. [*Ibid* 685, The fish seek food mainly on the bottoms of streams or lakes.]

c The longjaw goby (*Gillichthys mirabilis*) native to California. Also called **mudfish f**

1953 Roedel *Common Fishes CA* 143, *Mudsucker. Gillichthys mirabilis.* . . Common in Southern California bays and sloughs. . . Large quantities are used as bait, particularly by inland sport fishermen. . . The fish is extremely hardy. **1968** DARE (Qu. P7, *Small fish used as bait for bigger fish*) Infs **CA**36, 87, Mudsucker. **1983** *Audubon Field Guide N. Amer. Fishes* 677, Longjaw Mudsucker (*Gillichthys mirabilis*) has huge maxilla extending almost to rear edge of opercle. **1991** Amer. Fisheries Soc. *Common Names Fishes* 64, F[reshwater]-P[acific] Longjaw mudsucker.

2 Either the **least sandpiper** or the **semipalmated sandpiper.** [*OED* "an aquatic fowl that obtains its food from mud"; 1688]

1917 *Wilson Bulletin* 29.2.79, *Pisobia minutilla* and *Ereunetes pusillus.* . . Mud-suckers, little birds, bumblebees, Wallops Id., Va. **1923** U.S. Dept. Ag. *Misc. Circular* 13.55 **NJ, VA,** *Least Sandpiper.* . . *Vernacular Names.* . . In local use. . . Mud-suckers. *Ibid* 57 **NJ, VA,** *Semipalmated Sandpiper.* . . *Vernacular Names.* . . In local use. . . Mud-suckers. **1970** DARE (Qu. Q10, . . *Water birds and marsh birds*) Inf **VA**47, Big mudsucker—semipalmated sandpiper; little mudsucker—least sandpiper.

mud sunfish n

1 A **sunfish** (here: *Acantharcus pomotis*). Also called **mud bass 1**

1870 (1871) *Amer. Naturalist* 4.102, Professor S.F. Baird, during the summer of 1854, discovered, in New Jersey, . . the Mud Sunfish (*Ambloplites pomotis*). **1882** U.S. Natl. Museum *Bulletin* 16.469, *A[cantharchus] pomotis.* . . *Mud Sun-fish.* . . Color very dark greenish. . . Southern New York to South Carolina, in sluggish streams near the coast. **1902** Jordan-Evermann *Amer. Fishes* 338, The mud sunfish. . . is locally

common, especially in the lower Delaware. **1907** NJ State Museum *Annual Rept. for 1906* 169, Mud Sun Fish. In a pool near Pensauken, Burlington county, . . two were found with the cat-fish already mentioned. One was nearly 5 inches long and the other smaller. **1991** Amer. Fisheries Soc. *Common Names Fishes* 47, F[reshwater] . . Mud sunfish.

2 A **rock bass** (here: *Ambloplites rupestris*).

1905 NJ State Museum *Annual Rept. for 1904* 437, The Rock Bass. *Ambloplites rupestris.* . . Mud Sun Fish. From our sun fishes, . . this one approaches nearest the mud sun fish, *Acantharchus.* . . Introduced from the Great Lakes and Mississippi Valley. A gamy and valuable food-fish reaching a foot in length.

3 A **warmouth** (here: *Lepomis gulosus*).

1909 Webster 1418/1 (DA), Mud sunfish. . . The warmouth. **1935** Caine *Game Fish* 33 **Sth,** Warmouth. . . Synonyms . . Mud Sunfish. [*Ibid* 34, The warmouth prefers sluggish lowland streams and shallow mud-bottom ponds and lakes.]

mud swallow n chiefly West; also PA, NY, NJ See Map

=cliff swallow.

1873 (1874) Leland *Egyptian Sketch Book* 43 [Writer from **PA**], It is wonderfully startling to see camels in long strings . . and those curious little mud-swallow nests of little villages. **1874** NY Acad. Sci. *Annals Lyceum Nat. Hist.* 10.370 **IL,** *P[etrochelidon] lunifrons.* . . Cliff Swallow; . . "Mud Swallow." Summer sojourner. **1898** Deland *Old Chester* 181, Mud-swallows had built their nests in the corners. **1917** (1923) *Birds Amer.* 3.84, *Cliff Swallow.* . . *Other Names.* . . Mud Swallow. . . The early explorers of the far West were much impressed by the enormous collections of Cliff Swallow mud bottle nests that were plastered over the great perpendicular rocks in many places. . . As the settlements became established in the northwest the Cliff Swallow deserted the rocks in great numbers and became residents under the eaves of the farmers' barns. **1946** Goodrich *Birds in KS* 319, [Colloquial name:] swallow, mud—[common name:] swallow, northern cliff. **1950** WELS (*Kinds of swallows around your locality*) 1 Inf, **WI,** Mud swallow. **1953** Jewett *Birds WA* 449, *Oregon Cliff Swallow.* . . Other names . . Mud Swallow. . . The nest . . is a truly wonderful structure. Shaped like a bottle or purse, it is solidly constructed of mud and attached with wonderful efficiency to the perpendicular wall of cliff or cave, or the smooth side of a building. **1965–70** DARE (Qu. Q20, . . *Kinds of swallows and birds like them*) 25 Infs, **chiefly West, PA, NY, NJ,** Mud swallow.

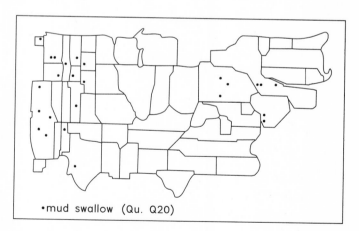

•mud swallow (Qu. Q20)

mud teal n

=green-winged teal.

1888 Trumbull *Names of Birds* 28, Green-winged teal. At Bath, Me. (To the older gunners at least), *Mud teal.* **1917** (1923) *Birds Amer.* 1.122, *Green-winged Teal.* . . Other Names . . Mud Teal. **1932** Howell *FL Bird Life* 139, *Mud Teal.* . . Resorts chiefly to fresh-water ponds and marshes, feeding in shallow water with Mallards, Widgeons, and other "puddle ducks." **1943** Musgrove-Musgrove *Waterfowl IA* 33, Mud teal. . . Their small size, and preference for small ponds and marshes, together with a rather dull coloration, make greenwings easy to identify. **1955** MA Audubon Soc. *Bulletin* 39.314 **MA,** *Green-winged Teal.* . . Mud Teal. . . It feeds much in very shallow water. **1982** Elman *Hunter's Field Guide* 178, (*Anas crecca carolinensis*) *Common & regional names* . . mud teal, congo, . . breakfast duck.

mud terrapin See **mud turtle**

mud thrush n [From the use of mud in constructing its nest] Cf **mud bird**

=**wood thrush.**

1938 Stuart *Dark Hills* 89 **KY,** The mud thrush would fly through the dark foliage of the water birches and hit her wings against the leaves.

mud time n Also *mud season* **NEng**

See quot 1941.

1934 in 1969 Frost *Poetry* 275 **NEng,** [Title:] "Two Tramps in Mud Time." . . The sun was warm but the wind was chill./ You know how it is with an April day. **1941** *AN&Q* 1.140, When I was a little girl in New England, the phrase "mudtime" was commonly used for a period of two or three weeks in spring, usually about April, when the roads were so muddy as to be almost impassable for any long-distance or heavy hauling. **1965** Needham–Mussey *Country Things* 15 **VT,** Mud time comes after sugaring. . . in mud time there's just nothing you can do except mend fences. **1967** *DARE* Tape **VT**1, I had a car, but I used it only in the summer, and sometimes in mud time a wagon with a horse. You couldn't get a car through. **1975** Gould *ME Lingo* 185, *Mud Season*—Since paved roads, this term has lost some of its pithiness. *Mud season* was Maine's fifth season (the others are Fall, Winter, Spring, and July). **1979** *Greenfield Recorder* (MA) 7 Apr, In Leverett the first Monday in March was "town meeting day" and as it was right in "mud time" nobody went out on the roads much unless it was quite necessary. **1989** Mosher *Stranger* 7 **nVT,** Summer crept north toward the Kingdom, always slowly and nearly always preceded by a month or more of immobilizing mudtime in lieu of spring. **1992** Phelps *Famous Last Words* 51 **NEng,** Mud season is a good time to work on equipment.

mud toad n

A **toadfish** (here: *Opsanus tau*).

1970 *DARE* (Qu. P4, *Saltwater fish that are not good to eat*) Inf **VA**79, Mud toad.

mud turtle n Also *mud terrapin, ~ tortoise*

1 Any of var freshwater turtles. Note: Some of these quots may refer specifically to senses below.

1785 (1930) Hazard *Jrl.* 87 **RI,** George found mudd tourtle. & I gave him ashilling for it. **1865** Byrn *Advent. Fudge Fumble* 71, He was seized, or hitched on to by what is called out west a "mud turtle." **1869** Twain *Innocents* 490, He was . . throwing a clod at a mud-turtle which was sunning itself on a small log in the brook. **1899** (1912) Green *VA Folk-Speech* 290, *Mud-turkle.* . . Mud-turtle; the name of various turtles that live in mud or muddy water. **1909** *DN* 3.351 **eAL, wGA,** *Mud-turkle.* . . The mud-turtle: chiefly among the negroes. **1946** *PADS* 6.21 **ceNC** (as of 1900–10), *Mud turkle* ['tɜˑkl]. . . A small turtle found in muddy bottoms, in either fresh or salt water. Pamlico. Mainly among Negroes. **1965–70** *DARE* (Qu. P24, . . *Kinds of turtles*) 207 Infs, **chiefly Nth, Midl,** Mud turtle; **KY**44, Mud turtle ['tɜkl]; (Qu. P18) Inf **NY**10, Mud turtle. **1986** Pederson *LAGS Concordance,* 47 infs, **Gulf Region,** Mud turtle(s); 1 inf, **cnTN,** Mud terrapin.

2 Spec: see below. Note: It is not always possible to be certain which senses the *DARE* Infs intended.

a A **snapping turtle** such as *Chelydra serpentina*.

1756 (1849) Darlington *Mem. John Bartram* 201, My son and I were both surprised at the sight of the great Mud Turtle. It is really a formidable animal. He bit very fierce at a stick. He had near bit my finger. **1792** Belknap *Hist. NH* 3.174, Mud Turtle, *Testudo denticulata*. **1796** *Aurora* (Phila.) 17 May *(DAE),* The crocodile throat of the gentle snappers or mud tortles in the Jersey market. **1838** Geol. Surv. OH *Second Annual Rept.* 188, C[helydra] serpentina. It is universally known as the *snapping turtle, the mud turtle, or the land turtle.* **1937** Cahn *Turtles IL* 34, *Chelydra serpentina* . . mud-turtle. [*Ibid* 40, A majority of the snappers go down into the mud at the bottom of the pond or slough, usually to a depth of ten to twelve inches, where they "mud up" for the winter. . . [W]hile the turtles are in hibernation . . the market catches are made by turtle hunters. **1966–70** *DARE* (Qu. P24, . . *Kinds of turtles*) Infs **GA**72, **ME**20, **NC**53, 80, **VA**8, Mud turtle [is the same as] snapping turtle; **NC**85, Mud turtle same as snapping turtle, shell about 14 or 15 inches; **OH**16, Mud turtle—that's a snapper—some are soft-shelled; good eating; **WI**26, Mud turtle, snapping turtle—I think they're really all the same.

b A turtle of the family Kinosternidae, as:

(1) also *mud box terrapin*: A turtle of the genus *Kinosternon.* Also called **kettlepot, killpot, musk turtle 2, skillpot,** **steelpot, stinkbox, stinking jim, stinkpot, stink(ing) turtle, tillpot.** For other names of var spp see **cow-dung cooter**

1787 Pennant *Arctic Zool. Suppl.* 80, Mud Tortoise. . . Inhabits *Pensylvania* and *Carolina.* **1829** in 1836 NY Acad. Sci. *Annals Lyceum Nat. Hist.* 3.120, *Terrapene pensylvanica,* Merrem. Mud tortoise. . . Mud tarapin of the southern states. . . Length four inches, height one inch and three quarters. Inhabits from New-Jersey to Florida in ditches and muddy streams: has a strong and not disagreeable odour of musk. **1839** MA Zool. & Bot. Surv. *Fishes Reptiles* 210, S[ternothaerus] odoratus. The mud Tortoise. . . is found burying itself in the mud in ditches and small ponds. **1842** DeKay *Zool. NY* 3.21, The Mud Tortoise. Kinosternon pensylvanicum. [*Ibid* 22, It inhabits ditches and muddy ponds, and often takes the hook.] **1891** in 1895 IL State Lab. Nat. Hist. Urbana *Bulletin* 3.238, *Cinosternum pennsylvanicum.* . . Mud Tortoise. . . In the form of its head it resembles the snapping turtle and, like that reptile, bites viciously, though from its small size it is less to be feared. . . Probably not common in this State away from the southern counties. **1908** Biol. Soc. DC *Proc.* 21.79 **TX,** *Kinosternon flavescens.* . . Yellow Mud Turtle. . . One of these was found half buried in the mud of a small prairie sink. **1928** Baylor Univ. Museum *Contrib.* 16.20, Louisiana Mud Turtle. . . East Texas negroes further vulgarize the name of this turtle by calling it *Mud Turkle.* **1932** *Copeia* 1.43, The "Mud Box" terrapin, *Kinosternon subrubrum subrubrum,* if entering New England at all, is only to be found in the southern counties of Connecticut. **1966–68** *DARE* (Qu. P24, . . *Kinds of turtles*) Inf **DC**2, Mud turtle = skillpot; **LA**14, Mud turtle—a small turtle that scavenges at the edge; stink turtles might be same thing as mud turtle; **LA**34, Stinking turtle also applied to mud turtle; **SD**3, Mud turtle—smooth top, dark green to black. **1979** Behler–King *Audubon Field Guide Reptiles* 438, Musk and mud turtles. . . are strongly aquatic and are usually seen crawling along the bottom.

(2) A **musk turtle 1,** usu *Sternotherus carinatus* or *S. odoratus.*

1842 DeKay *Zool. NY* 3.23, The *Musk Tortoise* or *Mud Turtle, Mud Terrapin* or *Stink-pot,* (with other equally savory popular names,) is to be found in most of our ponds and ditches. **1892** IN Dept. Geol. & Nat. Resources *Rept. for 1891* 593, *Aromochelys carinata.* . . Keeled Mud Turtle. . . This species is common in the streams and ponds of the Southern States from Georgia to Arizona. **1928** Pope–Dickinson *Amphibians* 73 **WI,** *Sternotherus odoratus.* . . Also called Stink-pot Turtle and Mud Turtle. . . Southern half of the state. **1969** *DARE* (Qu. P24, . . *Kinds of turtles*) Inf **IN**55, Mud turtle (gray, medium-sized).

c A turtle of the family Emydidae, as:

(1) A **box turtle** (here: *Terrapene carolina* or *T. ornata*).

1851 *De Bow's Rev.* 11.53 **LA,** *Hinge Mud Turtle,* or *Emys Clausa,* is also found here. They never exceed six inches in length (i.e. the shell) and close up like the *testudo clausa,* though not quite so completely. **1968** *DARE* (Qu. P24, . . *Kinds of turtles*) Inf **WI**17, Mud turtle, box turtle—same.

(2) A **red-bellied turtle,** usu *Chrysemys picta* or *C. concinna.*

1891 Jesup *Plants Hanover NH* 64, C[hrysemys] picta. . . Painted Turtle. Mud Turtle. Common. **1928** Pope–Dickinson *Amphibians* 80 **WI,** *Western Painted Turtle.* . . Known locally as "Mud Turtle" although this name is more correctly applied to *Kinosternon pennsylvanicum.* The shields of the carapace are dull olive-brown or black. . . The head is striped with yellow and the legs are touched with red. Averages five inches in length. **1950** *WELS* (*Kinds of turtles found in your neighborhood*) 33 Infs, **WI,** Mud turtle(s). **1966–69** *DARE* (Qu. P24) Inf **CT**31, Paint or mud turtle; **DC**8, Mud turtle—gets big; **MI**99, Mud turtle—large; **ND**3, Mud turtle—small, black; **VA**14, Mud turtle—up to 15–20 pounds. **1981** Vogt *Nat. Hist. WI* 203, *Turtles* . . mud. See Painted turtles.

(3) A **map turtle** (here: *Graptemys geographica* or *G. pseudogeographica*).

1890 in 1896 IL State Lab. Nat. Hist. Urbana *Bulletin* 3.186, *Malacoclemmys lesueuri,* Gray. Very abundant in all our rivers, where it is known as the mud turtle. **1891** in 1895 *Ibid* 3.237, It [=*Graptemys geographica*] is exceedingly common in the Illinois and Mississippi rivers, where it is known (with *M[alacoclemmys] lesueuri* [=*G. pseudogeographica*], from which it is not discriminated) as the mud turtle. It is timid and inoffensive in disposition, always sliding from bank or log when approached.

(4) A turtle of the genus *Clemmys:* usu the **spotted turtle** in the eastern US, or a **pond turtle** (here: *Clemmys marmorata*) in the Pacific states.

1947 Pickwell *Amphibians* 61 **Pacific,** *Clemmys marmorata.* . . is the Turtle known best to people in the Far West. It is commonly called "Mud Turtle." **1968–69** *DARE* (Qu. P24, . . *Kinds of turtles*) Infs **CA**105, 111, 114, 136, 141, 145, 171, Mud turtle; **CT**13, Mud turtle—small with yellow spots; **CT**14, Mud turtle—dark with yellow spots; **ME**8, Wood turtle commonly called a mud turtle; **NY**71, Mud turtle—has yellow spots onto him; **NY**207, Mud turtle—black with yellow spots; **NV**8, Mud turtle—in the rivers, sloughs, or the tule fields.

d =soft-shell turtle.

1966–67 *DARE* (Qu. P24, . . *Kinds of turtles*) Inf **CO**22, Mud turtle = leatherback (soft-shell); **IN**1, Mud turtle—black spots on back, . . = soft-shell.

mud up See **mud** v 3

mud wagon n

1 A lightweight stagecoach with open sides. **chiefly West** *hist*

1836 Latrobe *Rambler in N. Amer.* 2.259, We had to put up with an open 'mud-waggon,' with spring seats. **1868** Waters *Life Among Mormons* 43, The inferior coaches, commonly known on the plains as "mud wagons." **1872** Twain *Roughing It* 57 **NE,** For an hour we took as much interest in Overland City as if we had never seen a town before. The reason we had an hour to spare was because we had to change our stage (for a less sumptuous affair called a "mud wagon") and transfer our freight of mails. **1939** *Colorado Mag.* 16.177 **West,** The vehicle listed in the Abbot, Downing Co. catalogue as a Hack Wagon, better known in the West as the California Mud Wagon, did great work in carrying passengers and the mail, but got little credit. **1955** Lewis *High Sierra* 91 **CA,** Among the first to arrive was a type of vehicle that the Argonauts dubbed "mud wagons." These usually carried fourteen passengers, twelve on traverse seats behind and two up front with the driver. Sometimes extra "dickey seats" provided accommodations of a sort for six more. **1967** *DARE* Tape **NV**2, [Inf:] But this is a mud wagon; see this don't have the seat, has, . . a different seat. . . You get six inside and two is eight, sittin' up there with the driver. Sometimes if there was a lot of business, we had another seat that set right back here, and their limbs hung down over. [Aux Inf:] I think the reason they call it a mud wagon is because the old Concord stages were much heavier and they would sink in the ground, so you'd use this lighter wagon. [Inf:] That's the reason we call it a mud wagon, much, much lighter.

2 Fig: see quot. Cf **Lord's breadwagon**

1955 *Eaton Coll.* **Washington Is. WI,** There's the mud wagon . . said when rumble of thunder is heard.

3 See **mud boat 1.**

mud wasp n **chiefly NEast; also Inland Nth, N Midl, Pacific** See Map and Map Section Cf **dirt dauber 1, mud dauber 1**

A **mud dauber 1** of the family Sphecidae or Vespidae.

1824 *Old Colony Mem.* (Plymouth MA) 6 Mar [4]/1, [He was] a sort of would-be-dandy; having the bottom of his waist pinched up to the size of a quart pot, and thus resembling in shape what we call a mud wasp. **1852** Harris *Treatise Insects* 406 **NEng,** They will observe and admire . . the clay cells of the mud-wasp, plastered against the walls of our houses. **1909** Smith *Insect Friends* 115, That enormous series of solitary wasps, including the mud-wasps, . . all . . make cells of some kind. **1939** *LANE* Map 239 *(Wasp),* Mud wasp, widely current. **1950** *WELS,* 14 Infs, **WI,** Mud wasp(s). **1965–70** *DARE* (Qu. R20) 245 Infs, **chiefly NEast; also Inland Nth, N Midl, Pacific,** Mud wasp; **PA**126,

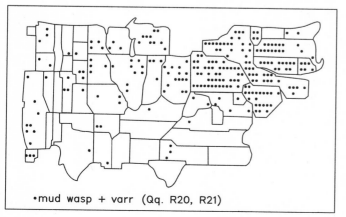

•mud wasp + varr (Qq. R20, R21)

Bluish mud wasp; **HI**2, Keyhole mud wasp—smaller [than a mud wasp]; (Qu. R21) Infs **GA**46, **PA**242, Mud wasp. **1986** Pederson *LAGS Concordance,* 8 infs, **Gulf Region,** Mud wasp(s).

‡mud whump n

A **minnow B1.**

1965 *PADS* 43.19 **seMA,** Small fish used for bait . . mud whumps [1 of 9 infs].

mudworm n Cf **muck worm**

=earthworm.

1907 *DN* 3.181 **seNH,** Mudworm. . . Common earthworm used in fishing. **1937** Crane *Let Me Show You VT* 35 **VT,** The earthworm is called *angleworm,* but several cases of *angledog* (a central Connecticut word) occur in western Vermont, and several cases of *mud-worm* (a northeastern Massachusetts word) in eastern Vermont. **1949** Kurath *Word Geog.* 74, Other expressions for the earthworm are local in character. *Mud worm* is common in the Merrimack Valley in New Hampshire and in Essex County, Massachusetts. **c1960** *Wilson Coll.* **csKY,** *Mud worm:* . . Earthworm. Rare. **1966–70** *DARE* (Qu. P5) Infs **FL**20, **NH**5, 10, **VA**73, Mudworm. **1967** Faries *Word Geog. MO* 135, *Missouri frequency of the dialect expressions used in the . . north*—mud worm 5 [of 700 infs]. **1986** Pederson *LAGS Concordance,* 3 infs, **GA, LA,** Mudworm(s); 1 inf, **nwFL,** Mudworms—long, big, wriggle a lot, low in ground.

mud yellow jacket See **yellow jacket**

mufalatta, muffa(letta) See **muffuletta**

muffed up See **muff-ups**

muffer-jawed See **muffle-jawed**

muffin n Also *cake muffin, muffin cake, sweet muffin* **chiefly Sth, S Midl**

A small cake; a cupcake.

1879 (1965) Tyree *Housekeeping in Old VA* 38, *Another Recipe for Muffins.* . . Make the batter the consistency of pound cake, and bake in snow-ball cups as soon as made. **1932** (1946) Hibben *Amer. Regional Cookery* 307 **CO,** *Muffin Cakes.* . . yolks 8 eggs . . flour . . sugar . . baking powder . . butter . . milk . . vanilla. Beat the yolks until they are thick and lemon colored; add the sugar gradually. . . Add the butter, creamed until soft and fluffy, then add flour. . . Grease muffin pans and dredge them with flour. . . Serve the same day as baked. The cakes will fall a little when taken from the oven, which is as it should be. **1956** Ker *Vocab. W. TX* 256, The term "small cake" implies a sweet, baked food. . . Muffin, with the greatest number of responses—seventeen—is ordinarily a bread . . but it is reported by all types of informants as a small cake or (sweet) *muffin.* Ibid 257, Closely related to *sweet muffin* . . is cupcake. **c1960** *Wilson Coll.* **csKY,** *Muffins* were common; what we now call cup cakes were sweet muffins. **1962** Atwood *Vocab. TX* 61, *Small Cake.* A rather unsystematic, and in general unsuccessful, attempt was made to elicit words for various small pastries. *Cookie* . . was the most common response followed by *muffin* . . *teacake* . . and *cupcake.* . . Of course, these do not all mean the same thing. **1966–70** *DARE* (Qu. H32, . . *Fancy rolls and pastries*) [Inf **FL**15, Cookies, tea cakes, muffins;] **FL**49, Muffins—cornbread muffins or cake muffins; **GA**88, Cupcakes—if bought; sweet muffins—if homemade; [they are the] same. **1969** *DARE* FW Addit **KY**5, Sweet muffins. . . A kind of cupcake eaten with preserves. **1971** *Today Show Letters* **seLA,** In New Orleans I was called upon to make some muffins. I'm sure I would have baked bran or blueberry muffins for the children's class party if the room mother had not insisted that they be frosted. Then I realized that she was referring to cupcakes. **1983** *MJLF* 9.1.58 **ceKY,** Sweet muffins . . sweetened cakes baked in a muffin pan. **1986** Pederson *LAGS Concordance,* 2 infs, **cMS, csLA,** (A) cake muffin; 1 inf, **ceAL,** Cake muffins; 1 inf, **swGA,** Sunday muffin = cupcake; "dress it" like a cake; 1 inf, **cAL,** Muffins—may or may not be iced; 1 inf, **cnGA,** Them little old muffin cakes; 1 inf, **swAL,** Muffin cakes—made like pound cake. **1994** *DARE* File, Any small cake that's baked in a muffin tin or one of those little fluted paper cups is a muffin. It doesn't matter whether it's a bran muffin on the breakfast table or a frosted cupcake at a birthday party—my family calls it a muffin. I don't remember where I first heard this; we moved all over the country when I was growing up.

muffle chops n Cf **chop** n[2], **muffle-jawed**

See quot 1904.

1904 *DN* 2.427 **Cape Cod MA** (as of a1857), *Muffle chops.* . . A person or animal with a swollen face or with a full lower face. **1916** *DN* 4.264 **Cape Cod MA,** If he is also heavy about the lower part of his face, he is "muffle-chops."

muffledice n [Var of **morphodite**]

1922 Gonzales *Black Border* 314 **sSC, GA coasts** [Gullah glossary], *Muffledice*—hermaphrodite. **1966** *DARE* (Qu. HH39, *A homosexual man*) Inf **SC26,** Muffledice ['mʌfədaɪs].

muffle-dun See **muckle-dun 1**

muffle-jaw adj See **muffle-jawed**

muffle-jaw n [Absol use of *muffle-jaw* adj (at **muffle-jawed**) in ref to the peculiar shape of the sculpin's head]

A **sculpin** (here: *Cottus* spp), usu **mottled sculpin.**

1877 *NY Acad. Sci. Annals Lyceum Nat. Hist.* 10.321 **GA,** It [=*Cottus bairdi*] is locally known as "Blob," and "Muffle-Jaw." **1882** U.S. Natl. Museum *Bulletin* 16.696, *Muffle-jaw.* . . Abounding in all clear rocky brooks and lakes; extending southward along the Alleghanies to Alabama. **1884** Goode *Fisheries U.S.* 1.259, In the lakes and streams of the Northern States are numerous species . . known in some localities . . [as] "Bull-heads," "Goblins," "Blobs," and "Muffle-jaws."

muffle-jawed adj Also *muffer-jawed, muffle-jaw* [*muffle* a muffler, scarf] Cf **muffle chops**

1 Having large or fleshy jaws. **esp S Atl**

1922 Gonzales *Black Border* 269 **sSC, GA coasts** [Gullah], De Jestuss sen' a mufflejaw' nigguh counstubble to my house. **1950** *PADS* 14.48 **SC,** *Muffle-jawed.* . . Having heavy, fleshy jaws. **1966–67** *DARE* (Qu. X6, *If a person's lower jaw sticks out prominently . . he's _____*) Infs **LA2, SC11,** Muffle-jawed; **GA11,** Muffle-jaw; **FL2,** Muffer-jawed ['mʌfɚ jɔd].

2 Of a chicken: having a ruff of feathers. [*EDD muffle* sb. 2 "A bunch of feathers under a hen's throat. . . Hence *Muffled* . . of a hen: tufted or having feathers protruding under the throat"]

1922 Gonzales *Black Border* 32 **sSC, GA coasts** [Gullah], 'E jaw look hebby 'tell 'e stan' lukkuh mufflejaw fowl. . . 'E tell me 'e hab uh teet'ache, en' dat w'ymekso 'e jaw swell.

muffuletta n Usu |məfə'lɑtə, -'lɛtə|; for addit varr see quots Abbr *muffa* Also sp *mufalatta, muffaletta* [Sicilian dial *muffuletta* a soft, spongy roll] **esp c,sLA** Cf **poor boy,** DS H42

A sandwich on a large, round, bun, consisting of var meats, cheeses, and olive salad with an oil dressing; the bun used for this sandwich.

1969 *AmSp* 42.283 **New Orleans LA,** Submarine sandwich. . . Musalatta [sic]. **1979** *DARE* File **cLA,** I also include the evidence on *muffaletta* from the Metairie restaurant. Apparently the artifact isn't known universally in New Orleans . . but it appears in Baton Rouge. Two restaurants in the 'Tigertown' area off the campus to the north advertise them—different spellings: one as *muffuleta* and the other just as *muffulett* (perhaps not enough room on the marquee). **1981** Pederson *LAGS Basic Materials,* 1 inf, **New Orleans LA,** [mæɨfə'la˃.ɪrəz]. Sandwich with different types of sausages. **1984** Stall *Proud New Orleans* 14, There was a time in the city's history when, because of economic conditions, Italians almost filled the French Quarter. . . Salvatore Tusa, owner of the Central Grocery on Decatur Street, began making a large sandwich. . . with a round bread called muffuletta and named it the "muffuletta sandwich." The eight-inch diameter bread topped with sesame seeds was cut in half and each side was coated with high-grade imported olive oil. . . To this were added generous layers of imported cheeses, ham and salami, then topped off with a homemade olive salad especially made by Central Grocery. **1990** Graham-Taylor *New Orleans* 47, [Title:] A Hero *Ain't* a Muffuletta! *Ibid,* The worst offense was saved for the summary: the N'awlins muffuletta, unique among the species dubbed "sandwich," the pride of the working class and elite alike, was classified by the world's most famous tabloid [=the *New York Times*] as a *Hero Sandwich!* **1991** *NADS Letters,* The French Quarter in New Orleans has several ethnic grocery stores that served po-boys and mufalattas. **1993** *DARE* File **sLA,** Spelled: *muffuletta;* said: *Muff-uh-Lot-uh;* made: one Italian roll (not French, but the big round one that looks like an overgrown hamburger bun)—olive salad, prosciutto, cappacola, salami, provolone. *Ibid* **csLA,** I'm in Lafayette, about 100 miles from the Big Easy, and we have some darn good muffulettas here too. *Ibid* **cTX,** I had wonderful muffaletta sandwiches in Austin back in 1970–76. *Ibid* **sLA,** Mickey's has been serving muffalettas [məfə'lɑtəz] since

1950. They started in 1927 at Central Grocery, in the Quarter, in downtown New Orleans. *Ibid,* It's a "Nawlins" poor boy. We said "muffa" [mʌfə]. We'd say, "Let's go get a muffa." *Ibid* **New Orleans LA,** They take this giant sandwich—a [məfə'lɛtə]—and cut it into halves or quarters and wrap it up in a great big piece of white paper.

muff-ups n Cf *DS* BB28

An imaginary illness; hence adj *muffed up* appearing to suffer from such an "illness."

1954 *Harder Coll.* **cwTN,** *Muff-ups.* . . A pretended illness; same as *lumbago laziness. Muffed-up.* "Act muffed-up, see if I keer nary bit."

mug n[1] [Prob abbr for **chamber mug** or **thunder mug**] Cf **chamber B4**

A chamber pot.

1950 *PADS* 14.48 **SC,** *Mug.* . . A chamber. **1965–69** *DARE* (Qu. F38, *Utensil kept under the bed for use at night*) Infs **IL61, MA40, NC55, RI16, SC26, 56, VA28,** Mug; **OK15,** Old mug. **1986** Pederson *LAGS Concordance* **nwFL,** Mugs [=bedroom conveniences].

mug v [*mug* face, mouth]

1 also with *up*: To engage in kissing and fondling; hence vbl n *mugging* necking, petting.

1932 *AmSp* 7.334 [Johns Hopkins jargon], *Mug* . . to kiss. **1956** Ker *Vocab. W. TX* 324, *Kissing* . . [3 infs] mugging. **1967–70** *DARE* (Qu. AA8, *When people make too much of a show of affection in a public place . . "There they were at the church supper _____ [with each other]."*) Infs **CA101, CT6, TX95, WI56,** Mugging; **TN14, RI6,** Muggin' (up). **1970** Major *Dict. Afro-Amer. Slang* 83, *Mugging:* . . making love. **1970** Tarpley *Blinky* 226 **neTX,** *Kissing* . . [1 inf] mugging. **1980** *Houston Chron.* (TX) 27 Jan 8, She is fascinated by "mugging"—used by college students [in Austin] to describe what they do on the couch. "I'm dying to know what they call the New York kind of mugging," she said. **1986** Pederson *LAGS Concordance* **cwLA,** Hugging and mugging [=fooling around when dancing].

2 also with *down*: To throw (an animal) to the ground by twisting its neck; see quot 1936. Cf **bulldog** v[1]

1936 McCarthy *Lang. Mosshorn West* [Rodeo terms], *Wild Cow Milkin'.* . . Two cowboys dash after each animal, one to rope the animal and then "mug" it and the other to obtain one inch of milk in a bottle. . . The term "mug" means to catch an animal around its head and place one hand on its nose, the other around its neck. **1944** Adams *Western Words* 102, *Mug*—To bulldog a calf. **1984** Lesley *Winterkill* 3 **neOR,** Hell, I can't even mug a steer much less a full-grown cow. *Ibid* 186, Throw your loop in front of the back feet so he can step into it. Once we've got him, I'll jump off the horse and mug him down. [*Ibid* 187, Danny grabbed the horns and twisted, digging his bootheels into the ground and putting his shoulder into the steer's neck. . . The steer's neck came around so far Danny thought it would break. "Now jerk," he said. As Jack tugged on the rope, the steer lost his balance and toppled.]

mug n[2] [Prob var of **meg 1** or **mig**]

In marble play: a marble.

c1970 Wiersma *Marbles Terms, Mugs*—marbles (slang).

mug down See **mug v 2**

mugging vbl n See **mug v 1**

mugging (up) See **mug-up n**

muggled up adj phr [Cf *EDD muggle* v.[1] 1 "*Muggled, pp.* in phr *muggled and huggled,* all in confusion"] Cf **muckle v 2,** *DS* GG2

1984 *DARE* File **seMA** (as of c1905), All muggled up—confused and irritated.

muggy adj Cf *mucky* (at **muck** n[1] **1a**)

Of land: marshy.

1966–68 *DARE* (Qu. C6, . . *A piece of land that's often wet, and has grass and weeds growing on it*) Infs **MS11, MO35,** Muggy land.

mug-in See **mug-up n**

mugs v [Etym unknown] Cf **boners, hosey**

To claim possession of.

1936 *AmSp* 11.191 **swWY,** To mugs. To choose, as in playing games (children's term). 'I mugs first shot.' **1992** *DARE* File **cnVT,** Other families in our town refer to it [=end slice of a loaf of bread] as the butt. An older lady in our area told me that when she was a child during the depression the children in her family used to sing out the phrase, "I mugs the butt!" The first one to finish the phrase was the winner, and recipient of the end slice.

mug up v phr[1]
To have a cup of coffee (and often a snack) between meals.
  1897 *KS Univ. Qrly.* (ser B) 6.89 **NEng,** *Mug up: "feed one's face."* **1901** *Scribner's Mag.* 29.498 **neMA,** Let Martin and me mug up and get over near the fire to dry out, and we'll have it again. **1905** Wasson *Green Shay* 242 **NEng,** In room of turning in, I jest set down and mugged-up [Footnote: Lunched] a grain with half a dezen doughnuts. **1930** [see **mug-up** n]. **1940** White *Wild Geese* 79 **NW** (as of 1890s), An invitation to "mug up" on coffee in thick cups. **1958** McCulloch *Woods Words* 119 **Pacific NW,** *Mug up*—To have a cup of coffee around a camp fire, or other than at regular meal times.

mug-up n Also *mugging (up), mug-in* [**mug up** v phr[1]] **scattered, but esp N Atl, Upper Missip Valley, AK** Cf **gam** n[1]
A cup of coffee (and often a snack, or even a meal) usu taken with others; a coffee break.
  1930 *AmSp* 5.391 [Language of N Atl fishermen], *Mug-up. . .* 1. To get a snack with tea or coffee between meals. 2. The snack itself, which is taken in the galley after each set if there is time. **1931–33** *LANE Worksheets* **RI,** *Mug up.* A snack taken between meals. Also *mugging up. . .* From a disabled seaman in the seaman's home in New York. **1932** Wasson *Sailing Days* 163 **cME coast,** Here the first food since the hasty afternoon "mug-up" of the day before was tasted. **1937** *AK Sportsman* 3.5.10 **AK,** Living on mug-ups and losing sleep on the trail is a severe drain on reserves of adipose tissue. **1939** (1962) Thompson *Body & Britches* 199 **NY,** A *mug-up* is a snack to eat. **1945** Colcord *Sea Language* 132 **ME, Cape Cod, Long Island,** *Mug up, a.* A hearty supper or between-meal snack, on fishing vessels. Occasionally heard on shore. **1947** *AK Sportsman* 13.6.36 **AK,** The cook had his work cut out for him, what with three square meals a day for the crew and mug-ups three times a day for good measure. [**1957** Beck *Folkl. ME* 167, An invitation to coffee is a "mug up."] **1965–70** *DARE* (Qu. O21, *When men out in seagoing boats get together for a visit and a cup of hot coffee . . a* _____) Infs **AK1, IL67, 77, 83, 84, ME16, 22, MA5, NC1, 12, RI6, WI61,** Mug-up; **IL78,** Mug-in; **IL86,** Mug-in [FW sugg]; **AL31,** Mugging [FW sugg]; [**OH20,** Mug of coffee]. [All IL Infs live on or near Missip R.] **1969** *Yankee* Aug 87 **NEng,** The skipper was seated at the galley table having a mug-up, one of the many cups of coffee he and the rest of the crew would drink during the long day. **1975** Gould *ME Lingo* 185, *Mug up*—Maine coastal perennial for the coffee break. Probably a *mug up* may be had in a lunch room or drug store, but the term means first of all the snack at any time of day when you stop by a fishing-village home in passing. *Mug up* suggests friendly hospitality to be shirked neither in the offering nor the accepting.

mug up v phr[2] See **mug** v 1

mugwort n Cf **sagebrush, wormwood**
Std: any of var plants of the genus *Artemisia*, but esp *A. vulgaris* in the eastern US and *A. ludoviciana* in the western US. For other names of *A. vulgaris* see **felon herb, sage**

muh n See **ma** n A4

-muh- infix See **-ma-** infix

muhdear See **mother dear**

muhly (grass) n
Std: a grass of the genus *Muhlenbergia*. Also called **dropseed 1, grama grass 2.** For other names of var spp see **aparejo grass, black grama 3, blowout grass 1, bullgrass 4, deer grass 4, gauze ~, hairgrass 1c, hoe grass, knotroot ~, marsh muhly, mat ~, mesquite grass 2g, mountain bunchgrass 2, nimble will 1, prairie rushgrass, pull-up muhly, ring grass, satin ~, scratch ~, spike muhly, tangle grass, tickle ~, white grama, wild timothy, wire grama, wire grass, wirestem muhly, wood grass**

muhself See **myself**

mukkle See **myrtle** n[1]

mukluk n Also sp *muckluck* [Yupik *maklak* bearded seal]
1 also *mukluk boot:* A warm, sturdy boot with the sole usu of sealskin and the high upper usu of fur. **chiefly AK**
  [**1868** Whymper *Travel AK* 136 **ceAK,** Their boots vary in length, and

in the material used for the sides, but all have soles of "maclock," or sealskin, with the hair removed.] **1904** (1969) Robins *Magnetic North* 31 **AK,** Nothing like mucklucks with a wisp of straw inside for this country. *Ibid* 190, When he pulled off his mucklucks his stockinged feet smoked in the frosty air. **1940** White *Wild Geese* 262 **AK** (as of 1890s), "Mukluks," said Len. "Leastwise a kind of what you'd call a slipper mukluk. The real mukluks got legs on 'em. That's whale gut—or walrus gut—they're made of. You wouldn't think it, but they'll wear like iron." **1947** *Chicago Daily Tribune* (IL) 11 Dec 20/3 **neIL,** He was presented with . . a pair of mukluk boots made to order for Paul Bunyan. **1957** *Seattle Daily Times* (WA) 4 Aug mag sec 5/3 **AK,** From St. Michael came what supplies we did get and our footwear, which we called mukluks. The bottoms or soles of these mukluks were made of the flippers of the seal. . . They were light and waterproof. **1959** Hart *McKay's AK* 32, *Mukluk:* A fur boot made by the Eskimo women skin sewers which has soles made of tough sealskin or sea-lion skin curled up at the edges and shaped to fit at the heels and toes by crimping the hide. . . The upper part of the boot is made of reindeer hide and other hardy furs. . . A removable inner sole of dried grass or baleen shavings is added for comfort, as well as for absorption, so no freezing moisture collects. **1965** Bowen *Alaskan Dict.* 22, *Mukluks* (muck-lucks)—Eskimo fur boots. Mukluks come in sets, inner and outer. The inner pair (sometimes called *fur socks*) are fur-in, and the outer pair fur-out. A thong wraps around the mukluk to keep it firm around the leg. Mukluks are moccasin-toed and are elegantly trimmed. They are the finest Arctic footgear in the world.
2 also *mudluck;* Transf: a house shoe or bedroom slipper with a knit top and a leather sole.
  1940 [see **1** above]. **1950** *WELS (Soft shoes, worn only inside the house)* 3 Infs, **WI,** Mukluks; 1 Inf, **seWI,** Mukluks—made of a felt sole with a knit stocking-like top. **1968–69** *DARE* (Qu. W21) Inf **CA58,** Mukluks—a leather sole and a knitted top; **CA85,** Mukluks—leather sole with a sock top; **WI47,** Mukluks; **MI102,** Mudlucks—a sock with a thin leather sole. **1986** Pederson *LAGS Concordance,* 1 inf, **seTN,** Mukluks—house shoes to him; socks and moccasins.

mukluk boot See **mukluk 1**

mukluk telegraph n Also *mukluk wireless* **chiefly AK** Cf **grapevine telephone, moccasin telegraph**
Word of mouth.
  1945 *AK Sportsman* 11.1.16 **AK,** It had been reported by mukluk wireless that a celebrated New york [sic] physician was aboard. *Ibid* 11.8.33, Through the good graces of Cho-ak, and through the mukluk telegraph, news concerning me had spread to all the village. This mouth-to-ear and ear-to-mouth communication seems about as rapid as the telephone or telegraph. **1946** *Ibid* 12.3.33, Whisperings of a romance between King and the substitute teacher went the rounds by mukluk wireless for days. **1963** *Ibid* 29.3.20, Word that went out recently via mukluk telegraph about Wien Alaska Airlines' taking delivery of a new bush plane from Switzerland caused more excitement among bush pilots than the first jet that zoomed over Alaska. **1966** Dufresne *My Way* 44 **AK,** News of the roundup had spread with incredible speed from mouth to ear—Mukluk Wireless, they called it—one fish camp and village to the next. **1981** *Fairbanks Daily News–Miner* (AK) 26 Apr 6 *(Tabbert Coll.),* What you said at the recent Foreman's meeting that was held in Fairbanks has travelled north, south, east and west via Mukluk Telegraph.

muktuk n Also *maktak, mungtuk* **AK**
Whale skin, usu with an attached layer of blubber, used as food; whale blubber.
  1910 in 1991 Tabbert *Dict. Alaskan Engl.* 77, He [Tabbert: "the Barrow native"] likes frozen fish and muk tuk (whale skin) better than ice cream, cake, or candy. **1937** *Alaska Sportsman* Oct 17 (Tabbert *Dict. Alaskan Engl.*), The outside skin, called "mungtuk," together with a layer of blubber two or three inches thick, is first removed. **1959** Hart *McKay's AK* 33, *Muktuk:* The rubbery outer layer of black or white whale skin and fat, usually two to three inches thick, is a popular Eskimo food. This chewy substance, similar to gristle, is cut into slabs or served in small squares which are chewed raw or served pickled. **1965** Bowen *Alaskan Dict.* 22, *Muktuk. . .* Whale blubber. The fibrous, fatty tissue between whale skin and the underlying muscle. . . The muktuk eater takes a good grip on his piece with his teeth, holds the free end straight out and cuts the bite off with his knife. After the oil is chewed out, only a clear, white fiber like cotton string is left. . . The tastes [sic] is slightly like walnut, but the content is pure whale oil. **1973** *Pioneer All-Alaska Weekly* (Fairbanks AK) 27 July 3/2, A food bar will sell both western

and native foods, including muktuk—whale skin and blubber. **1977** *Fairbanks Daily News–Miner* (AK) 13 Sept 9 (Tabbert *Dict. Alaskan Engl.*), Beluga muktuk consists of the outside skin of the beluga whale which is about ½ to ¾ inch thick with about ½-inch of blubber attached. It is considered a delicacy by the Eskimos who hunt this animal in Kotzebue sound. **1978** *AK Mag.* 44.7.82, When a boat captain got a whale in the spring, he filled out a poke with whale skin, which we called mungtuk, and cut the skin into bite size. **1980** *The Arctic Coastal Zone Management Newsletter* (Barrow) Sept 5 (Tabbert *Dict. Alaskan Engl.*), Frederick Brower. . . is shown here at the spring Nalukataq in Browerville with relatives of the Brower family in the background carving maktak and whale meat for distribution.

mulatto adj *chiefly Sth, S Midl*
Of soil: having a brown or reddish-brown color.
   1741 in 1940 *AmSp* 15.287 **VA,** A Tract of rich Mulattoe Land, lying in the County. **1789** Morse *Amer. Geog.* 447 **GA,** It changes into what is called the Mulatto soil, consisting of a black mould and red earth. **1837** (1962) Williams *Territory FL* 82, The surface is covered with a mulatto or chocolate colored loam. **1869** *Overland Mth.* 3.130 **TX,** Then there is the "chocolate" prairie, and the "mulatto." **1883** Smith *Rept. for 1881 & 1882* 435 **AL,** The red or mulatto lands are much the best for cotton. **1883** GA Dept. Ag. *Pub. Circular No. 35* 8.5, Soil—Mulatto, gravelly and rolling, with northeastern exposure; been in cultivation about 43 years; original growth oak and hickory. *Ibid* 10, Soil.—What is known as mulatto land. Has been in cultivation about fifty years. *Ibid* 11, Soil.—Light, inclined to mulatto, with red clay sub-soil; has been cleared probably eighty years. **1952** Callahan *Smoky Mt.* 76, The land which lay along the foot of the mountains was called "mulatto land," being a dark soil with a clay foundation.

mulatto rice n [Perh from the color] Cf **dirty rice**
A rice dish; see quots.
   1937 (1977) Hurston *Their Eyes* 15 **FL** [Black], Mah mulatto rice ain't so good dis time. Not enough bacon grease, but Ah reckon it'll kill hongry. **1966** *DARE* (Qu. H50, *Dishes made with beans, peas, or corn that everybody around here knows, but people in other places might not*) Inf **GA**12, Mulatto rice—stewed tomatoes and rice.

mulberry n **NEng** Cf **French mulberry, Texas mulberry**
Any of var **raspberries** of the genus *Rubus,* such as **flowering raspberry.**
   1672 Josselyn *New-Englands Rarities* 48, *Rasp-Berry,* here called Mul-berry. **1832** Williamson *Hist. ME* 1.114, High bush Blackberry is sometimes called "Mulberry." Rubus villosus. **1847** Wood *Class-Book* 249, R[ubus] odoratus. Rose-flowering Raspberry. Mulberry. *Ibid* 250, R. Chamaemorus. Dwarf Mulberry. Cloudberry. **1891** Jesup *Plants Hanover NH* 12, R[ubus] odoratus . . . (Purple Flowering Raspberry.) Often wrongly called Mulberry. **1892** *Jrl. Amer. Folkl.* 5.95, Rubus triflorus, mulberry. Washington Co., Me. **1898** *Ibid* 11.226 **sME coast,** Rubus odoratus . . mulberry. **1910** Graves *Flowering Plants* 237 **CT,** Rubus alleghaniensis. . . Mulberry Blackberry. . . One of our most valued wild berries. **1940** Clute *Amer. Plant Names* 8, R[ubus] chamaemorus. . . Low mulberry. . . R. odoratus. . . Thimbleberry, purple-flowering raspberry, mulberry. . . R. strigosus. . . Mulberry.

mulboard See **moldboard** n[1]

mulch worm n Cf **muck worm, mudworm**
   1966 *DARE* (Qu. P6, . . *Kinds of worms . . used for bait*) Inf **FL**16, Mulch worm.

mule n[1]
1 See **mule deer.**
2 =**white mule.**
   1926 *AmSp* 1.652 [Hobo lingo], Mule—corn alcohol. **1927** *DN* 5.456 [Underworld jargon], Mule. . . Corn whisky. **1929** *AmSp* 4.386 **KS,** Whiskey is sometimes called *donk* or *mule* because of its powerful "kick." **1968** *DARE* (Qu. DD21c, *Nicknames for whiskey, especially illegally made whiskey*) Inf **IN**13, Mule. **1969** Sorden *Lumberjack Lingo* 79 **NEng, Gt Lakes,** Mule—Alcohol or rotgut whisky—noted for its kick.
3 See quot. Cf **buck** n[1] **4,** DS L59
   1923 *DN* 5.236 **swWI,** Mule. . . A sawbuck.
4 See quot 1908. **Upper Missip Valley** Also called **mud sail**
   1908 Kunz–Stevenson *Book of the Pearl* 269 **Missip Valley,** Sometimes, when the current is light, the fisherman prepares a "mule" to assist the boat in towing the resisting drag. This "mule" consists of a wooden frame, hinged in V shape, and is fastened several feet in advance of the

boat with the V end pointed down the stream. It sinks low in the water, and the current pressing against the angle carries it along, and thus tows the skiff and the resisting drag at a uniform rate of speed. **1941** *AmSp* 16.155 **Missip R,** An essential feature of the [freshwater mussel and clam] fisher's outfit is the *under-water sail,* usually called a *mule* because of its 'kick.' **1953** (1977) Hubbard *Shantyboat* 236 **Missip-Ohio Valleys,** In the head wind we used a contrivance called a mule, or mud sail. It is really an underwater sail, used by shellers to drag their heavy brails over the bottom. Our mud sail was a square of canvas as wide as the boat. It was lowered into the water, over the end of the boat, an iron pipe on the lower edge to hold it down, the upper edge fastened to the deck. . . The boat was kept parallel with the current which exerted its force against the sail just as a wind would do. The mule carried us into a head wind very well. Another advantage was that it kept the end of the boat into the wind and waves. Without it our boat always turned broadside to the wind. **1966** *WI Conserv. Bulletin* 31.3.26 **swWI,** During 1965, between 50 and 75 boats worked the river out of Prairie du Chien. These wooden flatboats are . . drifted downstream over the clam beds. They are propelled by a device called a "mule," which is a piece of canvas rigged under the water to catch the current. **1968** *DARE* Tape **IL**29, You had what we called a mule. It was a big oblong board with a canvas on it. And you dropped your bar in the river, then you dropped this mule in . . and the water would run again' that and that's what pulled your boat downstream.

5 in phrr *as far as* (or *any further than*) *one can throw a mule* and varr: At all; to any degree. *chiefly Sth, S Midl* See Map
   1965–70 *DARE* (Qu. V2c, *About a deceiving person, or somebody that you can't trust . . "I wouldn't trust him any further than I could _____";* not asked in early QRs) 18 Infs, *chiefly Sth, S Midl,* Throw a mule (by the tail); **SC**19, Throw a greasy mule by the tail; (Qu. V2b, *About a deceiving person, or somebody that you can't trust . . "I wouldn't trust him _____";* not asked in early QRs) 12 Infs, *chiefly Sth, S Midl,* As far as I (*or* you) could throw a mule (by the tail); **GA**77, No further than I could throw a mule by the tail.

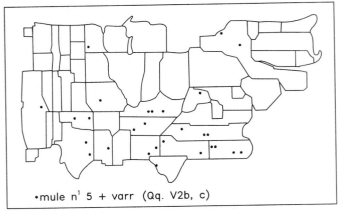

•mule n[1] 5 + varr (Qq. V2b, c)

6 in phr *sweat like a mule:* To sweat profusely. *chiefly Sth, S Midl* See Map Cf *sweat like a nigger* (at **nigger** n[1] **B11**), *sweat like a pig* (at **pig**)
   1965–70 *DARE* (Qu. X56b, *Expressions about sweating very heavily*) 65 Infs, *chiefly Sth, S Midl,* Sweat(ing) (*or* sweats) like a mule.

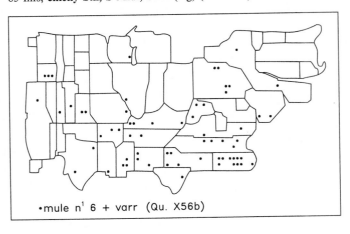

•mule n[1] 6 + varr (Qu. X56b)

7 In var phrr indicating that one's trouser fly is open: see quot. Cf **cow barn is open, horse B14**

1969–70 *DARE* (Qu. W24c, . . *To warn a man that his trouser-fly is open*) Inf **GA**77, Left your mule stable open; **TX**72, Mule's about to get out; **TX**89, Mule's liable to get out.

mule n² Also *mule cow*, *~ head* [**muley** adj **B1**] Cf **mull** adj, n¹
A hornless cow; hence adjs *muled, mule-headed* hornless.

1966–70 *DARE* (Qu. K12, *A cow that has never had horns*) Infs **CA**193, Mule cow; **GA**1, 5, Mule head; **GA**77, **LA**12, Mule-headed (cow); **IN**77, Mule; **MI**91, Muled cow.

mule ax n Cf **mad ax**

1968 *DARE* (Qu. L35, *Hand tools used for cutting underbrush and digging out roots*) Inf **OH**45, Mad ax, mule ax.

mule bird n
=**starling.**

1952 *AmSp* 27.295, A cross [*DARE* Ed: or hybrid], in the view of observers. . . *Mule bird* (starling, Tenn.)

mule corn n Cf **horse corn**
A var of **Indian corn 1;** see quot.

1967 *DARE* (Qu. I34, *If you don't have sweet corn, you can always eat young* _____) Inf **LA**2, Field corn, mule corn—occas.

mule cow See **mule** n²

mule-crippler cactus n Cf **horse crippler**
A **barrel cactus** (here: *Echinocactus horizonthalonius*).

1976 Bailey–Bailey *Hortus Third* 411, [*Echinocactus*] *horizonthalonius* . . Eagle-claws, mule-crippler cactus. . . spines straight or recurved, to 1–½ in. long, often stout and flattened.

muled See **mule** n²

mule deer n Also *mule, mule-ear(ed) deer, muletail (deer), muley (deer)* [See quot 1980]
A long-eared deer (*Odocoileus hemionus*) native to the western US. Also called **black-tailed deer, brush deer, burro deer, Pacific deer**

1805 (1965) Lewis–Clark *Hist. Lewis–Clark Exped.* 2.546, Our hunters returned soon after with two mule-deer and three common deer. **1843** (1960) Audubon *Audubon & His Jrls.* 2.167, Fresh signs of Indians. Saw many Antelopes and Mule Deer. **1893** Roosevelt *Wilderness Hunter* 16, The common blacktail or mule deer, which has likewise been sadly thinned in numbers . . extends from the great plains to the Pacific. **1965–70** *DARE* (Qu. P32, . . *Other kinds of wild animals*) 22 Infs, **chiefly West,** Mule deer; **CA**45, Mule deer—called the mule deer because it has such big ears; **CO**41, Mule deer—a black-tail deer; **NJ**56, Mule deer—big sticking-up ear; **NM**3, Blacktail or mule deer; **CA**3, 109, 120, 130, **MO**38, **OH**20, Mule-tail deer; **AZ**2, **CO**4, Mule-ear(ed) deer; **OK**52, Mule deer are called mule-ear deer; **KS**15, Muley deer; **HI**14, Black-tail mule deer; **WY**4, Mule. **1968** *DARE* Tape **CA**100, Ha! I've hunted elk in the coastal mountains. . . and have hunted muletail in southern Utah for my hunting trips. **1979** *NYT Article Letters* **Pacific NW** [Hunting terms], Muley: mule deer. **1980** Whitaker *Audubon Field Guide Mammals* 652, Mule Deer have a stiff-legged bounding gait, with back legs then front legs moving together. [*Ibid*, These deer have large ears that move independently and almost constantly and account for the common name.] **1982** Elman *Hunter's Field Guide* 480, A hunter from the East may be unprepared for his first glimpse of a mature muley buck across some high meadow in Montana's Rockies or on a sweeping Colorado plateau.

mule down v phr
To stop moving; to refuse to move.

1962 *Mt. Life* 38.1.19 **KY,** He begin to pull back, and I says, 'You want me to sqush yer head wi' this hyar .45?' He jest muled right down. I popped the handcuffs on 'im. **1991** *NADS Letters* e**VA,** To "mule down" is to dig in your heels and refuse to budge or relent. Stubborn.

mule duck n
1 =**shoveler.**

1932 Howell *FL Bird Life* 141, *Spatula clypeata.* . . Mule Duck. **1952** *AmSp* 27.295, A cross [*DARE* Ed: or hybrid], in the view of observers. . . *Mule duck* (shoveler, Fla.)

2 =**redhead.**

1982 Elman *Hunter's Field Guide* 199, Redhead . . Common & regional names . . mule duck.

mule-ear n [From the shape]
1 =**fried pie 1.**

1949 *AmSp* 24.111 **nwSC,** Mule ears. . . Fried pies (usually apple or peach).

2 pl; also *mule's ears:* A plant of the western genus *Wyethia.* For other names of var spp see **compass plant 2, dwarf sunflower 2, Indian wheat 2, poisonweed, sunflower, yellows**

1901 Jepson *Flora CA* 541, *W[yethia] glabra* . . Mule's Ears. **1937** U.S. Forest Serv. *Range Plant Hdbk.* W207, Mules-ears leaves, in shape like the ears of a mule, are dark green in color, smooth, somewhat stiff and leathery and are often covered with a resinous or waxy substance. **1961** Thomas *Flora Santa Cruz* 357 cw**CA,** *Wyethia* [spp] . . Mule Ears. . . *W[yethia] helenioides* . . Gray Mule Ears. . . *W[yethia] angustifolia* . . Narrow-leaved Mule Ears. **1966** *Julian Apple Day* 12 cs**CA,** She . . has the ability to see beauty in dock, a few stalks of wild oats and mule's ears. **1967** *DARE* (Qu. S26e) Inf **OR**10, Mule-ear—fuzzy leaf (large daisy). **1979** Spellenberg *Audubon Guide N. Amer. Wildflowers W. Region* 395, Mule's Ears (*Wyethia amplexicaulis*). . . Central Washington to western Montana; south to northwestern Colorado, northern Utah, and Nevada.

3 pl: See quot.

1967 Key *Tobacco Vocab.* **PA,** Mule ears—It [=a tobacco leaf] gets pointy . . in a dry year. *Ibid* **MO,** Mule ears—A cross between tobacco and mullen [sic].

mule-ear(ed) deer See **mule deer**

mule-eared rabbit n **TX** Cf **mule rabbit, narrow-gauge(d) mule, small mule**
=**jackrabbit 1.**

1885 Siringo *TX Cowboy* 142, I had just eaten a mule-eared rabbit. **1933** *AmSp* 8.1.31 nw**TX,** He don't know no more than a mule-yeared rabbit about brandin'. **1967** *DARE* (Qu. P30, . . *Wild rabbits*) Inf **TX**42, Mule-eared rabbit—same as jackrabbit.

mule-ear orchid n Cf **cowhorn orchid**
Prob an orchid of the genus *Cyrtopodium.*

1961 Douglas *My Wilderness* 147 **Everglades FL,** Lancewood, ironwood, inkwood, gumbo limbo—these were all new to me. So were the orchids that grow in them—grass pink orchid, cigar orchid, mule-ear orchid, butterfly orchid, shell orchid, penny orchid.

mule fat n [Prob **mule deer** + **fat** v] **CA**
A **groundsel tree** (here: *Baccharis viminea*). Also called **black willow 2**

1901 Jepson *Flora CA* 570, *B[accharis] viminea* . . Mule Fat. **1951** *PADS* 15.20 s**CA,** *Baccharis viminea* . . Mule-fat. **1961** Thomas *Flora Santa Cruz* 346 cw**CA,** Mule Fat. Occasional along dry stream beds in the Santa Clara Valley. **1981** Benson–Darrow *Trees SW Deserts* 336, *Baccharis viminea* . . Mule Fat. . . exceedingly common in north-central and central California.

mule-foot n¹, adj See **mule-footed 1**

mulefoot n² Also *mulefoot bonnet, mulefoot(ed) lily, muleshoe* [Appar from the shape of the leaf] esp **SE** Cf **bonnet B1a**
A **spatterdock** (here: *Nuphar luteum*).

1920 *Torreya* 20.21 nw**TN,** *Nymphaea advena* . . Mulefoot, mulefoot lily, mulefoot bonnet. **1933** Small *Manual SE Flora* 541, *Nuphar advena* . . Mulefoot-lily. **1941** *Torreya* 41.47 nw**TN,** *Nymphaea advena* . . Muleshoe. **1960** Williams *Walk Egypt* 127 **GA,** The banks were thick with cherrylaurel and fig, the water with mule-footed lily pads and bonnets, a fine docking place for snails.

mulefoot bonnet See **mulefoot** n²

mule-footed adj
1 also *mule-foot;* Of a hog or its foot: having a solid rather than a cloven hoof; hence n *mule-foot* a hog having such a hoof; the condition of having such a hoof.

1911 *Country Life* 19.231, One of the oddities in breeds of swine lately being urged upon public attention . . is the mule-foot hog. *Ibid*, Enthusiastic promoters of the mule-foots are tentatively putting forward statements that these swine "a hundred years or more ago are said to have been brought to this country from Norway, Denmark, Sweden, Scotland, Holland, South Africa, Mexico, and several other foreign countries." **1913** Rothert *Hist. Muhlenberg Co.* 393 **KY,** They are now not as well remembered on account of their connection with the mine as they are because they introduced into the neighborhood a breed of hogs known as "mule-footed hogs." . . Up to a few years ago one could see a hog with some of its hoofs "mule-footed" and the others "split." **1918** Babcock–Clausen *Genetics* 527, We refer particularly to such characters as the polled condition in cattle, hornlessness in sheep, mule-foot in hogs, taillessness in cats, and like characters. **1923** *DN* 5.236 **swWI**, *Mule-foot*. . . A one-toed hog, a hog with a solid hoof. "He's got a drove of mule-foots." . . Having only one toe (of a hog). **1986** Pederson *LAGS Concordance,* 1 inf, **ceAR**, Mule-foot hog—foot is solid, like a mule; 1 inf, **cwAR**, Mule-footed hog—hoof like mule; 1 inf, **ceTX**, Mule-footed hog—made track like a mule; 1 inf, **neAR**, A mule-footed hog = hog without cloven hoofs.

2 See quot. Cf **mountain hoof**

    1968 Adams *Western Words* 203, *Mule-footed*—A cowboy's term for a horse with round hoofs, a characteristic usually found in mountain horses.

mulefoot(ed) lily See **mulefoot** n²

mulehead n¹ Cf **gourdhead 1, ironhead 2**

=wood ibis.

    1913 *Auk* 30.491 **Okefenokee GA**, *Mycteria americana*. . . 'Mule-head'. . . This species is considered a game bird, and is eaten whenever it can be secured. **1955** *Oriole* 20.1.3 **GA**, *Wood Ibis*. . . *Mulehead* (probably as a synonym of "hardhead," the sense of several names of the bird).

mule head n² See **mule** n²

mule-headed See **mule** n²

mule-high adj [Var of **horse-high**]

Of a fence: too high for a mule to jump.

    1884 Smith *Bill Arp's Scrap Book* 69 **nwGA**, Fences are a big thing in these parts, and if a man aint careful it will take about half he makes on his farm to keep 'em mule high and bull strong and pig tight.

mule killer n

1 **=vinegarone.**

    1886 *Entomol. Amer.* 2.39, *T[helyphonus] giganteus* . . is found quite frequently in the Southern States, where it is much feared by the people who call it Nigger Killer, Mule Killer, Grampus, etc. **1950** *PADS* 14.76 **FL**, *Mule-killer*. . . A large scorpion found under trash piles.

2 **=praying mantis.** [See quot 1901]

    1899 Bergen *Animal Lore* 63 **KS**, Mule-killer, devil's war-horse, praying mantis. **1901** Howard *Insect Book* 327, In our Southern States they [=praying mantids] are known as "mule-killers," from the curious superstition that the brownish liquor which they exude from the mouth is fatal to mules. **1925** *Book of Rural Life* 4493, The mantis is at least two inches long when grown. . . Other names by which it is locally known are *devil's riding horse* . . and *mule killer*. **1949** Palmer *Nat. Hist.* 383, *Praying Mantis*. . . Known as rearhorses, mule killers, devil's horses, and soothsayers.

3 A **dragonfly.** Cf **horse stinger**

    1905 Kellogg *Amer. Insects* 76, Dragon-flies? Folks call 'em. . . 'snake-feeders,' 'horse-stingers,' 'mule-killers,' etc. **1940** Teale *Insects* 140, *Dragonflies*. . . are called . . devil's-darning-needles and mule-killers.

mule lightning See **lightning** n¹

mule pine n

A **juniper 1** (here: *Juniperus communis*).

    1947 (1976) Curtin *Healing Herbs* 18, When a horse is *malo* (suffering from a swollen neck), garlic is crushed with the twigs of *Sabino macho* (mule pine), and hot water is added. This is allowed to cool and is then administered.

mule rabbit n Cf **mule-eared rabbit**

A **jackrabbit 1** (here: *Lepus callotis*).

    1857 *Porter's Spirit of Times* 28 Feb 414, Some of our expedition formed themselves into a "Nimrod" party, and went farther out, for the purpose of *fetching* in some of the deer, bar, and mule rabbits. **1859** (1968) Bartlett *Americanisms* 218, *Jackass Rabbit. (Lepus callotis.)* A rabbit, found on the high plains of Texas and near the Rocky Mountains, so called from its very long ears and long and slender legs. It is known also by the names of Mule Rabbit, Texan Hare, and Black-tailed Hare.

mule's ear n

1 A children's game; see quot.

    1967 *Good Old Days* 3.9.41 (as of c1911), After supper they played Spin the Plate, Clap In and Clap Out, Blind Fold, Weevily Wheat, and Mule's Ear. . . Four boys and four girls would sit down in a circle, and

one would take two handkerchiefs and leave the corners protruding far enough for each one to get a corner. When a boy got a corner diagonally from a girl he got a kiss.

2 pl: See **mule-ear 2.**

muleshoe See **mulefoot** n²

muleshoe biscuit n

    1992 *DARE* File **AR**, A woman from Arkansas tells me her grandmother makes *muleshoe biscuits*. These biscuits are made of white flour and contain sugar, butter and a considerable dash of apple cider vinegar.

muleskinner n

1 See **skinner.**

2 A whip used in driving mules.

    1912 Wason *Friar Tuck* 71 **WY**, He would stand up an' yell, crack his mule-skinner, and send the ponies along on a dead run. **c1940** Eliason *Word Lists FL* 10 **wFL**, *Muleskinner:* A long whip used to drive mules. **1945** FWP *Lay My Burden Down* 169 **Sth** (as of c1860) [Black], So when Brother January he come home, the massa took down his long mule skinner and tied him with a rope to a pine tree. He strip his shirt off and said: "Now, nigger, I'm going to teach you some sense." With that he started laying on the lashes.

mule's tail See **muletail 2**

muletail n

1 See **mule deer.**

2 also *mule's tail:* A weedy plant such as **beggar ticks.**

    1966–68 *DARE* (Qu. S15) Inf **GA**25, Stickers—same as mule's tail—have three prongs, green, turn brown when ripe; (Qu. S21, . . *Weeds . . that are a trouble in gardens and fields*) Infs **IL**19, **IN**49, **NC**44, Mule('s) tail(s); **CO**20, Muletail—grows from cluster clump, then bushes out. **1991** Heat Moon *PrairyErth* 378 **ceKS**, We ride and he points out enemies—cheat grass, sourdock, mule tail, sunflower, cockleburr, velvet-leaf.

3 A **mullein** (here: *Verbascum thapsus*).

    1975 Hamel–Chiltoskey *Cherokee Plants* 45, Mullein, common; mule tail—*Verbascum thapsus*. . . Ingredient in drink for pains.

muletail deer See **mule deer**

muletail weed n

A **fleabane** (here: *Erigeron annuus*).

    1929 *Folk-Say* 75 **OK**, Summer complaint in children is cured by. . . the tea made of "mule tail" weed (common fleabane).

muley n¹ See **mule deer**

muley adj, n² For pronc varr see **A** below Also sp *mool(e)y, mull(e)y* [*EDD moiley* "A hornless cow or bullock," *mully* "A child's name for a cow or calf"; ult of Celtic origin. See **mull** adj, n¹ and 1984 *AmSp* 59.324]

A Forms. Note: Because many spp are ambiguous as to pronunciation, only those quots where it is explicit are given here; see **B** below for further exx of var spp.

1 |'mjuli, 'mɪuli, 'mjʊli|. **widespread exc Atlantic coast** See Map

    1893 Shands *MS Speech* 74, Muley cow ['mjulɪ]. **1901** *DN* 2.144 **IL**, *Muley-cow*, pron. [mjulɪ]. **1905** *DN* 3.88 **nwAR**, *Muley* ['mjulɪ]. . . A naturally hornless cow or calf. 'These calves are all natural muleys.' Universal. . . *Muley cow.* . . Universal. **1917** *DN* 4.396 **neOH**, *Muley*

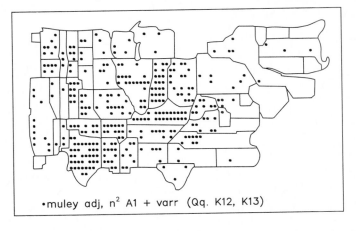

•muley adj, n² A1 + varr (Qq. K12, K13)

cow. . . A cow by nature without horns. Pronounced ['mjulɪ], not ['mjulɪ] or ['mulɪ]. M[edina Co.]. . . ['mulɪ] is reported from Ashtabula Co.; ['mulɪ] from Geauga Co. **1942** McAtee *Dial. Grant Co. IN* 44 (as of 1890s), *Muley-cow* . . one without horns. . . [O]ur pronunciation was as if the term were derived from mule; the prominence of the ears—a muley character—is enhanced by absence of horns. **1944** *PADS* 2.47 wNC, *Muley, mully* ['mjulɪ, 'mʌlɪ]: *n.* A cow that has never had any horns. **1965–70** *DARE* (Qu. K12) 330 Infs, **widespread exc Atlantic coast,** (Natural) muley ['mjulɪ, 'mɪulɪ] (cow); CT10, MI101, MS21, 39, ['mjulɪ] (cow); (Qu. K13) Infs CA87, NM13, OK43, VA33, Muley ['mjulɪ, 'mɪulɪ].

2 |'mulɪ|. **scattered, but less freq Atlantic coast, Gulf States** See Map

1917 [see **A1** above]. **1965–70** *DARE* (Qu. K12) 145 Infs, **scattered, but less freq Atlantic coast, Gulf States,** Mooley ['mulɪ] (cow); (Qu. K13) Inf CA131, Mooley ['mulɪ].

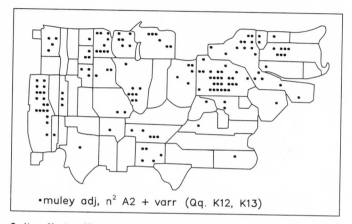

•muley adj, n² A2 + varr (Qq. K12, K13)

3 |'mulɪ, 'mʌlɪ|. **chiefly Upstate NY, nPA, wGt Lakes** See Map

1907 *DN* 3.194 NH, *Mooly, mooly cow.* . . Rimes with *bully.* **1910** *DN* 3.445 wNY, *Mŏŏly* . . *mŏŏly cow.* . . Cow without horns. Rimes with bully. **1917** [see **A1** above]. **1944** [see **A1** above]. **1965–70** *DARE* (Qu. K12) 36 Infs, 24 NY, PA, Mulley ['mʌlɪ]; 30 Infs, 14 NY, PA, Mooly ['mulɪ].

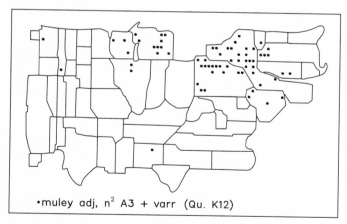

•muley adj, n² A3 + varr (Qu. K12)

4 other varr: See quot. Cf **molly** n¹ **2**

1966–69 *DARE* (Qu. K12) Infs HI2, MI2, NJ8, NY13, ['molɪ]; NY200, [mɪlɪ]; MO11, Mealy ['miˬiɫiˬi].

B As adj.

1 Of a cow (or other animal): hornless, esp naturally hornless as opposed to dehorned; hence n *muley (cow)* a hornless cow; also used as a nickname for a cow. **widespread, but less freq Atlantic coast** See Map For addit exx see **A** above See also **muley-head** Cf **butt-head, mule** n², **mull** adj, n¹, **noddle 1**

1838 (1843) Haliburton *Clockmaker* (2d ser) 41, Gives his Old Mooley a chance o' sneaking' into his neighbours' fields o' nights. **1840** *Daily Picayune* (New Orleans LA) 10 Sept 2/6, Brought to the Pound. . . A red and white mooley cow. **1853** (1928) Knight *Diary* 39 MA, Found the ox, and lost our muley cow. **1872** Powers *Afoot* 115 TX, P'raps you mout 'a seen a red mulley cow somewhar. **1892** *DN* 1.231 KY, *Muley*

cow: cow without horns. [*DN* Ed: Is the first syllable pronounced [mju] or [mu]? The latter is the pronunciation . . used in Michigan.] **1894** *DN* 1.342 wCT, *Mooley-cow:* cow without horns. [**1907** *DN* 3.194 NH, *Mooly, mooly cow.* . . Any cow. Used especially in talking to children, and hence by them. "That old mooly would hook you."] **1909** *DN* 3.351 eAL, wGA, *Muley(-cow).* **1912** *DN* 3.568 cNY, *Mooley-cow.* . . A cow that never had horns; one which has had her horns removed by sawing or clipping is called a dehorned cow. **1935** *AmSp* 10.172 PA, *Mooley cow* for a cow without horns, or a pet cow. **1936** Morehouse *Rain on Just* 314 NC, Dolly . . stopped . . to cover over the milk bucket, put it out of the black mooley's way. **1956** McAtee *Some Dialect NC* 30, *Muley.* . . hornless; a muley cow. **1965–70** *DARE* (Qu. K12, *A cow that has never had horns*) 513 Infs, **widespread, but less freq Atlantic coast,** Muley (and pronc varr); NM12, OK43, Natural muley; NY107, Muley—but I thought that was just a name; didn't know it meant they didn't have horns; 35 Infs, **scattered,** Muley (and pronc varr) cow; (Qu. K13, *A cow that has had her horns cut off*) Inf CA87, Muley—sometimes called by some people; NM13, Sometimes they refer to a natural muley and a muley (dehorned); OK43, VA33, Muley; CA131, Mooley. **1966–69** *DARE* Tape CA156, That's the breed of the stock, they ain't got no horn, never did have, muley cattle, they're just smooth heads, you know; NM3, [FW:] There's a lot of what? [Inf:] Muleys. A lot of 'em [=sheep] don't have horns anymore. **1977** *Foxfire 4* 261 wNC, Now if they don't have horns, that's muley cattle. . . They're born without any.

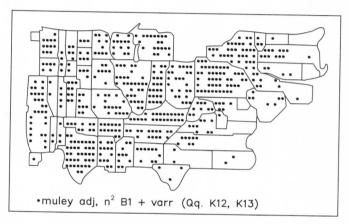

•muley adj, n² B1 + varr (Qq. K12, K13)

2 usu attrib: Lacking some projecting or prominent feature; bare, defective; hence n *muley (cow)* an implement lacking some projecting feature; see quots.

1884 Knight *New Mech. Dict.* 1.622, *Muley Axle.* (Railway.) One without collars on the outer ends of the axle. **1911** *Century Dict. Suppl.* (at *brick²* n), *Muley brick,* a brick-yard term for an imperfect brick. **1917** *DN* 4.396 neOH, *Muley hammer* (miuli). . . A hammer without claws. Familiar in the '80's in my father's family. **1918** in 1923 Mokler *Hist. Natrona Co. WY* 398 (as of 1865), A boy of about seventeen . . had what we called a "nuley [sic]," or "pepper box" revolver, the hammer being on the lower side of the weapon. **1923** Adams *Pioneer Hist. Ingham Co.* 319 MI, Then [came] the turkey-wing cradle, the grapevine, the mully, the man rake-off reaper [etc]. **1927** Van Wagenen *Golden Age* 26 NY, Old men speak of the "straight," the "grape vine," the "half grape vine," and the "mooley"—to which latter class belongs the rather unusual type pictured in Fig. 8. [Illustr shows grain cradle without nibs.] **1942** Warnick *Garrett Co. MD* 11 nwMD (as of 1900–18), *Muley* . . bare-looking, unadorned. . . "That tree (or this room) looks muley." **1944** Adams *Western Words* 101, *Muley saddle*—One without a horn. **1956** Ker *Vocab. W. TX* 182, *Muley saddle* is named ten times; informant 47b notes its use in Mississippi. (It is seldom used in the West, possibly because it has no horn.) **1956** Sorden–Ebert *Logger's Words* 7 Gt Lakes, Cant-hook, A tool like a peavey, but having a toe-ring and lip at the end instead of a pike. . . Same as . . mooley. **1961** [see **noway**]. **1968** Adams *Western Words* 203, *Muley cow*—A logger's term for his cant hook.

C As noun.

1 See **B1** above.

2 See **B2** above.

3a A fellow. [Cf *EDD moiley* sb. 2 "*Fig.* A mild, good-natured person."]

1948 Manfred *Chokecherry* 75 nwIA, Cor and Wilbur were good muleys to have come for him. He just couldn't turn down this proffer of friendship.

b Spec: a shiftless rustic.

1989 Baden-Hennessee *Unnatural Death* 167 **ceNY,** He and his cousin were the kind of people the police called "mullies," or "dirtbags," or "woodchucks"—rural people who grew up poor and ignorant, who wore the same dirty jeans covered with oil stains day after day, people who were constitutionally unable to stay out of trouble. **1991** *DARE* File **cnNY,** We [=state troopers] frequently, (no—regularly) encountered people—whole families—that are devoted to being on welfare. . . These are the type of people that have 2–3 junk cars on blocks in their front yards, no grass growing—a few mangy dogs—and some disability that prevents anyone from earning an honest wage. This word to describe these folks was confined to Zone 3 of Troop "D" of the NY State Police. These folks have been for years and continue to be called "mullys."

4 See **mule deer.**

muley carp n [**muley** adj **B2**] Cf **shorthead mullet**
Prob a **redhorse** such as *Moxostoma macrolepidotum*.
   1967 *DARE* (Qu. P3) Inf **SC31,** Muley ['muli] carp—short-headed.

muley cow See **muley** adj **B1, 2**

muley deer See **mule deer**

muley-head n [**muley** adj **B1**] **chiefly Sth** See Map Cf **mule** n[2], **mull** adj, n[1]
A naturally hornless cow (or other animal); hence adj *muley-head(ed)* hornless.
   1944 *PADS* 2.47 **sVA,** A cow that has never had any horns. . . In s. Va.: *mully-head.* **1954** *AmSp* 29.233, United States . . rare form, *muley-headed cow.* **1965–70** *DARE* (Qu. K12, *A cow that has never had horns*) Infs **GA80, MS46, 66, OK14, SC34, 39,** Muley-head; **AL11,** Mooley-head; **NJ45,** ['mjʊli]-head; **LA8,** Muley-head cow; **GA74, LA20, MS4, 28, SC32,** Muley-headed; **MS81, 87, NC63,** Mooley-headed; **NC49,** ['mʌlɪ]-headed; **NC87,** ['muli]-headed. **1967** *DARE* FW Addit **AR,** "Slick" or "muley-head" ['mjuli,hɛd]—doe shot illegally.

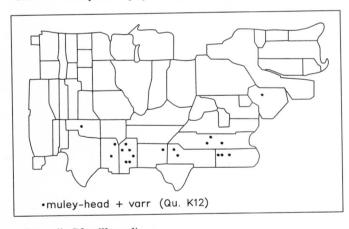

•muley-head + varr (Qu. K12)

mulky adj Cf **milky** adj
Of weather: **murky,** muggy.
   1965 *DARE* (Qu. B4, *A day when the air is very still, moist, and warm—it's _____*) Inf **OK13,** Sulky, sultry, mulky. **1981** Pederson *LAGS Basic Materials* (*It's a gloomy day*) 1 inf, **cLA,** ['mʌ<ə>lkɪ] day.

mull adj, n[1] |mʌl, mʊl| [*SND* mull adj "Hornless"; *EDD* moil sb.[1] "A cow without horns"; ult of Celtic origin] **Sth** Cf **mule** n[2], **muley** adj, n[2], **muley-head**
Hornless; a hornless cow; hence adj *mull-headed,* n *mull-head.*
   1956 McAtee *Some Dialect NC* 56, Mull, mull cow. . . A muley or hornless cow. Wake County. . . Mull-headed cow. . . From Lenoir County. **1966–70** *DARE* (Qu. K12, *A cow that has never had horns*) Inf **GA19,** Mull-head; **NC15,** ['mʊlhɛd]; **NC6,** ['mʌl'hɛdɪd]; **NC41,** Mull-headed cow; **VA70,** [mʊl'hɛdɪd].

mull n[2] [Prob < *mull* a mixture, muddle, mess] **esp GA** Cf **muddle**
A stew; see quots.
   1966 *DARE* (Qu. H45, *Dishes made with meat, fish, or poultry that*

everybody around here would know, but that people in other places might not) Inf **GA13,** Chicken, rabbit, squirrel, or turtle mull—stew (thickened with crackers). **1981** Pederson *LAGS Basic Materials,* 1 inf, **cnGA,** Rabbit mull = rabbit stew made with milk; [1 inf, **cwGA,** Mush, mull—synonyms]. **1984** Wilder *You All Spoken Here* 90 **Sth,** Muddle, mull: A stew, usually with fish or squirrel as the main ingredient; as in rockfish muddle or squirrel muddle.

mull n[3] Cf **fog mull**
A thick fog; fig: a state of depression.
   1975 Gould *ME Lingo* 185, *Mull*—The word most often used in Maine for *thick o' fog; a fog mull.* It suspends all harborfront activity and must be waited out. A simple fog will sometimes *scale off,* but a *fog mull* needs a change in weather. **1984** Doig *English Creek* 67 **nMT,** After this siege of black mull, a new thought did break through.

mull v[1] Often with *along, around*
To proceed in a lazy or aimless manner; to dawdle, loaf.
   1879 Webster *Amer. Dict.* 1568, *Mull.* . . To work steadily without accomplishing much. [*Colloq. Amer.*] **1892** *DN* 1.210 **RI,** *Mull:* to move sluggishly. "I went mulling along." "Let the fire mull along." **1966–69** *DARE* (Qu. KK31, *To go about aimlessly looking for distraction:* "He doesn't have anything to do, so he's just _____ around.") Inf **NC69,** Mulling; **MS6,** Melling [sic] along; [**KY28,** Molling ['molin]]. **1995** [see **mull** v[2]].

mull v[2] [Cf *SND* mull n.[2] 1 "The mouth, muzzle, or snout. . . Also *fig.* of a person, implying a pouting sulky expression"]
   1995 *NADS Letters, Mull* . . ='move sluggishly', but usually accompanied with *along* or *around,* as in "Quit mulling along, and finish reading the book so that I can return it to the library." . . Sometimes *mull* by itself: "Stop your mulling!" (said to someone pouting, also).

mullein n Also sp *mullen* Cf **mullein foxglove, ~ pink, turkey mullein**
Std: a plant of the genus *Verbascum.* Also called **mullet** n[2]. For other names of the common *V. thapsus* see **Aaron's rod 1, Adam's flannel, beggar's blanket, blanket leaf, candle-wick 1, coffee plant 3, coffeeweed 2c, cow mullein, devil's paintbrush 3, ~ tobacco 3, duffle, false tobacco, feltwort 1, fish poison 2, flannel flower, ~ leaf, ~ mullein, fluffweed 1, fuzzy mullein, hog taper, hung wort, Indian pipe 5, ~ tobacco 3, kinnikinnick 2d, lamb's tongue 3, ~ wool, lung-wort 2, miner's candle, muletail 3, musk mullein, old-field mullein, poultice weed, rouge plant, sheep mullein, sheep's ears, sheep tobacco, sheepweed, tickweed, tobacco plant, torchweed, velvet dock, velvetleaf, wild coffee, ~ tobacco, wood blade, woodman's Charmin, woolly mullein, wound-weed;** for other names of var spp see **bunny mullein, cactus n[1] B3, cherry bell, golden candlestick 3, greasy bacon, horse mullein, horseweed 10, slippery mullein, stickweed, white mullein, whitetop, yellowtop**

mullein bee n Also *mullein fly*
=**sweat bee.**
   1969 *DARE* (Qu. R21) Inf **NY211,** Mullein bee—same as mullein fly and sweat fly.

mullein foxglove n Also sp *mullen foxglove*
A tall, yellow-flowered plant (*Dasistoma macrophylla*).
   1857 Gray *Manual of Botany* 292, *S[eymeria] macrophylla.* . . *Mullein-Foxglove.* . . Shady riverbanks, Ohio, Kentucky, and southwestward. **1930** OK Univ. Biol. Surv. *Pub.* 2.80, *Seymeria macrophylla.* . . Mullein Foxglove. **1951** Voss-Eifert *IL Wild Flowers* 218, The deep shade of the river woods is one of the requirements of mullein foxglove. . . It is a pyramidal plant. It is very leafy, . . and . . often five feet tall. . . The throat of the flower is thickly furred with hairs and wool which prevent entry of most insects. **1970** Correll *Plants TX* 1431, *Mullein Foxglove.* . . In rich woods and on banks of streams in n.-cen. Tex.

mullein pink n Also sp *mullen pink*
1 The rose campion (*Lychnis coronaria*). [See quot 1840] Also called **dusty miller 1**
   1840 MA Zool. & Bot. Surv. *Herb. Plants & Quadrupeds* 87, *A[grostemma] coronaria.* . . Mullein Pink. Named from its woolly leaves. **1848** in 1850 Cooper *Rural Hours* 108 **NY,** Thus the corn-cockle bears a fine flower, not unlike the mullein-pink of the garden. **1938**

Madison *Wild Flowers OH* 50, Mullein Pink. *Lychnis coronaria.* **1949** Moldenke *Amer. Wild Flowers* 66, Outstandingly different from all previously mentioned pinks is the *mulleinpink,* . . whose densely white-woolly stems, leaves, and inflorescences are unmistakably characteristic. It has thoroughly acclimatized itself to roadsides and waste places in Washington and Oregon and from Michigan to Maine southward into New Jersey. **1969** *SC Market Bulletin* 11 Sept 4/3, Mullen Pinks, Rose Per. Phlox, Callicarpia [sic], Pink or Yellow Rain lily. **1976** Bailey-Bailey *Hortus Third* 688, *Mullein pink,* rose campion.

2 =corn cockle.

1900 Lyons *Plant Names* 20, *A[grostemma] Githago.* . . Mullen Pink.

mullen See **mullein**

mullen foxglove See **mullein foxglove**

mullen pink See **mullein pink**

mullet n[1] Cf **red mullet**

1 Std: a fish of the family Mugilidae. For other names of var fishes of the genus *Mugil* see **gannet-mullet, liza** n[2] **1, mulley** n[1] **2, shiteater, striped mullet, white ~**

2 A **sucker** of the family Catostomidae, esp a **white sucker** (here: *Catostomus commersoni*); by ext, see quot 1958. Cf **hog mullet, horn ~**

1818 *Amer. Monthly Mag. & Crit. Rev.* 3.447, Cyprinus fasciolaris [=*Erimyzon oblongus*]. . . Mullet. **1838** MA Zool. & Bot. Surv. *Repts. Zool.* 36, The most common Sucker in our market, *Catostomus Bostoniensis* [=*C. commersoni*], is yearly sold in large quantities as the "Mullet." **1896** U.S. Natl. Museum *Bulletin* 47.179, *Catostomus ardens.* . . *Mullet* of Utah Lake. . . Lakes and streams of great basin of Utah, swarming in myriads in Utah Lake. Also abundant in upper waters of Snake River in Idaho. **1905** NJ State Museum *Annual Rept. for 1904* 159, *Erimyzon sucetta oblongus.* . . Mullet. Chub Sucker. *Ibid* 162, [It is] equally abundant with the common sucker (*Catostomus commersonnii* [sic]), though distinguished by most fishermen as "mullet." **1947** Hubbs-Lagler *Fishes Gt. Lakes* 45, Suckers. . . are commonly called "mullet" by commercial fishermen. They afford some angling with doughballs and worms for bait. . . Suckers are palatable though bony. **1958** McCulloch *Woods Words* 119 **Pacific NW,** *Mullet*—A local term in the Klamath country to mean any fish found on the logger's table. The mullet is a large sucker-mouthed fish in Upper Klamath Lake, dried and used by the Indians in the early days for their winter food supply. **1968–70** DARE (Qu. P1, . . *Kinds of freshwater fish* . . *caught around here* . . *good to eat*) Inf **SC69,** Mullet—freshwater mullet caught with balls of dough; (Qu. P3, *Freshwater fish that are not good to eat*) Inf **PA83,** Mullets—look like a sucker. **1974** WI Univ. *Fish Lake MI* 30, The white sucker has never been a favored entree on the menu, perhaps because its name lacks market appeal. Yet the meat is firm and good tasting. . . White suckers are now being processed in a variety of ways for the market place. . . They are often sold under the name of "mullet." **1983** Becker *Fishes WI* 630, *Quillback—Carpiodes cyprinus.* . . Other common names . . broad mullet, mullet. *Ibid* 682, *White Sucker.* . . Other common names . . mullet, black mullet. *Ibid* 688, *Longnose Sucker—Catostomus catostomus.* . . Other common names . . mullet.

3 Any of var **redhorses,** but esp *Moxostoma macrolepidotum.* Cf **golden mullet, green ~, jumping ~ 2**

1842 DeKay *Zool. NY* 3.198, *Catostomus oneida* [=*Moxostoma macrolepidotum*]. . . Common in Lake Oneida, where it is called *Mullet,* and *Sucker. Ibid* 201, *The Mullet Sucker. Catostomus aureolus.* . . It is very common in Lake Erie, and at Buffalo passes under the various names of *Mullet, Golden Mullet,* and *Red Horse.* **1870** (1871) *Amer. Naturalist* 4.113 **NJ,** In other streams of New Jersey the fish [=*Hypentelium nigricans*] is less abundant, and found usually with the "mullet" (*Moxostoma oblongum*). **1878** U.S. Natl. Museum *Bulletin* 12.121, Examination of a very large series of "Mullet" and "Red Horse" from various parts of the country has led me to the conclusion . . that all the various forms . . belong to one . . species [=*Moxostoma macrolepidotum*]. . . It is sold commonly as a food-fish in the winter and spring in the markets of Washington and Philadelphia, as well as in the markets of those cities in the West which are supplied by the fisheries of the Great Lakes. **1902** Jordan-Evermann *Amer. Fishes* 63, *Common Redhorse.* . . This sucker has received many common names, among which are . . mullet. **1956** Harlan-Speaker *IA Fish* 71, Of the several species of redhorse or mullets, perhaps the northern redhorse is best known to most anglers by its large, bright silvery scales and blood-red tail and fins. **1957** Trautman *Fishes* 253, Since 1925 the Shorthead Redhorse and White Sucker have comprised almost the total commercial catch of

"mullets" for Lake Erie. **1983** Becker *Fishes WI* 665, *Shorthead Redhorse—Moxostoma macrolepidotum.* . . Other common names . . redhorse mullet, common mullet, shorthead mullet, mullet.

4 A **kingfish 1** (here: *Menticirrhus americanus*). Cf **black mullet 1, channel ~, sand ~, sea ~**

1968 DARE (Qu. P2, . . *Kinds of saltwater fish caught around here* . . *good to eat*) Inf **NC80,** Mullets: sea mullet; Sound mullet—different taste. **1973** Knight *Cook's Fish Guide* 385, Mullet . . see Kingfish, Southern.

mullet v

To fish for **mullet** n[1].

1969 DARE Tape **NC65,** We used to go a-nights a-mull'tin'.

mullet n[2] [*OED mullet* sb.[4] 1597–1750; *"Obs. rare";* this is prob an independent formation]

=mullein.

1968–70 DARE (Qu. S20) Infs **NY68, VA38,** Mullet; **VA52,** Old-field mullet.

mullet choker n Cf **herring choker**

1969 Lyons *My Florida* 29 (as of c1935), The father of the house was . . called back then a "mullet-choker," which meant that he was a gill-net fisherman for mullet.

mullet-head n

A stupid, ignorant person; by ext, an imaginary fish entirely lacking brains; hence adj *mullet-headed.*

1857 *Quindaro Chindowan* (KS) 6 June 1/3 **neKS,** The men, for the most part sleepy, ignorant, mullet-headed looking wretches, . . were engaged in cooking provisions either in the shanties of the Irish, . . or out of doors on the hill side. **1866** *Harper's New Mth. Mag.* 33.537, But in the stream was a large fish very unlike the rest. It partook freely of the bread and whisky, but with no perceptible effect. . . The other surveyed the wonder a moment, and then said: 'Sambo, I un'erstans dis case. Dat fish is a *mullethead; it hain't got any brains!'* In other words . . alcohol affects *only the brain;* and, of course, those having none may drink without injury! **1873** Beadle *Undeveloped West* 102, There is a fish called the mullet-head, that cannot be intoxicated by any amount of liquor. It can even swim in that fluid. Reason why: it has no brains, consequently nothing for the alcohol to act upon. In like manner some sects are invincible in argument. **1885** Twain *Huck. Finn* 336 **MO,** They're so confiding and mullet-headed they don't take notice of nothing at all. **1893** Twain in *St. Nicholas* Nov 24, It's enough to make a body sick, such mullet-headed ignorance. **1912** DN 3.583 **wIN,** *Mullethead.* . . A stupid or ignorant person. **1916** DN 4.278 **NE, IL, NC, KS,** *Mullet-head.* A know-nothing. Term of disparagement. "Look at that mullet-head of a Sam Smith. He don't know beans." **1935** Hurston *Mules & Men* 30 **FL,** Hey, you mullet heads! Get out de way. **1994** DARE File, [On a rerun of television show *Cheers:*] Don't you have customers to deal with, mullet-head?

mulley n[1]

1 See **mullikep.**

2 also *mullhead:* A **mullet** n[1] **1.**

1968–70 DARE (Qu. P2) Inf **MD36,** Jumping mulley; **SC69,** Saltwater mulley; (Qu. P3) Inf **VA8,** Mullheads.

mulley adj, n[2] See **muley** adj, n[2]

mulleyhead See **mullikep**

mullhead See **mulley** n[1] **2**

mull-head(ed) See **mull** adj, n[1]

mulli See **mullikep**

mulligan n Also *mulligan car, ~ wagon* [See quot 1958] Among loggers and railroad workers: see quots.

1938 (1939) Holbrook *Holy Mackinaw* 262, *Mulligan car.* Railroad car where midday lunch is served. **1950** *Western Folkl.* 9.119 **nwOR** [Logger speech], *Mulligan wagon.* The truck, flatcar, or other means of transportation to and from work. **1958** McCulloch *Woods Words* 119 **Pacific NW,** *Mulligan*—At one time hot noon meals were brought out to the men in the woods. A specially fitted railroad car was used for this purpose, known as a mulligan, from the mulligan or soup which it carried. Later the men were hauled to camp instead of taking the meal to the men at noon, and mulligan became any crew carrier. Now it is applied to trucks and busses. **1961** Labbe-Goe *Railroads* 259 **Pacific NW,** *Mulligan Car:* The crew car. Sometimes used in early days for

carrying hot meals (mulligan) to the woods crews at noon. **1962** *AmSp*
37.134 **nwCA**, *Mulligan*. . . Another name for a caboose. In the early
days of logging, the noon meals were taken out to the men in the woods
in a special car called the mulligan. The term referred to the mulligan
soup which was served. Later the term was applied to the caboose or
to any car that transported men from the woods to the cookhouse.

mulligrub n

1 A **tadpole.** [Transf from **mulligrubs**, appar infl by PaGer
mollekopp, mullikopp tadpole and std Engl *grub*] **PaGer area**
Cf **mullikep**

    1908 *German Amer. Annals* 10.35 **sePA**, *Mulligrub*. 1. Tadpole. 2.
Grub in decayed wood. "We caught some mulligrubs in the pond." **1913**
Johnson *Highways St. Lawrence to VA* 264 **nwMD**, Along the pool's
muddy borders were some lively colonies of polliwogs, or "mulligrubs"
as they were called locally. **1967–68** *DARE* (Qu. P20, *Very young
frogs—when they still have tails but no legs*) Infs **PA**17, 111, Mulligrubs.
1987 [see **mullikep**].

2 also *mollygrub:* An insect larva such as a **hellgrammite 1**
or a **white grub.**

    1890 *Century Dict.* 3892, *Mulligrubs*. . . The dobson or hellgramite.
[*Century* Ed: Local, U.S.] **1908** [see **1** above]. **1942** Warnick *Garrett
Co. MD* 11 **nwMD** (as of 1900–18), *Mulligrubs* . . white grubs, doubtless those of May beetles, found in land recently in sod such as was
used for potato patches. **1968** *DARE* (Qu. P6, . . *Kinds of worms . .
used for bait*) Inf **WV**3, Mollygrub; **MD**18, Mulligrub ['məli,grəb]—
white, about 2 inches long, thick as a pencil.

3 See **mulligrubs.**

mulligrubbing vbl n [**mulligrubs 1**]

    1984 Weaver *TX Crude* 118, *Mullygrubbing*. Sulking, petulant behav-
ior. "So your sister Darlene ran off with a albino motorcycle gang
president. Mullygrubbin' around the house ain't gonna help."

mulligrubs n pl Also *mollygrooms, mollygrubs, muddigrubs,
mullygrubs, mullygrumps;* rarely sg *mulligrub* [*OED* 1599 →]
Cf **collywobbles**

1 A condition of despondency or ill temper; a vague or imaginary unwellness. **scattered, but esp Sth** See Map

    1806 (1970) Webster *Compendious Dict.* 197, Mull'igrubs . . a twist-
ing of the guts, sullenness. [*DARE* Ed: This entry was carried over from
Webster's English model.] **1834** *Life Andrew Jackson* 95 **ME**, They was
sittin snug round their camp fires fillin their kittles and makin coffy when
another kind of Coffy [=General Coffy] was a preparin which giv'd
considerable of them the mulligrubs. **1838** Kettell *Yankee Notions* 96,
All the bitter diseases that flesh is heir to,— . . megrims, mulligrubs, . .
and all sorts of diabolical despondencies. **1898** Lloyd *Country Life* 131
AL, I had the mullygrubs and Sandy he had the botts. **1899** (1912)
Green *VA Folk-Speech* 291, *Mullygrubs*. . . Ill temper, sulkiness; the
sulks: as, to have the mullygrubs. **1909** *DN* 3.351 **eAL, wGA**, *Mulligrubs*. . . A fit of bad humor, the blues. **1913** Kephart *Highlanders* 297
sAppalachians, I knowed in reason she'd have the mullygrubs over them
doin's. **1944** *PADS* 2.25 **cwNC, cwOH**, *Mollygrubs, to have*. . . To be
slightly unwell or upset; to have the blues. In N.C.: mullygrubs. **1944**
PADS 2.30 **eKY**, *Mullygrubs* ['mʌlɪ'grʌbz]. . . Despondency. "He's in
the mullygrubs this morning." . . Common. **1950** *WELS* (*Joking or
fantastic names for imaginary diseases: "I guess he's got the _____."*)
1 Inf, **ceWI**, Mollygrooms. **1962** Steinbeck *Travels* 197, We'd be lousy
explorers. A few days out and we get the mullygrubs. **1965–70** *DARE*

(Qu. BB28, *Joking names . . for imaginary diseases: "He must have
the _____."*) 39 Infs, **chiefly Sth**, Mulligrubs; **GA**72, Mollygrubs;
NY205, He's got a mulligrub; (Qu. GG34a, *To feel depressed or in a
gloomy mood: "He has the _____ today."*) 21 Infs, **scattered, but
esp Sth**, Mulligrubs; **AL**41, Mulligrubs, muddigrubs; [**GA**74, Hubbi-
grubs]; (Qu. BB5, *A general feeling of discomfort or illness that isn't
any one place in particular*) Infs **AR**33, **GA**13, 33, 77, **MA**5, Mulligrubs; **NC**82, Got the mulligrubs; **AL**41, Muddigrubs; **AL**4, Mullygrumps; (Qu. BB39, *On a day when you don't feel just right, though not
actually sick . . "I'll be all right tomorrow—I'm just feeling _____
today."*) Inf **NC**72, Got the mulligrubs; (Qu. GG27b, *To get somebody
out of an unhappy mood . . "Don't _____."*) Infs **GA**77, **OK**9, Have
the mulligrubs; **GA**67, Give way to the mulligrubs; [(Qu. GG35b, *[To
sulk or pout:]* "Because she couldn't go, she's been _____ all day."*)
Inf **NY**1, Eating mulligrubs].

2 Spec:

a Pain in the stomach or intestines; diarrhea.

    1806 [see **1** above]. **1899** (1912) Green *VA Folk-Speech* 291, Mulli-
grubs. . . A pain in the intestines; colic. **1930** Shoemaker *1300 Words*
40 **cPA Mts** (as of c1900), *Mullygrumps*—An attack of indigestion or
stomach ache. **1966** *DARE* (Qu. BB19, *Joking names for looseness
of the bowels*) Inf **MS**33, Mulligrubs. **1990** Cavender *Folk Med. Lexicon* 27 **sAppalachians**, *Mullygrubs*—[sometimes pronounced as "mollygrubs"] . . hunger pains or growling sounds made by the stomach
when hungry.

b Menstruation.

    1966–67 *DARE* (Qu. AA27, . . *A woman's menstruation*) Infs **AL**30,
MS45, Mulligrubs.

mullikep n Also *mulley(head), mulli* [PaGer *mollekopp, mullikopp*] Cf **mulligrub 1**

A tadpole.

    1968 *DARE* (Qu. P20, *Very young frogs—when they still have tails
but no legs*) Inf **PA**157, Mulleys, mulleyheads. **1987** *Jrl. Engl. Ling.*
20.2.172 **ePA**, Despite the rarity of *mulli* as an alternate expression for
tadpole . ., the three informants [out of 100 total] represent different
generations of speakers, for their ages are 22, 47, and 77. . . Two of the
three informants supplied the term in the unclipped forms *mulligrub* and
mullikep.

mullinose See **maninose**

mully See **muley** adj, n[2]

mullygrubs, mullygrumps See **mulligrubs**

mully sobber See **malassada**

multiply, multiplying See **multiplying onion**

multiplying elder n

    =**box elder.**

    1966 *DARE* (Qu. T13) Inf **FL**32, Multiplying elder.

multiplying onion n Also *multiplying, multiply (onion)* [Varr
of *multiplier (onion)*] **chiefly Sth, S Midl** See Map

    An **onion B** (here: *Allium cepa* Aggregatum Group or *A. cepa*
Proliferum Group).

    1950 *WELS* (*The kind of onions that last from year to year*) 1 Inf,
WI, Multiply onions. **1965–70** *DARE* (Qu. I5, . . *Kind of onions that
keep coming up without replanting year after year*) 92 Infs, **chiefly Sth,
S Midl**, Multiplying onions; **MO**36, **SC**26, **WI**64, Multiply onions;

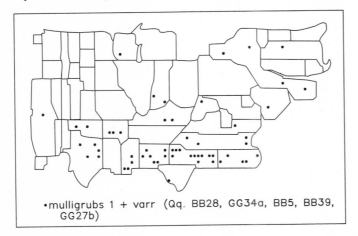

•mulligrubs 1 + varr (Qq. BB28, GG34a, BB5, BB39,
    GG27b)

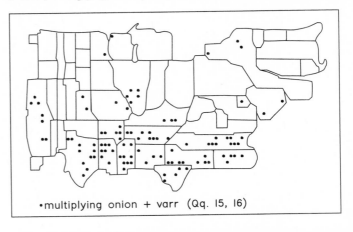

•multiplying onion + varr (Qq. I5, I6)

MN12, Multiplying; (Qu. I6, *The kind of onions that come up fresh early in the year, and you eat them raw*) Infs **GA**88, **KY**17, 22, **LA**2, 12, **NC**5, **SC**57, **TN**26, Multiplying onions; **TX**35, Multiplyings. **1983** *MJLF* 9.1.48 ceKY, Multiplying onions . . onions that keep coming up every year. **1986** Pederson *LAGS Concordance* **Gulf Region**, 58 infs, Multiplying (onion(s)); 7 infs, Multiply (onion(s)).

mum n[1] Also *muma, mumma(h), mummer, mummy* **chiefly NEng, wPA** See Map Cf **mam 1, mom** n[1]

A mother; occas a grandmother—often used as a quasi-personal name.

1834 *Life Andrew Jackson* 107 ME, The gineral's men retir'd from the battle well pleas'd. They had given them monkey's allowance, more kick's than cents, and had stopt their mummers from all future boastin. **1907** *DN* 3.194 seNH, Mumma. . . Mama. Mama' is a school-room word. **1915** *DN* 4.242 eTN, Any kind Mummy likes; that's the most [=usual] kind I gets. **1937** in 1976 *Weevils in the Wheat* 96 VA [Black], I 'bey my muma, an' tol' him so. **1941** *LANE* Map 372 *(Mother, ma)*, [*Mumma* (proncs of the type ['mʌmə]), but does not occur west of the Connecticut River. It is virtually the only reduplicated form in **ME** and eNH, but in **eMA** and **RI** it competes with *mama* (proncs of the type ['mɑmə, 'mamə]).] 9 infs, **chiefly eNEng**, Mum; 1 inf, **seMA**, Mummy. *Ibid* Map 383 *(Grandma)* 1 inf, **seNH**, Grammy, gram, affectionately; [maˑˑˑ·ᵊm, mʌˑ·m], sometimes in addressing her. **1950** *WELS Suppl.* cwWI, Mummah and papuh—mother and father. **1965–70** *DARE* (Qu. Z2, . . *'Mother'*) 16 Infs, **chiefly NEng, wPA**, Mum; 11 Infs, **chiefly eNEng**, Mumma; 10 Infs, **chiefly NEng, wPA**, Mummy; (Qu. Z8) Inf **PA**167, My mum and dad. **1973** Allen *LAUM* 1.340 (as of c1950), 2 infs, **nwNE**, Mum; 1 inf, **cwMN**, Mummy. **1989** Pederson *LAGS Tech. Index* 226 **Gulf Region**, *Mother* . . Mum (1 [inf]) . . Mummy (2). **1993** *DARE* File cwMI, Consultation . . reveals that I'm the only one in our transplanted family that pronounces it right—"mum"—rather than the affected "mahm." I, a native of Holland, Michigan, recall my way as being the standard there (no youthful deviant, I), whereas Doris, an immigrant from Illinois via Grand Rapids in junior high, can't believe my acquaintances could be so boorish as to pronounce it that way.

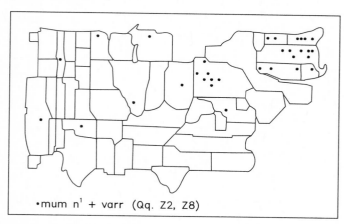

•mum n[1] + varr (Qq. Z2, Z8)

mum n[2] See **ma'am** n[1]

muma See **mum** n[1]

mumble v Also with *along* Pronc-sp *mummel* [*OED* (intr) c1325 →, (tr) 1591 →] *old-fash*

To eat by chewing with the gums; to gum (food).

1847 Paulding–Paulding *Amer. Comedies* 218, She devours horrors with as much relish as a butcher's dog mumbles a bloody calf's head. **1899** (1912) Green *VA Folk-Speech* 291, Mumble. . . To chew or bite softly with the gums; work food on account of lack of teeth or their defectiveness. **1959** *VT Hist.* 27.149 cn,neVT, Gladys Colburn, Unpublished article on Craftsbury Speech. "Without their teeth they manage to mummel along." Occasional. Orleans.

mumble peg See **mumblety-peg 2**

mumblety-peg n For varr see below Cf **knife, jackknife** n 1, **stick-knife, ~-frog**

Std sense, var forms.

1 *mumbledy-peg, mumble-the-~, mumblety-~, mummety-~*; for addit varr see quots. **widespread, but less freq Sth, S Midl** See Map

1845 Judd *Margaret* 1.130 NEng, Two boys sat . . playing mumble-the-peg. **1895** *Century Illustr. Mag.* 50.543 NEast, Those mysterious and irresistible forces which . . bind all boyish hearts to play mumble-the-peg at the due time. **1895** *DN* 1.398 IL, IA, MN, NY, Mumblety peg . . mummelty peg. . . [*DN* Ed: mubblety-peg, Conn.] **1899** (1912) Green *VA Folk-Speech* 291, Mumble-the-peg. . . A boy's game in which each player in turn throws a knife from a series of positions, continuing till he fails to make the blade stick in the ground. The last player to complete the series is compelled to draw out of the ground with his teeth a peg, which the others have driven in with a number of blows with the handle of the knife with which the game was played. **1920** Lewis *Main Street* 147 cwMN, While you're playing mumblety-peg with Mrs. Lym Cass, Pete and me will be rambling across Dakota. **1938** Rawlings *Yearling* 64 nFL, Jody and Fodder-wing . . went into a corner to play mumbledepeg. **1944** *PADS* 2.59 cwMO, VA, NC, SC, *Mumblety-peg* ['mʌmlti,peg]. . . A game played by tossing a two-bladed knife into the air and letting it fall on soft wood. **1965–70** *DARE* (Qu. EE5, *Games where you try to make a jackknife stick in the ground*) 273 Infs, **widespread, but less freq Sth, S Midl**, Mumbledy-peg; **WV**10, 18, Mumbledy-peg, also called (or heard) fumbledy-peg; 12 Infs, **scattered**, Mummety-peg; **CA**82, **CT**30, **MI**81, **PA**35, Mumblety-peg; **MA**14, **OH**8, Mummelty-peg; **PA**185, Mommety-peg; **NY**139, Mumbity-peg; **IN**39, Mumble-the-peg; **CA**8, Mumbledy-pegs; **NY**107, Mummeldy-peg; **CO**21, Nimblety-peg. [Of all Infs responding to the question, 29% were comm type 5, 33% coll educ, 44% male; of those giving these responses, 20% were comm type 5, 45% coll educ, 35% male.] **1967** Borland *Hill Country* 155 NE, Then we found a shady spot and played mumble-de-peg with the jackknives.

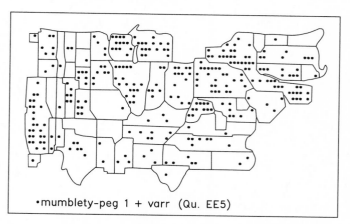

•mumblety-peg 1 + varr (Qu. EE5)

2 *mumble peg*; for addit varr see quots. **widespread, but less freq NEast, C Atl** See Map

1882 Sweet–Knox *Sketches TX Siftings* 75 (*DAE*), When other boys were engaged in mumble-peg and leap-frog pursuits, he was absorbed with division [etc.]. **1905** *DN* 3.88 nwAR, Mumble-peg. **1909** *DN* 3.351 eAL, wGA, Mumble-peg. . . Mumble-the-peg. The forms *mumblety-peg, mumbly-peg,* etc., are unknown to one. *Ibid* 413 nME, Mumblepeg. **1946** *PADS* 6.21 eNC (as of 1900–10), Mumble peg. . . A contest among boys as to who can throw his knife to make it stick in a wall. **1947** *PADS* 8.20 IA, Mumble peg: Game involves sticking knife in the ground. **1947** *PADS* 8.22 KY, Mumble peg: I heard this term as recently as September, 1946. The game was very popular twenty-five years ago.

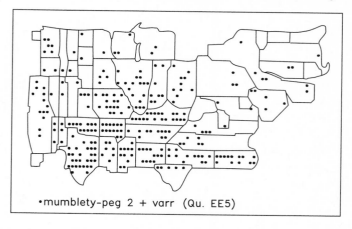

•mumblety-peg 2 + varr (Qu. EE5)

1965–70 *DARE* (Qu. EE5) 271 Infs, **chiefly SE, W Midl, Cent, West,** Mumble-peg; **AR**47, 51, **NY**75, **TN**59, Mummel-peg; **LA**6, 12, ['mʌmbə,pɛg]; **MO**18, Numble-peg. [Of all Infs responding to the question, 29% were comm type 5, 33% coll educ, 44% male; of those giving these responses, 38% were comm type 5, 21% coll educ, 49% male.] **1966** *DARE* Tape **AL**6, I used to play mumble peg but I've forgotten. All I know is you flip a knife in about an inch. **1983** *MJLF* 9.1.48 **ceKY** (as of 1956), *Mumblepeg.*

3 *mumbl(e)y-peg;* for addit varr see quots. **scattered, but esp Inland Nth, N Midl** See Map

1864 in 1989 Chisholm *Civil War Notebook* 12 **PA,** We had Sunday morning inspection, went to church, sit on the ground, most of the boys played Mumly Meg instead of listening to the sermon. **1933** Cheley *Camping Out* 300, What boy has not played mumbly peg? . . There are twenty-four different stunts in all, and . . a good deal depends upon both knife and sod, as well as the boy. **1944** Howard *Walkin' Preacher* 166 **Ozarks,** A group of men rolled a big log to a level spot at the edge of the school ground, peeled off the bark with their razor-sharp Barlow knives and started a game of mumbley-peg. The contestants straddled the log and played by flipping a knife in the air with the smaller of the two blades fully open and the larger blade half-opened. **1965–70** *DARE* (Qu. EE5) 118 Infs, **scattered, but esp Inland Nth, N Midl,** Mumbley-peg; 13 Infs, **scattered,** Mumley-peg; **OH**52, Mumbley-pegs; **NY**1, Mubley-peg. [Of all Infs responding to the question, 67% were old, 33% coll educ; of those giving these responses, 57% were old, 41% coll educ.] **1983** *DARE* File **CA,** Mumbly peg. *Ibid* **ID,** Mumly peg. **1983** *MJLF* 9.1.48 **ceKY** (as of 1956), *Mumblypeg* . . mumbletypeg.

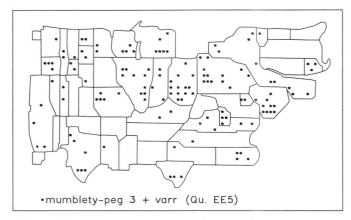

•mumblety-peg 3 + varr (Qu. EE5)

4 *mamma-peg, mumbling-~, mum(my)-~;* for addit varr see quots.

1954 *Harder Coll.* **cwTN,** Mama-peg . . mumble-peg. **1965–70** *DARE* (Qu. EE5) Infs **LA**11, **MO**23, 30, **TN**55, Mamma-peg; **VA**35, 39, 42, Mumbling-peg; **LA**8, 32, Mumma-peg; **FL**2, **MD**15, Mum-peg; **MO**1, Mumblem-peg; **VA**1, Mummy-peg; **MD**26, Mungdy-peg.

mumbl(e)y-peg See **mumblety-peg 3**

mumchimmee See **mummichog**

mumma See **mum** n[1]

mummachog See **mummichog**

mummah See **mum** n[1]

mummel See **mumble**

mummer n[1] [Engl dial]
See quot 1940.

1940 Writers' Program *Guide PA* 61, Among traditional holiday observances is the mummers' parade on New Year's Day in Philadelphia. This pageant resembles in spirit and form the old English Christmas season festivities, when a Lord of Misrule was chosen, and elaborately costumed revelers danced and paraded. **1968** *DARE* (Qu. FF16, . . *Local contests or celebrations*) Inf **PA**91, Mummers' Parade.

mummer n[2] See **mum** n[1]

mummety-peg See **mumblety-peg 1**

mummichim See **mummichog**

mummichog n Also *(chog-)mummy, mumchimmee, mummichug, mummychub, mumpchog, mumper;* for addit varr see quots [Of Algonquian orig; see quot 1902] **sNEng, Long Island**

Any of var **killifish 1,** but esp *Fundulus heteroclitus.* Also called **chim.** For other names of *F. heteroclitus* see **bull-head 1c, cobbler** n[1] **4a, dabbler, dogfish 7, minnow B2b, mudfish b, river minnow, saltwater ~**

1787 Pennant *Arctic Zool. Suppl.* 149, Inhabits *New York,* where it is known by the *Indian* name of *Mummy Chog.* **1807** in 1846 MA Hist. Soc. *Coll.* 2 ser 3.57 **MA,** The mumchimmee, a small fish, four or five inches long, resembling an eel in shape, is caught in summer. **1842** DeKay *Zool. NY* 4.219, To this [=*Fundulus heteroclitus*], and various other allied species, is applied the indian name of *Mummachog.* **1884** Goode *Fisheries U.S.* 1.466, In New England they [=*Cyprinodontidae*] are usually known by the Indian name "Mummichog". **1902** *Jrl. Amer. Folkl.* 15.250, *Mummychog (mummachog).* A name given in various regions of the North Atlantic coast of the United States to the barred killifish *(Fundulus pisculentus).* The word is derived from one of the eastern dialects, probably Narragansett (or Massachusetts). This word also appears in the decaudated form *mummy.* **1903** NY State Museum & Sci. Serv. *Bulletin* 60.309, The name bass mummy applied to the species [=*Fundulus majalis*] on Long Island, refers to its use in the capture of striped bass. *Ibid* 60.310, The killifish [=*Fundulus heteroclitus*]. . . is frequently called mummichog. . . On Long Island it is called mummy or chog-mummy. **1939** *LANE* Map 234, *Minnow* is applied . . to any small saltwater bait fish . . , which are also known as *mummychogs* [16 infs], *mummychugs* [7], *mummychubs* [5], *mummychims* [1], *mummies* [13], [etc]. [These resps are confined to **sNEng** and are most frequent in the vicinity of **seRI**.] **1949** Kurath *Word Geog.* 23 **MA,** *Mummichog* . . for the salt-water minnow (From New London to Martha's Vineyard). . . *Mummichims* or *chims* . . for the salt-water minnows, on Martha's Vineyard. **1962** Huden *Indian Place Names* 92 **RI,** Mamaquag Brook, Washington Co., R.I. *Eastern Niantic,* "small fish," called even now by children, "mummies." **1965** *PADS* 43.19 **seMA,** Small fish used for bait . . mumpchogs [1 of 9 infs]. . . Small fish used for bait . . mumpers [3 of 9 infs]. **1968–69** *DARE* (Qu. P4, *Saltwater fish that are not good to eat*) Inf **CT**13, Mummichogs; (Qu. P7, *Small fish used as bait for bigger fish*) Inf **RI**12, Mummichogs; **CT**29, 36, Mummichug; **CT**17, **RI**12, 15, Mummy. **1985** Rattray *Advent. Dimon* 259 **Long Is. NY,** The young ones were chasing mummychoggs and crabs, pantlegs rolled, in the dreen where the pond lets out into the Bay. **1991** Amer. Fisheries Soc. *Common Names Fishes* 34, *Fundulus heteroclitus* . . A[tlantic]-F[reshwater]. Mummichog.

mummick See **mammock** v

mummock n [Cf **mammock** n]
1895 *DN* 1.398 **cNY,** Mummock ['mumək]: a lummox.

mummock v, **mummox** See **mammock** v

mummy n[1] [*OED* 1601 →] *old-fash* Cf **pummy**
In phr *to (a) mummy:* Into (a) pulp.
1796 Morse *Amer. Universal Geog.* 2.680, The most horrible machines, calculated for grinding to mummy those unhappy criminals. **1899** (1912) Green *VA Folk-Speech* 292, *Mummy.* . . A pulpy mass. "The peaches in the basket were mashed to a mummy."

mummy n[2] See **mummichog**

mummy n[3] See **mum** n[1]

mummychog(g) See **mummichog**

mummy-peg See **mumblety-peg 4**

mump v Also with *around* [*OED mump* v.[1] 2.b "to sulk, mope. *arch.*"] **NEng**
To act dejected or ill-humored; hence ppl adj *mumping* dejected, unhappy; ppl adj phr *mumped up* irritable.
1887 (1895) Robinson *Uncle Lisha* 56 **wVT,** I'll be dum'd 'f I wouldn't druther hev Jozeff Hill's ol' yaller dawg for comp'ny 'n't hev sech a consarned mumpin' set as you be. *Ibid* 57, Wal, I do' know's I blame anybody much for mumpin' sech weather. . . sech weather 's turrible hefty on the sperits. **1903** *DN* 2.299 **Cape Cod MA** (as of a1857), *Mumped up.* . . In expression 'all mumped up,' like a setting hen. **1937** Crane *Let Me Show You VT* 35, Dull, depressing people are no longer said to 'mump'. **1959** *VT Hist.* 27.150 **c,ceVT,** *Mump around.* . . To be irritable. Occasional.

mumpchog See **mummichog**

mumped up See **mump**

mum-peg See **mumblety-peg 4**

mumper See **mummichog**

mumping See **mump**

mumsy n Also *mom(p)sy, momsey, momzey, mumpsy*
A mother.
1906 *DN* 3.147 **nwAR,** *Momsey, momzey. . .* Dear mother. "A boy's best friend is his momsey." **1941** *LANE* Map 372 *(Mother, ma)* 4 infs, Mumsy; 2 infs, Mumpsy; 1 inf, Mompsy. **1968–69** *DARE* (Qu. Z2, . . 'Mother') Infs **CA**80, 107, **CT**16, **NY**167, **OH**72, Mumsy; **MN**33, Momsy.

mumu See **muumuu**

mun See **man** n **A**

mundiner n
A **woodpecker.**
1946 *McDavid Coll.* **scSC,** [mən'daɪnəz] 'woodpecker.'

mung n[1] See **mang**

mung n[2] See **manglier**

munger See **mongrel**

mungofa See **magofer**

mungrel See **mongrel**

mung them pron [Var of **amongst (hands of) them**]
1954 *Sun* (Baltimore MD) 11 Nov 18/7 *(Hench Coll.),* He knew it [=the term *mung you*] well and contributed a variation "Mung 'em." His example was: "Mung 'em says taxes are going up next year." The meaning is obvious. "People say that. . ." or, perhaps, "It is rumored that. . ."

mungtuk See **muktuk**

mung you (all) pron [Var of **amongst you;** cf Suffolk dial *you mong she* (*EDD* at *mongs*)] **DE, MD**
=**you-all.**
1938 *FWP Guide DE* 356, If a man asks another "Mung-ye comin' to church?" he means "Are you and your family coming to church?" In the singular sense the expression may be: "Mung-ye go fodder them mules"; that means "Somebody out of a group" go do it. **1951** *DE Folkl. Bulletin* 1.7, *Mung you all* (all of you—as in "Mung you all let's pitch in," said at a meal, after grace). **1954** *Sun* (Baltimore MD) 11 Nov 18/7 *(Hench Coll.),* I read . . a novel the scene of which is laid on the Eastern Shore. The author, reporting on the speechways . . of the people there, frequently had them using a sentence like this: "Mung you going to shoot ducks this year?" It sounded a little strange to me but I finally concluded that "Mung you" is a contraction for "Among you," and that it is almost the exact equivalent of the Southern "You-all."

municipal n, adj Usu |ˌmjuˈnɪsəpəl|; also |ˌmjunəˈsɪpəl| Cf **discipline**
Std senses, var form.
1909 *DN* 3.351 **eAL, wGA,** *Municipal,* adj. With accent on third syllable. **1922** *DN* 5.134 **NE,** In the following words the accent is occasionally shifted to the penult:— . . muni'cipal. **1929** Wolfe *Look Homeward* 100 **NC,** The muni*ci*pal taxation . . was $2.25 the hundred. **1959** *VT Hist.* 27.150, *Municipal* [mū·nĭ·sĭ'pl]. . . pronc. Recent. Occasional. **1978** *DARE* File **cnMA** (as of 1920s), I remember that people were laughed at who said [mjunəˈsɪpəl].

munk n Also *monke(y)*
=**chipmunk.**
1961 Jackson *Mammals WI* 142, *Tamias.* . . In Wisconsin most commonly called chipmunk. Other names of general application include . . monke or munk. **1966** *DARE* (Qu. P28, . . *Names . . for the chipmunk;* total Infs questioned, 75) Inf **MS**11, Monkey.

munk up v phr [Perh var of *muck up* to botch, but cf **monk** v]
To make a mess of.
1994 NC Lang. & Life Project *Dial. Dict. Lumbee Engl.* 8 **seNC,** He tried to build his own house, but he munked up the job.

munny lite See **money light**

munny muss See **money musk**

munt See **month**

muracle See **miracle**

murderation exclam Cf **botheration** exclam, **darnation,** *DS* NN8a
Used as an exclam of surprise, annoyance, disgust, etc.

1924 *DN* 5.273 [Exclams in Amer Engl], *Murderation.* **1936** *WV Review* Aug 347, Vexation, for many, many years, has manifested itself in West Virginia in: . . Murderation. [**1942** McAtee *Dial. Grant Co. IN* 44 (as of 1890s), *Murderin' infants* . . man's exclamation.]

‡**murder in the gun room** n
A commotion.
1909 *DN* 3.421 **Cape Cod MA** (as of a1857), *Murder in the gun room.* . . A great catouse.

murder match n Cf **barn burner 1**
A wooden friction match.
1968 *DARE* (Qu. F46, . . *Matches you can strike anywhere;* not asked in early QRs) Inf **MN**37, Murder matches—men used to carry loose in pockets.

murdle See **myrtle** n[1]

murdock n
=**burdock 1.**
1966–68 *DARE* (Qu. I28a) Inf **AR**3, Murdock; (Qu. S13) Inf **PA**176, Murdock; (Qu. S21) Inf **MD**24, Murdock ['mɝ·dɑk]; (Qu. S26d) Inf **NE**9, Murdock.

murgens n Also sp *mergens, mergins* [Cf *SND* mirge (at **mird** n.[2]) "A tightly-packed crowd, throng, swarm" and *EDD* mirge sb. "A multitude, swarm"]
A great amount or number.
1952 Brown *NC Folkl.* 1.568, *Murgens, mergins:* . . A great many. "He has murgens of watermelons this year."—Central and east. **1984** Wilder *You All Spoken Here* 204 **Sth,** Mergens of medications: Enough medicines to cure a colicky colt.

murkle See **myrtle** n[1]

murky adj Cf **mucky** adj[2], **mulky**
Muggy, humid.
1965–70 *DARE* (Qu. B4, *A day when the air is very still, moist, and warm—it's _____*) Infs **AL**23, **DE**4, **IL**5, 26, **NY**87, **TX**11, 29, Murky. **1993** *DARE* File **csWI,** When the weather was hot and sticky, my mother-in-law said it was "mucky"—or sometimes "murky"—outside. She was born in 1908 in Evansville, Wisconsin, and spent almost all of her adult life in Madison.

murn See **murrain**

murp n
A playing marble.
1967 *DARE* (Qu. EE6b) Inf **PA**19, All marbles are called *murps.*

murphy n Also abbr *murph* [*OED* 1811 →] chiefly **Nth, N Midl** See Map Cf **Irish potato, Mick 3**
=**white potato.**
1835 Mahony *6 Months* 151 **eMA,** The murphies were much too large, and could not be swallowed at one mouthful. **1855** *SF Golden Era* 1 July 2/7 (*Mathews Coll.),* Which do you consider the correct way of spelling *murphies.* . . Pough-teigh-teaux. . . Pot-8-o's. . . Pot-oooooooo. **1950** *WELS* (Nicknames . . for potatoes) 18 Infs, **WI,** Murphies. **1956** Sorden–Ebert *Logger's Words* 24 **Gt Lakes,** Murphys, Potatoes. **1965–70** *DARE* (Qu. I9) 43 Infs, chiefly **Nth, N Midl,** Murphies; **CT**17, Irish murphies. **1993** *DARE* File **nOH** (as of c1930), "Pass the murphs" [in the student dining hall].

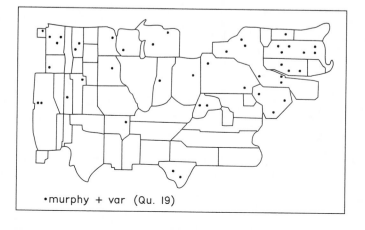

•murphy + var (Qu. I9)

murrah See **mother** n[1]

murrain n Usu |'mɜ·(ɪ)n|; for addit varr see quots Also sp *murren, murrin;* pronc-sp *murn* **chiefly S Midl** See Map

Any of var pestilent diseases of cattle; a physical manifestation of such a disease.

1859 Taliaferro *Fisher's R.* 258 **AL** (as of 1845), The murrin's bin mighty bad among cattle lately. **1933** Miller *Lamb in His Bosom* 146 **GA** (as of c1850), Not even hay would grow, nor grass, and the cows were like to die of dry murren. [**1944** Kenyon–Knott *Pronc. Dict.* 290, Murrain ['mɜ·ɪn]; E[astern and] S[outhern] ['mɜrɪn, 'mʌrɪn, 'mɜ·rɪn].] **1961** Adams *Old-Time Cowhand* 219, Rather than leave the water they [=cattle] ate the willow branches. This caked their stomachs with dry murrain which couldn't be cast off, and many died a horrible death. **1965–70** *DARE* (Qu. K28, . . *Chief diseases that cows have*) Infs **IN**13, **OK**52, **PA**187, 218, **WV**4, 8, Dry murn, **CO**33, Dry murn—don't get water enough, food dries up inside; **OK**1, Dry murn—when a cow is used to eating dry grass, then loads up on wet grass; **IN**8, **KY**39, **WV**7, Murn; **TN**24, [mɜn]—a kidney disease; **VA**38, Murn—cut hole in dewlap and put in twist of tobacco; old-fashioned; **WV**3, [mən]—lack of salt caused it; **NC**33, Murrain ['mə·ɪn]. **1981** Pederson *LAGS Basic Materials,* 1 inf, **cnAR,** The ['dra·ˌmən]. (Cattle died of this from eating too many acorns. Bowels were packed with the roughage.) **1982** Slone *How We Talked* 118 **eKY** (as of c1950), Cows had the "murn"—Symptoms were like a cold; cough, runny nose, fever. Cure: Poke root put inside an ear of corn.

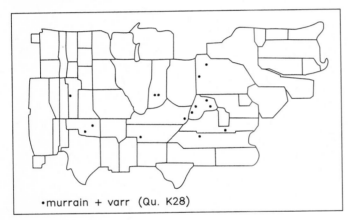

•murrain + varr (Qu. K28)

murre n

1 Std: any of var seabirds of the family Alcidae such as the black guillemot *(Cephus grylle)* or the **razor-billed auk,** but usu a guillemot of the genus *Uria.* For other names of this genus see **foolish guillemot, frowl;** for other names of *Uria aalge* see **ice bird;** for other names of *U. lomvia* see **crow duck 3, ice ~ 2, noddy 4, sea crow**

2 =**ruddy duck.**

1925 (1928) Forbush *Birds MA* 1.280, *Ruddy Duck.* Other names . . *Murre.*

murrell hen n [See quot]

=**black-crowned night heron.**

1951 *AmSp* 26.92, Thus *murrell hen,* for the black-crowned night heron (N.C.), was deemed by its users to refer to a family name, as they were familiar with a locality, Murrell's Inlet, South Carolina, designated in that fashion. However, the appellation seems much more interestingly and correctly explained as embodying a survival of the adjective *merle,* referring to the prevailing bluish-gray color of the bird.

murren See **murrain**

murricle See **miracle**

murrin See **murrain**

murruh See **mother** n[1]

murshroom See **mushroom**

muscadine (grape) n Usu |'mʌskəˌdaɪn|; also |'mʌskɪ-, 'mʌski-, -ˌdaɪm|; for addit varr see quot 1965–70 Also *muscardine, muscumdime, mustydine* **chiefly Sth, S Midl** See Map

An American **grape,** usu either a **frost grape** (here: *Vitis*

vulpina), or *Vitis rotundifolia,* which is also called **bullace 2, bullet grape, bull ~, fox ~ 3, mayhaw 2, scuppernong, sloe.**

c1785 Sarah Pears *Narrative* (MS.) 4 *(DAE),* Greenbrier berreys, honey locust pods, muskedines, a fruit like to fox graps [etc]. **1797** Imlay *Western Terr.* 266, Muscadine grapes, of an amber colour, of a very good kind, and very sweet, have been found upon declivities of a good exposure, even so far north as lat. 31. **1830** Rafinesque *Med. Flora* 2.132, *V[itis] vulpina* or *muscadina* . . Muscadine Grape. . . It bears a multitude of vulgar names such as Muscadine, Bullet, Fox and Scuppernong Grape: the confusion in the botanical names is as bad, and they do not apply, I have changed them all. [*Ibid,* Taste [of the fruit is] pleasant, sweet, and musky, makes a very good wine.] **1872** MO State Entomol. *Annual Rept.* 60, *V[itis] vulpina,* Linn. Southern Fox, or Muscardine. **1893** Shands *MS Speech* 46 [Black], *Muscumdime* [məskəmdaim]. Negro for *muscadine.* **1906** *DN* 3.147 **nwAR,** *Muscadine.* . . A kind of grape. **1913** *Auk* 30.485 **Okefenokee GA,** In many places the 'bamboo vine' . . and the muscadine *(Vitis rotundifolia)* bind the undergrowth into an impenetrable tangle. **1935** *Atlantic Mth.* 156.44 **nAL,** I just had to stop at a big mustydine vine up some pines before I'd made many steps. I shook the vine and they peppered to the ground. They was dead ripe and black as bess bugs. **1937** Thornburgh *Gt. Smoky Mts.* 23, A few of the more common vines you may encounter . . are . . woodbine, muscadine, and greenbrier. **1953** (1977) Hubbard *Shantyboat* 310 **Missip-Ohio Valleys,** One day I found a strange fruit, like a small plum or a large grape, under an elm tree. I asked Tom about it. He said it was a muscadine, and showed me the vine high in the elm. **1965–70** *DARE* (Qu. I46, . . *Kinds of fruits that grow wild around here*) 13 Infs, **chiefly Sth, AR, TN,** Muscadine(s); 21 Infs, **chiefly Sth, AR,** proncs of the type ['mʌskɪˌdaɪn]; 19 Infs, **chiefly Sth,** proncs of the type ['mʌskəˌdaɪn]; **GA**79, 81, 85, 88, ['mɪskəˌdaɪn]; **AL**6, 58, **SC**3, ['mʌskɪˌdaɪn]; **AL**46, 61, **LA**11, **TN**24, **VA**74, 78, ['mʌskəˌdaɪm, 'mʌskɪˌ 'mʌski-]; **TN**41, ['mʌsiˌdaɪm], (Qu. I44, *What kinds of berries grow wild around here?*) Infs **AL**6, **GA**1, 9, Muscadine(s); (Qu. I53, . . *Fruits grown around here . . special varieties*) Inf **SC**66, Muscadines. **1986** Pederson *LAGS Concordance* **Gulf Region,** 48 infs, Muscadine(s); 4 infs, Muscadine vine(s); 4 infs, Muscadine wine; 1 inf, Muscadine grapes; 1 inf, Green muscadine.

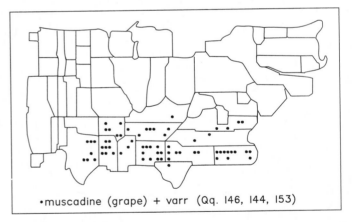

•muscadine (grape) + varr (Qq. I46, I44, I53)

muscag See **muskeg**

muscal(e) See **mescal**

muscalinga, muscallonge, muscallunge See **muskellunge**

muscardine See **muscadine (grape)**

muscheevous See **mischievous**

muschel See **mushle**

muschilongoe See **muskellunge**

muscle v

1 To lift or move (something heavy); hence vbl n *muscling.*

1913 Kephart *Highlanders* 282 **sAppalachians,** We can muscle this log up. **1926** *DN* 5.401 **Ozarks,** *Muscle.* . . To move or lift. "You-uns kin muscle thet leetle rock easy." **1931** *PMLA* 46.1320 **sAppalachians,** Muscle that log up, Mace. **1933** (1973) Sherman–Henry *Hollow Folk* 190 **cnVA,** In Oakton Hollow games make their appearance among adults as well as children. The most characteristic of these is "muscling rocks." Men and boys strive to lift the heaviest rocks. **1974** Fink *Mountain Speech* 17 **wNC, eTN,** Hit took four men to muscle that rock up.

1986 Pederson *LAGS Concordance,* 1 inf, **ceGA,** Muscle it up. **1993** *DARE* File **csWI,** If we get four men, do you think we can muscle it over? *Ibid* **CA, IA, MA, OH, WI,** To *muscle* something is to move it with effort.

2 often with *out:* To hold (something) with an outstretched arm; to lift something to shoulder level. **chiefly S Midl**

1940 in 1944 *ADD* **WV,** 'Can you muscle this stone?' = lift it shoulder high keeping a straight arm. **1941** *AmSp* 16.23 **sIN, MO,** *Muscle.* To hold an object straight out at arm's length. **1943** McAtee *Dial. Grant Co. IN Suppl.* 2 11 (as of 1890s), *Muscle out . .* lift a weight and hold it at arm's length; "How much can you muscle out?" **1946** *PADS* 6.21 **eNC** (as of 1900–10), *Muscle out. . .* To raise a weight in the hand with the arm extended till it is horizontal. Pamlico, 1900–05. Occasional. **c1960** *Wilson Coll.* **csKY,** *Muscle out. . .* Lift something to the level of the shoulders.

muscle-bill See **mussel-bill**

muscle-digger See **mussel-digger**

muscle-eater See **mussel-eater**

muscle knot See **knot** n[1] 3

muscle out See **muscle 2**

musclewood n Also *muscletree, musclewood tree* [From the smooth, corded appearance of the trunk]
=**hornbeam 1.**

1950 Moore *Trees AR* 37, *Carpinus caroliniana. . .* Local Names: Hornbeam, . . Ironwood, Musclewood. . . *Uses* Repair of agricultural implements and wagons, wedges, tool handles, [etc]. **1953** Strausbaugh–Core *Flora WV* 294, *American hornbeam. . . Muscletree.* A small tree to 12 m. high, . . common throughout the State. **1969** *DARE* FW Addit **Hatteras Is. NC,** Musclewood tree.

muscling See **muscle 1**

muscovy n Also *muscova, muscovey, muscovie, muscovite, 'scovy* [See quot 1953]
=**scoter.**

1923 U.S. Dept. Ag. *Misc. Circular* 13.27 **MD,** *Scoters. . . Collective Vernacular Names. . .* In local use.—Bay muscovies. *Ibid* 29 **OH,** *White-winged Scoter. . .* Vernacular Names. . . In local use. . . Muscova. **1943** Musgrove–Musgrove *Waterfowl IA* 65, *White-winged Scoter. . .* Other names . . muscovite. **1951** Martin *Amer. Wildlife & Plants* 73, *American Scoter. . .* This black marine diver, locally known as coot or muscovie, is like other scoters in being regarded as a third-rate game species. **1953** *AmSp* 28.276, In this type of folk naming, the domesticated varieties of ducks also are not wholly neglected, the large Muscovy, with distinctive head adornment, suggesting the scoters, sizable among wild ducks and with unusually shaped and colored bills. All of our three species are known as *bay muscoveys* in Maryland, and each has been recorded under cognate but distinct titles: the white-winged scoter as *muscovy* (Pa.) and *muscovite* (Iowa); the surf scoter as *'scovy* (Va.) and *wild muscovy* (Pa.); and the black scoter as *little muscovy* (Pa.).

muscumdime See **muscadine (grape)**

‡**musgo** n [Prob *must + go*]
1978 *DARE* File **cnAR,** *Musgo*—a meal of leftovers. "Come on over to my house for musgo."

mush n[1]

1 Ground cereal boiled to a soft consistency. [By ext from std *mush* boiled cornmeal] **widespread, but esp Pacific** See Map Note: Responses with the word *corn* have been excluded from quot 1965–70, as have those in which an Inf described *mush* as being made from cornmeal. It is possible that some other Infs are referring specifically to *mush* made of cornmeal.

1883 (1884) Howe *Story Country Town* 85 **Cent,** If you have cold oatmeal mush, or a bit of graham bread, I will refresh myself with that. **1887** Randall *Lady's Ranche Life* 65 **MT,** For breakfast we have porridge (which Americans call "mush"), eggs, fried potatoes. **1925** *AmSp* 1.150 **West,** There are other words, not sprung from custom but from a psychology that prompts the choice of a plain, meaty word for one more ornate. Here are a few examples . . "mush" for "cereal." **1965–70** *DARE* (Qu. H23, *. . Hot cooked breakfast cereal*) 141 Infs, **widespread, but esp West,** Mush; **OK**1, Cooked mush; **OH**78, **WA**1, Graham mush; **CA**126, 136, **NY**1, **TX**102, Hot mush; **DE**3, Milk and mush; **MI**106, **OH**80, Mush and milk; **NV**1, Oatmeal mush; **MI**106, **PA**163, Wheat

mush. **1983** *DARE* File **cUT,** Mush—any hot cereal (such as oatmeal or Cream Of Wheat). **1993** *Ibid* **cwCA** (as of 1950s), When I was growing up, *mush* referred to any hot cereal we might have for breakfast.

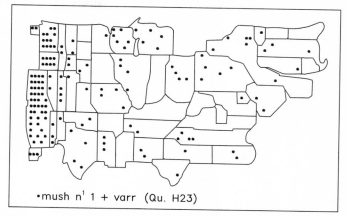

•mush n[1] 1 + varr (Qu. H23)

2 also *cornmeal mush, hog-head ~:* =**headcheese 1, scrapple,** or a similar food made of bits of head or organ meat mixed with boiled cornmeal; see quot. Cf **liver mush**
1986 Pederson *LAGS Concordance* (Scrapple) 4 infs, **AL, GA, TN,** Mush; 1 inf, **cAL,** Mush—head cheese or liver sausage and cornmeal; 1 inf, **ceGA,** Cornmeal mush; *(Headcheese)* 2 infs, **nwGA,** Hoghead mush; 1 inf, **ceMS,** Hoghead mush—feet, head, other parts; sliced; fried; *(Liver sausage)* 1 inf, **csAL,** Mush-cush; fried liver and meal.

3 also in combs *mush and milk, ~ molasses;* also attrib: Nonsense, twaddle; pap. **esp Sth, S Midl**
1866 in 1938 Twain *Letters Sandwich Is.* 151, I'm disgusted with these mush-and-milk preacher travels. **1905** *DN* 3.88 **nwAR,** *Mush and molasses. . .* Language indicating a weak intellect or a flabby character. 'He talked mush and molasses.' **1965–69** *DARE* (Qu. NN13, *When you think that the thing somebody has just said is silly or untrue: "Oh, that's a lot of _____."*) Infs **GA**13, **KY**65, **MS**30, **SC**3, **VA**2, Mush.

mush n[2] |mʌš, mᴜš| [Etym uncert; cf nEngl dial *muss* [mᴜs] the mouth] **esp Nth, West** Cf **bazoo 1**
A mouth; a face; by ext: excessive chatter.
[**1859** Matsell *Vocabulum* 127, *Mush.* The mouth.] **1912** *NY Eve. Jrl.* (NY) 6 Feb 17 *(Zwilling Coll.),* Take that cigar out of your mush. **1913** *DN* 4.27 **NW,** *Mush. . .* Mouth; talking to excess. **1919** *DN* 5.66 **NM,** *Mush,* the mouth. "Stop his mush and give us a rest." **1932** Farrell *Young Lonigan* 20 **Chicago IL,** That time he had pasted Weary in the mush with an icy snowball. *Ibid* 185 **Chicago IL** (as of 1916), Studs cracked Danny in the jaw with all his might, and the punk, holding his mush in his hands, bawled. **1935** Porter *Flowering Judas* 84, Aaah, shurrup yuh mush, I got plenty. **1950** *WELS* **WI** *(Joking . . names for a person's face)* 3 Infs, Mush; *(Joking . . names for a person's mouth)* 2 Infs, Mush. **1966–70** *DARE* (Qu. X9, *Joking or uncomplimentary words for a person's mouth . . "I wish he'd shut his _____."*) Infs **CA**15, 87, **OR**13, Mush; **AK**1, [mʌš]; **RI**12, [mᴜš]; (Qu. X29, *Joking or uncomplimentary words for a person's face)* Infs **CA**15, 208, 212, **MI**24, **NH**16, **PA**184, **RI**12, Mush; [**CA**36, Mush face].

mush v[1], hence vbl n *mushing*
Of a log in a stack: to give way, yield to pressure; hence n *mush log* the outermost log in a load.
1941 (1971) *MI Log Marks* 21, Suddenly, with a heavy rumble, the top of the pile sank, the lower logs "mushing out" toward the water. **1956** Sorden–Ebert *Logger's Words* 24 **Gt Lakes,** *Mush-log,* The outside log of a load of logs. **1958** McCulloch *Woods Words* 120 **Pacific NW,** *Mush log*—The outside log on a load. **1969** Sorden *Lumberjack Lingo* 79 **NEng, Gt Lakes,** *Mushing out*—Movement of lower logs in a pile at a rollway toward the water as the pile was broken out.

mush v[2] [Var of Fr imperative *Marche* Go! Get on! or *Marchons* Let's go! Move on! See quot 1940] **chiefly AK** Cf *DCan,* Tabbert *Dict. Alaskan Engl.*

1 also with *on:* To proceed, travel, usu on foot through snow; now esp, to travel with a dogsled; hence vbl n *mushing.* Cf **musher**
[**1862** in 1942 James *First Scientific Explor.* 99 **Yukon Terr. Canada,** Many a warning haul have my foregoer Nogah's lugs gotten because he would not "mouche" (go fast) when it was my spell ahead.] **1902**

(1906) Porter *4 Million* 105 **AK,** I never got off the train since I mushed out of Seattle, and I'm hungry. **1902** M. Clark *Roadhouse Tales, or Nome in 1900* 12 (Tabbert *Dict. Alaskan Engl.*), A returned Nomite was asked: "What do you mean by mushing?" It's taking a pack of fifty pounds on your back and starting over the tundra . . or it's taking a dog team in January with the temperature sixty below to go out on the creeks to re-locate claims. **1904** Schrader *Reconnaissance* 14 **AK,** Traveling by this means is known, in the language of the country, as "mushing," and the traveler is called a "musher." The "musher" does not ride on the sled . . but follows the sled afoot. **1915** Stuck *10000 Miles* 346 **AK,** The dogs were very weary with the eleven hours' mushing. **1933** Marshall *Arctic Village* 123, Winter travel, or mushing as it is generally called, is one of the genuine joys in the life of most of the Koyukukers. **1940** *AmSp* 15.326, *Mush.* . . Etymology usually given as abbr. from "mush on" from Fr. 'marchons.' . . Nobody mentions the imperative singular form 'marche,' which, however, is supported by the following: 'The French voyageur was in evidence in the early days, with his dog train. He would talk to his dogs in his own language and say "Marsh, marsh, marsh dog." Sometimes he would use stronger French language.' . . Superior [WI] *Telegram,* July 23, 1910. **1948** *Natl. Geogr. Mag.* Aug 235 **MD,** We . . then "mushed on" to Dam No. 5 [in a canoe]. **1949** *Anchorage Daily Times* 15 Jan 9 (Tabbert *Dict. Alaskan Engl.*), Linemen in parkas and on snowshoes were mushing over huge snowslides near Portage today restoring telephone communication lines. **1966** Huntington *On Edge of Nowhere* 25 **AK,** The people who stood watching as the team came mushing up from the bank stared at her as they would at a ghost. **1989** *Fairbanks Daily News-Miner* 19 Apr 13 (Tabbert *Dict. Alaskan Engl.*), We mush to town every spring. It makes a nice break for us.

2 also with *on:* Go! move on!—usu used as a command to a sled dog or team. *old-fash*

[**1862** in 1942 James *First Scientific Explor.* 113 **Yukon Terr. Canada,** One sees only a large cloud moving along the track, out of which come queer cries of . . "*Marche!*" "*Yeu!*" "*Chah!*" etc. . . The voyageur, be he English, Gaelic, Norwegian, or French, always addresses his dogs in a rubbaboo [=hodgepodge] sort of a language they call French here. *Ibid* 133, Some of the various words of command to their dogs are— spelled as they are pronounced here—*march!* (go on); *wo!* or *who!* (stop).] **1902** in 1904 U.S. Congress *Serial Set* 4599 Doc 155 158, The word in universal use throughout the country to start the dogs in motion is "mush," evidently a corruption of the French verb "*marcher,*" to march or walk, and has been obtained from the old Hudson Bay voyageurs. **1902** McKee *Land of Nome* 32 **cwAK,** The cry of encouragement to the dogs of "Mush on" (dog French for *Marchons*) was heard frequently. **1915** Stuck *10000 Miles* 200 **AK,** Nanook lunges forward at the command, "Mush!" and strains at the collar. **1943** Brandt *AK Bird Trails* 19 (as of 1924), To start the team the command is 'mush,' or 'mush on.' **1947** Jones *Evergreen Land* 86 **AK,** The idiom of Alaska and the Yukon Territory was a part of their speech. I can remember being told to "mush on" instead of to walk ahead. [**1980** Bills *Alaska* 23 **cnAK,** The term *mush* was not native to this area. I never heard that word in all my years of dog mushing. Everyone had his own means for speeding up the team.] **1995** *DARE* File **nMN,** Mushing is increasing in popularity all over the world. . . Nobody uses "mush" anymore [to start sled dogs]. . . The word most often used is "hike". It's a word you can hear better over the barking.

3 To drive (a dog team); to convey by dog team. Cf **dog musher, dog mushing, musher**

1934 *Anchorage Daily Times* 26 Mar 4 (Tabbert *Dict. Alaskan Engl.*), I've mushed the dogs from Nome to Valdez myself and know what heroic fellows those old mail carriers were. **1953** *Jessen's Weekly* (Fairbanks AK) 26 Feb 1/1 **AK,** Big Jeff . . has been mushing dogs since 1930 and at the age of 50 still gets out on the race trail every time there is a race. **1976** Hobbs-Specht *Tisha* 173 **AK,** There were always people . . who wanted to be mushed into the interior for one reason or another. **1979** *Fairbanks Daily News-Miner* 13 Jan sec B 3 (Tabbert *Dict. Alaskan Engl.*), In 1923 he mushed a five-dog team 2,500 miles along the Arctic Coast.

mush n[3] [**mush** v[2]] **AK**
A journey, esp over snow with a dog team and sled.

1902 McKee *Land of Nome* 76, They were making ready their packs for the "mush" to the auxiliary creeks. **1905** (1906) Beach *Spoilers* 248 **AK,** Let's hurry up. . . It's a long 'mush' and the mud is knee-deep. **1915** Stuck *10000 Miles* 148 **AK,** A day's mush brought us to "The Birches," and another to Gold Mountain. **1936** *Alaska Sportsman* Jan 9 (Tabbert *Dict. Alaskan Engl.*), After many grueling hours on the trail and the day's "mush" is ended, the stalwart malemute asks for nothing

more than a place to sleep, a piece of fish and a friendly word from his master. **1990** *Fairbanks Daily News-Miner* 26 Aug sec C 4 (Tabbert *Dict. Alaskan Engl.*), These strips . . will be nutritious trail snacks during the winter's long, cold mushes.

mush and milk (or molasses) See **mush** n[1] **3**

musharoom, musharoon See **mushroom**

musher n [**mush** v[2] 1, 3] chiefly **AK** Cf **dog musher**
One who travels on foot; a dog-team driver.

1900 in 1991 Tabbert *Dict. Alaskan Engl.* 201, Musher = one who travels on the trail, with or without dogs. **1902** in 1904 U.S. Congress *Serial Set* 4599 Doc 155 158, In Alaska the term "to mush" means to travel and a "musher" is a traveler on foot. **1902** McKee *Land of Nome* 178 **cwAK,** I felt that I had received a very high compliment, delicately expressed, when an old-timer in the party, with unnecessary calls on the Almighty, told me that I was a "musher from hell." **1904** [see **mush** v[2] 1]. **1948** *Time* 19 July 34/3, Klondike Mike, the greatest of the mushers, the sourdough who struck it rich and kept his poke, is a living legend. **1977** *Fairbanks Daily News-Miner* 18 Jan (Tabbert *Dict. Alaskan Engl.*), Musher Norman D. Vaughan, 71, . . will run his team of 12 dogs.

musheroom, mushero(o)n See **mushroom**

mush ice n Also *mushy ice* **scattered, but esp S Midl** Cf **slush ice**
A slushy mass of ice and water; a thin layer of ice on a body of water.

1815 *Niles' Natl. Reg.* 9.201/2 **csPA,** You may . . take a pole sixty feet long, and . . run it down the whole length, and find no termination of what is called the mush ice. **1905** (1966) London *White Fang* 218 **AK,** The fall of the year, when the first snows were falling and mush-ice was running in the river. **1964** O'Hare *Ling. Geog. E. MT* 62 **seMT,** The first thin coating of ice . . [1 inf] *mush ice* (salt water only). **1968–70** *DARE* (Qu. B33a, *The first thin ice that forms over the surface of a pond or pool: "There's just a _____ of ice."*) Inf **WV**13, Mush ice; [(Qu. B33b, *Talking about the first thin ice that forms over the surface of a pond or pool: "The pond is just _____ over."*) Inf **TN**37, Mushed [mʌšt];] (Qu. B35, *Ice that will bend when you step on it, but not break*) Inf **GA**71, Mush ice—not hard enough to cake; **KY**44, Mush ice—ice between snow and ice, not really ice yet; **VA**13, Mush ice; **KY**28, 84, **MO**37, Mushy ice. **1971** Wood *Vocab. Change* 33 **Sth,** When a thin covering of ice forms on ponds. . . Scattered instances of *anchor ice, mush ice* . . are recorded. **1973** Gawthrop *Dial. Calumet* 77 **nwIN,** First thin layer of ice on lake or pond: . . mush ice [5 infs, of 19 interviews, 125 mailed QRs]. **1983** *MJLF* 9.1.48 **ceKY** (as of 1956), *Mush ice* . . the very thin layer of ice that forms when a pond first freezes over.

mushing vbl n[1] See **mush** v[1]

mushing vbl n[2] See **mush** v[2] **1**

mushle v Also sp *muschel* [*mush* + frequentative *-le;* cf *SND mush* v[1] "Freq. forms *mus(c)hle.* . . II.1. . . to mix up or together in a confused manner. . . 2. To reduce to mush, . . to consume or eat by slow degrees"; cf also Ger *muscheln* to shuffle (cards)]
See quots.

1952 Brown *NC Folkl.* 1.568, Mushle. . . To shuffle cards. **1954** *WELS Suppl.* **seWI,** My husband who does not like the sound of people chewing seeds, as in straw- or raspberries, says "Don't chew, muschel." I have heard it used when someone mashes up his ice cream and chocolate sauce. "I like to muschel mine." I think it comes from mashing something to a mush. One cannot muschel hard things like nuts or candy, tho one can muschel a chocolate cream. *Ibid,* Muschel [is] said with *moo* as in cow—not quite as long—but not like *bushel.* . . We are not the only ones who use it.

mush log See **mush** v[1]

mushmelon, mushmillion See **muskmelon**

musho See **mashu**

mush oak n **CA**
=**valley oak.**

1910 Jepson *Silva CA* 209, A single tree [of *Quercus lobata*] often yields fifty to ninety cords of stovewood. . . The folk-name "Mush Oak" carries with it a species of contempt and tells a long story of its failure to meet the requirements of a tough, strong wood in a land where good oak is scarce and dear. **1968** *DARE* (Qu. T10) Infs **CA**99, 105, Mush oak.

mush on See **mush** v[2] 1, 2

mushoo See **mashu**

mush pop n Cf **ice pop**

   1971 *Today Show Letters* seNY, On Long Island we visited the ice cream Parlor. They had a flat top ice cream [cone] that was called a "mush pop." [*Ibid*, Regular cone on bottom.] [*DARE* Ed: Illustr shows a tapered ice cream cone with a wide, flat brim.]

mush pot exclam

   =**Antony-over B1.**

   1966 *DARE* (Qu. EE23b, *In the game of andy-over . . if you fail to get the ball over the building and it rolls back, what . . you call out*) Inf NC22, Mush pot.

mush rabbit See **marsh rabbit 2**

mushrat n

1 also rarely *mushrap:* =**muskrat 1. widespread exc West**
See Map

   1890 *DN* 1.74 NEng, Mushrat [məʃræt]: the muskrat or musquash. **1892** *DN* 1.234 KY, Mushrat. **1894** [see **muskrat 1**]. **1923** *DN* 5.215 swMO, Mush rat. **1937** *AmSp* 12.126 Upstate NY, Muskrat may have [sk] or [ʃ]. **1950** *WELS*, 2 Infs, WI, Muskrat, mushrat. **1961** [see **muskrat 1**]. **1965–70** *DARE* (Qu. P31, . . *Names or nicknames . . for the . . muskrat*) 217 Infs, **widespread exc West**, Mushrat(s); **GA72**, Musky, mushrat; **KY72**, Mushrat, water rat; **MI65**, Mushrat—most everybody calls 'em that; **MA42**, Always called 'em mushrats; when mushrats built their houses high, there was going to be high water that year; **NY48**, Mushrat—old-fashioned; **OK52**, Mushrat—old expression. **1966** *DARE* Tape ME26, We was trappin' mushrats. **1973** Allen *LAUM* 1.408 (as of c1950), 1 inf, MN, Mushrat. A muskrat. **1979** *DARE* File cnMA (as of c1915), I remember somebody's dog catching what people told me was a mushrat. It was some years later that I realized that dead animal was a muskrat, not a rat at all. **1991** *DARE* File ceNY (as of 1950s–60s), We used to get 50¢ apiece for a prime mushrat skin. **1993** Kingsolver *Pigs in Heaven* 221 OK, This one [=pond] they call the mushrat hole. I guess they used to trap a lot of mushrat and mink down here. **1995** *DARE* File csWI (as of c1930–50), Mushrap [for *muskrat*].

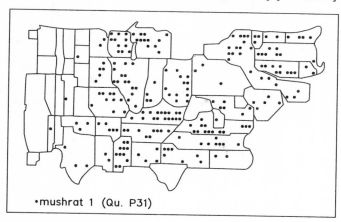

•mushrat 1 (Qu. P31)

2 See **muskrat 3.**

mushrat (around) v phr Cf **muskrat 3**

   1923 *DN* 5.236 swWI, Mushrat; mushrat around. . . To idle, to dawdle. "He don't seem to be doin' much—jest mushrattin' around."

mushrat clover n

   =**marsh hay.**

   1968 *DARE* (Qu. L8, *Hay that grows naturally in damp places*) Inf WI30, Mushrat [ˈmʌʃˌræt] clover—same as marsh hay.

mushroom n Usu |ˈmʌʃˌrum|; also **scattered, but esp Sth, S Midl** (See Map) |ˈmʌʃəˌrum| (pronc-sp *musheroom*); **chiefly NEast, Midl, N Cent** (See Map) |ˈmʌʃ(ə)ˌrun| (pronc-sp *mush(e)roon*); for addit pronc and sp varr see **A** below [Most of the var forms reflect to varying degrees survival of early forms such as *musseroun, muscheron* (15th cent) < OFr *mousseron.*]
A Forms.

   1899 (1912) Green *VA Folk-Speech* 292, Mushroon. . . Never with *m*, but a final *n*. . . Musheron. **1903** *DN* 2.323 seMO, Mushroom. . . Pronounced musharoom. **1907** *DN* 3.233 nwAR, Mushroom. . . Pronounced musharoom. **1915** *DN* 4.186 swVA, Mushyroom. **1917** *DN* 4.415 wNC, Mushyroom. **1940** in 1944 *ADD* 403 swPA, nWV, Moosharoons /muˈʃərunz/. **1941** *Ibid* WV, Murshroom. **1950** *WELS* (*Small plants, shaped like an umbrella, that grow in woods and fields*) 3 Infs, WI, Mushrooms. **1955** *PADS* 23.43 e,cSC, eNC, seGA, /-rum/ in *mushroom* (also Chesapeake Bay, e. New England). **1959** *IN Mag. Hist.* 55.220 (as of c1920), But the basket's load proved the point, for it was full of *musharoons!* **1961** Kurath–McDavid *Pronc. Engl.* 179, *Mushroom.* . . In summary one can say that disyllabic variants ending in /n/ are characteristic of the North, trisyllabic variants ending in /m/ or /n/ of the South and the Midland, though both types occur in all major areas. **1965–70** *DARE* (Qu. I37) 855 Infs, **widespread**, Mushrooms; 10 Infs, **scattered**, [ˈmʌʃˈrumz]; 9 Infs, **scattered**, [ˈmuʃrumz]; KS20, TX38, [ˈmuʃrumz]; AL14, [ˈmaʃrumz]; NJ17, [ˈmɔɪʃrumz]; CA70, [ˈmuʃˈrumz]; GA92, [ˈmʌθrum]; 28 Infs, **chiefly Sth, S Midl, nNEng**, Musherooms [proncs of the type [ˈmʌʃəˌrumz]]; 47 Infs, **chiefly Nth, Midl**, Mushroons [proncs of the type [ˈmʌʃrunz]]; AZ8, Mushroons [muʃrunz]; 32 Infs, **chiefly NEast, Midl, N Cent**, Musherooms [proncs of the type [ˈmʌʃəˌrunz]]; IN69, NC68, Musherooms [ˌmʌʃəˈrunz]; KY85, Mushrooms, [2nd resp] muskrooms; IN54, Muskrooms, [corr to] mushrooms; KY17, Musrooms [ˈmʌsrumz] [FW: sic] [Of all Infs responding to the question, 70% were old, 30% gs educ or less; of those giving the responses *mush(e)roons*, 84% were old, 48% gs educ or less.]; (Qu. H36) Inf VA13, Mushroom [ˈmʌʃrun] soup; (Qu. S18) Infs IN26, MD20, (Sponge) musheroon; MO2, 9, 16, 38, (Puff, red, *or* tremendous big) mushroon; (Qu. S19) Inf MO37, Musherooms; OH66, Tree musheroon; SC19, Musherooms. [Further exx of std *mushroom* throughout *DS*] **1983** *MJLF* 9.1.48 ceKY (as of 1956), Mushyroom . . mushroom.

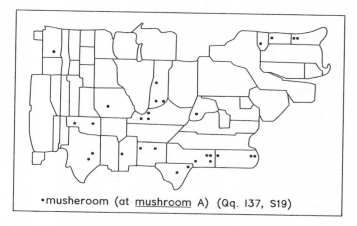

•musheroom (at <u>mushroom</u> A) (Qq. I37, S19)

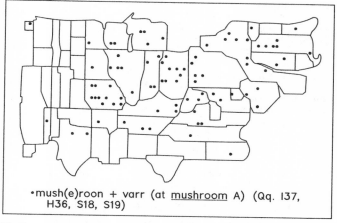

•mush(e)roon + varr (at <u>mushroom</u> A) (Qq. I37, H36, S18, S19)

B Senses.

1 Std: the fruiting body—often stalked, capped, and edible—of any of var fungi, usu included in Ascomycetes and Basidiomycetes. For other names of var of these see **barnacle mushroom, bay chicken, bear's head, beefsteak fungus, bolita, brain mushroom, buckhorn 6, catface 4, cat stool, cockscomb 5, comb n B8, conk** n[2] **1, dead-man's-fingers 1, death cap, deer head, desert inky cap, devil's bread, ~ cigar, ~ dust, ~ footstool, ~ umbrella, ~ urn, dunce cap, egg mushroom, fairy bread, ~ cup 2, ~ platform, ~ ring 1,**

~ umbrella, false chanterelle, ~ morel, ~ turkeytail, field mushroom, firefly 4, fried-chicken mushroom, frog bench, ~ house 2, ~ pillow, ~ plant 2, frogstool, frog table, ~ umbrella, fuzzy-foot, haymaker's mushroom, hen of the woods, hickory chicken, honeycomb 1, honey mushroom, horn mushroom, ~ of plenty 2, horsehair fungus, human ear, icicle mushroom, Indian bread 3, ~ paint fungus, inky cap, jack-o'-lantern 3, jelly drops, ~ fungus, lizard's claw, lobster mushroom, man-on-a-horse, milky cap, moose antlers, ~ mushroom, morel n², nigger's pipe, oak bonnet, orange peel, oyster mushroom, parasol ~, pig's ears, pine mushroom, pinecone ~, poison pie, puffball, quinine fungus, shaggymane, shelf mushroom, slippery jack, sticky bun, stinkhorn, stump mushroom, sulfur shelf, sweet knot, toadstool, turkeytail, winter mushroom, witches' butter Cf cedar apple, fox fire 1a, oak apple 2, swamp apple

2 in phr *go around the mushroom:* To do something in an indirect and complicated way.

1968 *DARE* (Qu. KK52, *To do something in an indirect and complicated way: "I don't know why he had to go _____ to do that."*) Inf **OH68**, Clear around the mushroom—very old-fashioned.

mushy ice See **mush ice**

mushyroom See **mushroom**

musical broom n Also *musical hats*
A children's game similar to **musical chairs**.

1969 *DARE* (Qu. EE2, *Games that have one extra player—when a signal is given, the players change places, and the extra one tries to get a place*) Inf **NJ54**, Musical broom; **PA177**, Musical hats.

musical chairs n pl but sg in constr Also rarely *musical chair* [*OEDS* 1877 →] **widespread, but somewhat less freq Sth, S Midl** See Map Cf **back man; bird, beast, or fish 2; Boston exchange; cakewalk 2b; chair walk; changing chairs; dropout** n 1; **fruit basket; hotel B3; in-and-out-the-window 2; Jerusalem, going to 1; kitchen furniture; marching through Georgia; musical broom; odd man out**
A game in which the players march around a circle of chairs (with one chair fewer than the number of players) while music is played; when it stops, each attempts to secure a chair, and the one who fails is eliminated; this is repeated until only one player remains.

1932 (1953) Smith *Games* 417, *Going to Jerusalem* . . (Musical Chairs). . . This ancient musical game, which is known under numerous titles, undoubtedly will always be popular. **1950** *WELS* **WI** (*Games with an extra player: at a signal the other players change places, and the extra tries to get a place*) 18 Infs, Musical chairs; 1 Inf, Musical chair; [1 Inf, Musical march; 1 Inf, Musical game]. **1953** Brewster *Amer. Nonsinging Games* 100 **AR**, Musical Chairs. . . A fairly large number of players, at least ten or twelve, is needed for this game. The only equipment required is chairs (one fewer than the number of players) and a piano or a record player. **1965–70** *DARE* (Qu. EE2) 666 Infs, **widespread, but somewhat less freq Sth, S Midl**, Musical chairs; 11 Infs, **scattered**, Musical chair. **1980** Oates *Bellefleur* 313, He slipped away, restless and bored with. . . [m]usical chairs and "The Needle's Eye" and charades and tag and hide-and-go-seek.

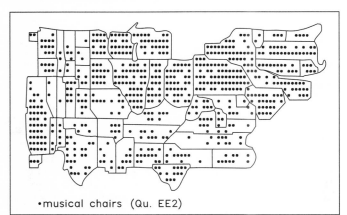

•musical chairs (Qu. EE2)

music bow n
=**mouth bow.**

1979 Irwin *Musical Instruments* 63 **neTN**, The late Lawrence Warwick of Dark Hollow . . is the only old-timer I have known who used a coin (a twenty-five cent piece) to strike the bow string. "I learnt to play the music bow from my Pap," he said. **1980** *Foxfire 6* 92 **neTN**, In the area surrounding Hancock County, Tennessee, they make instruments out of red cedar or hickory and wire and refer to them as "music bows," "mouth bows," or "tuning bows."

musicianer n Also sp *musicioner, musitioner* [*OED* 1540 →] **chiefly S Midl, formerly also NEng** Cf **-er** affix **1**
A musician.

1795 Dearborn *Columbian Grammar* 137, *List of Improprieties. . . Musicianer* for *Musician.* a1824 (1937) Guild *Jrl.* 261 **VT**, After I had ben introduced to the musitioners I began to nock round the tamborin while the people ware collecting. **1867** Lowell *Biglow* xlv **'Upcountry' MA**, "Musicianer" I had always associated with the militia-musters of my boyhood. **1891** *PMLA* 6.168 **WV**, A band of music is called *musicioners.* **1912** Green *VA Folk-Speech* 292, *Musicioner. . .* For *musician.* **1913** Kephart *Highlanders* 277 **sAppalachians**, Musicianer. **1927** [see **musicker**]. **1937** in 1976 *Weevils in the Wheat* 130 **VA** [Black], I went to dancin school wid de white folks an' can dance any kin' o' dance sets. My father was a musicianer. **1942** (1971) Campbell *Cloud-Walking* 145 **seKY**, The Old Man ain't again musicianers iffen they keep to their proper places. **1944** *PADS* 2.47 **NC**, Musicianer. **1971** Evans *Tommy Johnson* 24 **MS** (as of early 20th cent) [Black], I never did see no difference in 'em. They all was good musicianers. **1989** *DARE* File **cnNC**, The term "musicianers" is commonly and usually used in reference to fiddlers et al.

musicker n [*OED* 14 . . →]
A musician.

1927 *DN* 5.475 **Ozarks**, Musicker. . . A musician, one who plays a musical instrument. The term *musicianer* is also heard occasionally. **1940** *AmSp* 15.204, *Musickers.* The members of a dance orchestra. **1944** *PADS* 2.47 **NC**, Musicker. . . A musician. Less common than *musicianer.*

music root n [Perh in allusion to the ocarina, called also *sweet potato,* but see quots 1966–70, 1986]
A sweet potato.

1944 Adams *Western Words* 103, *Music roots*—A Westerner's name for sweet potatoes. **1966–70** *DARE* (Qu. I9, . . *Names [including nicknames] for potatoes*) Inf **SC26**, Music root [FW: "Potatoes" means sweet potato to her.]; **SC29**, Music root—sweet potatoes, joking; **TX89**, Music root—sweet potatoes, because they make you fart so bad. **1986** Pederson *LAGS Concordance* (*Sweet potatoes*) 2 infs, **cAL, cwAR**, Music roots; 1 inf, **cwMS**, Music roots—because they make you pass gas; 1 inf, **nwAR**, Music roots—he declines to explain; 1 inf, **nwAR**, Music roots—make you break wind.

musk n
1 pronc-sp *muss;* in phr *get one's musk up:* See quot. Cf **muck** n¹ **4**

1966 *DARE* (Qu. X56b, *Expressions about sweating very heavily*) Inf **NC6**, Getting his muss up.
2 See **musk plant.**

musk v Cf **musk cat 1**
To emit an odor; spec, of a skunk: to spray.

1968 *DARE* FW Addit **GA22**, ". . . when he musked." Inf describing the results of an encounter with a "polecat." **1986** Pederson *LAGS Concordance,* 1 inf, **ceFL**, Musk—to emit odor; intransitive.

muskallunge See **muskellunge**

musk bush n
A **ceanothus** (here: *Ceanothus jepsonii*).

1925 Jepson *Manual Plants CA* 624, *C[eanothus] jepsonii* . . Musk-bush. **1937** U.S. Forest Serv. *Range Plant Hdbk.* B39, Muskbush (*C. jepsonii*).

musk cat n
1 =**skunk.**

1843 (1916) Hall *New Purchase* 202 **IN**, Some secretly thought it would have been just as well if the musk-cats had been allowed to escape. **1909** *S. Atl. Qrly.* 8.48 **seSC**, That delicately-scented fop, the Skunk, is, with a sniff, entitled a *mus'cat, i. e. Musk-cat.* **1970** *DARE* (Qu. P31) Inf **TX96**, Musk cat |'məskæt|—used for skunk. **1986** Pederson *LAGS Concordance,* 1 inf, **cGA**, Musk cat = polecat.

2 See **muskrat 1.**

musk clover n [See quot 1906] **esp CA**
  A **storksbill:** usu *Erodium moschatum*, but also *E. cicutarium*.
  1901 Jepson *Flora CA* 247, E[rodium] moschatum. . . Filaree. Musk Clover. . . Abundant in rich lands of valley orchards and vineyards. **1906** (1918) Parsons *Wild Flowers CA* 200, E[rodium] moschatum . . is a coarser plant whose foliage has a musky fragrance, especially when wilted. It is also a valuable forage plant, and is commonly known as . . "musk clover." **1911** CA Ag. Exper. Sta. Berkeley *Bulletin* 217.1002, Erodium cicutarium . . Musk and Pin Clover. **1976** Bailey–Bailey *Hortus Third* 443, [Erodium] moschatum . . White-stemmed filaree, musk clover.

muskeag See **muskeg**

muskeeter See **mosquito** n[1]

muskeg n Also sp *muscag, muskeag, muskegg* [CanEngl < Algonquian (Ojibway *mashkig,* Cree *mashkek*)] **chiefly AK, MN**
  A marsh or bog; see quot 1959.
  1890 *Outing* 16.378, Both caribou and moose still exist . . among the pine barrens and *muskeags* of Northern Minnesota. **1895** Upham *Glacial Lake Agassiz* 29 **nMN,** Considerable tracts . . are tamarack swamps, morasses, and quaking bogs, called "muskegs." **1898** Green *Forestry MN* 16, On land that is very wet . . as the muskegs of northern Minnesota which are covered with Tamarack and Spruce the trees never get to be of large size. **1916** (1917) Eastman *From Deep Woods* 167, The great inland seas of northern Minnesota and the Province of Ontario are surrounded by . . the immense bogs called "muskeggs" filled with tamaracks. **1959** Anderson *Flora AK* 3, Muskeags or peat bogs. . . are areas of a few square meters up, characterized by a surface covering of sphagnum moss underlaid with moss and other vegetation in various stages of decay, merging gradually into black muck, and the whole saturated with water. **1962** Salisbury *Quoth the Raven* 47 **seAK,** We climbed up and up between the mountains and got among the muskegs with their coffee-colored water standing among the bogs. **1963** [see **mossberry 1**]. **1967–68** *DARE* (Qu. C6, . . *A piece of land that's often wet, and has grass and weeds growing on it*) Infs **AK**2, **MN**2, 38, Muskeg; (Qu. C7, . . *Land that usually has some standing water with trees or bushes growing in it*) Inf **AK**7, Muskeg. **1973** Allen *LAUM* 1.233 **nMN** (as of c1950), *Muskeg,* designating a particular type of swamp, is used only in the area where such swamps occur, i.e., northern Minnesota. **1984** Davis *Be Tough* 155 **AK,** My shortcut was full of muscag. A real bog! When the horses walked across it, the whole ground shook. **1994** *Nat. Hist.* 103.22 **nMI,** In northern Michigan, bogs eventually become dominated by black spruces, forming a type of swamp referred to as a muskeg. This process may take several thousand years.

muskeg berry n
  =**cloudberry.**
  1955 U.S. Arctic Info. Center *Gloss.* 54, Muskegberry. . . The baked-apple berry.

muskegg See **muskeg**

muskeg spruce n
  =**black spruce 1.**
  1894 *Garden and Forest* 7.504 **MN,** The Muskeag Spruce. Close to the open water that remains uncovered by the growth of sedges and sphagnum that is filling or covering many of the forest-lakes of Minnesota, little Spruce-trees are stubbornly existing, although they have no mineral earth to grow upon. **1916** Sudworth *Spruce & Balsam Fir* 4, "Swamp spruce," "bog spruce," and "muskeg spruce," are local names applied to it [=black spruce] when found growing in wet, marshy places.

muskellunge n Also *mascalonge, muscallunge, maskinonge;* for addit varr see quots [Algonquian; *DCan* (at *maskinonge*) 1761 →] Cf **saltwater muskellunge**
1 also abbr *muskie, musky:* A large freshwater game fish (*Esox masquinongy*). **chiefly Gt Lakes, OH, PA, Upstate NY** See Map Also called **blue pike 2, great northern ~ 2, great ~, jack** n[1] **24a(1), jackfish 1a, jack pike, ~ salmon 2, leopard muskellunge, lunge** n[2], **northern pike 2, pickerel, pike, tiger muskellunge**
  1777 in 1789 Anburey *Travels* 1.274 **NY,** It [=Lake Champlain] abounds with great quantities and variety of fish; sturgeon, black bass, masquenongez, pike of an incredible size, and many others. **1794** Williams *Nat. & Civil Hist. VT* 122, The *Pike* or *Pickerel* abounds much in Lake Champlain. It is there called by the name of Muschilongoe. **1796**

Morse *Amer. Universal Geog.* 1.351, Maskinungas, a very large species of pickerel. **1815** *Lit. & Philos. Soc. NY Trans.* 1.496 **NY,** The muscalinga, a species of pike, is greatly esteemed, and is generally caught in rivers emptying into the lakes. **1842** DeKay *Zool. NY* 4.223, The *Muskellunge,* or *Maskinonge,* for its orthography is not settled, occurs abundantly in Lake Erie, and is found also in the streams in the western district. **1849** (1851) Herbert *Frank Forester's Fish & Fishing* 152, The Mascalonge, which owes its name to the formation of the head—*masque allongè,* long face or snout, Canadian French—but which has been translated from dialect to dialect, maskinonge, muscalunge, and muscalinga, until every trace of true derivation has been lost, is said to be much more common in Lakes Erie and Ontario than in the more northern waters of Canada. **1886** Mather *Memoranda* 10 **NY,** The maskinonje, or muscallunge . . a species peculiar to the great lake system, and reaching a weight of forty pounds and upward. **1887** in 1991 Heat Moon *PrairyErth* 521 **ceKS,** [Union Hotel Bill of Fare:] Boiled—Cold ham. Cold beef tongue. Muskallonge. **1909** Holder–Jordan *Fish Stories* 285, A forty-two pound muskallunge is not caught every day on the St. Lawrence. **1949** Caine *N. Amer. Sport Fish* 98, Monarch of the pike family, heavyweight champ among fresh water game fish and the toast of nearly every northern sporting angler is the unpredictable powerhouse—the muskellunge. *Ibid, Colloquial Names.* . . Lunge, . . Spotted Muskellunge, Ohio Muskellunge, . . Great Lakes Muskellunge, . . Longe, Musky, . . Unspotted Muskellunge. **1950** *WELS* **WI** *(Fish that are good to eat)* 6 Infs, Muskellunge; 3 Infs, Muskie. **1965–70** *DARE* (Qu. P1, . . *Kinds of freshwater fish . . caught around here . . good to eat*) 15 Infs, **chiefly Gt Lakes, Upstate NY,** Muskellunge; 37 Infs, **chiefly Gt Lakes, OH, PA,** Muskie(s). **1967** *DARE* Tape IL9, We have most all the kinds of fish. . . we have a few muskies; **MI**65, [FW:] What does that grass pike look like? [Inf:] Well, the larger ones would look like a muskellunge; **WI**65, They have parades and a muskie festival each summer. **1972** Sparano *Outdoors Encycl.* 366, The muskellunge—whose name means "ugly fish" in Ojibway dialect—is green to brown to gray in overall color. **1975** Evanoff *Catch More Fish* 83, The muskellunge (*Esox masquinongy*) is also known as . . musky, and by various spellings of the name muskellunge. **1983** Becker *Fishes WI* 405, Muskellunge. . . *masquinongy*—in Cree "mashk" means deformed and "kinonge" is a pike. Other common names: Great Lakes muskellunge, Ohio muskellunge, . . muskie (musky), lunge, northern muskellunge, . . maskinonge. **1986** Pederson *LAGS Concordance,* 4 infs, 3 **TN,** Muskie(s).

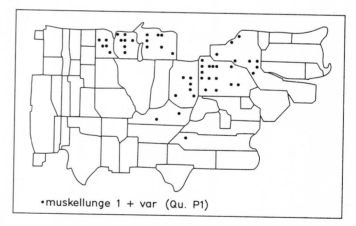

•muskellunge 1 + var (Qu. P1)

2 =**northern pike 1.** Cf **silver muskellunge**
  1886 Mather *Memoranda* 10 **NY,** This fish [=*Esox lucius*] is one of two species which are often confounded, especially in parts where the other does not exist. There it is sometimes termed muscallonge, mascallunge, maskinanga, or, what I believe to be the correct form of this variously spelled name, maskinonje. **1896** Robinson *In New Engl. Fields* 122, They were only pickerel at best, though some of them, bearing their spots on a green ground, are honored with the name of "maskalonge" by our fishermen. **1946** Dufresne *AK's Animals* 250, While there has been a tendency on the part of some Alaska residents to miscall this fish a "pickerel" or a "muskellunge," it can be very definitely stated that the Great Northern pike is the only member of the genus found in Alaska.

3 =**Missouri sucker.**
  1983 Becker *Fishes WI* 611, Missouri sucker, razorback, . . "muskellunge" in the lower Wabash River in Indiana.

muskete See **mesquite**

musk flower n

1 See **musk plant**.

2 =**devil's bouquet**.

1961 Wills–Irwin *Flowers TX* 107, Flowering from April until fall, especially after wet periods, the . . Musk-flower is an arresting plant. **1970** Correll *Plants TX* 576, *Nyctaginia capitata*. . . Scarlet musk-flower.

musk geranium n

=**herb Robert**.

1948 Wherry *Wild Flower Guide* 66, Musk Geranium *(G. robertianum)*. . . Leaves compound, the 3 leaflets deeply cut and toothed, musk scented.

musk grass n

Usu an alga of the genus *Chara*, but also of the genus *Nitella*. For other names of the former see **feather bed 2, fine moss 2, horse watertail, niggerwool 3, oyster grass 1, skunk ~, stonewort**

1913 *Torreya* 13.225 **FL**, *Chara* sp . . musk grass. **1933** *Ibid* 33.81 **NC**, *Chara* sp.—Musk grass. **1951** Martin *Amer. Wildlife & Plants* 6, The muskgrasses *(Chara* and *Nitella)* . . are aquatic plants that are important as duck food. *Ibid* 428, The muskgrasses (primarily *Chara*) are usually grouped with the algae. . . Their characteristic musky odor makes them a nuisance in city reservoirs, and the plants are reported to flavor the flesh of waterfowl that feed on them.

musk hog n [See quot 1917] Cf **Mexican hog 1**

=**jabalina**.

[**1773** *Gentleman's Mag.* 43.219, The Mexican Musk-Hog.] **1865** (1932) Pike *Scout & Ranger* 23 **TX**, We hunted deer, wild turkey, and musk hogs. **1917** Anthony *Mammals Amer.* 62, In the middle of the back the Peccary has a large gland containing an oily substance smelling somewhat like musk: hence the animal is sometimes called the Musk Hog. When in anger the Peccary ejects this substance, the odor emitted is very rank. **1929** Dobie *Vaquero* 209, Javelinas (peccaries, or musk hogs) were the most numerous forms of wild life in the brush. **1940** Writers' Program *Guide TX* 26, The muskhog or collared peccary, a vicious wild hog locally called javelina, is numerous from the Edwards Plateau to the Rio Grande, and also in the Big Bend. **1947** Cahalane *Mammals* 10, The musk is also an identification. As peccaries pass . . trees and shrubs, they may rub against these, leaving some of the musky odor behind. . . The human hunter, with his dull and limited faculties can only tell that one or more "musk hogs" have gone by. **1982** Elman *Hunter's Field Guide* 434, Peccary. . . Common & regional names . . musk hog.

muskick n [Pronc-sp for *musket;* cf Intro "Language Changes" IV.4]

1922 Gonzales *Black Border* 83 **sSC, GA coasts** [Gullah], He had implicit faith and infinite pride in the shooting powers of his old "muskick,"—"Ole Betsey." **1967** *DARE* (Qu. P37b) Inf **TX5**, Muskick—smooth bore.

muskie See **muskellunge 1**

muskie weed n [*muskie* (at **muskellunge 1**)]

A **pondweed** such as *Potamogeton amplifolius* or *P. praelongus*.

1937 *Torreya* 37.95 **WI**, *Potamogeton praelongus*. . . Muskie (i.e., muskellunge) weed. **1952** Strausbaugh–Core *Flora WV* 56, *P[otamogeton] amplifolius*. . . Muskie weed, bass weed, large-leaved pondweed.

muskit See **mesquite**

musk mare n Cf **devil's horse 4**

A **walkingstick** (here: *Phasmidae*).

1931 Blatchley *My Nature Nook* 70, I have seen . . numerous Orthoptera, for in Florida October is the heyday of their existence. Among them were . . a pair of thick-bodied walking-sticks or "musk-mares," *Anisomorpha buprestoides*. **1940** Teale *Insects* 116, In the Southeastern part of the United States you find a walking stick which is known as the "musk mare." It gives off an evil-smelling fluid which smarts like fire if it gets in your eyes.

muskmelon n **widespread, but less freq Sth, West** (See Map) |'mʌsk,mɛlən|; **widespread, but more freq Sth, S Midl, N Atl** (See Map) |'mʌʃ,mɛlən| Pronc-spp *mus(h)melon, mushmillion;* for addit pronc and sp varr see **A** below [Varr with *mush-* and *mus-* are attested in the *OED* from 16th and 17th centuries respectively] Cf **melon, muskrat**

A Forms.

1775 in 1963 Harrower *Jrl.* 112 **VA**, My Plantation for my Amusement consists of the following Articles Vizt. Water melons, Mush-melons, Cucumbers. **1837** Sherwood *Gaz. GA* 70, *Mushmillion,* for Muskmelon. **1871** (1892) Johnston *Dukesborough Tales* 60 **GA**, He have stob more saplin's! and more punkins! and more watermillions! and more mush-millions! **1890** *DN* 1.74 **NEng**, Mushmelon ['mʌʃmɛlən]. **1892** *DN* 1.217 **NY, NJ**, Mush-melon. **1893** Shands *MS Speech* 46, Musmelon or Mushmelon. . . The common names for the musk-melon. Mushmelon is used mostly by uneducated people. **1899** (1912) Green *VA Folk-Speech* 292, Mushmelon. **1909** *DN* 3.351 **eAL, wGA**, Mush-melon. . . Very common among all classes. Also *Mush-mil(li)on*. **1909** *DN* 3.400 **nwAR**, Mushmelon. **1923** *DN* 5.215 **swMO**, Mush melon. **c1940** Eliason *Word Lists FL* 10 **wFL**, Mushmelon. **1956** McAtee *Some Dialect NC* 30, Mushmelon. **1965–70** *DARE* (Qu. I26, . . *Kinds of melons*) 355 Infs, **widespread, but less freq Sth, West**, Muskmelons; **MI63, NH5**, Honey rock (*or* small) muskmelons; **MA122, NJ5, RI3**, [musk]melons; 207 Infs, **widespread, but more freq Sth, S Midl, N Atl**, Mushmelon; **IN35**, Banana mushmelons; **MS1, TX67**, [muʃ]melons; 21 Infs, **scattered**, Musmelons; **CA132**, ['mus,mɛlən, muʃ-]; **SC22**, [mʌst]melons; **VT16**, ['mʌsʔmɛlən]; **GA92**, ['mʌč'mɛlənz]; **IN19**, [mɝ·s]melons [Of all Infs responding to the question, 30% were gs educ or less; of those giving the response *mushmelon,* 50% were gs educ or less.]; (Qu. H56) Inf **IL55**, Muskmelon pickles; (Qu. H82a) Inf **KY34**, Mushmelon candy; (Qu. I4) Infs **CT2, MN3, NJ3, VA2**, Mushmelons; **VT2, 16**, Muskmelons; (Qu. I53) Inf **SC11**, Mushmelons; (Qu. L34) Inf **FL37**, Mushmelons. **1968** *PADS* 49.14 **Upper MW**, The schools tend to establish literary terms in place of or alongside indigenous folk terms. This influence is also evident in the following examples: . . the increasing use of *muskmelon* and the decline of *mushmelon*. **1983** *MJLF* 9.1.48 **ceKY** (as of 1956), Mushmellon.

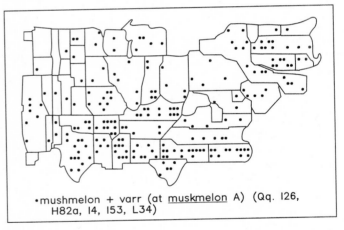

•mushmelon + varr (at <u>muskmelon</u> A) (Qq. I26, H82a, I4, I53, L34)

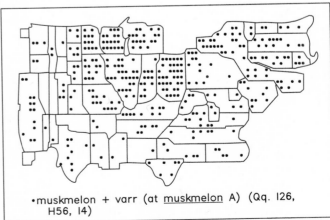

•muskmelon + varr (at <u>muskmelon</u> A) (Qq. I26, H56, I4)

B Std: a netted melon *(Cucumis melo* Reticulatus Group) which usu has a musky odor or flavor. For other names of varr or cultivars included in this Group see **banana melon, cue n[3] 2, French melon, guinea ~, honey rock ~** Cf **mango 1, 3, winter melon**

musk monkey flower See **musk plant**

musk mullein n Also *musk weed*

A **mullein** (here: *Verbascum thapsus*).

   1967–68 *DARE* (Qu. S20, *A common weed that grows on open hillsides: It has velvety green leaves close to the ground, and a tall stalk with small yellow flowers on a spike at the top*) Inf **PA**126, Fuzzy mullein; also called musk mullein. If you bend it down and touch the ground, and go back a week later, it will point towards your true love; **KS**5, Musk weed.

musk plant n Also *musk, ~ flower, ~ monkey flower* **scattered, but esp West**

A **monkey flower 1** (here: *Mimulus moschatus*).

   1857 Gray *Manual of Botany* 287, *M[imulus] moschatus*, the *Musk-plant*, from Oregon, [is] . . common in cultivation. **1900** Lyons *Plant Names* 249, *M[imulus] moschatus* . . Musk-flower, Musk plant, Vegetable musk. Plant has a musk-like odor. **1915** (1926) Armstrong–Thornber *Western Wild Flowers* 496, *Musk-plant*. . . This plant is more or less hairy and seems to be wet all over with slimy dew and smells of musk. **1937** St. John *Flora SE WA & ID* 374, Musk Flower. . . Introduced into cultivation . . because of its strong odor of musk, . . both the wild plants and the cultivated plants have now lost their odor. **1961** Peck *Manual OR* 706, *M[imulus] moschatus* . . Musk Monkey-flower. **1967** Gilkey–Dennis *Hdbk. NW Plants* 378, *Mimulus moschatus* . . Musk. **1970** *DARE* (Qu. S21, . . *Weeds . . that are a trouble in gardens and fields*) Inf **PA**234, Musk; (Qu. S26a, . . *Wildflowers . . Roadside flowers*) Inf **NY**232, Musk. **1979** Niering–Olmstead *Audubon Guide N. Amer. Wildflowers E. Region* 791, Muskflower (*Mimulus moschatus*).

musk rabbit See **marsh rabbit 2**

muskrat n Pronc-sp **chiefly Sth, S Midl** (See Map at **1** below) *musrat*; also *mussrat, mustrat* Cf Pronc Intro 3.I.14, 22

   1 also *musk cat*: An aquatic rodent (*Ondatra zibethica*) having a musky scent; also the fur or meat of this animal. Also called **bank rat, bottom cat, marsh hare, ~ rabbit 2, ~ rat 2, mud cat 2, ~ rat 2, mushrat 1, musky** n 1, **musquash, rat, water rat**

   1607 in 1910 Smith *Travels & Wks.* 1.lxix **VA**, There are Beares, . . Muskats [sic], and wild beasts vnknowne. **1666** (1972) Alsop *Character Province MD* 69, Furrs and Skins, as Beavers, Otters, Musk-Rats, . . were first made vendible by the *Indians* of the Country, and sold to the Inhabitant [sic]. **1688** in 1695 Royal Soc. London *Philos. Trans. for 1694* 18.123, *Musk-Rats*, in all things shaped like our Water-Rats, only something larger, and is an absolute Species of Water-Rats, only having a curious Musky scent. **1778** Carver *Travels N. Amer.* 455, The *Musquash*, or *Musk-rat*, is so termed for the exquisite musk which it affords. **1842** DeKay *Zool. NY* 1.76, The Musquash or Muskrat is so called from its strong musky odor, which is secreted from glands near the anus. It is a well-known inhabitant of our swamps and low grounds, and generally in every place in the vicinity of water. **1875** Holland *Sevenoaks* 237 **N Atl**, Ye couldn't eat 'im no more nor ye could a muss-rat. **1894** *Century Illustr. Mag.* 47.852, We have very naturally substituted "musk-rat" for [Indian] *musquash*. Many of the old writers say "musk-cat," and our frontiermen will have it "mush-rat." **1899** (1912) Green *VA Folk-Speech* 292, *Musrat*. . . Muskrat. A large, gnawing, fourfooted animal so called from its musky smell. Mussrat. Musquagh. *Musquash*. **1946** Dufresne *AK's Animals* 116, Food of the Alaska muskrats includes a wide variety of aquatic and marsh type vegetation. **1950** *WELS WI* (*Other names used locally for . . muskrat*) 32 Infs, Muskrat; 8 Infs, Muskrat, rat; 2 Infs, Muskrat, marsh rabbit(s); 2 Infs, Muskrat, mushrat; 1 Inf, Muskrat, water rat. **1961** Jackson *Mammals WI* 245, In Wisconsin usually called muskrat. Other names include . . mud cat, mushrat, musk beaver, musquash, mussacus [etc]. **1965–70** *DARE* (Qu. P31, . . *Names or nicknames . . for the . . muskrat*) 358 Infs, **widespread**, Muskrat; 17 Infs, **chiefly Sth, S Midl**, Musrat(s); **CA**195, Muskrat, mudrats; **DE**3, Muskrat, marsh rabbit, rat; **GA**18, Attic rat, muskrat; **IL**29, Muskrat—swamp rabbit used in southern Illinois; **MD**15, Muskrat—some people say marsh hare; **MD**26, Some people say muskrat, some say mushrat; **MD**40, Muskrat—most people say marsh rabbit; **NY**198, **VA**32, Muskrat, water rat; **NC**31, Mustrat ['mʌst,ræt]; **PA**58, Muskrats—eat them; **PA**121, Muskrat or musky; **PA**205, Muskrat, rat; **TN**65, Muskrat—called river rats by some; **WI**12, Muskrats—many times referred to as rats; **MA**55, Muskrat—real name; most of 'em call 'em musrat; (Qu. P29, . . *'Gophers' . . other name . . or what other animal are they most like*) Inf **TX**88, Muskrat; (Qu. P32, . . *Other kinds of wild animals*) Infs **IN**1, **OH**16, **PA**1, Muskrat. **1967** *DARE* Tape **MI**42, I sent the thing to E.W. Biggs down in Kansas City. . . I think I got 30 dollars out of that one. But a few muskrats and weasels and so forth—why, that was just

spending money! **1976** Garber *Mountain-ese* 59 **sAppalachians**, *Mussrat*. **1986** Pederson *LAGS Concordance* **Gulf Region**, 30 infs, Muskrat(s); 1 inf, Muskrat—has strong odor, but it's "sweet."

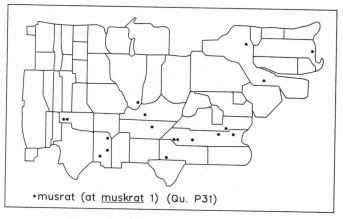

•musrat (at <u>muskrat</u> 1) (Qu. P31)

   2 =**round-tailed muskrat.**

   1917 Anthony *Mammals Amer.* 256, *Neofiber alleni*. . . While called a Musk-rat, this less familiar animal occupies a group by itself, intermediate between the smaller Mice and its big cousin the common Musk-rat. . . It is at home in both the fresh and salt-water marshes of Eastern Florida. **1927** Boston Soc. Nat. Hist. *Proc.* 38.360 **Okefenokee GA**, This unique little animal goes for the most part by the local names of 'Prairie-rat' and 'Water-rat'. . . Another name, used on Cowhouse Island, is 'Muskrat.' **1966–70** *DARE* (Qu. P31) Infs **FL**7, 20, 27, 51, Muskrat(s). [*DARE* Ed: Some of these Infs may refer instead to 1 above.]

   3 also attrib; also *mushrat*: Used as a derogatory term for a person; see quots. Cf **mushrat (around)**

   1845 Cist *Cincinnati Misc.* 1.240, The inhabitants of . . Delaware [are called] Muskrats. **1890** *Century Illustr. Mag.* 40.369 **seMI**, Her grandmother . . [had] a profound contempt for the "muskrats" as the Flats people are popularly called. **1915** *DN* 4.196, *Muskrat*, term of disparagement. "I am afraid you're a muskrat yourself." W. Lisenbee, *The Colonel's Experiment.* **1915** (1916) Johnson *Highways New Engl.* 268, She called me a mushrat and give me a slammin'. **1939** Faulkner *Wild Palms* 218 **MS**, If I took aboard every floating sardine can you son-abitchin mushrats want me to I wouldn't even have room forrard for a leadsman. **1967** Fetterman *Stinking Creek* 80 **seKY**, The "project work" is one of the many facets of the welfare program extended to the mountains. . . Its stated purpose was to provide aid for unemployed fathers. . . They are assigned to crews that clean up the creeks, cut weeds from the roads, and perform any other chores their assigned supervisors . . dream up. In the towns, the crews are called "muskrat gangs" or "happy pappies." **1979** *DARE* File **scMI**, A woman who grew up in Detroit, Michigan (born c1905) says when she was growing up that people who were part French and part Indian were called "muskrat French"—obviously a derogatory term. Probably suggested by the fact that they were said to eat muskrats. **1982** Slone *How We Talked* 43 **eKY** (as of c1950), A "happy pappy" or "mushrat" were [sic] men working on a government program for unemployed fathers. **1991** Kirlin–Kirlin *Smithsonian Folklife Cookbook* 175 **seMI**, Muskrat is trapped and eaten throughout the Great Lakes region, but perhaps nowhere with such significance and pride as in Monroe, Michigan. There, descendants of the area's early French community are known as "Mushrat French," a term that distinguishes them from Quebequois and French nationals.

muskrat duck n Cf **beaver duck**

=**ruddy duck.**

   1955 *AmSp* 30.178 **UT**, Muskrat duck . . this species [=*Oxyura jamaicensis*] reported from Utah. [*Ibid*, Because of the resemblance to . . fur of the thick down remaining on the bird's body after the ordinary feathers are plucked.]

muskrat mouse n

=**water shrew.**

   1961 Jackson *Mammals WI* 36, *Sorex palustris hydrobadistes*. . . Vernacular names.—In Wisconsin, when recognized, usually called water shrew. Other names include . . muskrat mouse.

muskrat potato n [See quot 1943]

An **arrowhead 1** (here: *Sagittaria latifolia*).

   1913 *Torreya* 13.227, *Sagittaria latifolia*. . . This is the famous wapato, wappatoo, or duck potato of the Northwestern States. It is known as the Chinese onion, and muskrat potato at Oshkosh, Wis. [**1943** Fernald–Kinsey *Edible Wild Plants E. N. Amer.* 87, All our species of *Arrow-head* produce late in the autumn hard, potato-like tubers at the ends of long, subterranean runners. *Ibid* 89, Ordinarily the tubers are so remote from the parent-plant that the Indians depended largely upon the stores of them which they found already assembled by muskrats.]

muskrat root n
=**sweet flag.**

> **1963** *DE Folkl. Bulletin* 1.37, I have watched them [=Nanticoke Indians] dig up muskrat root *(acorus calamus)* for use as a tea in curing colds.

muskrat weed n Also *musquash weed*

1 A **water hemlock** such as **spotted cowbane,** or a similar umbelliferous plant. Cf **musquash root**

> **1767** *Boston News-Letter* (MA) 21 May 3/1, Persons (especially Children) would do well to beware of this Weed: It is called wild Hemlock by some, and Musquash weed by others: It grows in low Lands, especially by running Water. **1830** Rafinesque *Med. Flora* 2.264, *Water Parsnep.* Several wild sp. . . *S[ium] rugosum* . . called *Muskrat weed,* because muskrats feed on it, and Indians bait the traps with it. Roots tuberose, poisonous to men, but boiled useful for tumors and bruises. **1964** Kingsbury *Poisonous Plants U.S.* 373, *Cicuta spp.* Water hemlock. The most useful common name of this genus is water hemlock. In appearance the plant is not easily distinguished from several other members of the family Umbelliferae. A profusion of common names, locally applied, has resulted. Among such names are . . muskrat weed, . . musquash root [etc].

2 A **meadow rue** (here: *Thalictrum pubescens*).

> **1892** *Jrl. Amer. Folkl.* 5.91 **MA,** *Thalictrum polygamum* . . muskrat-weed; musquash weed. **1896** *Ibid* 9.180 **ME,** *Thalictrum polygamum* . . musquash weed. **1900** Lyons *Plant Names* 368, *[Thalictrum] polygamum* . . Muskrat-weed, Musquash-weed, Rattlesnake-bite. **1976** Bailey-Bailey *Hortus Third* 1105, *[Thalictrum] polygamum* . . Muskrat weed.

muskroom See **mushroom**

musk root n
Moschatel *(Adoxa moschatellina).*

> **1906** Rydberg *Flora CO* 324, *Muskroot.* . . In shady, wet, rocky places. **1959** Anderson *Flora AK* 433, *A[doxa] moschatellina.* . . Moschatel. Musk Root. . . Circumpolar, south to Wis.—Iowa—Colo. **1973** Hitchcock–Cronquist *Flora Pacific NW* 454, Musk-root. . . Delicate herb with a musky odor.

musk turtle n Also *musk terrapin, ~ tortoise* [See quot 1979]

1 A turtle of the genus *Sternotherus,* esp *S. odoratus.* Also called **mud turtle 2b(2), skillpot, stinking jim, stinkpot.** For other names of var spp see **loggerhead musk turtle, razor-backed musk turtle**

> **1792** in 1849 Darlington *Mem. John Bartram* 474, Of these [=tortoises] I have gathered the shells, and would be exceeding glad to get some more. I have the Snapper, Land Turtle or *Carolina,* L., . . dotted, musk, Terrapin, the running, or your *cœlata* . . ; and miss one, which comes near to the Musk T., only that the under shell is wholly shut up. **1838** Geol. Surv. OH *Second Annual Rept.* 167, Emys odorata . . *Musk Tortoise.* **1842** DeKay *Zool. NY* 3.23, The *Musk Tortoise* . . is to be found in most of our ponds and ditches. It occurs from Maine to Florida, but its western limits are unknown. . . It appears to be an active, vigorous animal, biting with considerable vigor when irritated. **1868** (1869) *Amer. Naturalist* 2.330 **eMA,** The Turtle which you sent . . is the "Musk Turtle," *Aromochelys odoratum.* **1908** Biol. Soc. DC *Proc.* 21.79, *Texas Musk Turtle.* **1911** *Century Dict. Suppl.,* Musk-terrapin. . . The musk-turtle. . . The name includes several small ill-smelling fresh-water turtles of the genera *Aromochelys* and *Cinosternon,* widely distributed in the United States. **1926** TX Folkl. Soc. *Pub.* 5.58, The musk turtle. . . bears a rather unsavory reputation due to its mephitine odor. **1941** Writers' Program *Guide AR* 17, Reptiles other than snakes are the turtles—mud, snapping, box and musk (or stinkpot). **1968** *DARE* (Qu. P24, . . *Kinds of turtles)* Inf **LA**31, The musk turtle also has smell, but is not ill-tempered. **1968** *DARE* FW Addit **LA,** Musk turtle (with hinged undershell), tortue musquée, a small turtle not much favored for eating. **1979** Behler–King *Audubon Field Guide Reptiles* 438, All musk and mud turtles have 2 pairs of musk glands. . . The secretions are very offensive, thus the common names "stinkpot," . . "musk turtle." *Ibid* 443, *Razor-backed Musk Turtle.* . . Quite shy, unlike other musk turtles; it rarely

bites or expels musk. *Ibid* 445, *Sternotherus odoratus.* . . Also called Musk Turtle. . . Males are aggressive and bite readily. **1986** Pederson *LAGS Concordance,* 1 inf, **neFL,** Musk turtle.

2 =**mud turtle 2b(1).**

> [**1842** DeKay *Zool. NY* 3.22, Like the *odoratus,* it [=Kinosternon subrubrum ssp hippocrepis] has a strong musky smell.] **1911** [see **1** above]. **1930** *Copeia* 1.37 **OK,** *Kinosternon subrubrum hippocrepis* . . Musk-turtle; mud-turtle. . . Reported . . from Tulsa County. **1979** [see **1** above].

musk weed See **musk mullein**

musky adj [Cf Intro "Language Changes" IV.4] **chiefly Sth, S Midl; scattered NEast** See Map Cf **funky 1a**
Musty, moldy-smelling.

> **1965–70** *DARE* (Qu. X17, . . *A damp cellar that had been shut up for some time would smell* _____) 48 Infs, **chiefly Sth, S Midl; scattered NEast,** Musky.

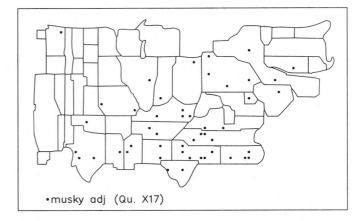

•musky adj (Qu. X17)

musky n

1 =**muskrat 1.**

> **1781** Pennant *Hist. Quadrupeds* 2.476, Shrew. . . Musky. . . Muscovy or Musk rat. **1967–69** *DARE* (Qu. P31, . . *Names or nicknames . . for the . . muskrat)* Inf **GA**72, Musky, mushrat; **MA**1, Muskies; **NE**11, Musky; **PA**121, Muskrat or musky.

2 See **muskellunge 1.**

musky mint n
A tall, aromatic plant *(Hyptis alata)* with small, dense heads of white flowers. Also called **desert lavender**

> **1976** Fleming *Wild Flowers FL* 27, *Hyptis alata.* . . Musky mint blooms all year, weather permitting, and grows in moist pinelands, swamps, and hammocks from Florida to Texas, North Carolina, and the West Indies. **1982** *Miami Herald* (FL) 24 Oct sec H 10 **FL,** We begin to cross the first prairie, and. . . we find musky mint, a square-stemmed plant with little white balls of flowers.

musmelon See **muskmelon**

musquash n Also aphet *squash;* for addit varr see quots [Algonquian] **chiefly C and N Atl, esp NEng**
=**muskrat 1.**

> [**1588** (1903) Hariot *Briefe Rept.* *VA* sig D2ʳ, *Saquenúckot & Maquo'woc;* two kindes of small beastes greater than conies which are very good meat.] **c1612** (1849) Strachey *Hist. VA Britannia* 123, Muscascus is a beast black in collour, proportioned like a water ratt. **1637** (1972) Morton *New Engl. Canaan* 80, The Muskewashe, is a beast that frequenteth the ponds. **1672** Josselyn *New-Englands Rarities* 53, There is a little Beast called a *Muskquash* . . their Cods sent as sweet and as strong as Musk. **1774** Goldsmith *Hist. Earth* 3.380, But the smell of our weasels, and ermines, and polecats, is fragrance itself when compared to that of the *squash,* and the *skink,* which have been called the Polecats of America. **1792** Belknap *Hist. NH* 3.161, The *musquash (castor zibethicus)* builds a cabin of sticks and mud in a shallow pond. **1838** Kettell *Yankee Notions* 127, Cotch [=caught] a 'tarnal great musquash this forenoon. **1842** DeKay *Zool. NY* 1.76, The Musquash or Muskrat is so called from its strong musky odor, which is secreted from glands near the anus. **1883** Eggleston *Hoosier Schoolboy* 175 **IN,** Jack, who had lived for years on the banks of the Wildcat, could swim and dive like a musquash. **1894** [see **muskrat 1**]. **1899** [see **muskrat 1**].

1904 *DN* 2.427 **Cape Cod MA** (as of a1857), *Musquash*. . . Muskrat. **1969** *DARE* (Qu. P31, . . *Names or nicknames . . for the . . muskrat*) Inf **MA**68, Indians called them ['mʌš,skwǒš].

musquash root n Also *musquash poison* Cf **beaver poison, muskrat weed 1**
=**spotted cowbane.**

    1807 *Thomas' MA Spy or Worcester Gaz.* (MA) 22 July [3]/4, Five children were lately poisoned in Scipio (Newyork) by eating *Wild Parsnip*, or *Musquash Root.* **1840** *MA Zool. & Bot. Surv. Herb. Plants & Quadrupeds* 16, *C[icuta] maculata* . . Water Parsnip. Musquash Root. **1900** Lyons *Plant Names* 101, *C[icuta] maculata*. . . Musquash-root, Beaver-poison, . . Musquash-poison. **1930** *OK Univ. Biol. Surv. Pub.* 2.74, *Cicuta maculata* L. Water Hemlock. Musquash-poison. **1955** U.S. Arctic Info. Center *Gloss.* 54, *Musquash root.* Spotted cowbane. **1975** Hamel–Chiltoskey *Cherokee Plants* 31, Musquash root, poison hemlock, water hemlock. . . *Suicide to eat large quantities.* Chew and swallow roots for four consecutive days to become sterile forever; old timers used this to find out how long they would live, if they got dizzy chewing the roots they would die soon, if not they would live a long time.

musquash weed See **muskrat weed**

musquet(o), musquit(e) See **mesquite**

musquito n[1] See **mesquite**

musquito n[2] See **mosquito** n[1]

musrat See **muskrat**

muss See **musk** n 1

mussel n

    1 Std: a marine bivalve mollusk of the family Mytilidae. See also **meadow mussel**

    2 also sp *muscle:* A **freshwater clam** of the family Unionidae. **chiefly Midl, Gulf States** See also **creek mussel**

      1804 (1904) Clark *Orig. Jrls. Lewis & Clark Exped.* 1.110, This creek [near Dakota City NE] . . is Crouded with large Musstles verry fat. **1820** Rafinesque *Ohio R. Fishes* 24, It feeds . . principally on the muscles, or various species of the bivalve genus *Unio* so common in the Ohio. **1843** DeKay *Zool. NY* 5.188, *Genus Unio*. . . The shells of this and the other genera are popularly known under the names of *Freshwater clams* and *mussels.* **1886** Mather *Memoranda* 42 **Adirondacks NY,** *Mussels.* (Unios.) . . I do not know the species and do not think they affect fish life in any way. . . Some of the specimens were quite large (four inches). **1908** Kunz–Stevenson *Book of the Pearl* 75, On the Atlantic seaboard of America, the Anodontas, or "mussels," as they are known locally, are more numerous than the Unios. **1933** LA Dept. of Conserv. *Fishes* 416, The Shovelnose happens to be the only fish host known to carry the parasitic glochidia stages of one of the Mississippi mussels. **1941** Writers' Program *Guide AR* 207, Dredging the White River and its tributaries for fresh-water mussels used for button making affords farmers a part-time occupation. **1950** *WELS* **WI** (*What kinds of shellfish are common in your neighborhood?*) 1 Inf, Freshwater mussel; [15 Infs, Clam]. **1953** (1977) Hubbard *Shantyboat* 211 **Missip-Ohio Valleys,** Fresh-water pearls are often found in mussel shells, occasionally one of considerable value. **1955** *AmSp* 30.75 **cwTN** [Musseling terms], *Drag*. . . A movement across the mussel beds. **1965–70** *DARE* (Qu. P18, . . *Kinds of shellfish*) 139 Infs, **chiefly Midl, Gulf States,** Mussel(s); **VA**8, Creek mussels; **ME**8, **MS**66, **OH**82, Freshwater mussels; **AR**41, Mussel shells. [*DARE* Ed: Included here are Infs who specifically identified these as freshwater mussels and those who did not identify them as saltwater mussels. A few Infs may refer instead to **1** above.]

mussel-bill n Also sp *muscle-bill*
=**surf scoter.**

    1888 Trumbull *Names of Birds* 103, *Surf scoter*. . . To some at Kennebunk, Me., *Muscle-bill.* **1925** (1928) Forbush *Birds MA* 1.277, *Surf Scoter.* Other names . . *Mussel-bill.* **1982** Elman *Hunter's Field Guide* 240, *Surf Scoter* . . Common & regional names . . mussel-bill.

mussel-digger n Also sp *muscle-digger*
=**gray whale.**

    1860 *Merc. Marine Mag.* 7.213 (*OED*), It being difficult to capture them, they have a variety of names among whalemen, as . . 'Muscle digger', 'Hard-head', &c. **1888** Kingsley *Riverside Nat. Hist.* 5.197 **Pacific,** The gray whale has received many curious titles, such as "hard-head," "mussel-digger," "devil-fish," and "gray-back." **1911** *Century Dict.* 3911, *Mussel-digger* . . The California gray whale, *Rhachianectes*

glaucus: so called from the fact that it descends to soft bottoms in search of food, or for other purposes, and returns to the surface with its head besmeared with the dark ooze from the depths.

mussel duck n [*EDD* 1862 →]
=**greater scaup.**

    1888 Trumbull *Names of Birds* 55 **seNY,** The greater scaup is distinguished on Long Island at Shinnecock Bay and Moriches as *Bay Broadbill.* . . Another name once common about Shinnecock Bay, but now seldom heard, is *mussel-duck.* **1917** (1923) *Birds Amer.* 1.135, Scaup Duck. . . *Other Names.*—Mussel Duck [etc]. **1982** Elman *Hunter's Field Guide* 206, Greater Scaup . . Common & Regional Names: . . laker, lake bluebill, mussel duck [etc].

mussel-eater n Also sp *muscle-eater* Cf **gaspergou 1**
=**freshwater drum.**

    1820 Rafinesque *Ohio R. Fishes* 24, Grunting Bubbler. *Amblodon grunniens*. . . The vulgar names of this fish are . . bubbling-fish, bubbler, and muscle-eater. . . It feeds on many species of fishes, Suckers, Catfishes, Sunfishes, &c., but principally on the muscles, or various species of the bivalve genus *Unio* so common in the Ohio, whose thick shells it is enabled to crush by means of its large throat teeth. **1890** *Century Dict.* 3911, *Mussel-eater*. . . The buffalo perch, *Aplodinotus grunniens*, of the Mississippi valley.

mussel-head n [Perh for *muscle-head;* cf *bonehead, meathead*]
See quots.

    1953 Randolph–Wilson *Down in Holler* 266 **Ozarks,** *Mussel-head*. . . One who is slow witted, not too intelligent. **1954** *Harder Coll.* **cwTN,** Mussel-head. . . A slow-witted person.

mussel-mucker n Cf **mudlark** v
One who drags for **freshwater clams.**

    1938 *FWP Guide IA* 328 **seIA,** The pearl trader was rarely honest; his tricks and deceptions were numerous. His business was conducted in any river town where the "mussel muckers" brought their pearls.

mussel worm n Cf **he-clam**
A marine worm of the genus *Nereis.*

    1967 *DARE* (Qu. P6, . . *Kinds of worms . . used for bait*) Inf **CA**23, Mussel worms—they grow under the rocks. **1989** Mickelson *Nat. Hist.* 36 **AK,** The "mat" of mussels provides a protective habitat for . . mussel worms (which look like foot-long centipedes).

mussrat See **muskrat**

mussy n [Prob var of *musty*]

    1966–70 *DARE* (Qu. X17, . . *A damp cellar that had been shut up for some time would smell* _____) Infs **MD**21, **MS**45, **VA**39, Mussy.

must vbl aux

    1 Shall, may—used in interrog constrs. [Cf *EDD must* v.³ "3. May. . . 4. Shall."] *old-fash*

      1895 *DN* 1.376 **seKY, eTN, wNC,** *Must* = shall. (Invariably used for questions.) **1905** *DN* 3.88 **nwAR,** *Must, aux. v.* Shall, am. . . to. 'Must I put the breakfast on now?' Not uncommon.

    2 Used as the first member of a multiple modal or a non-std multiple auxiliary. **chiefly Sth** *esp freq among Black speakers* Cf **ain't** v[1] **5, ain't must, may** v B, **must be**

      1943 Writers' Program NC *Bundle of Troubles* 68 [Black], Iffen you *got* to do it, then you jes *must kin.* **1967** *DARE* (Qu. P9) Inf **LA**7, Fish must ain't bitin'; (Qu. U17) Inf **LA**6, I'd say he must ain't gon' pay me. [Both Infs Black] **1971** Mitchell *Blow My Blues Away* 159 **nwMS** [Black], Well, that man must can do something. Them men's toting him in. **1972** Kochman *Rappin'* 206 [Black], Man, you must don't know who I am. **1986** Pederson *LAGS Concordance,* 1 inf, **swGA,** You must ain't never been around nobody crazy; 1 inf, **cwFL,** He must can smell; 1 inf, **swAL,** I must not can see = must not be able to see; 1 inf, **neLA,** My wife must ain't seen me; 1 inf, **ceTX,** I must don't = I must not. [4 of 5 infs Black] **1986** Montgomery–Bailey *Lang. Var. in South* 298 **TX,** He must wouldn't steal, would he? **1991** *DARE* File **SC,** That must didn't hurt him cause he's still in the lead.

mustang n

    1 A **blue curls 1** (here: *Trichostema lanceolatum*).

      1911 CA Ag. Exper. Sta. Berkeley *Bulletin* 217.1022, *Trichostema lancealatum* [sic]. . . Mustang (Sacramento County). . . The bulk of this honey goes to biscuit manufacturers.

    2 See **mustang grape.**

mustang clover n

A **gilia** (here: *Linanthus montanus*).

1925 Jepson *Manual Plants CA* 806, *L[inanthus] montanus* . . Mustang Clover. . . Sierra Nevada from Calaveras Co. to Tulare Co. **1959** Munz–Keck *CA Flora* 513, *L[inanthus] montanus.* . . Mustang-Clover.

mustang grape n Also *mustang* **chiefly TX, OK**

A **grape,** usu *Vitis mustangensis.* For other names of this sp see **leatherleaf grape**

1846 (1941) Gregg *Diary* 1.239 **TX,** There is a large species, called by the Americans, the *Mustang grape* which very much resembles the Muscadine of the western country, except in growing in large bunches or racemes. **1854** in 1878 Longfellow *Poems* 221, The red Mustang,/ Whose clusters hang / O'er the waves of the Colorado. **1860** Curtis *Cat. Plants NC* 113, *Muscadine.* (V[itis] vulpina . .). Known also . . in Florida, as *Mustang Grape.* **1886** Havard *Flora W. & S. TX for 1885* 511, *Vitis candicans* . . (Mustang Grape.) . . The best of the wild Texas Grapes. **1903** (1965) Adams *Log Cowboy* 6 **TX,** Though the fig tree was absent, along the river grew endless quantities of mustang grapes. **1920** Torreya 20.23, *Vitis munsoniana.* . . Everbearing, bird or mustang grape. **1953** Greene–Blomquist *Flowers South* 72, Mustang-grape *(V. candicans)* of Ark., Okla., and Tex. is represented in Fla. . . by the variety coriacea known as leather-leaf or caloosa-grape. **1960** Carpenter *Tales Manchaca* 100 **cTX** (as of 1958), Here is a list of the resources: wild pecans, mustang grapes, wild onions on the creek, [etc]. **1967–70** *DARE* (Qu. I46, . . *Kinds of fruits that grow wild around here*) Infs **TX**12, 13, 40, Mustang grapes; (Qu. I53, . . *Fruits grown around here . . special varieties*) Inf **TX**85, Mustang grapes. **1967** *DARE* Tape **TX**47, Mustang grapes grew better on live oak than anything else. **c1970** McDavid *Coll.* **csOK,** Mustang, post oak grapes. **1974** (1977) Coon *Useful Plants* 268, *V[itis] candicans:* Mustang grape—Arkansas to Texas.

mustang mint n

A **pennyroyal** (here: *Monardella lanceolata*).

1911 Jepson *Flora CA* 363, *M[onardella] lanceolata.* . . Mustang Mint. . . Sierra Nevada foothills. **1915** (1926) Armstrong–Thornber *Western Wild Flowers* 436, *Mustang Mint.* . . An attractive plant, pretty in color and form. **1949** Moldenke *Amer. Wild Flowers* 296, The *mustangmint.* . . The plants in full bloom resemble gorgeous, purple-tipped candelabra.

mustang persimmon n *obs*

=**black persimmon.**

1846 (1941) Gregg *Diary* 1.239 **TX,** Among other wild fruits of this vicinity, that called by Mexicans *chapote* and generally by Americans, black persimmon (or Mexican or Mustang persimmon) a black fruit about half the bulk of the common persimmon, much the same shape, and of very pleasant sweet flavor, when perfectly ripe.

mustard and pepper See **hot pepper**

mustard pickle n **chiefly Nth, N Midl, West** See Map

Pickled cucumbers, cabbage, or mixed vegetables flavored with mustard; the pickling medium itself.

1871 (1975) Levy *Jewish Cookery* 146, *Mustard pickle.*—Take a quarter of a pound of turmeric, one ounce of mace, one of cloves, one pound of English mustard, two gallons of the best vinegar, and one pint of mustard seed. . . [P]ut some cabbage in salt water for three days, then lay it in the sun for three days . . , and it is ready for the above pickle. **1932** Stieff *Eat in MD* 248, *Mustard Pickle* . . green tomatoes . . cauliflower . . green peppers . . small cucumbers . . small onions . . flour . . mustard . . turmeric. . . vinegar . . sugar. **1937** Sandoz *Slogum* 20 **wNE,** Usually she brought in a little something extra, perhaps a tall dish of wild-grape jelly or a glass of mustard pickles. **1939** Wolcott *Yankee Cook Book* 291 **cnCT,** *Mustard Pickles* . . green tomatoes . . cauliflower . . red peppers . . white pickling onions . . sweet gherkins . . mustard . . turmeric . . vinegar. **1965–70** *DARE* (Qu. H56, *Names for . . pickles*) 107 Infs, **chiefly Nth, N Midl, West,** Mustard (pickle(s)); **MI**96, Mixed mustard pickles; **MN**33, Sweet mustard pickles; [**CA**15, Pickles in mustard;] (Qu. H57, *Tasty or spicy side-dishes served with meats*) Infs **KY**63, **MA**48, **MN**11, **NJ**8, **RI**16, **SC**38, Mustard pickle(s). **1968** *DARE* Tape **NY**123, Some women, in cans, made mustard pickle, which denoted a little bit higher social strata because you could afford to have some cauliflower and some of the more unusual vegetables that you had to go out and buy. **1968** *DARE* FW Addit **cNY,** Mustard pickles—have yellowed tint—includes types with only sliced cucumbers and those with other vegetables included.

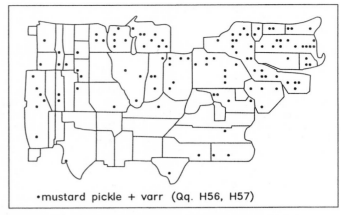

•mustard pickle + varr (Qq. H56, H57)

mustart n [Pronc-sp for *mustard;* cf Pronc Intro 3.I.15]

1988 Kingsolver *Bean Trees* 56 **KY,** The heat's done put that baby into a colic. He needs a mustart plaster to draw out the heat.

must be adv phr [By analogy with *maybe*] *among Black speakers* Cf **must 2**

Surely, certainly.

1927 Kennedy *Gritny* 13 **sLA** [Black], You mus' be got some news to tell. *Ibid* 149, Yo' stummic mus' be ain' workin' right. **1986** Pederson *LAGS Concordance,* 1 inf, **seGA,** His time must be was out. [Inf Black] **1994** *AmSp* 69.62 **seSC** [Gullah], [dɛ: mʌs bi dɪs put ʌm dɛ: ɪnɪ] . . 'They must have just put it there, mustn't they?' *Ibid* 69, [Footnote:] An alternative constituent order in this construction places [mʌs bi] sentence initially, which is not possible with the modal [mʌs] alone: [mʌs bi dɛ: dɪs put um dɛ: ɪnɪ]. *Ibid* 62, [dɛm gɛ˞ta mʌsbi kuda go fast] . . 'Those alligators must have been able to go ~ move fast.'

muster v [Cf *EDD muster* sb.[1] 4 "A litter."]

To give birth; hence nouns *(general) muster* childbirth.

1774 in 1915 *New Engl. Hist. & Geneal. Reg.* 69.122 **MA,** Jonas Parkers wife mustered & had a son Born. **1968** McPhee *Pine Barrens* 31 **NJ,** In the idiom of the community . . childbirth was spoken of as a muster or a general muster.

muster-John-Henry n

A naturalized marigold *(Tagetes minuta)* used as a seasoning.

1943 Fernald–Kinsey *Edible Wild Plants E. N. Amer.* 361, *Tagetes minuta.* . . *Muster John-Henry,* as it is universally called in southeastern Virginia and eastern North Carolina, . . is seen in the yards of most colored families . . ; it is generally used to season soups and broths. **1950** Gray–Fernald *Manual of Botany* 1514, *T[agetes] minuta.* . . *Muster John Henry.* . . Locally abundant, S.C. to se. Va. (where cult. for seasoning); occasionally n. to Mass. **1976** Bailey–Bailey *Hortus Third* 1095, *Muster-John-Henry.* . . Naturalized in e. U.S. . . Occasionally cult. for seasoning or medicinal uses.

must-marriage n Also *must-job, must-to* Cf **have-to**

See quot 1950.

1950 *WELS* (*A marriage that takes place because a baby is on the way*) 1 Inf, **ceWI,** Must-marriage; [1 Inf, **ceWI,** A must]. **1967–70** *DARE* (Qu. AA20) Inf **PA**243, Must-job; **TX**31, Must-marriage; **PA**139, Must-to; [**CA**53, **PA**110, A must].

mustrat See **muskrat**

must-to See **must-marriage**

musty adj[1] Also *musty-colored*

1966–69 *DARE* (Qu. K38, *A horse of a dirty white color*) Inf **FL**12, Smutty, musty; **GA**74, Musty-colored.

musty adj[2] *joc* Cf **moreish, taste like more**

1994 *DARE* File **IA,** "How is the pie?" our hostess asked. "It tastes musty," my father replied. When our hostess had registered a suitably shocked expression, Dad grinned and said, "Yep, tastes musty—must have more."

mustydine See **muscadine (grape)**

mutton See **mutton corn**

mutton bluegrass See **mutton grass**

Muttonburg See **Muttontown**

745

mutton cane / mutton-sass

mutton cane n [Cf **mutton corn**]
1 The young shoots of giant cane (*Arundinacea gigantea*) or **switch cane.**

1901 Mohr *Plant Life AL* 103, The seedlings [of *Arundinacea gigantea*] produce no branches during the first year. These simple sprouts, which are known as "mutton cane," are tender and sweet and afford the best of pasturage. **1908** *Sat. Eve. Post* 8 Aug 3 **LA**, Through the gentle springtime he finds little to eat except bugs, ash-buds and tender shoots called "mutton-cane." **1911** [see **2** below]. **1950** *PADS* 14.45 **SC**, *Mutton cane.* . . Early growth of cane, excellent for forage.
2 A **panic grass** (here: *Dichanthelium dichotomum*).

1911 *Century Dict. Suppl., Cane.* . . *Mutton cane. (a)* The seedlings of the large and small canes which furnish good pasture and which are specially sought by bears. [*Century* Ed: Alabama.] *(b)* A slender panic-grass, *Panicum dichotomum,* a valuable native forage for sheep in the southern United States.

mutton conductor See **mutton puncher**

mutton corn n Also *mutton (ear)* [Perh folk-etym form of Scots *mauten;* cf 1840 *DSL mauten, mawten* "Applied to grain that has sprung in the sheaf from damp"] **chiefly S Atl, esp SC** Cf **mutton cane**

Indian corn 1 that is just mature enough to be eaten.
[**1707** Sloane *Voyage* 1.xix **Jamaica**, *Indian* Corn or Maiz . . is fed on by the Slaves, especially the young Ears of it, before ripe, are rosted under the Coals and eaten; this is thought by them very delicious, and call'd Mutton.] **1821** James *Sketch* 139 **SC**, [Green corn is] commonly called *mutton* corn, a corruption of *matin,* that is *early* corn. **1859** O'Neall *Annals Newberry* 56 **SC**, Ears of green corn (called in the upper country roasting ears, in the lower country, mutton corn,) boiled, were on the table at dinner. **1897** (1952) McGill *Narrative* 44 **cSC**, Coons were caught in fields in mutton corn time. **1930** *DN* 6.82 **cSC**, *Mutton corn.* . . Green corn. . . The expression is used by even the most educated and cultured members of the community with no feeling that it is at all dialectically [sic] used. Its use is restricted to a locality having a diameter of about thirty miles. **1938** Rawlings *Yearling* 118 **nFL**, There was early mutton corn. The Baxters seldom ate new corn, for all that was raised seemed more desperately needed for the stock. **c1940** *LAMSAS Materials,* [12 infs, 5 **eGA**, 4 **c,eSC**, 3 **eNC**, Mutton corn; 1 inf, **eGA**, Mutton ears; 1 inf, **eSC**, Mutton.] **1945** *PADS* 3.11 **SC**, *Roasting-ear.* . . Is never heard; everyone says *mutton corn.* **1950** *PADS* 14.48 **SC**, *Mutton corn.* . . Early Indian corn, still in the milk used for the table; roasting ears. Old Santee French *matin,* i.e. early. **1955** *PADS* 23.45 **e,cSC, eNC, seGA**, *Mutton corn* 'green corn' (also n.e. Florida). **1966–67** *DARE* (Qu. I33, . . *Ears of corn that are just right for eating*) Infs **FL**19, **SC**19, 22, 26, 38, 43, 62, Mutton corn; **FL**36, Mutton ears. **1986** Pederson *LAGS Concordance* **AL, FL, GA** *(Sweet corn)* 3 infs, Mutton corn = roasting ears; 3 infs, Mutton corn; 1 inf, Mutton corn = young field corn; 1 inf, Mutton corn—grains smaller than on roasting ear; 1 inf, Mutton corn—heard of, it may be cut off the cob; 1 inf, Mutton corn—not sure what it is; heard of it.

mutton-cut (sail) See **mutton-ham sail**

mutton ear See **mutton corn**

muttonfish n
1 also *mutton snapper:* A **snapper** (here: *Lutjanus analis*). Also called **pargo, red snapper**
[**1735** Mortimer in Royal Soc. London *Philos. Trans.* 39.112, The Mutton-Fish. This is reckon'd one of the most delicate Fish of the Bahama Islands.] **1743** Catesby *Nat. Hist. Carolina* 2.25, *Anthea quartus Rondeletii.* . . The Mutton Fish. . . The Shape of this Fish in general resembles That of a Pearch; For the Excellency of it's Tast it is in greater Esteem than any other at the *Bahama Islands. Ibid* 2 [app] xliii, Mutton Snapper. **1775** (1962) Romans *Nat. Hist. FL* lii, These most commonly caught are such as seamen know by the following names, viz. *King-fish, baracoota,* . . *mutton-fish.* **1898** U.S. Natl. Museum *Bulletin* 47.1265, *Neomaenis analis* . . Mutton-fish; Pargo. **1939** Natl. Geogr. Soc. *Fishes* 194, The Muttonfish (*Lutianus analis*) attains a weight of 25 pounds. It is an excellent food fish known from Brazil to Florida. It strays as far north as Massachusetts. **1966** *DARE* (Qu. P2, . . *Kinds of saltwater fish caught around here* . . *good to eat*) Inf **FL**24, Mutton snapper. **1986** Pederson *LAGS Concordance,* 1 inf, **swFL**, Muttonfish. **1991** Amer. Fisheries Soc. *Common Names Fishes* 53, *Lutjanus analis* . . A[tlantic] . . mutton snapper.

2 An **eelpout 1** (here: *Macrozoarces anguillaris*). [See quot 1884]
1882 U.S. Natl. Museum *Bulletin* 16.784, *Z[oarces] anguillaris;* Eelpout; Mutton-fish; Mother of Eels. **1884** Goode *Fisheries U.S.* 1.247, It [=*Zoarces anguillaris*] is occasionally eaten by the Cape Ann fishermen, by whom it is known as the Mutton-fish, the name referring to a supposed resemblance of its flesh to mutton; and I can myself testify to the delicacy of its flavor. **1955** U.S. Arctic Info. Center *Gloss.* 54, Muttonfish. . . A name sometimes applied in error to the ling and eelpout. **1966** *DARE* (Qu. P4, *Saltwater fish that are not good to eat*) Inf **ME**22, Skates, eels, muttonfish. **1991** Amer. Fisheries Soc. *Common Names Fishes* 152, Muttonfish—see ocean pout.
3 =**Irish pompano.**
1896 U.S. Bur. Fisheries *Rept. for 1895* 392, Irish Pompano; Mutton Fish. West Indies north to southern Florida. **1898** U.S. Natl. Museum *Bulletin* 47.1376, *Gerres olisthostomus* . . Irish Pompano; Mutton Fish. **1902** Jordan–Evermann *Amer. Fishes* 448, *G[erres] olisthostomus,* the Irish pompano or mutton-fish, is abundant through the West Indies, south to Brazil and north to southern Florida. It reaches a foot in length and is of some value as a food-fish.
4 =**lingcod 1.**
1955 [see **2** above].

mutton grass n Also *mutton bluegrass* [See quot 1937]
A **bluegrass 1** (here: *Poa fendleriana*).
1911 *Century Dict. Suppl., Mutton-grass.* . . A blue-grass, *Poa Fendleriana,* found on mesas and dry hills from Colorado to Arizona and California. It is valuable for grazing, as is suggested by the name. **1912** Wooton–Standley *Grasses NM* 122, *Mutton Grass (Poa fendleriana)* is really the only native species . . that is of much economic value in New Mexico. **1937** U.S. Forest Serv. *Range Plant Hdbk.* G100, Muttongrass, also called . . mutton bluegrass, is one of the most widely distributed and important of native bluegrasses. . . The common name muttongrass is very appropriate, as it is one of the most nutritious forage plants in Arizona and New Mexico, being prized for fattening sheep. **1952** Davis *Flora ID* 121, *Mutton Grass.* . . South to S.D., Tex., and Calif. **1961** Douglas *My Wilderness* 29 **CO**, The canyons are thick with many grasses, sedges, and rushes. . . Timothy and mutton bluegrass are abundant. **1974** Munz *Flora S. CA* 994, Muttongrass. . . 3,000–10,100 ft.

mutton-ham sail n Also *mutton-ham, mutton-cut (sail)* [Varr of *leg-of-mutton sail*] **eNC**
A triangular sail; a boat with such a sail; hence n *mutton-ham boat.*
1899 *Atlantic Mth.* 84.197 **eNC**, In a Mutton-Ham Boat. . . Her mutton-ham fluttered as white as new cotton around her single mast. I more than once sought to learn why Albermarle and Pamlico fishing smacks call their huge sails "mutton-ham," and was invariably assured that "they was jes' named that-a-way, an' reckon tha' wa'n't no reason fo' it." **1946** *PADS* 6.21 **eNC** (as of 1900–10), *Mutton-ham sail.* . . A triangular sail used on a bug-eye boat. . . Common. **1966** *DARE* (Qu. O9, . . *Kinds of sailboats*) Inf **NC**21, Mutton-cut—named for the sails. **1966** *DARE* Tape **NC**21, I had a spritsail and then I had a mutton-cut sail . . and I thoroughly enjoyed 'em, in fact I never did capsize one but I came very near it several times.

mutton hound n
1968 *DARE* (Qu. J2, . . *Joking or uncomplimentary words* . . *for dogs*) Inf **WV**1, Mutton hounds—kill sheep; **WV**13, Mutton hound.

Muttonjerk See **Muttontown**

mutton puncher n Also *mutton conductor* [By analogy with **cowpuncher**] **West** *joc*
A sheepherder.
1936 McCarthy *Lang. Mosshorn* np **West** [Range terms], *Mutton Puncher.* . . A humorous term used to describe a sheepherder. **1984** Doig *English Creek* 30 **nMT**, I suppose that runs against the usual notion of the West, of cow chousers and mutton conductors forever at odds with each other. . . You could go into a bar and still find an occasional old hammerhead who proclaimed himself nothing but a cowboy and never capable of drawing breath as anything else, especially not as a mutton puncher.

mutton-sass n
A **glasswort.**
1937 Chapman *New Engl. Village Life* 73, *Salicornia* or marsh-sam-

phire commonly known as 'mutton-sass'. . . Books imply that it makes good pickles for man and fodder for cattle. The pickles I have never tried, nor do cattle favour it as forage though sheep are said to condescend so far as to provide its common name.

mutton snapper See **muttonfish 1**

mutton-tops n [*EDD* 1848]
A **goosefoot** (here: *Chenopodium album*).
   1900 Lyons *Plant Names* 95, C[*henopodium*] *album*. . . Mutton-tops, Muck-weed. **1959** Carleton *Index Herb. Plants* 85, *Mutton tops:* Chenopodium album.

Muttontown n Also *Muttonburg, Muttonjerk, Muttonville* Cf **jerk** n[1] **B5**
Used as a nickname for a small, out-of-the-way town.
   1951 Swetnam *Pittsylvania Country* 62 **wPA**, New Salem was a dirty little place of a dozen log houses . . and in derision called . . Muttontown. **1967** *DARE* (Qu. C33, *. . Joking names . . for an out-of-the-way place, or a very small or unimportant place*) Inf **OH**31, Crossroads, Muttonjerk; (Qu. C34, *Nicknames for nearby settlements, villages, or districts*) Inf **OH**36, Muttonjerk; **OH**41, Muttonburg; **MI**64, Muttonville.

mutual n Also *M.I.A.* [Abbr for *Mutual Improvement Association*] **chiefly Rocky Mts, Desert SW** *among Mormons*
A social organization of young adults (12 years and older) in the Mormon Church; a meeting of the organization.
   1942 Stegner *Mormon Country* 7 **UT**, The hall was already jammed for "Mutual," the weekly recreational and faith-promoting meeting that fills Tuesday night in every Ward of Zion. *Ibid* 16, Every Mormon child from the age of twelve upward is a member of either the Young Men's or the Young Ladies' Mutual Improvement Association—the M.I.A., or Mutual. *Ibid* 17, Especially in the smaller and more isolated towns, but to some extent in the cities as well, the M.I.A. focuses the social life of the Wards. **1959** Robertson *Ram* 162 **ID** (as of c1875), I always went to Sunday School, "Mutual," and Deacons' meetings, and took a part. **1966-68** *DARE* (Qu. FF1, *. . A kind of group meeting called a 'social' or 'sociable'. . . [What goes on?]*) Inf **NM**9, Mutual dance (Mutual Improvement Association)—12 years old and up; [(Qu. FF22a, *. . Clubs and societies . . for women*) Inf **UT**5, L.D.S. Young Women's Mutual Improvement Association; (Qu. FF22b, *. . Clubs and societies . . for men*) Inf **UT**5, Young Men's Mutual Improvement Association]. **1968** *Arco Advt.* (ID) 18 Jan, Tuesday, Mutual at 7:30 p.m. **1991** Isaacs *Magic Hour* 148, I remember her because she was friends with the boys and girls in my Eddie's Mutual [in Utah]. . . It's a group for Mormon junior high and high school kids. **1993** *DARE* File, Doris (who actually got more involved in Mormon domestic culture than I did [when we lived near Provo, Utah, for a year]) instantly recognized "Mutual." Short for "Mutual Improvement Society" or something like that, still active. I also asked one of our secretaries, a BYU grad who grew up in Utah. She smiled "of course" at "Mutual."

muumuu n Orig |'muʔu 'muʔu|; now usu |'mu,mu| Also sp *mumu;* abbr *muu* [Haw *muʻumuʻu*] **orig HI, now widely recognized** Cf **holoku, holomuu**
A loose-fitting dress usu made of bright-colored fabric; a shift, slip.
   1938 Reinecke *Hawaiian Loanwords* 25, *Muʻumuʻu* [muʔumuʔu], corrupted to mumu ['mu'mu]. . . A loose shift or undergarment worn by Hawaiian women; hence, a slip or underskirt. **1949** Clark *All the Best HI* v **HI**, The girl students were clad in the shapeless but many-colored muumuu whose somber sartorial ancestor was wished upon the Polynesian pagans by the Congregational missionaries arriving from Boston in 1820. **1965-70** *DARE* (Qu. W22, *. . A loose, full housedress*) 10 Infs, **esp West**, Muumuu; **CO**27, Muumuu; muus; **IL**63, Muu [mu]; **HI**1, Muumuu ['mu,mu]; muu [mu]; shortie muu—just below knee, normal; China muu—fitted and with the side slits, not belted; holomuu—fitted muumuu; **HI**6, Muumuu—doesn't tie; [,pɑ'ke] muumuu—with tight neck and form-fit bodice; **LA**14, Shell—just hangs from shoulders, not as voluminous as muumuu ['mu,mu]—doesn't tie; **LA**33, Muumuu ['mu,mu]—recent; **MD**17, Muumuu ['mu,mu]—modern word; **KS**6, ['mu,mɑz]—I'd call that a nickname, really; [**TX**95, ['mu,lə] [FW: Inf thinks this is a Hawaiian term];] (Qu. W16a, *The full-length garment that a woman wears under her dress*) Inf **HI**6, Muumuu used to be for *inside* slip, and the outside one was a holokuu. **1972** Carr *Da Kine Talk* 88 **HI**, *Hawaiian Words Commonly Heard In Hawaii's English:* . .

Muʻumuʻu. Loose Hawaiian gown without a train. **1984** Sunset *HI Guide* 85, *Muʻumuʻu*—long or short loose-fitting dress. **1993** *DARE* File **cwCA** (as of 1956), My grandfather spent a year as a minister in Hawaii, and sent muumuus to my mother, sister, and me. We called them ['mu,muz], as people did in California, until he told us that, properly, they were ['muʔu 'muʔuz]. They were made of cotton, in brightly colored floral prints.

muvver See **mother** n[1]

mux n[1] [Perh transf from swEngl dial *mux, mucks* mud, mire (regarded by *EDD* as pl of *muck*, or perh var of obs *mix* dung, filth < OE *meox*, infl by *muck*), but cf *EDD* mawks sb. 1 "A mess; a mixture; a state of decay."] **esp NEng** Cf **mux** v, **muxy**
A mess or state of confusion—usu in phrr *(all) in a mux.*
   1846 (1847) Moore *Fitzgerald & Hopkins* 127 **sePA**, "Gracious, mau! how I look! I'm all in a mux!" flutteringly ejaculated Cleopatra. **1848** in 1935 *AmSp* 10.41 **Nantucket MA**, *In a mux.* Confused, disarranged. **1865** Stoddard *2 Men* 32 **MA**, I knew you would come back. Now we are in a mux. **1910** *DN* 3.454 **seVT**, *Mux.* . . Confusion, "all in a mux." **1951** *DE Folkl. Bulletin* 1.7, *Mux* (a mess).

mux v [Engl dial; cf **mux** n[1]] **esp NEast**
1 often with *up;* rarely with *away:* To mess up; to paw over, maul; to botch, sully; hence ppl adj *muxed up* confused, messed up.
   1806 *Balance & Columbian Repository* (Albany NY) 26 Aug 272/2 **ceNY**, To do observance, make obliging mention,/ Wink lovingly, mux chastity away. **1859** (1968) Bartlett *Americanisms* 287, To *mux* is much used in New England for *muss;* as, "Don't mux my crinoline." **1877** J.M. Bailey *They all do It* 22 (*OEDS*), Stop muxin' that bread! . . you've eaten enough for twenty people. I shan't have you muxing and gauming up the victuals. **1893** *KS Univ. Qrly.* 1.141 **KS**, *Mux:* to mix, to confuse. **1895** *DN* 1.391 **csNY**, Mixed up , in confusion. . . *Muxed up.* **1910** *DN* 3.454 **seVT**, *Mux.* . . To confuse, disarrange. . . "All muxed up." Probably shortened from "flum*muxed*," which is also used. **1914** *DN* 4.77 **nNH, ME**, *Mux.* . . To handle, paw over, maul. **1926** Ashley *Yankee Whaler* 136, *Mux:* To botch a job. **1934** *WV Review* Dec 78, One may hear *muxed* in certain sections of West Virginia now and then. . . It is a term synonymous to *messed up,* rather than a form of *mixed,* as it might appear. **1943** Weslager *DE Forgotten Folk* 15, One of the old Nanticoke women told me: "Almost everybody of our class of people is kin to me. I get dizzy when I try to figger out how we are all related. We are all *muxed* up." **1979** *DARE* File **cnMA** (as of c1915), *Muxed* is a word I knew as a child—perhaps because children, properly dressed up to go somewhere, often get all muxed up before their parents are ready to start.
2 also with *around:* To mess around, do odd jobs.
   1969 *DARE* FW Addit **swNJ**, *Muxing around*—messing around. **1985** Rattray *Advent. Dimon* 236 **Long Is. NY**, I rowed out and muxed around, whipping some rope ends, splicing odd lengths of manila into something more useful, and tidying up. **1991** *DARE* File **seNY**, Mux = to putter. You mux around the house on a rainy day.

mux n[2] [Ger *Mucks* a slight sound]
   1950 *WELS Suppl.*, Not a [mʌks] out of him = not a sound, not a word.

mux around See **mux** v **2**

mux away, mux(ed) up See **mux** v **1**

muxy adj [Transf from swEngl dial *muxy, mucksy* muddy, miry; cf **mux** n[1]]
Mixed up, messy.
   [**1665** in 1899 Springfield MA *First Century* 2.218 **swMA**, And it is Ordered yt the Said six acres . . is soe to run to thorow along by the fence side to cover the muxy meddow.] **1893** *KS Univ. Qrly.* 1.141 **KS**, *Muxy:* awry, mixed. **1969** *DARE* FW Addit **swNJ**, *Muxy*—sloppy.

muz(dy), muzz See **muzzy**

muzzle n **esp Sth**
In phr *with a muzzle on* and varr: At all; to any degree.
   1965-69 *DARE* (Qu. V2b, *About a deceiving person, or somebody that you can't trust . . "I wouldn't trust him _____";* not asked in early QRs) Infs **FL**22, **GA**72, **NC**30, **SC**32, 43, **TX**54, In a meat house (*or* outhouse, shithouse) with a muzzle on; **LA**2, To the shithouse with a muzzle on; **TX**40, With a dog muzzle on.

muzzle loader n joc

Among loggers: see quot 1958.

1938 (1939) Holbrook *Holy Mackinaw* 262, *Muzzle loaders*. Old-fashioned bunks into which you crawled over the foot of the bed. **1958** McCulloch *Woods Words* 120 **Pacific NW**, *Muzzle loader*—Anything loaded or entered from the head end. In old time camps it referred to a bunk which had to be crawled into from the foot because the bunks were too close together to get into from the side. **1966** *DARE* Tape **MI**10, In the sleeping quarters or the men's camp, as it was generally called, the bunks were often called muzzle loaders because you went into them from the end. **1972** *Yesterday* 1.2.22, Those [bunks] which had to be entered from the end were called "muzzle loaders." **1975** Gould *ME Lingo* 185.

muzzy n Also *muzz, muz(dy)* [Varr of *(grand)mother*]

1950 *WELS* (*Affectionate words meaning: Mother*) 1 Inf, **cwWI**, Muzz. **1967–68** *DARE* (Qu. Z2, . . *'Mother'*) Inf **VA**11, Muzz; **ID**5, Muzdy, Muzzy; (Qu. Z4, . . *'Grandmother'*) Inf **MA**1, Muzzy.

-my- See **-ma-** infix

myah See **mare**

mycle See **miracle**

my daughter Jane n

1907 *DN* 3.247 **eME**, *My daughter Jane*. . . A game. A line of players and a single player, the *courtier*, stand facing each other. As the dialogue progresses the original line is depleted, until at the end it is, with the exception of one player, over on the side of the single player. Courtier: Here comes a courtier out of Spain / Inquiring for your daughter Jane. Line: My daughter Jane is yet too young / To be betrothed to anyone. Courtier: Be she young or be she old,/ It is for money she must be sold. Line: Come through my parlor and through my hall / And take the fairest one of all. Courtier: The fairest one that I can see / Is _____: come to me. Here the chosen one joins the *courtier*, and the game progresses as before.

my doggie won't bite you See **doggie 5**

my foot See **foot** n **C5i**

my grandmother doesn't like tea See **grandmother's tea**

my guns See **gun** n **2**

my lady's washbowl n
=**bouncing Bet 1.**

1920 Saunders *Useful Wild Plants* 183, In every-day speech the rustic English name, Soapwort, is more usual. In our Southern States a pretty local name that has come to my notice is "My lady's Wash-bowl." **1967** Borland *Hill Country* 235, Bouncing Bet. . . can be used for soap, and at one time its roots were in demand as a shampoo. . . In the South, it is often called My Lady's Washbowl.

my lost sheep n
=**run sheep run.**

1966 *DARE* (Qu. EE12, *Games in which one captain hides his team and the other team tries to find it*) Inf **NM**9, My lost sheep, run sheep run (same game).

my-nez See **mayonnaise**

myrtle n¹ Pronc-spp **chiefly Sth, S Midl** *merkel, merkle, mucker, murdle, murkle, myrkle;* also *mickle, muckle, mukkle* Cf Intro "Language Changes" IV.4

A Forms.

1899 (1912) Green *VA Folk-Speech* 292, *Murkle*. . . Myrtle, the name of a tree. **1916** *Torreya* 16.237 **VA**, *Myrica cerifera*. . . Merkle (myrtle) bushes, Wallops and Revels I[slan]ds. **1920** *Ibid* 20.20, *Myrica* sp.— Low mucker, undoubtedly a corruption of low myrtle, Goose Creek, S.C. **1922** Gonzales *Black Border* 314 **sSC, GA coasts** [Gullah glossary], *Mukkle*—myrtle, myrtles; myrtle thickets. **1927** Boston Soc. Nat. Hist. *Proc.* 38.220 **Okefenokee GA**, *Myrica* sp. 'Myrtle'; 'myrkle'. **1930** Stoney–Shelby *Black Genesis* 139 **seSC**, Not in swamp nor gall, nor pocosin, broom-grass, nor muckle, is anyt'ing dat so much as look like Br' Rabbit. *Ibid* 191, He git 'way ober in a corner o' de yard whe' he kin hide heself under a hebby muckle-bush. **1938** [see **myrtle vine**]. **1940** Clute *Amer. Plant Names* 159, *M[yrica] cerifera*. . . Myrkle-bushes. **1954** *PADS* 21.28 **SC**, *Gall*. . . A low wooded area; an area overgrown with bushes or low trees, as a *muckle (myrtle) gall*. Eastern and coastal region. *Ibid* 33, *Muckle gall*. **1966–70** *DARE* (Qu. T5, . .

Kinds of evergreens, other than pine) Inf **NC**21, Myrtle bush; **NC**76, ['mɜ˞kɨᵛl] bush; **NC**79, Myrtle; (Qu. T15, . . *Kinds of swamp trees*) Inf **SC**67, Sweet muckle (myrtle); **TX**106, ['mɜ˞kəl] bushes. **1967–69** *DARE* FW Addit **swAR**, Merkle ['mɜkl] = myrtle tree [among] Negroes; **GA**51, Myrtle bush ['mɑrdə ˌbuʃ]. **1974** Morton *Folk Remedies* 35 **SC**, Lowbush merkle, sea muckle. . . *Baccharis halimifolia*. *Ibid* 99 **SC**, "Merkel," "muckelbush," "mickleberry" . . *Myrica cerifera*. **1981** Pederson *LAGS Basic Materials*, 1 inf, **csMS**, Flea merkle—weed that gets rid of fleas.

B Senses. Cf **bee myrtle, crape ~, Florida ~, highland ~, Mexican ~**

1 Std: a shrub or tree of the genus *Myrtus*, esp *M. communis*. For other names of this sp see **maile haole 1**

2 also *myrtle bush, ~ tree:* =**wax myrtle.**

1634 Wood *New Engl. Prospect* 13, In the Woods, without eyther the art or the helpe of man, . . [grow] Mirtle, Saxifarilla, Bayes, &c. **1682** (1836) Ash *Carolina* 64, There are many other Fragrant smelling trees, the Myrtle, Bay and Lawrel. **1705** Beverley *Hist. VA* 2.22, The Myrtle, bearing a Berry, of which they make a hard brittle wax. **1775** (1962) Romans *Nat. Hist. FL* 6, Had not the clay been held fast by the roots of the black mangrove, and in some places the myrtle (*Myrica*) there would have been scarce a vestige of the island left. **1856** Simms *Eutaw* 555 **SC**, He stretched himself out, covered with a clump of myrtle, at the foot of a mighty sycamore. **1897** Sudworth *Arborescent Flora* 117, *Myrica cerifera*. . . *Common Names*. . . Myrtle (Fla.) Myrtletree (Fla.). . *Myrica californica*. . . *Common Names*. . . Myrtle (Nev.) . . California Myrtle (Cal.) **1927** [see **A** above]. **1938** Rawlings *Yearling* 48 **nFL**, Myrtle bushes brushed their legs. **1966–70** *DARE* (Qu. S11) Inf **NY**123, Myrtle; (Qu. S26e) Inf **CT**12, Myrtle; (Qu. T5, . . *Kinds of evergreens, other than pine*) Inf **NC**21, Myrtle bush; **NC**79, Myrtle; (Qu. T15, . . *Kinds of swamp trees*) Infs **SC**63, 67, Myrtle. **1986** Pederson *LAGS Concordance*, 1 inf, **swAL**, Myrtle bushes—some of them form trees; 1 inf, **neFL**, Myrtle swamps; 1 inf, **seLA**, Myrtle; 1 inf, **cnLA**, Myrtles; 1 inf, **cwLA**, Myrtle tree.

3 also *running myrtle:* A **periwinkle** (here: *Vinca minor*).

1890 *Century Dict.* 3923, *Running myrtle*, more often simply *myrtle*, a name of the common periwinkle. **1897** *Jrl. Amer. Folkl.* 10.50 **cME, swOH**, *Vinca minor* . . myrtle. **1931** Harned *Wild Flowers Alleghanies* 389, Periwinkle. . . Also called Myrtle and often used in funeral ceremonials. **1935** (1943) Muenscher *Weeds* 363, *Vinca minor*. . . Myrtle. . . *Control.*—In lawns raise the runner with a rake and mow them close. . . Dig out by hand. **1938** Madison *Wild Flowers OH* 88, Myrtle. *Vinca minor*. **1968** *DARE* (Qu. S3) Inf **MD**4, Myrtle; (Qu. S21, . . *Weeds . . that are a trouble in gardens and fields*) Inf **IN**17, Myrtle. **1976** Bailey–Bailey *Hortus Third* 1157, *[Vinca] minor* . . myrtle, running myrtle.

4 also *myrtle tree, myrtlewood:* =**California laurel. chiefly OR**

1897 Sudworth *Arborescent Flora* 203 **OR**, *Umbellularia californica*. . . Myrtle Tree. . . Myrtle. **1925** Jepson *Manual Plants CA* 397, In the woods of Mendocino and Humboldt the name "Pepperwood" is the only one in use, while in Oregon the name "Myrtle" replaces all others. **1961** Peck *Manual OR* 349, California Laurel. . . In Oregon misnamed Myrtle. **1967–69** *DARE* (Qu. T16) Infs **CA**111, **OR**3, Myrtlewood. **1974** Munz *Flora S. CA* 545 **swOR**, *U[mbellularia] californica*. . . Tree with broad crown and to 30 or 40 m high, or an erect shrub in dryer places. . . San Diego Co. n. to sw. Ore., where it is known as Myrtle. **1993** *DARE* File, When I lived in Oregon I discovered that one of the biggest products of the tourist trade was salad bowls made of myrtle—what I, as a Californian, would have called California bay or California laurel.

5 =**moneywort 1.**

1902 (1909) Mathews *Field Book Amer. Wild Flowers* 348, Moneywort or Myrtle—*Lysimachia nummularia*. **1916** *Torreya* 16.239 **cME coast**, *Lysimachia nummularia* . . Myrtle. **1959** Carleton *Index Herb. Plants* 85, *Myrtle:* Lysimachia nummularia.

6 =**ceanothus.** Cf **blue myrtle 1, island ~**

1920 Saunders *Useful Wild Plants* 142, There are a score or more of species of *Ceanothus* indigenous to the Pacific coast, where they are known as "myrtle" or "wild lilac". **1937** U.S. Forest Serv. *Range Plant Hdbk.* B39, Many species of *Ceanothus* have individual names. . . Unfortunately, however, there has never been general agreement as to a generic English name for this important group of woody plants. Probably the names in most general use have been bluebush (or bluebrush), buckbrush, lilac, and myrtle. **1979** Little *Checklist U.S. Trees* 79, *Ceanothus spinosus*. . *Common names* . . spiny-myrtle.

7 =**joewood.** Cf **sea myrtle**

    1938 Baker *FL Wild Flowers* 167, Like many other Florida shrubs, it [=*Jacquinia keyensis*] is locally called myrtle.

8 =**crape myrtle.**

    1942 (1960) Robertson *Red Hills* 60 **SC,** Our gardens were just a mass of myrtles and beautiful roses.

9 also *muckle mish:* A **groundsel tree.** Cf **lowbush merkle, saltwater myrtle, sand ~**

    [**1974** Morton *Folk Remedies* 36 **SC,** Branches [of *Baccharis halimifolia*] used as yard brooms in South Carolina.] **1986** Pederson *LAGS Concordance,* 1 inf, **swAL,** Yard brooms made of myrtle brush. **1987** Jones-Jackson *When Roots Die* 153 **sSC coast** [Gullah], When the tide comes up, you goes and cut muckle mish [bush] and drop em behind the wire to hold the fish on that side when e [the tide] goes down because we didn't had a gill net to put over river.

myrtle n[2] See **merkel** n[2]

myrtleberry n

1 The fruit of a **wax myrtle.** Cf **mickleberry**

    c1697 in 1835 MA Hist. Soc. *Coll.* 1st ser 5.127, There is great store of the myrtleberries, which being boiled up to a wax, make as good candles as the best wax candles whatsoever. **1954** Sprunt *FL Bird Life* 396, The food has a higher vegetable content than that of many other warblers because of the bird's fondness for myrtle . . berries.

2 =**farkleberry.** [Perh from the resemblance of the leaves to those of **myrtle** n[1] **B1**]

    1897 Sudworth *Arborescent Flora* 312 **LA,** *Vaccinium arboreum.* . . Myrtle Berries. **1908** Britton *N. Amer. Trees* 765, Tree Huckleberry. . . This small tree or shrub [=*Vaccinium arboreum*] is also called Farkleberry, Sparkleberry, Myrtleberry, Gooseberry, and Blueberry; it occurs in the sandy soils of the Gulf States from North Carolina to Florida and Texas.

myrtle bird See myrtle warbler

myrtle boxleaf (or boxwood) See myrtle bush 2

myrtle bush n

1 See **myrtle** n[1] **B2.**

2 also *myrtle boxleaf, ~ boxwood:* =**Oregon boxwood.**

    1938 Van Dersal *Native Woody Plants* 176, Myrtle boxleaf. . . A small evergreen shrub. **1960** Vines *Trees SW* 666, It [=*Pachystema myrsinites*] is also known under the vernacular names of Myrtle-bush, Myrtle-box-leaf, Mountain-lover, False-box, and Oregon-boxwood. **1963** Craighead *Rocky Mt. Wildflowers* 111, Oregon Boxwood, Myrtle Boxleaf, Mountain-hedge. **1973** Hitchcock–Cronquist *Flora Pacific NW* 288, *P[achistima] myrsinites* . . myrtle boxwood, Ore boxwood.

myrtle holly n

A **holly** n[1] **1** (here: *Ilex myrtifolia*).

    1960 Vines *Trees SW* 650, Common names [for *Ilex myrtifolia*] are Small-leaf Dahoon, Myrtle Holly, and Cypress Holly. **1970** Correll *Plants TX* 997, *Ilex myrtifolia* . . Myrtle holly. Shrub or small tree, evergreen.

myrtle nut n Cf myrtleberry 1

The fruit of **sweet gale.**

    [**1923** Abrams *Flora Pacific States* 1.508, Sweet Gale. . . Nutlet waxy-coated. . . In low moist situations.] **1935** Davis *Honey* 179 **OR,** The myrtle-nuts and wapato-root of the damp mud-flats.

myrtle oak n

A small, shrubby **oak** with dark, glossy leaves (here: *Quercus myrtifolia*). Also called **sand oak, scrub ~**

    1897 Sudworth *Arborescent Flora* 166, *Quercus myrtifolia.* . . *Myrtle Oak.* . . Usually a low, much-branched shrub. **1908** Britton *N. Amer. Trees* 308, *Myrtle Oak.* . . On dry sandy ridges along the coast and adjacent islands from South Carolina to Florida and Louisiana. **1946** West–Arnold *Native Trees FL* 45, *Myrtle Oak.* . . 20 to 40 feet, trunks 6 to 8 inches in diameter. . . The evergreen leaves are variable in size and form. **1962** Harrar–Harrar *Guide S. Trees* 202, *Myrtle Oak.* . . This small, evergreen oak, seldom found far from salt water, . . often forms extensive, nearly impenetrable thickets, and in exposed situations its grotesque wind forms lend added charm to the seascape. **1982** *Naples Now* May 37 **swFL,** In the same habitat grows the *myrtle oak* with gray, furrowed bark and smooth dark green leaves, shiny above and below.

myrtle-of-the-river n

A **spicewood** (here: *Calyptranthes zuzygium*).

    1919 Smithsonian Inst. *Annual Rept. for 1917* 384 **FL,** The myrtle-of-the-river . . (*Calyptranthes zuzygium*) with opposite glossy leaves and clusters of fruit resembling blueberries. **1933** Small *Manual SE Flora* 938, *Myrtle-of-the river.* . . Hammocks, Everglade Keys, pen. Fla. **1982** *Miami Herald* (FL) 24 Oct sec H 11 **FL,** Myrtle-of-the-river . . is. . . easy to recognize because the branches hold twigs that are upright, ridged and forked. Branch-branch-fork; branch-branch-fork.

myrtle tree See myrtle n[1] B2, 4

myrtle vine n

A **bittersweet** (here: *Solanum dulcamara*).

    1897 *Jrl. Amer. Folkl.* 10.52 **swOH,** *Solanum dulcamara* . . myrtle vine. **1938** Stuart *Dark Hills* 250 **neKY,** Son, them murdle vines is just full of copperheads.

myrtle warbler n Also myrtle bird [See quot 1844]

A **warbler** (here: *Dendroica coronata*). Also called **chee-chee, seedbird, teteet, yellow-crowned warbler, yellow-rumped ~**

    1810 Wilson *Amer. Ornith.* 2.139, Thro the whole of the lower parts of the Carolinas, wherever the myrtles grew, these birds [=yellow-rump warblers] were numerous. . . In those parts of the country they are generally known by the name of Myrtle-birds. **1844** DeKay *Zool. NY* 2.88, The . . *Myrtle-bird,* ranges from Mexico to the 65th degree of north latitude. . . [I]n the autumn and winter, [it feeds] on berries of the Juniper, and particularly the Myrtle-wax berries *(Myrica cerifera),* which has given rise to one of its popular names. **1890** Warren *Birds PA* 282, The Myrtle Warbler . . is the most abundant of all the family occurring in this state. It is one of the first to arrive from the south. **1934** Hanley *Disks* **neCT,** Two myrtle warblers came to a pasture of snow-covered bayberry bushes. **1968–70** *DARE* (Qu. Q14) Inf **VA**52A, Myrtle bird (myrtle warbler); (Qu. Q21, . . *Kinds of sparrows*) Inf **GA**18, Myrtle warbler. **1977** Bull–Farrand *Audubon Field Guide Birds* 692, In the East, the "Myrtle Warbler" is an abundant migrant, and the only warbler that regularly spends the winter in the northern states.

myrtlewood See myrtle n[1] B4

myself pron Also *meself;* pronc-spp *mahself, merse'f, m'se'f, muhself* [Cf *EDD myself* "Also in form *meself* Ir." and *OED meself* "*Obs.*"]

Std senses, var forms.

    1843 (1916) Hall *New Purchase* 439 **IN,** It a sort a couldn't be helped . . , says I to meself. **1899** Edwards *Defense* 163 **GA,** I'd er bounced 'im den and dere merse'f, but he had on es barkers. **1922** Gonzales *Black Border* 105 **sSC, GA coasts** [Gullah], Meself binnuh sleep. *Ibid* 313 [Gullah glossary], *Meself, muhself*—myself. **1923** *DN* 5.212 **swMO,** I made a jedge o' m'se'f. **1934** [see **least** adj 3].

my ship's come home from India n Also my ship (came in) Cf I went to Paris

Any of var games; see quots.

    1899 Champlin–Bostwick *Young Folks' Games* 500, My Ship, a game played by any number of persons, some of whom have not taken part in it before. Each player is asked what his ship is laden with, and is expected to mention an article beginning with the first letter of either of his names. . . Those who have not played before are not told of this condition, and whenever they mention something beginning with the wrong letter, are told that the ship cannot enter port with such a cargo. **1905** *DN* 3.88 **nwAR,** My ship's come home from India. . . Name of a game. **1940** Harbin *Fun Encycl.* 161, My ship came in.—The players are seated about the room or campfire. The leader says to the one seated next to him, "My ship came in." "What did it bring?" asks the second player. "A fan," replies the leader, whereupon he begins a fanning motion with his hand. The second person turns to the third and the conversation is repeated. And so it goes all the way around the circle. When it gets back to the leader he repeats, "My ship came in." "What did it bring?" this time brings the response, "A pair of scissors," and the leader uses the middle and index fingers of the other hand to imitate a pair of scissors. Next comes a pair of shoes with the feet being set in motion. Then a pair of glasses with the eyes blinking, followed by false teeth with an opening and closing of the mouth, the teeth being displayed. Finally, a hat with the head bobbing back and forth. That will probably leave the group limp, for all motions, once started, must be continued.

mystery grass n

=death camas.

1914 Georgia *Manual Weeds* 76, *Zygadenus venenosus* . . *Other English names* . . Hog's Potato, Mystery Grass. **1922** U.S. Dept. Ag. *Farmers' Bulletin 1273* 4, Other names occasionally applied [to *Zygadenus* spp] are . . "mystery grass," and "hog's potato."

mystery lily n

The fall crocus *(Colchicum autumnale).*

1960 Williams *Walk Egypt* 221 **GA,** A clump of mystery lilies blooming by the door. They appeared each October, tall leafless stems capped with red trumpet-shaped flowers. **1968** *DARE* Tape **WV**11, Mystery lily. . . Kind of wildflower. It's a beautiful lily. . . The foliage all dies down, every blade disappears, and then beautiful stems come up . . at least 18 inches tall. . . It has no green blades. . . And these mysterious stalks just pop up.

mystery lunch n

=box social.

1945 Saxon *Gumbo Ya-Ya* 571 **LA,** The Mystery Lunch (box social). Girls prepare lunches and pack them in elaboratedly [sic] decorated boxes. At the gathering the young men bid for these boxes, being able to identify their sweetheart's box by some peculiar article used in trimming.

mystery night n

=cabbage night.

1977–78 Foster *Lexical Variation* 76 **NJ,** *Mystery Night,* probably a reinterpretation of *Mischief Night,* is well attested among blacks in Essex and northern Middlesex, and it may also be used by blacks in other parts of North and Central Jersey.

N

n pron See **one** pron

-'n suff[1] See **-en** suff[1]

-'n suff[2] See **-en** suff[3]

-'n n See **ma'am**

-n suff[3] See **-ing**

-n conj[1] See **than**

'n' conj[2] See **and** conj

na adv See **no**

na conj See **nor**

na'ar See **narrow**

nabble, nabel, nable See **navel**

‡nabob n Cf **neighborhood** n 2
  1967 *DARE* (Qu. X34, . . *Names and nicknames for the navel*) Inf **CO**22, Nabob [nebɔb].

nachelly, nacherly, nachly See **naturally**

nachul See **natural**

nachully, nachurly See **naturally**

naer See **ne'er** adj[1]

naern See **nairn**

nag v [*OED nag* v. 1 "*dial*. . . To gnaw, to nibble." Cf also *EDD gnag* v. 1]
  To gnaw; to mark with the teeth.
  1938 Rawlings *Yearling* 101 **nFL**, Penny pointed out a bear gnaw. It was a clawed area on a tall pine tree, shoulder high to a man. . . "I've watched a bear at it. . . He'll stretch up and he'll claw. He'll turn his head sideways and he'll nag and gnaw."

nagelhawk n [See quot] Cf **eagle-hawk 2, winklehawk**, *DS* W27
  A rip or tear in a piece of clothing.
  1951 *NY Folkl. Qrly.* 7.190, The Adirondacks seem to have no characteristic vocabulary, but are noted chiefly for the preservation of occasional relics, some not found elsewhere: . . *nagelhawk* for a tear—probably from German *Nagelloch*, a reminiscence of the time when German was spoken in the Mohawk Valley.

nagent n [By metanalysis; see Intro "Language Changes" I.2]
  1890 *DN* 1.25, Strange, uncommon, or antiquated words or uses of words really current in any community. . . [include] *the nagent* for the agent.

nager See **nigger** n[1]

naggie n [By metanalysis; see Intro "Language Changes" I.2] =**aggie.**
  1968 *DARE* (Qu. EE6d, *Special marbles*) Inf **OH**47, Naggies.

nagoonberry n [Tlingit *neigóon*] **AK**
  A **dewberry 1** (here: *Rubus acaulis, R. arcticus,* or *R. stellatus*); also the fruit of such a plant. Also called **lagoonberry, wineberry**
  1914 Jones *Study Thlingets* 109 **AK**, Tons upon tons of the finest huckleberries, high-bush cranberries, nagoon berries, salmonberries, and other kinds go to waste every season. **1938** (1958) Sharples *AK Wild Flowers* 128, *R[ubus] stellatus.* "Nagoon or Lagoon Berry." A herbaceous species of swamp and tundra, producing a fragrant red berry

of excellent flavor. Much prized for jelly. **1952** Williams *AK Wildfl. Glimpses* 39, Nagoonberry. . . Two species of this delicious berry are found over all Alaska except the Arctic slope. One species of this berry touches the states in northern Minnesota but the other does not. . . The beautiful deep red fruit sometimes consists of only a few drupelets but in good years it forms a berry as large as a raspberry. **1961** *AK Sportsman* Sept 20, The nagoon berry belongs to the genus *rubus,* or raspberry. **1974** Welsh *Anderson's Flora AK* 393, *Rubus arcticus* . . Nagoon Berry. . . Plants herbaceous (rarely somewhat woody). *Ibid* 394, *Rubus stellatus* . . Nagoon Berry. **1988** *Homer News* 23 June 23 (Tabbert *Dict. Alaskan Engl.*), Nagoon berries, which are also called dew berries and wine berries.

nagrams n pl [Var of *megrims* low spirits, blues] Cf **megrim**
  1916 *DN* 4.278 **NE**, Nagrams. . . Blues, depression. "I have the nagrams." One contributor.

nah See **no**

naik See **neck** n

nail n
  1 =**coffin nail 1.** *esp* **NEast** Cf **casket nail**
    1942 Berrey–Van den Bark *Amer. Slang* 111.4, Cigarette. . . nail. **1965–70** *DARE* (Qu. DD6b, *Nicknames for cigarettes*) Infs **MA**35, **MI**76, 105, **MO**11, **NJ**8, 23, **PA**76, 94, 245, Nail(s).
  2 See quot. Cf **hammer** B
    1972 Claerbaut *Black Jargon* 73, Nail . . a male person; man.

nail bar n *scattered, but esp* **West, Gulf States** See Map
  An iron bar adapted for gripping and extracting nails.
  1965–70 *DARE* (Qu. L39, *An iron bar with a bent end, used for pulling nails, opening boxes, and so on*) 19 Infs, *scattered, but esp* **West, Gulf States,** Nail bar; **AL**2, Bought nail bars and sold them as wrecking bars [in hardware business]; **OK**18, Nail bar—same as crowbar; **OK**27, Nail bar, pinch bar, or crowbar are the same tool; **OK**52, Nail bar—same as nail puller. [19 of 23 Infs comm type 5] **1986** Pederson *LAGS Concordance,* 1 inf, **nwAR**, Nail bar. [*DARE* Ed: in a list of tools]

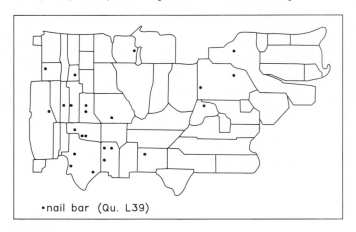

•nail bar (Qu. L39)

nail grass n
  A **teaweed** (here: *Sida spinosa*).
  1913 *Torreya* 13.232 **cLA**, *Sida spinosa.* . . Nail grass, Marksville, La.

nail hole, down to the last See **hole** n 10b

nail in one's coffin See **coffin nail 1**

‡nail keg n

1968 *DARE* (Qu. C35, *Nicknames for the different parts of your town or city*) Inf **GA**19, Nail keg ['nɛl ˌkæg]—colored section.

nail one to the cross v phr

In the game of **hat ball**: see quot.

1946 Wilson *Fidelity Folks* 145 **sKY**, In Hat Ball we "nailed to the cross" the loser, that is, the one who got the most forfeits or "pigs." . . The boy . . was stood against a sapling while all the boys took turns throwing a ball at him.

nail-pounder n Cf **hammerhead 6**

A **woodpecker**.

1969 *DARE* (Qu. Q18, *Joking names and nicknames for woodpeckers*) Inf **NY**198, Nail-pounder.

nail rod n

1 An aster (here: *Aster lateriflorus*).

1894 *Jrl. Amer. Folkl.* 7.91 **WV**, *Aster diffusus* . . nail-rod. **1940** Clute *Amer. Plant Names* 76, *A[ster] lateriflorus* . . nail-rod. **1959** Carleton *Index Herb. Plants* 85, Nail rod: Aster lateriflorus.

2 =**cattail 1.**

1959 Munz–Keck *CA Flora* 1367, *T[ypha] angustifolia*. . . Nail Rod. **1969** *DARE* (Qu. S20) Inf **KY**43, Nail rod. [*DARE* Ed: Inf may refer instead to **1** above.] **1976** Bailey–Bailey *Hortus Third* 1136, *T[ypha] latifolia* . . nail-rod.

nailsick adj [Cf *OED* iron sick "Now *rare* or *Obs.*"] **NEng**

Of wood or a wooden vessel: weakened by repeated nailing or by rusted iron parts; unsound.

1905 Wasson *Green Shay* 105 **NEng**, She's nail-sick [Footnote: Rusted out], and wormy and rotten besides, but she's all the boat you've got. **1914** *DN* 4.155 **Cape Cod MA**, Nail-sick. . . So weakened by repeated nailing that the nails no longer hold; less frequently applied to boards weakened by rot. "How can you expect the roof'll stay tight if you fix it with them nail-sick boards?" **1916** *DN* 4.266 **Cape Cod MA**, A board which through age or frequent use will no longer hold nails firmly is said to be "nail-sick." **1962** Morison *One Boy's Boston* 17 **eMA** (as of c1900), The skiff, though somewhat "nail-sick," is still doing duty today. **1975** Gould *ME Lingo* 143, *Iron sick*—Used to describe a wooden boat in which the metal fastenings are loose because of age and rust. Sometimes "nail sick."

nainaine See **nenaine**

nainy pron [Prob contr of *not* + *any*; but cf *OED* nany "*Obs.* . . Not any, no."] Cf **nairn**

1951 *PADS* 15.70 **nLA** [Speech of older rural speakers], *Nainy* ['nɛnɪ]. . . None.

naio n [Haw]

An evergreen tree (*Myoporum sandwicense*) native to Hawaii.

1836 *Sandwich Is. Gaz. & Jrl. of Commerce* (Honolulu HI) 17 Sept, Higher up the mountain the timber increases in size, being interspersed with Ohia, . . Koa, . . and Naiho [sic], (*Myoporum Tenui folium* [sic]). **1911** *Century Dict. Suppl.*, Naio. . . The bastard sandalwood of Hawaii, *Myoporum Sandwicense*. **1930** Degener *Ferns of HI* 261, The *naio* or false sandalwood is found exclusively in the Hawaiian Islands. **1948** Neal *In Gardens HI* 694, During the sandalwood trade, when the supply of sandalwood gave out, naio [=*Myoporum sandwicense*] was substituted. It is a small to large tree. **1970** Carlquist *Hawaii* 275, The naio, *Myoporum sandwicense*, is a common dry forest tree with relatives in New Zealand and on South Pacific islands. **1994** Stone–Pratt *Hawai'i's Plants* 279, Kamehameha butterflies are nectar and sap feeders and may be seen around koa, naio, and other native forest trees.

nair See **ne'er** adj[1]

nairn pron Also *na(e)rn* [Engl dial *narn, ne'ern, nern*, contrs of *ne'er (a) one* (see *EDD* never a one)] **Sth, S Midl** Cf **airn** pron, **nary** adj, **ne'er** adj[1]

Often with other negatives: Not a one, none.

1909 *DN* 3.351 **eAL, wGA**, *Nairn, nary one*. . . Not any, ne'er a one. **1915** *DN* 4.186 **swVA**, *Narn* [nɛəⁿ]. Contraction of *nairy one*. **1931** (1991) Hughes–Hurston *Mule Bone* 65 **cFL** [Black], [In a children's game:] "I must have a chick." . . "You shan't have n'airn." **1952** Brown *NC Folkl.* 1.568, *Narn* [nɑːn, nɛrn], *naern, nairn* [næən, nɛrn]. . . "I don't own a dog, and I don't want naern."—Illiterate. **1966** *DARE* (Qu. LL14, . . *"This pond used to be full of fish but now there's _____ left."*) Inf **MS**69, Narn [næəⁿ]—in the country. **1973** *Patrick Coll.*

Montgomery **AL**, Nair'n . . none at all. **1981** Pederson *LAGS Basic Materials* **coastal Gulf Region**, [6 infs gave proncs of the type [næə(r)n]; 1 said [nɛȳːɚn], 1 [nɛ̂ə̂]·] **1989** Nicholson *Field Guide S. Speech* 26, We seen bunches of deer, but we didn't shoot nairn.

nairy See **nary** adj

naiteral See **natural**

nake See **neck** n

naked adj Usu |'nekɪd|; also **scattered, but chiefly Sth, S Midl, TX** (See Map) |'nɛkɪd| Pronc-spp *nakid, nakit, necked, nek(k)id;* for addit varr see quots

A Forms.

1890 *DN* 1.41 **ME**, ['nekɪd]. **1891** *DN* 1.125 **cNY**, ['nekɪd]. **1892** *DN* 1.240 **wMO**, ['nekɪd]. **1893** Shands *MS Speech* 74, *Naked*. . . In Mississippi, as in Kansas City, this word is very generally pronounced [nɛkɪd]. **1899** (1912) Green *VA Folk-Speech* 295, *Neck'ed*. . . *Naked*; without any clothes on at all. **1905** *DN* 3.56 **eNE**, The vowel [e] is generally shortened in *take, plague* . . , sometimes also in . . *naked*. **1909** *DN* 3.351 **eAL, wGA**, *Necked. Ibid* 400 **nwAR**, *Nakid*. **1915** *DN* 4.186 **swVA**, *Necked*. **1922** Gonzales *Black Border* 222 **sSC, GA coasts** [Gullah], Strip nakit. *Ibid* 314 [Gullah glossary], *Nakid, Nakit*—naked. **1937** in 1976 *Weevils in the Wheat* 43 **VA** [Black], De overseer was jus' a layin' et on dat poor boy's necked back. **1942** Faulkner *Go Down* 53 **MS**, I dont need no razor. My nekkid hands will do. **1942** Hall *Smoky Mt. Speech* 18 **wNC, eTN**, *Naked* as ['nekɪd] . . is usual. **1949** *PADS* 11.8 **wTX**, *Naked* ['nɛkɪd]. **1952** Brown *NC Folkl.* 1.569, *Necked* ['nɛkɪd]. **c1960** *Wilson Coll.* **csKY**, *Naked* ['nɛkɪd]—regularly. **1965–70** *DARE* (Qu. W20) 575 Infs, **widespread**, Naked [also in var combs and phrr; see *DS*]; 145 Infs, **chiefly Sth, S Midl, TX**, Nekkid [also in var combs and phrr; see *DS*]; **IN**9, **LA**3, **MO**8, (Buck or stark) ['nɛkɪt]; **AR**27, **NY**219, (Buck) ['nɛkɪt]; **AR**18, ['nækɪd] as a jaybird; (Qu. C34) Inf **AR**55, [ˌnɛkɪd] City. **1976** Ryland *Richmond Co. VA* 374, Neck-ed—naked. **1981** Pederson *LAGS Basic Materials* **Gulf Region**, [For *naked*, 17 infs offered proncs of the type ['nɛ(ə)kɪd], 4 infs ['nɛɪkɪt], 1 inf ['neɪkɪd], and 1 inf ['neɪkɪt].]

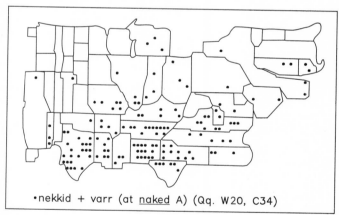

•nekkid + varr (at naked A) (Qq. W20, C34)

B Senses.

1 also *stark naked;* Of beverages: plain; undiluted. [Cf *OED* stark naked 2 1820 →] Cf **barefooted 1**

1942 Berrey–Van den Bark *Amer. Slang* 34.8, *Undiluted; unadulterated*. . . stark-naked. **1966–68** *DARE* (Qu. KK61, *Food taken alone, with nothing added: "Would you like milk or lemon in your tea?" "No thanks, I'll take it _____."*) Infs **IN**31, **MD**19, Naked; **MA**45, Naked—for whiskey; **MA**6, Stark naked. [All Infs old] **1986** Pederson *LAGS Concordance*, 1 inf, **swMS**, You best put naked water in it—plain water; 1 inf, **neTX**, Naked Coke—private slang, would order in a bar; *(Without milk)* 4 infs, 2 **MS**, Naked; 1 inf, **seMS**, Naked coffee; 1 inf, **cnMS**, Don't want it naked—of coffee. [5 of 8 total infs Black]

2 Of cattle: unbranded.

1967 *DARE* Tape **TX**24, Old-timers told me that they [=rustlers] took out worlds of big mavericks the first time. . . They took off a lots of naked calfs here, too. They didn't take off no mavericks after that . . when these birds in this country went to brandin' their mavericks.

naked as a jaybird See **jaybird 1b**

naked bed, (sick) in one's adj phr [Cf *OED* naked bed (at *naked* adj. A.2.b)] **NEng**

Ill; confined to bed.

1896 *Nation* 62.269 **Cape Cod MA,** There are many other terms used on "The Cape," which I have never heard elsewhere. When a person is ill, and confined to his bed, they speak of him as being "sick in his naked bed." **1914** *DN* 4.77 **nNH, ME,** *Naked bed, in one's.* . . Down sick. **1932** *DN* 6.284 **swCT,** When we first came to Danbury, people always said 'sick in your naked bed.'

naked bride n
=**naked lady 1.**
   1968 *DARE* FW Addit **PA**162, *Naked bride*—Fall crocus.

Naked City n Cf **Hungry Hill, Shall-I-go-naked**
   1967–70 *DARE* (Qu. C34, *Nicknames for nearby settlements, villages, or districts*) Inf **AR**55, Naked City.

naked Indian n [See quot 1980] **TX**
A **madrone** (here: *Arbutus texana*).
   1951 *PADS* 15.37 **TX,** *Arbutus texana.* . . Naked Indian; paper-bark tree. **1960** Vines *Trees SW* 805, Texas Madrone. . . Also known under the vernacular names of Texas Arbutus, Madroño, Naked Indian [etc]. **1970** Correll *Plants TX* 1174, *Arbutus xalapensis.* . . *Texas madrone, naked indian, Lady's Leg.* Small evergreen tree or rarely shrub. **1980** Little *Audubon Guide N. Amer. Trees W. Region* 579 **TX,** The local names, "Naked Indian" and "Lady's Leg," refer to the smooth flesh-colored bark.

naked lady n
1 Std: a plant of the genus *Colchicum*, esp *C. autumnale*. Also called **naked bride**
2 also *naked-lady lily*: An amaryllis (here: *Amaryllis belladonna*).
   1968 *DARE* (Qu. S26e, *Other wildflowers not yet mentioned;* not asked in early QRs) Inf **CA**105, Amaryllis or naked lady or resurrection flower. **1968** *DARE* Tape **MD**30, Hardy amaryllis is, I think, the catalog name, and the common name for them is naked ladies because the foliage comes up in the spring about twice as broad as a daffodil leaf, and then toward the latter part of May it's gone, it's dead and there's nothing there. . . Around the . . first week of August . . they start coming up out of the ground. There are no leaves whatever and they're a very lovely pink with a slight lavender stripe through them. **1976** Bailey-Bailey *Hortus Third* 66, [*Amaryllis*] *belladonna.* . . Belladonna lily, cape belladonna, naked-lady lily. **1986** *New Yorker* 17 Nov 48 **MS,** Red lilies sprang up in Anna Meredith's yard in King's Town around the end of September. The merest light rain that time of the year, and the bleached hot earth exploded with amaryllis. Naked ladies, the local people called them. **1986** *DARE* File **csWI,** Naked ladies—a type of amaryllis which produces copious leaves in spring, which die back completely. Then in late summer, tall, sleek stalks come out with pink (and white) blooms in profusion. **1989** *Ibid* **sCA,** As a teenager I remember encountering *naked lady* with some shock . . , when a matronly guest remarked at my aunt's centerpiece, "What lovely naked ladies!" I knew the flowers only as lilies of some kind or other. **1993** *Ibid* **nCA** (as of 1990), Naked ladies are pink, trumpet-shaped flowers like a lily. The foliage grows first, a clump of long blades, then it dies off completely. The flower stalk comes up out of bare ground later. They are bulb plants, and naturalize easily. *Ibid* **cwCA** (as of c1960), Amaryllis plants are called "naked ladies."

naked weed n [From the slender, nearly leafless stems]
=**gum succory.**
   1894 *Jrl. Amer. Folkl.* 7.91 **WV,** *Chondrilla juncea* . . naked weed. **1914** Georgia *Manual Weeds* 534, *Gum Succory—Chondrilla juncea.* . . Naked Weed. **1925** *Book of Rural Life* 6.3747, *Naked weed,* a common weed of wheat fields and meadows found in the Middle Atlantic states. It is commonly known as the *eastern skeleton weed.* **1959** Carleton *Index Herb. Plants* 86.

nakedwood n [From the shedding of the bark, which exposes the pinkish cambium layer] **FL**
1 A tree or shrub of the genus *Colubrina*. For other names of var spp see **hog plum 5, manzanita 3, snakewood, soldier wood, wild coffee**
   1884 Sargent *Forests of N. Amer.* 42, Naked wood. . . trunks 0.75 to 1 meter in diameter appear like a mass of braided serpents. On small trunks the bark breaks up into flakes which curl up and drop off. **1908** Britton *N. Amer. Trees* 682, The Nakedwood, or soldier wood, inhabits extreme southern Florida. . . The orange-brown bark is deeply irregularly furrowed and ridged, falling away in papery layers. **1942** Hylander *Plant Life* 369, Naked Wood (*Colubrina*) of the same region [=FL

Keys]. **1971** Craighead *Trees S. FL* 201, Nakedwood, *Colubrina reclinata.* **1979** Little *Checklist U.S. Trees* 94, *Colubrina arborescens* . . coffee colubrina . . nakedwood. . . *C. cubensis.* . . nakedwood. . . *C. elliptica.* . . nakedwood.
2 A **stopper** (here: *Myrcianthes fragrans*).
   1884 Sargent *Forests of N. Amer.* 88, *Eugenia dichotoma.* . . Naked wood. . . Wood very heavy, hard, close-grained. . . color, light brown or red. **1908** Britton *N. Amer. Trees* 728, Naked stopper. . . This evergreen tree is also known as Nakedwood. . . The bark is about 3 mm. thick, close, peeling off in thin scales of a red or reddish brown color. **1942** Hylander *Plant Life* 393, Two other trees in the Myrtle Family, native to Florida, are the Naked Wood (*Anamomis*), a tree of the Florida Hammocks, with fragrant white flowers, often attaining a height of sixty feet; and Spice Wood. **1962** Harrar-Harrar *Guide S. Trees* 545, The Nakedwoods—*Anamomis* [spp]. *Ibid* 547, Twinberry Nakedwood—*Anamomis dicrana.* . . occurs from the lower middle Florida peninsula south over the Keys to Key West and the West Indies. **1979** Little *Checklist U.S. Trees* 174, *Myrcianthes* [spp]. . . Other common name— nakedwood. *Ibid*, *Myrcianthes fragrans.* . . nakedwood, naked stopper.

nakedy adj, n Pronc-spp *nakity, nekkidy* Cf Intro "Language Changes" III.1
Naked; nakedness.
   1922 Gonzales *Black Border* 314 **sSC, GA coasts** [Gullah glossary], *Nakity*—naked; nakedness. **1968** *DARE* (Qu. W20, *If somebody has no clothes on at all*) Inf **MO**16, Nekkidy.

nakid, nakit See **naked**

nakity See **nakedy**

namaycush n Also *masamacush, namaycush salmon, ~ trout* [Algonquian; see quot 1993]
=**lake trout 1.**
   [**1743** (1949) Isham *Observations* 22 (*DCan*), Sammon—Ne ma cu sheeck.] [**1787** Pennant *Arctic Zool. Suppl.* 139, *Naymacush.* Inhabits the lakes of *Hudson's Bay.*] **1829** Richardson *Fauna Boreali-Amer.* 3.179 **Gt Lakes,** The *namaycush* is the tyrant of the lakes. *Ibid,* Salmo Namaycush. . . *The Namaycush.* . . is a denizen of all the great lakes that lie between the United States and the Arctic Sea. **1842** DeKay *Zool. NY* 4.240, The Namaycush Salmon. **1849** (1851) Herbert *Frank Forester's Fish & Fishing* 105, The term Namaycush, which Pennant adopted, and Dr. Richardson has retained, both as its English name and its scientific distinction, is no more than its denomination by the Cree Indians, who term it Nammecoos. *Ibid* 127, The Masamacush. **1879** U.S. Natl. Museum *Bulletin* 14.58, Namaycush Trout. **1896** *Ibid* 47.504, *Cristivomer namaycush.* . . Great Lake Trout; Mackinaw Trout; Longe (Vermont); Togue (Maine); Namaycush; Masamacush. **1902** *Jrl. Amer. Folkl.* 15.251, *Namaycush.* One of the names of the "lake trout" (*Salmo namaycush*). . . The word, as the Cree *namekus,* Ojibwa *namegos* indicate, is derived from one of the Algonkian dialects of the Great Lakes. The Cree *namekus* is perhaps the origin of this word, since it appears to have arisen in the Canadian Northwest. **1904** *Salmon & Trout* 287, This charr (*Cristivomer namaycush*) is rich in baptismal nomenclature . . it is called . . Mackinaw trout in the region of the Great Lakes. . . In other sections of the Northwest it is known as the "namaycush". **1975** Evanoff *Catch More Fish* 85, The lake trout (*Salvelinus namaycush*) is technically a char, but most anglers call it a trout. Other names include Great Lake trout, Mackinaw trout, salmon trout, namaycush, forktail trout, laker, and togue. [**1993** Hewson *Computer-Generated Dict. Proto-Algonquian* 128, [Proto-Algonquian] name·kwehsa . . trout . . C[ree] name·kus . . M[enomini] name·koh . . O[jibwa] name·koss.]

name v [Cf *OED name* v.[1] 6.b] **chiefly S Midl, esp sAppalachians**
To mention (something); with *about*: to talk about; hence n *name* a mention.
   1856 in 1956 Eliason *Tarheel Talk* 284 **ceNC,** Nelson named to me that master wishes. **1895** *DN* 1.373 **eTN, seKY, wNC,** *Name:* mention. "If you see him, name it to him." **1909** *DN* 3.400 **nwAR,** *Name.* . . To mention. "I just thought I'd name it to you for fear you might forget it." **1910** *DN* 3.456 **seKY,** *Name.* . . To tell, to mention. "I named that to him a week ago, but he didn't do it." **1915** *DN* 4.242 **eTN,** I told her not to name it to me again. **1919** *DN* 5.34 **seKY,** He never named it to me. **1923** (1946) Greer-Petrie *Angeline Steppin'* 31 **csKY,** Lum so sildom names workin' that I never like to dis-incurridge him. **1926** *DN* 5.401 **Ozarks,** *Name.* . . To mention. **1926** Roberts *Time of Man* 122 **cKY,** I studied a heap about the stars, since you named it, in my own mind I have. **1931** *PMLA* 46.1305 **sAppalachians,** He'll name it to

Jones, if so be he's there. **1942** (1971) Campbell *Cloud-Walking* 19 **seKY**, He never named it to his mammy, not knowing iffen she would whip him for being so bold. **1945** *Harder Coll.* **cwTN**, [Letter:] *Name about.* . . mention unwarrantedly. "Don't name about getting old for I feel like a 18 year old." **1957** *Sat. Eve. Post Letters* **cIN**, Fred "named it" (mentioned) to me. **1968** Haun *Hawk's Done Gone* 18 **eTN**, He found a dead rat in his basket. Of course he knowed Shorty Shipley put it in there but he didn't make any name of it. **1971** Mitchell *Blow My Blues Away* 32 **nwMS** [Black], Everybody likes the drums. You can name drums and get a bigger crowd with 'em at just a picnic or most any kind of entertainment.

name oneself Jeff See **jeff** n 2

nametake n [Perh folk-etym]
1966 *PADS* 46.27 **cnAR** (as of 1952), *Name-take.* . . Namesake.—"Ruth is a name-take."

nan n[1] See **nanny** n[2] **1**

nan n[2] See **nana** n[1]

nan intj See **anan**

nana n[1] Usu |'nænə|; also |'nɑnə|; for addit varr see quots Also *nanna, nan(-nan), nanaw, nanno* [Hypocoristic] **scattered, but chiefly Nth, esp NEast** See Map Cf **nanny** n[1]
A grandmother; rarely, an aunt—also used as a term of address.
  1899 in 1969 Cummings *Selected Letters* 3 **ceMA**, I am sorry dear Nana [=Grandmother] but I will be a good boy. **1941** *LANE* Map 383 *(Grandma)* 5 infs, **neMA, ceNH, swME**, Nana [nænə]; 1 inf, **neMA**, Nana [nɑnə]; 1 inf, **csCT**, *Nan,* used by the informant as a child on hearing her grandmother call sheep *nanny-nanny,* and adopted by the family. **1962** Atwood *Vocab. TX* 65, *Grandmother.* . . Many private nicknames show up, most of them only once or twice each: . . *Nanna.* **1965–70** *DARE* (Qu. Z4, . . *'Grandmother'*) 34 Infs, **scattered, but esp NEast**, Nana [no transcriptions recorded]; 19 Infs, **chiefly NEast**, ['nænə]; OK28, PA165, TX29, ['nɑnə]; IL47, CA170, [nɑnɑ]; SC40, VA5, [nænæ]; MA7, [nɑnə]; GA28, ['bɪg ˌnænə]; MS15, OH98, VA41, Nanaw ['nænə]; NE11, Nanno ['næno]—used an awful lot here; MD24, TN2, Nan-nan; MI89, MT1, Nan; (Qu. Z7, *Nicknames and affectionate words for any other relatives*) Infs **LA20, NE4**, Nana—aunt; **PA49**, Nana—used to be used for aunt, and now is used for grandmother. **1986** Pederson *LAGS Concordance (Grandmother)* 7 infs, **FL, AL, LA, TX**, ['nænə]; 2 infs, **AR, TX**, ['nænɒ]; 1 inf, **TX**, ['nænæ]. **1993** *DARE* File **FL**, I have heard *nana* when I have visited friends of the family in Florida. I am from Michigan and had never heard it. *Ibid* **Upstate NY**, Some of it [=*nana*] is German derivation. One parent's mother is *nana* or *nanny* and the other's is something else. *Ibid* **cwCA** (as of c1955), My neighbors called their grandmother *Nana* ['nænə]. *Ibid* **MA**, My cousins call their Polish-background maternal grandmother *Nana.*

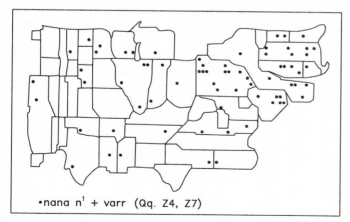
•nana n[1] + varr (Qq. Z4, Z7)

nana n[2] Also *nanna* [See quot 1949] *Gullah* Cf *DJE*
A mother or grandmother; an elderly woman.
  1892 (1893) Botume *First Days* 48 **seSC** (as of 1864) [Gullah], The terms "bubber" for brother, and "titty" for sister, with "nanna" for mother, and "mother" for grandmother . . were so generally used. **1949** Turner *Africanisms* 198 **sSC, GA coasts** [Gullah], [nɑ] (['nɑnɑ] . .) 'mother'; 'any elderly woman'. . . T[wi] [nɑnã] 'grandparent.' **1987** Jones-Jackson *When Roots Die* 137 **sSC coast** [Gullah], There are a host of African-derived words in Gullah, some of which are generally un-

known to inland black speakers, for example: . . *nana,* "elderly woman," "grandmother": Twi.

nanan See **nenaine**

nanaw See **nana** n[1]

‡**nancy** n Cf **nickie** n[1]
  1968 *DARE* (Qu. E20, *Soft rolls of dust that collect on the floor under beds or other furniture*) Inf **PA131**, Nancies.

Nancy Julia n
  1921 *DN* 5.114 **seCA**, *Nancy Julia.* . . Doe deer. Sierra Nevada.

Nancy-over-the-ground n [See quot 1934]
A **foamflower** (here: *Tiarella cordifolia* or *T. trifoliata*).
  1893 *Jrl. Amer. Folkl.* 6.142 **MA**, *Tiarella cordifolia,* Nancy-over-the-ground. **1934** Haskin *Wild Flowers Pacific Coast* 145, Foamflower—*Tiarella unifoliata.* . . A very abundant plant, sometimes completely carpeting the forest floor; from this it has earned another of its popular names, that of Nancy-over-the-ground. **1952** Taylor *Plants Colonial Days* 38, Foamflower [=*Tiarella cordifolia*]. . . Other common names are false miterwort . . coolwort, and Nancy-over-the-ground. **1956** St. John *Flora SE WA* 191, *Tiarella unifoliata.* . . Nancy-over-the-Ground.

nani adj |nɑni| [Haw] **HI**
Beautiful.
  1951 *AmSp* 26.23 **HI**, Other common Hawaiian words are *ae* (yes), . . *nani* (beautiful). **1954–60** Hance et al. *Hawaiian Sugar* 5, Nani . . [nɑni]—Beautiful. **1972** Carr *Da Kine Talk* 88 **HI**, *Hawaiian Words Commonly Heard In Hawaii's English.* . . Nani. Pretty, beautiful. **1984** Sunset *HI Guide* 85, *Nani*—beautiful.

nanna n[1], **nan-nan** See **nana** n[1]

nanna n[2] See **nana** n[2]

'**nanner** See **banana**

nannie n[1] See **nanny** n[1]

nannie n[2] See **nanny** n[2]

nanninose See **maninose**

nanno See **nana** n[1]

nanny n[1] Also sp *nannie* **scattered exc nNEng, Upper MW, Cent** See Map Cf **nana** n[1]
A grandmother; rarely, a mother or aunt—also used as a term of address.
  1941 *LANE* Map 383 *(Grandma)* 1 inf, **swME**, Nanny [næni]. **1962** Atwood *Vocab. TX* 65, *Grandmother.* . . Many private nicknames show up, most of them only once or twice each: . . *Nannie.* **1965–70** *DARE* (Qu. Z4, . . *'Grandmother'*) 51 Infs, **scattered exc nNEng, Upper MW, Cent**, Nanny; MI81, ['nɑni]; (Qu. Z2, . . *'Mother'*) Inf **TX35**, Nanny—long ago; (Qu. Z7, *Nicknames and affectionate words for any other relatives*) Inf **LA46**, Nanny; **MD7**, Nanny—for aunt; **PA63**, Aunt, also nanny. **1970** Tarpley *Blinky* 208, *Usual term of affection for grandmother* . . nanny [rare]. **1986** Pederson *LAGS Concordance (Grandmother)* 17 infs, **Gulf Region**, Nanny; *(Mother)* 1 inf, **swAL**, Nanny.

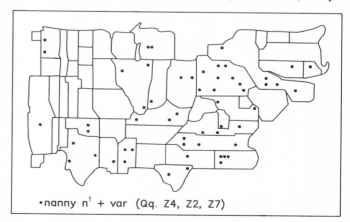
•nanny n[1] + var (Qq. Z4, Z2, Z7)

nanny n[2] Also sp *nannie* [Transf from *nanny* a female goat]
1 also *nan, nanny sheep*: A sheep, esp a female—also used as a call to sheep. Cf **co-nan(nie)**
  1896 *DN* 1.414 **n,cNY**, *Conan* . . for "Come, Nan"? *Ibid* 421 **cNY**,

Nan! nan!: a call for sheep. **1939** *LANE* Map 225 (*Calls to sheep in the pasture*) 10 infs, **CT, MA, ME,** Nannie; 8 infs, **CT, VT, ME,** Nan [næn]; 1 inf, **swCT,** [næ]; 1 inf, **seNY,** Nan, nan, nan. **1949** Kurath *Word Geog.* 65, Calls to Sheep. . . Of the New England calls, *nannie!* and its variants have the wider spread. It is (or was) current all the way from Maine and Cape Cod to the Western Reserve. . . In the South *nannie!* and its variants are in general use on both sides of Chesapeake Bay, on the Rappahannock, in coastal North Carolina, and on the Peedee. This coastal call has been carried westward into the Blue Ridge of North Carolina and westernmost Virginia. **1961** *AmSp* 36.28 **Cleveland OH,** *Nannie,* or *co-nannie,* was recorded in two of the field interviews. **1965–70** *DARE* (Qu. K62, . . *A female sheep*) Inf **LA12,** Nanny, [corr to] yo; **NC53,** [iv] [sic]; nanny; **TX13,** Nanny; **WA14,** Nanny, ewe; (Qu. K85, *The call to sheep to come in from the pasture*) Infs **NC60, WA2,** Nanny; **NY27, 102,** Nanny, nanny, nanny; **NY219,** Nan; **MI47, NY32, PA222,** Come nanny; **KY29,** Come on nanny; **MI40, NY27,** Here nanny (nanny, nanny); **TN14,** Sheep nanny. **1967** Faries *Word Geog.* MO 94, In Missouri approximately one-third of the [approx 230] informants seem never to have employed any sheep calls. . . However, of the calls that do exist in Missouri, the prevailing ones seem to be the Northern and Southern *nannie!* and its variants (227 occurrences). **1971** Wood *Vocab. Change* 46, The call to get sheep in from the pasture is . . *nan(nie)* in Louisiana. **1973** Allen *LAUM* 1.266 (as of c1950) 3 infs, **MN, SD,** Nanny, nanny. **1986** Pederson *LAGS Concordance* **Gulf Region** (*Sheep*) 22 infs, Nanny; 1 inf, Nanny sheep.

2 also *nanny plum:* Sheep manure; a pellet of sheep dung; hence nouns *nanny(-plum) tea, sheep-nanny tea* an infusion of sheep dung used as a remedy.

    1833 Greene *Life Dr. Dodimus* 1.93, Nanny tea—I took some when I had the weazles [sic]. **1869** (1921) Haycraft *Hist. Elizabethtown KY* 151 (as of c1790), Then sheep-nannie tea was prescribed; about a quart of that condiment swallowed down at night was certain to effect a cure. **1937** Coffin *Kennebec* 239 **ME,** One remedy there is, peculiar to the heart of Maine, I hope. That is the laxative nanny-plum tea. You find nanny plums where the sheep have marched on their narrow track through the ferns. **1944** Howard *Walkin' Preacher* 252 **Ozarks,** Wish't ye'd git me some dry sheep droppin's. . . Pick 'em up on the hard ground whar they ain't drawed no damp. I'm goin' to fetch them Davis young'uns some swallers of sheep-nanny tea. **1945** Pickard–Buley *Midwest Pioneer* 40 (as of c1820), The breaking out in eruptive fevers, such as measles, was hastened by the use of sheep-dung tea, popularly known as nanny tea. **1953** Randolph–Wilson *Down in Holler* 266 **Ozarks,** Nanny tea. . . A folk remedy, made by boiling sheep manure in water. **c1960** *Wilson Coll.* **csKY,** Nanny tea. . . tea made of sheep manure, supposed to be the best remedy to break out measles. **1964** *PADS* 42.21 **csKY,** *Nanny* (or *sheep-nanny*). Sheep manure made into a tea to break out measles. **1966** *Wilson Coll.* **csKY,** Nanny plum—pellet of sheep manure. [**1968** *DARE* (Qu. BB51a, . . *Cures for corns or warts*) Inf **NH14,** Sheep-shit tea.] **1975** Gould *ME Lingo* 187, *Nanny-plum tea*—A home remedy for measles whose efficacy was happily exploded long since: sheep droppings (*nanny plums*) steeped in rain water.

3 in phrr *get one's nanny (goat):* To irritate, annoy one; to get one's goat.

    1909 *NY Eve. Jrl.* (NY) 8 Dec 16 (*Zwilling Coll.*), Fedink's speed got Bunk's nanny something awful. **1914** *Sat. Eve. Post* 15 Aug 9, "Good night, Horseshoes!" he says. That got my nanny this time. "Shut up, you lucky stiff!" I says. **1966–69** *DARE* (Qu. Y5, . . *To urge somebody to do something he shouldn't:* "Johnny wouldn't have tried that if the other boys hadn't _____.") Inf **NM5,** Got his nanny; (Qu. GG13a, *When something keeps bothering a person*) Inf **GA72,** Gets my nanny goat; (Qu. II29b, . . *To explain the unpleasant effect that person has on you:* "He just _____.") Inf **GA72,** Gets my nanny goat. **1969** *DARE* File **neCT,** That gets my nanny—gets my goat; **swMA,** What gets my nanny—what makes me so angry; what irritates me. **1989** *Ibid* **Philadelphia PA,** They [=children with a water pistol filled with water] couldn't get her nanny with water so they switched to melted grape jelly as a shooting medium.

nanny n[3] [Prob var of **nenaine,** infl by **nanny** n[1]]
    A godmother.

    1967 LeCompte *Word Atlas* 267 **seLA,** Godmother . . nanny [3 of 21 infs]. **1981** Pederson *LAGS Basic Materials,* 1 inf, **seLA,** [nə'næ·ɛn] = godmother . . ['næ·ɛni] = godmother. [Inf is a French speaker.]

nannyberry n
    1 also *nannybush, nanny plum:* Any of several **viburnums,** but esp *Viburnum lentago* which is also called **black haw 1, ~ thorn 2, cowberry 4, doodlegee, sheepberry, sweetberry,**

sweet viburnum, tea plant, wild raisin; also the fruit of such a plant. [**nanny** n[2] 2; see quot 1954]

    1867 De Voe *Market Asst.* 384, *Partridge-berries,* or *nanny-berries.* These little black berries grow in clusters, on a tree-like bush, on uncultivated grounds or along hedges. **1874** *Shaker Med. Preparations* 209, Nanny Bush—*Viburnum lentago.* . . Nanny Berry. **1894** *Jrl. Amer. Folkl.* 7.90, *Viburnum nudum* . . nanny-berry, West Va., Livingston Co., N.Y., Ferrisburgh, Vt. **1898** *Ibid* 11.228, *Viburnum lentago.* . . Nanny-plum, Farmington, Me. **1931** Harned *Wild Flowers Alleghanies* 469, Sweet Viburnum. . . Fruit blue with a bloom, on reddish stems, ovoid, with a nipple-like tip which is responsible for the popular name Nanny-berry. **1931–33** *LANE Worksheets* **swMA,** Nannyberries got a pit in them, grow on a bush ten feet high. **1954** McAtee *Suppl. to Nomina Abitera* [4], Nannyberry, Nanny-Plum, Sheepberry (*Viburnum lentago* primarily, but applied also to *V. prunifolium*)—These names refer to a resemblance of the fruits (or blackhaws) to sheep turds. The latter are used in folk medicine to make nanny-tea or nanny-plum tea. **1960** Vines *Trees SW* 959, It [=*Viburnum prunifolium*] is also known under the vernacular names of Sheep-berry, Nanny-berry. *Ibid* 963, *Rafinesque Viburnum—Viburnum rafinesquianum.* . . The vernacular names of Hairy Nanny-berry and Downy Arrow-wood are used in some areas. **1968** *DARE* FW Addit **NY69,** Nannyberry bark—gargle for putrid sore throat. *Ibid* **NY91,** Nannyberry—*Viburnum dentatum*—locals may call other viburnums nannyberry. **1976** Bruce *How to Grow Wildflowers* 130, Five species comprise the purely American section Lentago: Nanny-berry, *V. lentago* [etc]. **1979** Little *Checklist U.S. Trees* 294, *Viburnum rufidulum* . . rusty nannyberry, southern nannyberry, nannyberry.

2 A **buffalo berry** (here: *Shepherdia canadensis*).
    1931 U.S. Dept. Ag. *Misc. Pub.* 101.119, Russet buffaloberry . . known locally as Canadian, or thornless buffaloberry, nannyberry [etc].

nannybush See **nannyberry 1**

nanny (goat), get one's See **nanny** n[2] 3

nannynose See **maninose**

nanny plum n
    1 See **nanny** n[2] 2.
    2 See **nannyberry 1.**

nanny(-plum) tea See **nanny** n[2] 2

nanny sheep See **nanny** n[2] 1

Nantucket sleighride n **chiefly NEng** *old-fash*
    A run of a whaling boat in tow by a harpooned whale; by ext: a run of a boat being towed by another vessel.

    1891 *Century Dict.* 5692, *Nantucket sleigh-ride,* the towing of a whale-boat by the whale. **1924** *DN* 5.287 **Cape Cod MA,** We find a ride in a small boat which is being towed behind a large boat referred to as a 'Nantucket sleigh ride', tho originally the phrase was used in the whaling industry. **1924** Anthony *Down to the Sea* 170 (as of 1850), The whale may . . take the boat for a 'Nantucket sleigh ride' charging off at a terrifying pace. **1938** Tripp *Flukes* 197, The animal was not mortally wounded, however, the whale line tightened like a fiddlestring and off he went towing the boat on its "Nantucket sleigh ride," as the whalemen say. **1938** *AmSp* 13.143 **MA,** 'Nantucket sleigh-ride.' . . Legends say that some rides have been so swift as to burn the paint off the boat or melt the nails. **1945** Colcord *Sea Language* 133 **ME, Cape Cod, Long Island,** *Nantucket sleigh-ride.* This term refers to a whaleboat fast to a whale, which sometimes runs away and tows the boat at a furious clip for miles. **1978** Whipple *Vintage Nantucket* 131 **MA,** Or the whale might try another tactic; it might take off on a 15-mile-an-hour dash across the surface of the Pacific, with the whaleboat rushing after in the famous "Nantucket Sleighride," the men snubbing the line when they could and letting it out when necessary, as if playing a giant trout.

nanu n
    A grandfather or grandmother—also used as a term of address.
    1969 *DARE* (Qu. Z3, . . '*Grandfather*') Inf **CA170,** Nanu ['nɑnu]. **1994** *DARE* File **cwMO** (as of 1950s), My cousins and I called our Kansas City grandmother *Nanu* ['nænu].

nanynose See **maninose**

nap n[1]
    1 A tight curl of hair. *among Black speakers* Cf **nappy** adj
    1931 (1991) Hughes–Hurston *Mule Bone* 115 **cFL** [Black], Git away from me before I knock every nap off yo' head, one by one. **1937** *Writer* 50.239 **neOH** [Black], *Naps* . . kinky hair common to most negroes. **1942** *Amer. Mercury* 55.223.95 **Harlem NYC** [Black], *Naps*—kinky

hair. **1970** Major *Dict. Afro-Amer. Slang* 84, *Naps:* kinky hair. **1994** Smitherman *Black Talk* 150, *Kinks*—Extremely curly hair, . . curled so tightly it appears "woolly". . . Also *naps*.
2 See quot.
   1966–68 *DARE* (Qu. E20, *Soft rolls of dust that collect on the floor under beds or other furniture*) Inf **DC**7, Nap; **NC**50, Nap [næb].

nap n[2] See **nape**

nap n[3] See **lagniappe**

nape n Usu |nep|; also **esp NEast, Sth, S Midl** |næp| Pronc-sp *nap*
Std sense, var form.
   1892 *DN* 1.240 **cwMO,** *Nape.* Almost universally [næp] in Kansas City. [*DN* Ed: So in New England.] **1893** Shands *MS Speech* 74, *Nape* [næp]. **1899** (1912) Green *VA Folk-Speech* 294, *Nap*. . . Nape. The back, upper part of the neck. **1906** *DN* 3.121 **sIN,** *Nap*. . . Regular form of *nape*. **1907** *DN* 3.194 **seNH,** The dog grabbed the woodchuck by the nap of the neck and shook him out. **1910** *DN* 3.445 **wNY,** *Nap of the neck*. **1928** *AmSp* 3.402 **Ozarks,** The *nape* of the neck is always made to rhyme with *cap*. **1954** *Harder Coll.* **cwTN,** 'At dog went 'n got 'im by nap o' the neck. **1959** *VT Hist.* 27.150 **nw,cnVT,** *Nape* [næp]. . . Occasional. **c1960** *Wilson Coll.* **csKY,** *Nape* . . always [næp]. **1965–70** *DARE* (Qu. X30, . . *The back part of the neck;* total Infs questioned, 75) 26 Infs, Nap (of the neck). **1983** *MJLF* 9.1.48 **ceKY,** *Nap* . . the nape.

napkin n Also *baby napkin, nappy* [*OEDS* napkin 1845 →, *nappy* 1927 →] Cf **hippen**
A diaper.
   1927 (1970) Sears *Catalogue* 562, [Index:] Napkins, Babies'. **1950** *WELS* (The folded cloth worn by a baby) 1 Inf, **ceWI,** Napkins—recent. **1965–70** *DARE* (Qu. W19) 27 Infs, **scattered,** Napkin; **VA**9, Baby napkin; **CO**27, **IL**113, Nappy.

napkin-ring buckwheat n
A **buckwheat 2** (here: *Eriogonum intrafractum*).
   1941 Jaeger *Wildflowers* 37 **Desert SW,** *Napkin-ring Buckwheat. Eriogonum intrafractum*. . . When old, as Gilman states, the bark of the stems falls away "leaving the stems made up of a series of white sections or joints looking like tiny napkin rings. The rings easily unjoint when weathered enough, and on the ground around old plants the fallen rings indicate the vintages of the different years' growth of stalks.[""] Grapevine Mt., Death Valley Nat. Mon.

nap of sleep n
A short sleep, doze.
   1931 *PMLA* 46.1310 **sAppalachians,** He tuk a nap o' sleep. **1944** *PADS* 2.47 **csVA,** *Nap o'sleep*. . . A little sleep. **1946** Stuart *Tales Plum Grove* 106 **seKY,** You waked me up. I was about to take a nap o' sleep.

napper's house, go to v phr Also *go to nappy's house* **esp Sth, S Midl**
To go to sleep.
   1944 *PADS* 2.47 **nwNC, csVA,** *Napper's house, to go to*. . . To go to sleep. **1954** *Harder Coll.* **cwTN,** [Letter:] Well I'm going to nappers house. **1956** McAtee *Some Dialect NC* 30, *Napper's house, go to*. . . go to sleep. **1966–67** *DARE* (Qu. X40, . . *Ways . . of saying, "I'm going to bed"*) Inf **SC**46, Go to nappy's house—children's word; **TX**35, Going to nappy's house; **AR**18, Time to go to nappy's house.

nappy n[1] Also *nappy dish* Also sp *nappie* [Scots dial dimin of *nap* bowl, basin] **chiefly NEng** See Map *somewhat old-fash*
A shallow dish used for baking or serving.
   1864 (1873) Webster *Amer. Dict.* 874, *Nappy*. . . A round earthen dish, with a flat bottom and sloping sides. [Written also *nappie*.] **1873** Whitney *Other Girls* 421 **Boston MA,** Kate . . producing some nice little stone-ware nappies hot from the hot closet, transferred the food from the china to these. **1895** *DN* 1.391 **neMA,** *Nappy:* round, shallow crockery dish used for baking pies. [*DN* Ed: A square vegetable dish was billed as a "nappie" from R.H. Macy & Co., New York, in July, 1895.] **1905** *DN* 3.14 **cCT,** *Nappy*. . . An earthen dish. **1922** (1926) Cady *Rhymes VT* 113, Ma unloads a nappy full / Of boiled New England dinner. **1927** (1970) Sears *Catalogue* 920, 6-Inch Handled Nappy. Cut with a rose and leaf design in silver gray finish on both sides. Pressed star bottom. **1947** Bowles-Towle *New Engl. Cooking* 77, Serve the [baked] beans in a large earthenware nappy. **1965–70** *DARE* (Qu. G6, . . *Dishes that you might have on the table for a big dinner or special*

occasion—for example, Thanksgiving) 14 Infs, **chiefly NEng,** Nappy (or nappies); **AL**21, Cut-glass nappies; **UT**6, Nappy dishes. [14 of 16 Infs old] **1969** *Oregonian* (Portland OR) 14 Dec mag sec 24/1 *(OEDS)*, Nappies (those flat bottomed, slope-sided little dishes for relish and a myriad of other uses). **1979** *DARE* File **cMA** (as of c1915), Nappy— rather like a large soup plate. This was a common term in central Massachusetts. I remember my aunt's telling that no one knew what a *nappy* was in Syracuse, New York. **1982** *Greenfield Recorder* (MA) 16 Jan sec A 4, There were . . cereal dishes, small nappies and china hatpin holders, which for a long time have been antiques selling for many times their original price.

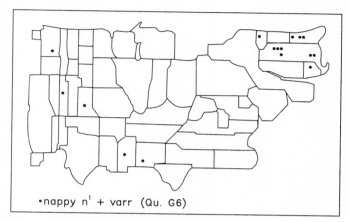

•nappy n[1] + varr (Qu. G6)

nappy n[2] See **napkin**

nappy adj [*OED* nappy a.[1] downy, shaggy; 1499 →] **chiefly Sth, S Midl** *esp freq among Black speakers; sometimes derog* Cf **kinky-head, nap** n[1]
Kinky, bushy—usu applied to a Black person's hair; hence adj *nappyblack* having a pronounced African appearance; n *nappy-head* someone with kinky hair; a Black person.
   c1937 in 1970 Yetman *Voices* 253 **OK** [Black], Niggers come up from the cabins nappy-headed, just like they gwine to the field. **1943** Writers' Program NC *Bundle of Troubles* 34 [Black], You git me them cardin' boards and lemme give yo'all's hair a good combin'. You sure a passel of nappy haids. **1950** Lomax *Mr. Jelly Roll* 80, Lightskinned Downtown shared the bandstand with 'real black and nappy-headed' Uptown. **1952** Brown *NC Folkl.* 1.568 **cnNC,** *Nappy*. . . Kinky-headed. "Colored folks comes into this world nappy, and they goes out nappy." **1956** Longstreet *Real Jazz* 150, To call a man *nappy* is to say his hair is kinky—a real insult. **c1960** *Wilson Coll.* **csKY,** *Nappy*. . . Kinky-headed. **1966** *Keystone Folkl. Qrly.* 11.81 **VA,** She used to say they would come up with black nappy-haired babies. **1966–70** *DARE* (Qu. X28, *Joking words . . for a person's head*) Infs **FL**48, **MS**6, Nappy head; **MO**23, Nappy-headed; (Qu. HH28, *Names and nicknames . . for people of foreign background*) Inf **GA**89, Nappy-heads—"nigger children." **1970** Major *Dict. Afro-Amer. Slang* 84, *Nappyblack:* (1960's) very African-looking. **1971** *Black World* June 71, Her hair . . was in the bushy style that the freedom riders had brought. They called it 'natural'; Bojack called it nappy. **1973** *Ibid* Apr 63 **sePA,** All them ol' nappy-heads runnin' up there tryin' to pull his clothes off. **1982** *Milwaukee Jrl.* (WI) 1 Aug Life Style sec 1, From the day the first strand of tightly curled (nappy, kinky, bushy) hair appeared on my head, I was taught that hair was good if it was long and straight. **1994** *WI State Jrl.* (Madison) 2 Oct sec G 1/2 [Black], I have thick, naturally kinky hair—in one politically incorrect word, it's *nappy*.

nappy dish See **nappy** n[1]

nappy-head See **nappy** adj

nappy's house, go to See **napper's house, go to**

nar adj[1] See **narrow**

nar adj[2] See **ne'er** adj[1]

n'ar adj, adv See **near**

nara See **ne'er** adj[1]

nard adj, also used absol Also sp *narr'd* [Appar pronc-spp for *narrowed;* cf *OED* narrow cloth (at **narrow** a. 1.c)]
See quot 1952.
   1933 Miller *Lamb in His Bosom* 30 **GA,** A length of narr'd homespun

that her mother had woven. **1952** Brown *NC Folkl.* 1.568, *Nard.* . . Yellow homespun cloth; said to be a corruption of "northern." I have heard [nɑːd] and [ˈnɑrə], which I took to be forms of "narrowed (cloth)" and "narrow (cloth)."—Illiterate.

nare See **ne'er** adj[1]

‡narely adv [Perh blend of *not* or **nary** adv + *barely*]
1968 *DARE* (Qu. LL14, *None at all, not even one: "This pond used to be full of fish but now there's _____ left."*) Inf **NJ**25, Narely [ˈnɛrli] one.

narn See **nairn**

narr adj[1] See **narrow**

narr adj[2] See **ne'er** adj[1]

narra See **ne'er** adj[1]

narr'd See **nard**

narrow adj, v, n Usu |ˈnæro, ˈnɛro|; less freq |ˈnɑro|; also **chiefly Sth, S Midl, less freq NEast** |-ə(r), -ɪ|; infreq |nɑr, nær|; for addit varr see quots Cf Pronc Intro 3.I.2.a, 3.I.12.d Pronc-spp *na'ar, nar(r), narrer, narr(e)y, norrer, norry* Cf **nard**
A Forms.
  1877 *Harper's New Mth. Mag.* 54.295 **CT,** What'd he want to be a-kitin' round in a narrer road this time o' night? **1884** Jewett *Country Dr.* 7 **ME,** They asked each other's advice from time to time about the propriety of "narrerin'" or whether it were not best to "widden" according to the progress their respective stockings had made. **1885** Murfree *Prophet of Smoky Mts.* 256 **eTN,** It looked mighty narrer. **1890** *DN* 1.71 **LA,** *Narrow* . . with *a* as in *father*. **1891** *DN* 1.118 **cNY,** [ˈnɑrwɪn] . . 'narrowing'. *Ibid* 164 **cNY,** Narrow [ˈnɑrɚ]. **1905** *DN* 3.103 **nwAR,** [ˈnærə]. **1914** *DN* 4.103 **cKS,** The sound [ɑ] occurs . . in *farrow, harrow,* . . *narrow.* **1919** *DN* 5.34 **seKY,** *Nars.* . . Narrows. **1923** *DN* 5.215 **swMO,** *Narrers.* . . A stretch of narrow road. **1923** (1946) Greer-Petrie *Angeline Steppin'* 34 **csKY,** Havin' to climb them norrer orn (iron) steps fastened to the *outside of the house.* **1926** *DN* 5.401 **Ozarks,** *Narr'.* . . Narrow. **1928** *AmSp* 3.401 **Ozarks,** In *narrow, arrow, barrel* and the like, the accented vowel has exactly the same sound as the *a* in *father;* such words are often reduced to monosyllables—*narr', arr', bar'l.* **1933** *AmSp* 8.1.24 **sAppalachians,** *Narrow,* besides having the correct pronunciation, is in some places *narrer* and other *narrey,* sometimes with the vowel of *father* and sometimes with the vowel of *hat.* **1935** *AmSp* 10.295 **Upstate NY,** *Narrow* . . 83 [ɛ], 164 [æ]. *Ibid* 296, *Narrow* appears twice with [a]. **1938** *FWP Guide DE* 500, The road is so norry I cain't hardly shun the ruts. **1941** Stuart *Men of Mts.* 248 **neKY,** Wagons with them nar-rimmed wheels cut down. **1942** Hall *Smoky Mt. Speech* 81 **wNC, eTN,** *Narrow* [ˈnɑrɪ] . . seems to be rare. **1954** *Harder Coll.* **cwTN,** He had a nar squeak 'at time. **c1960** *Wilson Coll.* **csKY,** *Narrow* is often [ˈnɑrə] or [ˈnærə]. **1967** *DARE* FW Addit **TN**15, Narrow-minded [ˌnɑrɪˈmɑndɪd]. **1972** Cooper *NC Mt. Folkl.* 94, *Narr*—narrow. **1974** Fink *Mountain Speech* 17 **wNC, eTN,** *Na'ar* . . narrow. "a na'ar bridge." **1976** Garber *Mountainese* 60 **sAppalachians,** *Narry* . . narrow. **1981** Pederson *LAGS Basic Materials,* 1 inf, **swFL,** [ə ˈnæːrəskeˑˀɪp] a narrow escape; 1 inf, **cTN,** [nɑˑə] narrow; 1 inf, **cTN,** [næɚˀ]—some of the old folks would use it; 1 inf, **nwAL,** [næˑɚ] = narrow; 1 inf, **neAR,** [soˀᵾ nɑˑəˀ] so narrow; 1 inf, **cnAR,** [nɑˑɚ] narrow; 1 inf, **cAR,** [nɑˑə roˀᵾd] = narrow [road]; 1 inf, **seTX,** [ˈnæˑˌmaˑɪndɪd] narrow-minded.
B Senses.
1 also *narrow-contracted,* *~-gutted:* Stingy, ungenerous. **chiefly NEng**
  1903 *DN* 2.299 **Cape Cod MA** (as of a1857), *Narrow gutted.* . . Mean, ungenerous. **1909** *DN* 3.414 **nME,** *Narrow contracted.* . . Narrow-minded; stingy. **1916** *DN* 4.264 **Cape Cod MA,** Joe Preston's nigher 'n the bark to a tree; he's so narrer-gutted he's let his own brother's wife come on the town. **1941** *LANE* Map 484, 1 inf, **seVT,** Narrow [=stingy]. **1944** *AmSp* 19.156 **IN,** *Narrow-contracted* . . straight-laced, sometimes stingy. **1968** *DARE* (Qu. U36b, . . *A person who saves in a mean way or is greedy in money matters: "She certainly is _____."*) Inf **NH**14, Narrow.
2 also *narrow-contracted,* *~-nebbed:* Stubborn, dogmatic; straitlaced; unsociable.
  1909 [see **1** above]. **1930** Shoemaker *1300 Words* 42 **cPA Mts** (as of c1900), *Narrow*—Cross, unsociable. . . *Narrow-nebbed*—Dogmatic, positive, peculiar. **1944** [see **1** above]. **1968** [see **narrow-neck**]. **1972**

NYT Article Letters **ME,** If we're stubborn in changing our minds, we're "narrow-contracted".

narrowback n *derog*
1 A second-generation American, esp one of Irish descent.
  [**1930** Shoemaker *1300 Words* 42 **cPA Mts** (as of c1900), *Narrowback*—A man too weak to engage in hard labor.] **1957** *NY Times* (NY) 29 Sept sec 2 3/1, William Joseph Patrick (Pat) O'Brien, a Milwaukee-born Irishman or narrowback. **1964** *PADS* 42.39 **Chicago IL,** *Irish* informants use *turkey* and *saltwater turkey* to designate a recent immigrant and *narrowback* for a second generation Irishman who has neither the need, the desire, nor the physical equipment to do the work his father had to do. **1968** *DARE* File **NYC,** Narrowback—a person born of parents in the United States. **1975** Higgins *City on Hill* 56 **eMA,** "You think it's maybe because he spent his whole life trying to make you into a Protestant and then you went out and married the same kind of commoner he always was himself, and a narrowback to boot?" . . "No, it's not the narrowback," she said, "he doesn't know what a narrowback is." "He knows what a mick is, though," Cavanaugh said.
2 See quot.
  1968 *DARE* File **Newport RI,** Narrowback—a Protestant.

narrow-contracted See **narrow B1, 2**

narrow dock n Also *narrow-leaf dock, narrow-leaved ~* Usu **curled dock,** occas another **dock** n[1].
  1784 in 1785 Amer. Acad. Arts & Sci. *Memoirs* 1.436, *Rumex floribus hermaphroditis: valvulis dentatis nudis, pedicellis planis reflexis.* . . *Narrow Dock.* . . The fresh roots bruised and made into an ointment, or decoction, cure the itch. **1859** (1880) Darlington *Amer. Weeds* 283, *Curled Rumex*—Sour Dock. Curled Dock. Narrow Dock. **1897** *Jrl. Amer. Folkl.* 10.54 **OH,** *Rumex crispus* . . narrow dock . . Sulphur Grove. **1903** *DN* 2.292 **Cape Cod MA** (as of a1857), *Dock* . . a kind of plant, as *burr-dock, narrow-dock.* **1947** (1976) Curtin *Healing Herbs* 113, *Lengua de vaca* . . narrow dock. **1949** Webber *Backwoods Teacher* 264 **Ozarks,** We picked . . shoots of lamb's-quarter and narrow dock. **c1960** *Wilson Coll.* **csKY,** *Narrow dock*—The narrow-leafed variety that is used regularly in wild greens or "sallet." **1961** Peck *Manual OR* 262, *R[umex] mexicanus* . . Narrow-leaved Dock. **1968–70** *DARE* (Qu. I28a, b, . . *Kinds of things . . you call 'greens'*) Infs **IN**3, 7, 39, **KY**74, 81, **MI**116, **PA**115, 119, Narrow dock; **MD**30, Narrow dock—long, narrow leaf, springs up from ground; **NY**75, **OH**72, Narrow-leaf dock; **KY**85, Narrow-leaf dock—cooked—wild green; (Qu. S21, . . *Weeds . . that are a trouble in gardens and fields*) Inf **NY**75, Narrow-leaf dock. **1973** Hitchcock–Cronquist *Flora Pacific NW* 92, Willow dock, narrow-l[ea]v[e]d d[ock]. . . *R[umex] salicifolius.*

narrow-gauge(d) mule n Cf **mule-eared rabbit** =**jackrabbit 1.**
  1882 *Ornith. & Oologist* 7.98 **swCA,** I have often found, in its burrows, portions of the large Jackass Hare (Lepus californicus) or "Narrow Gauged Mule,"—as popularly known in California. **1917** Anthony *Mammals Amer.* 274, As long ago as 1851, Audubon and Bachman, writing of a species found along the Mexican border, said: "This species [=the jackrabbit] is called the jackass rabbit in Texas, owing to the length of its ears." For the same reason, in certain parts of California they have been called "narrow-gauge mules" and "small mules." **1930** Henry *Conquering Plains* 294 **KS** (as of 1870s), Thus Quibbs informed himself on the Plains as to its famous narrow-gauged mules, of which he had heard so much.

narrow-gutted See **narrow B1**

narrow home n
=**long home.**
  1936 *AmSp* 11.201 [Euphemisms for the grave], Narrow home.

narrow-leaf dock, narrow-leaved dock See **narrow dock**

narrow-nebbed See **narrow B2**

narrow-neck n Cf **narrow B2**
  1968 *DARE* (Qu. CC4, . . *Nicknames . . for various religions or religious groups*) Inf **PA**79, Holy Rollers—for narrow ones; also narrow-necks.

narry adj[1] See **nary** adj

narry adj[2], v, n See **narrow**

narthing See **nothing**

narve See **nerve**

narvish See **nervish**

narvous See **nervous**

nary adj Also *nairy, narry, nory* [Engl, Ir dial forms of *never a* (*EDD* at *never a, never a one*); cf **ne'er** adj[1]]

1 often with other negatives: Not a single, no; hence pron *nary* none, nothing. Note: Although in origin *nary* is a var of *never a,* the presence of the indefinite article is often not recognized, and *nary* is followed by a pleonastic article, or, rarely, occurs in contexts where the article is not appropriate. *DARE* QR evidence shows that the comb *nary a one* (with pleonastic article) is **widespread,** while *nary one* is less common and **chiefly Sth, S Midl** (See Map). Cf **ary 1**

1843 Thompson *Major Jones' Courtship* 34 **GA,** Ther aint no mortgage on narry nigger nor foot of ground. **1851** Hooper *Widow Rugby's Husband* 45 **AL,** Thar's narry nuther like me! **1891** Johnston *Primes & Neighbors* 34 **GA,** I'm off to bed, a-hopin' in my soul that nary sech another day may bring forth. **1893** Shands *MS Speech* 47, Nary [næɾɪ]. Used by negroes and illiterate whites for *ne'er a...* Just as *ary, nary* always follows a negative; but, of course, the employment of a double negative is not unusual among the uneducated. **1895** *DN* 1.376, **eTN, seKY, wNC,** I never seen nary 'thout [=unless] that wasn't one. **1902** *DN* 2.239 **sIL,** Nary, pron. Not one. **1905** *DN* 3.14 **cCT,** Nary... Not one... *Nary red...* Not a red cent. *Ibid* 63 **eNE,** Nary a cent. *Ibid* 88 **nwAR,** Nary, pron[ominal] adj. No, none. **1906** *DN* 3.121 **sIN,** Nary, pron. Not any. **1909** *DN* 3.351 **eAL, wGA,** Nairy, adj. or pron. Ne'er a, neither, no. **1910** *DN* 3.456 **seKY,** He didn't do nary bit of that work. **1911** *DN* 3.539 **eKY,** I won't do it nary a step. **1914** *DN* 4.160 **cVA,** Ah aint got nairy a apple. **1915** *DN* 4.186 **swVA,** He wouldn't help nairy bit. *Ibid* 224 **wTX,** Airy, nairy... Quite common. *Ibid* 243 **cMT,** Was up in the mountains a week and got nary deer. **1916** *DN* 4.341 **seOH,** Nairy. Contraction of *ne'er a.* General. **1923** *DN* 5.215 **swMO,** I haint nary cent. **1927** *AmSp* 3.140 **eME,** "Nary" or "not ary"... "Nary fish did he catch." **1930** Williams *Logger-Talk* 26 **Pacific NW,** He said nary a word. **1936–56** *Hall Coll.* **wNC, eTN,** They wouldn't nary one of 'em go. *Ibid,* I ain't seed nary another'n [nɛɾɪ ənɑðɚn]. *Ibid,* Haint got nary pair? (of cards in poker). *Ibid,* I never seed a deer nor saw nary 'un's ['næɾɪənz] tracks. **1941** Stuart *Men of Mts.* 223 **eKY,** The girls didn't have nary two dresses the same color. **1950** *PADS* 14.48 **SC,** Nary, nairy ['næɾɪ]... "Don't you pay him nary red cent." **1954** *Harder Coll.* **cwTN,** Don't do that nary nother time. **1959** *VT Hist.* 27.150 **swVT,** *Not a nary...* Not anything. Rare. **1965–70** *DARE* (Qu. LL14, *None at all, not even one: "This pond used to be full of fish but now there's _____ left."*) 96 Infs, **widespread,** (Not) nary a one; 26 Infs, **chiefly Sth, S Midl,** (Not) nary one; **KY**30, **NC**38, **NJ**11, Nary a fish; **AR**51, Nary un; **MD**43, Nary—Inf reports that many say this; (Qu. LL29, *Any sign or trace: "He left last week, and nobody's seen _____ of him since."*) Infs **NY**241, **WI**61, Nary a hair; **MS**88, **WI**61, Nary a sign; (Qu. NN4, *... Ways of answering 'no': "Would you lend him ten dollars?" "_____."*) Inf **WV**1, Nary a one. **1967–69** *DARE* FW Addit **csKY,** They won't last nary a winter; **LA**12, I can't hardly see nary [nɛɾɪ] wink; **seLA,** It ain't on nary one [ˌnɛɾɪ 'wʌn] of 'em; **cLA,** Nary one ['nɛɾɪən]; **ceNC,** We don't have nary a one; **swNC,** There may not be nary anothern; **TN**27, Nary one [ˌnɛɾɪ 'wʌn]. **1974** Fink *Mountain Speech* 17 **wNC, eTN,** I ain't got nary none. **1976** Garber *Mountain-ese* 60 **sAppalachians,** We expected four men to work but nary'n showed up. **1983** *MJLF* 9.1.48 **ceKY** (as of 1956), *Nary'un...* nary one. **1986** Pederson *LAGS Concordance* **Gulf Region,** 48 infs,

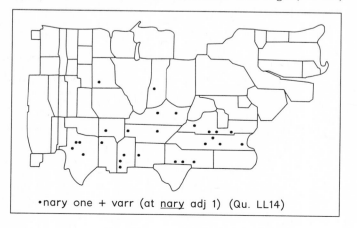

•nary one + varr (at <u>nary</u> adj 1) (Qu. LL14)

Nary a one; 21 infs, Nary one; 8 infs, Nary a (+ noun); 4 infs, Nary (+ noun); 1 inf, Nary (a)nother time. [Of the infs giving the resp *nary a one,* 15 indicated that they did not use it themselves and 11 that it was old-fashioned, rural, or uneducated; of infs giving the resp *nary one* 9 indicated that they did not use it, 7 that it was old-fashioned or rural.]

2 Neither. Cf **ne'er** adj[1] **2**

1746 in 1848 *New Engl. Hist. & Geneal. Reg.* 2.209, The Indians.. escaped them, and there was no "spile dunne on nary side." **1821** *Thomas' MA Spy or Worcester Gaz.* (MA) [3]/3 **seSC,** He asked her whether she was most fond of writing prose or poetry. "Nary one," says she, "I writes small hand." **1837** *Sherwood Gaz.* **GA** 71, *Provincialisms... Nary one,* neither. **1899** (1912) Green *VA Folk-Speech* 294, *Nary...* Neither; neither; none. **1903** *DN* 2.299 **Cape Cod MA** (as of a1857), I can't and I don't want to, nary one. **1909** [see 1 above]. **1923** (1946) Greer-Petrie *Angeline Steppin'* 38 **csKY,** Nory one of us can read a line, but I wasn't a-gwine to norate hit. **1930** Shoemaker *1300 Words* 42 **cPA Mts** (as of c1900), *Nary one*—Neither.

nary pron See **nary** adj **1**

nary adv [**nary** adj]

Not. Note: The comb *nary a* is treated at **nary** adj **1.**

1895 (1969) Crane *Red Badge* 102, There too much dependin' on me fer me t' die yit. No sir! Nary die! I *can't!* **1938** Matschat *Suwannee R.* 54 **neFL, seGA,** Hit's nary changed a-tall since a thousand years ago.

nasch See **nosh** v

nash adj See **nesh**

nash v See **nosh** v

nash n See **nosh** n

nas'ness See **nasty** adj

Nassau (nigger) n [*Nassau* capital of the Bahamas]
See quots.

1942 Kennedy *Palmetto Country* 109 **sFL,** Negroes.. from the Bahamas and Jamaica—who speak with a British accent—are indiscriminately lumped together as "Nassau niggers" by the crackers. **1987** *DARE* File **nwMS,** Here are words.. that I collected in interviews with Black people in Marks.. back in the sixties: Nassau—a "mixed nation" apparently a person of mixed Black and Indian ancestry. The person who used this word was a man born in Oklahoma in 1903, part Black and part Indian.

nastied (up) See **nasty** v

nasty adj **scattered, but esp Sth** See Map on p. 758 Note: In ref to bad weather and to mean-spirited behavior, *nasty* is not regional.

Filthy, foul, dirty; slovenly; lewd, dissolute; hence n *nastiness* (pronc-sp *nas'ness*) filth, excrement.

1758 in 1874 *Essex Inst. Coll.* 12.140 **NY,** The Dutch here have a nasty practice of yarding their cows in ye Street before their doors. **1840** (1847) Longstreet *GA Scenes* 56, Who do you call an impudent huzzy, you nasty, good-for-nothing, snaggle-toothed gaub of fat, you? **1872** Schele de Vere *Americanisms* 509, *Nasty...* denotes in America something disgusting in point of smell, taste, or even moral character, and is not considered a proper word to be used in the presence of ladies. **1899** (1912) Green *VA Folk-Speech* 294, *Nasty...* Filthy; dirty; foul; unclean. Physically filthy or dirty. *Ibid, Nastiness...* Disgusting taste; nauseousness. That which is filthy. Filth. *Nas'ness.* **1935** *AmSp* 10.95 **GA,** *Nasty* [considered obscene by 18 of 361 students]. *Ibid* 96, *Nasty...* I have no objection to reading the word or hearing another person use it. But it is one of the first conscious taboos I had. I now like the use of the word as applied to the weather, but not in any other sense. **1941** *LANE* Map 466 *(Slovenly)* **NEng,** 5 infs, Nasty; 1 inf, Nasty, 'the old slang word'; 1 inf, She's nasty as a slut; 1 inf, Slovenly, nasty, so strong as to be impolite; 1 inf, She's a nasty old slut; 1 inf, Nasty, in housekeeping. **1951** in 1977 Randolph *Pissing in the Snow* 215 **swMO,** Fetch the dishrag, and wipe that youngun's ass. If there's one thing I can't stand, it's nastiness! **1965–70** *DARE* (Qu. E22, *If a house is untidy*) Inf **FL**26, The house is nasty; (Qu. H12, *If somebody eating a meal takes little bits of food and leaves most of it on his plate, you say he _____*) Inf **MS**63, Acts like he thought it was nasty; (Qu. K14, *Milk that has a taste from something the cow ate in the pasture.. "That milk is _____."*) Inf **LA**7, Nasty; (Qu. U41b, *Somebody who has lost everything and is very poor: "He's poor as _____."*) Inf **OR**1, Pee and twice as nasty; (Qu. X9) Inf **MS**16, Nasty mouth; (Qu. X32) Infs **KY**84,

LA6, Nasty hands; (Qu. Y39, *To get something sticky or smeared up:* "The children have been eating candy and they've got their faces all _____.") Infs **CA**36, **LA**6, **TX**26, Nasty; (Qu. AA7b, *. . A woman who is very fond of men and is always trying to know more—if she's not respectable about it*) Inf **IL**57A, Nasty; **KY**40, Nasty about it [laughter]; **FL**48, Nasty woman; (Qu. DD4) Inf **LA**37, Nasty spit; **GA**3, Nastiness; (Qu. DD21b, *General words . . for bad liquor*) Inf **MI**85, Nasty; (Qu. HH36, *A careless, slovenly woman*) Inf **NC**87, Sloven, nasty woman [FW: conv]; **PA**247, Slut, slob, she's being nasty; (Qu. KK64, *Speaking of the part of a city that was once very fine, but isn't any more*) Inf **MS**80, Nasty; (Qu. NN15) Infs **FL**4, **MS**16, Nasty word. **1967** *DARE* FW Addit **GA**21, Go wash! Look how nasty you are [Inf to her son]; **GA**23, You've got nasty feet [Inf to his barefooted son]. **1971** *Today Show Letters,* In Detroit *nasty* was used as meaning bad or distasteful and used in referring to a person. But in New Orleans it was not as strong a word and could be used to describe an inanimate object. A skirt which is too short is nasty, not the person wearing it. **1982** Walker *Color Purple* 49 **GA** [Black], She ain't even clean. I hear she got the nasty woman disease. **1986** Pederson *LAGS Concordance* **Gulf Region,** [There were 79 responses with *nasty* (or *nastier, nastiest*) meaning greasy, dirty, messy, foul, unpleasant to the senses, morally reprehensible or obscene. Typical comments are: 1 inf, **seFL**, Nasty—filthy, not appetizing; 1 inf, **neAR**, Nasty—greasy from eating fried chicken; 1 inf, **cAL**, Nasty—unsanitary conditions; 1 inf, **swGA**, Nasty—shabby and dirty; 1 inf, **neAR**, Nasty—Coal is nasty because it smokes the house up; 1 inf, **cMS**, Nasty—A pigpen is a small open enclosure that's nasty; 1 inf, **seFL**, Using one another's toothbrush is nasty; 1 inf, **cLA**, Funky is a nasty word; 1 inf, **cnLA**, The term "smooching" sounds nasty; 1 inf, **ceAL**, A sexually indiscreet female is nasty.] **1988** Lincoln *Avenue* 225 **wNC** (as of c1940) [Black], You didn't walk all the way over here to tell me about somebody else's nasty house. At least I hope you didn't, because I ain't got time to listen to it. I'm busy trying to clean up my own.

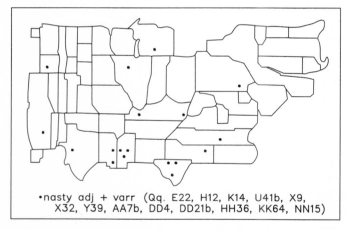

•nasty adj + varr (Qq. E22, H12, K14, U41b, X9, X32, Y39, AA7b, DD4, DD21b, HH36, KK64, NN15)

nasty v, hence ppl adj *nastied (up)* [*OED* "Obs. exc. *dial.*"] **esp S Midl** Cf **benasty**

To soil or make dirty; to defecate; also fig.

1863 in 1986 Messer *Civil War Letters* 16 **VT,** I had just as lives chaw him as not if it was not for nastying my mouth. **1867** Harris *Sut Lovingood Yarns* 235 **TN,** Lookin at his spread fingers like they warn't his'n, ur they wer nastied wif sumfin. **1930** *VA Qrly. Rev.* 6.246 **S Midl,** He fell down and nastied hisself. **1945** *Harder Coll.* **cwTN,** [Letter:] The little fellow nasted [sic] all over his clothes. **1949** Hornsby *Lonesome Valley* 191 (*Hench Coll.*) **eKY,** The cows hadn't caused him any trouble so far, but he'd have to watch out for them. If one of them started nastying, he might get his new clothes ruined. **c1960** *Wilson Coll.* **csKY,** *Nasty. .* To make filthy, to defecate in one's clothes or in bed. "The old fellow nastied his bed." **1966–67** *DARE* (Qu. Y37, *To make a place untidy or disorderly:* "I wish they wouldn't _____ the room so.") Inf **LA**8, Nasty [FW: sic—a verb]; (Qu. Y39, *To get something sticky or smeared up:* "The children have been eating candy and they've got their faces all _____.") Infs **FL**19, **TX**35, Nastied (up). **1986** Pederson *LAGS Concordance,* 1 inf, **cwMS**, Nastied up—dirty; (*Greased*) 1 inf, **cnAR**, Nastied up.

nasty adv Cf **filthy** adv

Extremely.

1966 *DARE* (Qu. U37, *. . Somebody who has plenty of money*) Inf

AL2, Nasty rich; (Qu. DD15, *A person who is thoroughly drunk*) Inf **MS**6, Nasty drunk. **1986** Pederson *LAGS Concordance,* 1 inf, **nwLA,** Knocked out, nasty drunk.

nasty-clean See **nasty-neat**

nasty-neat adj Also *nasty-clean* **scattered, but esp NEast** See Map Cf **nasty-nice, poison-neat**

Overly tidy; excessively fastidious.

1916 Macy-Hussey *Nantucket Scrap Basket* 28, Cousin Eunice, one of the Quaker housewives who had a reputation in her day for being what was called "nasty neat," once entertained several friends at "tea." **1943** Smiley *Gloss. New Paltz* **NY,** She is what you call *nasty* clean. **1947** Stegner *Second Growth* 226 **NH,** She had always been a tidy woman, almost nasty-neat about herself and her house. **1950** *WELS* (*If a house is very neat, with everything in its proper place, you say it's* _____) 1 Inf, **cwWI,** Nasty-neat—old-fashioned. **1959** *VT Hist.* 27.150 **neVT,** *Nasty neat. . .* religiously neat. Too particular; overly zealous in one's housekeeping. Common. **1960** Criswell *Resp. to PADS* 20 **Ozarks,** Nasty neat . . Too neat for comfort, at least to people around. Used of a meticulous housekeeper. Once common. **1965–70** *DARE* (Qu. HH11b, *Someone who is too particular or fussy—if it's a woman*) 16 Infs, **scattered, but esp NEast,** Nasty-neat; (Qu. KK34, *. . Very neat and clean:* "Her house always looks _____.") Infs **GA**36, **ME**11, **MA**5, **NY**105, Nasty-neat. [16 of 19 Infs old] **1968** Kellner *Aunt Serena* 42 **cIN** (as of c1920), My Aunt Love (who had the reputation of being "nasty clean") was the image of the energetic housewife on the Old Dutch Cleanser can. **1975** Gould *ME Lingo* 187, *Nasty-neat*—Neat and clean to the point of offensiveness; cleaner than clean and tidier than tidy. Said of a housewife over-zealous to the point that one is uncomfortable in her perfect parlor. **1986** Pederson *LAGS Concordance,* 1 inf, **AR,** Nasty clean—of mother, who was fastidious.

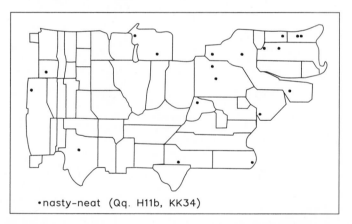

•nasty-neat (Qq. H11b, KK34)

nasty-nice adj Also *nice-nasty* **scattered, but less freq NEast** See Map

=nasty-neat.

1916 *DN* 4.335 **KS,** Disagreeably resolved on neatness. . . *nasty nice.* **1932** Wasson *Sailing Days* 6 **cME coast** (as of c1800), Others, however, suspicious of contamination [of the water] even at that day and ready to be thought "nasty-nice," would wisely have none of it for drinking purposes. **1941** *AmSp* 16.23 **sIN, MO,** *Nasty-nice.* **1942** (1971) Campbell *Cloud-Walking* 3 **seKY,** The neighbors said Sary was nasty-nice. She always hung up her dish rag all straight outside the cook room door. **c1960** *Wilson Coll.* **csKY,** *Nasty-nice*—Too particular about one's manners, too well-bred. **1965–70** *DARE* (Qu. HH11b, *Someone who is too particular or fussy—if it's a woman*) 17 Infs, **scattered, but less freq NEast,** Nasty-nice; **SC**7, Nice-nasty; (Qu. HH11a, *Someone who is too particular or fussy—if it's a man*) Infs **ID**5, **MD**49, **OH**49, 61, **OR**6, Nasty-nice; (Qu. U35, *. . Thrifty but not in a complimentary way:* "She's not a bad housekeeper, but very _____.") Infs **CO**11, **OR**17, Nasty-nice. [17 of 20 total Infs old] **1968** *DARE* FW Addit **GA**28, *Nice-nasty*—the kind of person who wipes off silverware before using it, asks if a drinking glass is clean, etc. . . Inf . . says they are "too nice to put up with poor people." **c1970** *Halpert Coll.* 44 **wKY, nwTN,** Nasty nice—so prudish as to be suggestive. **1980** *DARE* File **sIN** (as of c1910), There was a lady in our town who, every single morning, swept the alley behind her house. My mother called her a nasty-nice housekeeper. **1984** Santmyer *And Ladies* 230 **OH,** He was too much like his mother, who was what Sally called "nasty-nice."

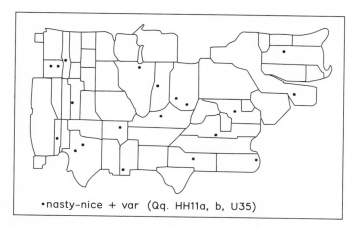

•nasty-nice + var (Qq. HH11a, b, U35)

natally, natchally See **naturally**

natchel See **natural**

natchelly, natcherly See **naturally**

natchie n [Pronc-sp for dimin of **natural** D; cf **natural** A]
  1972 Claerbaut *Black Jargon* 73, Natchie . . a poorly groomed black hairstyle; a sloppy natural.

natchul See **natural**

natchully See **naturally**

nater See **nature**

nateral See **natural**

naterally See **naturally**

naterel See **natural**

naterly See **naturally**

nation n[1] [Cf *OED* nation sb.[1] 8, →1765] **chiefly Sth, S Midl**
A great deal; a large amount or number; by ext: an impressive example.
  1775 in 1974 Winslow *Amer. Broadside* 141, A swamping gun . . makes a noise like a father's gun,/ Only a nation louder. 1930 *AmSp* 5.427 **Ozarks**, The word *nation* means simply a large amount. 1935 Hurston *Mules & Men* 64 **FL**, You hear dese hard ole coons lyin' up a nation and you stick in yo' bill. 1942 (1971) Campbell *Cloud-Walking* 86 **seKY**, And it's spread out more wider in a nation of books 'stead of being writ out in the Book like what you have to believe in whenever you get religion. 1952 Brown *NC Folkl.* 1.569 **c,eNC**, *Nation of a time, a*. . . A very good time. "We had a nation of a time at that party." 1986 Pederson *LAGS Concordance (Passel)* 1 inf, **cnAL**, A nation of them boogers.

nation n[2] [Euphem abbr, prob for *damnation*] Cf **tarnation**
1 with *the*: Used for emphasis or as a mild imprecation; see quots.
  1789 Dunlap *Father* 24, I guess she did mean so, for the nation knows she does'n't look much like hopping. 1858 Hammett *Piney Woods Tavern* 130, But the nation! jest to see the old critters [=women]. 1872 in 1917 Twain *Letters* 1.195, Where in the nation can I get that portrait? 1896 Harris *Sister Jane* 171 **GA**, Ma, what in the Nation do you reckon has got into the fire? 1911 (1916) Porter *Harvester* 54 **IN**, Why the nation did I admit anything to her? 1918 Lincoln *Shavings* 213 **Cape Cod MA**, Now how in the nation did I get it Wood? 1921 *DN* 5.116 **eKY**, *Nation, what in the*, a term of asseveration.
2 Used as a vaguely derog epithet; see quot.
  1934 Vines *Green Thicket* 49 **cnAL**, I call the noisy things [=pileated woodpeckers] Good-Gods. . . God dog, they make the woods ring for squirrel hunters. Yes, I like to see the old nations. *Ibid* 62, "They 'll eat right where you hold 'em, Uncle Greenberry. Where's Asbury? Ain't he helpin' Cora and Mina pick cotton?" "No, the old nation would n't help. And I tried my God damndest to get him to. Shore did."

nation adj [Cf **nation** n[1], n[2]] *arch* Cf **sight**
Great, large, impressive—usu in phr *a nation sight* a large amount or number.

  1765 in 1912 Thornton *Amer. Gloss.* 2.602 **CT**, I believe, my friend, you're very right,/ They'll get a nation profit by 't. 1809 (1814) Weems *F. Marion* 126 **SC**, Besides them plaguy guns, they have got a *tarnal nation sight* of pistols. 1810 Lambert *Travels* 3.486 **VT**, We have lost a *nation sight* of money by her. 1834 *Life Andrew Jackson* 7 **TN**, He will be a nation feller with a hickory. *Ibid* 15, He . . raised a nation site of game cox for the pit. 1838 (1843) Haliburton *Clockmaker* (2d ser) 239, The whole world might be stumped to produce such a factory stand as Niagara fall; what a nation sight of machinery that would carry, wouldn't it? 1858 Hammett *Piney Woods Tavern* 120, Some's got more'n their sheer [=share], and a nation sight's got none at all.

nation adv [Cf **nation** n[1], n[2]] *arch*
Very, extremely.
  1788 *Maryland Journal*, Feb. 26 (1912 Thornton *Amer. Gloss.*), So straightway they procession made,/ Lord! how *nation* fine, sir. 1800 *The Aurora*, Phila., Aug. 14 (1912 Thornton *Amer. Gloss.*), He'll read a speech—reads 'nation bad. 1815 Humphreys *Yankey in England* 106, [Glossary:] Nation, very, extraordinarily. 1834 *Life Andrew Jackson* 14 **TN**, He had nation good sense, and knew how tu employ it. 1834 Sands *Writings* 2.148 **NY**, I guess you've been a nation long time a writing that 'are answer. 1836 *Pub. Ledger* (Philadelphia PA) 27 July [4]/2, If I didn't look nation sheepish. 1859 Taliaferro *Fisher's R.* 43 **nwNC** (as of 1820s), "But how do you feel, Brother Snow?" "Ha! ha! nation hungry! I want some hog's gullicks and turnup greens right smack now." 1872 Twain *Roughing It* 30 **MO**, It's most uncommon lucky, becuz it's so nation dark I should 'a' gone by unbeknowns if that air thoroughbrace hadn't broke. 1884 (1958) Twain *Huck. Finn* 164 **MO**, I'm nation sorry for you, but you ain't the only person that's had troubles like that.

national adj Usu |ˈnæš(ə)nəl|; occas **NEng, NY** |ˈne(ɪ)šənəl|
Pronc-spp *nayshnul, naytional*
Std senses, var forms.
  1848 Lowell *Biglow* 70 '**Upcountry' MA**, Our eagle kicks yourn from the naytional nest. 1867 Lowell *Biglow* 30 '**Upcountry' MA**, We've entered on th' estate o' the late nayshnul eagle. [1890 *DN* 1.50 **Canada**, *National* . . is (rarely) pronounced [nešənəl].] *Ibid* 56 **NEng**, The pronunciation [=nešənəl] is] . . also known in New England. 1907 *DN* 3.194 **seNH**, *Naytional*. 1910 *DN* 3.445 **wNY**, *National*. . . First syllable pronounced *nei*. 1921–22 in 1944 *ADD* **cNY**, [ˈneɪšənəl]. . . pron. by an oldtime teacher.

nation bag See **nation sack**

‡**nation ball** n
  1970 *DARE* (Qu. EE33, . . *Outdoor games . . that children play*) Inf **CA182**, Nation ball—dodge ball in teams.

nation sack n Also *nation bag* [Perh var of *notion*] *among Black speakers*
See quots c1938, 1965.
  1936 in 1983 Taft *Blues Lyric Poetry* 147 [Black], I taken her last nickel: out of her nation sack. c1938 in 1970 Hyatt *Hoodoo* 2.1458 **swTN** [Black], De *nation bag* . . a belt aroun' dem an' dat bag hangs right down heah, an' dey tote dere money an' all dere diff'rent little concerns. . . Yo' know, a man bettah not try to put dere han' on dat bag. . . He goin' have some serious trouble wit dat old lady if he try to touch dat bag. . . She had dat *nation sack* an' done wore it. 1965 *DARE* FW Addit **MS60**, Nation sack—Used to carry pocketbook in it. A little cheese-cloth sack with a drawstring at the top. Tobacco, possibly snuff, came in it. [Inf Black]

native adj
Produced or cultivated locally.
  1965 *Amherst Rec.* (MA) 29 July sec Summer *Record* Week 5/5, Delicacies such as: light-as-a-feather corn fritters—dripping with butter and native maple syrup. 1981 *DARE* File **cnMA**, A cellophane package of asparagus in Stan's Sooper Market between Athol and Orange had a red sticker that said *Native*. It was used also on radishes and several other similarly packaged vegetables. 1995 *Ibid* **cwMA**, [Advt:] Native *Asparagus* Farm Fresh.

native n See **native trout**

native beef n Cf *DS* P35a
  1979 Lewis *How to Talk Yankee* [23] **nNEng**, *Native beef*. Moose, deer, when harvested out of season. Also known as "some of the Governor's meat."

native trout n Also *native*

Usu **brook trout** or **cutthroat trout,** but also a lake-dwelling Atlantic **salmon.**

1933 *NY Times* (NY) 9 Apr 3/5 *(Hench Coll.),* This special planting of 20,000 includes brown, rainbow and native trout. **1949** Caine *N. Amer. Sport Fish* 62, Sebago salmon. . . Native Trout. *Ibid* 84, Brook Trout. . . Other names derived from appearance and habitat are: Brookie. . . Native Trout. **1961** Douglas *My Wilderness* 38 **WY,** Carroll—indicating with his hands a mound about three feet high and as many feet wide— said, "I've seen offal that high on this lake's edge from the natives that were caught and cleaned here." When weather and water temperature are right, these "native" trout seem to march with abandon to man's guillotine. **1967–68** *DARE* (Qu. P1, . . *Kinds of freshwater fish . . caught around here . . good to eat)* Inf **CO22,** Native trout—pink meat; **CO41,** Cutthroat or native trout; **NY71,** Native trout or brook trout; **VA14,** Native trout. **1972** Sparano *Outdoors Encycl.* 356, *Cutthroat Trout* [=*Salmo clarki*] . . native trout, mountain trout . . harvest trout. **1983** Becker *Fishes WI* 316, Brook Trout—*Salvelinus fontinalis.* . . native trout, native.

natur See **nature**

natural adj, adv, n Usu |ˈnæč(ə)rəl|; also |ˈnætrəl|; also, **esp Sth,** |ˈnæčəl| Pronc-spp *na(i)teral, nat(e)rel, natchel, na(t)chul, nat'ral, nat'rul*

A Forms.

1823 *Natl. Intelligencer* (DC) 1 May *(DN* 4.47), [In list of "Yankee" provincialisms:] *Nateral.* . . Natural. **1825** Neal *Brother Jonathan* 1.143 **CT,** As naiteral, as *can* be. **1841** (1952) Cooper *Deerslayer* 307 **nNY,** In a nat'ral way. **1867** Lowell *Biglow* 24 'Upcountry' **MA,** 'T wuz nat'ral to expec'. *Ibid* 30, I nat'ral rights. **1867** Harris *Sut Lovingood Yarns* 100 **TN,** Ole Sock wer hurried on in this onnaterel an' onmanerly manner. *Ibid* 101, Hit gin him time tu turn roun' wif 'cumulated rath, the natrel bull fitein way. **1884** *Anglia* 7.274 **Sth, S Midl** [Black], *Des ez natchul ez de nex' one* = quite natural. **1891** Cooke *Huckleberries* 9 **CT,** Rum's kinder nateral to him. **1891** *DN* 1.121 **cNY,** [ˈnæčl]. **1899** Chesnutt *Conjure Woman* 72 **csNC** [Black], No 'lowance fer nachul bawn laz'ness. **1899** Edwards *Defense* 13 **GA,** Well, gentlemen, I reck'n 't was natchul at that time. **1909** *DN* 3.351 **eAL, wGA,** Nachul. **1932** Randolph *Ozark Mt. Folks* 56, I've saw fellers . . draw a bird . . a-lookin' so nateral you'd think it was a-goin' t' fly off. **1933** Rawlings *South Moon* 105 **nFL,** Hit's the most natchel thing in the world. **1942** Hall *Smoky Mt. Speech* 67 **wNC, eTN,** It is said that the old form of natural [ˈnætrəl] has not yet died out completely. **1969** Emmons *Deep Rivers* 51 **eTX** [Black], He wasn't scared o' the Devil hisself, . . he was so natchel born mean.

B As adj.

1 Of family relations: legitimate, legal. [*OED natural* a. 13 "*Obs.*"]

1899 (1912) Green *VA Folk-Speech* 295, *Natural.* . . Legitimate. Used in this sense in the County records; as, my "natural daughter." Also: "My natural mother." **1937** *AmSp* 12.232 **NJ** [Black], As late as the eighteenth century, *natural,* applied to family relationships, meant 'lawful, legitimate.' . . Negroes use it in the same way; by 'his natural wife' they mean his legally-married wife—not, as one might suppose, his common-law wife.

2 Familiar.

1946 *AmSp* 21.190 **seKY,** She's natural-lookin', but I don't know who she is.

3 Genuine, real. Cf **naturally B**

1970 *DARE* Tape **DC14,** She [=a woman on welfare] gittin' fo' hundred o' them natural [ˈnæčɚl] dollars a month. **1986** Pederson *LAGS Concordance (Genuine)* 4 infs, **Gulf Region,** Natural.

C As adv.

Naturally.

1931 (1991) Hughes–Hurston *Mule Bone* 62 **cFL** [Black], You couldn't lie dat good just natural. **1940** in 1944 *ADD* **AR,** Would I? Natural! . . Natural, she wants to show off. Radio. **1942** *Sat. Eve. Post* 5 Sept 57/2 **csFL** [Black], Natural, the future to me looks something different from the past. **1966–69** *DARE* (Qu. A24, . . *Someone who has always been the same way)* Inf **CT6,** He's just natural dumb, he's natural hot-tempered; (Qu. KK42a, *Expressions about a person who does something very easily: "For him that would be _____.")* Inf **OK31,** Come natural; (Qu. KK46, . . *Taking things as they come and not worrying)* Inf **IL59,** Taking things natural. **1971** Mitchell *Blow My Blues Away* 91 **nwMS** [Black], Hard to be a woman living alone? Wooh-wee, it's natural just miserable. It's miserable to live alone by yourself. **1986**

Pederson *LAGS Concordance,* 1 inf, **ceAL,** Come natural = naturally; 1 inf, **swGA,** Natural cool = quite cool; 1 inf, **neMS,** Took it natural.

D As noun.

=Afro n. *chiefly among Black speakers* Cf **natchie**

1965–70 *DARE* (Qu. X5, . . *Different kinds of men's haircuts)* 8 Infs, **scattered,** Natural; **AL60, 61, IL137, 140, OH102,** [ˈnætrəl]; **CA184,** Natural—Negroes; **IN75,** Natural—for Blacks. [13 of 15 Infs Black; 9 of 15 young] **1966** *DARE* FW Addit **PA66,** Natural—haircut worn by Negro males, long unstraightened, and without a part. **1969** *Ebony* Feb 27, There's a lean young cat wearing a natural who knows where it's at and tells it like it is. **1971** Malamud *Tenants* 42 **NYC,** She wore a natural of small silken ringlets, and a plain white mini with purple tights. **1972** Claerbaut *Black Jargon* 73, *Natural* . . the normal, unstraightened hairstyle of a black person . . a large, bushy hairstyle. **1972** (1973) Bullins *Theme is Blackness* 150, I love you, baby. . . I sure dig that sexy natural. **1986** Pederson *LAGS Concordance Gulf Region (Hairstyle)* 1 inf, A natural = braided; 1 inf, A natural is one that don't be comb and don't be cut; 2 infs, Natural = Afro; 2 infs, Natural—(woman's) hairstyle; 1 inf, Natural—hairstyle—black women; 2 infs, (The) naturals; 1 inf, Naturals—especially blacks; 1 inf, Naturals—black males and females. [All infs Black] **1994** Smitherman *Black Talk* 165, *Natural*— African American hair worn in its natural state, not *hotcombed* or treated with chemical straighteners.

naturalized ppl adj [*OED naturalize* v. 6 "To familiarize or accustom (one) *in* or *to* a thing. *Obs. rare.*"]

Accustomed.

1924 Raine *Land of Saddle-Bags* 102 **sAppalachians,** Our folks got *naturalized* to the doctor, and like him. **1930** *VA Qrly. Rev.* 6.249 **S Midl,** The gentleman of the backwoods . . may affirm . . that an outlander must get naturalized to the climate. **1940** (1968) Haun *Hawk's Done Gone* 156 **eTN,** It was hard for him to get naturalized to their ways.

natural leaf n Also *natural leaf plug*

Chewing tobacco that has had minimal cutting or sweetening.

[**1960** Heimann *Tobacco* 147, Some liked their "chaw" natural, others wanted it sweetened . . [with flavors such as] licorice, . . rum, sugar, tonka beans, cinnamon, nutmeg [etc.].] **1966–68** *DARE* (Qu. DD1, . . *Forms . . [of] chewing tobacco)* Infs **FL35, TX37, WY2,** Natural leaf; **IN18,** Natural leaf—twist; **LA15,** My grandfather used to chew natural leaf; **MD48,** Natural leaf—dried in twist. **1967** *DARE* Tape **TX43,** Nearest thing to that [=twist] was what they call a natural leaf. It had very little sweetening, but had a little moisture in it. . . The inside of that natural leaf plug was a greener tobacco that hadn't been thoroughly dried and compressed with this natural leaf on the outside. It had the same color as the twist and almost the same taste, but it did have a little bit of that juice in it, and that graduated on down to a almost coal black tobacco.

naturally adv Usu |ˈnæč(ə)rəli|; also |ˈnæčɚli|; **esp Sth** |ˈnæčəli| Pronc-spp *natally, na(t)chelly, na(t)cherly, naterally;* for addit pronc and sp varr see quots

A Forms.

1843 (1916) Hall *New Purchase* 78 **IN,** She "know'd we wanted over and so had hollored naterally." **1861** Holmes *Venner* 2.151 **NEng,** Massa Venner bright man naterally. *Ibid* 242 **wMA,** I naterally feel a graät responsibility. **1884** *Anglia* 7.263 **Sth, Midl** [Black], *To be natally or natchully live wid* = to swarm. **1887** (1967) Harris *Free Joe* 13 **cGA** [Black], Me en her wuz des natally raise up tergeer [=together]. **1893** Shands *MS Speech* 47, *Natcherly,* [ˈnæčəli]. Negro for *naturally.* **1896** Harris *Sister Jane* 169 **GA,** Lord knows my heart jest natchully yearns arter that gal. **1903** [see **B** below]. **1905** Chesnutt *Col.'s Dream* 148 **GA,** I ain't skeered er no ha'nt dat evuh walked, an' I sleeps in graveya'ds by pref'ence; fac', I jes nach'ly lacks ter talk ter ha'nts. **1907** Mulford *Bar-20* 10 **West,** He jest nachurly walks up to C 80. **1927** *AmSp* 2.285 **Ozarks,** *Naterly.* **1927** Kennedy *Gritny* 8 **sLA** [Black], Tom des natchally childish. **1933** Rawlings *South Moon* 144 **nFL,** Mister, we're here peaceable, but if you aim to act that-a-way, you'll jest natchelly find your fences cut. **1942** *New Yorker* 11 July 18/1 **sCA,** Nachelly my curiosity is up. **1961** Adams *Old-Time Cowhand* 269 **SW,** He jes' nacher'ly pokes his head through my loop. **1968** *DARE* FW Addit **GA22,** Naturally [ˈnæčɚlɪ].

B Sense.

Simply, really, actually; without further ado—often in phr *just naturally.* **Sth, S Midl** Cf **natural B3**

1884 Lanier *Poems* 170 **GA,** I caint see how to get out'n the muss,/ Except to jest nat'ally fail and bus'! **1884** [see **A** above]. **1887** [see **A**

above]. **1896** [see **A** above]. **1903** *DN* 2.322 **seMO**, *Naturally*. . . Actually. 'They were nachully driven outen house and home.' **1905** [see **A** above]. **1907** *DN* 3.233 **nwAR**, *Nachully*. . . Actually. **1907** Wright *Shepherd* 12 **Ozarks**, Ain't nothin' to a flat country nohow. A man jes naturally wears hisself plumb out a walkin' on a level 'thout ary hill t' spell him. **1913** Kephart *Highlanders* 78 **sAppalachians**, Thar come one turrible vyg'rous blow that jest nacherally lifted the ground. I went up in the sky . . and I went a-sailin' end-over-end. **1925** Dargan *Highland Annals* 206 **cwNC**, It wuz the law in them days that if a man an' his wife didn't live together fer three year they wuz nachally divorced 'thout goin' inter court. **1933** [see **A** above]. **1968** *DARE* FW Addit **GA22**, *Naturally*—used to mean "really"; e.g., "he naturally done that good"; heard several times in conversation. Old-fashioned.

nature n Usu |ˈneʧə(r)|; also **chiefly NEast, S Midl** |ˈneɪtə(r)| Pronc-spp *nater, natur*

A Forms.

1823 Cooper *Pioneers* 1.210 **nNY**, I don't think that by nater they are sitch tonguey speakers. **1834** Smith *Letters Jack Downing* 179 **NEng**, He banged away a spell agin like all natur. **1841** (1952) Cooper *Deerslayer* 269 **nNY**, Arbors raised by the hand of natur'. **1843** (1916) Hall *New Purchase* 174 **IN**, Proof from nater. **1861** Holmes *Venner* 1.125 **NEng**, Some thought it was in the natur' of a judgment. **1867** Harris *Sut Lovingood Yarns* 27 **TN**, Them words toch dad tu the hart, an' I felt they mus' be my las, knowin dad's unmollified nater. **1885** Murfree *Prophet of Smoky Mts.* 32 **eTN**, Nuthin' in natur' could hev held him. **1887** (1967) Harris *Free Joe* 107 **GA**, I know what human natur' on these hills is. **1891** *DN* 1.166 **cNY**, [ˈnetr]. **1907** *DN* 3.194 **seNH**, *Nater*. . . Now rare. **1930** *AmSp* 5.204 **Ozarks**, Noah Webster denounced the "affectation" of inserting a *y* sound before the *u* in such words as . . *nature*. The Ozark natives . . stand firm with . . Webster in the pronunciation of . . *nature*. **1942** Hall *Smoky Mt. Speech* 96 **wNC, eTN**, The older mountain forms of *pasture*, . . *nature*, and others, . . do not show [ʧ]. **1952** Brown *NC Folkl.* 1.568, *Nater* [ˈnetə, -ɚ]. . . *Nature*. So pronounced in the eighteenth century; Walker condemned it; Webster approved it. . . General. Illiterate. **c1960** *Wilson Coll.* **csKY**, *Nature* [ˈnetɚ]. Rare. **1982** Slone *How We Talked* 8 **eKY** (as of c1950), *Natur* (nature).

B Sense.

1 Sexual potency or desire; male or female ejaculate. [*MED natur(e* 6.(c) "sexual urge; the genitalia . . ; *sheden ~,* to ejaculate semen; also, of a woman: ejaculate fluid." Cf *OED nature* sb. 7 →1607] *chiefly among Black speakers* Cf **nature bump, ~-course**

1884 *Anglia* 7.261 **Sth, S Midl** [Black], To have er mighty young nater = to have youthful feelings. [Footnote: The English equivalents are far from conveying the pungent meaning of the Negro expressions.] **c1938** in 1970 Hyatt *Hoodoo* 1.402 **seSC**, And he won't have no *nature* for no other woman, just have to come back to you. *Ibid* 534 **ceVA**, Now, if a man want to break his wife from some man, he steals this dishcloth . . an' he ketches her *nachure* in this dishcloth. After he ketches this *nachure* in a dishcloth, he takes it home an' wraps it up tight an' buries it at his doah. *Ibid* 2.1394 **ceVA**, Now, this [counter-spell] is if she's got your *nature*. They generally wears it round their leg. Some of 'em, they may take it and ketch it on a piece of cotton and bottle it up. **1941** Percy *Lanterns* 305 **nwMS** [Black], He had placed a spell on her by means of a cunjer bag. . . Its effect was to rob her of connubial allure—in her words, "it stole her nature." **1946** (1972) Mezzrow–Wolfe *Really Blues* 274, Naturally, kids shouldn't have that kind of stimulus handy. . . But you take a guy thirty, forty, fifty years old, if he needs some Nature he sure can get it from marihuana, and no harm done. **1952** Brown *NC Folkl.* 1.569, *Nature, to take (one's).* . . To unsex a person or an animal. "If I have that operation, I'm afraid it will take my nature." **1968** Baldwin *Amen Corner* 36 **NYC** [Black], Oh sure, I knowed she'd been married and she had this boy. But, I declare, I thought that that was just a mistake and she couldn't wait to get away from her husband. There's women like that, you know, ain't got much nature to them somehow. **1969** Beck *Mama Black Widow* 93 **NYC** [Black], He ain't got no normul natchur. All he do is use his mouf on wimmen. **1970** *DARE* FW Addit **VA70**, Inf's wife once politely referred to "castration" as "taking its nature" (from an animal). **1974** (1975) Shaw *All God's Dangers* 67 **AL** [Black], The thing for a boy to do when he gets old enough that his nature to begin to teach him, don't make a dog of himself. So, I was afraid my nature would take over me and I stayed away from Hannah to a great extent. **1978** Dance *Shuckin' & Jivin'* 310 [Black], Wipe your man's discharge in a handkerchief and put it under your mattress, and he won't have no nature for nobody but you. **1990** Cavender *Folk Med. Lexicon* 27 **sAppalachians**, *Nature*—sexual drive, libido.

2 in phr *all nature:* Everyone; all the world; the whole creation.

1819 *Thomas' MA Spy or Worcester Gaz.* (MA) 3 Nov [3]/1 **CT**, Father and I have just returned from the balloon—all nature was there, and more too. **1878** *Atlantic Mth.* 42.472 **MA**, Cuff would prance round . . and seem to think he . . had the charge of all natur'. **c1960** *Wilson Coll.* **Mammoth Cave KY**, All nature . . All creation, everything.

3 in phr *like all nature:* To an extreme degree; like the dickens. *arch*

1824 *Woodstock* (Vt.) *Observer* 17 Feb. (*DA*), They said too 'twould shoot like *all nater*, 'Tis singlar what stories they tell. **1832** Paulding *Westward Ho* 1.173 **KY**, I had to wade through the creek, *and* I found the ball had entered in a hollow tree, after going right clean through the two deer, where there was a hive of honey, *and* the honey was running away like all natur. **1840** Hoffman *Greyslaer* 2.254 **Upstate NY**, The poor critter would have been sucked under, smashed on the rocky bottom, and dragged off like all natur. **1862** Lowell *Biglow Papers* 2nd Series, No. 1 (1912 Thornton *Amer. Gloss.*) **'Upcountry' MA**, He'd never thought o' borryin from Esau like all nater,/ An' then confiscatin' all debts to sech a small pertater.

4 in phr *beat all nature:* =**beat the Dutch**. *arch*

1825 Neal *Brother Jonathan* 2.93 **ME**, Hourra for you—that beats all nater! **1852** Watson *Nights Block-House* 47 **OH**, I know summut about red-skins. This 'ere beats all natur. **1864** Nichols *40 Yrs.* 1.386 **NEng**, It beats all natur heow he can go it when he gets his dander up. **1867** Lowell *Biglow* 13 **'Upcountry' MA**, Wal, it did beat all natur'. **1892** Duval *Young Explorers* 82 **csTX**, Well, I declar . . ef this don't beat all natur.

nature bump n Also *nature head* Cf **courage bump, fuck ~, love ~ 1** [**nature B1**]

A pimple.

1969–70 *DARE* (Qu. X59, . . *The small infected pimples that form usually on the face*) Infs **NJ56A, VA46**, Nature bumps; **MO29**, Nature heads. [All Infs Black]

nature-course n [**nature B1**]

Sexual intercourse.

1974 (1975) Shaw *All God's Dangers* 93 **AL** [Black], That night, that Sunday night I stood up and married her, I didn't know no more about bein with her in nature-course than I knowed about flying—it wouldn't have been no harm if I did. I meant to marry her and carry out the full obligation of my acts.

natured adj **Sth, S Midl**

Disposed, naturally inclined; in comb with adj: having the properties of (that adj). Note: In ref to disposition, as in *good-natured, bad-natured,* the term is widespread.

1927 *DN* 5.471 **Appalachians**, *Natured*. . . Formed or adopted by nature. "Land right natured for corn." "Sheep is natured like the deer." **1967** *DARE* (Qu. C6, . . *A piece of land that's often wet, and has grass and weeds growing on it*) Inf **NC46**, Wet-natured land. **1982** Slone *How We Talked* 8 **eKY** (as of c1950), *Natur* (nature) also means personality. . . "She is natured just like her mother." **1984** Wilder *You All Spoken Here* 135 **Sth**, *Natured:* Something come by naturally, as in "This river bottom is right natured for corn," and "Steers are sort of natured like horses— they work like horses," and "Snakes are natured that way, and that's why a snake is a damned snake." **1986** Pederson *LAGS Concordance*, 1 inf, **swTN**, Cold-natured land, soil that does not have heat; 1 inf, **cnLA**, Cold-natured land, needs manure to warm it up; (*Swamp*) 2 infs, **cwTN, cnAR**, Wet-natured land; (*Bottomland*) 1 inf, **seAL**, Wet-natured land; (*Loam*) 1 inf, **cTX**, Salty-natured. **1994** *DARE* File **csWI**, I heard a woman with a Southern accent tell a clerk that a jacket would be warm enough for her son because he was a hot-natured child.

nature head See **nature bump**

nature's mistake n

A **flowering dogwood** (here: *Cornus florida*).

1894 *Jrl. Amer. Folkl.* 7.90, *Cornus florida* . . nature's mistake. **1930** Sievers *Amer. Med. Plants* 28, Flowering Dogwood—*Cornus florida* . . nature's-mistake. **1951** Teale *North with Spring* 218 **NC**, The harvest of an American plant hunter may include badman's oatmeal, truelove, tread-softly, simpler's joy, lords-and-ladies, shoofly, nature's-mistake [etc]. **1960** Vines *Trees SW* 795, Flowering Dogwood—*Cornus florida.* . . Vernacular names are Arrowwood. . . Nature's Mistake . . and White Cornel.

naughts-and-crosses See **noughts-and-crosses**

nault n [Pronc-sp for *naught*] Cf **ault**

   1966 *DARE* (Qu. LL15, *To write ten . . what figure do you put after '1'?*) Inf **MS**49, Nault—heard.

nauseated ppl adj Usu |ˈnɔzietəd, ˈnɔsietəd|; also **esp NEast** |ˈnɔšietəd|; **esp Sth** |ˈnɔžietəd, ˈnɔze(ɪ)təd|; for addit varr see quots

Std sense, var forms.

   1943 *LANE* Map 503 *(Sick at his stomach)* 1 inf, **neRI**, [ˈnɒˆʃɪˌetɪd]; 1 inf, **neRI**, [ˈnɔʃɪˌetɪd]; 1 inf, **nwRI**, [ˈnæʃʃjuˌetɪd]; 1 inf, **seMA**, [ˈnaˆʃetɪd]; 1 inf, **csMA**, [ˈnɔʃĭˌeɪtɪd]; 1 inf, **csNH**, [ˈnɒˆʃtˌeɪˆtɪˇd]. *Ibid* Map 504 *(Vomit)* 1 inf, **ceCT**, Be [nosɪetɪd]; 1 inf, **neCT**, Was [nosɪetɪd]; 1 inf, **ceRI**, Be [nnsietɪd]; 1 inf, **seRI**, Be [nɒˆsetɪd]; 1 inf, **neRI**, Be [nɒˆʃɪetɪd]; 1 inf, **neRI**, Be [nɔʃɪetɪd]. [**1944** Kenyon–Knott *Pronc. Dict.* 292, [ˈnɔʒɪˌet, ˈnɔzi-, ˈnɔsi-, ˈnɔʃɪ-].] **1965–70** *DARE* (Qu. BB16b, *If something a person ate didn't agree with him, he might just feel a bit _____*) 196 Infs, **widespread**, Proncs of the type [ˈnɔzietəd, ˈnazietɪd]; 123 Infs, **scattered, but chiefly Nth,** Proncs of the type [ˈnɔsietəd, ˈnasietɪd]; 31 Infs, **scattered, but chiefly NEast,** Proncs of the type [ˈnɔšietəd, ˈnašietɪd]; 22 Infs, **chiefly Sth,** Proncs of the type [ˈnɔžietəd, ˈnažietɪd]; 13 Infs, **chiefly Sth,** Proncs of the type [ˈnɔze(ɪ)təd, ˈnaze(ɪ)tɪd]; 9 Infs, **chiefly Sth,** Proncs of the type [ˈnɔže(ɪ)təd, ˈnaže(ɪ)tɪd]; 6 Infs, **esp Sth,** Proncs of the type [ˈnauzietəd]; 6 Infs, **scattered,** Proncs of the type [ˈnausietəd]; **GA**12, **IN**73, **SC**11, [ˈnaušietɪd]; **PA**142, **SC**3, [ˈnauzietɪd]; **SC**4, 19, 46, [ˈnaužetɪd]; **AR**12, **MS**10, 71, [ˈnɔjietɪd]; **IN**82, [ˈnɔjietəd]; **MS**6, [ˈnaujetɪd]; **TN**30, [ˈnausəetɪd]; **IL**36, [ˈnɔšetɪd]; **NC**83, [ˈnošetɪd]; **SC**21, [ˈnaɪžetɪd]; **GA**77, [ˈnɔsəreɪtɪd]; **KY**84, [ˈnɔžueɪtɪd]; **TX**32, [ˈnɔziædɪd]; **NJ**2, [ˈnɔsietɪd]; **MS**45, [ˈnoɪzetɪd]; **FL**49, [ˈnoɪzɪ]; **MD**20, [ˈnɔši]; (Qu. BB16a) Inf **IL**15, [ˈnasietəd]; (Qu. BB17) Inf **LA**14, Became [ˈnɔzietɪd]; **MA**125, **MO**7, [ˈnɒziˈveɪrɪd]. **1981** Pederson *LAGS Basic Materials Gulf Region,* [Of 34 proncs of *nauseated,* 19 were of the type [ˈnɔzietɪd, ˈnɑ(ɔ)-]; 8 were of the type [ˈnɔžietɪd]; 1 inf, [ˈnɔˆʌˆsɪˆeˀɪtɪd]; 1 inf, [ˈnɔˇʊˇšieˀˀɪtɪd]; 1 inf, [ˈnɑˀozeˇɪtɪd]; 1 inf, [ˈnãˀžeˀɪtɪd]; 1 inf, [ˈnɔšˆžeˀɪtɪd]; 1 inf, [ˈnɔɔˀžeɪtɪd]; 1 inf, [ˈnɔˇosəreˀɪtɪd].]

nauseous adj Usu |ˈnɔšəs|; also |ˈnɔžəs, ˈnɔsiəs, ˈnɔziəs|; for addit var see quots **chiefly Nth, N Midl, esp NYC, NJ, PA** See Map Note: Proncs are attested for this sense only; their relative frequencies may vary where the word is used in other senses.

Affected by nausea; nauseated.

   1949 *Sat. Review* 7 May 41, After taking dramamine, not only did the woman's hives clear up, but she discovered that her usual trolley ride back home no longer made her nauseous. *Ibid* 4 June 25 **CT**, One of the minor crosses which any physician has to bear is the experience of hearing patient after patient say, "Doctor, I am nauseous." **1955** (1957) Wouk *Marjorie Morningstar* 125 **NYC**, They arrived back at Tamarack soaking wet, and nauseous from the tossing of the wind-whipped water. **1962** Baldwin *Another Country* 42 **NYC**, He wolfed down his sandwich. But the heavy bread, the tepid meat, made him begin to feel nauseous. **1965–70** *DARE* (Qu. BB16b, *If something a person ate didn't agree with him, he might just feel a bit _____*) 55 Infs, **chiefly Nth, N Midl, esp NYC, NJ, PA,** Nauseous [26 Infs gave proncs of the type [ˈnɔšəs, ˈnašɪs]; 6 Infs, Proncs of the type [ˈnɔsiəs, ˈnasiəs]; 5 Infs, Proncs of the type [ˈnɔžəs, ˈnažɪs]; **IL**98, **MD**27, **NJ**34, [ˈnɔziəs]; **NC**22, **VA**80, [ˈnɔž(i)jəs]; **PA**228, [ˈnɔzjəs]; **PA**130, [ˈnašjəs]; **WA**33, [ˈnɔšiəs]; **NY**235, [ˈnaušəs]; **PA**22, [ˈnɔjɛs]; for other Infs there were no transcriptions;] **NY**94, [ˈnošəes]; this means "causing nauseation"—read in the paper the other day; [**CT**8, Nauseated—for heaven's sake, not [ˈnɔžus]];

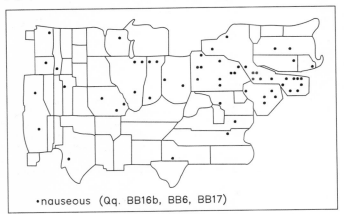

•nauseous (Qq. BB16b, BB6, BB17)

(Qu. BB6, *A sudden feeling of weakness, when sometimes the person loses consciousness*) Inf **NY**80, Nauseous; (Qu. BB17, *. . Vomiting*) Infs **IN**60, **PA**175, Nauseous. [Of all Infs responding to Qu. BB16b, 7% were comm type 1, 10% young; of those giving this response, 21% were comm type 1, 18% young.] **1975** Morris–Morris *Usage* 414, The use of the expression "I feel *nauseous*" instead of "I am *nauseated*" is increasingly widespread. At first we regarded it as an item of local dialect, typical of the speech of the Bronx and Brooklyn. Readers in all parts of the country have commented on it, however. **1981** Pederson *LAGS Basic Materials (Vomit)* 1 inf, neFL, [nɑ·ˀzias]; [34 infs, Nauseated]. **1984** *Annals Internal Med.* 100.6.900 cwAL, Nauseous has replaced nauseated nationwide: I am nauseous.

Navajo blanket flower n Cf **blanket flower, Indian blanket 1**
=**gaillardia B.**

   1959 Carleton *Index Herb. Plants* 86, *Navajo-blanket-flower:* Gaillardia [spp].

Nava-Joe n Also *Joe* [Joc pronc of *Navajo*]

   1963 *AmSp* 38.271 **KS** [Amer Indian student slang], Navaho students are called *Nava-Joes* or simply *Joes.* **1965** *Silver City Press Frontier* (NM) 32/5 (as of 1885), The mixologists [=bartenders] . . are linguists talking fluently Dutch, French, . . Pigeon English, Nava Joe, Army Joe, or Ho da do.

Navajo ruby n
=**Arizona ruby.**

   1912 *Out West Mag.* Mar 216 neAZ, [Advt:] I have constantly a very fine selection of Navajo silverware and jewelry, Navajo "rubies" cut and uncut, peridotes and native turquois.

Navajo tea n **SW**

   1 An **alumroot 1** (here: *Heuchera bracteata*).

   1936 Reichard *Navajo Shepherd & Weaver* 41 *(DA),* From the stems of the plant called 'Navajo tea' the pinkish tan may be obtained.

   2 A **greenthread** (here: either *Thelesperma ambiguum* or *T. megapotamicum*).

   1967 Dodge *Roadside Wildflowers* 86, Colorado greenthread. . . A close relative is known as "Navajo tea." **1970** Kirk *Wild Edible Plants W. U.S.* 135, *Thelesperma* species . . Navajo Tea, Cota, Greenthread. . . An excellent tea may be made by boiling the dried flowers and young leaves for several minutes. **1987** Bowers *100 Roadside Wildflowers* 52, A perennial herb, Navajo tea [=*Thelesperma megapotamicum*] grows along roadsides and in woodland openings from Nebraska and Wyoming to Texas, Arizona and Mexico. . . Navajo tea is a traditional medicinal herb among Hispanic New Mexicans, who call it *cota.* Tea made from the fried stems and leaves reportedly has a pleasantly piney, sweet flavor and can be used as a mild diuretic. Navajo tea blooms throughout the summer. **1990** *Plants SW* (Catalog) 39, *Thelesperma ambiguus* . . Showy Navajo Tea, Greenthread . . This lovely, bushy wildflower also makes a fine-tasting tea. Use the flowers, leaves and stems. . . Native to the plains and west to the eastern slope of Colorado and New Mexico. *Ibid, Thelesperma megapotamicum* . . Cota or Navajo Tea . . It has long been used as a tea because of its pleasant taste and reputed medicinal values.

Navajo time n
=**Indian time.**

   1978 Hillerman *Listening Woman* 21 neAZ, seUT [Navajo speaker], So now it's August, and somebody gets around to coming into Short Mountain and mentioning he's seen the damn thing. . . Nine months? That's about right for a Short Mountain Navajo. . . Three kinds of time. . . On time, and Navajo time, and Short Mountain Navajo time. **1990** *DARE* File cnAZ, Navajo time . . means lack of temporal consciousness or urgency. "He meant 4 p.m., Navajo time" may anticipate arrival at 6 p.m. or 10 p.m. or Thursday or February or March. Understand he *will arrive,* but if something comes up, or if he sees a clan cousin with a flat tire on the side of the road, and helps him, things in the immediate line of sight may preclude some abstract appointment. Current usage is a denigration for lack of punctuality. *Ibid* [see **Indian time**]. **1993** Hillerman *Sacred Clowns* 67 AZ, NM, "Eight minutes late," she said. . . "Eight minutes you don't mention," Chee said. "You have to be a lot later than that to claim you're working on Navajo time."

navel n Usu |ˈnevəl|; also **chiefly Sth, S Midl** (See Map) |ˈnebəl| Pronc-spp *nab(b)le, nabel*

Std sense, var forms.

   1890 *DN* 1.74 seMA, Nable. **1893** Shands *MS Speech* 47, Nable. . . Negro and illiterate white for *navel.* **1899** (1912) Green *VA Folk-Speech*

293, *Nabel*. . . *Nable*. **1903** *DN* 2.322 **seMO**, *Nabel*. **1906** *DN* 3.121 **sIN**, *Nabel*. **1909** *DN* 3.351 **eAL, wGA**, *Nabel*. **1912** *DN* 3.583 **wIN**, *Nabel*. **1913** Kephart *Highlanders* 278 **sAppalachians**, Most hillsmen say nabel (navel). **1934** Hurston *Jonah's Gourd Vine* 314 **AL**, *Nable-string*, umbilical cord. **1936** *AmSp* 11.250 **eTX**, *Navel* is still heard occasionally as ['nebəl] in the speech of unlettered people in the rural districts. This pronunciation is dying out. I am informed that it used to be the only colloquial pronunciation. **1944** Kenyon–Knott *Pronc. Dict.* 293, Navel ['nevl]. **1949** *PADS* 11.8 **wTX**, *Nabel*. . . Common among children and uneducated. **1950** *WELS* (Navel) 1 Inf, **cwWI**, Nabel. **1954** Harder Coll. **cwTN**, Nabel ['nebəl]—navel. **c1960** Wilson Coll. **csKY**, *Navel* . . sometimes ['nebəl]. **1965–70** *DARE* (Qu. X34, . . *Names and nicknames for the navel*) 16 Infs, **Sth, S Midl**, Nabel; (Qu. S7, *A kind of daisy, bright yellow with a dark center, that grows along roadsides in late summer*) Infs **AR**56, **KY**9, 77, 89, **LA**16, **TN**26, **TX**52, Nigger nabel; **GA**46, Nigger nabels—[FW: used by Inf's first-grade pupils]. **1968** *DARE* FW Addit **LA**31, Navel ['neɪbəl]. **1982** Slone *How We Talked* 119 **eKY** (as of c1950), Colic in horses or mules—Cure: hold a saucerful of turpentine under the "nabble" (navel). The turpentine will be drawn up inside to the stomach.

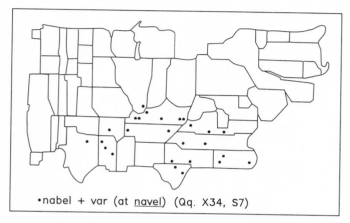

•nabel + var (at navel) (Qq. X34, S7)

navigate v

1 also with *about:* To loiter, hang around.

1893 Shands *MS Speech* 47, *Navigate*. . . This word is used by negroes to mean *to loiter, to linger around, to hang about;* as, "Dey was navigatin' about hyar all summer." In this use of the word there is no reference whatever either to the sea or to ships.

2 also with *along, around:* To get about, move around; to walk; also fig.

1844 Stephens *High Life in NY* 109, It warn't no easy matter tu navigate so as not tu git a second ducking, for every nigger in York seemed to be out a washing winders. **1846** *Spirit of Times* 11 July 234/3 *(OEDS)*, Well, by this time I began to think of navigating. **1881** (1883) Cooke *Somebody's Neighbors* 88 **NEng**, What are you navigating round me for so glib? **1909** *DN* 3.351 **eAL, wGA**, *Navigate*. . . To move about, guide oneself. "He was so drunk he couldn't navigate." Ibid 421 **Cape Cod MA** (as of a1857), *Navigate around*. . . To find one's way. "My kitchen is so small I can hardly navigate around in it." **1914** *DN* 4.110 **cKS**, *Navigate*. . . To move about. **1916** Macy–Hussey *Nantucket Scrap Basket* 139, *Navigate* . . This word is employed to express progress by any means of locomotion, walking, riding, driving, etc. Bad walking is called "bad navigating", and vice versa. **1930** *Randolph Enterprise* (Elkins WV) 13 Feb. 1/1 *(DA)*, The fellow was. . . hardly able to navigate as he was carrying a heavy load of Prohibition poison. **1965–70** *DARE* (Qu. Y23, . . *To move yourself or get yourself in motion:* "I was so stiff I could hardly _____.") 109 Infs, **widespread**, Navigate; (Qu. Y24, . . *To walk, to go on foot:* "I can't get a ride, so I'll just have to _____.") Inf **PA**130, Navigate along; **WA**28, Get up and get navigating.

navigate about See **navigate 1**

navigate along (or around) See **navigate 2**

navuh See **neighbor** n

navy bean n Also rarely *navy,* ~ *pea* (*bean*) **widespread, but less freq NEast** See Map Cf **great northern bean, pea bean**

A white dry bean (*Phaseolus vulgaris* cultivar).

1856 Kane *Arctic Explor.* 2.94, Coffee . . ; one part of the genuine berry to three of navy-beans. **1861** *S. Field & Fireside* 1 June 14, *White*

Navy Beans. Such of our readers as can procure seed of the small white Navy bean will find them a profitable crop for the army. **1896** *Daily News Cook Book* 53 **nwIL**, Soak over night one pint of small white or navy beans. **1903** (1965) Adams *Log Cowboy* 177 (as of c1880), Our supply of flour and navy beans was running rather low. **1910** Wickson *CA Vegetables* 199, *Small White Bean.*—This is the accepted local name for the variety which is called the Navy bean at the East. **1920** Kander *Settlement Cook Book* 180 **ceWI**, 1 qt. navy beans. **1949** Hedgecock *Gone Are the Days* 18 **swMO**, I think it was here on the Warren place that I first became conscious of the fact that we were poor folks. We ate more navy beans than the United States Navy itself. **1949** *Sat. Eve. Post* 22 Oct 128, A baby under a year old sucked a navy bean into its lung, where the bean immediately swelled from moisture. **1965–70** *DARE* (Qu. I18, *The smaller beans that are white when they are dry*) 648 Infs, **widespread, but less freq NEast**, Navy beans; **GA**79, **KY**69, **MO**5, 16, Navies; **GA**12, Navy peas; **VA**7, Navy pea beans. [Further exx throughout DS; all exx are mapped] **1968** *DARE* Tape **CA**63, Then they raise the small whites here, navy beans. **1978** *Wanigan Catalog* 15, *Navy pea* B[ush] More synonyms for this than space will permit. . . Many of the small white bush beans in this catalog qualify as Navy. **1988** Whealy *Garden Seed Inventory* (2d ed) 33, *Navy* (Boston Pea, White Navy, Small White Navy, White Bean) . . will not mush up when cooked[,] firm skins stand reheating well, excel. for baked beans or soup.

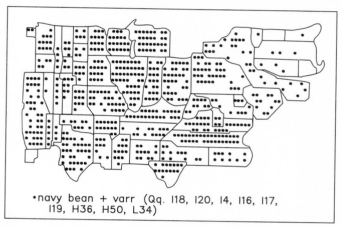

•navy bean + varr (Qq. I18, I20, I4, I16, I17, I19, H36, H50, L34)

naw See **no**

N'awlins See **New Orleans**

nawth See **north**

nawthin' See **nothing**

nawthun See **northern** adj

nayo See **no**

nayshnul, naytional See **national**

ne- See **never**

neager See **nigger** n[1]

neah See **near**

neap n[1] Also *ne(e)p* [*OED* 1553 →] **chiefly NEng, Upstate NY** See Map on p. 764 *old-fash* Cf **neb** n 3

The tongue of a cart or wagon; rarely, the iron at the end of the tongue.

1772 in 1947 *AmSp* 22.1.2.31 **CT**, 1 band for cart nep. **1828** Webster *Amer. Dict.*, *Neap*, the tongue or pole of a cart, sled or wagon. *N. England*. **1877** Warner *Being a Boy* 2 *(DAE)*, I rode on the neap of the cart, and drove the oxen . . to the cider mill. **1884** *Harper's New Mth. Mag.* 69.613 **NEng**, They had . . perched themselves on a cart neap. **1905** *DN* 3.14 **cCT**, *Neap*. . . The tongue or pole of a cart or wagon. **1934** *Hanley Disks* **neMA**, The neap is just the iron part where you slip it into the ring that's on the yoke. **1939** *LANE* Map 170 (*Wagon tongue*), [60 infs, **chiefly CT, eMA**, offered *neap*, occasionally in the combs *cart neap, horse* ~, *ox* ~, *wagon* ~. Some infs restricted its use to ox-drawn vehicles; 2 said it was (or was also) the tongue on an old-fashioned human-drawn fire engine; 1 that it could also refer to the tongue of a horse-drawn sled; 1 that it was the short tongue connecting the front and rear axles of a timber gear or dump cart.] **1951** *NY Folkl. Qrly.* 7.190, The St. Lawrence Valley has *neap* for the wagon tongue. **1965–70** *DARE* (Qu. L45, *The long piece of wood that sticks out in front of a* *wagon, and you put a horse on each side)* Infs **AL**20, **CT**4, **MA**15, **MO**5, **NY**13, 96, Neap; **CT**13, Neap—for an ox wagon; pole—for a horse wagon; **MA**5, Neap—has heard; **MA**16, Neap—old-fashioned; **VT**2, Neap—used especially on an ox cart. [9 of 10 Infs old] **1967** *Amer. Agric. & Rural New Yorker* June 30 **CT**, [In a list of old words not now commonly known:] Neap or neep—tongue or pole of a wagon. **1971** Wood *Vocab. Change* 51, The shaft between two horses hitched to a farm wagon is a *tongue.* In Mississippi that is the only word; in the other states *pole* is reported. *Neap, neb,* and *spear* occur in a few instances.

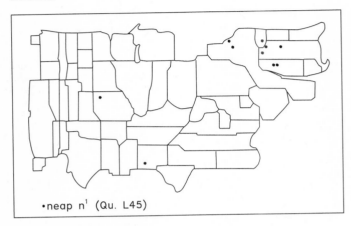

•neap n¹ (Qu. L45)

neap n² See **nip**

near adj, adv Pronc-spp *n'ar, neah, ne'er, neh-uh*

A Forms.

1843 [see **nearabout(s) 2**]. **1914** *DN* 4.160 [at *prong*], "Ovah neah thuh branch yo' kin find a prong foah my graveh-shootah" (gravel-shooter). **1927** Shewmake *Engl. Pronc. VA* 43, *Near.* The dialectal pronunciation is *neh-uh* (*e* as in *net*). **1938** in 1944 *ADD* **Boston MA,** [njɪə]. **1939** *Folk-Lore* (London) Sept 310 **nWV,** When the wheel [=a circle around the moon] is far, the storm is n'ar,/ When the wheel is n'ar, the storm is far.

B Gram forms.

Compar and superl: usu *nearer, nearest;* also **chiefly Sth, S Midl** *nearder, neardest.* Cf *farder, fardest* (at **far** adv, adj¹ **B1, C1**), **nighder,** Intro "Language Changes" I.8

1871 Eggleston *Hoosier Schoolmaster* 76 **sIN,** Stretch him to the neardest tree. *Ibid* 96, You come nearder to bein' kyind than anybody I know. **1897** *KS Univ. Qrly.* (ser B) 6.89 **neKS,** *Nearder:* nearer. **1903** *DN* 2.322 **seMO,** *Neardest.* . . Nearest. **1906** *DN* 3.121 **sIN,** *Neardest.* **1909** *DN* 3.400 **nwAR,** *Neardest.* **1914** *DN* 4.110 **cKS,** *Nearder.* . . Nearer. **1923** *DN* 5.215 **swMO,** *Nearder.* . . Nearer. . . *Neardest.* . . Nearest. "He come the neardest drown'din' I ever seed." **1936** *AmSp* 11.316 **Ozarks,** *Nearder.* . . Nearer. **1960** Criswell *Resp. to PADS 20* **Ozarks,** I have heard the . . form, *neardest.* **1968** *DARE* Tape **VA**27, They had near paths, when I was a boy. . . In place of going clear around the road you could cross over these here mountains and make it a heap nearder.

C As adj.

Also *near-sighted:* Stingy, frugal, parsimonious. [*OED* 1616 →] **chiefly Nth, esp NEast** Cf **nigh** adj **C3**

c1820 in 1941 *AmSp* 16.157 **NYC,** *Near*—close, avaricious. **1886** *S. Bivouac* 4.349 **sAppalachians,** *Near* (stingy). **1887** Kirkland *Zury* 538 **IL,** *Near.* . . Stingy, mean, penurious. **1899** (1912) Green *VA Folk-Speech* 295, *Near.* . . Economical; closely calculating; also close; parsimonious; stingy. **1914** Dickinson *WI Plays* 55, If you'd packed as many missionary barrels as I have you'd 'a' known it was Mis' Hemenway's without lookin'. Mis' Hemenway is a splendid cake-maker, but she *is* near-sighted about gifts she gives the poor. **1914** *DN* 4.77 **ME, nNH,** *Near.* . . Stingy, mean. Same as "close" or "cropin' ". **1923** *DN* 5.215 **swMO,** *Near.* . . Stingy. **1926** *DN* 5.388 **ME,** *Near.* . . Stingy. "The old man wouldn't give you anything; he's near." Common. **1944** Holton *Yankees Were Like This* 200 **Cape Cod MA** (as of c1890), Take Henry Goodwin, for instance. He was what we called *near,* with variations of *close as the bark to a tree.* One man, at least, called him plain mean, and did it to his face. **1947** Bowles-Towle *New Engl. Cooking* xi, Country cooks might be somewhat "near" with "boughten" things—but they were amazingly lavish with home-grown foods, and butter, cream,

and eggs. **1951** Johnson *Resp. to PADS 20* **DE** (*Names or nicknames for a stingy person*) Near with his money—(old-fashioned). **1959** *VT Hist.* 27.150, *Near.* . . Close; stingy. **1967–68** *DARE* (Qu. U33, *Names or nicknames for a stingy person*) Inf **NY**123, Near; (Qu. U35, . . *Thrifty but not in a complimentary way: "She's not a bad housekeeper, but very _____."*) Infs **MA**5, **NY**41, **PA**126, Near; **NJ**48, In New England you'd say "near"; **PA**135, Little bit nearer. **1975** Gould *ME Lingo* 188, *Near*—Reluctant to part with money; saving; not generous. A man who is "near with his money" will have the first nickel he ever earned. It can mean stingy and self-centered. Not unlike *tight* in "tight as the bark to a tree," but not so extreme sometimes; a person who is cautious and frugal, perhaps merely thrifty, would not be called *tight,* but will be said to be "a mite near." **1984** Santmyer *And Ladies* 444 **swOH,** To Sheldon's mother the pleasure of giving a party at someone else's expense (Mrs. Edwards was the least bit "near") prevented any objections or questions beyond a few murmurs.

nearabout(s) adv Cf **nighabout**

1 Close by; in the vicinity; hence prep (phr) *nearabout (to)* close to. [*OEDS* c1400 →; "*Obs.*"]

1934 (1970) Wilson *Backwoods Amer.* 186 **AR, MO,** They'd bend over a hickory sapplin' nearabouts. **1934** (1943) *W2, Nearabout.* . . Nearby. Now Dial. **1986** Pederson *LAGS Concordance,* 1 inf, **cwFL,** There was no low place nearabout to ditch it to; 1 inf, **nwMS,** Nearabout to the house; 1 inf, **cAL,** On the county line nearabout where he was born; 1 inf, **cwTN,** Everybody nearabout.

2 also *nearbout, nearly (a)bout, near on about:* Almost; nearly; approximately. **chiefly Sth, S Midl**

1702 in 1884 Boston Registry Dept. *Records* 11.20, The front of the Old house . . is neer abt Eleven foot from the Street. **1708** *Ibid* 81, The which mouth of the Said creek bears Neer about North East from ye Knowl of Trees. **1834** Caruthers *Kentuckian* 2.206, Yes, and I believe everybody's married, nearabouts, as far as I can learn. **1843** (1916) Hall *New Purchase* 432 **IN,** I kin a sort a pint out the course ne'er on about as well as Bill. **1890** *Harper's New Mth. Mag.* 82.103 **swME,** We'll have some o' your clam fritters, and near about stuff him to death. **1903** *DN* 2.299 **Cape Cod MA** (as of a1857), *Near bout.* . . Almost, used apologetically; as 'you foolhead, near bout.' **1909** *DN* 3.351 **eAL, wGA,** *Near(a)bout.* . . Almost, nearly. "We are near bout done this job." **1928** Green *In the Valley* 161 **eNC,** He took off near'bout all his clothes. **1938** Rawlings *Yearling* 9 **nFL,** "I near about give you out, son," he said. **1940** (1941) Bell *Swamp Water* 68 **Okefenokee GA,** Didn't you know I'd be worried near-bout to death? *Ibid* 90, I got to where I'm nearly-bout Indian myself. **1941** Faulkner *Men Working* 19 **MS,** We can make twelve bales of cotton, near 'bout, every year. **1941** Percy *Lanterns* 325 **nwMS** [Black], As how I near 'bout raised him. **1965–70** *DARE* (Qu. KK11, *To make great objections or a big fuss about something: "When we asked him to do that, he _____."*) Inf **TX**39, Nearabout had a fit; **MS**88, Nearabout went crazy; (Qu. LL30, . . '*Nearly' or 'almost': "He fell off the ladder and _____ [broke his neck]."*) Infs **LA**17, **MS**20, **SC**26, **VA**39, Nearabout; **LA**17, **MS**88, **SC**34, Nearbout; **VA**39, Nearly about; (Qu. LL32, *Expressions meaning that one man's ability is not nearly as great as another man's: "John can't [or doesn't, or isn't] _____ Bill."*) Inf **LA**17, Isn't nearbout the man Bill is. **1965–68** *DARE* FW Addit **DE**3, *Nearabout*—nearly or almost; **nwLA,** I begged him, nearabout; **MS,** *Nearbout*—almost or nearly. Common. **1966** Giles *Great Adventure* 15 **AR,** "You got some ponies?" "I got four." "They broke?" "Nearabout." **1986** Pederson *LAGS Concordance (Almost)* 69 infs, **chiefly coastal Gulf Region,** Nearabout; 10 infs, **Gulf Region,** Nearly (a)bout.

nearabout to See **nearabout(s) 1**

nearbout See **nearabout(s) 2**

near-by n

1938 *AmSp* 13.6 **AR** [Black], *Near-by.* . . Neighbor. 'Let's visit our near-bys.' A negro expression.

near cut n [nEngl, Scots dial; cf *EDD*] **chiefly S Midl** Cf **nigh cut**

A shortcut.

1915 *DN* 4.186 **swVA,** *Near cut.* . . A short by-way. Also *nighcut.* **1949** (1958) Stuart *Thread* 93 **KY,** I took the near cut across the Seaton Ridge. This would save me three miles. **1959** Hall *Coll.* **cwNC,** He thought he'd take a near cut through this laurel thicket and he didn't know what he was getting into. **1966** *PADS* 46.27 **cAR,** I takened a near cut. **1966** *DARE* (Qu. MM16, . . *"It'll be shorter if we _____."*) Infs **NC**30, 33, Take a near cut. **1981** *High Coll.* **ceKY** (as of c1930),

I'll take a near cut and beat you to the river. **1982** *Barrick Coll.* **csPA,** *Near-cut*—a short-cut.

nearder, neardest See **near** B

near hand adj phr [Scots dial]
Nearby, imminent.
   1958 *Hand Coll.* **neOH,** A far off ring around the moon is [=foretells] a near hand storm.

near horse n [*OED* (at *near* adj 3.b) c1611 →] Also called **boss horse, hand ~, haw ~, hither ~, inside ~, lagging ~, line ~, nearside ~, nigh ~, on ~, saddle ~** Cf **lead horse, off ~** 1
The left-hand horse of a pair; occas, the right-hand horse; similarly nouns *near mule, ~ ox, ~ wheeler*. Note: The occas attestations of *near horse* (and its synonyms) for the right-hand horse are probably simply errors based on unfamiliarity with, or imperfect recollection of, obsolete terminology. Though some investigators have assumed that the reversed sense reflects a change in usage, the evidence is not compelling.
   1876 Knight *Amer. Mech. Dict.* 3.1746, The Ohio plow is generally left-handed, that is, throws the furrow to the left; the near horse walks in the furrow, and the team is turned "gee" at the corners. **1935** Davis *Honey* 311 **OR,** The freighter sat in his saddle on the near-wheeler and threw rocks at them when they threatened to collapse. **1948** Davis *Word Atlas Gt. Lakes* 86, Terms of the North and Midland . . *near horse* [=the horse on the left side in plowing or hauling] . . Com[mon in the middle and southern parts of the Great Lakes Region]; fairly common [in the northern part of the Great Lakes Region]. **1949** Kurath *Word Geog.* 66, The left horse of a (plow) team is known as the *near-horse (near-side horse)* in a large area extending from the Connecticut River to the Potomac and the Kanawha, excepting only the southwestern half [sic] of Pennsylvania. In Eastern New England *nigh-horse* predominates (*near-horse* being uncommon), and this term, though yielding ground to *near-horse,* is still extensively used in Western New England and the entire New England settlement area. **1950** Stuart *Hie Hunters* 187 **eKY,** Old Dinah is the near mule when ye have 'em in the britchen. **1955** Potter *Dial. NW OH* 81, In these days of mechanized farming many informants are without terms for the left horse of a team. Only thirty-four responses were noted for this item [asked of 60 infs]. . . *Near horse* . . appeared in the data eight times. *Ibid* 126, *Near horse,* given 1 in 3 by the oldest people and 1 in 4 by the middle-aged, was not offered by the youngest group. **1961** Folk *Word Atlas N. LA* map 814, Horse on left side in hauling . . near horse [48% of 275 infs]. **1962** Atwood *Vocab. TX* 56, *Horse on the left*. . . Other terms [besides *haw horse*] for the left-hand horse are *near horse* . . and *lead horse. Ibid* 108, Decreasing familiarity with rural life and with premechanized days is most clearly evident in the waning knowledge of the horse and his uses. This is reflected in the obsolescence of the terms *nicker, near horse,* . . and *horse lot.* **1965–70** DARE (Qu. K32b, *The horse on the left side in plowing or hauling*) 125 Infs, **widespread,** Near horse; NY211, Near ox; (Qu. K32a, *With a team of horses, . . the horse on the driver's right hand*) 22 Infs, **chiefly Nth, N Midl,** Near horse. **1966** Dakin *Dial. Vocab. Ohio R. Valley* 2.292, Numerous comments in the field records make it evident that many informants are themselves uncertain about the usage of *near-horse* and *off-horse*. . . Only two terms—*near-horse* and *lead horse* . . are common. . . Other than in the *lead horse* area, Ohio usually has *near-horse* (rarely *nearside horse*), and this is the regular term in Indiana north and east of the hill triangle. *Near-horse* is also scattered in southern Indiana and appears along the line of the National Road west of the Kaskaskia in Illinois, but in Kentucky is known only rarely in the Bluegrass. *Ibid* 294, The field records do not indicate whether or not this reversal of terms is the reflection of a practice of driving horses from the opposite (right) side—in which case *near-horse* and *off-horse* would of course be reversed—but it seems that this must be the case. A few comments seem to suggest the possibility that this apparent reversal of the usual usage may have developed from the use of a two horse team with a hand plow. **1967** Faries *Word Geog. MO* 96, *Near Horse.* To distinguish the left from the right horse in a team, the Missouri informants use a variety of regional expressions, the most prevalent of which are *lead horse* (leader) (291 occurrences [among c700 infs]) and *near horse* (195 occurrences). . . *Near horse,* the common term in the North and North Midland, seems current in Missouri except in the extreme southern and eastern portions of the state. **1969** Sorden *Lumberjack Lingo* 80 **NEng, Gt Lakes,** *Near ox*—The left ox of a team

of oxen. Off ox was the one on the right. Oxen were driven from the left side. **1971** Bright *Word Geog. CA & NV* 173, The . . horse on the left . . *near horse* 34% [of approx 100 infs]. **1971** Wood *Vocab. Change* 45 **Sth,** For the horse on the left side of a team the general word is *lead horse.* In some states *leader* is the second preference; in others it is *wheel horse. Line horse, near horse, nigh horse,* and *saddle horse* are next. . . Responses to the questionnaire suggest that some informants were confused by the question or by actuality itself. **1986** Pederson *LAGS Concordance* **Gulf Region** (*Horse on the left*) 6 infs, Near horse; 1 inf, Near horse—on right, nearest to wagon driver.

nearly (a)bout See **nearabout(s)** 2

near mule See **near horse**

near on about See **nearabout(s)** 2

near onto adv phr
=**nigh onto** adv phr.
   1843 (1916) Hall *New Purchase* 261 **IN,** I allow that pianne [=piano] maybe perhaps cost near on to about half a quarter section. **1932** (1974) Caldwell *Tobacco Road* 11 **GA,** I been married to her near on to a whole year. **1966** DARE (Qu. X48a, *Expressions meaning that a person is not so young any more . . "She must be _____ sixty."*) Inf **AL24,** Near onto.

near ox See **near horse**

nearside horse n [*OED nearside* (at *near* a. 3) a1840 →] **chiefly Midl** See Map
=**near horse.**
   1949 Kurath *Word Geog.* fig 109, [The map shows 22 instances of near-side horse; except for 3 in swCT, they are concentrated in c,csPA and **MD,** with a scattering westwards.] **1965–70** DARE (Qu. K32b, *The horse on the left side in plowing or hauling*) 22 Infs, **chiefly Midl,** Nearside horse; (Qu. K32a, *With a team of horses, . . the horse on the driver's right hand*) Infs **MO38, TX6,** Nearside horse. **1966** [see **near horse**]. **1971** Wood *Vocab. Change* 45, Scattered reports of *near-side horse* occur in Tennessee, Florida, Arkansas, and Oklahoma.

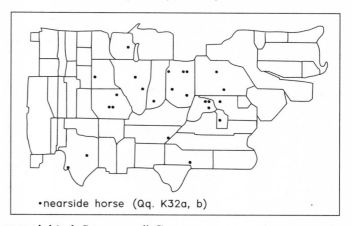
•nearside horse (Qq. K32a, b)

near-sighted See **near** adj C

near way n
=**near cut.**
   1836 in 1935 *Jrl. S. Hist.* 1.367 **VA,** I was directed for a near way, to go through the woods. Curse these near ways, they are always the longest. **1945** *Hench Coll.* **Richmond VA,** I asked a man how to get to a certain place and pointing in a direction he said "This is the near way to it." **1982** Powers *Cataloochee* 248 **cwNC,** My father built a near way from the old Indian trail that's on that map now. . . a near way coming off to the Grooms Boys Branch from the Asbury Trail.

near wheeler See **near horse**

neat-nice adj [Cf **nasty-neat, nasty-nice**]
   1951 Johnson *Resp. to PADS 20* **DE** (*Somebody who is very particular or fussy*) Women: neat-nice, nasty-nice.

neatrup See **netop**

neb n Cf **nib** n[1]
1a The nose. [*OED* c1000 →]
   1834 *Life Andrew Jackson* 70, Hit him in the pudding bag, make a pen of his neb, lush his muzzle with pokeberry juice. **1930** Shoemaker

1300 Words 43 **cPA Mts** (as of c1900), *Neb*—The nose. **1943** *Time* 15 Feb 8, In Birmingham, England, curve-beaked William Phillips, no money-worshipper, forfeited £100 by refusing to meet a condition in his brother-in-law's will. The condition: that he have his nose straightened. Observed Phillips of his neb: "I am not ashamed." **1968** *DARE* (Qu. X14, *Joking words for the nose*) Inf **WI**19, Neb. [Inf old]

b Transf: a busybody. Cf **neb** v, **nebby** adj, **neb-nose**

1968 *DARE* (Qu. GG36a, *The kind of person who is always poking into other people's affairs: "She's an awful _____."*) Inf **PA**167, Neb. **1982** *DARE* File **PA**, Don't be such a neb.

2 The point of a pen. [*OED* →1825] Cf **nib** n[1] **2**

1969 *DARE* (Qu. JJ10b, *Parts of an ink pen*) Inf **NY**209, Neb.

3 The tongue of a cart or wagon, esp one drawn by oxen; the iron at the end of the tongue; hence n **neb ox** a draft ox. [Engl dial; cf *EDD*] Cf **neap**

1710 in 1907 NH *Prov. & State Papers* 31.650 **NH**, All my houshold goods and four Cows, and a yoak of neb Oxen. **1865** Dodge *Skirmishes* 7 **MA**, Men left . . their oxen standing by the nebs. **1939** *LANE* Map 170 (*Wagon tongue*) 7 infs, 5 **neMA**, Neb [5 infs indicated that this is applied specifically to the tongue of an ox-drawn vehicle]; 1 inf, **csCT**, Neb—the iron at the end of the ox tongue; 1 inf, **neMA**, Long time since I see any oxen; but [nɛv] is what they used to call it ([*LANE* Ed: error for *neb?*]) **1967** Faries *Word Geog. MO* 82, *Tongue (of a wagon)*. . . neb (1 occurrence [among c700 infs]). **1968** *DARE* (Qu. L45, *The long piece of wood that sticks out in front of a wagon, and you put a horse on each side*) Inf **CT**17, Neb—for a cart. **1971** *Wood Vocab. Change* 51 **Sth**, The shaft between two horses hitched to a farm wagon is a *tongue*. . . *Neap, neb,* and *spear* occur in a few instances.

neb v Also *neb about* [**neb** n **1b**; cf *EDD* neb sb., and v. 16 "To put one's 'neb' into a discourse or argument intrusively or impertinently."] **PA** Cf **nib** v[1]

To pry; to nose around; hence v phr *neb out* to mind one's own business.

1928 *AmSp* 3.463 **wPA**, A friend reports "nebbin" as in use in Western Pennsylvania in the meaning of inquire into, nose about. "Your Christmas presents are in that room. Don't go nebbin," "Don't have *her*. She's always nebbin about." An adjective "nebby," ("She's a nebby child") is also used. **1931** *AmSp* 7.20 **swPA**, *To neb*. To be nosey, or inquisitive. **1968** *DARE* (Qu. II22, *Expressions to tell somebody to keep to himself and mind his own business*) Inf **PA**74, Neb out. **1982** *DARE* File **wPA**, You're always nebbing; don't neb!

neb adv, **nebbah, nebber** See **never**

nebbish n [Yiddish] esp **NYC**

An ineffectual, awkward, or hapless person; hence adj *nebbishe, nebbishy*.

1941 Schulberg *What Makes* 102 **NYC**, The Jewish language has the best word I have ever heard for people like Julian: *nebbish*. A *nebbish* person is not exactly an incompetent, a dope or a weakling. He is simply the one in the crowd that you always forget to introduce. **1960** *Commentary* June 530, *The nebbish,* the cynic, the sophisticate. *Ibid* 539 **Brooklyn NYC**, The sad *nebbishe* Podolsky is the owner of the building. **1967–70** *DARE* (Qu. HH5, *Someone who is queer but harmless*) Inf **MO**26, A nebbish—Yiddish; **NY**241, A nebbish; (Qu. HH21, *A very awkward, clumsy person*) Inf **MO**26, A nebbish. **1970** *AmSp* 45.106, The Yiddish slang words are probably traceable to New York literary circles, where use of Yiddish terms has long been favored for their expressiveness and as a means of spicing articles aimed at a rather sophisticated literary market. The most current Yiddish slang terms in the 1960s included *nebbish* 'a sad sack.' **1971** *AmSp* 46.300 **Los Angeles CA** [Yiddish in English], Nebbish . . ineffectual person. **1975** *New Yorker* 3 Feb 77 **NYC**, Mr. Antonacci is both antic and affecting as the jumpy, craven *nebbish* Honey Boy, and John Bottoms is superb in several roles. **1989** Piesman *Unorthodox Practices* 66 **NYC**, Deep in her heart she knew that some whiny nebbish with two-thirds her IQ could outargue her on any legal point by dint of sheer obstinacy. **1993** *NYT Mag.* 29 Aug 32, A bizarre feature of his attempted seductions . . is that they were less the actions of a sophisticated Lothario than of a shy and nebbishy teen-ager.

nebbuh See **never**

nebby adj Also *nebby-nosed* [**neb** n **1b**] chiefly **PA** Cf **neb-nose, nibby** adj
Snoopy, inquisitive.

1928 [see **neb** v]. **1930** Shoemaker *1300 Words* 42 **cPA Mts** (as of c1900), *Nebby*—Curious, inquisitive. **1931** *AmSp* 7.20 **swPA**, *Nebby*. Nosey, inquisitive. **1953** *AmSp* 28.251 **csPA**, *Nebby*. . Inquisitive. **1957** *Sat. Eve. Post Letters* **cwPA**, "Nebby" . . intrusive, nosey. **1968–70** *DARE* (Qu. GG36a, *The kind of person who is always poking into other people's affairs: "She's an awful _____."*) Inf **PA**135, Nebby person; (Qu. GG36b, *The kind of person who is always poking into other people's affairs: "She's the _____ person I know!"*) Infs **PA**93, 94, 167, Nebbiest; **PA**234, Nebby-nosed. **1970** *DARE* FW Addit **cwPA**, Nebby ['nɛbi]—nosey. **1972** *Atlanta Letters* **PA**, When I told a [Georgian] youngster to stop being nebby or being a nebbynose, they thought I was calling them dirty names instead of telling them to mind their own business. **1982** *DARE* File **PA**, Don't be so nebby! **1982** McCool *Sam McCool's Pittsburghese* 25 **PA**, *Nebby*: nosey as in "Aunt Edie is so nebby nobody can stand her."

nebby n, **nebby-nose** See **neb-nose**

nebby-nosed See **nebby** adj

neber, neb mine See **never**

neb-nose n Also *nebby(-nose)* chiefly **PA** See Map Cf **nib-nose, nibby-nose**
=**neb** n **1b**; also n *nebby-nosing* snooping.

1965–70 *DARE* (Qu. GG36a, *The kind of person who is always poking into other people's affairs: "She's an awful _____."*) Infs **PA**74, 76, 93, 94, 135, 164, Neb-nose; **FL**28, **PA**236, 242, Nebby-nose. [5 of 9 Infs young or mid-aged] **1972** [see **nebby** adj]. **1982** *DARE* File **PA**, Don't be such a nebby-nose! **1990** Murphy *Scorpion's Dance* 80 (*Poe Coll.*) **swPA**, No television set. Wait. He found one inside a cabinet. . . He decided to let himself feel a little guilty about what people in his hometown of Pittsburgh would call his "nebby-nosing." **1995** *DARE* File **swPA**, *[What do you call someone who is always poking into other people's affairs?]* A nebby. Another term we use for that is nebby nose.

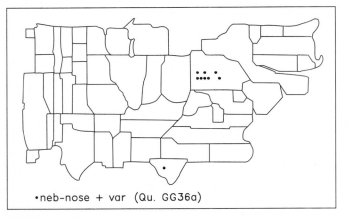

•neb-nose + var (Qu. GG36a)

neb out See **neb** v

neb ox See **neb** n **3**

Nebraska n Pronc-spp *Nebrasky, Newbrasky* Cf Intro "Language Changes" IV.1.b
Std sense, var forms.

1916 in 1944 *ADD* 408, Nebrasky. Somewhat common, but not among educated people. **1917** Garland *Son Middle Border* 134 **SD**, Newbrasky. **1929** *AmSp* 5.17 **Ozarks**, My kin-folks they went t' Newbrasky oncet. **1937** (1943) Dick *Sod-House Frontier* 511, Nebraska was widely pronounced "Newbrasky."

nebshit n [**neb** n **1b**] Cf **nibshit**

1968 *DARE* (Qu. GG36a, *The kind of person who is always poking into other people's affairs: "She's an awful _____."*) Infs **PA**93, 94, Nebshit.

necessary n Also *necessary house* [*OED necessary house* 1609 →] **scattered, but chiefly NEng, Mid and C Atl**
An outhouse; occas an indoor toilet.

1723 *Amer. Weekly Mercury* 4 July 3 **Philadelphia PA**, A new Brick House and Lot, with a good Kitchin, . . half of a Well, Necessary-House and a handsome Garden. **1788** (1925) Washington *Diaries* 3.318 **neVA**, In my Botanical Garden, next the Necessary house, was sown 3 Rows of Grass-seeds. **1810** in 1956 Eliason *Tarheel Talk* 284 **cn,cNC**, One of the public Necessaries. **1899** (1912) Green *VA Folk-Speech* 296, *Necessary. . .* A privy. Necessary-house. **1940** in 1944 *ADD* **swPA, nWV**, *Necessary. . .* A water closet. . . Old speaker. 'An older name.' **1949** Kurath *Word Geog.* 53, *Privy. . .* The more common regional terms [include] *. . necessary,* in the Boston area and in parts of the South. *Ibid* fig 55, [The map shows the following occurrences of *necessary* (or *necessary house*): 3 infs, **NH**; 7 infs, **ceMA**; 4 infs, **CT**; 4 infs, **WV**; 1 inf, **DE**; 5 infs, **VA**; 8 infs, **NC**]. **1950** *WELS* (An outside toilet building), 1 Inf, **swWI**, Necessary. c**1960** *Wilson Coll.* **csKY**, *Necessary. . .* Euphemism for privy. **1966–69** *DARE* (Qu. F37, *. . An indoor toilet*) Inf **CA21**, Necessary; (Qu. M21a, *An outside toilet building*) Infs **CT13, PA204**, Necessary house; (Qu. M21b, *Joking names for an outside toilet building*) Inf **MA11**, Necessary. **1967** Faries *Word Geog.* *MO* 74, *Privy.* The general term *privy . .* is common throughout Missouri. *. . Backhouse . . necessary, necessary house . .* appear to be in infrequent use in the state. **1979** *Blair & Ketchum's Country Jrl.* Jan 12 **ceVT**, The necessary house, so aptly named, is not so any more and almost none have survived. **1985** Rattray *Advent. Dimon* 174 **Long Is. NY**, In the winter, though, she'd wrap a muffler over her head, going out in the yard for wood or to the necessary. **1986** Pederson *LAGS Concordance* (Outhouse) 3 infs, **swAL, cwFL, cGA**, The necessary; 1 inf, **cwGA**, Necessary—not local; 1 inf, **swAR**, Necessary—also applies to one indoors; 1 inf, **neTN**, Necessary house; 1 inf, **ceGA**, In Virginia they call it a necessary house.

neck n Usu |nɛk|; also *esp Sth* |ne(ɪ)k|; for other varr see quot c1970 Pronc-spp *naik, nake, nick*

A Forms.

1867 Harris *Sut Lovingood Yarns* 100 **TN**, The shock fotch ole Burns outen the dorg wood saddil, an' ontu the naik. **1915** *DN* 4.186 **swVA**, *Nake* [nek]. Variant of *neck*. **1934** *AmSp* 9.211 **Sth**, Some words with standard [ɛ] before [g] or [k] change [ɛ] to [eɪ] or [e]. This pronunciation is decidedly vulgar. *. . Beg . . keg . . neck*. **1966–69** [see **nick and nick**]. c**1970** Pederson *Dial. Surv. Rural GA* **seGA**, *Neck* [Of 63 infs, 46 had proncs of the type [nɛk]; 10 [nɛɪk]; 6 [ne(ɪ)k]; 1 [næk]; 1 [nɛˆt]].

B Senses.

1 The throat.

1954 *Harder Coll.* **cwTN**, *Neck . .* throat. **1965–70** *DARE* (Qu. X7, *. . The throat: "Some food got stuck in his _____."*) 13 Infs, **scattered**, Neck. **1986** Pederson *LAGS Concordance,* 1 inf, **cAL**, Neck = goozle; 1 inf, **cLA**, Neck = throat.

2 =**red-neck.**

1966 *DARE* (Qu. HH1, *Names and nicknames for a rustic or countrified person*) Inf **MS8**, Neck. **1975** *AmSp* 50.63 **AR** (as of c1970), *Neck. . .* Redneck, person regarded as socially unacceptable, usually because of rural ways—"Look at that neck wearing white socks." **1991** *DARE* File, In the mid eighties in Austin, Texas, I heard *neck* used by the locals as a short form for *redneck*.

‡**3** A back road.

1968 *DARE* (Qu. N29, *. . Names . . for a less important road running back from a main road*) Inf **NJ16**, Neck.

neck v, hence vbl n *necking*

1 also with *up:* To catch or secure (an animal) by the neck; to fasten (an animal to another or to an object) by the neck; hence ppl adj *necked;* see quots. **chiefly West** Cf **gentle** v

1857 Gunn *Physiology Boarding-Houses* 133 **seNY**, The landlady *. .* necked the dog and bore him vengefully into the passage. **1858** Braman *Info. TX* 73, The usual practice of farmers, whenever they want work oxen, is to go to the prairie, and neck together, with ropes, as many pair of three and four-year-old steers as they desire. **1890** *Stock Grower & Farmer* 15 March 5/3 (*DAE*), The method [of weaning calves] generally followed in a hilly country is as follows, and is known as 'necking.' You drive the calf off, four or five miles and tie it up short to a bush. . . If some passing puncher should hear the peculiar bawl that a 'necked' calf makes, he is dead sure to investigate. **1907** White *AZ Nights* 153, Toward the middle of the morning the bull-doggers began to get a little tired. "No more necked calves," they announced. "Catch 'em by the hind legs, or bull-dog 'em yourself." And that went. Once in a while the rider, lazy, or careless . . dragged up a victim caught by the neck. The bull-doggers flatly refused to have anything to do with it. **1920** Hunter *Trail Drivers TX* 282 (as of 1873), Before we reached the Arkansas River, I killed a buffalo cow and roped her calf. Intending to take the calf with me, I necked it to a yearling, but it was so wild and stubborn it fought until it died. **1930** Dobie *Coronado* 102 **West**, They had been working for a month and had caught only about a car load

and a half of cattle. . . Every animal in the pen had been roped and led in necked to an old brindle ox. . . Some of the steers were necked together. **1941** Writers' Program *Guide WY* 463, *Neck. . .* To tie an unruly cow, or one with roving proclivities, to the neck of a more tractable animal. **1945** Thorp *Pardner* 261 **SW**, Shortly before moving camp, one of the boys would go to the ranch and bring back some gentle work oxen. We would neck up our mavericks to them, using twisted rawhide neckings made up during idle times, then turn them loose. . . Some mavericks lost many of their catch by necking two wild ones together. These would usually get to running. **1961** Adams *Old-Time Cowhand* 156 **West**, An unruly cow . . was often "necked" or tied to a more gentle animal, the animal used for this purpose bein' called a "gentler."

2 To pull (a sled or boat) by means of a line passed around the body or by a tumpline over the forehead. **AK** Cf *DCan*

1926 Willoughby *The Trail Eater* viii (Tabbert *Dict. Alaskan Engl.*), Necking a sled—hauling a sled by a rope about the neck. **1933** Marshall *Arctic Village* 128 **cnAK**, At other times you neck the boat up the river, that is, walk along the river bar some distance ahead of the boat, tugging against a rope which is attached on one end to the bow and the other to the stern. **1940** *AK Sportsman* Jan 18 (Tabbert *Dict. Alaskan Engl.*), In the following three days . . we "necked" our sled and outfit up to the Gold Creek cabin in two trips. **1963** *AK Sportsman* May 40 **swAK** (as of 1927), When we went to our second temporary camp I would help the dog pull the sled with a rope slung over my shoulder, a method called "necking" by prospectors and trappers. **1967** Heller *Sourdough Sagas* 119 **AK**, In the spring of 1887 they necked an outfit over to the Koyukuk River, a distance of two hundred miles, and landed there before the breakup. . . They wintered here and in the following spring outfitted again and returned by trail to the Koyukuk, necking their outfits as before. **1974** *AK Jrl.* 4.42 **AK**, When you use dogs, you have to pack along plenty of dog feed, and in breaking trail through new country the dogs eat more than they can haul. Instead, we "necked" our sleds over the pass. . . sledders rigged a tumpline, much like that used by many backpackers, and always pulled part of the load with the neck muscles. This developed the neck tremendously and it used to be said you could always spot an oldtime Alaska traveler because while he could wear a size 16 shirt, he needed a 19 collar. *Ibid* 44 **AK** (as of 1906), We replenished our supplies there, loaded the boat again and necked it up the Takotna River. **1983** Brown *Altona Brown* 24 **AK** (as of c1913), We watch all those people coming to the roadhouse. Some with a few dogs, but they always have to put on a harness and neck the sled with the dogs.

neck animal n [**neck** v 1]

A tame animal that is fastened by the neck to a wild one in order to render the latter more tractable; similarly n *neck mule*.

1944 Adams *Western Words* 103, A good neck animal is valued highly by its owner. **1952** Dobie *Mustangs* 232 **West**, Burros made good neck animals for wild horses as well as for wild cattle. A burro stands for no foolishness from an animal tied to his neck. **1964** Jackman–Long *OR Desert* 104, The neck mule was important. The neck chain was a foot and a half long, with a side strap on one end, a snap on the other. You buckle the strap around the mule's neck, and fasten the snap to the halter of the horse you want to stay with the bell mare. The strap gave the mule the advantage. He seemed fascinated by the bell. He would stay close to it, and the horse he was fastened to couldn't do much about it.

neck-cracker n

1967 *DARE* (Qu. N40a, *. . Sleighs . . for hauling loads*) Inf **NJ1**, Sled, jumper (nickname), neck-cracker (one set of runners, unpredictable over uneven ground).

necked adj See **naked**

necked ppl adj See **neck** v 1

necking vbl n See **neck** v

necking n

1 A neckstrap.

1945 [see **neck** v 1].

2 See quot.

1973 Allen *LAUM* 1.408 (as of c1950) 1 inf, **SD**, *Necking, sb.* A pillow or equivalent, even a round can, as used by a cowpuncher when sleeping outdoors.

necklace bean See **necklace pod**

necklace berry See **necklaceweed 1**

necklace pod n Also *necklace bean* [See quot 1938] Cf **necklace tree**

An evergreen shrub *(Sophora tomentosa)* native to southern Florida and southern Texas.

1933 Small *Manual SE Flora* 673, *S[ophora] tomentosa. . . Necklace-pod. . .* Coastal sand-dunes and shore-hammocks. **1938** Baker *FL Wild Flowers* 102, *Necklace-Pod . . Sophora tomentosa.* Shrub 3–10 ft. tall. . . Seedpod 2–4 in. long, constricted between the seeds. **1939** FWP *Guide FL* 346 **ceFL**, In this jungle, and elsewhere on southern Merritt Island where the land has not been cleared, are found trees growing more than 200 miles north of their native habitat on the Florida Keys. . . [A]mong others, ironwood, gumbo limbo, soapberry, torchwood, strangling fig, paradise tree, pond apple, and necklace bean. **1960** Vines *Trees SW* 570, *Necklace-pod Sophora. . .* is found on coastal dunes of Baja California, Florida, and south Texas. **1971** Craighead *Trees S. FL* 94, Some of the more characteristic trees and shrubs of the beaches and coastal ridges are randia, buttonwood, . . necklace pod.

necklace poplar n [From the resemblance of the seed pod to a small string of beads]
=**Carolina poplar 1.**

1847 Wood *Class-Book* 507, *P[opulus] monilifera. . .* Necklace Poplar. **1897** Sudworth *Arborescent Flora* 135 **CO, TX,** *Populus deltoides. . .* Necklace Poplar. **1939** Vestal–Schultes *Economic Botany* 19, *Populus balsamifera. . .* Necklace Poplar. . . Common from Quebec to North Dakota, south to Texas and Florida. **1947** Peattie *Sierra Nevada* 92 **eCA,** *Eastern Cottonwood—Populus deltoides. . .* Other Names: . . Carolina or Necklace Poplar. **1960** Vines *Trees SW* 92, *Eastern Cottonwood—Populus deltoides. . .* Other vernacular names are Carolina Poplar, Necklace Poplar . . and Alamo. **1976** Bailey–Bailey *Hortus Third* 901, *[Populus] deltoides. . .* Cottonwood, necklace poplar.

necklace tree n [From the resemblance of the seed pod to a string of beads] Cf **necklace pod**
=**Eve's necklace.**

1946 Reeves–Bain *Flora TX* 178, *S[ophora] affinis. . .* Necklace Tree. . . Shrub or small tree. . . Pods 3–12 cm. long, pubescent. Prairies and woods. Spring, summer.

necklaceweed n

1 also *necklace berry:* A **baneberry 1,** esp *Actaea pachypoda.* [From the round, beadlike berry]

1817 Eaton *Botany* 58, *[Actaea] spicata . .* neclace [sic] weed, or bane-berry. **1821** MA Hist. Soc. *Coll.* 2d ser 9.146 **cwVT,** Actaea . . alba. Necklace-weed. **c1830** in 1976 Miller *Shaker Herbs* 158, *Actea* [sic] *alba*—Necklace Weed. Bane Berry. **1896** *Jrl. Amer. Folkl.* 9.179 **ME,** *Actaea . .* necklace-weed. **1933** Small *Manual SE Flora* 513, *A[ctaea] alba. . .* Doll's-eyes. Necklace-weed. White-baneberry. White-berry. **1974** (1977) Coon *Useful Plants* 219, *Actaea* (various species)—Baneberry . . necklace berry.

2 A **false gromwell** (here: *Onosmodium virginianum*). Cf **marbleseed**

1900 Lyons *Plant Names* 266, *O[nosmodium] Virginianum. . .* False Gromwell. . . Necklace-weed. **1940** Clute *Amer. Plant Names* 227, *Onosmodium Virginianum.* Gravel-weed, necklaceweed.

3 A **speedwell** (here: *Veronica peregrina*). Cf **neckweed**

1970 Correll *Plants TX* 1428, *Veronica peregrina. . .* Necklace weed. . . Flowers in spiciform leafy-bracted terminal racemes.

neck mule See **neck animal**

necktie party n Also *necktie frolic, ~ sociable, ~ social* **chiefly West;** also **S Midl**

A lynching or hanging; hence v (phr) *necktie (party)* to hang (someone).

1871 *Harper's New Mth. Mag.* 53.949 **NV,** Mr. Jim Clemenston, equine abductor, was on last Thursday morning, at ten sharp, made the victim of a neck-tie sociable. **1876** *Carson Valley News* (Genoa, Nev.) 21 June 2/4 *(DA),* It's hard to leave ye, old hills, but it's either the States or a necktie frolic for me. **1882** in 1929 *Natl. Geogr. Mag.* Aug 247 **Las Vegas NV,** If Found within the Limits of this City after *Ten O'Clock P.M.* this Night, you will be Invited to attend a *Grand Neck-tie Party.* **1936** *AmSp* 11.201 [Euphemisms for hanging], Hold a necktie party (lynch). **1940** (1942) Clark *Ox-Bow* 47 **NV** (as of 1885), The only thing would get me out faster, would be your necktie party, Moore. **1952** Brown *NC Folkl.* 1.569, Necktie party. . . A hanging; a lynching. Sometimes used facetiously.—General. **c1960** *Wilson Coll.* **csKY,** Necktie

party. . . A hanging or lynching. **1966** Barnes–Jensen *Dict. UT Slang* 31, *Necktie frolic . .* a hanging. . . *Necktie sociable.* **1967–70** DARE (Qu. OO8a, *Talking about hanging a criminal: "Before the electric chair came in, a murderer would be _____.";* not asked in early QRs) Inf **CA**113, Necktied; **TN**23, Necktie-partied; (QR, near Qu. OO8a) Inf **CA**185, Necktie party. **1976** Garber *Mountain-ese* 60 **sAppalachians,** My uncle was a hoss-thief and lost his life at a necktie party.

neck up See **neck v 1**

neckweed n [See quot 1843] Cf **necklaceweed 3**

A **speedwell:** usu *Veronica peregrina,* but also *V. agrestis.*

1833 Eaton *Botany* 386, *Veronica agrestis . .* field speedwell, neck-weed. **1843** Torrey *Flora NY* 2.42, *Veronica peregrina. . .* Neck-weed. . . Formerly considered a valuable remedy for scrophulous affections, but probably of little value. **1870** MO State Entomol. *Annual Rept.* 35, Neckweed or Purslane—speedwell *(Veronica peregrina).* **1901** Mohr *Plant Life AL* 723, Neckweed . . [is found] throughout the continent. **1950** Gray–Fernald *Manual of Botany* 1284, *V[eronica] peregrina. . .* Neckweed, Purslane-Speedwell.

Ned n

1 See **Old Ned 1.**

2 See **Old Ned 3a.**

3 See quot.

1964 *PADS* 42.29 **IL,** Most of the terms [of abuse] collected exclusively from Negro informants are rare within the Caucasian social dialects of Chicago, e.g., *Cuff, Ned, blue, Uncle Tom,* and *black fay.*

nedcessity See **needcessity**

Neddy-jingo n Cf **jingo**

In phr *raise Neddy-jingo:* =**Old Ned 3b.**

1958 *Julian Apple Day* [28] **csCA,** When he [=the apple-farmer] has spare time, he can worry about frost in the spring and hail in the summer and wind in the fall, all of which can raise neddy-jingo with the fruit. **1961** *Ibid* [32] **csCA,** The birds raise neddy-jingo with fruit in dry years, and cause as much as 90% loss in peaches and early apples.

Neds See **Old Ned 3a**

nee- See **never**

need v
Syntax.

1 Used as neg aux verb foll by full infin (rather than bare infin); pronc-spp *neenter, neen to.* [Cf *OED need* v.² 8] **chiefly S Midl** Cf **to**

1884 *Anglia* 7.266 **Sth, S Midl** [Black], You neenter penter yo' mine = don't trouble yourself. **1899** Chesnutt *Conjure Woman* 92 **csNC** [Black], You neenter say nuffin 'bout dat. *Ibid* 151, You neenter come back ter see me. **1913** Kephart *Highlanders* 312 **sAppalachians,** I'm a hillbilly, all right, and they needn't to glory their old flat lands to me! **1943** in 1944 *ADD* 647 **WV,** You needn't to worry. **1949** Guthrie *Way West* 60, I'll see he's all right. You ne'en to worry. [**1952** Brown *NC Folkl.* 1.569 **wNC,** *Neen* ['ni:n], *neene* ['ninǝ]. . . *Needn't.* "You neene come for it; I'll take it to you."] **1966** *PADS* 46.27 **cnAR,** *Neen.* . . A pronunciation of *needn't* through loss of final *t* and the absorption of *d* into the adjacent alveolar nasal consonant.—"You neen to jump up." **1986** Pederson *LAGS Concordance,* 1 inf, **cAR,** I needn't to.

2 Foll by past pple without *to be.* [Prob of Scots, nIr origin; cf *SND need* v. 4, 1923 →] **chiefly Midl, esp PA** Cf **want** v

1954 *Harder Coll.* **cwTN,** Does my hair need combed? **1959** *AmSp* 34.69 **wPA,** Many western Pennsylvanians—educated as well as uneducated—often declare that the house *needs painted* or the television set *needs fixed* or the children *need spanked.* Certain radio and television announcers from Indiana, Johnstown, and Pittsburgh employ this construction, as do some newspaper writers and ministers. Numerous students at Indiana State Teachers College—and several indigenous professors—find it easy and appropriate to say that American education *needs improved* and that teachers' salaries *need raised.* As an eastern Pennsylvanian, I have met this usage only in the Allegheny Mountain region of the state; wide inquiries yield no evidence of its currency elsewhere in the land. . . If, as I am beginning to suspect, it is a western Pennsylvania localism, its origins *need traced.* **1970** DARE File, *Needs* and past participle: "The lawn needs mowed." Said to be a common type of usage in West Union, Ohio. **1973** *Ibid* **Pittsburg PA,** This needs fixed; these braces need lengthened; higher education in Pennsylvania needs upgraded. **1976** Wolfram–Christian *Appalachian Speech* 96 **sWV,** In

A[ppalachian] E[nglish], as in other regional varieties of English surrounding this general area, the *-ed* participial can occur without *be*. . . It *needs remodeled* all over it. . . I like my hair, except it *needs* trimmed right now. . . just about everything that *needs done*. **1982** McCool *Sam McCool's Pittsburghese* 26 **PA**, Needs: used for "needs to be" as in "The car needs washed." **1986** Pederson *LAGS Concordance*, 1 inf, **cLA**, You had cats, you don't *need bothered* with rats. **1987** Dillard *Amer. Childhood* 111 **cwPA**, We said, as Pittsburghers do say, "This glass needs washed." [**1989** *Ulster Folklife* 35.95, Modern Ulster-Scottish idioms . . [include] 'the car needs washed' (rather than standard English 'the car needs washing').] **1990** *DARE* File **sID** (as of c1965), A college friend used to say "All of my clothes need washed" or "My blouse needs ironed." **1992** Kincaid *Crossing Blood* 13 **nwFL**, He hoped to goodness that Mother and Walter got back home before Benny woke up from his nap and needed fed. **1993** *W3* File **CO, ID, MO, NJ, OH, VA, WV, WI**, [Constructions of the type "My car needs repaired."] **1993** *DARE* File **PA**, My wife's mother, b.1904 in sePA, always said "needs washed," etc. Her father, b. 1904, ncPA, did too. *Ibid*, [I am a native speaker of this [="needs washed"] dialect. . . born in 1969. . . Calgary in Alberta. I'm not sure if this is a local Calgary construction, however, since my parents were recent immigrants from Scotland, where the "needs washed" dialect is quite strong.] *Ibid*, In this morning's (Dec 5) *Macomb [IL] Journal*, I read this headline: "Zoning changes need stopped." *Ibid* **sIN, KS, c,sOH, ePA, eTN, wWV**.

3 Foll by adv of place, with ellipsis of infin. Cf **like v¹ C2, want**

1986 Pederson *LAGS Concordance*, 1 inf, **neGA**, That cat needs out.

need-be n Cf **needment**

1899 (1912) Green *VA Folk-Speech* 296, *Need-be*. . . Something compulsory, indispensable, or requisite; a necessity.

needcessity n Also *nedcessity, needsesity* [Brit, esp Scots, folk-etym for *necessity*] **chiefly S Midl** Cf **needment**

1795 in 1934 *NC Hist. Rev.* 11.307 **cPA**, He was then Riduced to the needcessity of take his shelter on a high Stump where he stood and wated his fate. **1853** Simms *Sword & Distaff* 285 **SC**, Yes, 'twas a needcessity. **1867** Harris *Sut Lovingood Yarns* 80 **TN**, Then hit wer that I'd a-cut ole Soul's froat wif a hansaw, an' never batted my eye, ef she'd a-hinted the needsesity. **1871** Eggleston *Hoosier Schoolmaster* 101 **sIN**, I find myself under the necessity—need-cessity the Rev. Mr. Bosaw would call it. **1872** Schele de Vere *Americanisms* 619, *Needcessity* . . is continually heard in the South and often so written. **1902** *DN* 2.239 **IL**, *Needcessity*. . . Always used. **1903** *DN* 2.322 **seMO**, *Needcessity*. **1906** *DN* 3.121 **sIN**, *Needcessity*. . . Usual form. **1907** *DN* 3.233 **nwAR**, *Needcessity*. **1909** *DN* 3.351 **eAL, wGA**, *Needcessity*. . . Occasional. **1911** *DN* 3.546 **ceNE**, *Needcessity*. **1915** *DN* 4.186 **swVA**, *Needcessity*. **1929** *WV Review* 7.1.9, *Nedcessity* for *necessity*. **1931** *PMLA* 46.1303 **sAppalachians**, Words of more or less Scottish tincture. . . *nee(d)cessity*. **1941** *Sat. Eve. Post* 10 May 36 **seKY**, No needcessity o'lock or key on Shoal Creek. **1952** Brown *NC Folkl.* 1.569, *Needcessity*. **c1960** *Wilson Coll.* **csKY**, [ˌnidˈsɛsɪtɪ]; usually humorous.

needer See **neither**

needle n

1 Std: a narrow, sharp-pointed leaf of a conifer. Also called **chaff n 2, diddledee, leaf n¹ B1, pin, shat, spike, spill, spine, straw, tag, twinkle**

2 also *needle burr*: The pointed or prickly fruit or seed of var plants. Cf **beggar's lice, crow needle, devil's darning ~, pin clover, Spanish needle**

1966–70 *DARE* (Qu. S14, . . *Prickly seeds, small and flat, with two prongs at one end, that cling to clothing*) Infs **FL1, IL138, MD39, PA77, VA46**, Needles; (Qu. S15, . . *Weed seeds that cling to clothing*) Infs **TN31, 34, 35**, Needles.

3 also *needle bug*, *~ fly*: A **dragonfly. chiefly Nth** Cf **darning needle 1**

1950 *WELS Suppl.* **seWI**, Needle fly—Dragon fly. **1967–69** *DARE* (Qu. R2, . . *The dragonfly*) Infs **MA3, 45, MI54**, Needle; **CA41, 141, MI96**, Needle fly; **PA225**, Needle bug; **MI63**, Didn't we call 'em "needle" or something? "Dragonfly" is all I ever knew. **1968** *AmSp* 43.53, *Others* (dragonfly). . . needle [1 of 1,518 infs]. **1971** Bright *Word Geog. CA & NV* 114, *Folk Terms* [for *dragonfly*]. . . Needle fly . . 1 [of 300 infs] . . San Bernardino; Needle bugs—1—Sierra. **1973** Allen *LAUM* 1.319 (as of c1950), *Dragonfly* . . needle [2 infs, **IA, ND**].

4 also *needle bug*: A **walkingstick.** Cf **darning needle 2**

1968 *DARE* (Qu. R9a, *An insect from two to four inches long that lives in bushes and looks like a dead twig*) Inf **WI68**, Needle bug. **1970** *DARE* FW Addit **OH**, *Needle*: an insect like (but smaller than) a walking stick, is common here.

5 See quot.

1899 (1912) Green *VA Folk-Speech* 296, *Needle*. . . Needlefull; the length of thread used at one time in a needle. "Give me a needle of black silk."

needle and thread n

1 also *needle-and-thread grass*: A **needlegrass 1** (here: *Stipa comata*). [See quot 1937]

1911 *Century Dict. Suppl.*, Needle-grass. . . One of several species of *Stipa*, especially *S. comata*. . . The awns of this grass. . . are long and flexuous and have suggested the name *needle-and-thread*. **1923** in 1925 Jepson *Manual Plants CA* 126, *S. comata*. . . Needle-and-Thread. . . Awn . . twice bent and flexuous. **1937** U.S. Forest Serv. *Range Plant Hdbk.* G116, Needle-and-thread, an erect leafy bunchgrass, 1 to 4 feet high, is so named because of its most distinguishing feature, the exceptionally long, twisted, and tapering beards (awns) which suggest a threaded sewing needle. **1965** Weaver *Native Vegetation* 122, Needle-and-thread is a perennial grass which becomes green late in March or early in April. **1966** *DARE* (Qu. S15, . . *Weed seeds that cling to clothing*) Inf **SD8**, Needle-and-thread grass. **1976** Bailey–Bailey *Hortus Third* 1076, *[Stipa] comata*. . . Needle-and-thread. . . Awn to 6 in. long. . . Ind[iana] to Yukon, s. to Tex. and Calif.

2 also *thread and needle*: An **Adam's needle (and thread)** (here: *Yucca filamentosa*). [See quot 1949]

1892 *Jrl. Amer. Folkl.* 5.104 **MA, NY**, *Yucca filamentosa*, thread-and-needle. **1910** Graves *Flowering Plants* 121 **CT**, *Yucca filamentosa*. . . Adam's Needle. Thread-and-Needle. **1940** Steyermark *Flora MO* 74, Adam's Needle, Needle-and-Thread, Spanish Bayonet *(Yucca filamentosa)*. . . native of the southeastern United States. **1949** Moldenke *Amer. Wild Flowers* 368, The *Adamsneedle* or *threadandneedle*, *Y. filamentosa*. . . is very widely cultivated for ornament. . . The leaves produce long and tough threads along their margins, with which the inrolled sharp tip of the leaf may be "threaded" to form a crude needle. **1968** Barkley *Plants KS* 100, Yucca filamentosa. . . Spanish Bayonet. Needle and Thread.

needle-and-thread grass See **needle and thread 1**

needle bug See **needle 3, 4**

needle burr See **needle 2**

needle bush n

=**chaparral pea.**

1898 *Jrl. Amer. Folkl.* 11.225 **CA**, *Pickeringia* (sp.), needle bush.

needle cushion n

1 A pincushion. [Cf Ger *Nadelkissen* pincushion, literally "needle cushion"]

1912 Green *VA Folk-Speech* 296, *Needle-cushion*. . . A small cushion filled with wool in which needles are stuck to keep from rust.

2 See **pincushion.**

needle-eyed adj phr [Cf *gimlet-eyed*]

1965–70 *DARE* (Qu. X21b, *If the eyes are very sharp or piercing*) 10 Infs, **scattered**, Needle-eyed.

needlefish n

1 A fish of the family Belonidae, usu of the genus *Strongylura*. [See quot 1960] Also called **gar n 2, silver gar.** For other names of *Strongylura* see **green gar, harvest pike**; for other names of var spp of this genus see **guardfish, houndfish 3, sea pike, ~ snipe, skippick, swordfish.** For other names of *Tylosurus acus* see **houndfish 3, sea needle**

1882 U.S. Natl. Museum *Bulletin* 16.374, *T[ylosurus] longirostris*. . . Needle-fish. . . *T. exilis*. . . Needle-fish. **1884** *Ibid* 27.450, *Tylosurus marinus*. . . Needle-fish. **1896** *Ibid* 47.710, *Tylosurus notatus*. . . Needle-fish. *Ibid* 714, *T. marinus*. . . Needlefish. **1926** Pan-Pacific Research Inst. *Jrl.* 1.1.6, Belonidae. The Needle Fishes. . . Platybelone platyura. . . Tylosurus giganteus. . . Tylosurus new species. . . Ablennes new species. **1929** *Ibid* 4.5, Belonidae. The Needle Fishes. . . Strongylura stolzmanni. . . Strongylura exilis. . . Strongylura petrura. . . Tyleosurus [sic] fodiator. **1939** Natl. Geogr. Soc. *Fishes* 226, Its [=California flying fish's] closest relatives are the halfbeaks, family Hemiramphidae, and needlefishes, family Belonidae, all of which can leap from the water for short intervals. **1953** Roedel *Common Fishes CA* 45, *The Needlefish Family, Belonidae—California Needlefish—Strongylura exilis*. . . The only member of the family found in California. . . Neither a commercial nor a game fish, it is caught accidentally throughout the year in round-haul nets and on hook and line. It has a fine flavor. **1955** Zim–Shoemaker *Fishes* 67, Needlefish have long bodies and very long, toothed jaws. **1960** Gosline–Brock *Hawaiian Fishes* 129, The needlefishes are the only Hawaiian fishes in which both jaws are extended forward into a long, sharp beak. . . *Belone platyura*. . . *Ablennes hians*. . . *Strongylura gigantea*. **1967–68** *DARE* (Qu. P4, *Saltwater fish that are not good to eat*) Infs **AL22, LA44, TX14**, Needlefish. **1991** Amer. Fisheries Soc. *Common Names Fishes* 33, Belonidae—needlefishes. . . *Ablennes hians*. . flat needlefish. . . *Platybelone argalus* . . keeltail needlefish. *Ibid* 34, *Strongylura exilis* . . California needlefish. . . *Strongylura marina* . . Atlantic needlefish.

2 A **pipefish**; see quot.

1931 *Copeia* 2.47 **TX**, *Syngnathus mackayi* . . A "needlefish" . . from Corpus Christi Pass.

3 A **sand lance** (here: *Ammodytes hexapterus*). [See quot 1937] **AK**

1937 *AK Sportsman* Feb 17 (Tabbert *Dict. Alaskan Engl.*), The needlefish, also known as candle fish and sand lance, is a slim silvery fellow averaging four or five inches long, but attaining an extreme length of seven inches. They are excellent eating. **1959** Murie *Fauna Aleutian Is.* 395, *Ammodytes tobianus personatus* is very common along the beaches and was often taken in large numbers with the seine; it is a bright silvery little fish that is called locally "needlefish".

4 A **stickleback** (here: *Gasterosteus aculeatus*). [See quot 1979] **AK**

1957 Butler–Dale *Alaska: The Land and the People* 76 (Tabbert *Dict. Alaskan Engl.*), Inland on the tundra small blackfish and still smaller needlefish are found at the bottom of streams, where the water remains unfrozen under many feet of ice and snow. **1968** *AK Sportsman* June 60, After freeze-up the men journey by snowmachine or dogteam to the sloughs near the mainland village of Chefornak. Here they use dip nets . . to capture blackfish and "needlefish" (stickleback). **1979** Pingayak in *Because We Are* 82 (Tabbert *Dict. Alaskan Engl.*), The needlefish are one to two inches in length and have sharp spines on them both on the back and front of their bodies. These needlefish are found in fresh-water rivers, and the older men know where to fish for them.

needle fly See **needle 3**

needle grama n

A **grama grass 1** (here: *Bouteloua aristidoides*).

1923 Abrams *Flora Pacific States* 1.177, *Bouteloua aristidoides*. . . Needle Grama. . . 3 awns longer than the spikelet. **1937** U.S. Forest Serv. *Range Plant Hdbk.* G31, It [=*Bouteloua rothrockii*] frequently grows in mixtures with . . needle grama . . , mesquites . . , and catclaw. **1950** Hitchcock–Chase *Manual Grasses* 533, *Needle Grama*. . . Mesas, deserts, and foothills in open ground, Texas to Nevada, southern California. **1970** Correll *Plants TX* 247, *Needle grama*. . . Frequent in the Trans-Pecos.

needlegrass n

1 A grass of the genus *Stipa*. [See quot 1925] **chiefly West** Also called **bunchgrass 4, darning needle 4, devil's darning ~ 6, feather grass 1, porcupine ~, spear ~**. For other names of var spp see **beargrass 3b, black oat grass, devil's knitting-needles, hairgrass 1e, mesquite grass 2d, needle and thread 1, oat grass d, sleepy ~, Texas winter ~, weather ~, wild oat**

1910 Graves *Flowering Plants* 60 **CT**, *Stipa avenacea*. . . Needle Grass. . . More frequent in southwestern Connecticut. . . The seeds of this grass are injurious to sheep by clinging to the wool and then penetrating the flesh. **1912** Baker *Book of Grasses* 101, The greater number of the species of this genus (*Stipa*) are found west of the Mississippi, and form the Bunch-grasses, Feather-grasses, and Needle-grasses of the plains. **1925** *Book of Rural Life* 6.3787, *Needle grass (Stipa comata)*, a perennial bunch grass which is native from British Columbia and Montana to California and New Mexico. It is so called from the fruits, which are narrow and very sharp-pointed, each having an awn four to six inches long. **1937** U.S. Forest Serv. *Range Plant Hdbk.* G114, *Needlegrasses—Stipa* spp. . . A number of our range species of *Stipa*, such as sleepygrass and needle-and-thread, have individual names, but most of them are called needlegrasses. **1954** Harrington *Manual*

Plants CO 93, *Stipa*. . . *Needlegrass*. . . The hard, sharp-pointed fruits of some species are injurious. **1965–70** *DARE* (Qu. S15, . . *Weed seeds that cling to clothing*) 10 Infs, **scattered**, Needlegrass; (Qu. L9a, . . *Kinds of grass . . grown for hay*) Inf **TX**42, Needlegrass; (Qu. S9, . . *Kinds of grass that are hard to get rid of*) Inf **NM**2, Needlegrass—native; (Qu. S14) Inf **NM**2, Needlegrass—a fall grass, a pest, especially to cotton growers; it grows short (6″–7″ high) and will release what may be a seed, with a sharp point and little "feathers" to guide it when blown by the wind. The "seeds" will stick in fenceposts, etc., and troubles cotton growers because they can't gin the "seeds" out of their cotton; (Qu. S14) Inf **OK**52, Pin grass or needlegrass (sticks to socks, etc). [*DARE* Ed: Some of the Infs at Qu. S15 may refer instead to **2** below.] **1976** Bailey–Bailey *Hortus Third* 1076, *Stipa*. . . *Needlegrass*. . . A widely distributed genus of . . tufted per[ennial] grasses.

2 A grass of the genus *Aristida*. Also called **dogtown grass, poverty ~, three-awn, wire grass**. For other names of var spp see **ant rice, arrowfeather, mesquite grass 2e, no-eat-um ~, sand ~, six-weeks ~, spider ~**

1879 McCook *Nat. Hist. Ag. Ant* 34 **TX**, Others were partially covered with a tall, yellowish grass, popularly known as the "needle-grass". . . This is probably the "ant-rice" . . ; at all events it is an Aristida, the plants gathered being identified . . as *A. oligantha*, but some of the seeds as probably *A. stricta*. **1884** (1885) McCook *Tenants* 341 **cTX**, Presently I saw an ant . . carrying in its jaws something which it . . dumped upon a heap of similar objects. . . I took up some of these, and found them to be the husks of a sort of grass known as ant-rice, or needle-grass. **1913** (1979) Barnes *Western Grazing* 246, These losses [of stock] are due to. . . bloat, death from corn smut, . . and needle grass (Aristida), whose sharp-pointed awns work their way into the lining of the mouth, lips, eyes and nostrils, . . frequently becoming so bad as to cause the death of the animal through starvation. **1937** U.S. Forest Serv. *Range Plant Hdbk.* G16, Three-awns—Aristida spp.—Three-awns, also commonly called needlegrasses, wiregrasses, and poverty grasses, constitute a large genus of the redtop tribe . . and are widely distributed throughout the Western States, being especially well represented in the Southwest. **1944** Barbour *Vanishing Eden* 124 **FL**, Most characteristic feature of Florida is the needle-grass pond of the open piney-woods prairie. **1950** Gray–Fernald *Manual of Botany* 174, *Aristida*. . . *Needlegrass*. . . Tufted annuals or perennials, chiefly of . . warm-temp[erature] reg[ions].

3 =**burro grass**.

1912 Wooton–Standley *Grasses NM* 114, *Scleropogon brevifolius* . . is locally called Needle Grass but is not related closely to the three-awned needle grasses of the genus *Aristida*.

4 also **needle rush**: A **rush** (here: *Juncus roemerianus*).

1942 *Torreya* 42.158, *Juncus roemerianus*. . . Needle grass . . coastal South Carolina. **1947** *Jrl. Wildlife Management* 2.55 **LA**, Other vegetation around the margins of the best local muskrat marshes . . include . . needlerush (*Juncus roemerianus*). . . The canes, saltgrass and needlerush marshes may be utilized by rats when better habitats become overpopulated.

needle man n

1 =**night doctor**.

1945 Saxon *Gumbo Ya-Ya* 75 **LA**, Them Needle Mens is medical students from the Charity Hospital tryin' to git your body to work on. That's 'cause stiffs is very scarce. . . If they ever sticks their needles in your arm you is jest a plain goner.

2 also **needle puncher, ~ pusher, ~ queen**: A doctor or nurse.

1965–70 *DARE* (Qu. BB53a, . . *Joking names . . for a doctor*) Inf **VA**105, Needle man; **MS**60, Needle puncher; **MO**18, Needle pusher; (Qu. BB53b, . . *A doctor who is not very capable or doesn't have a very good reputation*) Inf **MO**18, Needle pusher. **1976** Gould *Blackie's RR Hdbk.* 3, *Nurse*: Needle Queen—Pill Pusher—Pillow Flopper—Miss Nightingale.

needle palm n

1 also **needle palmetto**: =**blue palmetto 1**. [See quot 1924]

1903 Small *Flora SE U.S.* 224, *Rhapidophyllum Hystrix*. . . In shaded pine lands, South Carolina to Florida. . . Needle Palm. **1924** *Amer. Botanist* 30.125, The needle palm (*Rhapidophyllum hystrix*). . . has the leaf-sheaths thickly set with sharp spines which very effectively protect the fruits from the animals that might otherwise eat them and thus distribute the seeds. **1942** Kennedy *Palmetto Country* 5, Another low-lying palmetto—variously called the dwarf, needle, porcupine, blue, or creeping palmetto—has an even wider range than the saw palmetto, extending from Florida to North Carolina and Texas. **1966** Grimm

Recognizing Native Shrubs 68, *Needle-palm. . .* Distinguished by its short, thick . . trunklike stems covered with loose fibers and numerous long black spines. Mature fruits are red. **1975** Newell *If Nothin' Don't Happen* 9 **nwFL,** There's several kinds of scrub palmettos, including saw palmettos and needle palmettos. Either kind makes real rough goin' for a huntin' dog, because the stems of the saw palmettos will cut him and the spines of the needle palmettos will punch out his eyes if he ain't careful. **1976** Bailey–Bailey *Hortus Third* 946, *Needle palm. . .* The hardiest of palms, withstanding temperatures to -6° F.

2 A **yucca:** either *Yucca filamentosa* or *Y. schotti.*

1911 *Century Dict. Suppl., Needle-palm. . .* The short-leaved tree-yucca or Spanish bayonet, *Yucca Schottii,* of the southwestern United States and Mexico. **1976** Bailey–Bailey *Hortus Third* 1178, *[Yucca] filamentosa. . .* Needle palm.

needle palmetto See **needle palm 1**

needlepoint n Also *needle-point(ed) shoe, needletoe, needle-toed shoe*

A sharp-pointed shoe.

1965–70 *DARE* (Qu. W42a, . . *Nicknames . . for men's sharp-pointed shoes)* Infs **IA**32, **NY**145, **PA**177, **SC**32, **VA**102, Needle-points; **FL**25, **ID**5, **NJ**45, Needle-pointed (shoes); **IL**10, **VA**33, Needletoes; **MA**72, Needletoes: old expression from when I was a kid; **IL**7, **VA**78, Needle-point shoes; **TX**89, Needle-toed [shoes].

needle puncher (or pusher, queen) See **needle man 2**

needle rush See **needlegrass 4**

needles and pins exclam Cf **bread and butter** exclam

1984 *DARE* File **csWI** (as of c1920), *Needles and pins* was said when two people walking together were momentarily separated by someone or something coming between them, or when they accidentally spoke in unison. One would then say "needles" and the other "pins," then hook little fingers and make a silent wish. Accidental speaking in unison was considered good luck. When walkers were separated and did not use this phrase or "bread and butter," it was believed they would have a quarrel.

needle's eye n Cf **threading the needle**

A children's ring game; see quots.

a1874 in 1949 *PADS* 11.34 **cME,** And how we played the "needle's eye" / Which carries its tape so true,/ It has caught many a smiling lass,/ Now, lass, it has caught you. **1940** *Handy Play Party Book* 29 **OH,** "*Needle's Eye*" . . The needles [sic] eye that doth supply the thread that runs so truly;/ Many a lass have I let pass Because I wanted you. *Ibid* 30, *The Needle's Eye*—Needle's eye that doth supply The thread that runs so truly /. . . *Action:* In time to the music, the circle of players moves to the left. . . The person forming the inside half of the arch chooses someone from the line by lowering hands in front of the desired partner. He (or she) then joins right hands with the one chosen to make a new arch. . . This is practically the same version as that played in Central Ohio. . . The Arkansas version is slightly different. *Ibid* 91 **KY,** *Needle's Eye* . . Needle's eye, just so ply / The thread that runs so truly;/. . . A single circle; with one couple making an arch under which the circle marches. On the last line the bridge falls, and the one caught is given a choice (Ex. apple or pear). The one he selects is the side he joins, and at the end there is a tug-of-war. **1946** TN Folk Lore Soc. *Bulletin* 12.1.21, "Needle's Eye" always turned into a tug-of-war, the point of the game being to win this pull. **1949** (1958) Stuart *Thread* 6 **KY,** I heard the tenor of their uneven voices singing these familiar words: The needle's eye that does supply,/ The thread that runs so true/. . . I walked to the door and watched them. They had formed a circle, hand in hand, and around and around they walked and sang these words while two pupils held their locked hands high for the circle to pass under. Suddenly the two standing—one inside the circle and one outside—let their arms drop down to take a pupil from the line. . . When they had finished taking everybody from the circle, the two groups faced each other, lined up behind their captains. . . Each . . locked his hands. . . The first line to break apart or to be pulled forward lost the game. Fifteen minutes were all too short for them to play "the needle's eye." **1950** *WELS* (Games in which the players form a ring and either sing or recite a rhyme) 2 Infs, **WI,** Needle's eye. **1957** *Sat. Eve. Post Letters* **cIL, ME,** Needle's eye. **1966–69** *DARE* (Qu. EE1, . . *Games . . children play . . in which they form a ring, and either sing or recite a rhyme)* Infs **KY**41, **MN**12, **NY**88, Needle's eye; **MA**6, Needle's eye—The needle's eye you can't pass by / the one you love so truly./ He's kissed me once, he's kissed me twice / and I am his sincerely; (Qu. EE33, . . *Outdoor games . . that children play)* Infs **KY**5, **WI**66, Nee-

dle's eye. **1968–69** *DARE* Tape **KY**34, Needle's eye, thread running through . . you, just hold their hands up that way and line up and go through and then when one come through that you wanted to catch, why, just catch him in there, see? *Ibid* **KY**41, Needle's eye. That's an old, old game . . that we used to play at parties, and we played at school. . . Two people would . . put their hands together, I'd put my right hand to his left hand, and . . my left and his right, and hold our hands up over and make a bridge, and the rest of them would all line up and get hold of each other's hands, . . and they'd start round through saying "needle's eye, does supply, thread runs so truly, many a beau did I let go, 'cause I loved you truly." They'd sing that . . and then when they say that last word, "truly," whoever was in under the bridge they dropped down and caught it, . . they wanted a certain one, and at parties you'd catch somebody that's gonna be your girl friend, boyfriend, . . and then at parties we always, you got to kiss the girl, the boy did, when you played that, but at school it was just a game, they didn't allow that. *Ibid* **NY**88, [FW:] How about needle's eye? [Inf:] I could tell you the tune, but I can't quite recall how this was played either, but it went: [sings] "the needle's eye it does supply the thread that runs so freely, we have caught many a smiling lass, and now we have caught you." That was a ring game also. [FW:] Something the same as "go in and out the window?" [Inf:] Yes, similar, that's right. **1980** Oates *Bellefleur* 40, *The needle's eye that does supply / The thread that runs so truly / It has caught many a smiling lass / And now it has caught you./ Oh, it has caught one and it has caught two./ It has caught many a smiling lass / And now it has caught you. . .* Leah stood . . as the children sang "The Needle's Eye" through once again.

needletoe, needle-toed shoe See **needlepoint**

needle weed (plant) n Cf **needle 2, nettle rash**

A **storksbill** (here: *Erodium cicutarium*).

1967 *DARE* (Qu. S14, . . *Prickly seeds, small and flat, with two prongs at one end, that cling to clothing)* Inf **MO**2, Needle weed. **1982** Slone *How We Talked* 112 **eKY** (as of c1950), *Spring neddles* [sic]—Whelps and bumps that came in the spring. Probably from an allergy to weeds. Cure: make tea from the needle weed plant.

needle-wire n [Cf Scots *wire* a knitting needle]

A knitting needle.

1899 (1912) Green *VA Folk-Speech* 296, *Needle-wires. . .* Knitting-needles.

needment n Cf **needcessity**

A necessity.

1930 *AmSp* 5.427 **Ozarks,** Spenser also used the word *needments,* which still means necessities in the Ozark country. **1942** (1971) Campbell *Cloud-Walking* 69 **seKY,** They had borried Nelt's nags to ride to the store to get needments they wanted.

needmore n

1 A section of town, esp a poor or disadvantaged one. **esp S Midl**

1966–70 *DARE* (Qu. C34, *Nicknames for nearby settlements, villages, or districts)* Infs **KY**75, **MS**45, **MO**17, Needmore; (Qu. C35, *Nicknames for the different parts of your town or city)* Inf **TN**7, Needmore (colored section—old-fashioned); (Qu. II25, *Names or nicknames for the part of a town where the poorer people, special groups, or foreign groups live)* Inf **TN**6, Needmore (Negro section). **1986** Pederson *LAGS Concordance (Ethnic neighborhood)* 1 inf, **neMS,** Needmore—black.

2 See quot.

c1960 *Wilson Coll.* **csKY,** *Needmore. . .* Nickname for a ratty little country store.

3 An avaricious person.

1968 *DARE* (Qu. U36a, . . *A person who saves in a mean way or is greedy in money matters: "He's an awful _____.")* Inf **MD**31, A needmore.

needsesity See **needcessity**

needuh See **neither**

needy adj [*OED* "Obs."]

Necessary, required.

1939 *Atlantic Mth.* Oct 533 **eKY,** When they haf to sell a cow to get a little needy money, they know where to come.

neeger See **nigger** n¹

neelie n Also *kneelie* [Abbrs]

Prob =**carnelian.**

1976 *WI Acad. Rev.* June 20 (as of 1920s), The "cat's eyes" and red "kneelies" may have been polished stone. **1984** *WI State Jrl.* (Madison) 8 Apr sec 9 1/4, Dane County Supervisor Fred Raemisch tells about a "neelie" shooter he once owned when he played in the marbles tournaments in Madison back in the early 1940s.

nee-mind See **never**

neenter, neen to See **need 1**

neep See **neap**

ne'er adv¹ See **never**

ne'er adj¹ Pronc-spp *nair, naer, nar(r), nare, nere,* (for *ne'er a*) *nar(r)a* [Cf **never A** and *OED never one* (at *never* adv. 2.b) c1205 →, *never a* (at *never* adv. 3) c1250 →, *ne'er a* c1420 →] **chiefly Sth, S Midl** Cf **nary** adj, **nairn**

1 Also in comb *ne'er a:* Not any, not a single—used as an emphatic negative; hence pron *ne'er none.*

1795 Dearborn *Columbian Grammar* 137, *List of Improprieties,* commonly called *Vulgarisms,* which should never be used in *Speaking, Reading, or Writing.* . . Narra one for None. **1843** (1916) Hall *New Purchase* 365 **IN,** I say, Mister, you haint seen nara bonnit? **1862** *NY Daily Tribune* (NY) 4 Feb 4/3, There is not a Virginia abstractionist on earth who does not know that ne'er a negro who came over to us under such an act would ever be returned to Slavery. **1867** Harris *Sut Lovingood Yarns* 25 **TN,** Thars nara hoss ever foaldid durned fool enuf tu lope over eny sich place. **1884** Lanier *Poems* 177 **AL** [Black], As ef dat cabin hadn't nar' a plank upon de frame! [**1891** Johnston *Primes & Neighbors* 17 **GA,** She have told him *to* his face that he needn't pester hisself to come over here on sech a arrant not a nare another time.] **1899** Chesnutt *Conjure Woman* 45 **csNC** [Black], Atter Sandy got thoo talkin', Tenie did n' say naer word, but des sot dere. **1899** Edwards *Defense* 29 [Black], She ain't lak nair 'nother chile ever come ter dis house. **1926** Roberts *Time of Man* 62 **KY,** Ne'er one did I see. **1932** *Sat. Eve. Post* 3 Dec 6 **TN,** Hit ain't nere a hotel on the mou-tin. **1936** *AmSp* 11.245 **eTX,** In place of *any,* illiterate hill-type speakers frequently say ['ærɪ], [æɚ]; Negroes, [æːə]. For the negative form they use ['næɪrɪ], [næɚ]; and [næːə], respectively. **1936** (1951) Faulkner *Absalom* 290 **MS,** Better if narra one of them had ever rid back in '65. **1941** *AmSp* 16.5 **eTX** [Black], ['næːˌwʌn]. **c1960** *Wilson Coll.* **csKY,** Ne'er a one (or nary a one)—Not one; nary. . . ne'er a. **1968** *DARE* (Qu. LL14, *None at all, not even one: "This pond used to be full of fish but now there's _____ left."*) Inf **GA**45, [nær]—older people—"He ain't got nar left"; **GA**61, [nær] one. **1986** Pederson *LAGS Concordance* **Gulf Region,** 56 infs, Ne'er a one; 35 infs, Ne'er one; 24 infs, Ne'er a (+ noun); 12 infs, Ne'er (+ noun); 3 infs, Ne'er another; 1 inf, I ain't had a ne'er one killed since; 1 inf, She wasn't going to pick a ne'er one; 1 inf, I ain't never let ne'er of them bit me; 1 inf, I never made ne'er; 1 inf, I ain't caught ne'er; 1 inf, Didn't have ne'er; 1 inf, We ain't got ne'er here.

2 in comb *ne'er a:* Neither. Cf **nary** adj **2**

1867 Harris *Sut Lovingood Yarns* 30 **TN,** "Have you been beat playing cards or drinking?" "Nara wun, by geminy!"

ne'er adj², adv² See **near**

ne'er a See **ne'er** adj¹ **1, 2**

neetup See **netop**

neew See **new**

neffu See **nephew**

negar, neg(g)er See **nigger** n¹

negitimate See **illegitimate**

negra See **nigra**

negro bug n

A small, shiny, black bug of the genus *Corimelaena,* esp *C. pulicaria.*

1870 *MO State Entomol. Annual Report* 33, Third among the bogus Chinch Bugs may be mentioned the Flea-like Negro-bug *(Corimelæna pulicaria).* . . Its color is black with a white stripe each side. *Ibid* 35, There are two other species of Negro-bug which are common in this State. . . The first of these *(Corimelæna lateralis* . .) is . . fully one-half longer and wider [than *C. pulicaria*]. . The other Negro-bug *(Cor. unicolor* . .) is fully twice as long and wide. **1905** Kellogg *Amer.*

Insects 215, The flea-like negro bug . . is a tiny, very malodorous, polished black species often abundant on blackberries and raspberries, with which it often goes to market and even farther! **1926** Essig *Insects N. Amer.* 337, Cydnidae. Negro Bugs. . . The common negro bug, *Thyreocoris extensus* . . is a very small, shining black bug. **1954** Borror–DeLong *Intro. Insects* 241, The negro bugs are small . . shining black bugs that are very beetlelike in appearance. **1982** Entomol. Soc. Amer. *Common Names Insects* 26, Negro bug . . Corimelaena pulicaria.

negro chub See **nigger chub**

negro coffee n Also *nigger coffee*

=**senna,** usu *Cassia occidentalis;* also the seeds of this plant, or a beverage made from the seeds.

1889 *Century Dict.* 1088, Negro coffee, or *Mogdad coffee,* the seeds of *Cassia occidentalis,* which are roasted and used in the tropics as a substitute for coffee, though they contain no caffein. **1922** *Amer. Botanist* 28.30, *Cassia chamaecrista.* . . The seeds are known as "negro coffee." **1933** Small *Manual SE Flora* 661, *Ditremexa.* . . Nigger-coffees. Coffee-weeds. . . *D. occidentalis.* . . Coffee-weed. Coffee-senna. Nigger-coffee. **1949** Moldenke *Amer. Wild Flowers* 127, A cheap grade of coffee, called negro or magdad coffee, used occasionally by the southern Negroes, is made from the seeds of the *coffee senna.* **1953** Greene–Blomquist *Flowers South* 54, *C[assia] ligustrina,* closely related to coffee-weed or nigger-coffee *(C. occidentalis),* is large and partly woody with pointed leaflets. **1959** Carleton *Index Herb. Plants* 87, *Nigger-coffee:* Cassia occidentalis.

negro fish See **niggerfish** n **1**

negro goose See **niggergoose 1, 3**

negro killer See **nigger killer 1**

negro salmon n

=**humpback salmon.**

1902 Jordan–Evermann *Amer. Fishes* 150, The humpback salmon . . is often called "negro salmon" at the canneries, but when prepared, the name "pink salmon" is in common use, as distinguished from the "red salmon," *Oncorhynchus nerka.*

negro toe See **niggertoe 1**

negro toe rock See **niggertoe 8**

negro weed n Cf **negro coffee, niggerweed**

A **senna** (here: *Cassia* spp).

1922 *Amer. Botanist* 28.30, *Cassia occidentalis* is called . . "negro-weed." **1959** Carleton *Index Herb. Plants* 86, Negro-weed: Cassia (v).

negro wool n Cf **niggerwool**

1966 *DARE* (Qu. E20, *Soft rolls of dust that collect on the floor under beds or other furniture*) Inf **NC**11, Negro wool.

negur See **nigger** n¹

neh-o See **no**

neh-uh See **near**

neighbor n Usu |'nebə(r)|; also |nɛbə(r)|; pronc-spp, *Gullah, navuh, neighvuh* Cf Pronc Intro 3.I.17

A Forms.

1891 *DN* 1.156 **cNY,** More numerous are the examples of shortening . . [nebɚ], 'neighbor'; [nɛbɚhud] 'neighborhood'. **1922** Gonzales *Black Border* 314 **sSC, GA coasts** [Gullah glossary], *Navuh*—neighbor, neighbors. **1930** Woofter *Black Yeomanry* 50 **seSC,** *B* and *v* are interchanged, for *neighbor* is often *neighvuh.*

B Sense.

In phrr *live neighbor(s) to (or by):* To live near or next door to, be neighbors to.

1939 Aurand *Quaint Idioms* 29 [PaGer], We *live neighbors* to them. **1966–69** *DARE* Tape **KY**16, [Aux Inf:] We used to live neighbors to her. *Ibid* **SC**7, I lived neighbor . . by her for a year or two. **1994** *DARE* File **csWI,** We used to live neighbors to the Snyders.

neighbor v, hence vbl n *neighboring* [Brit dial]

To associate in a friendly way, esp by exchanging visits and assistance; to live on friendly terms with; hence v phr *neighbor it.*

1828 Webster *Amer. Dict.* np, Neighbor. . . *To neighbor it,* in colloquial language, to cultivate friendly intercourse by mutual visits. **1890** Holley *Samantha among Brethren* 177 **NY,** Yes, we neighbored with about all sorts of religius [sic] believers, and never disputed that they had a right to their own religion. **1893** *KS Univ. Qrly.* 1.141 **KS,** *Neighbor:* to be neighborly, as, 'He doesn't neighbor with anybody.' **1896** *DN* 1.421 **VA,** *Neighbor.* . . to be on friendly terms with. "I don't neighbor her, she's too proud." **1903** *DN* 2.323 **seMO,** They don't neighbor with any of their neighbors. **1907** *DN* 3.233 **nwAR,** *Neighbor, v.i.* To be on visiting terms with. **1909** *DN* 3.353 **cAL, wGA,** *Neighbor, v.i.* and *tr.* To send in occasional table delicacies, borrow small amounts of sugar, coffee, etc. Common. **1914** *DN* 4.110 **cKS,** *Neighbor with.* . . To be neighborly with. **c1920** in 1993 Farwell–Nicholas *Smoky Mt. Voices* 116 **sAppalachians,** I know in reason I cain't neighbor him. **1923** *DN* 5.215 **swMO,** Him an' me neighbored t'gether. **1940** Writers' Program *Guide TX* 115, Every county fair is the occasion of much "neighboring," feasting, friendly rivalry, and general enjoyment. **1944** *PADS* 2.25 **cwNC,** *Neighbor.* . . To exchange labor with, as in harvest time. **1960** McDavid *Coll.* **nwOK,** There wasn't anybody to neighbor with. **1967** *DARE* (Qu. L5, *When a farmer gets help on a job from his neighbors in return for his help on their farms later on*) Inf **CO7,** We neighbor together; **IL4, MI**67, Neighboring; (Qu. II13, *When you are friendly with people who live near you, and you do little things for each other* . . *"We've always _____ with them."*; total Infs questioned, 75) Infs **GA1, OK**20, Neighbored. **1975** Gould *ME Lingo* 188, *Neighbor*—"Folks don't neighbor same's they used to." To go *neighborin'* is to make an informal call in the vicinity. **1981** Bly *Letters* 46 **swMN,** Our general cultural stance in the countryside is that we wish people "neighbored" more, the way they used to, and we wish families were sticking together more, the way they used to. **1982** *Wall St. Jrl.* (NY NY) 9 Apr 1/1 **nwIA,** Financial distress has cut down on what they call here "neighboring back and forth," . . Dale Martin . . has noticed that "in a farming community, you don't have togetherness like you used to. You don't neighbor back and forth. You're a competitor. You're a business." **1986** Pederson *LAGS Concordance,* 1 inf, **ceTN,** We neighbored with each other; 1 inf, **cTX,** She loved to neighbor = visit with neighbors. **1992** Martone *Townships* 87 **swOH,** My mother's people . . more likely . . did the work themselves, or "neighbored it."

neighborhood n

1 A town.

1939 FWP *Guide NC* 303 **Hatteras Is. NC,** These people speak in broad Devon accents. Many older families believe they are descended from shipwrecked English sailors. . . Old words and phrases survive and the distinctive banker enunciation gives the speech a special quality. . . Towns are called *neighborhoods.*

2 The navel.

1966 *DARE* (Qu. X34, . . *Names and nicknames for the navel*) Inf **OK**42, The neighborhood; **SC**7, Neighborhood; belly button—can't stand that word; I don't like to hear it.

neighborhood road n Also *neighborhood lane* chiefly Sth, S Midl

A local road, esp one maintained by its users.

1835 Simms *Partisan* 2.266 **seSC,** A small track—a common wagon or neighbourhood road—wound into the forest. **1843** (1916) Hall *New Purchase* 77 **IN,** A neighborhood road does not imply necessarily much proximity of neighbors. I have travelled all day long upon a neighborhood or settlement road and seen neither neighbors nor neighbors' cabins. **1885** Cable *Dr. Sevier* 395 **LA,** The buggy was moving at a quiet jog along a "neighborhood road," with unploughed fields on the right and a darkling woods pasture on the left. **1903** *DN* 2.322 **seMO,** *Neighborhood road.* . . Byroad. **1907** *DN* 3.233 **nwAR,** *Neighborhood road.* . . A byroad. **1915** *DN* 4.186 **swVA,** *Neighborhood road.* . . A by-way,—distinguished from a public road. **1939** *LANE* Map 44 (*Side road; lane*) 1 inf, **RI,** Neighborhood road. **1967–70** *DARE* (Qu. N29, . . *Names . . for a less important road running back from a main road*) Infs **SC**43, 66, Neighborhood road. **1986** Pederson *LAGS Concordance* **Gulf Region** (*Byway, outside of town*) 5 infs, Neighborhood road(s); 1 inf, Neighborhood road—before paved; kept by neighbors; 1 inf, Neighborhood road—not usual term; circular road; 1 inf, Neighborhood road—two or three local families kept it up; 1 inf, Neighborhood road—local farmers had to keep up; 1 inf, Neighborhood road—on private property; (*Lane, from public road to house; from barn to pasture; across public road*) 2 infs, Neighborhood road; 1 inf, Neighborhood lane.

neighboring, neighbor it See neighbor v

neighbor Jones n

=Mrs. Jones.

1941 *LANE* Map 354 (*Privy*) 1 inf, **ceRI,** Neighbor Jones.

neighbor-people n pl Cf Intro "Language Changes" I.4

Neighbors.

1913 Kephart *Highlanders* 286 **sAppalachians,** Pleonasms are abundant. . . Everywhere in the mountains we hear of biscuit-bread . . granny-woman and neighbor-people. **1930** *VA Qrly. Rev.* 6.248 **S Midl,** There are the analogous compounds . . neighbor people, [etc]. **1972** Cooper *NC Mt. Folkl.* 94, *Neighbor-people*—neighbors.

neighvuh See neighbor n

neither adj, adv, pron, conj

Usu |ˈnɪðə(r)|; also |ˈnaɪðə(r)|; less freq |ˈnɪðə(r), ˈnʌðə(r)|; *esp freq among Black speakers* |ˈnidə| Pronc-spp *needer, n'er, nither, nithur, nother, nur, nuther;* for addit pronc and sp varr see **A** below.

A Forms.

1784 in 1967 *PADS* 48.39 **NC,** *Nither*—'neither'. **1789** Webster *Dissertations Engl. Lang.* 114, The words *either, neither* . . are generally pronounced, by the eastern people . . *ither, nither.* . . These are errors; all the standard authors agree to give *ei,* in these words, the sound of *ee.* **1815** Humphreys *Yankey in England* 107, *Nuther,* neither. **1818** Fessenden *Ladies Monitor* 172 **VT,** [In a list of provincialisms to be avoided:] *Nother* for neither. **1823** Cooper *Pioneers* 1.189 **nNY,** It's nather a Methodie, nor a Papish, nor Prasbetyrian, that he is. **1838** Cooper *Amer. Democrat* 119 **NY,** The polite pronunciation of "either" and "neither," is "i-ther" and "ni-ther," and not "eether" and "neether." This is a case in which the better usage of the language has respected derivations, for "ei," in German are pronounced as in "height." **1843** (1916) Hall *New Purchase* 113 **sIN,** That aint fair nither. *Ibid* 372, The Apostuls didn't nithur. **1844** Thompson *Major Jones's Courtship* 76 **GA,** Perliteness aint every thing, my child, and pearances aint every thing nother. **1883** (1971) Harris *Nights with Remus* 236 **GA** [Black], He aint hatter sell he ole mammy n'er. Dat he aint. **1884** *Anglia* 7.268 **Sth, S Midl** [Black], *Needer yer ner dar* = indifferent. **1884** (1958) Twain *Huck. Finn* 35 **MO,** I don't want it at all—nor the six thousand, nuther. **1891** Cooke *Huckleberries* 33 **CT,** 'T ain't best, nuther, to fight with the blacksmith, when there ain't but one handy. **1891** *DN* 1.135 **cNY,** [nɪðɚ] ([nʌðɚ]) . . 'neither.' **1893** Shands *MS Speech* 47, *Needer* [nidə]. Negro for *neither. Nuther* [nʌðə] is another form very largely used by negroes for *neither. Nuther* is generally employed at the end of sentences in constructions like the following: "No, I didn't do it nuther"; "An' I ain't goin' nuther"; etc. **1896** Harris *Sister Jane* 137 **GA** [Black], Dat ain't needer yer ner dar. **1899** Woerner *Rebel's Daughter* 110 **Ozarks,** "I'm real sorry," he said . . "'at nur me actions nur me words are to the likin' o' the ladies." **1899** (1912) Green *VA Folk-Speech* 301, *Nother.* . . Same as *neither.* **1903** *DN* 2.299 **Cape Cod MA** (as of a1857), *Nuther* . . Neither. **1906** *DN* 3.121 **sIN,** *Neither.* . . Usually pronounced *nither.* **1909** *DN* 3.353 **eAL, wGA,** *Nother.* . . Neither. "There ain't nobody there, and there ain't likely to be nuther." Both the conj. and the pron. are often contracted to *nur.* **1912** Green *VA Folk-Speech* 302, *Nuther* for *neither.* **1922** [see **E2** below]. **1942** *AmSp* 17.31 **seNY,** Other variations include . . [i] 12 [occurrences], [aɪ] 10, in *neither.* **1942** Hall *Smoky Mt. Speech* 20 **wNC, eTN,** Also *neither* and *rather* with [ʌ]. **1942** McAtee *Dial. Grant Co.* **IN** 45 (as of 1890s), *Neither* . . negative intensifier; "I didn't _____". Some pronounced the word, nither (short i). **c1960** Wilson *Coll.* **csKY,** *Neither* is regularly /ˈnɪðɚ/; half-jokingly it may be /ˈnʌðɚ/. **1961** Kurath–McDavid *Pronc. Engl.* 149, *Either, neither.* . . The vowel /i/ . . predominates on all social levels in all sections of the Eastern States (except parts of Pennsylvania, New Jersey, and Delmarva), and is almost the only pronunciation current in the North and the Lower South. The most frequent variant has the vowel /ɪ/ . . , which is rather common in . . Delmarva, New Jersey, central Pennsylvania, and the section of West Virginia adjoining the Ohio River. . . Though most frequent in folk speech, it is also used to some extent by the middle group. The second most common variant of the vowel . . is /ʌ/ . . , which is fairly common in the folk speech of North Carolina and occurs in scattered instances elsewhere in the South as well as in northeastern New England. The vowel /ɛ/ . . is rare in this word. . . The vowel /ai/ . . is distinctly a sporadic feature of the cultivated speech of Metropolitan New York and Philadelphia, although scattered instances occur elsewhere in the North Midland and the North, even among the less educated. **1967** *DARE* FW Addit **TN**23, [ˈnʌðɚ], meaning "neither" [used in conversation]. **1989** Pederson *LAGS Tech. Index* 257 **Gulf Region,** [In *neither,* 350 infs had the vowel [i], 6 [aɪ], 3 [ɪ], and 2 [ʌ]. 12 infs had [d] in place of [ð].]

B As adj.

With ref to more than two items: Not a single, not one. **Delmarva** Cf **D** below, **either B1**

1968 *DARE* FW Addit seMD, *Neither* for *none.* "There used to be a lot of crabs here, but now there's neither one." "You can't catch neither crab here." **1976** Warner *Beautiful Swimmers* 183 eMD, "Right now I don't owe Harris neither penny. Don't owe any man neither penny." *Ibid* 217, "When does _____ go out in the morning?" "Two-thirty most times, he do." "And then he stays out there even if there's neither crab in the county!" **1979** *Rappahannock Rec.* (Kilmarnock VA) 22 Nov 3/3 ceVA, On bad days he [=the Northern Neck native] is heard to complain that he hasn't caught "either" or "neither" oyster.

C As adv.

Following a negation: Either; moreover; likewise. [*OED neither* adv. A.3. 1551 →]

1834 *Life Andrew Jackson* 168, Some of the members treated him with their gloves off . . and warn't very pernickity about the severity of their languidge nother. **1843** (1916) Hall *New Purchase* 410 **IN,** Nor me nuther—bust my rifle if I do! **1867** Lowell *Biglow* 225 **'Upcountry' MA,** "You're a good lad; but 't ain't thet nuther," sez he. **1887** (1967) Harris *Free Joe* 126 **GA,** " 'Tain't me that's changed aroun'," he exclaimed passionately, "an' 'tain't the days nuther." **1907** (1970) Martin *Betrothal* 119 sePA, No, Sam, I don't think so nuther. **1919** Kyne *Capt. Scraggs* 22 **CA,** I'll have your ticket took away from you, an' that's no Chinaman's dream nuther. **1937** *Hall Coll.* ceTN, He weren't no hunter nuther /nʌðɚ/. **1963** Wright *Lawd Today* 18 **Chicago IL** [Black], I wouldn't've never married you, neither.

D As pron.

With ref to more than two items: Not one. [*OED neither* adj. B.2.c.] Cf **B** above, **either D**

1983 *DARE* File eMD, "Neither of those twenty never [did something]" said to be in popular use.

E As conj.

1 also in comb *or neither:* Nor. Cf **either E1**

1928 Peterkin *Scarlet Sister Mary* 36 **SC** [Gullah], You might could fool some people, but you can' fool me! Neither Gawd. *Ibid* 171, Night air ain' good nohow. Night air, or neither studyin. *Ibid* 208, We ought not to fret em if we can help it. Neither me, neither you.

2 in comb *neitherso . . neitherso:* Neither . . nor. Cf **either E2**

1922 Gonzales *Black Border* 235 sSC, GA coasts [Gullah], I yent know nutt'n' 'bout'um' . . nebbuh shum sence I bawn, ent know 'e name, needuhso 'e farruh, needuhso 'e murruh. [=I don't know anything about him . . never seen him since I was born, don't know his name, neither his father nor his mother.] *Ibid* 314, [Gullah glossary], *Needuhso*—neither so, neither, nor.

3 in comb *neither else:* Otherwise.

c1937 in 1972 *Amer. Slave* 2.246 **SC** [Black], Never couldn' go off de place widout dey get a mit (permit) from de overseer neither else dey tore up when dey come back.

neitherso See **neither** conj **E2**

nek(k)id See **naked**

nekkidy See **nakedy**

nellie n

A cow, esp a weak one.

1935 *AmSp* 10.271 [Stockyard language], *Nellies.* Old, *shelly* cows suitable for canning. **1937** *W. TX Today* Mar 7, They tell of an old cowman . . who got all of his "downers" up one frosty morning. . . Just after he rode over the hill he heard gun shots back in the direction of the cattle he had just left. . . "When you shot a while ago fifty-five head of my old "Nellies" tried to run and fell down." **1961** Adams *Old-Time Cowhand* 158, A weak cow was also a "rawhide," and a "Nellie". **1968–70** *DARE* (Qu. K8, *Joking terms for milking a cow: A farmer might say, "Well, it's time to go out and _____."*) Inf **MD**34, I have a date with the nellies; **CA**195, Pail the nellies.

Nellie's hideout See **hideout** n **2**

nellify See **nullify**

‡**Nell's bells** exclam *euphem*

1924 *DN* 5.274 [Exclams], *Nell's bells* (for hell's bells).

nem, ne(m)mind, ne(m)mine See **never**

nenaine n Usu |nəˈnæ(n)|; for addit varr see quots Also sp *nanan, nainaine, nenain* [LaFr] **LA**

A godmother; also used as a term of address.

1917 *DN* 4.420 **New Orleans LA,** *Nanan* [nɑˈnæ]. . . Godmother. **1961** *PADS* 36.11 sLA, The special Louisiana additions to the questionnaire produced a considerably longer list of terms which are almost surely confined to the area. . . That they could be generally current in other areas is extremely doubtful. . . *Nanan* (Godmother)—62.8 [percent of 70 informants]. **1967** LeCompte *Word Atlas* 267 seLA, Godmother . . *nenaine* [offered by 13 of 21 infs]. . . *Nenaine* is a childish or pet word which probably stems from the standard French *marraine* (godmother). **1968** *DARE* (Qu. Z7, *Nicknames and affectionate words for any other relatives*) Inf **LA**23, Nenain [nəˈnæn]—used without name following. **1968** *DARE* FW Addit LA39, Nenain [nəˈnæ] . . godmother. Common in the area including New Orleans and southwards; no matter whether the speaker is of French descent or not. **1981** Pederson *LAGS Basic Materials,* 1 inf, seLA, [nəˈnæˑɛn] (=godmother). **1983** Reinecke *Coll.* 7 **LA,** *Nainaine, nenaine.* . . godmother [nɑnæn, nɛnæn] "How you feel, nainaine?" "My big sister is junior's nainaine." Baby talk Fr. or Creole for Maraine, = godmother. . . Often the godmother of the eldest child becomes "Nainaine" to whole generation of a family. Common among non-French catholics, esp. Italians.

nene n |ˈne(ɪ)ne| Also *nene goose* [Haw]

A goose (*Branta sadvicensis*) native to Hawaii.

1902 Henshaw *Birds Haw. Is.* 103, *Bernicla sandvicensis.* . . Nene. Hawaiian Goose. . . Upon the island of Hawaii the haunts of the nene . . are the uplands. **1944** Munro *Birds HI* 41, Hawaiian Goose—*Nesochen sandvicensis.* . . Hawaiian name: *Nene.* **1967** *DARE* (Qu. Q6, . . *Kinds of wild geese*) Inf **HI**2, [ˈne͜ne]—native goose; almost extinct; London zoo furnished "gooslings" and now they're being revived; **HI**14, [ˈneme] goose. **1972** Berger *Hawaiian Birdlife* 73, *Nene* or *Hawaiian Goose.* . . The Nene, the State bird of Hawaii, is an attractive, medium-sized, heavily barred, gray-brown goose with a black face, head, and nape of the neck. . . The Nene is endemic to the island of Hawaii . . the Nene has the smallest range of any species of goose. **1975** *Natl. Geogr. Mag.* Mar 411 **HI,** A beautiful, unique species of goose called the nene (nay-nay) was being brought back from near extinction here. **1981** *Pidgin To Da Max* np **HI,** *Nene* (NAY nay). . . Goose (Hawaiian). **1994** Stone–Pratt *Hawai'i's Plants* 152, The nēnē has short wings, long legs, and reduced webbing on its toes, indications that it often walks and seldom swims. A low "nay-nay" call . . is the source of the Hawaiian name.

neon worm n [See quot]

A larviform female beetle (here: *Phengodes* spp).

1951 Teale *North with Spring* 150, We discovered a large, whitish grub bearing luminous spots along its sides. . . This glowing apparition was the wingless, larvaform [sic] female of a beetle, a relative of the familiar firefly. To scientists it is *Phengodes,* to people in parts of the South it is the 'neon worm'.

nep n See **neap**

nep n pl See **knepp**

nephew n Usu |ˈnɛfju|; also |ˈnɛvju|; less freq |ˈnɛfjə, ˈnɛv-, ˈnɛfi, ˈnɛv-|; for addit varr see **A** below Pronc-spp *neffu, nevue, nevy* **A** Forms.

1834 *Life Andrew Jackson* 27, He seconded his wifes neffu, A. Donaldson. **1843** (1916) Hall *New Purchase* 225 **IN,** The doctor's nevy is a most powerful clever feller. **1899** (1912) Green *VA Folk-Speech* 297, *Nevue* . . Form of *nephew.* **1911** *DN* 3.508 **Sth, S Midl,** Nephew— f 214 [infs]—v 22 [infs]. **1955** *PADS* 23.46 e,cSC, eNC, seGA, /nɛvjə/ 'nephew' (sporadic along the coast). **1961** Kurath–McDavid *Pronc. Engl.* 176, Nephew /nɛfju/ is the usual pronunciation . . throughout the Eastern States. Relics of /nɛvju/ survive, both in folk speech and in cultivated speech, in Eastern New England, on Chesapeake Bay, and especially in South Carolina, rarely elsewhere. Several instances of /nɛvi/ have been observed in the folk speech of New Hampshire. **1968** *DARE* (Qu. Z7, *Nicknames and affectionate words for any other relatives*) Inf **TN**24, Nephew—[ˈnɛvjə]—careful; [ˈnɛvɪ]—rapid. **1968** *DARE* FW Addit DE2, Nephew—[ˈnɛvjuw]. **1989** Pederson *LAGS Tech. Index* 235 (*Nephew*), [683 infs responded with proncs of the type [ˈnɛfju, ˈnɛf(j)ɪu]; other proncs include these types: 37 infs, [ˈnɛfjə]; 11 infs, [ˈnɛf(j)ɪ, ˈnɛf(j)ɪ]; 10 infs, [ˈnɪfju, ˈnɪf(j)ɪu]; 9 infs, [ˈnɛvju, ˈnɛv(j)ɪu].]

B Sense.

A niece. **esp S Midl** [Cf *OED nephew* 2 "*Obs.*"] Cf **niece**

1749 in 1965 *AmSp* 40.236 **VA,** To my nephew, Mary Cripps and nephew Ann Fields. **1950** *PADS* 14.48 **SC**, *Nephew. . . A nephew or a niece. Coastal Negro usage.* **c1960** [see **niece**]. **1986** Pederson *LAGS Concordance*, 1 inf, **neMS**, *Nephew—blacks sometimes use for "niece."*

nepushency n Also *nessipushety* Cf **compulshency, pushency**
   1934 in 1944 *ADD* 128 **NC**, *Compushency . . nepushency. From necessity, push, & urgency. Oral use reported.* **1942** *Ibid* **IN**, *Compushency . . nessipushety.*

ner See **nor**

n'er See **neither**

nere See **ne'er** adj¹

‡nerk up v phr [Perh *knock* with intrusive *r*]
   1969 *DARE* (Qu. W28, *When a woman is in a hurry and has to sew up a torn place quickly . . "I'll just _____."*) Inf **NY220**, Nerk [nɜ·k] it up.

nerve n, v Usu |nɜ(r)v|; also |nɜɪv|; *old-fash* |nɑ(r)v|; for addit varr see quots Pronc-sp *narve* Cf Pronc Intro 3.I.1.f, 3.II.12 Std senses, var forms.
   [**1789** Webster *Dissertations Engl. Lang.* 105, Another common error . . particularly in New England, is the pronouncing of *e* before *r*, like *a; as* marcy for mercy.] **1840** Cooper *Pathfinder* 1.48 **NY**, It isn't enough to know the channel, . . it needs narves and skill to keep the canoe straight. **1846** in 1848 Lowell *Biglow* 4 **'Upcountry' MA**, But my narves it kind o' grates. **1884** Jewett *Country Dr.* 16 **ME**, "I must say I can't a-bear to hear anything about ghosts after sundown," observed Mrs. Jake, who was at times somewhat troubled by what she and her friends designated as "narves." **1913** Kephart *Highlanders* 140 **sAppalachians**, Blockadin' is the hardest work a man ever done. And hit's wearin' on a feller's narves. Fust chance I git, I'm a-goin' ter quit! **1927** *AmSp* 2.482, Easily the most striking and frequent variation from the standard [in Cooper's Leather-Stocking series] is the substitution of *ar* for *er, ir, (sarmon, vartue),* that change which began in England toward the end of the fifteenth century and was completed in the next century. In the eighteenth century . . the educated usually have *er* and the uneducated *ar.* . . Instances of this substitution . . are: . . *Pathfinder: . . narves, narvous.* **1927** *AmSp* 3.140 **eME**, "Sence" (since) "narves" and "narvous," "duberous" (dubious) were often heard. **1941** in 1944 *ADD* 410 **MS**, *Nerve . .* steady |nɜɪvz|. [**1941** *LANE* Map 476–477 (*Excited, all nerved up*) 1 inf, **seNH**, [nɑˑvd], older pron[unciation].] **1981** Pederson *LAGS Basic Materials* **Gulf Region**, [8 infs, proncs of the type [nɜv]; 3 infs, proncs of the type [nɜv; 1 inf, [nʉɪv].]

nerved up adj phr **chiefly NEast** See Map Cf **nervoused up** Anxious; confused; agitated.
   1890 Holley *Samantha among Brethren* 62 **NY**, But though it [=one of the horses] didn't fall out only three times . . it kep' us all nerved up and uneasy. **1941** *LANE* Map 476–477 (*Excited, all nerved up*) **widespread NEng**, When a person is waiting in nervous suspense for an expected event, when he is 'on tenterhooks' with excitement (either pleasurable or apprehensive), he is said to be . . nerved up. **1951** Graham *My Window* 164 **ME**, Yesterday I was so "nerved up" that I hadn't the usual temptation to stop at the Turners. **1966–69** *DARE* (Qu. GG2, . . *'Confused, mixed up': "So many things were going on at the same time that he got completely _____."*) Inf **NH15**, Nerved up; (Qu. GG7, . . *Annoyed or upset: "Though we were only ten minutes late, she was all _____."*) Infs **CO4, ME1, 9, MA68, NY32, 126, 185, VT16**, Nerved up; (Qu. GG11, *To be quite anxious about something . . "The letter*

hasn't come and he's _____."*) Infs **CT37, NY70, VT16**, All nerved up; **MA46, NY75**, Nerved up; (Qu. GG15, . . *A person who became over-excited and lost control, "At that point he really _____."*) Inf **NY96**, [Was] nerved up.

nerveous See **nervous**

nerveroot n [From its use in making a tonic] Cf **nervine** =**lady's slipper 1.**
   1854 King *Amer. Eclectic Dispensatory* 424, *Cypripedium pubescens. Yellow Ladies' Slipper. . .* is an indigenous plant, known by various names, as *American Valerian, Umbel, Nerve-Root, Yellow-Moccasin Flower, Noah's Ark,* etc. **1873** in 1976 Miller *Shaker Herbs* 192, *Cypripedium acaule . . Nerve Root.* Beneficial in cases of nervous headache when administered with other remedies. *Ibid* 193, *Cypripedium pubescens*—Nerve Root. . . Useful in ordinary nervous headache. A gentle nervous stimulant or antispasmodic. **1892** (1974) Millspaugh *Amer. Med. Plants* 43–5, *Cypripedium pubescens. . .* Nerve-root. . . Cypripedium acts as a sedative to the nerves in general, causing a sense of mental quiet and lassitude, and subduing nervous and mental irritation. **1899** Bergen *Animal Lore* 115 **wMA**, The large lady's-slipper is often called "nerve-root" on account of its use as a nerve tonic. **1929** *Torreya* 29.149 **ME**, *Cypripedium acaule* [was called]. . . "Nerve-root," and much esteemed as a nerve-sedative, collected and used by the nervous. **1950** Correll *Native Orchids* 24, Yellow Lady's-slipper, Water Stealer . . Nerve Root. **1971** Krochmal *Appalachia Med. Plants* 106, *Cypripedium calceolus . .* nerve root. . . The plant is used as a sedative and in treating neuralgia. In Appalachia, a root is used to treat nervous ailments and headaches.

‡nerve-shake n
Delirium tremens.
   1966 *DARE* (Qu. DD22, . . *Delirium tremens*) Inf **SC10**, Nerve-shake.

nerve up to v phr
To gather the courage to try (something).
   1979 *NYT Article Letters* **Ozarks**, He expressed doubts about his ability to accomplish the job and questioned the clerk several times. The clerk's final reassurance: "Sure you can do it if you can *nerve* up to it."

nervine n Also *nervine root* [*OED nervine* sb. 1 "a nervetonic"; 1730 →] Cf **nerveroot** =**lady's slipper 1.**
   1828 Rafinesque *Med. Flora* 1.145, *C[ypripedium] spectabile,* or Red and White Ladies' Slipper, Female Nervine, &c. **1882** *Harper's New Mth. Mag.* 44.435 **nwMA**, I saw that she had been searching for nervine and sassafras. **1898** *Jrl. Amer. Folkl.* 11.280 **csWI**, *Cypripedium* (all species), nervine, Argyle, Wis. **1934** Haskin *Wild Flowers Pacific Coast* 61, Other names by which they [=lady's slippers] are locally known are "Venus' shoe,". . and from the medicinal properties of the root, "nervine," and "nerve-root." **1968** *Foxfire* 2.2.50 **sAppalachians**, The yellow ladyslipper (Cypripedium calcelarus). . . was sold under the name "nervine-root", . . and roots were gathered in late autumn. The roots have a barbituate [sic] effect. . . The roots were also a favorite medicine for female troubles.

nervious See **nervous**

nervish adj Also *narvish* [Engl, Scots, Ir dial; cf *EDD*] **chiefly S Midl**
   1913 Kephart *Highlanders* 224 **sAppalachians**, "Old Uncle Bobby Tuttle's got a pone come up on his side; looks like he mought drap off, him bein' weak and right narvish and sick with a head-swimmin'." **1917** *DN* 4.415 **wNC**, Nervish. **1919** *DN* 5.34 **seKY**, Narvish. **1926** *DN* 5.401 **Ozarks**, Narvish. **1928** Peterkin *Scarlet Sister Mary* 80 **SC**, She was nervish too. Her hands acted tremblish and her face had a twist-mouth look. **1966** *DARE* (Qu. DD22) Inf **SC10**, Nervish.

nervous adj Usu |'nɜ(r)vəs|; also |'nɜɪvəs, 'nɑrvəs| Pronc-spp *narvous, nerveous, nervious, nurvious* [*OED nervous* a., 18th cent *narvous*] Cf **nerve, nervish**
A Forms.
   1836 in 1956 Eliason *Tarheel Talk* 314 **nw,cwNC**, *Nervous*—nurvious. **1840** Cooper *Pathfinder* 1.45 **NY**, Though they may not be Niagara, nor the Genessee, . . they are narvous enough for a new beginner. **1858** in 1955 Lee *Mormon Chron.* 1.164, That verry Moment the Tempter aff[l]icted me with the Nervious Tooth ache. **1899** Chesnutt *Conjure Woman* 40 **csNC** [Black], No . . I ain' narvous. **1903** *DN* 2.290 **Cape Cod MA**, In 1840 the younger and older generations differed most noticeably in their pronunciation of the vowels before *r* plus a consonant.

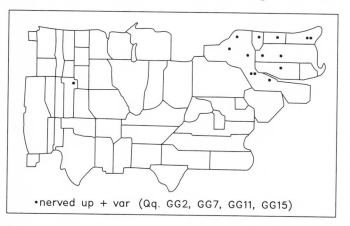

•nerved up + var (Qq. GG2, GG7, GG11, GG15)

Old folks still pronounced *er* as *ar.* Thus they said *parfectly . . narvous.* **1917** in **1944** *ADD* **sWV,** Narvous. **1927** Mason *Lure Great Smokies* 171, Dannel was all nerveous like. **1927** *AmSp* 3.140 **eME coast,** "Narves" and "narvous," . . were often heard. **1940** in **1944** *ADD* **AR,** *Nervous . .* |nɑrvəs|. Radio. **1967** *DARE* (Qu. DD22) Inf **LA6,** He done drank so much that he done got nervous ['nɜrvəs].

B Senses.

1 Of a dessert or salad: having a jelly-like consistency. *joc*

1936 *AmSp* 11.44 [Soda jerker jargon], *Nervous pudding.* Jello. **1944** *PADS* 2.11 **AL,** *Nervous salad. . .* Any gelatine salad. Alabama College slang. In use for at least ten years. **1945** *Eaton Coll.* **Milwaukee WI** (as of 1915), Nervous pudding . . gelatin dessert—family nickname.

2 Of a crop: easily spoiled by bad weather.

c1965 *DARE* File **csWI** (as of 1940s), *Nervous crop*—a crop (such as tobacco, cotton, etc) which may suddenly be spoiled by bad weather (hail, rain) before it can be harvested. Heard used by tobacco farmers in Dane County, Wisconsin, in the 1940s.

nervous n

Nervousness; an attack of mental distress.

1940 Harris *Folk Plays* 47 **NC,** I wish just one time you had to go through one *nervous* like mine. . . Nervous is worse'n anything you got in your body. *Ibid* 63, I'm goin' to pieces! I told you! I'm goin' to have a spell! . . Don't leave me, Etta. I'm goin' to have a *nervous! Ibid* 293, *Nervous,* an attack of nervousness.

nervoused up adj phr Also *nervous-upped*

=nerved up.

1931 Hannum *Thursday April* 227 **wNC,** Perk up now, honey; yo're all nervoused up over things and makin' 'em worse'n they are. **1942** (1971) Campbell *Cloud-Walking* 97 **seKY,** At houses along the way folks got Nelt all nervoused up. **1954** *Sun* (Baltimore MD) 27 Apr 9/3 (*Hench Coll.*), Corridi on several occasions hesitated in his testimony and told the judges: "I'm all nervous-upped." **1959** *VT Hist.* 27.150 **nwVT,** *All nervoused up. . .* Nervous. Occasional.

nes See **nest**

nesh adj Pronc-sp *nash* [Engl, Scots dial; cf *EDD nesh* adj]

Dainty, delicate; tender, sensitive; sickly.

1870 *Nation* 28 July 57 **sePA** (as of c1820), To be "nesh" (pr. "nash") was to be in delicate health. **1892** *DN* 2.227 **MA,** Mr. Chamberlain mentioned . . the word *nash,* 'dainty,' as familiar to him. **1905** Wasson *Green Shay* 56 **NEng,** You hain't need ever be the leastways scairt of gitting 'nash' [Footnote: Soft, tender] from settin' 'round the stove to home! I never knowed a Kentle yit with that failin'. **1931** *N. Amer. Rev.* 231.432 **NYC,** [In the speech of a cultivated woman practically deaf since 1826:] One of them [=words that have become obsolete in US] was *nesh.* Often she used it, apparently to express daintiness or fragility. **1975** Gould *ME Lingo* 187, *Nash*—Tender, of a sensitive disposition; ladylike and overly soft of temperament, perhaps sissified: "He's so nash you can't say 'damn' but he'll cry tears."

nessen conj Cf **lessen** conj[1]

1907 *DN* 3.232 **nwAR,** *Lessun* or *nessen. . .* Unless.

nesses See **nest**

nessipushety See **nepushency**

nessy n [Perh by syncope from **necessary;** but cf *EDD nessy* a privy]

1968 *DARE* (Qu. M21b, *Joking names for an outside toilet building*) Inf **PA158,** Nessy.

nest n Pl usu |nɛsts|; also esp **Sth, S Midl** |nɛs(t), 'nɛs(t)ɪz| Pronc-spp for pl *nes(ses), nestes, nesties* Cf Intro "Language Changes" IV.3, **-es** suff[1] **a**

A Forms.

1867 Harris *Sut Lovingood Yarns* 158 **TN,** I purvided about a dozen ho'nets' nestes. **1895** *DN* 1.375 **seKY, eTN, wNG,** Nestes. **1899** (1912) Green *VA Folk-Speech* 297, Two hen nesses full of eggs. **1902** *DN* 2.240 **sIL,** *Nestes.* . . always in two syllables. **1909** *DN* 3.352 **eAL, wGA,** *Nestes. Ibid* 401 **nwAR,** *Nestes* [nɛstɪz]. . . Nests. **1913** Kephart *High-landers* 285 **sAppalachians,** The ancient syllabic plural is preserved in . . nesties. **1915** *DN* 4.186 **swVA,** *Nest,* n. The dissylabic plural [nɛstɪz] is still heard. **1922** Gonzales *Black Border* 314 **sSC, GA coasts** [Gullah glossary], *Nes'* . . nest, nests. **1928** *AmSp* 3.404 **Ozarks** (as of 1916–1927), Such nouns as *post* and *nest* drop the *t* in the singular, but in the plural form the *t* is pronounced distinctly and an unaccented syllable added—*nestes* and *postes.* **1930** *VA Qrly. Rev.* 6.250 **S Midl,** Back-

woods speech shows an urge . . for the formation of regular plurals in 'es,' particularly for monosyllables ending in 'st,' as postes, nestes. **1934** *Natl. Geogr. Mag.* May 618 **Okefenokee GA,** Nex' time I found one er their nesties I taken some er the eggs. **1937** Thornburgh *Gt. Smoky Mts.* 14, The birds have been buildin' their *nestes* in that thar hemlock. **1949** Webber *Backwoods Teacher* 215 **Ozarks,** Granny was one of those who held to "Old Christmas" [=January 6], and she knew that was the right time "because at midnight on January fifth the bees always hum in their hives and nestes." **1954** Harder *Coll.* **cwTN,** Nesties. **1967** *DARE* FW Addit **seTN,** Plural of "nest" is ['nɛstɪz]—heard in conversation. **c1970** Pederson *Dial. Surv. Rural GA* **seGA** (*Before birds lay their eggs, they build* _____.), [Of 64 total infs, 30 had proncs of the type [nest]; 11 [nɛstɪz]; 10 [nɛ(ə)s]; 6 [nɛsts]; 3 [nɛstɪz].] **1986** Pederson *LAGS Concordance* **Gulf Region,** 78 infs, Nestes; 39 infs, Nest [with deleted plural marker].

B Senses.

1 also in combs *spider('s) nest:* A spider's web; a cobweb.

1903 *DN* 2.301 **Cape Cod MA** (as of a1857), *Spider's-nest. . .* Cobweb. **1909** *DN* 3.374 **eAL, wGA,** *Spider-nes(t). . .* A cobweb. Universal. **1966–68** *DARE* (Qu. R29a, . . *The thing that a spider spins and lives in—If it is indoors*) Infs **GA25, 72, LA37, MI80, MO26, OH77, WA30,** Nest; **OH82, SC57,** Spider('s) nest; (Qu. R29b, *What the spider spins—if it is outdoors*) Infs **GA25, 72, MN10, TN11,** Nest; **NC37,** Spider nest. **1986** Pederson *LAGS Concordance* **Gulf Region** (*Spider web*) 6 infs, Spider nest; 5 infs, (A) nest; 2 infs, Spider's nest; 1 inf, Spiders' nest; 1 inf, Spiders' nestes; 1 inf, Nestes.

2 in var phrr used to indicate that a woman is pregnant: See quots. Cf **hatch** v

1965–70 *DARE* (Qu. AA28, . . *Joking or sly expressions . . women use to say that another is going to have a baby . . "She['s]* _____.") 10 Infs, esp **Nth, N Midl,** On the nest; **CA201,** Feathering her nest; **OH60,** Setting on the nest; **OR6,** Sitting on a nest. **1986** Pederson *LAGS Concordance* (*Pregnant*) 1 inf, **csTX,** On the nest—has heard; doctor said of patients; 1 inf, **csMS,** She's watching his goose nest—grandmother said.

nest-egg onion See **nest onion**

nester n **chiefly West** *usu derog*

A squatter, homesteader, farmer, or small rancher, esp one who settles on established rangeland.

1880 *Ft. Griffin* (Tex.) *Echo* 3 Jan. *(DA),* [A sheep man is] a tramp, an ingrate, a 'Nester,' and a liar. **1907** Mulford *Bar-20* 289 **West,** Ain't th' Panhandle full of nesters (farmers)? **1921** Thorp *Songs Cowboys* 90, The nester came with his wife, his kids, his dogs, and his barbed-wire fence. **1929** Dobie *Vaquero* 167, I . . hung up my prized Stetson hat and in its place put on an old floppy piece of headgear that even a Kansas nester would have been ashamed to wear. **1935** Sandoz *Jules* 339 **wNE** (as of 1880–1930), The Spade ranch store presented every nester whose bill was paid up by New Year's with a ton of coal. **1936** McCarthy *Lang. Mosshorn* np **West** [Range terms], *Nesters. . .* A slang term applied to homesteaders, or a small stockman who settles close to a big outfit. **1939** (1973) FWP *Guide MT* 415, *Nester*—Homesteader. **1941** Writers' Program *Guide WY* 463, *Nester*—A man who squats on land and fences it in. **1944** Wellman *Bowl* 17 **KS** (as of c1890), We've combed this country for names until I think we've got just about every nester an' sand hill rat in the district. **1967–70** *DARE* [(Qu. C33, . . *Joking names . . for an out-of-the-way place, or a very small or unimportant place*) Inf **TX2,** Nestersville;] (Qu. HH18, *Very insignificant or low-grade people*) Inf **FL48,** Nesters—comes from back when people just took land and sat on it. **1970** *DARE* FW Addit **TX89,** *Nesters*—old-timers, original settlers.

nest(i)es See **nest**

nesting vbl n

Squatting, homesteading, settling in as a **nester.**

1918 Mulford *Man from Bar-20* 137 **West,** Not satisfied with nestin' on a man's range, you had to start a little herd. **1936** Barnard *Rider* 61 **OK,** We cowpunchers had no use for the boomers. They came into our country, plowed up good grass, and started to nesting and working like the devil.

nesting dory n

See quot 1957.

1957 Beck *Folkl. ME* 119, Dories were an improvement of the onshore fishing boats, with certain modifications to allow for easy stowage aboard the schooners and better handling in deep water. Eventually they became known as "banking" or "nesting" dories (the latter phrase evolving from the fact that they were stored one within another like Lily cups). [**1975** Gould *ME Lingo* 188, On trips to and from the fishing grounds, dories are *nested*.]

nest onion n Rarely *nest-egg onion* **chiefly Sth, esp GA**
A **multiplying onion** or similar **onion B**; see quots.
1966 Dakin *Dial. Vocab. Ohio R. Valley* 2.367, Spring onions. . . Miscellaneous terms . . *nest onions*. **1966** *DARE* Tape AL4, [FW:] Did you have a different name for that early onion? [Inf:] Onions were referred to as nest onions sometimes, or shallots. **1966–68** *DARE* (Qu. I5, . . *Kind of onions that keep coming up without replanting year after year*) Infs AL1, GA8, Nest onions; SC22, Nest onion—grows in clumps; (Qu. I6, *The kind of onions that come up fresh early in the year, and you eat them raw*) Infs GA9, 28, Nest onions; SC22, Nest onion— milder; for eating. **1970** GA Dept. Ag. *Farmers Market Bulletin* 5 Aug, Little red nest onions, $4 gal.; small white nest onions, $3.50 gal. **1971** Wood *Vocab. Change* 369 Sth, Early onions. . . Volunteered . . nest onions. **1986** Pederson *LAGS Concordance (Spring onions)* 29 infs, **chiefly GA,** Nest onion(s); 1 inf, **swGA,** White nest onions; 1 inf, **cnGA,** Nest onions—in cluster; 1 inf, **cwGA,** Nest onion—small variety; 1 inf, **swGA,** A little nest onion—in a little-old cluster; 1 inf, **cMS,** Little-old nest onion = multiplying onion; 1 inf, **cnGA,** Nest onions—very small; grow in bunches; 1 inf, **csGA,** Nest onions—in small clusters; 1 inf, **cAL,** Nest onions—small; 1 inf, **cAL,** Nest onions = shallots; 1 inf, **ceAL,** Nest onions—pencil size; for salad; 1 inf, **seAL,** Nest onions— many small onions together; 1 inf, **nwMS,** Nest-egg onions; [1 inf, **cAL,** Guinea-Nest onions—evergreens].

nest plant n Also *nestroot* [From the structure created by the rootlets]
=Indian pipe 1.
1830 Rafinesque *Med. Flora* 2.243, Monotropa uniflora . . Iceplant, Pipeplant, Nestroot, Fitroot. Ophthalmic and nervine. **1892** (1974) Millspaugh *Amer. Med. Plants* 28–1, Indian Pipe. . . Com[mon] names . . bird's nest, nest plant [etc]. . . *Rootlets* very numerous, forming a ball of densely-matted fibres. **1900** Lyons *Plant Names* 252, Indian-pipe, . . Nest-root, Bird's-nest plant.

nest robber n
Usu **=bluejay 1,** but see quots.
1917 (1923) *Birds Amer.* 2.217, Blue Jay—*Cyanocitta cristata cristata* . . Corn Thief; Nest Robber. **1946** Goodrich *Birds in KS* 318, Colloquial Name . . nest robber . . Common name . . northern blue jay. **1946** Hausman *Eastern Birds* 420, Northern Blue Jay—*Cyanocitta cristata cristata* . . Nest Robber. **1950** *WELS (Other names and nicknames for: Jays)* 1 Inf, **csWI,** Nest robber; *(Starlings)* 1 Inf, **cWI,** Nest robber. **1969** *DARE* (Qu. Q14, . . *Names . . for these birds: . . catbird*) Inf **PA225,** Nest robbers.

nestroot See **nest plant**

net-fly n [Folk-etym for **gnat-fly**]
1914 *DN* 4.155 Cape Cod MA, *Net fly—gnat fly.* "Haven't you ever seen them little net-flies all over old rotten nets? Well, that's what they come from."

netmeg See **nutmeg**

netop n Also sp *neatrup, neetup* [Cf **eatup**] **NEng, nNY** arch
Cf **meet-up**
A friend, esp a close one.
1643 in 1827 RI Hist. Soc. *Coll.* 1.27, What cheare *Nétop* is the general salutation of all English toward them [=American Indians]. *Nétop* is friend. **c1707** in 1895 Sheldon *Hist. Deerfield* 1.362 MA, She spake, saying, "Netop, Netop, my master." **1816** Pickering *Vocab.* 138, *Netop.* This *Indian* word (as a friend informs me) is still used, colloquially, in some towns in the interior of Massachusetts, to signify a *friend,* or (to use a cant word) a *crony.* **1890** *AN&Q* 4.237, *Netop.* Fifty years ago, in New England, this word was not very uncommon among the older people. It meant a close friend, a chum, a companion. **1898** Westcott *Harum* 289 cNY, Mr. Harum and I are great 'neetups,' . . It means 'cronies,' I believe, in his dictionary. **1932** *DN* 6.283 swCT, *Eat ups* or *neatrups.* A sudden and violent affection between two persons. "They are great eatups (or neatrups)."

netted globe-berry n Cf **globe-berry**
A slender annual plant *(Margaranthus solanaceus)* resembling **ground-cherry** and native to Arizona, New Mexico, and Texas.
1970 Correll *Plants TX* 1399, *Margaranthus solanaceus* . . Netted

globe-berry. . . berry small, entirely included in the globular-conical fruiting calyx.

netter rash See **nettle rash**

netting (wire) n, often attrib Rarely *steel netting, wire* ~
chiefly Upper Missip Valley, West See Map
=net wire.
1965–70 *DARE* (Qu. L63, *Kinds of fences made with wire*) Infs IL4, 142, MN16, WA31, WI70, WY4, Netting (fence); MN17, Netting—for keeping chicken [sic] in; NV9, Netting—impractical around cattle, a heavy net; TX38, Netting, chicken fence—the same; WI17, Netting fence, woven wire fence—same thing; ID3, TX13, Netting wire fence; CA124, Netting wire fence—a woven wire; MO21, WA18, Wire netting (fence); MO19, Wire netting—same as woven wire; CT10, Poultry netting or chicken wire; GA84, MI20, Poultry netting; MN34, Chicken netting; MI40, Netting fencing—poultry netting, mink netting, hardware netting; ½″ squares on it, for very small animals or for snakes; NV2, Sheep netting—closer mesh; (Qu. L65, . . *Kinds of fences*) Inf CA204, Netting fences; OR10, Netting wire—like chicken, not as fine, bigger squares, heavier gauge; CA131, Wire netting fence; OH27, Chicken netting. **1986** Pederson *LAGS Concordance (Other kinds of wire fences)* 1 inf, **seMS,** Netting—wire fence; 1 inf, **swLA,** Netting fence; 1 inf, **cTX,** A netting fence = hog-pasture fencing; 1 inf, **seAR,** Steel-netting fence; 1 inf, **swTN,** Netting fences—woven wire; to keep animals out; 1 inf, **swLA,** Garden netting; 1 inf, **swLA,** Hog netting; 1 inf, **ceMS,** Chicken netting.

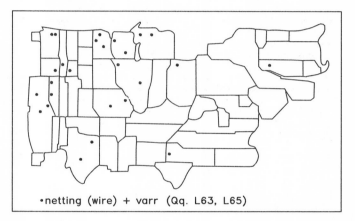

•netting (wire) + varr (Qq. L63, L65)

nettle n
1 Std: a plant of the genus *Urtica.* [*OED* 725 →] Also called **nettleweed.** For other names of var spp see **burning nettle, stinging** ~
2 often with modifier: A prickly **nightshade 1;** see quots. Cf **bull nettle 2, horse** ~ **1, Spanish** ~**, Texas** ~
1872 MO State Entomol. *Annual Rept.* 10, Upon the Nettle *(S[olanum] carolinense),* which is common with us but is mostly replaced in Kansas by the *S. rostratum,* it [=the Colorado Potato Beetle] seems to delight even more than upon the Potato. **1951** *PADS* 15.39 TX, *Solanum* spp.— All the prickly-leaved nightshades are either blue, purple, white, or yellow nettles. **1956** McAtee *Some Dialect NC* 31, Nettle. . . The nightshade ally, *Solanum carolinense.* Its fruits were called "nettle balls." **1964** Batson *Wild Flowers SC* 101, Silverleaf Nettle: *Solanum elaeagnifolium.* . . Prickly perennial herb. . . Introduced from the southwestern United States. **1979** Niering–Olmstead *Audubon Guide N. Amer. Wildflowers E. Region* 805, This plant [=*Solanum carolinense*] is not related to the true Nettles. Silverleaf Nettle *(S. elaeagnifolium),* a very similar plant with silvery foliage, occurs in the western United States.
3 A **spurge nettle** (here: *Cnidoscolus stimulosus*).
1926 *Torreya* 26.5 GA, *Cnidoscolus stimulosus.* . . Nettle, Jekyl Id.
4 also *nettle bush:* **=false nettle.**
1966–67 *DARE* Wildfl QR Pl.45 Infs MI57, WA10, Nettle; SC41, Nettle bush.
5 See **stinging nettle.**

nettleberry n
A **hackberry** (here: *Celtis tenuifolia*).
1960 Vines *Trees SW* 207, Small Hackberry—*Celtis tenuifolia.* . . Vernacular names are Sugarberry, Nettleberry, and Nettle-tree.

nettle bush See **nettle 4**

nettle cure n Cf **chaparral tea, prairie ~**
A croton (here: *Croton argyranthemus*).
 1938 Baker *FL Wild Flowers* 124, The unusual properties of *C[roton] argyranthemus* have won for it such various names as healing croton, nettle-cure, . . and cancer-weed. The sap is a country remedy for cuts and scratches. **1955** *S. Folkl. Qrly.* 19.234 **FL**, Crotons, from which the sap was formerly used as a remedy for cuts and scratches, are variously known as *Nettle Cure* (Croton argyranthemus), *Oil Weed, Cancer Weed,* [etc]. **1967** Jahoda *Other FL* 51, One of the most curious herbs of all in the dry woods is the healing croton. It is a perennial with minute, whitish flowers growing in short racemes, and in Florida it blooms nearly all year round. Florida crackers call it nettle-cure, oil weed, and cancer-weed, since its sap has long been a country remedy for cuts and scratches and sometimes, uselessly, for skin cancer lesions.

nettle rash n Also *nettles, netter rash, netty ~* [*OED nettle rash* 1740 →] **chiefly SE, Lower Missip Valley, TX** See Map
A skin irritation resembling that caused by a **nettle 1**; urticaria, hives.
 1890 *Century Dict.* 3976, *Nettle-rash.* . . An eruption on the skin like that produced by the sting of a nettle; urticaria. **1925** *Book of Rural Life* 7.3813, *Nettle rash,* a disease characterized by the sudden appearance of raised, white patches on the skin, so-called because they resemble the marks made by nettles. The usual name for the disorder is *hives.* **1946** *Harder Coll.* **cwTN,** [Letter:] Elsie has got something like nettle rash and some mornings her lips is swelled. **1950** *WELS (Other names for a rash on the skin, for example, with measles)* 1 Inf, **cwWI,** Nettle rash, eczema, scarlet-fever rash, prickly-heat rash, chicken-pox rash. **1965–70** *DARE* (Qu. BB24, . . *A rash that comes out suddenly—from hives or something else: "He's got some kind of _____ all over his chest."*) 21 Infs, **chiefly SE, Lower Missip Valley, TX,** Nettle rash; **MS**60, Netter rash; **AR**21, **TX**9, Nettles; (Qu. S17) Inf **AL**11, Nettle rash; (Qu. BB25, . . *Common skin diseases around here*) Infs **AR**3, 12, **MA**14, **TX**33, Nettle rash; [**NY**75, Rash from nettles]. **1986** Pederson *LAGS Concordance,* 2 infs, **neTN, nwGA,** Nettle rash. **1990** Cavender *Folk Med. Lexicon* 28 **sAppalachians,** *Nettle rash*—a heat rash on the neck and under the arms; sometimes referred to as "netty rash" or "heat in the skin folds."

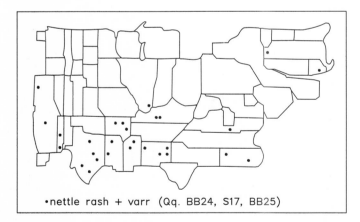

•nettle rash + varr (Qq. BB24, S17, BB25)

nettle tree n [*OED* 1548 →]
=**hackberry,** usu *Celtis occidentalis* or *C. tenuifolia*.
 1763 Catesby *Hortus* 41, Celtis [spp]. The Lote, or Nettle-tree of America. These trees are natives of Carolina and most of the northern colonies in America. **1819** (1821) Nuttall *Jrl.* 64 **seAR**, [In the cane-brake] I found abundance of the *Celtis integrifolia* (entire-leaved nettle tree). **1850** *New Engl. Farmer* 2.142, The Nettle-tree and the Hackberry are both found in Massachusetts. **1897** Sudworth *Arborescent Flora* 184 **DE, MI, MA, RI,** *Celtis occidentalis.* Hackberry. . . [Also called] Nettle tree. **1950** *WELS (Other names for . . Hackberry)* 1 Inf, **cWI,** Nettle tree, sugarberry. **1960** Vines *Trees SW* 207, Small Hackberry—*Celtis tenuifolia.* . . Vernacular names are Sugarberry . . and Nettle-tree. **1970** *DARE* (Qu. T13) Inf **MA**78, Nettle tree = sugarberry—not the same (as hackberry); is a tree with red berries. **1980** Little *Audubon Guide N. Amer. Trees E. Region* 414, "Nettletree"—*Celtis occidentalis.* . . Branches of this and other hackberries may become deformed bushy growths called witches'-brooms produced by mites and fungi. The leaves often bear rounded galls caused by tiny jumping plant lice.

nettleweed n esp **KY**
=**nettle 1.**
 1843 (1916) Hall *New Purchase* 136 **IN**, They gathered a peculiar species of nettle, (called there nettleweed,) which they succeeded in dressing like flax. **1867** Hill *Homespun* 18, Their blackened skeletons . . overgrown with the nettleweeds and long grasses that ever make haste to beautify these homestead desolations. **1966–69** *DARE* (Qu. S17, . . *Kinds of plants . . that . . cause itching and swelling*) Infs **KY**11, 34, 56, 63, **OK**20, Nettleweed.

netty rash See **nettle rash**

net wire n, often attrib **scattered, but chiefly Lower Missip Valley, TX** See Map Cf **hog wire, netting (wire), woven wire**
Fencing material made of wire mesh.
 1965–70 *DARE* (Qu. L63, *Kinds of fences made with wire*) 27 Infs, **scattered, but chiefly Lower Missip Valley, TX,** Net wire (fence); **AR**51, Net wire fence—more common than woven wire; **AR**52, Net wire fence—for pigs; **LA**2, Net wire fence—for hogs; **LA**3, Net wire fence—hog wire, sheep wire—taller than hog wire; **LA**7, Net wire fence—chicken wire, sheep wire—heavy, tall, hog wire—the usual kind, merely called "net wire" most of the time; **LA**12, Net wire fence—hog wire fence—synonyms; **LA**15, Net wire fence or hog wire fence; **LA**18, Net wire fence—used where they have sheep or goats; **LA**29, Net wire fence, woven wire fence—synonyms; **MD**15, Net wire—another name for hog fence; **NM**3, Net wire—with barb wire above for sheep; **OK**43, Net wire—also called hog wire; **TX**37, Net wire—5″ squares; **TX**43, Net wire fence—for sheep; **TX**69, [Aux Inf:] Net wire fence—wolf-proof fence; old-fashioned; **TX**99, Net wire, hog wire; (Qu. L65, . . *Kinds of fences*) Infs **AL**43, **VA**97, Net wire; **TX**29, Net wire for deer. **1986** Pederson *LAGS Concordance (Other kinds of wire fences)* 62 infs, **chiefly coastal Gulf Region, esp LA, MS,** Net wire; 6 infs, Net-wire fence(s). [*DARE* Ed: Numerous infs variously describe this style of fence as either chicken wire or hog wire.]

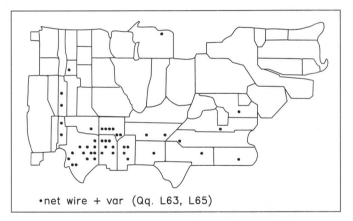

•net wire + var (Qq. L63, L65)

neuralgia n Usu |n(j)ur'æljə|; also |n(j)ur'ælji| Pronc-spp *neuralgy, neuralija;* for addit pronc and sp varr see quots
Std sense, var forms.
 1861 Holmes *Venner* 1.150 **NEng,** It was agreed that a man in an attack of neuralgy wasn't to be judged of by the rules that applied to other folks. **1863** in 1983 *PADS* 70.43 **ce,sePA,** Very pleasantly except some cold I suffered from, with Neiuraljah in my face. **1911** *DN* 3.546 **NE,** *Neuralija.* . . Frequent for *neuralgia.* **1920** in 1944 *ADD* **cNY,** *Neuralgia.* . . [nu'ræljə]. **1941** Faulkner *Men Working* 120 **MS,** I've seen him up there talking to the men and his neuralgy a-hurting him so bad he just had to stand there. **1950** *WELS (She's got the _____)* 1 Inf, **cwWI,** Neuralgy. **1955** McAtee *Dial. Grant Co. IN Suppl.* 6 [2], *Newraulgy* (neuralgia). **1959** *VT Hist.* 27.150, *Neuralgia* [nu'rælji]. . . pronc. Common. Rural sections. **1965–70** *DARE* (Qu. BB3a) Inf **LA**12, [,nju'rælji]; **TX**42, [,nju:'rælji]; (Qu. BB4a) Inf **VT**16, [nə'ælə,ji]; **KY**44, [,nu'rælji]; **LA**37, [,nur'ælji]; (Qu. BB5) Inf **IN**50, [,nu'rælji]; (Qu. BB8) Inf **IN**1, [nu'rælji]; **NJ**41, [nə'algiə].

neutral n Also *neutral rat* [Folk-etym]
The nutria (*Myocaster coypus*), naturalized in the Gulf States.
 1967–69 *DARE* (Qu. P32, . . *Other kinds of wild animals*) Inf **LA**22, ['nučrəl ,ræt]; **LA**34, ['nutrə] [FW: This is common among uneducated; also ['nutrəl ,ræts].]; **LA**37, The name is ['nutriə], but we call 'em ['nutrəl]; [**LA**20, 31, 40, **TX**11, 14, ['nutrə (,ræt)]; **LA**15, [njutrə]].

neutral ground n chiefly **LA, sMS** See Map Cf **neutral strip**
A grassy strip in the middle of a street, or between the sidewalk and the street.

c1950 *LANCS Checklists* (Grass strip between sidewalk and street) 1 inf, **csWI**, Neutral ground. **1965–70** *DARE* (Qu. N17, . . *The separating area in the middle [of a four-lane road]*) 12 Infs, **chiefly LA, sMS**, Neutral ground; (Qu. N25) Inf **LA20**, Neutral ground; (Qu. N44, *In a town, the strip of grass and trees between the sidewalk and the curb*) Infs **LA14, 20, 34, MS6, 8, 32**, Neutral ground. [7 of 14 total Infs young or mid-aged] **1970** Thompson *Coll.* **seLA** (as of 1960–61), Neutral ground . . highway median strip. **1979** *Times–Picayune* (New Orleans LA) 11 Feb mag sec 24/4, When Brad [=a fire department horse] died, he was buried in a strip of neutral ground between sidewalk and roadway. **1980** *DARE* File **New Orleans LA**, Neutral Ground is not the same as a median strip; it is wider. Louisiana is great on parades, and, formerly, political speeches, etc. The neutral ground provided a good wide place free from traffic for people—sort of like mini parks. Very popular in Louisiana. **1984** *Yeah You Rite* (Video recording) **New Orleans LA**, Since talking is something most of us take for granted, we . . forget that some of the words we use every day might not make sense to somebody from out of town: words like *neutral ground*. **1986** Pederson *LAGS Concordance* (The strip of green grass between the sidewalk and the street) 11 infs, **LA**, 3 infs, **swMS**, Neutral ground; (Grass that separate[s] two-way traffic) 2 infs, **seLA**, Neutral ground; 1 inf, **seMS**, Neutral ground—dividing streets in town; (Open place . . where . . green grass grows) 1 inf, **seLA**, Neutral ground—grassy spot in middle of street; (Strip of green grass) 1 inf, **swAL**, Neutral ground—median on boulevard. **1995** *DARE* File **LA**, New Orleans . . has a wide central grassy area between each direction of traffic. They call this area "the neutral ground," and it is wide enough to allow a safe u-turn.

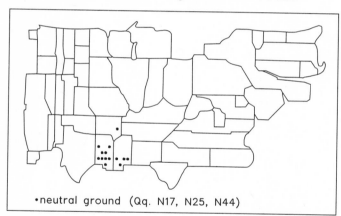

•neutral ground (Qq. N17, N25, N44)

neutral rat See **neutral**

neutral strip n **TN**
=**neutral ground.**

1968 *DARE* (Qu. N44, *In a town, the strip of grass and trees between the sidewalk and the curb*) Inf **TN24**, Neutral strip. **1986** Pederson *LAGS Concordance* (Grass that separate[s] two-way traffic) 1 inf, **swTN**, Neutral strip; (The strip of grass between the sidewalk and the street) 4 infs, **swTN**, Neutral strip.

neva See **never**

Nevada wild almond n
=**desert peach.**

1931 U.S. Dept. Ag. *Misc. Pub.* 101.70, Anderson peachbrush . . called also Anderson almond, Neveda [sic] wild almond, and wild peach(brush), is probably the nearest of the peachbrush species to the cultivated peach. **1941** Jaeger *Wildflowers* 92 **Desert SW**, Nevada Wild Almond. *Prunus Andersonii*.

never adv Pronc-spp *ne'er, nevah, nuv(v)er;* also *chiefly among Black speakers, neb(buh), nubbuh;* in phrr (e.g. *never mind*), often reduced to *neb-, nee-, ne(m)-, num-;* for addit varr see **A** below

A Forms.

1821 Cooper *Spy* 1.161, "I nebber tink Johnny Birch had such a big eye," said the African. **1829** Tenney *Female Quixotism* 2.84 **Philadelphia PA** [Black], I neber see such sight before. **1856** Simms *Eutaw* 209 **SC** [Gullah], You nebber bin do better, maussa, youse'f, in you best

days. **1858** Hammett *Piney Woods Tavern* 27 **TX** [Black], Mistiss done sent Rushey down to the grocery . . soon's neva she see you ride up. **1890** *DN* 1.68 **KY**, *Nebber* [nɛbə]: for *never*, by the old negroes. "Nebber min' dat, chile." **1891** Page *Elsket* 121 **VA** [Black], Dee 'ain' nuver had no 'quaintance wid it. **1899** (1912) Green *VA Folk-Speech* 302, *Nuver.* . . Never. "I nuver saw anything like that before." **1899** Chesnutt *Conjure Woman* 14 **csNC** [Black], Dey could n' nebber ketch none er de niggers. **1905** Chesnutt *Col.'s Dream* 145 **GA**, "Nem mine me, honey," said the old man, "dey can put me somewhar e'se." **1909** *DN* 3.345 **eAL, wGA**, *Lemine.* . . Never mind. . . "Bring me the ax. Lemine, I don't need it now." *Nemine* and *nummine* also heard. **1914** *DN* 4.77 **ME, nNH**, *Nemmind!* . . Contraction of *never mind!* **1922** Gonzales *Black Border* 314 **sSC, GA coasts** [Gullah glossary], *Nebbuh*—never. *Ibid* 315, *Nubbuh*—never. **1928** Peterkin *Scarlet Sister Mary* 129 **SC** [Gullah], You can' nebber blongst to nobody, honey. **1934** Hurston *Jonah's Gourd Vine* 151 **AL** [Black], Neb mine, Lucy, 'bout de words. **1937** in 1976 *Weevils in the Wheat* 135 **VA** [Black], Anyway he nevah 'ud come back. **1938** Matschat *Suwannee R.* 81 **neFL, seGA**, How come yer maw ain't nuvver larned ye sich as be of use? **1942** Faulkner *Go Down* 13 **MS**, And nem you mind that neither. **1953** [see **nevermind 1**]. **1960** (1966) Percy *Moviegoer* 96 **New Orleans LA**, "How much money do you have?" "Ne'mind." **1986** Pederson *LAGS Concordance*, 1 inf, **seAL**, Ne'er was afraid before; 1 inf, **neLA**, Hit wasn't ne'er [næ] at home.

B Senses.

1 Used to negate (often emphatically) a verb referring to a single past event. chiefly **S Midl**

1871 in 1983 *PADS* 70.43 **ce,sePA**, Papa was in the woods and never come in till one. **1886** *S. Bivouac* 4.343 **sAppalachians**, *Never* did it (didn't do it). **1902** *DN* 2.240 **sIL**, *Never.* . . Regularly used instead of the expression with 'did not,' as 'I never went,' for 'I didnt go.' **1903** *DN* 2.322 **seMO**, *Never.* . . Used as a common form of negation. 'He never touched me,' instead of 'he didn't touch me.' 'No I never!' is a very common expression corresponding to 'no I didn't!' **1906** *DN* 3.147 **nwAR**, *Never.* . . Not. "I never knew you got back from abroad." "I never told them all." **1909** *DN* 3.352 **eAL, wGA**, *Never.* . . Very commonly used for *not*. "I never done it." **1910** *DN* 3.456 **KY**, *Never.* . . Not. "I never did do that work yesterday." **1915** *DN* 4.186 **swVA**, *Never.* . . Intensive for *not*. "I never saw him to-day." **1926** Roberts *Time of Man* 60 **cKY**, "And so your pappy made the ax. . . What out of?" "He never made the blade. He made the handle outen hickory and wedged it in." **1939** *Hall Coll.* **cwNC**, George raised up with his Winchester and fired and he never touched a hair on that bear. **1968** *DARE* FW Addit **swLA**, Q: "How much feed do we need?" A: "I don't know. I never checked." **1976** Garber *Mountain-ese* 61 **sAppalachians**, *Never-done-it* . . didn't—Don't accuse me uv that cause I never done it, I never.

2 Not even.

1891 Ryan *Pagan* 271 **swPA**, There was a big spotted sow never ten feet away from the porch.

nevermind n Cf **never**

1 also *neverminds:* One's own business, affairs; a concern.

1935 Davis *Honey* 250 **OR**, That ain't no never-minds to me, though. **1949** Guthrie *Way West* 24, Leave the gentleman buy what he wants. It's none of your never-mind. **1953** Goodwin *It's Good* 39 **sIL** [Black], You was tole to go on 'bout yore nee-mind. **1954** in 1958 Brewer *Dog Ghosts* 118 **TX** [Black], Sifty bettuh go on 'bout his nevuhmin's. **1968** *DARE* (Qu. KK26, *Something that makes no difference at all to you:* "He can think what he likes, it _____ me.") Inf **NY22**, No nevermind to; **PA11**, 'S no neverminds to; **PA126**, Is my nevermind. **1984** Wilder *You All Spoken Here* 146 **Sth**, *Ain't no never mind:* The hell with it. Forget it.

2 in phrr *not pay nevermind* and varr: To regard with indifference; not to care.

1946 (1972) Mezzrow–Wolfe *Really Blues* 195, He pays it no nevermind. **1955** in 1958 Brewer *Dog Ghosts* 38 **TX** [Black], De Nigguhs don' gib a nevuhmin' 'bout dat. **1982** Slone *How We Talked* 6 **eKY** (as of c1950), "Pay that no never mind"; Don't let that bother you. **1982** [see **3** below]. **1991** *DARE* File **csWI**, This guy came over and sat down and the people didn't pay any nevermind.

3 also *neverminds;* in phrr *make no nevermind (to one), make one no nevermind* and varr: To be of no concern (to one); to affect or concern one not in the least; see also quot 1995.

1950 *WELS* (If you don't care what a person does, you might tell him: "You can go ahead and do it, _____.") 1 Inf, **ceWI**, It makes me no nevermind. **1956** Moody *Home Ranch* 162 **CO** (as of 1911), That don't make no never-minds! **1959** McAtee *Oddments* 5 **cnNC,** *Nevermind*. . . difference. "Hit don't make no never-mind." **1965–70** *DARE* (Qu. KK26, *Something that makes no difference at all to you: "He can think what he likes, it* _____ *me."*) 36 Infs, **scattered,** Makes (me) no nevermind(s); 10 Infs, **scattered,** Makes no nevermind(s) to; **GA**31, **LA**2, Don't make (me) no nevermind; **AK**5, Gives me no nevermind; **SC**45, Makes no nevermind to; (Qu. GG21a, *If you don't care what a person does* . . *"You can go ahead and do it* _____ *."*) Inf **GA**30, It don't make me no nevermind; **NJ**1, It make [sic] no nevermind to me; **LA**23, It makes no nevermind; **MA**58, Makes me no nevermind; **WA**1, Makes no nevermind to me. **1968** Kellner *Aunt Serena* 22 **IN,** Oh, he felt himself at home and he never saw a stranger, and it made no neverminds to him whether folks were good or bad. **1968** Moody *Horse* 213 **nwKS** (as of c1920), Oh well, it don't make no never-minds anyways. **1971** Malamud *Tenants* 177, Those are old books. . . Then it makes no nevermind if we burn them. **1982** *AmSp* 57.76, The expressions *That don't make me no never mind* and *I don't pay that no never mind*. . . occur in Ozark speech . . but . . are used too in Mississippi, South Carolina, Alabama, Kentucky, and West Virginia. **1984** Wilder *You All Spoken Here* 169 **Sth,** *It don't make no never mind:* It makes no difference. **1985** *DARE* File **cwIN,** Something of little consequence to a person . . "it don't make me no never-mind." **1995** *NADS* 27.2.7, The south central Pennsylvania Dutch equivalent [of "not for nothing"] is *makes no nevermind*. . . It is an appropriate response to all of the following questions [or comments]: "That's a lovely barn you've built." (in the sense of "Aw, shucks") "I'm so sorry I ran over your tulip bed." (in the sense of "That's OK") "Do you want scrapple or pork roll with your breakfast?"[ⁿ] (in the sense of "It doesn't matter to me one way or the other") "I'd like to be an astronaut someday." (in the sense of "It makes no difference what you want, you won't get it").

neverminds See **nevermind 1, 3**

never say dog See **dog n B9**

never-sweat n[1]

A person thought to dislike hard work; a bum or loafer.

1928 Ritchie *Forty-Niners* 196 **CA** (as of c1849), The lordly miners dubbed the farmers of Honey Lake Valley Never Sweats. *Ibid* 197, The Never Sweats of the Valley might have withstood the taunts of their mining town neighbors over the mountains with equanimity. **1944** Adams *Western Words* 104, *Never-sweat*—A slang name for the Mexican. **1958** McCulloch *Woods Words* 121 **Pacific NW,** *Never-sweat*—A lazy man or a bum. **1969** *DARE* (Qu. HH20a, *An idle, worthless person: "He's a* _____ *."*) Inf **IN**80, Never-sweat.

never-sweat n[2] [Folk-etym for *avocet*]
=bluestocking 2.

1923 U.S. Dept. Ag. *Misc. Circular* 13.48 **WA,** Avocet (*Recurvirostra americana*). . . Vernacular Names . . In local use . . never-sweat (no doubt a corruption of avocet).

neverwet n esp Okefenokee GA
=golden club 1.

1927 Boston Soc. Nat. Hist. *Proc.* 38.230, The plants recorded from this habitat [=Okefenokee GA] include the following: . . *Orontium aquaticum* 'Never-wet'; 'fire-leaf'. **1934** *Natl. Geogr. Mag.* May 599 **Okefenokee GA,** The swamp boatman amuses himself by pushing the dark-green blades of the bog torch beneath the water and watching them emerge to justify their local name of "never-wets". **1940** (1941) Bell *Swamp Water* 199 **Okefenokee GA,** Long before noon he was in the swamp, now poling, which was easier, the boat whispering against the pickerelweed and never-wet leaves. **1968–69** *DARE* Tape **GA**30, You can dip it down in the water—break off the leaves and dip it in the water, and take it up, and one side of it plumb dry and the other side wet. . . You can pull it in two and it's plumb full of silk threads. . . That's the never-wet. *Ibid* **GA**48, Never-wet, that's a flag bush. . . It come in bunches. . . You push it down under the water an' it come back up an' don't no water take to it a-tall, don't stick no water to it. **1968** McPhee *Pine Barrens* 59 **NJ,** There is a plant in the Pine Barrens that has velvety, magical leaves to which water absolutely will not adhere. Its common name is golden club. The pineys call it neverwet. **1976** Bruce *How to Grow Wildflowers* 278, *Orontium aquaticum*—Goldenclub. Like the above, an aroid, but lacking the spathe, its naked yellow and white spadix quite colorful in early spring. . . A folk name for the plant is "Never Wet."

nevue See **nephew**

nevy See **nephew**

new adj **widespread, but esp Nth, N Midl** |nu|; **widespread, but more freq Sth, S Midl** |nju|; **scattered** |nɪu|; for addit varr see quots Pronc-spp *neew, noo* Cf Pronc Intro 3.I.10
Std senses, var forms.

1789 Webster *Dissertations Engl. Lang.* 159, It is indifferent, as to pronunciation, whether we write *fuel* or *fewel*. And yet in this word, as also *new, brew,* &c. we do not hear the sound of *e,* except among the Virginians, who affect to pronounce it distinctly, *ne-ew, ne-oo, fe-oo.* **1861** Holmes *Venner* 1.107 **NEng,** This place was known as . . "the neew haouse" . . [by] old settlers. *Ibid* 2.302, I shell . . make sech noo arrangements as circumstahnces compel. **1867** Lowell *Biglow* xxiii **'Upcountry' MA,** Our "uplandish men" retain the soft or thin sound of the *u* in some words, such as *rule, truth* . . , while he says *noo* for *new,* and gives to *view* and *few* so indescribable a mixture of the two sounds with a slight nasal tincture that it may be called the Yankee shibboleth. **1874** (1895) Eggleston *Circuit Rider* 214 (as of early 19th cent), This vile vender of Yankee tins, who called a bucket a "pail," and said "noo" for new, and talked nasally. **1891** *DN* 1.149 **cNY,** [nu] . . 'new'. **1903** *DN* 2.291 **Cape Cod MA** (as of a1857), The long sound of [u] regularly took the place of [ɪu], as *noo* for *knew;* so in *new, news, Newton* . . etc. **1908** *DN* 3.281 **eAL, wGA,** [ɪu] is usually [u] . . , but [nɪu, nɪus] [sic] (never [nus] [sic]). **1913** Kephart *Highlanders* 279 **sAppalachians,** Some words . . are always sounded correctly in the southern highlands, as dew and new (never doo, noo). **1930** *AmSp* 5.345 **cGA,** The record is typical of the colloquial speech of a Southern gentleman of the cotton country south of Virginia. . . [ɪu] in *new, due, do.* **1931** *AmSp* 6.399 **eME coast,** [u] is usually fronted. . . *Do* and *due* are homonyms [du]. *New* is [nu]. **1931** *Ibid* 165 **seVA,** The vowel is often prolonged until it is difficult to tell whether [u] has become [ju] or [ɪu]. . . In some of the records the sound in *new* is longer and has more diphthongal character than the sound in *do* and *due.* This tense and fronted [u] is characteristic of all Southern speech. **1936** *AmSp* 11.29 **eTX,** Such words as *new* . . are always pronounced with [ju], never with [u] alone. **1942** Hall *Smoky Mt. Speech* 38 **wNC, eTN,** [u] is unusually tense and fronted and is always preceded by the palatal glide [j] . . [in the words] new, Newfound (Gap), Newport. **1950** Hubbell *Pronc. NYC* 72, The practice of many metropolitan speakers in the pronunciation of the classes of words represented by *new, tune,* . . is irregular. On the completely uncultivated level, the situation is not complicated: /uŭ/, not preceded by /j/, is as regular in these classes as in *noon, tool*. . . Among the cultivated and to some extent on the intermediate levels . . usage may be highly variable indeed. Some speakers pronounce the sequence /juŭ/ . . rather consistently; some do in certain words but not others of the same class; and many pronounce the same word now in one way and now in another. In this kind of speech, when /j/ is not pronounced, these words may have /uŭ/ or a diphthong distinct from /uŭ/, that is, with a more advanced first element. . . One factor in its use, I think, is the feeling that after certain consonants /juŭ/ is affected and /uŭ/ "not correct." . . In the speech of a person with such attitudes, /ɪŭ/ is likely to appear rather frequently as a conscious or unconscious compromise. **1952** *AmSp* 27.188 **WA,** Words like . . *new* . . are frequently pronounced [. . nⁱuw . .], sometimes with centralized vowel, but are also commonly heard as [. . nuw . .]. Speakers in southeastern Washington, and elegant speakers generally, distinguish the palatal glide regularly; others do not. **1961** Kurath–McDavid *Pronc. Engl.* 174, The type of /nu, du, tuzde/ is current throughout the North and the North Midland. . . [I]n the New England settlement area it is the predominant pronunciation, but not the only one. The type of /nju, dju, tjuzde/ has general currency in the South and the South Midland. . . Here the sporadic [iu] phone may be a prosodic variant of the /ju/ sequence. . . The type of /niu, diu, tiuzde/ . . is largely confined to New England and the Yankee settlements to the west. It is especially common in folk speech. **1976** Allen *LAUM* 3.306 **Upper MW** (as of c1950), For *new* the pronunciation /nu/ is well-nigh universal. . . The rare full variant /nju/ is recorded only [from 5 infs]. . . But a variant with a high mid vowel [ɨ] occurs much more frequently, though with fairly sharp restriction to the Midland speech area in Iowa and Nebraska. **1989** Pederson *LAGS Tech. Index* 100, [Pronunciations of *new* include 278 of the type [nɪu], 137 [nju], 98 [nu], 31 [njɪu], 1 [nu], 1 [njɪ], 1 [nju].]

Newbrasky See **Nebraska**

newby See **nubia**

Newcastle thorn n [See quot 1900]
=cockspur thorn.

1837 Darlington *Flora Cestrica* 290, *C[rataegus] crus galli*. . . Cockspur Thorn. New Castle Thorn. **1893** *Jrl. Amer. Folkl.* 6.141 **NY,** *Crataegus Crus-galli,* Newcastle thorn. **1897** Sudworth *Arborescent*

Flora 216 **DE, MS,** *Crataegus crus-galli.* . . Newcastle Thorn. **1900** (1927) Keeler *Our Native Trees* 140, Cockspur Thorn. Newcastle Thorn—*Crataegus crus-galli.* . . The name of Newcastle Thorn had its origin in the fact that this thorn was once largely used as a hedge plant by the farmers of Newcastle County, Delaware. **1950** Peattie *Nat. Hist. Trees* 364, Cockspur Thorn *Crataegus Crus-galli.* . . Newcastle . . Thorn. **1980** Little *Audubon Guide N. Amer. Trees E. Region* 468, Cockspur Hawthorn—"Hog-apple," "Newcastle-thorn."

New Christmas n Cf **Old Christmas**

December 25.

    [**1937** in 1976 *Weevils in the Wheat* 247 **VA** [Black], I knows too 'bout Old Christmas night dat come jus' fo' Christmas. Ain't many now dat knows 'bout Old Christmas fo' de new one.] **1955** Ritchie *Singing Family* 163 **seKY,** I reckon the New Christmas and the ideas of presents and the tree Mom read about in a paper or book of some kind. **1991** *DARE* File **wNC** (as of a1920), I remember occasional references to Old Christmas [=January 6] in conversation, but my memory is entirely of the New Christmas, with a tree, exchange of presents, etc.

New England aster n

An aster *(Aster nova-angliae).* Also called **farewell-summer 1, last-rose-of-summer 1, michaelmas daisy**

    1814 Bigelow *Florula Bostoniensis* 199, *Aster Novae Angliae.* New England Aster. . . A tall, and very beautiful plant. Stem three feet high, brown, very hairy. **1850** *New Engl. Farmer* 2.12 **MA,** The Trumpet Weed, and the New England Aster, having fine, sweet-scented, aromatic flowers, attract many insects. **1914** Georgia *Manual Weeds* 430, *New England Aster.* . . In spite of its name the plant is more common in the meadows and thickets of the Middle Western States than in New England. **1936** IL Nat. Hist. Surv. *Wildflowers* 350, *New England Aster.* . . One of the largest and most beautiful of the wild Asters, [it] is often cultivated. **1967** *DARE* Wildfl QR Pl.245 Inf **OH**37, New England aster. **1967–70** *DARE* (Qu. S25, . . *The small wild chrysanthemum-like flowers . . that bloom in fields late in the fall*) Infs **DE**3, **NY**21, **OH**37, **PA**234, New England asters; (Qu. S26a, . . *Wildflowers. . . Roadside flowers*) Inf **WI**64, New England asters. **1976** Bailey–Bailey *Hortus Third* 123, *New England a[ster].* . . Ray fl[ower]s usually deep violet-purple, but variable.

New England (boiled) dinner n Also *boiled New England dinner, New England stew* chiefly **NEast, N Cent** See Map Cf **boiled dinner**

A main dish consisting of meat (usu corned beef) and vegetables, boiled together.

    1896 *Daily News Cook Book* 53, New England boiled dinner. . . Corned beef. . . beets. . . turnips . . parsnips . . carrots . . potatoes. . . cabbage. **1907** *DN* 3.182 **seNH,** *Boil-dish.* . . New England boiled dinner. **1922** (1926) Cady *Rhymes VT* 112, You've got to have that home-corned beef / Of just the right complexion,/ A good square chunk—not jest a wing—/ And then a solid section / Of good saltpork—not jest enough / To tempt a new beginner—/ It's plenteous "private stock" that builds / A boiled New England dinner./ Then carrots, turnip, well dressed spuds,/ And cabbage cool and curly. **1929** *Mod. Priscilla Cookbook* 97, *New England boiled dinner*—Corned beef . . parsnips . . carrots . . turnips . . cabbage . . potatoes . . beets. **1950** *WELS (Dishes made with cooked cabbage)* 1 Inf, **csWI,** New England dinner. **1951** Johnson *Resp. to PADS* 20 **DE** *(Dishes made by boiling potatoes with other foods)* New England Boiled Dinner. **1960** Bailey *Resp. to PADS*

20 **KS,** New England boiled dinner. **1964** Amer. Heritage *Cookbook* 494, [Grover] Cleveland dined on the traditional New England Boiled Dinner and then exclaimed that it was "the best dinner I had had for months." **1965–70** *DARE* (Qu. H49, *Dishes made by boiling potatoes with other foods*) 49 Infs, **chiefly NEast, N Cent,** New England (boiled) dinner; **CA**64, Boiled New England dinner; **CT**42, New England stew; (Qu. H45, *Dishes made with meat, fish, or poultry that everybody around here would know, but that people in other places might not*) Infs **CT**29, **RI**3, New England boiled dinner; (Qu. H52, *Dishes made with fresh cabbage*) Inf **MI**102, New England boiled dinner.

Newer Leans See **New Orleans**

newfanglety adj [Var of *newfangled;* cf Intro "Language Changes" III.1]

    1922 Gonzales *Black Border* 221 **sSC, GA coasts** [Gullah], Clara hab on one deseyuh newfanglety kinduh t'ing dem call *'middle-blouse.'* **1930** Stoney–Shelby *Black Genesis* 9 **seSC,** For de mostest part, de more newfanglety dey git de worse off dey stan'.

new free issue See **free issue 3**

newground n, also attrib

1a also *new land:* Uncleared or recently cleared land; an area of newly cleared land. **chiefly C and S Atl, Gulf States** See Map on p. 782

    1619 in 1624 Smith *Genl. Hist. VA* 126, We haue ordinarily foure or fiue [barrels of produce an acre], but of new ground six, seuen, and eight. **1763** in 1889 Washington *Writings* 2.196, The arm of Dismal, which we passed through to get to this new land (as it is called) is 3¼ miles measured. . . This land . . became more dry and is now prodigious fine land. **1769** (1925) Washington *Diaries* 1.333 **VA,** That piece of New Ground containing 14 Acres. **1771** in 1919 *MD Hist. Mag.* 14.134, Our new ground tob[acc]o . . has been Housed 3 or 4 days past. **1857** in 1956 Eliason *Tarheel Talk* 285 **csNC,** The new ground. . . is not fiten for cotten. **1899** (1912) Green *VA Folk-Speech* 297, *New-ground.* . . New land clearing, but not fully cleared and ready for cultivation. **1902** *DN* 2.240 **sIL,** *New-ground.* . . Newly cleared land, the first crop on which is called *'New-ground corn.'* **1903** *DN* 2.322 **seMO,** *New-ground.* . . Newly cleared land. **1906** *DN* 3.121 **sIN,** *New-ground.* **1907** *DN* 3.233 **nwAR,** *New-ground.* **1908** *German Amer. Annals* 10.35 **sePA,** *New Land.* A clearing. "I'm going to plow up that new land." . . fr. Pa. Ger. *nei lönd.* **1909** *DN* 3.352 **eAL, wGA,** *New-ground.* . . A newly cleared tract of forest or swamp. Never called a *clearing* so far as I know. **1915** *DN* 4.186 **swVA,** *New-ground.* . . Virgin land prepared for cultivation. **1924** (1946) Greer-Petrie *Angeline Gits an Eyeful* 4 **csKY,** Stumble over a whole passle of clods in the *new ground.* **1943** Chase *Jack Tales* 4 **wNC,** Well, now, Jack, I have got a little piece of new-ground I been tryin' for the longest to get cleared. **1954** *Harder Coll.* **cwTN,** *New ground*—A field recently cleared. . . I have heard a field that had been cleared before the memory of my informant called a *new ground.* **1965–70** *DARE* (Qu. L36, . . *When you dig out roots and underbrush to make a new field*) 68 Infs, **chiefly C and S Atl, Gulf States,** Clearing (*or* breaking, cleaning up, etc) newground; **ME**24, **MD**20, **WI**77, Breaking up (*or* cleaning off, clearing up) a piece of newground; **AR**52, **DC**8, **GA**77, **NC**33, **SC**57, Clearing (*or* cleaning off, etc) a newground; **NC**37, Clearing the newground; In2, **MO**37, **NC**54, Newground; **AR**9, **MD**13, **MN**34, **MO**34, **NJ**58, Clearing (*or* breaking, cleaning up) new land; **TX**33, Making new land; (Qu. L19, *When you plow land or sod that has never been plowed before, you're* _____; total Infs questioned, 75) 16 Infs, Breaking (*or* plowing, turning, etc) newground; **MS**53, 74, Breaking new land; (Qu. B24, . . *A sudden, very heavy rain*) Inf **AL**52, Newground soaker; (Qu. C7, . . *Land that usually has some standing water with trees or bushes growing in it*) Inf **NC**49, Newground—not under cultivation; (Qu. C28, *A place where underbrush, weeds, vines and small trees grow together so that it's nearly impossible to get through*) Inf **AR**17, Newground; (Qu. C29, *A good-sized stretch of level land with practically no trees*) Inf **LA**9, When it's freshly cleared, why they say that's a newground; (Qu. II21, *When somebody behaves unpleasantly or without manners: "The way he behaves, you'd think he was* _____."*) Inf **GA**77, Raised in the newground; (Qu. KK52, *To do something in an indirect and complicated way: "I don't know why he had to go* _____ *to do that."*) Inf **VA**5, All way round Lindamood's newground. **1972** Jones-Hawes *Step it Down* 55 **GA,** "New ground" is ground where the trees have been cut off, but it's never been planted in. **1986** Pederson *LAGS Concordance* **Gulf Region,** 5 infs, (Made) new land; 1 inf, New land—just cleared; 1 inf, New land = newground—just cleared; 1 inf, New land—when stumps and roots are removed; 1 inf, New land—first put into cultivation; 2 infs, Cleared his (*or* some) new land.

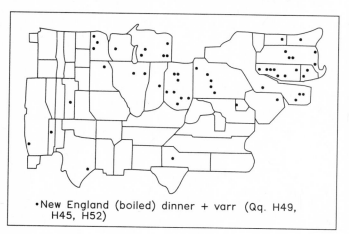

•New England (boiled) dinner + varr (Qq. H49, H45, H52)

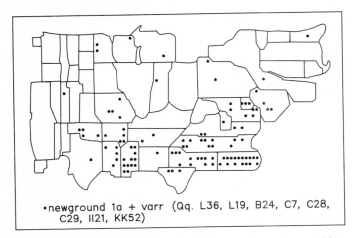

•newground 1a + varr (Qq. L36, L19, B24, C7, C28, C29, I121, KK52)

b in comb *newground plow:* A plow suitable for working

newground 1a. esp S Midl
    [**1838** in 1952 Green *Samuel Maverick* 82 **TX**, This last [=a bull-tongue plough] we want to break up a piece of new ground on the labors where the bushes grow.] **1893** Mansur & Tebbetts *Genl. Catalogue D* 75 (Mathews Coll.), This Plow will be found to meet the wants of the South and West for a first-class New Ground Plow. **1923** *DN* 5.215 swMO, New groun. . . -plow. . . See *Bull tongue* [=the simplest form of plow]. **1954** *Harder Coll.* cwTN, New ground plow—type of plow used for ground not plowed before. **1969–70** *DARE* (Qu. L18, *Kinds of plows*) Inf KY16, Newground plow—colters to cut roots; KY84, New-ground plow [drawing in text showing colter]. **1986** Pederson *LAGS Concordance* (Plows) 1 inf, **nwTN**, Newground plow; 1 inf, **nwTN**, Newground plow—throws dirt two ways, cuts roots; 1 inf, **nwTN**, Newground plow—used after clearing land; 1 inf, **cnMS**, Newground plow—to break newly cleared land; 1 inf, **nwMS**, Newground plow—for just cleared land.

2 in comb *newground pie:* A pumpkin pie.
    1960 in 1984 Gilmore *Ozark Baptizings* 205 **MO**, We called a pump-kin pie a "new-ground" pie because they always put out pumpkins on new ground.

newground plow See **newground 1b**

New Ground religion n
    1958 Randolph *Sticks* 121 **Ozarks**, One time there was a bunch of peckerwoods lived up on Panther Creek, and they belonged to the New Ground religion. Them people didn't build no regular church. Mostly they just visited around each others' houses, but sometimes there was big meetings out in the woods. Folks that came along the road would see men and women prancing around without a stitch of clothes on. They called it the Holy Dance. . . The respectable folks in town just laughed, because the New Ground community was mostly white trash anyhow.

New Jersey (mosquito) See **Jersey mosquito 1**

New Jersey pine See **Jersey pine**

New Jersey tea n [See quot 1974] Cf **Indian tea c, Oregon tea tree**
    A **ceanothus:** usu *Ceanothus americanus* of the eastern half of the US, but also occas *C. herbaceus* or other sp; see quots. Also called **Jersey tea, redroot.** For other names of *C. ameri-canus* see **redshank, spangles, wild pepper, ~ snowball**
    1785 Marshall *Arbustrum* 27, American Ceanothus . . or New-Jersey Tea-tree . . is a low shrub, growing common in most parts of North America. **1832** MA Hist. Soc. *Coll.* 2d ser 9.148 cwVT, Ceanothus americanus . . New Jersey tea. **1837** Darlington *Flora Cestrica* 148, American Ceanothus . . New Jersey Tea. . . This little shrub possesses considerable astringency. . . The *leaves* were used by the Whigs, as a substitute for *Tea,* during the American Revolution. **1870** MO State Entomol. *Annual Report* 35, The Red-root or New Jersey Tea-plant (*Ceanothus Americanus*). **1924** Hawkins *Trees & Shrubs* 97 wWY, Mountain balm (Ceanothus velutinus). . . Mountain laurel . . and New Jersey tea are other common names. **1941** Walker *Lookout* 59 seTN, The commonest shrub, perhaps, is New Jersey tea or redroot which grows profusely on the summit as well as on both sides of the mountain. **1960** Vines *Trees SW* 691, Desert Ceanothus—*Ceanothus greggii*. . .

Also known by the name of . . New Jersey-tea. . . some of the names should more properly apply to the related species *C. herbacea . .* which was used as a substitute for tea in Civil War days, and to *C. ameri-canus . .* which was similarly used. **1967** Borland *Hill Country* 334 **nwCT**, Some people also used New Jersey tea. . . You know, that wild plant with the little fluffy balls of white blossom. They picked the leaves and steeped a tea from them. **1968** *DARE* (Qu. S26a, . . *Wildflowers. . . Roadside flowers*) Inf **WI**12, New Jersey tea. **1974** (1977) Coon *Useful Plants* 234, *Ceanothus americanus . .* One of the most noteworthy of wild plants in colonial days, and one with much connection with the American Revolution, the New Jersey tea comes from a low shrub with downy leaves. . . After British tea was dumped in Boston Harbor, various substitutes were tried, principally the dried leaves of this plant. The knowledge of this was most likely taken from the Indians.

new land See **newground 1a**

New Leens See **New Orleans**

newlight n [See quot 1889] esp **KY** Cf **campbellite**
    The white **crappie.**
    1877 U.S. Natl. Museum *Bulletin* 9.21, *Pomoxys annularis. . .* Throughout Kentucky it is known as the "New Light", and sometimes as "Campbellite". **1887** Goode *Amer. Fishes* 71, *Pomoxys annularis* is also known by such names as "Bachelor" in the Ohio Valley, "New Light" and "Campbellite" in Kentucky, Illinois and Indiana, names given to it by the irreverent during the great Campbellite movement in the West nearly half a century ago. **1889** *Century Dict.* 780, *Campbellite. . .* "The names new-light and *Campbellite* are due to the fact that it became abundant and the subject of observation when the religious denomination bearing those names originated." **1946** LaMonte *N. Amer. Game Fishes* 143, White Crappie. . . Newlight, Campbellite, Lamplighter, and many other very localized names. **1969** *DARE* (Qu. P1, . . *Kinds of freshwater fish . . caught around here . . good to eat*) Inf KY60, Newlight—similar to bluegill; KY65, Newlight (old-fashioned) = croppie. **1975** Evanoff *Catch More Fish* 90, The white crappie has been called the Calico bass . . newlight . . and many other names.

New Mexican buckeye See **Mexican buckeye**

New Mexican duck See **Mexican duck 2**

New Mexican rain n Cf **Arizona cloudburst**
    1965 Teale *Wandering Through Winter* 97 **NM**, Dust clouds—"New Mexican rain"—swept in long tongues into the sky.

New Mexico buckeye See **Mexican buckeye**

new-milch adj, also used absol Pronc-sp *new-milks* [Cf *EDD new-melched cow* (at *new* 4.(7)); see also exx of *new-milched* (prob in same sense) at *OED milch* v. 1] chiefly **NEng** See Map *old-fash* Cf **milch cow**
    Of a cow: having recently begun to produce milk.
    1630 Winthrop *Let. in New Eng.* (1825) I.378 (*OED* at *meal* v. 2), Some more cows would be bought, especially two new milch, which must be well mealed and milked by the way. **1834** in 1988 Palmer *Lang. W. Cent. MA* 31, [For sale:] 10 cows, New Milch, or near calving. **1907** *DN* 3.247 eME, New-milks. . . New-milch. "I want a new-milks cow." **1917** *DN* 4.396 neOH, New-milk's cow. . . A fresh cow. . . Possibly a variant of *milch,* which is not very common on the W[estern] R[eserve]. Also N. Eng., N.Y. **1939** *LANE* Map 193 (*The cow is going to calve*) 4 infs, **NEng**, Be (or) become new-milks; 1 inf, **RI**, A new milch cow,

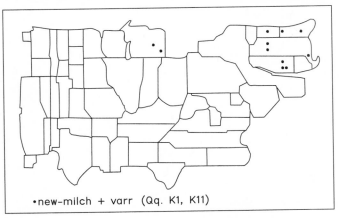

•new-milch + varr (Qq. K1, K11)

one that has freshened. **1948** *WELS Suppl.* **cwWI,** New milch (pron. milks) cows *freshen* or *come in.* **1965–70** *DARE* (Qu. K1, *A cow that is giving milk is a* _____) Infs **CT25, ME**1, New-milch (cow); **MA6,** When she's just calved she's a new-milks; **ME5,** New-milks cow—just had a calf; **MI71,** New-milks cow we called 'em if they had just come in with a calf; [**NH3,** Fresh-milch]; (Qu. K11, *When a cow has a calf . . she* _____) Infs **CT14, NH12,** She's a new-milch cow; **CT17,** She's new-milch; **MA32,** She's a new-milks; **MI64,** She's a new-milks cow; **ME5,** She's fresh; she's new-milks; **MA40,** New-milks. [All Infs old]

new-mown hay n

The leaves of **vanilla leaf** (here: *Achlys triphylla*).

1920 *DN* 5.83 **NW,** New mown hay. Achlys leaves.

newnited adj Also sp *nunited* [Cf quot 1949 and Intro "Language Changes" I.8] esp Sth

United—usu in comb *Newnited States.*

1922 *DN* 5.184 **GA,** *Nunited.* . . United, as in the "Nunited States." **1922** Gonzales *Black Border* 81 **sSC, GA coasts** [Gullah], Dis respected citizen ub de Newnited State. **1949** [see *nuse*]. **1968** *DARE* File **neAL,** I'll hand my hand to God on it, that I can read to you that the Newnited [ˈnɪɯˈnaːtɪd] States is Israel itself. **1976** Garber *Mountain-ese* 61 **sAppalachians,** She's the purtiest gal in the whole Newnited-States, bar none.

new of the moon n [*OED* →1805] Cf dark of the moon, old of the moon

The time of the new moon.

1939 *Hall Coll.* **seTN,** New of the moon—Corn planted on the new of the moon will grow tall. **1959** Roberts *Up Cutshin* 35 **seKY,** We would kill our hogs all the time on the old of the moon. Never would kill 'em on the new of the moon. **1972** *Foxfire Book* 190 **nGA,** If you kill a hog on th' new of th' moon, slice it and put it in a pan, it'll just blow you 'til you can't fry th' grease out of it hardly. *Ibid* 221 **nGA,** Dig a hole on th' new of th' moon and you will have dirt to throw away.

New Orleans n Usu |ˌn(ɪ)uˈɔ(r)liənz, -ˈɔ(r)lənz|; less freq |ˌn(ɪ)uɔrˈlinz|, |ˈnjɔ(r)lənz|; for addit varr see quots Pronc-spp *Newer Leans, New Leens, N'(y)awlins*

A Forms.

1916 *DN* 4.269 **New Orleans LA,** *New Orleans.* Pronounced [njuˈɔrlənz]. **1926** Ferber *Show Boat* 178, It was N'Yawlins as he said it. **1927** Kennedy *Gritny* 142 **sLA** [Black], I . . come hyuh to git my vegetables to carry over to New Leens to sell. **1940** *Sat. Eve. Post* 24 Feb 25 [Black], "Where were you born?" "Nyawlins." **1941** *AmSp* 16.15 **eTX** [Black], [ˌnjũɔ̃ˈliːnz]. **1944** *ADD* **cNY** (as of 1920s), [ˈnuɔrˈlinz]. **1969** *DARE* (Qu. H21) Inf **CT39,** [ˌnuəˈliənz]. **1975** *Times-Picayune* (New Orleans LA) 9 Jan sec 3 3/1, Sidewalks are called banquettes in Newer Leans. **1977** *MS Folkl. Reg.* 11.81, In *New Orleans* the first syllable has a pattern familiar to those who have charted the distribution of /u/, /ju/ and /iu/. . . The South and South Midland overwhelmingly have /nju/. Metropolitan New York, the Hudson Valley, Pennsylvania, and northern West Virginia strongly favor /nu/; there is divided usage in northeastern West Virginia and the Yankee Strip of Pennsylvania. Upstate New York is also divided. . . Forms with a reduced vowel, /njə/ or /nə/, appear . . in northern New York . . South Carolina, and . . northern Florida. . . A majority of informants pronounce *New Orleans* with a stressed final syllable. . . Pronunciations with primary stress on the penultimate syllable and secondary stress on the final syllable are most common in New York State, Pennsylvania, West Virginia, and western South Carolina. . . Pronunciations of *Orleans* with a reduced vowel . . are most common in the Hudson Valley and eastern Virginia. . . There are several types of pronunciations with reduced vowels following the stressed first syllable of *Orleans.* The commonest is a three-syllable form with two successive weakly stressed vowels. . . Also widespread, though most common in Georgia, are two syllable forms with a final weakly stressed syllable. . . A final /n/, with /z/ lacking, is widely distributed but nowhere common. . . A significant proportion of these forms are found in the speech of Black informants. . . The largest concentrations, however, are in the Appalachians. **1989** Pederson *LAGS Tech. Index* 329 **Gulf Region,** [For *New Orleans,* three-syllable proncs of the types [ˌnɪuˈɔ(ə)lnz] and [ˌnɪuˈɔrlnz] were most common and about equally frequent; four-syllable proncs of the type [ˈnɪuˈɔrlɪnz] and three-syllable proncs with stress on the final syllable, as [ˌnɪuɔrˈlinz], were occasional; proncs with first-syllable [nu-], as [ˌnuˈɔrlnz], [ˌnuˈɔ(ə)lnz], occurred frequently; variants with initial stress, as [ˈnjɔ(ə)lnz], were occasional, as were variants without a final

sibilant, as [ˌnɪuˈɔ(r)lṇ], [ˌnɪuɔ(r)ˈlin].] **1990** Graham–Taylor *New Orleans* 47, N'awlins. **1993** *DARE* File **sLA,** Nawlins.

B Sense.

Also *New Orleans tag;* a children's game: =**lemonade.**

1940 Marran *Games Outdoors* 144, *New Orleans Tag.* . . Here we come! . . Where from? . . New Orleans! . . What's your trade? . . Lemonade! . . Show us some. **1953** Brewster *Amer. Nonsinging Games* 4, *Lemonade.* . . other names . . New Orleans, New Orleans tag. **1957** *Sat. Eve. Post Letters* **Detroit MI,** *New Orleans*—Two sides chant: Here we come / Where from?/ New Orleans / What's your trade?/ Lemonade / Give me some./ Making houses or any occupation which is forthwith done as charades. If opposing side guesses it, they chase the New Orleaners. *Ibid* **MI,** *New Orleans*—(Choose sides:) Here we come / Where from / New Orleans / etc. Dramatize an action, which if guessed, the guessing side chases the performing side to goal, capturing as many as possible. **1967–68** *DARE* (Qu. EE33, . . *Outdoor games . . that children play*) Inf **CO21,** New Orleans; **IA7,** New Orleans or New York nigger nut town—like red rover. "Here I come," "Where you from," "New York nigger nut town." One side was New York nigger nut town, the other was New Orleans. The above is a rhyme recited responsively when playing the game New York nigger nut town; **NY120,** New Orleans—singing game—a type of charade. Here we come / Where from / New Orleans / What's your trade / Lemonade.

newraulgy See neuralgia

news bee n Also *news bug,* ~ *fly* chiefly Midl

A **hover fly** or similar insect.

1899 Bergen *Animal Lore* 40 **eKS,** If a beetle [sic], commonly called the "news-bug," fly through the house, the occupants are going to hear news. **1935** Hyatt *Folkl. Adams Co. IL* 60, When one of those 'news flies' *(any kind of large fly that continually darts about a person)* comes and buzzes around you, you are going to hear some good news. **1949** Webber *Backwoods Teacher* 201 **Ozarks,** When a yellow news bee hovers around you it means you'll get a letter with good news, and . . a black one foretells bad news. The news bee is as long as the finger. He can hover in one spot, with his wings making a high-pitched sound which can be heard for many yards, and then dart so fast that he is suddenly in another spot "without having moved." His abdomen does not appear to hold a stinger and perhaps he is not a bee at all. **1967** *DARE* FW Addit **AR46,** *News bee*—a buzzing, wasp-like insect that alternately hovers around in one spot and flies almost faster than the eye can see; its buzz sounds faintly like a human voice; **LA41,** News bee—a large yellowish bee that buzzes in a stationary position, then speeds away; it hums like a voice. **1967** in 1968 Haun *Hawk's Done Gone* x **TN,** A honeybee or newsbee flying around one's head means good luck. **1968** [see **letter carrier**]. **1971** *Foxfire* Winter 254 **nGA,** Nora Garland . . talked at length about the "news bees" that are so common around here: "Well, now, there's yeller ones—that's *good* news—and they's black ones, and that's bad news."

newspaper n

In var phrr indicating that someone or something is thin or transparent; see quots. esp Sth, S Midl

1951 TN Folk Lore Soc. *Bulletin* 17.52 **wTN,** She's so thin you can read a newspaper through her. **1966–69** *DARE* (Qu. H74b, . . *Coffee . . very weak*) Infs **IN30, NC82,** (I) can read a newspaper through it; **NC55,** You can read the newspaper through it; (Qu. X49, *Expressions . . about a person who is very thin*) Infs **AL30, GA77,** (One could) read a newspaper through him; **GA7,** So poor you could read a newspaper through him; **KY19,** Thin enough to read a newspaper through him. **1995** *DARE* File **csWI,** That slice of bread is so thin you can read a newspaper through it.

newsy adj [*EDD newsy* (at *news* sb. 2) "talkative; full of gossip; . . inquisitive"; *SND* (at *news* n. I). The meaning may have been infl by assoc with *nosy.*] chiefly C Atl, esp PA

Of a person: full of news, news-loving; inquisitive, prying.

1899 (1912) Green *VA Folk-Speech* 297, *Newsy.* . . Having the latest and fullest news: as, "it is a very newsy paper." "What a newsy woman she is." **1967–70** *DARE* (Qu. Y9, *Somebody who always follows along behind others: "His little brother is an awful* _____.") Inf **NJ69,** Tag-tail; awful newsy; (Qu. GG36a, *The kind of person who is always poking into other people's affairs: "She's an awful* _____.") Inf **DE3,** She's newsy; **PA135,** Newsy person; (Qu. GG36b, . . *"She's the* _____ *person I know!"*) Infs **CT23, DE3, MI45, PA245, TN35,** Newsiest. **1980** *DARE* File **sePA,** In the late Thirties among Black elementary school children in North Philadelphia, the form "newsy"

[nuzi] was commonly used according to my recollection, while "nosy" was either absent or rare. **1980** *NYT Article Letters* **NY,** It emerged that the youngsters did not care for those older folks they characterized as 'newsy.' It seems to mean snooping, prying into others' business, with the object of ferreting out and exchanging bits of gossip—i.e., nosy, but with an extra dimension. *Ibid* **PA,** Among native Philadelphians, however, both terms [=*nosy* and *nibby*] are unknown; their synonym is "Newsy," and only by context do they understand "nosy." **1980** *NADS Letters* **Philadelphia PA,** [I] grew up with "newsy" as an alternative to "nosy"; am surprised to find that this word is not a part of Standard speech, since it is simply so familiar to us. **1995** *DARE* File **Philadelphia PA,** Although my father (78 years old) has never heard the word *newsy,* my mother (76) knows this word well. *Newsy,* she says, describes "somebody who is into other people's business, a busybody." My aunt (86) has also often heard this word [=*newsy*] and condemns its use: "People who don't know any better use it for *nosy."* All three have always lived in Philly.

New Yawk See **New York**

New Year's gift exclam Also *New Year's give* **Sth, S Midl** Cf **Christmas gift**

Used as a greeting on New Year's Day—orig said in expectation of receiving a gift.

1903 *DN* 3.322 **seMO,** *Newyear's gift.* . . Corresponding to 'Happy new-year!' **1906** *DN* 3.147 **nwAR,** *New Year's gift.* . . Happy New Year. **1909** *DN* 3.352 **eAL, wGA,** *New-Year's gift.* . . A greeting on New Year's day, usually made with the hope of getting a present. The custom is passing. **1946** *PADS* 5.30 **VA,** *New year's gift!*: Happy new year!; not common. **1956** McAtee *Some Dialect NC* 31, *New Years gift!*: salutation on the pattern of "Christmas gift!" **1960** Criswell *Resp. to PADS 20* **Ozarks,** *New Year's gift.* . . Very common once. **1983** *MJLF* 9.1.48 **ceKY,** *New Year's Gift!* **1986** Pederson *LAGS Concordance* **Gulf Region** *(Happy New Year),* 51 infs, New Year's gift; 1 inf, New Year's gift—that's real common; 1 inf, New Year's gift—not expecting a gift; 1 inf, New Year's gift—not used often; no gifts involved; 1 inf, New Year's gift—rarely; only to good friends; 1 inf, New Year's gift—first response, but rejects gifts; 1 inf, New Year's gifts; 5 infs, New Year's give; 1 inf, New Year's give—you don't get nothing.

New York n Usu |,n(I)u 'jɔ(r)k, -'jɔ(r)k|; also |,nə-, ,nɪ-|; for addit varr see quots Pronc-spp *Ne' York, N(ew) Yawk, New Yo'k, Noo Yawk, ~ York*

A Forms.

1860 Holmes *Professor* 76 **eMA,** And what do you say to Ne' York?—asked the Koh-i-noor. **1937** NE Univ. *Univ. Studies* 37.110 [Terms from play-party songs], There's a building in Noo Yawk. **1944** *ADD* 411 **cNY** (as of 1920s), *New York.* . . |nu'jɔrk|, |nə'jɔrk|. *Ibid* (as of 1930s), New Yawk, Noo York. **1944** Kenyon–Knott *Pronc. Dict.* 295, *New York.* . . E[ast] S[outh]—'jɔək. **1965** Carmony *Speech Terre Haute* 83, *New York* [,nɨ 'jɔɚk]. **1968** Moody *Coming of Age MS* 157 [Black], Yeah, I wish I was one of them students sittin' out there. . . Got them rich-assed parents up there in New Yo'k. **1976** Allen *LAUM* 3.349 **Upper MW** (as of c1950), *New York.* . . *New* typically is /nu/ and *York* is typically /jɔrk/ or /jɒrk/. **1982** Chaika *Speaking RI* [7], N'yawk system. **1989** Pederson *LAGS Tech. Index* 315 **Gulf Region,** [For *New York,* the most common proncs are [,nnu'jork, -'jɔrk], followed by [,nu'jork, -'jɔrk]; less frequent proncs include [,nɪu'jɔk, -'jok], [,nu'jɔk, -'jok]; occasional proncs include [,nɪu'ja(r)k, ,nu'jark, -'jærk], [,nɪ'jɔ(r)k, -'jɔ(r)k], ['njɔk], [,nu 'jork, -'jork]. Note: Stress sometimes shifts from the second to the first syllable in the phrr *New York City* and *New York State.*]

B Senses.

1 also *New Yorker:* A marble game; see quots.

1905 *DN* 3.88 **nwAR,** *New York.* . . The name of a game of marbles. Common. **1968** *DARE* (Qu. EE7, . . *Kinds of marble games*) Inf **DE3,** New York—you put the marbles in a great big ring; **NJ18,** New Yorker—regular marbles—put commies in ring and knock them out. **1968** *DARE* Tape **DE3,** [FW:] We were talking about marble games . . and you mentioned the game New York. [Inf:] You make a big ring . . four or five foot round, and put the marbles, each one puts the same amount . . in the ring. And then you shoot from the edge . . Sometimes they're put in a bunch, and other times we used to pitch 'em in. We let 'em roll where they would and you shot from the edge of the ring and any part of the ring you wanted to shoot from.

2 also *New York nigger nut town;* A children's game: **=lemonade.**

1899 *Amer. Anthropologist* 1.265 **DC,** *New York.* . . One line turns around and advances, announcing, "Here we come." The children in the other line also turn and inquire, "Where from?" "New York." "What's your trade?" They imitate in dumb show the motions of any occupation which may have been agreed on. The others guess what it is. If right the imitating party cry, "Yes," and endeavor to escape to their own chalk line or base. The members of the other party pursue, making recruits of all prisoners. . . The name of any other place may be substituted for "New York." **1945** Boyd *Hdbk. Games* 106, *New York.* . . First group: Here we come. Second group: Where from? First group: New York. Second group: What's your trade? First group: Lemonade. Second group: Give us some. The players of the first group . . indicating their activity, act it in pantomime. . . The other players guess what is being acted; and when one of them guesses correctly, the first group run for their goal, and the second group try to tag them. **1964** Wallace *Frontier Life* 38 **OK** (as of 1893–1906), At recess and the noon hour, we staged such games as Blackman, Stink-Base, New York, or a ball game we called Two-Old-Cat. **1968–69** *DARE* (Qu. EE33, . . *Outdoor games . . that children play*) Inf **AK5,** New York—two teams lined up like charades: Where you from?/ New York / What's your trade?/ Lemonade / Show us some. Players act out something, if other side guessed what it was—climbing a tree—the guessing side ran and the others after them to catch them; **CA87,** New York—Where you from?/ New York / What's your trade?/ Lemonade / Show us some; pantomime; **IL35,** New York—charades; we called it New York; when person guessed he had to run and catch another; **IA7,** New Orleans or New York nigger nut town—like red rover.

3 in phrr referring to other children's games: See quots.

1957 *Sat. Eve. Post Letters* **eCO** (as of 1920s), Some of the games I remember . . are . . Going to New York; Fruit Basket Turn Over [etc]. . . An old man in his seventies, who grew up in Indian Territory, told me that the game I called Going to New York was to him and his childhood playmates called Going Out West. **1966–69** *DARE* (Qu. EE19, *The game in which children mark a 'court' on the ground or sidewalk, throw a flat stone in one section, then go on one foot and try to kick it or carry it out*) Inf **FL28,** Going to New York—old-fashioned; (QR, near Qu. EE39] Inf **IL35,** Trip to New York [FW: This was a box game according to Inf—not strictly a paper game.]

‡**4** in phr *going to New York:* See quot. Cf **Richmond, go to**

1970 *DARE* (Qu. AA28, . . *Joking or sly expressions . . women use to say that another is going to have a baby . . "She['s] _____."*) Inf **NC88,** Going to New York.

5 in var phrr indicating a roundabout route: See quot.

1968–70 *DARE* (Qu. KK52, *To do something in an indirect and complicated way: "I don't know why he had to go _____ to do that."*) Inf **PA247,** Through China to get to New York; **AL59,** To New York by way of California; **NY46,** To New York by way of New Jersey.

New Yorker n

1 A style of haircut; see quot.

1966–67 *DARE* (Qu. X5, . . *Different kinds of men's haircuts*) Inf **MI33,** New Yorker—"continental"—the top was a brush cut, the rest long and combed into a DA [=duck's ass]; **MI70,** New Yorker—a brush on top, long on sides.

2 See **New York B1.**

New York, holler v phr Also *holler New York* **E** Cf **york**

To vomit.

1968 *DARE* (Qu. BB17, . . *Vomiting*) Inf **WI24,** Hollering "New York E." **1976** *Webster's Collegiate Thesaurus* 915, *Vomit* . . idiom . . holler New York.

New York Indian n

1950 *WELS* (*Names and nicknames for people of foreign background: Jewish*) 1 Inf, **cwWI,** New York Indian.

New York minute n

A very short period of time; also fig.

1967 *DARE* (Qu. A14, . . *A very short period of time: "I'll be ready in _____." or "It won't take any longer than _____."*) Inf **TX37,** New York minute. **1984** Weaver *TX Crude* 116, *In a hot New York minute.* Immediately. Equates to a nanosecond, or that infinitesimal blink of time in New York after the traffic light turns green and before the ol' boy behind you honks his horn. **1987** *Isthmus* (Madison WI) 11 Sept 16, The experts aren't buying it for a New York minute. **1988** *DARE* File **PA,** You can do a search in a New York minute. [What's that?] Very, very quick.

New York nigger nut town See **New York B2**

New York system n RI

A frankfurter served with sauce or condiments; the restaurants that serve them.

  1982 Chaika *Speaking RI* [7], *N'yawk system* = restaurants famous faw wienies (q.v.) with sauce. New Yawkas claim neva to have heard of them. Unique taste reputed to come from bare ahm of cook as he puts several wienies on his ahm, from elbow to wrist, while ladling on sauce. **1989** *Providence Jrl.* (RI) 1 Jan sec C 1/1, Eating a New York system is Rhode Island. Eating an Oscar Meyer [sic] wiener isn't. **1989** *DARE* File **Newport RI** (as of 1950), New York System: I think a hot dog with everything.

New York turkey n Cf **Cape Cod turkey, Irish ~**

  1905 *DN* 3.88 **nwAR,** *New York turkey.* . . Bacon. Rare.

Ne' York See **New York**

ni See **nigh**

nib n[1] [Var of *neb*; *OED nib* sb.[1] 1585 →]

  1 See **nibby-nose.**

  2 also attrib: The point of a pen. [*OED nib* sb.[1] 2 1611 →] **chiefly Nth, N Midl, West** See Map Cf **neb** n **2**

  1806 (1970) Webster *Compendious Dict.* 201, *Nib.* . . a point of a pen. [*DARE* Ed: This entry was carried over from Webster's English model.] **1872** (1876) Knight *Amer. Mech. Dict.* 2.1525, *Nib.* . . One of the points of a pen. Pens have usually two nibs. . . A small pen adapted to be placed in a holder for use. The usual form of steel pens. **1965–70** *DARE* (Qu. JJ10b, *Parts of an ink pen*) 111 Infs, **chiefly Nth, N Midl, West,** Nib; **IA**9, **PA**190, Nib point; **NY**219, Pen nib; (Qu. JJ10a, *Different kinds of pens and pencils*) Inf **OR**10, Nib; **IL**92, Nib point; **NY**1, Steel nib.

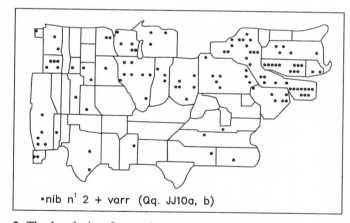

•nib n[1] 2 + varr (Qq. JJ10a, b)

  3 The handgrip of a scythe.

  1872 (1876) Knight *Amer. Mech. Dict.* 2.1525, *Nib.* . . The handle of a scythe-snath. It has a ring slipping on the snath and tightened by a bolt or wedge. **1964** (1974) Sloane *Museum Amer. Tools* 102, The first American grass blades were from England and matched to naturally bent "snaths" (handles) without "nibs" (handgrips). **1965** Needham–Mussey *Country Things* 25 **VT,** Gramp first taught me to mow when I wasn't hardly big enough to hold up the scythe. I stood in front of him, and hung on to the nibs, as he called them, that is, the handgrips of the scythe.

  4 =**pope's nose.**

  1957 Battaglia *Resp. to PADS 20* **eMD** (*The rump of a cooked chicken*) Nib.

  5 See quot 1958.

  1957 Clark *Song of the River* 49 **KY,** He figured that he had about enough money for a good line, a few extra hooks, and maybe a ball of staggon for nibs. **1958** *KY Folkl. Rec.* 4.112, *Nib.* . . A trot line . . is one long cord or wire . . on which many smaller lines are tied. The small lines hold the hooks. These small lines are known as nibs.

nib v[1] Also with *in* Cf **neb** v, **nibby** adj

To pry, meddle, interfere; hence v phrr *nib out (of)* to cease to meddle (in); n *nibber* one who meddles.

  1942 in 1944 *ADD* 408 **nWV,** *Nibbing,* ptc. = being nosy. *Nib, nibs,* present, not used. **1968–69** *DARE* (Qu. GG36a, *The kind of person who*

is always poking into other people's affairs: "She's an awful _____.") Inf **OH**44, Nibber; (Qu. II22, *Expressions to tell somebody to keep to himself and mind his own business*) Inf **PA**177, I'm tired of you nibbing in. **1979** *NYT Article Letters* **sOH,** "Nibby" means nosy, as in "Don't be so nibby," or "Nib out." **1980** *NYT Article Letters* **OH,** My father often used the expression, "Don't be nibbing in my business." **1995** *DARE* File **sNJ,** Where I came from (South Jersey), we would have said a [nosy] person is a "nib" [rather than a "neb"] or that my mother should "nib out" [rather than "neb out"] of my business. Of course, this was never written down, but we pronounced it more like *nib* than *neb.*

nib n[2] [Prob varr of **mib**]

  1 also *nimb:* A playing marble, esp a small or cheap one. **chiefly N Cent, NEast** See Map

  1896 *DN* 1.421 **wNY,** Nibs: for *mibs.* **1950** *WELS* **WI** (*Names and nicknames for different kinds of marbles: Small ones* _____) 6 Infs, Nibs; 1 Inf, Nimbs. **1950** *WELS Suppl.* **csWI** (as of 1935), *Nib*—small earthenware marble. **1957** *Sat. Eve. Post Letters* **WI,** *Nib,* a small marble. **1965–70** *DARE* (Qu. EE6b, *Small marbles or marbles in general*) 40 Infs, **chiefly N Cent, NEast,** Nibs; (Qu. EE6c, *Cheap marbles*) Infs **MI**34, **NY**36, Nibs. **c1970** Wiersma *Marbles Terms* **UT** (as of 1965), *Nib* . . small, opaque, dark-colored marble valued for its uniqueness. **1988** *DARE* Tape **WI**29, The main one I can remember is the nibs, and the shooters. . . The nibs were made of clay.

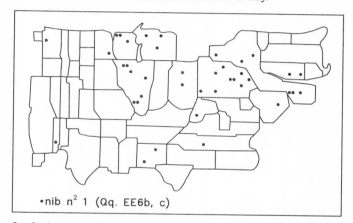

•nib n[2] 1 (Qq. EE6b, c)

  2 pl: A game of marbles.

  1968 *DARE* (Qu. EE7, . . *Kinds of marble games*) Inf **MD**16, Nibs— Player A shoots at B's shooter—if he hits it, he has nibbed it, and gets all the marbles that B has knocked out of [the] ring already.

nib v[2] [Prob < **nib** n[2]]

See quot.

  1968 [see **nib** n[2] 2].

nib n[3], v[3] [Abbr for *nibble*]

See quots.

  1909 *DN* 3.352 **eAL, wGA,** *Nib.* . . Nibble, a cautious bite. "I got a nib, but he wouldn't bite good." **c1938** in 1970 Hyatt *Hoodoo* 2.1085 **neFL,** They bites her skin inside and she got a sore there where done scratched it, trying to get in where they been nibbing her on the inside. She say they just nibbing her.

nibber See **nib** v[1]

nibbler n [See quots]

  =**cunner** n[1] **1.**

  1842 DeKay *Zool. NY* 4.173, The Bergall has various popular names: *Nibbler,* from its vexatious nibbling at the bait thrown out for other fishes, [etc]. **1872** Schele de Vere *Americanisms* 383, The *Blue Perch,* also known as *Nibbler,* from the wicked delight he seems to take in nibbling off the fisherman's bait, and as *Conner* on the coast of New England, is the *Burgall* mentioned elsewhere. **1906** NJ State Museum *Annual Rept. for 1905* 343, Bergall. Nibbler. [*Ibid* 344, Abundant along our coast, and a pest to wharf-fishermen, as it nibbles the bait off the hook.]

nibbling n esp Gulf States

A snack.

  1966–67 *DARE* (Qu. H5, . . *A small amount of food eaten between regular meals*) Infs **FL**6, **NY**12, Snack, nibbling; **FL**26, Nibbling, snack. **1970** Tarpley *Blinky* 188 **neTX,** *Food eaten between meals* . . nibblings

[rare]. **1986** Pederson *LAGS Concordance (Food taken between meals)* 4 infs, **LA, TN, MS,** Nibbling.

nibby adj, also used absol *esp N Midl* Cf **nebby** adj
Snoopy, inquisitive.
    1942 McAtee *Dial. Grant Co. IN* 73 (as of 1890s), *Nibby . .* nosey (the latter word used in the country). **1942** in **1944** *ADD* 408 **nWV,** *Nibby* ['nɪbi]. In general use. **1943** in **1944** *ADD* 408, One broken-down med student . . Is very nibby but motherlike. *Daily Athenaeum* W. Va. Univ., Mar. 3, p. 3. **1946** *PADS* 6.21 **eNC** (as of 1942), *Nibby. . .* Inquisitive. Used disparagingly. **1968–69** *DARE* (Qu. GG36a, *The kind of person who is always poking into other people's affairs: "She's an awful _____."*) Infs **IL**36, **NJ**18, **WV**3, Nibby; **OH**78, Nibby person; (Qu. GG36b, *. . "She's the _____ person I know!"*) Infs **NJ**33, **OH**44, 78, Nibbiest. **1982** [see **nibby-nose**]. **1984** Wilder *You All Spoken Here* 13 **Sth,** *Nibby:* Inquisitive; meddlesome. **1995** *DARE* File **sNJ** (as of c1955), Where I grew up, people said that a nosey person was "nibby."

nibby n[1] [Prob dimin of **nib** n[1]]
    1988 *DARE* File **Boston MA** (as of c1920), The bread [at a boys' school] was especially delicious, and the heels were coveted. "Nibby" was the boys' word for the heel.

nibby n[2] See **nubia**

nibby-nose n Also *nib* Cf **neb-nose**
=**neb** n **1b.**
    1980 *NYT Article Letters* **OH,** A friend of mine called a nosey neighbor "Miss Nib." . . My parents and grandparents have always used the expression [=*nibby*] and it seems to be fairly common in central and southeastern Ohio. A 'nib' or a 'nibby nose' was a person who was nosey. It was often used as a sort of mild reprimand to a child or puppy that was into something that he/she shouldn't be getting into. **1982** *DARE* File **neOH,** An informant from Youngstown, Ohio: *nibby* for . . [don't be so nebby!] and accepted *nibby-nose,* saying nevertheless, that it was less frequent. **1995** [see **nib** v[1]].

nib in See **nib** v[1]

nib-nose n Cf **neb-nose**
=**neb** n **1b.**
    1957 *Sat. Eve. Post Letters* **ceIN,** A busybody, or *nib-nose.* **1968–69** *DARE* (Qu. GG36a, *The kind of person who is always poking into other people's affairs: "She's an awful _____."*) Infs **IL**36, **NJ**23, **PA**182, Nib-nose.

nib out (of) See **nib** v[1]

nibs n pl Cf *dibs* (at **dib** n[1] **2**)
    A claim: a right of priority—often used as an exclam.
    1940 *Qrly. Jrl. Speech* 26.266 **VA,** What children in the North call "dibs on it," . . Virginia children may call . . "nibs on it." **1949** Hedgecock *Gone Are the Days* 19 **swMO,** I remember one time when Charley cried because somebody beat him to the brown bean after he had said nibs on it. **1950** *WELS Suppl. (Cries or calls used in playing marbles. . . To get the right to do something)* 1 Inf, **cwWI,** Nibs. **1957** *Sat. Eve. Post Letters* **sIN** (as of c1905), "Nibs" was another call that gave the shooter some advantage, but I forget what it was. **1968** *DARE* (Qu. V5b, *If you take something that nobody seems to own . . "Before anybody else gets it, I'm going to _____ this.")* Inf **MN**30, Put my nibs on. **1969** *AmSp* 44.21 **Pacific NW** [Painter jargon], *Nibs. . . A . .* warning [to] another [person] to "stay the hell off an area; that's mine; I'm going to work it": "I've got nibs on that job." **1977–78** Foster *Lexical Variation* 87 **NJ,** Claim calls. . . Nibs on. . . (1 [of 166 infs]).

nibshit v Cf **nebshit**
=**nib** v[1].
    1968 *DARE* (Qu. II22, *Expressions to tell somebody to keep to himself and mind his own business)* Inf **PA**165, Don't nibshit.

nicely adj **chiefly NEng**
    Well, very well; in good health.
    1815 Humphreys *Yankee in England* 107, *Nicely,* in good health. **1859** (1968) Bartlett *Americanisms* 292 **NEng,** *Nicely. . .* Well, very well. . . "How's your wife, Mr. Peabody, this fine morning?" "She's nicely." **1904** *DN* 2.427 **Cape Cod MA** (as of a1857), *Nicely. . .* Very well. 'How's your father? He's nicely.' **1907** *DN* 3.207 **nwAR,** *Nicely. . .* Well. "He has been real sick but is nicely now." *Ibid* 247 **eME,** *Nicely. . .* Very well. "Have you got nicely again?" **1975** Gould *ME*

Lingo 189, *Nicely*—Without complaint; used almost entirely in answer to a greeting: "How are you, Ben?" "Nicely, thank you."

nice-nasty See **nasty-nice**

nicey-nice adj Also *nicey-nicey* [Redup] Cf **nasty-nice**
    Affectedly proper; prissy.
    1930 Burnett *Iron Man* 228, This little kid here with all her nicey-nice talk. . . Why don't somebody ask her who got her a chance in Martin's show. I'll tell you. A guy seventy years old, and he ain't her grandpa! **1967–70** *DARE* (Qu. HH11a, *Someone who is too particular or fussy—if it's a man)* Inf **MD**49, Too nicey-nice; (Qu. HH11b, *Someone who is too particular or fussy—if it's a woman)* Inf **MI**113, Nicey-nice; (Qu. HH38, *A womanish man)* Inf **MI**92, Nicey-nice; (Qu. II33, *To get an advantage over somebody by tricky means: "I don't trust him, he's always trying to _____.")* Inf **MO**2, Be nicey-nicey. **1986** Pederson *LAGS Concordance,* 1 inf, **cnAR,** *Nicey-nice;* of euphemisms or circumlocutions.

nick n[1] **Delmarva** See Map Cf **kinick, nicker** n[2]
    A playing marble, esp a small or cheap one.
    1957 Battaglia *Resp. to PADS 20* **eMD** *(Kinds of marbles: Small ones)* Nick. **1968–70** *DARE* (Qu. EE6b, *Small marbles or marbles in general)* Infs **DE**3, **MD**38, 42, 46, **VA**50, Nicks; (Qu. EE6c, *Cheap marbles)* Inf **DE**1, Nicks; **DE**3, Nicks or commies—made out of clay. **1970** *DARE* FW Addit **ceVA,** *Marbles*—nicks (small marbles) put in *faddy* (a row) and shot out with shooter. Whoever hit the most out won.

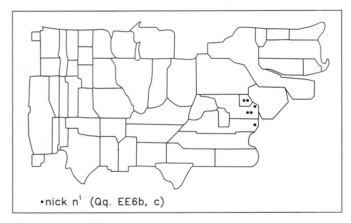

•nick n[1] (Qq. EE6b, c)

Nick n[2] See **Old Nick**

nick n[3], v See **nicker** n[1], v

nick n[4] See **neck** n

nick and nick adj [Var of *neck and neck*] Cf **neck** n **A**
    1966–69 *DARE* (Qu. KK54, *Just about equal, very close: "They were both fast runners and it was _____ all the way.")* Infs **FL**14, **KY**40, Nick and nick.

nick and tuck adj Also *nick or tuck* [Var of *nip and tuck,* infl by *neck and neck*] Cf **neck** n **A**
    1965–70 *DARE* (Qu. KK54, *Just about equal, very close: "They were both fast runners and it was _____ all the way.")* Infs **CO**15, **FL**48, **GA**61, **KY**21, 72, **ME**22, **MO**21, **PA**163, **TX**12, Nick and tuck; **KY**50, Nick or tuck.

nickar tree See **nicker tree**

nickel and dime n Also *nickel and dime store*
=**five and ten 1.**
    1965–70 *DARE* (Qu. U43, *. . The kind of store where most articles cost . . only five or ten cents;* not asked in early QRs) Infs **AL**10, **IL**44, **MI**68, **PA**142, 199, Nickel and dime store; **CA**49, **IL**39, **OH**44, **TN**11, Nickel and dime. **1972** *Times* (London) 16 May 1/3 **AL,** The first Mrs Wallace had worked in a nickel-and-dime store.

nickelette n Also *nicolet old-fash* Cf *nickelodeon*
    A theater or movie show to which the admission is (or was originally) five cents.
    1914 Grau *Theatre* 16 **seNY,** The "Nicolet," or five-cent store theatre, came into being. **1968** *DARE* (Qu. FF24, *The place or building where people go to see motion pictures)* Inf **PA**104, Nickelette—used to call

it; (Qu. FF25, *Joking names for motion pictures*) Inf **PA**81, Nickelette; **NJ**27, Nickelette—years ago.

nickels and dimes n

A **marsh pennywort** (here: *Hydrocotyle umbellata*).

1938 Baker *FL Wild Flowers* 158, *Hydrocotyle umbellata*, called pennywort from the shape of the small leaves has the more appropriate name in Florida of nickles [*sic*] and dimes, which takes note of their diversity in size.

nicker n[1], v Also *nick*; by lambdacism *nickle* [Scots, Ir, nEngl dial] **widespread exc NEast, Gt Lakes; less freq S Atl** See Map and Map Section Cf **whicker, whinner**

The sound made by a horse, esp a soft or low sound; to make this sound.

1867 Harris *Sut Lovingood Yarns* 168 **TN**, They . . roll'd over, run away, bawl'd, beller'd, nicker'd, screem'd, an' bray'd, till they farly shuck the leaves ontu the trees. **1899** (1912) Green *VA Folk-Speech* 298, *Nicker.* . . To make the cry of a horse; to neigh. **1902** *DN* 2.241 **sIL**, *Nicker.* . . To whinney as a horse. **1903** *DN* 2.322 **seMO**, *Nicker.* . . Neigh. **1906** Casey *Parson's Boys* 161 **sIL** (as of c1860), The boys soon christened him [=a horse] "Pe-coob-coob," this was the sound of a nicker he always gave when anyone approached the lot to feed him. **1906** *DN* 3.121 **sIN**, *Nicker.* . . To neigh. *Ibid* 149 **nwAR**, *Nicker.* . . To whinny. **1909** *DN* 3.352 **cAL, wGA**, *Nicker.* . . To neigh. **1912** *DN* 3.583 **wIN**, *Nicker.* . . To whinny. **1915** *DN* 4.186 **swVA**, *Nicker.* . . To whinny. **1923** *DN* 5.215 **swMO**, *Nicker*, n. or v. Whinny. **1941** *Language* 17.337 **WI**, [*LANCS* fieldwork:] *Nicker*—3 [of 50 infs]. . . [1 inf] says this is the oldest term and was once the most common; [2 infs] . . on hearing me mention the word, said they had heard it. . . *Nicker* is (and probably has been) hardly known at all in Wisconsin. [Footnote:] Work in the Great Lakes and Ohio River Valley region has shown *nicker* to be the most widely used term in Indiana and the adjoining southwest corner of Michigan. **1942** McAtee *Dial. Grant Co. IN* 45 (as of 1890s), *Nicker* . . neigh. My impression is that we used this word for . . some lesser sound than the full neigh of a horse, perhaps for what the dictionary calls whinny. **1949** Kurath *Word Geog.* 62, Terms . . for the gentle noise made by horses at feeding time . . [include] *nicker* (rarely *nickle*). *Ibid* 63, *Nicker* is in general use in a large area extending from Chesapeake Bay westward to southern Ohio and Kentucky and from there southward through the Appalachians as far as Georgia. It is in regular use in all of Virginia except the Norfolk area south of the lower James. The Virginia Piedmont would seem to be the original center from which *nicker* spread out. Interestingly enough, there are some relics of *nicker* in New England. **1965–70** *DARE* (Qu. K40, *The sound that a horse makes*) 182 Infs, **widespread exc NEast, Gt Lakes; less freq S Atl**; Nicker; **AR**55, Nicker—more common here [than *whinny*]; **AR**56, Nicker—just before he begins to whinny, which is louder and longer; **CA**87, Nicker—the waxing whicker; **CA**136, Nicker—we usually say [rather than *neigh*]; **CO**22, Nicker—for feed; **CO**38, Nicker [appar distinguished from *neigh/nigh* "the glad short sound" and *whinny* "the longer call, as from a mother to her colt"]; **CO**44, Nicker—a warning; the conversational horse talk; **GA**77, Nicker—in the stable; bray—outdoors; **IL**114, Neigh, nicker, and whinny represent different sounds: nicker—mare calls colt, [for] example; **IA**26, Nicker and whinny—same sound; **MA**58, Nicker—talking to self; **MI**64, Whicker, whinny, nicker—softer, sort of calling terms [in contrast to *neigh*]; **MO**18, Nickers, neigh—very similar, may be the same; **MO**25, Nickers; **NM**6, Nicker—more throaty than whinny, usually when you feed him; **OK**8,

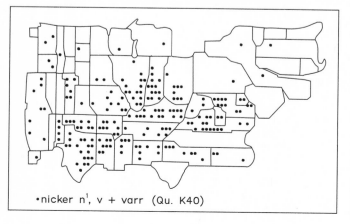

•nicker n[1], v + varr (Qu. K40)

Nicker—call to colt; **TX**11, Neigh, whinny, nicker—according to what he's saying; **WV**7, Nicker—old-fashioned [in contrast to neigh]; **OK**33, Nickering; **AL**11, Nick; **LA**33, Nicking; **VA**57, Nickle. **1983** *MJLF* 9.1.49 **ceKY**, *Nicker* . . the noise a horse makes when it is hungry. **1991** Pederson *LAGS Regional Pattern* 70, [The data show *nicker* (=whinny) to be particularly common in **eTX, AR, nLA, TN, nMS, nGA**, and particularly rare in **sAL, sGA, FL**.]

nicker n[2] Also sp *knicker* [Prob *OED* nicker sb.[3] 1 1675 →; but cf **kinick**] Cf **nick** n[1]

A playing marble; see quots.

1843 (1916) Hall *New Purchase* 42 **sePA**, "Hit black alley!—knock his nicker!—'tan't fair!" **1859** (1968) Bartlett *Americanisms* 231, *Knicker or Nicker.* . . A boy's clay marble; a common term in New York. **1890** *DN* 1.62 **wPA**, *Nicker*: the marble to be knocked out of the ring. **1922** [see **nicker tree**].

nicker tree n Also *nickar tree, nicor ~* [*OED* (at *nickar*) 1696 → for *Caesalpinia bonduc*; see quot 1922]

=**Kentucky coffee tree**; hence n *nicker nut*.

1763 in 1849 Darlington *Mem. John Bartram* 410, I should, in particular, be very glad to know if you saw anything of the Canada Bonduc, or Nickar-tree . . , and if you brought any of the seed home with you. **1785** Marshall *Arbustrum* 56, Guilandina dioica . . *Nickar Tree.* . . I have lately received several seeds from Kentucky, supposed to be of this tree, where it is said to grow plenty, and is called the Coffee or Mahogany tree. **1830** Rafinesque *Med. Flora* 2.226, Gymnocladus canadensis . . *Coffee tree, Mahogany, Nickar tree.* **1846** Browne *Trees* 219, *Gymnocladus canadensis.* . . Nicker-tree, Stump tree, Kentucky Coffee-tree. **1892** (1974) Millspaugh *Amer. Med. Plants* 53-1, American coffee bean, Kentucky mahogany, Nickar tree. **1922** *Amer. Botanist* 28.29, "Nicker-tree" and "nicker-nut" are terms supposed to have been applied to this species in allusion to the round seeds, like a "nicker" or marble. **1960** Vines *Trees SW* 531, Chicot, Luck-bean, Coffee-nut, Kentucky-mahogany, American Coffee-tree, Nicor-tree, and Stump-tree.

nicket n [Cf *EDD* nippet "A small quantity"]

A small amount.

1946 *PADS* 6.22 **eNC** (as of 1900–10), *Nicket.* . . A small amount of articles like sugar, coffee, flour, meal, etc. **1994** NC Lang. & Life Project *Harkers Is. Vocab.* 8 **eNC**, *Nicket.* . . A pinch of something (usually in cooking). *You should only use a nicket of paprika in you* [*sic*] *crab stew.*

nickety-tuck See **nippity-tuck**

‡nickie n[1] Cf **nancy**

See quot.

1968 *DARE* (Qu. E20, *Soft rolls of dust that collect on the floor under beds or other furniture*) Inf **OH**59, Nickies.

‡nickie n[2]

See quot.

1968 *DARE* (Qu. DD6b, *Nicknames for cigarettes*) Inf **PA**93, Nickies—from nicotine. [Laughter]

nick-knock See **knick-knock**

nickle See **nicker** n[1], v

nicknack See **knickknack** n[1]

nick or tuck See **nick and tuck**

nick-picker n [Var of *nit-picker;* cf Intro "Language Changes" IV.4]

1970 *DARE* (Qu. GG39, *Somebody who seems to be looking for reasons to be angry: "He's a _____."*) Inf **DC**11, Nick-picker.

nick-tailed adj esp Sth, S Midl

Of a horse: having the tail cut on the underside so that it is carried high; having the tail cut short; hence n *nicktail* a horse having such a tail.

1841 *S. Lit. Messenger* 7.219 **VA**, Brenda, mounted on Paul Clifford, nick-tailed sorrel pacer. **1852** *Ibid* 18.753 **VA**, The horse, a nick-tailed trotter, Tom had raffled off. **1867** Harris *Sut Lovingood Yarns* 19 **TN**, A nick tailed, bow necked, long, poor, pale sorrel horse. **1967–70** *DARE* (Qu. K41, *A horse with its tail cut short*) Infs **AR**55, **KY**35, **MS**87, Nicktail.

nickynack See **knickknack** n[1]

nic-nac, nicnacry See **knickknack** n[1]

nicolet See **nickelette**

nicor tree See **nicker tree**

nics cum arous See **nix** 2

niece n [Cf *OED niece* 3 → a1592; *"Obs. rare."*] **Sth, S Midl** Cf **nephew**

A nephew.

1671 in 1965 *AmSp* 40.236 **VA,** My loving neece, Charles Williams, son to my well-loved brother. **1950** *PADS* 14.48 **SC,** *Niece.* . . A niece or a nephew. Coastal Negro usage. **c1960** *Wilson Coll.* **csKY,** *Niece.* . . Referring to either male or female; nephew used in the same way. **1986** Pederson *LAGS Concordance,* 1 inf, **neMS,** *Niece*—used by Blacks to mean . . nephew. **1995** *DARE* File, "Niece" in Gullah is unmarked for sex (I [=a man] was referred to by a speaker in Colleton County, South Carolina, as my uncle's "niece").

niegor See **nigger** n[1]

nievitas n Also *nievita* [See quot 1934] **Pacific**

Usu =**forget-me-not 1f,** but also a **popcorn flower** (here: *Plagiobothrys nothofulvus*).

1897 Parsons *Wild Flowers CA* 30, *Pop-corn Flower. White Forget-me-not.* . . Though not showy, taken singly, they often cover the fields, presenting the appearance of a light snowfall, from which fact the Spanish-Californians have bestowed the pretty name, "nievitas," the diminutive of *nieve,* snow. **1901** Jepson *Flora CA* 444, *Cryptanthe . . Nievitas.* **1915** (1926) Armstrong–Thornber *Western Wild Flowers* 428, Nievitas—*Cryptanthe intermedia.* . . A rather attractive little plant, but inconspicuous except when it grows in patches, when it powders the fields with white, like a light fall of snow. **1934** Haskin *Wild Flowers Pacific Coast* 297, Nievitas—*Cryptanthe ambigua.* . . The name "nievita," from *nieve*—snow—is of Spanish-Californian origin, and refers to this sprinkling of the fields with flowery snow. **1961** Thomas *Flora Santa Cruz* 290 **cwCA,** *Cryptantha* . . Nievitas, White Forget-Me-Not. **1968** *DARE* (Qu. S26e, *Other wildflowers not yet mentioned;* not asked in early QRs) Inf **CA60,** Wild forget-me-not—nievitas—means "little snow"—they are white here.

niff n [*EDD niff* sb.[1] 1 "A quarrel; a silent, sullen feeling of resentment"]

See quots.

1914 *DN* 4.77 **ME, nNH,** *Niff.* . . A quarrel, grudge, or spite; also, dislike. **1953** *PADS* 19.12 **cwNC,** *Niff tree.* . . An imaginary tree up which one retreats when offended, i.e., a "miff" tree. "She did not like what I said, so she flew up the niff tree."

niff-naff n [Cf Scots, nEngl dial *niff-naff* a trifling or unimportant thing] Cf **nuff-nuff, DS** E20

1950 *WELS Suppl.* **eKS,** *Niff-naff.* . . Dust under a bed.

nig n [Abbr for **nigger** n[1] **B1** or **nigra, nigro**]

1 A Black person. **chiefly S Atl, Gulf States**

c1832 T.D. Rice *Jim Crow* x *(OEDS),* De Nigs in ole Virginny Be so black dey shine. **1865** in 1983 *PADS* 70.44 **ce,sePA,** I pity Sallie Cad's little Nigs; send them every stitch of clothing, overcoats, undercoats, pants, etc you can. **1872** in 1927 Jones *FL Plantation Rec.* 198, Perhaps it would pay to get some common whiskey for the nigs. **c1885** in 1981 Woodward *Mary Chesnut's Civil War* 828 **SC** (as of 1865), 'Respect the marriage tie.' Well, if he gets the nigs to do it, I hope he will proclaim awhile toward Utah. **1905** in 1913 Pringle *Woman Rice Planter* 160 **ceSC,** Her manner is what the "nigs" call "stiff." **1939** Griswold *Sea Is. Lady* 521 **csSC** (as of c1893), Well, wasn't nobody answerin' to that description got on [the train]. Only a couple of nigs, far as I know. **1941** *S. Rev.* 7.74 **TN,** The two nigs commenced to watch each other before their chickens had done scraping. **1956** Ker *Vocab. W. TX* 376, *Negro* . . nig. [1 of 67 infs] **1966–68** *DARE* (Qu. HH28, *Names and nicknames . . for people of foreign background: Black*) Infs **LA**17, **MS**8, 15, Nig. **c1970** Pederson *Dial. Surv. Rural GA* **seGA** (*What you [=a Black person] would not like to be called*) 1 inf, Nig. **1986** Pederson *LAGS Concordance (Black)* 1 inf, **cMS,** Nig—derogatory, used by children; 1 inf, **nwLA,** Nig. **1992** Hunter-Gault *In My Place* 242 **GA,** Dean Tate's message, which took several hours to deliver, was this: He was as sympathetic to the plight and aspirations of Black folks as anybody in the world ("I was asked one time to speak at a nig' funeral," Walter told me he said. "You know, they don't ask just any white man to speak at a nig' funeral").

2 See **nigger** n[1] **B5.**

nigger n[1] Usu |ˈnɪgə(r)|; infreq |ˈnegər| Also sp *negger, niggar, niggur;* arch spp *nager, ne(a)ger, neeger, negar, negur, niegor, niger* Pronc-spp *nigga(h), nigguh* [*nigger* < earlier *neger* < Fr *nègre* < Span, Port *negro; OED neger* "Now *north. dial.* and *Sc."* 1587 →; *nigger* 1786 →]

A Forms.

1619 in 1624 Smith *Genl. Hist. VA* 126, About the last of August came in a dutch man of warre that sold vs twenty Negars. **1676** (1872) Williams *George Fox* 5.425, The *Blackness* of the *Neger* comes not by Accident. **1700** [see **B1c** below]. **1701** (1879) S. Sewall *Diary* 2.43 **MA,** Mr. Cotton Mather . . talked very sharply against me as if I had used his father worse than a Neger. **1766** in 1894 *Harper's New Mth. Mag.* 88.535 **CT,** I, Governor Cuff of the Niegro's in the province of Connecticut, do resign my Governmentship to John Anderson Niegor man to Governor Skene. **1796** Barton *Disappointment* 34, You may tawk an tawk till you're as black as a nager. **1803** Davis *Travels* 383, I . . worked like a new negur. **1818** [see **B1a** below]. **1818** Fessenden *Ladies Monitor* 172 **NEng,** [In a list of words and phrases to be avoided:] *Neeger* for negro. **1843** (1916) Hall *New Purchase* 53 **IN,** Right hard to get gals here man—folks has to be their own niggurs. **1885** *Harper's New Mth. Mag.* 71.774 **CT** (as of 1644), She had abused the "neager" Anthony, and the other servants. **1894** Riley *Armazindy* 52 **IN,** Niggah in de roas'in'-yeers. **1922** Gonzales *Black Border* 273 **sSC, GA coasts** [Gullah,] I 'spec' you wouldn' uh fine yo' ole nigguh yuh [=here] teday. **a1930** [see **B1d** below]. **1967–68** *DARE* (Qu. FF5b, *More recent dance steps*) Inf **MN**15, Nigga dances; (Qu. HH28, *Names and nicknames . . for people of foreign background: Black*) Inf **GA**23, Nigger—*neger* [ˈnegə]—old-fashioned; **HI**6, Nigga. **1970** Tarpley *Blinky* 260 **neTX,** *Your everyday word for black people* . . 54.5% [of 200 infs] nigger . . 2.5% negger. **1994** [see **B1d** below].

B Senses.

1 A Black person, spec: see below. Note: The tone of the speaker or writer is not always possible to determine accurately; therefore, some of the quots below may be more appropriate at a different subsense.

a Used in a depreciatory sense by White speakers.

1818 Fearon *Sketches* 46 **NY,** The bad conduct and inferior nature of *niggars* (negroes). **1819** in 1823 Faux *Memorable Days* 9, Contempt of the poor blacks, or niggers, as they are there called, seems the national sin of America. **1867** Latham *Black & White* 127, Niggers (they are not 'coloured persons' yet in the South) are most artful flatterers. **1885** Twain *Huck. Finn* 280 **MO,** "Anybody hurt?" "No'm. Killed a nigger." "Well, it's lucky; because sometimes people do get hurt." **1897** *Outing* 29.333 **FL,** What is wanted is a genuine nigger—not a colored person, or an Afro-American, or a darkey—and one who has been there before. **1936** *AmSp* 11.11 **eTX,** The form universally used is *nigger,* pronounced [ˈnɪgə], [ˈnɪgɚ]. This pronunciation is maintained, I believe—though the reason is largely subconscious—because it expresses a racial and social distinction which [ˈniːgro] would not. [ˈnɪgə] may be flavored with genuine affection, or with contempt. But whatever the undertones, it is a means of keeping the black man in his place. The old slave-holding tradition still speaks in the pronunciation. **1966** Dakin *Dial. Vocab. Ohio R. Valley* 2.446, The status of *nigger* is much clearer, but positive statements about the present extent of its actual use are still uncertain. . . *Nigger* is mentioned with equal frequency everywhere, and it is quite certain that it is commonly used in all parts of the Valley. . . Numerous comments indicate that most people recognize that *nigger* is resented and that they use it as a derogatory term. At the same time, however, it is quite evident that this has not always been true and that the status of this term has changed within the lifetime of many speakers. . . The abandonment of the term represents a change of attitude which has resulted in *nigger* becoming "not a nice word" which many are not now willing to use. For them *Negro* or *colored (person)* has taken its place. Some older informants . . still use *nigger* in this neutral way. **1986** Pederson *LAGS Concordance* **Gulf Region,** [Of 281 infs who characterized *nigger* (and such phrases as *old nigger woman, nigger kids,* etc) as derogatory, insulting, abusive, offensive and the like, 72 were Black; of the 196 infs who characterized the same word and phrases as neutral or jocular, 24 were Black.]

b Used in a depreciatory sense by Black speakers.

1834 Lieber *Letters* 90 **sePA,** A negro boy under my window calls a lad of the same race, by way of reproach, *"nigger."* **1866** *Atlantic Mth.* July 79 **MD,** When they [=Black people] call each other "nigger," the familiar term of opprobrium is applied with all the malice of a sting. [**1927** Kennedy *Gritny* 29 **sLA** [Black], For a young ooman w'at bin well-raise', you sho kin make a whole lot o' nigger noise.] **1949** Botkin

Treas. S. Folkl. xxiii, In turning his laughter on himself as well as the whites, the Negro has taken over the objectionable word "nigger" (though not "darky") and made it a term of praise or blame, depending on the context. **1971** *Black World* Apr 56 **Philadelphia PA,** Who the hell you think, nigger? **1980** [see **B1d** below]. **1986** Pederson *LAGS Concordance,* 1 inf, **cwAL,** Damn nigger—they'd say to each other; 1 inf, **swAL,** Black nigger—blacks say to each other in anger. [Both infs White] **1994** Smitherman *Black Talk* 167, "A group of Brothas was buggin out, drinkin the forty ounce, goin the nigga route," a clearly negative use of the word, meaning, Some Black males were . . acting out the loud, vulgar stereotype of a *nigga.*

c Used in a relatively neutral or affectionate sense by White speakers.

1676 [see **A** above]. **1700** in 1879 *MA Hist. Soc. Coll.* 5th ser 6.19, [Footnote:] 'Tis to be feared, we have no other kind of Title to our *Nigers.* **1901** Harben *Westerfelt* 7 **nGA,** Mis' Simpkins was at Lithicum's when a nigger fetched the note. **1904** *DN* 2.419 **nwAR,** *Nigger. . .* Negro. The universal word in Arkansas, whether respect is intended or not. "I got a nigger to beat my carpets." **1933** Rawlings *South Moon* 61 **nFL,** The boy frowned blackly. "That ain't no tale. Tell me about niggers." The subject fascinated the child, for there was only one negro in the scrub, an ex-slave to whom his master had given land in Florida. The negro kept to himself in an old house. "Niggers," Lantry said, "is borned male and female, like squirrels and dogs and white folks. Niggers is all shade o' black and brown and yaller." **1936** [see **B1a** above]. **1958** Humphrey *Home from the Hill* 7 **neTX,** Now tell us, ma'am, where we might find a couple of niggers that'd like to make a dollar. **c1960** *Wilson Coll.* **csKY,** *Negro* is [ˈnɪgə] to most people, with no especially bad connotation. **1962** Atwood *Vocab. TX* 73, *Negro . .* is felt by most to be polite rather than neutral. *Nigger . .* is sometimes said to be neutral, but more often to be derogatory. **1966** [see **B1a** above]. **1966** *DARE* Tape **AL3,** He hired a nigger-preacher—something that you wouldn't think back then, but he was a jam-up good preacher—he was hard of hearing—he was very deaf, and he was kind of an old nigger, but he was a jam-up good carpenter, and he contracted to build that house for my daddy. **1967** Fetterman *Stinking Creek* 75 **seKY,** The Browns never had slaves. That was a hateful thing to own a nigger just like he was livestock. **1970** Tarpley *Blinky* 261 **neTX,** For more than half of the informants, the everyday word for a black person is *nigger. . . Nigger* is used most often by men, in non-city communities, and by a slightly higher percentage of members of the lowest educational division. . . Several informants say emphatically, "I call them *niggers,* 'cause that's what they really are." *Ibid* 263, Two non-rural informants in the two lowest educational groups say that *nigger* is the only word they ever use. **1981** Palmer *Deep Blues* 55 **MS,** Now in many cases, a nigger— and I don't mean anything by that, it's just what they called themselves—had his own eighty acres or hundred and twenty acres. **1986** [see **B1a** above].

d Used in a neutral or favorable sense by Black speakers.

1885 Twain *Huck. Finn* 72 **MO** [Black], Dey wuz a nigger name' Bob, dat had ketched a wood-flat. **1899** Chesnutt *Conjure Woman* 12 **csNC** [Black], Ef you . . doan' min' lis'nin' ter a ole nigger run on a minute er two. **a1930** in 1991 Hughes–Hurston *Mule Bone* 32 **cFL** [Black], "See whut you Meth'dis' niggahs will do?" asked Brazzle, a true Baptist. **c1937** in 1970 Yetman *Voices* 257 **GA** [Black], A nigger by name o' Enoch Golden married us. He was what we called a "double-headed nigger"—he could read and write, and he knowed so much. On his dyin' bed he said he been de death o' many a nigger 'cause he taught so many to read and write. **1939** in 1944 *AmSp* 19.166, It [=*nigger*] is a common expression among the ordinary Negroes and is frequently used in conversation between them. It carries no odium or sting when used by themselves, but they object keenly to whites using it because it conveys the spirit of hate, discrimination and prejudice. **1949** [see **B1b** above]. **1959** Lomax *Rainbow Sign* 76 **AL** [Black], The New World was where all the Negroes hang out—stores and cafés, you know, and barbershops, run by Negroes. They just call it a real *nigger* street. **1963** Wright *Lawd Today* 120 **Chicago IL** [Black], It was all right for one Negro to call another Negro "nigger"; but when in front of white folks one ought to be careful. *And that word ain't the same when a white man uses it. There's something he puts in it that ain't right.* **1970** Major *Dict. Afro-Amer. Slang* 85, *Nigger . .* used by black people among themselves, it is a racial term with undertones of warmth and good will—reflecting, aside from the irony, a tragicomic sensibility that is aware of black history. **1970** *DARE* (Qu. Z12, *Nicknames and joking words meaning 'a small child': "He's a healthy little _____."*) Inf **TN46,** Nigger; (Qu. AA3, *Nicknames or affectionate names for a sweetheart*) Inf **TN46,** My nigger; (Qu. AA15c, *. . Joking ways . . of saying that a woman is getting married. . . "She _____."*) Inf **TN46,** Got that nigger; (Qu.

AA23, *Joking names that a woman may use to refer to her husband: "It's time to go and get supper for my _____."*) Inf **TN46,** Nigger; (Qu. II1, *. . A close friend . . "He's my _____."*) Inf **NY239,** Nigger; (Qu. II10b, *Asking directions of somebody on the street when you don't know his name—what you'd say to a man: "Say, _____, how far is it to the next town?"*) Inf **FL48,** Nigger. **1971** Mitchell *Blow My Blues Away* 170 **nwMS** [Black], Mr. Walter [a white man] knocked that nigger just as flat, and that nigger knocked Mr. Walter just as flat. And they called it off right there. And that's the onliest fair fight I've seed. **1980** Folb *Runnin' Down* 37 **Los Angeles CA** [Black], "Nigger" can be a derogatory label, a neutral label, or a positive label—a term of endearment—when used by black people. Black comedian Dick Gregory once stated that he resented being called 'nigger' by whites because they 'didn't say it right.' What he meant is that the way whites used the word 'nigger' could not have a neutral or positive meaning as it can when blacks use it. **1986** Pederson *LAGS Concordance,* 1 inf, **nwAL,** Nigger—they call themselves that; 1 inf, **csAR,** Nigger—what blacks call one another; 1 inf, **cAR,** Nigger—used among friends; 1 inf, **seFL,** Nigger—blacks call each other; 1 inf, **seFL,** Nigger—neutral; jocular; from black to black; 1 inf, **nwLA,** Nigger—blacks used in joking; 1 inf, **cnMS,** They called each other niggers; 1 inf, **neMS,** Nigger—not derogatory if used black to black; 1 inf, **neMS,** Nigger—blacks use it in joking; 1 inf, **seMS,** Move out of the way nigger—parent to a child; 1 inf, **cnTN,** Nigger—Blacks don't say except joking; 1 inf, **swTN,** Nigger—derogatory or joking to each other; 1 inf, **cTX,** Nigger—among friends; said of himself; 1 inf, **csTX,** Nigger—insult; not when blacks use; a password; 1 inf, **cTX,** Nigger—use as a password among selves; 1 inf, **cTX,** Nigger—older blacks call each other. [13 of 16 infs Black] *Ibid* [see **B1a** above]. **1987** Rose *I Remember Jazz* 104 [Black], "You see that car, Honey?" she asked. "That niggah just gave me that car. . . That niggah gave me all those things. Now, *tonight,* after the show is over, where do you think that niggah's goin'? He's comin' right back here where he goes every night and," indicating the bedroom with her thumb, "gets into bed next to this niggah," indicating herself. **1994** Smitherman *Black Talk* 167, *Nigga*—Used with a variety of meanings, ranging from positive to negative to neutral. . . "She my main nigga," that is, She is my close friend. . . "That party was live; it was wall-to-wall niggas there," a generic, neutral use of the word, meaning simply that many African Americans were present.

e Used with a given name as an identifier; see quots.

1965 Durham–Jones *Negro Cowboys* 109, The most successful cowboys were those who stuck to the cattle business, staying out of saloon brawls and range wars. One of these was "Nigger Frank," who spent a lifetime wrangling horses for John Chisum. **1967** Fetterman *Stinking Creek* 75 **seKY,** They was slaves in Knox county. I knowed one—went by the name of Nigger Ned. **1973** McCarthy *Child of God* 53 **TN,** After a day or two Ballard fell into talking with him. He said: What's your name? John, said the nigger. Nigger John. **1993** *DARE* File **swID, seOR** (as of 1930s), I've heard livestock men speak in admiration of a black cowboy and noted rider in the Jordan Valley country simply as "Nigger Bill." Around New Plymouth there was another respected rider . . called "Nigger Abe." And there was a black settler in the hills . . who raised and sold good horses. He was simply "Nigger Ned." All of this is hard to accommodate, so sensitive have we become to the negative aspects of such language.

2 Transf:

a Used of any other non-White person, esp an American Indian.

1843 (1846) Haliburton *Attaché* (1st ser) 180 **NEng,** "Well, what's to prevent your boys gettin' those prizes, if colonists was made Christians of, instead of outlawed . . heathen Indgean niggers, as they be." **1848** (1855) Ruxton *Life Far West* 15 **Rocky Mts,** He throwed a Pueblo as had on poor Bent's shirt. I guess he tickled that niggur's hump-ribs. **1881** Greene *Cape Cod Folks* 146 **eMA,** The Indians rather set themselves up above the benighted Wallencampers, . . while they, in turn, made derisive allusions to the "Nigger-camp" minister. **1901** *N. Amer. Rev.* 172.174, Those 'niggers' [=Filipinos] spare their wounded, and the Americans massacre theirs! **1919** Kyne *Capt. Scraggs* 119 **CA,** On the island o' Aranuka, right under the Hakatuea volcano. There was some strappin' big buck native niggers there that would fetch $300 a head.

b Used of any person perceived as uncouth, immoral, or threatening, regardless of skin color. *esp freq among Black speakers; derog*

1839 (1840) Simms *Border Beagles* 2.85 **MS,** They[=White officers of justice]'re afraid of me [=a White man], the niggers. **1942** Hurston *Dust Tracks* 49 **FL,** "Don't be a nigger," he would say to me over and over. "Niggers lie and lie! . . People with guts don't lie." [Footnote to nigger:] The word Nigger used in this sense does not mean race. It means a weak, contemptible person of any race. **1971** Mitchell *Blow My Blues Away* 141 **nwMS** [Black], Like a person say, "You're a nigger." That don't mean nothing. Anybody can be a nigger. A nigger is just a slander word. Anybody, it don't make no difference what nationality and color you is, any-body can be a nigger. We have a lot of Negroes and we have some niggers. **1986** Pederson *LAGS Concordance,* 1 inf, **cnFL,** You don't have to be black to be a nigger; 1 inf, **nwFL,** Nigger = dirty; [a] low person of any race; pejorative; 1 inf, **cAL,** Nigger—a bad person; 1 inf, **cAL,** Nigger—can be of any race; 1 inf, **cAL,** Nigger—derogatory, but not racial; 1 inf, **cAL,** Color don't make a cracker, color don't make a nigger; 1 inf, **swGA,** Nigger—of a bad person, not necessarily a Negro; 1 inf, **swGA,** I don't care how white you is; I don't care how black you is or how yellow you is; any low-down, dirty person is a nigger; 1 inf, **cMS,** Nigger—of whites too; 1 inf, **cMS,** Nigger—any color; general pejorative; low-acting; 1 inf, **cMS,** Nigger—derogatory for anyone who is "low-down"; 1 inf, **cMS,** Nigger—of any race; silly, drunk conduct; 1 inf, **csMS,** Anybody can be a nigger; 1 inf, **swMS,** Them niggers—speaking of the "hillbillies"; 1 inf, **ceTX,** [I'm] scared of them niggers—of Mexicans; 1 inf, **ceTX,** Nigger—means a dirty person. [15 of 16 infs Black]

3 in combs *big* (or *head, lead*) *nigger:* An important, often self-important, person.

1942 Hurston *Dust Tracks* 224 **FL,** The humble Negro has a built-up antagonism to the "Big Nigger." . . He resents any lines between himself and the wealthy and the educated of his own race. **1966–70** *DARE* (Qu. GG19b, *When you can see from the way a person acts that he's feeling important or independent: "He seems to think he's _____."*) Inf **SC26,** The big nigger; (Qu. HH17, *A person who tries to appear important, or who tries to lay down the law in his community: "He'd like to be the _____ around here."*) Infs **MO29, OR1, TX37, 68,** Head nigger; **OH42,** Lead nigger; (Qu. HH43b, *The assistant to the top person in charge of a group of workmen*) Inf **NY241,** Head nigger in charge. **1975** King *S. Ladies & Gentlemen* 155, Anyone who lived in the segregated South knows who Big Nigger was. He was usually a preacher—and usually light-skinned—to whom the white pillars of the town turned whenever there was trouble. **1986** Pederson *LAGS Concordance,* 1 inf, **cAL,** The big nigger's car—the main man's car; 1 inf, **seAL,** That's Big Nigger's car—the patriarch.

4 attrib: Cheap; inferior; makeshift. Cf **Mexican B1, nigger v, nigger bath,** ~ **liquor,** ~ **pole,** ~ **rig,** ~ **runner**

1942 Berrey–Van den Bark *Amer. Slang* 784.6 [Railroad slang], *Tip. . . nigger tip,* any tip of an odd amount between fifteen and fifty cents. **1967** *DARE* (Qu. KK63, *To do a clumsy or hurried job of repairing something*) Inf **LA14,** Nigger work. **1967** *DARE* FW Addit **LA14,** *Nigger fixings*—careless or hasty work. Common. **1972** TN Folk Lore Soc. *Bulletin* 38.36, In some parts of the deep South, whites call some forbidden foods "nigger foods," meaning that these substances are fit only for blacks. **1988** *DARE* File **TX** (as of c1980), I heard the phrase "nigger brick" from a Houston heart surgeon who was showing me an old post office, the exterior of which was finished in tin painted to look like brick.

5 also *nig:* Used as a name for a black animal.

1858 (1966) Boller *MO Fur Trader* 161, It occurred to me that as the black ox was feeding near the "dead people" he might have gone down into the bottom—however I crept on, and getting nearer found that . . it *was* Nigger! [**1944** Adams *Western Words* 104, *Nigger horse*—One of black color.] **1967** Williams *Greenbones* 20 **GA** (as of c1910), [His mother slapped the black horse's neck. . . His father was running a hand down the red horse's neck.] *Ibid* 84, Nig and Apple cavorted as heavily as spring colts, throwing up their ragged old muzzles. **1968** *DARE* (Qu. K39, . . *Names . . for horses according to their colors*) Inf **UT4,** Black or nig; [**AL38,** Niggernose—black nose]. **1993** *DARE* File **swID, seOR,** In an earlier time it would appear that among many folk the word "nigger" meant only "black." I don't know how many horses I've driven and ridden that carried that word as a name simply because they were black. Often it was shortened to "Nig." It was also a popular name for dogs. **1994** *Ibid* **sNV,** When my grandfather and grandmother were building Boulder Dam . . on the Colorado River, they had a camp mascot. It was a jet black dog . . named "Nigger."

6 also *nigger engine:* A steam engine used to operate a capstan, esp on a riverboat. Cf **niggerhead 9**

1867 in 1932 *Frontier & Midland* 12.166, The boat . . struck the bar, they then began to work with the spars and nigger, and at two o'clock we got off. **1872** (1876) Knight *Amer. Mech. Dict.* 2.1526, *Nigger.* (Steam-engine.) A steam-engine employed in hoisting; especially on

shipboard and on the Western and Southern rivers. **1878** Beadle *Western Wilds* 378, Then oaths, spars, "nigger-engine" and all the other available machinery were set in operation. **1882** *Harper's New Mth. Mag.* 64.175, One of the 'nigger' engines [on a steamboat] is suddenly called into service to tighten a two-inch rope, or wind up a discarded cable. **1901** in 1952 Bissell *Monongahela* 181, There will be on the boat eight nigger engines and two doctors and much other machinery. **1903** *DN* 2.322 **seMO,** *Nigger.* . . A steam capstan used on river boats. **1923** *DN* 5.244 **LA,** *Nigger.* . . In logging, the engine that runs the capstan.

7 In logging: a device for lifting, turning, and adjusting logs in a sawmill.

1890 *Century Dict.* 3990, *Nigger.* . . A strong iron-bound timber with sharp teeth or spikes protruding from its front face, forming part of the machinery of a sawmill, and used in canting logs. **1906** *DN* 3.148 **nwAR,** *Nigger.* . . A mechanical contrivance in sawmills for turning and adjusting logs that are being sawed. **1909** *DN* 3.375 **eAL, wGA,** *Steamnigger.* . . A mechanical contrivance in saw-mills for turning logs that are being sawed. Also called simply *nigger.* **1941** Writers' Program *Guide WI* 351 **cWI,** A cradle-shaped "winch" releases the logs one at a time; two spiked arms called the "nigger" hoist them upon the carriage and roll them into the grip of the sharp-toothed, rachet-operated iron jaws known as "dogs." **1950** *Western Folkl.* 9.122 **nwOR** [Sawmill workers' speech], *Nigger.* Machinery used to turn logs on a carriage. **1969** Sorden *Lumberjack Lingo* 122 **NEng, Gt Lakes,** *Steam nigger*—The mechanism in the sawmill operated by the head sawyer, that turned the log for sawing.

8 See quot.

1948 *PADS* 9.40 **OK,** *Nigger.* . . A detachable length of heavy pipe made and sold as part of a large wrench; used in order to give added length and leverage to the wrench, thus allowing one to exert more pressure on the grip of the wrench.

9 See quot. Cf **nigger v 1**

1909 *DN* 3.414 **nME,** *Nigger.* . . A blackened brand [*DARE* Ed: =burnt stick].

10 =**cat and mouse 2.**

1905 *DN* 3.88 **nwAR,** *Nigger.* . . Boys' name of a game, identical with 'cat and mouse.'

11 in phrr *sweat like a nigger (at election)* and varr: To sweat profusely. **scattered, but chiefly Midl, Gulf States, TX** See Map Cf *sweat like a mule* (at **mule** n[1] **6**), *sweat like a pig* (at **pig**)

1906 *DN* 3.160 **nwAR,** *Sweat worse than a nigger at election.* . . To sweat copiously. **1939** *AmSp* 14.265 **IN,** Expressions relating to work are . . 'sweating like a nigger at election.' **1946** *PADS* 6.42 **eNC** (as of 1900–10), *Sweating like a Nigger going to 'lection.* (To be tired, sweaty, and out of breath.) . . Occasional. **1952** Brown *NC Folkl.* 1.450, Sweating like a Negro going to the 'lection. . . Sweating like a nigger at election. **1954** *Harder Coll.* **cwTN,** Sweat lak a nigger at a 'lection. **1956** McAtee *Some Dialect NC* 44, Sweating like a nigger going to election. **1965–70** *DARE* (Qu. X56b, *Expressions about sweating very heavily*) 50 Infs, **chiefly Midl, Gulf States,** Sweat (*or* sweating) like a nigger; 19 Infs, **esp Midl, TX,** Sweat (*or* sweating, sweats) like a nigger at (e)lection; **KY8, NC9, 22, PA14, 25, 175, 202, 205, 209, 214,** Sweat (*or* sweating, sweats) like (a) nigger going to (e)lection; **MD21, NJ67, OK20, TX13,** Sweat (*or* sweating) like a nigger on election day; **IN9, 45, KY70,** Sweat like a nigger at the election; **MS16, MO3,** Sweat (*or* sweating) like a nigger to election; **IL96, TN42,** (Sweat) like a nigger

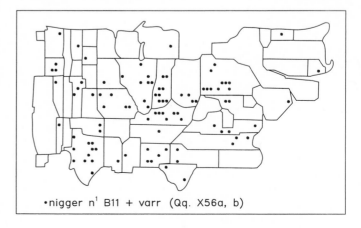

•nigger n[1] B11 + varr (Qq. X56a, b)

in church; **AL**43, Like a nigger; **MO**29, Sweat like a nigger at a county election; **IL**126, Sweating like a nigger at an election; **AL**22, Sweating like niggers going to 'lection; **TN**35, Sweating worse'n a nigger; **FL**22, Sweats like a nigger trying to tell the truth; (Qu. X56a) Inf **TX**95, Sweat like a nigger at election. **1967** *DARE* FW Addit **cMO**, Sweating like a nigger at an election; **cnTX**, Sweating like a nigger at an election—sweating very heavily. **1970** Tarpley *Blinky* 276 **neTX**, [He] sweated like a nigger preacher at election [1 of 200 infs]. **1986** Pederson *LAGS Concordance*, 1 inf, **seGA**, I sweat like [a] nigger at a county election; 1 inf, **neAL**, Sweating like a nigger.
12 See **nigger duck 1.**

nigger v

1 also with *off:* To divide (a log) into shorter lengths by burning it at the desired intervals; to divide a log in this way; hence vbl n *niggering (off).* **esp NEast, N Cent**

  1833 Smith *Life Jack Downing* 22 **ME**, He laid sticks across the large logs . . and *niggered* them off with fire. **1843** (1916) Hall *New Purchase* 204 **IN**, This is the niggering-off. . . A small space is hacked into the upper side of the trunk, and in that for awhile is maintained a fire fed with dry chips and brush; then at right angles, with the prostrate timber is laid in the fire a stick of some green wood, dry fuel being added at intervals, till the incumbent stick, sinking deeper and deeper into the burning spot, in no very long time . . divides or niggers the trunk asunder. *Ibid* 207, Very soon then . . were assembled about half a dozen men . . some with remnants of burning niggering sticks. **1887** Kirkland *Zury* 538 **IL**, Nigger. . . To burn logs into lengths. **1888** (1900) Sears *Woodcraft* 49 **Upstate NY**, It was easier to lay them on the fire and "nigger" them in two than to cut them shorter with light hatchets. **1903** *DN* 2.322 **seMO**, Nigger off. . . To burn logs in two by building small fires on them. **1909** *DN* 3.414 **nME**, Nigger. . . To burn a log off by piling brands crosswise of it. **1912** *DN* 3.584 **wIN**, Nigger (a log) off. . . To put one log across another at right angles and burn them in two at the cross. After this is done, the four parts are easily rolled together and burned. **1925** *Old-Time New Engl.* 15.4.172 **swPA**, Until about 1890, [they] sometimes bi-sected freshly felled trees . . by "niggering" them, as they called it; namely, by burning downward upon them, with fires carefully watched, spaced and restricted from spreading by mud and water.

2 also with *over, up:* To do, make, or repair (something) in a careless, haphazard, or tasteless manner; to mess (something) up. Cf **nigger rig**

  1967 *DARE* (Qu. W29, . . *Expressions . . for things that are sewn carelessly . . "They're _____."*) Inf **TX**35, Niggered up; (Qu. Y37, *To make a place untidy or disorderly: "I wish they wouldn't _____ the room so."*) Inf **LA**2, Nigger it up; (Qu. HH30) Inf **SC**26, Something that is gaudy or overdone may be occasionally said to be niggered up: "That was a nice car until he niggered it up"; (Qu. KK49, *When you don't have the time or ambition to do something thoroughly: "I'm not going to give the place a real cleaning, I'll just _____."*) Inf **TX**37, Nigger over it; (Qu. KK63, *To do a clumsy or hurried job of repairing something: "It will never last—he just _____."*) Inf **TX**11, Niggered it. **1986** Pederson *LAGS Concordance*, 1 inf, **cwLA**, Let's don't nigger it up—said to black workers.

3 also with *around:* To idle, laze around.

  1966–68 *DARE* (Qu. A10, . . *Doing little unimportant things: . . "What are you doing?" . . "Nothing in particular—I'm just _____."*) Inf **MS**16, Niggering around; (Qu. X43b, *If you sleep later than usual one day on purpose . . "I _____."*) Inf **PA**142, Niggered.

nigger n[2], hence adv *niggerly* [Folk-etyms for *niggard(ly)*; cf *EDD* nigger sb.[1]]

  1895 *DN* 1.398 **cNY**, Nigger: for niggard. **1909** *DN* 3.352 **eAL, wGA**, Niggerly. . . Niggardly. **1967** *DARE* (Qu. U36b, . . *A person who saves in a mean way or is greedy in money matters: "She certainly is _____."*) Inf **IA**7, Niggerly. [**1968** *DARE* FW Addit **swGA**, A middle-aged man (probably high school education or some high school) . . defined this [=['nɪgɚdlɪ]] as "cheap; tight; sorry." Says it comes from the word "nigger."]

nigger around See **nigger** v **3**

nigger baby n

1 A small, dark-colored candy in the shape of a baby. **scattered, but chiefly N Midl, seNY** See Map Also called **colored baby** Cf **niggerhead 7**

  1940 Mencken *Happy Days* 208 **Baltimore MD**, He much preferred

the black licorice nigger-babies sold by Old Man Kunker in Baltimore street, and commonly went about with his face mired by their exudations. **1957** *Sat. Eve. Post Letters* **NH** (as of c1895), Nigger babies—licorice dolls about ¾" long; **NY** (as of c1920), We call the tiny chocolate dolls "Nigger Babies." **1963** Burroughs *Head-First* 105 **CO**, Licorice "nigger babies" also were available (ten for a penny). **1965–70** *DARE* (Qu. H82b, *Kinds of cheap candy that used to be sold years ago*) 17 Infs, **esp N Midl, seNY**, Nigger babies; **CO**27, **IA**17, **OH**93, **PA**92, Nigger babies—licorice; **KY**79, Nigger babies—Licorice, one inch high, shaped like a baby; **LA**23, Nigger babies—licorice candy in oval shapes with cameo stamp; **LA**43, Nigger babies—shaped like a baby, made of licorice; **DE**2, Nigger babies—chocolate and shaped like little babies; **NY**34, Nigger babies—chocolate paste; **NY**53, Nigger babies—chocolate-covered baby faces; **NY**75, Nigger babies—these were chocolate; they used to have a penny in some of them; (Qu. H82a, *Cheap candies sold especially for schoolchildren*) Infs **ID**3, **NY**41, Nigger babies; **NY**48, Nigger babies—chocolates; **CT**5, Non-integrated nigger babies. **1975** King *S. Ladies & Gentlemen* 12, Inside the bin was a mountain of little licorice candies shaped like black children. Everyone privately called them "nigger babies."

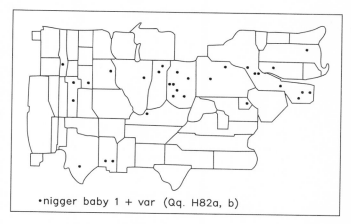

•nigger baby 1 + var (Qq. H82a, b)

2 Either of two children's games:

a A game played with a rubber ball and holes dug in the ground; a stick or stone used in the game. Cf **roly-poly**

  1901 *DN* 2.144 **FL, cNY**, Nigger-baby. . . Same as *roly-poly* [=A game played with a rubber ball and small holes dug in the ground]. **1906** *DN* 3.148 **nwAR**, Nigger-baby. . . A ball game, usually played with a rubber ball. If a player fails to hit the ball when thrown to him he must put a stick *(nigger-baby)* into the hole, which he guards. **1957** *Sat. Eve. Post Letters* **VA**, Nigger babies—Each person had a hole in the ground. The person "it" would roll a ball and try to get it in one of the holes. The person owning the hole would run to it and take out the ball and try to hit someone with all others having run as far as they could until the person taking the ball from the hole called halt. When a person was hit with the ball a stone or 'nigger baby' was placed in his hole. If the thrower missed he received a nigger baby. The one with the most nigger babies lost.

b also *nigger baby stop:* A children's game in which a player is hit with a rubber ball; a call in the game; see quots. Cf **spud**

  1957 *Sat. Eve. Post Letters* **WA**, "Nigger baby"—All participants used to lag at a target with marbles. The one farthest away had to stand facing a wall, bend over and present his posterior to one throw each, of a hard rubber ball, by each of the participants. **1968** *DARE* (Qu. EE33, . . *Outdoor games . . that children play*) Inf **LA**23, Nigger baby is called spud now. Everybody in a circle has a number; a ball is bounced and the one whose number is called catches it. If you miss three times in a row, they stand you against something and throw the ball at you; **LA**43, Nigger baby—take a ball; everybody has a number. You call a number and the person catches the ball. When somebody yells "Nigger baby," everybody stops and somebody gets hit with the ball. When one person is hit three times they stand him against the wall and everybody throws at him; **PA**76, Nigger baby stop—ball thrown in air, a number called. Player with that number must catch it. He then calls "Nigger baby stop" and the other players must stop. The one who caught the ball can take steps and throw the ball at the closest other player. If hit, one was retired from game. The last one left is winner; **PA**94, Nigger baby—ball thrown in air; a number called. Player with that number must catch it. He then calls "Nigger baby stop" and the other players must stop. The one who caught the ball can take three steps and throw the ball at the closest other player. If hit, one was retired from game. The last one left is winner. **1968** *DARE* Tape **LA**46, Nigger baby—it's played with a group of people. You assign a number to each person . . and you call a number while the ball's in the air. Now if the person catches the ball before it hits the ground, they can throw the ball up and call another number. Once the ball hits the ground, the number called to the person who catches the ball, he hollers "nigger baby, stop!" and everybody has to stop.

3 in phr *rain nigger babies* and varr: To rain heavily. **chiefly west of Appalachians** See Map

1965–70 *DARE* (Qu. B26, *When it's raining very heavily . . "It's raining _____."*) 30 Infs, **chiefly west of Appalachians,** Pitchforks and (little) nigger babies; 11 Infs, **scattered, but esp Sth, S Midl,** (Down) nigger babies; **NE**7, **PA**131, **WA**12, Cats and dogs and (little) nigger babies; **IL**50, Cats, dogs, and nigger babies; **MI**98, Nigger babies and pitchforks; **AZ**1, **VA**18, Tomcats (*or* puppy dogs) and nigger babies; (Qu. B25, *. . Joking names . . for a very heavy rain. . . "It's . . _____."*) Inf **AR**47, Raining pitchforks and nigger babies. **1986** Pederson *LAGS Concordance* (Heavy rain) 1 inf, **cAL,** Raining nigger babies; 2 infs, **ceMS, ceTX,** Raining pitchfork(s) and nigger babies.

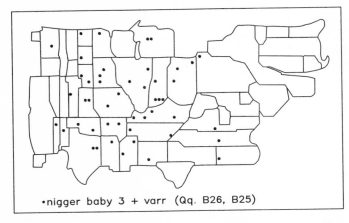

•nigger baby 3 + varr (Qq. B26, B25)

4 pl: A **blue-eyed grass 1** (here: *Sisyrinchium bellum*). [See quots 1897, 1915]

1897 Parsons *Wild Flowers CA* 284, Blue-Eyed Grass . . *Sisyrinchium bellum*. . . Owing to the quaint manner in which its petals kink up when they fade, these blossoms are called "nigger-babies" by the children. **1901** Jepson *Flora CA* 129, *S[isyrinchium] bellum. . . Blue-eyed Grass. Nigger-babies. . .* Very common throughout California. Mar.–Apr. **1915** (1926) Armstrong-Thornber *Western Wild Flowers* 70, Blue-Eyed Grass—*Sisyrinchium bellum*. . . The anthers are arrow-shaped, the style short, with three very small stigmas, and the small, oddly-shaped, little capsule is dark-brown when ripe, and perhaps suggested one of the common names, Nigger-babies. **1961** Thomas *Flora Santa Cruz* 127 **cwCA,** *S[isyrinchium] bellum* . . Nigger Babies, California Blue-eyed Grass.

5 also pl: A **sanicle** (here: *Sanicula bipinnatifida*).

1898 *Jrl. Amer. Folkl.* 11.227 **CA,** *Sanicula bipinnatifida* . . nigger babies. **1968** *DARE* (Qu. S26e, *Other wildflowers not yet mentioned;* not asked in early QRs) Inf **CA**60, Nigger baby—desert—so purple it's almost black—same as purple sanicle.

6 A large **channel catfish.**

1948 Hanna–Hanna *Lake Okeechobee* 185, Millions of pounds of "nigger babies," as the channel cats of the Mississippi Valley and Gulf States are called, were shipped annually from Louisiana and other centers. *Ibid* 186, Large channel cat or "nigger babies," weighing from five to thirty pounds and rarely as much as forty and fifty pounds. **1966** *DARE* (Qu. P1, *. . Kinds of freshwater fish . . caught around here . . good to eat)* Inf **FL**27, Nigger baby—large catfish, 60 pounds. **1973** *DARE* File **cwFL,** In Bartow . . a very large catfish, one 40 pounds or over, is called a nigger baby.

nigger baby stop See **nigger baby 2b**

nigger ball n

c1970 Wiersma *Marbles Terms, Nigger balls*—black marbles.

nigger bass n

Perh a **black bass 1.**

1965 *DARE* (Qu. P1, *. . Kinds of freshwater fish . . caught around here . . good to eat)* Inf **OK**11, Nigger bass.

nigger bath n Cf **bitch bath, cat ~, French dry clean**

1953 *AmSp* 28.145 **cFL,** A *nigger bath* is a talcum-powder bath; a *bitch bath* requires talcum powder, deodorant, and perfume.

niggerbelly n

=flathead catfish 1.

1908 Forbes-Richardson *Fishes of IL* 193, It [=*Leptops olivaris*] is perhaps best known to the fishermen of the Mississippi River as the "Morgan cat," and less often referred to as the "cushawn." . . Other local names are mud-cat, flat-belly, and nigger-belly. **1947** Dalrymple *Panfish* 291, *Pilodictis olivaris* . . is a very large fish inhabiting the muddy bottoms of large, deep rivers, particularly in the Mississippi system. . . Many are the colloquial names for it—Yellow Cat, Mud-Cat, Morgan Cat, Shovelhead Cat, Flat-belly, Nigger-belly, Goujon.

nigger black duck See **nigger duck 1**

nigger boy n [See quot 1932]

=limpkin.

1932 Howell *FL Bird Life* 201, The Limpkin rises from the marsh with a quick spring. . . The note of the bird is very characteristic—a loud, mournful wail suggesting the cry of a child. . . This explains the origin of the names "Crying Bird" and "Nigger Boy." **1946** Hausman *Eastern Birds* 233, Nigger Boy. . . *Notes*—Harsh, weird, mournful wailing cries, uttered both by day and by night, often sounding like the crying of a human voice. **1954** Sprunt *FL Bird Life* 138, *Limpkin. . . Local Names:* Nigger boy; Crying Bird.

nigger brand n

A sore on a horse's back caused by an ill-fitting saddle or by over-riding; hence adj *nigger branded.*

1936 Adams *Cowboy Lingo* 87, To ride a horse until his back became sore was to 'beefsteak' or 'gimlet' him, and such sores were called 'nigger brands.' **1961** Adams *Old-Time Cowhand* 113, Some saddles don't fit the hoss they're on, and cause sores . . and the hoss . . is said to be "nigger branded."

nigger catcher n

1936 Adams *Cowboy Lingo* 46, The small slotted leather flap on one or both sides of the saddle, usually at the base of the fork or cantle, or both, were called 'nigger catchers.' The purpose of these was to hold the long free end of the latigo through the slit when cinched up.

nigger chaser n

1 A type of firework that scoots along the ground. Cf **chaser 2, coon chaser, devil ~**

1883 (1958) Peck *Peck's Bad Boy & Pa* 36 **Milwaukee WI,** I had a lot of rockets and Roman candles, and six pin-wheels, and a lot of nigger chasers. . . A nigger chaser got after Ma and treed her on top of the sofa, and another one took after a girl that Ma had invited to dinner. **1894** Frederic *Marsena* 152 **nNY,** Their pockets literally bulging now with all sorts of portentous engines of noise and racket . . long, slim, vicious-looking "nigger-chasers." **1959** *IN Mag. Hist.* 55.229 (as of c1920), There I was with my puny packets of Chinese squibs compared with the neighbors' younguns' wealth of big Roman candles, pinwheels, nigger chasers, giant crackers, and the breath-taking splendor of sky-rockets. **1965–70** *DARE* (Qu. FF28, *. . Kinds of fireworks;* not asked in early QRs) 63 Infs, **scattered,** Nigger chasers; (Qu. FF14, *. . Kinds of firecrackers)* 10 Infs, **esp Sth, S Midl,** Nigger chasers; (Qu. FF15) Inf **CT**27, Nigger chaser. **1967** *DARE* FW Addit **cwLA,** *Nigger chaser*—Kind of fireworks that whizzes along the ground, then explodes. (The boys selling fireworks would not name this until Negroes were out of earshot. Until then they called it by its trade name, whistling chaser).

2 See **nigger-shooter.**

nigger choker See **nigger killer 1**

nigger chub n Also *negro chub* [See quot 1949]

=cutlips minnow.

1884 Goode *Fisheries U.S.* 1.618 **PA, MD,** The "Cut-lips," "Day Chub," or "Nigger Chub," has but a narrow distribution, being found in abundance only in the basin of the Susquehanna. It reaches a length of six or eight inches, and has no economic importance. **1896** U.S. Natl.

Museum *Bulletin* 47.327, *Exoglossum maxillingua* . . Cut-lips; *Nigger chub.* . . Color olivaceous, smoky or dark above. **1946** LaMonte *N. Amer. Game Fishes* 161, Cutlip Minnow—*Exoglossum maxillingua* . . Negro Chub. **1949** Palmer *Nat. Hist.* 444, Cutlips Minnow, Nigger Chub. *Exoglossum maxillingua* . . Breeding male dark to almost black and longer than female.

nigger coffee See **negro coffee**

nigger daisy n
=**black-eyed Susan 2.**
    1892 *Jrl. Amer. Folkl.* 5.98 **eMA,** *Rudbeckia hirta* . . nigger daisy. **1940** Clute *Amer. Plant Names* 86, *R[udbeckia] hirta* . . nigger-daisy. **1968** *DARE* (Qu. S7, *A kind of daisy, bright yellow with a dark center, that grows along roadsides in late summer*) Inf **IN48,** Nigger daisies.

nigger day n
1 =**Emancipation (Proclamation) Day.**
    1967 *DARE* (Qu. FF16, . . *Local contests or celebrations*) Inf **AR55,** Niggers used to have Emancipation Day when they all wore yellow. We called it "Nigger Day"; **TX16,** Nigger Day—or the 'Teenth of June. Negroes celebrate their emancipation day—19th of June—by getting all dressed up, drinking, and eating watermelons. **1967** *DARE* FW Addit **seTX,** June the 'teenth called nigger day by whites. 19th of June. Big celebration by Galveston Negro population. **1970** *Ibid* **KY92,** On August 8, Blacks in this area celebrate what they call their Independence Day. It is the Black equivalent to July 4th. It relates to the Emancipation Proclamation. The news was slow getting around, and evidently slaves in this area received the news on August 8. The holiday has over the years lost its historical significance and is now a Homecoming. . . The celebration has been called derogatorily by Whites "Nigger Day."
2 Saturday. Cf **nigger night**
    [**1889** Edwards *Runaways* 232 **GA,** Never before had Tom known of a church meeting on Saturday afternoon. It was the time universally claimed by the negroes for town shopping or loafing.] **1931** *AmSp* 7.51 **Sth, SW** [Lumberjack lingo], Almost every camp in the South has a negro section, usually off to one side of the main camp. . . Saturday night is "nigger day." **1966** *PADS* 46.27 **cnAR** (as of 1952), *Nigger day.* . . Saturday. The name comes from the type of crowd seen on the streets of the town. On other days of the week Negroes would be working at their jobs and not be free to do their shopping.

nigger dick n Also *nigger prick*
=**cutlips minnow.**
    1896 U.S. Natl. Museum *Bulletin* 47.327, *Exoglossum maxillingua* . . Cut-lips; *Nigger chub; Nigger Dick.* . . Color olivaceous, smoky or dark above. **1945** McAtee *Nomina Abitera* 20, Cut-lips Minnow *(Exoglossum maxillingua)*—Nigger-dick. . . The more literal form "nigger-prick" is reported to me . . as heard in the District of Columbia.

nigger duck n [From the color]
1 also *nigger (black duck):* A **black duck 1** (here: *Anas rubripes*).
    1876 *Fur, Fin, & Feather* Sep. 101/2 *(DA),* The gray-duck, shell-drake and teal . . are obliged to tolerate in their society that . . stupid, tough, shot-resisting thing, which is vulgarly called 'nigger duck.' **1917** *Wilson Bulletin* 29.2.77 **DE,** *Anas rubripes.* . . The black-legged form is known as nigger black duck, and the other as red paddle. **1923** U.S. Dept. Ag. *Misc. Circular* 13.9 **CT, Long Is. NY,** Black Duck. . niggerduck. **1955** *AmSp* 30.180 **CT, DE, MD,** *Nigger duck* has been applied to the black duck.
2 A scoter; see quot.
    1923 U.S. Dept. Ag. *Misc. Circular* 13.27 **KY,** Scoters. . . nigger ducks. **1949** Kitchin *Birds Olympic Peninsula* 53, *White-winged Scoter.* . . Other names: Nigger-duck. [*Ibid* 54, The male scoter has a solid black plumage with pure white speculum on the wings. . . Female, dark brown with white speculum.] *Ibid,* Surf-Scoter. . . Nigger duck. . . He, too, wears black plumage. *Ibid* 55, *American Scoter.* . . Other names: Nigger-duck. . . He is black all over, showing no white feathers like the other two varieties.

nigger engine See **nigger** n[1] **B6**

nigger fever n Cf **nigger** v **3**
    1969 *DARE* (Qu. Y21, *To move about slowly and without energy*) Inf **NY209,** Nigger fever.

niggerfish n
1 also *negro fish:* =**coney** n[2] **a.**
    1734 in 1735 Royal Soc. London *Philos. Trans. for 1733–34* 38.316 **SE,** *Perca marina puncticulata.* The *Negro Fish.* **1743** Catesby *Nat. Hist. Carolina* 2.7 **SE,** *Perca marina puncticulata.* The Negro Fish. This Fish was in Shape not unlike a Pearch, . . of a dark brown Colour. . . The Mouth wide, with a single Row of sharp Teeth. **1876** U.S. Natl. Museum *Bulletin* 5.59, *Enneacentrus punctatus.* . . Nigger-fish (red variety). *Ibid* 60, The red form corresponds to *Serranus ouatalibi,* and is known as the Nigger-fish. **1933** John G. Shedd Aquarium *Guide* 97, Epinephelidae—The groupers. . . *Cephalopholis fulvus punctatus*—Coney; Niggerfish.
2 A **winter flounder** (here: *Pleuronectes americanus*).
    1887 Goode *Amer. Fishes* 321, The Flat Fish, *Pseudopleuronectes americanus,* or Common Flounder, sometimes called the "Winter Flounder". . . New York anglers call it the "Nigger Fish."

nigger fish v phr, hence vbl n *nigger fishing* **scattered, but more freq Inland Nth, West** See Map Cf **nigger pole**
To fish by any of var simple and inactive methods, esp by using a cane pole and line.
    1933 Rawlings *South Moon* 231 **FL,** "I don't mean casting. My father fishes that way. I mean, with a pole." "Oh—nigger fishin'." **1965–70** *DARE* (Qu. P17, . . *When . . people fish by lowering a line and sinker close to the bottom of the water*) 49 Infs, **scattered, but more freq Inland Nth, West,** Nigger fishing; **FL39,** Nigger fishing—with a cane pole; always get catfish this way; **MI105,** Nigger fishing—you wouldn't dare say that today; **NY93,** Just plain fishing or nigger fishing; **NY233,** Nigger fishing—bait has to be *on* bottom; (Qu. P13, . . *Ways of fishing . . besides the ordinary hook and line*) Inf **AL31,** Nigger fishing—cane pole with line out; **CO4,** Nigger fishing—bamboo pole; **MN2,** Nigger fishing—using just the line through a hole in the ice; **ND1,** Nigger fishing—using 3 poles; **NJ41,** Regular hook and line is nigger fishing; **NY93,** Nigger fishing—with pole and line; **NY205,** Nigger fishing—just twine and pin; **SD3,** Nigger fishing—cane pole; sit on bank; **TX4,** Nigger fishing—cane pole; cork float to see what's biting; **TX37,** Nigger fishing—just set your pole and wait for days. **1968** *DARE* Tape **LA16,** [Inf:] We're not lure fishermen; we haven't practiced that. [FW:] What's your tackle like? [Inf:] Just a hook and a cane pole, string. [FW:] Do you have a particular name for that kind of fishing? [Inf:] Nigger fishin'. **1969** *DARE* FW Addit **AZ,** *Nigger fishin'*—propping the fishing pole up on a forked stick and sitting back drinking beer, waiting for the bobber to bounce. Used very derogatorily—a lazy, inferior way of fishing. **c1970** Halpert *Coll.* 45 **wKY, nwTN,** Nigger-fishin' = Fishing with bait, such as a worm or dough ball. **1986** Pederson *LAGS Concordance,* 1 inf, **ceLA,** They don't nigger fish—with pole or line; 1 inf, **cwAR,** Nigger fishing—with pole and line or trotlines; 1 inf, **cwAR,** Nigger fishing—with cane poles; 1 inf, **neTX,** Nigger fishing = cane pole and a bucket of minnows; 1 inf, **seTX,** Nigger fishing—cane fishing or with a hand line; 1 inf, **nwFL,** I done nigger fishing—fishing from the bank.

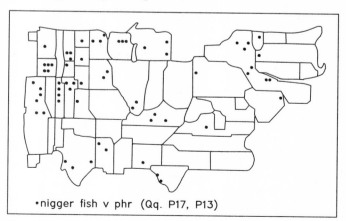

• nigger fish v phr (Qq. P17, P13)

nigger flea n
    1890 *DN* 1.65 **KY,** *Nigger-flea:* a broom-straw coated with the tallow of the tallow-candle. It was stuck on the "nigger's" flesh while he was asleep, and lighted.

nigger-flipper See **flipper** n[1] **3**

nigger gin See **nigger liquor**

niggergoose n

1 also *negro goose:* Usu =**double-crested cormorant,** but also a **Mexican cormorant** (here: *Phalacrocorax olivaceus*). [See quot 1955]

1909 Field Museum Nat. Hist. *Zool. Ser.* 9.309, *Phalacrocorax auritus* . . Double-crested Cormorant. . . Local name: Nigger Goose. **1911** *Forest & Stream* 77.174, *Phalacrocorax species.*—Cormorants go by the name of Nigger Geese at St. Vincent Island, Fla., and Chef Menteur and Mississippi Delta, La. **1916** *Times–Picayune* (New Orleans LA) 26 Mar mag sec 1/8, *Double-crested cormorant* . . "Nigger Goose." *Ibid, Florida cormorant.* . . In plumage the "nigger goose" (a name by which all of the cormorants are known locally) is greenish-black. *Ibid, Mexican cormorant.* . . This "nigger goose" has a white packet of feathers on each side of the head during the breeding season. **1939** FWP *Guide TN* 428 nwTN, More than 250 species of birds stop off here on their annual migrations. Among them are ducks, geese, water turkeys or cormorants ("nigger geese"), coots, and white herons. **1954** Sprunt *FL Bird Life* 18, Double-crested Cormorant: *Phalacrocorax auritus auritus.* . . Local Names: Nigger-Goose. . . Florida Cormorant: *Phalacrocorax auritus floridanus.* . . Local Names: Water-Turkey; Nigger Goose. **1955** *Oriole* 20.1.1, Double-Crested Cormorant.—Nigger Goose (in allusion to its black color and to its goose-like appearance, especially in flight in the V-formation so closely associated with the Canada goose). **1967–70** DARE (Qu. Q6, . . *Kinds of wild geese*) Inf **DE**1, Niggergeese—different from regular geese but you have to look close; **NY**47, Niggergeese—big, black geese; (Qu. Q10, . . *Water birds and marsh birds*) Inf **IL**14, Niggergeese—black as coal and not worth a damn; **VA**52A, Niggergeese—cormorant, probably double-crested cormorant; **VA**79, Niggergeese. [DARE Ed: Some of these Infs may refer instead to **2** below.] **1969** DARE FW Addit Hatteras Is. NC, ['nɪgrə] goose—local name for gannet. **1970** DARE Tape **VA**112, [FW:] So it's sort of a dark-colored bird? [Inf:] You're talking about a, let's see; we call 'em niggergeese too, 'cause they're black. Now that's just the language of old times, you know. **1981** Pederson *LAGS Basic Materials,* 1 inf, **swFL,** Niggergeese—black geese.

2 =**Canada goose.**

1913 Bailey *Birds VA* 28, Canada Goose . . Wild Goose. Honker. Nigger Goose.

3 also *negro goose:* =**anhinga.** Cf **nigger loon**

1931 Read *LA French* 5, American Snakebird (*Plotus anhinga* L.); in English commonly known as the "water turkey"—sometimes as the "negro goose" or "water crow." **1955** *AmSp* 30.180 **TX,** Nigger goose. . . is sometimes used for the anhinga or water turkey.

nigger guinea n Cf **guinea woodpecker**
=**ivory-billed woodpecker.**

1953 *AmSp* 28.277, Nigger guinea—Ivory-billed woodpecker—Texas. [Footnote to *nigger guinea:*] Ironical, as a bird used for food by Negroes, in the absence of a guinea.

nigger hair n Cf **nigger's hair**

1 A red alga (*Polysiphonia harveyi*).

1853 Smithsonian Inst. *Smithsonian Contrib.* 5.5.41 **Long Is. NY,** While dredging with Professor Bailey in Peconic Bay, our exclamations of delight on hauling up some specimens of it [=*Polysiphonia arietina*] attracted the notice of one of our boatmen, who took up a handful of what we seemed so eagerly hoarding, but immediately threw it down with a "Pooh! that's what *we* call *'nigger-hair.'* " **1884** U.S. Natl. Museum *Bulletin* 27.613, *Polysiphonia Harveyi.* . . Nigger-hair. Wood's Holl [sic], Massachusetts. **1901** Arnold *Sea-Beach* 88, *P[olysiphonia] harveyi.* Frond two to six inches high; grows in globose tufts, and has a bushy aspect. . . Common in Long Island Sound and northward. Called locally *niggerhair.*

2 A **reed grass** (here: *Calamagrostis rubescens*).

1937 St. John *Flora SE WA & ID* 37, *Calamagrostis rubescens.* . . Nigger Hair. Stems tufted, from creeping rhizomes. . . Somewhat rough, but a valuable forage plant.

3 Finely cut tobacco used for both chewing and smoking. **esp Gt Lakes**

1966–68 DARE (Qu. DD1, . . *Forms . . [of] chewing tobacco*) Inf **MI**24, Nigger hair; **MN**8, Nigger hair—same as fine-cut; **WI**30, Nigger hair—loose, stringy; **WI**48, Nigger hair—older name for bigger hair; **WI**60, Nigger hair—now called bigger hair—a loose tobacco used mostly for smoking but also for chewing. **1969** Sorden *Lumberjack*

Lingo 80 **NEng, Gt Lakes,** *Nigger hair*—A popular smoking and chewing tobacco in early days.

nigger hater n
=**mockingbird 1.**

1968 DARE (Qu. Q14, . . *Names . . for . . mockingbird*) Inf **MD**40, Nigger hater.

niggerhead n

1 A rock, stone, or boulder, esp one dark in color. **widespread exc Gulf States** See Map

1847 Howe *Hist. Coll. OH* 569 **cOH,** It was a saw mill, with a small pair of stones attached, made of boulders, or "nigger heads," as they are commonly called. **1889** Smithsonian Inst. *Annual Rept. for 1886* 2.523, *Nigger head.* (1) The black concretionary nodules found in granite; (2) Any hard, dark, colored rock weathering out into rounded nodules or bowlders; (3) Slaty rock associated with sandstone. A quarryman's term. **1906** DN 3.114 **sIN,** An aged Indian wandered through the neighborhood for days, searching among certain boulders, dark soft stones as large as a man's head and termed "niggerheads" by natives. **1936** McKenna *Black Range* 48 **swNM,** The hammers and war axes we took note of were nearly all made of a niggerhead rock not found in the vicinity. **1939** FWP *Guide KS* 8, Numerous boulders lie scattered over the pastures in this section of the State, most of them red or pinkish in color and hard as flint. These boulders of red quartzite have been used to some extent in building construction and are locally known as "niggerheads." **1948** Dick *Dixie Frontier* 4 **KY,** Bears rolled "nigger heads" stones over and ate the grubs and field mice. **1950** WELS **WI** *(A piece of stone that one person could move but not throw)* 1 Inf, Niggerhead; 1 Inf, Niggerhead—size of a human head and dark; *(Kinds of stones of particular size, shape, color)* 1 Inf, Niggerheads; 1 Inf, Niggerhead—dark, smooth, hard, large; 1 Inf, Niggerheads—black, small boulders left by glacial drift; 1 Inf, Niggerheads—dark colored, smooth surface; 1 Inf, Niggerheads—large round ones; 1 Inf, Niggerheads—black; 1 Inf, Niggerheads—depends on shape and hardness, not color; 1 Inf, Niggerhead—roundish, smooth, usually dark. **1960** Criswell *Resp. to PADS 20* **Ozarks,** *Niggerhead,* a round stone often approaching the size of a person's head, often rather dark because of the presence of iron ore. **1965–70** DARE (Qu. C25, . . *Kinds of stone . . about . . [. . size of a person's head], smooth and hard*) 154 Infs, **widespread exc Gulf States,** Niggerhead; **VA**5, Niggerhead rock; (Qu. C22, *A piece of stone too big for one person to move easily*) Infs **IA**24, **NY**66, Niggerhead; (Qu. C24a, *A small piece of stone that you could easily throw*) Infs **NM**1, **NY**59, Niggerhead; (Qu. C26, . . *Special kinds of stone or rock*) Inf **NC**52, Niggerhead—a black rock; **NY**93, Niggerhead—great big huge hard stone you have to blast out of the ground; **KY**1, Niggerheads. **1973** PADS 59.44 [Bituminous coal mining vocab], *Niggerhead* . . a small, hard ball of rock, often pressed slate. **1983** MJLF 9.1.49 **ceKY,** *Nigger head* . . a geode; a variety of round, very hard stones. **1991** DARE File **seWI** (as of 1950–60), I [=a steam fitter] have heard and used the term niggerhead when we were drilling holes in concrete and would run into black stones that were used in the mix. They were very hard and tough to get through.

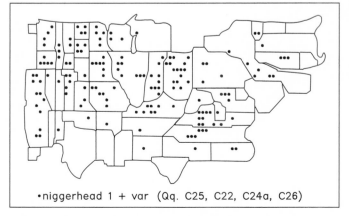

•niggerhead 1 + var (Qq. C25, C22, C24a, C26)

2 A mound of vegetation; a tussock; an area having many tussocks. **scattered, but esp AK**

1859 (1968) Bartlett *Americanisms* 292, *Nigger heads.* The tussocks or knotted masses of the roots of sedges and ferns projecting above the wet surface of a swamp. South. **1892** Lee *Hist. Columbus OH* 1.274,

Hummocks, called in the borough dialect "nigger-heads," formed by tufts of swamp grass. **1894** *DN* 1.342 **wCT,** *Nigger-head:* clump of fern-roots in swamps. When the land is reclaimed they remain for years undecayed, showing as black lumps in the ploughed field. **1898** Haskell *2 Yrs.* 192 **AK,** There are great stretches of tundra covered with clumps of grass which have sprung up sometimes on fields of solid ice. White people here call these grassy inventions of human torture "niggerheads." *Ibid* 194, The miners . . of that country keep as far away from a niggerhead swamp as they conveniently can. **1900** *Pop. Sci. Mth.* 52.637 **cwAK,** The surface is pre-eminently swampy during the warmer periods of the year, and walking over it means either wading through the water or risking continuous jumps to and from the individual clumps of matted grass and moss—the so-called "nigger-heads." **1901** Brooks et al. *Reconnaissances AK* 165 **swAK,** In many places these tundra grasses [=*Eriophorum* spp] grow in bunches, making hard lumps, known as "nigger heads," which turn under the feet in the more yielding moss and greatly increase the annoyance of tundra traveling. **a1922** (1953) Brooks *Blazing* 66 **AK,** There is also a variety of sedge known as tundra or cotton grass. This grows in thick tufts which project above the intervening moss carpet and forms the so-called "nigger head" which is so difficult to traverse. **1940** *AK Sportsman* Feb 23, The ground is moss covered . . and is very difficult to travel owing to the "niggerhead" formations and the boggy condition when thawed. **1947** *Jrl. Wildlife Management* 2.66 **sLA,** Muskrats can dig . . leaving clumps of cordgrass. This cordgrass produces an erect rather than prostrate growth, eventually forming "niggerheads." Cordgrass niggerheads only 8 inches across at the base may produce a canopy shading out all other vegetation within a radius of 4 feet. **1968** *DARE* (Qu. L8) Inf **CT**2, Niggerheads grow in bogs, usually in a marshy field. Heavy clumps of grass about a foot wide. **1976** Hobbs–Specht *Tisha* 20 **AK,** "Have you ever crossed a niggerhead flat?" . . He wheeled his horse and the pack train started forward. . . Then we hit swamp. Out of it grew great big hummocks of matted grass that looked like giant mops. They grew so thick that I thought of getting off Blossom and walking on them. Like the other animals, he wasn't having easy going. The mud sucked at his hoofs, and he kept slipping all over the place and stumbling over submerged roots.

3 Any of var plants, as:

a also *niggerhead cactus:* Usu a **barrel cactus** such as *Echinocactus polycephalus* or *Ferocactus wislizenii,* but also a **hedgehog cactus 3** such as *Echinocereus engelmanni* or *E. triglochidiatus.* [See quot 1941] esp **AZ**

1877 Hodge *Arizona* 244, The nigger head is round, of the size of a cabbage, and covered with large, crooked, catlike thorns. **1896** *Jrl. Amer. Folkl.* 9.188 **AZ,** *Echinocactus Wislizeni* . . niggerhead cactus, barrel cactus. **1924** Austin *Land of Journeys' Ending* 127 **AZ,** There are scores of variations of the bisnaga type, "niggerhead," "fish-hook," and "cushion" cacti, running to fat button shapes or short thickened cylinders, widely distributed through the Southwest. **1940** Benson *Cacti AZ* 109, *Echinocactus polycephalus* . . Nigger Heads. **1941** Jaeger *Wildflowers* 165 **Desert SW,** Niggerheads . . *Echinocactus polycephalus* . . Most commonly called "niggerheads," because of the general dark color of the melon-shaped heads. **1942** Whipple *Joshua* 189 **UT** (as of c1860), The niggerhead cactus pushing golden cups out of every rock crevice. **1951** Abrams *Flora Pacific States* 3.155, *Echinocereus Munzii.* . . Munz's Nigger-head. . . *Echinocereus mojavensis.* . . Mojave Nigger-heads. *Ibid* 156, *Echinocactus polycephalus.* . . Nigger-heads. **1974** Munz *Flora S. CA* 311, *E[chinocactus] polycephalus* . . Nigger-Heads.

b =**black-eyed Susan 2. chiefly TX, Lower Missip Valley** See Map Cf **nigger daisy, ~ heel b, ~ navel, ~ nose, niggerthumb, nigger tits, niggertoe 5**

1893 Price *Flora Warren Co. KY* 15, *Rudbeckia . . fulgida. . .* Cone Flower. "Nigger-head." **1894** *Jrl. Amer. Folkl.* 7.92, *Rudbeckia triloba* . . nigger-heads, Anderson, Ind. **1906** *DN* 3.148 **nwAR,** *Nigger-head.* . . Ox-eye daisy. "Nigger-heads have a large black centre and yellow petals." **1915** *DN* 4.227 **wTX,** *Nigger-head.* . . A peculiar six-petaled flower whose stamens and pistils form a long and narrow cone. **1920** *Torreya* 20.25, *Rudbeckia montana* . . Niggerhead, Uintah Mts., Utah. **1932** Rydberg *Flora Prairies* 835, *Rudbeckia.* . . Nigger-heads. **1937** U.S. Forest Serv. *Range Plant Hdbk.* W163, Niggerhead [=*Rudbeckia occidentalis*] is a coarse perennial herb of the aster or sunflower (composite) family. **1941** Writers' Program *Guide UT* 310, The delicate beauty of geraniums, violets, columbines, blue bells, daisies, and wild pansies is contrasted with the hardy and more colorful Indian paintbrush, yarrow, grape, "niggerhead," and wild mustard. **1954** Harder *Coll.* **cwTN,** *Nigger head*—flower: black-eyed Susan (Rudbeckia hirta). **1960** Criswell *Resp. to PADS* 20 **Ozarks,** Black-eyed Susan; com-

moner terms: niggerhead, nigger navel (pron. *nabel*). **1964** *PADS* 42.21 **wKY,** *Niggerhead.* . . The black-eyed Susan *(Rudbeckia hirta).* **1965–70** *DARE* (Qu. S7, *A kind of daisy, bright yellow with a dark center, that grows along roadsides in late summer*) 45 Infs, **chiefly TX, Lower Missip Valley,** Niggerhead.

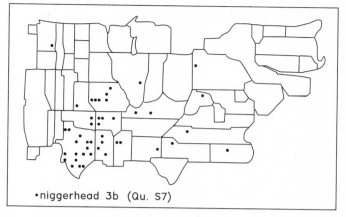
•niggerhead 3b (Qu. S7)

c =**buckhorn plantain.**

1897 *Jrl. Amer. Folkl.* 10.53 **seNY,** *Plantago lanceolata* . . nigger-heads . . Southold, L[ong] I[sland]. **1991** *DARE* File **seNY,** Niggerheads = narrow-leafed plantain.

d A **trillium** (here: *Trillium sessile*).

1897 *Jrl. Amer. Folkl.* 10.145 **IN,** *Trillium sessile,* . . nigger-heads.

e A **greenbrier** (here: *Smilax rotundifolia*).

[**1892** *Jrl. Amer. Folkl.* 5.104, *Smilax rotundifolia.* . . Nigger-head. Miramichi, N[ew] B[runswick].] **1900** Lyons *Plant Names* 348, *S[milax] rotundifolia.* . . Nigger-head. **1960** Vines *Trees SW* 75, Common Greenbrier—*Smilax rotundifolia.* . . Vernacular names for the plant are Biscuit-leaves . . Niggerhead . . and Sow-brier.

f A **zinnia** (here: *Zinnia elegans*).

1898 *Jrl. Amer. Folkl.* 11.230, *Zinnia elegans,* . . niggerheads, St. Joseph, Mo.

g A **yucca;** see quot.

1902 *Out West Mag.* Oct 452, He . . told her their many aliases of *maguey,* . . soapweed, "niggerhead," bear grass, Spanish dagger or bayonet. [*DARE* Ed: The term 'maguey' is generally used only of the genus *Agave*.]

h See quot. Cf **greasewood**

1907 White *AZ Nights* 23, "How's that?" he cried in triumph. "Found her just now while I was rustling nigger-heads for a fire." *Ibid* 40, After a moment we tore off long bundles of the nigger-head blades, lit the resinous ends at our fire, and with these torches started to make our way along the base of the cliff to the other cave.

i A **rush** (here: *Juncus effusus*).

1923 in 1925 Jepson *Manual Plants CA* 200, [*Juncus effusus*] Var. *brunneus.* . . Nigger Heads. . . Perianth and capsule dark brown.

j A **beggar ticks 1** (here: *Bidens polylepis*).

1926 *Torreya* 26.7 **MS,** *Bidens involucrata* . . Nigger-head, Pickens Miss.

k =**purple coneflower.**

1924 *Amer. Botanist* 30.33 **West,** I knew *Brauneria purpurea* as "nigger-head." **1929** *Folk-Say* 76 **OK,** A tea made of the root of "nigger head" would cure snakebite. This plant is better known farther afield as "purple rayed coneflower." **1930** Sievers *Amer. Med. Plants* 27 **KS,** *Echinacea angustifolia* . . niggerhead. **1940** Early *New Engl. Sampler* 317, Another remarkable weed is Echinacea (*Indian Head-root* or *Nigger-head*), a powerful drug, and an American cure-all for nearly three hundred years. Indians scraped the root, and used it as treatment for hydrophobia, insect, and snake bites. **1959** Carleton *Index Herb. Plants* 86, *Nigger-head:* Brauneria purpurea; . . Lepachys columnaris [=*Ratibida columnifera*]; Rudbeckia hirta.

l A **prairie coneflower:** usu *Ratibida columnifera,* but also *R. tagetes.*

1933 Small *Manual SE Flora* 1428, *R[atibida] columnaris.* . . Niggerhead. . . Dry soils, prairies, plains, and hills. **1936** Whitehouse *TX Flowers* 173, *Niggerhead.* . . *Ratibida columnaris.* . . is a very handsome plant. . . In South Texas it is at its best in April and May. . . The dwarf niggerhead (*Ratibida tagetes*) is quite similar to the large niggerhead in growth habit and coloring, but it is a smaller plant and has smaller flowers. **1959** [see **3k** above].

m A **cotton grass 1** (here: *Eriophorum vaginatum*).

1959 Anderson *Flora AK* 111, *E. vaginatum.* . . Niggerheads, Sheathed Cotton-grass. Densely tufted, forming "niggerheads".

4 Any of var **freshwater clams;** see quots. **chiefly Missip Valley**

1908 Kunz–Stevenson *Book of the Pearl* 72, The niggerhead (*Quadrula ebena*) is the most numerous in the Mississippi, and it is extensively used in button manufacture. The thick shell of this species is almost round, with a black outer surface and a pearly white interior. **1911** *Century Dict. Suppl.*, *Niggerhead.* . . A fresh-water mussel, *Quadrula ebena*, of the Mississippi River, used in the manufacture of pearl buttons. It is rather small with a thick shell and a black or dark brown outer skin. . . *Warty-back niggerhead, Quadrula metanerva* or *Q. pustulosa.* **1933** *LA Dept. of Conserv. Fishes* 416, The Shovelnose happens to be the only fish host known to carry the parasitic glochidia stages of one of the Mississippi mussels, the "Glassy-back" or Missouri "Niggerhead" (*Obovaria ellipsis*). **1938** *FWP Guide IA* 327, The fisherman's haul usually contained a wide assortment of shells: the niggerhead, with its round, flat exterior and milk-white interior, which would produce many blanks able to bear a bright, lustrous polish. **1940–41** Cassidy *WI Atlas*, 1 Inf, **WI**, Clam shells, niggerhead, oyster shell, mucket. **1941** *AmSp* 16.155 **Missip Valley**, [There are many varieties of fresh-water mussels, but the button-cutter is ignorant of any technical terminology for them. His names are mostly descriptive and frequently picturesque. . . Arkansas . . Elephant Ear.] *Ibid* 156, Niggerhead . . Washboard. **1941** Writers' Program *Guide AR* 207 **neAR**, Dredging the White River and its tributaries for fresh-water mussels for button making affords farmers a part-time occupation. . . Payment . . varies according to the type of shell, "grandmaws," "pocketbooks," and "cucumbers" bringing less than "elephant ears" and "niggerheads." **1953** (1977) Hubbard *Shantyboat* 211 **Missip-Ohio Valleys**, We learned that there are many classes of shells, of different value. Those called sand and niggerhead shells bring the highest price; then muckets and pigtoes. **1966** *WI Conserv. Bulletin* 31.3.26 **WI**, In the first decade of the 20th century. . . [C]lamming was big business. Hundreds of clam boats dragged the bottom . . bringing up mostly the valuable and abundant "niggerhead," as well as many other species.

5 =**rufous-sided towhee.**

1955 *AmSp* 30.180 **WA**, The spotted towhee is locally known as the *niggerhead* in the state of Washington.

6 A storm cloud. Cf **thunderhead**

1914 *DN* 4.110 **cKS**, Nigger-head. . . Dark cumulus clouds close to the horizon. **1929** Bell *Some Contrib. KS Vocab.* 241, Niggerhead. . . A name for one of the black-tipped cumulus clouds known also as "thunder heads." **1967–70** *DARE* (Qu. B9, . . *Big clouds that roll up high before a rainstorm*) Infs **IL**114, **TN**31, 34, 36, **WY**5, Niggerheads; **OH**31, Niggerheads—my grandmother said that.

7 A small black candy usu made from licorice; see quots. Cf **nigger baby 1, niggertoe 7**

1901 *DN* 2.144 **ePA**, Niggerhead. . . A kind of hard, black candy made both in spheres and in flat pieces. **1967–70** *DARE* (Qu. H82b, *Kinds of cheap candy that used to be sold years ago*) Infs **MO**12, 25, Niggerheads; **KY**84, Niggerheads—same as chocolate drops; **LA**33, Niggerheads—in the shape of a head made with licorice; **LA**40, Niggerheads—licorice in the shape of a head; **LA**43, Niggerheads—round with a head on it made of licorice; **PA**41, Niggerheads—black, face of a person, licorice.

8 In railroading:

a A steam dome, spec the one on top of a locomotive boiler; see quots.

1932 *RR Mag.* Oct 369, Niggerhead—Steam exit on top of boiler from which pipes to injector, etc., issue. **1940** Cottrell *Railroader* 133, *Niggerhead*—Steam dome on top of locomotive boiler from which issue pipes to injector, and other auxiliary equipment.

b See quot.

1916 *DN* 4.356 [Railroad terms], *Nigger-head.* . . In signals, a contrivance which trips to danger as the train passes over it.

9 A bollard or capstan. Cf **nigger** n[1] **B6**

1911 *Century Dict. Suppl.*, *Niggerhead.* . . A spool or capstan for lifting or hauling, formed on the end of a shaft which is turned by power: so called because it is usually black. **1927** (1942) Bradford *Gloss. Sea Terms* 119, *Nigger heads*, a name for bollards, and sometimes applied

to winch heads. **1965** Will *Okeechobee Boats* 136 **FL**, With a rope to that stationary engine's nigger head he got her into the lake again. **1966–67** *DARE* Tape **SC**18, They now have winches to pull the net in and let the net out. They used to use what's called a niggerhead because it was a hard piece of iron, a round spool that came from a shaft running to the engine and it would wrap the cables. *Ibid* **TX**14, We got the lazy line that goes to the net and we put it on what we call the niggerhead, which is a small rope capstan. **1968** *DARE* FW Addit **New Orleans LA**, *Niggerhead*—slanted iron post projecting from the curb at street corners to keep carriages from ruining the curb. Named for the rounded knob at top. Old-fashioned; item still seen at some street corners. **1984** *DARE* File **Chesapeake Bay** [Watermen's vocab], Cleat, niggerhead / samson post / dredge post.

10 See quot.

1959 *VT Hist.* 27.150, *Niggerhead.* . . A milk can.

11 See quot.

1968 *DARE* (Qu. H21, . . *The sweet stuff that's poured over these [pan]cakes*) Inf **DE**3, There used to be one they called niggerhead; right black molasses.

niggerhead cactus See **niggerhead 3a**

niggerheading vbl n Cf **nigger** v **3**

1968 *DARE* (Qu. A9, . . *Wasting time by not working on the job*) Inf **WV**13, Niggerheading.

nigger heaven n

1 also *niggers' heaven*: The highest balcony in a theater. **chiefly Nth, Plains States, Rocky Mts, CA** See Map

1878 in 1917 Daly *Life* 249 **ceNY**, There is a 'Nigger Heaven' (as the third tier is called in Troy) here. **1900** *DN* 2.47 **NY, OH, RI** [College slang], *Nigger-heaven.* . . Topmost gallery of a theatre. **1960** Criswell *Resp. to PADS 20* **Ozarks**, *Nigger heaven*—This was used mostly by hearsay because most of these people had never seen a standard theater, and they had no Negroes in their population who would go to theaters. I think I have heard the term for fifty years. **1965–70** *DARE* (Qu. D40, *Names and nicknames . . for the upper balcony in a theater*) 274 Infs, **chiefly Nth, Plains States, Rocky Mts, CA**, Nigger heaven; **MA**7, 44, 48, **MI**96, **NY**194, 209, **PA**234, **WI**72, Niggers' heaven; (QR, near Qu. FF25) Inf **NJ**58, Nigger heaven. **1979** *DARE* File **cnMA** (as of c1915), Sometimes people called the balcony in the movie theater in our town "nigger heaven." This made no sense to me, for there were no Negroes in town. Anybody could sit there. **1988** Lincoln *Avenue* 26 **wNC** (as of c1940) [Black], The local theater admitted colored patrons to its balcony, known colloquially as "Nigger Heaven" and reserved especially for colored citizens.

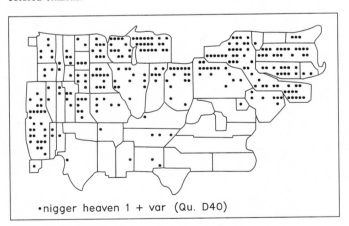

•nigger heaven 1 + var (Qu. D40)

2 =**Fiddler's Green.**

1906 *DN* 3.148 **nwAR**, *Nigger-heaven.* . . In the verb phrase, "to be in nigger-heaven," i.e., to enjoy one's self cheaply and vulgarly. "He's in nigger-heaven now."

nigger heel n

1 See **niggertoe 10.**

2 See quot. Cf **nigger liquor**

1968 *DARE* (Qu. DD21b, *General words . . for bad liquor*) Inf **CT**17, Nigger heel—seventy-five cents per quart gin.

3 See quot. Cf **long-heel**

1927 Ruppenthal *Coll.* **KS**, *Nigger heel*—An unusually long heel (of a person); a rearward projection of the heel beyond average.

4 A **purple coneflower** (here: *Echinacea angustifolia*).
1933 *Torreya* 33.84 **NE**, *Brauneria angustifolia.* . . Niggerheel, Valentine.

5 Any of var nuts; see quots. Cf **nigger nut, niggertoe 1, 6**
1906 *DN* 3.148 **nwAR**, *Nigger-heel, nigger-toe.* . . Brazil nut. **1949** *AmSp* 24.111 **nGA**, *Nigger heels.* . . Hazelnuts. **1986** Pederson *LAGS Concordance,* 2 infs, **AL**, Nigger heel(s) = Brazil nut(s); 1 inf, **AL**, Nigger heel—black, one end thick, other pointed; 2 infs, **AL, LA**, Nigger heels—butternuts; 4 infs, **AL, LA, MS, TN**, Nigger heel(s) [*DARE* Ed: It is impossible to determine what kinds of nuts these four infs are referring to.]

6 pronc-sp *nigger hill*: A **black-eyed Susan 2**. Cf **niggerhead 3b**
1969 *DARE* (Qu. S7, *A kind of daisy, bright yellow with a dark center, that grows along roadsides in late summer*) Inf **MO6**, Nigger hill ['nɪgɚˌhɪl].

nigger hill See **nigger heel 6**

nigger in a blanket See **niggers in a blanket**

niggering (off) See **nigger v 1**

‡**nigger in the barrel** n
=**nigger in the woodpile 1a.**
1967 *DARE* (Qu. V1, *When you suspect that somebody is trying to deceive you, or that something is going on behind your back* . . *"There's _____."*) Inf **SC43**, [A] nigger in the barrel.

nigger in the fence n esp Nth
=**nigger in the woodpile 1a.**
1847 *Yankee Doodle* 15 May 54/2 (*Mathews Coll.*), A Nigger in De Fence. This phrase was never so perfectly illustrated as by the law of Pennsylvania respecting the recovery of fugitive slaves. **1850** *CA Courier* (San Francisco CA) 4 Sept 2/6, The majority of the papers . . think that there "is a nigger in the fence" somewhere. **a1882** (1884) Weed *Life* 1.477 **NY** (as of 1839), I'll find out . . what this means. There's a nigger in the fence somewhere. **1887** (1888) Harte *Phyllis* 81 **CA**, Ef he ain't scooped up by Jenny Bradley he'll guess there's a nigger in the fence somewhere. **1911** Quick *Yellowstone Nights* 286, He's always looking for a nigger in the fence. **1933** Cheley *Camping Out* 167 (*DA*), The fox can reason too, and says to himself, 'What in thunder made that galoot set a trap as if it were a signpost? There's a nigger in that fence!'[¹] **1950** *WELS* **WI** (*When you suspect that somebody is trying to deceive you, or that something is going on behind your back, you say, "There's _____."*) 4 Infs, A nigger in the fence; (*If somebody has dishonest intentions, or is up to no good: "I think he's got _____."*) 1 Inf, A nigger in the fence. **1966–68** *DARE* (Qu. V1, *When you suspect that somebody is trying to deceive you, or that something is going on behind your back* . . *"There's _____."*) Infs **MI35, NY22, 96, 107, WI59**, Nigger in the fence.

nigger in the woodpile n For varr see quots

1a A concealed fact, factor, or motive; something suspicious. Cf **African n¹, adj C2, Ethiopian 2**
1846 *OH Statesman* 8 July 3/2 (*Mathews Coll.*), They smell a "rat." They talk as though there was a "nigger in the woodpile." **1852** in 1942 *KS Hist. Qrly.* 11.235, No "nigger in the woodpile" here. **1897** *Congressional Record* 18 Feb app 61 **ceKY**, Like a great many others ignorant of facts, he finds "a nigger in the wood pile" where there is neither wood pile nor nigger. **1903** *DN* 2.322 **seMO**, *Nigger in the woodpile.* . . An expression implying concealment. 'I suspicioned there was a nigger in the woodpile when I saw them collouing together.' **1907** *DN* 3.233 **nwAR**, *Nigger in the woodpile.* . . Something concealed. **1909** *DN* 3.352 **eAL, wGA**, *Nigger in the wood-pile.* . . Some concealed purpose or reason. "I thought there must be some nigger in the woodpile." Very common. **1912** *DN* 3.583 **wIN**, *Nigger in the wood-pile.* . . A treacherous, faithless person in the transaction. "As soon as he told me that, I knew there was a nigger in the wood-pile somewheres." **1927** *AmSp* 2.361 **cwWV**, *Nigger in the woodpile* . . some secret in the matter. "You may be sure the nigger in that woodpile will soon come out." **1958** Humphrey *Home from the Hill* 286 **neTX**, Then the baby, which even Fred acknowledged to be ahead of decent schedule, though he was pleased to think that he himself was the nigger in the woodpile. **1965–70** *DARE* (Qu. V1, *When you suspect that somebody is trying to deceive you, or that something is going on behind your back* . . *"There's _____."*) 336 Infs, **widespread**, [A] nigger in the woodpile (somewhere *or* someplace); **LA28, OR16, VA42, WY11**, [A] nigger in a woodpile; **LA2, TN24**, [A] dead nigger in the woodpile; **KY90**, [A] nigger behind the woodpile; **KY85**, [A] nigger in the brush pile; **KY59**,

[A] nigger in the woodshed; (Qu. JJ19, *If somebody has dishonest intentions, or is up to no good* . . *"I think he's got _____."*) Infs **DE1, MO13, OH45, OR4, 14**, [A] nigger in the woodpile. **1986** Pederson *LAGS Concordance,* 1 inf, **cnTN**, Nigger in the woodpile—something strange happens.

b Spec: a degree of Black ancestry in one who is apparently White.
1986 Pederson *LAGS Concordance* ([*Of a white person*] *with one black grandparent* . . *one black great-grandparent*) 1 inf, **neTN**, Nigger in the woodpile—a remote black ancestor; 3 infs, **LA, AR**, Nigger in the woodpile; 1 inf, **swGA**, Dead nigger in the woodpile. **1991** *DARE* File **eTN** (as of 1950s), I recall the expression "nigger in the woodpile" being used of white people with some suspiciously negroid physical feature implying the possibility of that person having had a Black ancestor, like saying of someone that they have "a touch of the tar brush."

2 An illegitimate child.
[**1958** see **1a** above.] **1968** *DARE* (Qu. Z11b, . . [*A child whose parents were not married*]) Inf **MD5**, Nigger in the woodpile. **1986** Pederson *LAGS Concordance* (*Bastard*) 2 infs, **MS**, Nigger in the woodpile.

nigger jigger See **nigger killer 3**

nigger killer n

1 also *negro killer, nigger choker*: A dark-skinned variety of **sweet potato. chiefly S Atl, AL** Cf **choker 2**
1855 Davis *Farm Bk.* 140 (*DA*) **AL**, Planted out in rows 7 bushels of Spanish potatoes & in the bed 10 Spanish—5 Negro killers & 23 of Yams. **1916** Massey *Reminiscences* 22 **swAL**, Yams, Spanish, white and red (called "nigger killers") potatoes were grown in abundance and put up. **c1940** Eliason *Word Lists FL* 10, *Niggerkiller:* A species of sweet potatoes that have a purple skin, and when cooked are very dry and mealy. **1956** Rayford *Whistlin' Woman* 33 **swAL**, Sweet potatoes were called "nigger killers." They had purple skins and stringy white meat. **1959** McAtee *Oddments* 5 **cNC**, *Nigger-choker* . . a sweet potato (or yam) low in moisture and sugar content, and therefore, hard to swallow. **1966–70** *DARE* (Qu. I9, . . *Names [including nicknames] for potatoes*) Inf **FL37**, Nigger chokers—sweet potatoes; **AL30**, Nigger killers; **FL49**, Used to have a long blue-skinned white potato called nigger killer; no longer grown; chokes the niggers to death. **1986** Pederson *LAGS Concordance,* 1 inf, **ceGA**, Nigger killer—sweet potato with purple skin; 1 inf, **neFL**, Nigger killer—large [sweet potato]: red outside, white inside; 1 inf, **swAL**, Nigger killer—sweet potato; 1 inf, **cwAR**, Nigger killer—a kind of yam; 1 inf, **seGA**, Nigger killer—a dry kind of potato; 1 inf, **ceGA**, Nigger killer potatoes; 1 inf, **nwFL**, Nigger killer(s)—dark, red-skinned; 1 inf, **ceGA**, Nigger choker—a big-old potato; 1 inf, **ceTN**, Nigger chokers—red Spanish sweet potatoes.

2 A **vinegarone** (here: *Mastigoproctus giganteus*).
1886 *Entomol. Amer.* 2.39, T[*helyphonus*] *giganteus* . . is found quite frequently in the Southern States, where it is much feared by the people who call it Nigger Killer, Mule Killer, Grampus, etc. **1890** *Century Dict.* 3990 **FL**, *Nigger-killer.* . . The whip-tailed scorpion.

3 also *nigger jigger,* ~ *sticker*: A large pocketknife.
1967–69 *DARE* (Qu. F39, *A large pocket knife with blades that fold in and out*) Inf **SC51**, Nigger jigger; **SC62**, Nigger killer; **NY210**, Nigger sticker. **1986** Pederson *LAGS Concordance,* 1 inf, **cAL**, Nigger stickers—big, wicked, mean looking.

4 See **nigger-shooter.**

nigger-knocker n

A **pigfish** (here: *Orthopristis chrysopterus*).
a1883 (1911) Bagby *VA Gentleman* 131, Another name for the nigger-knocker is hogfish, and it is by far the ugliest tenant of the Virginia waters.

nigger leg n

=**nigger killer 1.**
1986 Pederson *LAGS Concordance,* 1 inf, **swMS**, Nigger leg—purple peeling, long, sweet potato.

nigger lice n **MD** Cf **beggar's lice**
Usu a **burdock 1,** but also **tick trefoil;** also the prickly seed or fruit of either of these plants.
1933 *Sun* (Baltimore MD) 11 Sep 6/7 (*Hench Coll.*), What great clumps of "nigger lice," splendoring the landscape with its rich lavender bloom! **1940** Mencken *Happy Days* 43 **Baltimore MD** (as of c1890), Sometimes a black-hearted boy would sneak into the adjacent brickyard,

which was covered in large part with Jimpson weeds, plantains and other such vegetable outlaws, and return with a large ball of nigger-lice. [Footnote:] The burrs of the common burdock *(Arctium minus)*. **1946** *Sun* (Baltimore MD) 2 Oct 12/3 *(Hench Coll.),* I meant no offense to the members of the Negro race when I spoke the other day of "nigger lice." I was referring to the tick trefoil, its scientific name, which is commonly spoken of by everybody as I gave it in my former piece. **1968** *DARE* (Qu. S13, . . *A common wild bush with bunches of round, prickly seeds; when they get dry they stick to your clothing)* Inf **MD**9, Nigger lice.

niggerlip n
A **surfperch** (here: *Rhacochilus toxotes*).
1953 Roedel *Common Fishes CA* 107, Rubberlip Perch—*Rhacochilus toxotes.* . . Lips exceedingly thick. . . Unauthorized Names: Pile perch, porgy, niggerlip.

niggerlip cat n Also *niggerlips*
=**eel catfish.**
1878 U.S. Natl. Museum *Bulletin* 12.72 **cTN,** Nigger-lip Cat. **1908** Forbes–Richardson *Fishes of IL* 179, *Ictalurus anguilla.* . . is sometimes called "nigger-lips" by the fishermen.

nigger liquor n Also *nigger gin, ~ whiskey* Cf **nigger heel 2**
Bad liquor, esp when illegally distilled.
1929 *AmSp* 4.387 **KS,** *Nigger gin* . . means any sort of inferior synthetic gin. **1967–68** *DARE* (Qu. DD21b, *General words . . for bad liquor)* Inf **TX**11, Nigger whiskey; (Qu. DD28b, . . *Fermented drinks . . made at home)* Inf **GA**30, Nigger liquor—made with yeast and wheat bran. **1969** *DARE* Tape **GA**72, That kind of whiskey [=that made in a deadman still] is something I've never made in my life. . . It is made out of the siftings of wheat. *Nigger nabel* is much more common . . This is bolted and sifted 'til actually there's none of the heart of the grain left in it, it's nothing but the shuck of the grain . . and they cook that in this box. . . That is what is called nigger liquor. I can't think of a nigger. . . who'd want to drink this stuff. It's very mean. **1974** Dabney *Mountain Spirits* 107 (as of 1920s), In the black ghettos of Chicago, Washington, and New York's Harlem, "nigger gin," a low grade moonshine, sold for ten to fifteen cents a drink, but it was "awful tastin'." *Ibid* 225, Some of the redneck distillers, who know their product is destined for the black ghettos, seem to get a perverse pleasure in making their liquor as mean as possible. If it's an "especially good run", they'll share some of it with their friends. But most of it is what they call "nigger licker" which they ship off to Atlanta and to bootleggers in black ghettos in smaller cities.

nigger local n
In railroading: see quots.
1916 *DN* 4.356 [Railroad terms], *Nigger local.* A local freight train involving very hard work. **1969** *AmSp* 44.250 [Railroad terms], A fast freight is a *hotshot,* and a slow one . . a *nigger local.* On the Rock Island, the nigger local is a slow train that runs . . from Chicago to Peoria on Saturday nights only. In the days when riding the rails was more common, blacks frequently travelled on weekend freight trains to Peoria.

nigger loon n Also *nigger turkey* Cf **niggergoose 3**
=**anhinga.**
1955 *AmSp* 30.180, All of the other terms relating to man embody the opprobrious [sic] term *nigger,* but recording them here should not be taken in a bad sense by anyone. Such appellations invariably refer to the blackish or black coloration. . . *Nigger turkey* for this species [=*Anhinga anhinga*] also is heard in Louisiana, and *nigger loon* in Illinois.

nigger luck n Also *free nigger luck* Cf **mother luck**
Good luck, esp when unexpected.
1851 (1874) Glisan *Jrl. Army Life* 90 **KY,** I occasionally make him a little envious by my nigger-luck, as he is pleased to term it. **1870** Harte *Luck Roaring Camp* 31 **CA,** When a man gets a streak of luck,—nigger luck,—he don't get tired. **1909** *DN* 3.352 **eAL, wGA,** *Nigger-luck.* . . Fortunate chance. "You can't beat me playing dominoes. It's jest your nigger-luck that gets away with me." **1947** Chalfant *Gold* 7 **CA** (as of 1849), Mac [=a prospector from the east] told them their judgement was "free nigger luck, and that nothing more." **1966** *DARE* (Qu. HH30, *Things that are nicknamed for different nationalities—for example, a 'Dutch treat')* Inf **AR**12, Nigger luck.

niggerly See **nigger** n[2]

niggermouth n
=**jewbush.**
1942 Amer. Joint Comm. Horticult. Nomenclature *Std. Plant Names*

607, *Pedilanthus . . tithymaloides* . . Redbird S[lipperflower] *(Jewbush; Niggermouth).*

nigger navel n Also *nigger's navel* **chiefly Lower Missip Valley** See Map
=**black-eyed Susan 2.**
1942 Hall *Smoky Mt. Speech* 99 **wNC, eTN,** *Navel* ['neɪbəl] (usual); ['nɪgəᵊz 'neɪbəl] 'Black-eyed Susan'. **1949** *PADS* 11.9 **wTX** (as of 1911–29), *Nigger nabel, nigger toe:* . . A species of flower having a black button on top of a tall stem. *Nigger nabel* is much more common than *nigger toe.* **1960** Criswell *Resp. to PADS 20* **Ozarks,** Black-eyed Susan; commoner terms: nigger head, nigger navel (pron. *nabel*). **1965–70** *DARE* (Qu. S7, *A kind of daisy, bright yellow with a dark center, that grows along roadsides in late summer)* 18 Infs, **chiefly Lower Missip Valley,** Nigger navel; **AR**56, **KY**9, 77, 89, **LA**16, **TN**26, **TX**52, Nigger nabel; **AR**51, 52, 55, Nigger navel [laughter]; **KY**63, Nigger navel—some say; becoming old-fashioned; **LA**2, Nigger navel—larger than field daisy or black-eyed Susan; **GA**46, Nigger nabels [FW: used by Inf's first-grade pupils]; (Qu. S3) Inf **MO**39, Nigger navel; (Qu. S26a, . . *Wildflowers. . . Roadside flowers)* Inf **IL**119, Nigger navel; (Qu. S26b, *Wildflowers that grow in water or wet places)* Inf **OK**42, Nigger navel; (Qu. S26d, *Wildflowers that grow in meadows;* not asked in early QRs) Inf **IL**95, Nigger navels.

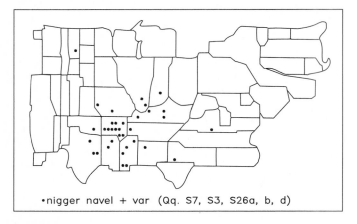

•nigger navel + var (Qq. S7, S3, S26a, b, d)

nigger news n
Gossip.
1859 in 1956 Eliason *Tarheel Talk* 150 **cNC,** The family . . depend upon Is . . to supply me with the latest *nigger news.* **c1960** *Wilson Coll.* **csKY,** *Nigger news.* . . Gossip, scuttlebutt, just such news as a servant might hint to her employer.

nigger night n Also *niggers' night* Cf **nigger day 2**
Saturday night.
1928 *Ruppenthal Coll.* **KS,** *Nigger night.* . . Saturday night. **1942** Berrey–Van den Bark *Amer. Slang* 604 [Miscellaneous theatrical terms], *Nigger night,* Saturday night. **1965** *DARE* File, *Niggers' night* = Saturday night. Used by my grandmother from Keene, N.H. (where there must have been very few Negroes). Her advice (this in Athol, Mass., where there were no negroes—or perhaps one): "Don't go uptown on Saturday night—it's niggers' night." **1968** Moody *Coming of Age MS* 261 [Black], Saturday night is Nigger Night all over Mississippi.

nigger nose n
A **black-eyed Susan 2.**
1967 *DARE* (Qu. S7, *A kind of daisy, bright yellow with a dark center, that grows along roadsides in late summer)* Inf **IL**25, Nigger nose.

nigger nut n Cf **nigger heel 5, niggertoe 1**
The Brazil nut *(Bertholletia excelsa).*
1986 Pederson *LAGS Concordance* **Gulf Region,** 1 inf, Nigger nuts— Brazil nuts—not raised locally; 1 inf, Nigger nuts—black nuts—white inside; 1 inf, Nigger nuts—not supposed to say.

nigger off See **nigger** v 1

nigger over See **nigger** v 2

‡**nigger pancake** n Cf **meadow muffin**
1968 *DARE* (Qu. L17, . . *Names . . for manure used in the fields: [Also joking names])* Inf **NY**87, Nigger pancake.

nigger pile n Cf **monkey pile**
= **buck buck 2.**

   1994 *DARE* File (as of 1970s), [What do you call it when a bunch of kids pile on top of each other?] This was a game the boys, no girls, played where I grew up—northeast Alabama, at the end of the Appalachias. It was called [blush] "nigger-pile." *Ibid* **Akron OH** (as of 1950s), Nigger Pile.

nigger-pill n
   A **hackberry** (here: *Celtis occidentalis*).

   1940 Clute *Amer. Plant Names* 164, C[*eltis*] *occidentalis* . . nigger-pill.

nigger pine n
   1 = **Jersey pine. chiefly C and Mid Atl, sAppalachians**

   1897 Sudworth *Arborescent Flora* 27 **NC**, *Pinus virginiana* . . Scrub Pine. . . Nigger Pine. **1908** Britton *N. Amer. Trees* 47, It [=Jersey pine] is also called by many other names, as Scrub pine . . Nigger pine . . and Shortshucks. **1950** Peattie *Nat. Hist. Trees* 27, Virginia Scrub Pine—*Pinus virginiana* . . Other Names: Jersey, Nigger, or River Pine. **1965–70** *DARE* (Qu. T17, . . *Kinds of pine trees; not asked in early QRs*) Infs **MD**24, **NJ**16, 21, **PA**17, **TN**22, Nigger pine; **GA**76, Nigger pine, short-needle pine—same; **MD**29, Nigger pine—same as jack pine; **NC**37, Jack or nigger pine; **TN**41, Nigger pine—limbs start at ground. **1981** Pederson *LAGS Basic Materials,* 1 inf, **cTN**, Colored pine (also called nigger pine); 1 inf, **cnTN**, Nigger pine.

   2 = **loblolly pine 1. Cf blackjack pine 3, longleaf ~ 2, slash ~**

   1981 Pederson *LAGS Basic Materials,* 1 inf, **neGA**, Slash pine—also called nigger pine; 1 inf, **cnGA**, Nigger pine = blackjack pine. **1992** *DARE* File **eNC**, I'm writing . . on the current cultural status of longleaf pines. Someone reported having heard them called "nigger pines."

nigger pole n **LA** Cf **nigger fish** v phr
   A simple fishing pole.

   1967 LeCompte *Word Atlas* **seLA**, (*Fishing pole made of bamboo and string*) 11 infs [of 21], Nigger pole. **1968** *DARE* (Qu. P13, . . *Ways of fishing . . besides the ordinary hook and line*) Inf **LA**20, Nigger pole—the ordinary hook and line is called 'nigger pole'; **LA**26, Nigger pole—simple rig with line and hook; **LA**34, Nigger pole—simple outfit with pole and string. **1986** Pederson *LAGS Concordance,* 1 inf, **seLA**, Nigger pole—bamboo fishing pole.

nigger prick See **nigger dick**

nigger quail n
   A **meadowlark 1** (here: *Sturnella magna*).

   1956 *AmSp* 31.181, Most of the monickers [for birds] in this division are derisive in another way, attaching the name of some race to a bird deemed inferior as food or game. Examples are: . . Nigger goose—Cormorants . . Nigger quail—Eastern meadow lark—Ala., Texas. **1970** *DARE* (Qu. Q15, . . *Kinds of larks*) Inf **TX**101, Nigger quail—same as field lark . . negroes eat them—they're size of quail.

nigger rich adj phr
   Foolishly or vulgarly extravagant.

   1930 Gowen *True Exposé Racketeers* 81 (*Tamony Coll.*), In those sections of the South where the old traditions of gentle birth and culture still assert their ancient authority and draw the lines of social demarcation, there is commonly in use a vivid, brutal phrase to describe ostentatious display by the merely vulgar wealthy. The phrase is 'nigger rich.' **c1930** Swann *Lang. Circus Lot* 13, Nigger rich: One who spends money foolishly. **1941** Corle *Desert Country* 49, There is in the temperament of the American Negro . . the urge and desire to burst forth from a more or less restricted social status into kingship—into being Caesar, czar, sultan, dictator. The stultified ego has, naturally, a tendency to express the counterpart. This manifestation of the human psyche has led to the vernacular expression "nigger rich." **1968–70** *DARE* (Qu. U37, . . *Somebody who has plenty of money*) Inf **CA**113, Nigger rich—somebody who's just made a lot and is flashing it around—common word here; (Qu. W40, . . *A woman who overdresses or . . spends too much on clothes*) Inf **KS**12, Nigger rich; (Qu. HH35, *A woman who puts on a lot of airs:* "*She's too _____ for me.*") Inf **PA**245, Nigger rich—acting like she just got rich but it's only a few bucks. **1986** Pederson *LAGS Concordance,* 1 inf, **nwMS**, Nigger rich—making money, spending it immediately. **1995** *DARE* File **KY**, [Nigger rich] refers to the racist notion that when black . . people get a paycheck they have lots of money but they quickly spend it. Thus to be "nigger-rich" is to have an infusion of money. *Ibid,* [Nigger rich] is a racial slur, but not about slaveowning. If you're used to having lots of money, and you find $5

on the sidewalk, it's no big deal; but if you win the lottery, you're rich. If you're used to getting by on next to nothing, and you find $5 on the sidewalk, you suddenly *feel* rich.

nigger rig v phr, hence ppl adj *nigger rigged,* vbl n *nigger rigging* Cf **nigger** v 3
   To make or repair (something) poorly or without proper materials; hence n *nigger rig(ging)* a makeshift.

   1965 *DARE* FW Addit **OK**, *Nigger-rigged*—rigging, etc., put together or repaired quickly and poorly. Inf says term is not used much anymore. "Now it has to be called 'Southern Gentleman's Engineering." **1969** *DARE* (Qu. HH30, *Things that are nicknamed for different nationalities—for example, a 'Dutch treat'*) Inf **TX**68, Nigger rig—anything poorly constructed. **1979** *Antioch Rev.* 37.58 **MS**, Don't it beat all for raising a shoat in a nigger-rigged crib? **1986** Pederson *LAGS Concordance (What might you call a makeshift lamp made with a rag, bottle, and kerosene)* 1 inf, **neMS**, Nigger rigging. **1991** *DARE* File **wKS**, A friend of mine in Topeka asked his landlord to come in and fix his commode, which wouldn't stop "running." The landlord, not having the necessary part, fixed it with a coat hanger. A few days later a friend of my friend, originally from west Kansas, came over to the apartment and when she saw what the landlord had done said, "Oh, he nigger rigged it." **1994** *Ibid* **Akron OH** (as of 1950s), The N-word showed up in a lot of places back home among the hillbillies (which is to say, us). To Nigger-rig was to improvise. . . as in "I had to nigger-rig that exhaust system, Cletus." **1995** *Ibid* **MS** (as of c1950s), "His car broke down, but he managed to nigger-rig it enough to get back to town." "Your fan is working again?" "Yeah, but it's just nigger-rigged." "He did a good job of nigger-rigging it."

nigger runner n
   1953 Randolph–Wilson *Down in Holler* 266 **Ozarks**, Nigger runner. . . A fox chaser of a trashy, ignorant type; such a man knows nothing of the fine points of a foxhound, and real fox hunters don't like to associate with him.

nigger's hair n Cf **nigger hair, niggerwool**
   = **ditch grass 2.**

   1909 *DN* 3.414 **nME**, Nigger's hair. . . A kind of wild grass growing in swampy places. The same as *devil's guts.*

nigger's heaven See **nigger heaven 1**

nigger-shooter n Also *nigger-chaser,* ~*-killer* **chiefly Gulf States, TX**
   A slingshot.

   1876 in 1969 *PADS* 52.53 **seIL**, I had a job on hand making Nigger shooters for Dr's children. **1883** Sweet–Knox *Mexican Mustang* 339 **TX**, Just about the time people have got used to tops buzzing about their ears, the "nigger-shooter" mania breaks out. **1909** *DN* 3.352 **eAL, wGA**, Nigger-shooter. . . A slingshot. **1915** *DN* 4.227 **wTX**, Nigger-shooter. . . A sort of sling shot, composed of a wooden handle and two rubber bands ending in a leather "pocket" from which stones are shot. Every boy in Texas is proficient in its use. **1940** Wilson *Wabash* 318 **IN**, It is barefoot boys on country roads, with nigger-killers dangling from the pockets of their overalls and strings of "yeller catfish" slung over their shoulders. **1941** O'Donnell *Great Big Doorstep* 2 **sLA**, 'Let me try!' Evvie whispered. 'Give me the nigger-shooter.' **1961** Folk *Word Atlas N. LA* map 1306, Boy's weapon made of rubber strips on a forked stick . . nigger shooter 46% [of 275 QRs] . . others 3% bean shooter, nigger killer, sling. **1965** *Western Folkl.* 24.192 **KS**, A forked stick, rubber bands, and an "apron" cut from an old shoe-tongue which could be used to project marble-sized stones with considerable force and accuracy and was most commonly known as a "nigger shooter," . . and . . as a slingshot. **1965** *DARE* FW Addit **ceOK**, A "nigger shooter" has one solid piece of rubber from post to post. **1967** *DARE* FW Addit **TX**, Nigger-shooter—name in Texas for what I call a sling shot. Device for shooting rocks or marbles, made with two strips of rubber, a piece of leather and a forked stick. **1968** Moody *Coming of Age MS* 16 [*Black*], Ed made us a "niggershooter" each. This was a little slingshot made out of a piece of leather connected to a forked stick by a thin slab of rubber. **1970** Tarpley *Blinky* 231 **neTX**, A favorite boyhood weapon . . is constructed by attaching two rubber strips to a forked stick. The majority of informants call this weapon a *nigger-shooter.* . . Another name . . is *nigger-killer.* **1970** *DARE* (Qu. F49) Inf **TX**85, Nigger shooter—a rubber band used to shoot at birds. **1983** *Capital Times* (Madison WI) 9 Aug 1/6 **TX**, [He] also reportedly referred to sling-shots as "nigger-shooters." **1986** Pederson *LAGS Concordance* **Gulf Region**, 11 infs, Nigger-shooter(s) = (homemade) slingshot(s). **1994** *DARE* File **cnOH** (as of 1920s), In Akron, I remember, a slingshot was called a *nigger-chaser*, but it may not have been the general term and there were many Southerners around. The term was also applied to a type of firework that whizzed along the ground.

niggers in a blanket n Also *nigger in a blanket*
See quots.
· **1941** Writers' Program *Guide LA* 229, Blackberries cooked in pastry turnovers are known as "niggers in a blanket." **1944** Adams *Western Words* 104, *Nigger-in-a-blanket*—A cowboy dessert, usually made of raisins in dough.

nigger's navel See **nigger navel**

nigger's night See **nigger night**

nigger's pipe n Cf **devil's snuff, ~ snuffbox 1**
Prob a **puffball.**
1969 *DARE* (Qu. S18, *A kind of mushroom that grows like a globe . . sometimes gets as big as a man's head*) Inf **KY40**, Nigger's pipe—old-fashioned.

nigger sticker See **nigger killer 3**

nigger teats See **nigger tits**

niggerthumb n
A **black-eyed Susan 2** (here: *Rudbeckia occidentalis*).
1936 McDougall-Baggley *Plants of Yellowstone* 128, Niggerthumb (*Rudbeckia occidentalis*). **1963** Craighead *Rocky Mt. Wildflowers* 225, Western Coneflower—*Rudbeckia occidentalis*. . . Other names: Nigger-thumb, Niggerhead.

nigger tits n Also *nigger teats*
=**black-eyed Susan 2.**
1903 Small *Flora SE U.S.* 1427, *R[udbeckia] bicolor* . . Nigger-teats. **1945** McAtee *Nomina Abitera* 15, Cone-flower (*Rudbeckia* sp.)—Nigger-tit (Texas Panhandle). **1950** Gray-Fernald *Manual of Botany* 1484, *R(udbeckia) bicolor* . . Nigger-teats. . . disk blackish, hemispherical, becoming conical. **1967** LeCompte *Word Atlas* 236 **seLA**, Black eyed susans . . nigger tits [5 of 21 infs]. **1968–70** *DARE* (Qu. S7, *A kind of daisy, bright yellow with a dark center, that grows along roadsides in late summer*) Infs **KY75, LA20, 43**, Nigger tit; **MO4**, Nigger tits. **1969** *DARE* FW Addit **MO**, I suspect she [=Inf **MO15**, who gave resps *niggerhead* and *nigger navel* to Qu. S7] wouldn't give what they were most commonly called: nigger tits.

niggertoe n
1 also *negro toe*: The Brazil nut (*Bertholletia excelsa*). Cf **nigger heel 5, nigger nut**
1896 *DN* 1.421 **NY, nOH, sePA**, Nigger toes: for Brazil nuts. **1906** *DN* 3.148 **nwAR**, Nigger-heel[·] nigger-toe—Brazil nut. **1909** *DN* 3.353 **eAL, wGA**, Nigger-toe. . . The Brazil nut: so called because of its dark rough shell. Never called *negro-toe*. **1915** *DN* 4.227 **wTX**, Nigger-toes. **1918** *DN* 5.19 **NC**, Nigger-toe. **1922** *DN* 5.171 **AR, NE, NY**, Nigger-toes. **1949** *PADS* 11.9 **wTX** (as of 1911–29), Nigger-toe. **1950** *PADS* 14.49 **SC**, Nigger toe. **1951** *PADS* 15.58 **neIN** (as of 1890s), Nigger-toe. **1965** *Western Folkl.* 24.193 **KS**, The name "nigger toes" [was] applied to one of the types of nuts which enriched our Christmas stockings; it was long before I discovered that properly they were Brazil nuts. **1967** *DARE* Tape **AL15**, [FW:] What sort of things did you used to get for Christmas? [Inf:] We didn't get too much. Just a little fruit, a few nuts . . nigger toes, we called 'em. They were Brazil nuts. **1967–69** *DARE* FW Addits **ID, IA, MN**, Niggertoes—Brazil nuts. **1976** Garber *Mountain-ese* 61 **sAppalachians**, We cracked a pound uv nigger-toes and a pound uv warnuts. **1986** Pederson *LAGS Concordance* **Gulf Region**, 49 infs, Niggertoe(s)—Brazil nut; 37 infs, Niggertoes; 2 infs, Niggertoes—Brazil nuts, butternuts; 1 inf, Niggertoes—cream nuts; 1 inf, Negro toe—facetious; 1 inf, Negro toe—Brazil nut. **1994** *DARE* File, When I was serving in the U.S. Army in Washington, D.C. in 1964, I asked a Black serviceman friend of mine what Blacks called the nuts I knew as "niggertoes." He replied, "We call them 'niggertoes,' just like you do!"
2 A **gaillardia B** (here: *Gaillardia pulchella*).
1898 *Jrl. Amer. Folkl.* 11.229 **KS**, *Gaillardia pulchella* . . niggertoe.
3 usu pl: A **brodiaea** such as **blue dicks. esp CA**
1908 Johnson *Highways Pacific Coast* 143 **nCA**, There were multitudes of delicate bluebells, and there were "nigger toes" and "popcorn" and dainty snowdrops and "little Johnnies" and many more. **1938** MacFarland et al. *Garden Bulbs* 176, Although native to the western part of our own country, Brodiæas are little known to eastern gardeners. The Indians of the West Coast call the bulbs "nigger-toes." **1968** *DARE*

File **swCA**, Niggertoes—another name for blue brodiaea. **1969** *DARE* (Qu. S23, *Pale blue flowers with downy leaves and cups that come up on open, stony hillsides in March or early April*) Inf **CA117**, Niggertoes—a beautiful little flower; (Qu. S26a, . . *Wildflowers. . . Roadside flowers*) Inf **CA127**, Niggertoes.
4 A **prickly pear** (here: *Opuntia fragilis*).
1926 *Torreya* 26.6, *Opuntia pes-corvi* . . Nigger-toes, Sapelo Id., Ga.
5 Any of var **coneflowers**, esp **black-eyed Susan 2. chiefly S Midl, TX** Cf **niggerhead 3b, 3k, 3l**
1936 Whitehouse *TX Flowers* 173, *Ratibida columnaris* . . is also called . . niggertoe. . . It is a very handsome plant. **1949** [see **nigger navel**]. **1965–70** *DARE* (Qu. S7, *A kind of daisy, bright yellow with a dark center, that grows along roadsides in late summer*) Infs **KY11, LA33, MO35, NC55, TX27, 28, 29**, Niggertoe(s); **TX68**, Niggerhead or niggertoe; (Qu. S26a, . . *Wildflowers. . . Roadside flowers*) Inf **CA127, TX28**, Niggertoes; (Qu. S26c, *Wildflowers that grow in woods*) Inf **IL19**, Niggertoes (has dark center); (Qu. S26d, *Wildflowers that grow in meadows;* not asked in early QRs) Inf **KY11**, Niggertoes. **1967–68** *DARE* Tape **TX28**, Niggertoes, which I think are sometimes called Indian paint; **LA33**, We have native Louisiana flowers growing here. . . Detonia is a very beautiful little flower that's . . two shades of orange; they look a little bit like the niggertoes that I told you about . . only the color is different and the foliage is different and they grow higher. **1969** *DARE* FW Addit **cwNC**, Nigger toes—a flower, possibly a black-eyed Susan. **1986** Pederson *LAGS Concordance*, 1 inf, **cnGA**, Niggertoes—orange-colored flower; black center.
6 Any of var nuts, but esp the fruit of the **butternut 1.** Cf **nigger heel 5**
1967 *DARE* (Qu. I43) Inf **KS4**, Niggertoes: a large, round, hard nut. **1981** Pederson *LAGS Basic Materials* **Gulf Region**, 3 infs, Niggertoes—butternuts; 2 infs, Niggertoes—Brazil nuts, butternuts; 1 inf, Niggertoes—filberts; 1 inf, Niggertoes—black with hard shells, round; 1 inf, Butternut, niggertoes—looks like a coconut, has an orange square at top.
7 also abbr *toe*: A small, chocolate-coated candy; also a licorice drop. **esp S Midl** Cf **niggerhead 7**
1966–69 *DARE* (Qu. H82a, *Cheap candies sold especially for school-children*) Inf **WV3**, Niggertoes—small chocolate drops, cream-filled; (Qu. H82b, *Kinds of cheap candy that used to be sold years ago*) Infs **KY22, MO20**, Niggertoes; **KY41, MO3**, Niggertoes—chocolate drops; **MO19**, Niggertoes—coconut-filled, with chocolate outside; **NC37**, Niggertoes—white cream with chocolate; **NY206**, Niggertoes—little drops of licorice; **TN5**, Niggertoes—same as chocolate cream drops. **1982** Mason *Shiloh* 95 **wKY**, Now he asked, "Who bought these 'toes'?" He would no longer say "niggertoes," the old name for the chocolate-covered creams. **1986** Pederson *LAGS Concordance*, 1 inf, **nwGA**, Niggertoes—small pieces of chocolate candy.
8 also *negro toe rock*: See quots. Cf **niggerhead 1**
1935 Hyatt *Folkl. Adams Co. IL* 393, I never cook white beans unless I drop three negro toe rocks *(small black rocks)* in them to cook. It makes them so much better. You can always go out and pick them up out of the gravel. And I never use the same three rocks over three times. **1968–69** *DARE* (Qu. C25, . . *Kinds of stone . . about . . [. . . size of a person's head], smooth and hard*) Inf **IL71**, Niggertoe—geodes, break open to get crystals inside; **KS8**, Niggertoes—in old days.
9 A man's sharp-pointed shoe.
1967 *DARE* (Qu. W42a, . . *Nicknames . . for men's sharp-pointed shoes*) Infs **MI70, PA42**, Niggertoes.
10 also *nigger heel*: A type of firework. Cf **nigger chaser**
1966–67 *DARE* (Qu. FF14, . . *Kinds of firecrackers*) Infs **AL37, MI16**, Niggertoes; **OH37**, Nigger heels.

nigger-toed adj phr
1968 *DARE* (Qu. X37, . . *Words . . to describe people's legs if they're noticeably bent, or uneven, or not right*) Inf **MD29**, Nigger-toed—toes point out.

nigger town n Also *niggerville* **chiefly Sth, S Midl** See Map
A Black neighborhood or district.
1857 Helper *Impending Crisis* 18, Like all other *niggervilles* in our disreputable part of the confederacy, the commercial emporium of South Carolina is sick and impoverished. **1942** Berrey-Van den Bark *Amer. Slang* 47.5, Negro district. . . Niggertown. **1945** Saxon *Gumbo Ya-Ya* 240 **LA**, Every big plantation was like a little ole nigger town, there was so many of us. **1958** Humphrey *Home from the Hill* 122 **neTX**, The band had been rounded up in niggertown. **1959** *Kenyon Rev.* 21.415

TN, Two white people passing each other on some desolate back street in the toughest part of nigger-town, each wondering what dire circumstances could have brought so nice a looking person as the other to this unlikely neighborhood. **1965** Little *Autobiog. Malcolm X* 148, Every Negro that lives in a city has seen the type a thousand times, the Northern cracker who will go to visit "niggertown," to be amused at "the coons." **1965–70** *DARE* (Qu. II25, *Names or nicknames for the part of a town where the poorer people, special groups, or foreign groups live*) 34 Infs, **chiefly Sth, S Midl,** Nigger town; **LA23,** Niggerville; (Qu. C35, *Nicknames for the different parts of your town or city*) 23 Infs, **scattered, but esp Sth, S Midl,** Nigger town; **FL27,** West Niggertown; **LA23,** Niggerville; (Qu. C34, *Nicknames for nearby settlements, villages, or districts*) Inf **MA53,** Nigger town. **1986** Pederson *LAGS Concordance* **Gulf Region,** 20 infs, Nigger town.

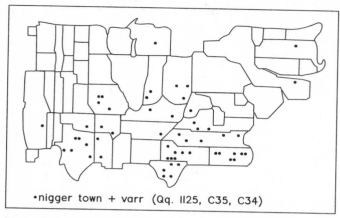

·nigger town + varr (Qq. II25, C35, C34)

nigger turkey See **nigger loon**

nigger up See **nigger** v 2

niggerville See **nigger town**

Nigger War n

The Civil War.

1943 *LANE* Map 551 (*The Civil War*) 1 inf, **ceME,** Abolition War, Nigger War, Abe Lincoln War; 1 inf, **seNH,** Abolition War, older term; Lincoln's Nigger War . . also used; 1 inf, **nwCT,** A Nigger War—that's virtually what it was.

niggerweed n [Prob from the dark color]

1 A **boneset 1** (here: *Eupatorium purpureum*).

1894 *Jrl. Amer. Folkl.* 7.92 **IN,** *Eupatorium purpureum,* nigger-weed, queen-of-the-meadow. **1967** Fetterman *Stinking Creek* 70 **seKY,** We call it niggerweed or sometimes iron blood. Dig the roots. It makes your iron blood. **1974** (1977) Coon *Useful Plants* 108, *Eupatorium purpureum* . . niggerweed.

2 A **blue curls 1** (here: *Trichostema lanceolatum*).

1911 CA Ag. Exper. Sta. Berkeley *Bulletin* 217.1022, *Trichostema lancealatum* [sic]. . . Nigger Weed (San Bernardino County). . . The bulk of this honey goes to biscuit manufacturers.

nigger whiskey See **nigger liquor**

niggerwool n

1 A **sedge** (here: *Carex filifolia*). [See quots 1894, 1950] **esp Upper MW Cf wool grass**

1894 *Jrl. Amer. Folkl.* 7.103 **NE,** *Carex,* sp., nigger-wool. . . From the blackish color of the leaves at the base. **1935** Sandoz *Jules* 20 **wNE** (as of 1880–1930), Where the occasional sunflower along the soldier trail reached to his shoulder, he sank his spade two blades deep through the tough nigger-wool sod. **1937** U.S. Forest Serv. *Range Plant Hdbk.* GL5, Threadleaf sedge, sometimes called niggerwool, . . is a small grasslike plant. . . Its many, black, fibrous roots are very tough and wiry and form a heavy sod which is highly resistant to heavy trampling. **1950** Stevens *ND Plants* 95, *Carex filifolia.* . . "Niggerwool." *Ibid* 96, The name "niggerwool" refers to black, kinky roots which are conspicuous when sod is turned over and are resistant to decay. **1952** FWP *Guide SD* 83, *Nigger wool:* a grass with tough fibrous roots that resist decay.

2 =**ditch grass 2.** Cf **nigger's hair**

1913 *Torreya* 13.226 **LA,** *Ruppia maritima* . . Nigger-wool, Chef Menteur, La. **1921** LA Dept. of Conserv. *Bulletin* 10.47, Widgeon-grass (*Ruppia maritima*), or niggerwool, . . is eaten by gadwalls, widgeons

and other ducks. **1935** *AmSp* 10.80, With its hills, hollows, and swamps, southeast Missouri is well adapted to propagation of the *Podunk* idea. . . Although one section is definitely referred to as *Swampeast* Missouri, not far away are some of the wild and woolly parts of the Ozarks. Emerging from *Nigger-Wool Swamp,* one is likely to find himself in the vicinity of *Gobbler's Knob,* or *Goose-Pond Hill.* **1951** *PADS* 15.27 **TX,** *Ruppia maritima.* . . Duck grass, nigger wool.

3 =**musk grass.**

1913 *Torreya* 13.225 **NC,** *Chara* sp. . . nigger-wool, Currituck Sound, N.C.

4 A **hornwort 1** (here: *Ceratophyllum demersum*).

1926 *Torreya* 26.5 **LA,** *Ceratophyllum demersum* . . Nigger wool, Mississippi Delta, La. **1940** Clute *Amer. Plant Names* 255, *Ceratophyllum demersum.* Nigger wool.

5 See quot.

1986 Pederson *LAGS Concordance,* 1 inf, **seAR,** Niggerwool—on a hog—can't be scraped off.

niggra See **nigra**

nigguh, niggur See **nigger** n[1]

nigh adv, prep, adj Also sp *ni*

A As adv.

1 In close proximity in space or time; near, close; hence prep phrr *nigh to,* rarely *nigh onto* close to. **chiefly S Midl** Note: Some of the glossary quots given here may belong instead (or also) at **B** below. Cf **anigh**

1867 Harris *Sut Lovingood Yarns* 243 **TN,** The road led ni ontu Wat's, ur the widder's. **1887** (1967) Harris *Free Joe* 109 **GA,** Some folks mought take a notion hit wuz a long ways off, an' then, ag'in, yuther folks mought take a notion that hit wuz lots nigher. **1901** Harben *Westerfelt* 136 **nGA,** He reckoned the nigher people got to the railroad the furder they wus from the cross [=Christianity]. **1902** *DN* 2.240 **sIL,** Nigh. . . Always instead of near, which is not used. **1906** *DN* 3.121 **sIN,** Nigh. . . Used exclusively as the positive of *near. Ibid,* Nigh onto. . . Near to. **1907** *DN* 3.225 **nwAR,** Nigh. . . Near. **1907** Wright *Shepherd* 18 **Ozarks,** There's them that 'lows Jim knows a heap more 'bout old man Dewey's cave . . his place bein' so nigh. **1915** (1916) Johnson *Highways New Engl.* 195, I felt his teeth graze my leg. I gorry! if he'd been a very little nigher he'd have got me! **1923** *DN* 5.215 **swMO,** Nigh. . . Near. **1934** Carmer *Stars Fell on AL* 156, The Lord tol' me to dress this way and go tell the Pope his time is nigh. **1954** [see **nigh onto** adv phr]. **1966–69** *DARE* (Qu. MM5, *When you're pointing out a house that's not far away: "The house is over _____."*) Inf **IL39,** Prit nigh; (Qu. MM6, . . *'Very close' or 'only a short distance away': "The house is _____ the park."*) Infs **CA3, MA38, TN20,** (Right) nigh to; **NY105,** Nigh onto. **1982** Slone *How We Talked* 4 **eKY** (as of c1950), If you hear someone say of another person, "He is nigh to me," it represents a closeness, a belonging to each other, that no one nor anything can come between, not even death. **1983** *MJLF* 9.1.49 **ceKY** (as of 1956), *Nigher* . . closer.

2 Almost, nearly; in neg contexts, at all.

1861 Holmes *Venner* 1.118 **NEng,** I'm pretty nigh beat out a'ready. **1867** Harris *Sut Lovingood Yarns* 218 **TN,** Everybody wer skar'd durn ni outen thar wits. **1871** Eggleston *Hoosier Schoolmaster* 165 **sIN,** Isn't nigh so good. **1884** *Anglia* 7.270 **Sth, S Midl** [Black], Mighty nigh = almost. **1887** (1967) Harris *Free Joe* 156 **GA,** I don't nigh like the style of that book. **1916** Lincoln *Mary-'Gusta* 64 **MA,** God would knock anybody's head off. Mine pretty nigh come off when she said that. **1942** Faulkner *Go Down* 125 **MS,** She dont weigh hardly nothing. Not nigh as much as that finding-box. **1942** (1971) Campbell *Cloud-Walking* 8 **seKY,** The little one was nigh tuckered out. **1965–70** *DARE* (Qu. LL30, . . *'Nearly' or 'almost': "He fell off the ladder and _____ [broke his neck]."*) 10 Infs, **scattered,** Dang (*or* damn, darn) nigh; **AR3, DC3, IN5, KY77, MA5, TN12, VA15,** Pretty (*or* purt[y]) nigh; **CA136, ID5, IL55, NC30, VA69,** Nigh; **KY25, LA8, NC82, VT6,** Mighty nigh; **IL97, LA40, PA190,** Well nigh; **AR35,** Most nigh; [**KY25, 77,** Come nigh]; (Qu. X48b, . . *If a person is not so young any more . . "He's _____."*) Inf **OK57,** Nigh seventy; (Qu. KK45, . . *A narrow escape*) Inf **TN23,** Purty nigh got hurt. **1969** *DARE* FW Addit **KY23,** Pert nigh nearly—heard by Inf.

B as quasi-prep or prep: Near, close to; hence v phr *come nigh* (foll by vbl n) to come close to, barely escape (doing something).

1859 (1922) Jackson *Col.'s Diary* 17 **PA,** I meet with difficulties I would not if I were nigh home. **1864** (1868) Trowbridge *3 Scouts* 16, Don't ye go nigh him. **1887** (1967) Harris *Free Joe* 85 **GA** [Black], I crope up nigher de aidge. **1899** (1912) Green *VA Folk-Speech* 298, We are nigh home now. **1906** Casey *Parson's Boys* 329 **sIL** (as of c1860), First, Blake, you go down nigh the top of the hill, and when ye see him comin' hurry back an' let us know. **1914** *DN* 4.155 **Cape Cod MA,** *Come nigh.* . . Come near, in the sense of barely to escape. (Used only with a verbal.) "I come nigh breaking my best china platter this morning." **1939** *Hall Coll.* **eTN,** "About how many bear have you got? . . Fifty or sixty?" "Why, . . fifty or sixty, yeh, I'd say nigher two hunderd would come a heap closer." **1950** *WELS* (*Something that is close:* "The farm is _____ the school.") 1 Inf, **swWI,** Nigh. **1956** *Hall Coll.* **eTN,** He was born over nigh the Chucky [Nolachucky] River. **1960** Criswell *Resp. to PADS 20* **Ozarks,** Came mighty nigh (*or* might nigh) falling off the cliff. **1962** Dykeman *Tall Woman* 95 **NC** (as of c1860), Mark's always speaking of her eyes, too; and the way she clings to him, the way she's so quick to walk, and talks already like a jaybird chattering—well, he thinks she's mighty nigh perfection itself. **1965–70** *DARE* (Qu. MM4, . . *A short distance past* . . "The mail box is just _____ the pine tree.") Inf **MA**58, Nigh; (Qu. MM6, . . *'Very close' or 'only a short distance away':* "The house is _____ the park.") Infs **IA**5, **KY**24, **MD**43, **MT**2, **TN**12, Nigh; **TN**20, Purty nigh; **VA**15, Very nigh; **DC**3, Pretty nigh the road. **1968** *DARE* FW Addit **csNC,** He'd come as nigh helping as anybody.

C As adj.

1 Near, close. See also **nigh cat**

1828 Cooper *Prairie* 1.23, What may a man call the distance, from this place to the nighest point on the main river. **1913** Kephart *Highlanders* 121 **sAppalachians,** The nighest State dispensary . . is sixty miles.

2 In ref to vehicles, draft animals, etc: left-hand. [*OED* 1722 →] See also **nigh horse**

1823 Cooper *Pioneers* 1.76 **NY,** It was only pulling hard on the nigh rein, and touching the off flank of the leader. **1840** (1934) Boynton *Jrl.* 34.346 **VT,** The nigh ones [=wheels] at the same time striking a knoll, and over we went. **1888** [see **jerk line 1**]. **1904** [see **jerk line 1**]. **1923** *DN* 5.215 **swMO,** *Nigh* . . *side*. . . The left side or near side. **1939** (1962) Thompson *Body & Britches* 503 **NY,** Presumably, if there is any difference in oxen, the off-ox is the stronger and more reliable of the pair—you drive oxen from the left (nigh) side.

3 Stingy, parsimonious. [*OED* 1555 →] **esp NEng** Cf **near C**

1899 (1912) Green *VA Folk-Speech* 298, *Nigh.* . . Penurious; stingy; close; near. **1916** in 1944 *ADD* **eMA,** Preston's nigher 'n the bark to a tree. **1927** *AmSp* 3.136 **ME,** A "croping" person was stingy, penurious or "nigh." **1936** Lutes *Country Kitchen* 216 **sMI,** My uncle Frank was what the neighbors called "a little nigh." He not only hated waste, as did all thrifty farmers, but he was a shade less generous in all his dealings than most. **1941** *LANE* Map 484 (*Miser, tightwad*) 1 inf, **ceMA,** Nigh, close as the bark of a tree. **1959** *VT Hist.* 27.150, *Nigh.* . . Stingy; close. Rare. Rural areas.

4 in phrr *nigh as a pea* and varr: See **pea.**

nigh n |naɪ| [Var of *neigh*]

1941 *Language* 17.337 **WI,** [*LANCS* fieldwork] *Nigh*—4 [of 50 infs]. . . *neigh* (and *nigh*) also have some currency. **1965–70** *DARE* (Qu. K40, *The sound that a horse makes*) 9 Infs, **scattered,** Nigh; **CT**7, **LA**44, **MO**17, **NC**10, **NJ**65, **OH**87, [naɪ(z)].

nighabout adv **chiefly Sth, S Midl**

1 =**nearabout(s) 1.**

1884 Murfree *TN Mts.* 249 **TN,** It's the onluckiest place ennywhar nigh about.

2 =**nearabout(s) 2.**

1857 *Putnam's Mag.* 10.352 **CT,** She allers was nigh about fit to get there. *Ibid* 353, I've nigh about swore agin'! **1899** Chesnutt *Conjure Woman* 13 **csNC** [Black], W'en de season is nigh 'bout ober. **1900** Day *Up in ME* 101, We was dobbin' along with dumpy sails in a nigh-about dead calm. **1907** Wright *Shepherd* 58 **Ozarks,** The girl was nigh about wild. **1913** Kephart *Highlanders* 94 **sAppalachians,** They mean nigh about the same thing. **1938** Rawlings *Yearling* 91 **nFL,** He left 'em to nigh about starve to death. **1960** Williams *Walk Egypt* 183 **GA,** This here judge was writing foreclosure orders and nigh-about hanged him. **c1960** *Wilson Coll.* **csKY,** *Nighabout* . . almost: "Nighabout eighty year old." **1966** *DARE* (Qu. LL30, . . *'Nearly' or 'almost':* "He fell off the ladder and _____ [broke his neck].") Inf **FL**38, Nigh about.

nigh-behind See **hide-behind 1**

nigh cut n Also *nigh way* **chiefly S Midl** Cf **near cut**

A shortcut; a bypath.

1848 *Yale Lit. Mag.* 13.281, Instead of plodding on foot along the dusty, well-worn McAdam of learning, why will you take nigh cuts on ponies? **1899** Chesnutt *Conjure Woman* 109 **csNC** [Black], Ez he come erlong back, he tuk a nigh-cut 'cross de cotton-fiel's. **1909** *DN* 3.352 **eAL, wGA,** *Nigh-cut.* . . A near cut, a by-path. **1915** [see **near cut**]. **1933** *AmSp* 8.1.51 **Ozarks,** *Nigh-cut.* . . A narrow trail or bridle path. **1937** (1963) Hyatt *Riverlid* 15 **KY,** Cut through the nigh way. **1939** *Hall Coll.* **wNC,** *Nigh way.* . . A short cut. I come back the nigh way to see if I could locate some bear sign. **1955** Roberts *S. from Hell-fer-Sartin* 101 **seKY,** After traveling a little ways he met up with some people. He asked if the road he had just passed was a nigh cut. **1966** *DARE* (Qu. MM16, *If you're walking with somebody to the other corner of a square, and you want to save steps* . . *"It'll be shorter if we _____."*) Inf **NC**33, Take a nigh cut. **1982** Slone *How We Talked* 34 **eKY** (as of c1950), *Nigh cut*—a shorter distance; "Take the nigh cut around the hill." **1986** Pederson *LAGS Concordance* (*Of walking across intersection or lot*) 1 inf, **neTN,** Going a nigh cut.

nighder adj, adv Cf *moreder* (at **more B1**), *nearder* (at **near B**), Intro "Language Changes" I.8

1936 *AmSp* 11.316 **Ozarks,** The form *nighder,* meaning nigher, is also common. Even *more nighder* is not unknown.

nigh horse n Also *nigh-side horse* **chiefly NEast, Gt Lakes** See Map Cf **eye horse, nigh** adj **C2**

=**near horse;** similarly n *nigh ox.*

1866 (1881) Whitney *Leslie Goldthwaite* 113 **NEng,** The nigh hoss was a res'less crittur. **1899** Garland *Boy Life* 65 **nwIA,** Unhitching with great haste, [he] climbed upon his nigh horse, and rode to the barn. **1907** *DN* 3.247 **eME,** *Nigh horse.* . . The left horse. **1910** *DN* 3.446 **wNY,** *Nigh horse.* . . The horse on the left. **1941** *Language* 17.335 **WI,** [*LANCS* fieldwork] *Near* and *nigh horse* both seem to be in current use through the state; but the former is less used. . . Some confusion, but not widespread, as to the position of horses; most mistakes are made by the middle generation (more familiar with tractors?) **1949** Kurath *Word Geog.* 14, The left-hand horse of a team is called the *nigh-horse* . . in all of the Northern area. In Eastern New England this term is universal; in Western New England, the Hudson Valley, and the New England settlements to the west it stands by the side of *near-horse,* which seems to be gaining ground. *Nigh-horse* . . is found also on Delaware Bay and, in scattering fashion, on Chesapeake Bay, surely as an independent derivative of British usage. **1950** Buley *Old NW* 1.475, [Footnote:] In many regions of the Midwest common usage later reversed the positions of the "nigh" and "off" horses. After a thorough investigation of the subject the author gives up; the only conclusion he can venture is that the "off" horse is the one farthest away from the observer. **1955** Potter *Dial. NW OH* 81, In these days of mechanized farming many informants are without terms for the left horse of a team. Only thirty-four responses were noted for this item [asked of 60 infs]. . . The New England *nigh horse* was counted ten times. *Ibid* 126, *Nigh horse,* offered by almost 1 in 2 of the oldest group, was given only once in each of the other two age groups. **1959** *VT Hist.* 27.151, The left horse is the nigh horse. **1961** Folk *Word Atlas N. LA* map 814, Horse on left side in hauling . . nigh horse 20% [of 275 infs]. **1962** Atwood *Vocab. TX* 56, Other terms for the left-hand horse are *near horse* . . and *lead horse.* . . *Nigh horse* . .

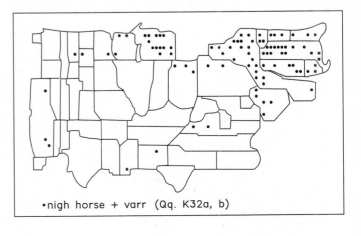

•nigh horse + varr (Qq. K32a, b)

is only a remnant. **1965–70** *DARE* (Qu. K32b, *The horse on the left side in plowing or hauling*) 59 Infs, **chiefly NEast, Gt Lakes,** Nigh horse; **MI**78, **NJ**1, **NY**32, 102, **VA**24, Nigh-side horse; **CT**17, **MA**68, 74, **NY**209, Nigh ox; (Qu. K32a, *With a team of horses, . . the horse on the driver's right hand*) 26 Infs, **NEast, MI,** Nigh horse. **1971** Wood [see **near horse**]. **1981** *PADS* 67.32 **Mesabi Iron Range MN,** Only five . . informants could provide terms for the left horse. Three . . use the Northern *nigh-horse,* which is frequent for other Minnesota informants. **1986** Pederson *LAGS Concordance,* 1 inf, **nwGA,** Nigh horse—right side.

nighly adv [*OED* 971 →] Cf **nigh** adv **A2**
Nearly.
  1843 (1847) Field *Drama Pokerville* 198 **IN,** I'm nighly dead a guessin'! **1968** *DARE* (Qu. LL30, . . 'Nearly' or 'almost': "He fell off the ladder and _____ [broke his neck].") Inf **VA**15, Nighly.

nigh onto adv phr Also *nigh (up)on* **scattered, but more freq S Midl** Cf **near onto**
Nearly, almost.
  1843 (1916) Hall *New Purchase* 147 **IN,** Squattertown, the county seat, was nigh on to twelve mile off. **1867** Harris *Sut Lovingood Yarns* 116 **TN,** Hit pester'd em ni ontu es bad as the eatch. **1871** Eggleston *Hoosier Schoolmaster* 87 **sIN,** Nigh upon twenty year ago they was a man lived over on Wild Cat Run. **1884** Murfree *TN Mts.* 250, Thar war a man hyar, nigh on ter fifty year ago. **1902** *DN* 2.241 **sIL,** Nigh on to. . . Nearly; the latter word is not used. **1905** *DN* 3.14 **cCT,** Nigh onto. . . Nearly, almost. **1907** *DN* 3.225 **nwAR,** Nigh on to. . . Nearly. **1950** *PADS* 14.49 **SC,** "He is nigh on to fifty." "It's nigh on to four miles from here." **1951** Johnson *Resp. to PADS 20* **DE,** (*I'd better go home, it's _____ bed time.*) Nigh onto—old-fashioned. **1953** Hall *Coll.* **wNC,** How long did Jake work for the lumber companies? . . Nigh on up til about nineteen and ten. **1954** Harder *Coll.* **cwTN,** Nigh on to. . . near, very nearly. **1960** Criswell *Resp. to PADS 20* **Ozarks,** Nigh onto a year. *Ibid,* Nigh on to . . getting on in years . . near (seventy). **1963** Owens *Look to River* 8 **TX,** "Nigh on time for quilting," she said. **1965–70** *DARE* (Qu. X48a, *Expressions meaning that a person is not so young any more . . "She must be _____ sixty."*) 15 Infs, **scattered,** Nigh onto; **NY**205, **OK**7, **RI**6, **VA**9, Nigh on; (Qu. X48b, . . *If a person is not so young any more . . "He's _____."*) Infs **OH**6, **FL**27, Nigh onto eighty (*or* ninety); (Qu. KK41, *Something that is very difficult to do:* "I managed to get through with it, but it was _____.") Inf **TX**33, Nigh onto impossible; (Qu. LL30, . . 'Nearly' or 'almost': "He fell off the ladder and _____ [broke his neck].") Inf **NY**105, Nigh onto. **1983** *MJLF* 9.1.49 **ceKY,** Nigh on to . . almost. **1986** Pederson *LAGS Concordance* **Gulf Region** (*Almost*) 6 infs, Nigh onto (it *or* midnight *or* twelve o' clock).

nigh onto prep phr See **nigh** adv **A1**

nigh ox See **nigh horse**

night n [*OED night* sb. 3 c1205 →] Cf **evening**
Nightfall.
  1903 *DN* 2.323 **seMO,** Night. . . Nightfall. 'I'll not get home till after night.' **1907** *DN* 3.233 **nwAR,** Night. . . Nightfall. c**1960** Wilson *Coll.* **csKY,** Night. . . Nightfall, twilight.

night bird n
Any of var largely nocturnal birds such as the **black-crowned night heron** or the **nighthawk** n **1.**
  1950 *WELS* (*Birds that come out only after dark*) 1 Inf, **cWI,** Night hawk [corr to:] Night bird. **1951** *AmSp* 26.278, *Night bird* (night-hawk, S.C., Wis.) **1955** MA Audubon Soc. *Bulletin* 39.312 **ME,** *Black-crowned Night Heron.* . . Night Bird. . A chiefly nocturnal species. **1968–70** *DARE* (Qu. Q3, . . *Birds that come out only after dark*) Inf **CT**42, Night bird—the bird you hear at night; **NY**231, Night bird—you just hear 'em at night; **PA**78, Night birds—catch insects; **WI**50, Night bird.

night-blooming catchfly See **night-flowering catchfly**

night-blooming cereus n
Std: a **cactus B1** (here: *Cereus greggi*) native to Arizona and Texas. Also called **deerhorn cactus 2, sweet-potato ~**

night bowl See **night glass**

night bug n
A night-flying insect such as a **June bug 1** or a **miller 1**; see quots.

1960 Criswell *Resp. to PADS 20* **Ozarks,** Night bugs are particularly bad around lights. **1960** Lee *Mockingbird* 161 **sAL,** He was reading, oblivious of the nightbugs dancing over his head. **1968** *DARE* (Qu. R5, *A big brown beetle that comes out in large numbers in spring and early summer, and flies with a buzzing sound*) Infs **NC**49, **NJ**52, Night bug. **1968** *DARE* Tape **IN**30, If we had little smoky lights like that, we would be afraid that maybe flies or nightbugs or something might get in the house.

nightcaps n Also *granny's nightcap* Cf **grandma's cap, grandmammy's nightcap**
A **wood anemone** (here: *Anemone quinquefolia*).
  1900 Lyons *Plant Names* 35, *A[nemone] nemorosa* . . Granny's-nightcap. **1931** Clute *Common Plants* 60, Among other names that seem to be more fanciful than real are rabbit-bells for *Crotalaria rotundifolia* . . and night caps for *Anemone nemorosa.* **1933** Small *Manual SE Flora* 517, *A[nemone] quinquefolia* . . Nightcaps. Snowboys. Wood-anemone. **1958** Jacobs–Burlage *Index Plants NC* 175, *Anemone quinquefolia.* . . granny's nightcap.

night chamber See **night glass**

night crane n
=**black-crowned night heron.**
  1913 Bailey *Birds VA* 50, *Nycticorax nycticorax naevius* . . Night Crane. **1951** *AmSp* 26.278 **ME,** *Night crane* . . black-crowned night heron.

night crawler n Rarely *night creeper* **widespread exc Sth** See Map
An **earthworm.** Also called **nighthawk** n **3, night prowler, ~ walker 1, ~ wiggler, nightworm**
  1924 *Collier's* 2 Feb 3, He could stay up till ten and hunt night crawlers in the garden with a lantern. **1933** *Sun* (Baltimore MD) 1 May 18/5 (*Hench Coll.*), "We're looking for night crawlers to go fishing with," one of the men said. . . "What are night crawlers?" asked the policeman. "Worms, of course," said one. **1939** *LANE* Map 236 (*Earthworm*) 36 infs, **NEng,** Night crawler. **1941** *Language* 17.330 **WI,** [*LANCS* fieldwork] Night-crawler—12 [of 50 infs]. . . All call it larger or heavier, but most think it not a different worm from the angleworm. **1965–70** *DARE* (Qu. P6, . . *Kinds of worms . . used for bait*) 408 Infs, **widespread exc Sth,** Night crawler; **OH**16, Red night crawler; (Qu. P5, . . *The common worm used as bait*) 116 Infs, **chiefly Nth, Midl,** Night crawler; (Qu. R27, . . *Kinds of caterpillars or similar worms*) Inf **MI**67, Big night crawler; **IL**143, Night crawlers. **1966** Dakin *Dial. Vocab. Ohio R. Valley* 2.394, Throughout the [Ohio] Valley . . this worm is regularly called a *night crawler.* . . *Night crawler* is frequently called a "new" name, but this probably means that only since the development of a practical flashlight have people commonly become familiar with them. **1973** Allen *LAUM* 1.327 **Upper MW** (as of c1950), Erroneously identified in the *W[ord] G[eography]* as applied to a "mature earthworm," the term *night crawler* actually refers to a particular variety known for its large size and its practice of coming out of its burrow at night. Most infs., especially non-anglers, do not recognize this as a special variety. . . Nearly all of those who do distinguish it use *night crawler. Night creeper* and *night worm* are singletons recorded in central Minnesota. **1982** Sternberg *Fishing* 56, Sometimes called the *dew* or *rain worm,* the native nightcrawler appears on roads and sidewalks after spring rains. Average length is 6 to 7 inches, but some are 10 inches or longer. Its color varies from brownish-pink to purplish-red. **1986** Pederson *LAGS Concor-*

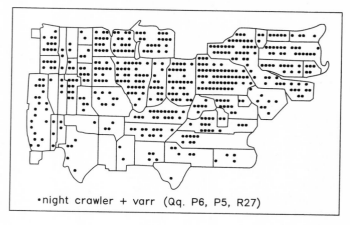

•night crawler + varr (Qq. P6, P5, R27)

dance, 1 inf **ceLA,** Night creeper—variety of earthworm. **1989** Mosher *Stranger* 65 **nVT** (as of 1952), He overturned a dead limb that had dropped off the soft maple tree behind us. He stooped and came up with a nightcrawler as long as a small snake. **1990** Pederson *LAGS Regional Matrix* 157 **Gulf Region,** [*Night crawler* was given by 80 of 914 infs; it was least common in the coastal area and most common in **TN.**]

‡night-did n
=**katydid B1.**

1981 *McDavid Coll.* **eKY,** I have been checking the extra pages of Ontario, Ohio and Kentucky records that were used in LAMSAS, and I found . . from one of the eKY informants (possibly Bell Co.), *night-dids* for 'katydids'.

night doctor n Also *night rider, ~ witch* chiefly among Black speakers Cf **needle man 1**
A person (or demonic figure) thought to kill people, esp Blacks, usu to obtain bodies for dissection; see quots.

1893 *Folk-Lorist* 1.161 **DC** [Black], The night doctor is the most dreaded of all creatures, whose name it is even dangerous to speak. He is a demon, with eyes of fire, who appears suddenly at the side of one who is walking in the dark. In utter silence, with irresistable strength, he wraps his long arms about his victim, upon whose mouth he forces a plaster, that no scream may be heard, then sinks with his prey into the ground, which has opened at their feet. . . I asked, what the doctor did with those, whom he took away? "Takes them down, and stews them up for medicine." **1896** *Jrl. Amer. Folkl.* 9.227 **GA,** On dark nights negroes in cities consider it dangerous to walk alone on the streets because the "night-doctor" is abroad. He does not hesitate to choke colored people to death in order to obtain their bodies for dissection. **1938** *Jrl. Amer. Folkl.* 51.92 **neDE,** During the days of slavery, they [=Blacks] believed that if they wandered out of the bounds of their master's place at night they would never be seen again, because the "night doctors" would get them. **1954** *Time* 4 Oct 61, Even today, in some southern states, mothers threaten naughty children with "the night doctor will get you"—a reference to the ante-bellum breed of burkers. **1970** *DARE* (Qu. EE41, *A hobgoblin that is used to threaten children and make them behave*) Inf **DC12,** Night doctor. [Inf Black] **1975** Fry *Night Riders* 171 [Black], The term "night doctor" (derived from the fact that victims were sought only at night) applies to both students of medicine, who supposedly stole cadavers from which to learn about body processes, and professional thieves, who sold stolen bodies—living and dead—to physicians for medical research. Night doctors were also known to Black folk as "student doctors" . . , "Ku Klux doctors," "night witches," and "night riders." The period of the night-doctor scare coincides with the great migration of Blacks to industrial centers, which lasted from about 1880 to the end of the First World War. *Ibid* 179, References by [Black] informants to fear of night travel . . all carried the same general meaning. . . "They used to say, 'You'd better not go out, the night doctors will catch you.'" *Ibid* 180, When whites first began to masquerade as night doctors in the rural South, their performance was not essentially different from the ghost routines acted out by slaveholders and overseers. In order to keep Blacks indoors at night, and therefore less able to escape undetected to the city, landowners regularly visited Black ghettoes dressed as night doctors.

night eye n Also *night light*
The callosity found on the inside of the leg of a horse or mule; see quots.

c1938 in 1970 Hyatt *Hoodoo* 1.453 **cSC,** These horses go up an' down the street. . . You see them little black places on em? . . Dat's wha' choo call horse *night-eyes. Ibid* 2.1259 **swTN,** It's a thing on de laigs, it's called a *night-eye.* **1943** *Hench Coll.* **cVA,** They . . explained that people often jokingly explain the fine vision horses have by saying that there are two oval spots on their legs which are their "night eyes." All talked as if everybody knew about these eyes. **1948** *Sat. Eve. Post* 29 May 117, Six photographs are taken . . of the horse's four "chestnuts," or "night eyes," which are the rough protrusions of scaly, hardened skin that are on the inner side of each leg. **1958** Browne *Pop. Beliefs AL* 109, Night eye (a sorelike growth on a mule's front leg) is good for toothache. *Ibid* 229, Horses with night lights on their legs (black wartlike patches) can see in the darkness. **1991** *DARE* File **seWI,** Night eyes are the horny growths on the inside of a horse's legs. They can be used as a means of identification.

night-flit n
A woodcock (here: *Philohela minor*).

1911 *Forest & Stream* 77.453, Local North Carolina names. . . Woodcock.—Night Flit, Currituck [NC].

night-flowering catchfly n Also *night-blooming catchfly, night-flowered ~*
A **catchfly 1** (here: *Silene noctiflora*). Also called **cockle 1, gentlemen's hats**

1822 Eaton *Botany* 459, *Silene. . . noctiflora* (night flowered catchfly.) **1847** Wood *Class-Book* 191, *S[ilene] noctiflora. Night-flowering Catchfly. . .* Flowers rather large, white, expanding only in the evening, and in cloudy weather. **1902** (1909) Mathews *Field Book Amer. Wild Flowers* 120, *Night-flowering Catchfly. . .* Probably it is exclusively fertilized by moths, as many such visitors may be seen sipping at the newly opened blossoms in the early evening. **1925** *Book of Rural Life* 7.3910, *Night-flowering catchfly,* an annual weed belonging to the pink family, which infests hay and clover fields. **1949** Moldenke *Amer. Wild Flowers* 67, Widespread over the continent is *S[ilene] noctiflora,* the nightblooming catchfly, a European immigrant with fragrant, white or pinkish flowers that open at dusk and remain open until daybreak. **1979** Niering–Olmstead *Audubon Guide N. Amer. Wildflowers E. Region* 460, Two . . white-flowered species found in our range are Night-Flowering Catchfly . . which is hairy, sticky and broader-leaved than Bladder Campion, and Forking Catchfly (*S[ilene] dichotoma*).

night flyer n
=**white-throated swift.**

1951 *AmSp* 26.278 **SD,** Night flyer . . white-throated swift.

night glass n Also *night bucket, ~ jar, ~ pot;* for addit varr see quots chiefly **Sth, S Midl** See Map
A chamber pot.

1899 (1912) Green *VA Folk-Speech* 299, *Night-glass. . .* A chamber-pot. **1950** *PADS* 14.49 **SC,** *Night glass. . . night jar. . .* Same as *mug* [=a chamber pot.] **1950** *WELS* (Utensil kept under a bed for use at night) 1 Inf, **seWI,** Night pail. **1954** *Harder Coll.* **cwTN,** *Night jar, night pot. . .* Chamber pot. **c1960** *Wilson Coll.* **csKY,** *Night jar. . .* A chamber pot. **1965** Guthrie *Blue Hen's Chick* 100 **KY,** On the last of her returns from the bottle Miss Minnie fell flat on the floor and cracked her skull on what Mary Lizzie in proper moments identified as the night urn. **1965–70** *DARE* (Qu. F38, *Utensil kept under the bed for use at night*) 17 Infs, chiefly **Sth, S Midl,** Night glass; 13 Infs, chiefly **Sth, S Midl,** Night pot; **PA**18, 167, **VA**45, Night bucket; **FL**26, **KY**8, **MS**60, Night jar; **KS**4, **VA**22, Night chamber; **OK**31, Night bowl; **NC**50, Night mug; **MO**35, Night pan.

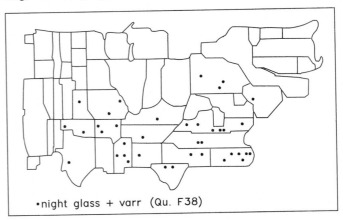

•night glass + varr (Qu. F38)

nighthawk n
1 A bird of the genus *Chordeiles.* Also called **bullbat 1, mosquito hawk 1a.** For other names of the common *C. minor* see **bat n¹ 1, burnt land bird, chimney bat 2, evening swallow, Florida nighthawk, flying bullfrog, haunt bird, mosquito catcher 2, night bird, nightjar 1, night owl 2, ~ swallow, piramidig, pisk, pope, pork-and-beans, shad-spirit, will-o'-the-wisp, woo**

1778 Carver *Travels N. Amer.* 466, The Night Hawk. This Bird is of the hawk species. **1792** Belknap *Hist. NH* 3.174, *Night hawk, Caprimulgus americanus.* **1812** Wilson *Amer. Ornith.* 5.65, Three species only, of this genus, are found within the United States; the *Chuck-will's-widow,* the Whip-poor-will, and the Night-hawk. *Ibid, Caprimulgus Americanus. . .* This bird, in Virginia and some of the southern districts, is called a bat; the name Night-hawk is usually given it in the middle and northern states. **1844** DeKay *Zool. NY* 2.34, The *Night Hawk,* in spite of its popular name, is scarcely nocturnal. It is seen in the afternoon, high in air; towards evening, and in the twilight, it skims over the ground, and is actively engaged in the search of winged insects. **1896** Robinson *In New Engl. Fields* 96, The nighthawk's monotonous cry and intermittent boom. **1913** *Pacific Coast Avifauna* 9.56 **CA**, *Chordeiles acutipennis texensis*. . . A glance . . revealed a Texas Nighthawk, flapping and tacking in the apparently aimless manner so characteristic of this species. This was not the first nighthawk that I had seen in Fresno County, as the birds are abundant summer visitants. **1932** *Sun* (Baltimore MD) 27 Aug 18/3 *(Hench Coll.)*, This is the slower, bigger bomber of the fleet, the nighthawk, or bullbat. It has a graceful, wheeling flight, and may be distinguished . . by the white bars on its wings. **1948** *Sierra Club Bulletin* Mar 11 **CA**, Even after dark, the yap of a coyote, the zoom of a nighthawk, and the rustle made by a scampering mouse are all familiar sounds. **1965–70** *DARE* (Qu. Q3, . . *Birds that come out only after dark*) 213 Infs, **widespread, but somewhat more freq Nth,** Nighthawk; (Qu. Q4, . . *Kinds of hawks*) 16 Infs, **chiefly Nth, N Midl,** Nighthawk; **MA5,** Nighthawks say, "Beef, beef so high; pork, pork so low"; (Qu. Q20, . . *Kinds of swallows and birds like them*) Infs **MI42, PA231,** Nighthawk; (Qu. Q2) Inf **NC44,** Nighthawk. **1977** Bull–Farrand *Audubon Field Guide Birds* 498, *Common Nighthawk. Ibid* 499, Its name is somewhat inappropriate, since it is not strictly nocturnal, often flying in sunlight, and it is not a hawk, although it does "hawk," or catch flying insects on the wing.

2 Any of several other birds such as the **black-crowned night heron,** the **white-tailed kite,** the **great horned owl,** the **whippoorwill,** or a **chicken hawk;** see quots. Cf **nighthawk owl, night owl 2**

[**1917** (1923) *Birds Amer.* 2.173, An old delusion—which is still a belief of many ignorant people, especially in the South—is that the Nighthawk and the Whip-poor-will are identical.] **1951** *AmSp* 26.277, Folk names alluding to nocturnal activity include . . *nighthawk* (the same species [=*Nycticorax nycticorax*], Ga.) . . and *nighthawk* (white-tailed kite, Calif., as it sometimes flies at dusk). **1955** *Oriole* 20.1.2 **GA,** Black-Crowned Night Heron . . Nighthawk (a bird active at night). **1969** *DARE* (Qu. Q2, . . *Kinds of owls*) Inf **GA72,** Horned owl—also called nighthawk. **1986** Pederson *LAGS Concordance,* 1 inf, **cnMS,** Nighthawk = chicken hawk.

3 also *nighthawker:* =**night crawler.**

1967–69 *DARE* (Qu. P6, . . *Kinds of worms . . used for bait*) Infs **PA38,** Nighthawk; **PA199,** Night crawler, nighthawker—same worm, different name.

4 A mosquito **B1.**

1968 *DARE* (Qu. R15a, . . *Names or nicknames . . for mosquitoes*) Inf **NC81,** Nighthawk.

5 A ranch hand in charge of horses or cattle at night; hence v *nighthawk* to herd or guard cattle at night. **West** Cf **night herd** v phr, **wrangler**

1903 Coburn *Rhymes* 18 **West,** Cotton-Eye, the night-hawk, Was then a top cow-hand. **1929** Dobie *Vaquero* 91, With some outfits a *remudero,* or wrangler—"night-hawk," he was often called—herded the horses; other outfits had no night-herder for the horses but simply hobbled them. **1940** (1966) Writers' Program *Guide AZ* 64, At sundown the wranglers were relieved by two nighthawks, who herded the ponies at night. **1940** Writers' Program *Guide NV* 75, The buckaroo who holds a large herd of cattle from straying at night, the *night herd,* is known as a *night hawk.* **1941** Writers' Program *Guide WY* 463, Nighthawk—cowboy on duty at night. **1952** FWP *Guide SD* 84, Night hawk: the man who watches the horse herd at night. **1964** Jackman–Long *OR Desert* 100, Anyone riding by was welcome to come in and eat, or to turn his horse into the cavvy for the grazing. If he didn't have a bed, knew the ropes, and wanted to help, he'd go out and night-hawk. *Ibid* 105, The saddle animals for night herding were brought in after the evening meal when each rider caught his most trustworthy animal, his "nighthawk horse." . . Number of nighthawks depended upon the size of the herd. There were at least two, and larger herds had five or six. **1966** *DARE* Tape **MT5,** They had night hawks that night hawked horses on these round-ups. . . He herded the horses every night; **NM13,** And then [they would] have a day horse wrangler and . . what they called a night hawk, a night horse wrangler; to take care of the horses. **1973** Allen *LAUM* 1.408 (as of c1950), Nighthawk. A horse wrangler on night duty [1 inf, **SD**].

6 also *night owl:* A chamber pot. [Prob euphem for **night glass** or varr]

1968 *DARE* (Qu. F38, *Utensil kept under the bed for use at night*) Inf **GA46,** Night hawk—colored people; **NC52,** Night owl.

nighthawk v See **nighthawk** n **5**

nighthawker See **nighthawk** n **3**

nighthawk owl n Cf **nighthawk** n **2, night owl** =**barn owl 1.**

1951 *AmSp* 26.277, This last species [=*Tyto alba*] is called also *nighthawk owl* in Tennessee.

night hen n

1 A **bittern** (here: *Botaurus lentiginosus*).

1834 Nuttall *Manual Ornith.* 2.61 **eMA,** During the day, the Night Hen, as it [=*Botaurus lentiginosus*] is here called, remains hid in the reeds and sedge, and rarely comes out till the approach of night.

2 =**black-crowned night heron.**

1890 Warren *Birds PA* 64, *Nycticorax nycticorax* . . Black-crowned Night Heron; Squawk; Night-hen.

night herd n See **night herder**

night herd v phr, hence vbl n *night herding* **West**

To herd or guard livestock at night; to herd (animals) at night.

1885 Siringo *TX Cowboy* 81, Finally the herd . . would arrive from camp, where we had been night-herding them. **1903** (1965) Adams *Log Cowboy* 11 **West,** We made twenty-five to thirty miles a day, giving the saddle horses all the advantage of grazing on the way. Rather than hobble, Forrest night-herded them, using five guards. **1920** Hunter *Trail Drivers TX* 471 (as of 1871), We could not night herd because we were afoot, and it took us six weeks to make the trip. **1929** *AmSp* 5.67 **NE,** Usually the "kept horses" or "herding horses" are also "night horses," those used for "night herding," though such use of them is infrequent nowadays. **1929** Dobie *Vaquero* 147 **West,** When we . . had no night-herding to do, we almost felt lost for a few days. **1936** McCarthy *Lang. Mosshorn* np **West** [Range term], *Night Herd.* . . Take charge of cattle on the bed-ground. **1964** [see **nighthawk** n **5**].

night herder n **West**

One who herds or guards livestock at night; hence n *night herd* nighttime herding duty.

1873 Beadle *Undeveloped West* 98, The "night herder" . . and two other drivers . . were Gentiles. **1884** (1966) Aldridge *Life on a Ranch* 62 **csKS,** When on night-herd the men usually keep singing all the time as they ride round. **1920** Hunter *Trail Drivers TX* 343 (as of 1885), The first bad thunderstorm I was in occurred on the Salt Fork of Red River when I was on night herd with the saddle horses. **1926** Lord *Frontier Dust* 132 **cnCO,** Patrick Cullen, Esq. graduated as a night herder. **1929** *AmSp* 5.60 **NE** [Cattle country talk], The heavy "stock-saddle" often served as a bed to the "night herder," especially when he was on a "drive" with cows to the "shipping point." *Ibid* 72, If there are few cattle, as is usually the case, or the cattle can be herded into a fenced piece of range, there may be no "night herd." **1939** FWP *ID Lore* 244, The following is reported as the talk of a southwest Idaho cowboy: In the mornun the night-herder rolls out of his soogan (bed-roll) and rolls a quirlie (cigarette). **1956** Ker *Vocab. W. TX* 187, One whose immediate duty is to herd the cattle at night is known as a *night herder* (1) [of 67 infs].

night herding See **night herd** v phr

night heron n

Either of two closely related birds: the **black-crowned night heron** or the **yellow-crowned night heron.** Also called **gaulding, gros-bec, Indian hen 2a, ~ pullet 1, moonshine n 3, night scoggins, quabird, quawk, squawk, shitepoke**

1785 Pennant *Arctic Zool.* 2.450, Night [Heron]. . . Inhabits *New York.* **1813** (1824) Wilson *Amer. Ornith.* 7.110, The food of the Night Heron, or Qua-bird, is chiefly composed of small fish, which it takes by night. **1844** Giraud *Birds Long Is.* 279, The migrations of the Night Heron [=*Nycticorax nycticorax*] seldom extend far into the interior, but on most parts of the sea coast of the United States it is common during summer. **1895** (1907) Wright *Birdcraft* 255, The Night Heron's [cry] merely suggests that he has half swallowed a particularly unappetizing frog, and wishes to unswallow it. **1923** U.S. Dept. Ag. *Farmers' Bulletin* 1375.19 **LA,** Open seasons: . . Gros-bec (night heron). . . July 1–Nov. 1. **1950** *WELS* (*Birds that come out only after dark*) 1 Inf, **cWI,** Night heron—same as grawk. **1967** *PA Game News* Aug 5 **PA,** Other than night herons, green herons, and big blues most herons and egrets nest south of Pennsylvania. **1967–70** *DARE* (Qu. Q3, . . *Birds that come out only after dark*) Infs **OH20, VA47,** Night heron; (Qu. Q10, . . *Water birds* *and marsh birds*) Infs **GA**20, **IN**39, Night heron; [**NY**53, Night-feeding heron].

night horse n **West** Cf **night herd** v phr, **nightmare**

A horse used for working at night, usu a sure-footed or keen-sighted one.

1908 *Sat. Eve. Post* 4 July 22 **nwTX,** They made Blackie a night horse, for his sure-footedness was remarkable. **1929** [see **nightmare**]. **1929** *AmSp* [see **night herd** v phr]. **1936** McCarthy *Lang. Mosshorn* np **West** [Range term], *Night Horse.* . . A saddle pony employed while a cowboy is on night guard. There is a wide variance in horses' sight. The cowboy generally picks the best in his string for this duty and often it is a white horse. The night horse is tied to the bed wagon as a free horse [is] often hard to find by a cowboy who must go on guard in the middle of the night. **1937** *DN* 6.619 **swTX,** The *night horse* is one staked near the cowpuncher's bed for immediate use in some such emergency as a stampede. **1946** Mora *Trail Dust* 149 **West,** While on guard they were mounted on their quietest and best ponies, their "night horses," and as they made their monotonous rounds they sang and crooned the while. **1966** *DARE* Tape **OK**30, A man's mount generally consisted of 'bout seven horses. . . In that, they would have one night horse that they always used to stand guard on. **1968** Adams *Western Words* 207, *Night horse*—A horse picketed so that he can be instantly caught for night use. A good night horse is of a special type, and in the days of the open range was one of the most essential horses. He was selected for his surefootedness, good eyesight, and sense of direction. He must not be high-strung, but must be gentle, unexcitable, and intelligent. He was never used except for night work, and during stampedes much depended upon him. His rider's life depended on his ability to see, run, dodge, and keep his footing. He could see an animal straying from the herd and turn it back without guidance, and he could find his way back to camp on the darkest night.

night-hunting vbl n **chiefly Sth, S Midl** See Map Cf **night-lighting, shining**

Hunting at night, esp with lights to blind the game; hence n *night-hunter.*

1965–70 *DARE* (Qu. P35b, *Illegal methods of shooting deer; not asked in early QRs*) 18 Infs, **chiefly Sth, S Midl,** Night-hunting; **AL**7, Night-hunting—shine light on them; **GA**25, Night-hunting—blinding them with light; **KY**11, Night-hunting—with lights at night; **KY**23, Night-hunting—with spotlights; **LA**14, Night-hunting—done with a light; **SC**69, Night-hunting or spotlighting; **VA**105, Night-hunting—with lights; **SC**21, Night-hunters.

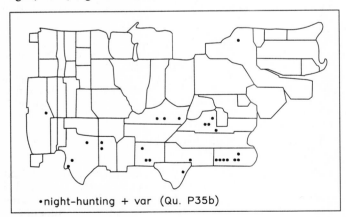

•night-hunting + var (Qu. P35b)

nightingale n

A bird thought to have a particularly melodious song and that often sings at night, such as:

a =**mockingbird 1.**

1649 in 1838 Force *Tracts* 2.8.15 **VA,** The Mock-bird . . will imitate all other Birds notes, and cries both day and night-birds, yea, the Owls and Nightingalls. **1804** (1904) Clark *Orig. Jrls. Lewis & Clark Exped.* 1.38 **MO,** Passed a Small Creek . . which we named Nightingale Creek from a Bird of that discription which Sang for us all last night. **1851** Woods *16 Months* 108, The notes of the robin, the thrush, and the American nightingale are heard, bringing back thoughts of the homes we have left. **1925** Bailey *Birds FL* 134, Mockingbird. . . *Mimus polyglottos polyglottos* (Southern nightingale). **1965–70** *DARE* (Qu. Q3, . . *Birds that come out only after dark*) 34 Infs, **scattered,** Nightingale;

FL26, Nightingale—like whippoorwill, but smaller; **MO**4, Mockingbird . . we'all most called it a nightingale; (Qu. Q14, . . *Names . . for these birds: . . mockingbird*) Infs **AL**25, **DC**8, **HI**2, **KY**43, **NE**11, **NC**35, Nightingale; **TX**33, Texas nightingale. [*DARE* Ed: Some of the Infs at Qu. Q3 may refer instead to **b** below.]

b Any of var other birds such as the **cardinal 1, hermit thrush 1, veery, whippoorwill,** or **white-throated sparrow;** see quots. Cf **Virginia nightingale**

1709 (1967) Lawson *New Voyage* 148, The Nightingales are different in Plumes from those in *Europe.* They always frequent the low Groves, where they sing very prettily all Night. **1759** in 1775 Burnaby *Travels* 10 **VA,** In the woods there are . . the mocking-bird, the red-bird or nightingale, [and] the blue-bird. **1806** *Balance* V.128 *(DA),* It is an attempt to rescue the honor of the American songster of the night, from the disgrace . . of calling the Whip-poor-will the 'American Nightingale.' **1836** Edward *Hist. TX* 75, Among the songsters are the thrush, the mocking-bird, the whippoorwill, and the nightingale. The notes of the last appear not to be so melodious, nor his strain so full as the same bird's at the north. **1895** Minot *Land-Birds New Engl.* 28, [*Catharus*] *fuscescens.* . . "Veery." "Nightingale." *Ibid* 30, In the summer evenings . . this song is somewhat prolonged, becoming more "glorious"; and the male [veery], when his mate is on her nest, sometimes repeats it at night, whence he is among the birds upon whom the epithet "Nightingale" has been bestowed. **1902** White *Blazed Trail* 139 **MI,** Down in the thicket, fine, clear, beautiful. . . came the notes of the white-throat—the nightingale of the North. **1917** (1923) *Birds Amer.* [3.37, *White-throated Sparrow.* . . *Other Names.* . . Nightingale (in Manitoba). *Ibid* 38, This is not only one of the handsomest of Sparrows; it is perhaps the sweetest singer of them all.] *Ibid* 3.151, *Oven-bird.* . . Nightingale. *Ibid* 3.228, *Veery.* . . Nightingale. *Ibid* 3.234, *Hermit Thrush.* . . American Nightingale. . . You have seen a Hermit Thrush, singer of the purest natural melody to be heard in this or, perhaps, any land. The "American Nightingale," he is sometimes called; but there are candid and competent critics who contend that in purity and sweetness of tone, as well as in technique, the Hermit's phrase is really finer than that of the celebrated English bird. **1929** Forbush *Birds MA* 3.403, The ineffable charm and sweetness of the Hermit's song has been the inspiration of many a gifted writer. . . Indeed, one of the names which the Hermit has earned is "American Nightingale." **1950** *WELS* (*Birds that come out only after dark*) 1 Inf, **seWI,** Nightingale. **1956** MA Audubon Soc. *Bulletin* 40.128, *Hermit Thrush.* . . Nightingale (Maine. Likening it to Europe's most noted songster is a tribute to its superior song, which is delivered both before sunrise and after sunset.) *Ibid* 129, *Veery.* . . Nightingale. *Ibid* 255, *White-throated Sparrow.* . . Nightingale (N.H. It sings at night.)

nightjar n [*OED* 1630 → for the related *Caprimulgus europaeus*]

1 A **nighthawk** n 1 (here: *Chordeiles minor*).

1832 Nuttall *Manual Ornith.* 1.619, Night-hawk, or Night-jar. . . Early in May they are first seen near the sea-coast of Massachusetts, which at all times appears to be a favorite resort. **1844** Giraud *Birds Long Is.* 33 **NY,** It [=*Chordeiles minor*] is known to many persons by the name of Night Jar, from the harsh noise it makes when flying about towards evening. **1904** Wheelock *Birds CA* 197, On the wing, Nighthawks are very sociable, circling in flocks and twittering after the manner of chimney-swifts, to which they are closely related, and uttering their characteristic "boom" which has given them the name of "night jar." **1923** WV State Ornith. *Birds WV* 32, *Chordeiles virginianus* . . Night Jar, Bull Bat. **1930** Giles *Enduring Hills* 96 **KY,** The nightjars started whining, and a bird in the hedge of trees cheeped fretfully. **1956** MA Audubon Soc. *Bulletin* 40.81 **VT,** Common Nighthawk . . Night Jar. . . By transfer of a British provincial name for a species of the same family, which is however, more like our Whip-poor-will. **1967–70** *DARE* (Qu. Q3, . . *Birds that come out only after dark*) Inf **CA**97, Nightjar—weird sort of creatures; **MA**78, Nighthawk, nightjars—same; **IL**26, Nightjar.

2 =**whippoorwill.**

1872 Coues *Key to N. Amer. Birds* 180, Whippoorwill. Night-jar. . . A nocturnal bird, rarely seen, but well known for its loud strange cry, whence its name is taken. **1903** Dawson *Birds OH* 1.338, Whip-poor-will . . *Antrostomus vociferus* . . Night-jar. **1917** *DN* 4.430 **NEng,** Whip-poor-will (*Antrostomus viciferus* [sic]). Night jar. **1946** Hausman *Eastern Birds* 369, Eastern Whippoorwill *Antrostomus vociferus vociferus.* . . Nightjar. **1950** *WELS* (*Other names . . for the whip-poor-will*) 3 Infs, **WI,** Nightjar.

3 See **night glass.**

night light See **night eye**

night-lighting vbl n Cf **lamp-lighting**
Hunting at night with a spotlight.

1967–69 DARE (Qu. P35b, *Illegal methods of shooting deer; not asked in early QRs*) Inf **TX**26, Night-lighting; **IL**41, Night-lighting—shining a light at night; **MA**26, Night-lighting—same as jacking.

night log n
A large log put on a fire and expected to burn all night.

1934 Minehan *Boy & Girl Tramps* 23, The fire flickers and ebbs. We pull a night log into the embers and prepare to join our companions in sleep. **1968–70** DARE (Qu. D33, *When you build a fire in the fireplace . . the big log that goes behind the others*) Infs **IL**69, **OK**53, Night log; **NY**92, Night log—used occasionally; **VA**38, Night log—old-fashioned.

night mackerel n
=**Pacific mackerel.**

1939 Natl. Geogr. Soc. *Fishes* 224, The Pacific mackerel. . . is similar to the chub mackerel. . . On the Pacific coast . . it is called greenback mackerel, stripe or zebra mackerel, and night mackerel.

nightmare n [Punning var of **night horse**] West
A horse or mule used on night duty.

1920 Hunter *Trail Drivers TX* 230 (as of 1880), One night I was on herd . . near the mouth of Cold Water Creek, and had for a night-mare a small Spanish mule. **1929** Dobie *Vaquero* 99, The cowboy on herd had one other possible source of time measurement—his night horse, or, as he sometimes called this important animal, his "nightmare." The night horse was generally the surest footed, the clearest sighted, and the most intelligent horse that a cowboy had in his string.

night mug See **night glass**

nigh to See **nigh** adv A1

night owl n

1 Any of var owls, but esp a **hoot owl 1** or a **screech owl** such as *Otus asio*. Cf **day owl**

1839 Audubon *Synopsis Birds* 24, Ulula Acadica. . . Acadian Night-Owl. . . Saw-whet. **1939** LANE Map 230 (*Screech owl*) 3 infs, **CT**, **NH**, **VT**, Night owl; 1 inf, **CT**, Night owl, small; 1 inf, **VT**, The night owl cries "hoot, hoo." **1951** AmSp 26.277, Most owls deserve the title *night owl,* and examples of this name are on hand for the great horned owl (N.C.), barred owl (N.J., S.C., Ky., Miss.), and barn owl (Miss.). The last species is called also *nighthawk owl* in Tennessee. *Night owl* (N.Y.) is perhaps as defensible for the bullbat as its most common book name, nighthawk. **1956** Ker *Vocab. W. TX* 235, A bird that hoots at night. . . [1 inf] *night owl.* **1965–70** DARE (Qu. Q2, . . *Kinds of owls*) 19 Infs, **scattered**, Night owl; **CO**20, Night owl—may be the same bird as hoot owl; **MT**4, Night owl—small; (Qu. Q1, . . *Kind of owl that makes a shrill, trembling cry*) Infs **CA**6, **DC**13, **NY**20, 57, **PA**162, **TN**53, **VT**16, Night owl; (Qu. Q3, . . *Birds that come out only after dark*) Infs **CT**7, **NY**41, 44, **TN**53, Night owl. **1973** Allen LAUM 1.316 **Upper MW** (as of c1950), *Screech owl.* . . The infrequent designation *night owl* . . seems to have a Northern orientation with the highest proportion in the Dakotas. Two of the three Nebraska infs. using it have New York state parents. **1981** PADS 67.36 **Mesabi Iron Range MN**, *Screech owl.* . . Other Range responses are . . the infrequent *Night owl* (3 occs.) and *Screech owl* (1 occ.) **1986** Pederson LAGS Concordance **Gulf Region,** 27 infs, Night owl; 1 inf, Night owl = hoot owl; 1 inf, Night owl—general term for all owls; 1 inf, Night owl—larger than hoot owl; 1 inf, Night owl—different from screech owls; 1 inf, Night owl—small, make noise at night; 1 inf, Night owl = hoot owl, big; 1 inf, Night owl = scrooch owl; 1 inf, Night owl = hoot owl.

2 Usu a **nighthawk** n **1** (here: *Chordeiles minor*), but also a **whippoorwill.** Cf **nightjar**

1951 [see **1** above]. **1966–68** DARE (Qu. Q3, . . *Birds that come out only after dark*) Inf **ME**12, Whippoorwill, night owl—same; nighthawk; **WV**3, Nighthawk, night owl—same bird. **1986** Pederson LAGS Concordance, 1 inf, **csLA**, Night owl = nighthawk.

3 See **nighthawk** n **6.**

night pail See **night glass**

night pan See **night glass**

night partridge n Also *night peck*
A **woodcock** (here: *Philohela minor*).

1888 Trumbull *Names of Birds* 153, At Pocomoke City (Worcester

Co.) Md., and Eastville (Northampton Co.), Va., [*Philohela minor* is called] *night partridge.* . . Dr. G.B. Grinnell . . tells us that the woodcock is known to some in the seaboard counties of Virginia as Night Partridge . . and also as *pewee,* and in portions of North Carolina as the *night peck.*

night pasture n **scattered, but esp eGt Lakes, Upstate NY**
See Map
See quots.

1965–70 DARE (Qu. M14, *The open area around or next to the barn*) 23 Infs, **esp eGt Lakes, Upstate NY,** Night pasture; (Qu. M13, *The space near the barn with a fence around it where you keep the livestock*) Inf **OH**10, Night pasture. **1970** Tarpley *Blinky* 130 **neTX,** *Small enclosure outside where horses are kept* . . other responses . . [with fewer than 1% of infs] horse stomp lot, night pasture, run-around.

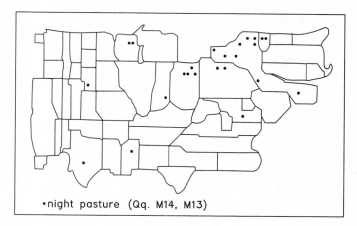

•night pasture (Qq. M14, M13)

night peck See **night partridge**

night peeper n
A tree frog.

1966 Dakin *Dial. Vocab. Ohio R. Valley* 2.388, *Spring frog.* . . In addition to the names mentioned . . Indiana has *night peepers.*

night prowler n
=**night crawler.**

1939 LANE Map 236 (*Earthworm*) 1 inf, **cVT**, Night prowler. **1941** *Nature Mag.* 34.137, A group of appellations employed in southern New England includes night-crawler, crawler, night-prowler, and night-walker. **1973** Allen LAUM 1.327 (as of c1950), One Minnesota inf. commented that his son had acquired in Minneapolis the equivalent *night prowler* [for *night crawler*].

night rail(e) n [OED 1554 →]
1899 (1912) Green *VA Folk-Speech* 299, *Night-rail.* . . Night-raile. A night gown.

night rainbow n
1954 WELS Suppl. **nwWI**, One of the school children here . . told me, last fall, when the whole sky on the northern horizon over Lake Superior pulsates with the northern lights, that many people call them the "night rainbow."

night raven n [OED c725 →]
=**black-crowned night heron.**

1890 *Century Dict.,* Night-raven. . . A bird that cries in the night; the night-heron. **1932** Bennitt *Check-list* 15, Black-crowned night heron. *Nycticorax nycticorax hoactli* . . Night raven; quawk; . . bittrun.

night rider See **night doctor**

night scoggins n Also sp *night skoggins* [**scoggin**]
=**night heron.**

1955 *Oriole* 20.1.2, Black-crowned Night Heron. . . *Nighthawk* . . *Night Skoggins.* Ibid, Yellow-crowned night heron. . . *Night Skoggins.*

night sergeant n
A **demoiselle 1** (here: *Abudefduf taurus*).

1960 Amer. Fisheries Soc. *List Fishes* 33, Night sergeant . . *Abudefduf taurus.* **1991** Amer. Fisheries Soc. *Common Names Fishes* 57, *Abudefduf taurus* . . night sergeant.

nightshade n

1 Std: a plant of the genus *Solanum*. For other names of var spp see **bittersweet, blue nettle, buffalo burr, bull nettle 2, deadly nightshade, fence-corner weed, garden huckleberry 1, horse nettle 1, Jerusalem cherry 1, love apple 1, Mexican nightshade, morel** n[1]**, nettle 2, poisonweed, potato jasmine, ~ tree, purple nightshade, soapberry, soda-apple, trompillo, turkeyberry, wild potato, ~ tomato**

2 A **trillium** (here: *Trillium cernuum*). Cf **three-leaved nightshade**

1967 *DARE* Wildfl QR Pl.24b Inf **MN37**, Nightshade.

nightshed n [Pronc-sp for *nightshade*]

=**nightshade 1.**

1967 *DARE* (Qu. S21, . . *Weeds . . that are a trouble in gardens and fields*) Inf **TX1**, Silver nightshed. **1982** Slone *How We Talked* 49 **eKY** (as of c1950), *Nightshed*—Very poison. Used mixed with milk on sores. *Ibid* 101, Fall or summer sores. . . Cure: . . a salve made from the nightshed plant (this plant was very poison and must be used with care) mixed with cream.

night-shining See **shining**

night skoggins See **night scoggins**

night's milk n Cf **morning's milk**

See quot 1917.

1899 [see **morning's milk**]. **1917** *DN* 4.396 **neOH, IL, KS, KY, NEng, NY,** *Night's milk*. . Milk that was milkt [sic] the evening of the same or previous day. **1927** *AmSp* 2.361 **cwWV,** *Night's milk* . . the milk given at night. "Did you strain any of the night's milk in the cream jar?" [**1929** *AmSp* 5.123 **ME,** "Morning's milk," "night's milk," "haying time," "planting time," . . were important times.]

night snake n

A small, spotted, nocturnal snake (*Hypsiglena torquata*) native chiefly to the southwestern US. Also called **rock snake**

1918 *Copeia* 61.83 **NV,** An example of the little spotted night snake . . was recently secured. **1947** Pickwell *Amphibians* 55 **Pacific,** Ditmars . . found a *Sceloporus* Lizard in the stomach of one of these Night Snakes. **1974** Shaw–Campbell *Snakes West* 171, Night snakes are actually quite common in the American West, but because they are nocturnal they are seldom encountered unless one is actively looking for them. **1979** Behler–King *Audubon Field Guide Reptiles* 616, *Night Snake*. . Patterned with numerous dark brown or gray blotches on back and side. . . *Eyes with vertical pupils.*

night squawk See **squawk**

nightstick n

A **walkingstick** of the family Phasmidae.

1968 *DARE* (Qu. R9a, *An insect from two to four inches long that lives in bushes and looks like a dead twig*) Inf **NY100**, Nightstick.

night swallow n Cf **evening swallow**

A **chimney swift**, a **nighthawk** n **1** (here: *Chordeiles minor*), or similar bird.

1967–69 *DARE* (Qu. Q3, . . *Birds that come out only after dark*) Inf **MA26**, Night swallow; (Qu. Q20, . . *Kinds of swallows and birds like them*) Inf **LA15**, Night swallow = chimney swift; **MN2**, Night swallow.

night's work See **night work**

night toad n Cf **night peeper**

A **treefrog**.

1994 Guterson *Snow Falling* 121 **nwWA,** Crickets and night toads, the brattle of a dog, laundry billowing on a line against the night breeze.

night urn See **night glass**

night walker n

1 =**night crawler. chiefly NEast** See Map

1894 *Outing* 24.137 **NEng,** The huge nightwalkers or bob worms. **1939** *LANE* Map 236 (*Earthworm*) 27 infs, **NEng,** Night walker. **1949** Kurath *Word Geog.* 75, *Night walker* and *night crawler* are applied to the mature earthworm over large areas. **1965** *DARE* FW Addit **ME,** *Nightwalker*—a nightcrawler. **1965–70** *DARE* (Qu. P6, . . *Kinds of worms . . used for bait*) 37 Infs, **NEast,** Night walker; **NJ8,** I've seen [a] sign for night walkers here—he said they were very large worms; (Qu. P5, . . *The common worm used as bait*) Infs **MA26, NY75, 191, 207, PA68,** Night walker; **NY93,** Night walker—this is most commonly seen on

roadside signs. **1980** *NYT Article Letters* **NY,** The large ones [=bait worms] are called "nightwalkers". **1986** Pederson *LAGS Concordance,* 1 inf, **cnGA,** Night walker—large worm. **1989** Mosher *Stranger* 331 **nVT** (as of 1952), At first I thought it was fishermen navigating around on the lawn and picking up nightwalkers, which they frequently do over in the churchyard. . . But this wasn't nightwalker pickers. **1994** *DARE* File **ceNY** (as of 1950s–60s), Night walkers is a common name for night crawlers. We used to go out at night with red cellophane over our flashlights to collect night walkers.

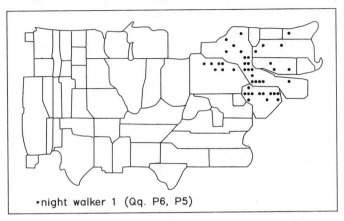

•night walker 1 (Qq. P6, P5)

2 =**ovenbird.** Cf **nightingale b**

1932 Howell *FL Bird Life* 411, Oven-bird: *Seiurus aurocapillus* . . Golden-crowned Thrush; Nightwalker. **1946** Hausman *Eastern Birds* 530, Ovenbird. . . Other Names—Teacher Bird . . Nightingale, Nightwalker. **1955** Forbush–May *Birds* 442, Oven-bird. . . Accentor; Nightwalker.

night water n

Urine excreted at night.

c1938 in 1970 Hyatt *Hoodoo* 2.1162 **seVA,** You kin break that up by using the stuff that is known as your *night water,* and with vinegar, and what is known as silver mullein. **1992** *DARE* File **wKY,** Even after he had plumbing my grandfather always had a piss pot next to his bed at night. In the morning, he would empty the night water. But he never used the term except in that context. . . One reason this sticks out in my mind is that both my grandparents used "night water" and would never refer to it as "piss" although they would both call the pot it was in a "piss pot" and not think twice about it.

night wiggler n

=**night crawler.**

1986 Pederson *LAGS Concordance,* 1 inf, **cnMS,** Night wiggler—large.

night willow-herb n

An **evening primrose a** (here: *Oenothera biennis*).

1791 in 1793 Amer. Philos. Soc. *Trans.* 3.168, Oenothera, Night-willowherb. **1837** Darlington *Flora Cestrica* 240, [*Oenothera*] *biennis* . . Evening Primrose. Night willow-herb. **1892** (1974) Millspaugh *Amer. Med. Plants* 60, *Oenothera biennis* . . common evening primrose, night willow-herb. **1914** Georgia *Manual Weeds* 295, Field Primrose . . Night Willow-Herb. **1940** Clute *Amer. Plant Names* 93, [*Oenothera*] *biennis* . . Common evening primrose. Night willow-herb.

night witch See **night doctor**

night work n Also *night's work* **chiefly Sth**

Farm chores, esp those done at the end of the day.

1909 *Atlantic Mth.* July 137 **VA,** Boys in . . *St. Nicholas* stories used to 'do chores' at the time when the Southern boy was 'doing his night's work.' **c1960** Wilson Coll. **csKY,** Nightwork. . . The farm chores. **1965–69** *DARE* (Qu. K8, *Joking terms for milking a cow: A farmer might say, "Well, it's time to go out and _____."*) Inf **NJ3,** Do the night work; (Qu. L4a, *A general word for work done every morning and evening on a farm; total Infs questioned, 75*) Inf **MS63,** Night work; (Qu. L4b, . . *The time early in the morning and at night when you have to feed livestock, clean stalls, and so on. A person might say, "I've got to go now, it's _____."*) Inf **GA87,** Night work—at night called night work, nothing called at mornings; **LA2,** Night work—old-fashioned; **NJ16,** Time to do morning or night work; **GA1,** Time to do my night work; **FL18,** Time to do night work—Negroes say. **1967** *Tyler Co. Booster* (Woodville TX) 10 Aug 5/4, Mr. and Mrs. Joe Barlow are getting in stove wood, tending to all the chores we use to call night work. **1986** Pederson *LAGS Concordance (Feeding time)* 4 infs, **GA, AL,** Night work; 1 inf, **seAL,** Night work = evening tasks; 1 inf, **nwFL,** Night work = chore time; 1 inf, **cwTN,** Night work = feeding time at night; 1 inf, **seMS,** Night work = what you did at feeding time; 13 infs, **chiefly coastal Gulf Region,** (Time to) do the (*or* his, up the, my, your) night work; 1 inf, **cwMS,** Night-work time; 1 inf, **ceAR,** Night work = "dirty work" cleaning outdoor toilets.

nightworm n
=night crawler.
1966 Dakin *Dial. Vocab. Ohio R. Valley* 2.395, Single instances of *night worm, creeper, shiner* . . , and *night hawk* are recorded. **1967–68** *DARE* (Qu. P6, . . *Kinds of worms* . . *used for bait*) Infs **OH**3, **VA**1, Nightworm. **1973** Allen *LAUM* 1.327 **cMN** (as of c1950), *Night creeper* and *night worm* [for *night crawler*] are singletons recorded in central Minnesota. **1984** *DARE* File **Boston MA, CO, UT, nCA, Seattle WA,** The common worm used as bait: nightworm.

nigh upon See nigh onto adv phr

nigh way See nigh cut

nigra n Usu |ˈnɪgrə|; also rarely |ˈni-| Pronc-spp negra, niggra, nigruh [Varr of **nigro** or *negro;* cf Pronc Intro 3.I.12.d] **chiefly Sth, S Midl** *sometimes derog* Cf **nigger, nigro**
A Black person.
1905 *DN* 3.103 **nwAR,** [ˈnɪgrə]. **1927** Shewmake *Engl. Pronc. VA* 32, The common Southern pronunciation of *negro,* which is *nigruh* (*i* being sounded as in *pin*) is all but universal in Virginia. **1938** Daniels *Southerner* 110 **nwAL,** And this planter was saving a little nigra girl for himself. **1941** Daniels *Tar Heels* 291 **NC,** The interesting thing has happened in the nigra schools. **1942** *New Yorker* 19 Sept 15 **NC,** Washington niggras are a bad, dangerous lot. I'm a Southerner. I know. **1945** *AmSp* 20.84 **TX,** A Negro man is . . on some formal occasions, a 'Nigruh.' **1959** McAtee *Oddments* 5 **cNC,** *Negra* . . pronunciation of "negro". **1959** *New Statesman* 6 June 800 **MS,** In the autumn of 1956 I asked a young plantation owner in Mississippi if he had noticed any change in his relations with Negro employees since the Supreme Court rulings against segregation. 'Well,' he said slowly, 'I guess you can say the nigra ain't loyal any more.' **c1960** *Wilson Coll.* **csKY,** *Negro* is [ˈnɪgrə] to many . . [ˈnɪgrə] very rare. **1964** *AmSp* 39.158 **Philadelphia PA,** Familiar variants of *negro* . . *nigra* and *nigger.* **1965–70** *DARE* (Qu. HH28) Infs **AR**52, **GA**36, 44, 67, **IL**50, **MO**9, **SC**26, 40, Nigra; **LA**2, 3, 16, 17, 32 [ˈnɪgrə]; (Qu. C35) Inf **MS**26, [ˈnɪgrə]; (Qu. U6) Inf **FL**27, Little nigra boys; (Qu. X56b) Inf **GA**17, [ˈnɪgrə]; (Qu. II25) Inf **SC**2, [ˈnɪgrə]. **1966** Dakin *Dial. Vocab. Ohio R. Valley* 2.448, The term *nigra* [nɪgrə] is fairly common in Kentucky and has scattered use in the more southern counties north of the Ohio—somewhat more commonly in Illinois. **1967–70** *DARE* Tape **AL**20, I don't believe the boys . . never ever went swimming back there in that creek, but the nigra [ˈnɪgrə] children did; **TX**99, Nigras [ˈnɪgrəz]. **1969** *DARE* FW Addit **MS**15, [ˈnɪgrə]; **GA**38, [ˈnɪgrə] quarters. **1973** Heren *Growing Up Poor* 109 **AL,** Several well-meaning whites, in spite of all the evidence, sought to persuade me that their niggers—or rather, nigras—were happy, well loved, and free to do whatever they wanted. **1973** *PADS* 60.47 **seNC,** *Negro.* . . The usual neutral pronunciation of this word is /nɪgrə/, with the vowel of *big.* **1981** *AmSp* 56.154, *LAGS* data shows that /ˈnɪgrə/ is common as a neutral or polite term among white Gulf States informants of both sexes and all social classes, particularly in Georgia, Alabama and Mississippi. Among black informants, however, the preferred pronunciations of *Negro* are /ˈnɪgro/ and /ˈnɪgro/; /ˈnɪgrə/ is rarely elicited and is usually glossed as a pejorative.

nigro n |ˈnɪgro(ʊ)| [Var of *negro;* cf *OED* nigro a1548–1618] **chiefly Sth, S Midl** Cf **nigger, nigra**
A Black person.
1893 Shands *MS Speech* 8, The short (i) sound is given to this long *e* in . . [nɪgro and nɪgə] for *negro.* Ibid 47, *Nigro* is sometimes used by educated people. **1941** in 1944 *ADD* **nWV,** *Negro.* . . [ˈnɪgro]. **1942** Hall *Smoky Mt. Speech* 13 **wNC, eTN,** The historical variation [i]/[ɪ] . . is reflected in . . *lief, negro,* which have [ɪ] in the Great Smokies. **1943** *Courier* (Pittsburgh PA) 15 May (*AmSp* 19.166), A great many professional Negro orators. . . make the one big noticeable error of pronouncing *Negro* as if it were spelled *nigro.* **1965–70** *DARE* (Qu. HH28) Infs **LA**8, 17, 25, 28, **MO**5, 26, **NY**96, [ˈnɪˌgrou(z)]; **MO**1, **VA**92, [ˈnɪgro]. **1981** *AmSp* 56.154, *LAGS* data shows that. . . Among black informants . . the preferred pronunciations of *Negro* are /ˈnɪgro/ and /ˈnɪgro/.

nigruh See nigra

---

nimb See nib n² 1

nimble pig See nimbly-peg

nimble will n
1 also *nimble weed, nimblewill muhly:* A **muhly (grass)** (here: *Muhlenbergia schreberi*).
1816 (1819) Thomas *Travels W. Country* 168 **swIN,** In his field he pointed out to me a grass, of which I had heard much, known through all the western country by the name of *nimble Will.* **1843** Torrey *Flora NY* 2.435, *Muhlenbergia diffusa* . . Drop-seed Grass. . . This is a very abundant grass in the Western States, and is the *"Nimble Will"* of Kentucky farmers. **1894** Coulter *Botany W. TX* 523, Nimble Will. . . Dry hills and woods, northern Texas and northward. **1914** Georgia *Manual Weeds* 44, Nimble Will, Drop-Seed Grass—*Muhlenbergia Schreberi.* **1925** *Book of Rural Life* 7.3912, *Nimble will,* or *dropseed grass (Muhlenbergia Schreberi),* a fine-stemmed very leafy perennial grass native from Maine to Minnesota, southward to the Gulf of Mexico. **1961** *Washington Post* (DC) 29 Jan sec G 10/1 (*Hench Coll.*), Early in the season nimblewill looks much like other grasses save, perhaps, for its gray-green foliage. **1966–69** *DARE* (Qu. S9, . . *Kinds of grass that are hard to get rid of*) Inf **NC**35, Nimber [sic] will; **OH**37, Nimble weed; (Qu. S21, . . *Weeds* . . *that are a trouble in gardens and fields*) Inf **IL**37, Nimble will—underground shoots; looks like grass. **1970** Correll *Plants TX* 230, *Muhlenbergia Schreberi* . . Nimblewill muhly.
2 =**black bindweed.**
1950 Gray–Fernald *Manual of Botany* 588, *Tiniaria* . . Climbing Buckwheat, Nimble-Will.

nimblewill muhly See nimble will 1

nimbly-peg n Also *nimble pig* [Varr of **mumblety-peg**]
1968 *DARE* (Qu. EE5, *Games where you try to make a jackknife stick in the ground*) Inf **NY**68A, Nimbly-peg. **1983** *DARE* File **MN,** (*Games where you try to make a jackknife stick in the ground*) Nimble pig.

nimshi n Also sp *nimshy* [*EDD* nimshie "A flighty girl"] Cf *Jehu Nimshi* (at **Jehu** 2) **chiefly NEng** *prob old-fash*
A person, esp a foolish one; a mischievous child.
1848 Bartlett *Americanisms* 233, Nimshi. A foolish fellow, or one who habitually acts in a foolish manner. Local in Connecticut. **1853** in 1915 *DN* 4.203 **NH,** Why any nimshi can jump across that little creek. **1914** *DN* 4.77 **ME, nNH,** Nimshy. . . A human being, creature, girl, young girl. "She was a smart young nimshy." Rather a laudatory sense. **1944** Holton *Yankees Were Like This* 230 **Cape Cod MA** (as of c1890), Like every other village in the world, too, our town had a group of those unfortunate beings nature has equipped with less than their full allotment of buttons. We called them the Nimshis and treated them with tolerance and kindness. **1947** *Sun* (Baltimore MD) 20 June 1/2 (*Hench Coll.*), A nimshi on the tikiteet—as any New Englander schooled in rare Yankee expressions knows—means a girl on the sofa. **1952** Brown *NC Folkl.* 1.569, Nimshi. . . A blockhead. In New England: a mischievous child. Central and east [NC].

‡nimwit n [Blend of *nitwit* + *dimwit*]
1968 *DARE* (Qu. HH3, *A dull and stupid person*) Inf **OH**65, Nimwit.

nina See ninny n²

nincker n [Var of **nicker** n¹, perh infl by **whinner**] Cf Intro "Language Changes" I.8
1969 *DARE* (Qu. K40, *The sound that a horse makes*) Inf **IL**69, Nincker.

ninebark n [So called from the exfoliating bark]
1 A shrub of the genus *Physocarpus.* For other names of var spp see **bridal wreath** 2
1785 Marshall *Arbustrum* 146, *Guelder Rose-leaved Spiraea,* or *Nine-Bark.* This rises with many shrubby branching stalks . . to the height of five or six feet. **1806** (1905) Lewis *Orig. Jrls. Lewis & Clark Exped.* 4.49, The seven bark or nine bark as it is called in the U'States is also common [near Ft. Clatsop OR]. **1830** Rafinesque *Med. Flora* 2.93, The *Spiraea opulifolia,* a larger shrub, growing on the banks of streams . . [is] commonly called *Ninebark.* . . But many shrubs bear the name of Nineback [sic] in the United States. **1860** Curtis *Cat. Plants NC* 104, *Nine Bark.* . . This is found upon river banks in the western part of the State, 6 to 10 feet high. . . The old bark peels off in thin layers. **1895** Gray–Bailey *Field Botany* 150, *P[hysocarpus]* . . *opulifolia* . . Ninebark. So-called from the loose bark, separating in thin annual layers from the stems. **1901** Lounsberry *S. Wild Flowers* 233, Of the rose family there are many children, some wildly gay and beautiful, others of

botanical interest only, and again others that are queer, very queer. The ninebark, however, is one of the large, rather gawky ones. **1937** U.S. Forest Serv. *Range Plant Hdbk.* B103, Mallow ninebark, mountain ninebark *(O. monogynus),* and Pacific ninebark *(O. capitatus)* are probably the most important among western ninebarks. **1944** Nute *Lake Superior* 322 **MI, WI, MN,** The rock shores abound in red wood lilies close to the forest, hedgerows of ninebark a little nearer the water, and rare butterworts with delicate violet blossoms. **1967** *DARE* (Qu. T15, . . *Kinds of swamp trees)* Inf **PA6,** Ninebark. **1976** Elmore *Shrubs & Trees SW* 144, Mountain Ninebark[,] low ninebark . . *Physocarpus monogynus. Ibid,* Ninebark receives its name from the fact that the old brownish bark is continually molting in thin, papery shreds, exposing each time a new layer of bark as if it had "nine lives."

2 A **hydrangea 1** (here: *Hydrangea arborescens*).
1901 Lounsberry *S. Wild Flowers* 221, Downy or Snowy Hydrangea. Nine Bark. *Hydrangea radiata.* . . In the mountains of the Blue Ridge and westward. . . the mountaineers call the plant, "nine bark." A name significant of the way its bark peels off in little layers. This they collect and steep for use in various medicinal ways. **1940** Clute *Amer. Plant Names* 59, *H[ydrangea] cinerea.* Nine-bark.

3 A **cinquefoil** (here: *Potentilla fruticosa*).
1931 U.S. Dept. Ag. *Misc. Pub.* 101.55, Bush cinquefoil . . often called shrub or shrubby cinquefoil and known locally also as buckbrush, ninebark, and yellow rose, is a much-branched, often sprawling, shreddy-barked shrub.

nine-men's morris n Also *nine-man morris, nine men of morse* [*OED* 1590 → (at *morris* sb.²)]
The game of **morris** played with nine pieces.
1899 Champlin-Bostwick *Young Folks' Games* 503, *Nine men's morris,* a game played by two persons, each of whom has nine pieces, or men. . . Each player's object, both in placing the men and in moving them, is to form a row of three of his own pieces; and when this is done, he may take from the board any hostile piece (called "pounding"); but he must not disturb a row of three, if there is any other that he can take. **1935** Sandoz *Jules* 212 **wNE** (as of 1880–1930), Often Susette played checkers or nine-men's morris in the kitchen. **1940** Harbin *Fun Encycl.* 66, Nine-Men's Morris. **1967–68** *DARE* (Qu. DD37, . . *Table games played a lot by adults)* Inf **MA5,** Nine-man morris; **MN12,** Nine men of morse—a variation using checkers and a different board—tried to get three in a row—if you did then you get to take one from your opponent. **1984** *Greenfield Recorder* (MA) 5 June [np; Ruby Hemenway column], When I was a child my Grandfather Hemenway used to show us a red board . . with a nine-men's morris game very carefully and accurately cut on it with a jackknife.

nine o cat n
=one old cat 2.
1968 *DARE* (Qu. EE10, *A game in which a short stick lying on the ground is flipped into the air and then hit with a longer stick)* Inf **NY36,** Nine o cat or one o cat.

nine-o'clock blues n Also *eight-o'clock fever, nine-o'clock bends*
1967–69 *DARE* (Qu. BB28, *Joking names . . for imaginary diseases: "He must have the _____."*) Inf **AL20,** Eight-o'clock fever; **NY37,** Nine-o'clock bends; **RI15,** Nine-o'clock blues—all right after nine o'clock because did not want to go to school.

nine o'clocks n Cf **four o'clock 3**
=spiderwort (here: *Tradescantia* spp).
1938 Baker *FL Wild Flowers* 33, *Nine O'clocks*—Genus *Tradescantia.* . . The local name of nine o'clocks . . [is] especially appropriate, as the flowers are open for only a few hours in the morning.

nine-pin n Cf **knee**
=cypress knee.
1938 FWP *Guide DE* 509, Cypresses. . . Their trunks rising straight to lofty crowns, their knees (here called "nine-pins") standing like elves above the black water.

nine-pin quadrille n
A quadrille performed with an extra man.
1966–69 *DARE* (Qu. FF5a, . . *Different steps and figures in dancing—in past years)* Inf **MA6,** Nine-pin quadrille—extra man supposed to step out and steal a partner; **MA73,** Nine-pin quadrille—an odd man put in the middle.

ninety to nothing adv phr
Extremely fast.
c1950 *Halpert Coll.* 45 **wKY, nwTN,** Going ninety-to-nothing = very fast. **1980** Banks *First-Person America* 4 **TX,** [Ref to riding a pony:] We were going ninety to nothing when I met my dad coming after me.

ninety ways to Dixie adv phr
=Sunday, forty ways till.
1967 *DARE* (Qu. MM12a, . . *'In all directions'* . . "He shot into a flock of birds and they went _____.") Inf **SC40,** Ninety ways to Dixie.

nine ways for Sunday See **Sunday, forty ways till**

ninna See **ninny** n²

ninny n¹ [*EDD* ninny v.² to whinny, sb.² a whinny] Cf **nicker** n¹, v
See quots.
1966 Dakin *Dial. Vocab. Ohio R. Valley* 2.255, [Whinny:] *Whimper* appears once in the Virginia Military District, and *ninny* (a compromise between *nicker* and *whinny?*) in Cincinnati. **1968–69** *DARE* (Qu. K40, *The sound that a horse makes)* Infs **OH45, PA232,** Ninny. **1986** Pederson *LAGS Concordance* (Whinny) 1 inf, **seAL,** Ninny; 1 inf, **cnLA,** Ninny—softer sound.

ninny n² Also *nin(n)a, ninny jug* [Etym uncert; perh hypocoristic, but see quot 1949] chiefly **Sth** See Map
The female breast; breast milk; rarely, a pacifier.
1909 *DN* 3.352 **eAL, wGA,** Ninny. . . Milk from the breast; also one of the breasts. **1946** McCullers *Member* 98 **AL,** She could feel Berenice's soft big ninnas against her back, and her soft wide stomach, her warm solid legs. **1949** Turner *Africanisms* 199 **sSC, GA coasts** [Gullah], [Words used in conversation:] [ˈɲini (ˈnini, ˈnini)] 'the female breast'—M[ende], ɲini (ɲini) 'female breast, udder'. **1950** *PADS* 14.49 **SC,** Ninny. . . Milk from the breast. Child's language. **1965–70** *DARE* (Qu. X31, . . *A woman's breasts)* Infs **AL24, GA33, IL26, MS16, PA248, SC40, 66, VA5,** Ninnies; **LA11,** Ninnies—what colored people call breasts; **CO20,** Ninas [ninaz]; **HI7,** [nini]; **GA89, MS86, MO29, TN52,** Ninny jugs. [6 of 15 Infs Black] **1970** *Thompson Coll.* **nwOH** (as of 1930s), *Ninny* . . sugar teat. [**1982** Holm-Shilling *Dict. Bahamian Engl.* 143, *Ninny.* . . breast. [Used by] White[s].] **1995** *DARE* File, In my family *ninny* was always associated with breast feeding. Both my grandmothers, one from Florida and one from Virginia, would say "Baby wants more ninny." (Sometimes one of them would say the baby wanted more *ninny-pie.*) My parents still use *ninny* in this context. Their friends from South Carolina say "Baby wants more ninnies." It's the kind of word babies can say easily, so they repeat [ˈnini] when they want more milk. The word may be from Gullah.

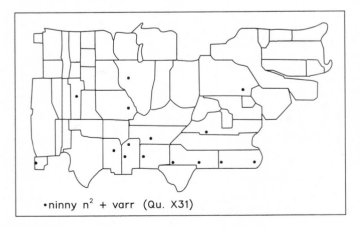

•ninny n² + varr (Qu. X31)

ninsin n Also *ninseng*
A **ginseng B1** (here: *Panax quinquefolium*).
1748 Catesby *Nat. Hist. Carolina* 2 app 16, The *Ginseng,* or *Ninsin* of the Chinese. . . That Father [=Jartoux] took the opportunity to make a draught of the Plant, and give an accurate description thereof, which . . gave light to the discovery of the same in *Canada* and *Pensylvania.* **1790** Deane *New Engl. Farmer* 203, *Panax, Ginseng,* or *Ninseng.* . . this plant is a native of our country, and is become a considerable article of commerce. **1830** Rafinesque *Med. Flora* 2.52, *Panax quinquefolium.* . . *Names* . . *Vulgar.* Ginseng-root, Ninsin, Garantogen. **1900** Lyons *Plant*

Names 273, *P[anax] quinquefolius* [sic] . . Ninsin. **1971** Krochmal *Appalachia Med. Plants* 186, *Panax quinquefolium* . . ninsin.

nint See **anoint**

ninth month See **first month**

ni'ntment See **ointment**

nip n[1] See **nipsy**

nip n[2] Also *blanket nip, neap* **esp Gt Lakes**
    See quot 1969; by ext, a sock.
    1906 *Superior Telegram* (WI) 22 Dec [20]/2, Adopting frontier life and habits, he wore blanket and moccasins, . . and . . somewhat absent-minded at times, the painter, on a cold winter day, complained of one foot being cold; whereupon it was found that he had put on one one of his feet three nips or neaps (blanket wraps), and on the other foot only one. **1911** (1913) Johnson *Highways Gt. Lakes* 166, I'd wrap up my feet in blanket nips, pull on moccasins, and nothing could be better to walk in dry snow. **1969** Sorden *Lumberjack Lingo* 81 **NEng, Gt Lakes,** *Nips*—Pieces of old blankets folded around the feet inside the shoe packs for warmth. **1993** *Detroit Free Press* (MI) 30 July sec F 3/3 **Upper Peninsula MI,** *Nips*: socks.

nip and frizzle adv phr [Var of *nip and tuck*]
    See quots.
    [**1895** *DN* 1.379 **eCanada,** *Nip and frizzle:* like nip and tuck, an even chance, a narrow escape, etc.] **1968** *DARE* (Qu. KK54, *Just about equal, very close: "They were both fast runners and it was _____ all the way."*) Inf **NJ53,** Nip and frizzle.

nip and go adv phr [Prob blend of *nip and tuck* + *touch and go*]
    1968 *DARE* (Qu. KK54, *Just about equal, very close: "They were both fast runners and it was _____ all the way."*) Inf **IA22,** Nip and go.

nipety-tuck, nipitytuck See **nippity-tuck**

nipper n
1 =**cunner** n[1] **1.** *old-fash* Cf **nibbler**
    1884 Goode *Fisheries U.S.* 1.273 **neMA,** At Salem they are called "Nippers," and occasionally here and elsewhere "Bait-stealers." **1911** U.S. Bur. Fisheries *Rept. for 1908* 308, Chogset (*Tautogolabrus adspersus*). . . is also called . . "nippers." **1986** *DARE* File **Bristol RI** (as of 1917), *Nipper*—Yankee chiefly—people older than my own . . contemporaries; I think it's now obsolete, giving way to chogshead or cunner.
2 A padded hand-covering used by fishermen; see quots. **NEng**
    1840 *Niles' Weekly Reg.* 15 Aug 376 **neME,** An article, neither mittens nor gloves, which he [=a Bay of Fundy fisherman] wears upon his hands, he calls "nippers." **1884** U.S. Natl. Museum *Bulletin* 27.794, *Fishermen's Nippers.* Knit of woolen yarn and stuffed with woolen cloth. Gloucester, Mass. . . Used on the hands of fishermen to enable them to grasp and hold a fishing-line better than they otherwise could do. **1896** (1897) Kipling *Captains Courageous* 67, A heavy blue jersey well darned at the elbows, a pair of nippers, and a sou'wester. **1926** Ashley *Yankee Whaler* 137, *Nipper:* A quilted piece of canvas eight or nine inches square which protects the boat-steerer's hand while throwing a turn of the line on or off the loggerhead. **1983** Hansen *Fox & Geese* 20 **ME,** Ask a Maine fisherman about Nippers today, and he'll probably tell you he doesn't use them. The hydraulic trap hauler . . has taken over most of the line hauling for fishermen, and what's left doesn't require Nippers. A Nipper looks like two stuffed tubes of knitting attached together along one side and at both ends. They were slipped on, one to a hand, over the palm, and cushioned the hand against the bite of the rope while actually providing more fetch and grip than the hand can manage on a narrow line.
3 A tooth.
    1968–69 *DARE* (Qu. X12, *. . Large front teeth that stick out of the mouth*) Inf **GA72,** Middle-nippers; (Qu. X13a, *. . Joking names . . for teeth*) Infs **GA72, VA24, WV3,** Nippers.
4 See **nipsy.**

nippety-nip See **nippity-nip**

nippety-tuck See **nippity-tuck**

‡**nippity-nice** adj Cf **nasty-nice**
    1967 *DARE* (Qu. HH11b, *Someone who is too particular or fussy—if it's a woman*) Inf **OH37,** Nippity-nice.

nippity-nip adj, adv, n Also sp *mippety-nip, nippety-nip* Cf **nippity-tuck**
    See quots.
    1953 Randolph–Wilson *Down in Holler* 266 **Ozarks,** *Nippety-nip:* adj. and *adv.* Implies an equal sharing, a division comparable to half and half or horse-and-horse. "*Nippety-nip* in rural central Missouri," says the Kansas City *Star* (April 26, 1935), "seems to be a phrase corresponding to fifty-fifty, even-Stephen or something of the sort." After a motor wreck, one of those concerned was asked who was to blame. "Well," was the answer, "he was a-goin' too fast an' I didn't have no lights. I guess it was just a case of *nippety-nip.*" One sometimes hears *nip-and-nip* and *nip-and-tuck* used to mean near equality in a contest, the equivalent of neck-and-neck. **1954** Harder *Coll.* **cwTN,** *Nippity-nip:* adj, adv. "Implies an equal sharing." **1978** Massey *Bittersweet Country* 207 **Ozarks,** *Mippety-nip* (equal sharing): We all pitched in mippety-nip.

nippity-tuck adv, adj Also *nickety-tuck* Also sp *nip(p)ety-tuck, nipitytuck* [Varr of *nip and tuck,* prob infl by *lickety-split*] **chiefly S Midl** See Map
    See quots.
    1901 Harben *Westerfelt* 222 **nGA,** Toot drove nipitytuck down the street from the Hawkbill as fast as he could lick it, and them a-gallopin' after 'im. **1912** *DN* 3.584 **wIN,** *Nippity-tuck.* . . Evenly. Same as *nip and tuck.* "They went nippity-tuck clear around the track." **1917** *DN* 4.415 **wNC,** *Nipety-tuck.* = *nip and tuck.* Also N.Y.—Also *nickety-tuck.* **1937** (1963) Hyatt *Kiverlid* 64 **KY,** An' thar they had it nippity-tuck. **1965–70** *DARE* (Qu. KK54, *Just about equal, very close: "They were both fast runners and it was _____ all the way."*) Infs **AL3, AR41, KY16, 41, 53, TN1, 4,** Nippity-tuck; **KY72, 75,** Nickety-tuck. **1993** Farwell–Nicholas *Smoky Mt. Voices* 116 **sAppalachians,** *Nipety-tuck, nickety tuck* . . living marginally. . . "It's just nickety tuck with 'em." [*DARE* Ed: Illustr example is from c1920 by Horace Kephart, author of quot 1917.] **1995** *DARE* File **eTN,** Nippity-tuck.

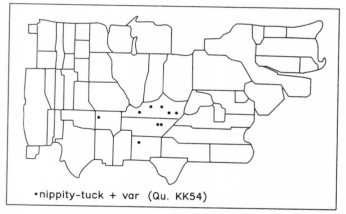

•nippity-tuck + var (Qu. KK54)

nipple cactus n [See quots 1920, 1967]
    Usu a **pincushion cactus** of the genera *Coryphantha* or *Mammillaria*, but also a **hedgehog cactus 3** (here: *Echinocereus triglochidiatus*).
    1920 Rice–Rice *Pop. Studies CA Wild Flowers* 67, *Mammillaria* is well translated by the English "Nipple Cactus," because of the protruding little nipples which cluster on the plant. **1936** Winter *Plants NE* 81, *C[oryphantha] missouriensis.* . . Missouri or Nipple Cactus. **1949** Moldenke *Amer. Wild Flowers* 101, Similar [to *Pediocactus simpsonii*] are the . . nipple cacti, *Neomammillaria,* including *N. missouriensis* [=*Coryphantha missouriensis*] and *N. similis* [=*Coryphantha missouriensis*]. **1967** Dodge *Roadside Wildflowers* 46 **SW,** *Nipple Cactus* [=*Echinocereus triglochidiatus melanacanthus*]. . . Flowers form a pink crown on top of the plant, maturing to nipple-shaped green fruits sometimes tinged with red. **1973** Hitchcock–Cronquist *Flora Pacific NW* 301, Nipple c[actus]. . . *C[oryphantha] missouriensis.* **1985** Dodge *Flowers SW Deserts* 52, *Mammillaria* . . Nipple Cactus.

nippleweed n
    A **greenthread** (here: *Thelesperma filifolium*).
    1936 Winter *Plants NE* 155, *T[helesperma] trifidum* . . Nipple-weed.

‡**nippling** n [Cf *nip* a hard frost]
    1969 Herndon *Wm. Tatham Tobacco* 476 **VA,** [Glossary:] Nippling. Nipping frost; a frost severe enough to damage vegetation susceptible to frostbite.

nipsy n Also *nip(s)*, *nipper* Also sp *nipsie* **chiefly NEast** Cf **cat** n **3a, b, cricket** n²

A game in which a player bats a small stick into the air with a large one; hence nouns *nips(y)*, *nipsie* the small stick itself.

1901 *DN* 2.144 **nePA**, *Nips*. . . A pussy, *q.v.* [*DARE* Ed: =**cat** n **3b.**] Schuyler Co., Pa. **1945** *CA Folkl. Qrly.* 4.84 **MA**, *Nipsy.*—John Russell Bartlett's *Dictionary of Americanisms* (New York, 1848) under the term *Catstick* has reference to a game which I played as a boy in western Massachusetts, although I knew the sport . . by the name of nipsy. . . After it was decided who was to bat first, . . the loser stood behind the line and tossed the short stick (the cat or nipsy) at the circle. **1950** *WELS Suppl.* **neWI**, *Nip*—Flipping a short stick into the air with a long one. **1957** *Sat. Eve. Post Letters* **Buffalo NY**, Now as to *"Nip."* We would take a stick maybe six inches long and about an inch thick. Whittle down both ends to a point—but not too much so. Then place the stick on the ground, and with a shingle or paddle whang it on one end. It should then fly in the air toward your partner and it was his job to catch it on the fly with his paddle and whang it back to you; **Philadelphia PA**, *Nipsie.* This is a game in which a small stick that had been carved to a point was put in a crack in the curb of a sidewalk and then kicked or hit with another stick. The smaller stick was the "Nipsie." **1970** *DARE* (Qu. EE10, *A game in which a short stick lying on the ground is flipped into the air and then hit with a longer stick*) Inf **PA**242, Nipper; **PA**245, Nips—4 sides, numbered, you get as many turns as numbered side facing up.

nip tide n [Var of *neap tide*]

1899 (1912) Green *VA Folk-Speech* 300, *Nip-tide.* . . Neap-tide. **1986** Pederson *LAGS Concordance,* 1 Inf, **seMS**, A nip [=neap] tide.

nirly See **knurl**

nit n

1 also *gnit*: A **midge 1** or **2.**

1903 *DN* 2.297 **Cape Cod MA** (as of a1857), *Gnit.* . . A small insect. **1950** *WELS* (*Very small flies that don't sting, often hovering in large groups*) 1 Inf, **cWI**, Gnats, gnits; bigger ones: lake flies. **1951** Johnson *Resp. to PADS 20* **DE**, (*Very small flies that don't sting, often seen hovering in large groups outdoors in the summer*) Nits. **1960** Bailey *Resp. to PADS 20* **KS**, Gnats, nits. **1965–70** *DARE* (Qu. R10) 13 Infs, **scattered**, Nit; **TX**33, Gnats are bigger than nits; (Qu. R11, *A very tiny fly that you can hardly see, but that stings*) Infs **NJ**27, **NY**100, 214, **PA**79, Nit; (Qu. R21, . . *Other kinds of stinging insects*) Inf **PA**242, Nit.

2 See **nit fly.**

nit adv [Ger dial *nit,* var of *nichts* nothing] Cf **aber nit**

No; definitely not!

1895 *Inlander* Nov 63, *Nit.* . . Not; sometimes an emphatic not. **1896** *DN* 1.421 **MA, MI, NY**, *Nit:* a decided negative, much stronger than *no.* **1897** *KS Univ. Qrly.* (ser B) 6.89, *Nit:* "over the left." **1905** *DN* 3.63 **eNE**, *Nit.* . . no. **1909** *DN* 3.352 **eAL, wGA**, *Nit.* . . no. **1927** *AmSp* 2.475 [Substitutes for "No"], Nit. **1960** Criswell *Resp. to PADS 20* **Ozarks**, *Nit,* a term of very short duration some years ago. Generally it meant "No." **1968** *DARE* (Qu. NN4, . . *Ways of answering 'no': "Would you lend him ten dollars?"* "_____.") Inf **MN**12, Nit. **1968** *DARE* FW Addit, [On a baseball poster advertising a game played June 13, 1906 at Windsor, New York:] "Old timer. Git a basket? Nit!"

nitchie n [Algonquian; *OEDS* 1791 →] Cf *DCan occas derog*

An American Indian.

[**1778** Carver *Travels N. Amer.* 422 **Gt Lakes, Upper MW**, Comrade *Neechee.*] **1950** *WELS Suppl.* **ceWI**, As long as 70 years ago the Indians about here were nicknamed "nitchies." . . It is scarcely used now . . except by real old-timers. **c1970** *DARE* File **cnWI**, *Nitchie*—an Indian (used humorously in the 1920's). Area of Ashland, WI, near Odanah Indian Reservation. I have even heard Indians call each other "nitchies" when kidding each other. You might call the term humorously derogatory.

nitchie adj [Prob **nitchie** n] Cf **bare-ass(ed), buck naked**

Naked.

1979 *NYT Article Letters* **MI**, When we were kids and at the cottage in the summer, we always went swimming "nitchie" after dark. That meant in the nude.

nit fly n Also *nit* **chiefly Sth, S Midl, esp KY** See Map Cf **chin fly, devil's nit ~**

The horse botfly (*Gasterophilus intestinalis*).

1926 Essig *Insects N. Amer.* 575, *The horse bot or nit fly, Gastrophilus*

[sic] *intestinalis.* . . These flies are slow of flight and are to be found about horses where they attach the minute, elongated, pale yellow nits or eggs to the hairs on the forelegs, hind legs, chest, stomach, and other parts of the [horse's] body. **1940** (1978) Still *River of Earth* 7 **KY**, A big house draws kinfolks like a horse draws nitflies. **1965–70** *DARE* (Qu. R12, . . *Other kinds of flies . . that fly around animals*) 36 Infs, **chiefly Sth, S Midl, esp KY**, Nit fly; **LA**8, Nit—mules and thing [sic] just hates 'em; (Qu. K47, . . *Diseases . . horses or mules commonly get*) Inf **VA**38, Grubs—eggs of nit fly; (Qu. R10, *Very small flies that don't sting, often seen hovering in large groups or bunches outdoors in summer*) Inf **GA**77, Nit fly; **TX**52, Nit fly—bothers horses, lays eggs under skin; (Qu. R11, *A very tiny fly that you can hardly see, but that stings*) Infs **KY**16, **VA**38, Nit fly; (Qu. R13) Inf **AR**35, Nit fly; (Qu. R21, . . *Other kinds of stinging insects*) Inf **KY**21, Nit—worse on horses; nit fly—same as nit. **1978** Massey *Bittersweet Country* 229 **Ozarks**, We traveled perhaps a mile and a half and the old horse was fighting nit flies and horseflies so I couldn't turn the lines loose.

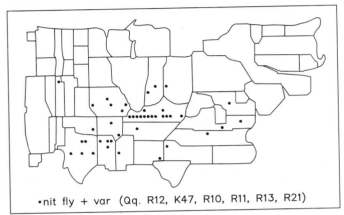

•nit fly + var (Qq. R12, K47, R10, R11, R13, R21)

nither, nithur See **neither**

nitname n [Var of *nickname;* cf Intro "Language Changes" IV.4]

1991 Still *Wolfpen Notebooks* 162 **sAppalachians**, *Nitname:* nick-name.

nits-and-lice n Cf **nitweed**

A **Saint-John's-wort** (here: *Hypericum drummondii*).

1950 Gray–Fernald *Manual of Botany* 1014, *H[ypericum] Drummondii.* . . *Nits-and-lice.* . . Bushy branches. **1970** Correll *Plants TX* 1065, *Nits-and-lice.* . . The stem and the alternate bushy branches rigidly erect, mostly densely punctate throughout. **1979** Niering–Olmstead *Audubon Guide N. Amer. Wildflowers E. Region* 560, *Nits-and-Lice.* . . occurs from Maryland to Florida, west to Texas, north to Iowa, southern Illinois, and West Virginia.

nitting vbl n

1968 *DARE* FW Addit **AL**, *Goosepicking* . . a term referring to . . a poor job of picking cotton. . . A cotton farmer in Florence AL is familiar with both *gooselocking* and *goosepicking,* but claims that the latter is more frequently used. He also mentioned two other terms for the same action: *tagging* and *nitting.* Where the fiber tuft is joined to the plant, there is a small, black speck which he calls the "nit" or the "tag." A good picker will take the entire fiber tuft from the boll, "nit" and all. Since the nit is the point of juncture between fiber and plant, careless pickers may frequently pull away the tuft, leaving the nit joined to the boll along with a good many strands of fiber. This is called *goosepicking.*

nitweed n Cf **louseweed, nits-and-lice**

A **Saint-John's-wort** (here: *Hypericum gentianoides*).

1822 Eaton *Botany* 447 **CT**, Nit-weed, false john's wort. . . On the sandy plain west of Ball's spring, New Haven. **1843** Torrey *Flora NY* 1.89, *Ground Pine. Nitweed. Pine-weed.* . . Leaves scarcely more than a line long, with scattered opake [sic] dots, closely appressed to the stem, so that the plant appears almost leafless. **1940** Clute *Amer. Plant Names* 133, *H[ypericum] gentianoides.* . . Knit-weed [sic].

nix adv [Ger *nichts* nothing]

1 No; definitely not! **chiefly Nth** See Map Cf **nit** adv, **nixie** adv

1909 *DN* 3.352 **eAL, wGA**, *Nix.* . . no. **1926** Black *You Can't Win* 67, "I'll go to the farmhouse . . and buy something." "Nix, nix," said one; "buy nothin'." **1927** *AmSp* 2.475 [Substitutes for "No"], Nix. **1928**

Lewis *Man Who Knew Coolidge* 152, He says they want the hero to come back—they'll make him sure-enough king, but he says, "Nix, not on your life." **1945** *Feathered Warrior* 44.6.13, Nix, men! **1950** *WELS* **WI** (*Ways of answering "no": "Would you lend him $10?" "_____!"*) 7 Infs, Nix. **1965–70** *DARE* (Qu. NN4) 25 Infs, **chiefly Nth,** Nix; **NY**132, Nix—used to be; **NY**236, Nixt, nix; (Qu. KK55c, . . *Expressions of strong denial*) Infs **NJ**25, **OH**24, **WA**1, Nix. [23 of 28 total Infs old]

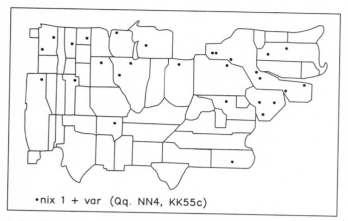

•nix 1 + var (Qq. NN4, KK55c)

2 in phr *nix come erouse* and varr: See quot 1970; also used as adj phr: finished, done for; irrelevant. [Ger *nichts kommt heraus* nothing will come of this]

1844 *Republican Sentinel* (Richmond, Va.) 27 July 1/1 *(DA)*, Clay must rest contented; For he's 'nics cum arous' at the old White House. **1856** *Sacramento Union* 29 March 1/7 *(DA)*, Our mouth watered for a whiff from the golden luxury, but it was 'Nix cum a rouse; nix for shtay, Mein Gott!' **1898** Westcott *Harum* 281 **cNY,** "Wa'al," said David, "as fur 's the bus'nis itself 's concerned, the hull thing's all nix-cum-rouse to me." **1907** Porter *Heart of West* 317, We will now pass you the time of day, as it is up to us to depart. Ausgespielt—nixcumrous, Dutchy. **1919** Kyne *Capt. Scraggs* 117 **CA,** Bull McGinty, roarin' like a sea lion, announces that all hands is doomed, because two of the pumps is nix comarous. **1931** Jacobson *Milwaukee Dial.* 16 **WI,** Nix come eraus. . . this is a byword in Milwaukee. **1970** *DARE* File **Akron OH** (as of c1920), Nix-come-erouse—It doesn't matter, nothing will come of it. (Fairly current in popular speech.)

3 in phr *nix on:* Enough of; no more of; "no" with respect to.

1902 Hobart *It's up to You* 55, We decided before we stepped on the Pullman that it would be nix on the sweetheart talk. **1911** Quick *Yellowstone Nights* 24 **nwWY,** Nix on this conversation game. **1950** *WELS* (*Ways of answering "no": "Would you lend him $10?" "_____!"*) 1 Inf, **csWI,** Nix on it. **1966** Barnes–Jensen *Dict. UT Slang* 32, *Nix on.* . . no more of, have done. "No hunting deer until November 15th—nix on that stuff; we want it in October." **1969–70** *DARE* (Qu. NN4) Infs **MI**103, 122, Nix on that; **NY**230, Nix on it.

4 Used as an exclam in games: Time out! [*OEDS nix* sb.¹ 3 1860 →]

1969 *DARE* (Qu. EE17, *In a game of tag, if a player wants to rest, what does he call out so that he can't be tagged?*) Inf **CA**133, Nix.

nix comarous, nix come erouse, nix cum a rouse, nix cum rous(e) See **nix 2**

nixie n

The young of the **chipping sparrow.**

1899 Bergen *Animal Lore* 61 **NEng,** Nixie, young chipping sparrow (or other sparrow), *Spizella socialis.* **1917** *Wilson Bulletin* 29.2.83 **NEng,** *Spizella passerina.*—Nixie (the young).

nixie adv Also sp *nixy*

=**nix** adv **1.**

1894 Frederic *Marsena* 178 **nNY,** He sniffed when Billy told him about the military company we were forming; he coldly shook his head with a curt "Nixie!" when invited to join it. **1902** (1906) Porter *4 Million* 121 **NYC,** One day she says she will; the same evenin' she says nixy. **1903** *Pedagogical Seminary* 10.373 [Slang terms used by children], Nixy. . . Don't you believe it. Not much. **1905** *DN* 3.63 **eNE,** Nixy. . . no. **1909** *DN* 3.352 **eAL, wGA,** Nix(y). . . no. **1914** *DN* 4.110 **cKS,** Nixie. . . No. **1914** Atherton *Perch of the Devil* 108 **swMT,** They're all

right to marry . . but to sacrifice your life for, nixie. **1927** *AmSp* 2.475 [Substitutes for "No"], Nixy.

nix on See **nix** adv **3**

nixy See **nixie** adv

no adv Usu |no|; also freq |nɔ:|; for addit varr see quots Pronc-spp *na(h), naw, nayo, neh-o, noi, nor, nuh(r)*

Std senses, var forms.

1891 Page *Elsket* 124 **VA** [Black], Nor, suh, dat he warn'! **1901** *DN* 2.144 **cwNY,** Noi. . . No. **1906** *DN* 3.147 **nwAR,** Naw [nɔ]. . . "Naw sir, we didn't do it." Common. **1908** Lincoln *Cy Whittaker* 22 **NEng,** "Expectin' anybody?" "Naw; nobody that I know of, special." **1909** *DN* 3.351 **eAL, wGA,** Naw. Ibid 353, Nuhr. **1916** *Scribner's Mag.* Mar 358 **Sth** [Black], "Was anything importan' gwine on lars' night?" . . "Nor'm," she sez, "nuthin' 't all." **1917** *DN* 4.396 **neOH,** Naw [nɔɔ]. . . No (in answer). Often connoting disgust that the question should be askt, whereas [no] is ordinarily used. General. **1926** Roberts *Time of Man* 193 **KY,** Who? That! Naw, not much! I know one that's prettier. **1927** Shewmake *Engl. Pronc. VA* 34, Negative forms . . besides *no, nuh* (*u* as in *hut,* but somewhat nasalized) and *neh-o* (*e* as in *men*). **1934** *AmSp* 9.212 **Sth,** *No* (also [nɔ], [nɑ], [nʌʊ]. **1936** *AmSp* 11.27 **eTX,** The sound of the vowel . . is [o] or [ou] in. . . no'm (no ma'am). **1941** Faulkner *Men Working* 17 **MS,** He said, 'Naw,' kind of madlike. **1941** Ward *Holding Hills* 45 **IA** (as of early 20th cent), "Na," he said, "stop here tonight, and we'll see what tomorrow'll be like." **1948** Manfred *Chokecherry* 215 **nwIA,** "Sure. But sometimes in your favor." "Nah." . . "Yeh." **1949** *PADS* 11.8 **wTX,** Naw. . . No in elliptical sentences: "Are you going?" "Naw." **1959** Mailer *Advt. for Myself* 53 **cwIN,** 'Does one of you want to go?' . . 'Naw.' **1960** (1966) Percy *Moviegoer* 118 **New Orleans LA,** Some old girl told me you were married to her. I said nayo indeed. **1965–70** *DARE* (Qu. NN4, . . *Ways of answering 'no': "Would you lend him ten dollars?" "_____."*) 23 Infs, **scattered, but esp Sth,** Naw; 20 Infs, **scattered,** Nah; **GA**91, 92, Hell, naw; **MS**4, Naw, I can't do it; **TX**26, Nuh; (Qu. KK55c, . . *Expressions of strong denial*) Infs **AL**59, **GA**91, 93, **OH**102, Hell, naw. **1966** Barnes–Jensen *Dict. UT Slang* 31, *Naw* . . no. **1977** Smitherman *Talkin* 145 [Black], Naw, it's the po-lice.

no-account adj, also used absol **scattered, but chiefly NEast, N Midl** See Map Cf **no-count**

Worthless; useless; good-for-nothing.

1845 Hooper *Advent. Simon Suggs* 39, The land I'm after is a . . no-account quarter section. **1878** Beadle *Western Wilds* 187 **UT,** Little Si Duvall, a splintery feller . . and . . no account. **1899** (1912) Green *VA Folk-Speech* 300, No-account. . . Worthless. "He is very no-account." **1903** *DN* 2.322 **seMO,** No-account. . . Worthless. 'He is a strickly no-account fellow.' **1906** *DN* 3.121 **sIN,** No-account. . . Worthless. **1909** *DN* 3.352 **eAL, wGA,** No-(ac)count. . . Worthless. **1940** (1968) Haun *Hawk's Done Gone* 183 **eTN,** All them girls had been no-account. **1965–70** *DARE* (Qu. HH20a, *An idle, worthless person: "He's a _____."*) 16 Infs, **scattered, exc Sth,** No-account; **NY**123, No-account loafer; (Qu. K55, *A pig that doesn't grow well and is not worth keeping*) Inf **MO**5, No-account; (Qu. U17, *Names or nicknames for a person who doesn't pay his bills*) Inf **OH**60, No-account; (Qu. V2a, *A deceiving person, or somebody that you can't trust*) Inf **RI**15, No-account; (Qu. Y28, *A person who loiters about with nothing to do*) Infs **KS**5, **MA**5, **NE**3, **OH**4, 53, **RI**15, No-account; (Qu. BB39, *On a day*

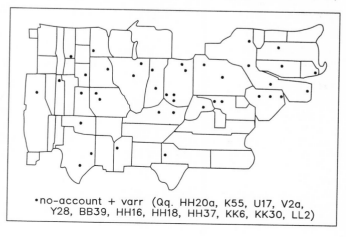

•no-account + varr (Qq. HH20a, K55, U17, V2a, Y28, BB39, HH16, HH18, HH37, KK6, KK30, LL2)

when you don't feel just right, though not actually sick . . "I'll be all right tomorrow—I'm just feeling _____ today.") Inf **TX**20, No-account; (Qu. HH16, *Uncomplimentary words with no definite meaning—just used when you want to show that you don't think much of a person: "Don't invite him. He's a _____."*) Infs **IA**17, **IL**61, **MN**38, **NJ**45, **RI**15, **TX**35, No-account; (Qu. HH18, *Very insignificant or low-grade people*) Infs **MD**17, **OH**68, **PA**219, No-account; **CT**37, **NY**54, No-accounts; **NJ**36, No-account people; (Qu. HH37, *An immoral woman*) Inf **IN**28, No-account; (Qu. KK6, *Something low-grade or of poor quality—for example, a piece of merchandise: "I wouldn't buy that, it's _____."*) Infs **GA**84, **UT**4, No-account; (Qu. KK30, *Feeling slowed up or without energy: "I certainly feel _____."*) Infs **GA**84, **KY**36, **MS**30, **WV**1, No-account; (Qu. LL2, *. . Too small to be worth much: "I don't want that little _____ potato."*) Infs **MO**11, **NY**22, No-account. **1986** [see **no-count**].

noach n, v Also sp *noatch* [Prob < PaGer *gnoche* bone]
See quots.
　　1963 in 1982 *Barrick Coll.* **csPA,** Noach doctor—chiropractor. **1982** *Ibid* **csPA,** Noach, noatch—massage; squeeze with the fingers; rub down.

Noah n Usu |ˈnoə|; for varr see quots Pronc-spp *Norah, Nowie* Cf Pronc Intro 3.I.12b, 3.I.23
Std sense, var forms.
　　1933 in 1944 *ADD,* Noah . . Nowie. **1941** *Ibid* Sth, [ˈnorə]. **1942** *Sat. Eve. Post* 3 Oct 68 **seSC,** Flood come a-creepin' up to Norah do' (door)/ Gawd tell Norah tek 'e chillun en' go. **1942** Hall *Smoky Mt. Speech* 77 **wNC, eTN,** The given name *Noah* always had [e] or [ɪ]: [ˈno,e]. **1967** *DARE* FW Addit **seAR,** Noah—[nɔɪ]. **1970** *DARE* (Qu. B25) Inf **VA**25, Noah's [ˈnowɪz] time. **1981** Pederson *LAGS Basic Materials,* 2 infs, **swAR, nwGA,** [noˤʊwɨ]; 1 inf, **neTN,** [nɔˤɚ]; 1 inf, **cnGA,** [noˤʊɨ].

Noah's ark n
1 =**lady's slipper 1.**
　　1826 Darlington *Florula Cestrica* 95, C[ypripedium] pubescens. . . Noah's ark. Yellow Mocasin [sic] flower. **1843** Torrey *Flora NY* 2.287, Cypripedium acaule. . . Noah's Ark. **1876** Hobbs *Bot. Hdbk.* 75, Noah's ark. . . Cypripedium pubescens. **1900** Lyons *Plant Names* 129, C[ypripedium] acaule. . . Other names applied indiscriminately to our native species, except . . [C. arietinum], are Moccasin-flower. . . Noah's-ark. [*DARE* Ed: Out of approx 11 spp in US, Lyons specifies here *C. candidum, C. parviflorum, C. reginae.*] **1924** *Amer. Botanist* 30.153, Cypripedium parvulum is the "yellow-" or "downy yellow Lady's slipper," "yellow moccasin flower," "whip-poor-will's shoes" . . and "Noah's ark," all ringing the changes on the shope [sic] of the lower lip. **1938** FWP *Guide DE* 13, Characteristic of the swamps are sphagnum or peatmosses, the swamp magnolia, and the pink ladyslipper, or Noah's Ark. **1951** Teale *North with Spring* 221, Also rapidly disappearing in the region is the Noah's ark, the yellow lady-slipper. **1960** Williams *Walk Egypt* 15 **GA,** Aunt Baptist liked to toll out the names of plants. "Adam's-flannel, Aaron's-rod, Noah's-ark, Jacob's-ladder, apple of Sodom." **1975** Dwyer *Thangs* 37 **Sth, S Midl,** Noah's Ark—Pink Lady's slipper.
2 =**white baneberry.**
　　c1830 in 1976 Miller *Shaker Herbs* 158, Cohosh, White—*Actea alba*—Necklace Weed. Bane Berry. Noah's Ark. **1959** Carleton *Index Herb. Plants* 87, Noah's ark: *Actea alba.*
3 A **gum elastic** (here: *Bumelia lanuginosa*).
　　1951 *PADS* 15.37 **TX,** Bumelia lanuginosa . . Noah's ark.

no aikie(s) See **aikie(s)**

noan See **none**

noatch See **noach**

noathe See **north**

nobbin n [Prob blend of *nob* + *noggin*]
The head.
　　1944 *Daily Progress* (Charlottesville VA) 22 Feb 12/5, Jerry would sit and wait until the quick attempt to pass the loop over his head, duck his nobbin, tear at the rope . . and leap to another spot. **1968–70** *DARE* (Qu. X28, *Joking words . . for a person's head*) Infs **CA**196, **KY**66, **MN**29, Nobbin.

no bears out tonight n Also *no buggers out tonight, no buggerbears* ~; for addit varr see quots
A children's hiding or chasing game; see quots.

1950 *WELS* (Games in which one captain hides his team and the other team tries to find it) 1 Inf, **swWI,** No bears tonight. **1967–70** *DARE* (Qu. EE16, *Hiding games that start with a special, elaborate method of sending the players out to hide*) Inf **GA**72B, There ain't no buggerbears out tonight; (Qu. EE33, *. . Outdoor games . . that children play*) Inf **AL**30, No buggers out tonight—a hiding game played at night; **UT**7, Beary ain't out today—one was the bear, everyone else was children; **VA**69, No bears out tonight—make a ring; several children would be in it. Those outside would sing, "No bears out tonight." Those in the ring would then break loose and try to catch those outside.

Nob Hill n Also rarely *Nob's Hill* [*nob* a swell, sophisticate; *Nob Hill* orig referred to a district in San Francisco] Cf **gold coast, main line 2**
Used as a nickname for an exclusive residential district.
　　[**1892** Stevenson–Osbourne *Wrecker* 124 **San Francisco CA,** Nor did I even neglect Nob Hill, which is itself a kind of slum, being the habitat of the mere millionaire. There they dwell upon the hill-top, high raised above man's clamour, and the trade-wind blows between their palaces about the deserted streets.] [**1912** Purdy *San Francisco* 24, The mansions on Nob Hill were built in the Seventies by millionaires created by the Central Pacific and the silver mines of Nevada. The hill acquired its present name through the universal adoption of the slang term given to it after these houses of the "nobs" were erected.] **1912** Thornton *Amer. Gloss.* 2.613, Nob Hill. A name sometimes applied to the aristocratic suburb of a city. **1965–70** *DARE* (Qu. II24, *Names or nicknames for the part of a town where the well-off people live*) 50 Infs, **scattered,** Nob Hill; **NY**111, Nob's Hill. [5 Infs, all in CA, indicated that *Nob Hill* is in San Francisco; 3 others, that the term was "after" or "taken from" the San Francisco *Nob Hill.*]

noble fir n Also *noble silver fir*
A Pacific timber tree (*Abies procera*) noted for its great height. Also called **larch 2, red fir, white ~**
　　1858 Warder *Hedges* 257, Picea nobilis, Noble Silver Fir. . . This majestic tree forms large forests in the northern part of California. **1885** Onderdonk *Idaho* 31, The Noble Fir. Inhabits all our mountain regions at an elevation of from 3,000 to 5,000 feet. **1897** Sudworth *Arborescent Flora* 57, Abies nobilis. . . "Larch" (Oreg. lumbermen). Noble Fir (Oreg.) **1917** (1923) Rogers *Trees Worth Knowing* 256, The noble fir or red fir is another giant of the Northwest. On the western slopes of the Cascade Mountains of Washington and Oregon it reaches occasionally two hundred and fifty feet in height. . . Its red-brown wood, furrowed bark and the red staminate flowers justify its name. **1959** Munz–Keck *CA Flora* 50, A[bies] procera. . . Noble Fir. . . The wood fairly hard and strong, of use for interior finish and packing cases. **1980** Little *Audubon Guide N. Amer. Trees W. Region* 255, Noble Fir. . . A handsome tree with large, showy cones mostly covered by papery bracts, Noble Fir was named by the Scottish botanical explorer David Douglas. . . It is the tallest true fir.

noble pine n Cf **prince's pine**
A **pipsissewa** (here: *Chimaphila umbellata*).
　　1892 *Jrl. Amer. Folkl.* 5.100 **NH,** Chimaphila umbellata . . noble pine. **1898** *Ibid* 11.273 **ME,** Chimaphila umbellata . . noble pine, South Berwick. **1930** Sievers *Amer. Med. Plants* 45, Pipsissewa . . *Chimaphila umbellata* . . noble pine. **1971** Krochmal *Appalachia Med. Plants* 90, Chimaphila umbellata . . Common Names: . . noble pine . . wintergreen.

noble silver fir See **noble fir**

nobody home (upstairs) phr Also *there is nobody home*
Used to describe someone considered to be dull or stupid, at least momentarily.
　　1914 *NY Eve. Jrl.* (NY) 11 Mar 14 (*Zwilling Coll.*), [In cartoon "Indoor Sports":] No he has no sense—nobody home nobody home. [*DARE* Ed: Speaker tapping his own head] **1919** *DN* 5.73 **NM,** Nobody home, a stupid, dull condition. "There is nobody home with you this morning." **1951** Johnson *Resp. to PADS 20* **DE** (*Someone who is queer but harmless*) Nobody home upstairs. **1960** Bailey *Resp. to PADS 20* **KS,** Tetched in the head, nobody home upstairs. **1960** Criswell *Resp. to PADS 20* **Ozarks,** Nobody home; saying to designate a person of little intelligence. Common. **1965–70** *DARE* (Qu. HH5, *Someone who is queer but harmless*) Infs **MI**4, 44, **NJ**61, **NY**34, **OR**15, **PA**175, **WI**52, 66, Nobody home; **AZ**15, **MI**17, 26, **NJ**8, **TN**48, 53, **TX**91, Nobody home upstairs; (Qu. HH3, *A dull and stupid person*) Inf **MI**44, Nobody home; (Qu. HH13, *Expressions meaning that a person is not very alert*

or not aware of things: "He's certainly _____.") Inf **CA**128, Nobody home.

Nob's Hill See **Nob Hill**

no bugger(bear)s out tonight See **no bears out tonight**

nocake n Also sp *nokick* [Narraganset *nokehick* parched corn meal] **NEng** *arch*

Parched corn crushed into meal.

    1634 Wood *New Engl. Prospect* 68, *Nocake* . . is nothing but *Indian Corne* parched in the hot ashes; the ashes being sifted from it, it is afterward beaten to powder, and put into a long leatherne bag. **1760** Hutchinson *Hist. MA Bay* 465, A small pouch of parched corn, ground or rather pounded into meal, and called Nuichicke, which is well enough translated Nocake. **1790** Deane *New Engl. Farmer* 141, When they eat it they reduce it to a paste with water. . . It is called *nocake*. **1859** (1968) Bartlett *Americanisms* 294, *Nocake*. An Indian word still used in some parts of New England. **1915** Hazard *Jonny-Cake Papers* 58 **RI** (as of c1880), I well remember the old no-cake mortar that used to stand in my grandfather's kitchen, upside down when not in use. . . I think it would hold a half gallon of parched corn, or more. **1977** Talman *How Things Began* 126, One of the most useful foods was called rockahominy in Virginia and nokick in New England.

nockaway See **anaqua**

no-count adj, also used absol [Aphet; cf Intro "Language Changes" I.7] **scattered, but chiefly Sth, S Midl** See Map =**no-account.**

    1853 Hammett *Stray Yankee in TX* 282 **seTX**, Dern no 'count calves done fool me agin. **1884** *Anglia* 7.273 **Sth, S Midl** [Black], To be no 'count = to be worthless. **1903** Murrie *White Castle LA* 214, Mr. Page said I was a pointer of fine breed, and if Victoria held on to me continuously like she promised I would either get sick or grow up a "no-count" dog. **1905** *DN* 3.89 **nwAR**, She married a no-'count man. **1906** *DN* 3.148 **nwAR**, He's the no-countest fellow in this township. **1909** *DN* 3.352 **eAL, wGA**, No-(ac)count. . . Sometimes *no-countest* supl. **1923** *DN* 5.215 **swMO**, No count. . . Of no account, worthless, lazy, shiftless, not respectable. **a1930** in 1991 Hughes–Hurston *Mule Bone* 32 **cFL** [Black], Theres jus' as many no count Baptists as anybody else. **1937** Sandoz *Slogum* 72 **NE**, You mind me of a girl I had once. . . No 'count half the time. **1953** Brewer *Word Brazos* 51 **eTX** [Black], He jes' lack some o' you no 'count triflin' membuhs; dis week you b'longs to St. John Chu'ch; nex' week you jines up wid Mount Moriah. **1965–70** *DARE* (Qu. HH20a, *An idle, worthless person: "He's a _____."*) 19 Infs, **esp Sth, S Midl**, No-count; **SC**40, **TN**62, No-count person; **CA**113, No-count bum; **KY**85, No-count for nothing; (Qu. HH18, *Very insignificant or low-grade people*) 11 Infs, **scattered**, No-count; **KY**84, No-count trash; **KY**42, No-count for anything; (Qu. J2, . . *Joking or uncomplimentary words . . for dogs*) Inf **OK**43, No-count dog; (Qu. K42, *A horse that is rough, wild, or dangerous*) Inf **TX**29, No-count horse; (Qu. U29, *Names or nicknames . . for worthless money*) Infs **CA**6, **MO**18, **TN**52, No-count money; (Qu. X47, . . *"I'm very tired, at the end of my strength"*) Inf **MS**68, No-count; (Qu. Y28, *A person who loiters about with nothing to do*) Infs **IN**60, **KY**80, No-count; (Qu. AA7b, . . *A woman who is very fond of men and is always trying to know more—if she's not respectable about it*) Inf **IN**60, No-count; (Qu. BB39, *On a day when you don't feel just right,*

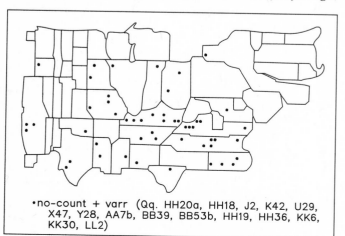

•no-count + varr (Qq. HH20a, HH18, J2, K42, U29, X47, Y28, AA7b, BB39, BB53b, HH19, HH36, KK6, KK30, LL2)

though not actually sick . . "I'll be all right tomorrow—I'm just feeling _____ today.") Infs **KY**24, **NC**16, **SC**44, **TX**3, **VA**23, No-count; (Qu. BB53b, . . *A doctor who is not very capable or doesn't have a very good reputation*) Inf **FL**49, No-count; (Qu. HH19, *Other words or nicknames for a tramp*) Inf **OR**4, No-count; (Qu. HH36, *A careless, slovenly woman: "She's just an old _____."*) Infs **NC**4, 34, No-count; (Qu. KK6, *Something low-grade or of poor quality—for example, a piece of merchandise: "I wouldn't buy that, it's _____."*) Inf **TX**29, No-count; (Qu. KK30, *Feeling slowed up or without energy: "I certainly feel _____."*) Infs **NC**7, **VA**29, 31, No-count; (Qu. LL2, . . *Too small to be worth much: "I don't want that little _____ potato."*) Infs **MD**49, **MO**17, **OH**63, No-count. **1966** Barnes–Jensen *Dict. UT Slang* 32, No count. . . worthless. **1986** Pederson *LAGS Concordance Gulf Region*, 79 infs, No-(ac)count [*DARE* Ed: =no-count]; 6 infs, No-account.

noculate v [Aphet form of *inoculate;* cf *EDD*, with one ex from sEngl]

    [**1925** *DN* 5.337 **Nfld**, *Nocklate*. Corruption of *inoculate*.] **1967** *DARE* FW Addit **ceTN**, If you don't [ˈnɑkəˌlet] it you cain't mend it [=a sick animal].

noddin' See **nothing**

nodding lily n esp **NEast**

Either the Canada lily *(Lilium canadense)* or a **turk's-cap lily** (here: *Lilium superbum*).

    1822 Eaton *Botany* 337, *Lilium. . . canadense* (nodding lily . .). Corol [sic] nodding, raceme spreading. **1832** Williamson *Hist. ME* 1.126, Of the *Lily* tribe, we have several species. . . Such as . . nodding-lily. **1892** *Jrl. Amer. Folkl.* 5.104 **MA**, *Lilium superbum*, nodding lilies; Turk's head. **1894** Ibid 7.102 **NY**, *Lilium Canadense*, . . . meadow lily, nodding lily. Ibid **MA**, *Lilium superbum*, . . nodding lilies. **1940** Clute *Amer. Plant Names* 12, *L[ilium] Canadense*. . . Nodding lily.

nodding mandarin See **mandarin**

nodding-nixie n

A small saprophytic plant *(Apteria aphylla)* native chiefly to the Gulf States.

    1933 Small *Manual SE Flora* 363, *Nodding-nixie*. . . Coastal Plain, Fla. to La. and Ga. **1970** Correll *Plants TX* 434, *Nodding-nixie*. . . Flowers small, nodding, with long pedicels. **1979** Ajilvsgi *Wild Flowers* 123, *Nodding-nixie*. . . Erect, delicate saprophytic annual to 8 in. tall. . . Plants usually in colonies. . . Uncommon or perhaps overlooked.

nodding trillium n

Std: a **trillium** (here: *Trillium cernuum*). Also called **benjamin, bethroot, birthroot, coughroot 1, ground lily, Indian balm, Jew's harp B2, lamb's quarters 2, nightshade 2, rattlesnake root, snakebite, three-leaved nightshade, wake-robin**

noddle n

1 also *noddle-head:* A person's head. [*OED* c1425 →] Cf **noggle 1**

    1806 (1970) Webster *Compendious Dict.* 202, *Noddle*. . . the head, *by way of contempt*. [*DARE* Ed: This entry was carried over from Webster's English model.] **1838** Kettell *Yankee Notions* 113, If a ghost wishes to give any person so sensible a token of his presence, let him bestow a sound bang upon his noddle. **1899** (1912) Green *VA Folk-Speech* 300, *Noddle*. . . The head. **1968–70** *DARE* (Qu. X28, *Joking words . . for a person's head*) Infs **CT**1, **NY**73, **RI**1, **VA**74, Noddle; **VA**35, 80, Noddle-head.

    2 in comb *noddle-head:* A naturally hornless cow. Cf **muley B1**

    1970 *DARE* (Qu. K12, *A cow that has never had horns*) Inf **VA**77, Noddle-head.

noddy n

1 Std: a tern of the genus *Anous*. Also called **noio**

2 =**ruddy duck.** [See quot 1917]

    1888 Trumbull *Names of Birds* 112 **NC**, At Newberne, N.C., [the ruddy duck is called] *paddy* and *noddy*. **1917** (1923) *Birds Amer.* 1.153, Other local names, such as Booby, Noddy, and Fool Duck, indicate a lack of respect for the birds' perspicacity. **1944** Hausman *Amer. Birds* 520, [In a list of other names of American birds:] Noddy—see Duck, Ruddy; see also Fulmar.

3 =**fulmar.** [See quot 1955] **NEast**

1910 Eaton *Birds NY* 1.154, The Fulmar, or Noddy, of the North Atlantic, has been taken in winter as far south as Massachusetts and New Jersey. **1917** (1923) *Birds Amer.* 1.81, To the crews of the whalers and sealers the bird [=the fulmar] is well known and to them it owes the names of "Mollimoke" and "Noddy." **1925** (1928) Forbush *Birds MA* 1.135, Noddy, marbleheader; white hagdon. **1955** MA Audubon Soc. *Bulletin* 39.310, Fulmar. . . Noddy (Some say because "they constantly nod their heads while flying").

4 Any of var other sea birds such as the **dovekie**, a **murre 1** (here: *Uria lomvia*), the common puffin (*Fratercula arctica*), or the **razor-billed auk.**

1956 MA Audubon Soc. *Bulletin* 40.79 **RI**, Razor-billed Auk. . . Noddy, Parrot-bill. *Ibid* 40.80 **MA**, Bruennich's Murre. . . Noddy. *Ibid* **MA**, Dovekie. . . Noddy, Pigeon Diver. *Ibid* **MA**, Common Puffin. Noddy.

node See **know B3a**

no-eat-um grass n

A **needlegrass 2** (here: *Aristida fendleriana*).

1937 U.S. Forest Serv. *Range Plant Hdbk.* G19, Fendler three-awn. . . is considered almost worthless, and stockmen sometimes call it "no-eat-um grass" because of its unpalatability.

no finger n Cf **dog finger, feeble man**

The ring finger.

1972 Jones–Hawes *Step it Down* 12 **eGA** [Black], You call 'em Tom Thumb, dog finger, middle finger, no finger. . . He give us to understand that the no finger [ring finger] is called that because it isn't much help.

no force See **force 1, 2**

nogal n [Span] **SW**

Usu a **walnut** (here: *Juglans* spp), occas a **hickory B1** such as a **pecan**; also the nut of such a tree.

1869 Browne *Adventures* 262 **csAZ**, We returned to our pleasant camping-place under the wide-spreading nogales, or walnut-trees. **1892** *DN* 1.192 **TX**, *Nogál:* properly the walnut tree, in Texas the pecan tree (*Carya olivæformis*), as *nuez* (*nuéces*), in Spanish walnut(s), applies in Texas to the pecan nut, and is found in the proper names of rivers and creeks; as *Nueces* river. The hickory is called *nogal encarcelado*. **1904** NM Ag. Exper. Station *Bulletin* 51.20, The Walnut or Nogal (*Juglans rupestris*) is a native tree. . . [which] resembles the black walnut of the Mississippi valley states in most respects, except that . . the "nuts" are only about half to two-thirds as large as the black walnut. **1913** Wooton *Trees NM* 48, This family contains the well known walnut or *nogal*, the English walnut of commerce, the hickory nut, and the pecan. **1960** Vines *Trees SW* 125, *J[uglans] microcarpa*. . . Vernacular names used are Dwarf Walnut, Little Walnut, Nogal. **1967** *DARE* (Qu. I43, *What kinds of nuts grow wild around here?*) Inf **TX5**, Nogals ['no͵gælz]—very small walnut, not good to eat. **1970** Correll *Plants TX* 458, *Juglans*. Walnut. Nogal. *Ibid* 460, *Carya myristicaeformis*. . . Nutmeg hickory, nogal. **1975** Lamb *Woody Plants SW* 151, Little walnut—*Juglans microcarpa* "Nogal". **1976** Elmore *Shrubs & Trees SW* 87, Arizona black walnut, nogal. . . *Juglans major*.

nogger See **noggle 2**

noggin n

1 A bowl or small vessel for liquids, usu made of wood; see quots. [*OED* 1630 →] *old-fash*

1766 in 1912 Augusta Co. *VA Chronicles* 1.127, Four wooden noggins. **1824** Doddridge *Notes Indian Wars* 109, The furniture for the table . . consisted . . mostly of wooden bowls, trenchers and noggins. **1895** *DN* 1.383 **NJ**, *Noggin:* a wooden dipper. **1930** (1935) Porter *Flowering Judas* 124 **TX**, Her father had lived to be one hundred and two years old and had drunk a noggin of strong hot toddy on his last birthday. **1939** *LANE* Map 133 *(Tin cup)* 1 inf, **ceNH**, Noggin, old name for a two-quart dipper. **1939** Wolcott *Yankee Cook Book* 367, *Noggin:* small bowl or mug with a short heavy handle whittled at the side. **1947** Croy *Corn Country* 280, *Noggin:* A small cup for drinking. **1951** Johnson *Resp. to PADS 20* **DE**, A beer mug: noggin. **1968** *DARE* FW Addit **VA31**, *Noggin*—in New Market, Virginia, a small dipper or water dipper. **1968** *DARE* FW Addit **swVA**, [From a museum director:] *Noggin*—a tree knot [=burl] made into a cup. The lump was cut off, debarked, and hollowed out to form a cup.

2 also *noggin tub:* A pail or small tub. Cf **piggin**

1843 *Amer. Pioneer* 2.424 **IL**, *Noggins;* these were small vessels shaped like a pail, made from small cedar staves, and held about a quart.

1885 Murfree *Prophet of Smoky Mts.* 175, Mirandy Jane, seated on an inverted noggin, listened tamely to the conversation. **1890** *Century Dict.* 4007, *Noggin*. . . One end of a keg that has been sawn into halves, used for various purposes on shipboard. **1899** (1912) Green *VA Folk-Speech* 300, *Noggin*. . . A vessel of wood, with iron or brass hoops that is kept near a tub of water, used for washing hands, mostly for children. **1941** *Sat. Eve. Post* 1 Mar 82 **MO**, The noggin tub that they were filling. **1968** *DARE* FW Addit **VA31**, *Noggin*—in Stephen City, Frederic County, Virginia, a small tub used for washing or soaking the feet.

3 See quot. [Cf *EDD nog* sb.[1] 1 "A small log, or rough block of wood"]

1967 *DARE* (Qu. D34, . . *The small pieces of wood and other stuff that are used to start a fire*) Inf **WY4**, Noggin—full sized piece of stove wood, unsplit.

4 See quot. [Prob transf from *noggin* head] Cf **noggle 2**

1969 *DARE* (Qu. X60, . . *A lump that comes up on your head when you get a sharp blow or knock;* not asked in early QRs) Infs **CA170, NY166**, Noggin.

noggin v

1899 (1912) Green *VA Folk-Speech* 300, *Noggin*. . . To cut the hair straight round as if a noggin had been turned over the head to cut by; the blue-law cap method.

noggin-head n [Redund]

1970 *DARE* (Qu. X28, *Joking words . . for a person's head*) Infs **IL116, TX86**, Noggin-head.

noggin tub See **noggin n 2**

noggle n [Prob var of *noggin* head]

1 also *noggle-head:* A person's head. [Cf *EDD noggle-head* (at *noggle* v.) a blockhead] Cf **noddle 1**

1966 *DARE* FW Addit **WA**, Joking words for a person's head—noggle. **1970** *DARE* (Qu. X28, *Joking words . . for a person's head*) Inf **MS86**, Noggle-head.

2 also *nogger:* See quot.

1968 *DARE* (Qu. X60, . . *A lump that comes up on your head when you get a sharp blow or knock;* not asked in early QRs) Inf **WI50**, Noggle; **NY197**, Nogger.

noggle-head See **noggle 1**

no hide off one's back See **hide n[2] 5**

no hill for a stepper See **hill n 4**

no-horn n

1968–69 *DARE* (Qu. K12, *A cow that has never had horns*) Infs **CT29, NJ50, RI16**, No-horn; **MA66**, No-horns.

no-host adj phr Also *no-hostess* **chiefly West**

Of a dinner, reception, etc: requiring those attending to pay for their own food or drink.

1967 *Raymond Herald & Advt.* (WA) 9 Mar 13/3, Members of the Willapa Harbor Past Presidents Club of Eagles Auxiliary met at Bridges Inn March 1 for a no-host dinner. **1967** *Independence Enterprise* (OR) 12 Jan 6/2, The World War I Veterans . . met . . , with twenty four attending a no host dinner. **1968** *Hungry Horse News* (Columbia Falls MT) 20 Dec 2/5, A no-hostess luncheon opened the Christmas party. **1968** *Mt. Home News* (ID) 8 Feb 1/6, A no-host reception will be held . . where U.S. Rep. James McClure will speak to a group of his constituents. *Ibid* 4/1, There will be a no-host dinner. **1970** *DARE* (Qu. FF1, . . *A kind of group meeting called a 'social' or 'sociable'. . . What kinds are there?*) Inf **CA81**, No-host bar: liquor served but people buy chips to exchange for drinks. Money and chips are kept in separate places—no money given to bartender. **1975** Morris–Morris *Usage* 422, In many parts of the not-so-wild West today, what many Easterners call a "Dutch treat" lunch or dinner is called a *no host* affair. . . Each person pays for his own meal and doesn't have to pick up the tab. **1991** *San Francisco Examiner* (CA) 29 Dec sec D1, On Monday, when it's time to go home, some convention-goers will still be looking for the host hotel. . . Followed by "welcome" cocktail party. No-host bar. No-host peanuts. No-hope job hunting. **1992** *El Paso Herald–Post* (TX) 26 June B2, *No-Host Dinner.* The Widowed Persons Service is scheduled to have a no-host dinner at 5 p.m. Saturday at Luby's Cafeteria.

nohow adv

1 In no way, by no means—usu used redundantly to emphasize a negation. Cf *any how you can fix it* (at **fix v B8**)

1833 Hall *Harpe's Head* 91 **VA**, They don't raise such humans in the old dominion, no how. **1843** (1916) Hall *New Purchase* 121 **IN**, I . . couldn't read a chapter in the Bible no how you could fix it. **1857** *Putnam's Mag.* 10.353 **CT**, Can't a feller help himself nohow? **1899** (1912) Green *VA Folk-Speech* 300, Nohow. . . In no manner; not in any way; not at all. **1905** *DN* 3.15 **cCT**, Nohow. . . by no means. **1907** *DN* 3.215 **nwAR**, Nohow. . . By no means. **1928** Peterkin *Scarlet Sister Mary* 171 **sSC** [Gullah], Night air ain' good nohow. **1938** Rawlings *Yearling* 33 **nFL**, Don't seem to me like he's headin' acrost it, nohow. **1942** McAtee *Dial. Grant Co. IN* 45 (as of 1890s), *Nohow* . . in any event; negative intensifier as in the expression, "I wouldn't believe you _____". **1950** *PADS* 14.49 **SC**, Nohow. . . In no way. Usually at the end of a negative sentence, making a double negative. "I couldn't fix it nohow." **1954** *Harder Coll.* **cwTN**, Nohow. . . In no way. **1967–69** *DARE* (Qu. V2b, *About a deceiving person, or somebody that you can't trust . . "I wouldn't trust him _____.";* not asked in early QRs) Infs **MI55, NY40, OH25, PA205, WI12**, Nohow; (Qu. HH16, *Uncomplimentary words with no definite meaning—just used when you want to show that you don't think much of a person: "Don't invite him. He's a _____."*) Inf **TN26**, Not right bright nohow; (Qu. II29a, *An unexplainable dislike that you feel from the first moment you meet a person: "I don't know why, but I just can't _____ him."*) Inf **WI12**, Stand him nohow. **1986** Pederson *LAGS Concordance* **Gulf Region**, [Of 73 exx of *nohow*, most are used to emphasize negation. Typical uses include these: "I don't want to run the heat all night nohow"; "Ain't nothing nowhow"; "Had no business noway, nohow"; "I ain't scared of nothing nohow"; "I don't (al)low no children standing around me nohow."]

2 In any case; anyway.   esp S Midl

1926 Roberts *Time of Man* 30 **KY**, You keep down along the branch nohow. **a1930** in 1991 Hughes–Hurston *Mule Bone* 37 **cFL** [Black], Never mind bout dem white folks laws at O'landa, Brother Long. Dis is a colored town. Nohow we oughter run by de laws uh de Bible. **1931** (1991) *Ibid* 51 **cFL** [Black], Yo' husband done bought you plenty meat, nohow. **1934** (1970) Wilson *Backwoods Amer.* 171 **Ozarks**, People is jest bound to know a mighty lot about moonshiners, nohow. **1938** in 1972 *Amer. Slave* 2.1.102 **SC**, Dere, you want a piece of bread fore you is dress. Who undressed you last night nohow? **1942** Thomas *Blue Ridge Country* 108 **sAppalachians**, "No how," Jorde was off on another defense, "land up here and in lots of places in these mountains is not fitten to farm so we have allus made whiskey of it." **1986** Pederson *LAGS Concordance* **Gulf Region**, [Of 73 exx of *nohow*, 12 are explicitly glossed by *LAGS* Eds as "= anyway," e.g., "Ain't got no hogs to go in it nohow"; "He's not very stout nohow"; "He didn't care nohow." Other exx that seem to have the same sense are these: "Why bother to call police? They never come nohow"; "You ain't got but one time to die nohow."]

nohu n [Haw] **HI**

1 A low-growing plant *(Tribulus cistoides)* with yellow flowers and thorny fruits. Also called **mahukona violet, puncture weed**

1836 *Sandwich Is. Gaz. & Jrl. of Commerce* (Honolulu HI) 17 Sept, The eye is only relieved by the yellow blossoms of the Nohu, *(Tribulus.)* **1900** Lyons *Plant Names* 375, *T[ribulus] cistoides.* . . Nohu, Mahukona Violet (Hawaii). **1924** [see **mahukona violet**]. **1929** Pope *Plants HI* 126, Nohu attains its full beauty of form and color on the leeward side of most of the islands of the Hawaiian group. The low spreading growth of shiny green leaves often completely carpets considerable areas, hence it is sometimes called "Carpet Weed". Nohu, the Hawaiian name, has reference to it as such. **1948** Neal *In Gardens HI* 417, Nohu. *Tribulus cistoides.* . . A prostrate or low-spreading, hairy perennial . . considered a weed, because its spiny fruits stick to the coats of animals and also injure their feet.

2 A scorpionfish of the family Scorpaenidae such as *Scorpaenopsis cacopsis* or *S. gibbosa.*

1926 Pan-Pacific Research Inst. *Jrl.* 1.1.10 **HI**, Scorpaenidae. The Scorpion-Fishes. Nohu. . . Merinthe macrocephala. . . Nohu. . . Scorpaenopsis catocala. . . Nohu Omakaha. **1960** Gosline–Brock *Hawaiian Fishes* 287, *Scorpaenopsis gibbosa (Nohu* . .)—An ugly gray fish with numerous flaplike appendages. . . We know of no records of ill effects from being spined by the nohu. . . A common inshore species. *Ibid* 288, *Scorpaenopsis cacopsis (Nohu)*—This fish . . is never found in less than 20 feet of water. . . It attains a size of at least 20 inches and is much sought after as food.

noi See **no**

noint See **anoint**

noio n [Haw] **HI**

A **noddy 1**, usu *Anous minutus.*

1944 Munro *Birds HI* 63, [Noddy Tern. . . Hawaiian name: *Noio koha.* (According to Francis Gay (1891) the name is probably a shortened form of *Noio kohaha,* the large *noio.*)] *Ibid* 64, Hawaiian Noddy. Hawaiian names: *Noio.* . . I have seen a group of noio fishing where the sea was breaking on rocks. **1994** Stone–Pratt *Hawai'i's Plants* 69, Noio have lighter caps . . and a faster, more "fluttery" flight than the larger noio koha or brown (common) noddy . . which nests on offshore islands. . . Noio nest on rocky cliffs or in caves on the main Islands. . . Noio need large fishes to drive the small fishes upon which they feed to the surface of the sea.

noise v

1917 *DN* 4.415 **wNC**, Noise. . . To make the sound of. "Any kind of thing ever heered tell of, he can noise it."

noisy duck n

=**old-squaw.**

1838 Audubon *Ornith. Biog.* 4.105, Long-tailed duck. *Fuligula glacialis.* . . Owing to their reiterated cries these birds are named "Noisy Ducks;" but they have various appellations, among others those of "old wives," and "old squaws." **1898** Elliot *Wild Fowl* 191, In various parts of the land, . . it [=the old-squaw] has many names, some of which are . . Old Wife, Old Injun, Old Molly . . and Noisy Duck. **1923** U.S. Dept. Ag. *Misc. Circular* 13.25. [**1977** Bull–Farrand *Audubon Field Guide Birds* 352, Oldsquaw. . . These very noisy birds are noisiest in early spring, when males gather and utter their mellow, barking courtship calls; this pleasing sound is audible for a mile or two on a still, spring morning.]

noisy plover n

=**killdeer 1.**

1917 (1923) *Birds Amer.* 1.259, Killdeer. . . Other names.—Killdeer Plover; Noisy Plover [etc.]. [**1923** Dawson *Birds CA* 3.1299, *Oxyechus vociferus vociferus earsplitterus ananias!* The books concede only the first three epithets: we add the others upon our own authority. *Oxyechus* is the noisemaker extraordinary, the professional scold, the yap yap artist, the irrepressible canine of the bird world.] **1946** Hausman *Eastern Birds* 256, Killdeer Plover, Meadow Plover, Noisy Plover, Chattering Plover. **1953** Jewett *Birds WA* 245, Kildee Plover; Chattering Plover; Noisy Plover. [*Ibid* 247, Though the bird with its strident calls is sometimes a little exasperating, its presence is in the highest degree beneficial economically.]

nokick See **nocake**

no lay See **lay** n[1] **3**

nole See **knoll**

noll n [*OED noll* c825 →; "Now *dial.*"]

1969 *DARE* (Qu. X28, *Joking words . . for a person's head*) Inf **IN56**, Noll.

no-manners adj Pronc-sp *nomannus* Also *no-mannered, no-mannersable* **sSC, GA coasts** *Gullah*

Ill-mannered; rude; hence n *no-manners* lack of manners, rudeness.

1922 Gonzales *Black Border* 265 **sSC, GA coasts** [Gullah], You gots de nomannus to come een de Lawd' house wid t'ree aig' en' one leetle fo'punce chickin. *Ibid* 268, W'en I see de 'ceitfulness en' de ondeestunt gwinin' en' gwinin' uh dese nomannus nigguh', I git disgus' wid de nigguh'. *Ibid* 315 [Gullah glossary], Nomannus, nomannussubble—impolite, without manners, rude. **1928** Peterkin *Scarlet Sister Mary* 200 **sSC** [Gullah], The children were his and Doll's no-mannered bunch. *Ibid* 281, You low-down no-manners gal. **1930** Woofter *Black Yeomanry* 212 **seSC**, "Manners" are emphasized. To be "no-manners" is disgraceful. **1930** Stoney–Shelby *Black Genesis* 106 **seSC**, How you mek bol' to come here, an' set yo' self down on me house door, you no-manners t'ing?

no-nation adj Cf **darnation**

1914 *DN* 4.77 **ME, nNH**, No-nation. . . Worthless. "You no-nation cuss!"

nondo n

A **lovage** (here: *Ligusticum canadense*).

1791 Bartram *Travels* 45, I observed . . the carminative Angelica lucida. [Footnote:] Called Nondo in Virginia: by the Creek and Cherokee traders, White Root. **1848** Gray *Manual of Botany* 160, *L[igusticum]* *actaefolium. . . Nondo. Angelico. . .* I have not seen it from N[ew] England: it doubtless grows in S.W. Pennsylvania, as it abounds in the mountains southward. **1901** Mohr *Plant Life AL* 643, *Canada Lovage. Nondo. . .* The root, called "white root," is used in domestic medicine. **1903** Porter *Flora PA* 232, *Nondo. . .* In rich woods, southern Pa. to Ga., Mo. and Ky. **1974** (1977) Coon *Useful Plants* 261, Nondo. . . The seeds . . were used by Indians as a cough remedy. **1975** Hamel–Chiltoskey *Cherokee Plants* 61, Lovage, nondo. . . Cooked greens for food.

none pron Usu |nʌn|; also, esp **NEast** |non, nɔn| Pronc-spp *noan, noon*

A Forms.

1860 Holmes *Professor* 262 **eMA,** Our landlady said to me, one day, that though it was noon of her business, them that had eyes couldn't help seein' that there was somethin' goin' on between them two young people. **1890** *DN* 1.40 **ME,** None. . . originally [nən]; [nɛn]. **1938** Matschat *Suwannee R.* 15 Okefenokee **GA,** 'T won't hurt ye noan, ma'am. Hain't no call to be skeert. **1940** in 1944 *ADD* **cNY,** [non]. **1941** *LANE* Map 320 *(I don't care for any)* 3 infs, **sME, seNH,** [noˀˑən]; 1 inf, **seNH,** [nɔˑ.ˀn]; 1 inf, **ceVT,** [non].

B Sense.

In phr *none of:* Not, not at all; spec: see below. [*OED none* pron. A.3.c **1571** →] Note: This sense is std in phr *none of one's business* and varr.

a in phr *none of one's funeral:* See **funeral B3a.**

b in phr *none of (someone or something):* Certainly not—often used redundantly after a negation. *now esp freq among Black speakers*

1910 in 1931 Lomax *Cowboy Songs* 87, Whoopee ti yi yo, git along little dogies,/ It's your misfortune and none of my own. **1931** (1991) Hughes–Hurston *Mule Bone* 66 **cFL** [Black], You ain't none of my mama. My mama in the store and she told me to wait out here. **1971** Mitchell *Blow My Blues Away* 21 **nwMS** [Black], He turned his head and he said, "This ain't none of my baby." She say, "It is." **1986** Pederson *LAGS Concordance,* 1 inf, **ceGA,** This ain't none me = none of me; i.e., not I; 1 inf, **swMS,** It was none of me = it wasn't me; 1 inf, **seAR,** It wasn't none of my house = it wasn't my house; 1 inf, **nwLA,** It wasn't none of me = it wasn't me. [3 of 4 infs Black]

none of one's funeral See **funeral B3a**

none-so-pretty n

1 A **pearly everlasting** (here: *Anaphalis margaritacea*).

1830 Rafinesque *Med. Flora* 2.224, The *Gn[aphalium] margaritaceum* also called *Silver leaf, None so pretty,* is anodyne and pectoral, used in colds and coughs, pains in the breast. . . Also in the diseases of sheep. One of the good substitutes for tobacco in smoking. **1876** Hobbs *Bot. Hdbk.* 75, None so pretty . . Pearl flow[ere]d life everlasting. **1900** [see **moonshine 1**]. **1940** Clute *Amer. Plant Names* 74, *A[naphalis] margaritacea.* Pearly Everlasting. . . none-so-pretty.

2 Esp a **johnny-jump-up 1** (here: *Viola tricolor*), but also the related garden **pansy.**

1844 [see **jump-up-johnny**]. **1896** *Jrl. Amer. Folkl.* 9.182 **MA,** *Viola tricolor* . . none-so-pretty, Abington, Mass. **1902** Earle *Old Time Gardens* 134, In Breck's *Book of Flowers,* 1851, is the first printed reference I find to the flower [=*Viola tricolor*] under the name Ladies' Delight. In my childhood I never heard it called aught else; but it has a score of folk names, all testifying to an affectionate intimacy: Bird's-eye; Garden-gate; Johnny-jump-up; None-so-pretty [etc]. **1922** *DN* 5.181 **ID,** *None-so-pretties.* . . Pansies. . . Rare. **1959** Carleton *Index Herb. Plants* 87, *None-so-pretty:* Saxifraga umbrosa; Silene armeria; Viola tricolor.

3 =**garden catchfly.**

1892 *Jrl. Amer. Folkl.* 5.93 **MA,** *Silene Armeria.* . . none-so-pretty. Hatfield, Mass. **1950** Gray–Fernald *Manual of Botany* 633, *S[ilene] armeria* . . Garden- or Sweet-William-Catchfly, None-so-pretty.

no nothing See **nothings**

no not one n

An unlimited extent.

1952 Brown *NC Folkl.* 1.569, *No not one, to.* . . Indefinitely. "This rubber band will stretch to no not one."

nonpareil n

A painted bunting (here: *Passerina ciris*).

[**1758** G. Edwards *Gleanings* I.132 *(OED),* The Painted Finch . . , more generally known to the curious in London by the name of Non-

pareil and Mariposa.] **1791** Bartram *Travels* 11 **GA,** Moon-light nights, filled with the melody of the chearful mockbird, warbling nonpareil, and plaintive turtle dove, . . present a view of magnificence and joy. **1811** Wilson *Amer. Ornith.* 3.68, Painted Bunting. . . One of the most numerous of the little summer birds of Lower Louisiana . . known [as] . . the *Nonpareil.* **1887** *Harper's New Mth. Mag.* 74.349 **LA,** There was the lively little nonpareil, which seems to change its color, and is red and green and blue. **1895** *Outing* 26.70 **sME,** Cane-brakes gay with cardinals and nonpareils. **1916** *Times–Picayune* (New Orleans LA) 23 Apr mag sec 21/5 **LA,** *Painted bunting* (Passerina ciris). Nonpareil; Painted Finch; Pape doux; Sweet "Pop." . . The painted bunting is undoubtedly the most gaudily-colored bird of Louisiana. **1954** Sprunt *FL Bird Life* 455, Having been "born and raised" with the bird, the writer has never yet tired of it, . . though it is literally, a "yardbird" with him. It is known as "Nonpareil" throughout most of its range. **1977** Bull–Farrand *Audubon Field Guide Birds* 587, Its other well-known name is "Nonpareil," meaning "without equal." . . Common in parts of the Deep South. . . the female is one of the few truly green birds in North America.

noo See **new**

nooby See **nubia**

no occasion See **occasion B**

noodle n

1 also *noodle shock:* A small haystack. Cf **doodle** n[1] **1**

1928 *AmSp* 4.132 **cnNE,** A "doodle," "noodle," or "shock" is a small hay stack made by gathering the hay and piling it by hand. **1986** Pederson *LAGS Concordance,* 1 inf, **csTN,** *Noodle shocks*—small piles raked from windrows.

2 See quot.

1966–68 *DARE* (Qu. K73, . . *Names . . for the rump of a cooked chicken*) Infs **IN8, MS46,** Noodle.

noodle v[1], hence ppl adj *noodled,* vbl n *noodling,* n *noodler* [Etym unknown; cf Scots, nEngl dial *guddle,* and similar frequentative forms **canoodle, doodle, grabble**] esp **Ozarks** Cf **noodling hook**

To catch (fish, or occas turtles) with the bare hands or with a gaff; to fish in this way.

1923 *DN* 5.215 **swMO,** Noodle. . . To catch fish with the bare hand or with a long-handled barbed hook. **1933** Williamson *Woods Colt* 9 **Ozarks,** I'm aimin' to help noodle that catfish. *Ibid* 13, You git things ready, an' the rest of us can go noodle that cat [=catfish]. **1937** *Esquire* Apr 130 **swMO,** If the larder is replenished by a noodled or jumped fish . . so much the better. **1937** *AmSp* 12.162 **AR,** In the state of Arkansas . . *noodling* is the process of catching fish by reaching into the water and grasping them by the gills with the thumb and forefinger. **1951** Conant *Reptiles OH* 160, Professional turtle collectors take them [=softshell turtles] by "noodeling," [sic] in traps, nets or on set lines. **1957** McMeekin *Old KY Country* 205, Noodling is the sport of catching snapping turtles barehanded. **1960** Criswell *Resp. to PADS 20* **Ozarks,** Noodle. . . To catch catfish nesting in holes in a bank with bare hands. **1968–69** *DARE* (Qu. P13, . . *Ways of fishing . . besides the ordinary hook and line*) Inf **KS10,** Noodling—dive in under a bank and catch fish with your hands, usually done in August; **MO39,** A-noodlin'. **1987** Childress *Out of the Ozarks* 28, There were two kinds of noodling practiced during my Midwest childhood—one using an encircling seine and bare hands and another with a breakable stick attached to a hook and line. **1988** *DARE* File **csOK,** Some friends who grew up in Garvin County, Oklahoma . . told me that people wade out into creeks and rivers and reach in mud holes in the banks to pull out catfish. This is called *noodlin'.* **1989** *Yankee* June 66 **ME,** A few turtle hunters. . . flop down in the mud and feel around blindly under riverbanks till they find a snapper to pull out, preferable tail-first—a method known as "noodling," the practitioners of which can be numbered even on the fingers of *their* hands. **1991** *Kirksville Express & News* (MO) 1 Sept 12, [Headline:] "Noodling" Hurts Duo's Pocketbook. *Ibid* 12/1, Good behavior might get a pair of Monroe County men $100 of their fines back, but their illegal behavior cost the two "noodlers" $600 each. The duo pled guilty in . . Court on charges of taking fish by illegal methods. Specifically, they were handfishing in the Salt River.

noodle v[2], hence vbl n *noodling,* n *noodler* [Ger *nudeln* to force-feed geese] **WI** Cf **noodle-goose**

To feed (geese) forcibly to increase body weight or liver size.

1941 Writers' Program *Guide WI* 519, Another transplantation is the "noodling", or force-feeding of geese for a period of a month before they are brought to market. Large quantities of cooked noodles made of wheat, corn, and barley are shoved down the birds' throats with a wooden pestle; the geese grow to uncommon size, and their livers become greatly enlarged. Watertown geese are raised chiefly for these livers which are made into pâté de foie gras. **1956** *Daily Progress* (Charlottesville VA) 5 Jan 14/4, If you like goose liver you'll appreciate Fred Rumler of Watertown, Wis. He's a "noodler" and there aren't many more of them in the United States. "Noodling" is a process of force-feeding geese to enlarge their livers. **1986** *WI Alumnus Letters* **WI,** In the earlier part of the century (about 1910) I remember well hearing (and using) the Badger phrase "genoodlete gans" or also the "water-towner goose." It was a special Christmas delicacy whose preparation began around Thanksgiving time when the Wisconsin farmer would cage his geese to be noodled and stuff them daily with home-made noodles. This produced an enlarged goose liver for foie gras which was prized for the holidays by the New York market. The region around Watertown was the choice source of this luxuriance, but I believe the market faded when the State enacted opposing-cruelty legislation. *Ibid* **WI** (as of c1927), As a boy in Wisconsin (1924 to 1930) I saw "noodle-ing" many times in Watertown, Wisconsin. To enlarge the liver was a very second-ary-reason. Keynote-reason was to tremendously increase body-weight for greater sales-price-weight. . . A goose is one vertebrate that abso-lutely cannot vomit—Thus huge volumes of noodles were digested, after being "ramrodded" down with a solid rubber hose. . . Only "old-fash-ioned" German immigrants knew this "art."

noodled See **noodle** v[1]

noodle-goose n [**noodle** v[2]]
A force-fed goose.
   1980 *DARE* File **csWI,** I ate a lot—I felt as full as a noodle-goose.

noodler n[1] See **noodle** v[1]

noodler n[2] See **noodle** v[2]

noodle shock See **noodle** n 1

noodling vbl n[1] See **noodle** v[1]

noodling vbl n[2] See **noodle** v[2]

noodling hook n Also *noodle hook* **Ozarks** Cf **noodle** v[1]
A gaff used for fishing.
   1923 *DN* 5.215 **swMO,** *Noodlin' hook.* . . A long-handled, barbed hook used for catching fish. **1929** *AmSp* 4.204 **Ozarks,** Thet 'ar pore . . woman o' hisn was . . a-scrunchin' cheenches on th' punch'on 'ith a antiganglin noodle-hook. **1931** Randolph *Ozarks* 270, Many an Ozark boy . . "noodles" his fish—pulls them out from under the rocks with his bare hands, or with a short gaff known as a "noodlin' hook." Some of these hooks are made of steel . . but the average noodler prefers to make his own by lashing a big fishhook to a wooden handle. **1933** Williamson *Woods Colt* 11 **Ozarks,** Boys, you cut yourself a stick, while I wade across to my boat an' git me my noodlin' hook.

noogie n |'nᴜgi, 'nugi| Also sp *nouggie* **chiefly Nth** Cf **Dutch rub, knuck** n[1] **4**
An act of striking or vigorously rubbing someone (usu on the head) with the knuckles.
   1988 *DARE* File **cwMA,** The young woman who cuts my hair says a noogie (['nugi] or ['nᴜgi]) is a "real rough scalp massage done with the knuckles hard enough to hurt." The kids do it to each other for a punishment, she says. My paper boy (age nine) says "That's when the guys rub another guy's head with their knuckles and it hurts." **1988** *Springfield Sunday Republican* (MA) 26 June comics sec, ["Calvin and Hobbes" cartoon:] "There aren't any penalties" [in a game of tag]. "None?? Don't I even get free hits? . . Well, what about an Indian burn then? Or noogies? Can I give you noogies? . . If you ask *me,* . . any game without push-ups, hits, burns, or noogies is a sissy game." **1991-93** *DARE* File **NYC** (as of 1950s), In the Bronx a noogie was a sharp blow to the crown of the head administered with the joint between the first and second phalanges of the middle finger, the hand having been made into a fist with the middle finger protruding. *Ibid* **MA** (as of 1948-50), From about [age] 12 through 14: If you said something "corny" (not all that funny) or blatantly stupid . . you got a certain number of *noogies,* which were raps on the arm. They were gentle raps. If they weren't, they were illegal. *Ibid* **Upstate NY** (as of 1968-69), Oh! noogies are . . applied by placing the fisted knuckles to the other person's head and rubbing like crazy in a very limited space, not only causing the scalp to burn but the hair to pull in several directions. . . It

seemed to be a boy thing. **1993** *Capital Times* (Madison WI) 28 May sec D 6/6 **RI,** If Vince in fact had tried to shampoo me and any of my friends had walked in, I'd have been an outcast: "Did y'hear Patinkin has his barber shampoo him? What a geek. Next time we see him, let's give him some head nouggies and a wedgie." **1995** *DARE* File **cwCA** (as of c1960), A noogie was a rub on the head with the knuckles. It led to the phrase "Tough noogies," which meant, sarcastically, "Too bad for you." *Ibid* **csWI,** A noogie is a hard rub on the head.

noon v, hence vbl n *nooning* Also with *it, up*
To take a midday break from work or travel for food and rest; hence n *nooning* a midday break.
   1687 in 1940 *AmSp* 15.290 **VA,** At ye head of a bottom tending to ye aforesaid Nooning place. **1805** (1904) Lewis *Orig. Jrls. Lewis & Clark Exped.* 2.9, We nooned it just above the entrance of a large river. **1828** (1936) McCoy *Jrl. Exped.* 240 **PA,** We nooned in the woods. **1853** (1928) Knight *Diary* 53 **MA,** Have just halted at the first farm to noon and rest awhile. **1854** (1932) Bell *Log TX-CA Trail* 35.293, We are nooning it about seven miles from last camp. **1859** (1965) Marcy *Prairie Traveler* 45, Starting with the dawn, and making a "nooning" during the heat of the day. **1865** (1889) Whitney *Gayworthys* 52 **NEng,** Baskets were opened and the simple nooning meal . . was eaten. **1867** Lowell *Biglow* lxxiii '**Upcountry**' **MA,** I am carried back . . to long-ago noon-ings in my father's hay-fields, and to the talk of Sam and Job over their jug of *blackstrap.* **1877** in 1937 Ruede *Sod-House* 106 **PA,** By 10 o'clock we had to quit, as it was too hot. . . We took about four hours for nooning, and then went back and worked till after sunset. **1895** Wiggin *Village Watch-Tower* 59, It was used as a "nooning" tree by all the men at work in the surrounding fields. **1930** *AmSp* 5.419 **csNH,** *Nooning:* intermission for rest in the middle of the day. "The hired man took an hour's nooning." **1937** Sandoz *Slogum* 140 **NE,** The yellow sun of a quiet morning rose on a dull day at Slogum House. Two freighters stopped for the nooning and a dusty cowboy or two loped through. **1959** *VT Hist.* 27.150, *Nooning.* . . A noon hour rest. Occa-sional. **1977** *Greenfield Recorder* (MA) 19 Mar 8 **MA,** By grabbing our coats we managed to slide twice down the Chestnut Hill road at recess and all the time during the hours nooning. **1985** Ehrlich *Solace* 24 **WY,** John pulled the wagon ahead with his pickup, meeting the herders at a prearranged spot to "noon up." . . By the time a herder arrived at the wagon with his sheep, John would have lunch ready.

noon pron See **none**

noon-bird n
An imaginary bird; see quot.
   1951 Randolph *We Always Lie* 68 **wAR,** Along the western border of Arkansas . . many old-timers remember the noon-bird, said to inhabit the Kiamichi Mountains of Oklahoma. It whistles like a fire engine exactly at noon.

nooning vbl n, n See **noon** v

noon it See **noon** v

noon mark n Also *noon stone* **esp NEng** *hist*
A mark or object that indicates the noontime position of a shadow.
   1842 Kirkland *Forest Life* 2.164 **MI,** All this . . took a good hour in the telling; and the poor woman had removed her wheel and I my seat several times to avoid the encroachments of the sun, which now ap-proached the noon-mark. **1853** (1860) Taylor *January & June* 131, The sun has . . reached the noon-mark on the threshold. **1884** Baldwin *Yankee School-Teacher* 52 **MA,** That same midday sun streamed through the doorway of a log cabin, touching the "noon mark"—a nail driven in one of the warped floor-boards. **1891** (1902) Earle *Sabbath New Engl.* 77, The time of the day was indicated to our forefathers in their homes by "noon marks" on the floor or window-seats. **1926** *DN* 5.401 **Ozarks,** *Noon mark.* . . A stake so placed as to mark the edge of the shadow cast by the cabin at noon. The clock, if there is one, is set according to the noon mark. **1938** FWP *Guide CT* 488, In the center of the cemetery is a 'noon stone,' a crude Colonial sundial, made of an upright stone and a chiseled mark on a flat rock beneath it. When the shadow of the vertical stone 'lines up' with the straight mark, it is noon by sun time. **1947** *VT Life* Autumn 20 **cwVT,** Visitors at noon of a sunny day . . may see the "noon mark," a dimple in the window-sill of the dining room (originally, the kitchen) so placed that the two shadows of the window sash cross the noon mark at exactly twelve o'clock. **1983** *Greenfield Recorder* (MA) 18 June [Ruby Hemenway column], Sometimes early settlers found just where the sun was at noon and made a mark on their

door sill. That marked [sic] was called the "noon mark" and that was all the time piece they had.

noon up See **noon** v

nooshni(c)k See **nushnik**

Noo Yawk (or York) See **New York**

nopal n Also *nopal cactus* [MexSpan *nopalli,* ult < Nahuatl; *OED* 1730 → for *Nopalea cochinellifera*] **SW**
=**prickly pear,** esp the flattened joint of this plant; see quots.

    1823 James *Acct. of Exped.* 2.209 **CO,** The nopals are considered characteristic of warm and dry climates. **1836** Latrobe *Rambler in Mexico* 67, The whole of the stony surface . . is covered with a profusion of maguey, mimosa, cactus, and gigantic nopal or prickly pear. **1842** in 1952 Green *Samuel Maverick* 183 **TX,** Old mine—fine garden—grape vines—nopal—cigaritos. **1875** Bourke *Diary* 31 May **wSD, eWY,** A plant, plentiful in this country [=along the South Cheyenne River] called the nopal, or Tuña cactus, plate cactus or Indian fig, is employed with success to clarify the water for drinking purposes. **1886** Havard *Flora W. & S. TX for 1885* 520, This and other species of flat-jointed *Opuntia,* known under the name of Nopal, abound all over Southern and Western Texas. . . I have seen cattle eating Nopal leaves with great relish in the open field. . . Nopal . . refers to the leaves. **1891** *Century Illustr. Mag.* 41.386 **cwCA,** More nopal hedges were planted, and the old ones extended. **1891** Coulter *Botany W. TX* 134, The joints [of prickly pear] are commonly spoken of as "leaves," and form an important food for grazing animals, under the name of "nopal." The "nopal leaf" is also much used for poultices, etc. **1892** *DN* 1.192 **TX,** *Nopál:* a cactaceous plant belonging to the prickly pear, or *Opuntia* tribe. **1932** Bentley *Spanish Terms* 172, *Nopal.* . . The flat-leaved prickly pear (*Opuntia chorotica*). Although the term "prickly pear" is more frequently used by English speaking people along the border, *nopal* seems to be regarded as a bit more learned. **1962** Balls *Early Uses CA Plants* 35, Another use for these plants [=prickly pear] . . is to gather the young joints . . to serve as a vegetable. . . The young growths are known as nopales. **1988** Schoenhals *Span.-Engl. Gloss.* 153, *Opuntia* spp . . "nopal cactus", "prickly pear", "flat-pad cactus".

nor adv See **no**

nor conj Pronc-spp *na, ner, nuh* [*OED* nor conj.² c1400 →] *old-fash*
Following a comparative adj or adv: Than.

    1823 Cooper *Pioneers* 1.17 **nNY,** I have yarbs that will heal the wound quicker nor all his foreign 'intments. **1834** Caruthers *Kentuckian* 1.103, I'll be bound you'd look at somebody else's pretty cheeks more nor you would at the parson's chaw-tobacco. **1845** Thompson *Pineville* 74 **cGA,** Pete Hopkins aint no better nor he should be. **1858** Hammett *Piney Woods Tavern* 129, What he minded wus [=worse] ner all. **1859** Taliaferro *Fisher's R.* 53 **nwNC** (as of 1820s), On I went wusser nur an old buck fur 'bout a quarter. **1862** (1864) Browne *Artemus Ward Book* 213 **NEng,** New England Rum. . . is wuss nor the korn whiskey of Injianny, which eats through stone jugs. **1864** Sargent *Peculiar* 106 **VA,** My father owned more slaves nor he could count. **1874** (1895) Eggleston *Circuit Rider* 92 **sOH** (as of early 1800s), They do say he *does* hate the Methodis' worse nor copperhead snakes, now. **1888** Jones *Negro Myths* 55 **GA coast** [Gullah], Eh tek down de pan gen, an eat mona half de butter. *Ibid* 69, Mo na dat, eh prummus um big money if eh git back de Ring. **1909** *DN* 3.401 **nwAR,** *Nor.* . . Than. "He can't do more nor I can." **1911** *DN* 3.539 **eKY,** He's better nor you. **1922** Gonzales *Black Border* 189 **sSC, GA coasts** [Gullah], W'en me ten toe' dig een de du't, 'e t'row de san' mo'nuh half uh acre behin' me! **1927** *AmSp* 2.360 **cwWV,** I bought those shoes no longer nor three weeks back.

Norah See **Noah**

norard See **northward**

norate v Also with *about, around* Also sp *norrate* [Prob back-formation from **noration,** though perh blend of *narrate* + *orate*] **chiefly S Midl, Sth**
To report; to advertise; to spread by word of mouth; to depreciate.

    1851 Hooper *Widow Rugby's Husband* 96 **AL,** I'll norate it to you. **1851** Burke *Polly Peablossom* 144 **GA,** Of course it was "norated in the settlement" that old man Crump had bought a whole barrel. **1884** Smith *Bill Arp's Scrap Book* 13 **nwGA,** Along in the evenin it was norated around that Ike was goin to banter [=challenge] me for a rassel [=wres-

tling contest]. **1893** Shands *MS Speech* 47, *Norate* [noret]. To make widely known, to spread abroad, as of a rumor or report. In this sense it is used by educated people as well as by illiterate. **1895** *DN* 1.373 **seKY, eTN, wNC,** *Norate.* . . "We will norate the preaching" (i.e. announce the services to be held). **1899** (1912) Green *VA Folk-Speech* 301, *Norate.* . . To rumour; spread by report. **1903** *DN* 2.322 **seMO,** He norated all over the settlement that I was going to leave. **1906** *DN* 3.148 **nwAR,** He norated it around some. **1908** *DN* 3.353 **eAL, wGA,** It got norated around that there was to be a frolic at Ward's mill. **1914** *DN* 4.110 **cKS,** He norated how the trouble started. **1914** Furman *Sight* 72 **KY,** A-taking my stand by the grave-houses in these resurrection gyarments, for to norate the wonders of my experience. **1915** *DN* 4.186 **swVA,** *Norate.* . . It is norated around that Bill and Sallie's a-goin' to get married. **1923** *DN* 5.215 **swMO,** *Norate.* . . To make public by word of mouth. Applicable chiefly to the spreading of unpleasant or depreciatory rumors of a personal nature. **1938** *AmSp* 13.6 **seAR,** *Norate.* . . 'It is norated about that he is a crook.' **1941** Skidmore *Hawk's Nest* 22 **WV,** Norratin' it round bout them wanten men to work . . , he had some mighty strange tales to tell. **1946** *PADS* 6.22 **eNC** (as of 1900–10), *Norate.* . . To bruit around. . . Rare. **1949** Webber *Backwoods Teacher* 112 **Ozarks,** The news had been "norated around" and we were hopeful that many women and girls would be here with boxes, and as many men and boys with money to buy them. **1954** *PADS* 21.33 **SC,** *Norate.* . . To depreciate. Usually of persons. **1983** *MJLF* 9.1.49 **ceKY** (as of 1956), *Norate* . . to deprecate by gossip.

noration n Also sp *norration* [Prob by metanalysis of *an oration,* infl by *narration;* cf *EDD* oration 1823 → "A confused noise or uproar; a clamour, disturbance; noisy public talk or rumour"; *EDD* n-oration "Loud or prolonged talking, a great noise or clamour; a disturbance, fuss" 1825 →] **chiefly S Midl, Sth**
An announcement, rumor, or account.

    1853 Page *Uncle Robin* 231 **VA,** Der's some folks who tells de people, dar, dat massers in dis country, when der niggers runs away, puts out a noration, dat dey will give four hundred dollar' to anybody who will bring one o' der runaway niggers to um, dead or 'live. **1859** Taliaferro *Fisher's R.* 235 **nwNC** (as of 1820s), Go on with your noration. **1899** (1912) Green *VA Folk-Speech* 301, *Noration.* . . A rumour; a long, rambling account. "She put out the noration that there would be a dance there next week." **1905** *DN* 3.89 **nwAR,** *Noration.* . . Announcement. 'A French specialist has given out the 'noration' that kissing is not a hurtful process.' Rare. **1914** *DN* 4.110 **cKS,** *Norration.*

nor'east See **northeast**

nor'easter See **northeaster**

norf See **north**

norrate See **norate**

norration See **noration**

norrer See **narrow**

norrud See **northward**

norry See **narrow**

no'rs See **nowheres**

Norski n, also attrib |ˈnɔrski| Also sp *Norsk(i)e, Norsky* [Norw *norsk* adj Norwegian + -y] **chiefly MI, WI, Upper MW, Pacific NW** See Map *chiefly in Norwegian settlement areas*
A person of Norwegian (rarely other Scandinavian) descent.

    1929 (1982) Rölvaag *Peder Victorious* 142 **SD,** [There was a picture of] a combat between a man and an infuriated bear. . . The title of the paragraph accompanying the picture was the single word: *Norway.* Under the picture someone had written in pencil: "A Norskie." **1950** *WELS* **WI** (*People of foreign background: Norwegian*) 25 Infs, Norski; (*Nicknames for people living in nearby settlements or places*) 1 Inf, The Norskis—people from the Scandinavian areas north of Waupaca; 1 Inf, Norskis. **1964** *PADS* 42.39 **Chicago IL,** *Herring choker, herring destroyer,* and *Norski* were restricted to Norwegians. **1965–70** *DARE* (Qu. HH28, *Names and nicknames . . for people of foreign background*) 44 Infs, **chiefly MI, WI, Upper MW, Pacific NW,** Norski; **MI**67, [ˈnɔrskɪ]; **MI**13, Norski [ˈnɔrskɪ]—Norwegians, Swedes and Danish would come under Norski; **[MI**17, Norsk]; **MN**6, [ˈnorski]; **[WI**22, A norski fillyfonts [*DARE* Ed: =Norw *fillefant* "ragged bum"]]; (Qu. H74a, . . *Coffee . . very strong*) Inf **MI**13, Norski coffee. **1983** Allen *Lang. Ethnic Conflict* 63, *Norwegians . .* norsky. **1989** Karni-Jarvenpa *Sampo* 165, **neMN** (as of c1930), Many of the various [Iron] Range nationalities engaged to some degree in name-calling . . : Italians were Wops or Dagos . . ; Swedes were dumb Swedes; Norwegians, Herring Chokers or Norskies. **1991** *DARE* File **cwWI**, Norske ['nɔrski] Nook—name of a restaurant; **csWI**, The Norske Fourske [nɔrski fɔrski]—name of a local musical group. **1995** *WI State Jrl.* (Madison) 25 Mar sec A 7/3, [Headline:] Norskis learned English, why not African-Americans?

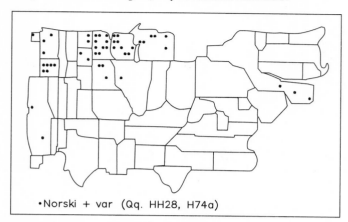

•Norski + var (Qq. HH28, H74a)

Norski coffee See **Norwegian coffee**

Norskie, Norsky See **Norski**

north adv, adj, n Usu |nɔ(r)θ, no(r)θ|; for addit varr see quots Pronc-spp *nawth, noathe, norf, noth* Cf Pronc Intro 3.I.1.e, 3.I.17 Cf **northeaster, northwester**
Std senses, var forms.
  1808 in 1956 Eliason *Tarheel Talk* 314 **c,cwNC**, Noth. **1884** *Anglia* 7.263 **Sth, S Midl** [Black], *Fum up Norf.* **1899** Chesnutt *Conjure Woman* 28 **csNC** [Black], He come down to Norf C'lina. **1903** *DN* 2.292 **Cape Cod MA** (as of a1857), *North* [noθ]. **1905** Chesnutt *Col.'s Dream* 24 **GA** [Black], Young Mars Henry went ter de Norf, and dey say he's got rich. **1908** Fox *Lonesome Pine* 27 **KY**, He lives over on the Nawth Fork. **1916** *DN* 4.335 **Nantucket MA**, *North.* Pron. [noθ] unless modifying a noun. So northeast [noθist] and north-northeast [nonoθist]; but northwest [nɔrwɛst] and north-northwest [nɔr-nɔrwɛst]. **1937** in 1983 Beyle *How Talk Cape Cod* 12, 'North' is said 'noathe,' like 'loathe'. **1939** *LANE* Map 13 *(North Carolina)* **NEng**, [In the pronunciation of *north*, proncs of the type [noθ, nɒθ] are about equally represented; those of the type [nɔrθ, nɒrθ] are much less freq, occurring esp in **wMA, wCT.**] **1940** *Morgantown Post* (WV) in 1944 *ADD* 417 **OH**, Certain Southern college gentlemen have invaded the 'Nawth' again. **1942** Hall *Smoky Mt. Speech* 90 **wNC, eTN**, *North* [noθ], [noθ]. **1989** Pederson *LAGS Tech. Index* 316 **Gulf Region**, [In the pronunciation of *North Carolina* the predominant pronc of *north* was [nɔrθ] with 228 infs so responding; other proncs were [no(ə)θ] 178 infs; [nɔ(ə)θ] 165 infs; [nɔrθ] 90 infs; [nɑrθ] 12 infs; [nɑ(ə)θ] 7 infs; [norf] 2 infs; [nɔɔf] 1 inf.]

northard See **northward**

North Carolina poplar See **Carolina poplar**

North Carolina robin n Cf **Cape Cod turkey**
  1912 Green *VA Folk-Speech* 301, *North Carolina robin.* . . A salted roe-herring.

North Caroline poplar See **Carolina poplar**

northeast adv, adj, n Usu |nɔ(r)θ'ist|; also |noθ'ist|; for addit varr see quots Pronc-spp *nor'east, noth(e)east* Cf **northeaster, northwest, northwester**
Std senses, var forms.
  1878 *Appletons' Jrl.* 5.415 **NEng**, "Day before yesterday," he [=a New Englander living alongshore] will tell you, "the wind was blowing *nōthe-*east, while yesterday it had hauled to *sou-*west." **1916** *DN* 4.335 **Nantucket MA**, *Northeast* [noθist]. **1937** in 1983 Beyle *How Talk Cape Cod* 12, On the Cape, the pronunciation is always 'no'theast' (not 'nor'east'). **1966–69** *DARE* (Qu. O19, . . *Kinds or degrees of wind that are important when you're in a boat*) Inf **CT39**, Nor'east; (Qu. O20, *Winds from particular directions;* total Infs questioned, 75) Inf **MS72**, Nor'east ['nɔr,ist]. **1968** *DARE* Tape **MD**14, [nɔ'θist]. **1975** Gould *ME Lingo* 190, *Northeast*—Correctly, this is pronounced know-theast, with the *th* sound of those, instead of the *th* of thing. The four quarter-points

in boxing the Maine compass are spoken thus: know-theast, sow-theast, sow-west, and norwest. . . The dictionary-sanctioned nor-east and nor-easter are absolutely in error, and shouldn't be spoken anywhere.

northeaster n Pronc-spp *nor'easter, no'theaster* **chiefly Atlantic; also Gt Lakes** See Map Cf **northwester**
A strong northeasterly wind, usu with heavy rain.
  1774 (1957) Fithian *Jrl. & Letters* 177 **NJ**, Still stormy. . . This is a true August Northeaster, as we call it in Cohansie. **1865** *Atlantic Mth.* 15.546 **NJ**, A bleak morning wind mingled with the fierce, incessant nor'easter. **1899** (1912) Green *VA Folk-Speech* 301, Northeaster. . . A wind or gale from the northeast. **1929** Starbuck *My House* 146 **Nantucket MA**, The weather had cleared during the night, and the wind had settled to a 'dry no'theaster,' the one perfectly satisfactory wind at any season of the year, sweet smelling and with the atmosphere always of crystal clearness. **1954** *WELS Suppl.* **cwWI**, I asked a herring fisherman about some ways to describe wind, and he said . . "a nor'easter." I was surprised at the salty sound of that, here in Wisconsin! **1957** Battaglia *Resp. to PADS 20* **eMD**, *(Kinds of wind)* Noreaster = heavy from the NE. **1965** *PADS* 43.17 **seMA**, A destructive windstorm with high wind and rain . . northeast [1 of 9 infs]. **1965–70** *DARE* (Qu. B18, . . *Special kinds of wind*) 41 Infs, **chiefly Atlantic, Gt Lakes**, Northeaster; 30 Infs, **chiefly Atlantic**, Nor'easter; 12 Infs, **Atlantic**, [nɔ(r)'θistə(r), nɔ(r)θ'istə(r)]; **MA**27, 34, 72, [nɒθ'istə]; **MA**2, 3, [norθ'istɚ]; **MA**7, 50, [nɒ'θistə(r)]; **CT**13, ['nɔθistər]; **ME**22, [noð'istə]; **MA**5, [nɒ'θistə]; **MA**44, ['nɒθistə]; **ME**5, [nɔristə]; **MA**55, Dry northeaster; (Qu. O19, . . *Kinds or degrees of wind that are important when you're in a boat*) 11 Infs, **Atlantic**, Northeaster; **GA**11, 12, **NJ**55, Nor'easter; (Qu. B17, *A destructive wind that blows straight*) Infs **NH**10, **NJ**22, 55, **RI**1, Northeaster; (Qu. B25, . . *Joking names . . for a very heavy rain.* . . *"It's a regular _____."*) Infs **MA**125, **NJ**19, Northeaster; **NH**16, Nor'easter; (Qu. O20, *Winds from particular directions; total Infs questioned, 75*) Infs **FL**16, 20, **MS**73, Northeaster. **1966–68** *DARE* Tape **FL**15, We have some northeasters in the wintertime that are not hurricane winds, but are . . storms. *Ibid* **MD**14, If you have northeasters ['nɔr,θistəz], now, our northeasters last three days here, you know, the northeast [nɔ'θist]. And after the northeaster ['nɔ,'θistə] begins to break the clouds, and the breeze begins to drift towards the southwest, look for good weather. *Ibid* **NH**19, A northeaster [nɑ'θistɚ]? A strong northeast wind, and usually rainy and foggy, it's very cold, always very, very cold and it always lasts for three days. . . Come all year round. It's usually down around or fifty or forty, very cold. **1978** *Yankee* Nov 46 **ME**, Dear Oracle: Where does the expression "Nor'easter" originate? I've heard it on T.V. and even read it in *Yankee.* I've lived in New England all my life and the old-timers always say "No'theaster." Answer: Your Maine accent is entirely correct. The heft of coastal New England says "No'theaster." Any human parsnip who says "Nor'easter" is a pilgrim and a stranger—don't trust such a specimen. **1986** Pederson *LAGS Concordance* **chiefly coastal Gulf Region**, 16 infs, Northeaster; 1 inf, **neFL**, Northeaster—heavy wind and rain from northeast; 1 inf, **neFL**, Northeaster—a wind with rain, damages beach; 1 inf, **ceFL**, Northeaster—term used "out in the water."

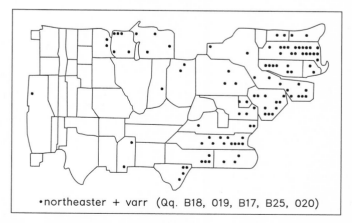

•northeaster + varr (Qq. B18, O19, B17, B25, O20)

Northeast Kingdom n Often with *the;* also *the Kingdom* **VT**
The northeastern part of Vermont.
  1967 *DARE* Tape **VT**1, [FW:] I was talking . . to a man . . down in Gill, just across the border in Massachusetts, and he was talking about some of this border territory between Vernon and Gill . . and he spoke of it as the kingdom, but he didn't know why it was called the kingdom,

do you? [Inf:] No, I've never heard that called the kingdom. We have . . the Northeast Kingdom up in the northern part of Vermont . . up through Essex County. . . It's very wild, and has a number of lakes. **1969** *DARE* (Qu. C34, *Nicknames for nearby settlements, villages, or districts*) Inf **VT**16, Northeast Kingdom—Orleans, Essex, Caledonia counties. **1977** Swift *VT Place-Names* 195, Essex County makes up much of the area referred to as the Northeast Kingdom, a name that is generally considered to have been given to the area by the distinguished Vermont statesman, George D. Aiken, governor from 1937–41 and for thirty-four years thereafter a United States Senator. The first known record of this designation occurred in the report of a speech by the Senator at Lyndonville (Caledonia County) in November 1949. **1977** *Yankee* Jan 50, The Northeast Kingdom [=Orleans, Essex, and Caledonia counties] never turns up in the handsome four-color brochure advertising Vermont's charm. . . When "the Northeast Kingdom" drops into a Vermonter's conversation, it elicits a reflexive giggle that is both amusement and embarrassment. **1986** Strickland *Vermonters* 61, [Subtitle:] Oral Histories from Down Country to the Northeast Kingdom. **1989** Mosher *Stranger* 4 **nVT,** We lived as far away from Boston as it's possible to live and still be in Vermont and not Canada. . . I often drove up the logging road above our place into the high wild country known as the Kingdom gore. *Ibid* 9, The tragedy. . . wrenched the Kingdom—tucked off between the Green Mountains to the west and the White Mountains to the east . . —out of the past. *Ibid* 268, Often my father had said and written in the *Monitor* that there was little or no law in the Kingdom.

north end of a chicken flying south *n* Also *north end (of a chicken), south end (of a chicken going north);* for addit varr see quot **scattered, but esp Sth, S Midl** See Map

1965–70 *DARE* (Qu. K73, . . *Names . . for the rump of a cooked chicken*) Infs **CO**47, **IN**35, **TX**78, North end of a chicken; **WV**2, 4, 10, North end of a chicken flying (*or* heading) south; **CO**38, **SC**34, North end going south; **AR**56, North end of southbound chicken; **GA**72, North end; **CA**195, **NC**38, **WI**61, South end of a (*or* the) chicken going north; **MT**3, South end of a hen going north; **GA**84, South end of a northbound chicken; **AR**52, **TN**14, South end.

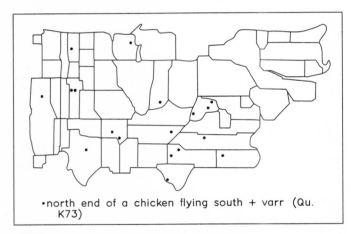

•north end of a chicken flying south + varr (Qu. K73)

norther *n* **chiefly TX** See Map Cf **blue norther**
A usu strong northerly wind that often brings a sudden decrease in the temperature.
1820 in 1858 Dewees *Letters TX* 17, A heavy storm of rain and sleet, together with a furious "norther" overtook us. **1834** (1928) Underwood *Jrl.* 32.129 **TX,** We were much in fear that a norther would spring up, in which case all of us must have been consigned to a watery grave. **1835** in 1952 Green *Samuel Maverick* 36 **TX,** Yesterday at about same hour a norther blew up, bringing the thermometer down 20°, from 75° to 55°. **1845** in 1868 McCall *Letters Frontiers* 431 **csTX,** If the Norther is accompanied by rain in the form of sleet, it is of course the more severe. Not a fortnight since, we had one of these Wet Northers, as they are called. **a1861** (1880) Eastman *Poems* 174 **VT,** And the Norther! see! on the mountain peak,/ In his breath, how the old trees writhe and shriek! **1873** in 1909 Roe *Army Letters* 87, Then we knew that we were having a "Texas norther," a storm that is feared by all old frontiersmen. **1888** Lindley–Widney *CA of South* 42, The norther is, owing to the topographical configuration of the country, less felt in Southern California than in the northern portion of the State. **1899** Garland *Boy Life* 45 **nwIA,** They [=the days] could be terrible when the Norther was abroad in his wrath. **1920** Hunter *Trail Drivers TX* 108 **TX** (as of 1877), On the 8th of June, . . a cold norther blew up, accompanied by rain, and it

soon became so cold we had to stop driving [cattle] about three o'clock in the afternoon. **1923** *DN* 5.215 **swMO,** *Norther.* . . A period of cold, blustery weather, preceded usually by strong north winds. **1962** Atwood *Vocab.* TX 39, *North wind.* The most dramatic weather phenomenon in Texas (aside from an occasional tornado) is the sudden sharp wind from the north which can reduce temperatures many degrees in a few hours or even minutes. This is universally known as a *norther.* **1962** Steinbeck *Travels* 220 **TX,** At this time the winter which had been following my track ever since I left home suddenly struck with a black norther. It brought ice and freezing sleet and sheeted the highways with dark ice. **1965** Teale *Wandering Through Winter* 168 **TX,** That afternoon the norther blew itself out. **1965–70** *DARE* (Qu. B18, . . *Special kinds of wind*) 28 Infs, **chiefly TX,** Norther; **TX**22, 29, 33, 45, 56, 73, Dry norther; **TX**11, 13, 22, Wet norther; **LA**14, Texas norther; (Qu. B5, *When the weather looks as if it will become bad . . it's* _____) Inf **TX**36, Gonna come a norther; **OK**25, Looks like it's going to be a norther; **OK**13, Norther coming up; (Qu. B11, . . *Other kinds of clouds that come often*) Inf **TX**73, Dry norther; (Qu. B12, *When the wind begins to increase . . it's* _____) Infs **AR**56, **LA**15, Coming a norther; (Qu. B24, . . *A sudden, very heavy rain*) Inf **OK**13, Norther; (Qu. O20, *Winds from particular directions;* total Infs questioned, 75) Infs **FL**24, **OK**25, Norther. **1967** *DARE* Tape **TX**32, When a norther comes up and the hogs are ready to kill, it's the time to kill 'em then. They need to be killed because the northers don't come when *you're* ready everytime, so you have to work with the weather. **1986** Pederson *LAGS Concordance* (*Any bad winds*) 1 inf, **swAL,** A norther; 1 inf, **swFL,** A norther—any winter storm from the north.

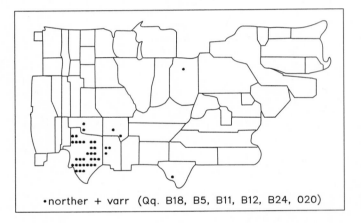

•norther + varr (Qq. B18, B5, B11, B12, B24, O20)

northern *adj* Usu |ˈnɔ(r)ðɚn|; also |ˈnɔ(r)ðən|; for addit varr see quots Pronc-spp *nawthun, norv'n, nothe(r)n*
Std senses, var forms.
1821 in 1956 Eliason *Tarheel Talk* 285 **NC,** 9 yds of Nothern Homespun. **1829** *Ibid* 314 **NC,** Nothen. **1899** Chesnutt *Conjure Woman* 10 **csNC** [Black], Is you de Norv'n gemman w'at's gwine ter buy de ole vimya'd [=vineyard]? **1936** Greene *Death Deep South* 84 [Black], He a Nawthun man. **1936** *AmSp* 11.313 **nNY,** In the following . . I have italicized the *r* which is last by dissimilation. . . norther*n*—[r] *included* 10 [r] *omitted* 3. **1939** *LANE* Map 230 (*Screech owl*) 1 inf, **neMA,** [nʊðən ɑˆʊɫ]. **1942** *AmSp* 17.153 **seNY,** Northern—*Both r's pronounced* 6—*First r omitted* 0—*Second r omitted* 3—*Both r's omitted* 2. **1969** *DARE* FW Addit **ceNC,** [ˈnaðɚn]. **1976** Allen *LAUM* 3.325 (as of c1950), [nɔðɚn] *northern* [1 inf, **cMN**].

northern *n*

1 also *northerner:* =**northern pike 1. chiefly MN, WI** See Map
1949 Caine *N. Amer. Sport Fish* 107, *Colloquial Names.* . . Northerner [etc]. **1950** *WELS* **WI** (*Kinds of fish that are good to eat, commonly caught in your neighborhood*) 1 Inf, Northern; 1 Inf, Northern, Northern pike. **1965–70** *DARE* (Qu. P1, . . *Kinds of freshwater fish . . caught around here . . good to eat*) 18 Infs, **chiefly MN, WI,** Northern(s); **MN**2, **WI**72, Northerns, northern pike; (Qu. P14, . . *Commercial fishing . . what do the fishermen go out after?*) Inf **MN**16, Northerns. [12 of 20 total Infs mid-aged or young] **1966** *DARE* Tape **MI**27, We fish for perch and walleyes and Northerns. **1968** *Cook Co. News–Herald* (Grand Marais MN) 9 May 3/1, The northerns are working up creeks to shallow ponds to carry on their spawning activities as well as along the shallow bays. **1972** [see **northern pike 1**].

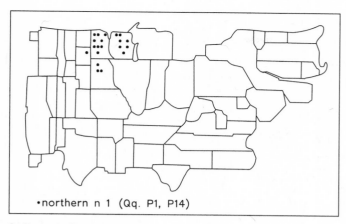

•northern n 1 (Qq. P1, P14)

2 See **northern bean.**

northern bean n Also *big northern bean, white ~, northern*
scattered, but esp Sth, Missip-Ohio Valleys See Map
=**great northern bean.**

  1950 *WELS (The large flat beans that are not eaten in the pod)* 1 Inf,
  cWI, Northern beans. **1965–70** *DARE* (Qu. I18, *The smaller beans*
  that are white when they are dry) 12 Infs, **scattered,** Northern beans;
  TX99, White northern beans; (Qu. I20, . . *Kinds of beans)* Infs **FL**51,
  IL31, **IN**35, **KY**77, Northern beans; **AL**30, Big northern beans; **IN**27,
  Northerns.

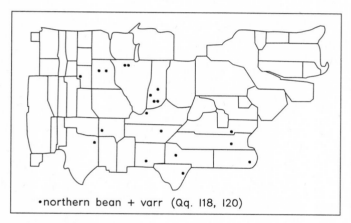

•northern bean + varr (Qq. I18, I20)

northern coffee n
  See quots.
  1939 in 1944 *ADD* **New Orleans LA,** *Southern coffee* = coffee mixed
  with chicory. *Northern coffee* = pure coffee. Restaurant signs. **1968**
  DARE (Qu. H74b, . . *Coffee . . very weak)* Inf **LA**23, Hot colored water
  in town [*DARE* Ed: =New Orleans] . . is called Northern Coffee or
  Yankee Coffee.

northerner See **northern** n **1**

northern lily n
  A **bead lily** (here: *Clintonia borealis*).
  1894 *Jrl. Amer. Folkl.* 7.101, *Clintonia borealis* . . Northern lily,
  Penobscot Co., Me. **1900** Lyons *Plant Names* 108, *C[lintonia] bore-*
  alis . . Northern Lily. **1911** *Century Dict. Suppl., Northern lily.* Same as
  Clinton's lily. Ibid, Clinton's lily, Clintonia borealis, a plant of northeastern North America related to the lily-of-the-valley.

northern mallard n Also *big northern mallard*
  =**mallard 1.**
  1943 Musgrove–Musgrove *Waterfowl IA* 17, Common Mallard . .
  Anas platyrhynchos platyrhynchos. . . Other names: French duck . .
  northern mallard, [etc]. *Ibid* 19, Sportsmen commonly believe that there
  are several species of mallards found in our state, calling them the big
  northern mallards, grass mallards, cornfield mallards, and red-legged
  mallards. Actually they are all one species.

northern phalarope n
  Std: a **phalarope** (here: *Phalaropus lobatus*). Also called
  fairy duck, gale bird, harbor goose, herring bird, Jersey
  goose, mackerel ~, red-necked phalarope, rock old-squaw,

sea goose, ~ plover, ~ snipe, squeaker, web-footed peep,
whalebird, whirligig bird

northern pike n
  1 also *northern pickerel:* A large freshwater game fish *(Esox*
  lucius). **chiefly Gt Lakes** See Map Also called **dogfish 9,**
  duck-billed pike 2, grass pickerel 2, ~ pike 1a, Great
  Lake(s) pike, great northern ~ 1, jack n[1] **24a(1), jack-**
  fish 1a, jack pike, lake pickerel 1, muskellunge 2, northern
  n 1, pickerel, pike, shovelnose pike, silver muskellunge, ~
  pike, slinker, snake, ~-eater, ~ pickerel
  1849 (1851) Herbert *Frank Forester's Fish & Fishing* 154, The Northern Pickerel is taken up to the weight of sixteen or seventeen pounds,
  but rarely, I believe, exceeds that weight. **1856** *Porter's Spirit of Times*
  1 Nov 142 **IL, IN,** *Esox Boreus,* or the northern pike . . ranks next to
  the muscalonge among our lake fishes. **1933** LA Dept. of Conserv.
  Fishes 373, The Northern Pike attains a weight of 25 pounds and is
  highly regarded for its food value. **1949** Caine *N. Amer. Sport Fish* 107,
  Its powerful, acrobatic struggles place the northern pike high on the list
  of worth-while sport fish. **1949** *Chicago Tribune* (IL) 23 Sept sec 3 5/1,
  Will an Illinois fisherman fishing thru the ice for northern pike be likely
  to catch a pickerel? **1950** *WELS* **WI** *(Kinds of fish that are good to eat,*
  commonly caught in your neighborhood) 6 Infs, Northern pike; 1 Inf,
  Northern pike (often called pickerel); *(What kinds of fish do commercial*
  fishermen go out for in your section?) 1 Inf, Lake trout, northern pike,
  bass. **1965–70** *DARE* (Qu. P1, . . *Kinds of freshwater fish . . caught*
  around here . . good to eat) 30 Infs, **chiefly Gt Lakes,** Northern pike.
  1966 *DARE* Tape **MI**12, [FW:] What's the biggest fish you ever caught
  in Sixteen-Mile? [Inf:] Oh, seven pounds, Northern pike. **1972** Sparano
  Outdoors Encycl. 367, Northern Pike—*Common Names:* Northern pike,
  pike, northern, snake, great northern, jackfish, jack. **1983** Becker *Fishes*
  WI 398, In Wisconsin the northern pike occurs in the Mississippi River,
  Lake Michigan, and Lake Superior drainage basins. **1986** Pederson
  LAGS Concordance, 1 inf, **ceAL,** Northern pike—some locally; 1 inf,
  ceTX, Northern pike—imported from lakes up north.

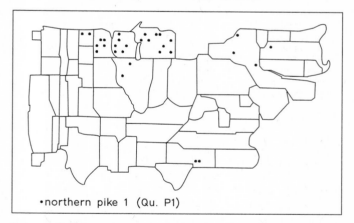

•northern pike 1 (Qu. P1)

  2 =**muskellunge 1.**
  1949 Caine *N. Amer. Sport Fish* 99, The muskellunge, especially
  smaller ones, is often mistakenly called northern pike. Although very
  similar in shape, the muskellunge can readily be identified by the
  distribution of scales on its cheeks and gill covers.

northern pine n Cf **southern pine**
  A **white pine** (here: *Pinus strobus*).
  1863 Porcher *Resources* 505 **Sth,** *Pinus strobus.* . . White or Wey-
  mouth pine, northern pine. Found in the declivities of the mountains of
  South Carolina, in the dark, sphagnous swamps along rivulets. **1897**
  Sudworth *Arborescent Flora* 13, *Pinus strobus* . . White Pine. . . Northern Pine (S.C.) **1930** Sievers *Amer. Med. Plants* 61, White Pine *Pinus*
  strobus . . Northern pine . . spruce pine. **1965–70** *DARE* (Qu. T17, . .
  Kinds of pine trees; not asked in early QRs) 10 Infs, **chiefly Gt Lakes,**
  Northern pine(s). **1979** Little *Checklist U.S. Trees* 199, *Pinus strobus* . .
  eastern white pine . . northern pine . . Weymouth pine. **1994** *DARE* File
  WI, I frequently inspected right-of-way covered by stands of northern
  pine, a kind of white pine.

northern shrike n Cf **loggerhead shrike, southern ~**
  Std: a bird *(Lanius excubitor)* known for impaling its prey.
  Also called **crazy jay, kite** n **1, mock hawk, mockingbird 4,**
  shamble-sticker, winter shrike

northin' See **nothing**

northward adv, adj, n Usu |'nɔ(r)θwə(r)d|; for addit varr see quots Pronc-spp *norard, northard, norrud, no'th'ard*
Std senses, var forms.

   1818 in 1956 Eliason *Tarheel Talk* 314 **ceNC,** Northardly. **1837** Sherwood *Gaz. GA* 71, *Norard,* northward. **1851** Hooper *Widow Rugby's Husband* 89 **AL,** He was a Norrud raised man and talked mighty proper. **1903** *DN* 2.291 **Cape Cod MA** (as of a1857), The *w*-sound frequently assimilated or disappeared after a consonant: *ekal = equal . . innards = inwards, norðard . . = northward. Ibid* 294, It blowed fresh from the northeast all day, then moderated and backened round to the northard and into the norwest. **1916** *DN* 4.335 **Nantucket MA,** Northward [nɔrðard]. **1945** Colcord *Sea Language* 134 **ME, Cape Cod, Long Island,** *Northward* (Pronounced no'th'ard; "th" as in clothing).

northwest adv, adj, n Usu |'nɔ(r)θ'wɛst|; in **NEng** also |nɔ(r)'wɛst|; for addit varr see quots Pronc-sp *norwest*
Std senses, var forms.

   1903 *DN* 2.291 **Cape Cod MA** (as of a1857), The *w*-sound frequently assimilated or disappeared after a consonant. . . But *Harwich* was never *Harrich,* and *northwest, southwest* were *norwest, souwest. Ibid* 294, [see **northward**]. **1916** [see **north**]. **1966–69** *DARE* (Qu. B18, . . *Special kinds of wind*) Inf **ME16,** Norwest—in winter; (Qu. O19, . . *Kinds or degrees of wind that are important when you're in a boat*) Inf **CT39,** Norwest; **LA45,** ['nɔət,wɛst] wind—never get caught in this; (Qu. O20, *Winds from particular directions;* total Infs questioned, 75) Inf **FL24,** Norwest; **MS72,** ['nɔr,wɛst]. **1975** [see **northeast**].

northwester n Also *nor'wester* **chiefly Atlantic, Gulf States, Gt Lakes** See Map Cf **northeaster**
A northwesterly wind, esp a strong one.

   1733 (1876) Byrd *Journey to Eden* 13, Towards the Evening, a Strong Norwester was so kind as to sweep all the Clouds away. **1751** in 1887 Franklin *Complete Wks.* 2.215, I question whether the strongest dry north-wester would dissipate it. **1823** Cooper *Pioneers* 1.110 **cNY,** This damned nor-wester is enough to whiten the skin of a blackamoor. **1855** in A. Lawrence *Diary & Corr.* 123 (*DAE*), A long trot . . in the face of a keen winter north-wester. **1965–70** *DARE* (Qu. B18, . . *Special kinds of wind*) Infs **MI47, SC69, TX12, VA77, WI58, 71,** Northwester; **FL24, GA11, MI44, MS72, NH16, NY37,** Nor'wester; **CT7,** Northwester—storm winds, as a rule; **DE4,** A heavy blow is a nor'wester or a northeaster, but the wind is from the no'theast; **IA4,** Northwester—cold in winter; **MD43,** Northwester; son-in-law [says] 'nor'wester'; **MI14,** Northwester is the prevailing wind; **FL21,** Nor'wester—cold wind out of northwest; **ME22,** [nɔrwɛstə]; **MI54,** There's a saying here, since if you get a storm from the southeast, it'll be followed by one from the northwest: "A nor'wester don't take nothin' from a southeaster"; (Qu. B17, *A destructive wind that blows straight*) Infs **CO7, MI44,** Nor'wester; (Qu. O19, . . *Kinds or degrees of wind that are important when you're in a boat*) Inf **LA26,** Northwester, **MI47,** Old northwester; (Qu. O20, *Winds from particular directions;* total Infs questioned, 75) Infs **FL13, 21, MS73,** Nor'wester; **FL10, 39,** Northwester(s). **1966** *DARE* Tape **MI21,** Coming in . . the boat would just lay right over on her side and the white foam would just curl off of the sides, you'd be travelin' that fast in a northwester, see, but you're goin' with the wind. **1986** Pederson *LAGS Concordance (Northwest wind)* 12 infs, **esp coastal Gulf Region,** Northwester.

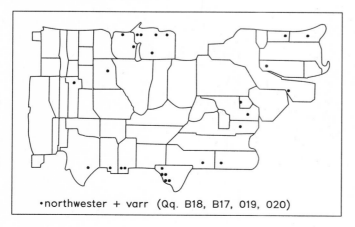

•northwester + varr (Qq. B18, B17, O19, O20)

northwestern crow n
Std: a crow *(Corvus caurinus)* native to the Pacific Northwest. Also called **beach crow, fish ~ 2, tidewater ~**

norv'n See **northern** adj

Norway pine n Also *Norway jack pine, Norwegian pine* [See quot 1980] **chiefly NEast, Gt Lakes, esp MI, WI, MN** See Map
A northern **pine** (here: *Pinus resinosa*). Also called **hard pine 2, red ~, yellow ~**

   1784 in 1888 Cutler *Life* 1.99, We rode five miles over pitch and Norway-pine plains. **1810** Michaux *Histoire des Arbres* 1.45, Dans la partie la plus septentrionale des Etats-Unis, qui comprend le District de Maine, le New-Hampshire et l'Etat de Vermont, il est désigné sous celui de *Norway pine,* Pin de Norwège, quoi qu'il en diffère totalement, puisque ce dernier est l'*Abies picea,* espèce de Sapin qui croît en Europe. [=In the northernmost part of the United States, which comprises the District of Maine, New Hampshire, and the State of Vermont, it is called by the name of *Norway pine,* from which it is entirely different, since the latter is *Abies picea,* a species of fir-tree which grows in Europe.] **1847** Wood *Class-Book* 514, *P[inus] resinosa . . Norway Pine. Red Pine. . .* abounds in the northern parts of the U.S. and in Canada. **1885** *Bot. Gaz.* 10.209 **Upper Peninsula MI,** The soil is either sandy, forming pine plains covered with an almost exclusive growth of *Pinus resinosa,* the so-called "Norway Pine" of the lumbermen, or a light clay loam, devoted to the hard woods. **1950** *WELS* **WI,** 23 Infs, Norway pine; 1 Inf, Norway pine—red bark—3 needles; 1 Inf, Norway or red pine; 1 Inf, Red or Norway pine—tall, red bark, dark green; 1 Inf, Norway pine—has long, large needles in bunches; has reddish bark. **1961** Douglas *My Wilderness* 108 **MN,** The red or Norway pine, whose color had been lost in the rain we experienced on Robinson Lake, now stood in full glory. Its tall, bare trunks with red-brown bark and its sparse graceful limbs gave color and character to many points and cliffs. **1965–70** *DARE* (Qu. T17, . . *Kinds of pine trees;* not asked in early QRs) 57 Infs, **chiefly NEast, Gt Lakes, esp MI, WI, MN,** Norway pine; **MN14,** Norway jack pine; **WI66,** Norway; **NH16, NY109,** Norwegian pine; (Qu. T5, . . *Kinds of evergreens, other than pine*) Inf **OH88,** Norway pine; (Qu. T15, . . *Kinds of swamp trees*) Inf **MI36,** Norway pine; (Qu. T16, . . *Kinds of trees . . 'special'*) Inf **MI26,** Norway pine. **1980** Little *Audubon Guide N. Amer. Trees E. Region* 293, The misleading name "Norway Pine" for this New World species may be traced to confusion with Norway Spruce by early English explorers. Another explanation is that the name comes from the tree's occurrence near Norway, Maine, founded in 1797. Because the name was in usage before this time, the former explanation is more likely.

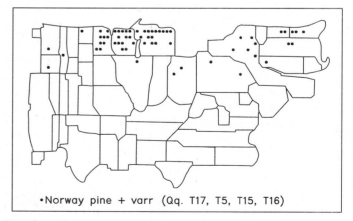

•Norway pine + varr (Qq. T17, T5, T15, T16)

Norway rat n
Std: the common brown rat *(Rattus norvegicus).* Also called **gopher rat 1, gray ~, sewer ~, water ~, wharf ~**

Norwegian n [See quot 1951] Cf **Norwegian widgeon**
=**baldpate 1.**

   1923 U.S. Dept. Ag. *Misc. Circular* 13.12 **UT,** Baldpate *(Mareca americana). . .* Norwegian. **1951** *AmSp* 26.90, From the word *widgeon* came *Norwegian* for the American widgeon in Utah.

Norwegian coffee n Also *Norski coffee*
See quots.

   1966 *DARE* (Qu. H74a, . . *Coffee . . very strong*) Inf **MI13,** Norwegian coffee, Norski coffee. **1970** *DARE* File **csWI** (as of 1930s), *Norwegian coffee*—strong coffee; **nWI**, *Norwegian coffee*—lumberjack coffee. Coffee made with an egg in it (not merely eggshells).

Norwegian duck See **Norwegian widgeon**

Norwegian herring n

A **gizzard shad 1** (here: *Dorosoma cepedianum*).

1943 Eddy–Surber *N. Fishes* 72, Gizzard Shad (Hickory Shad, Mud Shad, Hairy Back, Norwegian Herring). **1983** Becker *Fishes WI* 273, Gizzard Shad—*Dorosoma cepedianum.* . . Other common names: eastern gizzard shad . . Norwegian herring.

Norwegian pine See **Norway pine**

Norwegian snowstorm n Cf *Irish snowstorm*

See quots.

1950 *WELS* (Things nicknamed for particular nationalities—*[Norwegian])* 1 Inf, **cwWI**, Norwegian snowstorm—a bunch of lumberjacks shoveling snow on to the logging road. **1969** Sorden *Lumberjack Lingo* 81 **NEng, Gt Lakes,** *Norwegian snowstorm*—The shoveling of snow by hand when the snow road was getting bare.

Norwegian summer n

1950 *WELS Suppl.* **neWI, Chicago IL,** *Norwegian Summer* = Mild winter.

Norwegian widgeon n Also *Norwegian duck* [See quot 1951] Cf **Norwegian**

=**European widgeon.**

1911 *Forest & Stream* 77.173, European Widgeon. . . this species is known as . . Norwegian Widgeon on the eastern shore of Virginia. **1923** U.S. Dept. Ag. *Misc. Circular* 13.11, European Widgeon *(Mareca penelope)* . . In local use . . Norwegian duck, Norwegian widgeon (Va.) **1951** *AmSp* 26.90, From the word *widgeon* came *Norwegian* for the American widgeon in Utah and *Norwegian duck* and the tautonym *Norwegian widgeon* for the European widgeon in Virginia.

norwest See **northwest**

nor'wester See **northwester**

nory See **nary** adj

nose v Cf **snipe** v

In logging: to round or bevel the end of (a log); hence n *nosing* the part of a log so rounded.

1905 U.S. Forest Serv. *Bulletin* 61.43 [Logging terms], *Nose.* . . To round off the end of a log in order to make it drag or slip more easily. (Gen.) **1913** Bryant *Logging* 105, Previous to skidding, the forward end of a large log is "sniped" or "nosed." This consists of rounding off the under side of the log so that it will not catch on obstructions. **1958** McCulloch *Woods Words* 122 **Pacific NW,** Nose. . . To snipe a log, putting a bevel on the front end. *Ibid, Nosing*—The sniped part of a donkey sled, or front part of a sniped log.

nose n Cf **jaw** n

In phr *one's nose is getting hard:* See quot.

1931 *AmSp* 7.53 **Sth, SW** [Lumberjack lingo], "Your nose is gettin' hard" means one is getting angry.

nose bag n [Transf from std sense "a feed bag fastened over an animal's muzzle"] Cf **feed bag**

A meal, esp one carried along to be eaten away from home; a lunch pail or similar container—also in phrr *put on the* (or *a*) *nose bag* to eat a meal.

1921 Lardner *Big Town* 201 **cnIN,** We couldn't stop to put on the nose bag at the Graham. **1925** *AmSp* 1.139 **Pacific NW** [Logger Talk], The use of . . "nose-bag" for lunch has also come down from the old teaming days. The logger "puts on a nose-bag" at the lunch hour. **1927** *DN* 5.456 [Underworld jargon], *Nosebag.* . . A lunch carried in a paper bag. **1930** Williams *Logger-Talk* 26 **Pacific NW,** *Nosebag:* Lunch-pail. **1938** (1939) Holbrook *Holy Mackinaw* 262, *Nosebag.* Lunch bucket. *Nosebag show.* A camp where midday meal is taken to the woods in lunch buckets. Not highly thought of in these latter days. **1945** Hubbard *Railroad Ave.* 353, *Nosebag*—Lunch carried to work. *Put on the nosebag* means to eat a meal. **1956** Sorden–Ebert *Logger's Words* 24 **Gt Lakes,** *Nose-bag.* . . Lunch bucket carried by river drivers. Generally made of tin and was strapped to the back of the driver. **1966–67** *DARE* Tape **ID**2, Some of 'em won't even feed you at noon; they want you to carry one them lunch buckets. We call 'em a nose bag if you know what I

mean. *Ibid* **WA**30, She made these sandwiches—homemade bread you know—they'd come right to the top of your nose bag—one sandwich. [FW:] What's a nose bag? [Inf:] That's your lunch pail. **1968** *E. Liverpool Rev.* (OH) 19 June 9/3, Girls are asked to bring a nosebag lunch. **1975** Gould *ME Lingo* 191, *Nose bag*—A chopper's dinner pail. . . "To put on the *nose bag*" is a common Maine expression for pausing to eat, whether from a dinner bucket or at the kitchen table.

nosebleed n

1 An **Indian paintbrush 1** (here: *Castilleja coccinea*).

1869 Fuller *Uncle John* 102, Old Rose said it was 'Nose-bleed,' and an aged squaw who used to bring around roots for small beer, called it *Indian pink.* **1894** *Jrl. Amer. Folkl.* 7.95, *Castillea coccinea* . . bloody warrior, Minn.—nosebleed, Conn.

2 also *nosebleed plant, ~ weed:* A **yarrow** (here: *Achillea millefolium*). [*OED* c1450 →]

1876 Hobbs *Bot. Hdbk.* 75, Nosebleed . . Yarrow . . Achillea millefolium. **1892** (1974) Millspaugh *Amer. Med. Plants* 85-1, Common yarrow, milfoil, nosebleed. **1914** Georgia *Manual Weeds* 486, Milfoil, Thousand-leaf, Sanguinary, Bloodwort, Soldier's Woundwort, Nosebleed Weed. **1929** *Torreya* 29.151 **ME,** Achillea millefolium was "*Nosebleed plant.*" **1947** (1976) Curtin *Healing Herbs* 159, The Spanish Californians still steep its leaves in water to prepare a healing application for cuts and bruises, and to stop the flow of blood—which may be the reason why the plant has the colloquial name of nosebleed. **1979** Spellenberg *Audubon Guide N. Amer. Wildflowers W. Region* 342, Among this species' several common names . . Sneezeweed and Nosebleed may derive from the irritating odor.

3 A **trillium,** esp *Trillium erectum.* Cf **bloody nose**

1894 *Jrl. Amer. Folkl.* 7.102 **NY,** Trillium erectum . . nosebleed. **1901** Lounsberry *S. Wild Flowers* 62, *T[rillium] erectum,* ill-scented wakerobin, or nose bleed, is known by its handsome nodding flower, reddish in its gayest form, or sometimes pink, or white. **1940** Clute *Amer. Plant Names* 14, *T[rillium] erectum* . . nose-bleed. *Ibid* 15, *T. reflexum* . . nose-bleed. . . *T. sessile* . . Nose-bleed. **1949** *WELS Suppl.* **neIL,** We used to go [there] in the spring, looking for "Nose Bleeds," the very unpleasant name we had for the red trillium! **1965–70** *DARE* (Qu. S2, . . *The flower that comes up in the woods early in spring, with three white petals that turn pink as the flower grows older*) 10 Infs, **scattered,** Nosebleed; **CT**26, Nosebleed—doesn't turn red, starts out that way. **1971** Krochmal *Appalachia Med. Plants* 256, Trillium Erectum . . Purple trillium . . nosebleed . . wood lily. **1975** Dwyer *Thangs* 37 **Sth, S Midl,** Nosebleed—*Trillium (erectum).*

4 A **cardinal flower** (here: *Lobelia cardinalis*).

1901 Lounsberry *S. Wild Flowers* 486, *L[obelia] cardinalis,* cardinal-flower, red lobelia. . . Old men, urchins, and little maids all seek it by the brook's side. Some among them call the flowers "nosebleed," not, however, a pretty name.

nosebleed plant (or weed) See **nosebleed 2**

nose bot(fly) See **nose fly**

nose box n [**box** n 5a]

1968–70 *DARE* (Qu. GG36a, *The kind of person who is always poking into other people's affairs: "She's an awful _____."*) Infs **PA**66, **VA**46, Nose box; (Qu. II20a, *A person who tries too hard to gain somebody else's favor: "He's an awful _____."*) Inf **NC**79, Nose box.

nose-drops exclam Cf **drop** C7a, **dropsie** 2, **eye-drops**

In marble play: see quot.

1958 *PADS* 29.37 **WI,** *Nose-drops.* . . A call claiming the right to drop one's marble from one's nose, in the game of *chase*.

no-see-um n Cf **can't-see-um**

1 also *no-see (fly), no-see-em, no-see-um bug, ~ fly:* A biting dipterous insect: either a **black fly** or a **punkie** (here: family Ceratopogonidae). **chiefly Nth, Pacific** See Map on p. 826

1842 Harris *Treatise Insects* 405 **ME,** They [=black flies] are followed, however, by swarms of midges, or sand-flies . . called no-see-'em, by the Indians of Maine, on account of their minuteness. **1848** *Union Mag.* (NY NY) 3.29 **MA,** In the summer myriads of black flies, or, as the Indians call them, "no-see-ems," make travelling in the woods almost impossible. **1886** *Forest & Stream* 26.349 **Gt Lakes,** The [mosquito] bar is no protection, however, from sandflies or "no-see-ems" and the black fly. **1905** Kellogg *Amer. Insects* 310, The females [of the family Ceratopogonidae], except in the case of the minute punkies or "no-see-ums" of the New England and Canadian mountains and forests, and their near relatives in the western forests, are not blood-suckers. **1916** Kephart *Camping & Woodcraft* 1.255, *Punkies.*—The punkie or "no-see-um" of our northern wildwoods, and its cousins the biting gnats and stinging midges of southern and western forests, are minute blood-suckers. **1940** White *Wild Geese* 125 **NW** (as of 1890s), "You're worse than a no-seeum," he complained. **1949** *WELS Suppl.* **neWI,** No-see-ums = sandflies = gnats. **1950** *Ibid* **nWI,** Have heard the word "no-see-ems" used many times in northern Wisc. where they are. You don't notice them until they bite. *Ibid* **cWI,** I was raised in Marathon county and lived long in Lincoln county. I always have heard the small black flies you spoke of called "no-see-ums." In fact, I've never heard them called by any other name, and it is still the name. *Ibid* **cWI,** The little biting insect here is called by some no-see-ems and by some punks and I can assure you that it is no larger than a mosquito. *Ibid* [see **2** below]. **1950** *WELS* **WI** (*A very tiny fly that you can hardly see but that stings sharply*) 18 Infs, No-see-um; (*Very small flies that don't sting, often seen hovering in large groups outdoors in the summer*) 1 Inf, Gnats, no-see-ums—they don't sting, they bite. **1962** Salisbury *Quoth the Raven* 252 **seAK,** I . . got gnat bites. . . The pests got in my eyes . . up my sleeves. . . They are called "no-see-ums" by the Indians, but they are "sure-feel-ems." **1965–70** *DARE* (Qu. R11, *A very tiny fly that you can hardly see, but that stings*) 117 Infs, **chiefly Nth, Pacific,** No-see-um; **NH14, VA101,** No-see; **CA207,** No-see fly; **OR1,** No-see-um bug; **OR3,** No-see-um fly; (Qu. R10) Inf **WA28,** No-see-ums—they sting. **1975** *New Yorker* 24 Feb 82 **nME,** No-see-ums are so small they go right through the screening of the tent. They home on flesh. **1979** Lewis *How to Talk Yankee* [23] **nNEng,** *No-see-um.* . . When you're off on a fishing trip . . and the exposed parts of your body feel dozens of fiery nips, you've made acquaintance with the *no-see-ums* or minges. Mere specks, they are practically invisible, but their bites smart like the dickens. As a nuisance, they're much worse than black flies or mosquitoes. **1981** Pederson *LAGS Basic Materials,* 1 inf, No-see-ums—a friend from California called them this.

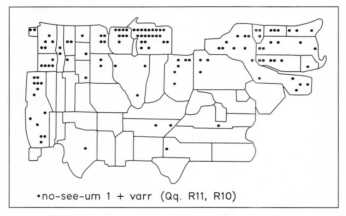

•no-see-um 1 + varr (Qq. R11, R10)

2 also *no-see:* =**midge 1.**

1950 *WELS* **WI** (*Very small flies that don't sting, often seen hovering in large groups outdoors in the summer*) 3 Infs, No-see-ums. **1950** *WELS Suppl.* **cWI,** My father-in-law used to call those little knats [sic] that buzz around a person's ears and eyes while perspiring and working in the garden about the middle of June "No See ums." *Ibid* **seWI,** We used the term "no-see-ums" in Milwaukee to refer to a tiny black insect which sometimes came in through the screens on summer nights and which bit or stung. I think we also used the same name for little green insects which did the same. [*DARE* Ed: The "little green insects" are prob midges of the genus *Tanytarsus.*] **1966–69** *DARE* (Qu. R10, *Very small flies that don't sting, often seen hovering in large groups or bunches outdoors in summer*) Inf **MA1,** No-see-um; **MN2,** No-sees, no-see-um; (Qu. R15a, . . *Names or nicknames . . for mosquitoes*) Inf **FL39,** Blind mosquitoes or no-see-ums—they don't bite; **MA30,** No-see-um—old Indian name for mosquitoes; **WA20,** No-see-um. [*DARE* Ed: Midges of the family Chironomidae are very similar in appearance to mosquitoes and often mistaken for them.]

3 Either the **harvest mite** or the grain thrips (*Limothrips cerealium*). Cf **oats bug**

1967–69 *DARE* (Qu. R12, . . *Other kinds of flies*) Inf **IL56,** We call the oats bug "no-see-ums" because they fly right through the screen and you don't see them come in; (Qu. R22, *Very small red insects, almost too small to see, that get under your skin and cause itching*) Inf **IL64,**

That's what I mean by no-see-ums; **MN7,** No-see-ums; **WI23,** Jiggers—Indians used to call them no-see-ums; (Qu. R21, . . *Other kinds of stinging insects*) Inf **IL64,** No-see-um—little stinging things you can't see. **1982** Slone *How We Talked* 110 **eKY** (as of c1950), Chiggers were called "the no see um, big feelum bug."

nose fly n Also *nose bot(fly)* [See quots 1890, 1925; *OED* a1793 →] Cf **chin fly, heel ~, nit ~**
Usu a horse botfly (*Gasterophilus haemorrhoidalis*), but also the sheep botfly (*Oestrus ovis*) or a **warble fly.**

1890 *Century Dict.* 4020, *Nose-fly.* . . The bot-fly, *Œstrus ovis,* which infests the nostrils of sheep, in which are deposited its living larvæ. **1925** *Book of Rural Life* 2666, There are . . two other kinds of botflies that attack horses. One is known as the *chin bot,* or *throat bot,* and the other as the *nose bot.* *Ibid,* The nose botfly attaches its eggs usually on the hairs of the lips and nostrils. **1949** Swain *Insect Guide* 208, The nose bot fly larvae attach first to the walls of the stomach, then the rectum, and finally, just before dropping to the ground, the anus. **1965–70** *DARE* (Qu. R12, . . *Other kinds of flies*) Infs **IN69, MN16, MT3, NE8, OK42, WY5,** Nose fly; **IL11,** Nose fly—called sweat bee, too; **IL14,** Bot—same as nose fly; **MI27,** Nose fly—I've seen 'em around sheep; **MN23,** Nose fly—used to bother the horses—half as big as a sweat bee; **MN42,** Horse fly or nose fly; **NY233,** Head fly, nose fly—same—around face of cattle; **ND5,** Nose fly—horse's nose. **1967** *Merck Vet. Manual* 717, The eggs of *G. haemorrhoidalis* (the nose or lip bot) are attached to the hairs of the lips. *Ibid* 804, *Sheep Nose Bots*—The larva of the fly *Oestrus ovis.* . . is one of the most widely distributed of the parasites of sheep in the United States. **1989** *Entomol. Soc. Amer. Common Names Insects* 92, *Gasterophilus haemorrhoidalis* . . nose bot fly.

nose open, get one's v phr Also *have one's nose wide open* and var [Prob in ref to the flaring nostrils characteristic of the sexually aroused stallion] *among Black speakers*
To be infatuated or in love; to cause someone to be infatuated or in love.

1963 Mencken–McDavid *Amer. Lang.* 745 [Black], A *cat* in hot pursuit of a *chick* or *fox* is said to *have his nose wide open.* **1970** *DARE* (Qu. AA1, *When a man goes to see a girl often and seems to want to marry her, he's _____ her*) Inf **NY241,** Getting his nose open; (Qu. AA4a, . . *A man who is very eager to get married. . . "He's _____."*) Inf **DC11,** His nose is wide open—recent expression; **SC69,** Got his nose open; (Qu. AA10, *A very special liking that a boy may have for a girl [or the other way round] . . "He _____ her."*) Inf **NY241,** Got his nose open for her; [**NY250,** Has his (her) nose;] (QR, near Qu. AA15c) Inf **FL48,** To be in love is to "have one's nose open." [All Infs Black] **1970** Major *Dict. Afro-Amer. Slang* 85, *Nose wide open:* to have one's "nose wide open" is to be in love. **1971** Roberts *Third Ear* np [Black], *Nose open* . . 1. . . . strongly influenced by; e.g. ["]He sure got your nose open.[*] 2. in love. **1972** Claerbaut *Black Jargon* 49, *Get your . . nose open* . . Allude[s] to the male condition of being in love or strongly infatuated with a woman to a degree which makes him unable to exercise his own will in the relationship. He has a ring in his nose. **1994** Smitherman *Black Talk* 128, Got his/her nose open—Refers to a person who is vulnerable and helpless because of being deeply in love. *Nose open* derives from the idea of the scent or smell of sex; it is this that "opens the nose."

nose-to-nose adj phr
Antagonistic.

1967 *DARE* (Qu. II11b, *If two people can't bear each other at all . . "Those two are _____."*) Inf **PA55,** Nose-to-nose. **1967** *DARE* FW Addit **cePA,** We were nose-to-nose = at odds.

nosh v, hence vbl n *noshing* Also sp *nas(c)h* [Ger *naschen* to nibble on, *Nascher* a nibbler; also Yiddish *nashn, nasher* in same senses]
To snack (on); to nibble between meals; to eat; hence *nosher* a nibbler.

1947 *WELS Suppl.,* 1 Inf, **csWI,** Harold has always called me a "nascha." He too likes to "nasch." This expression . . he told me was Yiddish—or Jewish. . . This word he used at home in New York & New Jersey. Many of our Jewish friends used the word; 1 Inf, **seWI,** Here are the forms in which I overheard and used the word—to naasch—naashing [sic]; 1 Inf, **seWI,** "Nash." We have always used it with the meaning that we nibbled food delicacies between meals. **1963** [see **nosh** n]. **1968** Rosten *Yiddish* 267, To *nosh* is to "have a little bite to eat before dinner is ready," or to "have a little something between meals." **1975** *Los Angeles Times* (CA) 19 Oct calendar sec 51, A vegetarian who noshes nuts and raisins during the day, Ashby came up as a film editor. **1978** *Sunset* Jan 30 *(Random House Coll.),* No other street in Los Angeles has the variety of eating experiences you'll find packed into Fairfax Avenue near Framer's Market. It's where "noshing," Yiddish for nibbling at tidbits of food, becomes almost an art. **1982** *Sunset* Jan 26 *(Random House Coll.),* Great noshers, otters consume 25 percent of their body weight every day. **1986** Chapman *New Dict. Amer. Slang* 295, *Nosh* or *nash.* . . v To have a snack. . . n . . *He always liked a little nosh between meals.*

nosh n Also sp *nash* [Yiddish *nash* a snack]
A snack; a tidbit; also fig.
1953 *NY Times* (NY) 1 Feb sec 6 pt 2.76/4, On the lower East Side, dominated by Delancey Street and Second Avenue—"Knish Alley"—the week-end [sic] sees the streets crowded with people from uptown and out of town, enjoying a "nosh" at Yonah Shimmel's Knishery, a leading dispenser of the potato, cheese or groat-filled delicacies. **1963** Mencken–McDavid *Amer. Lang.* 261, Many of these expressions [=New York Yiddishisms] . . are originally German, [and] are familiar to non-Jews as well; among them are. . . *nash:* a bit of food between meals. *nasher:* one who habitually eats between meals. . . [Footnote:] *Nash* . . [is] pronounced and often spelled *nosh.* **1965** *NY Times* (NY) 9 Apr 40/3, Advertising copy will stress that the company makes everything from "soup to nosh." (A nosh is a snack). **1966–68** *DARE* (Qu. H5, . . *A small amount of food eaten between regular meals*) Infs IL50, PA171, WI11, Nosh; CA4, Nosh—in childhood. **1968** Rosten *Yiddish* 267, Many delicatessen counters display plates with small slices of salami, or pieces of halvah, with a legend affixed to a toothpick: "Have a *nosh.*" **1970** *AmSp* 45.106, Yiddish slang words are probably traceable to New York literary circles. . . The most current Yiddish slang terms in the 1960s included . . *nosh* 'a snack'. **1971** *DARE* File **Atlanta GA,** Nosh Corner: name of a small eating place on Peachtree St. **1982** *Los Angeles Times* (CA) 9 May Book Rev. 9, It's a pity that low-salt dieting hasn't become a craze like designer jeans or jogging . . bemoans Corinne T. Netzer in another nosh from the organic circuit, *The Low-Salt Diet Counter.* **1986** [see **nosh** v].

nosher See **nosh** v

noshery n Also *nosherye* [Prob **nosh** v + *-ery,* by analogy with *eatery,* perh infl by Yiddish *nasherei* snacks]
A snack bar, restaurant.
1963 Mencken–McDavid *Amer. Lang.* 261, [Footnote:] *Nash* (pronounced and often spelled *nosh*) has yielded *noshery* as a designation for a snack bar. Miami Beach and similar outposts of civilization are full of *nosheries.* . . [A] *Chinese Noshery* was opened in the posh Georgetown section of the District of Columbia, c. 1955. **1985** *WI Alumnus Letters* **neIL,** Chicago has both *Noshery Deli* and *Nosherye Deli* (Yiddish). **1986** Chapman *New Dict. Amer. Slang* 295, *Noshery.* . . A restaurant or delicatessen, esp for snacking.

noshing See **nosh** v

nosing See **nose** v

nosy around v phr Also sp *nosey around* [Cf *DBE nosey around* (at *nosey* v. "to pry")]
To go about inquisitively; to idle about.
1940 Faulkner *Hamlet* 267 **MS,** That durn vote-sucking sheriff noseying around out here. **1969** *DARE* (Qu. KK31, *To go about aimlessly looking for distraction: "He doesn't have anything to do, so he's just _____ around."*) Inf **KY**60, Nosying.

nosy Rosy n Also *Rosy nosy*
1965–70 *DARE* (Qu. GG36a, *The kind of person who is always poking into other people's affairs: "She's an awful _____."*) Infs **CA**81, 117, **LA**28, **MS**80, 88, **OH**45, Nosy Rosy; **IL**28, Rosy nosy; (Qu. FF1, . . *A kind of group meeting called a 'social' or 'sociable'. . . [What goes on?]*) Inf **CA**81, The Nosy Rosies—gossipers that meet to chat; a "social" time; (Qu. II18, *Someone who joins himself on to you and your group without being asked and won't leave*) Inf **MS**84, Nosy Rosy. [4 of 8 total Infs Black]

not interrog exclam [Ger *nicht (wahr),* PaGer *net (wor)*] Cf **ain't** v[2] **1, huh not, isn't it**
Used as a tag question; see quots.
1908 *German Amer. Annals* 10.36 **sePA,** Not. . . Used at end of

interrogative sentence. "Have you seen it, *not?*" **1948** *AmSp* 23.237, *Not,* as an interrogative. P[ennsylvania] G[erman] *net,* when used with a rising inflection, is meant to anticipate an affirmative answer. . . 'This is bound to be true, not?'

no-tail n
=**pied-billed grebe.**
1955 MA Audubon Soc. *Bulletin* 39.310 **NH,** *Pied-billed Grebe.* . . No-tail. . . All of the grebes have rudimentary tails.

not by a jugful See **jugful(l), not by a**

notch n
1 A mountain pass or **gap** n[1] **1. chiefly NEast** See Map
1718 in 1882 MA Hist. Soc. *Coll.* 5th ser 7.195 **CT,** Lodg'd with Col. Quincy at Olcot's, about ½ way between the Notch of the Mountains and Hartford. **1888** Stockton *Dusantes* 12 **CA,** The other road pursued its way along a valley or notch in the mountain. **1903** (1984) Ayer *Autobiog.* 6 **NEng,** It was twenty miles to the "Notch" of the White Mountains. **1932** *DN* 6.231, *Notch.* This word is heard in New England for a depression between hills or mountains. In New York, *pass* is more usual—in the Adirondacks, at least—and farther south *gap.* All three words may be heard in the West, though *notch* is not very common. **1943** Peattie *Great Smokies* 40, A pass is usually a gap or, rarely, a notch. **1950** *WELS* (A low place in mountains or high hills where you can get through without climbing over) 1 Inf, **seWI,** Notch. **1951** Johnson *Resp. to PADS 20* **DE,** Notch. c**1955** Reed-Person *Ling. Atlas Pacific NW* (Notch between mountains) 11 [of c50] infs, Notch. **1965–70** *DARE* (Qu. C15, *A place in mountains or high hills where you can get through without climbing over the top*) 30 Infs, **chiefly NEast,** Notch; (Qu. C19, . . *Low land running between hills*) Inf **CT**2, Notch; (Qu. C21, *A deep place cut in sloping ground by running water*) Inf **MD**7, Notch. **1986** Pederson *LAGS Concordance* (Notch between mountains) 48 infs, **Gulf Region,** (A) notch. [*DARE* Ed: 304 infs defined *notch* as something other than a topographical designation, e.g., a cut made in wood, on the handle of a gun, in a belt, etc, suggesting that many infs may have been prompted by use of the word by the fieldworker.]

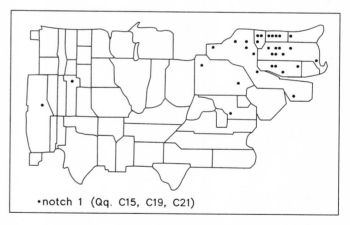

•notch 1 (Qq. C15, C19, C21)

2 in phrr *(up* or *down) to the (last) notch:* To the proper standard; to perfection; to the limit. **scattered, but less freq NEast, West** See Map on p. 828 *old-fash* Cf **topnotch**
1790 Tyler *Contrast* 69 **NYC,** There the old man was even with her; he was up to the notch. **1837** Smith *Col. Crockett's Exploits* 32, Every thing was cooked to the notch precisely. **1843** (1916) Hall *New Purchase* 116 **IN,** It's my opinyin this stranger's acted up, clean up, to the notch, and is most powerful clever. **1888** Jones *Negro Myths* 82 **GA coast** [Gullah], May Belle . . farruh [=father] bin rich, an eh dress um up ter de notch. **1897** *Outing* 30.466, When you have girded yourself up to the last notch, so to speak. **1965–70** *DARE* (Qu. KK50, *When something is planned out carefully, down to the last detail: "He had it all worked out _____."*) 30 Infs, **scattered, but less freq NEast, West,** (Down) to the last notch; **SC**3, To the last notch; down to a [sic] notch; **NC**26, Right down to the notch; (Qu. KK1b, . . *'In the very best condition': "His farm is _____."*) Inf **NJ**8, Up to the notch; (Qu. KK3b, *Something done perfectly—for example, a piece of work: "It's done to _____."*) Infs **CA**101, **MS**49, **NY**131, **OH**72, **SC**24, **VA**15, Last notch. [34 of 37 total Infs old]

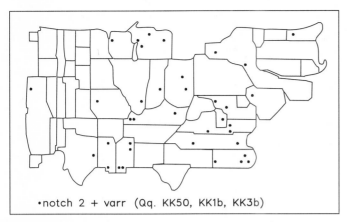

•notch 2 + varr (Qq. KK50, KK1b, KK3b)

notchweed n [*OED* 1736 →]

A **goosefoot** (here: *Chenopodium vulvaria*).

1900 Lyons *Plant Names* 95, C[*henopodium*] *Vulvaria*. . . Notchweed.

note v

1 To put into musical notation. [*W3* "*archaic*"]

1974 Fink *Mountain Speech* 17 **wNC, eTN,** *Note* . . write music for. "Can he note a song?" **1976** Garber *Mountain-ese* 62 **sAppalachians,** *Note* . . write music. She got a musicianer to note the song ballet fer her.

2 To stop (the strings of a musical instrument); to produce the desired tone when stopped; hence n *noter* an implement for stopping the strings of a **dulcimer. S Midl**

1956 McAtee *Some Dialect NC* 31, *Note*. . . Finger a musical instrument. "He had rheumatism so bad he couldn't note his fiddle." **1959** Roberts *Up Cutshin* 9 **seKY,** I'd just watch . . my daddy note the strings and his fingers strike the chords, and then I'd grab the old banjer. I first learnt to play tunes by picking the strings while he noted 'em for me. **1964** *Mt. Life* Summer 25 **sAppalachians,** Dad used a stick to note with and a goose feather to strum with. **1975** *Foxfire 3* 205 **nGA,** Pick the melody by noting the first string only. Strum the other three strings; they are the drone strings. *Ibid* 206, Mark off the frets *exactly* as they are here, or the dulcimer will not note properly. **1978** Massey *Bittersweet Country* 385 **Ozarks,** The purpose of the noter is to hold down the melody string. On a four-string dulcimer, there are two melody strings which are played as one. . . The noter may be any of several materials, but most players use a piece of wood that is tapered on the end to move smoothly up and down the fretboard, and carved to fit the hand.

note up for v phr

To indicate, point toward (some outcome).

1974 Fink *Mountain Speech* 17 **wNC, eTN,** Them colouds [sic] don't note up for rain. **1976** Garber *Mountain-ese* 62 **sAppalachians,** The signs jist don't note up fer a very mild winter this year.

noth See **north**

no'th'ard See **northward**

not hardly See **hardly** adv A2

notheast See **northeast**

no'theaster See **northeaster**

notheeast See **northeast**

nothen See **northern** adj

nother adj[1], adv, pron, conj See **neither**

nother adj[2] See **another**

nother pron, adj[3] [By metanalysis of *an other*; *OED nother* pron.[1], a.[1] a1300 →] Cf **another**

Other—often in phr *a whole nother.*

1899 (1912) Green *VA Folk-Speech* 301, *Nother*. . . "You are a nother." **1909** *DN* 3.353 **eAL, wGA,** *Nother* . . pron. adj. . . The *n* is clearly detached from the *a* and attached to the following word in many similar cases. **1954** *Harder Coll.* **cwTN,** [Letter:] Will try to drop you a nother card. **1969** *DARE* File, It will take a whole nother day. A group of nother people will take over. *Ibid* **CA,** There's a whole nother storm coming. **1982** *Ibid* **LA,** Making it is one thing; it's a whole nother effort selling it. **1989** *Daily Hampshire Gaz.* (Northampton MA) 2 Aug 14/2, It's crazy because it presents a whole 'nother problem.

nothern See **northern** adj

nothing n Usu |'nʌθɪŋ|; also |'nʌtn̩, 'nɒθɪn, 'nɔ-, 'nɑ-|; also *chiefly among Black speakers* |'nʌfn̩| (cf Pronc Intro 3.I.17); for addit varr see quots Pronc-spp *narthing, nawthin', noddin', northin', nothink, nothun, nuffin, nuthin', nuttn(g), nuttn(e)*

Std sense, var forms.

1843 (1916) Hall *New Purchase* 404 **IN,** It's a robbin a boy of his money by keepin him out a school for nothun no how. **1853** Simms *Sword & Distaff* 200 **SC** [Black], Who could b'lieb dat a pusson could lib so long and grow so big, and nebber l'arn nutting! **1884** *Anglia* 7.278 **Sth, S Midl** [Black], *Nuthin' or nuffin'* comes up ter = nothing is equal to. **1888** Jones *Negro Myths* 82 **GA coast** [Gullah], Day yent nuttne wuh de Debble cant do ef eh mek up eh mine ter um. **1890** *DN* 1.40 **ME,** *Nothing:* originally perhaps ['nɔθɪn] or ['nɔθɪn]; now ['nʌθɪŋ]. *Ibid* 68 **KY,** *Nothing* ['nʌθɪn]. [*DN* Ed: In New England also pronounced [nɔθɪn].] **1893** Shands *MS Speech* 47, *Nuffin* [nʌfn̩]. Negro for *nothing*. **1899** Chesnutt *Conjure Woman* 19 **csNC** [Black], Sayin' nuffin ter nobody. **1901** *DN* 2.183 **neKY** [Black], *Nothing—nuffin*. **1904** Day *Kin o' Ktaadn* 31 **ME,** Plum fizzle in life—wuss off 'n northin'. **1909** *DN* 3.400 **nwAR,** *Nawthin'*. . . Nothing. **1910** *DN* 3.445 **wNY,** ['nɒθɪn]. . . Nothing. Often so pronounced. **1914** *DN* 4.74 **ME, nNH,** Hain't got nawthin' on yer hip, hev ye? **1922** Gonzales *Black Border* 315 **sSC, GA coasts** [Gullah glossary], *Nutt'n'*—nothing. **1934** Carmer *Stars Fell on AL* 182 [Black], Don' drap noddin' on de big road. **1935** *AmSp* 10.165 **PA** [Engl of PA Germans], Another matter of pronunciation attributable to the German influence is the substitution of [aː] for [ʌ], noticeable especially in the words *nothing, comfortable,* and *country*. **1936** Reese *Worleys* 13 **MD** (as of 1865) [Black], All dat fightin' and bloodsheddin' fo' nuttin'. **c1937** in 1976 *Weevils in the Wheat* 223 **VA** [Black], I jus' begged him, "Hubban', please don' do nuffin." **1938** Liebling *Back Where* 34 **NY,** The river men. . . say "narthing" when they mean "nothing." **1961** Kurath–McDavid *Pronc. Engl.* 145, *Nothing*. . . In the North, the vowel of *lot, rod* competes in this word with the vowel /ʌ/ of *nut*. In folk speech, /ɑ ~ ɒ/ predominate decidedly over /ʌ/ in most of New England and Upstate New York and the greater part of New Jersey and Pennsylvania, as well as the Yankee settlements of Northern Ohio. In middle-class speech they are largely confined to northeastern New England and some rural sections of the New England settlement area. **1966** *DARE* Tape **ID2,** They'd extend credit to poor people and they never got ['nɑθɪn]. **1966** *DARE* File **Baltimore MD,** *Nothink* . . nothing. **1967–68** *DARE* FW Addit **LA3,** ['nʌtn̩]; **NY68,** ['nɑθɪn]. **1989** Pederson *LAGS Tech. Index* 363 **Gulf Region,** [802 infs offered proncs of the type ['nʌθn̩, -ŋ]; 52 infs, ['nʌtn̩]; 24 infs, ['nʌθɪn, -ɪŋ]; 22 infs, ['nɑθn̩, -ŋ]; 10 infs, ['nʌɾn̩]; 9 infs, ['nʌðn̩, -ŋ]; 5 infs, ['nʌfn̩].]

nothing off of one's hide See **hide** n[2] 5

nothings exclam Also *no nothing*

In marble play: used as a call to prevent another player from claiming any special privileges.

1922 *DN* 5.187 **MA,** *Nothings*. . . A call which gave no privileges, whereas *everythings* gave all. **1950** *WELS* (Cries or calls used in playing marbles: To stop another player from doing something) 1 Inf, **seWI,** Nothings. **1958** *PADS* 29.37 **WI,** *No nothing*. . . Same as *nothings*. . . *Nothings*. . . A call (the opposite of *anythings*) which, if said first, denied any advantages to one's opponents. **c1970** Wiersma *Marbles Terms* **swMI,** *Nothings:* a call to counteract another player's call for special privileges.

nothing, to know from See **from** B10

nothink See **nothing**

nothuh See **another**

nothun See **nothing**

notice v

1 To watch over; to look after. [Cf *SND notice* v. 1 "To watch, tend, take care of, see to, look after"] **Sth, S Midl**

1944 *TN Folk Lore Soc. Bulletin* 10.10 **nGA,** He decided to take a stroll about the station, and asked his new friend if she would watch his possessions. "I'll be glad to notice them for you," she replied. **1966–70** *DARE* (Qu. Z13, *If a mother has to leave her baby for a little while, she might ask a neighbor, "While I'm gone, will you _____ the baby for me?"*) Infs **FL2, GA6, LA8, MS90, SC40, TN52, TX32,** Notice. [4 of 7 Infs Black]

2 See quot.

1952 Brown *NC Folkl.* 1.570 **wNC,** *Notice.* . . To court. "I hear Clem is noticing again."

notify oneself v phr [Cf *OED* notify v. 2 quot 1718]
To make one's presence known (to the authorities).

1962 Faulkner *Reivers* 173 **MS,** "Who's he?" he [=a deputy] said. "As a general rule, we dont take to strange niggers around here. We dont object though, providing they notify themselves and then keep their mouths shut."

notion n

1 A liking or fancy, esp for a person of the opposite sex. [nEngl, Scots dial; cf *SND* notion n. 1]

1864 Nichols *40 Yrs.* 1.386, A plain girl is as homely as a hedge-fence, but a Yankee may have a kinder sneakin' notion arter her. **1902** *DN* 2.240 **sIL,** *Notion.* . . A liking or fancy, as 'I've tuck a powerful notion to you.' **1907** *DN* 3.224 **nwAR,** *Notion.* . . A liking or fancy. **1916** Lincoln *Mary-'Gusta* 330 **MA,** They thought as much of Farmer as they did of themselves. He was that kind—you couldn't help takin' a notion to him. **c1960** *Wilson Coll.* **csKY,** *Notion*—A fancy. . . "He tuck a notion to Sally but she wouldn't go with him."

2 in phr *to one's notion:*

a To one's liking, up to one's expectations or standards.

1909 *DN* 3.382 **eAL, wGA,** *To one's notion.* . . To suit one, according to one's desire. "He didn't do that to my notion." **1915** *DN* 4.186 **swVA,** *Notion, to (one's).* . . So as to suit or please one. "He's not doin' that to my notion."

b In one's opinion.

1903 *DN* 2.323 **seMO,** *Notion (to my).* . . In my opinion. 'To my notion the jury ought to turn him loose.' **1907** *DN* 3.233 **nwAR,** *Notion, to my.* . . In my opinion. **1968** *DARE* FW Addit **IA**31, It seems that way to my notion. **1986** Pederson *LAGS Concordance,* 1 inf, **nwLA,** Not to my notion = not in my opinion; 1 inf, **ceFL,** Them was the good days, to my notion; 1 inf, **ceTX,** The best kind to my notion = in my opinion; 1 inf, **cnAR,** To my notion.

3 in phr *in the notion:* in the mood, inclined; in favor (of something); similarly *out of (the) notion* disinclined; not in favor (of something). [Cf *OED* notion sb. 7 quot 1774]

1871 in 1983 *PADS* 70.44 **ce,sePA,** Mary and I in the notion of going to see Hettie tomorrow. *Ibid,* Men come from the woods & said we could go to Hetties. I was nearly out of the notion. **1887** (1967) Harris *Free Joe* 103 **GA,** Don't set her atter me, Abe,—don't fer mercy's sake. Get her in the notion, an' she'll be a-yerkin' me aroun' thereckly like I wuz a rag-baby. [**1906** *DN* 3.126 **nwAR,** *Be the notion.* . . To intend. "Are you still the notion to go?"] **1929** in 1952 Mathes *Tall Tales* 129 **sAppalachians,** Me an' Phrony's been talkin' it over an' we're might' nigh in the notion, but I aimed to ax you afore we done anything. [**1967** *DARE* FW Addit **LA**12, *Notion* = mood. "Just whatever notion he was in." Common.] **1969** *DARE* Tape **CA**156, That'll get 'em out of the notion of trying to buck. **1986** Pederson *LAGS Concordance (She turned him down)* 1 inf, **csLA,** Got out of notion—changed her mind after engaged.

notionable adj [Cf *EDD* notionable "Having a fancy or inclination to a thing"] Cf **notional 2**
Of people: queer, odd, strange.

1967–68 *DARE* (Qu. HH4, *Someone who has odd or peculiar ideas or notions*) Infs **DC**1, **IN**14, Notionable. **1973** Allen *LAUM* 1.356 (as of c1950), Synonyms of *queer.* . . notionable [1 inf, **cnND**].

notional adj *old-fash*

1 foll by n clause: Inclined to believe; of the opinion.

1823 Cooper *Pioneers* 1.125, I'm glad if the Judge is pleased; but I'm notional that you'll find the sa'ce overdone. **1913** (1919) *WNID, Notional.* . . [H]e's notional that he'll win.

2 Strange, having odd ideas; fanciful; opinionated; temperamental. **chiefly Nth, esp NEng** Cf **notionate**

1791 *Gaz. U.S.* (Philadelphia PA) 9 Feb 733/2, If a man is a little *odd in his way* . . his friends say he is a *notional creature.* **1819** *Niles' Weekly Reg.* 16.224, A somewhat similar occurrence [took place] among the *notional folks* of Boston. **1859** (1968) Bartlett *Americanisms* 296 **NEng,** *Notional.* Fanciful, whimsical. Applied to persons; as, "He's a very notional man." **1884** Jewett *Country Dr.* 16 **ME,** He always used to be tellin' what everything was the sign of, when we was first married, till I laughed him out of it. It made me kind of notional. There's too much now we can't make sense of without addin' it out o' our own

heads. **1894** *Outing* 24.96 **ND,** He did think he would have to get the room cleaned and whitewashed as his wife was rather notional. **1905** *DN* 3.15 **cCT,** *Notional.* . . Fanciful. **1907** *DN* 3.215 **nwAR,** *Notional.* . . Fanciful. **1941** *LANE* Map 471 *(Obstinate)* 1 inf, **cwCT,** He's a notional jigger: if he gets a notion you can't knock it out with a sledge-hammer. **1966–69** *DARE* (Qu. K16, *A cow with a bad temper*) Inf **MA**42, Notional; (Qu. HH4, *Someone who has odd or peculiar ideas or notions*) Inf **CA**87, Notional; (Qu. HH11a, *Someone who is too particular or fussy—if it's a man*) Inf **NY**195, Notional; (Qu. HH12, *A person who is always finding fault about unimportant things*) Inf **WA**13, Notional. [All Infs old] **1969** *DARE* Tape **VT**14, Model-T Ford . . they could be balkier than a mule, notional as anything that you could think of. **1975** Gould *ME Lingo* 191, *Notional*—Said of an animal given to caprice. A cow that won't eat certain things is said to be *notional* about them. A horse that won't step across a wooden bridge because he doesn't like the noise of his own hoofs is said to be *notional* about bridges. The word is sometimes applied to persons, too, but a *notional* child is more likely than a *notional* adult. An adult would be "opinionated."

notionate adj [Cf *SND* notionate (at notion n. 2) "obstinate, headstrong"] **chiefly Sth, S Midl**
=**notional 2.**

1850 Northall *Life Yankee Hill* 127, Samuel Winston . . was considered a 'notionate critter,' and one of his notions was *Cabala.* **1859** (1968) Bartlett *Americanisms* 297, *Notionate.* Fanciful, whimsical. West. **1872** (1973) Thompson *Major Jones's Courtship* 119 **GA,** She's as notionate as a child here lately. Sometimes she cries, and ses I don't love her like she does me, and sich nonsense; and then agin she's as bright and happy as a lark. *Ibid* 161, It's monstrous strange to me how wimin can have so much imagination and be so dredful scary and notionate. **1880** *Scribner's Mth.* 20.21, She's mighty still, an' sits an grieves a heap, but she aint ever notinate. **1903** *DN* 2.323 **seMO,** *Notionate.* . . Notional. 'She's mighty notionate when she's sick.' **1906** *DN* 3.123 **sIN,** *Notionate.* . . Notional, peevish. "He's notionate when he's ailin'." **1907** *DN* 3.233 **nwAR,** *Notionate.* . . Notional. **1909** *DN* 3.353 **eAL, wGA,** *Notionate.* . . Notional, changeable, given to hobbies. Universal. **1909** *DN* 3.401 **nwAR,** *Notionate.* . . Notional, peevish. "She is so notionate [sic] I can't do anything with her." **1915** *DN* 4.186 **swVA,** *Notionate* . . = notional, given to hobbies, impulses, or whims. "He's such a notionate man." **1945** FWP *Lay My Burden Down* 40 **Sth** [Black], A old man named Josh, he pretty old and notionate.

no-top buggy n Also *no-top*
An open buggy.

1827 *Harvard Reg.* Oct 247, He who desires to be a *big-/ Bug,* rattling in a natty gig,/ *No-top,* or chaise. **1894** Chopin *Bayou Folk* 14 **LA,** [At] Natchitoches . . they found Pierre's no-top buggy awaiting them. **1966–69** *DARE* (Qu. N41a, . . *Horse-drawn vehicles . . to carry people*) Inf **KY**49, No-top buggy; **SC**3, No-top buggy—with no cover.

not to do a thing with See **do a thing to, not to**

not to have much for See **much** n 3

notty(head) See **knothead 4**

not worth hell room See **hell room**

nouggie See **noogie**

nough See **enough**

noughts-and-crosses n Also *naughts-and-crosses, noughts-and-x's*
Tick-tack-toe.

1899 Champlin–Bostwick *Young Folks' Games* 727, Tit-tat-to, or Noughts and Crosses. **1909** (1923) Bancroft *Games* 229, *Naughts and Crosses*—2 players. Indoors; out of doors. A diagram is drawn on a slate, paper, or the ground. . . One player chooses to write "naughts" (o) and the other "crosses" (x). . . [T]he object being to get three naughts or three crosses in a row. **1953** Brewster *Amer. Nonsinging Games* 128 **IN,** Noughts and X's. **1968–70** *DARE* (Qu. EE38a, *A game played with pencil and paper where the players try to get three X's or three O's in a row*) Infs **IL**78, 83, **MA**100, **WV**14, Noughts-and-crosses; (Qu. EE39, . . *Games played on paper by two people*) Inf **OH**90, Noughts-and-crosses; **OH**71, Noughts-and-crosses—that's like tick-tack-toe.

noung See **nyoung**

nourish v [*OED* nourish v. 5.a *"Obs."*]
To suck.

1938 Stuart *Dark Hills* 353 **eKY,** He even said I wasn't worthy of your milk I nourished as a baby.

noway adv **chiefly Sth, S Midl** Cf **nohow 2**
Anyhow; in any case.
    1946 Caldwell *House in the Uplands* 51 **Sth** [Black], Me and my wife ain't got much longer to live, noway. **1946** *Encore* July 6 (*W3* File), You ain't goin' to git in noway, so you've got all the time there is to tell me what you would do if you could get in. **1961** in 1995 *Montgomery Coll.* **wNC, eTN,** You know a muley bed has post-es, but them post-es ain't very high, not at the foot noway, bein' not much above a man's waist. **1969** *DARE* FW Addit **eNC,** *Noway*—used for *anyway* in negatives. **1986** Pederson *LAGS Concordance* **Gulf Region,** [Numerous exx of *noway* occur, but in the absence of full context and indication of tone of voice it is often impossible to determine which mean 'anyway' and which mean 'in no way' or 'at all.' Many resps occur in the frame "I didn't like it _____" or, more specifically, "Someone apologizes for breaking your rake, and you say, 'That's all right. I didn't like it _____.' " Other typical exx in the *Concordance* are "I don't talk real loud noway," "I don't wash in hot water noway," "My family never did care much about sweetening noway," and "I wasn't drinking coffee noway."] **1988** Naylor *Mama Day* 254 **GA, SC coast** [Black], Wouldn't be no telephones no way till long after the bridge was up.

noways adv [Cf *-s* adv-forming suff]
1 In no way, by no means; in any case, anyhow. Cf **anyways 1, 2, nohow 1, 2**
    1867 Lowell *Biglow* 22 'Upcountry' **MA,** Other nations all, ef sot 'longside o' us, . . ain't noways wuth a cuss. **1871** [see **leastways**]. **1899** (1912) Green *VA Folk-Speech* 301, *Noways.* . . In no way, respect, or degree; not at all. **1919** Mencken *Amer. Lang.* 229, It goes without saying that the common American tendency to add *-s* to such adverbs as *towards* is carried to full length in the vulgar language. One constantly hears, not only *somewheres* and *forwards,* but even *noways* and *anyways.* **1931** Randolph *Ozarks* 68, He aint got nary smidgin' o' mother-wit, an' he aint nothin' on'y a tie-whackin' sheer-crapper noways. **1953** Brewer *Word Brazos* 12 **eTX** [Black], He hab a haa'd time gittin' to preach, 'caze de boss-mens don' relish no preachin' in de cotton pickin' season noways. **1986** Pederson *LAGS Concordance,* 4 infs **ceAR, ce,seMS, ceTX,** Noways; 1 inf, **cnTN,** Noways—heard; 1 inf, **nwFL,** Local people say noways; 1 inf, **cAR,** It wouldn't have stayed noways; 1 inf, **swGA,** Didn't like it noways; 1 inf, **seLA,** I couldn't find it noways; 1 inf, **ceAR,** I didn't care for it noways; [1 inf, **swGA,** That don't mean noways like;] 1 inf, **cAL,** They ain't going do [*sic*] nothing about it noways.
2 =**nowheres.**
    1942 [see **keep v B1a**].

nowdays adv Also *nowday* [Varr of *nowadays*]
    1864 (1868) Trowbridge *3 Scouts* 19 **TN,** "*I* don't have the ordering of anything, now-days." **1928** Aldrich *Lantern* 259 **NE,** Girls now-days . . do things immediately. . . right off the bat. **1941** Smith *Going to God's Country* 104 **MO** (as of 1895), They had some toys . . but not like the children have now days. **1965–70** *DARE* (Qu. A26, *Talking about the past: "People used to walk a lot, but everybody drives a car _____."*) 122 Infs, **widespread,** Nowdays; 1 inf, **VA53,** Nowday. **1966** *Pike Co. Courier* (Murfreesboro AR) 19 Aug 3/4, You didn't hear any fussing among the children, as so many do in large families now days. **1967–69** *DARE* Tape CA137, It's funny now, nowdays everybody has to work for a living and work steady. Them days they didn't make any money at all; TX8, It's not only plowin' nowdays, it's preparin' the land by levelin' it, plowin' it. **1976** *Sublette Co. Artist Guild More Tales* 115 **WY** (as of c1900), What he did to the seat of my pants a teacher would go to jail for now days.

nowheres adv Also sp *no'rs, nowers, nowhars* [*-s* adv-forming suff] Cf **anywheres, somewheres**
Nowhere—often used with redund negative.
    1847 Hurd *Grammatical Corrector* 54, [Common Errors of Speech:] *Nowheres,* for *nowhere;* as, "It is nowheres to be found." **1848** Lowell *Biglow* 145 'Upcountry' **MA,** Nowers, *nowhere.* **1885** Twain *Huck. Finn* 349 **MO,** "*I* hain't been nowheres," I says, "only just hunting for the runaway nigger." **1891** *DN* 1.169 **cNY,** In unstressed syllables *hw* is sometimes reduced to *w,* sometimes lost, as is *h.* Examples are: [noərz] < *nowheres.* **1909** *DN* 3.353 **eAL, wGA,** Nowheres. . . Nowhere. **1936** *AmSp* 11.352 **eTX,** An *-s* ending is added regularly to *somewhere, anywhere, nowhere:* 'I ain't goin' nowheres.' These forms are used chiefly by those who lack formal training. **1936** Reese *Worleys* 8 **MD** (as of 1865) [Black], Dey ain nowheres 'bout heah, honey. **1937** Sandoz *Slogum* 346 **NE,** Hell, but they'd never get away. With no money to

plunk down in advance on a new lease nowheres else. **1953** Brewer *Word Brazos* 51 **eTX** [Black], Nex' minnit he's in de air. He don' stay nowhars. **1955** Roberts *S. from Hell-fer-Sartin* 127 **seKY,** Mike he was purty smart and he worked and he could get a job anywheres. But old Pat he couldn't do any good, he wouldn't work and couldn't hold a job nowheres. **1969** *DARE* FW Addit **eNC,** Nowheres. **1970** *DARE* (Qu. LL32, *Expressions meaning that one man's ability is not nearly as great as another man's*) Inf **PA**240, Nowheres nears. **1986** Pederson *LAGS Concordance,* 1 inf, **cTX,** Nowheres; 1 inf, **neTN,** Nowheres = nowhere; 1 inf, **csLA,** You can't put a hog nowheres; 1 inf, **swLA,** We couldn't find it nowheres; 1 inf, **seAR,** We didn't have a swimming pool nowheres close; 1 inf, **neMS,** She didn't have to move nowheres else; 1 inf, **neAL,** Couldn't get nowheres; 1 inf, **cMS,** Not nowheres; 1 inf, **cAR,** Not going nowheres; 1 inf, **ceAR,** Don't never go nowheres; 1 inf, **csLA,** You couldn't buy no wine nowheres; 1 inf, **cTX,** Didn't see no car nowheres; 1 inf, **nwFL,** Nowheres else; [1 inf, **neTX,** They didn't have nowheres to go;] 1 inf, **cLA,** I ain't ever been nowheres. **1994** NC Lang. & Life Project *Dial. Dict. Lumbee Engl.* 8 **seNC,** Harley couldn't find the hog no'rs.

Nowie See **Noah**

noxvomik(y), nox vomit See **nux vomica**

nub n
In marble play: a shooter.
    1967–70 *DARE* (Qu. EE6a, . . *Different kinds of marbles—the big one that's used to knock others out of the ring*) Infs **MO**7, **PA**242, Nub.

nub v
1 also *nubbin:* To remove the small kernels from an ear of corn.
    1912 Green *VA Folk-Speech* 302, *Nubbin.* . . To *nubbin* corn is to shell off the small grains from the two ends of the ear so as to have good corn for bread, or seed-corn. **1986** Pederson *LAGS Concordance,* 1 inf, **cAL,** Nub the end off—remove small kernels; 1 inf, **ceMS,** Nubbed it—removed end part of corn for stock.
2 ppl adj; Of the horn of a cow: reduced to a stub.
    1966 *DARE* (Qu. K13, *A cow that has had her horns cut off*) Inf **SC**12, Nubbed.

nubbie n [*EDD nobby* sb.² "*Dev. Cor.* . . A small cake or bun"]
A saffron bun.
    1939 (1973) FWP *Guide MT* 138, Cornish (Cousin Jack) miners of earlier days contributed the pasty, or meat pie, to Butte cuisine. . . Saffron buns or "nubbies" are another Cornish food.

nubbin n
1 in combs *nubbin strangler, ~ stretcher:* A heavy rain that comes when corn is immature, causing the nubbins to develop fully; also *nubbin killer* thunder that signifies such a rain. **esp eKY**
    1915 *DN* 4.186 **swVA,** *Nubbin killer.* . . Thunder:—because the rain develops the nubbin into a full grown ear of corn. *Facetious.* **1966** Dakin *Dial. Vocab. Ohio R. Valley* 2.21, [Terms for severe rainstorms:] *Nubbin stretcher, nubbin strangler* (three times, Kentucky Mountains). **1969** *DARE* (Qu. B25, . . *Joking names . . for a very heavy rain.* . . "*It's a regular _____.*") Inf **KY**26, Nubbin stretcher—makes corn grow. [**1982** Slone *How We Talked* 9 **eKY** (as of c1950), "Nubbin"—an ear of corn that is very small, but that did mature. Usually fed to the cows or calves with the shuck or husk attached [*sic*]. Phrase: "This good weather is going to spile (spoil) my nubbin crop, it's making big ears out of them."] **1984** Wilder *You All Spoken Here* 141 **Sth,** *Nubbin stretcher.* . . A pour down. **1991** Still *Wolfpen Notebooks* 92 **eKY,** Pretty good rain last night on the corn. What you would call a 'nubbin-stretcher.'
2 also *nummin:* An antler bud; hence nouns *nummin, nubbin buck* a buck fawn.
    1978 *NADS Letters* **cwWI,** I heard a new term the other day for a buck fawn or "button buck." It is *nubbin,* . . from a man about 40 years old who grew up near Knapp, in Dunn County, Wisconsin. **1979** *DARE* File **nMI,** I heard another term meaning "buck fawn" the other day. It is nummin or nummin buck, and I heard it from Dan Reynolds . . [who] learned the word in the Upper Peninsula of Michigan, where he hunts deer. He also referred to the antler buds themselves as nummins. **1992** *Ibid* **ceNY** (as of 1960s), Nubbin buck was the common term for a first year buck. About all they get for antlers are bumps on their heads. *Ibid* **WI,** A nubbin buck is a first year buck, then comes a spike buck, then

a forkhorn, in ascending order by age. **1995** *WI State Jrl.* (Madison) 27 Nov sec B 1/2 **swWI,** She and her husband had shot a doe and a nubbin buck.

nubbin v See **nub** v **1**

nubbin buck See **nubbin** n **2**

nubbin killer (or strangler, stretcher) See **nubbin** n **1**

nubbiny See **nubby** adj[1]

nubble n esp coastal ME
A small hill or mountain; an islet—also used in place names.
   1890 *Century Dict.* 4034, The name *nubble* is applied to a rocky promontory on the coast of Maine, at York. **1946** Attwood *Length ME* 15 [Geographical terms], *Nubble*—A rounded hill or small mountain, often a foothill of a mountain. **1950** Moore *Candlemas Bay* 256 **ME,** Eleven lost here. Four on Little Nubble Shoals. Two on Grindstone. Twenty traps left out of thirty-seven. **1977** *Yankee* June 159 **seMA,** Once past the "nubble" guarded by swift tidal currents, the [Westport] river broadens into a wide channel. **1978** *Ibid* June 1 **seME,** [Cover painting of the "Nubble Lighthouse," also known as the "Nubble Light," off Cape Neddick.]

nubbuh See **never**

nubby adj[1] Also *nubbiny* Cf **nubbin** n **1**
Of corn: having or consisting of small or immature ears.
   1942 Warnick *Garrett Co. MD* 11 **nwMD** (as of 1900–18), *Nubby* . . descriptive of inferior corn; "all the corn that was left was little nubby stuff." **c1960** *Wilson Coll.* **csKY,** *Nubbiny corn.* . . Having small or immature ears.

nubby adj[2] [Perh var of *nobby* smart, elegant]
   1946 *AmSp* 21.235 **csOH,** *Nubby* . . 'clever.' People here apply it to a situation as well as a person, and invariably to a situation or a person that is humorous as well as clever. For example, of an anecdote that contained a clever, humorous twist, my friends would say that it was nubby.

nubia n [*OED* 1881 →; < Span *nube* shawl, literally "cloud"] Also *newby, nibby, nooby, nube, nubi, nuby* Cf **fascinator, zephyr**
A scarf.
   1856 *Harper's New Mth. Mag.* 13.448, The lake was entirely hidden by a thick coverlet of white mist, which lay upon its surface almost as palpable as if it had been . . an extensive worsted nube. **1864** *Hist. North-Western Soldiers' Fair* 126 *(DAE),* 1 elegant worsted nubia. **1904** Glasgow *Deliverance* 29, "The same evening that I got this pink crochetted [sic] nuby." She touched a small pointed shawl about her shoulders. **1914** *DN* 4.161 **KS,** *Nubi.* . . Some article of wearing apparel, perhaps a fascinator. **1927** *DN* 5.476 **Ozarks,** *Newby, nooby.* . . A long knit scarf or muffler, usually wrapped twice around the neck. **1930** *Atlantic Mth.* May 681 **ME,** She always wore a white nubia an' a real lace kerchief. **1966–68** *DARE* (Qu. W3, *A piece of cloth that a woman folds over her head and ties under her chin*) Infs **NJ4, 24, NM12, PA90, 96, TX1,** Nuby; **PA26,** Nibby. **1968** *DARE* FW Addit **PA169,** *Nooby*—head scarf. **1977** *Greenfield Recorder* (MA) 5 Mar 8 **MA,** The 1870's or 80's, women had long, rather narrow, soft scarves. They were machine made and wound around the neck, with an end thrown over the shoulder. They were called "nubias."

nubtail n Cf **dock** n[2] **2, nick-tailed**
A bobtailed horse.
   1970 *DARE* (Qu. K41, *A horse with its tail cut short*) Inf **VA70,** Nubtail.

nuby See **nubia**

nucks See **knuck** n[1] **2a**

nuder See **another**

nudges n Also *nudging, nuggin* Cf **fudge** v, n, **hunch** v **2a**
In marble play: the act of moving the hand or marble forward when shooting; hence n *nudgie* a marble so played.
   1896 *DN* 1.412 **cwNY,** *Ben nuggins* [ˈnʌjɪnz]: A term in marbles. **1963** *KY Folkl. Rec.* 9.3.65, *Trying to get closer shot by placing the hand in a position nearer to the marble being shot at:* . . nudges. **c1970** *Wiersma Marbles Terms* **swMI** (as of c1953), *Nudging* (from to *nudge*, push): a. to carry the marble forward instead of snap-shooting it. Mostly illegal. b. fudging. c. travelling. Noun. Ex: a. "If you don't quit your nudging,

you're going to quit, period." *Ibid, Nudgie* . . a marble played with illegal wrist action.

nudget n [Var of *nugget*]
   1969 *DARE* (Qu. C25, . . *Kinds of stone*) Inf **KY68,** Nudget [ˈnʌjɪt]—some say. **1979** *AmSp* 54.99 **sME** (as of 1899–1910), *Nudget.* . . Nugget [common usage].

nudgie, nudging See **nudges**

nuf(f) See **enough**

nuffin See **nothing**

nuff-nuff n Cf **gnir, niff-naff**
   1973 *San Francisco Sun. Examiner & Chron.* (CA) 2 Dec Sunday Punch sec 1/1, The stuff that collects in the pockets of old suits and overcoats . . [is also called] "nuff-nuff."

nug See **knuck** n[1] **2b**

nugget n [Perh by metanalysis of *an agate*] Cf **agate 1**
   1968 *DARE* (Qu. EE6a, . . *Different kinds of marbles—the big one that's used to knock others out of the ring*) Inf **IN13,** Nugget [ˈnʌgɪt].

nuggin See **nudges**

nuh See **nor**

nuh(r) adv See **no**

nui adj [Haw] **HI**
See quot 1938.
   1938 Reinecke *Hawaiian Loanwords* 26, *Nui.* . . Big; great. . . Many. (This word is not much used except in phrases with other Hawaiian words.) . . *Okole.* . . Arse. . . (The phrase *okole nui* is sometimes heard in English speech.) . . *Opu nui.* . . Big paunch. . . Also, pregnant. *Ibid* 23, *Mahalo.* . . Thanks. . . *Mahalo nui.* . . Many thanks; thanks very much indeed. **1984** Sunset *HI Guide* 85, *Nui*—big, large, great.

null n, v[1] Also sp *knull* [Varr of *knur(l)* a protuberance; cf *OED null* sb.[3]] esp **GA**
See quots.
   1909 *DN* 3.353 **eAL, wGA,** *Null.* . . The iron point or spinner of a top. Universal among boys. *Null.* . . To strike the spinner of a top into another top. Also used absolutely as the name of a game. "Le's play null." **1957** *Sat. Eve. Post Letters* **GA** (as of c1905), Tops: the object was to hit a spinning top of the opposing player with your own top. You never "hit" his top; you "knulled" or "nulled" it. **1986** Pederson *LAGS Concordance,* 1 inf, **cnGA,** Null the tops—hit one spinning top with another.

null v[2], hence vbl n *nulling* Also *null down* [Cf *EDD nool* v. 2 "To benumb, to allay or assuage pain."]
To abate; to alleviate pain.
   1984 *Annals Internal Med.* 100.6.899 **cwAL,** The pain nulled down, or *Give me some nulling medicine.*

nullify v Also *nellify* [By ext from *nullify* to suspend a federal law, prob alluding esp to the South Carolina Ordinance of Nullification (enacted 1832, rescinded 1833)] esp **eNC**
Of a horse: to balk.
   1918 *DN* 5.19 **NC,** *Nellify,* variant of *nullify.* *Ibid, Nullify,* to balk. "Does this horse nullify?" **1946** *PADS* 6.21 **ceNC** (as of 1900–10), *Nellify.* . . To rise on the hind legs and then come back on all fours repeatedly, meanwhile refusing to move forward. Said of a horse. . . Occasional. **1952** Brown *NC Folkl.* 1.569 **eNC,** *Nellify.* . . Variant of *nullify;* to balk. *Ibid* 570, *Nullify.* . . Variant of *nellify;* to balk.

nulling See **null** v[2]

num- See **never**

numb adj Also *numby* [*EDD num(b* adj. 1 "Clumsy; stupid; dull, heavy, insensible"; *numb-head* (at *numb* adj. 2(5)); *numby* sb. "A dolt."] chiefly **NEng**
Dull, stupid; clumsy; hence nouns *numbhead* (rarely *numb, numby* [also sp *nummy*]) a dull or stupid person, fool; adj *numbheaded* stupid.
   1856 Whitcher *Bedott Papers* 98, The old coot was so awful numbheaded I couldent beat anythin' into him. **1941** *LANE* Map 465 *(Fool)* [Numbhead is widely scattered across **NEng.**]; 1 inf, **seNH,** Numbhead, numskull . . older terms; 1 inf, **seNH,** Numb creature. **1966–70** *DARE* (Qu. HH3, *A dull and stupid person*) Inf **NH14,**

Numbhead, numb nut; **NY**249, Ignorant, stupid, numby; (Qu. HH13, *Expressions meaning that a person is not very alert or not aware of things: "He's certainly _____."*) Inf **MA**71, Numb; (Qu. HH21, *A very awkward, clumsy person*) Inf **ME**19, Numb, like a bull in a crockery shop; (Qu. HH24, *Somebody who doesn't talk very much*) Inf **ME**6, Numb, close; (Qu. KK30, *Feeling slowed up or without energy*) Inf **ME**19, Logy, numb. **1971** Roberts *Third Ear* np [Black], *Numb . . dumb; stupid.* **1975** Gould *ME Lingo* 192, *Numb*—A mild version of dumb, in the sense of somewhat stupid. A *numb*-head doesn't know enough to come in out of the rain. Physical numbness, transferred to intelligence, is suggested by "as numb as a pounded thumb." A Mainer might call somebody dumb behind his back, but to his face he'd use *numb*: "You seem a little numb about learnin' how to do that!" **1979** Lewis *How to Talk Yankee* [24] **nNEng**, *Number'n a hake. . .* Stupid. Why the poor hake—which is delicious corned and served with potatoes and salt pork scraps—is so singled out is unknown to this writer. A *lumper's helper* would certainly be *number'n a hake.* **1982** *DARE* File **coastal ME**, Number than a hake: really dumb. **1986** Pederson *LAGS Concordance (That fool!)* 1 inf, **swMS**, A numb doesn't have good sense. **1995** *DARE* File **cME** (as of 1980), "I saw you out in the truck today and I waved, but you didn't wave back." "Oh, I'm number than a pounded thumb when I'm driving."

numberbelly, numberell See **umbrella**

number plate n **NEng**
An automobile license plate or license tag.
1933 *AmSp* 8.3.78, *Jitney . .* hasn't gone out in Rhode Island, but appears, spelled out, on the number plates of busses. **1967** *DARE* File **csMA** (as of c1947), *Number plate*—for license plate or license tag. **1972** *Ibid* **MA, NH, RI**, Number plate—auto license plate. **1981** [see **marker 2**]. **1994** *DARE* File **nwMA**, My parents now have the number plate that my grandfather had. It is a very low number that his father had on the first car he ever owned, one of the first cars in his town.

numbers n
1 See quot.
1966–69 *DARE* (Qu. EE39, *. . Games played on paper by two people*) Inf **MA**24, Numbers [FW: Inf not sure of details]; **NH**5, Numbers—two players take turns writing numbers on paper. The other player tries to guess number. Player number one marks down each incorrect guess. First to get all of a certain series of numbers (one to ten, one to fifteen, etc) wins; [**CA**8, Number games; **PA**28, Number game—numbers up to ten; secretly make a number and others guess].
2 See quot.
1968 *DARE* (Qu. EE33, *. . Outdoor games . . that children play*) Inf **PA**167, "Sheepie," also "babies" and "numbers." Throw ball at wall, call number. He has to catch it. First one to miss 3 times puts fanny [=buttocks] out. Others throw ball at wall.
3 in phr *you play the numbers:* Used to warn a woman that her slip is showing.
1968 *DARE* (Qu. W24a, *. . Expressions . . to warn a woman slyly that her slip is showing*) Inf **NJ**39, You play the numbers; I see your slip.

number two (walker) n Cf **ankle express, footmobile**
Transportation by foot.
1969 *DARE* (Qu. Y24, *. . To walk, to go on foot: "I can't get a ride, so I'll just have to _____."*) Inf **KY**19, Go on number two—go on your two legs. **1976** *Harper's Weekly* 26 Jan 18 **swTN** [Black], We call a car a "ride." What you catch to go somewhere when you don't have carfare is a "No. 2 Walker"—in other words, feet.

numbhead(ed) See **numb**

numble peg See **mumblety-peg 2**

numbrell' See **umbrella**

numbskull n
=**popskull.**
1968–69 *DARE* (Qu. DD21b, *General words . . for bad liquor*) Infs **AL**56, **NC**49, Numbskull.

numby See **numb**

nummin See **nubbin** n **2**

nummine See **never**

nummy See **numb**

numpy n [Cf *EDD* numps "A dolt, a fool"] Cf **numb**
1941 *LANE* Map 465 *(Fool)* 1 inf, **seNH**, Numbhead, numskull, numpy, older terms.

nun n
1 A female **scaup.**
1951 Pough *Audubon Water Bird* 338, Nun. *See* Scaup ducks (female).
2 pl: A **bluet 2** (here: *Houstonia caerulea*).
1892 *Jrl. Amer. Folkl.* 5.97, *Houstonia cærulea,* blue-eyed babies . . Nuns. **1959** Carleton *Index Herb. Plants* 87, *Nuns:* Houstonia caerulea.

nuncle n Also hypocoristic *nunk(s), nunky* [Varr of *uncle; OED* c1589 →; the resps of the Louisiana *DARE* Infs may instead be from LaFr *noncle.*]
1839 *Spirit of Times* 23 Mar 27, Just such is the condition of Uncle Sam. We doubt whether Nunky, though, escapes with his scalp. **1883** (1971) Harris *Nights with Remus* 188 **GA** [Black], You' gran'daddy foller at' me nuncle wit' 'e dog. *Ibid* 314 **GA** [Black], I bin-a tell you' nunk Jeem' how fine noung màn you is. **1942** Berrey–Van den Bark *Amer. Slang* 446.2, Nunks . . uncle. **1966–68** *DARE* (Qu. Z7, *Nicknames and affectionate words for any other relatives*) Inf **LA**20, Nunk—for an uncle; **LA**31, Uncle or nunk—in French; **LA**35, Uncle—country people say [nɔ̃k] So-and-so; **SC**46, Nunk—for uncle; **IL**50, **SC**2, Nunky. [**1983** *Reinecke Coll.* 12 **LA**, *Nonc'* [nɔ̃k] . . form of address to an uncle or courtesy uncle. So in Cajun and N[ew] O[rleans] French. . . Pretty common in Cajun country.]

nunder See **in under**

nunited See **newnited**

nunk(s), nunky See **nuncle**

nuns See **nun 2**

nur See **neither**

nurky n Also sp *nurkey* Cf **lurky**
=**kick the can 1**—also used as a call in the game; hence v *nurky* see quot 1957.
1957 *Sat. Eve. Post Letters* **KS**, *Nurky. . .* A tin can is set up in the center of the ring. Prisoners are in the prison, someone kicks can out of circle and prisoners escape and hide. "It" hunts them and sends them into prison. If someone can sneak in from hiding and kick the can out of the ring, every prisoner again escapes while "it" returns to the prison, replaces can in circle, places foot on can, counts to ten and then "nurkys" any prisoner he can see; i.e. "Nurky John." *Ibid* **MT** (as of c1904), "Nurkey"—for kick-the-can. **1965–68** *DARE* (Qu. EE12, *Games in which one captain hides his team and the other team tries to find it*) Inf **KS**20, Nurky [nɝki]; (Qu. EE18, *Games in which the players set up a stone, a tin can, or something similar, and then try to knock it down*) Inf **FL**22, Nurky—hit can with a broomstick and holler "nurky!"; **KS**20, Nurky—one person is "it" and he sets up a can while the rest hide, and then he starts out to look for the other players. In the meantime, a player tries to come in and kick the can so "it" will have to come back and set the can up again. **1967** *DARE* FW Addit **CO**31, Nurky—kick the can. [**1969** Opie–Opie *Children's Games* 166 **Engl**, 'Kick the Can'. . . 'Tin Can Nurky' (Barrow-in-Furness and Wolverhampton). *Ibid* 167, 'Nurky' (Windermere, c. 1900).]

nurly See **knurl**

nurse n Pronc-sp *nuss*
1 A woman who lives in a household and has primary care of the children, orig esp a Black woman on a plantation. *old-fash* Cf **nurse** v
1835 Ingraham *South-West* 2.92 **swMS**, Southerners . . have been familiar with Africans from childhood; whom they have had for their nurses, play-fellows, and "bearers." **1853** Simms *Sword & Distaff* 349 **SC**, It's you own ole Sappho, my chile! You no know you own nuss; you own good ole woman, old Sappho, my son! **1890** *Century Illustr. Mag.* 41.46, It was Tante Jantje, the old darky nurse, who had educated him to a gruesome terror of that ancient Church of St. Bartholomew and the graveyard beside it. **1907** *St. Nicholas* Aug 879, Promptly at three the little guests began to arrive, some of them in charge of nurses. **1984** Joyner *Down by Riverside* 77 **SC coast** (as of a1866), The term nurse was used to designate two plantation occupations—those who cared for the sick and those who cared for the children. *Ibid* 78, The job of children's nurse was typically assigned to slave women who were either too old or too young to work in the fields.

2 also *nursement:* Breast milk. Cf **-ment B**

1927 *DN* 5.476 **Ozarks**, *Nursement*. . . Milk. When a young mother says "th' nursement is a-comin' on fine now" she means simply that her milk is flowing freely. The word *nurse* is sometimes used in the same sense: "Th' baby done spit up his nurse again, Doc." **1965** Hyatt *Folkl. Adams Co. IL* 155 (as of c1905), Years ago . . I thought my baby was dying with a spasm. She was turning black. . . I had plenty of nurse, and I was so scared I lost every bit of it; didn't have a drop to give the baby when she came out of the spasm. Then my neighbor told me about wetting the middle finger and making the cross over my forehead to bring back my nurse. I did just what she told me and it came right back.

nurse v, hence vbl n *nursing* Also *baby-nurse* Pronc-sp *nuss* [**nurse** n 1; cf *OED nurse* v. 6.b] **chiefly Sth, S Midl**
To hold and comfort, rock in one's arms (a small child); by ext, to take care of (a child or, rarely, an animal).

1900 in 1995 Millersville Univ. Center for PA Ger. Studies *Jrl.* Winter 15 **sePA**, In the afternoon I nursed Minnie's baby while she cleaned her garret. **1902** *DN* 2.240 **sIL**, *Nurse*. . . To fondle or coddle. **1905** *DN* 3.89 **nwAR**, *Nurse a baby*. . . To take care of a baby. 'Mr. Brown will nurse your baby.' Universal. **1923** *DN* 5.215 **swMO**, *Nuss*. . . To . . take care of or amuse a child. "He nussed the young-un to sleep." **1923** (1946) Greer-Petrie *Angeline Doin' Society* 19 **csKY**, [She] nusses one of them little, bitty flat nosed dogs. *Ibid* 20, Why on 'arth don't she 'dopt a little orphint and nuss hit? **1929** Ellis *Ordinary Woman* 217 **CO** (as of c1900), Mr. Mahoney 'nusses' Joy, pillowing her little sore head in his shoulder and his white beard. **1939** *Hall Coll.* **ceTN**, *Nussed*. . . fondled (a child), holding the child on one's lap. "I nussed your child." **1945** FWP *Lay My Burden Down* 147 **AR** (as of c1860) [Black], All the grown folks went to the field to work, and the little children would be left at a big room called the nursing-home. All us little ones would be nursed and fed by an old mammy, Aunt Mandy. **1950** WELS *Suppl.* **Sth**, *Nuss*. . . To hold and love a child. [Inf's grandmother "Southern born and raised"] **1954** *Harder Coll.* **cwTN**, *Nuss*. . . hold a child on the lap. Dontchie nuss 'at young'um [sic] too much. **1966–68** *DARE* (Qu. Z13, *If a mother has to leave her baby for a little while, she might ask a neighbor, "While I'm gone, will you _____ the baby for me?"*) Infs **FL2, 8, GA67, LA11, MO36, SC40**, Nurse; **LA12**, Baby-nurse. **1972** *Atlanta Letters* **cnGA**, Southern Colloquialisms. . . Have you ever seen a man "Nuss" the baby, meaning to hold it on his lap? **1986** Pederson *LAGS Concordance*, 1 inf, **seAL**, Nursing—speaking of his tending local children.

nursement See **nurse** n **2**

nursing See **nurse** v

nurvious See **nervous** adj

nuse n, v Also sp *nyuse, nyuze* [Varr of *use;* see quot 1949] *among Black speakers* Cf **nusen, nyoung**

1888 Jones *Negro Myths* 29 **GA coast** [Gullah], Buh Rabbit run Buh Wolf down dat eh nebber bin nuse no sich wud. **1909** *S. Atl. Qrly.* 8.51 **sSC, GA coasts** [Gullah], An odd euphonic use of extraneous . . *n,* in . . *nuse* for *use.* **1922** Gonzales *Black Border* 244 **sSC, GA coasts** [Gullah], Him en' me alltwo nyuse to smoke de same pipe befo' him dead. *Ibid* 315 [Gullah glossary], *Nyuse* . . n. and v. *Ibid* 316, *Nyuze* . . used. **1927** Adams *Congaree* 9 **cSC** [Black], He say it one time he ain' grudge nusin' a little extra fire. **1929** Sale *Tree Named John* 106 **MS**, Ax 'im ef de elefunts is still skeered uv mices lak dey nuseter [=used to] be. *Ibid* 110, Big Man, fetch me dem shoes 'fo' you w'ars 'em plum out; den d'won't be no nuse t'shine 'em. **1930** Woofter *Black Yeomanry* 50 **seSC** [Gullah], *Nused* for *used.* **c1938** in 1970 Hyatt *Hoodoo* 1.428 **cAR**, It's good take hives offa babies, or eithah nuse [Hyatt: use] for jis' any kinda bumps. *Ibid* 587 **seGA**, She would not let anybody nuse it but her, an' see she'd nuse it. **1949** Turner *Africanisms* 243 **seSC** [Gullah], The palatal nasal [ɲ] (not to be confused with *n* + *y*) is very common in Gullah. It is heard in many words in which *y* and *n* would be used in cultivated English: e.g., [ɲuz] 'use,' [ɲɒɲ] 'young,' [nu'nɒɪtɪd] 'united.' *Ibid* 274, [de ɲus tu bi kʌmɪn ɪn dɪ rum ɪn yo slɪp. . . dɪ hɑg ɲus tə reɪd əm]. [=They used to be coming in the room in your sleep. . . The hag used to ride him.]

nusen v past [Var of *usen;* cf **nuse**] *among Black speakers*
Used, were accustomed.

c1885 in 1981 Woodward *Mary Chesnut's Civil War* 374 **SC** (as of 1862) [Black], All the people has fine fat hogs, but you see our people n'usen to salt as much as they choose—and now they will grumble.

1888 Jones *Negro Myths* 92 **GA coast** [Gullah], Weneber dem meet, dem nusen fuh pass de time er day.

nuseter See **nuse**

nushnik n Also *nooshni(c)k* [Russ *nuzhnik*] **AK**
A privy.

1945 *AK Sportsman* Feb 32 (Tabbert *Dict. Alaskan Engl.*), Tardily, we picked up some of the more obvious trash littering our spacious yard, and laid a graceful, curving path of shells to our "nooshnick." By way of explanation, "nooshnick" is the Russian name for the outhouses made necessary by the lack of a modern sewer system. **1965** Bowen *Alaskan Dict.* 23, *Nooshnik.* An outdoor privy. A common term in the old Russian sections of Alaska such as the Kenai Peninsula. **1983** *Cama-i Book* 43 **swAK**, And just a little further is the banya [steam bath] and the nushnik [outhouse]. **1991** Tabbert *Dict. Alaskan Engl.* 109, *Nushnik . . nooshnik.* This term meaning 'outhouse' is from Russian *nuzhnik* 'outhouse, latrine, toilet'. . . The word was borrowed by several Alaska Native languages . . and is used in English contexts in the Aleutian, Alaska Peninsula, Kodiak, and Kenai Peninsula areas.

nuss n See **nurse** n

nuss v See **nurse** v

nut v, hence ppl adj *nutted,* vbl n *nutting* [*nut* testicle] **scattered, but chiefly Nth, N Midl** See Map Cf **mark** v[1] **2, nut horse**
=**de-nut;** hence n *nutter* one who castrates animals.

1950 *WELS* (A castrated pig) 1 Inf, **csWI**, Nutted pig. **1965–70** DARE (Qu. K70, *Words used . . for castrating an animal*) 45 Infs, **chiefly Nth, N Midl**, Nut; (Qu. K25, *What is a 'steer'?*) Inf **MI120**, Nutted bull; (Qu. K58, *A castrated pig*) Inf **IA19**, Nutted pig. **1968** Adams *Western Words* 208, *Nutter*—In sheep raising, a man who castrates the young males of the lamb crop. *Nutting*—Castrating young male lambs. **1973** Allen *LAUM* 1.251 **Upper MW** (as of c1950), The incidence of the more frequently used terms is: *alter* 11%, *castrate* 81%, *cut* 37%, *nut* 5%, and *trim (up)* 7%.

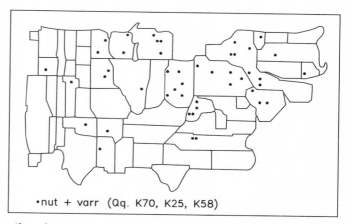

•nut + varr (Qq. K70, K25, K58)

nutbrush n
=**jojoba.**

1931 U.S. Dept. Ag. *Misc. Pub.* 101.94, Jojoba (*Simmondsia californica*) . . known by a variety of vernacular names, including bushnut, coffee berry, coffee bush, goat-berry, nutbrush and pignut. . . The seeds of jojoba have an agreeable nutty flavor, and are a rather important source of food supply among certain Indians. **1938** Van Dersal *Native Woody Plants* 345, Nutbrush (*Simmondsia chinensis*).

nutcake n Also *Yankee nutcake* **chiefly NEng** Cf **friedcake 1, fried nut**
A doughnut; a cake formed in various shapes and fried.

1801 *Spirit Farmers' Museum* 235 **NH**, Heap the nutcakes, fried in butter. **1823** Cooper *Pioneers* 1.126, The four corners were garnished with plates of cake. On one was piled certain curiously twisted and complicated figures, called "nut-cakes." **1853** Webster *Improved Housewife* 122, Yankee Nut Cakes. **1857** *Quinland* 1.36 **NY**, The 'nut-cakes' are an institution of the country. Some call 'em 'dough-nuts' and some 'fried cakes.' **1897** Robinson *Uncle Lisha's Outing* 253 **wVT**, "Come right in . . an' have a fried cake an some cider." . . "I wouldn't go ag'in a nut cake." **1949** Kurath *Word Geog.* 69, The unraised variety [of doughnut] has . . other names: *fried-cake* . . *nut cake* (New Hampshire and Maine). **1950** *WELS Suppl.* **WI,** *Nutcake* . . was her Vermont grandfather's name for what I call *fried-cakes.* Says they didn't have nuts in them that she remembers. **1967** Faries *Word Geog. MO* 135, (*Doughnut*) . . *nut cake* 1 [inf of c700]. **1971** Wood *Vocab. Change* 45 **Sth,** Doughnuts. . . *nut cake* [is] scattered . . east of the Mississippi. **1974** *DARE* File **csWI,** A friend born in the 1890s says her grandfather, who came to Wisconsin from Vermont, called doughnuts *nutcakes.*

nutcrack n [*OED* →1806] Cf Intro "Language Changes" III.4
An implement for cracking nutshells.
   1892 *DN* 1.236 **MI, MO,** *Nut-crack:* nut-cracker. **1906** *DN* 3.148 **nwAR,** Please pass the nut-cracks.

nutcracker n
Either of two western birds that feed chiefly on **pine nuts:**
a usu in comb *Clark('s) nutcracker:* A gray bird (*Nucifraga columbiana*) with black-and-white patterned wings and tail, native chiefly to the Pacific Northwest. Also called **gray crow, meatbird 2, mountain parrot, pine crow, rain ~**
   1838 Audubon *Ornith. Biog.* 4.459, *Clarke's* [sic] *Nutcracker. Nucifraga columbiana.* . . "We first observed this species . . on the borders of Bear River." **1874** Coues *Birds NW* 207, *Picicorvus Columbianus* . . Clarke's [sic] Crow; American Nutcracker. . . The range of this species is nearly coincident with the zone of coniferous vegetation in the West. **1904** Wheelock *Birds CA* 330, "As black as a crow" loses its significance when one looks at the soft gray plumage of the Clarke [sic] Crow, or Nutcracker, of the California mountains. **1917** (1923) *Birds Amer.* 2.233, The Clarke [sic] Crow or Nutcracker was first discovered by Captain William Clarke [sic] near the site of Salmon City in Idaho, August 22, 1805. **1928** Bailey *Birds NM* 503, When walking about before you in crow-like pose, the Clark Crow or Nutcracker with his sharply contrasted plumage seems the most conspicuous and striking of birds. **1953** Jewett *Birds WA* 473, The nutcracker, while ranging west to Whatcom Pass and Mt. Rainier, is much more common than elsewhere on the east slopes of the Cascade Mountains. **1977** Udvardy *Audubon Field Guide Birds* 727, An erratic winter wanderer, this nutcracker's periodic irruption in great numbers, bringing it all the way to the Pacific Coast, is related to failure of the pine seed crop.
b =**piñon jay.**
   1904 Wheelock *Birds CA* 494, The Piñon Jay is also called Nutcracker, Blue Crow, and Piñario by the Mexicans, in reference to its fondness for the nuts of the variety known as piñon. **1953** Jewett *Birds WA* 471, *Gymnorhinus ceanocephalus* . . Nutcracker.

nut grass n
1 also *nut sedge,* ~ *weed:* A **galingale 1:** usu *Cyperus esculentus* or *C. rotundus,* rarely *C. strigosus.* [From the edible tubers] **scattered, but chiefly S Atl, Gulf States** See Map For other names of *C. esculentus* see **chufa, grassnut 1, groundnut B5, nut rush 2, sweet coco;** for other names of *C. rotundus* see **bitter coco, coco grass 1;** for other names of *C. strigosus* see **ground moss 3**
   1775 (1962) Romans *Nat. Hist. FL* 129, In Carolina it [=*herbe au cheval*] is called *nutt grass* from a nutt found at its root. **1830** Rafinesque *Med. Flora* 2.215, *C[yperus] hydra* (Nut grass, or Horse grass of the South) is a bad weed, roots like horse hair, with round nuts . . , it spoils fields, but consolidates sandy soils. **1859** (1880) Darlington *Amer. Weeds* 359, *C[yperus] phymatodes* . . "Nut Grass," of Florida. **1890** *FL Ag. Exper. Sta. Gainesville Bulletin* 8.15, Rating weeds in order of badness, I would give the Sandspurs the first place . . Nut grass ranks third, and once well established in a field, usually outlives the owner. **1894** *Jrl. Amer. Folkl.* 7.103, *Cyperus strigosus* . . nut-grass [Footnote: The tubers are eaten by children], Concord, Mass. **1894** Coulter *Botany W. TX* 463, *C[yperus] rotundus.* . . From the South Atlantic and Gulf States to the Texan coast. . . Often called "nut grass." **1935** (1943) Muenscher *Weeds* 174, *Cyperus esculentus* . . Yellow nutgrass . . Northern nut-grass . . Nut sedge. . . *Cyperus rotundus* . . Nutgrass, Nut sedge. **1953** *Sun* (Baltimore MD) 2 Aug sec B 11/1 (Hench Coll.) **CA,** The gardener's headache, nutgrass, can be controlled by fumigating soil with the herbicide C.B.P. **1960** Lee *Mockingbird* 49 **sAL,** If she found a blade of nut-grass in her yard it was like the Second Battle of the Marne. **1965–70** *DARE* (Qu. S9, . . *Kinds of grass that are hard to get rid of*) 139 Infs, **scattered, but chiefly S Atl, Gulf States,** Nut grass; **HI**11, Nut weed; (Qu. S21, . . *Weeds . . that are a*

trouble in gardens and fields) 15 Infs, **scattered, but esp S Atl,** Nut grass; (Qu. S8, *A common kind of wild grass that grows in fields: it spreads by sending out long underground roots, and it's hard to get rid of*) 11 Infs, **scattered, but esp S Atl,** Nut grass; (Qu. I43, *What kinds of nuts grow wild around here?*) Inf **GA**62, Nut grass. **1986** Pederson *LAGS Concordance* **Gulf Region,** 34 infs, Nut grass(es); 1 inf, Nut grass—similar to chufas; 1 inf, Nut grass—been giving me fits; 1 inf, The only way you can get rid of nut grass is move.

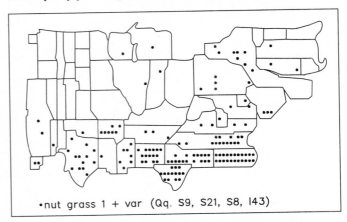

•nut grass 1 + var (Qq. S9, S21, S8, I43)

2 Any of var plants that resemble **nut grass 1,** such as a bulrush (*Scirpus* spp), **black grass,** or a **nut rush 1;** see quots.
   1916 *Torreya* 16.237, *Scirpus robustus* . . Nut grass, Santee Club, S.C. **1933** *Ibid* 33.82, *Scirpus campestris* . . Nut grass, Carson Sink, Nev. *Ibid* 83, *Juncus gerardi* . . Nut grass, Cambridge, Md. **1940** Gates *Flora KS* 120, *Scleria pauciflora* . . Nutgrass. . . *Scleria triglomerata* . . Tall Nutgrass. **1968** Barkley *Plants KS* 85, *Scleria pauciflora* . . Nutgrass. Nut-rush. . . *Scleria triglomerata* . . Tall Nutgrass. Nut-rush.

3 A **pondweed** (here: *Potamogeton pectinatus*).
   1941 *Torreya* 41.45, *Potamogeton pectinatus* . . Bay grass, Norfolk, Va. . . nut grass, Suisun Marshes, Calif. . . In this series and elsewhere, the writer has recorded 18 different terms for this plant, most of them in genuine vernacular use.

nuthatch n
Std: a bird of the genus *Sitta.* Also called **ass-up, creeper 2, flycatcher 1c, nuthatcher, sapsucker, topsy-turvy bird, upside-down ~.** For other names of var spp see **cardy bird, cha-cha 2, chay-chay 2, hominy bird 2, devil-downhill, flutterbutt, jizibee, quick-quick, red-breasted nuthatch, talala bird, tomtit, white-breasted nuthatch**

nuthatcher n [Cf -er affix **1**]
=**nuthatch.**
   1862 in 1865 *IL Dept. Ag. Trans.* 5.731 **seWI,** Even the *Nuthatchers,* are, by many, indiscriminately called Sap-Suckers. **1967–70** *DARE* (Qu. Q23, *The insect-eating bird that goes headfirst down a tree trunk*) Infs **CT**42, **IA**43, **KS**7, **OH**49, **TN**6, Nuthatcher.

nuther adj[1], adv, pron, conj See **neither**

nuther adj[2] See **another**

nuthin' See **nothing**

nut horse n Cf **nut** v
   1960 Criswell *Resp. to PADS 20* **Ozarks,** *Nut horse*—A horse not yet cut but destined for it was called a *nut horse.*

nutmeat See **meat** n **1**

nutmeg n
Pronc-spp *netmeg, nuttenmeg, nutten-egg;* for addit varr see quots.
Std sense, var forms.
   1909 *S. Atl. Qrly.* 8.44 **seSC** [Gullah], She had supplied the place of the missing chicken-eggs with *nutmegs;* in Gullah known as *nutten-eggs.* **1912** Green *VA Folk-Speech* 302, *Nutmeg.* . . Nuttenmeg. Nutmeg. **1922** (1926) Cady *Rhymes VT* 212, She knows that pickle does for hash / What netmeg does for custard. **1933** *N. Amer. Rev.* 236.541 **seSC** [Gullah], Nutmegs, [becomes] *nuttin'-aigs.* **1933** *AmSp* 8.2.44 **neNY,**

[eɪ] is usually found in place of [ɛ] in . . *nutmeg* [nʌtmeɪg]. **1934** *AmSp* 9.211 **Sth,** Some words with standard [ɛ] before [g] or [k] change [ɛ] to [eɪ] or [e]. This pronunciation is decidedly vulgar. . . *Nutmeg.* **1936** *AmSp* 11.15 **eTX,** Before [g] the sound [=[ɛ]] usually appears as [e], [eɪ], though sometimes as [ɛ]: . . *nutmeg.* **1966–70** *DARE* (Qu. I35) Inf **DC8,** [ˈnʌtn‚mɛg]; **NY235,** [ˈnʌtəm ‚ɛg]. **1968** *DARE* FW Addit **LA15,** Nutmeg [ˈnʌt‚nɛg].

nutmeg hickory n [From the shape of the nut]
A **hickory B1** (here: *Carya myristiciformis*). Also called **bitter water hickory, ~ waternut, nogal, swamp hickory**

    1810 Michaux *Histoire des Arbres* 1.21, J[uglans] myristicaformis. *Nutmeg hickery nut . .* , nom donné par moi à cette espèce, qui n'en a aucun dans les Etats du midi. [= . . , name given by me to this species, which has none in the southern states.] **1897** Sudworth *Arborescent Flora* 112 **NC, SC, AL,** *Hicoria myristicæformis. . . Common Names.* Nutmeg Hickory. **1930** OK Univ. Biol. Surv. *Pub.* 2.1.57, *Carya myristicaeformis . .* Nutmeg Hickory. **1970** Correll *Plants TX* 460, *Carya myristicaeformis . .* Nutmeg hickory, nogal. **1980** Little *Audubon Guide N. Amer. Trees E. Region* 351, *Nutmeg Hickory. . .* The common and scientific names of this patchily distributed hickory refer to the nutmeg-like shape of the nut. Nutmeg Hickory is easily recognized by the brownish hue produced by numerous tiny scales on various parts.

nutmeg tree See **California nutmeg**

nutnmeg See **nutmeg**

nut pine n
Any of var pines with edible seeds, as:
a A **piñon,** esp *Pinus edulis.*

    1845 Frémont *Rept. Rocky Mts.* 221, A pine tree . . which Dr. Torrey has described as a new species, under the name of *pinus monophyllus;* in popular language, it might be called the *nut pine.* **1877** Wright *Big Bonanza* 384 **NV,** For many miles in all directions about the town they have dug up and hacked to pieces the stumps left by the white men who first denuded the hills of their sparse covering of cedar and nut-pine. **1884** Sargent *Forests of N. Amer.* 9, The foot-hills [of the southern Rocky Mountains] . . are covered with scant groves of the nut-pine (*Pinus edulis*). *Ibid* 189, *Pinus Parryana. . .* Piñon. Nut pine. *Ibid* 190, *Pinus cembroides. . .* Nut pine. . . *Pinus edulis. . .* Piñon. Nut pine. . . *Pinus monophylla. . .* Piñon. Nut pine. **1894** *Jrl. Amer. Folkl.* 7.100, *Pinus edulis . .* nut-pine of New Mex., or simply nut-pine (Americans), Tex. to Cal. **1897** Sudworth *Arborescent Flora* 17, *Pinus cembroides . .* Mexican Piñon. . . Nut Pine (Ariz., N. Mex.) . . *Pinus edulis . .* Piñon. . . Nut Pine (Tex., Colo.) **1908** Britton *N. Amer. Trees* 14, It [=*Pinus cembroides*] . . is variously known as Mexican piñon or pinyon, Nut pine, Pinyon and Stone pine. *Ibid* 16, One-leaved Nut Pine—*Pinus monophylla. . .* It is also called . . Piñon nut pine, Nevada nut pine . . and Fremont's nut pine. *Ibid* 17, This [=*Pinus edulis*] is also called Piñon, Nut pine, Piñon pine, and New Mexican Pinyon. **1938** Van Dersal *Native Woody Plants* 348, Pine, . . Nut (*Pinus cembroides, Pinus edulis, Pinus monophylla, Pinus parryana*). **1960** Vines *Trees SW* 15, Mexican Pinyon Pine—*Pinus cembroides. . .* Other vernacular names are Nut Pine . . and Ocote. . . The tree is valued for its edible seeds which are gathered and sold in great quantities by the Mexican and Indian people. The seeds are eaten raw or roasted and have an excellent flavor. **1980** Little *Audubon Guide N. Amer. Trees W. Region* 272, "Nut Pine" . . *Pinus cembroides. . .* The hard seeds are the main commercial pinyon nuts (*piñones*) of Mexico. However, in the United States this species has limited distribution and usually bears light cone crops. *Ibid* 282, "Nut Pine" . . *Pinus monophylla. . .* The large, edible, mealy seeds are sold locally as pinyon or pine nuts and used to be a staple food of Indians in the Great Basin region. *Ibid* 287, "Nut Pine"—*Pinus quadrifolia. . .* The edible seeds are not gathered commercially because of the tree's limited distribution.
b The Coulter **pine** (*Pinus coulteri*).

    1897 Sudworth *Arborescent Flora* 24 **CA, ID,** *Pinus coulteri. . .* Nut Pine. **1908** Britton *N. Amer. Trees* 39, This pine [=*Pinus coulteri*] grows over much the same area [of CA] as the Digger pine, but at higher altitudes. . It is also known as Pitch pine, Big cone pine, Large cone pine, and Nut pine. [**1962** Balls *Early Uses CA Plants* 28, In the areas where they are abundant, the seeds of all the large-seeded Pines were used as an important item of food. The Coulter Pine *Pinus Coulteri,* was used in the south; the Digger Pine *Pinus Sabiniana,* in the foothills and the Coast Ranges on either side of the San Joaquin Valley; and the

Sugar Pine, *Pinus Lambertiana,* throughout its wide range from southern California to Oregon.]
c =**digger pine.**

    1898 *Jrl. Amer. Folkl.* 11.280 **CA,** *Pinus Sabiniana . .* nut pine, bull pine, digger pine. **1902** U.S. Natl. Museum *Contrib. Herbarium* 7.307 **CA,** *Pinus sabiniana. . .* The well-known round-topped nut or digger pine. . . The nuts are about three-quarters of an inch in length and are very sweet and oily. . . At present the supply of flour and cultivated products renders it unnecessary for the Indians to go through the laborious process of collecting the cones and extracting the seeds, but they are often collected as a pastime both by natives and whites. **1910** Jepson *Silva CA* 90, This species [=*Pinus sabiniana*] is one of the "nut pines." The "nuts" or seeds were a favorite article of food with the native tribes and they had no more useful tree save the oaks. **1920** [see **d** below]. [**1962** see **b** above.]
d =**sugar pine.**

    1920 Saunders *Useful Wild Plants* 75, The most esteemed nut-pines are the Two-leaved Pine . . the closely related One-leaved Pine . . the Digger Pine . . and the stately Sugar Pine (*P[inus] lambertiana . .*), whose huge cones are frequently a foot and a half long or more. [**1962** see **b** above.]
e =**limber pine 1.**

    1966 Barnes–Jensen *Dict. UT Slang* 32, *Nut pine. . .* A name sometimes given the Limber pine (*Pinus flexilis*) which grows in the high mountains, and has cones as much as 10 inches long which bear seeds ½ inch long, angled and flattened. It is a favorite food of the Clark nutcracker.

nut rush n
1 Std: a plant of the genus *Scleria.* For other names of var spp see **nut grass 2, whip ~**
2 also *rush nut:* A **nut grass 1** (here: *Cyperus esculentus*).

    1863 Burr *Field & Garden* 34, Nut Rush. *Cyperus esculentus. . .* The flesh of these roots, or tubers, is of a yellowish color, tender, and of a pleasant, sweet, and nut-like flavor. The leaves are rush-like, about eighteen inches high. **1900** Lyons *Plant Names* 129, *C[yperus] esculentus. . . Tubers . .* Earth or Ground Almond, Rush-nut. **1935** (1943) Muenscher *Weeds* 174, *Cyperus esculentus . .* Rush nut. **1945** Wodehouse *Hayfever Plants* 60, Nutgrass . . also called galingale, chufa and nutrush, though it is neither a grass nor a rush. It is a low tufted sedge with extensive slender rootstocks, bearing edible nut-like tubers. **1951** Martin *Amer. Wildlife & Plants* 443, The wildlife value of chufa, also known as nutgrass, nutrush, or ground almond, is probably much greater than that of all other species of *Cyperus* combined. **1974** (1977) Coon *Useful Plants* 124, Rush-nut. . . If found to be growing in the reader's garden, they should be dug and used, for, as a weed, it is otherwise perhaps the most difficult-to-eradicate garden pest known.

nut sedge See **nut grass 1**

nutted See **nut**

nutten-egg, nuttenmeg See **nutmeg**

nutter See **nut**

nuttin See **nothing**

nuttin-aig See **nutmeg**

nutting vbl n See **nut**

nutting n, **nuttn(e)** See **nothing**

nut weed See **nut grass 1**

nuv(v)er See **never**

nux vomica n Also *noxvomik(y); by folk-etym, nox vomit, ox vomit*
Std sense, var forms.

    1895 *DN* 1.392 **wFL,** *Ox vomit:* popular etymology for *nux vomica.* **1909** *DN* 3.353 **eAL, wGA,** *Noxvomik(y). . . Nox vomit. . .* Nux vomica.

nyam v Also *nyam-nyam, yam* [Of W Afr origin; see quot 1949; cf *DBE, DJE*] chiefly Gullah
To eat—used in var inflections of the verb.

    1922 Gonzales *Black Border* 315 **sSC, GA coasts** [Gullah glossary], *Nyam*—eat, eats, eating, ate; sometimes "nyam-nyam," a repetition for emphasis. **1930** Stoney-Shelby *Black Genesis* 6 **seSC** [Gullah], He sure did tek a whole lot o' interest in de way God nyam (ate) his bittles. *Ibid*

19, Tis only because dey aint find out yet much 'bout bein' hongry dat keep Br' Wolf, an' Br' Lion, an' dem, from nyamin' Br' Goat, an Br' Cow. **1930** Woofter *Black Yeomanry* 54 **seSC,** African words which are more or less confined to the low country are *buckra* . . and possibly . . *nyam* (to eat). **1933** *N. Amer. Rev.* 236.540 **SC coast** [Gullah], From the West African that was his forefathers' speech, this unique American has preserved such useful words as *nyam,* meaning to eat (also I eat, you eat, he eats, they have eaten, will eat, etc.) **1949** Turner *Africanisms* 199, *West African Words In Gullah* . . [ɲam (ˈɲamɲam)] 'to eat, to eat up' W[olof], [ɲam (ɲamɲam)] 'to eat'; Fu[la], [ɲama (ɲamgo)] 'to eat' [etc]. **1970** Major *Dict. Afro-Amer. Slang* 125, *Yam:* (1940's) to eat.

N'Yawk See **New York**

N'yawlins See **New Orleans**

nyoung adj Also sp *noung, nyung* [Varr of *young;* see quot 1949] *among Black speakers*

1883 (1971) Harris *Nights with Remus* 136 **GA** [Black], Wut noung gal gwan do wit' ole Chris'mus' 'cep 'e do 'joy 'ese'f? **1888** Jones *Negro Myths* 82 **GA coast** [Gullah], Day was a berry pooty noung ooman name May Belle. **1892** (1969) Christensen *Afro-Amer. Folk Lore* 10, Well, dere was a beautiful nyung lady. **1909** *S. Atl. Qrly.* 8.51 **sSC, GA coasts** [Gullah], An odd euphonic use of extraneous . . *n,* in . . *nyoung* for *young.* **1922** Gonzales *Black Border* 315 **sSC, GA coasts** [Gullah glossary], *Nyoung, nyung*—young. **1930** Woofter *Black Yeomanry* 50 **seSC** [Gullah], *Nyoung* for *young.* **1949** [see **nuse**].

nyuse, nyuze See **nuse**

o See **of** prep

oaf See **off**

oak n

Std: a tree or shrub of the genus *Quercus*. Also called **acorn tree.** For other names of var spp see **ash oak, basket ~, bastard ~, bear ~, blackjack ~, black ~, bluejack 1, blue oak, branch ~, burr ~, canyon ~, chair bark ~, chaparro** n[1], **cherrybark oak, chestnut ~, chestnut white ~, chinquapin ~, deer ~, Durand ~, encino, evergreen oak, evergreen white ~, Gambel ~, gray ~, ground ~ 1, hard ~, huckleberry ~, jack ~, Lacey ~, laurel ~, live ~, mesa ~, moss ~, myrtle ~, oracle ~, Oregon ~, overcup ~, pin ~, post ~, quercitron ~, red ~, roble, running oak, Spanish ~, scarlet ~, scrub ~, shingle ~, shinnery ~, shin ~, Shumard ~, striped , swamp chestnut ~, swamp white ~, Texas ~, turkey ~, valley ~, water ~, whiteleaf ~, white ~, willow ~** Cf also **bitter oak 1, golden ~ 1, ground ~ 2, hedgehog ~, Jerusalem ~, poison ~, running ~, silver ~, swamp ~, tanbark ~**

oak apple n Also *oak ball*

1 A gall on **oak** twigs caused by the larvae of gall wasps (family Cynipidae). [*OED* 14 . . →] Cf **cedar apple, huckleberry ~, swamp ~**

1842 Harris *Treatise Insects* 397 **NEng,** The largest galls found in this country are commonly called oak-apples. They grow on the leaves of the red oak, are round and smooth, and measure from an inch and a half to two inches in diameter. . . A single grub lives in the kernel, becomes a chrysalis in the autumn, when the oak-apple falls from the tree, changes to a fly in the spring, and makes its escape. . . The name of this insect is *Cynips confluentus.* **1850** Emerson *Rept. Trees & Shrubs* 143, Upon the leaves of the black oak, as also those of the red and scarlet, are often found smooth, round, light excrescences, called oak apples. **1890** (1904) Hyatt–Arms *Insecta* 233, *Cynipidæ.* These gall-flies are small insects. . . The larva produces an irritation in the living tissues [of a plant], and an abnormal growth or a gall is the result. . . The nut-galls, or "oak-apples," so common on oak trees, are familiar. **1899** (1912) Green *VA Folk-Speech* 302, Oak-apple. . . The oak gall. **1911** *Century Dict. Suppl.,* Oak-ball. . . Same as *nutgall:* used especially of those borne by the California white oak, *Quercus lobata.* **1926** Essig *Insects N. Amer.* 803 **West,** The *California gallfly, Andricus californicus* . . produces the largest and best known gall in the west. . . The galls begin to form on the twigs in the spring . . and are frequently called oak apples. **1968** *PA Game News* Aug 19 **PA,** Several "oak apples," the spherical galls found on oak foliage, were lying in the path. . . They were . . perfectly round and smooth, pale greenish-white delicately marbled with reddish. . . Oak apples like the ones I found are formed by a small tiny insect called a gall-wasp, or Cynipid. I cut one gall open, . . and curled up in the center was . . a little white grub. . . It will pupate there, then chew a hole through its spherical house to emerge as an adult. **1980** Milne–Milne *Audubon Field Guide Insects* 814, Larvae [of *Andricus quercuscalifornicus*] tunnel inward, causing tree to form hard galls, known as "oak apples." Galls are green at first, then turn red or brown, growing to 4″ in width.

2 Appar a **mushroom B1;** see quot.

1967–70 *DARE* (Qu. S18, *A kind of mushroom that grows like a globe . . sometimes gets as big as a man's head*) Inf **NJ4,** Oak ball; **PA245,** Oak apples.

oak-barked cedar See **oak-barked juniper**

oak-barked juniper n Also *oak-barked cedar, oakbark juniper* =**alligator juniper.**

1897 Sudworth *Arborescent Flora* 98 **AZ,** *Juniperus pachyphloea* . . Oak-barked Cedar . . Oakbark Juniper. **1908** Britton *N. Amer. Trees* 113, Thick-barked Juniper. . . also known as . . Alligator juniper, Oak-barked juniper, Oak-barked cedar [etc].

oak bonnet n

A **mushroom B1** such as *Collybia dryophila.*

1968 *DARE* (Qu. S19, *Mushrooms that grow out like brackets from the sides of trees*) Inf **VA25,** Oak bonnet—one old West Virginian gathers them in the fall and eats them.

oak fungus n Cf **oak bonnet** =**honey mushroom.**

1938 Boyce *Forest Pathology* 110, *Shoestring Root Rot.* . . The causal fungus has also been referred to as honey agaric, oak fungus, and shoestring fungus. . . The fungus causes rotting of the bark and wood of the roots and root collar, followed by death of the tree.

oakhead n *joc*

1966–68 *DARE* (Qu. K50, *Joking nicknames for mules*) Inf **NC13,** Oakheads [laughter]; **NC81,** Oakhead.

oakiedoke See **okeydoke**

oak Jerusalem See **Jerusalem oak 1**

oakleaf (moccasin) snake See **oak snake**

oak leech n

A **false foxglove** parasitic on **oak** trees.

1948 Wherry *Wild Flower Guide* 120, *Lace-leaf Oak-leech (Aureolaria pedicularia).* . . The common name refers to the fact that the plant sends down stalks which suck sap from the oak roots. . . *Smooth Oak-leech (A. flava).* . . *Habitat:* Open oak woods, sucking sap from the tree roots. . . *Virginia Oak-leech (A. virginica)* has hairy herbage.

oak of Jerusalem See **Jerusalem oak 1**

oak opening n chiefly **wGt Lakes, esp WI, MI** Cf **bald, park** An open stand of **oak** trees, esp **burr oak,** often adjoining a prairie or interspersed with prairie vegetation; the land supporting such a stand.

1830 in 1892 *WI State Hist. Soc. Coll.* 12.185, From that up, on the right bank, it is oak openings. **1833** in 1934 *MI Hist.* 18.55, "Oak Openings" . . a light sandy soil, poor, on which nothing but burr oak will grow. **1835** Hoffman *Winter in West* (NY) 1.148, These fires . . seize upon the large prairies, and consuming every tree in the woods, except the hardiest, cause the often-mentioned oak openings, so characteristic of Michigan scenery. **1842** Kirkland *Forest Life* 1.131 **MI,** Immense tracts are covered but thinly with scattered oaks, and these are almost exclusively of the different kinds of oak. By contrast with the heavily timbered land these tracts seem almost bare, and they have received the appropriate name of "oak-openings." **1846** Lapham *Wisconsin* 134 **seWI,** The country consists of oak openings, interspersed with small prairies, except in the town of Oconomowoc [sic]. The oak most usual on the openings, are the white oak and burr oak, *(Quercus macrocarpa;)* but these species are seldom mixed, and the kind of tree gives name to the openings; thus we say "white oak openings," or "burr oak openings." There is believed to be a difference in the character of the soil on the different kinds of openings, as well as on the prairies. **1850** Chamberlain *IN Gaz.* 154, In the north-western part of the country are many oak openings, or barrens, all very fertile and easily brought into cultivation. **1868** IA State Ag. Soc. *Rept. for 1867* 175, It [=sugar sorghum] grows well here on all our soils, high prairie, low bottom, oak openings, timber lands. **1908** Rogers *Tree Book* 201, This tree [=**burr oak**]. . . forms the "oak openings" of Minnesota and Dakota. **1947** Homme *Oak Opening* 4 **csWI,** Our oak openings were nothing like a forest. They were rather groves consisting only of oaks and hickories growing comparatively far apart. **1950** Peattie *Nat. Hist. Trees* 215, True that other Oaks are often found in the Oak openings, or prairie groves, of the Middle West, but ecologists consider them secondary successors; they have come in only after the Bur Oak has conquered the prairie for them. **1968** *DARE* (Qu. C29, *A good-sized stretch of level land with practically no trees*) Inf **WI5,** Oak openings; **WI12,** Oak opening—a grove of trees in the prairie where the grass would be shorter.

oak petal n
An unidentified plant; see quot.
　　1961 Douglas *My Wilderness* 83 **AZ,** The path hugs the dark rock and climbs to a saddle where the steep pitch of a staircase against a wall. On this section of the trail in March are patch after patch of the oak petal. The petals are bright white and lobed like miniature oak leaves. The plant stands a foot or so high. The flowers are in crowded clusters.

oak runner n
Either a **live oak 1** (here: *Quercus minima*) or a **running oak** (here: *Quercus pumila*).
　　1797 Smith *Nat. Hist. GA* 2.157, The caterpillar feeds on the Oak Runner. . . This Oak can scarcely be referred to any thing else than the Water Oak, of which it is probably a variety. **1927** Boston Soc. Nat. Hist. *Proc.* 38.213 **Okefenokee GA,** *Quercus pumila*—'oak runner' . . *Quercus minima*—'Oak runner.'

oak snake n Also *oakleaf (moccasin) snake*
A **rat snake** (*Elaphe obsoleta spiloides*).
　　1908 *Country Life* Nov 67 (Mathews Coll.), Oak leaf moccasin snake. **1958** Conant *Reptiles & Amphibians* 162, Gray Rat Snake—*Elaphe obsoleta spiloides* . . Called the "oak snake" in some parts of the South. **1965–70** *DARE* (Qu. P25, . . *Kinds of snakes*) Inf **FL17,** Oak snake—not poisonous; **GA7,** Oak snake; **SC69,** Oakleaf [snake].

oak winter n Cf **blackberry winter**
　　1936 *AmSp* 11.316 **Ozarks,** Oak-winter. . . A late spring frost, after the oak leaves have appeared.

oar v
To row (a boat).
　　1912 Green *VA Folk-Speech* 302, Oar. . . To row with oars. **c1970** Pederson *Dial. Surv. Rural GA,* 1 inf, **seGA,** You have to oar those boats. **1986** Pederson *LAGS Concordance,* 1 inf, **cTN,** Oaring the boat = rowing the boat; 1 inf, **neTX,** Oared them = rowed.

oaster See **oyster**

oat beetle See **oats bug 1**

oat bird n Also *oats bird*
=**bobolink B.**
　　1923 U.S. Dept. Ag. *Misc. Circular* 13.75 **FL,** Bobolink (*Dolichonyx oryzivorus*). . . In local use . . oats-bird. **1955** Forbush-May *Birds* 459, Bobolink—*Dolichonyx oryzivorus*. . . Other names: Reed-bird . . Oat Bird. **1962** Imhof *AL Birds* 497, Bobolink—*Dolichonyx oryzivorus* . . Other Names: Oatbird, Ricebird . . Ortolan.

oat bug See **oats bug 1**

oatburner n Also *oatsmobile;* for addit varr see quots *joc* Cf **fish burner, hayburner 5,** DS K44
A horse.
　　1916 *DN* 4.341 **seOH,** Oatsmobile. . . A horse. **1941** *Sun* (Baltimore MD) 21 July 11/4 (*OEDS*), There isn't a galloper in the lot who can say 'I'm the boss', so your milkman's oat burner might do just as well as any of 'em. **1942** Berrey-Van den Bark *Amer. Slang* 120.39, Horse. . . Oats consumer, -destroyer, -grinder or muncher, oatsmobile. **1951** *PADS* 16.45 [Argot of the racetrack], Oat muncher (burner). . . 1. A horse which does not pay for his feed with his winnings. 2. Any worthless horse. **1952** in 1960 Wentworth-Flexner *Slang* 361, Oat-burner. . . When the time comes. . . that even an oat-burner must sport a tax stamp on its stem or stern. *Letter,* N.Y. *Daily News,* Aug. 20, C11/4. **1955** Stong *Blizzard* 15 **IA,** Direct line from old Dan Patch—the best oatburner that ever trotted.

oat fly See **oats bug 1**

oat grass n [*OED* 1578 → for *Avena* spp] Cf **wild oat, ~ oat grass**
Any of var grasses which are related to or are thought to resemble those of the genus *Avena,* such as:

a A meadow grass (*Arrhenatherum elatius*) naturalized chiefly in the eastern half of the US. Also called **evergreen grass 2, meadow oat grass**
　　1795 Winterbotham *Amer. U.S.* 3.401, The States of New-England abound with. . . Millet, . . Fescue grass, . . Oat grass. **1822** (1972) Deane *New Engl. Farmer* 171, Tall-oat-grass, *Avena elatior.* This kind of grass was imported from England, and has been cultivated in Massachusetts, as well as in the State of New-York, and the southern States. **1869** Porcher *Resources* 682 **Sth,** Consult Dr. Lee's editorials. . . He recommends the "tall Oat grass" (*Arrhenatherum avenaceum*). **1891** Jesup *Plants Hanover NH* 53. **1903** Small *Flora SE U.S.* 130, *Arrhenatherum elatius.* . . In fields and waste places, Maine and Ontario to Georgia, Tennessee and Nebraska. Also on the Pacific Coast. . . *Oat Grass.* **1940** Gates *Flora KS* 123. **1968** *PA Game News* Apr 16 **PA,** Tall oat grass provided the best quick cover but is gradually thinning out. **1973** Hitchcock-Cronquist *Flora Pacific NW* 622, Oatgrass. . . Widely intro[duced] as a meadow grass and now estab[lished] from sw BC to Cal, mostly w Cas[cades], as well as in many other states. **1976** Bailey-Bailey *Hortus Third* 111, [*Arrhenatherum*] *elatius.* . . Tall o[at] g[rass]. . . Cult. in the n. humid region of the U.S. as a meadow grass; escapes frequently from cult., especially in the n. and e. states.

b A grass of the genus *Trisetum.* Also called **wild oat grass.** For other names of *T. pennsylvanicum* see **marsh oats, swamp oat grass**
　　1802 Drayton *View of SC* 61, Oat grass. (*Avena Caroliniana.*) Grows in rich tide lands. **1881** Phares *Farmer's Book of Grasses* 79, *T[risetum] pubescens.* Downy Oat Grass is a valuable forage plant, but has not been introduced in the south. **1901** Mohr *Plant Life AL* 372, *Trisetum pennsylvanicum.* . . Swamp Oat Grass. . . Alleghanian and Carolinian areas. **1923** Abrams *Flora Pacific States* 1.168, *Trisetum spicatum.* . . Downy Oat-grass. . . A characteristic grass of high altitudes. **1960** Williams *Walk Egypt* 7 **GA,** No one knew why the trees stopped at an invisible line, and oatgrass and sedge took over. **1974** Welsh *Anderson's Flora AK* 605, *Trisetum cernuum* . . Nodding Oatgrass. . . Woods, thickets, and marshes; in coastal south-central and southeastern Alaska . . southward to California, Idaho, and Montana. . . *Trisetum spicatum* . . Downy Oatgrass. . . Spits, tundra, heathlands, rock outcrops, bars, snow flushes, river banks, roadsides, landing strips, ridge tops, moraines, and open woods; in most of Alaska and Yukon.

c A grass of the genus *Danthonia,* native chiefly to the western US. Also called **wild oat grass;** for other names of the common eastern sp, *D. spicata,* see **cunt-hair grass, June ~ 1c, moonshine ~, poverty oat ~, poverty ~, wildcat ~, wire ~, witchgrass, turkey-strip, white horse, whitetop**
　　1824 Bigelow *Florula Bostoniensis* 32, Spiked Oat grass. . . *Danthonia spicata.* . . A common grass in dry sunny pastures. **1837** Darlington *Flora Cestrica* 66, *Danthonia spicata* . . Spiked Danthonia . . Vulgo—Oat-grass. Wild oats. **1891** Jesup *Plants Hanover NH* 54, *Danthonia.* . . Oat-Grass. **1911** *Century Dict. Suppl.,* Oat-grass. . . California oat-grass, *Danthonia Californica,* . . in Wyoming and Montana forming a considerable part of the meadow vegetation at altitudes from 5,500 to 8,000 feet. . . *Parry's oat-grass, Danthonia Parryi.* . . resembles the California oat-grass and replaces it farther southward.—*Rocky Mountain oat-grass, Danthonia intermedia,* a species occurring with the California oat-grass, but ascending to higher altitudes. . . *Tennessee oat-grass,* . . *Danthonia compressa,* common in hilly country in North Carolina and Tennessee and farther north forming the bulk of the forage of 'balds' or parks. **1937** U.S. Forest Serv. *Range Plant Hdbk.* G45, It is a bit unfortunate that the common name, oatgrass, has become so firmly intrenched in western range usage for this genus [=*Danthonia*] as the western species show no great resemblance to oats (*Avena* spp.) **1952** Davis *Flora ID* 99, *Danthonia.* . . Oatgrass. Tufted, low or medium tall perennials. **1974** Welsh *Anderson's Flora AK* 567, *Danthonia intermedia* . . Timber Oatgrass. . . Meadows; in south-central and continental southeastern Alaska and southern Yukon; eastward to Newfoundland and south to California, Utah, Colorado, and Michigan. **1976** Bailey-Bailey *Hortus Third* 362, *Danthonia.* . . Oat grass, wild o. g.

d A similar oatlike grass such as *Avenochloa hookeri,* a **needlegrass 1** (here: *Stipa avenacea*), or a **spike-grass** (here: *Uniola* spp); see quots. Cf **black oat grass, sea oat**
　　1837 (1962) Williams *Territory FL* 82, Oat grass. Uniola paniculata.

1884 Vasey *Ag. Grasses* 92, *Uniola latifolia.* (Broad-flowered Fescue grass.) . . It is called by some *wild fescue* or *oat grass.* **1906** Rydberg *Flora CO* 23, *Stipa.* . . Oat-grass. **1911** *Century Dict. Suppl.,* Oatgrass. . . *American oat-grass, Avena Hookeri* [=*Avenochloa hookeri*], a species resembling the European *A. pratensis,* found on the eastern slopes of the Rocky Mountains. It is useful for grazing where abundant and may deserve cultivation.

oather See **other**

oatlage n [Blend of *oats* + *silage*] Cf **haylage**
Silage made from oats; oats grown for silage.
   1968 WI Statist. Reporting Serv. *Report* 29 July [2] neWI, Put our oats in Harvestore as oatlage. **1972** *Ibid* 22 May 2, Discing over 40 acres of alfalfa and reseeding to alfalfa and oatlage.

oat midget, oat mite See **oats bug 1**

oats n pl, but sg in constr
1 Porridge made from ground or rolled oats; oatmeal. **chiefly W Midl** See Map Note: *Oatmeal* in this sense is not regional.
   [**1902** *DN* 2.240 sIL, *Oats,* n. pl. as sg. Shown to be singular by pronoun, as 'that oats.'] **1954** *Harder Coll.* cwTN, Oats. . . A hot, cooked breakfast cereal. **c1960** *Wilson Coll.* csKY, Oats, or *rolled oats,* or *oatmeal.* . . Common as a "cooked cereal." **1965–70** *DARE* (Qu. H23, . . *Hot cooked breakfast cereal*) 43 Infs, **chiefly W Midl,** Oats; 26 Infs, **chiefly W Midl,** Rolled oats; IA13, Bowl of oats; MO36, Cooked oats; MA1, Cracked oats. [Of all Infs responding to the question, 27% were gs educ or less; of those giving these responses, 52% were gs educ or less.]

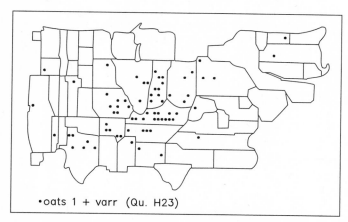

•oats 1 + varr (Qu. H23)

2 Boldness, assertiveness. [Prob < *feel one's oats* to feel energetic]
   1970 *DARE* (Qu. GG5, *When someone does something unexpectedly bold or forward* . . *"Well, she certainly has a lot of _____."*) Inf NJ69, Oats.

3 A wild rice (here: *Zizania aquatica*). Cf **duck oats, water oat, wild ~**
   1982 Elman *Hunter's Field Guide* 326, When an old Connecticut pusher mentions oats, he means wild rice. The best way to hunt soras is to push through rice at high tide.

oats bird See **oat bird**

oats bug n
1 also *oat beetle, ~ bug, ~ fly, oats louse, oat(s) midget, oat mite, ~ thrips:* The grain thrips (*Limothrips cerealium*) or a similar insect; see quots. **chiefly N Midl** See Map
   1939 *Hench Coll.* ePA, Jack Finley was talking about these small flies and how they sting. Here he calls them harvest flies. But in eastern Penna., where he worked once, he says they were called interchangeably harvest or oat flies. They are small and on your hand look like a piece of string. **1954** Borror–DeLong *Intro. Insects* 197, The corn or oat thrips, *Limothrips cerealium* . . , is a dark brown to black thrips, 1.2 to 1.4 millimeters in length, that feeds on various cereals and grasses; it is sometimes quite abundant, and may bite man. **1966–70** *DARE* (Qu. R10, *Very small flies that don't sting, often seen hovering in large groups or bunches outdoors in summer*) Inf IL130, Oat bugs—get on your skin; PA44, Oat flies; PA1, Oats midget; (Qu. R11, *A very tiny fly that you can hardly see, but that stings*) Inf MI116, Oat beetle—crawls and bites; IL130, IN14, Oat bug(s); MO10, We have what we call an oat bug here; OH90, Oat bug—very small, out in the field; OH4, Oat fly;

PA246, Oat midget—black, one-eighth inch long, bites; IL76, I don't know a name for them—might be oat mite; IN35, Oats lice; (Qu. R12, . . *Other kinds of flies*) Inf MO15, Oat bug; IL56, We call the oats bug no-see-um because they fly right through the screen and you don't see them come in; (Qu. R13, *Flies that come to meat or fruit*) Inf PA202, Oats bug; (Qu. R27) Inf MD29, Oats midget; (Qu. R30, . . *Kinds of beetles;* not asked in early QRs) Inf NJ48, Oats bug—has funny smell when squashed; PA210, Oats bug. **1982** *Barrick Coll.* csPA, Oats bug—small insect prevalent at time of oats harvest.

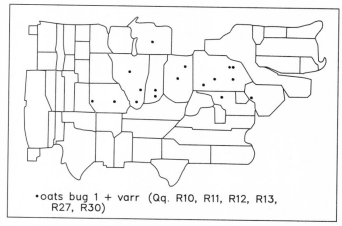

•oats bug 1 + varr (Qq. R10, R11, R12, R13, R27, R30)

2 Prob a **cicada.** Cf **harvest fly**
   1968 *DARE* (Qu. R8, . . *Kinds of creatures that make a clicking or shrilling or chirping kind of sound*) Inf PA143, Oats bug.

oats louse, oats midget See **oats bug 1**

oatsmobile See **oat burner**

oats, pease(e), beans, and barley grow(s) n Also *oats, peas, beans; old sweet beans and the barley grows* [*EDD oats and beans and barley* (at *oat* sb. 1.(20))]
A children's singing game played in a circle.
   1883 Newell *Games & Songs* 80, *Oats, Pease, Beans, and Barley Grows.* . . The ring circles, singing, about a child in the centre. **1909** (1923) Bancroft *Games* 287, *Oats, Peas, Beans.* . . The players form a ring, clasping hands, and circle about one of their number who has been chosen to stand in the center. **1950** *WELS* (*Games in which the players form a ring and either sing or recite a rhyme*) 1 Inf, csWI, Oats, peas, beans, and barley grows. **1957** *Sat. Eve. Post Letters* NY, "Oats, pease, beans & barley grows / Where you nor I nor nobody knows["] repeated ad infinitum then "a-waiting for a partner" repeated until a selected girl stands before a boy—then "Now you're married you must obey / You must be true to all you say / And live together all your life / And now pronounce you man and wife." **1967–69** *DARE* (Qu. EE1) Infs CA8, PA181, Oats, peas, beans, and barley grow; (Qu. EE33, . . *Outdoor games* . . *that children play*) Inf AL37, Old sweet beans and the barley grows—a piece of nonsense verse that children sang while playing a game very much like ring-around-the-rosy. The circle was formed around a couple in the middle who went through a mock wedding while the others sang.

oat thrips See **oats bug 1**

ob See **of** prep

obedient plant n Also *obedience* [See quots 1901, 1949] **Sth** =**false dragonhead 1.**
   1900 Lyons *Plant Names* 287, *P[hysostegia] Virginiana* . . False Dragon-head, Obedient-plant. **1901** Lounsberry *S. Wild Flowers* 452, Obedient Plant. . . A curious point about the delicate flowers is that they seem to be overpowered by lassitude. They have no elasticity. So when one is turned with the thumb and finger to another than its original position in the spike, it makes no effort to rebound, but remains most obediently wherever it is put. **1949** Moldenke *Amer. Wild Flowers* 297, In the southeastern part of our area the naturalist is sooner or later shown certain curious plants which the natives call *obedient-plants.* The purplish pink flowers, about an inch long, are borne in rather dense, terminal wands. If a flower is unobtrusively pressed out of position it will speedily return to its former position as though in obedience to the command of the demonstrator who pretends vociferously that the elaborate beckoning motion of his finger brings it back! **1955** *S. Folkl. Qrly.* 19.235, *Obedient Plant* (Physostegia denticulata) obeys the touch of hand or wind, the

flowers changing their position at the slightest pressure. **1972** Brown *Wildflowers LA* 159, Obedient Plant—*Physostegia digitalis. Ibid,* Obedient Plant—*Physostegia virginiana.* **1976** Bailey-Bailey *Hortus Third* 869, *Physostegia. . .* Obedience, obedient plant.

o-be-joyful n Also sp *oh-be-joyful;* for addit varr see quots **scattered, but esp NEast** *somewhat old-fash*

Liquor, wine.

  1830 *Greensborough* (N.C.) *Patriot* 4 Aug. 4/2 *(DA),* They didn't come to, till the old woman and her darter poured some o be joy full down their throates. **c1830** in 1939 NY Hist. Soc. *Qrly.* 23.16 **NY,** Most people supply themselves with these cakes . . (and also a good share of the "O! be joyful") wherewith to regale themselves and friends. **1846** Crawford *Hist. White Mts.* 45 **NH,** There I was loaded . . with a plenty of what some call . . "O be joyful." **1884** Hill *Tales Pioneers* 100 **cCO,** They joined in a little 'O-be-joyful,' to bind the bargain. [**1894** *DN* 1.332 **NJ,** *O be joyful:* hilariously drunk.] **1912** *DN* 3.568, *O-be-joyful. . .* Humorous for intoxicant. Reported from Long Island [NY], Missouri, and Vermont, but not from Illinois or Pennsylvania. **1914** *DN* 4.77 **ME, nNH,** *Oh-be-joyful.* Also, *oh-be-rich-an'-happy.* Hard liquor. **1922** (1926) Cady *Rhymes VT* 131, A black and tan / Container 'neath his lift-up seat / With Oh-be-joyful ran. **1932** *DN* 6.283 **swCT,** *O-be-joyful.* Intoxicating liquor. **1968–70** *DARE* (Qu. DD21a, *General words . . for any kind of liquor*) Inf **NY202,** O-be-joyful; (Qu. DD27, *. . Nicknames . . for wine*) Infs **NY202, WV3, 13,** O-be-joyful; **VA69,** O-be-happy. **1984** Gilmore *Ozark Baptizings* 170 **MO,** One issue of the *Houston Herald,* that of December 29, 1898, . . [reported that] Two Taney County boys took on a "little too much of the 'oh-be-joyful' " . ., but the only person injured was an onlooker.

obelia n [Var of **lobelia**] Cf **highbelia**

=**Indian tobacco 1.**

  1971 Krochmal *Appalachia Med. Plants* 164, *Lobelia inflata . .* Common Names: Indian tobacco, asthma weed, . . Indian Tobacco lobelia, lobelia, obelia, pukeweed [etc].

ober See **over**

obfusticated adj [Var of *obfuscated; EDD* 1888] Cf **busticate, confisticate, discomgollifusticated,** *exfluncticated* (at **exflunct**), **flusticated**

See quots.

  1909 *DN* 3.353 **eAL, wGA,** *Obfusticated. . .* Excited, flustrated. Facetious. **1966** Barnes–Jensen *Dict. UT Slang* 32, *Obfusticated . .* bewildered, overshadowed, eclipsed. "When she got up to speak in tongues she seemed obfusticated." The expression is obsolescent.

obispo pine n [From its discovery in 1835 near the mission of San Luis *Obispo* de Tolosa, California]

=**bishop pine.**

  1884 Sargent *Forests of N. Amer.* 200, *Pinus muricata. . .* Obispo Pine. **1890** *Century Dict.* 4496, *Obispo pine,* a local Californian tree, *Pinus muricata,* of no great value. **1897** Sudworth *Arborescent Flora* 28 **CA,** *Pinus muricata . .* California Swamp Pine . . Obispo Pine. **1908** Britton *N. Amer. Trees* 49, Prickle Cone Pine—*Pinus muricata. . .* It is said to be a very desirable pine for planting in the Pacific States and is known by many names, as: California swamp pine . . Obispo pine . . Bishop's pine, and Anthony's pine.

oblige v, hence adj *obliged* Usu |ə'blaɪʤ|; also **chiefly Sth, S Midl** |ə'bliʤ|, aphet |bliʤ|, and assim |(ə)'bliʤ| (for *obliged*) Pronc-spp *obleege, obleadge;* for past ppl, pronc-sp *ableeze;* aphet *bleedged, blee(d)st, bleedzed, bleege(d), bleeze, blidge(d), blige* [Until at least the end of the 18th cent [ə'bliʤ] competed with [ə'blaɪʤ] as the std English pronunciation.]

Std senses, var forms.

  1767 in 1956 Eliason *Tarheel Talk* 315 **cNC,** Obleadge. **1828** Webster *Amer. Dict., Oblige, . .* pronounced as written, not *obleege.* **1840** (1847) Longstreet *GA Scenes* 61, *Lay* still and take it! you *bleege* to have it! **1851** Hooper *Widow Rugby's Husband* 40 **AL,** He's obleeged to stay 'bout home. **1861** Holmes *Venner* 1.121 **NEng,** Very well, much obleeged to you. **1871** Eggleston *Hoosier Schoolmaster* 45 **sIN,** I'm obleeged to Mr. Means fer this honor. **a1883** (1911) Bagby *VA Gentleman* 262, "This here ridge ar called 'Venjunce Ridge.' " "Indeed! Why so?" "They was bleest to name it somethin', I reckon, and that's what it took its name from." **1887** (1967) Harris *Free Joe* 57 **GA** [Black], But I 'uz mos' 'blige' ter do it. *Ibid* 87, De Tomlinsons is bleeze to do like Christun people. *Ibid* 110, You'd be ableeze to ketch 'em ef

you went thar. **1893** Shands *MS Speech* 20, *Bleedged* or *bleedzed. . .* Negro for *obliged.* These forms are common in the majority of the Southern States. **1899** Chesnutt *Conjure Woman* 42 **csNC** [Black], He wuz bleedst ter make de trade. **1899** (1912) Green *VA Folk-Speech* 303, *Obleege. . .* To oblige. **1908** *DN* 3.291 **eAL, wGA,** *Bleege(d). . .* Obliged. A negroism, but used by illiterate whites. Also *blidge(d)* [blaɪʤ]. **1928** *AmSp* 3.403 **Ozarks,** *Little, itch, inch, idiot,* and *oblige* have the sound of *ee,* while such words as *bitch, hitch,* and *pitch* keep the standard vowel. **1930** Stoney–Shelby *Black Genesis* 6 **seSC,** I is jis' bleege to cut you a mout'. **1934** *WV Review* Dec 78 **WV,** *Obleege* for *oblige,* as we still hear it now and then, was formerly the only English pronunciation of that word. **1952** Brown *NC Folkl.* 1.570, *Obleege* [o'bliʤ]. . . General. Illiterate.

oblige n Also *obligement* Also, prob by metanalysis, *blige*

An obligation.

  1903 *DN* 2.307 **seMO,** *Blige. . .* Obligation. 'I had a blige to go.' **1913** Kephart *Highlanders* 285 **sAppalachians,** We have oblige to take care on him. **1985** *NC Folkl. Jrl.* 33.39 **wNC** (as of c1920) [Black], "Well, Miz Wyman, I had an obleegement to go to myself," meaning she had a sudden call of nature.

obsquatulate, obsquotulate See **absquatulate**

obstropolous adj Also *obstriperous, obstroperous* Also sp *obstropelous, obstropulous, upstropolis, upstroppelous* [Varr of *obstreperous; OED* (at *obstreperous*) 1727 →] *old-fash*

  1795 Dearborn *Columbian Grammar* 139, *List of Improprieties. . .* Upstroppelous for Obstreperous. **1815** Humphreys *Yankey in England* 107, *Obstropulous,* obstreperous. **1818** Fessenden *Ladies Monitor* 172 **VT,** *Provincial words and phrases . .* to be avoided. . . *Obstropolous* for obstreperous. **1848** in 1935 *AmSp* 10.42 **Nantucket MA,** *Obstriperous.* Bad, obstinate. **1856** Simms *Eutaw* 59 **SC,** We're only taking care of you in these obstropolous times of needcessity. **1858** Hammett *Piney Woods Tavern* 291, You needn't tell me that, you obstropelous young sinner. **1890** *DN* 1.68 **KY,** *Obstroperous:* for *obstreperous.* **1912** Green *VA Folk-Speech* 303, *Obstropolous. . .* Obstinate; resisting. **1977** *Yankee* Jan 73 **csME,** But if you're really upstropolis you might muckle a hold on the scruff of his neck and hist him.

obuh See **over**

ocateo See **ocotillo**

occasion n, v Also aphet form *'casion*

A Form.

  1843 (1916) Hall *New Purchase* 153, Sheepish young chaps usually hang back, however hungry, and say, "Oh! there's no 'casion:" after which they give an acquiescing cough or two . . and then drop, as if shot down, into a seat [at the dinner table]. **1899** Chesnutt *Conjure Woman* 17 **csNC** [Black], Mars Dugal' did n' hab no 'casion ter fine no mo' fault. **1927** Adams *Congaree* 14 **cSC** [Black], Dey tells me it was folks like Ole Sister 'casion Christ to be crucify.

B As noun.

In phrr *(there's) no occasion:* Used as a formulaic expression of good manners; see quots. Cf **care** v **B1**

  1843 [see **A** above]. **1952** Brown *NC Folkl.* 1.570, *Occasion, no. . .* Equivalent to "You're welcome," "Don't mention it," etc. Used in response to "Thank you."—General. Old people.

occomy See **alchemy**

ocean catfish n

1 The Atlantic wolffish *(Anarhichas lupus).*

  1933 John G. Shedd Aquarium *Guide* 152, *Anarhichas lupas* [sic]—Common Wolffish. . . They are sold under the name "Ocean Whitefish" or "Catfish." It is a northern fish, fairly common on the fishing banks off the New England shore. When caught, it viciously snaps at everything within reach and unless quickly dispatched by the fisherman, can inflict considerable damage with its tusk-like teeth. **1955** Zim–Shoemaker *Fishes* 146, The Atlantic Wolffish is. . . good eating; it is caught commercially in quantity and often sold as "ocean catfish."

2 The California **scorpion fish** *(Scorpaena guttata).*

  [**1953** Roedel *Common Fishes CA* 137, *Scorpaena guttata. . .* Of minor commercial significance with heaviest landings in the Los Angeles region. Sold entirely in the fresh fish markets. . . *Unauthorized Name:* Bullhead.] **1967** *DARE* (Qu. P2, *. . Kinds of saltwater fish caught around here . . good to eat*) Inf **CA23,** Bullhead or ocean catfish.

ocean foam See **sea foam**

ocean goldfish See **goldfish 1**

ocean is stormy, the n

A children's game; see quot.

1968 *DARE* (Qu. EE2, *Games that have one extra player—when a signal is given, the players change places, and the extra one tries to get a place*) Inf **GA**18, The ocean is stormy.

ocean perch n

A **rockfish** (here: *Sebastes* spp): usu the **rosefish** of the Atlantic coast or *S. alutus* of the Pacific coast, but see quot 1991.

1955 Zim–Shoemaker *Fishes* 129, Ocean Perch, sometimes called Rosefish, grows to about 20 in. and weighs to 5 lb. It is very abundant and recently has become an important commercial species—more valuable than cod and a source of frozen filets and fish-sticks. **1960** Amer. Fisheries Soc. *List Fishes* 37, Redfish or ocean perch . . *Sebastes marinus*. . . Pacific ocean perch . . *Sebastes alutus*. **1966–67** *DARE* (Qu. P2, . . *Kinds of saltwater fish caught around here . . good to eat*) Infs **CA**25, 31, **ME**16, 22, Ocean perch. **1991** Amer. Fisheries Soc. *Common Names Fishes* 39, *Sebastes alutus* . . Pacific ocean perch. *Ibid* 85, The market names redfish and ocean perch apply to all Atlantic species of *Sebastes* including the three [=*Sebastes fasciatus, S. mentella,* and *S. norvegicus*] in our region.

oceans n pl [Engl dial] **scattered, but less freq S Midl, SW** See Map

Large quantities or numbers.

1899 (1912) Green *VA Folk-Speech* 303, Oceans. . . A very large quantity. "Oceans of money." **1905** *DN* 3.63 **eNE**, Oceans, oodles, oogens, or *dead oogens*. . . Large quantities. "Oceans of money." **1912** *DN* 3.584 **wIN**, Oceans. . . Lots; a great deal. **1941** *LANE* Map 416 *(A lot of fun)* 2 infs, **cs,seNH**, Oceans of fun. **1942** ME Univ. *Studies* 56.79, "Enough to sink a ship." A hyperbolic expression for a large quantity. "Oceans." **1950** *WELS (A large amount or number, more than enough: "He's got _____ of time.")* 3 Infs, **WI**, Oceans. **1965–70** *DARE* (Qu. LL8a, *A large amount or number: More than enough . . "He's got _____ of time.")* 51 Infs, **scattered, but less freq S Midl, SW**, Oceans; (Qu. U38a, . . *A great deal of money: "He's got _____ [of money].")* 15 Infs, **chiefly Nth, Mid Atl**, Oceans; (Qu. LL9a, *As much as you need or more . . "We've got _____ of apples.")* 12 Infs, **esp Nth**, Oceans; (Qu. LL8b, . . *A large number . . "She has a whole _____ of cousins.")* Inf **DC**3, Oceans; (Qu. LL9b, . . *All you need or more . . "She's got clothes _____.")* Inf **MO**9, Oceans. [61 of 74 total Infs old]

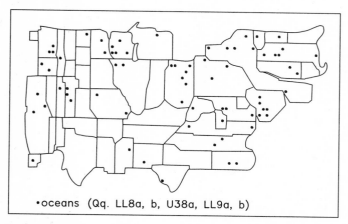

•oceans (Qq. LL8a, b, U38a, LL9a, b)

ocean spray n

A white-flowered shrub of the genus *Holodiscus*, native chiefly from the Rocky Mountains westward. Also called **creambush, mountain spray, rock spirea.** For other names of var spp see **arrowwood g, false meadowsweet, foam bush, meadowsweet 3**

1906 U.S. Natl. Museum *Contrib. Herbarium* 11.330 **WA**, *Schizonotus discolor*. . . Ocean spray. **1937** U.S. Forest Serv. *Range Plant Hdbk.* B147, Oceanspray ranges from British Columbia to western Montana and California. In California it is distributed from Los Angeles northward through the Coast Range, with occasional occurrence in the Sierra Nevada Mountains. **1940** Writers' Program *Oregon* 20, In the spring and early summer . . sweet syringa, ocean spray, and Douglas spirea form streamside thickets of riotous blossom. **1960** Vines *Trees SW* 428,

Holodiscus dumosus. . . is also known under the vernacular names of Cream-bush, Foam-bush, Ocean-spray, and Mountain-spray. **1976** Elmore *Shrubs & Trees SW* 145, *Holodiscus dumosus*. . . When it grows on the coast it is known as ocean-spray. **1976** Bailey–Bailey *Hortus Third* 567, [*Holodiscus*] *discolor* . . Creambush, ocean-spray. . . S. Ore. to s. Calif.

ocean sunfish n

=**mola,** usu *Mola mola* which is also called **globefish 2.**

1906 NJ State Museum *Annual Rept. for 1905* 368, *Mola mola* . . Ocean Sun Fish. **1911** U.S. Bur. Census *Fisheries 1908* 317, The ocean sunfish *(Mola mola)* is found off the entire coast of the United States; also called "headfish." It reaches a weight of 500 pounds, and yields a large quantity of valuable oil. **1955** Zim–Shoemaker *Fishes* 139, The Ocean Sunfish is also called Headfish, for its head dominates the entire body. **1960** Gosline–Brock *Hawaiian Fishes* 303, Family *Molidae* (Ocean Sunfishes). . . The ocean sunfishes are peculiar oceanic fishes that look as if they had had their tails bitten off. **1983** *Audubon Field Guide N. Amer. Fishes* 766, Ocean Sunfish *(Mola mola)*. . . These fishes . . are a familiar sight drifting lazily on the surface of the water during the late summer. **1991** Amer. Fisheries Soc. *Common Names Fishes* 70, *Mola mola* . . ocean sunfish.

‡**ocean tea** n Cf **branch water 2**

1966 *DARE* (Qu. H74b, . . *Coffee . . very weak*) Inf **NC**44, Ocean tea.

ocean trout n

A **menhaden 1** (here: *Brevoortia tyrannus*).

1878 *Amer. Naturalist* 736, Among the manufacturers in Port Monmouth, N.J., who prepare the menhaden as an article of food, a number of . . names are in use, such as . . "ocean trout." **1884** Goode *Fisheries U.S.* 1.569, The Menhaden has at least thirty popular names, most of them limited in their use within narrow geographical boundaries. . . A number of trade names are employed by the manufacturers in New Jersey who can this fish for food; these are "American Sardine," "American Club-fish," "Shadine," and "Ocean Trout." **1906** NJ State Museum *Annual Rept. for 1905* 103, *Brevoortia tyrannus* . . Menhaden. Bunker . . Ocean Trout . . Banker. **1984** *DARE* File **Chesapeake Bay** [Watermen's vocab], Ocean trout.

ocean wave n Also *ocean well* [Perh infl by *ocean wave* a square dance step with undulating motions]

See quots.

1966–67 *DARE* (Qu. EE32, *A homemade merry-go-round*) Infs **AZ**8, **MS**8, Ocean wave. **1967** *DARE* Tape **AZ**8, The ocean wave is a homemade or welded together circular sort of swing thing that is assembled so that there is a seat made in a circular form that many children can sit on. It is attached to a center post with bearings at the top so that the circle may swing and go as a merry-go-round would go. **1986** Pederson *LAGS Concordance,* 1 inf, **csTX**, Ocean well = merry-go-round.

ocelot n [*OED* 1774 →]

Std: a wild, spotted cat *(Felis pardalis)* native to the southwestern US. Also called **leopard cat 1, tiger cat**

ocochilla See **ocotillo**

Oconee bells n [Prob in ref to the *Oconee* River in Georgia]

A wildflower *(Shortia galacifolia)* native to the southern Appalachians. Also called **coltsfoot 6, jackscrew-root**

1933 Small *Manual SE Flora* 1019, *S[herwoodia] galacifolia* . . Shortia. Oconee-bells. One-flower Coltsfoot. **1949** Moldenke *Amer. Wild Flowers* 158, Every naturalist traveler in the mountains of North and South Carolina looks forward with keen anticipation to seeing the famous oconee-bells . . in its native haunts. **1953** Greene–Blomquist *Flowers South* 93, Oconee-Bells. . . Only 3 species of this interesting genus exist in the world, 2 in the Orient and one in the gorges of the s. Appalachian Mountains on both sides of the border between N.C. and S.C. **1956** Savage *River* 275, A farm boy brought home to his amateur botanist father a clump of galaxlike plants he had dug from the banks of the Catawba near Marion, North Carolina. So the lovely plant commonly known as Oconee Bells was rediscovered. **1964** Batson *Wild Flowers SC* 89, Oconee-bells, Jackscrew-root. . . On wooded banks of mountain streams in a few little-frequented areas. Spring. North and South Carolina. **1967** *DARE* (Qu. S26e) Inf **SC**32, Oconee bells—a mountain flower. **1967** *DARE* FW Addit **SC**41, Oconee bells—also called shortia. **1975** Duncan–Foote *Wildflowers SE* 118, Oconee-bells. One of our rarest wildflowers. . . Rich mountain woods of only seven counties in Ga, SC and NC. **1979** Niering–Olmstead *Audubon Guide*

N. Amer. Wildflowers E. Region 490, *Oconee Bells.* . . White, bell-shaped, *solitary flowers* hang from erect, leafless stalks.

ocote n [MexSpan < Nahuatl *ocotl* torch] Cf **torch pine**
A **piñon** (here: *Pinus cembroides*) or other resinous **pine**; also the wood of such a tree.

   1911 *Century Dict. Suppl.*, *Ocote.* . . The common Mexican or candlewood pine. . . In New Mexico the word is used to designate very resinous pine-wood. **1932** Bentley *Spanish Terms* 173, Ocote (*Spanish* [o:'ko:te:]; *English, the same and* [o:'ko:ti:]). A resinous species of pine found in parts of Mexico. The word, being a specialized name, is not encountered frequently. **1946** Waters *Colorado* 316, Now in the flicker of ocote torches at the street turnings. **1960** Vines *Trees SW* 15, Mexican Pinyon Pine—*Pinus cembroides.* . . Other vernacular names are Nut Pine . . and Ocote.

ocotillo n Also *ocateo, ocochilla, ocotilla* [MexSpan *ocotillo, ocotilla, ochotilla,* dimins of **ocote**]
A spiny resinous shrub (*Fouquieria splendens*) native to the desert Southwest. Also called **candle cactus, candlewood 3, coachwhip, flaming sword, Jacob's staff 1, Joseph's ~, slimwood, vine cactus, wolf's candle**

   1856 *Wide West* (San Francisco CA) Oct 4/6, Aside from the grass, there is a shrub called the . . *Ocetilla* [sic]. **1864** *Harper's New Mth. Mag.* 29.697 **AZ,** Passing through some dense thickets of mesquit and ocochilla, the struggling family found themselves at the foot of a rocky bluff. **1887** in 1921 Thorp *Songs Cowboys* 93 **SW,** *Little Adobe Casa* [title]. . . The roof is ocateo,/. . . In my little adobe casa on the plains. **1892** *DN* 1.192 **TX,** *Ocotillo:* a tree or shrub of the tamarisk family with long racemes of bright scarlet flowers (*Fouquiera splendens*). **1919** Chase *CA Desert* 50, The ocotillo, *Fouquieria splendens* (commonly but wrongly taken for a cactus), is to me the most striking and characteristic of the desert plants. **1929** Dobie *Vaquero* 202, Again, far out in the sandy draws of the Sonoran desert against the Gulf of California the mesquite's leaves are very small. . . [H]ere, too, the top of the tree is a bunch of dozens of stems, or limbs, that run up from the trunk-base, sprangle out like the stem of the *ocotillo* and, when the tree . . attains age and size, bend over like the limbs of a weeping willow or a pepper tree. **1939** Pickwell *Deserts* 65, Ocotillo (*Fouquieria splendens*) is a Spanish word meaning "little pine," but to the ordinary observer the thorny stems of this most unusual plant look more like a very queer cactus than a pine. **1948** *Nat. Hist.* 57.181 **Desert SW,** The Ocotillo is frankly red. **1949** Curtin *By the Prophet* 89 **AZ,** The term *ocotl* is Aztec, *illo* the Spanish diminutive. . . [A]s pitch pine, *ocote,* was made into torches by the Mexicans, so were the thin dry wands of ocotillo. **1961** Douglas *My Wilderness* 81 **AZ,** There are scatterings of ocotillo, a dozen or more stalks bending gracefully outward from a common root and some of them even in February showing their first green leaves. **1967–69** *DARE* (Qu. S26a, . . *Wildflowers.* . . *Roadside flowers*) Inf **CA**94, Ocotillo; (Qu. S26b, *Wildflowers that grow in water or wet places*) Inf **TX**66, Ocotilla; (Qu. S26e, *Other wildflowers not yet mentioned;* not asked in early QRs) Infs **CA**4, 91, Ocotillo; (Qu. L65, . . *Kinds of fences*) Inf **CA**87, Ocotilla—in the desert—a willow-like stick with thorns, threaded into chicken wire. **1967** *DARE* Wildfl QR (Wills–Irwin) Pl.26A Inf **TX**44, Ocotillo. **c1979** TX Dept. Highways *Flowers* 4, Ocotillo (oh-ko-TEE-yo). . . a native of West Texas, . . blooms in April and May, sporadically thereafter following rains.

ocra See **okra**

ocred See **awkward**

ocry See **okra**

October n
1 See **October bean.**
2 See **October rose.**

October bean n Also *October* chiefly **sAppalachians, IN** See Map Cf **cornfield bean, cranberry ~**
A cultivated bean (*Phaseolus vulgaris* var).

   1937 *Hall Coll.* **wNC,** *Octobers.* . . late beans, shelled. "October beans" or "Octobers" are "cornfield beans," according to [an informant]. **1954** *Harder Coll.* **cwTN,** October beans. . . White with a red eye. **1965–70** *DARE* (Qu. I15, *Some of the beans that you eat in the pod have yellow pods; you call these* ——) Inf **NC**34, October bean; (Qu. I17, *Beans* . . *that are dark red when they are dry*) Infs **IN**19, **NC**63, October (beans); **VA**9, Octobers; (Qu. I19, *Small white beans with a black spot where they were joined to the pod*) Inf **NC**55, Octobers; (Qu. I20, . . *Kinds of beans*) Infs **IN**7, 30, **VA**19, 24, October

beans; **KY**50, October beans—good green, also good dried and then [they] were gray with dark brown specks; larger than navy [beans], round, and very rich; ripen late; **TN**11, October bean (dry bean); he eats very good while he's in the shelly stage; **VA**7, October beans—tender; **VA**42, October beans—pink hulls with green stripes; are shelled though can be eaten as snaps. **1978** *Wanigan Catalog* 15, *October bean.* . . This strain is a white, size 5 seed on short poles. A North Carolina home saved bean, it is late here [=MA]. **1982** *Smithsonian Letters* **cnWV,** Enclosed please find evidence for cranberry bean, alias October beans. One of my students found this in a supermarket in Morgantown. **1990** *Seed Savers Yearbook* 47, [Dry pole bean:] *October* . . pink-tan background with maroon specks and stripes, prolific vines with 6-7 beans per pod, good flavor, cooked beans have very tender skin, . . require strong support, often planted in corn, . . known in VA area for 60 years.

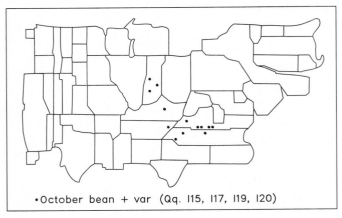

•October bean + var (Qq. I15, I17, I19, I20)

October berry n
A blackberry (here: *Rubus canadensis*).
   1916 *Torreya* 16.238 **NC,** *Rubus canadensis.* . . Bear berry, October berry.

October bloom(er) See **October rose**

October duck n Also *October redlegs*
A **black duck 1** (here: *Anas rubripes*).
   1955 MA Audubon Soc. *Bulletin* 39.314 **MA,** *Black Duck.* . . October Duck, October Redlegs.

October flower n
1 A **jointweed 1** (here: *Polygonella polygama*). [See quot 1901]
   1901 Mohr *Plant Life AL* 486, *Polygonella polygama.* . . October Flower. . . Flowers white to pink. October, November. **1933** Small *Manual SE Flora* 449, *P[olygonella] polygama* . . October-flower. **1953** Greene–Blomquist *Flowers South* 28, Joint-Wood, October-Flower. . . The copiously branched plants of *Polygonella* covered with white, persistent flowers are attractive on open shrubby pinelands and sandhills in the autumn when most plants are through blooming. **1975** Duncan–Foote *Wildflowers SE* 28, October-flower—*Polygonella polygama.*
2 A **milkwort** (here: *Polygala polygama*).
   1940 Clute *Amer. Plant Names* 267, *Polygala polygama.* October flower.
3 See **October rose.**

October grape n Cf **coon grape 1, fall ~, frost ~, raccoon ~**
A **fox grape 1** or **2.**
   1970 *DARE* (Qu. I46, . . *Kinds of fruits that grow wild around here*) Inf **VA**42, October grapes—small and sour, [same as] coon grapes.

October peat (or pink) See **October rose**

October redlegs See **October duck**

October rose n Also *October, ~ bloom(er), ~ flower, ~ peat, ~ pink* Cf **fall rose**
Usu a chrysanthemum (*Chrysanthemum* spp), but also occas an aster (*Aster* spp) or similar composite plant.
   [**1914** Saunders *With Flowers in CA* 190, Her chrysanthemum plants just started into vigorous growth had, in her speech, a more understandable name—*octubres,* or as we should say, Octobers.] **1949** *WELS Suppl.* **seMI,** Small chrysanthemums. . . I first heard them called October roses in Holland, Mich. 25 years ago where the population is nearly 100% of Holland Dutch descent. *Ibid* **cwWI,** Small mums—often

called October roses by older people. **1950** *Ibid* **csWI,** October roses = small white late-blooming chrysanthemums. Term esp. common among older people. **1950** *WELS (Other names you have for small chrysanthemums that bloom late in the fall)* 3 Infs, **WI,** October rose(s). **1954** *PADS* 21.33 **SC,** *October flowers. . .* Chrysanthemums. Also *Octobers.* **1965–70** *DARE* (Qu. S25, *. . The small wild chrysanthemum-like flowers . . that bloom in fields late in the fall)* 12 Infs, **scattered, but esp Sth, S Midl,** October roses; **SC67,** Octobers; **SC70,** October blooms; **IL95,** October bloomer [FW sugg]; **VA69,** October peats; **NC6,** October pink; (Qu. S26c, *Wildflowers that grow in woods)* Inf **FL22,** October flowers. **1967** *DARE* FW Addit **LA1,** *October pinks*—old-fashioned for chrysanthemum.

octopus n Cf **spider**

An elastic cord with hooks on either end, used to strap things in place.

1981 *DARE* File **Chicago IL,** Surely everyone knows that what is described [=a bungee cord] is properly known as an octopus! Long live the whatchamacallit.

octopus bite n

=monkey bite 1.

1970 *DARE* (Qu. X39, *A mark on the skin where somebody has sucked it hard and brought the blood to the surface)* Inf **NJ63,** Octopus bite.

octopus tree n Also *octopus plant* [See quot 1948] **esp HI**

An introduced red-flowered evergreen tree (*Brassaia actinophylla*).

1948 Neal *In Gardens HI* 575, *Octopus tree. Brassaia actinophylla. . .* Like arms of an octopus, stiff, radiating, floral branches to 2 feet long spread widely, bearing sucker-like prominences or heads of small red flowers, which usually can be found in Hawaii from April to October. **1967** *DARE* (Qu. T16, *. . Kinds of trees . . 'special')* Inf **HI2,** Octopus plant (because inflorescence has tentacle-like branches). **1976** Bailey-Bailey *Hortus Third* 177, *Australian umbrella tree, . . octopus tree. . .* Widely cult. as a landscape tree in Hawaii, s. Fla., and Calif.

ódale See **ándale**

odd and even See **odd or even**

odd as Dick's hatband See **Dick's hatband 1**

odd-come-short n [Cf *EDD* odd-come-short-lies "an occasion or day close at hand," *odd-come-shorts* "small miscellaneous articles; odd fragments"] *old-fash*

1 An idle moment; an unspecified day or time—usu in phrr *one* (or *some) of these odd-come-shorts* sometime, one of these days. **chiefly Sth, S Midl**

1883 (1971) Harris *Nights with Remus* 5 **GA** [Black], Some er dese odd-come-shorts he gwine ter call en pay he 'specks. *Ibid* 170, One time, endurin' [=during] de odd-come-shorts, ole Jedge B'ar sont wud dat one er his chilluns done bin tooken wid a sickness. [Footnote to *odd-come-shorts:*] Sometime, any time, no time. Thus: "Run fetch me de ax, en I'll wait on you one er deze odd-come-shorts." **1899** (1912) Green *VA Folk-Speech* 303, *Odd-come-short. . .* Some day soon to come; . . some time; any time. "I'll give it back to you some of these odd-come-shorts." **1953** Randolph-Wilson *Down in Holler* 267 **Ozarks,** *Odd-come-short. . .* An indefinite time, an odd moment. "Thanks for the loan of the book; I'll fetch it back, one of these odd-come-shorts." **1984** Wilder *You All Spoken Here* 63 **Sth,** *Odd come shorts:* An indefinite period; an odd moment.

2 An eccentric person.

1967 Williams *Greenbones* 195 **GA** (as of c1910), People come off and on, the curious, the out-of-place, the odd-come-shorts, the lonely.

odd corner n

=long corner.

1958 McCulloch *Woods Words* 125 **Pacific NW,** *Odd corner*—A long corner of timber; a hard-to-reach spot on a logging show.

odder See **other**

‡odd house n

1969 *DARE* (Qu. M21b, *Joking names for an outside toilet building)* Inf **MI93,** Odd house.

oddling n

See quot 1953.

1941 Stuart *Men of Mts.* 85 **neKY,** That's why I said you was one of God's oddlings, son. You won't even drink the licker like your Pap

drinks. . . You won't smoke the weed that we are plowin. You ain't like your people. *Ibid* 89, I told him I didn't chew terbacker nor smoke it. He called me a oddlin. **1953** Randolph-Wilson *Down in Holler* 268 **Ozarks,** *Oddling. . .* Something peculiar or abnormal in a harmless, inoffensive way. A pious eccentric is sometimes called "God's oddlin'." So is an agreeable, even-tempered half-wit. **1985** *DARE* File **KY,** Oddling: In Kentucky, a person different from ordinary people. **1991** Heat Moon *PrairyErth* 363 **ceKS,** I've wondered whether I could ever set this quad before you in some fairness to it and its oddlings, things I've had a hard time finding.

odd man out n

Any of var children's games; see quot.

1965–70 *DARE* (Qu. EE2, *Games that have one extra player—when a signal is given, the players change places, and the extra one tries to get a place)* 16 Infs, **scattered,** Odd man out; **IN39,** Odd man out—same as circle tag; **OK42,** Odd man out—played with chairs—same as musical chairs; **PA35,** Odd man out—a counting game; (Qu. EE1, *. . Games . . children play . . in which they form a ring, and either sing or recite a rhyme)* Inf **CA114,** Odd man out.

odd or even n Also *even or odd, odd(s) and even(s)*

[*OED* even and odd (at *odd* a. 2.d) 1552 →; odd and even 1836 →] Cf **hull-gull**

A children's guessing game; see quots.

1883 Newell *Games & Songs* 147, *Odd or Even.* A small number of beans or other counters are held in the hand, and the question is, Odd or Even? If the guess is even, and the true number odd, it is said "Give me one to make it odd," and *vice versa.* The game is continued until all the counters belong to one or other of the two players. **1897** (1952) McGill *Narrative* 32 **SC,** Also the game "Even or Odd," in closed hands. These games may have been a species of childish gambling, tho' none of our crowd ever indulged in it to any extent. **1953** Brewster *Amer. Nonsinging Games* 7 **IN,** *Odd or Even. . .* This game is to be found in all parts of the country. It is played by two children, both of whom have the same number of counters (buttons, beans, grains of corn, pebbles, or the like). Each in turn holds out to the other his clenched hand containing a number of the counters. **1955** *PADS* 23.26 **cwTN,** *Odd and even. . .* A game in which one player attempts to guess whether another has one or two marbles in his closed hand. . . *Heard: odd or even.* **1966–69** *DARE* (Qu. EE33) Inf **FL33,** Even or odd—grab a handful of peanuts, other [player] must guess even or odd number, if he's right he wins; (Qu. EE7, *. . Kinds of marble games)* Infs **VT16, WY1,** Odd and even; **MI49,** Odd or even—one player would hide a certain number of marbles in his hand; others try to guess how many; **IN39,** Odds and evens. **1967** *DARE* Tape **WY1,** Odd and even—you took a handful of marbles and said "Odd or even?" Your opponent guessed odd or even. Well, if he guessed even, and you opened your hand and counted eleven, he had to give you eleven marbles. And if he guessed odd and they were odd, you had to give him that handful of marbles.

odds n pl, but sg in constr

Difference, importance.

1899 (1912) Green *VA Folk-Speech* 303, *Odds. . .* Difference: as, "What's the odds?" **1909** *DN* 3.353 **eAL, wGA,** *Odds. . .* Difference, hindrance. "That ain't no odds to me," i.e., "I can do it with perfect ease." **1943** *LANE* Map 688, 1 inf, **ceMA,** It doesn't make no odds. **1966** *DARE* (Qu. KK26, *Something that makes no difference at all to you: "He can think what he likes, it _____ me.")* Inf **ME22,** Makes no odds to.

odds and endments n pl [Prob blend of *odds and ends* + *oddments*]

1953 Randolph-Wilson *Down in Holler* 268 **Ozarks,** *Oddments. . .* Odds and ends. [An informant] referred to "some odds and endments of handkerchief linen that she got out of her big old trunk."

odds and evens See **odd or even**

odduh, oder See **other**

odorless onion n

A **false garlic** (here: *Nothoscordum bivalve*).

1961 Wills-Irwin *Flowers TX* 94, Crow-poison looks very much like wild onion but lacks the characteristic odor. . . Crow-poison, sometimes known as False-garlic or Odorless-onion, ranges over most of East, Central, and South Texas.

of prep Pronc-spp *a, av, er, o, ob, ove, ub, uh;* eye-dial sp *uv*

A Forms.

1662 in 1922 **RI** (Colony) *Court of Trials Records* 2.21, William marble of Boston being . . found guilty a Riott. **1795** Dearborn *Columbian Grammar* 137, *List of Improprieties*. . . O for Of. **1843** (1916) Hall *New Purchase* 79 **IN,** Then sort a turn to the left. *Ibid* 146, Plenty a fish, and plenty a wood. **1848** Lowell *Biglow* 65 'Upcountry' **MA,** A Kind uv Poetikul lie. **1867** Harris *Sut Lovingood Yarns* 172 **TN,** I hes the longes' par ove laigs ever hung tu eny cackus. **1888** Jones *Negro Myths* 27 **GA coast** [Gullah], Eh sorter courage bofe er um [=encouraged both of them]. **1894** Riley *Armazindy* 63 **IN,** The black wings av night are a-droopin' an' trailin'. **1898** Westcott *Harum* 345 **cNY,** What do you say? . . 'll you make it a couple a hundred? **1899** Chesnutt *Conjure Woman* 13 **csNC** [Black], De grapes begin ter swivel [=shrivel] up . . wid de wrinkles er ole age. **1899** Garland *Boy Life* 132 **nwIA** (as of c1870s), Mr. Stewart considered him the "measliest critter that ever punished a hunk o' meat." **1922** Gonzales *Black Border* 336 **sSC, GA coasts** [Gullah glossary], *Ub uh*—of a—"Uh debble ub uh mule"—a devil of a mule. **a1930** in 1991 Hughes–Hurston *Mule Bone* 31 **cFL** [Black], You'd be world's champeen 'stead uh Jack Dempsey. **1931** (1991) *Ibid* 68 **cFL** [Black], Seem like everybody's scared a us. **1936** Reese *Worleys* 13 **MD** (as of 1865) [Black], She ain' glad on 'count ob dem po' daid boys. **1938** Rawlings *Yearling* 23 **nFL,** You and them hounds and all the rest o' the stock. **1976** Garber *Mountain-ese* 98 **sAppalachians,** *Uv* (prep) of—One uv us has gotta go.

B Gram function.

Used redund:

a after verbs of sense, esp *feel, taste,* and *smell.* **scattered, but esp Sth, S Midl** See also **feel of, taste of, smell of**

1817 in 1866 Essex Inst. *Coll.* 8.249 **MA,** My ears were frozen; and . . I felt of them. **1843** Perkins *Residence in Persia* 103, In the course of the forenoon, a few women came around our tent—felt of it—and peeped through the cracks, to see Mrs. Perkins. **1848** Bartlett *Americanisms* 238, Some people . . supply . . the verbs *to feel, to taste, to smell,* with the preposition *of,* to signify a voluntary act. Hence, to feel, taste, smell *of* a thing, is to do so intentionally. This corruption is rarely met with in writing. **1871** Eggleston *Hoosier Schoolmaster* 15 **IN,** Bull [=a dog] smelled of the new-comer again. **1899** Garland *Boy Life* 18 **nwIA,** With all their treasures under the seat, where they could look at them or feel of them. **1905** *DN* 3.15 **cCT,** *Of.* . . Used in the phrases 'to feel of,' 'to taste of,' ['to smell of,' signifying a voluntary act. **1907** *DN* 3.215 **nwAR. 1936** *AmSp* 11.352 **eTX,** The use of the preposition *of* after verbs which in standard speech take the object directly is almost universal: *Taste of it, smell of it, feel of it.* **1937** Hall *Coll.* **wNC,** Feel of it now. **1946** *PADS* 6.22 **NC, VA** (as of 1900–10), *Of.* . . Used after the verbs *feel, smell,* and *taste.* . . Common. **c1960** Wilson *Coll.* **csKY,** *Of*—superfluous [in] feel of, smell of, taste of. **1986** Pederson *LAGS Concordance,* 50 infs, **chiefly Inland Gulf Region exc GA, eTN,** Smell(ed) of it (*or* that, them, this); 22 infs, **Gulf Region,** Taste(d) of it (*or* them, this, those things); 1 inf, **ceAR,** I could see of it now; 1 inf, **ceAR,** When you feel of it; 1 inf, **seMS,** Don't touch of it.

b after *remember,* also *recollect, recall, mind.* **esp Appalachians, Lower Missip Valley, SW** See Map

1856 in 1862 Colt *Went to KS* 150 **NY,** I then remembered of reading of such a practice among Southern ladies. **1876** in 1983 *PADS* 70.48 **ce,sePA,** Today I think has been the windiest day I ever recollect of seeing. **1903** (1984) Ayer *Autobiog.* 3 **NEng,** I cannot remember of learning my letters, or of learning to spell easy words. **1905** *DN* 3.92 **nwAR,** 'I don't remember of you saying it.' Common. **1907** (1970) Martin *Betrothal* 105 **sePA,** "Do you mind [=remember] of him, pop?" she asked her husband. **1909** *DN* 3.363 **eAL, wGA,** I don't remember of it now. **1918** *DN* 5.20 **NC,** *Remember of,* remember. **1927** *AmSp*

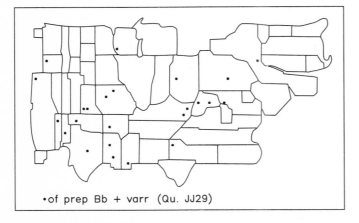

•of prep Bb + varr (Qu. JJ29)

3.11 Ozarks, *Of* . . is used superfluously in such statements as *I don't remember of it.* **1934** Stribling *Unfinished Cathedral* 349 **AL,** Yes, an' I allow, too, you remember of puttin' Pap in jail. **1965–70** *DARE* (Qu. JJ29, . . *Something that may have happened in the past: "Have you met him before?" "Not that I _____."*) 23 Infs, **esp Appalachians, Lower Missip Valley, SW,** (Can) remember of; **MD**24, Recollect of. [19 of 24 Infs old, 5 mid-aged] **1986** Pederson *LAGS Concordance,* 1 inf, **cwAR,** I don't remember of ever seeing one; 1 inf, **seGA,** Not that I remember of; 1 inf, **cnLA,** I remember of seeing one or two; 1 inf, **ceAR,** I can't recall of a skunk doing it.

c after other finite verbs.

1842 Kirkland *Forest Life* 1.113 **MI,** I wouldn't ha' missed of it for a cow! **1861** Holmes *Venner* 2.239 **NEng,** He would consider of the matter. **1870** in 1968 *Filson Club Hist. Qrly.* 161 **csKY,** We accepted of the invitation. **1887** Freeman *Humble Romance* 252 **MA,** Alferd won't last long ef he don't hev somethin' pretty soon to strengthen of him up. **1887** *Scribner's Mag.* 2.475 **AR,** She done hilt Bulah en her arms ever sence she dressed of her.

d after vbl nouns without a preceding possessive or *the.* [*OED of* prep. 31.b c1340 →; "still in archaic and dial. use"]

1859 (1968) Bartlett *Americanisms* 300, In the colloquial language of New England, this preposition [=*of*] . . is used after a gerund or active participle; as, "Ebenezer is coming to stick our pig; but he'll want a quarter for doin' of it (or *on* it)." **1871** Eggleston *Hoosier Schoolmaster* 100 **sIN,** is selfish . . in takin' of you. **1884** *Anglia* 7.272 **Sth, S Midl** [Black], *Stidder mindin' uv his biznis* = instead of minding his business. **1884** Murfree *TN Mts.* 252 **eTN,** We quit burnin' of lime on T'other Mounting. **1890** Holley *Samantha among Brethren* 170 **NY,** How folks will get to tellin' things, and . . finally they will get to believin' of 'em themselves. **1921** Haswell *Daughter Ozarks* 27 (as of 1880s), Doc let me read his books and holp me a heap about understandin' of 'em.

e after pres pples. [*OED of* prep. 32 "After what was formerly a verbal sb. governed by *in* or *a,* but is now identified with a present participle. The use of *of* is now *dial.* or *vulgar.*"; 1563–87 →] **chiefly Sth, S Midl**

1650 (1923) Bland *Discovery New Brittaine* 9 **VA,** The King of *Pawhatan* went to salute and embrace the King of *Chawan,* and stroaking of him after their usuall manner, he whipt a bow string about the King of *Chawans* neck, and strangled him. **1751** *Maryland Statutes* (1859 Bartlett *Americanisms* 300), Whereas, many negroes and other slaves absent themselves from their masters' service, and run out into the woods and there remain, killing and destroying of hogs and cattle belonging unto the people of this province. **1870** in 1945 Lanier *Poems & Outlines* 25 **GA,** Jones was settin' in it, *so:/* A-readin' of a paper. **1884** Murfree *TN Mts.* 250 **eTN,** I clar forgits what horses thems Jeemes boys war a-ridin' of. *Ibid* 251, What did Tony Britt say he war a-doin' of when ye kem on him? **1896** Harris *Sister Jane* 148 **GA,** I'm a-payin' of the fiddler. **1907** Wright *Shepherd* 57 **Ozarks,** He was always drawin' of her. **1907** White *AZ Nights* 33, "That lets you out," growls Pete, gettin' hostile and handlin' of his rifle. **1915** *DN* 4.186 **swVA,** *Of.* . . Used redundantly with verbs, especially present participles following *keep.* "He kept a runnin' of, (botherin' of, a-callin' of, scoldin' of, etc.)" **1916** *DN* 4.317 [Folk-song dialect], *Of.* . . Redundant, as in: "Concerning of Hiram Hubbert." **1918** *DN* 5.20 **NC,** *Reading of,* reading. **1921** Haswell *Daughter Ozarks* 27 (as of 1880s), And follerin' of a big meetin' down to Bar Den Camp, I tuk up to preach. **1926** *AmSp* 1.412 **seGA,** An' when 'e come down, the dog jest covered 'im, a-gnawin' uv 'im, an' the Tiger hugged 'im. **1932** (1974) Caldwell *Tobacco Road* 55 **GA,** You and him has been squatting there, hugging and rubbing of the other, for near about half an hour. **1938** Rawlings *Yearling* 76 **FL,** Jody's been a-wanting of a leetle knapsack. **1944** *PADS* 2.20 **sAppalachians,** *Of.* . . Used redundantly with transitive verbs. Cf.: " . . I will not go to old Jo Clark's,/ A-stealing of his rye."

f after words denoting quantity (without a following determiner); see quots. Cf **considerable** n

1739 in 1969 *AmSp* 44.304 **GA,** One thousand of planks. **1965** *DARE* (Qu. LL9a, *As much as you need or more* . . *"We've got _____ of apples."*) Inf **MS**56, Enough of. **1968** *DARE* FW Addit **NY**68, Fifteen dozen of eggs.

g after an adjective that is modified by any of the adverbs (chiefly *as, how, that, this, too*) that normally cause the adj to precede the indefinite article, if it is present (as in *how big a piece, this good a price*); see quots. [Prob a remodeling of the order adj + indef art + noun by analogy with the common pattern noun + *of* + indef art + noun (as in *a whale of a deal* or *not much of a bargain*)] For addit exx, see 1991 *AmSp* 66.213–220 Cf *no such of a* (at **such**)

[**1914** *DN* 4.77 **ME, nNH,** He wa'n't no gret of a hand to wuk.] **1942** Rawlings *Cross Creek* 4 **nFL,** I wondered if ary one in that big of a hurry knowed where he was going. **1948** Mencken *Amer. Lang. Suppl. 2* 394, How old of a mule have you ever saw? **1970** *DARE* (Qu. LL2) Inf **TN65,** I don't want that small of a potato. **1980** *NYT Mag.* 10 Feb 29, Is "honesty" too strong of a word? **1982** *Barrick Coll.* **csPA,** How big of an engine is that? **1984** in 1991 *AmSp* 66.216, [Sports announcer:] Will judge how good of skaters they are. **1986** Pederson *LAGS Concordance* **Gulf Region,** 1 inf, Too fine of a hair; 1 inf, We haven't got that big of a backyard; 1 inf, Too large of a population; 1 inf, I wasn't in too good of health; 1 inf, There [sic] not that big of lakes. **1987** *WI State Jrl.* (Madison) 26 Mar sec 1 12, [Editorial:] Four years ago, Harley-Davidson . . was on the verge of bankruptcy. . . Its "hogs" carried too fat of a price tag. **1988** Kingsolver *Bean Trees* 156 **KY,** If anything, Lou Ann, you're just too good of a mother. **1989** Gurganus *Oldest Confederate Widow* 7 **Sth,** I've had hints it looks, well, cheap. Is it too bright of a yellow for you? **1989** in 1991 *AmSp* 66.215, [Sports announcer:] She doesn't have as flat of a groundstroke. *Ibid,* [Sports announcer:] The Cowboys are in as good of health as anyone else in the league. *Ibid* 216 **MI,** Not so good of a play, though.

h after preps: See quots. **chiefly Sth, S Midl, NEast** See also **aside (of), behind of, enduring** prep, **excusing, off** C1

1830 (1930) Phelps *Diary* 209 **IL,** You . . put them aboard of the boat. **1857** *Putnam's Mag.* 10.347 **CT,** There he was, fast asleep on the bed beside of the corpse. **1865** in 1983 *PADS* 70.44 **ce,sePA,** At ½ past 12 we shouldered knapsacks and started for the dock to get on board of a steamboat. **1939** *Hall Coll.* **cwNC,** We all nine of us just had a mess around of that bear. **1940** *Harder Coll.* **cwTN,** [Letter:] He has had something wrong with his back, neck, and shoulders he is over of that now. **1941** Stuart *Men of Mts.* 131 **neKY,** Flint was standin' beside of him. **1943** in 1944 *ADD* 422 **sPA,** [The lightning comes down] beside of her. **1965** Needham–Mussey *Country Things* 57 **sVT,** After Gramp had rolled the big stones off into the ditch, and set them to suit him, he would draw the boat beside of it. **1967** *DARE* Tape **AR47,** I have a piece of ground right beside of it. **1968–69** *DARE* (QR, near Qu. C16) Inf **IL42,** The water was right down beside of us; (QR, near Qu. MM17) Inf **PA150,** Sit aside of each other. **1976** Wolfram–Christian *Appalachian Speech* 128, The river was right beside of the railroad. . . A real old guy that lived beside of us. **1984** Wilder *You All Spoken Here* 125 **Sth,** *About to git above of herself:* She served a six-course dinner, if you count the mints. **1985** Rattray *Advent. Dimon* 140 **Long Is. NY,** The Cuban disappeared behind of the house. **1986** Pederson *LAGS Concordance,* 1 inf, **neTX,** Underneath of it; 1 inf, **cwTN,** Underneath of the pump; 1 inf, **csGA,** And he laid down aside of this one.

C Senses.

1 With ref to distance: from, away from; see quots.

1794 in 1936 *KY Hist. Soc. Register* 34.384 **PA,** I . . was informed that on his place, about one fourth of a mile of his house, there was a family murdered by the indns. **1939** *Hall Coll.* **eTN,** [He] heard something holler and thought it was a man. But in a few minutes it hollered about fifty yards of him.

2 usu after *buy, borrow:* Used to indicate the source from which something is obtained. **chiefly NEast**

1799 Hunt in 1898 *Chester Co. Hist. Soc. Bulletins* 2 **PA,** This Day bought a Watch of Thomas Crow. **1800** in 1907 *Columbia Hist. Soc. Records* 10.179 **PA,** The property was bought of the State. **1846** in 1940 *VT Hist.* 8.174, Took my mare of Mr. Gilbert. **1860** in 1937 *Colorado Mag.* 14.215 **PA,** Borrowed 19 lbs. of sugar of Graves. **1864** in 1983 *PADS* 70.44 **ce,sePA,** Bought a horse of Ben Doan. **1866** in 1983 *Lutz Coll.* **neNJ,** Bought a coat and some cloth of Pedlar Jacob. *Ibid,* Bought a hat of Mr Mason for $2. **1899** Garland *Boy Life* 15 **nwIA** (as of c1870s), He was sent to borrow a sand-sieve of neighbor Jennings. **1903** (1984) Ayer *Autobiog.* 19 **NEng,** We always bought one in the fall of Mr. Ranney. **1966** *DARE* Tape **MO1,** He steals you blind if you do buy anything of him. **c1976** *DARE* File **swVT,** For years a sign near a maple sugar house on Rt. 9 near Brattleboro, VT read "Buy Of The Producer." **1979** *Ibid* **MA,** A house . . , he had it in the summer. . . He hired it of the Commission.

3 Used to indicate the time of a regular or habitual action. **scattered, but chiefly Sth, S Midl**

1814 in 1916 *Columbia Hist. Soc. Records* 19.181 **PA,** Many poor fellows dying . . laying out of nights without tents. **1843** (1916) Hall *New Purchase* 427 **sIN,** It's raythur more hardish to strike the course of a dark night. **1871** Eggleston *Hoosier Schoolmaster* 159 **IN,** Your run-

ning about of nights is likely to get you into trouble. **1884** Smith *Bill Arp's Scrap Book* 79 **GA,** He kept 'em at home of nights, and he made good men of them. **1899** Garland *Boy Life* 32 **WI,** The cattle stood in narrow, ill-smelling stalls, close and filthy, especially of a morning. **1911** Dreiser *Jennie* 267 **IN,** There was a place out in one corner of the veranda where he liked to sit of a spring or summer evening. **1917** Garland *Son Middle Border* 47 **WI,** Often of an evening, especially in winter time, father took his seat beside the fire. **1932** (1974) Caldwell *Tobacco Road* 75 **GA,** She used to tell me how pretty I looked when I combed my hair of mornings and put on a clean apron and sunbonnet. **1942** Rawlings *Cross Creek* 223 **FL,** Don't you go pickin' 'em of an evenin' when the sun's low and the day's coolin'. **1953** *Hall Coll.* **wNC,** I've set down and read by firelight of a night. *Ibid,* He'd coon hunt of a night. **1955** Ritchie *Singing Family* 263 **seKY,** [It] wasn't long fore the boys of a Sunday, sitting around with their banjers, were singing "John Henry" as pyert as you please. **1966–69** *DARE* Tape **AL2,** We usually started about five o'clock of a morning; **NC54,** Of a night people would go there and stay all night; **OK19,** She would stir this [=yeast for bread] of an evening; **TX70,** You couldn't start 'em [=cars] of a morning. **1967–69** *DARE* FW Addit **eMD,** "He usually stays home of a Thursday." "He often goes fishing of a morning." *Ibid* **ceTN,** "Of a night," "of a morning" (meaning generally "at night," "in the morning"), e.g., "Of a morning we do this." *Ibid* **swMO,** She works all day, so of an evening she must be pretty tired. *Ibid* **ceNC,** "Of a morning," meaning "in the morning." **1986** Pederson *LAGS Concordance,* [*Of an afternoon, of an evening, of a night, of a summer, of a Sunday, of a winter,* etc, occur freq throughout the **Gulf Region.**]

4 In expressions of time between the half hour and the hour: before, until. [Though first attested in the US, this may be from Scots, nIr dial; cf *SND o* prep. 1.(6)(v), *of* 4.(4)(ii), *EDD of* prep. 14] **widespread, but esp NEast, eN Midl** Cf **till**

1817 in 1918 *IN Hist. Soc. Pub.* 6.278 **cNY,** At 15 minutes of 10 A.M. Paul Dick arrived. **1857** Holmes *Meadow Brook* 47 **NEng,** Five minutes of nine, and round the corner at the foot of the hill appeared a group of children. **1879** Stockton *Rudder Grange* 10, We ceased to call it a boat at about a quarter of eleven. **1949** Kurath *Word Geog.* 50, *Quarter of eleven. . .* In the Northern area, on Delaware Bay, and on Chesapeake Bay *of* and *to* stand side by side in this expression. *Quarter of* predominates in the Boston area and in the Hudson Valley, elsewhere *of* and *to* seem to be in balance. **1960** *PADS* 34.64 **CO,** *Younger speech. . . Quarter of.* **1965–70** *DARE* (Qu. A6, *What time is this? [. . clock face at 10:45]*) 316 Infs, **widespread, but esp NEast, eN Midl,** Quarter of (eleven); 11 Infs, **scattered,** Fifteen (minutes) of (eleven); (Qu. II3, *Expressions to say that people are very friendly toward each other: "They're _____."*) Inf **PA151,** Like five minutes of eleven. **1975** Allen *LAUM* 2.67 **Upper MW** (as of c1950), Quarter *of* eleven. . . More than one-half of the informants have *to;* one-third use competing *of.* Each manifests a regional pattern, *to* being stronger in Northern speech territory and *of* in Midland. **1989** Pederson *LAGS Tech. Index* 21 **Gulf Region,** 87 infs, (A) quarter of (eleven).

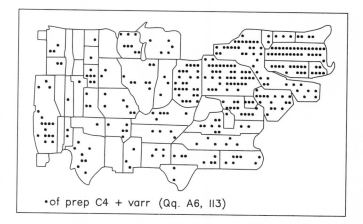

•*of* prep C4 + varr (Qq. A6, II3)

5 On—usu in phr *flat of one's back.* **chiefly Sth, S Midl**

1871 Eggleston *Hoosier Schoolmaster* 112 **sIN,** I'll lay you out flat of your back afore you can say Jack Robinson. **1871** in 1983 *PADS* 70.44 **ce,sePA,** I left about four for I had to go to Wiggins of an arrend. **1933** Miller *Lamb in His Bosom* 102 **GA,** She was tired of lying flat of her back, or sitting carefully in a chair. **1938** Stuart *Dark Hills* 224 **neKY,** He laid right there flat of his back. **1941** Nixon *Possum Trot* 42

neAL, To get the best light on his book, he sometimes lay flat of his back on the floor with his head toward the fire. **1946** Stuart *Tales Plum Grove* 97 **seKY,** I laid flat of my stummick and watched 'em. **1952** Brown *NC Folkl.* 1.570, *Of. . . On,* upon. "He put that fellow flat of his back." **1966–67** DARE (Qu. BB41, *Not seriously ill, but sick enough to be in bed: "He's been _____ for a week."*) Infs **FL**19, **OR**3, Flat of his back; (Qu. BB43, *A person who has to stay in bed all the time: "For two years now he's been _____."*) Infs **MS**51, **OR**3, Flat of his (or her) back. **1986** Pederson *LAGS Concordance,* 1 inf, **neFL,** Fell flat of his back; fell flat of his belly; (*He fell _____*) 1 inf, **cAL,** Flat of his face.

6 With; spec:

a in phr *the matter of:* The trouble with. **chiefly S Midl**

1896 Twain *Tom Sawyer Abroad; Detective* 123 **MO,** I wouldn't give a dern to know what's the matter of Phillips, I says to myself. **1896** DN 1.421 **c,n,seNY,** *Of:* for *with.* "What's the matter of him?" **1901** DN 2.144 **c,eNY,** *Of. . .* For *with,* as in "what's the matter of it." **1906** DN 3.146 **nwAR,** *Matter of. . .* "What's the matter of him?" **1907** (1970) Martin *Betrothal* 103 **sePA,** What 's the matter of you, Ellie? **1911** DN 3.539 **eKY,** *Of. . .* With; as in, "What's the matter of you?" **1914** DN 4.110 **cKS,** *Of. . .* With. "What is the matter of him?" **1915** DN 4.186 **swVA,** *Of. . .* "What's the matter of him?" **1921** Haswell *Daughter Ozarks* 107 (as of 1880s), Now what's the matter of usin' hit fur yer theayter fur the one night? **1927** AmSp 3.11 **Ozarks,** *Of* replaces *with* in the sentence *whut's th' matter of you?* **1944** PADS 2.20 **sAppalachians,** *Of. . .* With. "What's the matter of that child?" **1956** McAtee *Some Dialect NC* 31, *Of . .* with. "What's the matter of that child?" *Obs. exc. Dial.*

b in var other collocations: See quots.

1895 Brown *Meadow-Grass* 127 **NH,** Cyrus, if you knew how you looked with your face plastered over o' lather, you'd wipe it off. **1937** in 1944 ADD 421 **eTN, wNC,** Hit was thick of houses, thick of people up thar then. **1942** Hale *Prodigal Women* 214 **MA,** I know you aren't satisfied with the way we brought you up. I know you are impatient of us. **1967–69** DARE (Qu. X56b, *Expressions about sweating very heavily*) Infs **AL**33, **KY**40, Wet of sweat; (Qu. AA12, *If a man loses interest in a girl and stops seeing her . . he _____*) Inf **NC**49, Lost contact of her.

7 For, with respect to; see quots.

1858 Hammett *Piney Woods Tavern* 120, I was dreadful small of my age. **1937** Esquire 7.171 **neKY,** He's getting too smart of his pants. **1941** LANE Map 461 *(Lively, spry)* 1 inf, **CT,** She's smart of her age; 1 inf, **csMA,** She's spry of her age; 1 inf, **cnVT,** He's smart of his age.

8 In honor of.

c1970 Pederson *Dial. Surv. Rural GA,* 1 inf, **seGA,** General Blackshear, it [=the town of Blackshear] was named of him.

9 About, because of.

1949 Dean *Diamond Bess* 111 **GA,** Ellen was sorry of her bargain. **1954** *Harder Coll.* **cwTN,** I am so excited of your coming home I haven't done a thing all day but bawl.

10 in phr *sick of one's stomach:* Nauseated. Cf **at prep 2, on B9, to**

1965–70 DARE (Qu. BB16a, *If something a person ate didn't agree with him, he might be sick _____ his stomach*) Infs **IN**41, **LA**35, **MS**80, **MO**18, **OR**4, **TX**28, 31, **UT**4, Of. **1966** Dakin *Dial. Vocab. Ohio R. Valley* 2.485, [4 of 207 infs, **sIL, sIN, KY,** Sick of the stomach.] **1971** Wood *Vocab. Change* 302 **Sth,** Of his stomach [25 of approx 1000 infs]. **1972** PADS 58.23 **cwAL,** Sick at the stomach. At (19 [infs]) is in common use. Pennsylvania and Coastal Southern *in . . ,* Pennsylvania and Southern *on* (2), Northern and Coastal Southern *to* (2, one of whom labeled it correct usage as opposed to the more natural *at*), and *of* (1) also occur. **1975** Allen *LAUM* 2.65 (as of c1950), Sick *at* the stomach. . . *of his stomach* [1 inf, **seIA**]. **1986** Pederson *LAGS Concordance (He is sick _____)* 9 infs, **Gulf Region,** Sick of his (or a, my) stomach.

of v[1] See **have** v[1] **A1a, c**

of v[2] See **have** v[2]

ofay n Also sp *offay* [Etym uncert. African sources have been proposed (see quot 1932 and 1975 AmSp 50.87–89), but the lack of early attestations weakens the hypothesis of African origin (cf the evidence for **buckra**). If the word originated in Harlem c1920 it may be, as has often been asserted, pig Latin for *foe.*] *among Black speakers; chiefly urban; derog* Cf **fay** n

A White person.

1925 *Inter-State Tattler* 6 Mar 8/1 **Harlem NYC** [Black], We hear that "Booker Red" has three ofays on his staff. **1926** Van Vechten *Nigger Heaven* 46 **Harlem NYC,** You know as well as I do that practically every other ofay in the South has a coloured half-brother. **1928** Fisher *Walls Jericho* 299 **NYC** [Black], *Ofay*—A person who, so far as is known, is white. *Fay* is said to be the original term and *ofay* a contraction of "old" and "fay." **1928** McKay *Home to Harlem* 22 **Harlem NYC** [Black], I ain't told no nigger but you, boh. Nor ofay neither. **1932** *Africa* (London) 5.506, The last of the five words contributed indirectly by Ibibio to the English language is *Offay. . .* The root of the word appears to come from the Ibibio *Afia,* white or light-coloured. Hence in Harlem *Offay* means any light-coloured person and therefore a European. **1937** *Writer* 50.239 **neOH** [Black], *Ofay*—a white person. **1946** (1972) Mezzrow-Wolfe *Really Blues* 192, Take the word 'ofay.' Ninety million white Americans right now probably don't know that that means 'a white,' but Negroes know it. . . Ofay, of course, is pig Latin for *foe.* **1954** Armstrong *Satchmo* 147 **LA,** Those rich ofay (white) business men and planters would come from all over the South. *Ibid* 238, He had the features and even the voice of a white boy—an ofay, or Southern, white boy at that. **1961** (1962) Griffin *Black Like Me* 121 **TX,** You white bastard, you ofay sonofabitch, what are you doing walking these streets? **1963** Mencken-McDavid *Amer. Lang.* 388, *Ofay,* an urban word, is less frequently used than it used to be. **1964** PADS 42.44 **Chicago IL,** *Ofay. . .* All five [Black] informants in Chicago assumed it to be pig Latin. **1965** Bradford *Born with the Blues* 49 **Sth** [Black], Mamie Smith cut her first record . . with Fred Hager's ofay orchestra (meaning white group of musicians in theatrical slang). **1970** Bullins *Electronic* 11 **sCA** [Black], A lot of the ofays start in sayin' things they had held back before. **1986** Pederson *LAGS Concordance,* 1 inf, **ceTN,** Ofay—white person, poor white, or rustic; 1 inf, **csTN,** Ofay—Black term; 1 inf, **ceAL,** Ofay—has become derogatory; 1 inf, **seAL,** Ofay; 1 inf, **cAR,** Ofay—derogatory, used by Blacks; 1 inf, **cTX,** Ofay—derogatory; 1 inf, **ceTX,** Ofay—not insulting, just a member of the white race. [5 of 7 infs from cities of more than 100,000 inhabitants] **1987** Rose *I Remember Jazz* 48, I guess we've got room on the paper for one ofay reporter.

ofen See **offen**

off adv, prep, adj, v, n Usu |ɔf|; also |ɑf, ɒf|; for addit varr see quots Pronc-spp *auf, oaf* Cf Pronc Intro 3.II.9

A Forms.

1899 (1912) Green *VA Folk-Speech* 70, Christmas is a long way *auf.* **1930** AmSp 5.340 **neMA,** [ɔ] is noticeably unrounded . . in *loft, long, off. Ibid* 342 **ceVA,** [ɔ] in . . *off. Ibid* 343 **cnTX,** [ɔ] is . . rounded in *log, loft, off. Ibid* 344 **cwPA, OK,** [ɔ] . . slight rounding in . . *off. Ibid* 345 **cGA,** [ɔ] is . . rounded in *log, loft, off. Ibid* 346 **cNY,** [ɔ] occurs in . . *off. Ibid* 355 **NYC,** [ɔ] . . a trace of vowel glide in *walk, off.* **1931** AmSp 6.164 **seVA,** There is a tendency to unround [ɔ] to [ɑ]. . . We have examples . . in *off, all* and *always.* In some examples of Williamsburg speech, the vowel is half-rounded and may be transcribed [ɒ]. **1942** AmSp 17.36 **seNY,** Off . . [ɒ] 5 [infs] . . [ɔ] 66 [infs] . . [ɔˠ] 5 [infs]. **1943** LANE Map 724 *(Off),* [widespread NEng, but esp **RI, NH, ME,** [ɒᵊf]; widespread NEng, but esp **VT, MA, CT,** [ɔf]; 4 infs, **seCT, swRI, csMA,** [ɔᵊf]; 7 infs, **wMA, cnCT, cnVT,** [ɑf].] **1990** Amory *Cat & Curmudgeon* 192 **eTX,** On the way to our first pasture I kept thinking about that East Texas accent. . . I am not just talking here of "all" for oil, . . I am also talking about "bard" for buried, . . "own and oaf" for on and off, . . and "tarred" for tired.

B As adv.

Away, at a place away from home—often in phr *from off* from a different or distant place. Cf **off-island**

1848 in 1935 AmSp 10.41 **Nantucket MA,** Come from off. From abroad. **1916** Macy-Hussey *Nantucket Scrap Basket* 140 **seMA,** "*Off*"—An abbreviation of "off-island," is very frequently heard. One often hears such a remark as "I haven't seen you lately. Have you been Off?" Still more odd is the expression "when did you come On from Off?" **1935** AmSp 10.167 **PA** [Engl of PA Germans], He is off this morning (he is away). **1942** Rawlings *Cross Creek* 124 **nFL,** My car is either under its shelter, . . and I am at home, or it is not under the cashay and I am simply "off." **1946** AmSp 21.190 **seKY,** *Off,* away, absent from home. 'She works off.' **1947** AmSp 22.157 **sIN,** The word *off* usually is accompanied by *away.* For instance, a woman will tell a neighbor, 'Her boy's workin' off away from here somewhere.' **1952** DE *Folkl. Bulletin* Oct 11, "She comes from off"—that is, from far away. **1952** Giles *40 Acres* 5 **KY,** To my chagrin I learned that allowances were made for me because I was "from off," I had not been properly "raised up" and I therefore could not be expected to know much. **1955** Ritchie *Singing Family* 249 **seKY,** Newspapers from off said it was the first settlement school ever built or even thought of, out in the country like that. **1959** *VT Hist.* 27.151, *Off. . . Away;* another town or state. He's from *off.* Occasional.

C As prep.

1 In phr *off of:* Off; from. **widespread, but more freq Sth, Midl** See Map

1843 (1846) Haliburton *Attaché* (1st ser) 2.210, The groom has stole her oats, forgot to give her water, and let her make a supper sometimes off of her nasty, mouldy, filthy beddin'. **1885** Twain *Huck. Finn* 45 **MO,** I'd borrow two or three dollars off of the judge for him. **1918** *DN* 5.20 **NC,** Keep off of the fence. **1932** Stong *State Fair* 98 **IA,** I took most of this stuff off of him. **1942** McAtee *Dial. Grant Co.* **IN** 46 (as of 1890s), *Off of* . . "of" was very generally used after "off"; "I won't take nothin' _____ you". Now illiterate. **1945** *AmSp* 20.19, Informants who were asked to indicate their familiarity with the phrases *off of* and *off from* in the informal speech of their home speech areas. . . Both idioms . . seem to be familiar in all of the major speech areas, with *off of* the more common of the two. *Off from* appears to be strongest in the North Central area, especially in Michigan, Wisconsin, and Minnesota. **1956** McAtee *Some Dialect NC* 31, *Off of* . . "of" an expletive. "I won't take nothin' off of you." *Now Illiterate.* **1965–70** *DARE* (Qu. MM20, *"So that she could sit down, he took his coat _____ the chair.")* 220 Infs, **widespread, but more freq Sth, Midl,** Off of; (Qu. MM21, *'Off':* "Get _____ my land."; total Infs questioned, 75) 33 Infs, Off of; (Qu. Y51, . . *Ways of saying 'to avoid' things or people* . . *"He's not your kind—you'd better _____ him.")* Inf **CA**107, **IA**15, **LA**11, **MO**17, 19, **TX**42, Lay off of; (Qu. AA12, *If a man loses interest in a girl and stops seeing her* . . *he _____)* Inf **AL**26, Shied off of her; (Qu. GG15, . . *A person who became over-excited and lost control, "At that point he really _____.")* Inf **SC**3, Flew off of the handle; (Qu. GG20, . . *'Very much surprised':* "When those two got married, I was certainly _____.")* Infs **KY**24, **NC**84, **SC**34, Knocked (*or* swept) off of my feet; (Qu. GG21a, *If you don't care what a person does* . . *"You can go ahead and do it _____.")* Inf **OK**31, It's no meat off of my bones; **NJ**18, No skin off of my nose; **OK**48, Nothing off of my hide; (Qu. HH6, *Someone who is out of his mind)* Inf **GA**77, Off of the beam; (Qu. JJ7, . . *Cheating in school examinations)* Infs **FL**14, **LA**17, Copying off of the other (*or* someone else); (Qu. JJ26, *If somebody has been doing poor work or not enough, the boss might say, "If he wants to keep his job he'd better _____.")* Inf **LA**16, Get off of it; (Qu. LL18, *To do no work at all, not even make any effort:* "She hasn't _____ all day.")* Inf **OR**3, Been off of it; (Qu. MM6, . . *'Very close' or 'only a short distance away':* "The house is _____ the park.")* Inf **AR**39, Off of; (Qu. NN22c, *Expressions used to drive away a dog)* Inf **LA**8, Git off of here. **1966** Dakin *Dial. Vocab. Ohio R. Valley* 2.235, He fell *off.* . . The inland counties of Ohio, Kentucky, and most of Illinois have *off* and *off of*—usually pronounced ['ɔf,ə]—in about equal numbers but with a somewhat different social distribution. . . *Off* is more characteristic of the middle-aged and more educated speakers (although these speakers frequently use both expressions) while *off of* is more often the only usage of the oldest informants. **1968** *PADS* 49.14 **Upper MW,** The schools tend to establish literary terms in place of or alongside indigenous folk terms. This influence is also evident in the following examples: . . the use of *off* in place of *off of.* **1975** Allen *LAUM* 2.68 (as of c1950) 26 infs, **Upper MW,** He fell *off of* the horse. **1989** Pederson *LAGS Tech. Index* 130 **Gulf Region,** 59 [of 914] infs, (Fell/was thrown) off of (the horse); 2 infs, Slid off of (it); 34 infs, (Fell) off of (the bed); 5 infs, Rolled off of (the bed).

2 Out of; spec: not in attendance in (class); out of fellowship with (a church). Cf **on B10**

1927 [see **on B10**]. **1929** [see **on B10**]. **1935** *AmSp* 10.169 **PA** [Engl of PA Germans], Two special expressions, for which there are no good American equivalents, are in use among the 'plain' people . . : *to go gay,* meaning to become worldly in the sense of attending dances, card parties, movies, or participating in other forbidden pleasures; and *to put off the church,* meaning to excommunicate. One who is *off the church* is probably one who has *gone gay* once too often.

D As adj.

1 Being on the right (rarely left) side, usu of an animal or vehicle. See note at **off horse**

1823 Cooper *Pioneers* 1.51 **NY,** I knew just the spot where to touch the off-leader. **1840** (1934) Boynton *Jrl.* 43.346 **VT,** By and by, the off wheels went into a deep hollow. **1897** *Outing* 30.254, Take up about six or seven inches of your off-leader's rein. . . Take the off-lead and off-wheeler's reins in right hand. **1923** *DN* 5.216 **swMO,** *Off side.* . . The right side of an animal. **1929** (1978) Watt *Mule Train* 41 **eWA** (as of 1860s), The men who worked in pairs were called the 'near' and the "off" packer. **1946** Mora *Trail Dust* 119 **West,** In this operation [=earing down], a twister reaches either over or under the horse's head for his off ear, and grabs it with his right hand, while he likewise fastens to the near one with his left. **1956** Ker *Vocab. W. TX* 218, *Off side*—the wrong side; opposed to near [1 of 67 infs]. **1959** *VT Hist.* 27.151 **cn,neVT,** *Off.* . . Farther. The *off* runner of a sled. Rare. **1965–70** *DARE* (Qu. K32a, *With a team of horses,* . . *the horse on the driver's right hand)* Infs **DC**8, **MD**20, 26, 30, 48, **TN**24, Off wheelhorse; **AR**51, **CA**23, 199, Off-wheeler; **MD**20, **TN**56, Off-lead horse. **1986** Pederson *LAGS Concordance* (The lead horse/horse on the left) 4 infs, **cwGA, cwMS, csTN, cTX,** (On the) off side—on the right; 4 infs, **cwTN, seMS, cwMS, cLA,** (He's on the) off side—on the left; 1 inf, **ceMS,** Off side—mule other than lead mule was on; 1 inf, **seLA,** Off side is the passenger side of the car; 1 inf, **seAR,** Off wheel; 1 inf, **neLA,** Off-wheeler—the horse on the right; 1 inf, **cnLA,** The off-wheeler—the one on the other side; 3 infs, **swAL, cwAR, nwLA,** Off lead—on left, nearest wagon; 1 inf, **nwLA,** Off leader; 1 inf, **swAR,** Off leader—on right; (Left ear) 1 inf, **nwLA,** Off side—left side of the head.

2 also *off-flavor, off-taste, off-tasting:* Tainted; distasteful, sour—used of meat or milk. [*OEDS off* adj. 1.g.(b) 1952 →] **scattered, but somewhat more freq NEast, N Cent** See Map Cf **blinky 1, 2, turned**

1941 *LANE* Map 306 *(Spoiled),* The map shows the terms applied to meat that has begun to decay or 'go bad'; 1 inf, **seCT,** A little off = not quite spoiled; 1 inf, **swVT,** Off = spoiled. **1965–70** *DARE* (Qu. K14, *Milk that has a taste from something the cow ate in the pasture* . . *"That milk is _____.")* 56 Infs, **scattered, but more freq NEast, N Cent,** Off-flavor; 12 Infs, **scattered,** Off-taste; **CT**13, **MI**116, **MA**27, **NY**109, **RI**7, Off; **AR**40, Off-flavor milk; **FL**27, Off-tasting; **OK**10, The cow's been eating a certain kind of a weed that gives the milk an off taste; (Qu. H46, *When meat begins to go bad, so that you can't eat it* . . *it's _____)* Inf **NY**144, Off; (Qu. H58, *Milk that's just beginning to become sour)* Inf **MI**66, A little off; **NY**105, Off. **1967** *DARE* FW Addit **cOR,** *Off odor*—smell of tainted meat; heard in conversation.

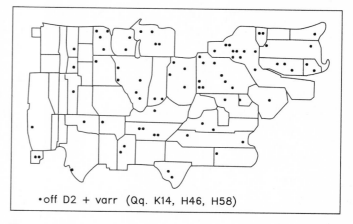

•off D2 + varr (Qq. K14, H46, H58)

E As verb.

To beat severely; to kill. *orig among Black speakers*

1968 *Negro Digest* June 77, The only way we can ever justify offing a brother is if we have already offed twenty whiteys. **1971** Roberts *Third*

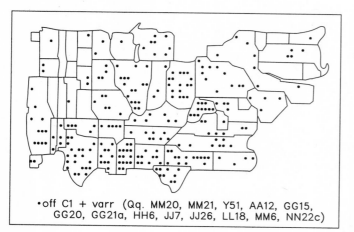

•off C1 + varr (Qq. MM20, MM21, Y51, AA12, GG15, GG20, GG21a, HH6, JJ7, JJ26, LL18, MM6, NN22c)

Ear np [Black], *Off* . . to beat severely; to kill; e.g. Did he really off him last night? **1972** Claerbaut *Black Jargon* 74, *Off* . . 1. to maul; beat up someone: *I'll off that dude.* 2. to kill; take another's life. **1973** Walker *In Love* 32 [Black], She heard "slave trade" and "violent overthrow" and "off de pig," an expression she'd never heard before. **1979** Gillespie–Fraser *To Be Or Not To Bop* 377, I asked this dude, "Man, what are you in here [=jail] for?" "I offed eight people." **1980** *Capital Times* (Madison WI) 20 Dec 10/3, "My main concern," he says, "was whether I would be able to continue my career [after an accident]. One day, I wanted to off myself."

F As noun.

1 A vacation; a day away from work. **chiefly PaGer area**
1927 *AmSp* 3.463 cnPA, By "My off is all," a sentence heard in North Central Pennsylvania, the speaker meant that his vacation was over. **1935** *AmSp* 10.167 sePA, Today is my off (my day off). **1937** *AmSp* 12.205 [Engl in PaGer area], The average speaker will employ in speech . . 'the cookies are all' (all gone), . . and 'my off is all' (my vacation is over). Many of these usages may be noticed in the speech of high school and college students. **1939** Aurand *Quaint Idioms* 25 [PaGer], How long is your *off* (vacation)? *Ibid* 31, An item was handed to us for publication, viz: "One of the women in the office was away on her vacation, and was about due to come back to work. Another woman was discussing her with the balance of the office force, and with a show of pity, remarked: 'Poor Miss Smith, her off's about all.'" **1954** *WELS Suppl.* ceWI, I wonder if you have ever come across the expressions "my off is on" and "my off is all." They are quite common in the Manitowoc–Sheboygan area, and have always been a source of amusement to me. **1982** *Barrick Coll.* csPA, *Off*—vacation; leave. Humorous. "He's on his off; his off is all." **1987** *Jrl. Engl. Ling.* 20.2.172 sePA, *Off*—'day off.' . . Only a 52-year-old, high-school educated female from Lancaster County acknowledged using *off.*

2 The land to the right of a furrow being plowed. [*off* D1]
1981 Pederson *LAGS Basic Materials* (*The lead horse/horse on the left*) 1 inf, neTN, Leader [walks] in the furrow, [the off horse walks] in the off; 1 inf, cnAR, The off horse was on the off [FW: Not sure if it's this way or the other way around. Old people talked about "the off horse; I work him on the off."]

off Adam n
=Adam's off-ox 1.
1963 Owens *Look to River* 52 TX, We didn't know you from off Adam when you come up the road.

off against prep phr Cf against B3, DS MM1
1946 *PADS* 6.22 eNC (as of 1900–10), *Off against.* . . Opposite, in front of, near. Pamlico. Common.

offals n pl Also *off alls* [Prob by reanalysis of *offal* as mass noun; but cf *OED offal* sb. 1.b "In collective sing. and pl. . . Obs." and 2.a "Formerly also in *pl.*"] Cf **off-fall** n[1]
Scraps, crumbs; esp, meat scraps or internal organs left after butchering.
1939 *LANE* Map 216 (*Giblets*) 1 inf, neMA, Offals, all the interior organs. **1966** Dakin *Dial. Vocab. Ohio R. Valley* 2.262, The edible internal organs of a pig or calf. . . A related term, apparently of North Midland origin and not a comprehensive term for internal organs, is occasional and scattered from Pennsylvania to the Mississippi and also known on the lower Kentucky. Several variations occur: *off fall(ing)(s)*, *off all(s)*, and *offal(s)*. For some speakers this was a comprehensive term for the ribs, backbone, and trimmings—the edible scraps from the less desirable parts of the animal—and for others a term for the internal organs, both edible and inedible. **1971** Dwyer *Dict. for Yankees* 30 Sth, S Midl, *Offals*—Pieces of food fallen from the table. **1986** Pederson *LAGS Concordance* (*Comprehensive term for edible "insides" of a pig or calf*) 3 infs, neTN, cwGA, cwAR, Offals; (*Second cutting*) 1 inf, cnTN, Offals—dead grass.

offay See ofay

off-bar v, hence vbl n *off-barring*
=bar off.
1905 U.S. Dept. Ag. Div. Entomol. *Bulletin* 54.16, On two large plantations at Broussards [LA] it was suggested by the writer that the owners "offbar" the cane in April and May and keep the dirt away from it as late as possible. **c1926** in 1995 *W3* File, [From an agricultural implement catalog:] When equipped with two single mouldboard bottoms the No. 10 [cane cultivator] can be adjusted for wide or narrow offbarring. **1938** U.S. Dept. Ag. *Leaflet* 138.4, When the garlic is planted

on single ridges some growers off-bar the ridge to facilitate pulling. **1954** *Harder Coll.* cwTN, *Off-bear* [sic]. . . To disk earth away from corn in rows; also *bar-off.*

off-bear n Cf off-fall n[2]
1953 Randolph–Wilson *Down in Holler* 268 **Ozarks,** *Off-bear.* . . Progeny, offspring. "Doc Yokum has got off-bears on every creek in this county."

off-brand adj
1 Unconventional, unusual, strange. [By ext from *off brand* an unfamiliar or inferior brand]
1960 Carpenter *Tales Manchaca* 109 cTX, There was a sprinkling of Cumberland Presbyterians and Campbellites; but these off-brand folk attended our Sunday-school meetings and church services. **1965** *DARE* FW Addit seNM, *Off-brand*—unconventional, strange. **1967–70** *DARE* (Qu. CC4, . . *Nicknames* . . *for various religions or religious groups*) Inf SC31, Off-brand—any different or strange one, e.g., Jehovah's Witnesses; TN48, Off-brand churches; (Qu. CC10, . . *An unprofessional, part-time lay preacher*) Inf KY70, Off-brand [laughter]. **1967** *DARE* File, *Off-brand* = non-standard. Used, among other things, of grammatical uses. Heard from a Southern (Black) speaker at ADS meeting. [An informant] says it's "common in the South—all over Texas." Familiar to [informants from Idaho, California, Nebraska, and Boston, Massachusetts, but not known to informants from Michigan and Buffalo, New York].

2 Illegitimate; not intentionally bred.
1966–70 *DARE* (Qu. K43, *A horse that was not intentionally bred, or bred by accident*) Inf LA8, Off-brand horse; (Qu. Z11b, . . *[A child whose parents were not married]*) Infs MS23, SC70, Off-brand child. [**1986** Pederson *LAGS Concordance* (*Mongrel* . . , *dogs of mixed breeds*) 1 inf, cnAR, Off brands.]

off-breed n Cf field bred, off-brand 2
A person or animal of mixed or indeterminate ancestry; similarly adj *off-bred* of an animal: not intentionally bred, mongrel.
1965–70 *DARE* (Qu. J1, . . *A dog of mixed breed*) Inf NY209, Off-bred (dog); KY62, Off-breed; (Qu. J5, *A cat with fur of mixed colors*) Inf IA47, Off-breed; (Qu. K37, . . *A horse of mixed colors*) Infs NE8, OR17, Off-breed; (Qu. K43, *A horse that was not intentionally bred, or bred by accident*) Infs CO19, IA26, MO9, NC26, 52, OH20, Off-breed; MS21, Off-bred colt; (Qu. HH29a, . . *People of mixed blood—part Indian*) Inf NC52, Off-breed; (Qu. HH31, *Somebody who is not from your community, and doesn't belong*) Inf OK48, Off-breed. **1986** Pederson *LAGS Concordance* (*Mongrel*) 4 infs, sAL, csGA, cMS, (He's a) off breed; 1 inf, csAR, Off breed—mixed.

offcast n [*OED* 1587 →; but perh reversed compound; cf Intro "Language Changes" I.1]
See quot 1953.
1854 Kane *Grinnell Exped.* 30, This wood . . is the offcast of the great Siberian and American rivers. **1953** Randolph–Wilson *Down in Holler* 268 **Ozarks,** *Off-casts.* . . Castoffs, something discarded. I have heard a woman, formerly a mistress of William Jones, described as "one of Bill Jones' off-casts." **1954** *Harder Coll.* cwTN, *Off-cast.* . . Castoff, something discarded.

off-color adj esp Nth
Not in good health, slightly sick.
1876 Harte *Gabriel Conroy* 215, Mr. Hamlin had not been well, or as he more happily expressed it, had been "off color." **1880** *Scribner's Mth.* 19.680, He looked rather "off color." **1943** *LANE* Map 493 (*Feeling bad*) 1 inf, ceMA, Off color. **1950** *WELS* (*When you are only a little bit sick, you might say "I'm _____."*) 2 Infs, WI, (A little) off-color. **1966–69** *DARE* (Qu. BB39, *On a day when you don't feel just right, though not actually sick . . "I'll be all right tomorrow—I'm just feeling _____ today."*) Inf IL97, Little off-color; CT23, PA115, Off-color; (Qu. BB41, *Not seriously ill, but sick enough to be in bed: "He's been _____ for a week."*) Inf MI24, Off-color.

offen prep Also sp *ofen, off on, of(f')n*; pronc-sp *off'm* [Chiefly Scots, nEngl dial; see *SND affin, EDD off* prep. 2.(14)] *chiefly among speakers with little formal educ; somewhat old-fash* Cf **-en** suff[3]
Off of; off.
1841 *Spirit of Times* 27 Mar 42 AR, It took two men to hold Sam off on him, for that ar hat cost Sam a mortal sight of Peltry. **1867** Harris *Sut Lovingood Yarns* 34 TN, I hearn a nise like tarin a shingle ruff ofen

a hous' at wun rake. **1869** in 1884 Lanier *Poems* 173 **GA,** He picked up all the rocks from off'n the groun'. **1871** Eggleston *Hoosier Schoolmaster* 216 **IN,** The master had jist knocked the hind-sights offen that air young lawyer. **1887** Kirkland *Zury* 109 **IL,** Git daown offen that stule. **1892** *DN* 1.213 **VT,** I have a neighbor, unschooled but intelligent, a native of Vermont, who says "get offn that grass," "take the harness offn the horse." **1893** Frederic *Copperhead* 82 **nNY,** He'll boot you off'm the place if you try it. **1893** Shands *MS Speech* 48, *Offen. . .* Negro and illiterate white for *off of,* exactly analogous to *outen* for *out of.* **1899** Garland *Boy Life* 159 **nwIA** (as of c1870s), I'll knock the everlasting spots offen 'im f'r two cents. **1899** (1912) Green *VA Folk-Speech* 304, The shell isn't ofn their heads yet. **1901** *DN* 2.144 **ME,** *Off'n. . .* Off from, as in "The leaves are off'n the trees." **1903** *DN* 2.322 **seMO,** *Offen. . .* Off of. 'I can't make good corn offen that land.' **1906** *DN* 3.148 **nwAR,** He fell offen the roof. **1909** *DN* 3.353 **eAL, wGA,** He couldn't make nothin offen me. **1911** *DN* 3.546 **NE,** Get offn that grass. *Ibid* 550 **WY,** He got the dirt offn my father to fix his dike. **1917** *DN* 4.397 **neOH,** "He got off'n the wagon." "Get off'n that fence." **1919** *DN* 5.76 **wMA,** *Off'n the.* Probably from *off'm,* weakened form of *off from. Off'm* is common in Western Massachusetts. **1940** Faulkner *Hamlet* 51 **MS,** He clumb down offen the fence and went across. **1943** *LANE* Map 724 **NEng,** [In contexts "He fell _____ the horse" and "He was thrown _____ his horse," *off* occurs frequently; *off'n* is common, but occurs less frequently; *off of* is much less common.] **1965–70** *DARE* (Qu. MM20, *"So that she could sit down, he took his coat _____ the chair."*) 27 Infs, **scattered,** Offen; (Qu. H74a, . . *Coffee . . very strong*) Inf **CO**11, Take the hair offen your tongue; (Qu. K16, *A cow with a bad temper*) Inf **WI**30, Offen her rocker; (Qu. X56b, *Expressions about sweating very heavily*) Inf **OH**12, Water run offen him; (Qu. Z10, *If a child looks very much like his father . . "He _____ his father."*) Inf **ME**21, Is a chip offen the old block; (Qu. AA8, *When people make too much of a show of affection in a public place*) Inf **KY**42, Couldn't keep their hands offen each other; (Qu. DD9a, . . *A person who smokes a great deal*) Inf **NY**96, Lights one offen the other; (Qu. DD11, *When somebody gives up drinking: "I hear he _____ ."*) Inf **SC**3, Swore offen the jug; (Qu. HH5, *Someone who is queer but harmless*) Infs **GA**19, **MD**40, Offen his marbles (*or* rocker); (Qu. HH22c, . . *A very mean person . . "He's mean enough to _____ ."*) Inf **SC**3, Steal the money offen a dead person; (Qu. II22, *Expressions to tell somebody to keep to himself and mind his own business*) Inf **NM**9, Keep offen my back; (Qu. KK42a, *Expressions about a person who does something very easily: "For him that would be _____ ."*) Inf **MO**15, Like falling offen a log; (Qu. KK59, *To have a mistaken idea, or to be quite wrong about something: "If he thinks she'll help him, he's _____ ."*) Inf **AR**51, Offen his rockers; (Qu. MM21, . . *'Off': "Get _____ my land."*; total Infs questioned, 75) Infs **MS**7, 42, 64, 71, **NM**9, **OK**45, Offen. [Of 40 total Infs, 33 were old, 21 gs educ or less, 34 comm type 4 or 5.] **1966** Dakin *Dial. Vocab. Ohio R. Valley* 2.236, *Off from* is very rare, but *off'n* is fairly common in eastern Kentucky and is scattered north of the [Ohio] river. This usage is limited to those of little education. **1966–68** *DARE* Tape **AK**9, They'd . . unload the boat offen there; **SD**3, They mostly lived offen the eggs. **1986** Pederson *LAGS Concordance* (He fell _____ the horse) 16 infs, Offen; (He fell _____ bed) 9 infs, **Gulf Region,** Offen; 1 inf, **cwMS,** The pantry was offen the porch; pulling slabs offen the corn; whipped the clothes offen the line; 1 inf, **neTN,** They go and scrape the seed offen that; 1 inf, **seGA,** Offen the land; 1 inf, **nwAR,** Fallen offen the log; 1 inf, **seMS,** Chip offen the old block; 1 inf, **nwTN,** To eat the insects offen the water; 1 inf, **swGA,** Drag the hair offen them; 1 inf, **csGA,** Fall offen them; 1 inf, **cTN,** Up offen the ground right smart; 1 inf, **cAL,** Fell offen the bed; 1 inf, **cGA,** Have fun offen that; 1 inf, **cnLA,** I bought them offen my cousin; 1 inf, **cnLA,** Clip the feathers offen one of the wings; 1 inf, **cAL,** Wash that salt offen it; 1 inf, **ceMS,** Offen; 1 inf, **seGA,** Offen it; 1 inf, **nwAR,** A lot of that money come offen us [22 of 32 total infs have 8th-grade educ or less].

offen adv See **often** adv

offer v, n [*OED offer* v. 5.b 1540–1 →, sb. 3 1581 →]
To attempt, try; an attempt.

1871 Eggleston *Hoosier Schoolmaster* 127 **sIN,** Ef anybody offers to trouble you, do you let off a yell and I'll be thar in no time. **1899** (1912) Green *VA Folk-Speech* 303, *Offer. . .* To make as though you were going to do a thing; an attempt. "He made an offer to hit him." "If he offers to walk his legs give way and he falls down." **1937** *Hall Coll.* **eTN, wNC,** *Offer. . .* To try; to attempt. "I didn't offer to kill it." **1976** Ryland *Richmond Co. VA* 374, *Offer*—try; "As sick as he was, that dog offered to stand up."

off-fall n[1] Also *off-falling* [Cf *EDD off-fall* (at *off* adv. 1.(6)) "a scrap fallen off", *off-falling* (at *off* adv. 1.(8)(b)) "obs., a scrap, anything cast off and thrown on one side"] Cf **offals**
A scrap, bit of waste.

1946 *AmSp* 21.193, The waste from the distillation of beer into high wines isn't offal but 'off-falls,' the still operator insists. **1966** [see **offals**]. **1968** *DARE* (Qu. W25, *When a woman is cutting out a dress to sew . . the little scraps of cloth left over*) Inf **VA**2, Off-fallin's.

off-fall n[2] [Perh < Ger *Abfall* defection, apostasy] Cf **off-bear**
An offshoot, a separate branch.

1967 *DARE* Tape **PA**30, The black-bumper [branch of the Mennonite Church] is, if you want to use the term, [an] off-fall of the original team or horse-and-wagon Mennonites.

off-falling See **off-fall** n[1]

off-flavor See **off** D2

off-floor adj
=off the roof.

1967 *DARE* (Qu. AA27, . . *A woman's menstruation*) Infs **OR**1, **WA**28, Off-floor [FW: sic]; [**OR**15, Falling off the floor].

off from See **from** B5

off-hand horse (or mule) See **off horse 1**

off-hand ox See **off ox 1**

off horse n

1 also *off-hand horse:* The right-hand horse of a pair; occas the left-hand horse; similarly nouns *off(-hand) mule, off steer.* [**off** D1] Also called **blind horse, far ~, gee ~, offside ~** Cf **lead horse, near horse** Note: The occas attestations of *off horse* (and its synonyms) for the left-hand horse are probably simply errors based on unfamiliarity with, or imperfect recollection of, obsolete terminology (see note at **near horse** and commentary to 1939 *LANE* Map 175). In evaluating the quots, it is important to note that the Linguistic Atlas worksheets, on which quots 1941, 1961, 1962, 1966, 1971, 1973, and 1986 are directly or indirectly based, ask only for terms for the left-hand horse.

1898 Lloyd *Country Life* 62 **AL,** "Boys growin up in the country has powerful hard times, don't they?" says the old man as he laid his whip down on the off mule. **1907** *DN* 3.247 **eME,** *Off horse. . .* The horse on the right and next to the driver. **1910** *DN* 3.446 **wNY,** *Off horse. . .* The horse on the right. **1925** *Book of Rural Life* 5.2674, In putting a pair of horses together, the heavier one should be put on the off (right) side, because in turning out to the right . . the off horse does most work, especially if the road is well crowned to the center. He goes a longer distance and pulls more in returning the load to the center of the road after turning out for a passing vehicle. **1941** *Language* 17.335 **WI** [*LANCS* fieldwork], *Off horse*—27 [of 50 infs]. . . This is the complementary term [to *near horse*], but not all informants mentioned it. Most say it means the right horse; but [4 infs] . . say left, and [1 inf] . . was uncertain. **1950** *WELS* **WI** (*The horse on the driver's right hand in a team*) 18 Infs, Off (horse); (*The horse on the driver's left*) 16 Infs, Off (horse). **1954** *Harder Coll.* **cwTN,** *Off mule. . .* The right hand mule of a team. **1961** *AmSp* 36.268 **CO,** A further example of confusion in terms of uncertain application is the occurrence in the foothills and the West of *off horse* for the left-hand horse of a team. Since the expression usually means the right-hand horse, the response is surprising. **1962** Atwood *Vocab. TX* 56, *Horse on the left. . .* The other horse is most commonly the *off horse.* **1965–70** *DARE* (Qu. K32a, *With a team of horses, . . the horse on the driver's right hand*) 269 Infs, **widespread,** Off horse; **CA**205, **IN**32, Off-hand mule; **NC**49, Off-hand mule; (Qu. K32b, *The horse on the left side in plowing or hauling*) 101 Infs, **widespread,** Off horse. **1966** Dakin *Dial. Vocab. Ohio R. Valley* 2.294, *Off-horse* is usually a term for the horse on the right, but despite the uncertainty expressed by some informants, it is certain that the contradictory usage [=for the horse on the left] is fairly common in some sections. The field records do not indicate whether or not this reversal of terms is the reflection of a practice of driving horses from the opposite (right) side. . . A few comments seem to suggest the possibility that this apparent reversal of the usual usage may have developed from the use of a two horse team with a hand plow. **1971** Bright *Word Geog. CA & NV* 173, The *near horse*/horse on the left . . *off horse* 18% [of 300 infs]. **1973** Allen *LAUM* 1.268 **Upper MW** (as of c1950), As the comments reveal, however, some infs. are unsure whether *near* means right or left; and as many as 22% of the total number have switched referents and now use *off horse* to indicate the horse on [the] left instead of on the right. . . Eleven [of 750 checklist] respondents wrote in *off horse* as their term to describe the horse on the left. Since 9 of them are in the Midland zone and since a similar contrast appears in the field data, this reversal of meaning does seem to be correlated with Midland speech. **1986** Pederson *LAGS Concordance (The lead horse/horse on the left)* 9 infs, **chiefly inland Gulf Region,** (The) off horse; 9 infs, **chiefly inland Gulf Region,** Off horse—on the right; 8 infs, **chiefly inland Gulf Region,** Off horse—on the left; 3 infs, **cnAR, MS,** Off horse—unsure; 2 infs, **TN,** Off horse—the horse that does not walk in the furrow; 2 infs, **TN,** Off horse—in the furrow; 1 inf, **swMS,** Off horse—could be in furrow or outside; 1 inf, **cwAR,** Off horse—and near horse; has forgotten positions; 1 inf, **cTN,** No, the off horse—corrected from "lead"; 1 inf, **cnAR,** The off horse—old people talked about; 1 inf, **swGA,** Off horse—heard; probably partner of lead horse; 1 inf, **cnAR,** Off horse—on the left; walks off the furrow; 1 inf, **neAR,** The off—the other horse, not the lead; 1 inf, **cnAR,** The off—on the left; 1 inf, **cwTN,** "A lead mule," as opposed to the off mule; 1 inf, **nwMS,** Off mule—in plowing; to your right; 1 inf, **csLA,** Off mule—on right side; 3 infs, **AR, cwLA,** Off mule—on the left; 1 inf, **nwAR,** Off steer.

2 An odd or eccentric person; hence adj *off-horseish*. Cf **off ox 2**

1879 *Harper's Weekly* 30 Aug 682, There is often within the party itself a troublesome body of "off-horses," which is roundly cursed as impractical and "sore-headed," but which, nevertheless, must be considered. **1967–69** *DARE* (Qu. II7, *Somebody who doesn't seem to 'fit in' or to get along very well . . "He's kind of a _____."*) Inf **MA71,** Off horse ['ɒf hɒs]; (Qu. GG18, . . *'Obstinate': "Why does he have to be so _____."*) Inf **RI15,** Off-horseish [-'hɔsɪš]; (Qu. HH4, *Someone who has odd or peculiar ideas or notions*) Inf **RI15,** On the offside, off-horseish.

office n

1 See quot. [Cf *OED office* sb. 9.a "*pl.* The parts of a house, or buildings attached to a house, specially devoted to household work or service"]

1895 *DN* 1.391, *Office:* small house of one or two rooms, built to accommodate overflow of large family. N.C. (and South generally?)

2 A toilet, esp one outdoors. [Cf *OED office* sb. 9.b "A privy" 1727 →] *euphem* Cf **post office**

1941 *LANE* Map 354 **NEng,** Jocular euphemisms and circumlocutions offered for the terms *privy, back house,* etc. . . *The office* [3 infs] . . *Arthur's office* [1 inf]. **1942** Berrey-Van den Bark *Amer. Slang* 84.11, *Toilet*. . . Office, . . private office, . . the warden's office. **1950** *WELS (An outside toilet building: Joking names)* 4 Infs, **WI,** Office. **1950** *WELS Suppl.* **csWI,** Office—outdoor toilet. **1968** *DARE* (Qu. M21b) Inf **NJ16,** Out in the office; **AR51,** Outhouse; the offices. **1973** Allen *LAUM* 1.181 **cIA** (as of c1950), *Privy*. . . [1 inf] Office.

3 A post office.

1858 in 1956 Eliason *Tarheel Talk* 285 **cn,cNC,** I . . asked . . if he had been to the office [Eliason: Office—post office]. **1986** Pederson *LAGS Concordance (You mail a package at the _____)* 33 infs, **Gulf Region,** Office.

officer n

=redwing blackbird.

1955 *Oriole* 20.1.12 **GA,** Red-winged blackbird.—Officer (the red patches on the wing of the male suggest military insignia).

offin See **orphan**

offish adj

1 Inclined to stand off, reserved, unapproachable; shy; hence adv *offishly* in a reserved or aloof manner. **chiefly S Midl, NEng**

1831 in 1834 Smith *Life Jack Downing* 146 **ME,** I find some [folks] . . ready to shoulder their guns and march to-morrow if I say the word, and others are a little offish. **1861** *NY Daily Tribune* (NY) 17 June 6/6, A majority of the people in our neighborhood regard us very offishly. **1873** Twain-Warner *Gilded Age* 377 **eTN,** Do not be offish and unsociable. **1899** (1912) Green *VA Folk-Speech* 304, *Offish*. . . Distant in manner; reserved; inclined to keep aloof; shy. **1905** *DN* 3.15 **cCT,** *Offish*. . . Distant or unapproachable in manners. **1907** *St. Nicholas* Aug 905 **seNY,** It was so hard for loyal, fun-loving Rob to be "offish" with one who was so kind to those she loved. **1926** *AmSp* 2.78 **ME,** You

must be duly impressed, or you will be regarded as "tony" or "offish." **1939** FWP *Guide TN* 134, Backcountry folk are prone to use parts of speech in strange ways. . . If a man is reserved, he is "offish" or "uncomeatable." **1952** Brown *NC Folkl.* 1.570, *Offish*. . . Shy, not sociable. **c1960** *Wilson Coll.* **csKY,** *Offish*—Unsociable, shy, sometimes arrogant, self-important. **1966–69** *DARE* (Qu. GG7, . . *Annoyed or upset: "Though we were only ten minutes late, she was all _____."*) Inf **IA17,** Confused, offish, miffed, huffy; (Qu. HH35, *A woman who puts on a lot of airs: "She's too _____ for me."*) Infs **TN31, 33,** Offish; (Qu. II7, *Somebody who doesn't seem to 'fit in' or to get along very well . . "He's kind of a _____."*) Infs **VA18, WA6,** Offish. **1968** *DARE* FW Addit **CT15,** *Bit offish*—slightly haughty.

2 **=off-color.**

1952 Brown *NC Folkl.* 1.570, *Offish*. . . Sick.

offishly See **offish 1**

off-island adv, adj **chiefly Nantucket MA** Cf **off B, off-islander**

Away from the island of which one is resident; originating or produced away from the island.

1916 Macy-Hussey *Nantucket Scrap Basket* 140, "*Off-Island and Off-Islander*"—Words in constant local use, and of too obvious a meaning to require definition. **1916** *DN* 4.335 **Nantucket MA,** *Off island*. . . Elsewhere than on the island (Nantucket). "What would I want to go off island for?" **1941** *LANE* Map 285 **Nantucket MA,** Bread that is not baked in the home. . . [1 inf] *Off-island bread*, usually. **1971** *NY Times* (NY) 27 June sec 10 3/2, One [Martha's Vineyard] islander was heard to remark recently that he never carried more than 30 cents in his pocket unless he planned to go off-island. **1994** NC Lang. & Life Project *Dial. Vocab. Ocracoke* 14 **eNC,** *Off island*—Not from the island. *Walt is an off-island person who studies dialects.*

off-islander n [**off-island**] **NEng, esp Nantucket MA**

One who is not a native of a particular island; an outsider.

1882 (1883) Austin *Nantucket Scraps*, [Subtitle:] *Being the experiences of an off-islander, in season and out of season, among a passing people.* **1914** *DN* 4.156 **Nantucket MA,** *Off-Islander*. . . A stranger visiting the island. **1916** *DN* 4.335 **Nantucket MA,** *Off-islander*. . . One not a Nantucketer. "He [=Napoleon] was a great soldier and a great statesman, but he was an off-islander." **1921** Anderson *An Off-Islander* [title]. **1929** Starbuck *My House* 268 **Nantucket MA,** Then an off-islander started a shoe factory. **1935** *AmSp* 10.38 **seMA,** The inhabitants of . . Nantucket have long been known for their quaint and salty speech. . . The old residents maintain their identity strictly apart from the *off-islanders*. . . A linguistic effect of this detachment is to be found in a locution recorded in 1902 as prevailing among the older inhabitants: "They speak of the continental . . United States as America. . . Perhaps this custom arose from the prudent neutrality of the islanders during the Revolutionary war." **1968–69** *DARE* (Qu. HH31, *Somebody who is not from your community, and doesn't belong*) Inf **CT16,** Outsider, outlander, off-islander; **RI17,** Off-islander. **1975** Gould *ME Lingo* 194, *Off-islander*—A term used by residents of Maine islands to describe anybody who doesn't live on their particular island. Basically, it is not snobbish; but when picked up by summer people to describe other summer people on the mainland it achieves a disparaging nuance never intended by the originators.

off-keel adj [By analogy with *on an even keel* in a sound condition; cf *off-key, off-kilter*]

=off-color.

1968 *DARE* (Qu. BB39, *On a day when you don't feel just right, though not actually sick . . "I'll be all right tomorrow—I'm just feeling _____ today."*) Inf **OH60,** A little off-keel.

off-kilter adj [Var of *out of kilter*]

See quots.

1930s in 1944 *ADD* **eWV,** Off kilter = out of kilter, awry, askew. **1992** Martone *Townships* 168 **cwIA,** We were the fallen ones, always a little behind, a little off-kilter.

offlike adv

Casually, offhandedly.

1949 Arnow *Hunter's Horn* 43 **KY,** When you're as old as I am, man, an if'n you've still not give your heart to God, you won't be a talken so easy an offlike about hell an them that's dead cain't hep theirselves.

off'm See **offen**

off mule See **off horse 1**

off'n See **offen**

off of See **off C1**

off on See **offen**

off one's soundings See **off soundings**

off ox n [**off D1**] chiefly Nth, esp NEast See also **Adam's off-ox, God's off-ox** Cf **off horse**

1 also *off-hand ox:* The right-hand ox in a yoke of oxen.
    1807 *Balance* (Hudson NY) 25 Aug 267 (1912 Thornton *Amer. Gloss.* 2.620), We behold a clumsy, awkward off ox trying the tricks of a kitten. **1855** Douglass *My Bondage* 209 seMD, I was introduced to this huge yoke of unbroken oxen, and was carefully told . . which was the "in hand," and which was the "off hand" ox. **1899** *South Dakotan* 1.176, [He] walked slowly 'round and lovingly rubbed the brockeled face of the off ox. [**1931–33** *LANE Worksheets* ceMA, The nigh ox would be lashed with the whip; the off one prodded with the goad.] **1959** [see **2** below]. **c1960** *Wilson Coll.* csKY, Off ox. . . The one to the right of the driver. **1969** Sorden *Lumberjack Lingo* 82 **NEng, Gt Lakes,** Off ox— The right ox of a team of oxen. Near ox was the one on the left side. Oxen were driven from the left side. **1969** *DARE* (Qu. K32a, *With a team of horses, . . the horse on the driver's right hand*) Inf **MA68,** Off ox—used for oxes; **MA74,** Off ox—expression used more for ox; **NY209,** Off ox—not horse; **NY211,** Off ox—ox, never heard of with horses. **1986** Pederson *LAGS Concordance,* 1 inf, **swMS,** Off ox— walked on side of path away from plowman; 1 inf, **csMS,** The off ox—she thinks it was the one on the right.

2 A stubborn or headstrong person. *old-fash*
    1848 Lowell *Biglow* 90 'Upcountry' MA, Ez to the answerin' o' questions, I'm an off ox at bein' druv. **1867** Lowell *Biglow* lviii 'Up-country' MA, *Off-ox:* an unmanageable, cross-grained fellow. **1903** *DN* 2.352, *Off ox.* . . One who is usually on the opposite side of a popular movement. **1950** *WELS* (*Someone who doesn't seem to "fit in" or get along very well: "He's kind of a _____."*) 1 Inf, **cwWI,** Off ox. **1956** Moody *Home Ranch* 71 **CO** (as of 1911), You could learn a lot from Zeb [=a ranch hand]. . . Kind of an off-ox old critter, . . but a plumb good one. **1959** *VT Hist.* 27.151, *Off ox.* . . 1. The right ox in a pair of oxen. 2. A person contrary to others. Common.

offset v
    To deceive or harm (someone).
    c1938 in 1970 Hyatt *Hoodoo* 1.401 **cSC** [Black], Dere's anothah superstition among men dat if yo' urinate an' don't spit in it. . . somebody kin do somethin' tuh offset chew. . . (To harm you?) Yes, to harm yo'. **1970** *DARE* (Qu. KK36, *Talking about a person who is easily fooled: "It's easy to _____."*) Inf **MO22,** Betray him, offset him. [Inf Black]

offset n Also *offset kitchen* Cf **summer kitchen**
    An outbuilding, esp one used as a kitchen.
    1981 Pederson *LAGS Basic Materials,* 1 inf, **csTN,** Summer kitchen— not a room; an "offset" for warming food; 1 inf, **swGA,** Offset kitchen [=label given, in a sketch, to a small building separate from the "single pen" house of inf's childhood]; 1 inf, **cLA,** Kitchen (was) an offset [illustration shows a small, separate building].

offshore adj
    Fig: see quots.
    1994 NC Lang. & Life Project *Dial. Vocab. Ocracoke* 14 **eNC,** *Offshore*—Crazy, silly or outlandish. . . *Those dingbatters* [=non-natives] *are offshore.* **1994** NC Lang. & Life Project *Harkers Is. Vocab.* 8 **eNC,** *Off-shore.* . . Soundly sleeping. *Jake's been off-shore in bed all morning.*

offside horse n Also *offside worker, offsider* [**off D1**] scattered, but esp nAppalachians See Map
    =**off horse 1.**
    1950 *WELS* **WI** (*The horse on the driver's right hand in a team*) 1 inf, Offside [horse]; (*The horse on the driver's left*) 2 Infs, Offside [horse]. **1965–70** *DARE* (Qu. K32a, *With a team of horses, . . the horse on the driver's right hand*) 29 Infs, esp **wPA, WV, wMD,** Offside horse; **MD29,** Offside worker; **PA163,** Offsider; (Qu. K32b, *The horse on the left side in plowing or hauling*) 9 Infs, **scattered,** Offside horse. **1967** Faries *Word Geog. MO* 96, *Near horse.* . . Substitute expressions offered by Missouri informants are *off horse* (18 occurrences [from c700 written QRs]) . . and *off side horse* [1 occurrence]. **1967** *DARE* FW

Addit **sePA,** You're all dressed out like Mrs. Astor's offside horse. **1986** Pederson *LAGS Concordance* (*Horse on the left*) 1 inf, **nwGA,** The off side [horse]; 1 inf, **swMS,** Off side [horse]—in the furrow; on the left; 1 inf, **ceTX,** Off side [horse], as opposed to "gee side" [horse].

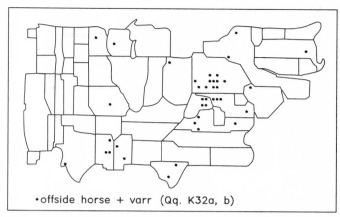

•offside horse + varr (Qq. K32a, b)

offside, on the adj phr Also *on offsides* Cf **off horse 2, off ox 2**
    Of a person: peculiar; irritable.
    1969 *DARE* (Qu. HH4, *Someone who has odd or peculiar ideas or notions*) Inf **RI15,** On the offside. **1986** Pederson *LAGS Concordance* (*Touchy, easily offended, irritable*) 1 inf, **neAR,** On offsides.

offsider, offside worker See **offside horse**

off soundings adv phr Also *off one's soundings* chiefly NEng
    In deep water; also fig: beyond one's capabilities or knowledge.
    1849 Melville *Mardi* 1.6, Like many others, they were keepers of a secret: had doubtless contracted a disgust for some ugly craft still afloat and hearty, and stolen away from her, off soundings. **1899** (1912) Green *VA Folk-Speech* 41, There is no Sunday off soundings. **1916** Macy-Hussey *Nantucket Scrap Basket* 140 seMA, "*Off-Soundings*"—In deep water. One who gets beyond his capacity in an argument is said to be off-soundings, that is, he can't "touch bottom." **1926** Ashley *Yankee Whaler* 137, *Off soundings:* Water too deep for a hand lead. **1942** ME Univ. *Studies* 56.17, When the water is too deep to *fathom* he is *off his soundings* [Footnote: Out of touch, lacking information to guide one]. **1963** Haywood *Yankee Dict.* 113, *Off soundings*—A sailor's term meaning well out to sea. A ship is "off soundings" when she is far enough at sea so she is beyond the relatively shallow waters . . where it is possible to use the lead line to ascertain depth.

offspring n [*OED* a1548–1808; "*obs.*"] Cf Intro "Language Changes" II.7
    Used as count noun rather than mass noun.
    1943 in 1944 *ADD* 423 csPA, 'He had several offsprings.' Used seriously. **1966** *DARE* Tape AL3, There was a white man in the neighborhood. He has some offsprings here. **1968** *DARE* (Qu. K43, *A horse that was not intentionally bred, or bred by accident*) Inf **NH14,** Off-spring; (Qu. Z11b, . . *[A child whose parents were not married]*) Inf **CA59,** Poor little offspring; **NH14,** Offspring. **1986** Pederson *LAGS Concordance* (*Our _____ are still in school*) 4 infs, **neAL, csGA, cMS, csTX,** Offsprings; (*Calf, a little one when it's first born*) 1 inf, **csTX,** Calves, offsprings—plural; (*She is pregnant*) 1 inf, **nwAL,** Looking for an offspring.

offstart n *old-fash*
    The outset, beginning.
    1889 Johnston *Ogeechee Cross-Firings* 23 cGA, Sech idees does a man good in the first off-start. **1898** Johnston *Pearce Amerson's Will* 156 cGA, As for where'd he got his ideas he had at the offstart, . . he never got 'em from nobody but Wile Amerson hisself.

off steer See **off horse 1**

off-taste, off-tasting See **off D2**

off the high end See **high** adj B8

off-the-point n NYC
    A game similar to **stoopball;** see quot 1975; hence adj phr *off-the-point* having struck a corner.
    1968 *DARE* (Qu. EE33, . . *Outdoor games . . that children play*) Inf

NY119, Off-the-point. **1968** *DARE* Tape **NY**118, We used to play like stoopball and off-the-point. You'd have to hit the ball off the sidewalk or off a point of the building and it had to go past a certain place and once it went past a certain place, depending on how many times it bounced, that would be how much it would be. **1975** Ferretti *Gt. Amer. Book Sidewalk Games* 140 **NYC**, There is no way of telling just how the spaldeen will fly out in Off the Point because it is thrown high against a decorative cornice of a building . . . In this game, the onus is on the thrower. He has to throw his spaldeen and catch the rebound on a fly in order to remain up. Even if he fields it cleanly on one bounce, which is something admired in other Stoopball games, he loses his turn at bat. . . A successful catch on the fly gives the thrower 1 point, and 21 points wins. **1995** *DARE* File **NYC**, An informant who was a notable fan of spaldeen-based games . . says that "off-the-point" was a term used . . to describe a throw that bounced directly off the corner (of a building, step, etc.), thus rocketing away unexpectedly.

off the roof adj phr [*fall off the roof*] Cf **off-floor**
Of a woman: menstruating.
    1954 *Harder Coll.* **cwTN**, Off the roof. . . Menstruating. **1968–69** *DARE* (Qu. AA27, . . *A woman's menstruation*) Inf **GA**55, I fell off the roof, I'm off the roof; **GA**89, Got the pip, off the roof, got her monthlies. **1969** *Current Slang* 3.3.9 **FL**, Off the roof, adj. Menstruating.—High school and college students, both sexes.

off, want See **want**

ofn See **offen**

oft and on adv phr Also *often and on* [Varr of *off and on*]
    1909 *DN* 3.353 **eAL, wGA**, Oft and on. . . Off and on. Occasionally heard, as is also a distinct *t* sound in *often*. **1986** Pederson *LAGS Concordance* (*How often do you go to town?*) 1 inf, **ceAL**, Often and on—blend from "off and on."

often adv Usu |'ɔf(ə)n, 'af(ə)n|; also |'ɔft(ə)n|; for addit varr see quots Pronc-sp *offen* Cf Pronc Intro 3.III.4 [*OED* "The pronunciation ['ɔftən], which is not recognized in the dictionaries, is now frequent in the south of England, and is often used in singing."]
    Std senses, var forms.
    1848 Lowell *Biglow* 145 **'Upcountry' MA**, Offen, often. **1891** *DN* 1.165 **cNY**, In [ɔftn̩] it [=excrescent *t*] has probably always remained in common speech. **1905** *DN* 3.101 **nwAR**, [ɔftn̩] (not [ɔfn̩]). **1909** [see **oft and on**]. **1928** *AmSp* 3.405 **Ozarks**, The Ozarker nearly always pronounces the *t* in *often*. **1936** *AmSp* 11.312 **Upstate NY**, In *often*, the historical loss of [t] has usually been accepted as 'standard'; in my records it occurs 209 times in the 'standard' form, and 51 times with [t] retained or restored. **1940** *AmSp* 15.369 **nePA**, Often ['ɔfn], ['ɒfn]. **1942** Hall *Smoky Mt. Speech* 32 **wNC, eTN**, Often ['ɒºftən]. **1942** *AmSp* 17.36 **seNY**, Often . . [ɒ] 1 [inf] . . [ɔ] 25 [infs] . . [ɔ‧] 3 [infs]. *Ibid* 156, Downstate dialect . . occasionally restores the [t] to *often*. **1943** *LANE* Map 711 (*How often?*), [*Often* is commonly pronc, esp **wNEng**, [ɔf(ə)n], and, **esp eNEng**, [ɒf(ə)n]; also, **chiefly eMA, NH, eVT, ME**, [ɒfm, ɔ-]; occas, **chiefly wMA**, [afn], and, **esp s,wNEng**, [ɒft(ə)n, ɔ-]; rarely [af(t)tn].] **c1960** *Wilson Coll.* **csKY**, Often ['ɔfn]. Less frequently ['ɔftən]. *Often* in "How often?" is usually the former. In singing or trying to be "proper" some people say the latter. **1965–70** *DARE* (Qu. A15) 10 Infs, **scattered**, ['ɔftən, -ɪn, -ɪn, -ɛn]; (Qu. KK40) Infs **MO**5, 9, ['ɒftɪn]; **LA**6, ['ɔftən]. **1989** Pederson *LAGS Tech. Index* 257 **Gulf Region**, 369 infs [ɔftn]; 257 infs, [ɔfn]; 40 infs, [ɒftn]; 31 infs, [ɒfn]; 34 infs, [af(t)n]; 10 infs, [af(t)n]; 1 inf, **swLA**, [ɑrfn]; 1 inf, **cnTN**, [aufn].

often and on See **oft and on**

oftenly adv [*OED* 1577; "*Obs. rare*"] Cf Intro "Language Changes" II.8
    1916 *DN* 4.278 **NE**, Oftenly. . . Often.

often usually adv phr [Redund; cf Intro "Language Changes" I.4] Cf **generally always, usually ~**
Usually.
    1930 *VA Qrly. Rev.* 6.247 **S Midl**, Backwoods speech abounds in pleonasms . . often usually.

oftin See **orphan**

ofttimes adv [*OED* 1382 →; "Now *arch*. and *poet*."] Cf **most time(s)**
Often, frequently.

1806 (1970) Webster *Compendious Dict.* 207, Oft, Oft'en, Oft'entimes, Oft'times. [*DARE* Ed: This entry was carried over from Webster's English model.] **1899** (1912) Green *VA Folk-Speech* 304, Oftentimes. . . Ofttimes; frequently; many times; often. **1943** *LANE* Map 711 (*How often?*) 2 infs, **ceCT, cwRI**, Ofttimes. **1967–68** *DARE* Tape **AZ**8, In the more modern dishes a garnish of lettuce is ofttimes used; **IN**30, Ofttimes there would be two rooms; **MI**66, Ofttimes. **1968** *DARE* FW Addit **PA**142, We ofttimes would go to Coburn. **1986** Pederson *LAGS Concordance*, 2 infs, **ceAL, ceTX**, Ofttimes.

Ogeechee lime n Also *geechy lime, Ogeche plum;* for addit sp varr see quots [From the *Ogeechee* R., Georgia]
A Southern **tupelo** (here: *Nyssa ogeche*); also its acid fruit. Also called **gopher plum 1, lime tree** n[2], **Ogeechee tupelo, sour ~, white ~, wild lime**
    1775 (1962) Romans *Nat. Hist. FL* 23, These savannahs . . are overgrown with different species of the *cratægus*, or hawthorn, as also very often a species of shrub much resembling the *Laurus* in appearance . . its fruit . . is a bacca with several cells full of an agreeable acid like the common lime from the West Indies; it is of the size of a large pigeon's egg, but more oblong; we also find it on the low banks of rivers in Georgia, and know it by the name of the Ogeechee lime. **1785** Marshall *Arbustrum* 97, The Ogeche Lime Tree. . . The fruit is nearly oval, of a deep red colour, of the size of a Damascene Plumb. **1791** Bartram *Travels* 17, The most northern settlement of this tree, yet known, is on Great Ogeeche, where they are called Ogeeche limes, from their acid fruit being about the size of limes, and their being sometimes used in their stead. **1819** (1821) Nuttall *Jrl.* 71, In this swamp, I also observed the *Nyssa aquatica, N. pubescens* (Ogeechee lime, the fruit being prepared as a conserve). **1908** Britton *N. Amer. Trees* 740, Ogeche Plum—*Nyssa Ogeche.* . . This is a round-headed tree, known also as the Ogeche lime, Gopher plum, Wild lime tree, and Tupelo. **1943** Fernald–Kinsey *Edible Wild Plants E. N. Amer.* 302, The well known Ogeechee Lime of wooded swamps from Florida to South Carolina has large red fruits up to 1½ inches long. **1950** *PADS* 14.32 **SC**, Geechy limes. . . Preserved limes, said to be from the Ogeechee river of Georgia. **1979** Little *Checklist U.S. Trees* 179, *Nyssa ogeche* . . Ogeechee tupelo. . . Other common names—Ogeechee-lime, sour tupelo, sour tupelo-gum, white tupelo.

Ogeechee tupelo n
=**Ogeechee lime.**
    1946 West–Arnold *Native Trees FL* 162, The Ogeechee tupelo is distributed sporadically from Dixie and St. Johns counties to western Florida, typically on river banks. The sour, juicy fruits of this small, irregular tree are occasionally used to prepare a cooling summer beverage. **1962** Kurz–Godfrey *Trees N. FL* 238, The Ogeechee tupelo is common throughout our area in sloughs, bayous, on river banks, in swamps, and on pond and lake shores. **1980** Little *Audubon Guide N. Amer. Trees E. Region* 619, Ogeechee Tupelo "Ogeechee-lime" "Sour Tupelo"—*Nyssa ogeche.* . . Ogeechee-lime preserve is made from the edible but sour fruit, and the juice is used like that of limes.

ogle eye n
A bulging or round eye; hence adj **ogle-eyed** having such eyes.
    1966–69 *DARE* (Qu. X21a, . . *Words . . used to describe people according to their eyes . . if they stick out*) Inf **PA**188, Ogle eyes; (Qu. X21b, *If the eyes are very sharp or piercing*) Inf **NM**12, Ogle-eyed [FW: Inf queries]; (Qu. X21c, *If the eyes are very round*) Infs **MN**37, **WI**68, Ogle-eyed.

oh-be-joyful See **o-be-joyful**

oh dear (me) See **dear** intj

ohelo n [Haw *'ōhelo*] **HI** Cf **ohelo-kai**
A Hawaiian plant of the genus *Vaccinium*, esp *V. reticulatum;* also the fruit of such a plant. For other names of *V. reticulatum* see **Hawaiian huckleberry**
    1825 Ellis *Jrl. HI* 128, By the way side, we saw a number of low bushes, bearing beautiful red and yellow berries in clusters, each berry being about the size and shape of a large currant. . . The native name of the plant is *ohelo*. **1873** in 1966 Bishop *Sandwich Is.* 71 **HI**, I notice that the foreigners never use the English or botanical names of trees or plants, but speak of *ohias, ohelos, kukui* (candle-nut) . . &c. **1896** *Pop. Sci. Mth.* 48.757, On the island of Hawaii are great thickets of the *ohelo*, or Hawaiian huckleberry (*Vaccinium reticulatum*). **1929** Pope *Plants HI* 163, The Ohelo is a native Hawaiian fruit-plant which grows mainly on the islands of Hawaii and Maui at elevations ranging from 3500 to 6000

feet. . . The Hawaiian name, Ohelo, means berry. **1930** Degener *Ferns of HI* 244, The high-bush *ohelo* . . is *Vaccinium calycinum*. . . It may be found on all the larger islands in this group in the more open rain forest. . . Its bitter berries. . . are sometimes added in small numbers to the true *ohelo* berry before cooking to impart a special flavor to them. **1967** *DARE* (Qu. 144, *What kinds of berries grow wild around here?*) Inf **HI**1, [oˈhɛlo]—related to cranberry, on other islands, edible, used for jam; **HI**3, [oˈhɛlo]—similar to blueberry but orange-red all over. **1970** Carlquist *Hawaii* 320, Most kinds of ohelo *(Vaccinium)* grow in open places. . . However, the large-leaved *V. calycinum* is common in the undergrowth of wet forest. *Ibid* 364, Two ohelos can be found on the floor of Haleakala Crater: *Vaccinium reticulatum* . . and *V. berberidifolium*. **1994** Stone–Pratt *Hawai'i's Plants* 135, 'Ōhelo fruits may be distinguished from 'ākia by their many tiny seeds and round disk at the tip bearing the calyx lobes of the flower.

ohelo-kai n [See quot 1929] **HI** Cf **ohelo**
A **wolfberry** (here: *Lycium sandwicense*) native to Hawaii.
   1911 *Century Dict. Suppl.*, Aeae. . . A name in Hawaii of *Lycium Sandwicense*, an erect shrub from two to three feet high, with stiff, smooth branches. It grows along the sea-coast, and bears a red berry which is edible but not very palatable. Also called *ohelo-kai*. **1929** Pope *Plants HI* 207, The fleshy leaves of Ohelo-kai are eaten by livestock in times of scarcity of green forage. . . The native name Ohelo-kai means the Ohelo near the sea. It is in no way related to the true Ohelo, *Vaccinium reticulatum*. **1948** Neal *In Gardens HI* 652, 'Ohelo kai. . . A small spreading shrub a few inches to 3 feet high, growing near salt marshes and among rocks near the sea. . . The berries are shiny, red, globose . . and contain salty-tasting pulp with many flat seeds. **1970** Carlquist *Hawaii* 273, The aeae (or ohelo kai) occurs on Hawaiian coasts.

oh for exclam
1 with primary stress on *oh;* foll by adj: How. Cf **for** prep **B4c**
   1981 Bly *Letters* 50 **swMN,** If whoever of us, like Hamlet, should now wonder aloud how it is without the mortal coil, no one need kill that with "Oh, for morbid!" because the house is full of confidence. **1987** Mohr *How Minnesotan* 70, The *oh, for* construction is used mostly by women to describe a person, thing, or animal, including oneself. For example, if a kitten climbs into somebody's shoe, you would say *Oh, for cute.* If the baby smiles and waves its arms, you would say *Oh, for darling.* . . If you were supposed to bring . . salad to the potluck and you forgot it, you would say—"Oh, for dumb." **1988** *DARE* File **cnUT** (as of c1965), My mother, who has lived most of her life in Ogden, Utah, uses the exclamatory formula "Oh for _____" to emphasize a particular quality. She would say, for example, "Oh for cute!" if something struck her as remarkably adorable or cute, and "Oh for rude!" when someone was especially impolite or rude. *Ibid* **cnUT,** Oh for, a Utahism, meaning "oh how" followed by an adjective, as in "Oh for ignorant!" = How ignorant!, that is, how can one be so ignorant? Or "Oh for fun" = Oh how amusing or fun. Reported from Provo.
2 with equal stress on both words; foll by a person's name: Used as a call to someone.
   1981 *DARE* File **seWI** (as of c1950), When we were kids in Brookfield and West Allis, if we wanted someone else to come out and play, we'd go to the back screen door and yell "Oh for Jimmy!" ['oː ˈfɔːr ˈʤɪmiː] or whatever his name was, and he'd come out. **1992** *Ibid* **seWI** (as of c1945), When I was growing up in "west Racine" or "Kringleville", children stood out in front of a playmate's house and called "Oh for Janet!" ['oː ˈfɔːr ˈʤæːnɪt] or "Oh for Junior!" in order to get the friend to come out to play. As far as I know, this form of address was only used in this part of Racine and nowhere else.

ohia n[1] **HI**
1 also *ohia-ai:* =**Malay apple.** [Haw *'ōhi'a, 'ōhi'a-'ai* literally "edible ohia"]
   1824 (1970) Stewart *Jrl. Sandwich Is.* 305 **HI,** The only trees and plants known to us, which we saw . . were the koa, *acacia,* a large and beautiful tree of dark, hard wood, . . the Ohia, *eugenia malaccensis,* bearing a beautifully tufted crimson flower, and a fruit called by foreigners, the native apple. **1825** Ellis *Jrl. HI* 27, Here they enjoyed the agreeable shade of bread-fruit and *ohia* trees. The latter is a deciduous plant, bearing a beautifully red, pulpy fruit, of the size and consistency of an apple. **1833** in 1934 Frear *Lowell & Abigail* 74 **HI,** The "Ohia" or native apple tree yields a fruit resembling in form and color like our American apple, although inferior in taste. It contains a stone like the

peach instead of seeds like our apple. **1896** *Pop. Sci. Mth.* 48.757, The *ohia,* or Malay apple, is a common timber tree of the Hawaiian Islands. . . On the Island of Maui is a mammoth orchard of wild ohias. **1911** *Century Dict. Suppl.*, It [=the Malay apple] is often called *ohia-ai* (edible ohia) in distinction from *ohia-lehua* (flowering ohia). **1924** *Amer. Botanist* 30.20, Another tree, doubtless imported like the bread fruit, by the aborigines, although now one of the most common of the forest trees, is the ohia or mountain apple. **1948** Neal *In Gardens HI* 559, 'Ohi'a 'ai. . . A handsome tree . . found on many islands of the Pacific. **1980** Bushnell *Water of Kane* 413 **HI,** Henry descended amid the crowns of leaves, into the green half-light beneath the spreading kukui trees and tall ohia-ai and ohia-lehua.
2 also *ohia-lehua,* abbr *lehua:* A tree *(Metrosideros macropus)* native to Hawaii. [Haw *'ohi'a, 'ohi'a-lehua*]
   1836 *Sandwich Is. Gaz. & Jrl. of Commerce* (Honolulu HI) 10 Sept, The Northern mountains [of Hawaii] . . are thickly wooded, abounding with large trees . . , but the largest and most plentiful is the Ohia rehua; here this species . . appears generally to take root on the top of the fern trees at a height of 20 or 30 feet from the ground, the roots shoot downward and reach the earth, the fern tree thus trampled on gradually decays and leaves the tree supported on a number of arching trunks with a vaulted space beneath. [*DARE* Ed: Haw has only one liquid consonant, which early writers often represented with *r* rather than *l*.] **1866** in 1966 Twain *Letters HI* 99, Shady groves of forest trees . . and, handsomest of all, the ohia, with its feathery tufts of splendid vermilion-tinted blossoms. **1888** Hillebrand *Flora Hawaiian Is.* 125, M[etrosideros] *polymorpha*. . . The most generally prevailing tree on all Islands between 1500 and 6000 ft., usually gregarious. Nat[ive] name: 'Ohia lehua', or simply 'Lehua'. **1917** *Nature* (London) 20 Sept 57, The ohia *(Matrosideros polymorpha)*. . . also called ohia lehua and lehua, resembles . . our white oak, but bears beautiful clusters of scarlet flowers with long, protruding stamens. **1930** Degener *Ferns of HI* 232, The flowers of the *ohia lehua,* which in exceptional cases may vary from the usual scarlet to yellow, were formerly much used by the Hawaiians in the weaving of garlands, or *lei.* **1970** Carlquist *Hawaii* 350, [Caption:] A typical scene in the central part of Alakai Swamp . . shows standing water, low vegetation, and pockets of ohia forest. **1980** [see **1** above]. **1994** Stone–Pratt *Hawai'i's Plants* 11, The 'ōhi'a is the most abundant and widespread native tree in the Hawaiian Islands. . . A morphologically variable species, 'ōhi'a has eight varieties. . . All varieties bear clusters of pompom-shaped flowers [which]. . . are usually red. . . 'Ōhi'a flowers (lehua) produce large amounts of sweet nectar. . . Many 'ōhi'a trees . . bear clusters of reddish aerial roots hanging from main branches.

Ohia n[2] See **Ohio**

ohia-ai See **ohia 1**

ohia-lehua See **ohia 2**

Ohio n Usu |oˈhaɪo|; also |oˈhaɪə, (ə)ˈhaɪə| Pronc-spp *Hiah, Hio, Ohia*
Std senses, var forms.
   1810 (1912) Bell *Journey to OH* 11 **MA,** We were going to the Hio. **1890** *DN* 1.17 neOH, The generation has passed away here that pronounced *hiah* for *Ohio*. **1891** *DN* 1.158 cNY, [haɪə] < *Ohio*. **1892** *DN* 1.240 cwMO, Ohio. The every-day pronunciation in Kansas City is [əhaɪə]. [*DN* Ed: of course accented on the second syllable. This is also known in New England.] **1940** in 1944 *ADD* swPA, nWV, [əˈhaɪə]— Old speaker. **1942** *Ibid* **WV,** [Radio:] [əhaɪə]. **1943** *Ibid* nWV, [oˈhaɪə]. . . Educated. **1979** *NYT Article Letters* **sOH,** My uncle . . is now 73 and was raised in rural southern Ohio (that's "Ohi-uh," like "Cincinnat-uh" . . and "pie-an-uh"). **1987** Kytle *Voices* 202 **NC,** White and black, both, put on a show in Ohio, which they call Ohia.

Ohio buckeye n [See quot 1813]
A **buckeye 1** (here: *Aesculus glabra*). Also called **horse chestnut 2, stinking buckeye**
   1810 Michaux *Histoire des Arbres* 1.34, Ohio buck eye. **1813** *Ibid* 3.242, The American Horse Chesnut. Or Ohio Buckeye. . . Je l'ai seulement vue au-delà des montagnes, et plus particulièrement sur les bords de l'Ohio, entre Pittsburgh et Marietta, où elle est extrêmement commune. . . Les habitans lui donnent le nom de *Buckeye;* mais cette dénomination étant la même que celle qui a été donnée au *Pavia lutea,* qui croît plus au Sud, dans la Virginie et les Hautes-Carolines, j'ai cru devoir, pour éviter toute confusion, y ajouter le nom d'*Ohio,* par la seule raison que cet arbre est peut-être, sur les rives de cette rivière, plus multiplié que partout ailleurs. [=The American Horse Chestnut. Or Ohio buckeye. . . I have seen it only beyond the mountains, and especially

on the banks of the Ohio, between Pittsburgh and Marietta, where it is extremely common. . . The inhabitants there give it the name of *Buckeye,* but since that name is the same as that given to *Pavia lutea,* which grows further south, in Virginia and the High Carolinas, I have thought it necessary, in order to avoid any confusion, to add the name *Ohio,* simply because this tree is perhaps more numerous on the banks of that river than anywhere else.] **1847** Wood *Class-Book* 214, *Ohio Buckeye.* . . A small, ill-scented tree, along the banks of the Ohio and its tributaries. **1897** Sudworth *Arborescent Flora* 294, *Ohio Buckeye* (Miss., Ga., Ark., Mo., Ohio). **1908** Britton *N. Amer. Trees* 659, Ohio Buckeye—*Aesculus glabra.* . . This tree grows best in moist soil, especially along and near rivers, and is distributed from western Pennsylvania to Alabama, Illinois, Iowa, and the Indian Territory. **1917** (1923) Rogers *Trees Worth Knowing* 53, The Ohio buckeye has . . bitter nuts in spiny husks. . . The great abundance of this little tree in the Ohio Valley accounts for Ohio being called the "Buckeye State." **1948** *Chicago Sun-Times* (IL) 20 Apr 32/2, The Ohio buckeye . . is the first of all the big trees to burst forth with leaves. **1960** Vines *Trees SW* 680, Ohio Buckeye. . . The wood is used for fuel, paper pulp, artificial limbs, splints, woodenware, boxes, crates, toys, furniture, veneer for trunks, drawing boards, and occasionally for lumber. **1980** Little *Audubon Guide N. Amer. Trees E. Region* 583, Ohio Buckeye—"Fetid Buckeye."

Ohio curcuma n [Because the rootstock has similar uses to that of *Curcuma longa,* the source of turmeric]
=goldenseal 1.

1876 Hobbs *Bot. Hdbk.* 29, Ohio Curcuma . . Goldenseal . . *Hydrastis Canadensis.* **1900** Lyons *Plant Names* 195, *H[ydrastis] Canadensis.* . . Golden-seal . . Ohio Curcuma, Indian Turmeric . . Indian dye. **1930** Sievers *Amer. Med. Plants* 31, Goldenseal . . Other common names . . Ohio curcuma, ground raspberry [etc]. **1971** Krochmal *Appalachia Med. Plants* 144, Ohio curcuma. . . In Appalachia, a root tea is used as a tonic. **1974** (1977) Coon *Useful Plants* 220, Ohio curcuma. . . The roots are the part used, either as a source for a yellow dye, or in reputable medical practice as an alterative and bitter tonic.

Ohio pike n Cf Ohio salmon
A **pike perch** such as a **walleye** (here: *Stizostedion vitreum vitreum*); see quots.

1856 *Porter's Spirit of Times* 20 Sept 40, The Pike-perch, *Lucioperca Americana,* variously known as the Glass-eye, the Ohio Pike, the Yellow Pike, and possibly also, as the Ohio salmon. **1927** Weed *Pike* 46 **OH,** *Stizostedion*—Common names of this group are so confused that no attempt has been made to separate names belonging only to the Saugers from those belonging only to the Walleye. It is probable that practically all the names are applied to either. . . Ohio Pike.

Ohio River pigtoe n Cf pigtoe
A **freshwater clam** (here: *Pleurobema cordatum*).

1982 U.S. Fish & Wildlife Serv. *Fresh-Water Mussels* [Wall chart], Ohio River Pigtoe . . *Pleurobema cordatum* . . Shell brown or black, heavy. . . Jeopardized. *Ibid,* Ohio River Pigtoe. Historically widespread, uncommon; recent living records . . Nearly extirpated.

Ohio salmon n Also *salmon of the Ohio* Cf Ohio pike, salmon
=walleye (here: *Stizostedion vitreum*).

1820 Rafinesque *Ohio R. Fishes* 21, Salmon Perch. *Perca Salmonea.* . . It has received the vulgar names of *Salmon, White Salmon,* and *Ohio Salmon.* It is not a common fish, but is occasionally caught all over the Ohio and in the Kentucky, Licking, Wabash, and Miami rivers during the spring and summer. **1838** Geol. Surv. OH *Second Annual Rept.* 190, The *salmon of the Ohio, pike of the lake,* . . and *Perca salmonis* of Raf[inesque]. . . is one of the most valuable fishes for the table found in the western waters, and sells readily at a high price in the markets of the towns on the banks of the Ohio. Those taken in Lake Erie are less esteemed. **1865** Norris *Amer. Angler's Book* 120, Ohio Salmon. *Lucioperca Americana.* . . Of the many misnomers given to fish, [this] . . is the most inappropriate. . . Still we are not disposed to find fault with rustic anglers because, in the absence of scientific knowledge, they have given what seemed to them the most fitting name for it. **1872** *Fur, Fin, & Feather: Game Laws* 131 (*DA* at glass-eyed pike), The Mohawk River is stocked with black and Oswego bass and the Ohio salmon, or glass-eyed pike. **1927** Weed *Pike* 46, Ohio Salmon; Ohio River valley.

Ohio shad n
Either a **skipjack** (here: *Alosa chrysochloris*) or a related **shad** (here: *A. alabamae*).

1820 Rafinesque *Ohio R. Fishes* 39, *Pomolobus chrysochloris.* . .

Greenish-gold above, silvery beneath. . . A fine fish from twelve to eighteen inches long. Flesh esteemed, white and with less bones than the shad. . . Its vulgar names are Ohio Shad, Gold Shad, Green Herring, &c. **1882** U.S. Natl. Museum *Bulletin* 16.266, *C[lupea] chrysochloris* . . Ohio Shad; Skipjack. . . Gulf of Mexico and Mississippi Valley; abundant, and resident in all the larger streams, and introduced through the canals into Lake Erie and Lake Michigan. A handsome fish, not valued for food. **1884** *Ibid* 27.455, *Clupea chrysochloris.* . . Ohio shad; Skipjack; Blue Herring. **1956** Harlan–Speaker *IA Fish* 60, *Ohio Shad—Alosa ohiensis* [=*A. alabamae*]. . . Included as an Iowa species on the basis of those collected in the Mississippi River at Keokuk [in 1930]. **1991** Amer. Fisheries Soc. *Common Names Fishes* 169, Shad, . . Ohio—see Alabama shad [=*Alosa alabamae*].

oh my dear See **dear** intj

oil n[1], v Usu |ɔɪl|; also chiefly Sth, S Midl, NEng |aɪl|; chiefly Midl |ɔ(r)l|; chiefly NYC |ʌɪl, ɜɪl|; occas |ɝl|; for addit varr see quots Pronc-spp *all, awl, e(a)rl, ile, i'll* See Pronc Intro 3.I.11 Cf **boil** n[1], v
Std senses, var forms.

1795 Dearborn *Columbian Grammar* 136, *List of Improprieties.* . . I'll for Oil. **1815** Humphreys *Yankey in England* 106 **NEng,** *Ile,* oil. **1858** Hammett *Piney Woods Tavern* 281, I took them locks off to clean and ile. **1871** Eggleston *Hoosier Schoolmaster* 87 **sIN,** A black dog's ile a'n't worth no more nor a white one's. **1893** Shands *MS Speech* 39, *Ile* [aɪl]. Negro for *oil.* **1904** Day *Kin o' Ktaadn* 87 **ME,** There's nothin' saves the doctor's bills like ile upon his boots. **1908** *DN* 3.322 **eAL, wGA,** *Ile.* **1923** *DN* 5.211 **swMO,** *Ile.* **1925** Krapp *Engl. Lang.* 2.199, It is not improbable also that the pronunciation of words like *oil* [ʌɪl], [əɪl] which is common in the popular dialect of New York City and elsewhere, is merely a survival from an earlier more general pronunciation. **1928** *NY Times* (NY) 12 Aug sec 8 6/2 **NYC,** The specialists of the Department of English at Columbia seem to think that the spread of . . "erl" for "oil" is comparatively recent, though both can be traced back to eighteenth-century English. **1931** *PMLA* 46.1317 **sAppalachians,** *Oil* is usually "awl." **1937** *AmSp* 12.170 **NYC,** The pronunciation [əɪl] for *earl* is by no means limited to the East Side and the Bowery. A New Yorker might have this pronunciation in the *r*-words and consider the same sound in *oil, boil* a crude pronunciation, since he would use [ɔɪ] in these words. A New Yorker untrained in phonetics who declares or writes that some New Yorkers say *earl* for *oil* is thus giving a correct analysis from the point of view of his own pronunciation, but one that, seen in print, would be a misleading analysis to a speaker of General American. *Ibid* 286 **wVA,** Occasionally [ɔrl], [tɔrlət] . . are heard for *oil, toilet.* **1939** *LANE* Map 187 *(Oil),* [**Widespread NEng,** [ɔɪl, ɔ-]; chiefly eNEng, esp NH, ME, [aɪl, ɑɪl, ɐɪl], often said by infs to be obsolete or old-fashioned; CT, RI, c,wMA, wVT, [ɔəl, ɔ-, oɛl, ɔ-]; chiefly sNEng, [oɪəl, ɔ-, ojəl, ɔ-]; 7 infs, eMA, seNH, eME, [owɪl, ɔ-].] **1940** *AmSp* 15.374 **NYC,** In the speech of certain less-educated New Yorkers. . . [əɪ]. The first element of this diphthong may vary between the limits of the [ʌ] in *cut* and a vowel which is considerably higher and farther forward. This group includes . . *spoil, oil,* . . *ointment.* **1944** Wellman *Bowl* 190 **KS,** You, Gary, fetch some coal ile. **1950** Hubbell *Pronc. NYC* 69, [Among cultivated speakers] even when /ɜɪ/ appears in their speech in *curl, earl, learn,* such words are not homonyms of *coil, oil,* and *loin. Ibid* 142, I have several times heard pronunciations like /ɜɪl/ *oil* from elderly speakers of a cultivated sort, but their practice was quite unusual. **c1960** *Wilson Coll.* **csKY,** *Oil*—[ɑɪl] sometimes; also [ɔrl]. **1961** Kurath–McDavid *Pronc. Engl.* 167, As far as . . *oil,* and *boil* are concerned, a rather important deviation exists. . . The earlier /ɔi/ has either been merged with the /ɔ/ of *dog* . . , as in the western part of the Carolinas (where *oil* rimes with *all*), or developed into the sequence /ər/ . . , as in scattered instances in the Midland. . . *Oil* predominantly has the vowel /ɔi/ of *boy* on all social levels in the Eastern States, the /ai/ of *five* being exceedingly rare, except in parts of New Hampshire and Maine; scattered instances of it occur chiefly in coastal communities from Chesapeake Bay to Georgia. . . In Metropolitan New York /ɜ/ appears. *Ibid* map 145 **chiefly Appalachians, Delmarva,** Incidence of /ɔ/ and /ɔr/ in *boiled, spoiled,* and *oil.* **1965** Carmony *Speech Terre Haute* 114 **cwIN,** /ɔi/ . . is the usual syllabic of *oysters* and *oil,* the exceptions occurring in the records of the Negro informants. . . [1 inf] has /ɔr/ . . in *oil.* **1965–70** *DARE* (Qu. F45, . . *Fuel that's used in an ordinary lamp*) Inf **GA**72, [ˈkoʊl ɔ˅·l]; **IL**63, [ˈkoʊɔɪl] [FW: pronounced as one word]; **LA**33, [ˈkoʊl,ɔɪəl], also [ˈko,lɔɪ]; **LA**43, [ɪnˈsʊrənts,ɜəl]; **MD**21, [ˈkol,ɔrl]; **MD**24, [ˈkol,ɔɪl] [FW: [ɔrl] in conv]; **MD**28, [ɔrl]; **MO**38, [ˈfjuˑuɫ,oɪɫ]; **NY**70, [ˈfju,lɔɪəl]; **PA**77, [ɔrl]; **SC**6, [aʊjəl]; **SD**1, [ɪˈlumə,netɪŋ ,ɔɪl]. **1966** Labov *Social Stratification NYC*

231, The upgliding central diphthong may be written phonetically as [ə͡ɪ], and as /ʌy/ in the phonemic notation. . . A few lower class and working class respondents used this diphthong for *oil* and *voice,* as well as *Earl* and *verse*. But this merger of word classes is rare today; middle class speakers have apparently never used /ʌy/ for the *voice* group of words, even when they used it regularly for *verse*. **1967** *DARE* FW Addit **eTN,** *Oil* [ɑ·l]. **1976** Allen *LAUM* 3.28 **IA, eNE** (as of c1950), Before /l/ in the monosyllables *oil* and *boil(ed)* it [=the diphthong] may be so protracted before the onset of /l/ that there is produced a two-syllable word with a weak intervening /j/ glide, e.g., [ɔjəl] and [ʋijəl]. This disyllabic form for either or both *oil* and *boil* is recorded in the speech of . . [27 infs] in Iowa and eastern Nebraska. **1989** Pederson *LAGS Tech. Index* 91 **Gulf Region,** 867 infs, [ɔɪl]; 18 infs, [ɔl]; 12 infs, [ɔɪ]; 8 infs, [aɪl]; 6 infs, [ɔrl]; 1 inf, [ɑrl]; 3 infs, [ʌrl]; 2 infs, [ow(ɛ)l]. **1990** Amory *Cat & Curmudgeon* 192 **eTX,** I kept thinking about that East Texas accent. . . "all" for oil, or "are" for hair.

oil n² See **earl** n¹

oilan See **island**

oil bag n Also *oil can, ~ pot*
The oil gland of a bird.

    1806 (1970) Webster *Compendious Dict.* 207, *Oilbag . .* a gland in birds containing an oil. **1954** *Harder Coll.* **cwTN,** The rump of a cooked chicken: "Got oil bag back there. I just call it the back; also the oil bag. Runs oil down; keeps lice off 'im. Heerd called last part through the fence." **1966–68** *DARE* (Qu. K73, . . *Names . . for the rump of a cooked chicken*) Inf **AL33,** Tail, oil bag—where the feathers came out; **NM3,** Oil bag; **NJ17,** Oil can; **NJ22,** Oil pot.

oil-base road See **oiled road**

oil bean n

The soybean *(Glycine max)* or a var thereof.

    1970 *DARE* (Qu. I20, . . *Kinds of beans*) Inf **MS87,** Oil beans—people raise beans around here that are used in making oil; (Qu. L34, . . *Most important crops grown around here*) Infs **KY84,** Oil beans—variety of soybean; **MS87,** Oil beans.

oilbird n [See quots 1925, 1955]
=**fulmar.**

    1917 *Wilson Bulletin* 29.2.76, *Fulmarus glacialis . .* Noddy . . oil-bird, North-eastern Banks. [**1925** (1928) Forbush *Birds MA* 1.137, Large numbers of the birds [=fulmars] are taken annually for their oil which is used for lighting as well as for medicinal purposes. . . The clear, yellowish or amber-colored Fulmar oil is one of the principal products of the island [=St. Kilda].] **1955** MA Audubon Soc. *Bulletin* 39.310 **NEng,** Fulmar. . . Oil Bird (from the oily substance it spews upon provocation).

oil can See **oil bag**

oiled road n Also *oil-base road, oiled highway, oil-surfaced road, oil-top ~, oil(y) ~* **scattered, but chiefly West, NEast** See Map Cf **oil mat (road), tarred road**
An unpaved road graded and bound by a thin layer of crude petroleum or other bitumen.

    [**1913** (1919) *WNID, Oiled. . . Road making*. Designating a kind of road made by spreading a layer of crude petroleum or asphalt residuums heated to a high temperature on a roadbed of dirt and sand. It is esp. suitable for hot, dusty countries.] **1939** FWP *Guide MT* 226, Left from Scobey on State 13, an oiled road traversing grain- and cattle-raising country. *Ibid* 240, At 8.1 *m.* is the junction with an unnumbered oil-sur-faced road. **1952** FWP *Guide SD* 297, Left on this oiled highway is *Scotland. Ibid,* Right on this oil-surfaced road is *Armour. Ibid* 326, At 28.2 *m.* is the junction with an oiled road. **1965–70** *DARE* (Qu. N21, *Roads that are surfaced with smooth black pavement*) 14 Infs, **esp West,** Oiled (road *or* roads); **CO22, WA8,** Oil (road); (Qu. N23, *Other kinds of paved roads*) 11 Infs, **chiefly West, NEast,** Oiled road; **WA1,** Oiled road—gravel and oil; **MO11,** Oil; **IL41,** Oil—they call it a three-A road: one layer of gravel, one of oil; gravel, oil; gravel, oil; in the summer all the oil comes to the top and we say the road bleeds; **IL104,** Oil roads—gravel roads, graded up and oiled; **CA189,** Oil road; **NY142,** Oil-base; **NY206,** Oil-top road; **AR3,** Oily road; [**IA11,** Gravel and oil; **MN2,** Hard rock, oil-dressed; **NY206,** Oil and gravel; **NJ39, NY123,** Oil and stone; **TX51,** Oil mixed with dirt;] (Qu. N27a, *Names . . for different kinds of unpaved roads*) Infs **IL11, 108, 144, MO11, NY80, PA165, TX89,** Oil road; **WA11,** Oil road—treated road; **CA86,** Oil road—grade, harrow, cover with oil, drag pulled over; **TX72,** Oil road—

sand and oil mixed; **CA17, 36, ND3, 20, NY92,** Oiled road; **CA200,** Oiled road—gets pitted; **ME19,** Oiled roads—not many now; **NJ18,** Oiled road—also a hard surface road; gravel with oil on, to run water off to sides; [**NY123,** Oil-and-stone road]. **1968** *Times–News* (Twin Falls ID) 12 Feb 12/1, 320 acres on oiled highway. **1971** Bright *Word Geog. CA & NV* 167, Black top (bituminous) . . oil(ed) road 19% [of 300 infs]. **1971** Wood *Vocab. Change* 383 **Sth,** Oiled road . . : tar road [offered by 49 of 1000 infs]. **1973** Allen *LAUM* 1.239 **Upper MW** (as of c1950), *Blacktop road. . . Oil(ed) road* [26 infs, **scattered**], though not unknown in Minnesota and Iowa, is most popular in South Dakota and Nebraska. This term apparently sometimes refers also to a rolled road surface compounded of heavy oil and clay or earth. **1986** Pederson *LAGS Concordance,* 1 inf, **cTN,** Blacktop or oil road; 1 inf, **nwLA,** Oil roads, oil road—paved roads; 1 inf, **ceTX,** Oil roads—covered with asphalt, not "paved." **1995** *DARE* File, *Oil road*—This is the common term for a tar or blacktop road in western Minnesota and adjacent Dakotas.

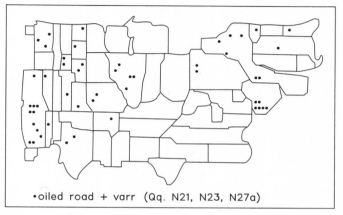

•oiled road + varr (Qq. N21, N23, N27a)

oiled up See **oil up**

oil mat (road) n Also *mat* [See quot 1973] **esp NE**
=**oiled road.**

    1941 Writers' Program *Guide IN* 326, Concrete roadbed . . between Ohio line and Farmland; asphalt between Farmland and Muncie . . oil mat to Crawfordsville. *Ibid* 391, Concrete and high type bituminous roadbed to Mt. Vernon; oil stone and oil mat to Illinois line. *Ibid* 401, The route continues to the junction with State 245, an oil mat road. **1958** *PADS* 30.11, Within . . the eastern two-thirds of Nebraska the familiar *blacktop* and *tarvia* (or *tarvy*) of other parts of the Upper Midwest are frequently replaced by the distinctive *oil mat*. This term is reported by 17% of the Nebraska informants [in the *Linguistic Atlas of the Upper Midwest* survey], all of them in the east. "If you drive a mile north, you can take the mat back into town," one farmer told me when I mentioned that I had come out to his place over a pretty dusty road. **1968** *DARE* (Qu. N21, *Roads that are surfaced with smooth black pavement*) Inf **KS12,** Mat, oiled road. **1973** Allen *LAUM* 1.239 (as of c1950), *Blacktop road. . . Mat* [2 infs, **csNE**] and *oil mat* [5 infs, **eNE**], not hitherto recorded, are familiar in eastern and southern Nebraska, where the sense appears to be an extension of *mat* designating a concrete slab or the base of such a slab.

oil nut n

1 =**butternut 1;** also the fruit of this tree. **chiefly NEng**

    1694 in 1897 Topsfield Hist. Soc. *Hist. Coll.* 3.86 **neMA,** From thence on a straight line to an oylenut tree which is Isaac Burtons tree marked. **1758** in 1874 Essex Inst. *Coll.* 12.147 **MA,** Observed the leaves begin to fall . . chiefly from ye Oyl Nutt tree. **1778** Carver *Travels N. Amer.* 500, The *Butter* or *Oilnut. . .* The tree grows in meadows, where the soil is rich and warm. **1810** Michaux *Histoire des Arbres* 1.165, *Juglans cathartica*. The Butter Nut . . Cette espèce est connue dans l'Amérique septentrionale, sous différentes dénominations. Dans les Etats de New-Hampshire, de Massachussett et de Vermont, elle porte le nom de *Oil nut*. [=This species is known in North America by various names. In the States of New Hampshire, Massachusetts and Vermont, it has the name of *Oil nut*.] **1824** Bigelow *Florula Bostoniensis* 352, *Juglans cinerea*. Butternut, Oilnut. . . It contains a nut which is of a dark colour. . . The kernel is more regular than in most nuts of its kind, is very oily, pleasant to the taste when fresh, but acquires a rancid taste by age. **1866** Whittier *Prose Wks.* 1.79 **MA,** We passed many trees, well loaded with walnuts and oilnuts. **1908** Rogers *Tree Book* 128, The frugal housewife in the country looks with interest upon the butternut when it is half grown. . . If a knitting needle goes through husk and nut without hindrance, it is not too late to make "pickled oil nuts," which are a delectable relish with meats in winter. **1950** Grimm *Trees PA* 118, The Butternut is also known as . . the Oilnut. . . The nuts have sweet, edible, and very oily kernels. **1971** Krochmal *Appalachia Med. Plants* 148, Oilnut. . . Oil extracted from the fruit is reportedly valuable in treating tape worms and fungus infections.

2 also *Allegheny oil nut:* A shrub of the eastern US (*Pyrularia pubera*); also the fruit of this plant. Also called **buffalo nut 1, ~ tree 1, colic ball, mountain coconut, rabbitwood, thunderwood**

1813 Muhlenberg *Catalogus Plantarum* 96, Oil nut, Elk nut. **1847** Wood *Class-Book* 479, P[yrularia] oleifera . . Oilnut. **1883** Hale *Woods NC* 154, Oil-nut. . . The leaves are . . rather acrid to the taste, and oily. The fruit is . . pear-shaped or roundish, with a thin shell and large oily kernel. **1933** Small *Manual SE Flora* 1250, Oil-nut. . . An oil, resembling olive oil, but ill-scented and poisonous, has been pressed from the drupes. **1952** Blackburn *Trees* 224, Deciduous shrub with a pungent oil, inconspicuous flowers, and pear-shaped fruits . . *Pyrularia pubera*—Allegany oilnut (s Appalachian area to Pennsylvania). **1973** Wharton–Barbour *Trees KY* 107, *Pyrularia pubera* . . Buffalo-nut, Oilnut . . a straggling shrub parasitic on roots of various trees from which it obtains water and minerals. . . The plant contains an acrid oil which is most concentrated in the fruit and the endosperm of the seed.

oil of hazel n Also *oil of birch, ~ hickory, ~ walnut* [*OED* c1678 →] **esp NEast** Cf **hickory** n B3

A whipping.

1907 *DN* 3.195 **seNH**, Oil of birch. . . A whipping. "That young one needs oil of birch the worst way." **1930** Shoemaker *1300 Words* 44 **cPA Mts** (as of c1900), Oil of hazel—A sound whipping. **1939** Coffin *Capt. Abby* 5 **ME** (as of 1860s), She had a long birch switch in her hand. . . They didn't hear the whistle of birch now . . but they heard their mother's tongue. . . If oil of birch could do it, the baby would take his place and tend to business beside his brothers. **1941** *LANE* Map 398 *(Switch [for punishing children])* 1 inf, **swCT**, A little oil of walnut; 1 inf, **ceRI**, A little oil of birch will be good for him, said of a naughty boy; 1 inf, **seNH**, Oil of birch. **1942** Berrey–Van den Bark *Amer. Slang* 322.3, *Beating; thrashing*. . . oil of birch, -hazel, -hickory &c.

oil pot See **oil bag**

oil road See **oiled road**

oil sausage n

See quots.

1966 *DARE* (Qu. H39, *Kinds of sausage;* total Infs questioned, 75) Inf **FL**11, Oil sausage—in oil, come in links. **1978** *DARE* File **neSC**, Oil sausage: made from both choice and less choice parts of both swine and beef, packed in links in buckets of oil.

oil station n

A gas station.

1967–70 *DARE* (Qu. N14, *The place where you go to get gasoline put into a car*) Infs **CA**6, 189, **IN**34, **MI**93, **MO**17, Oil station. [4 of 5 Infs old; the one mid-aged Inf considered this old-fash.]

oil-surfaced road, oil-top road See **oiled road**

oil tree n Cf **oil weed 2**

Perh a croton (*Croton* spp).

1945 Saxon *Gumbo Ya-Ya* 170 **LA**, Other things used for cure and prevention of illness included . . oil tree, bite of the devil, angel's balm and mouse's eyes. [**1976** Bailey–Bailey *Hortus Third* 337, The seeds of *C[roton] Tiglium* L. yield croton oil, a powerful purgative.]

oil up v phr

To put on oilskins or other waterproof clothing; hence ppl adj *oiled up* wearing waterproof clothing.

1969 *DARE* File **seME**, Oiled up—having on a complete set of oilskins: coat, pants, sou'wester (hat), and long rubber boots. **1975** Gould *ME Lingo* 194, Oil up—To put on weather gear, or oilskins. To dress for foul weather. Early rain suits were impregnated with linseed oil, but today neoprene and other treated fabrics are used.

oil weed n

1 See quot. Cf **greasewood 1**

1885 Siringo *TX Cowboy* 231, We had to make a fire out of a bush called the "oil weed" to keep warm by.

2 A croton such as *Croton argyranthemus;* see quots. **FL**

1938 Baker *FL Wild Flowers* 124, The unusual properties of *C[roton] argyranthemus* have won for it such various names as healing croton, . . oil-weed, and cancer-weed. The sap is a country remedy for cuts and scratches. For this purpose the stems are broken and the sap is allowed to drip on the cut, where it forms a thin, tenacious coating. **1955** *S. Folkl. Qrly.* 19.234 **FL**, Crotons, from which the sap was formerly used as a remedy for cuts and scratches, are variously known as . . *Oil Weed, Cancer Weed,* and *Healing Croton*. **1967** Jahoda *Other FL* 51, One of the most curious herbs of all in the dry woods is the healing croton. . . Florida crackers call it . . oil weed.

oil willow n [See quot]

A **groundsel tree** (here: either *Baccharis angustifolia* or *B. halimifolia*).

1951 *PADS* 15.42 **TX**, *Baccharis angustifolia* . . Oil willow. . . *Baccharis halimifolia* . . Oil willow. . . It so happens that oil has been found by drilling in many of the flats where these bushes are abundant; hence a legend has grown up to the effect that they indicate oil-sand areas.

oily adj[1] Cf *DS* K16, 42

Mean tempered, **ornery B3**.

1936 Adams *Cowboy Lingo* 86, Bad horses were variously referred to as 'oily broncs,' or 'salty broncs.' **1958** *AmSp* 33.271 **eWA** [Ranching terms], *Oily*. Tough or mean.

oily adj[2] See **early**

oily road See **oiled road**

ointment n Usu |ˈɔɪntmənt|; also |ˈaɪnt-, ˈəɪnt-, -mɪnt|; for addit varr see quots Pronc-spp *aintment, 'intment, ni'ntment* Cf Pronc Intro 3.I.11

Std senses, var forms.

1884 *Anglia* 7.243 [Black], 'Intment. **1891** *DN* 1.152 **cNY**, [ˈaɪntmənt] . . 'ointment.' **1899** (1912) Green *VA Folk-Speech* 63, Aintment. . . For ointment. *Ibid* 241, Intment. . . Ointment. **1899** Chesnutt *Conjure Woman* 175 **csNC** [Black], She gun 'im a' 'intment ter kyo de rheumatiz. **1927** Kennedy *Gritny* 147 **sLA** [Black], I bin rubbin' my back an' my two knees wid some ni'ntment Unc' Bendigo gimme. **1940** [see **oil A**]. c**1960** Wilson *Coll.* **csKY**, Ointment is sometimes [ˈaɪntˌmɪnt] among the elderly; [ˈɔɪntmənt] among others. **1967–70** *DARE* (Qu. BB50b) Inf **MO**38, [ɔɪntˈmɪnt]; **TX**32, [ˈɔɪntˌmɛnt]; (Qu. BB50c) Inf **KY**74, [ˈɔɚntmɛnt]; **MO**9, [ˈɔɪntmɪnt]. **1981** Pederson *LAGS Basic Materials*, 1 inf, **neMS**, [ˈɔˬɪntmĩt].

oio n [Haw *ʻōʻio*] **HI**

A **bonefish 1** (here: *Albula vulpes*).

1926 Pan-Pacific Research Inst. *Jrl.* 1.1.5, Albula virgata. . . Oio; Lady-fish. **1955** Day *HI People* 255, The sandy beaches . . are dotted with fishermen . . hoping to hook a hundred-pound ulua (jack crevally) or a sixteen-pound *oio* (bonefish). **1960** Gosline–Brock *Hawaiian Fishes* 95, *Albula vulpes* . . The 'o'io. . . occurs along open, sandy shores where it is sometimes taken by surf fishermen. Formerly, it was brought into the markets in some abundance. The maximum length attained is about 3 feet. **1967** *Honolulu Star–Bulletin* (HI) 31 May sec F 1/4, Oio—Bonefish. Used to make fishcake. **1967** *DARE* (Qu. P2, . . *Kinds of saltwater fish caught around here . . good to eat*) Inf **HI**14, Oio [oʔio]—bonefish. **1984** *Sunset HI Guide* 145, ʻOʻio—bonefish.

oisland See **island**

oke See **okolehao**

oker See **okra**

okeydoke adj, adv Also *okeydokey, okledokle,* rarely *oksydoksy, okumsdokums* Also sp *o(a)kiedoke;* for addit varr see quots [Varr of *OK*] Cf **hokey-dokey**

Fine, o.k., yes, all right.

1932 *AmSp* 7.334 [Johns Hopkins jargon], Okey-dokey—O.K. **1934** (1940) Weseen *Dict. Amer. Slang* 190, Okey dokey—O.K. *Ibid* 373, Okay doke—Satisfactory; agreeable; all right. **1935** *Sun* (Baltimore MD) 7 Feb 7/1 (*OEDS*), An attorney asked Carl Bush, witness, to answer a 'yes or no' question. 'Oakie-Doke,' replied Bush. **1942** Berrey–Van den Bark *Amer. Slang* 279.7, *Satisfactory, correct, good*. . . okey-dokey, okie-dokie. **1947** Schulberg *Harder They Fall* 121 **NYC**, "Hey, Killer, tell Jack to pick me up in front of the door right away." "Okle-dokle," the Killer said. **1949** Pound *Selected Writings* 329 **NE**, The progeny hatched out by O.K., oky-doky, oksy-doksy, okums-dokums, and oke. **1964** *AmSp* 39.95, The stretch forms [of o.k.] okie-doke and okie-dokie are whimsical variants that gained considerable currency in the 1930s.

Ibid 96, Another stretch form was *okle-dokle,* memorialized in a popular song of 1947. **1965–70** *DARE* (Qu. KK4, *When things turn out just right . . "Everything is _____ now."*) 23 Infs, **scattered,** Okeydoke(y); **FL**22, **LA**11, Okeydough; (Qu. GG29, *To be in a good or pleasant mood: "This morning he seems to be feeling _____."*) Inf **MO**35, Okeydoke; (Qu. NN1, *. . Words like 'yes': "Are you coming along too?"*) Inf **GA**83, Okeydoke; (Qu. NN2, *Exclamations of very strong agreement: Somebody says, "I think Smith is absolutely right," and you reply, "_____."*) Inf **MA**30, Okeydoke. **1968** *Esquire* Apr 162, There are certain classic soul terms. . . Among the classical expressions are: "solid," "cool," . . "okee doke." **1977** *New Yorker* 16 May 33/1 **NYC,** Now, if for any reason you lose your paper clips, you're in big trouble. Okeydoke. **1986** Pederson *LAGS Concordance,* 3 infs, **seAR, cGA, neMS,** Okeydoke.

Okie n **chiefly Pacific, esp CA** See Map *often derog* Cf **Arkie**
A person (esp a migrant worker) from Oklahoma; a descendant of such a person; transf: a rustic; a boor; a newcomer.
1938 *Forum* Jan 12, About a fifth of them [=the migratory workers in California] are Okies. **1939** Steinbeck *Grapes* 280 **CA,** Okie use' ta mean you was from Oklahoma. Now it means you're a dirty son-of-a-bitch. **1949** *AmSp* 24.26, *Okie* first became familiar during the great drought of 1936, when thousands of Oklahoma small farmers began scurrying out of the Dust Bowl. . . Most of them headed for California. . . In a little while *Okie* began to be used to designate any bankrupt and mendicant farmer. **c1955** Reed-Person *Ling. Atlas Pacific NW,* 2 infs, Okie [=a rustic]. **1957** Kerouac *On Road* (1958) 167 *(OEDS),* This was an Okie from Bakersfield, California. **1960** *AmSp* 38.271, Oklahoma Indians like to be called *Okies.* **1965–70** *DARE* (Qu. HH1, *Names and nicknames for a rustic or countrified person*) 9 Infs, **chiefly CA, OR,** Okie; [(Qu. C34, *Nicknames for nearby settlements, villages, or districts*) Inf **CA**117, Part of Clovis was called Okieville before [it was called] Beanville;] (Qu. W41, *. . Expressions . . for someone whose clothes never look right or who always dresses carelessly*) Inf **CA**59, Okie; (Qu. HH2, *Names and nicknames for a citified person*) Inf **CA**137, Okie—a reference to Oklahoman or anyone from South, but means any newcomer, whether from Maine or San Francisco or Georgia; (Qu. HH18, *Very insignificant or low-grade people*) Infs **CA**142, 154, 169, **CO**34, **WA**30, Okies; (Qu. HH19, *Other words or nicknames for a tramp*) Inf **CA**154, Okie; (Qu. HH28, *Names and nicknames . . for people of foreign background*) Inf **CA**113, Okie—loud mouth, hillbilly type; **CA**158, Okies—from Oklahoma; **WA**3, Okies—Oklahomans; (Qu. II21, *When somebody behaves unpleasantly or without manners: "The way he behaves, you'd think he was _____."*) Inf **CA**147, Okie. **1970** Hansen *Fadeout* 67 **swCA,** I'm a dirty, ignorant Okie to him. **1971** Bright *Word Geog. CA & NV* 72, Only seven items were found to be predominantly urban in distribution, some rather surprisingly so, as *Okies* and *Arkies* [=rustics; used by 12% of 300 infs]. *Ibid* 194, *Migratory worker. . .* Ten percent [of 300 infs] gave *Okies* in this category; again over half were urban, 12 of which were from San Francisco.

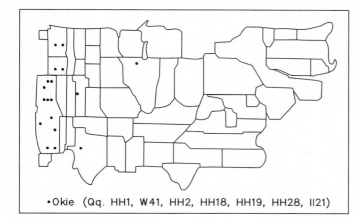

•Okie (Qq. HH1, W41, HH2, HH18, HH19, HH28, II21)

okiedoke See **okeydoke**

Oklahoma n Usu |ˌoklə'homə|; also **chiefly S Midl** |-'homɪ|; occas |-'homər|; for addit varr see quot 1989 Pronc-sp *Oklahomy* Cf Pronc Intro 3.I.12.b
Std sense, var forms.
1916 in 1983 Truman *Dear Bess* 205 **MO,** One hind tire came off and spoiled a brand new tube (rear tire? I've been in Oklahomy so long I talk like 'em—be saying you'ens and us'ens pretty soon). **1932** Ran-

dolph *Ozark Mt. Folks* 56, Thar warn't no Oklahomy then, an' th' Injun Territory didn't have no cap'tal, seemed like. **1940** in 1944 *ADD* **AR,** Oklahomy. **1989** Pederson *LAGS Tech. Index* 322 **Gulf Region,** 572 infs, [ˌoklə'homə, ˌoklɪ-]; 28 infs, ['oklə,homə]; 17 infs, [ˌokə'homə, ˌokɪ-]; 6 infs, [oklə'homɚ, oklɪ-]; 2 infs, ['oklə,homɪ, ˌokɪ'homɪ]; 2 infs, [ˌoklɪ'hʌmə].

Oklahoma rain n **chiefly SW, Plains States**
=**Idaho rain.**
1919 *DN* 5.37 **OK,** Oklahoma rain. . . A sand storm, common in that State. **1941** Vestal *Short Grass Country* 206 **nTX, neNM, seCO, swKS, wOK,** Everyone jestingly referred to a dust storm as an "Oklahoma rain." **1941** Writers' Program *Guide WY* 463, Oklahoma rain—Sandstorm.

Oklahoma son-of-a-bitch n
A **log perch** or similar fish; see quot.
1945 McAtee *Nomina Abitera* 20, Log-perch (*Percina caprodes*)—This species, and also other darters, according to Philip F. Allan, are called "Oklahoma son-of-a-bitch" in that State.

Oklahomy See **Oklahoma**

okledokle See **okeydoke**

okole n, adv |ˌo'kole, -lɪ| [Haw] **HI**
The anus, buttocks, rear end.
1938 Reinecke *Hawaiian Loanwords* 26, Okole. . . 1. Arse, in the sense of either anus or buttocks, or both. 2. Of inanimate things, the rear or bottom end. **1954–60** Hance et al. *Hawaiian Sugar* 5, Okole. . . the rearend, bottom, "fanny." **1967** *DARE* (Qu. K73, *. . Names . . for the rump of a cooked chicken*) Inf **HI**3, Okole [ˌo'kole] moa [*DARE* Ed: *moa* is Haw for chicken]; **HI**14, [o'koulɪ]; (Qu. X35, *Joking words for the part of the body that you sit on . . "He slipped and came down hard on his _____."*) Infs **HI**8, 9, [o'kole]. **1969** *DARE* FW Addit **HI,** Okole [ˌou'koule]—rear end, ass. **1981** *Pidgin To Da Max* np **HI,** Okole . . What you sit on in Hawaii. **1991** Saiki *From the Lanai* 103 **HI,** Maybe [there will be] somethin in the paper if the cops aren't sitting on their *okoles.*

okolehao n Also abbr *oke* [Haw *'ōkolehao* try-pot still (literally "iron buttocks")]
An alcoholic liquor usu distilled from the ti root.
1924 *Amer. Botanist* 30.21 **HI,** The principal use made of it [=*Cordyline fruticosa*] by the native is to produce okolehao, a kind of whiskey. **1938** Reinecke *Hawaiian Loanwords* 26, Okolehao. . . A distilled liquor manufactured in Hawaii. It is made from several materials, the best "oke" [ok], and the only kind truly entitled to the name, being that distilled from *ti* root. **1955** Day *HI People* 92, Hawaiians. . . used for the purpose [=distilling] not only sugar cane and sweet potatoes but particularly the roasted root of the ti plant. The resulting brew, called okolehau, or "iron bottom," derived its name from the fact that the primitive still consisted of a musket barrel draining into an iron pot. **1965** Krauss–Alexander *Grove Farm* xvi **HI** [Glossary], Okolehao—whiskey made by distilling ti root. **1967** *DARE* (Qu. DD21c, *Nicknames for whiskey, especially illegally made whiskey*) Inf **HI**1, Oke ['ouki], okolehao [oˌkolɪ'au]—a distilled liquor made from ti-root when properly made; modern substitutes are common; **HI**6, Okolehao, also oke [ouk]. **1980** Bushnell *Water of Kane* 371 **HI,** Many celebrants, although not all, sustained themselves through the afternoon with sips of okolehao, or gin, or whisky, or with long pulls upon bottles of imported American beer cooled in the ditch. **1984** Sunset *HI Guide* 85, 'Okolehao—ti-root liquor.

okole maluna exclam [See quot 1967 Reinecke-Tsuzaki] **HI**
Cheers! Bottoms up!—used as a drinking toast.
1938 Reinecke *Hawaiian Loanwords* 26, Okole maluna. . . Bottoms up!—a toast. **1967** Reinecke-Tsuzaki *Hawaiian Loanwords* 106, Okole maluna. . . [Reinecke-Tsuzaki: *'Okole,* bottom, and *maluna,* up.] Bottoms up! A toast. (Considered vulgar by older native Hawaiians.) V[ery] F[requent]. **1967** *DARE* (QR, near Qu. X35) Inf **HI**7, [o'kole ma'luna] = bottoms up. **1984** Sunset *HI Guide* 85, 'Okole maluna—bottoms up.

okra n Usu |'okrə|; also **chiefly Sth, S Midl** *esp freq among older speakers and among speakers with little formal educ* |'okri, -ɪ, 'okər|; for addit varr see quots Also sp *ocra;* pronc-spp *ocry, oker, okry, w'uckra* Cf Pronc Intro 3.I.12.b
A Pronc varr.
1909 *S. Atl. Qrly.* 8.52 **seSC,** The introduction of an extraneous initial *w,* as in . . w'uckra, (okra), [etc] . . are all characteristics of *Gullah.*

1909 *DN* 3.353 **eAL, wGA,** *Okry.* . . the common pronunciation of *okra*. **1916** *DN* 4.345 **nwTN, LA,** *Ocry.* . . Ocra. **1934** *AmSp* 9.213 **TX,** So well established as to be called "old-fashioned" are: . . *irrevelant* for *irrelevant*[?], *oker* for *okra*. **1936** *AmSp* 11.159 **eTX,** The vowel in the final syllable of all the words listed below is usually [ə]. . . okra, Ola, opera. *Ibid* 160, Among older or less well educated people in rural districts, *algebra,* . . *okra,* . . are pronounced with [ɪ] in the final syllable. **1938** Rawlings *Yearling* 393 **nFL,** The cotton's up. Hit looks like okry, don't it? **1942** Hall *Smoky Mt. Speech* 76 **wNC, eTN,** In the speech of most old people, of many middle-aged and young, both *-a* and *-ia* . . appear as [ɪ]. . . The words in which [ɪ] was heard [in final position] are. . Martha, Nora, okra. . . A man in his twenties may say ['oʊkrɪ] for *okra*, but he may regard [nu'moʊnɪ] as old-fashioned. *Okra* is a word which is largely limited to use within the family and hence less subject to changing modes of pronunciation. **1943** in 1944 *ADD* 424 **sGA,** *Okry.* . . ['okri]. **c1960** *Wilson Coll.* **csKY,** Okra is ['okə˞], ['okrə˞], or ['okrɪ]. **1965–70** *DARE* (Qu. I4, . . *Vegetables . . less commonly grown around here*) 173 Infs, **widespread,** Okra; **IN**12, **KY**17, **NM**8, **TX**105, ['okri]; **LA**2, 15, **TX**54, ['oʊkri]; **MO**18, ['oʊkri]; **NC**50, ['oʊkrɪs]; **LA**37, [okrɨ]; **IL**63, ['oʊkər]; (Qu. Y22) Inf **AR**51, Strutting his ['oʊkrɪ]. [Of the 12 Infs for whom proncs are given, 9 were old, 8 gs educ or less.] **1966–67** *DARE* Tape **AL**4, Later on . . we'd plant beans, and okra ['oʊkrɪ] and corn . . vegetables of that nature; **AL**14, The okra ['okrɪ] would be fried, of course. **1968** *DARE* FW Addit **LA**37, Okra ['okrɪ]. **1989** Pederson *LAGS Tech. Index* 190 **Gulf Region,** [Proncs of the type ['okrɨ, -i] are most common, with ['okrə] also very common;] 3 infs, ['okwe, 'okwi, 'okwə]; 2 infs, ['okə˞]; 4 infs, ['okre]; 1 inf, ['olkrɨ]. **1991** Pederson *LAGS Social Matrix* 143 **Gulf Region,** [Of 209 infs responding ['okrɨ], 141 (67%) were 66 years of age or older, 166 (79%) were lower or lower-middle class, and 148 (71%) had 10 years or less of formal educ.]

B Gram form.

Used as count noun rather than mass noun.

1968 *DARE* (Qu. I28b, *Kinds of greens that are cooked*) Inf **NC**50, Okras. **1986** Pederson *LAGS Concordance,* 6 infs, **GA, FL, LA,** Okras.

C Phrases.

1 *strut one's okra:* To swagger, show off.

1953 Randolph–Wilson *Down in Holler* 102 **Ozarks,** Okra is another vegetable which often carries a sexual significance. A man in Carroll County, Arkansas, was swaggering around with some young girls. "Look at old Sam, *a-struttin' his okra* for them town gals," a country woman said scornfully. **1967** *DARE* (Qu. Y22, *To move around in a way to make people take notice of you: "Look at him _____."*) Inf **AR**51, Strutting his okra ['oʊkrɪ].

2 *lose one's okra:* To vomit. Cf **cookie** n[1] **3**

1967 *DARE* (Qu. BB17, . . *Vomiting*) Inf **LA**14, Lost his okra.

okra soup n Also *okra and tomato soup* **chiefly SC** See Map Cf **gumbo 2**

A thick soup consisting primarily of okra and tomatoes.

1845 (1852) Simms *Wigwam & Cabin* (2d ser) 127 **seSC,** It was a confident faith among the old ladies, that okra soup was always inferior if cooked in any but an Indian pot. **1847** (1979) Rutledge *Carolina Housewife* 43, Okra Soup. . . A peck of okra; . . a peck of tomatoes, . . a shin or leg of beef. **1961** Folk *Word Atlas N. LA* map 1110, Thick soup usually containing okra . . [infreq responses include] okra soup. **1965–70** *DARE* (Qu. H36, *Kinds of soup*) Infs **CA**97, **GA**15, **SC**4, 19, 34, 43, 67, 70, Okra (and tomato) soup; **SC**21, 22, Okra soup—okra and tomatoes; **SC**26, Okra soup—okra and tomatoes, corn, bell pepper;

SC62, Okra and tomatoes—corn, okra, tomatoes, beans; (Qu. H45, *Dishes made with meat, fish, or poultry that everybody around here would know, but that people in other places might not*) Inf **SC**4, Gumbo—okra, tomato, but very thick, thicker than okra soup. **1970** Tarpley *Blinky* 198 **neTX,** *Thick soup, usually containing okra* . . okra soup [7 of 200 infs]. **1973** *News & Courier* (Charleston, S. Carolina) 4 Nov. 3-E/1 *(OEDS),* A lunch of sandwiches and okra soup will be served from noon to 1 p.m.

okry See **okra**

oksydoksy, okumsdokums See **okeydoke**

old adj

1 in var combs referring to the devil, or sometimes a hobgoblin or **boogerman 1:** See quots. [*OED* "orig. in reference to his primeval character;" a1000 →] See also **dragon B1, Old Billy 2, ~ Boy, ~ Harry, ~ Horny, ~ Ned 3, ~ Nick, ~ Rip, ~ Scratch**

1790 Tyler *Contrast* 74 **NEast,** Is the old one in you? **1805** in 1857 Dow *Hist. Cosmopolite* 230 **CT,** The young woman was turbulent, I told her Old Sam would pay her a visit. *Ibid* 248, He ran, and I after him, crying, "run, run, Old Sam is after you." **1825** Neal *Brother Jonathan* 1.253 **NEng,** His Master—the Evil One; or Old One. **1830** in 1957 Old Farmer's Almanac *Sampler* 52 **NEng,** It is said that Old Splitfoot has always hated asses since the affair of Balaam. **1867** Harris *Sut Lovingood Yarns* 270 **TN,** Ole Smutty's arter, wif a torch ove hell-fire. **1909** *DN* 3.421 **Cape Cod MA** (as of a1857), *Old round foot.* . . The devil. **1930** Shoemaker *1300 Words* 44 **cPA Mts** (as of c1900), *Old Sanko*—A mountaineer name for the deil, or satan. **1937** Gardner *Folkl. Schoharie* 108 **ceNY,** When asked who the other young man was, she replied in a whisper, "Why, the Old Un," a local term for the devil. **1942** Berrey–Van den Bark *Amer. Slang* 329.4, *Devil.* . . Harry, Ned, Nick, Nickey, Old Bendy, –Blazes, –Cain, –Clootie, –Gentleman, –Gooseberry, –Hallelujah, –Harry, –Ned, –Nick, –One, –Poker, –Scratch, –Scratcher, –Serpent, –Split-foot or Round-foot, Old Man Satan, Sam Hill. **1943** *LANE* Map 532 *(The Devil)* 4 infs, **ce,seNH, ceME,** The old serpent; 2 infs, **cwVT, seNH,** Old cloven-foot. **1950** *WELS (The devil)* 1 Inf, **csWI,** Old Man, Old One. **1953** [see **Old Scratch**]. **1954** Forbes *Rainbow* 20 **NEng,** Old Split Foot, by the way, is a country word for the devil. **1965–70** *DARE* (Qu. EE41, *A hobgoblin that is used to threaten children and make them behave*) Inf **MS**1, Old Aunt Dinah; **AR**13, Old Aunt Violet; **MS**46, Old Biting Dick; **NY**89, Old Black Joe; **GA**13, **OK**48, Old Booger; **OK**6, Old Boogerman; **GA**33, Old Corker; **NY**205, Old Cratch; **FL**37, **GA**13, **MS**38, Old Devil; **GA**77, Old Dinah Flow; **AL**32, Old Goblin; **GA**13, Old Imp; **SC**58, Old Jack; **NC**16, Old Scrooge; **VA**46, Old White Horse; (Qu. HH22b, . . *A very mean person . . "He's meaner than _____."*) Inf **NY**232, Old Coot; **AZ**6, **VA**5, Old Devil (himself); **MO**34, Old Devil hisself; **PA**242, Old Dick; **NY**96, Old Rot; **FL**26, **KS**6, **TN**33, **TX**104, **VA**50, Old Satan; **OH**49, Old Scrooge; **MD**26, Old Varmint; (Qu. CC8) Inf **MI**67, Old 'Un; **AR**3, Old Adam; **KY**84, Old Dickens; **NY**88, Old Enemy; **OR**6, Old Imp; **OK**18, Old Lutherfud; **NY**70, Old Pitchfork; **NC**49, Old Serpent; **ID**5, Old Sin. **1967** *DARE* FW Addit **ceTN,** Old forked toes ['fɔrkɪd,toz]—common term for the Devil. **1986** Pederson *LAGS Concordance (Devil)* 1 inf, **nwFL,** Old deluder; 1 inf, **cnLA,** Old Haggy, Old Haggy Bill; 1 inf, **swGA,** Old Jack; 1 inf, **swGA,** Old Scrooge; 1 inf, **ceGA,** Old serpent.

2 in phr *any old:* Any whatever—used dismissively to express indifference or lack of interest.

1896 (1898) Ade *Artie* 171 **Chicago IL,** Any old farmer . . could buy up him and a hundred more like him. **1897** *KS Univ. Qrly.* 6.85 **neKS,** Any old _____: used in "any old thing," "any old street," etc., to express indifference, or absence of choice.—General. **1911** Chambers *Common Law* 63 **NYC,** "Would you like to have a chance to study?" . . "Study? What?" "Sculpture—any old thing!" **1927** *AmSp* 3.218 **KS** [University slang], *Any old punk.* . . Any man who happens to be available. To say that a girl "will go with any old punk" means that she is not very particular in her choice of associates. **1943** *LANE* Map 709 **NEng,** The phrases *any place, any old place,* stressed on the first syllable, are in general use as synonyms of *anywhere.* **1948** *Chicago Tribune* (IL) 16 May 6, [Comic strip:] I'll take on guys my size any old time. **1965–70** *DARE* (Qu. A26) Inf **WA**2, Any old way; (Qu. W28) Inf **MI**33, Sew it up any old way; (Qu. W29) Inf **CA**144, Whipped up any old way; (Qu. KK42b) Inf **CO**29, Any old time, any old way; (Qu. KK48) Infs **NJ**64, **PA**181, **TX**90, Any old way; (Qu. KK62) Inf **OH**71, Any old thing; (Qu. MM11) Inf **VA**11, Most any o' where. **1986** Pederson *LAGS Concordance (You can find that _____)* 1 inf, **csLA,** Any old place.

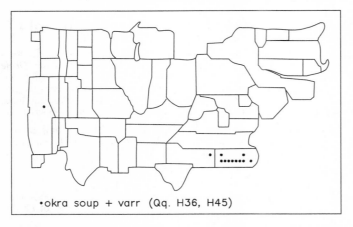

•okra soup + varr (Qq. H36, H45)

3 Used as a generalized adj of respect, admiration, approval. Note: The use of *old* as a generalized adj of affection, endearment, or familiarity (as in "good old Mom" or "that little old kitten") is widespread.

1958 Humphrey *Home from the Hill* 53 **neTX,** Chauncey had been Old Chauncey even as a young man, for it was a title he had earned early, a certificate of reliability. **1963** Carson *Social Hist. Bourbon* 53, "Old" was the important qualifying word associated with excellence. One said Old Woodford County, Old Virginia Military Institute where one had gone to school, old bourbon whiskey, as already noted, and of course Old Kentucky. **1967** *DARE* FW Addit **CO**21, "Old John Coe"—regardless of age, [*old* is] applied to all men with large land holdings.

Old Adam See **old 1**

Old Al n Also *Al*

A mythical alligator of the Mississippi River; see quot.

1938 Burman *Blow for a Landing* 284, Faint patches of fog appeared on the water. . . 'Looks like old Al, the big alligator that's boss of the river, is a-smoking up his pipe, don't it? . . I'm sure going to give Al some tobacco, so he'll smoke his pipe good and make a real fog.'

Old Arthur n Cf **arthuritis**

Arthritis personified.

1968–70 *DARE* (Qu. BB8, *When a person's joints and muscles ache and sometimes swell up, especially in damp weather, he may have* _____) Inf **TX**51, Old Arthur's after me again; **IL**130, Old Arthur's got me. **1986** Pederson *LAGS Concordance (Arthritis)* 1 inf, **ceLA,** Old Arthur's—they used to say; 1 inf, **ceTX,** Old Arthur's got me. **1990** Cavender *Folk Med. Lexicon* 28 **sAppalachians,** *Old Arthur*—arthritis.

Old Aunt Dinah (or Violet) See **old 1**

old bachelor n

1 also *old batch(elor):* A confirmed bachelor; a solitary or reclusive rustic. [By analogy with *old maid*]

1867 Harris *Sut Lovingood Yarns* 263 **TN,** "Stop a moment, Mr. Lovingood," said an old batchelor, an old field schoolmaster, who was one of Sut's auditory. **1899** (1912) Green *VA Folk-Speech* 304, *Old batch.* . . An "old batchelor." "Bachelor" is nearly always preceeded by *old.* **1966** Dakin *Dial. Vocab. Ohio R. Valley* 2.454 **IN,** A rustic. . . *Hermit* (Ill., Ind.), *recluse* (Ind.), *old bachelor* (Ind.) are apparently primarily terms for one who leads a solitary rural life. **1968** Kellner *Aunt Serena* 143 **cIN** (as of c1920), I knew Doc was an Old Batch and once said, "Too bad he hasn't got any folks." **1968** *DARE* FW Addit **NY**96, *Old batch* = confirmed bachelor. **1973** Allen *LAUM* 1.351 (as of c1950), A rustic (neutral and derogatory terms). . . *Old bachelor:* A hermit [1 inf, **neMN**]. **1986** Pederson *LAGS Concordance (A rustic)* 1 inf, **seAL,** Old bachelor; 1 inf, **nwMS,** An old bachelor—man who lives by himself.

2 also *bachelor, old bachelor's piece:* =**old maid 4.**

[**1950** *WELS* (The last piece of something on a plate) 1 Inf, **seWI,** If you take the last piece you will be an old maid or bachelor.] **1966–68** *DARE* (Qu. H71) Infs **MD**19, **NY**109, (Old) bachelor; **MI**34, Old bachelor's piece.

Old bad man See **bad man 2**

old batch(elor) See **old bachelor 1**

old belt n Also *belt*

The piedmont tobacco-growing region of Virginia and North Carolina; the **flue-cured** tobacco grown in this region.

1933 *Sun* (Baltimore MD) 12 Sept 6/6 *(Hench Coll.),* Virginia must postpone the opening date of its 'old belt' warehouses. . . They must give the buyers opportunity to get up to the 'old belt.' **1940** *AmSp* 15.134 [Tobacco market language], *Old belt leaf.* Leaf of flue-cured type, grown principally in Piedmont sections of Virginia and North Carolina. **1960** *Daily Progress* (Charlottesville VA) 29 Sept 44/3, The North Carolina-Virginia Old Belt was the only flue-cured tobacco selling area in the Carolinas and Virginia reporting an increase in price. . . The Old Belt's average Tuesday was $59.62. . . For the season, the belt has averaged $59.98. **1970** *DARE* Tape **VA**38, We here in the old belt will soon be cut clean out of our crop of tobacco.

Old Betsy n

=**Old Hannah.**

1939 *AmSp* 14.91 **eTN,** *Old Betsy.* The sun. 'Old Betsy didn't shine today.'

Old Billy n

1 =**old-squaw,** usu the drake. Cf **old molly**

1888 Trumbull *Names of Birds* 88, In New Jersey . . the drake [is] . . distinguished at Pleasantville as old Billy. **1917** (1923) *Birds Amer.* 1.141, Old-Squaw—*Harelda hyemalis* . . Other Names.—Long-tailed Duck . . Old Billy . . Hound. **1946** Hausman *Eastern Birds* 160, Old Squaw. . . Other Names—Old Wife . . Old Billy . . Scolder.

2 also *Old Billy Hell:* =**Old Scratch.** [Cf **billy hell**] **KY** Cf **old 1**

1966 Dakin *Dial. Vocab. Ohio R. Valley* 2.520, The devil. . . Kentuckians say *old Billy hell* (Owsley County). **1969** *DARE* (Qu. HH22b, . . *A very mean person . . "He's meaner than* _____.") Inf **KY**11, The devil, Old Billy, Old Billy Hell. **1983** *MJLF* 9.1.49 **ceKY** (as of 1956), *Old Billy Hell* . . Satan.

Old Biting Dick, Old Black Joe See **old 1**

old blade See **blade 4**

Old Booger(man) See **old 1**

Old Boy n Usu with *the* Also *Old Fellow, ~ Man* **esp east of Missip R** See Map
=**Old Scratch.**

1782 in 1976 Freneau *Poems* 216 **ceNJ,** 'Till they all get as black as they paint the *old Boy.* **1843** (1916) Hall *New Purchase* 388 **IN,** But a few (*friends* doubtless of the *old fellow*), cried out . . "Bite him! devil—bite him!" **1871** (1882) Stowe *Fireside Stories* 244 **MA,** Tam was ahead of them all, sure enough, and was snorting and snuffling as if he'd got the very old boy in him. **1887** (1967) Harris *Free Joe* 17 **cGA,** When Spite Calderwood meets the Old Boy in the road they'll be a turrible scuffle. **1899** (1912) Green *VA Folk-Speech* 304, *Old boy.* . . The devil. **1916** Lincoln *Mary-'Gusta* 313 **MA,** It's Isaiah, and runnin' as if the Old Boy was after him! **1941** *LANE* Map 473, 1 inf, **seNH,** Mad as the Old Boy. *Ibid* Map 474, 1 inf, **swCT,** He ran like the Devil. . . Like the Old Boy; 2 infs, **neMA,** He ran as though the Old Boy was after him. **1943** *Ibid* Map 532 *(The Devil)* **scattered NEng,** (The) old boy; 2 infs, **ceMA,** The old man; 2 infs, **seCT, sRI,** The old fellow. **1950** *WELS* **WI** *(Names for the devil)* 1 Inf, Old Boy, Old Harry, Old Scratch; 1 Inf, Old Man, Old One. **1958** Babcock *I Don't Want* 23 **eSC,** The devil is, after all, a pretty influential fellow. 'Tis a great pity Martin Luther missed the Old Boy when he threw that ink bottle at him. **1965–70** *DARE* (Qu. CC8) 22 Infs, **chiefly east of Missip R,** Old Boy (himself); 9 Infs, **scattered,** Old Man; **GA**74, **LA**11, Old Man with the horns; **VA**50, Old Fellow; **LA**11, Old Man down below; (Qu. HH22b, . . *A very mean person . . "He's meaner than* _____.") Infs **AR**22, **VA**11, Old Boy (hisself). [30 of 35 total Infs old] **1973** Allen *LAUM* 1.385 (as of c1950), *Devil.* . . old boy himself [1 inf, **csNE**]. . . old fellow himself [1 inf, **swND**]. . . old man (below) [3 infs, **seMN, neSD, cNE**]. **1986** Pederson *LAGS Concordance (Devil)* 1 inf, **cnFL,** Old boy; 1 inf, **neTN,** Old man.

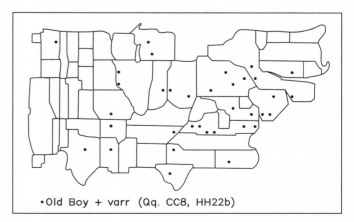

•Old Boy + varr (Qq. CC8, HH22b)

old brass wagon n

1969 *DARE* (Qu. EE1, . . *Games . . children play . . in which they form a ring, and either sing or recite a rhyme*) Inf **CA**133, Old brass wagon.

Old Buck n [Cf **buck** n[1] **1e**] **Outer Banks NC**

A mythical bull-like creature associated with the celebration of **Old Christmas.** Note: The representation of Old Buck by a man or men in costume clearly reflects English morris dance traditions.

1949 *Sun* (Baltimore MD) 6 Jan 2/8 **ceNC** *(Hench Coll.),* "Old Christmas" came to this fishing village [=Rodanthe] on North Carolina's outer banks today. . . The Old Buck appeared. He is as much a part of the Old Christmas mythology as is Santa Clause himself. **1956** *Sun* (Baltimore MD) 5 Jan 3/2 *(Hench Coll.),* Why residents of the Outer Banks celebrate Epiphany or Old Christmas, as well as December 25, and why they do so on January 5 instead of January 6, is something lost in antiquity. Also going back to antiquity is the appearance of Old Buck, a mythical bull of the woods, who materializes once a year and frightens children who have been bad. . . he also praises children who have been good. . . He used to be represented by a resident dressed in the hide and head of an Outer Banks steer. But now he has been put on wheels. He is a life sized reproduction of a pasture bull. **1968–69** *DARE* Tape **NC**58, They have a rather unique way of distributing the gifts [at the Old Christmas celebration]. Old Buck comes riding out of the woods, and Old Buck and his rider presents the presents to the children. . . Old Buck sort of looks like a four-legged animal; **NC**76, There's a part in it [=Old Christmas celebration] where the Ol' Buck would come in. What it consists of is, they would have two men inside of a wooden frame that was covered with a blanket, something like a horse blanket and it's got a set of horns and a head of an old steer, and they would come in and run through the audience. . . They used to say that Ol' Buck used to come out of Cape Woods every January fifth, every Old Christmas and go to Rodanthe. **1969** *DARE* (Qu. CC17, *Imaginary animals or monsters that people . . tell tales about*) Inf **NC**77, Ol' Buck—at Old Christmas, has a bull's head, said to come out of Trent woods, tell kids that if they weren't good Ol' Buck would get them at Christmas. **1974** [see **Old Christmas**]. **1983** *Salt Lake Tribune* (UT) 6 Jan sec C 2/5 **NC**, Old Christmas will be celebrated at Rodanthe with . . Santa Claus, a dance and the appearance of "Old Buck."

old cat n

1 also *one old cat, three old cats:* The game of tick-tack-toe. **N Cent, Plains States** See Map Cf **cat and mouse 1**

1950 *WELS* (Tick-tack-toe) 3 Infs, **WI**, Old cat. **1965–70** *DARE* (Qu. EE38a, *A game played with pencil and paper where the players try to get three X's or three O's in a row*) Infs **IN**69, **MI**75, 101, **OH**70, Old cat; **IL**130, Old cat [FW: Inf corrected this to tick-tack-toe]; **OH**8, Old cat, tick-tack-toe; **KS**15, **MI**8, **NE**3, One old cat; **MI**92, Three old cats.

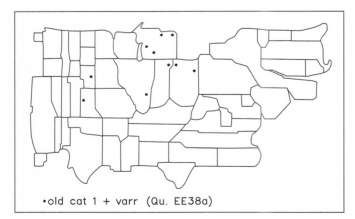

•old cat 1 + varr (Qu. EE38a)

2 also *one old cat:* An imaginary character credited with the win when a game of tick-tack-toe ends in a tie; a tie game. Cf **jack** n[2] **2b**

1950 *WELS* (Neither "x" nor "o" wins [at tick-tack-toe], you say it's _____) 3 Infs, **WI**, Old cat's (game); 1 Inf, **csWI**, One for the old cat; 1 Inf, **seWI**, The old cat wins. **1968–70** *DARE* (Qu. EE38b) Inf **WI**66, Old cat; **KS**15, One old cat; **MI**114, The old cat wins; **NY**232, The old cat got it.

3 See **one old cat 1**.

Old Christmas n [From its being reckoned by the "old style" or Julian calendar; see quot 1974] **chiefly Mid Atl, S Midl** Cf **Little Christmas, Old Buck**

Twelfth Night (January 5) or Twelfth Day (January 6); occas associated with New Year's Eve.

1895 *DN* 1.373 **seKY, eTN, wNC**, *Old Christmas:* January 6th. (The day is remembered by those who never heard of Twelfth Night or

Epiphany.) **1905** *DN* 3.89 **nwAR**, *Old Christmas.* . . Twelfth night. **1930** Shoemaker *1300 Words* 43 **cPA Mts** (as of c1900), *Old Christmas*—Celebrated by some mountaineers in January. **1932** *Sun* (Baltimore MD) 2 Jan 4/2 *(Hench Coll.),* Twelfth Night . . throughout many sections of the Delmarva Peninsula . . is known as Old Christmas or Little Christmas. **1938** Matschat *Suwannee R.* 152 **neFL, seGA**, The sixth day of January. Some fowkses, they say, calls hit Ole Christmas, but most fowkses calls hit Twelfth-night. **1940** (1978) Still *River of Earth* 223 **eKY**, The cold spells at Old Christmas and during the week Ruling Day fell were the only times I had need to put on my red woven coat. **c1940** Hall *Coll.* **eTN**, [Clipping, nd:] Newport (Tenn.) *Plain Citizen:* Don't carry ashes out between Christmas and Old Christmas. **1944** *PADS* 2.20 **sAppalachians**, *Old Christmas.* . . January 6. Still observed here and there in spite of the changes which took place with the introduction of the Gregorian calendar. On the eve of Old Christmas, at midnight, the elder is said to blossom, cows to kneel in prayer, and the cock to crow all night. . . [*PADS* Ed: Still observed in some parts of e. N.C.] **1954** *Harder Coll.* **cwTN**, *Old Christmas.* . . The night of December 31st, now called New Year's Eve. **1956** [see **Old Buck**]. **c1960** *Wilson Coll.* **csKY**, *Old Christmas.* . . January 6, still remembered by older people as told to them by their parents. My mother always reminded us of the day and said that her mother always regarded it as the real Christmas. **1966–67** *DARE* (Qu. FF11, . . *The night of December 31st*) Infs **MO**8, **NC**33, (That's) Old Christmas; **TN**6, Old Christmas [FW: Inf not sure]. **1968–69** *DARE* Tape **NC**58, The people of the little village of Rodanthe do celebrate what they call Old Christmas around January the first. They have quite a festive affair. . . A Christmas program, and gifts of candy and apples or fruit is exchanged . . [followed by] . . a oyster roast or something like that out on the beach; **NC**76, [FW:] Tell us about Old Christmas as it used to be celebrated. [Inf:] It's celebrated on January the fifth and used to be more or less a get-together of the people of the three villages and usually a few of the other villages on the island and the mainland would join in. There'd be usually a play, a colored master, and they'd have square dances or whatever dance was in style. And usually it would end up in a brawl. **1974** Betts–Walser *NC Folkl.* 4, In 1752 England officially adopted the Gregorian calendar. Some people continued to celebrate Christmas according to the old Julian calendar, making their Yule holiday January 5. The tradition of Old Christmas came to North Carolina with its English settlers. And although Old Christmas is no longer widely celebrated, the people of Rodanthe on the Outer Banks still have an observance of the original holiday. One feature of their celebration is the appearance of Old Buck, a fierce bull-like creature (really two men in a costume). Every year he cavorts about, trying to frighten the children. **1981** Mebane *Mary* 49 **cnNC**, After Christmas we clustered at recess. "What you get?" . . I asked one girl. . . "I didn't get anything," she said. "I'll get mine 'Old Christmas'." . . I asked. "What's 'Old Christmas'?" "It's after Christmas and I'm going to get something then," she answered. (Old Christmas, I have since learned, is Epiphany, January 6.) **1986** Pederson *LAGS Concordance,* 1 inf, **seMS**, Old Christmas Day—celebration on January 6.

Old Cloven-foot See **old 1**

old coaley n [Cf **coaly** n **1** quots 1953, 1975]

1986 *Barrick Coll.* **csPA** (as of 1940s), *Old coaley*—the anus[.] Rare euphemism used in the Carlisle area in the 1940s.

Old Coffinhead n

1940 Writers' Program *Guide TX* 378 **ceTX** [Black], Mammies still frighten children with tales of Old Coffinhead, giant rattlesnake of Texas folklore, pictured as "eight feet long and so ole he done got whiskers."

Old Coot (or Corker, Cratch) See **old 1**

‡**old dad** n [Cf *OEDS* old man 1.i; 1902 →] Cf **daddy** v **1**

1969 *DARE* FW Addit **ceNC**, Old dad—penis.

old daddy n Also *old pap(py),* ~ *pop* [*SND* auld daddy, auld father (at *auld* adj. 2)] Cf **big daddy, daddy 2, old mamma, pappy**

One's grandfather.

1967–70 *DARE* (Qu. Z3, . . *'Grandfather'*) Inf **KY**74, Old daddy; **NC**40, Old pap; **GA**28, Old pappy; **NC**61, Old pop.

Old Deluder (or Devil, Dick, Dickens, Dinah Flow) See **old 1**

old dragon See **dragon B1**

old drum n
=**red drum**.

1969 *DARE* FW Addit **Roanoke Is. VA**, *Old Drum*—Type of fish. Also called red drum. Same as channel bass.

Old Enemy See **old 1**

old-England robin n Cf **English robin 1**
=**Baltimore oriole.**

1894 *Century Illustr. Mag.* 47.849, In the matter of the American redbreast there seems to have been a suspicion that he was only an upstart robin, for in the North-country our farmers call this same mellifluous Baltimore oriole, "Old-England robin." **1956** MA Audubon Soc. *Bulletin* 40.130 **MA,** Baltimore Oriole . . Old-England Robin (Mass. As a familiar bird different from the common Robin; it is not at all like any bird called "Robin" in England.)

old English hake n
A **hake 2** (here: *Urophycis chuss*).

1873 in 1878 Smithsonian Inst. *Misc. Coll.* 14.2.17 **MA,** *Phycis chuss* . . old English hake. **1884** Goode *Fisheries U.S.* 1.234, Owing to their great similarity, *Phycis chuss* and *P. tenuis* are usually known indifferently by the name "Hake"; the former, however, is sometimes called the Old English Hake. **1911** U.S. Bur. Census *Fisheries 1908* 311, Hake (*Urophycis*).—Not true hakes. A food fish found off the Atlantic coast from Newfoundland to Cape Hatteras. Different species are known as "old English hake," [etc].

Old English humbug See **humbug** n **1**

oldenmost See **oldermost**

older n [*OED older* B.2 1483–1562; *"Obs."*] Cf **oldermost**
One who is older or senior; an elder.

1986 Pederson *LAGS Concordance,* 1 inf, **cwAR,** The olders [=older people]. **1989** Gurganus *Oldest Confederate Widow* 569 **Sth** (as of 1865) [Black], Tribe olders point, "Look what's happening here."

older head See **old head**

oldermost adj Also *oldenmost arch* or *obs*
Oldest.

1843 (1916) Hall *New Purchase* 258 **IN,** Them two likely young gals, your two oldenmost daters. *Ibid* 313, Ain't that oldermost stranger a kinder sort a preacher? **1872** Schele de Vere *Americanisms* 621, *Oldermost,* made after the model of *furthermost* and *hindermost,* is quite common in the West, where it takes the place of *oldest.* **1934** (1943) *W2, Oldermost. . .* Eldest. *Dial. U.S.*

oldfangled adj [By analogy with *newfangled*]
Old-fashioned; hence *oldest-fangled* most old-fashioned.

1894 *Harper's Weekly* 7 Apr 315 **NY,** Repelling the new-fangled remedy, [he] resorts to the oldest-fangled known. **1955** Stong *Blizzard* 55 **IA,** His faithful old-fangled windmill. **1991** Still *Wolfpen Notebooks* 54 **sAppalachians,** In their home everything is old-fangled.

old-fashion adj [*OED "Obs.";* but many quots may be pronc-spp instead: cf Pronc Intro 3.I.22]
Old-fashioned.

1848 Bartlett *Americanisms* 394 **OH,** The whole caboodle will . . endeavor to secure a triumph in the old fashion way. **1949** in 1986 *DARE* File **MI,** I saw *old fashion* baked beans on a menu in a drug store on South State Stree, Ann Arbor. **1967–69** *DARE* (Qu. H36, *Kinds of soup*) Infs **AL**25, 38, Old-fashion vegetable soup; (Qu. H47, *Kinds of fried potatoes*) Inf **PA**41, Old-fashion raw fried; (Qu. BB9, *A sickness in which you have a severe cough and difficult breathing—it often starts with a cold, and lasts a week or two*) Inf **CA**134, Old-fashion flu. **1986** Pederson *LAGS Concordance,* 10 infs, **Gulf Region,** Old-fashion (consumption, disc, furniture, house, iron pots, quilt, etc).

old-fashioned bay grass n
A **pondweed** (here: *Potamogeton pectinatus*).

1926 *Torreya* 26.4 **VA,** *Potamogeton pectinatus.* . . Old-fashioned baygrass, Ragged Id., Back Bay, Va.

old-fashioned potato beetle n Also *old-fashioned potato bug*
Cf **potato bug**
A **blister bug** (here: *Epicauta* spp).

1949 Swain *Insect Guide* 137, Before effective insecticides were as available as they are now, children used to drive blister beetles or "old-fashioned potato beetles" by beating on pans and threshing the ground and plants with leafy branches. When the insects had been herded into the grass at the fence row, a fire was set to destroy them. **1952** *Natl. Geogr. Mag.* Aug. 257 **NY, NJ,** The *Blister Beetle* is often called the "old-fashioned potato bug" because it fed on that plant until the Colorado potato beetle drove it off. **1954** Borror–DeLong *Intro. Insects* 372, Several species of blister beetles are important pests, feeding on

potatoes, tomatoes, and other plants. Two of these are often called the "old-fashioned potato beetles," *Epicauta vittata* (Fabricius) (with orange and black longitudinal stripes) and *E. marginata* (Fabricius) (black, with the margins of the elytra and the sutural stripe gray).

Old Fellow See **Old Boy**

old field n

1 An open area, usu of formerly cultivated land, that has been allowed to become overgrown. **chiefly Sth, S Midl** Cf **field B5, Indian field**

1635 in 1954 VA Co. Court *Co. Court Rec. Accomack–Northampton* 31 **VA,** Mr. John wilkins made suit . . for a neck of land . . boundeth . . northerly on Cugleyes ould field. **1656** in 1886 Braintree MA *Records* 7, A highway layd out in the old feild for goodman Hoydin to bring his corne out. **1748** in 1954 *AmSp* 29.226 **SC,** There are . . several large Indian Old fields which are Lands that have been cleared by the Indians, and remain now just as they left them. **1791** Bartram *Travels* 54 **S Atl,** Their old field and planting land extend up and down the river. **1833** Kercheval *Hist. Valley VA* 55, When the country was first discovered, there were considerable openings of the land, or natural prairies, which are called "the Indian old fields," to this day. **1856** in 1956 Eliason *Tarheel Talk* 285 **c, csNC,** I have broke about ten ackors of old field. **1884** Baldwin *Yankee School-Teacher* 11 **VA,** When dey don't raise nuffin f'r years an' years, an' de pines done spring up eb'rywhar . . , dey calls it ole field. **1895** (1896) Bruce *Economic Hist. VA* 1.427, In the records of deeds in the country courts, as well as in the original patents, the references to old fields are very numerous; these were lands which, after passing out of cultivation, had at first been given up as pastures to roaming cattle, but which in a few years relapsed into thickets, and finally into forests of a second growth. **1903** *DN* 2.322 **seMO,** *Old-field.* . . Land formerly in cultivation but now abandoned. It has been very common to cultivate land without fertilizing until exhausted and then abandon it, or 'turn it out' clearing new-ground in its stead. Many parts of the South abound in 'old-fields.' **1907** *DN* 3.234 **nwAR. 1909** *DN* 3.353 **eAL, wGA,** *Ol(d)-fiel(d).* . . Worn-out or abandoned farm lands. Often used attributively as "old-field pines," i.e., short-leafed pines grown up in old fields. **1930** *DN* 6.84 **cSC. 1939** Hall Coll. **wNC,** (We) trailed one (a bear) . . back down to the Dowdle place and all around through them old fields. **1968–70** *DARE* (Qu. P25) Inf **GA**80, Old-field ground rattler; **VA**47, Old-field snake; (Qu. T2b) Inf **NC**49, Old-field land. **1986** Pederson *LAGS Concordance,* 1 inf, **cnGA,** Old field—abandoned land.

2 A graveyard.

1942 (1965) Parrish *Slave Songs* 108 **GA coast,** In ante-bellum days the slaves called the graveyard "the ole field." **1969** *DARE* (Qu. BB56, *Joking expressions for dying: "He _____."*) Inf **GA**72, Gone to the old field; (Qu. BB61b, . . *Joking names for a cemetery*) Inf **GA**72, Old field.

old-field adder See **field viper**

old-field aster n [old field 1]
An aster (here: *Aster pilosus*).

1953 Greene–Blomquist *Flowers South* 135, Old-field aster (*A[ster] pilosus*) is a white-flowered aster flourishing in autumn along roadsides and in waste places but especially in abandoned fields where it may grow in pure stands. It is quite ornamental . . , but because of its weedy nature it is not often admired.

old-field balsam n [old field 1]
=**cudweed 1.**

1873 in 1976 Miller *Shaker Herbs* 132, Balsam, Sweet—*Gnaphalium polycephalum* . . White Balsam. . . Old Field Balsam. **1892** *Jrl. Amer. Folkl.* 5.98 **NEng,** *Gnaphalium polycephalum* . . old field balsam. **1938** FWP *Guide DE* 107, "Old field balsam" and "horse mint" are fever cures. **1968** *DARE* (Qu. S26d, *Wildflowers that grow in meadows;* not asked in early QRs) Inf **DE**3, Old-field balsam—white, something like ageratum. **1974** Morton *Folk Remedies* 65 **SC,** *Old field balsam.* . . (Current use); Dry plant is sold in market in the fall. Bundles are kept in household for winter use. . . "Tea" is the most popular native cold remedy in South Carolina.

old-field birch n [old field 1] **chiefly NEng**
=**gray birch a.**

1810 Michaux *Histoire des Arbres* 1.26, *Old field birch.* **1812** *Ibid* 2.139, Aux environs de New-York et de Philadelphie, on donne à cet arbre le nom de *White birch,* Bouleau blanc: ce nom est aussi en usage dans le district de Maine, où cependant il est fréquemment désigné sous celui de *Old field birch,* Bouleau des champs abandonnés, pour le distinguer du Bouleau à canot. Les situations peu garnies de bois, ou le sol est sec et maigre, sont celles où le *Betula populifolia* se rencontre le plus souvent. [=In the area around New York and Philadelphia, this tree is called *White birch* . . this name is also used in the district of Maine, though there it is frequently called *Old field birch,* 'birch of abandoned fields,' to distinguish it from the Canoe birch. Scantly wooded places, where the soil is dry and thin, are those where the *Betula populifolia* is most often found.] **1884** Sargent *Forests of N. Amer.* 159, *Betula alba,* var. *populifolia.* . . White Birch. Old-field Birch. Gray Birch. . . A small, short-lived tree of rapid growth . . now generally springing up upon abandoned or burned land in eastern New England. **1900** (1927) Keeler *Our Native Trees* 300, *Betula populifolia.* . . The tree loves rocky barren woods, old fields and abandoned farms, and in New England has the familiar name of Old Field Birch. **1947** Collingwood–Brush *Knowing Trees* 175, The wings, slightly broader than the seeds, enable them to be carried far by the wind. This accounts for the tree quickly taking possession of burned-over, cutover and abandoned land, which has given it the name "oldfield birch." **1979** Little *Checklist U.S. Trees* 63, *Betula populifolia* . . gray birch . . oldfield birch.

old-field cinquefoil n [old field 1]
A **cinquefoil:** usu *Potentilla simplex,* but also *P. canadensis.*
   1937 U.S. Forest Serv. *Range Plant Hdbk.* W155, As much as 13 percent of tannin has been obtained from the dried leaves of oldfield cinquefoil (*P. canadensis*). **1948** Stevens *KS Wild Flowers* 242, *Potentilla simplex* . . Oldfield Cinquefoil. **1976** Bailey–Bailey *Hortus Third* 906, [*Potentilla*] *simplex* . . Old-field c[inquefoil].

old-field clover n [old field 1]
1 =rabbit-foot clover.
   1900 Lyons *Plant Names* 377, *T[rifolium] arvense* . . Old-field Clover. **1922** *Amer. Botanist* 28.33, The soft furry covering of *Trifolium arvense* seems to have caught the fancy of nature-lovers. . . "Old field clover", "stone clover" and "poverty grass" allude to the habit this grass has of growing in sterile soil. **1971** Kieran *Nat. Hist. NYC* 140, Then there is the Rabbit-foot or Old Field Clover (*Trifolium arvense*) that grows in poor ground or waste places and hangs out grayish-pink woolly heads of flowers that resemble miniature powder puffs.
2 A **lespedeza** (here: *Lespedeza striata*).
   1942 *Torreya* 42.161, *Lespedeza striata* . . oldfield clover, southeastern States.

old-field colt See **field colt**

old-field daisy n [old field 1] Cf **field daisy**
=oxeye daisy 1.
   1969 *DARE* FW Addit **KY**47, Old-field daisies: Bookname oxeye daisy (*Chrysanthemum leucanthemum*).

old-field kid See **field colt 2**

old-field lark n [old field 1] Cf **fee lark, field lark**
=meadowlark 1.
   1805 (1904) Lewis *Orig. Jrls. Lewis & Clark Exped.* 2.180 **VA,** There is a kind of larke here that much resembles the bird called the oldfield lark with a yellow brest and a black spot on the croop. **1811** Wilson *Amer. Ornith.* 3.22, Their general name is the *Meadow Lark;* among the Virginians they are usually called the Old field Lark. **1898** (1900) Davie *Nests N. Amer. Birds* 343, *Sturnella magna* . . The Old Field Lark is a well-known bird in the United States east of the Mississippi . . As its name implies, the meadows and fields are its home. **1899** (1912) Green *VA Folk-Speech* 305, Old-field lark . . field-lark. **1923** Dawson *Birds CA* 1.129, Western Meadowlark . . *Sturnella neglecta* . . Field Lark. Old-Field Lark. **1955** *Oriole* 20.1.12 **GA,** Meadowlark.—Field Lark (often pronounced fee-lark; from its habitat; it is, however, no lark); Lark, Old-field Lark. **1956** MA Audubon Soc. *Bulletin* 40.130 **MA,** Meadowlark . . Old-field Lark.

old-field lettuce n [old-field 1]
A **wild lettuce** (here: *Lactuca canadensis*).
   1967 *DARE* Tape **KY**34A, [FW:] What kinds [of greens] do they pick? [Inf:] Well, they pick old-field lettuce . . Field lettuce, you ever seen it? [**1979** Niering–Olmstead *Audubon Guide N. Amer. Wildflowers E. Region* 392, Young leaves [of *Lactuca canadensis*] can be used in salads or as cooked greens, but have a slightly bitter taste.] **1983** *MJLF* 9.1.49 **ceKY,** *Old field lettuce* . . a wild green.

old-field mullein n Also *old-field mullet* [old field 1] Cf **mullet** n[2]
The common **mullein** (*Verbascum thapsus*).

1951 *DE Folkl. Bulletin* Oct 8/1, Old field mullin [sic] was boiled into a tea and used as a medicine for fever and ague (ager) chills. **1968** Harris *S. Home Remedies* 24 **Sth,** Old field mullein, of a genus of herbs of the figwort family, grew wild on the edge of fields and was tolerated in vegetable gardens because of its medicinal properties. **1970** *DARE* (Qu. S20, *A common weed that grows on open hillsides: It has velvety green leaves close to the ground, and a tall stalk with small yellow flowers on a spike at the top*) Inf **VA**52, Old-field mullet [mʌlɪt]—poultices made for boils.

old-field pea See **field pea**

old-field pine n chiefly **Sth, S Midl** Cf **field pine**
A pine growing in an **old field 1**; any of several **pines** that typically grow in this environment, but esp **loblolly pine 1**.
   1797 in 1916 Hawkins *Letters* 89 **Sth,** The whole grown up with old field pine, some of them a foot and an half diameter. **1841** *S. Lit. Messenger* 7.452 **VA,** The old-field pine had not intruded so largely on the domain of the ploughman and reaper. **1856** Olmsted *Journey Slave States* 89 **VA,** Cannot some Yankee contrive a method of concentrating some of the valuable properties of this old-field pine, so that they may be profitably brought into use in more cultivated regions? **a1883** (1911) Bagby *VA Gentleman* 51, The road leads apparently nowhere, through thickets of old-field pine and scrub-oak. **1894** Coulter *Botany W. TX* 554, *P[inus] Taeda.* . . A tree 15 to 45 m. high. . . Extending from the Gulf States to the valley of the Colorado. "Loblolly pine." "Old-field pine." **1896** Mohr–Roth *Timber Pines* 87 **AL, MS,** The Shortleaf Pine . . *Pinus echinata* . . Oldfield Pine. **1897** Sudworth *Arborescent Flora* 28 **FL,** Sand Pine. . . Oldfield Pine. *Ibid* 29 **AL, MS,** Shortleaf Pine. . . Oldfield Pine. **1899** (1912) Green *VA Folk-Speech* 305, Old-field pine. . . Second growth pine. **1903** *DN* 2.322 **seMO,** Old-field pine. . . Pine trees growing on abandoned land. Second growth pine. **1911** *Century Dict. Suppl.,* Old-field pine. . . In Florida, same as cedar pine [=*Pinus glabra*]. **1922** U.S. Dept. Ag. *Farmers' Bulletin* 1256.2, Slash or "yellow slash" pine was formerly referred to in forestry literature as Cuban pine. . . In its younger stages on abandoned fields it is somewhat widely known as "oldfield," and even as "shortleaf" pine. **1960** Vines *Trees SW* 22, Loblolly Pine—*Pinus taeda* . . Other vernacular names are Frankincense Pine . . and Old-field Pine. *Ibid* 25, Shortleaf Pine—*Pinus echinata* . . Vernacular names are Yellow Pine . . Old-field Pine . . and Carolina Pine. **1968** Harris *S. Home Remedies* 62 **NC,** Pulverized wood from a rotten stump, preferably oldfield pine, sifted through muslin rag and dusted on the affected parts was widely used as a cure for chafing. **c1974** Jones *Ozark Hill Boy* 42 **AR** (as of c1930), I personally have been subjected to . . cow dung for stone bruises, pine resin and whiskey for cough, old field pine for dog bites. **1986** Pederson *LAGS Concordance,* 1 inf, **csMS,** Old field pine—bush, makes tea to sweat off fever.

old-field plover n [old field 1] Cf **field plover**
=black-bellied plover.
   1888 Trumbull *Names of Birds* 190, *Charadrius squatarola.* . . Dr. Lewis, in his American Sportsman, tells of its returning from the South early in May, and soon after retiring to the "high upland districts to breed," and of its being known "at this time more particularly as the old field-plover or whistling plover."

old-field preacher n Cf **cornfield preacher**
An old-fashioned rural preacher.
   1904 (1905) Watson *Bethany* 168 **Sth,** The tremendous emphasis with which the old field preacher uttered the words . . I shall never forget.

old-field salvia See **salvia**

old-field school n **Sth, S Midl** *hist* Also called **cornfield school**
A rural elementary school often situated on an **old field 1**; hence n *old-field schoolmaster.*
   1809 Weems *Life George Washington* 10 **ceVA,** The first place of education to which George was ever sent was a little *"old field school."* **1834** Caruthers *Kentuckian* 1.26, He sold his horse and cart too, and then turned in to keepin a little old-field school. **1853** (1854) Baldwin *Flush Times* 106 **AL,** He had been an old-field schoolmaster. *Ibid* 125, The master of the old field school was one of the regular faculty. **1867** Harris *Sut Lovingood Yarns* 37 **TN,** He cum amung us a ole field school-marster. **1885** Green *Memoir Otey* 3 **VA,** In his early boyhood, James was sent . . to an "old-field school," a short distance from their home. **1889** Jones *Educ. in GA* 24, There was no examination of teachers, no issuing of license as a condition precedent to obtaining a school, and no supervision. . . 'old field school-masters,' . . they were called. **1940** Writers' Program *Guide TX* 100, Many private schools

appeared during the period 1823–36. They were called "old field" or "cornfield" schools. **1941** Writers' Program *Guide WV* 116 **ceWV** (as of 1750s), *West Virginia's* free school system . . evolved from log structures built by early settlers to serve as both schools and churches. . . The buildings were usually situated on hard-scrabble or worn-out lands and were called 'old field schools.'

old-fields colt See **field colt 2**

old-field snipe n [old field 1] Cf **snipe**
=**killdeer 1.**
> **1955** *Oriole* 20.1.7 **GA**, Killdeer . . Old-field Snipe (any shore bird may be called a snipe; this one inhabits drier places than most of them do).

old-field toadflax n [old field 1]
=**blue toadflax.**
> **1948** Stevens *KS Wild Flowers* 196, *L[inaria] canadensis*—Oldfield Toadflax. . . Sandy soil of thickets or open ground. **1970** Correll *Plants TX* 1426, *Linaria canadensis* . . Old field toad-flax. . . In sandy-grassy areas in open woodlands . . widespread over much of U.S. and s. Can. **1979** Ajilvsgi *Wild Flowers* 263, Old-field toad-flax—*Linaria canadensis.*

Old Forked-toes See **old 1**

old fort comfort See **old point comfort**

old free issue See **free issue 2**

Old Gentleman n
1 See **old man 2.**
2 =**Old Scratch.**
> **1984** Gilmore *Ozark Baptizings* 68 **MO**, Evidences of the "old gentleman's" efforts to corrupt were seen principally in certain amusement activities and . . in the intemperate consumption of alcoholic beverages.

Old Goblin See **old 1**

old goose n
=**lady's slipper 1.**
> **1900** Lyons *Plant Names* 129, *C[ypripedium] acaule* . . Other names applied indiscriminately to our native species . . Moccasin-flower . . Old-goose, Two-lips. **1924** *Amer. Botanist* 30.153, The genus *Cypripedium* ends the list of orchid genera in North Eastern America . . the "stemless Lady's slipper" (*C. acaule*) covers most of the ground we have already traversed being "pink moccasin flower," "pink lady slipper," "Indian moccasin" and "Noah's ark," and in additional [sic] "camel's foot," "old goose" (instead of duck), "purple cypripedium" and "squirrel's shoes." **1950** Correll *Native Orchids* 20, *Cypripedium acaule* . . Old Goose. . . It is as much at home in the sand hills of the low Coastal Plain of eastern North Carolina and in the pine barrens of New Jersey as it is on the higher mountain slopes of North Carolina, New England, and Canada.

old granddad n Also *old granddad hippety hop* Cf **grand-daddy 3, horse racer 2**
=**praying mantis.**
> **1969** *DARE* FW Addit **NC**, Old granddad, old granddad hippety hop: some kind of insect—some green, some brown, no wings—similar to a grasshopper and a horseracer.

old grandma gray See **grandma gray**

old granny See **granny 8**

old granny Bess n
=**betsy bug.**
> **1894** *S. Workman* 23.66 **DC** [Black], For earache—find a beetle that lives in rotten wood called Old Granny Bess, pull its head off and drop the one drop of blood that comes out into the aching ear.

old granny hibble-hobble n Also *old man hippety hop*
=**old witch 1.**
> **1952** Brown *NC Folkl.* 1.52, 'Old Granny Hibble-Hobble.' . . This particular version [of the game 'Old Witch'] is from Abingdon, Virginia. . . The mother goes to look, and Granny steals the child. *Ibid* 53, 'Old Man Hippety Hop.' . . A Negro version. . . The mother steals her children one at a time from Old Man Hippety Hop. . . The Negro version is most interesting in that it takes the child-eating demon of folklore and makes him an overseer forcing the children to work in the fields.

old granny hobble gobble (or hubbub) See **old mother hobble gobble**

old granny tippy-toes n Also *grand mammy tipsy-toe, old mother tipsy-toe;* for addit varr see quots
=**old witch 1.**
> **1883** Newell *Games & Songs* 144 **ceMA, sePA**, "Old mother Tipsytoe" [Footnote: Or . . *Old mother Cripsy-crops.* The name "Tipsy-toe" is derived from the limping gait supposed to belong to witches.] . . "Old mammy Tipsy-toe" . . makes preparations to depart. . . The children, of course, pursue her with shouts of defiance, upon which she turns and chases them, while they rush to their places. . . Any child she catches is out of the game which is continued until all are captured. **1945** Boyd *Hdbk. Games* 112, *Grand Mammy Tipsy Toe*—The mother gives each of the children a blade of grass and says, "Now you sew your clothes and don't go out after the old witch." They sew; the mother goes away and is transformed into a witch. She hobbles back in front of the house. . . the children . . go out tagging after her as she hobbles along. They chant, "Grand mammy tipsy toe, lost my needle and cannot sew." They repeat this until she turns and tags as many of them as possible as they run for home. All she catches, she put [sic] in her den. **1966** *DARE* Tape **IN1**, Ol' granny tippy-toes. . . much like mother, may I. There's one leader. . . The leader stands in front of the entire group that is spread out lengthwise behind her or him . . and she sings "ol' granny tippy-toes, lost her needle and couldn't sew" over and over again, the children following, and all of a sudden she turns around with no warning . . and runs toward the crowd. And whoever she can catch becomes ol' granny tippy-toes with her. . . The last person to be caught gets to be ol' granny tippy-toes the next time.

old gray coot See **gray coot**

old gray mare n Also *old horse* Cf **gray-mare** v, exclam, **Jack-in-the-bush 2**
A guessing game similar to **hull-gull.**
> **1953** Goodwin *It's Good* 195 **sIL**, After we had eaten our fill we would divide the remaining grains equally and play "Old Horse," a game in which the participants tried to guess the number of grains of corn in each other's hand. **1968** *DARE* Tape **VA9**, Chinquapin games. . . I got the game of old gray mare. He'd say "Old gray mare, ride him to mill, how many miles." I'd say 'bout fifteen and then he'd open up his hand and say "Well, you little devil you, you did get it this time."

old gray wolf in the woodshed See **gray wolf 3**

Old Haggy (Bill) See **old 1**

Old Hairy (man or toe) See **Old Harry**

old hand n Cf **han** n[1], **white old-hand**
=**great blue heron.**
> **1955** MA Audubon Soc. *Bulletin* 39.312 **ME**, Great Blue Heron. . . Old Hand.

Old Hannah n Also *Hannah* esp **TX** Also called **Old Betsy, Old Huldy**
The sun personified.
> **1934** Hurston *Jonah's Gourd Vine* 152 **AL** [Black], When Lucy woke up, old Hannah was riding high. The light was strong in her face. **1947** Lomax *Advent. Ballad Hunter* 173 **TX** [Black] (as of 1933), One day his song was an appeal to "Ol' Hannah" (the sun) to go down. As he explained, "About three o'clock on a long summer day, de sun forgits to move an' stops. Den de mens sings dis song": Been a great long time since Hannah went down / Oh, Hanna [sic], go down. **1956** Ker *Vocab. W. TX* 55, *Time when the sun comes up.* . . [1 inf] Old Hannah's open'd her eyes agin. **1970** Tarpley *Blinky* 46 **neTX**, Time when the sun comes up. . . Ole Hanner's coming over the hill [rare].

Old Harry n Freq with *the* Also *Harry, Old Harry man* (or *toe*) Also sp *Old Hairy toe* Cf **Harry Dick 1**
=**Old Scratch.**
> **1838** Kettell *Yankee Notions* 154, A charming songe, but it all wente wronge /. . . / and next I tried "The Tongs and the Bones,"/ But the verie Olde Harrie was in the tones. **1843** (1916) Hall *New Purchase* 149 **sIN**, I gits bodaciously sker'd and hollows agin like the very ole Harry! **1872** [see **Old Nick**]. **1895** *DN* 1.399 **seMN, NEng, c,swNY**, Raise the Old Harry. **1903** *DN* 2.298 **Cape Cod MA** (as of a1857), *Harry.* . . In expression 'Old Harry,' a rough-looking-strange man. 'The Old Harry's come now.' **1916** Lincoln *Mary-'Gusta* 383 **MA**, You couldn't be wicked if you was apprenticed to the Old Harry for ten years. **1939** Coffin *Capt. Abby* 46 **ME** (as of c1860s), They were full of the Old Hairy. **1939** *AmSp* 14.268 **IN**, Referring to the Devil: . . 'old Hairy,' 'the Old Scratch,' [etc]. **1941** *LANE* Map 473 (*Mad as a wet hen*) 6 infs, **chiefly sNEng**, Mad as (the) Old Harry. *Ibid* Map 474 (*He*

ran like a house afire) 12 infs, **chiefly sNEng,** [He ran] Like the Old Harry; 1 inf, **ceMA,** He ran as though the Old Harry was after him. **1943** *Ibid* Map 532 *(The Devil)* **widespread NEng,** (The) Old Harry. **1944** *PADS* 2.34 **NC, VA,** *Harry, Old .* . The devil, the Old Scratch. Common. **1945** *PADS* 3.10 **Atlanta GA,** *Old Hairy-* (or *Harry-*) *toe,* meaning Satan. **1948** Manfred *Chokecherry* 26 **nwIA,** [On a service station sign:] Get new pep, new zip, new speed-up. . . from *Arctic* gas. With *Arctic* you can go like The Old Harry. **1965–70** *DARE* (Qu. CC8, . . *The devil)* 27 Infs, **scattered, but esp NEast, N Cent, WV,** Old Harry; **SC**46, Old Harry man; (Qu. E22, *If a house is untidy and everything is upset . . "It's a _____!" or "It looks like _____.")* Infs **NY**188, 205, (Old) Harry; (Qu. EE41, *A hobgoblin that is used to threaten children and make them behave)* Infs **AL**37, **CT**35, **KY**66, Old Harry; (Qu. HH22b, . . *A very mean person . . "He's meaner than _____ ."*) Infs **CT**35, **KY**65, Old Harry; (Qu. NN26c, *Weakened substitutes for 'hell': "What the _____!"*) Inf **PA**29, Harry; (Qu. OO14a, *About the wind blowing hard: "Last night the wind _____ [very hard]."*) Inf **CT**36, Blew like the Old Harry. [31 of 34 total Infs old] **1969** *DARE* Tape **MA**40, They would go down and they'd raise the Old Harry with those rabbits. **1986** Pederson *LAGS Concordance (Devil)* 3 infs, **c,cnGA,** Old Harry. **1991** *DARE* File **seNY,** The Old Harry = euphemism for the devil. "Rained like the Old Harry."

old head n Also *older head* [**head** n B3] **chiefly Sth, S Midl**
An elderly person, old-timer.

 1891 Harris *Balaam* 15 **cGA,** Some of the older heads predicted that he would come to the gallows. **1899** (1912) Green *VA Folk-Speech* 305, *Old-heads.* . . The old people of the neighborhood. "I have always heard the old-heads say so." **1937** in 1976 *Weevils in the Wheat* 42 **VA** [Black], On a neighboring plantation when the old heads died out it was necessary to divide up the slaves among the children. **1938** FWP *Guide DE* 363, [At] *Delmarva Camp* . . [i]n the evenings the "old heads" like to sit in rocking-chairs, talk with visitors, read papers, or watch the promenaders. **1942** Hurston *Dust Tracks* 235 **FL** [Black], Some of the older heads held that it [=education] was too much for Negroes to handle. **1954** *DE Folkl. Bulletin* 1.15, Granny Hessy . . hexed a man to death. According to the "old heads," the man stole one of Granny Hessy's piglets. **1958** McCulloch *Woods Words* 126 **Pacific NW,** *Old head*—An old timer, a man who has been around the camp for a long time. **1963** *AmSp* 38.272 **KS** [Amer Ind student slang], During a student's first year, he will be referred to as *new meat.* . . All other students are *old head.* **1976** Ryland *Richmond Co. VA* 374, *Old-heads*—older, wiser people of the community. **1986** Pederson *LAGS Concordance,* 1 inf, **cLA,** Older heads—older people in the community; 1 inf, **seAR,** Old heads—old-timers.

old hen n [See quot 1954] **esp VA** Cf *DS* DD28b
A homemade alcoholic beverage; see quots.

 1930 *DN* 6.88 **cWV,** *Old hen,* corn mash fermented and fortified with fruit juice or birch candy. **1944** Hench Coll. **VA,** Her cook said of some home-brew: "I've got some old hen that's been settin' a good while." **1954** *Daily Progress* (Charlottesville VA) 30 Nov 5/6, "Old hen" (so called because the mixture from which the beverage was made had to "sit" for 21 days). **1971** Hench Coll. **nwVA,** Wine run—the first run in making moonshine. Old hen—this is the liquor from which whiskey is made.

old hen curlew n [See quot 1955]
=**long-billed curlew.**

 1888 Trumbull *Names of Birds* 198, *Numenius longirostris.* . . In Massachusetts at Rowley and New Bedford, Hen Curlew, or Old-Hen Curlew. **1917** (1923) *Birds Amer.* 1.251, Long-Billed Curlew—*Numenius americanus* . . Old Hen Curlew. **1946** Hausman *Eastern Birds* 267, Long-Billed Curlew . . Old Hen Curlew. **1955** MA Audubon Soc. *Bulletin* 39.446, Long-Billed Curlew . . Old Hen Curlew (Mass. From its speckled brown color and its large size.)

old Henry See **Henry** B1

Old Hickory n [Because it carries the picture of Andrew Jackson (US President, 1829–37), whose nickname was *Old Hickory*]
A twenty-dollar bill.

 1966 *DARE* (Qu. U28c, . . *A twenty-dollar bill)* Inf **MI**1, Old Hickory.

old hog n Cf **hog** B10, **old horsey**
 1950 *PADS* 14.49 **SC,** *Old hog.* . . A half-pint bottle of corn whiskey with the palmetto blown in the glass, said to have been formerly sold by the S.C. dispensary at ten cents a bottle. Obsolete.

Old Home Day n Also *Home Day* [By analogy with *Old Home Week*] **esp NEng, NY**
A day of celebration when former residents of a community return for a reunion.

 1966–69 *DARE* (Qu. FF16, . . *Local contests or celebrations)* Inf **NY**111, Home Days; **OH**8, Home Day—Everybody comes home; **NY**146, Old Home Day; **CT**12, Old Home Day—on July 4; **MA**6, Old Home Day—all former residents, all invited; **MA**24, Old Home Day—old friends invited back; **MA**48, Old Home Day—has gone on for 13 years, a reunion for natives and other residents. [All Infs old] **1989** Mosher *Stranger* 129 **nVT,** What I'd like to propose is that we combine a celebration of the church sesquicentennial with an Old Home Day on the common. **1990** *Yankee* Jan 123 **NEng,** Many of us are familiar with Old Home Week, or now more commonly Old Home Day, celebrations that are still held each summer in a number of towns in New England. **1993** *DARE* File **MA,** *Old Home Day* (equal stress on all three words) continues in many New England rural communities, sometimes in summer, also occasionally in fall during "the color" or if the town is celebrating an anniversary. It usually involves a community picnic, often including visits to old graveyards. Descendants of people who left Southampton, Pelham, Windsor, Northampton in covered wagons come back. *Ibid* **nwMA,** Old Home Day? Oh, yes, we all have 'em. We [=a square and contra dance band] played at the Guilford Old Home Day last year. All the small towns have 'em. They are like a fair or festival: horse drawing, square dances, pie baking contests, frog jumping contests, and, starting up recently, tractor pulls, which don't do much for me.

old homeplace See **homeplace** 2

old hook n
=**devil's-claw** 4.
 1933 Small *Manual SE Flora* 489, *P[isonia] aculeata* . . Old-hook. **1960** Vines *Trees SW* 252, Devils-claw Pisonia—*Pisonia aculeata* . . Vernacular names are Garabato Prieto . . Old Hook, and Pull-and-hold back.

Old Horny n Also *Old Horns* Also sp *Auld Hornie* [Scots *Auld Hornie*] Cf **horny man**
=**Old Scratch.**
 1853 Simms *Sword & Distaff* 529 **SC,** With the help of Old Horny, I tried it; and sure enough, off she went, ship and all. *Ibid* 572, The old Horny swore it should be so, and I told him! **1943** *LANE* Map 532 *(The Devil)* 1 inf, **ceVT,** Old Horny. **1950** *WELS (Names for the devil)* 1 Inf, **cwWI,** Auld Hornie. **1953** [see **Old Scratch**]. **1956** Ker *Vocab. W. TX* 435, The Devil: an imaginary bad man that "gets" little children. . . [1 inf] Old Horns. **1967** *DARE* (Qu. CC8) Infs **MI**67, **NY**30, Old Horny.

old horse See **old gray mare**

old horsey n Cf **corn** n B1, **old hog**
Corn liquor, moonshine.
 1985 Wilkinson *Moonshine* 28 **neNC,** "After that they'd serve you North Carolina Corn." It is called . . old horsey.

Old Huldy n
=**Old Hannah.**
 1943 TN Folk Lore Soc. *Bulletin* 9.4.10, After several days of overcast skies last February a friend said to me one morning "Well, I see Old Huldy is out again." *Old Huldy,* it developed, is the sun. But my friend, nor any one else of whom I have inquired, knows anything [sic] about the meaning or currency of the term. He insists he had known it all his life.

old hundred See **hundred** B2b

Old Imp See **old** 1

old Indian squash See **Indian squash**

old Injun n
=**old-squaw,** usu the drake.
 1888 Trumbull *Names of Birds* 87, Known all along the New England coast as *old squaw,* the full-feathered drake being sometimes distinguished, as at West Barnstable and Fairhaven, Mass., Stonington and Essex, Conn., as *old injun.* **1898** Elliot *Wild Fowl* 191, In various parts of the land, . . it [=the Old Squaw] has many names, some of which are . . Old Wife, Old Injun, Old Molly [etc]. **1917** (1923) *Birds Amer.* 1.141, Old Wife; Old Injin; Old Granny; Old Molly; Old Billy.

Old Jack See **old** 1

old Jersey bull pine n Cf **bull pine 1c, d, Jersey ~**
A **pitch pine** (here: *Pinus rigida*).
    1967 *New Yorker* 25 Nov 128 **cNJ,** The trees themselves—the pre-
dominant pitch pines, at any rate—are called Old Jersey Bull Pines.

old Jerusalem weed See **Jerusalem weed**

Old Job's turkey (hen) See **Job's turkey 1**

old joe n [Cf *DJE old Joe* the pelican] Cf **old hand, poor joe**
=**great blue heron.**
    1966 *DARE* FW Addit **SC,** *Old joe*—water bird (heron), but everybody
calls him po-Jo.

old Kate See **Kate**

old Kentucky girl n Also *Kentucky girl*
A children's singing game played in a ring.
    1968 *DARE* (Qu. EE1, . . *Games . . children play . . in which they
form a ring, and either sing or recite a rhyme*) Inf **LA37,** Old Kentucky
girl. **1968** *DARE* Tape **LA36,** [The game] Kentucky girl. . . [Song
lyrics:] They had a girl in Kentucky / This old Kentucky girl. . . How
we play this is . . somebody spins around and she stops at somebody
and . . they gotta get in and we start singin' the song and they gotta
dance and you dance and then when we say "around and around you
go and where you stop nobody knows" she turns around, she picks
somebody else.

old-ladies'-clothespins n Also *old-lady's-clothespin* [From the
shape of the achene]
A **beggar ticks 1** (here: *Bidens frondosa*).
    1896 *Jrl. Amer. Folkl.* 9.191 **MA,** *Bidens frondosa . .* old ladies'
clothes-pins. **1959** Carleton *Index Herb. Plants* 88, *Old-Lady's-Clothespin:* Bidens frondosa.

old-lady's-darning needle See **darning needle 1**

old-lady's-tobacco See **ladies'-tobacco b**

old lighthouse shitter n Cf **flying shit-house**
A **gull;** see quot.
    1945 McAtee *Nomina Abitera* 38, Gulls *(Larus),* not further iden-
tified.—Old lighthouse shitter, Northwest coast.

old logger n
=**Canada jay.**
    1919 Gilmore *Birds of Field* 295, He [=the old guide] tells me that
in the early days in the lumber camps the Canada Jay bore the name of
"The Old Logger." The legend is that when an aged lumberman died
his spirit at once took possession of a Jay, and if the bird was killed the
spirit, too, died with it. **1959** [see **lumberjack**].

Old Lutherfud See **old 1**

old ma See **old mamma**

old maid n

1 also *old-maid-flower:* A **zinnia** (here: *Zinnia elegans*).
chiefly Sth, S Midl See Map Cf **old maid's pink 4**
    1839 *S. Lit. Messenger* 5.751, A particular spot in his garden was
appropriated to the culture of old maids, whose stiff stems and dusky
red petals occupied a small space of earth. **1888** *Century Illustr. Mag.*
36.896 **GA,** The flower-garden overrun with . . four-o'clocks, old-maids,

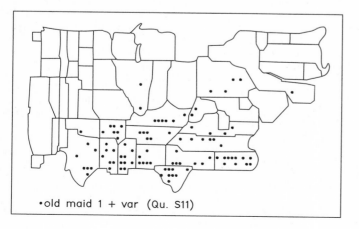
•old maid 1 + var (Qu. S11)

and sunflowers. **1909** *DN* 3.353 **eAL, wGA,** *Ol(d) maid. . .* A cultivated
flower, the zinnia. Common. **1940** (1978) Still *River of Earth* 104 **KY,**
Before frost fell we went to Grandma's flower bed in a corner of the
garden and picked the dry seeds. We broke off the brown heads of old
maids and the smooth buttons of Job's tears hanging on withered stalks.
1950 *WELS (Zinnia)* 1 Inf, **cWI,** Old maids. [*DARE* Ed: Both sides of
Inf's family from KY] **1965–70** *DARE* (Qu. S11, . . *Zinnia)* 71 Infs,
chiefly Sth, S Midl, Old maid(s); 19 Infs, **chiefly Sth, S Midl,** Old-
maid-flower; **AL19,** Old maid—older people use it; **KY5,** Old maids—
old-fashioned; **OK28,** Old maids (old term); **SC11,** Old-maid-flower—a
way old-time name—all "zinnias" now; **TX53,** Old maid—years ago we
called them that. **1982** *Smithsonian Letters* **NC,** Old maids—zinnias in
Georgia. **1986** Pederson *LAGS Concordance,* 1 inf, **cnGA,** Old maids—
their name for zinnias.

2 A **periwinkle** (here: *Catharanthus roseus*). [*OED* 1884]
esp FL
    1916 *DN* 4.345 **FL,** *Old maid.* = *graveyard flower:* among 'crackers.'
1933 Small *Manual SE Flora* 1060, Periwinkle. Old-maid. . . This
showy plant has taken possession of acres of scrub land in southern
peninsular Florida. **1953** Greene-Blomquist *Flowers South* 101, Rose-
Periwinkle, Old-Maid *(Vinca rosea)*—This erect herb which was introduced from Madagascar has become naturalized in hammocks, pinelands, waste places, and roadsides in peninsular Fla. and the Keys. **1979**
Niering-Olmstead *Audubon Guide N. Amer. Wildflowers E. Region* 336,
In the southern United States the erect Old Maid *(Vinca rosea),* with
either pink or white flowers, often becomes well established. **1982**
Perry-Hay *Field Guide Plants* 114, *Catharanthus roseus . .* old maid.

3 A **velvetleaf** (here: *Abutilon theophrasti*).
    1880 *Scribner's Mth.* 20.101 **NY,** In my section an annoying weed is
Abutilon, or velvet-leaf, also called "old maid."

4 also *old maid('s) piece;* for addit varr see quots: The last
piece of food left on a plate. **widespread, but more freq Nth,
N Midl** See Map Cf **last button on Gabe's coat 1, manner** n **3**
    1950 *WELS (The last piece of something on a plate)* 7 Infs, **WI,** Old
maid; 6 Infs, **WI,** Old maid's piece; 1 Inf, **swWI,** The old maid's bit;
[6 Infs, **WI,** You'll be an old maid (if you take the last piece)]. **c1960**
Wilson Coll. **csKY,** *Old maid. . .* Humorous name for the last piece of
bread or part of other food. The folk saying had it that the person who
took the last piece on a plate would never marry. **1965–70** *DARE* (Qu.
H71) 209 Infs, **widespread, but more freq Nth, N Midl,** Old maid; 12
Infs, **scattered,** Old maid('s) piece; 8 Infs, Old maid's (bit, dish, portion,
share); **NE11,** Old maid choice; **MD30,** Old maid—for next-to-last
piece; [**AL30,** If you ate it you'd be an old maid; **MN3,** Wind up an
old maid; **PA126,** If you eat it you will be an old maid; **FL21, PA234,**
Old maid if you take it].

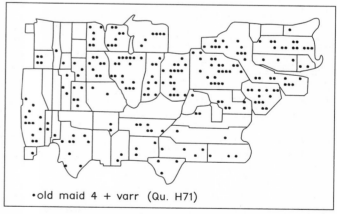
•old maid 4 + varr (Qu. H71)

5 A kernel of popcorn that fails to pop. **chiefly Nth, N Midl**
    1947 Bowles-Towle *New Engl. Cooking* 6, When the kernels begin to
pop, cover the kettle. Shake rapidly until the kettle is filled with fluffy
white kernels. Discard any old maids left in the bottom of the kettle.
1949 *Sat. Eve. Post* 21 May 36, All hands kept right on pitching in, and
munching, until there was nothing left but a few unpopped kernels
derisively known as old maids. **1967** *DARE* FW Addit **swWI,** "Old
maids"—kernels of corn that do not pop and are left in the bottom of
the pot after making popcorn. **1970** *DARE* File **seWI,** Old maids—the
unpopped kernels of popcorn that are left in the popping pan. I've heard
two different people from Milwaukee say this. **1972** *NYT Article Letters*

ePA, We all called the unpopped corn "old maids." *Ibid* **IL**, As a native of Ill. I have known *old maids* for unpopped popcorn kernels all my life. **1982** *DARE* File **cwIL**, *Old maids*. Kernels of popcorn that do not pop. Term used by adult volunteers running the refreshment stand at Jacksonville, Ill. Pony-Colt baseball park. Appears on posted list of instructions for making popcorn. *Ibid* **cwCA** (as of c1950). **1995** *Ibid* **sCA, IL, KS, cnKY, ceMO, MT, NEng, ceNY, SD, UT, eWA.** *Ibid* **ceAL,** Of the 23 students . . in my class at Auburn, only 1—a 24-year-old female from Jacksonville, Florida (parents from Iowa and South Dakota)—was familiar with 'old maid' in this context.

6 See quot. Cf *DS* M21a-b

1950 *WELS Suppl.* **WI,** Old maid—euphemism for an outdoor toilet.

7 See quot.

1968 *DARE* (Qu. EE2, *Games that have one extra player—when a signal is given, the players change places, and the extra one tries to get a place*) Inf **NY84,** Musical chairs, old maid.

8 See quot.

1967 *DARE* (Qu. EE11, *Bat-and-ball games for just a few players [when there aren't enough for a regular game]*) Inf **OR6,** Old maid, catch flies.

old-maid-flower See **old maid 1**

old maid piece See **old maid 4**

old-maid-pink See **old-maid's pink 1**

old-maid's-bonnet n

A **lupine** (here: *Lupinus perennis*).

1896 *Jrl. Amer. Folkl.* 9.186, *Lupinus perennis* . . old maids' bonnets, Southampton, Mass., Southold, L[ong] I[sland]. **1922** *Amer. Botanist* 28.76, "Quaker bonnets" and "old maids bonnets" are probably . . names imposed for the fancied resemblance of the keel of the flower to the head-gear mentioned. **1959** Carleton *Index Herb. Plants* 88, Old-Maid's Bonnets: Lupinus perennis. **1969** *DARE* (Qu. S26a, . . *Wildflowers. . . Roadside flowers*) Inf **NY205,** Old-maid's-bonnet—blue bonnets.

old-maid's-breastpin n

A **tickseed** (here: *Coreopsis* spp).

1894 *Jrl. Amer. Folkl.* 7.92, *Coreopsis*, sp., old maid's breastpin, Plymouth, O[hio].

old-maid's-hair n Cf **maidenhair 2, old-man's-whiskers 1**

A **prairie smoke** (here: *Geum triflorum*).

1950 FWP *Guide ID* 72, Old maid's hair . . also called prairie smoke, is typical of the great prairie regions of the United States. Its red, budlike flowers sprout in groups from a crimson stalk, and in late summer the silky plumed heads shimmer like pale purple mist in the distance.

old-maid's-nightcap n Cf **grandmammy's nightcap, lady's-nightcap, nightcaps**

A **cranesbill 1** (here: *Geranium maculatum*).

1896 *Jrl. Amer. Folkl.* 9.184, Old maids' night-caps, Madison, Wis. **1930** Sievers *Amer. Med. Plants* 62, *Geranium maculatum.* . . Old-maid's-nightcap. **1971** Krochmal *Appalachia Med. Plants* 134, Old maid's-nightcap. . . Produces 3 to 5 loose, rosy-purple to white flowers, 1 inch across.

old-maid's-paintbrush n Cf **devil's paintbrush 1**

A **hawkweed** (here: prob *Hieracium pratense*).

1969 *DARE* (Qu. S21, . . *Weeds . . that are a trouble in gardens and fields*) Inf **NY222,** Devil's paintbrush (burnt orange), old-maid's-paintbrush (paler, towards yellow)—both tall, rough stalk with small pointed leaves.

old maid's piece See **old maid 4**

old-maid's-pink n

1 also *old-maid-pink:* =**bouncing Bet 1.** scattered but esp **MA**

1876 Hobbs *Bot. Hdbk.* 84, Old maids' pink, Soapwort, Saponaria officinalis. **1892** Torrey *Foot-Path Way* 79 **Cape Cod MA,** Across the road from the old house . . stood a still more ancient-seeming barn . . but with old maid's pinks, catnip, and tall, stout pokeberry weeds yet flourishing beside it. **1892** *Jrl. Amer. Folkl.* 5.92 **MA,** *Saponaria officinalis,* old maid's pink; London pride. **1901** Lounsberry *S. Wild Flowers* 158, The homely bouncing bet, or old maid's pink, Saponaria officinalis. . . was once exclusively a garden plant. One day a young lad in the Alleghanies handed me one of the flowers with the quaint remark: "that's a tame flower." **1910** Graves *Flowering Plants* 180 **CT,** Sapo-

naria officinalis . . Old-maid's or Hedge Pink. **1958** Jacobs–Burlage *Index Plants* NC 35, Saponaria officinalis. . . Old maid's pink. . . The inspissated juice is said to be a cure for gonorrhoea. **1967** *DARE* (Qu. S26a, . . *Wildflowers. . . Roadside flowers*) Inf **MA5,** Old-maid-pinks (Saponaria). **1982** *Greenfield Recorder* (MA) 11 Sept 4/1, "Old maid pinks," which you may know as "Bouncing Bet," . . still persists even in poor, dry soil.

2 =**corn cockle.** Cf **corn pink, French ~ 2, mullein ~ 2**

1892 *Jrl. Amer. Folkl.* 5.93 **NH,** *Lychnis Githago,* old maid's pink. **1900** Lyons *Plant Names* 20, *A[grostemma] Githago* . . Old-maid's Pink. **1995** Brako et al. *Scientific & Common Names Plants* 195, Old-maid's-pink—*Agrostemma githago*.

3 =**garden catchfly.** Cf **mice pink**

1893 *Jrl. Amer. Folkl.* 6.138 **wMA,** *Silene Armeria* . . old maid's pink.

4 A **zinnia** (here: *Zinnia elegans*). Cf **old maid 1**

1896 *Jrl. Amer. Folkl.* 9.193, *Zinnia elegans* . . old maid's pink, Sulphur Grove, Ohio.

old-maid's-pins n Cf **old-ladies'-clothespins**

A **beggar ticks 1** (here: *Bidens leucantha*).

1955 *S. Folkl. Qrly.* 19.232 **FL,** Old Maid's Pins (Bidens leucantha) . . and *Pine Cone Lily* (Zingibar [sic] zerumbet) are named from the objects they most resemble.

Old Maker n

=**Old Master 1.**

1942 Hurston *Dust Tracks* 75 **FL** [Black], One day He called everybody and gave out feet and eyes. Another time he give out toe-nails that Old Maker figured they could use. *Ibid* 180, Old Maker had left out the steering gear when He gave Papa his talents.

old mamma n Also *old ma, ~ mom* [Cf *SND auld-mither* (at *auld* adj. 2(5))] Cf **big mamma, mamma n[1] 3, old daddy**

One's grandmother.

1967–70 *DARE* (Qu. Z4, . . 'Grandmother') Inf **NC40,** Old ma; **NC61,** Old mom; **KY74,** Old mamma.

old mammy See **mammy duck**

old man n

1 Any of var plants: see below.

a also *old man plant, ~ sage:* Either of two related plants: usu **southernwood** in the eastern US, but also **sand sage** of the western US. [*OED* 1824 → for *Artemisia abrotanum;* cf quot 1968] Cf **old woman**

1837 Darlington *Flora Cestrica* 491, *A[rtemisia] abrotanum* . . Southern-wood. Old Man. **1839** *S. Lit. Messenger* 5.751, Bachelor's hat, with southernwood or old man, were conspicuous embellishments to almost every parterre. **1853** in 1908 Handsaker *Pioneer Life* 58 **cwNE,** Here may be seen acres of that beautiful shrub, old man. **1892** *Jrl. Amer. Folkl.* 5.99 **OH, IL,** *Artemisia abrotanum* . . old man. **1910** Graves *Flowering Plants* 401 **CT,** *Artemisia Abrotanum* . . Old Man. Southernwood. **1929** *Torreya* 29.151, Artemisia Abrotanum, *Southernwood,* "Old Man," "Old Woman," a sprig of which was carried to church and to funerals. **1935** Hyatt *Folkl. Adams Co. IL* 353, During the Civil War there was a plant that grows in the garden called old man plant, and if you would take a piece of that and a horseshoe and hang them both over your door, your man was sure to come under that door you would marry. **1942** Whipple *Joshua* 95 **UT** (as of c1860), Healthy growth of 'old man' sage, always a sign of good land. He chewed one of the threadlike leaves, puckered over the bitter flavor. **1968** Abbey *Desert Solitaire* 28 **seUT,** Sand sage or old man sage, a lustrous windblown blend of silver and blue and aquamarine, gleams in the distance, the feathery stems flowing like hair.

b A **yarrow** (here: *Achillea millefolium*).

1897 Parsons *Wild Flowers CA* 97, Yarrow. Milfoil. *Achillea Millefolium.* . . Among children the yarrow is commonly known as "old man." **1947** (1976) Curtin *Healing Herbs* 158, Plumajillo—*Achillea lanulosa* . . Milfoil . . Old Man.

c usu *old-man-in-the-ground:* =**bigroot 1.**

1911 Jepson *Flora CA* 270, *Echinocystis* . . Big Root. . . Our species are all perennial from exceedingly large, often deep-seated, fusiform or globose roots, sometimes as large as and not unlike the shape of a man's body, whence the common name, "Old Man in the Ground." **1934** Haskin *Wild Flowers Pacific Coast* 355, Wild Cucumber *Micrampelis oregana* . . The roots of this plant attain a great size, and from them the plant is sometimes given the name of "old man," and "man-in-the-ground." **1967** Gilkey–Dennis *Hdbk. NW Plants* 409, *Marah oreganus* . . Old man-in-the-ground. Wild cucumber. **1967** *DARE* FW Addit **WA**, Old-man-in-the-ground—parsnip-like root, sometimes two feet long, found around Washington ocean beaches.

d also *old man of the desert:* A **prickly pear** (here: either *Opuntia erinacea* or *O. bigelovii*). Cf **old-man cactus**

1924 Austin *Land of Journeys' Ending* 128 **AZ**, Among the chollas, the unaccustomed eye will distinguish the "old-man," having a silvery-haired appearance from the sheaths of its dense covering of spines, from the deer-horn type. **1939** Pickwell *Deserts* 48 **Desert SW**, The cactus with the numerous joints is the notorious cholla *(Opuntia bigelovii)*, the "Old Man of the Desert," that grows at times to a height of four feet. *Ibid* 65, So notorious is Cholla that in the desert it is known by many different names: "Silver Cactus" (the new stems at the top are silvery in color, older stems nearly black); "Jumping Cactus" . . and most picturesquely, "Old Man of the Desert." **1951** Corle *Gila* 348 **AZ**, A host of others [=cacti] that seem endless—the old man, the rainbow . . the deerhorn. **1974** Munz *Flora S. CA* 317, *O[puntia] erinacea*. . . Old Man. Mojave Prickly-Pear.

e A **virgin's bower.** Cf **old man's beard 3**

1967 *DARE* (Qu. S26e, *Other wildflowers not yet mentioned;* not asked in early QRs) Inf **IA**13, Wild clematis—also called "old man."

f A **ragwort** (here: *Senecio longilobus*). Cf **old-man-in-the-spring**

1976 Elmore *Shrubs & Trees SW* 74, *Threadleaf Groundsel* . . old man, squawweed, yerba cana [gray-hair plant].

2 also cap: =**Old Master 1.**

1902 *DN* 2.240 **sIL**, Old man. . . The very ignorant thus commonly designate the deity. **1906** *DN* 3.122 **sIN**, Old Man. . . Used commonly for the deity. **1942** (1971) Campbell *Cloud-Walking* 128 **seKY**, Iffen the Old Man wanted them flower blooms and garden truck to be wetted He'd a-sent rain down on them. **1953** Randolph–Wilson *Down in Holler* 268 **Ozarks**, The *Old Man,* or the *Good Man,* or the *Old Gentleman*—these names for God are used even by deeply religious hillfolk.

3 also cap: See **Old Boy.**

4 A bull. *euphem* Cf **gentleman n B2**

1939 *LANE* Map 190 *(Bull)* 1 inf, **seMA**, Old man. **1970** *DARE* (Qu. K22, *Words used for a bull)* Inf **CA**195, Old man.

5 =**bald eagle 1.**

1953 Jewett *Birds WA* 176, Northern Bald Eagle . . Other names: White-headed Sea Eagle; Old-man.

old-man-and-woman n

=**houseleek 1.**

1948 Neal *In Gardens HI* 330, *S[empervivum] tectorum* . . was believed to protect houses from lightning. Other names are houseleek, live-forever, old-man-and-woman. **1976** Bailey–Bailey *Hortus Third* 1034, *Sempervivum tectorum* . . old-man-and-woman. . . This most variable sp. is the most widely grown, appearing in many forms and under many names.

old-man beard See **old-man's-beard 1**

old-man cactus n

1 also *old-man-of-the-mountain:* A **cactus B1** (here: *Cephalocereus senilis*) native to Mexico and freq cult in the southwestern US.

1858 in 1859 U.S. Congress *Serial Set* 862 Doc 135 3.44, [Footnote:] *Cereus Schottii* . . leaves no doubt in my mind about the propriety and necessity of a reunion of the "Old man Cactus" and its allies with *Cereus.* **1868** (1870) Gray *Field Botany* 155, *C[ereus] senilis*, Old-Man Cactus. Cult. for its singular appearance, the long white hanging bristles at the top likened to the locks of an aged man. **1876** Hobbs *Bot. Hdbk.* 84, Old man cactus, Cereus senilis. **1936** Shiner Cactus Nursery *Illustr. Catalog* 11, Cephalocereus senilis. . . One of most famous of Mexican species. White spines are intermixed with long white bristly hairs like an old man's beard, hence the popular name "Old Man of the Mountain." **1942** Hylander *Plant Life* 333, [Caption:] Old Man Cactus *(Cereus senilis)* grows a tawny wool among the long spines, forming a tangled mass which gives the species a venerable and hoary appearance. **1948** Neal *In Gardens HI* 534, The old-man cactus [*C. senilis* . .], from Mexico, may attain a height of 45 feet.

2 also *old-man whiskers:* =**senita.**

1948 *So. Sierran* May 5/2 *(DA)*, The Organ Pipe and Senita (Old Man) Cacti are similar except that the Senita has whiskers. **1967** *DARE* (Qu.

S26e, *Other wildflowers not yet mentioned;* not asked in early QRs) Inf **CA**4, Old-man whiskers or old-man cactus.

old man hippety hop See **old granny hibble-hobble**

old man, I'm on your land n

A children's game: see quot.

1969 *DARE* (Qu. EE33, . . *Outdoor games . . that children play)* Inf **RI**17, Old man, I'm on your land—only we'd say "old man mony ['moni] land," one guy would jump on land, other had to catch him.

old-man-in-the-ground See **old man 1c**

old-man-in-the-spring n Also *old-man-of-spring* **Pacific** Cf **old man 1f**

A **ragwort** (here: *Senecio vulgaris*).

1911 Jepson *Flora CA* 428, *S[enecio] vulgaris*. . . Sometimes called "Old Man of Spring." **1960** Abrams *Flora Pacific States* 4.452, Common Groundsel or Old Man in the Spring. **1961** Thomas *Flora Santa Cruz* 374 **cwCA**, Old-Man-in-the-Spring. A very widespread and common weed in disturbed areas. **1973** Hitchcock–Cronquist *Flora Pacific NW* 544, Old-man-in-the-spring, common g[roundsel].

old man of the desert See **old man 1d**

old-man-of-the-mountain n

1 See **old-man cactus 1.**

2 as *old-man-of-the-mountains:* A **pasqueflower** (here: *Pulsatilla occidentalis*); also its seed head. Cf **little dish mops**

1949 Peattie *Cascades* (plate facing page 261) **OR**, Seed pods of western anemone—Called "old men of the mountains." **1967** Gilkey–Dennis *Hdbk. NW Plants* 138, *Anemone occidentalis* . . Pasque flower. Old man of the mountains.

3 A **bitterweed** (here: *Hymenoxis grandiflora*).

1963 Craighead *Rocky Mt. Wildflowers* 221, Alpine Sunflower. . . Old-Man-of-the-Mountain. **1973** Hitchcock–Cronquist *Flora Pacific NW* 532, Old-man-of-the-mt. . . [*Hymenoxys] grandiflora.* **1979** Spellenberg *Audubon Guide N. Amer. Wildflowers W. Region* 373, Old Man of the Mountain . . *Hymenoxys grandiflora.* . . A *whitish, hairy* plant with feather-like leaves mostly near the base. . . In a complicated genus of about 20 species in western North America, this has the largest and prettiest heads.

4 A **virgin's bower.** Cf **old-man's-beard 3**

1967 *DARE* FW Addit **CO**29, Clematis gets white fuzzy seed balls and is then called Old Man of the Mountain.

old-man-of-the-mountains See **old-man-of-the-mountain 2**

old-man-of-the-woods n

A **pinecone mushroom:** usu *Strobilomyces floccopus,* but also *S. confusus.*

1972 Miller *Mushrooms* 159, *Strobilomyces floccopus.* . . *Cap shaggy from gray-black scales; stalk also shaggy.* . . The . . "Old Man of the Woods" is very distinctive . . , but its taste is not outstanding. **1981** Lincoff *Audubon Field Guide Mushrooms* 580, Old Man of the Woods—*Strobilomyces floccopus.* . . On the ground; among hardwoods (oak) and mixed hardwoods and conifers (pine); also in pine barrens. Range: Nova Scotia to Florida, west to Michigan and Texas. **1987** McKnight–McKnight *Mushrooms* 112, *Old-Man-of-the-Woods* . . *Strobilomyces floccopus.* . . Surface breaks into dark . . shaggy scales at a very early stage, exposing lighter, dingy flesh between scales. *Ibid* 113, *Strobilomyces confusus* . . is another shaggy bolete that cannot be distinguished from *S. floccopus* without examining the spores. . . Both species are called Old-Man-of-the-Woods and are very easily distinguished from all other boletes.

old man on the mountain n

=**king of the mountain 1.**

1967 *DARE* FW Addit **ceNC**, Old man on the mountain—leader on top of hill, other players try to replace him.

old man plant (or sage) See **old man 1a**

old-man's-beard n [See quot 1836] Cf **old-man's-whiskers**

1 also *old-man beard:* A **Spanish moss** (here: *Tillandsia usneoides*). [*DJE* 1696 →]

[**1756** Browne *Civil & Nat. Hist. Jamaica* 2.193, Old-man's Beard. . . is frequently imported to *Jamaica* From North America, for the use of the sadlers and coach-makers.] **1836** (1840) Phelps *Lectures on Botany* app 144, *Tillandsia usneoides*. . . Parasitic. From its peculiar appearance, suspended from trees to which it has fastened itself, it is called *old man's* *beard.* **1877** Bartlett *Americanisms* 790, *Old Man's Beard,* A moss hanging from the boughs of most trees in Louisiana and Texas. **1974** Morton *Folk Remedies* 153 **SC**, *Spanish Moss;* . . *Old Man's Beard.* . . Plant reaches 10 or 12 ft. or even 25 ft. in length, its strands wavy and curling. Leaves threadlike, 1 to 3 in. long. . . Occurs in masses on shrubs and trees, especially oaks, cypresses, pines, and pecans, in low woods, hammocks, and swamps. **1981** Pederson *LAGS Basic Materials,* 1 inf, **seGA**, That old-man-beard—a medicine used for appetite and blood—high blood pressure.

2 =**fringe tree.**
1797 Smith *Nat. Hist. GA* 1.67, The caterpillar feeds on the Fringe-tree, called old man's beard from its clusters of white blossoms. **1855** Simms *Forayers* 485 **SC**, Don't forget the "wake robbin," and the "old man's beard," the leafy green look of the one, and the snow-white fringes of the other. **1860** Curtis *Cat. Plants NC* 95, *Fringe Tree.* . . Sometimes called Old Man's Beard. We have no shrub of softer and more delicate beauty than this, when draped in its clusters of snow-white, fringe-like flowers. **1901** Mohr *Plant Life AL* 668, Fringe tree. Old Man's Beard. . . New Jersey . . south to Florida and Texas. **1941** Walker *Lookout* 61 **TN**, Fringe-tree, or Old Man's Beard . . builds snowlike spots in many places on top of the mountain. **1955** *S. Folkl. Qrly.* 19.232 **FL**, *White Lady* (Chionanthus Virginica), also called *Finger Tree, Old Man's Beard, Fringe Tree,* and *Sunflower Tree,* is a sheet of pure white color from top to bottom in early March before the foliage appears. **1969** *DARE* FW Addit **GA**51, Old man's beard—A bush with a flower which is like a beard, bushy, hanging down several inches from stem. Bush does not grow over eight feet high; has smooth white bark and blue berry.

3 =**virgin's bower.** [*OED* 1760 →]
1876 Hobbs *Bot. Hdbk.* 84, Old man's beard, Travellers' Joy. **1902** (1909) Mathews *Field Book Amer. Wild Flowers* 130, In October the flowers are succeeded by the gray plumy clusters of the withered styles . . which appear under the glass like many tiny twisted tails. The plants presenting this hoary appearance gave rise to the popular name, Old Man's Beard. **1920** Rice–Rice *Pop. Studies CA Wild Flowers* 78, "Old Man's Beard" is a name commonly applied to the vine at seed time. **1936** Whitehouse *TX Flowers* 28, Old Man's Beard (*Clematis drummondii*) is a vine growing in great profusion, covering shrubs and fences from Central Texas to Arizona and Mexico. . . The seeds mature in a few weeks, and soon the vine is covered with iridescent masses of silky, feathery plumes, 2–4 in. long, which grow out from the seed cover. These plumes are elongated, persistent styles and are responsible for many common names given to the vine, including grandfather's beard, gray beard, goat's beard, and love-in-the-mist. **1949** *Nature Mag.* Apr 187, As the days shorten, fluffy old man's beard is white against the blue October sky. **1966** *DARE* Wildfl QR (Wills–Irwin) Pl.73 Inf **TX**44, Old-man's-beard—virgin's bower. **1967** *DARE* (Qu. S26e) Inf **MA**5, Wild clematis—old-man's-beard. **1967** Borland *Hill Country* 288 **nwCT**, We saw the fantastic tangle of ripe stamens on the wild clematis which gave it the autumn name Old Man's Beard—in midsummer it is Virgin's Bower. **1976** Elmore *Shrubs & Trees SW* 24, Western Virgin's Bower—traveler's-joy, old-man's-beard [etc.].

4 =**horsetail 1.** [*EDD* 1886 →]
1890 *Century Dict.* 4100, *Old-man's-beard.* . . A species of *Equisetum.* **1959** Carleton *Index Herb. Plants* 88, *Old-man's-beard:* Equisetum.

5 =**black gum 1.**
1894 *Jrl. Amer. Folkl.* 7.90, *Nyssa sylvatica* . . old man's beard, Lincolnton, N.C.

6 A **hydrangea 1** (here: *Hydrangea quercifolia*).
1903 Small *Flora SE U.S.* 506, *Hydrangea quercifolia* . . middle Georgia to Florida and Mississippi. Gray-beard. Old-Man's-beard. **1960** Vines *Trees SW* 305, Vernacular names are Sevenbark, Gray Beard, and Old Man's Beard.

7 The beard lichen (*Usnea barbata*) or a related lichen. **esp West** Cf **goatsbeard lichen**
1907 Marshall *Mosses* 20, Old Man's Beard (*Usnea barbata* . .) was used to promote the growth of hair. *Ibid* 84, Old Man's Beard, *Usnea longissima.* . . Used to promote the growth of hair. **1941** Writers' Program *Guide WY* 25, On the northern slopes the Douglas firs are often covered with green lichen known as 'old man's beard,' and with black, hanging lichen. **1949** Palmer *Nat. Hist.* 56, *Old-man's-beard—Usnea barbata.* . . Found hanging on bark and branches of living or dead trees in all parts of North America. . . Fibers to over 4 inches long. **1975** Zwinger *Run River* 25 **UT**, This is my idea of the forest primeval: filled with deadfall, very still, ground soft and cushioned, a windrow of porcupine needles, big circles of dog lichen, trees festooned with old man's beard. **1995** *DARE* File **nwCA** (as of 1976), Old-man's-beard is

a gray-green moss that hangs from the branches of trees. I used it to make a pale green-yellow dye.

8 An unidentified seaweed; see quot. Cf **niggerhair 1**
1937 *Natl. Geogr. Mag.* Feb 210 **FL**, A curious spreading seaweed known as "old man's beard" grows over the muddy bottom, and here and there are outcrops and ledges of old limestone rock.

9 A **goatsbeard 1** (here: *Tragopogon dubius*).
1957 Roberts–Nelson *Wildflowers CO* 56, Salsify, *Tragopogon dubius.* . . Goatsbeard or "old man's-beard" are not attractive names for these fluffy seed heads, but the fluff picks up the fine dust of the roadside, and often they look dirty and unkempt.

10 Prob a **crabgrass 1.**
1970 *DARE* (Qu. S9, . . *Kinds of grass that are hard to get rid of*) Inf **MA**78, Poor man's grass—another name for old-man's-beard or crabgrass.

old-man's-britches n
=**Dutchman's breeches 1.**
1970 *DARE* (Qu. S26e, *Other wildflowers not yet mentioned;* not asked in early QRs) Inf **PA**235, Old-man's-britches—in woods, white—looks like britches.

old-man's-cologne n [Prob from the scent of the root] Cf **candyroot**
=**orange milkwort.**
1927 Boston Soc. Nat. Hist. *Proc.* 38.7.213 **Okefenokee GA**, *Polygala lutea* 'Old man's cologne'.

old-man's-hand n
A **prickly pear** (here: *Opuntia humifusa*).
1898 *Jrl. Amer. Folkl.* 11.227 **KS**, *Opuntia Rafinesqueii,* . . old man's hand. **1914** Georgia *Manual Weeds* 288, *Opuntia humifusa.* . . Old Man's Hands. . . Joints usually about two to six inches long and two to four inches wide . . ; in the axil of each leaf is a small rounded elevation, usually somewhat woolly.

old-man's-root n
A **spikenard** (here: *Aralia racemosa*). [From its supposed tonic effects] Cf **life-of-man 1**
1894 *Jrl. Amer. Folkl.* 7.90 **ME**, *Aralia racemosa* . . old man's root, Buckfield, Me. **1896** *Ibid* 9.189 **ME**, Old man's root, spikenard, Oxford County, Me. **1930** Sievers *Amer. Med. Plants* 63, The American spikenard . . known also as spignet, spiceberry . . and old-man's root. **1968** *Foxfire* Summer 49 **nwGA**, Aralia, along with several closely allied species, is a "cure-all". . . With ginseng it "eases ills of old age and prolongs life," but only for men, giving it such names as "life-of-man," or "old man's roots." **1971** Krochmal *Appalachia Med. Plants* 56, *Aralia racemosa.* . . Old man's root [etc.]. . . Roots and rhizomes have been used to treat rheumatism, syphilis, coughs, and shortness of breath. In Appalachia, a tea made of roots is used for backache. **1975** Sweet *Common Edible & Useful Plants* 9, American Spikenard, Old Man's Root, *Aralia racemosa* (Ginseng Family).

old-man's-snuffbox n Cf **devil's snuffbox 1**
A **puffball.**
1931 Clute *Common Plants* 89, Several of the puff-balls are called old man's snuffboxes.

old-man's-whiskers n
1 also *old-man whiskers:* A **prairie smoke** (here: *Geum triflorum*). **esp West**
1925 Jepson *Manual Plants CA* 497, *G[eum] triflorum.* . . Old Man's Whiskers. . . Tails of the achenes plumose, at length ¾ to 1½ in. long. **1932** Rydberg *Flora Prairies* 424, *Old Man's Whiskers.* . . Fruit a hairy achene. **1950** Stevens *ND Plants* 171, *Geum triflorum.* . . is an attractive and popular wild flower. Also called . . Old Man's Whiskers. **1970** Kirk *Wild Edible Plants W. U.S.* 92, Oldman-whiskers. . . The roots may be boiled to produce a tea. . . The plant is . . covered with soft hairs. **1979** Spellenberg *Audubon Guide N. Amer. Wildflowers W. Region* 723, *Old Man's Whiskers.* . . Fruit: seed-like, bearing reddish plumes to 2" (5 cm) long, many in a head. **1995** Brako et al. *Scientific & Common Names Plants* 195, Old-man's-whiskers—*Geum triflorum*.

2 A **Spanish moss** (here: *Tillandsia usneoides*).
1929 Neal *Honolulu Gardens* 61, Hanging like gray veils from branches of trees in Florida, the moisture-loving Spanish moss is commonly seen. Locally its appearance has won it the name of "old man's whiskers."

3 A **virgin's bower** such as *Clematis hirsutissima.* **West** Cf **old-man's-beard 3**

1932 Rydberg *Flora Prairies* 335, *Viorna* [=*Clematis*]. . . *Old Man's Whiskers* or *Lion's Beard* (Fruit). **1963** Craighead *Rocky Mt. Wildflowers* 57, *Clematis hirsutissima.* . . Old-man's Whiskers. *Ibid* 58, Each flower produces numerous seeds, the styles of which become feathery, attaining a length of 2½ in.

old-man whiskers n

1 See **old-man's-whiskers 1.**

2 See **old-man cactus 2.**

Old Master n

1 God. **chiefly Sth, S Midl** Cf **Old Maker**

1849 in 1952 Green *Samuel Maverick* 347 **SC,** For some time past Old Master has offered me hollerday & had filled my wallet wt ginger-bread & gave me plenty of spending money, but still I persisted to ware my harness. **1884** Baldwin *Yankee School-Teacher* 67 **VA,** "She's de Lawd's chile" (meaning one deficient in intellect), "an' ole Mas'r am boun' f'r t' take keer o' His own." **1903** *DN* 2.322 **seMO,** *Old-Mahster* (Master). . . God. 'I expect to live right here till Old-Mahster calls me.' **1912** Green *VA Folk-Speech* 305, Old Marster. . . God. **1953** Randolph–Wilson *Down in Holler* 268 **Ozarks,** *Old Master.* . . God, or sometimes Jesus Christ, used without any intention of irreverence. **1954** *Harder Coll.* **cwTN,** *Old Master.* . . God. **1959** Faulkner *Mansion* 5 **MS,** He didn't believe in any Old Moster. *Ibid* 398, *Old Moster jest punishes; He dont play jokes.* **c1960** *Wilson Coll.* **csKY,** *Old Master.* . . God. Probably an echo from slavery times. **1986** Pederson *LAGS Concordance,* 1 inf, **cAL,** Old Master—grandfather's term for God; 1 inf, **csAR,** Me and Old Master—referring to God.

2 See quot. Cf **old daddy**

1970 *DARE* (Qu. Z3, . . 'Grandfather') Inf **NY241,** The old master [Inf Black].

Old Mexico n chiefly SW Cf Mexico

Mexico.

1863 *Rio Abajo Weekly Press* (Albuquerque NM) 28 Apr 1/3, Those whose business called them to old Mexico were often obliged to "camp out." **1890** *Stock Grower & Farmer* 11 Jan 6/2 (*DA* at *old* 3.c), The sign riders cut the trail, going in the direction of Old Mexico. **1905** *DN* 3.89 **nwAR,** *Old Mexico.* . Mexico. 'Mr. Brown has returned from his trip to Old Mexico.' Very common. **1966** [see **Mexico**]. **1993** *NADS Letters* **eTX** (as of 1930s), My parents [were] . . born . . in 1888 and 1895 in East Texas near Nacogdoches. . . As a child, I remember these same parents often calling the country "Old Mexico," but the state, always "New Mexico." *Ibid* **TX** (as of 1960s), My friends at that time from Oklahoma were always confused when the rest of us referred to *Mexico.* They always wanted to know if we were saying *New Mexico* or *Old Mexico. Ibid* **OK,** "My grandmother used to say 'Old Mexico' all the time," she said. While it is still heard, she would say that her parents' generation was the last to use it regularly.

old mill n

=**miller boy.**

1939 *Hall Coll.* **eTN,** The Old Mill—girls and boys swingin' around together. "Hands on the hopper," were some of the words of this play-party song. **1961** Sackett–Koch *KS Folkl.* 211, To occupy the long winter evenings there were indoor games which reveal the settlers' remarkable capacity to devise entertainment from very simple material. "Fox and Geese" (the indoor version) and "Old Mill" were two of this type.

Old Miss Wit n Cf little Sally Water(s)

A children's game.

1968 *DARE* Tape **VA9,** Then we played "Old Miss Wit, not a soul can she get, and she's tired of living all alone, all alone. She's tired of living all alone. Won't some young man take pity on her, and make her a home of her own, of her own, and make her a home of her own." Then they'd say, "Rise up Miss Wit, take the first one you meet," then she'd take the first young man she met, and they'd have children in there, and babies in there, and everything. Said "Worried Miss Wit for to hear the baby cry and the children all a-singen lully-by, lully-by." . . I never did want to be Miss Wit.

old Molly n Cf knock Molly

=**old-squaw.**

1841 *S. Lit. Messenger* 7.220 **VA,** An old molly has her nest in the inside. **1888** Trumbull *Names of Birds* 88, In New Jersey, at Pleasant-

ville (Atlantic Co.), and Somers Point, Old Molly. **1898** Elliot *Wild Fowl* 191, In various parts of the land . . it [=the Old Squaw] has many names, some of which are, South Southerly . . Old Molly . . Scolder, and Noisy Duck. **1917** (1923) *Birds Amer.* 1.141, Old-Squaw—*Harelda hyemalis* . . Old Molly. **1946** Hausman *Eastern Birds* 160, Old Squaw *Clangula hyemalis* . . Old Molly.

old mother hobble-gobble n Also *old mother hobgobble, old granny hobble gobble, ~ hubbub* Cf grandmother humbum

See quot 1953.

1897 (1952) McGill *Narrative* 137, Another play is called for when everybody is seeming drowsy and sleepy. All are again in a circle with their partners and are seated, when the head one says to his right hand girl: "Old Mother Hobgobble sends me to you," who inquires: "What for to do?" "To beat one pestle as I do," using one hand. This goes round . . and the last order from Old Mother Hobgobble is to beat five pestles as I do, using both hands, both feet and the body rising and beating the chair. **1905** *DN* 3.89 **nwAR,** *Old Granny Hobble Gobble.* . . The name of a game. *Old Granny Hubbub.* The name of a game. 'Old granny Hubbub sent me to you.' **1953** Brewster *Amer. Nonsinging Games* 32 **TX,** *Old Mother Hobble-Gobble.* . . Players are seated. . . The leader says to the player next to him, "Old Mother Hobble-Gobble sent me to you, sir." "What for to do, sir?" asks the other. The leader replies, "Do as I do, sir," and performs some action. . . Each of the other players must imitate the action of the leader. . . For failure to perform any or all of the actions called for by the leader, penalties are imposed.

old mother tipsy-toe See old granny tippy-toes

old mother witch See old witch 1

Old Ned n

1 also rarely *Ned:* Bacon, salt pork. **chiefly Sth, S Midl** Cf *DS* H38

1833 Alexander *Transatlantic Sketches* 260 **TN,** A snow-white cloth was spread, on which were placed bacon, or "Old Ned," as it is called in Tennessee. **1850** Garrard *Wah-to-yah* 155, Among many farmers, pork is familiarly called 'Ned.' *Ibid* 286, They were entitled every day to three-fourths of a pound of messpork or 'Ned.' **1869** *Overland Mth.* 3.129 **TX,** Southern smoke-cured pork, in distinction from the Northern salted article, in allusion to the famous negro song, was termed "Old Ned," from its sable appearance. **1909** *DN* 3.353 **eAL, wGA,** *Ol(d) Ned.* . . Bacon, "We had plenty of Old Ned and corn dodger." **1913** Kephart *Highlanders* 75 **sAppalachians,** "Bill, hand me some Old Ned from out of that suggin o' mine." . . On inquiry I learned that "Old Ned" is merely slang for fat pork. **1931** *PMLA* 46.1304 **Appalachians,** Tutor hit up jist right, this old Ned (bacon) orter last a good span. **1936** *AmSp* 11.316 **Ozarks,** *Old Ned.* . . Home-cured bacon.

2 See quot. Cf *DS* K52

1936 *AmSp* 11.316 **swMO,** *Old Ned.* . . The term is used to mean *boar* in Taney county, Mo.

3a also *Ned(s):* =**Old Scratch;** also used in exclams.

1853 Hammett *Stray Yankee in TX* 227 **TX,** 'By Ned,' says he, 'if it aint that owdacious critter of Miss Mash's.' **1939** *AmSp* 14.268 **swIN,** Euphemisms . . referring to the Devil: 'the Old Scratch,' 'old Nick,' . . and 'old Ned.' [Footnote:] Found, for example, in the expression 'to raise old Ned' (i.e. to create a disturbance of some kind). **1942** [see **old 1**]. **1943** McAtee *Dial. Grant Co. IN Suppl.* 2 11 (as of 1890s), *Old Ned* . . the devil. **1949** *Jrl. Amer. Folkl.* 62.63 **CT,** The devil was referred to as "Old Ned" or "Old Scratch." **1952** Brown *NC Folkl.* 1.569, *Ned, by.* . . A mild oath.—General. *Ibid* 571, *Old Ned.* . . The devil—General. **1953** [see **Old Scratch**]. **1959** *VT Hist.* 27.150, *Full of the old Ned.* . . Mischievous; troublesome. . . Common. Older people. **c1960** *Wilson Coll.* **csKY,** *Ned.* . . The Devil. **1965** Will *Okeechobee Boats* 9 **FL,** And then, by Neds, he hired the Menge brothers from Louisiana. **1967–69** *DARE* (Qu. CC8, . . *The devil*) Infs **LA14, NY59,** Old Ned; (Qu. NN8a, *Exclamations of annoyance or disgust: "Oh _____. I've lost my glasses again."*) Inf **MD26,** Golly Ned; (Qu. NN29a, *Exclamations beginning with 'great': "Great _____!"*) Inf **PA91,** Ned; (Qu. NN29c, *Exclamations beginning with 'holy': "Holy _____!"*) Infs **AZ11, NY102, SC44, WI51,** Ned.

b in phrr *raise (Old) Ned* and varr: To create a commotion, disturbance, or trouble; by ext: to have a rousing good time.

1848 Lowell *Biglow* 69 **'Upcountry' MA,** Your fact'ry gals . . 'll make head, / An' gittin some Miss chief or other to lead 'em,/ 'll go to work raisin' promiscoous Ned. **1870** Logan *Before Footlights* 165 **cnMA,** We are real smart girls . . and can raise ned and keep folks A laughing. **1897** *KS Univ. Qrly.* (ser B) 6.55 **KS,** *Ned* . . a disturbance, as, 'to raise Ned.' **1906** Quick *Double Trouble* 223 *(DA),* You've been raising merry Ned, Florian, in your Brassfield capacity. **1939** [see **3a** above]. **1942** Warnick *Garrett Co. MD* 12 nwMD (as of 1900–1918), *Raise old Ned . .* to make a row (Slang). **1948** Manfred *Chokecherry* 75 nwIA, C'mon, get yer duds on. Let's raise Old Ned. **1965–70** *DARE* (Qu. FF18, *Joking words . . about a noisy or boisterous celebration or party: "They certainly _____ last night."*) Inf **AZ**11, Raised Ned; **CO**35, Raised Old Ned; (Qu. GG35b, *[To sulk or pout:] "Because she couldn't go, she's been _____ all day."*) Inf **MI**68, Raising Ned; (Qu. KK11, *To make great objections or a big fuss about something: "When we asked him to do that, he _____."*) Infs **MO**10, **VA**26, Raised Ned.

c in phrr *give one (Old) Ned* and varr: To berate or disparage someone.

1897 *KS Univ. Qrly.* (ser B) 6.55 KS, *Ned:* a scolding; as "She gave him Ned, (or, the very Ned, or particular Ned)." **1970** *DARE* (Qu. Y3, *To say uncomplimentary things about somebody*) Inf **KY**94, Giving him Old Ned.

Old Nick n Also *Nick* Occas with *the*
=Old Scratch.

1764 in 1957 Dunbar *Paxton Papers* 177 PA, By which, they with a Magic Trick / Could shew white Folks as black's Oldnick. **1809** (1814) Weems *F. Marion* 110, Tom is a negro, and as black as Old Nick. **1856** Cary *Married Not Mated* 231 OH, As proud as old Nick. **1872** Schele de Vere *Americanisms* 595, The devil is . . concealed behind . . Old *Nick,* Old *Harry,* Old *Scratch,* and Old *Splitfoot.* **1899** (1912) Green *VA Folk-Speech* 298, *Nick. . . Old Nick,* the devil. **1909** *DN* 3.353 eAL, wGA, *Ol(d) Nick. . .* Satan. "He was as mad as the Old Nick." **1914** *DN* 4.123, *Nick,* probably from *Nicholas.* The devil. Usually *Old Nick.* **1941** *LANE* Map 474 *(He ran like a house afire)* 3 infs, seNH, neMA, nwVT, He ran like . . Old Nick. **1943** *Ibid* Map 532 *(The devil)* widespread NEng, (The) Old Nick. **c1955** Reed–Person *Ling. Atlas Pacific NW,* 8 infs, Old Nick. **1965–70** *DARE* (Qu. CC8, *. . The devil*) 115 Infs, **widespread,** Old Nick; **OH**20, 68, 71, Nick; (Qu. BB47, *Feeling in the best of health and spirits: "I'm feeling _____!"*) Inf **CO**27, Full of the Old Nick; (Qu. EE41, *A hobgoblin that is used to threaten children and make them behave*) Infs **AL**6, 10, **IN**10, **NY**232, **OH**15, Old Nick; (Qu. GG32b, *To habitually play tricks or jokes on people: "He's an awful _____."*) Inf **WA**28, Full of the Old Nick; (Qu. HH22b, *. . A very mean person . . "He's meaner than _____."*) Inf **MD**12, Old Nick; (Qu. KK28, *Feeling ambitious and eager to work*) Inf **IA**5, Full of the Old Nick; (Qu. KK41, *Something that is very difficult to do: "I managed to get through with it, but it was _____."*) Inf **NC**82, Hard as Old Nick. **1986** Pederson *LAGS Concordance (Devil)* 9 infs, **Gulf Region,** Old Nick.

Old Night n With *the* Cf **Old Year's Eve(ning)**
New Year's Eve.

1966 *DARE* (Qu. FF11, *. . The night of December 31st*) Inf **ND**1, The Old Night.

old of the moon n [*OED old* sb.² 3 *"Obs."*] **esp S Midl** Cf **new of the moon**
The period of the waning moon.

1904 (1913) Johnson *Highways South* 165 KY, You boil meat killed in the old of the moon, and it will all shrivel up and there won't be none of it. **1959** Roberts *Up Cutshin* 35 seKY, We would kill our hogs all the time on the old of the moon. **1968** Kellner *Aunt Serena* 103 cIN (as of c1920), "Take timber," Lawnie would tell me. "If it ain't cut in the old of the moon, it'll warp and curl and never age right." **1969** *Foxfire* Summer 12 nGA, Timber was cut, for example, only on the "old of the moon" . . when the sap was down so that it would cure correctly. **1972** *Foxfire Book* 221 nGA, Take taters. On th'dark of th'moon or th'old of th'moon—that's th'last quarter . . they make less vine. **1975** Dwyer *Thangs* 26 Sth, S Midl, Set fence posts in the old of the moon to prevent loosening.

old one n

1 An adult. Cf **older, young one**
1942 McAtee *Dial. Grant Co. IN* 46 (as of 1890s), *Old ones . .* adults in contrast to young ones; applied to animals; the term "younguns" as a rule was restricted to children. **1942** Warnick *Garrett Co. MD* 11 nwMD (as of 1900–18), *Old ones . .* adults as contrasted to young. **c1960** *Wilson Coll.* csKY, *Old ones, old-uns. . .* The mature people as contrasted with young-uns.

2 also cap: See **old 1.**

old one-one See **one-one 3**

old orchard pie n
A pie made from various kinds of apples taken from abandoned orchards.

1985 Clark *From Mailbox* 163 ME, Finding different kinds of apples—at least five different kinds—and tossing . . these into the pie basket. . . [for] that first Old Orchard pie made just hours after clambering over stone walls . . seeking trees left from orchards planted by long-gone farmers.

old pap(py) See **old daddy**

Old Pitchfork See **old 1**

old plainsman n
A **woolly-white:** usu *Hymenopappus scabiosaeus var corymbosus,* but also *H. artemisiifolius.*

1948 Stevens *KS Wild Flowers* 389, *Hymenopappus corymbosus. . .* In 'Old Plainsman' we have a common name rich in fancy and atmosphere, but notice that the scientific name has the virtue of precise description. **1961** Wills–Irwin *Flowers TX* 238, *Old-plainsman—Hymenopappus artemisiaefolius. . .* Old-plainsman is found in Texas from Wood, Williamson, Wilson and Hidalgo counties eastward to the Gulf Coast and the Louisiana border, and is in flower from March to July. **1970** Correll *Plants TX* 1703, *Hymenopappus scabiosaeus . .* var. *corymbosus. . . Old plainsman. . .* tomentose to nearly glabrate. **1995** Brako et al. *Scientific & Common Names Plants* 195, Old-plainsman—*Hymenopappus scabiosaeus* var. *corymbosus.*

Old Point Comfort n Also *Old Fort Comfort* [Cf quot 1970] *joc*
An outhouse.

1967–68 *DARE* (Qu. M21b, *Joking names for an outside toilet building*) Inf **IN**32, Old Fort Comfort; **PA**10, Old Point Comfort. [Both Infs old] [**1970** Stewart *Amer. Place-Names* 108, On April 26, 1607, the Virginia colonists anchored safely, 'which put us in good comfort. Therefore we named that point of land Cape Comfort.' This naming has survived as *Point Comfort,* or *Old Point Comfort* VA.]

old pop See **old daddy**

old preacher See **preacher**

Old Rip n Also with *the*
=Old Scratch.

1905 *DN* 3.89 nwAR, *Old Rip (himself). . .* The (very) Devil. **1909** *DN* 3.354 eAL, wGA, *Ol(d) Rip. . .* A bad tempered man, the devil. **1932** Stong *State Fair* 96 IA, Blue Boy's madder'n the old rip about something. **1953** [see **Old Scratch**]. **1968** *DARE* (Qu. CC8, *. . The devil*) Inf **GA**56, Old Rip. **1973** Allen *LAUM* 1.385 (as of c1950), *Devil. . .* old Rip [1 inf, cIA]. **1993** *DARE* File csMA (as of c1950), "Old Rip" was the name of the Devil, or of someone who behaved like the Devil.

Old Rot (or Round-foot) See **old 1**

old sailor's soul n
A petrel (family Procellariidae); see quot.

1917 *Wilson Bulletin* 29.2.76, Petrels.—Old sailors' souls; so-called by down-east mariners.

old Sal See **sow and pigs**

Old Sam (or Sanko, Satan) See **old 1**

Old Scholar n
=Old Master 1.

1975 Gould *ME Lingo* 195, *Old Scholar*—The seafaring man's affectionate term for God. **1979** *AmSp* 54.99 sME (as of 1899–1910), *Old Scholar. . .* God.

Old Scratch n Also with *the* Also *Old Scratcher, (Mr.) Scratch* **chiefly Sth, S Midl; also NEng** See Map Also called **Old Billy 2, ~ Boy, ~ Gentleman 2, ~ Harry, ~ Horny, ~ Ned 3, ~ Nick, ~ Rip** Cf **old 1**
The devil; a hobgoblin or **boogerman 1;** also fig.

1824 Irving *Tales of a Traveller* 2.261 eMA, If I mistake not, . . you are he commonly called old Scratch. **1825** Neal *Brother Jonathan* 1.254 CT, He "cleared out," in a hurricane; as the Marble-Head fishermen do, when they have made a league with Old Scratch. **1854** (1923) Holmes *Tempest & Sunshine* 13 KY, You old torment! I wish the Old Scratch had got you before you ever came here. **1899** (1912) Green *VA Folk-*

Speech 305, *Old scratch. . .* The devil. **1901** Harben *Westerfelt* 250 **nGA**, She's had the very old scratch in 'er ever since Toot was run off. **1909** *DN* 3.367 **eAL, wGA**, *Scratch. . .* The devil: often with *Old.* "He is as mean as the Old Scratch." **1914** *DN* 4.79 **ME, nNH**, *Scratcher, the Old. . .* The devil. **1915** (1916) Johnson *Highways New Engl.* 146, You must excuse my clothes. I've been fishing today and I look like the old scratch. **1916** Lincoln *Mary-'Gusta* 384 **MA**, The Old Scratch ain't sacred. **1917** *DN* 4.397 **neOH**, *Old Scratch, the. . .* In the phrase, *like the old scratch,* "like the Devil." General. **1927** *AmSp* 3.139 **eME**, [Common expressions included] the old scratch. **1941** *LANE* Map 473 *(Mad as a wet hen)* 1 inf, **csME**, Mad as Old Scratch. *Ibid* Map 474 *(He ran like a house afire)* 3 infs, **csRI, seNH, neMA**, Like (the) Old Scratch; 1 inf **swMA**, He run like as if the Old Scratch was after him. **1943** *Ibid* Map 532 *(The Devil)* **scattered NEng**, (The) Old Scratch; 1 inf, **cnCT**, The Old Scratcher. **1944** *PADS* 2.36 **wNC, VA, SC, TN**, *Scratch, the Old. . .* The devil, the boogey man. . . Common. **1950** *PADS* 14.49 **SC**, *Old scratch. . .* The devil. This term is not used in a jocular tone as is *Old Nick,* but is rather an evasion of the word *devil,* and is used seriously. **1952** Brown *NC Folkl.* 1.588, If you aren't a good boy, *Old Scratch* will get you. **1953** Randolph–Wilson *Down in Holler* 268 **Ozarks**, Other terms for the Devil are *Old Red, Old Rip, Old Sam, Old Coaley, Old Ned, . . Old Scratch, Old Horny, Old Blackie, Old Samson, Old Simpson,* and *Old Jimson.* **1954** Harder *Coll.* **cwTN**, *Old Scratch. . .* The devil. **c1955** Reed–Person *Ling. Atlas Pacific NW,* 1 inf, Mr. Scratch. **1960** Carpenter *Tales Manchaca* 164 **cTX**, He was his own former self—brawny, hearty, and not afraid of Old Scratch himself. **1965–70** *DARE* (Qu. CC8, *. . The devil*) 46 Infs, **chiefly Sth, S Midl**, Old Scratch; **IL135, VT12**, The Old Scratch; **GA56, WI57**, Scratch; (Qu. HH22b, *. . A very mean person . . "He's meaner than _____."*) 10 Infs, **esp Sth, S Midl**, Old Scratch; **IN23, KY78**, The Old Scratch; **TN15**, Scratch; (Qu. EE41, *A hobgoblin that is used to threaten children and make them behave*) 9 Infs, **esp Inland Sth**, Old Scratch; (Qu. E22, *If a house is untidy and everything is upset . . "It's a _____!" or "It looks like _____."*) Inf **MA**18, The Old Scratch; (Qu. GG40, *Words or expressions meaning violently angry*) Inf **VA**21, Mad as Old Scratch. **1986** Pederson *LAGS Concordance* (Devil) 22 infs, **Gulf Region**, Old Scratch.

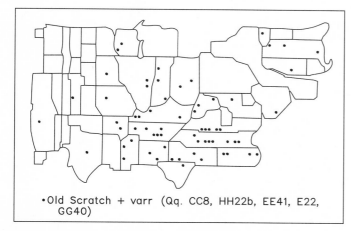

•Old Scratch + varr (Qq. CC8, HH22b, EE41, E22, GG40)

Old Scrooge (or Serpent, Sin, Smutty) See **old 1**

old soak n
=**bullpen.**

1961 *AmSp* 36.299 **ceIN**, *Bull pen. . .* The Grant County version of this game in my youth was called *old soak,* and the ball was thrown at an opponent.

old sol n [Abbr for *solitaire*]
A card game that requires only one player.

1966 *DARE* (Qu. DD35, *. . Card games*) Inf **OK**25, Old sol—for one player. **1977** Taylor *Miro District* 22 **TN**, He . . wasn't on the wicker settee in the sun parlor, with a game of old sol going on the cushion beside him.

old soldier n *old-fash* Cf *DS* DD8
A cigar or cigarette butt; a used quid of tobacco.

1834 Caruthers *Kentuckian* 1.12 **MD** [Black], I smokes the old sodgers what the gentlemen throws on the bar-room floor. **1899** (1912) Green *VA Folk-Speech* 305, *Old-soldiers. . .* Ends of cigars and quids of tobacco that have been used. **1935** Horwill *Mod. Amer. Usage* 213, A

partly-smoked cigar is sometimes called colloq. an *old soldier.* **1942** Berrey–Van den Bark *Amer. Slang* 111.10, Cigar or cigarette stub. . . Old soldier.

old sow See **sow and pigs**

Old Split-foot See **old 1**

old-squaw n Also *old-squaw duck* [See quots 1876, 1977] Cf **rock old-squaw**
A sea duck *(Clangula hyemalis)* of the northern Pacific and northern and central Atlantic coasts. Also called **butterfly coot, callithumpian duck, creamy ass, Florida longtail, granny 8, ice duck 1, jack owly, knock Molly, long-tailed duck, lord and lady 2, mammy duck, mommy 4, noisy duck, old Billy 1, ~ Injun, ~ Molly, oldwife 2, organ duck, pine knot, pintail, quandy, scoldenore, scolder, singing duck, sou-sou-sally ~, south-southerly, squaw, squeaking duck, swallow-tailed ~, teet, uncle huldy, winter duck**

1834 Nuttall *Manual Ornith.* 2.454, This elegant and noisy duck, known so generally in the Southern States by the nickname of 'South-Southerly,' from its note, and, in most other parts by the appellation of 'Old Squaws' or 'Old Wives,' is an Arctic inhabitant of both continents, and abounds in the glacial seas of America. **1838** Audubon *Ornith. Biog.* 4.105, They [=long-tailed ducks, *Fuligula glacialis*] have various appellations, among others those of "old wives," and "old squaws." **1844** Giraud *Birds Long Is.* 338 **seNY**, This hardy bird at the South is known by the name of "South Southerly;" in this vicinity it is called by our gunners "Old Wife," or "Old Squaw." **1870** [see **oldwife 2**]. **1876** *Forest & Stream* 7.245 **MA**, The "quaudie," [sic] (long-tailed duck) is also called the "old squaw," (never "old wife" hereabout) from its constant chattering. **1892** *Auk* 9.330, This sprightly little salt water Duck frequents the New England coast . . where it is well known under the cognomens of Oldsquaw, Oldwife, and Quandy. **1924** in 1931 McCorrison *Letters Fraternity* 60 **NEng**, You mentioned "old squaws"—a bird I had not thought of for many years. . . "whenever an old Indian squaw dies, her spirit goes into a coot, and that's why they call them old squaws." **1950** *WELS,* 1 Inf, **seWI**, Old-squaw. **1955** *AmSp* 30.184, Old squaw duck. **1966–67** *DARE* (Qu. Q5, *. . Kinds of wild ducks*) Infs **ME**12, **MI**2, Old-squaw; **MI**53, Squaw duck—barred gray and white, many call 'em old-squaw; (Qu. Q7, *Names and nicknames for . . game birds*) Inf **ME**22, Old-squaw; (Qu. Q10, *. . Water birds and marsh birds*) Inf **ME**12, Old-squaw—a duck. **1977** Udvardy *Audubon Field Guide Birds* 494, Oldsquaw. . . In courting, several males display around a female, calling noisily. This phase of the courtship behavior gave rise to their American name.

old squint-eye See **squint-eye**

old stager n [*OED* (at *stager*) 1570 →]
An experienced person, veteran, old hand.

1841 in 1886 Longfellow *Life of H.W. Longfellow* 1.394, I do not know that an old stager in authorship, like you, cares for anybody's opinion. **1848** (1855) Ruxton *Life Far West* 26 **Rocky Mts**, At intervals his keen gray eye glanced piercingly around, particularly toward an old, weather-beaten, and grizzled mule, who now, old stager as she was, having filled her belly, stood lazily over her picket pin. **1859** Taliaferro *Fisher's R.* 139 **nwNC**, Larkin Snow was a graduate—an old stager—in milling when I was a mill-boy. *Ibid* 237 **nwNC** (as of 1820s), An "old stager" in camp-meetings once told me of an incident which clearly outdid him. **1899** (1912) Green *VA Folk-Speech* 305, *Old-stager. . .* Some person, animal, or thing that has been long in use. **1927** *DN* 5.457 [Underworld jargon], *Old stager. . .* A master tramp. **1930** Shoemaker *1300 Words* 44 **cPA Mts** (as of c1900), *Old stager*—An experienced person, someone from an earlier generation.

‡**Old Stony Lonesome** n Cf **rock garden, silent city**
Prob a graveyard personified.

1948 Hurston *Seraph* 225 **FL**, You're all that stood between me and Old Stony Lonesome.

old Susie n Cf **biscuit B3, grandma B2**
1940 Writers' Program *Guide NV* 75, The horn of the saddle, called the *biscuit, grandma, old Susie,* the *handle,* or the *pig,* all indicative of the contempt of true cowhands for the flat-heeled *peeler* who must *pull leather* (grasp the saddle horn) in order to remain with his mount.

old sweet beans and the barley grows See **oats, peas(e), beans, and barley grow(s)**

old-timer's disease n [Folk-etym for *Alzheimer's disease*]

1989 *DARE* File **cwWI**, "My brother has that old-timer's disease." This was said by a 67-year-old, white male, from the Tomah area. One frequently hears "old-timer's disease" for Alzheimer's disease from older patients at the V.A. Hospital. **1990** *Capital Times* (Madison WI) 4 July sec A 7/2, There were many clues that I now realize I missed as my . . friends took advantage of my early stages of oldtimer's disease. **1990** Cavender *Folk Med. Lexicon* 28 **sAppalachians**, Old timer's disease— Alzheimer's disease. **1993** *DARE* File, My Grandma, on the Eastern Shore of Maryland, says "old-timer's disease." **1995** *Ibid* **OH**, My neighbor . . was telling me about someone suffering from old-timer's disease.

old-timey adj Also rarely *old-timesy* Rarely sp *old-timy* **chiefly Sth, S Midl**

Old-fashioned, out-of-date; hence n *old-timey* something that is old-fashioned.

1850 *Horticulturist & Jrl. Rural Art* 5.265, The terraced garden, too, is quaint and "old-timey." **1879** Stockton *Rudder Grange* 246 **sePA**, Things that were apparently so 'old-timey' . . that David Dutton did not care to take them with him. **1892** Harris *Uncle Remus & Friends* 151 **GA** [Black], We'll have a reg'lar ole-timey camp-meetin' gwine on here 'fo' you know it. **1932** *Scribner's Mag.* 91.288 **FL**, Thet's the ol'-timey way. Don't nobody hide their money these days. **1939** FWP *Guide NC* 95, In town as well as country may be seen . . the "old-timey" hickory cane-bottomed chair tilted back on two legs against the porch for perfect comfort. **1942** Hall *Smoky Mt. Speech* 73 **wNC, eTN**, Old-timey ('old-fashioned'). **1959** Lomax *Rainbow Sign* 113 **AL** [Black], That's when those old-timey songs was fixed out. **1965–68** *DARE* (Qu. F46, . . *Matches you can strike anywhere;* not asked in early QRs) Inf **NC79**, Old-timey matches; (Qu. W2, . . *A cloth bonnet worn by women for protection from the sun*) Inf **VA9**, Old-timey bonnet; (Qu. FF21a, *A joke that is so old it doesn't seem funny any more: "His jokes are all _____."*) Infs **AL20, MS63, TX3**, Old-timey; (Qu. HH1, *Names and nicknames for a rustic or countrified person*) Inf **TX29**, Country, old-timey. **1966–69** *DARE* Tape **GA25**, You know the old-timey remedy for that was to go in the chicken house; **GA48**, I remember a song I tried to learn to sing a long time ago from mother, old-timey song; **NC25**, Them old-timey houses had wooden corner blocks. **1967** Fetterman *Stinking Creek* 127 **seKY**, Daddy's old-timey. He said he didn't want boys coming around here. **1967–68** *DARE* FW Addit **GA25**, A old-timey gopher had a shell, looked similar to a turtle; **TN23**, "Old-timey" used frequently by Inf; heard it also from the country people. **1984** *Grandfather Tell Me a Story* 54 **OK**, We used to sing all the old timey songs though, like Suwannee River and Old Black Joe, My Old Kentucky Home and all those old timies. They were very popular then. **1986** Pederson *LAGS Concordance*, 63 infs, **Gulf Region**, Old-timey (ceilings, chimney, corn bread, cracker, dish, farm house, fellows, fireplace, etc); 1 inf, **ceGA**, Old-timesy.

Old Varmint See **old 1**

Old War n

1 The American Revolutionary War.

1960 Hall *Smoky Mt. Folks* 50 **ceTN** (as of 1937), She was proud of the fact her "gramp" came to this country from across the waters about the time of the "Old War" (the Revolution). **1962** Dykeman *Tall Woman* 38 **NC** (as of 1860s), They came taking up some vague land grant from the days of the old war, the Revolution.

2 The American Civil War.

1937 *Hall Coll.* **wNC**, The Old War. . . The Civil War. "Doc . . says that most migration to Texas from the Smokies took place 'after the Old War.'" **1969** Gt. Smoky Mt. Natl. Park *Recordings* 37:2:5 (*Montgomery Coll.*) **wNC, eTN**, He was born right there in that time of the old war right yonder. **1986** Pederson *LAGS Concordance (Civil War)* 2 infs, **cMS, nwAR**, (The) Old War.

old wench n [See quot 1939] Cf **oldwife 1b**

A **triggerfish** (here: *Balistes vetula*).

1898 U.S. Natl. Museum *Bulletin* 47.1703, *Balistes vetula* . . Old Wife; Old Wench; Conchino. **1939** FWP *Guide FL* 30, And there are queen triggerfish, commonly called 'old wenches' because of shrewish wrinkles etched in blue on the background of their yellow faces.

old whiskers n

A **channel catfish** (here: *Ictalurus punctatus*).

1956 Harlan–Speaker *IA Fish* 212, Just why "Old Whiskers" gets cagey about taking the hook in response to falling water stages is not fully understood.

Old White Horse See **old 1**

oldwife n

1 pronc-sp (for pl) *o'wise:* Any of var fishes:

a A **herring** n^1 **1**, esp an **alewife** (here: *Alosa* spp), **hickory shad**, or **menhaden 1. chiefly Mid Atl**

1588 (1903) Hariot *Briefe Rept.* **VA** sig D3[r], There are also *Troutes: Porpoises: Rayes: Oldwiues: Mullets: Plaice.* **1671** in 1897 SC Hist. Soc. *Coll.* 5.336, Fish there are in both riuers multitudes, As Bass, mullets, Old Wiffes; &c. **1705** Beverley *Hist. VA* 2.31, The Old-Wife, a Fish not much unlike an Herring. **1709** (1967) Lawson *New Voyage* 163 **NC, SC**, *Old-Wives*—These are a bright scaly Fish, which frequent the Swamps, and fresh Runs; they seem to be between an *English* Roach and a Bream, and eat much like the latter. **1787** Gesellschaft Naturforschender Freunde *Schriften* 8.158, Der Fisch, welcher in Virginien und den übrigen südlichen Gegenden *Old Wife* (Altes Weib) genant [sic] wird, mir aber nicht vorgekommen ist, mag vielleicht zu diesem Geschlecht gehören; wenigstens läßt sich vermuthen, daß ihm einige Aehnlichkeit mit dem *Labrus Tincta* . . welcher in England *Old Wife* genannt wird, diesen Namen erworben haben. [=The fish, which in Virginia and other southern regions is called *Old Wife* . . is however not known to me; it may perhaps belong to this family; in any case it can be assumed that its likeness to the *Labrus tincta*, which in England is called *Old Wife*, has earned it this name.] **1805** (1904) Lewis *Orig. Jrls. Lewis & Clark Exped.* 2.143, The other species is precisely the form . . of the well known fish called the *Hickary Shad* or *old wife.* **1899** (1912) Green *VA Folk-Speech* 305, *Old-wife.* . . Alewife; a fish. Of the herring tribe. **1951** *DE Folk. Bulletin* 1.8 (as of c1870–1900), Old wives (ale-wives) were caught in seines at the Fenwick inlet and then cooked or allowed to decay and used as fertilizer. **1976** Warner *Beautiful Swimmers* 127 **eMD**, On the Eastern Shore the menhaden rather confusingly becomes the alewife or "old wife." **1984** *DARE* File **Chesapeake Bay** [Watermen's vocab], Alewives, o'wise.

b A **triggerfish** (here: *Balistes vetula*). Cf **old wench**

1743 Catesby *Nat. Hist. Carolina* 2.22, *Turdus oculo radiato* [=*Balistes vetula*] . . The Old Wife. . . All the Fish of this Form I have observed to be slow Swimmers, and that they are a Prey to the larger and voracious Kinds. **1879** U.S. Natl. Museum *Bulletin* 14.24, *Balistes vetula*, Linn.—Oldwife. **1933** John G. Shedd Aquarium *Guide* 156, *Balistes vetula*—Queen Triggerfish; Old Wife. This prettily marked species is common in the West Indies, occasionally straying to our shores. Although it is a tropical fish, the writer once received at Boston an adult of this species, which was captured in a pound net in Narraganset [sic] Bay. **1976** Tryckare et al. *Lore of Sportfishing* 129, *Queen Triggerfish* . . Other common names . . old-wife.

c Either of two **pompano:** *Trachinotus falcatus* or *T. glaucus.*

1896 U.S. Natl. Museum *Bulletin* 47.940, *Trachinotus glaucus* . . Gaff-topsail Pampano; Old Wife; Palometa. **1911** U.S. Bur. Census *Fisheries 1908* 314, Other species [of pompano] found on our eastern coast are the "old-wife," or "gaff-topsail pampano;" [etc]. **1935** Caine *Game Fish* 112, Round Pompano. . . *Synonyms:* Alewife . . Old Wife.

d A **spot** (here: *Leiostomus xanthurus*).

1882 U.S. Natl. Museum *Bulletin* 16.574, *L[eiostomus] xanthurus* . . Oldwife. . . Cape Cod to Florida; a valuable food-fish southward. **1933** LA Dept. of Conserv. *Fishes* 180, The Spot. . . Additional popular names for the species are Oldwife, Yellowtail and Goody. **1949** Brown *Amer. Cooks* 833 **VA**, Spots are thick-bodied, firm-fleshed little sea fish, distinguished by a black spot just behind the shoulders and 15 oblique dark bars. They seldom grow more than 9 inches long. . . Spots are sometimes called "goodies" and "old wives," in the interesting local fish nomenclature.

2 =**old-squaw.** Cf **alewife**

1634 Wood *New Engl. Prospect* 31, The Oldwives, be a foule that never leave tatling day or night, something bigger than a Ducke. **1709** (1967) Lawson *New Voyage* 151 **NC, SC**, Old Wives are a black and white pied Gull with extraordinary long Wings, and a golden colour'd Bill and feet. He makes a dismal Noise, as he flies, and ever and anon dips his Bill in the Salt-Water. **1792** Belknap *Hist. NH* 3.168, *Oldwife, Anas strepera?* **1834** [see **old-squaw**]. **1844** DeKay *Zool. NY* 2.329, The *Old-wife*, or *Old-squaw*, is one of the most common and least valued of the genus. **1870** *Fur Fin & Feather* 119, For instance, the long-tailed duck (Fluligula Glaciates [sic]) has its own specific name at different points of the coast. Along the coast of New England it is generally called the quondy; at other New England points and on Long Island and Jersey it is known as the old wife or old squaw; while at the South it is called the South southerly. **1892** [see **old-squaw**]. **1940** Weygandt *Down Jersey* 30 **sNJ**, We saw . . offshore in the sea, some kind of fish duck, but whether sheldrakes or old wives I couldn't tell at the distance. **1955** MA Audubon Soc. *Bulletin* 39.375, Old Squaw. . . In allusion to its "talkativeness". . Old Wife (N.H., Mass., Conn., R.I. Same note.) **1982** Elman *Hunter's Field Guide* 232, *Oldsquaw* . . Common & Regional Names . . jack-owly, old-wife, [etc.]

old-wife's shirt tree n Also *old-wife's shirttail*
=tulip tree.

1897 Sudworth *Arborescent Flora* 198 **TN**, *Liriodendron tulipifera*. . . Old-Wife's-Shirt Tree. **1945** McAtee *Nomina Abitera* 12, Tulip Tree . . Peter Kalm, early Swedish botanical explorer of the American colonies, wrote: "The leaves have likewise something peculiar; the English therefore in some places call the tree the old woman's smock, because their imagination finds something like it below the leaves" (Forster Transl., 1770, 1, p. 203). The plant is known in Tennessee as "old wife's shirttail." These names may refer to the shape of the leaf, but again, as Kalm implies, they may have a deeper meaning.

old winter duck n Cf **winter duck**
A **black duck 1** (here: *Anas rubripes*).

1923 U.S. Dept. Ag. *Misc. Circular* 13.9 **ME**, *Anas rubripes*. . . *Vernacular Names*. . . In local use. . . Old winter duck.

old witch n

1 also *old mother witch, old witch by the wayside, (the) witch*: Any of var children's chasing games, usu involving a "witch" who "steals" children; see quots. Cf **chickamy chickamy craney crow; mother, mother, the pot boils over; old granny hibble-hobble; old granny tippy-toes; prisoner's base**

1881 *Harper's New Mth. Mag.* 62.184, The young folks . . played at "prisoner's base," or "old witch by the wayside." **1883** Newell *Games & Songs* 215 **NYC**, *Old Witch*. . . Ten girls, a mother, a witch, and eight children. **1897** (1952) McGill *Narrative* 34 **SC**, The girls played "Old Witch" by themselves. One of them, getting into a ditch or old clay hole, would act an old witch . . , while the other girls would caper around, inquiring of her, "What o'clock, old witch?" who . . would announce twelve o'clock and dinner time. Then she would ask, "How many chicks you got," and when told, "None for your pot," she says, "I will have a chick," and when told "you shan't have a chick," being repeated by both in a prancing and chanting manner . . , the old witch, yet unable to get one, leaps out and the scramble begins with increased "I will have a chick;" "You shan't have a chick," and as the old hen and her brood swing around, vigorously defending themselves, suddenly some part of their dress gives away, and thus separated and alone, the old witch seizes one of the brood and runs away with a chick for her dinner. **1906** *DN* 3.148 **nwAR**, *Old witch*. . . An out-door game. The players circle around one of their number, the old witch, to whom the following is addressed: "Chickamy, chickamy, crany-crow,/ Went to the well to wash my toe;/ When I got back my (black-eyed) chickens were gone./ What time is it, old witch?" **1909** *DN* 3.354 **eAL, wGA**, *Ol(d) witch*. . . A children's outdoor game. **1945** Boyd *Hdbk. Games* 113, *Old Mother Witch*. . . The children mark off a space for their home. The old witch comes by, and they follow her, chanting. . . They run for home while the old witch tags as many as possible and puts those caught in her den. **1952** Brown *NC Folkl.* 48, 'Old Witch' and 'Chickamy, Chickamy, Craney Crow' have the same theme and the differences between them are only superficial. [*Ibid* 49, Children's games have retained . . the tradition of the child-stealing witch.] **1957** *Sat. Eve. Post Letters* **csIL**, Old-Witch and Grand-Ma's-Darning-Needle was played by my own Grandmother when she was a child, over one hundred years ago. *Ibid* **NJ** (as of c1900), Old mother witch was another chasing game, but set to shouts of "Old mother witch / Couldn't sew a stitch / When she had a penny / She thought she was rich." The gang stood in a line with mother witch about 20 feet away, and after that delightful poem was completed . . they would rush past her and she would try to catch one. *Ibid* **NYC** (as of c1950), *Old Mother Witch*—a tame game. We followed "it" singing "Old Mother Witch, couldn't sew a stitch, she picked up a penny and she thought she was rich." Upon completion of song or any time before, the witch chased us back to "safe." *Ibid* **swWI** (as of a1901), We girls had a game we called "*Old Witch*." . . The two largest girls were Mother and Old Witch, respectively. All the smaller children . . were named for days of the week. There would be a knock at the door, and while the mother was called to answer it, the old witch slipped in and snatched away one of her children. Mother returned and began to wail, "Where is my little Friday?" or whichever child was missing. "The old witch stole her," would be the chorus. Then mother had to walk a crooked trail, as a witch never walked a straight path, seeking her lost child. From that point on, my memory is hazy. **1965–70** *DARE* (Qu. EE33, . . *Outdoor games* . . *that children play*) 20 Infs, **scattered, but esp Nth,**

N Midl, West, Old mother witch; **IN39, IA34**, Old witch; **KY17**, Witch; (Qu. EE2, *Games that have one extra player—when a signal is given, the players change places, and the extra one tries to get a place*) Inf **CO21**, Old witch—old witch had a home, used to get kids who had to be touched to be freed, like dare-base or prisoner's base; (Qu. EE12, *Games in which one captain hides his team and the other team tries to find it*) Inf **PA247**, Old mammy witch. **1986** Pederson *LAGS Concordance*, 1 inf, **ceTN**, Old witch—a game they made up, with home base.

‡2 See quot. Cf **emptins 1**

1973 Allen *LAUM* 1.284 (as of c1950), *Yeast*. . . A few scattered infs. preserve various terms for the kinds of homemade liquid or sponge yeast used before the advent of the commercial cake variety. . . Older names include: *emptyings, old witch* [1 inf, **eNE**].

old witch by the wayside See **old witch 1**

old-witch grass n Cf **witchgrass**
A **panic grass** (here: *Panicum capillare*).

1859 (1880) Darlington *Amer. Weeds* 403, *P[anicum] capillare*. . . Old-witch Grass. . . Sandy pastures, cultivated grounds: throughout the United States. **1892** IN Dept. Geol. & Nat. Resources *Rept. for 1891* 157, *P[anicum] capillare* . . Old-witch Grass. Tickle-Grass. **1894** Coulter *Botany W. TX* 2.508, *P[anicum] capillare* (Old witch grass). **1911** Jepson *Flora CA* 38, *P[anicum] capillare* . . Old-witch-grass. . . sheathes and often the blades hirsute with stiff, spreading hairs. **1914** Georgia *Manual Weeds* 28, Old Witch Grass—*Panicum capillare*. . . When mature, the branches become very stiff and brittle and the large panicles break away and are driven before the winds for long distances, often piling in thick windrows against fences. **1925** *Book of Rural Life* 7.4055, *Old witch grass* . . (*Panicum capillare*), a common annual grass found throughout the United States and southern Canada. Upon maturity the stem breaks at the base and the plant becomes a typical tumbleweed. **1976** Bailey–Bailey *Hortus Third* 816, *P[anicum] capillare* . . Witch-grass, old-witch grass.

old woman n [Cf quot 1930] Cf **old man 1a**
A **wormwood**, esp *Artemisia absinthium*.

1892 *Jrl. Amer. Folkl.* 5.99 **nOH**, *Artemisia* sp., old woman. **1900** Lyons *Plant Names* 46, *A[rtemisia] Absinthium* . . Old-woman. **1910** Graves *Flowering Plants* 401 **CT**, *Artemisia Stelleriana* [sic] . . Dusty Miller . . Old Woman. . . Sometimes cultivated for ornament. **1911** Henkel *Amer. Med. Leaves* 41, Wormwood.—*Artemisia absinthium* . . old-woman . . mugwort. **1929** [see **old man 1a**]. **1930** Sievers *Amer. Med. Plants* 65, Wormwood—*Artemisia absinthium* . . old woman. . . The growing shoots are silvery white with fine silky hairs. **1974** (1977) Coon *Useful Plants* 104, *Artemisia absinthum* [sic]—Wormwood . . old woman. **1976** Bailey–Bailey *Hortus Third* 112, [*Artemisia*] *Stellerana* [sic] . . Beach w[ormwood], old-woman, dusty-miller.

old woman is picking her geese, the phr For varr see quots [*OED goose sb.* 1.d, *EDD* (at *old* adj. 1.154.d)] esp **Appalachians** Cf **devil n B4**
It is snowing.

1899 (1912) Green *VA Folk-Speech* 305, *Old-woman picking her geese*. . . Snowing. **1931** *PMLA* 46.1307 **sAppalachians**, The old woman's a-losin' her feathers. (Snow is falling.) The old woman's a-pickin' her geese. (Snow is falling.) **1942** Warnick *Garrett Co. MD* 11 **nwMD** (as of 1900–18), *Old woman picking her geese*, an expression used when large flakes of snow were falling fast. **1942** McAtee *Dial. Grant Co. IN* 46 (as of 1890s), "*Old woman's pickin' her geese*", said when snow was falling in large flakes. **1952** Brown *NC Folkl.* 1.499, The old woman is picking her geese. (It is snowing.) **1968** *DARE* FW Addit **PA169**, "Old woman is picking her geese"—snow. **1983** De Vries *Slouching* 51 **ND**, Come in and have some coffee and pfeffernuesse that I made myself. The old woman is plucking the geese this day.

old-year-out n Also *old-year-gone*
December 31st, New Year's Eve.

1967–68 *DARE* (Qu. FF11, . . *The night of December 31st*) Infs **TX43, 51**, Old-year-out, New Year's Eve; **TX35**, Old-year-gone; **AL32**, Old-year-out party.

Old Year's Eve(ning) n Also *Old Year's Night* [Cf *SND auld* adj 6] Cf **Old Night**
New Year's Eve.

[**1897** Stuart *Simpkinsville* 14 **AR**, They got him to come to the old-year party one year, jest for the fun of it.] **1966–69** *DARE* (Qu. FF11, . . *The night of December 31st*) Infs **MI93, 103, MO36, WA18**, Old Year's Eve; **WA18**, Old Year's Evening; **MI103**, Old Year's Night.

old yellow n

1923 *DN* 5.239 **swWI,** *Old yellow.* . . A powerful purgative, probably jalap. "Ol' doc come an' give her a dose of ol' yaller."

oleaster n

=buffalo berry.

1931 U.S. Dept. Ag. *Misc. Pub.* 101.119, Buffaloberries (*Lepargyrea* Spp., syn. *Shepherdia* Spp.) . . *Russet buffaloberry (L. canadensis)* . . known locally as . . wild oleaster, and wild olive. **1942** *Torreya* 42.163, *Elaeagnus argenta* [=*Shepherdia argentea*] . . silvery oleaster.

olecoke, olekoek See **olykoek**

Ole Ole Olson all in free exclam For varr see quots [Prob folk-etym for **all-ee all-ee out(s) in free**] **chiefly N Cent, Pacific; also NEast** See Map Cf **all (in) free**

In var hiding and chasing games: =**home free.**

1950 *WELS Suppl.* **WI,** Ole Ole Olson all come free—signal for remaining players to come in free in hide and go seek; **nWI,** Ole Ole out's in free. **1961** *Chicago Daily News* (IL) 4 Apr 18/3, On this tour of Chicago I saw some children on the Southwest Side playing a game around a tree. . . They were playing . . "Tap the Icebox," a game Chicago children have played for generations. But when it came time to call in all players who were in hiding, a boy hollered something that sounded like: "Ow-wee, Ow-wee yow-shun pree." I laughed because in the 1920s in one section of the South Side kids playing games hollered: "All-ee, All-ee Oceans Free." Four miles away kids hollered: "Ole, Ole Olson's Free." . . [A] nice lady who was a child in Brighton Park in the 1890s . . recalled the same games and said the proper call then was: "All ye, All ye outs in free." **1965–70** *DARE* (Qu. EE15, *When he has caught the first of those that were hiding what does the player who is 'it' call out to the others?*) 10 Infs, **esp IL,** Ole Ole Olson free (free); **AZ**11, **IL**85, 86, **PA**68, **WA**9, **WI**64, Ole Ole Olson all in free; **MA**6, Ole Ole all (in) free; **OR**14, Ole Ole in come free; **CA**99, Ole Ole; **MA**1, Ole Ole in free; **NY**199, Ole Ole Olson all in; **IL**102, Ole Ole Olson all's out; **WI**68, Ole Ole Olson come in free; **IL**27, Ole Ole Olson outs in free; **PA**247, Ole Ole oops all in free; **OH**57, Ole Ole otsen free; **AK**9, Ole Ole outs all in free; **WA**13, Ole Ole outs in free; **AZ**8, **IN**1, Ole Ole ox in free; **UT**3, Ole Ole oxen (or Oxford) come in free; **WI**50, Ole Ole oxen free; **MD**34, Ole Ole-o. **1975** Ferretti *Gt. Amer. Book Sidewalk Games* 144, Ring-a-levio. . . A player who is captured can be freed. . . In the Bronx . . the rescuing member of the Hunted team has to race to the Jail, put his foot on a step, and shout, "Oley, Oley in free!"

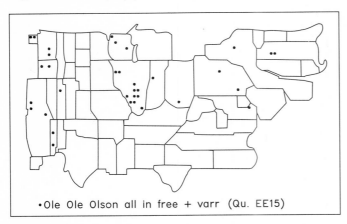

•Ole Ole Olson all in free + varr (Qu. EE15)

olicook See **olykoek**

oliebollen n pl [Du *oliebol(len)* oil dumpling(s)] **Du settlement areas** Cf **olykoek**

Small deep-fried cakes often made with raisins or currants. Note: *DARE* Infs may be construing pl as sg.

1941 Writers' Program *Guide WI* 337 **seWI,** Sunday dinners are prepared on Saturday by Dutch housewives who still cook the good things their mothers made—*khuete,* a vegetable and pork roast stew; *oliebollen,* fried dumplings. **1952** Tracy *Coast Cookery* 116 **MI,** *Olie Bollen* (Dutch Fritters). . . flour . . eggs . . seedless raisins. . . Spoon the dough by tablespoonfuls into hot fat. **1969** *DARE* (Qu. H26, *A round cake of dough, cooked in deep fat, with a hole in the center*) Inf **MI**102, Oliebollen ['olibələn]—used by the Dutch, like a doughnut, but no hole; (Qu. H28, *Different shapes or types of doughnuts*) Inf **IL**51, Oliebollen

['ouli 'boulən]—a Dutch food, doughnut-like batter, drop a spoonful of it in hot fat or oil, has raisins or currants in them.

oliekoek See **olykoek**

Olive Oyl n [From the character *Olive Oyl* in E.C. Segar's comic strip *Thimble Theater,* 1919–, better known as *Popeye,* 1929–]

A very thin woman.

1970 *DARE* (Qu. X49, *Expressions . . about a person who is very thin*) Inf **PA**248, Olive Oyl—the kids used to call me Olive Oyl; **TN**50, Olive Oyl—Popeye's old lady. [Both Infs Black]

olive tree See **wild olive**

olla n [Span] **SW**

An earthenware jar usu used as a container for water.

[**1844** Farnham *Travels in Calif.* 367 *(DA),* The matrimonial alliance formed, the suitor presents his lady love with a jug, in their [i.e. Indian] language an *olo,* the acceptance of which denotes her consent.] **1846** (1962) Magoffin *Down Santa Fé* 94 **cnNM,** A cheese . . and two earthen *jollas* [*ollas*—jugs] of a mixture of meat, *chilly verde* [green pepper] & onions boiled together completed course No. 1. **1872** Powers *Afoot* 231 **SW,** Under this hangs the great olla, full of water. **1894** *DN* 1.325 [Spanish words used in TX], *Ólla.* . . Pronounced ['oʝa]. **1929** Ellis *Ordinary Woman* 278 **CO** (as of early 20th cent), She . . stopped at the olla jar, left out at night with a wet cloth around it to keep it cool, and took a big drink. **1944** (1967) McNichols *Crazy Weather* 1 **SW,** He ducked out into the blinding, stunning glare of the sun and headed for the olla that hung in the grape arbor alongside the summer kitchen. **1962** Atwood *Vocab.* TX 47, *Large jar for drinking water.* . . Of those who gave the response *olla* (pronounced *oya*) [8% of 273 infs], nearly all were in Southwest or West Texas.

ollers See **always**

olly-olly-over See **alley(-alley)-over**

olomea n

A small tree *(Perrottetia sandwicensis)* native to Hawaii.

1930 Degener *Ferns of HI* 216, A pointed stick, . . of some hard wood such as that of the *olomea (Perrottetia sandwicensis* . .) was rapidly rubbed in the groove of a block . . of soft *hau* wood. **1948** Neal *In Gardens HI* 464, The olomea is a shrub or small tree native in forests of Hawaii. **1970** Carlquist *Hawaii* 458, *Perrottetia sandwicensis,* the olomea. **1980** Bushnell *Water of Kane* 414 **HI,** Below these, lesser trees sought the sun: olopua with their dark fruits like blue olives; red-veined, red-stemmed, red-berried olomea; ever-green kawauu with hanging panicles of white flowers not yet turned to small round fruits packed with seeds. **1994** Stone–Pratt *Hawai'i's Plants* 173, Other rain forest understory trees that are typically small when mature include . . olomea *(Perrottetia sandwicensis).*

olona n

A shrub *(Touchardia latifolia)* native to Hawaii that produces a fiber formerly much used in cordage.

1911 *Century Dict. Suppl.,* Olona . . [Hawaiian name.] A Hawaiian fiber-plant. **1933** Bryan *Hawaiian Nature* 110, Olona plants . . formerly grew more abundantly in the lower and middle forest zones of the Hawaiian Islands, between 800 and 1,000 feet elevation. **1955** Day *HI People* 302, The finest fiber for nets and fishlines, one of the strongest in the world, was made from the inner bark of the olona, a plant of the nettle family growing in the rain forest. **1980** Bushnell *Water of Kane* 414 **HI,** And below those, closer to the ground, grew olona, mountain ginger, and ferns of many kinds. **1994** Stone–Pratt *Hawai'i's Plants* 251, Olona is a sprawling shrub restricted to rain forests.

olykoek n Also sp *olecoke, olekoek, olicook, oliekoek, olycoke* [Du *oliekoek* oil cake] **chiefly Hudson Valley NY** *old-fash* Cf **cruller, oliebollen,** DS H26-28

A small sweetened cake fried in deep fat.

1809 Irving *Hist. NY* 1.149 **seNY,** The table . . was always sure to boast an enormous dish of balls of sweetened dough, fried in hog's fat, and called dough nuts, or oly koeks. **1848** Bartlett *Americanisms* 240, *Olycoke.* . . A cake fried in lard. A favorite delicacy with the Dutch, and also with their descendants, in New York, There are various kinds, as dough-nuts, crullers, etc. **1848** in 1850 Cooper *Rural Hours* 433 **ceNY,** Cake-jars are filling up . . with raisined olecokes. **1881** *Harper's New Mth. Mag.* 62.533 **ceNY,** His favorite city has surpassed all others in . . oliekoeks, and New Year cookies. **1889** Cooke *Steadfast* 78 **NY,** Refreshing him with hot flip, oly keoks [sic], or Indian preserves and arrack punch. **1932** (1946) Hibben *Amer. Regional Cookery* 28, *Ole Koeks*

(Albany, New York). . . Dough for Cinnamon Buns . . raisins . . cognac. **1949** Kurath *Word Geog.* 24 **Hudson Valley NY,** Some food terms of Dutch origin have spread beyond the Dutch area, . . but others, such as *olicook* for a doughnut. . . have probably always been Dutch family words and are disappearing fast.

oma n [Ger] **esp in Ger settlement areas** Cf **opa**
One's grandmother.

    1962 Atwood *Vocab. TX* 65, *Grandmother*. . . Fourteen informants of German background give *Oma.* **1967–68** DARE (Qu. Z4, . . 'Grandmother') Inf **CA**6, Oma ['ouma]; **IA**32, Oma ['omə]. [1 Inf of Ger background] **1986** Pederson *LAGS Concordance (Grandmother)* 2 infs, **cwFL, cTX,** Oma. [1 inf of Ger background] **1987** Dillard *Amer. Childhood* 57 **cwPA,** Our grandmother's name was Meta Waltenburger Doak. We children called her Oma, accenting both syllables. She was . . heir of well-to-do Germans in Louisville, Kentucky.

omadhaun n Pronc-sp *omathon, omathan* [OED 1818 →; < Ir *amadan* fool]
A fool, simpleton.

    [**1925** *DN* 5.337 **Nfld,** Omadaun. . . A lazy, good-for-nothing fellow; fool.] **1941** Ward *Holding Hills* 5 **IA** (as of early 20th cent), Any child in any family, unless he was an omathon, would find out by hard knocks. *Ibid* 173, After all, it was only an omathon, hardly ever mentioned in our neighborhood, that got married and got divorced; and he had to leave the community. **1966** DARE (Qu. HH3, *A dull and stupid person*) Inf **MI**26, Omadhaun ['omə͵ðɑn].

Omahog n [See quot 1949]
A resident of Omaha, Nebraska.

    1876 *Silver City* (Ida.) *Avalanche* 8 Feb. 2/2 *(DA),* A party of eight . . Omahogs, or, in other words, citizens of Omaha, left Cheyenne Wednesday for the Black Hills. **1889** *Sporting Life* (Phila.) 3 July 1/5 *(heading) (DA),* The 'Omahogs' Closing In On the Leader—Great Work All Round. **1933** *AmSp* 8.4.80, Out-state newspapers often call the inhabitants of Omaha, Nebraska, *Omahogs.* **1949** *AmSp* 24.25, *Omahog* for a citizen of Omaha. . . It referred, of course, to Omaha's large packing industry.

omathan, omathon See **omadhaun**

ombray See **hombre**

‡omelette-eyed adj Cf **egg-eyed**

    1969 DARE (Qu. X21c, *If the eyes are very round*) Inf **MO**6, Omelette-[eyed].

ommalie See **hommilie**

ompen See **open**

on prep, adv **chiefly Inland Nth, West** |ɑn|; **chiefly Sth, Midl, eNEng** |ɒn, ɔn|; also **chiefly Sth, S Midl** |on| Pronc-spp *awn, own*

    A Forms.

    1825 in 1956 Eliason *Tarheel Talk* 315 **nw,cwNC,** On—own. **1893** Shands *MS Speech* 16, Ag on [æg ɒn] [=to egg on]. **1909** *DN* 3.354 **eAL, wGA,** On, prep. Pronounced [ɒn]. **1909** *Atlantic Mth.* 104.138 **VA,** Awn . . a fairly just reproduction of the sounds. **1950** Hubbell *Pronc. NYC* 81, /ɑə/ may appear, but there is a great deal of irregularity: . . on (when stressed; the unstressed form has /ɑ/). **1952** Brown *NC Folkl.* 1.571, On [on]. . . Robeson and Sampson counties. All classes. **1961** Kurath–McDavid *Pronc. Engl.* 164, The adverb *on,* as in *put it on!* . . The phoneme /ɑ/ is confined to a single area extending from Western New England to the New England settlements on the Great Lakes. It includes Metropolitan New York and the Hudson Valley. . . In the South and the South Midland the phoneme /ɔ/, always well rounded and often an upgliding diphthong, is nearly universal in the adverb *on* . . [and] has general currency also in Eastern Pennsylvania and adjoining sections of New Jersey and Maryland; it is universal in northern West Virginia and in all of Ohio, except for a narrow belt along Lake Erie. In Western Pennsylvania, the phoneme /ɒ/, usually only slightly rounded (if at all), occurs . . in *on.* . . In Eastern New England, *on* . . the vowel being a more or less rounded [ɒ] sound. **1965** Carmony *Speech Terre Haute* 75 **cwIN,** An ingliding allophone of /ɔ/ occurs frequently in the record in the pronunciation of the word *on* [ɔən], [ɒən], as in the expression *put it on. Ibid* 113, /ɔ/, phonetically [ɔᵛ] or [ɒ], is the usual vowel of . . *on,* . . in Terre Haute speech. **1973** *PADS* 60.53 **seNC,** [Ref to quot 1961 above:] On. . . PEAS finds that /ɔ/, "always well rounded," is nearly universal in the South and South Midland. This is true for our informants, all of whom said [ɔ] or [ɔə]. **1973** Thompson *Coll.* **cAL** (as of 1920s), You cayn't hardly go down that way no more thout steppin

own third base [=cow dung]. **1976** Allen *LAUM* 3.265 (as of c1950), Stressed *on,* as in *Put it on!* . . In the U[pper] M[idwest], unround /ɑ/, with some instances of slightly backed /ɑ/, persists as a distinctive Northern dialect marker. It almost completely dominates Minnesota, North Dakota, and the northern third of Iowa. The rounded /ɔ - ɒ/, on the contrary, is strongest in southern Iowa, Nebraska, and, less so, South Dakota. . . No instances of Southern /on/ occur. **1987** Childress *Out of the Ozarks* 15 **eTX** (as of c1945), First off, the rich farmer talked the way we did. . . "Less go own in th' porler," he said in his East Texas accent. **1989** Pederson *LAGS Tech. Index* 362 **Gulf Region,** [*On* in the phrase *put it on,* is pronounced [ɔn] by 375 infs; [on] by 216 infs; [ɑn] by 39 infs; [ɒn] by 24 infs.]

    B As prep.

    1 Of. [OED on prep. 27 1258 →; "now *dial.* or *vulgar*"] **chiefly NEng, Sth, S Midl** *old-fash* Cf **-en** suff³

    1781 *PA Jrl. & Weekly Advt.* (Philadelphia) 16 May [1]/3, Some on'em, one on'em, many on'em. This, though frequent in the northern parts of England, and some parts of America, perhaps is rather local and general. **1815** Humphreys *Yankey in England* 107, On't, on it, of it. **1834** Smith *Letters Jack Downing* 194 **ME,** But some on you say the bank has too much power. **1848** Lowell *Biglow* 145 **'Upcountry' MA,** On, of; used before *it* or *them,* or at the end of a sentence, as, *on 't, on 'em, nut ez ever I heerd on.* **1859** Taliaferro *Fisher's R.* 90 **nwNC** (as of 1820s), It was onpossible almost to git enuff fur her to make a meal on. **1861** Holmes *Venner* 2.187 **NEng,** Glad on 't! **1867** Harris *Sut Lovingood Yarns* 25 **TN,** The balance on em, ni ontu a gallun, kep' on wif dad. **1894** *DN* 1.342 **wCT,** On is used often for *of* with a pronoun object: *on't* for *of it,* as in Shakspere, is common. *Ibid* 343 **MA,** On (for *of*). **1895** *DN* 1.373 **seKY, eTN, wNC,** On: for *of* or *from.* "I won't take it on him." **1899** (1912) Green *VA Folk-Speech* 467, Un um. . . Of them. "He is one un um." **1907** *DN* 3.195 **seNH,** On, prep. Often used where *of* is used by the younger generation. "What are you thinking on?" **1910** *DN* 3.454 **seVT,** I found ten on 'em. **1923** *DN* 5.216 **swMO,** On, prep. Of. **1927** Adams *Congaree* 24 **cSC** [Black], Dey get rid on her. **1945** FWP *Lay My Burden Down* 27 **Sth** (as of c1865) [Black], All on a sudden he started running. **1968** DARE Tape **AK**6, Some on 'em here all right. **1969** DARE FW Addit **ceNY,** He could tell you the history on it. **1975** Gould *ME Lingo* 195, On—Sometimes meaning *of:* "I bought four new tires, and one on 'em blew out before I got home!" **1986** Pederson *LAGS Concordance,* 1 inf, **cTX,** Can't think on it.

    2 Used redund:

    a after pres pples. [Cf EDD on prep. II.2] Cf **of Be**

    1821 Howison *Upper Canada* 294 **NY,** I fear that little shaver (child) is troubling on you, sir. **1840** *Daily Picayune* (New Orleans LA) 21 Aug 2/5, If I could larn to cook that are hominy! and there always havin' on't every mornin' for breakfast. **1843** (1916) Hall *New Purchase* 212 **IN,** I actually seed him a readin on it. *Ibid* 227, He sees me . . a bekenin on him to stop. **1861** Holmes *Venner* 2.181 **NEng,** The' a'nt no use in lettin' on 'em spile. *Ibid* 186, I shouldn' min' keepin' on 'em. *Ibid* 187, What is't the chap's been a-doin' on? **1871** (1882) Stowe *Fireside Stories* 81 **MA,** He brought down them colts to-day, and I worked the biggest part o' the mornin' shoein' on 'em. **1883** (1971) Harris *Nights with Remus* 38 **GA** [Black], I dunner w'at Miss Sally wanter be sendin' un you down yer fer, ef you gwine ter be stirr'n' en bodderin' 'longer dem ar doin's. **1894** *DN* 1.342 **wCT,** Often used redundantly with verbs and present participles; *e.g.* "What ye duin' on? Hayin' on't?" Also with reflexive verbs . . "Mr. ——— can't come jes' now; he's a-shavin' on him." **1914** *DN* 4.77 **ME, nNH,** On, prep. Of. Redundantly used in innumerable ways. "Doin' on it," "Seein' on 'em home," etc. **1980** *NADS Letters,* On marker of the accusative pronoun in Black and Street English. Examples: kissin on you = kissin you. **1986** Pederson *LAGS Concordance,* 1 inf, **cwLA,** They went to cutting on him = began stabbing him; 2 infs, **cnLA, nwMS,** Doctoring on (him).

    b after finite verbs. [Cf EDD on prep. II.2] Cf **of Bb, c**

    1906 *DN* 3.153 **nwAR,** Remember on. . . To remember. "That's all I remember on." **1926** Roberts *Time of Man* 256 **cKY,** Wherever I happen on to be they always like my way with a harp. **1942** (1971) Campbell *Cloud-Walking* 76 **seKY,** Squire and the Little Teacher begged on her to sing again. *Ibid* 84, They begged on the teacher women to let them learn to sing school song ballets. **1967** Williams *Greenbones* 211 **GA** (as of c1910), Remember how I nursed on you all the time when we were traveling, how bad I felt when you were sick?

    c in phrr *on yesterday, on tomorrow,* etc. [Cf EDD on prep II.3] **esp VA**

    1829 *VA Lit. Museum* 1.459, On. As "on tomorrow;" a mere expletive. *Common.* **1848** *S. Lit. Messenger* 14.636 **VA,** "On" yesterday, (another

Southern emendation of the Queen's English, which is funny enough,) I was so unfortunate as to be grounded by a colt of the tavern-keeper's whom I most insanely mounted. **1852** *NY Tribune* (NY) 9 Jan 6/1, It was the intention to send in the Treasury Report . . on yesterday. **1914** *DN* 4.160 **cVA**, On, prep. "On yesterday"; "on last week." **1922** *Congressional Record* 27 Dec 64.1.931 **MA**, I took occasion to ask the Secretary of State on yesterday. **1945** Mencken *Amer. Lang. Suppl. 1* 122, But he [=W.C. Bryant, editor of the *NY Evening Post*, 1829–1878] also prohibited such terms as . . *on yesterday. On yesterday* still appears every day in the *Congressional Record.*

3 In contexts where *for* would be expected:

a in phr *wait on:* To wait for (someone or something). [Cf *EDD on* prep II.10, *SND wait* v. I.B.1.(3)(i)] **widespread, but more freq Sth, Midl** See Map and Map Section

1817 (1930) Sewall *Diary* 14 **ME**, I proceeded to the Academy and agreed to enter there upon the condition that the Professor would wait on me until the next winter for the tuition. **1865** (1922) Jackson *Col.'s Diary* 227 **PA**, We have been waiting on the Pay Department. **1878** *Appletons' Jrl.* 5.413 **PA**, The Pennsylvanian . . says he will wait *on* you when he means that he will wait *for* you. **1886** *S. Bivouac* 4.345 **sAppalachians**, Wait on (wait for.) **1901** *DN* 2.150 **ceNY, e,sePA**, *Wait on.* . . "Wait on me" = wait for me. **1903** *DN* 2.353 **seIA**. **1905** *DN* 3.100 **nwAR**, *Wait on.* . . To wait for, to await. . . Universal. **1908** *German Amer. Annals* 10.50 **sePA**, *Wait on.* Wait for. "I'll go along if you wait on me a few minutes." . . fr. Pa. Ger. *wawrtă uf;* Ger. *warten auf.* **1909** *DN* 3.386 **eAL, wGA**. **1914** *DN* 4.160 **cVA**. **1916** *DN* 4.270 **New Orleans LA**. **1918** *DN* 5.21 **NC, SC**. **1923** *DN* 5.224 **swMO**. **1926** *DN* 5.394 **KS**, *Wait on,* meaning "wait for." I am inclined to think that the *on* has better standing here than in the East. "Flour mills wait on Senate."—Kansas City Star. "Won't wait on a treaty."—Ibid. **1931** Jacobson *Milwaukee Dial.* 19 **WI**, Wait on me after school. **1932** (1974) Caldwell *Tobacco Road* 180 **GA**, Bessie and Dude stayed a while, too; they had to wait on Lov. **1933** in 1942 Handy *Father of Blues* vii **Chicago IL** [Black], I had to wait on Bill, and consequently when Miss Tyler did arrive with the check it was almost train time. **1942** Faulkner *Go Down* 59 **MS**, If I can wait on that milk, I reckon the cow can too. **1945** *PADS* 3.12 **cwNY**, *Wait on.* . . Not common here; but my Scottish housekeeper, who, despite a thirty-year residence in Rochester, clings to her native idiom, uses it. **1965–70** *DARE* (Qu. A12, *When somebody keeps you waiting . . "Hurry up! I don't have all day to _____ you!"*) 358 Infs, **widespread, but more freq Sth, Midl,** Wait on; **TN66**, Wait around on; **IL113**, Wait on slow motion; **GA4**, Keep waiting on; (Qu. GG11, *To be quite anxious about something*) Inf **GA91**, Waiting on the baby; (Qu. GG17, *Other words for longing . . "She had been so lonely— she was really _____ [to see him]."*) Inf **KY17**, Waiting on him to come in. **1968** *DARE* Tape **AL43**, They had held Bob more than three weeks because they were waiting on his folks. **1975** Allen *LAUM* 2.66 (as of c1950), I'll wait *for* you. After *wait* only four U[pper] M[idwest] infs., all in Midland speech territory, have the preposition *on.* **1989** Pederson *LAGS Tech. Index* 354 **Gulf Region**, ([Wait] for) 509 infs, For; 154 infs, On. **1990** Brown *Big Bad Love* 58 **MS**, I knew she was sitting out on the porch, waiting on me.

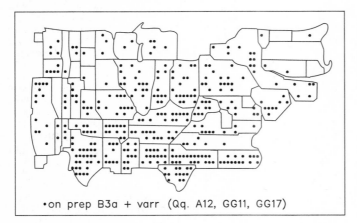

•on prep B3a + varr (Qq. A12, GG11, GG17)

b See quots.

1966–70 *DARE* FW Addit **ceOK**, [Sign in grocery store:] We do not cash checks on strangers; **cePA**, That's a good name *on* it—i.e., *for* it. **1968** Kellner *Aunt Serena* 103 **IN**, The neighbors . . went together and had a Surprise Party on her.

c See quot. Cf **for** prep **B4c**

1921 Thorp *Songs Cowboys* 95 **SW**, We ain't jest much on stylish,/ But we got a good Home Ranch.

4 Toward, in the direction of; to, at.

1836 (1928) Underwood *Jrl.* 32.143 **MA**, But I succeeded allthough I had on a very heavy lot of clothing ammunition &c with a rifle to swim on shore not even losing my rifle. **1916** *DN* 4.347 **cnTX** (as of 1896), *On,* prep. Up to. "He rode on me and invited me to dinner." **1925** in 1944 *ADD* **cWV**, I will holler on 'em [the children]. **1928** *DN* 6.4 **MA** (as of c1850), *On,* prep. At;—written as dialect. And him inside barkin' *on* us. **c1938** in 1970 Hyatt *Hoodoo* 1.625 **ceSC**, When de [=the jurors] come out yo' *hol'* dat judge.

5 In; into. [*OED on* prep. 5 → c1375; "*Obs.*"; *EDD on* prep. II.6 1806 →] Cf **B8, 11, 12a** below

1836 in 1934 Frear *Lowell & Abigail* 103 **MA**, They came and returned on my canoe. **1938** Stuart *Dark Hills* 396 **neKY**, They took fourteen stitches on the other fellow. **1944** *PADS* 2.11 **seAL**, Ride on a car (automobile). **1972** Carr *Da Kine Talk* 142 **HI**, I got on the Ford, drove to town, and got off. **1972** *DARE* File **nwFL**, Let's don't use your car. We can go to the show on mine. **1981** Jenkins *Baja OK* 81 **TX**, "Can I get you some juice, Momma?" "Oh, I couldn't put anything on my stomach today." **1986** Pederson *LAGS Concordance,* 1 inf, **ceTN**, He been on bed all morning—in bed, sick.

6 About, concerning, with regard to. [Cf *EDD on* prep. II.7] **scattered, but chiefly Sth, S Midl**

1899 (1912) Green *VA Folk-Speech* 444, *Think on.* . . To consider carefully. "I'll think on it." **1940** Stuart *Trees of Heaven* 251 **neKY**, I can't kick on their work. **1941** Smith *Going to God's Country* 167 **MO** (as of 1901), It was lots of fun to see how the people would lie on each other just for the sake of an office. **1945** FWP *Lay My Burden Down* 125 **LA** [Black], And I tells you that Marse William am the greatest man what ever walk this earth. That's the truth. I can't lie on him when the poor man's in he grave. **1952** Brown *NC Folkl.* 1.571, *On.* . . About, concerning. "She knows a right smart on gardening." **1967–68** *DARE* Tape **GA35**, Naw, I wouldn't know too much on that; **SC43**, Doctors talk on it. **1967–68** *DARE* FW Addit **seMI, cnMI, ceNY, seOR**, I'll have to (*or* let me) think on that; **MD31**, Tell lies on—tell lies about. **1968–70** *DARE* (Qu. U35, . . *Thrifty but not in a complimentary way: "She's not a bad housekeeper, but very _____."*) Inf **PA240**, Tight on her money; (Qu. JJ18, *If you want to have time to think about something before you make a decision: "Give me till tomorrow, I'd like to _____."*) Inf **WI13**, Think on it—heard. **1974** Fink *Mountain Speech* 18 **wNC, eTN**, *On* . . about. "I'll think on it." **1982** Barrick *Coll.* **csPA**, *Lie on*—lie about. **1986** Pederson *LAGS Concordance,* 1 inf, **csTN**, I been thinking on it; 1 inf, **cTN**, Study on it; 1 inf, **ceAL**, I'm not bragging on myself; 1 inf, **cwGA**, Thinking on it; 1 inf, **cMS**, Thinking on things; 1 inf, **swGA**, I'm really thrilled on seeing you now; 1 inf, **cwLA**, Talking on someone else—gossiping; 1 inf, **cwAL**, My grandmamma was tight on me (=strict on me); 1 inf, **nwMS**, He was very tight on loans—of a banker.

7 As an accompaniment to (a main dish).

1980 *NY Times* (NY) 20 July 55/5 **NYC**, I should like to add a favorite New York idiom . . : "On" for "with," as in "Would you like turnips on your flounder?" . . Years ago at a restaurant near Penn Station I ordered spaghetti. The waitress asked what I wanted on it. . . "Do you want beans or salad on your spaghetti?"

8 in phr *believe on:* To believe in (someone or something). [Cf *OED believe* v. 1 "No difference can be detected between the use of 'believe *in*' and 'believe *on,*' in the 16th c. versions of the Scriptures, except that the latter was more frequent".]

1953 Brewer *Word Brazos* 10 **eTX** [Black], Dem what b'lieve on 'im gonna be saved. **1986** Pederson *LAGS Concordance,* 1 inf, **csTX**, A few old people might believe on it.

9 in phrr *sick on one's stomach* and varr: Nauseated. **chiefly S and Mid Atl, PA** See Map Cf **at** prep **2, of** C10, **to**

1940 Tresidder *Reading to Others* 433 **Sth**, The Southerner may say . . "I'm sick on my stomach" where a Northerner will say . . "I'm sick to my stomach." **1944** *PADS* 2.11 **seAL**, *On:* prep. Substituted for *in* or *at* in some phrases; specifically, *ride on a car* (automobile) *sick on his stomach.* **1944** *ADD* **eWV**, Sick on one's stomach. Usual. *At* is heard, but not *to.* **1949** Kurath *Word Geog.* 78, The variant *on the stomach* is also current in two detached areas: (1) the Pennsylvania German settlement area of Eastern Pennsylvania and the Shenandoah Valley; (2) the Pennsylvania German settlements on the Yadkin in North Carolina, and from there between the Cape Fear and the Peedee all the way down to the coast. This use of *on* in the phrase *sick on the stomach* may rest upon the corresponding German idiom *etwas auf dem Magen haben,* but it may also have been introduced from the synonymous English expression *to have something on the stomach.* **1955** Potter *Dial. NW OH* 94, Putnam [County] shows about equal favor for *to his stomach, at his stomach,* and *in his stomach,* and even offered the one instance of *on his stomach.* **1965–70** *DARE* (Qu. BB16a, *If something a person ate didn't agree with him, he might be sick _____ his stomach*) 72 Infs, **chiefly S and Mid Atl, PA,** On (the); (Qu. BB16b, *If something a person ate didn't agree with him, he might just feel a bit _____*) Inf **GA8,** About half-sick on his stomach; **SC7,** Nauseated on your stomach; **GA42,** Sick on the stomach; **GA23,** Urpish on his stomach; (Qu. BB17, . . *Vomiting*) Inf **VA35,** He's been sick on his stomach; **VA46,** Sick on his stomach. **1967** Faries *Word Geog. MO* 117, *On the stomach* (25 [of c700] occurrences), current in the German settlements of Pennsylvania and North Carolina, occurs mainly in the Ozark Highland. **1971** Wood *Vocab. Change* 304 **chiefly AL, FL, GA, MS,** [Of 1000 infs, 69 reported *on his stomach.*] **1975** Allen *LAUM* 2.65 **seIA** (as of c1950), Pennsylvania *on the stomach* is used by only three Midland speakers, two in Iowa and one in Nebraska. **1991** Pederson *LAGS Regional Pattern* 294, [81 of 914 infs, chiefly **sMS, sAL, sGA, FL,** offered the construction *(sick) on (his stomach).*]

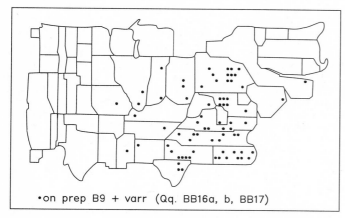

•on prep B9 + varr (Qq. BB16a, b, BB17)

10 in phr *on class:* In attendance in a classroom. **NC** Cf **off** C2

   1927 *AmSp* 3.463 **NC,** The expressions "on class" and "off class" are current in the college slang of North Carolina. "Grace is on class now and can't go," "I'll be off class at three o'clock." **1929** *AmSp* 4.331, "On class" and ["]off class" . . are provincialisms, but they should not be classed as slang. They are used widely in North Carolina among teachers and students alike. **1930** *AmSp* 6.130 **NC** [Campus expressions], *On class*—At this institution the students and the instructor are not "at class" nor "in class," but "on class." "Where is Smith?" "He is on class." **1932** *AmSp* 7.386 **NC,** At Davidson College *on class* has long been in use among the students, and it is also heard in the speech of many members of the faculty. A student may confess that he "wasn't on class last Tuesday," and . . may say that a professor told him he had better "sit on class." . . [In eNC a high school] pupil said, by way of indicating the time of some incident, that it happened while he was "sitting on an English period." **1944** *PADS* 2.33, *Class, on.* . . In class. Some parts of N.C. All classes of people. Common.

11 in phr *on line:* In line. **chiefly NYC, nNJ**

   [**1949** in 1986 *DARE* File **seMI,** Seen on sign in cafeteria in Michigan League: "No smoking on the line, please."] **1958** Francis *Structure of Amer. Engl.* 518, *New York City and Hudson Valley. . . Morphology and Syntax.* [H]e lives *in* King Street. . . we stood *on* line. **1968** *DARE* Tape **NY81,** People who came early have to wait on line. . . We have to wait on line. **1975** *NY Times* (NY) 1 Apr 35/5 **seNY,** It's to stand silently on unemployment lines with other surplus members of America's work force, waiting to sign for your unemployment check. **1977–78** Foster *Lexical Variation* 33 **NJ,** The distribution of *(stand) on line,* long familiar as a New York City phrase, illustrates the loss of a New York focus for such items. *On line* is rare among blacks and somewhat less common among non-college educated informants, but the geographic distribution among college-educated whites . . , as well as the absence of variation by age, shows that *(stand) on line* is well-established in North and Central Jersey, only slightly more common in the counties adjacent to New York City than in the outlying suburbs. **1988** *DARE* File, [News-

paper clipping:] Yes, I've encountered "stand on line" in San Francisco, but only from former New Yorkers. . . I have lived and worked in Manhattan myself, and lived or vacationed in Maryland, Pennsylvania, Oklahoma, Missouri, Michigan, upstate New York, Cape Cod and Kitty Hawk; and New York City seems to be alone in this usage. **1992** *Ibid* **NYC,** My midtown Manhattan husband always stood on line at the movies. *Ibid* **NYC** (as of 1950s–60s), In the Bronx we always "stood on line."

12 In var uses appar infl by non-English languages:

a In, at; into. [Prob calque of Ger *auf, an*] **Ger settlement areas**

   1931 Jacobson *Milwaukee Dial.* 16 **WI,** Look on me. . . for look at me. Ansehen is the influence. **1935** *AmSp* 10.167 **sePA** [English of PA Germans], We have an old bed on the attic. **1968** *Budget* (Sugarcreek OH) 18 July 2/5 **OH,** Most of the wheat is on shock. **1971** *Today Show Letters* **cePA,** In this particular small area of Pennsylvania, people say "on" the attic, "Go up on the attic, Mary, and bring down the high chair, Jane is bringing the baby here this afternoon." . . They also say. . . "I was just up on the cemetary [sic], putting flowers on Mamma's grave." **1985** *DARE* File, Only in the Pennsylvania Dutch country will you hear folks say—It's "on the attic"—she sings "on the choir"—the band played "on the park." **1995** *Ibid* **Chicago IL,** One thing I picked up from my grandparents (born in Chicago) was saying "on the attic" instead of "in."

b In phr *on the table:* At the table. [Usu calque of Ger *an;* in quot 1972 perh calque of Haw *ma* on, at]

   1914 *DN* 4.110 **cKS,** *On, prep.* At. "He sat on the table." [*DN* Ed: Ger., *an dem Tisch.*] **1939** Aurand *Quaint Idioms* 23 [PaGer], Fitzie, come in to eat; Ma and Pa are on the table and Johnny has *et himself already.* **1944** *ADD* **sePA,** Paw's on the table, & Maw's half et. **1972** Carr *Da Kine Talk* 142 **HI,** I sat on the table and had my lunch.

on- *pref* See **un-**

ona See **una**

on a drag See **drag** n 16

o'nary See **ornery**

once *adv* Usu |wʌn(t)s|; also **chiefly Sth, S Midl** |wʌnst|; occas |wɔn(t)s|; for addit varr see quots Pronc-spp *onced, onc(e)t, on(e)st, wancet, wonst, wunst* Cf **twice**

A Forms.

   1818 in 1956 Eliason *Tarheel Talk* 315 **nw,cnNC,** Onest. **1827** (1939) Sherwood *Gaz. GA* 139, Onct, for once. **1851** Burke *Polly Peablossom* 141 **MS,** He was at my ferry wonst, and I refused to set him over the river. **1867** Harris *Sut Lovingood Yarns* 24 **TN,** He lit ontu his hans agin, an kick'd strait up onst. **1871** Eggleston *Hoosier Schoolmaster* 34 **sIN,** Ef Bull wunst takes a holt. **1894** Riley *Armazindy* 136 **IN,** Wunst he bringed us some. **1895** *DN* 1.375 **seKY, eTN, wNC,** Onct, twict. **1896** *DN* 1.421 **NY,** Once: to oncet [təwʌnst]. For *at once.* **1899** Chesnutt *Conjure Woman* 14 **csNC** [Black], He en de oberseah sot up nights once't er twice't. **1902** *DN* 2.249 **sIL,** Wunst. **1902** Wister *Virginian* 251, I couldn't be so good if I wasn't bad onced in a while. **1903** *DN* 2.299 **Cape Cod MA** (as of a1857), . . Pronounced onct [wʌnst] in expression 'all to onct.' *Ibid* 323 **seMO,** Onct, twict. **1909** *DN* 3.354 **eAL, wGA,** Onct (wunst). **1911** *DN* 3.539 **eKY,** Onct. **1912** *DN* 3.584 **wIN,** Onct. . . Once. Very frequently heard. **1915** *DN* 4.186 **swVA,** Oncet. **1915** *DN* 4.230 **wTX,** Wunst. **1923** Sinclair *Parowan Bonanza* 52 **SW,** Beans is never the same, wancet they've been wrinkled wit' rain water an' dried again. **1938** Rawlings *Yearling* 14 **nFL,** I got to fool you oncet. **1949** Kurath *Word Geog.* 179, An added /t/ occurs in *once* and *twice* throughout the Midland and the South, excepting only the piedmont of Virginia. It is more frequent in *once* than in *twice.* Though most common in folk speech, it is widely used by middle-class speakers, especially in the South Midland. **1951** West *Witch Diggers* 200 **IN,** I thought about it once or twice. **1955** Roberts *S. from Hell-fer-Sartin* 108 **seKY,** And they'd go back ever oncet in a while. **1965–70** *DARE* Tape **AL14,** Every oncet [wʌnst] in a while you had to clean the tank out; **NC1,** We'd go out oncet [wɔnst] a day; **GA23,** Oncet [wʌnst] a week, it runs; **GA25,** About oncet [wʌnst] a year; **FL10,** They are not as good as they oncet [wɔnst] have been; **FL36,** I know some horses it [=snake bite] killed right at oncet [wʌnst]; **IN3,** Once [wʌnst] upon a time. **MS1,** Once [wʌnst] upon a time. **1967–69** *DARE* FW Addit **neNC,** Oncet used for 'once;' **wNC,** Oncet [wunst]—once. Common pronc in highlands of N.C.; **sLA,** Oncet; **IA31,** Oncet or twicet; **eKY,** Once [wʌnst]. **1968–69** *DARE* (Qu. A13, *When something needs to be done* *immediately . . "I'll do it _____!"*) Inf **GA**22, Right at oncet; (Qu. A15, *Something that happens only occasionally: "He comes around _____."*) Inf **KY**20, Oncet a year; (Qu. KK49, *When you don't have the time or ambition to do something thoroughly: "I'm not going to give the place a real cleaning, I'll just _____."*) Inf **KY**21, Give it a oncet-over. **1982** *Barrick Coll.* **csPA**, Oncet in a while. **1989** Pederson *LAGS Tech. Index* 10 **Gulf Region** (Once) 556 infs, [wʌn(t)s]; 133 infs, [wʌn(t)st]; 39 infs, [wɑn(t)s]; 7 infs, [wɑnst]; 4 infs, [wɔn(t)s]; 1 inf, [wɔnst]. **1989** Gurganus *Oldest Confederate Widow* 222 **Sth**, Onct our armoire was locked shut.

B Sense.

Used, esp in imper sentences, with a vague emphatic or limiting force; see quots. [Prob calque of Ger *einmal,* but cf *EDD*] **chiefly German settlement areas**

1872 Haldeman *PA Dutch* 57 [English influenced by German], The German idiom of using *einmal* (once) as an expletive, is common, as in, "Bring me a chair once." **1882** (1971) Gibbons *PA Dutch* 390, A scientific friend, wishing to examine a specimen, said, "Let me see it once." Of the same kind are these: "When we get moved once," "You'll know what it is when you hain't got no father no more once." **1886** *Amer. Philol. Assoc. Proc.* 17.xiii **ePA**, A remark in the nature of a request or an invitation always ends with the word "once." e.g. "Let me see 'once,' " "John, come here 'once,' " etc. This is simply the German idiom *ein Mal,* anglicized. **1908** *German Amer. Annals* 10.36 **sePA**, Once. Expletive. "Rosina, will you marry me *once?*" "Where were you?" "I was at the store once." fr. Pa. Ger *amol;* Ger. *ein mal.* **1916** *DN* 4.338 **PA**, Once. . . [Cf. German *einmal.*] Used expletively. "Come here once." In La., among German settlers. Neb., Mich. **1931** Jacobson *Milwaukee Dial.* 17 **WI**, Once. . . is another word that makes Milwaukee distinct. "Come once! Look at this once!" **1935** *AmSp* 10.167 **PA** [Engl of PA Germans], Come here once (*often* oncet). *Ibid,* I will read you now once a small story. **1942** Warnick *Garrett Co. MD* 11 **nwMD** (as of 1900–1918), Once . . used for emphasis, in expressions "come here once", "let me see once." **1948** *AmSp* 23.109 **swIL** [German language influences], Give me the knife once. *Ibid* 237 **sePA** [English spoken by Pennsylvania Germans], Once, as an adverb used most freely and tortuously. It is used locally as a translation of *einmal* or *mal,* . . which has lost any real meaning of time, and functions rather as a stylistic intensifier, with the meaning of *indeed, really, actually,* or *as a matter of fact.* **1950** *WELS Suppl.* **WI**, "Come here once." "Do it once." **1953** *AmSp* 28.246 **csPA**, The pleonastic *once,* as in 'Will you hand me that hammer once?' is deeply imbedded in the speech of the area. **1978** Kalibabky *Hawdaw* 2 **neMN**, Nancy, come here once. . . lemme fix dat hem on yer dress. **1981** *WI Acad. Trans.* 69.84 **WI**, The use of 'once' to mean 'right now' or 'right away'. The sentence presented to the speaker was, "Come here once, I gotta tell you something." 67% of the young group admitted using this construction, 45% of the middle-aged group, and 25% of the older group. . . [T]his construction is spreading in Wisconsin. . . from Milwaukee, as a focal area, to the developing speech of the young in the state as a whole. **1983** *Barrick Coll.* **csPA**, Once—sometime. "Why don't you bring him along once?"

once and occasionally adv phr Also *every once an occasion, once in occasion* **Sth, S Midl**

Now and again, once in a while.

1953 Randolph–Wilson *Down in Holler* 268 **Ozarks**, Once and occasionally. . . Now and then. I asked a rabbit hunter if he ever killed 'em a-runnin'. "Yes, once an' occasionally," he answered, "but mostly I just arkansaws 'em." **1954** *Harder Coll.* **cwTN**, Once and occasionally. . . Now and then. **c1960** *Wilson Coll.* **csKY**, Once and occasionally. . . Now and then, at times. **1966** *DARE* (Qu. A15, *Something that happens only occasionally: "He comes around _____."*) Inf **GA**9, Every once an occasion. **1967** *DARE* FW Addit **seGA**, Once in occasion—meaning 'once in a while.' Old man in conversation.

onced See **once**

once in a miracle See **miracle B**

once in occasion See **once and occasionally**

oncer n

See quots.

1916 *DN* 4.327 **KS**, Oncer. . . He who (or that which) does a thing but once, esp. a church member who attends service but once on Sunday. **1950** *WELS Suppl.* **nwIA**, Oncer—one who attends church only once per Sunday. Services are held twice in all Dutch Reformed Churches. A term of mild stigma. "He's a good man to do business with, but he is a oncer." **1950** *WELS* (Nicknames for someone who goes to church

seldom or not at all) 1 Inf, **cnWI**, Oncer. **1968** *DARE* (Qu. CC7) Inf **NJ**39, Oncer—goes once a year on Easter or Christmas.

oncet See **once**

on class See **on** prep **B10**

onct See **once**

ondly See **only**

one pron, adv, indef art Usu |wʌn|; also rarely |wɔn|; also, in unstressed position following a pronoun or adj, |-ən| Pronc-spp *en, wa(u)n, -(u)n* See also **you-uns, we-uns, them-uns** Cf **big one, least** adj 2, **old one, young ~**

A Forms.

1826 Royall *Sketches* 58 **csWV**, Not waun hate will ye's do. **1902** *DN* 2.240 **sIL**, One [ən], *pron.* The reduced form, especially in expressions 'we uns,' 'you uns.' **1907** *DN* 3.224 **nwAR, sIL**, One, *pron.* Pronounced [ən], especially when preceded by an adjective, as young 'un. **1908** *DN* 3.284 **eAL, wGA**, Thisn, thatn, this here, that there, emphatic demonstratives. **1914** *DN* 4.78 **ME, nNH**, Reg'lar he-un. . . A big, strong specimen of man or beast. **1932** in 1944 *ADD* **nVA**, |wɔn|. Speaker aged 17. 'Waun out o' 13.' **1938** Rawlings *Yearling* 103 **nFL**, That un there's a buck big enough to ride. **1941** [see **one C1**]. **1942** Hall *Smoky Mt. Speech* 40 **eTN, wNC**, An occasional tendency to lower and retract [ʌ] to [ɔ] has been observed in *hungry* ['hɔŋgrɪ], *one* [wɔːən], *until* [ɔn'tɪl]. **1942** Faulkner *Go Down* 324 **MS**, Genl Cawmpson guv me this un'. **1942** McAtee *Dial. Grant Co. IN* 7 (as of 1890s), Such pronouns as . . thatn, thisn, were the rule. **1965–70** *DARE* (Qu. B3) Infs **MS**55, **NC**31, Hot un; (Qu. R15b) Inf **MS**63, Big un; (Qu. X50), Inf **NC**68, Fat un; (Qu. Y14a) Inf **CT**36, Poked him a good un; (Qu. Z12) Infs **AR**55, **GA**28, 82, **KY**44, **NC**86, 88, **VA**109, Young un; (Qu. CC8) Inf **VA**5, Bad un; **MI**67, Old un. **1967** *Mt. Life* 43.1.16 **sAppalachians**, He didn't have sense a nough abaout meetin haouses to know whichens had shet daown and whichens 'uz still open. **1984** Burns *Cold Sassy* 28 **nGA** (as of 1906), "We never knowed which'n he meant," Granny said. . . I knew which'n. It was Granny.

B As pron.

Ellip for *one or the other.* **chiefly Sth, S Midl**

1845 Thompson *Pineville* 30 **cGA**, I paid my half dollar to come in here; and I'm gwine to have a ride or a fight, one. **1895** *DN* 1.373 **seKY, eTN, wNC**, One seems to be superfluous or else 'or the other' is omitted. "I will see you or send word, one." **1902** *DN* 2.240 **sIL**. **1905** *DN* 3.89 **nwAR**. **1909** *DN* 3.354 **eAL, wGA**. **1913** in 1983 Truman *Dear Bess* 114 **MO**, I am positively confident mine will look very scared or very mulish, one. **1915** *DN* 4.186 **swVA**. **1917** *DN* 4.415 **wNC**. **1930** *DN* 6.84 **cSC**. **1934** *AmSp* 9.152 **ceFL**. **c1937** in 1976 *Weevils in the Wheat* 125 **VA** [Black], He jes' had to hide or die one, 'cause his marster was gonna kill him. **1939** *Hall Coll.* **wNC, eTN**, "He was in Tennessee or Kentucky, one." . . 'One' in such an instance is uttered with a peculiar emphasis, and is usually somewhat drawled with a down glide. A high-frequency expression. **1944** *PADS* 2.11 **AL, NC, VA, SC**. **1946** *PADS* 6.22 **ceNC**. **1952** Brown *NC Folkl.* 1.572, "Jane or Mary one went to see her."—Polk county. **1954** *Harder Coll.* **cwTN**, I got to shit or git off the pot, one. **1955** Roberts *S. from Hell-fer-Sartin* 123 **seKY**, I'm goin' to throw you right out that winder if you don't hush, or holler out loud one. **1958** *PADS* 29.13 **TN**, I got to mow or plow, one. **1967–69** *DARE* FW Addit **seTX**, I'll either quit or be fired, one; **ceNC**, Hit a car or wire, one; **AL**, I'm going to the movies or to bed, one; **NC**, "He was stabbed or shot, one." This method of expressing two possibilities is very common. **1970** *DARE* Tape **VA**38, Now most everybody cure [tobacco] by oil or gas one, but the old way was cure by wood. **1984** Burns *Cold Sassy* 6 **nGA** (as of 1906), I got to hire me a colored woman or get married, one. **1987** Kytle *Voices* 10 **NC**, I reckon he has bad dreams or wants attention, one.

C As adv.

1 usu following a pronoun: By oneself; only. **chiefly coastal SC** *among Black (esp Gullah) speakers* Cf *DJE*

1867 Allen *Slave Songs* xxvii **ceSC**, One for alone. "Me one, and God." . . "Gone home one in de dark." **1908** *S. Atl. Qrly.* 7.341 **seSC** [Gullah], One is used to mean *only,* or *alone: "Who's there?"* you call into the darkness. *"Me, one!"* is the quick reply. **1922** Gonzales *Black Border* 316 **sSC, GA coasts** (Gullah glossary), One—only; "me one," I only. **1941** Writers' Program SC *Folk Tales* 78 [Black], He wife bin dere ter dat hant house—she wan. **1950** *PADS* 14.50 **ceSC**, One: adj. Alone, only. "Nobody here but me one." Negro usage of Charleston. **1986** Pederson *LAGS Concordance,* 1 inf, **nwMS**, Because if I cook, you see, me one, I don't eat much nohow—cook for myself alone. [Inf white]

2 For each; singly. **HI**

1972 Carr *Da Kine Talk* 142 **HI,** *One* vs. *a, each.* . . "Da candy bah cos' fi' cent one." 'The candy bars cost five cents each.'

D As indef art.

A. [See quot 1972] Cf *DBE, DJE*

1888 Jones *Negro Myths* 65 **GA coast** [Gullah], Dem haffer go tru one tick swamp. **1908** *S. Atl. Qrly.* 7.342 **seSC** [Gullah], Dem [=they] kill one cow an' git de mores' pa't 'im libbah [=largest part of its liver] fuh brile [=to broil]. **1972** Carr *Da Kine Talk* 142 **HI,** *One* vs. *a, each*—"I thirsty, an' I drink jus' like one horse." . . The use of *one* for *a*, very common in Hawaii, has parallels in all areas of pidgin English. **1981** *Pidgin To Da Max* np **HI,** *One* "A." Haole: "Do you have a car?" Pidgin: "You get one cah?" **1991** Saiki *From the Lanai* 4 **HI,** If the morning was rainy, cloudy or windy, I took Mrs. Finch her breakfast tray in bed like one queen. I mean it. *Ibid* 33, Folks say it's in the blood, like one disease.

one-a-baby phr

In childrens' games: used as a counting-out rhyme.

1967 *DARE* (Qu. EE33, . . *Outdoor games . . that children play*) Inf **NY**30, One a baby, two a baby, three a baby, four, five a baby, six a baby, seven and no more.

one a cat See **one old cat 1, 2**

one-a-cat-out See **one-cat-out**

one-and-over n

1 See quot. Cf **anti-over**

1966 *DARE* (Qu. EE22, . . *The game in which they throw a ball over a building . . to a player on the other side*) Inf **MS**71, One-and-over.

2 A children's game of leapfrog.

1953 Brewster *Amer. Nonsinging Games* 106 **IL,** *One and Over.* . . One of the players bends over, with his hands on his knees. The rest in turn jump over him, placing their hands on his back or shoulders as they go over. After each has jumped, the player who is "down" moves up to where the leader jumped. Then the latter must decide whether the next jump is to be a "one" (a single leap from the rising-place) or a "one and over" (a hop from the rising-place and then a jump). **1966** *DARE* (Qu. EE33, . . *Outdoor games . . that children play*) Inf **MS**71, One-and-over—leapfrog.

one-base n

1968–70 *DARE* (Qu. EE11, *Bat-and-ball games for just a few players [when there aren't enough for a regular game]*) Inf **LA**37, One-base—the base is right in back of the pitcher; **MO**23, One-base.

one-berry n

1 also *one-berry leaf*: A **partridgeberry** (here: *Mitchella repens*).

1873 in 1976 Miller *Shaker Herbs* 239, Squaw Vine—*Mitchella repens* . . Partridge Berry . . One Berry. **1876** Hobbs *Bot. Hdbk.* 84, One berry leaves, Squaw vine, *Mitchella repens.* **1896** *Jrl. Amer. Folkl.* 9.190 **cNY,** *Mitchella repens* . . one berry. **1911** Henkel *Amer. Med. Leaves* 34, Squaw Vine.—*Mitchella repens* . . Other common names.—Checkerberry . . oneberry . . squaw-plum. **1971** Krochmal *Appalachia Med. Plants* 176, *Mitchella repens* . . Partridgeberry . . one berry . . winter clover.

2 A **hackberry** (here: *Celtis occidentalis*).

1897 Sudworth *Arborescent Flora* 185 **RI,** *Celtis occidentalis* . . Hackberry. . . One Berry. **1960** Vines *Trees SW* 206, Common Hackberry—*Celtis occidentalis.* . . Vernacular names are Nettle-tree . . and One-berry.

3 A **jack-in-the-pulpit 1** (here: *Arisaema triphyllum*).

1877 Bartlett *Americanisms* 319 **CT,** *Jack-in-the-Pulpit. (Arisæma triphyllum).* . . In Connecticut, it is called *One-berry.*

4 A **wintergreen** (here: *Gaultheria procumbens*).

1892 *Jrl. Amer. Folkl.* 5.100, *Gaultheria procumbens,* one-berry.

one-berry leaf See **one berry 1**

one-brain n

1916 *DN* 4.278 **NE,** One-brain. . . Term of disparagement. "That fellow is a one-brain." . . Also, a *single-thought.* . . Same meaning and usage.

one-cat-out n Also *one-a-cat-out, one-cat-up* Cf **one-old-cat 1**

1967–70 *DARE* (Qu. EE11, *Bat-and-ball games for just a few players [when there aren't enough for a regular game]*) Infs **IL**116, 122, **NY**162, **VA**69, One-cat-out; **OH**25, One-cat-up. **1994** *DARE* File

cnOH (as of 1921), *One-a-cat-out*—Name of a reduced form of baseball played in Akron. "Let's play one-a-cat-out."

‡**one-day clothes** n pl

1969 *DARE* (Qu. W39, *Joking ways of referring to a person's best clothes*) Inf **GA**77, One-day clothes—old-fashioned.

one-er-scrub n Cf **one old cat 1**

A baseball game in which the team at bat has only two players; see quot.

1946 *Greenville Advocate* (AL) 26 Sept [7]/1, Never having heard of "four-hole cat" . . , we were impressed with the similarity to the game played in Greenville under the title: "One-er-Scrub." (It might have been "One or Scrub"—we never knew which it was when we played the game, and still don't.) . . Only two boys constituted the ever-changing "in" team. The boy who got his hands on the bat first was "One-er-Scrub." The other was "Other." [The "out" team had a full complement of players.] . . If the batted ball was not caught, the runner advanced just as far as he could on the hit. Then "Other" came to the bat. It was up to him to bring his partner in home. . . If there were too few players for "One-er-Scrub," a game of "One-eyed Cat" was resorted to.

one-eye aggie n Also *one-eyed grubbing* (or *sprouting*) *hoe* =**eye hoe.**

1935 *Yale Rev.* new ser 25.176 **KY,** Dig all the loose roots out with one-eyed sproutin' hoes. **1937** *Natl. Geogr. Mag.* Mar 271 **MS,** Shouldering their "one-eye aggies," or hoes, convicts heed the call to pork, pone, and greens. **1938** Stuart *Dark Hills* 332 **eKY,** Get back in the old saw-briars and sassafras sprouts with a big one-eyed grubbing hoe!

one-eyed cat n

1 also *one-eyed catch, one-eye cat*: =**one-old-cat 1. chiefly S Midl, TX** See Map

1946 *Greenville Advocate* (AL) 26 Sept [7]/3, A game of "One-eyed Cat" was resorted to. As few as three could play this game, and as many as five. There were only two bases. . . The batter played the rest of the group. To remain "in" he had to hit a homerun every time. **1947** Lomax *Advent. Ballad Hunter* 14 **TX** (as of c1880), We children never played games on Sunday, not even . . one-eyed cat. **1957** *Sat. Eve. Post Letters* **NC,** I can look back and recall . . one-eyed cat and work up as baseball games. *Ibid* **cnTN,** Our three man ball game was "one eyed cat." **1965–70** *DARE* (Qu. EE11, *Bat-and-ball games for just a few players [when there aren't enough for a regular game]*) 14 Infs, **chiefly S Midl, TX,** One-eyed cat; **MS**8, One-eyed catch; (Qu. EE33, . . *Outdoor games . . that children play*) Inf **AR**47, One-eyed cat—form of catball; with a baseball, three bases. **1966–69** *DARE* Tape **AL**4, Then that one-eyed cat where there'd be one batter in the middle; **TN**37, You had a batter and a pitcher, and the . . pitcher pitched the ball to the batter, and the batter would score by running to first base and back to home plate. And if he didn't get back and was put out, the other boy came to bat. You only had one out and the game was called one-eyed cat. **1967** *DARE* FW Addit **swIN,** One-eye cat—a type of children's game. **1969** O'Connor *Horse & Buggy West* 83 **AZ,** Baseball games . . were generally of the informal variety, such as One-Eyed Cat, with only a pitcher, a catcher, and a first baseman, and where the batter could continue to bat as long as he could hit the ball far enough . . [to] make it to first base and back to home plate before he was thrown out.

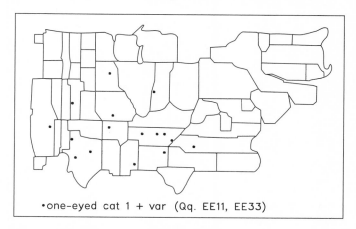

•one-eyed cat 1 + var (Qq. EE11, EE33)

2 A marble game: see quot. Cf *DS* EE7

1957 *Sat. Eve. Post Letters* **OK,** The same children had a marble game called one-eyed-cat. Each player put a stipulated number of marbles in an eye-shaped ring and the one who got most out was winner.

one-eyed catch See **one-eyed cat 1**

one-eyed gravy n

Perh =**red-eye gravy.**

1953 Brewer *Word Brazos* 16 **eTX** [Black], So when his pappy call 'im to come to breakfast, he comes on in an' staa't to soppin' his biscuits in his 'lasses an' one-eyed gravy.

one-eyed grubbing hoe See **one-eye aggie**

‡**one-eyed mabel** n *joc* [Cf *nabel* at **navel**]

1969 *DARE* (Qu. X34, . . *Names and nicknames for the navel*) Inf **GA77**, One-eyed mabel.

one-eyed monster n

1965–70 *DARE* (Qu. FF27, *Joking names and nicknames for television*) 26 Infs, **scattered**, One-eyed monster.

one-eyed sprouting hoe See **one-eye aggie**

one-eyed Susan n

A fried egg.

1950 *WELS* (*Other ways of cooking eggs*) 1 Inf, **ceWI**, Fried, sunny side up, one-eyed Susans.

one-finger poi n [See quot 1972] **HI**

Poi that is thick enough to be dipped up and eaten with one finger; similarly nouns *two-finger poi, three-finger poi* progressively thinner mixtures.

1940 Bazore *Hawaiian Foods* xxi, I have learned to manage "one finger," "two finger," and even "three finger" poi. One finger poi is so thick that enough for a mouthful clings to the forefinger when it is expertly twirled in the mass. **1955** Day *HI People* 297, Taro. . . was then peeled, pounded with stones into a thick paste . . and mixed with water to the proper stiffness—"one-finger poi" is thicker than "three-finger poi." **1972** Carr *Da Kine Talk* 116 **HI**, One-finger poi (English + Hawaiian). *Poi* that is thick enough to be scooped up with one finger from the calabash. *Poi*, the Hawaiian staff of life, is made from cooked taro corms, pounded and thinned with water. For *two-finger poi*, a thinner mixture, two fingers are needed to transport it from the calabash to the mouth.

one-foot-off-the-gutter n **CA**

A children's running game; see quots.

1967–69 *DARE* (Qu. EE19) Inf **CA15**, One-foot-off-the-gutter—boys' game, advance against person who has one foot off gutter on other side; (Qu. EE33, . . *Outdoor games . . that children play*) Inf **CA166**, One-foot-off-the-gutter. **1968** *DARE* Tape **CA72**, It was usually in the early evening that we played one-foot-off-the-gutter, all the boys and girls together. We'd form two teams and then race from one side of the sidewalk to sidewalk across the street and try not to be caught. **1975** Ferretti *Gt. Amer. Book Sidewalk Games* 207, A San Francisco innovation called *One Foot off the Gutter* . . begins with the player designated "It" standing on one sidewalk and all other players standing across the street. . . "It" . . has to race across the street and break through the other players' linked arms anywhere he can. If he fails he goes back and tries again. If he is successful, all members of the human chain have to free themselves quickly and race across to the other sidewalk. . . [Whoever finishes] last becomes "It".

one-gallus(ed) adj Also sp *one-gallows* [**gallus** n 1] **Sth, S Midl** *usu derog*

Of people: rustic, poor, low-class; hence, typical of such people.

1882 *Congressional Record* 19 July 6194 **KY**, I can see in my mind's eye . . those one-gallows, straw-hatted fellows flying from the revenue officials to their mountain fastnesses. **1892** *DN* 1.230 **KY**, "A one-gallus'd fellow" is a worthless man. **1899** (1912) Green *VA Folk-Speech* 190, "He belongs to the one gallus crowd," speaking of an "ornary person." **1904** *DN* 2.418 **nwAR**, You one-gallused hill billies, behave yourselves. **1905** *DN* 3.89 **nwAR**, One gallussed feller. . . A worthless poor man. Common. **1909** *DN* 3.354 **eAL, wGA**, One-gallused. . . Wearing only one "gallus" or suspender strap. Used of primitive or simple rustics. "The little freckled, barefooted one-gallused boys of the country school house will make the best citizens of the state." **1933** Williamson *Woods Colt* 168 **Ozarks**, What the hell air you Claggetts, anyhow, nothin' but a one-gallus family, an' you never will be nothin' else. **1934** *Sun* (Baltimore MD) 1 May 8/2 (*Hench Coll.*) **VA**, These one-gallus sportsmen outnumber their more fortunate friends at least

three to one throughout the South. **1950** *PADS* 14.50 **SC**, One-gallus. . . Having only *one gallus*, hence not fastidious in dress; applied only to country people, and connoting closely the expression "grass roots." Not ordinarily used in derision. Often with political implications: "the one-gallus crowd," "the one gallus vote." **1953** Randolph–Wilson *Down in Holler* 268 **Ozarks**, Them Tylers is a one-gallus family, an' always was. **1957** Faulkner *Town* 278 **MS**, Every other one-galluscd share-cropper in the county whose sole cash value was the October or November sale of the single bale of cotton which was his tithe. **c1960** *Wilson Coll.* **csKY**, One-gallus. . . Referring to a type of person who wore just one "gallus" through poverty or just to be a durned fool; mostly used to refer to the philosophy of such a feller. **1966** *DARE* (Qu. CC10, . . *An unprofessional, part-time lay preacher*) Inf **AL4**, One-gallus preacher.

one hole cat See **one old cat 1**

one-holer See **-holer**

one-hop n

1970 *DARE* (Qu. EE11, *Bat-and-ball games for just a few players [when there aren't enough for a regular game]*) Inf **GA90**, One-hop.

one-horse adj

1 Of a farm, farmer, or crop: requiring only one work animal. **esp S Midl** Cf **four-horse**

1903 *DN* 2.323 **seMO**, One-horse crop. . . A small crop. 'I am tending only a one-horse crop this summer.' It is not uncommon for a poor man to do all his plowing with one horse or mule. He is sometimes called (and often calls himself) a 'one-horse farmer.' **1907** *DN* 3.234 **nwAR**, One-horse farmer. . . A poor farmer who does all his plowing with one horse or mule. Hence, a one-horse crop is a small crop. [**1958** Babcock *I Don't Want* 82 **eSC**, Po' Chance was a back province, a checkerboard of cypress bays and small fields which had been "one-hoss"-farmed for uncounted years.] **1966** *DARE* Tape **GA4**, People . . run three-horse farm, four-horse farm, I run one farm [=one-horse farm]. . . That's just enough for one mule can tend. **1969** *State* (Raleigh, N.C.) 15 Mar 28/3 (*Mathews Coll.*), So you see what could be called a "One Horse" farming [sic] is fastly disappearing from this hilly country. *Ibid* 1 Aug 17/1 (*Mathews Coll.*), But the smaller one hoss farmer had a much humbler building.

2 Small and insignificant; second-rate, inferior.

1853 *Oregonian* (Portland OR) 19 Nov 2/1 (*DA*), These *one-horse* meetings are got up by men whose capital consists in *brass*. **1862** in 1962 Truxall *Respects To All* 69 **PA**, The towns down here are one horse concerns every one of them. **1867** Lowell *Biglow* 20 '**Upcountry**' **MA**, A one-hoss, starn-wheel chaplin. **1884** *Anglia* 7.278 **Sth, S Midl** [Black], *Er one-horse scrub* = a worthless creature. **1899** (1912) Green *VA Folk-Speech* 306, One-horse. . . Petty; on a small scale; of limited capacity or resources; inferior. **1899** (1977) Norris *McTeague* 82 **San Francisco CA**, I'm sorry I ever lowered myself to keep company with such dirt. Ah, one-horse dentist! Ah, ten-cent zinc-plugger—hoodlum—mucker! **1909** *DN* 3.354 **eAL, wGA**, One-horse. . . Second or third rate, small, insignificant. **1910** *DN* 3.446 **cwNY**, One horse. . . Small and insignificant. **1913** Wharton *Custom of Country* 486 **NY**, They certainly do things with style over here—but it's kinder one-horse after New York. **1965–70** *DARE* (Qu. C33, . . *Joking names . . for an out-of-the-way place, or a very small or unimportant place*) 37 Infs, **scattered**, One-horse (town); (Qu. C34, *Nicknames for nearby settlements, villages, or districts*) Infs **ND3, OH66**, One-horse town; (Qu. N37, *Joking names for a branch railroad that is not very important or gives poor service*) Infs **IL126, NJ54, TX74, 95, VA13**, One-horse (railroad, stop, train); **TX86**, One-horseshoe train; (Qu. BB53a, . . *Joking names . . for a doctor*) Inf **MO2**, One-horse doc; (Qu. BB53b, . . *A doctor who is not very capable or doesn't have a very good reputation*) Infs **IN32, 61**, One-horse doctor; (Qu. CC10, . . *An unprofessional, part-time lay preacher*) Infs **CA158, IL15, 143, IN32, KY41, OH74, VA13, WV3**, One-horse (preacher); (Qu. HH44, *Joking or uncomplimentary names for lawyers*) Infs **CA158, KY42, 65**, One-horse lawyer. **1985** Ladwig *How to Talk Dirty* 4 **Ozarks**, It's as useless as two buggies in a one-horse town.

one hundred See **hundred B2b**

one-inner See **inners** n pl²

one-knocker See **knocker 7c**

one-man baseball n

See quots.

1967 *DARE* (Qu. EE11, *Bat-and-ball games for just a few players [when there aren't enough for a regular game]*) Inf **SC40**, One-man baseball. **1967** *DARE* Tape **SC**40A, One-man baseball. Each man had one out. There was one man in the field—one pitcher—and one batter. . . If I were playing you. . . If it were my turn to bat, you would pitch to me . . and I'd hit the ball. You'd go get it. If you could catch me before I went to the base and got back to the home base, I was out and then it was your turn to bat.

one-man-in-town n Cf *round-town*, *town ball*

1983 *MJLF* 9.1.49 **ceKY** (as of 1956), *One man in town* . . a ball game, in which only one man is at bat at one time, the rest of the players being in the field.

one-man match n Cf *DS* F46

1950 *PADS* 14.50 **SC**, *One-man match.* . . Safety match. It strikes only on its own box. . . Negro, coastal area.

one-man-out n

The children's game of **hide-and-seek A.**

1967 *DARE* (Qu. EE13a, *Games in which every player hides except one, and that one must try to find the others*) Inf **IA**3, One-man-out.

one-man-stand-the-gang n

1901 *DN* 2.144 **cwNY**, *One man stand the gang.* . . Name of a game. Buffalo, N.Y.

one more adj phr **sAppalachians**

Being a remarkable or outstanding example of a (person or thing).

1913 Kephart *Highlanders* 286 **sAppalachians**, The mountaineers have some queer ways of intensifying expression. . . "We had one more *time*" means a rousing good time. **1939** *Hall Coll.* **wNC**, *One more time.* . . A hard time, usually said with a humorous inflection; a wonderful time. Common. "We had one more time with that devilish infernal thing (a cub bear), and I pulled my shoe strings out and tied it." *Ibid*, *One more time.* . . A wonderful time. "We had one more time in this world a-bear-huntin'." **c1940** *Ibid* **wNC, eTN**, "Ain't that one more sight!" Isn't that a remarkable sight? **1967** *Ibid* **eTN**, *One more sight.* . . said of a humorous or a comic character. "John, he was one more sight, he was." **1986** Wear *Sugarlands* 68 **eTN**, December 15th Jeanette was born. I had worked so hard my muscles would not give, so I had one more time having her.

one o cat See *one old cat* **1, 2**

one o'clock n

1 =dandelion **1.**

1900 Lyons *Plant Names* 365, T[araxacum] Taraxacum . . One-o'clock. **1904** Henkel *Weeds Used in Med.* 13, Dandelion—Taraxacum taraxacum . . *Taraxacum officinale* . . Blow-ball . . Irish daisy . . one o'clock. **1930** Sievers *Amer. Med. Plants* 26, Dandelion—*Leontodon taraxacum* . . *Taraxacum officinale* . . Blowball . . horse gowan . . one-o'clock.

2 See quot. Cf **one-eyed cat 1, one old cat 1**

1968 *DARE* (Qu. EE11, *Bat-and-ball games for just a few players [when there aren't enough for a regular game]*) Inf **NJ**48, One o'clock.

one o'clock, it's phr Also *it's one o'clock at the button factory, it's two* (or *three*) *o'clock (at the button factory);* for addit varr see quots

Used to indicate that a man's trouser fly is open.

1916 *DN* 4.327 **KS, PA, neOH, MA, MI**, *One o'clock.* Secret code word, warning that a fly is unbuttoned. Also *two o'clock* should two buttons be unbuttoned. **1927** *AmSp* 2.361 **cwWV**, *One o'clock* . . warning that the fly of the trousers is unbuttoned. "Excuse me; it is one o'clock." **1942** McAtee *Dial. Grant Co. IN* 46 (as of 1890s), *O'clock.* . . "It's one _____, two _____", etc., were euphemisms to call attention to unfastened buttons of a pants fly. **1944** *PADS* 2.20 **Sth**, *One o'clock* (etc.): A euphemistic hint that one's trousers are unbuttoned one (etc.) button(s). "Hit's one o'clock, Rafe." **1950** *WELS* (*Expressions or sly words of warning for: A trouser fly open*) 9 Infs, **WI**, (It's) one o'clock; 7 Infs, **WI**, (It's) one o'clock at the button factory. **c1960** *Wilson Coll.* **csKY**, *One o'clock:* signal to a boy that one button of his pants is undone. **1965–70** *DARE* (Qu. W24c, *. . To warn a man that his trouser-fly is open*) 24 Infs, **scattered**, (It's) one o'clock; **NY**232, **OK**7, It's one o'clock or two o'clock; **GA**1, It's one o'clock or two o'clock—depending on which button is open; **CA**15, One o'clock—according to number of buttons; **CA**208, One o'clock—two o'clock if two buttons are open, etc.; **MA**64, When they had buttons, we used to say it was one or two o'clock; **RI**1, One or two o'clock to designate the

number of buttons; **CA**165, **KY**71, **ME**6, **MA**69, (It's) two o'clock; **GA**59, It's three o'clock—or two o'clock, depending on how many buttons; **CA**2, It's four o'clock—or two o'clock; **PA**2, Papa, it's six o'clock—could be two, three, etc o'clock; 10 Infs, **scattered**, One o'clock at the button factory; **AR**33, ? o'clock at the button factory; **AR**37, One, two, three o'clock at the button factory; **OH**16, One o'clock at the button factory—two o'clock is two of 'em; **TX**1, One o'clock at the button factory—however many buttons are showing; **TX**40, One o'clock at the button factory—or two, or three—however many buttons are showing; **WI**8, One o'clock at the button shop; **IL**39, One o'clock at the zipper factory; **TX**28, One o'clock in the button factory; **MO**21, It's one o'clock, close up; **MN**42, One o'clock in Watertown; **WA**33, It's one o'clock in Petersburg.

one of these odd-come-shorts See **odd-come-short 1**

one old cat n

1 also *one a cat, ~ hole cat, ~ o cat, old cat;* for addit varr see quots: A baseball game with few players in which the batter runs to a single base and back to home. **chiefly Nth, N Midl, West** See Map Cf **cat** n **3c, five old cat, four-cornered cat, four old cat, long ball, one-er-scrub, one-eyed cat 1, three-cornered cat, three old cat, two-cornered cat, two old cat**

1850 *Knickerbocker* 35.84 **NY**, [We] never indulged in a game of chance of any sort in the world, save the 'bassball,' 'one' and 'two-hole-cat,' and 'barn-ball' of our boyhood. **1860** *Harper's New Mth. Mag.* 21.195 **seNY**, Mrs. Tyler Todd caught the toss, like a skillful player at "one old cat," on the edge of her . . bonnet. **1883** Newell *Games & Songs* 185, We need only mention the game of "Old Cat," in which there are two goals—the striker's and the pitcher's—and the run is made from the former to the latter and return. The game is then named from the number of batters, "One Old Cat," or "Two Old Cat." **1891** *Jrl. Amer. Folkl.* 4.231 **Brooklyn NYC**, One o' cat. **1907** *DN* 3.195 **seNH**, *Old cat.* . . A simple game of ball with two, three, or four players; hence called *two old cat, three old cat,* and *four old cat* respectively. **1908** *DN* 3.297 **eAL, wGA**, *Cat, one (two, or three) ole.* . . A ball game in which the batters stand at one, (two, or three) points or holes. **1910** *DN* 3.446 **cwNY**, *Old cat.* . . A simple game of ball, played usually by either three or four boys. If there is one batter (with a pitcher and a catcher), it is called *one old cat.* If there are four players, two of them batters, the batters exchanging bases when one hits the ball, the game is called *two old cat.* **1912** *DN* 3.568 **cNY**, *One-old-cat.* . . Game of ball played by three boys or more using only one base and batting in turn. Called *three-holed* on Long Island and *rounds* in Illinois and Missouri. **1940** *Hench Coll.,* After [he] had described his boyhood game of "holt" [*DARE* Ed: See **hold** n B2], another member of the group said he knew the game as "one hold cat." **1950** *WELS* **WI** (*Bat-and-ball games for a few players [when you don't have enough for a regular game]*) 10 Infs, One o cat; 8 Infs, One old cat; 1 Inf, One old black cat; 1 Inf, Old cat. **1961** Sackett-Koch *KS Folkl.* 211, Before baseball was introduced, one-hole cat was very popular; T.W. Wells of Hays, who was born in Russell County in 1877, recalls playing one-hole cat as a boy. **1965–70** *DARE* (Qu. EE11) 78 Infs, **chiefly Nth, N Midl, West**, One old cat; 14 Infs, **esp Nth, N Midl, West**, One a cat; 11 Infs, **esp Nth, N Midl, West**, One o cat; **IN**69, **PA**234, **WA**9, 13, Old cat; **CA**107, One o cat [FW sugg "one old cat" but Inf changed his response to this]; **SC**32, One o cat—one base, run from home to base without being put out; **CA**20, One old cat—a keep-away with three players; **CA**51, One old

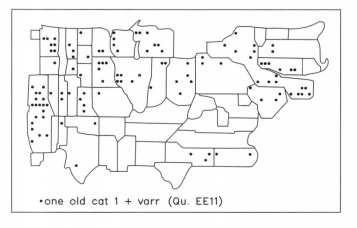

•one old cat 1 + varr (Qu. EE11)

cat—ran to one base only; **CO**28, One old cat—a pitcher, catcher, ran to first base and back; **NY**52, One old cat—could be played with three players, he had to go to the single base and return before the pitcher could return the ball to the catcher; **MI**24, One a cat knocks; **NM**9, One old cat and my bat; **MN**37, One old catch. [Of all Infs responding to the question, 63% were old; of those giving these resps, 79% were old.]

2 also *one a cat, one o cat:* =**cat** n **3a.** **seNY** Cf **cricket** n²,
nine o cat

1968–69 *DARE* (Qu. EE10, *A game in which a short stick lying on the ground is flipped into the air and then hit with a longer stick*) Infs **NY**37, 60, One a cat; **NY**36, 51, One o cat; **NY**209, One old cat or shinny—puck was pointed on each end like a peggy and hit on one end and then swatted when in the air.

3 See **old cat 1, 2.**

one-one adv, adj, n [Redup] *among Gullah speakers* Cf *DBE*, *DJE*

1 as adv; also *oney-oney:* One at a time.

1908 *S. Atl. Qrly.* 7.342 **seSC** [Gullah], Solitary swallows which come in advance of the spring flights are described as coming *oney-oney*. . . Where fish are biting slowly, yet steadily, they are said to bite *one-one.*

2 as adj: See quot.

1950 *PADS* 14.50 **SC**, One-one. . . Normal; as usual. "How you stan' today?" "Kinda one-one." Negro usage.

3 as noun; also *old one-one:* =**redwing blackbird.**

1908 *S. Atl. Qrly.* 7.342 **seSC** [Gullah], *The swamp black-bird,* from his solitary habit during certain seasons of the year, is called by the negroes *One-one.* **1950** *PADS* 14.49 **SC**, *Old one-one:* . . The eastern red-winged blackbird. So called from the habit of the two sexes to gather into separate flocks in the fall and winter seasons.

one-out n Cf **one old cat 1**

1969 *DARE* (Qu. EE11, *Bat-and-ball games for just a few players [when there aren't enough for a regular game]*) Inf **IN**73, One-out.

one poster n

See quot 1936.

1936 *AmSp* 11.316 **Ozarks**, *One-poster*. . . A bed built into the corner of a cabin, in such a fashion that only one post is necessary. **1954** *Harder Coll.* **cwTN**, *One-poster*. . . Used "way back yonder." **1975** McDonough *Garden Sass* 46 **AR**, He made two holes in the wall for every bed he needed. Side rails were put into these holes and legs were placed at the other end, with the wall of the cabin becoming the headboard of the bed. Ropes were strung between the rails to hold the cornshuck ticks and feather beds. When this same type of bed was built into a corner it was called a "one-poster" since only one leg was needed.

oner n Usu |ˈwʌnə(r)|; see also quot 1966–70 [*OED* 1862 →]
A hard blow; the result of such a blow.

1942 Berrey–Van den Bark *Amer. Slang* 702.2, *Hard blow*. . . Oner. **1950** *WELS* (*A very hard blow:* "You should have seen Bill go down! Joe really hit him a _____.") 1 Inf, **ceWI**, Oner. **1966–70** *DARE* (Qu. X20, . . *A black eye*) Inf **NC**88, Shiner, oner [ˈwʌnə]; (Qu. Y11) Inf **CT**23 [ˈwanɚ]—crossword puzzle word; **MI**46, [ˈwʌnɚ]—I think I got that in a crossword puzzler; **MS**23, [ˈwʌnɚ]; **SC**46, [ˈonə]—newer; **TN**12, [ˈonɚ].

onery See **ornery**

one-sided adj, adv Also *one-side* **chiefly Sth, S Midl** See Map
Askew, awry; diagonally, crookedly.

1883 (1971) Harris *Nights with Remus* 138 **GA**, De gal w'at git ole Brer Jack 'ull git a natchul pacer, sho'. He move mo' one-sideder dan ole Zip Coon, w'ich he rack up de branch all night long wid he nose p'int lak he gwine 'cross. **1947** *True* 32.102 **New Orleans LA** [Black], He wore his mouth onesided all the time. . . Evidently he must have had a stroke somewhere through life. **1965–70** *DARE* (Qu. MM13, *The table was nice and straight until he came along and knocked it _____*) Infs **GA**1, 77, **KY**91, **NC**4, 40, **SC**3, 26, **TX**36, One-sided; **SC**9, One-side; (Qu. W23, *When a collar or other clothing works itself up out of place* . . "It's _____."; total Infs questioned, 75) Inf **MS**72, One-sided; (Qu. KK70, *Something that has got out of proper shape:* "That house is all _____.") Infs **KY**33, **LA**37, **NC**88, **NY**14, 24, **TX**35, **VA**46, One-sided; **GA**77 Warped one-sided. [13 of 18 Infs grade school or less educ] **1986** Pederson *LAGS Concordance* (Kitty-corner) 1 inf, **nwLA**, Sitting one-sided to the corner.

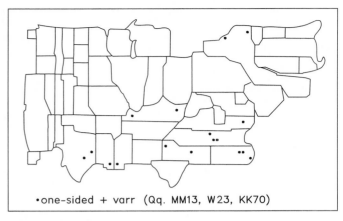

•one-sided + varr (Qq. MM13, W23, KK70)

onesie n Cf **twosie**
In marble play: see quot.

1957 *Sat. Eve. Post Letters* **GA**, "Onesies", also known as "chalkies," were the least expensive marbles, and were rarely played with. They were a grayish white, decorated with fine lines running around the marbles, usually red or blue. Unglazed.

onest See **once**

one step, two step n Cf **hundred steps**
1968 *DARE* (Qu. EE16, *Hiding games that start with a special, elaborate method of sending the players out to hide*) Inf **KS**8, One step, two step.

one-three-one(-one) n
A bat-and-ball game; see quots.

1934 *Hanley Disks* **ceMA**, One-three-one-one was the old game the boys used to play when I went to school. . . Regular baseball—very similar to 'stub one.' **1969** *DARE* (Qu. EE11, *Bat-and-ball games for just a few players [when there aren't enough for a regular game]*) Inf **NY**228, One-three-one.

onetime adv Cf *DJE, DBE*

1 Simultaneously, at the same time.

[**1870** *Appletons' Jrl.* 3.161 [Black], And then you would have one brought after the other, unless accompanied by the request, "all at the same time," or in their own language [=Pidgin English of Liberia], *"go fetch 'em come; both two; one time!"*] **1922** Gonzales *Black Border* 168 **sSC, GA coasts** [Gullah], Uh 'membuh de time w'en uh could'uh box'um en' kick'um alltwo one time.

2 All at once, as a single action.

1967 *DARE* Tape **HI**7, The best way to get up, you just jump up one time. If you get up slowly, you're gonna rock the thing.

one-two n [Prob transf from *one-two (punch)* in boxing: two short blows delivered rapidly with alternate hands]
A hasty departure; quick dispatch.

1942 Berrey–Van den Bark *Amer. Slang* 58.2, *Hasty or unceremonious departure*. . . One-two. *Ibid* 498.1, The one-two, *flight*. **1950** *WELS* (*Expressions . . about getting away from someone whose company you don't like:* . . "I'd like to give him the _____.") 1 Inf, **csWI**, One-two. **1968** *DARE* (Qu. W28, *When a woman is in a hurry and has to sew up a torn place quickly* . . "I'll just _____.") Infs **NY**39, **OH**76, Give it a one-two; (Qu. II5b, *When you don't want to have anything to do with a certain person because you don't like him* . . "I'd certainly like to give him the _____.") Inf **CA**66, One-two, heave-ho.

one-two adj
Of equal ability, on par (with).

1969 *DARE* (Qu. LL32, *Expressions meaning that one man's ability is not nearly as great as another man's:* "John can't [or doesn't, or isn't] _____ Bill.") Inf **CT**29, Isn't one-two with Bill.

one-two-three exclam For varr see quot Cf **all (in) free, home free**

In var phrr, often foll by *for* (or *on*) plus a player's name; used in the children's games of **hide-and-seek** and **I spy** n **1** when the seeker ("it") sees a hider; the call used by hiders who reach base without being caught.

1883 Newell *Games & Songs* 160, *I Spy*. . . The "home" is usually a tree. When the seeker catches sight of any of the players, he (or she) runs to the tree, and touches it thrice, saying, "One, two, three, for _____" (naming the child). On the other hand, if the latter can reach the tree first, he touches it, saying, "One, two, three, for myself." **1953** Brewster *Amer. Nonsinging Games* 42, Hide and Seek. . . One player is counted out to be "It." . . If he finds a player, there is a race between them back to a preannounced spot. If the player who is "It" succeeds in reaching the spot first, he strikes it and says, "One, two, three for _____!" If the other is the first to reach it, he calls, "One, two, three for me!" or simply "Home free!" **1965–70** DARE (Qu. EE15, *When he has caught the first of those that were hiding what does the player who is 'it' call out to the others?*) 26 Infs, **scattered,** One-two-three for (*or* on) [name]; **GA**77, **IL**130, **KY**17, **MN**37, **VA**54, One-two-three you're out; **IA**29, I spy one-two-three on [name]; **NY**172, One-two-three; **KY**41, One-two-three [name]; **VA**30, One-two-three etcetera; **IL**130, One-two-three home free; **NY**84, One-two-three I see you; **MN**12, One-two-three in free; **MI**89, One-two-three no free; **PA**16, One-two-three on Jimmy; **GA**72, One-two-three one-two-three; **IN**16, One-two-three you're it; **OK**42, One-two-three, all that's out come in free; **LA**37, One-two-three, caught, caught; **VA**27, One-two-three, I catched [name]; **MA**8, Somebody's goose, one-two-three; **NY**119, Tap, tap [name] behind the tree, one-two-three.

one-two-three-fifty-o See **fifty-o**

one-two-three for (or on) See **one-two-three**

one-two-three-four cake n [See quot 1847]

A kind of cake; see quot 1847.

1847 (1852) Crowen *Amer. Cookery* 294 **NY,** *One-two-three-four Cake.*—One cup of butter, two cups of sugar, three cups of flour, and four eggs. . . [R]oll the cake to rather more than a quarter of an inch thick; stick each with a fork, and bake fifteen minutes in a quick oven. **1932** (1946) Hibben *Amer. Regional Cookery* 300 **TN,** *1,2,3,4 Cake.* **1939** Wolcott *Yankee Cook Book* 251 **MA,** *1-2-3-4 Cake.* **c1965** Randle *Cookbooks* (Ask Neighbor) 3.48 **OH,** *1-2-3-4 Cake.* **1977** Anderson *Grass Roots Cookbook* 55 **cMD,** At Christmas. . . We'd make one-two-three-four cakes—that's the only kind of cake most people made around here in those days. **1993** Thomas Co. Hist. Soc. (KS) *Prairie Winds* Mar 7 (as of c1890), Mother made a '1, 2, 3, 4 cake'. It was . . white and had the whites of four eggs in it.

one-two-three red light See **red light, green light**

one-while adv

Once, formerly.

1906 Johnson *Highways Missip. Valley* 129 **Ozarks,** Things ain't bringin' as much as they did one while. **1908** Johnson *Highways Pacific Coast* 92 **sCA,** One while we lived in Los Angeles.

oney See **only**

oney-oney See **one-one 1**

onfare See **infare 1**

on halvers See **halvers 2b**

on horse n [By analogy with **off horse 1**]

=near horse.

1967–68 DARE (Qu. K32b, *The horse on the left side in plowing or hauling*) Infs **MI**94, **NJ**4, **VA**33, **WY**4, On horse. **1981** PADS 67.32 **neMN,** Terms for the left horse. . . One [informant] . . says *on horse* in contrast to *off horse*.

onion n Usu |ˈʌnjən, -jn̩|; also **chiefly Sth, S Midl** old-fash |ˈɪŋə(r)n|; infreq |ˈʌnjən, -jn̩| Pronc-spp *engern, inge(r)n, ingun, in(g)yon;* for addit pronc and sp varr see **A** below

A Forms.

1793 in 1794 Drayton *Letters* 58 **Boston MA,** They . . are taught to pronounce the word first in its proper way, and then to contrast it with the mode in which it is miscalled. . . Onions, [are called] Onions, [and not] *Inions.* **1795** Dearborn *Columbian Grammar* 136, *List of Improprieties.* . . Ingyons for Onions. **1815** Humphreys *Yankey in England* 106, *Inyons.* **1837** Sherwood *Gaz. GA* 70, *Provincialisms.* . . *Ingon.* **1843** (1916) Hall *New Purchase* 155 **IN,** And there were "bil'd ingins!"—"fried ingins!"—and "ingins out of this here pie!" **1853** Simms *Sword & Distaff* 237 **SC,** I'll send the peas and inyons (onions) over to her. **1867** Harris *Sut Lovingood Yarns* 26 **TN,** Thar wer dad's bald hed fur all the yeath like a peeled inyin. *Ibid* 164, More disagreabil than

whisky an' inyuns. **1884** *Anglia* 7.273 **Sth, S Midl** [Black], *To weed yo' inguns (onions)* = to be industrious. **c1885** in 1981 Woodward *Mary Chesnut's Civil War* 717 **SC** (as of 1865) [Black], I never did eat raw ingins, and I won't begin now. **1887** Eggleston *Graysons* 134 **sIL,** The only real luxuries affected were onions and watermelons—"ing-uns and watermillions," in Broad Run phrase. **1888** Stockton *Dusantes* 120 **PA,** We'll plant inyans for ye. **1899** (1912) Green *VA Folk-Speech* 240, *Ingun.* **1906** DN 3.142 **nwAR,** *Ingern.* . . Used facetiously. **1908** DN 3.323 **eAL, wGA,** *Ingun.* . . *Ingun-set.* **1911** DN 3.538 **eKY,** *Engern.* **1912** DN 3.593 **wIN,** Yingin. **1915** DN 4.184 **swVA,** *Ingern,* [ɪŋərn]. **1923** DN 5.211 **swMO,** *Ingern.* **1929** Sale *Tree Named John* 89 **MS,** De ingon gits hit's strengt' f'um de ye'th. **1934** AmSp 9.213 **Sth,** *Onion* (vulgar [iːnjən]). **1937** Hall Coll. **eTN,** Engern [ɛŋən]. . . Reported to me by a mountain man as an old pronunc[iation] and I heard one use of it by a 13 yr. old boy who at once corrected himself. **1939** AmSp 14.90 **cTN,** *Engern.* **1941** LANE Map 257 (Onions) [Most proncs are of the type [ˈʌnjən, -jn̩]. 8 infs, **eNEng,** give proncs with [ŋ] rather than [n], and one gives [ˈʌŋɪn]. [ˈɪŋjən] was identified by one inf as an older pronc, and one reported [ˈɪŋjn̩] as the " 'uneducated' pron. used by a local family."] **1944** PADS 2.57 **Ozarks,** Ingern [ˈɪŋəʳn] [PADS Ed: in Va. and N.C.: [ˈɪŋən].] **1950** PADS 14.40 **SC,** Ingans, inguns. . . Onions. Seldom heard in singular form. **1952** Brown *NC Folk.* 1.554, *Ingen* [ˈɪŋən], *ingern* [ˈɪŋəʳn]. **1966–67** DARE (Qu. S21) Inf **GA**7, Wild inions; (QR near Qu. I25) Inf **KY**34, Onions [ɪŋəʳnz]—old fashioned. **1972** Cooper *NC Mt. Folkl.* 89, *Aingern*—onion. **1976** Allen *LAUM* 3.333, Five U[pper] M[idwest] infs. have |ʌŋjn̩|. **1989** Pederson *LAGS Tech. Index* 188 **Gulf Region,** [The great majority of infs gave proncs of the type [ˈʌnjn̩(z)]; varr include 20 of the type [ˈʌnjn̩(z)]; 16 [ˈʌɲ(j)n̩(z)], 15 [ˈʊnjn̩(z)], 4 [ˈɔnjn̩(z)], 3 [ˈhʌnjn̩(z)], 3 [ˈonjn̩(z)], 2 [ˈʌɲn̩(z)], 2 [ˈɪŋə˞nz], and one each of [ˈʌnn̩z, ˈʌnɪjn̩z, ˈʌndjn̩z, ˈɛnjn̩z, ˈɝnjn̩z, ˈʌɲjn̩z].]

B Sense.

Std: a plant of the genus *Allium.* For other names of cultivated spp and varr see **bull onion, bunch ~, butter ~, courting apple, cow onion, cullion, Egyptian onion, evergreen ~, everlasting ~, French lozenger, fresh onion, fruit n 3, gloria 2, grass onion, green ~ 1, 2, ground keeper, hill onion, Irish plum, live-forever 5, multiplying onion, nest ~, onion grass 2, potato ~, pull ~, rareripe, salad onion, scallion, schnittlauch, scullion, seed onion, seven-year ~, shallot (~), shive, silverskin onion, spring ~, summer ~, top ~, tree ~, volunteer ~, walking ~, Welsh ~, winter ~, young ~;** for other names of wild spp see **wild onion** Cf also **bog onion, Chinese ~, false ~, hog ~, Indian ~ 1, 2, odorless ~, oyster ~, prairie ~, wild ~**

onion exclam Cf **cucumber** exclam, **tobacco**

In children's games: see quot.

1957 *Sat. Eve. Post Letters* **wNY,** I can recount a few Western New York games that we fellers used to play . . fifty and sixty years ago. One-two-three and so on to ten. . . Stillwater!! Then you had to stand absolutely still. . . If you got home free, and the "It" went hunting, we could call "Onion-onion" or "Tobacco"—words that obviously meant come or go back!

onion button n Also *button onion*

The bulblet of a **top onion** used for planting.

1967–69 DARE (Qu. I5, . . *Kind of onions that keep coming up without replanting year after year*) Inf **AL**14, Onion buttons; **GA**72, Onion buttons—on top of plant—used to replant. **1986** Pederson *LAGS Concordance,* 1 inf, **cwGA,** Button onion; 2 infs, **neGA, neLA,** Onion buttons.

onion eye n

1968 DARE (Qu. EE6d, *Special marbles*) Inf **KS**16, Onion eyes.

onion fish n

A grenadier of the family Macrouridae, usu *Macrourus berglax.*

1884 Goode *Fisheries U.S.* 1.244, The Grenadiers, or, as the fishermen frequently call them, on account of the size and shape of their eyes, "Onion-fishes," inhabit the deep parts of the ocean. They are particularly abundant in the Western Atlantic. . . The largest species, and the one best known to the fishermen, is *Macrurus rupestris* [=*Macrourus berglax*] called "Rat-tail Fish" as well as "Onion-fish." It is exceedingly abundant on all of our off-shore banks, attaining a length of three feet and a weight of four or five pounds. **1890** *Century Dict.* 4113 **MA,**

Onion-fish. . . The grenadier, *Macrurus rupestris:* so called from a fancied likeness of its eyes to onions.

oniongrass n

1 =melic grass.

1923 in 1925 Jepson *Manual Plants CA* 97, *M[elica] spectabilis*. . Showy Onion Grass. . *M. bella*. . Onion Grass. **1937** U.S. Forest Serv. *Range Plant Hdbk.* G78, Oniongrass, often called purple melic, is a rather tall perennial, with the base of the stalks frequently enlarged or swollen into a bulblike growth. The common name oniongrass, as well as the specific name *bulbosa,* refer to this basal enlargement. *Ibid,* Oniongrass, showy oniongrass, or melic (*M[elica] spectabilis*), and little oniongrass *(M. fugax)* rank as good to excellent forage. **1950** Hitchcock–Chase *Manual Grasses* 195, *Melica subulata*. . Alaska oniongrass. . *Melica geyeri*. . Geyer oniongrass. . *Melica spectabilis*. . Purple oniongrass. . *Melica bulbosa*. . Oniongrass. . *Melica fugax*. . Little oniongrass. **1966–70** *DARE* (Qu. S9, . . *Kinds of grass that are hard to get rid of*) Inf **SC**21, Oniongrass; (Qu. S21, . . *Weeds* . . *that are a trouble in gardens and fields*) Inf **CA**179, Oniongrass. **1970** Correll *Plants TX* 122, *Melica bulbosa*. . Onion grass. **1995** Brako et al. *Scientific & Common Names Plants* 195, Alaska onion grass—*Melica subulata*. . onion grass—*Melica bulbosa.*

2 A chive *(Allium schoenoprasum)* or similar **onion B.** Cf **grass onion**

1948 *WELS Suppl.* **cnWI,** I was told as a child it [=chives] was "onion grass." **1950** *WELS* (*The small plants like onions with hollow green leaves that are cut up in salad*) **WI,** 2 Infs, Onion grass. **1959** Carleton *Index Herb. Plants* 88, *Onion-Grass:* Allium schaenoprasum. **1966–69** *DARE* (Qu. I5, . . *Kind of onions that keep coming up without replanting year after year*) Inf **NJ**54, Scallions [corr to] oniongrass; **NY**65, Oniongrass [FW: Inf can't remember the name she uses—might be grass onions, but she really isn't sure]; (Qu. I7, *The small plants like onions with hollow green leaves that are cut up in a salad*) Infs **SD**5, **VT**13, Oniongrass; **MN**23, Chives; some call oniongrass; **MA**13, Oniongrass is much coarser than chives.

onion orchid n [Prob from its growth habit]

A **tree orchid** (here: *Encyclia tampensis*).

1975 Natl. Audubon Soc. *Corkscrew* 26, *(Epidendrum tampense)*— These small orchids growing in clusters up and down the trunk of a cypress are the commonest and most hardy of Florida's tree orchids. . . They are sometimes called onion orchids.

onion rain See **onion snow**

onion skin n Cf **veil**

A **caul.**

1990 Cavender *Folk Med. Lexicon* 28 **sAppalachians,** Onion skin— amniotic sac.

onion snow n **chiefly PA** Cf **blackberry storm**

A light snowfall late in the spring; similarly *onion rain.*

1930 Shoemaker *1300 Words* 44 **cPA Mts** (as of c1900), *Onion snow*—A late snow in Spring after the onions have been set out. **1937** *AmSp* 12.238 **sePA,** 'Onion snow' is one that falls after the onions are planted. Generally it is a storm of short duration, coming after days of balmy spring weather—'false spring,' about the time these folks begin to plow. **1943** *Sun* (Baltimore MD) 22 Apr 16/5 **MD** (*Hench Coll.*), The prolonged spell of abnormal spring cold weather had at last eventuated in the usual "onion rain" of the srping [sic] season. . . I call it the "onion rain" because that is the general designation truck growers in Maryland have for it, and it is supposed not only to start crops generally to growing but to be especially beneficial to the onion cdop [sic]—though all crops are going to be late this year. **1953** *AmSp* 28.251 **csPA,** Onion snow. . . A late, short-lived snow in the spring, after the onion sets are in. **1963** Teller *Area Code 215* 79 **cePA,** A wind-driven northeaster brings onion snow but I have not put out my onion sets. . . A fine April day follows, forty degrees by the radio . . , clearing and promising warmer. . . Come to think of it, was that the onion snow? Onion snow should follow a spell of mild weather, come after the onions are planted, and run a brief course. This snow met none of the specifications. **1967** *DARE* FW Addit **nwNJ,** Onion snows—last snows of spring, the light overnight snows that melt first thing in the morning, snows come after onions have been planted. Also seems to be common in coal regions of Pennsylvania. **1968–70** *DARE* (Qu. B39, *A very light fall of snow*) Inf **PA**126, Onion snow—in spring, last snow, called onion because the onions were already planted; **PA**156, Onion snow—in spring, the last snow; **PA**242, Onion snow—a snow in the late spring, unexpected, the last snow of

the season. **1982** McCool *Sam McCool's Pittsburghese* 27 **PA,** Onion snow: a light, late spring snow, just enough to cover the ground but not hide the onion shoots.

oniony adj **chiefly NC, VA** See Map and Map Section =**garlicky.**

c1960 *Wilson Coll.* **csKY,** Oniony milk. . . Milk with the flavor of wild onions that have been eaten by the cows; also weedy milk. **1965–70** *DARE* (Qu. K14, *Milk that has a taste from something the cow ate in the pasture* . . *"That milk is _____."*) 17 Infs, **chiefly NC, VA,** Oniony; [62 Infs, **chiefly Sth, S Midl,** Has (*or* tastes like) (wild) onions [and var phrr: see *DS*]].

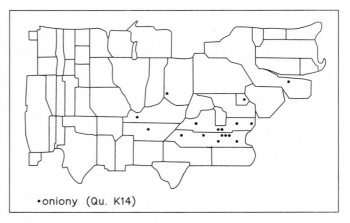

•oniony (Qu. K14)

on it adj phr

1916 *DN* 4.326 **KS,** On it. . . Lustful, esp. at the immediate time of desire.

onliest adj Also sp *onlest, only-est* **chiefly Sth, S Midl** Cf **-est 1b**

Only; also used absol: the only one; spec, a sweetheart.

1890 *DN* 1.70 **LA,** Onliest. . superlative of *only.* Common among the ignorant. **1892** *DN* 1.234 **KY,** Onliest ("that's the onliest one there"). **1893** Shands *MS Speech* 48, Onliest. . . Superlative of *only,* used mostly by negroes. **1906** (1908) Lorimer *Jack Spurlock* 63, The Onliest snuggled up against you and intimated that you were Alpha and Omega, the dearest and the duckiest. **1906** *DN* 3.149 **nwAR,** Onliest. . . Only. "These methods are commonly accepted as the onliest nowadays."— Fayetteville Daily. **1909** *DN* 3.354 **eAL, wGA,** Onliest. . . Only. Facetiously or consciously used, especially as a noun for sweetheart. "She's my onliest." **1923** *DN* 5.216 **swMO,** Onliest. . . Only. "That's the onliest ax I got." **1927** *AmSp* 3.9 **Ozarks,** The peculiar form *onliest* is very common—*thet 'ar is th' onliest axe we-all has got.* **1929** Sale *Tree Named John* 37 **MS,** De onliest way you ever *is* t' git loose is fer me to break dem teethes. **a1930** in 1991 Hughes–Hurston *Mule Bone* 29 **cFL** [Black], He aint de onliest one Ah got mah eye on neither. **1940** in 1976 *Weevils in the Wheat* 336 **VA** [Black], I wuz the onliest man on the place after my master went ter de war. **1942** Faulkner *Go Down* 139 **MS,** You's de onliest least thing whut ever kep up wid me one day. **1950** *PADS* 14.50 **SC,** Onliest. . . Only. **1951** *DE Folkl. Bulletin* 1.7, Onliest (often pronounced without the "l"; used instead of "only"). **c1960** *Wilson Coll.* **csKY,** Onliest. . . The only one, an intensive now rarely used. **1966–70** *DARE* Tape **AL**1, He's the onliest man there that kept . . cheap caskets; **LA**5, The onliest kind commercial fishermen use around here; **VA**75, It's the onliest kind I ever 'member seeing; **VA**73, The onliest thing I'd like to have is . . half-and-half in each school. **1966–68** *DARE* FW Addit **MS,** Onliest one—another way of saying "only one"; primarily used by uneducated people or in a joking manner; **GA**22, Onliest = only, "the onliest ones"—heard in conv; **MD**42, Onliest for "only." **1971** Mitchell *Blow My Blues Away* 70 **nwMS** [Black], I'm the onliest man, me and that colored man over yonder—we the only two people on this place. **1984** Wilder *You All Spoken Here* 197 **Sth,** Only-est, onlest: The only one. **1986** Pederson *LAGS Concordance,* 128 infs, **Gulf Region,** Onliest (auntie, boy, child, name, one, person, place, problem, etc).

on line See **on prep B11**

only adj, adv, prep Pronc-spp *ondly, on(e)y, unly*

A Forms.

1834 [see **B** below]. **1837** Sherwood *Gaz. GA* 72, *Unly,* for only. **1848**

Lowell *Biglow* 145 '**Upcountry**' **MA**, On'y, *only*. **1858** Hammett *Piney Woods Tavern* 40, I ain't the ondly one. *Ibid* 230, There's ony two more [=houses] on your road afore ye get to Houston. **1893** Shands *MS Speech* 48, *Only* ['ɒnlɪ]. Some well-educated people make a point of pronouncing this word with short *o* [ɑnlɪ]. **1894** Riley *Armazindy* 136 **IN**, Slaves wuz on'y ist before / The War wuz—an' *ain't* no more. **1898** Westcott *Harum* 136 **nNY**, He wa'n't the unly man that needed my kind o' work. **1899** (1967) Chesnutt *Wife of Youth* 14 [Black], I dremp three nights runnin' on'y dis las' week dat I foun' him. **1917** *DN* 4.397 **neOH, MA, KY**, On'y. . . Only. **1931** Randolph *Ozarks* 68, He aint nothin' on'y a tie-whackin' sheer-crapper noways. **1932** Farrell *Young Lonigan* 81 **Chicago IL** (as of 1916), It's ony right, and I say, I say, that when yuh do the right thing, ye're happier. **1982** *Barrick Coll.* **csPA**, *Only*—pron. ōny.

B As prep.

Except. [*OED only* B.2 "Now only *dial.*"] **scattered, but esp Sth, S Midl**

1782 in 1906 Franklin *Writings* 8.606 [Black], *Boccarorra* [=buckra] . . make ebery ting workee; only de Hog. He, de hog, no workee. **1834** *Life Andrew Jackson* 57, That they wou'dn't du oney when they cou'dn't help it. *Ibid* 149, He didn't never seem in his proper ilement only when he was ramshacklin 'em are Inglish or Ingins. **1858** Hammett *Piney Woods Tavern* 280 **TX**, Every settler, ondly no 'count whelps, has gone to jine the army. **1913** Johnson *Highways St. Lawrence to VA* 17, He never was to home only a few days at a time. **1931** [see **A** above]. **1936** *Esquire* Sept 32 **KY**, My old woman won't feed me only when I got company. **1941** Ward *Holding Hills* 19 **IA** (as of early 20th cent), But a good crop of corn and oats, everything good only potatoes; they're poor and no good. **1950** *WELS* **WI** (*They don't sell anything there _____ groceries*) 4 Infs, Only; 1 Inf, Only a few; 1 Inf, If there is a pause after the word *there*, the words *just* or *only* would be used rather than *but*. **1953** Brewer *Word Brazos* 41 **eTX** [Black], Dey husban's don' relish dis heah servus, and don' line up wid dey wives only of occasion. **1966** *Arcadian* (Arcadia FL) 31 Mar sec A 4/3, Notice—Not responsible for any debts incurred only by me. **1967–68** *DARE* (Qu. LL31, . . *All but one: "Everybody's here now, _____ John."*) Inf **IL**15, Only; **MO**11, Except, only; **VT**6, But, except, only. **1967–68** *DARE* Tape **AR**55, And they all lived to be fairly old people, only my oldest uncle—he died of pneumonia in the Civil War; **IN**20, [He] wouldn't plant corn only in the dark of the moon. **c1970** Pederson *Dial. Surv. Rural GA*, 1 inf, **seGA**, I don't call it anything only mantel-piece. **1986** Pederson *LAGS Concordance*, 1 inf, **nwFL**, She don't be there only at night; 1 inf, **nwFL**, Hit don't be there, only every four years; 1 inf, **cwGA**, Nothing only—nothing except; 2 infs, **nwAR, ceMS**, Nothing only—nothing but; 1 inf, **ceTX**, They didn't use to teach out here only to about the six grade; 1 inf, **csGA**, He didn't have any schooling only what little I taught him; 1 inf, **ceGA**, I sleep pretty well, only when she talks in her sleep; 1 inf, **csMS**, Don't never empty the ashes only when they're cold.

only-est See **onliest**

ono n [Haw *ono;* despite quots 1955 and 1960, this word is not related to **ono** adj, v] **HI**

A **wahoo** (here: *Acanthocybium solandri*).

1926 Pan-Pacific Research Inst. *Jrl.* 1.1.8 **HI**, Acanthocybium solandri. . . Ono. **1946** LaMonte *N. Amer. Game Fishes* 25 **HI**, Wahoo—*Acanthocybium solandri* . . Ono. **1955** Day *HI People* 254, They bring in not only ahi but most of the marlin, swordfish, *ono* (whose name means "delicious"), dolphin or *mahimahi*, ulua, and other food fish found in local markets. **1960** Gosline–Brock *Hawaiian Fishes* 255, *Acanthocybium solandri* (Ono, Wahoo)—A long, slender mackerel or tuna-like fish, dark blue in color on the back with about 30 irregular dark purplish gray bars on the sides. . . The ono is a pelagic species. . . The ono is taken usually by trolling and is regarded as a fine food fish; one meaning of the Hawaiian word ono is "to have sweet taste." **1967** *Honolulu Star–Bulletin* (HI) 31 May, Ono—wahoo. . . Good for sashimi; fry, steam, boil. **1967** *DARE* (Qu. P2, . . *Kinds of saltwater fish caught around here . . good to eat*) Inf **HI**2, Ono. **1984** Sunset *HI Guide* 145, Ono—wahoo.

ono adj, v Also *onoono* [Haw *'ono*] **HI**

Delicious, sweet; to crave, relish.

1938 Reinecke *Hawaiian Loanwords* 26, Ono. . . Palatable; sweet; delicious. . . To be hungry for or wish for a certain food, as in the statement: "I am [sic] ono for ice cream." V[ery] F[requent] *Onoono*. . . [Reinecke: Intensive of *ono*.] The same as *ono*. **1951** *AmSp* 26.23 **HI**, Ono (sweet). **1954–60** Hance et al. *Hawaiian Sugar* 5, Ono. . . ['ono]

Sweet, good. **1969** *DARE* FW Addit **HI**, Ono ['ounou]—good, tasty—most commonly used in reference to food. **1972** Carr *Da Kine Talk* 116 **HI**, 'Ono 'delicious', as an adjective, enters into many expressions such as an '*ono-looking strawberry* ' a delicious-looking strawberry'. A sign recently seen in a supermarket of Honolulu read: "Ruby-red Texas grapefruit—so *ono!*" **1981** *Pidgin To Da Max* np **HI**, Ono. . . Delicious. "Wow, ono da malasadas [=a kind of doughnut], yeah?" **1984** Sunset *HI Guide* 85, 'Ono—delicious, tasty.

on offsides See **offside, on the**

on one's ear See **ear** n[1] **B**

‡**on one's feet** adj phr [Var of *on one's uppers* (at **upper**)] Broke; down and out.

1967 *DARE* (Qu. U41a, *Somebody who has lost everything and is very poor: "He's _____."*) Inf **SC**55, On his feet, that is, his shoes are worn out and he can't buy any more; a joking statement.

on one's foot See **foot** n **C5i**

on one's head See **head** n **D3**

on one's hip, have something See **hip** n[1] **1**

on one's man See **man** n **C7**

onoono See **ono** adj, v

on outs See **out** **F2b**

on pump See **pump** n

onry See **ornery**

onst See **once**

onsurance See **insurance**

onswoggled See **hornswoggle 1**

on tew See **onto**

on the drag(s) See **drag** n **16**

on the fin See **fin** n **3**

on the flakes See **flake** n[1] **2**

on the fritz See **fritz, on the**

on the hack See **hack** n[1] **1**

on the halves See **halves 2b**

on the hummer See **hummer 4a**

on the hump See **hump** n **6**

on the knot See **knot** n[1] **7**

on the out(s) See **out** **F2b**

on the table See **on** prep **B12b**

onto prep Pronc-sp *on tew;* eye-dial *ontu*

1 On, upon.

1867 Harris *Sut Lovingood Yarns* 27 **TN**, A pow'ful fat man wer a lyin in the yard ontu his belly. **1883** Twain *Life on Missip.* (Boston) 374 **MO**, You get a leetle too much constumery on to your statements. **1887** Kirkland *Zury* 52 **IL**, That'll take th' last quarter [of land] but th' one we're on tew, Zury. **1907** White *AZ Nights* 84, We run on a four-months' calf all by himself, with the T O iron onto him. **1930** *AmSp* 6.99 **cNY**, Onto: On. "There ain't a single mark onto his face." **1938** Liebling *Back Where* 31 **NYC**, She was so deep in the water with coal, and no deck onto her. **1941** *Sat. Eve. Post* 5 Apr 10, Junior kept a holt onto him. *Ibid* 116, They wasn't a bruise onto him. **1942** McAtee *Dial. Grant Co. IN* 78 (as of 1890s), On to. . . redundant, for "on." **1954** *AmSp* 29.228 **csNJ**, As long ago as 1925 I first noticed the use of *onto* in place of *on*. People say, 'This coat has big buttons onto it; her hat has a feather onto it.' **1959** *AmSp* 34.148 **cePA**, 'The boat was floating onto the river'; 'There is plenty of snow onto the roof'; 'Down onto the turnpike several hundred people were stranded into a roadside restaurant.' **1966** *DARE* Tape **NC**1, It has what we call doors onto it. **1986** Pederson *LAGS Concordance*, 1 inf, **swGA**, You don't see those onto houses now; *(The coat has buttons _____ it)* 11 infs, **Gulf Region**, Onto (it).

2 With regard to, concerning.

1939 Smiley *Gloss. New Paltz* **seNY**, I smoke all the time. I ought to cut down *onto* it.

on tomorrow See **on** prep **B2c**

on top of one's head See **head** n D3

ontu See **onto**

onus child n Cf *DS* Z11a-b
1986 Pederson *LAGS Concordance (Illegitimate child)* 1 inf, **seAL**, Onus child.

ony See **only**

on yesterday See **on** prep **B2c**

onyx n
In marble play: a marble made of onyx or similar material.
1950 *WELS (Names and nicknames for different kinds of marbles: . . Large ones: _____)* 1 Inf, **cnWI**, Onyxes. 1967–69 *DARE* (Qu. EE6d) Infs **MO**37, **UT**4, **WY**1, Onyx(es).

oo n |ʔoʔo| [Haw *ʻōʻō*]
A Hawaiian bird of the genus *Moho.*
1890 *Ibis* (London) 2.179 **HI**, Large numbers of the O-o must have been taken in old days. 1902 Henshaw *Birds Haw. Is.* 70, The brilliant shining black body feathers of the o-o were . . in great demand for making cloaks. 1915 Bryan *Nat. Hist. HI* 95, The oo was found only on the Island of Hawaii, but it had relatives, with much inferior yellow feathers, on Maui, Molokai and Kauai. 1944 Munro *Birds HI* 85, The yellow feathers on the leg [of *Moho braccatus*] were. . . smaller and not nearly so fine as the plumes of the other oos and their gathering was early discontinued. 1955 Day *HI People* 205, A cloak of Kamehameha I, made of five thousand tuft feathers of the o-o bird. 1972 Berger *Hawaiian Birdlife* 18, The only known surviving species of Oo (*Moho braccatus* on Kauai) has fewer yellow feathers than any of the other three species. *Ibid* 121, *Moho nobilis.* . . was the largest of the four species of Oo, males being between 12 and 13 inches in length. 1994 Stone–Pratt *Hawaiʻi's Plants* 23, These birds [=*Acridotheres tristis*] were common even in the deep forests, where they nested in cavities, perhaps in direct competition with cavity-nesting native birds (such as the now-extinct ʻōʻō) on several islands. 1994 *DARE* File **HI**, While we were visiting the Bishop Museum in Honolulu, a local ornithologist told us the oo [ʔoʔo] no longer survives.

ooch v[1] |uč, ŭč| Usu with *over, up* [*EDD* hootch v "[ūtʃ.] To crouch, sit huddled up."] Cf **hooch** v, **oonch, oontz out, ootz 2**
To crowd together, move oneself over to make room for someone else; to slide or push (something) up or along.
1930 Burnett *Iron Man* 184, He lay down on the lounge with Rose. "Ooch over," he said. "God, do you want all the room," said Rose. 1967–68 *DARE* (Qu. Y32, *To squeeze yourself into a small space: "If you're going to fit in there you'll have to _____."*) Inf **TX**29, Ooch up [laughter]; (Qu. Y52, *To move over—for example on a long bench: ". . . Can you _____ [a little]?"*) Infs **TX**29, **WI**19, Ooch over. 1968 Moody *Horse* 99 **nwKS** (as of c1920), He ooched his behind up onto the bench beside the coil I was winding. 1992 *DARE* File **cIA**, In my family [Jewish] we'd tell each other to ooch [uč] or [ŭč] over. *Ibid* **NYC**, I use *ooch* [uč], with the vowel of *good*, rather than *scooch*, which is totally alien to me.

ooch n Also *ooch and an eek*
A very short distance, very small margin.
c1960 *DARE* File **cnWV**, We made it by an ooch. . . We made it by an ooch and an eek. . . It's just an ooch away from here.

ooch v[2] See **ootz 1**

ooch and an eek See **ooch** n

ooch over (or up) See **ooch** v[1]

oodle-talk n Cf **tut language**
1966 *DARE* FW Addit **csWI**, Oodle-talk—a child's (language) game. Put an "oodle" before the vowel in each syllable, for example: poodleapoodler (paper), boodleook (book), poodlencoodleil (pencil). Used by 10–12 year olds.

oodlins n pl, but sg or pl in constr [Var of *oodles*] **S Midl, esp KY, TN** See Map Cf **dead oodles**
A great quantity.
1886 *S. Bivouac* 4.350 **sAppalachians**, Oodlins or oodles (large quantity). 1895 *DN* 1.392 **cKY**, *Oodlins*: abundance, a large quantity; "dead oodlins" = a very great quantity. [1909 *DN* 3.354 **eAL, wGA**, *Oodles.* . . Quantities. *Oodlins* is not used.] c1960 Wilson *Coll.* **csKY**, *Oodles, oodlins.* . . Plenty, lots, many. 1965–70 *DARE* (Qu. U38a, . . *A*

great deal of money: "He's got _____ [of money]."*) Infs **GA**77, **TN**1, 14, 15, Oodlins; (Qu. FF26, . . *A large group of people at a public gathering* . . *"There was quite a _____ at the auction."*) Inf **GA**77, Oodlins of people; (Qu. LL8a, *A large amount or number: More than enough* . . *"He's got _____ of time."*) Infs **AR**31, **GA**77, **KY**5, 36, 53, **TN**1, 6, **VA**2, Oodlins; (Qu. LL9a, *As much as you need or more* . . *"We've got _____ of apples."*) Infs **KY**5, 11, 19, 53, **TN**1, 23, Oodlins; **TN**14, Oodlins and oodlins. 1967 *DARE* Tape **TN**6, Up there I keep my stamps, and I just have oodlins and oodlins.

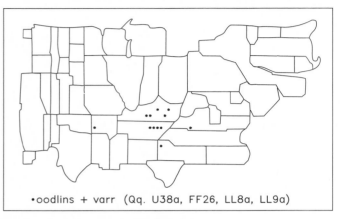

•oodlins + varr (Qq. U38a, FF26, LL8a, LL9a)

oods n pl [Cf *EDD odds* sb.[5]] Cf **oodlins**
1927 *AmSp* 3.140 **eME**, "Oodles," "oods," "odds" is old English for odds and ends, miscellaneous small articles, excessive in quantity or number.

ooey See **oo-wee**

oogarook See **oogruk**

oogens n [Prob var of **oodlins**] Cf **dead oodles**
1905 *DN* 3.63 **NE**, Oceans, oodles, oogens, or dead oogens. . . Large quantities. "Oceans of money."

oogles n pl Also *oozles* [Varr of *oodles*]
1969 *DARE* (Qu. U38a, . . *A great deal of money: "He's got _____ [of money]."*) Inf **IN**79, Oozles; **MA**59, Oogles [ˈuglz].

oogruk n [Inupiaq *ugruk*] Also *oog(a)rook, ugruk;* for addit varr see quots **AK**
The bearded seal (*Erignathus barbatus*).
1891 in 1976 Thornton *Among Eskimos* 11 **AK**, Yonder is a line of ten, tugging away at some heavy burden. It is a large *oogarook*, or big seal, that one of them has killed. 1893 in 1991 Tabbert *Dict. Alaskan Engl.* 113, The skins of the large seal (oogrook or maklak) are the kind preferred for coverings [of boats]. 1920 Stuck *Winter Circuit* 142 **AK**, Other sources of meat there are: the whale, . . the ooguruk (or giant seal) and many varieties of fish. 1948 Helmericks–Helmericks *Our Summer* 170 **AK**, I imagine most of us will soon be familiar with the term *ugrug.* . . We have no English word for this animal—the giant bearded seal of the arctic, which is so important in the arctic economy. 1958 Carrighar *Moonlight* 62 **AK**, The animals now most plentiful were the white beluga whales and the large bearded *oogruks.* 1959 Hart *McKay's AK* 33 [Glossary], Oogruk: Also ugrook and ugruk. The seal-skin or sea-lion skin used for making mukluks and moccasins. It is also an Eskimo food. 1965 Bowen *Alaskan Dict.* 24, Oogruk (oog-rook)—The bearded seal, which is larger than the hair seal and smaller than a walrus. 1974 Wells *Ipani Eskimos* 44 **AK**, The Ipani Eskimo also uses a strong rawhide snare made from a big seal (ugruk) to catch bear.

ooh-wee See **oo-wee**

oojit-nawsty adj [See quot]
1929 *AmSp* 5.19 **swMO**, Oojit-nawsty. . . Good or pleasing. Used in describing anything from music to corn whiskey. It is in common use near Southwest City, Mo., and is said to be derived from a Cherokee Indian word.

ookey See **hookey**

ookow n [Etym uncert]
A **brodiaea**: esp *Brodiaea congesta* or a **blue dicks** (here: *Dichelostemma pulchellum*).
[1897 Parsons *Wild Flowers CA* 264, B[rodiaea] congesta . . another

similar species, is often four feet tall. . . This is called "ookow" by the Indians.] **1923** Abrams *Flora Pacific States* 1.408, *Dichelostemma pulchellum.* . . Ookow. . . Open hillsides. **1949** Moldenke *Amer. Wild Flowers* 355, Differing from all the species previously mentioned in having very dense, headlike, flower clusters is the bluedicks, *Dichelostemma capitatum.* . . The ookow, *D. pulchellum,* . . ranges from California to Washington, flowering later than the bluedicks. **1979** Spellenberg *Audubon Guide N. Amer. Wildflowers W. Region* 576, Forktooth Ookow—*Dichelostemma congestum.* . . Western Washington to central California. *Ibid* 577, Roundtooth Ookow (*D. multiflorum*) . . grows from southern Oregon to central California.

‡oolie oop n, exclam [Var of **alley oop(s)**]

1966 *DARE* (Qu. EE22, . . *The game in which they throw a ball over a building . . to a player on the other side*) Inf **WA**1, Oolie oop ['uli 'up]—that's what they'd holler; (Qu. EE23a, *In the game of andy-over . . what . . you call out when you throw the ball*) Inf **WA**1, Oolie oop ['uli 'up].

oona See **una**

oonch v |unč| Usu with *along, over* [Cf *EDD hunch* v.¹ "[unʃ.] . . To push, *gen.* with the shoulder or elbow"] Cf **hunch** v **1a, 3c** =**ooch** v¹.

1993 *DARE* File **csWI**, For me, the natural way to ask someone to move over without getting up is to say "*oonch* [unč] *over.*" *Oonch* is also a transitive verb, meaning to move something by sliding it in jerks. You usually *oonch* something *over* or *along.*

oontz out v phr Cf **ooch** v¹

To crowd (something) out.

1947 in 1960 Wentworth–Flexner *Slang* 368, I don't think any wire-and-glass dingbat is going to oontz out cheek-to-cheek dancing.

oopu n [Haw *'o'opu*] **HI**

A fish of the family Gobiidae.

1960 Gosline–Brock *Hawaiian Fishes* 269, *Chonophorus genivittatus* ('O'opu). . . A common form in streams and estuaries. **1967** *DARE* (Qu. P1, . . *Kinds of freshwater fish . . caught around here . . good to eat*) Infs **HI**4, 14, Oopu; **HI**4, Chinese oopu. **1984** Sunset *HI Guide* 144 [Game fish species], 'O'opu . . goby. **1994** Stone–Pratt *Hawai'i's Plants* 81, Two species of small native 'o'opu or gobies (family Gobiidae) prey on crustaceans, and native waterbirds probably prey on the fishes.

oose n Also *oose root,* ~ *weed* [Per var of **ooze**] **UT**

A **yucca** (here: *Yucca glauca*).

1866 in 1955 Lee *Mormon Chron.* 2.31 **UT**, I went up comances Kanyon with a Horse Team . . for oose or soap root. **1942** Whipple *Joshua* 190 **UT**, He found a blossoming oose for her—a panicle of creamy blooms that shot out of its nest of dark green swords a dozen feet into the air. **1946** in 1957 *Western Folkl.* 16.155 **UT**, So I went out and got a bunch of soapweed leaves and made a tea. . . And I've never been bothered with rheumatism since. The true name is "oose weed." Some old codger told me about it. It looks like the yucca plant. **1982** Brooks *Quicksand* 11 **swUT** (as of c1903), When she scrubbed it [=the floor] with her bar of oose-root soap, she worked the sudsy water lengthwise, then threw clear water on and swept it crosswise.

oot See **out**

ootz v [Cf Ger *uzen* to tease, chaff]

1 also *ooch:* To pressure, urge.

1958 Smith *How to Do Nothing* 10, For [a spool tank] you need an empty spool. Here's one place your mother can be ootzed into the deal. You can ask her for a spool. **1979** *DARE* File **cTX**, They kept on gradually ooching ['u:čɪŋ] me to do the work, and at last I accepted. [*DARE* Ed: Speaker has known term since the 1920s.]

2 To move (something) slightly. Cf **ooch** v¹

1958 Smith *How to Do Nothing* 42, [In the game mumbly-peg] there will be arguments . . [if] the knife won't stick straight up. If it leans over . . [but] you can get two fingers under it, it counts. The reason why there'll still be arguments . . is that sometimes it looks as if the guy is ootzing the knife up with his two fingers.

oo-wee exclam Usu |'u:ˌ(w)i, ˌu'wi:| Also sp *ooey, ooh-wee;* for addit pronc and sp varr see quots **chiefly Sth, S Midl** See Map

Used to express surprise, joy, pain, or similar emotions.

1961 (1963) Gover *100 Dollar Misunderstanding* 21 [Black], What the fug the looks o'the place got t'do wiff it? Ooh-wee! I do me some

more considerin. **1965–70** *DARE* (Qu. NN6a, *Exclamations of joy . . when somebody gets a pleasant surprise, he might shout "_____.*") Inf **MO**30, Ooh-wee! (Qu. NN6b, *Expressions of joy used mostly by children*) Inf **GA**31, Oo-wee ['uˌwi]; (Qu. NN20a, *Exclamations caused by sudden pain—a blow on the thumb*) Inf **LA**8, Ohwee [ouuwi:]; (Qu. NN20b, *Exclamations caused by sudden pain—a slight burn*) Inf **AL**6, Ooey ['u:i]; **DE**3, Oo-wee ['uwˌi]; **SC**24, Ooey; (Qu. NN21a, *Exclamations caused by sudden pain—a pinched finger*) Infs **KY**92, **SC**45, Oo-wee; **SC**40, Ooey ['uɨ]; **SC**69, Ooey [u'i]; (Qu. NN21b, *Exclamations caused by sudden pain—a hard blow on the chest*) Inf **MO**12, Ooey [ʔʊːɪ]; (Qu. NN21c, *Exclamations caused by sudden pain—a twisted ankle*) Inf **IN**1, Ooey [u-i], that smarts; **FL**52, Ohwee [ou'wi]; **LA**3, Oo-wee [uwi] [FW: Inf's daughter says]; **KY**11, Oo-wee ['u:wi]; (Qu. NN23, *Exclamations when people smell a very bad odor*) Inf **GA**77, Ooey [ˌu:'i:]; **MI**66, Oo-weoo ['u:'wiu]; **SC**9, Oo-wee [u:wi]; **TN**46, Oo-whew; **TX**5, 54, Oo-wee; **TX**36, Oo-wee [u'wi]—falsetto. [12 of 22 Infs young or mid-aged, 7 Black] **1970** Major *Dict. Afro-Amer. Slang* 88, *Oowee:* (1940's) an expression of shock or delight or excitement. **1981** Pederson *LAGS Basic Materials* (*Exclamations of surprise*) 1 inf, **cwGA**, [ˌɵʊɵ'wi˞.ᵊ]; (*Exclamations of impatience*) 1 inf, **csTX**, [ˌu:'ɾi·]. **1985** Wilkinson *Moonshine* 142 **neNC**, Ooo-wee, somebody's been in the woods.

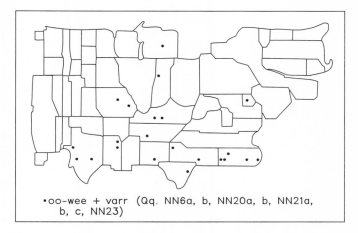

•oo-wee + varr (Qq. NN6a, b, NN20a, b, NN21a, b, c, NN23)

ooze n [By ext from *ooze* a decoction of vegetable matter used in tanning leather] **chiefly S Midl, esp KY** Cf **oose**

A medicinal liquid or paste made from boiled herbs, bark, roots, etc.

1937 (1963) Hyatt *Kiverlid* 45 **KY**, The best thing fer a snake bite is strong ooze biled from rattle snakemaster. **1953** Randolph–Wilson *Down in Holler* 169 **Ozarks**, Ooze is a noun, which usually means some kind of medicine made by concentrating herb teas or decoctions. *Slippery-ellum ooze,* for example, is made by macerating the inner bark of the elm in water and then boiling it down to a thick paste. *May-apple ooze,* a violent purgative, is similarly derived from mandrake roots. **1959** Roberts *Up Cutshin* 95 **seKY**, Now if one had the misfortune of catching something like the eetch, she would take this old pokeroot and make a ooze out of it and boil it and wash you with it and kill that eetch dead as a nit. **1966** *DARE* (Qu. BB50c, *Remedies for infections*) Inf **AL**4, Red oak poultice—bark ooze they call it. **1981** *High Coll.* **ceKY** (as of c1930), *Ooze:* n. medicine made from red oak bark which has been chipped and boiled, and is used in the Gorge to cure sores, cuts, and snake bite. **1983** *MJLF* 9.1.49 **ceKY**, *Ooze* . . the syrup made by boiling down medicinal herbs.

oozles See **oogles**

oozy adj [Prob var of *woozy*] **Nth, N Midl** See Map on p. 888

Nauseated, weak, dizzy.

1965–70 *DARE* (Qu. BB6, *A sudden feeling of weakness, when sometimes the person loses consciousness*) Inf **MN**16, Had an oozy feeling; (Qu. BB16b, *If something a person ate didn't agree with him, he might just feel a bit _____*) Infs **CA**148, **IA**22, **IL**29, **IN**79, **MA**14, 51, **RI**4, Oozy; (Qu. BB39, *On a day when you don't feel just right, though not actually sick . . "I'll be all right tomorrow—I'm just feeling _____ today.*") Inf **PA**214, Oozy; (Qu. DD13, *When a drinker is just beginning to show the effects of the liquor . . he's _____*) Inf **AK**8, Oozy.

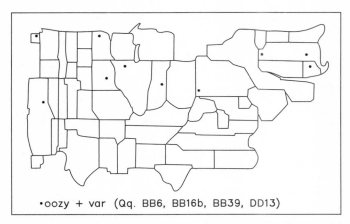

•oozy + var (Qq. BB6, BB16b, BB39, DD13)

opa n Also *opi* [Ger, Du] **esp in Ger settlement areas** Cf **oma**

One's grandfather.

1962 Atwood *Vocab. TX* v, To Tad and Laurie who may possibly take after their Opa. *Ibid* 66, *Grandfather.* . . Fourteen informants of German origin give *Opa;* another *Grosspapa.* **1967–68** *DARE* (Qu. Z3, . . *'Grandfather'*) Inf **CA**6, Opa ['oʊpa]—German; **IA**32, Opa ['ɔpə]—it's an affectionate German word. **1970** *DARE* Tape **MI**122, We called him *opa,* which is Dutch for grandfather. **1986** Pederson *LAGS Concordance (Grandfather)* 2 infs, **cwFL, cTX,** Opa. [Both infs have Ger grandparents.] **1995** *DARE* File **csWI,** We "adopted" John McGalliard as the children's grandfather since they otherwise had none. They called him "Opi." They still talk about their opi. He was wonderful.

opah n [*OED* 1750 →]

A deepwater marine fish *(Lampris regius)* conspicuous for its rich colors. Also called **glance fish, Jerusalem haddock, mariposa 2, moonfish 3**

1872 Schele de Vere *Americanisms* 385, There are few more splendidly-colored creatures in the world than some of our American fish, and among them the Southern *King-Fish* (Lampris guttatus), or *Opah,* stands foremost. Its steel-blue back contrasts strangely with its bright green sides, while the remaining parts are of a delicate rose-color; its flesh is as palatable as its appearance is gorgeous. On the coast of New Jersey the fish is known by its more modest name of *Hake.* **1902** Jordan–Evermann *Amer. Fishes* 326, The single known species is the opah, mariposa or moonfish, *Lampris luna.* **1933** LA Dept. of Conserv. *Fishes* 272, The Opah, . . usually a fish of more northern open seas which may reach a length of as much as six feet and attracts instant attention because of its body, metallic silver and gold, spotted with white and adorned with bright red fins. **1953** Roedel *Common Fishes CA* 48, The Opah Family, Lampridae—Opah—*Lampris regius.* . . Taken uncommonly in California by both sport and commercial fishermen. The flesh is good to eat and smokes well. **1991** Amer. Fisheries Soc. *Common Names Fishes* 36, *Lampris guttatus* . . opah.

opakapaka n [Haw *'ōpakapaka*] **HI**

A **snapper** (here: family Lutjanidae) such as *Pristipomoides microlepis.*

1926 Pan-Pacific Research Inst. *Jrl.* 1.1.9 **HI,** Pristipomoides violescens. . . Opakapaka. **1960** Gosline–Brock *Hawaiian Fishes* 182, Family Lutjanidae ('Opakapakas or Snappers). *Ibid* 186, *Pristipomoides microlepis* ('Opakapaka). . . A very important market species, attaining a length of at least 3 feet. **1967** *DARE* (Qu. P2, . . *Kinds of saltwater fish caught around here . . good to eat*) Inf **HI**2 [o'paka'paka]; **HI**4, Opakapaka. **1984** Sunset *HI Guide* 144 [Game fish species], 'Opakapaka . . pink snapper.

opal n

1967 *DARE* (Qu. EE6d, *Special marbles*) Inf **NE**3, Agates, opals.

opala n [Haw] **HI**

See quots.

1938 Reinecke *Hawaiian Loanwords* 26, Opala [o'pala]. . . Refuse; trash; cane trash. . . Compost *(opala lepo)* or compost pit. V[ery] F[req]. **1954–60** Hance et al. *Hawaiian Sugar* 5, Opala. . . Trash, cane trash.

opaleye n

A marine fish *(Girella nigricans)* of California waters. Also called **bluefish 2, greenfish 2, green perch 2**

1933 John G. Shedd Aquarium *Guide* 112, *Girella nigricans*—

Greenfish; Opal Eye. The Greenfish is a fair food fish. It grows to be about a foot long and is abundant on rocky shores of southern California. **1946** LaMonte *N. Amer. Game Fishes* 74, Opal-eye—*Girella nigricans* . . This rudderfish is also found on rocky shores from San Francisco, California, southward. . . It . . is further distinguished by its opalescent blue eyes. **1991** Amer. Fisheries Soc. *Common Names Fishes* 55, *Girella nigricans* . . opaleye.

opedildoc(k) See **opodeldoc**

opelo See **opelu**

opelousa, opelousas cat See **appaloosa** n²

opelu n Also *opelo* [Haw *'ōpelu*] **HI**

A **mackerel scad,** esp *Decapterus pinnulatus.*

1926 Pan-Pacific Research Inst. *Jrl.* 1.1.8 **HI,** Decapterus pinnulatus . . Opelu. **1960** Gosline–Brock *Hawaiian Fishes* 171, The 'opelu is one of the two species of the genus *Decapterus* in Hawaii. . . *Decapterus maruadsi* ('Opelu) . . is very similar to the common 'opelu, *Decapterus pinnulatus.* **1967** *DARE* (Qu. P2, . . *Kinds of saltwater fish caught around here . . good to eat*) Inf **HI**14, Opelu [o'pɛlu]; (Qu. P7, *Small fish used as bait for bigger fish*) Inf **HI**14, Opelo [opɛlo]. **1984** Sunset *HI Guide* 145, 'Opelu—mackerel scad.

open adj, v Usu |'opən|; also **esp Sth, S Midl** |'opm̩|; occas |'omp(ə)m| Pronc-spp *ompen, op(e)m*

A Forms.

1785 in **1956** Eliason *Tarheel Talk* 315 **nw,cwNC,** Opem. **1905** *DN* 3.58 **eNE,** The "nasal infix," occurs in . . o(m)pen . . but it is rare. **1908** *DN* 3.282 **eAL, wGA,** *N* has become vocalic *m* after *p* or *b,* as in . . [op-m]. **1927** Shewmake *Engl. Pronc. VA* 43, Opened. Very often *opemed,* or *op'md* is heard, especially in informal or illiterate speech. **1936** *AmSp* 11.162 **eTX,** Open . . is sometimes pronounced ['opən], but more often ['opn], ['opm]. **1941** *AmSp* 16.10 **eTX** [Black], *Eleven, even, . . open,* . . show the assimilation usual in southern illiterate speech: ['lɛbm], ['ibm], etc. **1954** *WELS Suppl.* **ceWI,** ['ompm̩], ['empɾən]—intrusive [m]—or at least nasalization—reported as commonly heard in Oconto, Wis. **1967** *DARE* (Qu. M1) Inf **LA**7, Open barn ['oʊpm̩ ˌbɑːn].

B As adj.

1 also *open top;* Of a conveyance: without a top; topless. **chiefly Nth**

1771 in **1968** CT (Colony) *Pub. Rec.* 13.514, Every open chair and other open top riding wheel-carriage [shall be rated] three pounds. **1873** Holland *A. Bonnicastle* iii (*DAE*) **NEng,** We saw before us a light, open wagon drawn by two gray horses. **1884** Rittenhouse *Maud* 319 (*DAE*), Mr. Butler came here and we were both whirled off in an open carriage. **1889** Brayley *Boston Fire Dept.* 323 (*DAE*), One open buggy, one top-buggy, and water-tower were purchased during the year. **1902** (1969) Sears *Catalogue* 363, Our new $27.27 open buggy. **1910** *DN* 3.446 **cwNY,** Open-buggy. . . Buggy without a top. **1944** Holton *Yankees Were Like This* 106 **Cape Cod MA** (as of c1890), This open buggy puzzled me at first. . . It was a long time before I could be made to see that it really was just a buggy body with the top left off. **1965–70** *DARE* (Qu. L42, . . *What kind of thing do you call a 'rig'?*) Inf **OH**15, Something on wheels, pulled by horse, open; (Qu. N40b, . . *Sleighs for carrying people*) Infs **MO**12, **VA**8, **VT**16, (One-horse) open sleigh; **MI**11, Open cutter; **MI**20, Open two-seater; (Qu. N41a, . . *Horse-drawn vehicles . . to carry people*) Infs **ME**5, **OH**82, Open buggy; **NJ**16, **RI**15, Open wagon; (Qu. N41b, *Horse-drawn vehicles to carry heavy loads*) Inf **MI**67, Open van; (Qu. N41c, *Horse-drawn vehicles to carry light loads*) Inf **NY**233, Open buggy.

2 Of a female domestic animal: capable of being bred; not currently bred. [Cf *EDD* open adj. 4 "Of a sow (more rarely of a heifer): unspayed"; *SND* open adj. 2 "Of female animals: ready to bear young or bearing young . . unspayed."]

1843 (1844) Johnson *Farmer's Encycl.* 862, Open. A term frequently applied to cows or heifers, signifying that they are not in calf. **1857** in 1956 Eliason *Tarheel Talk* 286 **c,csNC,** 1 young open sow $5.00. **1899** (1912) Green *VA Folk-Speech* 307, Open-sow. . . A sow left unspayed to breed. **1934** (1943) *W2,* Open. . . Stock breeding. Not with young. **1944** Adams *Western Words* 108, Open heifer—One not spayed. **1947** in 1948 *AmSp* 23.50 **NY,** It is better though to breed them a little too young than after they have attained an age of six or more, because when mares are left open that long, they may never settle or at best may become shy breeders. **1966** Monroe *Eve. Times* (WI) 16 Aug 7/2, Holstein heifers wanted, 900 to 1,100 pounds, just bred or open. [**1968** *DARE* (Qu. K10, *Words used about a cow that is going to have a calf*) Inf **NY**123, Open.] **1969** *SC Market Bulletin* 11 Sept 1/4, Bred gilts, open gilts and boars selected from the best Hampshire herds in the state. **1986** Pederson *LAGS Concordance,* [1 inf, **cnGA,** Open—bred, of a sow;] 1 inf, **neTN,** Open gilts. **1994** *WI State Jrl.* (Madison) 4 Oct sec D 2, [Advt:] Open Heifers, 139 head, 700 lbs. **1995** *DARE* File **csWI,** [From the newsletter of a local veterinary clinic:] If your mare was open this year the fall is a good time to do cultures, biopsies, and cytology of the uterus.

3 also used absol; Of a hunting dog: that readily gives tongue. **[open C1]**

    1984 Wilder *You All Spoken Here* 58 **Sth,** Free tonguer; open dog: Barks muchly. **1985** Wilkinson *Moonshine* 78 **neNC,** Bigfoot had hardly made a sound, and Garland said that for the moment at least he wasn't likely to. "He's a semi-silent," he said. "There's also a silent and an open. A dog that's an open barks as soon as he strikes the track."

C As verb.

1 Of a hunting dog: to bay, bark, esp on first finding a scent. [*OED* 1565 →]

    1828 (1970) Webster *Amer. Dict., Open.* . . To bark; *a term in hunting.* **1923** *DN* 5.216 **swMO,** *Open.* . . To give tongue, to bay, as a hound. **1939** *Hall Coll.* **wNC, eTN,** *Open.* . . (Of dogs in trailing) To bark or yelp at finding indications of a good trail. "Some old trained bear hounds . . picked up a cold trail. And started out up th'u the Bear Creek a-trailin', openin' along." **1966** *DARE* Tape **DC9,** Once a hound opens, the idea is to have all the other hounds . . honor that hound; they all come running in and they all get on the line and go away together. **1972** *Foxfire Book* 274 **nGA,** When dogs "open on a track," they find the scent they're looking for and charge ahead.

2 To dig (a grave).

    1946 *PADS* 6.22 **swVA,** *Open a grave.* . . To dig a grave.

3 To turn on (a light). [Prob by analogy with **close** v] Cf *DS* Y411b

    1972 Carr *Da Kine Talk* 127 **HI,** *Close the light* and *open the light* vs. *turn out the light* and *turn on the light*—These loan translations have apparently entered Hawaii's English from a language that uses the verbs *close* and *open* for electric switches. **1995** *DARE* File **nwMA** (as of 1960s), My friend who has lived in the US since age 3, has always said "open" or "close" the light, meaning to turn it on or off. Her parents are Czech, and Czech and French were both spoken at home when she was growing up.

open-and-shut adj Also *opening-and-shutting* **chiefly N Atl** See Map Cf **light and shut**

Of the weather: alternately cloudy and sunny; variable.

    1890 *DN* 1.19 **seNH,** *Light and shut:* of the weather. 'It lights and shuts,' that is, the sun peeps out at intervals. The common New England maxim is "Open and shet's a sign of wet." **1929** *AmSp* 5.123 **ME,** The weather was much spoken of. A fine day was a "weather breeder," "Open and shet" is a sign of wet. **1941** *LANE* Map 347 **neMA,** Open and shet, more wet—'a Marblehead phrase' referring to the prediction of rain in the opening and shutting of clouds. **1951** Johnson *Resp. to PADS 20* **DE** *(When clouds come and go all day, you say it's _____)* Open and shet—old-fashioned; *(When the weather seems likely to become bad, you say it's _____)* Open and shet, sign of wet. **1965–70** *DARE* (Qu. B8, *When clouds come and go all day . . it's _____*) 17 Infs, **chiefly N Atl,** Open-and-shut (day); **NY53,** Open-and-shet; **CT2,** Opening-and-shutting. **1975** Gould *ME Lingo* 196, *Open and shut*—Threatening weather with quick changes from sunshine to clouds. The adage runs: "Open and shet; sign o' wet."

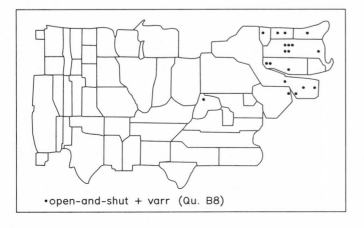

•open-and-shut + varr (Qu. B8)

---

open barn n esp **Sth, S Midl**

See quots.

    1967–70 *DARE* (Qu. M1, . . *Kinds of barns . . according to their use or the way they are built*) Infs **GA19, VA97,** Open barn; **LA7,** Open barn ['oupm ,ba:n]—for loading corn into each end; [**WI66,** Open-housing barn; **IN59,** Open-shed barn; **KS17,** Open-sided hay barn]. **1986** Pederson *LAGS Concordance,* 2 infs, **neTN, swAL,** Open barn; 1 inf, **cwMS,** Open barn—for hay, open on sides to shelter cows.

open church adj phr, also used absol

Requiring no personal invitation for attendance.

    1926 Bennet *Boss Diamond A* 286 **West,** That means plenty for your open-church wedding. **1968** *Ironton Tribune* (OH) 1 Apr 5/3, The custom of open church will be observed for the wedding. **1968** *Daily News* (Port Clinton–Oak Harbor OH) 26 June 5/3, Attendants for the open-church ceremony were: Ruth Ann Gulas . . Patricia Krupp. **1995** *DARE* File **nwOH,** An open church wedding means that anyone in that particular church community can attend. An announcement would appear in the bulletin saying that it would be an open church wedding. Also, the announcement in the newspaper of weddings that week might state that a certain ceremony would be open church; or an engagement announcement might state "an open church wedding is planned." In those cases, anyone in the community that reads the announcement, knows the couple, and wants to come—even if they're not members of that church—can come.

open clock n Cf **nine o'clocks, one o'clock 1, twelve o'clock**

    1899 (1912) Green *VA Folk-Speech* 306, *Open-clock.* . . A flower, open at some hours of the day and closed at others. The blooms open in the morning and close at 12 o'clock.

open-heart (peach) See **open peach**

open house n Cf **barn door 2b**

Used to indicate that a man's trouser fly is open.

    1950 *WELS (Expressions or sly words of warning for: A trouser fly open)* 1 Inf, **ceWI,** Open house. **1969** *DARE* (Qu. W24c) Inf **NY226,** Open house.

opening-and-shutting See **open-and-shut**

opening peach See **open peach**

open-mouth n

A **warmouth** (here: *Lepomis gulosus*).

    1972 *Living Museum* 34.127 **IL,** The warmouth, often known as the warmouth bass, wood bass, open-mouth, goggle-eye, and by other local names, is one of the less familiar members of the Illinois fish fauna.

open-mouthed grunt n

A **grunt** n **1** (here: *Haemulon flavolineatum*).

    1898 U.S. Natl. Museum *Bulletin* 47.1306, *Haemulon flavolineatum* . . French Grunt; Open-mouthed Grunt. **1946** LaMonte *N. Amer. Game Fishes* 63, French Grunt—*Haemulon flavolineatum* . . Open-mouthed Grunt. **1973** Knight *Cook's Fish Guide* 382, Openmouthed Grunt.

open one's head See **head** n **B2**

open peach n Also *open-heart (peach), opening ~, open-stone ~, open-seed ~, open-rock ~* **chiefly sAppalachians, Mid Atl** See Map on p. 890 Cf **clingstone** =**freestone 2.**

    1899 (1912) Green *VA Folk-Speech* 307, *Open-peach.* . . A peach that leaves the seed easily. **1949** Kurath *Word Geog.* 72, *Free-stone peach.* . . Maryland west of the Bay regularly has *open-stone peach* or *open-seed peach,* and this term has taken hold in northern West Virginia, probably as a Baltimore trade name; the Eastern Shore has *opening peach* and *open peach. Open peach* is found also in a coastal belt extending from the lower James to the Peedee, as well as on the Yadkin in North Carolina. Curiously enough *open-stone peach* and *open-seed peach* turn up again in Western North Carolina. **1954** *PADS* 21.24 **SC,** Freestone as applied to peaches. Also . . *open stone.* **c1960** Wilson Coll. **csKY,** *Freestone peach* . . also open or soft peach. **1964** *PADS* 42.17 **cwKY,** *Freestone peach.* The kind in which the seed is easily removed. *Soft peach* and *open peach* are occasionally heard. **1965–70** *DARE* (Qu. I51, *The kind of a peach where the hard center is loose*) 17 Infs, **GA, KY, MD, NC, SC,** Open-stone; **NC52, 68, SC3, VA48, 69,** Open peach; **MD28, 30,** Open-seed. **1966** Dakin *Dial. Vocab. Ohio R. Valley* 2.361, 26 infs, **chiefly eKY,** Open-stone *or* open-seed peach; 6 infs, **sIL, sIN, KY,** Open peach; 1 inf, **seKY,** Open-rock peach. **1972** *PADS* 58.21 **cwAL,** *Freestone peach.* . . Virginia Piedmont *soft peach* (1), and Coastal Southern *open-seed* (1 [of 27 infs]) also occur. **1986** Pederson

LAGS Concordance (Freestone peach) 29 infs, **chiefly eTN, neGA,** Open stone; 5 infs, **cnGA, nwLA, TN,** Open (peach); 3 infs, **c,neTN, ceLA,** Open seed; 1 inf, **neTN,** Open heart.

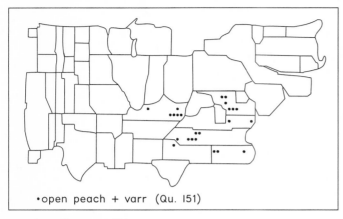

•open peach + varr (Qu. I51)

open top See **open B1**

opera n Usu |ˈɑp(ə)rə|; also |ˈɑpri|; for addit varr see quots Pronc-spp *op(e)ry*

A Forms.

1891 *DN* 1.117 **cNY,** [ɑpəri, ɑpri] < opera. **1906** *DN* 3.149 **nwAR,** *Opera.* . . Pronounced by the illiterate *op'ry* [ɑpri]. **1931** *AmSp* 6.332 [Circus and carnival slang], Jig-opry. . . A negro minstrel. **1943** *Grand Ole Opry Specials* [title]. **1967** *DARE* (Qu. FF24) Inf **CO**35, Tabor Opera [ˈɑpɚi] House. **1985** [see **B** below]. **1986** Pederson *LAGS Concordance* **Gulf Region,** [31 infs offered proncs of the type [ˈɑprə], 5 of the type [ˈɑpri], 1 [ˈɐpri] and 1 [ˈɐpɚrə]. According to 1 inf, "operys" [ɐpriz] are country music, "operas" [ɐprəz] are classical.]

B Sense.

Fig: the "performance" of cowboys working horses in a corral; hence *opera house, ~ seat* the top fence rail of a corral.

1929 *AmSp* 5.54 **NE** [Cattle country talk], When horses are being "broke," trained for riding, in the corrals, some of the men might perch themselves on the fence to watch the activities and are at the "opera," or are "fence riding." They are facetiously called "fence riders." **1944** Adams *Western Words* 108, *Op'ra*—The riding of a wild horse, branding. *Op'ra house*—The top rail of the corral fence where one can watch the riding of a bucking horse. It is also a time-honored conference place for all true range men. **1985** McMurtry *Lonesome Dove* 130 **TX,** Wilbarger paused . . to look at the stream of horses trotting past, then went back to his cutting. Since there was already enough help in the pen, there was nothing for Newt to do but stand by the fence and watch. Pea had already climbed up on what they called the "opry seat"—the top rail of the corral—to watch the proceedings.

opera drop n

A type of chocolate candy; see quots.

1992 *Berkshire Eagle* (Pittsfield MA) 11 Mar np **NY** (as of early 20th cent), By the time all these objects were distributed around the kitchen, only basics were left in the drawer: potholders "too good to use" . . , an envelope of gelatin, uncancelled stamps torn off letters, stray gray chocolate opera drops, . . old pennies [etc]. **1992** *DARE* File **Boston MA** (as of 1940s), Opera drops were chocolates with vanilla cream filling, kind of conical, haystack shaped. You would buy them at intermission at the opera. There was a British brand called Between the Acts that you could buy at Bailey's in Boston.

opera house (or seat) See **opera B**

opery See **opera**

opi See **opa**

opihi n [Haw *'opihi*] **HI**

A limpet of the family Patellidae, esp of the genus *Cellana.*

1915 Bryan *Nat. Hist. HI* 466, To the old-world limpets belong the opihi of the natives. It is a favorite food with the Hawaiians. . . This knee-cap or umbrella limpet is roughly though evenly ribbed without and pearly white within. **1967** *DARE* (Qu. P18, . . *Kinds of shellfish*) Infs **HI**4, 14, Opihi. **1968** *Jrl. Engl. Ling.* 2.83 [Common Hawaiian loanwords], *Opihi* /ʼopihi/. . . Any of several species of limpet (Helcioniscus), some of which are popular for food. **1972** Carr *Da Kine Talk* 116

HI, *'Opihi pants* (Hawaiian + English). Blue jeans, cut off above the knees, worn for the job of picking *'opihi* 'limpets'. **1979** Bushnell *Stone of Kannon* 384 **HI,** Then the woman . . showed them how to gather pipipi and opihi, the limpets small and big. **1994** Stone–Pratt *Hawai'i's Plants* 79, 'Opihi are a highly prized delicacy, and regulations by the state of Hawaii are enforced to protect this Hawaiian-style escargot from being overharvested.

opiopio adj [Haw]

1938 Reinecke *Hawaiian Loanwords* 26, Opiopio. . . Young, immature. . . F[req].

opm See **open**

opodeldoc n Also sp *opedildoc(k), opydildock;* for addit varr see quots [*OED* 1656 →; prob reinforced by comic strip character *Ole Opey Dildock*—see quot 1976] *old-fash*

A soap liniment; transf: any medicine; alcohol; in phr *on one's opodildocs* spirited.

1830 in 1938 Gardiner–Gardiner *Chron. Old Berkeley* 310 **VA,** Bought 1 vial of appodell-dock at 25 cents. **1851** Hooper *Widow Rugby's Husband* 91 **AL,** He axed me if I had enny opydildock in the wagin box, that he could rub his side with. **1892** Johnston *Mr. Fortner's* 86 **GA,** He never was without a small vial of camphor, and one of opodeldoc, or other salve for healing. **1892** *DN* 1.210 **seMA,** Opodildocs [ɔpəˈdɪl-]. "He's on his opodildocs" (said of a spirited horse). **1899** (1912) Green *VA Folk-Speech* 307, Opodeldoc. . . Soap-liniment. **1911** (1913) Johnson *Highways Gt. Lakes* 77, Usually they're fair sort of workers, but they went to town last night and took a little too much opedildoc. So they're grouchy and cranky today. **1922** (1926) Cady *Rhymes VT* 131, They 'rested him in Taftsville once / Because a black and tan / Container 'neath his lift-up seat / With Oh-be-joyful ran;/ The Army Boys, they paid his fine—/ Good Opedildock Man. **c1965** *DARE* File **CT,** A long time ago my husband . . would say whenever he had to take any medicine . . "Wall, I will take a little opadilldock." The saying amused us and it became a familiar one in our household. **1976** Horn *World Encycl. Comics* 323, Soon Howarth emerged in the *Chicago Tribune* comic section, doing *Ole Opey Dildock—the Storyteller.* . . This strip about a teller of tales didn't last long—at least with Howarth as artist, for he died in 1908. An artist named Wells continued the strip for the *Tribune.*]

opopanax n

A **huisache** (here: *Acacia farnesiana*).

1889 *Boston Morning Jrl.* (MA) 30 Nov 2/3, [Quotation from the *News & Courier* (Charleston SC):] There are a score or more of ladies in Charleston who actually get all their winter dresses from the opoponax [sic] trees in their gardens. . . The flowers are made up in tiny button-hole bouquets and are. . . [sold] to Northern tourists. **1908** Britton *N. Amer. Trees* 525, *Vachellia Farnesiana . . Mimosa Farnesiana . . Acacia Farnesiana.* . . Also called Yellow opopanax, Sponge wood, Cassie, and Huisache, this is a small monotypic tree or shrub, probably native in Texas . . and occurs in our area from Florida to southern California. **1937** U.S. Forest Serv. *Range Plant Hdbk.* B1, The huisache, or sweet acacia *(A. farnesiana),* native from western Texas south to northern Chile, is widely cultivated at home and abroad and, under the (unfortunately misleading) names cassie and opopanax, is an aristocrat among commercial perfumery plants. **1953** Greene–Blomquist *Flowers South* 53, Sweet-Acacia, Popinack, Yellow-Opopanax *(Vachellia Farnesiana).* . . Fla. to Tex. **1972** Brown *Wildflowers LA* 72, Opopanax, Sweet-acacia, Huisache. . . A large shrub to small tree with the numerous branches armed with paired spines.

opossum n

Std: the North American marsupial *Didelphis virginiana.* Also called **blue-cod possum, eggeater, gravedigger 2, file-tail, poor Sam, possum, Sambo, slick-tail, slowpoke, sundowner, woolly shoat** Cf **blackjack possum**

opossum on the half shell n Cf **hard-shelled possum, iron-plated ~**

The armadillo *(Dasypus novemcinctus).*

1995 *Smithsonian* Dec 22 **GA,** [Letter:] Many people know armadillos by the moniker "opossum on the half shell." Besides sharing similar size, shape and gait, both creatures are notorious for being found dead along Southern roads. In fact, their respective ranges can be determined by the highway sightings where one replaces the other as victim.

opossum tree n

=**sweet gum.**

1876 Hobbs *Bot. Hdbk.* 84, Opossum tree, Sweet gum tree, Liquidambar styraciflua. **1900** Lyons *Plant Names* 227, *L[iquidambar] Styraciflua.* . . Connecticut to Florida, west to Missouri and Mexico. . . Opossum tree. **1960** Vines *Trees SW* 325, Vernacular names [for *Liquidambar styraciflua*] are . . Opossum-tree . . and Star-leaf Gum. . . At least 25 species of birds are known to feed upon the fruit, as well as the gray squirrel and Eastern chipmunk.

opossum wood n Cf **possum wood**

A **silver bell** (here: *Halesia carolina*).

1897 Sudworth *Arborescent Flora* 323 **AL,** *Mohrodendron carolinum.* . . Opossum-wood. **1903** Small *Flora SE U.S.* 915, *Mohrodendron Carolinum.* . . In woods, Virginia to Illinois, south to Florida and Texas. . . *Opossum Wood.* **1950** Peattie *Nat. Hist. Trees* 545, *Common Silverbill* . . *Other Names* . . Opossumwood. **1970** Correll *Plants TX* 1190, *Halesia carolina.* . . O'possum-wood. **1980** Little *Audubon Guide N. Amer. Trees E. Region* 637, "Opossum-wood"—*Halesia carolina.*

‡**oppastrouder** n Cf *DS* NN12b

1970 *DARE* File **csNE,** Oppastrouder—layovers to catch meddlers: "What are you making?" "Oppastrouders."

oppsies exclam

In marble play: see quot.

1950 *WELS* **ceWI** *(Cries or calls used in playing marbles: To stop another player from doing something)* 1 Inf, No oppsies; *(To get the right to do something)* 1 Inf, Oppsies on all.

opry See **opera**

optriculum n *joc* Cf *DS* NN12b

1916 *DN* 4.278 **NE,** Optriculum. . . About the same as *doodad, thingumbob,* etc. "Where is that optriculum?" (Referring to a dish towel.)

opu n [Haw] **HI**

The stomach, belly; hence n, adj *opu nui* big belly; having a big belly, pregnant.

1836 in 1934 Frear *Lowell & Abigail* 107 **HI,** The great argument with them all was that it [=smoking] warmed the mouth and the *opu* (stomach) after eating. **1938** Reinecke *Hawaiian Loanwords* 26, Opu. . . Stomach; belly, paunch. . . V[ery] F[req]. **1954–60** Hance et al. *Hawaiian Sugar* 5, Opu. . . The stomach. Opu nui. . . Pot-bellied. **1967** Reinecke–Tsuzaki *Hawaiian Loanwords* 106, Opu nui. . . ['Ōpū and nui, big]. 1. Big paunch (used jestingly). 2. Pregnant. F[req]. **1967** Clark *All the Best HI* 55, Opu—like our "tummy" or "bay window." **1969** *DARE* FW Addit **Honolulu HI,** Opu [ouʻpu]—stomach. **1984** Sunset *HI Guide* 85, 'Opu—belly, stomach.

opydildock See **opodeldoc**

oquassa n Also *oquassa trout, quasky* [See quot 1896]

The Arctic char *(Salvelinus alpinus).* Also called **blueback trout**

1879 U.S. Natl. Museum *Bulletin* 14.58, *Salvelinus oquassa* . . Oquassa Trout . . Rangely Lake, Me., and vicinity. **1882** *Ibid* 16.318, *S[alvelinus] oquassa* . . Oquassa Trout; Blue-back Trout. **1896** U.S. Natl. Museum *Bulletin* 47.514, Oquassa Trout; Blueback Trout; Quasky. . . Smallest and handsomest of the charrs, as yet known only from the Rangely Lakes in western Maine. . . (Oquassa or Oquassoc, name of one of the Rangely Lakes.) **1925** *Book of Rural Life* 9.5608, A third fish of this group [=the chars] is the *sea trout* of eastern Canada, called also the *oquassa,* or *Arctic char.*

or conj Pronc-spp *a, aer, er, ur*

A Forms.

a1824 (1937) Guild *Jrl.* 3.252 **VT,** I came to a poor house where they wanted a needle atoo [=or two] or a few pins. **1843** (1916) Hall *New Purchase* 145 **sIN,** Jist then I hears somethin a nuther in the beech above. **1867** Harris *Sut Lovingood Yarns* 158 **TN,** Hit am es true es sayin yas, when a man axes yu ur me. **1894** Riley *Armazindy* 157 **IN,** Fer any boy 'at's little as me,/ Er any little girl. **1908** *DN* 3.309 **eAL, wGA,** Er, conj. Or. The r is usually lost. **1939** Cheney *Lightwood* 5 **GA,** It didn't last more'n seven aer eight year.

B Sense.

Except, other than. Cf **only B**

c1970 *Halpert Coll.* 17 **wKY, nwTN,** What shall we do—or stay here? = Is there anything we can do except stay home?

orach n Also sp *orache*

Std: a plant of the genus *Atriplex.* For other names of var spp see **fogweed, French spinach, redscale, rillscale, sea purslane.** For other names of chiefly western spp see **saltbush**

oracle oak n

A natural hybrid **oak** (here: *Quercus* x *moreha*) native to California. Also called **Spanish oak**

1923 in 1925 Jepson *Manual Plants CA* 277, *Q[uercus] morehus* . . Oracle Oak. **1959** Munz–Keck *CA Flora* 903, *Q[uercus] morehus* . . Oracle Oak. **1979** Little *Checklist U.S. Trees* 223, Another hybrid of wider distribution in California is *Q.* x *moreha* Kellogg (*Q. kelloggi* x *wislizeni*), oracle oak.

Orah-gone See **Oregon**

orainge See **orange**

orance n Cf *DS* CC17

1951 Randolph *We Always Lie* 53 **swMO,** Oddly enough, the name orance is still known to some old settlers in southwest Missouri, but nowadays it means only a peculiar sort of legendary wildcat, more commonly called the wampus.

orange n, adj Usu |ˈɔrɪnǰ|; also |ˈɑr-|; less freq |ɔrnǰ, ˈɔɨnǰ|; for addit varr see quots Pronc-spp *aw'inge, orainge*

Std senses, var forms.

1789 in 1956 Eliason *Tarheel Talk* 315 **cNC,** Orainge. **1927** Kennedy *Gritny* 109 **sLA** [Black], To bring you dis aw'inge-rine purzerve I made for you. *Ibid* 51, Settin' in de aw'inge tree in de moonlight. **1936** *AmSp* 11.73 **Upstate NY,** [In the first vowel in *orange,* there were 39 instances of [ɑ], 48 of [ɒ] and 164 of [ɔ] among speakers in upstate NY.] **1939** *AmSp* 14.175, My own record, started in 1932, shows the following instances of [ɑ], [ɒ], and [ɔ] for those parts of the United States in which I have heard *orange* pronounced frequently enough to warrant an estimate of regional preference: New England 46 7 8—Lower New York 185 2 3—Upper New York 115 180 467—New Jersey 83 6 0—Pennsylvania 59 21 37—Virginia 63 0 0—Florida 50 3 5—Tennessee 71 5 2—Ohio 2 11 29—Illinois 1 15 16—Louisiana 59 8 1—Texas 43 13 8—Colorado 1 13 17—Arizona 3 20 34—California 7 21 43. **1941** *LANE* Map 273 *(The oranges),* [The first vowel in *orange* is usually [ɔ] or [ɒ]; [ɑ] is fairly common in **sNEng,** esp the western two thirds of **MA;** it does not occur in **nNEng** except sporadically in **wVT.**] **1955** *PADS* 23.44 **e,cSC, eNC, seGA,** /ɔ/ as well as /a/ in *pot, crop, borrow, orange,* etc. **1961** Kurath–McDavid *Pronc. Engl.* 125, The vowels in *tomorrow, borrow, orange.* . . The South and the South Midland have /ɑ ~ ɑ/ regularly [in *tomorrow*], with the possible exception of the Low Country of South Carolina. *Ibid* 126, New England predominantly has a more or less rounded [ɒ] sound in *tomorrow. Ibid, Orange,* . . though it follows the same pattern [as *tomorrow*] in the South and the South Midland and to some extent also in New England, exhibits a decided predominance of rounded [ɒ ~ ɔ] . . in Upstate New York and the adjoining counties of Pennsylvania . . and is widely current in the Ohio Valley, including the greater part of West Virginia. **c1970** Pederson *Dial. Surv. Rural GA* **seGA** *(A round fruit about the size of a baseball that grows in Florida is an _____)* [31 [of 64] infs gave proncs of the type [ˈɑɚnǰ, ˈɑɚɨnǰ]; 10 [ˈɑ-ɨnǰ, ˈɔɨnǰ]; 8 [ˈɔɚnǰ]; 4 [ˈɔɚnǰ, ɑɚnǰ]; 1 [ɑ-nǰ]; 1 [ɔ^Uɛn].] **1976** Allen *LAUM* 3.36 (as of c1950), *Orange.* The stronger position of a rounded vowel in this word in the East is the basis for its strength in the U[pper] M[idwest], where only nine infs. have /ɑrɪnǰ/, six of them in Minnesota. *Ibid* 298, The reduction of dissyllable *orange* /ɔrɪnǰ/ to a monosyllabic /ɔrnǰ/ has been accepted by more than one-third of all infs., actually nearly one-half in Type II [=mid-aged, with approx hs educ]. A likely Midland orientation of the single syllabic form appears in its higher frequency in Iowa, particularly in the southern two-thirds, and also in Nebraska. **1989** Pederson *LAGS Tech. Index* 183 **Gulf Region,** [Of the 822 proncs recorded for *orange(s),* 47% have [ɑ] in the first syllable, 13% [ɑ], 23% [o], and 16% [ɔ]. 36% of the singular forms are monosyllabic, but 53% of the plural forms have two (rather than three) syllables.]

orange borer n Also *orange sapsucker* [See quots 1890, 1955] chiefly **FL**

=**red-bellied woodpecker.**

1890 Warren *Birds PA* 174, In various sections of Florida where the Red-bellied Woodpeckers are exceedingly numerous . . , the common names of "Orange Sapsucker" and "Orange-borer" are universally applied to them. On making inquiry of farmers and others, I learned that the names were given because these woodpeckers "sucked the sap" of orange trees and fed on oranges. **1930** OK Univ. Biol. Surv. *Pub.* 2.146, *Red-bellied Woodpecker. . . Local Names . .* orange "sapsucker" and orange borer. **1955** Forbush–May *Birds* 297, *Centurus carolinus. . .* Orange Sucker. . . It has a habit of boring into oranges, either on the ground or growing on the tree, and eating both juice and pulp. **1969** Longstreet *Birds FL* 89, *Red-bellied Woodpecker—Other names . .* Orange Sapsucker. [*Ibid* 90, The one criticism against the [red-bellied woodpecker] . . is its fondness for oranges. But as it pecks holes only in dead ripe fruit, and patrols the ground under the trees to consume whole dropped and decaying oranges, it is a valuable grove and forest scavenger, as well as a truck crop protector.]

orange-breast n

A **merganser** (here: *Mergus merganser*).

1955 MA Audubon Soc. *Bulletin* 39.379 **MA,** American Merganser. . . Orange-breast. . . The under plumage of the adult male is creamy white to salmon buff, the salmon, however, fading after death.

orange crab n Cf **lemon-belly**

=**bally** n[1].

1984 *DARE* File **Chesapeake Bay** [Watermen's vocabulary], Sponge crab, brood crab, cushion crab, lemon, orange crab.

orangecup lily n Also *orangecup* Cf **orange lily**

A **wood lily** (here: *Lilium philadelphicum*).

1933 Small *Manual SE Flora* 291, *L[ilium] philadelphicum. . .* Orange-cup lily. . . Thickets and open woods, often in acid soil. **1963** Craighead *Rocky Mt. Wildflowers* 26, *Lilium umbellatum* [=*L. philadelphicum* var *andinum*]. . . Orange-cup. . . This is the only large red-to-orange lily with purple-spotted sepals and petals in the Rockies. . . Goblet-shaped blossom is 3–4 in. deep and generally solitary. **1976** Bailey–Bailey *Hortus Third* 663, *[Lilium] philadelphicum. . .* Orange-cup l[ily]. . . Me. to s. Ont., s. to Del., Ky. and N.C. Var. *andinum. . . Western orange-cup l[ily]. . .* Smaller; . . W. Que. to B.C., s. to Ky., Nebr., New Mex.

orange dog n

1 also *orange puppy:* Usu the larva of the giant swallowtail *(Papilio cresphontes),* but also the adult butterfly. [See quots 1890, 1960] **esp FL**

1881 U.S. Dept. Ag. *Rept. of Secy. for 1880* 247, Mr. A.T. Harvey, of . . Sumter County, Florida, informs me that he has had many orange seedlings completely defoliated by these larvae—"orange dogs" as they call them in that part of the country. **1890** (1893) Ballard *Among Moths* 142 **FL,** The common name in Florida for this caterpillar is "the orange dog," from a fancied resemblance of its most curious head to that animal. **1902** Holland *Butterfly Book* 311, It [=*Papilio cresphontes*] is very common in the orange-groves of Florida, where the people call the caterpillar the "orange-puppy," and complain at times of the ravages perpetrated by it upon their trees. **1939** FWP *Guide FL* 29, Butterflies frequently seen are . . orange dogs, which are citrus pests. **1954** Borror–DeLong *Intro. Insects* 494, The giant swallowtail or orange-dog . . is a large dark-colored butterfly with rows of large yellow spots on the wings; the larva feeds largely on citrus in the South and on prickly ash in the North. **1960** Barker *Famil. Insects Amer.* 115, In the South the caterpillar of the giant swallowtail is called "orange dog" or "orange puppy" because it feeds on the leaves of citrus trees. . . But North or South, the caterpillar of *Papilio cresphontes* is undoubtedly one of the ugliest of all butterfly larvae. **1972** Swan–Papp *Insects* 206, Orange-dog. . . Our largest butterfly, often referred to as the giant swallowtail. The caterpillar is also called orange puppy. **1972** Harris *Butterflies GA* 162, The caterpillar—especially in Florida, where it is found on citrus trees—is known as the "orange dog." **1986** Scott *Butterflies N. Amer.* 177, Larvae (Orange Dogs) eat new shoots and young and older leaves. **1989** Entomol. Soc. Amer. *Common Names Insects* 43, Orangedog—*Papilio cresphontes.*

2 in comb *California orange dog:* The western swallowtail *(Papilio zelicaon)* or its larva.

1913 Essig *Injurious Insects CA* 198, *The California Orange Dog. Papilio zolicaon. . .* The adult butterfly is one of the smaller swallowtails. [*Ibid* 199, In the Porterville section, as well as in the vicinity of Riverside, the larvae feed upon orange trees and in the former district promise to be a pest.] **1926** Essig *Insects N. Amer.* 634, *The western parsley caterpillar, Papilio zelicaon. . .* is yellow or orange and black. . . Also known as the . . California orange dog. [**1986** Scott *Butterflies N. Amer.* 171, *P[apilio] zelicaon* invaded lowland Calif. after *Foeniculum* was introduced, and now larvae eat *Citrus* there, and are pests within orange groves.]

orange-flower tree n [See quot 1942]

A **mock orange 1b** (here: *Philadelphus coronarius*).

1900 Lyons *Plant Names* 284, Syringa, Mock Orange, Orange-flower tree. **1942** Tehon *Fieldbook IL Shrubs* 89, The Syringa is an introduced shrub that has escaped somewhat sparingly from cultivation in Illinois. The appearance of the flowers, which bloom in May and June, gives rise to the occasionally used name Orange Flower Tree.

orange grass n [So called from its yellow-orange flowers and grasslike appearance]

A **Saint-John's-wort:** usu *Hypericum gentianoides,* occas *H. drummondii.*

1833 Eaton *Botany* 324, *[Sarothra] gentianoides . .* orange grass. . . Flowers on the branchlets alternate, solitary. **1882** Godfrey *Is. Nantucket* 36 **seMA,** The orange-grass with its fragrance, now greeting us at every turn. **1901** Lounsberry *S. Wild Flowers* 344, *Sarothra gentianoides, . .* orange grass, is the wiry, grass-like looking little plant with minute leaves which occurs in sandy fields. . . In a scattered way its tiny deep orange flowers grow along the filiform, erect branches. **1931** Harned *Wild Flowers Alleghanies* 300, *Orange Grass. . .* An annual, with threadlike branches. **1932** Rydberg *Flora Prairies* 546, Orange-grass. . . *S[arothra] Drummondii. . . S. gentianoides.* **1968** Barkley *Plants KS* 238, Hypericum drummondii. . . Orange Grass. Dry soil, fields, barrens and open woods.

orange hawkweed n [From the color]

A **hawkweed** (here: *Hieracium aurantiacum*). Also called **devil's hawkweed, ~ paintbrush 1, ~ weed c, fairy's paintbrush, fireweed h, Flora's paintbrush 1, hawkbit 2, Indian paintbrush 4, Italian daisy, king devil, missionary weed, mouse-ear 1d, orange paintbrush, paintbrush, red daisy, redweed**

1822 Eaton *Botany* 306, *Hieracium . . aurantiacum* (orange hawkweed). **1836** (1840) Phelps *Lectures on Botany* 104, *[Hieracium] aurantiacum* (orange hawkweed). **1914** Georgia *Manual Weeds* 556, If possible, the sentiment of an entire neighborhood should be aroused against Orange Hawkweed, for, with a plant of this quality, the careful farmer is largely at the mercy of any slovenly cultivator who chooses to be regardless of communal welfare. **1937** U.S. Forest Serv. *Range Plant Hdbk.* W94, Several of the hawkweeds are serious pests in the Eastern States, the leading one being orange hawkweed *(H. aurantiacum),* which has become one of the most troublesome weeds ever introduced into America. **1949** Moldenke *Amer. Wild Flowers* 180, The *orange hawkweed* or *devilspaintbrush. . .* have become thoroughly acclimated to fields, woods, and roadsides from New Brunswick and Ontario south to New Jersey and Pennsylvania and west to Iowa. **1961** Douglas *My Wilderness* 231 **White Mts NH,** The coarse orange hawkweed with its hairy stems (sometimes called devil's paintbrush) and a large-leafed plant called Indian poke are constant companions. **1966** *DARE* Wildfl. QR Pl.223B Inf **MI**7, Orange hawkweed. **1966–70** *DARE* (Qu. S26a, . . *Wildflowers. . . Roadside flowers)* Inf **MI**2, Orange hawkweed; **WI**58, Paintbrush—right name is orange hawkweed; (Qu. S26d, *Wildflowers that grow in meadows;* not asked in early QRs) Inf **MA**78, Orange hawkweed; same as devil's paintbrush. **1968** WI Statist. Reporting Serv. *Report* 25 June 2, Orange hawkweed (Indian paint brush) in full bloom—makes for colorful roadsides.

orange jasmine See **orange jessamine**

orange jelly n

A **jelly fungus** (here: *Dacrymyces palmatus*).

1981 Lincoff *Audubon Field Guide Mushrooms* 381, Orange Jelly—*Dacrymyces palmatus. . .* The Orange Jelly is edible, but should be boiled or steamed, rather than sautéed.

orange jessamine n Also *orange jasmine*

=**mock orange 1g.**

1929 Neal *Honolulu Gardens* 167, Mock orange, orange jessamine *(Murraya exotica).* **1953** Greene–Blomquist *Flowers South* 169, Others often confused with jasmines are . . *Murraya paniculata,* not orange-jasmine [etc]. **1976** Bailey–Bailey *Hortus Third* 745, *[Murraya] paniculata . .* Orange jasmine, orange jessamine.

orange lily n

A **lily 1** such as *Lilium bulbiferum,* or a **day lily 1;** see quots.

1822 Eaton *Botany* 337, *[Lilium] bulbiferum* (orange lily). **1840** MA Zool. & Bot. Surv. *Herb. Plants & Quadrupeds* 215, *L[ilium] bulbiferum . .* Orange Lily. From Italy, is another beautiful plant in gardens. **1891** Jesup *Plants Hanover NH* 45, *L[ilium] Philadelphicum. . .* (Orange

Lily.) Common in sandy, open woods. **1952** Gleason *New Britton & Brown* 1.417, *Lilium bulbiferum* . . Orange Lily. **1967–69** *DARE* (Qu. S26a, . . *Wildflowers. . . Roadside flowers*) Inf **OH**21, Orange lily; **VT**13, Orange lily (wild Canada lily). **1968** *DARE* Tape **IN**14, I do have some flower seed planted, but I like the flowers that you can put out and come up every year. I do have a lemon lily and an orange lily that a lot of people have not seen. **1979** Niering–Olmstead *Audubon Guide N. Amer. Wildflowers E. Region* 602, The Orange Lily . . , a European native, has sepals and petals downy within.

Orangeman n Also *Orangey* [William III, King of England and Prince of *Orange*]

A Protestant Irishman; a Netherlander.

1895 in 1976 Dunne *Mr. Dooley & Chicago Irish* 422 **Chicago IL,** Th' day come f'r th' Orangeys to cillybrate th' time whin King Willum . . got a stand-off. **1967–69** *DARE* (Qu. HH28, *Names and nicknames . . for people of foreign background . . Irish*) Inf **NJ**61, Orangeman; [**PA**199, County-Orange]; (Qu. HH28, . . *Hollanders*) Inf **NY**34, Dutchmen, Orangemen.

orange milkweed n

A **milkweed 1:** usu **butterfly weed 1,** but occas *Asclepias lanceolata.*

1892 (1974) Millspaugh *Amer. Med. Plants* 135-1, *Asclepias tuberosa,* pleurisy-root. . . orange swallow-wort, orange milk-weed. **1914** Georgia *Manual Weeds* 315, Butterfly Weed. . . Orange Milkweed. **1925** *Book of Rural Life* 7.4086, *Orange milkweed,* a beautiful wild flower, reddish-orange in color, belonging to the milkweed family. See *Butterfly Weed.* **1936** Whitehouse *TX Flowers* 101, Butterfly-Weed. . . Other common names include orange milkweed, orange-root, Indian posy, and orange swallow-wort. **1946** Tatnall *Flora DE* 210, *A[sclepias] lanceolata. . . Orange Milkweed.* Frequent on beaches and in salt marshes. . . Late June, July. **1951** Hough *Singing in Morning* 70 **Martha's Vineyard MA,** Along the roadsides of Chappaquiddick blooms the gayest of wild flowers, the orange milkweed or butterfly weed. **1968** *DARE* (Qu. S7) Inf **NJ**24, Orange milkweed. **c1979** TX Dept. Highways *Flowers* 3, Orange milkweed or Butterfly Milkweed blooms in spring and summer in East and Central Texas. The leaves are poisonous to livestock, but the nectar attracts Monarch butterflies.

orange milkwort n

A **milkwort** (here: *Polygala lutea*). Also called **bachelor wort, candyroot, candyweed 1, old-man's-cologne, red bug plant, thimbles, wild bachelor's button, yellow ~, yellow clover, ~ milkwort**

1900 Lyons *Plant Names* 299, *P[olygala] lutea* . . eastern U.S., Orange Milkwort. **1919** (1923) House *Wild Flowers NY* 160, Orange Milkwort; Wild Bachelor's-button. . . In pine-barren depressions and swamps, Long Island to New Jersey and eastern Pennsylvania to Florida and Louisiana. **1946** Tatnall *Flora DE* 165, Orange Milkwort. Common in moist, sandy places, Caroline and Sussex Counties, and southward to Cape Charles. **1964** Batson *Wild Flowers SC* 69, Orange Milkwort. . . Open, wet sandy woods, eastern half of state. **1976** Bruce *How to Grow Wildflowers* 169, In open bogs . . grows one of the most spectacular but, alas, uncultivated of all native plants: *Polygala lutea,* the Orange Milkwort or "Bachelor's Button." **1979** Niering–Olmstead *Audubon Guide N. Amer. Wildflowers E. Region* 700, Orange Milkwort. . . The species name, Latin for "yellow," refers to the flower's distinctive color when dried; when fresh, it is bright orange, differing from most of the Milkworts, which are pinkish, yellow, or white.

orange mustard n

A **wallflower** (here: *Erysimum asperum*).

1896 *Jrl. Amer. Folkl.* 9.181 **CA,** *Erysimum asperum,* . . orange mustard. **1923** *Amer. Botanist* 29.150, *Erysimum asperum* is the . . "orange mustard." **1959** Carleton *Index Herb. Plants* 88.

orange paintbrush n

=**orange hawkweed.**

1935 (1943) Muenscher *Weeds* 499, *Hieracium aurantiacum* . . Orange hawkweed, Orange paintbrush. . . Very abundant from New Brunswick to Ontario, southward to New Jersey and Pennsylvania, infrequent in the north central states and rare in the Pacific Northwest. **1940** Clute *Amer. Plant Names* 261.

orange peel n [See quot 1981]

A **mushroom B1:** usu *Aleuria aurantia,* but also *Caloscypha fulgens.*

1972 Miller *Mushrooms* 219, *Caloscypha fulgens* . . "Orange Peel". . .

Cups . . pale orange with blue-green stains. . . *Aleuria aurantia* . . "Orange Peel". . . Cups . . bright orange. **1981** Lincoff *Audubon Field Guide Mushrooms* 349, Orange Peel—*Aleuria aurantia.* . . In color and shape, this species resembles an orange peel. **1987** McKnight–McKnight *Mushrooms* 59, *Orange Fairy Cup (Orange Peel).* . . Common across the continent from Tennessee and California north to southern Canada.

orange plume n

A **fringed orchid** (here: *Platanthera ciliaris*).

1933 Small *Manual SE Flora* 370, *B[lephariglottis] ciliaris.* . . Orange plume. . . Fla. to Tex., Mich., and Vt. **1950** Correll *Native Orchids* 64, *Habenaria ciliaris.* . . Yellow Fringed-orchid, Orange-fringe, Orange-plume, Rattlesnake's Master. **1976** Bailey–Bailey *Hortus Third* 533, *[Habenaria] ciliaris.* . . orange-plume, orange-fringe.

orange puccoon n Cf **red puccoon, yellow ~**

A **gromwell** (here: either *Lithospermum canescens* or *L. carolinense*).

1936 Whitehouse *TX Flowers* 114, *Orange puccoon (Lithospermum gmelinii)* is a striking woodland plant of the Eastern States which is widespread in East Texas. **1940** Steyermark *Flora MO* 450, Orange Puccoon. . . Throughout Mo., but commonest in the Ozarks. The red juice from the roots . . was at one time used by the Ozark people as a dye for coloring cloth. **1951** *PADS* 15.39 **TX,** *Lithospermum gmelinii* . . Orange, musky, piney-wood, or dye-root, puccoon; Indian 'bokay.' **1959** Carleton *Index Herb. Plants* 88, *Orange puccoon:* Lithospermum canescens.

orange puppy See **orange dog 1**

orange rockfish n

A **rockfish** (here: *Sebastes pinniger*) of the Pacific coast.

1882 U.S. Natl. Museum *Bulletin* 16.662, *S[ebastichthys] pinniger.* . . Orange Rock-fish. . . Ground color light olive-gray, profusely blotched with bright clear orange-red or with light orange-yellow, the red shades predominating above, the pale below. **1902** Jordan–Evermann *Amer. Fishes* 497, Another abundant species is the orange rockfish, . . found from Puget Sound to San Diego. It reaches 2 feet in length and is a common market-fish. **1953** Roedel *Common Fishes CA* 126, Orange Rockfish. . . The most important species in the State in recent years. Dominates the catch at Eureka, but is of lesser importance in Central and Southern California. **1991** Amer. Fisheries Soc. *Common Names Fishes* 164, [Rockfish,] orange—see canary rockfish.

orangeroot n Cf **climbing orangeroot**

1 =**goldenseal 1.**

1817 Eaton *Botany* 62, *[Hydrastis] canadensis,* (orange-root). **1844** Lapham *Geogr. Descr. WI* 77, Some of the more useful or interesting plants of Wisconsin [include]. . . Hydrastis Canadensis . . orange root, golden seal [etc]. **1903** Porter *Flora PA* 134, *Hydrastis canadensis* . . Golden Seal. Orange-root. **1942** Hylander *Plant Life* 220, Orange Root *(Hydrastis),* or Goldenseal, is a flower of rich woods, with one American species found from New England to Kansas and Georgia. . . It is a low-growing plant with a thick yellow rootstock containing substances of medicinal value. **1968** *Foxfire* Summer 15, Best known as sang-sign is the "little brother of the ginseng," the golden seal (Hydrastis canadensis). Other names include tumeric-root, tonic-root, ohio curcuma, orange-root, and jaundice-root. **1971** GA Dept. Ag. *Farmers Market Bulletin* 15 Sept 8, Goldenseal is often known as Orange-root or Ground-raspberry according to the part of the country you are from. **1974** (1977) Coon *Useful Plants* 220, *Hydrastis canadensis*—Golden seal, orange-root, Indian turmeric. . . The roots are the part used, either as a source for a yellow dye, or in reputable medical practice as an alterative and bitter tonic.

2 =**butterfly weed 1.**

1900 Lyons *Plant Names* 50, Butterfly-weed, Canada-root, Indian Posy, Orange-root. **1914** Georgia *Manual Weeds* 315, Butterfly-weed, Pleurisy root, Orange milkweed, Orange root, White root. **1936** [see **orange milkweed**]. **1974** Morton *Folk Remedies* 33 **SC,** Butterfly weed; Orange milkweed; Orange root; Canada root.

orange sapsucker See **orange borer**

orange sneezeweed n

A composite plant *(Dugaldia hoopesii)* of the western US. Also called **owl's claws, sneezeweed, sunflower, yellowweed**

1937 U.S. Forest Serv. *Range Plant Hdbk.* W88, Wherever good forage plants are plentiful orange sneezeweed is so low in palatability as to be scarcely grazed. **1949** Moldenke *Amer. Wild Flowers* 195, The *orange* *sneezeweed* . . has orange-colored rays and lives in wet places from the Mackenzie basin and Saskatchewan to British Columbia, south to Oregon and Wyoming. **1968** Schmutz et al. *Livestock-Poisoning Plants AZ* 90, Orange sneezeweed . . (*Helenium hoopesi*). . . Sheep are the principal animals poisoned on the range and some losses may be expected in Arizona. **1979** Spellenberg *Audubon Guide N. Amer. Wildflowers W. Region* 370, Orange Sneezeweed, which has become increasingly frequent in heavily grazed areas, causes the sheep poisoning called "spewing sickness."

orangespotted sunfish n Also *orangespot (sunfish), orange-spotted*

A small **sunfish** (here: *Lepomis humilis*) common in the Mississippi and Ohio River basins. Also called **dwarf sunfish, pumpkinseed, red-spotted sunfish**

    1908 Forbes–Richardson *Fishes of IL* 255, *Lepomis humilis* . . Orange-spotted sunfish. **1929** OK Univ. Biol. Surv. *Pub.* 1.107, *Allotis humilis* . . (Orange-spotted sunfish). **1943** Eddy–Surber *N. Fishes* 216, The orange-spot sunfish is found from North Dakota and western Ohio southward to Texas and the Gulf States. **1957** Trautman *Fishes* 507, Throughout the 1925–50 period I attempted to follow the Orangespotteds as they moved eastward across western Ohio. Almost invariably the first specimens collected along the then-existing eastern frontier were hybrids between the Orangespotted and some other sunfish species. **1967** Cross *Hdbk. Fishes KS* 266, The Orange-spotted sunfish occurs throughout Kansas, rivaling the green sunfish in ubiquity and abundance. *Ibid*, The orangespot sometimes gains access to lakes and ponds. **1983** Becker *Fishes WI* 840, In Wisconsin, the orangespotted sunfish is known only from the Mississippi River drainage basin. **1991** Amer. Fisheries Soc. *Common Names Fishes* 47, *Lepomis humilis* . . orangespotted sunfish.

orange-throated warbler n

The Blackburnian warbler (*Dendroica fusca*).

    1907 Anderson *Birds IA* 355, The Orange-throated or Blackburnian Warbler is a tolerably common spring and fall migrant in eastern Iowa. **1917** (1923) *Birds Amer.* 3.137, *Blackburnian Warbler. . . Other Names. . .* Orange-throated Warbler. [*Ibid* 138, The crown, sides of face, throat and breast are of a most vivid flame color—a most astonishing combination of orange, black and white.] **1936** Roberts *MN Birds* 2.229, *Orange-throated Warbler. . .* A summer resident in the northern evergreen forests, where it breeds as far south as the spruce swamps of northern Isanti [County] and . . as far west as northeastern Otter Tail [County]. **1955** Forbush–May *Birds* 431, Orange-throated Warbler. . . This little bird is the most brilliant of all our warblers.

orange weed n

A **glasswort** (here: *Salicornia europaea*).

    1966 *DARE* Wildfl. QR Pl.49B Inf **NC**28, Orange weed.

Orangey See **Orangeman**

orchard n

See quots.

    1943 Peattie *Great Smokies* 163, At high altitudes certain of these trees—the beech, yellow birch, and buckeye, northern red oak, scarlet and white oaks, and the dotted haw—become curiously dwarfed in stature, with thick stems when old, and the wide crowns that trees may develop when they are spaced far apart. They resemble old apple trees in outline, and for this reason the mountain people call them "orchards." In general there are no shrubs or understory trees in these sub-alpine orchards; the flowering herbs and ferns, growing shoulder-high, fill up the "orchards" the way timothy and daisies do in a real orchard. **1979** *S. Living* May 105 **NC**, Certain sections of the parkway [=Blue Ridge Parkway] are bordered by a mixed hardwood forest whose appearance is unique because of the severity of the climate. The trees are slow growing and have the withered character of old fruit trees—thus the local designation of "orchard."

orchard beef n Cf **government beef**, *DS* P35a

    1987 *DARE* File **ME** (as of 1980), The word venison was rarely heard in Maine. Deermeat was universally used and in the south-central apple-growing country "orchard beef" was standard.

orchard grass n [See quot 1922] **chiefly Nth, Midl, esp S Midl** See Map

A grass of the genus *Dactylis*, usu *D. glomerata*. For other names of this sp see **archy grass, cocksfoot ~ 1, dogfoot, hard grass**

    1765 *Ann. Reg.* II.144/2 (*OED*), A seed of the plant which they call orchard grass. **a1782** (1788) Jefferson *Notes VA* 40, Our grasses are lucerne, st. foin, burnet, timothy, ray and orchard grass. **1800** (1907) Thornton *Diary* 10.190, A Man brought some Orchard Grass Seen [sic] from Virginia a *Guinea* a Bushel. **1824** Bigelow *Florula Bostoniensis* 32, *Dactylis glomerata* . . *Orchard grass.* . . A coarse, but extremely hardy and productive grass, said to be much more luxuriant here than in Europe. **1880** VT State Bd. Ag. *Report* 6.34, Other varieties, such as orchard grass, blue grass, etc., [should] be added. **1884** (1885) McCook *Tenants* 153 **PA**, It [=a bumblebee's nest] was prettily embowered beneath the tufts of orchard grass and sprigs of red clover. **1901** Mohr *Plant Life AL* 384, Orchard Grass. . . Alleghenian to Louisianian area. From Canada to the Gulf. **1922** U.S. Dept. Ag. *Farmers' Bulletin* 1254.13, Orchard grass is readily distinguished by its large circular bunches, folded leaf blades, and compressed sheaths, and very easily by the peculiar form of its flower heads. . . Its ability to grow in the shade of trees is responsible for the name orchard grass. **1925** *Book of Rural Life* 7.4087, Orchard grass is more or less cultivated in nearly every state, but is most important in Maryland, Virginia, North Carolina, West Virginia, Tennessee, Kentucky and Indiana. **1940** Stuart *Trees of Heaven* 129 **neKY**, I'd corn this land three years, then I'd sow it in wheat and orchard grass. **1959** Anderson *Flora AK* 69, *D[actylis] glomerata* . . Orchard Grass. **1965–70** *DARE* (Qu. L9a, . . *Kinds of grass . . grown for hay*) 101 Infs, **chiefly Nth, Midl, esp S Midl**, Orchard (grass); (Qu. S9, . . *Kinds of grass that are hard to get rid of*) 19 Infs, **chiefly Nth, Midl,** Orchard grass; (Qu. L8, *Hay that grows naturally in damp places*) Infs **NH**3, **NY**66, **PA**234, **TN**1, **VA**97, **WI**63, Orchard grass; (Qu. L9b, *Hay from other kinds of plants [not grass]; not asked in early QRs*) Infs **PA**21, 80, Orchard (grass); (Qu. L34, . . *Most important crops grown around here*) Inf **KY**64, Orchard grass; (Qu. S8, *A common kind of wild grass that grows in fields: it spreads by sending out long underground roots, and it's hard to get rid of*) Infs **IL**4, **MO**13, **NJ**45, **OH**18, **PA**3, 89, Orchard grass.

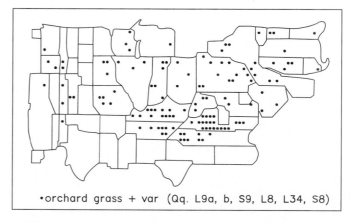

•orchard grass + var (Qq. L9a, b, S9, L8, L34, S8)

orchard oriole n [See quot 1890]

An oriole (*Icterus spurius*) native chiefly to the eastern half of the US. Also called **basket bird, bastard Baltimore, chookee 1, English mockingbird 3, ~ robin 4, figeater 2, firebird 1, garden oriole, hangnest, Mexican canary 2, sanguillah, swinger**

    1808 Wilson *Amer. Ornith.* 1.71, The Orchard Oriole . . is no sneaking pilferer. **1844** Giraud *Birds Long Is.* 144, The Orchard Oriole arrives among us in the latter part of May. **1857** U.S. Patent Office *Annual Rept. for 1856: Ag.* 130, The orchard oriole enters the Southern States from South America early in March, and continues there until October. **1872** Coues *Key to N. Amer. Birds* 157, *Orchard Oriole.* . . Eastern U.S., very abundant in parks, orchards, and the skirts of woods. **1890** Warren *Birds PA* 214, The Orchard Oriole, as its vernacular name would indicate, is a common inhabitant of orchards, particularly apple orchards. **1946** Kopman *Wild Acres* 45 **LA**, Orchard orioles were very animated but in a less roisterous way than the redhead [=woodpecker]. **1961** Ligon *NM Birds* 261, Where other Orioles show yellow in flight, the Orchard exhibits rich chestnut, and appears black when seen through heavy foliage. **1977** Bull–Farrand *Audubon Field Guide Birds* 652, Orchard Oriole. . . Southeastern Louisiana seems to be the heart of this oriole's nesting country since the highest densities have been recorded there.

orchard thrush n

A **wood thrush** (here: *Hylocichla mustelina*).

1969 *DARE* (Qu. Q14, . . *Names* . . *for* . . *thrush*) Inf **NY**209, Orchard thrush.

order n

1 In tobacco curing: =**case** n[1] **2;** hence *high order* a condition of excess moisture, *low order* a condition of insufficient moisture.

1897 U.S. Dept. Ag. *Farmers' Bulletin* 60.4, "Order" or "case" in tobacco curing means a moist condition in which the tissue will not break. **1940** *AmSp* 15.134 [Tobacco market language], *In case* or *in order.* In pliable condition (with reference to leaves). **1944** *PADS* 2.68 **sVA,** *Order, to be* (or *get*) *in.* . . To be in a state of pliancy because of moisture. Tobacco must be "in order" before it can be stripped or otherwise handled. Same as *in case.* **1966** *Wilson Coll.* **sw,wKY,** *In order.* . . When tobacco is in right condition for stripping in dark-tobacco belt, southwest and western Kentucky. **1966** *PADS* 45.18 **cnKY,** The tobacco has to be in order before it can be stripped. **1966** *DARE* FW Addit **MD,** Tobacco is "in order" when it can be stripped (the leaves removed from the stem). Usually humid weather, when leaves are pliable, not brittle. The leaves are then made up into fan-shaped "hands" for storage and marketing. **1966–70** *DARE* Tape **NC**7, You can't handle it [=tobacco] until . . we get it in order. It has to get soft enough to take it down and not crumble; **SC**17, You've got to have it in order [FW:] That means its got the right amount of dampness so it's not brittle. [Inf:] No, it's not brittle; **VA**38, If you had a good [ordering] pit maybe the next morning it [=tobacco] would be in order to tie. **1967** *Key Tobacco Vocab.* **CT,** Order—high order (too damp), low order (too dry), medium order, prime order; **MD,** In order—"(when stripping) it has to be in order, because otherwise it would just crumble up"; **NC,** "Too much order"; high order = wet; **GA,** "In too high order"; **PA,** Not here, inf says order is "a manufacturer's term"; **KY,** "It has to come in order"; too much order.

2 in phr *in good order:* See quot. Cf **case** n[1] **1**

1929 *AmSp* 5.121 **ME,** One putting on much weight was "in good order" or "fat enough to kill" or "fat as a hog in bootcherin' time" or "big as all outdoors."

3 See quot.

1901 *DN* 2.144 **ME,** *Order.* . . Program for a dance. Portland, Me.

order v[1]

In tobacco curing: to bring (tobacco leaf) into **order** n **1;** hence nouns *ordering house, ~ pit.*

1944 *PADS* 2.68 **sVA,** *Order: tr. vb.* To induce pliableness in tobacco by hanging it in damp air or by hanging it in an "ordering-house." . . *Ordering-house.* . . A small tight house, generally daubed, in which tobacco is hung and steam applied to induce pliancy. . . *Ordering-pit.* . . A large hole, or cellar, dug under a packhouse (or some other house) in which tobacco is hung to get it "in order" by means of the moisture from the earth. **1968–70** *DARE* Tape **NC**51, The night air circulatin' through that barn for, say, two nights, will order it—as they call it. It'll put enough moisture back in that leaf and stem to where you can handle it; **VA**38, And then we'd have a orderin' pit—hole dug in the ground. . . Most of the people would try to have the orderin' pit right next to the pack barn—maybe all built together.

order v[2] See **ought**

order house n

A mail-order company.

1970 *DARE* (Qu. X13b, *Joking names for false teeth*) Inf **NJ**67, Sears and Roebuck teeth, order-house teeth. **1995** *NADS Letters* **cWI** (as of 1950s), *Order house:* heard in Wisconsin, but I have only heard it used specifically to modify "catalogue": "Did you get the new order-house catalogue from Sears yet?" A mail-order company was also termed a *mail-order house.*

ordering house (or pit) See **order** v[1]

ordinary n Pronc-sp *ornary* [*OED* 1590 →] esp **VA** *old-fash*

A tavern or inn.

1637 in 1869 *Essex Inst. Coll.* 9.1.55 **neMA,** Mr. John Holgraue . . hath undertaken to keepe an ordinary for the entertainm[en]t of strangers. **1774** (1957) Fithian *Jrl. & Letters* 177 **eVA,** All Taverns they call "Ordinary's." **1784** Smyth *Tour U.S.A.* 1.49 **VA,** There is no distinction here between inns, taverns, ordinaries, and public-houses; they are all in one, and are known by the appellation of taverns, public-houses, or

ordinaries, which, in the general acceptance of the names here, are synonymous terms. They are all very indifferent indeed, compared with the inns in England: and three-fourths of them are in reality little better than mere shelters from the weather; yet the worst of them is by no means deficient in charging high. **1899** (1912) Green *VA Folk-Speech* 307, *Ordinary.* . . *Ornary.* A tavern; an eating-house where there is a fixed price for meals. They used to be found on the old stage roads where horses were changed, and meals served. [**1950** Kimbrough *Innocents* 21 **Chicago IL,** Brother was not allowed in the dining room [of a "family hotel"]. Children his age had to eat apart from us [=in a separate room] in what was called, for some reason, the Ordinary.] **1956** Settle *Beulah Land* 281 **WV** (as of 18th cent), Solomon yearned for an ordinary where he could find a little argument. **1967** *DARE* FW Addit **cwVA,** Ordinary—inn.

ordinary adj [Cf *OED ordinary* a. 6. 1659 →; "Of low degree; . . common, vulgar; unrefined, low, coarse. *Obs.*" The strongly derog senses are now usu attached to *ornery,* orig representing a colloq pronc of *ordinary*]

=**ornery B2, 3.**

1800 *Aurora Genl. Advt.* (Philadelphia PA) 1 May 2/3 (*OEDS*), This ordinary drunken wretch is supposed to be the perpetrator. **1847** [see **ornery B2**]. **1966–68** *DARE* (Qu. HH18, *Very insignificant or low-grade people*) Inf **SC**54, Very ordinary—below average; **TX**29, Ordinary; (Qu. HH37, *An immoral woman*) Inf **ME**22, Ordinary woman; (Qu. NN17) Inf **WI**12, No-good son-of-a-bitch, ordinary son-of-a-bitch. **1986** Pederson *LAGS Concordance (Common)* 1 inf, **neAL,** Ordinary means plain or immoral; 1 inf, **ceAR,** Ordinary girl—rough language, higher than common; 1 inf, **cTX,** Ordinary = common; pejorative of a girl.

orean(n)a See **orejana**

Oregon n Usu |ˈɔrɪˌɡan, ˈar-, ˈɔrɪɡən|; for addit varr see quots

Pronc-spp *Orah-gone, Orygun*

Std sense, var forms.

1829 in 1938 *AmSp* 13.264 [Frontier place names], I [=Representative Edward Everett] have never heard Or'-e-gon pronounced otherwise, than as you [=Joseph Worcester] have marked it. **1906** *DN* 3.149 **nwAR,** *Oregon.* . . Pronounced [ɔrɪɡṇ]. **1944** Kenyon–Knott *Pronc. Dict.* 307, Oregon [ˈɔrɪˌɡan, ˈar-, ˈɒr-, -ɡən]. **1950** Hubbell *Pronc. NYC* 82, In *authority, borrow, Florence,* . . *Oregon,* . . the most usual vowel is /ɑ/. **1986** Pederson *LAGS Concordance,* [5 infs **AL, LA, MS, TN, TX,** offered proncs of the type [ˈɑɚɪɡn]; 2 infs, **LA,** [ˈɔɚɪɡn]; 1 inf, **nwLA,** [ˈɑɚɡn]; 1 inf, **ceAL,** [ˈɔˀɡn]; 1 inf, **cwAR,** [ˈɔɚogɪn]; 1 inf, **cnAR,** [ˈɔɚɪɡɪn].] **1993** Eggers–Jaynes *Against the World* 154, Not only have Portland players often felt unpublicized and underappreciated, Oregon residents often feel the same way. . . Most people in the East still pronounce it "Orah-gone" instead of the proper, "Ory-gun." **1995** *DARE* File, Westerners pronounce the state name [ˈɔɚɪɡən] or [ˈɔɚəɡən], while Easterners often say, based on the spelling, [ˈɔɚəˌɡɔn] or [ˈɑɚəˌɡɑn]. The University of Oregon has bumper stickers that say "Orygun," to set the visitors straight. *Ibid* **csWI,** The Village of Oregon is locally pronounced [ˈɔɚɪˌɡɑːn].

Oregon alder n

A **red alder** (here: *Alnus rubra*).

1874 Glisan *Jrl. Army Life* 480, Thus the Coast Range [of Oregon] . . is covered with evergreen forests . . intermixed at places with . . Oregon alder, balsam tree, [etc]. **1908** Rogers *Tree Book* 178, The *Oregon* . . *Alder* . . is a large tree for an alder, sometimes 80 feet in height, with a narrow pyramid of drooping branches about a trunk that may exceed 3 feet in diameter. . . This is the alder of the Western coast that climbs mountains until it leaves the spruces behind, but reaches its greatest size about Puget Sound. **1923** Abrams *Flora Pacific States* 1.513, Oregon or Red Alder. . . Southern Alaska south in the coastal region to Santa Barbara County, California. **1959** Anderson *Flora AK* 188, Oregon Alder. . . A medium to large tree with gray bark. **1980** Little *Audubon Guide N. Amer. Trees W. Region* 377, "Oregon Alder" . . *Alnus rubra.* . . The leading hardwood in the Pacific Northwest.

Oregon apple n

=**squaw apple.**

1931 U.S. Dept. Ag. *Misc. Pub.* 101.66, *Squaw-apple (Peraphyllum ramosissimum).* . . is often known locally . . in Oregon as Oregon apple.

Oregon boxwood n Also *Oregon box* Cf **boxwood**

A **mountain lover** (here: *Paxistima myrsinites*) native to the western US. Also called **false box 3, mountain box 2, ~ hedge, ~ myrtle 1, myrtle bush 2**

1925 Jepson *Manual Plants CA* 610, *P[achystima] myrsinites* . . Oregon Boxwood . . Densely branched, very leafy, 1 to 3 ft. high. **1945** Benson–Darrow *Manual SW Trees* 237, Bittersweet Family. . . best known in the United States for . . *Pachystima*, including the Oregon box [etc]. **1963** Craighead *Rocky Mt. Wildflowers* 111, Oregon Boxwood, Myrtle Boxleaf, Mountain-hedge. **1976** Bailey–Bailey *Hortus Third* 827, *[Paxistima] Myrsinites* . . Oregon boxwood . . B.C. to Calif., e. to Mont., Colo., New Mex.

Oregon cedar n

A **white cedar** (here: *Chamaecyparis lawsoniana*).

1872 Victor *All Over OR & WA* 279, The Oregon cedar *(Thuya Gigantea)* grows very abundantly near the coast. **1894** *Jrl. Amer. Folkl.* 7.99 **OR, nCA,** *Chamaecyparis Lawsoniana,* . . Oregon cedar, white cedar, ginger-pine. **1910** Jepson *Silva CA* 152, Some woodsmen use the names "Oregon Cedar" and "White Cedar" [for *Chamaecyparis lawsoniana*]. **1980** Little *Audubon Guide N. Amer. Trees W. Region* 303, "Oregon-cedar". . . Large evergreen tree with enlarged base, narrow, pointed spirelike crown, and horizontal or drooping branches.

Oregon char n Also sp Oregon charr

=Dolly Varden 1.

1896 Jordan–Evermann *Check List Fishes* 293, *Dolly Varden Trout; Oregon Charr.* . . Streams west of the Cascade Range, from the upper Sacramento to Montana, Alaska, and Kamchatka; in the Columbia basin as far up as Montana and Idaho. **1904** *Salmon & Trout* 286, The Dolly Varden trout; Oregon charr. **1911** *Century Dict. Suppl., Oregon char.* Same as *Dolly Varden trout.* **1946** LaMonte *N. Amer. Game Fishes* 118, *Dolly Varden.* . . Western Charr, Malma, Oregon Charr [etc]. **1949** Caine *N. Amer. Sport Fish* 89, Dolly Varden. . . Oregon Charr.

Oregon coltsfoot n Cf coltsfoot

A **false lily of the valley** (here: *Maianthemum bifolium* var *kamtschaticum*).

1923 in 1925 Jepson *Manual Plants CA* 250, *M[aianthemum] bifolium* . . var *kamtschaticum* . . Oregon Coltsfoot. . . Woods near the coast from Marin Co. to Humboldt Co.; n. to Alas. **1949** Moldenke *Amer. Wild Flowers* 334, Oregon coltsfoot, *M[aianthemum] bifolium var. kamtchaticum* [sic] . . is known from northern California eastward to Idaho and north far into Alaska.

Oregon dew See Oregon mist 1

Oregon fir n Cf Oregon pine

=Douglas fir.

1904 *NM Ag. Exper. Station Bulletin* 51.15, The *Douglas Spruce* or *Oregon fir (Pseudotsuga taxifolia)* and the *Bull Pine* . . would well repay the care necessary to getting them established. **1958** McCulloch *Woods Words* 127 **Pacific NW,** *Oregon fir*—Douglas fir. **1966** DARE (Qu. T5, . . *Kinds of evergreens, other than pine*) Inf **MT**4, Oregon fir.

Oregon grape n Cf agarita

Any of several **barberries** native chiefly to the Pacific NW, but usu *Berberis aquifolium, B. repens,* or *B. nervosa;* also the fruit of such a plant. For other names of these plants see **hollygrape, mountain grape 2, ~ holly 1**

1851 *OR Statesman* (Oregon City OR) 27 June [3]/1, Oregon Grape, so called, is not a grape, but resembles the grape in size and appearance. **1893** *Jrl. Amer. Folkl.* 6.136 **OR,** *Berberis aquifolium,* Oregon grape. **1896** *Ibid* 9.180 **OR, WA,** *Berberis aquifolium* . . Oregon grape. **1898** *Ibid* 11.222 **WA, WY,** *Berberis nervosa,* . . Oregon grape, Pierce Co., Wash. *Berberis repens,* . . Oregon grape, Wyo. **1915** (1926) Armstrong–Thornber *Western Wild Flowers* 154, Oregon Grape, Trailing Barberry—*Berberis repens.* . . The fruit is a handsome blue berry with a "bloom," the color of wild grapes, contrasting well with the foliage when it turns red in the autumn, and delicious jelly is made from them. **1929** Ellis *Ordinary Woman* 43 **CO** (as of early 20th cent), Then there was Oregon grape root, brewed with rock candy, supposed to be fine for the kidneys, when juniper and a lot of whiskey were added to it. **1946** Peattie *Pacific Coast* 68, Still I have said nothing of Oregon's State flower, the Oregon grape, so-called. It may be known to you already in eastern or European gardens, where under the nurseryman's name of mahonia, it is a favorite plant. . . In its native state, however, the leaves of this evergreen barberry are picked like holly by the country people and sold at Christmas. **1965–70** DARE (Qu. I44, *What kinds of berries grow wild around here?*) Inf **WA**13, Oregon grape; (Qu. I46, . . *Kinds of fruits that grow wild around here*) Infs **CO**11, **ID**4, 5, **MT**4, 5, **WA**6, Oregon grape(s); **CO**45, Oregon grape—on a vine along the ground; **SD**5, Oregon grapes—grow close to the ground—blue; (Qu. S26e) Inf **CO**22, Oregon

grapes—on a may-apple-size plant—small grapes; (Qu. T5, . . *Kinds of evergreens, other than pine*) Inf **ID**5, Oregon grape; **OH**65, Mahonia—an Oregon grape holly; (Qu. BB50c, *Remedies for infections*) Inf **CA**199, Oregon grapes—take roots and boil them; drink it—cures boils. **1967** DARE Wildfl QR (Craighead) Pl.7.8 Inf **CO**29, Oregon grape. **1969** DARE FW Addit **Weaverville CA,** For a spring tonic—take oregon grape fruit, mountain balm, and spignit [sic] root (plant growing along streams and gulches) and brew them all together. **1976** Elmore *Shrubs & Trees SW* 123, Creeping holly-grape, "Oregon grape," yerba de la sangre, sangre de Cristo.

Oregon jay n

A **Canada jay** (here: *Perisoreus canadensis obscurus*).

1898 (1900) Davie *Nests N. Amer. Birds* 330, Oregon Jay. *Perisoreus obscurus.* . . Mr. A.W. Anthony . . characterizes it as a bird utterly devoid of fear. While dressing deer in the thick timber he has been almost covered with these Jays. **1904** Wheelock *Birds CA* 327, *Oregon Jay.* . . Northern California, Oregon, and Washington to British Columbia. **1917** (1923) *Birds Amer.* 2.227, The Oregon Jay *(Perisoreus obscurus obscurus)* and his variant form, the Gray Jay . . look like Canada Jays, with the wrong color of plumage. . . Both are familiarly known as "Camp Robbers." **1940** Gabrielson *Birds OR* 416, The first Oregon record of the Oregon Jay . . was made near the mouth of the Columbia, January 2, 1806, by members of the Lewis and Clark Expedition. **1949** Kitchin *Birds Olympic Peninsula* 6, The Oregon jay feeds on beetles and larvae found in the festooned moss on fir branches.

Oregon junco n

A western **junco** n[1]: usu *Junco hyemalis oregonus,* but often also another race such as *J. h. simillimus.*

1898 (1900) Davie *Nests N. Amer. Birds* 382, Oregon Junco. . . One of the most common birds of Northwestern Oregon, rearing three and often four broods in a season. **1904** Wheelock *Birds CA* 333, Oregon Junco. . . Nest: of dry grasses loosely put together; lined with cow hair; placed generally on or near the ground. **1917** (1923) *Birds Amer.* 3.47, Maybe the handsomest is the Oregon Junco *(Junco hyemalis oreganus)* with a black head and breast, sharply defined against a mahogany-brown back, white under parts, and pinkish-brown sides. **1948** *Pacific Discovery* Mar–Apr 15 **cwCA,** A female Oregon junco scurried into a fuchsia bush at the southeast side of the Aquarium. **1964** Phillips *Birds AZ* 204, *J[unco] h[yemalis] simillimus.* . . "Oregon Junco." . . Breeds on the northwest coast of Washington and Oregon. (The term "Oregon" or "Pink-sided Junco" is often applied to the several races from this one to *mearnsi,* collectively.) . . *J.h. oregonus.* . . "Oregon Junco." Like *simillimus* but darker, with a very black hood and a richer, redder brown back. It breeds in coastal British Columbia. **1967** DARE (Qu. Q21, . . *Kinds of sparrows*) Inf **OR**4, Oregon junco. **1977** Udvardy *Audubon Field Guide Birds* 731, *Junco hyemalis.* . . This species shows much geographic variation in color. Typically, males of western populations ("Oregon Junco") have *black hood, chestnut mantle,* white under-parts with buff sides.

Oregon lily n

The Columbia **lily 1** *(Lilium columbianum).* Also called **tiger lily**

1923 in 1925 Jepson *Manual Plants CA* 245, *Oregon Lily.* . . Bright reddish orange, thickly spotted with purple. **1949** Moldenke *Amer. Wild Flowers* 323, The *Oregon lily* . . ranges from northern California to British Columbia. **1973** Hitchcock–Cronquist *Flora Pacific NW* 692, Tepals yellow-orange to reddish-orange, strongly reflexed . . Ore[gon] l[ily]. **1979** Spellenberg *Audubon Guide N. Amer. Wildflowers W. Region* 584, *Oregon Lily.* . . This is one of the most popular western wildflowers, often dug for the garden, and in some areas now uncommon.

Oregon maple n

=big-leaf maple.

1897 Sudworth *Arborescent Flora* 283 **OR, WA,** *Acer macrophyllum* . . Oregon Maple. **1931** U.S. Dept. Ag. *Misc. Pub.* 101.100, Bigleaf maple . . often called Oregon maple, occurs from extreme southeastern Alaska along or near the Pacific coast to California. This most valuable Pacific coast hardwood is the largest of the Pacific maples and one of the largest maples in the world, and reaches its maximum size in the rich bottom lands of humid southwestern Oregon. **1961** Peck *Manual OR* 510, Oregon Maple. . . Alaska to southern Calif., mainly west of Cascade Mts. **1967** DARE (Qu. T14, . . *Kinds of maples*) Inf **OR**4, Oregon maple. **1980** Little *Audubon Guide N. Amer. Trees W. Region* 532, Bigleaf maple . . Broadleaf Maple . . Oregon Maple.

Oregon mist n Cf **California mist,** *DS* B21, 23

1 also *Oregon dew:* A light rain or mist; used ironically—a prolonged rain.

1965 *Western Folkl.* 24.198, *Oregon mist*—San Francisco's wet fog. **1966** *Oregonian* (Portland OR) 31 Dec sec A 12, Portland is moist with rain, or what you call "Oregon mist." **1967** *Western Folkl.* 26.190, *Oregon mist (dew)*—the protracted winter rains of the state. **1967** *DARE* FW Addit **seOR,** Oregon mist—a fine mist that generally misses Oregon and ends up in Idaho. **1996** *DARE* File, A colleague who lived in Oregon from 1971–77 . . identified "Oregon mist" as a light rain that Oregonians would ignore, but that would be sufficient to bring out umbrellas in any other part of the country. . . [H]e said that "Oregon mist" was widely used. *Ibid* **eWA,** I recall my father calling a heavy rain (in eastern Washington) "Oregon mist."

2 =**Idaho rain.**

1993 *DARE* File **swID,** What is identified in your letter as a *Mormon rainstorm* I have heard called an *Oregon mist,* with specific reference to the huge clouds of dust blowing across the Snake River from Malheur County, Oregon.

Oregon myrtle n
=**California laurel.**

1908 Sudworth *Forest Trees Pacific* 327, California Laurel; Oregon Myrtle. . . an evergreen tree, distinguished at once from all others of its range by the strong camphoric-pungent odor of its crushed leaves or green bark. **1940** Writers' Program *Oregon* 20, Near the southern coast are extensive groves of Port Orford cedar, redwood, and the rare Oregon myrtle found nowhere else in America. **1949** Peattie *Cascades* 188 **Pacific NW,** This is the California laurel, according to California chambers of commerce and curio dealers; or the Oregon myrtle, according to Oregon chambers of commerce and curio dealers. **1980** Little *Audubon Guide N. Amer. Trees W. Region* 434, California-laurel—"Oregon-myrtle." . . Prized for novelties and woodenware, it is often marketed as "Oregon-myrtle," though a member of the Laurel Family.

Oregon oak n

An **oak** (here: *Quercus garryana*) native to the Pacific NW. Also called **mountain white oak, post ~, shin ~, white ~**

1897 Sudworth *Arborescent Flora* 153 **CA, OR,** *Quercus garryana.* . . Oregon White Oak (Cal.) . . Oregon Oak (Oreg.) **1926** Essig *Insects N. Amer.* 805, [It] produces . . galls on the undersides of the leaves of blue oak, Oregon oak, and valley oak throughout the Pacific Coast States. **1937** U.S. Forest Serv. *Range Plant Hdbk.* B117, Garry oak *(Quercus garryana),* the Oregon white oak of the lumber trade and sometimes called Oregon oak, is a Pacific tree or shrub ranging from British Columbia to California, and is the only native oak in the State of Washington. **1970** *DARE* (Qu. T10, . . *Kinds of oak trees*) Inf **CA208,** Oregon [oak]. **1980** Little *Audubon Guide N. Amer. Trees W. Region* 399, Oregon White Oak . . Oregon Oak. . . The sweetish acorns, often common in alternate years, are relished by livestock and wildlife and were eaten by Indians.

Oregon pine n Cf **Oregon fir**
=**Douglas fir**—often used as a trade name for the lumber.

1845 *N. Amer. Rev.* 60.166, One of those gigantic Oregon Pines . . whose prostrate trunk Douglas found to be two hundred and fifty feet in length. **1897** Sudworth *Arborescent Flora* 47 **CA, WA, OR,** Douglas Spruce. . . Oregon Pine. **1910** Jepson *Silva CA* 115, When . . the log has passed through the sawmill and comes out as lumber, the manufactured product is universally known in the trade as "Oregon Pine." **1947** Peattie *Sierra Nevada* 148 **CA,** When it is made into lumber . . it is known in the trade as Oregon pine. It is called Douglas fir or Douglas spruce indiscriminately. **1958** McCulloch *Woods Words* 127 **Pacific NW,** *Oregon pine*—The name given to Douglas fir by Dr. John McLoughlin as early as 1833 when shipping timber to the Sandwich Islands. He felt that fir was an unknown word, whereas pine was a well-understood term and would make the cargo sell better. Oregon pine was used by loggers and lumbermen as late as 1910, and the term is still known in foreign ports. **1980** Little *Audubon Guide N. Amer. Trees W. Region* 294, Douglas-spruce . . Oregon-pine.

Oregon robin n
=**varied thrush.**

1860 in 1861 U.S. Congress *Serial Set* 1058 Doc 90 5.5, *Turdus naevius,* . . Oregon robin. Colorado river. **1874** Coues *Birds NW* 2, *Varied Thrush; Oregon Robin.* [*Ibid* 3, This species . . is essentially a west-coast bird.] **1917** (1923) *Birds Amer.* 3.240, The Varied Thrush,

Alaska Robin, or Oregon Robin, as it is sometimes called, lives back in the mountains in the wilder sections where the timber is most dense. **1923** Dawson *Birds CA* 2.768, *Oregon Robin.* . . *Nest:* Of sticks, twigs, grasses, and rotten wood, smothered in moss.

Oregon spruce n
=**Sitka spruce.**

1958 McCulloch *Woods Words* 127 **Pacific NW,** *Oregon spruce*—Sitka spruce.

Oregon tea n

1 =**yerba buena.**

1891 Victor *Atlantis Arisen* 225 **NW,** Botanists call it *Micromeria Douglassi,* after David Douglass, Oregon's first explorer in this field of science. . . The early settlers used its aromatic leaves in place of tea, which caused it to be called Oregon tea. **1940** Writers' Program *Oregon* 23, So often did our forebears substitute the dried leaves of the *yerba buena* for "store tea" that the plant has become known by the common name of Oregon tea. **1967** Gilkey–Dennis *Hdbk. NW Plants* 360, *Satureja douglasii*—Oregon tea. . . Common in open woods. Deliciously fragrant, it is one of our most-loved Pacific Coast herbs. **1970** Kirk *Wild Edible Plants W. U.S.* 198, Yerba buena, Oregon Tea. . . The dry leaves may be steeped for fifteen to twenty minutes in hot water to make a good tea said to be stimulating to the digestion.

2 See **Oregon tea tree.**

Oregon tea tree n Also *Oregon tea*

A **buckbrush 3c** (here: *Ceanothus sanguineus*). Also called **chaparral B1, snowbrush, soapbloom, wild lilac**

1925 Jepson *Manual Plants CA* 619, *C[eanothus] sanguineus* . . Oregon Tea-tree. **1931** U.S. Dept. Ag. *Misc. Pub.* 101.110, Red soapbloom *(C. sanguineus),* sometimes called Oregon tea-tree, a red-stemmed, white-flowered species of the Northwest, ranging from British Columbia to western Montana, and northern California . . is of fair to fairly good palatability. **1942** Hylander *Plant Life* 369, The Snow Brush of the prairie states, (known as Oregon Tea farther west). **1973** Hitchcock–Cronquist *Flora Pacific NW* 290, Ore[gon] tea-tree . . *(C. sanguineus).*

Oregon white pine n
=**ponderosa pine.**

1958 McCulloch *Woods Words* 127 **Pacific NW,** *Oregon white pine*—Ponderosa pine.

or either(wise) See **either** conj **E1**

orejana n Also sp *orean(n)a* Also *orejano* [Span *orejano, -na,* adj also used absol, of an animal: unmarked < *oreja* ear] **West** Cf **longear 2**
=**maverick** n **1.**

1924 James *Cowboys N. & S.* 25 **CA, OR, NV,** A "remuda" changes to "caviada," "slick ear" to "Orejana," . . but it all goes to the same critter and the same things and the same work. **1932** Bentley *Spanish Terms* 174, Orejano. . . From *oreja,* ear. A longear; that is, an animal usually cow, calf or steer, that has not been branded or earmarked. Its use at present is less frequent than formerly. **1940** Writers' Program *Guide NV* 77, An *oreana* is an unbranded animal old enough to have strayed from its mother, making identification impossible. The finder usually brands it for himself. **1981** *KS Qrly.* 13.2.69, Oreanna (n.) any unbranded cow loose in the country and fair game for any rancher; in earlier times, a rancher could get started in the cattle business by collecting up oreannas and branding them; "maverick" elsewhere.

oreo n [*Oreo,* tradename for a cookie with chocolate wafers on the outside and vanilla cream filling] *esp freq among Black speakers*

See quots 1968–70, 1971.

1970 *Current Slang* 4.3–4.21 **NM,** Oreo. . . A black who thinks like a white or tries to join white society. (Blacks on the outside but whites on the inside.) **1971** Roberts *Third Ear* np [Black], Oreo . . a black person with white-oriented attitudes; i.e. like an Oreo cookie. . . black outside, white inside. **1973** Walker *In Love* 110 [Black], She was heard from coast to coast blasting the genteel Southern college she had attended for stunting her revolutionary growth and encouraging her incipient whiteness, and striking out at black preachers, teachers and leaders for being "eunuchs", "Oreos", and "fruits". **1982** Heat Moon *Blue Highways* 101 **AL** [Black], Those black motherheads'll manhandle you. Nothin' but Oreos—black out, white in. **1986** Pederson *LAGS Concordance (Negro)* 1 inf, **cwFL,** Oreo—Uncle Tom, "chocolate" outside, white inside; 2 infs, **seFL, ceAL,** Oreo—black on the outside, white on the inside; 3 infs, **cnAL, swAL, nwLA,** Oreos [2 call it pejorative or derogatory]. [3 infs Black]

orey-eyed adj Also *awry-eyed* Also sp *orie-eyed, orry-eyed* [Perh var of *awry,* but cf *SND oorie* adj 1. "Of persons and things: dismal, gloomy. . . 'having a debauched or dissipated look' "] Having bleary or wild-looking eyes, esp as a result of drunkenness; drunk; enraged.

    1919 Mencken *Amer. Lang.* 85, Common American synonyms for *drunk,* for example, *piffled. . . awry-eyed.* **1926** Nason *Chevrons* 107, He's the man that brought you home the night you got orey-eyed at Cokeydawn. **1928** *AmSp* 4.102 [Slang synonyms for "drunk"], Orie-eyed. **1939** (1962) Thompson *Body & Britches* 234 **NY,** For a time he traveled with Sullivan the uproarious, . . trying to keep his friend sober. When the Strong Boy of Boston fell off a rear platform, it was Paddy who stopped the train and hastened back to find his pal, "orry-eyed" but uninjured. **1941** Cleaveland *No Life* 190, I do not know what arrangements Ray made for quitting before the term expired, but I know that he arrived in Datil orey-eyed. **1942** *Time* 9 Mar 62, [West Coast fishermen] roared around the water fronts orie-eyed with Napa Valley red. **1943** (1945) Smith *Life Putty Knife* 33, He would be orry-eyed before nightfall. **1946** *PADS* 6.22 **swVA,** Orey-eyed. . . Blear-eyed. **1950** *Western Folkl.* 9.119 **nwOR** [Logger speech], Orey-eyed. Very angry. **1966-69** *DARE* (Qu. DD15, *A person who is thoroughly drunk*) Inf **IL4,** Orey-eyed ['ɔrɪ,aɪd]—glaze in the eye; **NM11,** Orey-eyed [oɚ-ijɑɪd]; **NY213,** Orey-eyed [ɔri]. [**1986** *DARE* File, 'Aw-ry' may indeed be jocular, but the situation in which it occurred in my youth doesn't sound that way. It was 'that *aw-ry* eyed bastard.' I, and I believe other boys took it to be an imprecation.]

orflin(g) See **orphan**

organ v Also *org* [*OED* 1827 →]
To play an organ.

    1893 Shands *MS Speech* 74, Organ. This word is used by the illiterate whites of Mississippi as a regular verb, meaning to play on the organ. **1911** *DN* 3.549 **NE,** Some common cases of "back-formations," or "back-shortenings," are. . . (2) verbs:—*batch* (< *bachelor*), *burgle* (< *burg(u)lar*), *org* (< *organ*) . . and *insurge* (< *insurgent*). **1914** *DN* 4.138, *Org,* from *organ.* To play the organ. "She orgs at the First Christian Church."

organ cactus n [See quot 1911] Cf **organ-pipe cactus**
=**saguaro.**

    1883 *Harper's New Mth. Mag.* 66.502 **AZ,** The enormous saguaras, the organ-cactus, which . . bristle over the landscape like masts or columns. **1895** *Jrl. Amer. Folkl.* 8.51 **SW,** The true Pitahaya is the Candelabrum, the Organ, the Giant, or the Saguara cactus of various writers. **1911** *Century Dict. Suppl., Organ-cactus.* . . [which] takes its common name from the resemblance of its rows of parallel stems to the pipes of an organ, . . [is] a name given to . . the giant saguaro of the south-western United States, *Cereus giganteus.* **1947** Curtin *Healing Herbs* 158 **NM,** Misappropriation of the word *pitajaya* has resulted in a great deal of confusion, since it is applied by many writers to signify the organ, or giant, cactus.

organ duck n
=**old-squaw.**

    1923 U.S. Dept. Ag. *Misc. Circular* 13.24 **AK,** Old-squaw. . . organ duck. **1982** Elman *Hunter's Field Guide* 232, Oldsquaw . . Common & Regional Names . . organ duck.

organ-pipe cactus n Also *organ pipe, pipe-organ cactus* [See quot 1942] Cf **organ cactus**
A **cactus B1** (here: *Cereus thurberi*).

    1854 *Colburn's United Serv. Mag.* Feb 274, A specimen of [cactus] . . which from its shape is commonly called "the organ pipe" rose to the height of about twenty feet. **1908** Hornaday *Camp-Fires* 352 **AZ,** The mines are quite the northern limit of the organ-pipe cactus. **1940** Benson *Cacti AZ* 76, *Cereus Thurberi. . . Organ pipe cactus.* . . Arizona plants are more branched than those . . occurring in Sonora where the climate is milder. The organ pipe cactus is sensitive to frost, and although the plant seldom is killed, the tender growing tips may be. **1942** Hylander *Plant Life* 330, Next in size to the Sahuaro is the Pipe Organ Cactus . . of extreme southern Arizona and Mexico. . . It looks like a slender Sahuaro, branching however at the ground to form a dense mass of erect cylindrical stems six to eight inches in diameter, ten to twenty feet high. . . Pipe Organ Cactus is the aristocrat of the arid rocky mesas.

Ibid 660, Organ Pipe Cactus—Cereus thurberi. **1957** Kerouac *On the Road* 276, We began to see the ghostly shapes of yucca cactus and organpipe on all sides. **1965** Teale *Wandering Through Winter* 73 **sAZ,** Although nesting holes are numerous in saguaros, only once did we see one excavated in an organ-pipe cactus. . . It appears in clusters like the tubes of a pipe organ. **1977** *Times* (London) 21 Apr 16/8 **AZ,** Organ-pipe cacti still grow alongside . . golf course greens. **1985** Dodge *Flowers SW Deserts* 51, Stenocereus thurberi. . . Lophocereus schottii. . . These two spectacular desert giants with their clumps of erect branches are sufficiently similar to be readily confused at first glance. However, the stems of the Organpipe *(Stenocereus thurberi)* are longer and contain more but much smaller edges than do the stems of the senita or "whisker cactus" [=*L. schottii*].

organ-pipe mud dauber n Also *pipe-organ mud dauber* [See quot 1972]
A **mud dauber 1** of the subfamily Trypoxyloninae.

    1954 Borror–DeLong *Intro. Insects* 744, The Trypoxylinae, or organ-pipe mud-daubers, are elongated, slender, usually shining-black wasps. . . Some species make their nests of mud, with the cells arranged in the form of a long tube, hence the common name for this group. **1971** *Living Museum* 33.4 **IL,** But the common mud-daubers (*Sciliphron cementarium* (Drury)), the organ-pipe mud-daubers (*Trypoxylon politus* Say.), and the jug-makers or potter wasps (*Eumenes fraternus* Say.) are outstanding artists of the clay-working wasps. **1972** Swan–Papp *Insects* 563, Pipe Organ Mud Dauber: *Trypoxylon politum.* Wasps in this genus . . build mud nests of long parallel tubes on exposed surfaces, or use open plant stems or twigs [etc]. [*Ibid* 564, Its nest is a series of parallel mud tubes of varying length (like a pipe organ), with several or many tubes in a row.]

orie-eyed See **orey-eyed**

original n Pronc-spp *richinal, ridgnal, ridinel, rig(i)nal* [Prob folk-etyms for *ridgel* in same sense] Cf **rig**
=**ridgeling.**

    1887 *Amer. Philol. Assoc. Trans. for 1886* 17.42, *Ridgling* or *ridgil* . . is still used in Tennessee and the West in the sense given by Webster [="the male of any beast half gelt"], but has been corrupted into *riginal,* and would-be correct people say *original.* **1897** *KS Univ. Qrly.* (ser B) 6.55, *Original:* one-testicled stallion. Gen'l in country. **1916** *DN* 4.327 **KS,** Original. . . A stallion whose testicles have remained, congenital, in the abdomen. Also *'rig'nal, riginal.* **1917** *DN* 4.397 **neOH, IL,** *Original, 'riginal* [ə'rɪjɪn̩]. . . Ridgeling, a horse whose testicles have not descended into the scrotum at the proper time. **1927** *AmSp* 2.361 **cwWV,** Original . . an animal whose testicles have never descended. "Did you know that hog is an original?" **1942** McAtee *Dial. Grant Co. IN Suppl. 1* 8 (as of 1890s), Ridgnal (from original? cf. ridgling) . . man or animal in which the testicles have not descended into the scrotum; a cryptorchid. **1965-70** *DARE* (Qu. K31, *A horse that's only partly castrated;* total Infs questioned, 75) Infs **ME19, NM13, OK8,** 18, 27, Original; **MS1,** Richinal ['rɪčnəl]; **AR4,** Ridinel; **NM10,** Riginal ['rɪgɪnəl]; (Qu. K43, *A horse that was not intentionally bred, or bred by accident*) Inf **NY163,** Original—if it only has one testicle. **1968** Adams *Western Words* 213, Original—A cowman's name for an imperfectly castrated horse.

oriole basket n
A kind of baby carriage; see quot 1974.

    1941 *Yankee* Dec 39 **ceTN,** One fascinating Oriole Basket costs only $1. **1969** *DARE* (Qu. N42, *Vehicles for a baby or small child—the kind it can lie down in*) Inf **MI106,** Oriole basket—shaped like an oriole nest; two-wheeled. **1974** *DARE* File **MA** (as of early 20th cent), *Oriole basket*—A child's light-weight wicker carriage with an adjustable handle, shaped rather like an oriole nest. Handle releases wheels to bring basket to an upright position or tilts basket for pushing.

or less conj Also *ornelse* [Prob blend of *or else + unless*]
Or else; unless.

    1908 *German Amer. Annals* 10.36 **sePA,** Orless.—Unless. "I'll speak to him, orless you will." . . The form *ornelse* is also found. **1950** *WELS Suppl.* **swWI,** "You can take the highway or less you can come from Muscoda on the Black River road." This was also used by a former teacher of mine . . from Livingston.

orn See **iron**

ornary adj See **ornery**

ornary n See **ordinary** n

or neither See **neither** conj **E1**

ornelse See **or less**

orneriness See **ornery B3**

ornery adj Usu |ˈɔ(r)n(ə)ri, ˈɑn(ə)ri| Also sp *awnry, o'nary, onery, onry, ornary, ornry* For addit pronc and spp varr see **A** below [Originally, pronc-spp representing informal proncs of *ordinary;* now usu considered a separate word, to which the extended, mostly derog, senses of *ordinary* have become attached. The semantic split is not yet complete; see **B1** below for exx of *ornery* in the std sense of *ordinary,* and **ordinary** adj for exx of extended senses now usu confined to *ornery.*]

A Forms.

1816 [see **B2** below]. **1829** Kirkham *Engl. Grammar* 192, *Vulgarisms. Common . . In Pennsylvania.* [Improper:] or na ry [Pronounced:] or di na ry. **1836** *Pub. Ledger* (Philadelphia PA) 22 Aug [2]/2, One instance [of Philadelphia pronunciation] is in *ornary.* We have been taught to pronounce this *ordinary;* but our teachers were bombastic fellows. **1837** *Knickerbocker* 9.68 **NY,** You're all a pack of poor, or'nary common people. **1890** [see **B2** below]. **1892** [see **B2** below]. **1893** [see **B2** below]. **1905** [see **B3** below]. **1917** [see **B3** below]. **1926** [see **B1** below]. **1936** Reese *Worleys* 11 **MD** (as of 1865) [Black], Dem awnry niggahs dey done all runs away. **1939** [see **B1** below]. **1961** *Mt. Life* 37.1.6 **sAppalachians,** In a few words, however, *r* is omitted: . . *fust, hathrock* (hearthrock), and *onery* (ordinary). **1965–70** *DARE* (Qq. B2, J2, K16, 42, V6, Z16, BB5, 39, GG18, 32a, 35b, 38, 39, 41, HH18, 22a, KK11, 30, NN17) [Proncs were recorded from 104 Infs; of these, 40, **chiefly Nth, Midl,** were of the type [ˈɔrn(ə)ri, ˈbrn-, ˈɑrn-, ˈorn-]; 34, **scattered, but less freq Nth, N Midl,** of the type [ˈɔn(ə)ri, ˈbn-, ˈon-]; 35, **scattered, but less freq N Cent, Inland Sth, S Atl,** of the type [ˈɑn(ə)ri]; **VA7,** [ˈorni]. For two Infs, pronc-spp with initial *h-* were recorded: Inf **NJ69,** Hornery; **PA247,** Honery [ˈhɑnəri].]

B Senses.

1 Ordinary, commonplace, plain.

1838 Neal *Charcoal Sketches* 55 **PA,** When I condescend to unbuzzum myself . . to folks of ornery intellect—and caparisoned to me, I know very few people that ar'n't ornery as to brains— . . they ludicrate my sitiation. **1867** Lowell *Biglow* 127 'Upcountry' **MA,** Poor shotes thet ye could n't persuade us to tech,/ Not in ornery times. **1899** (1912) Green *VA Folk-Speech* 307, *Ornary.* . . Ordinary; ugly; not handsome. . . (2) . . mean. **1926** Roberts *Time of Man* 63 **KY,** He must like me, even if my dress is old-styled and o'nary. **1939** *Natl. Geogr. Mag.* Aug 144 **IA,** Wild sweet williams in the wood lot were much more alluring than the "o'n'ry" weeds. **1954** Tolbert *Bigamy Jones* 3 **wTX,** Jones was tall and red-haired and ornery-looking. He was usually clean-shaven, in a land where most men ran to scratchy whiskers. He might have been all-around handsome if he hadn't been a kind of gotch-eyed man.

2 Inferior, poor, worthless, contemptible, immoral. [Cf **ordinary** adj]

1816 in 1915 *MD Hist. Mag.* 10.369, The Land is old completely worn out, the farming extremely ornary in general. **1830** *MA Spy & Worcester Co. Advt.* (Worcester MA) 28 July 4/1, *Southerner.* You ornery fellow! do you pretend to call me to account for my language? *Yankee.* I did but drop a hint. **1847** Hurd *Grammatical Corrector* 54, *Ornary,* for *ordinary;* as, "He is a very ornary fellow." "I never listened to a more ornary address." *Penn.* This word, . . though often used by persons of education, is not only very *ordinary,* but very *low and barbarous.* **1851** Hooper *Widow Rugby's Husband* 46 **AL,** We had an old one-horned cow, mighty onnery (ordinary) lookin', old as the North Star, and poor as a black snake. **1877** Twain in *Atlantic Mth.* 40.723, I proved by eleven witnesses that the cat was of a low character and very ornery and warn't worth a cancelled postage-stamp, any way. **1890** *DN* 1.65 **KY,** *Onery* [ˈɔnəri]: for *extremely ordinary.* "What onery looking chap is that?" "He is an onery 'cuss'." [*DN* Ed: Also in the Middle States (*orn'ry* = mean, or vile. Professor J. Henry Thayer). How wide-spread is this use?] **1892** *DN* 1.217 **swMA,** *Ornery.* . . [Ref to quot 1890 above:] "This is familiar in New England, but is it a native word or an imported one?" *Ibid* 236 **cwMO,** [Ref to quots 1890, 1892 above:] *Onery* [ˈɔnəri], in the well-known sense. **1893** Shands *MS Speech* 48, *Onery* [ˈɔnəri]. Used to some extent by all classes to mean *extremely ordinary, poor, mean.* **1894** *DN* 1.332 **NJ,** [Ref to quot 1890 above:] *Ornery:* common in use. **1899** [see **1** above]. **1902** [see **3** below]. **1903** *DN* 2.323 **seMO,** *Ornary* (often *onery*). . . Inferior. 'That's a mighty onery horse.' **1905** *DN* 3.89 **nwAR,** *Onery.* . . Worthless. 'That's an onery crowd.' **1907** [see **3** below]. **1913** Kephart *Highlanders* 169 **sAppalachians,** "Torn

down scoundrels, every one." "Oh, come, now!" "Yes, they are; plumb onery—lock, stock, barrel and gun-stick." **1914** *DN* 4.77 **ME, nNH,** *Ornery.* . . No good. "An ornery squirt." *Ibid* 110 **cKS,** *Ornery.* . . Bawdy; as, ornery houses. **1915** *DN* 4.227 **wTX,** *Onery.* . . Insignificant, worthless. "He is an onery cuss." **1920** *DN* 5.86 **NC,** *Ornery,* ordinary, common, contemptible. "measly." **1923** *DN* 5.216 **swMO,** *Orn'ry.* . . Worthless, shiftless, lazy. **1926** Roberts *Time of Man* 9 **KY,** It's o'nary to steal. . . It's right low down. **1930** Shoemaker *1300 Words* 44 **cPA Mts** (as of c1900), *Ornery*—Mean, contemptible, immoral. **1942** Warnick *Garrett Co. MD* 11 **nwMD** (as of 1900–18), *Onry* (ornery) . . immoral. **1942** McAtee *Dial. Grant Co. IN* 47 (as of 1890s), *Ornery* (sometimes *onry*) . . mean, no good, worthless, but not as in some places, immoral. **1953** Randolph–Wilson *Down in Holler* 269 **Ozarks,** *Ornery, onery.* . . Inferior, mean, worthless. A stronger word than *sorry.* Applied to a human being, *ornery* generally means lazy and shiftless; sometimes it means ill-tempered. **1962** Atwood *Vocab. TX* 72, When a person lacks energy, ambition, and probably other traits valued by his community, he is referred to as . . *o(r)nery* (25[% of all resps]). [Footnote:] This often implies other traits, such as stubbornness or contrariness. **1965–70** *DARE* (Qu. J2, . . *Joking or uncomplimentary words . . for dogs*) Inf **OK14,** Ornery cuss; **OK43,** Ornery; (Qu. V6, . . *Words . . for a thief*) Inf **IL126,** Ornery; (Qu. X43b, *If you sleep later than usual one day on purpose . . "I _____."*) Inf **CA113,** Made yourself ornery; (Qu. AA6b, . . *A man who is fond of being with women and tries to attract their attention—if he's rude or not respectful*) Inf **MO23,** He's ornery; (Qu. HH18, *Very insignificant or low-grade people*) Inf **MO38,** Ornery class of people; (Qu. LL2, . . *Too small to be worth much: "I don't want that little _____ potato."*) Inf **MO39,** Ornery. **1986** Pederson *LAGS Concordance (Poor whites)* 2 infs, **neAR, nwAR,** Ornery; 1 inf, **cAR,** Tramps are ornery; *(Caucasian)* 1 inf, **cnAR,** Why you ornery sapsucker; *(One who tattles)* 1 inf, **csAL,** Ornery; *(Skunk)* 1 inf, **csTN,** Calling a person "peckerwood" means kind of ornery; *(Obstinate)* 1 inf, **nwAR,** Ornery—dishonest, lazy, worthless.

3 Unpleasant, troublesome, unruly, obstinate, ill-tempered; hence n *orneriness,* also sp *orneryness.*

1862 Winthrop *John Brent* 71, Good company betters the orneriest sort er weather. **1891** (1900) French *Otto* 174 **AR,** My foot got cotched in the elbow-brush. . . Say, kin ye cut the orney branch off? **1899** Tarkington *Gentleman* 45, They . . let loose their deviltries just for pure orneriness. **1902** *DN* 2.240 **sIL,** *Ornery.* . . 1. Refractory or disobedient. 2. Of poor quality, as 'Ornery meat.' **1905** *DN* 3.63 **eNE,** *Ornery, orneriest, onnery, oniest.* . . Disagreeable. "The onriest critter." **1906** *DN* 3.122 **sIN,** *Ornery.* . . Bad, unmanageable. "He's an ornery boy." **1907** *DN* 3.224 **nwAR,** *Or'nary* (orn'ry). . . 1. Refractory, disobedient. 2. Of poor quality. **1917** *DN* 4.397 **neOH,** *Ornery* [ˈɔrnəri]. . . Generally bad, stubborn, unruly. . . The sense "ordinary," "inferior" seems to have disappeared here. "That horse is an ornery cuss." **1938** *Sun* (Baltimore MD) 28 Jan 10/3 *(Hench Coll.),* We are forced to spend all this money [on defense] solely because mankind up to now is too ornery to organize international life on some more sensible basis. **1941** Faulkner *Men Working* 201 **MS,** Mules is the orneriest critters when they takes a notion. **1953** [see **2** above]. **1959** Thurber *Years with Ross* 87, Some orneriness of mood aggravated by . . peptic ulcers. **1965–70** *DARE* (Qu. K16, *A cow with a bad temper*) 133 Infs, **widespread, but less freq Sth, S Midl,** Ornery (cow, critter, etc); **AZ15,** Plain ornery; **DE5,** Damned ornery cow; (Qu. GG18, . . *'Obstinate': "Why does he have to be so _____."*) 74 Infs, **widespread, but less freq S Midl,** Ornery; **UT4,** Cockeyed ornery; **PA247,** Honery; (Qu. NN17, *Something that keeps on annoying you—for example, a fly that keeps buzzing around you: "That _____ fly won't go away."*) 31 Infs, **scattered, but more freq S Midl,** Ornery; (Qu. Z16, *A small child who is rough, misbehaves, and doesn't obey, you'd call him a _____*) 18 Infs, **chiefly N Midl, West,** Ornery (brat, child, etc); (Qu. GG38, *Somebody who is usually mean and bad tempered: "He's an awful _____."*) 18 Infs, **scattered,** Ornery (cuss, person, etc); **PA29,** Mean and ornery; (Qu. K42, *A horse that is rough, wild, or dangerous*) 14 Infs, **chiefly Nth, N Midl,** Ornery (horse); **MD32,** Damned ornery horse; (Qu. GG35b, *[To sulk or pout:] "Because she couldn't go, she's been _____ all day."*) 14 Infs, **chiefly Nth,** Ornery; **WA28,** Ornery as the devil; (Qu. B2, *If the weather is very unpleasant . . it's a _____ day*) Inf **PA29,** Ornery; (Qu. K50, *Joking nicknames for mules*) Inf **NY219,** Ornery; (Qu. K68, . . *A goat that habitually strikes people with its horns*) Infs **DE3, MI74, WA18,** Ornery (goat); **MN16,** Ornery old billy goat; (Qu. R15a, . . *Names or nicknames . . for mosquitoes*) Inf **IA11,** Ornery pest; (Qu. Z14b, *If a child expects to have its own way or have too much attention . . "That child is _____."*) Infs **CA94, OK31,** Ornery; (Qu. BB57, *If someone committed suicide . . he _____*) Inf **CA199,** Too ornery to keep on livin'; (Qu. GG4, *Stirred up, angry*) Inf **CO**7, Ornery; (Qu. GG16, . . *Finding fault, or complaining*) Inf **CT**37, Ornery; **IA**30, Plain right ornery; (Qu. GG32a, *To habitually play tricks or jokes on people*) Infs **OH**22, **PA**29, Ornery (son of a bitch); (Qu. GG39, *Somebody who seems to be looking for reasons to be angry*) Infs **MN**36, **NJ**53, Ornery; (Qu. GG40, *Violently angry*) Inf **CA**211, Ornery as a bull; (Qu. GG41, *To lose patience easily*) Infs **CA**73, 134, **IL**28, Ornery; (Qu. HH16, *Uncomplimentary words with no definite meaning . . "Don't invite him. He's a _____."*) Inf **MS**21, Ornery, crumb, jerk; (Qu. HH22a, *A mean or disagreeable person;* total Infs questioned, 75) Infs **FL**4, 18, 36, **UT**3, Ornery; (Qu. HH22b, . . *A very mean person*) Inf **CA**201, Ornery old devil; (Qu. HH26, *A person who is always ready to stir up trouble*) Inf **OK**31, Ornery; (Qu. II7, *Somebody who doesn't seem to 'fit in' or to get along very well*) Inf **NJ**69, Hornery; (Qu. KK11, *To make great objections or a big fuss about something*) Inf **CT**10, Got ornery. **1967** Will *Dredgeman* 52 **FL**, I've fought mosquitoes in the Everglades . . , but for numbers, voracity and year 'round orneryness, I'm here to state that there has never been a match for the species at Cape Sable. **1967–69** *DARE* Tape **CA**90, My brother and I got kind of ornery ['ɔrnə·i]; **CA**160, Apparently, right here was a group of Indians that were pretty ornery ['oə·nə·i]; **IL**7, A boar can get pretty ornery ['ɑə·nrɪ]; **IA**8, They [=mules] can be the orneriest ['oə·nrɪəst] damn things you ever got into. **1986** Pederson *LAGS Concordance* **Gulf Region** (*Obstinate*) 30 infs, Ornery; (*Touchy*) 1 inf, Ornery; (*Angry*) 1 inf, Ornery.

4 Tired or vaguely unwell. **esp MO** See Map

1965–70 *DARE* (Qu. BB5, *A general feeling of discomfort or illness*) Infs **MO**18, 37, 39, Ornery; **MD**20, Feeling ornery; (Qu. BB39, *On a day when you don't feel just right, though not actually sick*) Infs **IL**17, **IN**13, **MO**9, 15, 18, 20, 37, Ornery; (Qu. KK30, *Feeling slowed up or without energy*) Infs **IL**143, **MO**3, Ornery; **VA**31, Ornery—meaning tired. **1986** Pederson *LAGS Concordance* (*Peaked*) 1 inf, **cnAR**, Ornery—not feeling well.

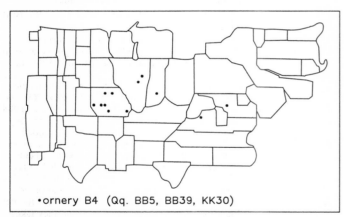

•ornery B4 (Qq. BB5, BB39, KK30)

orneryness See **ornery B3**

ornry See **ornery**

orphan n Usu |'ɔ(r)fən|; also freq |'ɔ(r)fənt|; less freq |'ɔ(r)frən, 'ɔ(r)fə·n, 'ɔ(r)flən| Pronc-spp *orphant, orflin(g), orphing, oftin* For addit pronc and sp varr see quots [The form *orphant* is attested from the 16th cent (*OED orphan* sb. 1). The appar excrescent *l* of *orfling*, etc, may represent a survival of *orphelin* (*OED* →1652, *EDD orf'lin*).]

A Forms.

1733 in 1965 *AmSp* 40.237 **seVA**, Orphant. **1851** Hooper *Widow Rugby's Husband* 128 **AL**, Keep still, you poor . . clay-eatin' offin. **1885** *Indianapolis Jrl.* (IN) 15 Nov 10/4, Little Orphant Annie's come to our house to stay. **1899** (1912) Green *VA Folk-Speech* 307, Orphline. . . Orflin. An orphan. **1903** *DN* 2.323 **seMO**, I was left an orphant when I was six years old. **1907** *DN* 3.234 **nwAR**, Orphant. **1909** *DN* 3.354 **eAL, wGA**, Orphant. **1912** *DN* 3.584 **wIN**, Orphant. . . Very common. **1915** *DN* 4.187 **swVA**, Orphant. **1923** *DN* 5.216 **swMO**, Orphant. **1931** *AmSp* 6.347, The following are examples of what may be called Regressive Assimilation. A final *n* is assimilated to a preceding labial. . . orphm. **1940** in 1944 *ADD* **wAR**, [Radio:] A orphings' home. **1940** *Sat. Eve. Post* 6 Apr 17 **GA**, I reckon I'm just a oftin boy now. **1941** *LANE* Map 390 (*Orphan*), [Pronunciations of the types [ɔ(r)fən, ɒ(r)fən] are widespread; 13 infs offered proncs with a final dental, and 7 offered proncs of the types [ɔ(r)frn, ɔ(r)frən].] **1942** Hall *Smoky Mt. Speech* 33

eTN, wNC, ['ɑə·fənt]. **1965** Carmony *Speech Terre Haute* 122 **cwIN**, An added /t/ occurs in the record of informant 3 in words such as *once, twice,* and *orphan.* **1967** *DARE* Tape **KY**2, [Inf:] I's raised orphant. . . [FW:] And the mother you're talking about was not your own mother? [Inf:] Yes, she's my mother, . . but all that didn't have a daddy was called orphant ['ɔə·fɪnt]. **1968** *DARE* (Qu. Z11b) Inf **NC**49, ['ɔˇftɪn] children. **c1970** *Halpert Coll.* 46 **wKY, nwTN**, She's an orfling. **1976** Allen *LAUM* 3.301 **Upper MW** (as of c1950), After homorganic /n/ in *orphan* 26 infs. add /t/. **1989** Pederson *LAGS Tech. Index* 236 **Gulf Region**, [Most infs gave proncs of the types ['ɔ(r)fn̩, 'o(r)fn̩]. 40 infs gave proncs with a final [-t]. 28 gave proncs with an *r* in the second syllable (e.g., ['ɔfə·n] or ['ɔfrən]). 7 inserted a *t* in the second syllable (e.g., ['ɔə·ftn̩]); 2 had an *l* in the same position (['ɔflɪnz, 'oflɛn]), and one gave ['ɔə·flt].]

B Sense.

Also *orphan child:* An illegitimate child. [By ext from *orphan* a child whose father has died]

1966 Dakin *Dial. Vocab. Ohio R. Valley* 2.438, Bastard. . . The variants *unlawful child, illegal* ~, and *fatherless* ~ appear occasionally, as well as a less precise *orphan* and *waif* used in this sense. **1966–69** *DARE* (Qu. Z11a, . . *A child whose parents were not married—serious words*) Infs **LA**37, **ME**4, **NY**80, 209, Orphan; (Qu. Z11b, . . *Joking words for a child of unwed parents*) Inf **NC**49, Orphan ['ɔˇftɪn] children; **NC**72, Orphan child; **WA**18, Orphan. [**1975** Morgan *Amer. Slavery* 168 **VA** (as of 17th cent), As women in Virginia generally became widows sooner or later, children generally became "orphants," as fatherless children were called in Virginia even when their mothers were still alive.] **1986** Pederson *LAGS Concordance,* 1 inf, **nwLA**, Orphan child—born to mother who's unmarried.

orpine n

Std: a **stonecrop**, usu *Sedum telephium*. For other names of this sp see **Aaron's rod 2, bag leaves, ~ plant, blow-leaf, evergreen 3, everlasting, frog plant 1, houseleek 2, leeks, life everlasting 3, life-of-man 4, live-forever 2, toad-bellies, witches' moneybags**

orry-eyed See **orey-eyed**

orsanberg See **osnaburg**

orse See **horse**

orsenberg See **osnaburg**

Orsh See **Irish** n[1], adj

ort n Pronc-sp *ought* chiefly **NEng**

A leftover (esp of food), scrap; refuse, offal, trash.

1828 (1970) Webster *Amer. Dict.,* Ort. . . A fragment; refuse. **1900** Day *Up in ME* 102, He got the orts of the fish we caught. **1909** *DN* 3.414 **nME**, Orts. . . The leavings of cattle in their manger. **1914** *DN* 4.77 **ME, nNH**, Orts. . . Guts of a fish. Entrails of animals. **1927** *AmSp* 3.139 **ME coast**, "Orts," . . is archaic for refuse. **1941** *LANE* Map 346 (*Rubbish*), [*Orts* is recorded from 33 infs, esp **nNEng**, usually either in the sense "leavings from the table, garbage" or "scraps of hay left by cattle (or by sheep . .)." One inf applies the word to scraps of paper, and one says it also means "manure."] **1947** *Hench Coll.,* [He] has friends or relatives in Northeastern Penna. and in spots eastward to the Hudson River. He hears them say: "Take this ought and throw it out." "Put these peelings in the ought can." **1950** Moore *Candlemas Bay* 200 **ME**, "Take the orts out to the hens, Neal," Jen said. . . He picked up the refuse dish and started for the barn. **1959** *VT Hist.* 27.151, Orts. . . Coarse hay or straw butts which the cattle do not eat. Common. **1966–70** *DARE* (Qu. H71, . . *The last piece of food left on a plate*) Inf **ME**1, Orts—table scraps; **TX**1, Leavings, ort; **TX**35, Ort [ɔ·t]; **VA**66, Ort; (Qu. F24, *The container for kitchen parings and scraps—inside the kitchen*) Inf **MA**40, Orts bag—old-fashioned. **1966** *DARE* FW Addit **ME**15, Orts—word always(?) used for garbage near Friendship and Long Island, Maine. **1973** Allen *LAUM* 1.198 **MN** (as of c1950), One Minnesota respondent [to a written checklist], of Scottish and Canadian parentage, checked *ort pail,* which in the eastern atlas study appeared only in Essex county, Massachusetts. **1986** Pederson *LAGS Concordance* (*Comprehensive term for edible "insides" of a pig or calf*) 1 inf, **cAL**, Orts and offal—words I've learned; 1 inf, **ceTX**, Orts—all edible organs collectively.

ort v, **orta** See **ought** v

orten(t) See **ought** v C2a

orter v See **ought** v

orter n See **otter**

orther, orthor See **author**

ortn't See **ought** v **C2a**

ortolan n [From similarity to the European ortolan *(Emberiza hortulana)*]

1 A **sora** (here: *Porzana carolina*). Cf **king ortolan**

1836 (1935) Holley *Texas* 100, Ortolans, which form so celebrated a dish in Europe, are abundant in Texas. **1859** Turnbull–Turnbull *Amer. Photographs* 2.194 (as of c1854), There is also a small bird, seen only in September and October, which is much sought for, and is considered a great delicacy. It is less than a snipe, and is called in Pennsylvania the Rail, in Virginia the Sora, and in some States the Ortolan. **1874** *Forest & Stream* 1.411 **Baltimore MD,** I am glad to see that sportsmen are awaking to the idea that birds, fish and animals, should be called by their right names. I think it would be a good plan to introduce into the schools a hand-book of Natural History, and teach the growing ones at least what is correct. Here they call . . the rail an ortolan. **1888** Trumbull *Names of Birds* 132, At Washington, D.C., and Pocomoke City (Worcester Co.), Md., [the sora is called] *ortolan.* **1897** *Auk* 14.287 **LA,** *Porzana carolina.* Sora. Commonly known as Ortolan. **1916** *Times–Picayune* (New Orleans LA) 2 Apr mag sec 5/6, Sora rail . . Rice Rail, Carolina Rail, Ortolan. **1936** Roberts *MN Birds* 1.448, It [=the sora] shares with the Bobolink the name Ortolan, and both birds are considered great delicacies when broiled and served on toast, tiny morsels though they are. **1955** *Oriole* 20.1.6, Sora.—*Coot; Ortolan* (the name of a gastronomically famous European finch that has been transferred to numerous species of excellent table birds).

2 =**bobolink B.**

1859 (1968) Bartlett *Americanisms* 41, Bobolink. . . A lively little bird . . which in the fall frequents the wild rice of shallow rivers and marshes, where it becomes very fat. It is highly esteemed by epicures. Other popular names by which it is known in different parts of the country are Rice-bird, . . American Ortolan [etc]. **1872** Coues *Key to N. Amer. Birds* 154, The name "ortolan," applied by some to this bird, by others to the Carolina rail, is a strange misnomer, the ortolan being a fringilline bird of Europe. **1888** Trumbull *Names of Birds* 132, [Footnote to *reed-bird*:] Our Reed-bird—*Dolichonyx oryzivorus*—termed also Bobolink, Rice-bird, Skunk Blackbird, Ortolan, etc., . . is shot only for the "pot," having nothing more gamy about it than the English Sparrow has. I will add that I have nowhere found it called "Ortolan" but in print, and that the far-famed and delicious little ortolan of Europe, from which the name is borrowed, is known to scientists as *Emberiza hortulana.* **1923** U.S. Dept. Ag. *Misc. Circular* 13.75, Bobolink. . . [Vernacular names in local use:] ortolan (N.J. to La.) **1936** [see **1** above]. **1962** Imhof *AL Birds* 497, Bobolink . . other names: Oatbird, Ricebird, Reedbird, Maybird, Ortolan.

Orygun See **Oregon**

Osage See **Osage orange**

Osage apple n

=**Osage orange.**

1804 (1905) Lewis *Orig. Jrls. Lewis & Clark Exped.* 6.172, No appearance of the buds of the Osage apple. *Ibid* 7.296, The *Osage Apple* is a native of the interior of the continent of North America. . . Mr. Peter Coteau, who first introduced this tree in the neighbourhood of St. Louis, about five years since, informed me, that he obtained the young plants at the great Osage vilage [sic] from an Indian of that nation. . . The fruit is the size of the largest orange, of a globular form, and a fine orange colour. **1817** *Amer. Monthly Mag. & Crit. Rev.* 2.118, Description of the *Ioxylon Pomiferum,* a new genus of North American Tree. . . discovered by Captain Lewis, and called by him the *Osage-apple* or *Arrow-wood of the Missouri.* **1897** Sudworth *Arborescent Flora* 190 **TN,** Osage Apple Tree. **1940** Clute *Amer. Plant Names* 164, Osage Orange. Hedge apple, mock orange, . . osage apple. **1952** Taylor *Plants Colonial Days* 63, Osage orange, a member of the mulberry family, Moraceae, is also called . . Osage apple tree, and hedgetree.

Osage orange n Also *Osage* [See quot 1846] **widespread exc S Atl, Inland Sth, Gulf States** See Map Cf **Osage apple, bois d'arc, hedge apple**

A spiny tree *(Maclura pomifera)* formerly much planted for hedges; also the fruit or wood of this tree. Also called **bois d'arc, bowwood, brass wood, Chinese orange, hedge, ~ apple, ~ orange, horse apple 2, Indian ~ 5, ironwood a(5), milkball tree, mock orange 1c, Osage apple, wild orange, yellowwood;** for other names of the fruit see **green ball, hedge ~, monkey ~ 1**

1817 Bradbury *Travels* 160, It bleeds an acrid milky juice when wounded, and is called by the hunters the Osage orange. **1846** Browne *Trees* 465, *Maclura aurantiaca,* The Osage Orange-tree. [*Ibid* 466, This species was first noticed by the travellers, Hunter and Dunbar, on the banks of the Red River. . . It was first cultivated among the white settlers of the west, in about the year 1800, in the garden of M. Chouteau, at St. Louis, on the Mississippi, where it was propagated from some seeds procured from a village of Osage Indians; whence it obtained its popular name.] **1855** *Chi. W. Times* 29 March 3/2 *(DA),* The introduction of the Osage orange hedges, as a substitute for fences on the Western prairies. . . is becoming very general. **1859** (1965) Marcy *Prairie Traveler* 26, Wheels made of the bois-d'arc, or Osage orangewood, are the best for the Plains, as they shrink but little, and seldom want repairing. **1868** (1870) Gray *Field Botany* 299, *Osage-orange. . . M[aclura] aurantiaca,* Common O[sage-orange], or Bois d'arc (Bow-wood, the tough yellow wood used for bows by the Indians). Low bushy tree from Arkansas, &c.: multiplying rapidly by its running roots; planted for hedges, especially W.; armed with slender and very sharp spines. **1897** Sudworth *Arborescent Flora* 190 **IA,** *Toxylon pomiferum* . . Osage Orange. . . Osage. **1940** Fergusson *Our Southwest* 157, Mrs. Hayden found a stately adobe house with water piped in, an osage orange hedge around an orchard, [etc]. **1948** *WELS Suppl.,* Osage Orange fence is extremely common from central Ill. up to the Wis. border. These trimly cut bushes seem to be a feature of prairie farming. **1965–70** *DARE* (Qu. T13) 81 Infs, **widespread exc S Atl, Inland Sth, Gulf States,** Osage orange; **MO25, VA**100, Osage tree; (Qu. I46, . . *Kinds of fruits that grow wild around here*) Inf **OH**3, Osage orange; (Qu. L65, . . *Kinds of fences*) Infs **MD**34, **OH**78, Osage orange hedge; **CA**79, Osage orange fence; **IA**8, Osage fence; **MN**40, Osage hedge fence; **IL**24, Osage orange hedge fence. **1986** Pederson *LAGS Concordance,* 1 inf, **ceTX,** Osage orange—proper name of bois d'arc.

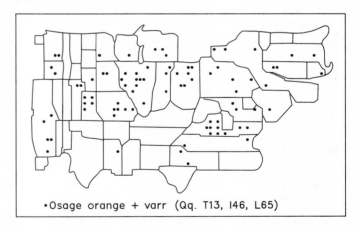

•Osage orange + varr (Qq. T13, I46, L65)

Osceola's plume n [Perh after the well-known painting by George Catlin which shows the Seminole chief *Osceola* (1804–38) wearing a hat with prominent plumes]

A **death camas** (here: *Zigadenus densus*).

1939 FWP *Guide FL* 423, Among them [=flowers] is Osceola's plume, also known as 'crow poison', identified by its slender leafless stem. It bears a conical cluster of small white flowers which change to pink and purple before seeding. **1953** Greene–Blomquist *Flowers South* 7, The thick, candle-like racemes of Osceola's-plume are the most conspicuous of our Coastal Plain flowers during April and May. **1955** *S. Folkl. Qrly.* 19.233, The cylindrical white racemes of *Osceola's Plume* (Tryacanthus angustifolius) change to pink and purple and remain on fluted pedicels while the buds above them are opening in pure white, a blossom that waves as proudly, as gracefully, and as colorfully as did the Indian chieftain's plume in his heyday.

osha n SW

A **lovage** (here: either *Ligusticum filicinum* or *L. porteri*).

1900 Lyons *Plant Names* 223, *L[igusticum] filicinum* . . Colorado Cough-root, Osha. **1923** Smith *Ethnobotany* 55 **WI,** Osha or *Colorado Root (Ligusticum filicinum . .).* This is not native to Wisconsin, still quantities are used by the Menomini, who buy it from the Shawano druggists under the name of Colorado root. **1937** U.S. Forest Serv. *Range Plant Hdbk.* W107, Fernleaf loveroot, also called fernleaf lovage, osha, wildcelery, and wildparsnip, is one of the most abundant of the western loveroots. *Ibid,* Porter loveroot *(L. porteri),* also called osha and chuchupate, may be regarded as a more southern and coarser-leaved sister species of fernleaf loveroot. **1947** (1976) Curtin *Healing Herbs* 139, *Oshá. . .* The popular names *chuchupate* and *oshá* are of Indian origin. . . Oshá, highly-valued mountain herb, occurs as a dwarf and also as a plant of considerable size. The larger plant, which has broad dark leaves variously serrated and wide umbels of yellow terminal flowers, often reaches six feet in height. The smaller kind has white flowers, thinner, paler leaves much more jagged at the edges, and its growth never exceeds three feet. **1966** *DARE* Tape **NM**6, Nowadays the Spanish people like to use a root called osha ['ošjə], which is boiled up and sugar and a little whiskey added and some other ingredients and they use this for coughs and for the warding off of colds. **1988** Crawford *Mayordomo* 5 **nNM**, A fertile clay soil . . supports an abundant growth of willow, wild rose, . . squawberry bush, . . hemlock, *oshá,* . . and innumerable types of grass.

oshtuh See **oyster**

osnaburg n Pronc-spp *ansenberg, ausenburg, aznaburgh, eizen-burg, orsanberg, orsenberg;* for addit varr see quots [Varr of *Osnabrück,* Germany, where it was orig made] **chiefly Sth**
A thick, coarse fabric, orig made of linen but now usu of cotton.
    1660 in 1885 Suffolk Co. MA *Deeds* 3.382, Three smale packetts Conteining three peices of ozenbrigs. **1709** (1967) Lawson *New Voyage* 94 **NC, SC**, The Commodities, which are necessary to carry over to this Plantation . . are . . Linnens of all sorts, but chiefly ordinary Blues, *Osnabrugs . .* , *Scotch* and *Irish* Linnen. **a1711** in 1965 *AmSp* 40.236, As much ozenbrigs as will make her a bed. **1792** in 1956 Eliason *Tarheel Talk* 286 **neNC**, Oznaburgs [also] oznaburghs. **1828** (1938) Bolling *Diary* 46.238 **VA**, The boat arrived with my iron, salt, aznaburgh, whiskey, . . etc. **1859** (1965) Marcy *Prairie Traveler* 27, Every wagon should be furnished with substantial bows and double osnaburg covers, to protect its contents from the sun and weather. **1899** (1912) Green *VA Folk-Speech* 307, Osnbrigs. . . A kind of coarse, unbleached cotton cloth. **c1937** in 1970 Yetman *Voices* 56 **AL** [Black], Our clothes weren't many. Us chillens wore a one piece suit made outen ausenberg, and us would have to take dat off at night, wash it, and put it back on de next day. **1937–38** in 1977 *Amer. Slave Suppl. 1* 1.151 **AL**, The cheapes' cloth that could be bought. Unbleached ausenburg cloth, coarse, but made to las'. *Ibid* 301, Our dresses were plain ansenberg an' we would dye it wid cherry bark. *Ibid* 117, Us wore mostly slips woven in homemade looms and hit wus orsanberg and homespun. *Ibid* 166, Our orsenberg clothes wus dyed brown wid walnut leaves and hazelnut bush. *Ibid* 420, De shirts wuz made of os'enberg. **1966** *DARE* (Qu. F23, *A container made of rough, loosely-woven, brown cloth; commonly used for potatoes, etc*) Inf **AR**7, Eizenburg sack—a cotton sack, a lighter sack [than a gunny sack]. **1986** Pederson *LAGS Concordance,* 1 inf, **swGA**, Osnaburg—cotton sack for picking; 1 inf, **cwAL**, Osnaburg—heavy cloth, rough; 1 inf, **ceMS**, We made our own cotton sacks of osnaburg; 1 inf, **seLA**, Osnaburg—for sugar, covers for parlor furniture; 1 inf, **seAL**, Osnaburg sacks.

osoberry n
A shrub or small tree *(Oemleria cerasiformis)* native to Washington, Oregon, and California; also its fruit. Also called **Indian peach 2, ~ plum 2, skunkbush, squawberry, squaw plum**
    1884 Miller *Dict. Engl. Names of Plants* 223, *Nuttallia cerasiformis. Oso-berry-tree,* of California. **1888** Lindley–Widney *CA of South* 332, The white-blossomed "Oso berry." **1896** *Jrl. Amer. Folkl.* 9.187 **CA, OR**, *Nuttallia cerasiformis . .* oso berry. **1931** U.S. Dept. Ag. *Misc. Pub.* 101.70, Osoberry *(Osmaronia cerasiformis . .*), often called Indian plum, is an ornamental shrub, or rarely a small tree, 2 to 15 feet high, with deciduous leaves 2 to 4 inches long having a peculiar, rather disagreeable odor when first appearing. Essentially a Pacific species, it ranges from British Columbia to California, mainly in the coastal region. **1961** Thomas *Flora Santa Cruz* 200 **cwCA**, *O[smaronia] cerasiformis . .* Oso Berry. Shaded slopes and canyons throughout the Santa Cruz Mountains, but more common on the eastern slopes than on the western. **1974** (1977) Coon *Useful Plants* 227, *Osmaronia cerasiformis*—Oso berry, Indian plum. A shrub belonging to the rose family, it is found on the West Coast with rather poorly-flavored fruit.

ostkaka n |'ust(ə)ˌkɑkə| Also sp *ostakaka* [Sw *ostkaka,* Norw *ostekake*] **esp MN**
A type of cheesecake or pudding; see quots.
    1940 Tufford *Scandinavian Recipes* 44 **MN**, Ost Kaka (Swedish Cheese Dessert). . . Drain off whey and turn cheese into a baking dish. Beat eggs well and add rest of ingredients. . . Bake in a slow oven. . . Serve cold. **1967–68** *DARE* (Qu. H63, *Kinds of desserts*) Inf **KS**7, Ostkaka—kind of a cheese pudding or cheesecake; **MN**14, Ostkaka; (Qu. H65, *Foreign foods favored by people around here*) Inf **MN**14, Ostkaka; **MN**17, Ostkaka ['ustˌkɑkə]; **MN**23, Ostakaka ['ustəˌkɑkə]—a Swedish dish: one gallon of milk, one-half rennet tablet, one cup of cream, one cup of flour, two eggs, one cup sugar. Add flour to a little milk, making smooth; beat into gallon lukewarm milk, add dissolved rennet a little at a time. Let set a few minutes, stir, drain whey, add cream, sugar, eggs. Bake in slow oven till well browned; **NE**3, Ostakaka ['ustəˌkɑkə]—a milk base with clabber in it. **1989** *Country* June/July 17 **KS**, The taste of Sweden is as close as mid-Kansas. . . [D]on't forget the ostkaka (a Swedish cheesecake-like dessert).

ostrich fern n [See quot 1911]
An edible fern *(Matteucia struthiopteris).* Also called **buck's horn brake, fiddlehead n 1**
    1833 Eaton *Botany* 358, *Struthiopteris. . . pennsylvanica, . .* ostrich fern. **1843** Torrey *Flora NY* 2.486, *Struthiopteris Germanica. . .* Common Ostrich-fern. . . Low grounds and borders of rivers. **1868** (1869) *Amer. Naturalist* 2.528, [In] the majestic Ostrich Fern, beauty, elegance, grace and novelty will be found. **1911** Waters *Ferns* 273, The common name has been given to the fern from the resemblance of the sterile fronds to ostrich-plumes. . . Several common ferns somewhat resemble the ostrich-fern. **1943** Fernald–Kinsey *Edible Wild Plants E. N. Amer.* 74, Few other substitutes for asparagus ever graced a slice of toast with as much promise of furnishing a substantial meal as lies in the thick, succulent, young unrolled fronds of the *Ostrich-Fern. Ibid* 75, Canned Ostrich-Fern has recently come into the market. In one case, at least, a novice, eating the canned product, was somewhat poisoned. **1961** Douglas *My Wilderness* 277 **ME**, If the fiddlehead ferns were right, we had a real feast. These fiddleheads—or "fiddlehead greens" as some say—are from the ostrich fern *(Pteretis nodulosa),* though other ferns are also used at times. **1966** *DARE* Tape **ME**8, As the young leaves come up through the ground, before they open up, they're tightly coiled, shaped like the head of a fiddle. That's why they call 'em fiddleheads. Ostrich fern and lady fern produce these.

Oswego bass n Also *Oswego* [From the city or river so named in New York] **chiefly NY**
A **black bass 1**: usu **largemouth bass** or **smallmouth bass.**
    1751 in 1881 Essex Inst. *Coll.* 18.112, The Lake affords plenty of a Fish call'd Oswego Bass. **1787** Gesellschaft Naturforschender Freunde *Schriften* 8.166, Oswego-Bass, oder Pertschen der innländischen Seen. [=Oswego-Bass, or perch of the inland lakes.] **1815** De Witt Clinton in *Lit. & Philos. Soc. NY Trans.* 1.496, It affords fine amusement to trail for the black or Oswego basse [sic], when passing over the Oneida lake: Even when the boat is in full motion, they bite with avidity at a red rag tied to a hook. **1840** Cooper *Pathfinder* 1.130 **NY**, Even the Major himself . . will sometimes swear an oat-meal cake is better fare than the Oswego bass. **1884** [see **Otsego (Lake) bass**]. **1897** NY Forest Fish & Game Comm. *Annual Rept. for 1896* 176, There are two species of black bass, the small mouth, with the Latin name *Micropterus dolomieu,* sometimes called the "true black bass;" and the large mouth, *M. salmoides,* improperly called "Oswego" bass. **1921** *Outing* 78.108, I can't remember ever having caught one which really put up a battle, even a big Oswego. **1967** *DARE* (Qu. P1, *. . Kinds of freshwater fish . . caught around here . . good to eat*) Inf **NY**10, Oswego bass; **IA**17, Oswego or largemouth bass. **1968** *DARE* Tape **NJ**41, Especially the black bass up in Maine. . . I'd rather catch one black bass than I would ten of the Oswego or largemouth bass, as they call them. **1974** *DARE* File, A northern name for the largemouth bass is Oswego bass, after a lake in New York.

Oswego tea n [See quot 1988]
A **horsemint 1**: usu *Monarda didyma,* but also *M. fistulosa.* For other names of the former see **balm B1b, beebalm 1, bergamot, fireweed l, fragrant balm, horseradish 2, Indian plume 2, monkey's face, mountain balm 1, ~ mint 1, sweet Mary, torch flower, wild bergamot**
    1752 Miller *Gardeners Dict.* (at *Monarda*), This Plant is very common in most of the Northern Parts of *America,* where the Inhabitants drink

an Infusion of this Herb as Tea, and call it *Ozweega Tea.* **1806** McMahon *Amer. Gardener's Calendar* 604, [*Monarda*] *dydima* [sic]— . . Oswego-Tea. **1822** Eaton *Botany* 356, [*Monarda*] *kalmiana* . . Oswego tea, Oswego county. **1830** Rafinesque *Med. Flora* 2.38, It [=*Monarda coccinea*] has been called Oswego tea, because first used by the Indians near Oswego lake. **1848** in 1850 Cooper *Rural Hours* 117 **NY**, Humming-birds. . . are partial, to the bee larkspur also, with the wild bergamot or Oswego tea. **1937** U.S. Forest Serv. *Range Plant Hdbk.* W132, The volatile oil present in *Monarda* yields, in the case of both spotted beebalm . . and Oswego beebalm *(M. didyma),* also called Oswego tea, the valuable antiseptic drug, thymol. **1948** Wherry *Wild Flower Guide* 114, Lavender Wild-bergamot *(M. fistulosa).* . . These plants are sometimes called *Oswego-tea, bee-balm,* etc. **1967–68** *DARE* (Qu. S26a, . . *Wildflowers. . . Roadside flowers)* Inf **PA**104, Oswego tea; (Qu. S26b, *Wildflowers that grow in water or wet places)* Inf **TN**11, Oswego tea. **1967** *DARE* Wildfl QR Pl.189 Infs **AR**44, **OH**14, Oswego tea. **1988** Werner *Life & Lore* 91 **IL**, It is called Oswego Tea because it was discovered in 1743 by John Bartram while on a trip to Oswego, New York, on Lake Ontario. The Indians of that region used the plant in a medicinal tea.

other adj, n, pron, conj Pronc-spp *edder, ither, od(d)er, udder, yudda;* for addit varr see quots

A Forms.

1821 Cooper *Spy* 2.188 [Black], A tongue like *oder* folk. **1857** in 1956 Eliason *Tarheel Talk* 315 **cnNC**, Oather. **1858** *Ibid* 315 **c,csNC**, Urthes [for *others*]. **1887** (1967) Harris *Free Joe* 109 **nwGA**, Some folks mought take a notion hit wuz a long ways off, an' then, ag'in, yuther folks mought take a notion that hit wuz lots nigher. **1888** Jones *Negro Myths* 63 **GA coast**, De soup wuh mek long dat rock sweeter den all edder soup. **1901** *DN* 2.183 **neKY** [Black], Other—*uddah.* **1904** Day *Kin o' Ktaadn* 111 **ME**, Mike wor slow in figgers like ither men that take leanin's to great doin's. **1905** Chesnutt *Col.'s Dream* 29 **GA** [Black], Dey got mo' dan any yuther colored folks roun' hyuh. **1922** Gonzales *Black Border* 316 **sSC, GA coasts** [Gullah glossary], *Odduh*—other, others. **1929** Sale *Tree Named John* 7 **MS** [Black], En whut wid dat, en de udder things Um gwi do m'se'f, dat chile sho gwi have a good start. **1937** [see **michael tea**]. **c1937** in 1976 *Weevils in the Wheat* 222 **VA** [Black], He say dat odder night I dreamed o' a open drawer at home what somebody done put dere. **1941** O'Donnell *Great Big Doorstep* 41 **sLA** [Black], Nen de [=And then the] yudda day Ah was passin Chippy's Saloon . . an dey's playin a piece on de reckid. **1952** Brown *NC Folkl.* 1.570, *Oder* ['ʌdə], *anoder* [ə'nʌdə]: . . *Other; another.*

B As adj.

1 Else, different.

1947 Williams *Streetcar* 71 **LA**, *Blanche:* You're so—matter of fact about it, Stella. *Stella:* What other can I be?

2 also *tother;* Of clothes: best, dressiest.

1831 in 1956 Eliason *Tarheel Talk* 301 **cwNC**, The whole town were putting on their "tother clothes." **1839** Kirkland *New Home* 228 **MI**, A dozen other Mistresses shone in their " 'tother gowns," and their tamboured collars. **1966–67** *DARE* (Qu. W38, *When a man dresses himself up in his best clothes . . he's* _____) Inf **AR**27, Got on his other clothes; (Qu. W39, *Joking ways of referring to a person's best clothes)* Inf **TX**33, Other suit. **1975** Gould *ME Lingo* 197, *Other ones*—A man's best suit of clothes. Instead of saying he's about to dress up, a Mainer is quite likely to excuse himself while he puts on his *other ones.*

C As conj. Cf **except(ing) B**

Unless.

1950 *WELS Suppl.,* You don't have to sign for anything, other it's registered mail.

other room n Cf **front** adj

See quots.

1973 Allen *LAUM* 1.159 **csMN** (as of c1950), *Sitting room* (where guests are entertained). . . *Other room:* Used in youth. **1983** *NADS Letters* **Sth, S Midl**, *Other room*—Perfectly familiar to me, though I am not sure whether I set it down very often [in field collecting], since it seemed to me more of a description than a specific name. That is, one named the *kitchen,* for its specific function; everything else went on in the other room. This would seem to derive from the practice of S. & S.M. small farmers, etc., of building as their first abode two structures, often connected but sometimes not (for fear of fire), with the larger serving all functions other than cooking and eating (the *dining room* was a symbol of prosperity). *Ibid* **seGA**, Other room: Sam says this meant specifically "living room" in their family. I think in ours it meant any

room that wasn't regularly used (the upstairs bedroom at my grandmother's for instance was always "the other room"). *Ibid* **eVA**, I also grew up using "the other room" for *living room.* **1986** Pederson *LAGS Concordance (Make a floor plan of the house and name the rooms)* 4 infs, **swGA, cw,nwTN**, The other room; 1 inf, **swAL**, The other room— t.v. room, has water bed. **1996** *DARE* File **csWI** (as of c1968), Besides bedrooms and a bath, the house I grew up in had three rooms—the kitchen, the dining room, and what my mother and grandmother usually referred to as "the other room." They seldom called it the living room.

otherways adv [*OED* →1808; "*Obs. exc. dial.*"] Cf **elseways**
Otherwise.

1899 (1912) Green *VA Folk-Speech* 301, *Other ways, adv.* Otherwise.

otie n [Aphet form of **coyote** n pronc |ˌkaɪ'(j)oti|]
1931 *AmSp* 6.358 **West** [Sheep ranching lingo], Lighted lanterns are set around the various flocks. These have sufficient force to ward off "oties" (coyotes) from attacking.

Otsego (Lake) bass n [From *Otsego Lake,* New York] **chiefly NY**

A **whitefish** (here: *Coregonus clupeaformis*).

1822 De Witt Clinton in *Amer. Med. Philos. Reg.* III.188 *(caption) (DA),* Account of the Salmo otsego or the Otsego basse [sic]. **1844** DeKay *Zool. NY* 4.248, The Otsego Shad Salmon. *Coregonus otsego. Salmo otsego,* The Otsego Bass. **1857** *Porter's Spirit of Times* 5 Dec 209, The famous Otsego bass, of that lake, is a *Corre gonus* [sic]. **1884** Goode *Fisheries U.S.* 1.401, The Large-mouth is known in the Great Lake region, especially in Northern New York, as the "Oswego Bass." This name should not be confounded with "Otsego Bass," a local name for the common whitefish. **1911** U.S. Bur. Census *Fisheries 1908* 318, The common whitefish *(C[oregonus] clupeaformis)* is the most valued of the tribe, although the others ar[e] highly esteemed as a food. It is found in the Great Lakes region and is known as "humpback," "bowback," and "highback" whitefish; also as "Otsego bass" in the neighborhood of Otsego Lake, N.Y. **1940** Brown *Amer. Cooks* 615 **NY**, The Cooper Inn serves a fish you can't get anywhere else in America. It's the self-same Otsego Lake bass that [James Fenimore] Cooper praised in *The Pioneers.* **1969** *DARE* (Qu. P1, . . *Kinds of freshwater fish . . caught around here . . good to eat)* Inf **NY**191, Otsego bass. **1972** Sparano *Outdoors Encycl.* 358, Lake Whitefish—Common Names . . Great Lakes whitefish, Labrador whitefish, Otsego bass.

otter n Usu |'ɑtə(r)|; also |'ɔtə(r), ɔrtɚ|; for addit varr see quots Pronc-spp *auter, orter*

Std sense, var forms.

1912 Green *VA Folk-Speech* 307, Orter. . . For *Otter.* **1926** *AmSp* 1.420 **Okefenokee GA**, The Auter's a feller that's got a wide range. **1965–70** *DARE* (Qu. P32) Infs **MA**68, **NC**80, ['ɔtə(r)]; **MA**80, ['ɔdə]; **GA**25, ['ɒtə]; **GA**34, **MI**99, ['ɔrtə(z)]; **MS**16, ['ɒrtəz]; **NC**87, ['aʊdə]; (Qu. P31) Inf **MD**13, ['ɔtə]. **1969** *DARE* Tape **GA**51, The otters [ɔdəˌz] and other stuff use that too. **1981** Pederson *LAGS Basic Materials,* [Of 18 infs from whom proncs of *otter* were recorded, 10 had vowels of the type [ɑ], 8 (6 **GA, FL**) had [ɔ] or [ɒ].] **1994** *DARE* File **Okefenokee GA** (as of 1968), *Otter*—pronounced ['oʊtɚ]—I heard this pronunciation frequently from elderly local people.

otter-drizzle n Cf **otter weather**
See quot.

1933 Rawlings *South Moon* 193 **FL**, A mist sifted through the air, fine and sharp as myriads of broken needle points. Lant said, "I don't keer for this ol' otter-drizzle."

otter weather n Cf **bluebird weather**
1967 *DARE* FW Addit **NC**, Otter weather [ɔtə wɛðə]—a season of comfortable weather "before it be spring."

ottymobile See **automobile**

ouah See **our**

ouch n Also *ouchie, ouchy* Cf **owie**
A pain or injury.

1962 *AmSp* 37.271 **sCA**, Ouch. . . An injury. A very serious injury is a *big ouch.* **1966–67** *DARE* (Qu. BB3c, *A sudden pain that comes in the side)* Inf **NV**2, An ouch; (Qu. BB4, . . *A pain . . "He's had a _____ in his arm for a week.")* Inf **FL**28, An ouch [laughter]. **1972** Cooper *NC Mt. Folkl.* 94, Ouches—aches; pains. **1988** [see **owie**]. **1995** *NADS Letters* **cWI**, "Ouch", as a noun, has been in my vocabulary ever since I can remember, so I must have learned it in Wisconsin. The "precious" diminutive "ouchie" is far more prevalent: "I have an ouchie!" *Ibid,* Familiar to me are owey and ouchy, slight variants of ooey and ouch.

ouch v esp PaGer area

To hurt, cause pain to.

1952 *Word Study* 27.4.4, Dr. Samuel Wehr . . reports two Pennsylvania Dutch coinages: "His tooth ouches him" and "It wonders me." **1969** *DARE* File, [Reported as appearing in the Fort Wayne IN *News-Sentinel* in late 1968 or early 1969:] His rheumatic ouches him so in the back. **1985** *Ibid* [List of "PA Dutch" expressions], Salome's tooth ouches her somesing wonderful.

ouchie See ouch n

ouchy adj [ouch n]

Unwell; irritable, touchy.

1966–70 *DARE* (Qu. BB5, *A general feeling of discomfort or illness that isn't any one place in particular*) Inf **PA**214, Feeling ouchy; (Qu. GG8, *When a person is very easily offended: "Be careful what you say to him, he's _____."*) Infs **IL**126, **OR**1, Ouchy; (Qu. II11b, *If two people can't bear each other at all . . "Those two are _____."*) Inf **ND**5, Little bit ouchy at each other. **c1970** *DARE* File **nwOH**, Ouchy— sensitive, intolerant. Oldest generation, woman. **1973** Allen *LAUM* 1.358 **cnNE** (as of c1950), *Touchy . .* A person who is easily offended is describable by a variety of terms. . . Feisty. . . Ouchy. **1978** *DARE* File, Ouchy—cross, short-tempered, hard to get along with. I remember it as a favorite word of a woman born c1880 in the La Crosse, Wisconsin, area, probably on the Minnesota side of the Mississippi.

ouchy n See ouch n

oudacious See audacious(ly)

ought v Pronc-sp chiefly Sth, S Midl ort; in phr ought to: pronc-spp awda, order, orta, orter, oughta, oughter; for addit varr see quots

A Pronc varr.

1815 Humphreys *Yankey in England* 107, Ort, ought. **1829** Kirkham *Engl. Grammar* 193, [Pennsylvania provincialisms:] He ort to go; so he ort. **1867** Harris *Sut Lovingood Yarns* 25 **TN**, Dad warn't actin muel, tho' he orter tuck that karacter. **1871** Eggleston *Hoosier Schoolmaster* 135 **sIN**, What ort I to do? **1884** *Anglia* 7.265 **Sth, S Midl** [Black], *He jes' oughter* = he just ought to. **1898** Westcott *Harum* 7 **nNY**, You ort to 've hed the law on him. **1904** *DN* 2.423 **Cape Cod MA** (as of a1857), *Ought to* (oughty). **1911** *DN* 3.539 **eKY**, Ought. Pronounced [ort]. **1922** Gonzales *Black Border* 317 **sSC, GA coasts** [Gullah glossary], *Oughtuh.* **1923** *DN* 5.216 **swMO**, Ort. **1927** *DN* 5.470 **Appalachians**, Orter. **1931** *AmSp* 7.91 **eKY**, Ater Maud's death he orter do better'n' he use' to. **1931** (1991) Hughes–Hurston *Mule Bone* 54 **cFL** [Black], He was too contrary to lay down on his side like a mule orter and die decent. **1935** *Sun* (Baltimore MD) 21 Apr 21/7 *(Hench Coll.),* [Headline for Letter to Ed:] Orta Be a Law. [Text:] There certainly oughta be a law. **1939** Faulkner *Wild Palms* 214 **MS**, Maybe I awda sockm, Pete. Whadya think? **1942** Hall *Smoky Mt. Speech* 32 **wNC, eTN**, An intrusive [ɚ] frequently appears in . . ought [ɔɚt], [ɒɚt]. **1959** *VT Hist.* 27.151, *Ought to* ['ortər]. . . Rare. Rural areas. **1976** Garber *Mountain-ese* 64 **sAppalachians**, *Order* (v) ought to.

B Gram form.

Pres 3rd pers sg: Usu *ought;* also rarely *oughts.*

1927 Adams *Congaree* 18 **cSC** [Black], Ellen oughts to love you.

C Syntax.

1 Used with var auxiliaries: see below. Note: The corresponding negative forms are treated separately at **2** below.

a *(ha)d ought.* [Cf *EDD ought* v. II.1] **widespread, but chiefly Nth** Cf **2b** below

1829 Kirkham *Engl. Grammar* 192, [New England provincialisms:] You haddent ought to do it. Yes I had ought. **1830** *MA Spy & Worcester Co. Advt.* (Worcester MA) 28 July 4, Yankee. Now I *swow,* Mr. South- erner, you *hadn't ought* to open your mouth about Yankee talk, unless you can talk better yourself. *Southerner.* And harkee, sir, you never ought to open your mouth *from July to eternity,* unless you can leave off using such phrases as, hadn't ought, *et cetera. Yankee.* In the first place, learn to talk as *you'd ought* to yourself, and then correct me. **1835** Crockett *Account* 87 **Boston MA**, One actress, who, it was very plain, was either a married woman or "had ought to be," as they say there, was playing the character of a young lady. **1871** Eggleston *Hoosier Schoolmaster* 91

sIN, May be a'n't no better'n he had orter be. **1887** Kirkland *Zury* 89 **IL**, Smart Aleck 'd oughter be his other name. **1899** Garland *Boy Life* 192 **nwIA** (as of c1870s), Well, you d'oughto. **1905** *DN* 3.15 **cCT**, Ought. . . In the expressions *had ought* and *hadn't ought,* for *ought* and *ought not.* **1910** Hart *Vigilante Girl* 77 **nCA**, The boys had oughter had this case tended to by the regular county judge. **1929** (1951) Faulkner *Sartoris* 68 **MS**, She'd ought to have had it. **1940** *AmSp* 15.214 **TX**, You are doubtless quite familiar with the common Middle Western *had ought.* As *had ort* it occasionally occurs in Texas. **1949** Webber *Backwoods Teacher* 18 **Ozarks**, Last year they had a little ol' flippety-snippet that I don't reckon was no better'n she'd ort to abeen. **1960** Criswell *Resp. to PADS 20* **Ozarks**, Had ought. . . Even high school seniors say this here now, some of them. **1966–68** *DARE* Tape **CA5**, Yes, that's the way we'd ought all be; **SD8**, What else do you think we'd ought to cover?

b *should ought.* [Cf *EDD ought* v. II.1] Cf **2d** below and Intro "Language Changes" I.4

1916 Lardner *You Know Me Al* 144, I should ought to have 1 day of rest at home. **1931** Randolph *Ozarks* 69, He should orter be bored fer th' simples!

2 Negative constrs: see below. Note: Many speakers avoid negating *ought* altogether.

a *ought not, oughtn't;* rarely foll by pleonastic neg; pronc- spp *ortn't, orten(t), ought(e)n.* **widespread, but more freq S Midl, Sth**

1847 Hurd *Grammatical Corrector* 55, Ort, and *ortn't,* for *ought* and *ought not.* **1918** *DN* 5.20 **NC**, Ought'n not, ought not. **1938** in 1983 Taft *Blues Lyric Poetry* 95, Oh babe ; you oughtn't be so doggone wise. **1952** Giles *40 Acres* 163 **csKY**, He ortent to ever do a day's work in the sun. **1953** Atwood *Survey of Verb Forms* 33, In the southern two thirds of Pa. and nearly everywhere to the southward *oughtn't* /ɔtənt/ is in universal use in all types. In the South Midland and throughout N.C. phonetic, and probably phonemic, /r/ very generally appears in this form. . . In N. Eng., N.Y., n. Pa., and most of N.J. the usual form is *hadn't ought. . .* Throughout most of this area nearly all the uncultured informants use this form; however, in s. N. Eng. only about half the informants use it, often alongside *oughtn't* or *ought not. . .* There are only three instances of *didn't ought* in N. Eng. In a small area of s. Ohio . . and in part of n.e. N.C. *hadn't ought* is also current, though not universal. **c1955** [see **2b** below]. **1956** Ker *Vocab. W. TX* 415, *Oughtn't . .* is recorded by the interviewers as *oughtn't* and *orten'* for twenty-three (of 67] informants. . . *Hadn't ought* is reported by four- teen. . . *Shouldn't ought* is used by [1 inf]. **c1960** *Wilson Coll.* **csKY**, *Hadn't ought to*—rare; oughtn't t'ave is more common. **1962** Atwood *Vocab. TX* 76, Ought not. Oughtn't (23 [infs]) is slightly more prevalent than *hadn't ought* (20), but both of these forms seem to be giving way to *shouldn't* (27). **1966** Dakin *Dial. Vocab. Ohio R. Valley* 2.384, The only usage other than *ought not (oughtn't)* that is common enough on all social levels to be of significance is . . *hadn't ought to. . . Hadn't ought to* has much currency in Ohio and even Type III [=cultured] informants . . attest this usage with no apology. Beyond Ohio *hadn't ought to* is used by scattered speakers in Indiana. **1966–70** *DARE* (Qu. N12) Inf **TN**6, He oughtn't to be allowed on the road; (Qu. NN3, . . *"We ought to come back here again, _____?"*) Infs **GA**18, **MA**4, **TN**44, Oughtn't we? **1975** Allen *LAUM* 2.42 **Upper MW** (as of c1950), Nearly one-half use the full *ought not,* but only one-tenth the contracted *oughtn't. . .* At least one-fourth can express the negative only by resort- ing to *shouldn't. . . Ought not* itself occurs fairly uniformly throughout the U[pper] M[idwest], with greatest frequency in Minnesota and least in Iowa. The Midland orientation of *oughtn't* does not appear in the UM. **1976** Garber *Mountain-ese* 64 **sAppalachians**, You oughten to do that sonny, you may git whupped fer it. **1981** *PADS* 67.49 **neMN**, The majority of the Iron Range informants responding (six of nine) do not have a negative for *ought:* they say *shouldn't,* which is an infrequent response of other Minnesota informants (6/45). The remaining three Range informants who responded say *oughtn't,* which is usual with other Minnesota informants (33 occs.) **1986** Pederson *LAGS Concordance,* 2 infs, **cAL, cTN**, Oughtn't not to do(ne); 1 inf, **neLA**, Oughtn't to not did. **1989** Pederson *LAGS Tech. Index* 199 **Gulf Region**, [Of 914 infs, 371 gave *shouldn't* as the negative of *ought;* 44 gave *should not,* 219 *ought not,* and 91 *oughtn't.*]

b *had not ought, hadn't ought.* **widespread, but more freq Nth** Cf **1a** above

1816 in 1824 Knight *Letters* 30 **sePA**, They say . . had not ought [in Philadelphia]. **1829** [see **1a** above]. **1830** [see **1a** above]. **1837** Sherwood *Gaz.* GA 70, *Hadn't ought,* for ought not. **1847** Hurd *Grammatical Corrector* 39, *Hadn't ought,* for *ought not; as,* "You hadn't ought to address one in so rude a manner." This gross abuse of *ought* is, I believe, peculiar to New Englanders. **1872** Schele de Vere *Americanisms* 608, *Hadn't ought,* an utterly inexcusable combination of the two verbs, standing for "ought not to have," is, nevertheless, common in all parts of the Union among the uneducated. **1905** [see **1a** above]. **1910** *DN* 3.442 **cwNY,** I hadn't ought to have went. **1913** Kephart *Highlanders* 85 **sAppalachians,** You hadn't orter a-told. **1930** (1935) Porter *Flowering Judas* 63 **TX,** Oh, Mrs. Whipple, you hadn't ought to let Him do that. **1932** *Hanley Disks* **Farmington CT,** I ha'nt ought to really been frightened. **1949** Faulkner *Knight's Gambit* 104 **MS,** He turned the mule and rid back up the road toward them hills he hadn't ought to never have left. **1953** [see **2a** above]. c**1955** Reed–Person *Ling. Atlas Pacific NW,* 18 infs, Shouldn't; 10 infs, Hadn't ought to do that; 9 infs, Ought not to; 2 infs, Oughtn't to. **1956** [see **2a** above]. **1962** [see **2a** above]. **1966** [see **2a** above]. **1973** *PADS* 60.77 **seNC,** All our informants [=12] but one said *hadn't ought to.* The exception said *shouldn't.* **1975** Allen *LAUM* 2.42 **Upper MW** (as of c1950), One-fifth have *hadn't ought.* . . *Hadn't ought,* presumably Northern in orientation, turns up occasionally in southern Iowa. It is consistently more common in North Dakota than in Nebraska. **1989** Pederson *LAGS Tech. Index* 199 **Gulf Region,** [Of 914 infs, 9 used *hadn't ought.*]

c *didn't ought, don't ought.* [Cf *EDD* ought v. II.1]

    1847 Hurd *Grammatical Corrector* 29, *Don't ought,* for *ought not; as,* "You don't ought to return evil for evil." **1953** [see **2a** above]. **1966** Dakin *Dial. Vocab. Ohio R. Valley* 2.382, *Shouldn't ought to, shouldn't never* . . and *didn't ought to* are all attested, but only the latter appears in more than one record. Two of the oldest generation of informants in Illinois . . use this expression. **1986** Pederson *LAGS Concordance,* 3 infs, **neGA, cnLA, cTN,** Didn't ought.

d *shouldn't ought, shouldn't have ought.* Cf **1b** above

    1913 *DN* 4.5 **ME,** Shouldn't ought to have. . . Ought not to have. **1940** Chandler *Farewell* 30, I shouldn't ought to barber with you. **1956** [see **2a** above]. **1966** [see **2c** above]. **1968** *DARE* FW Addit **cwNY,** I shouldn't have ought to do it—I shouldn't have done that. **1989** Pederson *LAGS Tech. Index* 199 **Gulf Region,** [Of 914 infs, 5 gave *shouldn't ought* as the negative of *ought,* and 3 gave *shouldn't have ought.*]

e *ought to not.* Cf **2a** above

    1967 LeCompte *Word Atlas* 336 **seLA,** Oughta not [1 of 21 infs]. **1975** Allen *LAUM* 2.42 **MN** (as of c1950), One Minnesota inf. solves the problem [of negating *ought*] by putting the negative marker in the following infinitive phrase, e.g., "She ought to not play." **1986** Pederson *LAGS Concordance* **Gulf Region,** 10 infs, Ought to not. [Typical constrs are: "You ought to not do that," "He ought to not to do that," "I ought to not said that."]

3 Used in multiple modal constrs:

a *ought to could:* Should be able to. **chiefly Sth, TX** Cf **may** v **B1**

    1848 (1855) Ruxton *Life Far West* 201 **Rocky Mts,** If thar's game afoot, this child knows 'bull' from 'cow,' and ought to could. **1938** in 1972 *Amer. Slave* 2.23 **SC,** I ought to could fetch back more to speak to you bout. **1940** *AmSp* 15.214 **TX,** There is an appalling use of other double auxiliaries here even among educated people who should, and frequently do, know better. . . The most commonly heard examples: . . *he ought to could.* **1958** Latham *Meskin Hound* 47 **cTX,** Sugar figured that late of an evening like this, he ought to could locate a deer feeding on that tender rescue grass. **1963** Wright *Lawd Today* 106 **Chicago IL** [Black], Doc sure ought to could do something. **1967** *DARE* Tape **TX37,** It's just the little things that people thinks that I ought to could do. **1986** Pederson *LAGS Concordance,* 1 inf, **cnLA,** They ought to could do; 1 inf, **swMS,** You ought to could see God.

b *might ought:* See **may** v **B4.**

ought n See **ort**

oughta See **ought** v

oughten See **ought** v **C2a**

oughter See **ought** v

oughtn See **ought** v **C2a**

oughts See **ought** v **B**

oulachan See **eulachon**

oule n |'ula| [See quot 1949] *Gullah*
A **louse B1** or similar insect.

    1930 Stoney–Shelby *Black Genesis* 65 **seSC,** While dem turrah creeter is rastlin' in de dus' wid flea an' mite an' oule (lice), dis one kin tek he ease. **1949** Turner *Africanisms* 203 **sSC, GA coasts** [Gullah], [Words used in conversation:] ['ula] 'louse, bedbug, insect'—Cf. U[mbundu], *ola (ona)* 'louse.'

ounty tounty See **ownty do(w)nty**

our adj Usu |ɑr, ɑʊə(r), ɑʊr|; also |æʊə(r), ɛr|; for addit proncs see quots Pronc-spp *aour, ar(e), ouah* Similarly pron *ours* Std senses, var forms.

    1861 Holmes *Venner* 2.64 **NEng,** She was genteel enough for him and . . born the same year we buried aour little Anny Marí'. **1891** *DN* 1.156 **cNY,** [ɑr] < our. **1905** Chesnutt *Col.'s Dream* 29 **NC,** She's de barbuh's wife, suh, w'at bought ouah ole house. **1905** *DN* 3.55 **eNE,** *Our* is likely to become *ar,* as "ar house". **1935** in 1942 *AmSp* 17.51 **eKS,** ['ɑˠ 'kʌntrɪ]. **1936** *AmSp* 11.309 **Upstate NY,** *Our* and *ours* occur regularly as [ɑr] and [ɑrz]. **1939** *AmSp* 14.125 **neTN,** [ɑr kɑr. . . ɑr hændz. . . ɑr we]. **1943** *AmSp* 18.268 **VA,** The word *our* had peculiar variations: [ɑʊr], [ɑʊə] . . [æʊə] . . [æə] . . [ɑr] . . [ɑʊr], [ɑʊə] . . [ɑʊ]. **1943** *LANE* Map 615 *(Ours; yours)* **NEng,** [For *ours,* proncs of the type [awəz, ɑwəz, ɑʊə(r)z, æwə(r)z] predominate throughout the region, while proncs with loss of the inglide such as [arz, ɑrz, ɑʊrz] are rare.] **1950** Hubbell *Pronc. NYC* 71, In *our* . . /aɑ̆/ often occurs, making the word a rime of *car* rather than of *power.* **1959** *VT Hist.* 27.151, *Our* [ɑr] . . pronc. Also [æɑʊr] in some rural areas. Common. Rural areas. **1976** Allen *LAUM* 3.33 **Upper MW** (as of c1950), Supplementary data for generally recorded *ours* suggest that the tendency to simplify the /ɑʊ/ diphthong before /r/ is affecting speakers outside the Midland speech area. Loss of rounding, as in [ɑˠz], occurs [with 9 infs out of 208]. Weakening of the offglide as in [ɑᵁɚ, ɑˠɚz] is evinced in the pronunciation of [12] infs . . Complete loss, yielding [ɑˠz], appears in the field records of [26] . . infs. . . But it is my opinion that a current survey would reveal this pronunciation to be spreading rapidly, as it is now fairly common in the Twin Cities and among students at the University of Minnesota. **1982** *Barrick Coll.* **csPA,** "Are father, which art in heaven. . ." **1986** *DARE* File **ceKY,** Dialect and vocabulary items from Martin County, Kentucky. . . Standard 'our' (possessive pronoun) is /ɛr/, identical with standard 'air'.

our beauties See **arbutus**

Our Lady's bedstraw See **lady's bedstraw**

Our Lord's candle(stick) n Also *candle of the Lord, Lord's candlestick, Lord's candle yucca* [See quots 1915, 1985] Cf **God's candle, Madonna ~**
A **yucca,** esp *Yucca whipplei;* also the flowering stalk of such a plant.

    1888 Lindley–Widney *CA of South* 330, One sees "Our Lord's Candlestick," the stately *Yucca.* **1915** (1926) Armstrong–Thornber *Western Wild Flowers* 40, Our Lord's Candle. Spanish Bayonet. *Yucca Whipplei.* White. Spring, summer. Cal., Ariz. . . After they have blossomed, the tall, white stalks remain standing for some time, so that the hills look as if they had been planted with numbers of white wands. **1948** *Nat. Hist.* 57.180, The *"Candle of the Lord"* sends up its triumphant banner to tell the desert traveler that spring has come. **1949** Moldenke *Amer. Wild Flowers* 370, In the chaparral belt of western Arizona and southern California grows the famous *quixoteplant* or *Our-Lords-candle, Hesperoyucca whipplei.* . . The flower stalk rises 8 to 14 feet and is terminated by a 3- to 6-foot panicle of creamy white flowers. **1967** *DARE* (Qu. S26a, *. . . Wildflowers. . . Roadside flowers*) Inf **CA4,** Lord's candle yucca or Whipple yucca. **1976** Bailey–Bailey *Hortus Third* 1178, *[Yucca] gloriosa. . . Lord's-candlestick. . .* Fl[ower]s greenish-white to reddish. . . N.C. to Fla. *Ibid* 1179, *[Yucca] Whipplei. . . Our-Lord's-candle. . .* Fls. fragrant, creamy-white, sometimes tinged with purple. . . Calif. **1985** Dodge *Flowers SW Deserts* 28, *Yucca whipplei,* a much smaller plant than yucca elata, produces a stouter flower stalk with a great spreading plume of small, delicate flowers. These graceful plumes appear at night as if aglow with an inner light, hence the name "Our Lord's Candle."

ourn pron Also *ourns* [*OED* c1380 →; prob *our/ourn* by analogy with *my/mine*] **chiefly Sth, S Midl, NEng** *somewhat old-fash* Cf **hern** pron, **hisn, mines, yourn**
Ours.

1795 Dearborn *Columbian Grammar* 137, *List of Improprieties. . .* Ourn for Ours. **1818** Fessenden *Ladies Monitor* 172 **VT**, *Ourn* for ours. **1859** (1968) Bartlett *Americanisms* 304, *Ourn,* for *ours.* A vulgarism frequently heard, which is also common in the local dialect of London. **1899** (1912) Green *VA Folk-Speech* 307, *Ourn.* **1903** *DN* 2.292 **Cape Cod MA** (as of a1857), *Ourn.* **1905** *DN* 3.15 **cCT**, *Ourn.* **1907** *DN* 3.215 **nwAR**, *Ourn. Ibid* 248 **eME**, *Ourn.* **1909** *DN* 3.354 **eAL, wGA**, *Ourn.* **1919** Kyne *Capt. Scraggs* 58 **CA**, This well-known peculiarity of ourn. **1924** (1926) Vollmer *Sun-Up* 3 **wNC**, A city man has bought the land next to ourn. **1926** *DN* 5.388 **ME**, *Ourn. . .* Obsol[ete]. **1934** *WV Review* Dec 79, We still hear this form of the possessive in our *. . yourn . .* and *ourn.* **1938** Rawlings *Yearling* 327 **nFL**, He likes dogs. He plays with ourn. **1940** Faulkner *Hamlet* 344 **MS**, "Watch out, paw!" the boy said. "There he is! There's ourn!" **1943** *LANE* Map 615, Only forms currently used by the informants in their own speech are shown on the map. [The map shows 45 instances of *ourn* throughout **NEng**.] *. . Ourn* and *yourn* were reported as heard in the speech of others by . . [19 infs]. They are described as older though still in use by . . [38 infs]. They are described as obsolete or as heard only from very old people by . . [22 infs]. **1952** Brown *NC Folkl.* 1.572, *Ourn* ['ɑwən, ɑrn, aʊrn]. *Ibid, Ourns* ['ɑwənz, ɑrnz, aʊrnz]. *. . Ours.—Illiterate.* **1958** Humphrey *Home from the Hill* 7 **neTX**, How do we know it's one of our'n? **1960** Lee *Mockingbird* 129 **sAL**, They got their church, we got our'n. **1967** *DARE* Tape **KY2**, [FW:] Do you go to church every Sunday? [Inf:] No, not every Sunday. Ourn don't hold every Sunday. [**1975** Allen *LAUM* 2.54 (as of c1950), In the U[pper] M[idwest] the normalizing power of the schools apparently has extinguished *ourn.*] **1986** Pederson *LAGS Concordance* **Gulf Region**, 16 infs, Ourn; 1 inf, Ourn—her grandmother's form; 1 inf, Ourn—heard; not lately; 1 inf, Ourn—folks say; 1 inf, Ourn—facetiously; 1 inf, Ourn—uses jokingly; 1 inf, Ourn—country people; 1 inf, Ourn—in "cute, kidding" conversation. [21 of 23 infs old]

ours See **our**

out adv, v, adj, prep, n, exclam Usu |aut, ɑut|; also |æut|; also **chiefly nNEng, nNY, Mid Atl, esp eVA** |əut, ʌut|; also **chiefly Upstate NY, wNEng** |ɛut|; occas eVA, SC |ut|; for addit varr see quots Pronc-spp *aout, eout, ert, oot* Cf Pronc Intro 3.II.14, **about**

A Forms.

1861 Holmes *Venner* 1.56 **NEng**, Put him aout y'rself. **1871** Eggleston *Hoosier Schoolmaster* 12 **IN**, Git aout, you pup! **1881** (1883) Cooke *Somebody's Neighbors* 273 **CT**, Git aout! Git aout! **1898** Westcott *Harum* 304 **nNY**, The's some folks eout in front wants you to come eout an' see 'em. **1914** *DN* 4.68 **ME, nNH**, He hypered like all git aout! *Ibid* 159 **cVA**, Ah might a could found aout. **1919** *DN* 5.40 **VA**, *Out*, adv., pronounced *ow-oot. . . Oot,* adv. Out—a word, along with "a-boot," with which the Virginian is sometimes twitted. Yet it is actually heard in that State. **1930** *AmSp* 5.342 **cnNH**, [aʊ] appears as [aʊ] in *ground, house, out. Ibid* **ceVA**, [ɑʊ] appears in *in out. Ibid* 345 **cGA**, [ɑʊ] occurs in *out. Ibid* 347 **cSC**, [æʊ] in *scouts, out. Ibid* 354 **ceSC**, The [ɑʊ] diphthong is practically [oʊ] with the second element very short—*scouts, out.* **1930** *AmSp* 6.94 **eVA**, In the Tidewater *out . .* [is] [əut] or [ut]. **1931** *AmSp* 6.167 **seVA**, The diphthong [ɑʊ] appears as [əu] *. .* in *out. . .* Though common among the negroes, the diphthong [oʊ] in *out . .* is rare among the white people. [oʊ] is heard in the speech of white people and negroes in Charleston, S.C. *. . .* Sometimes in *about* and *out,* it tends to lose its diphthongal character and appear as [u] or [ʊ]. *Ibid* 400 **eME**, Down the Maine coast, [ɑʊ] may be replaced by a diphthong of uncertain quality [ʌu] or [əu] or [oʊ], in *out.* **1934** *AmSp* 9.213, Along the coast of Virginia and South Carolina the diphthong in *about* and *out* tends to become the vowel [u] or [ʊ]. **1939** in 1976 *Weevils in the Wheat* 303 **VA** [Black], She den went ert an' brought ole Missie in. **1955** *PADS* 23.43 **e,cSC, eNC, seGA**, Centered beginning of /ai, au/ [əi, əu] before voiceless consonants, as in *knife, ice, out, house* (also e. Virginia and Canada). **1961** Kurath–McDavid *Pronc. Engl.* Map 29, *Out.* [Chiefly N Atl, PA, nWV, scattered NC, SC, GA, [aut ~ ɑut]; chiefly nMD, VA, nNC, eSC, scattered nNEng, nwNY, [əut ~ ʌut]; scattered NY, wCT, wMA, [ɛut]; chiefly nNEng, sNJ, sePA, DE, nMD, WV, NC, SC, [æut].] **1967–68** *DARE* FW Addit **seAR**, Out [æɔt]—heard from a poor White; **seMD**, Out—some say [æʊ], some say [əʊ], and some say [əi]; also in words like *about, house,* etc. FW could find no way of predicting which people would use which pronunciation. Variations occur in all ages, sexes, and geographical locations, and no social class could be distinguished; **MD**, Out [ut]. **1976** Allen *LAUM* 3.25 (as of c1950), The vowel in *house, out, down, mountain. . .* As in the North and North Midland areas of the eastern states, the

dominant variety is a diphthong with an onset ranging from [a] to [ɑ], that is, from low-front to low-central.

B As adv.

1 Away from or out of a relatively remote area; esp, away from or out of Alaska. **West, esp AK** Cf **go out 4, in C, outside** adv

1899 Hitchcock *2 Women in Klondike* 42 **AK**, There are so many prognostications that we may not be able to get "out" (entering Alaska is always spoken of as "going in;" leaving it, as "going out"). **1904** Lynch *3 Yrs. Klondike* 164 **AK**, The many cabins to the left near its junction with the Yukon were empty and deserted. They had only formed [a] portion of the city of refuge for those who wintered there in 1897, and who by now had either gone 'out' or were distributed over the country. **1925** *AmSp* 1.149 **NV**, "Out" and "in" are used with peculiar beauty. In the mining camps men ask, "Are you going out tomorrow?" When they say "going out," there is still a savor of those days when going out from the shelter of the camp was like leaving this planet for Mars. **1928** *AmSp* 4.131 **cnNE**, On leaving the "hills" one goes "out." **1983** *Tundra Drums* (Bethel) 5 May 16 (Tabbert *Dict. Alaskan Engl.*), Of course, now that we're ready to go back Out, all of our children are back in Alaska!

2 Of the wind: away from the sea and toward the land. Cf **outwind**

1890 *DN* 1.19 **seNH**, *Out:* of the wind. Along the seaboard, the wind 'is out' or 'has got out' when it blows from the sea. The expression is known in Portsmouth, Salem, and Plymouth. I do not think it is common in Boston. **1892** *DN* 1.217 **neMA**, "The wind is out" is common in North Andover, Mass.

3 Forward in time. [Ir dial]

1855 (1940) Chambers *Jrl.* 137 **MT**, I apprehend but little danger from this out. **1867** (1930) Buck *Yankee Trader* 214 **NEng**, Now, I am going to try to be a Jew from this out. **1899** Edwards *Defense* 197 **GA**, Mr. Linkum tuk er pen an' writ down dese two lines . . , 'Niggers ez free fum ter-day out.' **1940–41** Cassidy *WI Atlas* **nwWI**, From now out. **1941** *Morgantown Post* (WV) 3 June 6/1 **nWV**, He has run the race and is fairly entitled to sit on the sidelines from here out.

4 At an end—used in contexts where *up* or *over* would be std.

1800 (1907) Thornton *Diary* 10.125 **PA**, Our gardiner came from the farm, his time is out today—and he will not stay without higher wages. **1912** Green *VA Folk-Speech* 96, Don't come back till your broad [=trip] is out. **1928** Peterkin *Scarlet Sister Mary* 193 **SC**, Winter makes them run slow and cold, but, thank God, winter's time was out. **c1938** [see **outen v 2**]

5 also *outs:* In disagreement, at odds, in a state of opposition. [*OED* 1565–72 →] Cf **F2** below

1834 (1961) Strang *Diary* 38 **NY**, Mr. Smith says I tell a falsehood when I say the last year of my life was the happiest, and when I say I enjoy more happiness than I endure misery he is nearly out upon me. **1838** Walker in 1940 Drury *Pioneers Spokanes* 81 **ME**, Mrs. Smith very much out with Dr. Gray, in a fret all the time. **1941** *LANE* Map 483 *(He queered himself with me)* 1 inf, **ceMA**, He's out with me; 1 inf, **csMA**, I'm out with him, 'slang.' **1965–70** *DARE* (Qu. III11b, *If two people can't bear each other at all . . "Those two are _____."*) Inf **CA136**, Plumb outs; **IN49**, Outs; **NJ68**, Way out; **TN66**, Out with each other; (Qu. KK68, *. . "We agree on most things, but on politics we're _____."*) Infs **KY60, MN33, PA185**, Way out; **MD19, SD5**, Out; **IN73**, Out together.

6 To a point of completion or exhaustion; fully, completely. Note: Std v phrr with *out* as the second element are not treated; those that are regionally distributed are entered separately. The distinction between this sense and **7** below is not always clear.

1921 (1923) Greer-Petrie *Angeline Seelbach* 25 **KY**, I didn't half git my broad [=trip] out. **1965–70** *DARE* (Qu. L11) Infs **MA42, NH14**, Tedder it out; **GA87**, It cures out; **KY43**, Let it lay and cure out; **NY219**, Dry it and stir it out; (Qu. N27b, *When unpaved roads get very rough, you call them _____*) Inf **IL26**, Potted out; **MO10**, Rutted out; (Qu. U39, *Somebody who has lost all his money: "During the depression he _____."*) Inf **FL19**, Spent out; (Qu. U40, *. . "At the moment he's _____."*) Infs **NC68, SC42**, Spent out; (Qu. X47, *. . "I'm very tired, at the end of my strength"*) Infs **LA11, SC7, 26, 44**, Whipped out; **CT27**, All frazzled out; **GA77**, Fatigued out; **NC33**, Bushed out; **NC88**, Flagged out; (Qu. GG13a) Inf **KY40**, It worries me out; (Qu. JJ46, *. . To pretend: "Let's _____ we don't know a thing about it."*) Inf **MO3**,

Play out. **1986** Pederson *LAGS Concordance* **Gulf Region,** 12 infs, Cure (*or* cured, curing) out [used of hay, potatoes, sausage, meat, onions]; 1 inf, Cooked out—syrup; 1 inf, To cook out a barn of tobacco; 1 inf, Fatigue out; 1 inf, Finished out = completely finished; 1 inf, Let him chill out good—of hog after slaughter; 1 inf, Grow them out—of calves—letting them grow up; 1 inf, It rains out—rains hard for a while, then quits; 1 inf, It won't drought out—of sandy loam; 1 inf, Mature out = tassel out; 1 inf, They might quilt out two a day = produce; 1 inf, Let the hay season out = air out; *(Worn out)* 4 infs, Whipped out.

7 Added with little semantic force to var verbs, often where other advs would be expected; see quots. Note: Std v phrr with *out* as the second element are not treated; those that are regionally distributed are entered separately.

1914 *DN* 4.77 **ME, nNH,** *Out.* . . For "up" in familiar phrases. "Wash out the dishes," etc. **1954** *Harder Coll.* **cwTN,** 'At teacher's good at showin' 'im scholars how to add out. **1965–70** *DARE* (Qu. E21, . . *About a room that needs to be put in order* . . "*I'm just going to* _____ *this room.*") 31 Infs, **esp NEast,** Straighten (it) out; (Qu. L43a, . . *To get horses ready to work* . . "*I'll* _____ *the horses.*") Infs **AL2, SC**57; **GA**17, Ketch out; (Qu. M19, *A place for keeping carrots, turnips, potatoes, and so on over the winter*) Inf **AR**56, Hill them out; (Qu. X47, . . "*I'm very tired, at the end of my strength*") Infs **ID**5, **MI**20, **MT**1, **NJ**48, **NY**20, 103, **TN**34, Done out; (Qu. Y5, . . *To urge somebody to do something he shouldn't: "Johnny wouldn't have tried that if the other boys hadn't* _____.") Inf **OK**7, Egged him out; (Qu. Y47, *To hide something away for future use: "I know he's got it* _____ *somewhere."*) Inf **TX**83, Stashed out; (Qu. Y48, *To look in every possible place for something you've mislaid* . . "*I've* _____ *[the house looking for them].*") Inf **NC**37, Searched the house out; (Qu. BB21, . . *Being constipated*) Inf **MO**26, Stuffed out; (Qu. OO19b, *Talking about stretching out to rest: "He'll feel better after he has* _____ *[down a while].*") Inf **VA**39, Rest out. **1969** Emmons *Deep Rivers* 4 **eTX** [Black], In spite of the fact that she had so roundly "'bused him out," it seemed that she still had his love and respect. **1986** Pederson *LAGS Concordance* **Gulf Region,** 1 inf, And the reason I had to quit out = quit school; 1 inf, Catch them out; 1 inf, Catch them out = get them [=horses] out to go; 1 inf, Go catch them out—to bridle mules; 1 inf, Go catch out my horse and hitch him up; 1 inf, Caught out; 1 inf, Candle them out; 1 inf, You're all done out; 1 inf, Fancy it out = build in a fancy way; 1 inf, He used to trip me out = amuse me greatly; 1 inf, Peddle them out; 1 inf, Ruins it out—of tool left out in weather; 1 inf, Scalded out—the dishes; 1 inf, Land that was subject to drowning out; 1 inf, When it drown out—floods; 1 inf, It's drowned out your crop; 1 inf, Kicked out the bucket [=died]; 1 inf, The North whipped out the South—in the Civil War; 1 inf, Whisper out—of butter old or turning bad; 1 inf, Shrink out; 1 inf, Stop out—of school to work in the fields; 1 inf, Study that out = figure that out; 1 inf, Study it out—i.e., think about; 1 inf, Sun him out.

8 Fully. [Scots, Engl dial; cf *SND out* adv. II.4, *EDD out* adv. 13] Cf **long** adj **B4**

1946 *PADS* 6.22 **ceNC,** *Out.* . . Already. Used only in stating ages. "I'm twenty-one out and in my twenty-two."

9 Used with compass directions to indicate distance or direction away from the speaker; see quots. Cf **back East, down** adv **B1**

1857 in 1924 *Jrl. Amer. Hist.* [New Haven] 18.41 **RI,** A game universally in vogue "out West". **1965** *Bee* (Phillips WI) 19 Aug [3/5], Mr. and Mrs. Ed Rhody left Saturday for a week's vacation out east. They were . . to attend the World's Fair in New York for several days. **1966** *DARE* (Qu. BB56, *Joking expressions for dying: "He* _____.") Inf **MI**24, Is going out north; the cemetery is out north. **1975** Gould *ME Lingo* 197, *Out East*—To Maine's blue-water sailors of the later 1800s *Out East* meant Australian, East Indian, and Chinese ports of call. *Out West* meant any part of present U.S.A. beyond the Mississippi, but not as far as the coast, which in Maine parlance was the Pacific Coast. *Ibid* 198, *Out West* is used in Maine with the same generalization implied by down South and up North when used in New York or Georgia. **1979** *DARE* File **cnMA** (as of c1915), *Out west* covered a good deal of territory. My mother had two half-brothers who had gone out west when she was a child, one to Minnesota and one to California. . . As I recall, it was much more common to speak of someone's going out west than just going west. **1986** Pederson *LAGS Concordance* **Gulf Region,** 33 infs, Out west; 3 infs, Out east; 2 infs, (A place) out east here; 1 inf, The school was 5 or 6 miles away, right out east. **1995** *DARE* File, In California in the 1950s we talked of going "back East," or said that someone was from "back East." When I moved to Wisconsin in 1975 I

was surprised to hear people use "out East" instead of "back East" in those contexts. I would have said "out West," but not "out East."

C As verb.

1 To eject, expel. [*OED out* v. 1.a 1008 →]

1952 Brown *NC Folkl.* 1.572, *Out.* . . To put out. "Out that wet dog before he shakes hisself."—General. Rare.

2 To deprive (of a possession); to cheat, defraud. [*OED out* v. 1.a 1602 →]

1691 Mather *Life of John Eliot* 66, But our *Eliot* was in such ill terms with the Devil, as to . . make some noble and zealous attempts towards outing him of his ancient Possessions here. **1927** *DN* 5.476 **Ozarks,** *Out.* . . To cheat, to defraud. "He don't need no pension, nohow—he's jes' a-tryin' t' out th' Gov'ment."

3 To extinguish (a fire or lamp). **chiefly eSC, eGA** See Map Cf **outen** v **1,** *DJE*

1888 Jones *Negro Myths* 93 **GA coast** [Black], Eh roll ober an try fuh out de fire. **1892** (1969) Christensen *Afro-Amer. Folk Lore* 109, You leetle raskil, you out dat fire 'cause you see me da cook an' you wan' me for gib you some. **1910** *DN* 3.458 **FL, GA,** *Outed.* . . Extinguished, as "He has outed the fire." **1950** *PADS* 14.50 **SC,** *Out.* . . To extinguish, as a lamp, a fire. **1966–70** *DARE* (Qu. Y43b, . . *To put out a fire*) Infs **FL**31, **GA**7, 19, **OK**54, **SC**7, 19, 24, 70, Out the fire; **NC**49, **SC**10, Out it; **GA**30, Out that fire; (Qu. Y42, *Expressions for putting out a lamp or light*) Infs **NY**199, **SC**7, 44, 66, 70, Out the light. **1986** Pederson *LAGS Concordance,* 1 inf, **cnFL,** He could have throwed a bucket of water on it and outed it. **1987** Jones-Jackson *When Roots Die* 139 **sSC coast** [Gullah], Out the light: turn the light out.

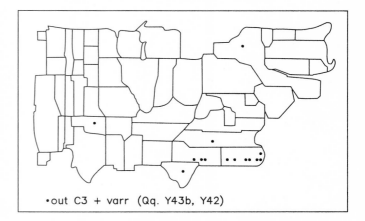

•out C3 + varr (Qq. Y43b, Y42)

4 in phr *out with:* To bring out; to utter. Cf **outen** v **3**

1833 in 1834 Davis *Letters Downing* 39 **NY,** I out with my seal-skin wallet, and I showed him a mess on 'em. **1851** Burke *Polly Peablossom* 118 **KY,** Arter apparently considering awhile, he outs with his jack-knife, and . . made a rip at the sole of his left boot. **1864** (1868) Trowbridge *Cudjo's Cave* 17 **TN,** "I've been deceived in him," said a third. . . "I never suspected he was anti-slavery till I talked with him t'other day about joining us; then he out with it." **1912** Green *VA Folk-Speech* 308, *Out.* . . To draw out: "He out with his sword and smote off the chains." **1942** Faulkner *Go Down* 235 **MS,** The negro he was shooting at outed with a dollar-and-a-half mail-order pistol . . only it never went off.

5 See quot.

1884 *Anglia* 7.272 **Sth, S Midl** [Black], *To gwinter* [=be going to] *out er man* = to get him out, to baffle.

D As adj.

1 Empty. [Cf *SND out* adv. II.3 "Of a cup, glass, etc. or its contents: emptied, drained, consumed"]

1821 Howison *Upper Canada* 294 **cNY,** 'Squire, is your cip [sic for *cup*] out?—It will be so right off, ma'am. **1995** *DARE* File **csWI,** My gas tank is nearly out—I'd better stop at the station.

2 Consumed, used up. **chiefly Sth, S Midl** See Map on p. 908 Cf **all** adj[2]

1928 Peterkin *Scarlet Sister Mary* 21 **SC,** When de kerosene is out. **1943** *LANE* Map 557 *(The oranges are all gone)* 1 inf, **seMA,** Are out; 1 inf, **sVT,** The tripe's out (i.e. The tripe is all gone) heard from a lunchroom attendant. **1965–70** *DARE* (Qu. LL17, . . *There's no more of something: "The potatoes are* _____.") 23 Infs, **chiefly Sth, S Midl,** Out. [*DARE* Ed: In the phrr *all out, fresh out,* and *slap out,* the

Infs are not regionally distributed.] **1986** Pederson *LAGS Concordance*, 2 infs, **ceTN, cwMS**, The oranges are (*or* was) out.

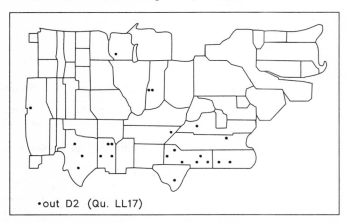

•out D2 (Qu. LL17)

3 In children's games: temporarily safe or immune—also used as a call claiming immunity.

1965–70 *DARE* (Qu. EE17, *In a game of tag, if a player wants to rest, what does he call out so that he can't be tagged?*) Infs **CA**73, **MD**25, **VA**75, Out; **GA**77, **KY**17, **MO**15, **NJ**3, **NY**162, **TN**46, I'm out; (Qu. EE20, *When two boys are fighting, and the one who is losing wants to stop, he calls out, "_____."*) Infs **NY**205, **PA**221, Out; **NY**152, I'm out [aʊt].

E As prep.

From; out of. **chiefly Sth, Midl; also NEast** See Map Note: *Out* in the sense "out through," as in *out the door,* is widespread and not treated here.

1955 *PADS* 23.44 **e,sSC, eNC, seGA**, He fell) *out the bed*. (Also e. Virginia.) **1959** Lomax *Rainbow Sign* 30 **AL** [Black], You wait and I'll get us some syrup out the smokehouse. **1965–70** *DARE* (Qu. MM19, *"He took the letter _____ his pocket."*) 26 Infs, **scattered, but esp Sth, Midl**, Out; (Qu. U2) Inf **NY**61, Bought it out the store; (Qu. W24c) Inf **SC**70, Cow's out the stable; hog's out the pen; **SC**68, Horse 'bout to come out the stable; (Qu. II11a) Inf **NC**84, See out the same eye; (Qu. JJ15a) Infs **DC**8, **LA**25, **NY**93, **SC**5, 24, 26, Come (in) out the rain; **SC**26, Come in out the cold; **SC**40, Get out a shower of rain; **NC**17, Get in out the rain; **MO**21, **SC**21, Pour piss out a boot; (Qu. KK43) Inf **SC**65, Out the hard part; (Qu. KK48) **TN**46, Out the blue; (Qu. NN22b) Inf **CT**25, Get out here; **MA**56, Get out the way; **MO**23, Y'all get out here. **1986** Pederson *LAGS Concordance* **Gulf Region**, 47 infs, (Fell, fall, fallen, fellen, have fell, *or* rolled) out the bed; 15 infs, Out the east (*or* north, northwest, south, west); 13 infs, Out the way; 48 infs, Out the pot (*or* road, top, woods, world [and var similar phrr]).

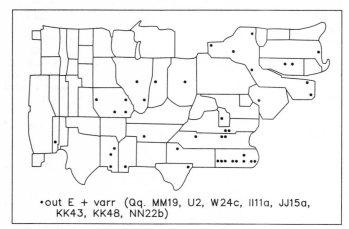

•out E + varr (Qq. MM19, U2, W24c, II11a, JJ15a, KK43, KK48, NN22b)

F As noun.

1 A showing, outcome; (great or little) success, progress—freq in phr *make a poor out* to have little success in an endeavor, to do a poor job. [Engl dial] **chiefly Sth, S Midl**

1843 in 1951 *AmSp* 26.183 **NC**, A man . . that made half as many good resolutions as I have or made a worse out in sticking to them. **1853** (1854) Baldwin *Flush Times* 31 **AL**, I might have made a pretty good *out* of it, if I had thrown myself upon the merits of my case. **1899**

(1912) Green *VA Folk-Speech* 307, He has not made much out towards making a living. **1904** (1972) Harben *Georgians* 176, Warren got down on his knees then and actually tried to pray; but he made a pore out. **1909** *DN* 3.348 **eAL, wGA**, *Make a poor out*. . . To do poorly, make a failure. **1912** *DN* 3.582 **wIN**, He tried to make a speech, but he made a poor out at it. *Ibid* 586, *Pretty out*. . . A sorry state of affairs. **1914** *DN* 4.110 **cKS**, If she married him to reform him, she made a poor out of it. **1915** *DN* 4.187 **swVA**, *Poor out*, weak effort without success; *purty out*, blunder; matter of embarrassment or annoyance. **1923** *DN* 5.216 **swMO**, He made a pore out o' farmin'. **1938** Rawlings *Yearling* 347 **FL**, I often figger I made a sorry out of it, not encouragin' you. **1943** *Hench Coll.* **VA**, She made an out at cleaning the shavings. But it was a very poor out. **1944** *PADS* 2.47 **NC, VA**, He made a hell of a out trying to raise them boys. **1953** *PADS* 19.13 **sAppalachians**, I tried to make a cake by your rule, but I made a poor out of it. **1959** Faulkner *Mansion* 63 **MS**, Montgomery Ward hoed out the vegetable rows, not making much of a out at it maybe, but anyhow swinging the hoe. **1977** Norman *Kinfolks* 3 **eKY**, "Wilgus Collier's my name. I don't have a middle name." The fat man shook his head and sucked his teeth. "Well," he said. "Either way, it's a poor out for a name." **1982** *Smithsonian Letters* **cnKY** (as of 1930s), If she tried to cut out a dress and did it wrong, she "made a bad out."

2 usu pl; in adv phrr: At odds, on bad terms. Cf **B5** above

a *at outs,* rarely *at the outs*. [Engl dial] **scattered exc NEast, C Atl** See Map

1884 *Congressional Record* 23 Apr 15.4.3326, His church and the Unitarians [were] very much at outs. **1914** *DN* 4.102 **cKS**, *At outs*. . . At odds; 'out of sorts.' "They were good neighbors, but got at outs over the chickens." **1929** *AmSp* 5.125 **ME**, Persons might be "at outs" or variance. **1940** (1968) Haun *Hawk's Done Gone* 27 **TN**, I never have heard tell of Dona and the truth being very far at outs. **1941** *Esquire* May 13 **KY**, Families used to be at the outs. Now it would all be healed. **1959** Lahey–Hogan *As I Remember It* 129 **swKS** (as of early 20th cent), The whole caboodle of them were "at outs." The parents had been feuding over ranges, fences, and cattle from time unknown. **c1960** *Wilson Coll.* **csKY**, *At outs*. . . In disagreement, on bad terms. **1965–70** *DARE* (Qu. II11b, *If two people can't bear each other at all . . "Those two are _____."*) 14 Infs, **scattered exc NEast, C Atl**, (Really *or* sure-nuff) at outs; **MI**110, **TX**29, At (the) outs with each other; (Qu. KK68, *When people don't think alike about something: "We agree on most things, but on politics we're _____."*) Infs **CA**87, **CO**7, At outs. [16 of 18 Infs old]

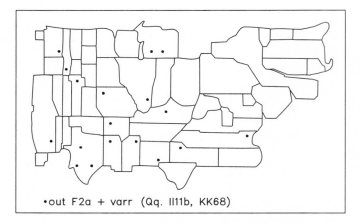

•out F2a + varr (Qq. II11b, KK68)

b *on the outs,* rarely *on the out, on outs*. **scattered, but less freq NEng, Sth** See Map

1917 McCutcheon *Green Fancy* 87 **NY**, My daughter and I are . . what you might say 'on the outs' at present. **1922** (1950) Grey *To the Last Man* 22 **West**, I reckoned you belonged to the sheep raisers who're on the outs with my father. **1951** *PADS* 15.58 **neIN** (as of 1890s), *Outs, on the*. . . In disagreement; hostile toward. Slang. **1965–70** *DARE* (Qu. II11b, *If two people can't bear each other at all . . "Those two are _____."*) 22 Infs, **scattered, but less freq NEng, Sth**, (Really) on the outs; **GA**7, On the out; **KY**85, On outs with each other; (Qu. GG16, . . *"You just can't please him—he's always _____."*) Infs **NY**223, **OH**80, On the outs; (Qu. II11a, *If two people don't get along well together . . "They don't _____."*) Inf **KY**19, On the outs; (Qu. KK68, *When people don't think alike about something: "We agree on most things, but on politics we're _____."*) Inf **MI**18, On the outs.

1976 Garber *Mountain-ese* 64 **sAppalachians,** The Smiths have been on the outs with Chad ever since he sold them a stripper fer a milk cow.

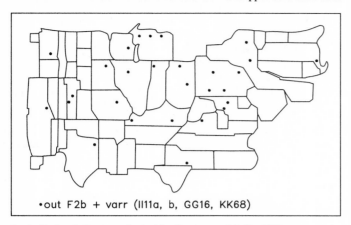

•out F2b + varr (II11a, b, GG16, KK68)

3 A fault, defect, undesirable feature. **chiefly NEast**
1885 (1897) Ward *Old Maids* 2.48 **MA,** Sound as sense! Hadn't an out about him. **1901** *Scribner's Mag.* 29.418 **NEast,** There were horses of every kind—except the right kind. Each one had his own peculiar "out." **1914** *DN* 4.77 **ME, nNH,** Out. . . In *pl.* unpleasant or difficult features. "There's lots of outs about his goin' down t' Boston." **1917** Garland *Son Middle Border* 129 **SD,** Even hostling had its "outs," especially in spring when the horses were shedding their hair. **1929** *AmSp* 5.125 **ME,** "No outs about her" meant she was without any faults or deformities (both disposition and physique included).

4 pl: A hiding game; see quot.
1957 *Sat. Eve. Post Letters* **ceWI** (as of 1890s), *Outs:* Outdoor game at night. Much like Hide and Seek, except that those in hiding may run from place to place, but every one in hiding must shout occasionally, *"Outs,"* while trying to get back to the goal. One of those caught by the seeker becomes the seeker for the next round.

out-and-down See **down-and-out 1**

outarde n [LaFr < Fr *outarde* bustard] **LA**
=**Canada goose.**
1898 Elliot *Wild Fowl* 68, In Louisiana it [=*Branta canadensis*] is known as Outarde. **1911** *Forest & Stream* 77.173, *Branta canadensis.*— Outarde, . . Mississippi Delta, La. . . It is of interest that the English counterpart of this word, i.e. Bustard, was applied to this species at Hudson Bay in early days. **1916** *Times–Picayune* (New Orleans LA) 26 Mar mag sec 2, *Canada Goose.* . . Outarde. . . The best-known and most widely distributed of the geese and the commonest of these that visit Louisiana each winter. **1917** *Wilson Bulletin* 29.2.77, *Branta canadensis.*—Outarde, brant, Marksville, La.

outards See **outwards**

outberry n
=**cloudberry.**
1933 *Torreya* 33.83, *Rubus chamaemorus* . . Outberry.

out-come-shout n
1927 *AmSp* 3.139 **eME,** The older people. . . spoke of . . "out-come-shout" for a noisy disturbance.

outcry n [*OED* c1600 →; "*Obs.* or *local*"] Cf **cry** v **1**
An auction.
1712 (1901) Hempstead *Diary* 5 Aug 13 **seCT,** I went into town & brought 2 Cows yt were Sold att an outcry. **1719** in 1965 *AmSp* 40.236 **seVA,** My goods to be sold by way of outcry. **1896** (1968) Earle *Colonial NY* 270, The meeting-house sometimes bore other decorations,—often "Billets of sales," and notices of vendues or "outcrys." **1899** Green *VA Folk-Speech* 308, *Outcry.* . . An auction. "To be sold at public outcry." **1931** *AmSp* 7.20 **swPA,** Public outcry. An auction sale. **1974** *News & Reporter* (Chester, S. Carolina) 15–A/6 (Advt.) (*OEDS*), I, the undersigned Special Referee will sell at public outcry to the highest bidder . . the following described real estate.

outdacious See **audacious(ly)**

outdoingest adj, also used absol *esp* **S Midl** Cf **outingest**
Most remarkable, most extraordinary.
1909 *DN* 3.355 **eAL, wGA,** *Out-doin(g)est.* . . Most surprising, most difficult to manage. "He's the out-doinest child I ever saw." **1925**

Dargan *Highland Annals* 190 **cwNC,** By the end of the summer Serena would be as duckless as at its beginning, but she had had many a pleasant, shady jaunt in search of them "outdoin'est things." **1942** (1971) Campbell *Cloud-Walking* 88 **seKY,** But the outdoinest thing Nelt done for learning was when he brought on a grist mill. *Ibid* 193, "Now ain't that the outdoinest?" the women said. **1943** in 1944 *ADD* **AR,** [Radio:] That's the outdoin'est thing I ever heerd.

outdone adj **chiefly Sth, S Midl**
Put out, perplexed, exasperated; disappointed, overcome.
1816 in 1915 *MD Hist. Mag.* 10.362, Now again we feel out done in finding it has left the Books & for what Cause we know not. **1888** Jones *Negro Myths* 113 **GA coast,** Buh Rabbit fool Buh Wolf so many time, an een sich diffrunt fashion, dat eh outdone wid um. **1903** *DN* 2.323 **seMO,** *Outdone.* . . Put out; nonplussed. 'I never was so outdone before: I don't know which way to turn.' **1907** *DN* 3.234 **nwAR,** *Outdone.* . . Perplexed, nonplussed. **1909** *DN* 3.355 **eAL, wGA,** *Outdone.* . . Put out, displeased, flustrated. **1923** *DN* 5.216 **seMO,** *Out done.* . . Beaten, overcome, humiliated, embarrassed. **1929** Ellis *Ordinary Woman* 70 **CO,** Mama was . . 'outdone' to think he would run them so hard. **1935** Hurston *Mules & Men* 52 **FL,** She was mighty tired but she was more out-done than she was tired so she climbed all night. **1942** (1971) Campbell *Cloud-Walking* 49 **seKY,** Marthy borned two babies . . and Sary was so outdone it took her mind clean away from studying. **1946** *PADS* 6.22 **seNC,** *Outdone.* . . Disappointed, exasperated. . . Common. **1960** Williams *Walk Egypt* 269 **GA,** She was weepy and fanciful and spoke of herself in the third person. . . until Toy was out-done with her. **1965–70** *DARE* (Qu. GG6, *Talking about a person's feelings being hurt: "When she said she wouldn't go with him, he was quite _____."*) Inf **SC**40, Outdone; (Qu. GG41, *To lose patience easily: "You never did see such a _____ person."*) Inf **LA**40, Outdone; (Qu. LL37, *To make a statement as strong as you can: "I could have wrung her neck, I was so _____ mad."*) Inf **DC**1, I sure was outdone. **1966** Maddux *Spring Rain* 19 **WV,** There would be a drawn look to his face. . . "Oh, me," he would say then, "sometimes I am just outdone." And then would come forth what The Wife had done. **1976** Ryland *Richmond Co. VA* 374, *Outdone*—annoyed, frustrated, disappointed. **1986** Pederson *LAGS Concordance,* 1 inf, **csAL,** Say "I swanny" when outdone with yourself. **1994** NC Lang. & Life Project *Dial. Dict. Lumbee Engl.* 9 **seNC,** *Outdone.* . . Disappointed. . . *I was so outdone I couldn't go to town.*

outdoor adv [Var of *outdoors*]
1903 *DN* 2.299 **Cape Cod MA** (as of a1857), *Out door.* . . Out of doors. **1926** in 1983 Taft *Blues Lyric Poetry* 119, Never has a baby : put me outdoor. **1929** *Ibid* 262, You know you shout at me : you throwed my trunk outdoor. **1966** *DARE* (Qu. MM18, *"Going from the kitchen to the back steps, he walked _____ the door."*) Inf **ME**22, Outdoor, out. **1966** *DARE* FW Addit **ME**10, Outdoor—outdoors (heard two or three times).

outdoor kitchen See **outside kitchen**

outdoor library See **library 2**

out-dugan v
See quots.
1923 *DN* 5.216 **swMO,** *Out duganed.* . . Circumvented by questionable means. "He jest plumb out duganed me." "I felt plumb out duganed." **1953** Randolph–Wilson *Down in Holler* 269 **Ozarks,** *Out-dugan.* . . To outwit, to get the better of, to cheat. "Tom Fitzhugh will be out-duganed in no time, if he tries to trade with them Lassiter boys."

outed adj Cf **outdone**
1903 *DN* 2.323 **seMO,** *Outed.* . . Disappointed.

outen prep[1] Also sp *out(i)n, outten* [Scots, nEngl dial; *OEDS* 1854 →, "chiefly *U.S.* and *Sc.*"; cf **-en** suff[3]] **chiefly Sth, Midl**
Occas with redund *of:* Out of.
1867 Harris *Sut Lovingood Yarns* 34 **TN,** I flung the hammer outen my reach. **1867** Twain *Jumping Frog* 38, He'd yank a sinner outen (Hades),/ And land him with the blest. **1871** (1892) Johnston *Dukesborough Tales* 59 **GA,** I'll paddle you as long as thar's poplars to make paddles outen. **c1885** in 1981 Woodward *Mary Chesnut's Civil War* 376 **SC** [Black], Overseer and Claiborne, head of the plows [=plowmen], connive together to cheat master "outin everything." **1899** Chesnutt *Conjure Woman* 23 **csNC** [Black], De knots begun ter straighten out'n Henry's ha'r. **1903** *DN* 2.323 **seMO,** *Outen.* . . Out of. 'We are clean outen anything to eat.' **1906** *DN* 3.149 **nwAR,** *Outen.* . . Out of. "He come outen the door." **1908** Fox *Lonesome Pine* 76 **KY,** That's the only way I've kept outen of it fer thirty years. **1909** *DN* 3.355 **eAL, wGA,** *Outen.* . . Out of. **1931** *PMLA* 46.1304 **sAppalachians,** Steve ups and

runs like a bat shot outn hell. **1940** Faulkner *Hamlet* 16 **MS**, Flem . . watched them . . take a wore-out broom and a lantern outen the wagon. **1945** FWP *Lay My Burden Down* 107 **AR** [Black], I seen the blood running outen many a back, all the way from the neck to the waist. **1952** Brown *NC Folkl.* 1.572, Out'n. . . "My wife kin throw more out'n the window than I can bring in at the door." **1955** Roberts *S. from Hell-fer-Sartin* 98 **seKY**, Run 'em outen town and they come back. **1963** Owens *Look to River* 8 **TX**, We kind of run out'n work. **1965–70** *DARE* (Qu. MM18, *"Going from the kitchen to the back steps, he walked _____ the door."*) Infs **GA**31, **NC**22, 26, **PA**245, Outen; (Qu. MM19, *"He took the letter _____ his pocket."*) Infs **GA**31, **IL**135, **IN**32, **NY**75, 96, **VA**15, Outen. **1986** Pederson *LAGS Concordance,* 1 inf, **nwTN**, It was outen doors; 1 inf, **nwGA**, Cut a notch outen it; 1 inf, **cTN**, So I wouldn't fall outen the bed.

outen prep[2] Cf **-en** suff[1], **withouten**

Without.

   1895 *DN* 1.373 **seKY, eTN, wNC**, Outen. . . without. "I can't go outen my sunbunnit." **1909** *DN* 3.401 **nwAR**, Outen. . . Without. "I won't go outen you."

outen v Cf **-en** suff[5]

1 To extinguish (a fire); to turn off (a light). **chiefly PA; also SC** See Map *somewhat old-fash* Cf **out C3**

   1878 Pinkerton *Molly Maguires* 364 **cePA**, I was just outening the light when two men made up to me and fired! **1908** *German Amer. Annals* 10.37 **sePA**, Outen (out'n). Extinguish. "It's time to outen your light." **1916** *DN* 4.338 **PA**, Outen. . . to extinguish. "Be sure to outen the light when you go to bed." Esp. Pa. Dutch. **1935** *AmSp* 10.167 [Engl of PA Germans], Outen the light. **c1938** in 1970 Hyatt *Hoodoo* 2.1184 **GA** [Black], After yo' do dat yo' go outen dese candles. **1942** Warnick *Garrett Co. MD* 11 **nwMD** (as of 1900–18), Outen . . extinguish a fire. **1947** Hench Coll. **cSC**, Let's outen the fire. He is outening the light. The fire has been outened. **1948** *WELS Suppl.* **seWI**, Other German expressions frequently heard are: "outen the light" . . "deaden the mouse." *Ibid* **seWI**, I grew up in the German section of Milwaukee and we sometimes use the German expressions for fun, such as "I'll learn you" or "outen the light." **1950** *Ibid* **ceWI**, Your talk . . reminds me of a term used by the older Germans around Oshkosh. . . "Outen the light." **1950** *PADS* 14.50 **SC**, Outen. . . to extinguish, as a fire. **1956** *DE Folkl. Bulletin* 1.24, Outen, as a fire. **1957** *Sat. Eve. Post Letters* **PA**, "Outen the light." . . I understand this is Pennsylvania Dutch and was handed down to me by my mother, who is from Pennsylvania Dutch country. **1965–70** *DARE* (Qu. Y42, *Expressions for putting out a lamp or light*) 15 Infs, **chiefly PA**, Outen; **MI**110, Outen—kerosene; **MN**24, Outen—a German gentleman here says; **PA**152, Used to say outen; **PA**161, Outen—older people; **PA**243, Outen—old Dutch one; **SC**19, 26, Outen [FW sugg]; **SC**40, 58, Outen—(especially) of a kerosene lamp [FW sugg]; **SC**2, Outen—heard; none of us would have said that; an uneducated person or a colored person might use it; **SC**24, Outen—hears it from Negroes [FW sugg]; **SC**44, Outen—old-fashioned [FW sugg]; **VA**31, Outen—electric light or fire; (Qu. Y43b, . . *To put out a fire*) 17 Infs, **chiefly PA**, Outen; **OH**28, Outen—my cousin used that; **SC**46, 58, Outen [FW sugg]; **SC**2, Outen—an uneducated person could use this; **SC**11, Outen—Negroes say that; **SC**44, Outen—old-fashioned [FW sugg]; **SC**55, Outen—heard [FW sugg]; **VA**31, Outen—common; if a brush fire, they'll say someone didn't outen his fire. **1969** *DARE* FW Addit **cNC**, Outen the light. **1982** Barrick Coll. **csPA**, Outen—put out, extinguish, turn off (a light)[-] Common. **1987** *Jrl. Engl. Ling.* 20.2.172 **ePA**, Outen 'to extinguish'. . . 14% [of total responses] ([used actively by]

18 [of 100 infs]), ages 19–85. . . Younger informants are generally residents of Berks or Lebanon County and/or members of the Mennonite Church or the Church of the Brethren.

2 To take out, remove (something); in imperative, also intrans: see quot 1928.

   1928 Chapman *Happy Mt.* 273 **seTN**, "Boys both, outen yourself! 'Tain't fitten such goings-on should happen before women. Outen!" **c1938** in 1970 Hyatt *Hoodoo* 2.1196 **GA** [Black], After dem 120 seconds [of obligatory waiting] is out, yo' taken an' outen de splinters. **1950** *PADS* 14.50 **SC**, Outen. . . To erase, as writing on a slate. **1968** *DARE* FW Addit **GA**28, That would outen your eye.

3 To utter, say. Cf **out C4**

   1951 Craig *Singing Hills* 68 **sAppalachians**, Outen it, fellow. Give out what you know. *Ibid* 126, There are words we want to outen and we can't.

outen adv

Out.

   1895 *DN* 1.373 **seKY, eTN, wNC**, Outen . . out. "I can't get the sliver outen."

outerds See **outwards**

outer road n Also *outer lane* **MO, AR** Cf **out road**

An access or frontage road.

   1967–69 *DARE* (Qu. N28, *A road that connects a big highway with stores and business places set back from it*) Infs **MO**19, 21, 33, Outer road; **MO**11, Up there [=on Highway 70] they say outer road; **MO**27, Outer roads—this term is used only of those attached to I-70, though such roads exist locally; **AR**47, Outer lane. **1977** *DARE* File **AR**, Outer road—an access or frontage road.

outfavor v [**favor C1**] esp **S Midl**

See quots.

   1912 *Jrl. Amer. Folkl.* 25.139 **sAppalachians**, Outfavor . . to be better looking than. **1936** *AmSp* 11.368 **nLA**, Out-favor. To be better looking, more handsome, etc.; as, 'Mary outfavors Sarah.' **1944** *PADS* 2.47 **cnNC**, Outfavor. . . To be better looking than some one else. Remark to a new-born infant: "You do outfavor your daddy, don't you?" . . Rare. **1954** Harder Coll. **cwTN**, Outfavor. . . To be better looking than someone else.

outfit n **chiefly West**

1 Personal equipment or accoutrements; an item of such gear. Cf **fitout**

   1828 (1936) McCoy *Jrl. Exped.* 239 **PA**, I had a hard days work of it, procuring my out-fit, &c. *Ibid* 341, We are packed with flour, bacon, and all our out-fit. **1869** McClure *3000 Miles* 211 **West**, Everything is an "outfit," from a train on the plains to a pocket-knife. It is applied almost indiscriminately,—to a wife, a horse, a dog, a cat, or a row of pins. **1887** *Scribner's Mag.* 2.510 **West**, How much of the pastoral life of old Spain adheres to the cow-boy's language appears most plainly when he talks of animals, particularly of his horse, his horse's trappings, and his personal "outfit." **1925** *AmSp* 1.149 **West**, "Outfit" is very common and may have originated in the big cattle companies or "outfits." A prominent Californian tells how once, when his wife had gone back to visit her folks in New Haven, he wired ahead that "Elizabeth and outfit arrive Saturday," and that her Yankee relatives inferred that the "outfit" meant babies, though to others it suggested a circus. **1941** Writers' Program *Guide WY* 463, Outfit. . . Also means cowboy equipment. **1958** *AmSp* 33.271 **eWA**, Outfit. . . A man's equipment. **1958** McCulloch *Woods Words* 128 **Pacific NW**, Outfit. . . A man's personal gear. . . A line up of equipment and materials for a job. **1981** *KS Qrly.* 13.2.69, Outfit . . an individual's personal collection of gear and furnishings.

2 A person.

   1867 (1868) Meline *2000* 74, To cross the plains, or go to the mountains, every one must get an outfit; and, having outfitted, you become yourself an outfit. **1869** [see **1** above]. **1924** C.E. Mulford *Rustlers' Valley* xi.130 (*OEDS*), You ain't believin' everythin' *this* outfit tells you, are you? **1967–70** *DARE* (Qu. HH7a, *Someone who talks too much, or too loud: "He's an awful _____."*) Inf **WY**1, Mouthy outfit; (Qu. HH24, *Somebody who doesn't talk very much, who keeps his thoughts to himself*) Inf **TX**95, Close-mouth outfit.

out from here (or there) See **from B3**

‡outhandle v

   1968 *DARE* (Qu. GG3, *To tease: "See those big boys trying to _____ [that little one]."*) Inf **NC**49, Pick on, outhandle.

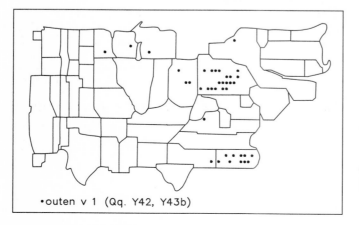

•outen v 1 (Qq. Y42, Y43b)

out hog n
1949 *AmSp* 24.111 **ceSC,** *Out hogs.* . . Hogs allowed to forage for themselves in woods or swamps, as contrasted with *fattening hogs.*

outin See **outen** prep[1]

outingest adj Pronc-sp *outnes'*
=**outdoingest.**
1884 *Anglia* 7.275 **Sth, S Midl** [Black], *De outnes' man* = the cleverest man. **1887** *Amer. Philol. Assoc. Trans. for 1886* 17.40 **Sth,** "Brer Rabbit wuz de out'nes' man." Uncle Remus.

out kitchen See **outside kitchen**

outland adj [*OED* c1425 →]
Foreign, alien.
1942 (1971) Campbell *Cloud-Walking* 106 **seKY,** We never had no girls to learn cooking up victuals in the outland fashion.

outland adv
To a foreign or alien place.
1938 Matschat *Suwannee R.* 36 **neFL, seGA,** They took him outland [=away from the swamp] and doomed him to die by fire. *Ibid* 106, And she made up her mind, right then, that one of these days she was going outland.

outlander n [*OEDS* 1598 →] **chiefly east of Missip R** See Map
Cf **flatlander**
An outsider; a stranger, foreigner.
1904 Twain in *Harper's Weekly* 2 Jan 18, One relative or neighbor mixed up in a scandal is more interesting than a whole Sodom and Gomorrah of outlanders gone rotten. **1929** *AmSp* 4.203 **Ozarks,** For the past ten years I have spent a large part of my time in the Ozarks, and I am still, linguistically speaking, a *furriner*—an *outlander*. **1937** Thornburgh *Gt. Smoky Mts.* 49, Gatlinburg. . . is named for an "outlander." **1940** *Sat. Eve. Post* 20 Jan 12 **FL,** Don't . . get no idee we're goin' to look at no outlander. **1940** *Sun* (Baltimore MD) 9 Sept 10/2 *(Hench Coll.),* This Pennsylvania ignorance no longer surprises us. . . Outlanders are outlanders and so they remain. **1965–70** *DARE* (Qu. HH31, *Somebody who is not from your community, and doesn't belong*) 28 Infs, **chiefly east of Missip R,** Outlander. [17 of 28 Infs coll educ] **1975** [see **outlandish**]. **1986** Pederson *LAGS Concordance (Stranger, foreigner, newcomer)* 2 infs, **ceGA, seAL,** Outlander.

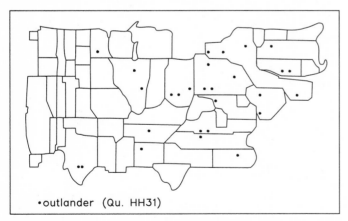

•outlander (Qu. HH31)

outlandish adj, also used absol [*OED* c1000 →; "Now *arch.*"] **esp NEng**
Foreign; from outside one's own community.
1815 Humphreys *Yankey in England* 107, *Outlandish,* strange, foreign. **1913** Kephart *Highlanders* 17 **sAppalachians,** Whether you come from Boston or Chicago, Savannah or New Orleans, in the mountains you are a "furriner." A traveler . . asked a native of the Cumberlands what he would call a "Dutchman or a Dago." The fellow studied a bit and then replied: "Them's the outlandish." **1914** *DN* 4.77 **ME, nNH,** *Outlandish.* . . Foreign. "He was some kind of an outlandish man." **1931–33** *LANE Worksheets* **neMA,** *Outlandish man.* . . Stranger. Old-fashioned. **1946** *Hench Coll.* **NH, VT,** He said that in Vermont and New Hampshire he has heard people call people from over the mountains or from another county outlandish people. **c1960** *Wilson Coll.* **csKY,** *Outlandish.* . . Foreign, in any sense; not familiar; from up the creek or over across the river. **1975** Gould *ME Lingo* 198, *Outlander*—Used in Maine with the meaning of the German *Ausländer* but more often embellished into the adjective form, *outlandish:* "He's an outlandish man." It is reserved for

somebody who has moved in *from away* to make his home, and is not applied to casual or seasonal people.

outlandisher n [**outlandish**]
1895 *DN* 1.392 **seMA,** *Outlandishers:* foreigners.

outlaw n
1 An animal, esp a horse, that is unmanageable or untamable. [*OED* 1599 →] **formerly chiefly West, now widespread**
1885 in 1909 Roe *Army Letters* 337 **MT,** Many a fine, spirited animal is ruined, made an "outlaw" that no man can ride, just by the fiendish way in which they are first ridden. **1903** *Out West Mag.* Feb 187 **SW,** They'll take outlaws all right, but no broncos. **1914** *DN* 4.163 **NW,** *Outlaw.* . . A horse shrewd and vicious from years of running wild. **1915** *DN* 4.244 **MT,** *Outlaw.* . . A wild horse. "I got an outlaw for $55 at Fred Warren's sale." **1920** Hunter *Trail Drivers TX* 199 (as of 1884), In this drive we rounded up one of those notorious outlaw steers which were to be found in the country at that time. **1929** *AmSp* 5.64 **NE** [Cattle country talk], Generally an "outlaw" is a horse (possibly one in several hundred or more) that cannot be "broke." **1937** *DN* 6.618 **swTX,** Other terms about horses. . . An *outlaw* is a killer. **1945** Mathews *Talking Moon* 5 **OK,** I remembered the colt, an iron-gray and a veritable outlaw that only a bolt of lightning had been able to subdue. **1965–70** *DARE* (Qu. K42, *A horse that is rough, wild, or dangerous*) 230 Infs, **widespread,** Outlaw; **AR9,** Outlaw horse; (Qu. K16, *A cow with a bad temper*) Infs **IL**87, 104, **MS**1, **NY**163, 182, **TX**22, **VA**14, Outlaw; (Qu. K68, . . *A goat that habitually strikes people with its horns*) Inf **CA**195, Outlaw. **1966** *DARE* Tape **MS**61, Horses. . . they ain't going to hurt you unlessen's just a real outlaw. **1986** Pederson *LAGS Concordance,* 1 inf, **nwMS,** A outlaw—a troublesome mule.

2 One who is crude or ill-mannered; a misfit.
1965–70 *DARE* (Qu. Z16, *A small child who is rough, misbehaves, and doesn't obey, you'd call him a _____*) Infs **AR**51, **LA**11, **MO**39, **MT**3, **NY**232, **OK**15, **TX**35, (Little) outlaw; (Qu. AA6b, . . *A man who is fond of being with women and tries to attract their attention—if he's rude or not respectful*) Infs **AL**33, **IN**3, 13, **MS**84, **OK**15, Outlaw; (Qu. AA7b, . . *A woman who is very fond of men and is always trying to know more—if she's not respectable about it*) Inf **MS**84, Outlaw woman; (Qu. HH16, *Uncomplimentary words with no definite meaning*) Inf **LA**6, Outlaw; (Qu. HH18, *Very insignificant or low-grade people*) Infs **MN**12, **OH**81, Outlaws; (Qu. HH37, *An immoral woman*) Inf **GA**7, Outlaw woman; (Qu. II7, *Somebody who doesn't seem to 'fit in' or to get along very well* . . *"He's kind of a _____."*) Infs **NJ**36, **TX**33, Outlaw; (Qu. II21, *When somebody behaves unpleasantly or without manners: "The way he behaves, you'd think he was _____."*) Inf **LA**3, An outlaw; **LA**6, Raised a perfect outlaw. [15 of 18 total Infs old]

3 One who hunts or fishes illegally; hence v *outlaw* to hunt or fish illegally; vbl n *outlawing.* **Nth**
1954 White *Adirondack Country* 38 **NY,** Out in the woods men . . speak of an "outlaw," one who gets game illegally. **1965** Bowen *Alaskan Dict.* 24, *Outlaw.* . . A man *outlaws* a moose when he kills it without a license, or an *outlaw* fisherman takes salmon in the closed periods or on *outlaw* gear. **1967–68** *DARE* (Qu. P13, . . *Ways of fishing* . . *besides the ordinary hook and line*) Inf **OH**22, Outlaw fly—dynamite; (Qu. P35b, *Illegal methods of shooting deer;* not asked in early QRs) Inf **PA**147, Outlawing; (Qu. P37a, *Nicknames for a rifle*) Inf **WA**30, Outlaw gun—illegal guns, too small to kill. **1968** McPhee *Pine Barrens* 93 **NJ,** If you want to get some food, you just take your gun and go out and get it—in season. I don't outlaw. I used to. My son does a little outlawing.

4 =**outlander.**
1968 *DARE* (Qu. HH31, *Somebody who is not from your community, and doesn't belong*) Inf **NJ**36, Outlaw.

5 A child of unwed parents. Cf **illegal, outside child**
[**1966–70** *DARE* (Qu. Z11a, . . *A child whose parents were not married—serious words*) Infs **SC**7, Born unlawfully; **LA**11, Unlawful child.] **1973** Allen *LAUM* 1.344 **seMN** (as of c1950), *Illegitimate child.* . . Outlaw baby. **1986** Pederson *LAGS Concordance (Illegitimate child)* 1 inf, **cTN,** Outlaw.

6 A mongrel; a dog of mixed breed. Cf *DS* J1, 2
1986 Pederson *LAGS Concordance (Mongrel)* 1 inf, **seAL,** Outlaw dog; 1 inf, **csLA,** A outlaw—if you didn't know the breed.

7 =**blue goose 1.** [See quot 1952]
1923 U.S. Dept. Ag. *Misc. Circular* 13.33 **NE,** Blue Goose. . . [Local vernacular names:] outlaw. **1932** Bennitt *Check-list* 18 **MO,** Blue goose . . Blue brant; bald brant . . outlaw [etc]. **1952** *AmSp* 27.295, It seems certain also that the cognomen *outlaw* for the blue goose (Nebr.)

has similar significance [to *mongrel*], as belief in its hybrid nature prevailed for years and may not yet have been entirely abandoned.

outlaw v, **outlawing** See **outlaw** n 3

outlay n [Prob reversed compound; cf **layout** n 2]
See quots.
1909 *DN* 3.355 **eAL, wGA,** Outlay. . . The lot, the crowd. **1969** *DARE* (Qu. FF26, . . *A large group of people at a public gathering . .* "*There was quite a _____ at the auction.*") Inf **IN**73, Outlay.

outlet n Cf **out road**
An access road or driveway.
1940 in 1944 *ADD* **swPA, nWV,** Outlet. . . A small road from a country house to a main road. . . Old speaker. 'We call 'em outlets a heap o' times. It's deeded that way.' **1967–68** *DARE* (Qu. N27a, *Names . . for different kinds of unpaved roads*) Inf **MD**13, Outlet—road running from main road back into farm; (Qu. N28, *A road that connects a big highway with stores and business places set back from it*) Inf **MI**67, Exit road, outlet road; (Qu. N29, . . *Names . . for a less important road running back from a main road*) Inf **MD**18, Outlet. **1968** *DARE* FW Addit **seOH,** Outlet—driveway, especially driveway for a carport rather than a garage. Used regularly in Longbottom, Ohio. **1986** Pederson *LAGS Concordance (Driveway)* 1 inf, **cwLA,** Outlet.

outline n Cf **setline, trotline**
A fishing line set across a stream or anchored on one side.
1890 *Century Dict.* 4185, Outline. . . In *angling,* a set-line. **1940** Weygandt *Down Jersey* 181 **sNJ,** In my boyhood, in a summer's fortnight on the Tuscarora, it was my chore to set the outlines across the stream at nightfall and to take them up in the morning twilight. I had as many water-snakes as eels to take off the hooks. **1968–69** *DARE* (Qu. P13, . . *Ways of fishing . . besides the ordinary hook and line*) Inf **NY**93, Outline—goes all the way across; **PA**121, Snood—the short line you put on an outline; same as a trotline; (Qu. P17, . . *When . . people fish by lowering a line and sinker close to the bottom of the water*) Inf **IL**29, Outline, trout line; **MD**31, Outline fishing—anchor placed on line, floater above to hold line up.

outlookingest adj [*OED* outlook v. 4 "To outdo in looks or appearance. *Obs.*"]
Prettiest.
1975 Thomas *Hear the Lambs* 295 **nwAL** [Black], You gittin' mo' prettier by de day, chile. You de out-lookin'est gal I ever did see.

outn See **outen** prep[1]

outnes' See **outingest**

out of bank(s) adj phr *esp S Midl*
Of a river or stream: uncontained by its normal channel; overflowing.
1940 *Esquire* Sept 44 **neKY,** The river is out of banks. *Ibid* 132, Whetstone creek. . . was almost out'n banks. **c1960** *Wilson Coll.* **csKY,** Out of banks. . . Overflowing the stream banks; 'out of low banks,' 'out of high banks.' **1965–70** *DARE* (Qu. C9, *Water from a river that comes up and covers low land when the river is high*) Infs **MD**20, **TX**80, Out of bank(s); **GA**71, River is out of banks; **TX**51, River's out of banks; **TN**7, Water's out of bank; (Qu. KK39, *Stirred up, upset:* "*Because of the storm, the pond was all _____.*") Inf **MO**8, Out of bank. **1967** Green *Horse Tradin'* 241 **TX,** When the river was out of banks, the fences would be washed away and we would have steers in the bog.

out of fix See **fix** n 2

out of heart adj phr [*OED* heart sb. 38 1586 →] *esp S Midl*
Downhearted.
1925 Dargan *Highland Annals* 59 (Montgomery Coll.) **wNC,** I finds ol' Jim so out o' heart about her, I stays to help him put over a couple o' hours. **1933** *AmSp* 8.1.51 **Ozarks,** Out of heart. . . Downcast, discouraged. **c1960** *Wilson Coll.* **csKY,** Out of heart. . . Downcast, discouraged. **1990** Cavender *Folk Med. Lexicon* 28 **sAppalachians,** Out of heart—low in spirit or deep mental depression: "I've been out of heart ever since my mother died."

out of kin See **kin** 2

out of (the) pocket See **pocket**

out of the way adj phr
Out of line, irregular, inappropriate.
1899 (1912) Green *VA Folk-Speech* 308, Out of the way. . . Not well

done; vicious. "He has never done anything out of the way." **1906** *DN* 3.149 **nwAR,** Out of the way. . . Not in possession of one's senses, intoxicated. "Them two boys wasn't out of the way," (said of boys accused of intoxication). **1972** Cooper *NC Mt. Folkl.* 91, Done nothing *out of the way*—did no wrong or immoral. **1976** Ryland *Richmond Co. VA* 374, Out-of-the-way—unsuitable, gauche.

outpatience v
To cause to lose patience.
c1950 *Halpert Coll.* 46 **wKY, nwTN,** Outpatience. . . put or get (me) out of patience. "Quit, 'fore you outpatience me."

‡**outrageable** adj
1952 Brown *NC Folkl.* 1.572, Outrageable. . . Outrageous.—Rare.

outrider n **chiefly West** Cf **fence rider 1, line rider**
A cowboy who rides with a herd or around the range, keeping an eye out for trouble and attending to it; see also quot 1872; hence n *outriding* performing this duty.
1872 *KS Mag.* 1.319, Where the grower does not drive his own stock to market, the buying and driving is done by a class of speculators known in Texas as "outriders." **1892** *Scribner's Mag.* 11.740, A herd of buffalo roaring and tearing its way across the plain was almost certain to cause a panic, if within hearing, and outriders were necessary to watch for these enemies and turn their course from the trail. **1907** White *AZ Nights* 117, We saw in clarity the whole herd and the outriders and the mesas far away. **1929** *AmSp* 5.55 **NE** [Cattle country talk], In the "old days" there were "line camps," far-off outpost cabins of cowboys working out from the ranch. These cowboys might be "line riders" or "outriders," men who look for "breaks" in fences and repair them, "round them up," inspect the "dogies" on the range to see how the "feed" is lasting, and "tail 'em down," if necessary, drive them to better "grass." **1936** Adams *Cowboy Lingo* 24 **West,** 'Line-riders' were men who patrolled a prescribed boundary to look after the interests of their employer. These men were interchangeably called 'line-riders' or 'outriders,' though, strictly speaking, a 'line-rider' had a regular beat while an 'outrider' was commissioned to ride anywhere. **1968** Adams *Western Words* 214, Outriding—Performing the duties of an *outrider, q.v.;* also called *range riding.* **1977** Watts *Dict. Old West* 231, Outriders—Cowboys who rode a general circuit of inspection around a range. The term was mostly replaced by *line riders, fence riders.*

out road n Cf **outer road,** *DS* N28
A byroad.
1986 Pederson *LAGS Concordance (Byway)* 2 infs, **cnGA, nwAR,** Out road; 1 inf, **cwTN,** Out road—off a main road; 1 inf, **csAL,** Out road = lane; from house to highway.

outs See **out** B5

outset n [Du *uitzet* trousseau]
1977 Talman *How Things Began* 266 **seNY,** Sometimes heard until recent years was an expression such as "That is my grandmother's outset furniture." The Dutch word is "uitzet," meaning trousseau, or the articles with which a couple began their marriage.

outshore adj [By analogy with *inshore*]
Offshore.
1969 *DARE* Tape **NC**76, You'll kill your marsh ducks in your inshore blinds, your outshore blinds you'll kill divers.

outside n
1 also attrib: The world outside of Alaska; esp, the rest of the United States. [From earlier use in ref to northern Canada] **AK** Cf **inside** n, **lower** adj 2, **outside** adv
1900 Spurr *Through Yukon Diggings* 156 **AK,** "When did you leave the Outside?" . . (The Outside means anywhere but Alaska—a man who has been long in the country falls into the idea of considering himself in a kind of a prison, and refers to the rest of the world as lying beyond the door of this.) **1901** in 1991 Tabbert *Dict. Alaskan Engl.* 31, Today the mail contractor . . arrived, bringing outside papers. **1915** Stuck *10000 Miles* 54 **AK,** From an "outside" point of view they may appear rough. **1935** *Anchorage Daily Times* (AK) 27 July (Tabbert *Dict. Alaskan Engl.*), John Staller of Oklahoma left for the Outside today and will return the last part of August. **1944** Williamson *Far North* 209 **AK,** Outside is either the States or some other place beyond the confines of Alaska. **1953** *AK Sportsman* Oct 14, The trading company's little railroad was no monstrous undertaking by Outside standards. **1959** Hart *McKay's AK* 33, Outside: Means anywhere except Alaska and usually refers to any of the other states. **1987** *Fairbanks Daily News–Miner* (AK) 30 Dec 9 (Tabbert *Dict. Alaskan Engl.*), Most people now have

telephones and can call almost anywhere in the world, except on Christmas when all the lines to the Outside are always busy.

2 See **outside child.**

outside adj

Situated or taking place in the open sea; from the ocean (as opposed to water near the shore or in a bay).

1932 Wasson *Sailing Days* 66 **cME coast,** Low, overhanging sponsons and guards extended on each side to the full width of the enormous paddle-wheel boxes, and made the deck and most of the top of the vessel many feet wider than the actual hull, which feature alone rendered the craft unfit for any outside work. **1966** *DARE* Tape ME17, Then there's the outside scallops, which ain't so sweet as the bay scallops are; **SC**18, [Inf:] There used to be small boats here before they cracked down on inside shrimping. [FW:] What do you mean, "inside shrimping"? [Inf:] Not in the ocean, in the creeks—inside, as opposed to outside, in the ocean.

outside adv esp AK Cf inside adv 2, outside n 1

Away from some relatively isolated area; esp, out of Alaska.

1896 in 1904 *Judge Amer. Missionary* 196 **AK,** The excitement is very high here now; and when the news gets outside, no doubt there will be a great rush for these parts. **1909** *DN* 3.414 **nME,** Outside. . . Beyond the limits of Aroostook County. **1915** Stuck *10000 Miles* 49 **AK,** Again and again the unfortunate victim of accident or disease has been sent outside for treatment. **1931** *Anchorage Daily Times* (AK) 1 Dec 1 (Tabbert *Dict. Alaskan Engl.*), She leaves here soon for her first trip outside. **1951** Craig *Singing Hills* 83 **sAppalachians** (as of 1930s), My boy went outside and he ain't come back. Will you find him and tell him to come home? **1987** *Fairbanks Daily News–Miner* (AK) 29 Dec 9 (Tabbert *Dict. Alaskan Engl.*), Customers want a quality of grain-fed beef raised Outside.

outside child n Also outside (boy), ~ chap, outsider chiefly Sth See Map esp freq among Black speakers Cf outside man 2

A child of unwed parents.

1913 Kephart *Highlanders* 294 **sAppalachians,** A bastard is a woodscolt or an outsider. **1927** *AmSp* 2.361 **cwWV,** Outsider . . an illegitimate child. "He cannot help being an outsider." **1950** Lomax *Mr. Jelly Roll* 35 **LA,** Maybe some of us is 'outside' children, because I don't know for *sure* that Mama was really married to Jelly's daddy or to mine. **1952** Brown *NC Folkl.* 1.572, Outsider. . . An illegitimate child. "That oldest youngun of hern is an outsider."—West. **1965–70** *DARE* (Qu. Z11b, . . *[A child whose parents were not married]*) 19 Infs, chiefly **Sth,** Outside child; **FL**18, Outside children—Negroes; (Qu. Z11a, . . *A child whose parents were not married—serious words*) Inf **SC**26, Outside child. [11 of 21 Infs Black, 11 coll educ] **1968** *DARE* FW Addit **neLA,** Outside child—illegitimate. Negro usage. **1974** (1975) Shaw *All God's Dangers* 5 **AL** [Black], My daddy had a outside chap by one of Aunt Eva's daughters. *Ibid* 22, Bein his outside boy my daddy had great sympathy for him. **1986** Pederson *LAGS Concordance (Illegitimate child)* 15 infs, 11 **AL, MS,** Outside child(ren); 1 inf, **cnGA,** We'd call him an outside; 1 inf, **seMS,** Outside = outside wedlock; less insulting. [10 of 17 infs Black]

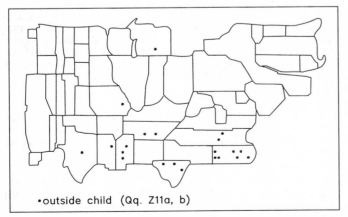

• outside child (Qq. Z11a, b)

outside kitchen n Also out kitchen, outdoor ~ Cf summer kitchen

A separate addition to a house or a small separate building used as a kitchen in the summer.

1966–68 *DARE* (Qu. D16, . . *Parts added on to the main part of a*

house) Inf **MD**8, Outside kitchen; **MO**3, Outdoor kitchen; (Qu. M22, . . *Kinds of buildings . . on farms*) Inf **WI**52, Outdoor kitchen. **1973** Allen *LAUM* 1.169 **cnMN, cNE** (as of c1950), Room used as kitchen in summer. . . Outside kitchen [2 infs]. **1986** Pederson *LAGS Concordance,* 1 inf, **nwLA,** Outdoor kitchen—in old houses, to prevent fire; 1 inf, **nwGA,** Outside kitchen—years ago; 1 inf, **ceGA,** Outside kitchen— separate building; 1 inf, **cAL,** Outside kitchen—at grandparents' place; 1 inf, **neTX,** Outside kitchen; 1 inf, **ceTX,** Outside kitchen—separate, country, especially Louisiana; 1 inf, **seAL,** Outside kitchens—she is familiar with these; 1 inf, **cnAL,** Out kitchen—separate from house.

outside man n

1 See quots. **West**

1929 Dobie *Vaquero* 293 **West,** He had for several years been "outside man"—a man who attends roundups on ranges away from those of the home ranch. **1944** Adams *Western Words* 109, Outside man—A man who represents his brand at outside ranches during a general roundup. He is usually at the top of the cowboy profession and is a riding encyclopedia on brands and earmarks. His work is done in following the roundups of other ranges and turning back strays of his brand. **1945** Thorp *Pardner* 17 **SW,** His first year with the Bar W he worked as a plain cowhand, the next year as an outside man. In the latter capacity, he rode the range on horses not bearing the Bar W brand, to look at other herds and strays and see if he could spot any "burnt" cattle.

2 A married woman's lover; similarly nouns *outside woman* (or *wife*) a married man's lover. *esp freq among Black speakers* Cf **outside child**

1923 in 1983 Taft *Blues Lyric Poetry* 219, Papa likes his outside women : mama likes his outside men. **1930** *Ibid* 224, You can't watch your wife : and your outside woman too / While you're off with your woman : your wife could be at home beating you doing buddy what you trying to do. **1937** *Ibid* 299, Oh you're the married woman : ooo well well but you have your outside man. **1967** *DARE* FW Addit **swAL,** Outside woman—a mistress. **1968** *DARE* (Qu. AA19, . . *A man and woman who are not married but live together as if they were*) Inf **GA**44, That's his outside wife—Inf's Negro yard worker. **1974** (1975) Shaw *All God's Dangers* 22 **AL** [Black], My daddy had another boy by a outside woman. *Ibid* 24, My dear lovin mother never come up with such a thing as that against her as to have a young-un by a outside-man.

outsiden prep Cf -en suff³, outen prep¹

Outside of.

1887 *Scribner's Mag.* 2.363 **Sth,** Mr. Rife 'lows ye'd better see ef ye can't settle it outside'n the law.

outsider See outside child

outside wife (or woman) See outside man 2

outstart n [*OED* 1866 →]

The outset.

1906 *DN* 3.149 **nwAR,** Outstart. . . Outset, start. "This is what was gathered at the outstart."

outten See outen prep¹

out, want See want

outward Adam n

One's body, exterior, appearance.

1837 Smith *Col. Crockett's Exploits* 23, He could not conceive how his outward Adam could make him ridiculous in the eyes of another. *Ibid* 33, I had no sooner elongated my outward Adam [=stood up], than they at it again.

‡outwardly adj

Self-important, forward.

1968 *DARE* (Qu. GG19a, *When you can see from the way a person acts that he's feeling important or independent: "He surely is _____ these days."*) Inf **IA**22, Being outwardly.

outwards adv, n Pronc-spp outards, outerds Cf inwards

Std senses, var forms.

1887 (1967) Harris *Free Joe* 126 **GA,** Ever'thing's turned wrong-sud-outerds. **1941** Percy *Lanterns* 83 **nwMS,** The obvious connection between the innards and out'ards of red-heads is generally conceded. [**1942** Hall *Smoky Mt. Speech* 88 **wNC, eTN,** [w] is generally absent in a number of words with the suffix *-ward*: . . *outward.*] **1969** *DARE* FW Addit **neNC,** Outards [æʊdɚdz]. When fishermen's nets changed around with the current and turned inside out: "Turn it inside outards."

outwind n [*OED* 1676 →] Cf **out B2**
See quots.
  1905 Wasson *Green Shay* 187 **NEng,** That vessel is goin' to fetch up on the laidge all solid enough, unless'n this heavy out-wind [Footnote: A wind from the eastern board] shoves in the tide out of all reason to-night. **1932** Wasson *Sailing Days* 29 **cME coast,** In any "out-wind," from southwest to northeast, dense fog, that summer curse of the Maine coast, . . added greatly to the difficulties of navigation.

out with See **out** v **C4**

ova(h), ove adv, prep[1], adj, v, n, exclam See **over**

ove prep[2] See **of** prep

oven n

1 also *oven-and-lid:* A covered cast-iron cooking vessel, often with legs, used esp over an open fire. [Prob abbr for *Dutch oven* or **bake oven 2**] **chiefly Sth, S Midl**
  1902 (1969) Sears *Catalogue* 582, *Bake Oven,* deep pattern, with bails and covers. These ovens are *designed for camp use;* can be set in center of wood fire without injury to contents. **1937** *Hall Coll.* **wNC, eTN,** *Oven.* . . A cast iron pan used for baking before the introduction of stoves. Had a cover and legs, and was set among the hot coals. **1958** *PADS* 29.13 **TN,** *Oven:* A covered iron vessel. "A cast iron oven about 14 inches in diameter, 3 inches deep with legs about 1½ inches long and ears for pothooks, and a cast lid with a turned up rim and [a] loop on top to lift by. . . Put the lid and cover it with live coals." Known to the older generation. *Ibid, Oven bread.* . . A kind of corn bread. "Oven bread [was ca. 1890] corn bread baked in an iron vessel complete with lid and legs . . in hot coals before open fireplaces." **1966** Dakin *Dial. Vocab. Ohio R. Valley* 2.121, *Frying pan.* . . *Baker* . . more often seems to be the name for a somewhat deeper utensil with straight sides, short legs (usually), a lid, and no handle. In the Mountain counties . . and scattered elsewhere throughout Kentucky, Illinois, and Indiana the same vessel seems to be called simply *oven,* or . . rarely *oven and lid.* **1967–70** *DARE* (Qu. F1, . . *A heavy metal pan that's used to fry foods*) Inf **FL49,** Spider—some have legs and a top; if it doesn't have legs, call it an oven ['ʌbn̩]; **LA12,** Skillet, one with legs on it was an oven [ʌbm̩], also oven-and-lid; **SC29,** Oven—a skillet about 5 inches deep used for baking, had a cover and legs and you banked coals about it for heat. **1968** *DARE* FW Addit **TN26,** Oven = skillet-like utensil with legs and a recessed cover for charcoal. Used in a fireplace. Sometimes called Dutch oven. **1986** Pederson *LAGS Concordance* **Gulf Region** *(Frying pan)* 66 infs, Oven; 2 infs, Bread oven; 2 infs, (Po)tato oven; 1 inf, Iron oven—three legs and lid; 1 inf, Old time oven; 1 inf, Oven skillet—with legs, heavy iron lid; *(Kettle)* 15 infs, Oven; 1 inf, Roasting oven—larger than dinner kettle.

2 in phrr *have a bun in the oven, have one in the oven,* and varr: To be pregnant. **chiefly NEast, OH, MI, CA** See Map
  1965–70 *DARE* (Qu. AA28, . . *Joking or sly expressions . . women use to say that another is going to have a baby . . "She['s] _____."*) 14 Infs, **esp NEast, OH, MI,** Got a bun (*or* bean, duck, potato, turkey) in the oven; 11 Infs, **esp OH, MI, CA,** (Has *or* got) one in the oven; **CT21, PA167, MA12, NY94,** Got something (cooking) in the oven; **PA225,** Has bread in the oven; [**PA76,** Oven's full]. **1986** Pederson *LAGS Concordance* (*Pregnant*) 3 infs, **seAL, seAR, cwFL,** Bun in the oven. **1990** Cavender *Folk Med. Lexicon* 17 **sAppalachians,** Baby in the oven—pregnancy.

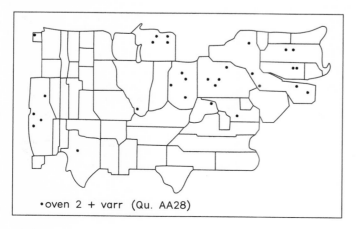

•oven 2 + varr (Qu. AA28)

3 also *oven tomb:* One of a group of aboveground burial vaults arranged in tiers. **New Orleans LA**
  1851 Stuart-Wortley *Travels U.S.* 1.237 **New Orleans LA,** The graves are also elevated. The dead are buried in sepulchral houses, which are termed here "ovens." These often contain three or four tiers. Those belonging to the wealthy are frequently very handsome, and built with marble walls. **1893** *Harper's New Mth. Mag.* 86.374 **New Orleans LA,** The tombs are houses built upon the ground, and provided with cubby-hole or drawerlike compartments, to be sealed with a marble slab as each coffin is put in place. The term "oven tombs" describes them well. **1906** Johnson *Highways Missip. Valley* 11 **New Orleans LA,** These tombs usually consist of two vaults well cemented to prevent exhalations from interred bodies; but sometimes the vaults are built in a solid mass in tiers and are then called ovens. **1945** Saxon *Gumbo Ya-Ya* 321 **New Orleans LA,** For the poor, crypts were erected, vaults built tier upon tier, usually into the cemetery wall, looking not unlike ovens in some gigantic bakery, and therefore becoming known locally as 'ovens.' **1946** Roberts *Lake Pontchartrain* 167 **sLA,** New Orleans had always had trouble with its cemeteries. . . So vaults were built above ground. . . [O]vens . . were brick structures with horizontal cells into which the coffins were thrust from the outside and the open ends sealed.

4 See quot.
  1913 *DN* 4.5 **ME,** *Oven.* . . Cavernous holes in the rocks on the seashore.

oven-and-lid See **oven 1**

ovenbird n [See quot 1911]
A wood warbler (*Seiurus aurocapillus*) noted for its distinctive nest. Also called **golden-crowned thrush, nightingale b, night walker 2, teacher bird, wagtail**
  1841 (1949) Thoreau *Jrl.* 1.260, The oven-bird and plover are heard in the horizon. **1844** DeKay *Zool. NY* 2.79, The Oven-bird. *Seiurus aurocapillus.* . . One of its trivial names is derived from its sinking a curious oven-shaped nest in the ground. **1868** (1869) *Amer. Naturalist* 2.182 **NEng,** The Golden-crowned Thrush (*Seiurus aurocapillus*). . . Its curious nest has long been known; from it, it derives its name of "Oven-bird." **1902** White *Blazed Trail* 296 **MI,** Oven birds, peewits, blue jays, purple finches, passed silently or noisily, each according to his kind. **1911** Howell *Birds AR* 80, The ovenbird, so named from the fancied resemblance of its domed nest to an old-fashioned oven, is one of the ground warblers. **1925** *Book of Rural Life* 7.4115, *Ovenbird.* . . a ground warbler, known to most country folk as the *teacher bird.* . . The "oven" is its nest, well hidden and secure. **1968** *DARE* (Qu. Q14) Inf **IN39,** Ovenbird. **1977** Bull-Farrand *Audubon Field Guide Birds* 667, *Ovenbird.*

oven tomb See **oven 3**

over adv, prep, adj, v, n, exclam Pronc-spp *ober, obuh, ova(h), ovuh, ove* Cf Pronc Intro 3.I.17
A Forms.
  1854 in 1956 Eliason *Tarheel Talk* 315 **cnNC,** Over—ove. **1884** *Anglia* 7.255 **Sth, S Midl** [Black], Prepositions. . . ova. **1888** Jones *Negro Myths* 33 **seGA,** Dem tell um de dinner done ober, an eh mights well tun back. **1899** (1967) Chesnutt *Wife of Youth* 13 [Black], Den de wah broke out, an' w'en it wuz ober de cullud folks wuz scattered. **1922** Gonzales *Black Border* 316 **sSC, GA coasts** [Gullah glossary], *Obuh*—over, above. **1936** Reese *Worleys* 9 **MD** (as of 1865) [Black], De fightin's ovah, yas, Gawd. **1946** in 1958 Brewer *Dog Ghosts* 56 **TX** [Black], All de cowboys comed ovuh to see de red toro.

B As prep.
Because of.
  1946 *Harder Coll.* **cwTN,** [Letter:] Eddie looks bad over the measles. **1953** Johnson *Sullivan* 31 **ceME,** While eating his dinner in a restaurant in New York, he choked over a piece of meat, died from the effects and was buried there.

C As adj.
In combs with terms for var types of **earmark** n: Made in the upper edge of the ear. **Sth, S Midl, West** See also **slope, split** Cf **crop** n **B1, figure seven, hack** n[1] **4, half-crop, lower** adj **1, round, square, under, upper**
  [**1647** in 1887 *Archives of MD* 4.310, One red heyfer Calfe. . . both eares overkeeld.] **1677** in 1904 New Castle DE *Court Records* 79, In each Eare a swallow forke and in the Right Eare an overkeel. **1869** *Overland Mth.* 3.126 **TX,** I had seen a brown-and-white-pied calf, with

an overslope and a slit in the right, and a swallow-fork in the left. **1887** *Scribner's Mag.* 2.508 **CO,** Other marks signifying ownership [of cattle] are *over-bit, over-hack, over-half-crop, over-slope, swallow-fork, under-bit, under-hack,* etc. **1894** in 1975 *Foxfire 3* 87 **nwGA,** Personally appeared before the undersigned John W. Hollifield who being duly sworn says on oath that his stock mark is a swallow fork in the left ear and and [sic] an over-bit in the right ear. **1906** *DN* 3.149 **nwAR,** *Overbit. . .* A semicircular cut taken from the upper part of an animal's ear. **1908** *DN* 3.303 **eAL, wGA,** There are the *undercrop* (a piece cut off on the lower side of the ear), and the *over-crop* (from the upper side of the ear). Other marks are the *over-square . . ,* the *over-bit . . ,* etc. . . The custom of marking is still in vogue though not so common since the advent of hog-proof fences. **1915** *DN* 4.185 **swVA,** *Under-bit,* a triangular cut from the lower side [of the ear of a hog, sheep, or cow]. *Over-bit,* the same from the upper side. **1920** Hunter *Trail Drivers TX* 298, Some of the terms used in marking are "crop," "under bit," "over bit," "half crop," "split," "over slope," "under slope," etc. **1936** Adams *Cowboy Lingo* 130, Each mark had a name that formed a part of the cowboy's language. The 'over-bit' was a V-shaped mark. . . The 'over-split' was made by making the split from the upper edge of the ear to about the middle. . . An 'over-slope' was made by cutting the ear about two thirds of the way back from the tip straight to the center of the ear at its upper side. . . The 'over-hack' was made by simply cutting down on the upper side of the ear. . . The 'over-round' was made by cutting a half-circle from the top of the ear. **1956** Gipson *Old Yeller* 94 **TX,** First I folded his [=a pig's] right ear and sliced out a three-cornered gap in the top side, a mark that we called an overbit. **1967-69** *DARE* (Qu. K18, *. . Kind of mark . . to identify a cow*) Infs **KY**29, **LA**18, **TX**43, Overbit; **LA**7, Over figure seven, under figure seven; **TX**22, Overslope [*DARE* Ed: Illustr shows a slanted cut across the top of the ear]. **1982** Ginns *Snowbird Gravy* 129 **nwNC,** Ours was a swallow fork in the left and a overslope in the right.

D As verb.

1 To recover from. [*OED* 1825 →; "*dial.*"] **chiefly Sth**

1870 *Nation* 28 July 57 **sePA,** To be "overing the bilious" is to be getting well of the bilious fever. **1933** Miller *Lamb in His Bosom* 24 **GA,** He believed that she would over it [=a snakebite]. **1936** *AmSp* 11.368 **nLA,** I have overed my trouble all right. **1944** *PADS* 2.35 **GA,** I can't over his marrying that old woman. **1949** *AmSp* 24.111 **cSC,** *Over. . .* To recover from, as a disease or an injury. **1956** *DE Folkl. Bulletin* 1.24, Over (get over—as in "I thought I would over it by now.") [**1968** *DARE* (Qu. BB54, *When a sick person is past hope of recovery . . he's [a]* _____) Inf **GA**28, About overed his troubles.] **1968** *DARE* FW Addit **GA**30, Heard in conversation [about] Inf's wife's cancer operation: " . . and she never overed it good." **1972** *Atlanta Letters* **csGA,** *Over. . .* Overcome. "Did you over it?" (recover from an illness). **1975** Newell *If Nothin' Don't Happen* 75 **nwFL,** Old Rambler was wobblin' around like a drunk feller when we found him. Uncle fed him a bellyful of pot likker and greased him with lard and sulphur and he overed it. I do believe a hound dog can get well quicker'n anything in the world. **1986** Pederson *LAGS Concordance,* 1 inf, **nwFL,** She overed it—of diphtheria; 1 inf, **cwLA,** She overed it = she recovered from diphtheria.

2 See quot.

1956 McAtee *Some Dialect NC* 57, *Over. . .* To pass over. "The bird overed the house." . . Knott's Island, Upper Currituck Sound.

E As noun.

1 also *over-ball, over-handy, over-rover, over-the-hill, over-the-roof,* and varr: **=Antony-over A. chiefly Sth, Midl** Cf **F** below

1965-70 *DARE* (Qu. EE22, *. . The game in which they throw a ball over a building . . to a player on the other side*) Infs **LA**25, 28, **SC**26, **VA**1, Over; **PA**206, Over-ball; **SC**58, Over-handy; **TN**27, Over-rover; **NC**1, Over-the-hill; **NC**14, **TX**13, Over-the-house; **NY**190, **SC**65, Over-the-roof; **LA**11, Over-the-top.

2 A surplus; a leftover. Cf **coldover**

1960 Williams *Walk Egypt* 239 **GA,** "It run much?" "Thirty-two gallons. I gave John the over for grinding." **1986** Pederson *LAGS Concordance* (Perhaps you had something more than you could eat for Sunday dinner. Monday you'd eat it, and you'd say you were having _____) 1 inf, **seLA,** Overs.

F As exclam.

Also *over-handy, over-rover, over-the-roof:* **=Antony-over B1, 2. chiefly Sth, S Midl** See Map Cf **E1** above

1965-70 *DARE* (Qu. EE23a, *In the game of andy-over . . what . . you*

call out when you throw the ball) 31 Infs, **chiefly Sth, S Midl,** Over; **AL**30, One throwing calls "over"; one catching calls "handy-over"; **KY**80, The one throwing the ball yelled "Annie," the receiver yelled "over," and he threw the ball; **OH**8, If you catch it, you say "over"; **OK**42, "Anti"; the other calls out "over"; **VA**30, "Antny"—call; "over"—answer; **NY**190, Over-the-roof; **SC**58, Over-handy; **TN**27, Over-rover—recent; (Qu. EE23b, *In the game of andy-over . . if you fail to get the ball over the building and it rolls back, what . . you call out*) Inf **NC**2, Call "over" again.

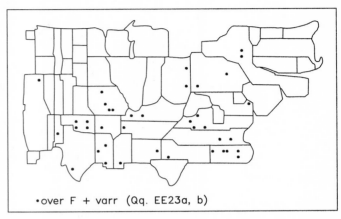

•over F + varr (Qq. EE23a, b)

over and above adv phr [*OED* 1749 →]

Excessively.

1905 *DN* 3.15 **cCT,** *Over and above. . .* Excessively. 'She is not over and above particular in her housekeeping.' **1907** *DN* 3.215 **nwAR,** *Over and above. . .* Excessively. **1914** *DN* 4.77 **ME, nNH,** *Over 'n' above. . .* Very. "He ain't over 'n' above smart." **1946** *AmSp* 21.308 **MA, eIA,** *Over and above.* A phrase expressing degree, as in the sentence, 'He's not over and above smart,' meaning, he was not smart at all, he was something of a dullard.

over-ball See **over E1**

overbit See **over C**

overboard adv

In marble play: see quot.

c1970 Wiersma *Marbles Terms* **swMI** (as of 1924), *Overboard. . .* When your meg goes outside the area formed by the person's legs on the pavement, you are overboard and the person sitting down gets to keep your marble.

overbridge n Also *oversection, overway* [*OED* 1878 →]

=overhead 4.

1967-68 *DARE* (Qu. N19, *. . A structure that carries a road above railroad tracks, or above another road or a deep gully*) Inf **NC**55, Overbridge, oversection; **CA**6, Overway.

overcast n Also *overpass, overthrow* Cf **air bridge**

In bituminous coal mining: see quots.

1918 Peele *Mining Engineers' Hdbk.* 1028, *Overcasts* (overthrows or bridges) carry one air current across another. They are usually made by blasting down part of the haulage road roof, and building an airtight conduit in the space so formed. **1947** Natl. Coal Assoc. *Gloss.* 16, *Overcast*—The passageway through which air is conveyed over another airway or over a haulageway. **1973** *PADS* 59.45 [Bituminous coal mining vocab], *Overcast . .* a crossover between two *air courses* in which the two are not permitted to mix; usually built of stone and completely insulated. *Ibid, Overpass* n, = *overcast.*

overcrop See **over C**

overcup See **overcup oak 1, 2**

overcup oak n [From the cup which encloses or nearly encloses the acorn]

1 also *overcup:* A chiefly Southern **oak** (*Quercus lyrata*) with narrow, lyre-shaped leaves and acorns set deep in their cups. Also called **post oak, Spanish ~, swamp post ~, swamp white ~, water white ~, white ~**

1797 Smith *Nat. Hist. GA* 2.165, Feeds on the Over-cup Oak, and other kinds of the same genus. **1804** in 1930 Dunbar *Life* 240 **MS,** The margin of the river is clothed with . . a species of the white oak called vulgarly the overcup-oak. **1812** Michaux *Histoire des Arbres* 2.42, Le *Quercus lyrata* n'est pas très-multiplié dans la Basse-Caroline et la Basse-Géorgie, ce qui fait que, jusqu'à présent, il n'a été remarqué que des habitans qui demeurent à proximité des lieux où il croît. Ils le connoissent sous les noms d'*Over cup oak,* . . de *Swamp post oak,* . . et plus rarement sous celui de *Water white oak.* . . [La première dénomination] indique une particularité fort remarquable de cet arbre, qui est d'avoir un gland entièrement renfermé dans sa cupule. . . Le premier de ces noms . . est plus usité dans la Caroline méridionale. [=The *Quercus lyrata* is not widely distributed in Lower Carolina and Lower Georgia, so that up to now it has not been much noticed except by those who live close to the places where it grows. They know it by the names *Over cup oak,* . . *Swamp post oak,* . . and more rarely *Water white oak.* . . [The first name] points to a very remarkable peculiarity of this tree: that it has an acorn entirely covered by its cap. . . The first of these names . . is most current in Southern Carolina.] **1831** Peck *Guide for Emigrants* 122 **IL,** The growth of the bottom lands consists of . . over cup, bur oak, swamp or winter oak, [etc]. **1854** (1874) Glisan *Jrl. Army Life* 152 **AR,** The following are some of the principal trees observed along our route . . sweet-gum, over-cup, cottonwood. **1868** (1870) Gray *Field Botany* 2, *Q[uercus] lyrata*, Southern Overcup Oak. **1946** West–Arnold *Native Trees FL* 42, The overcup oak, an uncommon species, is confined to wet river bottoms from the Suwannee River westward. The divided leaves, often with a narrow waist effect near the middle, and the acorns, nearly enclosed in their cups, are unmistakable characteristics by which this species is distinguished from other Florida species. **1967–70** *DARE* (Qu. T10, . . *Kinds of oak trees*) Infs **IL**119, **LA**10, 15, 18, **TX**32, Overcup oak; **MS**21, Overcup oak—same as water oak. [*DARE* Ed: Some of these Infs may refer instead to other senses below.] **1981** Pederson *LAGS Basic Materials,* 1 inf, **neAR,** Overcup; 1 inf, **csAR,** ['oᵁvə‚kʌ<ᵊf]; 1 inf, **swMS,** Overcup oak—a low grade of oak, and the acorn just overlaps the acorn shell. [*DARE* Ed: Some of these infs may refer instead to other senses below.]

2 also *overcup (white oak):* =**burr oak.**

1795 Michaux in 1889 *Amer. Philos. Soc. Proc.* 26.118, Overcup White Oak. **1812** Michaux *Histoire des Arbres* 2.34, Les cantons les plus fertiles des Etats du Kentucky et de l'ouest Ténessée, ainsi que de la partie de la Haute-Louisiane qu'avoisine le Missouri, sont, au-delà des monts Alléghanys, les endroits où cette espèce intéressante est le plus multipliée. Elle est connue dans ces contrées, des Américains, sous le nom d'*Over cup white oak.* [=The most fertile parts of the states of Kentucky and west Tennessee, as well as the part of Upper Louisiana which borders the Missouri, are the places beyond the Alleghenies where this interesting species is most abundant. In these regions Americans know it by the name of *Over cup white oak.*] **1817** Bradbury *Travels* 288, Of the oak only, there are fourteen or fifteen species, of which the over cup (*Quercus macrocarpa*) affords the best timber. **1851** *De Bow's Rev.* 11.46 **LA,** The *over-cup* is so called from the fact that the cup or shell nearly completely covers the acorn. **1868** (1870) Gray *Field Botany* 303, *Q[uercus] macrocarpa*, Bur-Oak, Over-cup or Mossy-cup White Oak. **1897** Sudworth *Arborescent Flora* 155, *Common Names* [of *Quercus macrocarpa*]. . . Overcup Oak (R.I., Del., Pa., Miss., La., Ill., Minn.) **1908** Britton *N. Amer. Trees* 335, It [=*Quercus macrocarpa*] is also called Mossy cup oak, Overcup oak, Blue oak, Scrub oak, Overcup white oak [etc]. **1966** *DARE* (Qu. T10, . . *Kinds of oak trees*) Inf **AR5,** Overcup oak—big acorn.

3 A post oak (here: *Quercus stellata*).

1897 Sudworth *Arborescent Flora* 154, *Common Names* [of *Quercus minor* [=*Q. stellata*]]. . . Overcup Oak (Fla.) **1908** Britton *N. Amer. Trees* 342, It [=*Quercus stellata*] is also known as Box white oak, Iron oak, Overcup oak [etc]. [**1952** *Argosy* (NY) June 25/3 **LA,** The post oaks drop a bounteous mast of overcup acorns.]

overcup white oak See **overcup oak 2**

over-date n [*date*]
In marble play: see quots.

1942 Berrey–Van den Bark *Amer. Slang* 665.3, "Ante." (*Marbles put in the ring as a stake.*) . . Over-dates, *more marbles won than one had "dated" up.* **1955** *PADS* 23.26 **cwTN,** Over-dates. . . A situation [sic] occurring when a player has won more marbles than he had originally or at the beginning of play. **c1970** Wiersma *Marbles Terms* **cMI,** Over-dates. . . Marbles won in excess of the number which one dated.

overden n [PaGer *owwerdenn* < *denn* (Ger *Tenne*) threshing floor] **chiefly sePA** Cf **overhead 1,** *DS* M3
A **loft** n 1.

1940 Yoder *Rosanna* 106 **PA,** Reuben had swept the barn floor and had hung lanterns from the "overden," for he knew that as soon as supper

was over, the young folks would want to go to the barn and play party games. **1949** Kurath *Word Geog.* 53, In most of Pennsylvania the loft is called the *overhead,* in the Pennsylvania German sections also the *over-den* (cf. German *Tenne* 'barn floor'). **1968** *DARE* Tape **MD**18, You don't need the space for the barn floor above the square; therefore, you fix that so you can store grain up there and call that the overden. It's one of the best places to dry damp grain or hay or anything. You put it on the overden, it's always air under it. **1985** *AmSp* 60.233 **sePA,** *Overden*—Upper part of a barn. . . Obviously Kurath's claim . . that "*loft* is not current in central Pennsylvania". . and is infrequent in other parts of Pennsylvania" no longer holds true. In fact, *overhead* was marked only by an eighty-year-old male, while *overden* was marked only by a twenty-one year old female from Ephrata, Lancaster County—a community which probably constitutes a relic area.

over figure seven See **over C**

overglad adj Cf **overhappied**
Overjoyed.

1934 Hurston *Jonah's Gourd Vine* 294 **FL** [Black], Deacon Turner and dem wuz overglad tuh know youse in town. Dey wants yuh tuh run our revival meetin'.

overgrow v [*OED* c1536 →]
To outgrow.

1968 *DARE* (Qu. OO23a, *About a child growing:* "Billy has to have new clothes—during the summer he _____ [two inches].") Inf **NC**49, Overgrowed his clothes.

overhack, over half-crop See **over C**

overhall See **overhaul** v

overhalls See **overhauls**

over-handy See **over E1, F**

overhappied adj Cf **overglad**
1931 *AmSp* 6.271 **KY,** Overhappied (overjoyed and happy).

overhaul v Also sp *overhall, overhawl*
To scold or discipline; hence nouns *overhaul(ing)* a reprimand, dressing-down; a thrashing.

1797 J. Pettigrew *Lett.* 27 June (Univ. N.C. MS) *(DA),* The steward has provided very poorly untill lately, when the Trustees gave him a severe over-hall, and I believe threatened him severely. **1833** in 1834 Davis *Letters Downing* 156 **NEast,** Such an overhawlin I never see. **1942** Berrey–Van den Bark *Amer. Slang* 295.2, *Scold; reprimand.* . . Overhaul. **1967–69** *DARE* (Qu. Y6, . . *To put pressure on somebody to do something he ought to have done but hasn't:* "He's a whole week late. I'm going to _____.") Inf **PA**231, Give him a good overhauling; **NJ**21, Overhaul him; (Qu. Y16, *A thorough beating:* "He gave the bully an awful _____.") Infs **AK**1, **AZ**16, Overhauling; (Qu. II27, *If somebody gives you a very sharp scolding . .* "I certainly got a _____ for that.") Inf **CO**3, Overhauling. **1981** *AmSp* 56.156 **swIL** (as of c1845), Mr. Wyland, a favorite teacher . . *overhauled* some of the boys for misbehaving.

overhaul n
1 See **overhauls.**
2 See **overhaul** v.

overhauling See **overhaul** v

overhauls n pl (rarely sg exc in attrib use) Also sp *overhalls, overhawls* [Folk-etym for *overalls*] Cf **coverhauls**

[**1781** in 1883 *Mag. Amer. Hist.* 10.498, They received at Morristown two pair shoes, a waistcoat and overhalls, and a few of them had coats.] **1845** (1969) Hooper *Advent. Simon Suggs* 144 **AL,** But Jim, son, get out from the fire!—you'll set your over-halls afire! **1894** *DN* 1.342 **wCT,** *Overhauls* is the universal word. I heard a dispute as to this word settled summarily in a country store as follows: "Of course they're overhauls; you haul 'em on over your pants, don't you?" **1903** *DN* 2.299 **Cape Cod MA** (as of a1857), Overhawls. **1907** *DN* 3.207 **nwAR,** *Overhauls.* **1910** *DN* 3.446 **cwNY,** Overhauls. **1912** Green *VA Folk-Speech* 308, Over-hauls. **1915** *DN* 4.227 **wTX,** Overhalls. . . The usual term for *overalls.* **1917** *DN* 4.397 **neOH,** Overhauls. . . The popular etymology in this word noted in . . [quot 1894] is familiar in Medina and Ashtabula Cos. General. **1923** *DN* 5.216 **swMO,** Overhauls. **1940** Faulkner *Hamlet* 62 **MS,** The fellow had just begun to unbutton his over-halls. **1944** *PADS* 2.59 **cMO,** Overhalls ['ovə‚hɔlz]. **1945** *PADS* 3.11 **cwNY,** Overhalls. . . Common here some years ago among workmen. **1949** Webber *Backwoods Teacher* 44 **Ozarks,** A body can wear his Sunday overhalls three-four months fer nice. **1965–70** *DARE* (Qu. W9, *A work garment, usually of blue cloth, covering the legs and sometimes the chest, worn by farmers*) 155 Infs, **widespread,** (Bib) overhalls; **WI**27, 32, (Blue) denim overhauls [Of all Infs responding to the question, 68% were comm type 4 or 5, 27% gs educ or less; of those giving these responses, 81% were comm type 4 or 5, 44% gs educ or less.]; (Qu. W4, . . *Men's coats or jackets for work and outdoor wear*) 14 Infs, **scattered,** Overhaul (jacket *or* jumper); **WI**32, Pair of overhauls; (Qu. W10, *Work trousers made of rough cloth, usually blue*) 9 Infs, **scattered,** Overhaul; **MN**12, **VA**4, (Bibless *or* denim) overhauls; **WA**24, Striped overhauls; **SC**10, ['obəhaul] got no top; **KY**19, **MI**29, **MD**26, **ND**1, **NH**14, Overhaul (material *or* pants). **1968** *DARE* Tape **CA**89, Good overalls . . they were 85 cents a pair. . . [I]f you could get that kind of an overhaul, . . it'd cost you somewhere between six and seven dollars. **1986** Pederson *LAGS Concordance,* 98 infs, **Gulf Region,** Overhauls; 3 infs, **csTN, swGA, swMS,** Overhaul pants; 2 infs, **eTN,** Overhaul suit.

overhawl See **overhaul** v

overhawls See **overhauls**

overhead n

1 A loft n **1.** *orig esp* PA, *now more widespread* Cf **overden**
    1949 [see **overden**]. **1951** *NY Folkl. Qrly.* 7.187 **wNY,** The Genesee Valley proper has its characteristic infiltrations from other sections, notably the widespread use of the Pennsylvania *overhead* for the hayloft. **1966** Dakin *Dial. Vocab. Ohio R. Valley* 2.68, The common Pennsylvania term *overhead* has not become established with any significant currency in the Ohio Valley. Only three Ohio informants use it—two in the interior counties between the Scioto and the Muskingum and one . . in Darke County. *Overhead* also appears twice in Illinois—once on the National Road, once in Egypt. Two eastern Kentucky speakers use the word. **1966–68** *DARE* (Qu. M1, . . *Kinds of barns . . according to their use or the way they are built*) Inf **FL**7, Overhead barn—stock kept below, feed above; (Qu. M3, *The place inside a barn for storing hay*) Inf **PA**71, Overheads. **1967** Faries *Word Geog. MO* 75, *Loft.* . . Two instances of the Pennsylvania *overhead* appear on the Missouri checklists. **1971** Wood *Vocab. Change* 299 **AL, GA, OK, TN,** Upper part of barn, used for storing hay. . . Overhead [6 of 1094 infs]. **1986** Pederson *LAGS Concordance (Loft)* 5 infs, **GA, neFL, cAL,** Overhead; 1 inf, **cnFL,** Call it "loft," really the overhead.
2 An attic.
    1986 Pederson *LAGS Concordance* **seMS** *(Attic)* 1 inf, That's the overhead; 1 inf, Overhead—attic.
3 See quot.
    1986 Pederson *LAGS Concordance,* 1 inf, **swGA,** The overhead—older term for ceiling.
4 *also overhead bridge, ~ crossing, ~ pass;* for addit varr see quots: An overpass or bridge. Cf **overbridge**
    1965–70 *DARE* (Qu. N19, . . *A structure that carries a road above railroad tracks, or above another road or a deep gully*) 46 Infs, **scattered, but esp Inland Nth, N Midl,** Overhead; 25 Infs, **chiefly Sth, Midl,** Overhead bridge; 11 Infs, **scattered,** Overhead pass; **IA**30, **NY**68, 134, 195, 219, **PA**218, Overhead crossing; **MA**13, Overhead and underpass; **SC**43, Overhead road [FW: Inf queries]; **GA**77, Overhead trestle. **1967** *DARE* FW Addit **MI**47, Overhead bridge—for "overpass," where one highway crosses over another. **1986** Pederson *LAGS Concordance,* 1 inf, **swTN,** Overhead—road over the tracks; [1 inf, **neMS,** Overhead—tracks go over the road;] 2 infs, **cnGA, seAL,** Overhead bridge(s); 1 inf, **cnAL,** An overhead ramp—not really sure of term.

over head and ears See **head over ears**

overhead bridge (or crossing, pass) See **overhead 4**

overjet n

1 *also overject:* See quots 1919, 1966. *old-fash*
    1919 *DN* 5.37 **OK,** *Over-jet.* . . A sort of wooden frame fitting over a wagon bed, in which to place a bed for sleeping. Long used, especially by pioneers and immigrants. **1966** *DARE* FW Addit **OK**18, *Overjet*—a cover of canvas (similar to those on covered wagons) made to fit over the top of a spring wagon. **1967** *Good Old Days* 3.11.11 **OK** (as of 1900), That door frame . . was made from the overject of the covered wagon the family had come to the country in.
‡2 =**loft** n **1.**
    1966 Dakin *Dial. Vocab. Ohio R. Valley* 2.68 **cwOH,** Only three Ohio informants use it [=*overhead*]—two in the interior counties . . and one (who also was the only informant to say *overjet*) in Darke County.

overkeel See **over C**

overland trout n *joc* Cf **mountain trout 4**
See quots.
    1942 *AmSp* 17.75 **NE** [Cowboy talk], Bacon is *overland trout.* **1942** Berrey–Van den Bark *Amer. Slang* 816.35 [Restaurant slang], Overland trout, *roast pork.* **1958** McCulloch *Woods Words* 128 **Pacific NW,** *Overland trout*—Bacon. **1967** *DARE* (Qu. H38, . . *Words for bacon [including joking ones]*) Inf **WA**30, Overland trout.

overlay v

1 See quots. [*OED* 1557 →]
    1953 Randolph–Wilson *Down in Holler* 269 **Ozarks,** *Overlay.* . . To kill by crushing or suffocation, as when a sleeping mother rolls over on her babe. When a small man in our town married a very large woman, one of my neighbors said, "Don't you reckon that feller will get overlaid?" **c1960** *Wilson Coll.* **csKY,** *Overlay.* . . To kill by crushing or stifling. "Our old sow overlaid two of her pigs."
2 To oversleep.
    1969 *DARE* (Qu. X43a, *If you sleep later than usual one day by accident . . "I _____."*) Inf **GA**72, Overslept, overlaid, I laid over this morning.

overlay n [Reversed compound; cf Intro "Language Changes" I.1]
    1967–69 *DARE* (Qu. N38, *On a trip when you have to change trains and wait a while between them . . "I have a two-hour _____ in Chicago."*) Inf **KY**6, Overlay—corrected to "layover"; **SC**40, Overlay [FW: sic].

overlook v [*OED* v. 7 1596 →] Cf *DJE* overlook vb[2]
To bewitch.
    1912 Green *VA Folk-Speech* 308, *Overlook.* . . To conjure; bewitch. "He has been overlooked." **1930** Shoemaker *1300 Words* 44 **cPA Mts** (as of c1900), *Overlooked*—Bewitched, "hechsed."

overlooker n [*OED* 1387–8 →]
A supervisor, overseer.
    1772 in 1910 Commons *Doc. Hist. Amer. Industrial Soc.* 1.328 **VA,** His brother, the overlooker there, may be miffed at it. **1792** in 1985 Lederer *Colonial Amer. Engl.* 162 **VA,** All the articles in the world would not enforce the measure longer than he himself was under the observation of an overlooker. **1854** in 1870 Hawthorne *Passages Engl. Note-Books* 1.96 **MA,** About in the centre of the garden there was an actual, homely-looking, small dwelling-house, where perhaps the overlookers of the place live. **c1937** in 1977 *Amer. Slave Suppl. 1* 1.156 **AL,** Jake—he was the over-looker. **c1937** in 1970 Yetman *Voices* 94 **OK** [Black], De next day he played sick along in de evening and de black overlooker . . sent him back to de quarters. . . We called a white man boss the "overseer," but a nigger was a overlooker.

overly adj
Of an amount or quantity: large.
    1969 *DARE* (Qu. LL4, *Very large:* "He took a _____ helping of potatoes.") Inf **CA**133A, Overly amount.

overnight adv
In the preceding evening.
    1899 (1912) Green *VA Folk-Speech* 308, *Overnight.* . . The night before. "The dough should be made up overnight." **1995** *DARE* File **NY,** Thanks to Alison . . , who puts up coffee overnight as she puts out cats.

overnight n

1 The preceding evening or night. [*OED* 1581 →; "Now chiefly *U.S.*"]
    1705 in 1870 Perry *Hist. Coll.* 1.170 **VA,** Came to Town the over night before that general meeting. **1770** (1925) Washington *Diaries* 1.423 **VA,** After much Councelling the overnight, they all came to my fire the next morning. **1803** (1965) Lewis *Jrls.* 46 **VA,** Having had every thing in readiness the over night we set out before sunrise. **1871** (1968) Howells *Wedding Journey* 14, The air, . . freshened by the over-night's storm. **1898** Lloyd *Country Life* 14 **AL,** So I packed my saddle bags and got everything ready the over night, and by the crack of day the next mornin I was straddle of the old gray. *Ibid* 20, The overnight was windy and there didn't any dew fall.
2 in phr *for the overnight:* Until the next morning.
    1865 (1889) Whitney *Gayworthys* 129 **NEng,** Mrs. Gair put the letter in her pocket. She went round, presently, . . looking to the window fastenings, for the night. Fastening something else, also, back in her own

knowledge, for the over-night, at least. Should she tell Gershom, in the morning, of this that his mother had written?

overnight weed n Cf **foot-a-night**

Perh **kudzu;** see quot.

1968 *DARE* (Qu. S21, . . *Weeds . . that are a trouble in gardens and fields*) Inf **VA**26, Overnight weed.

overpass See **overcast**

overplush n [Folk-etym for *overplus* n; *EDD* 1838 →]

A surplus.

1837 Sherwood *Gaz. GA* 71, Overplush, overplus. **1903** *DN* 2.323 **seMO,** Overplush. . . Overplus; surplus.

overround See **over** C

over-rover See **over** E1, F

overs exclam, n Also *oversies*

In children's games: used as a call to claim the right to do something again; the right so claimed.

1942 Berrey–Van den Bark *Amer. Slang* 663.2, *Hopscotch.* . . Overs, *throwing the "lagger" over again, a second opportunity to toss the "lagger."* Ibid 664.2, *Jacks.* . . Overs, *throwing the jacks over again, having a second chance.* Ibid 665.6, *Marbles.* . . Overs!, *called for permission to shoot over.* **1955** *PADS* 23.26 **cwAL** [Marble terms], *Overs.* . . A call allowing the player to shoot again. **1962** *PADS* 37.2 **cKS** [Marble terms], *Overs.* **1968** *DARE* FW Addit **swCA,** *Oversies—a* call like dibs, etc. This one means the contestant wishes to do it over. **c1970** Wiersma *Marbles Terms* **swMI** (as of c1955), *Overs* . . the option to shoot over again.

oversection See **overbridge**

overseer n

1 also *overseer of the poor:* A public official responsible for the care of the poor. [*OED* overseer sb. 1.c 1601 →] **chiefly NEng**

1647 in 1856 RI (Colony) *Records* 1.185, Each Towne shall provide carefully for the reliefe of the poore, . . and shall appoint an overseer for the same purpose. **1686** in 1845 Coffin *Sketch Hist. Newbury* 147 **MA,** Deacon Nicholas Noyes, deacon Robert Long and deacon Tristram Coffin were . . chosen standing overseers of the poore for the town of Newbury. **1760** *Boston–Gaz. & Country Jrl.* (MA) 13 Feb [3]/1, Yesterday there was a general Visitation of the Town by the Justices of the Peace, Selectmen and Overseers of the Poor. **1824** in 1925 Longyear *Hist. of a House* 17 **MD,** I am this year, Selectman, Assessor, Overseer of Poor, Representative. **1854** Adams *In Doors & Out* 52 **MA,** She ought to go to the poorhouse; the overseers offered to take her. **1934** *Hanley Disks* **neMA,** He used to keep a store here. . . Then he was overseer of the poor . . for fifty odd years. **1954** Forbes *Rainbow* 18 **NEng** (as of early 19th cent), [In] his Thanksgiving at the Poor Farm [=a painting], you could guess the turkey was a stuffed pauper. And the overseers of the poor gathered about "the festive board" looked real heedless of Christian charity. **1970** *DARE* Tape **MA**79, The selectmen are also overseers of the poor.

2 also *overseer of the road(s), ~ highway(s), road* (or *route*) *overseer:* A person responsible for supervision of roads and highways. **formerly chiefly NEast; now scattered, but less freq N Cent, NEast** See Map Cf **maintainer**

1637 in 1869 Essex Inst. *Coll.* 9.1.67 **neMA,** There was a warrant graunted out vnder or hands for the mending of high wayes. . . There are appointed 3 men for overseers. **1704** in 1886 NC *Colonial Rec.* 1.607, Wm Jackson presents George Gordon overseer of the High Wayes in his Room for the year Ensuing. **1751** in 1975 N. Castle NY *N. Castle Hist. Rec.* B17 **seNY,** Nathan Kniffin Overseer of the roads for that part of West Pattent that lies on the east side of the Middle of the long bridge. [*DARE* Ed: In the records of previous years this official is called *highway master.*] **1828** Cooper *Notions of Americans* 1.258 **NY,** The overseers of the highway are the men who lay out the ordinary roads of the town. **1834** in 1870 *Atlantic Mth.* 26.334, For mending roads, two instruments are used here, which many road-overseers in Virginia have long been vainly urged to employ. **1857** in 1941 Raymond *Bark Shanty Times* 6 Mar **seMI,** There is to be elected. . . one overseer of the highways in each district which is a very essential office and should be filled by a good man. **1965–70** *DARE* (Qu. N33, *A man whose job is to take care of roads in a certain locality*) 55 Infs, **scattered, but less freq N Cent, NEast,** (Road) overseer; **MS**72, **NJ**20, Overseer of the road; **MO**4, Route overseer. [52 of 58 Infs old]

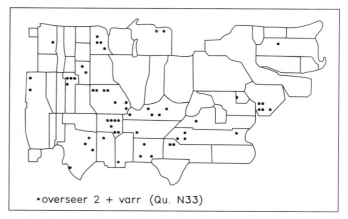

•overseer 2 + varr (Qu. N33)

overseer of the poor See **overseer 1**

overseer of the road(s) See **overseer 2**

overshoot See **overshot** n 1

overshot adj esp NW, Rocky Mts

Of a hay stacker: designed to lift the hay over the frame backward onto the stack.

1919 U.S. Dept. Ag. *Farmers' Bulletin* 1009.4, The overshot stacker . . is so called because the hay is carried up and over the stacker frame and delivered at one point on the stack. *Ibid* 5, The "overshot" stacker is in general use in the Middle West, and can be used for large or small stacks. **1925** *Book of Rural Life* 4.2535, This fork is lifted in such a way as to discharge the hay backward on the stack, as in the case of the *over-shot* stacker. **1929** *AmSp* 5.56 **NE** [Cattle country talk], During the "haying season," . . the rancher generally adds many "hay waddies," . . to help cut and stack hay, to his "ranch hands." . . The "stacker" might be of the "over-shot" variety which shoots rather than piles the hay into stacks; the "stack-horse" (or horses) pulls, and an enormous wooden fork "shoots" the hay up. **1958** *AmSp* 33.271 **eWA** [Ranching terms], *Overshot stacker.* A fork-like arrangement, used in conjunction with a buck rake, which throws the hay backward onto the stack. **1984** Doig *English Creek* 223 **nMT,** An overshot stacker worked as its name suggests, tossing a load of hay up over a high wide framework which served as a sort of scaffolding for the front of the haystack. **1985** Attebery *ID Folklife* 10 **UT, seID, wWY,** Finally, we wish to note the recent intrusion from other areas of two stacker types into the region of our investigation: the "beaverslide" and the "overshot." **1986** Klinkenborg *Making Hay* 25 **wMT,** A hundred and fifty horses . . [were] used to pull Case or McCormick and Deering mowers or push buckrakes or draw haywagons or work the Mormon derricks or overshot stackers or beaverslides.

overshot n

1 also *overshoot;* also attrib: =**forebay. chiefly PA**

1940 Yoder *Rosanna* 39 **PA,** Cristal joined a good-sized group of men who had gathered under the "overshot" waiting until it was time to go into the house and begin the services. **1967** Sloane *Age of Barns* 48, The grain bin or granary was placed at the end of one mow, often in an overshoot or cantilevered bay to keep it high and dry. **1967–68** *DARE* (Qu. M1, . . *Kinds of barns* . . *according to their use or the way they are built*) Inf **PA**13, Overshot barn—in Lancaster County called forebay barns [FW illustr: barn with overhanging section]; **PA**72, Barn with overshot roof. **1976** Wells *Barns U.S.A.* [np; in PA section], In Pennsylvania, the Dutch . . built big, beautiful barns on their farms. . . A typical one is 50′ wide and 80′ to 100′ long, with a gable roof and a seven foot "overshot" over the entrance doors along one side. **1982** *Barrick Coll.* **csPA,** Overshot—forebay of a barn.

2 in phr *overshot barn:* =**bank barn. esp NY**

1968–69 *DARE* (Qu. M1, . . *Kinds of barns . . according to their use or the way they are built*) Inf **NY**69, Overshot barn—you drive in to the second floor from the hillside above; **NY**72, Overshot barn—three stories, two top floors on a hillside, and you can drive in on the third floor, built on the side of a hill; **NY**75, Overshot barn—you went in up high so you could drop the hay; **NY**187, Overshot barn—three story barn.

oversies See **overs**

overslope, oversplit See **over** C

oversport v

To overplay; to exaggerate the importance of.

1937 (1977) Hurston *Their Eyes* 268 **FL** [Black], Everytime Ah see uh patch uh roses uh somethin' over sportin' they selves makin' out they pretty, Ah tell 'em 'Ah want yuh tuh see mah Janie sometime.' **1988** Lincoln *Avenue* 164 **wNC** (as of c1940) [Black], He was even tempted to think that sometimes God oversported his hand.

oversquare See **over C**

overstreet adv **chiefly NEast** Cf **downstreet** adv, **overtown**

Across the street; to a nearby street; see quots.

1901 *DN* 2.144 **cNY**, *Over-street, adv.* So pron. with accent on first syllable in Otsego Co., N.Y. **1959** *VT Hist.* 27.151, *Over-street.* . . Across the street; to the shopping district of a town. Common. **1967–68** *DARE* FW Addit **csOH**, Overstreet—meaning neither uptown or downtown, but one block over; **neNY**, Overstreet—downtown, uptown, anywhere as opposed to one's present position in the street; **cNY**, Overstreet—downtown. **1968–69** *DARE* (Qu. MM23) Inf **VT**16, Overstreet; **MA**14, Overstreet—toward the business district. **1970** *DARE* File **cnMA**, *Overstreet*—uptown, downtown. [The word is] used currently in Athol, MA. Not a separate shopping area. There is a long hill between uptown and downtown, 1 to 2 miles. You go overstreet when you shop on the level where you live. Recent. Not used, so far as I recall in my childhood, W[orld] W[ar] I, except by a woman from Syracuse, NY. **1990** *DARE* File **ceNY**, Another interesting expression from Montgomery County in the Mohawk Valley involves the concept of going "overstreet." As far as I know it is only used in two situations, i.e., in talking about going from Nelliston across the Mohawk River bridge to Fort Plain on the south side and also from Palatine Bridge across the river to Canajoharie on the south side; it is never used from south to north. The reason for this being that the larger more important villages, originally grew in importance along the Erie Canal, which was on the south side of the river. When I talk to my mother (who lives in Nelliston) on the phone and she informs me that she was just "overstreet," I know exactly that she has just come back from Fort Plain.

over-the-bay See **bay** n[1]

over-the-hill See **over E1**

over the left eye (or shoulder) See **left, over the**

over-the-roof See **over E1, F**

overthrow See **overcast**

overtop of prep phr

On top of, on the outside of.

1982 *Barrick Coll.* **csPA**, *Overtop of*—"He put his shirt on overtop of his suspenders."

overtown adv, n **chiefly NEast, N Cent** Cf **overstreet**

In, to, or toward the center of a city; across the city; the business section of a city.

1901 *DN* 2.144 **cwNY, nwMO**, *Over-town, adv.* So pron. with accent on first syllable. **1932** *Hanley Disks* **neMA**, I started from over town that morning. **1965–70** *DARE* (Qu. MM23, *Do you use 'uptown' and 'downtown' around here?*) Infs **MI**82, **NY**114, **OH**80, Overtown—toward the business district; **ME**22, **PA**175, Overtown; **FL**52, Overtown is the most frequently used down there; the Blacks in the residential town of Gifford go overtown to Vero Beach, where the Whites live and where the stores are; **IL**37, Overtown—because most people have to go over a river to get to the business district; [**KY**40, Over town—two words; they go over the mountains to town;] **ME**6, Generally downtown or overtown; **ME**9, Overtown—occasionally used; **NC**88, Overtown—over to downtown; **NY**30, Overtown—across town; **OH**45, You go overtown around here; **OH**65, Eastsiders say overtown [=toward the business district]. **1966** *N. Berwick Enterprise* (ME) 29 Apr 1/5, Kennedy took his bicycle and rode over town to Cressey's Store to get some comic books. **1966–69** *DARE* FW Addit **nME**, I'm going overtown = I'm going to town; **cnNY**, Overtown—I'm going over *to* town. **1968** *DARE* Tape **MD**25, You can stand on our main street which at one time was crowded up till nine, ten o'clock at night and stores were open, and now then you can go overtown and there's about a half a dozen people there. **1994** *DARE* File, I left there [=cWV] when I was a teenager, and have lived in northern New England for about 30 years. So, I occasionally find myself (shudder) 'packing' my 'caa' in the 'dowah yad,' going 'overtown' to the store, [etc]. **1995** *Ibid* **csMA**, Intown ['ɪnˌtaʊn] and *overtown* ['ovɚˌtaʊn] [both mean 'in, to, or toward the

business section']. *Overtown* [is used by] West Springfield residents who have to cross the bridge to get to Springfield.

overway See **overbridge**

ovuh See **over**

owdacious(lee) See **audacious(ly)**

owenda(w) See **awendaw**

owie n |ˈaʊwi| Also sp *owey* Cf **ouch** n

A hurt, pain; a minor injury.

1967–68 *DARE* (Qu. BB4, . . *A pain* . . *"He's had a _____ in his arm for a week."*) Inf **MN**38, Owie—children say; (Qu. NN20b, . . *A slight pain.*) Inf **OR**15, Is an owie ['aʊwi]. **1979** *NYT Article Letters* **OR**, There are two words that Oregonians and West Virginians do not . . agree upon. . . Oregon . . owie—W.Va. . . a hurt. **1987** *New Yorker* 30 Nov 33, Diane Carty was wearing an Owie Wowie on the middle finger of her right hand. . . "I have an owie right here," she said. **1988** *Discover* 9.1.7 (*W3* File), So I find myself saying to the patient, "There's going to be an *owie*"—or an *ouchie* or a boo-boo or a pokie. And when the child screams, I find myself repeating, as if it were an exceptionally comforting thought, "You know, I don't like owies either!" **1988** *DARE* File **csWI**, By a nurse at Jackson Clinic, Madison: Which is your owie foot? I'll try not to touch the owie foot. **1995** *NADS Letters*, Familiar to me are owey and ouchy, slight variants of ooey and ouch. **1995** *WI State Jrl.* (Madison) 31 Dec sec G 3/4, This is part of the make-it-all-better powers we [=parents] possess to heal "owies" and emotional wounds with our lips.

owing to prep phr **scattered, but esp Sth, S Midl**

According to; depending or contingent on.

1887 Kirkland *Zury* 131 **IL**, But *then.* It's all owin' t' haow ye look at it. *Ibid* 319 **IL**, Wal, that's owin' t' haow the cat jumps. [**1925** *DN* 5.338 **Nfld**, *Owin'.* According to. "It's all owin' how plenty de fish is."] **1946** *McDavid Coll.* **seGA**, Owing to the recipe—'according to.' **1967–68** *DARE* FW Addit **cnLA**, It's owing to = It depends on. "I think it's owing to what kind of a place they have to build in." Common; **neLA**, It's owing to = It depends on. "It's owing to who you are and who you know"; **swAR**, It's owing to = It depends on; **seNY**, It's owing to = It depends on. "It's owing to when we have a frost, actually." **1986** Pederson *LAGS Concordance,* 1 inf, **neTN**, It's owing to how a man looks—it depends on; 1 inf, **ceTX**, Owing to how big you want to build it [=a haystack]; 1 inf, **cwTN**, Just owing to how—depending on how; 1 inf, **nwTN**, Just owing to—just depending upon; 1 inf, **cnGA**, There [are] some made out of cork, it's owing to kind, you know; 1 inf, **neMS**, Owing to the age—ma'am and sir, respect for age; 1 inf, **cnGA**, Owing to the cow—depending on its temper; 1 inf, **seTN**, Owing to the state—strong or spoiled; 1 inf, **nwTN**, Back stick lasted 2–3 days, owing to the weather; 1 inf, **nwTN**, It's owing to the weather = it depends upon; 1 inf, **csAL**, It's owing to what kind you got; 1 inf, **csAL**, You got them in the field owing to what time; 1 inf, **nwLA**, Just owing to what time you got up; 1 inf, **cwAL**, Just owing to whatever a fellow thought about saying—on selection of usage forms; 1 inf, **csTN**, Owing to who's putting them down = depending on; 1 inf, **cMS**, Owing to you.

o'wise See **oldwife 1**

owl v, hence vbl n *owling*

1 To hoot like an owl.

1941 Writers' Program *Guide AR* 77, To demonstrate more artistic inflections the hunters urge the best of their group to "owl for the stranger," and looking as solemn as the bird itself, the expert, with hoots that echo eerily down the valleys, will proceed to raise one of the great gray ghosts. "Owling" is helpful in hunting crows. **1965** *Clarke Co. Democrat* (Grove Hill AL) 19 Aug 6/2 (*Mathews Coll.*), The hunter who can "owl" properly is thus able to locate the position of the gobbler.

2 with *around:* See quot.

1975 Gould *ME Lingo* 199, *Owlin' 'round*—Night roving, but not always the kind with dalliance in mind; a gentleman who can't sleep and gets up to make a glass of warm milk is *owlin' 'round,* too.

owl claws See **owl's claws**

owl clover (or flower) See **owl's clover**

owl gull n

=glaucous gull.

1925 (1928) Forbush *Birds MA* 1.64, *Glaucous Gull.* Other names: burgomaster; ice gull; owl gull; white minister. **1946** Hausman *Eastern Birds* 309, *Glaucous Gull.* . . Other Names . . Owl Gull [etc]. **1956** MA

Audubon Soc. *Bulletin* 40.22, Glaucous Gull. . . Owl Gull (Mass. Perhaps from sharing white coloration with another winter visitant, the Snowy Owl.)

owl hawk See **hawk owl 1**

owlhead n

1 =**black-bellied plover.** [See quot 1955] Cf **bullhead 2a**
  1888 Trumbull *Names of Birds* 191, In New Jersey at Pleasantville (Atlantic Co.), and Atlantic City, [the black-bellied plover is called] *hollow-head;* and again at Pleasantville, *owl-head.* **1917** (1923) *Birds Amer.* 1.256, Black-Bellied Plover. . . Other Names . . Chuckle-head; Hollow-head; Owl-head. **1944** Hausman *Amer. Birds* 521, Owl-head. **1955** *AmSp* 30.181, *Owlhead,* for the black-bellied plover (N.J.), probably is only another of several names alluding to the large head of this species.

2 also *owl's head (pistol):* See quot 1927. **esp Sth, S Midl**
  1927 *DN* 5.457 [Underworld jargon], *Owl's head.* . . A short, heavy revolver, frequently having a finger hole in the grip allowing it to be used in addition as a *knuckle duster.* **1944** Clark *Pills* 130 **Sth,** Competing with the "nigger killer" was the well-known Iver-Johnson "owl head" which was a double-acting piece of unreliable rubber-stocked artillery. **1969** Emmons *Deep Rivers* 8 **eTX** [Black], He had taken along with him a little old owl's head pistol. **1972** in 1982 Powers *Cataloochee* 186, **cwNC,** This Indian had what we call an owlhead pistol. I don't know why they call them that. **a1975** Lunsford *It Used to Be* 172 **sAppalachians,** "Owl head" is a cheap pistol. They used to have one with an owl head on it. **1976** Garber *Mountain-ese* 65 **sAppalachians,** *Owl-head.* . . small cheap pistol—Slim never goes to town without takin' his ole owlhead along. **1985** Wilkinson *Moonshine* 38 **neNC,** So he ran into the house and came back with a damn old owl's head pistol, a cheap worthless brand of gun. . . I said, 'You can't hit me with that owl's head, I know because I've had two or three of them.'

3 See quot.
  1937 *DN* 6.618 **swTX** [Cowboy lingo], The greater share of the cowpuncher's inventiveness has been expended in developing . . vocabulary about the horse. For example, an *owl head* is an animal that can not be trained either to work or to ride.

owling See **owl**

owl manure See **owl shit**

owl, poor as an adj phr Also *poor as owl shit* **GA** Cf **Job's turkey 1**
  1968 *DARE* (Qu. U41b, *Somebody who has lost everything and is very poor: "He's poor as _____."*) Infs **GA**19, 30, A owl; **GA**23, Owl shit.

owl's claws n Also *owl claws* [Calque of the Navaho name; see quot 1943]
=orange sneezeweed.
  1937 U.S. Forest Serv. *Range Plant Hdbk.* W88, Orange sneezeweed, sometimes also called . . owls-claws, . . is one of the important western poisonous plants. . . The greenish, leaflike bracts (phyllaries) that encircle the flower head are in two rows and, at maturity, curve outward at their tips, a characteristic that has given rise to a Navajo name for the plant, meaning owl's claws. **1943** Elmore *Ethnobotany Navajo* 87, Orange Sneezeweed, Owl's Claws. Ne'éctjaa' yil khee'éh (tuft, ear, like, foot; i.e. [plant whose leaves look] like [the] foot [of the] owl). **1968** Schmutz et al. *Livestock-Poisoning Plants AZ* 90, Western sneezeweed, orange sneezeweed, owl-claws. **1979** Spellenberg *Audubon Guide N. Amer. Wildflowers W. Region* 369, Orange Sneezeweed; Owlclaws (*Helenium hoopesii*).

owl's clover n Also *owl clover, ~ flower, owl's foot clover* [See quot 1979]
A plant of the genus *Orthocarpus* native chiefly to the western US. For other names of var spp see **butter-and-eggs 3, escobita, gold tongue, johnny-nip, johnny-tuck, mossy pink, paintbrush, pelican flower, popcorn beauty, ~ flower, scrambled eggs, snaps, valley tassels**
  1897 Parsons *Wild Flowers CA* 52, During the spring the meadows about San Francisco are luxuriantly covered with the pretty blossoms of the owl's clover, which make snowy patches in some places. . . I do not know why this plant should be accredited to the owl and called clover, unless the quizzical-looking little blossoms are suggestive of the wise bird. **1915** (1926) Armstrong–Thornber *Western Wild Flowers* 496, Perhaps it is called Owl's-clover because, in some kinds, the flowers look

like the faces of owls. **1923** Dawson *Birds CA* 1.236, Elsewhere all is green, green save for the glowing pink of owl's-foot clover. **1934** Haskin *Wild Flowers Pacific Coast* 333, White Owl's Clover—*Orthocarpus hispidus.* . . Just why these plants have received their curious name is not known, but it is probable that the peculiar, two-lipped corolla is supposed to suggest the face of an owl. **1950** FWP *Guide ID* 72, Owl-clover, a member of the figwort and not of the clover family, is also widely distributed. **1959** Carleton *Index Herb. Plants* 89, Owl-flower: Orthocarpus [spp]. **1966–69** *DARE* (Qu. S26a, . . *Wildflowers. . . Roadside flowers*) Infs **CA**4, 60, 87, Owl's clover; (Qu. S26e, *Other wildflowers not yet mentioned;* not asked in early QRs) Inf **CA**2, Owl's clover—desert; **CA**115, Owl clover—not a clover at all but that's the popular name for it, sort of a magenta color, cluster of fine little flowers. **1966** *DARE* FW Addit **WA**10, Orthocarpus—Owl clover—similar to Indian paintbrush. **1967** *DARE* Wildfl QR (Craighead) Pl.18.1 Inf **CA**24, Owl clover. **1979** Spellenberg *Audubon Guide N. Amer. Wildflowers W. Region* 764, The name Owl's Clover may refer to the eye-like spots on the petals of some species or, picturesquely, to the swollen head-like ends of the erect corollas that seem to peer from the bracts as owls peer from the leaves of a tree. **1985** Dodge *Flowers SW Deserts* 40, In the desert, goldpoppies are sometimes mixed with owlclover.

owl's dung See **owl shit**

owl's foot clover See **owl's clover**

owl's head (pistol) See **owlhead 2**

owl shit n Also *owl manure, owl's dung, ~ shit* Cf **cat shit**
The most worthless or despicable thing.
  1967–68 *DARE* (Qu. U41b, *Somebody who has lost everything and is very poor: "He's poor as _____."*) Inf **GA**23, Owl shit; (Qu. HH20c, *Of an idle, worthless person . . "He isn't worth _____."*) Inf **OR**1, Sour owl shit; (Qu. HH22b, . . *A very mean person . . "He's meaner than _____."*) Inf **NJ**20, Owl's dung, owl's shit. **1985** Ladwig *How to Talk Dirty* 4 **Ozarks,** That's as worthless as a pinch of sour owl manure.

owl skull n Cf **popskull**, *DS* DD21a–c
  c1970 Pederson *Dial. Surv. Rural GA* (*What do you call cheap whiskey?*) 1 inf, **seGA,** Owl skull.

owl's shit See **owl shit**

owly adj **chiefly Upper MW, Gt Lakes** See Map
Angry, cross, irritable; also fig, of weather: threatening.
  1950 WELS (*Somebody who is usually in a bad temper: "She's always _____."*) 2 Infs, **ce,seWI,** Owly. **1950** WELS Suppl. **csWI,** To look owly—to appear angry, irritated. **1957** *Sat. Eve. Post Letters* **MA,** Old New England "Sayings." . . Owly—irritable, cross. **1958** in 1973 Allen *LAUM* 1.359 **nwMN,** The weather, getting gradually owlier the past few days, broke loose today. . . Thunderstorms passed over the Twin Cities during the night, and a lightning strike or two was reported during the morning. **1965–70** *DARE* (Qu. B5, *When the weather looks as if it will become bad . . it's _____*) Inf **NJ**39, Owly; **WI**66, Owly-looking; (Qu. GG4, *Stirred up, angry: "When he saw them coming he got _____."*) Inf **MI**26, Owly; (Qu. GG8, *When a person is very easily offended: "Be careful what you say to him, he's _____."*) Infs **IL**11, **OH**16, Owly; (Qu. GG16, . . *Finding fault, or complaining: "You just can't please him—he's always _____."*) Infs **SD**2, 3, Owly; (Qu. GG18, . . *'Obstinate': "Why does he have to be so _____."*) Infs

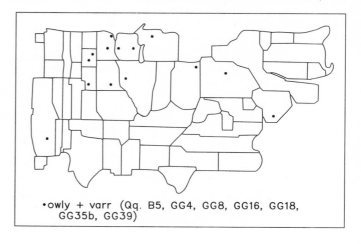

•owly + varr (Qq. B5, GG4, GG8, GG16, GG18, GG35b, GG39)

MI26, MN3, SD3, WI49, Owly; (Qu. GG35b, [To sulk or pout:] "Because she couldn't go, she's been _____ all day.") Infs CA36, MN18, PA69, Owly; (Qu. GG39, Somebody who seems to be looking for reasons to be angry: "He's a _____.") Inf IA25, Owly; NE11, Owly person. **1971** Wood Vocab. Change 41 Sth, Obstinate. . . One word, owly, was given both for this concept and that of anger. In each instance its reported use is slight. **1973** Allen LAUM 1.358 (as of c1950), Touchy. . . A person who is easily offended. . . 3 infs, ceMN, ne,ceND, Owly. Ibid 359, Angry. . . Returns from 1,040 respondents . . in the checklist. . . Owly . . has a much higher frequency, enough so as to suggest a Northern orientation. **1985** Kidder House 94 MA, Suddenly, as it seemed to him, he was deposited back in Shelburne Falls, in a little town beside the Deerfield River, and he was bored, among other things. "I was owly. I'd fight with Lindy and take off through the woods for half a day." **1993** DARE File, Another Mom-word for "weird" is owly. Ibid, Owly was always used by my mom to denote crabby, grumpy or that sort of behavior from us kids.

own adj

1 also own born: Directly related by blood—used with kinship terms, esp in comb own cousin first cousin. [OED own a. 2. 1671 → (in this sense)] chiefly NEng, S Midl
1690 in 1878 MA Hist. Soc. Coll. 5th ser 5.335 ceMA, Mr. Laurence . . is buried this day; so that Five own Sisters are now Widows. **1810** (1912) Bell Journey to OH 37 MA, She is not own mother to these children. **1855** Douglass My Bondage 82 eMD, This young woman was the daughter of Milly, an own aunt of mine. **1899** (1912) Green VA Folk-Speech 309, Own. . . Showing nearest relationship: as, "Own cousin," for, first cousin; "own brother;" "own uncle." "The young people just married were own cousins." **1903** (1984) Ayer Autobiog. [Foreword] NEng, Arthusa Ann Hibbard Ayer was an own cousin of Amelia Gregory Hall. . . Arthusa's father, Silas, and Amelia's mother, Delia, were two of the twelve children of Deacon David Hibbard. **1932** Randolph Ozark Mt. Folks 112, Isham Lane's widow—she was a Morgan before her marriage, own cousin to Aunt Elvy Hatfield—told me. **1941** LANE Map 387, Own cousin, in the meaning 'first cousin' (i.e. father's or mother's nephew or niece) was incidentally recorded in three cases: . . [1 inf, ceMA,] He was my own cousin; . . [1 inf, cwVT,] Own cousin; . . [1 inf, nwVT,] He was own cousin to my father. **1954** Harder Coll. cwTN, Own cousins. . . First cousins. "We're own cousins." **1959** VT Hist. 27.151, Own cousins. . . First cousin or near cousin. Common. **1966** PADS 46.28 cnAR (as of 1952), Own cousin (sometimes own born cousin). . . First cousin. "Their mammy and daddy was own born cousins." **1970** DARE (Qu. Z9, General word for others related to you by blood) Inf OH98, "Own cousin" or "own uncle" is used to distinguish those related by marriage. **1976** Ryland Richmond Co. VA 374, Own—as in "my own cousin" means "my first cousin." **1986** Pederson LAGS Concordance, 1 inf, neAR, Own cousins = blood cousins. **1988** DARE File NEng, My New England genealogy freak friends use own cousin for first cousin.

2 pronc-spp ahn, ownt: Used to mark the absolute possessive of pronouns and nouns. [By ext from the optional, emphatic use of own in std Engl] Gullah
1917 Torrence Granny Maumee 71 [Black], De house is youah'n. . . I shorely goin' to put dis man er youah'n th'oo er tes'. **1922** Gonzales Black Border 314 sSC, GA coasts [Gullah glossary], My'own—mine, my. **1927** Adams Congaree 19 cSC [Black], Brother, you is a little 'lated. Dat ole gal of yourownt is jes lef' we. **1928** Peterkin Scarlet Sister Mary 282 sSC [Gullah], "E ain' my own," Seraphine declared . . , and Keepsie echoed, "I know e ain' my own." Ibid 295, Dey ain' none o you-own. **1930** in 1944 ADD ceSC, 'Who own dat?' = Whose is that?, not Who owns that? 'Dat Doctor own' = That is Doctor's. 'Dat he own?' = Is that his? Illit[erate] negro & white. Better usage has whose own, Doctor's own. **1950** PADS 14.50 SC, Own: adj. Used in a redundant possessive, not emphatic: "Mary's own is better than yours." Ownt: adj. Same as own, q.v. "Who ownt dis is?" Whose is this? **1971** Cunningham Syntactic Analysis Gullah 22, The attributive genitive may be optionally followed by the form, own. The absolute form of the genitive, however, is formed by the obligatory addition of own. . . Y'all fry y'all own. . . The other children could keep them own on.

own v

1 Of a mother animal: to nurse and care for (her young).
1925 Book of Rural Life 9.5040, For reasons that are not fully understood, ewes sometimes refuse to own their lambs. . . Keeping a ewe and her lamb together in a four-by-four-foot lambing pen . . often brings the ewe to own her offspring. **1952** Brown NC Folkl. 1.573, Own. . . Of a

mother animal: to nurse and take care of her young, thus acknowledging them as hers; frequently in the negative. "That old sow wouldn't own her pigs; just fought them and threw them around."—Granville county. **1968** DARE Tape NJ10, Two or three years ago they had one [=a lamb] that the mother wouldn't own.

2 To give birth to.
1952 Brown NC Folkl. 1.573, Own. . . To give birth to. "I've owned nine children, and didn't have no trouble when they come."—Duplin county. **1959** Lomax Rainbow Sign 26 AL [Black], Mama never did own but just three childrens—well, she owned four— . . but the boy died just a tiny baby.

own prep, adv See **on** prep, adv

own-alone adj

1 =**own** adj **1.**
1883 (1971) Harris Nights with Remus 220 GA [Black], Aint you 'shame' yo'se'f fer ter be talkin' dat a-way, en 'bout yo' own-'lone blood kin too?

2 in phr own-alone self: =**own self.**
1883 (1971) Harris Nights with Remus 77 GA [Black], Brer Tarrypin crope inter de hole en gobble up de las' drop er de bumbly-bee honey by he own-alone se'f. Ibid 214, He des went off some'rs by he own-alone se'f en tuck a big laugh. **1892** (1969) Christensen Afro-Amer. Folk Lore 26, So Br'er Wolf gone fishin' by his own-alone-self.

own born (or cousin) See **own** adj **1**

own self pron [OED at self CI1a c1400 →] chiefly Sth, S Midl Used instead of -self to form reflexive and emphatic personal pronouns.
1905 (1975) Miles Spirit of Mts. 107, You may see for your own self. **1913** Kephart Highlanders 122 sAppalachians, I gather the corn, and shuck hit and grind hit my own self. **1945** FWP Lay My Burden Down 103 AR [Black], I was one of them little slave gals my own self, and I never seen nothing but work and tribulations till I was a grownup woman, just about. **1950** Stuart Hie Hunters 244 eKY, Sparkie wants booklarnin' so he can write fancy and speak proper like ye do yer ownself. **1967–70** DARE (Qu. X19b, . . If a person's hearing is very bad . . he's _____) Inf TX98, He can't hear his own self fart; (Qu. BB57, If someone committed suicide . . he _____) Inf FL49, Killed his own self; (Qu. HH10, A very timid or cowardly person: "He's _____.") Inf SC34, Scared of his own self; (Qu. HH22c, . . A very mean person . . "He's mean enough to _____") Inf NC84, Bite him own self; (Qu. II22, Expressions to tell somebody to keep to himself and mind his own business) Infs OH72, 87, Mind your own self. **1982** Walker Color Purple 20 GA [Black], I feel like I want to talk about her my own self. **1986** Pederson LAGS Concordance, 5 infs, Gulf Region, Your own self; 8 infs, Gulf Region, Their own self; 8 infs, Gulf Region, My own self; 2 infs, cnGA, cwTN, For my own self; 1 inf, neTN, He hung his own self; 2 infs, swGA, nwLA, Help your own self; 1 inf, seGA, Her own self; 1 inf, neFL, It can do that its own self; 1 inf, seGA, I've forgotten my own self; 1 inf, csAL, Killing your own self; 1 inf, cnGA, He's going [to] kill his own self off; 1 inf, neMS, Clean its own self out; 1 inf, csAL, It burns its own self out; 1 inf, cLA, Parch it your own self; 1 inf, cMS, Put a shoe [=horseshoe] on your own self—by self; 1 inf, cnMS, Clover would sow its own self; 1 inf, cwMS, Take care your own self; 1 inf, neFL, My father fixed a trough his own self; 1 inf, cnLA, Wait on your own self; 1 inf, cLA, You'll kill your own self; 1 inf, cLA, Our own self; 1 inf, swFL, We never killed them for our own selves; 2 infs, ceGA, nwMS, Their own selves; 1 inf, cwLA, Our own selves.

ownt See **own** adj **2**

own the corn See **acknowledge the corn**

ownty do(w)nty n, adj phr Also owntsy dontsy; for addit varr see quots [Redup] esp NEng
Prec by a possessive pron: (One's) own abilities or resources; (one's) own.
1815 Humphreys Yankey in England 19 (OEDS), My owny, towny, Lydy Lovett. Ibid 107, Owny towny (owny downy, ounty tounty) peculiarly belonging to one. **1871** Alcott Little Men 77 NEng, How nice it is to do it all my ownty donty self. **1882** in 1907 Brown Letters 359, It is told, the story, without any affectation, but so lovingly that the blessed little creature becomes our own child, our "ownty-downty," as New England nursery small talk has it. **1907** Lincoln Cape Cod 248 MA, The air had affected the colonel's head till he imagined he could

sail a boat all by his ownty-donty. **1970** *DARE* File, Owntsy-dontsy ['oʊntsɪ 'doʊntsɪ]. "If I had to do it on my owntsy-dontsy" = on my own responsibility, by my own decision.

ox n

A Gram forms.

1 sg: usu *ox;* also *oxen* (pronc-sp *oxin*). **chiefly Sth, S Midl**
1893 Shands *MS Speech* 48, Oxen. . . This form is largely used, even by educated people, for *ox.* **1903** *DN* 2.323 **seMO,** He is a mighty good oxen. **1907** *DN* 3.234 **nwAR,** Oxen, *n. sg.* Ox. **1909** *DN* 3.355 **eAL, wGA,** Oxen. . . Ox. **1922** Gonzales *Black Border* 317 **sSC, GA coasts** [Gullah glossary], Oxin—ox. **1937** (1977) Hurston *Their Eyes* 130 **FL,** Something stood like an oxen's foot on her tongue. **1944** *PADS* 2.20 **S Midl,** Oxen. . . Ox. **1965–67** *DARE* (Qu. K22, *Words used for a bull*) Inf **OK**1, Old oxen; (Qu. K23, *Words used by women or in mixed company for a bull*) Inf **SC**30, Oxen. **1969** [see **jenny 1**]. **1986** [see **2a** below].

2 pl: usu *oxen;* also: see below. **chiefly Sth, S Midl**

a *oxens.*
1827 (1939) Sherwood *Gaz. GA* 139, Oxens, for Oxen. **1869** *Overland Mth.* 3.127 **TX,** With the Texan driver all oxen are "steers". . . He never uses the former word in the singular, and very seldom in the plural, when it is almost invariably "oxens." **1902** *DN* 2.240 **sIL,** Oxens, *n. pl.* Always for oxen, when used, which is seldom. The word ox is not used at all, but steer. **1903** *DN* 2.323 **seMO,** I own two fine oxens. **1907** *DN* 3.224 **nwAR,** Oxens, *n. pl.* For oxen. The word *steer* used instead of *ox.* **1909** *DN* 3.355 **eAL, wGA,** Oxens. **1937** *Hall Coll.* **eTN,** Used oxen myself when up agin it. Had two yoke of oxens. **1944** *PADS* 2.20 **S Midl,** The plural is oxens. **1966–69** *DARE* (Qu. K24, *What does the word 'ox' mean?*) Inf **KY**43, Oxens; (Qu. K26, *If six oxen are hitched together two and two, you have three* _____) Infs **GA**39, **SC**57, Team(s) of oxens; **NC**12, Two oxens; **AK**8, Yoke of oxens. **1966–69** *DARE* Tape **FL**36, [Aux Inf:] Maybe we'd have about four oxens; **GA**1, It was hauled in by mules and oxens; **KY**14, They'd hook these oxens to 'em; **WV**2, It were four oxens to a plow. **1968** [see **2c** below]. **1986** Pederson *LAGS Concordance,* 148 infs, **Gulf Region,** (A yoke of, pair of, team of, them two, etc.) oxens; 25 infs, **Gulf Region,** Oxes; 2 infs, **se,cTN,** Ox—plural; 1 inf, **csGA,** Two ox; 1 inf, **cnGA,** A couple of ox; 4 infs, **MS, cTX, cwLA,** Team of ox; 2 infs, **csLA,** Them (two) ox; 3 infs, **MS, cTX,** Two ox; 4 infs, **eGA, cMS, neTX,** An oxen; 1 inf, **cwTN,** Yoke of ox; 1 inf, **seGA,** An oxen is a bull that's been castrated; 13 infs, **Gulf Region,** An oxen; *(A pair of* _____) 16 infs, **Gulf Region,** Ox. **1987** Jones–Wheeler *Laughter* 131 **Appalachians,** Went down to the barn and got a team of oxens.

b *oxes.*
1905 Culbertson *Banjo Talks* 41, Hitch my oxes / To de plow. **1906** *DN* 3.122 **sIN,** Oxes, *pl.* Regular plural of *ox; oxen* not used. **1968** *DARE* (Qu. H74a, . . *Coffee . . very strong*) Inf **IN**7, Strong as forty oxes. **1968** *DARE* FW Addit **VA,** Oxes pl. form of ox. **1968** [see **2c** below]. **1986** [see **2a** above].

c *ox.*
1922 Gonzales *Black Border* 317 **sSC, GA coasts** [Gullah glossary], Ox—oxen. **1954** *Harder Coll.* **cwTN,** Ox. Plural. "Six ox hitched together." **1966** *DARE* (Qu. K26, *If six oxen are hitched together two and two, you have three* _____) Inf **SC**9, Yoke of ox. **1968** *PADS* 50.33 **swTN** [Black], For *ox,* nine of the fourteen informants for whom responses were recorded have the plural form /ɑksən/. Five, all type I [=old, with little educ], form the plural differently. . . [One] has the plural /ɑksɪz/. . . [One] has /ɑksənz/. Three . . have /ɑks/. **1986** [see **2a** above].

B Senses.

1 A bull. **scattered, but more freq Sth, S Midl** *euphem* Cf **male** adj, **seed ox**
1931 Randolph *Ozarks* 79, The names of male animals must not be mentioned when women are present. . . Many Southerners use *ox* . . instead of the English word *bull.* **1946** *PADS* 5.30 **VA,** Ox . . : Bull; on the lower Rappahannock, in the presence of women. **1949** Kurath *Word Geog.* 62, Bull. . . Ox [is used] in the Virginia Tidewater, central West Virginia, and sporadically elsewhere. **c1960** *Wilson Coll.* **csKY,** Ox. . . A sort of generic name for any male member of the cattle tribe, bull or steer. **1965–70** *DARE* (Qu. K22, *Words used for a bull*) 15 Infs, **scattered, but esp Appalachians,** Ox; **OK**1, Old oxen; (Qu. K23, *Words used by women or in mixed company for a bull*) Infs **GA**80, **MO**1, **OK**18, **PA**103, **WV**3, 8, Ox; **SC**30, Oxen. [16 of 19 total Infs old] **1966** Dakin *Dial. Vocab. Ohio R. Valley* 2.230 **scattered sIN, sOH, nKY,** Ox [as a polite term for a bull] has some currency on both sides of the lower Wabash Valley, and is mentioned one time each in the Indiana Hills, in

the Northern Mountain-Knobs margin, and on the Ohio side of the river a short ways above the Kanawha. **1972** *PADS* 58.17 **cwAL,** Most of the informants (18) could recall a time when *bull* was taboo in the presence of women. . . The alternate terms given are Southern *male (cow)* (9) . . and *ox* (1). **1973** Allen *LAUM* 1.244 **IA, NE** (as of c1950), Bull. . . South Midland *ox* survives with seven infs, five of whom deem the term old-fashioned. **1989** Pederson *LAGS Tech. Index* 124, (Bull) 12 infs, **Gulf Region,** Ox(en).

2 in phr *the ox is in the ditch* and varr: See quots. [Cf Luke 14:5 "Which of you shall have an . . ox fallen into a pit, and will not straightway pull him out on the sabbath day?"]
1967 *DARE* FW Addit **cnNC,** To get the ox out of the ditch—to get something done that has to be done but that you don't much want to do. After church someone had to go home and make a casserole for the church supper that evening: "I gotta get home and get the ox outa the ditch." **1978** Wiersma *Purpaleanie* 53 **IA,** Were my parents right or wrong / not to mow the ripe oats that Sunday morning / with the rainstorm threatening?/ I reminded them that the Sabbath was made for man / and of the ox fallen into the pit. **1984** Wilder *You All Spoken Here* 156 **Sth,** The ox in the ditch: An emergency has arisen, requiring top priority. **1992** Mieder *Dict. Amer. Proverbs* 445 **KY, TN,** When the ox is in the ditch, pull him out.

ox balm n Also *ox weed*
A **horse balm** (here: *Collinsonia canadensis*).
1787 *Columbian Mag.* Dec 807, Horse balm, or Ox-weed, smells like balm, but more mild, grows in moist, rich, new grounds and woods, to the height of two feet, or more. **1854** MI State Ag. Soc. *Trans. for 1853* 5.130, The plants were very numerous, among which were oxbalm . . and marsh grass. **1900** Lyons *Plant Names* 111, C[ollinsonia] Canadensis. . . Horse-weed, Ox-balm, [etc.] **1974** (1977) Coon *Useful Plants* 156, *Collinsonia canadensis*—Horse or ox balm.

oxbird n [*OED* a1547 → for *Calidris alpina* and var similar birds] Cf **oxeye 1a**
=red-backed sandpiper.
1834 Nuttall *Manual Ornith.* 2.106, Dunlin, or Ox-Bird. . . Met with throughout the northern hemisphere. **1839** MA Zool. & Bot. Surv. *Fishes Reptiles* 367, The *Red backed Sandpiper, Tringa alpina,* is called . . in this country the Red-back, or the Ox-bird. **1956** MA Audubon Soc. *Bulletin* 40.19, Red-backed Sandpiper. . . Ox-bird (Maine, N.H., Mass., Conn. Also in British provincial use. From the prominent eyes.)

oxbow stirrup n Also *oxbow, ox yoke* **chiefly West**
A wooden stirrup shaped like an oxbow.
1902 (1969) Sears *Catalogue* 420, S., R. & Co.'s Special Ox-bow Stirrup, made of the best quality of choice white ash timber. **1907** White *AZ Nights* 245, They were good men, addicted to the grassrope, the double cinch, and the ox-bow stirrup. **1927** (1970) Sears *Catalogue* 1050, Ox bow stirrups, brass bound. **1933** White *Dog Days* 197 **CA,** Are we plunging on "ox-bow" stirrups or hooded? **1936** Adams *Cowboy Lingo* 46, In the old days they were of wood, extremely wide, and were known as 'ox yokes,' or 'ox bows.'

oxen See **ox A1**

oxens See **ox A2a**

oxes See **ox A2b**

oxeye n

1 Any of var shorebirds, as: See below. [See quot 1955 at **1a**]
a folk-etym sp *oxide;* Any of several **sandpipers,** but esp the **least sandpiper** and the **semipalmated sandpiper. chiefly Atl coast** Cf **meadow oxeye, oxbird, oxheart, sand oxeye, winter ~**
1612 Smith *Map VA* 1.15, In winter there are great plentie of . . Oxeies, Parrats and Pigeons. **1649** in 1844 Force *Tracts* 3.10.24, I fired at a great flight of small birds called *Oxeyes,* and made great slaughter among them, which gave refreshment to all our company. **1832** Williamson *Hist. ME* 1.147, The *Oxeye* is a little tottering shore-bird, large as a martin. **1876** *Forest & Stream* 7.149 **NY,** The little oxeye is the smallest of all. He has dark legs, and brown predominates in his feathers. If he was scarce he wouldn't be worth hunting, for his body isn't much, if any, bigger than your thumb, but he is very sweet and delicate eating. **1895** Elliot *N. Amer. Shore Birds* 97, Semipalmated Sandpiper. The Peep, or Ox-eye, as it is often called, is one of the best known and most abundant of the Sandpipers, being seen everywhere on our eastern coast in places frequented by waders. **1910** Eaton *Birds NY* 1.313, The Least

sandpiper, Little peep, or Oxeye, is a common migrant along our coast and inland waters. **1925** (1928) Forbush *Birds MA* 1.419, *Semipalmated Sandpiper.* Other names: peep . . oxeye. **1951** *AmSp* 26.93, Various shore birds bear the name *ox-eye,* from their prominent eyes. The pronunciation of this word has been noted as slipping to 'oxide' (N.C.; N.Y.) and in the latter state was explained as referring to the color of the breast and sides, 'ox-sides,' as it were. **1955** *AmSp* 30.177, The term *oxeye,* applied to several shore birds, apparently refers to the full, round eye, made more prominent by a white ring in many species. This is an imported name, having long been used for the dunlin in Great Britain. It denotes the same species on this side (Mass., Conn.), and in addition the black-breasted plover (Maine, Mass., Pa., N.J.), piping plover (Maine, Mass.), ruddy turnstone (N.C.), spotted sandpiper (Mass.), pectoral sandpiper (Pa.), white-rumped sandpiper (N.Y.), least sandpiper (Maine, N.Y., Md., Va.), and semipalmated sandpiper (Maine, Mass., R.I., N.Y., N.J., Md., Nova Scotia). **1956** MA Audubon Soc. *Bulletin* 40.19 **CT**, *Red-backed sandpiper.* . . Oxeye. *Ibid* 21 **MA**, *Sanderling.* . . Oxeye.

b Usu the **black-bellied plover**; rarely the **piping plover**.

1839 Audubon *Synopsis Birds* 221, Charadrius Helveticus . . Black-bellied Plover.—Bull-head. Ox-eye. **1880** *Forest & Stream* 15.4, In New Jersey and Pennsylvania it [=the black-bellied plover] is called both bull-head and beetle-head, and also, in the latter, ox-eye. **1904** (1910) Wheelock *Birds CA* 76, Black-bellied Plover . . Common names: Beetle-head; Oxeye [etc]. **1923** Dawson *Birds CA* 3.1290, Beetle-head. Bull-head. Ox-eye. **1953** Jewett *Birds WA* 248, Whistling Plover; Ox-eye; Chuckle-head. **1955** [see **1a** above].

2 Any of several composite plants; see below. Cf **sea oxeye**

a =**oxeye daisy 1.** [OED 1625 →]

1790 Deane *New Engl. Farmer* 313, Of the upland-weeds those which have proved to be the most troublesome are . . the greater-daisy, ox-eye, or piss-abed. **1900** Lyons *Plant Names* 99, C[hrysanthemum] Leucanthemum. . . Great White Ox-eye. **1959** Carleton *Index Herb. Plants* 124, *White oxeye:* Chrysanthemum leucanthemum. **1966–69** *DARE* (Qu. S7, *A kind of daisy, bright yellow with a dark center, that grows along roadsides in late summer*) Inf **MI**2, Black-eyed Susan, oxeye daisy. [FW: But wife insists "oxeye" not right; oxeye a white daisy.]; (Qu. S26a, . . *Wildflowers.* . . *Roadside flowers*) Inf **KY**11, Butter daisies (oxeye)—white with yellow center.

b A plant of the genus *Heliopsis.* Also called **false sunflower 2;** for other names of *H. helianthoides* see **brown-eyed Susan 3**

1822 Eaton *Botany* 302, [Heliopsis] laevis . . ox-eye. . . Tall, resembling the sunflowers, for which it is often mistaken by botanists. **1843** Torrey *Flora NY* 1.378, *Heliopsis* [spp] . . Ox-eye. *Ibid* 379, *Heliopsis laevis* . . Ox-eye. **1861** Wood *Class-Book* 445, *Heliopsis* [spp] . . Ox-eye . . flowers radiant like the sun. **1903** Porter *Flora PA* 330, *Heliopsis scabra* . . Rough Ox-eye. **1939** *Natl. Geogr. Mag.* Aug 262, Oxeyes . . are tall, leafy plants bearing numerous attractive bright-orange flower heads that come into bloom in late summer. . . They might easily pass for sunflowers, except . . that the ray flowers, instead of falling back from the head, turn dry and persist as they do in zinnias of the garden. **1949** Moldenke *Amer. Wild Flowers* 195, The oxeyes (*Heliopsis*) comprise another small group of perennial plants often mistaken for sunflowers. . . Best known is the smooth oxeye or falsesunflower, *H. helianthoides.* **1968** *DARE* (Qu. S11) Inf **IN**35, Oxeyes. **1972** Courtenay–Zimmerman *Wild Flowers* 116, *Ox eye* . . Dry woods, dry to wet prairies, disturbed ground. **1995** Brako et al. *Scientific & Common Names Plants* 37, [Heliopsis] helianthoides . . sweet-ox-eye, sunflower-everlasting.

c A **sneezeweed** (here: *Helenium autumnale*).

1828 Rafinesque *Med. Flora* 2.235, Sneezeweed, Sneezewort, Swamp Sunflower, False Sunflower, Yellow Star, Oxeye. **1876** Hobbs *Bot. Hdbk.* 85, Oxeye, Sneezewort, Helenium autumnale. **1903** Porter *Flora PA* 336, *Helenium autumnale* . . Sneezeweed. Ox-eye. **1940** Clute *Amer. Plant Names* 83, H[elenium] autumnalis. . . swamp sunflower, ox-eye [etc]. **1958** Jacobs–Burlage *Index Plants NC* 54, *Helenium autumnale.* . . ox-eye [etc].

d See **oxeye daisy 2.**

oxeye camomile n

=**dog fennel 1.**

1959 Carleton *Index Herb. Plants* 89, *Ox-eye-chamonile* [sic]: Anthemis cotula.

oxeye daisy n

1 also *ox-eyed daisy:* A widespread, naturalized plant (*Leu-*

canthemum vulgare, formerly *Chrysanthemum leucanthemum*) with flower heads of white rays and a yellow center. [*OED* 1753 →] Also called **bull daisy 2, bull's-eye 6a, ~ daisy 2, chiggerweed 5, daisy 2a, dog daisy 2, Dutch cuss, ~ morgan, field daisy, golden ~ 1, horse ~ 1, June ~, love-me 2, old-field daisy, oxeye 2a, poor-land daisy, povertyweed, pismire, piss-a-bed, Rhode Island clover, sheriff pink, white daisy, whiteweed**

1813 Muhlenberg *Catalogus Plantarum* 77, Chrysanthemum [spp]—ox-eye daisy. a**1820** in 1832 *Mass. Hist. Soc. Coll.* 2d ser 9.148, Chrysanthemum leucanthemum—Ox-eyed daisy. **1837** Darlington *Flora Cestrica* 490 **PA**, White-flowered Chrysanthemum. *Vulgò*—Daisy. Ox-eye Daisy. . . This vile foreign weed, from the culpable negligence of the farmers, has become a serious nuisance in many neighborhoods; and threatens to overrun the whole country. **1850** U.S. Patent Office *Annual Rept. for 1849: Ag.* 374, In southern Pennsylvania . . the "ox-eye-daisy," a species of wild camomile, (*Chrysanthemum leucanthemum,*) [is] very often nipped by cows when the herbage is short or scarce. **1895** U.S. Dept. Ag. *Farmers' Bulletin* 28.27, Ox-eye daisy, bull's-eye, whitedaisy, whiteweed. **1931** Clute *Common Plants* 97, The bull daisy (*Chrysanthemum leucanthemum*), which is also called ox-eye daisy, is one of the largest and commonest of daisies. **1961** Douglas *My Wilderness* 117 **MN**, In addition to the tall purple and white asters already mentioned were extensive stands of the large white oxeye daisies. **1968** *DARE* (Qu. S26a, . . *Wildflowers.* . . *Roadside flowers*) Inf **OH**78, Oxeye daisy—it's white; (Qu. S26e, *Other wildflowers not yet mentioned;* not asked in early QRs) Inf **CA**40, Oxeye daisy is white with a yellow center. **1968** *DARE* FW Addit **VA**15, Oxeye daisy—polite term for bull's-eye daisy. **1979** Niering–Olmstead *Audubon Guide N. Amer. Wildflowers E. Region* 372, Though an extremely common, even weed-like species, the Oxeye Daisy was originally introduced in North America from Europe. **1995** Brako et al. *Scientific & Common Names Plants* 44, [Leucanthemum] vulgare . . field daisy, marguerite, ox-eye daisy.

2 also *oxeye, ox-eyed daisy:* =**black-eyed Susan 2. chiefly NEast, N Cent, sAppalachians** Cf **yellow oxeye daisy**

1894 *Jrl. Amer. Folkl.* 7.92 **MA**, *Rudbeckia hirta* . . ox-eye daisy, somewhat general in Mass. **1896** *Ibid* 9.193 **ME**, *Rudbeckia hirta* . . bull's eyes, ox-eyed daisies, Paris, Me. **1906** *DN* 3.148 **nwAR**, *Niggerhead* . . Ox-eye daisy. "Nigger-heads have a large black centre and yellow petals." **1929** *Torreya* 29.151 **ME**, Rudbeckia hirta was *"Ox-eye Daisy."* **1950** *WELS* **WI** (Bright yellow daisy-like flower with a dark center; grows along roadsides in the fall) 1 Inf, Oxeye (or ox-eyed) daisy; (Other weeds common in your locality) 2 Infs, Ox-eyed daisy. **1965–70** *DARE* (Qu. S7, *A kind of daisy, bright yellow with a dark center, that grows along roadsides in late summer*) 46 Infs, **chiefly NEast, N Cent, sAppalachians,** Oxeye (or ox-eyed) daisy; **NC**24, **OH**6, 44, Oxeye; (Qu. S21, . . *Weeds . . that are a trouble in gardens and fields*) Infs **TN**6, **WI**58, Oxeye daisy; (Qu. S26a, . . *Wildflowers.* . . *Roadside flowers*) Inf **VA**101, Ox-eyed daisies; **IN**17, Oxeye daisy; (Qu. S26c, *Wildflowers that grow in woods*) Inf **PA**99, Oxeye daisy; (Qu. S26e, *Other wildflowers not yet mentioned;* not asked in early QRs) Infs **IN**3, **SC**46, Oxeye daisy. [*DARE* Ed: Some of these Infs may refer instead to **1** above.]

3 A **fleabane** (here: *Erigeron philadelphicus*).

1976 Miller *Shaker Herbs* 252, White Root—*Erigeron philadelphicus*—White Weed. Ox Eye Daisy. White Daisy.

ox-eyed daisy See **oxeye daisy 1, 2**

ox-eyed Susan n

=**black-eyed Susan 2.**

1969 *DARE* (Qu. S7, *A kind of daisy, bright yellow with a dark center, that grows along roadsides in late summer*) Inf **VT**17, Ox-eyed Susan.

oxheart n [Blend of **oxeye 1a** + **blackheart 1**]

=**red-backed sandpiper.**

1956 MA Audubon Soc. *Bulletin* 40.19 **MA**, *Red-backed Sandpiper.* . . Ox-heart (Mass. Apparently from a mingling of the names "Oxeye" and "Black-heart.")

oxide See **oxeye 1a**

oxin See **ox A1**

ox-joint n

An **ironweed 1;** see quot.

1969 *DARE* (Qu. S26a, . . *Wildflowers.* . . *Roadside flowers*) Inf **KY**47, Queen of the meadow = ox-joint (Joe-Pye).

ox shovel n

See quot 1969.

1823 *New Engl. Farmer* (Fessenden) 2.9, The most expeditious, effectual, and economical mode of making a drain would undoubtedly be to use oxen, and a *scraper* or ox-shovel, as it is sometimes called. **1852** *Plow* Dec. 385/2 *(Mathews Coll.),* New-Oreleans [sic] Agricultural Warehouse, comprising a large assortment of Plows, Harrows, . . Ox Shovels, . . and other Agricultural Implements. **1969** *DARE* FW Addit **CT,** Ox shovel—a large scoop, wheelbarrow-shaped, used to dig a cellar or drain along side of a road—old-fashioned.

ox-tongue n

An aquatic plant such as **burr reed** or **tape grass; see quots.**

1913 *Torreya* 13.226, *Sparganium* sp.—Ox-tongue, Santee Club, S.C. Sold to the Club as *Vallisneria spiralis.* *Ibid* 227, *Vallisneria spiralis* . . ox-tongue, Chef Menteur, La.

ox vomit See **nux vomica**

ox weed See **ox balm**

ox yoke See **oxbow stirrup**

oy See **I** pron

oyster n Usu |ˈɔɪstə(r)|; also |ˈos-, ˈɔrs-, ˈaɪ-, ˈɜ-, -što̅(r), -sč-|; for addit varr see quots Pronc-spp *aister, a(u)rster, erster, is(h)ter, oaster, oshtuh, oyrster, oystcher, w'osteh*

A Forms.

1864 in 1986 Messer *Civil War Letters* 29 **VT,** They had a dance up to Bens the other night. Swallow was going to find oasters Colbern the rum. **1887** Page *In Ole VA* 227, Dat lamb over dyah maybe got oystchers waitin' for him. **1903** *DN* 2.291 **Cape Cod MA** (as of a1857), *Aisters* for *oysters.* **1909** *DN* 3.355 **eAL, wGA,** Oyster. . . Commonly called [ɔɪstšə]. **1909** *S. Atl. Qrly.* 8.52 **seSC,** The introduction of an extraneous initial *w,* as in *w'osteh, (oyster)* . . are all characteristics of *Gullah.* **1922** Gonzales *Black Border* 317 **sSC, GA coasts** [Gullah glossary], *Oshtuh*—oyster, oysters. **1928** *NY Times* (NY) 12 Aug sec 8 6/2, The specialists of the Department of English at Columbia seem to think that the spread of "erster" for "oyster" . . is comparatively recent, though [it] can be traced back to eighteenth-century English. **1940** *Sat. Eve. Post* 20 July 55 **GA,** Lay out my erster-gray suit. **1941** Writers' Program SC *Folk Tales* 101, He lib where dere's ister en swimps en crabs. **1941** *LANE* Map 289, 1 inf, **nwCT,** [ɔɔstr frɪtr]. *Ibid* Map 360, 1 inf, **swCT,** [ɔɪstr bæskɪt]. **1950** *PADS* 14.40 **SC,** *Ishters* [ˈaɪštəz]. . . Oysters. Beaufort, and probably along the coast. **1950** Hubbell *Pronc. NYC* 142, The occurrence of /ɔɪ/ in *join, oil, oyster* is much less frequent, although not unknown. **c1960** Wilson *Coll.* **csKY,** Oysters is sometimes [ˈɔɪstjəz]. **1961** Kurath–McDavid *Pronc. Engl.* Map 146, Incidence of Vowels other than /ɔɪ/ in *oyster* [**scattered eGA, SC, NC, VA, eMD, eWV,** /os ~ oš/; **scattered eGA, SC, WV, PA, NY,** /ɔrs ~ ɔrš/; **scattered,** /ai/; **seNY, neNJ,** /ɜ/]. **1965** Carmony *Speech Terre Haute* 88 **cwIN,** A more open onset sometimes occurs initially or in alveolar or palatal environments, as in *oysters* [ˈɔˇɪstə·z]. *Ibid* 114, /ɔi/ . . is the usual syllabic of *oysters* . ., the exceptions occurring in the records of the Negro informants. . . Informant 3 has /ɔr/ in *oysters.* **1965–70** *DARE* (Qu. P18, . . *Kinds of shellfish*) 124 Infs, **chiefly Atlantic, Gulf States, Pacific NW,** Oysters [Proncs of the type [ˈɔɪstə(r)z, ˈɔɪs-] are recorded for 99 of these Infs.]; **SC**43, **VA**110, [ˈɔɪstə]; **SC**66, [ˈɔɪštɚ]; **FL**48, [ˈɔɪšstəz]; **SC**9, [ˈašta]; **NC**87, [ˈɔɪščɚz]; **SC**69, [ˈɔɪsčɚ·z]; **VA**84, [ˈɔɚštəz]; **IL**14, **MD**42, 45, [ˈɔrstə·(z)]; **MD**15, 40, **NY**236, [ˈɔstɚ·(z)]; **LA**44, [ˈɜɪstəz]; **NY**59, [ˈɜɪrstɚ·z]; **AL**10, [ˈo·stɚ·z]; **VA**73, [ˈbstɚ]; **DC**2, [ˈɔɪsəz]. **1967** LeCompte *Word Atlas* 214 **seLA,** Oysters, 9 infs, [ˈɔ·štə]; 7 infs, [ˈɔɪšta]; 4 infs, [ˈɔɪstɚ·]; 1 inf, [ˈɔ·štə]. **1968** *DARE* FW Addit **ceMD,** Oyster—[ˈɔɪstɚ·] or [ˈɔrstɚ·]; **ceVA,** Oysters [ˈɔɪstɚ·z]. **1969** *DARE* Tape **GA**79, Oysters [ˈɔɪsčɚz]. **1976** Ryland *Richmond Co. VA* 374, *Oyrsters.* **1976** Warner *Beautiful Swimmers* 30 **eMD,** Soon be time you was out drudging arsters with your daddy. **1989** Pederson *LAGS Tech. Index* 207, [Proncs of the type [ɔɪstə(r)z, ɔɪšta(r)z] are common; somewhat less commonly [ɔɪšča(r)z, ɔɪsča(r)z, ɔɔstə(r)z]; occas [ɔɔštə(r)z, ɔɔsča(r)z, aɪstə(r)z, aɪš(s)tə(r)z, ɔɪsjə(r)z, ɔɚ-]; infreq [ɔrštə(r)z, orstə(r)z].] **1989** (1990) Baden *Maryland's E. Shore* 109, An enterprising skipper . . plans to take a group of landlubbers to catch a bushel or two of "aursters."

B Senses.

1 Std: a marine bivalve mollusk of the family Ostreidae, esp *Crassostrea virginica;* also a mollusk of any of the families Isognomonidae, Pteriidae, or Spondylidae, which resemble Ostreidae. For other names of var mollusks of the family

Ostreidae see **bluepoint 1, cat-tongue, coonheel, coon oyster, hard ~, rabbit-ear, razor blade, sand oyster, shanghai, soft oyster, strap ~** Cf **rock oyster**

2 also *oyster shell:* A **freshwater clam** of the family Unionidae. **chiefly Upper Missip Valley**

1940–41 Cassidy *WI Atlas,* 1 inf, Oyster shells—local shellfish; 1 inf, Oyster—"not very plenty" around here; 1 inf, Clams, oysters—hunted for pearls here, some around Fort Atkinson; 1 inf, Clam shells, niggerhead, oyster shell, mucket; 1 inf, Oysters—used for shellfish in general—mussels, etc. **1950** *WELS (What kinds of shellfish are common in your neighborhood?)* 1 Inf, **ceWI,** Clams, crabs, . . oysters. [**1967–68** *DARE* (Qu. P18, . . *Kinds of shellfish*) Inf **IL**14, Clams, oysters; **MN**5, Oysters, crabs—not edible; **NY**205, Clams, oysters; **WI**22, Oyster. [*DARE* Ed: 143 Infs gave the resp *oysters* to this question; their locations, however, suggest that they were referring instead to **1** above.]] [**1979** *WI Week-End* Apr 6, Some clams contain pearls, which form around an irritant such as a grain of sand. But clams in the Mississippi River produce only imperfect or baroque pearls, known as "blisters" or "slugs". They are seldom of gem quality.]

3 A small piece of food resembling an oyster in size, shape, taste, or texture; see quots.

1847 Rutledge *Carolina Housewife* 101 **SC,** *Corn Oysters*—Grate the corn . . in a deep dish. To two ears of corn allow one egg; beat the whites and yolks separately, and add them to the corn, with one tablespoonful of wheat flour and one of butter. **1883** *Harper's New Mth. Mag.* 67.456 **NEng,** He rolled under his tongue the sweet morsel of the oyster out of a side bone. **1896** *Daily News Cook Book* 388, Veal Oysters—Get one and one-half pounds of tender veal from the leg, cut into pieces size and shape of an oyster, dip in olive oil and roll in fine cracker crumbs. **1936** Lutes *Country Kitchen* 162 **sMI,** The leg [of a young rooster] yielded drumstick and upper joint; the back, for a pie, was deftly split down the centre, leaving an "oyster" of meat on either side. **1966–69** *DARE* (Qu. H50, *Dishes made with beans, peas, or corn*) Inf **PA**74, Corn oysters; (Qu. H52, *Dishes made with fresh cabbage*) Inf **NH**11, Cabbage oyster—cut cabbage fine, cook in salt water, add salt, pepper and butter and milk, tastes like oyster stew with cabbage in place of oysters; (Qu. K73, . . *Names . . for the rump of a cooked chicken*) Inf **TX**33, Oyster; **NY**163, Two oysters in the rungs. **1979** *DARE* File **cnMA** (as of c1915), The little pieces of meat shaped like and the size of oysters in the back bone of a chicken, one on each side, were referred to as "oysters." *Ibid,* My mother made both corn fritters and corn oysters.

4 See **oyster mushroom.**

oysterbird n

1 An **oyster-catcher** (here: *Haematopus palliatus*).

1890 *Century Dict.* 4219, *Oyster-bird.* . . An oyster-catcher. **1923** U.S. Dept. Ag. *Misc. Circular* 13.72 **FL, SC,** American Oyster-catcher. . . *Vernacular names* . . oyster-bird. **1949** Sprunt–Chamberlain *SC Bird Life* 208, American Oyster-catcher. . . Local Names: Oyster Bird.

2 =**ruddy turnstone.**

1911 *Forest & Stream* 77.174, *Arenaria interpres.*—Oyster Bird, Matagorda, Tex.

oyster-catcher n

Either of two related, red-billed shorebirds: *Haematopus palliatus* native chiefly to the Atlantic coast, or *H. bachmani* of the Pacific coast. For other names of the former see **flood gull 1, oysterbird 1, oyster-cracker 1, pill-willet, redbill snipe, sea crow;** for other names of the latter see **redbill**

1731 Catesby *Nat. Hist. Carolina* 1.85, The Oyster Catcher. . . In Rivers and Creeks near the Sea there are great quantities of Oysterbanks, which at low Water are left bare: On these Banks of Oysters do these Birds principally, if not altogether, subsist. **1814** Wilson *Amer. Ornith.* 8.17, The Oyster-catcher will not only take to the water when wounded, but can also swim and dive well. **1844** Giraud *Birds Long Is.* 222, The Oyster-catcher is generally confined to the sea-coast. . . At low water it is said to visit the oyster-beds, awaiting a favorable opportunity, when the shells open, to thrust in its hard and strong bill, and rob them of their tenants. **1869** (1870) *Amer. Naturalist* 3.232 **MA,** The Oyster-catcher, a Southern coast-bird . ., occasionally wanders as far north as Marshfield. **1886** Turner *Contribs. AK* 151, The Black Oyster-catcher is universally detested by both white and native hunters, as it frequents just those places most resorted to by seals and sea-otters, so that on the approach of a hunter to obtain those animals the bird is certain to give the alarm and cause the animal to disappear into the water. **1916** *Times-*

Picayune (New Orleans LA) 9 Apr mag sec 2/2, *American Oyster Catcher* (Haematopus palliatus). . . Their common name comes from the tale that oyster catchers pry open oysters to obtain their food—something, however, no self respecting oyster would allow. **1918** Grinnell *Game Birds CA* 501, The name Oyster-catcher, as applied to these birds [=*Haematopus bachmani*] is somewhat of a misnomer. . . [O]n this coast, they frequent localities where these bivalves are rare or absent. **1967** *Rockport Pilot* (TX) 30 Mar sec 1 1/5, Many common loons and mergansers . . were observed. . . [S]omeone noted three young oyster-catchers with one of their parents. **1977** Bull–Farrand *Audubon Field Guide Birds* 377, Oystercatchers insert their long, bladelike bills into mussels and other bivalves, severing the powerful adductor muscles before the shells can close.

oyster crab n [*DJE* 1756 for *Pinnotheres geddesi*]
Either of two crabs: esp the edible *Pinnotheres ostreum* which is commensal on an **oyster B1** (here: *Crassostrea virginica*), but also a mud crab *(Panopeus herbsti);* see quots.
[**1817** Acad. Nat. Sci. Philadelphia *Jrl.* 1.4.58, *C[ancer] Panope* [=*Panopeus herbsti*]. . . The young of this species are often found on oysters . . in our markets, secreting themselves about the hinge of such as are not perfectly divested of the mud in which they had been imbedded. *Ibid* 1.5.68, A very common inmate of the oyster of our markets, . . though small, it [=*Pinnotheres ostreum*] is excellent food, and those who eat oysters seldom reject it. Where the fresh oyster is opened in considerable numbers, the crabs are often collected and served apart, for the palates of the luxurious.] **1843** DeKay *Zool. NY* 6.5, *Panopeus herbsti*. . . This species is commonly known on our shores by the names of *Mud Crab* and *Oyster Crab*. It is frequently taken while dredging for oysters, and is almost invariably found on oyster beds. It is also supposed to be injurious to the Oyster, by feeding on the young spawn. *Ibid* 12, The *P[innotheres] depressum* of Say, is . . the male, or as we suppose the young, of the *Common Oyster Crab*. **1884** U.S. Natl. Museum *Bulletin* 27.127, *Pinnotheres ostreum*. . . Oyster Crab. Atlantic coast, Massachusetts to South Carolina; living as a messmate in the shells of the oyster, *Ostrea virginiana*. Used as food. **1901** Arnold *Sea-Beach* 287, The oyster-crab. The female . . lives in the gill-cavity of the oyster, and is particularly abundant in oysters from the Chesapeake. The males are seldom seen, and rarely occur in the oyster, but swim freely about. **1938** Bemelmans *Life Class* 49 **NYC,** All maîtres d'hôtel. . . are especially fond of little fried things . . whitebait, oyster crabs, fried scallops. **1970** *DARE* FW Addit **VA**47, Oyster crab—small crab found among oysters. One kind is found in the oyster; another kind is found among the oysters.

oyster-cracker n
1 An **oyster-catcher** (here: *Haematopus palliatus*).
1937 (1965) Stone *Bird Studies* 1.367 **NJ,** In August, 1928, two [oyster-catchers] were seen by Oscar T. Sayre near Barnegat Inlet "in late summer." He knew them as "Oyster-crackers."
2 A **toadfish** (here: *Opsanus tau*). **C Atl** Cf **oysterfish 1, oyster toad**
1958 *Washington Post* (DC) 15 Aug sec A 21/4 **Chesapeake Bay,** It was only an unloved oyster cracker ("mud trout" to you). **1968** *DARE* (Qu. P4, *Saltwater fish that are not good to eat*) Infs **DE**1, 3, 4, **NJ**21, 22, Oyster-cracker(s).

oyster duck n
1 =**hooded merganser.**
1918 Grinnell *Game Birds CA* 89, Hooded Merganser . . Other names—Hooded Sheldrake; Oyster Duck (Napa County).
2 =**goldeneye 1.** [From its winter diet of crabs, mollusks, etc]
1923 U.S. Dept. Ag. *Misc. Circular* 13.22, Goldeneye. . . *In local use.* . . oyster duck (N.C., Miss.) **1982** Elman *Hunter's Field Guide* 218, American Goldeneye . . Common & Regional Names . . oyster duck [etc].

oysterfish n
1 A **toadfish:** usu *Opsanus tau,* occas also *O. beta.* Cf **oyster-cracker 2, oyster toad**
[**1842** DeKay *Zool. NY* 3.170, *The Two-spined Toadfish.* . . This little fish . . is usually found on muddy bottoms. It has frequently been brought to me, included between the two valves of an oyster.] **1855** Smithsonian Inst. *Annual Rept. for 1854* 340 **NJ,** *Batrachus variegatus, Les.* . . The toad-fish, or, as it is called at Beesley's point, the oyster-fish, . . is one of the fishermen's pests. **1884** U.S. Natl. Museum *Bulletin* 27.433, *Batrachus tau* L. subsp. *beta* [=*Opsanus beta*]. . Oyster-fish;

Toad-fish. . . Gulf of Mexico. This is the common form of toad-fish in shoal water, replacing the typical *B. tau* of more northern waters. **1884** Goode *Fisheries U.S.* 1.251, The Toad-fish, *Batrachus tau,* called also on the coast of New Jersey and in some parts of the Southern States "Oyster-fish," is one of the most repulsive looking fishes upon our coast. . . In the South it . . [is] frequently found on the oyster-beds, hiding between the valves of empty oyster-shells. **1940** *Sun* (Baltimore MD) 30 Apr 6/3 (*OEDS*), The oyster fish, sometimes called 'devil fish' by local fishermen, has a big head and mouth with which it crushes oysters for food. **1968–69** *DARE* (Qu. P4, *Saltwater fish that are not good to eat*) Inf **LA**37, Oysterfish; **LA**44, Oysterfish—an ugly fish with strong jaws—it is about eight or ten inches long; **NJ**55, Oysterfish. **1969** *DARE* FW Addit **Hatteras Is. NC,** Oysterfish. **1991** Amer. Fisheries Soc. *Common Names Fishes* 155, Oysterfish—see oyster toadfish.
2 =**tautog.**
1878 U.S. Natl. Museum *Proc.* 1.374 **NC,** *Tautoga onitis.* . . *Oyster-fish.* Rather common. The young abundant about the wharves at Beaufort. **1884** Goode *Fisheries U.S.* 1.270, At Cape Lookout, North Carolina, Jordan records this species [=*Tautoga onitis*], under the name "Oyster-fish," as rather common. . . As might be inferred from its haunts and from the character of its strong, sharp teeth, the food of this fish consists of the hard-shelled mollusks and crustaceans which are so abundant among the rocks. **1903** NY State Museum & Sci. Serv. *Bulletin* 60.598, This [=*Tautoga onitis*] is better known in New York as the blackfish; farther south it is styled chub . . , Moll, Will George and oyster fish. **1946** LaMonte *N. Amer. Game Fishes* 92, *Tautoga onitis.* . . Oysterfish. . . New Brunswick to South Carolina. . . Food: Chiefly mollusks. **1973** Knight *Cook's Fish Guide* 386, Oysterfish—Tautog or see Toadfish, Oyster.
3 The naked goby *(Gobiosoma bosc).*
1903 NY State Museum & Sci. Serv. *Bulletin* 60.656, *Gobiosoma bosci* . . *Oysterfish.* [*Ibid* 657, Some large individuals were secured in empty oyster shells off Duncan's creek. . . [Others were] taken in moderate numbers in oyster dredges at Eaton's Neck Long Island, in the fall of 1896.] **1933** John G. Shedd Aquarium *Guide* 148, *Gobiosoma bosci* . . *Oysterfish.* These little gobies are fairly common along the south Atlantic coast in grassy bays.

oyster fungus See **oyster mushroom**

oyster grass n
1 =**musk grass.**
1913 *Torreya* 13.225, *Chara* sp. . . oyster grass, nigger-wool, Currituck Sound, N.C.
2 A **cordgrass** (here: *Spartina alterniflora*) common in salt marshes.
1913 *Torreya* 13.227, *Spartina glabra* . . oyster grass, Mississippi Delta, La. **1958** Grau *Hard Blue Sky* 286 **seLA,** He had nothing to look at but alligator grass and salt cane and oyster grass and cattails waving in the wind.

oyster loaf n Also *oyster poor boy, ~ sandwich* **chiefly LA**
A baked sandwich made with oysters, cream, and other ingredients; the bread for such a sandwich.
1893 *Harper's New Mth. Mag.* 86.378 **New Orleans LA,** "Oyster loaves" . . are among the queer edibles of [New Orleans]. **1932** Stieff *Eat in MD* 22, *Oyster Loaf*—Cut an oblong slice . . of bread. . Fill with raw oysters . . cream . . butter. . Bake. **1932** (1946) Hibben *Amer. Regional Cookery* 94 **New Orleans LA,** *Oyster Loaf.* . . This loaf is never served at a meal, but is eaten as a midnight snack, or . . as buffet refreshment. The oyster loaf was originally made only at saloons for husbands to take home as a peace offering to their wives, and was known in old New Orleans as *La Médiatrice.* **1941** Writers' Program *Guide LA* 237, Today (1940) Antonio Colomb and his mother make bread in the same way as did Jean Boyance almost a century ago—twisted French loaves, round "all-crusts" (called Old Mother's Bread), French "flutes," rolls, and "oyster loaves." **1946** Farmer *Boston Cook Book* 283, *Oyster Loaf.* Slice off top of small loaf of bread. Cut out center. . Fill with creamed oysters, put on top, and bake in moderately hot oven. **1967–68** *DARE* (Qu. H41, . . *Kinds of roll or bun sandwiches* . . *in a round bun or roll*) Inf **LA**24, Oyster sandwich; (Qu. H42, . . *[A sandwich]* . . *in a much larger, longer bun, that's a meal in itself*) Inf **LA**9, Oyster loaf—old-fashioned; take a loaf and split it, put all kinds of things inside including oysters. **1968** *DARE* Tape **LA**22, If you want you can get this French bread, you know, and run it into the stove, you see. And leave it bake a little and spread your butter on it. Put your oysters and your pickles—stuff like that—maybe a lettuce, you

know. Fix it up, you see. . . We call that a oyster loaf. **1979** *DARE* File **cLA,** The New Orleans *oyster loaf* is dispensed here (at least at the best place for finding it) as an *oyster po' boy.* **1993** *DARE* File **New Orleans LA,** A real Yat [=a native of New Orleans] can hold an oyster (pronounced *erster)* po boy in one hand and in the other hand hold and open a bottle of Crystal Hot Sauce without spilling a drop.

oyster mushroom n Also *oyster,* ~ *fungus,* ~ *shell* [From the cap, which resembles an oyster in shape; *OED* 1875] Cf **dry-land fish 1**

A **mushroom B1** of the genus *Panellus* or *Pleurotus,* but esp *Pleurotus ostreatus.*

    1890 *Century Dict.* 4219, Oyster-mushroom. . . *Agaricus ostreatus,* an esculent fungus with a large, thick, fleshy pileus. **1908** Hard *Mushroom Edible* 155, If one will locate a few logs or stumps upon which the Oyster mushroom grows, he can find there an abundant supply. **1925** *Book of Rural Life* 6.3722, The *oyster mushroom* . . [is] common on decaying logs in rich woods and one of the most delicious of all wild mushrooms. **1948** Boyce *Forest Pathology* 392, *Pleurotus ostreatus* . . , the oyster mushroom, causes a white, flaky rot. . . The fleshy annual conks are shelving structures, either sessile or with a short, stout, excentric stalk. . . The upper surface is smooth, white or grayish. **1950** *WELS* WI *(Mushrooms that grow out like shelves from the sides of trees)* 3 Infs, Oyster; 1 Inf, Oyster mushroom; 1 Inf, Several small ones in groups: oyster mushrooms. **1961** Douglas *My Wilderness* 169 **wNC,** Oyster mushrooms grew like tiny shelves from the sides of down logs. **1965–70** *DARE* (Qu. S19, *Mushrooms that grow out like brackets from the sides of trees)* Infs **IN**38, 67, **MI**42, **NH**4, **NY**160, Oyster mushroom(s); **WA**12, Oyster fungus; **MI**108, Oyster; **MI**26, Oyster shells. **1981** Lincoff *Audubon Field Guide Mushrooms* 790, Also called the "Green Oyster," . . the Late Fall Oyster [=*Panellus serotinus*] is edible, but requires long, slow cooking. *Ibid* 793, The Veiled Oyster [=*Pleurotus dryinus*] grows on alder on the Pacific Coast, and on hickory and maple in the East. **1987** McKnight–McKnight *Mushrooms* 179, Oyster Mushrooms: Genus *Panellus. Ibid* 180, Late oyster—*Panellus serotinus.* . . Bitter oyster—*Panellus stipticus. Ibid* 181, Oyster Mushrooms: Genus *Pleurotus. Ibid,* Oyster—*Pleurotus ostreatus.* [*Ibid* 182, This popular and widespread edible mushroom [=*Pleurotus ostreatus*] is named for its shape rather than its taste.]

oyster onion n
Prob an **oyster plant 1.**
    1968 *DARE* (Qu. I4, . . *Vegetables . . less commonly grown around here)* Inf **CT**6, Oyster onion; (Qu. I5, . . *Kind of onions that keep coming up without replanting year after year)* Inf **CT**6, Oyster onions.

oyster plant n
1 A **goatsbeard 1,** usu *Tragopogon porrifolius.* [From the taste]
    1821 Cobbett *Amer. Gardener* 257, *Salsafy,* called, by some, *oyster plant,* is good in soups, or to eat like the *parsnip.* **1837** Darlington *Flora Cestrica* 443 **PA,** Leek-leaved Tragopogon. Vulgò—Oyster-plant. *Salsify.* . . Cultivated for the root, which, when properly cooked, has something of the flavor of oysters—whence a common name of the plant. **1884** Roe *Nature's Serial Story* 205 **seNY,** Will your nose become *retroussé* if I ask you to aid me in planting parsnips, oyster-plant, carrots, and . . onions? **1909** *DN* 3.355 **eAL, wGA,** Oyster-plant. . . Salsify. Also called *vegetable-oyster.* **1911** Jepson *Flora CA* 411, Salsify. . . Root edible, tasting like oysters and so called "Oyster Plant." **1950** *WELS (Other names in your neighborhood for: Salsify)* 8 Infs, **WI,** Oyster plant. **c1960** *Wilson Coll.* **csKY,** Oyster plant. . . Salsify. Grown by a very few people. **1963** Craighead *Rocky Mt. Wildflowers* 232, Meadow Salsify—*Tragopogon pratensis* . . Other names: Goatsbeard, Oysterplant. **1965–70** *DARE* (Qu. I4, . . *Vegetables . . less commonly grown around here)* 16 Infs, 7 **MD,** Oyster plant; **DE**3, Oyster plant—bulb something like an onion; the stew is like oyster stew—really more like a carrot but white; **MD**19, Oyster plant—used to raise, not now; **WI**13, Salsify or "oyster plant" in old times; (Qu. I7, *The small plants like onions . . that are cut up in a salad)* Inf **OH**48, Oyster plant; (Qu. I35, . . *Kitchen herbs . . grown and used in cooking around here)* Inf **OH**75, Oyster plant; (Qu. S21, . . *Weeds . . that are a trouble in gardens and fields)* Inf **AZ**2, Oyster plant—because it tastes like oysters. **1970** Correll *Plants TX* 1729, Oyster plant. . . The somewhat oyster-flavored napiform taproot of this plant is cooked, often as a stew.

2 The eggplant (*Solanum melongena* var *esculentum).* Cf **mock oyster**

1941 *Hench Coll.* **LA,** The Garrisons [from LA] . . were visiting here yesterday and we saw them on a picnic. Two terms they used were 1. lighterwood . . [and] 2. oyster plant. What we [in VA] call egg plant.

3 =**Moses-in-the-bulrushes 1.** [*DJE* 1811 →]
    1933 Small *Manual SE Flora* 262, R[hoeo] discolor. . . Boat-lily. Oyster-plant. **1971** Gantz *Naturalist in S. FL* 92, I have always known it [=*Rhoeo spathacea*] as the oyster plant, but here [=Miami FL] it has the more colorful name of Moses-in-the-bulrushes. **1976** Bailey–Bailey *Hortus Third* 966, [*Rhoeo*] spathacea. . . oyster plant, boat lily [etc].

oyster poor boy See **oyster loaf**

oyster sale n [Folk-etym for *hoist the sail* (at **hoist the (green) sail**)]
Also pl: A children's hiding game played in teams.
    1909 (1923) Bancroft *Games* 7 **NY,** This same game [=run sheep run] was found in the city environment of New York under the name of Oyster Sale, and the signals had become pickles, tomatoes, and other articles strongly suggestive of a delicatessen store. **1957** *Sat. Eve. Post Letters* **seMA** (as of c1900), We played Hoist the Sails which I thought for many years was Oyster Sales.

oyster sandwich See **oyster loaf**

oyster shell n
1 See **oyster B2.**
2 See **oyster mushroom.**

oyster toad n Also *oyster toadfish* **Chesapeake Bay** Cf **oyster-cracker 2, oysterfish 1**
A **toadfish** (here: *Opsanus tau).*
    1936 *Hench Coll.,* On a guided fishing trip in Chesapeake Bay we heard a guide call a certain fish an "oyster toad." It is a hideous, large-eyed . . fish with powerful jaws that can crack oyster shucks and feed on oysters. **1940** Writers' Program *Guide MD* 116 **cnMD,** The production limit of the Chesapeake fishing grounds has not nearly been reached and it abounds with more than 200 different species of fish. . . Others caught are the oyster toad, bonito, skate, black sea bass, cod, mackerel. **1968–70** *DARE* (Qu. P4, *Saltwater fish that are not good to eat)* Infs **MD**36, **VA**55, Oyster toad. **1968** *DARE* Tape **VA**112, Now oyster toads, they live on crabs too in the summertime. . . They will swim around in the grass. . . He'll go up an' he'll swaller the whole thing. . . They got bristles on them like the spurs on a rooster. **1970** *DARE* FW Addit **ceVA,** Oyster toad—toadfish. **1976** Warner *Beautiful Swimmers* 23 **eMD,** Amazing what comes up in pots, besides crabs. Huge gaping-mouthed oyster toadfish, slimy-skinned and with wickedly sharp dorsal spines. **1984** *DARE* File **Chesapeake Bay** [Watermen's vocab], Brown toad fish, oyster toad. **1991** Amer. Fisheries Soc. *Common Names Fishes* 32, *Opsanus tau* . . oyster toadfish.

oysterwood n
=**crabwood.**
    1946 West–Arnold *Native Trees FL* 109, The range of oysterwood, a subtropical tree, is limited in its distribution to the Florida Keys and southern coastal areas. **1979** Little *Checklist U.S. Trees* 143, Oyster-wood. . . S. Fla. incl. Fla. Keys.

oyt n [See quot 1956]
=**least tern.**
    1925 (1928) Forbush *Birds MA* 1.122, Least Tern. *Other names:* Little striker; oyt; pond tern. **1956** MA Audubon Soc. *Bulletin* 40.22, Least tern. . . Oyt (Mass. Sonic for some tern if not for this.)

ozark v Cf **arkansaw v 1**
    1953 Randolph–Wilson *Down in Holler* 269 **Ozarks,** *Ozark.* . . To cheat, to defraud. A woman in Branson, Mo., said: "I've been ozarked out of my property," meaning that she was cheated by a realtor.

Ozark date n Cf **date plum**
=**persimmon.**
    1984 Wilder *You All Spoken Here* 177 **Sth,** Ozark dates, dog apples: Persimmons.

Ozark holly n Cf **Georgia holly, mountain** ~ **3**
A **holly** n[1] **1.**
    1949 Webber *Backwoods Teacher* 238 **Ozarks,** Now it was time to bring bittersweet and limbs of thornless Ozark holly, bare except for glowing orange-red berries, and mistletoe, and sprigs of real holly if a tree could be found.

Ozark minnow n

A **minnow B1** (here: *Notropis nubilus*).

   1943 Eddy–Surber *N. Fishes* 146, The Ozark minnow is a dusky, silvery minnow with a yellow belly. **1956** Harlan–Speaker *IA Fish* 99, *Ozark Minnow*. . . This species is confined to small, lime-rock creeks or to the upper lime-rock reaches of major streams in northeast Iowa. **1965** IL Nat. Hist. Surv. *Biol. Notes* 54.7, Ozark minnow. Occasional in the extreme northern part of the state; sporadic in the lower Mississippi River. **1983** *Audubon Field Guide N. Amer. Fishes* 440, Ozark Minnow. . . One of the most common minnows in the Ozark Uplands. **1991** Amer. Fisheries Soc. *Common Names Fishes* 22, *Notropis nubilus* . . Ozark minnow.

Ozark snowdrops n Also *Ozark sundrop(s)* Cf **snowdrop, sundrops**

An **evening primrose a** (here: *Oenothera macrocarpa*).

   1940 Clute *Amer. Plant Names* 265, *Oenothera Missouriense*. Ozark snowdrops, glade flower. **1948** Stevens *KS Wild Flowers* 310, Oenothera missouriensis—Ozark Sundrops. **1961** Wills–Irwin *Flowers TX* 164, The Flutter-mill, known also as Ozark-sundrop, Missouri-primrose, or Buttercup is found from Grayson, McLennan, and Bexar counties north-westward through the Panhandle.

ozenbrig, oznaburg See **osnaburg**

‡**ozzy** adj

   1950 *WELS (Strange-looking, peculiar: "She wears the most _____ clothes you ever saw)* 1 Inf, **ceWI**, Ozzy.